ART BOOKS 1950 1979

This edition of ART BOOKS 1950-1979 was prepared
by the R. R. Bowker Company's Department of
Bibliography in collaboration with the
Publication Systems Department.

Senior staff of the Department of Bibliography includes:
Gertrude Jennings, Editor-In-Chief, Department of Bibliography,
Debra K. Brown, Manager, Product Development,
Peter Simon, Product Manager, Subject Bibliographies,
Scott MacFarland, Project Coordinator, Product Development,
William Garbe, Assistant Editor.

Michael B. Howell, Business Systems Manager.

Marc Weinstein, Vice President and Publisher,
Data Services Division.

ART BOOKS

1950 1979

Including an International Directory of Museum Permanent Collection Catalogs

SUBJECT INDEX

AUTHOR INDEX

TITLE INDEX

ART BOOKS IN PRINT INDEX

GEOGRAPHIC GUIDE TO MUSEUMS

PERMANENT COLLECTION CATALOG INDEX

R.R. BOWKER COMPANY

New York & London

Published by the R. R. Bowker Company (a Xerox Publishing Company)
1180 Avenue of the Americas, New York, N.Y. 10036
Copyright © 1979 by Xerox Corporation

International Standard Book Number 0-8352-1189-4
International Standard Serial Number 0000-0418
Printed and bound in the
United States of America

CONTENTS

FOREWORD

Art Books 1950-1979 is an idea whose time has come. Long before it became a reality, the plan for this bibliography on the visual arts was enthusiastically applauded by art librarians, art historians and others who realized how valuable a reference work, acquisitions tool, and research aid it would be. The finished work lives up to its promise.

In this first compilation, some 37,000 books on the visual arts are indexed under approximately 14,000 subject headings, with full searching information for each title listed. There are, as well, separate author and title indexes, each of which refers to the complete entries in the subject index.

An unusual and innovative feature of this bibliography is the "Guide to Museum Permanent Collection Catalogs". This section, which is international in coverage, is arranged by the name of the institution and supplies the title of the permanent collection catalog or catalogs, with publication date and price provided by the museums themselves. The "Guide" alone is worth the price of the book, as far as I am concerned. To be able to find in one place the answers to those perennial and persistent questions—"How can I find out what that museum has?" and "Is there a catalog available for that museum's collection or any part of it?"—and to be able to do so on a worldwide basis will make life enormously easier.

Art Books 1950-1979 also contains a geographic index to museum names and addresses with descriptive annotations of the permanent collections and a "subject area outline" which is a topical index to the main body of subject heading entries. This "outline" is designed to provide general access to the more specific subject headings under which the books are classified.

Another feature of ART BOOKS 1950-1979 is the inclusion of an art books in print index drawn from the BOOKS IN PRINT 1979-80 database. This index, arranged by title, will provide current acquisitions information for cataloged titles listed in the subject index. A symbol denoting 'BIP' at the end of the cataloged title in the subject index refers the user to this art books in print index.

To produce *Art Books 1950-1979*, the R. R. Bowker Company was able to identify and draw on the tens of thousands of entries which appear in its research files and in *Books in Print*. The data base for this volume was also enriched by the responses to Bowker's questionnaires which went to 7,000 art museums around the world — questionnaires which verified the existence of the institutions, to begin with, and asked for a description of its collection as well as for a list of its published catalogs. Those museums which did not answer their mail, received telephone calls, and sometimes more than one.

With this volume, the R. R. Bowker Company once again confirms its unique place in the publishing world and its remarkable ability to satisfy the need for special services. Its service to art libraries does not end here, however, for Bowker is already thinking of the next steps which, among other things, will include the listing of art exhibition catalogs, will provide up-to-date coverage, and which will be published in cumulative form.

J. M. Edelstein
Chief Librarian
  National Gallery of Art
    Washington, D. C.

PREFACE

The R.R. Bowker Company's principal aim has always been to provide superior reference tools to libraries and booksellers. The tradition of BOOKS IN PRINT, SUBJECT GUIDE TO BOOKS IN PRINT, AMERICAN BOOK PUBLISHING RECORD, and WEEKLY RECORD is indicative of Bowker's successful effort in providing quality reference materials.

ART BOOKS 1950-1979 further demonstrates Bowker's committment to publish specialized research tools for librarians and booksellers in special areas. ART BOOKS 1950-1979 provides in one volume cataloged books and in-print books on the visual arts. New international indexes of museum permanent collection catalogs, and a geographic guide to the world's art museums, with descriptive annotations of their permanent collections, were especially compiled for this work.

ACQUISITION OF DATA

ART BOOKS 1950-1979 began with a survey of 1700 librarians and booksellers in the visual arts. The survey represented a broad cross-section of the potential audience: public libraries, college and university libraries, junior college libraries, art and architecture libraries, historical societies, museum libraries, museum bookstores, art bookstores and selected large trade bookstores.

This edition of ART BOOKS 1950-1979 was produced from records stored on magnetic tape, edited by computer programs and set in type by computer-controlled photocomposition.

In order to produce the subject, author and title indexes, we examined the databases of cataloged entries used to produce the AMERICAN BOOK PUBLISHING RECORD CUMULATIVE 1950-1977, AMERICAN BOOK PUBLISHING RECORD CUMULATIVE 1978 and AMERICAN BOOK PUBLISHING RECORDs January-June 1979. From these combined databases, in excess of 1,000,000 cataloged entries, some 36,400 titles on the visual arts were selected. In addition, the in-print index, containing 11,600 entries, was produced from the BOOKS IN PRINT 1979-1980 database. Entries in the in-print index contain complete acquisitions information. A code, BIP, appears on those cataloged entries, in the subject index, which were identified on the BOOKS IN PRINT database. Our first consideration was to add the acquisitions information to the cataloged entries, but upon further examination, it was decided to retain the integrity of the original cataloging.

Complete entries appear in the subject index, arranged by main entry within the subject. Some 36,400 entries are classified under some 14,000 Library of Congress subject headings. The author and title indexes contain page references to the full entries in the subject index. Descriptions of all indexes can be found in the "How to Use" section.

FOUR UNIQUE FEATURES

ART BOOKS 1950-1979 has four unique features designed to make it a more useful reference tool. The first is the *Subject Area Directory*. This Directory gives a broad overview of the more than 14,000 subjects covered in the subject index of ART BOOKS 1950-1979. The Library of Congress classification scheme was used to assign the various subjects to broader topical Areas with which they are associated. Since some subject headings contain listings for books concerning different aspects of the subject, these headings may appear under more than one Area. Cross-references are also provided for alternate forms of the main Area headings.

The Directory may be used by those wishing to know the range of information available regarding a topic. When looking at a particular Area, one is given a thorough guide to the subject headings containing books which pertain to that Area. Additionally, the Directory serves as a guide to the broad areas with which a specific subject is concerned. Further examination of the headings within the various Areas give an indication of other headings which also encompass the subject.

Some Areas are necessarily broad, due to the use of the Library of Congress classification scheme. In preparing this Directory, a chronological approach to materials having a historical perspective was used. When a heading was too general to be placed chronologically (e.g. in Art, Modern - 19th & 20th Centuries) a general category such as Art History (General) may have been used.

The second unique feature of ART BOOKS 1950-1979 is the *Art Books In Print Index*. This index, arranged by title, was prepared from a computer-controlled comparison between the cataloged entries selected from the AMERI-

CAN BOOK PUBLISHING RECORD databases and the BOOKS IN PRINT 1979-1980 database. This process identified those books on the visual arts which are in print. A code, BIP, in the subject index catalog entries refers the user to the in-print index for current acquisitions information. Complete acquisitions information is provided with each in-print entry: title, subtitle, edition statements, price with type of binding if other than cloth over boards, International Standard Book Number, publisher's order number, and publisher's or distributor's name abbreviation.

The third unique feature of ART BOOKS 1950-1979 is the *Geographic Guide to Museums*. This Guide is an international listing of 7000 of the world's art museums, arranged by country and including descriptive annotations of their permanent collections provided by the museums. Entries include institution name, address, telephone number, cable address, telex number, and permanent collection annotation.

The *Geographic Guide* was compiled from a newly created database of 7000 of the world's art museums. This database was used for special mailings to art museums to solicit listings of their permanent collection catalogs and/or descriptions of their permanent collections. A marked effort was made to reach all art museums to at least get descriptions of their permanent collections.

This Guide can be used to verify location of particular museums, and in many cases, provides an opportunity to peruse their permanent collections.

The fourth feature of ART BOOKS 1950-1979 is the *Museum Permanent Collection Catalogs Index*. Arranged by museum name and providing location information with cross-references for alternate forms of institution name, over 3300 permanent collection catalogs are listed with full bibliographic information. Entries are for catalogs currently available, and include prices, which are given in the respective foreign currency when applicable. The publisher or distributor is also given so that full ordering information can be obtained from the "Key to Publisher's and Distributor's Directory." Since all art

museums do not publish permanent collection catalogs we decided that the Guide should contain all museums in the database whether they publish permanent collection catalogs or not.

We extend a very special thanks to our Advisory Board members, who so willingly assisted us with their expertise in their areas of specialization. Members of the Advisory Board were J.M. Edelstein, Chief Librarian, National Gallery of Art; Joanne Polster, Chairperson, Art Library Society, NA (ARLIS) and Chief Librarian, Museum of Contemporary Crafts; Donald Anderle, Art and Architecture Librarian, New York Public Library; Robert Cahn, Art Historian and reviewer of art books for LIBRARY JOURNAL. We also extend special gratitude to J.M. Edelstein, Chief Librarian, National Gallery of Art for his encouraging and splendid Foreword.

Gertrude Jennings, Editor-in-Chief, Department of Bibliography, Data Services Division, was responsible for the concept of ART BOOKS 1950-1979. Debra K. Brown, Manager, Product Development, was responsible for the design. She and Peter Simon, Product Manager, Subject Bibliographies, prepared the Subject Area Directory, Geographic Guide to Museums and International Directory of Museum Permanent Collection Catalogs.

Special thanks to Scott MacFarland, Project Coordinator, Product Development. Also, William Garbe, Assistant Editor, Subject Bibliographies and Mark Lademann, for their contributions in the preparation of this first edition.

Gertrude Jennings, Editor-in-Chief,
    Department of Bibliography,
        Data Services Division
Debra K. Brown, Manager,
    Product Development
Peter Simon, Product Manager,
    Subject Bibliographies

HOW TO USE
ART BOOKS 1950-1979

GENERAL EDITORIAL POLICIES:

In order to insure that the integrity of original Library of Congress cataloging is maintained in the subject index, and that entries are uniform and easy to find, the following editorial policies have been maintained:

Subject headings were made uniform whereas the entries listed within may contain variant forms of the tracing.

Dual listings are provided when an entry contains both subject and uniform name tracings.

Entries without subject or name tracings in the original cataloging were assigned by editorial staff to appropriate subject headings.

Entries for which acquisitions information can be found in the Art Books In Print index contain the symbol *BIP*. This was placed at the end of the entry to preserve the original format of the cataloged entries.

Similarly, to insure that critical information can be found in the Art Books In Print and Permanent Collection Catalog indexes, editorial policies consistent with the *Books In Print* line of products have been maintained. Every effort is made by most contributing publishers and institutions to prepare their material with consideration for its accuracy throughout the life of this edition of ART BOOKS 1950-1979. In spite of these efforts, a number of changes in price will occur and a number of titles in this edition will become unavailable before the new edition is published. All prices are subject to change without notice.

Most prices are list prices. Lack of uniformity in the individual catalogs prohibits indicating trade discounts. A lower case "t" indicates a tentative price; a lower case "x" indicates a short discount, 20% or less.

The names of publishers, distributors, and institutions, in most cases, are abbreviated. A key to these abbreviations, with the addresses of the publishing or distributing firms whose titles are listed in the Art Books In Print or Permanent Collection Catalog indexes will be found in the "Key to Publisher's and Distributor's Directory," at the end of this volume. Here is an example of an entry in this key:

> SIRAUDEAU
>   Siraudeau Cie
>   Pl. de la Visitation, F-49000 Angers
>   France
>   (2-85672)
>   ▲ THIS IS THE PUBLISHER'S INTERNATIONAL STANDARD BOOK NUMBER PREFIX.

Above the full name of any publisher, distributor, or institution represented in this book, the name or abbreviation for that publisher, distributor, or institution is given as it is used in the Art Books In Print or Permanent Collection Catalog index entries.

SUBJECT INDEX

Entries are arranged alphabetically by main entry within subject.

Headings were derived from the primary subject and uniform name tracings in the original cataloging entries. Some of these headings were made uniform due to variances in the styling of tracings in these entries.

Subject headings are arranged alphabetically.

> *Antiques*
> *Beads*
> *Castles*

Many of the main headings are broken down still further:

> *Antiques*
> *Antiques* - Bibliography
> *Antiques* - Catalogs
> *Antiques* - Conservation and Restoration

Headings, as used in Library of Congress cataloging practice, are explicit rather than general—thus books on *Chairs* are under *Chairs*, not under *Furniture*.

The Subject Area Directory was designed to provide a complete overview of the Subject Index, and can be used to discern the relationships between specific headings.

AUTHOR AND TITLE INDEXES

The author and title indexes are alphabetically arranged by their authors and titles respectively. Page references are provided to the main entries in the subject index.

ART BOOKS IN PRINT INDEX

The *Art Books In Print Index* is alphabetically arranged by title. Entries include the following bibliographic information, when available: title, subtitle, edition statement, price with type of binding if other than cloth over boards, International Standard Book Number, publisher order number and publisher's or distributor's name abbreviation.

GEOGRAPHIC GUIDE TO MUSEUMS

This *Guide* is arranged by institution name within country. Cross-references provide access from variant forms of the institution name, when applicable. Entries include: institution name, address, telephone number, cable, telex, International Standard Book Number Prefix, and descriptive annotation of the permanent collections, when provided by the institution.

PERMANENT COLLECTION CATALOG INDEX

This index is arranged alphabetically by title within headings for institution names. These headings also provide the location of the institutions. Cross-references have been included for variant forms of institution names, when applicable.

Entries include the following, when available: title, subtitle, author, co-author, editor, co-editor, translator, co-translator, number of volumes, edition, Library of Congress number, series, illustration statement (including number and types), language, year of publication, price with proper currency, type of binding if other than cloth over boards, publisher's order number, International Standard Book Number, and abbreviation for publisher, distributor, or institution name.

KEY TO ABBREVIATIONS

GENERAL

a	after price, specially priced library edition available
a.	annual
abr.	abridged
abstr.	abstracts
adpt.	adapted
adv.	advertising
Amer.	American
annot.	annotation(s), annotated
ans.	answer(s)
app.	appendix
approx.	approximately
assn.	association
auth.	author
Ave.	Avenue
bd.	bound
bdg.	binding
bds.	boards
bi-m.	every two months
bibl(s).	bibliography (ies)
BIP	Books in Print
bk(s).	book, books
bk. rev.	book reviews
bklet(s)	booklets
Blvd.	Boulevard
Bro.	Brother
c/o	care of
charts	charts (diagrams, graphs, tables)
circ.	circulation
coll.	college
comm.	commission, committee
co.	company
comp(s).	compiler(s)
cond.	condensed
contr.	controlled
corp.	corporation
cum. ind.	cumulative index
Cy.	county
d.	daily
dept.	department
diag(s).	diagram(s)
dir.	director
dist.	distributed
Div.	Division
doz.	dozen
Dr.	Drive
ea.	each
ed.	editor, edited, edition
Ed. Bd.	Editorial Board
eds.	editions, editors
educ.	education
elem.	elementary
ency.	encyclopedia
Eng.	English
enl.	enlarged
exp.	expurgated
fac.	facsimile
fasc.	fascicle
fict.	fiction
fig(s).	figure(s)
film rev.	film reviews
for.	foreign
fortn.	fortnightly
Fr.	French
frwd.	foreword
g	after price, guaranteed juvenile binding
gen.	general
Ger.	German
Gr.	Greek
gr.	grade, grades
hdbk.	handbook
Heb.	Hebrew
i.t.a.	initial teaching alphabet
Illus.	illustrated, illustration(s), illustrator(s)
in prep.	in preparation
incl.	includes, including
inst.	institute
intro.	introduction
ISSN	International Standard Serial Number
irreg.	irregular
It.	Italian
Jr.	Junior
jt. auth.	joint author
jt. ed.	joint editor
k	kindergarten audience level
l.p.	long playing
ltd. ed.	limited edition
lab.	laboratory
lang(s).	language(s)
Lat.	Latin
lea.	leather
lib.	library
lit.	literature, literary
m.	monthly
math.	mathematics
mkt.	market prices
mod.	modern
mor.	morocco
MS, MSS	manuscript, manuscripts
music rev.	music reviews
N.S.	New Series
natl.	national
no., nos.	number, numbers
o.p.	out of print
orig.	original text, not a reprint
pap.	paper
pat.	patents
photos	photographs, photographer
play rev.	play reviews (theatre reviews)
PLB	publisher's library binding
P.O.	Post Office
Pol.	Polish
pop. ed.	popular edition
Port.	Portuguese
prep.	preparation
probs.	problems
Prof	Professor
prog. bk.	programmed book
ps	preschool audience level
pseud.	pseudonym
pt(s).	part, parts
pub.	published, publisher, publishing
pubn.	publication, publications
q.	quarterly
record rev.	record reviews
ref(s).	reference(s)
repr.	reprint
reprod(s).	reproduction(s)

rev.	revised	suppl.	supplement
rpm.	revolution per minute (phono records)	t	after price, tentative price
Rte	Route	tech.	technical
Rus.	Russian	tele. rev.	television reviews
s-a.	twice annually	text ed.	text edition
s-m.	twice monthly	3/m.	3 times a month
s-w.	twice weekly	3/yr.	3 times a year
s.p.	school price	tr.	translator, translated, translation
sec.	section		
sel.	selected	tr. lit.	trade literature (manufacturers' catalogues, etc.)
ser.	series		
s & l	signed & limited		
Soc.	Society	tr. mk.	trade marks
sols.	solutions	univ.	university
Span.	Spanish	vol(s).	volume, volumes
Sr. (after given name)	Senior	w.	weekly
		wkbk.	workbook
Sr. (before given name)	Sister	x	after price, short discount (20% or less)
St.	Saint, Street	YA	young adult audience level
stat.	statistics	yrbk.	yearbook
subs.	subsidiary	‡	not available from a subscription agency
subscr.	subscription		

KEY TO CURRENCY SYMBOLS

SYMBOL	UNIT	COUNTRY
Arg.$	peso	Argentina
As.	annas	Pakistan
Aus.$	dollars	Australia
B.	bahts	Thailand
B.$	dollars	Borneo (Brunei)
Bl.	balboas	Panama
Bol.$	peso	Bolivia
Bs.	bolivares	Venezuela
C.$	cordobas	Nicaragua
Can.$	dollars	Canada
Col.	colones	Costa Rica, El Salvador
Col.$	peso	Colombia
Cr.$	cruzeiros	Brazil
ctms.	centimes; centimos; centesimos	various
cvs.	centavos	various
d.	pence	Great Britain
DH.	dirhams	Morocco
DM.	marks	West Germany
din.	dinars	Yugoslavia
$	dollars; pesos	various
Dr.	drachmas	Greece
E.	pounds	Gt. Britain
EAs.	shillings	East Africa
Esc.	escudos	Portugal
Eth.$	dollars	Ethiopia
F.	franc	France
fl.	florins or guilders	The Netherlands, Surinam
FMG.	francs	Malagasy Republic
Fmk.	marks; markkas	Finland
Fr.	francs	Belgium, Switzerland
Fr. CFA	francs	African Financial Community
Ft.	forints	Hungary
Gde.	gourdes	Haiti
G.$	dollars	Guyana
g.	guaranies	Paraguay
HK.$	dollars	Hong Kong
I.D.	dinars	Iran, Iraq
Jam.$	dollar	Jamaica
K.	kwacha	Zambia
Kcs.	koruny	Czechoslovakia
Kop.	kopecks	U.S.S.R.
Kr.	kroner; kronor	Scandinavian countries
L.	lempira; lira	Honduras, Italy
Le.	Leones	Sierra Leone
lei	lei	Romania
lv.	leva	Bulgaria
M.	marks	East Germany
M.$	dollars	Malaya
Mex.$	pesos	Mexico
Mils.	mils	Cyprus
$m.n.	moneda nacional	various
n.	ngwee	Zambia
NC.	New Cedis	Ghana
NT.$	dollars	Taiwan
N.Z.$	dollars	New Zealand
p.	pesewas; pence	Ghana, Gt. Britain
P.	pesos	various
P.T.	piasters	Egypt, Syria, Turkey
pf.	pfennigs	Germany
£E	pounds	Egypt
I£	pounds	Israel
£L	pounds	Lebanon, Libya
£N	pounds	Nigeria
£S	pounds	Syria
ptas.	pesetas	Spain
Q.	quetzales	Guatemala
R.	rands	South Africa
RD.$	peso	Dominican Republic
Rhod.$	dollars	Rhodesia
Rps.	rupiahs	Indonesia
Rs.	riels; rupees; rials	Cambodia, Ceylon, India, Pakistan, Iran
Rub.	rubles	U.S.S.R.
S/	sucres, soles	Ecuador, Peru
S.	schillings	Austria
S.$	dollars	Singapore
s.	shillings	Gt. Britain
TL.	pounds	Turkey
T.T.$	dollars	Trinidad
Urg.$	Pesos	Uruguay
VN.$	dollars	Vietnam
Won	won (hwan)	Korea
Yen	yen	Japan
Zl.	zlotys	Poland

ISBN
INTERNATIONAL STANDARD
BOOK NUMBER

ART BOOKS 1950-1979 is the first edition where each title or edition of a title is listed with an ISBN. All publishers were notified and requested to submit a valid ISBN for their titles.

During the past decade, the majority of the publishers complied with the requirements of the standard and implemented the ISBN. At present, approximately 93% of all new titles and all new editions are submitted for listing with a valid ISBN.

To fulfill the responsibility of accomplishing total book numbering, the ISBN Agency allocated the ISBN prefixes 0-685 and 0-686 to number the titles in the BOOKS IN PRINT database without an ISBN. Titles not having an ISBN at the closing date of this publication were assigned an ISBN with one of these prefixes by the International Standard Book Numbering Agency.

Titles numbered within the prefixes 0-685 and 0-686 are:
— Publishers who did not assign ISBN to their titles.
— Distributors with titles published and imported from countries not in the ISBN system, or not receiving the ISBN from the originating publisher.
— Errors from transposition and transcription which occurred in transmitting the ISBN to the BOOKS IN PRINT database.

All the ISBN listed in ART BOOKS 1950-1979 are validated by using the check digit control, and only valid ISBN are listed in the BIP database.

All publishers participating in the ISBN system having titles numbered within the prefixes 0-685 and 0-686 will receive a computer printout, requesting them to submit the correct ISBN.

Publishers not participating in the ISBN system may request from the ISBN Agency the assignment of an ISBN Publisher Prefix, and start numbering their titles.

By having an ISBN for each title and edition of a title, order fulfillment and inventory control systems will be able to operate more efficiently and economically. The ISBN Agency will produce and publish an ISBN Index on microfiche. Users encountering an ISBN in the range of 0-685 and 0-686 who are unable to identify the title in their file, will be able to refer to the ISBN microfiche Index. Each ISBN in the Index will have the information on title, author and publisher, or a cross reference to another ISBN. When publishing rights are sold and the title is published under the new imprint with a separate ISBN, the ISBN Index will carry a cross reference from the previous ISBN to the new one.

The Book Industry System Advisory Committee (BISAC) developed a standard format for data transmission, and many companies are already accepting orders transmitted on magnetic tape using the ISBN. Another standard format by BISAC for title updating is under development.

The ISBN Agency and the Data Services Division of the Bowker Company wish to express their appreciation to all publishers who collaborated in making the ISBN system the standard of the publishing industry.

For additional information related to the ISBN total numbering, please refer to Emery Koltay, Director of the ISBN Agency or Enea Bacci, Manager of Publisher's Information and Services, both of the R. R. Bowker Co.

SUBJECT AREA DIRECTORY

The *Subject Area Directory* provides a topical outline to the Library of Congress subject tracings listed in *Art Books 1950-1979*. The *Subject Area Directory* is designed to provide general access to all topics found in the *Subject Index*. The more than 14,000 subjects were classified under the 35 major areas or topics derived from the Library of Congress Classification scheme. For instance, all subjects within *Art Books 1950-1979* which deal with the topic of *Architecture* or *Drawing* would be alphabetically arranged under their respective topic. This index is intended to provide the user with an overall view of the general topic with specific Library of Congress subjects used in the *Subject Index* that relate to the area listed. Therefore, a user wishing to approach a topic, e.g. *Architecture*, can scan this topic and isolate specific subjects for review of the cataloging records within the subject index.

AESTHETICS
Aesthetic Movement (British Art)
Aesthetics.
Aesthetics -- Addresses, Essays, Lectures.
Aesthetics, American.
Aesthetics, Ancient.
Aesthetics, British.
Aesthetics, British-Addresses, Essays, Lectures.
Aesthetics--Collected Works.
Aesthetics-Collections.
Aesthetics-Congresses.
Aesthetics-Early Works to 1800.
Aesthetics, French.
Aesthetics-History.
Aesthetics, Japanese-Addresses, Essays, Lectures.
Aesthetics, Modern.
Aesthetics, Modern-18th Century.
Aesthetics, Modern-18th Century-Addresses, Essays, Lectures.
Aesthetics, Modern-20th Century.
Aesthetics, Modern-20th Century-Addresses, Essays, Lectures.
Aesthetics, Modern-20th Century-Collected Works.
Aesthetics, Oriental.
Aesthetics -- Period.
Aesthetics--Philosophy.
Aesthetics-Physiological Aspects.
Aesthetics, Polish.
Aesthetics, Russian.
Art Appreciation.
Art Appreciation-Juvenile Literature.
Art Appreciation-Study and Teaching (Elementary)
Avant-Garde (Aesthetics)
Barber Bottles-Catalogs.
Benn, Gottfried, 1886-1956-Aesthetics.
Black in Art.
Color.
Color-Bibliography.
Color in Art.
Color in Art-Juvenile Literature.
Color-Psychology.
Color-Psychology-Bibliography.
Color Sensitometry (Photography)
Color-Study and Teaching.
Colors.
Colors-Juvenile Literature.
Communist Aesthetics-Addresses, Essays, Lectures.
Creation--Art.
Creation in Art.
Creation (Literacy, Artistic, Etc.)--Psychological Aspects.
Creation (Literary, Artistic, Etc.)
Creation (Literary, Artistic, Etc.)-Addresses, Essays, Lectures.
Creative Ability.
Form (Aesthetics)
Form (Aesthetics)--Addresses, Essays, Lectures.
Form Perception-Juvenile Literature.
Fuller, Richard Buckminster, 1895- -Bibliography.
Information Theory in Aesthetics.

Judgment (Aesthetics)
Kant, Immanuel--Aesthetics.
Kierkegaard, Soren Aabye, 1813-1855--Aesthetics.
Meaning (Psychology)
Modernism (Aesthetics)-Addresses, Essays, Lectures.
Mondriaan, Pieter Cornelius, 1872-1944- Aesthetics.
Movement, Aesthetics of.
Nature (Aesthetics)
Nietzsche, Friedrich Wilhelm, 1844-1900- Aesthetics.
Poetics.
Poetry.
Ruskin, John, 1819-1900-Aesthetics.
Ut Pictura Poesis (Aesthetics)-Bibliography.

ANCIENT ART
see Art, Ancient, Classical, and Medieval

ANTIQUES
Airplanes-Restoration.
Alexander Doll Company.
Alexander Doll Company-Catalogs.
Antique Dealers.
Antique Dealers-New York (City)-Directories.
Antique Dealers-United States-Directories.
Antiques.
Antiques-Australia.
Antiques-Bibliography.
Antiques-Catalogs.
Antiques-Collectors and Collecting-Directories.
Antiques-Conservation and Restoration-Handbooks, Manuals, Etc.
Antiques-Dictionaries.
Antiques-England-Dictionaries.
Antiques-Europe.
Antiques-Expertising.
Antiques, French.
Antiques-Great Britain.
Antiques-Handbooks, Manuals, Etc.
Antiques in Interior Decoration.
Antiques-Japan.
Antiques-New England.
Antiques-New England-Directories.
Antiques-New England-Prices.
Antiques-New Jersey-Directories.
Antiques-New York (City)-Directories.
Antiques-Pennsylvania-Directories.
Antiques-Pennsylvania-Perry Co.
Antiques-Prices-Canada.
Antiques-Private Collections-Australia.
Antiques-Southern States.
Antiques-United States.
Antiques-United States-Catalogs.
Antiques-United States-Conservation and Restoration-Directories.
Antiques, Victorian.
Art Objects, American.
Art Objects, American-Catalogs.
Art Objects, American-Dictionaries.
Art Objects, American-Exhibitions.
Art Objects, American-History.
Art Objects, Ancient-Exhibitions.

Art Objects-Catalogs.
Art Objects, Chinese.
Art Objects, Chinese-Catalogs.
Art Objects, Chinese-Exhibitions.
Art Objects--Collectors and Collecting.
Art Objects-Collectors and Collecting-Dictionaries.
Art Objects-Collectors and Collecting-Handbooks, Manuals, Etc.
Art Objects--Collectors and Collecting--Juvenile Literature.
Art Objects--Dictionaries.
Art Objects, Egyptian-Exhibitions.
Art Objects-Europe.
Art Objects, European-Catalogs.
Art Objects-Exhibitions.
Art Objects, French-Canadian.
Art Objects-Gt. Brit.-Directories.
Art Objects-History.
Art Objects, Islamic.
Art Objects, Japanese-Catalogs.
Art Objects, Korean.
Art Objects-Limited Editions-Collectors and Collecting.
Art Objects-Limited Editions-Collectors and Collecting-Handbooks, Manuals, Etc.
Art Objects-New England.
Art Objects-New York (City)-Catalogs.
Art Objects-Nigeria-Benin City-Catalogs.
Art Objects-Oceanica-Catalogs.
Art Objects, Oriental-Catalogs.
Art Objects-Packing.
Art Objects-Prices.
Art Objects-United States.
Art Objects, Victorian.
Art Objects, Victorian-Dictionaries.
Art Objects, Victorian-Great Britain.
Art Objects, Victorian-Handbooks, Manuals, Etc.
Avon Products, Inc.
Avon Products, Inc.-Catalogs.
Ball Corporation.
Barber and McMurry.
Barber Bottles-Catalogs.
Baseball Cards.
Baseball Insignia.
Baston, Eng. Tinker's Urn.
Beer Bottles-Catalogs.
Beer Cans-Collectors and Collecting.
Beer Cans-United States.
Beer Cans-United States-Collectors and Collecting.
Beer-Posters-Catalogs.
Bells-Collectors and Collecting.
Bitters Bottles.
Bitters Bottles-Catalogs.
Bonnin and Morris.
Book Ends.
Bookmarks-Collectors and Collecting.
Boots and Shoes.
The Borden Limner.
Bottles.
Bottles, American.
Bottles, American-Catalogs.
Bottles, American-Colorado.

Bottles, American-Dictionaries.
Bottles, American-Exhibitions.
Bottles-Catalogs.
Bottles-Chemung Co., N.Y.
Bottles-Chicago.
Bottles-Collectors and Collecting.
Bottles-Collectors and Collecting-Caricatures and Cartoons.
Bottles-Collectors and Collecting-Great Britain.
Bottles-Collectors and Collecting-United States.
Bottles-Colorado.
Bottles-Columbia, S.C.
Bottles-Conservation and Restoration.
Bottles-Florida Keys-Catalogs.
Bottles-Great Britain.
Bottles, Hawaiian.
Bottles-Long Island-Catalogs.
Bottles-Marks.
Bottles-New England.
Bottles-New England-Catalogs.
Bottles-Orange Co., N.Y.-Catalogs.
Bottles-Prices.
Bottles-Private Collections-United States.
Bottles-South Carolina.
Bottles-The West-Catalogs.
Bottles-United States.
Bottles-United States-Catalogs.
Bottles-United States-Collectors and Collecting-Catalogs.
Boxes.
Boxes-Collectors and Collecting.
Boxes in Art.
Buttonhooks-Collectors and Collecting.
Buttons--Collectors and Collecting.
Buttons, American.
Buttons-Europe-Collectors and Collecting-Dictionaries.
Buttons-United States.
Cambridge Glass Company, Cambridge, Ohio.
Cameo Glass, French-Catalogs.
Carnival Glass.
Carnival Glass-Catalogs.
Carnival Glass-Collectors and Collecting.
Carnival Glass-Collectors and Collecting-Catalogs.
Carriages and Carts--Bibl.
Children's Paraphernalia-Collectors and Collecting-U.S.
Children's Paraphernalia-Collectors and Collecting.
Clock and Watch Makers-Vermont.
Clock and Watch Making--Japan.
Clocks and Watches.
Clocks and Watches, American.
Clocks and Watches, American--New Jersey.
Clocks and Watches-Catalogs.
Clocks and Watches--Collectors and Collecting.
Clocks and Watches -- England.
Clocks and Watches, English.
Clocks and Watches, French.
Clocks and Watches-Great Britain.
Clocks and Watches-History.
Clocks and Watches, History.
Clocks and Watches-Malibu, Calif.-Catalogs.
Clocks and Watches-Michigan-Dearborn-Catalogs.

Architecture--Societies.
Architecture-Socorro, N.M.-History.
Architecture-Sonora Desert-History.
Architecture-South Carolina.
Architecture -- Southern States.
Architecture -- Southwest, New.
Architecture--Spain--Outlines, Syllabi, Etc.
Architecture--Spanish America.

Architecture-Spokane.
Architecture-Springfield, Ill.
Architecture-Staffordshire, Eng.
Architecture-Study and Teaching.
Architecture-Study and Teaching (Elementary)
Architecture-Study and Teaching-Great Britain.
Architecture-Study and Teaching-Texas.
Architecture-Study and Teaching-United States.
Architecture, Sukiya.
Architecture--Sweden.
Architecture--Switzerland.
Architecture--Tasmania.
Architecture-Tempsford, Eng.-Conservation and
   Restoration.
Architecture-Tennessee-Clarksville-Guide-Books.
Architecture-Tennessee, Middle.
Architecture--Terminology.
Architecture-Texas.
Architecture-Texas-Pictorial Works.
Architecture-Toddington, Eng.-Conservation and
   Restoration.
Architecture-Toledo-Guide-Books.
Architecture-Toronto-History.
Architecture, Tropical.
Architecture, Tropical-Bibliography.
Architecture--Turkey.
Architecture-Ulster Co., N.Y.
Architecture-United States.

Architecture -- U.S. -- Addresses, Essays,
   Lectures.
Architecture-United States-Bibliography.
Architecture-United States-Conservation and
   Restoration.
Architecture-United States-Conservation and
   Restoration-Bibliography.
Architecture-United States-Designs and Plans.
Architecture-United States-Examinations.
Architecture-United States-Exhibitions.
Architecture--United States--History.

Architecture-United States-Pictorial Works.
Architecture-U.S.-Juvenile Literature.
Architecture--Venezuela.
Architecture--Venice.

Architecture-Venice-Guide-Books.
Architecture, Victorian.
Architecture, Victorian-Chicago.
Architecture, Victorian-Colorado.
Architecture, Victorian-Great Britain.
Architecture, Victorian-Great Britain-Addresses,
   Essays, Lectures.
Architecture, Victorian-Hamilton, Ont.
Architecture, Victorian, in Art.
Architecture, Victorian-Iowa.
Architecture, Victorian-London.
Architecture, Victorian-Louisville, Ky.
Architecture, Victorian-Portsmouth, Eng.
Architecture, Victorian-South Africa.
Architecture, Victorian-The West.
Architecture, Victorian-U.S.
Architecture-Virgin Islands of the United States.
Architecture--Virginia.
Architecture-Virginia-Catalogs.

Architecture-Virginia-Danville.
Architecture-Vocational Guidance.
Architecture-Vocational Guidance-Addresses,
   Essays, Lectures.
Architecture-Wales.
Architecture-Warren Co., Ohio.
Architecture-Warwickshire, Eng.
Architecture-Washington, D. C.

Architecture-Washington, D.C.-Bibliography.
Architecture-Washington, D.C.-Catalogs.
Architecture-Washington, D.C.-Guide-Books.
Architecture-Washington, D.C.-History.
Architecture-Washington-Skagit Co.-Guide-Books.
Architecture-West Indies, British-Conservation
   and Restoration.
Architecture-Western Reserve.
Architecture-Westminster, Eng. St. Margaret's
   Parish.
Architecture-Wilmington, N.C.
Architecture--Wisconsin--Hist.
Architecture-Yearbooks.
Architecture-Yorkshire, Eng. North Riding.
Architecture-Yorkshire, Eng. West Riding.
Archive Buildings.
Asolo Theater, Sarasota, Fla.
Assisi. San Francesco (Church)
Astronomy, Prehistoric.
Athens, Acropolis.
Athens. Agora.

Athens. Parthenon.

Athens. Parthenon-Juvenile Literature.

Atlanta. Hyatt Regency Atlanta.
Auditorium.
Auditoriums.
Autun, France. SaintLazare (Cathedral)
Baileys Harbor, Wis. Chapel.
Baltimore-Buildings.
Bamberg. Dom.
Bank of the United States (1816-1836)-Buildings.
Barfreston, Church.
Barns.
Barns-Designs and Plans.
Barns-England-Norfolk (County)
Barns-Massachusetts-Martha's Vineyard.
Barns-Northeastern States.
Barns-Pennsylvania-Chester Co.
Barns-United States.
Bartiesville, Okla. Price Tower.
Basements.
Baton Rouge, La. State Capitol.
Bauhaus.
Beacon Hill, Boston.
Bergdorf Goodman, New York.
Bergenfield, N.J. South Presbyterian Church.
Bernini, Givovanni Lorenzo, 1598-1680.
Beth-El Synagogue, New Rochelle, N.Y.
Blount Family.
Bognor Regis, Eng. Hotham Park House.
Bonfire Shelter Site, Texas.
Boston-Buildings-Juvenile Literature.
Boston University. Marsh Chapel.
Bourges. Saint-Etienne (Cathedral)
Bricklaying.
Bridges -- Design -- Addresses, Essays, Lectures.
Bridges--Gt. Brit.
Bridges--Hist.
Bridlington, Eng. (Yorkshire). St. Mary the Virgin
   (Church)
Buckingham Palace.
Building, Adobe.
Building-Bibliography.
Building, Brick.
Building, Brick-History.
Building-Details.
Building-Details-Drawings.
Building-Dictionaries.
Building-Egypt-History.
Building-Estimates.
Building-Handbooks, Manuals, Etc.
Building-History.
Building, Iron and Steel.
Building Materials.
Building Sites.
Building-Tropics.
Building, Wooden.
Building, Wooden-British Columbia.
Buildings-Energy Conservation.
Buildings-Energy Conservation-Bibliography.
Buildings-Energy Conservation-Case Studies.
Buildings in Art.
Buildings, Octagonal.
Buildings, Prefabricated.
Buildings-Repair and Reconstruction.
Building--Tables, Calculations, Etc.

Buildings-United States-Remodeling for Other
   Use.
Buildings, Wooden.

Bungalows.
Cambridge, Eng.-Description-Guide-Books.
Candilis-Josic-Woods.

Canterbury Cathedral.

Capitols-United States-History.
Castelseprio, Italy. Santa Maria (Church)
Castles.

Castles-England.
Castles-England-Guide-Books.
Castles-Europe.

Castles -- France -- Hist.
Castles-Great Britain.
Castles-Great Britain-History.

Castles -- Gt. Brit. -- Juvenile Literature.

Castles--Ireland.
Castles-Japan.
Castles-Juvenile Literature.
Castles-Latin Orient.
Castles-Loire Valley.
Castles-Netherlands.
Castles-Spain.

Castles-United States.
Cathedrals.
Cathedrals--England.
Cathedrals-Europe.
Cathedrals-France.
Cathedrals--Germany.

Cathedrals-Great Britain.
Cathedrals-Italy.
Cathedrals-Juvenile Literature.
Cathedrals--Spain.
Catholic Institutions-Buildings.
Cave Churches.

Cave Churches-Cappadocia.
Cave Churches-Ethiopia.
Cave Temples.
Cave Temples, Buddhist-India-History.
Ceilings.
Chantries.
Charlwood, Eng. (Surrey)-Buildings.
Chartres, France. Notre-Dame (Cathedral)
Chartres, France. Saint Pierre (Church)
Chesterfield, Eng. St. Mary and All Saints
   (Church)
Chicago. Frederick C. Robie House.
Chicago School of Architecture.
Chicago. World's Colombian Exposition, 1893.
Chidabaram, India. Temple.
Chiesa Della Madonna Dell'Orto Di Venezia.
Chiropractic Clinics-United States-Design and
   Construction.
Choir-Stalls-Gt. Brit.-Catalogs.
Choir-Stalls-Lincoln, Eng.
Church Architecture.
Church Architecture-Boston.
Church Architecture-California.
Church Architecture-Cotswold Hills.
Church Architecture-Designs and Plans.
Church Architecture-Dorset, Eng.
Church Architecture--England.
Church Architecture-England-Essex-Conservation
   and Restoration.
Church Architecture--England--Hist.
Church Architecture--England--Juvenile
   Literature.
Church Architecture-England-Suffolk-Addresses,
   Essays, Lectures.
Church Architecture-Europe.
Church Architecture-France.
Church Architecture-France-Nivernais.
Church Architecture-Germany.
Church Architecture-Great Britain.
Church Architecture--Gt. Brit.--Juvenile
   Literature.
Church Architecture-History.
Church Architecture-Ireland.
Church Architecture-Italy.
Church Architecture-Italy-Venice-Conservation
   and Restoration.
Church Architecture-Jolf a (Ost an-E Dahom)
Church Architecture-Macedonia.
Church Architecture-Mexico.
Church Architecture-Mexico-History.
Church Architecture-New England-History.
Church Architecture--New Mexico.
Church Architecture-Norfolk, Eng. (County)
Church Architecture-Oaxaca, Mexico (State)
Church Architecture-Ravenna.
Church Architecture-Rhine Valley.
Church Architecture-Russia-History.
Church Architecture--Scotland--History.
Church Architecture--Southern States.
Church Architecture-Spain.
Church Architecture-United States.
Church Architecture-United States-Bibliography.
Church Facilities.
Church of the Holy Cross, Aktamar Island.
Church of the Holy Trinity, Stratford-Upon-Avon.
Churches.
Churches, Catholic.
Churches --England.
Churches-England-Essex.
Churches--England--Somerset.
Churches--Gt. Brit.
Churches--Melbourne.
Churches-Mexico-Sonora.
Churches -- New England.
Churches-Palestine.
Churches, Protestant.
Churches-U.S.
Churches -- Virginia.
Churches-Wight, Isle of.
Cincinnati. Union Terminal Station.
Ciudad Rodrigo, Catedral.
Ciudad Rodrigo, Spain.
Club-Houses.
Cobblestone Buildings-New York (State)
Colledi, Italy. Castello Garzoni.
Colonial Revival (Architecture)-United States.
Colonial Williamsburg, Inc.
Colonial Williamsburg, Inc. Dept. of Collections.
Color in Architecture.
Columbia University. Libraries. Avery
   Architectural Library.
Columbia University. School of Architecture.
Columbus, Ohio-Dwellings.
Columns.
Comacine Masters (Builders)
Communication in Architectural Design.
Concrete Blocks.
Concrete Construction.
Connecticut-Capital and Capitol.
Constructivism (Architecture)-Russia.
Cordoba. Catedral.
Correctional Institutions-Design and
   Construction-Competitions.
Cottages.
Country Homes.

Country Homes-Gt. Brit.
Country Homes-Spain.
Country Homes-United States.
Country Houses-England.
Court-Houses-Iowa.
Court-Houses-Michigan.
Court-Houses-United States.
Court-Houses-United States-Conservation and
   Restoration.
Courtyards-United States-Bibliography.
Covent Garden, London.
Coventry Cathedral.
Covered Bridges.
Cram, Ralph Adams, 1863-1942.
Cret, Paul Philippe, 1876-1945.
Croton-on-Hudson. N. Y. Van Cortlandt Manor.
Crypts-Lorraine.
Cubitt, Thomas, 1788-1855.
Curtain Walls.
Cyane (Sloop of War)
Dakin, James H.
Daland, John Tucker, 1795-1858.
Dallas-Buildings.
Dartington Hall, Totnes, Eng.
Decatur House, Washington, D.C.
Decatur, Stephen, 1779-1820.
Decision-Making in Architecture.
Delaware-Capital and Capitol.
Domes.
Dormitories--Designs and Plans.
Dover Castle.
Dunstaffnage Castle.
Dunster Castle.
Dwellings.
Dwellings-Case-Studies.
Dwellings-England-London Metropolitan Area-
   Designs and Plans.
Dwellings-Europe-Remodeling.
Dwellings-Ghana.
Dwellings--Gt. Brit.
Dwellings--Greece.
Dwellings-Illinois-Vermilion Co.
Dwellings-Lighting.
Dwellings-Netherlands.
Dwellings-New England.
Dwellings-North Carolina-Franklin Co.
Dwellings-Remodeling.
Earth Sheltered Houses.
Eclecticism in Architecture.
Eclecticism in Architecture-France.
Eclecticism in Architecture-United States.
Egyptian Revival (Architecture)-United States.
Eiffel Tower, Paris.
El Bersheh, Egypt-Tombs.
Electric Insulators and Insulating-Collectors and
   Collecting.
Electric Insulators and Insulation-Collectors and
   Collecting.
Electric Insulators and Insulation-Catalogs.
Electric Insulators and Insulation-Prices.
Electric Power-Plants-Connecticut-Design and
   Construction.
Electronic Data Processing-Architectural Design.
Electronic Data Processing-Architectural Practice.
Electronic Data Processing-Architecture.
Electronic Data Processing-Architecture-
   Bibliography.
Electronic Data Processing-Arts.
Electronic Data Processing-Museums.
Ellwood, Craig.
Engineering--Rome.
Engineering Design.
Engineering Schools-Buildings.
Engineers -- Legal Status, Laws, Etc. -- U.S.
England. Architecture.
Environmental Engineering (Buildings)
Epiphanius, Monastery of.
Escorial.
Exeter Cathedral.
Facades.
Facades-Great Britain.
Facades-New York (City)
Factories.
Factories-- Design and Construction.
Farm Buildings.
Farm Buildings-U.S.
Farmhouses.
Farmhouses--England.
Farmhouses-United States.
Fences.
Florence. Bigallo.
Florence. Campanile.
Florence-Fountains.
Florence. San Giovanni (Baptistery)
Florence. San Miniato Al Monte (Church)
Florence. Santa Maria Del Fiore (Cathedral)-
   Juvenile Literature.
Florence. Santa Trinita (Church)
Florida. University, Gainesville. Dept. of
   Architecture.
Follies.
Forde Abbey.
Fort Lauderdale, Fla. Second Presbyterian
   Church.
Fortification.
Fortification-America-History-Exhibitions.
Fortification-United States-History.
Fountains.
Fountains-France.
Fratta Polesine, Italy. Villa Badoer.

ART, MODERN–19TH AND 20TH CENTURIES

Barber, Philip, 1946-
Barchus, Eliza Rosanna, 1857-1959.
Barker, Alfred Charles, 1819-1873.
Barlow, Francis, 1626?-1702.
Barnabe, Duilio, 1914-1961.
Barnes, Albert Coombs, 1872-1951.
Barnes, Burt, 1872-1947.
Barnet, Will, 1911-
Barnsley, Ernest, 1863-1926.
Bartlett, John Russell, 1805-1886.
Baskin, Leonard, 1922-
Battiss, Walter, 1906-
Baudelaire, Charles Pierre, 1821-1867.
Bauer, John Albert, 1882-1918-Juvenile Literature.
Bauer, Marius Alexander Jacques, 1864-1932.
Bauer, Rudolf, 1889-1953.
Baumeister, Will, 1889-1955.
Bayer, Herbert, 1900-
Beal, Jack, 1931-
Beals, Jessie Tarbox.
Bearden, Romare, 1914-
Beaux, Cecilia, 1863-1942.
Bechtle, Robert, 1932-
Beck, Rosemarie.
Beckmann, Max, 1884-1950.
Beeler, Joe.
Bell, Clive, 1881-1964.
Bell, Vanessa Stephen, 1874-1961.
Bellows, George Wesley, 1882-1925.
Bender, Albert Maurice, 1866-1941.
Benitez Sanchez, Jose, 1938-
Bennett, Paul A., 1897-1966.
Benson, John Howard, 1901-1956.
Benton, Thomas Hart, 1889-1975.
Benziger, August, 1867-1955.
Berard, Christian, 1902-1949.
Berkowitz, Leon, 1919-
Berman, Eugene, 1899-1972.
Bernaldo, Allan T., 1900-
Berthon, Paul, 1872-1909.
Bertini, Aldo.
Bertini, Gianni, 1922-
Bertrand, Raymond.
Bevan, Robert, 1865-1925.
Bianconi, Piero, 1899-
Biehn, Betty.
Bietry-Salinger, Jehanne.
Biggers, John Thomas, 1924-
Bill, Max, 1908-
Binder, Joseph, 1898-1972.
Bireline, George, 1923-
Bischof, Werner Adalbert, 1916-1954.
Bishop, Bernice Pauahi, 1831-1884-Portraits, Etc.
Bishop, Isabel, 1902-
Bissier, Julius, 1893-1965.
Blackman, Charles Raymond. 1928-
Blaine, Nell, 1922-
Blakelock, Ralph, Albert, 1847-1919.
Block, Leigh B., 1905- -Art Collections.
Bloedel, Lawrence Hotchkiss, 1902-1976-Art Collections.
Bloom, Hyman, 1913-
Bluemner, Oscar, 1867-1938.
Bluhm, Norman, 1920-
Boccioni, Umberto, 1882-1916.
Bochner, Mel, 1940-
Boehm, Edward Marshall, 1912-
Boehm, Edward Marshall, 1913-1969.
Boer, Saskia De, 1945-
Bok, Hannes, 1914-1964.
Bollinger, James Wills, 1867-
Bolotowsky, Ilya, 1907-
Bonheur, Rosa, 1822-1899.
Bonheur, Rosa, 1822-1899-Juvenile Literature.
Bonnard, Pierre, 1867-1947.
Boonzaier, Gregoire, 1909-
Booth, Franklin, 1874-1948.
Borein, Edward, 1872-1945.
Borglum, John Gutzon De la Mothe, 1867-1941.
Borglum, Solon Hannibal, 1868-1922.
Botero, Fernando, 1932-
Boubat, Edouard, 1923-
Bouguereau, William Adolphe, 1825-1905.
Bourdelle, Emile Antoine, 1861-1929.
Bourke-White, Margaret, 1906-1971.
Bourke-White, Margaret, 1906-1971-Juvenile Literature.
Boyd, Guy Martin a Beckett, 1923-
Boydell, John, 1719-1804.
Boynton, Ray, 1883-1951.
Brach, Paul, 1924-
Brackman, Robert, 1898-
Bradley, Will H., 1868-1962.
Brady, James, 1928-
Brady, Mathew B., 1823 (Ca.)-1896.
Brady, Mathew B., 1823 (Ca.)-1896-Juvenile Literature.
Brancusi, Constantin, 1876-1957.
Brandegee, Robert Bolling, 1849-1922.
Braque, Georges, 1882-1963.
Brasher, Rex, 1869-1960.
Braynard, Frank Osborn, 1916-
Brendel, Otto, 1901-1973.
Breton, Andre, 1896-1966.
Brevoort, James Renwick, 1832-1918.
Bricher, Alfred Thompson, 1837-1908.
Britt, Peter, 1819-1905.
Brock, 1912-
Broderson, Morris, 1928-
Brooks, James, 1906-
Brown, Ford Madox, 1821-1893.
Brown, Joan, 1938-
Brown, Oliver Madox, 1855-1874.
Browne, Hablot Knight, 1815-1882.
Brumidi, Constantine, 1805-1880.
Brun Charles Frederic, D. 1871.
Brush, George De Forest, 1855-1941.
Bryant, Harold, 1894-1950.
Bryce, David, 1803-1876.
Buell, Abel, 1742-1882.
Bufano, Beniamino, 1898-1970.
Buffet, Bernard, 1928-
Bulfinch, Charles, 1763-1844.
Bunker, Dennis Miller, 1861-1890.
Bunny, Rupert Charles Wulsten, 1864-1947.
Burchfield, Charles Ephraim, 1893-1967.
Burford, Byron, 1920-
Burne-Jones, Edward Coley, Sir, Bart., 1833-1898.
Burnham, Daniel Hudson, 1846-1912.
Burns, William, 1921-1972.
Burr, George Elbert, 1859-1939.
Burri, Alberto, 1915-
Butler, Howard Russell, 1856-1934.
Butler, Maude Kimball, 1880-
Buttersworth, James Edward, 1817-1894.
Bye, Ranulph, 1916-
Cage, John -- Bibl.
Caldecott, Randolph, 1846-1886.
Calder, Alexander Milne, 1846-1923.
Calder, Alexander, 1898-1976.
Callahan, Kenneth, 1905-
Callender, Bessie (Stough) 1889-1951.
Calvert, Edward, 1799-1883.
Cameron, Julia Margaret Pattle, 1815-1879.
Camesi, Gianfredo, 1940-
Candedo, Eulogio,1924-
Cantor, B. Gerald, 1916- -Art Collections.
Capa, Robert, 1913-1954.
Caparn, Rhys, 1909-
Capp, Al, 1909-
Cardew, Michael, 1901-
Cardew, Michael, 1901- -Addresses, Essays, Lectures.
Carles, Arthur B., 1882-1952.
Carlisle, George James Howard, 9th Earl of, 1843-1911.
Carlson, George, 1940-
Carmean, Hary, 1922-
Caro, Anthony, 1924-
Carpenter, James, 1949- -Exhibitions.
Carrier-Belleuse, Albert Ernest, 1824-1887.
Carriere, Eugene, 1849-1906.
Carter, Jimmy, 1924-
Cartier, Edd, 1914-
Carvalho, Solomon Nunes, 1815-1897.
Cassatt, Mary, 1844-1926.
Casson, Alfred Joseph, 1898-
Castelfranco, Giorgio, 1896-
Catherwood, Frederick.
Catlin, George, 1796-1872.
Caulfield, Patrick, 1936-
Cecchi. Emilio, 1884-
Cesnola, Luigi Palma Di, 1832-1904.
Cezanne, Paul, 1839-1906-Addresses, Essays, Lectures.
Chagall, Marc, 1887-
Champney, Benjamin, 1817-1907.
Chang, Ta-Chien, 1899-
Channon, Howard.
Chapman, Conrad Wise, 1842-1910.
Charles, Prince of Wales, 1948-
Charlot, Jean, 1898-
Chase, John Churchill.
Chase, William Merritt, 1849-1916.
Chateauneuf, Alexis De, 1799-1853.
Chen, Chi, 1912-
Chenavard, Paul Marc Joseph, 1807-1895.
Chesney, Lee, 1920- -Exhibitions.
Chi, Pai-Shih, 1861-1957.
Chillida, Eduardo, 1924-
Chirico, Giorgio De, 1888-
Christo, 1935-
Christy, Howard Chandler, 1873-1952-Exhibitions.
Chryssa, Varda, 1933-
Chumley, John, 1928-
Chun, Soo Ja, 1942-
Church, Frederick Edwin, 1826-1900.
Church, William, 1779-1863.
Cisneros, Jose, 1910-
Citron, Minna, 1896-
Ciurlionis, Mikalojus Konstantinas, 1875-1911.
Cizek, Franz, 1865-
Clark, Bill, 1926-
Clark, Kenneth McKenzie, Baron Clark, 1903-
Clark, Russell, 1905-1966.
Claypoole, Johnny.
Cleland, Thomas Maitland, 1880-1964.
Cloar, Carroll.
Clough, Prunella, 1919-
Clymer, John, 1907-
Cober, Alan E.
Coburn, Alvin Langdon, 1882-1966.
Cockburn, James Pattison, 1779?-1847.
Codman, Ogden.
Cogswell, Arthur Edward, 1858-1934.
Cole, Thomas, 1801-1848.
Colin, Paul, 1892- -Catalogs.
Coll, Joseph Clement, 1881-1921.
Collins, Jess.
Collins, Paul.
Colman, Samuel.
Combs, Ann, 1935-
Computer Animation.
Computer Art.
Computer Art-Exhibitions.
Computer Drawing.
Computer Graphics.
Conceptual Art.
Conceptual Art-Addresses, Essays, Lectures.
Conceptual Art-Exhibitions.
Conceptual Art-United States.
Conceptual Art-United States-Addresses, Essays, Lectures.
Conde, Miguel.
Conder, Charles, 1868-1909.
Conlon, William, 1941-
Connard, Philip, 1876-1958.
Conner, Bruce.
Constable, John, 1776-1837.
Constructivism.
Constructivism (Art)
Constructivism (Art)-Addresses, Essays, Lectures.
Constructivism (Art)-Exhibitions.
Constructivism (Art)-History.
Constructivism (Art)-Russia-Catalogs.
Cooke, Jean, 1927-
Coomaraswamy, Ananda Kentish, 1877-1947-Addresses, Essays, Lectures.
Cooper, Ron, 1943-
Cooper, Thomas Sidney, 1803-1902.
Copy Art-United States-Addresses, Essays, Lectures.
Corne, Michele Felice, 1752-1845.
Cornell, Joseph.
Cornwell, Dean, 1892-1960.
Corot, Jean Baptiste Camille, 1796-1875.
Coughtry, John Graham, 1931-
Counihan, Noel, 1913-
Courbet, Gustave.
Courbet, Gustave, 1819-1877.
Couture, Thomas, 1815-1879.
Coye, Lee Brown.
Crane, Walter, 1845-1915.
Cropsey, Jasper Francis, 1823-1900.
Crosby, Percy Leo, 1891-1964.
Cruikshank, Isaac, 1756?-1811?
Cruise, Boyd.
Cubism.
Cubism-Exhibitions.
Cubism-Paris-History.
Cumming, Charles Atherton, 1858-1932.
Currey, Thomas Lane, 1922-
Curtis, Philip C.
Czobel, Bela, 1883-
Dadaism.
Dadaism-Addresses, Essays, Lectures.
Dadaism-Berlin-Exhibitions.
Dadaism-History-Sources.
Daingerfield, Elliott, 1859-1932.
Dali, Salvador, 1904-
Danby, Francis, 1793-1861.
Danby, Ken, 1940-
Dantan, Jean Pierre, 1800-1869.
Darley, Felix Octavius Carr, 1822-1888.
Daubigny, Charles Francois, 1817-1878.
Daumier, Honore Victorin, 1808-1879.
Davies, Arthur B.
Davies, Ken, 1926-
Davis, Gene, 1920-
Davis, Ronald, 1937-
Davis, Stuart, 1894-
Day, Worden, 1916-
Dayez, Georges, 1907-
De Creeft, Jose.
De Forest, Lockwood, 1850-1932.
De Forest, Roy, 1930-
De Grazia, Ted Ettore, 1909-Portraits, Etc.
De Kooning, Willem, 1904-
De Morgan, William Frend, 1839-1917.
De Wint, Peter, 1784-1849.
Decamps, Alexandre Gabriel, 1803-1860.
Degas, Hilaire Germain Edgar, 1834-1917.
DeGrazia, Ted Ettore, 1909-
Delacroix, Eugene, 1798-1863.
Delaroche, Hippolyte, Called Paul, 1797-1856.
Delaunay, Robert, 1885-1941.
Delaunay, Sonia.
Deming, Edwin Willard, 1860-1942.
Demuth, Charles, 1883-1935.
Denes, Agnes.
Denny, Robyn, 1930-
Derain, Andre, 1880-1954.
Design, Industrial.
Design, Industrial-Addresses, Essays, Lectures.
Design, Industrial-Australia.
Design, Industrial-Exhibitions.
Design, Industrial-Finland.
Design, Industrial-Great Britain.
Design, Industrial-Italy.
Design, Industrial-Juvenile Literature.
Design, Industrial-Pictorial Works.
Design, Industrial-Social Aspects-Congresses.
Design, Industrial-Study and Teaching-Directories.
Design, Industrial-Study and Teaching-Great Britain-Congresses.
Design, Industrial-United States.
Design, Industrial-United States-History.
Design, Industrial-Vocational Guidance.
Design, Industrial--Yearbooks.
Dessau Bauhaus.
Dexter, Henry, 1806-1876.
Dickinson, Edwin Walter, 1891-
Die Brucke (Dresden)
Diebenkorn, Richard, 1922-
Diehl, Gaston.
Dine, James 1935-
Dinnerstein, Harvey.
Dixon, Maynard, 1875-1946.
Dodgson, Campbell, 1867-1948.
Doesburg, Theo Van, 1883-1931.
Dombrowski, Ernest, Ritter Von, 1896-
Domestic Animals-U.S.-Pictorial Works.
Domjan, Joseph, 1907-
Domjan, Jozsef, 1907-
Domsaitis, Pranas, 1880-1965.
Dongen, Kees Van, 1877-1968.
Dore, Gustave, 1832-1883.
Dorflinger, Hans, 1941-
Dorner, Alexander, 1893-1957.
Doughty, Thomas, 1793-1856.
Douglass, Frederick, 1817?-1895.
Dove, Arthur Garfield, 1880-1946.
Doxiades, Konstantinos Apostoiou, 1913-
Dozier, Otis, 1904-
Drake, Gordon, 1917-1952.
Drexel, Francis Martin, 1792-1863.
Du Tilleux, Jean, 1903-
Dubuffet, Jean, 1901-
Duchamp, Marcel, 1887-1968.
Duchamp-Villon, Raymond, 1876-1918.
Dufy, Raoul, 1877-1953.
Dulac, Edmund, 1882-1953.
Durand, Asher Brown, 1796-1886.
Durieux, Caroline, 1896-
Duveen, Joseph Duveen, Baron, 1869-1939.
Duveneck, Frank, 1848-1919.
Dwiggins, William Addison, 1880-1956.
Dzubas, Friedel, 1915-.
Eakins, Thomas, 1844-1916.
Eastlake, Charles Lock, Sir, 1793-1865.
Eastlake, Charles Lock,E 1833-1906-Influence.
Eastman, George, 1854-1932.
Eastman, Seth, 1808-1875.
Eaton, Norman, 1902-1966.
Eddy, Oliver Tarbell, 1799-1868.
Edmonds, Francis William, 1806-1863.
Edmondson, William, 1883?-1951.
Edoart, Augustin Amant Constance Fidele. 1789-1861.
Edward VIII, King of Great Britain, 1894-
Eggenhofer, Nicholas, 1897.
Eichenberg, Fritz, 1901-
Eichholtz, Jacob, 1776-1842.
Eickemeyer, Rudolf, 1862-1932.
Eide, Palmer, 1906-
Eilshemius, Louis Michwel, 1864-1941.
Electronic Data Processing-Arts.
Eliot, Charles, 1859-1897.
Elizabeth II, Queen of Great Britain, 1926-
Ellsworth, Clarence, 1885-1961.
Ellsworth, James Sanford, 1802-1873 Or 4.
Embry, Norris, 1921-
Emerson, Peter Henry, 1856-1936.
Emerson, William Ralph, 1833-1917.
Emmons, Chansonetta Stanley, 1858-1937.
England-Social Life and Customs-1945- -Pictorial Works.
England-Social Life and Customs-20th Century-Pictorial Works.
English Literature--Selections: Extracts, Etc.
English Literature-19th Century-History and Criticism.
Enneking, John J., 1841-1916.
Ensor, James Baron, 1860-1949.
Environment (Art)-Exhibitions.
Environments (Art)-Exhibitions.
Epstein, Jacob, Sir, 1880-1959.
Erickson, Carl Ebert, 1899-1966.
Ericson, Augustus William, 1848-1927.
Ernst, Max, 1891.
Escher, Maurits Cornelis, 1898-1971.
Etook, Tivi, 1928-
European War, 1914-1918-Art and the War.
European War, 1914-1918-Pictorial Works.
European War, 1914-1918-Posters.
European War, 1914-1918-Posters-Exhibitions.
Evans, Bob, 1947-
Evans, Garth, 1934-
Evans, Walker, 1903-1975.
Evenepoel, Henri Jacques Edouard, 1872-1899.
Evergood, Philip, 1901-
Eyerly, Ray, 1894-
Ezekiel, Moses, Sir, 1844-1917.
Faberzhe, Karl Gustavovich, 1846-1920.
Fabian, Stephen E., 1930-
Fairbanks, Avard Tennyson, 1897-
Fairlie, Reginald, 1883-1952.
Fales, Douglas A., 1929-
Farnsworth, Lizzie Amelia, 1865-1941.
Farny, Henry Francois, 1847-1916.
Faulkner, Barry, 1881-1966.

Kollwitz, Kathe (Schmidt) 1867-1945.
Konti, Isidore, 1862-1938.
Krakel, Dean Fenton, 1923-
Krans, Olof, 1838-1916.
Kranz, Kurt.
Krebs, Patsy, 1940-
Krebs, Rockne, 1938-
Krenkel, Roy G., 1918-
Krimpen, Jan Van, 1892-1958.
Kruse, Werner, Fl. 1959-
Kubin, Alfred, 1877-1959.
Kuhn, Walt. 1877-1949.
Kuniyoshi, Yasuo, 1893-1953.
Kupka, Frantisek, 1871-1957.
Kurelek, William, 1927-
Kurokawa, Noriaki, 1934-
La Farge, John, 1835-1910.
Laboureur, Jean Emile, 1877-1943.
Lachiase, Gaston, 1882-1935.
Ladell, Edward, 1821-1886.
Lafever, Minard.
Lalique, Rene, 1860-1945.
Land, Edwin Herbert, 1909-
Landsberger, Franz, 1883-1964-Bibliographhy.
Landseer, Edwin Henry, Sir, 1802-1873.
Lane, Fitz Hugh, 1804-1865.
Lane, Hugh Perry, Sir, 1875-1915.
Lang, Gerhard, 1916-
Lapinski, Tadeusz, 1928-
Larcher, Jean, 1947-
Lardera, Berto, 1911-
Larsson, Carl Olof, 1853-1919.
Larsson, Carl Olof, 1853-1919-Juvenile Literature.
Lasansky, Mauricio, 1914-
Lasers-Congresses.
Lasers in Art.
Lassaw, Ibram, 1913-
Last, Clifford, 1918-
Latham, John, 1921-
Laurence, Sydney, 1868-1940.
Laurencin, Marie, 1885-1956.
Laurens, Henri, 1885-1954.
Lawrence, David Herbert, 1885-1930.
Lawrence, Jacob, 1917-
Lawrence, Thomas, Sir, 1796-1830.
Lax, David, 1910-
Le Brocquy, Louis, 1916-
Le Pautre, Antoine,1614-1691.
Lea, Tom, 1907-
Leach, Bernard Howell, 1887-
Lear, Edward, 1812-1888.
Lear, Edward, 1812-1888-Juvenile Literature.
Lebenstein, Jan, 1930-
Ledivelec, Madeleine.
Lee, Arthur Tracy, D. 1879.
Lee-Johnson, Eric, 1908-
Lee, Russell, 1903-
Leech, John, 1817-1864.
Leetag, Edgar William, 1904-1953.
Leger, Fernand, 1881-1955.
Lehmbruck, Wilhelm, 1881-1919.
Leigh, William Robinson, 1866-1955.
Leighton, Clare, 1899-
Leighton, Clare, 1899- -Exhibitions.
Leighton, Frederic Leighton, Baron, 1830-1896.
Lelooska, 1934-
Leslie, Alfred, 1927-
Lessing, Carl Friedrich, 1808-1880.
LeVan, Susan, 1947-
Levine, David, 1926-
Levy, Benjamin, 1786-1860.
Lewis, Martin, 1881-1962.
Lewis, Wyndham, 1862-1957.
Lewitt, Jan, 1907-
Lewitt, Sol, 1928-
Leyendecker, J. C., 1874-1951.
Liardet, Wilbraham Frederick Evelyn, 1799-1878.
Lichtenstein, Roy, 1923-
Lilien, Ephraim Mose, 1874-1925.
Lincoln, Abraham, Pres. U. S., 1809-1865.
Lincoln, Abraham, Pres. U. S., 1809-1865-Assassination.
Lincoln, Abraham, Pres. U. S., 1809-1865-Autographs.
Lincoln, Abraham, Pres. U. S., 1809-1865-Bibliography-Catalogs.
Lincoln, Abraham, Pres. U. S., 1809-1865-Iconography.
Lincoln, Abraham, Pres. U. S., 1809-1865-Quotations.
Lindner, Richard, 1901-
Lindsay, Norman, 1879-1969.
Lindsay, Sir Daryl, 1890-
Lissim, Simon, 1900-
Lloyd, Reginald J., 1926-
Locke, William M., 1894-1972.
Locker, Thomas, 1937-
Loewy, Raymond Fernand, 1893-
Longo, Vincent, 1923-
Looby, Keith Ronald, 1940-
Loos, Adolf, 1870-1933.
Loudon, John Claudius, 1783-1843.
Louis, Morris, 1912-1962.
Love, Jim, 1927-
Lovet-Lorski, Boris, 1894-
Low, Will Hicok, 1853-1932.
Lowry, Laurence Stephen, 1887-1976.
Luiken, Jan, 1649-1712.
Lukacs, Gyorgy, 1885-1971.
Luks, George Benjamin, 1867-1933.
Lutyens, Edwin Landseer, Sir, 1869-1944.
Luxardo Girolamo, S.P.A.
McAdoo, Donald, 1929-
McBey, James, 1883-1959.
McCarthy, Frank C., 1924-
McClusky, John, 1914-
McCurdy, John Derrickson, 1940-1974.
MacDonald, Angus Snead, 1883-1961.
MacDonald, Thoreau, 1901-
McGowan, Harold, 1909-
McGrew, Ralph Brownell, 1916- -Exhibitions.
McGugan, Ian, 1932-
Machetanz, Frederick, 1908-
MacIver, Loren, 1909-
Macke, August, 1887-1914.
Mackennal, Edgar Bertram, Sir, 1863-1931.
McKenzie, Robert Tait, 1867-1938.
McKim, Charles Follen, 1847-1909.
Mackintosh, Charles Rennie, 1868-1928.
Mackintosh, Charles Rennie, 1868-1928-Catalogs.
McLaren, Norman, 1914-
McLaughlin, John, 1898-
McManus, James W., 1942-
McMurtry, John, 1812-1890.
Macpherson, Duncan Ian, 1924-
Maekawa, Kunio, 1905-
Magritte, Rene, 1898-1967.
Maillol, Aristide Joseph Bonaventure, 1861-1944.
Maison, K. E.
Makowski, Tadeusz, 1882-1932.
Maldarelli, Oronzio, 1892-
Maler, Leopoldo, 1937-
Malone, Blondelle Octavia Edwards, 1877-1951.
Man, Felix H., 1893-
Manessier, Alfred, 1911-
Manet, Edouard, 1832-1883.
Manet, Edouard, 1832-1883-Catalogs.
Mangold, Robert, 1937-
Manguin, Henri, 1874-1949.
Manning, Reg, 1905-
Mansbendel, Peter, 1883-1940-Exhibitions.
Manzu, Giacomo, 1908-
Marc, Franz, 1880-1916.
Marden, Brice, 1938-
Marini, Marino, 1901-
Mark, Mary Ellen, 1940-
Marks, Saul, 1905-1974.
Marsh, Reginald, 1898-1954.
Marshall, John, 1936-
Marston, William Moulton, 1893-1947.
Martienssen, Rex Distin, 1905-1942.
Martin, Agnes, 1912-
Martin, Fletcher, 1904-
Martin, Fred, 1927-
Martin, John, 1789-1854.
Martin, Keith, 1911- -Exhibitions.
Martin, Paul, 1864-1944.
Martinez, Xavier, 1869-1943.
Marx, Karl, 1818-1883.
Marx, Robert Burle, 1909-
Masereel, Frans, 1889-1972.
Mason, Benjamin Franklin, 1804-1871.
Masson, Andre, 1896-
Mastroianni, Umberto, 1910-
Mathews, Alfred Edward, 1831-1874.
Mathieu, Georges, 1921-
Matisse, Henri, 1869-1954.
Matta Echaurren, Roberto Sebastian, 1911-
Matthews, John, 1933-
Mauzey, Merritt, 1898-
Maverick, Peter, 1780-1881.
Maxwell, John, 1905-1962.
Mears, Norman B., 1904-
Meegeren, Han Van, 1889-1947.
Meier, Richard, 1934-
Meissner, Kurt, 1909-
Melchers, Gari, 1860-1932.
Melnikov, Konstantin Stepanovich, 1890-
Mendelsohn, Erich, 1887-1953.
Mercer, Henry Chapman, 1856-1930.
Meryon, Charles, 1821-1868.
Meszaros, Andor, 1900-1972.
Michael, Marjorie M., 1920-
Michalczyk, Casimer, 1914-
Michelson, Leo, 1887-.
Mies Van der Rohe, Ludwig, 1886-1969-Bibliography.
Miley, Michael, 1841-1918.
Millais, John Everett, Sir, Bart., 1829-1896.
Millares, Manolo, 1926-1972.
Miller, Kenneth Hayes, 1876-1952.
Milles, Carl, 1875-1955.
Millet, Jean Francois, 1814-1875.
Mills, Donald, 1896-
Mills, Robert, 1781-1855.
Milne, David Browne, 1882-1953.
Milton, Peter, 1930- -Exhibitions.
Minimal Art-Addresses, Essays, Lectures.
Minimal Art-Exhibitions.
Minkkinen, Arno Rafael, 1945-
Minter, Marilyn, 1948-
Minton, John, 1917-1957.
Miro, Joan, 1893-
Mocsanyi, Paul.
Modotti, Tina, 1896-1942.
Moholy-Nagy, Laszlo, 1895-1946.
Molas.
Molas-Exhibitions.
Molinari, Guido, 1933-
Monachesi, Sante, 1910-
Mondriaan, Pieter Cornelius, 1872-1944.
Monet, Claude, 1840-1926.
Monnier, Henri Bonaventure, 1799-1877.
Monticelli, Adolphe, 1824-1886.
Moon, Jeremy, 1943-1973.
Moon, Michael, 1937-
Moore, Bruce, 1905-
Moore, Charles Herbert, 1840-1960.
Moore, Gary E., 1942-
Moore, Henry Spencer, 1898-
Moran, Thomas, 1837-1926.
Morandi, Giorgio, 1890-1964.
Morassi, Antonio, 1892-
Moreau, Gustave, 1826-1898.
Morgan, Julia, 1872-1957.
Morgan, Peter, 1951-
Morison, Stanley, 1889-1967.
Morison, Stanley, 1889-1967-Bibliography.
Morris, Carl.
Morris, Jane Burden.
Morris, Robert, 1931-
Morris, Thomas Francis, 1852-1898.
Morris, William, 1834-1896.
Morris, William, 1834-1896-Exhibitions.
Morrison, George, 1919-
Morrison, George, 1919-Juvenile Literature.
Morrow, Stanley J., 1843-1921.
Morse, Samuel Finley Breese, 1791-1872.
Morse, Samuel Finley Breese, 1791-1872-Juvenile Literature.
Mosaics-Beverly Hills, Calif.-Catalogs.
Moses, Anna Mary (Robertson) 1860-1961.
Moses, Anna Mary (Robertson) 1860-1961-Juvenile Literature.
Moses, Robert, 1888-
Mother Lode (The Phrase)
Mount, William Sidney, 1807-1868.
Moustakas, Evangelos, 1930-
Mucha, Jiri, 1915-
Muller, Jan. 1922-1958.
Mullins, Patricia, 1952-
Multiple Art-Exhibitions.
Munakata, Shiko, 1903-1975.
Munch, Edvard, 1863-1944-Catalogs.
Munsell, Joel, 1808-1880.
Murphy, Gerald, 1888-1964.
Muybridge, Eadweard, 1830-1904.
Nabi.
Nadelman, Elie, 1882-1946.
Nahl, Charles, 1818-1878.
Namatjira, Albert, 1902-1959.
Nampeyo, Daisy Hooee, 1910- -Juvenile Literature.
Nash, Paul, 1889-1946.
Nason, Thomas Willoughby, 1889-
Nast, Thomas, 1840-1902.
Natkin, Robert, 1930-
Nauman, Bruce, 1941-
Negre, Charles, 1820-1880.
Neillot, Louis, 1898-
Neiman, LeRoy, 1927-
Neizvestnyi, Ernest, 1926-
Neo-Impressionism (Art)
Nesbitt, Lowell, 1933-
Nesch, Rolf, 1893-
Nevelson, Louise, 1900-
New York School.
Newhall, Beaumont, 1908-
Newman, Arnold, 1918-
Newman, Barnett, 1905-1970.
Nicholson, Ben, 1894-
Niemeyer Soares, Oscar, 1907-
Nimschke, Louis Daniel, 1832-1904.
Niven, Thornton MacNess, 1806-1895.
Noguchi, Isamu, 1904-
Noguchi, Isamu, 1904-Juvenile Literature.
Nolan, Sidney, 1917-
Noland, Kenneth, 1924-
Nolde, Emil, 1867-1956.
Norman, Henry C., 1850-1913.
Nowicki, Matthew, 1910-1950.
Ochikubo, Tetsuo, 1923-
Ofek, Avraham, 1935-
Ogata, Korin, 1658-1716.
O'Keefe, Georgia, 1887-
Oldenburg, Claes, 1929-
O'Leary, Dennis, 1945-
Oliveira, Nathan, 1928-
Olmstead, Frederick Law, 1822-1903.
Olmstead, Frederick Law, 1822-1903-Archives.
Olmstead, Frederick Law, 1822-1903-Collected Works.
Olmstead, Frederick Law, 1822-1903-Juvenile Literature.
Olovson, Gudmar, 1936-
O'Neill, Rose Cecil, 1874-1944.
Oppenheim, Moritz, D. 1882.
Oprescu, George, 1881-
Orozco, Jose Clemente, 1883-1949.
Orphism (Art)-France-Paris.
Orr, Chris, 1943-
Osbourne, Lloyd, 1868-1947.
Ossorio, Alfonso, 1916-
Otto, Frei, 1925-
Overstreet, Joe.
Ozenfant, Amedee, 1886-1966.
Page, William 1811-1885.
Palmer, Frederick, 1944-
Palmer, Samuel, 1805-1881.
Paolozzi, Eduardo, 1924-
Paris. Salon.
Park, David, 1911-1960.
Parker, Raymond, 1922-
Parks, Charles C., 1922-
Parrish, Maxfield, 1870-1966.
Pascin, Jules, 1885-1930.
Patchen, Kenneth, 1911-1972.
Patri, Giacomo, 1898-
Paulson, Ronald, Comp.
Pavia, Phillip.
Paxson, E. S., 1852-1919.
Peake, Mervyn Laurence, 1911-1968-Biography.
Peale, Sarah Miriam, 1800-1885.
Pearce, Bryan.
Pearson, John, 1934-
Peck, Sheldon, 1797-1868.
Peiffer-Watenphul, Max, 1896-1976.
Peladan, Josephin, 1859-1918.
Penelon, Henri, 1827?-1885.
Peploe. Samuel John, 1871-1935.
Perates, John.
Perceval, John, 1923-
Perez, Luis, 1934-
Perret, Auguste, 1874-1954.
Petersen, Christian, 1884 or 5-1961.
Petri, Friedrich Richard.
Pfahl, Charles Alton, 1946-
Philipson, Robin.
Phillips, Coles, 1880-1927.
Phillips, Duncan, 1886-1966.
Phillips, Harry, 1911-
Picabia, Francis, 1879-1953.
Picasso, Pablo, 1881-1973.
Pippin, Horace, 1888-1946.
Pissarro, Lucien, 1863-1944.
Plamondon, Antoine, Ca.1802-1895.
Platner, Warren, 1919-
Polasek, Albin, 1879-1965.
Pollak, Max.
Polland, Don, 1932-
Pollock, Jackson, 1912-1956.
Pop Art.
Pop Art-England-Exhibitions.
Pop Art -- Exhibitions.
Pop Art-Gt. Brit.
Pope, Arthur, 1880-
Porter, Arthur Kingsley, 1883-1933.
Porter, Katherine, 1941-
Porter, Rufus, 1792-1884.
Posada, Jose Guadalupe, 1852-1913.
Potter, Beatrix, 1866-1943.
Potter, Beatrix, 1866-1943-Biography.
Pousette-Dart, Richard, 1916-
Powers, Asamel, 1759-1841.
Powers, Hiram, 1805-1873.
Pozzatti, Rudy, 1925-
Prang, Louis, 1824-1909.
Prassinos, Mario, 1916-
Project Apollo in Art.
Prudhomme, Edward C.
Puccinelli, Raimondo, 1904-
Pugh, Clifton Ernest, 1924-
Pugin, Augustus Welby Northmore, 1812-1852.
Purcell, Roy, 1936-
Pushkin, Aleksandr Sergeevich, 1799-1837.
Puy, Jean, 1876-1960.
Puzinas, Paul, 1907-1967.
Pyle, Howard, 1853-1911.
Pyne, William Henry, 1769-1843.
Quaytman, Harvey, 1937-
Quinn, John, 1870-1924.
Quinn, Wayne, 1941-
Radford, Albert, 1862-1904.
Ramirez, Eduardo, 1923-
Ramos, Mel, 1935-
Ranney, William, 1813-1857.
Rathbone, Perry Townshend, 1911-
Rauschenberg, Robert, 1925-
Raverat, Gwendolen Mary Darwin, 1885-1957.
Ray, Man, 1890-1976.
Raymond, Antonin, 1888-
Reaugh, Frank, 1860-1945.
Reder, Bernard, 1897-
Redon, Odilon, 1840-1916.
Redoute, Pierre Joseph, 1759-1840.
Rees, Lloyd Frederic, 1895-
Reid, Neel, 1885-1926.
Reinhardt, Adolph Frederick.
Reiss, Winold, 1886-1953.
Rejlander, Oscar Gustav, 1813-1875.
Remington, Frederic, 1861-1909.
Renoir, Auguste, 1841-1919.
Renoir, Auguste, 1841-1919. Full Name: Georges Albert Edouard De Traz.
Reynal, Jeanne, 1903-
Reynard, Grant T., 1887-1968.
Rice, David Talbot, 1903-1972.
Richards, Ceri, 1903-1971.
Richards, William Trost, 1833-1905.
Richardson, Henry Hobson, 1838-1886.
Richardson, Sam, 1934-
Richardson, Sam, 1934- -Exhibitions.
Richier, Xavier, 1922-
Rietveld, Gerrit Thomas, 1888-1964.
Rifesser, Joseph, 1921-
Riis, Jacob August, 1849-1914.
Riley, Bridget, 1931-
Rimmer, William, 1816-1879.
Ritman, Louis, 1889-1963.
Rivera, Diego, 1886-1957.

Zavaro, Albert, 1925-
Zemach, Margot-Juvenile Literature.
Zerbe, Jerome, 1904-
Zerbe, Karl, 1903-
Zigrosser, Carl, 1891-
Zimmerman, John, 1927-
Zogbaum, Wilfrid, 1915-1965.
Zox, Larry, 1936-

ART, PREHISTORIC
Adena Culture.
Akenfield.
Alabama--Antiq.
Altamira Site, Mexico.
Altar De Sacrificios Site, Guatemala.
Amapa Site, Mexico.
Amasis, 6th Cent. B. C.
America--Antiquities.
Amistad Reservoir Region-Antiquities.
Arizona -- Antiq.
Arkansas--Antiq.--Yearbooks.
Armin a West Site, Egypt.
Art, Maya.
Art-Mesopotamia.
Art-Meuse Valley.
Art, Prehistoric.
Art, Prehistoric-Africa, Southern.
Art, Prehistoric-Australia.
Art, Prehistoric-Dictionaries.
Art, Prehistoric-Europe.
Art, Prehistoric-Exhibitions.
Art, Prehistoric-Greece, Modern.
Art, Prehistoric-History.
Art, Prehistoric-Juvenile Literature.
Big Bean Site, Ill.
Big Horn Basin-Antiquities.
Big Horn Co., Mont.-Antiquities.
Black Partizan Site.
Blain Site.
Bowen Site, Ind.
Bronze Age.
Bronze Age-Aegean Sea Region.
Bronze Age-England.
Bruce Co., Ont. -- Antiq.
Buffalo Site, W. Va.
Caddo Parish, La. -- Antiq.
Cameron Creek Village Site, N.M.
Casas Grandes, Site, Mexico.
Cascade Range-Antiquities.
Casper Site, Wyo.
Central America--Antiq.
Chalchuapa, Salvador-Antiquities.
Chavin, Peru.
Chihuahua, Mexico-- (State)--Antiq.
China-Antiquities.
Christian Antiquities.
Cirencester, Eng.-Antiquities-Addresses, Essays, Lectures.
Cohonina Culture.
Colorado -- Antiq. -- Addresses, Essays, Lectures.
Colorado -- Antiq. -- Collected Works.
Colorado--Antiq.--Collections.
Columbia River Valley--Antiq.
Copan, Honduras.
Dead Sea Scrolls-Juvenile Literature.
Death Valley, Calif.--Antiq.
El Bersheh, Egypt-Tombs.
En Medio Shelter, N.M.
Evolution-Pictorial Works.
Excavations (Archaeology)-Colorado.
Excavations (Archaeology)-Egypt.
Excavations (Archaeology)--Florida.
Excavations (Archaeology)-Oklahoma-McCurtain Co.
Excavations (Archaeology)--Utah.
Excavations (Archaeology) -- Utah -- Sevier Co.
Fire Heart Creek Site.
Grant Lake Site, N.W.T.
Grayson Site, Calif.
Herzog Site, Wash.
Ibaugh Site.
Iron Gate Site.
Jeffers Petroglyph Site, Minn.
John Ischy Site.
Kaminaljuyu, Guatemala-Addresses, Essays, Lectures.
Kaminaljuyu, Guatemala-Antiquities-Addresses, Essays, Lectures.
Karnak, Egypt.
Kentucky--Antiq.
Kentucky -- Antiqu. -- Bibl.
Kerkeosiris, Egypt.
Kermah, Sudan-Antiquities.
Khmers--Antiq.
Kodiak, Alaska--Antiq.
Kyle Site.
La Roche Site.
LAn-2 Site.
Latin America-Antiquities.
Lindenmeier Site, Colo.
Little Tennessee River Watershed-Antiquities.
Livingston Co., N. Y.--Antiq.
London-Antiquities.
London-Antiquities-Addresses, Essays, Lectures.
Louisiana--Antiq.
Mai-Chi Shan Caves.
Man, Prehistoric--England--Derbyshire.
Man, Prehistoric-Siberia, Western.

Man, Prehistoric-Tools-Addresses, Essays, Lectures.
Marion County, Tenn.-Antiquities.
Martha's Vineyard, Mass.-Antiquities.
Martime Province, Siberia--Antiq.
Maskwa River Site, Man.
Megalithic Monuments-Ireland.
Michigan. Northern Peninsula--Antiq.
Mississippian Culture.
Missouri -- Antiq.
Mogollon Culture.
Murlo, Italy-Antiquities.
Napata Site, Sudan.
Near East-Antiquities-Pictorial Works.
Paleography. English.
Paleography, German.
Paleography, Greek.
Paleography-Handbooks, Treatises, Etc.
Paleography, Italian.
Paleography, Latin.
Paleontology-Pictorial Works.
Peck Village Site, La.
Pecos, N.M.
Peru--Antiq.
Peru--Antiq.--Juvenile Literature.
Petroglyphs.
Petroglyphs-California.
Petroglyphs-Klamath Valley.
Petroglyphs-North Dakota.
Petroglyphs-Saudi Arabia.
Picture-Writing, Indian.
Picture-Writing, Indian-Exhibitions.
Projectile Points-Prices-United States.
Qasr-E Ab U Nasr Site, Iran.
Sakkara-Antiquities.
Sakkara-Tombs.
Salinas De los Nueve Cerros Site, Guatemala.
Seibal Site, Guatemala.
Southern States--Antiq.
Southwest New--Antiq.
Spiro Mound.
Spiro Site, Okla.
Stele (Archeology)
Stonehenge.
Tamaulipas, Mexico--Antiq.
Tehuacan Valley--Antiquities.
Tepexi El Viejo Site, Mexico.
Tlapacoyan, Mexico (Mexico)--Antiq.
Tonala Ruin, Mexico.
Tula De Allende, Mexico-Antiquities-Addresses, Essays, Lectures.
Underwater Archaeology.
United States--Antiquities.
United States-Antiquities-Addresses, Essays, Lectures.
United States-Antiquities-Bibliography.
United States-Antiquities-Collection and Preservation.
United States-Antiquities-Collection and Preservation-Congresses.
United States-Antiquities-Congresses.
U.S.-Antiquities.
Washington (State)--Antiquities.
Wenos Creek Site, Wash.
West Virginia-Antiq.

ART, PRIMITIVE
Afo-A-Kom (Statue)
Africa-Social Life and Customs.
Apache Indians-Art.
Art, Abelam (New Guinea Tribe)-Exhibitions.
Art--Africa.
Art--Africa, South.
Art-Africa, Sub-Saharan.
Art-Africa, West.
Art-Africa, West-Addresses, Essays, Lectures.
Art, African.
Art, African--History.
Art, African--Juvenile Literature.
Art, African-Catalogs.
Art, African-Exhibitions.
Art, African-History.
Art, Amlash.
Art, Amlash -- Exhibitions.
Art-Arnhem Land, Australia.
Art, Australian (Aboriginal)
Art, Australian (Aboriginal)-Congresses.
Art, Australian (Aboriginal)-Exhibitions.
Art, Australian (Aboriginal)-Kimberley, Western Australia (Division)
Art-Benin, Nigeria (Province)-Bibliography.
Art, Cameroon-Exhibitions.
Art-Central Asia.
Art, Chilean.
Art, Dogon.
Art, East African.
Art-Easter Island-History.
Art, Fan (African People)-Exhibitions.
Art. -- Hartford -- Catalogs.
Art, Hausa-Exhibitions.
Art, Liberian-Exhibitions.
Art, Maori.
Art, Massim (Melanesian People)
Art, Melanesian-Exhibitions.
Art-Melbourne-Catalogs.
Art, Mende-Exhibitions.
Art, Negro.
Art -- New Guinea.
Art--Nigeria.

Art-Northwest, Pacific.
Art Objects--Benin, Nigeria (Province)
Art Objects-Benin City, Nigeria.
Art-Oceania.
Art-Oceania-Exhibitions.
Art-Pagan, Burma.
Art--Papua.
Art, Parthian.
Art, Primitive.
Art, Primitive--Addresses, Essays, Lectures.
Art, Primitive--Catalogs.
Art, Primitive-Africa.
Art, Primitive-Africa, West.
Art, Primitive-Africa, West-Exhibitions.
Art, Primitive-America.
Art, Primitive-America.
Art, Primitive-Benin, Nigeria (Province)
Art, Primitive-Congresses.
Art, Primitive-Exhibitions.
Art, Primitive-New Ireland (Island)
Art, Primitive-Oceanica.
Art, Primitive-Papua-New Guinea (Ter.)
Art, Primitive-Sepik Valley.
Australian Aborigines-New South Wales-Antiquities.
Bambara Tribe-Rites and Ceremonies.
Benin City, Nigeria.
Benin City, Nigeria-Antiquities.
British Guiana-Antiquities.
Cahokia Mounds, Ill.
Cherokee Indians-Industries.
Cheyenne Indians-Art.
Chichen Itza, Mexico.
Chippewa Indians.
Chippewa Indians-Juvenile Literature.
Cliff-Dwellings-Colorado-Mesa Verde.
Crazy Horse, Ogala Indian, 1842 (Ca.)-1877-Juvenile Literature.
Dakota Indians-Art-Exhibitions.
Elema (Papuan People)-Religion.
Eskimos-Alaska.
Eskimos-Alaska-Art.
Eskimos-Alaska-Art-Exhibitions.
Eskimos-Art.
Eskimos-Art-Catalogs.
Eskimos-Art-Directories.
Eskimos-Art-Exhibitions.
Eskimos-Canada.
Eskimos-Canada-Pictorial Works.
Eskimos-Pictorial Works.
Ethiopian Magic Scrolls.
Ethnology-Africa, West-Juvenile Literature.
Ethnology-New Guinea-Pictorial Works.
Ethnology-Oceania-Exhibitions.
Ethnology-Polynesia.
Ethnology Polynesia--Exhibitions.
Fan (African People)
Fiji Islands--Antiq.
Florida-Antiquities.
Hopi Indians-Art.
Hopi Indians-Art-Exhibitions.
Hopi Indians-Biography.
Hopi Indians-Biography-Juvenile Literature.
Hopi Indians-Painting.
Hopi Indians-Social Life and Customs-Pictorial Works.
Huichol Indians-Art-Exhibitions.
Indians--Art.
Indians-Art-Catalogs.
Indians-Art-Congresses.
Indians-Art-Exhibitions.
Indians of Central America-Collected Works.
Indians of Central America-Panama-Antiquities.
Indians of Central America-Panama-Art.
Indians of Central America-Panama-Chiriqui (Province)-Antiquities.
Indians of Central America-Panama-Cocle (Province)-Pottery-Pictorial Works.
Indians of Central America-Sculpture.
Indians of Mexico-Antiquities.
Indians of Mexico-Antiquities-Addresses, Essays, Lectures.
Indians of Mexico-Art.
Indians of Mexico-Art-Bibliography.
Indians of Mexico-Art-Congresses.
Indians of Mexico-Art-Exhibitions.
Indians of Mexico-Baja California.
Indians of Mexico-Baja California-Antiquities.
Indians of Mexico -- Congresses.
Indians of Mexico-Durango (State)-Implements.
Indians of Mexico-Veracruz-Art.
Indians of North America-Alabama-Antiquities-Exhibitions.
Indians of North America--Antiquities.
Indians of North America-Antiquities-Congresses.
Indians of North America-Arizona-Antiquities.
Indians of North America-Arizona-Grand Canyon-Antiquities-Collected Works.
Indians of North America-Art.
Indians of North America-Art-Bibliography.
Indians of North America-Art-Exhibitions.
Indians of North America-Art-Juvenile Literature.

Indians of North America-British Columbia-Antiquities.
Indians of North America-British Columbia-Art-Pictorial Works.
Indians of North America-California-Alameda Co.-Antiquities.
Indians of North America-California-Antiquities.
Indians of North America-California-Fresno Valley-Antiquities.
Indians of North America-California-Glenn Co. -Antiquities.
Indians of North America-California-Marin Co.-Antiquities.
Indians of North America-California-Pictorial Works.
Indians of North America-California-Tuolumne Valley-Antiquities.
Indians of North America-Culture.
Indians of North America-Florida-Antiquities.
Indians of North America-Great Basin-Antiquities.
Indians of North America-Great Lakes Region-Art-Exhibitions.
Indians of North America-Great Plains-Art-Exhibitions.
Indians of North America-Great Plains-Art-Juvenile Literature.
Indians of North America-Great Plains.
Indians of North America-Great Plains-Art.
Indians of North America-Louisiana-Antiquities.
Indians of North America-Montana-Art.
Indians of North America-Montana-Art-Exhibitions.
Indians of North America-Nevada-Pictorial Works.
Indians of North America-New Mexico.
Indians of North America-New Mexico-Antiquities.
Indians of North America-New York (State)
Indians of North America-North Carolina-Antiquities.
Indians of North America-Northwest Coast of North America-Art.
Indians of North America-Northwest Coast of North America-Art-Catalogs.
Indians of North America-Northwest Coast of North America-Art-Exhibitions.
Indians of North America-Northwest Coast of North America-Art-Juvenile Literature.
Indians of North America-Northwest Pacific-Art.
Indians of North America-Northwest, Pacific-Pictorial Works.
Indians of North America-Pictorial Works-Exhibitions.
Indians of North America-Pictorial Works-Juvenile Literature.
Indians of North America-Pictorial Works.
Indians of North America-Southern States-Pictorial Works.
Indians of North America-Southwest, New-Art-Juvenile Literature.
Indians of North America-Southwest, New.
Indians of North America-Southwest, New-Art.
Indians of North America-Southwest, New-Arts.
Indians of North America-Southwest, New-Pictorial Works.
Indians of North America-Southwest, Old.
Indians of North America-Texas.
Indians of North America-Texas-Pictorial Works.
Indians of North America-The West.
Indians of North America-The West-Antiquities-Addresses, Essays, Lectures.
Indians of North America-Utah-Art.
Indians of South America-Brazil.
Indians of South America-Art.
Indians of South America-Ecuador-Antiquities.
Indians of South America-Peru.
Indians of South America-Peru-Art.
Indians of South America-Peru-Art-Exhibitions.
Indians of the West Indies-Antiquities-Bibliography.
Iron Age-India-South India.
Iroquois Indians-Art-Catalogs.
Isleta Indians-Art.
Kivas.
Kwakiutl Indians--Art--Exhibitions.
Lummi Indians-Art.
Masks.
Masks-Africa, Sub-Saharan-Catalogs.
Masks, African.
Masks, African-Africa, West.
Masks, African-Exhibitions.
Masks-Congo.
Masks-Exhibitions.
Masks-Japan.
Masks-Juvenile Literature.
Masks (Sculpture)
Mayas.
Mayas-Antiquities.
Mayas-Antiquities-Addresses, Essays, Lectures.
Mayas-Antiquities-Collections.
Mayas-Antiquities-Pictorial Works.
Mayas-Architecture.
Mayas-- Art.
Mayas-Art-Exhibitions.
Mayas-Kings and Rulers.
Mayas-Pottery.
Mayas-Pottery-Exhibitions.
Mayas-Sculpture.
Mayas-Writing.

CITY PLANNING AND BEAUTIFICATION

Havasupai Indians-Basket Making.
Home Workshops.
Hooking.
Ice Carving.
Indian Craft.
Indian Craft-Juvenile Literature.
Indians-Basket Making.
Indians of Mexico-Textile Industry and Fabrics.
Indians of North America-Alaska-Basket Making.
Indians of North America-Basket Making-
  Exhibitions.
Indians of North America-Basket Making.
Indians of North America-California-Basket
  Making-Exhibitions.
Indians of North America-Implements.
Indians of North America-Industries.
Indians of North America-Industries-Juvenile
  Literature.
Indians of North America-Leather Work.
Indians of North America-Northwest Coast of
  North America-Basket Making.
Indians of North America-Southwest, New-Basket
  Making.
Indians of North America-Southwest, New-Basket
  Making-Exhibitions.
Indians of North America-Southwest, New-
  Industries.
Indians of North America-Southwest, New-Textile
  Industry and Fabrics-Catalogs.
Indians of North America-Washington (State)-
  Basket Making.
Industrial Arts.
Industrial Arts-Early Works to 1800.
Industrial Arts-Examinations, Questions, Etc.
Industrial Arts-Juvenile Literature.
Industrial Arts-Study and Teaching.
Industrial Arts-Study and Teaching-Congresses.
Industrial Arts-Study and Teaching (Elementary)
Industrial Arts-Study and Teaching-Louisiana.
Industrial Arts-Study and Teaching (Secondary)-
  Maryland.
Industrial Arts-Study and Teaching (Secondary)-
  United States.
Industrial Arts-Study and Teaching-United States-
  Congresses.
Inkle Weaving.
Jewish Crafts.
Jig Saws.
Johnboats.
Katcinas.
Katcinas-Collectors and Collecting.
Kites.
Kites-Juvenile Literature.
Knitted Lace-Patterns.
Knitting.
Knitting-Bibliography.
Knitting-History.
Knitting-Juvenile Literature.
Knitting, Machine.
Knitting, Machine-Dictionaries.
Knitting-Patterns.
Knitting-Patterns-Indexes.
Knitting-Scandinavia-Patterns.
Knots and Splices.
Lace and Lace Making.
Lace and Lace Making-History.
Lace and Lace Making-Patterns.
Lace and Lacemaking.
Lathes.
Leather Carving.
Leather Industry and Trade-Bibliography-
  Catalogs.
Leather Work.
Leather Work-Juvenile Literature.
Looms.
Luggage.
Macaroni Craft-Juvenile Literature.
Machine Quilting.
Machine-Tools.
Macrame.
Macrame-Juvenile Literature.
Macrame-Patterns.
Manual Training.
Model Houses.
Modeling.
Modeling-Juvenile Literature.
Models and Model Making.
Models and Modelmaking.
Models and Modelmaking-Juvenile Literature.
Models and Modelmaking-- Period.
Models and Modelmaking-Periodicals-Indexes.
Models and Modelmaking--Radio Control
  Systems.
Mosaics-Handbooks, Manuals, Etc.
Mountain Artisans.
Nail Craft.
Nailsea Glassworks.
Nature Craft.
Nature Craft-Juvenile Literature
Needlepoint.
Needlepoint Lace.
Needlework.
Needlework Boxes-History.
Needlework-Dictionaries.
Needlework-Great Britain.
Needlework-Great Britain-History.
Needlework-History.
Needlework-Implements and Appliances-History.

Needlework, Jewish.
Needlework-Juvenile Literature.
Needlework-Miscellanea.
Needlework-Nova Scotia-Patterns.
Needlework-Patterns.
Needlework-Pennsylvania.
Needlework-Study and Teaching.
Needlework, Turkoman.
Needlework-United States.
Needlework-United States-History.
Needlework--Yearbooks.
Netting.
Netting-Juvenile Literature.
Origami.
Origami--Juvenile Literature.
Pairpoint Glass Works.
Palm Frond Weaving.
Papago Indians-Industries.
Paper Airplanes.
Paper Airplanes-Juvenile Literature.
Paper-Cutting, Japanese.
Paper Doll Making-Collected Works.
Paper Doll Making-Juvenile Literature.
Paper Dolls.
Paper-Exhibitions.
Paper Flowers.
Paper--Juvenile Literature.
Paper Making and Trade-Bibliography.
Paper Making and Trade-History-Bibliography.
Paper Toy Making-Juvenile Literature.
Paper Work.
Paper Work-China.
Paper Work--Juvenile Literature.
Paper Work-Study and Teaching (Elementary)
Paperboard.
Paperwork.
Papier-Mache.
Papier-Mache-Juvenile Literature.
Papier-Mache-Study and Teaching.
Party Decorations.
Patchwork.
Patchwork-Exhibitions.
Patchwork-Juvenile Literature.
Patchwork-Patterns.
Peanut Craft.
Peanut Craft-Juvenile Literature.
Penland School of Handicrafts, Penland, N.C.
Pet Supplies-Juvenile Literature.
Pewtercraft.
Pincushion Dolls-Collectors and Collecting.
Pincushions.
Pine Needle Crafts.
Pins and Needles.
Plaster Craft.
Plastic Foams.
Plastic Sculpture.
Plastics.
Plastics As Art Material.
Plastics Craft.
Plastics Craft-Juvenile Literature.
Plywood.
Pressed Flower Pictures.
Pressed Flower Pictures-Juvenile Literature.
Punched Work.
Puppet Craft.
Puppet Making.
Puppet Making-Juvenile Literature.
Puppets and Puppet-Plays.
Quilting.
Quilting-Canada-History.
Quilting-Kentucky.
Quilting-Patterns.
Quilting-Texas.
Quilting-United States.
Quilting-United States-Patterns.
Raffia Work.
Repairing-Amateurs' Manuals.
Reweaving.
Rock Craft.
Rock Craft-Juvenile Literature.
Rugs, Braided.
Rush-Work.
Salish Indians-Basket Making.
Samplers.
Samplers-Germany-Exhibitions.
Samplers-Lawrence, Kan.-Exhibitions.
Samplers-United States.
Sand Craft.
Saws.
Scrimshaw.
Sewing.
Sewing-Dictionaries.
Sewing-Equipment and Supplies-Catalogs.
Sewing-Study and Teaching.
Seymour, John, Cabinetmaker.
Seymour, Thomas, Cabinetmaker.
Shakers-Industries.
Shellcraft.
Shellcraft-Juvenile Literature.
Shells.
Siletz Indians-Basket Making.
Smocking.
Soft Toy Making.
Soft Toy Making-Juvenile Literature.
Spinning.
Sporting Goods.
Sprang.
Stone Implements.
Stone Implements-Congresses.
Straw Work.

Straw Work-Exhibitions.
String Craft.
String Craft-Juvenile Literature.
String-Figures.
String-Figures-Juvenile Literature.
Tanning-Juvenile Literature.
Tatting.
Tatting-Patterns.
Textile Craft-Juvenile Literature.
Textile Crafts.
Textile Crafts-Africa.
Textile Crafts-Bibliography.
Tie-Dyeing.
Tie-Dyeing-Juvenile Literature.
Tile Craft.
Tools--Hist.
Tools-Handbooks, Manuals, Etc.
Toy Making.
Toy Making-Amateurs' Manuals.
Trapunto.
Treenware.
Treenware-United States.
Turning.
Twinrocker Handmade Paper Mill.
Violin Makers-Biography.
Weavers-United States.
Weaving.
Weaving-Patterns.
Weeks and Gilson.
Whips.
Wire Craft.
Wire Craft-Juvenile Literature.
Wirecraft.
Wood.
Wood-Carvers-United States-Biography.
Wood-Carving.
Wood-Carving-Africa, West-Catalogs.
Wood-Carving, African-Catalogs.
Wood-Carving, American.
Wood-Carving, Asmat.
Wood-Carving-England.
Wood-Carving, English.
Wood-Carving-Juvenile Literature.
Wood-Carving-Karawari Region.
Wood-Carving, Maori.
Wood-Carving, Medieval-England-Winchester.
Wood-Carving, Primitive-History-Juvenile
  Literature.
Wood-Carving, Romanesque-Auvergne.
Wood-Carving-Technique.
Wood-Carving-Texas-Exhibitions.
Wood-Carving-United States.
Wood-Carving-Zambia.
Wood-Carvings, American.
Wood Finishing.
Wood-Handbooks, Manuals, Etc.
Wood-Work.
Wooden Toy Making.
Woodwork.
Woodwork--Amateurs' Manuals.
Woodwork-Bibliography.
Woodwork-Dictionaries.
Woodwork-Handbooks, Manuals, Etc.
Woodwork-Japan.
Woodwork-Kentucky.
Woodwork (Manual Training)
Woodwork (Manual Training)-Juvenile Literature.
Woodwork (Manual Training)-Pictorial Works.
Woodwork-New England.
Woodwork-Study and Teaching.
Woodworking Tools.
Woodworking Tools-Catalogs.
Woodworking Tools-Dictionaries.
Woodworking Tools-History.
Workbenches.
Workshop Receipts.
Workshops.
Workshops--Equipment and Supplies.
Workshops-Designs and Plans.
Wreaths.

HISTORY OF ART
see Art History (General)

ILLUSTRATION
Animal Painting and Illustration.
Animal Painting and Illustration-Juvenile
  Literature.
Arabian Nights-Illustrations.
Archaeological Illustration.
Barbier, George.
Beardsley, Aubrey Vincent, 1872-1898.
Beardsley Limner.
Becca, R. G.
Bicycles and Tricycles-Posters.
Biological Illustration.
Biological Specimens-Collection and Preservation.
Biology in Art.
Biology-Laboratory Manuals.
Birds.
Birds-Addresses, Essays, Lectures.
Birds-Caricatures and Cartoons.
Birds-Dictionaries.
Birds-Habits and Behavior.
Birds in Art.
Birds-Juvenile Literature.
Birds-North America.
Birds-North America-Exhibitions.
Birds-Pictorial Works.
Birds-Pictorial Works-Juvenile Literature.

Birds-Pictures, Illustrations, Etc.
Birds-Tropics-Pictorial Works.
Blair, Robert, 1699-1746-Illustrations.
Blake, William, 1757-1827 -- Religion and Ethics.
Blake, William, 1757-1827--Dictionaries, Indexes,
  Etc.
Blake, William, 1757-1827. Illustrations to the
  Divine Comedy of Dante.
Botanical Illustration.
Botanical Illustration-Exhibitions.
Burroughs, Edgar Rice, 1875-1950-Illustrations.
Cats--Pictures, Illustrations, Etc.
Children's Literature-Illustrations-Juvenile
  Literature.
Chisholm Trail-Poetry.
Coleridge, Samuel Taylor, 1772-1834-Illustrations.
Crawford, Ralston, 1906-
Crests.
Crutchfield, William, 1932-
Crutis, Edward S., 1868-1952.
Darling, Jay Norwood, 1876-1962.
Davenport, Homer Calvin, 1867-1912.
Davis, Paul, 1938-
Denslow, William Wallace, 1856-1915.
Detmold, Edward Julius, 1883-1957.
Dickens, Charles--Illustrations.
Dickens, Charles, 1812-1870-Illustrations.
Drayton, John Grimke, 1815-1891.
Entomology.
Flowers-U.S.
Folk-Lore-China.
France--Soc. Life & Cust.--Illustrations.
France-Social Life and Customs.-Pictorial Works.
Frost, Robert, 1874-1963-Quotations.
Gladys English Memorial Collection of Original
  Illustrations for Children's Books.
Glaser, Milton.
Gorey, Edward St. John.
Gray, Thomas,1716-1771-Illustrations.
Greek Drama (Comedy) -- Illustrations.
Greenaway, Kate, 1846-1901.
Homerus. Ilias--Illustrations.
Horror Tales-Illustrations.
Horses-Pictures, Illustrations, Etc.
Illustrated Books.
Illustrated Books, Children's.
Illustrated Books, Children's-History and
  Criticism.
Illustrated Books-19th Century.
Illustrated Books-19th Century-Catalogs.
Illustrated Books--20th Cent.
Illustrated Periodicals.
Illustrated Periodicals-Indexes.
Illustration of Books
Illustration of Books-Addresses, Essays, Lectures.
Illustration of Books-Bibliography-Catalogs.
Illustration of Books-England.
Illustration of Books-England-Catalogs.
Illustration of Books-Exhibitions.
Illustration of Books-France.
Illustration of Books-Germany.
Illustration of Books-Great Britain.
Illustration of Books-Handbooks, Manuals, Etc.
Illustration of Books-History.
Illustration of Books-United States.
Illustration of Books-United States-Exhibitions.
Illustrators.
Illustrators, American.
Illustrators-Biography.
Illustrators-Biography-Dictionaries.
Illustrators, British.
Illustrators-Dictionaries.
Illustrators-England-Biography.
Illustrators-France-Biography.
Illustrators-Great Britain.
Illustrators-Great Britain-Correspondence.
Illustrators-United States.
Illustrators-United States-Biography.
Indians of North America-Pictures, Illustrations,
  Etc.
Knowles, Charles, 1939-1958.
Konica Camera.
Letter-Pictures.
Literature-Illustrations.
Love Poetry, American.
M Ah Abh Arata-Illustrations.
Magazine Illustration-England.
Martha's Vineyard, Mass.
Mathematical Recreations.
Milne, Alan Alexander, 1882-1956.
Mohawk Valley, N. Y.--Hist.--Revolution-Fiction.
Orchids-Indexes.
Ornithologists-South Africa-Biography.
Ornithologists-United States-Biography.
Ornithologists-United States-Juvenile Literature.
Oxford Almanac-Illustrations.
Picture-Books.
Picture-Books for Children.
Poets, English-19th Century-Biography.
Rackham, Arthur, 1867-1939.
Religions-Pictures, Illustrations, Etc.
The Saturday Evening Post-Illustrations.
Science Fiction-Illustrations.
Scientific Illustration.
Shakespeare, William, 1564-1616-Illustrations.
Sick Children-Juvenile Literature.

PHOTOGRAPHY

PICTORIAL HUMOR AND SATIRE

SCULPTURE

SUBJECT INDEX

Aalto, Alvar, 1898-1976.

AALTO, Alvar 1898-   720.9471
Alvar Aalto. [New York] Wittenborn [1963] 271p. illus., ports., plans (pt. col.) 24x29cm. German, French, and English. 63-25167 16.75
I. Title.

AALTO, Alvar, 1898-   720'.92'4
Alvar Aalto / [edited] by Karl Fleig. New York : Praeger Publishers, 1975, c1974. 208 p. : ill. ; 21 cm. Includes index. [NA1455.F53A239] 74-5568 ISBN 0-275-49660-0 : 10.00. ISBN 0-275-63610-0 pbk. : 4.95
1. Aalto, Alvar, 1898- I. Fleig, Karl, Architekt, ed.

AALTO, Alvar, 1898-   720'.924
Alvar Aalto, 1963-1970. [Editor: Karl Fleig. Translated by Henry A. Frey. New York, Praeger [1971] 248 p. illus. 24 x 29 cm. Published also in Zurich as Alvar Aalto, v. 2 (1971) Text and captions in English, French, and German. "Index of works, 1918-1971": p. 246-247. [NA1455.F53A218132] 73-158095 29.50
I. Fleig, Karl, Architekt, ed.

BORRAS, Maria Lluisa.   720.9471
Arquitectura finlandesa en Otaniemi: Alvar Aalto, Heikki Siren, Rema Pietila [Texto: Maria Lluisa Borras; fotos: Matti I. Jaatinen; seleccion y secuencia: J. Prats Valles. Barcelona. Ediciones Poligrafas 1967 or 8] Stamped on p. [7]: Amer. dist., Wittenborn, New York. 60p. 116 plates (pt. col.) 21cm. Spanish. English French and German. [NA1198.B6] 68-3067 15.00
1. Aalto Alvar, 1898- 2. Siren, Heikki, 1918- 3. Pietila, Reima, 1923- 4. Architecture—Otaniemi. I. Jaatinen, Matti II. Title.

GUTHEIM, Frederick   720.9471
Albert, 1908-
Alvar Aalto. New York, G. Braziller, 1960. 128 p. plates, ports., plans. 26 cm. (The Masters of world architecture series) Bibliography: p. 122-123. [NA1199.A2G8] 60-6080
1. Aalto, Alvar, 1898- I. Title. II. Series.

NEUENSCHWANDER, Eduard,   720.94895
1924-
Alvar Aalto and Finnish architecture [by] Eduard and Claudia Neuenschwander. London, Architectural Press; New York, Praeger [1954] 192p. illus., plans. 28cm. German, French, and English. Published also in Switzerland under title: Finnische Bauten. Batiments finnois. Atelier Alvar Aalto, 1950, 1951. [NA1193.M45 [NA1196.N45 1954b] 720. 9471 55-2530 55-2530
1. Aalto, Alvar, 1898- 2. Architecture—Finland. I. Neuenschwander, Claudia, 1927- joint author. II. Title.

NEUENSCHWANDER, Eduard,   720.94895
1924-
Finnish architecture, and Alvar Aalto [by] Ed. and Cl. Neuenschwander. New York, Praeger [1954] 192p. illus. plans. 28cm. (Books that matter) On spine: Ateller Alvar Aalto 1950/1951. German, French, and English. Published also in Switzerland under title: Finnische Bauten. Batlements finnois. Finnish buildings. Ateller Alvar Aalto, 1950, 1951. [NA1193.N45 1954a] [NA1193.N45 1954a] 720.9471 54-9527 54-9527
1. Aalto, Alvar, 1898- 2. Architecture—Finland. I. Neuenschwander, Claudia, 1927- joint author. II. Title.

PEARSON, Paul David,   720'.92'4 B
1936-
Alvar Aalto and the international style / by Paul David Pearson. New York : Whitney Library of Design, 1978. 240 p. : ill. ; 29 cm. Includes index. Bibliography: p. 236. [NA1455.F53A255] 77-20029 ISBN 0-8230-7023-9 : 27.50
1. Aalto, Alvar, 1898-1976. 2. International style (Architecture) I. Title.
Distributed by Watson Guptill.   **BIP**

Aalto, Alvar, 1898-1976— Bibliography,

MILLER, William   016.3092 s
Charles, 1945-
Alvar Aalto : a bibliography / William C. Miller. Monticello, Ill. : Council of Planning Librarians, 1976. 51 p. ; 28 cm. (Exchange bibliography - Council of Planning Librarians ; 1190) Cover title. [Z5942.C68 no. 1190] [Z8003.2] [NA1455.F5] 016.72'092'4 77-351345 pbk. : 5.00
1. Aalto, Alvar, 1898—Bibliography. I. Series: Council of Planning Librarians. Exchange bibliography ; 1190.   **BIP**

Aaron, Jesse J.

PURSER, Stuart R.   730'.92'4
Jesse J. Aaron, sculptor / by Stuart R. Purser ; drawings by the author. Gainesville, Fla. : Purser Publications, [1975] 28 p., 14 leaves of plates : ill. ; 24 cm. [NB237.A23P87] 74-15649
1. Aaron, Jesse J. I. Aaron, Jesse J. II. Title.

'Abbas I, the Great, Shah of Iran, 1571-1629—Art patronage.

WELCH, Anthony.   709'.55
Shah 'Abbas & the arts of Isfahan. [New York] The Asia Society; distributed by New York Graphic Society [Greenwich, Conn., 1973] 152 p. illus. (part col.) 29 cm. "An Asia House Gallery publication."

Catalogue of an exhibition shown at Asia House Gallery, New York, Oct. 11-Dec. 2, 1973, and Fogg Art Museum, Harvard University, Jan. 19-Feb. 24, 1974. Bibliography: p. 150-151. [N7287.183W44] 73-76938 ISBN 0-87848-041-2 19.95
1. 'Abbas I, the Great, Shah of Iran, 1571-1629—Art patronage. 2. Art, Iranian—Exhibitions. 3. Art, Islamic—Isfahan. I. Asia House Gallery, New York. II. Harvard University. William Hayes Fogg Art Museum. III. Title.   **BIP**

Abbett, Robert K.

ABBETT, Robert K.   759.13
The outdoor paintings of Robert K. Abbett / introd. by Gene Hill. Toronto ; New York : Peacock Press/Bantam Book, c1976. [95] p. : chiefly col. ill. ; 23 x 28 cm. [ND237.A18A53 1976] 76-7155
1. Abbett, Robert K. I. Title.

Abbey, Edwin Austin, 1852-1911.

ABBEY, Edwin Austin,   741.9'73
1852-1911.
Edwin Austin Abbey (1852-1911). An exhibition organized by the Yale University Art Gallery [and held at] Yale University Art Gallery, New Haven, Dec. 6, 1973-Feb. 17, 1974. Pennsylvania Academy of the Fine Arts, Philadelphia, Mar. 9-Apr. 14, 1974; [and] Albany Institute of History and Art, Albany, Sept. 6-Oct. 27, 1974. [New Haven, Yale University Art Gallery, 1973] iiij, 112 p. illus. (part col.) 28 cm. Bibliography: p. 109-112. [N6537.A28Y24] 73-87154 5.50 (Pbk.)
1. Abbey, Edwin Austin, 1852-1911. I. Yale University. Art Gallery. II. Pennsylvania Academy of the Fine Arts, Philadelphia. III. Albany Institute of History and Art.

Abbey, John Roland, 1896- —Library.

ALEXANDER, Jonathan   016.091'0945
James Graham.
The Italian manuscripts in the library of Major J. R. Abbey, by J. J. G. Alexander and A. C. De la Mare. New York, Praeger [1969] xliv, 187 p. facsims., 86 plates (incl. facsims.; 6 col.) 32 cm. A catalogue of 63 MSS. dating from the early 12th to the late 16th century. Includes bibliographies. [Z6623.A39 1969b] 69-15589 40.00
1. Abbey, John Roland, 1896- —Library. 2. Manuscripts—Catalogs. I. De la Mare, Albinia Catherine, joint author. II. Title.

Abbey, Rita Deanin.

†ABBEY, Rita Deanin.   759.13
Rivertrip / Rita Deanin Abbey ; foreword

---

by Frank Waters. 1st ed. Flagstaff, Ariz. : Northland Press, 1976, c1977 69 p. : ill. (some col.) ; 24 x 31 cm. [ND1839.A18A55] 77-371305 ISBN 0-87358-152-0 : 14.95
1. Abbey, Rita Deanin. 2. Colorado River in art. 3. Colorado River—Poetry. 4. Poetry of places—Colorado River. I. Title.   **BIP**

Abbeys—England.

COOK, Olive   726.70942
English abbeys and priories. Text by Olive Cook. 136 pictures in photogravure by Edwin Smith, with 2 ground plans, 11 engravings, and 4-colour plates. New York, Viking Press [1960] 62p. Bibl.: p.61. plates (part col.) map, plans 31cm. (A Studio book) 60-50995 12.00
1. Abbeys—England. 2. Priories—England. 3. Church architecture—England. I. Smith, Edwin, photographer. II. Title.

Abbreviations, Greek.

OIKONOMIDES, Al N., comp.   481'.7
Abbreviations in Greek inscriptions : papyri, manuscripts, and early printed books : a manual / compiled by Al. N. Oikonomides. Chicago : Ares Publishers, 1974. ix, 204 p. ; 24 cm. On spine: Greek abbreviations. Contents.Contents.—Avi-Yonah, M. Abbreviations in Greek inscriptions.—Kenyon, F. G. Abbreviations and symbols in Greek papyri.—Allen, T. W. Abbreviations in Greek manuscripts.—Von Ostermann, G. F. and Giegengack, A. E. Abbreviations in early Greek printed books. Includes bibliographical references. [Z111.O54] 75-302478
1. Abbreviations, Greek. I. Title. II. Title: Greek abbreviations.

Abbreviations, Latin.

CHASSANT, Alphonse Antoine   413
Louis, 1808-1907.
Dictionnaire des abreviations latines et francaises usitees dans les inscriptions lapidaires et metalliques, les manuscrits et les chartes du Moyen Age. 5. ed. New York, B. Franklin [1973] p. Reprint of the 1884 ed. published by J. Martin, Paris. [Z111.C48 1973] 73-3365 ISBN 0-8337-0547-4 16.50
1. Abbreviations, Latin. 2. Abbreviations, French. 3. Paleography. I. Title.

Abby Aldrich Rockefeller Folk Art Collection, Williamsburg, Va.

ABBY Aldrich   709'.73'07401554252
Rockefeller Folk Art Collection, Williamsburg, Va.
The Abby Aldrich Rockefeller Folk Art

Collection : a gallery guide / by Beatrix T. Rumford. Williamsburg, Va. : The Collection, c1975. 31 p. : col. ill. ; 26 cm. Bibliography: p. 30-31. [NK807.A35 1975] 75-36926 ISBN 0-87935-033-4 : 2.00
1. Abby Aldrich Rockefeller Folk Art Collection, Williamsburg, Va. 2. Folk art—United States—Catalogs. I. Rumford, Beatrix T.

ABBY Aldrich Rockefeller Folk Art Collection, Williamsburg, Va. 708.155'4252
American folk art from the Abby Aldrich Rockefeller Folk Art Collection. [Catalogue. Rev. ed.] Williamsburg,Va. [1966] 47 p. illus. (part col.) 24 cm. Originally issued as the catalogue of a traveling exhibition arranged in cooperation with the American Federation of Arts. [NK460.W46A63 1966] 66-23513
1. Abby Aldrich Rockefeller Folk Art Collection, Williamsburg, Va. 2. Folk art—Exhibitions. I. Title.

Abdell, Douglas, 1947—

ABDELL, Douglas, 1947- 730'.92'4
The sculpture of Douglas Abdell : January 14th to February 5th, 1977, Andrew Crispo Gallery, New York. New York : The Gallery, c1977. [32] p. : ill. ; 26 cm. [NB237.A26A52] 76-52293
1. Abdell, Douglas, 1947- I. Andrew Crispo Gallery. II. Title.

Abeita, Jim.

ABEITA, Jim. 759.13
The American Indians of Abeita : "his people" / introd. by Joseph Stacey ; special dedication and song by Johnny Cash. 1st U.S. ed. Scottsdale, Ariz. : Rick Tanner Publications, c1976. [72] p. : all col. ill. ; 30 cm. [ND237.A23A43 1976] 76-27119
1. Abeita, Jim. 2. Navaho Indians—Portraits. 3. The West in art. I. Title.

Aberdeen Art Gallery, Aberdeen, Scot.

ABERDEEN Art Gallery, Aberdeen, Scot. 759.2'074'0941235
Catalogue : oil paintings, water colours, drawings, sculpture / Aberdeen Art Gallery. 3d ed. [Aberdeen, Scot.] : The Gallery, 1950. 84 p. ; 21 cm. [N1185.A53 1950] 75-319377
1. Aberdeen Art Gallery, Aberdeen, Scot. 2. Art—Aberdeen, Scot.—Catalogs.

Abigail Adams Smith Mansion, New York (City)

COLONIAL Dames of America. 974.7'1'03
The Abigail Adams Smith house. New York [1968] 16 p. illus. (part col.), facsims., col. ports. 21 cm. Cover title. Text about the house by Mrs. George F. B. Johnson, Jr. Text about the garden by Mrs. Madison H. Lewis and Mrs. L. Whittington Gorham. Includes bibliographical references. [F128.8.A2C6] 68-29091
1. Abigail Adams Smith Mansion, New York (City)

Abraham Lincoln Birthplace National Historic Site.

PETERSON, Gloria. 973'.074'016971
An administrative history of Abraham Lincoln Birthplace National Historic Site, Hodgenville, Kentucky. [Washington] Division of History, Office of Archeology and Historic Preservation, 1968. 107 l. illus. 26 cm. Bibliography: leaf 107. Bibliographical footnotes. [E457.32.P43] 73-601791
1. Abraham Lincoln Birthplace National Historic Site. I. Title.

Abrams, Maida—Art collections.

ROBINSON, Franklin Westcott. 741.9492
Selections from the collection of Dutch drawings of Maida & George Abrams; a loan exhibition [by Franklin W. Robinson] Wellesley, Mass., Wellesley College Museum, 1969. xi, [132] p. illus. 22 cm. Cover title: Dutch drawings from the Abrams collection. Catalog of an exhibition held at Hopkins Center art galleries, Dartmouth College, Hanover, N.H., March 27-April 28, 1969; and at other museums. [NC261.R6] 78-77279
1. Abrams, Maida—Art collections. 2. Abrams, George—Art collections. 3. Drawings, Dutch—Exhibitions. I. Dartmouth College. Hopkins Center. II. Wellesley College. Jewett Arts Center. III. Title. IV. Title: Dutch drawings from the Abrams collection.

STERLING and Francine Clark Art Institute, Williamstown, Mass. 741.9'492
Things of this world; a selection of Dutch drawings from the Collection of Maida and George Abrams. Williamstown [1973] 67 p. illus. 21 cm. Catalog of an exhibition held at the Institute, Oct. 31, 1972-Feb. 25, 1973. "This is the second catalogue of drawings selected from the collection of Maida and George Abrams; all entries have been written by the students under the supervision of professor Franklin W. Robinson." Includes bibliographical references. [NC261.S74] 73-160648
1. Abrams, Maida—Art collections. 2. Abrams, George—Art collections. 3. Drawings, Dutch—Exhibitions. I. Robinson, Franklin Westcott. II. Title.

Abstract expressionism.

ALDEN, Richard, 1942- 709'.04
Abstract expressionism / by Richard Alden. [State College, Pa.?] : Alden, c1976. 8 p. ; 28 cm. Cover title. Includes bibliographical references. [N7432.5.A2A73] 76-8796
1. Abstract expressionism. I. Title.

Abstract expressionism—Exhibitions.

INTERIOR vision; European abstract expressionism, 1945-1960. 759.06 [Santa Barbara, Calif., Santa Barbara Museum of Art, 1972] [36] p. illus. 28 cm. Exhibition held March 25 to May 18, 1972, at the Santa Barbara Museum of Art. Bibliography: p. [8] [ND196.A25I57] 72-82205
1. Abstract expressionism—Exhibitions. 2. Abstract expressionism—Europe. 3. Painting, Modern—20th century—Europe. I. Santa Barbara, Calif. Museum of Art.

Abstract expressionism—San Francisco.

MCCHESNEY, Mary Fuller. 759.194'61
A period of exploration, San Francisco, 1945-1950. [Oakland, Calif.] Oakland Museum, Art Dept. [1973] 87 p. illus. 22 x 34 cm. [N6535.S3M32] 73-176054
1. Abstract expressionism—San Francisco. 2. Art, Modern—20th century—San Francisco. I. Title.

Abstract expressionism—United States—Exhibitions.

HOBBS, Robert Carleton, 1946- 759.13'074'014771
Abstract expressionism, the formative years / by Robert Carleton Hobbs and Gail Levin. Ithaca, N.Y. : Herbert F. Johnson Museum of Art, Cornell University, c1978. 140 p. : ill. (some col.) ; 28 cm. "Published in conjunction with an exhibition organized by the Herbert F. Johnson Museum of Art and the Whitney Museum of American Art." Includes bibliographical references. [ND212.5.A25H63] 77-29204 ISBN 0-87427-017-0 : 7.50
1. Abstract expressionism—United States—Exhibitions. 2. Painting, American—Exhibitions. 3. Painting, Modern—20th century—United States—Exhibitions. 4. Painters—United States—Biography. I. Levin, Gail, 1948- joint author. II. Herbert F. Johnson Museum of Art. III. Whitney Museum of American Art, New York. IV. Title.

Abstract expressionism—U.S.—History.

SANDLER, Irving, 1925- 759.13
The triumph of American painting; a history of abstract expressionism. New York, Praeger [1973, c1970] xv, 301 p. illus. (part col.) 31 cm. (Praeger paperbacks, P388) Bibliography: p. 281-298. [ND212.5.A25S2] 75-124607 9.95 (pbk.)
1. Abstract expressionism—U.S.—History. I. Title. BIP

Abstract impressionism.

MOISE, William S. 751.4
The taste of color, a touch of love; the creative world of abstract impressionism, by William S. Moise. [Hancock, Me., 1970] iii, 72 p. illus. (part col.), port. 23 x 25 cm. [ND196.A25M6] 76-18013
1. Abstract impressionism. I. Title.

Abydos, Egypt.

SIMPSON, William Kelly. 913.32
The terrace of the great God at Abydos: the offering chapels of dynasties 12 and 13. New Haven, Peabody Museum of Natural History of Yale University, 1974. viii, 30 p., 84 plates. 35 cm. (Publications of the Pennsylvania-Yale Expedition to Egypt, no. 5) Includes bibliographical references. [DT73.A16S57] 73-88231 20.00
1. Abydos, Egypt. 2. Stele (Archaeology) 3. Tombs—Egypt. I. Title. II. Series: Pennsylvania-Yale Expedition to Egypt, 1961-1962. Publications, no. 5. BIP

Abydos, Egypt. Temple of Rameses I.

WINLOCK, Herbert Eustis, 1884-1950. 732'.8'0932
The temple of Rames[s]es I at Abydos. [New York] Arno Press, 1973. 54, 20 p. illus., 16 plates. 29 cm. Reprint of the 1921 ed. of Bas-reliefs from the temple of Rameses I at Abydos, published by the Metropolitan Museum of Art, New York, and issued as v. 1, pt. of the Papers of the Metropolitan Museum of Art; and of the 1937 ed. of The temple of Ramesses I at Abydos, published by the Metropolitan Museum of Art, New York, and issued as no. 5 of the Papers of the Metropolitan Museum of Art. Includes bibliographical references. [NB75.W53 1973] 75-168411 ISBN 0-405-02247-6 35.00
1. Abydos, Egypt. Temple of Rameses I. 2. Bas-relief. 3. Sculpture, Egyptian. I. Winlock, Herbert Eustis, 1884-1950. Bas-reliefs from the temple of Rameses I at Abydos. 1973. II. Title. III. Series: New York (City). Metropolitan Museum of Art. Papers v. 1, pt. 1 [etc.]

Academie des sciences, Paris. Description des arts et metiers.

COLE, Arthur Harrison, 1889- 745
The handicrafts of France as recorded in the Descriptions des arts et metiers 1761-1788. By Arthur H. Cole and George B. Watts. Boston, Baker Library, Harvard Graduate School of Business Administration [1952] 43 p. plates, port. 28 cm. (Publication of the Kress Library of Business and Economics, no. 8) Includes bibliographies. [NK947.C6] 52-10731
1. Academie des sciences, Paris. Description des arts et metiers. 2. Art industries and trade—France. I. Watts, George Byron, 1890- joint author. II. Title. III. Series: Harvard University. Graduate School of Business Administration. Baker Library. Kress Library of Business and Economics. Publication no. 8

Acoma Indians—Pottery—Exhibitions.

A Tribute to Lucy M. Lewis, Acoma potter / commentary by John E. Collins ; foreword by Frederick J. Dockstader. Fullerton, Calif. : Museum of North Orange County, c1975. 75 p. : ill. (some col.) ; 27 cm. "This catalog was published in conjunction with the Lucy M. Lewis show, September 27-November 30, 1975." Bibliography: p. 73. [E99.A16T75] 75-26373 738.3'7
1. Lewis, Lucy M.—Exhibitions. 2. Acoma Indians—Pottery—Exhibitions. 3. Pueblo Indians—Pottery—Exhibitions. 4. Indians of North America—Southwest, New—Pottery—Exhibitions. I. Lewis, Lucy M. II. Collins, John E. III. Museum of North Orange County.

Acoustic holography—Congresses.

ACOUSTIC imaging : cameras, microscopes, phased arrays, and holographic systems / edited by Glen Wade. New York : Plenum Press, c1976. xiv, 325 p. : ill. ; 24 cm. "Lectures on acoustical holography and imaging presented at the University of California in Santa Barbara, California, March, 1975." Includes bibliographical references and index. [TA1550.A26] 76-21 ISBN 0-306-30914-9 : 25.00 774
1. Acoustic holography—Congresses. I. Wade, Glen.

Acoustical materials.

AMERICAN Society for Testing Materials. 693.83
Symposium on acoustical materials, presented at the fifty-fourth annual meeting, American Society for Testing Materials, Atlantic City, N. J., June 22, 1951. Philadelphia [1952] 35 p. illus. 23 cm. (Its Special technical publication no. 123) Bibliography: p. 10. [TH1725.A6 1951] 52-4395
1. Acoustical materials. I. Title. II. Series.

RANNEY, Maurice William, 1934- 691'.9
Soundproof building materials, 1970 [by] M. W. Ranney. Park Ridge, N.J., Noyes Data Corp. [1970] vi, 217 p. illus. 28 cm. [TH1725.R36] 70-126127 ISBN 0-8155-0325-3 35.00
1. Acoustical materials. 2. Soundproofing. I. Title.

Action in art.

BRODATZ, Phil. 704.942
The human form in action and repose; a photographic handbook for artists [by] Phil Brodatz & Dori Watson. New York, Reinhold Pub. Corp. [1966] 1 v. (chiefly illus., photos.) 32 cm. [NC785.B7] 66-14432
1. Action in art. 2. Human figure in art. I. Watson, Dori, joint author. II. Title.

Actors—Caricatures and cartoons.

FRUEH, Alfred Joseph, 1880-1968. 741.5'973
Frueh on the theatre; theatrical caricatures, 1906-1962. Compiled, with an introd., by Maxwell Silverman; and with a pref. by Brendan Gill. [New York] New York Public Library, 1972. xvii, 108 p. illus. 28 cm. [NC1429.F78S54 1972] 72-83887 ISBN 0-87104-241-X 12.50
1. Actors—Caricatures and cartoons. I. Silverman, Maxwell, comp. II. Title. BIP

NERMAN, Einar, 1888- 741.5'9485
Caught in the act / by Nerman ; [selected] with foreword by Sandy Wilson. London : Harrap, 1976. 72 p. : chiefly ill. ; 23 cm. Includes index. [NC1629.N4A42 1976] 76-375280 ISBN 0-245-52981-0 : £2.95. ISBN 0-245-52950-0 pbk.
1. Actors—Caricatures and cartoons. 2. Actresses—Caricatures and cartoons. 3. Swedish wit and humor, Pictorial. I. Title.

Actors—Japan—Portraits.

SUZUKI, Juzo, 1919- 769'.924
Sharaku, translation by John Bester. [1st ed.] Tokyo, Palo Alto, Calif., Kodansha International [1968] 96 p. col. illus., ports. 27 cm. (Masterworks of ukiyo-e, 2) [NE1325.T65S9] 68-13740 unpriced
1. Toshusai Sharaku, fl. 1794. 2. Actors—Japan—Portraits. I. Title. II. Series. BIP

SUBJECT INDEX ADVERTISING CARDS—ENGLAND—YORKSHIRE—CATALOGS.

Actors—Portraits.

BASSHAM, Ben L. 770'.92'4 [B]
The theatrical photographs of Napoleon Sarony / by Ben L. Bassham. Kent, Ohio : Kent State University Press, c1978. p. cm. Bibliography: p. [TR140.S37B37] 78-4933 ISBN 0-87338-213-7 : 8.50
1. Sarony, Napoleon, 1821-1896. 2. Actors—Portraits. I. Title. BIP

Adam, Robert, 1728-1792.

ADAM, Robert, 1728-1792 720.942
The works in architecture of Robert and James Adam. Biog. tribute by John Swarbrick. London, A. Tiranti [Hollywood-by-the-Sea, Fla., Transatlantic, 1964] iv, 24p. plates, plans. 29cm. (Precepts in art, v.5) 61-34916 18.75
I. Adam, James, d. 1794 II. Swarbrick, John, 1879- III. Title. BIP

BEARD, Geoffrey W. 720'.92'4
The work of Robert Adam / Geoffrey Beard. New York : Arco, [1978] p. cm. [NA997.A4B4] 78-641 ISBN 0-668-04535-3 : 16.95
1. Adam, Robert, 1728-1792. 2. Neoclassicism (Architecture)—Great Britain. I. Adam, Robert, 1728-1792. II. Title. BIP

HARRIS, Eileen 749.22
The furniture of Robert Adam. London, A. Tiranti [dist. Hollywood-by-the-Sea, Fla.. Transatlantic, 1964, c.1963] viii, 110p. illus.; plates.s 19cm. (Chapters in art ser., v. 38) Bibl. 64-56194 12.00
1. Adam, Robert, 1728-1792. 2. Furniture, English. I. Title.

MUSGRAVE, Clifford. 749.22
Adam and Hepplewhite and other neo-classical furniture. [1st American ed.] New York, Taplinger Pub. Co. [1966] 223, [96] p. illus. (part col.) 26 cm. Bibliography: 175-178. [NK2542.A3M8 1966] 66-11302
1. Adam, Robert, 1728-1792. 2. Hepplewhite, George, d. 1786. 3. Furniture, English. I. Title.

ROWE, Robert, 1902- 739.23742
Adam silver, 1765-1795. [1 st American ed. New York Taplinger Pub. Co. [1965] 94 p. 97 plates (1 col.) 26 cm. (Faber monographs on silver) Bibliography: p. 89. [NK7143.R6] 65-20355
1. Adam, Robert, 1728-1792. 2. Silversmithing — Gt. Brit. — Hist. 3. Plate, English. I. Title. BIP

STILLMAN, Damie. 745.4'4924
The decorative work of Robert Adam. [1st American ed.] New York, Transatlantic Arts, 1966. viii, 119 p. illus., plans, 174 plates (1 col.) 26 cm. Bibliography: p. 57-58. [NK1535.A3S8 1966] 67-3495
1. Adam, Robert, 1728-1792. I. Title. BIP

YARWOOD, Doreen. 720'.924 B
Robert Adam. New York, Scribner [1970] x, 221 p. illus. 26 cm. Bibliography: p. 211-213. [NA997.A4Y3] 73-108198 7.95
1. Adam, Robert, 1728-1792.

Adams, Ansel Easton, 1902—

ADAMS, Ansel Easton, 1902- 779'.092'4
The portfolios of Ansel Adams / introd. by John Szarkowski ; [edited by Tim Hill]. Boston : New York Graphic Society, c1977. xii, 124 p. : chiefly ill. ; 28 cm. [TR654.A34] 77-71628 ISBN 0-8212-0723-7 : 19.50
1. Adams, Ansel Easton, 1902- 2. Photography, Artistic. I. Title. BIP

NEWHALL, Nancy (Wynne) 927.7
Ansel Adams. San Francisco, Sierra Club [1964, c1963- v. illus. (part fold.), ports. 35 cm. (Sierra Club exhibit format series, 7) Contents.Contents.—v. 1. The eloquent light. [TR140.A55N4] 63-23019
1. Adams, Ansel Easton, 1902- 2. Photography, Artistic. I. Sierra Club. II. Title: The eloquent light.

Adams, Earl C.—Art collections.

BAIRD, Joseph Armstrong. 704.94'9'978
The West remembered : artists and images, 1837-1973 : selections from the Collection of Earl C. Adams, exhibited at the Old Mint, San Francisco, June 16, 1973, through September 15, 1973, and the Santa Barbara Museum of Art, November 10 to January 6 / compiled by Joseph A. Baird, Jr. ; photos. by Armando Solis. San Francisco : California Historical Society, 1973. 88 p. : ill. (some col.) ; 27 cm. Includes index. Bibliography: p. 85-87. [N8214.5.U6B34] 75-318276
1. Adams, Earl C.—Art collections. 2. The West in art. 3. Art, Modern—19th century—Exhibitions. 4. Art, Modern—20th century—Exhibitions. I. Santa Barbara, Calif. Museum of Art. II. California Historical Society. III. Title.

Adams, Henry, 1838-1918.

SCHEYER, Ernst, 1900- 709.24 B
The circle of Henry Adams: art & artists. Detroit, Wayne State University Press, 1970. 309 p. illus., ports. 24 cm. "Bibliography of Ernst Scheyer": p. 289-298. [N7483.A3S3 1970] 72-79478 ISBN 0-8143-1418-X 8.95
1. Adams, Henry, 1838-1918. I. Title.

Adams, James Frederick, 1927- —Art collections.

COLONIAL 755'.2'098074014816
Spanish art of the Americas : [exhibition] Reading Public Museum. [Reading, Pa. : Reading Public Museum and Art Gallery], c1975. 141 p. : chiefly ill. ; 22 cm. "The illustrations in this book came entirely from the Collection of Dr. James F. Adams ... displayed for the first time in its entirety at the Reading Public Museum in the Spring of 1975. The ... essay about the collection was ... written by Dr. Adams who also supplied all the identifying captions for the illustrations." Bibliography: p. 141. [N6502.C57] 75-34692
1. Adams, James Frederick, 1927- —Art collections. 2. Art, Colonial—Latin America—Exhibitions. 3. Art, Latin American—Exhibitions. 4. Art, Colonial—Central America—Exhibitions. 5. Art, Central American—Exhibitions. I. Reading, Pa. Public Museum and Art Gallery.

Adams, John, Pres. U.S., 1735-1826—Portraits, etc.

OLIVER, Andrew, 1906- 757'.9'0973
Portraits of John and Abigail Adams. Cambridge, Mass., Belknap Press of Harvard University Press, 1967. xxxvi, 284 p. illus., geneal. table, ports. 26 cm. (The Adams papers. Series IV: Portraits) Bibliographical footnotes. [N7628.A3O55] 67-11863
1. Adams, John, Pres. U.S., 1735-1826—Portraits, etc. 2. Adams, Abigail (Smith) 1744-1818—Portraits, etc. I. Title. II. Series. BIP

Adams, John Quincy, Pres. U.S., 1767-1848—Portraits, caricatures, etc.

NATIONAL Portrait Gallery, Washington, D.C. 704.94'23
The life portraits of John Quincy Adams. Washington, 1970. 1 v. (unpaged) illus., ports. 28 cm. Catalog of a loan exhibition. [E377.N37] 71-134241
1. Adams, John Quincy, Pres. U.S., 1767-1848—Portraits, caricatures, etc. I. Title.

OLIVER, Andrew, 1906- 704.94'2
Portraits of John Quincy Adams and his wife. Cambridge, Mass., Belknap Press of Harvard University Press, 1970. xli, 335 p. illus., ports. 26 cm. (The Adams papers. Series IV: Portraits) Includes bibliographical references. [E377.O4] 70-128349 ISBN 0-674-69152-0 15.00
1. Adams, John Quincy, Pres. U.S., 1767-1848—Portraits, caricatures, etc. 2. Adams, Louisa Catherine (Johnson) 1775-1852—Portraits, caricatures, etc. I. Title. II. Series. BIP

Adams revolvers.

CHAMBERLAIN, William Henry Jason. 683'.43
Adams' revolvers / by W. H. J. Chamberlain and A. W. F. Taylerson. London : Barrie and Jenkins, 1976. 240 p. : ill., facsims., ports. ; 31 cm. Includes index. Bibliography: p. 224-235. [TS537.C4] 77-357036 £15.00
1. Adams revolvers. I. Taylerson, A. W. F., joint author. II. Title. BIP

Addison, Robert William, 1924—

NORTON (R. W.) Art Gallery. 759.13
Robert W. Addison; a retrospective exhibition, Mar. 7-May 2, 1971. [1st ed.] Shreveport, La. [1971] 28 p. illus., port. 22 cm. Catalog. [ND237.A27N6] 73-155783 ISBN 0-9600182-2-0
1. Addison, Robert William, 1924-

Adena culture.

WEBB, William Snyder, 1882-1964. 970.4'7
The Adena people, by William S. Webb and Charles E. Snow. With a chapter on Adena pottery and a foreword to the new ed. by James B. Griffin. [Knoxville] University of Tennessee Press [1974] xix, 369 p. illus. 23 cm. Reprint of the 1945 ed. published by the University of Kentucky, Lexington, which was issued as v. 6 of its Dept. of Anthropology and Archaeology Reports in anthropology and archaeology. Bibliography: p. [344]-356. [E78.O4W38 1974] 74-10598 ISBN 0-87049-159-8 10.75
1. Adena culture. I. Snow, Charles Ernest, 1910- joint author. II. Title. III. Series: Kentucky. University. Dept. of Anthropology. Reports in anthropology, v. 6. BIP

Adhemar, Jean.

TOULOUSE-LAUTREC MONFA, Henri Marie Raymond de, 1864-1901 769.924
Toulouse-Lautrec; his complete lithographs and drypoints [by] Jean Adhemar. New York. Abrams [1965] xxxviiip., 370 illus. (pt. col.)) 34cm. Bibl. [NE2451.T64] 65-21831 18.50
1. Adhemar, Jean. I. Title.

Adirondack Mountains in art.

TAIT, Arthur Fitzwilliam, 1819-1905. 759.13
A. F. Tait: artist in the Adirondacks; an exhibition of paintings and other works by the sporting and animal artist Arthur Fitzwilliam Tait (1819-1905). [Blue Mountain Lake, N.Y., Adirondack Museum, 1974] 73 p. illus. (1 col.) 21 x 23 cm. Catalogue of an exhibition held at the Adirondack Museum, June 15-Oct. 15, 1974. [ND237.T323A65] 74-182318 ISBN 0-910020-30-2
1. Tait, Arthur Fitzwilliam, 1819-1905. 2. Adirondack Mountains in art. I. Adirondack Museum, Blue Mountain Lake, N.Y.

Adkins, Eugene B.—Art collections.

WESTERN art 759.13'074'019173
from the Eugene B. Adkins Collection; [exhibition] Phoenix Art Musuem, Western Art Associates, November 1971-January 1972. [Phoenix, Ariz., 1971] [40] p. illus. (part col.) 26 cm. [N8214.5.U6W4] 72-175442
1. Adkins, Eugene B.—Art collections. 2. The West in art. 3. Art—Exhibitions. I. Western Art Associates.

Adler, David, 1882-1949.

PRATT, Richard. 720'.924
David Adler. With photos. by Ezra Stoller and others. New York, M. Evans; distributed by Lippincott, New York [1969, c1970] xii, 227 p. illus., plans, port. 29 cm. "Adler's architectural library": p. 203-217. [NA737.A3P7] 68-11187 20.00
1. Adler, David, 1882-1949. BIP

Adnet, Francoise.

ADNET, Francoise. 759.4
Francoise Adnet / par Louis Pauwels. Paris : Editions Art et industrie, [1976?] 79 p. : ill. (some col.) ; 32 cm. French and English. [ND553.A32P37] 76-466920 120F
1. Adnet, Francoise. I. Pauwels, Louis, Aug. 2, 1920-

Adobe houses.

MCHENRY, Paul Graham. 690'.8
Adobe; build it yourself. Tucson, University of Arizona Press [1973] x, 157 p. illus. 31 cm. Bibliography: p. 151. [TH4818.A3M32] 72-92105 ISBN 0-8165-0370-2 7.95
1. Adobe houses. 2. Building, Adobe. I. Title.

MUD, space & spirit : 690'.8
handmade adobes / text, Virginia Gray and Macrae ; photography, Wayne McCall. Santa Barbara, Calif. : Capra Press, 1976. 93 p. : ill. ; 21 x 26 cm. Bibliography: p. 91. [TH4818.A3M8] 76-7958 ISBN 0-88496-059-5 pbk. : 8.95
1. Adobe houses. I. Gray, Virginia, 1933- II. Macrae, Alan, 1943- III. McCall, Wayne. BIP

Advertising cards

DUVALL, Edward J. 659.134
The show card writer. Wilmette, Ill., F. J. Drake [1950] 158 p. illus. 21 x 28 cm. [TT360.D82] 51-9218
1. Advertising cards I. Title.

Advertising cards—Collectors and collecting.

BURDICK, Jefferson R 741.67
The American card catalog; [the standard guide on all collected cards and their values. Published by J. R. Burdick, managing editor, and associate editors: Charles R. Bray and others. East Stroudsburg? Pa., 1960] 240p. illus. 23cm. [NC1280.B87 1960] 60-31578
1. Advertising cards—Collectors and collecting. 2. Cards—Collectors and collecting. I. Title.

BURDICK, Jefferson R 741.67
The American card catalog. [The standard guide on all collected cards and their values] Published by J. R. Burdick, managing editor [and others] Syracuse, N. Y., 1953. 168p. (p. 148-168 advertisements) illus. 22cm. Bibliography: p. 134-136. [NC1280.B87] 741.68 53-25798
1. Advertising cards—Collectors and collecting. 2. Cards—Collectors and collecting. I. Title.

HEAL, Ambrose, Sir 1872- 769'.5
London tradesmen's cards of the XVIII century; a account of their origin and use. New York, Dover [1968] vi, 110p. illus. facsims. 24cm. (Dover pictorial archive ser.) Unabridged & unaltered repubn. of the work orig. pub. in 1925. [NE965.H4 1968] 67-19613 2.50 pap.,
1. Advertising cards—Collectors and collecting. I. Title. II. Title: Tradesmen's cards of the XVIII century. III. Series.

Advertising cards—England—Yorkshire—Catalogs.

LEEDS Art Galleries. 769'.5
The Leeds Art Galleries take this opportunity to acquaint the publick with a large sortment of engrav'd cards embellish'd in the most elegant & ornamental manner, of trades-men ... in the County of Yorkshire : likewise with some others from London ... / compil'd, with an introd. ... by Terry Friedman. Bradford [Eng.] : Lund Humphries, 1976. [33] p. : chiefly facsims. ; 28 x 12 cm. Bibliography: p. [33] [NE965.3.G7L43 1976] 77-351302 £0.50
1. Advertising cards—England—Yorkshire—Catalogs. I. Friedman, Terry. II. Title: Engraved cards ... of trades-men ... in the County of Yorkshire ...

Advertising—Drug trade.

NEUBURG, Hans, 1904- 741.6'7
Chemie-Werbung und Graphik. Publicite et graphisme dans l'industrie chimique. Publicity and graphic design in the chemical industry. Mit Beitragen von Rene Rudin, Victor N. Cohen [und] Josef Muller-Brockmann. (Franzosische Ubersetzung: Denise Schai, Monique Picard. Englische Ubersetzung: M J. Wynne.) Zurich. ABC Verlag (1967). 239p. illus. 26cm. [HF6161.D7N4] 68-80434 27.50
1. Advertising—Drug trade. 2. Advertising—Chemical industries. I. Title. II. Title: Publicity and graphic design in the chemical industry.
Distributed by Hastings, New York.

Advertising layout Practical—Make-up.

BUTLER, Kenneth B 016.051
Practical handbook on display typefaces for publication layout, by Kenneth B. B. Butler, George C. Likeness and Stanley A. Kordek. Mendota, Ill., Butler Typo-Design Research Center [1956] 89p. illus. 28cm. 'No. 7 in a series of handbooks.' [Z253.5B8] 56-2905
1. Advertising layout Practical—Make-up. I. Title. II. Title: Double-spreads in publication layout.

Advertising novelties—Catalogs.

DIETZ, Lawrence. 659.1'9'663620973
Soda pop; the history, advertising, art, and memorabilia of soft drinks in America. [New York] Simon and Schuster [1973] 184 p. illus. 26 cm. "A Subsistence Press book." [NK1125.D43] 72-83895 ISBN 0-671-21442-X 14.95
1. Advertising novelties—Catalogs. 2. Advertising—Carbonated beverages. I. Title.

Advertising, Outdoor.

ASSOCIATION of National Advertisers. Outdoor Advertising Committee. 659.134
Essentials of outdoor advertising. New York, Association of National Advertisers [1952] 128 p. illus. 22 cm. [HF5843.A8] 52-1326
1. Advertising. Outdoor. I. Title.

HOUCK, John W. 659.13
Outdoor advertising; history and regulation, edited by John W. Houck. Notre Dame [Ind.] University of Notre Dame Press, 1969. v, 250 p. illus. 27 cm. Bibliographical footnotes. [HF5843.H57] 79-75155 15.00
1. Advertising, Outdoor. 2. Advertising, Outdoor—U.S. BIP

HOYLE, John T 659.134
Outdoor and transportation advertising, by John T. Hoyle, in collaboration with C. D. McCormick and Philip J. Everest. Serial 5720-1. [Ed. 2] Scranton, International Correspondence Schools, c1959. 90p. illus. 20cm. [HF5843.H59] 59-44100
1. Advertising, Outdoor. 2. Advertising cards. I. International Correspondence Schools, Scranton, Pa. II. Title.

Advertising, Outdoor—Tennessee.

LOWRY, Paul R. 338.4
Economic effects of the control of highway signs in Tennessee, by Paul R. Lowry, Harry H. Summer [and] P. Charles [i.e. Charles P.] Cartee. Prepared for Tennessee Dept. of Highways in cooperation with the U.S. Dept. of Transportation, Federal Highway Administration, Bureau of Public Roads. Memphis, Bureau of Business and Economic Research, Memphis State University, 1967. xii, 157 p. illus., maps. 28 cm. Bibliographical footnotes. [HF5843.L68] 68-66689
1. Advertising, Outdoor—Tennessee. 2. Motels—Tennessee. I. Summer, Harry H., joint author. II. Cartee, Charles P., joint author. III. Tennessee. Dept. of Highways. IV. Tennessee. State University, Memphis. Bureau of Business and Economic Research. V. Title.

Advertising, Outdoor—U.S.

HILL, Richard, 1934- 659.13'42'0973
Highway aesthetics; new directions for outdoor advertising. [Notre Dame, University of Notre Dame, Dept. of Architecture, 1970] 30 p. illus. 22 cm. Thesis (M.S.)—University of Notre Dame. Bibliography: p. 29-30. [HF5843.5.H55] 70-139959
1. Advertising, Outdoor—United States. I. Title.

TENNESSEE. State University, Memphis. Bureau of Business and Economic Research. 659.13'4
A survey of the standard poster outdoor advertising industry, by Paul R. Lowry [and others. Prepared for the Bureau of Public Roads, U.S. Dept. of Transportation by Bureau of Business and Economic Research, Memphis State University and Texas Transportation Institute, Texas A & M University] Memphis, 1967. v, 45 p. forms. 28 cm. [HF5843.T45] 68-66688
1. Advertising, Outdoor—U.S. I. Lowry, Paul R. II. U.S. Bureau of Public Roads. III. Texas Transportation Institute, College Station. IV. Title.

Advertising—Photographic apparatus.

GILBERT, George, 1922- comp. 771.3
Photographic advertising from A-to-Z, from the Kodak to the Leica, actual size from the pages of the leading magazines of America from the 1880's to the 1920's; reproduced in exact detail: cameras, plates, novelties, schools, shutters, more. [1st ed. Riverdale, N.Y.] Yesterday's Cameras, [1970-72] 2 v. (390 p.) illus., facsims. 24 cm. Vol. 2 has title: More photographic advertising from A-to-Z, from the Kodak to the Leica. "A unique compilation for the photographic historian and collector of camera curiosa." [HF6161.P5G55] 78-143903
1. Advertising—Photographic apparatus. I. Title.

Advertising, Point of sale.

OFFENHARTZ, Harvey. 659.15'7
Point-of-purchase design. New York, Reinhold Book Corp. [1968] 224 p. illus. 31 cm. [HF5845.O37] 68-16028
1. Advertising, Point of sale. 2. Display of merchandise. I. Title.

Advertising specialties.

ANDERSON, Will, 1939or40- 659.1'9'663420973
The beer book; an illustrated guide to American breweriana. [1st ed.] Princeton [N.J.] Pyne Press [1973] 199 p. illus. 28 cm. Bibliography: p. 196. [NK1125.A57] 73-79519 ISBN 0-87861-057-X 17.50
1. Advertising specialties. 2. Advertising—Brewing industries. I. Title. BIP

COPE, Jim. 338.43'741'67
Soda water advertising, with current prices and photographs. Orange, Tex. [1971] 80 p. illus., ports. 22 cm. [NK1125.C642] 73-31502 3.95
1. Advertising specialties. 2. Advertising—Carbonated beverages. I. Title.

Advertising specialties—Catalogs.

GOLDSTEIN, Shelly. 741.6'7
Coca-cola collectibles; with current prices and photographs in full color [by Shelly and Helen Goldstein] Woodland Hills, Calif. [1971] 78 l. col. illus. 26 cm. [NK1125.G56] 76-31385 10.00
1. Advertising specialties—Catalogs. 2. Advertising—Carbonated beverages. 3. Advertising specialties—Collectors and collecting. I. Goldstein, Helen, joint author. II. Coca-Cola Company, Wilmington, Del. III. Title. BIP

MUNSEY, Cecil. 659.1'9'66362
The illustrated guide to the collectibles of Coca-Cola. New York, Hawthorn Books [1972] xv, 333 p. illus. 29 cm. Bibliography: p. 322-326. [NK1125.M88 1972] 71-39276 12.95
1. Advertising specialties—Catalogs. 2. Advertising—Carbonated beverages. I. Coca-Cola Company, Wilmington, Del. II. Title.

Advertising specialties—Collectors and collecting.

HAMMOND, Dorothy M. 659.1
Advertising collectibles of times past, by Dorothy Hammond, with Robert Hammond. [Des Moines] WH Books [1974] 128 p. illus. (part col.) 28 cm. Cover title: Collectible advertising. Includes bibliographical references. [NK1125.H315] 74-75950
1. Advertising specialties—Collectors and collecting. I. Hammond, Robert, 1924- joint author. II. Title. III. Title: Collectible advertising.

Aerial photographs—Catalogs.

ILLINOIS. University at Urbana-Champaign. Committee on Aerial Photography. 016.779'9'77835
University of Illinois Air Photo Repository; catalog. Urbana, 1967. 1 v. (various pagings) map, photos. 28 cm. [TR810.I47 1967] A 68
1. Illinois. University at Urbana-Champaign. Air Photo Repository. 2. Aerial photographs—Catalogs.

Aeronautics in art.

O'DEA, William T. 704.94962913
Aeronautica: objects d'art, prints, air mail, by W. T. O'Dea. London, H. M. S. O. Obtainable in the U.S.A. from British Info., New York. 1966. 48p. 20col. illus. 15cm. (Sci. Mus. iddus. bklet) Title. (Series: London. Science Museum. A Science Museum illustrated booklet) [N8217.A4O3] 66-78943 1.00
1. Aeronautics in art. I. Title. II. Series.

Aeronautics — Pictorial works.

BOWERS, Peter M. 629.13'0022'2
Aircraft photo album, compiled by Peter M. Bowers and Paul R. Matt. Temple City, Calif., Historical Aviation Album [1970, c1969- v. illus. 28 cm. [TL549.B67] 79-109593 3.50 (v. 1)
1. Aeronautics—Pictorial works. I. Matt, Paul R., joint author. II. Title. BIP

GABRIELSON, Walter. 741.9'73
41 airplanes, crew wt. 200 lbs. [by W. Gabrielson. [Pasedena, Calif., Dawson Aircraft; distribution by the Aviation Book Co., Glendale, Calif., 1970] 41 l. (chiefly illus.) 19 x 29 cm. [TL549.G3] 76-18265
1. Aeronautics—Pictorial works. 2. Aeroplanes in art. I. Title.

PALMER, Henry Robinson, 1911- 629.1309
This was air travel. [1st ed.] Seattle, Superior Pub. Co. [c1960] 190p. illus. 28cm. [TL549.P3] 60-14423
1. Aeronautics—Pictorial works. 2. Aeronautics, Commercial— Hist. I. Title.

TAYLOR, John William Ransom. 629.1084
A picture history of flight. New York, Pitman Pub. Corp. [1956] 192 p. illus. 29 cm. [TL549.T3] 629.13084 56-2130
1. Aeronautics — Pictorial works. 2. Aeronautics — Hist. I. Title.

Aeroplanes — Hist.

BOWERS, Peter M. 387.7
Antique plane guide. New York, Modern Aircraft Series, a division of Sports Car Press [1962] 130 p. illus. 21 cm. (Modern aircraft series) [TL671.B58] 62-18920
1. Aeroplanes — Hist. 2. Used aircraft. I. Title.

Aeroplanes in art.

DUNAVENT, Jim. 743'.8'962913334
How to draw airplanes. New York [Sports Car Press; distributed by Crown Publishers, 1973] 92 p. illus. 14 x 21 cm. (Modern aircraft series) [NC825.A4D86 1973] 72-77646 ISBN 0-87112-061-5 2.95
1. Aeroplanes in art. 2. Drawing—Instruction. I. Title.

Aertsen, Pieter, 1508-1575.

MOXEY, Keith P. F., 1943- 759.9493'2
Pieter Aertsen, Joachim Beuckelaer, and the rise of secular painting in the context of the Reformation / Keith P. F. Moxey. New York : Garland Pub., 1977. xii, 284 p., [37] leaves of plates : ill. ; 21 cm. (Outstanding dissertations in the fine arts) Thesis—Chicago, 1974. Bibliography: p. 269-284. [ND623.A32M68] 76-23656 ISBN 0-8240-2715-9 : 35.00
1. Aertsen, Pieter, 1508-1575. 2. Beuckelaer, Joachim, ca. 1533-ca. 1575. 3. Reformation and art. I. Title. II. Series. BIP

Aesthetic movement (British art)

HAMILTON, Walter , 1844-1899. 700'.942
The aesthetic movement in England. New York, AMS Press [1971] viii, 127 p. 23 cm. Reprint of the 1882 ed. [NX543.A1H3 1971] 76-144633 ISBN 0-404-03091-2
1. Aesthetic movement (British art) I. Title. BIP

SEDDING, John Dando, 1838-1891. 709'.42
Art and handicraft / John Sedding. New York : Garland Pub., 1977. 179 p. : port. ; 23 cm. (The Aesthetic movement & the arts and crafts movement) Reprint of the 1893 ed. published by Kegan Paul, Trench, Trubner, London. [N6767.5.A3S43 1977] 76-17777 ISBN 0-8240-2482-6 lib.bdg. : 35.00
1. Aesthetic movement (British art) 2. Architecture—England. 3. Arts and crafts movement. I. Title. II. Series. BIP

Aesthetics.

AESTHETIC concepts and education. Edited by Ralph A. Smith. Urbana, University of Illinois Press [1970] xv, 455 p. 24 cm. Includes bibliographical references. [BH41.A36] 75-94401 9.50 370.1
1. Aesthetics. 2. Education—Philosophy. I. Smith, Ralph Alexander, ed.

AESTHETICS: problems in the philosophy of criticism. New York, Harcourt, Brace [1958] 614p. illus. 24cm. Includes bibliography. [BH201.B4] [BH201.B4] 701.17 58-5919 58-5919 101
1. Aesthetics. I. Beardsley, Monroe C

AESTHETICS and criticism. New York, Philosophical Library [1955] 341p. 23cm. [BH39] [BH39] 701.17 55-14497 55-14497 101
1. Aesthetics. 2. Criticism. I. Osborne, Harold, 1905-

ALEXANDER, Samuel, 1859-1938. 111.8'5
Beauty and other forms of value. Introd. by Ralph Ross. New York, Crowell [1968] xxiv, 305 p. 20 cm. (Apollo editions, A-199) Bibliographical footnotes. [BH201.A47 1968] 68-31775 2.25
1. Aesthetics. 2. Worth. I. Title. BIP

AMES, Van Meter, 1898- 700'.1
Introduction to beauty. Freeport, N.Y., Books for Libraries Press [1968, c1958] xii, 280 p. 22 cm. (Essay index reprint series) First published 1931. Bibliography: p. 265-269. [BH201.A5 1968] 68-14895
1. Aesthetics. I. Title. BIP

ASCHENBRENNER, Karl. 700'.1
The concepts of criticism / Karl Aschenbrenner. Dordrecht ; Boston : D. Reidel Pub. Co., [1975] c1974. x, 549 p. ; 25 cm. (Foundations of language : Supplementary series ; v. 20) Includes index. Bibliography: p. [537]-540. [BH39.A725] 74-80523 ISBN 90-277-0482-1 lib.bdg. : 55.00
1. Aesthetics. 2. Criticism. I. Title. II. Series. BIP

BATTCOCK, Gregory, 1937- 701'.17
Why art : casual notes on the aesthetics of the immediate past / by Gregory Battcock. 1st ed. New York : Dutton, c1977. viii, 134 p. : ill. ; 21 cm. Includes

the Univ. of Cincinnati by Wayne State. [c.] 1965. 201p. 24cm. Bibl. [BH201.M33] 65-10949 9.00
1. Aesthetics. I. Title.

MAURON, Charles. 701.15
Aesthetics and psychology. Translated from the French by Roger Fry and Katherine John. Port Washington, N.Y., Kennikat Press [1970] 110 p. 19 cm. Reprint of the 1935 ed. [BH202.M33 1970] 79-102576
1. Aesthetics. 2. Art—Psychology. I. Title. BIP

MEAD, Hunter. 101
An introduction to aesthetics. New York, Ronald Press Co. [1952] 307 p. 22 cm. [BH201.M4] 701 52-6199
1. Aesthetics.

METZGER, Charles Reid, 1921- 101
Emerson and Greenough, transcendental pioneers of an American esthetic. Berkeley, University of California Press, 1954. 153p. 22cm. Includes bibliographies. [PS1633.G67M4] [PS1633.G67M4] 701.17 54-10438 54-10438
1. Emerson. Ralph Waldo. 1803-1882. 2. Greenough, Horatio, 1805-1852. 3. Aesthetics. I. Title.

MORAWSKI, Stefan. 111.8'5
Inquiries into the fundamentals of aesthetics. Cambridge, Mass., MIT Press [1974] xviii, 408 p. 23 cm. Includes bibliographical references. [BH39.M618] 74-6123 ISBN 0-262-13096-3 25.00
1. Aesthetics. I. Title. BIP

NAHM, Milton Charles, 701.17
1903-
Aesthetic experience and its presuppositions [by] Milton C. Nahm. New York, Russell & Russell [1968, c1946] xiii, 554 p. 22 cm. Bibliography: p. 519-540. [BH201.N27 1968] 68-10933
1. Aesthetics. 2. Art—Philosophy. I. Title. BIP

NAHM, Milton Charles, 701.17
1903-
The artist as creator; an essay of human freedom. Baltimore, Johns Hopkins Press, 1956. 352p. 24cm. [BH201.N32] 56-8241
1. Aesthetics. 2. Creation (Literary, artistic, etc.) 3. Art—Philosophy. I. Title. BIP

NAHM, Milton Charles, 701'.17
1903-
The artist as creator : an essay of human freedom / by Milton C. Nahm. [Ann Arbor : University Microfilms International, 1978] c1956. xi, 352 p. ; 23 cm. (Books on demand : Series 10) Reprint of the ed. published by Johns Hopkins Press, Baltimore. Includes index. Bibliography: p. 331-343. [BH201.N32 1978] 78-7316 ISBN 0-8357-0317-7 pbk. : 18.25
1. Aesthetics. 2. Creation (Literary, artistic, etc.) 3. Art—Philosophy. I. Title.

OGDEN, Charles Kay, 1889- 111.8'5
1957.
The foundations of aesthetics [by] I. A. Richards, C. K. Ogden [and] James Wood. [2d ed.] New York, Haskell House, [1974] 92 p. illus. 23 cm. Reprint of the 1925 ed. published by Lear Publishers, New York. Richards' and Ogden's names in reverse order in 1922 London ed. Includes bibliographical references. [BH201.O5 1974] 74-1364 ISBN 0-8383-2046-5 11.95 (lib. bdg.).
1. Aesthetics. I. Richards, Ivor Armstrong, 1893- joint author. II. Wood, James Edward Hathorn, joint author. III. Title.

ONSLOW-FORD, Gordon. 750.1
Painting in the instant. New York, H. N. Abrams [1964] 92 p. illus. 26 cm. "This book is written entirely by hand as handwriting is a form of drawing." [N70.O68] 64-16802
1. Aesthetics. 2. Painting. 3. Art and society. I. Title.

ORTEGA y Gasset, Jose, 700'.1
1883-1955.
The dehumanization of art; and other essays on art, culture, and literature. Princeton, N.J., Princeton University Press, 1968 [c1948] 204 p. 21 cm. (Princeton paperbacks, 128) Translation of La deshumanizacion del arte. Bibliographical footnotes. [BH205.O713 1968] 68-8963 2.45
1. Aesthetics. 2. Fiction. I. Title.

ORTEGA y Gasset, Jose, 701.17
1883-1955.
The dehumanization of art, and other writings on art and culture. [Translated from the Spanish by Willard R. Trask] Garden City, N.Y., Doubleday, 1956. 187 p. 18 cm. (Doubleday anchor book, A72) Contents.Contents.—The dehumanization of art.—Notes on the novel.—On point of view in the arts.—In search of Goethe from within.—The self and the other. [BH205.O717] 56-5590
1. Aesthetics. 2. Fiction. I. Title.

ORTEGA Y GASSET, Jose, 701.17
1883-
The dehumanization of art, and other writings on art and culture. [Translated from the Spanish by Willard R. Trask] Garden City, N. Y., Doubleday, 1956. 187p. 18cm. (Doubleday anchor book, A72) [BH205.O717] 56-5590
1. Aesthetics. 2. Fiction. I. Title.

OSBORNE, Harold, 1905- 111.8'5
Aesthetics and criticism. Westport, Conn., Greenwood Press [1973] vii, 341 p. 22 cm. Reprint of the 1955 ed. published by Routledge & Paul, London. Bibliography: p. 325-334. [BH39.O78 1973] 73-3756 ISBN 0-8371-6847-3 13.75
1. Aesthetics. 2. Criticism. I. Title.

OSSOWSKI, Stanislaw. 111.8'5
The foundations of aesthetics / Stanislaw Ossowski ; translated from the Polish by Janina and Witold Rodzinski ; the pref. by Stefan Nowak. Dordrecht, Holland ; Boston : D. Reidel Pub. Co., c1978. xxx, 386 p., [49] leaves of plates : ill. ; 23 cm. Translation of U podstaw estetyki. Includes index. [BH39.O85213] 77-26213 ISBN 9-02-770551-8 : 42.15
1. Aesthetics. I. Title.

PAGET, Violet, 1856-1935. 111.8'5
The beautiful : an introduction to psychological aesthetics / by Vernon Lee [i.e. V. Paget]. Folcroft, Pa. : Folcroft Library Editions, 1974. p. cm. Reprint of the 1913 ed. published by the University Press, Cambridge, in series: The Cambridge manuals of science and literature. Bibliography: p. [BH41.P26 1974] 74-22079 ISBN 0-8414-5673-9 lib. bdg. : 10.00
1. Aesthetics. 2. Psychology, Applied. 3. Form (Aesthetics) I. Title. BIP

PARKER, DeWitt Henry, 111.8'5
1885-1949.
The principles of aesthetics / DeWitt H. Parker. 2d ed. Westport, Conn. : Greenwood Press, 1976, [c1946] p. cm. Reprint of the 2d ed. published by Appleton-Century-Crofts, New York. Includes index. Bibliography: p. [BH201.P35 1976] 76-40928 ISBN 0-8371-9279-X lib.bdg. : 18.00
1. Aesthetics. I. Title. BIP

PEPPER, Stephen Coburn, 111.8'5
1891-
Aesthetic quality; a contextualistic theory of beauty, by Stephen C. Pepper. Westport, Conn., Greenwood Press [1970, c1965] ix, 255 p. 23 cm. [BH201.P4 1970] 79-110052
1. Aesthetics. I. Title. BIP

PRALL, David Wight, 1886- 701.17
1940
Aesthetic judgement [by] D. W. Prall, Introd. by Ralph Ross. New York, Apollo eds. [1967] xxix, 378p. 20cm. (Apollo eds. A-149) Reprint of the 1929 ed. [BH201.P7 1967] 67-9025 1.95 pap.,
1. Aesthetics. I. Title.

RADER, Melvin Miller, 111.8'5
1903-
Art and human values / by Melvin Rader and Bertram Jessup ; with a foreword by Virgil C. Aldrich. Englewood Cliffs, N.J. : Prentice-Hall, [1975] p. cm. Includes index. Bibliography: p. [BH201.R28] 75-22486 ISBN 0-13-046821-5 : 9.95
1. Aesthetics. 2. Worth. 3. Art—Philosophy. I. Jessup, Bertram Emil, 1899- joint author. II. Title. BIP

RADER, Melvin Miller, •101 701.17
1903- ed.
A modern book of esthetics, an anthology. Rev. ed. New York, Holt [1952] 602 p. 22 cm. [BH21.R3 1952] 52-7015
1. Aesthetics. I. Title. BIP

REID, Louis Arnaud, 1895- 111.8'5
A study in aesthetics. Westport, Conn., Greenwood Press [1973] 415 p. 22 cm. Reprint of the 1954 ed. published by Macmillan, New York. [BH201.R4 1973] 70-114546 ISBN 0-8371-4794-8 15.50
1. Aesthetics. I. Title.

REYNOLDS, Frances. 701'.17
An enquiry concerning the principles of taste and of the origin of our ideas of beauty. New York, Garland Pub., 1972. v, 49 p. 21 cm. Facsim. reprint of the 1785 ed. [N70.R43 1972] 74-112116
1. Aesthetics. 2. Art—Philosophy. I. Title. Sold only as part of the 225 title series, English Literary Criticism of the 18th century, for 3900.00.

REYNOLDS, Frances. 701.17
An enquiry concerning the principles of taste, and of the origin of our ideas of beauty, etc. (1785) With an introd. by James L. Clifford. Los Angeles, William Andrews Clark Memorial Library, University of California, 1951. xi p., facsim.: v, 49 p. 21 cm. (Augustan Reprint Society. Publication no. 27) [N70.R43] 51-13000
1. Aesthetics. 2. Art — Philosophy. I. Title. II. Series.

SANTAYANA, George, 1863-1952. 101
The sense of beauty; being the outline of aesthetic theory. New York, Dover Publications [1955, c1896] ix, 275 p. 21 cm. [N66.S23 1955] 701.17 55-14673
1. Aesthetics. I. Title.

SANTAYANA, George, 1863- 701.17
1952.
The sense of beauty, being the outlines of aesthetic theory. With a foreword by Philip Blair Rice. New York, Modern Library [1955] xii, 268 p. 19 cm. (The Modern library of the world's best books, 292) [N66.S23 1955a] 101* 55-10656
1. Aesthetics. I. Title.

SARTRE, Jean Paul, 1905- 701.17
Essays in aesthetics. Selected and translated by Wade Baskin. Freeport, N.Y., Books for Libraries Press [1970, c1963] ix, 94 p. 23 cm. (Essay index reprint series) Contents.Contents.—The Venetian pariah. Jacopo's shenanigans. The puritans of the Rialto. Man at bay. A mole in the sun.—The paintings of Giacometti.—The unprivileged painter: Lapoujade.—The mobiles of Calder.—The quest for the absolute. [N67.S243 1970] 73-117755
1. Aesthetics. I. Title.

SAW, Ruth Lydia. 701.17
Aesthetics: an introduction, by Ruth L. Saw. [1st ed.] Garden City, N.Y., Anchor Books, 1971. 231 p. 18 cm. (New introductions to philosophy) Bibliography: p. [219]-225. [N66.S34] 71-144309 1.95
1. Aesthetics. 2. Art—Psychology. I. Title.

SCHILLER, Johann Christoph 100
Friedrich von, 1759-1805.
On the aesthetic education of man, in a series of letters. Translated with an introd. by Reginald Snell. New Haven, Yale University Press, 1954. v, 146p. 22cm. (Rare masterpieces of philosophy and science) 'Text ... followed is that of the earliest edition of the Letters in book form, in a volume of Lesser prose writings by Schiller ... (Lcipzig, 1801); Bibliographical footnotes. [N70.S32] A54
1. Aesthetics sArt—Philosophy. I. Title. II. Series.

SCHNEIDER, Elisabeth 111.8'5
Wintersteen, 1897-
Aesthetic motive, by Elisabeth Schneider. New York, Octagon Books, 1974 [c1939] 136 p. 21 cm. Reprint of the ed. published by Macmillan, New York. [BH201.S42 1974] 73-159226 ISBN 0-374-97127-7 7.75
1. Aesthetics. I. Title. BIP

SELIGMAN, Germain. 701.17
Oh! tickle taste; or, Objectivity in art. Pref. by Rene Huyghe. [New York] B. Wheelwright Co., 1952. 180 p. illus. 24 cm. [N75.S44] 52-4726
1. Aesthetics. 2. Collectors and collecting. I. Title. II. Title: Objectivity in art.

SHAW, Theodore L * 101
War on critics. Boston, Stuart Art Gallery [1952] 206 p. 21 cm. [BH221.U54S37] 701.17 52-7566
1. Aesthetics. I. Title.

SIEGEL, Eli, 1902- 111.8'5
The opposites class : aesthetic realism class on opposites / conducted by Eli Siegel ; [edited by Martha Baird and Dorothy Koppelman]. New York : Terrain Gallery, Aesthetic Realism Foundation, 1975. 26 p. ; 22 cm. [BH39.S53] 75-31346 ISBN 0-911492-20-8 pbk. : 1.25
1. Aesthetics. 2. Opposition, Theory of. 3. Realism in art. I. Title. BIP

SINGER, Irving. 101
Santayana's aesthetics; a critical introduction. Cambridge, Harvard University Press, 1957. ix, 235p. 22cm. Bibliographical references included in 'Notes' (p. [225]-232) Bibliographical footnotes. [B945.S24S55] [B945.S24S55] 701.17 57-9079 57-9079
1. Santayana, George, 1863-1952. 2. Aesthetics. I. Title. BIP

SIRCELLO, Guy. 111.8'5
A new theory of beauty / Guy Sircello. Princeton, N.J. : Princeton University Press, [1975] vi, 141 p. ; 25 cm. (Princeton essays on the arts ; 1) Includes bibliographical references and index. [BH39.S54] 75-3475 ISBN 0-691-07211-6 : 9.50 ISBN 0-691-01987-8 pbk. : 3.95
1. Aesthetics. I. Title. BIP

SLATTERY, Mary Francis, 111.8'5
Sister, 1909-
Hazard, form, & value. Detroit, Wayne State University Press, 1971. 127 p. 24 cm. Includes bibliographical references. [BH301.F6S57] 77-161073 ISBN 0-8143-1455-4 7.50
1. Aesthetics. 2. Form (Aesthetics) 3. Worth. I. Title.

SPARSHOTT, Francis Edward, 100
1926-
The structure of aesthetics. Toronto, University of Toronto Press, 1963. xiii, 471 p. diagrs. 24 cm. Bibliography: p. [437]-457. [BH201.S53] 64-966
1. Aesthetics. 2. Art—Philosophy. I. Title. BIP

STEDMAN, John, d.1791. 701.17
Laelius and Hortensia; or, Thoughts on the nature and objects of taste and genius. New York, Garland Pub., 1970. xiv, 536 p. 22 cm. Facsim. of the Yale University Library copy with imprint: Edinburgh, Printed for F. Balfour, and T. Cadell, London, 1782. [AC7.S67 1782a] 73-112243
I. Title.

STILL, Colin, 1888- 111.8'5
The timeless theme; a critical theory formulated and applied. [Folcroft, Pa.] Folcroft Library Editions, 1973. viii, 244 p. 29 cm. Reprint of the 1936 ed. published by I. Nicholson & Watson, London. Contents.Contents.—The theory formulated: Art, myth, ritual and experience.—The theory applied: An interpretation of Shakespeare's "Tempest." Includes bibliographical references. [BH39.S83 1973] 73-1310 17.50 (lib. bdg.)
1. Shakespeare, William, 1564-1616. The tempest. 2. Aesthetics. I. Title. BIP

THEORY of beauty; 101
an introduction to aesthetics. New York, Philosophical Library [1953] 220p. 23cm. [BH39.O8 1953] [BH39.O8 1953] 701.17 53-1197 53-1197
1. Aesthetics. I. Osborne, Harold, 1905-

TILGHMAN, Benjamin R. 111.8'5
Language and aesthetics; contributions to the philosophy of art. Edited by Benjamin R. Tilghman. Lawrence, University Press of Kansas [1973] 165 p. 23 cm. Includes bibliographical references. [BH39.T53] 73-75383 ISBN 0-7006-0104-X 8.00
1. Aesthetics. 2. Art—Philosophy. I. Title. BIP

Beitrag zur Begriffsgeschichte der alteren Kunsttheorie.(Studien der Bibliothek Warbug, Nr. 5) Bibliography references included in Notes (p. 181-253) [N68.P313] ISBN 0-06-430049-8 4.95 (pbk.)
1. Aesthetics, Ancient. 2. Idealism. 3. Art—History. I. Title.
L.C. card no. for hardcover: 67-29380.

Aesthetics, British.

MALEK, James S. 700'.1
The arts compared, an aspect of eighteenth-century British aesthetics, by James S. Malek. Detroit, Wayne State University Press, 1974. 175 p. 24 cm. Includes bibliographical references. [BH221.G73M33 1974] 74-11088 ISBN 0-8143-1519-4 10.95
1. Aesthetics, British. I. Title.

Aesthetics, British—Addresses, essays, lectures.

NATURE and the Victorian 941'.081 *imagination* / edited by U. C. Knoepflmacher and G. B. Tennyson. Berkeley : University of California Press, c1977. xxiii, 519 p. : ill. ; 26 cm. Includes bibliographical references and index. [BH221.G73N37] 76-7761 ISBN 0-520-03229-2 : 25.00
1. Aesthetics, British—Addresses, essays, lectures. 2. Nature (Aesthetics)—Addresses, essays, lectures. 3. Painting, Victorian—England—Addresses, essays, lectures. 4. English literature—19th century—History and criticism—Addresses, essays, lectures. 5. Nature photography—Addresses, essays, lectures. 6. Science—England—History—Addresses, essays, lectures. I. Knoepflmacher, U. C. II. Tennyson, G. B. BIP

Aesthetics—Collected works.

AESTHETICS : 111.8'5
a critical anthology / George Dickie, R. J. Sclafani, editors. New York : St. Martin's Press, c1977. ix, 898 p. : ill. ; 25 cm. Includes index. Bibliography: p. [871]-887. [BH21.A35] 76-28127 ISBN 0-312-00910-0 : 13.95
1. Aesthetics—Collected works. I. Dickie, George, 1926- II. Sclafani, R. J.

CARRITT, Edgar Frederick, 111.8'5
1876- ed.
Philosophies of beauty from Socrates to Robert Bridges : being the sources of aesthetic theory / selected and edited by E. F. Carritt ; with a foreword by D. W. Prall. Westport, Conn. : Greenwood Press, 1976. xxix, 334 p. ; 23 cm. Reprint of the 1931 ed. published by Oxford University Press, New York. Includes bibliographical references and index. [BH21.C3 1976] 76-5885 ISBN 0-8371-8812-1 : 18.75
1. Aesthetics—Collected works. I. Title. BIP

ISENBERG, Arnold. 111.8'5
Aesthetics and the theory of criticism; selected essays of Arnold Isenberg. Edited by William Callaghan [and others] With an introd. by Mary Mothersill and a biographical sketch by William Callaghan. Chicago, University of Chicago Press [1973, i.e.1974] xxxix, 322 p. port. 24 cm. Includes bibliographical references. [BH39.I83] 73-77133 ISBN 0-226-38511-6 12.50
1. Isenberg, Arnold. 2. Aesthetics—Collected works. 3. Criticism—Collected works. I. Title.
Contents omitted. BIP

NAHM, Milton Charles, 700'.1
1903- comp.
Readings in philosophy of art and aesthetics [compiled by] Milton C. Nahm. Englewood Cliffs, N.J., Prentice-Hall [1974, c1975] xvi, 587 p. 25 cm. Includes bibliographical references. [BH21.N33] 72-11659 ISBN 0-13-760892-6 12.95
1. Aesthetics—Collected works. 2. Art—Philosophy—Collected works. I. Title. BIP

Aesthetics—Collections.

ASCHENBRENNER, Karl, 111.85082
ed.
Aesthetic theories; studies in the philosophy of art, edited by Karl Aschenbrenner [and] Arnold Isenberg. Englewood Cliffs, N.J., Prentice-Hall [c1965] xi, 491 p. illus. 26 cm. (Prentice-Hall series in philosophy) Bibliographical footnotes. [BH21.A8] 64-11554
1. Aesthetics — Collections. I. I. Isenberg, Arnold, joint ed. II. Title.

HOFSTADTER, Albert, 111.85082
1910- ed.
Philosophies of art and beauty; selected readings in aesthetics from Plato to Heidegger. Edited by Albert Hofstadter and Richard Kuhns. New York [Modern Library,] [1964] xix, 701 p. 21 cm. (The Modern library of world's best books. Modern library giants, G90) [BH21.H6] 64-18941
1. Aesthetics—Collections. I. Kuhns, Richard Francis, 1924- joint ed. II. Title.

HOFSTADTER, Albert, 111.8'5'08
1910- ed.
Philosophies of art and beauty; selected readings in aesthetics from Plato to Heidegger. Edited by Albert Hofstadter and Richard Kuhns. New York, Vintage Books [1973] p. Reprint of the 1964 ed., which was issued as no. G90 of The Modern library of the world's best books. Modern library giants. [BH21.H6 1973] 72-10071 ISBN 0-394-71910-7
1. Aesthetics—Collections. I. Kuhns, Richard Francis, 1924- joint ed. II. Title. BIP

LEVICH, Marvin, ed. 111.85
Aesthetics and the philosophy of criticism. New York, Random House [c1963] xv, 649 p. 22 cm. Bibliography: p. [631]-637. [BH21.L4] 62-16202
1. Aesthetics — Collections. 2. Criticism — Collections. I. Title.

OSBORNE, Harold, 1905- 700'.1
comp.
Aesthetics; edited by Harold Osborne. London, Oxford University Press, 1972. [5], 186 p. 21 cm. (Oxford readings in philosophy) Contents.Contents.—Valery, P. The idea of art.—Sartre, J.-P. The work of art.—Ingarden, R. Artistic and aesthetic values.—Merleau-Ponty, M. Eye and mind.—Moore, G. E. Wittgenstein's lectures in 1930-33.—Findlay, J. N. The perspicuous and the poignant.—Hungerland, I. C. Once again, aesthetic and non-aesthetic.—Wollheim, R. On drawing an object.—Elliott, R. K. Aesthetic theory and the experience of art.—Savile, A. The place of invention in the concept of art.—Bibliography (p. [178]-184) [BH21.O7] 73-156482 ISBN 0-19-875020-X £0.75
1. Aesthetics—Collections. 2. Art—Philosophy—Collections.

RADER, Melvin Miller, 111.85
1903- ed.
A modern book of esthetics; an anthology. Edited with introd. and notes by Melvin Rader. 3d ed. [New York] Holt, Rinehart, and Winston [1960] xxxii, 540 p. 25 cm. Bibliography: p. 505-533. [BH21.R3 1960] 60-8597
1. Aesthetics—Collections. I. Title.

RADER, Melvin Miller, 111.8'5
1903- ed.
A modern book of esthetics; an anthology. Edited with introd. and notes by Melvin Rader. 4th ed. New York, Holt, Rinehart and Winston [1973] viii, 568 p. illus. 24 cm. Bibliography: p. 535-560. [BH21.R3 1973] 72-86536 ISBN 0-03-001756-4 9.95
1. Aesthetics—Collections. I. Title.

RICHTER, Peyton E., ed. 701.17
Perspectives in aesthetics, Plato to Camus, edited by Peyton E. Richter. New York, Odyssey Press [1967] xiv, 472 p. 21 cm. Includes bibliographical references. [BH21.R5] 66-19066
1. Aesthetics—Collections. I. Title.

SESONSKE, Alexander, 111.85082
ed.
What is art? Aesthetic theory from Plato to Tolstoy. New York, Oxford University Press, 1965. xvi, 428 p. 26 cm. Bibliography: p. [419]-428. [BH21.S4] 65-12469
1. Aesthetics—Collections. I. Title.

STOLNITZ, Jerome, ed. 701.17
Aesthetics. New York, Macmillan [c.1965] 115p. illus. 22cm. (Sources in phil.) Bibl. [BH21.S8] 65-11070 1.50 pap.,
1. Aesthetics—Collections. I. Title. II. Series.

TILLMAN, Frank A., 701.17'08
1923-
Philosophy of art and aesthetics, from Plato to Wittgenstein [by] Frank A. Tillman [and] Steven M. Cahn. New York, Harper & Row [1969] xiii, 791 p. 25 cm. Bibliography: p. 742-791. [BH21.T5] 69-11946
1. Aesthetics—Collections. 2. Art—Philosophy—Collections. I. Cahn, Steven M., joint author. II. Title.

Aesthetics—Congresses.

CENTER for Hermeneutical 111.8'5
Studies in Hellenistic and Modern Culture.
Art as a hermeneutic of narrative : protocol of the twentyfourth colloquy, 14 November 1976 / The Center for Hermeneutical Studies in Hellenistic and Modern Culture ; John W. Dixon, Jr. Berkeley, CA : The Center, c1977. 56 p. ; 21 cm. (Protocol series of the colloquies of the Center ; 24) "Select bibliography of John W. Dixon, Jr.": p. 56. [BH39.C4 1977] 77-4346 ISBN 0-89242-023-5 pbk. : 3.00
1. Aesthetics—Congresses. 2. Art—Philosophy—Congresses. 3. Art and religion—Congresses. 4. Hermeneutics—Congresses. 5. Narration (Rhetoric)—Congresses. I. Dixon, John W. II. Title. III. Series: Center for Hermeneutical Studies in Hellenistic and Modern Culture. Protocol series of the colloquies ; no. 24.

Aesthetics—Early works to 1800.

BURKE, Edmund, 1729?- 111.8'5
1797.
A philosophical enquiry into the origin of our ideas of the sublime and beautiful. New York, Garland Pub., 1971. ix, 342 p. 21 cm. "Facsimile ... made from a copy in the Yale University Library [originally published in 1759]" [BH181.B8 1759aa] 70-112087
1. Aesthetics—Early works to 1800. 2. Sublime, The. I. Title.

BURKE, Edmund, 1729-1797. 701
A philosophical enquiry into the origin of our ideas of the sublime and beautiful. Edited with an introd. and notes by J. T. Boulton. London, Routledge and Paul; New York, Columbia University Press, 1958. cxxx, 197p. 23cm. Bibliographical footnotes. [BH181.B8 1958] 58-9089
1. Aesthetics—Early works to 1800. 2. Sublime, The. I. Title.

DONALDSON, John, 1737- 701.17
1801.
The elements of beauty. Also, Reflections on the harmony of sensibility and reason. New York, Garland Pub., 1970. 119 p. 22 cm. Facsim. of a Yale University Library copy with imprint: Edinburgh, Printed for Charles Elliot; and T. Cadell, London, 1780. [N62.D67 1780a] 70-112112
1. Aesthetics—Early works to 1800. 2. Ethics. I. Title. II. Title: Reflections on the harmony of sensibility and reason.

GERARD, Alexander, 1728- 700.17
1795.
An essay on taste. New York, Garland Pub., 1970. viii, 298 p. 22 cm. Facsim. of the Yale University Library copy of the 2d ed. with corrections and additions. To which are annexed three dissertations by Mr. De Voltaire, Mr. D'Alembert, and Mr. De Montesquieu. Edinburgh: Printed for A. Millar, London; and A. Kincaid and J. Bell, Edinburgh, 1764. [N75.G3 1970] 72-112129
1. Aesthetics—Early works to 1800. I. Voltaire, Francois Marie Arouet de, 1694-1778. II. Alembert, Jean Lerond d', 1717-1783. III. Montesquieu, Charles Louis de Secondat, baron de La Brede et de, 1689-1755. IV. Title.

GERARD, Alexander, 1728- 701.17
1795
An essay on taste (1759), together with observations concerning the imitative nature of poetry. Facsimile reproduction of the 3d ed. (1780); introd by Walter J. Hipple, Jr. Gainesville, Fla., Scholars' Facsimiles & Reprints, 1963. xxviii p., facsim.: xi, 284 p. 22 cm. 63-7081 7.50
1. Aesthetics—Early works to 1800. I. Title.

HOGARTH, William, 1697- 701.17
1764.
The analysis of beauty. With the rejected passages from the manuscript drafts and autobiographical notes. Edited with an introd. by Joseph Burke. Oxford, Clarendon Press, 1955. ixii, 244p. plates, facsims. 26cm. With facsimile reproduction of original title page. Bibliography: p. 232-234. [N70.H7 1955] 55-13860
1. Aesthetics—Early works to 1800. I. Title.

HOGARTH, William, 1697- 111.8'5
1764.
The analysis of beauty. New York, Garland Pub., 1973. xxii, 153 p. 21 cm. Plates wanting. Facsim. reprint of the 1753 ed. printed by J. Reeves for the author, London. [BH181.H6 1753a] 73-112227
1. Aesthetics—Early works to 1800. I. Title.
Sold only as part of the 208 title series, English literary criticism of the 18th century, for 3900.00. BIP

LESSING, Gotthold Ephraim, 701.17
1729-1781.
Laocoon; an essay upon the limits of painting and poetry. Translated by Ellen Frothingham. New York, Noonday Press, 1957. xi, 245p. 19cm. [N64.L742 1957] 57-8048
1. Aesthetics—Early works to 1800. I. Title. BIP

LESSING, Gotthold Ephraim, 701.17
1729-1781.
Laocoon; an essay on the limits of painting and poetry. Translated with an introd. and notes by Edward Allen McCormick. Indianapolis, Bobbs-Merrill [1962] 259 p. illus. 21 cm. (The Library of liberal arts, 78) [N64.L742 1962] 62-21259
1. Aesthetics — Early works to 1800. I. Title.

LESSING, Gotthold Ephraim, 701.17
1729-1781.
Laokoon. Ed. by Dorothy Reich. [New York] Oxford [c.]1965. 323p. illus., port. 19cm. (Clarendon German ser.) Bibl. [N64.L6] 65-58371 2.20
1. Aesthetics—Early works to 1800. I. Reich, Dorothy, ed. II. Title.

THE Polite arts; 701.17
or, A dissertation on poetry, painting, musick, architecture, and eloquence. New York, Garland Pub., 1970. xii, 160 p. 21 cm. Facsim. of the Yale University Library copy with imprint: London, Printed for J. Osborn and T. Lownds, 1749. [BH181.P6 1749a] 78-112204
1. Aesthetics—Early works to 1800.

SPENCE, Joseph, 1699- 111.8'5
1768.
Crito; or, A dialogue on beauty. New York, Garland Pub., 1970. 61 p. 21 cm. "Facsimile ... made from a copy loaned by Stephen Weissman of Ximenes: Rare Books [originally published in 1752.]" [BH181.S64 1752a] 72-112240
1. Aesthetics—Early works to 1800. I. Title.

THOMSON, William, 1726- 111.8'5
1798.
An enquiry into the elementary principles of beauty in the works of nature and art. New York, Garland Pub., 1972. xx, 214 p. illus. 26 cm. Original t.p. has imprint: London, Printed for J. Johnson, St. Paul's Church Yard, 1798. [BH181.T48 1798a] 75-112249
1. Aesthetics—Early works to 1800. 2. Nature (Aesthetics) I. Title.

USHER, James, 1720-1772. 710.17
Clio: or, A discourse on taste. New York, Garland Pub., 1970. xiii, 247 p. 22 cm. Facsim. "made from a copy loaned by Stephen Weissman of Ximenes: Rare Books, inc." with imprint: London, Printed for T. Davies, in Russel-Street, Covent-Garden, 1769. [N75.U8 1769a] 74-112254
1. Aesthetics—Early works to 1800. I. Title.

Aesthetics, French.

COLEMAN, Francis X. J. 111.8'5
The aesthetic thought of the French Enlightenment [by] Francis X. J. Coleman. [Pittsburgh] University of Pittsburgh Press [1971] xxi, 167 p. 22 cm. Bibliography: p. 161-164. [BH221.F83C64] 76-136570 ISBN 0-8229-3221-0 7.95
1. Aesthetics, French. 2. Enlightenment. 3. Philosophy, French—18th century. I. Title. BIP

SAISSELIN, Remy Gilbert, 1925- 701.17
Taste in eighteenth century France. Critical reflections on the origins of aesthetics; or, An apology for amateurs [by] R. G. Saisselin. [1st ed. Syracuse, N. Y.] Syracuse University Press [1965] vii, 161 p. 22 cm. "Bibliographical notes": p. 135-145. [BH221.F8S3] 65-23460
1. Aesthetics, French. 2. Eighteenth century. I. Title. II. Title: Critical reflections on the origins o aesthetics. III. Title: An apology for amateurs. BIP

Aesthetics—History.

BEARDSLEY, Monroe C. 111.85
Aesthetics from classical Greece to the present; a short history. New York, Macmillan [c.1966] 414p. 21cm. (Fields of Phil. ser.) Bibl. [BH81.B4] 65-24765 7.95
1. Aesthetics — Hist. I. Title.

BOSANQUET, Bernard, 1848-1923. 701.1709
A history of aesthetic. New York, Meridian Books, 1957. 502p. 21cm. (The Meridian library, ML8) Includes bibliography. [BH81.B6 1957] 57-10845
1. Aesthetics— Hist. I. Title.

BOSANQUET, Bernard, 1848-1923. 701.17'09
A history of aesthetic, 2nd ed. London, Allen & Unwin; New York, Humanities P., 1966. xxiii, 502 p. 22 cm. (The Muirhead library of philosophy) unpriced Bibliography: p. 495-498. [BH81.B6] 66-27376
1. Aesthetics—Hist. I. Title. II. Series: Library of philosophy

GILBERT, Katharine (Everett) 1886-1952. 101
A history of esthetics, by Katherine Everett Gilbert and Helmut Kuhn. Rev. and enl. Bloomington, Indiana University Press, 1953. xxi, 613p. 22cm. Includes bibliogra7hpes. [BH81.G5 1953] 701.17 53-7022
1. Aesthetics—Hist. I. Kuhn, Helmut, 1899- joint author. II. Title. BIP

HIPPLE, Walter John. 101
The beautiful, the sublime, & the picturesque in 18th century british aesthetic theory. Carbondale, Southern Illinois University Press, 1957. vi, 390p. illus. 24cm. Bibliography: p. 377-384. [BH221.G72H5] 701.17 57-9535
1. Aesthetics—Hist. 2. Sublime, The. I. Title.

Aesthetics—History.

BATE, Walter Jackson, 1918- 701.17
From classic to romantic premises of taste in eighteenth-century England [Gloucester, Mass., Peter Smith, 1961, c.1946] 197p. (Harper Torchbk., Academy lib. TB 1036 rebound) 'Presented as the Lowell Institute lectures, Boston, 1945.' (Harper Torchbk., Academy lib. TB1036 rebound) 3.35
1. Esthetics—Hist. 2. Classicism. 3. Romanticism—England. I. Lowell Institute lectures 1945. II. Title.

BEARDSLEY, Monroe C. 111.8'5
Aesthetics from classical Greece to the present / Monroe C. Beardsley. University : University of Alabama Press, [1975, i.e.1976] p. cm. Reprint of the 1966 ed. published by Macmillan, New York. Includes bibliographies and index. [BH81.B4 1976] 75-20138 ISBN 0-8173-6623-7 pbk. : 6.50
1. Aesthetics—History. I. Title. BIP

CHAMBERS, Frank Pentland, 1900- 701.17
The history of taste; an account of the revolutions of art criticism and theory in Europe, by Frank P. Chambers. Westport, Conn., Greenwood Press [1971, c1932] ix, 342 p. illus. 23 cm. Bibliography: p. 307-312 [N61.C48 1971] 76-136057 ISBN 0-8371-5207-0
1. Aesthetics—History. 2. Art—Europe. 3. Art criticism—History. I. Title. BIP

GILBERT, Katharine (Everett) 1886-1952. 111.8'5
A history of esthetics, by Katharine Everett Gilbert and Helmut Kuhn. Rev. and enl. Westport, Conn., Greenwood Press [1972, c1953] xxi, 613 p. 23 cm. Includes bibliographies. [BH81.G5 1972] 76-163548 ISBN 0-8371-6207-6
1. Aesthetics—History. I. Kuhn, Helmut, 1899- joint author. II. Title.

GILBERT, Katharine (Everett) 1886-1952. 111.8'5
A history of esthetics, by Katharine Everett Gilbert and Helmut Kuhn. Rev. and enl. New York, Dover Publications [1972, c1953] xxi, 613 p. 21 cm. Includes bibliographical references. [BH81.G5 1972b] 71-188811 ISBN 0-486-22829-0 5.00
1. Aesthetics—History. I. Kuhn, Helmut, 1899- joint author. II. Title.

KALLEN, Horace Meyer, 1882- 701.17
Art and freedom; a historical and biographical interpretation of the relations between the ideas of beauty, use, and freedom in Western civilization from the Greeks to the present day [by] Horace M. Kallen. New York, Greenwood Press [1969, c1942] 2 v. (xvii, 1006 p.) 23 cm. Bibliographical references included in "Notes" (p. 965-978) [BH81.K3 1969] 77-90538
1. Aesthetics—History. 2. Art—Philosophy—History. 3. Literature—Aesthetics. I. Title. BIP

OSBORNE, Harold, 1905- 701.17'09
Aesthetics and art theory: an historical introduction. New York, E. P. Dutton, 1970 [c1968] 320 p. illus. 21 cm. Bibliography: p. 308-313. [N66.O8 1968b] 74-87205 iSBN 5-250-51031- 7.95
1. Aesthetics—History. I. Title. BIP

Aesthetics, Japanese—Addresses, essays, lectures.

WATTS, Alan Wilson, 1915-1973. 111.8'5
Uncarved block, unbleached silk : the mystery of life / Alan Watts ; photos and introd. by Jeff Berner ; calligraphy by Renee Locks. New York : A&W Visual Library, c1978. [107] p. : col. ill. ; 28 cm. [BH221.J33W37] 78-53063 ISBN 0-89104-103-6 : 20.00. ISBN 0-89104-102-8 pbk. : 10.00
1. Aesthetics, Japanese—Addresses, essays, lectures. I. Berner, Jeff. II. Title. BIP

Aesthetics, Modern.

LISTOWEL, William Francis Hare, Earl of, 1906- 701'.17
A critical history of modern aesthetics / by the Earl of Listowel. New York : Haskell House, 1974. 288 p. ; 21 cm. Reprint of the 1933 ed., which was originally presented as the author's thesis, University of London. Includes index. Bibliography: p. [279]-284. [BH151.L5 1974] 75-1009 ISBN 0-8383-1958-0 : 13.95
1. Aesthetics, Modern. I. Title.

Aesthetics, Modern—18th century.

MOORE, Robert Etheridge, 1920- 701'.17
Changing taste in eighteenth-century art and literature; papers read at a Clark Library seminar, April 17, 1971, by Robert E. Moore and Jean H. Hagstrum. With an introd. by Earl Miner. Los Angeles, William Andrews Clark Memorial Library, University of California, 1972. iv, 67 p. illus. 23 cm. (William Andrews Clark Memorial Library seminar papers) Contents.Contents.—The art of Piranesi: looking backward into the future, by R. E. Moore.—"Such, such were the joys": the boyhood of the man of feeling, by J. H. Hagstrum. Includes bibliographical references. [NX452.M6] 72-181945
1. Aesthetics, Modern—18th century. 2. The arts. I. Hagstrum, Jean H. II. California. University. University at Los Angeles. William Andrews Clark Memorial Library. III. Title. IV. Series.

Aesthetics, Modern—18th century—Addresses, essays, lectures.

ARMSTRONG, John, 1709-1779. 701.17
Miscellanies in Cooper, John Gilbert, 1723-1769. Essays on taste, from Letters concerning taste, 3d ed. (1757) Los Angeles, William Andrews Clark Memorial Library, Univ. of California, 1951. [N75.C6 1951] 51-12964
I. Title.

GILMORE, Thomas B., comp. 709'.03'3
Early eighteenth-century essays on taste; facsimile reproductions, with an introduction, by Thomas B. Gilmore, Jr. Delmar, N.Y., Scholars' Facsimiles & Reprints, 1972. xi, 350 p. illus. 23 cm. Includes bibliographical references. [NX452.G5] 78-161932 ISBN 0-8201-1092-2 20.00
1. Aesthetics, Modern—18th century—Addresses, essays, lectures. 2. The arts—Addresses, essays, lectures. I. Title. BIP

Aesthetics, Modern—20th century.

BOLAM, David W. 111.8'5
Art and belief, by David W. Bolam and James L. Henderson. New York, Schocken Books [1970, c1967] 206 p. illus. 23 cm. Includes bibliographies. [BH201.B67 1970] 69-12904 5.95
1. Aesthetics, Modern—20th century. 2. Religions. 3. Philosophy, Modern—20th century. I. Henderson, James Lewis, 1910- joint author. II. Title. BIP

KAELIN, Eugene Francis, 1926- 700'.1
Art and existence: a phenomenological aesthetics [by] Eugene F. Kaelin. Lewisburg [Pa.] Bucknell University Press [1971, c1970] 357 p. col. illus. 22 cm. Bibliography: p. 340-347. [BH201.K34 1971] 74-101236 ISBN 0-8387-7582-9 12.00
1. Husserl, Edmund, 1859-1938. 2. Heidegger, Martin, 1889- 3. Aesthetics, Modern—20th century. 4. Phenomenology. I. Title. BIP

Aesthetics, Modern—20th century—Addresses, essays, lectures.

ESTHETICS contemporary / edited by Richard Kostelanetz. Buffalo : Prometheus Books, 1978. 444 p. ; 24 cm. Bibliography: p. 428-438. [BH201.E84] 77-73848 ISBN 0-87975-105-3 : 19.95 111.8'5
1. Aesthetics, Modern—20th century—Addresses, essays, lectures. 2. Avant-garde (Aesthetics)—Addresses, essays, lectures. 3. Arts, Modern—20th century—Addresses, essays, lectures. 4. Art—Philosophy—Addresses, essays, lectures. I. Kostelanetz, Richard. BIP

THE Quest for imagination; essays in twentieth century aesthetic criticism. Edited by O. B. Hardison, Jr. Cleveland, Press of Case Western Reserve University, 1971. xiv, 286 p. 24 cm. Includes bibliographical references, [BH201.Q47 1971] 70-145425 ISBN 0-8295-0207-6 12.95 801
1. Aesthetics, Modern—20th century—Addresses, essays, lectures. 2. Criticism (Philosophy)—Addresses, essays, lectures. 3. Imagination. I. Hardison, O. B., ed.

Aesthetics, Modern—20th century—Collected works.

LIPMAN, Matthew, comp. 111.8'5
Contemporary aesthetics. Boston, Allyn and Bacon [1973] x, 505 p. 24 cm. Includes bibliographical references. [BH201.L53] 73-76197 10.50
1. Aesthetics, Modern—20th century—Collected works. 2. Art—Philosophy—Collected works. I. Title. BIP

Aesthetics, Oriental.

MUNRO, Thomas, 1897- 701.17
Oriental aesthetics. Cleveland, Press of Western Reserve University [1965] ix, 138 p. illus. (part col.) 23 cm. Bibliographical footnotes. [BH101.M8] 65-13908
1. Aesthetics, Oriental.

Aesthetics — Period.

ILLINOIS. University. 701.1707
Illinois. Dept. of Public Instruction. *The Journal of aesthetic education.* spring 1966- [Champaign, Ill.] v. 23 cm. Issued by the University of Illinois and the Illinois Dept. of Public Instruction (called Office of the Superintendent of Public Instruction) [N1.J58] 66-9897
1. Aesthetics — Period. 2. Education. Secondary — Curricula — Period. I. Title.

Aesthetics—Physiological aspects.

BERLYNE, D. E. 701.17
Aesthetics and psychobiology [by] D. E. Berlyne. New York, Appleton-Century-Crofts [1971] xiv, 336 p. illus. 25 cm. (The Century psychology series) Bibliography: p. 297-321. [NX165.B387] 70-165204 ISBN 0-390-08670-3
1. Aesthetics—Physiological aspects. 2. The arts—Psychology. I. Title.

Aesthetics, Polish.

HARRELL, Jean Gabbert, 1921- comp. 111.8'5
Aesthetics in twentieth-century Poland; selected essays. Edited by Jean G. Harrell and Alina Wierzbianska. Lewisburg [Pa.] Bucknell University Press [1973] 285 p. 22 cm. Includes bibliographical references. [BH221.P63H37] 78-38984 ISBN 0-8387-1100-6 15.00
1. Aesthetics, Polish. 2. Aesthetics, Modern—20th century. I. Wierzbianska, Alina, joint comp. II. Title.
Contents omitted. BIP

Aesthetics, Russian.

FILIPOV, Aleksandr Pavlovich, 1891- 100
Origin and principles of Soviet aesthetics, unitl N. Krushchev, by Alexander Philipov. [1st ed.,] New York, Pageant Press [c1964] 161 p. 21 cm. Includes bibliographical references. [BH221.R93F5] 64-25292
1. Aesthetics, Russian. 2. Communism and art. I. Title.

WEST, James D. 891.7'09'003
Russian symbolism; a study of Vyacheslav Ivanov and the Russian symbolist aesthetic [by] James West. London, Methuen [1972, c.1970] vii, 250 p. port. 22 cm. (University paperbacks, UP 453) Bibliography: p. 231-245. [BH221.R93W47] 79-139834 ISBN 0-416-19350-1 pap., 4.50
1. Ivanov, Viacheslav Ivanovich, 1866-1949. 2. Aesthetics, Russian. 3. Symbolism in art. I. Title.
Dist. by Barnes & Noble, New York.

Aethelwold, Saint, Bp. of Winchester.

WORMALD, Francis. 096
The Benedictional of St. Ethelwold; with an introd. and notes. New York, T. Yoseloff [1960, c1959] 30 p. 8 mounted col. illus. 29 cm. (The Library of illuminated manuscripts) The illuminated miniatures reproduced are from the ms. in the British Museum. [ND3362.5.W6] 60-1239
1. Aethelwold, Saint, Bp. of Winchester. 2. Illumination of books and manuscripts—Winchester, Eng. 3. Benedictionals. I. Title. II. Series.

Afghanistan — Antiq.

ROWLAND, Benjamin, 1904- 709.581
Ancient art from Afghanistan; treasures of the Kabul Museum, by Benjamin Rowland, Jr. [New York] Asia Society; distributed by H. N. Abrams [1966] 144 p. illus. (part col.) map, port. 28 cm. Catalog of a traveling exhibition shown at the Asia House Gallery, New York, the Los

Angeles County Museum of Art, Lytton Gallery, and the National Collection of Fine Arts, Smithsonian Institution, Washington, D.C., from Jan. 13 to Aug. 23, 1966. [N5335.K3R6] 66-11137
1. Afghanistan — Antiq. 2. Art, Ancient — Exhibitions. I. Kabul, Afghanistan (City) Museum. II. Asia Society. III. Asia House Gallery, New York. IV. Los Angeles County Museum, Los Angeles. V. Smithsonian Institution. National Collection of Fine Arts. VI. Title. BIP

Afo-A-Kom (Statue)

FERRETTI, Fred. 732'.2'096711
Afo-A-Kom : sacred art of Cameroon / by Fred Ferretti. New York : Third Press, c1975. 145 p. : ill. ; 27 cm. [NB1255.C17F47] 73-92800 ISBN 0-89388-134-1 : 12.95
1. Afo-A-Kom (Statue) 2. Sculpture—Cameroon. 3. Sculpture, Primitive—Cameroon. 4. Art thefts—Cameroon. 5. Kom (African people) I. Title. BIP

Africa—Social life and customs.

BIGGERS, John Thomas, 1924- 916
Ananse, the web of life in Africa. Drawings and text by John Biggers. Austin, University of Texas Press [1962] 119 p. illus. 29 cm. (The Blaffer series of southwestern art, no. 3) [NC1075.B54A42] 62-9269
1. Africa—Social life and customs. I. Title.

Africa, South—Descr. & trav.

MORRIS, Wilson Major, 1884- 916.66
Africa, the great continent. New York, North River Press [1954] 80p. illus. 26cm. [DT626.M62] 54-4420
1. Africa, South—Descr. & trav. 2. Liberia—Descr. & trav. I. Title.

Afro-American art.

LEWIS, Samella S. 790'.73
Art : African American / Samella Lewis. New York : Harcourt Brace Jovanovich, c1978. x, 246 p. : ill. (some col.) ; 25 cm. Includes index. Bibliography: p. 233-239. [N6538.N5L39] 77-78732 ISBN 0-15-503410-3 pbk. : 11.95
1. Afro-American art. I. Title.

Afro-American art—Exhibitions.

AMISTAD II, 709'.73'074016855
Afro-American art / [edited by] David C. Driskell. Nashville : Dept. of Art, Fisk University, c1975. 92 p. : ill., facsims. ; 29 cm. Exhibition held at Van Vechten Gallery, Fisk University. "Catalogue:" p. 69-88. [N6538.N5A45] 75-7466
1. Afro-American art—Exhibitions. 2. Art, Modern—20th century—United States—Exhibitions. I. Driskell, David C. II. Van Vechten Gallery.

DRISKELL, David C. 709'.73
Two centuries of Black American art : [exhibition], Los Angeles County Museum of Art, the High Museum of Art, Atlanta, Museum of Fine Arts, Dallas, the Brooklyn Museum / David C. Driskell ; with catalog notes by Leonard Simon. Los Angeles : Los Angeles County Museum of Art, c1976. Includes index. Bibliography: p. [N6538.N5D74] 76-20479 ISBN 0-87587-070-8 : 5.00
1. Afro-American art—Exhibitions. I. Simon, Leonard, 1936- II. Los Angeles Co., Calif. Museum of Art, Los Angeles. III. Title. BIP

AN Exhibition 709'.73'074'09491
of Black women artists : [an exhibition on the occasion of the fourth annual Black Culture Festival, May 5-17, 1975, UCEN Art Gallery, University of California, Santa Barbara] / by Nanette Hayles ... [et al.]. Santa Barbara : Committee for Black Culture, University of California, Santa Barbara, [1975] p. cm. [N6538.A35E93] 75-26604
1. Afro—American art—Exhibitions. 2. Afro—American artists. 3. Afro—American women. I. Hayles, Nanette. II. Black Culture Festival, 4th, University of California, Santa Barbara, 1975. III. California. University, Santa Barbara.

NEW Muse 709'.73'074014723
Community Museum of Brooklyn.
The Black artists in the WPA, 1933-1943 : [an exhibition of drawings, paintings, and sculpture, February 15-March 30, 1976 / Charlene Claye Van Derzee, curator, George Carter, assistant curator]. [1st ed.]. [Brooklyn, N.Y. : New Muse Community Museum of Brooklyn, 1976] [23] p. : ill. ; 21 cm. Cover title. [N6538.N5N37 1976] 76-3078
1. United States. Work Projects Administration. 2. Afro-American art—Exhibitions. 3. Art, Modern—20th century—United States—Exhibitions. 4. Politics in art. I. Van Derzee, Charlene Claye. II. Carter, George, 1931- III. Title.

THE Pittsburgh 709'.73'074014886
Chapter of Links presents Black American art from the Barnett Aden Collection : Frick Fine Arts Museum, University of Pittsburgh, September 17 thru October 23, 1977. Pittsburgh : The Chapter, c1977. 56 p. : chiefly ill. ; 23 cm. An exhibition of a portion of the collection of the Barnett-Aden Gallery. Includes index. [N6538.N5P5] 77-153782
1. Afro-American art—Exhibitions. I. Links, inc. Pittsburgh Chapter. II. Barnett-Aden Gallery. III. Frick Art Museum, Pittsburgh. IV. Title: Black American art from the Barnett Aden Collection.

Afro-American artists—Biography.

FAX, Elton C. 709'.2'2 B
Black artists of the new generation / Elton C. Fax ; foreword by Romare Bearden. New York : Dodd, Mead, c1977. xiv, 370 p., [8] leaves of plates : ill. ; 22 cm. Includes index. [N6538.N5F29] 77-7053 ISBN 0-396-07434-0 : 8.95
1. Afro-American artists—Biography. 2. Afro-American art. 3. Art, Modern—20th century—United States. I. Title. BIP

HASKINS, James, 1941- 770'.92'4 B
James Van DerZee, the picture-takin' man / by Jim Haskins. New York : Dodd, Mead, [1979] p. cm. Includes index. A biography of the black photographer who has received acclaim for his prints of Harlem. [TR140.V37H37] 92 78-22431 ISBN 0-396-07678-5 : 8.95
1. Van DerZee, James—Juvenile literature. 2. Afro-American photographers—New York (City)—Biography—Juvenile literature.

Afro-Americans in art.

WHITE, Charles, 1918- 760'.092'4
The work of Charles White : an American experience : an exhibition / organized by the High Museum of Art, Atlanta, Georgia, 1976. Atlanta : The Museum, 1976. 23 p. : ill. ; 21 cm. Catalogue of an exhibition held at the High Museum of Art, Atlanta, Sept. 4-Oct. 3, 1976, and at other museums, Oct. 23, 1976-Aug. 14, 1977. [N6537.W44H53] 76-26396
1. White, Charles, 1918- 2. Afro-Americans in art. I. High Museum of Art.

Afro-Americans—Portraits—Exhibitions.

SCURLOCK, Addison N., 1883-1964. 779'.9'9753030924
The historic photographs of Addison N. Scurlock : June 19-August 29, 1976, The Corcoran Gallery of Art, Washington, D.C. Washington : The Gallery, c1976. [21] p. : ill. ; 21 cm. "Catalogue of the exhibition": p. [20]-[21] [E185.96.S423] 76-20428
1. Afro-Americans—Portraits—Exhibitions. I. Corcoran Gallery of Art, Washington, D.C. II. Title.

Agam, Yaacov, 1928—

AGAM, Yaacov, 1928- 730'.924
Yaacov Agam: transformable transformables. [New York, Galerie Denise Rene, 1971] [52] p. illus. (part col.), ports. 27 cm. Catalog of an exhibition held May 1971. [NB979.A4G3] 74-198262
I. Galerie Denise Rene.

AGAM, Yaacov [name orig.: Yaacov Gipstein] 1928- 759.95694
Yaacov Agam. Texts by the artist. [Ed. with Paul Kanelski. Tr. from French by Haakon Chevalier]Neuchatel, Switzerland, Editions du Griffon [dist. New York, Universe, 1963, c.1962] 128p. illus. (pt. col.) port., music. 31cm. and phonodisc. (2 s. 7 in. 45 rpm.) in pocket. (Sculpture of the twentieth cent.) Introd. in Eng. and Hebrew. 63-4166 20.00
I. Title.

METKEN, Gunter, 1928- 709'.2'4
Yaacov Agam. New York, H. N. Abrams [1974] p. cm. [N7279.A4M47] 74-5115 ISBN 0-8109-4408-1 7.50
1. Agam, Yaacov, 1928- I. Agam, Yaacov, 1928-

POPPER, Frank, 1918- 709'.2'4
Agam / by Frank Popper. New York : H. N. Abrams, [1976, i.e.1975] p. cm. Includes index. Bibliography: p. [N7279.A4P66] 75-5580 ISBN 0-8109-0294-X : 7.95
1. Agam, Yaacov, 1928- I. Agam, Yaacov, 1928- II. Title. BIP

Aged—Dwellings.

GREAT Britain. Dept. of the Environment. 728
Housing the elderly. Lancaster : M.T.P. Construction, 1974 [i.e.,1975] 227 p. : ill. ; 31 cm. (Design bulletins) Includes bibliographical references and index. [NA7195.A4G73 1974] 74-193638 ISBN 0-904406-01-6 : 18.50
1. Aged—Dwellings. 2. Architecture, Domestic—Designs and plans. I. Title. II. Series.
Distributed by Herman Publishing.

MCGUIRE, Marie C., 1904- 728
Design of housing for the elderly: a checklist, by Marie C. McGuire. Washington, National Association of Housing and Redevelopment Officials, 1972. 19 p. 22 cm. "NAHRO publication number N560." "Edited version of Mrs. McGuire's address at the NAHRO National Housing Workshop in San Antonio on September 22, 1972." [NA7195.A4M32] 74-173132 1.50
1. Aged—Dwellings. I. National Association of Housing and Redevelopment Officials. II. Title.

MATHIASEN, Geneva, 1898- ed. 728.2
Planning homes for the aged. Geneva Mathiasen [and] Edward H. Noakes, editors. New York, F. W. Dodge Corp. [1959] 119 p. illus. 30 cm. Includes bibliography. [NA7195.A4M45] 59-8314
1. Aged—Dwellings. I. Noakes, Edward H., joint ed. II. Title.

MUSSON, Noverre. 725.56
Buildings for the elderly [by] Noverre Musson and Helen Heusinkveld. New York, Reinhold Pub. Corp. [1963] 216 p. illus. 22 x 27 cm. [NA7195.A4M8] 62-19489
1. Aged—Dwellings. 2. Architecture, Domestic—Designs and plans. 3. Architecture, Domestic—U.S. I. Heusinkveld, Helen, joint author. II. Title.

NIERTRASZ, Frits H. J., 1926- ed. 725.56
Building for the aged. [dist. Princeton, N. J., Van Nostrand, 1961] ix, 187p. illus. 31cm. Bibl. 60-15522 16.50
1. Aged—Dwellings. I. Title.

RUTHERFORD, Robert B., ed. 725.56
Architectural designs: homes for the aged; the European approach, compiled and edited by Robert B. Rutherford and Arthur J. Holst. Peoria, Ill., Howard Co., 1963. 102 p. illus. (part col.) ports, plans. 29 x 36 cm. Page 102 blank for "notes." [NA7195.A4R8] 63-3829
1. Aged—Dwellings. 2. Architecture, Domestic—Designs and plans. I. Holst, Arthur J., joint ed.

Aged—Dwellings—Bibliography.

CASTO, Marilyn Dee. 016.3092 s
Housing for the elderly : design, economics, legislation, and socio-psychological aspects / Marilyn Dee Casto and Savannah S. Day. Monticello, Ill. : Council of Planning Librarians, 1976. 30 p. ; 29 cm. (Exchange bibliography ; 1128) Cover title. [Z5942.C68 no. 1128] [Z7164.O4] [HD7287.9] 016.3015'4 76-381108 pbk. : 3.00
1. Aged—Dwellings—Bibliography. I. Day, Savannah S., 1927- joint author. II. Title. III. Series: Council of Planning Librarians. Exchange bibliography ; 1128.

Aged—Portraits.

SIMMONS, Patricia Worth. 779'.2'0924
Yesterday's children; a photographic essay. [Nashville, Tenn., Aurora Publishers, c1972] 265 p. illus. 29 cm. [TR681.A35S55] 72-85164 ISBN 0-87695-158-2 10.00
1. Aged—Portraits. I. Title.

Agrella, Len, 1939—

AGRELLA, Len, 1939- 709'.2'4
Agrella, born February 14, 1939; an aesthetic appreciation, by David W. Linscott. Edited by William Wilborn. Photography by Michael Morgan [Reno, Davidpressinc., 1974] p. cm. [N6537.A38L54] 74-10916 ISBN 0-914786-00-8 3.00
1. Agrella, Len, 1939- I. Linscott, David W., 1940-

Agricultural exhibitions—Iowa—Pictorial works.

WOOLSTON, Bill. 779'.9'977703
Iowa's fair : photographs / by Bill Woolston. Genesee, Idaho : Thorn Creek Press, c1975. [106] p. : chiefly ill. ; 24 x 26 cm. [S555.I8W66] 75-9404 ISBN 0-915664-01-1
1. Agricultural exhibitions—Iowa—Pictorial works. 2. Iowa—Fairs—Pictorial works. I. Title.

Agricultural machinery—Seats—Catalogs.

SITES, Donald E. 739'.48
An illustrated guide for collecting cast iron implement seats [by] Donald E. Sites. Donald and Alberta Sites: photography. [Grinnell? Kan., 1968] 1 v. (unpaged) illus. 21 cm. [NK8459.S4S5] 76-699 4.00
1. Agricultural machinery—Seats—Catalogs. I. Title.

SITES, Donald E. 739'.48
An illustrated guide for collecting cast iron implement seats, Donald E. Sites, author. Donald and Alberta Sites, photography. [Grinnell? Kan., 1969] 1 v. (chiefly illus.) 21 cm. "An identification guide for cast iron implement seat collectors." [NK8459.S4S5 1969] 73-8593 4.00
1. Agricultural machinery—Seats—Catalogs. I. Title.

SITES, Donald E. 739'.48
More cast iron implement seats; an identification and price guide for cast iron implement seat collectors. Donald E. Sites, author. [Grinnell? Kan., 1972] 1 v. (chiefly illus.) 22 cm. [NK8459.S4S52] 72-170082 5.25 (pbk)
1. Agricultural machinery—Seats—Catalogs. I. Title.

Air conditioning.

ROBINSON, Karl Davis. 628.8
What the lithographer should know about air conditioning; superseding Handbook of air conditioning for lithographers, 1929. New York, Lithographic Technical Foundation [1950] iv, 92 p. illus., diagrs. (1 fold., laid in) 22 cm. [Lithographic Technical Foundation, inc. Technical bulletin] 309 [i.e. 9] Bibliography: p. 90. [NE2250.L77 no. 9] 50-4460
1. Air conditioning. 2. Lithography. I. Title. II. Series.

Air guns.

BEEMAN, Robert. 683
Air gun digest / by Robert Beeman ; edited by Jack Lewis. Northfield, Ill. : DBI

Books, c1977. 256 p. : ill. ; 28 cm. [TS537.5.B43] 76-50750 ISBN 0-695-80764-1 : 6.95
1. Air guns. I. Lewis, Jack P., 1924- II. Title.

DUNATHAN, Arni T. 683'.42
The American B. B gun: a collector's guide [by] Arni T. Dunathan. South Brunswick, A. S. Barnes [1971] 154 p. illus. 29 cm. [TS537.5.D86] 77-146752 ISBN 0-498-07803-5 10.00
1. Air guns. I. Title.

SMITH, Walter Harold 623.44
Black, 1901-
Gas, air, and spring guns of the world. Harrisburg, Pa., Military Service Pub. Co. [1957] 279 p. illus. 29 cm. [TS535.S518] 57-8696
1. Air guns. 2. Rifles. 3. Pistols. I. Title.

WESLEY, Leslie. 623.44
Air-guns and air pistols. New York, Barnes [1956, c1955] 178 p. illus. 20 cm. [SK274.W4] 56-1660
1. Air guns. I. Title. BIP

WESLEY, Leslie. 684
Air-guns and air-pistols / by L. Wesley. Rev. and enl. ed. South Brunswick [N.J.] : A. S. Barnes, 1977, c1971. xiv, 224 p., [12] leaves of plates : ill. ; 21 cm. Includes index. [TS537.5.W4 1977] 76-42137 ISBN 0-498-02042-8 : 9.95
1. Air guns. I. Title.

Air guns—History.

WOLFF, Eldon G. 623.4'4
The Scheiffel and Kunitomo air guns, by Eldon G. Wolff. [Milwaukee] Milwaukee Public Museum [1967?] 55 p. illus. 23 cm. (Milwaukee. Public Museum. Publications in history 8) Page 55, blank for "Notes." [TS537.5.W6] 68-5340
1. Air guns—History. I. Title. II. Title: Kunitomo air guns. III. Series.

Air mail service.

SMITH, Stephen H 769'.563
Rocket mail catalogue and historical survey of first experiments in rocketry. 2d rev. ed.; corrections and additions by Max Kronstein and J. Dellenbag. Jamaica, N.Y., F. Billig, 1955. 68 p. illus. 23 cm. (Billig's specialized catalogues, v. 8) [HE6238.S6 1955] 58-18134
1. Air mail service. 2. Rockets (Aeronautics) 3. Covers (Philately) I. Title. II. Series.

Air mail service—Great Britain.

SMITH, Leonard H. 769'.563
The Ross Smith England-Australia flight: a postal history, by Leonard H. Smith, Jr. 1st ed. Clearwater, Fla., N. H. Smith, 1968. xiv, [64] p., [65]-177 l. illus., facsims., map. 28 cm. Bibliography: leaves 167-168. [HE6238.S57] 68-4116
1. Air mail service—Great Britain. 2. Air mail service—Australia. I. Title.

Air mail stamps—Albums.

SCOTT Publications, inc., 383.22
New York.
Scott's international air post album. Contains spaces for every major variety of government air post stamps listed in Scott's standard postage stamp catalogue. New York, c1961. 5 v. illus. 30 cm. Vols. [2]-[5] without title pages. [HE6230.S29] 62-50440
1. Air mail stamps—Albums. I. Title. II. Title: International air post album.

Air mail stamps—U. S.

GOODKIND, Henry M. 769.56973075
United States: the 5 cents beacon air mail stamp of 1928. New York Collectors Club, 22 E. 35th St., c.1965. 61p. illus. 25cm. (Collectors Club handbk. 19) Pub. under the auspices of the Theodore E. Steinway Memorial Pubn. Fund. [HE6185.U6G67] 65-9701 2.00 pap.,
1. Air mail stamps—U. S. I. Title. II. Title: The 5cents beacon air mail stamp of 1928.

GOODKIND, Henry M. 769.56973075
United States: the 5 cent beacon air mail stamp of 1928 by Henry M. Goodkind New York, Collectors Club [1965] 61 p. illus. 25 cm. (A Collectors Club handbook, 19) "Published under the auspices of the Theodore E. Steinway Memorial Publication Fund." [HE6185.U6G67] 65-9701
1. Air mail stamps — U.S. I. Title. II. Title: The 5 cent beacon air mail stamp of 1928

Airbrush art.

ALLEN, James Zellers 738.15
1913-
Air brush in ceramics. Illus. by the author. Ferndale, Mich., Graphicraft [1955] 59p. illus. 31cm. [NC915.A35A5] 56-21093
1. Airbrush art. 2. Ceramics. I. Title.

DEMBER, Sol. 741.2'9
Complete airbrush techniques for commercial, technical, & industrial applications / Sol Dember. 1st ed. Indianapolis : H. W. Sams, 1974. v, 122 p. : ill. (some col.) ; 28 cm. Includes index. [NC915.A35D45] 74-79841 ISBN 0-672-21119-X pbk. : 9.95
1. Airbrush art. 2. Technical illustration. I. Title. BIP

HAYNES, Michael D. 579'.4
Haynes on airbrush taxidermy painting / by Michael D. Haynes, with the collaboration of Charles L. Haynes, Lola R. Haynes, Nadine Haynes Roberts ; foreword by George Fox Mott. New York : Arco Pub. Co., 1979. p. cm. Includes index. [QL63.H38] 78-23578 ISBN 0-668-04634-1 : 12.50
1. Taxidermy. 2. Airbrush art. I. Title.

MAURELLO, S Ralph, 1911- 741.29
The complete airbrush book. New York, W. Penn Pub. Corp. [c1955] 159p. illus. 29cm. [NC915.A33M3] 55-14221
1. Airbrush art. I. Title. BIP

MICKLUS, Samuel, 1934- 741.2'9
Teacher guide for airbrush, prepared by Samuel Miklus [i.e. Micklus] New Brunswick, N.J., Vocational-Technical Curriculum Laboratory, Rutgers, The State University, 1967. 76 p. illus. 28 cm. At head of title: State of New Jersey, Department of Education, Division of Vocational Education. Bibliography: p. 76. [NC915.A35M5] 68-65030
1. Airbrush art. I. New Jersey. Division of Vocational Education. II. Vocational-Technical Curriculum Laboratory. III. Title.

MUSACCHIA, John B., 1916- 741.29
Airbrush techniques for commercial art, by John B. Musacchia, Henri A. Fluchere [and] Melvin J. Grainger. New York, Reinhold Pub. Corp. [c1953] 128p. illus. 22x27 cm. [NC915.A35M8] 53-5566
1. Airbrush art. 2. Commercial art. I. Title.

MUSACCHIA, John B., 1916- 741.29
Airbrush techniques for commercial art, by Henri A. Fluechere, Melvin J. Grainger, John B. Musachia, Rev. [i.e. 2d] ed. New York, Reinhold [1961, c.1953] 64p. illus. 27cm. 61-14821 5.95
1. Airbrush art. 2. Commercial art. I. Fluchere, Henri Andre, 1914- II. Title.

Airbrush art—Exhibitions.

SANTA Barbara, 759.13'074'019491
Calif. Museum of Art.
Spray. [Santa Barbara, 1971] 30 p. illus. 28 cm. Catalog of "an exhibition presented by the Santa Barbara Museum of Art, April 24 - May 30, 1971." [NC915.A35S2] 75-164743
1. Airbrush art—Exhibitions. 2. Airbrush art—U.S. I. Title.

Aires camera

SIMMONS, Robert, 1931- 770.2
fullname:RobertPrestonSimmons
Aires guide [1st ed.] Philadelphia, Chilton Co. [1958] 128 p. illus. 20 cm. (The Modern camera guide series) [TR263.A5S5] 58-13696
1. Aires camera I. Title.

Airplanes in art.

WOOTTON, Frank A. A. 759.2
The aviation art of Frank Wootton / edited by David Larkin ; introd. by John Blake. 1st U.S. ed. Bearsville, N.Y. : Peacock Press, 1976. [16] p., [40] leaves of plates : ill. (some col.) ; 23 x 28 cm. [ND497.W77A43 1976] 76-15475 6.95
1. Wootton, Frank A. A. 2. Great Britain. Royal Air Force—Pictorial works. 3. Airplanes in art. I. Title. BIP

Airplanes in art—Catalogs.

FERRIS, Keith. 759.2
The aviation art of Keith Ferris / introd. by Keith Ferris ; [edited by Ian Ballantine]. 1st ed. New York : Peacock Press/Bantam Books, 1978. [95] p. : ill. (some col.) ; 23 x 29 cm. [ND237.F38A4 1978] 78-105758 7.95
1. Ferris, Keith—Catalogs. 2. Airplanes in art—Catalogs. 3. Airplanes—Pictorial works—Catalogs. I. Ballantine, Ian. II. Title. BIP

Airplanes in art—Juvenile literature.

AMES, Lee J 743'.8'96291
Draw 50 airplanes, aircraft, & spacecraft / Lee J. Ames. 1st ed. Garden City, N.Y. : Doubleday, c1977. [62] p. : chiefly ill. ; 32 cm. Step-by-step instructions for drawing fifty different aircraft and spacecraft including a Boeing 747, a U-2, and a hang glider. [NC825.A4A46] 76-51554 ISBN 0-385-12235-7 : 5.95. ISBN 0-385-12236-5 lib.bdg. : 7.00
1. Airplanes in art—Juvenile literature. 2. Space vehicles in art—Juvenile literature. 3. Drawing—Instruction—Juvenile literature. I. Title.

Airplanes—Miscellanea.

HATFIELD, David 387.7'33'43
Daniel, 1903-
Aeroplane : historical data and reproductions / compiled by D. D. Hatfield. Inglewood, Calif. : Northrop University Press, c1975. vi, 246 p. : ill. ; 22 cm. On spine: Aeroplane scrap book no. 3, 1911-1941. Includes index. [TL671.H374] 75-331607
1. Airplanes—Miscellanea. I. Title. II. Title: Aeroplane scrap book no. 3, 1911-1941.

Airplanes—Restoration.

DWIGGINS, Don. 629.134'6
Restoration of antique & classic planes / Don Dwiggins. New York : Sports Car Press ; [distributed by Crown Publishers], c1975. 110 p. : ill. ; 21 cm. (Modern aircraft series) Bibliography: p. 103-104. [TL671.9.D9 1975] 75-12423 ISBN 0-87112-073-9 pbk. : 3.95
1. Airplanes—Restoration. I. Title. BIP

Airports—Design and construction.

BLANKENSHIP, Edward G. 711'.78
The airport: architecture—urban integration—ecological problems [by] Edward G. Blankenship. New York, Praeger [1974] 159 p. illus. 29 cm. English and German. [TL725.3.P5B55] 72-92495
1. Airports—Design and construction. I. Title.

MICHIGAN. Aeronautics 711'.78
Commission.
Master plan guide for airports. [Lansing] 1966. 16, 14 l. illus., plans. 28 cm. [TL725.3.P5M53] 67-65153
1. Airports—Design and construction. 2. Airports—Planning. I. Title.

WENGATZ, Gunter F. 711'.78
Design concept of a high capacity airport, by Gunter F. Wengatz and Rolf P. Krischer. Boston, Mass., Transportation Dept., Alonzo B. Reed [1970] [15] p. illus. 22 x 28 cm. [TL725.W45] 76-13695
1. Airports—Design and construction. I. Krischer, Rolf P., joint author. II. Title.

Airports—Illinois—Planning.

JOYCE, John J. 711'.78'0977311
Planning general aviation airports. Report prepared by John J. Joyce. [Chicago] Chicago Area Transportation Study, 1970. 19, 4, 3 p. illus. 29 cm. [TL725.3.P5J68] 72-192145
1. Airports—Illinois—Chicago metropolitan area—Planning. I. Chicago Area Transportation Study. II. Title.

Ake, Mexico.

ROYS, Lawrence, 1884- 917.26
Preliminary report on the ruins of Ake, Yucatan [by] Lawrence Roys and Edwin M. Shook. Salt Lake City [Society for American Archaeology] 1966. x, 54 p. illus. 26 cm. (Memoirs of the Society for American Archaeology, no. 20) "Issued as American antiquity, volume 31, number 3, part 2, January 1966." Errata slip inserted. Bibliography: p. 53-54. [E51.S7 no. 20] 67-186
1. Ake, Mexico. I. Shook, Edwin M., joint author. II. Title. III. Series: Society for American Archaeology. Memoirs, no. 20

Akeley, Carl Ethan, 1864-1926.

CLARK, James Lippitt, 069'.0924 B
1883-
In the steps of the great American museum collector Carl Ethan Akeley by James L. Clark. Illus. by Matthew Kalmenoff. New York, M. Evans; distributed in association with Lippincott, Philadelphia [1968] 127 p. illus. 21 cm. Bibliography: p. 127. A biography of the museum specialist who invented an inexpensive method of stuffing and displaying animals to make them look natural in a natural setting. [QL31.A5C6] 92 AC 68
1. Akeley, Carl Ethan, 1864-1926. 2. Zoological speciments—Collection and preservation. I. Kalmenoff, Matthew, illus. II. Title.

Akeley, Carl Ethan, 1864-1926—Juvenile literature.

CLARK, James Lippitt, 590'.924
1883-
In the steps of the great American museum collector Carl Ethan Akeley by James L. Clark. Illus by Matthew Kalmenoff. New York, M. Evans; distributed in association with Lippincott, Philadelphia [1968] 127 p. illus. 21 cm. Bibliography: p. 127. [QL31.A5C6] 67-28198
1. Akeley, Carl Ethan, 1864-1926—Juvenile literature. 2. Zoological specimens—Collection and preservation—Juvenile literature. I. Title.

Akenfield.

BLYTHE, Ronald, 1922- 914.26'4
Akenfield; portrait of an English village. New York, Pantheon Books [1969] 286 p. 25 cm. Bibliography: p. 11-12. [DA690.A28B55 1969b] 69-15471 6.95
1. Akenfield.

BLYTHE, Ronald, 1923- 914.26'4
Akenfield: portrait of an English village, by Ronald Blythe. [New York] [Dell] [1973, c.1969] 351 p. 18 cm. (Laurel edition, 0202) Bibliography: p. [5]-[6] [DA690.A28B55 1969b] pap., 1.50
1. Akenfield. I. Title.

Akin, Louis, 1868-1913.

BABBITT, Bruce E. 759.13
Color and light: the southwest canvases of Louis Akin, by Bruce E. Babbitt. [1st ed.] Flagstaff, Ariz., Northland Press [1973] xiv, 76 p. illus. 27 cm. Bibliography: p. 75-76. [ND237.A28B32] 73-79778 ISBN 0-87358-111-3 12.50
1. Akin, Louis, 1868-1913. 2. Southwest, New, in art. I. Title.

Akro Agate Company.

FLORENCE, Gene, 748.2'9171'36
1944-
The collectors encyclopedia of Akro Agate glassware / by Gene Florence. 1st ed.

Paducah, Ky. : Collectors Books, c1975. 80 p. : ill. ; 28 cm. [NK5198.A39F56] 75-323832 ISBN 0-89145-000-9 : 8.95
1. Akro Agate Company. 2. Glassware—United States—Catalogs. I. Title. II. Title: Akro Agate glassware.

Alabama—Antiq.

MCMICHAEL, Edward V 970.4
Archaeological salvage in the Oliver Basin, by Edward V. McMichael and James H. Kellar. Athens, Laboratory of Archeaology. Dept. of Sociology and Anthropology, University of Georgia, 1960. iii, 221p. illus., maps (1 fold.) 28cm. (University of Georgia Laboratory of Archaeology series. Report no. 2) Includes bibliography. [E78.A28M3] 61-63001
1. Alabama—Antiq. 2. Georgia—Antiq. 3. Indians of North America—Alabama. 4. Indians of North America—Georgia. I. Kellar, James H., joint author. II. Title. III. Series: Georgia. University. Laboratory of Archaeology. Report no. 2

Alabama — History.

GRIFFITH, Lucile Blanche, 1905- 611.018.'1
History of Alabama, 1540-1900 as recorded in diaries, letters, and papers of the times. Northport, Ala., Colonial Press [1962] x, 457 p. 24 cm. [NUC] 63-14373
1. Alabama — History. I. Title.

Alabama—Maps—Bibliography—Union lists.

MASON, Sara Elizabeth. 016.912'761
A list of nineteenth century maps of the State of Alabama. [1st ed.] Birmingham, Ala., Birmingham Public Library, 1973. 253 p. 23 cm. [Z6027.A25M37] 73-87421
1. Alabama—Maps—Bibliography—Union lists. I. Birmingham, Ala. Public Library. II. Title.

Alabaster sculpture, English—England—Yorkshire.

ROUTH, Pauline E. 730'.942'0740281
Medieval effigial alabaster tombs in Yorkshire / [by] Pauline E. Routh. Ipswich : Boydell Press, 1976. 155 p. : ill. ; 23 cm. Includes index. Bibliography: p. 10-11. [NB1210.A4R68] 77-374768 ISBN 0-85115-073-X : £7.50
1. Alabaster sculpture, English—England—Yorkshire. 2. Alabaster sculpture—Medieval, 500-1500—England—Yorkshire. 3. Sepulchral Monuments—England—Yorkshire. I. Title.

Alaska—Capital and capitol.

BOEING Computer Services. 711'.551
Alaska State capital relocation study / Boeing Computer Services, inc., Naramore Bain Brady & Johanson. Seattle : The Services, 1974. 81 leaves : ill., maps ; 33 cm. Cover title. Bibliography: leaves 77-81. [JK9587.B64 1974] 74-623306
1. Alaska—Capital and capitol. I. Naramore, Bain, Brady, & Johanson. II. Title.

Alaska—Description and travel—1959- —Views.

COOPER, Ed, 1937- 779'.9'91798045
Beautiful Alaska / featuring Ed Cooper and Bob Spring, photography ; text by Paul M. Lewis. Portland, Or. : Beautiful West Pub. Co., c1977. 71 p. : col. ill. ; 29 cm. [F905.C66] 78-102338 ISBN 0-915796-14-7 : 12.95.
1. Alaska—Description and travel—1959- —Views. I. Spring, Robert, 1918- joint author. II. Lewis, Paul M. III. Title.

Alaska in art.

MACHETANZ, Frederick, 1908- 759.13
The Alaskan paintings of Fred Machetanz / introd. by Russ Riemann. 1st U.S. ed. New York : Peacock Press/Bantam Book, 1977. [16] p., [40] leaves of plates : ill. (some col.) ; 23 x 28 cm. [ND237.M2125A42 1977] 76-54104 ISBN 0-553-01061-1 : 6.95
1. Machetanz, Frederick, 1908- 2. Alaska in art. I. Title. BIP

Alazard, Jean, 1887-

JEANNERET-GRIS, Charles Edouard, 1887- 720.944
Le Corbusier [by] Jean Alazard New York, Universe Books [1960] [19]p. illus. 96 plates (part col.) 17cm. (Universe architecture series) Bibl.: p.[15]-[16] 60-12420 1.50 pap.,
1. Alazard, Jean, 1887- I. Title.

Albany. New York State Education Building.

NEW York (State). University. 759.13
Mural paintings in the rotunda of the State Education Buildings, Albany, [designed and painted in the years 1913-18 by Will H. Low. Text by Leonard Freedman and Beverly Burke] Albany, 1967. iii, 32 p. illus. 14 x 22 cm. [ND2638.A3N4 1967] 68-64266
1. Albany. New York State Education Building. 2. Mural painting and decoration—Albany. I. Low, Will Hicok, 1853-1932. II. Freedman, Leonard. III. Burke, Beverly. IV. Title.

Albers, Anni—Exhibitions.

ALBERS, Anni. 760'.092'4
Anni Albers / [organized] by Gene Baro ; with an essay by Nicholas Fox Weber. Brooklyn, N.Y. : Brooklyn Museum, Division of Publications and Marketing Services, c1977. 96 p. : ill. (some col.) ; 26 cm. "Published for the exhibition Anni Albers: drawings and prints, the Brooklyn Museum, October 1-November 11, 1977." Bibliography: p. 96. [N6888.A48A4 1977] 77-82324 pbk. : 5.95
1. Albers, Anni—Exhibitions. I. Baro, Gene. II. Brooklyn Institute of Arts and Sciences. Museum. BIP

Albers, Josef.

ALBERS, Josef. 760'.092'4
Formulation, articulation / Josef Albers. New York : H. N. Abrams, c1972. 2 portfolios ([14] p., [113] leaves of plates : 127 col. ill. ; 52 x 40 cm. [ND588.A34A45] 72-2150 ISBN 0-8109-4752-8
1. Albers, Josef. 2. Art—Philosophy. I. Title.

ALBERS, Josef. 759.3
Josef Albers at the Metropolitan Museum of Art; an exhibition of his paintings and prints. [New York, Metropolitan Museum of Art, c1971] 76 p. illus. (part col.) 26 cm. Bibliography: p. 74-76. [N6888.A5N4] 73-175486 ISBN 0-87099-114-0
I. New York (City). Metropolitan Museum of Art. II. Title. BIP

ALBERS, Josef. 759.3
Paintings; [Exhibition] October 5-through October 31, 1970. New York, S. Janis [1970] 1 v. (chiefly col. illus.) 22 x 29 cm. [ND588.A34A55] 75-198194
I. Sidney Janis Gallery.

BUCHER, Francois. 741.973
Josef Albers: despite straignt lines; an analysis of his graphic constructions. Captions by Josef Albers. New Haven, Yale University Press, 1961. 87 p. illus. 24 cm. Errate slip inserted. Bibliography: p. 86-87. [NE2415.A45B8] 61-66789
1. Albers, Josef. I. Title.

BUCHER, Francois. 769'.92'4
Josef Albers : despite straight lines : an analysis of his graphic constructions / by Francois Bucher ; statements and poems by Josef Albers. Rev. ed. Cambridge : MIT Press, c1977. 111 p. : ill. ; 24 cm. Bibliography: p. 107-109. [NE2350.5.A4B8 1977] 77-76462 ISBN 0-262-01049-6 : 6.95.
1. Albers, Josef. I. Albers, Josef.

LOS Angeles Co., Calif. Museum of Art, Los Angeles. 769.924
Josef Albers: white line squares. [Los Angeles, Gemini G.E.L., c1966] 66 p. illus., col. plates. 19 cm. English, German, and French. "This exhibition will be circulated internationally by the Los Angeles County Museum of Art." Bibliography: p. 56-63. [ND588.A34L6] 66-29124
1. Albers, Josef. I. Title: White line squares.

NORTH Carolina. Museum of Art, Raleigh. 741.973
Josef Albers. [Exhibition] Feb. 3-Mar. 11, 1962. Raleigh [1962] 50p. illus. 26cm. [ND588.A34N65] 62-63049
1. Albers, Josef. I. Title. BIP

SPIES, Werner, fl.1965- 759.3
Albers [by] Werner Spies. New York, H. N. Abrams [1971] 79 p. illus. (part col.) 21 x 23 cm. (Modern artists) Bibliography: p. 75-79. [N6888.A5S613 1971b] 75-125777 ISBN 0-8109-4400-6
1. Albers, Josef. BIP

Albers, Josef—Art collections—Catalogs.

ALBERS, Anni. 732.2
Pre-Columbian Mexican miniatures: the Josef and Anni Albers collection. Foreword by Ignacio Bernal. Introductory text by Michael D. Coe. Photos. by John T. Hill. New York, Praeger [1970] [32] p. illus., map, 84 plates. 32 cm. Bibliography: p. [23] [F1219.3.A7A38 1970] 70-99925 15.00
1. Albers, Josef—Art collections—Catalogs. 2. Albers, Anni—Art collections—Catalogs. 3. Terra-cottas, Mexican—Catalogs. 4. Indians of Mexico—Sculpture. I. Coe, Michael D. II. Title.

Albert, consort of Queen Victoria, 1819-1861.

AMES, Winslow. 704'.31'42
Prince Albert and Victorian taste. New York, Viking Press [1968] xvii, 238 p. illus., ports. 25 cm. Bibliographical footnotes. [DA559.A1A8] 68-10867
1. Albert, consort of Queen Victoria, 1819-1861. 2. Windsor, House of—Art collections. I. Title.

Albert Kahn Associates.

KING, Sol. 338.7'61'720922
Creative-responsive-pragmatic; 75 years of professional practice, Albert Kahn & Associates, architects-engineers. New York, Newcomen Society in North America, 1970. 36 p. illus. 23 cm. (Newcomen address, 1970) [NA737.A4K5] 73-135591
1. Albert Kahn Associates. I. Title. II. Series.

Alberti, Leone Battista, 1404-1472.

GADOL, Joan. 709'.24 B
Leon Battista Alberti: universal man of the early Renaissance. Chicago, University of Chicago Press [1969] xv, 266 p. illus. 22 x 23 cm. Bibliography: p. 245-257. [NA1123.A5G3] 72-75811 14.50
1. Alberti, Leone Battista, 1404-1472. I. Title.

IVINS, William Mills, 1881-1961. 742
On the rationalization of sight : with an examination of three Renaissance texts on perspective / William M. Ivins, Jr. De artificiali perspectiva : reproducing both the first edition (Toul, 1505) and the second edition (Toul, 1509) / Viator. New York : Da Capo Press, [1975] c1973. 43, [116] p., : ill. ; 26 cm. (A Da Capo paperback) Bibliography: p. 43-[44] [NC749.I94 1975] 74-22066 ISBN 0-394-71571-3 pbk. : 2.95
1. Alberti, Leone Battista, 1404-1472. Della pittura libri tre. 2. Pelerin, Jean, d. 1524. De Artificiali perspectiva. 3. Durer, Albrecht, 1471-1528. Underweysung der Messung. 4. Perspective—Early works to 1800. I. Pelerin, Jean, d. 1524. De artificiali perspectiva. 1975. II. Title. BIP

IVINS, William Mills, 1881-1961. 742
On the rationalization of sight, with an examination of three Renaissance texts on perspective [by] William M. Ivins, Jr. De artificiali perspectiva [by] Viator, reproducing both the 1st ed. (Toul, 1505) and the 2d ed. (Toul, 1509) New York, Da Capo Press, 1973. 44 p., [116] p. (chiefly illus.) 28 cm. (Da Capo Press series in graphic art, v. 13) Bibliography: p. 43-44. [NC749.I94 1973] 68-54843 ISBN 0-306-71189-3 15.00 (lib. bdg.)
1. Alberti, Leone Battista, 1401-1472. Della pittura libri tre. 2. Pelerin, Jean, d. 1524. De artificiali perspectiva. 3. Durer, Albrecht, 1471-1528. Underweysung der Messung. 4. Perspective. I. Pelerin, Jean, d. 1524. De artificiali perspectiva. 1973. II. Title. III. Title: De artificiali perspectiva.

WESTFALL, Carroll William. 711'.4'0945632
In this most perfect paradise; Alberti, Nicholas V, and the invention of conscious urban planning in Rome, 1447-55. University Park, Pennsylvania State University Press [1974] xvi, 228 p. illus. 28 cm. Bibliography: p. [185]-214. [NA9204.R7W47] 73-3352 ISBN 0-271-01175-0
1. Alberti, Leone Battista, 1404-1472. 2. Nicolaus V, Pope, d. 1455. 3. Cities and towns—Planning—Rome (City) I. Title. BIP

Albertinelli, Mariotto, 1474-1515.

BORGO, Ludovico. 759.5
The works of Mariotto Albertinelli / Ludovico Borgo. New York : Garland, 1976. 585 p., [97] leaves of plates : ill. ; 21 cm. (Outstanding dissertations in the fine arts) Originally presented as the author's thesis, Harvard, 1968. Includes documents in Italian and Latin (p. 478-567) [ND623.A4712B67 1976] 75-23781 ISBN 0-8240-1978-4 lib.bdg. : 40.00
1. Albertinelli, Mariotto, 1474-1515. 2. Bartolommeo, Fra, 1475-1517. I. Title. II. Series.

Albright, Ivan, 1897—

CROYDON, Michael. 759.13 B
Ivan Albright / by Michael Croydon. New York : Abbeville Press, c1978. p. cm. Includes index. Bibliography: p. [ND237.A32C76] 78-5369 65.00 limited deluxe edition : 1500.00
1. Albright, Ivan, 1897- 2. Painters—United States—Biography. BIP

Alcorn, Thomas John, 1956-1974.

ALCORN, Thomas John, 1956-1974. 779'.092'4
Photographs / Thomas Alcorn. New York : Rizzoli, 1976. [76] p. : chiefly ill. ; 28 cm. Title on cover: Thomas John Alcorn, New York, 28-4-1956—Firenze, 13-3-1974. Introd. in English and Italian. [TR654.A46 1976] 76-377961 ISBN 0-8478-0057-1 pbk. : 8.95
1. Alcorn, Thomas John, 1956-1974. 2. Photography, Artistic. I. Title.

Alden House, Duxbury, Mass.

ROBBINS, Roland Wells, 1908- 917.44'82
Pilgrim John Alden's progress; archeological excavations in Duxbury. With Evan Jones. Plymouth, Mass., Pilgrim Society, 1969. 63 p. illus., plans. 23 cm. Report of the archeological excavation conducted for the Alden Kindred of America, inc. [F74.D95R6] 70-22219
1. Alden House, Duxbury, Mass. I. Alden Kindred of America, inc. II. Title.

Alden, James Madison, 1834-1922.

STENZEL, Franz. 759.13
James Madison Alden : Yankee artist of the Pacific coast, 1854-1860 : [catalog] accompanying exhibition presented at Amon Carter Museum, Fort Worth ... [et al.] / by Franz Stenzel. Fort Worth [Tex.] : The Museum, [1975] xiii, 209 p. : ill. (some col.) ; 25 cm. Includes index. Bibliography: p. 200-202.

SUBJECT INDEX ALLSTON, WASHINGTON, 1779-1843.

[ND1839.A44S83] 74-18766 ISBN 0-88360-011-0 : 25.00
1. Alden, James Madison, 1834-1922. 2. Pacific coast in art. I. Alden, James Madison, 1834-1922. II. Amon Carter Museum of Western Art, Fort Worth, Tex. BIP

Aldershot, Eng.

COLE, Howard N 942.27
The story of Aldershot; a history and guide to town and camp. Aldershot, Gale & Polden, 1951. 406p. illus. 23cm. [DA690.A32C63] 53-22264
1. Aldershot, Eng. I. Title.

Aldrich, Larry—Art collections.

WHITNEY Museum 759.13'074'01471 of American Art, New York.
Lyrical abstractions. [New York, 1971] 46 p. illus. 19 x 21 cm. Catalogue of an exhibition held May 25-July 6, 1971. [ND212.5.A25W48] 73-162569
1. Aldrich, Larry—Art collections. 2. Paintings, American—Exhibitions. 3. Abstract expressionism—U.S. I. Title.

Aldridge, Mont. — Hist.

WHITHORN, Bill. 978.66603
A photo history of Aldridge, coal camp that died a-bornin', by bill and Doris Whithorn. Minneapolis, Printed by Acme Printing and Stationery [1965?] 200 p. illus., maps, ports. 22 x 30 cm. Bibliography: p. 200. [F739.A47W5] 66-1504
1. Aldridge, Mont. — Hist. I. Whithorn, Doris, joint author. II. Title.

Alechinsky, Pierre.

ALECHINSKY, Pierre. 741'.0924
The future of property; fourteen specimen[s] re-evaluated. [New York, Lefebre Gallery, c1970] [20] p. illus. 19 cm. Caption title. Label mounted on p. [1]: Supplied by Worldwide Books, Boston. Catalogue of 14 drawings from an exhibition, Oct. 20-Nov. 14, 1970, in celebration of the 10th anniversary of the Lefebre Gallery. [NC266.A45A44] 70-21952
I. Lefebre Gallery. II. Title.

ALECHINSKY, Pierre. 769'.92'4
Les estampes de 1946 [a 1972.] [Paris?] Y. Riviere [1973] 225 p. illus. (part col.) 28 cm. [NE674.A4A45] 74-183201
1. Alechinsky, Pierre. I. Title.

Alexander Doll Company.

WATSON, Eleanor 688.7'22 Schwingle.
Wee friends : a collection of 8" Madame Alexander dolls / by Eleanor Schwingle Watson. [Little Rock, Ark.] : Watson, [1974] v, 81 p. : ill. ; 27 cm. Includes index. [NK4894.2.A44W37] 75-300677
1. Alexander Doll Company. 2. Dolls, American. I. Title. II. Title: Madame Alexander dolls.

Alexander Doll Company—Catalogs.

SMITH, Patricia R. 688.7'22
Madame Alexander collector's dolls / by Patricia R. Smith ; editors, Beatrice Alexander, Karen Penner. Paducah, Ky. : Collector Books, [c1978] 315 p. : ill. ; 29 cm. & price guide. Includes index. [NK4894.2.A44A4 1978] 78-103728 19.95
1. Alexander Doll Company—Catalogs. 2. Dolls—United States—Collectors and collecting—Catalogs. I. Alexander, Beatrice. II. Penner, Karen. III. Title.

Alexander the Great, 356-323 B.C.

NEWELL, Edward 737.4'9'3937 Theodore, 1886-1941.
Some Cypriote "Alexanders" / by E. T. Newell. Chicago : Obol International, 1974. 29 p., [3] leaves of plates : ill. ; 22 cm. Pages also numbered 294-322. Reprinted from the Numismatic chronicle and journal of the Royal Numismatic Society, 4th series, v. 15, no. 59, 1915. Includes bibliographical references. [CJ684.N37 1974] 74-188861
1. Alexander the Great, 356-323 B.C. 2. Coins, Greek—Cyprus. I. Title. BIP

UNDERWOOD, Paul Atkins, 1902- 246
The mosaics of Hagia Sophia at Istanbul, the portrait of the Emperor Alexander; a report on work done by the Byzantine Institute in 1959 and 1960[by] Paul A. Underwood and Ernest J. W. Hawkins. Cambridge, Mass. 30 cm. no. 15 (1961) p. [187]-217. illus., plates) (In Dumbarton Oaks papers. Bibliographical footnotes. [N5970.D8 no. 15] A65
1. Alexander the Great, 356-323 v. c. 3. Mosaics. 2. Istanbul. Ayasofya Muxesi. I. Bysantine Institute of America. II. Hawkins, Ernest J. W., joint author. III. Title.

Alexander the Great, 356-323 B.C.—Portraits.

BIEBER, Margarete, 1879- 731.823
Alexander the Great in Greek and Roman art. Chicago, Argonaut, 1964. 98 p. 63 plates. 22 cm. (Argonaut library of antiquities) Bibliographical footnotes. [DF234.3.B5] 64-23430
1. Alexander the Great, 356-323 B.C.—Portraits. I. Title.

Alexander the Great, 356-323 B.C.—Romances—Illustrations.

ROSS, David John 745.6'7'0943 Athole.
Illustrated medieval Alexander-books in Germany and the Netherlands : a study in comparative iconography / by D. J. A. Ross. Cambridge : Modern Humanities Research Association, 1971. xvii, 202 p., [79] leaves of plates ; 32 cm. (Publications of the Modern Humanities Research Association ; v. 3) Includes indexes. Bibliography: p. [187]-190. [ND3151.R67] 75-320144 £18.00 ($54.00 U.S.)
1. Alexander the Great, 356-323 B.C.—Romances—Illustrations. 2. Illumination of books and manuscripts, Medieval—Germany. 3. Illumination of books and manuscripts, German. 4. Illumination of books and manuscripts, Medieval—Netherlands. 5. Illumination of books and manuscripts, Dutch. I. Title. II. Series: Modern Humanities Research Association. Publications ; v. 3.

Alexandria, Egypt.

FORSTER, Edward Morgan, 916.2'1 1879-
Alexandria: a history and a guide, by E. M. Forster. Gloucester, Mass., P. Smith, 1968 [c1961] xxvi, 243 p. illus., maps, plans. 21 cm. [DT73.A4F6 1968] 68-7844
1. Alexandria, Egypt. 2. Alexandria, Egypt—Description—Guide-books. I. Title.

FORSTER, Edward Morgan, 962.1 1879-1970.
Alexandria: a history and a guide. Garden City, N. Y., Anchor Books, 1961. 243 p. illus. 18 cm. (A Doubleday anchor original, A231) [DT73.A4F6 1961] 61-7648
1. Alexandria, Egypt. 2. Alexandria, Egypt—Description—Guide-books.

FORSTER, Edward Morgan, 916.2'1 1879-1970.
Alexandria : a history and a guide / by E. M. Forster. Woodstock, N.Y. : Overlook Press, 1974, c1961. xxvi, 243 p. : ill. ; 25 cm. Includes index. [DT73.A4F6 1974] 74-78549 ISBN 0-87951-023-4 : 10.00
1. Alexandria, Egypt. 2. Alexandria, Egypt—Description—Guide-books. I. Title. BIP

Alexandria, Va.—Hotels, motels, etc.—Conservation and restoration.

FAUBER, J. Everette. 728.5
Restoration, "Gadsby's Tavern" in Old Town at Alexandria, Virginia / J. Everette Fauber, Jr. Lynchburg, Va. : Fauber, 1976. v, 78 leaves, [35] leaves of plates : ill. ; 29 cm. Cover title. Bibliography: leaves 72-78. [NA7845.A433F38] 76-151664
1. Gadsby's Tavern, Alexandria, Va. 2. Alexandria, Va.—Hotels, motels, etc.—Conservation and restoration. I. Title. II. Title: "Gadsby's Tavern" in Old Town at Alexandria, Virginia.

Algonquin Provincial Park—Antiquities.

HURLEY, William 970.4'713'147 Michael.
Algonquin Park archaeology 1970 [by W. M. Hurley and I. T. Kenyon [Toronto] Dept. of Anthropology, University of Toronto, 1970. v, 174 p. illus., maps. 29 cm. (University of Toronto. Dept. of Anthropology. Research report no. 3) Bibliography: p. 167-174. [E78.O5H93] 73-855272
1. Algonquin Provincial Park—Antiquities. 2. Indians of North America—Ontario—Antiquities. I. Kenyon, I. T., joint author. II. Title. III. Series: Toronto. University. Dept. of Anthropology. Research report no. 3

Alhambra.

BARGEBUHR. FREDERICK P., 723.3 1904-
El palacio de la Albambra en el siglo XI [por] Frederick P. Bargebuhr. [1. ed.] Mexico, 1966. 176p. illus. 23cm. (State Univ. of Iowa studies in Spanish lang. lit. 15) Bibl. [NA387.B3] 66-31245 4.50 pap.,
1. Alhambra. I. Title. II. Series: Iowa. University. Studies in Spanish language and literature 15
Distributed by the University of Iowa Pr. in Iowa City.

GRABAR, Oleg. 728.8'2'094682
The Alhambra / Oleg Grabar. Cambridge, Mass. : Harvard University Press, 1978. 230 p. : ill. ; 24 cm. Includes index. Bibliography: p. 211-215. [NA387.G73] 77-24555 ISBN 0-674-01556-8 : 15.00
1. Alhambra. I. Title. BIP

Allegories.

KAUFMANN, Thomas 704'.35'11 DaCosta.
Variations on the Imperial theme : studies in ceremonial art and collecting in the age of Maximilian II and Rudolf II / Thomas Da Costa Kaufmann. New York : Garland Pub., [1978] p. cm. (Outstanding dissertations in the fine arts) Originally presented as the author's thesis, Harvard University, 1977. Bibliography: p. [ND623.A7K38 1978] 77-94699 ISBN 0-8240-3231-4 : lib.bdg. : 20.00
1. Arcimboldi, Giuseppe, 1527?-1593. 2. Maximiliam II, Emperor of Germany, 1527-1576—Art patronage. 3. Allegories. 4. Festivals in art. 5. Festivals—Germany. I. Title. II. Series. BIP

WITTKOWER, Rudolf. 704.94'6
Allegory and the migration of symbols / Rudolf Wittkower. Boulder, Colo. : Westview Press, 1977. 223 p. : ill. ; 26 cm. (The Collected essays of Rudolf Wittkower) Includes bibliographical references and index. [N7710.W775 1977] 76-18969 ISBN 0-89158-627-X lib.bdg. : 32.75
1. Allegories. 2. Symbolism in art. I. Title.

Allen and Wheelock firearms.

THOMAS, H H 623.44
The story of Allen and Wheelock firearms, by H. H. Thomas. Pref. by Harold L. Peterson. Cincinnati, Printed by the C. J. Krehbiel Co., 1965. xiv, 125 p. illus., port. 24 cm. [TS535.T54] 66-80695
1. Allen and Wheelock firearms. I. Title.

Allen, Harry Frederick, 1878-1965.

LANE, Maryette B. 769'.56973
The Harry F. Allen collection of Black Jacks : a study of the stamp and its use / by Maryette B. Lane (Mrs. Arthur G.) ; Elliott Perry, consultant. 1st ed. State College, Pa. : American Philatelic Society, c1969. x, 148 p. : ill. ; 26 cm. (A.P.S. handbook series) Spine title: Black Jacks. Bibliography: p. 147-148. [HE6207.A37L36] 75-322350
1. Allen, Harry Frederick, 1878-1965. 2. Postage-stamps—Collectors and collecting. 3. Postage-stamps—United States—History. I. Perry, Elliott. II. Title. III. Title: Black Jacks. IV. Series: American Philatelic Society. A.P.S. handbook series.

Allen, Louis A.—Art collections.

DAVIDSON, James A. 709.01'1
Australian aboriginal art; Louis A. Allen Collection. Text by James A. Davidson. [Exhibition] The Art Galleries, University of California, Santa Barbara, January 6 to February 1, 1970. [Santa Barbara, 1970] 21 p. illus., map. 22 x 23 cm. [N7401.D3] 71-629584
1. Allen, Louis A.—Art collections. 2. Art, Australian (Aboriginal)—Exhibitions. I. California. University, Santa Barbara. Art Gallery. II. Title.

ELSASSER, Albert B. 709.01'1
Australian aboriginal art; the Louis A. Allen collection. An exhibition at the Robert H. Lowie Museum of Anthropology of the University of California, Berkeley, January 17—August 25, 1969. Text by Albert B. Elsasser and Vivian Paul. [Berkeley, 1969?] 18 p. illus., map (on cover) 24 cm. Bibliography: p. 17. [N7401.E4] 79-632468
1. Allen, Louis A.—Art collections. 2. Art, Australian (Aboriginal)—Exhibitions. I. Paul, Vivian, joint author. II. California. University. Robert H. Lowie Museum of Anthropology. III. Title.

Allen, Natasha—Art collections.

DUBLIN. 704.948'4'074094183 National Gallery of Ireland.
Icons; the Natasha Allen Collection, catalogue [by] David Talbot Rice [and] Tamara Talbot Rice. 1968. 62 p. illus. (some col.) 26 cm. Label on t.p.: Supplied by Worldwide Books, Inc. New York. Bibliography: p. 62. [N7827.D78] 68-30495 unpriced
1. Allen, Natasha—Art collections. 2. Icons—Dublin—Catalogs. I. Rice, David Talbot, 1903- II. Rice, Tamara (Abelson) Talbot.

Alley, Ronald.

NICHOLSON, Ben, 1894- 759.02
Ben Nicholson [Text] by Ronald Alley [London, Beaverbrook Newspapers, [dist. Chester Springs, Pa., Dufour, 1965, c.1962] [38]p. illus. (15 mounted col.) 36cm. (British painters ser. Express art bk.) On spine: Daily Express [ND497.N58A8] 65-4082 6.95 bds.,
1. Alley, Ronald. I. Title.

Alloys.

SHEARMAN, William Morgan. 739'.5
Metal alloys and patinas for castings : for metalsmiths, jewelers, and sculptors / William Morgan Shearman. Kent, Ohio : Kent State University Press, c1976. p. cm. Bibliography: p. [TS650.S47] 76-28729 ISBN 0-87338-193-9 pbk. : 4.50
1. Alloys. 2. Metals—Coloring. I. Title.

Allston, Washington, 1779-1843.

FLAGG, Jared Bradley, 759.13 1820-1899.
The life and letters of Washington Allston. New York, Kennedy Galleries, 1969 [c1892] xvii, 435 p. illus., ports. 27 cm. (Library of American art) [ND237.A4F5 1969b] 68-27719
1. Allston, Washington, 1779-1843. I. Title.

FLAGG, Jared Bradley, 759.13 1820-1899.
The life and letters of Washington Allston. With reproductions from Allston's pictures. New York, B. Blom [1969] xiii, 435 p. illus., ports. 24 cm. Reprint of the 1892 ed. [ND237.A4F5 1969] 72-82002
1. Allston, Washington, 1779-1843. II. Title. BIP

Alma-Tadema, Lawrence, Sir, 1836-1912.

SHEFFIELD, Eng. City Art Galleries. 759.2
Sir Lawrence Alma-Tadema, OM, RA, 1836-1912 : [catalogue of an exhibition held at] Mappin Art Gallery, Weston Park, Sheffield, 3rd July-8th August 1976 [and] Laing Art Gallery, Higham Place, Newcastle, 21st August-13th September 1976 : [organized by Sheffield City Art Galleries]. Sheffield : [Sheffield City Art Galleries], [1976] [37] p. : ill., 2 ports. ; 26 cm. Bibliography: p. [36] [ND497.A4S53 1976] 77-354819 ISBN 0-905577-01-9 : £0.75
1. Alma-Tadema, Lawrence, Sir, 1836-1912. I. Mappin Art Gallery, Sheffield, Eng. II. Laing Art Gallery, Newcastle-upon-Tyne.

SWANSON, Vern G. 759.2 B
Alma-Tadema : the painter of the Victorian vision of the ancient world / by Vern G. Swanson. New York : Scribner, 1977. 144 p. : ill. (some col.) ; 31 cm. Includes index. Bibliography: p. 132-134. [ND497.A4S9] 77-77549 ISBN 0-684-15304-1 : 15.95
1. Alma-Tadema, Lawrence, Sir, 1836-1912. 2. Painters—Great Britain—Biography. 3. Egypt in art. 4. Greece in art. 5. Rome in art.

Almagia family—Art collections.

SPEAR, Richard E., 1940- 759.03'074'05632
Renaissance and baroque paintings from the Sciarra and Fiano collections [by] Richard E. Spear. University Park, Pennsylvania State University Press [1972] 111 p. illus. (part col.) 27 cm. Includes bibliographical references. [ND170.S63] 72-1141 ISBN 0-271-01156-4
1. Almagia family—Art collections. 2. Paintings, Renaissance—Catalogs. 3. Paintings, Baroque—Catalogs. I. Title. BIP

Alnwick, Eng.—Description.

DAVISON, William, 1781-1858. 914.28'2
Descriptive and historical view of Alnwick / by William Davison. 2nd ed. Newcastle upon Tyne : Graham, 1973. [2], 334 p., 22 leaves : ill., plans ; 22 cm. Reprint of the 2d ed. published in 1822 by W. Davison, Alnwick. Includes index. [DA690.A4D38 1973] 74-188373 ISBN 0-902833-97-9 : £2.75
1. Alnwick, Eng.—Description. 2. Alnwick, Eng.—History. I. Title.

Alphabet.

COPELAND, L'Harl. 655.10872
Design of the Roman letters. New York, Philosophical Library [1966] ix, 66 p. illus. 22 cm. [Z114.C75] 65-23492
1. Alphabet. I. Title. BIP

GOUDY, Frederic William, 1865-1947 745.6
The alphabet and Elements of lettering. Rev., enl., with many full-page plates and other illus. drawn & arr. by the author. New York. Dover [1963, c.1918, 1942] 101p. illus. 28cm. (T792) 2.00 pap.,
1. Alphabet. 2. Alphabets. 3. Type and type-founding. 4. Printing—Hist. 5. Lettering. I. Goudy, Frederic William, 1865-1947. Elements of lettering. II. Title. BIP

TORY, Geoffrey, 1480-1533 741
Champ Fleury Tr. into English and annotated by George B. Ives [Magnolia, Mass., P. Smith, 1968] xxii, 208p. illus. 28cm. (Dover bk. rebound) Unabridged, unaltered repubn. of the English tr. pub. in 1927 [NK3615.T6213 1967] 6.00
1. Alphabet. 2. French language—Pronunciation. 3. French language—Provincialisms. I. Title.

TORY, Geoffroy, 1480-1533. 741
Champ Fleury. Translated into English and annotated by George B. Ives. New York, Dover Publications [1967] xxiii, 208 p. illus. 28 cm. "An unabridged and unaltered republication of the English translation published ... in 1927." [NK3615.T6213 1967] 66-30378
1. Alphabet. 2. French language—Pronunciation. 3. French language—Provincialisms. I. Title. BIP

Alphabets.

ANGEL, Marie. 769'.92'4
An animated alphabet. [Cambridge, Harvard College Library, Dept. of Print. and Graphic Arts, 1971] 1 v. (chiefly illus.) 14 cm. [NK3631.A5A4] 72-177752
1. Alphabets. I. Title.

ATCHLEY, Dana 744.43
ABC design; a modular alphabet book. New York, Wittenborn, 1966. [33] p. (chiefly illus. (pt. col.))24cm. 200 copies. Plastic stencil inserted. [NK3630.A8] 66-7710 9.00
1. Alphabets. I. Title.

BERGLING, John Mauritz, 1866-1933. 745.6
Art alphabets and lettering, by J. M. Bergling. 9th ed., rev. and enl. Coral Gables, Fla., V. C. Bergling, 1967. 108 p. illus. 28 cm. [NK3620.B4 1967] 67-29582
1. Alphabets. 2. Lettering. I. Title. BIP

BETTI, Giovanni Battista. 769'.924
A' dilettanti delle bell'arti; a decorated alphabet engraved by Giovanni Battista Betti, Florence, 1785. Cambridge, Harvard College Library, Dept. of Printing and Graphic Arts, 1969. [5] p., 25 plates. 22 x 26 cm. Facsim. of a copy of the 2d ed., in the Harvard College Library, published in 1785. Cf. Pref., signed: Eleanor M. Garvey. [NK3631.B4A43 1969] 76-27132
I. Harvard University. Library. Dept. of Printing and Graphic Arts. II. Title.

BIEGELEISEN, Jacob Israel, 1910- 745.6'1
Antique alphabets, compiled and edited by J. L. Biegeleisen. [Cincinnati] Signs of the Times Pub. Co. [1969] 50 p. illus. 22 cm. [NK3630.B48] 77-103109
1. Alphabets. I. Title. BIP

A Book of art nouveau alphabets and ornamental designs / compiled by the Main Street Press. New York : Main Street/Universe Books, 1977. 112 p. : all ill. ; 22 x 28 cm. [NK3625.A73B66] 76-55866 ISBN 0-87663-958-9 pbk. : 4.50 745.6'197
1. Alphabets. 2. Decoration and ornament—Art nouveau. I. Main Street Press. BIP

CATICH, Edward M. 745.6'1
Reed, pen, & brush alphabets for writing and lettering / Edward M. Catich. Davenport, Iowa : Catfish Press, c1972. 32 p. ; 26 cm. & portfolio ([2] p., 27 leaves of plates : ill. ; 30 cm.) [Z43.C36] 72-87877
1. Alphabets. 2. Calligraphy. 3. Lettering. I. Title.

COHN, Raymond, comp. 745.6
101 ornamental alphabets / collected, and with notes by Raymond Cohn and Michael Estrin New York, Wm. Penn Pub. Corp. [1956, c1955] 96p. illus. 29cm. [NK3630.C6] 56-2328
1. Alphabets. I. Estrin, Michael, joint comp. II. Title.

COHN, Raymond, comp. 745.6
101 ornamental alphabets, collected, and with notes, by Raymond Cohn and Michael Estrin. New York, Wm. Penn Pub. Corp. [1956, c1955] 96p. illus. 29cm. [NK3630.C6] 56-2328
1. Alphabets. I. Estrin, Michael, joint comp. II. Title.

DAY, Lewis Foreman, 1845-1910. 745.6'1
Alphabets old and new, for the use of Craftsmen, with an introductory essay on art in the alphabet. 3d ed., rev. & enl. London, B. T. Batsford, 1910. Detroit, Gale Research Co., 1968. xxx, 256 p. illus., facsims. 20 cm. [NK3600.D22 1968] 68-23148
1. Alphabets. I. Title. BIP

DOVER Publications, inc., New York. 745.6'197
Florid and unusual alphabets / by Midolle, Silvestre and others. New York : Dover Publications, 1976. 89 p. : chiefly ill. ; 31 cm. (Dover pictorial archive series) [NK3620.D64 1976] 75-30175 ISBN 0-486-23304-9 pbk. : 3.00
1. Alphabets. 2. Design, Decorative. I. Title. BIP

FISHER, Leonard Everett. 745.6'1
Alphabet art : thirteen ABCs from around the world / written and illustrated by Leonard Everett Fisher. New York : Four Winds Press, c1978. p. cm. [NK3600.F6] 78-6148 ISBN 0-590-07520-9 : 8.95
1. Alphabets. 2. Lettering. I. Title. BIP

HISTORIC alphabets & initials, woodcut & ornamental / edited by Carol Belanger Grafton. New York : Dover Publications, 1977. 175 p. : chiefly ill. ; 29 cm. (Dover pictorial archive series) [NK3630.H5] 77-72183 ISBN 0-486-23480-0 pbk. : 4.00 686.2'17
1. Alphabets. 2. Lettering. 3. Decoration and ornament. I. Grafton, Carol Belanger.

HUNT, Walter Bernard, 1888- 745.6
101 alphabets, by W. Ben Hunt and Ed. C. Hunt. Milwaukee, Bruce Pub. Co. [1954] 1 v. (unpaged) typog. specimens. 23 cm. [NK3630.H78] 54-7739
1. Alphabets. I. Hunt, Edwin Cornelius, 1892- joint author. II. Title.

HUNT, Walter Bernard, 1888-1970. 745.6
101 alphabets, by W. Ben. Hunt and Ed. C. Hunt. Milwaukee, Bruce Pub. Co. [1958] 183 p. illus. 23 cm. [NK3630.H78 1958] 58-13897
1. Alphabets. I. Hunt, Edwin Cornelius, 1892- joint author. II. Title.

LARCHER, Jean, 1947- 686.2'17
Fantastic alphabets / by Jean Larcher. New York : Dover Publications, 1976. 72 p. : chiefly ill. ; 29 cm. (Dover pictorial archive series) [NK3631.L37A45] 76-24153 ISBN 0-486-23412-6 pbk. : 3.00
1. Larcher, Jean, 1947- 2. Alphabets. I. Title. BIP

LOEB, Marcia. 745.6'1'0904
New art deco alphabets / by Marcia Loeb. New York : Dover Publications, 1975. 75 p. : all ill. ; 29 cm. (Dover pictorial archive series) [NK3625.A7L63 1975] 74-29015 ISBN 0-486-23149-6 pbk. : 3.00
1. Alphabets. 2. Art deco. I. Title. BIP

LOISY, Jean, ed. 745.6
Advanced style in lettering. Pref. by Maximilien Vox. New York, Sterling Pub. Co. [1953] 110p. (chiefly illus.) 32cm. Translation of Letters. [NK3620.L613] 53-10407
1. Alphabets. 2. Lettering. I. Title.

MORISON, Stanley, 1889-1967. 745.6'1
Fra Luca de Pacioli of Borgo S. Sepolcro. New York, Grolier Club, 1933. [New York, Kraus Reprint Co. 1969] vii, 105 p. illus., port. 32 cm. "Bibliographical notes on the works of Luca de Pacioli, by Philip Hofer": p. [91]-98. Bibliography: p. [99]-100. "Selected recent publication on Pacioli and on geometric alphabets, compiled by James Wells": p. [101]-102. [NK3615.P34 1969] 68-58494
1. Pacioli, Luca, d. ca. 1514. De divina proportione. 2. Alphabets. 3. Lettering. BIP

NERDINGER, Eugen. 745.6
Alphabets: alphabets and their roman, sans serif, and italic modifications for use in advertising, the applied arts, and architecture [by] Eugen Nerdinger [and] Lisa Beck. New York, Reinhold Pub. Corp. [1965] 127 p. 27 x 41 cm. Translation of Alphabete fur Werbung und Gebrauchsgrafik. [NK3630.N4] 65-13369
1. Alphabets. 2. Lettering. I. Beck, Lisa, joint author. II. Title.

NESBITT, Alexander, 1901- ed. 745.6
Decorative alphabets and initials. New York, Dover Publications [1960, c.1959] 1 v. (unpaged, chiefly typog. specimens) 28cm. Includes bibliography. 59-65116 2.25 pap.,
1. Alphabets. 2. Initials. I. Title. BIP

RYDER, John, 1917- 745.61
Lines of the alphabet in the sixteenth century. London. Stellar Pr., 1965. 79p. facsims. 26cm. Erratum slip mounted on p. 6 [Z43.R9] 66-4204 18.50 bds.,
1. Alphabets. I. Title.
Available from Dufour, Chester Springs, Pa.

SIEGL, Helen. 759.13
An alphabet book; a portfolio of wood engravings. [Philadelphia] Print Club Philadelphia, 1967. 1 portfolio ([2] l., 26 plates) 23 cm. "Limited to 300 numbered copies signed by the artist ... number 105." [NE1215.S5A43] 68-4849
I. Title.

THE Studio book of alphabets. London, New York, Studio Publications [1953] 72 p. 19 cm. [NK3630.S8] 53-2028 655.24
1. Alphabets. 2. Lettering.

THE Studio book of alphabets. [Rev. ed.] London, Studio Vista; New York, Viking Press [1965, c1963] 80 p. 19 cm. [NK3630.S8] 63-25569 655.24
1. Alphabets. 2. Lettering.

SVENNAS, Elsie. 746.4'4
A handbook of lettering for stitchers. New York, Van Nostrand Reinhold Co. [1973] 92 p. illus. 15 x 21 cm. "This book was originally published in Swedish in two volumes, entitled Markbok and Markbok 2." [TT773.S814] 72-5278 ISBN 0-442-28085-8 3.95
1. Alphabets. 2. Embroidery—Patterns. I. Title. II. Title: Lettering for stitchers.

TORY, Geoffroy, 1480-1533 745.61
Champ fleury, by Geoffroy Tory, tr. into English and annotated by George B. Ives. New York, The Grolier Club. 1927; New York, Kraus Reprint, 1967. 3p. l., xxiii, 208p. 1 l., illus. 28cm. Colophon with design of Bruce Rogers: At the printing house of William Edwin Rudge, Mount Vernon, N. Y., Oct. 1927. [NK3615.T62] 28-4222 58.50
1. Alphabets. 2. French language—Pronunciation. 3. French language—Provincialisms. I. Ives, George Burnham., 1856- tr. II. Grolier Club, New York. III. Title.

WEINBERGER, Norman S. 745.6'1'03
Encyclopedia of comparative letterforms for artists & designers, by Norman S. Weinberger. New York, Art Direction Book Co. [1971] vi, 416 p. 23 x 29 cm. Introductory matter in English, French, and German. [NK3600.W4] 79-158572
1. Alphabets. 2. Lettering. I. Title. BIP

Alphabets—Specimens.

SPECIAL-EFFECTS and topical alphabets : 100 complete fonts / selected and arranged by Dan X. Solo from the Solotype typographers catalog. New York : Dover Publications, 1978. 100 p. : chiefly ill. ; 28 cm. (Dover pictorial archive series) [NK3630.S67 1978] 78-52150 ISBN 0-486-23657-9 pbk. : 3.50 686.2'17
1. Alphabets—Specimens. 2. Lettering—Specimens. I. Solo, Dan X. BIP

Alpuy, Julio, 1919—

JULIO Alpuy. 730'.92'4
[Exhibition held Jan. 26-Mar. 5, 1972, Center for Inter-American Relations] New York, Center for Inter-American Relations [1971] [28] p. illus. (part col.) 26 cm. "In the world and workshop of Julio Alpuy, an interview, by Ronald Christ": p. [5]-[23] "Checklist": p. [26]-[27] [NB429.A4J8] 72-198179
1. Alpuy, Julio, 1919- I. Christ, Ronald J. II. Center for Inter-American Relations.

Altamira site, Mexico.

GREEN, Dee F. 732.2
Altamira and Padre Piedra, early Preclassic sites Chiapas, Mexico, by Dee F. Green abd Gareth W. Lowe. Provo, Utah, New World Archaeological Foundation, Brigham Young University, 1967. xiii, 133 p. illus. 27 cm. (New World Archaeological Foundation. Publication no. 15. Papers, no. 20) Bibliography: p. 131-133. [E51.N38 no. 20] [F1219.1.C45] 301.2'4 72-183670
1. Altamira site, Mexico. 2. Padre Piedra

1967. ix, 162 p. 25 cm. (Temple University publications) "A day long session ... held at the University of Pennsylvania Museum on October 12, 1962." Includes bibliographies. [E51.P52] 67-26963
1. America—Antiq.—Addresses, essays, lectures. 2. Indians—Addresses, essays, lectures. 3. Anthropology—Addresses, essays, lectures. I. Title.
Contents omitted

HARVARD University, 301.2'4
Robert Woods Bliss Collection of Pre-Columbian Art, Washington, D.C.
Studies in pre-Columbian art and archaeology. no. 1- Washington, Dumbarton Oaks Trustees for Harvard University, 1966- v. illus. 27 cm. "A new series . . . concerned chiefly with objects in the Robert Woods Bliss Collection." [E51.S85] 66-1543
1. America — Antiq. — Collected works. 2. Indians — Antig. — Collected works. 3. Indians — Art — Collected works. I. Title.

*SOCIETE des 970/.005
americanistes de Paris
Journal de la Societe des americanistes de Paris. t. 1-5; nouv. ser. t. 1-20 Paris, 1895-19-; New York, Johnson Reprint, 1967 v. illus., plates, ports., maps, geneal. tables. 28cm. First ser., v. 5, has added t.-p.: Les voyages du naturaliste Ch. Alex. Lesueru dans l'Amerique du Nord (1815-1837) ... par E. T. Hamy. 1904 [E51.S68] 9-875 555.00 set,
1. America—Antiq.—Societies. 2. American—Disc. & explor.—Societies. 3. Indians I. Title.

America—Antiquities.

ANTON, Ferdinand. 709'.8
Pre-Columbian art and later Indian tribal arts. Texts by Ferdinand Anton and Frederick J. Dockstader. New York, H. N. Abrams [1968] 264 p. illus. (part col.), col. maps. 23 cm. (Panorama of world art) Contents.Contents.—Pre-Columbian art of Middle and South America, by F. Anton, translated by R. E. Wolf.—Later Indian tribal arts, by F. J. Dockstader. Bibliography: p. 258-261. [E59.A7A5] 68-11509
1. America—Antiquities. 2. Indians—Art. I. Dockstader, Frederick J., joint author. II. Title.

America—Antiquities.

THE Philadelphia 572'.097
Anthropological Society: papers presented on its golden anniversary, edited by Jacob W. Gruber. New York, Distributed by Columbia University Press, 1967. ix, 162 p. 25 cm. (Temple University publications) "A day long session ... held at the University of Pennsylvania Museum on October 12, 1962." Contents.Contents.—Anthropology in Philadelphia, by A. I. Hallowell.—The American Philosophical Society in American anthropology, by J. F. Freeman.—The direction of physical anthropology, by H. L. Shapiro.—The paleo-indian, by H. M. Wormington.—Mesoamerican archaeology, by G. F. Ekholm.—Arctic anthropology in America, by C. S. Chard.—Northern woodland ethnology, by F. Eggan.—A challenge for lingusitics today, by W. L. Chafe.—Anthropology and the museum, by F. J. Dockstader. Includes bibliographies. [E51.P52] 67-26963
1. America—Antiquities—Addresses, essays, lectures. 2. Indians—Addresses, essays, lectures. 3. Anthropology—Addresses, essays, lectures. I. Gruber, Jacob W., ed.

America — Bibl. — Catalogs.

HEARD, Joseph Norman, 016.9173
1922-
Bookman's guide to Americana. 3d ed. New York, Scarecrow Press, 1964. 424 p. 22 cm. [Z1207.H43 1964] 64-11780
1. America — Bibl. — Catalogs. 2. U.S. — Imprints. 3. Books — Prices. I. Title. BIP

STREETER, Thomas 016.973
Winthrop, 1883-
Americana-beginnings; a selection from the library of Thomas W. Streeter, shown in honor of a visit of the Hroswitha Club on May 3, 1951. Morristown, N.J., 1952. xix, 97 p. facsims. 26 cm. "325 copies printed." [Z1207.S86] 52-38540
1. America — Bibl. — Catalogs. I. Title.

WEMYSS, Stanley. 016.9731
The general guide to rare Americans, with auction records and prices; a hand book and guide to the rare and notable books relating to America. With chronological and regional inventories of early printed books in the United States, and a key to American imprints, 1639-1889. New, enl. ed. Philadelphia, 1950. 323 p. 23 cm. Bibliography: p. 11-13. [Z1207.W4] 50-12158
1. America — Bibl. — Catalogs. 2. U.S. — Bibl. — Catalogs. 3. Bibliography — Rare books. 4. Books — Prices. I. Title.

America—Bibliography.

BROWN University. John 016.09
Carter Brown Library.
Rare Americana : a selection of one hundred & one books, maps, & prints not in the John Carter Brown Library. Providence : Associates of the John Carter Brown Library, 1974. 77 p. (p. 74-77 advertisements) ; 23 cm. Includes bibliographical references and index. [Z1201.B75 1974] [E18] 74-79027
1. America—Bibliography. 2. Bibliography—Rare books. I. Title.

RICH, Obadiah, 1783?- 016.917
1850.
Bibliotheca Americana nova; a catalogue of books in various languages relating to America, printed since the year 1700, including voyages to the Pacific and round the world and collections of voyages and travels. Compiled principally from the works themselves by O. Rich. Rev. by the addition of two supplements. New York, B. Franklin [1967] 2 v. 24 cm. (Burt Franklin bibliography and reference series, #43) "First published London 1835-1846." Contents.Contents.—pt. 1. 1701-1800.—pt. 2. Printed since the year 1800. [Z1207.R5 1967] 74-6307
1. America—Bibliography. I. Title. BIP

THOMPSON, Lawrence 016.9173'03
Sidney, 1916-
The new Sabin; books described by Joseph Sabin and his successors, now described again on the basis of examination of originals, and fully indexed by title, subject, joint authors, and institutions and agencies, by Lawrence S. Thompson. Troy, N.Y., Whitston Pub. Co., 1974- v. 24 cm. [Z1201.T45] 73-85960
1. America—Bibliography. I. Sabin, Joseph, 1821-1888. A dictionary of books relating to America. II. Title.
Volume 1, pt. 1, 25.00, ISBN 0-87875-049-5; vol. 1, pt. 2, 10.00, ISBN 0-87875-050-9.

America—Bibliography—Catalogs.

BRINLEY, George, 1817- 017'.7
1875.
Catalogue of the American library of the late Mr. George Brinley, of Hartford, Conn. New York, AMS Press [1968] 5 pts. in 2 v. 23 cm. Reprint of the 1879-93 ed. Each part has also special t.p. On spine: Brinley American library auction catalogue. Consists of the catalogs for the 5 auctions at which the library was sold, an index, and a price list. [Z1207.B8592] 68-54529
1. America—Bibliography—Catalogs. 2. America—Imprints. I. Title. II. Title: Brinley American library auction catalogue.

BROWN University. John 016.917
Carter Brown Library.
A collection's progress: two retrospective exhibitions. Providence, Associates of the John Carter Brown Library, 1968. 79 p. illus., facsims., maps. 27 cm. Supplements the library's catalog of an exhibition, In retrospect, 1923-1949, held in 1949. Catalogue of two exhibitions; one held at the Grolier Club, New York, Apr. 16-June 1, 1968; the other at the library, Providence, Apr. 5-Sept. 1, 1968. [Z1207.B872] 68-25685
1. America—Bibliography—Catalogs. I. Grolier Club, New York. II. Brown University. John Carter Brown Library. In retrospect, 1923-1949. III. Title.

EBERSTADT (Edward) 016.9173'03
and Sons, New York.
Americana; being a collection of rare & important books & manuscripts relating to the history of America, including a choice selection of Lincolniana. New York [1964] 171 p. illus., facsims. 23 cm. (Its Catalogue 165) [Z1207.E2] 73-238163
1. Lincoln, Abraham, Pres. U.S., 1809-1865—Bibliography—Catalogs. 2. America—Bibliography—Catalogs. I. Title.

GOODSPEED'S Book Shop, 017'.4 s
Boston.
Americana: books, pamphlets, broadsides, maps. Boston [1972?] 33 p. 23 cm. (Its Catalogue 574) Cover title. [Z999.G655 no. 574] [Z1207] 016.9173 74-173111
1. America—Bibiography—Catalogs. 2. Catalogs, Booksellers'—Massachusetts—Boston. I. Title. II. Series.

NEWBERRY Library, 016.973
Chicago. Edward E. Ayer Collection.
Dictionary catalog of the Edward E. Ayer Collection of Americana and American Indians in the Newberry Library. Boston, G. K. Hall, 1961. 16 v. (8062 p.) 37 cm. Introd. signed: Ruth Lapham Butler. "A reproduction of the entire Ayer dictionary card catalogue, i.e. author and subject entries for all printed material with the exception of the Indian, Philippine, and Hawaiian collections, checklists of which have been published earlier ... The Greenlee and Graff collections, both of which are housed within the Ayer collection, will not be found in the present catalogue." [Z1201.N45] [E18] 76-4986
1. Newberry Library, Chicago. Edward E. Ayer Collection. 2. America—Bibliography—Catalogs. 3. Indians—Bibliography—Catalogs. I. Butler, Ruth (Lapham) 1896- II. Title.

STEVENS, Henry, 1819- 016.9173
1886.
Historical nuggets. Bibliotheca Americana; or, A descriptive account of my collection of rare books relating to America. New York, B. Franklin [1971] xii, 805 p. 19 cm. (Burt Franklin bibliography & reference series, 410. American classics in history and social science, 154) Half-title and running title: Bibliotheca Americana. Reprint of v. 1-2 (1862) of the original. [Z1207.S8432 1971] 77-154649 ISBN 0-8337-3407-5
1. America—Bibliography—Catalogs. I. Title. II. Title: Bibliotheca Americana. BIP

America—Bibliography—Exhibitions.

THE British look at 016.9173'03'2
America during the age of Samuel Johnson; an exhibition. Providence, Associates of the John Carter Brown Library, 1971. vi, 55 p. illus., facsims., map, ports. 27 cm. Catalogue, by T. R. Adams and J. D. Black, of an exhibition shown in the John Carter Brown Library beginning in April 1971. "Address by Herman W. Liebert delivered at the 28th annual meeting of the Associates of the John Carter Brown Library April 30, 1971": p. [1]-16. [Z1201.B73] 72-190326 10.00
1. America—Bibliography—Exhibitions. I. Adams, Thomas Randolph, 1921- II. Black, Jeannette Dora, 1909- III. Liebert, Herman W. IV. Brown University. John Carter Brown Library. V. Associates of the John Carter Brown Library.

America—Discovery & exploration—Bibliography.

CHURCH, Elihu Dwight, 016.9731
1835-1908.
A catalogue of books relating to the discovery and early history of North and South America, forming a part of the library of E. D. Church; compiled and annotated by George Watson Cole. New York, P. Smith, 1951. 5 v. (vi, 2635 p.) illus., facsims. 27 cm. Reprint of the 1907 ed. The Church collection, now in the Henry E. Huntington Library and Art Gallery, was acquired in 1911 by Henry E. Huntington. Contents.v. 1. 1482-1590.--v. 2. 1590-1625.--v. 3. 1626-1676.--v. 4. 1677-1752.--v. 5. 1753-1884. Index. [Z1203.C55 1951] 51-4055
1. America—Disc. & explor.—Bibl. 2. Bibliography—Rare books. 3. America—Bibl.—Catalogs. I. Cole, George Watson, 1850-1939. II. Henry E. Huntington Library and Art Gallery, San Marino, Calif. III. Title.

HARRISSE, Henry, 1829- 016.9731
1910.
Bibliotheca Americana vetustissima: a description of works relating to America, published between the years 1492 and 1551. Chicago, Argonaut, 1967. liv. 519, xl, 199 p. facsims. 23 cm. Reprint of the 1866 New York ed. and its Additions published in Paris, 1872. [Z1202.H3] 67-21041
1. America — Disc. & explr. — Bibl. 2. Bibliography — Rare books. I. Title.

America—History—Medals.

BETTS, Charles Wyllys, 737'.2
1845-1887.
American colonial history illustrated by contemporary medals, by C. Wyllys Betts. Edited, with notes, by William T. R. Marvin and Lyman Haynes Low. Glendale, N.Y.,' Benchmark Pub. Co., 1970. v, 332 p. illus., ports. 23 cm. Reprint of the 1894 ed. Includes bibliographical references. [CJ5811.B5 1970] 73-22599 9.50
1. America—History—Medals. I. Title. BIP

America—History—To 1810—Medals.

BETTS, Charles Wyllys, 737'.2
1845-1887.
American colonial history illustrated by contemporary medals. Boston, Quarterman Publications [1972] v, 369 p. illus. 24 cm. Reprint, with a new foreword and price guide, of the 1894 ed. Includes bibliographical references. [CJ5793.A4B48 1972] 72-85121 ISBN 0-88000-004-X 15.00
1. America—History—To 1810—Medals. I. Title.

America—Maps—Bibliography—Catalogs.

MICHIGAN. University. 016.912'73
William L. Clements Library.
Research catalog of maps of America to 1860 in the William L. Clements Library, University of Michigan, Ann Arbor, Michigan. Edited by Douglas W. Marshall. Boston, G. K. Hall, 1972. 4 v. 37 cm. Bibliography: v. 1, p. viii. [Z6027.A5M53] 73-157170 ISBN 0-8161-1003-4 240.00
1. Michigan. University. William L. Clements Library. 2. America—Maps—Bibliography—Catalogs. I. Marshall, Douglas W., ed. II. Title. BIP

American Academy in Rome.

VALENTINE, Lucia 707'.01045'632
N.
The American Academy in Rome, 1894-1969 [by] Lucia Valentine [and] Alan Valentine. Charlottesville, University Press of Virginia [1973] viii, 237 p. illus. 25 cm. [DG12.A8V34] 72-92663 ISBN 0-8139-0444-7 10.00
1. American Academy in Rome. I. Valentine, Alan Chester, 1901- joint author. BIP

American Academy of the Fine Arts, New York.

COWDREY, Mary Bartlett, 706.273
1910-
American Academy of Fine Arts and American Art-Union, 1816-1852. With a history of the American Academy by Theodore Sizer and a foreword by James Thomas Flexander. New York, New-York Historical Society, 1953- v. illus., ports. 25cm. (Collections of the New-York Historical Society for the year 1943. The John Watts De Peyster publication fund series, 76) 'Publications of the American Art-Union': v. 1, p. 241-293. Includes bibliographical references. [F116.N63] 57-23841
1. American Academy of the Fine Arts, New York. 2. American Art-Union New York. I. Title. II. Series: New York Historical Society. Collections, 1943. The

[NC1429.S568A4 1979] 78-22023 ISBN 0-394-72543-3 pbk. : 5.95
1. American wit and humor, Pictorial. I. Title. BIP

SOREL, Edward, 1929- 741.5'973
Superpen : the cartoons and caricatures of Edward Sorel / edited and designed by Lidia Ferrara. 1st ed. New York : Random House, c1978. ca. 150 p. : ill. ; 29 cm. [NC1429.S568A4 1978] 77-90236 ISBN 0-394-50002-4 : 8.95
1. American wit and humor, Pictorial. I. Title.

STEIG, William, 1907- 741.5
The agony in the kindergarten; foreword by Arthur Steig. [1st ed.] New York, Duell, Sloan and Pearce [1950] 1 v. (chiefly illus.) 25 cm. [NC1429.S5775] 50-7028
1. American wit and humor, Pictorial. I. Title.

THURBER, James, 1894- 741.5
The seal in the bedroom & other predicatments. With an "Author's memoir" and an introd. by Dorothy Parker. New York, Harper [1950] 1 v. (chiefly illus.) 23 cm. Full name: James Grover Thurber. [NC1429.T5] 50-9838
I. Title.

THURBER, James, 1894-1961. 741.5973
The last flower; a parable in pictures. New York, Harper [1962, c1939] unpaged. illus. 21 x 28 cm. Full name: James Grover Thurber. [NC1429.T47 1962] 62-575
I. Title. BIP

THURBER, James, 1894-1961. 741.5'973
Men, women, and dogs / James Thurber ; with a new introd. by Wilfrid Sheed. New York : Dodd, Mead, [1975] c1943. p. cm. Includes index. [NC1429.T48 1975] 75-24914 ISBN 0-396-07206-2 : 8.95
I. Title. BIP

THURBER, James, 1894-1961. 741.5973
Thurber & company. Introd. by Helen Thurber. [1st ed.] New York, Harper & Row [1966] 208 p. (chiefly illus.) 27 cm. [NC1429.T53 1966] 64-18067
I. Thurber, Helen, comp. II. Title. BIP

THURBER, James [Grover] 1894- 741.5973
The seal in the bedroom. and other predicaments. New York, Grosset and Dunlap [1961. c.1932, 1950] unpaged (mostly illus.) (Grosset s universal lib., UL85 1.25 pap.,
I. Title.

THURBER, James Grover, 1894-1961 741.59
The seal in the bedroom, and other predicaments. With an Author's memoir, and introd. by Dorothy Parker. New York, Harper [1965, c.1932, 1950] 1v. (unpaged) chiefly illus. 18cm. (Perennial lib., P65A) [NC1429.N5] .50 pap.,
I. Title.

WANAMAKER and Brown, Philadelphia. 741.9'73
Art in outline; sketches of life and character. Philadelphia, v. illus. 19-22 cm. [NC1070.W3] 56-51666
1. American wit and humor, Pictorial. I. Title.

American wit and humor, Pictorial—Hist & crit.

BECKER, Stephen D 1927- 741.5973
Comic art in America; a social history of the funnies, the political cartoons, magazine humor, sporting cartoons, and animated cartoons. With an introd. by Rube Goldberg. New York, Simon and Schuster, 1959. xi, 387p. illus. 29cm. [NC1420.B4] 59-13140
1. American wit and humor, Pictorial—Hist & crit. 2. Caricature—U. S.—Hist. I. Title.

MURRELL, William, 1889- 741.573
A history of American graphic humor. New York, Cooper Square Publishers, 1967 [c1933-38] 2 v. illus. 29 cm. Contents.Contents.—v. 1. 1747-1865.—v. 2. 1865-1938. Includes bibliographies. [NC1420.M82] 67-20784
1. American wit and humor, Pictorial—History. 2. Caricatures and cartoons—U.S. 3. U.S.—History, Comic, satirical, etc. I. Title. II. Title: American graphic humor. BIP

Americana—Catalogs.

HORNUNG, Clarence Pearson, comp. 745.1'0973
A source book of antiques and jewelry designs : containing over 3800 engravings of Victorian Americana, including jewelry, silverware, clocks, cutlery, glassware, musical instruments, etc., etc., etc. / by Clarence P. Hornung. 1st paperback ed. New York : Da Capo Press, 1977, c1968. x, 244 p. : ill. ; 28 cm. (A Da Capo paperback) Reprint of the ed. published by G. Braziller, New York. [NK807.H6 1977] 77-10003 ISBN 0-306-80070-5 pbk. : 6.95
1. Americana—Catalogs. 2. Antiques—United States—Catalogs. 3. Art industries and trade, Victorian—United States—Catalogs. I. Title. II. Title: Antiques and jewelry designs.

RAYCRAFT, Donald R. 745.1'0973'075
Wallace-Homestead price guide to American country antiques / by Don and Carol Raycraft ; [photography, Hayes & Benedict]. Des Moines, Iowa : Wallace-Homestead Book Co., c1978. 178 p. : ill. ; 23 cm. Bibliography: p. 178. [NK805.R4] 78-112687 ISBN 0-87069-230-5 : 8.95
1. Americana—Catalogs. 2. Antiques—United States—Catalogs. I. Raycraft, Carol, joint author. II. Wallace-Homestead Book Co. III. Title. BIP

Americana—Collectibles.

BOWYER, Mathew J. 745.1'0973
Collecting Americana / by Mathew J. Bowyer. South Brunswick [N.J.] : A. S. Barnes, c1977. p. cm. Includes index. [NK805.B69] 76-58589 ISBN 0-498-02081-9 : 20.00
1. Americana—Collectibles. I. Title. BIP

Americana—The West.

BEITZ, Lester V. 745.1'0978'075
Treasury of frontier relics : a collector's guide / by Les Beitz. 2d ed., rev. South Brunswick, [N.J.] : A. S. Barnes, c1977. 142 p. : ill. ; 29 cm. Includes index. [NK823.B44 1977] 75-20587 ISBN 0-498-01688-9 : 12.00
1. Americana—The West. 2. Implements, utensils, etc.—The West. 3. Frontier and pioneer life—The West. I. Title. BIP

Americans in Japan—Caricatures and cartoons.

SCKLAREWITZ, Norm 741.5973
Bamboo shoots for Breakfast Words by Norm Sklarewitz; cartoons by Sanae Yamazaki. Rutland, Vt., Tuttle [c.1962] 64p. illus. 22cm. 62-18034 1.50 pap.,
1. Americans in Japan—Caricatures and cartoons. 2. Americans in Japan—Anecdotes, facetiae, satire, etc. I. Yamazaki, Sanae, 1929- II. Title.

Ames, Ezra, 1768-1836.

BOLTON, Theodore, 1889- 927.5
Ezra Ames of Albany, portrait painter, craftsman, Royal Arch Mason, banker, 1768-1836, by Theodore Bolton and Irwin F. Cortelyou; and a catalogue of his works by Irwin F. Cortelyou with the collaboration of Theodore Bolton. New York, New-York Historical Society, 1955. xix, 398p. illus., ports. 24cm. Bibliography: p.359-370. [ND237.A58B6] 55-27077
1. Ames, Ezra, 1768-1836. I. Cortelyou, Irwin F. II. Title. BIP

Amherst, Mass.—Hist.

RAND, Frank Prentice, 1889- 974.423
The village of Amherst, a landmark of light. Amherst, Mass., Amherst Historical Society, 1958. 337p. illus. 24cm. Includes bibliography. [F74.A5R3] 58-49300
1. Amherst, Mass.—Hist. I. Title.

Amish in art.

WHITE, Stephen. 769'.92'4
Amish. [Chapel Hill? N.C., 1968-69] 3 v. illus. 30 cm. Issued in a case. Artist's proof ed. of 25: no. 1. [NE1112.W46A57] 74-176355 180.00
1. White, Stephen. 2. Amish in art. I. Title.

Amish—Social life and customs—Pictorial works.

ZIELINSKI, John M. 779'.9'917303
The Amish, people of the soil, by John M. Zielinski. [Kalona, Iowa, Photo-Art Gallery Publications, 1972] 1 v. (chiefly illus.) 30 cm. Includes bibliography. [E184.M45Z53] 72-193143
1. Amish—Social life and customs—Pictorial works. I. Title.

Amistad Reservoir region—Antiquities.

COLLINS, Michael B. 917.64'88
Test excavations at Amistad International Reservoir, fall, 1967 [by] Michael B. Collins. Austin [Available for purchase through the Texas Memorial Museum, University of Texas] 1969. viii, 103 p. illus. 28 cm. (Papers of the Texas Archeological Salvage Project, no. 16) Bibliography: p. 102-103. [E78.T4T44 no. 16] 79-15202 3.00
1. Amistad Reservoir region—Antiquities. 2. Texas—Antiquities. 3. Indians of North America—Texas—Antiquities. I. Title. II. Series: Texas Archeological Salvage Project. Papers, no. 16

Amman, Jost, 1539-1591.

LEHMANN-HAUPT, Hellmut, 1903- 769'.4'930155
The book of trades in the iconography of social typology / by Hellmut Lehmann-Haupt. Boston : Trustees of the Public Library of the City of Boston, [1976] p. cm. (Maury A. Bromsen lecture in humanistic bibliography ; no. 1) [NE1150.5.A45L43] 76-8399 ISBN 0-89073-010-5
1. Amman, Jost, 1539-1591. 2. Sachs, Hans, 1494-1576. Das Standebuch—Illustrations. 3. Occupations in art. I. Title. II. Series. BIP

Ammannati, Bartolommeo, 1511-1592.

KINNEY, Peter. 730'.92'4
The early sculpture of Bartolomeo Ammanati / Peter Kinney. New York : Garland, 1976. xx, 356 p. : ill. ; 21 cm. (Outstanding dissertations in the fine arts) Originally presented as the author's thesis, New York University, 1974. Bibliography: p. 269-275. [NB623.A46K56 1976] 75-23798 ISBN 0-8240-1993-8 : 27.50
1. Ammannati, Bartolommeo, 1511-1592. I. Title. II. Series. BIP

Amon Carter Museum of Western Art, Fort Worth, Tex.

AMON Carter Museum of Western Art, Fort Worth, Tex. 708'.1764'5315
Catalogue of the collection, 1972. Fort Worth [Tex., c1973] v, 602 p. illus. 23 cm. [N8214.5.U6A48 1973] 73-84472 ISBN 0-88360-000-5
1. Amon Carter Museum of Western Art, Fort Worth, Tex. 2. The West in art. 3. Art—Forth Worth, Tex.—Catalogs. I. Title.

Amphoras—New York (City)—Catalogs.

NEW York (City). Metropolitan Museum of Art. 738.3'82'093 s
Attic black-figured neck-amphorae / Mary B. Moore and Dietrich von Bothmer. New York : Metropolitan Museum of Art, c1976. 1 portfolio (76 p., 52 leaves of plates) : ill. ; 33 cm. (Corpus vasorum antiquorum : United States of America ; fasc. 16 : The Metropolitan Museum of Art, New York ; fasc. 4) At head of title: Union academique internationale. Includes bibliographical references and indexes. [NK4640.C6U5 fasc. 16] [NK4650.A6] 738.3'82 75-25613 ISBN 0-87099-134-5 30.00
1. New York (City). Metropolitan Museum of Art. 2. Amphoras—New York (City)—Catalogs. I. Moore, Mary B. II. Von Bothmer, Dietrich, 1918- III. Title. IV. Series: Corpus vasorum antiquorum : United States of America ; fasc. 16. BIP

Amshewitz, John Henry, 1882-1942.

AMSHEWITZ, Sarah Briana. [759.2]
The paintings of J. H. Amshewitz, R. B. A. London, New York, Batsford [1951] 66 p. illus. 29 cm. [ND497.A5A58] 927.5 52-42562
1. Amshewitz, John Henry, 1882-1942. I. Title.

Amsterdam. Rijks-Museum.

MEIJER, Emil R. 708.9/492/3
The Rijksmuseum, Amsterdam. Text by E. R. Meijer. [Tr. from the Italian by James Brockway] New York, Meredith [1967] 160p. illus. (pt. col.) 28cm. (Great galleries ser.) [N2460.M413 1967] 68-21901 8.95 bds.,
1. Amsterdam. Rijks-Museum. I. Title.

MEIJER, Emil R. 708.9'492'3
The Rijksmuseum, Amsterdam. Text by E. R. Meijer. [Translated from the Italian by James Brockway] New York, Meredith Press [1967] 160 p. illus. (part col.) 28 cm. (Great galleries series) Translation of Het Rijksmuseum. [N2460.M413 1967] 68-31901
1. Amsterdam. Rijks-Museum. I. Title.

Amulets.

LIPPMAN, Deborah. 745.59'3
How to make amulets, charms, and talismans; what they mean and how to use them, by Deborah Lippman and Paul Colin. New York, M. Evans; [distributed by Lippincott, Philadelphia, 1974] 208 p. illus. 29 cm. [BF1561.L54] 73-89758 ISBN 0-87131-135-6 8.95
1. Amulets. 2. Talismans. I. Colin, Paul, 1946- joint author. II. Title. III. Title: Amulets, charms, and talismans.
Pbk. 4.95, ISBN 0-87131-151-8. BIP

Anaconda Company—History.

POWELL, Peter J., 1928- 741'.092'2
Montana, past and present : papers read at a Clark Library seminar, April 5, 1975 / by Peter J. Powell, Michael P. Malone. Los Angeles : William Andrews Clark Memorial Library, University of California, 1976. vi, 84 p. : ill. ; 23 cm. (William Andrews Clark Memorial Library seminar papers) Contents.Contents.—Powell, P. J. They drew from power.—Malone, M. P. Montana as a corporate bailiwick. Includes bibliographical references. [E99.C53P58] 77-621076
1. Anaconda Company—History. 2. Cheyenne Indians—Art. 3. Cheyenne Indians—Wars. 4. Indians of North America—Great Plains—Art. I. Malone, Michael P., joint author. II. California. University. University at Los Angeles. William Andrews Clark Memorial Library. III. Title. IV. Series.

Anamorphic art.

BALTRUSAITIS, Jurgis, 1903- 760
Anamorphic art / by Jurgis Baltrusaitis ; translated by W. J. Strachan. New York : Harry N. Abrams, 1977. viii, 182 p. : ill. ; 29 cm. Translation of Anamorphoses. Includes bibliographical references and index. [N7433.6B3413 1977] 77-73789 ISBN 0-8109-0662-7 : 20.00
1. Anamorphic art. I. Title.

Anastaise.

MINER, Dorothy Eugenia. 745.6'7
Anastaise and her sisters : women artists of the Middle Ages / Dorothy Miner. Baltimore : Walters Art Gallery, 1974. 24 p. : ill. ; 22 cm. Includes bibliographical references. [ND2920.M54] 75-309852
1. Anastaise. 2. Illumination of books and manuscripts, Medieval. 3. Women painters. I. Title.

Anastasius I, Emperor of the East, 430 (ca.)-518.

METCALF, David Michael. 737.49'495
The origins of the Anastasian currency reform, by D. M. Metcalf. Chicago, Argonaut, 1969. vi, 105 p. illus. 26 cm. Bibliography: p. 103-105. [HG237.M43 1969] 78-4555
1. Anastasius I, Emperor of the East, 430 (ca.)-518. 2. Coinage—Byzantine Empire. 3. Coinage—Rome—History. I. Title.

Anatomy, Artistic.

BARCSAY, Jeno. 743
Anatomy for the artist, drawings and text by Jeno Barcsay. Budapest, Corvina [1955] 316p. illus. 34cm. [NC760.B33] 56-796
1. Anatomy, Artistic. I. Title. BIP

BARCSAY, Jeno. 743'.4
Anatomy for the artist; drawings and text. [Medical revision and contribution to the drawings illustrating the muscular system, by Barnabas Somogyi. 2d rev. ed.] New York, Tudor Pub. Co. [1973] p. "Appendix: Movements drawn in 1952-53 by students of the Budapest Academy of Fine Arts": p. [NC760.B33 1973] 73-1885 ISBN 0-8148-0010-6
1. Anatomy, Artistic. I. Title.

BASKIN, Leonard, 1922- 741.9'73
Ars anatomica : a medical fantasia, thirteen drawings / Leonard Baskin. New York : Medicina Rara, c1972. [7] p., 13 leaves of plates in portfolio : ill. ; 56 cm. [NC139.B37A47] 75-315752
1. Baskin, Leonard, 1922- 2. Anatomy, Artistic. I. Title.

BRIDGEMAN, George Brant, 1864-1943 743.4
The human machine. New York, Sterling [1961, c.1959] 143p. illus. (Worthwhile how-to paperbacks, 503) 1.00 pap.,
1. Anatomy, Artistic. I. Title.

BRIDGMAN, Brant, 1864-1943. 743.4
Complete guide to drawing from life, with drawings and text by George B. Bridgman. Edited by Howard Simon. New York, Sterling Pub. Co. [1952] 350p. illus. 30cm. (A Bridgman art book) [NC765.B775] A53
1. Anatomy, Artistic. 2. Human figure in art. I. Title. II. Title: Drawing from life.

BRIDGMAN, George Brant, 1864-1943 743.4
Book of 100 hands. London, W. Foulsham. New York, Sterling [c.1962] 128p. illus. 19cm. (Worthwhile how to paperbacks, 505) First pub. in 1920 under title: The book of a hundred hands. 62-18645 1.00 pap. sHand.
1. Anatomy, Artistic. I. Title.

BRIDGMAN, George Brant, 1864-1943. 743'.4
Bridgmans life drawing. New York, Dover Publications [1971, c1961] 169 p. illus. 24 cm. Reprint of the 1924 ed. [NC760.B85 1971] 74-182098 ISBN 0-486-22710-3 £2.00
1. Anatomy, Artistic. I. Title: Life drawing.

*BRIDGMAN, George Brant. 1864-1943 743.4
Constructive anatomy. New York, Barnes & Noble [1966.c.1920.1960] 160p. illus. 21cm. (Everyday handbks. 302) 1.00 pap.,
I. Title. BIP

BRIDGMAN, George Brant, 1864-1943. 743'.4
Constructive anatomy. [Rev. ed.] New York, Sterling Pub. Co. [1968, c1960] 160 p. illus. 21 cm. [NC760] 68-18692
1. Anatomy, Artistic. I. Title.

BRIDGMAN, George Brant, 1864-1943. 743.4
Constructive anatomy; abridged. New York, Sterling Pub. Co. [c.1920, 1960] 160p. illus. 20cm. (Worthwhile how-to paperbacks, 501) 1.00 pap.,
1. Anatomy, Artistic. I. Title.

BRIDGMAN, George Brant, 1864-1943. 743'.4
Constructive anatomy. New York, Dover Publications [1973, c1920] ix, 170 p. illus. 24 cm. "Unabridged republication of the work first published in 1920 ... The present edition has been repaginated, and a new table of contents has been added." [NC760.B83 1973] 72-95434 ISBN 0-486-21104-5 2.00 (pbk.)
1. Anatomy, Artistic. I. Title.

*BRIDGMAN, George Brant. 1864-1943 743.4
The human machine. New York. Barnes & Noble [1966. c.1939] 143p. illus. 21cm. (Everyday handbks. 303) 1.00 pap.,
I. Title. BIP

BRIDGMAN, George Brant, 1864-1943. 743.4
The human machine. New York, Sterling Pub. Co. [1961, c1939] 143p. illus. 20cm. (Worthwhile how-to paperbacks, 503) [NC760.B854 1961] 62-5148
1. Anatomy, Artistic. I. Title.

BRIDGMAN, George Brant, 1864-1943. 743'.4
The human machine; the anatomical structure & mechanism of the human body. New York, Dover Publications [1972, c1939] 143 p. illus. 24 cm. [NC760.B854 1972] 70-187018 ISBN 0-486-22707-3 2.00
1. Anatomy, Artistic. I. Title.

BRIDGMAN, George Brant, 1864-1943. 743.4
Life drawing. [Rev. ed.] New York, Sterling Pub. Co. [1961, c.1924, 1961] 159p. illus. (Worthwhile how-to paperbacks, 502) First ed published in 1924 under title: Bridgman's life drawing. 61-3082 1.00 pap.:
1. Anatomy, Artistic. I. Title. II. Title: Life drawing.

BROOKS, Walter, 1921- 743.49
The art of drawing heads and hands. [Designed and edited by Walter Brooks. New York, 1966] 48 p. illus. (part col.) 32 cm. (A Grumbacher library book) [NC770.B75] 66-19000
1. Anatomy, Artistic. 2. Head. 3. Hand. I. Title. II. Title: Drawing heads and hands.

BUONARROTI, Michel Angelo, 1568-1646. 730'.92'4
Michelangelo : a lesson in anatomy / James Beck. New York : Viking Press, 1975. 31 p., [32] leaves of plates : ill. ; 31 cm. (A Studio book) [NB623.B9B34 1975] 74-29472 ISBN 0-670-47396-0 : 12.95
1. Buonarroti, Michel Angelo, 1568-1646. 2. Anatomy, Artistic. 3. Artists' preparatory studies. I. Beck, James H. II. Title.

DAVY, Don, 1927- 743'.4
Anatomy and life drawing / Don Davy. New York : Taplinger Pub. Co., 1978, c1975. 96 p. : ill. ; 25 cm. "A Pentalic book." [NC765.D38 1978] 77-91042 ISBN 0-8008-0196-2 pbk. : 4.95.
1. Anatomy, Artistic. 2. Human figure in art. I. Title. BIP

FARRIS, Edmond John, 1907- 743.4
Art students' anatomy, by Edmond J. Farris. 2d ed. rev. 158 illustrations, drawings by L. Augusta S. Farris. New York, Dover [1961, c.1935, 1944] x, 159p. illus. (T744) 1.45 pap.,
1. Anatomy, Artistic. I. Title.

FARRIS, Edmund John, 1907- 743.4
Art students' anatomy. Drawings by L. Augusta S. Farris 2d ed., rev. New York, Dover Publications [1961, c1944] 150 p. illus. 22 cm. [(NC760)] A 62
1. Anatomy, Artistic. I. Title. BIP

HALE, Robert Beverly, 1901- 743'.4
Anatomy lessons from the great masters / by Robert Beverly Hale and Terence Coyle. New York : Watson-Guptill Publications, 1977. p. cm. Includes index. Bibliography: p. [NC760.H27 1977] 77-12810 ISBN 0-8230-0222-5 : 15.00
1. Anatomy, Artistic. I. Coyle, Terence, joint author. II. Title. BIP

HILL, Adrian Keith Graham, 1895- 743.4
The beginners' book of basic anatomy. New York, Reinhold Pub. Corp. [1962] 64p. illus. 18 x 20cm. [NC760.H49] 62-12997
1. Anatomy, Artistic. I. Title.

HOGARTH, Burne. 743
Dynamic anatomy. New York, Watson-Guptill Publications [1958] 232 p. illus. 29 cm. Bibliography: p. 225-226. [NC760.H63] 57-10690
1. Anatomy, Artistic. I. Title. BIP

JACKSON, Arthur Gladstone. 743.4
The right way to human figure drawing and anatomy. New York, Emerson Books [1952] 139p. illus. 19cm. [NC760.J3 1952] 52-11379
1. Anatomy, Artistic. 2. Figure drawing. I. Title.

KNIGHT, Charles Robert, 1874-1953 743.6
Animal drawing. Anatomy and action for artists, with illustrations by the author. New York, Dover Publications [c.1947] vii, 149p. illus. 22x28cm. (first published under the title: Animal anatomy and psychology for artists and layman.) 2.00 pap.,
1. Anatomy, Artistic. 2. Animal painting and illus. I. Title.

KNIGHT, Charles Robert, 1874-1953. 743.6
Animal drawing, anatomy and action for artists. With illus. by the author. New York, Dover Publications [1959. c1947] 149p. illus. 22x28cm. First published in 1947 under title: Animal anatomy and psychology for artists and laymen. [NC780] A62
1. Anatomy, Artistic. 2. Animal painting and illustration. I. Title. BIP

KNOX, Robert, 1791-1862. 709'.2'2
Great artists and great anatomists : a biographical and philosophical study / by R. Knox. New York : AMS Press, 1977. xii, 213 p. ; 18 cm. Reprint of the 1852 ed. published by J. Van Voorst, London. [N7570.K57 1977] 75-23734 18.00
1. Anatomy, Artistic. 2. Human figure in art. 3. Artists—Biography. I. Title. BIP

LENSSEN, Heidi. 743.4
Art and anatomy. Text edited by Lancaster M. Greene. N[ew] Y[ork] Barnes & Noble [1955] 80 p. illus. 28 cm. [NC760.L54 1955] 55-12083
1. Anatomy, Artistic. I. Title.

LENSSEN, Heidi 743.4
Art and anatomy. Text ed. by Lancaster M. Greene. N[ew] Y[ork] Barnes & Noble [1961, c.1946] 80p. illus. (part col.) (Everyday handbk. 278) 1.75 pap.,
1. Anatomy, Artistic. I. Title.

MARSH, Reginald, 1898-1954. 743'.4
Anatomy for artists. New York, Dover Publications [1970] 209 p. illus. 28 cm. (Dover art instruction and reference books) "These drawings consist of free adaptations, combinations, abbreviations and copies of works of the old masters, chiefly from the Italian and Flemish schools before the advent of academicism." [NC760.M38 1970] 75-129078 ISBN 4-86226-131-
1. Anatomy, Artistic. I. Title.

PANOFSKY, Erwin, 1892-1968. 701
The Codex Huygens and Leonardo da Vinci's art theory; the Pierpont Morgan Library, Codex M.A. 1139. Westport, Conn., Greenwood Press [1971] 138, [90] p. 117 illus. 24 cm. Reprint of the 1940 ed. Includes bibliographical references. [N65.L4P3 1971] 79-109814 ISBN 0-8371-4306-3
1. Leonardo da Vinci, 1452-1519. 2. Huygens, Constantijn, heer van Zuilichem, 1628-1697. 3. Anatomy, Artistic. 4. Proportion (Art) 5. Perspective. I. Pierpont Morgan Library, New York. Mss. (M.A. 1139) II. Title. BIP

PECK, Stephen Rogers, 1912- 743.4
Atlas of human anatomy for the artist. New York, Oxford University Press, 1951. xv, 272 p. illus. 26 cm. [NC760.P35] 51-10735
1. Anatomy, Artistic. I. Title. BIP

PERARD, Victor Semon, 1870-1957. 743
Anatomy and drawing. [4th ed.] New York, Pitman Pub. Corp. [1955] unpaged (chiefly illus.) 24 cm. [NC760.P4 1955] 55-11899
1. Anatomy, Artistic. 2. Human figure in art. I. Title.

RICHER, Paul Marie Louis Pierre, 1849-1933. 743'.4
Artistic anatomy. Translated and edited by Robert Beverly Hale. New York, Watson-Guptill Publications [1971] 255 p. illus. 32 cm. Translation of Anatomie artistique. [NC760.R4813] 73-146794 ISBN 0-8230-0220-9 15.00
1. Anatomy, Artistic. I. Title. BIP

RIMMER, William, 1816-1879. 743.4
Art anatomy. [Rev.] New York, Dover Publications [1962] xiii, 153p. illus. 28cm. [NC760.R573] 62-3152
1. Anatomy, Artistic. I. Title. BIP

SCHIDER, Fritz, 1846-1907. 743.4
An atlas of anatomy for artists. Rev. by M. Auerbach and translated by Bernard Wolf. New bibliography by Adolf Placzek. Additional illus. from the old masters and historical sources. With a new section on hands selected by Heidi Lenssen. 3d American ed. [New York] Dover Publications [c1957] 1v. (chiefly illus., part col.) 29cm. Translation of Plastisch-anatomischer Handatlas. Bibliography: [3] p. at end. [NC760.S32 1957] 58-3622
1. Anatomy, Artistic. 2. Anatomy, Human—Atlases. I. Auerbach, Max, 1879- II. Title. BIP

SHEPPARD, Joseph, 1930- 743'.4
Anatomy : a complete guide for artists / by Joseph Sheppard. New York : Watson-Guptill Publications, 1975. 222 p. : chiefly ill. ; 32 cm. [NC760.S53 1975] 74-31404 ISBN 0-8230-0218-7 : 18.50
1. Anatomy, Artistic. I. Title. BIP

TAUBES, Frederic, 1900- 743'.4
Anatomy for artists. New York, Pitman [1969] 48 p. illus., port. 20 x 26 cm. [NC760.T28] 71-94652
1. Anatomy, Artistic. I. Title. BIP

TAUBES, Frederic, 1900- 743'.4
The human body : aspects of pictorial anatomy / Frederic Taubes. 1st ed. New York : C. N. Potter : distributed by Crown Publishers, [1975] c1974. [95] p. : chiefly ill. ; 32 cm. [NC760.T32 1974] 74-75053 ISBN 0-517-51534-2 : 8.95
1. Anatomy, Artistic. I. Title.

TAUBES, Frederic, 1900- 743
Pictorial anatomy of the human figure. New York, Studio-Crowell [1956] unpaged (chiefly illus.) 26 cm. [NC760.T3] 56-6238
1. Anatomy, Artistic. I. Title.

THOMSON, Arthur. 743.4
A handbook of anatomy for art students. 5th ed [Gloucester, Mass., P. Smith, 1965] xx, 459p. illus., plates. 22cm. (Dover bk. rebound) First pub. in 1896 by Oxford. Bibl. [NC760.T48] 5.00
1. Anatomy, Artistic. I. Title. BIP

THOMSON, Arthur, 1858-1935 743.4
A handbook of anatomy for art suudents. 5th ed. New York, Dover [1964] xx, 459p. illus., plates. 22cm. unabridged unaltered repubn. of the 5th (1929) ed. pub. by Oxford. Bibl. 64-15507 3.00 pap.,
1. Anatomy, Artistic. I. Title.

WARREN, Henry, 1794-1879. 743'.4
Artistic anatomy of the human figure / Henry Warren. [Albuquerque, N.M.] : Gloucester Art Press, 1978. p. cm. Reprint of the 1868 ed. published by Winson & Newton, London, which was issued as no. 19 of One shilling hand-books on art. Bibliography: p. [NC760.W33 1978] 78-21476 ISBN 0-930582-12-8 : 31.50
*1. Anatomy, Artistic. I. Title. II. Series: One shilling hand-books on art ; no. 19.*BIP

Anatomy Artistic—Exhibitions.

LEONARDO da Vinci, 1452-1519. 741.9'45
Leonardo da Vinci, anatomical drawings from the Queen's Collection at Windsor Castle. Los Angeles : Los Angeles County Museum of Art, c1976. 60 p. : ill. (some col.) ; 30 cm. "Exhibition dates: National Museum of History and Technology, Smithsonian Institution, July 2-August 1, 1976; Los Angeles County Museum of Art, August 5-September 5, 1976." Bibliography: p. 60. [NC257.L4N37] 76-19378 ISBN 0-87587-072-4 pbk. : 4.00
1. Leonardo da Vinci, 1452-1519. 2. Windsor, House of—Art collections—Exhibitions. 3. Anatomy Artistic—Exhibitions. I. National Museum of History and Technology. II. Los Angeles Co., Calif. Museum of Art, Los Angeles. III. Title. IV. Title: Anatomical drawings from the Queen's Collection at Windsor Castle.

Anatomy—Exhibitions.

TATE Gallery, London. 599'.04'0222
George Stubbs, anatomist and animal painter / [by] Judy Egerton ; [photographs by A. C. Cooper Ltd. et al.]. London : Tate Gallery Publications, 1976. 64 p., plate : ill., port. ; 25 cm. Published for an exhibition held at the Tate Gallery, 25 Aug.-3 Oct., 1976. Distributed in France and Italy by Idea Books, Paris and Milan. Includes reprint of an article by B. Taylor written for the Arts Council's exhibition catalogue, 1958 and excerpts from O. Humphry's ms. Memoir of George Stubbs. Includes bibliographical references. [QL31.S82T37 1976] 77-359204 ISBN 0-905005-55-4. ISBN 0-905005-50-3 pbk.
1. Stubbs, George, 1724-1806. 2. Tate Gallery, London. 3. Anatomy—Exhibitions. 4. Animal painting and illustration—Exhibitions. 5. Anatomists—England—Biography. I. Stubbs, George, 1724-1806. II. Egerton, Judy. III. Taylor, Basil. IV. Humphry, Ozias, 1743-1810.

Anatomy, Human—History.

STUDIES in pre-Vesalian anatomy : biography, translations, documents / L. R. Lind. Philadelphia : American Philosophical Society, 1975. 344 p. : ill. ; 31 cm. (Memoirs of the American Philosophical Society ; v. 104 ISSN 0065-9738s) Includes index.lBibliography: p. 331-336. [Q11.P612 vol. 104] [QM11] 611 74-78093 ISBN 0-87169-104-3 : 18.00 081 s
1. Anatomy, Human—History. 2. Anatomy, Human—Early works to 1800. 3. Anatomists—Biography. I. Lind, Levi Robert, 1906- II. Series: American Philosophical Society, Philadelphia. Memoirs ; v. 104.
Contents omitted. BIP

Andersen, Arthur Olaf, 1880-1958—Art collections.

LOS Angeles Co., Calif. Otis Art Institute, Los Angeles. 709'.52
Japanese art: the Arthur Olaf Andersen Japanese Print Collection [and the] Mr. and Mrs. Maurice K. Grossman Japanese Ceramic Collection. Los Angeles [1966?] [28] p. illus. 23 cm. Catalog of an exhibition held Sept. 8 to Oct. 23, 1966, at the Otis Art Institute of Los Angeles County. [NE771.L6] 68-2638
1. Andersen, Arthur Olaf, 1880-1958—Art collections. 2. Grossman, Maurice K.—Art collections. 3. Grossman, Maurice K., Mrs.—Art collections. 4. Art, Japanese—Exhibitions. I. Title.

Anderson, Eleanor Cleveland.

ANDERSON, Eleanor Cleveland. 759.13
Muses first; an exhibition of paintings and eleven poems. Presented May 11th through June 30th, 1973 by the Monterey Peninsula Museum of Art. Monterey, Calif. [Monterey Peninsula Museum of Arts, 1973] [22] l. 30 cm. "Fifty copies ... copy no. 50." "Catalogue of paintings": leaves [16]-[21]. [NX512.A52M66] 73-173364
1. Anderson, Eleanor Cleveland. 2. Mythology, Classical, in art. I. Monterey Peninsula Museum of Art. II. Title.

Anderson, Guy, 1906—

ANDERSON, Guy, 1906- 759.13
Guy Anderson : Modern Art Pavilion, Seattle Art Museum, June 30-September 11, 1977, with the Henry Art Gallery, University of Washington, July 28-September 18, 1977. Seattle : Seattle Art Museum, c1977. 35 p. : ill. (some col.) ; 26 cm. [ND237.A642S4] 77-152316
1. Anderson, Guy, 1906- I. Seattle. Art Museum. II. Henry Art Gallery. BIP

Anderson, Harry, 1906—

WOOLSEY, Raymond H. 759.13 B
Harry Anderson : the man behind the paintings / Raymond H. Woolsey and Ruth Anderson. Washington : Review and Herald Pub. Association, c1976. 127 p. : ill. (some col.) ; 26 cm. [ND237.A6423W66] 76-15700 5.95
1. Anderson, Harry, 1906- 2. Painters—United States—Biography. I. Anderson, Ruth, 1911- joint author. II. Title. BIP

Ando, Hiroshige, 1797-1858.

ANDO Hiroshige, 1797-1858. Text by Sei-iehiro Takahashi: English adaptation by Charles S. Terry. [1st English ed.] Tokyo. Rutland, Vt., C.E. Tuttle Co. [1956] 1v. (chiefly plates, part col.) 18cm. (Kodansha library of Japanese art, no. 3) Includes bibliography. [NE1325.A5T3] [NE1325.A5T3] 927.61 56-6808 56-6808 761.283
I. Ando, Hiroshige, 1797-1858. II. Takahashi, Seiichiro, 1884- III. Terry, Charles S. IV. Series.

ANDO, Hiroshige, 1797-1858. 769.952
Hiroshige. New York, Crown Publishers [1958] 18 p. illus., 23 col. plates (1 fold.) 18 x 19 cm. (Art of the East library) Text by Takashi Suzuki. [NE1325.A5S8] 59-620
I. Suzuki, Takashi. II. Series.

ANDO, Hiroshige, 1797-1858. 769.952
Hiroshige. [Text by] Walter Exner. With an introd. by Werner Speiser. Translated [from the German] by Marguerite Kay. New York, Crown Publishers [1960] 112p. mounted col. illus. (1 fold-out) 33 cm. 60-12248 10.00 half cloth,
I. Exner, Walter, ed. II. Title.

ANDO, Hiroshige, 1797-1858 769'.924
Hiroshige famous views, by Muneshige Narazaki. English adaptation by Richard L. Gage. [1st ed.] Tokyo, Palo Alto, Calif. Kodansha Intl. [c1968] 96p. col. illus., maps. (pt. col.) 27cm. (Masterwords of Ukiyo-e, 5) [NE1325.A5N33] 68-26557 4.75; 3.50 pap.,
I. Narazaki, Muneshige, 1904- II. Title. III. Series.

ANDO, Hiroshige, 1797-1858. 769.952
Hiroshige; the 53 stations of the Tokaido, by Muneshige Narazaki. English adaptation by Gordon Sager. Tokyo, Palo Alto, Calif., Kodansha International [1969] 92 p. map, col. plates. 26 cm. (Masterworks of Ukiyo-e, 10) [NE1325.A5A53 1969] 79-82655 ISBN 0-87011-100-0 3.50
1. Ando, Hiroshige, 1797-1858. 2. Tokaido in art. I. Narazaki, Muneshige, 1904- II. Title. III. Title: The 53 stations of the Tokaido. IV. Series.

ROBINSON, Basil William 769.952
Hiroshige. New York, Barnes & Noble [1964, c. 1963] 90p. illus. (pt. col.) port. 18cm. (Barnes & Noble art ser., No. 615) 64-1804 .75 pap.,
1. Ando, Hiroshige, 1797-1858. I. Title.

Andre, Carl, 1935—

CORCORAN Gallery of Art, Washington, D.C. 709'.73'0740153
Andre, Leva, Long : [catalogue of the exhibition], Corcoran Gallery of Art, December 11, 1976-January 30, 1977. [Washington] : The Gallery, [1977] 32 p. : ill. ; 22 x 27 cm. Includes bibliographies. [N6494.S7C67 1977] 77-73028
1. Andre, Carl, 1935- 2. Leva, Barry, 1941- 3. Long, Richard. 4. Spatialism (Art)—Exhibitions. I. Title.

WALDMAN, Diane. 730'.924
Carl Andre. New York, Solomon R. Guggenheim Museum [1970] 82 p. illus. (part col.) 26 cm. "Exhibition 70/5." Includes bibliographical references. [N6537.A5W3] 79-138305
1. Andre, Carl, 1935- I. Solomon R. Guggenheim Museum, New York.

Andrews, Benny, 1930—

ANDREWS, Benny, 1930- 759.13
Benny Andrews : the bicentennial series : ... exhibition ... organized by the High Museum of Art, Atlanta / with an essay by Lawrence Alloway. Atlanta : The Museum, 1975. 31 p. : ill. (some col.) ; 22 x 28 cm. Exhibition held Jan. 18-Feb. 23, 1975. Bibliography: p. 29-31. [ND237.A643H54] 74-30684
1. Andrews, Benny, 1930- I. High Museum of Art.

Anecdotes.

ARVINE, Kazlitt, 1819-1851. 700'.3
The cyclopaedia of anecdotes of literature and the fine arts. Detroit, Gale Research Co., 1967. xxiv, 698 p. illus. 24 cm. Title page includes original imprint: Boston, Gould and Lincoln, 1851. [PN6261.A65 1967] 67-14020 14.50
1. Anecdotes. 2. Literature—Anecdotes, facetiae, satire etc. 3. Art—Anecdotes, facetiae, satire etc. I. Title.

Angel, Marie.

ANGEL, Marie. 759.2
Beasts in heraldry / [ill. by] Marie Angel ; [text by] J. P. Brooke-Little. Brattleboro, Vt. : S. Greene Press, [1974] [93] p. : col. ill. ; 21 cm. [ND497.A52B76] 74-10577 ISBN 0-8289-0213-5 : 20.00
1. Angel, Marie. 2. Animals in art. 3. Heraldry. I. Brooke-Little, John Philip. II. Title. BIP

Angels—Art.

TATIC-DJURIC, Mirjana 704.9486
Image of the angels. Tr. by George H. Genzel. Hans Rosenwald. [n. p.] Catholic Art Bk. Guild. [New York dist. Taplinger, 1966,c.1964] 71p. illus. (pt. col.) 18cm. (pictorial lib. of Eastern Church art, v. 4) [N8090.T313 1966] 66-9078 2.50 bds.,
1. Angels—Art. I. Title.

Angels in art.

CAMERON, Ann, 1943- 704.948'6
The angel book / Ann Cameron. 1st ed. New York : Ballantine Books, 1977. p. cm. [NX652.A55C35] 77-78332 ISBN 0-345-27263-3 : 6.95
1. Angels in art. 2. Arts. I. Title. BIP

Anglo-Saxons.

MAYES, Philip. 942.5'38
An Anglo-Saxon cemetery at Baston, Lincolnshire / [by] P. Mayes and the late M. J. Dean ; with a report on the pottery by J. N. L. Myres. Sleaford : Society for Lincolnshire History and Archaeology, 1976. 63 p. : ill., maps, plans ; 30 cm. (Occasional papers in Lincolnshire history and archaeology ; 3 ISSN 0307-2797s) Includes bibliographical references..[DA690.B296M38] 77-372997 ISBN 0-904680-05-3 : £1.40
1. Baston, Eng. Tinker's Urn. 2. Anglo-Saxons. 3. Baston, Eng.—Antiquities, Saxon. 4. England—Antiquities, Saxon. I. Dean, M. J., joint author. II. Myres, John Nowell Linton. III. Title. IV. Series: Occasional papers in Lincolnshire history and archaeology ; 3.

Angstadt, Jacob, 1809—

HOLROYD, Ruth N. 746.1'4
Jacob Angstadt designs, drawn from his weavers patron book / Ruth N. Holroyd, with Ulrike L. Beck. [Pittsford, N.Y.] : Holroyd, c1976. 28, [256] p. [2] leaves of plates : chiefly ill. ; 30 cm. [TS1490.H57] 76-9402
1. Angstadt, Jacob, 1809- 2. Weaving—Patterns. I. Beck, Ulrike L., joint author. II. Title.

Animal housing.

HANCOCKS, David. 727'.5'59
Animals and architecture. New York, Praeger [1971] 200 p. illus. (part col.), plans, ports. 26 cm. (Excursions into architecture) [NA8230.H33] 70-101251 13.95
1. Animal housing. 2. Zoological gardens. I. Title. BIP

Animal painting and illustration.

BROOKS, Walter, 1921- ed. 701
The art of drawing animals; horses, zebras, lions, tigers, dogs, cats, cows, bears, bison, elephants, and others. [Designed and edited by Walter Brooks. New York, Odyssey, 1965] 1 v. (unpaged) illus. (part col.) 32 cm. (A Grumbacher library book) [NC780.B66] 65-15430
1. Animal painting and illustration. 2. Drawing — Instruction. I. Title.

BROOKS, Walter, 1921- 743'.6
Creative ways with drawing dogs and cats. Designed and edited by Walter Brooks. [Artist: Lorence Bjorklund] New York, Golden Press [1974] 32 p. illus. 29 cm. (The Golden Press art instruction series) [NC780.B67] 73-88431 1.25 (pbk.)
1. Animal painting and illustration. 2. Dogs in art. 3. Cats in art. I. Bjorklund, Lorence F., illus. II. Title. BIP

CALDER, Alexander, 1898- 743'.6
Animal sketching. 3d ed. New York, Dover Publications [1973, c1941] 62 p. illus. 22 cm. (Dover art instruction and reference books) [NC780.C3 1973] 73-75876 ISBN 0-486-20129-5 1.25 (pbk.)
1. Animal painting and illustration. I. Title. BIP

CALDER, Alexander, 1898- 743'.6
Animal sketching. Illus. by Alexander Calder. Text by Charles Liedl. New York, Sterling Pub. Co. [1972] 63 p. illus. 22 cm. A well-known artist's sketches of animals are accompanied by brief text explaining how to capture some of the elusive qualities of wildlife. [NC780.C3 1972] 74-180460 ISBN 0-8069-5190-7 3.95
1. Animal painting and illustration. I. Liedl, Charles. II. Title.

CALDER, Alexander, 1898- 743.6
Drawing animals, by Alexander Calder, Charles Liedl [and] Diana Thorne. London, Oak Tree Press. New York, Sterling Pub. Co. [1963] 128 p. illus. 28 cm. (A Bridgman giant) "Abridged and revised from Diana Thorne's 101 favorite animals and birds ... and from Animal sketching, by Alexander Calder and Charles Liedl." [Animal painting and illustration.] [NC780.C32 1963] 63-6256
I. Title.

CALDERON, William Frank, 1865-1943. 743'.6
Animal painting & anatomy / by W. Frank Calderon. New York : Dover Publications, 1975. 336 p. : ill. ; 24 cm. (Dover art instruction and reference books) Reprint of the 1936 ed. published by Seeley, Service, London, which was issued as v. 18 of the New art library, 2d ser. Includes index. [NC780.C35 1975] 72-75583 ISBN 0-486-22523-2 pbk. : 5.00
1. Animal painting and illustration. I. Title. BIP

CHRISTENSEN, Gardell Dano. 743.69
Animal art. Serial 6331. [Ed. 1] Scranton, International Correspondence Schools, c1960. 70p. illus. 19cm. [NC780.C57] 60-31579
1. Animal painting and illustration. I. International Correspondence Schools, Scranton, Pa. II. Title.

96 p. : ill. (some col.) ; 42 cm. [N7660.A67] 76-366403 ISBN 0-7148-1669-8 : pbk. : 7.95
1. Animals in art. 2. Art—Catalogs. I. Dent, Anthony Austen.
Distributed by Dutton.

BERRY, Ana M. 704.94'32
Animals in art, by Ana M. Berry. London, Chatto and Windus. Detroit, Tower Books, 1971. xviii, 83 p. 32 plates. 23 cm. [N7660.B45 1971] 79-162506
1. Animals in art. BIP

BUNKER, Emma C. 704.94'32
Animal style art from East to West [catalogue of an exhibition. By] Emma C. Bunker, C. Bruce Chatwin [and] Ann R. Farkas. [New York] Asia Society; Distributed by New York Graphic Society [1970] 185 p. illus. (part col.), maps. 28 cm. "An Asia House Gallery publication." "Asia House Gallery, New York, January 15-March 15, 1970; The University Museum, University of Pennsylvania, Philadelphia, April 2-May 31, 1970; M. H. de Young Memorial Museum, San Francisco, June 12-July 19, 1970." Bibliography: p. 185. [N7260.B75] 72-103164
1. Animals in art. 2. Art, Asian—Exhibitions. I. Chatwin, C. Bruce, joint author. II. Farkas, Ann R., joint author. III. Asia House Gallery, New York. IV. Pennsylvania. University. University Museum. V. De Young Memorial Museum, San Francisco. VI. Title.

CARL Battaglia Galleries. 704.94'32
Art and the animal : a collection of paintings, drawings, sculpture, and graphics from our contemporary roster, with a selection of works from the early 20th, 19th, 18th, and mid 17th centuries. New York : Carl Battaglia Galleries, c1974. 103 p. : chiefly ill. ; 29 cm. Includes indexes. [N7660.C28 1974] 74-22620
1. Animals in art. 2. Art—Exhibitions. I. Title.

CARTER, Dagny (Olsen) 704.9432
The symbol of the beast; the animal-style art of Eurasia. New York, Ronald Press Co. [1957] ix, 204p. illus., map. 27cm. Bibliography: p. 173-191. [N7660.C3] 57-6799
1. Animals in art. 2. Symbolism in art. 3. Art, Primitive. I. Title.

CETTO, Anna Maria, 1898- 704.9432
Animal drawings of eight centuries. With 59 illus. [Translated by Eveline Winkworth] New York, Harper [1950] 90 p. illus. 25 cm. (Master drawings) Harper's art library. [N7660.C43 1950] 50-10511
1. Animals in art. I. Title. II. Series.

COOKE, Hereward Lester. 704.94'32'074'0153
Dogs, horses, cats and other animals in the National Gallery of Art. Book design by Sylvan Jacobson. [1st ed.] Richmond, Westover Pub. Co. [1970] [63] p. illus. 23 cm. [N7660.C74] 70-133458
1. Animals in art. 2. Art—Washington, D.C.—Catalogs. I. U.S. National Gallery of Art. II. Title.

CUSHION, John Patrick. 738.09
Animals in pottery and porcelain [by] John P. Cushion. New York, October House [1966] viii, 72 p. illus. (part col.) 23 cm. (Collectors guidebooks) Bibliography: p. 67. [NK3780.C8 1966a] 66-23888
1. Animals in art. 2. Pottery—History. 3. Porcelain—History. I. Title. II. Series.

DAVY, Don, 1927- 743'.6
Drawing animals and birds / Don Davy. New York : Taplinger Pub. Co., 1978, c1977. 96 p. : ill. ; 25 cm. "A Pentalic book." [NC780.D38 1978] 77-91048 ISBN 0-8008-2268-4 pbk. : 4.95
1. Animals in art. 2. Birds in art. 3. Drawing—Technique. I. Title. BIP

DETMOLD, Edward Julius, 1883-1957. 759.2
The fantastic creatures of Edward Julius Detmold / edited by David Larkin ; introd. by Keith Nicholson. 1st U.S. ed. New York : Scribner, 1976. [96] p. : col. ill. ; 31 cm. [NC978.5.D47L37 1976c] 76-378147 ISBN 0-684-14587-1 : 12.00
1. Detmold, Edward Julius, 1883-1957. 2. Animals in art. I. Title. BIP

DETMOLD, Edward Julius, 1883-1957. 759.2
The fantastic creatures of Edward Julius Detmold / edited by David Larkin ; introd. by Keith Nicholson. Toronto ; New York : Peacock Press/Bantam Book, c1976. [14] p., [40] leaves of plates : col. ill. ; 30 cm. [NC978.5.D47L37 1976] 76-372121 6.95
1. Detmold, Edward Julius, 1883-1957. 2. Animals in art. I. Larkin, David. II. Title.

FULLER, Catherine Leuthold, comp. 769
Beasts; an alphabet of fine prints. [1st ed.] Boston, Little, Brown [1968] xii, 59 p. illus. 23 x 25 cm. Bibliography: p. 55-56. [NE962.A5F8] 68-15557 4.95
1. Animals in art. 2. Prints—Catalogs. I. Title.

KLINGENDER, Francis Donald. 704.94'32
Animals in art and thought to the end of the Middle Ages. Edited by Evelyn Antal and John Harthan. Cambridge, Mass., M.I.T. Press [1971] xxviii, 580 p. illus. 29 cm. Bibliography: p. 540-564. [N7660.K55 1971] 77-123254 ISBN 0-262-11040-7
1. Animals in art. 2. Animals in literature. I. Title. BIP

LONGSTREET, Stephen, 1907- 704.94'32
The Animal in art. Introd. by Stephen Longstreet. [1st ed.] Alhambra, Calif., Borden Pub. Co. [1966] 1 v. (chiefly illus.) 31 cm. (Master draughtsman series) [N7660.A65] 67-2875
1. Animals in art. I. Title. BIP

RIEGER, Shay. 731.8'3'2
Animals in wood. New York, Scribner [1971] [46] p. illus. 27 cm. [NK9798.R5A4] 70-143928 ISBN 0-684-12322-3 4.95
1. Animals in art. I. Title.

ROTHAMSTED Experimental Station, Harpenden, Eng. Library. 769.942
Printe and paintings of British farm livestock, 1780-1910; a record of the Rothamsted collection, by D. H. Boalch, librarian. With an historical sketch of the development of British farm livestock breeds as represented in the collection by John Hammond. Harpenden, 1958. xxxiv, 126p. 32plates, 25cm. Bibliography: p. 101-102. [N7660.R6] 59-46694
1. Animals in art. 2. Art, British. 3. Stock and stock-breeding—Gt. Brit.— Hist. I. Boalch, Donald Howard. II. Title.

SETON, Ernest Thompson, 1860-1946. 743'.69'7
Art anatomy of animals / Ernest Thompson Seton. Philadelphia : Running Press, c1977. p. cm. Reprint of the 1896 ed. published by Macmillan, London, under title: Studies in the art anatomy of animals. Includes index. [NC780.S5 1977] 77-12234 ISBN 0-89471-005-2 lib. bdg. : 15.90. ISBN 0-89471-004-4 pbk. : 5.95
1. Animals in art. 2. Anatomy, Artistic. I. Title. BIP

VIRCH, Claus, 1927- 704.94'32'07401471
The artist and the animal; a loan exhibition for the benefit of the Animal Medical Center, May 7-24, 1968. New York, M. Knoedler [1968] 80 p. illus. (part col.) 22 cm. [N7660.V47] 68-29943
1. Animals in art. 2. Art—Exhibitions. I. Animal Medical Center. II. Title.

WORLD Confederation of organizations of the Teaching Profession 704.9432
Man and animal [Eds.: Anil de Silva. others] Greenwich. Conn.. N. Y. Graphic [c.1965] 64p. illus. plates (pt. col.) 32cm. (Man through his art. v.3) Bibl. [N7660.W6] 65-29172 7.95: 5.25 schl. ed.,
1. Animals in art. 2. Animals and civilization. I. De Silva. Anil. ed II. Title. III. Series.

Animals in art—Catalogs.

STUBBS, George, 1724-1806. 759.2
Stubbs / [text by] William Gaunt. Oxford : Phaidon, 1977. 16 p., 28 p. of plates : chiefly col. ill. ; 32 cm. Bibliography: p. 14. [ND497.S93A4 1977] 78-313922 ISBN 0-7148-1808-9 : 7.95
1. Stubbs, George, 1724-1806—Catalogs. 2. Animals in art—Catalogs. I. Gaunt, William, 1900- BIP

Animals in art—Juvenile literature.

BEHRENS, June. 704.94'32
Looking at beasties / by June Behrens ; illustrated with art reproductions ; pictures collected by Bernard Shapiro. Chicago : Childrens Press, [1977] p. cm. (Adventures in art series) "A Golden Gate junior book." Pictures of fifteen works of art which portray animals, with explanations of the animals, the artists, and the time periods of each. [N7660.B364] 77-6331 ISBN 0-516-08823-8 lib.bdg. : 6.60
1. Animals in art—Juvenile literature. 2. Animals, Mythical, in art—Juvenile literature. 3. Art. I. Title. BIP

BELVES, Pierre, 1909- 704.94'32
Animals in art: a practical introduction to seventy of the principle techniques of art [by] Peter Belves and Francis Mathey; editor Denys Kay-Robinson. Feltham, Odhams Books, 1968. 4-109 p. of illus. (some col.). 22 x 26 cm. Illus. on lining papers. Translation of Portraits d'animaux. [N7660.B3713 1968b] 75-481888 35/-
1. Animals in art—Juvenile literature. I. Mathey, Francois, joint author. II. Kay-Robinson, Denys, ed. III. Title.

BELVES, Pierre, 1909- 704.94'32
How artists work; an introduction to techniques of art, by Pierre Belves and Francois Mathey. English adaptation by Alice Bach. New York, Lion Press [1968] 107 p. illus. (part col.) 22 x 26 cm. Translation of Portraits d'animaux. Brief text and photographs introduce representations of various animals in different artistic media and styles from prehistory to the present. [N7660.B3713] 68-20450 6.50
1. Animals in art—Juvenile literature. 2. Art—Technique—Juvenile literature. I. Mathey, Francois, joint author. II. Title. BIP

Animals (in numismatics)

SCHON, Gunter. 737.4
Animals, birds & fishes on coins, by Gunther Schon, assisted by A. V. Ziegesar. New York, Sterling Pub. Co. [1971] 48 p. illus. 20 cm. (Topical coin library) Adapted from Tiermotiv Katalog. Briefly describes some of the land animals, fish, birds, and insects that appear on various coins. Includes illustrations of many of the coins. [CJ161.A6S36 1971] 79-126854
1. Animals (in numismatics) I. Ziegesar, A. V. II. Title.

Animals, Mythical.

VINYCOMB, John. 704.94'6
Fictitious & symbolic creatures in art with special reference to their use in British heraldry. London, Chapman and Hall, 1906. Detroit, Gale Research Co., 1969. xvi, 276 p. illus., coats of arms. 22 cm. [N7690.V75 1969] 76-89300
1. Animals, Mythical. 2. Symbolism in art. 3. Heraldry—Gt. Brit. I. Title. BIP

Animals, Mythical, in art—Juvenile literature.

MULLINS, Patricia, 1952- 759.994
Fabulous beasts / [by] Patricia Mullins. Sydney : Collins, 1976. [30] p. : col. ill. ; 30 cm. [ND1105.M84A45] 77-352653 ISBN 0-00-185019-9
1. Mullins, Patricia, 1952- 2. Animals, Mythical, in art—Juvenile literature. 3. Animals, Mythical—Juvenile literature. I. Title.

WILLIAMS, Diane. 704.947
Demons and beasts in art. Designed by Linda Stewart. Minneapolis, Lerner Publications Co., 1970. 67 p. illus. (part col.) 27 cm. (Fine art books for young people) Describes the appearance and the symbolic meaning of beasts, demons, and mythical creatures in paintings, drawings, and sculpture from various eras and cultures. [N7745.A5W53] 75-84407
1. Animals, Mythical, in art—Juvenile literature. I. Title. BIP

Anonima Group.

ANONIMA Group retrospective, 1960-1971; 759.13'074'014317 October 28-November 26, 1971. Burlington, Robert Hull Fleming Museum, University of Vermont, 1971. 24 p. illus. 28 cm. Includes bibliographical references. [ND212.5.A5A5] 72-198088
1. Anonima Group. I. Anonima Group. II. Vermont. University. Robert Hull Fleming Museum.

Anonymous paintings—Exhibitions.

FINCH College, New York. Museum of Art. 759.94'074'01471
Sixty-six paintings in search of their authors; a loan exhibition, Nov. 21, 1969-Jan. 20, 1970. New York [1969?] [40] p. illus. 23 cm. Introd. by Robert L. Manning. [ND454.F5] 70-23311
1. Anonymous paintings—Exhibitions. 2. Anonymous painters—Europe. I. Manning, Robert L. II. Title.

Anschutz, Philip—Art collections.

SCHRIEVER, George. 758
American masters in the West : selections from the Anschutz Collection : the Boise Gallery of Art, Boise, Idaho, April 26 to June 16, 1974, Utah Museum of Fine Arts, University of Utah, Salt Lake City, Utah, June 30 to September 1, 1974 / catalog text by George Schriever ; with an introd. by E. F. Sanguinetti. Boise, Idaho : Boise Gallery of Art, c1974. 48 p. : ill. (some col.) ; 22 x 28 cm. Includes index. [ND1441.5.S37] 76-359327
1. Anschutz, Philip—Art collections. 2. The West in art. 3. Paintings, American—Exhibitions. 4. Paintings, Modern—19th century—United States—Exhibitions. 5. Paintings, Modern—20th century—United States—Exhibitions. I. Boise Gallery of Art. II. Utah Museum of Fine Arts. III. Title.

Antietam, Battle of, 1862.

FRASSANITO, William A. 779'.9'9737336
Antietam : the photographic legacy of America's bloodiest day / William A. Frassanito. New York : Scribner, c1978. 304 p. : ill. ; 23 cm. Includes bibliographical references and index. [E474.65.F7] 78-2336 ISBN 0-684-15659-8 : 14.95
1. Antietam, Battle of, 1862. I. Title. BIP

Antique dealers.

COWIE, Donald. 658'.91'7451
How to deal in antiques, by Donald Cowie and John Mebane. Dubuque, Iowa, Babka Pub. Co. [1972] 108 p. illus. 21 cm. Bibliography: p. 94-107. [NK1133.C68] 72-83651 3.50
1. Antique dealers. I. Mebane, John, 1909- joint author. II. Title.

SOMMER, Elyse. 381'.45'7410973
How to make money in the antiques-and-collectibles business / by Elyse Sommer ; illustrated with photos. Boston : Houghton Mifflin, 1979. p. cm. Bibliography: p. [NK1133.S65] 78-24351 ISBN 0-395-27758-2 : 10.95
1. Antique dealers. 2. Antiques—Marketing. 3. Antiques as an investment. I. Title. BIP

SWINDELL, Deane F. 708.051
Antics of antiquers. New York, Vantage Press [c.1959] 191p. 22cm. 3.00 bds.,
I. Title.

WEISS, Mark M. 381'.45'74510973
501 valuable free tips and things for people who want to make money with antiques. Compiled and edited by Mark Weiss. [New York, Greystone Press, 1973] 50 p. 18 cm. [NK1133.W44] 73-158786
1. Antique dealers. 2. Art objects—Collectors and collecting—Catalogs. 3. Free materials. I. Title.

Antiques—Conservation and restoration—Handbooks, manuals, etc.

DOUSSY, Michel. 745.1'028
The art of restoring antiques / Michel Doussy ; translated from the French by Patrick Evans. New York : Times Books, [1978] c1973. p. cm. Translation of Guide des secrets de l'antiquaire. [NK1125.D6513 1978] 78-18003 ISBN 0-8129-6302-4 pbk. : 5.95
1. Antiques—Conservation and restoration—Handbooks, manuals, etc. I. Title. BIP

GROTZ, George. 745.1'028
The antique restorer's handbook : a dictionary of the crafts & materials used in restoring antiques and works of art / by George Grotz. 1st ed. Garden City, N.Y. : Doubleday, 1976. x, 206 p. : ill. ; 22 cm. Includes index. [NK1127.5.G74] 75-40702 ISBN 0-385-05302-9 : 8.95
1. Antiques—Conservation and restoration—Handbooks, manuals, etc. I. Title. BIP

Antiques—Dictionaries.

MOUNTFIELD, David, 1938- 745.1'03
The antique collectors' illustrated dictionary / compiled by David Mountfield. London ; New York : Hamlyn, 1974. 3-273 p. : ill. (some col.) ; 31 cm. On jacket: Distributed in the U.S.A. by Crown Publishers. [NK1125.M845] 75-329775 ISBN 0-600-30154-0 : £3.95
1. Antiques—Dictionaries. I. Title.

Antiques—England—Dictionaries.

WILLS, Geoffrey. 745.1'03
A concise encyclopedia of antiques / [by] Geoffrey Wills. Reading : Osprey, 1975. 303 p. : ill. (some col.), geneal. table, ports. ; 23 cm. Includes index. [NK928.W53 1975] 76-353947 ISBN 0-85045-063-2 : £5.50
1. Antiques—England—Dictionaries. I. Title.

WILLS, Geoffrey. 745.1'03
A concise encyclopedia of antiques / Geoffrey Wills. New York : Van Nostrand Reinhold Co., [1976] p. cm. Includes index. [NK928.W53] 75-22082 ISBN 0-442-29488-3
1. Antiques—England—Dictionaries. 2. Antiques—United States—Dictionaries. I. Title. BIP

Antiques—Europe.

KENNEDY, Carol. 745.1'094
Buying antiques in Europe : what to buy and where / Carol Kennedy. London ; New York : Bowker, 1977 xv, 397 p. : ill. ; 23 cm. Includes bibliographical references and index. [NK925.K46 1976] 76-49706 ISBN 0-85935-018-5 : 23.00
1. Antiques—Europe. 2. Antique dealers—Europe—Directories. I. Title. BIP

WILSON, Doris C. 745.1'075
Parlez-vous antiques? The when, where, and how of buying antiques in Europe [by] Doris C. Wilson. South Brunswick [N.J.] A. S. Barnes [1970, c1969] 154 p. illus., maps. 22 cm. [NK1127.W5 1970] 68-27828 ISBN 0-498-06806-4 5.95
1. Antiques—Europe. 2. Antique dealers—Europe—Directories. I. Title.

Antiques—Expertising.

GILBERT, Anne, 1927- 745.1'075
How to be an antiques detective / by Anne Gilbert. New York : Grosset & Dunlap, c1978. 179 p. : ill. ; 29 cm. Includes index. [NK1125.G48] 77-72621 ISBN 0-448-14276-7 : 14.95. ISBN 0-448-14277-5 pbk. : 7.95
1. Antiques—Expertising. I. Title. BIP

Antiques, French.

COSTANTINO, Ruth T. 709.44
How to know French antiques. Illus. by Helen Costantino [New York] New Amer. Lib. [c.1961] 256p. illus. (Signet key bk., KT378) Bibl. .75 pap.,
1. Antiques, French. I. Title.

Antiques—Great Britain.

BENEDICTUS, David. 745.1'0941
Junk! : how and where to buy beautiful things for next to nothing / [by] David Benedictus. London : Macmillan, 1976. 192 p. : ill. ; 23 cm. Includes bibliographies and index. [NK928.B46] 77-350739 ISBN 0-333-19616-3 : £2.95
1. Antiques—Great Britain. 2. Antique dealers—Great Britain. I. Title.

FLETCHER, Edward, fl.1970- 745.1'0941
Digging up antiques / [by] Edward Fletcher. London : Pitman, 1975. viii, 120 p., [4] p. of plates : ill. (some col.), facsims., port. ; 25 cm. Includes index. Bibliography: p. 117. [NK928.F54] 75-325717 ISBN 0-273-00494-8 : 10.95
1. Antiques—Great Britain. 2. Treasure-trove. I. Title.

FLETCHER, Edward, fl.1970- 745.1'0941'075
Where to dig up antiques / E. Fletcher ; photographs M. J. Coffin ; illustrations A. Payne. Southampton : Southern Collectors Publications, 1976. [3], 55 p. : ill. ; 21 cm. [NK928.F545] 77-365124 ISBN 0-905438-04-3 : £1.35
1. Antiques—Great Britain. I. Title.

WINTERSGILL, Donald. 745.1'0942
English antiques, 1700-1830 / Donald Wintersgill. New York : Morrow, c1975. 256 p., [8] leaves of plates : ill., (some col.) ; 27 cm. Includes index. Bibliography: p. [246]-247. [NK928.W55 1975] 75-4162 ISBN 0-688-02931-0 : 18.00
1. Antiques—Great Britain. 2. Decoration and ornament, Georgian. 3. Decoration and ornament—Regency style. I. Title.

Antiques—Handbooks, manuals, etc.

THE Antique dealers pocketbook. New York : Scribner, [1974] c1972. 158 p. : chiefly ill. ; 16 cm. Includes index. [NK1125.A142] 74-3739 ISBN 0-684-13828-X : 4.95 745.1
1. Antiques—Handbooks, manuals, etc.

BOGUE, Dorothy McGraw. 745.1'02'02
Understanding yesterday's antique treasures : a self-taught course in antiques in ten chapters / Dorothy McGraw Bogue. [Colorado Springs, Colo. : Bogue, c1975] iv, 265 p. : ill. ; 29 cm. [NK1125.B565] 75-28588
1. Antiques—Handbooks, manuals, etc. I. Title.

COHEN, Hal L. 745.1'075
Official guide to popular antiques, curios; the price to buy & sell, by Hal L. Cohen. 3d ed. New York, HC Publishers [1971] 415 p. illus. 19 cm. Beginning with the 4th ed. (1973) published under title: Antiques, curios. Title on spine: Official guide to antiques. [NK1125.C57 1971] 73-158144 5.00
1. Antiques—Handbooks, manuals, etc. I. Title.

MULLENIX, Dennis. 745.1
Antiques : a browser's handbook / Dennis Mullenix. 1st ed. New York : Harper & Row, c1977. vii, 214 p. : ill. ; 21 cm. Bibliography: p. [209]-214. [NK1125.M875 1977] 76-47264 ISBN 0-06-013109-8 : 8.95
1. Antiques—Handbooks, manuals, etc. I. Title. BIP

Antiques in interior decoration.

GROSS, Leslie, 1927- 749.2
Housewives' guide to antiques : how to get the most for your money when furnishing your home with antiques / by Leslie Gross ; illustrated by the author. New York : Galahad Books, [1975] c1959. 180 p., [2] leaves of plates : ill. ; 21 cm. [NK2115.5.A5G76 1975] 73-91800 ISBN 0-88365-142-4 : 5.95
1. Antiques in interior decoration. 2. Antiques. I. Title.

SCHULER, Josef Egon. 747
Old art in new rooms. Introd. and accompanying text by Olga Soden. Edited by J. E. Schuler. Translated from the German by William and Jane Wolf. South Brunswick [N.J.] A. S. Barnes [1969] 146 p. illus. (part fold., part col.) 27 cm. Translation of Alte Kunst in neuen Raumen. [NK2113.S3713] 70-82134 ISBN 0-498-07464-1 15.00
1. Antiques in interior decoration. I. Title.

WILLIAMS, Henry Lionel. 747
Antiques in interior design, by Henry Lionel Williams and Ottalie K. Williams. South Brunswick [N.J.] A. S. Barnes [1966] 387 p. illus. 29 cm. [NK2130.W5] 66-28022
1. Antiques in Interior decoration. I. Williams, Ottalie Kroeber, 1901- joint author. II. Title.

Antiques—Japan.

SALMON, Patricia. 745.1'0952
A guide to Japanese antiques / by Patricia Salmon. New York : Van Nostrand Reinhold Co., 1976. 256 p. : ill. ; 19 cm. Published in 1975 under title: Japanese antiques. Includes index. Bibliography: p. 241-242. [NK1071.S255 1976] 75-27186 ISBN 0-442-25091-6 : 8.95
1. Antiques—Japan. I. Title.

SALMON, Patricia. 745.1'0952
The price guide to Japanese antiques / by Patricia Salmon. [New ed.]. Woodbridge : Antique Collectors' Club, [1976] 255 p. : ill. ; 21 cm. Originally published under title: Japanese antiques. Includes index. [NK1071.S255 1976b] 77-358579 ISBN 0-902028-49-9 : £6.95
1. Antiques—Japan. 2. Antique dealers—Japan—Directories. I. Title.

Antiques—New England.

MICHAEL, George, 1919- 745.1'0974
The treasury of New England antiques / by George Michael. New York : Galahad Books, [1975] c1969. x, 210 p. : ill. ; 26 cm. Includes index. [NK810.M5 1975] 74-15430 ISBN 0-88365-296-X : 12.50
1. Antiques—New England. I. Title.

Antiques—New England—Directories.

HITCHCOCK, Anthony, 1940- 380.1'45'74502574
Country New England antiques, crafts, and factory outlets / by Anthony Hitchcock and Jean Lindgren. New York : Artemis Books, c1978. 156 p., [12] leaves of plates : ill. ; 17 cm. (The Compleat traveler's companion) Includes index. [NK810.H57] 78-6502 ISBN 0-89102-141-8 : 6.95. ISBN 0-89102-137-X pbk. : 3.95
1. Antiques—New England—Directories. 2. Handicraft—New England—Directories. 3. Shopping—New England—Directories. I. Lindgren, Jean, 1941- joint author. II. Title. III. Series. BIP

Antiques—New England—Prices.

HUDSON, William Norman. 745.1'075
Antiques illustrated and priced / Norman Hudson. Cranbury, N.J. : A. S. Barnes, [1977] p. cm. [NK810.H82 1977] 76-58584 ISBN 0-498-02109-2 : 25.00
1. Antiques—New England—Prices. I. Title.

Antiques—New Jersey—Directories.

JACOBS, Muriel. 338.4'7'741525749
Antiquing in New Jersey and Bucks County, Pennsylvania / Muriel Jacobs, Doris Ballard. New Brunswick, N.J. : Rutgers University Press, c1978. lxiv, 439 p. : ill. ; 24 cm. Includes indexes. Bibliography: p. 413-418. [NK835.N45J33] 78-9471 ISBN 0-8135-0853-3 : 12.95. ISBN 0-8135-0863-0 pbk. : 5.95
1. Antiques—New Jersey—Directories. 2. Antiques—Pennsylvania—Bucks Co.—Directories. I. Ballard, Doris, joint author. II. Title.

Antiques—New York (City)—Directories.

GARDNER, Arron. 745.1'025'7471
Gardner's guide to antiques and art buying in New York City. Indianapolis, Bobbs-Merrill [1969] xiii, 204 p. 22 cm. [NK1127.G3] 69-13091 5.95
1. Antiques—New York (City)—Directories. 2. Antique dealers—New York (City)—Directories. I. Title.

Antiques—Pennsylvania—Directories.

HARTLER, Arthur L. 745.1'025'748
Penn's countrie : the antique directory guide / by Arthur L. Hartler. Philadelphia : Franklin Pub. Co., [1975] ix, 68 p. : maps ; 19 cm. Includes index. [NK1127.H37] 75-260 ISBN 0-87133-051-2 pbk. : 1.95
1. Antiques—Pennsylvania—Directories. I. Title. BIP

Antiques—Pennsylvania—Perry Co.

CHANDLER, Roy F. 745.1'09748'45
Antiques of Perry County, Pa. / Roy F. Chandler. Deer Lake, Pa. : Bacon and Freeman Publishers, 1976, c1975. 200 p. : ill. ; 29 cm. Includes index. [NK835.P42P473 1976] 75-18264 12.90
1. Antiques—Pennsylvania—Perry Co. I. Title.

Antiques—Prices—Canada.

UNITT, Peter, 1914- 745.1'02'9
Unitt's Canadian price guide to antiques and collectables; an illustrated guide to price trends in Canada for dealer and collector [by Peter and Doris Unitt] Peterborough, Ont., Clock House Publications, 1968. 200 p. illus. 22 cm. [NK1133.U5 1968] 73-414168 6.00
1. Antiques—Prices—Canada. 2. Art objects—Canada—Catalogs. I. Unitt, Doris Joyce, joint author. II. Title: Canadian price guide to antiques and collectables.

Antiques—Private collections—Australia.

ROGAN, John P. 745.1'075
Antiques in Australia from private collections / [by] John P. Rogan ; photographs, John H. Gumley ; foreword, Joseph Burke. Milton, Q. : Jacaranda, 1975. xii, 244 p. : ill. (some col.) ; 32 cm. Includes index. Bibliography: p. 233-235. [NK560.R63] 76-354270 ISBN 0-7016-0784-X : 25.00
1. Antiques—Private collections—Australia. I. Gumley, John H. II. Title.

Antiques—Southern States.

MORTON, Robert, 1934- 745.1'0975
Southern antiques & folk art / by Robert Morton ; design by Ladislav Svatos. 1st ed. Birmingham, Ala. : Oxmoor House, c1976. 251 p. : ill. (some col.) ; 31 cm. Bibliography: p. 243-244. [NK811.M67] 76-14114 ISBN 0-8487-0420-7 : 31.95
1. Antiques—Southern States. 2. Folk art—Southern States. I. Title. BIP

Antiques—United States.

BEITZ, Lester V. 745.1'075
Overlooked treasures / Les Beitz. South Brunswick : A. S. Barnes, c1975. p. cm. Bibliography: p. [NK805.B44] 74-30715 ISBN 0-498-01672-2 : 9.95
1. Antiques—United States. I. Title. BIP

MICHAEL, George, 1919- 745.1
George Michael's treasury of Federal antiques. New York, Hawthorn Books [1972] xviii, 235 p. illus. 26 cm. Bibliography: p. 223-225. [NK806.M5] 72-158025 10.00
1. Antiques—United States. 2. Decoration and ornament—Federal style. I. Title. II. Title: Treasury of Federal antiques.

NOSTALGIC treasures from America's past. Fort Atkinson, Wis. : Home Library Pub. Co., c1976. 96 p. : ill. (some col.) ; 32 cm. [NK805.N63] 76-370921 4.98 745.1'0973

1. Antiques—United States. I. Home Library Publishing Company. BIP

ROCKMORE, Cynthia. 745.1'0973
The room-by-room book of American antiques / by Cynthia & Julian Rockmore. New York : Galahad Books, c1970. 240 p. : ill. (some col.) ; 29 cm. Includes index. [NK805.R6 1970b] 75-12264 ISBN 0-88365-319-2 : 12.50
1. Antiques—United States. I. Rockmore, Julian, joint author. II. Title.

Antiques—United States—Catalogs.

HAMMOND, Dorothy M. 745.1'075
Pictorial price guide to American antiques and objects made for the American market : over 5000 objects in 300 catagories illustrated and priced / by Dorothy Hammond. 1st ed. New York : Dutton, c1977. 224 p. : ill. ; 28 cm. [NK805.H328 1977] 77-72038 ISBN 0-525-47445-5 : 8.95
1. Antiques—United States—Catalogs. 2. Americana—Catalogs. I. Title.

HAMMOND, Dorothy M. 745.1'075
Pictorial price guide to American antiques and objects made for the American market : almost 6000 objects in 300 categories illustrated and priced / by Dorothy Hammond. 2d ed. New York : Dutton, c1979. 224 p. : ill. ; 28 cm. Includes index. [NK805.H328 1979] 78-74223 ISBN 0-525-47517-6 : 8.95
1. Antiques—United States—Catalogs. 2. Americana—Catalogs. I. Title.

HAMMOND, Dorothy M. 745.1'0973
Price guide to country antiques & American primitives / Dorothy Hammond. New York : Funk & Wagnalls, [1975] 280 p. : ill. ; 22 cm. [NK805.H33] 75-13602 ISBN 0-308-10183-9 10.00 ISBN 0-308-10184-7 pbk. : 6.95
1. Antiques—United States—Catalogs. I. Title. BIP

KETCHUM, William C., 1931- 745.1'0973
The catalog of American antiques / by William C. Ketchum, Jr. ; photography by John Garetti. New York : Rutledge Books, [1977] p. cm. Includes index. Bibliography: p. [NK805.K47] 77-1118 ISBN 0-87469-011-0 : 24.95
1. Antiques—United States—Catalogs. I. Garetti, John. II. Title. BIP

Antiques—United States—Conservation and restoration—Directories.

PORTER, Arthur. 702'.8
Directory of art & antique restoration / editors, Arthur Porter, Elizabeth Taylor. [New ed.]. San Francisco : [s.n., 1975?] 251 p. ; 21 cm. Includes index. [NK1127.5.P6 1975] 75-325504
1. Antiques—United States—Conservation and restoration—Directories. I. Taylor, Elizabeth, joint author. II. Title.

Antiques, Victorian.

DREPPERD, Carl William, 1898-1956. 708.051
Victorian, the Cinderella of antiques. [1st ed.] Garden City, N.Y., Doubleday, 1950. xxi, 260 p. illus. 22 cm. Includes bibliographies. [NK1125.D67] 50-11085
1. Antiques, Victorian. 2. Furniture, American. 3. Art objects—Collectors and collecting. I. Title. BIP

LATHAM, Jean. 745.1'0942
Victoriana. New York, Stein & Day [1971] 158 p. illus. (part col.) 22 cm. Bibliography: p. 149-150. [NK775.L36 1971] 76-148833 ISBN 0-8128-1372-3 7.95
1. Antiques, Victorian. I. Title.

Antiquities—Collection and preservation.

ORGAN, R. M. 069'.4
Design for scientfic conservation of antiquities [by] R. M. Organ. Washington, Smithsonian Institution Press [1969, c1968] xi, 497 p. illus. 23 cm. "Published with the approval of ... IIC [i.e. International Institute for Conservation of Historic and Artistic Works]" Includes bibliographies. [CC135.O7] 68-8260 16.00
1. Antiquities—Collection and preservation. I. International Institute for Conservation of Historic and Artistic Works. II. Title. III. Title: Scientific conservation of antiquities.

Antiquities—Collectors and collecting.

EDE, Charles. 730'.093
Collecting antiquities : an introductory guide / [by] Charles Ede. London : Dent, 1976. xviii, 142 p. : ill., maps ; 26 cm. Includes index. Bibliography: p. 134. [N5340.E33] 76-362589 ISBN 0-460-04240-8 : £9.50
1. Antiquities—Collectors and collecting. 2. Art, Ancient—Collectors and collecting. I. Title. BIP

Antoninianus (Coin)

EDDY, Samuel Kennedy, 1926- 737.49'39'23
The minting of Antoniniani A. D. 238-249, and the Smyrna hoard, by Samuel K. Eddy. New York, Amer. Numismatic Soc., 1967. vii, 133p. illus. 23cm. (Numismatic notes and monographs, no. 156) Bibl. [CJ1005.E3] 67-5498 4.50 pap.,
1. Antoninianus (Coin) 2. Coin hoards—Izmir (City) I. Title. II. Series. BIP

Antwerp. St. Charles Borromeo (Church)

MARTIN, John Rupert. 759.9493
The ceiling paintings for the Jesuit Church in Antwerp. London, New York, Phaidon, 1968. xvii, 241 p. illus., plan. 27 cm. (Corpus Rubenianum Ludwig Burchard, pt. 1) Bibliography: p. 13-17. [ND673.R9C63 pt. 1] 68-21258 1500.00
1. Antwerp. St. Charles Borromeo (Church) 2. Mural painting and decoration—Antwerp. I. Title. II. Series.

Anuszkiewicz, Richard.

ANUSZKIEWICZ, Richard. 759.13
Anuszkiewicz / Karl Lunde. New York : H. N. Abrams, 1977. 207 p. : ill. (some col.) ; 28 x 30 cm. Includes index. Bibliography: p. 200-204. [ND237.A645L86] 76-28230 ISBN 0-8109-0363-6 : 45.00
1. Anuszkiewicz, Richard. I. Lunde, Karl. BIP

ANUSZKIEWICZ, Richard. 759.13
New paintings by Anuszkiewicz. [New York? c1967] [20] p. illus. (part col.) 28 cm. On label on t.p.: Supplied by Worldwide Books, New York. "An exhibition ... opening ... October 2-25, 1967, at Sidney Janis ... New York." [ND237.A645S5] 68-30094
I. Sidney Janis Gallery. II. Title.

ANUSZKIEWICZ, Richard. 759.13
Richard Anuszkiewicz : an exhibition / organized by the La Jolla Museum of Contemporary Art. La Jolla, Calif. : The Museum, c1976. [40] p. : ill. (some col.) ; 23 cm. Bibliography: p. [38]-[39] [ND237.A645L34] 76-43241
1. Anuszkiewicz, Richard. I. LaJolla Museum of Contemporary Art.

Apache Indians—Art.

WAYLAND, Virginia. 769'.5
Apache playing cards from the Wayland collection. Pasadena, Calif., H & V Wayland, 1972. 10 p. illus. 25 cm. and portfolio (4 col. plates) 27 x 41 cm. (Her The Wayland playing card monograph, no. 3) [E99.A6W37] 72-169527
1. Apache Indians—Art. 2. Cards—Art. I. Title.

Apartment houses.

ARCHITECTURAL record. 728.2
Apartments and dormitories. [New York] F. W. Dodge Corp., c1958. vii, 232p. illus., plans. 30cm. (An Architectural record book) Articles previously published in Architectural record. [NA7860.A7] 58-13443
1. Apartment houses. 2. Dormitories. 3. Architecture, Domestic—Designs and plans. I. Title.

HABRAKEN, N. J. 301.5'4
Supports: an alternative to mass housing [by] N. J. Habraken. Translated from the Dutch by B. Valkenburg. New York, Praeger Publishers [1972] viii, 97 p. 22 cm. Translation of De dragers en de mensen. [NA7860.H2513 1972b] 76-180868 7.95
1. Apartment houses. 2. Architecture and society. I. Title.

HOUSING / 728.3'1
John Macsai ... [et al.] ; illustrator, Alfred J. Hidvegi. New York : Wiley, c1976. ix, 483 p. : ill. ; 29 cm. "A Wiley-Interscience publication." Includes bibliographical references and index. [TH4820.H68] 75-38736 ISBN 0-471-56312-9 : 30.00
1. Apartment houses. 2. Architecture, Domestic. I. Macsai, John, 1926- II. Hidvegi, Alfred J. BIP

PAUL, Samuel, 1912- 728'.2
Apartments: their design and development. New York, Reinhold Pub. Co. [1967] 308 p. illus. 29 cm. Bibliography: p. 297-298. [NA7860.P3] 67-27430
1. Apartment houses. 2. Architecture, Domestic—Designs and plans. I. Title.

YORKE, Francis Reginald Stevens, 1906- 728.2
Masterworks of international apartment building design [by] F. R. S. Yorke [and] Frederick Gibberd. New York, Praeger [1959] 211 p. illus., plans. 31 cm. "The English edition, entitled Modern flats [was] published [in 1958]" [NA7860.Y62 1958] 59-7393
1. Apartment houses. I. Gibberd, Frederick, joint author. II. Title.

Apartment houses—Exhibitions.

NEW York (City). Museum of Modern Art. 728.3'1
Another chance for housing: low-rise alternatives; Brownsville, Brooklyn, Fox Hills, Staten Island. [Catalogue of] an exhibition at the Museum of Modern Art, June 12-August 19, 1973, designed by the Institute for Architecture and Urban Studies for the New York State Urban Development Corporation. New York [1973] 38 p. illus. (part col.) 24 cm. [NA7860.N48 1973] 73-78278
1. Apartment houses—Exhibitions. 2. Apartment houses—New York (City) 3. Architecture, Domestic—Designs and plans. I. Institute for Architecture and Urban Studies. II. Urban Development Corporation. III. Title.

Apartment houses—Landscape architecture.

GREAT Britain Ministry of Housing and Local Government. 712'.6
Landscaping for flats: the treatment of ground space on high density housing estates. 2nd ed. London. H.M.S.O., 1967. 68p. illus., tables, diagrs. 30cm. (Its. Design bulletin 5) Bibl. [TH6010.G7 no.5] 67-81075 1.70 pap.,
1. Apartment houses—Landscape architecture. I. Title. II. Series.
Available from British Info. New York

Apartment houses—New York (City)

ALPERN, Andrew. 728.3'1
Apartments for the affluent : a historical survey of buildings in New York / Andrew Alpern ; with a foreword by Harmon H. Goldstone. New York : McGraw-Hill, [1975] 159 p. : ill. ; 29 cm. Includes indexes. [NA7860.A497 1975] 75-17692 19.95
1. Apartment houses—New York (City) 2. Architecture and society—New York (City) 3. Interior decoration—New York (City) I. Title. BIP

Apartments.

NAAR, Jon. 747'.8'831
Living in one room / Jon Naar and Molly Siple ; photos. by Jon Naar. New York : Random House, 1976. p. cm. [NK2195.A6N22 1976b] 76-14167 ISBN 0-394-40846-2 : 10.95 ISBN 0-394-72076-8 pbk. :
1. Apartments. 2. Interior decoration. I. Siple, Molly, joint author. II. Title.

NAAR, Jon. 747'.8'831
Living in one room / Jon Naar and Molly Siple ; photos. by Jon Naar. 1st Vintage Books ed. New York : Vintage Books, 1976. p. cm. [NK2195.A6N22 1976] 76-10579 ISBN 0-394-72076-8 pbk. : 5.95
1. Apartments. 2. Interior decoration. I. Siple, Molly, joint author. II. Title. BIP

Apocalyptic art.

BLAKE, William, 1757-1827. 760'.92'4
The apocalyptic vision. Pref. and catalogue by Harvey Stahl. Introd. by Bruce Daryl Barone. [An exhibition at Reid Hall, Manhattanville College, April 21 to May 13, 1974] Purchase, N.Y., Manhattanville College [1974] [74] p. illus. 23 cm. Bibliography: p. [73]-[74] [N6797.B57S82] 74-175885
1. Blake, William, 1757-1827. 2. Apocalyptic art. I. Stahl, Harvey. II. Manhattanville College of the Sacred Heart, Purchase, N.Y. III. Title.

NOLAN, Barbara, 1941- 700'.9'02
The Gothic visionary perspective / by Barbara Nolan. Princeton, N.J. : Princeton University Press, c1977. xviii, 268 p., [12] leaves of plates : ill. ; 24 cm. Includes bibliographical references and index. [NX650.A6N64] 76-56241 ISBN 0-691-06337-0 : 16.50
1. Apocalyptic art. 2. Arts, Gothic. I. Title. BIP

PARKINSON, Ronald. 759.2
Samuel Colman, fl. 1816-1840 : four apocalyptic themes / [by Parkinson] [London] : Tate Gallery Publications, [1976] [12] p. : ill. ; 21 cm. Cover title. Catalogue of an exhibition held at the Tate Gallery. [ND497.C644P37] 76-383871 ISBN 0-905005-40-6 : £0.25
1. Colman, Samuel. 2. Apocalyptic art. I. Colman, Samuel. II. Tate Gallery, London.

Apocalyptic art—Exhibitions.

HENKEL, Kathryn. 760
The Apocalypse. [Exhibition at] University of Maryland Art Gallery, March 22-April 29, 1973. Introductory notes by Don Denny and James D. Farquhar. Text by Kathryn Henkel. [College Park] University of Maryland Dept. of Art [1973] 103 p. illus. (part col.) 28 cm. "University of Maryland Department of Art, Museum Training Program, 1972-1973." Catalogue: p. 95-101. Bibliography: p. 79-81. [N8180.H37] 72-619727 6.00
1. Apocalyptic art—Exhibitions. I. Maryland. University. Art Gallery. II. Maryland. University. Dept. of Art. III. Title.

Apollonio di Giovanni, 1415?-1465.

CALLMANN, Ellen. 759.5
Apollonio di Giovanni. Oxford, Clarendon Press, 1974. xiii, 98, [93] p. illus. (1 col.) 30 cm. (Oxford studies in the history of art and architecture) Based on the author's thesis, New York University. Bibliography: p. 88-90. [ND623.A658C34] 74-185679 ISBN 0-19-817196-X
1. Apollonio di Giovanni, 1415?-1465.
Distributed by Oxford University Press New York; 48.00. BIP

Apostles—Art.

LOESCHCKE, Walter 704.9486
Apostles and evangelists. Tr. by Giovanni Rossetti, Marguerite Buchloh. Recklinghausen, A. Bongers; dist. Taplinger [New York. 1958] 78p. 16 col. plates. 18cm. (Pictorial lib. of Eastern Church art, v. 14) Cover title Icons: apostles and evangelists. Tr. of Apostel und Evangelisten. [N8080.L5813] 67-16577 2.50 bds.,
1. Apostles—Art. I. Title. II. Title: Icons: apostles and evangelists.

Appel, Karel, 1921-

APPEL, Karel, 1921- 759.9492
Karel Appel, [n. p., 1961?] [52] p. illus. (part col.), facsims., ports. 27 cm. Cover title. Catalog of an exhibition held at the Stedelijk Van Abbe-Museum, Eindhoven. Apr. 29-June 4, 1961 and Haags Gemeentemuseum, Den Haag, June 9-July 9, 1961. "Beknopte bibliografie": p. [49] [ND653.A65E35] 67-111840
I. Eindhoven. Stedelijk Van Abbe-Museum. II. Hague. Gemeentemuseum. III. Title.

APPEL, Karel, 1921- 730.9492
The sculpture of Karel Appel. [Tr. from Italian by Olga Ragusa] New York, Abrams [1964] [70]p. illus. (pt. col.) ports. 28x30cm. Bibl. 63-14759 15.00
I. Title.

CLAUS, Hugo, 1929- 759.9492
Karel Appel, painter. [Tr.: Cornelis de Dood] Amsterdam, A. J. G. Strengholt; New York, Abrams [1963] 178p. illus. (pt. mounted, pt. col.) ports., facsims. 31cm. Bibl. 63-2627 30.00
1. Appel, Karel, 1921- I. Title.

Applique.

ANDERS, Nedda (Casson) 746.4'4
Applique, old and new, including patchwork and embroidery, by Nedda C. Anders. Drawings 4-10 by Bucky King. New York, Hearthside Press [1967] 128 p. illus. 25 cm. Bibliography: p. [125] [TT779.A5] 67-17832
1. Applique. 2. Patchwork. 3. Embroidery. I. Title.

ANDERS, Nedda Casson. 746.4'4
Applique, old and new, including patchwork and embroidery / Nedda C. Anders. New York : Dover Publications, 1976. 128 p., [1] leaf of plates : ill. ; 23 cm. Includes index. Bibliography: p. [125] [TT779.A5 1976] 75-19756 ISBN 0-486-23246-8 pbk. : 2.50
1. Applique. 2. Patchwork. 3. Embroidery. I. Title. BIP

ANDERS, Nedda (Casson) 746.4
Applique, old and new, including patchwork and embroidery, by Nedda C. Anders. Drawings 4-10 by Bucky King. New York, Hearthside Press [1967] 128 p. illus. 25 cm. Bibliography: p. [125] Covers materials; ways of transferring designs; different types and methods of both onlay and inlay applique; bead, braid, ribbon and cord applique; applique and patchwork quilts; teaching applique to children; and embroidery stitches. [TT779.A5] AC 68
1. Applique. 2. Patchwork. 3. Embroidery. I. Title.

AULD, Rhoda L. 746.4
Molas : what they are, how to make them, ideas they suggest for creative applique / Rhoda L. Auld ; photos. by Lawrence Auld. New York : Van Nostrand Reinhold Co., 1977. 112 p., [5] leaves of plates : ill. ; 29 cm. Includes index. Bibliography: p. 109-110. [TT779.A84] 76-17156 ISBN 0-442-20379-9 : 15.00
1. Applique. 2. Molas. 3. Cuna Indians—Textile industry and fabrics. I. Title. BIP

AVERY, Virginia. 746.4'4
The big book of applique / Virginia Avery. New York : Scribner, [1978] p. cm. [TT779.A93] 78-6547 ISBN 0-684-15623-7 : 14.95
1. Applique. I. Title. BIP

BALLARIAN, Anna. 746.4'4
Fabric collage : contemporary stitchery and applique / Anna Ballarian. Worcester, Mass. : Davis Publications, 1977,c1976. 80 p., [4] leaves of plates : ill. ; 27 cm. Bibliography: p. [77] [NK9104.B34] 76-29553 ISBN 0-87192-089-1 : 9.95
1. Applique. 2. Needlework. I. Title. BIP

BETTER homes and gardens 746.4'4
applique. 1st ed. Des Moines : Meredith Corp., c1978. 96 p. : ill. ; 27 cm. (Better homes and gardens books) [TT779.B47] 77-85853 ISBN 0-696-00435-6 : 3.95
1. Applique. I. Better homes and gardens. II. Title: Applique. BIP

LAURY, Jean Ray. 746.44
Applique stitchery. New York, Reinhold Pub. Co. [1966] 135 p. illus. (part col.) 26 cm. [TT779.L3] 66-24542
1. Applique. 2. Embroidery. I. Title.

PATERA, Charlotte, 1927- 746.4'4
The applique book. [New York] Creative Home Library [1974] 264 p. illus. 27 cm. Bibliography: p. 264. [TT779.P37 1974] 73-19920 ISBN 0-696-11000-8 9.95
1. Applique. I. Title.

PULS, Herta. 746.4'4
The art of cutwork and applique : historic, modern and Kuna Indian / Herta Puls. Newton Centre, Mass. : C. T. Branford Co., 1978. 240 p., [2] leaves of plates : ill. (some col.) ; 26 cm. Includes index. Bibliography: p. 237-238. [TT779.P84 1978b] 79-101006 ISBN 0-8231-4256-6 : 19.50
1. Applique. I. Title. II. Title: Cutwork and applique. BIP

RAYMO, Anne. 746.4'4
Sew up art : how to do it : 26 applique projects / by Anne Raymo and Holly Vose ; photos. by Jim Raymo. New York : Quick Fox, c1976. 95 p. : ill. (some col.) ; 28 cm. [TT779.R38] 75-45768 ISBN 0-8256-3065-7 pbk. : 4.95
1. Applique. I. Vose, Holly, joint author. II. Raymo, Jim. III. Title. BIP

SHEARS, Evangeline. 746.4'4
Applique, by Evangeline Shears and Diantha Fielding. New York, Watson-Guptill Publications [1972] 142 p. illus. (part col.) 27 cm. Bibliography: p. 137. [TT779.S5] 75-190520 ISBN 0-8230-0240-3 10.95
1. Applique. I. Fielding, Diantha, joint author.

SILVERSTEIN, Mira. 746.4'4
Fun with applique. New York, Scribner [1973] 56 p. illus. 24 cm. [TT779.S55] 72-11144 ISBN 0-684-13193-5 5.95
1. Applique. I. Title.

Applique.—Juvenile literature.

ALLENDORF, Katherine. 746.4'4
Applique. Pictures by George Overlie. Minneapolis, Lerner Publications Co. [1973] 32 p. illus. 19 cm. (An Early craft book) Introduces the tools, materials, and stitches used for applique and suggests various projects. [TT779.A44] 72-13333 ISBN 0-8225-0851-6 3.95 (Lib. bdg.)
1. Applique.—Juvenile literature. I. Overlie, George, illus. II. Title.

CHRISTENSEN, Jo Ippolito. 746.4'4
Applique & reverse applique / by Jo Ippolito Christensen & Sonie Shapiro Ashner. New York : Sterling Pub. Co., [1974] 48 p. : ill. (some col.) ; 20 cm. (Little craft book series) Includes index. Introduces the necessary materials and techniques of applique and offers suggestions for a variety of projects. [TT779.C48 1974] 73-83445 ISBN 0-8069-5274-1. ISBN 0-8069-5275-X lib. bdg.
1. Applique—Juvenile literature. I. Ashner, Sonie Shapiro, joint author. II. Title. BIP

Apprentices—Italy—Venice—Biography.

FISHER, M. Roy. 759.5 B
Titian's assistants during the later years / M. Roy Fisher. New York : Garland Pub., 1977. xxii, 148, 133 p. : ill. ; 21 cm. (Outstanding dissertations in the fine arts) Originally presented as the author's thesis, Harvard, 1958. Bibliography: p. 141-148. [ND623.T7F53 1977] 76-23618 ISBN 0-8240-2689-6 lib.bdg. : 40.00
1. Tiziano Vecelli, 1477-1576. 2. Apprentices—Italy—Venice—Biography. I. Title. II. Series. BIP

Aprons.

WRIGHT, Roxa. 646.48
How to make aprons, by Roxa Wright, assisted by Margot Knox. Sketches by Catherine Karuschkat. New York, M. Barrows [1953] 128 p. illus. 22 cm. [TT560.W7] 53-5032
1. Aprons. I. Title.

Apulia—Antiquities.

WILLEMSEN, Carl Arnold, 1902- 913.4575
Apulia, imperial splendor in southern Italy [by] C. A. Willemsen and D. Odenthal. [Translated from the German by Daphne Woodward] With 231 plates in monochrome. New York, Praeger [1959] 257 p. plates, map, plans. 29 cm. (Books that matter) Translation of Apulien, Land der Normannen, Land der Staufer. Bibliography: p. 252-254. [DG975.A65W513] 59-8408
1. Apulia—Antiquities. I. Odenthal, Dagmar, joint author.

Arabesques.

WADE, David, fl.1976- 745.4'49'17671
Pattern in Islamic art / David Wade. London : Studio Vista, 1976. 144 p. : chiefly ill. (chiefly col.) ; 29 cm. [NK1575.W3] 77-358512 ISBN 0-289-70719-6 : £7.50
1. Arabesques. 2. Design, Decorative—Islamic countries. 3. Decoration and ornament, Islamic. I. Title.

Arabian nights—Illustrations.

NIELSEN, Kay Rasmus, 1886-1957. 759.89
The unknown paintings of Kay Nielsen / edited by David Larkin ; with an elegy by Hildegarde Flanner. 1st ed. Toronto ; New York : Peacock Press/Bantam Book, 1977. [19] p., 42 leaves of plates : col. ill. ; 29 cm. [ND723.N54A52] 77-366097 7.95
1. Nielsen, Kay Rasmus, 1886-1957. 2. Arabian nights—Illustrations. I. Title. BIP

Archaeological illustration.

BRODRIBB, Arthur Charles Conant. 743'.8'9913031
Drawing archaeological finds, by Conant Brodribb. [1st American ed.] New York, Association Press [1971, c1970] 96 p. illus. 20 cm. [CC77.B73 1971] 74-129434 ISBN 0-8096-1806-0 4.95
1. Archaeological illustration. I. Title.

PIGGOTT, Stuart. 743'.8'99301
Antiquity depicted : aspects of archaeological illustration / Stuart Piggott. New York : Thames and Hudson, c1978. 64 p. : ill. ; 22 cm. (Walter Neurath memorial lectures ; 10) Includes bibliographical references. [CC75.7.P53] 78-62805 ISBN 0-500-55010-7 : 9.95
1. Archaeological illustration. I. Title. II. Series. BIP

Archer, John F., 1946—

ARCHER, John F., 1946- 769'.973
Susohn : a personal journey / John F. Archer. San Diego, Calif. : Atavistic Press, 1976. 1 portfolio ([4] leaves of plates : 17 ill.) ; 23 cm. "Of an edition of 30, this is number 29." [NE2232.5.A72A57] 75-40290 ISBN 0-915718-01-4 : 150.00
1. Archer, John F., 1946- 2. Nude in art. 3. Women in art. I. Title. BIP

Archer, Thomas, 1668 or 9-1743.

WHIFFEN, Marcus. 720'.92'4
Thomas Archer, architect of the English baroque. [New ed.] Los Angeles, Hennessey & Ingalls, 1973. 96 p. illus. 22 cm. (Architectural monographs, 1) First published in 1950 under title: Thomas Archer. Includes bibliographical references. [NA997.A82W45 1973] 72-93734 ISBN 0-912158-23-9 5.95
1. Archer, Thomas, 1668 or 9-1743. 2. Architecture, Baroque—England.

Archer, William George, 1907- —Art collections.

ARCHER, William George, 1907- 751.7'7'0954074
Visions of courtly India : the Archer collection of Pahari miniatures / introd. and catalogue by W. G. Archer ; circulated by International Exhibitions Foundation, Washington, D.C., 1976-1978. Washington : Foundation, c1976. xiii, 156 p. : ill. (some col.) ; 26 cm. Bibliography: p. 155-156. [ND1337.I5A74] 76-18030 ISBN 0-85667-032-4
1. Archer, William George, 1907- —Art collections. 2. Archer, Mildred—Art collections. 3. Pahari painting—Exhibitions. 4. Miniature painting, Indic—Exhibitions. I. International Exhibitions Foundation. II. Title. BIP

Architecture, Domestic — Designs and plans.

HOMEMASTER; 728.084
a book of home planning. [New York] v. illus. 31cm. [NA7127.H59] 56-17610
1. Archiecture, Domestic—Designs and plans. 2. Architecture, Domestic—U. S.

Archipenko, Alexander, 1887-1964.

ARCHIPENKO, Alexander, 1887- 730.973
Archipenko: fifty creative years, 1908-1958, by Alexander Archipenko and fifty art historians [New York] [TEKHNE] [1960] 109 p. illus., plates (part col.) port. 32 cm. Includes bibliography. [NB699.A7A45] 60-3406

ARCHIPENKO, Alexander, 1887-1964. 730'.924
Archipenko; international visionary. Edited by Donald H. Karshan. Pref. by S. Dillon Ripley. Foreword by David W. Scott. Essay by Guy Habasque. Washington, Published for the National Collection of Fine Arts by Smithsonian Institution Press, 1969. 116 p. illus. (part col.), facsims., ports. 26 cm. Bibliography: p. 116. [NB237.A7K32] 71-77509 10.00
I. Karshan, Donald H., ed. II. Smithsonian Institution. National Collection of Fine Arts.

ARCHIPENKO, Alexander, 1887-1964. 730'.924
Archipenko: the American years, 1923-1963. New York, Bernard Danenberg Galleries [1970?] 36 p. illus., ports. 28 cm. Exhibition held July 23-Aug. 15, 1970, at the Bernard Danenberg Galleries. Bibliography: p. 32. [NK7998.A7A42] 74-198010
I. Bernard Danenberg Galleries.

KARSHAN, Donald H. 709'.2'4
Archipenko : the sculpture and graphic art : including a print catalogue raisonne / Donald Karshan. Boulder, Colo. : Westview Press, [1975] c1974. p. cm. Includes indexes. Bibliography: p. [N6537.A64K37 1975] 75-19245 ISBN 0-89158-500-1 : 27.50
1. Archipenko, Alexander, 1887-1964. I. Archipenko, Alexander, 1887-1964. BIP

MICHAELSEN, Katherine Janszky, 1944- 730'.92'4
Archipenko : a study of the early works, 1908-1920 / Katherine Janszky Michaelsen. New York : Garland Pub., 1977. 419 p. : ill. ; 21 cm. (Outstanding dissertations in the fine arts) Reprint of author's thesis, Columbia University, 1975. Bibliography: p. 415-419. [NB699.A7M5 1977] 76-23644 ISBN 0-8240-2712-4 : 42.50
1. Archipenko, Alexander, 1887-1964. I. Title. II. Series. BIP

Architect-designed houses—Prices.

AFFORDABLE houses designed 728.3
by architects / [edited] by Jeremy Robinson and the editors of Architectural record. New York : McGraw-Hill, c1979. p. cm. "An Architectural record book." Includes index. [NA7125.A35] 78-11471 ISBN 0-07-002341-7 : 18.95
1. Architect-designed houses—Prices. I. Robinson, Jeremy, 1940- II. Architectural record.

AFFORDABLE houses designed 728.3
by architects / [edited] by Jeremy Robinson and the editors of Architectural record. New York : McGraw-Hill, c1979. p. cm. "An Architectural record book." Includes index. [NA7125.A35] 78-11471 ISBN 0-07-002341-7 : 18.95
1. Architect-designed houses—Prices. I.

Robinson, Jeremy, 1940- II. Architectural record.

Architects.

BLOMFIELD, Reginald   780'.922
Theodore, Sir, 1856-1942.
Six architects. Freeport, N.Y., Books for Libraries Press [1969] ix, 198 p. ports. 23 cm. (Essay index reprint series) Reprint of the 1935 ed. Contents.Contents.—Andrea Palladio.—Lorenzo Bernini.—Inigo Jones.—Jacques Francois Mansart.—Ange Jacques Gabriel.—Christopher Wren.—Bibliography (p. 187-189) [NA40.B55 1969] 78-99682
1. Architects. I. Title.   BIP

BRIGGS, Martin Shaw, 1882-   720'.9
The architect in history, by Martin S. Briggs. New York, Da Capo Press, 1974. xii, 400 p. illus. 21 cm. (Da Capo Press series in architecture and decorative art) Reprint of the 1927 ed. published by Clarendon Press, Oxford. Includes bibliographies. [NA203.B7 1974] 69-15613 ISBN 0-306-70584-2 15.00
1. Architects. 2. Architecture—History. I. Title.   BIP

FORSEE, Aylesa   720.922
Men of modern architecture; giants in glass, steel, and stone. Philadelphia, McCrae [c.1966] 223p. illus., ports. 24cm. Bibl. [NA40.F6] 65-24901 4.50
1. Architects. 2. Architecture, Modern—20th cent. I. Title.

Architects, American.

LAVINE, Sigmund A.   720'.922
Famous American architects, by Sigmund A. Lavine. New York, Dodd, Mead [1967] 158 p. illus. 22 cm. (Famous biographies for young people) Contents.Contents.—Introduction: Amateur architects in early America.—Charles Bulfinch (1763-1844).—Benjamin Henry Latrobe (1764-1820).—Henry Hobson Richardson (1838-1886).—Daniel Hudson Burnham (1846-1912).—Charles Follen McKim [1847-1909].—William Rutherford Mead (1846-1928).—Stanford White (1853-1906.).—Louis Henri Sullivan (1856-1924).—Eliel Saarinen (1873-1950).—Eero Saarinen (1910-1961).—Walter Adolph Gropius (1883-).—Richard Joseph Neutra (1892-).—Richard Buckminster Fuller (1895-).—Marcel Lajos Breuer (1902-) [NA736.L3] 67-14309
1. Architects, American. I. Title.   BIP

WALKER, Ralph, 1889-   720.973
Ralph Walker, architect, of Voorhees, Gmelin & Walker; Voorhees, Walker, Foley & Smith; Voorhees, Walker, Smith & Smith. New York, Henahan House, 1957. 259p. illus. (part col.) port., plans. 30cm. 'Omissions and errors' slip inserted. [NA737.W26A53]   [NA737.W26A53] 720.81 57-3840 57-3840
I. Title.

WALKER, Ralph   *720.973 720.81
Thomas, 1889-
Ralph Walker, architect, of Voorhees, Gmelin & Walker; Voorhees, Walker, Foley & Smith; Voorhees, Walker, Smith & Smith. New York, Henahan House, 1957. 259 p. illus. (part col.) port., plans. 30 cm. "Omissions and errors" slip inserted. [NA737.W26A53] 57-3840
I. Title.

Architects, American—Biography— Juvenile literature.

LEIPOLD, L. Edmond,   720'.92'2 B
1902-
Famous American architects, by L. E. Leipold. Minneapolis, T. S. Denison [1972] 77 p. 25 cm. (Famous American heroes and leaders series) Contents.Contents.—Charles Bulfinch—Frank Lloyd Wright.—Louis Sullivan.—Eero Saarinen.—Edward Durell Stone.—Eric Mendelsohn.—Mies van der Rohe.—Paul Williams.—Robert G. Cerny. [NA736.L44] 920 70-178992 ISBN 0-513-01163-3
1. Architects, American—Biography—Juvenile literature. I. Title.

Architects—Bibl.

COLUMBIA University.   016.72
Libraries. Avery Architectural Library.
Avery obituary index of architects and artists. Boston, G. K. Hall, 1963. 338 p. 37 cm. [Z5941.C64] 64-7017
1. Architects — Bibl. 2. Artists — Bibl. 3. Obituaries — Indexes. I. Title. II. Title: Obituary index of architects and artists. BIP

SHARP, Dennis   016.72
Sources of modern architecture; a bibliography. [1st ed.] New York, Wittenborn [1967] 56p. facsims., ports. 30cm. (Architectural Association, London. Paper no. 2) [Z5941.S48] 67-19697 4.75 pap.,
1. Architects—Bibl. I. Title. II. Series. BIP

Architects—Biography.

WHO'S who in   720'.92'2 B
architecture : from 1400 to the present day / edited by J. M. Richards, American consultant, Adolph K. Placzek. 1st ed. New York : Holt, Rinehart and Winston, c1977. 368 p. : ill. ; 26 cm. Includes index. [NA40.W48] 76-44323 ISBN 0-03-017381-7 : 19.95
1. Architects—Biography. I. Richards, James Maude, Sir, 1907-   BIP

Architects, British.

JENKINS, Frank.   720.69
Architect and patron; a survey of professional relations and practice in England from the sixteenth century to the present day. London, New York, Oxford University Press, 1961. xvi, 254p. plates. 23cm. (University of Durham publications) 'An earlier form of this book was submitted in ... 1953 as a dissertation for the degree of master of arts in the University of Durham.' Bibliographical footnotes. [NA964.J4 1961] 61-19793
1. Architects, British. 2. Art patronage. 3. Architecture—England— Hist. I. Title. II. Series: Durham, Eng. University. Publications

REILLY, Charles Herbert,   720'.942
Sir 1874-
Representative British architects of the present day, by C. H. Reilly. Freeport, N. Y., Books for Libraries Press [1967] 172 p. illus., ports. 22 cm. (Essay index reprint series) Reprint of the 1931 ed. [NA996.R4 1967] 67-26774
1. Architects, British. 2. Architecture—Gt. Brit. I. Title.
Contents omitted   BIP

Architects—California—Biography.

CARDWELL, Kenneth H.,   720'.92'4 B
1920-
Bernard Maybeck : artisan, architect, artist / Kenneth H. Cardwell. Santa Barbara : Peregrine Smith, 1977. p. cm. Includes index. Bibliography: p. [NA737.M435C37] 77-13773 ISBN 0-87905-022-5 : 24.95
1. Maybeck, Bernard R. 2. Architects—California—Biography.   BIP

Architects—Chicago.

PEISCH. MARK L.   720.973
The Chicago school of architecture; early followers of Sullivan and Wright. New York, Random [1965] xiii, 177p. illus., plans, ports. 21cm. (Columbia Univ. studies in art, hist. and archaelogy no. 5) Bibl. [NA735.C4P4] 64-15895 2.95 pap.,
1. Architects—Chicago. 2. Architecture—Chicago 3. Cities and towns—Planning. I. Title. II. Series.

Architects—Correspondence, reminiscences, etc.

BENDINER, Alfred.   720'.924
Translated from the Hungarian; notes toward an autobiography. South Brunswick [N.J.] A. S. Barnes [1967] 317 p. illus. 25 cm. [NA737.B45A2] 67-22886
1. Architects—Correspondence, reminiscences, etc. I. Title.

MENDELSOHN, Erich, 1887-   720'.924
1953.
Eric Mendelsohn: letters of an architect. Edited by Oskar Beyer. Translated by Geoffrey Strachan. With an introd. by Nikolaus Pevsner. London, New York, Abelard-Schuman [1967] 192 p. illus., ports. 26 cm. Translation of Briefe eins Architekten. [NA1088.M57A313 1967] 66-15598
1. Architects—Correspondence, reminiscences, etc. I. Beyer, Oskar, 1882- ed.

*MOSCOWITZ, Leopold   720.924
Solomon.
Adventures in selfhood architecture [Imperial Beach. Calif., Selfhood Architecture Pr. 1968?] 294p. 14cm. (B) 5.85
1. Architects—Correspondence, reminiscences, etc. I. Title.
Publisher's address: 208 Palm Ave., Imperial Beach, Calif. 92032.

Architects—Education—England.

DU PREY, Pierre de la   720'.92'4 B
Ruffiniere.
John Soane's architectural education, 1753-80 / Pierre de la Ruffiniere du Prey. New York : Garland Pub., 1977, i.e.1978 xxxv, 565, 299 p. : ill. ; 22 cm (Outstanding dissertations in the fine arts) Originally presented as the author's thesis, Princeton, 1972. Bibliography: p. 557-565. [NA997.S7D86 1977] 76-23615 ISBN 0-8240-2686-1 lib.bdg. : 62.50
1. Soane, John, Sir, 1753-1837. 2. Architects—Education—England. 3. Architecture—England—Biography. I. Title. II. Series.   BIP

Architects—Education—France.

TURNER, Paul V.   720'.92'4 B
The education of Le Corbusier / Paul Venable Turner. New York : Garland Pub., 1977. p. cm. (Outstanding dissertations in the fine arts) Thesis—Harvard, 1971. Bibliography: p. [NA1053.J4T87] 76-23658 ISBN 0-8240-2732-9 lib.bdg. : 35.00
1. Jeanneret-Gris, Charles Edouard, 1887-1965—Knowledge and learning. 2. Architects—Education—France. I. Title.   BIP

Architects—England—Biography.

SCOTT, George   720'.92'4 B
Gilbert, Sir, 1811-1878.
Personal and professional recollections / by George Gilbert Scott ; edited by his son, G. Gilbert Scott ; with an introd. by John Williams Burgon. New York : Da Capo Press, 1977. xx, 436 p., [1] leaf of plates : port. ; 23 cm. (A Da Capo Press reprint series in architecture and decorative arts) Reprint of the 1879 ed. published by S. Low, Marston, Searle & Rivington, London. [NA997.S4A25 1977] 77-1202 ISBN 0-306-70873-6 : 27.50
1. Scott, George Gilbert, Sir, 1811-1878. 2. Architects—England—Biography.   BIP

Architects—Fees.

CASE and Company.   331.2'8'172
Methods of compensation for architectural services. Washington, 1969. ii, 104 p. illus. 28 cm. "Prepared ... for the American Institute of Architects. [NA2570.C38] 70-93128
1. Architects—Fees. I. American Institute of Architects. II. Title.

Architects—Great Britain.

REILLY, Charles Herbert,   720'.942
Sir, 1874-1948.
Representative British architects of the present day, by C. H. Reilly. Freeport, N.Y., Books for Libraries Press [1967] 172 p. illus., ports. 22 cm. (Essay index reprint series) Reprint of the 1931 ed. Contents.Contents.—Professor S. D. Adshead.—Robert Atkinson.—Sir Herbert Baker.—Sir Reginald Blomfield.—Arthur J. Davis.—E. Guy Dawber.—Clough Williams-Ellis.—W. Curtis Green.—H. V. Lanchester.—Sir Edwin L. Lutyens.—Sir

Giles Gilbert Scott.—Walter Tapper. [NA996.R4 1967] 67-26774
1. Architects—Great Britain. 2. Architecture—Great Britain. I. Title.

Architects—Great Britain— Correspondence, reminiscences, etc.

FRY, Edwin Maxwell,   720'.92'4
1899-
Autobiographical sketches / [by] Maxwell Fry ; with twenty-six illustrations by the author. London : Elek, 1975. 167 p. : ill. ; 23 cm. [NA997.F78A22] 76-361717 ISBN 0-236-40010-X : 14.95
1. Fry, Edwin Maxwell, 1899- 2. Architects—Great Britain—Correspondence, reminiscences, etc. I. Title.
Distributed by Technical Impex   BIP

Architects—Homes and haunts.

PLUMB, Barbara.   728'.092'2 B
Houses architects live in / Barbara Plumb. New York : Viking Press, 1977. 168 p. : ill. ; 29 cm. (A Studio book) [NA7195.A7P59 1977] 77-6350 ISBN 0-670-38038-5 : 14.95
1. Architects—Homes and haunts. I. Title.

PLUMB, Barbara.   720'.92'2
Houses architects live in / Barbara Plumb. Harmondsworth, Eng. ; New York : Penguin Books, 1978, c1977. 168 p. : ill. (some col.); 28 cm. Reprint of the 1977 ed. published by Viking Press, New York. [NA7195.A7P59 1978] 78-3649 ISBN 0-14-004986-X pbk. : 6.95
1. Architects—Homes and haunts. I. Title.   BIP

Architects—Homes and haunts— United States.

WAGNER, Walter F.,   728'.0973
comp.
Houses architects design for themselves. Edited by Walter F. Wagner, Jr., and Karin Schlegel. New York, McGraw-Hill [1974] x, 230 p. illus. 31 cm. "An Architectural record book." [NA7208.W27] 74-2485 ISBN 0-07-002214-3
1. Architects—Homes and haunts—United States. 2. Architecture, Domestic—United States. I. Schlegel, Karin, joint comp. II. Title.

Architects—Honduras—Roatan Island.

WIEBACH, Carl M.   728'.092'4 B
Heinz.
Escape from rat-race / by Carl M. Heinz Wiebach ; collaborator, Barbara Hopfinger ; ill. Hein Wiebach. Los Angeles : Cultural Exchange Center, c1975. 140 p. : ill. ; 23 cm. [NA781.W53] 76-16889
1. Wiebach, Carl M. Heinz. 2. Architects—Honduras—Roatan Island. 3. Bay Islands—Description and travel. I. Title.

Architects—Illinois—Chicago.

COHEN, Stuart E., 1942-   720.977
Chicago architects : documenting the exhibition of the same name organized by Laurence Booth, Stuart E. Cohen, Stanley Tigerman, and Benjamin Weese / by Stuart E. Cohen ; with an introd. by Stanley Tigerman. Chicago : Swallow Press, c1976. 120 p. : ill. ; 24 x 31 cm. Includes bibliographical references. [NA722.C63] 76-2194 ISBN 0-8040-0731-4 pbk. : 6.95
1. Chicago School (Architecture) 2. Architects—Illinois—Chicago. I. Title. BIP

Architects—Iowa.

IOWA. Board of   720.69
Architectural Examiners.
Report. Des moines. v. illus. 28cm. annual. Report year ends June 30. [NA124.I8A32] 55-37586
1. Architects—Iowa. I. Title.

Architects—Israel—Biography.

SHARON, Aryeh, 1900- v. 12
Kibbutz + Bauhaus : an architect's way in a new land / by Arieh Sharon. Stuttgart : Kramer Verlag, 1976. 267 p. : chiefly ill. ; 29 cm. Text in English, French, and German. Includes index. Bibliography: p. 267. [NA1479.S5A48] 77-365331 ISBN 3-7828-1430-4
1. Sharon, Aryeh, 1900- 2. Architects—Israel—Biography. 3. Architecture—Israel. 4. Architecture, Modern—20th century—Israel. 5. Bauhaus—Influence. I. Title.

Architects—Italy—Biography.

BLUNT, Anthony, Sir, 1907- 720'.92'4
Borromini / by Anthony Blunt. Cambridge, Mass. : Harvard University Press, [1979] p. cm. Includes index. Bibliography: p. [NA1123.B6B56] 78-11320 ISBN 0-674-07925-6 : 15.00
1. Borromini, Francesco, 1599-1667. 2. Architects—Italy—Biography. 3. Architecture, Baroque—italy. BIP

Architects—Kentucky.

KENTUCKY. State Board of Examiners and Registration of Architects. 720.69
Report. [Frankfort?] v. ports. 28 cm. annual. [NA124.K4A3] 50-63128
1. Architects—Kentucky. I. Title.

Architects—Maine.

MAINE, State Board of Architects. 720.69
Report. [n. p.] v. 23cm. annual. Report year ends June 30. [NA124.M2A36] 57-49711
1. Architects—Maine. I. Title.

Architects—Mexico—Biography.

SMITH, Clive Bamford. 720'.9'72
Builders in the sun; five Mexican architects. Foreword by Jose Villagran Garcia. New York, Architectural Book Pub. Co. [1967] 224 p. illus., facsims., plans, ports. 28 cm. [NA758.S6] 66-27873
1. Architects—Mexico—Biography. 2. Architecture—Mexico. I. Title.

Architects — Michigan.

MICHIGAN. State Board of Registration for Architects, Professional Engineers and Land Surveyors. 720.69
Roster of architects, professional engineers [and] land surveyors. Detroit. v. 23 cm. [NA124.M53] 51-62217
1. Architects — Mighigan. 2. Engineers — Michigan. 3. Surveyors — Michigan. I. Title.

Architects—Russian Republic—Biography.

STARR, S. Frederick. 720'.92'4 B
Melnikov : solo architect in a mass society / S. Frederick Starr. Princeton, N.J. : Princeton University Press, c1978. xvii, 276 p. : ill. ; 29 cm. Includes index. Bibliography: p. [263]-270. [NA1199.M37S7] 77-85566 ISBN 0-691-03931-3 : 25.00
1. Mel'nikov, Konstantin Stepanovich, 1890- 2. Architects—Russian Republic—Biography. I. Title. BIP

Architects—United States.

HEYER, Paul. 720.973
Architects on architecture; new directions in America. New York, Walker [1966] 415 p. illus. 32 cm. Bibliography: p. 404-405. [NA736.H4] 66-22504
1. Architects—United States. 2. Architecture, Modern—20th century—United States. I. Title. BIP

KATSELAS, Tasso, 1927- 720'.924
Tasso Katselas: architect, planner. [Edited by Edith Wile and Jules Ehrman. Pittsburgh, Geyer Print. Co.; distributed by Stricker Associates, c1969] [58] p. illus. (part col. (1 fold.)), plans, col. port. 30 cm. Cover title. [NA737.K36A55] 77-248134
I. Title.

SKIDMORE, Owings & Merrill. 720'.973
Skidmore, Owings & Merrill. Introd. and notes by Christopher Woodward. With 73 photos. by Yukio Futagawa. New York, Simon and Schuster [1970] 136 p. illus. (part col.), plans. 27 cm. (Library of contemporary architects) "First published in Japan in 1968 ... [under title: SOM] New texts have been provided for the English language edition." Includes bibliographical references. [NA737.S53W613 1970] 79-120905 7.50
1. Woodward, Christopher. II. Futagawa, Yukio, 1932-

Architects—United States—Biography.

GILLER, Norman M. 720'.92'4 B
An adventure in architecture / Norman M. Giller. Miami Beach, Fla. : Virgo Press, c1976. 248 p. : ill. ; 26 cm. Includes index. [NA737.G534A43] 76-28287 12.50
1. Giller, Norman M. 2. Architects—United States—Biography. I. Title. BIP

LAPIDUS, Morris. 720'.92'4 B
An architecture of joy / Morris Lapidus. Miami, Fla. : E. A. Seemann, [1977] p. cm. Includes index. [NA737.L32A42] 77-9090 ISBN 0-912458-96-8 : 14.95
1. Lapidus, Morris. 2. Architects—United States—Biography. I. Title. BIP

LATROBE, Benjamin Henry, 1764-1820. 720'.92'4 B
The Virginia journals of Benjamin Henry Latrobe, 1795-1798 / Edward C. Carter II, editor, Angeline Polites, associate editor ; Lee W. Formwalt and John C. Van Horne, editorial assistants. New Haven : Published for the Maryland Historical Society by Yale University Press, 1977. p. cm. (The papers of Benjamin Henry Latrobe : Series I, Journals) Includes index. Contents.Contents.—v. 1. 1795-1797.—v. 2. 1797-1798. [NA737.L34C37] 77-12101 ISBN 0-300-02198-4 : 60.00
1. Latrobe, Benjamin Henry, 1764-1820. 2. Architects—United States—Biography. 3. Virginia—Social life and customs—Colonial period. I. Carter, Edward Carlos, 1928- II. Maryland Historical Society. III. Title. IV. Series. BIP

RANSOM, David F. 720'.92'4
George Keller, architect / David F. Ransom ; introd. by Barry Hannegan. Hartford, Conn. : Stowe-Day Foundation, c1978. xxxiii, 218 p. : ill. (some col.) ; 28 cm. Includes index. Bibliography: p. 208-210. [NA737.K44R36] 77-14060 ISBN 0-917482-14-X pbk. : 9.95
1. Keller, George W., 1842-1935. 2. Architects—United States—Biography. I. Title. BIP

TAFEL, Edgar. 720'.92'4 B
Apprentice to genius : years with Frank Lloyd Wright / Edgar Tafel. New York : McGraw-Hill, c1979. 228 p. : ill. (some col.) ; 29 cm. Includes index. [NA737.W7T33] 78-18504 ISBN 0-07-062815-7 : 19.50
1. Wright, Frank Lloyd, 1867-1959. 2. Tafel, Edgar. 3. Architects—United States—Biography. I. Title. BIP

WRIGHT, Frank Lloyd, 1867-1959. 720'.92'4 B
An autobiography / Frank Lloyd Wright. New York : Horizon Press, c1977. 620 p., [20] leaves of plates : ill. ; 24 cm. Includes index. [NA737.W7A3 1977] 72-86739 ISBN 0-8180-0222-0 : 17.50
1. Wright, Frank Lloyd, 1867-1959. 2. Architects—United States—Biography.

Architects—U.S.—Correspondence, reminiscences, etc.

BUSH-BROWN, Harold Bushbrown harold 720'.92'4 B
Beaux arts to Bauhaus and beyond : an architect's perspective / by Harold Bush-Brown. New York : Whitney Library of Design, 1976. 128 p. : ill. ; 26 cm. Includes bibliographical references and index. [NA737.B87A22] 76-17005 ISBN 0-8230-7067-0 : 12.95
1. Bush-Brown, Harold. 2. Architects—United States—Correspondence, reminiscenses, etc. 3. Architecture, Modern—20th century. I. Title. BIP

STONE, Edward Durell. 720.973
The evolution of an architect. New York, Horizon Press, 1962. 288 p. illus., ports, plans. 27 cm. Autobiographical. [NA737.S66A3] 62-18208
I. Title.

STONE, Harris, 1934- 720'.92'4
Workbook of an unsuccessful architect. New York, M[onthly] R[eview Press, 1974, c1973] 192 p. illus. 25 cm. Includes bibliographical references. [NA737.S67A27] 73-8052 ISBN 0-85345-294-6 8.95
1. Stone, Harris, 1934- 2. Architects—United States—Correspondence, reminiscences, etc. I. Title.

STONE, Harris, 1934- 720.924
Workbook of an unsuccessful architect. New York, Monthly Review Press [1974, c1973] 192 p. illus. 24 cm. Includes bibliographical references. [NA737.S67A27] ISBN 0-85345-294-6 3.45 (pbk.)
1. Stone, Harris, 1934- 2. Architects—U.S.—Correspondence, reminiscences, etc. I. Title.
L.C. card number for cloth edition: 73-8052.

Architects—U.S.—Direct.

AMERICAN architects directory. 1st-ed.; 1956- New York, Published under the sponsorship of American Institute of Architects by R.R. Bowker. v. 29 cm. [NA53.A37] 55-12270 720.69
1. Architects—U.S.—Direct. I. American Institute of Architects.

AMERICAN architects directory. Ed. by George S. Koyl. 2d ed. New York, Bowker, pub. under the auspices of Amer. Inst. of Architects [c.] 1962. 919p. 29cm. 55-12270 25.00 720.69
1. Architects—U.S.—Direct. I. American Institute of Architects. II. Koyl, George S., ed.

Architectural acoustics.

BERANEK, Leo Leroy, 1914- 729.2
Music, acoustics & architecture. New York. Wiley [1962] 586p. illus. 28cm. [NA2800.B4 1962] 62-19866
1. Architectural acoustics. 2. Music—Acoustics and physics. 3. Music-halls. I. Title.

BERANEK, Leo Leroy, 1914- 729.2
Music, acoustics & architecture. New York, Wiley [c.1962] 586p. illus. 28cm. 62-19866 17.50; 15.00
1. Architectural acoustics. 2. Music—Acoustics and physics. 3. Music-halls. I. Title. BIP

BURRIS-MEYER, Harold 1902- 729.21
Acoustics for the architect [by] Harold Burris-Meyer & Lewis S. Goodfriend. New York, Reinhold Pub. Corp. [1957] 126 p. illus. 27 cm. [NA2800.B8] 57-9462
1. Architectural acoustics. 2. Sound. I. Goodfriend, Lewis S., joint author. II. Title.

DOELLE, Leslie L. 729'.29
Environmental acoustics [by] Leslie L. Doelle. New York, McGraw-Hill [1972] x, 246 p. illus. 28 cm. Includes bibliographies. [NA2800.D62] 70-159320 ISBN 0-07-017342-7
1. Architectural acoustics. I. Title.

EGAN, M. David. 729'.29
Concepts in architectural acoustics [by] M. David Egan. 2d ed. [New Orleans] Tulane University, School of Architecture [1971] 194 p. illus. 28 cm. Bibliography: p. 175. [NA2800.E34 1971] 78-172918
1. Architectural acoustics. I. Title.

EGAN, M. David. 729'.29
Concepts in architectural acoustics [by] M. David Egan. New York, McGraw-Hill [1972] xvii, 200 p. illus. 29 cm. Includes bibliographies. [NA2800.E34 1972] 72-39 ISBN 0-07-019053-4 16.50
1. Architectural acoustics. I. Title. BIP

FURRER, Willi, 1906- 729.2
Room and building acoustics and noise abatement. Translated by Evelyn R. Robinson and Peter Lord. Washington, Butterworths, 1964. vii, 226 p. illus., plans. 26 cm. Translation of 2d German ed., 1961; 1st German ed. had title: Raum-und Bauakustik fur Architekten. [NA2800.F813] 65-1446
1. Architectural acoustics. I. Title.

KNUDSEN, Vern Oliver, 1893- 729.21
Acoustical designing in architecture [by] Vern O. Knudsen [and] Cyril M. Harris. New York, Wiley, 1950. x, 457 p. illus. 22 cm. [NA2800.K58] 50-6152
1. Architectural acoustics. I. Harris, Cyril M. joint author. II. Title. BIP

KUTTRUFF, Heinrich. 729'.29
Room acoustics. New York, Wiley [1973] xxi, 298 p. illus. 23 cm. "A Halsted Press book." Includes bibliographical references. [NA2800.K87] 73-16149 ISBN 0-470-51105-2 29.75
1. Architectural acoustics. 2. Sound. I. Title. BIP

LAWRENCE, Anita. 620.2'2
Architectural acoustics. Amsterdam, New York, Elsevier Pub. Co., 1970. xii, 219 p. illus. 22 cm. (Elsevier architectural science series) Includes bibliographical references. [NA2800.L38] 79-99799
1. Architectural acoustics.

PARKIN, Peter Hubert. 729.21
Acoustics, noise and buildings [by] P. H. Parkin and H. R. Humphreys. With a foreword by Hope Bagenal. New York, F. A. Praeger [1958] 331p. illus. 26cm. (Books that matter) [NA2800.P3] 58-11402
1. Architectural acoustics. 2. Sound. 3. Noise. I. Humphreys, Henry Robert, joint author. II. Title. BIP

PURKIS, Hubert John 693.834
Building physics: acoustics. 1st ed. Oxford. New York [etc.] Pergamon, 1966. vii. 141p. plate. tables. diagrs. 21cm. (Commonwealth & intl. lib. Physics div.) Bibl. [TH1725.P8 1966] 65-27379 price unreported
1. Architectural acoustics. 2. Soundprofing. I. Title. BIP

UNITED States Gypsum Company. 729.2
Sound control in design. [Chicago? c1959] 83 p. illus. 21 cm. [NA2800.U65] 60-29686
1. Architectural acoustics. I. Title.

Architectural acoustics—Addresses, essays, lectures.

ARCHITECTURAL acoustics / edited by Thomas D. Northwood. Stroudsburg, Pa. : Dowden, Hutchinson & Ross ; New York : exclusive distributor, Halsted Press, c1977. xv, 428 p. : ill. ; 26 cm. (Benchmark papers in acoustics ; 10) Articles chiefly in English, some in French or German, with English summaries. Includes bibliographical references and indexes. [NA2800.A68] 76-54182 ISBN 0-87933-257-3 : 36.00 729'.29
1. Architectural acoustics—Addresses, essays, lectures. I. Northwood, Thomas D.

Architectural acoustics—Congresses.

INTERNATIONAL Symposium on Architectural Acoustics, Heriot-Watt University, 1974. 729'.29
Auditorium acoustics : the proceedings of an International Symposium on Architectural Acoustics, held at Heriot-Watt University, Edinburgh, Scotland / edited by Robin Mackenzie. New York : Wiley, [1975] xii, 231 p. : ill. ; 23 cm. "A Halsted Press book." Includes bibliographical references and index. [NA2800.I56 1974] 75-16445 ISBN 0-470-56284-6 : 30.00
1. Architectural acoustics—Congresses. I. MacKenzie, Robin. II. Title. BIP

Architectural Association, London.

A Continuing experiment : learning and teaching at the 720'.7'1142142

Architectural Association / edited by James Gowan. London : Architectural Press, 1975. 175 p. : ill. ; 22 cm. Includes bibliographical references. [NA2310.G74A73] 75-311694 ISBN 0-85139-131-1 : 8.00
1. Architectural Association, London. 2. Architecture—Study and teaching—Great Britain. I. Gowan, James.
Distributed by Intl. Publication Service. Available from Northwestern Univ. School of Education. 2003 Sheridan Rd. Evanston, Ill. 60201

Architectural criticism.

ATTOE, Wayne. 720'.1
Architecture and critical imagination / Wayne Attoe. Chichester ; New York : Wiley, c1978. xx, 188 p. : ill. ; 26 cm. Includes index. Bibliography: p. 169-183. [NA2599.5.A88] 77-22016 ISBN 0-471-99574-6 : 19.95
1. Architectural criticism. I. Title. BIP

Architectural criticism—Data processing.

HASSID, Sami, 1912- 029'.9'72
Development and application of a system for recording critical evaluations of architectural works / by Sami Hassid. [Berkeley, Calif. : Hassid], 1964. iii, 37 leaves, [10] leaves of plates : graphs ; 28 cm. [NA2599.5.H37] 75-330331
1. Architectural criticism—Data processing. I. Title: System for recording critical evaluations of architectural works.

Architectural design.

ALDEN, Richard, 1942- 720'.92'4
Unity and diversity : on Gropius' problem of unity in diversity / by Richard Alden. [State College? Pa.] : s.n., [1974] iv, 17 p. : ill. ; 28 cm. Cover title. Includes bibliographical references. [NA1088.G85A79] 74-84643
1. Gropius, Walter, 1883-1969. 2. Architectural design. 3. Architecture—Composition, proportion, etc. I. Title.

BROADBENT, Geoffrey. 729
Design in architecture; architecture and the human sciences. London, New York, John Wiley & Sons [1973] xiv, 504 p. illus. 23 cm. Bibliography: p. 453-480. [NA2750.B73] 71-39233 ISBN 0-471-10583-X 19.95
1. Architectural design. 2. Structural design. 3. Environmental engineering. I. Title. BIP

BUILDING Performance Research Unit. 729
Building performance. Edited by Thomas A. Markus. New York, Wiley [1972] xii, 281 p. illus. 26 cm. "A Halsted Press book." Bibliography: p. 274-276. [NA2750.B8] 72-7275 ISBN 0-470-58020-8 26.00
1. Architectural design. 2. Decision-making in architecture. I. Markus, Thomas A., ed. II. Title.

DESIGNING for human 720.18
behavior: architecture and the behavioral sciences. Edited by Jon Lang [and others] Stroudsburg, Pa., Dowden, Hutchinson & Ross [1974] xiii, 353 p. illus. 25 cm. (Community development series) Bibliography: p. 341-350. [NA2750.D42] 73-22208 ISBN 0-87933-054-6 20.00 (text ed.)
1. Architectural design. 2. Architecture—Psychological aspects. I. Lang, Jon T., comp.

GREENE, Herb. 729
Mind & image : an essay on art & architecture / Herb Greene. Lexington : University Press of Kentucky, c1976. xii, 210 p. : ill. ; 23 x 29 cm. Includes bibliographical references and index. [NA2750.G72] 74-18932 ISBN 0-8131-1323-7 : 22.50
1. Architectural design. 2. Visual perception. 3. Architecture—Psychological aspects. I. Title. BIP

HERBERT, Lynden. 729
A new language for environmental design. [New York] New York University Press, 1972. vi, 215 p. illus. 25 cm. Bibliography: p. 205-209. [NA2750.H4] 77-145511 ISBN 0-8147-3361-1
1. Architectural design. 2. Architecture and society. I. Title. BIP

KNOWLES, Ralph L. 711'.55
Energy and form; an ecological approach to urban growth [by] Ralph L. Knowles. Cambridge, Mass., MIT Press [1974] ix, 198 p. illus. 22 x 26 cm. Bibliography: p. 194-196. [NA2750.K56] 74-3003 ISBN 0-262-11050-4
1. Architectural design. 2. Energy conservation. I. Title. BIP

MARCH, Lionel, 1934- 721'.01'516
The geometry of environment : an introduction to spatial organization in design / Lionel March and Philip Steadman. 1st U.S. ed. Cambridge, Mass. : M.I.T. Press, 1974, c1971. 360 p. : ill. ; 24 cm. Includes index. Bibliography: p. 336-350. [NA2750.M26 1974] 74-9144 ISBN 0-262-63055-9 : 7.95
1. Architectural design. 2. Environmental engineering (Buildings) 3. Geometry. I. Steadman, Philip, 1942- joint author. II. Title. BIP

OAKLEY, David. 729
The phenomenon of architecture in cultures in change. [1st ed.] Oxford, New York, Pergamon Press [1970] xiii, 375 p. illus. 25 cm. (The Commonwealth and international library) Includes bibliographies. [NA2543.S6O15 1970] 77-128372
1. Architectural design. 2. Architecture and society. I. Title. BIP

PEARCE, Peter. 729
Structure in nature is a strategy for design / Peter Pearce. Cambridge : MIT Press, c1978. xvii, 245 p. : ill. ; 29 cm. Bibliography: p. 240-245. [NA2750.P4] 77-26866 ISBN 0-262-16064-1 : 45.00
1. Architectural design. 2. Nature (Aesthetics) 3. Form (Aesthetics) I. Title. BIP

†STUBBINS, Hugh, 1912- 720'.6'57444
Architecture, the design experience / Hugh Stubbins ; editing by Susan Braybrooke ; book design by Hugh Stubbins and Merle Westlake ; foreword by Marcel Breuer ; introd. by Mildred Schmertz. New York : Wiley, c1976. xv, 190 p. : ill. ; 29 cm. "A Wiley-Interscience publication." Includes index. [NA2750.S88] 75-42173 ISBN 0-471-83482-3 : 18.95
1. Hugh Stubbins and Associates. 2. Architectural design. 3. Architecture, Modern—20th century—United States—Case studies. I. Title.

TZONIS, Alexander. 729
Towards a non-oppressive environment; an essay. [Boston, i Press; distributed by G. Braziller, New York, 1972] 124 p. 21 cm. (i Press series on the human environment) On spine: Non-oppressive environment. Includes bibliographical references. [NA2750.T9] 79-189033 3.75
1. Architectural design. I. Title. II. Title: Non-oppressive environment. BIP

VAN DER RYN, Sim. 729
Natural energy designer's handbook [by] Sim Van der Ryn and Jim Campe. [New York] Random House [1975] p. cm. "A Random House/Bookworks book." [NA7125.V25 1975] 74-7470 ISBN 0-394-49451-2 11.95
1. Architectural design. 2. Architecture, Domestic. 3. Energy conservation. I. Campe, Jim, joint author. II. Title.

WADE, John William, 1925- 729
Architecture, problems, and purposes : architectural design as a basic problem-solving process / John W. Wade. New York : Wiley, [1976] p. cm. Includes bibliographies and index. [NA2750.W3] 76-27280 ISBN 0-471-91305-7 : 20.00
1. Architectural design. 2. Problem solving. I. Title. BIP

WONG, Wucius. 701'.8
Principles of three-dimensional design / Wucius Wong. New York : Van Nostrand Reinhold Co., 1977. 112 p. : ill. ; 20 cm. [NA2750.W66] 76-54669 ISBN 0-442-29561-8 pbk. : 4.50
1. Architectural design. 2. Design. 3. Visual perception. I. Title. BIP

Architectural design—Addresses, essays, lectures.

THE Architecture of form / 721
edited by Lionel March. Cambridge ; New York : Cambridge University Press, 1976. xv, 490 p. : ill. ; 24 cm. (Cambridge urban and architectural studies ; 4) Bibliography: p. 482-490. [NA2750.A6815] 74-80354 ISBN 0-521-20528-X : 49.50
1. Architectural design—Addresses, essays, lectures. 2. Architecture—Composition, proportion, etc.—Addresses, essays, lectures. I. March, Lionel, 1934- II. Series.

DESIGN Methods in Architecture Symposium, Portsmouth School of Architecture, 1967. 729
Design methods in architecture. Edited by Geoffrey Broadbent and Anthony Ward. [1st ed.] New York, G. Wittenborn [1969] 204 p. illus. (part col.) 31 cm. (Architectural Association. Paper no. 4) Includes bibliographical references. [NA2750.D4] 78-111684 14.50
1. Architectural design—Addresses, essays, lectures. I. Broadbent, Geoffrey, ed. II. Ward, Anthony, ed. III. Portsmouth College of Technology. School of Architecture. IV. Series: Architectural Association, London. Paper no. 4 BIP

Architectural design—Bibliography—Catalogs.

HARVARD University. Graduate School of Design. Library. 019'.1
Catalogue of the Library of the Graduate School of Design, Harvard University. Boston, Mass., G. K. Hall, 1968. 44 v. 37 cm. [Z5945.H28 1968] 73-169433
1. Harvard University. Graduate School of Design. Library. 2. Architectural design—Bibliography—Catalogs. 3. Engineering design—Bibliography—Catalogs. I. Title.

Architectural design—Computer programs.

SANOFF, Henry. 720'.28'542
Methods of architectural programming / Henry Sanoff. Stroudsburg, Pa. : Dowden, Hutchinson & Ross, c1977. xi, 184 p. : ill. ; 24 cm. (Community development series ; 29) Includes index. Bibliography: p. 177-178. [NA2728.S26] 76-13231 ISBN 0-87933-253-0 : 18.00
1. Architectural design—Computer programs. 2. Architecture—Research. I. Title. BIP

Architectural design—Data processing.

CAMPION, David. 721'.018
Computers in architectural design. Amsterdam, New York [etc.] Elsevier Pub. Co., 1968. xii, 320 p. with illus. 21 1/2 cm. (Elsevier architectural science series) Bibliography: p. 301-305. [NA2005.C3] 68-17574 35.00
1. Architectural design—Data processing. I. Title.

LEE, Kaiman. 729'.028'54
Computer programs in environmental design. Boston, Environmental Design & Research Center [1974] 5 v. (1308 l.) illus. 29 cm. [NA1996.5.L43] 74-169212
1. Architectural design—Data processing. I. Title. BIP

LEE, Kaiman. 729'.01'83
Interactive computer graphics in architecture / Kaiman Lee. Boston : Environmental Design & Research Center, c1976. 108 leaves (2 fold.) : ill. ; 29 cm. Bibliography: leaves 106-108. [NA2728.L436] 76-366950 30.00
1. Architectural design—Data processing. I. Title. BIP

LEE, Kaiman. 720'.28'54
State of the art of computer aided environmental design / Kaiman Lee. Boston : Environmental Design & Research Center, [1975] 309 leaves : ill. ; 29 cm. Based on the first part of the author's thesis, Texas A & M University, with title: Performance specification of computer aided environmental design. [NA2728.L437 1975b] 76-358975 50.00
1. Architectural design—Data processing. I. Title. BIP

MITCHELL, William John, 1944- 721'.028'54
Computer-aided architectural design / William J. Mitchell. New York : Petrocelli/Charter, 1977. xiii, 573 p. : ill. ; 26 cm. Includes index. Bibliography: p. 515-559. [NA2728.M58] 76-50663 ISBN 0-88405-323-7 : 24.95
1. Architectural design—Data processing. I. Title. BIP

SPATIAL synthesis in 729'.028'54
computer-aided building design / edited by Charles M. Eastman. New York : Wiley, [1975] xii, 333 p. : ill. ; 23 cm. "A Halsted Press book." Includes index. [NA2728.S65] 75-7416 ISBN 0-470-22946-2 : 37.50
1. Architectural design—Data processing. I. Eastman, Charles M.
Contents omitted. BIP

Architectural design—Data processing—Congresses.

YALE Conference on Computer Graphics in Architecture, New Haven, 1968. 720'.18
Computer graphics in architecture and design; proceedings. Edited by Murray Milne. New Haven, Yale School of Art and Architecture [1969] 116 p. illus. 26 cm. Bibliography: p. [105]-111. [NA21.Y34 1968] 76-8847 3.95
1. Architectural design—Data processing—Congresses. I. Milne, Murray, ed. II. Yale University. School of Art and Architecture. III. Title.

Architectural drawing.

ATKIN, William Wilson. 744.42
Pencil techniques in modern design [by] William W. Atkin, Raniero Corbelletti [and] Vincent R. Fiore. New York, Reinhold [1953] vi, 122 p. illus. 30 cm. (Presentation methods, v. 1) [NA2700.A85] 52-11825
1. Architectural drawing. I. Title. II. Series.

BELLIS, Herbert F 744.424
Architectural drafting, by Herbert F. Bellis and Walter A. Schmidt. New York, McGraw-Hill, 1961. 118p. illus. 28cm. [NA2700.B44] 60-15281
1. Architectural drawing. I. Schmidt, Walter A., 1918- joint author. II. Title.

BELLIS, Herbert F. 720'.28
Architectural drafting [by] Herbert F. Bellis [and] Walter A. Schmidt. 2d ed. New York, McGraw-Hill [1971] xiii, 175 p. illus. 28 cm. Bibliography: p. 169. [NA2700.B44 1971] 77-133389
1. Architectural drawing. I. Schmidt, Walter A., 1918- joint author. II. Title. BIP

BURGE, Henry Charles. 744.424
Architectonics: accenting contract drawings [by] Henry Charles Burge [and] Arthur F. O'Leary. [Los Angeles? 1963] 164 l. illus. 28 cm. (Their Architectonics, 1) [NA2700.B78] 63-2078
1. Architectural drawing. I. O'Leary, Arthur F., joint author. II. Title.

CHING, Frank, 1943- 720'.28
Architectural graphics / Frank Ching. New York : Van Nostrand Reinhold Co., [1975] 128 p. : ill. ; 22 x 28 cm. Includes index. [NA2700.C46] 74-15248 9.95 pbk. : 4.95
1. Architectural drawing. I. Title. BIP

COULIN, Claudius. 720.28
Step-by-step perspective drawing for architects, draftsmen, and designers. Translated by John H. Yarbrough. New York, Van Nostrand Reinhold Co. [1971, c1966] 112 p. illus. 29 cm. Translation of Zeichenlehre fur Architekten, Bauzeichner und Designer. [NA2710.C613] 67-24692
1. Architectural drawing. 2. Perspective. I. Title.

DAGOSTINO, Frank R. 720'.28
Contemporary architectural drawing / Frank R. Dagostino. Reston, Va. : Reston Pub. Co., c1977. p. cm. Includes index. [NA2700.D17] 76-8896 ISBN 0-87909-132-0 : 15.95
1. Architectural drawing. 2. Drawing materials. I. Title. BIP

DALZELL, James Ralph, 1900- 744.5
Building trades blueprint reading, 3d [rev.]

ed. by Rex Battenberg and W. Rahy Paul. Contributor, chapter 7: William Woltjes. Chicago, American Technical Society, 1956-59. 2 v. illus. 28 cm. Vol. 2 of this ed. by Elmer W. Sundberg, Rex Battenberg, and W. Rahy Paul. [TH431.D34] 57-843
1. Architectural drawing. 2. Drawing—Instruction. 3. Blue-prints. I. Battenberg, Rex. II. Sundberg, Elmer W. III. Title.

DALZELL, James Ralph, 1900-1970. 744.532
Blueprint reading for home builders. New York, McGraw-Hill, 1955. 133 p. illus. 31 cm. [TH431.D32] 54-9693
1. Architectural drawing. 2. Blue-prints. I. Title.

DUNNING, William J. 728
Home planning and architectural drawing: an illustrated guide for the correlation of planning principles and drafting techniques [by] W. J. Dunning, L. P. Robin. New York, Wiley [c.1966] vii, 81p. illus., plans. 29cm. Bibl. [NA2700.D8] 66-16141 4.95
1. Architectural drawing. 2. Architecture, Domestic—Designs and plans. I. Robin, Lewis P., joint author. II. Title.

DUNNING, William J. 728.3
Home planning and architectural drawing / W. J. Dunning, L. P. Robin. Huntington, N.Y. : R. E. Krieger Pub. Co., [1976] c1966. p. cm. Reprint of the ed. published by Wiley, New York. Includes index. Bibliography: p. [NA2700.D8 1977] 76-13029 ISBN 0-88275-400-9 : 7.50
1. Architectural drawing. 2. Architecture, Domestic—Designs and plans. I. Robin, Lewis P., joint author. II. Title. BIP

ELWOOD, Franklin George. 744.42
Problems in architectural drawing. [Rev. and reset ed.] Peoria, Ill., C. A. Bennett Co. [1950] 160 p. illus., plans. 26 cm. [NA2700.E53 1950] 50-14826
1. Architectural drawing. I. Title.

GOODBAN, William T. 720'.28
Architectural drawing and planning [by] William T. Goodban [and] Jack J. Hayslett. 2d ed. New York, McGraw-Hill [1972] xvi, 320 p. illus. 29 cm. Bibliography: p. 316-317. [NA2700.G6 1972] 79-179883 ISBN 0-07-023751-4
1. Architectural drawing. I. Hayslett, Jack J., 1928- joint author. II. Title. BIP

GOODBAN, William T. 744.424
Architectural drawing & planning [by] William T. Goodban [and] Jack J. Hayslett. New York, McGraw-Hill [1965] viii, 232 p. illus., maps, plans. 29 cm. (McGraw-Hill technical education series) Bibliography: p. 227-228. [NA2700.G6] 64-21630
1. Architectural drawing. I. Hayslett, Jack J., 1928- joint author. II. Title.

GUIDELINES Publications. 720'.28
Architectural working drawing check list. Orinda, Calif. : Guidelines Publications, 1975, c1974. 2 v. ; 29 cm. Contents.Contents.—v. 1. Commercial, institutional, and other heavy frame construction. v. 2. Residential and other light frame construction. [NA2700.G83 1974] 75-326320
1. Architectural drawing. 2. Architecture—Details. I. Title.

*HELPER, Donald E. 744.4'24
Architectural drafting transparencies; creative architectural drafting [by] D. E. Hepler, P. I. Wallach [others] New York, McGraw 1967. 1v. 28cm. Nine transparencies directly correlatedwith illus. found in pt. 4 of Architecture: drafting and design, by Donald E. Helper, Paul L. Wallach, pub. by Webster-McGraw in 1965. 38.00
1. Architectural drawing. 2. Architecture—Designs and plans. I. Wallach, Paul I., joint author. II. Title.

HEPLER, Donald E. 744.424
Architecture; drafting and design [by] Donald E. Hepler and Paul I. Wallach. St. Louis, Webster Division, McGraw Hill [1965?] vii, 472 p. illus., plans. 25 cm. [NA2700.H4] 64-66271
1. Architectural drawing. 2. Architecture—Designs and plans. I. Wallach, Paul I., joint author. II. Title.

HEPLER, Donald E. 720'.28
Architecture : drafting and design / Donald E. Hepler, Paul I. Wallach. 3d ed. New York : McGraw-Hill, c1977. viii, 568 p. : ill. ; 26 cm. Includes index. [NA2700.H4 1977] 76-19073 ISBN 0-07-028291-9 : 13.28
1. Architectural drawing. 2. Architectural design. I. Wallach, Paul I., joint author. II. Title.

HEPLER, Donald E. 720'.28
Architecture; drafting and design [by] Donald E. Hepler and Paul I. Wallach. 2d ed. New York, McGraw-Hill [1971] vii, 568 p. illus. (part col.), plans (part col.) 24 cm. [NA2700.H4 1971] 70-20336 ISBN 0-07-028290-0
1. Architectural drawing. 2. Architectural design. I. Wallach, Paul I., joint author. II. Title. BIP

HOGARTH, Paul, 1917- 720'.28
Drawing architecture: a creative approach. New York, Watson-Guptill Publications [1973] 191 p. illus. 27 cm. [NA2700.H72] 72-8820 ISBN 0-8230-1363-4 14.50
1. Architectural drawing. I. Title.

HORNUNG, William J. 744.424
Architectural drafting. 4th ed. Englewood Cliffs, N.J., Prentice [1966] 277p. illus. 29cm. [NA2700H73] 66-4344 10.25
1. Architectural drawing. I. Title. BIP

HORNUNG, William J. 744.424
Architectural drafting. [3d ed.] Englewood Cliffs, N. J., Prentice-Hall [1960] 230 p. illus. 29 cm. (Prentice-Hall technical-industrial-vocational series) [NA2700.H73 1960] 60-6116
1. Architectural drawing.

HOWARD, Herbert Seymour. 744.424
Useful curves and curved surfaces. [Brooklyn 5, New York, Pratt Institute, 1959] unpaged. 'Reprinted from Architectural record, by the School of Architecture, Pratt Institute.' illus. diagrs. 28cm. 59-65268 2.00 pap.,
1. Architectural drawing. I. Title.

JONES, William T. 720'.28
Elementary architectural drawing, by William T. Jones. [Ed. 4] Scranton, Pa., International Correspondence Schools, 1974- v. illus. 27 cm. "5893A-8." [NA2700.J62] 74-174357
1. Architectural drawing. I. Title.

JONES, William T. 744.4'24
Elementary architectural drawing, by William T. Jones. Scranton, International Correspondence Schools, c1966- v. illus. 23 cm. "Serial 5893A-6, edition 3." [NA2700.J6] 67-2688
1. Architectural drawing. I. International Correspondence Schools, Scranton, Pa. II. Title.

KEMMERICH, Carl. 744.4'24
Graphic details for architects. [Translation into English by E. Rockwell. Translation into French by Paul Gratwohl.] New York, Praeger [1968] 1 v. (chiefly illus.) 29 cm. English, French, and German. [NA2700.K38] 68-31524 7.50
1. Architectural drawing. I. Title.

LASEAU, Paul, 1937- 720'.28
Graphic problem solving for architects & builders / Paul Laseau. Boston : Cahners Books, [1975] 159 p. : ill. ; 23 x 27 cm. Includes index. Bibliography: p. [156] [NA2705.L37] 75-8607 ISBN 0-8436-2065-X : 14.50
1. Architectural drawing. 2. Architectural design. I. Title. BIP

LIEBLING, Ralph W. 1935- 720.28
Architectural working drawings / Ralph W. Liebling, Mimi Ford Paul. New York : Wiley, 1977. p. ; cm. A Wiley-Interscience Publication Includes index Bibliography [NA2700.L474] 76-48154 ISBN 0-471-53432-3 : 14.95
1. Architectural drawing. 2. Architecture-Designs and plans. I. Paul, Mimi Ford, 1925- joint author. II. Title. BIP

LOCKARD, William Kirby, 1929- 720'.28
Design drawing / William Kirby Lockard. Tucson, Ariz. : Pepper Pub., [1974] 267 p. : ill. ; 22 x 30 cm. Bibliography: p. 264-267. [NA2705.L62] 74-16003 ISBN 0-914468-01-4 : 10.00
1. Architectural drawing. 2. Architectural rendering. 3. Drawing. I. Title. BIP

LOCKARD, William Kirby, 1929- 720'.28
Design drawing experiences / William Kirby Lockard. 3d ed., rev. Tucson, Ariz. : Pepper Pub., 1976. 111, [14] leaves : ill. ; 22 x 28 cm. [NA2705.L622 1976] 76-47136 ISBN 0-914468-02-2 : 8.00
1. Architectural drawing. 2. Architectural rendering. 3. Drawing. I. Title.

LOCKARD, William Kirby, 1929- 720'.28
Design drawing experiences / William Kirby Lockard. Tucson, Ariz. : Pepper Pub., 1975. 101, [20] leaves : ill. ; 22 x 29 cm. Companion to the author's Design drawing. [NA2705.L622] 74-16002 ISBN 0-914468-00-6 : 8.00
1. Architectural drawing. 2. Architectural rendering. 3. Drawing. I. Title. BIP

LOCKARD, William Kirby, 1929- 744.4'24
Drawing as a means to architecture. New York, Reinhold Book Corp. [1968] 96 p. illus. (part col.), plans. 23 x 32 cm. [NA2700.L55] 67-24696
1. Architectural drawing. 2. Architecture—Composition proportion, etc. I. Title. BIP

LOCKARD, William Kirby, 1929- 720'.28
Drawing as a means to architecture / William Kirby Lockard. Rev. ed. Tucson, Ariz. : Pepper Pub., 1977. 112 p. : ill. (some col.) ; 22 x 27 cm. [NA2700.L55 1977] 76-47137 ISBN 0-914468-03-0 : 15.00. ISBN 0-914468-04-9 pbk. : 10.00
1. Architectural drawing. 2. Architecture—Composition, proportion, etc. I. Title.

LOWNDES, William Shepherd, 1866- 604'.2'69
Architectural drawing, by William S. Lowndes and Frederick Fletcher. Serial 5637A-4. [Ed. 4] Scranton, International Correspondence Schools, 1963- v. illus., diagrs., plans. 19 cm. [NA2700.L573] 64-468
1. Architectural drawing. I. Fletcher, Frederick, joint author. II. International Correspondence Schools, Scranton,Pa. III. Title.

LOWNDES, William Shepherd, 1866- 744.4'24
Elementary architectural drawing, by William S. Lowndes and William T. Jones. Ser[i]al 5893C-6 [Ed. 4] Scranton, Pa., International Correspondence Schools [1969- pts. illus. 23 cm. [NA2700.L583] 75-17281
1. Architectural drawing. I. Jones, William T., joint author. II. International Correspondence Schools, Scranton, Pa. III. Title.

MCHUGH, Robert C. 720'.28
Working drawing handbook : a guide for architects & builders / Robert C. McHugh. New York : Van Nostrand Reinhold Co., c1977. p. cm. Includes bibliographical references and index. [NA2700.M32 1977] 77-23157 ISBN 0-442-25283-8 : 12.95 ISBN 0-442-25284-6 pbk. : 7.95
1. Architectural drawing. I. Title. BIP

MARTIN, C Leslie. 744.42
Architectural graphics. New York Macmillan [1952] 213 p. illus. 28 cm. [NA2700.M37] 52-4674
1. Architectural drawing. I. Title. BIP

MARTIN, C. Leslie. 744.4'24
Architectural graphics [by] C. Leslie Martin. 2d ed. [New York] Macmillan [1970] xiv, 239 p. illus. 29 cm. [NA2700.M37 1970] 72-89929
1. Architectural drawing. I. Title.

MORAN, Earl. 741.4'24
Practical architectural drawing. New Brunswick, N.J., Curriculum Laboratory, 1965. 158 p. illus., plans. 28 cm. At head of title: Department of Vocational-Technical Education, Rutgers, the State University, Graduate School of Education. [NA2700.M66] 68-65818
1. Architectural drawing. I. Rutgers University, New Brunswick, N.J., Graduate School of Education. Dept. of Vocational-Technical Education. II. Title.

MORGAN, Sherley W., 1892- 744.42
Architectural drawing; perspective, light and shadow rendering. Illus. executed by William Feay Shellman, Jr. [1st ed.] New York, McGraw-Hill, 1950. 227 p. illus., diagrs. 32 cm. Bibliography: p. 225. [NA2700.M68] 50-6716
1. Architectural drawing.

MULLER, Edward John, 1916- 744.424
Architectural drawing and light construction [by] Edward J. Muller. Englewood Cliffs, N.J., Prentice-Hall [1967] xii, 450 p. illus., plans. 29 cm. Bibliography: p. 415-416. [NA2700.M8] 67-10749
1. Architectural drawing. I. Title. BIP

MULLER, Edward John, 1916- 720'.28
Architectural drawing and light construction / Edward J. Muller. 2d ed. Englewood Cliffs, N.J. : Prentice-Hall, c1976. xiv, 498 p. : ill. ; 28 cm. Includes index. Bibliography: p. 451-454. [NA2700.M8 1976] 75-23212 ISBN 0-13-044578-9 : 13.95
1. Architectural drawing. 2. Building—Tools and implements—Drawings. I. Title.

MULLER, Edward John, 1916- 692'.1
Reading architectural working drawings [by] Edward J. Muller. Englewood Cliffs, N.J., Prentice-Hall [1971] xiii, 352 p. illus. 28 cm. [NA2700.M82] 75-150991 ISBN 0-13-753913-4
1. Architectural drawing. I. Title. BIP

OLES, Paul Stevenson. 720'.28
Architectural illustration / Paul Stevenson Oles. New York : Van Nostrand Reinhold, [1978] p. cm. Includes index. [NA2700.O43] 78-15323 ISBN 0-442-26274-4 : 24.95
1. Architectural drawing. 2. Architectural rendering. 3. Communication in architectural design. I. Title. BIP

PATTEN, Lawton M 744.424
Architectural drawing, by Lawton M. Patten and Milton L. Rogness. Rev. ed. Dubuque, Iowa, W. C. Brown [1962] 1v. illus. 29cm. [NA2700.P3 1962] 62-21426
1. Architectural drawing. I. Rogness, Milton L., joint author. II. Title. BIP

PATTEN, Lawton M. 744.4'24
Architectural drawing, by Lawton M. Patten and Milton L. Rogness. Rev. ed. Dubuque, Iowa, W. C. Brown Co. [1968] 1 v. (various pagings) illus. 29 cm. [NA2700.P3 1968] 68-17698
1. Architectural drawing. I. Rogness, Milton L., joint author.

PATTEN, Lawton M. 720'.28
Architectural drawing / by Lawton M. Patten and Milton L. Rogness. Rev. ed. Dubuque, Iowa : Kendall/Hunt Pub. Co., c1977. 187 p. in various pagings : ill. ; 29 cm. Includes bibliographical references. [NA2700.P3 1977] 77-154743 ISBN 0-8403-1809-X : 8.95
1. Architectural drawing. I. Rogness, Milton L., joint author. II. Title.

PRESENTATION drawings by American architects / [compiled by] Alfred Kemper. New York : Wiley, c1977. 380 p. : chiefly ill. ; 29 cm. "A Wiley-Interscience publication." Includes indexes. [NA2700.P73] 76-40891 ISBN 0-471-01369-2 : 20.00 720'.28
1. Architectural drawing. 2. Architectural rendering. 3. Architecture—Sketches. 4. Architecture—Designs and plans. 5. Graphic arts—Technique. 6. Architects—United States. I. Kemper, Alfred M., 1933-

RAY, Jesse Edgar, 1888- 744.42
Graphic architectural drafting. Bloomington, Ill., McKnight & McKnight Pub. Co. [1954] 256p. illus. 27cm. [NA2700.R36] 54-83850
1. Architectural drawing. I. Title.

RAY, Jesse Edgar, 1888- 744.424
Graphic architectural drafting. [2d ed.] Bloomington, Ill., McKnight & McKnight Pub. Co. [1960] 256p. illus. 27cm. Includes bibliography. [NA2700.R36 1960] 60-3832
1. Architectural drawing. I. Title.

REEKIE, Ronald Fraser. 720'.28
Draughtsmanship : drawing techniques for graphic communication in architecture and

SUBJECT INDEX ARCHITECTURAL METAL-WORK.

building / [by] Fraser Reekie. 3rd ed. London : Edward Arnold, 1976. [9], 250 p. : ill., maps, plans, port. ; 21 cm. On cover: Metric units. Includes index. Bibliography: p. 248. [NA2700.R44 1976] 76-381170 ISBN 0-7131-3368-6 : £2.40
1. Architectural drawing. I. Title.

ROGNESS, Milton L. 744.424
Architectural drawing problems [workbk.] by Milton L. Rogness, Robert I. Duncan. Dubuque, Iowa, 0 3.25, pap., wire bdg.
1. Architectural drawing. I. ccompany Architectural drawing problems, by Lawton M. Patten, Milton L. Rogness. II. Duncan, Robert I., joint author. III. Title. **BIP**

SCHAARWACHTER, Georg. 744.4'24
Perspectives for architecture. New York, F. A. Praeger [1967, c1964] 119 p. illus., plans. 23 x 29 cm. Translation of Perspektive fur Architekten. [NA2710.S313] 67-20404
1. Architectural drawing. 2. Perspective. I. Title.

STEGMAN, George K. 744.424
Architectural drafting; functional planning and creative design [by] George K. Stegman [and] Harry J. Stegman. Chicago, American Technical Society [1966] 455 p. illus., plans. 21 x 26 cm. Bibliography: p. 435-437. [NA2700.S75] 65-24313
1. Architectural drawing. I. Stegman, Harry J., joint author. II. Title. **BIP**

STEGMAN, George K. 720'.28
Architectural drafting; functional planning and creative design [by] George K. Stegman [and] Harry J. Stegman. 2d ed. Chicago, American Technical Society [1974] 632 p. illus. 22 x 27 cm. Bibliography: p. 622-624. [NA2700.S75 1974] 73-75303 ISBN 0-8269-1042-4
1. Architectural drawing. I. Stegman, Harry J., joint author. II. Title.

SUNDBERG, Elmer W. 744.5
Building trades blueprint reading [by] Elmer W. Sunberg. 4th ed. [rev.] Chicago, American Technical Society. [1967- v. illus., plans (part fold.) 28 cm. Previous ed. by J. R. Dalzell. Contents.Contents.—pt 1. Fundamentals. [TH431.S8] 67-16046
1. Architectural drawing. 2. Blue-prints. I. Dalzell, James Ralph, 1900- Building trades blueprint reading. II. Title. **BIP**

TURNER, William Wirt. 744.43
Shades and shadows their use in architectural rendering. New York, Ronald Press Co. [1952] 115 p. illus. 24 cm. [NA2715.T8] 52-6206
1. Architectural drawing. I. Title.

WAFFLE, Harvey W 744.424
Architectural drawing. Rev. ed. Milwaukee, Bruce Pub. Co. [1962] 582 p. illus. 27 cm. Previous ed. published in 1939 under title: Architectural drawing for high schools. [NA2700.W3 1962] 62-19085
1. Architectural drawing. 2. Architecture — Details. 3. Architecture, Domestic. I. Title. **BIP**

WALKER, Theodore D. 720'.28
Plan graphics : drawing, delineation, lettering / Theodore D. Walker. West Lafayette, Ind. : PDA Publishers, [1975] 219 p. : chiefly ill. ; 23 x 29 cm. [NA2700.W34] 75-12051 ISBN 0-914886-05-3 : 18.00 ISBN 0-914886-04-5 pbk. : 12.00
1. Architectural drawing. I. Title. **BIP**

WEIDHAAS, Ernest R. 720'.28
Architectural drafting and construction [by] Ernest R. Weidhaas. Boston, Allyn and Bacon [1974] viii, 550 p. illus. 29 cm. Bibliography: p. 525-528. [NA2700.W39] 73-88065 14.95
1. Architectural drawing. 2. Architecture—Designs and plans. 3. Building materials. I. Title. **BIP**

WEIDHAAS, Ernest R. 720'.223
Architectural drafting and design [by] Ernest R. Weidhaas. Boston, Allyn and Bacon [1968] 309 p. illus. (part col.), plans. 29 cm. Bibliography: p. 289-292. [NA2700.W4] 67-29943
1. Architectural drawing. 2. Architecture—Design. I. Title. **BIP**

WEIDHAAS, Ernest R. 720'.28
Architectural drafting and design [by] Ernest R. Weidhaas. 2d ed. [Boston] Allyn and Bacon [1972] ix, 390 p. illus. 29 cm. Bibliography: p. 369-372. [NA2700.W4 1972] 72-75066
1. Architectural drawing. 2. Architecture—Designs and plans. I. Title.

WEIDHAAS, Ernest R. 720'.28
Architectural drafting and design / Ernest R. Weidhaas. 3d ed. Boston : Allyn and Bacon, c1977. p. cm. Includes index. Bibliography: p. [NA2700.W4 1977] 76-16077 ISBN 0-205-05624-5 : 16.95
1. Architectural drawing. 2. Architecture—Designs and plans. I. Title.

WYATT, William E. 720'.28
General architectural drafting / William E. Wyatt. Peoria, Ill. : C. A. Bennett Co., c1976. 572 p. : ill. ; 25 cm. Edition for 1968 published under title: General architectural drawing. Includes indexes. [NA2700.W9 1976] 75-964 ISBN 0-87002-072-2 : 13.28
1. Architectural drawing. I. Title. **BIP**

WYATT, William E. 744.4'24
General architectural drawing [by] William E. Wyatt. Peoria, Ill., C. A. Bennett [1968, c1969] 556 p. illus., plans (both part col.) 25 cm. [NA2700.W9] 67-10061
1. Architectural drawing. I. Title.

Architectural drawing—Catalogs.

KOYL, George S., 016.744.4'24
1885-
American architectural drawings; a catalog of original and measured drawings of buildings of the United States of America to December 31, 1917. Compiled and edited by George S. Koyl. Assistant editor: Moira B. Mathieson. Foreword by John F. Harbeson. [Philadelphia, Philadelphia Chapter, American Institute of Architects, 1969] 5 v. (unpaged) 28 cm. [NA2605.K6] 74-87938
1. Architectural drawing—Catalogs. 2. Architecture—U.S.—Catalogs. I. Mathieson, Moira B. II. American Institute of Architects. Philadelphia Chapter. III. Title.

Architectural drawing—Detailing.

WAKITA, Osamu A. 720'.28
The professional practice of architectural detailing / Osamu A. Wakita, Richard M. Linde. New York : Wiley, [1977] p. cm. Includes index. [NA2718.W34] 77-7658 ISBN 0-471-91715-X : 18.95
1. Architectural drawing—Detailing. I. Linde, Richard M., joint author. II. Title. **BIP**

Architectural drawing—Exhibitions.

O'NEAL, William Bainter. 744.4'24
Architectural drawing in Virginia, 1819-1969. Exhibition and catalogue [compiled] by William B. O'Neal. [Exhibition] School of Architecture, University of Virginia [Oct. 18-26, 1969, and] Virginia Museum [Nov. 3-30, 1969. Charlottesville, School of Architecture, University of Virginia, 1969] 154 p. illus., plans. 22 cm. [NA2700.O5] 79-98306
1. Architectural drawing—Exhibitions. I. Virginia. University. School of Architecture. II. Virginia Museum of Fine Arts, Richmond. III. Title.

Architectural drawing—Handbooks, manuals, etc.

PRESTRESSED Concrete 720'.28
Institute. Committee on Architectural Precast Concrete Shop Drawings.
Architectural precast concrete drafting handbook / prepared by PCI Committee on Architectural Precast Concrete Shop Drawings, Robert W. Johnson, chairman ... [et al.]. Englewood Cliffs, N.J. : Prentice-Hall, [1975] xiii, 208 p. : ill. ; 29 cm. Includes index. [NA2705.P73 1975] 74-26663 ISBN 0-13-044602-5 : 16.00
1. Architectural drawing—Handbooks, manuals, etc. 2. Precast concrete construction—Handbooks, manuals, etc. I. Title. **BIP**

Architectural drawing—Juvenile literature.

SPENCE, William Perkins, 720'.28
1925-
Construction—architectural drawing / William P. Spence. Englewood Cliffs, N.J. : Prentice-Hall, c1976. 119 p. : ill. ; 24 cm. (Modular exploration of technology series) Includes index. Discusses such topics as drawing tools and techniques, room planning, exterior design, construction details, and working drawings. Includes activities to provide architectural drawing experiences. [NA2750.S63] 75-22084 ISBN 0-13-169433-2 : 5.95 ISBN 0-13-169425-1 pbk. : 2.60
1. Architectural drawing—Juvenile literature. I. Title.

Architectural drawing—Technique.

THOMAS, Marvin L., 1922- 720'.28
Architectural working drawings : a professional technique / Marvin L. Thomas. New York : McGraw-Hill, c1978. xiv, 207 p. : ill. ; 29 cm. Includes index. [NA2708.T46] 77-26084 ISBN 0-07-064240-0 : 17.50
1. Architectural drawing—Technique. I. Title. **BIP**

WANG, Thomas C. 720'.28
Plan and section drawing / Thomas C. Wang. New York : Van Nostrand Reinhold, [1979] p. cm. Includes index. [NA2708.W36] 78-12269 ISBN 0-442-29178-7 pbk. : 7.00 ISBN 0-442-26127-6 : 12.95
1. Architectural drawing—Technique. 2. Architectural rendering—Technique. 3. Communication in architectural design—Technique. I. Title. **BIP**

Architectural drawings.

DALZELL, James Ralph, 744.532
1900-
Building trades blueprint reading. [2d] rev. ed. Chicago, American Technical Society, 1951 [c1949] [TH431.D33 1951] 53-3873
1. Architectural drawings. 2. Drawing—Instruction. 3. Blueprints. I. 2v. illus. 28 cm. II. Title.

JACOBY, Helmut 720.973
Architectural drawings. Architekturzeichnungen. Introd., Claudius Coulin. New York, Praeger [1965] 107p. (chiefly illus. (pt. col.)) 29cm. [NA1088.J3A43] 65-25834 13.75
I. Title. II. Title: Architekturzeichnungen.

JACOBY, Helmut. 744.4'24
New architectural drawings. New York, Praeger [1969] 97 p. (chiefly illus.) 29 cm. Text in English and German. [NA1088.J3A53] 69-19618 14.00
I. Title.

Architectural historians—Great Britain—Biography.

LEESMILNE, James 828'.9'1403 B
Ancestral voices / James Lees-Milne. New York : Scribner, 1978. x, 301 p. ; 23 cm. Autobiographical. Continued by: Prophesying peace. Includes bibliographical references and index. [NA2599.8.L43A2 1975] 77-92997 ISBN 0-684-15647-4 : 10.95
1. Lees-Milne, James. 2. Architectural historians—Great Britain—Biography. I. Title. **BIP**

LEES-MILNE James. 828'.9'1403 B
Prophesying peace / James Lees-Milne. New York : Scribner, 1978. 253 p. : port. ; 23 cm. Includes index. [NA2599.8.L43A2 1977b] 77-92996 ISBN 0-684-15646-6 : 10.95
1. Lees-Milne, James. 2. Architectural historians—Great Britain—Biography. I. Title. **BIP**

Architectural inscriptions.

ANDRIOT, John L 729
Guide to the building inscriptions of the Nation's Capital. Arlington, Va., Jay- Way Press, 1955. 57p. illus. 23cm. [NA4050.I5A55] 55-4977
1. Architectural inscriptions. 2. Washington, D. C.—Public buildings. 3. Quotations. I. Title. II. Title: Building inscriptions of the Nation's Capital.

BARTRAM, Alan. 729
Lettering on architecture / Alan Bartram. New York : Whitney Library of Design, 1976. 176 p. : ill. ; 28 cm. Includes indexes. Bibliography: p. [6] [NA4050.I5B37 1976] 75-20337 ISBN 0-8230-7340-8 : 22.50
1. Architectural inscriptions. I. Title.

GRAY, Nicolette Mary (Binyon) 729
Lettering on buildings. New York, Reinhold Pub. Corp. [1960] 191p. Includes bibliography. illus. 23cm. 60-8936 7.50
1. Architectural inscriptions. 2. Signs and signboards. 3. Lettering. I. Title. **BIP**

Architectural ironwork.

BARNETT, Cara Chastang. 739.4
Facsinating New Orleans and its iron lacework; romance, history. Pictures by Roy C. Meates. [New Orleans? 1953] unpaged. illus. 24 cm. [NA3950.B33] 54-23235
1. Architectural ironwork. 2. Architecture— New Orleans. I. Title.

GEERLINGS, Gerald Kenneth, 729
1897-
Wrought iron in architecture ... [by] Gerald K. Geerlings. New York, Scribner [1972, c1929] v, 202 p. illus. 29 cm. Bibliography: p. 199-200. [NA3950.G4 1972] 72-183895 ISBN 0-684-12842-X 10.00
1. Architectural ironwork. 2. Decoration and ornament, Architectural. I. Title.

MAGNANI, Franco. 721'.8
Ornamental metalwork. [1st American ed.] New York, Universe Books [1967] 144 p. illus. (part col.) 22 cm. Translation of Lavori in metallo. [NA3950.M313] 67-26915
1. Architectural ironwork. I. Title.

ROBERTSON, Edward Graeme. 739'.47
Cast iron decoration : a world survey / E. Graeme and Joan Robertson. New York : Whitney Library of Design, 1977. 336 p. : ill. ; 29 cm. Includes index. Bibliography: p. 324-331. [NA3950.R6 1977] 76-27355 ISBN 0-8230-7122-7 : 27.50
1. Architectural ironwork. I. Robertson, Joan, joint author. II. Title. **BIP**

Architectural ironwork—England—Leamington.

ROTH, Daniel. 739'.47424'87
Early nineteenth century decorative ironwork : a study based on Leamington Spa / by Daniel Roth. Leamington Spa : The author, 1976. [2], 104 leaves : chiefly ill. ; 30 cm. Limited ed. of 100 copies. [TH1651.R63] 76-382861 ISBN 0-9504954-0-9 : £4.50
1. Architectural ironwork—England—Leamington. I. Title.

Architectural ironwork—United States.

SOUTHWORTH, Susan. 739'.4773
Ornamental ironwork : an illustrated guide to its design, history & use in American architecture / by Susan and Michael Southworth ; photos. by Charles C. Withers. Boston : D. R. Godine, 1978. 202 p. : ill. ; 24 cm. Includes index. Bibliography: p. 197-199. [NA3503.S68] 77-94111 ISBN 0-87923-233-1 : 20.00
1. Architectural ironwork—United States. 2. Decoration and ornament, Architectural—United States. I. Southworth, Michael, joint author. II. Withers, Charles C. III. Title. **BIP**

Architectural metal-work.

NATIONAL Association of 729.9
Architectural Metal Manufacturers.
Architectural metal handbook [by] Earl P. Baker [and] Harold S. Langland. [2d ed. Washington] 1952. 219p. illus. 29cm. [TH1651.N38 1952] 54-23015
1. Architectural metal-work. 2. Metals. I. Baker, Earl P., 1882- II. Langland, Harold S., 1898- III. Title.

NICHOLSON, Durward E 739'.47424'87
Architectural metalwork, by Durward E. Nicholson and David T. Jones. Serial 6320A--1-- [Ed. 2] Scranton, International Correspondence Schools, c1961- v. illus. 19cm. [TH1651.N48] 61-37848
1. Architectural metal-work. I. Jones, David Thomas, joint author. II. International Correspondence Schools, Scranton, Pa. III. Title.

Architectural metal-work—Congresses.

SYMPOSIUM on Stainless Steel for Architecture, San Francisco, 1968. 691'.7
Stainless steel for architectural use; a symposium presented at the seventy-first annual meeting, American Society for Testing and Materials, San Francisco, Calif., 23-28 June 1968. Philadelphia, American Society for Testing and Materials [1969] 140 p. illus. 24 cm. (ASTM special technical publication 454) "Sponsored by Committee A-10 on Iron-Chromium, Iron-Chromium-Nickel, and Related Alloys." Includes bibliographies. [TH1651.S94 1968] 70-78440 9.75
1. Architectural metal-work—Congresses. 2. Building, Iron and steel—Congresses. 3. Steel, Stainless—Congresses. I. Title. II. Series: American Society for Testing and Materials. Special technical publication 454

Architectural models.

JANKE, Rolf. 720'.18
Architectural models. [Translated from the German by James Palmes] New York, F. A. Praeger [1968, c1962] 139 p. illus. 21 x 23 cm. Bibliography: p. 134-135. [NA2790.J313 1968b] 67-10688
1. Architectural models. BIP

SMITH, Jackie Lee. 721'.022'8
Building to scale; a manual for model home construction [by] Jackie Lee Smith and Theodore Hoppe, Jr. Englewood Cliffs, N.J., Prentice-Hall [1971] xii, 158 p. illus. 24 cm. [NA2790.S6] 75-144334 ISBN 0-13-087585-6 12.00
1. Architectural models. I. Hoppe, Theodore, joint author. II. Title. BIP

TAYLOR, John Rueger, 1934- 721'.022'8
Model building for architects and engineers [by] John R. Taylor. [New York] McGraw-Hill [1971] vii, 152 p. illus., plans. 28 cm. [NA2790.T38] 73-136189 ISBN 0-07-062938-2
1. Architectural models. I. Title. BIP

TAYLOR, Norman G. 721
Architectural modelling and visual planning. London, Cassell [dist. Chester Springs, Pa., Dufour, 1965, c.1959] xiii, 161p. illus., plans. 21cm. [NA2790] 64-57292 3.50
1. Architectural models. I. Title.

Architectural practice.

DIBNER, David R., 1926- 658.1'144
Joint ventures for architects and engineers [by] David R. Dibner. New York, McGraw-Hill [1972] xiii, 205 p. illus. 23 cm. [NA1996.D5] 73-39902 ISBN 0-07-016760-5
1. Architectural practice. 2. Joint adventures—United States. 3. Engineering—United States. 4. Contractors' operations. I. Title. BIP

ROSSMAN, Wendell E. 658'.91'72
The effective architect [by] Wendell E. Rossman. Englewood Cliffs, N.J., Prentice-Hall [1972] xv, 182 p. illus. 29 cm. [NA1996.R6] 77-168618 ISBN 0-13-240754-X
1. Architectural practice. 2. Architectural services marketing. I. Title. BIP

Architectural practice—Costs.

CASE and Company. 720
The economics of architectural practice. Washington, American Institute of Architects [1968] ix, 65 p. illus. 28 cm. Prepared for the American Institute of Architects. [NA2570.C37] 68-19047
1. Architectural practice—Costs. I. American Institute of Architects. II. Title.

Architectural practice—Data processing.

EVANS, Benjamin H. 720'.18
Architectural programming; emerging techniques of architectural practice—a continuing study by the Committee on Research for Architects [i.e. Architecture] by Benjamin H. Evans and C. Herbert Wheeler, Jr. Washington, American Institute of Architects [1969] 68, [2] p. illus., maps. 22 x 28 cm. (Emerging techniques, 2) "References": p. [69]-[70] [NA1996.E95] 68-59553
1. Architectural practice—Data processing. I. Wheeler, Clarence Herbert, 1915- joint author. II. Title. III. Series.

Architectural practice—Handbooks, manuals, etc.

CURRENT techniques in architectural practice 658'.91'720973 / Robert Allan Class, Robert E. Koehler, editors. Washington : American Institute of Architects, c1976. xi, 275 p. : ill. ; 29 cm. Includes index. Bibliography: p. 265. [NA1996.C87] 76-5887 ISBN 0-07-002324-7 : 25.00
1. Architectural practice—Handbooks, manuals, etc. I. Class, Robert Allan. II. Koehler, Robert E. BIP

Architectural rendering.

ATKIN, William Wilson. 720'.28
Architectural presentation techniques / William Wilson Atkin. New York : Van Nostrand Reinhold Co., 1976. 196 p. : ill. ; 24 cm. Includes index. Bibliography: p. 194. [NA2780.A84] 73-16697 ISBN 0-442-20361-6 : 15.95
1. Architectural rendering. 2. Architectural drawing. 3. Photography, Architectural. 4. Computer drawing. 5. Architectural models. I. Title. BIP

BURDEN, Ernest E., 1934- 721'.022
Architectural delineation; a photographic approach to presentation [by] Ernest Burden. New York, McGraw-Hill [1971] vii, 310 p. illus. 29 cm. [NA2780.B87] 77-145617 ISBN 0-07-008924-8
1. Architectural rendering. I. Title. BIP

DUDLEY, Leavitt. 720'.28
Architectural illustration / Leavitt Dudley. Englewood Cliffs, N.J. : Prentice-Hall, [1976] p. cm. Includes index. Bibliography: p. Describes different types of architectural illustrations, their uses, the techniques used in their execution, and how to master those techniques. [NA2780.D82] 75-45472 ISBN 0-13-044610-6 : 25.00
1. Architectural rendering. I. Title. BIP

HALSE, Albert O., 1910- 744.424
Architectural rendering; the techniques of contemporary presentation. New York, F. W. Dodge [1960] x, 277 p. illus., 16 col. plates, diagrs. 30 cm. Bibliography: p. 272-273. [NA2780.H3] 59-8313
1. Architectural rendering. I. Title. BIP

HALSE, Albert O., 1910- 720'.28
Architectural rendering; the techniques of contemporary presentation [by] Albert O. Halse. 2d ed. New York, McGraw-Hill [1972] x, 326 p. illus. 31 cm. Bibliography: p. 320-321. [NA2780.H3 1972] 76-39900 ISBN 0-07-025628-4 21.50
1. Architectural rendering. I. Title.

JACOBY, Helmut. 720'.28
New techniques of architectural rendering. New York, Praeger Publishers [1971] 143 p. illus. 23 x 29 cm. English and German. [NA2780.J34 1971b] 78-136742 18.50
1. Architectural rendering. I. Title.

Architectural rendering—United States.

KEMPER, Alfred M., 1933- comp. 720'.28
Drawings by American architects [by] Alfred M. Kemper. Associates: Sam Mori & Jacqueline Thompson. New York, Wiley [1973] 613 p. (chiefly illus.) 28 cm. "A Wiley-Interscience publication." [NA705.K45] 72-13428 ISBN 0-471-46845-2 30.00
1. Architectural rendering—United States. 2. Architecture—United States. I. Title. BIP

Architectural services marketing.

COOPER, David G. 658'.09'72
Architectural and engineering salesmanship / David G. Cooper. New York : Wiley, [1978] p. cm. "A Wiley-Interscience publication." Includes index. [NA1996.C56] 78-15367 ISBN 0-471-03642-0 : 15.00
1. Architectural services marketing. 2. Engineering services marketing. I. Title. BIP

COXE, Weld. 658.8'09'72
Marketing architectural and engineering services. New York, Van Nostrand Reinhold Co. [1971] xvi, 195 p. 24 cm. Bibliography: p. 178-180. [NA1996.C6] 75-164987
1. Architectural services marketing. 2. Engineering services marketing. I. Title. BIP

JONES, Gerre L., 1926- 659.2'9'72
How to market professional design services [by] Gerre L. Jones. New York, McGraw-Hill [1973] ix, 354 p. illus. 23 cm. Includes bibliographical references. [NA1996.J66] 73-12032 ISBN 0-07-032800-5 17.00
1. Architectural services marketing. 2. Engineering services marketing. I. Title. BIP

Architecture.

ADAM, Robert 720.942
The works in architecture of Robert and James Adam. Biographical tribute by John Swarbrick. Chicago, Quadrangle Books, 1959[ ] iv, 24p. plates, plans. 29cm. 59-15549 12.50
1. Architecture. I. Adam, James, d. 1794 II. Swarbrick, John. III. Title. BIP

ALEXANDER, Christopher. 720'.1
The timeless way of building / Christopher Alexander. New York : Oxford University Press, 1978. p. cm. [NA2500.A45] 76-42650 ISBN 0-19-502248-3 : 20.00
1. Architecture. 2. Pattern perception. I. Title. BIP

ANGERER, Fred. 624.177
Surface structures in building; structure and form. [Translated into English by W. Redlich] New York, Reinhold Pub. Corp. [1961] 142p. illus. 21cm. Translation of the author's thesis, Technische Hochschule. Munich. [NA2500.A573] 61-11600
1. Architecture. 2. Structures, Theory of. I. Title.

BRAGDON, Claude Fayette, 1866-1946. 720'.1
The beautiful necessity : seven essays on theosophy and architecture / by Claude Bragdon. Wheaton, Ill. : Theosophical Pub. House, 1978, c1939. 111 p. : ill. ; 23 cm. (Quest books) [NA2500.B8 1978] 77-17454 ISBN 0-8356-0507-8 pbk. : 3.75
1. Architecture. 2. Theosophy. I. Title. BIP

CHANG, I-t'iao. 720.1
The existence of intangible content in architectonic form based upon the practicality of Laotzu's philosophy, by Amos Ih Tiao Chang. Princeton [Princeton University Press] 1956. 72p. illus. 26cm. [NA2500.C45] 56-6543
1. Lao-tzu. 2. Architecture. I. Lao-tzu. Tao te ching. II. Title.

COOK, John Wesley, 1933- 720'.92'2
Conversations with architects: Philip Johnson, Kevin Roche, Paul Rudolph, Bertrand Goldberg, Morris Lapidus, Louis Kahn, Charles Moore, Robert Venturi & Denise Scott Brown, by John W. Cook and Heinrich Klotz. Foreword by Vincent Scully. New York, Praeger [1973] 272 p. illus. 25 cm. [NA2540.C63] 72-85972 13.50
1. Architecture. 2. Architects, American—Interviews. I. Klotz, Heinrich, joint author. II. Johnson, Philip Cortelyou, 1906- III. Title.

DALZELL, William Ronald. 720'.9
Architecture, by W. R. Dalzell. Illustrated by Harry Green. New York, Grosset & Dunlap [1971] 159 p. col. illus. 22 cm. (The Grosset all-color guide series, 30) Bibliography: p. 156. Describes the techniques used for constructing buildings in various mediums—timber, stone, brick, etc.—and discusses changes in man's philosophy which have prompted changes in architecture. [NA200.D3 1971] 77-135001 ISBN 0-448-00863-7 3.95
1. Architecture. I. Green, Harry, illus. II. Title.

•DALZELL, William Ronald. 720'.9
Architecture. Illus. by Harry Green. Toronto, New York, Bantam Books [1974, c.1971] 169 p. col. illus. 18 cm. (Knowledge through color series, no. 46) Bibliography: p. 156. Summary: Describes the techniques used for constructing buildings in various mediums—Timber, stone, brick, etc.—And discusses changes in man's philosophy which have prompted changes in architecture. [NA200.D3] 1.45 (pbk.)
1. Architecture. I. Green, Harry, illus. II. Title.
L.C. card no. for the hardbound edition: 77-135001.

DANBY, Miles. 720.9
Grammar of architectural design, with special reference to the tropics. London, New York, Oxford University Press, 1963. 243 p. illus. 23 cm. Includes bibliography. [NA2540.D25 1963] 63-5838
1. Architecture. 2. Architecture, Tropical. I. Title.

DE ZURKO, Edward Robert. 724.91
Origins of functionalist theory. New York, Columbia University Press, 1957. 265p. illus. 25cm. 'An earlier version ... was submitted as a doctoral dissertation [New York University]' Bibliography: p.[243]-255. [NA2500.D4 1957] 57-8448
1. Architecture. 2. Aesthetics. I. Title.

EDWARDS, Arthur Trystan, 1884- 720.1
Good & bad manners in architecture, by A. Trystan Edwards. London, J. Tiranti ltd, 1944 [New York, Transatlantic, 1966] xvi, 176p. illus., plates. 19cm. First pub. in 1924. New ed.[2d] 1944. [NA2550.E4 1944] 45-5418 2.50
1. Architecture. I. Title.

EIDLITZ, Leopold, 1823-1908. 720
The nature and function of art, more especially of architecture / by Leopold Eidlitz. New York : Da Capo Press, 1977, [c1881]. xxii, 493 p. ; 23 cm. (Da Capo Press series architecture and decorative art) Reprint of the ed. published by A. C. Armstrong, New York. Includes index. [NA2520.E38 1977] 77-4765 ISBN 0-306-70898-1 : 32.50
1. Architecture. 2. Art. 3. Aesthetics. I. Title. II. Series. BIP

ENGEL, Heinrich. 721
Structure systems. With a pref. by Ralph Rapson, and an article by Hanns-karl Bandel. New York, Praeger [1968, c1967] 261, [19] p. illus. 30 cm. English and German. Published in 1967 under title: Tragsysteme. Structure systems. Bibliography: p. [280] [TH845.E54 1968] 68-16801
1. Architecture. 2. Structural engineering. I. Title.

ENGEL, Heinrich. 721
Tragsysteme. Structure Systems. Mit einem Vorwort von Ralph Rapson und einem Beitrag von Hannskarl Bandel. Stuttgart, Deutsche Verlags Anstalt (1967). 261p. with illus. 30cm. English and German [TH845.E54] 68-83443 22.50
1. Architecture. 2. Structural engineering. I. Bandel, Hannskarl. II. Title. III. Title: Structure Systems.
American distributor: Wittenborn, New York.

FIEDLER, Konrad, 1841-1895. 624.177
Essay on architecture, with notes by Victor Hammer. [Lexington?Ky., 1954] v, 56p. 26cm. 'One hundred copies printed.' Edited by Carolyn Reading. Translation of uber Wesen und Geschichte der Baukunst. [NA2500.F5313] 54-43071
1. Architecture. I. Title.

FILARETE, Antonio Averlino, known as, 15th cent. 720
Treatise on architecture; being the treatise by Antonio di Piero Averlino, known as

Filarete; 2v. Tr., introd., notes by John R. Spencer. New Haven, Yale [c.]1965. 2v. illus. 37cm. (Yale pubns. in the hist. of art, 16) Includes facsim. of the Magliabecchiana ms. in Florence (Bib. Naz., Magl. II. I. 140) Contents.v.1 The translation.--v.2. The facsimile. [NA2515.F493] 65-12547 60.00 set,
1. Architecture. 2. Drawing—Instruction. 3. Medici, House of. I. Spencer, John Richard, ed. and tr. II. Title. III. Series.

FOERSTER, Bernd. 624.177
Man and masonry. (Washington? 1960] 59 p. (chiefly illus.) 29 cm. and phonodisc. L. C. copy imperfect: phonodisc wanting. (2 s. 10 in. 33 1/2 rpm microgroove) in pocket. [NA2500.F6] 60-11593
1. Architecture. 2. Architecture, Modern — 20th cent. I. Title.

FRIEDMAN, Yona, 1923- 720'.1
Toward a scientific architecture / Yona Friedman ; translated by Cynthia Lang. Cambridge, Mass. : MIT Press, [1975] xii, 169 p. : ill. ; 21 cm. Translation of Pour une architecture scientifique. [NA2500.F7413] 75-8769 ISBN 0-262-06058-2 : 12.50
1. Architecture. I. Title. BIP

GAULDIE, Sinclair. 720
Architecture. London, New York, Oxford U.P., 1969. [11], 193 p. illus., plans. 22 cm. [NA2520.G3] 78-109897 42/- ($8.50)
1. Architecture. I. Title. BIP

GEDAT, Gustav Adolf. 720.9
They built for eternity, translated by Roland H. Bainton. New York, Abingdon-Cokesbury Press [1953] 175 p. illus. 29 cm. [NA2550.G413] 53-10010
1. Architecture. I. Title. BIP

GEDAT, Gustav Adolf. 720'.9
They built for eternity. Translated by Roland H. Bainton. Freeport, N.Y., Books for Libraries Press [1971, c1953] 175 p. illus. 29 cm. (Essay index reprint series) Translation of Sie bauten fur die Ewigkeit. [NA2550.G413 1971] 72-167345 ISBN 0-8369-2451-7
1. Architecture. I. Title.

HAMLIN, Talbot Faulkner, 720'.1
1889-1956.
Architecture, an art for all men / Talbot Hamlin. Westport, Conn. : Greenwood Press, 1975, c1947. xxii, 279 p., [16] leaves of plates : ill. ; 23 cm. Reprint of the ed. published by Columbia University Press, New York, which was a revision of the author's The enjoyment of architecture. Includes index. Bibliography: p. [257]-261. [NA2550.H3 1975] 75-3798 ISBN 0-8371-8079-1 : 17.50
1. Architecture. I. Title. BIP

HAMMER, Victor Karl, 1882- 720
A theory of architecture; the second chapter from A platonic dialog. New York, Wittenborn, Schultz [1952] 4, 35-93. [2]p. illus. 17cm. 'Two hundred and fifty numbered copies . . . Number 251.' Bibliographical references included in 'Notes and comments' (p.[90]- [94] [NA2500.H35] 52-67702
1. Architecture. I. Title.

HITCHCOCK, Henry Russell. 724.9
1903-
The international style [by] Henry-Russell Hitchcock. Philip Johnson. A New foreword. appendix by Henry-Russell Hitchcock. New York. Norton [c.1932-1966] xiii. 260p. illus., plans. 20cm. (Norton lib., N311) First pub. in 1932 under the title: The international style: architecture since 1922. 'The international style twenty years after' by H. R. Hitchcock. an article written for the Architectural record of August 1951: p. 237-255. [NA680.H5 1966] 66-15312 2.95 pap.,
1. Architecture. 2. Architecture—Design and plans. I. Johnson. Philip Cortelyou. 1906- joint author. II. Title.

HUDNUT, Joseph, 1886-1968. 720'.1
Architecture and the spirit of man. New York, Greenwood Press [1969, c1949] 301 p. 23 cm. [NA2500.H8 1969] 77-95124
1. Architecture. I. Title. BIP

INTRODUCTION to architecture 720
/ edited by James C. Snyder, Anthony J. Catanese. New York : McGraw-Hill, c1979. p. cm. Includes index. [NA2500.I57] 78-12808 ISBN 0-07-059547-X : 23.50
1. Architecture. I. Snyder, James C. II. Catanese, Anthony James.

JEANNERET-GRIS, Charles 720
Edouard, 1887-1965.
Towards a new architecture, by Le Corbusier. Translated from the French by Frederick Etchells. New York, Praeger [1970] 269 p. illus., plans. 22 cm. Reprint of the 1927 ed. Translation of Vers une architecture. [NA2520.J4 1970] 76-92371 7.50
1. Architecture. I. Title.

LETHABY, William Richard, 720'.1
1857-1931.
Architecture, mysticism, and myth / by W. R. Lethaby ; with ill. by the author. New York : G. Braziller, 1975. xxiv, 280 p. : ill. ; 22 cm. Reprint of the 1891 ed. published by Percival, London, with new introd. and bibliography. Bibliography: p. [273]-280. [NA2500.L54 1975] 74-25316 ISBN 0-8076-0783-5 : 10.00
1. Architecture. 2. Symbolism in architecture. I. Title. BIP

MAKI, Fumihiko, 1928- 711'.4
Investigations in collective form. St. Louis, School of Architecture, Washington University, 1964. vii, 87 p. illus., plans. 21 cm. (Washington University, St. Louis. School of Architecture. A special publication, no. 2) [NA2500.M27] 73-5429
1. Architecture. 2. Cities and towns—Planning—1945- I. Title. II. Series.

MUSCHAMP, Herbert. 720
File under architecture. Cambridge, Mass., MIT Press [1974] 117 p. 23 cm. [NA2500.M83] 74-3297 ISBN 0-262-13110-2
1. Architecture. I. Title. BIP

NORBERG-SCHULZ, Christian 720.1
Intentions in architecture. Cambridge, Mass., M.I.T. Pr. [1968,c.1965] 242p. illus. plans. 22cm. (MIT 100) Bibl. [NA2500.N6] 65-23862 4.95 pap.,
1. Architecture. 2. Aesthetics. I. Title. BIP

PARKER, Alfred Browning 720
You and architecture; a practical guide to the best in building. [New York, Delacorte Pr.]; dist. Dial [c.1965] 277p. illus. 28cm. [NA2550.P35] 63-17221 10.00; 12.50 after 12/25/65.
1. Architecture. 2. Architecture, Domestic. I. Title.

PONTI, Giovanni, 1891- 720
In praise of architecture. Translated by Giuseppina and Mario Salvadori. Pref. by Mario Salvadori. New York, F. W. Dodge Corp. [1960] 270 p. illus. 20 cm. Translation of Amate l'architettura. [NA2500.P613] 59-11727
1. Architecture. I. Title.

RASKIN, Eugene. 720.1
Architecturally speaking. Illus. by Robert Osborn. [New York] Reinhold [1954] 129p. illus 23cm. [NA2500.R35] 54-11962
1. Architecture. I. Title. BIP

RASKIN, Eugene. 720'.1
Architecturally speaking. Illus. by Robert Osborn. [2d ed.] New York, Bloch Pub. Co. [1966] xvi, 129 p. illus. 20 cm. [NA2500.R35 1966] 78-19418 ISBN 0-8197-0003-7 1.95
1. Architecture. I. Title.

RASMUSSEN, Steen Eiler 720
Experiencing architecture. [Translation from Danish by Eve Wendt. Cambridge, Mass.] Technology Press of Massachusetts Institute of Technology and N.Y., Wiley [1959] 251p. illus. (part col.) diagrs. 24cm. 59-16495 4.50 bds.,
1. Architecture. I. Title. BIP

RASMUSSEN, Steen Eiler, 1898- 720
Experiencing architecture. [Translation from Danish by Eve Wendt. 2d United States ed.] Cambridge [Mass.] M.I.T. Press, Massachusetts Institute of Technology, 1962. 245 p. illus. 25 cm. [NA2550.R313 1962] 62-21637
1. Architecture. I. Title.

RICCI, Leonardo, 1918- 720.1
Anonymous (20th century) New York, G. Braziller, 1962. 254 p. 21 cm. [NA1123.R5A3] 61-15494
1. Architecture. 2. Cities and towns—Planning. 3. Art—Philosophy. I. Title.

ROSENGARTEN, Albert, 720'.9
b.1809.
A handbook of architectural styles / translated from the German of A. Rosengarten by W. Collet-Sandars. Boston : Longwood Press, 1977. p. cm. Translation of Die architektonischen Stylarten. Reprint of the 1878 ed. published by Chatto and Windus, London. [NA204.R6713 1977] 77-23404 ISBN 0-89341-206-6 lib.bdg. : 55.00
1. Architecture. I. Title. BIP

RUDOFSKY, Bernard, 1905- 720
The prodigious builders : notes toward a natural history of architecture with special regard to those species that are traditionally neglected or downright ignored / Bernard Rudofsky. New York : Harcourt Brace Jovanovich, [1979] c1977. p. cm. Includes bibliographical references and index. [NA200.R76 1979] 78-23534 ISBN 0-15-674625-5 pbk. : 7.95
1. Architecture. I. Title.

RUDOFSKY, Bernard, 1905- 720
The prodigious builders : notes toward a natural history of architecture with special regard to those species that are traditionally neglected or downright ignored / Bernard Rudofsky. New York : Harcourt Brace Jovanovich, [1979] c1977. p. cm. Includes bibliographical references and index. [NA200.R76 1979] 78-23534 ISBN 0-15-674625-5 pbk. : 7.95
1. Architecture. I. Title.

RUSKIN, John, 1819-1900. 720'.94
The poetry of architecture: or, The architecture of the nations of Europe considered in its association with natural scenery and national character. With illus. by the author. Sunnyside, Orpington, G. Allen, 1893. [New York, AMS Press, 1971] xii, 261 p. illus. 24 cm. [NA2550.R7 1971] 74-148294 ISBN 0-404-05463-3
1. Architecture. I. Title. BIP

RUSKIN, John, 1819-1900. 728'.094
The poetry of architecture; or, The architecture of the nations of Europe considered in its association with natural scenery and national character. Sunnyside, Orpington, G. Allen, 1893. St. Clair Shores, Mich., Scholarly Press, 1972. xii, 261 p. illus. 22 cm. Includes bibliographical references. [NA2550.R7 1972] 78-115265 ISBN 0-403-00305-9
1. Architecture. I. Title. II. Title: The architecture of the nations of Europe considered in its association with natural scenery and national character.

RUSKIN, John, 1819-1900. 720
The seven lamps of architecture. Including illus. drawn and etched by the author. New York, Noonday Press [1961] 210p. illus. 21cm. (Noonday [paperbacks] N215) [NA2550.R75 1961] 61-4427
1. Architecture. I. Title. BIP

RUSKIN, John, 1819-1900. 720
The seven lamps of architecture. With illus. drawn by the author, and an introd. by Charles Eliot Norton. Brantwood ed. New York, Merrill, 1892. St. Clair Shores, Mich., Scholarly Press, 1972. p. (The works of John Ruskin) [NA2550.R75 1972] 72-8328 ISBN 0-403-02058-1
1. Architecture. I. Title.

SCOTT, Geoffrey, 1885-1929 724.
The architecture of humanism: a study in the history of taste.[2d ed.] Gloucester, Mass., P. Smith, 1965. 197p. 21cm. Bibl. [NA2500.S4] 65-3506 3.00
1. Architecture. 2. Aesthetics. I. Title. BIP

SCOTT, Geoffrey, 1885-1929. 720.1
The architecture of humanism; a study in the history of taste. Garden City, N. Y., Doubleday, 1954. 197p. 18cm. (Doubleday anchor books, A33) [NA2500] 54-14934
1. Architecture. 2. Aesthetics. I. Title.

SCOTT, Geoffrey, 1885-1929. 724
The architecture of humanism; a study in the history of taste. New York, Norton [1974] 197 p. illus. 20 cm. (The Norton library, N734) Includes bibliographical references. [NA2500.S4 1974] 74-14765 ISBN 0-393-00734-0
1. Architecture. 2. Aesthetics. I. Title.

SCOTT, Geoffrey, 1885-1929. 724
The architecture of humanism; a study in the history of taste. New York, Charles Scribner's Sons [1969] 197 p. 21 cm. (The Scribner library, SL183. Lyceum editions) Reprint of the 2d ed. published in 1924, with a new foreword by Henry Hope Reed. Bibliographical footnotes. [NA2500.S4 1969] 72-77528 2.25
1. Architecture. 2. Aesthetics. I. Title.

SULLIVAN, Louis Henry, 720.1
1856-1924.
The testament of stone; themes of idealism and indignation from the writings of Louis Sullivan. Edited, with an introd., by Maurice English. [Evanston, Ill.] Northwestern University Press, 1963. xxvii, 227 p. 24 cm. [NA737.S9A33] 63-15297
1. Architecture. 2. Art and society. 3. Democracy I. Title. BIP

VIOLLET-LE-DUC, Eugene 720.4
Emmanuel 1814-1879.
Discourses on architecture. Translated from the French by Benjamin Bucknall. New York, Grove Press [1959] 2 v. illus. 29 cm. [NA2520.V7 1959] 59-6254
1. Architecture.

VIOLLET-LE-DUC, Eugene 720
Emmanuel, 1814-1879.
Discourses on architecture. Translated from the French of Eugene Emmanuel Viollet-Le-Duc, by Benjamin Bucknall. Illustrated by 37 steel engravings and 200 woodcuts. Boston, Milford House [1973] p. Reprint of the 1889 translation of Entretiens sur l'architecture published by Ticknor, Boston. [NA2520.V7 1973] 73-10209 ISBN 0-87821-063-6 65.00 (lib. bdg.)
1. Architecture. I. Title.

WASS, Alonzo. 721
Manual of structural details for building construction. Englewood Cliffs, N.J., Prentice-Hall [1968] xiv, 386 p. illus., plans. 29 cm. [TH845.W3] 68-23547
1. Architecture. 2. Building—Details. I. Title.

WRIGHT, Frank Lloyd 720.81
Frank Lloyd Wright on architecture; selected writings, 1894-1940. Edited, with an introd., by Frederick Gutheim. New York, Grosset & Dunlap [1959, c.1941] xviii, 275p. 21cm. (The Universal library, UL-70) 60-90 1.65 pap.,
1. Architecture. I. Title.

WRIGHT, Frank Lloyd, 720.973
1867-1959.
Architecture: man in possession of his earth. Biography by Iovanna Lloyd Wright. Designer and editor: Patricia Coyle Nicholson. [1st ed.] Garden City, N. Y., Doubleday, 1962. 127 p. illus. (part col.) ports., plans. 33 cm. "Books by Frank Lloyd Wright ... Books about Frank Lloyd Wright": p. [6] [NA737.W7N5] 62-15928
1. Architecture. I. Wright, Iovanna Lloyd. II. Nicholson, Patricia Coyle, ed. III. Title.

WRIGHT, Frank Lloyd, 1867- 720'.1
1959.
An organic architecture; the architecture of democracy. Cambridge, M.I.T. Press [1970, c1939] viii, 56 p. illus. 29 cm. Facsim. of the Sir George Watson lectures of the Sulgrave Manor Board for 1939. Bibliography: p. 48-49. [NA2500.W7 1939ab] 77-105749 ISBN 0-262-23044-5
1. Architecture. 2. Form (Aesthetics) I. Title. II. Series: Sir George Watson Foundation for American History, Literature and Institutions. Lectures, 1939.

WRIGHT, Frank Lloyd, 720.973
1867-1959.
Writings and buildings. Selected by Edgar Kaufmann and Ben Raeburn. [New York] Horizon Press [1960] 346 p. illus. 22 cm. [NA737.W7A48 1960a] 60-8166
1. Architecture. I. Kaufmann, Edgar, 1910- comp. BIP

ZEVI, Bruno, 1918- 720
Architecture as space : how to look at architecture / by Bruno Zevi ; edited by Joseph A. Barry ; translated by Milton Gendel. Rev. ed. New York : Horizon

Press, [1974] 310 p. : ill. ; 26 cm. Translation of Saper vedere l'architettura. Includes index. Bibliography: p. 245-284. [NA2500.Z413 1974] 74-15386 ISBN 0-8180-0024-4 : 15.00. ISBN 0-8180-0025-2 pbk. : 8.95
1. Architecture. 2. Space (Architecture) I. Title.

Architecture—Addresses, essays, lectures.

AIA-ACSA Teacher Seminar. 720.8
Cranbrook Academy of Art, 1964
The history, theory. and criticism of architecture; papers, ed. by Marcus Whiffen. Foreword by Buford L. Pickens. Cambridge. Mass., M.I.T. Pr. [1966 ,c.1965] x, 112p. illus. 24cm. Bibl. [NA2560.A2] 65-23081 3.95
1. Architecture—Addresses, essays, lectures. I. Whiffen, Marcus, ed. II. American Institute of Architects. III. Association of Collegtate Schools of Architecture. IV. Cranbrook Academy of Art. Bloomfield Hills, Mich. V. Title.

BRAGDON, Claude Fayette, 720
1866-1946.
Architecture and democracy. Freeport, N.Y., Books for Libraries Press [1971, c1918] 213 p. illus. 23 cm. (Essay index reprint series) Contents.Contents.—Architecture and democracy.—Ornament from mathematics.—Harnessing the rainbow.—Louis Sullivan, prophet of democracy.—Color and ceramics.—Symbols and sacraments.—Self-education. [NA2560.B7 1971] 70-156617 ISBN 0-8369-2386-3
1. Sullivan, Louis Henri, 1856-1924. 2. Architecture—Addresses, essays, lectures. 3. Architecture—United States. 4. Decoration and ornament. I. Title. BIP

BRYAN, James, comp. 720
Structures implicit and explicit. Edited by James Bryan and Rolf Sauer. [Philadelphia, Graduate School of Fine Arts, University of Pennsylvania; distributed by Wittenborn, New York, 1973] 203 p. illus. 31 cm. (Via, no. 2) Includes bibliographical references. [NA2500.B84] 73-96896 6.00 (pbk.)
1. Architecture—Addresses, essays, lectures. 2. Structural engineering—Addresses, essays, lectures. I. Sauer, Rolf, joint comp. II. Title. III. Series.
Contents omitted.

CRAM, Ralph Adams, 1863- 720'.9
1942.
Six lectures on architecture, by Ralph Adams Cram, Thomas Hastings [and] Claude Bragdon. Freeport, N.Y., Books for Libraries Press [1968] x, 172 p. illus. 22 cm. (Essay index reprint series) Reprint of the 1917 ed., issued as the Scammon lectures for 1915. Contents.Contents.—The beginnings of Gothic art and The culmination of Gothic architecture, by R. A. Cram.—Principles of architectural composition and Modern architecture, by T. Hastings.—Organic architecture and The language of form, by C. Bragdon. [NA2560.C83 1968] 68-57314
1. Architecture—Addresses, essays, lectures. I. Hastings, Thomas, 1860-1929. II. Bragdon, Claude Fayette, 1866-1946. III. Title. BIP

CREIGHTON, Thomas Hawk, ed. 724.9
Building for modern man; a symposium, edited by Thomas H. Creighton. Freeport, N.Y., Books for Libraries Press [1969, c1949] xv, 219 p. 23 cm. (Essay index reprint series) Papers prepared in connection with conference 5 of series 2 of the conferences that marked Princeton's bicentennial celebration. Bibliographical footnotes. [NA2560.C85 1969] 74-80385
1. Architecture—Addresses, essays, lectures. 2. Cities and towns—Planning—1945- I. Princeton University. II. Title. BIP

HUDNUT, Joseph, 1886- 720.4
The three lamps of modern architecture; lectures delivered at College of Architecture and Design, University of Michigan, May 12-16, 1952. Ann Arbor, University of Michigan Press, 1952. 57p. 23cm. (Architecture and planning series, no.1) [NA2563.H82] 53-6427
1. Architecture—Addresses, essays, lectures. I. Title. II. Series.

HUXTABLE, Ada Louise. 720
Kicked a building lately? / Ada Louise Huxtable. New York : Quadrangle/The New York Times Book Co., c1976. p. cm. Includes index. [NA2563.H88 1976] 75-36276 ISBN 0-8129-0630-6 : 12.50
1. Architecture—Addresses, essays, lectures. 2. Architecture, Modern—20th century—Addresses, essays, lectures. I. Title. BIP

JENCKS, Charles. 720'.1
Meaning in architecture. Edited by Charles Jencks and George Baird. New York, G. Braziller [1970, c1969] 288 p. illus. 26 cm. Includes bibliographical references. [NA2500.J43 1970] 73-83404
1. Architecture—Addresses, essays, lectures. 2. Architecture—Psychological aspects—Addresses, essays, lectures. I. Baird, George, joint author. II. Title.

MAGINNIS, Charles Donagh, 720.4
1867-1955.
Charles Donagh Maginnis, FAIA, 1867-1955: a selection of his essays and addresses. Selected and edited by Robert P. Walsh and Andrew W. Robert. New Haven, Conn., 1956. 51p. illus. 26cm. [NA2560.M3] 58-15757
1. Architecture—Addresses, essays, lectures. I. Title.

MUMFORD, Lewis, 1895- 720.4
From the ground up; observations on contemporary architecture, housing, highway building, and civic design. New York, Harcourt, Brace [c1956] 243p. 19cm. (A Harvest book, 13) [NA2560.M8] 56-13736
1. Architecture—Addresses, essays, lectures. 2. Cities and towns—Planning—Addresses, essays, lectures. 3. Cities and towns—Planning—New York (City) 4. Housing. 5. Traffic engineering. I. Title.

MUMFORD, Lewis, 1895- 720'.8
Lewis Mumford : architecture as a home for man / edited by Jeanne M. Davern. New York : Architectural Record Books, 1975. p. cm. Twenty-one of the 24 essays included originally appeared in Architectural record, 1928-1968; 3 appeared in Architecture, 1928. [NA2560.M82] 75-21382
1. Architecture—Addresses, essays, lectures. 2. Cities and towns—Planning—Addresses, essays, lectures. I. Title.

PEVSNER, Nikolaus, Sir, 720'.9
1902-
Some architectural writers of the nineteenth century. Oxford, Clarendon Press, 1972. xiv, 338 p. illus. 25 cm. "A considerably, enlarged version of the Slade Lectures ... [given] at Oxford in the session 1968-9." Includes bibliographical references. [NA25.P48] 72-170683 ISBN 0-19-817315-6 £8.50
1. Architecture—Addresses, essays, lectures. I. Title. BIP

POWYS, Albert Reginald, 720'.8
1881-1936.
From the ground up, collected papers of Albert Reginald Powys, architect, writer, and secretary of the Society for the Protection of Ancient Buildings, 1882-1936. With an introd. by John Cowper Powys and two photos. Freeport, N.Y., Books for Libraries Press [1971] xvi, 179 p. 23 cm. (Essay index reprint series) Reprint of the 1937 ed. [NA27.P6 1971] 77-156706 ISBN 0-8369-2292-1
1. Architecture—Addresses, essays, lectures. I. Title.

RUSKIN, John, 1819-1900. 720
Lectures on architecture and painting, delivered at Edinburgh in Novermber 1853. With an introd. by Charles Eliot Norton. Brantwood ed. New York, Merrill, 1892. St. Clair Shores, Mich., Scholarly Press, 1972. p. (The works of John Ruskin) [N7445.2.R78 1972] 72-8233 ISBN 0-403-02051-4
1. Turner, Joseph Mallord William, 1775-1851—Addresses, essays, lectures. 2. Architecture—Addresses, essays, lectures. 3. Preraphaelitism—Addresses, essays, lectures. I. Title.

SMITHSON, Alison Margaret, 720.9
comp.
Team 10 primer, edited by Alison Smithson [for Team 10]. Cambridge, MIT Press, [1974, c1968]. 112 p. illus. 26 cm. Bibliography: p. 106-112 [NA2560.S55] 68-25990 ISBN 0-262-69047-0 4.95 (pbk.)
1. Architecture—Addresses, essays, lectures. I. Title. II. Title: Team 10.

STREET, Arthur 720'.92'4 B
Edmund, 1855-
Memoir of George Edmund Street, R.A., 1824-1881. New York, B. Blom, 1972. 441 p. port. 21 cm. Reprint of the 1888 ed. Includes lectures given before students of the Royal Academy in the spring of 1881. [NA997.S8S8 1972] 70-173141
1. Street, George Edmund, 1824-1881. 2. Architecture—Addresses, essays, lectures. BIP

SUMMERSON, John Newenham, 720.4
1904-
Heavenly mansions, and other essays on architecture. New York, Scribner [1950] ix, 253 p. illus. 22 cm. [NA2563.S8] 50-561
1. Architecture—Addresses, essays, lectures. I. Title.

WALKER, Ralph Thomas, 1889- 720.4
The fly in the amber; [comments on the making of architecture. New York? 1957] 160 p. illus. 25 cm. [NA2560.W3] 57-42306
1. Architecture — Addresses, essays, lectures. I. Title.

WRIGHT, Frank Lloyd, 1869- 720.81
1959.
Writings and buildings. Selected by Edgar Kaufmann and Ben Raeburn. New York, Meridian Books [1960] 346 p. illus. 21 cm. (Meridian books, MG22) [NA737.W7A48] 60-11169
1. Architecture—Addresses, essays, lectures. I. Title.

Architecture—Adelaide.

MORGAN, Edward James 720'.994'2
Ranembe, Sir, 1900-
Early Adelaide architecture 1836 to 1886 [by] E. J. R. Morgan and S. H. Gilbert. Melbourne, New York, Oxford University Press [1969] 169 p. chiefly illus. 24 cm. Bibliography: p. 161-162. [NA1603.A4M6] 79-464238 8.50
1. Architecture—Adelaide. 2. Architecture, Victorian—Adelaide. 3. Adelaide—Historic houses, etc. I. Gilbert, Stephen Hamilton, 1910- joint author. II. Title. BIP

Architecture, Aeolic—Palestine.

BETANCOURT, Philip P., 1936- 722
The Aeolic style in architecture : a survey of its development in Palestine, the Halikarnassos peninsula, and Greece, 1000-500 B.C. / by Philip P. Betancourt. Princeton, N.J. : Princeton University Press, c1977. viii, 169 p., [12] leaves of plates : ill. ; 29 cm. Includes index. Bibliography: p. 157-162. [NA245.P34B47] 76-45890 ISBN 0-691-03922-4 : 25.00
1. Architecture, Aeolic—Palestine. 2. Architecture—Palestine. 3. Palestine—Antiquities. 4. Architecture, Aeolic—Mugla, Turkey (Province) 5. Architecture—Mugla, Turkey (Province) 6. Mugla, Turkey (Province)—Antiquities. 7. Architecture, Aeolic—Greece. 8. Architecture—Greece. 9. Greece—Antiquities. I. Title. BIP

Architecture — Africa.

KULTERMANN, Udo. 720.96
New architecture in Africa. [Translated from the German by Ernst Flesch] New York, Universe Books [1963] 26 p. 180 p. of illus., plans. illus. 28 cm. Errata slip inserted. [NA1580.K813] 63-12537
1. Architecture — Africa. 2. Architecture, Modern — 20th cent. I. Title.

KULTERMANN, Udo. 720'.96
New directions in African architecture. [Translated by John Maass] New York, G. Braziller [1969] 128 p. illus. 25 cm. (New directions in architecture) Bibliography: p. 116-119. [NA1580.K8213] 70-87062 5.95
1. Architecture—Africa. 2. Architecture, Modern—20th century. I. Title. BIP

Architecture—Allegheny Co., Pa.

VAN TRUMP, James 720'.9748'85
Denholm, 1908-
Landmark architecture of Allegheny County, Pennsylvania, by James D. Van Trump, Arthur P. Ziegler, Jr. Pittsburgh, Pittsburgh Hist. & Landmarks Found., 1967. viii, 294p. illus., maps. 27cm. (Stones of Pittsburgh, no. 5) [NA25.S7 no.5] 67-26459 8.50
1. Architecture—Allegheny Co., Pa. 2. Allegheny Co., Pa.—Historic houses etc. I. Ziegler, Arthur P. joint author. II. Pittsburgh History and Landmarks Foundation. III. Title.
Publisher's address: 900 Benedum-Tree Building, Pittsburgh, Pa. 15222.

Architecture, American.

EARLY, James, 1923- 720.973
Romanticism and American architecture. New York, A. S. Barnes [1965] 171 p. illus., plans. 26 cm. Includes bibliographical references. [NA710.E2] 65-20532
1. Architecture, American. 2. Romanticism in art. I. Title.

SAARINEN, Eliel, 1873-1950 729.38
The Saarinen door: Saarinen, architect and designer at Cranbrook [Comp. ed. by the Public Relations Office, the Cranbrook inst. Bloomfield Hills, Mich., Cranbrook Acad. of Art, 1963] 63p. illus., ports. 28cm. Bibl. 63-21759 price unreported
I. Cranbrook Foundation, Bloomfield Hills, Mich. II. Title.

*WESTERN architect (The) 720.973
The work of Purcell and Elmslie. architects. New introd. by David Gebhard. [Park Forest, Ill., 60466, The Prairie Sch. Pr., 117 Fir St., 1966, c.1965] 96p. illus., plans. 32cm. A reissue from Prairie Sch. Pr. Includes all of the text and plates orig. contained in the pages of the Jan. issues of Western Architect for 1913 & 1915, and July, 1915. 6.50; 4.00 pap.,
1. Architecture, American. I. Title.

Architecture, American — Exhibitions.

NEW York. Museum of Modern 720.69
Art.
Modern architecture U.S.a. Presented by the Museum of Modern Art and the Graham Foundation for Advanced Studies in the Fine Arts. [New York, 1965] [39] p. (incl. cover) illus., plans. 21 cm. Cover title. "Exhibition reviews sixty-five years of modern architecture in the United States." [NA712.N48] 65-26065
1. Architecture, American — Exhibitions. 2. Architecture, Modern — 20th cent. — Exhibitions. I. Graham Foundation for Advanced Studies in the Fine Arts. II. Title.

Architecture—Amherst, Mass.—Guide-books.

NORTON, Paul F. 917.44'23
Amherst : a guide to its architecture / by Paul F. Norton. [Amherst, Mass.] : Amherst Historical Society, 1975. 175, [3] p. : ill. ; 22 cm. Bibliography: p. [177]-[178] [NA735.A52N67] 75-18147
1. Architecture—Amherst, Mass.—Guide-books. I. Title.

Architecture, Ancient.

BADAWY, Alexander. 722.5
Architecture in ancient Egypt and the Near East. Cambridge, M.I.T. Press [1966] x, 246 p. illus., maps, plans. 27 cm. Bibliographical footnotes. [NA215.B285] 66-22351
1. Architecture, Ancient. 2. Architecture, Egyptian. 3. Architecture—Near East. I. Title. BIP

CICHY, Bodo, 1924- 722
Architecture of the ancient civilizations in color; Mesopotamia, Egypt, the Indus Valley, the Megaliths, the Hittites, the Minoans, the Mycenaeans, the Etruscans, Central and South America. [Translated from the German by A. K. Bakker] New York, Viking Press [1966] 424 p. 108 col. plates. 29 cm. (A Studio book) [NA210.C513 1966a] 66-22245

1. Architecture, Ancient. I. Title.

DONALDSON, Thomas Leverton, 1795-1885. 722
Architectura numismatica; ancient architecture on Greek and Roman coins and medals. Chicago, Argonaut Publishers, 1966. A-M, xxxi, 361 p. illus., plans. 24 cm. (Argonaut library of antiquities) Includes bibliographies. [NA260.D7 1966] 65-15464
1. Architecture, Ancient. 2. Medals. I. Title. II. Title: Ancient architecture on Greek and Roman coins and medals.

Architecture, Ancient—Addresses, essays, lectures.

ANCIENT art : 709 s
pre-Greek and Greek architecture. New York : Garland Pub., 1976. 304 p. : ill. ; 29 cm. (The Garland library of the history of art ; v. 1) Includes bibliographical references. [N5300.G32 vol. 1] [NA210] 722'.8 76-14062 ISBN 0-8240-2411-7 lib.bdg. : 35.00
1. Architecture, Ancient—Addresses, essays, lectures. 2. Architecture, Greek—Addresses, essays, lectures. I. Series.

Architecture, Ancient—Near East.

LLOYD, Seton. 722
Ancient architecture: Mesopotamia, Egypt, Crete, Greece [by] Seton Lloyd, Hans Wolfgang Muller [and] Roland Martin. New York, H. N. Abrams [1974] 415 p. illus. 29 cm. (History of world architecture) Bibliography: p. 397-399. [NA210.L58] 73-2843 ISBN 0-8109-1020-9
1. Architecture, Ancient—Near East. 2. Architecture—Near East. 3. Architecture, Greek. I. Martin, Roland. II. Muller, Hans Wolfgang. III. Title.

Architecture and climate.

ARONIN, Jeffrey Ellis, 1927- 729
Climate & architecture. New York, Reinhold [1953] x, 304 p. illus., charts, plans. 30 cm. (Progressive architecture book) Bibliography: p. 282-296. [NA2540.A65] 53-9171
1. Architecture and climate.

ARONIN, Jeffrey Ellis, 1927- 729
Climate & architecture / Jeffrey Ellis Aronin. New York : AMS Press, [1979] c1953. p. cm. Reprint of the ed. published by Reinhold Pub. Corp., New York, in series: Progressive architecture book. Includes index. Bibliography: p. [NA2541.A76 1979] 77-10218 ISBN 0-404-16200-2 : 28.50
1. Architecture and climate. I. Title. **BIP**

ASSOCIATION for Applied Solar Energy. 728.6
Living with the sun. Phoenix, Ariz., 1958- v. illus., map, diagrs., plans. 37cm. Contents.v. 1. Sixty plans selected from the entries in the 1957 international architectural competition to design a solar-heated residence. Bibliography: v.1, p.xii. [NA2540.A68] 57-14476
1. Architecture and climate. 2. Solar houses. I. rchitecture, Domestic—Designs and plans. II. Title.

GIVONI, B. 720
Man, climate, and architecture, by B. Givoni. Amsterdam, New York, Elsevier, 1969. xiii, 364 p. illus. 22 cm. (Elsevier architectural science series) Bibliography: p. 344-354. [NA2541.G58] 69-15822 ISBN 0-444-20039-8
1. Architecture and climate. I. Title. **BIP**

LICKLIDER, Heath. 720
Appearance of climate and place / Heath Licklider. Princeton, N.J. : Research Center for Urban and Environmental Planning, School of Architecture and Urban Planning, Princeton University, 1975. 29 leaves : ill. ; 28 cm. (Working paper - Research Center for Urban and Environmental Planning, Princeton University ; 12) Includes bibliographic references. [NA2541.L52] 76-355630
1. Architecture and climate. I. Title. II. Series: Princeton University. Research Center for Urban and Environmental Planning. Working paper — Research Center for Urban and Environmental Planning, Princeton University ; 12.

NATIONAL Research Council. 624.177
Housing and building in hot-humid and hot-dry climates. [Conference] Nov. 18 and 19, 1952, conducted by the Building Research Advisory Board. Washington, 1953. iv, 177p. illus., maps, diagrs. 28cm. (Its Research conference report no.5) uilding Research Advisory Board. [NA2540.N3 1952] 55-61079
1. Architecture and climate. 2. Architecture, Domestic. I. Title. II. Series.

NATIONAL Research Council. Building Research Institute. Conferences. Washington, D.C., Spring, 1962. 729
Solar effects on building design; report of a program held as part of the BRI 1962 Spring Conferences. [Washington, D.C.] Bldg. Res. Inst. [c.1963] iii, 174p. illus., diagrs. 23cm. (Bldg. Res. Inst. Pubn. no. 1007) Bibl. 63-62130 10.00 pap.,
1. Architecture and climate. 2. Windows. I. Title. II. Series.

NATIONAL Research Council. Building Research Institute. Conferences. Washington, DC., Spring, 1962. 729
Solar effects on building design; report of a program held as part of the BRI 1962 Spring Conferences. [Washington] Building Research Institute [1963] iii, 174 p. illus., diagrs. 23 cm. (Building Research Institute. Publication no. 1007) Includes bibliographies. [NA2540.N37] 63-62130
1. Architecture and claimte. 2. Windows. I. Title. II. Series.

OLGYAY, Aladar, 1910- 729
Solar control & shading devices [by] Olgyay & Olgyay. Princeton, Princeton University Press, 1957. 201p. illus., charts, diagrs., plans, tables. 23 x 29cm. Bibliography: p. 200. [NA2540.O4] 57-5455
1. Architecture and climate. I. Olgyay, Victor, 1910- joint author. II. Title. **BIP**

OLGYAY, Citor, 1910- 729
Design with climate: bioclimatic approach to architectural regionalism. Some chapters based on cooperative research with Aladar Olgyay. Princeton, N.J., Princeton University Press, 1963. v, 190 p. illus. 28 x 28 cm. "Bibliography and references": p. 186-188. [NA2540.O44] 61-7423
1. Architecture and climate. I. Olgyay, Aladar, 1910- II. Title. **BIP**

UNITED Nations. Dept. of Economic and Social Affairs. 300'.8 s
Climate and house design. New York, United Nations, 1971. vii, 93 p. illus. 28 cm. (Design of low-cost housing and community facilities, v. 1) ([United Nations. Document] ST/SOA/93) "United Nations publication. Sales number: E.69.IV.11." Part 1, prepared by the Center for Housing, Building, and Planning of the United Nations Dept. of Economic and Social Affairs: p. 3-8. Part 2, prepared by O. Koenigsberger, C. Mahoney, and M. Evans: p. 11-93. Plastic shadow-angle protractor in pocket. Bibliography: p. 85. [JX1977.A2 St/SOA/93] 728.1 72-187187 2.50
1. Architecture and climate. 2. Architecture, Domestic. I. Koenigsberger, Otto H. II. Mahoney, Carl. III. Evans, Martin. IV. United Nations. Centre for Housing, Building, and Planning. V. Title. VI. Series.

Architecture and energy conservation.

CAUDILL, William Wayne. 729
A bucket of oil; the humanistic approach to building design for energy conservation [by] William Wayne Caudill, Frank D. Lawyer [and] Thomas A. Bullock. [Boston] Cahners Books [1974] 87 p. illus. 23 cm. [NA2542.3.C38] 74-789 ISBN 0-8436-0126-4 10.95
1. Architecture and energy conservation. I. Lawyer, Frank D., joint author. II. Bullock, Thomas A., joint author. III. Title. **BIP**

DAVIS, Albert J. 721
Alternative natural energy sources in building design / Davis & Schubert. [Blacksburg, Va. : Davis, 1974] 252 p. : ill. ; 22 x 29 cm. Cover title: Energy in building design. Includes bibliographies and index. [NA2542.3.D38] 74-196849
1. Architecture and energy conservation. I. Schubert, Robert P., joint author. II. Title. III. Title: Energy in building design. **BIP**

DAVIS, Albert J. 721
Alternative natural energy sources in building design / Davis & Schubert. New York : Van Nostrand Reinhold, [1977], c1974. 252 p. : ill. ; 22 x 28 cm. Cover title: Alternate natural energy sources in building design. Includes bibliographical references and index. [NA2542.3.D38 1977] 76-54002 ISBN 0-442-22008-1 pbk. : 6.95
1. Architecture and energy conservation. I. Schubert, Robert P., joint author. II. Title.

GRIFFIN, Charles William, 1925- 729
Energy conservation in buildings : techniques for economical design / by C. W. Griffin, Jr. Washington : Construction Specifications Institute, [1974] 183 p. : ill. ; 24 cm. Includes index. Bibliography: p. 171-175. [NA2542.3.G74] 74-18630
1. Architecture and energy conservation. I. Title.

STEIN, Richard G. 721
Architecture and energy / Richard G. Stein. 1st ed. Garden City, N.Y. : Anchor Press, 1977. x, 322 p. : ill. ; 27 cm. Includes bibliographical references and index. [NA2542.3.S73] 76-42401 ISBN 0-385-04250-7 : 12.50
1. Architecture and energy conservation. I. Title. **BIP**

Architecture and energy conservation—Bibliography.

LEE, Kaiman. 016.721
Bibliography of energy conservation in architecture : keyword searched / by Kaiman Lee. Boston : Environmental Design and Research Center, c1977. 428 columns ; 29 cm. [Z5943.E5L4] [NA2542.3] 77-362422 ISBN 0-915250-19-5 : 50.00
1. Architecture and energy conservation—Bibliography. I. Title. **BIP**

POLLOCK, Peter Lewis. 016.3092 s
Strategies for the implementation of energy conservation in architecture : a bibliographic guide / Peter Lewis Pollock. Monticello, Ill. : Council of Planning Librarians, 1976. 18 p. ; 29 cm. (Exchange bibliography - Council of Planning Librarians ; 1182) Cover title. [Z5942.C68 no. 1182] [Z5943.E5] [NA2542.3] 016.721 77-355432 pbk. : 2.00
1. Architecture and energy conservation—Bibliography. I. Title. II. Series: Council of Planning Librarians. Exchange bibliography ; 1182.

Architecture and energy conservation—United States.

BUILDING Systems Information Clearinghouse. 690.7'08 s
Energy conservation and the building shell. Menlo Park, Calif. : Building Systems Information Clearinghouse, Educational Facilities Laboratories, 1974. 22, [6] p. : ill. ; 28 cm. (Its BSIC/EFL energy workbook ; section 1) Bibliography: p. [26] [LB3218.A1B8 1974 vol. 1] [NA2542.3] 690.7'0973 74-84131
1. Architecture and energy conservation—United States. 2. School buildings—United States. I. Title.

Architecture and handicapped children—Bibliography.

BARTHOLOMEW, Robert. 016.3092'08 s
Indoor and outdoor space for mentally and physically handicapped children. [Monticello, Ill., Council of Planning Librarians] 1973. 9 p. 29 cm. (Council of Planning Librarians. Exchange bibliography 503) Cover title. [Z5942.C68 no. 503] [Z5943.H3] 016.725'54 75-309069 1.50
1. Architecture and handicapped children—Bibliography. I. Title. II. Series.

Architecture and history.

ABRAMOVITZ, Anita. 701
People and spaces : a view of history through architecture / Anita Abramovitz ; illustrated by Susannah Kelly. New York : Viking Press, [1979] p. cm. [NA2543.H55A27] 78-24555 ISBN 0-670-54705-0 : 14.95
1. Architecture and history. 2. Architecture and society. I. Kelly, Susannah. II. Title. **BIP**

GLOAG, John, 1896- 720'.9
The architectural interpretation of history / John. Gloag. New York : St. Martin's Press, [1977] p. cm. Includes bibliographical references and index. [NA2543.H55G56 1977] 77-74665 ISBN 0-312-04812-2 : 18.95
1. Architecture and history. I. Title. **BIP**

Architecture and mentally handicapped children—Denmark.

BEDNAR, Michael J. 725'.53
Architecture for the handicapped in Denmark, Sweden, and Holland : a guidebook to normalization / Michael J. Bednar. [Ann Arbor : University of Michigan, 1974] 68 p. : illus. ; 28 cm. Includes bibliographical references. [NA2545.M4B42] 74-186473
1. Architecture and mentally handicapped children—Denmark. 2. Architecture and mentally handicapped children—Sweden. 3. Architecture and mentally handicapped children—Netherlands. I. Title.

Architecture and religion—Congresses.

INTERNATIONAL Congress on Religion, Architecture, and the Arts, 3d, Jerusalem, 1973. 291.3'5
Sacred space, meaning and form : the Third International Congress on Religion, Architecture, and the Arts / Moshe Davidowitz, general chairman ; edited by David James Randolph. New York : United Church Board for Homeland Ministries, c1976. iii, 131 p. : ill. ; 23 cm. [NA4595.I57 1973] 76-21385
1. Architecture and religion—Congresses. 2. Space (Architecture)—Congresses. 3. Symbolism in architecture—Congresses. 4. Arts and religion—Congresses. I. Davidowitz, Moshe. II. Randolph, David James, 1934- III. United Church Board for Homeland Ministries. IV. Title.

INTERNATIONAL Congress on Religion, Architecture, and the Visual Arts, 1st, New York and Montreal, 1967. 726'.0631
Revolution, place, and symbol; journal. [Edited by Rolfe Lanier Hunt. New York, 1969] xiv, 318 p. 24 cm. Bibliographical footnotes. [NA21.I615 1967] 70-80740
1. Architecture and religion—Congresses. 2. Church architecture—Philosophy. I. Hunt, Rolfe Lanier, 1903- ed. II. Title.

Architecture and society.

ALLSOPP, Bruce 724.9
Towards a humane architecture [London] Fredrick Muller [1974] vii, 111 p. ill. 22 cm. Includes index [NA2543] 74-162002 ISBN 0-584-10301-8
1. Architecture and society. 2. Architects and community. I. Title.
Distributed by Transatlantic Arts Inc. for 7.50 **BIP**

BAUM, Andrew. 729
Architecture and social behavior : psychological studies of social density / Andrew Baum, Stuart Valins. Hillsdale, N.J. : L. Erlbaum Associates ; New York : distributed by the Halsted Press Division of Wiley, 1977. ix, 112 p. : ill. ; 24 cm. (Complex human behavior) Includes index. Bibliography: p. 107-110. [NA2543.S6B35] 77-11133 ISBN 0-470-99300-6 : 10.95
1. Architecture and society. 2. Architecture—Environmental aspects. I. Valins, Stuart, joint author. II. Title. **BIP**

BURCHARD, John Ely, 1898- 720'.1'9
Bernini is dead? : Architecture and the social purpose / John Burchard. New York : McGraw-Hill, [1975] p. cm. Includes index. Bibliography: p. [NA2543.S6B78] 74-31263 ISBN 0-07-008922-1 : 25.00

1. Architecture and society. 2. Architecture—Psychological aspects. I. Title. BIP

BURNS, Jim, 1926- 724.9
Arthropods: new design futures. New York, Praeger [1972] 167 p. illus. 31 cm. Includes bibliographical references. [NA2543.S6B813] 79-166513 12.50
1. Architecture and society. 2. Architects and community. I. Title.

CONWAY, Donald, 1931- 720
Social science and design : a process model for architect and social scientist collaboration and report of a conference, October 1973, Coolfont Conference Center, Berkeley Springs, West Virginia / edited by Donald Conway. Washington : American Institute of Architects, [1973?] vi, 66, 20 p. : diagrs. ; 29 cm. (Research report - American Institute of Architects) [NA2543.S6C66] 75-324568
1. Architecture and society. 2. Human engineering. I. Title. II. Series: American Institute of Architects. Research report — American Institute of Architects.

DEASY, C. M. 720'.1'9
Design for human affairs [by] C. M. Deasy. [Cambridge, Mass., Schenkman Pub. Co.; distributed by Halsted Press, New York, 1974] 183 p. illus. 26 cm. "A Schenkman publication." Bibliography: p. 180-183. [NA2543.S6D38] 74-5198 ISBN 0-470-20454-0 15.00
1. Architecture and society. 2. Architecture—Psychological aspects. I. Title. BIP

FEIN, Albert. 712'.092'4
Frederick Law Olmsted and the American environmental tradition. New York, G. Braziller [1972] xi, 180 p. illus. 26 cm. (Planning and cities) "Selected list of the writings of Frederick Law Olmsted": p. 171-176. [NA737.O4F4 1972] 72-75831 ISBN 0-8076-0650-2 10.00 3.95 (pbk)
1. Olmsted, Frederick Law, 1822-1903. 2. Architecture and society. 3. Urban beautification. I. Title.

POOLE, Gray. 720'.92'2
Architects and man's skyline, by Gray Johnson Poole. New York, Dodd, Mead [1972] ix, 176 p. illus. 21 cm. (Makers of our modern world books) [NA2543.S6P66] 72-1532 ISBN 0-396-06435-3 5.95
1. Architecture and society. 2. Architecture—Psychological aspects. I. Title. BIP

QUANTRILL, Malcolm, 1931- 720
Ritual and response in architecture / [by] Malcolm Quantrill. London : Lund Humphries, 1974. 151 p. : ill., plans ; 21 cm. Includes bibliographical references and index. [NA2543.S6Q36] 75-309665 ISBN 0-85331-287-7 : 15.00
1. Architecture and society. 2. Architecture—Psychological aspects. I. Title.
Distributed by International Publications Service. BIP

RASKIN, Eugene. 720
Architecture and people. Englewood Cliffs, N.J., Prentice-Hall [1974] xiii, 191 p. illus. 24 cm. (Prentice-Hall international series in architecture) Includes bibliographical references. [NA2543.S6R37] 73-9832 ISBN 0-13-044594-0 8.95
1. Architecture and society. I. Title. BIP

SOMMER, Robert. 301.15'43'729
Design awareness. San Francisco, Rinehart Press [1971, c1972] ix, 142 p. illus. 24 cm. Includes bibliographical references. [NA2543.S6S64] 77-179628 ISBN 0-03-080298-9
1. Architecture and society. 2. Man—Influence of environment. I. Title. BIP

SPYER, Geoffrey. 711'.4
Architect and community: environmental design in an urban society. London, Owen, 1971. 3-168, [12] p. illus., maps, ports. 22 cm. (Contemporary issues series, 4) Bibliography: p. 159-160. [NA2543.S6S643 1971] 72-188544 ISBN 0-7206-0290-4
1. Architecture and society. 2. Cities and towns—Planning. I. Title.
Distributed by Humanities 11.00 BIP

STEVENS, Mary Otis. 711'.13
World of variation, by Mary Otis Stevens and Thomas F. McNulty. New York, G. Braziller [1970] xviii, 158 p. illus. 22 cm. (The i Press series on the human environment) "An i Press book." Bibliography: p. 148-157. [NA2543.S6S68] 79-129359 ISBN 0-8076-0574-3 6.95
1. Architecture and society. I. McNulty, Thomas F., 1919- joint author. II. Title. BIP

TAFURI, Manfredo. 720
Architecture and utopia : design and capitalist development / Manfredo Tafuri ; translated from the Italian by Barbara Luigi La Penta. Cambridge, Mass. : MIT Press, c1976. xi, 184 p. : ill. ; 19 cm. Translation of Progetto e utopia. Includes bibliographical references. [NA2543.S6T3313] 75-33128 ISBN 0-262-20033-3 : 9.95
1. Architecture and society. 2. Cities and towns—Planning. 3. Form (Aesthetics) I. Title. BIP

WILSON, Forrest, 1918- 720'.1
The joy of building : restoring the connection between architect and builder / Forrest Wilson. New York : Van Nostrand Reinhold, [1979] p. cm. Includes index. Bibliography: p. [NA2543.S6W54] 78-31710 ISBN 0-442-29521-9 : 14.95
1. Architecture and society. 2. Technology—Social aspects. I. Title. BIP

Architecture and society—Addresses, essays, lectures.

GUTMAN, Robert, comp. 729'.01
People and buildings. New York, Basic Books [1972] xix, 471 p. illus. 24 cm. Bibliography: p. 435-461. [NA2543.S6G8] 75-174827 ISBN 0-465-05456-0 12.50
1. Architecture and society—Addresses, essays, lectures. 2. Architecture—Psychological aspects—Addresses, essays, lectures. I. Title. BIP

ZUCKER, Paul, 1889- ed. 711'.4
New architecture and city planning; a symposium. Freeport, N.Y., Books for Libraries Press [1971, c1944] xv, 694 p. illus. 23 cm. (Essay index reprint series) Includes bibliographical references. [NA25.Z8 1971] 76-128337 ISBN 0-8369-2035-X
1. Architecture and society—Addresses, essays, lectures. 2. Cities and towns—Planning—Addresses, essays, lectures. I. Title. BIP

Architecture and society—Bibliography.

KLEEMAN, Walter. 016.3092'08 s
Interior ergonomics—significant dimensions in interior design and planning: a selected bibliography [by] Walter Kleeman, Jr. [Monticello, Ill., Council of Planning Librarians] 1972. 43 p. 29 cm. (Council of Planning Librarians. Exchange bibliography, 286) Cover title. [Z5942.C68 no. 286] [Z5941] 016.72 74-157566 4.50
1. Architecture and society—Bibliography. 2. Design—Bibliography. 3. Human engineering—Bibliography. I. Title. II. Series.

Architecture and society—San Francisco Bay region.

FREUDENHEIM, Leslie Mandelson, 1941- 720.97946
Building with nature; roots of the San Francisco Bay region tradition [by] Leslie Mandelson Freudenheim & Elizabeth Sussman, with photographs by Ambur Hiken. Santa Barbara, Peregrine Smith, 1974. xii, 112 p. illus. 27 cm. Includes bibliographical references. [NA735.S35F73] 74-19328 ISBN 0-87905-021-7. 12.95.
1. Architecture and society—San Francisco Bay region. I. Sussman, Elisabeth Sacks, 1939-, joint author. II. Title.
Publisher's address: P.O. Box 11606 Salt Lake City, Utah 84111

Architecture and society—United States.

FITCH, James Marston. 720'.973
American building : the environmental forces that shape it / James Marston Fitch. New York : Schocken Books, [1975] p. cm. Reprint of v. 2 of the 2 vol. ed. published by Houghton Mifflin, Boston, 1966-1972, under title: American building. Companion vol. to American building: the historical forces that shaped it. [NA2543.S6F54] 75-10857 ISBN 0-8052-0503-9 pbk. : 5.95
1. Architecture and society—United States. I. Title.

Architecture and solar radiation.

BRADLEY, Quinton M. 729
Solar primer one : solar energy in architecture : a guide for the designer / by Quinton M. Bradley and James F. Carlson. 2d ed. Whittier, Calif. : SOLARC, c1975. v, 101 leaves : ill. ; 22 x 30 cm. Bibliography: leaves 90-94. [NA2542.S6B72 1975] 76-353872
1. Architecture and solar radiation. 2. Architecture and energy conservation. I. Carlson, James F., joint author. II. Title. BIP

DANZ, Ernst. 729'.2
Sun protection; an international architecturalsurvey. [Translation into English by E. Rockwell] New York, F. A. Praeger [1967] 149 p. illus., plans. 26 cm. English, German and Spanish. Originally published under title: Sonnenschutz. [NA2542.S6D3] 67-27948
1. Architecture and solar radiation. 2. Architecture—Designs and plans. I. Title.

Architecture and the aged.

KONCELIK, Joseph A. 016.3092'08 s
Considerate design and the aging: review article with a selected and annotated bibliography [by] Joseph A. Koncelik. [Monticello, Ill., Council of Planning Librarians] 1972. 12 p. 29 cm. (Council of Planning Librarians. Exchange bibliography 253) Cover title. [Z5942.C68 no. 253] [NA2545.A3] 725'.56 73-150709 1.50
1. Architecture and the aged. 2. Architecture and the aged—Bibliography. I. Title. II. Series.

Architecture and the aged—Bibliography.

HARRIS, Howard. 016.725'56
An annotated bibliography on the architectural design implications of residential homes for old people / prepared by Howard Harris and Anne Griffiths .... Cardiff : Welsh School of Architecture, Research and Development, UWIST, [1976] [1], 63 p. ; 30 cm. [Z5943.A4H37] [NA2545.A3] 77-364641 £1.00
1. Architecture and the aged—Bibliography. I. Griffiths, Anne, joint author. II. Title. BIP

Architecture and the aged—U.S.

WEISS, Joseph Douglas, 1895- 725'.56'0973
Better buildings for the aged. New York, Hopkinson and Blake [1969] 286 p. illus., plans. 31 cm. Bibliography: p. 282-285. [NA2545.A3W4] 76-87854
1. Architecture and the aged—U.S. I. Title. BIP

Architecture and the handicapped—Addresses, essays, lectures.

BARRIER-FREE environments / 720
edited by Michael J. Bednar. Stroudsburg, Pa. : Dowden, Hutchinson & Ross, c1977. xiv, 278 p. : ill. ; 24 cm. (Community development series ; 33) Includes bibliographical references and index. [NA2545.A1B36] 76-54798 ISBN 0-87933-277-8 : 22.00
1. Architecture and the handicapped—Addresses, essays, lectures. I. Bednar, Michael J. BIP

Architecture and the handicapped—Bibliography.

MOE, Christine. 016.3092
Planning for the removal of architectural barriers for the handicapped / Christine Moe. Monticello, Ill. : Council of Planning Librarians, 1977. 48 p. ; 28 cm. (Exchange bibliography - Council of Planning Librarians ; 1337) Cover title. [Z5942.C68 no. 1337] [Z5943.H3] [NA2545.A1] 720 77-375633 pbk. : 4.50
1. Architecture and the handicapped—Bibliography. I. Title. II. Series: Council of Planning Librarians. Exchange bibliography ; 1337.

Architecture and the handicapped—Ohio.

OHIO. Governor's Committee on Employment of the Handicapped. 720
Access for all : an illustrated handbook of barrier free design for Ohio / by the Ohio Governor's Committee on Employment of the Handicapped ; Elizabeth A. Aino, project director, and Schooley Cornelius Associates ; Robert D. Loversidge, Jr., editor. [Columbus] : The Committee, c1977. viii, 192 p. : ill. ; 28 cm. Includes index. Bibliography: p. 188-190. [NA2545.A1O37] 77-156152
1. Architecture and the handicapped—Ohio. I. Aino, Elizabeth A. II. Loversidge, Robert D. III. Schooley Cornelius Associates. IV. Title.

Architecture and the handicapped—United States.

SORENSON, Robert J. 720
Design for accessibility / Robert J. Sorenson. New York : McGraw-Hill, c1979. Includes index. Bibliography: p. [NA2545.A1S67] 78-11801 ISBN 0-07-059680-8 : 21.50
1. Architecture and the handicapped—United States. I. Title. BIP

Architecture and the physically handicapped.

CARY, Jane Randolph. 728
How to create interiors for the disabled : a guidebook for family and friends / by Jane Randolph Cary ; with a foreword by Howard A. Rusk and Sharon Wright ; ill. by Philip F. Farrell, Jr. 1st ed. New York : Pantheon Books, c1978. xvi, 127 p. : ill. ; 29 cm. Includes index. Includes bibliographical references and index. [NA2545.P5C37] 77-88781 ISBN 0-394-41376-8 : 15.00. ISBN 0-394-73595-1 pbk. : 5.95
1. Architecture and the physically handicapped. I. Title. BIP

GOLDSMITH, Selwyn. 720
Designing for the disabled. 2d ed., rev. and expanded. New York, McGraw-Hill [1968, c1967] 207 p. illus. 31 cm. "Sponsored by the RIBA." Bibliography: p. 193-202. [NA2545.P5G6 1968] 68-27354 15.00
1. Architecture and the physically handicapped. I. Royal Institute of British Architects, London. II. Title. BIP

GOLDSMITH, Selwyn. 720
Designing for the disabled / [by] Selwyn Goldsmith. 3rd ed., fully revised / diagrams by Louis Dezart. London : RIBA Publications, 1976. 525 p. : col. ill., col. plans ; 31 cm. Includes index. Bibliography: p. 481-509. [NA2545.P5G6 1976] 77-362487 ISBN 0-900630-50-7 : £20.00
1. Architecture and the physically handicapped. I. Title.

GUTMAN, Ernest M. 720
Wheelchair to independence; architectural barriers eliminated, by Ernest M. Gutman with Carolyn R. Gutman. With a foreword by Howard A. Rusk. Springfield, Ill., Thomas [1968] xviii, 136 p. illus. 24 cm. Bibliography: p. 129-130. [NA2545.P5G8] 68-13757
1. Architecture and the physically handicapped. I. Gutman, Carolyn R., joint author. II. Title.

HARKNESS, Sarah P., 1914- 720
Building without barriers for the disabled / by Sarah P. Harkness, James N. Groom, Jr. New York : Whitney Library of Design, 1976. p. cm. Includes index. Bibliography: p. [NA2545.P5H37] 76-20691 ISBN 0-8230-7082-4 : 10.95
1. Architecture and the physically handicapped. I. Groom, James N., 1941- joint author. II. Title. BIP

UNITED States. Congress. 725
House. Committee on Public Works. Subcommittee on Public Buildings and Grounds.
Building design for the physically handicapped. Comprehensive plan for the U.S. Capitol grounds. Hearings, Ninetieth Congress, second session, on H.R. 6589 and S. 222 ... [and] H.J. Res. 914 and S.J. Res. 74 ... March 19, 1968. Washington, U.S. Govt. Print. Off., 1968. v, 139 p. 24 cm. "90-25." [NA2545.P5U5] 68-61572
1. United States. Capitol. 2. Architecture and the physically handicapped. I. Title. II. Title: Comprehensive plan for the U.S. Capitol grounds.

U.S. National Commission on 725
Architectural Barriers to Rehabilitation of the Handicapped.
Message from the President of the United States; transmitting a report entitled "Design for all Americans." Washington, U.S. Govt. Print. Off., 1968. v, 28 p. 23 cm. (90th Congress, 2d session. House document no. 324) [NA2545.P5U56] 68-62333
1. Architecture and the physically handicapped. I. Title. II. Title: Design for all Americans. III. Series: U.S. 90th Congress, 2d session, 1968. House. Document no. 324

WHEELER, Virginia Hart. 747'.797
Planning kitchens for handicapped homemakers. [New York] Institute of Physical Medicine & Rehabilitation, New York University Medical Center [196-] 82 p. illus., plans. 29 cm. (Rehabilitation monograph 27) [NA2545.P5W45] 77-232869 2.00
1. Architecture and the physically handicapped. 2. Kitchens. I. New York University Medical Center. Institute of Physical Medicine and Rehabilitation. II. Title. III. Series.

Architecture and the physically handicapped—Bibliography.

BARTHOLOMEW, Robert. 016.3092 s
Planning considerations in designing facilities for the physically handicapped / by Robert Bartholomew. Monticello, Ill. : Council of Planning Librarians, 1976. 9 p. ; 29 cm. (Exchange bibliography ; 1046) Caption title. [Z5942.C68 no. 1046] [NA2545.P5] 016.72 76-376384 pbk. : 1.50
1. Architecture and the physically handicapped—Bibliography. I. Title. II. Series: Council of Planning Librarians. Exchange bibliography ; 1046.

CASTO, Marilyn Dee. 016.3092'08 s
Adaptive housing for the physically handicapped / Marilyn Dee Casto, Savannah S. Day. Monticello, Ill. : Council of Planning Librarians, 1975. 27 p. ; 29 cm. (Exchange bibliography - Council of Planning Librarians ; 933) Cover title. [Z5942.C68 no. 933] [Z5943.H3] 016.72 76-353421 2.50
1. Architecture and the physically handicapped—Bibliography. I. Day, Savannah S., 1927- joint author. II. Title. III. Series: Council of Planning Librarians. Exchange bibliography ; 933.

Architecture and the physically handicapped—Cheshire, Eng.

CHESHIRE, Eng. Dept. of 728.3
Architecture.
Made to measure : domestic extensions and adaptions for handicapped persons / Cheshire County Council, Department of Architecture. [Chester] : The Council, [197-] 44 p. : ill. ; 21 x 30 cm. Cover title. Bibliography: p. 44. [NA2545.P5C45 1970z] 75-318320
1. Architecture and the physically handicapped—Cheshire, Eng. 2. Architecture, Domestic—Cheshire, Eng. I. Title.

Architecture and the physically handicapped—Illinois.

ILLINOIS. Dept. of General 729
Services.
State of Illinois standard specifications for facilities for the handicapped, authorized and enforceable under H.B. 2416, Illinois 75th General Assembly. [Springfield, 1968?] 37 l. plans. 23 cm. Cover title. [NA2545.P5I4] 73-627727
1. Architecture and the physically handicapped—Illinois. 2. Building—Contracts and specifications—Illinois. I. Title. II. Title: Standard specifications for facilities for the handicapped.

Architecture and the physically handicapped—New Jersey.

NEW Jersey. Treasury Dept. 725
Division of Building and Construction.
Barrier-free design for providing facilities for the physically handicapped in public buildings / State of New Jersey, Department of the Treasury, Division of Building and Construction. Trenton, N.J. : The Division, 1976. 37, 4 p. ; 29 cm. [NA2545.P5N48 1976] 77-622266 2.00
1. Architecture and the physically handicapped—New Jersey. 2. New Jersey—Public buildings. I. Title.

Architecture and the physically handicapped—United States.

AMERICAN Society of Landscape 720
Architects Foundation.
Access to the environment : a series of reference documents on the design and development of site facilities to make them barrier free to the physically handicapped and disabled / prepared by the American Society of Landscape Architects Foundation. [Washington] : Dept. of Housing and Urban Development, Office of Policy Development and Research, 1977. 3 v. : ill. ; 26 cm. "Contract no. H-2002-R." "HUD-PDR-163-1." Contents.Contents.—v. 1. Introduction.—v. 2. Case studies of barrier free sites.—v. 3. Appendices. [NA2545.P5A45 1977] 77-603362
1. Architecture and the physically handicapped—United States. I. Title.

LIFCHEZ, Raymond, 1932- 643
Design for independent living : the environment and physically disabled people / by Raymond Lifchez and Barbara Strong Winslow. New York : Whitney Library of Design, 1979. p. cm. Includes index. Bibliography: p. [NA2545.P5L5] 78-21273 ISBN 0-8232-7140-5 : 25.00
1. Architecture and the physically handicapped—United States. I. Winslow, Barbara Strong, 1941- joint author. II. Title. **BIP**

Architecture and the physically handicapped—United States—Bibliography.

WILD, Lynn Charles. 016.3092 s
An annotated bibliography of current sources and guidelines on architectural accessibility for the physically handicapped / Lynn Charles Wild. Monticello, Ill. : Council of Planning Librarians, 1978. 12 p. ; 29 cm. (Exchange bibliography — Council of Planning Librarians ; 1489) Cover title. [Z5942.C68 no. 1489] [Z5943.H3] [NA2545.P5] 016.72 78-105205 1.50.
1. Architecture and the physically handicapped—United States—Bibliography. I. Title. II. Series: Council of Planning Librarians. Exchange bibliography ; 1489.

Architecture, Anglo-Saxon.

TAYLOR, Harold 726.50942
McCarter, 1907-
Anglo-Saxon architecture; 2v. by H. M. Taylor, Joan Taylor [New York] Cambridge [c.]1965. 2v. (734p.) illus., maps, plans, plates. 29cm. Bibl. [NA963.T3] 65-3244 35.00 set,
1. Architecture, Anglo-Saxon. I. Taylor, Joan (Sills) joint author. II. Title. **BIP**

TAYLOR, Harold 726.50942
McCarter, 1907-
Why should we study the Anglo-Saxons [by] H. M. Taylor. Cambridge, Cambridge U.P., 1966. 50 p. plan, diagrs. 18 1/2 cm. (B 66-9605) (Rede lecture[s]1966) [NA963.T36] 66-71857
1. Architecture, Anglo-Saxon. 2. Civilization, Anglo-Saxon—Study and teaching. I. Title. II. Series.

Architecture, Anonymous.

MOHOLY-NAGY, Dorothea 720'.9
Maria Pauline Alice Sibylle (Pietzsch)
Native group genius in anonymous architecture. New York, Horizon Press, 1957. 223p. illus. 27cm. [NA203.M6] 57-10081
1. Architecture, Anonymous. 2. Architecture—America. I. Title.

MOHOLY-NAGY, Dorothea 720'.9
Marie Pauline Alice Sibylle (Pietzsch)
Native genius in anonymous architecture in New York, Horizon Press, 1957. 223p. illus. 27cm. [NA203.M6] 57-10081
1. Architecture, Anonymous. 2. Architecture—America. I. Title.

VAN DINE, Alan. 720'.9
Unconventional builders / by Alan Van Dine ; design by Ron Villani ; Holly Harrington, picture editor. Chicago : J. G. Ferguson Pub. Co., c1977. 184 p. : ill. (some col.) ; 27 x 32 cm. [NA203.V36] 76-44587 ISBN 0-89434-001-8 : 19.95
1. Architecture, Anonymous. I. Title. **BIP**

Architecture, Anonymous—America.

MOHOLY-NAGY, Dorothea 720'.973
Maria Pauline Alice Sibylle Pietzsch.
Native genius in anonymous architecture in North America / Sibyl Moholy-Nagy. New York : Schocken Books, 1976, c1957. 190 p. : ill. ; 24 cm. Reprint of the ed. published by Horizon Press, New York. [NA203.M6 1976] 75-37290 ISBN 0-8052-0512-8 : 6.50
1. Architecture, Anonymous—America. 2. Architecture—America. I. Title.

Architecture—Argentine Republic.

BULLRICH, Francisco 720.982
Arquitectura argentine contemporanea; panorama de la arquitectura argentina 1950-63. Buenos Aires, Ediciones Nueva Vision [dist. New York, Wittenborn, 1964, c.1963] 164p. illus., plans, 23cm. (Colleccion Arquitectura contemporanea) 64-4947 7.00 pap.,
1. Architecture—Argentine Republic. I. Title.

Architecture as a profession.

GRAD, Bernard John, 1908- 720'.23
Adventure into architecture. New York, Arco Pub. Co. [1968] 189 p. illus. 32 cm. [NA1995.G7] 68-20406 ISBN 0-668-01763-5 12.50
1. Architecture as a profession. I. Title.

HUNT, William Dudley, ed. 720
Comprehensive architectural services: general principles and practice. New York, McGraw-Hill [1965] xiii, 241 p. illus., plans. 28 cm. Most of the material originally appeared in AIA journal. [NA1995.H8] 65-14701
1. Architecture as a profession. I. American Institute of Architects. II. Title. **BIP**

KAYE, Barrington 720.69
The development of the architectural profession in Britain; a sociological study. London, G. Allen & Unwin [dist. Hollywood-by-the-Sea, Fla., Transatlantic Arts 1960] 223p. (Bibl. p.179-200) tables. 23cm. 60-3404 6.25
1. Architecture as a profession. 2. Architects—Gt. Brit. 3. Architecture—Gt. Brit. I. Title.

LAPIDUS, Morris. 720'.23
Architecture: a profession and a business. New York, Reinhold Pub. Corp. [1967] xv, 207 p. illus. 27 cm. [NA1995.L3] 67-15831
1. Architecture as a profession. 2. Architecture—Handbooks, manuals, etc. I. Title.

MCLAUGHLIN, Robert 720.69
William, 1900-
Architect, creating man's environment. New York, Macmillan, 1962. 201p. illus. 22cm. (Macmillan career book) [NA1995.M3] 61-15183
1. Architecture as a profession. I. Title. **BIP**

MEINHARDT, Carl, 1907- 720'.23
So you want to be an architect [by] Carl and Carolynn Meinhardt and Alan E. Nourse. [1st ed.] New York, Harper & Row [1969] 201 p. 22 cm. Includes bibliographical references. [NA1995.M4] 68-15994 4.95
1. Architecture as a profession. I. Meinhardt, Carolynn, joint author. II. Nourse, Alan Edward, joint author. III. Title.

NEWCASTLE-UPON- 720'.71'14282
TYNE. University. School of Architecture.
The art and profession of architecture; a handbook produced at the School of Architecture, University of Newcastle upon Tyne. 4th ed. Newcastle upon Tyne, Oriel P. [1967] 19 p. 4 plates. 21 cm. Bibliography: p. 16. [NA1995.N4 1967] 68-101114 3/6
1. Architecture as a profession. I. Title.

PATTRICK, Michael 720.69
A career in architecture, by Michael Pattrick, Michael Tree. London, Museum Press [dist. New Rochelle, N.Y., SportShelf, 1964, c.1961] 127p. illus. 23cm. Bibl. 62-383 4.25
1. Architecture as a profession. I. Tree, Michael, 1926- joint author. II. Title.

PIPER, Robert J 720'.23
Opportunities in an architecture career, by Robert J. Piper. New York, Educational Books Division, Universal Pub. and Distributing Corp. [1966] 120 p. 20 cm. (VGM career series, V160) Includes bibliographies. [NA1995.P5] 66-28818
1. Architecture as a profession. I. Title.

PIPER, Robert J. 720'.23
Opportunities in architecture today / Robert Piper. Rev. ed. Louisville, Ky. : Vocational Guidance Manuals, [1975] 115 p. : ill. ; 20 cm. (VGM career series ; V202) Previous editions published in 1966 and 1970 under title: Opportunities in an architecture career. Includes index. Bibliography: p. [106]-110. [NA1995.P5 1975] 75-3794 ISBN 0-89022-202-9 lib.bdg. : 4.25 ISBN 0-89022-015-8 pbk. : 2.45
1. Architecture as a profession. I. Title. **BIP**

RESOURCE Publications, 720'.23
inc.
Index of opportunity in architecture & design. 1969 ed. Princeton, N.J. [1969] 32 p. 28 cm. (Career resource series) (A Resource publication.) Caption title. [NA1995.R4 1969] 71-78660
1. Architecture as a profession. 2. Design, Industrial—Vocational guidance. I. Title: Architecture and design.

RICHARDS, James Maude, 720'.23
Sir
Architecture [by] J. M. Richards. Newton Abbot, David & Charles [1974] 151 p. 23 cm. (The Professions) Bibliography: p. 141-143. [NA1995.R52] 74-169010 ISBN 0-7153-6422-7
1. Architecture as a profession. I. Title.
Distributed by David and Charles, Vermont, 9.95.

ROTH, Richard, 1904- 720.69
Your future in architecture. [1st ed.] New York, R. Rosen Press, 1960. 159 p. 20 cm. (Careers in depth, 2) Includes bibliography. [NA1995.R65] 60-11116
1. Architecture as a profession. I. Title. **BIP**

VREELAND, Frank, 1891- 720.69
1946.
Opportunities in architecture, by William Thorpe [pseud.] New York, Grosset & Dunlap [1951] 112 p. 20 cm. (Vocational manuals) [NA2540.V7] 52-292
1. Architecture as a profession. I. Title.

Architecture as a profession—Florida.

MITCHELL, Bruce. 331.1'1
A study of Florida's future needs for architects, 1973 / by Bruce Mitchell, Dennis Wittenberg. Tallahassee : Academic Affairs, Florida Board of Regents, State University System of Florida, 1974. 144 p. : 28 cm. Includes bibliographical references. [NA1995.M57] 74-623599
1. Architecture as a profession—Florida. I. Wittenberg, Dennis, joint author. II. Title.

Architecture as a profession—Juvenile literature.

BAKER, Eugene H. 720'.23
I want to be an architect, by Eugene Baker. Illus. by Felix Palm. Chicago, Childrens Press [1969] [32] p. col. illus. 25 cm. Two boys discover they want to be architects when Mr. Jones shows them how to plan a play house. [PZ10.B1472Ig] 70-79575
1. Architecture as a profession—Juvenile literature. I. Palm, Felix, illus. II. Title. III. Title: Architect.

SETZEKORN, William David, 1935- 720'.23
Architecture. Minneapolis, Dillon Press [1974] 90 p. illus. 24 cm. (Looking forward to a career) Bibliography: p. [87]-88. Discusses different careers in architecture and the training and educational requirements for each. [NA1995.S47] 74-4725 ISBN 0-87518-072-8
1. Architecture as a profession—Juvenile literature.

Architecture—Asia.

WHEELER, Robert Eric Mortimer, Sir 1890- ed. 720.95
Splendors of the East; temples, tombs, palaces and fortresses of Asia Photos. by Ian Graham. New York, Putnam [c.1965] 288p. illus. (pt. col.) 32cm. [NA1460.W5] 65-19762 25.00; 20.95 until Jan. 1.
1. Architecture—Asia. 2. Art, Asiatic. I. Graham, Ian, illus. II. Title.

Architecture—Athens.

PENROSE, Francis Cranmer, 1817-1903. 726'.1'20809385
An investigation of the principles of Athenian architecture; or, The results of a survey conducted chiefly with reference to the optical refinements exhibited in the construction of the ancient buildings at Athens. New and enl. ed. Washington, McGrath Pub. Co., 1973. xii, 128, [97] p. illus. 48 cm. Reprint of the 1888 ed. published by Macmillan, London. [NA280.P4 1973] 71-119273 ISBN 0-8434-0142-7 175.00
1. Architecture—Athens. 2. Architecture, Greek. I. Title.

STUART, James, 1713-1788. 722'.8
The antiqvities of Athens, measvred and delineated by James Stvart and Nicholas Revett. New York, B. Blom, 1968- v. illus., plans. 34 cm. Reprint of the 1762-1830 ed. [NA280.S913] 68-21230
1. Architecture—Athens. 2. Architecture—Greece. I. Revett, Nicholas, 1720-1804, joint author. II. Title.

TRAULOS, Ioannes N., 1908- 913.38'5
Pictorial dictionary of ancient Athens [by] John Travlos. [Prepared in collaboration with the] German Archaeological Institute. New York, Praeger [1971] xvi, 590 p. illus., maps, plans. 30 cm. Includes bibliographical references. [NA280.T68] 70-89608 70.00
1. Architecture—Athens. 2. Architecture, Greek—Athens. I. Deutsches Archaologisches Institut. II. Title.

Architecture—Athens, Ga.

MARSH, Kenneth Frederick 720.975818
Athens, Georgia's columned city. Photogs. by Kenneth Frederick Marsh. Commentary by Blanche Marsh. [Asheville, N. C., Biltmore Pr., 9 Valley St., c.]1964. 84p. illus., ports. 24cm. 64-3022 3.75
1. Architecture—Athens, Ga. 2. Athens, Ga.—Historic houses, etc. I. Marsh, Blanche. II. Title.

Architecture—Austin, Tex.

WILLIAMSON, Roxanne Kuter, 1928- 720'.9764'31
Austin, Texas; an American architectural history. San Antonio, Trinity University Press [1973] xxii, 161 p. illus. 23 x 29 cm. Includes bibliographical references. [NA735.A85W49] 72-86263 ISBN 0-911536-48-5 12.00
1. Architecture—Austin, Tex. 2. Austin, Tex.—Historic houses, etc.

Architecture—Austin, Tex.—History.

WILLIAMSON, Roxanne Kuter, 1928- 720'.9764'3
Victorian architecture in Austin. Austin, University of Texas, 1967. 249 l. illus., maps. 27 cm. Vita. Thesis (M.A.)—University of Texas. Bibliography: leaves 236-249. [NA735.A85W5] 67-8344
1. Architecture—Austin, Tex.—History. 2. Architecture—Details. I. Title.

Architecture—Australia.

BOYD, Robin, 1923- 720.994
The Australian ugliness. Foreword by John Betjeman. Rev. ed. [Melbourne] Penguin, in assn. with F. W. Cheshire [1968] 256p. illus. 19cm. (Australian Pelican, AU6) [NA1600.B6] 5.00 bds.,
1. Architecture—Australia. 2. National characteristics, Australian. I. Title.
Order from Verry, Mystic, Conn.

HEE, David. 720'.994
Architectural survey : interim report to June 1976. [Melbourne] : Urban Conservation Projects, University of Melbourne, [1976] 34 leaves ; 30 cm. (Urban conservation working papers ; no. 14) Caption title. Project staff: D. Hee, T. Sawyer and K. Lee. "National estate project 244." [NA1600.H43] 77-365399 ISBN 0-86904-025-1
1. Architecture—Australia. 2. Architects—Australia. I. Sawyer, Terry, joint author. II. Lee, Ken, joint author. III. Melbourne. University. IV. Title. V. Series.

Architecture—Australia—Conservation and restoration—Congresses.

URBAN conservation : 720'.28
proceedings of a seminar conducted at the University of Melbourne, 25th February, 1976 / edited by Miles Lewis, Alison Blake. Melbourne : Urban Conservation Projects, 1976. vi, 186 p. : ill. ; 30 cm. (Urban conservation working papers ; no. 9) "National estate project 130." Includes bibliographical references. [NA109.A8U7] 77-365400 ISBN 0-86904-019-7 : 7.00
1. Architecture—Australia—Conservation and restoration—Congresses. I. Lewis, Miles. II. Blake, Alison. III. Melbourne. University. IV. Title. V. Series.

Architecture—Australia—History.

FREELAND, John Maxwell, 1920- 720'.994
Architecture in Australia; a history [by] J. M. Freeland. Melbourne, Canberra [etc.] Cheshire [1968] 328 p. illus. 27 cm. [NA1600.F7] 68-16539 9.95
1. Architecture—Australia—History. I. Title. **BIP**

Architecture—Australia—Juvenile literature.

BOYD. ROBIN 720.994
The walls around us: the story of Australian architecture, told and illustrated for young readers. Melbourne. Children's Library Guild of Australia: [dist. by Australian Children's Lib. Distributors. 1962] 90p. col. illus. 25cm. [NA1600] 66-5335 2.95
1. Architecture—Australia—Juvenile literature. I. Title.
Available from Ginn in Boston.

Architecture—Australia—Sydney—Guide-books.

BAGLIN, Douglass. 994.4
Sandstone Sydney / [photographs by] Douglass Baglin & [text by] Yvonne Austin. Adelaide : Rigby, 1976. 191 p. : ill. ; 30 cm. [NA1603.S9B34] 77-363903 ISBN 0-7270-0153-1
1. Architecture—Australia—Sydney—Guide-books. 2. Architecture—Details. 3. Sydney—Description—Views. 4. Sandstone—Australia—Sydney. I. Austin, Yvonne. II. Title.

Architecture—Baltimore.

DORSEY, John R., 1938- 917.52'2'043
A guide to Baltimore architecture, by John R. Dorsey and James D. Dilts. Foreword by John Dos Passos. Introductions by Wilbur Harvey Hunter and Alexander S. Cochran. Cambridge, Md., Tidewater Publishers, in cooperation with the Peale Museum, 1973. L, 246 p. illus. 18 cm. [NA735.B3D67] 73-12576 ISBN 0-87033-187-6 4.95
1. Architecture—Baltimore. I. Dilts, James D., 1936- joint author. II. Baltimore. Municipal Museum. III. Title.

HOWLAND, Richard Hubbard. 720.9752
The architecture of Baltimore, a pictorial history. Text by Richard Hubbard Howland and Eleanor Patterson Spencer; edited by Wilbur Harvey Hunter, Jr. Introd. by Henry-Russell Hitchcock. [1st ed. Baltimore, Johns Hopkins Press, 1953. xx, 149p. illus., maps, plans. 29cm. 'Sponsored by the Peale Museum.' [NA735.B3H68] 53-7465
1. Architecture—Baltimore. I. Spencer, Eleanor Patterson, joint author. II. Title.

Architecture, Baroque.

BRIGGS, Martin Shaw, 1882- 724'.19
Baroque architecture. New York, Da Capo Press, 1967. 238 p. illus. 24 cm. (Da Capo Press series in architecture and decorative art, v. 2) (A Da Capo Press reprint edition.) Reprint of the 1913 ed. Bibliographical footnotes. [NA590.B7 1967] 67-23634
1. Architecture, Baroque. I. Title.

KAUFMANN. EMIL, 1891-1953 724.19
Architecture in the Age of Reason: baroque and postbaroque in England, Italy. and France. [Hamden. Conn.] Archon [dist. Shoe String] 1966 [c.1955] xxvi. 293p. illus. 25cm. Bibl. [NA590.K3 1966] 66-18643 12.50
1. Architecture, Baroque. I. Title.

KAUFMANN, Emil, 1891-1953. 724.199
Architecture in the age of reason; baroque and post-baroque in England, Italy, and France. Cambridge, Harvard University Press, 1955. xxvi, 293p. illus. 25cm. Bibliographical references included in 'Notes' (p. 219-279) [NA590.K3] 52-10753
1. Architecture, Baroque. I. Title. **BIP**

KAUFMANN, Emil, 1891-1953 720.9'4
Architecture in the age of reason; baroque and post-baroque in England, Italy, and France. New York, Dover [1968,c1955] xxvi, 293p. illus., plans. 24cm. An unabridged, unaltered repubn. of the work orig. pub. in 1955. Bibl. [NA590.K3 1968] 68-17252 3.50 pap.,
1. Architecture, Baroque. I. Title.

MILLON, Henry A. 724.19
Baroque & rococo architecture. New York, G. Braziller, 1961. 127 p. 100 illus. 26 cm. (The Great ages of world architecture) Bibliography: p. 113-122. [NA590.M5] 61-15492
1. Architecture, Baroque. 2. Architecture, Rococo. I. Title. II. Series. **BIP**

NORBERG-SCHULZ, Christian. 724'.19
Late Baroque and Rococo architecture. New York, H. N. Abrams [1974] 415 p. illus. 29 cm. (History of world architecture) Bibliography: p. 399-400. [NA590.N63] 73-980 ISBN 0-8109-1012-8
1. Architecture, Baroque. 2. Architecture, Rococo. I. Title. **BIP**

POWELL, Nicolas. 724.19
From baroque to rococo; an introducation to Austrian and German architecture from 1580 to 1790. New York, Praeger [1959] 184p. plates (part col.) maps, plans. 26cm. (Books that matter) Bibliography: p. 157-162. [NA1006.P6] 59-3561
1. Architecture, Baroque. 2. Architecture, Rococo. 3. Architecture—Austria—Hist. 4. Architecture—Germany—Hist. I. Title.

REYNOLDS, James, 1891- 724.1992
Baroque splendour. Paintings in sanguine by the author. New York, Creative Age Press [1950] 271 p. illus. 26 cm. Bibliography: p. 263-264. [NA590.R4 1950] 50-6635
1. Architecture, Baroque. 2. Art, Baroque. I. Title.

SITWELL, Sacheverell, Sir, bart., 1897- 724'.19
Spanish baroque art, with buildings in Portugal, Mexico, and other colonies. New York, B. Blom, 1971. 112 p. illus. 24 cm. Reprint of the 1931 ed. Bibliography: p. 109-112. [NA5806.S5 1971] 71-175874
1. Architecture, Baroque. 2. Church architecture—Spain. 3. Church architecture—Portugal. 4. Church architecture—Mexico. 5. Church architecture—Latin America. I. Title. **BIP**

Architecture, Baroque—England.

WHIFFEN, Marcus. 720'.92'4
Thomas Archer, architect of the English baroque. [New ed.] Los Angeles, Hennessey & Ingalls, 1973. 96 p. illus. 22 cm. (Architectural monographs, 1) First published in 1950 under title: Thomas Archer. Includes bibliographical references. [NA997.A82W45 1973] 72-93734 ISBN 0-912158-23-9 5.95
1. Archer, Thomas, 1668 or 9-1743. 2. Architecture, Baroque—England.

Architecture, Baroque—Europe.

BUSCH, Harald, 1904- ed. 724.19094
Baroque Europe. With an introd. by James Lees-Milne. Edited by Harald Busch and Bernd Lohse. With commentaries on the illus. by Eva-Maria Wagner. [Translated by Peter Gorge] New York, Macmillan, 1962 [c1961] xxiii p., 240 p. of illus. plans. 27 cm. (Buildings of Europe) Captions to the plates in German and English. Translation of Baukunst des Barock in Europa. [NA590.B813 1962] 62-51825
1. Architecture, Baroque—Europe. 2. Architecture—Europe. I. Lohse, Bernd, joint ed. II. Title.

Architecture, Baroque—History.

NORBERG-SCHULZ, Christian. 724'.19
Baroque architecture. New York, H. N. Abrams [1972, c1971] 407 p. illus. 29 cm. (History of world architecture) Bibliography: p. 392-393. [NA590.N6] 74-149851 ISBN 0-8109-1002-0 25.00
1. Architecture, Baroque—History. I. Title. **BIP**

Architecture, Baroque—Italy.

CHARPENTRAT, Pierre 720'.94
Living architecture: Baroque, Italy and central Europe. Photos. by Peter Heman. Pref. by Hans Scharoun. Ehg. tr.: Carol Brown New York, Grosset [1967] 192p. illus., maps, plans (pt. fold.) 21cm. (Living architecture) Cover title: Baroque architecture. Tr. of Baroque; Italie et Europe centrale. Bibl. [NA1116.C513 1967b] 67-20408 7.95
1. Architecture, Baroque—Italy. 2. Architecture, Baroque—Central Europe. 3. Architecture —Italy. 4. Architecture—Central Europe. I. Heman, Peter, illus. II. Title.

WITTKOWER, Rudolf. 720'.945
Studies in the Italian Baroque / Rudolf Wittkower. Boulder, Colo. : Westview Press, 1975. p. cm. (The Collected essays of Rudolf Whittkower) Includes bibliographical references and index. [NA1116.5.B3W57] 75-22083 ISBN 0-89158-506-0 : 32.75
1. Architecture, Baroque—Italy. 2. Architecture—Italy. I. Title.

Architecture, Baroque—Sicily.

BLUNT, Anthony, Sir, 1907- 720'.9458
Sicilian baroque. With photos. by Tim Benton. [1st American ed.] New York, Macmillan [1968] 160 p. illus., map, plans.

State University Press [1971] xviii, 194, [60] p. illus. 27 cm. A revision of the author's thesis, New York University. Bibliography: p. [181]-187. [NA5870.I7M3] 78-111972 ISBN 0-271-00108-9 19.50
1. Architecture, Byzantine—Istanbul. 2. Church architecture—Istanbul. 3. Liturgy and architecture. I. Title.

Architecture—California.

BANGS, Edward Geoffrey, 1889- 720.9794
Portals West; a folio of late nineteenth century architecture in California. Pref. by Robert Gordon Sproul. [San Francisco] California Historical Society [1960] 86p. 36 illus. 32cm. (California Historical Society. Special publication no. 35) [NA730.C2B3] 60-53593
1. Architecture -California. I. Title. II. Series.

GEBHARD, David. 720'.9794
Architecture in California, 1868-1968; an exhibition organized by David Gabhard and Harriette Von Breton [Santa Barbara, Calif., Printed by Standard Printing of Santa Barbara, 1968] 107 p. illus. 26 cm. Held Apr. 16-May 12, 1968, at the Art Gallery, University of California, Santa Barbara, to celebrate the centennial of the University of California. Bibliography: p. 32-34. [NA730.C2G38] 68-63037
1. Architecture—California. 2. Architecture—Exhibitions. I. Von Breton, Harriette, joint author. II. California. University, Santa Barbara. Art Gallery. III. Title.

HONNOLD, Douglas. 720.9794
Southern California architecture, 1769-1956. New York, Reinhold Pub. Corp. [1956] 96p. illus. 22cm. On cover: A guide to the architecture of southern California, 1769-1956. [NA730.C2H6] 56-9615
1. Architecture—California. I. Title. II. Title: A guide to the architecture of southern California, 1760-1956.

KIRKER, Harold. 720'.9794
California's architectural frontier; style and tradition in the nineteenth century. New York, Russell & Russell [1970, c1960] xiv, 224 p. illus. 24 cm. Bibliography: p. 203-216. [NA730.C2K5 1970] 70-102512
1. Architecture—California. 2. Architecture, Modern—19th century—California. I. Title. BIP

KIRKER, Harold. 720'.9794
California's architectural frontier; style and tradition in the nineteenth century. Santa Barbara [Calif.] Peregrine Smith, 1973. xxii, 224 p. illus. 21 cm. Bibliography: p. 197-216. [NA730.C2K5 1973] 73-77786 ISBN 0-87905-011-X 4.95
1. Architecture—California. 2. Architecture, Modern—19th century—California. I. Title.

KIRKER, Harold. 720.9794
California's architectural frontier; style and tradition in the nineteenth century. San Marino, Calif., Huntington Library, 1960. xiv, 224p. illus. 24cm. (Huntington Library publications) 'Bibliographical notes': p. 197-202. Bibliographical footnotes. [NA730.C2K5] 60-11898
1. Architecture—California. I. Title. II. Series: Henry E. Huntington Library and Art Gallery, San Marino, Calif. Huntington Library publications

LONGSTRETH, Richard W. 720'.92'4
Julia Morgan, architect / Richard W. Longstreth. [Berkeley, Calif.] : Berkeley Architectural Heritage Association, 1977. 35 p. : ill. ; 19 x 22 cm. (Berkeley Architectural Heritage publication series ; no. 1) "Originally appeared in Perspecta 15: Yale papers on architecture under the title Julia Morgan: some introductory notes." [NA737.M68L66] 77-152920
1. Morgan, Julia, 1872-1957. 2. Architecture—California. I. Title. II. Series.

MCCOY, Esther. 720'.9794
Five California architects / Esther McCoy ; chapter on Greene and Greene By Randell L. Makinson. New York : Praeger Publishers, 1975, c1960. vii, 200 p. : ill. ; 27 cm. Originally published by Reinhold Book Corp., New York. Includes index. [NA730.C2M3 1975] 74-19818 ISBN 0-275-46690-6 : 17.50 ISBN 0-275-71720-8 pbk. : 9.95
1. Greene & Greene. 2. Architecture—California. 3. Architects—California. I. Title.

MAKINSON, Randell L., 1932- 728.3
Greene & Greene / Randell L. Makinson ; with new photos. by Marvin Rand ; and an introd. by Reyner Banham. Salt Lake City : Peregrine Smith, c1977- v. : ill. ; 24 cm. Includes index. Contents.Contents.—1. Architecture as a fine art. Bibliography: v. 1, p. 269-273. [NA737.G73M33] 76-57792 ISBN 0-87905-023-3 (v. 1) : 24.95
1. Greene & Greene. 2. Architecture—California. 3. Architecture, Modern—20th century—California. BIP

Architecture—California—Catalogs.

MAKINSON, Randell L., 1932- 720'.92'2
A guide to the work of Greene and Greene, by Randell L. Makinson. Salt Lake City, Peregrine Smith, 1974. 65 p. illus. 22 cm. [NA737.G73M34] 74-19386 ISBN 0-87905-015-2 4.95 (pbk.).
1. Greene & Greene. 2. Architecture—California—Catalogs. 3. Architecture, Modern—20th century—California. I. Title.

Architecture—California—Los Angeles—Guide-books.

GEBHARD, David. 917.94'9'045
A guide to architecture in Los Angeles & southern California / David Gebhard, Robert Winter ; Julius Shulman, photographic consultant ; designed by Marc Treib. Santa Barbara [Calif.] : Peregrine Smith, 1977. p. cm. Includes index. Bibliography: p. [NA735.L55G4] 77-7317 ISBN 0-87905-049-7 pbk. : 9.95
1. Architecture—California—Los Angeles—Guide-books. 2. Architecture—California—California, Southern—Guide-books. I. Winter, Robert, joint author. II. Title. BIP

Architecture—California, Southern.

HARRIS, Frank, 1922- ed. 724.91
A guide to contemporary architecture in southern California, edited by Frank Harris [and] Weston Bonenberger. Forword by Arthur B. Gallion, photos. by Julius Shulman, designed by Alvin Lustig. Los Angles, Watling, 1951. 91 p. illus., maps, plans. 23 cm. Bibliography: p. 90-91. [NA730.C2H35] 51-3582
1. Architecture—California, Southern. I. Bonenberger, Weston David, 1923- joint ed. II. Title. III. Title: Contemporary architecture in southern California.

SILLO, Terry. 720'.9794'9
Excerpts from southern California's architectural heritage / Terry Sillo. Pasadena, Calif. : Gallery Productions, c1976. 111 p. : ill. ; 25 cm. Includes index. Bibliography: p. 109. [NA730.C22S687] 76-151714
1. Architecture—California, Southern. 2. Architecture—Details. 3. California, Southern—History, Local. I. Title.

Architecture — California, Southern — Direct.

GEBHARD, David. 917.48'21'00222
A guide to architecture in southern California [by] David Gebhard [and] Robert Winter. [Los Angeles] Los Angeles County Museum of Art, 1965. 164 p. maps. 80 plates. 17 cm. Bibliography: p. 19-22. [NA730.C2G4] 67-5136
1. Architecture — California, Southern — Direct. I. Winter, Robert, joint author. II. Title. III. Title: Architecture in southern California.

Architecture—Cambridge, Mass.

CAMBRIDGE, Mass. Historical Commission. 720.973
Survey of architectural history in Cambridge. Cambridge [1965- v. illus., maps. 23 x 82 cm. Includes bibliographies. [NA735.C28A5] 65-6778
1. Architecture—Cambridge, Mass. 2. Cambridge, Mass.—Historic houses, etc. I. Title.
Contents omitted. BIP

RETTIG, Robert B. 917.44'4
Guide to Cambridge architecture; ten walking tours [by] Robert Bell Rettig. Cambridge, Mass., MIT Press [1969] 1 v. (various pagings) illus. 15 x 22 cm. [NA735.C28R47] 69-14407
1. Architecture—Cambridge, Mass. I. Title. BIP

Architecture—Cambridgeshire, Eng.

PEVSNER, Nikolaus, 1902- 720.942
Cambridgeshire. [Harmondsworth, Middlesex] Penguin Books [1954] 453p. illus., 72 plates, maps, plans. 19cm. (His The buildings of England, 10) [NA969.C35P4] 56-1345
1. Architecture—Cambridgeshire, Eng. I. Title.

Architecture—Canada—Conservation and restoration—Handbooks, manuals, etc.

FALKNER, Ann. 301.5'4
Without our past? : A handbook for the preservation of Canada's architectural heritage / Ann Falkner. Toronto ; Buffalo : University of Toronto Press, c1977. x, 242 p. : ill. ; 24 cm. Bibliography: p. [235]-242. [NA109.C2F34] 76-28544 ISBN 0-8020-2239-1 : 15.00. ISBN 0-8020-6298-9 pbk. : 5.00
1. Architecture—Canada—Conservation and restoration—Handbooks, manuals, etc. I. Title. BIP

Architecture— Canada—Hist.

GOWANS, Alan 720.971
Building Canada; an architectural history of Canadian life. [Rev. and enl. ed.] Toronto, Oxford Univ. Pr., 1966. xx, 412p. illus. 27cm. First ed. 1958, under title: Looking at architecture in Canada. Bibl. [NA740.G6 1966] 67-72595 15.95
1. Architecture— Canada—Hist. I. Title.
Available from the publisher's New York office.

Architecture—Canton, Ohio—Guide-books.

ALBACETE, M. J. 720'.9771'62
Architecture in Canton, 1805-1976 / by M. J. Albacete ; photography by Edward L. Hickson. 1st ed. [Canton, Ohio] : Canton Art Institute, 1976. xii, 91 p. : ill. ; 28 cm. "A joint project of the Canton Art Institute and the Junior League of Canton, inc." Errata slip inserted. [NA735.C315A42] 76-373989
1. Architecture—Canton, Ohio—Guide-books. I. Hickson, Edward L. II. Canton Art Institute, Canton, O. III. Junior League of Canton. IV. Title.

Architecture—Cape May, N.J. (City)—History.

THOMAS, George E. 974.9'98
Cape May, queen of the seaside resorts : its history and architecture / George E. Thomas and Carl Doebley ; photos. by George E. Thomas. Philadelphia : Art Alliance Press, c1976. p. cm. Includes bibliographical references and index. [NA735.C32T45] 75-18239 ISBN 0-87982-016-0 : 20.00
1. Architecture—Cape May, N.J. (City)—History. 2. Cape May, N.J. (City)—History. I. Doebley, Carl, joint author. II. Title.

Architecture—Caricatures and cartoons.

DUNN, Alan, 1900- 741.59'73
Architecture observed. [Limited 1st ed.] New York, Architectural Record Books [1971] 144 p. (chiefly illus.) 23 x 24 cm. [NC1429.D76A44] 75-165515 ISBN 0-07-018305-8 6.95
1. Architecture—Caricatures and cartoons. I. Title. BIP

MACAULAY, David. 720'.9
Great moments in architecture / David Macaulay. Boston : Houghton Mifflin, 1978. [116] p. : chiefly ill. ; 23x30 cm. [NC1429.M15A46] 77-15490 ISBN 0-395-25500-7 : 9.95 pbk. : 5.95
1. Architecture—Caricatures and cartoons. 2. American wit and humor, Pictorial. I. Title. BIP

Architecture, Carlovingian.

CONANT, Kenneth John, 1894- 723'.4
Carolingian and Romanesque architecture, 800 to 1200. [2d ed.] Baltimore, Penguin Books [1966, c1959] xxxviii, 326, 176, 331-343 p. illus., maps, plans, plates. 27 cm. (The Pelican history of art, Z13) Bibliography: p. 320-326. [NA365.C6 1966] 67-2222
1. Architecture, Carlovingian. 2. Architecture, Romanesque. I. Title. II. Series. BIP

CONANT, Kenneth John, 1894- 723'.4
Carolingian and Romanesque architecture, 800 to 1200 / Kenneth John Conant. 3rd ed. Harmondsworth ; Baltimore [etc.] : Penguin, 1973. xxxix, 345 p., leaf of plate, [184] p. of plates : ill. (incl. 1 col.), maps (some col.), plans ; 27 cm. (The Pelican history of art) Includes index. Bibliography: p. 321-328. [NA365.C6 1973] 76-354254 ISBN 0-14-056013-0 : £12.50
1. Architecture, Carlovingian. 2. Architecture, Romanesque. I. Title. II. Series.

Architecture—Carson City, Nev.

CHAMBERS, S. Allen. 917.3'03 s
The architecture of Carson City, Nevada, by S. Allen Chambers, Jr. Washington, Historic American Buildings Survey [1972?] v, 194 p. illus. 28 cm. (Selections from the Historic American Buildings Survey, no. 14) Includes bibliographical references. [NA705.A25 no. 14] [NA735.C34] 720'.9793'57 73-602805
1. Architecture—Carson City, Nev. 2. Carson City, Nev.—Historic houses, etc. I. United States. Office of Archaeology and Historic Preservation. II. Title. III. Series: Historic American Buildings Survey. Selections, no. 14.

Architecture—Charleston, S.C.

SIMONS, Albert, 1890- ed. 720'.9757'915
The early architecture of Charleston. Edited by Albert Simons and Samuel Lapham, Jr. With an introd. by Samuel Gaillard Stoney. [2d ed.] Columbia, University of South Carolina Press [1970] 223 p. (chiefly illus., facsims., maps, plans, port.) 34 cm. First ed. published in 1927 under title: Charleston, South Carolina. Bibliography: p. 219. [NA735.C35S5 1970] 77-120918 ISBN 8-7249-1978- 12.95
1. Architecture—Charleston, S.C. 2. Architecture, Colonial—Charleston, S.C. 3. Charleston, S.C.—Historic houses, etc. I. Lapham, Samuel, 1892- joint ed. II. Title.

STONEY, Samuel Gaillard, 1891- 720'.9757'915
This is Charleston; a survey of the architectural heritage of a unique American city. Charleston, S.C., Carolina Art Association [1970] x, 137 p. illus., maps. 23 cm. [NA735.C35S8 1970] 73-15222
1. Architecture—Charleston, S.C. 2. Charleston, S.C.—Historic houses, etc. I. Carolina Art Association, Charleston, S.C. II. Title. BIP

STONEY, Samuel Gaillard, 1891- 720.975791
This is Charleston; a survey of the architectural heritage of a unique American city. [2d ed., rev.] Charleston, S.C., Carolina Art Association [1960, 1944] x, 137 p. illus., maps. 23 cm. [NA735.C35S8 1960] 61-1230
1. Architecture — Charleston, S.C. 2. Charleston, S.C. — Historic houses, etc. I. Carolina Art Association, Charleston, S.C. II. Title.

Architecture—Chelsea, Eng. (Parish)

GODFREY, Walter Hindes, 1881- 914.21'34
The Parish of Chelsea, by Walter H. Godfrey. New York, AMS Press [1971- v. illus. 29 cm. (The Survey of London, v. 2,) Reprint of the 1909- ed. Includes bibliographical references. [DA685.C53G632] 71-138271 ISBN 0-404-51652-1 (v. 2)
1. Chelsea, Eng. (Parish)—Historic houses, etc. 2. Architecture—Chelsea, Eng. (Parish) I. Title. II. Series: Joint Publishing Committee Representing the London County Council and the London Survey Committee. Survey of London, v. 2, etc. BIP

Architecture—Cheshire, Eng.

PEVSNER, Nikolaus, Sir, 1902- 914.27'1'0485
Cheshire, by Nikolaus Pevsner and Edward Hubbard. Harmondsworth, Penguin, 1971. 442 p., 64 plates. illus., map. 19 cm. (His The buildings of England) [NA969.C45P4] 72-193419 ISBN 0-14-071042-6 £2.25
1. Architecture—Cheshire, Eng. I. Hubbard, Edward, joint author.

Architecture—Chicago.

ANDREWS, Wayne. 720'.977
Architecture in Chicago & mid-America; a photographic history. [1st ed.] New York, Atheneum, 1968. xviii, 186 p. illus. 30 cm. [NA735.C4A65] 68-23511 20.00
1. Architecture—Chicago. 2. Architecture—Middle West. I. Title. BIP

ANDREWS, Wayne. 720.977
Architecture in Chicago & mid-America; a photographic history. New York, Harper and Row [1973, c1968] xviii, 186 p. illus, ports., 28 cm. (Icon editions) Originally published in hardcover by Atheneum Publishers Bibliography: p. 181-182. [NA735.C4A65] ISBN 0-06-430043-9 4.95 (pbk.)
1. Architecture—Chicago. 2. Architecture—Middle West. I. Title.
L.C. card number for hardcover: 68-23511

RANDALL, John D 720.977311
A guide to significant Chicago architecture of 1872 to 1922. [Limited ed. Glencoe, Ill., 1958] 59p. illus. 28cm. Includes bibliography. [NA735.C4R3] 58-59746
1. Architecture— Chicago. I. Title.

SIEGEL, Arthur S ed. 720.977311
Chicago's famous buildings; a photographic guide to the city's architectural landmarks and other notable buildings. Edited by Arthur Siegel. [Chicago] University of Chicago Press [1965] ix, 230 p. illus., maps, plans. 21 cm. Project of the Commission on Architectural Landmarks. "Bibliography [compiled by Ruth Schoneman]": p. 219-220. [NA735.C4S5] 64-15803
1. Architecture—Chicago. 2. Chicago—Public buildings. I. Chicago. Commission on Architectural Landmarks. II. Title. BIP

SIEGEL, Arthur S., ed. 720'.9773'11
Chicago's famous buildings; a photographic guide to the city's architectural landmarks and other notable buildings. Edited by Arthur Siegel. Descriptive text by J. Carson Webster. With contributions by Carl W. Condit, Hugh Dalziel Duncan [and] Wilbert R. Hasbrouck. 2d ed. rev. and enl. Chicago, University of Chicago Press [1969] xiv, 272 p. illus., maps, plans. 22 cm. Bibliography: p. 261-262. [NA735.C4S5 1969] 69-15367 4.50
1. Architecture—Chicago. 2. Chicago—Public buildings. I. Webster, James Carson, 1905- II. Title.

Architecture—Chicago—Conservation and restoration.

MILLER, Hugh C. 720'.9773'11
The Chicago School of Architecture; a plan for preserving a significant remnant of America's architectural heritage, by Hugh C. Miller. [Washington, U.S. National Park Service, 1972?] v, 36, [2] p. illus. 27 cm. "Study was prepared by the Office of Archeology and Historic Preservation, National Park Service, Department of the Interior." Bibliography: p. [38] [NA2300.C4M54] 73-601208
1. Chicago School of Architecture. 2. Architecture—Chicago—Conservation and restoration. I. United States. Office of Archeology and Historic Preservation.

Architecture—Chicago—History.

CONDIT, Carl W. 725.0977311
The Chicago school of architecture; a history of commercial and public building in the Chicago area, 1875-1925. Chicago, Univ. of Chic. Pr. [c.1952, 1964] xviii, 238p. 196 illus. 25cm. Bibl. 64-13287 8.50
1. Architecture—Chicago—Hist. 2. Architecture—U. S.—Hist. I. Title. BIP

Architecture—Chicago—History.

LOWE, David, 1933- 720'.9'77311
Lost Chicago / David Lowe. Boston : Houghton Mifflin, 1975. xii, 241 p. : ill. ; 29 cm. Includes bibliographical references and index. [NA735.C4L68] 75-19181 ISBN 0-395-20726-6 : 20.00
1. Architecture—Chicago—History. I. Title. BIP

Architecture—Chicago metropolitan area—Guidebooks.

WEBSTER. JAMES CARSON. 1905- 720.977311
Architecture of Chicago and vicinity [Media Pa., Box 94 Soc. of Architectural Historians.] 1965. 72p. illus., plans. 22cm. August tour 1965. Soc. of Arch. Historians. Bibl. [NA735.C4W4] 65-26429 2.50
1. Architecture—Chicago metropolitan area—Guidebooks. I. Society of Architectural Historians. II. Title.

Architecture—China.

CHAMBERS, William, Sir, 1726-1796. 709'.51
Designs of Chinese buildings, furniture, dresses, machines, and utensils. New York, B. Blom, 1968. 19 p. 21 plates (incl. 2 plans) 34 cm. Reprint of the English text and the plates of the 1757 ed. which was published with text in English and French. [NA1540.C5 1968] 68-17156
1. Architecture—China. 2. Costume—China. 3. Gardens—China. I. Title. BIP

WU, Nelson Ikon, 1919- 720.95
Chinese and Indian architecture; the city of man, the Mountain of God, and the realm of the immortals, by Nelson I. Wu (Wu No-sun) New York, G. Braziller, 1963. 128 p. illus., map, plans. 26 cm. (The Great ages of world architecture) Bibliography: p. 122-123. [NA1543.W8] 63-7513
1. Architecture—China. 2. Architecture—India. I. Title. II. Series. BIP

Architecture—China—Bibliography.

HUGO-BRUNT, Michael. 016.3092'08 s
Bibliography of architecture, planning and landscape in China : including materials on Hong Kong, Korea, Manchuria, Mongolia and Tibet / Michael Hugo-Brunt. Monticello, Ill. : Council of Planning Librarians, 1974. 68 p. ; 28 cm. (Exchange bibliography - Council of Planning Librarians ; 535) Cover title. [Z5944.C5H84] [NA1540] 016.951 75-309695 7.00
1. Architecture—China—Bibliography. 2. Cities and towns—Planning—China—Bibliography. 3. Landscape gardening—China—Bibliography. I. Title. II. Series: Council of Planning Librarians. Exchange bibliography ; 535.

Architecture—China—Hist.

BOYD, Andrew Charles Hugh. 720.951
Chinese architecture and town planning 1500 B.C.-A.D. 1911. [Chicago] University of Chicago Press [c1962] vi, 166 p. illus., maps. plans. 20 cm. Bibliography: p. 160-161. [NA1540.B68] 63-9735
1. Architecture — China — Hist. 2. Cities and towns — Planning — China. I. Title.

BOYD, Andrew Charles Hugh 720.951
Chinese architecture and town planning, 1500 B.C.--A.D. 1911 [by] Andrew Boyd. London, Tiranti, 1962. Label pasted on t.p. dist. Transatlantic, New York [1967] vi, 166p. illus. (inc. 158 plates) diagrs., map. 20x17cm. (Chapters in art ser., v. 36) Bibl. 10.00
1. Architecture—China—Hist. 2. Cities and towns—Planning—China. I. Title.

SU, Gin-djih, 1908- 720.951
Chinese architecture, past and contemporary. Hong Kong, Sin Poh Amalgamated (H. K.) [dist. S. Pasadena, Calif., Hutchins, 1965] vii, 281p. illus. facsims. 20cm. [NA1540.S8] 65-1289 12.50 bds.,
1. Architecture—China—Hist. I. Title.

Architecture—Chios (Island)

SMITH, Arnold Clarence 720.9495
The architecture of Chios; subsidiary buildings, implements, and crafts. Ed. by Philip P. Argenti. London, A. Tiranti [Hollywood-by-the-Sea, Fla., Transatlantic, 1964, c.1962] viii, 171p. 7 maps (pt. fold.) 226 plates (incl. illus., plans) 26cm. (Tiranti lib. ser.) Bibl. 64-4669 26.75
1. Architecture—Chios (Island) 2. Art industries and trade—Chios (Island) I. Argenti, Philip Pandely, 1891- ed. II. Title.

Architecture—Cincinnati—Exhibitions.

CINCINNATI. Art Museum. 720'9771'78
Cincinnati landmarks : a Bicentennial exhibition, Cincinnati Art Museum, July 2-August 22, 1976. Cincinnati : The Museum, c1976. 55 p. : ill. ; 26 cm. Includes bibliographies. [NA735.C5C56 1976] 76-375319
1. Architecture—Cincinnati—Exhibitions. 2. Cincinnati—Buildings—Exhibitions. 3. Historic buildings—Ohio—Cincinnati—Exhibitions. I. Title.

Architecture, Cistercian—Italy—Florence.

LUCHS, Alison. 726'.5'094551
Cestello, a Cistercian church of the Florentine renaissance / Alison Luchs. New York : Garland Pub. Co., 1977. xix, 443 p. : ill. ; 21 cm. (Outstanding dissertations in the fine arts) Originally presented as the author's thesis, Johns Hopkins University, 1975. Bibliography: p. 421-443. [NA5621.F748L8 1977] 76-23642 ISBN 0-8240-2706-X lib.bdg. : 45.00
1. Santa Maria Maddalena dei Pazzi (Church), Florence. 2. Architecture, Cistercian—Italy—Florence. 3. Art, Italian—Italy—Florence. 4. Art, Renaissance—Italy—Florence. I. Title. II. Series.

Architecture—Cleveland.

AMERICAN Institute of Architects. 720.9771
Cleveland architecture, 1796-1958. New York, Reinhold Pub. Corp. [1958] leveland Chapter. 64p. illus. 22cm. [NA735.C6A7] 58-11229
1. Architecture—Cleveland. 2. Cities and towns—Planning—Cleveland. I. Title.

Architecture—Clinton Co., N.Y.—Conservation and restoration.

EVEREST, Allan Seymour. 917.47'53
Our North Country heritage; architecture worth saving in Clinton and Essex Counties [by] Allan S. Everest. [Plattsburgh, N.Y.] Tundra Books, 1972. 143 p. illus. 18 x 27 cm. Bibliography: p. 143. [NA107.N7E94] 72-83652 ISBN 0-912766-05-0 4.95
1. Architecture—Clinton Co., N.Y.—Conservation and restoration. 2. Architecture—Essex Co., N.Y.—Conservation and restoration. I. Title.

Architecture, Cluniac.

EVANS, Joan, 1893- 726'.77'1
The Romanesque architecture of the order of Cluny. New York, AMS Press [1971] xxxviii, 256 p. maps, 259 plates. 27 cm. Reprint of the 1938 ed. Bibliography: p. [xxvii]-xxxviii. [NA4828.E9 1971] 75-136385 ISBN 0-404-02358-4 42.00
1. Architecture, Cluniac. 2. Architecture, Romanesque. I. Title. BIP

Architecture—Collected works.

AALTO, Alvar, 1898-1976. 720
Sketches / Alvar Aalto ; edited by Goran Schildt ; translated from the Swedish by Stuart Wrede. Cambridge, Mass. : MIT Press, c1978. ix,, 172 p. : ill. ; 23 cm. Translation of Skisser. [NA2500.A2213] 78-6155 ISBN 0-262-01053-4 : 25.00
1. Architecture—Collected works. 2. Architecture, Modern—20th century—Collected works. I. Schildt, Goran, 1917- II. Title.

Architecture, Colonial.

HOWELLS, John Mead, 1868-1959 720.973
Lost examples of colonial architecture; buildings that have disappeared or been so altered as to be denatured. Introd. by Fiske Kimball [Gloucester, Mass. P. Smith, 1964, c.1963] 244p. of illus. 28cm. (Dover bk. T1143 rebound) [NA707.H75] 5.00
1. Architecture, Colonial. 2. Architecture—U. S. I. Title.

MARKMAN, Sidney David, 1911- 720.97281
Colonial architecture of Antigua, Guatemala. Philadelphia, Amer. Philosophical Soc. [c.]1966. xviii, 335p. illus., maps, plans. 29cm. (Memoirs of the Amer. Philosophical Soc., v.64) Title. (Series: American Philosophical Society, Philadelphia. Memoirs, v.64) Bibl. [NA777.A6M3] 66-13634 10.00
1. Architecture, Colonial. 2. Architecture—Antigua. Guatemala. I. Title. II. Series.

Architecture, Colonial—Bibliography.

ROOS, Frank John, 1903-1966. 016.720'973
Bibliography of early American architecture; writings on architecture constructed before 1860 in Eastern and Central United States. Urbana, University of Illinois Press, 1968. 389 p. 24 cm. 1943 ed. published under title: Writings on early American architecture. [Z5944.U5R6 1968] 68-24624 ISBN 0-252-72680-4 12.50
1. Architecture, Colonial—Bibliography. I. Title. BIP

Architecture, Colonial—Dictionaries.

ISHAM, Norman Morrison, 1864-1943. 720'.973
A glossary of colonial architectural terms, by Norman Morrison Isham. With a bibliography of books, 1880-1930. The dating of old houses, by Henry C. Mercer. [Watkins Glen, N.Y.] American Life Foundation, 1968. [64] p. illus. 23 cm. (Classic guidebooks to the visual arts) Bibliography: p. [59]-[64] [NA707.I68] 72-197309
1. Architecture, Colonial—Dictionaries. 2. Pennsylvania—Historic houses, etc. 3. Art, Colonial—Bibliography. I. Mercer, Henry Chapman, 1856-1930. The dating of old houses. 1968. II. Title.

Architecture, Colonial—Georgia.

NICHOLS, Frederick Doveton. 720'.9758
The architecture of Georgia / text by Frederick Doveton Nichols ; photos. by Van Jones Martin and Frances Benjamin Johnston ; drawings by Frederick Spitzmiller ; special research by Elizabeth MacGregor ; edited by Mills Lane. Savannah : Beehive Press, c1976. 436 p. : ill. ; 30 cm. Includes bibliographical references and index. [NA730.G4N48] 76-16226 30.00
1. Architecture, Colonial—Georgia. 2. Architecture, Modern—19th century—

Georgia. 3. Architecture—Georgia. I. Martin, Van Jones. II. Johnston, Frances Benjamin, 1864-1952. III. Title.

Architecture, Colonial—Maryland.

COFFIN, Lewis Augustus, 1892- 720'.9752
Brick architecture of the colonial period in Maryland & Virginia, by Lewis A. Coffin, Jr. [and] Arthur C. Holden. New York, Dover Publications [1970] viii, 29 p., 118 plates. illus., plans. 28 cm. Reprint of the 1919 ed. Bibliography: p. 28-29. [NA730.M3C6 1970] 73-125625 ISBN 0-486-22488-0 3.50
1. Architecture, Colonial—Maryland. 2. Architecture, Colonial—Virginia. 3. Architecture—Maryland. 4. Architecture—Virginia. I. Holden, Arthur Cort, 1890- joint author. II. Title.

Architecture, Colonial—New England.

†*COLONIAL architecture in New England :* from material originally published as the White pine series of architectural monographs, edited by Russell F. Whitehead and Frank Chouteau Brown / prepared for this series by the staff of the Early American Society, Robert G. Miner, editor ... [et al.]. New York : Arno Press, c1977. 223 p. : ill. ; 29 cm. (An Early American Society book) (Architectural treasures of early America ; v. 3) [NA715.C63] 77-14466 ISBN 0-405-10066-3 : 10.95 720'.974
1. Architecture, Colonial—New England. 2. Architecture—New England. I. Miner, Robert G. II. Early American Society. III. The Monograph series, records of early American architecture. IV. Series. BIP

CUMMINGS, Abbott Lowell, 1923- 728
The framed houses of Massachusetts Bay, 1625-1725 / Abbott Lowell Cummings. Cambridge, Mass. : Harvard University Press, 1979. p. cm. Includes bibliographical references and index. [NA730.M4C85] 78-8390 ISBN 0-674-31680-0 : 35.00
1. Wooden-frame houses—Massachusetts (Colony) 2. Architecture, Modern—17th-18th centuries—Massachusetts (Colony) 3. Architecture, Colonial—Massachusetts (Colony) 4. Architecture, Domestic—Massachusetts (Colony) 5. Architecture—United States—English influences. 6. Historic building—Massachusetts. I. Title.

Architecture, Colonial—United States.

GREAT Georgian houses of America Published for the Benefit of the Architects' Emergency Comm. by the Edit. Comm. & the Pub. Comm. Magnolia, Mass Peter Smith [1973, c1970] 2 v. (chiefly illus., facsims., plans) (Dover bk rebound) Reprint of the 1933-37 ed. [NA707.G67] 71-105663 ISBN 0-8446-4502-8 15.00 set. 728.8'3'0973
1. Architecture, Colonial—U.S. 2. Architecture, Domestic—U.S. 3. U.S.—Historic houses, etc. I. Architects' Emergency Committee BIP

GUINNESS, Desmond. 720'.92'4
Mr. Jefferson, architect [by] Desmond Guinness & Julius Trousdale Sadler, Jr. New York, Viking Press [1973] 177 p. illus. 29 cm. (A Studio book) [NA737.J4G84 1973] 72-12057 ISBN 0-670-49261-2 14.95
1. Jefferson, Thomas, Pres. U.S., 1743-1826. 2. Architecture, Colonial—United States. I. Sadler, Julius Trousdale, joint author. II. Title.

HOWELLS, John Mead, 1868-1959. 720.973
Lost examples of colonial architecture; buildings that have disappeared or been so altered as to be denatured. With an introd. by Fiske Kimball. New York, Dover Publications [1963] 244 p. of illus. 28 cm. "T1143." [NA707.H75 1963] 63-21679
1. Architecture, Colonial—United States. 2. Architecture—United States. I. Title.

MILLAR, John Fitzhugh. 720'.922
The architects of the American Colonies; or, Vitruvius Americanus. With drawings rendered by Suzanne Carlson. [Barre, Mass.] Barre Publishers, 1968. 205 p. illus. 37 cm. Bibliography: p. 196-197. [NA707.M53] 68-17068 20.00
1. Architecture, Colonial—United States. 2. Architecture—United States. 3. Architects—United States. I. Carlson, Suzanne, illus. II. Title.

SHURTLEFF, Harold Robert, 1883-1938. 728.6'0973
The log cabin myth; a study of the early dwellings of the English colonists in North America. Edited with an introd. by Samuel Eliot Morison. Gloucester, Mass., P. Smith, 1967. xxi, 243 p. illus., plates. 21 cm. Reprint of the 1939 ed. Bibliographical footnotes. [NA707.S47 1967] 67-5735
1. Architecture, Colonial—United States. 2. Architecture, Domestic—United States. I. Morison, Samuel Eliot, 1887- ed. II. Title. BIP

Architecture, Colonial—U.S.—Juvenile literature.

FISHER, Leonard Everett. 720'.973
The architects, written & illustrated by Leonard Everett Fisher. New York, Watts [1970] 48 p. illus., plans. 23 cm. (Colonial Americans) Traces the history of architecture in the American colonies describing the influence of existing styles and the needs of environment. [NA707.F58] 70-101748
1. Architecture, Colonial—U.S.—Juvenile literature. I. Title. BIP

Architecture—Columbus, Ind.—Guide-books.

COLUMBUS, Indiana, a look at architecture. Columbus, Ind. : Visitors Center, [1974] 100 p. : ill. ; 28 cm. On cover: A Look at architecture, Columbus, Indiana. [NA735.C64C64] 75-301364 917.72'24'043
1. Architecture—Columbus, Ind.—Guide-books. I. Visitors Center, Columbus, Ind. II. Title: A look at architecture, Columbus, Indiana.

Architecture—Commonwealth of Nations.

RICHARDS, James Maude, ed. 724.9
New buildings in the Commonwealth. New York, Praeger [1962, c.1961] 240p. illus. (col. front.) 29cm. 62-8291 14.50
1. Architecture—Commonwealth of Nations. 2. Architecture, Modern—20th cent. I. Title.

Architecture—Competitions.

BIRMINGHAM-JEFFERSON Civic Center Authority. 725'.8
Birmingham-Jefferson Civic Center national architectural competition. [Editor: Les Adams. Birmingham] 1969. vi, 314 p. illus., plans. 25 x 34 cm. [NA2340.B5] 68-9481
1. Birmingham, Ala. Birmingham-Jefferson Civic Center (Proposed) 2. Architecture—Competitions. I. Adams, Les, ed. II. Title.

MOORE, Charles Willard, 1925- comp. 727'.4'51097468
The Yale Mathematics Building competition : architecture for a time of questioning / Charles W. Moore and Nicholas Pyle, editors. New Haven : Yale University Press, 1974. viii, 117 p. : ill. ; 23 x 29 cm. Includes index. [LD6342.M37M66] 73-77162 ISBN 0-300-01621-2 : 15.00
1. Yale University. Mathematics Building. 2. Architecture—Competitions. 3. Architecture—Designs and plans. I. Pyle, Nicholas, joint comp. II. Title. BIP

UNITED States. Dept. of Housing and Urban Development. 720'.973
1966 honor awards for design excellence. [Washington, U.S. Govt. Print. Off., 1967] 36 p. illus., plans, ports. 24 x 29 cm. (Its HUD MP -50) [HT175.U6A2 no. 50] 68-60378
1. Architecture—Competitions. 2. Architecture, Domestic—Designs and plans. I. Title. II. Series.

Architecture—Competitions—Handbooks, manuals, etc.

STRONG, Judith. 658'.91'72079
Participating in architectural competitions : a guide for competitors, promoters, and assessors / Judith Strong. London : Architectural Press, 1976. ix, 151 p., [4] leaves of plates : ill. ; 22 cm. [NA2335.S75] 76-379126 ISBN 0-85139-514-7 : £5.50
1. Architecture—Competitions—Handbooks, manuals, etc. I. Title. BIP

Architecture — Competitions — Yearbooks.

NATIONAL Institute for Architectural Education. 720.973
Scholarships, fellowships, prizes. 1964- New York. v. illus., plans. 29 cm. Cover title, 1964- : NIAE yearbook. Each vol. accompanies by a separate collection of glossy photographs. [NA2340.N35] 66-59309
1. Architecture — Competitions — Yearbooks. 2. Architecture — U.S. Yearbooks. I. National Institute for Architectural Education. Yearbook. II. Title. III. Title: NIAE yearbook.

Architecture—Composition, proportion, etc.

ARNHEIM, Rudolf. 729
The dynamics of architectural form : based on the 1975 Mary Duke Biddle lectures at the Cooper Union / Rudolf Arnheim. Berkeley : University of California Press, c1977. vi, 289 p. : ill. ; 25 cm. Includes index. Bibliography: p. 279-283. [NA2760.A74] 76-19955 ISBN 0-520-03305-1 : 16.95 ISBN 0-520-03551-8 pbk. : 4.95
1. Architecture—Composition, proportion, etc. 2. Architecture—Psychological aspects. 3. Visual perception. I. Title. BIP

BORISSAVLIEVITCH, Miloutine. 729.2
The golden number and the scientific aesthetics of architecture. With pref. by Louis Hautecoeur. [1st English ed.] New York, Philosophical Library, 1958. 91p. illus. 19cm. [NA2760.B673 1958] 58-14795
1. Architecture—Composition, proportion, etc. 2. Proportion (Art) 3. Aesthetics. I. Title.

CENTER, Ronald A. 744.4'24
Architectural shadow projection, by R. A. Center. [Melbourne] Cassell Australia [1967] 80 p. illus. 25 cm. [NA2710.C4] 73-356077 unpriced
1. Architecture—Composition, proportion, etc. 2. Perspective. I. Title.

COOK, Peter 720
Architecture: action and plan. London, Studio Vista; New York, Reinhold [1967] 96p. front., illus., plans, diagrs. 22cm. Bibl. [NA2760.C57] 67-14164 5.50; 2.45 pap.,
1. Architecture— Composition, proportion, etc. I. Title.

GOODOVITCH, I. M. 720/.1
Architecturology; an interim report, by I M. Goodovitch. New York, Wittenborn [1967] 119p. illus., maps. 23x25cm. [NA2760.G6] 67-30097 8.00 bds.,
1. Architecture—Composition, proportion, etc. 2. Design. I. Title. BIP

ISAAC, Alan Reginald George. 729
Approach to architectural design [by] A. R. G. Isaac. [Toronto] University of Toronto Press [1971] 112 p. illus. 22 x 31 cm. Bibliography: p. 109. [NA2760.187 1971] 79-166931 ISBN 0-8020-1801-7 15.00
1. Architecture—Composition, proportion, etc. I. Title. BIP

JEANNERET-GRIS, Charles Edouard, 1887- 720
The modulor; a harmonious measure to the human scale universally applicable to architecture and mechanics, by Le Corbusier [pseud. Translated by Peter de Francia and Anna Bostock. 2d ed.] Cambridge, Harvard University Press, 1954. 243p. illus., diagrs. 20cm. [NA2760.J] A 54
1. Architecture— Composition, proportion, etc. I. Title.

LICKLIDER, Heath 729.13
Architectural scale. New York, Braziller [1966] 232p. illus., plans. 23cm. Bibl. [NA2760.L5 1966] 66-14230 5.00
1. Architecture—Composition, proportion, etc. I. Title. BIP

MARTIENSSEN, Heather. 729
The shapes of structure / Heather Martienssen. London ; New York : Oxford University Press, 1976. x, 166 p. : ill. ; 21 cm. Includes index. Bibliography: p. [155]-156. [NA2760.M37] 76-378346 ISBN 0-19-217646-3 : 10.50 pbk. : 5.95
1. Architecture—Composition, proportion, etc. 2. Space (Architecture) 3. Form (Aesthetics) I. Title. BIP

POPKO, Edward. 721'.46
Geodesics. Detroit, School of Architecture, University of Detroit [1968] 1 v. (chiefly illus.) 22 cm. (Industrialization and technology course supplement no. 1) Includes bibliography. [NA2890.P6] 77-675
1. Architecture—Composition, proportion, etc. 2. Domes. I. Title. II. Series.

RASCH, Heinz. 720'.1
Some roots of modern architecture. Translated and edited by George and Joan Jelinek. [1st American ed.] New York, Transatlantic Arts, 1967. 92 p. illus., plans. 22 cm. A collection of the author's lectures. [NA680.R3513 1967b] 67-66281
1. Architecture—Composition, proposition, etc. 2. Architecture, Modern—20th century. I. Title. BIP

ROOT, John Wellborn, 1850-1891. 720'.973
The meanings of architecture; buildings and writings. Collected and with an introd. by Donald Hoffmann. New York, Horizon Press [1967] 238 p. illus., plans. 30 cm. [NA2760.R76] 67-27906
1. Architecture—Composition, proportion, etc. 2. Architecture—United States. 3. Decoration and ornament, Architectural. I. Hoffmann, Donald. II. Title.

SCHOLFIELD, P H 729.13
The theory of proportion in architecture. Cambridge [Eng.] University Press, 1958. xi, 155p. illus., diagrs. 26cm. 'In its original form this book was written as a thesis for the degree of M. A. at Liverpool University.' Bibliography p. 147-150. [NA2760.S35] 58-14746
1. Architecture—Composition, proportion, etc. I. Title. II. Title: Proportion in architecture.

SOLOMON, Daniel, 1939- 745'.05 s
Five and dime architects, DQ 97 : a recession catalogue / by Daniel Solomon Minneapolis : Walker Art Center, c1975. 32 p. : ill. ; 28 cm. (Issues in architecture ; 1) [NK1.E9 no. 97] [NA2760] 729 76-357092 1.60
1. Architecture—Composition, proportion, etc. 2. Harmony (Aesthetics) I. Title. II. Series. III. Design quarterly ; 97

STULINSKY, J. A. 720'.1
Form in architecture : bineral and analogo-contrasting principles in composition, gonio-space, and architecture / J. A. Stulinsky. Greensboro : Engineering News Bulletin, School of Engineering, N.C. A & T State University, 1974. vi, 95 [i.e. 223] leaves : ill. ; 28 cm. Errata sheet inserted. Includes bibliographical references. [NA2760.S88] 75-622085
1. Architecture—Composition, proportion, etc. 2. Space (Architecture) I. Title.

UNRAU, John. 720'.9
Looking at architecture with Ruskin / John Unrau. Toronto ; Buffalo : University of Toronto Press, 1978. 180 p., [2] leaves of plates : ill. (some col.) ; 25 cm. Includes index. Bibliography: p. 172-174. [NA2760.U57] 78-318139 ISBN 0-8020-2284-7 : 15.00
1. Ruskin, John, 1819-1900. 2. Architecture—Composition, proportion, etc. 3. Decoration and ornament, Architectural. 4. Architecture—Psychological aspects. I. Title. BIP

VENTURI, Robert. 721
Complexity and contradiction in

architecture. With an introd. by Vincent Scully. New York Museum of Modern Art; distributed by Doubleday, Garden City, N.Y. [c1966] 135 p. illus., plans. 21 cm. (Museum of Modern Art papers on architecture, 1) Bibliographical references included in "Notes" (p. 134-135) [NA2760.V46] 66-30001
1. Architecture — Composition, proportion, etc. I. New York. Museum of Modern Art. II. Title. BIP

VENTURI, Robert. 720'.1
Complexity and contradiction in architecture / Robert Venturi ; with an introd. by Vincent Scully. 2d ed. New York : Museum of Modern Art ; Boston : distributed by New York Graphic Society, 1977. 132 p. : ill. ; 23 x 29 cm. (The Museum of Modern Art papers on architecture) Includes bibliographical references. [NA2760.V46 1977] 77-77289 ISBN 0-87070-281-5 : 12.95. ISBN 0-87070-282-3 pbk. : 7.95
1. Architecture—Composition, proportion, etc. I. New York (City). Museum of Modern Art. II. Title. III. Series: New York (City). Museum of Modern Art. Papers on architecture.

Architecture—Congresses.

AIA-NSF Conference on 720.82
Research for Architecture, Ann Arbor, Mich., 1959.
Research for architecture: proceedings. Edited by Eugene F. Magenau. Washington, American Institute of Architects, Documents Division, 1959. 127p. (incl. cover) diagrs. 28cm. [NA21.A5 1959] 61-1649
1. Architecture—Congresses. I. Magenau, Eugene F., ed. II. Title.

ROYAL Institute of British 720
Architects, London.
Architecture : opportunities, achievements : a report of the Annual Conference of the Royal Institute of British Architects held at the University of Hull, 14 to 17 July 1976 / edited by Barbara Goldstein. London : RIBA Publications, 1977. [1], 120, [1] p. : ill., plans, ports. ; 30 cm. [NA21.R68 1977] 77-376880 ISBN 0-900630-59-0 pbk. : 7.00
1. Architecture—Congresses. I. Goldstein, Barbara. II. Title.
Distributed by International Scholarly Book Service, Forest Grove, OR.

Architecture—Connecticut—Pictorial works.

TRAGER, Philip, 1935- 779'.4'0924
Philip Trager photographs of architecture. Middletown, Conn. : Wesleyan University Press, [1977] p. cm. Includes index. [NA730.C8T73] 76-41483 ISBN 0-8195-5003-5 : 25.00
1. Architecture—Connecticut—Pictorial works. I. Title.

Architecture—Conservation and restoration.

HARVEY, John Hooper. 720'.28
Conservation of buildings [by] John Harvey. [Toronto] University of Toronto Press [1972, i.e. 1973] 240 p. illus. 24 cm. Bibliography: p. 222. [NA105.H28 1972b] 72-90749 ISBN 0-8020-1937-4 15.00
1. Architecture—Conservation and restoration. I. Title. BIP

MASSEY, James C. 720'.72'3
The architectural survey [by] James C. Massey. Washington, National Trust for Historic Preservation [1969?] [19] p. illus. 28 cm. (Preservation leaflet series) Caption title. Bibliography: p. [13]-[18] [NA105.M3] 79-21283
1. Architecture—Conservation and restoration. I. Title. II. Series.

SCHMIDT, Carl Frederick, 720'.28
1894-
Restoration and preservation / by Carl F. Schmidt. [s.l. : s.n.], c1976. 272 p. : ill. ; 29 cm. Includes index. [NA105.S35] 76-373085
1. Architecture—Conservation and restoration. 2. Historic buildings—Conservation and restoration. I. Title.

Architecture—Conservation and restoration—Addresses, essays, lectures.

THE Future of the past 720'.28
: attitudes to conservation 1174-1974 / Nikolaus Pevsner ... [et al.] ; edited by Jane Fawcett. London : Thames and Hudson, c1976. 160 p. : ill. ; 25 cm. Includes bibliographical references and index. [NA105.F87 1976b] 76-373613 ISBN 0-500-23231-8 : £7.50
1. Architecture—Conservation and restoration—Addresses, essays, lectures. I. Pevsner, Nikolaus, Sir, 1902- II. Fawcett, Jane.

†THE Future of the past 720'.28
: attitudes to conservation, 1174-1974 / Nikolaus Pevsner ... [et al.] ; edited by Jane Fawcett. New York : Whitney Library of Design, 1976. 160 p. : ill. ; 25 cm. Includes bibliographical references and index. [NA105.F87 1976] 76-18 ISBN 0-8230-7184-7 : 15.95
1. Architecture—Conservation and restoration—Addresses, essays, lectures. I. Pevsner, Nikolaus, Sir, 1902- II. Fawcett, Jane.

Architecture—Conservation and restoration—Handbooks, manuals, etc.

GLENN, Marsha. 720'.28
Historic preservation : a handbook for architecture students / by Marsha Glenn. [Washington : American Institute of Architects, 1974] iv, 60 p. ; 29 cm. Bibliography: p. 51-59. [NA105.G5] 75-318238
1. Architecture—Conservation and restoration—Handbooks, manuals, etc. I. American Institute of Architects. II. Title.

Architecture—Contra Costa Co., Calif.

BOHN, Dave. 720'.9794'63
East of these golden shores; architecture of the earlier days in Contra Costa and Alameda Counties. [Oakland, Calif.] Junior League of Oakland [1971] 124, [4] p. illus. 26 cm. Bibliography: p. [127] [NA730.C22C62] 73-175896 ISBN 0-912020-18-0
1. Architecture—Contra Costa Co., Calif. 2. Architecture—Alameda Co., Calif. I. Junior League of Oakland. II. Title. BIP

Architecture — Cornwall.

PEVSNER, Nikolaus, 1902- 720.942
Cornwall. Harmondsworth, Middlesex, Penguin Books [1951] 251 p. illus., map. 18 cm. (The Buildings of England, BE 1) [NA969.C67P48] 52-44143
1. Architecture — Cornwall. I. Title. II. Series.

Architecture—Coventry, Eng.

LEWISON, Grant, ed. 720.942'48
Coventry new architecture: a guide to the post war buildings; [edited by] Grant Lewison [and] Rosalind Billingham. Warwick, The editors, 33 High St., 1969. 157 p. illus., maps, plans. 15 x 21 cm. [NA971.C6L4] 79-470635 12/6
1. Architecture—Coventry, Eng. 2. Architecture, Modern—20th century—Coventry, Eng. I. Billingham, Rosalind, joint author. II. Title.

Architecture—Czechoslovak Republic—Hist.

STARY, Oldrich, ed. 720.9437
Ceskoslovenska architektura od nejstarsi doby po soucasnost. Zpracl. MarieBenesova [et al. Vyd. 1.] Praha, Nakl. ceskoslovenskych uytvarnvch umelcu [dist. New York, Vanous, c.]1962. xxxvii, 267p. illus. 27cm. (ceska architektura. Velka. rada, sv. 6) Summaries in Russian, German, French, English. Bibl. 63-2035 13.90
1. Architecture—Czechoslovak Republic—Hist. I. Benesova, Marie. II. Title.

Architecture—Czechoslovakia—Prague.

UHER, Vladimir, 720'.9437'12
1925-
Dialogue of forms / introd. and commentary by Milan Pavlik ; photos. by Vladimir Uher. New York : St. Martin's Press, 1977, c1975. ca. 200 p. : ill. ; 32 cm. Translation of Dialog tvaru. Includes a bibliography. [NA1033.P7U3313 1977] 74-21651 ISBN 0-900997-92-3 : 17.50
1. Architecture—Czechoslovakia—Prague. 2. Architecture, Baroque—Czechoslovakia—Prague. I. Pavlik, Milan, 1930- II. Title. BIP

Architecture—Dallas

AMERICAN Institute of 720.976428
Architects Dallas Chapter.
The prairie's yield: forces shaping Dallas architecture from 1840 to 1962. New York, Reinhold [c.1962] 72p. illus., maps. 14x22cm. 62-15235 2.50 pap.,
1. Architecture—Dallas I. Title.

Architecture—Data processing.

PENA, William. 720'.28'542
Problem seeking : an architectural programming primer / by William Pena, with William Caudill and John Focke. Boston : Cahners Books International, c1977. 202 p. : ill. ; 23 cm. Includes index. Bibliography: p. 192-194. [NA2728.P46] 77-73637 ISBN 0-8436-2172-9 : 14.95
1. Architecture—Data processing. I. Caudill, William Wayne, joint author. II. Focke, John, joint author. III. Title. BIP

Architecture—Delaware.

EBERLEIN, Harold 720.9751
Donaldson
Historic houses and buildings of Delaware, by Harold Donaldson Eberlein, Cortlandt V. D. Hubbard [2d ed.] Dover, Del., Public Archives Comm., 1963 [c.1962] 227p. illus., maps (on lining papers) plans 31cm. 63-2364 10.00 lim. ed.
1. Architecture—Delaware. 2. Delaware—Historic houses, etc. I. Hubbard, Cortlandt Van Dyke, joint author. II. Title.

Architecture—Denmark.

FABER, Tobias, 1915- 720'.9489
New Danish architecture. [Translation into English and German by E. Rockwell] New York, Praeger [1968] 219 p. illus. 26 cm. [NA1218.F313] 68-31670 17.50
1. Architecture—Denmark. 2. Architecture, Modern—20th century—Denmark. I. Title.

MONIES, Finn. 720.9489
Wood in architecture. Layout: Gunnar Jensen and Finn Monies.iNew York, F. W. Dodge Corp., c1961. 107p. illus. 23cm. 'The translation from the Danish was done by Doreen Malling Petersen, Sally Jacob, and Charles Jacob. [NA1218.M613] 61-8089
1. Architecture—Denmark. 2. Woodwork—Denmark. I. Title.

Architecture—Derbyshire, Eng.

PEVSNER, Nikolaus, 1902- 720.942
Derbyshire. London, Baltimore, Penguin Books [1953] 282p. illus. 18cm. (The Buildings of England, BE8) [NA969.D37P4] 53-4310
1. Architecture—Derbyshire, Eng. I. Title.

Architecture—Design and plans.

DIXON, John Morris, 1933- 729
Architectural design preview, U.S.A. New York, Reinhold [c.1962] 224p. illus., 27cm. 62-17173 15.00
1. Architecture—Design and plans. 2. Architecture —U.S. I. Title.

Architecture—Designs and plans.

BREUER, Marcel, 1902- 720.973
Buildings and projects, 1921-1961. Captions and introd. by Cranston Jones. New York, Praeger [1963, c1962] 262 p. illus. (part col.) port., plans. 23 x 29 cm. (Books that matter) [NA737.B68A45 1963] 62-21001
I. Title.

GIBBS, James, 1682-1754. 720'.223
A book of architecture, containing designs of buildings and ornaments. New York, B. Blom, 1968. xxviii, 150 p. (chiefly illus., plans) 34 cm. Reprint of the 1728 ed. [NA2620.G5 1968] 68-17153
1. Architecture—Designs and plans. 2. Sepulchral monuments. I. Title.

[JEANNERET-GRIS, Charles 720.944
Edouard] 1887-
Oeuvre complete, 1938-1946 [par] Le Corbusier [pseud. et Pierre Jeanneret] Publie par Willy Boesiger. 4th ed. [dist. Wittenborn 1961, c.1946] 207p. illus. (part col.) maps (part col.) 24x29cm. Text in French, with some English Translations. 12.00
1. Architecture—Designs and plans. 2. Cities and towns—Planning. I. Jeanneret, Pierre, 1896- II. Title.

JEANNERET-GRIS, Charles 720.924
Edouard, 1887-1965.
Oeuvre complete 1957-1965 Le Corbusier et son atelier, rue de Sevres 35. Edited by W. Boesiger New York, G. Wittenborn [1966, c1965] 239 p. illus. (part col.) facsims., plans (part col.) ports. 24 x 29 cm. French, English and German. Forms the seventh volume of Le Corbusier et Pierre Jeanneret, Oeuvres completes: the first volume includes the period 1910-1929, the second, 1929-1934, the third, 1934-1938, the fourth, 1938-1946, the fifth, 1946-192, the sixth 1952-1957. [NA1053.J4A53] 66-7277
1. Architecture—Designs and plans. 2. Cities and towns—Planning. I. Boesiger, Willy, ed. II. Title.

JEFFERSON, Thomas, Pres. 720.973
U.S., 1743-1826.
Architectural drawings. Compiled and with commentary and a check list by Frederick Doveton Nichols. [Rev. and enl. 2d ed.] Boston, Massachusetts Historical Society [1961] 46 p. facsims. 22 x 28 cm. "Checklist of Thomas Jefferson's architectural drawings": p. 31-44. [NA737.J4M3 1961] 62-3311
1. Architecture—Designs and plans. I. Nichols, Frederick Doveton. II. Title.

JEFFERSON, Thomas, 720'.924
Pres. U. S., 1743-1826.
Thomas Jefferson, architect; original designs in the Coolidge Collection of the Massachusetts Historical Society, with an essay and notes, by Fiske Kimball. New York, DaCapo Press, 1968. xi, vii, 205 p., [101] p. of illus., xi p. 40 cm. (Da Capo Press series in architecture and decorative art, v. 5) $80.00 A Da Capo Press reprint edition. Reprint of the 1916 ed. with a new introd. by F. D. Nichols. Includes bibliographical references. [E332.J48 1968] 67-27459
1. Architecture—Designs and plans. 2. Monticello, Va. I. Kimball, Sidney Fiske, 1888-1955. II. Title. BIP

LOWNDES, William Shepherd, 725
1866-
Examples of architectural design. 6587 [Ed. 1] Scranton, International Correspondence Schools, c1961. 50p. illus. 19cm. [NA2605.L76 1961] 61-46015
1. Architecture—Designs and plans. I. International Correspondence Schools, Scranton, Pa. II. Title.

LOWNDES, William Shepherd, 725
1866-
Examples of architectural design. Serial 2565-2. [Ed. 3] Scranton, International Correspondence Schools, c1959. 58p. illus. 19cm. [NA2605.L76 1959] 59-3964
1. Architecture—Designs and plans. I. International Correspondence Schools. Scranton. Pa. II. Title.

MEYER, Hannes, 1889-1954 724.9
Hannes Meyer: Bauten. Projekte und Schriften. Buildings, projects, and writings [Von] Claude Schnaidt [English version by D. Q. Stephenson] Teufen AR/Schweiz, A. Niggli [New York, Architectural Bk. [dist. Fasting, c.1965] 59, 123p. illus., plans., ports. 23x29cm. German and English. Bibl. [NA1353.M4S3] 65-5936 16.50

1. Architecture—Designs and plans. I. Schnaidt, Claude. 1931- ed. II. Title.

NERVI, Pier Luigi 720.945
Buildings, projects, structures, 1953-1963. [Tr. by Giuseppe Nicoletti] New York, Praeger [1963] 167p. illus., plans. 23x29cm. 63-14050 15.00
I. Title.

NEUTRA, Richard Joseph, 1892-1970. 720'.924
Building with nature. New York, Universe Books [1971] 223 p. illus., plans. 31 cm. Translation of Naturnahes bauen. [NA737.N4A5313] 79-93953 ISBN 0-87663-133-2 18.50
I. Title.

OEUVRE complete 1952-1957. 720.944 Le Corbusier et son atelier rue de Sevres 35, par W. Boesiger. New York, G. Wittenborn [1957] 223p. illus. (part col.) plans. 24x28cm. French, English and German. Forms the sixth volume of Le Corbusier et Pierre Jeanneret, OEeureres completes: the first volume includes the period 1910-1929, the second, 1929-1964, the third, 1964-1968, the forth, 1938-1946, the fifth, 1946-1952. [NA1053.J4A46] 720.81 57-38938
1. Architecture— Designs and plans. I. Jeanneret-Gris, Charles Educuard, 1887- II. Boesiger, Willy.

REIDY, Affonso Eduardo 720.981
The works of Affonso Eduardo Reidy. Introd. by S. Giedion. Text by Klaus Franck. [Introd. translated by Mary Hottinger. Text translated by D. Q. Stephenson] New York, Praeger [1960] 143p. illus., plans. 23 x 27cm. English and German 60-6997 11.50
I. Franck, Klaus. II. Title.

SEIDLER, Harry, 1923- 720.994
Houses, buildings and projects; 1955/63. Maisons, realisations et projets. Hauser, Bauten und Grossprojekte. [French tr.: Emmanuel de Maurepas. German tr.: Sergio Buzzolini, Gerd Hatje] Sydney, Horwitz Pubns. [dist. New York, Wittenborn, 1964] 216p. illus., plans. 24x 29cm. 64-4134 15.00
I. Title. II. Title: Maisons, realisations et projets. III. Title: Hauser, Bauten und Grossprojekte.

SKIDMORE, Owings & Merrill. 720.973
Architecture of Skidmore, Owings & Merrill, 1950-1962. Introd. by Henry Russell Hitchcock. Text by Ernst Danz. (Translation into English: Ernst van Haagen. Translation of introd. into German: Antje Pehnt New York, Praeger [1963, c1962] 231 p. illus., plans. 29 cm. (Books that matter) English and German. [NA737.S53D3] 63-8834
1. Architecture—Designs and plans. I. Danz, Ernst.

SPECIFIC Development 720'.924 Consultants, inc., Sherman Oaks, Calif.
Land of the Navajo. [Sherman Oaks? Calif., 1963] 1 v. (chiefly illus., plans) 36 x 44 cm. Includes bibliography. [NA737.S6A49] 66-81788
1. Architecture — Designs and plans. 2. Navaho Indians. 3. Indians of North America — Dwellings. I. Title.

Architecture—Designs and plans—Catalogs.

MASSEY, James C. 016.72'028
Sources for American architectural drawings in foreign collections; a preliminary survey carried out under a grant from the Ford Foundation [by] James C. Massey. Washington, 1969. 140 l. illus. 28 cm. Includes bibliographical references. [NA705.M36] 73-158773
1. Architecture—Designs and plans—Catalogs. 2. Cities and towns—United States—Maps—Catalogs. 3. Architecture—United States—Manuscripts—Catalogs. 4. Archives—Directories. I. Title.

Architecture—Details.

GATZ, Konrad, ed. 729.3
Modern architectural detailing: v.2. Tr. from German by Thomas E. Burton. New York, Reinhold [c.1965] 284p. illus. (part. col.) plans. 31cm. [NA2840.G313] 62-19480 17.50
1. Architecture—Details. 2. Architecture, Modern—20th cent. I. Title.

GATZ, Konrad, ed. 729.3
Modern architectural detailing; v. 1. Tr. from German by Thomas E. Burton. New York, Reinhold [1963, c.1961] 299p. illus. (pt. col.) plans. 31cm. Orig. pub. in the magazine Detail--Zeitschrift fur Architektur + Baudetail. 62-19480 16.50
1. Architecture—Details. 2. Architecture, Modern— 20th cent. I. Title.

GATZ, Konrad, ed. 729.3
Modern architectural detailing. v.3. Tr. from German by Thomas E. Burton. New York, Reinhold [1967] v. illus. (pt. col.) plans. 31cm. V. 3 tr. by P. Browning, L. Fuller. Orig. pub. in the magazine Detail [NA2840.G313] 62-19480 18.50
1. Architecture—Details. 2. Architecture, Modern—20th cent. I. Title. BIP

LAFEVER, Minard. 721
The beauties of modern architecture. New introd. by Denys Peter Myers. New York, Da Capo Press, 1968. xii, [105], [65]-139 p. illus. 26 cm. (Da Capo Press series in architecture and decorative art, v. 18) Reprint of the 1835 ed. Bibliography: p. [ix]-xii. [NA2840.L18 1968] 68-29602
1. Architecture—Details. 2. Architecture—History. I. Title. BIP

LANGLEY, Batty, 1696-1751. 729'.3
The builder's jewel; or, The youth's instructor and workman's remembrancer [by] Batty and Thomas Langley. New York, B. Blom, 1970. 34, 99 p. 100 plates. 17 cm. Reprint of the 1757 ed. [NA2840.L2 1970] 69-16325
1. Architecture—Details. 2. Architecture—Orders. I. Langley, Thomas, 1702-1751, joint author. II. Title. BIP

PARENT, David C. 729'.3
Peaks, parapets, and steeples, by David C. Parent. Lawrence, Mass., Glenridge Associates [1970] [60] p. (chiefly illus.) 23 cm. [NA2840.P36] 72-20524 1.85
1. Architecture—Details. I. Title.

POTHORN, Herbert. 720
Architectural styles. New York, Viking Press [1971, c1970] 187 p. illus. (part col.), plans (part col.) 25 cm. (A Studio book) Translation of Baustile. [NA2840.P7313] 77-101774 ISBN 0-670-13100-8 7.95
1. Architecture—Details. 2. Decoration and ornament, Architectural. 3. Architecture—Terminology. I. Title.

PROGRESSIVE architecture. 720
Selected architectural details for architects, engineers, designers & draftsmen. New York, Reinhold [196-?] 128p. illus. 28cm. [NA2840.P77] 62-6156
1. Architecture—Details. I. Title.

SCHMIDT, Carl Frederick, 1894- 728.3
Colonial and post-Colonial details, by Carl F. Schmidt. [Scottsville, N.Y., 1969] 61, 103 p. illus., plans. 29 cm. [NA707.S3] 77-6695
1. Architecture—Details. 2. Architecture—U.S. I. Title.

SCHMIDT, Carl Frederick, 1894- 720.9'73
Greek revival details, by Carl F. Schmidt. [Scottsville, N.Y., 1968] 144 p. (chiefly illus., plans) 29 cm. "No. 114 of 350 copies." [NA710.S3] 68-4183
1. Architecture—Details. 2. Greek revival (Architecture)—United States. I. Title.

TUTHILL, William Burnet, 1855-1929. 728
Interiors and interior details : fifty-two large quarto plates, comprising a large number of original designs of halls, staircases, parlors, libraries, dining rooms, &c. ... / by Wm. B. Tuthill. New York : Da Capo Press, 1975. [84] p. : ill. ; 35 cm. (Da Capo Press series in architecture and decorative art) Reprint of the 1882 ed. published by W. T. Comstock, New York. [NA2851.T9 1975] 75-4785 ISBN 0-306-70747-0 lib.bdg. : 22.50
1. Architecture—Details. I. Title. BIP

Architecture—Detroit.

DETROIT architecture; 720'.9774'34 A.I.A. guide. Katharine Mattingly Meyer, editor. With an introd. by W. Hawkins Ferry. [Prepared under the sponsorship of] the American Institute of Architects, Detroit Chapter. Detroit, Wayne State University Press, 1971. 202 p. illus., col. maps. 19 cm. "The material in this guide was drawn largely from the book by W. Hawkins Ferry, The buildings of Detroit: a history." [NA735.D4D4 1971] 74-157267 2.95
1. Architecture—Detroit. 2. Detroit—Description—Guide-books. I. Meyer, Katharine Mattingly, ed. II. Ferry, W. Hawkins. The buildings of Detroit. III. American Institute of Architects. Detroit Chapter.

Architecture—Detroit—History.

FERRY, W. Hawkins. 720'.9774'34
The buildings of Detroit; a history, by W. Hawkins Ferry. Detroit, Wayne State University Press, 1968. xxii, 479 p. 466 illus., maps. 32 cm. "A centennial publication." Bibliography: p. 455-456. [NA735.D4F4] 68-20167 10.00
1. Architecture—Detroit—History. I. Title. BIP

Architecture—Devon, Eng.

PEVSNER, Nikolaus, 1902- 720.942
North Devon. Harmondsworth, Middlesex. Penguin Books [1952] 200p. illus., fold. map. 18cm. (The Buildings of England, BE 4) [NA969.D4P4] 53-33171
1. Architecture—Devon, Eng. I. Title. II. Series.

PEVSNER, Nikolaus, 1902- 720.942
South Devon. Harmondsworth, Middlesex, Penguin Books [1952] 351p. illus., 80 plates, fold. map. 18cm. (The Buildings of England, BE5) [NA969.D4P4] 53-27386
1. Architecture—Devon, Eng. I. Title. II. Series.

Architecture—Dictionaries.

BRIGGS, Martin Shaw 720.3
Everyman's concise encyclopaedia of architecture. With line-drawings by the author and 32p. of photos. New York, Dutton [1959] xi, 372p. illus. 20cm. (Everyman's reference library) 59-5837 5.00
1. Architecture—Dictionaries. I. Title.

BURKE, Arthur E. 690.3
Architectural and building trades dictionary [by] Arthur E. Burke, J. Ralph Dalzell [and] Gilbert Townsend. Edited by Pearl Jenison. Chicago, American Technical Society, 1950. 377 p. illus. 22 cm. [NA31.B84] 50-8147
1. Architecture—Dictionaries. 2. Building—Dictionaries. I. American Technical Society, Chicago. II. Title.

BURKE, Arthur Edward, 1909- 690.3
Architectural and building trades dictionary [by] Arthur E. Burke, J. Ralph Dalzell [and] Gilbert Townsend. Edited by Pearl Jenison. Chicago, American Technical Society, 1955. xxxviii, 377p. illus. 22cm. [NA31.B84 1955] 56-433
1. Architecture-Dictionaries. 2. Building-Dictionaries. I. Title.

COWAN, Henry J. 721'.03
Dictionary of architectural science [by] Henry J. Cowan. New York, Wiley [1973] xi, 354 p. illus. 23 cm. "A Halsted Press book." Bibliography: p. 301-311. [NA31.C64] 73-15839 ISBN 0-470-18070-6 10.95
1. Architecture—Dictionaries. 2. Building—Dictionaries. I. Title. BIP

DICTIONARY of architectural abbreviations, signs, and symbols. 720.3 Ed.: David D. Polon. Managing ed.: Herber W. Reich. Project director: Marjorie B. Witty. Assoc. ed.: William H. Walker. New York, Odyssey [1966, c.1965] xvii, 595p. illus. 26cm. (Odyssey sci. lib.) At head of title: DAA. [NA31D53] 65-18847 20.00
1. Architecture—Dictionaries. I. Polon, David D., ed. II. Title: DAA.

ENCYCLOPEDIA of architectural technology 720 / Pedro Guedes, editor in chief. New York : McGraw-Hill, c1979. p. cm. Includes index. [NA31.E58] 78-16571 ISBN 0-07-051740-1 : 21.00
1. Architecture—Dictionaries. I. Guedes, Pedro.

FLEMING, John 1919- 720.3
The Penguin dictionary of architecture [by] John Fleming. Hugh Honour. Nikolaus Pevsner. Drawings by David Etherton. Baltimore, Penguin [1966] 247p. illus., plans. 20cm. (Penguin ref. bks. R13) [NA31.F55] 66-2846 1.95 pap.,
1. Architecture—Dictionaries. I. Honour, Hugh. joint author. II. Pevsner. Nikolaus. 1902- joint author. III. Title. IV. Title: Dictionary of architecture.

FLEMING, John, 1919- 720.3
The Penguin dictionary of architecture, [by] John Fleming, Hugh Honour, Nikolaus Pevsner; drawings by David Etherton. Harmondsworth, Penguin, 1966. 248 p. illus., plans, diagrs. 20 cm. (Penguin reference books, R13) 8/6 (B66-2039) [NA31.F55 1966a] 66-70279
1. Architecture — Dictionaries. I. Honour, Hugh. II. Pevsner, Nikolaus, 1902- III. Title. IV. Title: Dictionary of architecture. BIP

FLEMING, John, 1919- 720'.3
The Penguin dictionary of architecture [by] John Fleming, Hugh Honour [and] Nikolaus Pevsner; drawings by David Etherton. 2nd ed. Harmondsworth, Penguin, 1972. 315 p. illus., plans. 20 cm. (Penguin reference books) [NA31.F55 1972] 73-156287 ISBN 0-14-051013-3 2.10
1. Architecture—Dictionaries. I. Honour, Hugh. II. Pevsner, Nikolaus, 1902- III. Title.
Distributed by Penguin Baltimore, Md.

HARRIS, Cyril M. 720'.3
Dictionary of architecture and construction / edited by Cyril M. Harris. New York : McGraw-Hill, [1975] xv, 553 p. : ill. ; 25 cm. [NA31.H32] 74-30219 35.00
1. Architecture—Dictionaries. 2. Building—Dictionaries. I. Title. BIP

HARRIS, John, 1931- 720'.3
Illustrated glossary of architecture, 850-1830 [by] John Harris & Jill Lever. New York, C. N. Potter [c1966] xi, 78 p. 224 illus., plans. 26 cm. Bibliography: p. 77-78. [NA31.H34] 67-22528
1. Architecture — Dictionaries. I. Lever, Jill, joint author. II. Title. BIP

HISTORIC architecture sourcebook 720'.3 / edited by Cyril M. Harris. New York : McGraw-Hill, 1976c1977 p. cm. Includes index. [NA31.H56] 76-39802 ISBN 0-07-026755-3 : 15.95
1. Architecture—Dictionaries. I. Harris, Cyril M. BIP

OSBORNE, Arthur Leslie. 728
A dictionary of English domestic architecture. New York, Philosophical Library [1956] 111p. illus., plans. 26cm. [NA31] 57-926
1. Architecture—Dictionaries. 2. Architecture, Domestic —England. I. Title. II. Title: English domestic architecture.

SAYLOR, Henry Hodgman, 1880- 720.3
Dictionary of Architecture. New York, Wiley [1952] xi, 221 p. illus. 18 cm. [NA31.S25] 52-8260
1. Architecture — Dictionaries. I. Title. BIP

STURGIS, Russell, 1836-1909 720'.3
A dictionary of architecture and buildings biographical, historical, and descriptive, by Russell Sturgis and many architects, painters, engineers, and other expert writers, American and foreign. Detroit, Gale, 1966. 3 v. illus. 24cm. Reprint of the 1902 ed. Bibl. [NA31.S84 1966] 66-26997 45.00 set,
1. Architecture—Dictionaries. 2. Architecture—Bibl. 3. Architects. I. Title.

†WHITE, Norval. 720'.3
The architecture book / by Norval White. 1st ed. New York : Knopf, 1976. 343 p. : ill. ; 24 cm. [NA31.W45 1976] 76-13713 ISBN 0-394-49326-5 : 15.00
1. Architecture—Dictionaries. I. Title. BIP

SUBJECT INDEX

ARCHITECTURE, DOMESTIC— AUSTRALIA.

Architecture—Dictionaries—Polyglot.

ZBOINSKI, A., ed. 721.03
Dictionary of architecture and building trades in four languages: English, German, Polish, Russian. Ed. by A. Zboinski, L. Tyszynski [Oxford] Pergamon Press; New York, Macmillan [c.] 1963. 491p. 25cm. Based on the card register of the Tech. Terminology Div. of Wydawnictwa Naukowo-Techniczne, Warsaw. 63-22975 20.00
1. Architecture—Dictionaries—Polyglot. 2. Building Dictionaries—Polyglot. I. Tyszynski, L., joint ed. II. Title.

ZBOINSKI, A., ed. 720'.3
Dictionary of architecture and building trades in four languages: English, German, Polish [and] Russian, edited by A. Zboinski and L. Tyszynski. New York, Macmillan [1963] 491 p. 25 cm. "A Pergamon Press book." [NA31.Z34 1963b] 62-22062
1. Architecture—Dictionaries—Polyglot. 2. Building—Dictionaries—Polyglot. I. Tyszynski, L., joint ed. II. Title.

Architecture—Diyala, Mesopotamia.

DELOUGAZ, Pinhas. 722'.51
Private houses and graves in the Diyala region, by Pinhas Delougaz, Harold D. Hill, and Seton Lloyd. Chicago, University of Chicago Press [1967] xvii, 361 p. illus., maps (part fold.), plans. 30 cm. (The University of Chicago Oriental Institute publications, v. 88) "This publication is one of a group planned to present as a whole the work of the Oriental Institute's Iraq Expedition in the Diyala region." Contents.Contents.—Khafaja, by P. Delougaz.—Tell Asmar: The private house area, by H. D. Hill. The northern palace area, by S. Lloyd. Remarks concerning dating and function of the northern palace, by P. Delougaz. The town wall, by S. Lloyd. Soundings made in the search for Esikil, by S. Lloyd. Catalogue of objects.—Tell Agrab, by S. Lloyd.—Concluding remarks, by P. Delougaz. [NA221.D5D4 1967] 64-8911
1. Architecture—Diyala, Mesopotamia. 2. Diyala, Mesopotamia—Antiquities. I. Hill, Harold D. II. Lloyd, Seton. III. Chicago. University. Oriental Institute. Iraq Expedition, 1930-1937. IV. Title. V. Series: Chicago. University. Oriental Institute. Publications, v. 88. BIP

Architecture, Domestic.

BEAZLEY, Elizabeth 728
Designed to live in. London, Allen & Unwin [Dist. New Rochelle, N.Y., SportShelf, 1963 c.1962] 198p. illus. 22cm. Bibl. 63-3375 8.50 bds.,
1. Architecture, Domestic. 2. Architecture, Domestic—England. I. Title.

BEYER, Glenn H 728
Houses are for people; a study of home buyer motivations [by] Glenn H. Beyer, Thomas W. Mackesey [and] James E. Montgomery. [Ithaca] Cornell University Housing Research Center [1955] 58p. illus. 29cm. ([Cornell University. Housing Research Center] Research publication no. 3) [NA7115.B4] 55-12061
1. Architecture, Domestic. I. Title.

COREY, Paul, 1903- 728.6
Homemade homes. New York, Sloane [1950] viii, 309 p. illus. 22 cm. [NA7120.C725] 50-11160
1. Architecture, Domestic. I. Title.

FOWLER, Orson Squire, 1809-1887. 728'.3
The octagon house; a home for all. With a new introd. by Madeleine B. Stern. New York, Dover Publications [1973] xii, 192 p. illus. 22 cm. Reprint of the 1853 ed. published by S. R. Wells, New York, under title: A home for all. Bibliography: p. xii. [NA7125.F775 1973] 72-93768 ISBN 0-486-22887-8 3.00 (pbk.)
1. Architecture, Domestic. 2. Buildings, Octagonal. I. Title. BIP

GOTTLIEB, Lois Davidson. 728.6024
Environment and design in housing. Julius Shulman, photography consultant. New York, Macmillan [1965] xiv. 258 p. illus. (part col.) 27 cm. Bibliography: p. 255-258. [NA7115.G6] 65-16560
1. Architecture, Domestic. 2. Architecture and climate. I. Title.

GRESSWELL, Peter 728.6
Houses in the country; a primer for those who live in or look at new houses in the country. London, Batsford [dist. New Rochelle, N.Y., SportShelf, 1965, c.1964] 160p. illus., plan. 26cm. [NA7560.G7] 64-6665 14.00
1. Architecture, Domestic. I. Title.

GUIDELINES Publications. 720'.28 s
Residential and other light frame construction. Orinda, Calif. : Guidelines Publications, 1975, c1974. 66 p. ; 29 cm. (Its Architectural working drawing check list ; 2) [NA2700.G83 1974 vol. 2] [NA7110] 728'.3 75-326322 pbk. : 6.00
1. Architecture, Domestic. 2. Architecture—Details. I. Title.

KASSIER, Elizabeth (Bauer) 1911- 728.6
If you want to build a house by Elizabeth B. Mock. Illustrated by Robert C. Osborn. [New York] Museum of Modern Art [1946] 96 p. illus. 26 cm. [NA7120.K23] 46-4224
1. Architecture. Domestic. 2. Architecture, Domestic — Designs and plans. I. New York. Museum of Modern Art. II. Title.

KEISER, Marjorie B. 728
Housing : an environment for living / Marjorie Branin Keiser. New York : Macmillan, c1978. ix, 358 p. : ill. ; 26 cm. Includes bibliographies and index. [NA7125.K44] 77-1259 ISBN 0-02-362230-X : 13.95
1. Architecture, Domestic. 2. Architecture—Environmental aspects. I. Title.

KENNEDY, Robert Woods. 728
The house and the art of its design. New York, Reinhold [1953] ix, 550 p. illus. 24 cm. (Progressive architecture library) Bibliography: p. 535-539. [NA7110.K28] 53-9169
1. Architecture, Domestic. I. Title. II. Series. BIP

KENNEDY, Robert Woods. 728
The house and the art of its design / by Robert Woods Kennedy. Huntington, N.Y. : R. E. Krieger Pub. Co., 1975, c1945. ix, 550 p. : ill. ; 24 cm. Reprint of the ed. published by Reinhold, New York, in series: Progressive architecture library. Includes bibliographical references and index. [NA7110.K28 1975] 74-32250 ISBN 0-88275-275-8 : 16.50
1. Architecture, Domestic. I. Title.

KING, A. Rowden. 728.084
Realtors' guide to architecture; how to identify and sell every kind of home. New York, Prentice-Hall, 1954. 234 p. illus. 24 cm. [NA7120.K5] 54-6122
1. Architecture, Domestic. I. Title.

KIRKPATRICK, Waldo Adams. 728.6084
The house of your dreams: how to plan and get it. New York, McGraw-Hill [1958] 198 p. illus. 26 cm. [NA7115.K5] 58-7420
1. Architecture, Domestic. 2. Interior decoration. I. Title.

MCCONNELL, Pauline. 643.7
George Washington's horse slept here. New York, T.Y. Crowell [c1956] 218p. illus. 21cm. Autobiographical. [NA7120.M23] 56-9792
1. Architecture, Domestic. 2. Architecture—Conservation and restoration. I. Title.

MOORE, Charles, 1925- 728.3
The place of houses [by] Charles Moore, Gerald Allen [and] Donlyn Lyndon. With axonometric drawings by William Turnbull. [1st ed.] New York, Holt, Rinehart and Winston [1974] ix, 278 p. illus. 25 cm. [NA7125.M66] 70-182776 ISBN 0-03-007726-5
1. Architecture, Domestic. 2. Architecture and climate. 3. Architecture and society. I. Allen, Gerald, joint author. II. Lyndon, Donlyn, joint author. III. Title. BIP

NEUTRA, Richard Joseph, 1892- 728.084
Life and human habitat. Mensch und Wohnen. Stuttgart, A. Koch [1956] 317p. illus. (part col) ports., plans. 31cm. Text in English: illus. have descriptive legends in English and German. Bibliography: p. 314. [NA7110.N38] 56-2606
1. Architecture, Domestic. 2. Architecture, Domestic—Designs and plans. 3. Architecture, Domestic—California I. Title.

OSMOND, Edward, 1900- 728
Houses. written and illustrated by Edward Osmond. New York, Macmillan [1956] 80p. illus. 21cm. (Junior heritage books) [NA7120.O73] 56-14132
1. Architecture, Domestic. I. Title.

ROBERTS, Rex. 728.6
Your engineered house. New York, M. Evans; distributed in association with Lippincott, Philadelphia [1964] 237 p. illus., plans. 26 cm. [NA7115.R6] 64-20782
1. Architecture, Domestic. 2. House construction. I. Title. BIP

ROYAL Barry Wills Associates. 728'.022'2
More houses for good living, by Royal Barry Wills associates: Richard Wills, Robert E. Minot [and] Warren J. Rohter. New York, Architectural Book Pub. Co. [1968] 128 p. illus. 29 cm. [NA7120.R75] 68-31686 ISBN 0-8038-0162-9 7.95
1. Architecture, Domestic. 2. Architecture, Domestic—Designs and plans. I. Wills, Richard II. Minot, Robert E. III. Rohter, Warren J. IV. Title. BIP

SEYMOUR, Robert Grimmer, 1913- ed. 728
When I have a house: a guide to decisions about home building and remodeling. Authors: Raymon H. Harrell [and others] Champaign, Ill., Guideways [1961] 152 p. illus. 30 cm. Includes bibliography. [NA7120.S19] 61-10741
1. Architecture. Domestic. 2. Dwellings — Remodeling. I. Harrell, Raymon H. II. Title.

SUNSET. 728.6
Sunset ideas for hillside homes; ideas compiled from Sunset magazine. [2d ed.] Menlo Park, Calif., Lane Pub. Co. [1956] 88 p. illus. 28 cm. [NA7110.S88 1956] 56-8589
1. Architecture, Domestic. I. Title. II. Title: Hillside homes.

THORNDIKE, Joseph J., 1913- 909
The magnificent builders and their dream houses / by Joseph J. Thorndike Jr. and the editors of American Heritage. New York : American Heritage Pub. Co. : book trade distribution by Simon and Schuster, c1978. 352 p. : ill. (some col.) ; 29 cm. Includes index. [NA7120.T46] 78-18371 ISBN 0-8281-3064-7 : 34.95. ISBN 0-8281-3072-8 de luxe : 39.95
1. Architecture, Domestic. 2. Biography. I. American heritage. II. Title.

TOWNSEND, Gilbert, 1880- 728
How to plan a house, by Gilbert Townsend and J. Ralph Dalzell. 2d ed. Chicago, American Technical Society, 1952. 584 p. illus. 22 cm. [NA7115.T6] 52-10904
1. Architecture, Domestic. I. Title.

TOWNSEND, Gilbert, 1880- 728
How to plan a house, by Gilbert Townsend and J. Ralph Dalzell. Contributor to 3d ed.: Rexford Battenberg. [3d ed., rev.] Chicago, American Technical Society, 1958. 591 p. illus. 22 cm. (Books of the building trade series) [NA7115.T6 1958] 58-8306
1. Architecture, Domestic. I. Dalzell, James Ralph, 1900- joint author. II. Title.

YORKE, Francis Reginald Stevens, 1906- 728.6084
The modern house. [8th ed., rev.] London, Architectural Press [1957] 228p. illus., plans. 26cm. [NA7110.Y6 1957] 57-43093
1. Architecture, Domestic. 2. Architecture, Domestic—Designs and plans. I. Title.

Architecture, Domestic—Addresses, essays, lectures.

ROWE, Colin. 720'.8
The mathematics of the ideal villa, and other essays / Colin Rowe. Cambridge, Mass. : MIT Press, c1976. p. cm. Contents.Contents.—The mathematics of the ideal villa.—Mannerism and modern architecture.—Character and composition.—Chicago frame.—Neo-classicism and modern architecture I.—Neo-classicism and modern architecture II.—Transparency: literal and phenomenal (with R. Slutsky).—La Tourette.—The architecture of utopia. Includes bibliographical references. [NA7110.R68] 75-33908 ISBN 0-262-18077-4 : 15.95
1. Architecture, Domestic—Addresses, essays, lectures. I. Title. BIP

Architecture, Domestic—Alabama.

HAMMOND, Ralph Charles, 1916- 728.37
Ante-bellum mansions of Alabama. Photos-by the author;plans by Edwin B. Lancaster New York, Architectural Book Co. [1951] 196 p. illus., maps, plans. 29 cm. [NA7235.A6H3] 52-191
1. Architecture, Domestic—Alabama. I. Title.

Architecture, Domestic—Amateurs' manuals.

GODDARD, Murray. 728
How to be your own architect / by Murray Goddard. Blue Ridge Summit, Pa. : Tab Books, [1977] p. cm. Includes index. [NA7111.G54] 77-15481 ISBN 0-8306-7988-X : 8.95. ISBN 0-8306-6988-4 pbk. : 5.95
1. Architecture, Domestic—Amateurs' manuals. 2. Architecture, Domestic—Designs and plans. I. Title. BIP

WALKER, Les. 728.3
Designing houses : an illustrated guide / by Les Walker and Jeff Milstein. 1st ed. Woodstock, N.Y. : Overlook Press, 1976. 153 p. : ill. ; 24 cm. Bibliography: p. 148. [NA7115.W34] 75-7684 ISBN 0-87951-035-8 : 10.00
1. Architecture, Domestic—Amateur's manuals. 2. Architecture, Domestic—Designs and plans. I. Milstein, Jeff, joint author. II. Title. BIP

Architecture, Domestic — Antioch.

STILLWELL, Richard, 1899- 246
Houses of Antioch. In Dumbarton Oaks papers. Cambridge, Mass. 30 cm. no. 15 (1961) p. [45]-57. plates) Bibliographical footnotes. [N5970.D8 no. 15] A65
1. Architecture, Domestic — Antioch. I. Title.

Architecture, Domestic—Austin, Tex.

HARRIS, August Watkins. 728.084
Minor and major mansions & their companions in early Austin... [Austin? Tex., 1958] [52]p. illus. plans. 33cm. [NA7238.A8H28] 58-6923
1. Architecture, Domestic— Austin Tex. 2. Architecture, Domestic— Designs and plans. I. Title.

HARRIS, August Watkins. 728.084
Minor and major mansions in early Austin. An edition composite. [Austin? Tex., 1958] [116]p. illus., plans. 33cm. Includes the 1955 ed. of this work and the author's Minor andmajor mansions & their companions in early Austin, 1958, with special t.p. [NA7238.A8H3 1958] 58-7255
1. Architecture, Domestic—Austin, Tex. 2. Architecture, Domestic—Designs and plans. I. Harris, August Watkins. Minor and major mansions their companions in early Austin. II. Title.

Architecture, Domestic— Australia.

BOYD, Robin. 728
Australia's home; its origins, builders, and occupiers. [Carlton] melbourne University Press [1952] 287p. illus. 22cm. [NA7469.B6] 52-39322
1. Architecture, Domestic— Australia. I. Title.

BOYD, Robin. 728'.0994
Australia's home; its origins, builders and occupiers. [Rev., i.e. 2nd ed. Ringwood, Vic.] Penguin Books [1968] 316 p. illus., diagrs. 19 cm. (Australian pelican books, AU 21) [NA7469.B6 1968] 76-417456 1.75

1. Architecture, Domestic—Australia. I. Title.

LIVING & partly living: 728.3
housing in Australia [by] Ian Mackay — [and others]. Melbourne, Thomas Nelson (Australia), 1971 [i.e. 1972]. 195 p. illus. (part col.) 25 cm. Title on two consecutive recto pages. Index. [NA7469.L58] 73-169216 ISBN 0-17-001908-X
1. Architecture, Domestic—Australia. 2. Architecture, Modern—20th century—Australia. 3. Architecture and society—Australia. I. McKay, Ian David.

Architecture, Domestic—Avoyelles Parish, La.

DECUIR, Randy P. 976.3'71
Avoyelles homes : a history of Avoyelles Parish as seen through its architecture ... / by Randy P. DeCuir ; co-edited by Blanche Arceneaux Swann and Marion H. Gremillion ; with photos by Randy P. DeCuir. Marksville, La. : Gremillion Print. Co., 1975. 56 p. : ill. ; 28 cm. [NA7235.L82A864] 75-322578
1. Architecture, Domestic—Avoyelles Parish, La. I. Title.

Architecture, Domestic—Boston—History.

BUNTING, Bainbridge. 728.3'1'0974461
Houses of Boston's Back Bay; an architectural history, 1840-1917. Cambridge, Belknap Press of Harvard University Press, 1967. xvii, 494 p. illus., maps, plans. 25 cm. Bibliographical references included in "Notes" (p. [463]-484) [NA7237.B65B8] 66-21334
1. Architecture, Domestic—Boston—History. 2. Decoration and ornament—Boston. I. Title. BIP

Architecture, Domestic — Brooklyn.

BROOKLYN Institute of Arts and Sciences. Museum. 720.973
The Jan Martense Schenk house, by Marvin D. Schwartz, curator of decorative arts. [Brooklyn, 1964] 39 p. illus., plans. 23 cm. Bibliographical references included in "Notes" (p. 38-39) [NA735.B74B7] 65-1291
1. Architecture, Domestic — Brooklyn. 2. Schenk, Jan Martense. I. Schwartz, Marvin D. II. Title.

Architecture, Domestic—California.

BAYLIS, Douglas. 728.6
California houses of Gordon Drake [by] Douglas Baylis and Joan Parry. New York, Reinhold Pub. Corp. [1956] 91 p. illus. 23 cm. [NA737.D7B3] 56-11751
1. Drake, Gordon, 1917-1952. 2. Architecture, Domestic—California. I. Parry, Joan, joint author. II. Title.

CRANDALL, Chuck. 728.3
They chose to be different; unusual California homes. San Francisco, Chronicle Books [1972] 131 p. illus. 27 cm. [NA7235.C2C72] 72-85174 9.95
1. Architecture, Domestic—California. 2. Architecture, Modern—20th century—California. I. Title.

FENYES, Eva Scott, d.1930. 751.42
Thirty-two adobe houses of old California, reproduced from watercolor paintings by Eva Scott Fenyes. Descriptive text by Isabel Lopez de Fages. A special publication of the Southwest Museum. Los Angeles, 1950. 76 p. illus. 18 x 27 cm. [ND1839.F4L6] 52-1164
1. Architecture, Domestic—California. 2. Building, Adobe. I. Lopez de fages, Isabel. II. Title. III. Title: Adobe houses of old California. BIP

LEWIS, Oscar, 1893- 728
Here lived the Californians. New York, Rinehart [1957] 265 p. illus. 26 cm. [NA7235.C2L45] 57-5058
1. Architecture, Domestic—California. I. Title.

MCCOY, Esther. 728.64084
Modern California houses; case study houses, 1945-1962. New York, Reinhold Pub. Corp. [1962] 215 p. illus., ports., plans. 19 x 26 cm. [NA7235.C2M2] 62-17174
1. Architecture, Domestic—California. 2. Architecture, Domestic—Designs and plans. I. Title.

NEWSOM, Samuel. 728.3
Picturesque California homes / by Samuel Newsom, Joseph Cather Newsom ; with an introd. by David Gebhard. Los Angeles : Hennessey & Ingalls, 1978. p. cm. Facsim. of v. 1 of the work published by the authors in 4 v. in 1884. [NA7235.C2N472 1884a] 78-4248 ISBN 0-912158-82-4 pbk. : 12.95
1. Architecture, Domestic—California. 2. Architecture, Victorian—California. 3. Dwellings—California. I. Newsom, Joseph Cather, joint author. II. Title.
Publisher's address : 11833 Wilshire Blvd., Los Abngeles, Calif. 90025 BIP

WEISSKAMP, Herbert. 728.64
Beautiful homes and gardens in California. [Translated from the German by Herbert Weisskamp] New York, H. N. Abrams [1965, c1964] 211 p. illus. (part col.) 23 cm. Translation of: Hauser und Garten in Kalifornien. [NA7235.C2W43] 65-19223
1. Architecture, Domestic — California. 2. Architecture, Domestic — Designs and plans. 3. Gardens — California. I. Title.

Architecture, Domestic—California—Case studies.

MCCOY, Esther. 728.3
Case study houses, 1945-1962 / by Esther McCoy. 2d ed. Los Angeles : Hennessey & Ingalls, 1977. p. cm. First ed. published in 1962 under title: Modern California houses. Bibliography: p. [NA7235.C2M2 1977] 77-14499 ISBN 0-912158-70-0 : 28.50 pbk. : 14.95
1. Architecture, Domestic—California—Case studies. 2. Architecture, Modern—20th century—California—Case studies. 3. Architecture—California—Case studies. I. Title. BIP

Architecture, Domestic—California—San Francisco.

BAER, Morley. 728.3'7'0979461
Painted ladies : San Francisco's resplendent Victorians / Morley Baer, Elizabeth Pomada, Michael Larsen. 1st ed. New York : Dutton, 1978. 80 p. : col. ill. ; 29 cm. Bibliography: p. 80. [NA7238.S35B33] 78-59312 ISBN 0-525-17441-9 : 19.95. ISBN 0-525-47523-0 pbk. : 10.95
1. Architecture, Domestic—California—San Francisco. 2. Architecture, Victorian—California—San Francisco. 3. San Francisco—Dwellings. 4. Decoration and ornament, Architectural—California—San Francisco. I. Pomada, Elizabeth, joint author. II. Larsen, Michael, joint author. III. Title. BIP

OLWELL, Carol, 1944- 728.3
A gift to the street / photos. by Carol Olwell ; commentary by Judith Lynch Waldhorn. San Francisco : Antelope Island Press, 1976. xv, 195 p. : ill. ; 31 cm. Includes index. [NA7238.S35O48] 76-26576 pbk. : 10.95
1. Architecture, Domestic—California—San Francisco. 2. Architecture, Victorian—San Francisco. 3. Architecture, Domestic—United States. 4. Architecture, Victorian—United States. I. Waldhorn, Judith Lynth. II. Title. BIP

Architecture, Domestic—California—San Francisco bay region.

BAY area houses / 728.3
edited by Sally Woodbridge ; introd. by David Gebhard ; photos. by Morley Baer, Roger Sturtevant, and others ; architectural drawings by Randolph Meadors and Floyd Campbell. New York : Oxford University Press, 1976. 329 p. : ill. ; 29 cm. Includes bibliographical references and index. [NA7235.C22S353] 76-9261 ISBN 0-19-502084-7 : 29.95
1. Architecture, Domestic—California—San Francisco bay region. 2. Dwellings—California—San Francisco bay region. I. Woodbridge, Sally Byrne. II. Baer, Morley. III. Sturtevant, Roger. BIP

Architecture, Domestic—California—San Francisco Bay region—Guide-books.

WALDHORN, Judith Lynch. 917.94'6'045
Victoria's legacy : tours of San Francisco Bay Area architecture / Judith Lynch Waldhorn and Sally Woodbridge ; drawings by Wendy Wheeler. San Francisco : 101 Productions, c1978. p. cm. Includes index. Bibliography: p. [NA7238.S35W34] 78-18350 ISBN 0-89286-139-8 : 5.95
1. Architecture, Domestic—California—San Francisco Bay region—Guide-books. 2. Architecture, Modern—19th century—California—San Francisco Bay region—Guide-books. 3. Architecture, Victorian—California—San Francisco Bay region—Guide-books. 4. San Francisco—Dwellings—Guide-books. I. Woodbridge, Sally Byrne, joint author. II. Title. BIP

Architecture, Domestic—California, Southern.

NEFF, Wallace 728.6
Architecture of southern California; a selection of photographs, plans, and scale details from the work of Wallace Neff. Chicago, Rand McNally [c.1964] 144p. chiefly illus. (pt. col.) plans 27cm. [NA7235.C2N4] 64-24392 14.95
1. Architecture, Domestic—California, Southern. I. Title.

Architecture, Domestic—Calticugan, Philippines.

HART, Donn Vorhis, 1918- 728.6099145
The Cebuan Filipino dwelling in Caticugan: its construction and cultural aspects. [New Haven] Yale University, Southeast Asia Studies, 1959 [c1958] 148p. illus. 28cm. (Yale University. Southeast Asia Studies. Cultural report series) [NA7444.C3H3] 59-4281
1. Architecture, Domestic—Calticugan, Philippines. 2. Caticugan, Philippines—Soc. life & cust. I. Title.

Architecture, Domestic — Case Studies.

ILLINOIS. University. Small Homes Council-Building Research Council. 728.6084
Contemporary houses developed from room units; a report of an architectural investigation in house design making use of improved building techniques. Rev. ed. [Urbana, 1951] 62p. illus., plans. 28cm. (Its Technical series. Index no. C2.2R) Issued by the council under its earlier name: Small Homes Council. [TH4811.I53 no. C2.2R 1951a] 51-3435
1. Architecture, Domestic—Cesignsand plans. I. Title. II. Series.

Architecture, Domestic—China.

INN, Henry, 1899- 722.11
Chinese houses and gardens; edited by Shao Chang Lee. [2d ed.] New York, Hastings House [1950] xii, 148 p. illus. 51 cm. Added t.p. in Chinese and English: A choice collection of garden and house pictures, by Henry Inn; edited by Shao Chang Lee, characters by Ch'en Shou-yi. Contents.Contents.—Introduction, by E. C. Schenck.—Chinese houses and gardens in retrospect, by Ch'en Shou-yi.—Foreign influence in Chinese architecture, by Chuin Tung.—Chinese gardens: contrasts, designs, by Chuin Tung.—Man and nature in the Chinese garden, by Wing-tsit Chan.—The Chinese love of home and symbolism, by Shao Chang Lee.—Photographic illustrations and drawings, by Henry Inn. [NA7448.I5 1950] 50-7017
1. Architecture, Domestic—China. 2. Gardens—China. I. Li, Shao-ch'ang, 1891-ed. II. Title. III. Title: A choice collection of garden and house pictures.

Architecture, Domestic—Connecticut.

GARVAN, Anthony N. B. 720.9746
Architecture and town planning in colonial Connecticut. New Haven, Yale University Press, 1951. xiv, 166 p. illus., maps. 28 cm. (Yale historical publications. History of art. 6) "Bibliographical note": p. 152-159. Bibliographical footnotes. [NA7235.C8G3] 51-14684
1. Architecture, Domestic—Connecticut. 2. Cities and towns—Planning—Connecticut. I. Title. II. Series.

ISHAM, Norman Morrison, 1864-1943. 728.09746
Early Connecticut houses; an historical and architectural study, by Norman M. Isham and Albert F. Brown. New York, Dover Publications [1965] xiv, 303 p. illus., map, plans. 24 cm. "An unabridged and unaltered republication of the work first published ... in 1900." Bibliographical footnotes. [NA7235.C817 1965] 65-26654
1. Architecture, Domestic—Connecticut. 2. Connecticut—Historic houses, etc. I. Brown, Albert Frederic, 1862- joint author. II. Title.

KELLY, John Frederick, 1888-1947. 728.3709746
Connecticut's old houses, a handbook and guide, by J. Frederick Kelly. With an introd. by Orrin P. Kilbourn. [Stonington, Published for the Antiquarian & Landmarks Society of Connecticut by the Pequot Press, 1963] 73 p. illus. plans. 23 cm. (Connecticut booklet no. 4) Cover title. "Reprinted from the Tercentenary pamphlets series, Connecticut Tercentenary Commission, 1933-36." [NA7235.C8K39] 63-16431
1. Architecture, Domestic — Connecticut. 2. Architecture — Connecticut. I. Title. II. Series.

KELLY, John Frederick, 1888-1947. 728.09746
The early domestic architecture of Connecticut. New York, Dover Publications [1963] xvi, 210 p. illus., diagrs., plans. 28 cm. "T1136." "Unabridged and unaltered republication of the work first published ... in 1924." [NA7235.C8K42 1963] 63-20249
1. Architecture, Domestic—Connecticut. 2. Architecture, Colonial—Connecticut. 3. Architecture—Details. I. Title. BIP

Architecture, Domestic—Connecticut—Stonington.

TRASK, John J. 974.6'5
Stonington houses : a panorama of New England architecture, 1750-1900 / by John J. Trask. New York : Ivy Press, c1976. 95 p. : ill. ; 20 x 23 cm. Includes index. [NA7238.S83T7] 76-383694
1. Architecture, Domestic—Connecticut—Stonington. I. Title.

Architecture, Domestic—Conservation and restoration—England.

WHITTAKER, Neville. 728.3
The house and cottage handbook / [by] Neville Whittaker ; foreword by Sir John Summerson. Durham : Civic Trust for the North East, 1976. 120 p. : ill. (some col.), plans ; 20 x 23 cm. Bibliography: p. 114. [NA7328.W47] 77-361064 ISBN 0-905516-00-1 : £2.50
1. Architecture, Domestic—Conservation and restoration—England. 2. Architecture—Details. I. Title.

Architecture, Domestic — Designs and plans.

THE American home. 728.084
The American home book of house plans. [Forest Hills? N. Y., 1955?] 90p. illus. 32cm. [NA7127.A44 1955] 55-1221
1. Architecture, Domestic—Designs and plans. 2. Architecture, Domestic—U. S. 3. Interior decoration—U. S. I. Title.

THE American lumberman & building products merchandiser. 728.084
Old homes made new: comfort, convenience, beauty. v.1- [Chicago, 1924-v. 27 illus. 20x25cm. Published by the periodical under its earlier name: American lumberman. [NA7127.A52] 26-11799

1. Architecture, Domestic—Designs and plans. I. Title.

AMERICA'S guide to   728.6084
family homes. [East Detroit, Mich.] Homegraf. v. illus. 31cm. [NA7127.A532] 58-24758
1. Architecture Domestic—Designs and plans. I. Homograf Company, East Detroit, Mich.

ARCHITECTS Home Plan   728.6084
Institute, Minneapolis.
52 small homes [Minneapolis, 1952] unpaged. illus. 28 cm. [NA7127.A537] 52-2791
1. Architecture, Domestic—Designs and plans. 2. Architecture, Domestic—U. S. I. Title.

ARCHITECTURAL record.   728.084
The second treasury of contemporary houses. [New York] F. W. Dodge Corp., c1959. viii, 216p. illus., col. plates, plans. 30cm. [NA7127.A6615] 59-14353
1. Architecture, Domestic—Designs and plans. 2. Architecture, Domestic—U. S. I. Title.

ASSOCIATED Plan Service,   728.6084
inc., Huntington, N.Y.
This year's best homes, by America's leading architects. [New York, Universal Pub. and Distributing Corp.] v. illus., plans. 28cm. Title varies slightly. [NA7127.A78] 56-58044
1. Architecture, Domestic—Designs and plans. 2. Architecture, Domestic—U.S. I. Title.

BETTER homes and   728.6084
gardens.
Home plans. Des Moines Meredith Pub. Co. v. illus. 32cm. [NA7127.B5283] 54-4220
1. Architecture, Domestic—Designs and plans. 2. Architecture, Domestic—U. S. I. Title.

BETTER homes and gardens.   728
Remodeling ideas [by] John Normile, Guy M. Neff [and] John Mack Carter. Rev. ed. Des Moines, Meredith Pub. Co., '1951. 201 p. illus. (part col.) 32 cm. Published in 1945 under title: New ideas for remodeling your home. [NA7127.B529 1951] 51-7110
1. Architecture, Domestic—Designs and plans. 2. Interior decoration. 3. Dwellings. I. Normile, John. II. Title.

BLACKSHAW, B. B.   728
Utilization of space in dwellings; report presented by the Secretariat of the Economic Commission for Europe, prepared by M. B. Blackshaw in collaboration with P. Blokhine and M. Lebegge in consultation with the International Union of Architects. [New York, Columbia University Press. 1959] various pagings diagrs., plans, tables. 28cm. (United Nations publication. Sales no.: 59. IIE/-Mim.9.) 60-595 1.50 pap.,
1. Architecture, Domestic—Designs and plans. I. United Nations. Economic Commission for Europe. II. Title. III. Series: United Nations. Document E/ECE/350 [etc.]

THE Book of duplexes.   728.22
1st–ed.; 1951- [St. Paul] Home Plan Book Co. v. illus. 28 cm. [NA7127.B583] 51-37076
1. Architecture, Domestic—Designs and plans. I. Home Plan Book Company, St. Paul.

THE Book of rambler and   728.6084
ranch-type homes, 1st- ed.; 1951- [St. Paul] Home Plan Book Co. v. illus. 28 cm. [NA7127.B5865] 51-7348
1. Architecture, Domestic—Designs and plans. I. Home Plan Book Company. St. Paul.

BROWN-BLODGETT, inc., St.   728.084
Paul.
The book of 100 homes; designs and floor plans of more than one hundred homes. St. Paul [1952] 100 p. illus. 30 cm. Previous editions published by the firm's predecessor, Brown-Blodgett Company. [NA7127.B84 1952] 52-36738
1. Architecture, Domestic—Designs and plans. I. Title.

BURROWS, John Shober,   728.6084
1911-
Your new home... 1950 ed. [New York, Archway Press, 1950] 64 p. illus. 27 cm. (Know-how books) Cover title. [NA7127.B946 1950] 50-5383
1. Architecture, Domestic—Designs and plans. I. Title.

BURROWS, John Shober,   728.6084
1911-
Your new home ... [by John S. Burrows, Jr., and others] 1952 ed. [New York, Archway Press, 1952] unpaged. illus. 27 cm. (Know-how books, 33) [NA7127.B996 1952] 52-68922
1. Architecture, Domestic—Designs and plans. I. Title.

CANTACUZINO, Sherban.   728.37
Modern houses of the world. [London, Studio Vista; New York, Dutton, 1964] 160 p. illus., plans. 19 cm. (A Dutton Vista pictureback, 3) "Bibliographical note": p. 160. [NaA7126.C3] 64-4438
1. Architecture, Domestic—Designs and plans. I. Title.

CASSENS, Alwin.   728.6084
Ranch homes for today; house plans, including split-level houses, expandable houses, colonial houses, etc., for every income, every climate. [New York, Archway Press, 1953] unpaged. illus. 28cm. (Know-how books, 41) [NA7127.C33] 53-24156
1. Architecture, Domestic —Designs and plans. 2. Architecture, Domestic—U. S. I. Title.

CHIRGOTIS, William G   728.6084
1910-
New homes, house plans; popular homes, featuring ranch houses, ramblers, new split-level houses, Cape Cod, and many others in practical sizes, for the best in today's living. [New York, Archway Press, 1952-v. illus. 28cm. (Know-how books) Subtitle varies slightly. [NA7127.C48] 52-1932
1. Architecture, Domestic–Designs and plans. 2. Architecture, Domestic—U. S. I. Title.

CURRAN, June, 1923-   728'.3
Drawing plans for your own home / June Curran ; designs and ill. by the author. New York : McGraw-Hill, c1976. ix, 180 p. : ill. ; 29 cm. Includes 6 plastic drawing plan scales and ruler in pocket. Includes index. [NA7115.C87] 75-45313 ISBN 0-07-014925-9 : 19.95
1. Architecture, Domestic—Designs and plans. I. Title.

DONNELLY, Dorothy   811'.5'4
(Boillotat) 1903-
Houses [by] Dorothy Donnelly. Providence, Burning Deck [1970] [12] l. 25 cm. Label mounted on t.p.: American distributor: Wittenborn and Company, New York, N.Y. 150 copies printed. No. 26. [PS3554.O52H6] 73-17783 2.50
I. Title.

ESTES, Hiawatha Thompson   728.084
Ranch and modern homes. [Los Angeles 28, Nationwide Plan Book Co., P.O. Box 948, Calif. c1960] 64p. illus., diagrs. 27cm. 60-4954 2.00 pap.,
1. Architecture, Domestic—Designs and plans. I. Title.   **BIP**

FARMER, William Davis.   728.6084
Homes for pleasant living, by W. D. Farmer, residence designer. 6th ed. Atlanta, 1964. 1 v. (chiefly illus., part col.) 28 cm. Cover title. [NA7127.F19] 64-55419
1. Architecture, Domestic — Designs and plans. 2. Architecture, Domestic — U.S. I. Title.   **BIP**

FORD, Katherine (Morrow)   728.6084
1905-
Quality budget houses; a treasury of 100 architect-designed houses from $5,000 to $20,000 by Katherine Morrow Ford and Thomas H. Creighton New York, Reinhold Pub. Corp. [1954] 224p. illus. 27cm. [NA7127.F59] 54-6003
1. Architecture, Domestic—Designs and plans. 2. Architecture, Domestic—U. S. I. Creighton, Thomas Hawk, joint author. II. Title.

FOSTER, George G   728.6084
Spacious homes you can afford. [New York, Universal Pub. and Distributing Corp. by special arrangement with Associated Plan Service, 1956] 64p. illus. 28cm. [NA7127.F63] 57-19537
1. Architecture, Domestic—Designs and plans. 2. Architecture, Domestic—U. S. I. Title.

GA houses /   728'.09'04
[edited and photographed by Yukio Futagawa]. [Tokyo : A.D.A. Edita, c1976] 2 v. : chiefly ill. (some col.) ; 30 cm. (Global architecture) Cover title. English and /or Japanese. [NA7126.G13] 77-373487
1. Architecture, Domestic—Designs and plans. 2. Architecture, Modern—20th century—Designs and plans. I. Futagawa, Yukio, 1932-

GRAF, Jean.   728
Practical houses for contemporary living, by Jean Graf [and] Don Graf. New York, F. W. Dodge Corp. [1953] xiii, 174 p. (chiefly illus., plans) 30 cm. [NA7127.G65] 53-7215
1. Architecture, Domestic—Designs and plans. 2. Architecture, Domestic—U.S. I. Graf, Donald Thornton, joint author. II. Title.

GUERTNER, Beryl   728.6
Gregory's 200 home plan ideas Sydney, Gregory's Guides & Maps [New Rochelle. N.Y., SportShelf. 1966] 191p. illus., plans. 24cm. (Homemaker ser., no. 1) [NA7469.G8] 66-2752 4.00 pap.,
1. Architecture, Domestic—Designs and plans. 2. Architecture. Domestic—Australia. I. Title. II. Title: 200 home plan ideas.

HALFPENNY, William, fl.1750.   720
Rural architecture in the Chinese taste [by] William and John Halfpenny. New York, B. Blom, 1968. 4 pts. in 1 v. illus. 22 cm. "Reprinted from the third edition, London 1755." Includes reproduction of original t.p. Each part has also special t.p. Contents.Contents.—pt. 1. New designs for Chinese temples, triumphal arches, garden-seats, palings, &c. 1750.—pt. 2. New designs for Chinese bridges, temples, triumphal arches, garden-seats, palings, obelisks, termini's, &c. 1751.—pt. 3. New designs for Chinese doors, windows, piers, pilasters, garden seats, green-houses, summer-houses, &c. 1751.—pt. 4. New designs for Chinese gates, palisades, staircases, chimney-pieces, ceilings, garden-seats, chairs, temples, &c. 1752. [NA8450.H17 1968] 68-58993
1. Architecture, Domestic—Designs and plans. 2. Architecture—Details. 3. Architecture, Chinese. I. Halfpenny, John, fl. 1750, joint author. II. Title.   **BIP**

HARVARD University.   728.084
Graduate School of Design.
Comparative housing study; analyses of housing types and comparative designs of dense urban residential sectors, one of a continuing series of studies in environmental design. Cambridge, 1958. 163 l. illus., maps, plans 29 x 38 cm. Cover title. "A compilation of work produced by the Master in architecture class at the Harvard Graduate School of Design, with the collaboration of students in landscape architecture and city planning." [NA7127.H32] 67-40586
1. Architecture, Domestic — Designs and plans. I. Title.

HELICK, R. Martin.   728'.022'2
Varieties of human habitation, by R. Martin Helick. Pittsburgh, Pa., Regent Graphic Services Co. [1970] 1 v. (various pagings) illus. 28 x 44 cm. Includes bibliography. [NA7126.H4] 73-19343
1. Architecture, Domestic—Designs and plans. I. Title.

HOFFMANN, Hubert.   728.3'1
Row houses and cluster houses; an international survey. New York, Praeger [1967] 175 p. illus., plans. 26 cm. [NA7126.H613 1967] 66-18903
1. Architecture, Domestic—Designs and plans. I. Title.

HOME Builders Plan   728.6084
Service, Atlanta.
Designs for better living. Atlanta, '1951. unpaged. illus. 28 cm. [NA7127.H7278] 51-33977

1. Architecture, Domestic—Designs and plans. I. Title.

HOME Building Plan   728.6084
Service, Portland, Or.
115 selected homes; a selection of home plans... [Portland, 1955] 64p. illus., plans. 28cm. Cover title. [NA7127.H72915] 55-23649
1. Architecture, Domestic—Designs and plans. 2. Architecture, Domestic— U. S. I. Title.

HOME Building Plan   728.6084
Service, Portland, Or.
New trends in home plans; more than 100 designs, many never before published in book form. [Portland, 1954] 72p. illus. 21x28cm. [NA7127.H55] 54-23241
1. Architecture, Domestic—Designs and plans. 2. Architecture, Domestic—U. S. I. Title.

HOME Building Plan   728.6084
Service, Portland, Or.
Planning or dreaming? 75 individual designs, over 135 floor plans [of] homes; complete working blueprints and material lists available. [Portland, 1950] 73 p. (incl. cover) illus., plans. 22 x 28 cm. Cover title. [NA7127.H58] 50-13574
1. Architecture, Domestic—Designs and plans. 2. Architecture, Domestic—U. S. I. Title.

HOME Planners Clinic,   728.6084
Portland, Or.
Ranch homes for the West, featuring daylight basements. Portland [1951] 40 p. illus. 22 x 18 cm. [NA7127.H6] 51-6718
1. Architecture, Domestic—Designs and plans. 2. Architecture, Domestic—U.S. I. Title.

HOME Planners, inc.,   728.6
Detroit
150 popular homes / by Richard B. Pollman, Irving E Palmquist. Rev. ed. [New York, Universal Pub. Dist., c1963] 96p. illus. 28cm. (Its Designs for convenient living, bk. no. 43) 63-1604 1.00 pap.,
1. Architecture, Domestic—Designs and plans. I. Pollman, Richard B., 1914- II. Title.

HOME Planners, inc.,   728.6
Detroit.
68 custom homes for all budgets. Charles W. Talcott, editor. Richard B. Pollman, designer. Irving E. Palmquist, architect. 1st rev. ed N[ew] Y[ork] Universal Pub. and Distributing Corp. for Home Planners [1965] 45, [14] p. illus., plans. 28 cm. (Its Designs for convenient living, book no. 58) [NA7127.H79177] 66-2697
1. Architecture, Domestic — Designs and plans. I. Talcott, Charles W., ed. II. Pollman, Richard B. III. Palmquist, Irving E. IV. Title.

HOME Planners, inc.,   728.3
Detroit.
98 homes for good living, by Richard B. Pollman,designer. N[ew] Y[ork] Universal Pub. and Distributing Corp. [1967] 96 p. illus., plans. 28 cm. (Its Designs for convenient living, book no. 62) [NA7127.H79132] 68-1176
1. Architecture, Domestic—Designs and plans. I. Pollman, Richard B., 1914- II. Title.

HOME Planners, Inc., Detroit.   728
405 homes, all sizes and types. Richard B. Pollman, designer. Palmquist & Wright, architects. New York, Arco Pub. Co. [1960?] 96, 96 p. illus., plans. 29 cm. (The Do-it-yourself series) Contains two works: 202 homes, all sizes and types, published in 1958, and 203 homes, published in 1959. [NA7127.H6253] 60-1427
1. Architecture, Domestic—Designs and plans. I. Pollman, Richard B., 1914- II. Title.

HOME Planners, inc.,   728.6084
Detroit
115 homes for family living. Richard B. Pollman, designer, Palmquist & Wright, architects. New York, Arco Pub. Co. [c1956] 128p. illus., plans. 28cm. (The Do-it-yourself series) Issued also as Designs for convenient living, book no. 17. [NA7127.H7916] 58-3251
1. Architecture, Domestic—Designs and

plans. I. Pollman, Richard B., 1914- II. Title.

HOME Planners, inc., Detroit. 728.084
150 popular homes. Richard B. Pollman, designer and Irving e. Palmquist. N[ew] Y[ork] Universal Pub. and Distributing Corp., for Home Planners, 1961. 96p. illus. 28cm. (Its Designs for convenient living, book no. 33) [NA7127.H7917] 61-19561
1. Architecture, Domestic—Designs and plans. I. Pollman, Richard B., 1914] II. Title.

HOME Planners, inc., Detroit. 728.084
142 popular designs. Richard B. Pollman, designer. Irving E. Palmquist [architect] 1st rev. ed. [New York, Universal Pub. and Distributing Corp., 1964?] 94 p. illus., plans 28 cm. (Its Designs for convenient living, book no. 48) Cover title. [NA7127.H791714] 65-1199
1. Architecture, Domestic — Designs and plans. I. Pollman, Richard B., 1914- II. Title.

HOME Planners, inc., Detroit. 728.6084
101 homes for every purse and person / Richard B. Pollman, designer. N[ew] Y[ork] Published by Universal Pub. and Distributing Corp. for Home Planners, Detroit, c1957. 96p. illus. 28cm. (Its Convenient living, book no. 19) [NA7127.H626] 57-43326
1. Architecture, Domestic—Designs and plans. 2. Architecture, Domestic—U. S. I. Poliman; Richard B., 1914- II. Title.

HOME Planners, inc., Detroit. 728.084
199 plans you can build. Richard B. Pollman, designer and Irving E. Palmquist, architect. N[ew] Y[ork] Published by Universal Pub. and Distributing Corp. for Home Planners, 1954. 96 p. illus., plans. 28 cm. (Its Designs for convenient living, book no. 51) [NA7127.H79172] 64-56863
1. Architecture, Domestic — Designs and plans. I. Pollman, Richard B., 1914- II. Title.

HOME Planners, inc., Detroit. 728.084
102 plans for every need. Richard B. Pollman, designer, Irving E. Palmquist architect. New York, Universal Pub. and Distributing Corp., 1964?] 95 p. illus., plans. 28 cm. (Its Designs for convenient living, book no. 49) Cover title. [NA7127.H79174] 64-4671
1. Architecture. Domestic — Designs and plans. I. Pollman, Richard B., 1914- II. Title.

HOME Planners, inc., Detroit. 728.6084
75 homes for convenient living [by] Richard B. Pollman, designer N[ew] Y[ork] Published by Universal Pub. and Distributing Corp. for Home Planners, Detroit, c1956. 64p. illus., plans. 28cm. (Its Convenient living, book no. 18) [NA7127.H628] 57-433281
1. Architecture, Domestic— Designs and plans. 2. Architecture, Domestic—U. S. I. Pollman, Richard B., 1914- II. Title.

HOME Planners, inc., Detroit. 728.084
60 plans, featuring ranch, two-story & multi-level homes. Special section on homes of brick [and] vacation homes. Richard B. Pollman, designer and Irving E. Palmquist, architect N[ew] Y[ork] Published by Universal Pub. and Distributing Corp. for Home Planners, 1964. 61 p. illus., plans. 28 cm. (Its Designs for convenient living, book no. 50) [NA7127.H79182] 64-56811
1. Architecture, Domestic — Designs and plans. I. Pollman, Richard B., 1914- II. Title.

HOME Planners, inc., Detroit. 728.084
61 plans for building. Charles W. Talcott, editor. Richard B. Pollman, designes. Irving E. Palmquist, architect. T[ew] Y[ork] Universal Pub. and Distributing Corp. [1965] 63 p. illus. 28 cm. (Its Designs for convenient living, book no. 54) [NA7127.H791816] 65-1600
1. Architecture, Domestic — Designs and plans. I. Talcott, Charles W., ed. II. Pollman, Richard B., 1914- III. Palmquist, Irving E. IV. Title.

HOME Planners, inc., Detroit. 728.6084
201 homes for every budget [by] Richard B. Pollman, designer, Irving E. Palmquist and Clifford N. Wright. [New York, Universal Pub. and Distributing Corp., 1958] 96p. illus., plans. 28cm. (Its Library series, no. 1) Designs for convenient living, book no. 22. Cover title. [NA7127.H792] 58-2033
1. Architecture, Domestic—Designs and plans. I. Pollman, Richard B., 1914- II. Title.

HOME Planners, inc., Detroit. 728.64084
202 homes, all sizes and types. New York, Published by Universal Pub. and Distributing Corp. for Home Planners, c1958. 96p. illus., plans. 28cm. (Its Library series, no. 2) Designs for convenient living, book no. 24. [NA7127.H633] 59-20693
1. Architecture, Domestic—Design and plans. I. Title.

HOMES and plans for building. 728.6084 [Greenwich, Conn., Fawcett Publications, 1951] 144 p. illus. 24 cm. (A Fawcett book, no. 128) [NA7127.H64] 51-8545
1. Architecture, Domestic—Designs and plans. 2. Architecture, Domestic—U. S. I. Fawcett Publications, inc.

HOMES for living. 728.084 [New York, Universal Pub. and Distributing Corp., 19 v. illus. 28cm. [NA7127.H643] 56-40739
1. Architecture, Domestic—Designs and plans. 2. Architecture, Domestic— U. S.

HOUSE & garden. 728.084
Best home plans. Greenwich, Conn., Fawcett Publications [1964?] 112 p. illus. 24 cm. "No. 563." [NA7127.H822] 64-7205
1. Architecture, Domestic — Designs and plans. I. Title.

HOUSE & garden. 728.084
Book of building, by the editors of House & garden. New York, Conde Nast Publications, '1951. 194 p. illus. (part col.) 83 cm. [NA7127.H66] 51-10522
1. Architecture, Domestic—Designs and plans. 2. Architecture, Domestic—U. S. I. Title.

HOUSE & garden 728.6
Book of modern houses and conversions; ed.: Robert Harling: art ed.: Alex Kroll; edit. assistants: Leonie Higton, Martin Simmons, Caroline Willcox. London, Conde Nast [1967] 256p. 2 col. fronts., illus. (same col.) plans (some col.) diagrs. 30cm. [NA7132.H58] 66-68465 22.50
1. Architecture, Domestic— Designs and plans. 2. Architecture, Modern—20th cent. 3. Dwellings— Remodelling. I. Harling, Robert, ed. II. Title.

HOUSE & garden Best home plans. 728.37 Greenwich. Conn., Fawcett [c.1961-1964] 112p. illus. 24cm. (563) 64-7205 .75 pap.,
1. Architecture, Domestic—Designs and plans.

HOUSE & garden book of plans. 728.084 [New York, Conde Nast Publications] v. illus. 32 cm. annual. [NA7127.H823] 63-4169
1. Architecture, Domestic — Designs and plans.

HOUSE and garden book of plans. 1963. 728.3705873 Ed.: William E. Hague Conde Nast Pubns. [dist. greenwich, conn., house & garden bk. of plans, c.1957-1963] 136 p. illus. (pt. col.) 32 cm. annual 63-4169 pap., 1.25
1. Architecture, Domestic—Designs and plans.

HOUSE & Garden's book of building. 728.084 [1st]- issue;1951- [Greenwich, Conn.] Conde Nast Publications. v. illus. (part col.) plans. 33cm. annual. [NA7127.H66] 51-10522
1. Architecture, Domestic—Designs and plans. 2. Architecture, Domestic—U. S.

HOUSE beautiful. 728.6084
Handbook for home planners. [New York, 1950] 68 p. illus. 32 cm. Cover title. [NA7127.H68] 50-6678
1. Architecture, Domestic—Designs and plans. 2. Architecture. Domestic—U. S. I. Title.

HOUSE plan favorites. 728.37
New York [Archway] c.1964. unpaged. illus. 28cm. annual. 63-1458 1.00 pap.,
1. Architecture, Domestic—Designs and plans.

HOUSE plan favorites. 728.37
[New York, Illustrated Publications] v. illus. 28 cm. annual. [NA7127.H832] 63-1458
1. Architecture, Domestic — Designs and plans.

IDEAS for planning your new home. 728.6 By the editors of Sunset magazine and Sunset books. [2d ed.] Menlo Park, Calif., Lane Books [1967] 128 p. illus., plans. 28 cm. [NA127.I43 1967] 67-15741
1. Architecture, Domestic—Designs and plans.

JONES, Willam T 728
House planning. Serial 6442A[-B. Ed. 1] Scranton. International Correspondence Schools, c1959-61. 2v. illus. 19cm. Part 2 by William T. Jones and David T. Jones. [NA7127.J7] 59-52938
1. Architecture, Domestic—Designs and plans. I. Jones, David Thomas, joint author. II. International Correspondence Schools, Scranton, Pa. III. Title.

JONES, William T 728.084
House planning. Serial 6442A-1- [Ed. 2] Scranton, International Correspondence Schools, c1962- v. illus. 19 cm. [NA7127.J72] 63-1624
1. Architecture, Domestic—Designs and plans. I. International Correspondence Schools, Scranton, Pa. II. Title.

†KICKLIGHTER, Clois E. 728.3
Architecture : residential drawing and design / by Clois E. Kicklighter ; Ronald J. Baird, consulting editor. South Holland, Ill. : Goodheart-Willcox Co., c1976. 492 p. : ill. (some col.) ; 29 cm. Includes index. [NA7115.K46 1976] 76-368557 ISBN 0-87006-198-4 : 11.92
1. Architecture, Domestic—Designs and plans. I. Title.

KICKLIGHTER, Clois E. 728.3
Architecture: residential drawing and design, by Clois E. Kicklighter. Ronald J. Baird, consulting editor. South Holland, Ill., Goodheart-Willcox Co. [1973] 492 p. illus. 29 cm. [NA7115.K46] 73-84691 ISBN 0-87006-170-4
1. Architecture, Domestic—Designs and plans. I. Title. BIP

KOCH, Carl, 1912- 728.6084
At home with tomorrow, by Carl Koch with Andy Lewis. New York, Rinehart [1958] 208p. illus. 20x27cm. [NA7127.K65] 58-5160
1. Architecture, Domestic—Designs and plans. 2. Architecture, Domestic—U. S. I. Lewis, Andy, joint author. II. Title.

LASSON, Robert, 1922- ed. 728.6084
Homes you can build. Greenwich, Conn., Fawcett Publications, c1953. 144p. illus. 24cm. (A Fawcett book, no. 186) [NA7127.L35] 53-34133
1. Architecture Domestic —Designs and plans. 2. Architecture, Domestic—U. S. I. Title.

LINDMAN, W E. 728.6084
Wisdom in homes. Hollywood, Calif. [1951] 96 p. illus., plans. 28 cm. "An International Correspondents publication." [NA7127.L63] 51-1662
1. Architecture. Domestic—Designs and plans. 2. Architecture, Domestic—U. S. I. Title.

MCCALL'S magazine. 728.6084
McCall's book of modern houses, by Mary Davis Gillies. New York, Simon and Schuster [1951] 191 p. illus. 34 cm. [NA7127.M13] 51-14069
1. Architecture, Domestic—Designs and plans. 2. Architecture, Domestic—U. S. I. Gillies, Mary (Davis) II. Title. III. Title: Book of modern houses.

MCCALL'S Magazine. 728.6084
McCall's book of modern houses, by the architectural editor of McCall's, Mary Davis Gillies. New York, Simon and Schuster [1959] 191p. illus. (part col.) plans. 34cm. 'The revised McCall's book of modern houses.'-- Dust jacket. [NA7127.M13 1959] 59-16338
1. Architecture, Domestic—Designs and plans. 2. Architecture, Domestic—U. S. I. Gillies, Mary (Davis) II. Title. III. Title: Book of modern houses.

MATERN, Rudolph Albert, 1912- 728.6084
51 house plans for 1951; construction-tested house designs of designs of proven popularity. [New York, Archway Press, 1951] [52] p. (incl. cover) illus. 27 cm. (Know-how books, 32) Cover title. [NA7127.M36] 51-10870
1. Architecture, Domestic—Designs and plans. I. Title.

MATERN, Rudolph Albert, 1912- 728.6084
52 house plans for 1952; construction-tested house designs of proven popularity... [New York, Archway Press, 1952] unpaged. illus. 26 cm. (Know-how books) [NA7127.M37] 52-6815
1. Architecture, Domestic—Designs and plans. I. Title.

MORAND, Francois C 728.6
Small homes in the new tradition. New York, Sterling Pub. Co. [1959] 143p. illus., plans. 29cm. [NA7127.M713] 59-9012
1. Architecture, Domestic—Designs and plans. I. Title.

NATIONAL Homes Corporation. 728.6084
Your national home magazine. [1st]-ed. [Muncie, Ind., National Homes Corp., 1951- v. illus., plans. 33 cm. [NA7127.Y59] 51-26738
1. Architecture, Domestic — Designs and plans. 2. Buildings, Prefabricated. 3. Interior decoration. I. Title.

NEW homes and plans for building. 728.6084 Greenwich, Conn., Fawcett Publications, c1955. 146p. illus. 24cm. (A Fawcett book, no. 253) A Fawcett how-to book, 253. [NA7127.N53 1955] 55-27075
1. Architecture, Domestic—Designs and plans. 2. Architecture. Domestic— U. S. I. Fawcett Publications, inc.

NORRIS, Henry D. 728.0973
Architecture for contemporary living: 59 distinguished houses. Commentary and foreword by Joseph B. Mason, Harriet S. Mason; renderings by Jack Cavender. [New York, Simmons-Boardman, c.1961] unpaged illus. 29cm. 61-11868 6.00
1. Architecture, Domestic—Designs and plans. 2. Architecture, Domestic—U.S. I. Title.

120 houses and plans. 728.6084
v. 1, 1957- [New York, Hearst Corp.] v. illus. 32cm. annual. [NA7130.O6] 57-1559
1. Architecture. Domestic—Designs and plans. 2. Architecture, Domestic—U. S.—Period.

PAUL, Samuel, 1912- 728.6084
Homes for living; the giant book of house plans, from the works of Samuel Paul, architect. New York, Simmons-Boardman Books [1952] 192 p. illus. 29 cm. [NA7127.P352] 52-14702
1. Architecture, Domestic—Designs and plans. 2. Architecture, Domestic—U.S. I. Title.

PAUL, Samuel, 1912- 728.6
Homes for living, from the works of Samuel Paul, architect. Jamaica, N.Y., Architectural Plan Service, c1950-51. 2 v. illus., port., plans. 29 cm. [NA7127.P35] 50-50066
1. Architecture. Domestic — Designs and plans. 2. Architecture, Domestic — U.S. I. Architectural Plan Service, inc., Jamiaca, N.Y. II. Title.

PAUL, Samuel, 1912- 728.6084
New split level homes. [Jamaica, N. Y.] [Architectural Plan Service] [1953] 48 p. illus. 28 cm. [NA7127.P38] 53-10057
1. Architecture, Domestic—Designs and plans. 2. Architecture, Domestic—U.S. I. Title.

PAUL, Samuel, 1912- 728.6084
3 and 4 bedroom homes; selected homes for growing families. [Jamaica, N. Y., Homes for Living, 1956] 62p. illus. 28cm. [NA7127.P393] 56-1631
1. Architecture, Domestic—Designs and plans. 2. Architecture, Domestic—U. S. I. Title.

PIDGEON, Monica, ed. 728
An anthology of houses, edited and introduced by Monica Pidgeon and Theo Crosby. New York, Reinhold Pub. Corp. [1960] 174p. illus., plans. 26cm. [NA7126.P5] 60-15826
1. Architecture, Domestic—Designs and plans. I. Crosby, Theo, joint ed. II. Title.

PLANS for building 728.60223
homes and vacation cabins. [Greenwich. Conn.] Fawcett [1966] 112p. illus., plans. 24cm. Cover title [NA7127.P58] 66-6992 .95 pap.,
1. Architecture, Domestic—Designs and plans I. Fawcett Publications, Inc.

POLLMAN, Richard B., 1914- 728.6
Homes for family living; 93 designs for the seventies, by Richard B. Pollman. Detroit, Home Planners, c1969. 93 p. illus., plans. 28 cm. (Convenient living, book no. 72) [NA7127.P5915] 74-13054 1.00
1. Architecture, Domestic—Designs and plans. I. Home Planners, inc., Detroit. II. Title.

POLLMAN, Richard B., 1914- 728.6
94 plans for building. Richard B. Pollman, designer. [Detroit, Home Planners 1968] 96 p. illus. 28 cm. (Home Planners designs for convenient living, book no. 66) Cover title. [NA7127.P592] 68-44190
1. Architecture, Domestic—Designs and plans. I. Home Planners, inc., Detroit. II. Title.

POLLMAN, Richard B., 728.6'022'3
1914-
116 homes for town and country living, by Richard B. Pollman. [New York, Published by Universal Pub. and Distributing Corp. for Home Planners, c1968] 112 p. illus. 28 cm. (Designs for convenient living, book no. 68) [NA7127.P5925] 70-6917 1.00
1. Architecture, Domestic—Designs, and plans. I. Home Planners, inc., Detroit. II. Title.

POLLMAN, Richard B., 1914- 728.3
116 homes for town and country living, by Richard B. Pollman. 1st rev. ed. [New York, Published by Universal Pub. and Distributing Corp. for Home Planners, Detroit, c1970] 104 p. illus. 28 cm. (Designs for convenient living, book no. 76) At head of title: Home Planners. [NA7570.P6 1970] 71-25394 1.25
1. Architecture, Domestic—Designs and plans. I. Home Planners, inc., Detroit. II. Title.

POLLMAN, Richard B., 1914- 728.6
103 homes; all-American selection for the seventies, by Richard B. Pollman. 1st rev. ed. [New York, Published by Universal Publishing and Distributing Corp. for Home Planners, inc., Detroit, 1969] 96 p. (p. 89-96 advertisements) illus., plans. 28 cm. (Designs for convenient living, book no. 69) Cover title. [NA7127.P59213 1969] 73-5804 1.00
1. Architecture, Domestic—Designs and plans. I. Home Planners, inc., Detroit. II. Title.

POPULAR homes and 728.6084
plans; 12th ed. New York, Archway Press, 117 W. 48 St. [c.1959] 48p. illus., plans. 28cm. .50 pap.,
1. Architecture, Domestic—Designs and plans.

PROGRESSIVE architecture. 728.084
100 houses : selected designs from pencil points-Pittsburgh architectural competition for a house for cheerful living. New York, Reinhold Pub. Corp., 1947. vi, 114p. illus., plans. 29cm. [NA7127.P75] 47-3236
1. Architecture, Domestic—Designs and plans. 2. Architecture, Domestic— U. S. I. Title.

ROBUCK (B. E.) INC., 728.6084
College Park, Ga.
Southernair dream homes; your personalized book of home planning. 4th ed. [College Park, Ga., 1950] 73 p. illus., plans. 28 cm. Cover title. [NA7127.R62 1950] 50-38250
1. Architecture, Domestic — Designs and plans. I. Title.

ROGERS, Kate Ellen. 643
The modern house, U.S.A.: its design and decoration. New York, Harper [1962] 292 p. illus. 26 cm. (Harper's home economics series) Includes bibliography. [NA7127.R64] 61-14739
1. Architecture, Domestic—Designs and plans. 2. Architecture, Domestic—U.S. 3. Interior decoration. I. Title.

ROGERS, Tyler Stewart. 728
Plan your house to suit yourself. 2d ed., rev. and enl. New York, Scribner, 1950. 313 p. illus. 24 cm. [NA7120.R65 1950] 50-6236
1. Architecture, Domestic — Designs and plans. 2. Dwellings. I. Title.

SHERWOOD, Roger. 728.3'1'0222
Modern housing prototypes / by Roger Sherwood. Cambridge, Mass. : Harvard University Press, c1978. p. cm. Bibliography: p. [NA7126.S48] 78-15508 ISBN 0-674-57941-0 : 25.00
1. Architecture, Domestic—Designs and plans. 2. Architecture, Modern—20th century—Designs and plans. I. Title. BIP

SMALL home plans 728.6084
[1965 ed. New York. Science & Mechanics] 1965, c.1964. 1v. (various p.) illus. (pt. col.) plans. 29cm. (Science & mechanics annual) [NA7127.S685] 65-908 1.00 pap.,
1. Architecture, Domestic—Designs and plans. 2. Architecture, Domestic—U.S. I. Science and mechanics.

STILLWELL, Walter Abel, 728.6084
1889-
25 homes and how to build them ; an informal, non-technical book on small house construction in plain, simple American. Norristown, Pa., 25 Homes Builders [1950] 219 p. illus., diagrs., plans. 28 cm. Cover title. [NA7127.S843] 51-1129
1. Architecture, Domestic — Designs and plans. 2. Architecture, Domestic — U.S. I. Title.

STONE, Robert B ed. 728.6084
Approved homes; selected new plans you can custom build; beautiful ranches, charming colonials, striking split-levels, cozy cape cods -- all by leading American architects. [New York, Universal Pub. and Distributing Corp. 1956] 56 p. illus. 28 cm. [NA7127.S845] 56-58560
1. Architecture. Domestic — Designs and plans. 2. Architecture, Domestic — U.S. I. Title.

STONE, Robert B ed. 728.6084
The complete book of home plans. [New York, Universal Pub. and Distributing Corp., 1955] 96p. illus. 28cm. [NA7127.S846] 55-4348
1. Architecture, Domestic—Designs and plans. I. Title.

STONE, Robert B ed. 728.6084
Selected plans for new air conditioned homes by leading American architects, edited by Robert B. Stone and George F. Robinson. [New York, Universal Pub. and Distributing Corp., c1955] 55p. illus. 28cm. [NA7127.S847] 56-797
1. Architecture, Domestic—Designs and plans. 2. Architecture, Domestic—U. S. 3. Air conditioning. I. Robinson, George F., joint ed. II. Title.

SUNSET. 728.084
New homes for western living, by the editorial staff of Lane Pub. Co. and based upon recent articles in Sunset magazine. [1st ed.] Menlo Park, Calif., Lane Pub. Co. [1956] 94 p. illus. 28 cm. (A Sunset book) [NA7127.S89-728.6084] 56-11876
1. Architecture, Domestic—Designs and plans. 2. Architecture, Domestic—U.S. I. Lane Publishing Company, Menlo Park, Calif. II. Title.

SUNSET. 728.084
Planning and landscaping hillside homes, by the editorial staffs of Sunset books and Sunset magazine. Menlo Park, Calif, Lane Books [1965] 128 p. illus., plans. 28 cm. (A Sunset book, 540) [NA7127.S894] 65-16751
1. Architecture, Domestic — Designs and plans. 2. Landscape gardening. I. Title.

SUNSET. 728
Sunset ideas for remodeling your home, by the editorial staff of Lane Pub. Co. and based upon recent articles in Sunset magazine. [1st ed.] Menlo Park, Calif., Lane Pub. Co.[1958] 160 p. illus. 28 cm. [NA7127.S914] 58-13247
1. Architecture, Domestic—Designs and plans. 2. Dwellings—Remodeling. 3. Building—Repair and reconstruction. 4. Interior decoration. I. Lane Publishing Company, Menlo Park, Calif. II. Title. III. Title: Remodelling your home.

SUNSET. 728
Western ranch houses by Cliff May, by the editorial staff of Sunset magazine and books, under the direction of Paul C. Johnson, editor of Sunset books. [1st ed.] Menlo Park, Calif., Lane Pub. Co. [1958] 176 p. illus. 28 cm. (A Sunset book) [NA7127.S926] 58-10876
1. Architecture, Domestic—Designs and plans. 2. May, Cliff. I. Title.

TODAY'S woman. 728.6084
Approved homes. Greenwich, Conn., Fawcett Publications, c1952. 144 p. illus. 24 cm. (A Fawcett book, no. 142) [NA7127.T56] 52-1934
1. Architecture, Domestic — Designs and plans. 2. Architecture, Domestic — U.S. I. Title.

TODAY'S woman. 728.6084
Low cost homes. New York, Arco Pub. Co. [1954] 144p. illus., plans. 25cm. (Arco handi-books for better living) Fawcett book no. 217. [NA7127] 54-9270
1. Architecture, Domestic—Designs and plans. I. Title.

TODAY'S woman. 728.6084
Low cost homes, approved by Today's woman magazine. [Greenwich, Conn., Fawcett Publications, 1951] 144 p. illus., ports., plans. 24 cm. (A Fawcett book, no. 115) Cover title. [NA7127.L8] 51-3584
1. Architecture. Domestic—Designs and plans. I. Fawcett Publications, inc. II. Title.

TODAY'S woman. 728.6084
Low cost homes; illustrated by Henry Clark. Cover photos, by Robert Scharff. New York, Published by Fawcett for Sterling Pub. Co., c1953. 143p. illus. 24cm. (A Fawcett book, no. 115) [NA7127.T563 1953] 53-8216
1. Architecture, Domestic—Designs and plans. 2. Architecture, Domestic—U. S. I. Title.

TODAY'S woman. 728.6084
Low cost homes: ranch, split-level, expansion attic. Greenwich, Conn., Fawcett Publications, c1954. 144p. illus. 24cm. (A Fawcett book, no. 217) [NA7127.T564] 54-1547
1. Architecture, Domestic—Designs and plans. 2. Architecture, Domestic—U.S. I. Title.

TODAY'S woman. 728.6084
Small ranch homes, with plans for building. [Greenwich, Conn., Fawcett Publications, 1952] 144p. illus. 24cm. (A Fawcett book, no. 160) [NA7127.T565] 53-16482
1. Architecture, Domestic—Designs and plans. 2. Architecture, Domestic— U. S. I. Title.

TODAY'S woman low cost 728.6084
homes. New York, Arco Pub. Co. [1954] 144p. illus., plans. 25cm. (Arco handi-books for better living Fawcett book no. 217. First published in 1951 under title: Low cost homes. [NA7127] 54-9270
1. Architecture, Domestic—Designs and plans.

VAUX, Calvert, 1824- 728'.0973
1895.
Villas and cottages; a series of designs prepared for execution in the United States. New York, Dover Publications [1970] 348 p. illus., plans. 22 cm. Reprint of the 1864 ed. [NA7120.V3 1970] 70-124181 3.00
1. Architecture, Domestic—Designs and plans. I. Title. BIP

VAUX, Calvert, 1824- 720'.973
1895.
Villas and cottages. New introd. by Henry Hope Reed. New York, Da Capo Press, 1968. xiv, 318 p. illus., plans. 24 cm. (Da Capo Press series in architecture and decorative art, v. 12) (Da Capo Press reprint edition.) Reprint of 1857 ed. [NA7120.V3 1968] 68-29858 15.00
1. Architecture, Domestic—Designs and plans. I. Title.

VOWELL, Jim D 1914- 728.6084
Homes for the Southwest. 5th ed. Fort Worth, Tex., 1952 unpaged (chiefly illus.) 22 x 28 cm. [NA7127.V8] 52-28652
1. Architecture, Domestic — Designs and plans. 2. Architecture, Domestic — U.S. I. Title.

WALSH, Harold Vandervoort. 643
Your house begins with you. New York, G. W. Stewart [1950] 248 p. illus., plans. 26 cm. [NA7127.W23] 50-3812
1. Architecture, Domestic — Designs and plans. 2. Interior decoration. I. Title.

*WALTON, Harry 728.7
How to build your cabin or modern vacation home. New York, Harper [1964] 1v. illus., diagrs. 24cm. 2.95
I. Title. BIP

WEIDERT, Werner. 728.6
Private houses, an international survey. [Translation into English: E. Rockwell] New York, Praeger [1967] 165 p. illus., plans. 29 cm. English and German. [NA7132.W413 1967] 67-29466
1. Architecture, Domestic—Designs and plans. I. Title.

WEIDHAAS, Ernest R. 728'.022'3
Reading architectural plans for residential and commercial construction / Ernest R. Weidhaas. Boston : Allyn and Bacon, c1977. x, 464 p. : ill. ; 28 cm. Includes index. [NA7115.W44] 76-48085 ISBN 0-205-05730-6 : 16.95
1. Architecture, Domestic—Designs and plans. 2. Mercantile buildings—Designs and plans. 3. Architecture—Details. I. Title.

WILLS, Royal Barry, 1895- 728.084
Living on the level; one-story houses. Boston, Houghton Mifflin, 1955 [c1954] viii, 120 p. illus. (part col.) plans. 31 cm. [NA7127.W6185] 54-107585
1. Architecture, Domestic—Designs and plans. 2. Architecture, Domestic—U.S. I. Title.

WRIGHT, Frank Lloyd, 728.084
1869-
Taliesin drawings; recent architecture of Frank Lloyd Wright, selected from his drawings. Comments by Edgar Kaufmann, Jr. [New York] Wittenborn Schultz [1952] 62 p. illus., plans, 23 x 29 cm. (Problems of contemporary art. no. 6) [NA7127.W945] 52-14907
1. Architecture, Domestic — Designs and plans. 2. Architecture, Domestic — U.S. I. Kaufmann, Edgar, 1910- II. Title. III. Series.

WURMAN, Richard Saul, 1934- 728
ed.
Various dwellings described in a comparative manner, being a collection of comparative descriptive drawings in perspective of thirty-five dwellings of significance from around the world...Drawn by 15 2d year architectural students of the Sch. of Design, N.C. State of the Univ. of N.C. at Raleigh: [by] Joseph Allan Courter, Jr. [others] Philadelphia [Joshua Pr., 1964. 64]p. illus., plans. 23x29cm. 64-21895 price unreported
1. Architecture, Domestic—Designs and plans. 2. North Carolina. University. State College of Agriculture and Engineering, Raleigh. School of Design. I. Title.

Architecture, Domestic—Designs and plans.

BAKER, John Milnes, 1932- 728.3
How to build a house with an architect / John Milnes Baker. Philadelphia : Lippincott, 1979, c1977. p. cm. Bibliography: p. [NA7115.B28 1979] 79-203 ISBN 0-397-01325-6 pbk. : 4.95
1. Architect-designed houses. I. Title. BIP

HENNESSEY, William James, 1901- 728.7
Vacation houses. [1st ed.] New York, Harper [1962] viii, 109 p. illus., plans. 24 cm. [NA7575.H4] 62-7902
1. Architecture, Domestic—Designs and plans. 2. Architecture, Domestic—U.S. 3. Summer homes. I. Title.

HOFFMANN, Kurt, 1923- 728.64
Neue Einfamilienhauser. Zweite folge. 95 Beispiele aus 12 Landern. Mit 317 Lichtbildern und 209 Grundrissen und Schnitten. Alle texte in deutsche, englische und franzosisch. Stuttgart, Julius Hoffmann [dist. New York, Efron, c.1962] 159p. illus. 30cm. 57-3015 14.00
1. Architecture, Domestic— Designs and plans. 2. Architecture, Domestic. I. Title.

HOME Planners, inc., Detroit. 728.64084
203 homes: split-level, contemporary, ranch, low cost, hillside, traditional, custom-deluxe, frame-brick, 2 and 2 story, Charles W. Talcott, editor. Richard B. Pollman, designer. N[ew] Y[ork] Universal Pub. and Distributing Corp., c1959. 96p. illus. 28cm. (Its Designs for convenient living, book no. 25. Library series, no. 3) [NA7127.H634] 59-3759
1. Architecture, Domestic—Designs and plans. I. Pollman, Richard B., 1914- II. Title.

HOME Planners, inc., Detroit. 728.640223
64 homes for delightful living, by Richard B.Pollman, designer. New York, Published by Universal Pub. and Distributing Corp. for Home Planners [1966] 64 p. illus., plans. 28 cm. (Its Designs for convenient living, book no. 60) [NA7127.H79179] 66-5277
1. Architecture, Domestic — Designs and plans. I. Pollman, Richard B., 1914- II. Title.

HOME Planners, inc., Detroit. 728.640223
97 homes for family living fun. Richard B. Pollman, designer. Irving E. Palmquist architect. Detroit, 1966] 96p. illus., plans. 28cm. (Designs for convenient living bk. no. 59) [NA7127.H7913] 66-5278 1.00 pap.,
1. Architecture, Domestic—Designs and plans. I. Pollman, Richard B., 1914- II. Palmquist, Irving E. III. Title. IV. Series.
Distributed by Universal Pub., New York.

HOME Planners, inc., Detroit. 728.64
Family room homes. N[ew] Y[ork] Published by Universal Pub. and Distributing Corp. for Home Planners, Detroit [1965] 64 p. illus., plans 28 cm. (Its Designs for convenient living. book no. 57) [NA7127.H787] 65-6895
1. Architecture, Domestic — Designs and plans. 2. Recreation rooms. I. Title.

HOMOGRAF Company, East Detroit, Mich. 728.6084
Parade of homes: 140 home designs for today & tomorrow; plans, specifications and material lists. [East Detroit, Mich., 1961] 56p. illus. 28cm. [NA7127.H7945] 62-880
1. Architecture, Domestic—Designs and plans. I. Title. II. Title: 140 home designs.

ILLINOIS. University. Small Homes Council. 728.6084
Contemporary houses developed from room units; a report of an architectural investigation in house design making use of improved building techniques. Rev. ed. [Urbana, 1951] 62 p. illus., plans. 28 cm. (Its Technical series. Index no. C2.2R) [NA7208.I 4 no. C2.2R 1951a] 51-3435
1. Architecture, Domestic—Designs and plans. I. Title. II. Series.

ILLINOIS. University. Small Homes Council-Building Research Council. 728.6084
Contemporary houses developed from room units; a report of an architectural investigation in house design making use of improved building techniques. [Urbana, 1951] 62p. illus., plans. 28cm. (Its Technical series. Index no. C2.2R) Issued by the council under its earlier name: Small Homes Council. [TH4811.I53 no. C2.2R] A 51
1. Architecture, Domestic—Designs and plans. I. Title. II. Series.

ILLUSTRATED ranch homes, 17th issue. 728.64084 [New York,] Archway Press, 117 W. 48th St., c.1960 48p. illus., diagrs. 28cm. quarterly. 60-446 .50 pap.,
1. Architecture, Domestic—Designs and plans.

ILLUSTRATED ranch homes; 16th series. 728.64084 [New York, Archway Press] 48 p. illus., diagrs. 28 cm. 60-446 pap., .50
1. Architecture, Domestic—Designs and plans.

LUMPKINS, William T 728.64
La casa adobe. Santa Fe, N. M., Ancient City Press, 1961. 1v. (unpaged, chiefly illus., plans) 37cm. [NA7165.L8] 61-18753
1. Architecture, Domestic—Designs and plans. 2. Architecture, Domestic—Southwest, New. 3. Building, Adobe. I. Title.

MORLEY-FLETCHER, Hugo. 728.64
Ebenerdig wohnen; der Flachbau als Wohnform und als stadtebauliches Element, Low-level group housing. Habitations de plain-pied. Stuttgart, J. Hoffmann [dist. New York, Efron, c.1963] 135p. illus., maps, plans. 30cm. 63-5453 12.50
1. Architecture, Domestic—Designs and plans. 2. Cities and towns—Planning. I. Title. II. Title: Lowlevel group housing.

POLLMAN, Richard B., 1914- 728.6'4
Contemporary one-story homes under 1,600 sq. ft. Richard B. Pollman, designer [Detroit] Home Planners, 1966. 1 v. of illus. 28 cm. (Designs for convenient living. Portfolio no. 47) [NA7127.P589] 68-3394
1. Architecture, Domestic—Designs and plans. I. Home Planners, inc., Detroit. II. Title.

POLLMAN, Richard B., 1914- 728.6'4
Home Planners 84 home designs for traditional and contemporary tastes, by Richard B. Pollman, designer. New York, Published by Universal Pub. and Distributing Corp. for Home Planners, inc., Detroit [1969] 93 p. (p. 92-93 advertisements) illus. (part col.), plans. 28 cm. (Designs for convenient living, book no. 70) [NA7127.P5914] 71-13387 1.00
1. Architecture, Domestic—Designs and plans. I. Home Planners, inc., Detroit. II. Title. III. Title: 84 home designs for traditional and contemporary tastes.

POLLMAN, Richard B., 1914- 728.6'4
Multi-level homes. Richard B. Pollman, designer. [Detroit] Home Planners [1966] 2 v. of illus. 28 cm. (Designs for convenient living. Portfolio no. 48-49) [NA7127.P5917] 68-3896
1. Architecture, Domestic—Designs and plans. I. Home Planners, inc., Detroit. II. Title.

POLLMAN, Richard B., 1914- 728.6'4
Traditional one-story homes under 1,600 sq. ft. Richard B. Pollman, designer. [Detroit] Home Planners, 1966. 1 v. of illus. 28 cm. (Designs for convenient living. Portfolio no. 46) [NA7127.P593] 68-3235
1. Architecture, Domestic—Designs and plans. I. Home Planners, inc., Detroit. II. Title.

PRATT Institute, Brooklyn. School of Architecture. 728.6084
An investigation of the small house. Brooklyn [c1957] 1 v. (unpaged) illus., diagrs. 28x44cm. Contents.pt. 1. The function makes the plan, by C. J. Spaulding.--pt. 2. Small house structure, by M. A. Goldwasser. --pt. 3. Mechanical equipment, by R. E. Ancipink. [NA7127.P73] 58-24007
1. Architecture, Domestick —Designs and plans. I. Title.

STICKLEY, Gustav, 1858-1942. 728.3
The best of Craftsman homes / Gustav Stickley. Santa Barbara : Peregrine Smith, inc., 1979. p. cm. Includes plans from the author's Craftsman home (1909) and More Craftsman homes (1912) [NA737.S65A4 1979] 79-14082 ISBN 0-87905-058-6 pbk. : 9.95
1. Stickley, Gustav, 1858-1942. 2. Architecture, Domestic—United States—Designs and plans. 3. Arts and crafts movement. I. Stickley, Gustav, 1858-1942. Craftsman homes. II. Stickley, Gustav, 1858-1942. More Craftsman homes. III. Title. BIP

SUNSET. 728.7
Sunset ideas for cabins and beach houses. [1st ed.] Menlo Park, Calif., Lane Pub. Co. [1952] 112 p. illus. 28 cm. "Part of the material published in this book was copyrighted in 1938 and in 1948 under the title, Sunset cabin plan book." [NA8470.S8] 52-9027
1. Architecture, Domestic — Designs and plans. 2. Log cabins. I. Title.

Architecture, Domestic—Designs and plans—Juvenile literature.

MYLLER, Rolf. 728
From idea into house. House designed by Myller & Szwarce. Drawings for this book prepared by Henry K. Szwarce. [1st ed.] New York, Atheneum, 1974. 64 p. illus. 29 cm. Describes the process of building a house including buying the land, drawing up plans, and the actual construction. [NA7120.M95] 73-84832 ISBN 0-689-30144-8 6.95
1. Architecture, Domestic—Designs and plans—Juvenile literature. 2. House construction—Juvenile literature. I. Szwarce, Henry K., illus. II. Title.

Architecture, Domestic—Dorset, Eng.

OSWALD, Arthur 728.8094233
Country houses of Dorset. [2d, rev. and enl. ed.] London, Country Life, ltd. [label: Hollywood-by-the-Sea, Fla., Transatlantic Arts [1959, i.e., 1960] 184p. Includes bibliography illus. 26cm. 60-2258 15.75
1. Architecture, Domestic—Dorset, Eng. 2. Castles—England—Dorset. I. Title.

Architecture, Domestic—England.

BARLEY, Maurice Willmore, 1909- 728.670942
The English farmhouse and cottage [New York, Hillary, 1962, c.1961] xxi, 297p. illus., maps. 26cm. Bibl. 61-19981 10.00
1. Architecture, Domestic—England. 2. Farmhouses—England. 3. Cottages. I. Title. BIP

BATSFORD, Harry. 728.68
The English cottage, by Harry Batsford and Charles Fry. 3d ed., rev. London, New York, Batsford [1950] viii, 119 p. illus. 22 cm. (The "British heritage" series) [NA7562.B33 1950] 50-12589
1. Architecture, Domestic—England. 2. Cottages. I. Fry, Charles, 1903- joint author. II. Title. III. Series.

HUSSEY, Christopher, 1899- 728.8
English country houses [v. 1. Rev. ed] London. Country Life, ltd. [New York, Oxford, c.1965] 258p. illus., plans. ports. 32cm. Contents.1. Early Georgian, 1715-1760. [NA7620.H82] 66-814 20.20
1. Architecture, Domestic—England. 2. England—Historic houses. etc. I. Title.

HUSSEY, Christopher, 1899- 914.2
English country houses open to the public. [2d ed., rev. and enl. [London] Country Life; New York, Scribner [1953] 208p. illus. 30cm. [NA7328.H83 1953] 53-3646
1. Architecture, Domestic—England. I. Title.

KERR, Robert, 1823-1904. 728'.0942
The gentleman's house. Introd. by J. Mordaunt Crook. New York, Johnson Reprint Corp., 1972. xviii, 26, xiv, 477 p. illus. 23 cm. Reprint of the 1871 ed. published by J. Murray, London. [NA7620.K39 1972] 72-4312 30.00
1. Architecture, Domestic—England. 2. Architecture, Domestic—Designs and plans. I. Title.

NASH, Joseph, 1809-1878. 720'.942
The mansions of England in the olden time. With a pref. by George B. Tatum and an introd. by C. Harrison Townsend. [New York] Bounty Books [1970] vi p., 100 plates. 41 cm. Based on the 1906 facsim. ed. [NA7328.N3 1970] 71-108062
1. Architecture, Domestic—England. 2. Historic buildings—England. I. Title.

PENOYRE, John. 728.3
Houses in the landscape : a regional study of vernacular building styles in England and Wales / John and Jane Penoyre ; with ill. by the authors. London ; Boston : Faber, 1978. 175 p., [16] leaves of plates : ill. (some col.) ; 20 cm. Includes index. Bibliography: p. [165]-166. [NA7328.P28] 78-326923 ISBN 0-571-11055-X : 15.95
1. Architecture, Domestic—England. 2. Vernacular architecture—England. 3. Architecture, Domestic—Wales. 4. Vernacular architecture—Wales. I. Penoyre, Jane, joint author. II. Title. BIP

POTTER, Margaret 728.0942
Houses, being a record of the changes in construction, style, and plan of the smaller English home from mediaeval times to present day [2d ed. Dist. Hollywood-by-the- Sea, Fla., Transatlantic, 1962, c.1960] 47p. illus. (pt. col.) 29cm. (Changing shape of things ser.) 61-2677 3.75 bds.,
1. Architecture, Domestic—England. I. Potter, Alexander, joint author. II. Title. III. Series. BIP

YARWOOD, Doreen 728.0942
English houses. London, Batsford, 1966. 48p. 187 illus., plans. 31cm. Companion to the author's Outline of English architecture. Bibl. [NA7328.Y3] 66-78634 4.00 bds.,
1. Architecture, Domestic—England. 2. Architecture, Domestic—Designs and plans. I. Title.
Distributed by Verry, Mystic, Conn.

Architecture, Domestic—England—Breckland.

POVEY, Terence. 728.3
Design in Breckland : individual houses / [prepared by Terence Povey and Peter Tolhurst]. [2d ed.]. Dereham [Eng.] : Breckland District Council, [1976] 27 p. : ill. ; 30 cm. Caption title. [NA7331.B73P68 1976] 77-350850
1. Architecture, Domestic—England—Breckland. I. Tolhurst, Peter, joint author. II. Title.

Architecture, Domestic—England—Conservation and restoration.

PAGE, Marian, 1918- 728'.028
Historic houses restored and preserved / by Marian Page. New York : Whitney Library of Design, 1976. p. cm. Includes index. Bibliography: p. [NA7328.P22] 76-18966 ISBN 0-8230-7275-4 : 25.00
1. Architecture, Domestic—England—Conservation and restoration. 2. Historic buildings—England—Conservation and restoration. 3. Architecture, Domestic—United States—Conservation and restoration. 4. Historic buildings—United States—Conservation and restoration. 5. Architecture—United States—English influences. I. Title. BIP

Architecture, Domestic—England—Hist.

BRAUN, Hugh Stanley 728.60942
Old English houses. London, Faber & Faber [Mystic, Conn., Verry, 1966, c.1962] 168p. illus. 23cm. [NA7328.B67] 63-2906 5.00
1. Architecture, Domestic—England—Hist. 2. Farm-houses—England—Hist. I. Title.

HENDERSON, Andrew, 1919- 728.60942
The family house in England, written, illus. by Andrew Henderson. London, Phoenix [dist. Mystic, Conn., Verry. 1965, c.1964] 96p. illus. 26cm. [NA7328.H417] 65-2105 5.00
1. Architecture, Domestic—England—Hist. I. Title.

JORDAN, Robert Furneaux 728.0942
A picture history of the English house. New York, Macmillan [1959 i.e. 1960]

160p. illus. 29cm. (Hulton's picture histories) 60-1730 7.00
1. Architecture, Domestic—England—Hist. I. Title.

WOOD, Margaret E. 728.0942
The English mediaeval house [by] Margaret Wood (Mrs. E. G. Kaines-Thomas) London. Phoenix House [Mystic. Conn., Verry. c.1965] xxx, 448p. illus., plans. 26cm. Bibl. [NA7328.W64] 66-485 32.50
1. Architecture, Domestic—England.—Hist. 2. Architecture. Medieval. I. Title.

Architecture, Domestic—England—History.

INNOCENT, Charles Frederick. 690'.0942
The development of English building construction, by C. F. Innocent. [1st ed.] new impression; with new introduction and bibliography by Sir Robert de Z. Hall. Newton Abbot, David and Charles, 1971. [26], 294 p. illus., map, plan. 24 cm. Facsimile reprint of 1st ed., Cambridge, Cambridge University Press, 1916. Bibliography: p. [12-18] [NA7328.I5 1971] 71-886093 ISBN 0-7153-5299-7 15.00
1. Architecture, Domestic—England—History. 2. Building—Great Britain. I. Title.
Distributed by David & Charles. BIP

Architecture, Domestic—England—Kent—Designs and plans.

HOUSING design guide / Kent Planning Officers. 711'.58'094223
[Maidstone] : [Kent County Planning Department], 1976. [1], 59 p. : ill. (some col.), map, plans (some col.) ; 30 cm. Includes index. Bibliography: p. 57. [NA7331.K3H68] 77-367507 ISBN 0-900947-99-3 : £2.00
1. Architecture, Domestic—England—Kent—Designs and plans. 2. Kent, Eng.—Dwellings. I. Kent, Eng. Planning Dept.

Architecture, Domestic—England—Suffolk.

SANDON, Eric. 728'.09426'4
Suffolk houses : a study of domestic architecture / by Eric Sandon, with contributions by Stanley West and Elizabeth Owles ; drawings by John Western ; photos. by Helen Sandon, Liza Whipp & Baron Publishing. Woodbridge [Eng.] : Baron Pub., c1977. 344 p. : ill. (some col.) ; 31 cm. Bibliography: p. 341-344. [NA7331.S7S26] 77-370576 ISBN 0-902028-68-5 : £15.00
1. Architecture, Domestic—England—Suffolk. I. West, Stanley E., joint author. II. Owles, Elizabeth, joint author. III. Title.

Architecture, Domestic—Europe.

DAL LAGO, Adalberto. 728.8'2
Villas and palaces of Europe [by] Adalbert Dal Lago. London, New York, P. Hamlyn [1969] 157 p. 67 col. illus. 20 cm. (Cameo) Translation of Ville antiche. [NA7580.D2813] 70-20809 ISBN 0-600-01235-2
1. Architecture, Domestic—Europe. 2. Historic buildings—Europe. I. Title.

Architecture, Domestic—Fayette Co., Ky.

LANCASTER, Clay 728.0976947
Ante bellum houses of the Bluegrass; the development of residential architecture in Fayette County, Kentucky. Lexington, Univ. of Ky. Pr. [c.1961] xiii, 186p. illus., map (fold. in pocket) plans. 29cm. Bibl. 61-15624 12.50
1. Architecture, Domestic—Fayette Co., Ky. 2. Fayette Co., Ky.— Historic houses, etc. I. Title.

Architecture, Domestic—Frascati.

FRANCK, Carlludwig. 728.84094563
The villas of Frascati, 1550-1750 [by] Carl L. Franck. With drawings by the author. [Translated into English, rev. and enl. 1st American ed. New York, Transatlantic Arts, 1966. vi, 174 p. illus., plans, col. plate. 26 cm. Translation of Die Barockvillen in Frascati. Bibliography: p. 170-172. [NA7594.F713 1966] 66-9838
1. Architecture, Domestic—Frascati. 2. Architecture, Baroque—Frascati. 3. Suburban homes—Frascati. I. Title. BIP

Architecture, Domestic—Grahamstown, South Africa—History.

REYNOLDS, Rex. 728'.09687
Grahamstown from cottage to villa / photographs by Rex & Barbara Reynolds ; text by Eily Gledhill ; design by Ken Robinson ; foreword by Ronald Lewcock. Claremont, South Africa : D. Philip, 1974. 109 p. : ill. ; 25 cm. (South African yesterdays ; no. 5) [NA7468.6.S63G727] 75-320206 ISBN 0-949968-29-3. ISBN 0-949968-30-7 (de luxe)
1. Architecture, Domestic—Grahamstown, South Africa—History. I. Reynolds, Barbara. II. Gledhill, Eily. III. Title.

Architecture, Domestic—Great Britain.

BARLEY, Maurice Willmore, 1909- 728.0942
The house and home [London] Vista Bks. [dist. Chester Springs, Pa., Dufour, 1965, c.1963] 208p. illus. 26cm. (Visual hist. of mod. Brit.) Bibl. [NA7328.B24] 65-8056 6.95 bds.,
1. Architecture, Domestic—Gt. Brit. 2. Gt. Brit.—Historic houses, etc. 3. Gt. Brit.—Soc. life & cust. I. Title. II. Series.

BARLEY, Maurice Willmore, 1909- 392'.36'00942
The house and home; a review of 900 years of house planning and furnishing in Britain [by] M. W. Barley. Greenwich, Conn., New York Graphic Society [1971, c1963] 208 p. illus. 26 cm. Bibliography: p. 75-76. [NA7328.B24 1971] 72-162716 ISBN 0-8212-0351-7 12.50
1. Architecture, Domestic—Great Britain. 2. Architecture and society—Great Britain. I. Title.

BRUCKMANN, Hansmartin 728.0942
New housing in Great Britain [by] Hansmartin Bruckman [and] David L. Lewis. [German/English trans. by Sylvia Roberts; English/German trans. by Hansmartin Bruckmann] New York, Universe Bks. [1960] 131p. Bibl. and bibl. notes, p.128-131. illus., maps, plans, charts, tables 27cm. 60-12423 9.50
1. Architecture, Domestic—Gt. Brit. 2. Cities and towns—Planning —Gt. Brit. I. Lewis, David L., joint author. II. Title.

BRUNSKILL, R. W. 728
Illustrated handbook of vernacular architecture [by] R. W. Brunskill. New York, Universe Books [1971, c1970] 229 p. illus., maps, plans. 22 cm. Includes bibliographical references. [NA7328.B83 1971] 71-134757 ISBN 0-87663-138-3 8.95
1. Architecture, Domestic—Gt. Brit. I. Title. BIP

GREAT Britain. Dept. of the Environment. 728.3
Housing the family. Lancaster : MTP Construction, 1974. v, 264 p. : ill. ; 31 cm. (Design bulletins) Includes index. Bibliography: p. 259. [NA7328.G83 1974] 74-193750 ISBN 0-904406-00-8 : £5.25
1. Architecture, Domestic—Great Britain. 2. Space (Architecture) I. Title. II. Series.

HOUSE & garden 728.60942
Small houses. Eds.: Robert Harling, Joyce Lowrie, Alex Kroll. [Dist. New York, St. Martin's, 1962]c.1961[ ] 208p. illus. (pt. col.) 30cm. 62-1152 12.00
1. Architecture, Domestic—Gt. Brit. 2. Architecture, Domestic—Designs and plans. I. Harling, Robert, ed. II. Title.

LIVERPOOL daily post and echo. 728.3
Country heritage; the stately homes of the north west counties and north Wales. [Liverpool] 1951. 112 p. illus. 28 cm. [NA7328.L58] 52-41954
1. Architecture, Domestic—Gt. Brit. I. Title.

NICOLSON, Nigel. 728.80942
Great houses of Britain. Photos. by Kerry Dundas. New York, Putnam [1965] 288 p. illus. (part col.) 33 cm. [NA7620.N5] 65-19760
1. Architecture, Domestic—Gt. Brit. 2. Gt. Brit.—Historic houses, etc. I. Title.

WOODFORDE, John. 728'.0941
Georgian houses for all / John Woodforde. London ; Boston : Routledge and Kegan Paul, 1978. xiv, 177 p. ; 22 cm. Includes index. Bibliography: p. 168-170. [NA7328.W66] 78-310018 ISBN 0-7100-8680-6 : 10.75
1. Architecture, Domestic—Great Britain. 2. Architecture, Georgian—Great Britain. I. Title. BIP

Architecture, Domestic—Hamburg.

HIPP, Hermann. v. 12
Colonnaden / Hermann Hipp. Hamburg : Christians, 1975. 63 p. : 41 ill., maps, plans (1 fold. in pocket) ; 30 cm. (Arbeitshefte zur Denkmalpflege in Hamburg ; Nr. 2) Includes bibliographical references. [NA7351.H34H56] 76-459642 ISBN 3-7672-0366-9 : DM14.00
1. Architecture, Domestic—Hamburg. 2. Architecture, Modern—19th century—Hamburg. 3. Hamburg—Streets—Colonnaden. I. Title.

Architecture, Domestic—Hampshire, Eng.

HAMPSHIRE, Eng. County Council. 728'.09422'7
Better design, 66: some recent examples in Hampshire. Winchester [1966] [21] p. illus., maps, plans. 21 x 30 cm. [NA7333.H3A5] 67-86089
1. Architecture, Domestic—Hampshire, Eng. I. Title.

Architecture, Domestic—Handbooks, manuals, etc.

BAKER, John Milnes, 1932- 728.3
How to build a house with an architect / John Milnes Baker. 1st ed. Philadelphia : Lippincott, c1977. 190 p. : ill. ; 26 cm. Bibliography: p. 189-190. [NA7115.B28] 76-49974 ISBN 0-397-01124-5 : 14.95
1. Architecture, Domestic—Handbooks, manuals, etc. 2. Architectural practice—Handbooks, manuals, etc. I. Title.

HARRISON, Henry S. 728.3
Houses : the illustrated guide to construction, design, and systems / Henry S. Harrison ; ill., Peter A. Farbach ... [et al.] ; editing, Helene Berlin, Llani O'Connor, Peg Keilholz ; design, Sherman Mutchnick, Libby Marschke. 1st rev. ed. Chicago : Realtors National Marketing Institute of the National Association of Realtors, 1976. 435 p. : ill. ; 24 cm. Includes index. Bibliography: p. 394-403. [NA7110.H33 1976] 76-150371 ISBN 0-913652-05-9
1. Architecture, Domestic—Handbooks, manuals, etc. 2. Building materials—Handbooks, manuals, etc. I. Farbach, Peter A. II. Title.

Architecture, Domestic—History.

CAMESASCA, Ettore, 1922- comp. 690'.8
History of the house. With a foreword by Sir Robert Matthew. Translated by Isabel Quigly. [1st American ed.] New York, Putnam [1971] 432 p. illus. (part col.) 32 cm. Translation of Storia della casa. [NA7105.C313] 73-141310 25.00
1. Architecture, Domestic—History. I. Title.

GARDINER, Stephen. 728'.09
Evolution of the house; an introduction. New York, Macmillan [1974] 298 p. illus. 24 cm. [NA7105.G37] 73-10784 ISBN 0-02-542500-5 8.95
1. Architecture, Domestic—History. I. Title.

†RIDLEY, Anthony. 909
At home : an illustrated history of houses and homes / by Anthony Ridley. New York : Crane Russak, 1976. 190 p. : ill. ; 24 cm. Includes index. Bibliography: p. 181-182. [NA7105.R5 1976b] 77-371314 ISBN 0-8448-0916-0 : 9.95
1. Architecture, Domestic—History. 2. Dwellings—History. 3. Interior decoration—History. I. Title.

RIDLEY, Anthony. 643'.09
At home : an illustrated history of houses and homes / [by] Anthony Ridley. London : Heinemann, 1976. 191 p. : ill., facsims., plans ; 24 cm. Includes index. Bibliography: p. 181-182. [NA7105.R5 1976] 76-373610 ISBN 0-434-95961-8 : £3.60
1. Architecture, Domestic—History. 2. Dwellings—History. 3. Interior decoration—History. I. Title.

VIOLLET-LE-DUC, Eugene Emmanuel, 1814-1879. 728'.09
The habitations of man in all ages. Translated by Benjamin Bucknall. Ann Arbor, Mich., Gryphon Books, 1971. xvi, 394 p. illus. 22 cm. "Facsimile reprint of the 1876 edition." Translation of Histoire de l'habitation humaine depuis les temps prehistoriques jusqu'a nos jours. [NA7105.V5513 1876a] 71-146922
1. Architecture, Domestic—History. 2. Dwellings—History. I. Title. BIP

Architecture, Domestic—Hudson Valley.

*REYNOLDS, Helen Wilkinson 728.6097473
Dutch houses in the Hudson Valley before 1776. Introd. by Franklin D. Roosevelt, Photography by Margaret De M. Brown [Gloucester, Mass., P. Smith, 1966] 467p. illus., map. 24cm. (Dover bk. T1469 rebound) Prepd. under the auspices of the Holland Soc. of New York. First pub. by Payson & Clarke in 1929 [NA7235.N7H6] 6.00
1. Architecture, Domestic—Hudson Valley. 2. Architecture, Colonial. 3. Hudson Valley—Historic houses, etc. 4. New York (State)—Historic houses, etc. I. Holland Society of New York. II. Title.

REYNOLDS, Helen Wilkinson. 728.6097473
Dutch houses in the Hudson Valley before 1776. With an introd. by Franklin D. Roosevelt. Photography by Margaret De M. Brown. New York, Dover Publications [1965] 467 p. illus., map. 24 cm. "Prepared under the auspices of the Holland Society of New York." "An unabridged and unaltered republication of the work first published ... in 1929." [NA7235.N7H6 1965] 65-26075
1. Architecture, Domestic—Hudson Valley. 2. Architecture, Colonial—Hudson Valley. 3. Hudson Valley—Historic houses, ect. 4. New York (State)—Historic houses, etc. I. Holland Society of New York. II. Title. BIP

Architecture, Domestic—Indiana.

PEAT, Wilbur David, 1898- 728.3709772
Indiana houses of the nineteenth century. Indianapolis, Ind. Hist. Soc. [1963, c.1962] xiv, 195p. illus., plans. 29cm. 63-2411 12.50
1. Architecture, Domestic—Iindiana. I. Title.

Architecture, Domestic in art.

SWANN, Don, 1889- 769'.92'4
Colonial and historic homes of Maryland : one hundred etchings / by Don Swann ; text by Don Swann, Jr. ; foreword by F. Scott Fitzgerald. Baltimore : Johns Hopkins University Press, [1975] 211 p. : ill. ; 29 cm. Includes index. [NE2012.S92A43 1975] 75-9722 ISBN 0-8018-1727-7 : 35.00
1. Swann, Don, 1889- 2. Architecture, Domestic, in art. 3. Historic buildings—Maryland—Pictorial works. 4. Architecture, Colonial—Maryland—Pictorial works. I. Swann, Don, 1911- joint author. II. Title. BIP

WRIGHTSON, Priscilla. 708'.172'52 s
The English picturesque: villa and cottage, 1760-1860. Introd., catalogue, and notes by Priscilla Wrightson. Pref. by Carl J. Weinhardt. [Indianapolis, Indianapolis Museum of Art, 1973] 136-205 p. illus. 26 cm. (Indianapolis Museum of Art. Bulletin/catalogue, v. 1, no. 3 (new ser.))

Errata slip inserted. [N577.A4 n.s. vol. 1, no. 3] [NE628] 769'.4'40942 74-152795
1. Indianapolis Museum of Art. 2. Architecture, Domestic, in art. 3. Prints, English—Catalogs. 4. Prints—Indianapolis—Catalogs. I. Title. II. Series: Indianapolis Museum of Art. Bulletin/catalogue. New ser., v. 1, no. 3.

Architecture, Domestic—Ireland.

CRAIG, Maurice James. 728.8'3'09415
Classic Irish houses of the middle size / by Maurice Craig. London : Architectural Press ; New York : Architectural Book Pub. Co., 1977, c1976. 170 p. : ill. ; 31 cm. Includes index. Bibliography: p. 167. [NA7337.C73 1977] 76-49536 ISBN 0-8038-0044-4 : 17.95
1. Architecture, Domestic—Ireland. 2. Neoclassicism (Architecture)—Ireland. 3. Architecture, Domestic—Designs and plans. I. Title. BIP

DE BREFFNY, Brian. 941.5
The houses of Ireland : domestic architecture from the medieval castle to the Edwardian villa / Brian de Breffny and Rosemary Ffolliott ; photos. by George Mott. New York : Viking Press, 1975. 240 p. : ill. (some col.) ; 26 cm. (A Studio book) Includes index. Bibliography: p. 233. [NA7337.D42] 74-7509 ISBN 0-670-38102-0 : 16.95
1. Architecture, Domestic—Ireland. I. Ffolliott, Rosemary, joint author. II. Title.

IDE, John Jay, 1892- 728.8309415
Some examples of Irish country houses of the Georgian period. New York, 1959. 66p. illus. 19cm. [NA7337.I3] 59-12388
1. Architecture, Domestic—Ireland. 2. Architecture, Georgian. I. Title. II. Title: Irish country houses of the Georgian period.

Architecture, Domestic—Italy.

MASSON, Georgina. 728.80945
Italian villas and palaces. New York, H. N. Abrams [1959] 244 p. 193 plates, maps. 33 cm. Bibliography: p. 238-239. [NA7594.M3 1959] 59-13062
1. Architecture, Domestic—Italy. 2. Palaces—Italy. I. Title. BIP

WHARTON, Edith Newbold Jones, 1862-1937. 945
Italian villas and their gardens / by Edith Wharton ; illustrated with pictures by Maxfield Parish and by photos. New York : Da Capo Press, 1976, c1904. xii, 270 p., [8] leaves of plates : ill. ; 24 cm. (Da Capo Press series in architecture and decorative art) Reprint of the ed. published by the Century Co., New York. Includes index. Bibliography: p. 251-252. [NA7594.W46 1976] 76-10865 ISBN 0-306-70817-5 : 35.00 ISBN 0-306-80048-9 pbk. : 8.95
1. Architecture, Domestic—Italy. 2. Landscape architecture—Italy. I. Title. BIP

Architecture, Domestic— Japan.

BLASER, Werner, 1924- 722.12
Japanese temples and tea-houses. [English version by D. Q. Stephenson] New York, F. W. Dodge Corp. [1957, c1956] 156 p. illus. (part col.) plans. 33 cm. Picture captions in German, French, and English. Bibliography: p. 156. [NA7451.B564] 57-7727
1. Architecture, Domestic—Japan. 2. Temples—Japan. 3. Japan—Social life and customs. 4. Tea. I. Title.

BLASER, Werner, 1924- 722.12
Tempel and Teehaus in Japan. Olten, Urs.-Graf-Verlag, 1955. 156 p. illus. (part col.) plans. 32 cm. Picture captions in German, French, and English. Bibliography:p. 156. [NA7451.B56] 56-58176
1. Architecture, Domestic— Japan. 2. Temples—Japan. 3. Japan—Soc. life & cust. 4. Tea. I. Title.

FUTAGAWA, Yukio, 1932- 728'.0952
The essential Japanese house; craftsmanship, function, and style in town and country. Text and commentaries: Teiji Itoh. Tokyo, J. Weatherhill [1967] 419p. (chiefly illus.) plans. 36cm. (Weathermark ed.) Tr. of (romanized: Nihon no minka) [NA1451.F813 1967 fol] 67-15270 25.00
1. Architecture, Domestic—Japan. I. Ito Teiji, 1922- II. Title.

ISHIMOTO, Tatsuo. 728.0952
The Japanese house, its interior and exterior, by Tatsuo and Kiyoko Ishimoto. New York, Crown [1963] 128 p. illus. 29 cm. [NA7451.I8] 63-12066
1. Architecture, Domestic — Japan. 2. Interior decoration — Japan. I. Ishimoto, Kiyoko, joint author. II. Title.

ITO, Teiji, 1922- 728'.0952
Traditional domestic architecture of Japan, by Teiji Itoh. Translated by Richard L. Gage. [1st ed.] New York, Weatherhill [1972] 150 p. illus. 24 cm. (The Heibonsha survey of Japanese art, 21) Translation of Minka. [NA7451.I8413] 76-183520 ISBN 0-8348-1004-2 7.95
1. Architecture, Domestic—Japan. 2. Architecture, Japanese. I. Title. II. Series. BIP

MORSE, Edward Sylvester, 1838-1925. 728.0952
Japanese homes and their surroundings. Illus. by the author. New introd. by Clay Lancaster. New York, Dover Publications [1961] 372p. illus. 61-2262 2.00 pap.,
1. Architecture, Domestic—Japan. 2. Interior decoration—Japan 3. Japan—Soc. life & cust. I. Title. BIP

MORSE, Edward Sylvester, 1838-1925 728.0952
Japanese homes and their surroundings. Illus. by the author. New introd. by Clay Lancaster. [Gloucester, Mass., Peter Smith, c. 1961] 372p. illus. (Dover bk. rebound) 4.01
1. Architecture, Domestic—Japan. 2. Interior decoration—Japan. 3. Japan—Soc. life & cust. I. Title.

MORSE, Edward Sylvester, 1838-1925. 728.6'4
Japanese homes and their surroundings. With an introd. to the new ed. by Terence Barrow. Rutland, Vt., C. E. Tuttle Co. [1972] xliii, 372 p. illus. 19 cm. (Tut books. A) [NA7451.M6 1972] 76-157262 ISBN 0-8048-0998-4 2.95
1. Architecture, Domestic—Japan. 2. Interior decoration—Japan. 3. Japan—Social life and customs. I. Title.

NISHIHARA, Kiyoyuki, 1930- 728.3'7'0952
Japanese houses; patterns for living. Translated by Richard L. Gage. Tokyo, Japan Publications; [distributed by Japan Publications Trading Co., New York, 1968, c1967] 276 p. illus., maps, plans. 31 cm. Bibliography: p. 269-270. [NA7451.N5313] 66-22390
1. Architecture, Domestic—Japan. I. Title.

YOSHIDA, Tetsuro, 1894-1956. 728
The Japanese house and garden. Translated from the German by Marcus G. Sims. New York, Praeger [1955] 204 p. illus., map, plans. 28 cm. (Books that matter) Translation of Das japanische Wohnhaus. Bibliography: p. 204. [NA7451.Y615] 55-8110
1. Architecture, Domestic—Japan. I. Title.

YOSHIDA, Tetsuro, 1894-1956. 728
The Japanese house and garden. Translated from the German by Marcus G. Sims, with an epilogue by Udo Kultermann. [Rev. ed.] New York, Praeger [1969] 224 p. illus. (part col.), map, plans. 28 cm. Translation of Das japanische Wohnhaus. Bibliography: p. 224. [NA7451.Y613 1969] 76-89607 15.00
1. Architecture, Domestic—Japan. I. Title.

Architecture, Domestic — Juvenile literature.

ADLER, Irving. JUV
Houses [by] Irving and Ruth Adler. New York, John Day Co. [1964] 48 p. illus. (part col.) 22 cm. (Their The reason why books) [PZ10.A3Ho] j728 64-20708
1. Architecture, Domestic — Juvenile literature. I. Adler, Ruth, joint author. II. Title.

Architecture, Domestic—Kansas City, Mo.

MULKEY Square, Kansas City, Missouri, 1869-1973; a survey of the city's first suburb. Researched and compiled by Milton F. Perry [and others] Kansas City, Mo., Museums Council of Mid-America, 1973. 42 p. illus. 24 cm. [NA7238.K36M84] 74-184590 728.3
1. Architecture, Domestic—Kansas City, Mo. 2. Kansas City, Mo.—Plazas—Mulkey Square. I. Perry, Milton F.

Architecture, Domestic—Kentucky.

MONTELL, William Lynwood, 1931- 728
Kentucky folk architecture / William Lynwood Montell and Michael Lynn Morse. Lexington : University Press of Kentucky, c1976. xii, 104, [1] p. : ill. ; 21 cm. (The Kentucky bicentennial bookshelf) Bibliography: p. 101-[105]. [NA7235.K4M66] 76-4437 ISBN 0-8131-0230-8 : 3.95
1. Architecture, Domestic—Kentucky. 2. Architecture, Anonymous—Kentucky. 3. Barns—Kentucky. I. Morse, Michael Lynn, joint author. II. Title. III. Series. BIP

Architecture, Domestic—Lawrence, Kan.

KANSAS. University. Museum of Art. 728.6'09781'65
Nineteenth century houses in Lawrence, Kansas; [exhibition] September 22-October 27, 1968. [Lawrence, Kan., 1968] 1 v. (unpaged) illus, maps. 23 cm. (Its Miscellaneous publications, no. 72) [NA7238.L33K3] 68-65918
1. Architecture, Domestic—Lawrence, Kan. 2. Architecture, Domestic—Exhibitions. 3. Architecture, Modern—19th cent.—Lawrence, Kan. I. Title.

Architecture, Domestic—Lima.

TROY, Robert D. 720'.985
Lima, Peru; a study of housing in an arid coastal region, 1967-1968, by Robert D. Troy. [Lubbock, Tex.] International Center for Arid and Semi-arid Land Studies [1969] 55 p. illus., map. 28 cm. (International Center for Arid and Semi-arid Land Studies. Special report, no. 13) Sponsored by the American Institute of Architects and the Texas Technological Foundation. Bibliography: p. 54-55. [NA7318.L5T7] 76-628032
1. Architecture, Domestic—Lima. I. Title. II. Series.

Architecture, Domestic—Louisiana.

OVERDYKE, William Darrell. 728.8309763
Louisiana plantation homes, colonial and ante bellum, by W. Darrell Overdyke. New York, Architectural Book Pub. Co. [1965] 206 p; illus., map (on lining papers) 28 cm. [NA7235.L8O9] 65-23195
1. Architecture, Domestic—Louisiana. 2. Louisiana—Historic houses, etc. I. Title.

Architecture, Domestic—Louisville, Ky.

OLD Louisville. 728.084
Louisville, Ky., University of Louisville [1961] 68p. illus., map. 25cm. [NA7238.L8O4] 62-1294
1. Architecture, Domestic—Louisville, Ky. 2. Louisville, Ky.—Soc. life & cust. I. Brown, Theodore M. II. Bridwell, Margaret Morris, 1905-
Contents omitted.

Architecture, Domestic—Lydia.

RAMAGE, Andrew. 728.3'09392'2
Lydian houses and architectural terracottas / Andrew Ramage. Cambridge : Harvard University Press, 1978. p. cm. (Monograph - Archaeological exploration of Sardis ; 5) Includes index. Bibliography: p. [NA251.L9R35] 78-15507 ISBN 0-674-53959-1 : 14.00
1. Architecture, Domestic—Lydia. 2. Decoration and ornament, Architectural—Lydia. 3. Terra-cotta sculpture—To 500—Lydia. 4. Lydia. I. Title. II. Series: Archaeological exploration of Sardis. Monograph ; 5. BIP

Architecture, Domestic — Maryland.

WILSON, Everett Broomall, 1900- 728.309752
Maryland's colonial mansions and other early houses, by Everett B. Wilson. New York, A. S. Barnes [1965] 249 p. (chiefly illus.) 26 cm. Bibliography: p. 249. [NA7235.M3W5 1965] 65-17510
1. Architecture, Domestic — Maryland. 2. Architecture, Colonial. 3. Maryland — Historic houses, etc. I. Title.

Architecture, Domestic—Massachusetts.

†*EARLY homes of Massachusetts* : from material originally published as the White pine series of architectural monographs, edited by Russell F. Whitehead and Frank Chouteau Brown / prepared for this series by the staff of the Early American Society, Robert G. Miner, editor ... [et al.]. New York : Arno Press : distributed to the book trade by Crown Publishers, c1977. 223 p. : ill. ; 28 cm. (An Early American Society book) (Architectural treasures of early America) [NA7235.M4E18] 77-104 ISBN 0-405-10064-7 : 10.95 728.3
1. Architecture, Domestic—Massachusetts. 2. Architecture, Colonial—Massachusetts. 3. Architecture—Massachusetts. I. Miner, Robert G. II. Early American Society. III. The Monograph series, records of early American architecture. IV. Series. BIP

Architecture, Domestic—Mediterranean region.

BRANCH, Daniel Paulk. 720.91822
Folk architecture of the east Mediterranean. New York, Columbia University Press, 1966. 145 p. illus., maps. 25 cm. (The William Kinne Fellows studies in architecture, no. 1) Bibliography: p. 141-142. [NA7450.B7] 66-17586
1. Architecture, Domestic—Mediterranean region. I. Title. II. Series.

Architecture, Domestic—Mexico.

SHIPWAY, Verna (Cook) 1890- 728.0972
The Mexican house, old & new, by Verna Cook Shipway and Warren Shipway. New York, Architectural Book Pub. Co. 1960 187 p. illus. 29 cm. [NA7244.S45] 60-14620
1. Architecture, Domestic—Mexico. I. Shipway, Warren, joint author. II. Title.

Architecture, Domestic—Miami metropolitan area.

THE Villagers (Organization) 728.3
The Villagers' book of outstanding homes of Miami / sponsored by The Villagers ; with text by Patricia Gabriel. Coral Gables, Fla. : University of Miami Press, c1975. 159 p. : ill. ; 29 cm. [NA7238.M52V54] 75-31851 ISBN 0-87024-296-2
1. Architecture, Domestic—Miami metropolitan area. I. Gabriel, Patricia, 1922- II. Title. III. Title: Book of outstanding homes of Miami. BIP

Architecture, Domestic—Nantucket, Mass.

DUPREY, Kenneth. 728.0974497
Old houses on Nantucket. New York, Architectural Book Pub. Co. [1959] xii, 242 p. illus., plans. 28 cm. Bibliography: p. 235-236. [NA7238.N3D8] 59-10847
1. Architecture, Domestic—Nantucket, Mass. 2. Interior decoration—Nantucket, Mass. I. Title. BIP

Architecture, Domestic— Natchez, Miss.—Historic houses, etc.

TYREE, Irene S. 728.80976226
Natchez ante-bellum homes, comp. by Mrs. Raymond Tyree. Natchez, Miss., T.

SUBJECT INDEX

ARCHITECTURE, DOMESTIC—TEXAS.

L. Ketchings Co. [c.1964] 128p. illus. 29cm. 64-2810 7.95
1. Architecture, Domestic— Natchez, Miss.—Historic houses, etc. I. Title.

Architecture, Domestic—New England.

BAKER, Norman B. 728'.0974
Early houses of New England, by Norman B. Baker. [1st ed.] Rutland, Vt., C. E. Tuttle Co. [1967] 144 p. illus., plans. 29 cm. [NA7210.B34] 67-11935
1. Architecture, Domestic—New England. 2. New England—Historic houses, etc. 3. Architecture, Domestic—Designs and plans. I. Title. BIP

†*EARLY homes of New England* 728.3
: from material originally published as the White pine series of architectural monographs, edited by Russell F. Whitehead and Frank Chouteau Brown / prepared for this series by the staff of the Early American Society, Robert G. Miner, editor ... [et al.]. New York : Arno Press : distributed to the book trade by Crown Publishers, c1977. 223 p. : ill. ; 28 cm. (An Early American Society book) (Architectural treasures of early America) [NA7210.E18] 77-14469 ISBN 0-405-10068-X : 10.95
1. Architecture, Domestic—New England. 2. Architecture, Colonial—New England. 3. Architecture—New England. I. Miner, Robert G. II. Early American Society. III. The Monograph series, records of early American architecture. IV. Series. BIP

MCARDLE, Alma 1924- 728'.0974
Carpenter Gothic : 19th-century ornamented houses of New England / by Alma deC. McArdle and Deirdre Bartlett McArdle ; photos. by Frederick L. Hamilton. New York : Whitney Library of Design, 1978. p. cm. Includes index. Bibliography: p. [NA7210.M3 1978] 78-8034 ISBN 0-8230-7121-9 : 24.50
1. Architecture, Domestic—New England. 2. Gothic revival (Architecture)—New England. 3. Architecture, American—New England. 4. Decoration and ornament, Architectural—New England. 5. Decoration and ornament, American—New England. 6. Historic buildings—New England. 7. New England—Dwellings. I. McArdle, Deirdre Bartlett, 1954- joint authors. II. Hamilton, Frederick L., 1900- III. Title.
Distributed by Watson-Guptill, New York BIP

PILLSBURY, Richard. 728.3
A field guide to the folk architecture of the northeastern United States [by] Richard Pillsbury [and] Andrew Kardos. [Hanover, N.H., Dartmouth College, Dept. of Geography, 1970] 99 p. illus. 26 cm. (Geography publications at Dartmouth, no. 8) "Special edition on geographical lore." Bibliography: p. 98-99. [NA7206.P54] 72-187626
1. Architecture, Domestic—New England. 2. Architecture, Domestic—Middle Atlantic States. I. Kardos, Andrew, joint author. II. Title. III. Series.

UNDERWOOD, Francis H. 728.3
The colonial house then and now : a picture study of the early American house adapted to modern living / by Francis H. Underwood. Rutland, Vt. : C. E. Tuttle Co., 1977. 172 p. : ill. ; 27 cm. [NA7210.U5] 75-28720 ISBN 0-8048-1150-4 : 17.50
1. Architecture, Domestic—New England. 2. Architecture, Colonial—New England. 3. Architecture, Domestic—Designs and plans. I. Title. BIP

Architecture, Domestic—New Harmony, Ind.

BLAIR, Don, 1909- 728.3'7'977234
Harmonist construction, principally as found in the two-story houses built in Harmonie, Indiana, 1814-1824. Indianapolis, Indiana Historical Society, 1964. 45-82 p. illus., map. 23 cm. (Indiana Historical Society. Publications, v. 23, no. 2) [F521.I41 vol.23.no 2] 64-64334
1. Architecture, Domestic—New Harmony, Ind. I. Title. II. Series.

Architecture, Domestic—New York (State)

†*EARLY homes of New York* 728.3
and the Mid-Atlantic States : from material originally published as the White pine series of architectural monographs, edited by Russell F. Whitehead and Frank Chouteau Brown / prepared for this series by the staff of the Early American Society, Robert G. Miner, editor ... [et al.]. New York : Arno Press : distributed to the book trade by Crown Publishers, c1977. 223 p. : ill. ; 28 cm. (An Early American Society book) (Architectural treasures of early America) [NA7235.N7E18] 77-14467 ISBN 0-405-10069-8 : 10.95
1. Architecture, Domestic—New York (State) 2. Architecture, Colonial—New York (State) 3. Architecture—New York (State) 4. Architecture, Domestic—Middle Atlantic States. 5. Architecture, Colonial—Middle Atlantic States. 6. Architecture—Middle Atlantic States. I. Miner, Robert G. II. Early American Society. III. The Monograph series, records of early American Architecture. IV. Series. BIP

SCHMIDT, Carl Frederick, 1894- 729.6
Cobblestone masonry, by Carl F. Schmidt. Scottsville, N. Y., 1966. 326 p. illus., plans. 29 cm. [NA7235.N7S38] 66-4144
1. Architecture, Domestic—New York (State) 2. New York (State)—Historic houses, etc. 3. Building stones—New York (State) I. Title.

Architecture, Domestic—New York (State)—Hudson Valley.

VILLAS on the 728.8'4'097473
Hudson : a collection of photo-lithographs of thirty-one country residences. New York : Da Capo Press, 1977, c1860. [10] p., [53] leaves of plates : chiefly ill. ; 32 x 42 cm. (Da Capo Press series in architecture and decorative art) Reprint of the ed. published by B. Appleton, New York. [NA7586.V54 1977] 76-41854 ISBN 0-306-70800-0 : 65.00
1. Architecture, Domestic—New York (State)—Hudson Valley. BIP

Architecture, Domestic—North Carolina.

ALLCOTT, John V. 728.609756
Colonial homes in North Carolina. Raleigh, N.C., Carolina Charter Tercentenary Commn. [dist. State Dept. of Archives & History, 1964] 103p. illus., maps, diagrs., plans. 24cm. Bibl. 64-63141 .50 pap.,
1. Architecture, Domestic—North Carolina. 2. Architecture Colonial. 3. North Carolina —Historic houses, etc. I. Carolina Charter Tercentenary Commission, Raleigh, N.C. II. Title. BIP

Architecture, Domestic—Norwich, Vt.

WHITE, Philip Aylwin, 1915- 728.3'7'0974365
Early houses of Norwich, Vermont [by] Philip Aylwin White [and] Dana Doane Johnson. Edited by Marjorie Yule Butler and Abbie H. Metcalf. 2d rev. ed. [Norwich, Vt., Norwich Historical Society, 1973] xi, 88 p. illus. 23 cm. Bibliography: p. 82. [NA7238.N7W5 1973] 73-173472 1.90
1. Architecture, Domestic—Norwich, Vt. 2. Architecture—Norwich, Vt. 3. Architecture, Colonial—Norwich, Vt. I. Johnson, Dana Doane, 1914- joint author. II. Butler, Marjorie Yule. III. Metcalf, Abbie H. IV. Title.

Architecture, Domestic—Paris.

GALLET, Michel. 728'.0944
Stately mansions; eighteenth century Paris architecture. New York, Praeger [1972] xiv, 196 p. illus. 26 cm. Translation of Demeures parisiennes. Bibliography: p. 189-190. [NA7348.P2G313 1972] 75-166512 25.00
1. Architecture, Domestic—Paris. 2. Architecture, Modern—17th-18th centuries—Paris. 3. Decoration and ornament—Louis XVI style. I. Title.

Architecture, Domestic—Pennsylvania.

RAYMOND, Eleanor. 720'.9748
Early domestic architecture of Pennsylvania : photographs and measured drawings / by Eleanor Raymond ; with an introd. by R. Brognard Okie. Exton, Pa. : Schiffer, c1977. [19] p., [79] leaves of plates : ill. ; 29 cm. [NA7235.P4R3 1977] 77-92980 ISBN 0-916838-11-0 ; 15.00
1. Architecture, Domestic—Pennsylvania. 2. Architecture, Colonial—Pennsylvania. I. Title.

RAYMOND, Eleanor. 720'.9748
Early domestic architecture of Pennsylvania. Introd. by R. Brognard Okie. With a new introd. by John Milner. Princeton, Pyne Press [1973, c1931] 1 v. (unpaged) illus. 28 cm. Reprint of the ed. published by W. Helburn, New York. [NA7235.P4R3 1973] 73-79526 ISBN 0-87861-047-2 6.95 (pbk.)
1. Architecture, Domestic—Pennsylvania. I. Title.

Architecture, Domestic—Period.

INTERNATIONAL Union of Architects 728
Habitation [International documentation; ser. 3, Rotterdam, Bouwcentrum, New York, Amer. Elsevier, 1964. 250p. illus., maps, plans. 31cm. French and English. 64-55157 29.50
1. Architecture, Domestic—Period. 2. Architecture— Designs and plans—Period. I. Title.

LIVING for young 728.605
homemakers. v. 1- New York, Street & Smith Publications. autumn 1947- v. illus. (part col.) 33 cm. Frequency varies. Title varies: 1947-Apr. [NA7100.L5] 51-17541
1. Architecture, Domestic—Period. 2. Interior decoration—Period.

LIVING'S new guide to 728.6084
home planning [and] remodeling. [New York, Street & Smith Publications] v. illus. (part col.) 34cm. [NA7100.L52] 58-26512
1. Architecture, Domestic—Period. 2. Interior decoration—Period. 3. Dwellings—Remodeling—Period.

Architecture, Domestic—Quebec (Province)

WILSON, P. Roy, 1900- 971.4
The beautiful old houses of Quebec / P. Roy Wilson ; with a foreword by Jean Palardy. Toronto ; Buffalo : University of Toronto Press, [1975] 125 p. : ill. ; 23 x 27 cm. Includes index. [NA7242.Q3W54] 75-8501 ISBN 0-8020-2146-8 : 12.50
1. Architecture, Domestic—Quebec (Province) I. Title. BIP

Architecture, Domestic—Rhode Island.

†*EARLY homes of Rhode* 728.3
Island : from material originally published as the White pine series of architectural monographs, edited by Russell F. Whitehead and Frank Chouteau Brown / prepared for this series by the staff of the Early American Society, Robert G. Miner, editor ... [et al.]. New York : Arno Press : distributed to the book trade by Crown Publishers, c1977. 223 p. : ill. ; 28 cm. (An Early American Society book) (Architectural treasures of early America ; v. 4) [NA7235.R4E18] 77-14470 ISBN 0-405-10067-1 : 10.95
1. Architecture, Domestic—Rhode Island. 2. Architecture, Colonial—Rhode Island. 3. Architecture—Rhode Island. I. Miner, Robert G. II. Early American Society. III. The Monograph series, records of early American architecture. IV. Series. BIP

Architecture, Domestic—Rome.

MCKAY, Alexander Gordon, 1924- 728
Houses, villas, and palaces in the Roman world / A. G. McKay. Ithaca, N.Y. : Cornell University Press, 1975. 288 p., [24] leaves of plates : ill. ; 23 cm. (Aspects of Greek and Roman life) Includes index. Bibliography: p. [259]-268. [NA324.M32] 74-20425 ISBN 0-8014-0948-9 : 19.75
1. Architecture, Domestic—Rome. I. Title. II. Series.

Architecture, Domestic—St. Louis—Conservation and restoration.

CONLEY, Timothy G., 1947- 917.78'66
Lafayette Square : an urban renaissance / by Timothy G. Conley ; photos. by Barbara Elliott Martin. [St. Louis?] : Lafayette Square Press, [1974] 116 p. : ill. ; 23 cm. Bibliography: p. 115-116. [NA7238.S28C66] 74-21699 ISBN 0-9600796-1-0. ISBN 0-9600796-2-9 pbk.
1. Architecture, Domestic—St. Louis—Conservation and restoration. 2. St. Louis—Plazas—Lafayette Square. I. Title.

Architecture, Domestic—Saratoga Springs, N.Y.

PROKOPOFF, Stephen S. 728
The nineteenth-century architecture of Saratoga Springs; architecture worth saving in New York State. Text by Stephen S. Prokopoff and Joan C. Siegfried. Photos. by Joe Alper. [New York, New York State Council on the Arts] 1970. 104 p. illus. 21 cm. [NA7238.S37P7] 75-109052
1. Architecture, Domestic—Saratoga Springs, N.Y. 2. Saratoga Springs, N.Y.—Historic houses, etc. I. Siegfried, Joan C., joint author. II. New York (State). State Council on the Arts. III. Title. BIP

Architecture, Domestic—Southern States.

†*COLONIAL homes in the* 728.3
Southern States : from material originally published as the White pine series of architectural monographs, edited by Russell F. Whitehead and Frank Chouteau Brown / prepared for this series by the staff of the Early American Society, Robert G. Miner, editor ... [et al.]. New York : Arno Press : distributed to the book trade by Crown Publishers, c1977. 223 p. : ill. ; 28 cm. (An Early American Society book) (Architectural treasures of early America) [NA7211.C7] 77-14465 ISBN 0-405-10070-1 : 10.95
1. Architecture, Domestic—Southern States. 2. Architecture, Colonial—Southern States. 3. Architecture—Southern States. I. Miner, Robert G. II. Early American Society. III. The Monograph series, records of early American architecture. IV. Series. BIP

FIRST American National Bank. 728.8'3'09768
Interesting homes of middle Tennessee. [Enl. 3d ed.] Nashville [1966] 1 v. (unpaged) illus. 21 x 28 cm. Cover title. First ed., 1941, published under the bank's earlier name, American National Bank, has title: Historic homes of the "Old South." The 2d ed., 1956, was published under the bank's later name, and has title: Homes of Tennessee. [NA7214.A5 1966] 70-12341
1. Architecture, Domestic—Southern States. 2. Historic buildings—Southern States. I. American National Bank, Nashville. Historic homes of the "Old South." II. Title.

Architecture, Domestic — Taos, N.M.

BUNTING, Bainbridge. 728.64
Taos adobes; Spanish colonial and territorial architecture of the Taos Valley. Illus. by Jean Lee Booth and William R. Sims, Jr. [1st ed.] Santa Fe, Museum of New Mexico Press, 1964. 80 p. illus. 29 cm. (Fort Burgwin Research Center. Publication no. 2). "Bibliographical note": p. 80. [NA7165.B8] 64-54700
1. Architecture, Domestic — Taos, N.M. 2. Building, Adobe. 3. Sims, William R., illus. I. Title. II. Series. BIP

Architecture, Domestic—Texas.

ALEXANDER, Drury Blakeley. 728'.09764
Texas homes of the nineteenth century. Photos. by Todd Webb. Foreword by Harry H. Ransom. Austin [tex.] Published for the Amon Carter Museum of Western Art by the University of Texas Press

[c1966] Amon Carter Museum of Western Art, Fort Worth, Tex. xiv, 276 p. illus., 201 plates. 32 cm. (The Texas architectural survey, publication no. 1) Bibliography: p. 267. [NA7235.T4A54] 66-27416
1. Architecture, Domestic—Texas. 2. Texas—Historic houses, etc. I. -Webb, Todd, illus II. Title. III. Series. **BIP**

BRACKEN, Dorothy Kendall. 728
Early Texas homes, by Dorothy Kendall Bracken and Maurine Whorton Redway. Dallas, Southern Methodist University Press, 1956. xii, 188p. illus. 29cm. [NA7235.T4B7] 56-12565
1. Architecture, Domestic—Texas. I. Redway, Maurine Whorton, joint author. II. Title. **BIP**

Architecture, Domestic—The West.

THOMPSON, Elisabeth Kendall. 728'.09182'1
Houses of the West / by Elisabeth Kendall Thompson. New York : McGraw-Hill, 1978, c1977. p. cm. "An Architectural record book." Includes index. [NA7223.T48 1978] 77-15106 ISBN 0-07-002339-5 : 18.95
1. Architecture, Domestic—The West. 2. Architecture, Anonymous—The West. I. Title. **BIP**

Architecture, Domestic—Tuscany.

ACTON, Harold Mario Mitchell, 1904- 728.8'4'09455
Great houses of Italy the Tuscan villas [by] Harold Acton. With photos. by Alexander Zielcke. New York, Viking Press [1973] 288 p. illus. 32 cm. (A Studio book) [NA7594.A38 1974] 73-1637 ISBN 0-670-34971-2 28.50
1. Architecture, Domestic—Tuscany. 2. Tuscany—Historic houses, etc. I. Title.

Architecture, Domestic—U. S.

ALSWANG, Betty. 728.0973
The personal house; homes of artists and writers [by] Betty Alswang and Ambur Hiken. New York, Whitney Library of Design [1961] 80p. illus. (part mounted col.) ports., map. 40cm. [NA7205.A63] 61-16681
1. Architecture, Domestic—U. S. 2. Interior decoration—U. S. 3. Artists, American. 4. Authors, American. I. Hiken, Ambur, joint author. II. Title.

THE American home. 728
The American home book of home improvement ideas. [Garden City? N. Y., 1955?] 106p. illus. 33cm. [NA7205.A65] 55-1845
1. Architecture, Domestic—U. S. I. Title. II. Title: Home improvement ideas.

ARTISTIC houses; 728.8'0973
being a series of interior views of a number of the most beautiful and celebrated homes in the United States, with a description of the art treasures contained therein. New York, B. Blom, 1971. 184, 184 p. illus. 27 cm. "First published New York, 1883." [NA7207.A72] 69-18531
1. Architecture, Domestic—U.S. 2. Interior decoration—U.S.

ASSOCIATED Plan Service, inc., Huntinglon, N. Y. 728.6084
Architect's 1957 selection of new home plans [New York] Universal Pub. and Distributing Corp., c 1956] 56p. illus., plans. 28cm. (Associated plan book no. 11 [sic]) [NA7127.A766] 57-498
1. Architecture, Domestic—U. S. 2. Architecture, Domestic—Designs and plans. I. Title.

ASSOCIATED Plan Service, inc., Huntington, N. Y. 728.6084
Prize winning homes for nineteen fifty-seven by leading architects [New York, Universal Pub. and Distributing Corp., c1956] 56p. illus. 28cm. [NA7127.A774] 57-497
1. Architecture, Domestic—U. S. 2. Architecture, Domestic—Designs and plans. I. Title.

BALLINGER, Richard M. 728'.0973
The illustrated guide to the houses of America, edited by Richard M. Ballinger and Herman York. New York, Hawthorn Books [1971] xii, 260 p. illus., plans. 29 cm. [NA7205.B34 1971] 73-130710 13.95
1. Architecture, Domestic—U.S. I. York, Herman H., 1908- joint author. II. Title.

BALLINGER, Richard M. 728'.0973
The illustrated guide to the houses of America / edited by Richard M. Ballinger and Herman York. New York : Galahad Books, c1971. xii, 260 p. : ill. ; 29 cm. Includes index. [NA7205.B34 1971b] 73-92079 ISBN 0-88365-177-7 : 13.95
1. Architecture, Domestic—United States. I. York, Herman H., 1908- joint author. II. Title.

BETTER homes and gardens. 643.7
Home improvement ideas. Des Moines, Meredith Pub. Co. v. illus. 32cm. [NA7205.B45] 53-3856
1. Architecture, Domestic—U. S. 2. Building—Repair and reconstruction. I. Title.

CALLENDER, John Hancock. 728.6084
Before you buy a house. New York, Crown Publishers [1953] 160 p. illus. 29 cm. [NA7208.C3] 53-5685
1. Architecture, Domestic—U.S. 2. Architecture, Domestic—Designs and plans. I. Title.

CREIGHTON, Thomas Hawk 728.0973
Contemporary houses evaluated by their owners [by] Thomas H. Creighton, Katherine M. Ford. New York, Reinhold [c.1961] 224p. illus. 27cm. 61-13198 10.95
1. Architecture, Domestic—U.S. 2. Architecture, Domestic— Designs and plans. I. Ford, Katherine (Morrow) 1905- joint author. II. Title.

CURRENT, William. 728'.0973
Greene & Greene; architects in the residential style. Photos. by William R. Current. Text by Karen Current. Fort Worth [Tex.] Amon Carter Museum of Western Art [1974] 128 p. illus. 24 x 28 cm. [NA737.G73C87] 74-76989 ISBN 0-88360-005-6 15.00
1. Greene & Greene. 2. Architecture, Domestic—United States. I. Current, Karen. **BIP**

FIVE architects : 728.3
Eisenman, Graves, Gwathmey, Hejduk, Meier. New York : Oxford University Press, 1975. 137 p. : ill. ; 27 cm. "This book is to some extent the outcome of a meeting of the CASE group (Conference of Architects for the Study of the Environment) held at the Museum of Modern Art in 1969." Erratum slip inserted. [NA7208.F54 1975] 74-16658 ISBN 0-19-519794-1 : 25.00. ISBN 0-19-519795-X pbk. : 9.95
1. Architecture, Domestic—United States. 2. Architecture, Modern—20th century—United States. I. New York (City). Museum of Modern Art.

FIVE architects: Eisenman, 728.3
Graves, Gwathmey, Hejduk, Meier. [New York] Wittenborn [1972] 137 p. illus. 27 cm. "This book is to some extent the outcome of a meeting of the CASE group (Conference of Architects for the Study of the Environment) held at the Museum of Modern Art in 1969." [NA7208.F54] 72-91948 ISBN 0-8150-0422-2 17.50
1. Architecture, Domestic—United States. 2. Architecture, Modern—20th century—United States. 3. Architecture, Domestic—Designs and plans. I. New York (City). Museum of Modern Art.

FORD, Katherine (Morrow) 1905- 728.6084
Designs for living; 175 examples of quality home interiors, by Katherine Morrow Ford and Thomas H. Creighton. New York, Reinhold Pub. Corp. [1955] 215p. illus. 27cm. [NA7208.F57] 55-7617
1. Architecture, Domestic—U. S. 2. Interior decoration. I. Creighton, Thomas Hawk, joint author. II. Title.

GOULD, Mary Earle 917.3032
The early American house; household life in America, 1620-1850. With special chapters on the construction and evolution of old American homes, fireplaces & iron utensils, [and] hearthside & barnyard activities [Rev. ed.] Rutland, Vt., Tuttle [1965, c.1949] 152p. illus. 29cm. [NA7206.G6] 66-255 8.95
1. Architecture, Domestic—U.S. 2. Architecture, Colonial. 3. U. S.—Soc. life & cust.—Colonial period. 4. Kitchen utensils. 5. Fireplaces. I. Title.

GROW, Lawrence. 728.3
Old house plans : two centuries of American domestic architecture / Lawrence Grow. New York : Universe Books, 1978. 127 p. : ill. ; 22 x 29 cm. "A Main Street Press book." [NA7205.G77] 77-91927 ISBN 0-87663-981-3 pbk. : 4.95
1. Architecture, Domestic—United States. 2. Architecture, Domestic—Designs and plans. 3. Architecture—Details. I. Title. **BIP**

HAAGEN, Paul T. 728.6
How to have a better house; a helpful guide, Based on experience, for those who wish a better house. Wilmette, Ill., F. J. Drake [1950] 312 p. illus., plans. 23 cm. [NA7208.H3] 50-6388
1. Architecture, Domestic—U. S. I. Title.

HOMES for living. 728.6
57 builder tested ranch and split level homes. [New York, Universal Pub. and Distributing Corp., c1957] 56p. illus. 28cm. Contents.24 spilt level designs from Samuel Paul, A. I. A.--8 custom fabricated homes by Fabricators, inc.--25 ranch designs from Samuel Paul, A. I. A. [NA7127.H644] 57-899
1. Architecture, Domestic—U. S. 2. Architecture, Domestic—Designs and plans. I. Paul, Samuel, 1912- II. Title.

HOUSE Plan Headquarters. 728.3
Beautiful home plans. New York [1972] [80] p. illus. 28 cm. [NA7208.H66] 73-157152 1.00
1. Architecture, Domestic—United States. 2. Architecture, Modern—20th century—United States. 3. Architecture, Domestic—Designs and plans. I. Title.

HOUSE Plan Headquarters. 728.3
Beautiful home plans. 16th ed. New York : House Plan Headquarters, c1978. [80] p. : ill. ; 29 cm. [NA7208.H66 1978] 78-106296 pbk. : 1.50
1. Architecture, Domestic—United States. 2. Architecture, Modern—20th century—United States. 3. Architecture, Domestic—Designs and plans. I. Title.
Publisher's address : 48 W. 48th St., New York, NY 10036

ISHAM, Norman Morrison, 1864-1943. 728'.0974
Early American houses; the seventeenth century. [Watkins Glen, N.Y.] American Life Foundation, 1968. 61, [19] p. illus., plans. 23 cm. (Classic guide books to the visual arts) "Quest of the colonial; a biography [i.e. bibliography] of books, 1880-1930 [by Hugh Guthrie]": p. [65]-[70] [NA7206.I7 1968] 68-20804 2.45
1. Architecture, Domestic—United States. 2. Architecture, Colonial—United States. I. Title.

ISHAM, Norman Morrison, 1864-1943 728/.0972
Early American houses; and, A glossary of colonial architectural terms. New York, Da Capo, 1967. 61, 37p. illus., plans. 33 plates. 24cm. (Da Capo ser. in architecture and decorative art, v. 10) Da Capo Pr. reprint ed. Reprint of two works pub. orig. by the Walpole Soc.: Early American houses, pub. in 1928, and A glossary of colonial architectural terms, pub. in 1939. [NA7206.I 7 1967] 67-27457 10.00
1. Architecture, Domestic—U. S. 2. Architecture, Colonial—U. S. 3. Architecture, Colonial—Dictionaries. I. Title. II. Title: A glossary of colonial architectural terms.

JONES, Archie Quincy, 1913- 728.6084
Builders' homes for better living [by] A. Quincy Jones [and] Frederick E. Emmons. John L. Chapman, associate. Sketches by Rudy Veland. New York, Reinhold Pub. Corp. [1957] 220 p. illus. 27 cm. [NA7208.J56] 57-11776
1. Architecture, Domestic—U.S. 2. Architecture, Domestic—Designs and plans. I. Emmons, Frederick Earl, 1907- joint author. II. Title.

KATZ, Robert D. 711.58
Design of the housing site, a critique of American practice [by] Robert D. Katz. Urbana, [Dept. of Urban Planning, University of Illinois] distributed by Small Homes Council-Building Research Council, University of Illinois, 1966. 223 p. illus., map. 23 x 30 cm. Bibliography: p. 216-218. [NA7208.K3] A 67
1. Architecture, Domestic—U. S. 2. Homesites. I. Illinois. University. Small Homes Council-Building Research Council. II. Title.

KIMBALL, Sidney Fiske, 1888-1955 728/.0973
Domestic architecture of the American colonies and of the early republic [Magnolia, Mass., P. Smith, 1967, c.1922] xx, 314p. illus., plans. 28cm. (Dover bk. rebound) Lect. delivered at the Metropolitan Mus. of Art in 1920, pub. under the auspices of its Comm. on Educ. Unabridged, corrected repubn. of the work orig. pub. in 1922 Bibl. [NA707.K45 1966] 7.50
1. Architecture, Domestic—U. S. 2. Architecture, Colonial. 3. U.S.—Historic houses, etc. I. New York, Metropolitan Museum of Art. Committee on Education. II. Title. **BIP**

KIMBALL, Sidney Fiske, 1888-1955. 728'.0973
Domestic architecture of the American colonies and of the early Republic. New York, Dover Publications [1966, c1922] xx, 314 p. illus., plans. 28 cm. Lectures delivered at the Metropolitan Museum of Art in 1920, published under the auspices of its Committee on Education. "An unabridged and corrected republication of the work originally published ... in 1922." Bibliographical footnotes. [NA707.K45 1966] 66-29154
1. Architecture, Domestic—United States. 2. Architecture, Colonial—United States. 3. United States—Historic houses, etc. I. New York. Metropolitan Museum of Art. Committee on Education. II. Title.

NEUTRA, Richard Joseph, 1892- 728
Mystery and realities of the site. Scarsdale, N. Y., Morgan & Morgan [1951] 64 p. illus. 21 cm. At head of title: Richard Neutra on building. [NA7208.N4] 51-6414
1. Architecture, Domestic — U.S. 2. Homesites. I. Title.

NEUTRA, Richard Joseph, 1892- 720.973
World and dwelling. New York, Universe Bks. [c.1962] 159p. illus., plans. 31cm. 62-12005 15.00
1. Architecture, Domestic—U.S. 2. Architecture. I. Title.

PALLISER, Palliser & Co., firm, Architects. 728.3'7
Palliser's model homes : showing a variety of designs for model dwellings .... [Felton, Calif. : Glenwood Publishers, 197-] c1878. 96 p. (p. 89-96 advertisements) : ill. ; 23 cm. Reprint of the ed. published by Palliser, Palliser, Bridgeport, Conn. [NA7205.P26 1970z] 75-319988 ISBN 0-911760-07-5 : 4.95
1. Architecture, Domestic—United States. 2. Architecture, Domestic—Designs and plans. I. Title. II. Title: Model homes. **BIP**

PALLISER, Palliser & Co., firm, architects. 728'.022'2
Palliser's new cottage homes and details .... New York : Da Capo Press, 1975. ca. 150 p. : ill. ; 35 cm. (Da Capo Press series in architecture and decorative art) Reprint of the 1887 ed. published by Palliser, Palliser, New York. [NA7205.P34 1975] 75-4887 ISBN 0-306-70744-6 lib.bdg. : 35.00
1. Architecture, Domestic—United States. 2. Architecture, Domestic—Designs and plans. I. Title. **BIP**

PICKERING, Ernest, 1893- 728
The homes of America, as they have expressed the lives of our people for three centuries. New York, Crowell [1951] 284 p. illus., map. 24 cm. (The Growth of America series) [NA7205.P5] 51-4857
1. Architecture, Domestic—U.S. 2. U.S.—Historic buildings. I. Title. II. Series.

PIERCE, Mary Knowles. 747.88
An acquired taste; American houses, rooms, and gardens explained in a rapid primer. New York, Vantage Press [1952] 140 p. illus. 22 cm. [NA7205.P53] 52-6962
1. Architecture, Domestic—U.S. 2. Landscape gardening—U.S. I. Title.

POLLMAN, Richard B., 1914- 728'.0973
154 homes, by Richard B. pollman. Detroit, Home Planners, inc. [1971] 129 p. illus. 28 cm. (Designs for convenient living, book no. 77. Design series, v. 3) Cover title. [NA7208.P6] 75-30125 1.25
1. Architecture, Domestic—U.S. 2. Architecture, Domestic—Designs and plans. I. Title.

POLLMAN, Richard B., 1914- 728.3
152 homes, by Richard B. Pollman. Detroit, Home Planners [1970] 129 p. illus. 28 cm. (Design series, v. 1) (Designs for convenient living, book no. 73) Cover title: Home Planners 152 homes. [NA7205.P64] 74-184389
1. Architecture, Domestic—United States. 2. Architecture, Domestic—Designs and plans. I. Home Planners, inc., Detroit. II. Title.

PRATT, Dorothy. 728
A guide to early American homes [by] Dorothy & Richard Pratt. New York, McGraw-Hill [1956] 2 v. illus. 26 cm. Contents.—[1] North.—[2] South. [NA7205.P68] 56-10867
1. Architecture, Domestic—United States. 2. United States—Historic houses, etc. 3. Museums. I. Pratt, Richard, joint author. II. Title: Early American homes.

RANLETT, William H. 728.3
The architect : a series of original designs, for domestic and ornamental cottages and villas, connected with landscape gardening, adapted to the United States / by William H. Ranlett ; illustrated by drawings of ground plots, plans, perspective views, elevations, sections, and details. New York : Da Capo Press, 1976. p. cm. (Da Capo Press series in architecture and decorative art) Reprint of the 1849-1851 ed. published by Dewitt & Davenport, New York. [NA7205.R36 1976] 76-21851 ISBN 0-306-70799-3 : 75.00(2 vol. set)
1. Architecture, Domestic—United States. 2. Architecture, Domestic—Designs and plans. I. Title.

ROBSJOHN-GIBBINGS, Terence Harold, 1905- 728
Homes of the brave. With drawings by Mary Petty. [1st ed.] New York, Knopf, 1954. 113 p. illus. 24 cm. [NA7208.R6] 53-6859
1. Architecture, Domestic—U.S. 2. Interior decoration. I. Title.

SCULLY, Vincent Joseph, 1920- 728
The shingle style; architectural theory and design from Richardson to the origins of Wright. New Haven, Yale University Press, 1955. 181p. illus. 28cm. (Yale historical publications. History of art, 10) Based on thesis, Yale University. Bibliography: p.165-174. Bibliographical footnotes. [NA7207.S38] 55-5988
1. Architecture, Domestic—U. S. I. Title. II. Series.

SCULLY, Vincent Joseph, 1920- 728'.0973
The shingle style today : or, The historian's revenge / Vincent Scully. New York : G. Braziller, [1974] 118 p. : ill. ; 25 cm. "Written and expanded from a lecture [given] ... at Columbia University in September, 1973." Includes bibliographical references and index. [NA7208.S38 1974] 74-79058 ISBN 0-8076-0759-2 : 7.95. ISBN 0-8076-0760-6 pbk. : 4.95
1. Architecture, Domestic—United States. 2. Architecture, Modern—20th century—United States. 3. Shingles. I. Title.

SLOAN, Samuel, 1815-1884. 728'.0973
The model architect : a series of original designs for cottages, villas, suburban residences, etc., accompanied by explanations, specifications, estimates, and elaborate details prepared expressly for the use of projectors and artisans throughout the United States / by Samuel Sloan. New York : Da Capo Press, 1975. 2 v. : ill. ; 36 cm. (Da Capo Press series in architecture and decorative art) Reprint of the 1852 ed. published by E. S. Jones, Philadelphia. [NA7207.S6 1975] 75-4698 ISBN 0-306-70746-2
1. Architecture, Domestic—United States. 2. Architecture, Domestic—Designs and plans. I. Title. BIP

STONE, Robert B ed. 728.6084
Treasury of new homes. [New York, Universal Pub. and Distributing Corp. 1956] 56 p. illus. 28 cm. (Associated plan book no. 11 [sic]) [NA7127.S848] 57-496
1. Architecture, Domestic — U.S. 2. Architecture, Domestic — Designs and plans. I. Title.

A Treasury of contemporary houses / [edited] by Walter F. Wagner, Jr. 728.3
New York : McGraw-Hill, c1978. 184 p. : ill. ; 31 cm. "An Architectural record book." Includes index. [NA7208.T73] 78-1448 ISBN 0-07-002330-1 : 18.95
1. Architecture, Domestic—United States. 2. Architecture, Modern—20th century—United States. 3. Dwellings—United States. I. Wagner, Walter F. II. Architectural record. BIP

WATERMAN, Thomas Tileston, 1900- 728
The dwellings of colonial America. Chapel Hill, University of North Carolina Press [1950] 312 p. illus., maps (on lining papers) plans. 27 cm. Bibliography: p. 291-293. [NA707.W42] 50-14735
1. Architecture, Domestic — U.S. I. Title.

WATERMAN, Thomas Tileston, 1900- 728
The dwellings of colonial America / by Thomas Tileston Waterman ; with an introd. and expanded bibliography by Nancy Halverson Schless. Chapel Hill : University of North Carolina Press, [1975] c1974. p. cm. Includes index. Bibliography: p. [NA707.W42 1975] 74-26844
1. Architecture, Domestic—United States. 2. Architecture, Colonial—United States. I. Title.

WEBBER, Joan, 1933- 728.3
How old is your house? : A guide to research / Joan Webber. 1st ed. Chester, Conn. : Pequot Press, c1978. 101 p. : ill., plans ; 23 cm. Bibliography: p. 100-101. [NA7205.W4] 77-88359 ISBN 0-87106-092-2 pbk. : 3.95
1. Architecture, Domestic—United States. 2. Dwellings—United States. 3. Historical research—United States—Handbooks, manuals, etc. I. Title. BIP

WILLIAMS, Henry Lionel. 728
Old American houses: how to restore, remodel, and reproduce them [by] Henry Lionel Williams & Ottalie K. Williams. Drawings and photos. by the authors except where noted. New York, Coward-McCann [1957] 190 p. illus. 26 cm. [NA7206.W5] 57-7066
1. Architecture, Domestic—United States. 2. Dwellings—Remodeling. 3. Architecture, Domestic—Conservation and restoration. I. Williams, Ottalie Kroeber, 1901- joint author. II. Title.

WOODWARD, George Evertson. 728'.0973
Woodward's National architect : containing 1000 original designs, plans, and details, to working scale, for the practical construction of dwelling houses for the country, suburb, and village, with full and complete sets of specifications and an estimate of the cost of each design / by Geo. E. Woodward and Edward G. Thompson. New York : Da Capo Press, 1975 [c1869] ca. 200 p. : ill. ; 30 cm. (Da Capo Press series in architecture and decorative art) Reprint of the ed., published by G. E. Woodward, New York. [NA7205.W66 1975] 75-23066 ISBN 0-306-70748-9 lib.bdg. 29.50
1. Architecture, Domestic—United States. 2. Architecture, Domestic—Designs and plans. I. Thompson, Edward G., joint author. II. Title. III. Title: National architect. BIP

WRIGHT, Frank Lloyd, 1869-1959. 728.081
The natural house. New York, Horizon Press, 1954. 223 p. illus., port., plans. 26 cm. [NA7208.W68] 54-12278
1. Architecture, Domestic—United States. 2. Architecture, Modern—20th century. 3. Architecture, Domestic—Designs and plans. I. Title.

WRIGHT, Frank Lloyd, 1869-1959 728.081
The natural house. [New York] New Amer. Lib. [1963. c.1954] 224p. illus., port., plans. 18cm. (Mentor Bk., MT469) .75 pap.,
1. Architecture, Domestic—U. S. 2. Architecture, Modern—20th cent. 33. Architecture, Domestic—Designs and plans. I. Title. BIP

Architecture. Domestic—U.S. Cottages.

DOWNING,Andrew Jackson, 1815-1852. 728.6'4'0973
Cottage residences, rural architecture & landscape gardening. With a new introd. by Michael Hugo-Brunt. [Watkins Glen, N.Y.] Library of Victorian Culture, 1967. 200 p. illus., plans. 24 cm. Includes bibliographies. [NA7561.D8] 6730049
1. Architecture. Domestic—U.S. Cottages. I. Title.

Architecture, Domestic—United States—Designs and plans.

†POLLMAN, Richard B., 1914- 728.3
Book of successful home plans / designs by Richard Pollman. Farmington, Mich. : Structures Pub. Co., 1976. 191 p. : ill. ; 28 cm. Prepared by Structures Publishing Company in cooperation with Home Planners, inc. Includes index. [NA7205.P63] 76-23485 ISBN 0-912336-34-X : 12.00 pbk. : 4.95
1. Architecture, Domestic—United States—Designs and plans. I. Home Planners, inc., Detroit. II. Structures Publishing Company. III. Title. IV. Title: Successful home plans. BIP

STICKLEY, Gustav, 1858-1942. 728.3
Craftsman homes : architecture and furnishings of the American arts and crafts movement / by Gustav Stickley. New York : Dover Publications, 1979. 205 p., [1] leaf of plates : ill. ; 28 cm. Reprint of the 2d ed. published in 1909 by Craftsman Pub. Co., New York. [NA737.S65A4 1979b] 78-73519 ISBN 0-486-23791-5 : 6.00
1. Stickley, Gustav, 1858-1942. 2. Architecture, Domestic—United States—Designs and plans. 3. Arts and crafts movement. I. Title. BIP

200 most popular home plans / New York : Bantam/Hudson Plan Books, 1978. 256 p. : ill. ; 18 cm. [NA7205.T86] 77-93586 ISBN 0-553-11758-0 pbk. : 2.25 728
1. Architecture, Domestic—United States—Designs and plans. I. Hudson home guides.

Architecture, Domestic — U.S. — History.

HOAG, Edwin. 728.0973
American houses: colonial, classic, and contemporary. Philadelphia, Lippincott [1964] 160 p. illus. 27 cm. Bibliography: p. 155-156. [NA7205.H6] 64-19042
1. Architecture, Domestic — U.S. — Hist. — Juvenile literature. I. Title. BIP

WILLIAMS, Henry Lionel. 728.0973
A guide to old American houses, 1700-1900, by Henry Lionel Williams and Ottalie K. Williams. New York, A. S. Barnes [1962] 168 p. illus., map, plans. 29 cm. [NA7205.W5] 62-18145
1. Architecture, Domestic—United States—History. I. Williams, Ottalie Kroeber, 1901- joint author. II. Title: Old American houses, 1700-1900.

Architecture, Domestic—U. S.—Period.

ARCHITECTURAL record. 728.6084
Record houses. 1956- New York, F. W. Dodge. v. illus. (part col.) plans. 30cm. [NA7100.A67] 56-14033
1. Architecture, Domestic—U. S.—Period. 2. Interior decoration—U. S.—Period. I. Title.

ARCHITECTURAL record. 728.6084
Record houses. 1956- New York, F. W. Dodge. v. illus. (part col.) plans. 30cm. [NA7100.A67] 56-14033
1. Architecture, Domestic—U. S.—Period. 2. Interior decoration— U. S.—Period. I. Title.

ARCHITECTURAL record 728.6084
Record houses of 1966 [New York, McGraw, c.1966] 166p.illus. (pt. col.) plans. 30cm. [NA7100.A67] 56-14033 2.95 pap.,
1. Architecture, Domestic—U.S.—Period. 2. Interior decoration—U.S. Period. I. Title.

ARCHITECTURAL RECORD. 728.6084
Record houses. 1967- New York, McGraw. v. illus. (pt. col.) plans. 30cm. [NA7100.A67] 56-14033 2.95 pap.,
1. Architecture, Domestic—U. S.—Period. 2. Interior decoration—U. S. Period. I. Title.

MODEL homes.1954 /55- 728
Atlantic City [Central Pier Co.] v. 31cm. [NA7100.M53] 54-43565
1. Architecture, Domestic—U. S.— Period. 2. Architecture, Domestic—Designs and plans.

Architecture, Domestic—Venezuela.

GASPARINI, Graziano 728.0987
La casa colonial venezolana. Caracas, Centro Estudiantes de Arquitectura, Universidad Central de Venezuela, [dist. New York, Wittenborn, 1963] 187p. illus. 22cm. 63-32851 7.50 pap.,
1. Architecture, Domestic—Venezuela. I. Title.

Architecture, Domestic—Vermont.

CONGDON, Herbert Wheaton, 1876- 728.370943
Early American homes for today; a treasury of decorative details and restoration porcedures. Rutland, Vt., Tuttle [c.1963] 236p. illus. 27cm. 62-18936 12.50
1. Architecture, Domestic—Vermont. 2. Architecture—Details. 3. Buildings—Repair and reconstruction. I. Title.

Architecture, Domestic—Virginia.

GLASSIE, Henry H. 975.5
Folk housing in middle Virginia : structural analysis of historic artifacts / by Henry Glassie ; photos. and drawings by the author. 1st ed. Knoxville : University of Tennessee Press, [1975] p. cm. Includes index. Bibliography: p. [NA7235.V5G55] 75-11653 ISBN 0-87049-173-3 : 12.50
1. Architecture, Domestic—Virginia. 2. Folk art—Virginia. I. Title. BIP

WATERMAN, Thomas Tileston, 1900- 728'.3'709755
Domestic colonial architecture of Tidewater Virginia, by Thomas Tileston Waterman and John A. Barrows. With an introd. by Fiske Kimball. New York, Dover Publications [1969] xvii, 191 p. illus., map. 31 cm. Reprint of the 1932 ed. [NA7235.V5W3 1969] 79-91975 4.00
1. Architecture, Domestic—Virginia. 2. Architecture, Colonial—Virginia. 3. Virginia—Historic houses, etc. I. Barrows, John A., joint author. II. Title. BIP

WATERMAN, Thomas Tileston, 1900- 728'.3'709755
Domestic colonial architecture of Tidewater Virginia, by Thomas Tileston Waterman and John A. Barrows. Introd. by Fiske Kimball. New York, Da Capo Press, 1968 [c1932] xvii, 191 p. illus., map. 29 cm. (Da Capo series in architecture and decorative art, v. 24) (A Da Capo Press reprint edition.) [NA7235.V5W3 1968] 69-11290 27.70
1. Architecture, Domestic—Virginia. 2. Architecture, Colonial—Virginia. 3. Virginia—Historic houses, etc. I. Barrows, John A., joint author. II. Title.

Architecture, Domestic—Western Mediterranean.

SERT, Jose Luis, 1902- 720'.92'4
Sert, Mediterranean architecture / edited by Maria Lluisa Borras [translated by Kenneth Lyons]. Boston : New York

Graphic Society, 1975. 25, 226 p., [3] leaves of plates : chiefly ill. (some col.) ; 21 cm. Translation of Sert, arquitectura mediterranea. Includes index. [NA737.S4A8513] 75-9108 ISBN 0-8212-0675-3 : 19.50
1. Sert, Jose Luis, 1902- 2. Architecture, Domestic—Western Mediterranean. I. Title.

Architecture, Domestic— Williamsburg Va.

WHIFFEN, Marcus 728.097554252
The eighteenth-century houses of Williamsburg; a study of architecture and building in the colonial capital of Virginia. Williamsburg, Va., Published by Colonial Williamsburg; distributed by Holt, Rinehart, and Winston, New York [c.1960] xx, 223p. (Bibl. notes: p.201-216) illus., map (on lining papers) diagrs., facsim., plans. 26cm. (Williamsburg architectural studies [v. 2]) 60-13174 10.00
1. Architecture, Domestic— Williamsburg Va. 2. Architecture, Colonial. I. Title. II. Series.

Architecture, Domestic—Woodstock, N.Y.

HANEY, Robert. 728.3
Woodstock handmade houses / Robert Haney and David Ballantine ; Jonathan Elliott, photographer. New York : Ballatine Books, 1974. [96] p. : col. ill. ; 25 cm. [NA7238.W66H36 1974] 75-308390 5.95
1. Architecture, Domestic—Woodstock, N.Y. 2. Architecture, Anonymous—New York (State)—Woodstock. I. Ballantine, David, joint author. II. Elliott, Jonathan. III. Title. BIP

Architecture—Dorset, Eng.

NEWMAN, John, 1936- 914.23'3'0485
Dorset, by John Newman and Nikolaus Pevsner. Harmondsworth, Penguin, 1972. 554, [64] p. illus., facsim., map. 19 cm. (The Buildings of England) [NA969.D67N48] 73-165945 ISBN 0-14-071044-2 £2.50
1. Architecture—Dorset, Eng. 2. Dorset, Eng.—Historic houses, etc. I. Pevsner, Nikolaus, Sir, 1902- II. Title.

Architecture—Dubuque, Iowa—History.

SOMMER, Lawrence J. 977.7'39
The heritage of Dubuque : an architectural view / by Lawrence J. Sommer ; illustrated by Carl H. Johnson, Jr. 1st ed. Dubuque, Iowa : First National Bank, 1975. xii, 172 p. : ill. ; 21 x 27 cm. 500 copies printed. No. 377. Includes index. Bibliography: p. 167-170. [NA735.D82S65] 75-29909
1. Architecture—Dubuque, Iowa—History. I. Johnson, Carl H. II. Title.

Architecture— Durham, Eng. (County)

BILLINGS, Robert William, 942.8'6
1813-1874.
Architectural antiquities of the county of Durham / Robert William Billings. Newcastle upon Tyne : Graham, 1974. [6], 64 p., [66] leaves of plates : ill. ; 29 cm. Reprint of original 1846 ed. published under title: Illustrations of the architectural antiquities of the County of Durham. [NA969.D9B6 1974] 75-323710 ISBN 0-85983-090-X : £5.00
1. Architecture—Durham, Eng. (County) I. Title.

PEVSNER, Nikolaus, 1902- 720.942
County Durham. London, Baltimore, Penguin Books [1953] 279p. illus. 18cm. (The Buildings of England, BE9) [NA969.D9P4] 54-28475
1. Architecture— Durham, Eng. (County) I. Title.

Architecture, Early Christian.

KRAUTHEIMER, Richard, 1897- 723.1
Early Christian and Byzantine architecture. Baltimore, Penguin Books [1965] xxv, 390 p. illus., maps, plans, 193 plates (1 col.) 27 cm. (The Pelican history of art, Z24) Bibliography: p. 365-367. [NA360.K7] 66-3419
1. Architecture, Early Christian. 2. Architecture, Byzantine. 3. Church architecture — Hist. I. Title. II. Series. BIP

KRAUTHEIMER, Richard, 1897- 723.1
Early Christian and Byzantine architecture. Harmondsworth, Penguin, 1965. xxx, 390 p. col. front., illus., 192 plates, 3 maps, plans, diagr. 27 cm. (B66-4222) (The Pelican history of art, Z24) Bibliography: p. 365-367. [NA360.K7] 66-70773
1. Architecture, Early Christian. 2. Architecture, Byzantine. 3. Church architecture — Hist. I. Title. II. Series.

KRAUTHEIMER, Richard, 1897- 726
Early Christian and Byzantine architecture / Richard Krautheimer. Harmondsworth, Eng. ; Baltimore : Penguin Books, 1975. 575 p. : ill. ; 21 cm. (The Pelican history of art ; PZ24) Includes index. Bibliography: p. 539-541. [NA4817.K7 1975] 72-93453 ISBN 0-14-056124-2 : 15.00
1. Architecture, Early Christian. 2. Architecture, Byzantine. 3. Church architecture—History. I. Title. II. Series.

Architecture—Early works to 1800.

ALBERTI, Leone Battista, 720
1404-1472
Ten books on architecture. Tr. into Italian by Cosimo Bartoli and into English by James Leoni. Ed. by Joseph Rykwert, [1st Amer. ed.] New York, Transatlantic, 1966. xx, 256p. 68 illus. 26cm. Complete reprint from the 1755 ed., with the addition of the Life from the 1739 ed. Tr. of De re aedificatoria. [NA2515.A32 1966] 66-6446 12.00
1. Architecture—Early works to 1800. I. Title. BIP

ANDROUET du Cerceau, 720.9
Jacques. fl.1549-1584.
Les trois lives d'architecture. Paris, 1559, 1561, 1582. Ridgewood, N. J., Gregg Pr. Inc., 1966. 3 v. in 1. illus., plans. 41cm. [NA2515.A4714] 66-59146 45.00
1. Architecture—Early works to 1800. I. Title.
171 E. Ridgewood Ave., Ridgewood, N.J., 07450

BENJAMIN, Asher, 1773-1845. 720
The country builder's assistant; containing a collection of new designs of carpentry and architecture, which will be particularly useful to country workmen in general. New York, Da Capo Press, 1972. xiv [61] p. 30 plates. 27 cm. (The Works of Asher Benjamin, 1) (Da Capo Press series in architecture and decorative art, 14) Reprint of the 1797 ed. [NA2520.B4 1972] 68-18611 ISBN 0-306-71027-7 29.50
1. Architecture—Early works to 1800. I. Title.
Part of a 7 vol. series selling for 195.00.

CETIUS Faventinus, Marcus. 690
Vitruvius and later Roman building manuals, by Hugh Plommer. London, Cambridge University Press, 1973. vii, 117 p. illus. 23 cm. (Cambridge classical studies) "An edition and translation of Faventinus' compendium of Vitruvius' De architectura."—Dust jacket. Translation of De diversis fabricis architectonicae. Parallel Latin text and English translation; English introd., notes and commentary. Includes bibliographical references and index. [NA2515.C4213] 72-90487 ISBN 0-521-20141-1
1. Architecture—Early works to 1800. I. Plommer, William Hugh. II. Vitruvius Pollio. De architectura. III. Title. IV. Series.
Distributed by Cambridge University Press, New York, 11.50. BIP

CORDEMOY, J. L. de. 720
Nouveau traite de toute l architecture, ou, L art de bastir avec un dictionnaire des termes d'architecture, etc., par M. De Cordemoy. Earnborough (Hants.), Gregg, 1966 [i.e.1967] [18], 291p. illus., 10 plates (incl. diagrs.), tables. 28cm. Facsim. reprint of 1st ed. Paris, Coignard, 1714. [NA2515.C651714a] 67-87849 31.50
1. Architecture—Early works to 1800. 2. Architecture—Dictionaries. I. Title.

HALFPENNY, William, 774.4'24
fl.1750.
The art of sound building. New York, B. Blom, 1968. 56 p. illus., plans. 31 cm. Reprint of the 1725 ed. [NA2515.H34 1968] 69-13236
1. Architecture—Early works to 1800. 2. Architectural drawing. I. Title. BIP

HALFPENNY, William, 728.8'3'0924
fl.1750.
Chinese and Gothic architecture properly ornamented. Correctly engr. from the designs of William and John Halfpenny. New York, B. Blom, 1968. 16 p., [12] p. of illus. 31 cm. Reprint of the 1752 ed. [NA996.H28 1968] 69-13237
1. Architecture—Early works to 1800. 2. Architecture—Details. I. Halfpenny, John, fl. 1750, joint author. II. Title.

LAUGIER, Marc-Antoine, 1711- 720
1769.
An essay on architecture / by Marc-Antoine Laugier ; translated and with an introd. by Wolfgang and Anni Herrmann. Los Angeles : Hennessey & Ingalls, 1975. p. cm. (Documents and sources in architecture ; no. 1) Translation of Essai sur l'architecture. [NA2515.L2913] 75-28448 ISBN 0-912158-55-7
1. Architecture—Early works to 1800. I. Title. BIP

LAUGIER, Marc Antoine, 1711- 721
1769
Observations sur l'architecture, par M. L'Abbe Laugier. [Facsimile reprint of 1st ed.] Farnborough (Hants.), Gregg Pr., 1966. xvi, 326p. 18cm. First ed. pub. in 1765. [NA2515.L3 1765b] 67-82521 21.00
1. Architecture—Early works to 1800. I. Title.
Available from Gregg Pr., Ridgewood, N.J.

MORRIS, Robert, 1701- 720'.942
1754.
Select architecture; being regular designs of plans and elevations well suited to both town and country. New foreword by Adolf K. Placzek. New York, Da Capo Press, 1973. 8 p., 50 plates. 27 cm. (Da Capo Press series in architecture and decorative art, v. 36) Reprint of the 1757 ed. [NA997.M67A55 1973] 72-87427 ISBN 0-306-71573-2
1. Architecture—Early works to 1800. 2. Architecture—Designs and plans. I. Title.

PALLADIO, Andrea, 1508-1580 720
The four books of architecture. New introd. by Adolf K. Placzek. New York, Dover [1965] vii, 110p. 212 plates. 33cm. Unabridged. unaltered repubn. of the work first pub. by Isaac Ware in 1738 [NA2515.P253] 64-18862 10.00
1. Architecture—Early works to 1800. 2. Rome—Antiq. I. Title. BIP

PRATT, Roger, Sir, 1620- 720'.942
1684.
The architecture of Sir Roger Pratt, Charles II's commissioner for the rebuilding of London after the great fire: now printed for the first time from his note-books. Edited by R. T. Gunther. New York, B. Blom, 1972. xi, 312 p. illus. 26 cm. Half title: Sir Roger Pratt on architecture. Reprint of the 1928 ed. [NA997.P7G8 1972] 72-177516 15.75
1. Architecture—Early works to 1800. I. Title. II. Title: Sir Roger Pratt on architecture.

SERLIO, Sebastiano, 1475- 720
1552.
The book of architecture by Sebastiano Serlio, London, 1611. Introd. by A. E. Santaniello. New York, B. Blom, 1970. 1 v. (unpaged) illus., plans. 37 cm. A facsim. of the 1611 ed., with a new introd., bibliography, and publisher's note, published under title: The first[-fift] booke of architecture. Contents.Contents.—The first booke of architecture, entreating of geometrie.—The second booke of architecture, entreating of perspectiue ...—The third booke, intreating of all kind of excellent antiquities ...—The fourth booke, rules for masontry ...—The fift booke of architecture, wherein there are set downe certayne formes of temples, according to the ancient maner; and also seruing for Christians. [NA2517.S5 1970] 68-56509
1. Architecture—Early works to 1800. I. Santaniello, A. E. II. Title. BIP

SUGER, Abbot of 726'.5'0944362
Saint Denis, 1081-1151.
Abbot Suger on the Abbey Church of St.-Denis and its art treasures / edited, translated, and annotated by Erwin Panofsky. 2d ed. / by Gerda Panofsky-Soergel. Princeton, N.J. : Princeton University Press, c1978. p. cm. Latin and English. Includes index. Bibliography: p. [NA5551.S2S8 1978] 78-51186 ISBN 0-691-03936-4 : 22.50. ISBN 0-691-10068-3 pbk. : 9.95
1. Saint-Denis, France (Benedictine abbey). 2. Architecture—Early works to 1800. 3. Art—Early works to 1800. I. Panofsky, Erwin, 1892-1968. II. Panofsky-Soergel, Gerda, 1929- III. Title.

SWAN, Abraham 721
The British architect. New York, Da Capo, 1967. viii, viii, 16 p., 60 plates. 42cm. (Da Capo ser. in architecture and decorative art, v. 3) Da Capo reprint ed. Unabridged repubn. of the 1758 ed. pub. in London. [NA2517.S9 1967] 67-25995 45.00
1. Architecture—Early works to 1800. 2. Stair building. 3. Staircases. I. Title.
Available from Plenum, New York. BIP

VASARI, Giorgio 701.8
Vasari on technique; being the introduction to the three arts of design, architecture, sculpture and painting, prefixed to the lives of the most excellent painters, sculptors and architects...now for the first time translated into English [from the Italian] by Louisa S. Maclehose, ed. with introd. by Professor G. Baldwin Brown. New York, Dover Pubns. [1960] 328p. illus. (Dover T717) Bibl. footnotes 2.00 pap.,
1. Architecture—Early works to 1800. 2. Sculpture—Early works to 1800. 3. Painting—Early works to 1800. 4. Art—Technique. I. Maclehose, Louisa S., tr. II. Brown, Girard Baldwin, 1849-1932, ed. III. Title.

VASARI, Giorgio, 1511-1574 702.8
Vasari on technique; being the introduction to the three arts of design, architecture, sculpture and painting, prefixed to the Lives of the most excellent painters, sculptors, and architects. Tr. into English by Louisa S. Maclehose. Ed., introd., notes by G. Baldwin Brown. [Gloucester, Mass., Peter Smith, 1961] xxiv, 328p. illus., map. (Dover bk. rebound) 4.01
1. Architecture—Early works to 1800. 2. Sculpture—Early works to 1800. 3. Painting—Early works to 1800. 4. Art—Technique. I. Maclehose, Louisa S., tr. II. Brown, Gerard Baldwin, 1849-1932, III. Maclehose, Louisa S., tr. IV. Brown, Gerard Baldwin, 1849-1932, ed. V. Title.

VASARI, Giorgio, 1511-1574. 702.8
Vasari on technique; being the introduction to the three arts of design, architecture, sculpture and painting, prefixed to the Lives of the most excellent painters, sculptors, and architects. Now for the first time translated into English by Louisa S. Maclehose. Edited, with introd. & notes, by G. Baldwin Brown. New York, Dover Publications [1960] xxiv, 328 p. illus., ports., map. 21 cm. "An unabridged and unaltered republication of the work first published by J. M. Dent & Company in 1907, except that the frontispiece, plate XII, which appeared in color in the original edition, are here reproduced in black and white." Includes bibliographical references. [N7420.V3] 61-460
1. Architecture — Early works to 1800. 2. Sculpture — Early works to 1800. 3. Pointing — Early works to 1800. 4. Art — Technique. I. Maclehose, Louisa S., tr. II. Brown, Gerard Baldwin, 1849-1932 ed. III. Vasari, Giorgio, 1511-174. Le vite de' plu eccelenti pittori, scultori e architetti. IV. Title. BIP

VITRUVIUS, Pollio 720
Vitruvius: the ten books on architecture. Translated by Morris Hicky Morgan. With illus. and original designs prepared under the direction of Herbert Langford Warren. New York, Dover Publications [1960] 331 p. illus. 21 cm. "An unabridged and unaltered republication of the first edition of the English translation by Morris Hicky Morgan, originally published ... in 1914." [NA2515.V73 1960] 60-50037
1. Architecture—Early works to 1800. I. Morgan, Morris Hicky, 1859-1910, tr.

YARWOOD: DOREEN 720.942
Outline of English architecture. London. B. T. Batsford [Mystic, Conn., Verry] c.1965. 47p. illus., plans 31cm. Bibl. [NA961.Y32] 66-2828 4.00
1. Architecture—England. 2. Architecture—Outlines. syllabi. etc. I. Title.

Architecture—England—Addresses, essays, lectures.

EMMETT, John T. 720'.942
Six essays, by John T. Emmett. Introd. by J. Mordaunt Crook. New York, Johnson Reprint Corp., 1972. 1 v. (various pagings) illus. 23 cm. Reprint of 6 articles from the Quarterly review and the British quarterly review first published as a collection in 1891. Contents.Contents.—The state of English architecture.—The hope of English architecture.—The profession of an architect.—The bane of English architecture.—The ethics of urban leaseholds.—Religious art. Includes bibliographical references. [NA961.E45 1972] 72-4311 15.00
1. Architecture—England—Addresses, essays, lectures. I. Title. BIP

Architecture—England—Dales Way.

RAISTRICK, Arthur. 942.8'4
Buildings in the Yorkshire Dales : who built them, when and how? / by Arthur Raistrick. Clapham, N. Yorkshire : Dalesman, 1976. 88 p. : ill., plans ; 21 cm. (A "Dalesman" paperback) (The Yorkshire Dales library ; 4) Bibliography: p. 88. [NA995.D34R34] 77-359769 ISBN 0-85206-367-9 : £1.00
1. Architecture—England—Dales Way. I. Title. II. Series.

Architecture—England—Dictionaries.

CURL, James Stevens, 1937- 720'.942
English architecture : an illustrated glossary / James Stevens Curl ; with a foreword by Lord Muirshiel ; and drawings by John J. Sambrook. Newton Abbot ; North Pomfret, Vt. : David & Charles, c1977. 192 p. : ill. ; 26 cm. Bibliography: p. 189-191. [NA961.C87] 78-308092 ISBN 0-7153-7110-X : 22.50
1. Architecture—England—Dictionaries. I. Title.

Architecture—England—History.

BRAUN, Hugh Stanley 720.942
The story of English architecture. London, Faber & Faber [Mystic, Conn., Verry, 1965] 200p. plates. 23cm. First pub. in England in 1950 [NA961.B66] 51-4543 4.00
1. Architecture—England—Hist. I. Title.

DUTTON, Ralph, 1898- 720.942
The age of Wren. London, New York, Batsford [1951] 136 p. illus., ports. (1 col.) 25 cm. [NA997.W8D8] 720.81 A52
1. Wren, Sir Christopher, 1632-1723. 2. Architecture—England—Hist. I. Title.

GLOAG, John, 1896- 720.942
The English tradition in architecture. New York, Barnes & Noble [1963] 158 p. illus. 24 cm. Full Name: John Edward Gloag. [NA961.G56 1963] 63-3091
1. Architecture — England — Hist. I. Title.

GLOAG, John Edward, 1896- 720.942
The English tradition in architecture. New York, Barnes & Noble [c.1963] 258p. illus. 24cm. 63-3091 8.50
1. Architecture—England—Hist. I. Title.

KIDSON, Peter 720.942
A history of English architecture. Part I, by Peter Kidson; part II, by Peter Murray. New York, Arco [1963, c.1962] 256p. illus. 23cm. Bibl. 63-8794 5.95
1. Architecture—England—Hist. I. Murray, Peter, joint author. II. Title.

KIDSON, Peter. 720'.942
A history of English architecture [by] Peter Kidson, Peter Murray, and Paul Thompson. Rev. ed. [Harmondsworth, England, Penguin Books [1965] 352 p. illus. 20 cm. (A Pelican book, A759) Bibliography: p. 331-333. [NA961.K5 1965] 67-4538
1. Architecture — England — Hist. I. Murray, Peter. II. Thompson, Paul Richard, 1935- III. Title.

LITTLE, Bryan D. G. 720.942
English historic architecture. New York, Hastings [1964] 256p. illus., plans. 23cm. Bibl. 64-25991 5.95
1. Architecture, English—Hist. I. Title. BIP

PETTER, Helen Mary 726.50942
Churches and public buildings [New York] Oxford [c.]1963. 95p. illus. 24cm. Bibl. 64-1192 2.20
1. Architecture—England—Hist. 2. Churches—England. 3. England—Public buildings. I. Title.

WEST, T W 720.9'42
A history of architecture in England [by] T. W. West. [2d ed.] New York, D. McKay Co. [1966] 176 p. illus., map. 23 cm. Includes bibliographies. [NA961.W46] 68-4108
1. Architecture—England—Hist. I. Title. II. Title: Architecture in England.

YARWOOD, Doreen. 720.942
The architecture of England, from prehistoric times to the present day. London, B. T. Batsford; New York, Putnam [1963] xvi, 672 p. illus., 70 plates (part col.) plans. 26 cm. Bibliography: p. [640]-646. [NA961.Y3] 64-11567
1. Architecture — England — Hist. I. Title.

Architecture—England—History.

BETJEMAN, John, Sir, 1906- 720'.942
A pictorial history of English architecture [by] John Betjeman. Photos. by Julian Barnard [and others] Notes on the illus. by Nicholas Taylor. [1st American ed.] New York, Macmillan [1972] 112 p. illus. (part col.) 27 cm. [NA961.B43 1972b] 78-189049 12.95
1. Architecture—England—History. I. Title. BIP

EASTLAKE, Charles Locke, 1833-1906. 720'.942
A history of the Gothic revival. By Charles L. Eastlake; with an introduction by Alan Gowans. [Watkins Glen, N.Y.], American Life Foundation 1975, [c1969] xxi, 439 p., illus., 23 cm. [NA988.E17] 5.95 (pbk.)
1. Architecture—England—History. 2. Gothic revival (Architecture) I. Title. II. Title: Gothic revival.
L.C. card no. for original ed.: 71-69637. BIP

Architecture—England—Juvenile literature.

FLETCHER, Geoffrey S. 720.942
Town's eye view. Written and illus. by Geoffrey S. Fletcher. Introd. by A. E. Richardson. [dist. SportShelf, New Rochelle, N. Y., 1961, c.1960] 91p. 61-1416 4.25 bds.,
1. Architecture—England—Juvenile literature. 2. England—Descr. & trav.—Juvenile literature. I. Title.

Architecture—England—London.

SUMMERSON, John Newenham, Sir, 1904- 720'.9421
Georgian London / John Summerson. 3d ed. Cambridge, Mass. : MIT Press, 1978. 348 p., [24] leaves of plates : ill. ; 22 cm. "1st MIT Press ed." Includes index. Bibliography: p. 329-331. [NA970.S8 1978] 78-53798 ISBN 0-262-19173-3 : 15.00
1. Architecture—England—London. 2. Architecture, Georgian—England—London. I. Title.

Architecture—England—Mutilation, defacement, etc.

GREAT Britain. Royal Commission on the Ancient and Historical Monuments and Constructions of England. 720'.942
Monuments threatened or destroyed, 1963-74 / the Royal Commission on the Ancient and Historical Monuments and Constructions of England. London : H.M.S.O., [1976] 48 p. ; 25 cm. (Interim report - Royal Commission on the Ancient and Historical Monuments and Constructions of England) (Cmnd. ; 6382) [NA961.G73 1976] [NA961] 76-374126 ISBN 0-10-163820-5 : £0.55
1. Architecture—England—Mutilation, defacement, etc. I. Title. II. Series: Great Britain. Royal Commission on the Ancient and Historical Monuments and Constructions of England. Interim report — Royal Commission on the Ancient and Historical Monuments and Constructions of England. III. Series: Great Britain. Parliament. Papers by command, cmnd. ; 6382.

Architecture—England—Totnes.

THEN & now : 942.3'592
the architectural heritage of Totnes & district / [illustrations brought together by Totnes and District Society et al. ; written and edited by Michael Dower]. [Dartington] : [Dartington Amenity Research Trust for the Society et al.], [1976] [1], 32 p. : chiefly ill. ; 15 x 21 cm. (Publication - Dartington Amenity Research Trust ; no. 17) Cover title. Bibliography: p. 32. [NA995.T67T47] 77-363468 ISBN 0-9500410-5-X : £0.50
1. Architecture—England—Totnes. 2. Totnes, Eng.—Description—Views. I. Dower, Michael. II. Totnes and District Society. III. Series: Dartington Amenity Research Trust. Publication ; no. 17.

Architecture—England—Tunbridge.

DAVIS, Terence, 1924- 942.2'3
Tunbridge Wells : the gentle aspect / Terence Davis ; photos. by Charles Saumarez Smith. London : Phillimore, 1976. xvi, 72 p. : ill. ; 25 cm. Includes bibliographical references and index. [NA971.T86D38] 77-359064 ISBN 0-85033-250-8 : £4.95
1. Architecture—England—Tunbridge. 2. Tunbridge Wells, Eng.—Description. I. Title.

Architecture—Environmental aspects.

CONTI, Flavio, 1943- 720
Architecture as environment / by Flavio Conti. New York : Harcourt Brace Jovanovich, 1978. p. cm. (His The Grand tour ; 5) Translation of L'architettura, l'uomo, e l'ambiente. [NA2542.35.C6613] 78-51425 ISBN 0-15-003728-7 : 11.95
1. Architecture—Environmental aspects. 2. Architecture—Human factors. I. Title. II. Series.

CROSBY, Theo. 720
The pessimist utopia / by Theo Crosby. London : Pentagram Design, [1976] 24 p. : ill. ; 21 cm. (Pentagram papers ; 2 ISSN 0309-2135s) (The Lethaby lectures are delivered annually at the Royal College of Art ; in 1975 the lectures ... were delivered in two parts under the single title The pessimist utopia.) [NA2542.35.C76] 77-373492 ISBN 0-905739-01-9 : £1.00
1. Architecture—Environmental aspects. I. Title.

LUDWIG, Richard L. 720
Research needs in environmental design and continuity : summary of the conference sponsored by the National Science Foundation & the College of Architecture & Urban Planning, University of Washington. [Seattle : University of Washington], 1976. iv, 35 p. ; 28 cm. "NSF/RA-760210." "Prepared by Richard Ludwig and Dennis Ryan." "The Conference on Research Needs in Environmental Design and Continuity [was] held at Issaquah, Washington on June 1-3, 1976". [NA2542.35.L8] 76-151685
1. Architecture—Environmental aspects. I. Ryan, Dennis M., joint author. II. United States. National Science Foundation. III. Washington (State). University. College of Architecture and Urban Planning. IV. Conference on Research Needs in Environmental Design and Continuity, Issaquah, Wash., 1976. V. Title.

WIEDENHOEFT, Ronald V. 711'.4
Readings in architecture and urban design / by Ronald V. Wiedenhoeft. Dubuque, Iowa : Kendall/Hunt Pub. Co., c1978. v, 66 p. : ill. ; 28 cm. Includes bibliographies. [NA2542.4.W53] 78-56721 ISBN 0-8403-1883-9 pbk. : 4.95
1. Architecture—Human factors. 2. Architecture—Environmental aspects. I. Title. BIP

Architecture—Environmental aspects—United States.

FRIEDMANN, Arnold. 729
Environmental design evaluation / Arnold Friedmann, Craig Zimring, and Ervin Zube. New York : Plenum Press, c1978. p. cm. Includes index. Bibliography: p. [NA2542.35.F75] 78-24252 ISBN 0-306-40092-8 : 22.50
1. Architecture—Environmental aspects—United States. I. Zimring, Craig, joint author. II. Zube, Ervin, joint author. III. Title. BIP

Architecture—Essex, N.Y.

MCNULTY, George F. 720'.9747'53
Essex; the architectural heritage. [Photos. & text by George F. McNulty. Historical text by Margaret Scheinin. Essex? N.Y., c1971] 52 p. illus. 22 x 28 cm. Cover title. Includes bibliographical references. [NA735.E87M32] 72-193497
1. Architecture—Essex, N.Y. I. Scheinin, Margaret. II. Title.

Architecture, Etruscan.

BOETHIUS, Axel, 1889-1969. 722'.7
Etruscan and Roman architecture, by Axel Boethius [and] J. B. Ward-Perkins. Harmondsworth, Penguin, 1970. xxxiii, 622 p., 183 plates. illus. (incl. 1 col.), maps, plans. 27 cm. (The Pelican history of art) Bibliography: p. 587-601. [NA295.B6] 70-20510 ISBN 0-14-056032-7 £8/10/- ($29.50 U.S.)
1. Architecture, Etruscan. 2. Architecture, Roman. I. Ward-Perkins, John Bryan, 1912- joint author. II. Title. III. Series.

Architecture — Europe.

DAMAZ, Paul. 729
Art in European architecture. Synthese des arts. Pref. by Le Corbusier. New York, Reinhold Pub. Corp. [1956] xii, 228 p. illus., col. plates. 27 cm. 'Dollie Plerre Chareau ... made the English translation. Bibliography : p. 228. [NA958.D3] 56-5603
1. Architecture—Europe. 2. Art—Europe. 3. Art, Modern—20th cent. I. Title. II. Title: Synthese des arts.

DAMAZ, Paul F 729
Art in European architecture. Synthese des arts. Pref. by Le Corbusier. New York, Reinhold Pub. Corp. [1956] xii, 228 p. illus., col. plates. 27 cm. "Dollie Pierre Chareau ... made the English translation." Bibliography: p. 228. [NA958.D3] 56-5603
1. Architecture — Europe. 2. Art, European. 3. Art, Modern — 20th Cent. I. Title. II. Title: Synthese des arts.

DORGELO, A. 720.94
Modern European architecture. Amsterdam, New York, Elsevier Pub. Co., 1960. 242 p. illus., plans. 36 cm. Includes bibliographies. [NA958.D6] 60-1650
1. Architecture—Europe. 2. Architecture—Designs and plans. 3. Architecture, Modern—20th century. I. Title.

SMITH, George Everard Kidder, 1913- 720.94
The new architecture of Europe. [Harmondsworth], Penguin Books [1962, c1961] 351 p. illus. 20 cm. (Pelican books, A518) Includes bibliography. [NA958.S6 1962] 63-3585
1. Architecture — Europe. I. Title.

SMITH, George Everard Kidder, 1913- 720.94
The new architecture of Europe, an illustrated guidebook and appraisal. Cleveland, World Pub. Co. [1961] 361 p. illus., maps. 21 cm. (Meridian books,

SUBJECT INDEX ARCHITECTURE, GEORGIAN.

MG33) Bibliography: p. 335-340. [NA958.S6] 61-11474
1. Architecture — Europe. 2. Architecture, Modern — 20th cent. I. Title.

UNIVERSITY Prints, Boston. 720.94
University prints. Series G: European architecture, edited by Professors Chase, Pope and Post. Boston, 1950. xxiv p. 509 p. of illus., plans. 21 cm. [NA950.U5] 51-2973
1. Architecture — Europe. I. Chase, George Henry, 1874- ed. II. Title.

Architecture—Europe—History.

JORDAN, Robert Furneaux. 720.94
The world of great architecture, from the Greeks to the nineteenth century. New York, Viking Press [1961] 460p. 112col. plates. 29cm. (A Studio book) 'Notes on the plates by Dr. Bodo Cichy translated [from Baukunst in Europa] and adapted by C. Ligota.' [NA950.J6 1961] 61-8828
1. Architecture— Europe—Hist. I. Cichy, Bodo. 1924- Balkunst in Europa. II. Title.

MUSCHENHEIM, William. 720
Elements of the art of architecture. New York, Viking Press [1964] 200 p. illus. 22 cm. (A Studio book) Bibliography: p. 187-188. [NA204.M8] 64-24875
1. Architecture, European—History. 2. Architecture, American—History. 3. Architecture—Views. I. Title. BIP

PEVSNER, Nikolaus, 1902- 720.94
An outline of European architecture. [6th, Jubilee ed.] Baltimore, Penguin Books [1960] 740p. illus., plans. 26cm. Bibl.: p.727-731. 60-52016 30.00, bxd.
1. Architecture—Europe—Hist. I. Title. BIP

PEVSNER, Nikolaus, 1902- 720.94
An outline of European architecture. [2d rev. ed.] Harmondsworth, Middlesex, Penguin Books [1951] 301 p. illus. 18 cm. (Pelican books, A 109) [NA950.P4 1951] 52-23617
1. Architecture — Europe — Hist. I. Title.

PEVSNER, Nikolaus, 1902- 720.94
An outline of European architecture. [Harmondsworth, Middlesex] Penguin Books [1954] 317p. illus., plans. 19cm. (Pelican books, A 109) Bibliography: p. [287]-297. [NA950.P4 1954] 56-1815
1. Architecture—Europe— Hist. I. Title.

Architecture—Europe—History.

WHITTICK, Arnold, 1898- 720'.94
A history of European architecture in the twentieth century. New York, Abelard-Schuman [1973] p. Bibliography: p. [NA958.W49 1973] 73-13637 ISBN 0-200-04017-0 30.00
1. Architecture—Europe—History. 2. Architecture, Modern—20th century—Europe. I. Title.

YARWOOD, Doreen. 720'.94
The architecture of Europe. New York, Hastings House [1974] 598 p. illus. 26 cm. Bibliography: p. 565-572. [NA950.Y37] 73-11105 ISBN 0-8038-0364-8 18.95
1. Architecture—Europe—History. I. Title. BIP

Architecture - Europe, Western - Historiography.

WATKIIN, David. 720'.7'22
Morality and architecture / David Watkin. Oxford : Clarendon Press, 1977. 126p. ; 22 cm. bibliography p. 117-121. [NA190] ISBN 0-19-817350-4 : 7.50
1. Architecture — Europe, Western — Historiography. 2. Historicism. I. Title.
Distributed by Oxford University Press, New York.

Architecture—Exhibitions.

THE 720'.9747'25074014725
Architecture of Suffolk County. [Historical selection and essay by Denys Peter Myers. Modern selection and essay by Eva Ingersoll Gatling. Huntington? N.Y., 1971. 35 p. illus. 28 cm. Catalog of an exhibition held at the Heckscher Museum, Huntington, N.Y., Apr. 25-May 30; Parrish Art Museum, Southampton, N.Y., June 5-July 13; and Guild Hall of East Hampton, N.Y., Oct. 9-Nov. 5, 1971. [NA730.N42S82] 70-162946
1. Architecture—Exhibitions. 2. Architecture—Suffolk Co., N.Y. I. Heckscher Art Museum, Huntington, N.Y. II. Parrish Art Museum. III. Guild Hall of East Hampton.

COOPER Union for the Advancement of Science and Art, New York. School of Art and Architecture. 720'.71'17471
Education of an architect: a point of view. An exhibition by the Cooper Union School of Art & Architecture at the Museum of Modern Art, New York City, November 1971. [New York, 1971] 323 p. illus. (part col.) 31 cm. [NA2440.N47M873 1971] 74-184158
1. Cooper Union for the Advancement of Science and Art, New York. School of Art and Architecture. 2. Architecture—Exhibitions. 3. Architecture—Study and teaching—New York (City) I. New York (City). Museum of Modern Art. II. Title.

KELEMEN, Pal. 726'.59
Folk baroque in Mexico; [exhibition of] mestizo architecture through the centuries. Photos. by Judith Hancock de Sandoval, with text by Pal Kelemen. [Orlando, Fla., Brewton Co., 1974] [92] p. illus. 23 cm. Catalog. "Circulated by the Smithsonian Institute Traveling Exhibition Service." [NA753.K44] 74-77544
1. Architecture—Exhibitions. 2. Architecture—Mexico. 3. Architecture, Colonial—Mexico. 4. Decoration and ornament, Architectural—Mexico. 5. Folk art—Mexico. I. Sandoval, Judith Hancock de. II. Smithsonian Institution. Traveling Exhibition Service. III. Title.

MARCHAEL, James. 720'.9'074017866
The architecture of St. Louis. Photography: James Marchael. Commentary: George McCue. [St. Louis, City Art Museum, c1971] 47 p. illus. 25 cm. Prepared for the exhibition held Nov. 19, 1971-Jan. 9, 1972 at the City Art Museum of Saint Louis. [NA735.S2M36] 72-176244
1. Architecture—Exhibitions. 2. Architecture, Modern—19th century—St. Louis. 3. Architecture, Modern—20th century—St. Louis. I. McCue, George. II. St. Louis. City Art Museum. III. Title.

RUDOFSKY, Bernard, 1905- 720.9
Architecture without architects, an introduction to nonpedigreed architecture. New York, Museum of Modern Art; distributed by Doubleday, Garden City, N.Y. [1964] 1 v. (unpaged) illus. 25 cm. [NA2430.R8] 64-8755
1. Architecture—Exhibitions. 2. Architecture, Primitve. I. Title. BIP

Architecture—Falls Church, Va.—Awards.

FALLS Church Village Preservation and Improvement Society. 711'.4'09755293
"Award for excellence in design". [Falls Church, Va., 1971] [24] p. illus. 29 cm. Cover title. [NA2340.F34 1971] 74-184402
1. Architecture—Falls Church, Va.—Awards. I. Title.

Architecture—Finland.

NEUENSCHWANDER, Eduard, 1924- 720.94895
Alvar Aalto and Finnish architecture [by] Eduard and Claudia Neuenschwander. London, Architectural Press; New York, Praeger [1954] 192p. illus., plans. 28cm. German, French, and English. Published also in Switzerland under title: Finnische Bauten. Batiments finnois. Finnish buildings. Atelier Alvar Aalto, 1950, 1951. [NA1193.M45 1954a] [NA1196.N45 1954b] 720. 9471 55-2530 55-2530
1. Aalto, Alvar, 1898- 2. Architecture—Finland. I. Neuenschwander, Claudia, 1927- joint author. II. Title.

NEUENSCHWANDER, Eduard, 1924- 720.94895
Finnish architecture, and Alvar Aalto [by] Ed. and Cl. Neuenschwander. New York, Praeger [1954] 192p. illus. plans. 28cm. (Books that matter) On spine: Atelier Alvar Aalto 1950/1951. German, French, and English. Published also in Switzerland under title: Finnische Bauten. Batlements finnois. Finnish buildings. Ateller Alvar Aalto, 1950, 1951. [NA1193.N45 1954a] [NA1193.N45 1954a] 720.9471 54-9527 54-95277
1. Aalto, Alvar, 1898- 2. Architecture—Finland. I. Neuenschwander, Claudia, 1927- joint author. II. Title.

RICHARDS, James Maude, Sir. 720'.9471
800 years of Finnish architecture / J. M. Richards. Newton Abbot [Eng.] : David & Charles, c1978. 191 p. : ill. ; 30 cm. Based on the author's 1966 ed. of Guide to Finnish architecture. Includes index. Bibliography: p. 188. [NA1455.F5R5] 78-319214 ISBN 0-7153-7512-1 : 24.00
1. Architecture—Finland. 2. Church architecture—Finland. I. Richards, James Maude, Sir. Guide to Finnish architecture. II. Title.
Distributed by David & Charles,North Pomfret,VT

RICHARDS, James Maude. 720'.9471
A guide to Finnish architecture, by J. M. Richards. New York, Praeger [1967, c1966] 112 p. illus., plans. 26 cm. Bibliography: p. 99-100. [NA1193.F5 1967] 67-25565
1. Architecture—Finland. I. Title.

SALOKORPI, Asko. 720'.9471
Modern architecture in Finland. New York, Praeger [1970] 64 p. plans, plates (part col.) 20 cm. (Modern arts in Finland) [NA1455.F5S2] 78-111290 4.50
1. Architecture—Finland. 2. Architecture, Modern—20th century—Finland. I. Title.

TEMPEL, Egon. 720'.9471
New Finnish architecture. [Translation into English by James C. Palmes] New York, F. A. Praeger [1968] 192 p. illus., map, plans. 26 cm. English and German. [NA1193.T413] 68-19863 17.50
1. Architecture—Finland. 2. Architecture, Modern—20th century—Finland. I. Title.

Architecture—Florence.

ANTHONY, Edgar Waterman, 1890-1947. 726'.5'094551
Early Florentine architecture and decoration / Edgar W. Anthony. New York : Hacker Art Books, 1975. xii, 108 p., [41] leaves of plates : ill. ; 23 cm. Reprint of the 1927 ed. published by Harvard University Press, Cambridge. Includes index. Bibliography: p. [97]-[104] [NA1121.F7A6 1975] 78-143335 ISBN 0-87817-055-3 : 35.00
1. Architecture—Florence. 2. Architecture, Medieval—Florence. 3. Decoration and ornament—Italy—Florence. 4. Decoration and ornament, Architectural—Florence. 5. Sculpture, Medieval—Florence. 6. Sculpture, Florentine. 7. Florence—Churches. I. Title. BIP

Architecture—Florence—Guide-books.

ARTIGIANATO fiorentino. 914.5'51
History of Florence and of its handicraft. [Florence, Italy, 1953?] 52 p. illus. 22 cm. [N6921.F7A68 1953] 75-304437
1. Architecture—Florence—Guide-books. 2. Art industries and trade—Florence. I. Title.

Architecture—France.

BLOMFIELD, Reginald Theodore, Sir, 1856-1942. 720'.944
Three hundred years of French architecture 1494-1794. Freeport, N.Y., Books for Libraries Press [1970] x, 129 p. illus. 22 cm. Reprint of the 1936 ed. [NA1044.B55 1970] 70-124233
1. Architecture—France. 2. Architecture, Renaissance—France. 3. Architecture, Modern—17th-18th centuries—France. I. Title. BIP

†WARD, William Henry, 1865-1924. 720'.944
The architecture of the Renaissance in France : a history of the evolution of the arts of building, decoration, and garden design under classical influence from 1495 to 1830 / by W. H. Ward. 2d ed., rev. and enl. New York : Hacker Art Books, 1976. xxvi, 533 p. : ill. ; 25 cm. Reprint of the 1926 ed. published by Scribner, New York. Includes bibliographical references and indexes. [NA1045.W37 1976] 70-147040 ISBN 0-87817-097-9 : 40.00
1. Architecture—France. 2. Architecture, Renaissance—France. 3. Classicism in architecture—France. I. Title. BIP

Architecture—France—Hist.

ALLSOPP, Bruce 720.944
Architecture of France. by Bruce Allsopp and Ursula Clark. [London] Oriel Pr. [1963, Chester Springs, Pa., Dufour. 1966] 96p. illus., map. 17cm. (Oriel guides) [NA1041.A7] 65-29907 3.25
1. Architecture—France—Hist. I. Clark, Ursula, joint author. II. Title.

LAVEDAN, Pierre, 1885- 720.944
French architecture. [Harmondsworth, Middlesex] Penguin Books [1956] 394p. illus. 19cm. (Pelican books, A329) [NA1041.L343 1956] 61-19875
1. Architecture—France—Hist. I. Title.

Architecture—France—Provence.

MACGIBBON, David, d.1902. 720'.944'9
The architecture of Provence and the Riviera / by David MacGibbon. Boston : Longwood Press, 1978. p. cm. Reprint of the 1888 ed. published by D. Douglas, Edinburgh. Includes index. [NA1049.P8M3 1978] 78-16237 ISBN 0-89341-356-9 : 50.00
1. Architecture—France—Provence. 2. Architecture—Riviera. I. Title. BIP

Architecture—Georgia.

LINLEY, John. 720'.958
Architecture of middle Georgia: the Oconee area. [Athens] University of Georgia Press [1972] 194 p. illus. 31 cm. Bibliography: p. [189]-190. [NA730.G4L56] 72-188569 ISBN 0-8203-0295-3 17.50
1. Architecture—Georgia. 2. Georgia—Historic houses, etc. I. Title.

NICHOLS, Frederick Doveton. 720.9758
The early architecture of Georgia. With a pictorial survey by Frances Benjamin Johnston. Chapel Hill, University of North Carolina Press, 1957. xvi, 292p. illus., maps. 34cm. Bibliographical footnotes. [NA730.G4N5] 57-14027
1. Architecture— Georgia. I. Johnston, Frances Benjamin, 1864-1952. II. Title.

REID, Neel, 1885-1926. 720'.92'4
Architecture of Neel Reid in Georgia [by] James Grady. Photography by Kenneth Kay. Special photography by Josephine von Miklos. Color photography by Carey Sutlive. [Athens] University of Georgia Press [1973] xxii, 204 p. illus. (part col.) 29 cm. "Commissioned by Peachtree-Cherokee Trust." Bibliography: p. 200-201. [NA737.R44G72] 73-85027 ISBN 0-8203-0323-2 29.75
1. Reid, Neel, 1885-1926. 2. Architecture—Georgia. I. Grady, James H. II. Peachtree-Cherokee Trust. III. Title.

Architecture, Georgian.

HARRIS, John, 1931- 728.8
Georgian country houses. Feltham, Country Life Books, 1968. [1], 64 p. (chiefly illus., plans) 23 cm. (RIBA drawings series) Bibliography: p. 64. [NA7620.H3] 70-437298 10/6
1. Architecture, Georgian. 2. Country homes—England. I. Title.

RICHARDSON, Albert Edward, 1880- 724.14207
Georgian architecture. New York, Pellegrini & Cudahy [1950] 256 p. illus. 24 cm. [NA966.R5] 50-13639
1. Architecture, Georgian. 2. Architecture — Gt. Brit. I. Title.

Architecture, Georgian—Dublin.

CLARKE, Harold. 914.18'3'04
Georgian Dublin [by Harold Clarke. Norwich, Eng., Jarrold, c1972] 25 p. col. illus. 25 cm. Cover title. [NA991.D82C55] 74-157456
1. Architecture, Georgian—Dublin. 2. Architecture—Dublin—Guide-books. I. Title.

Architecture, Georgian—England.

RAMSEY, Stanley Churchill. 728.3
Small Georgian houses and their details, 1750-1820; by Stanley C. Ramsey and J. D. M. Harvey. With a foreword by J. M. Richards. New York, Crane, Russak [1972] 1 v. (various pagings) illus. 30 cm. Published in 1919-23 under title: Small houses of the late Georgian Period, 1750-1820. [NA7328.R322] 72-81193 ISBN 0-8448-0055-4 17.50
1. Architecture, Georgian—England. 2. Architecture, Domestic—England. I. Harvey, John Dean Monroe, illus. II. Title.

RAMSEY, Stanley Churchill. 728.3
Small Georgian houses and their details, 1750-1820, by Stanley C. Ramsey and J. D. M. Harvey. With a foreword by Sir James Richards. London, Architectural Press. New York, Architectural Book Pub. Co. [1974, c1972] 1 v. (chiefly illus.) 30 cm. Reprint of the ed. published by Crane, Russak, New York. The 1st ed. (1919-1923) was published in 2 v. under title: Small houses of the late Georgian period, 1750-1820. [NA7328.R324] 74-655 ISBN 0-8038-0235-8 17.95
1. Architecture, Georgian—England. 2. Architecture, Domestic—England. I. Harvey, John Dean Monroe, illus. II. Title.

Architecture, Georgian—United States.

EBERLEIN, Harold Donaldson. 720'.973
American Georgian architecture / by Harold Donaldson Eberlein and Cortlandt VAn Dyke Hubbard ; line drawings by John B. Lear, Jr. New York : Da Capo Press, 1976. p. cm. (Da Capo Press series in architecture and decorative art) Reprint of the 1952 ed. published by Indiana University Press, Bloomington. [NA707.E29 1976] 76-22726 ISBN 0-306-70796-9 : 29.50
1. Architecture, Georgian—United States. 2. Architecture—United States. I. Hubbard, Cortlandt Van Dyke, joint author. II. Title.
BIP

Architecture—Germany.

BEYER, Gunther 720.943
Baroque architecture in Germany [by] Beyer [and] Mielke [Tr. from German by Lena Jaeck] London, Studio Bks. [dist. Chester Springs, Pa., Dufour, 1965.c.1961] 200p. illus. (pt. col.) map, plans. 29cm. [NA1066] 65-7754 8.50
1. Architecture—Germany. 2. Architecture, Baroque. I. Mielke, Georg. II. Title.

BURCHARD, John Ely, 1898- 720.943
The voice of the phoenix; postwar architecture in Germany. Cambridge, Mass., M. I. T. Pr. [c.1966] xii, 179p. illus., plans. 23x25cm. Bibl. [NA1068.B86] 65-24414 12.50
1. Architecture—Germany. 2. Architecture, Modern—20th cent. I. Title.

BURCHARD, John Ely, 1898- 720.943
The voice of the phoenix; postwar architecture in Germany [by] John Burchard. Cambridge,Mass., M.I.T. Press [1966] New York, St Martin's Press [1965] xii, 179 p. illus., plans. 23 x 25 cm. x 168 p. illus. maps. port. 22 cm. Bibliographical footnotes. [NA1068.B86] [E513.5 54th.B8] 973.7415 65-24414 65-18643
1. Shaw, Robert Gould, 1837-1863. 2. Architecture — Germany. 3. Architecture, Modern — 20th cent. 4. Massachusetts Infantry. 54th Regt., 1863-1865. 5. U.S. — Hist. — Civil WarPregimental histories — Massachusetts Infantry — 54th. I. Burchard, Peter. II. Title. III. Title: One gallant rush;

FEUERSTEIN, Gunther. 720'.943
New directions in German architecture. [Translated by Thomas E. Burton] New York, G. Braziller [1968] 128 p. illus., plans. 25 cm. ([New directions in architecture]) Bibliography: p. 120-121. [NA1068.F413] 68-56282 5.95
1. Architecture—Germany. 2. Architecture, Modern—20th century—Germany. I. Title. **BIP**

JOSEF CLEMENS. Abp. and elector of Cologne, 1671-1723. 725.17
Letters of the Archbishop-Elector Joseph Clemens of Cologne to Robert de Cotte, 1712-1720; with supplementary letters from the architect Guillaume d'Hauberat to De Cotte, 1716-1721. Edited by John Finley Oglevee. [Bowling Green? Ohio] 1956. xxiv, 190p. illus. 29cm. Letters in French. [NA1053.C64J6] 56-4956
1. Architecture—Germany. I. Cotte, Robert de, 1656-1735. II. Hauberat, Guillaume di, d. 1749? III. Oglevee, John Finley, ed. IV. Title.

NEW German architecture. 724.91
Selected by Gerd Hatje, Hubert Hoffmann [and] Karl Kaspar. Introd. by Hubert Hoffmann. Text and captions by Karl Kaspar. Translated by H. J. Montague. New York, Praeger [1956] xx, 219p. illus. 27cm. (Books that matter) [NA1068.N413] 56-9675
1. Architecture—Germany. 2. Architecture, Modern—20th cent. I. Hoffmann, Hubert. II. Kaspar, Karl. III. Hatje, Gerd.

Architecture—Germany—Addresses, essays, lectures.

POSENER, Julius. 720'.943
From Schinkel to the Bauhaus; five lectures on the growth of modern German architecture. With a pref. by Dennis Sharp. [1st ed.] New York, G. Wittenborn [1972] 48 p. illus. 30 cm. (Architectural Association. Paper no. 5) [NA1068.P68] 78-145975 ISBN 0-8150-0012-X pap $6.50
1. Architecture—Germany—Addresses, essays, lectures. 2. Architecture, Modern—19th century—Germany—Addresses, essays, lectures. 3. Architecture, Modern—20th century—Addresses, essays, lectures. I. Title. II. Series: Architectural Association, London. Paper no. 5.
BIP

Architecture—Germany (Federal Republic, 1949-)

PEHNT, Wolfgang. 720'.943
German architecture: 1960-1970. [Translation into English by E. Rockwell] New York, Praeger [1970] 239 p. illus., plans. 26 cm. English and German. Bibliography: p. 44. [NA1068.P43 1970] 78-89610 20.00
1. Architecture—Germany (Federal Republic, 1949-) 2. Architecture, Modern—20th century—Germany (Federal Republic, 1949-) I. Title.

Architecture, Gothic.

ACLAND, James H. 721'.43'094
Medieval structure: the gothic vault [by] James H. Acland. [Toronto] University of Toronto Press [1972] viii, 254 p. illus. 31 cm. Bibliography: p. 246-249. [NA440.A24] 72-76769 ISBN 0-8020-1886-6 25.00
1. Architecture, Gothic. 2. Vaults (Architecture) I. Title. **BIP**

BRANNER, Robert. 723.5
Gothic architecture. New York, G. Braziller, 1961. 125 p. 104 illus., maps. 26 cm. (The Great ages of world architecture) Bibliography: p. 115-118. [NA440.B68] 61-13690
1. Architecture, Gothic. I. Title. II. Series.

CARTER, Harry Graham 761.2
Orlando Jewitt. [New York] Oxford [c.] 1962. 48p. illus. 22cm. Bibl. 63-1345 3.40
1. Jewitt, Thomas Orlando Sheldon, 1799-1869. 2. Architecture, Gothic. I. Title.

*CLARK, Kenneth. 724.3
The gothic Revival; an essay in the history of taste. New York Harper & Row [1974, c1962] xii, 236 p. illus. 22 cm. (Icon Editions) [NA963] 73-21308 ISBN 0-06-430048-X 4.95 (pbk.)
1. Architecture, Gothic. I. Title.

CLARK, Kenneth McKenzie Sir 1903- 720.942
The Gothic revival; an essay in the history of taste. [3d ed.] New York, Holt [1963] 236p. illus. 23cm. 63-12745 5.00
1. Architecture, Gothic. 2. Architecture—England. I. Title.

FITCHEN, John 726.6
The construction of Gothic cathedrals; a study of medieval vault erection. [dist. New York, Oxford Univ. Press, c.]1961[ ] xxi, 344p. illus. 28cm. Bibl. 61-1182 10.10
1. Architecture, Gothic. 2. Vaults. 3. Cathedrals. I. Title. **BIP**

FRANKL, Paul, 1878- 723.5
The Gothic literary sources and interpretations through eight centuries. Princeton, N.J., Princeton Univ. Press [c.] 1960. 916p. illus. Bibl. 57-5471 17.50
1. Architecture, Gothic. 2. Art, Gothic. I. Title.

GILCHRIST, Agnes Eleanor (Addison) 1907- 724'.3
Romanticism and the Gothic revival, by Agnes Addison. New York, Gordian Press, 1967 [c1938] viii, 187 p. front. 23 cm. Bibliography: p. 157-183. [NA645.G5 1967] 67-18439
1. Architecture, Gothic. 2. Romanticism in art. I. Title. **BIP**

GOTHIC design techniques 723'.5
: the fifteenth-century design booklets of Mathes Roriczer and Hanns Schmuttermayer / edited, translated, and introduced by Lon R. Shelby. Carbondale : Southern Illinois University Press, c1977. xiii, 207 p. : ill. ; 24 cm. Text of the booklets in German and English; introd. and editorial matter in English. Includes index. Bibliography: p. 193-202. [NA480.G67] 77-2598 ISBN 0-8093-0810-X : 15.00
1. Architecture, Gothic. 2. Architecture—Details. 3. Architecture—Early works to 1800. 4. Geometry—Early works to 1800. I. Roritzer, Matthaus, d. 1495? II. Shelby, Lonnie Royce, 1935- III. Schmuttermayer, Hanns. Fialenbuchlein. English and German. c1977.
Contents omitted **BIP**

GRODECKI, Louis, 1910- 723'.5
Gothic architecture / Louis Grodecki, in collaboration with Anne Prache and Roland Recht ; translated from the French by I. Mark Paris. New York : H. N. Abrams, 1977, c1976. 442 p. : ill. ; 29 cm. (History of world architecture series) Translation of L'architecture gothique. Includes index. Bibliography: p. 423-427. [NA480.G7613 1977] 77-4853 ISBN 0-8109-1026-8 : 37.50
1. Architecture, Gothic. I. Prache, Anne, joint author. II. Recht, Roland, joint author. III. Title. **BIP**

HOFSTATTER, Hans Hellmut, 1928- 723'.5
Living architecture: Gothic. Text: Hans H. Hofstatter. Photos.: Rene Bersier. Foreword: Guy Desbarats. English translation. A. N. Wells. New York, Grosset & Dunlap [1971, c1970] 191 p. illus. 22 cm. (Living architecture) Translation of Gotik. Bibliography: p. 189-191. [NA440.H613 1971] 68-10649 7.95
1. Architecture, Gothic. I. Title.

JACKSON, Thomas Graham, Sir, bart., 1835-1924. 723'.5
Gothic architecture in France, England, and Italy / Sir Thomas Graham Jackson. New York : Hacker Art Books, 1975. 2 v. : ill. ; 25 cm. Reprint of the 1915 ed. published by the University Press, Cambridge, Eng. Includes bibliographical references and index. [NA440.J3 1975] 77-158333 ISBN 0-87817-106-1 lib.bdg. : 50.00
1. Architecture, Gothic. I. Title. **BIP**

JANTZEN, Hans, 1881- 723.5
High Gothic; the classic cathedrals of Chartres, Reims, Amiens. Translated from the German by James Palmes. [New York] Pantheon Books [1962] 181 p. illus. 23 cm. Translation of Kunst der Gotik. [NA453.J23] 59-11958
1. Architecture, Gothic. 2. Art, Gothic. 3. Chartres, France. Notre-Dame (Cathedral) 4. Reims. Notre-Dame (Cathedral) 5. Amiens. Notre-Dame (Cathedral) I. Title.

JANTZEN, Hans, 1881- 723.5
High Gothic; the classic cathedrals of Chartres. Reims. Amiens. Tr. from the German by James Palmes. [New York] Minerva Pr. [1967, c.1957] 181p. illus. 21cm. (Minerva Pr., M11) Tr. of Kunst der Gotik. Orig. pub. in 1962. [NA453.J23] 2.50 pap.,
1. Architecture, Gothic. 2. Art, Gothic. 3. Chartres, France. Notre-Dame (Cathedral) 4. Reims, Notre-Dame (Cathedral) 5. Amiens. Notre-Dame (Cathedral) I. Title.
Available from Funk & Wagnalls.

LANGLEY, Batty, 1696-1751. 724'.3
Gothic architecture, improved by rules and proportions; in many grand designs of columns, doors, windows, chimney pieces, arcades, colonnades, porticoes, umbrellas, temples, and pavilions [by] Batty Langley and Thomas Langley. New York, B. Blom, 1972. 1 v. (chiefly illus.) 32 cm. Reprint of the 1747 ed. [NA440.L27 1972] 73-172512
1. Architecture, Gothic. 2. Architecture—Early works to 1800. I. Langley, Thomas, 1702-1751, joint author. II. Title. **BIP**

LANGLEY, Batty, 1696-1751 724'.3
Gothic architecture improved by rules and proportions. In many grand designs of columns, doors, windows, chimney-pieces, arcades, colonades, porticos, umbrellos, temples and pavillions, & c., with plans, elevations and profiles; geometrically explained, by B. & T. Langley. Farnborough (Hants.), Gregg. 1967. [2f.] 64f, illus., plans, diagrs. 21cm. Facsimile reprint of 1747 ed. [NA440.L27 1747a] 68-77847 28.00
1. Architecture, Gothic. 2. Architecture—Early works to 1800. I. Langley, Thomas, 1702-1751, joint author. II. Title.
Available from Gregg, Kenifield, Calif.

LESSER, George 726.6
Gothic cathedrals and sacred geometry. v.3. London, A. Tiranti [dist. Levittown, L.I., N.Y., Transatlantic, 1965, c.] 1964. 167-203p. illus. diagrs. (pt. col., pt. fold) Bibl. [NA440.L43] 57-4509 9.00
1. Architecture, Gothic. 2. Cathedrals. 3. Architecture—Composition, proportion, etc. I. Title.

MOORE, Charles Herbert, 1840-1930. 723'.5
Development & character of Gothic architecture / by Charles Herbert Moore. Boston : Longwood Press, 1978. p. cm. Reprint of the 1890 ed. published by Macmillan, London and New York. Includes index. [NA440.M66 1978] 78-15867 ISBN 0-89341-358-5 : 35.00
1. Architecture, Gothic. I. Title. **BIP**

PANOFSKY, Erwin, 1892- 723.5
Gothic architecture and scholasticism. New York, Meridian Books, 1957. 156p. illus. 19cm. (Meridian books, M44) [NA440.P23 1957] 57-6681
1. Architecture, Gothic. 2. Scholasticism. I. Title. **BIP**

PANOFSKY, Erwin, 1892-1968. 723.5
Gothic architecture and scholasticism. New York, Meridian Books, 1957. 156 p. illus. 19 cm. (Meridian books, M44) [NA440.P23 1957] 57-6681
1. Architecture, Gothic. 2. Scholasticism. I. Title.

RUSKIN, John, 1819-1900. 723'.5
The nature of Gothic : a chapter of The stones of Venice / John Ruskin ; edited by William Morris. New York : Garland Pub., 1977. iv, 127 p. : ill. ; 22 cm. (The Asthetic movement & the arts and crafts movement) Reprint of the 1892 ed. printed by W. Morris at the Kelmscott press, Hammersmith, and published by G. Allen, London. [NA440.R8 1977] 76-17747 ISBN 0-8240-2450-8 lib.bdg. : 35.00
1. Architecture, Gothic. I. Title. II. Series.
BIP

Architecture, Gothic—England.

BOND, Francis, d.1918. 726'.5'0942
Gothic architecture in England; an analysis of the origin & development of English

SUBJECT INDEX
ARCHITECTURE, GRECO-ROMAN—EXHIBITIONS.

church architecture from the Norman conquest to the dissolution of the monasteries. Freeport, N.Y., Books for Libraries Press [1972] xxii, 782 p. illus. 27 cm. Reprint of the 1905 ed. Bibliography: p. viii-xii. [NA5463.B59 1972] 70-39656 ISBN 0-8369-9931-2
1. Architecture, Gothic—England. 2. Architecture—England. 3. Church architecture—England. I. Title. BIP

PUGIN, Augustus Welby Northmore, 1812-1852. 726'.5'0942
Contrasts. New York, Humanities Press, 1969. 18, v, 104, [31] p. illus. 29 cm. (The Victorian library) Reprint of the 1841 ed., with a new introd. by H. R. Hitchcock. [NA440.P85 1969] 78-7888 6.75
1. Architecture, Gothic—England. 2. Church architecture—England. I. Title.

Architecture, Gothic—Hist.

FRANKL, Paul, 1878-1962. 723.5
Gothic architecture. [Tr. from German by Dieter Pevsner] Baltimore, Penguin [1963, c.1962] xxii, 315p. illus., 192 plates, maps, plans. 27cm. (Pelican hist. of art. Z19) Bibl. 63-2733 16.50
1. Architecture, Gothic—Hist. I. Title. II. Series.

Architecture, Gothic—Noyon, France.

SEYMOUR, Charles, 1912- 726'.6'094435
Notre-Dame of Noyon in the twelfth century; a study in the early development of gothic architecture New York, Norton [1968] xx, 202 p. illus., plans. 20 cm. (The Norton library, N464) Reprint of the 1939 ed. Includes bibliographical references. [NA5551.N6S4 1968] 77-683 2.95
1. Noyon, France. Notre-Dame (Cathedral) 2. Architecture, Gothic—Noyon, France. I. Title. BIP

Architecture—Gt. Brit.

BETJEMAN, John, 1906- 720.942
First and last loves. Drawings by John Piper. [dist. by New Rochelle, N. Y., SportShelf 1961] 191p. illus. (Grey arrow, G53) 61-2065 1.50 pap.,
1. Architecture—Gt. Brit. 2. Gt. Brit.—Descr. & trav.—1946- I. Title.

BETJEMAN, John, 1906- 720.942
First and last loves. With drawings by John Piper. [Grey Arrow ed. London] ArrowBooks; stamped; distributed by Sportshelf, New Rochelle, N.Y. [1960] 191p. illus. 18cm. (A Grey arrow, G53) [NA961.B383 1960] 61-2065
1. Architecture—Gt. Brit. 2. Gt. Brit.—Descr. & trav.—1946- I. Title.

CONWAY, William Martin Conway, Baron, 1856-1937. 759.9493'1
The Van Eycks and their followers / by Sir Martin Conway. New York : AMS Press, 1979. p. cm. Reprint of the 1921 ed. published by J. Murray, London. Includes indexes. [ND669.F5C66 1979] 75-41065 ISBN 0-404-14657-0 : 37.50
1. Eyck, Hubert van, 1366-1426. 2. Eyck, Jan van, 1390-1440. 3. Painting, Flemish. 4. Painting, Gothic—Belgium—Flanders. 5. Painting, Renaissance—Belgium—Flanders. I. Title. BIP

GLOAG, John Edwards, 1896- 720.942
Victorian taste; some social aspects of architecture and industrial design from 1820-1900. [v.3] New York, Macmillan [1962] xvi, 175p. illus. 26cm. The third volume of a trilogy, the first of which is Georgian grace and the second of which is Victorian comfort. Bibl. 62-6802 8.00
1. Architecture—Gt. Brit. 2. Design, Decorative—Gt. Brit. 3. Design, Industrial. I. Title.

HITCHCOCK,Henry Russell, 1903- 724.142081
Early Victorian architecture in Britain. New Haven, Yale University Press, 1954. 2v. illus., maps, plans. 28cm. (Yale historical publications. History of art, 9) Contents.v.1. Text.--v.2. Illustrations. [NA967.H55] 54-5085
1. Architecture—Gt. Brit. I. Title. II. Series. BIP

HITCHCOCK, Henry Russell, 1903- 720'.942
Early Victorian architecture in Britain. New York, Da Capo Press, 1972 [c1954] v. 27 cm. (Da Capo Press series in architecture and decorative art, 41) Original ed. issued as no. 9 of Yale historical publications. History of art. Contents.Contents.—v. 1. Text. [NA967.H55 1972] 72-151765 ISBN 0-306-70195-2 45.00
1. Architecture—Great Britain. 2. Architecture, Victorian—Great Britain. I. Title. II. Series: Yale historical publications. History of art, 9.

HITCHCOCK, Henry Russell, 1903- 720.942
Early Victorian architecture in Britain (abridged) / by Henry-Russell Hitchcock. New York : Da Capo Press, 1976, c1954. p. cm. (A Da Capo paperback) [NA967.H552 1976] 75-35908 ISBN 0-306-80036-5 : 45.00(2 vol. set)
1. Architecture—Great Britain. 2. Architecture, Victorian—Great Britain. I. Title.

JACKSON, Anthony, 1926- 720'.942
The politics of architecture; a history of modern architecture in Britain. [Toronto] University of Toronto Press [1970] 219 p. illus., maps, plans. 23 cm. Includes bibliographical references. [NA968.J3] 76-483503 ISBN 0-8020-1663-4 8.50
1. Architecture—Great Britain. 2. Architecture, Modern—20th century—Great Britain. I. Title. BIP

LANCASTER, Osbert, 1908- 720.9
Here, of all places. Illustrated by the author. Boston, Houghton Mifflin, 1958. 189 p. illus. 25 cm. [NA961.L296] 58-11501
1. Architecture—Gt. Brit. 2. Interior decoration—Gt. Brit. 3. Architecture—U.S. 4. Interior decoration—U.S. I. Title.

MAXWELL, Robert. 720'.942
New British architecture. New York, Praeger Publishers [1973, c1972] 199 p. illus. 27 cm. [NA968.M34] 72-77547 25.00
1. Architecture—Great Britain. 2. Architecture, Modern—20th century—Great Britain. I. Title.

MILLS, Edward David. 724.91
The new architecture in Great Britain, 1946-1953. With a forword by Sir William Holford. New York, Reinhold [1954] 209p. illus, ports., plans. 33cm. Bibliography: p. 209. [NA968.M5 1954] 54-3734
1. Architecture—Gt. Brit. 2. Architecture—Designs and plans. I. Title.

PENOYRE, John, 1870- 720.942
The observer's book of British architecture, written and illustrated by John Penoyre and Michael Ryan, describing and indexing the development of building in Britain from Saxon times to the present day. Foreword by F. R. S. Yorke. London, New York, F. Warne [1951] 218 p. illus. (part col.) 15 cm. (The Observer's pocket series, 13) [NA961.P4] 51-12746
1. Architecture — Gt. Brit. I. Ryan, Michael, joint author. II. Title. III. Series.

ROYAL Institute of British Architects, London. 720
Architectural drawings from the collection of the Royal Institute of British Architects. [London] 1961. [New York, Transatlantic, 1966] 18p. 54 plates. 21cm. Cover title [NA964.R68] 62-51832 1.40 pap.,
1. Architecture—Gt. Brit. 2. Architecture. I. Title.
Available from Transatlantic, New York.

THREE centuries of architectural craftsmanship early 19th centuries / edited by Colin Amery. 720'.941
London : Architectural Press ; New York : Nichols Pub. Co., 1977. xiv, 3 p. [iii] leaves of plates : ill. ; 31 cm. [NA966.T48 1977] 76-48734 ISBN 0-89397-004-2 (Nichols) : 17.50
1. Architecture—Great Britain. 2. Architecture, Modern—17th-18th centuries—Great Britain. 3. Architecture, Modern—19th century—Great Britain. 4. Architecture—Details. I. Amery, Colin.

TURNOR, Reginald. 724.142
Nineteenth century architecture in Britain. London, New York, Batsford [1950] x. 118 p. illus. 23 cm. (The British art and building series) [NA967.T8] 51-5636
1. Architecture — Gt. Brit. I. Title. II. Series.

Architecture—Great Britain—Bibliography.

WODEHOUSE, Lawrence. 016.72'0941
British architects, 1840-1976 : a guide to information sources / Lawrence Wodehouse. Detroit : Gale Research Co., [1978] p. cm. (Art and architecture information guide series ; v. 8) Includes indexes. Bibliography: p. [Z5944.G7W66] [NA961] 78-54116 ISBN 0-8103-1393-6 : 18.00
1. Architecture—Great Britain—Bibliography. 2. Architects—Great Britain—Bibliography. I. Title.

Architecture—Gt. Brit.—Conservation and restoration.

BARNETT, Winston, 1935- 711'.4'0942784
A study in conservation / by Winston Barnett and Cyril Winskell. Stocksfield ; Boston : Oriel Press, 1977. [6], 46 p. : ill., maps, plans ; 26 cm. English, French, and German. Includes bibliographical references. [NA109.G7B37] 78-315756 ISBN 0-85362-168-3 : 11.95 ISBN 0-85362-172-1 pbk. : 8.25
1. Architecture—Great Britain—Conservation and restoration. I. Winskell, Cyril, joint author. II. Title. BIP

ENTWISLE, Frank, 1927- 711'.0942
Rape or marriage? the relationship of town and country, by Frank Entwisle; based on the T.V. film featuring Bruce Allsopp and produced by Frank Entwisle. Newcastle upon Tyne, Oriel, 1970. [32] p. illus. 22 cm. Book of a film in the Tyne Tees Television series, The way I see it. [NA109.G7E5] 71-122522 ISBN 0-85362-092-X 6/-
1. Architecture—Gt. Brit.—Conservation and restoration. I. Allsopp, Bruce. II. Tyne Tees Television. III. Title.

MADSEN, Stephan Tschudi, 1923- 720'.28
Restoration and anti-restoration : a study in English restoration philosophy / Stephan Tschudi Madsen. Oslo : Universitetsforl., [1976] 164 p., [8] leaves of plates : ill. ; 23 cm. Includes index. Bibliography: p. 147-[156] [NA109.G7M32] 77-463850 ISBN 8-200-01501-7 : 12.00
1. Architecture—Great Britain—Conservation and restoration. I. Title.
Distributed by Columbia University Press

Architecture—Great Britain—History.

COLVIN, Howard Montagu, ed. 720.942
The history of the King's works. [2v. & boxed plans] London, H.M.S.O. [dist. N.Y., British Info., c.1963] v. illus., plates (pt. col.) maps, plans (pt. fold.) and portfolio (4 fold. plans) (pt. col.) 25 cm. This work was commissioned in 1951 by the Ministry of Public Building and Works under its earlier name: Ministry of Works. Contents.v.1-2. The Middle Ages, by R. A. Brown, H. M. Colvin. A. J. Taylor.--Box of architectual plans. Bibl. 64-1679 50.40 set,
1. Architecture—Gt. Brit.—Hist. 2. Gt. Brit.—Kings and rulers. I. Gt. Brit. Ministry of Public Building and Works. II. Title.

LANCASTER, Osbert, 1908- 720.942
A cartoon history of architecture. Illus. by the author. Introd. by John Coolidge. Boston, Houghton, 1964[c.1958-1964] xxi, 199p. illus. 21cm. (Sentry ed., SE27) 64-4862 1.95 pap.,
1. Architecture—Gt. Brit.—Hist. 2. Interior decoration—Gt. Brit.—Hist. 3. Architecture—U.S.—Hist. 4. Interior decoration—U.S.—Hist. I. Title. BIP

NELLIST, John Bowman. 720'.942
British architecture and its background [by] John B. Nellist. London, Macmillan; New York, St. Martin's P., 1967. xvii, 361 p. illus., plans, tables, diagrs. 25 1/2 cm. (B67-19627) Bibliography: p. [331]-334. [NA961.N4] 67-11466
1. Architecture — Gt. Brit. — Hist. I. Title.

TRENT, Christopher. 720.942
Looking at buildings. With 25 photos. by the author and 10 drawings. London, Phoenix House; New York, Roy Publishers [1960] 160p. illus. plans. 20cm. (Excursions series) 60-7677 2.75 bds.,
1. Architecture—Gt. Brit.—Hist. I. Title.

WEBB, Geoffrey Fairbank, 1898- 720.942
Architecture in Britain: the Middle Ages. [Harmondsworth, Middlesex] Penguin Books [1956] xxi, 234p. illus., 192 plates, plans. 27cm. (The Pelican history of art, Z12) Bibliography: p. 222-224. [NA963.W4] 57-927
1. Architecture—Gt. Brit.—Hist. 2. Architecture, Medieval. I. Title. II. Series.

Architecture—Great Britain—History.

SUMMERSON, John Newenham, Sir, 1904- 720'.942
Architecture in Britain, 1530-1830 [by] John Summerson. [Harmondsworth, Eng.] Penguin Books [1970] 611 p. illus., maps. 21 cm. (Pelican history of art, PZ3) Bibliography: p. [569]-576. [NA964.S85 1970] 76-128006 ISBN 0-14-056103-X ($8.95 pbk.)
1. Architecture—Gt. Brit.—History. I. Title. II. Series.

SUMMERSON, John Newenham, 1904- 720.942
Architecture in Britain, 1530 to 1830 London, Baltimore, Penguin Books [1953] xviii, 372 p. 192 plates, plans. 27 cm. (The Pelican history of art, Z3) Bibliography: p. 349-355. [NA964.S85] 54-2199
1. Architecture—Gt. Brit.—History. I. Title. II. Series.

SUMMERSON, John Newenham, Sir, 1904- 720.942
Architecture in Britain, 1530 to 1830. [4th rev. and enl. ed.] Baltimore, Penguin Books [1963, c1953] xx, 391 p. illus., 224 plates, plans. 27 cm. (The Pelican history of art, Z3) Bibliography: p. 363-370. [NA964.S85 1963] 63-4924
1. Architecture—Great Britain—History. I. Title. II. Series.

SUMMERSON, John Newenham, Sir, 1904- 720'.942
Architecture in Britain, 1530 to 1830 [by] John Summerson. 5th ed. Harmondsworth, Penguin, 1969. xx, 391 p., 224 plates. illus. (incl. 1 col.) plans. 27 cm. (The pelican history of art) Bibliography: p. 363-370. [NA964.S85 1969] 74-482866 ISBN 1-405-60033- 6/10/-
1. Architecture—Gt. Brit.—History. I. Title.

WEBB, Geoffrey Fairbank, 1898- 726'.0941
Architecture in Britain : the Middle Ages / Geoffrey Webb. 2d ed. Harmondsworth, Middlesex ; Baltimore : Penguin Books, 1965, c1956. xxi, 234 p., [97] leaves of plates : ill. (some col.) ; 27 cm. (The Pelican history of art ; Z 12) Bibliography: p. 222-224. [NA963.W4 1965] 75-327274 38.00
1. Architecture—Great Britain—History. 2. Architecture, Medieval—Great Britain—History. I. Title. II. Series.

YARWOOD, Doreen. 720'.941
The architecture of Britain / Doreen Yarwood. New York : Scribner, 1976. 276 p. : ill. ; 26 cm. Includes index. Bibliography: p. [263]-266. [NA961.Y29] 76-380350 ISBN 0-684-14729-7 : 14.95
1. Architecture—Great Britain—History. I. Title.

Architecture, Greco-Roman—Exhibitions.

BLESSING, Charles A. 741.9'73
The form of cities in perspective; the Graeco-Roman world—500 B.C. to A.D. 200. An exhibition of drawings, March, 1973; a guide, by Charles A. Blessing. Ann Arbor, Center for Coordination of Ancient and Modern Studies, University of Michigan [1973] iv, 39 p. illus. 28 cm. Exhibition held at the University of

Michigan Art Museum. [NC139.B53M52] 73-161629
1. Blessing, Charles A. 2. Architecture, Greco-Roman—Exhibitions. I. Michigan. University. Center for Coordination of Ancient and Modern Studies. II. Michigan. University. Museum of Art. III. Title.

Architecture—Greece.

ANDERSON, William James, 1864-1900. 722'3.8
The architecture of Ancient Greece : an account of its historic development, being the first part of The architecture of Greece and Rome / by William J. Anderson and R. Phene Spiers ; revised and rewritten by William Bell Dinsmoor. 1st AMS ed. New York : AMS Press, 1978. x, 241 p., [40] leaves of plates (2 fold) : ill. ; 22 cm. Reprint of the 1927 ed. published by B. T. Batsford, London. Includes index. Bibliography: p. [201]-211. [NA270.A6 1978] 75-41010 ISBN 0-404-14725-9 : 30.00
1. Architecture—Greece. I. Spiers, Richard Phene, 1838-1916, joint author. II. Dinsmoor, William Bell, 1886- III. Title.

ANDERSON, William James, 1864-1900. 722'.8
The architecture of Greece & Rome; a sketch of its historic development, by William J. Anderson and R. Phene Spiers. With 255 illus. 2d ed., rev. and enl., by R. Phene Spiers. London, B. T. Batsford; New York, Scribner, 1907. St. Clair Shores, Mich., Scholarly Press, 1974. p. cm. [NA260.A5 1974] 74-3184 ISBN 0-403-03078-1
1. Architecture—Greece. 2. Architecture—Rome. I. Spiers, Richard Phene, 1838-1916, joint author. II. Title.

BELL, Edward, 1844-1926. 722'.8
Hellenic architecture; its genesis and growth. Freeport, N.Y., Books for Libraries Press [1972] xx, 185 p. illus., fold. map. 23 cm. Reprint of the 1920 ed. which was issued as v. 2 of the author's The origins of architecture. [NA270.B4 1972] 73-39657 ISBN 0-8369-9928-2
1. Architecture—Greece. I. Title.

COULTON, J. J. 722'.8
Ancient Greek architects at work : problems of structure and design / J. J. Coulton. Ithaca, N.Y. : Cornell University Press, 1977. 196 p., [4] leaves of plates : ill. ; 25 cm. Includes index. Bibliography: p. [182]-188. [NA270.C65 1977] 76-44117 ISBN 0-8014-1077-0 : 15.00
1. Architecture—Greece. I. Title. **BIP**

DINSMOOR, William Bell, 1886- 722.8
The architecture of ancient Greece; an account of its historic development. Rev. and enl. ed. based on the first part of The architecture of Greece and Rome by William J. Anderson and R. Phene Spiers. [3d ed.] London, New York, Batsford [1950] xxiv, 424 p. illus., maps (1 fold.) 24 cm. Bibliography: p. 341-386. [NA270.D5 1950] 51-6495
1. Architecture—Greece. I. Anderson, William James, 1864-1900. II. Title. III. Title: The architecture of Greece and Rome.

DINSMOOR, William Bell, 1886- 722'.8
The architecture of ancient Greece; an account of its historic development. Rev. and enl. ed. based on the first part of the Architecture of Greece and Rome, by William J. Anderson and R. Phene Spiers. New York, Biblo and Tannen, 1973. xxiv, 424 p. illus. 23 cm. Reprint of the 1950 3d ed. rev., published by B. T. Batsford, London. First published as the Architecture of ancient Greece and Rome, 1902; second ed., the Architecture of ancient Greece, 1927; 3d ed., rev., 1950. Bibliography: p. 341-385. [NA270.D5 1973] 73-12401 ISBN 0-8196-0283-3
1. Architecture—Greece. I. Anderson, William James, 1864-1900. The architecture of ancient Greece. II. Title.

LEACROFT, Helen. 722.8
The buildings of ancient Greece [by] Helen and Richard Leacroft. New York, W. R. Scott [1966] 40 p. illus. (part col.) 25 cm. A detailed explanation, in word and pictures, of the evolution of Greek architecture from prehistoric to classical times. Describes specific building processes and materials. [NA270.L42] AC 67
1. Architecture—Greece. 2. Civilization, Greek. I. Leacroft, Richard, joint author. II. Title. **BIP**

Architecture—Greece—History.

DINSMOOR, William Bell, 1886- 722'.8
The architecture of ancient Greece : an account of its historic development / William Bell Dinsmoor. New York : Norton, [1975] xxiv, 424 p. : ill. ; 24 cm. Reprint of the 1950 3d ed. rev., published by B. T. Batsford, London, with a new pref. and new photos. First published in 1902 under title: The architecture of ancient Greece and Rome. Includes index. Bibliography: p. 341-386. [NA270.D5 1975] 75-6960 ISBN 0-393-04412-2 : 18.95.
1. Architecture—Greece—History. I. Title. **BIP**

LAWRENCE, Arnold Walter, 1900- 722'.8
Greek architecture / A. W. Lawrence. 2d ed. Harmondsworth, Middlesex ; Baltimore : Penguin Books, 1967, c1957. xxxiv, 338 p., [76] leaves of plates : ill. ; 27 cm. (The Pelican history of art ; Z11) Includes index. Bibliography: p. 315-326. [NA270.L36 1967] 75-310468
1. Architecture—Greece—History. I. Title. II. Series.

ROBERTSON, Donald Struan, 1885-1961. 722'.6
Greek and Roman architecture [by] D. S. Robertson. 2nd ed. reprinted. London, Cambridge U.P., 1969. xxiv, 407 p. 24 plates, illus., plans. 23 cm. First published in 1929 under title: A handbook of Greek and Roman architecture. Bibliography: p. [347]-378. [NA260.R6 1969] 76-407810 25/- ($3.95)
1. Architecture—Greece—History. 2. Architecture—Rome—History. I. Title. **BIP**

Architecture—Greece (Modern)—Collections.

ARCHITECTURE in Greece. 720'.995
annual review. 1968 Greece. 1968 v. illus., maps, plans. 28cm. annual. Summaries in English Title romanized; Architektoniak themata. [NA6.A67] 67-9595 15.00 pap.,
1. Architecture—Greece (Modern)—Collections. I. Title: Architecture in Greece.
U.S. distributor: Wittenborn, New York.

Architecture, Greek.

ALLSOPP, Bruce 722.6
A history of classical architecture from its origins to the emergence of Hellenesque and Romanesque architecture. New York, Pitman [1966. c.1965] xiii. 215p. illus. 26cm. Bibl. [NA260.A35] 66-2284 10.95
1. Architecture, Greek. 2. Architecture. Roman. I. Title.

BROOKS, Alfred Mansfield, 1870- 722.6
Architecture. New York, Cooper Square Publishers, 1963. xix, 189 p. 19 cm. (Our debt to Greece and Rome) Bibliographical references included in "Notes" (p. 175-178) Bibliography: p. 179-182. [NA260.B7] 63-10303
1. Architecture, Greek. 2. Architecture, Roman. I. Title. II. Series.

ELDERKIN, George Wicker, 1879- 726'.1'09385
Problems in Periclean buildings, by G. W. Elderkin. Washington, McGrath Pub. Co., 1973 [c1912] 58 p. illus. 24 cm. Reprint of the ed. published by Princeton University Press, Princeton, N.J., in series: Princeton monographs in art and archaeology, 2. [NA280.E5 1973] 73-119260 ISBN 0-8434-0130-3 28.00
1. Architecture, Greek. 2. Athens. Propylaea. 3. Athens. Erechtheum. I. Title. II. Series: Princeton monographs in art and archaeology, 2.

MARTIN, Roland. 722'.8
Living architecture: Greek. Text by Roland Martin. Photos. by Henri Stierlin. Pref. by Max Bill. New York, Grosset [c.1967] 192p. illus., map, plans. 22cm. (Living architecture) Cover. title: Greek architecture. Tr. of Monde grec. Bibl. [NA270.M323 1967b] 67-20409 7.95
1. Architecture, Greek. 2. Architecture—Details. I. Title. II. Title: Greek architecture.

SCRANTON, Robert Lorentz, 1912- 722.8
Greek architecture. New York, Braziller, 1962. 128p. 111 illus. (incl. plans) 26cm. (Great ages of world architecture) Bibl. 62-7532 4.95 bds.,
1. Architecture, Greek. I. Title. **BIP**

SCULLY, Vincent Joseph, 1920- 726.1
The earth, the temple, and the gods; Greek sacred architecture. New Haven, Yale University Press, 1962. xxvi, 257p. illus., maps, plans. 20cm. Bibliographical references included in 'Notes' (p. 215-238) [NA275.S3] 62-8262
1. Architecture, Greek. 2. Temples—Mediterranean region. 3. Mediterranean region—Descr. & trav. 4. Gods in art. I. Title.

SCULLY, Vincent Joseph, 1920- 726.1'2'08
The earth, the temple, and the gods; Greek sacred architecture [by] Vincent Scully. Rev. ed. New York, Praeger [1969] xxxii, 271, [192] p. illus., maps, plans. 26 cm. "Illustrations": p. [1]-[192] (3d group) Bibliographical references included in "Notes" (p. 227-251) [NA275.S3 1969] 69-15754 16.00
1. Architecture, Greek. 2. Temples, Greek. 3. Gods in art. I. Title.

TAYLOR, William, 1921- 722'.8
Greek architecture. New York, John Day Co. [1971] 96 p. illus. (part col.), plans. 25 cm. (The World of architecture) Bibliography: p. 95. [NA270.T3] 74-117171 4.95
1. Architecture, Greek.

Architecture, Greek—History.

LAWRENCE, Arnold Walter, 1900- 722.8
Greek architecture. [Harmondsworth, Middlesex] Penguin Books [1957] xxxiv, 327 p. illus., 152 plates, maps. 27 cm. (The Pelican history of art, Z11) Bibliography: p. 307-316. [NA270.L36] 722.6* 57-59193
1. Architecture, Greek—History. I. Title. II. Series.

Architecture—Hampshire, Eng.

PEVSNER, Nikolaus, Sir, 1902- 720'.9422'7
Hampshire and the Isle of Wight, by Nikolaus Pevsner and David Lloyd. Harmondsworth, Penguin, 1967. 832 p. front. (map), illus., 64 plates, map, plans, diagrs. 19 cm. (His Buildings of England, 32) [NA971.H3P4] 67-85075
1. Architecture—Hampshire, Eng. 2. Architecture—Wight, Isle of. I. Lloyd, David Wharton, joint author. II. Title.

Architecture—Handbooks, manuals, etc.

AMERICAN Institute of Architects. 720.2
The handbook of architectural practice. [6th ed.] Washington [1951] 234 p. 27 cm. [NA2570.A6 1951] 51-8474
1. Architecture—Handbooks, manuals, etc. 2. Building—Contracts and specifications—U.S. I. Title.

AMERICAN Institute of Architects. 720.69
Handbook of architectural practice. [8th ed. Washington] 1958. 1v. illus. 29cm. [NA2570.A6 1958] 58-59866
1. Architecture—Handbooks, manuals, etc. 2. Building—Contracts and specifications—U.S. I. Title.

AMERICAN Institute of Architects. 720.2
The handbook of architectural practice. [7th ed.] Washington [1953] 255p. illus. 28cm. [NA2570.A6 1953] 54-446
1. Architecture—Handbooks, manuals, etc. 2. Building—Contracts and specifications—U. S. I. Title.

AMERICAN Institute of Architects. 720.2
The handbook of architectural practice. [5th ed.] Washington [1950, '1949] 222 p. forms. 28 cm. [NA2570.A6 1950] 50-14547
1. Architecture—Handbooks, manuals, etc. 2. Building—Contracts and specifications. I. Title.

BENJAMIN, Asher, 1773-1845. 720
The practical house carpenter. Being a complete development of the Grecian orders of architecture, each example being fashioned according to the style and practice of the present day. New York, Da Capo Press, 1972. 119 p. illus. 27 cm. (The Works of Asher Benjamin, 4) (Da Capo Press series in architecture and decorative art, 14) Reprint of the 1830 ed. [NA2520.B45 1972] 68-18614 ISBN 0-306-71029-3
1. Architecture—Handbooks, manuals, etc. 2. Architecture—Orders. 3. Carpentry. I. Title. **BIP**

BENJAMIN, Asher, 1773-1845. 720
Practice of architecture; containing the five orders of architecture and an additional column and entablature, with all their elements and details explained and illustrated, for the use of carpenters and practical men. New York, Da Capo Press, 1972 [c1833] 116 p. 60 plates 27 cm. (The Works of Asher Benjamin, 5) (Da Capo Press series in architecture and decorative art, 14) [NA2520.B48 1972] 68-18615 ISBN 0-306-71030-7 29.50
1. Architecture—Handbooks, manuals, etc. 2. Architecture—Orders. 3. Carpentry—Tables, calculations, etc. I. Title.

BENJAMIN, Asher, 1773-1845. 720
The rudiments of architecture; being a treatise on practical geometry, Grecian and Roman mouldings, the origin of building, and the five orders of architecture. New York, Da Capo Press, 1972. 96 p. plates. 27 cm. (The Works of Asher Benjamin, 3) (Da Capo Press series in architecture and decorative art, 14) Reprint of the 1814 ed. [NA2520.B5 1972] 68-18616 ISBN 0-306-71031-5 29.50
1. Architecture—Handbooks, manuals, etc. 2. Architecture—Orders. 3. Architecture—Details. I. Title.

LAFEVER, Minard. 720
The modern builder's guide. New York, Dover Publications [1969] xv, 146 p. illus., 89 plates (incl. plans) 31 cm. "An unabridged and unaltered republication of the first edition as published ... in 1833, to which have been added three plates from the third (1846) edition, a new introduction by Jacob Landy, and ten illustrations of buildings by Minard Lafever." [NA2520.L25 1969] 68-54518 4.00
1. Architecture—Handbooks, manuals, etc. 2. Building—Handbooks, manuals, etc. I. Title. **BIP**

NEW York City Housing Authority. 720.2
Memo to architects. [New York, 1952- 1 v. (loose-leaf) illus. 29 cm. [NA2540.N4] 52-26660
1. Architecture — Handbooks, manuals, etc. 2. Building. I. Title.

SPENCE, William P. 721
Architecture; design, engineering, drawing [by] William P. Spence. [1st ed.] Bloomington, Ill., McKnight [1967] xx, 582p. illus., plans. 27cm. Bibl. [NA2540.S6] 66-29017 9.40; 7.05 sch. ed.,
1. Architecture—Handbooks, manuals, etc. I. Title.
Distributed by Taplinger in New York.

SPENCE, William Perkins, 1925- 721
Architecture: design, engineering, drawing [by] William P. Spence. [2d ed.] Bloomington, Ill., McKnight & McKnight [1972] xvi, 636 p. illus. 27 cm. Bibliography: p. 618-622. [NA2540.S6 1972] 76-182042 ISBN 0-87345-068-X
1. Architecture—Handbooks, manuals, etc.

Indexes: Vols. 4-7, 1944-48. 1v [NA1.A327] 177.00 set, pap.,
1. Architecture—Hist.—Period. 2. Architecture—Period. I. Title.

STATHAM, Henry Healthcote, 1839-1924. 720.9
A history of architecture, Rev. by Hugh Braun. [3d, rev. ed.] London, New York, Batsford [1950] viii, 206 p. illus. 23 cm. First ed. published in 1912 under title: A short critical history of architecture. [NA200.S7] 50-9665
1. Architecture — Hist. I. Title.

VALMARANA, Mario 720.9
Architecture. Illus. by Peter Spier. New York, Odyssey [1964] 41p. illus. (part col.) 11x17cm. (Odyssey lib. 8) 64-12882 .95 bds.,
1. Architecture—Hist. I. Title.

WATERHOUSE, Percy Leslie, 1864- 720.9
The story of architecture. [3d ed.] rev. by R. A. Cordingley. London, New York, Batsford, [1950] xii, 228 p. illus. 19 cm. First published under title: The story of the art of building. Bibliography: p. 212-215. [NA200.W3] 51-6416
1. Architecture — Hist. I. Title.

WATTERSON, Joseph. 720.9
Architecture; five thousand years of building. [1st ed.] New York, Norton [1950] xix, 399 p. illus., plans. 25 cm. Bibliography: p. 389-390. [NA200.W413] 50-10999
1. Architecture — Hist. I. Title.

WATTERSON, Joseph. 720'.9
Architecture; a short history. Rev. ed. New York, W. W. Norton [1968] xiv, 402 p. illus., plans. 24 cm. Bibliography: p. 389-391. [NA200.W4 1968] 67-12453
1. Architecture—History. I. Title.

WORLD architecture; 720.9
an illustrated history. Introd. by H. R. Hitchcock. [Test by] Seton Lloyd [and others. Editor: Trewin Copplestone. New York] McGraw-Hill [1963] 348 p. illus. (part col.) maps, plans. 35 cm. [NA201.W6] 63-15582
1. Architecture—History. I. Hitchcock, Henry Russell, 1903- II. Lloyd, Seton.

Architecture—History—Anecdotes, facetiae, satire, etc.

WILSON, Forrest, 1918- 720'.9
A history of architecture on the disparative method, with apologies to Sir Banister Fletcher (all eighteen editions) Written and illustrated by Forrest Wilson. New York, Van Nostrand Reinhold [1974] 80 p. illus. 24 cm. [NA2599.W54] 74-11594 ISBN 0-442-29544-8
1. Architecture—History—Anecdotes, facetiae, satire, etc. I. Title.

Architecture—History—Bibliography.

PARK, Helen. 016.72
A list of architectural books available in America before the Revolution. New ed., rev. and enl., with a foreword by Adolf K. Placzek. Los Angeles, Hennessey & Ingalls, 1973. xv, 79 p. illus. 24 cm. (Art & architecture bibliographies, 1) Originally appeared as an article in the Journal of the Society of Architectural Historians. Includes bibliographical references. [Z5941.P35 1973] 76-189461 ISBN 0-912158-21-2 7.95
1. Architecture—History—Bibliography. 2. Bibliography—Early printed books—17th century. 3. Bibliography—Early printed books—18th century. 4. United States—Imprints. I. Title. II. Series. BIP

Architecture—History—Outlines, syllabi, etc.

ALLSOPP, Bruce. 720'.94
The great tradition of Western architecture, by Bruce Allsopp, Harold W. Booton [and] Ursula Clark. [New York] Architectural Book Pub. Co. [1967, c1966] 319 p. illus., maps, plans. 26 cm. [NA2530.A4 1967b] 67-9119
1. Architecture—History—Outlines, syllabi, etc. I. Booton, Harold W., joint author. II. Clark, Ursula, joint author. III. Title.

RAEBURN, Michael. 720'.9
Architecture of the world / Michael Raeburn. New York : Galahad Books, 1975, c1973. 128 p. : ill. (some col.) ; 33 cm. "Originally published as 'An outline of world architecture.'" Includes index. [NA203.R33 1975] 75-325037 15.00
1. Architecture—History—Outlines, syllabi, etc. I. Title.

Architecture—Houston, Tex.

HOUSTON; 720'.9764'1411
an architectural guide. [Houston, Tex.] Houston Chapter, American Institute of Architects [1972] 168 p. illus. 23 cm. [NA735.H68H6] 72-189286
1. Architecture—Houston, Tex.

Architecture—Human factors.

BECHTEL, Robert B. 720
Enclosing behavior / Robert B. Bechtel. Stroudsburg, Pa. : Dowden, Hutchinson & Ross, c1977. x, 192 p. : ill. ; 24 cm. (Community development series ; v. 31) Includes bibliographical references and index. [NA2542.4.B42] 77-2850 ISBN 0-87933-069-4 : 20.00
1. Architecture—Human factors. 2. Architecture—Environmental aspects. I. Title. BIP

BENNETT, Corwin. 721
Spaces for people : human factors in design / Corwin Bennett. Englewood Cliffs, N.J. : Prentice-Hall, c1977. x, 195 p. : ill. ; 21 cm. Includes bibliographies and index. [NA2542.4.B46] 76-30847 ISBN 0-13-823963-0 : 9.95 ISBN 0-13-823955-X pbk. : 3.95
1. Architecture—Human factors. I. Title. BIP

BLOOMER, Kent C., 1935- 720
Body, memory, and architecture / Kent C. Bloomer and Charles W. Moore ; with a contribution by Robert Yudell. New Haven : Yale University Press, 1977. p. cm. Includes index. Bibliography: p. [NA2542.4.B57] 77-76304 ISBN 0-300-02139-9 : 15.00. ISBN 0-300-02142-9 pbk. : 6.95
1. Architecture—Human factors. 2. Architectural design. I. Moore, Charles Willard, 1925- joint author. II. Title. BIP

FRY, Edwin Maxwell, 1899- 720
Architecture and the environment / Maxwell Fry and Jane Drew. London : Allen & Unwin, 1976. 94 p. : ill. ; 26 cm. Includes index. [NA2542.4.F78] 76-381123 ISBN 0-04-720020-0 : 7.50
1. Architecture—Human factors. I. Fry, Jane Beverly Drew, joint author. II. Title. Distributed by Allen & Unwin 198 Ash St. Reading, Mass. 01867 BIP

HEIMSATH, Clovis. 729
Behavioral architecture : toward an accountable design process / Clovis Heimsath. New York : McGraw-Hill, c1977. x, 230 p. : ill. ; 25 cm. Includes index. Bibliography: p. 189-192. [NA2542.4.H44] 76-47673 ISBN 0-07-027890-3 : 13.50
1. Architecture—Human factors. 2. Architectural design. I. Title. BIP

LERUP, Lars. 720'.1
Building the unfinished : architecture and human action / Lars Lerup ; introd. by Roger Montgomery. Beverly Hills, Calif. : Sage Publications, c1977. p. cm. (Sage library of social research ; v. 53) [NA2542.4.L47] 77-12370 ISBN 0-8039-0921-7 : 14.00. ISBN 0-8039-0922-5 pbk. : 6.95
1. Architecture—Human factors. I. Title. BIP

Architecture—Human factors—Bibliography.

PREISER, Wolfgang F. E. 016.3092 s
Behavior and design : a selected bibliography / Wolfgang F. E. Preiser. Monticello, Ill. : Council of Planning Librarians, 1978. 12 p. ; 28 cm. (Exchange bibliography - Council of Planning Librarians ; 1508) Cover title. [Z5942.C68 no. 1508] [Z5943.H84] [NA2542.4] 016.72'01 78-103380 1.50
1. Architecture—Human factors—Bibliography. I. Title. II. Series: Council of Planning Librarians. Exchange bibliography ; 1508.

Architecture—Illinois.

BROWN, William T. 720'.9773
Architecture evolving : an Illinois saga / by William T. Brown ; edited by Marilyn Hasbrouck. Collectors' 1st ed. Chicago : Teach'em, inc., c1976. 188 p. : ill. ; 22 x 28 cm. [NA730.I3B76] 76-45690
1. Architecture—Illinois. 2. Architecture, Modern—19th century—Illinois. 3. Architecture, Modern—20th century—Illinois. I. Title. BIP

KOEPER, Frederick. 720'.9773
Illinois architecture from territorial times to the present; a selective guide. Chicago, University of Chicago Press [1968] xv, 304 p. illus. 21 cm. [NA730.I3K6] 68-16700
1. Architecture—Illinois. 2. Illinois—Historic houses, etc. I. Title. BIP

Architecture—Illinois—Chicago—Exhibitions.

GRUBE, Oswald W. 720'.9773'11
100 years of architecture in Chicago : continuity of structure and form : exhibited at the Museum of Contemporary Art, Chicago / by Oswald W. Grudde, Peter C. Prom, and Franz Schulze; translations and additional text by David Norris. Chicago : Follett, c1977. 191 p. : ill. ; 22 x 29 cm. German version published in 1973 under title: 100 [i.e. Hundert] Jahre Architektur in Chicago. "The American version ... presented ... in May and June of 1976, has been expanded to include new buildings planned and erected between 1973 and the present." Includes index. Bibliography: p. 181-184. [NA735.C4G8513] 77-608287 ISBN 0-695-80837-0 : 14.95
1. Architecture—Illinois—Chicago—Exhibitions. 2. Architecture, Modern—19th century—Illinois—Chicago—Exhibitions. 3. Architecture, Modern—20th century—Illinois—Chicago—Exhibitions. 4. Chicago—Buildings—Exhibitions. I. Pran, Peter C., joint author. II. Schulze, Franz, 1927- joint author. III. Museum of Contemporary Art, Chicago. IV. Hundert Jahre Architektur in Chicago. V. Title.

Architecture—Illinois—Chicago—Guide-books.

BACH, Ira J. 917.73'11'044
Chicago on foot : walking tours of Chicago's architecture / by Ira J. Bach. Completely rev., 3d ed. Chicago : Rand McNally, c1977. xiii, 392 p. : ill. ; 27 cm. Includes index. [NA735.C4B32 1977] 77-369195 ISBN 0-528-81793-0 : 12.50. ISBN 0-528-81794-9 pbk. : 7.95
1. Architecture—Illinois—Chicago—Guide-books. I. Title. BIP

Architecture—Illinois—Guide-books.

ILLINOIS. Division of Instruction. 977.3
Illinois architecture. [Springfield] : Office of the Superintendent of Public Instruction, Division of Instruction, [1974?] ix, 67 p. : maps ; 28 cm. (Monograph - Office of the Superintendent of Public Instruction ; 4) Cover title: State resources in architecture; Illinois architectural list. Bibliography: p. 66-67. [NA730.I3I44 1974] 74-623990
1. Architecture—Illinois—Guide-books. I. Title. II. Title: State resources in architecture. III. Series: Illinois. Dept. of Public Instruction. Monograph — Office of the Superintendent of Public Instruction ; 4.

Architecture—Illinois—Oak Park—Guide-books.

SPRAGUE, Paul E. 917.73'1
Frank Lloyd Wright and Prairie School architecture in Oak Park / Paul E. Sprague. 2d ed. Oak Park, Ill. : Oak Park Bicentennial Commission of the American Revolution ; Chicago : distributed by Follett Pub. Co., 1978. 96 p. : ill. ; 23 cm. On cover: Guide to Frank Lloyd Wright and Prairie School architecture in Oak Park. Includes index. [NA735.O24S67 1978] 78-54948 ISBN 0-695-81213-0 : 3.50
1. Wright, Frank Lloyd, 1867-1959. 2. Architecture—Illinois—Oak Park—Guide-books. 3. Prairie School (Architecture) I. Title.

Architecture—India.

FERGUSSON, James, 1808-1886 720'.954
History of Indian and eastern architecture. Rev., ed. with additions [on] Indian arch. by James Burgess, & Eastern architecture, by R. Phene Spiers. Delhi, Munshiram Manoharlal [1968,c.1967] 2 v. illus., maps. (pt. fold.), plans, plates, port. 22cm. First pub. in 1876. This ed. is reprinted from the rev. ed. of 1910. Select bibl. of Fergusson's works: v. 1, p. vii-ix. Bibl. footnotes. [NA1460.F3 1967] SA 67 30.00 set,
1. Architecture—India. 2. Architecture, Oriental. I. Burgess, James, 1832-1916, ed. II. Spiers, Richard Phene, 1838-1916, ed. III. Title.
Distributed by Verry, Mystic, Conn.

Architecture—India—Bibliography.

HUGO-BRUNT, Michael. 016.3092'08 s
Architecture and planning in the Far East—India, east Pakistan, and Bangladesh / Michael Hugo-Brunt. Monticello, Ill. : Council of Planning Librarians, 1974. 47 p. ; 28 cm. (Exchange bibliography - Council of Planning Librarians ; 537) Cover title. [Z5942.C68 no. 537] [Z5961.I4] [NA1501] 016.954 75-312976 4.50
1. Architecture—India—Bibliography. 2. Cities and towns—Planning—India—Bibliography. 3. Architecture—Bangladesh—Bibliography. 4. Cities and towns—Planning—Bangladesh—Bibliography. I. Title. II. Series: Council of Planning Librarians. Exchange bibliography ; 537.

Architecture—India—History.

FABRI, Charles Louis, 1899- 720.954
An introduction to Indian architecture. New York, Asia Pub. [dist. Taplinger. c.1963] 104p. illus. 25cm. (Aligarh Muslim Univ. General educ. reading material ser. 5. Art and philosophy) 63-1872 7.00
1. Architecture—India—Hist. I. Title.

FABRI, Charles Louis, 1899- 720.954
An introduction to Indian architecture. Bombay, New York, Asia Pub. House [1963] 104 p. illus. 25 cm. (Aligarh Muslim University. General education reading material series. no. 5) [NA1501.F3] SA63
1. Architecture — India — Hist. I. Title.

Architecture—Indianapolis—Guide-books.

INDIANAPOLIS 977.2'52
architecture. [Indianapolis?] : Indiana Architectural Foundation, c1975. 261 p., [3] leaves of plates (1 fold.) : ill. ; 23 cm. "Authors, Rick A. Ball ... [et al.]" Bibliography: p. 260-261. [NA735.I5I53] 76-360439
1. Architecture—Indianapolis—Guide-books. I. Ball, Rick A. II. Indiana Architectural Foundation.

Architecture, Industrial.

GRUBE, Oswald W. 725'.4'09046
Industrial buildings and factories [by] Oswald W. Grube. New York, Praeger Publishers [1971] 199 p. illus. 29 cm. English and German. Stuttgart ed. (G. Hatje) has title: Industriebauten international. [NA6400.G78 1971b] 72-111069 25.00
1. Architecture, Industrial. I. Title.

Architecture, Industrial—Designs and plans.

ALOI, Giampiero. 725'.2
Architetture industriali contemporanee. (Seconda serie) Con un saggio di Carlo Bassi; testo e didascalie in italiano e inglese. 304 illustrazioni in nero, 511 disegni. Milano, Hoepli [1966] Label mounted on t. p.: W. S. Heinman, New York, [NA6400.A49] 66-5987 22.50
1. Architecture, Industrial—Designs and plans. 2. Architecture, Modern—20th cent. I. Title.

Architecture, Industrial—Germany (Federal Republic, 1949-)

WILD, Friedemann. 725'.35'0943
Centers for storage and distribution. New York, Van Nostrand Reinhold Co. [1972] 134 p. illus. 26 cm. (Design & planning) [NA6400.W4713] 77-163488
1. Architecture, Industrial—Germany (Federal Republic, 1949-) I. Title. II. Series.

Architecture—Iowa City.

LAFORE, Laurence Davis. 917.77'65
American classic / by Laurence Lafore. Iowa City : State Historical Society of Iowa, [1975] p. cm. [NA735.I58L33] 75-9698 ISBN 0-89033-001-8
1. Architecture—Iowa City. I. Title.

Architecture—Iran.

WILBER, Donald Newton. 720.9'55
The architecture of Islamic Iran; the Il Khanid period, by Donald N. Wilber. New York, Greenwood Press [1969, c1955] xi, 208 p. illus., maps, plans. 27 cm. Bibliography: p. 192-200. [NA1483.W5] 72-88972
1. Architecture—Iran. 2. Architecture, Islamic—Iran. I. Title. II. Title: Islamic Iran. BIP

WILBER, Donald Newton. 723.33
The architecture of Islamic Iran; the Il Khanid period. Princeton, N. J., Princeton University Press, 1955. xi, 268p. illus., maps. plan. 31cm. (Princeton monographs in art and archaeology, 29) Oriental studies, 17. Bibliography: p. 192-200. [PJ25.P7 vol. 17] 55-5010
1. Architecture-Iran I. Title. II. Title: Islamic Iran. III. Series: Princeton Oriental studies, 17

Architecture—Iran—History.

POPE, Arthur Uphan, 1881-1969. 720'.955
Introducing Persian architecture. London, Oxford University Press, 1971. [8], 119 p. illus. (some col.), plans. 22 cm. (Library of introductions to Persian art) [NA1480.P58 1971] 73-154914 ISBN 0-19-647629-1 £1.25
1. Architecture—Iran—History. 2. Architecture, Islamic—Iran. I. Title. II. Title: Persian architecture.

POPE, Arthur Upham, 1881- 720.955
Persian architecture; the triumph of form and color. New York, Braziller [c.1965] 288p. illus., map, plans, 33 col. plates. 28cm. Bibl. [NA1480.P6] 65-10275 25.00; pre-Xmas 20.00
1. Architecture—Iran—Hist. 2. Architecture, Islamic. I. Title.

POPE, Arthur Upham, 1881-1969. 720.955
Persian architecture; the triumph of form and color. New York, G. Braziller [1965] 288 p. illus., map, plans, 33 col. plates. 28 cm. Bibliographical references included in "Notes": p. [272]-280. "Selected bibliography": p. 281-283. [NA1480.P6] 65-10275
1. Architecture—Iran—History. 2. Architecture, Islamic—Iran.

Architecture—Ireland.

STALLEY, R. A. 720'.9415
Architecture and sculpture in Ireland, 1150-1350 [by] R. A. Stalley. Dublin, Gill and Macmillan. New York, Barnes & Noble Books [1972, c1971] 149 p. illus. 26 cm. [NA984.S82 1972] 72-197179 ISBN 0-06-496500-7 11.00
1. Architecture—Ireland. 2. Architecture, Gothic—Ireland. 3. Sculpture, Irish. 4. Sculpture, Gothic—Ireland. I. Title.

Architecture—Ireland—Guide-books.

ROTHERY, Sean. 720'.9415
Everyday buildings of Ireland : an illustrated introduction to some of the ordinary buildings of town and countryside / text, Sean Rothery ; ill., David Gallagher ... [et al.]. Dublin : Dept. of Architecture, College of Technology : distributed by J. Duffy, c1976. 31 p. : ill. ; 15 x 22 cm. [NA982.R67] 76-373662 £0.78
1. Architecture—Ireland—Guide-books. 2. Architecture—Details. I. Gallagher, David. II. Title.

Architecture—Isfahan.

BLUNT, Wilfrid, 1901- 709.5595
Isfahan, pearl of Persia. Photos. by Wim Swaan. New York, Stein and Day [1966] 208 p. illus. (part col.) 28 cm. Bibliography: p. 201. [NA1487.I8B55] 66-17157
1. Architecture—Isfahan. 2. Architecture, Islamic—Isfahan. I. Swaan, Wim, illus. II. Title.

Architecture, Islamic.

GARLAKE, Peter S. 720.967
The early Islamic architecture of the East African coast. by Peter S. Garlake. Nairobi, London, pub. for the Inst. by Oxford Univ. Pr., 1966. x, 207p. 12 plates, plans. tables. diagrs. 29cm. (British Inst. of Hist. and Archaeology in East Africa. Memoir no. 1) Bibl. [NA1597.E2G3] 66-74919 15.20
1. Architecture, Islamic. 2. Architecture—Africa, East. I. Title. II. Series.
Available from the publisher's New York office.

HOAG, John D. 720'.917'671
Islamic architecture / John D. Hoag. New York : H. N. Abrams, [1977] p. cm. (History of world architecture) Includes index. Bibliography: p. [NA380.H58] 76-41805 ISBN 0-8109-1010-1
1. Architecture, Islamic. I. Title. BIP

RIVOIRA, Giovanni Teresio, 1849-1919. 726'.09'021
Moslem architecture, its origins and development / by G. T. Rivoira ; translated from the Italian by G. McN. Rushforth. New York : Hacker Art Books, 1975. xvii, 383 p. : ill. ; 29 cm. Translation of Architettura musulmana. "First published 1918 by Oxford University Press, London." Includes bibliographical references and indexes. [NA380.R5413 1975] 73-76790 ISBN 0-87817-136-3 : 35.00
1. Architecture, Islamic. I. Title.

SCERRATO, Umberto. 720'.917'671
Islam / Umberto Scerrato ; foreword by Richard Ettinghausen. London : Cassell, 1976. 192 p. : (col.) ill., map, plans ; 33 cm. (Monuments of civilization) Translated from the Italian. Includes index. Bibliography: p. 188. [NA380.S313 1976] 77-370465 ISBN 0-304-29695-3 : L7.95
1. Architecture, Islamic. I. Title. II. Series. BIP

Architecture, Islamic—Africa, North.

HILL, Derek. 720'.917'671
Islamic architecture in North Africa : a photographic survey / by Derek Hill ; with notes on the monuments and a concluding essay by Lucien Golvin ; and an introd. by Robert Hillenbrand. Hamden, Conn. : Archon Books, 1976. p. cm. Includes index. Bibliography: p. [NA1587.H54 1976] 76-7233 ISBN 0-208-01599-X
1. Architecture, Islamic—Africa, North. 2. Architecture—Africa, North. 3. Decoration and ornament, Architectural—Africa, North. I. Golvin, Lucien. II. Title. BIP

Architecture—Islamic—History.

HILL, Derek 720.956
Islamic architecture and its decoration, A. D. 800-1500; a photographic survey. Introductory text by Oleg Grabar. Chicago. Univ. of Chic. Pr. [1965, c.1964] 88p. map, plates (pt. col.)26cm. Bibl. [NA380.H5] 64-19844 17.50
1. Architecture, Islamic—Hist. 2. Decoration and ornament, Architectural—Hist. I. Grabar, Oleg. II. Title.

Architecture, Islamic—Morocco.

LANDAU, Rom, 1899- 916.4'03
Morocco; Marrakesh, Fez, Rabat. Photos. by Wim Swaan. [1st American ed.] New York, Putnam [1967] 160 p. illus. (part col.), map. 29 cm. Bibliography: p. 159. [NK1270.L3 1967] 67-23125
1. Architecture, Islamic—Morocco. 2. Decoration and ornament, Architectural. 3. Decoration and ornament, Islamic—Morocco. I. Swaan, Wim, illus. II. Title.

Architecture, Islamic—Turkey.

GOODWIN, Godfrey. 720'.9561
A history of Ottoman architecture. Baltimore, Johns Hopkins Press [1971] 511 p. illus., maps, plans, col. plates. 29 cm. Bibliography: p. 496-502. [NA1364.G6 1971b] 79-124947 ISBN 0-8018-1202-X 30.00
1. Architecture, Islamic—Turkey. 2. Architecture—Turkey. I. Title.

Architecture—Israel.

HARLAP, Amiran. 720'.95694
New Israeli architecture / Amiram Harlap. Rutherford [N.J.] : Fairleigh Dickinson University Press, [1975] c1974. p. cm. Includes index. Bibliography: p. [NA1477.H37 1975] 73-8291 ISBN 0-8386-1425-6 : 25.00
1. Architecture—Israel. 2. Architecture, Modern—20th century—Israel. I. Title. BIP

Architecture—Italy.

BRUNO, Fabrizio. 720'.924
Fabrizio Bruno, architetture 1960-1967. Con un testo di Giuseppe Mazzariol e una nota dell'editore. Venezia, Alfieri, 1967. Stamped on t. p.: Amer. dist. Wittenborn. New York. 113p. illus. 24x25cm. Introduction in Italian & English. [NA1123.B84M3] 68-97155 9.00
I. Mazzariol, Giuseppe. ed. II. Title.

FEININGER, Andreas, 1906- 720.94
Man and stone: a journey into the past. Introd. by Kasimir Edschmid. New York, Crown [c.1961] xvi, 128p. (chiefly illus.) 31cm. 61-15791 7.50 bds.,
1. Architecture—Italy. 2. Architecture—France. 3. Building, Stone. 4. Decoration and ornament, Architectural. I. Title.

GREGOTTI, Vittorio. 720.9'45
New directions in Italian architecture. [Translated by Giuseppina Salvadori.] New York, G. Braziller [1968] 128 p. illus., plans. 25 cm. ([New directions in architecture]) Bibliography: p. 120-121. [NA1118.G6813] 68-57723 5.95
1. Architecture—Italy. 2. Architecture, Modern—20th century—Italy. I. Title.

HEYDENREICH, Ludwig Heinrich, 1903- 720'.945
Architecture in Italy, 1400 to 1600 [by] Ludwig H. Heydenreich and Wolfgang Lotz. Translated by Mary Hottinger. [Harmondsworth, Eng., Baltimore] Penguin Books [1974] xxvii, 432 p. illus. 27 cm. (The Pelican history of Art) Bibliography: p. 397-412. [NA1115.H4913] 74-179842 ISBN 0-14-056038-6 49.50
1. Architecture—Italy. 2. Architecture, Renaissance—Italy. 3. Mannerism (Architecture)—Italy. I. Lotz, Wolfgang, 1912- II. Title.

ITALIAN Renaissance; 720.94
photographs and measured drawings with details, from the thirteenth to the sixteenth century. New York, Architectural Book Pub. Co. [19- v. plates. 47cm. In portfolio. [NA1115.I 8] 61-49281
1. Architecture—Italy. 2. Architecture, Renaissance. I. Architectural Book Publishing Company, New York.

MEEKS, Carroll Louis Vanderslice, 1907- 720.945
Italian architecture, 1750-1914 [by] Carroll L. V. Meeks. New Haven, Yale University Press, 1966. xxviii, 546 p. illus. 29 cm. "Chronological list of publications, 1700-1800": p. [463]-505. Bibliography: p. [507]-525. [NA1116.M4] 65-22334
1. Architecture—Italy. 2. Church architecture—Italy. I. Title.

MURRAY, Peter. 720-945
The architecture of the Italian Renaissance. New York, Schocken Books [1964, c9163] xviii, 268 p. illus., plans. 23 cm. Bibliography: p. 257-260. [NA1115.M8] 64-11469
1. Architecture—Italy. 2. Architecture, Renaissance. I. Title. BIP

PICA, Agnoldomenico 720.945
Recent Italian architecture [Translated from the Italian. Milan, Edizioni del Milione [dist. New York, W. S. Heinman] 1959[ ] lviii, 139p. Bibliography: p.[xli]-[liii] 323 illus., diagrs. 23cm. (il Dittamondo, 4) 60-1742 5.50 pap.,
1. Architecture—Italy. 2. Architecture, Modern—20th cent. I. Title.

SMITH, George Everard Kidder, 1913- 724.91
Italy builds: its modern architecture and native inheritance. L'Italia costruisce. Photos. by the author. New York, Reinhold [1955] 264p. illus., maps. plans. 29cm. Bibliography: p. 261-263. [NA1111.S5] 55-6278
1. Architecture—Italy. I. Title. II. Title: L'Italia costruisce.

YARWOOD, Doreen. 720'.945
The architecture of Italy. [1st U.S. ed.] New York, Harper & Row [1970, c1969] 127 p. illus. 26 cm. Bibliography: p. 123. [NA1111.Y3 1970] 70-92723 ISBN 0-06-014769-5 7.95
1. Architecture—Italy. 2. Architecture—Outlines, syllabi, etc. I. Title.

Architecture—Italy—Bibliography.

ACKERMAN, James S. 016.72'0945
A bibliography of Italian Renaissance and baroque architecture, with classification numbers of volumes in the Harvard University collections / compiled by James S. Ackerman and John A. Pinto. Cambridge, Mass. : [s.n.], 1974. 31 p. ; 28 cm. Cover title. [Z5944.I8A35] [NA1115] 75-321160
1. Harvard University. Library. 2. Architecture—Italy—Bibliography. 3. Architecture, Renaissance—Italy—Bibliography. 4. Architecture, Baroque—Italy—Bibliography. 5. Classification—Books—Architecture. I. Pinto, John A., joint author. II. Title: A bibliography of Italian Renaissance and baroque architecture ...

Architecture—Italy—History.

ALLSOPP, Bruce 720.945
Architecture of Italy, by Bruce Allsopp, Ursula Clark. [Newcastle upon Tyne] Oriel Pr. [1964, Chester Springs, Pa., Dufour, 1966] 95p. illus., maps. plans. 17cm. (Oriel guides) [NA1111.A38] 65-29906 3.25
1. Architecture—Italy—Hist. I. Clark, Ursula, joint author. II. Title.

BRIGGS, Martin Shaw, 1882- 720.945
Architecture in Italy, a handbook for travellers and students. Drawings by the author. New York, Dutton [c.1961] 179p. illus. Bibl. 61-66002 3.75
1. Architecture—Italy—Hist. I. Title.

GODFREY, Frederick M. 720'.945
Italian architecture up to 1750 [by] F. M. Godfrey. [1st American ed.] New York, Taplinger Pub. Co., 1971. vi, 340 p. illus. (part col.), map. 22 cm. Bibliography: p.

310-311. [NA1111.G58 1971] 75-137662 ISBN 0-8008-4270-7 8.50
1. Architecture—Italy—History. I. Title.

Architecture—Japan.

BLASER, Werner, 1924- 720.952
Structure and form in Japan: architectural reflections. [English translation by D. Q. Stephenson] Scarsdale, N.Y., Wittenborn [1964] 207 p. illus., plans. 25 cm. German and English. [NA1550.B553] 64-233
1. Architecture—Japan. I. Title. BIP

CRAM, Ralph Adams, 1863-1942 709.52
Impressions of Japanese architecture and the allied arts [Magnolia, Mass., P. Smith, 1968] 242p. illus. 21cm. (Dover bk. rebound) Unabridged, corrected repubn. of the work pub. in 1930 [N7350.C8 1966] 4.00
1. Architecture—Japan. 2. Art—Japan. I. Title.

CRAM, Ralph Adams, 1863-1942 709.52
Impressions of Japanese architecture and the allied arts. New York, Dover [1966, i.e., 1967 242p. illus. 21cm. Unabridged & corrected repubn. of the work pub. in 1930. [N7350.C8 1966] 66-25705 2.00 pap.,
1. Architecture—Japan. 2. Art—Japan. I. Title. BIP

CRAM, Ralph Adams, 1863-1942. 709.52
Impressions of Japanese architecture and the allied arts. New York, Dover Publications [1966] 242 p. illus. 21 cm. "Unabridged and corrected republication of the work published ... in 1930." [N7350.C8 1966] 66-257051
1. Architecture—Japan. 2. Art—Japan. I. Title.

FUTAGAWA, Yukio, 1932- 720.952
The roots of Japanese architecture; a photographic quest. Text, commentaries by Teiji Itoh; foreword by Isamu Noguchi. New York, Harper [c.1963] 207p. illus. 35cm. Present text, entirely rewritten by the author for this English ed. has been tr. by Paul Konya, and adapted for Western readers by the edit. staff of John Weatherhill, inc., Tokyo. 63-16240 25.00
1. Architecture—Japan. I. Ito, Teiji, 1922- II. Title.

HARADA, Jiro, 1878- 720.952
The lesson of Japanese architecture. Rev. ed. Boston, C. T. Branford Co. [1954] 192 p. illus., plans. 29 cm. [NA1550.H3 1954] 55-1321
1. Architecture—Japan. I. Title.

ISHIKAWA, Tadashi, 1908- 728.8'2'0952191
Palaces of Kyoto. Photos. by Bin Takahashi. [1st ed.] Tokyo, Palo Alto, Calif., Kodansha International [1968] 157 p. col. illus., maps. 18 cm. (This beautiful world, 2) Translation of Kyoto no Gosho (romanized form) [NA1557.K91783 1968] 68-17461
I. Title. BIP

ISHIMOTO, Yasuhiro. 1921- 720.952
Katsura: tradition and creation in Japanese architecture. Architecture in Japan [by] Walter Gropius. Tradition and creation in Japanese architecture [by] Kenzo Tange. Photos [by] Yasuhiro Ishimoto [Translated from the Japanese. Charles S. Terrv.] New Haven. Conn., Yale University Press. 1960[ ] vi, 36p. text [148]p. plates & plans (part col.) 29cm. 60-51016 15.00
1. Kyoto, Katsura Rikyu. 2. Architecture—Japan. I. Gropius, Walter, 1883- II. Tange, Kenzo. 1913- III. Title.

JAPANESE gardens & architecture. 717 Tokyo, Japan Travel Bureau [dist. New York, Perkins, 1963, c.1962] 138p. illus. (pt. col.) maps. 18cm. 62-21699 3.00 pap.,
1. Architecture—Japan. 2. Gardens—Japan. I. Nihon Kotsu Kosha.

KULTERMANN, Udo 720.952
New Japanese architecture. New York, Praeger [1960, i.e., 1961] 37p. text: 180p. plates. illus., plans. 28cm. 60-15601 13.75
1. Architecture—Japan. I. Title.

KULTERMANN, Udo. 720.952
New Japanese architecture. Rev. ed. New York, Praeger [1967] 180p. illus., plans. 28 cm. (Bks. that matter) [NA1555.K8] 60-15601 13.50
1. Architecture—Japan. I. Title.

NEW York. Museum of modern Art. 720.952
The architecture of Japan, by Arthur Drexler. New York [1955] 286p. illus., map. 27cm. 'Supplement: Japanese exhibition house': p. 262-286. [NA1550.N4] 55-5987
1. Architecture—Japan. I. Drexier, Arthur. II. Title. BIP

ROSS, Michael Franklin, 1945- 722'.1
Beyond metabolism : the new Japanese architecture / Michael Franklin Ross. New York : Architectural record books, c1978. 200 p. : ill. (some col.) ; 29 cm. (A McGraw-Hill publication) Includes bibliographical references and index. [NA1555.R67] 77-13696 ISBN 0-07-053893-X : 19.95
1. Architecture—Japan. 2. Architecture, Modern—20th century—Japan. 3. Metabolism in architecture (Movement) I. Title. BIP

TEMPEL, Egon. 720'.952
New Japanese architecture. New York, Praeger [1969, i.e. 1970] 220 p. illus., plans. 26 cm. "Translation into English by E. Rockwell." [NA1555.T4] 69-19187 18.50
1. Architecture—Japan. 2. Architecture, Modern—20th century—Japan. I. Title.

Architecture—Japan—Bibliography.

HUGO-BRUNT, Michael 016.3092 s
Architecture, planning, and landscape architecture in Japan / Michael Hugo-Brunt. Monticello, Ill. : Council of Planning Librarians, 1978. 26 p. ; 28 cm. (Exchange bibliography - Council of Planning Librarians ; 1447) Cover title. [Z5942.C68 no. 1447] [Z5944.J3] 016.3092'3'0952 78-304665 pbk. : 2.50
1. Architecture—Japan—Bibliography. 2. City planning—Japan—Bibliography. 3. Landscape architecture—Japan—Bibliography. I. Title. II. Series: Council of Planning Librarians. Exchange bibliography ; 1447.

Architecture—Japan—Edo period, 1600-1868.

OKAWA, Naomi, 1929- 722'.1
Edo architecture, Katsura and Nikko / by Naomi Okawa ; with photos. by Chuji Hirayama ; translated by Alan Woodhull and Akito Miyamoto. 1st English ed. New York : Weatherhill, 1975. 162 p., [2] fold. leaves of plates : ill. (some col.) ; 24 cm. (The Heibonsha survey of Japanese art ; v. 20) Translation of Katsura to Nikko. [NA1553.5.O3713] 74-23786 ISBN 0-8348-1027-1 : 12.50
1. Kyoto. Katsura Rikyu. 2. Nikko, Japan (Torhigi Prefecture). Toshogu. 3. Architecture—Japan—Edo period, 1600-1868. I. Title. II. Series.

Architecture—Japan—History.

ALEX, William. 720.952
Japanese architecture. New York, G. Braziller, 1963. 127 p. illus., map, plans. 26 cm. (The Great ages of world architecture) Bibliography: p. 120-121. [NA1550.A75] 63-7516
1. Architecture—Japan—History. I. Title. II. Series. BIP

KIRBY, John B. 720.952
From castle to teahouse; Japanese architecture of the Monoyama period. Rutland, Vt., Tuttle [1962] xv, 222p. illus. 27cm. Bibl. 62-9361 12.50, bxd.
1. Architecture—Japan—Hist. I. Title.

SADLER, Arthur Lindsay, 1882- 722.1
A short history of Japanese architecture. Rutland, Vt., Tuttle Co. [1963, c. 1962] xvi, 140p. 123 plates (incl. plans) 26cm. Bibl. 62-21539 7.50
1. Architecture—Japan—Hist. I. Title.

Architecture—Japan—Yearbooks.

ANNUAL of architecture in Japan, 720.952058 1962. Tokyo, Bijutsu Shupapnsha [dist. New York, Perkins Oriental, 1962, c.1961] various p. illus. 30cm. J62 17.50
1. Architecture—Japan—Yearbooks.

Architecture, Japanese.

BOYD, Robin. 720'.952
New directions in Japanese architecture. New York, G. Braziller [1968] 128 p. illus., plans. 25 cm. ([New directions in architecture]) Includes bibliographical references. [NA1555.B6] 68-29665 5.95
1. Architecture, Japanese. 2. Architecture, Modern—20th century—Japan. I. Title. BIP

Architecture, Jesuit—Mexico—Chihuahua (State)

ROCA, Paul M. 972'.1
Spanish Jesuit churches in Mexico's Tarahumara / Paul M. Roca. Tucson : University of Arizona Press, c1978. p. cm. Includes index. Bibliography: p. [NA5256.C45R6] 78-14467 ISBN 0-8165-0651-5 : 18.50 ISBN 0-8165-0572-1 pbk. : 11.50
1. Architecture, Jesuit—Mexico—Chihuahua (State) 2. Church architecture—Mexico—Chihuahua (State) 3. Architecture, Colonial—Mexico—Chihuahua (State) 4. Tarahumare Indians—Architecture. 5. Indians of Mexico—Mexico—Chihuahua (State)—Architecture. I. Title. BIP

Architecture—Juvenile literature.

CLARK, Evelyn Vallentin. 720
A guide to architecture for young people; exploring old buildings. New York, Roy Publishers [1955] 231p. illus. 23cm. First published in 1952 under title: Exploring old buildings; every child's guide to architecture. [NA2555] 55-9141
1. Architecture—Juvenile literature. I. Title.

COPPLESTONE, Trewin. 720
Architecture: the great art of building; illustrations by Harry and Gwen Green [and others] London, New York, Hamlyn, 1969. 3-93 p. illus., col. maps, plans, ports. 31 cm. (Learning with colour) Illus. on lining papers. Examines the purpose, methods, and styles of architecture from prehistoric constructions to those of present day. [NA2555.C6] 72-497293 17/6
1. Architecture—Juvenile literature. I. Title.

HILLYER, Virgil Mores, 1875-1931. 720.9
Architecture, by V. M. Hillyer and E. G. Huey. New ed. designed and rev. by Children's Press, Chicago. Consultants: Howard Dearstyne [and] H. F. Koeper. New York, Meredith Press [1966] 127 p. illus. (part col.) 29 cm. (Young people's story of our heritage) Cover title: Young people's story of architecture, 3,000 B.C.-Gothic period. Originally published as a part of the author's A child's history of art. [NA2555.H5] 66-11326
1. Architecture—Juvenile literature. I. Huey, Edward Greene, 1899- joint author. II. Children's Press, inc., Chicago. III. Title. IV. Title: Young people's story of architecture, 3,000 B.C.-Gothic period.

HILLYER, Virgil Mores, 1875-1931. 720.9
Architecture; [Gothic-modern] by V. M. Hillyer and E. G. Huey. New ed. designed and rev. by Childrens Press, Chicago. Consultants: Howard Dearstyne [and] H. F. Koeper. New York, Meredith Press [1966] 127 p. illus. 29 cm. (Young people's story of our heritage) Cover title: Young people's story of architecture; Gothic-modern. Originally published as a part of the author's A child's history of art. [NA2555.H52] 66-11327
1. Architecture—Juvenile literature. I. Huey, Edward Greene, 1899- joint author. II. Childrens Press, inc., Chicago. III. Title. IV. Title: Young people's story of architecture; Gothic-modern.

MOORE, Lamont. 720
The first book of architecture. New York, F. Watts [1961] 82 p. illus. 23 cm. [The First books, 135] [PZ10.M822Fi] 61-5552
1. Architecture—Juvenile literature. I. Title.

PAINE, Roberta M. 720
Looking at architecture [by] Roberta M. Paine. New York, Lothrop, Lee & Shepard [1974] 127 p. illus. 29 cm. Bibliography: p. 125. An introduction to architecture which examines some of the great buildings of the world, from the Egyptian pyramids to modern skyscrapers. [NA2555.P34 1974] 73-17718 ISBN 0-688-41553-9 5.95
1. Architecture—Juvenile literature. I. Title.
Library binding; 5.11, ISBN 0-688-51553-3. BIP

ROBBIN, Irving 720
The how and why wonder book of caves to skyscrapers. Illus. by Robert Doremus. [Deluxe ed.] New York, Grosset [c.1963] 48p. illus. (pt. col.) 29cm. (4042) 63-16314 bds., 1.00; pap., .50; lib. ed. net, 2.08
1. Architecture—Juvenile literature. 2. Dwellings—Juvenile literature. I. Title. II. Title: Caves to skyscrapers.

SULLIVAN, George, 1927- 720
Understanding architecture. New York, F. Warne [1971] 108 p. illus. 24 cm. Discusses the history of architecture from the ancient Greek era to the present day emphasizing the structural and aesthetic aspects characteristic of each period. [NA2555.S94] 79-150365 3.95
1. Architecture—Juvenile literature. I. Title. BIP

WILSON, Forrest, 1918- 721
Architecture; a book of projects for young adults, written and illustrated by Forrest Wilson. New York, Reinhold Book Corp. [1968] 96 p. illus. 21 cm. Bibliography: p. 95-96. Thirty-three architectural projects explain the principles of structure, classic symmetry, scale and space. [NA2555.W5] 67-24701 6.95
1. Architecture—Juvenile literature. 2. Architecture—Composition, proportion, etc. I. Title.

Architecture—Lancashire, Eng.

PEVSNER, Nikolaus, Sir, 1902- 914.27'2'0485
Lancashire. Harmondsworth, Penguin, 1969. 2 v. plates, illus., maps. 19 cm. (His The buildings of England, 36-37) Contents.Contents.—1. The industrial and commercial south.—2. The rural north. [NA969.L3P4] 79-591689 ISBN 0-14-071036-1(v.1) 35/- (v. 1) 30/- (v. 2)
1. Architecture—Lancashire, Eng.

Architecture—Las Vegas, Nev.

VENTURI, Robert. 720.9'793'13
Learning from Las Vegas [by] Robert Venturi, Denise Scott Brown, and Steven Izenour. Cambridge, Mass., MIT Press [1972] xvi, 188 p. illus. 37 cm. [NA735.L3V4] 74-169014 ISBN 0-262-22015-6 25.00
1. Architecture—Las Vegas, Nev. 2. Symbolism in architecture. I. Brown, Denise Scott, 1931- joint author. II. Izenour, Steven, joint author. III. Title. BIP

Architecture—Latin America.

BULLRICH, Francisco. 720'.98
New directions in Latin American architecture. New York, G. Braziller [1969] 128 p. illus., plans. 25 cm. (New directions in architecture) Bibliography: p. 121. [NA702.B77] 71-85698 5.95
1. Architecture—Latin America. 2. Architecture, Modern—20th century—Latin America. I. Title.

HITCHCOCK, Henry Russell, 1903- 724'.098
Latin American architecture since 1945. New York, Museum of Modern Art. [New York] Published for the Museum of Modern Art by Arno Press, 1972 [c1955]

203 p. illus. 26 cm. [NA702.H5 1972] 71-169304 ISBN 0-405-01563-1
1. Architecture—Latin America. 2. Architecture, Modern—20th century—Latin America. 3. Architecture—Designs and plans. I. New York (City). Museum of Modern Art. II. Title.

Architecture—Lexington, Va.

LYLE, Royster, 1933- 720'.9755'852
The architecture of historic Lexington / Royster Lyle, Jr., and Pamela Hemenway Simpson ; photos. by Sally Munger Mann. Charlottesville : Published for the Historic Lexington Foundation by the University Press of Virginia, 1977. xi, 314 p. : ill. ; 26 cm. Includes index. Bibliography: p. 303-307. [NA735.L48L95] 76-49890 ISBN 0-8139-0647-4 : 15.00
1. Architecture—Lexington, Va. 2. Lexington, Va.—Buildings. I. Simpson, Pamela Hemenway, 1946- joint author. II. Title. BIP

Architecture—Liverpool.

HUGHES, Quentin 711.4094272
Seaport: London, 1. humphries [1964] xi, 180p. illus., maps. 27cm. Bibl. [NA9188.L5H8] 66-38241 13.50
1. Architecture—Liverpool. 2. Cities and towns—Planning—Liverpool. I. Title. II. Title: Architecture and townscape in Liverpool,
Available from Transatlantic Arts. New York. BIP

Architecture, Lombard.

PORTER, Arthur Kingsley, 1883-1933. 720'.945'2
Lombard architecture. New York, Hacker Art Books, 1967. 4 v. 244 plates (incl. plans) 27 cm. v. 4: 37 cm. Reprint of the 1917 ed. Vol. 4: Atlas. Bibliography: v. 1, p. [441]-483. [NA1119.L8P6 1967] 67-8936
1. Architecture, Lombard. 2. Church architecture—Lombardy.

RIVOIRA, Giovanni Teresio, 1849-1919. 726'.5'094
Lombardic architecture, its origin, development, and derivatives / by G. T. Rivoira. New York : Hacker Art Books, 1975. 2 v. : ill. ; 27 cm. Translation of Le origini della architettura lombarda. Reprint of the 1933 ed. published by Clarendon Press, Oxford. Includes indexes. Bibliography: v. 1, p. [xxvii]-xxviii. [NA1119.L8R613 1975] 73-76789 ISBN 0-87817-137-1 : 75.00(2 vols.)
1. Architecture, Lombard. 2. Architecture—Italy. 3. Church architecture. I. Title.

Architecture—London.

PEVSNER, Nikolaus, 1902- 720.942
London, except the cities of London and Westminster. Harmondsworth, Middlesex, Penguin Books [1952] 496p. illus., 64 plates, fold, map. 18cm. (The Buildings of England, BE 6) [NA969.L6P4] 53-26502
1. Architecture—London. I. Title. II. Series.

PEVSNER, Nikolaus, Sir, 1902- 720'.9421
London / by Nikolaus Pevsner. 3rd ed. extensively revised / by Bridget Cherry. Harmondsworth : Penguin, 1973- v. : ill., maps, plans ; 19 cm. (The Buildings of England) Includes index. Contents.—v. 1. The cities of London and Westminster. [NA970.P42] 75-313782 ISBN 0-14-071012-4 (v. 1) : £4.75 (v. 1)
1. Architecture—London. I. Cherry, Bridget.

SUMMERSON, John Newenham, Sir 1904- 720.9421
Georgian London. [Rev. ed.] Baltimore, Penguin [1963] 348p. illus. 19cm. (Pelican bks. A574) Bibl. 63-2734 1.65 pap.,
1. Architecture—London. 2. Cities and towns—Planning—London. 3. Architecture Georgian. I. Title. BIP

SUMMERSON, John Newenham, Sir, 1904- 720'.9421
Georgian London; an architectural study [by] John Summerson. New York, Praeger Publishers [1970, c1962] 348 p. illus., maps, plans, plates. 23 cm. Bibliography: p. 329-331. [NA970.S8 1970] 76-114297 8.50
1. Architecture—London. 2. Cities and towns—Planning—London. 3. Architecture, Georgian. I. Title.

Architecture—London—Bibliography.

MADOX, Dawn. 016.3092'08 s
The history of London from the seventeenth century to the present / Dawn Madox and Michael Hugo-Brunt. Monticello, Ill. : Council of Planning Librarians, 1974. $4.00 Cover title. [Z5942.C68 no. 536] [Z5944.G7] [NA970] 016.9421 75-312975
1. Architecture—London—Bibliography. 2. Cities and towns—Planning—London—Bibliography. I. Hugo-Brunt, Michael, joint author. II. Title. III. Series: Council of Planning Librarians. Exchange bibliography ; 536.

Architecture—London—Guide-books.

CRAWFORD, David, 1940- 914.21'2'04855
The City of London : its architectural heritage : the book of the City of London's heritage walks / David Crawford. Cambridge [Eng.] : Woodhead-Faulkner, 1976. 143 p. : ill. ; 16 x 22 cm. Bibliography: p. 143. [NA970.C76] 76-378433 ISBN 0-85941-049-8 : £4.25. ISBN 0-85941-043-9 pbk.
1. Architecture—London—Guide-books. 2. London—Buildings. I. Title. BIP

Architecture—London—Hist.

GODFREY, Walter Hindes, 1881- 720.9421
A history of architecture in and around London; arranged to illustrate the course of architecture in England until the end of the nineteenth century, with a list of principal twentieth-century buildings. London, Phoenix House [New York, Hillary House, 1966, c.1962] xvii, 264p. illus. 22cm. First pub. in 1911 under title: A history of architecture in London. [NA970.G6] 63-2855 8.50
1. Architecture—London—Hist. 2. Architecture—England—Hist. I. Title.

Architecture—Long Island—Guide-books.

VIEMEISTER, August, 1893- 917.47'21'044
An architectural journey through Long Island / August Viemeister ; edited with an introd. by Marian Leifsen. Port Washington, N.Y. : Kennikat Press, c1974. x, 150 p., [3] leaves of plates : chiefly ill. ; 29 cm. Includes index. [NA730.N42L668] 75-304886 ISBN 0-8046-9109-6 : 12.50
1. Architecture—Long Island—Guide-books. I. Title. BIP

Architecture—Los Angeles.

BANHAM, Reyner. 720'.9794'94
Los Angeles: the architecture of four ecologies. [Harmondsworth, Eng.] Penguin Books [1973, c1971] 256 p. illus. 20 cm. (The Architect and society) (Pelican books, A1178) Bibliography: p. 247-252. [NA735.L55B3 1973] 74-155302 ISBN 0-14-021178-0 3.95
1. Architecture—Los Angeles.
Distributed by Penguin, Baltimore, Md.

BANHAM, Reyner. 720'.9794'94
Los Angeles; the architecture of four ecologies. [1st U.S. ed.] New York, Harper & Row [1971] 256 p. illus., maps. 23 cm. [NA735.L55B3] 72-148430 6.95
1. Architecture—Los Angeles.

GEBHARD, David. 720'.9'79494
L.A. in the thirties, 1931-1941 / David Gebhard and Harriette Von Breton. [Layton, Utah] : Peregrine Smith, 1975. 165 p. : ill. ; 28 cm. Includes index. Bibliography: p. 159-160. [NA735.L55G42] 75-14026 ISBN 0-87905-039-X : 8.50
1. Architecture—Los Angeles. 2. Architecture, Modern—20th century—Los Angeles. I. Von Breton, Harriette, 1910- joint author. II. Title.

Architecture—Louisiana.

DESMOND, John. 720'.9763
Louisiana's antebellum architecture, in text and sketches. Baton Rouge, Claitor's Pub. Div., 1970. 97 p. illus. 24 x 32 cm. Bibliography: p. 97. [NA730.L8D47] 71-143691
1. Architecture—Louisiana. 2. Architecture, Colonial—Louisiana. 3. Architecture, Modern—19th century—Louisiana. 4. Louisiana—Historic houses, etc. I. Title.

Architecture—Louisiana—New Orleans.

KIRK, Susan Lauxman. 976.3'35
The architecture of St. Charles Avenue / by Susan Lauxman Kirk, Helen Michel Smith ; photos. by Thomas G. Krentel ; architectural consultant, Monroe Labouisse, Jr. ; edited by Jerry Snider. Gretna, La. : Pelican Pub. Co., [1977] p. cm. Bibliography: p. [NA735.N4K57] 77-23486 ISBN 0-88289-174-X : 15.00
1. Architecture—Louisiana—New Orleans. 2. New Orleans—Streets—Saint Charles Avenue. I. Smith, Helen Michel, joint author. II. Title. BIP

Architecture—Lowell, Mass.

COOLIDGE, John Phillips, 1913- 720'.9744'4
Mill and mansion; a study of architecture and society in Lowell, Massachusetts, 1820-1865 [by] Joyn Coolidge. New York, Russell & Russell [1967,c1942] xi, 261p. illus., maps, plans. 24cm. (Columbia studies in Amer. culture, no. 10) Bibl. [NA735.L9C61967] 66-27058 15.00
1. Architecture—Lowell, Mass. 2. Lowell, Mass.—Hist. I. Title. II. Series.
Originally published by Columbia. BIP

Architecture—Maine—History.

HISTORIC American Buildings Survey. 720'.9'741
Maine catalog : a list of measured drawings, photographs, and written documentation in the survey, 1974 / Historic American Buildings Survey, National Park Service, Department of the Interior ; compiled with an introductory essay "The historic architecture of Maine" by Denys Peter Myers. [Augusta] : Maine State Museum, c1974. vii, 254 p. : ill. ; 23 cm. Includes index. Bibliography: p. 194-197. [NA730.M2H57 1974] 74-84742 ISBN 0-913764-05-1
1. Architecture—Maine—History. 2. Historic buildings—Maine. I. Myers, Denys Peter, 1916- The historic architecture of Maine. 1974. II. Title.

Architecture—Malta.

HUGHES, James Quentin 720.9458
The building of Malta during the period of the Knights of St. John of Jerusalem. 1530-1795. London, A. Tiranti. 1956 [New York. Transatlantic. 1966] xiii. 241p. illus., maps. plans. 22cm. (Tiranti lib.) Bibl. [NA1455.M3HH] 56-14515 2.50
1. Architecture—Malta. 2. Knights of Malta. I. Title.

Architecture—Maryland.

FORMAN, Henry Chandlee, 1904- 720'.9752
Old buildings, gardens, and furniture in Tidewater Maryland, by H. Chandlee Forman. Drawings, photos. by author except where noted. Cambridge, Md., Tidewater Pubs., 1967. xi, 326p. illus., plans. 26cm. Bibl. [NA730.M3F58] 67-17538 12.50
1. Architecture—Maryland. 2. Gardens—Maryland. 3. Furniture—Maryland. I. Title. BIP

FORMAN, Henry Chandlee, 1904- 728.6
Tidewater Maryland architecture and gardens. New York, Architectural Book Pub. Co. [c1956] xv, 208p. illus., plates, plans. 26cm. 'A sequel to Early manor and plantation houses of Maryland.' Bibliography: p. 201. [NA730.M3F6] 56-11068
1. Architecture—Maryland. 2. Architecture, Colonial. 3. Gardens—Maryland. I. Title.

Architecture—Maryland—History.

FORMAN, Henry Chandlee, 1904- 720.9'752
Maryland architecture; a short history from 1634 through the Civil War, by H. Chandlee Forman. Cambridge, Md., Tidewater Publishers, 1968. xvi, 102 p. illus., plans. 26 cm. "Reprinted and expanded ... from Chapter XIV, 'Maryland Architecture; the first two centuries,' by Henry Chandlee Forman ... in The Old Line State: a history of Maryland (Vol. I), edited by M. L. Radoff ... 1956." Bibliography: p. 87-88. [NA730.M3F56] 68-58449 6.00
1. Architecture—Maryland—History. I. Radoff, Morris Leon, 1905- ed. The Old Line State. II. Title. BIP

Architecture—Massachusetts—Boston.

TUCCI, Douglass Shand. 720'.9744'61
Built in Boston : city and suburb, 1860-1940 / Douglass Shand Tucci ; with a foreword by Walter Muir Whitehill. 1st ed. Boston : New York Graphic Society, 1978. p. cm. [NA735.B7T8] 78-7072 ISBN 0-8212-0741-5 : 22.50
1. Architecture—Massachusetts—Boston. 2. Boston—Buildings. 3. Architecture, Victorian—Massachusetts—Boston. 4. Architecture, Modern—20th century—Massachusetts—Boston. I. Title. BIP

Architecture—Mathematical models.

MARCH, Lionel, 1934- 721'.01'84
Some elementary models of built forms. Cambridge, University of Cambridge Department of Architecture, 1971. [5], 56 p. illus. 30 cm. (Land use and built form studies. Working paper no. 56) Bibliography: p. 56. [NA2750.M27] 73-175027 ISBN 0-903248-35-2
1. Architecture—Mathematical models. I. Title. II. Series.

Architecture, Maya.

STIERLIN, Henri 722.91
Living architecture: Mayan. Text, photos. by Henri Stierlin. Preface by Pedro Ramirez Vasquez. New York, Grosset [1965, c.1964] 192p. illus., maps, plans (pt. fold.) 22cm. (Living architecture) Bibl. [F1435.3.A6S8] 65-7595 6.95
1. Architecture, Maya. 2. Mayas—Antiq. I. Title.

Architecture, Medieval.

GIMPEL, Jean 726.60902
The cathedral builders. Tr. [from French] by Carl F. Barnes, Jr. [Gloucester, Mass., Peter Smith, 1962] 192p. illus. (Evergreen profile bk. 21 rebound) Bibl. 3.35
1. Architecture, Medieval. 2. Building. I. Title.

GIMPEL, Jean 726.60902
The cathedral builders. Tr. [from French] by Carl F. Barnes, Jr. New York, Grove Press [1961] 192p. illus. (Evergreen profile book P 21) Bibl. 60-6216 1.35 pap.,
1. Architecture, Medieval. 2. Building. I. Title.

HARVEY, John Hooper. 723
The mediaeval architect [by] John Harvey. New York, St. Martin's Press [1972] 296 p. illus. 25 cm. Bibliography: p. [262-278. [NA350.H26 1972b] 79-190103
1. Architecture, Medieval. 2. Architecture as a profession. I. Title.

HONNECOURT, Villard de. 723.1
The sketchbook of Villard de Honnecourt.

Ed. by Theodore Bowie. [Magnolia, Mass.] [Peter Smith] [1973, c1959] 144 p. facsims. 21 cm. (Indiana University paperback rebound) Includes bibliographies. [NA1053.V6A423] 68-14615 ISBN 0-8446-4427-7 3.50
1. Architecture, Medieval. 2. Drawings, French. I. Title.

MACDONALD, William Lloyd 723.1
Early Christian & Byzantine architecture. New York, Braziller, 1962. 128p. 100 illus. 26cm. (Great ages of world architecture) Bibl. 62-7531 4.95 bds.,
1. Architecture, Medieval. 2. Architecture, Byzantine. I. Title. II. Series. BIP

PORTER, Arthur Kingsley, 1883-1933. 723
Medieval architecture; its origins and development, with lists of monuments and bibliographies. New York, Hacker Art Books, 1966. 2 v. illus., plans. 28 cm. Reprint of the 1909 edition. Contents.Contents.—v. 1. Origins.—v. 2. Normandy and the Ile de France. Bibliography: v. 1, p. 335-467; v. 2, p. 419-479. [NA350.P8 1966] 67-4391
1. Architecture, Medieval. 2. Architecture, Medieval—France. 3. Architecture—France. I. Title.

SAALMAN, Howard. 723.4
Medieval architecture; European architecture, 1600-1200. New York, G. Braziller, 1962. 127 p. 100 illus. 26 cm. (The Great ages of world architecture) Bibliography: p. 113-119. [NA350.S2] 62-7530
1. Architecture, Medieval. I. Title. II. Series. BIP

VILLARD de Honnecourt, 13thcent. 741.944
The sketchbook of Villard de Honnecourt. Edited by Theodore Bowie. Bloomington, Indiana University; distributed by G. Wittenborn, New York, c1959. 80 p. (p. 16-78 facsims.) facsim. 23 cm. The drawings, which are arranged by subject in this edition, have been reproduced from Ms. 19093 of the French collection in the Bibliotheque nationale in Paris. Bibliography: p. 6. [NA1053.V6A423 1959] 59-1208
1. Architecture, Medieval. 2. Drawings, French. 3. Manuscripts, French — Facsimiles. I. Bowie, Theodore Robert, ed. II. Paris, Bibliotheque nationale. Mss. (Fr. 19093) III. Title.

VILLARD de Honnecourt, 13th cent. 741.944
The sketchbook of Villard de Honnecourt. Ed. by Theodore Bowie. 2d ed., rev. [Bloomington] Indiana Univ. dist. Wittenborn, New York [1962]c.1959. 80p. 63 plates. 23cm. The drawings, which are arranged by subject in this edition, have been reproduced from Ms. 19093 of the French collection in the Bibliotheque nationale in Paris. Bibl. 62-6877 3.00 pap.,
1. Architecture, Medieval. 2. Drawings, French. 3. Manuscrepts,French—Facsimiles. I. Bowie, Theodore Robert, ed. II. Paris. Bibliotheque nationale. Mss. (Fr. 19093) III. Title.

Architecture, Medieval—Addresses, essays, lectures.

MEDIEVAL architecture. 709 s
New York : Garland Pub., 1976. 268 p. : ill. ; 29 cm. (The Garland library of the history of art ; v. 4) Includes bibliographical references. [N5300.G32 vol. 4] [NA350] 723 76-14066 ISBN 0-8240-2414-1 lib.bdg. : 35.00
1. Architecture, Medieval—Addresses, essays, lectures. I. Series.
Contents omitted BIP

Architecture—Mediterranean region.

ARENDT, Erich. 709'.18'22
Art and architecture on the Mediterranean Islands. Translated [from the German] by Edith Andersen. London, New York [etc.] Abelard-Schuman, 1968. 37 p. 211 plates, illus. (some col.) 31 cm. Translation of Saule-Kubus-Gesicht. [NA950.A7213 1968] 68-14887 ISBN 0-20071547X 63/-
1. Architecture—Mediterranean region. 2. Art—Mediterranean region. I. Title.

BENY, Roloff. 722.6
The thrones of earth and heaven. Photographs and notes on the plates by Roloff Beny. Foreword by Herbert Read. Texts by Freya Stark [and others] New York, H. N. Abrams [1958] 181 p. 183 illus., maps. 32 cm. [NA202.B36] 58-13484
1. Architecture—Mediterranean region. 2. Sculpture—Mediterranean region. I. Stark, Freya. II. Title.

Architecture—Melbourne.

CASEY, Male, ed. 720'.994'2
Early Melbourne architecture, 1840-1888. Compiled and edited by Maie Cases [and others. 2d ed.] Melbourne, New York, Oxford University Press [1963] 184 p. illus., map. 24 cm. Bibliography: p. 179. [NA1603.M4E2 1963] 65-9547
1. Architecture—Melbourne. I. Title.

CASEY, Male, ed. 720'.994'2
Early Melbourne architecture, 1840-1888. Compiled and edited by Maie Cases [and others. 2d ed.] Melbourne, New York, Oxford University Press [1963] 184 p. illus., map. 24 cm. Bibliography: p. 179. [NA1603.M4E2 1963] 65-9547
1. Architecture—Melbourne. I. Title.

EARLY Melbourne architecture, 1840-1888 / compiled and editedby Maie Casey et al 3rd ed. Melbourne ; New York : Oxford University Press, 1975. 184 p. : chiefly ill. ; 24 cm. Includes index. Bibliography: p. 179. [NA1603.M4E2 1975] 75-332133 ISBN 0-19-550049-0 : 8.75 720'.9945
1. Architecture—Melbourne. I. Casey, Maie, Lady.

EARLY Melbourne architecture, eighteen forty to eighteen eighty-eight. Melbourne, Oxford University Press, 1953. 184p. illus. 24cm. Edited by Male Casey and others. [NA1603.M4E2] 54-15092 720.994
1. Architecture—Melbourne. I. Casey, Male, ed.

Architecture—Mexico.

BEACHAM, Hans. 720'.972
The architecture of Mexico; yesterday and today. Introd. by Mathias Goeritz. New York, Architectural Book Pub. Co. [1969] 254 p. illus. 29 cm. Imperfect copy: pages 161-191 duplicated; 31 pages wanting. [NA750.B4] 69-15058 12.95
1. Architecture—Mexico. I. Title. BIP

CETTO, Max L 720.972
Modern architecture in Mexico. Arquitectura moderna en Mexico. [Translated from the German into English by D. Q. Stephenson. Translated from the German into Spanish by Francisco Maigler] New York, Praeger [1961] 224p. illus., map, plans. 29cm. (Books that matter) [NA755.C413] 61-7600
1. Architecture—Mexico. 2. Architecture, Modern—20th cent. I. Title. II. Title: Arquitectura moderna en Mexico.

KILHAM, Walter Harrington, 1868-1948. 720'.972
Mexican architecture of the vice-regal period. New York, AMS Press [1971] 221 p. illus. 23 cm. Reprint of the 1927 ed. [NA753.K5 1971] 75-137252 ISBN 0-404-03675-9
1. Architecture—Mexico. 2. Architecture, Colonial—Mexico. I. Title. BIP

KUBLER, George, 1912- 720'.972
Mexican architecture of the sixteenth century. Westport, Conn., Greenwood Press [1972- c1948- v. illus. 26 cm. Original ed. issued as no. 5 of History of art. Yale historical publications. Includes bibliographical references. [NA753.K8 1972] 70-171517 ISBN 0-8371-6256-4 (set)
1. Architecture—Mexico. 2. Architecture, Colonial—Mexico. I. Title. II. Series: Yale historical publications. History of art, 5.

MYERS, Irving Evan, 1918- 724.91
Mexico's modern architecture, by I. E. Myers in cooperation with the National Institute of Fine Arts of Mexico. New York, Architectural Book Pub. Co. [1952] 264 p. illus. 27 cm. English and Spanish. [NA755.M94] 52-12831
1. Architecture — Mexico. 2. Architecture — Designs and plans. I. Title.

Architecture—Michigan.

ANDREW, Wayne. 720/.9774
Architecture in Michigan; a representative photographic survey. Detroit, Wayne State Univ., 1967. 1v. (unpaged) illus. 16x23cm. Bibl. [NA730.M5A55] 67-26428 6.95; 2.95 pap.,
1. Architecture—Michigan. 2. Michigan—Historic houses, etc. I. Title.

ANDREWS, Wayne. 720'.9774
Architecture in Michigan; a representative photographic survey. Detroit, Wayne State University, 1967. 1 v. (unpaged) illus. 16 x 23 cm. Includes bibliography. [NA730.M5A55] 67-26428
1. Architecture—Michigan. 2. Michigan—Historic houses, etc. I. Title. BIP

Architecture—Milan.

ALOI, Roberto 720.94521
Nuove architetture a Milano. Didascalie in italiano e inglese. Milano, U. Hoepli [dist. New York, W. S. Heinman] 1959[ ] xxvi, 385p. illus. (part col.), maps (part col.), diagrs. 28cm. 59-16939 20.00 bds.,
1. Architecture—Milan. 2. Architecture—Designs and plans. I. Title.

Architecture— Minnesota.

MINNEAPOLIS. Institute of Arts. 720.9776
A century of Minnesota architecture. Organized by the Minneapolis Institute of Arts as a contribution to the Minnesota Statehood Centennial for showings at the Minneapolis Institute of Arts, Rochester Art Center, Winona County Art Committee, the Saint Paul Gallery and School of Art, Tweed Gallery of the University of Minnesota, Duluth Branch. Selection of architectural monuments and text by Donald R. Torbert. Photos. by Jerome Liebling. [Minneapolis] Minneapolis Society of Fine Arts, c1958. unpaged. illus. 26cm. [NA730.M5] 58-2392
1. Architecture— Minnesota. I. Torbert, Donald R. II. Title.

Architecture, Minoan.

BELL, Edward, 1844-1926. 722'.61
Prehellenic architecture in the Aegean. Washington, McGrath Pub. Co. [1971] xvi, 213 p. illus. 23 cm. Reprint of the 1926 ed., issued in the author's series: The origins of architecture. Includes bibliographical references. [NA267.B44 1971] 77-119253 ISBN 0-8434-0125-7
1. Architecture, Minoan. 2. Architecture, Mycenaean. 3. Crete—Antiquities. I. Title.

Architecture—Mississippi—Biloxi—Guide-books.

THE Buildings of Biloxi : an architectural survey. Biloxi, Miss. : City of Biloxi, 1976. 172 p. : ill. ; 22 x 29 cm. Includes index. Bibliography: p. 157-160. [NA735.B5B84] 76-45993 720'.9762'13
1. Architecture—Mississippi—Biloxi—Guide-books. 2. Biloxi, Miss.—Buildings. I. Biloxi, Miss.

Architecture, Modern—19th century.

BEHRENDT, Walter Curt, 1884-1945. 720'.9'04
Modern building, its nature, problems, and forms / by Walter Curt Behrendt. Westport, Conn. : Hyperion Press, 1979. p. cm. Reprint of the 1937 ed. published by Harcourt, Brace, New York. Includes index. Bibliography: p. [NA642.B39 1979] 78-59005 lib.bdg. : 23.50
1. Architecture, Modern—19th century. 2. Architecture, Modern—20th century. I. Title.

BENEVOLO, Leonardo. 724
History of modern architecture. Cambridge, Mass., M.I.T. Press [1971] 2 v. (xxxiv, 868 p.) illus. 25 cm. Translation of Storia dell'architettura moderna. Contents.Contents.—v. 1. The tradition of modern architecture.—v. 2. The modern movement. Bibliography: v. 2, p. 850-858. [NA642.B413 1971b] 77-157667 ISBN 0-262-02080-7 (v. 1) 35.00
1. Architecture, Modern—19th century. 2. Architecture, Modern—20th century. I. Title.

BRADBURY, Ronald, 1908- 724
The Romantic theories of architecture of the nineteenth century, in Germany, England, and France (together with a brief survey of the Vitruvian school) / [Ronald Bradbury]. New York : AMS Press, [1976] p. cm. Reprint of the 1934 ed. published by the Dorothy Press, New York. Originally presented as the author's thesis, Columbia, 1934. Bibliography: p. [NA645.B7 1976] 75-28994 ISBN 0-404-14005-X : 9.00
1. Architecture, Modern—19th century. I. Title: The Romantic theories of architecture ...

HITCHCOCK, Henry Russell, 1903- 724
Architecture: nineteenth and twentieth centuries. [3d ed. Harmondsworth, Middlesex, Baltimore] Penguin Books [1968] xxix, 520 p. illus., 196 plates. 27 cm. (The Pelican history of art, Z15) Bibliographical references included in "Notes" (p. 439-478) Bibliography: p. 479-492. [NA645.H55 1968] 75-8765
1. Architecture, Modern—19th century. 2. Architecture, Modern—20th century. I. Title. II. Series.

HITCHCOCK, Henry Russell, 1903- 724.9
Architecture: nineteenth and twentieth centuries. [Harmondsworth, Middlesex] Penguin Books [1958] xxix, 498 p. illus., 192 plates, plans. 27 cm. (The Pelican history of art, Z15) Bibliographical references included in "Notes" (p. 431-461) Bibliography: p. 463-472. [NA645.H55 1958] 61-45138
1. Architecture, Modern—19th century. 2. Architecture, Modern—20th century. I. Title. II. Series.

HITCHCOCK, Henry Russell, 1903- 724.9
Architecture: nineteenth and twentieth centuries. [2d ed.] Baltimore, Penguin Books [1963, c1958] xxix, 510 p. illus., 192 plates, plans. 27 cm. (The Pelican history of art, Z15) Bibliographical references included in "Notes" (p. 439-471) Bibliography: p. 473-483. [NA645.H55 1963] 63-5619
1. Architecture, Modern—19th century. 2. Architecture, Modern—20th century. I. Title. II. Series.

HITCHCOCK, Henry Russell, 1903- 724
Architecture, nineteenth and twentieth centuries / Henry-Russell Hitchcock. 4th ed. Harmondsworth, Eng. ; New York : Penguin Books, 1977. 688 p. : ill. ; 21 cm. (The Pelican history of art ; PZ15) Includes index. Bibliography: p. [631]-648. [NA642.H56 1977] 75-128606 ISBN 0-14-056115-3 : 15.00
1. Architecture, Modern—19th century. 2. Architecture, Modern—20th century. I. Title. II. Series.

HITCHCOCK, Henry Russell, 1903- 724
Modern architecture: romanticism and reintegration. New York, Hacker Art Books, 1970. xvii, 252 p. illus. 29 cm. "First published ... 1929." Includes bibliographical references. [NA642.H57] 73-116356 ISBN 0-87817-044-8
1. Architecture, Modern—19th century. 2. Architecture, Modern—20th century. I. Title.

HITCHCOCK, Henry Russell, 1903- 724
Modern architecture; romanticism and reintegration. New York, Payson & Clarke, 1929. [New York, AMS Press, 1972] xvii, 252 p. illus. 24 cm. Includes bibliographical references. [NA642.H57 1972] 74-137241 ISBN 0-404-03276-1 12.00
1. Architecture, Modern—19th century. 2. Architecture, Modern—20th century. I. Title.

HOFMANN, Werner, 1928- 724.9
Modern architecture in color [by] Werner

Hofmann and Udo Kultermann. [Translated from the German by Peter Usborne] New York, Viking Press [1970] 528 p. plans, 112 col. plates. 29 cm. (A Studio book) Translation of Baukunst unserer Zeit. Bibliography: p. 518-521. [NA642.H6413] 72-125823 ISBN 0-670-48265-X 30.00
1. Architecture, Modern—19th century. 2. Architecture, Modern—20th century. I. Kultermann, Udo, joint author. II. Title.

PEVSNER, Nikolaus, Sir, 1902- 709.04
The sources of modern architecture and design. New York, F. A. Praeger [1968] 216 p. illus. (part col.) 22 cm. (Praeger world of art series) Includes bibliographies. [NA645.P4 1968] 68-19137
1. Architecture, Modern—19th century. 2. Art nouveau. I. Title. BIP

Architecture, Modern—19th century—Addresses, essays, lectures.

NINETEENTH and twentieth 709 s
century architecture. New York : Garland Pub., 1976. (The Garland library of the history of art ; v. 11) Includes bibliographical references. [N5300.G32 vol. 11] [NA642] 724 76-14074 ISBN 0-8240-2421-4 lib.bdg. : lib.bdg. : 35.00
1. Architecture, Modern—19th century—Addresses, essays, lectures. 2. Architecture, Modern—20th century—Addresses, essays, lectures. I. Series.
Contents omitted Contents omitted BIP

Architecture, Modern—19th century—Catalogs.

ROTH, Leland M. 720'.6'57471
The architecture of McKim, Mead & White, 1870-1920 : a building list / Leland M. Roth. New York : Garland Pub., 1978. p. cm. (Garland reference library of the humanities ; v. 114) Includes index. Bibliography: p. [NA737.M4A4 1978] 77-83368 ISBN 0-8240-9850-1 : lib.bdg. : 40.00
1. McKim, Mead & White—Catalogs. 2. Architecture, Modern—19th century—Catalogs. 3. Architecture, Modern—20th century—Catalogs. I. Title. BIP

Architecture, Modern—19th century—United States—Addresses, essays, lectures.

VAN BRUNT, Henry, 1832-1903. 720
Architecture and society; selected essays of Henry Van Brunt. Edited with an introductory monograph by William A. Coles. Cambridge, Mass., Belknap Press of Harvard University Press, 1969. xvi, 562 p. illus. 27 cm. Includes bibliographical references. [NA710.V3 1969] 69-18028 15.00
1. Architecture, Modern—19th century—United States—Addresses, essays, lectures. 2. Architecture—United States—Addresses, essays, lectures. 3. Architecture and society—United States—Addresses, essays, lectures. I. Coles, William A., ed. BIP

Architecture, Modern—20th century.

BANHAM, Reyner 724.9
Guide to modern architecture. Princeton, N.J., Van Nostrand [1963, c.1962] 159p. illus. 20cm. 63-24051 6.75
1. Architecture, Modern—20th cent. I. Title.

BANHAM, Reyner. 724.9
Theory and design in the first machine age. 2d ed. New York, Praeger [1967, c1960] 338 p. illus., plans, 23 cm. Bibliographical footnotes. [NA680.B25 1967] 67-16449
1. Architecture, Modern—20th cent. I. Title.

BARRAN, Fritz Richard 724.9
Kunst am Bau heute; Wanbild, Relief und Plastik in der Baukunst der Gegenwart. Art and architecture today. Einfuhrung von Walter Muller. Stuttgart, J. Hoffmann [dist. New York. Efron. 1965, c.1964] 168p. (p.10--134 illus., plans) 27cm. Captions and pt. of text also in English and French [NA680.B34] 65-1662 14.00
1. Architecture. Modern—20th cent. 2. Art, Modern—20th cent. I. Title. II. Title: Art and architecture today.

BOYD, Robin. 724.9
The puzzle of architecture. [Carlton, Australia] Melbourne University Press; New York, Cambridge University Press [1965] 188 p. illus., plans. 25 cm. [NA680.B6] 65-25314
1. Architecture, Modern — 20th cent. I. Title. BIP

BREUER, Marcel, 1902- 720'.924
Marcel Breuer: new buildings and projects [by] Tician Papachristou. New York, Praeger [1970] 239 p. illus. (part col.), plans, port. 28 cm. [NA737.B68P3 1970b] 71-136743 22.50
I. Papachristou, Tician.

BRIMELOW, E. I. 691.8
Aluminium in building. London, Macdonald [Boston, Ginn, 1966] 378p. illus. 23cm. [NA4140.B7] 58-49289 6.80
1. Architecture, Modern—20th cent. 2. Aluminum, Structural. 3. Building. I. Title.

CANTACUZINO, Sherban. 724.9
Great modern architecture. London, Studio Vista; New York, Dutton [1966] 160 p. front., illus., plans, diagrs. 18 1/2 cm. (A Dutton Vista pictureback) 10/6 (B66-8505) Includes bibliographies. [NA680.C28] 67-82828
1. Architecture, Modern—20th cent. 2. Architecture—Sketchbooks. I. Title.

CONRADS, Ulrich 724.9
The architecture of fantasy; utopian building and planning in modern times [by] Ulrich Conrads, Hans G. Sperlich. Tr., ed., expanded by Christiane Crasemann Collins, George R. Collins. New York, Praeger [1963, c.1960] 187p. illus., plans. 29cm. 62-8740 16.00
1. Architecture, Modern—20th cent. 2. Grotesque. I. Sperlich, Hans Giinther, joint author. II. Title.

DONAT, John, ed. 724.9
World architecture today. New York, Viking [c.1964] 255p. illus., plans. 29cm. (Studio bk.) 64-11432 15.00
1. Architecture, Modern—20th cent. I. Title.

DOXIADES, Konstantinos Apostolou, 1913- 724.9
Architecture in transition. New York, Oxford [c.1963] 199p. illus., diagrs., plans. 24cm. 63-6915 7.50
1. Architecture, Modern—20th cent. I. Title. BIP

DOXIADES, Konstantinos Apostolou, 1913- 724.9
Architecture in transition. New York, Oxford, [1968,c.1963] 200p. illus., diagrs., plans. 21cm. [NA680] 63-6915 1.75 pap.,
1. Architecture, Modern—20th cent. I. Title.

GROPIUS, Walter. 1883- 720.904
Scope of total architecture. New York. Collier [1962, c.1943-1955] 158p. illus. 18cm. (AS191X) .95 pap.,
1. Architecture, Modern—20th cent. I. Title. BIP

GROPIUS, Walter, 1883- 720.904
Scope of total architecture. [1st ed.] New York, Harper [1955] 185p. illus. 20cm. (World perspectives, v.3) [NA680.G73] 54-12179
1. Architecture, Modern—20th cent. I. Title.

GROUP for the Research of Social and Visual Inter-relationships. 724.9
New frontiers in architecture; CIAM '59 in Otterlo [by] Oscar Newman, by order of Jacob B. Bakema for the Otterlo 1959 participants. [1st American ed.] New York, Universe Books [1961] 224p. illus. ports., maps, plans. 28cm. (Documents of modern architecture, 1) English, French, or German. Errata slip inserted. [NA680.G75 1961] 61-14470
1. Architecture. Modern—20th cent. 2. Architecture—Designs and plans. I. Newman, Oscar, ed. II. Title. III. Series.

HILBERSEIMER, Ludwig. 724.9
Contemporary architecture: its roots and trends [by] L. Hilberseimer. Chicago, P. Theobald, 1964. 221 p. illus., plans. 29 cm. Bibliographical footnotes. [NA680.H44] 64-55788
1. Architecture, Modern — 20th cent. I. Title. BIP

JOEDICKE, Jurgen. 724.9
A history of modern architecture. [Translated from the German by James C. Palmes] New York, Praeger [1959] 243p. illus. 26cm. (Books that matter) [NA680.J613] 59-7459
1. Architecture, Modern—20th cent. I. Title.

JONES, Cranston. 724.9
Architecture today and tomorrow. New York, McGraw-Hill [1961] 243p. illus. (part col.) ports. 32cm. Bibliography: p. 241-243. [NA680.J64] 60-14222
1. Architecture, Modern—20th cent. I. Title.

KULTERMANN, Udo. 724.9
Architecture of today; a survey of new building throughout the world. [Translated by E. H. W. Priefert] New York, Universe Books [1959] 236p. (chiefly plates) 28cm. Bibliography: p. 49-51. [NA680.K813] 59-7234 riefert]
1. Architecture, Modern—20th cent. I. Title.

KULTERMANN. UDO 724.9
New architecture in the world. [Tr. from German by Ernst Flesch] New York, Universe [1966. c.1965] xxviii. 208p. illus., plans. 28cm. [NA680.K8213] 65-24565 10.50
1. Architecture. Modern—20th cent. I. Title.

L'OEIL 724.9
The best in 20th century architecture; pictures, texts chosen from L'Oeil, the intl.art review [Tr. from French] Ed. by Georges and Rosamund Bernier. New York, Reynal [dist. Morrow, 1964] 278p. illus. (pt. col.) port. 32cm. (Selective eye V; Bernier bk.) 64-64 15.00 bds.,
1. Architecture, Modern—20th cent. I. Bernier, Georges, ed. II. Bernier, Rosamond, ed. III. Title.

MARSCHALL, Werner. 720.943
Contemporary architecture in Germany. Introd. by Ulrich Conrads. Translated by James Palmes. New York, Praeger [1962] 231p. illus., plans. 26cm. (Books that matter) German and English. [NA1068.M3 1962] 62-13860
1. Architecture, Modern—20th cent. 2. Architecture—Germany (Federal Republic, 1949-) I. Title.

PETER, John, 1917- 724.91
Masters of modern architecture. New York, G. Braziller, 1958. 230p. illus. 33cm. Includes bibliography. [NA680.P374] 58-11897
1. Architecture, Modern—20th cent. 2. Architects. I. Title.

REYNOLDS Metals Company. 721.998
Aluminum in modern architecture, by John Peter. Associate editor, Edward A. Hamilton. Louisville, Ky.; distributed by Reinhold Pub. Corp., New York [1956] [n. p.] 2v. illus., ports., diagrs., tables. 24cm. v. illus., ports., diagrs. 23cm. Vol. 2, by Paul Weldlinger, has also special title: Engineering design and details. Includes bibliographies. [NA4140.R4] 56-6114
1. Architecture, Modern-20th cent. 2. Aluminum, Structural. I. Peter, John, 1917- II. Weidlinger, Paul. III. Title. IV. Title: — Supplement.

RICHARDS, James Maude 724.9
An introduction to modern architecture. London, Cassell [dist. New York, Barnes & Noble, 1964, c.1940, 1961] 175p. illus., 48 plates. 21cm. (Belle sauvage lib.) Bibl. 64-571 5.00
1. Architecture, Modern—20th cent. I. Title.

ROGERS, William Garland, 1896- 724.9
What's up in architecture; a look at modern building. New York. Harcourt [c.1965] 192p. illus. 21cm. Bibl. [NA680.R6] 65-21702 3.95
1. Architecture, Modern—20th cent. I. Title.

SIEGEL, Curt, 1911-. 721
Structure and form in modern architecture. Translated by Thomas E. Burton. New York, Reinhold Pub. Corp. [1962] 308 p. illus., diagrs. 27 cm. Translation of Strukturformen der modernen Architekur, Bibliography: p. 305-308. [NA680.S533] 62-13689
1. Architecture, Modern — 20th cent. 2. Building. I. Title. BIP

STONE, Edward Durell. 720'.924
Recent & future architecture. New York, Horizon Press [1967] 136 p. illus. (part col.), plans, port. 35 x 38 cm. [NA737.S66A53] 67-25682
1. Architecture, Modern—20th cent. I. Title.

WORLD architecture; 724.9
2. Ed.: John Donat. New York, Viking [1965] 219p. illus., plans. 29cm. (Studio bk.) v.1 entitled World architecture today [NA680.D58] 64-11432 15.00
1. Architecture, Modern—20th cent.

WORLD architecture. 724.9
3. Ed.: John Donat. New York. Viking [c.1966] 215p. illus., plans. 29cm. (Studio Vista bk.) v.1. entitled World architecture today [NA680.D58] 64-11432 16.50
1. Architecture, Modern—20th cent.

WORLD architecture. 724.9
4. New York, Viking 1967. v. illus., plans. 29cm. (Studio vista bks.) Ed.: 1965- J. Donat v.1. entitled World architecture today [NA680.D58] 64-11432 16.95
1. Architecture, Modern—20th cent. I. Donat, John, ed.

WRIGHT, Frank Lloyd, 1869- 724.91
The future of architecture. New York, Horizon Press, 1953. 326p. illus., port. 26cm. [NA680.W7] 53-3814
1. Architecture, Modern—20th cent. I. Title.

WRIGHT, Frank Lloyd, 1869-1959 724.91
The future of architecture [New York] New Amer. Lib. [1963, c.1953] 352p. illus., ports. 18cm. (Mentor Bk., MQ471) .95 pap.,
1. Architecture, Modern—20th cent. I. Title. BIP

Architecture, Modern—20th century—Addresses, essays, lectures.

JEANNERET-GRIS, Charles Edouard, 1887- 720.944
Le Corbusier talks with students from the schools of architecture. Translated from the French by Pierre Chase. New York, Orion Press [1961] 83p. 21cm. 'First published in France under the title Entretien ... 1943.' [NA2560.J413] 61-9299
1. Architecture, Modern—20th cent.—Addresses, essays, lectures. I. Title.

Architecture, Modern—20th century.

BANHAM, Reyner. 724.9
Age of the masters : a personal view of modern architecture / Reyner Banham. 1st U.S. ed. New York : Harper & Row, c1975. 170 p. : ill. ; 22 cm. (Icon editions) Edition for 1962 published under title: Guide to modern architecture. Includes index. [NA680.B248 1975b] 74-25276 ISBN 0-06-430369-1 : 15.00. ISBN 0-06-430064-1 pbk. : 5.95
1. Architecture, Modern—20th century. I. Title. BIP

BANHAM, Reyner. 724.9
Theory and design in the first machine age. New York, Praeger [1960] 338 p. illus. 23 cm. (Books that matter) Includes bibliographies. [NA680.B26 1960] 60-8831
1. Architecture, Modern—20th century. I. Title.

BLAKE, Peter, 1920- 724.9
The master builders. [1st ed.] New York, Knopf, 1960. 399 p. illus. 25 cm. [NA1053.J4B55] 60-10276
1. Jeanneret-Gris, Charles Edouard, 1887- 2. Mies van der Rohe, Ludwig, 1886- 3. Wright, Frank Lloyd, 1867-1959. 4. Architecture, Modern—20th century. I. Title. BIP

BLAKE, Peter, 1920- 724.9
The master builders : Le Corbusier, Mies van der Rohe, Frank Lloyd Wright / by Peter Blake. New York : Norton, c1976. p. cm. (The Norton library) Includes index. [NA680.B52 1976] 76-7067 ISBN 0-393-00796-0 pbk. : 5.95
1. Jeanneret-Gris, Charles Edouard, 1887-1965. 2. Mies van der Rohe, Ludwig, 1886-1969. 3. Wright, Frank Lloyd, 1867-1959. 4. Architecture, Modern—20th century. I. Title.

BREUER, Marcel, 1902- 720.973
Sun and shadow, the philosophy of an architect. Editing and notes by Peter Blake; book design and cover by Alexey Brodovitch. New York, Dodd, Mead [1955] 205 p. illus., port. 28 cm. [NA737.B68B56] 55-9928
1. Architecture, Modern—20th century. I. Blake, Peter, 1920- ed. II. Title.

BROLIN, Brent C. 724.9
The failure of modern architecture / Brent Brolin. New York : Van Nostrand Reinhold Co., 1976. 127 p. : ill. ; 24 cm. Includes index. Bibliography: p. 125-126. [NA680.B76] 75-23922 ISBN 0-442-21070-1 : 9.95
1. Architecture, Modern—20th century. 2. Architecture—Psychological aspects. 3. Architecture and society. I. Title.

BROLIN, Brent C. 724.9
The failure of modern architecture / Brent C. Brolin. London : Studio Vista, 1976. 128 p. : ill. ; 24 cm. Includes index. Bibliography: p. 125-126. [NA680.B76 1976b] 77-361063 ISBN 0-289-70753-6 : £6.00
1. Architecture, Modern—20th century. 2. Architecture—Psychological aspects. 3. Architecture and society. I. Title. BIP

CHENEY, Sheldon, 1886- 724.9
The new world architecture. New York, AMS Press [1969] ix, 404 p. illus. 24 cm. Reprint of the 1930 ed. [NA680.C5 1969] 72-100513
1. Architecture, Modern—20th century. I. Title. BIP

COOK, Peter. 724.9
Experimental architecture. New York, Universe Books [1970] 160 p. illus., map. 26 cm. Includes bibliographical references. [NA680.C63] 78-122016 6.95
1. Architecture, Modern—20th century. 2. Cities and towns—Planning—1945- I. Title.

DOW, Alden B., 1904- 720'.924
Reflections [by] Alden B. Dow. [Midland, Mich., Northwood Institute, c1970] 192 p. illus. (part col.), plans. 35 x 38 cm. [NA737.D67A55] 75-109044
I. Title. BIP

DOXIADES, Konstantinos Apostolou, 1913- 724.9
Architecture in transition [by] Constantinos A. Doxiadis. New York, Oxford University Press [1968, c1963] 200 p. illus., plans. 21 cm. (A Galaxy book, GB238) Bibliography: p. 197. [NA680.D65 1968] 68-3218
1. Architecture, Modern—20th century. I. Title.

DREW, Peter Philip. 720'.92'2
Third generation; the changing meaning of architecture [by] Philip Drew. New York, Praeger [1972] 175 p. illus. 26 cm. Bibliography: p. 173-175. [NA680.D72] 72-77545 25.00
1. Architecture, Modern—20th century. 2. Architects—Biography. I. Title.

GIEDION, Sigfried, 1888- ed. 720.904
A decade of contemporary architecture. [2d ed.] New York, G. Wittenborn, 1954 [c1951] viii, 271 p. illus., ports., maps, plans. 25 cm. Title in English, French and German; text in English and French. "Material for the book was contributed by CIAM groups and from this a selection was made by the editor." "French translations by Jean-Paul Haymoz." First ed. published in 1951 under title: A decade of new architecture. [NA680.G52 1954] 54-14272
1. Architecture, Modern—20th century. I. International Congresses for Modern Architecture. II. Title.

GROPIUS, Walter, 1883-1969. 724.9
The new architecture and the Bauhaus. Translated from the German by P. Morton Shand, with an introd. by Frank Pick. Cambridge, Mass., M.I.T. Press [1965] 112 p. illus 21 cm. (The M.I.T. paperback series, MIT21) [NA680.G7 1965] 65-10279
1. Bauhaus. 2. Architecture, Modern—20th century. 3. Industrial arts—Study and teaching—Germany. I. Title. BIP

JACOBUS, John M. 724.9
Twentieth-century architecture; the middle years, 1940-65, [by] John Jacobus. New York, Praeger [1966] 215 p. illus., plans. 26 cm. Bibliographical references included in "Notes" (p. 203-209) [NA680.J3] 66-12526
1. Architecture, Modern—20th century. I. Title.

JENCKS, Charles. 724.9
Architecture 2000; New York, Praeger [1971] 128 p. illus. 22 cm. Bibliography: p. 124-126. [NA680.J45 1971b] 76-128597 7.50
1. Architecture, Modern—20th century. 2. Cities and towns—Planning—1945- I. Title.

JENCKS, Charles. 724.9
The language of post-modern architecture / Charles A. Jencks. New York : Rizzoli, 1977. 104 p. : ill. (some col.) ; 31 cm. Includes bibliographical references and index. [NA680.J457] 76-62545 ISBN 0-8478-0071-7 : 18.50. ISBN 0-8478-0087-3 pbk. : 10.00
1. Architecture, Modern—20th century. 2. Communication in architectural design. I. Title. BIP

JENCKS, Charles. 724.9
Modern movements in architecture / Charles Jencks. Harmondsworth ; Baltimore [etc.] : Penguin, 1973. 432 p. : ill., plans ; 20 cm. Includes index. Bibliography: p. 397-398. [NA680.J46 1973b] 75-310406 ISBN 0-14-021534-4 : £1.50
1. Architecture, Modern—20th century. I. Title. BIP

*JENCKS, Charles, 1939- 724.9
Modern movements in architecture. Garden City, N.Y., Anchor Press/Doubleday, 1973. 432 p. illus. 22 cm. Bibliography: p. 397-398. [NA642] 72-86674 ISBN 0-385-02555-6 10.00
1. Architecture, Modern—20th century. I. Title.
Pbk. 4.95. ISBN 0-385-02554-8

JOEDICKE, Jurgen. 724.9
Architecture since 1945; sources and directions. [Translated by J. C. Palmes] New York, Praeger [1969] 179 p. illus., plans. 29 cm. Bibliography: p. 172-176. [NA680.J5713] 68-31523 18.50
1. Architecture, Modern—20th century. I. Title.

JOHNSON, Philip Cortelyou, 1906- 720.924
Architecture 1949-1965. Introd. by Henry-Russell Hitchcock. New York, Holt [1966] 115p. illus. (pt. col.) plans. 29cm. Bibl. [NA737.J6A42] 66-13559 15.00
I. Hitchcock, Henry Russell, 1903- II. Title.

JOHNSON, Philip Cortelyou, 1906- 720.924
Architecture 1949-1965 [by] Philip Johnson. Introd. by Henry Russell Hitchcock. [1st ed.] New York, Holt, Rinehart and Winston [1966] 115 p. illus. (part col.) plans. 29 cm. "Writings by Philip Johnson": p. 30-31. "Works about Philip Johnson": p. 32-33. [NA737.J6A42] 66-13559
I. Hitchcock, Henry Russell, 1903- II. Title.

KULSKI, Julian Eugene, 1929- 724.9
Architecture in a revolutionary era. Nashville, Tenn., Aurora [1971] 303 p. illus. (part col.) 32 cm. [NA680.K78] 70-114779 ISBN 0-87695-016-0 30.00
1. Architecture, Modern—20th century. I. Title.

KULTERMANN, Udo. 724.9
New architecture in the world / Udo Kultermann. Rev. and updated ed. Boulder, Colo. : Westview Press, 1976. xxix, 144 p. : chiefly ill. ; 28 cm. Translation of Neues Bauen in der Welt. [NA680.K8213 1976] 76-17545 ISBN 0-89158-621-0 : 27.50
1. Architecture, Modern—20th century. I. Title.

RICHARDS, James Maude, Sir. 724.9
A critic's view [by] J. M. Richards. Melbourne, Royal Australian Institute of Architects, 1971] [53] p. illus. 23 cm. (Architecture in the seventies, 1) [NA680.R49] 77-153842 ISBN 0-909825-00-9
1. Architecture, Modern—20th century. 2. Harmony (Aesthetics) 3. Cities and towns—Planning—1945- I. Title. II. Series. III. The Melbourne architectural papers

SCULLY, Vincent Joseph, 1920- 724.9
Modern architecture; the architecture of democracy. New York, G. Braziller, 1961. 128 p. illus., plans. 26 cm. (The Great ages of world architecture) "Bibliographical note": p. 113-114. Bibliographical references included in "Notes" (p. 115-121) [NA680.S395] 61-13689
1. Architecture, Modern—20th century. I. Title. II. Series. BIP

SCULLY, Vincent Joseph, 1920- 724.9
Modern architecture; the architecture of democracy, by Vincent Scully, Jr. Rev. ed. New York, G. Braziller [1974] ix, 158 p. illus. 26 cm. (The Great ages of world architecture) Includes bibliographical references. [NA680.S395 1974] 74-157053 ISBN 0-8076-0159-4 8.95
1. Architecture, Modern—20th century. I. Title. II. Series.

SHARP, Dennis. 724.9
A visual history of twentieth-century architecture. [Greenwich, Conn.] New York Graphic Society [1972] 304 p. illus. (part col.) 32 cm. Bibliography: p. 10. [NA680.S52 1972b] 78-177906 ISBN 0-8212-0425-4 27.50
1. Architecture, Modern—20th century. I. Title. II. Title: Twentieth-century architecture. BIP

SIEGEL, Curt, 1911- 724.9
Structure and form in modern architecture. Translated by Thomas E. Burton. Huntington, N.Y., R. E. Krieger Pub. Co., 1975 [c1962] 308 p. illus. 27 cm. Reprint of the ed. published by Reinhold, New York. Translation of Strukturformen der modernen Architektur. Includes bibliographical references. [NA680.S533 1975] 74-16416 ISBN 0-88275-192-1 22.50
1. Architecture, Modern—20th century. 2. Building. I. Title.

SMITH, C. Ray. 720'.973
Supermannerism : new attitudes in post-modern architecture / C. Ray Smith. 1st ed. New York : Dutton, c1977. xxviii, 354 p., [12] leaves of plates : ill. (some col.) ; 21 cm. Includes index. Bibliography: p. 339-343. [NA680.S56 1977] 76-44664 ISBN 0-525-47424-2 : 9.95
1. Architecture, Modern—20th century. 2. Architecture—Psychological aspects. I. Title. BIP

SMITHSON, Alison Margaret. 724.9
Without rhetoric; an architectural aesthetic, 1955-1972 [by] Alison & Peter Smithson. Cambridge, Mass., M.I.T. Press [1974, c1973] 97 p. illus. 22 cm. [NA680.S59 1974] 73-11737 ISBN 0-262-19119-9 6.95
1. Architecture, Modern—20th century. 2. Form (Aesthetics) 3. Architecture—Details. I. Smithson, Peter, joint author. II. Title. BIP

SOMMER, Robert. 720'.1
Tight spaces; hard architecture and how to humanize it. Englewood Cliffs, N.J., Prentice-Hall [1974] ix, 150 p. illus. 21 cm. (A Spectrum book) Includes bibliographical references. [NA680.S65 1974] 73-21844 ISBN 0-13-921346-5 6.95
1. Architecture, Modern—20th century. 2. Architecture and society. 3. Architecture—Psychological aspects. I. Title.
Pbk. 2.45; ISBN 0-13-921338-4.

VON ECKARDT, Wolf. 724.9
A place to live; the crisis of the cities. Foreword by August Heckscher. New York, Delacorte Press [1968, c1967] xviii, 430 p. illus. 24 cm. "A Seymour Lawrence book." Bibliography: p. 409-414. [NA680.V6] 67-20653
1. Architecture, Modern—20th century. 2. Cities and towns—Planning. I. Title.

WINTER, John. 724.9
Modern buildings. London, New York, Hamlyn, 1969. 4-189 p. illus. (some col.), plans. 23 cm. (Great buildings of the world) Illus. on lining papers. Bibliography: p. 187. [NA680.W53] 71-481974 25/-
1. Architecture, Modern—20th century. I. Title.

Architecture, Modern—20th century—Addresses, essays, lectures.

ARCHIGRAM. 720'.942
Edited by Peter Cook [and others] New York, Praeger Publishers [1973] 144 p. illus. 29 cm. [NA680.A68 1973] 72-92494 12.50
1. Architecture, Modern—20th century—Addresses, essays, lectures. 2. Cities and towns—Planning—1945- —Addresses, essays, lectures. I. Cook, Peter, ed.

BENTON, Timothy, comp. 724.9
Architecture and design, 1890-1939 : an international anthology of original articles / New York : Whitney Library of Design, 1975. xxiii, 252 p., [6] leaves of plates : ill. ; 25 cm. Includes bibliographical references and index. [NA680.B48 1975] 74-30215 ISBN 0-8230-7045-X pbk. : 12.50
1. Architecture, Modern—20th century—Addresses, essays, lectures. 2. Architectural design—Addresses, essays, lectures. I. Benton, Charlotte, joint comp. II. Sharp, Dennis. III. Title.

BLAKE, Peter, 1920- 720
The new forces [by] Peter Blake. Melbourne: Royal Australian Institute of Architects, Victorian Chapter, 1971. [47] p. ill. 23 cm. (Melbourne architectural papers) [NA680.B53] 70-153843 ISBN 0-909825-01-7 1.50
1. Architecture, Modern—20th century—Addresses, essays, lectures. 2. Architecture and society—Addresses, essays, lectures. I. Title. II. Series. III. Architecture in the seventies, 2

CONRADS, Ulrich, comp. 724.9'01
Programs and manifestoes on 20th-century architecture. Translated by Michael Bullock. [1st English language ed.] Cambridge, Mass., MIT Press [1970] 192 p. illus. 22 cm. Translation of Programme und Manifeste zur Architektur des 20. Includes bibliographical references. [NA680.C6213 1970b] 71-143178 ISBN 0-262-03039-X
1. Architecture, Modern—20th century—Addresses, essays, lectures. I. Title. BIP

THE Open hand : 720'.92'4
essays on Le Corbusier / edited by Russell Walden. Cambridge : MIT Press, c1977. xiv, 484 p. : ill. ; 24 cm. Includes bibliographical references and index. [NA1053.J4O63] 76-40046 ISBN 0-262-23074-7 24.95
1. Jeanneret-Gris, Charles Edouard, 1887-1965—Addresses, essays, lectures. 2. Architecture, Modern—20th century—Addresses, essays, lectures. I. Walden, Russell.

Architecture, Modern—20th century—California, Southern.

STRAND, Janann, 1921- 720'.92'2
A Greene & Greene guide. Sketches by Gregory Clond. [Pasadena, Calif., G. Dahlstrom, 1974] ix, 112 p. illus. 22 x 23 cm. Includes bibliographical references. [NA737.G73S87] 74-15804 ISBN 0-9600780-1-0 8.00
1. Greene & Greene. 2. Architecture, Modern—20th century—California, Southern. 3. Architecture—California, Southern—Guide-books. I. Title. BIP

Architecture, Modern—20th century—Collected works.

JOHNSON, Philip Cortelyou, 1906- 724.9
Writings / Philip Johnson ; edited by Robert Stern, Peter Eisenman ; foreword by Vincent Scully. New York : Oxford University Press, 1978. p. cm.

Architecture, Modern—20th century—United States—Exhibitions.

BARBER and McMurry. 720'.6'576885
The architecture of Barber and McMurry, 1915-1940 : an exhibition of photographs and drawings, September 20-October 15, 1976, Dulin Gallery of Art, Knoxville, Tennessee / exhibition organization and catalog text, W. R. McNabb ; design by Ronald Childress. Knoxville : Dulin Gallery of Art, c1976. 92 p. : ill. ; 19 x 27 cm. Includes bibliographical references. [NA737.B25M32] 76-150412
1. Barber and McMurry. 2. Architecture, Modern—20th century—United States—Exhibitions. I. McNabb, W. R. II. Dulin Gallery of Art. III. Title.

Architecture, Modern—Dictionaries.

ENCYCLOPEDIA of modern architecture, edited by Wolfgang Pehnt. 724.903
Contributors: Kyosti Alander [and others] New York, H. N. Abrams [1964] 336 p. illus., plans, ports. 27 cm. Translations from various languages by Harold Meek and others. Bibliography: p. 327. [NA680.E5] 63-14758
1. Architecture, Modern—Dictionaries. I. Pehnt, Wolfgang, ed. BIP

Architecture, Mogul.

MEHTA, Rustam Jehangir. 722'.4
Masterpieces of Indo-Islamic architecture / introd. and notes by Rustam J. Mehta. Bombay : Taraporevala, 1976. viii, 70, 100 p. : chiefly ill. ; 28 cm. Includes bibliographical references. [NA1502.M4] 77-903173 Rs75.00
1. Architecture, Mogul. 2. Architecture, Islamic—India. I. Title.

SARASVATI, Sarasi Kumar. 723.34
Glimpses of Mughal architecture. Introd. with historical analysis by Sir Jadunath Sarkar text by S. K. Saraswati edited, compiled and surveyed by A. Goswami. Published in co-operation with the Govt. of India and the Govt. of West Bengal. New York, G. Wittenborn [1953] xi, 56p. illus., 14 col, plates. 35cm. Bibliographical footnotes. [N7302.S3 1953] 58-799
1. Architecture, Mogul. 2. Decoration and ornament, Mogul. 3. Decoration and ornament, Architectural. I. Goswami, A., ed. II. Title.

Architecture, Mohammedan.

CRESWELL, Keppel Archibald Cameron 723.31
The Muslim architecture of Egypt. [New York, Oxford University Press] 1959 various pages. illus., 2 fold. col. maps. (in pocket) plans 46 cm. Contents.[v.] 2. Ayyubids and Early Bahrite Mamluks, A.D. 1171-1326. 52-2664 80.00
1. Architecture, Mohammedan. 2. Architecture—Egypt. I. Title.

Architecture, Moravian—Bethlehem, Pa.

MURTAGH, William J. 720.9748'22
Moravian architecture and town planning; Bethlehem, Pennsylvania, and other eighteenth-century American settlements, by William J. Murtagh. Chapel Hill, University of North Carolina Press [1967] viii, 145 p. illus., plans. 29 cm. Bibliography: p. 135-139. [NA735.B4M8] 67-26034
1. Architecture, Moravian—Bethlehem, Pa. 2. Architecture, Moravian—United States. I. Title. BIP

Architecture—Moscow.

VOYCE, Arthur. 708'.7
The Moscow Kremlin: its history, architecture, and art treasures. Westport, Conn., Greenwood Press [1971, c1954] xiii, 147 p. illus. 27 cm. Bibliography: p. 139-142. [N6997.M7V6 1971] 74-138135 ISBN 0-8371-5708-0 31.50
1. Moscow. Kremlin. 2. Architecture—Moscow. 3. Art—Moscow. I. Title.

Architecture, Mozarabic.

FERNANDEZ Arenas, Jose. 726'.5'0946
Mozarabic architecture. Greenwich, Conn., New York Graphic Society [1973, c1972] 281 p. illus. (part col.) 28 cm. Text in English, French, Spanish, and German. Bibliography: p. 280-281. [NA1303.F4 1972] 72-87498 ISBN 0-8212-0504-8 37.50
1. Architecture, Mozarabic. I. Title.

Architecture—Nantucket, Mass.

LANCASTER, Clay. 720'.9744'97
The architecture of historic Nantucket. Introd. by James C. Massey. [1st ed.] New York, McGraw-Hill [1972] xxxiii, 286 p. illus. 25 cm. Pages [280]-286, blank for "Notes". Bibliography: p. 263-271. [NA735.N2L3] 72-37747 ISBN 0-07-036120-7
1. Architecture—Nantucket, Mass. 2. Nantucket, Mass.—Historic houses, etc. I. Title.

RAMIREZ, Constance Werner. 720'.9744'97
The historic architecture and urban design of Nantucket. [Washington] Circulated by the Smithsonian Institution [1970] 1 v. (unpaged) illus. 23 cm. [NA735.N2R3] 77-135036
1. Architecture—Nantucket, Mass. 2. Cities and towns—Planning—Nantucket, Mass. I. Smithsonian Institution. II. Title.

Architecture—Nepal—Kathmandu Valley.

KORN, Wolfgang. 954'.008 s
The traditional architecture of the Kathmandu valley / Wolfgang Korn. 1. Aufl. Krefeld, Gustav-Wilhelm-Str. 47 : W. Korn (Selbstverl.], 1976. xix, 125 p. : ill., graph. ; 27 cm. (Bibliotheca Himalayica : Ser. 3 ; v. 11) Imprint from label mounted on t.p. Includes index. Bibliography: p. 115-116. [DS485.H6B52 Ser. 3, vol. 11] [NA1510.8.N42] 720'.951'5 77-375059
1. Architecture—Nepal—Kathmandu Valley. 2. Kathmandu Valley—Buildings. 3. Architecture—Details. I. Title. II. Series. BIP

Architecture—Nevada—Las Vegas.

VENTURI, Robert. 720'.9793'13
Learning from Las Vegas : the forgotten symbolism of architectural form / Robert Venturi, Denise Scott Brown, Steven Izenour. Cambridge, Mass. : MIT Press, c1977 xvii, 192 p. : ill. ; 24 cm. Bibliography: p. [167]-189. [NA735.L3V4 1977] 77-1917 pbk. : 9.95
1. Architecture—Nevada—Las Vegas. 2. Symbolism in architecture. I. Scott Brown, Denise, 1931- joint author. II. Izenour, Steven, joint author. III. Title.

Architecture—New England.

ANDREWS, Wayne. 720'.974
Architecture in New England; a photographic history. Brattleboro, Vt., S. Greene Press [1973] vi, 202 p. (chiefly illus.) 32 cm. Bibliography: p. 199-200. [NA715.A83] 72-91797 ISBN 0-8289-0178-3 16.95
1. Architecture—New England. I. Title. BIP

BRUCE, Curt. 720'.974
Revelations of New England architecture : people and their buildings / photos. by Curt Bruce ; text by Jill Grossman. New York : Grossman Publishers, 1975. p. cm. Includes index. Bibliography: p. [NA715.B78] 75-14354 ISBN 0-670-59615-9 : 15.00
1. Architecture—New England. 2. Architecture and society—New England. 3. New England—Social life and customs. I. Grossman, Jill, 1939- II. Title. BIP

Architecture—New Haven.

HISTORIC American Buildings Survey. 720'.9746'8
New Haven architecture. Washington, 1970. v, 159 l. illus., maps, plans. 28 cm. (Its Selections, no. 9) Includes bibliographical references. [NA705.A25 no. 9] 73-608429
1. Architecture—New Haven. I. Title. II. Series.

METZ, Don. 720'.9746'8
New architecture in New Haven. Rev. ed. Cambridge, MIT Press [1973] 88 p. illus. 19 cm. [NA735.N39M4 1973] 72-5839 3.95 (pbk.)
1. Architecture—New Haven. 2. Architecture, Modern—20th century—New Haven. I. Title.

METZ, Don. 720.97468
New architecture in New Haven. Text: Don Metz. Photos.: Yuji Noga. Cambridge, M.I.T. Press [1966] 80 p. illus., maps, plans. 20 cm. [NA735.N39M4] 66-26015
1. Architecture—New Haven. 2. Architecture—Designs and plans. I. Noga, Yuji, illus. II. Title. BIP

Architecture—New Haven—Guide-books.

KELLEY, Brooks Mather. 917.46'8
New Haven heritage; an area of historic houses on Hillhouse Avenue and Trumbull Street. [New Haven] New Haven Preservation Trust, 1974. 59 p. illus. 27 cm. Errata slip inserted. Bibliography: p. 59. [NA735.N39K44] 74-173517
1. Architecture—New Haven—Guide-books. 2. New Haven—Dwellings. 3. New Haven—Streets—Hillhouse Avenue. 4. New Haven—Streets—Trumbull Street. I. Title.

Architecture—New Jersey.

DE LAGERBERG, Lars. 720.9749
New Jersey architecture, colonial & federal. [1st ed.] Springfield, Mass., Priv. print. by W. Whittum, 1956. 1v. (various pagings, chiefly illus. (part col.)) maps. 30cm. [NA730.N36D4] 57-1134
1. Architecture—New Jersey. 2. Architecture, Colonial. I. Title.

Architecture — New Jersey — Hist.

GOWANS, Alan. 720.9749
Architecture in New Jersey, a record of American civilization. Princeton, N.J., Van Nostrand, 1964. xiii, 161 p. illus., col. maps (on lining papers) 22 cm. (The New Jersey historical series, v. 6) "Bibliographical note": p. 153-155. [NA730.N36G6] 64-7134
1. Architecture — New Jersey — Hist. I. Title. II. Series.

Architecture—New Mexico.

LAZAR, Arthur. 720'.9789
Of earth and timbers made; New Mexico architecture [Text by] Bainbridge Bunting. Photos. by Arthur LaZar. [1st ed.] Albuquerque, University of New Mexico Press [1974] vii, 85 p. illus. 28 cm. [NA730.N38L39] 73-91766 ISBN 0-8263-0318-8 6.95
1. Architecture—New Mexico. 2. Decoration and ornament, Architectural—New Mexico. I. Bunting, Bainbridge. II. Title.

Architecture—New Mexico—History.

BUNTING, Bainbridge. 720.9789
Early architecture in New Mexico / Bainbridge Bunting. 1st ed. Albuquerque : University of New Mexico Press, c1976. p. cm. Includes index. Bibliography: p. [NA730.N38B86] 76-21511 ISBN 0-8263-0424-9 : 12.95. ISBN 0-8263-0435-4 pbk. : 6.95
1. Architecture—New Mexico—History. I. Title. BIP

Architecture—New Orleans—Conservation and restoration.

LEMANN, Bernard, 1905- 720.9763'35
The Vieux Carre—a general statement. With a foreword by John W. Lawrence. New Orleans, School of Architecture, Tulane University [1966] 91 p. illus. 26 cm. [NA735.N414] 720.973 78-294654
1. New Orleans. Vieux Carre. 2. Architecture—New Orleans—Conservation and restoration. I. Title.

Architecture—New York (City)

AMERICAN Institute of Architects. New York Chapter. 917.47'2
AIA guide to New York City. Norval White, Elliot Willensky, editors. New York, Macmillan [1968] xii, 464 p. illus., maps, port. 26 cm. [NA735.N5A78 1968] 68-58489 6.95
1. Architecture—New York (City) 2. New York (City)—Description—1951- —Guide-books. I. White, Norval, ed. II. Willensky, Elliot, ed. III. Title. IV. Title: Guide to New York City. BIP

BURNHAM, Alan, ed. 720.97471
New York landmarks; a study & index of architecturally notable structures in greater New York. [1st ed.] Middletown, Conn., Published under the auspices of the Municipal Art Society of New York by the Wesleyan University Press [1963] xiv, 430 p. illus. 29 cm. Bibliography: p. 391-412. [NA735.N5B8] 63-17794
1. Architecture — New York (City) 2. New York (City) — Descr. — Views. I. Municipal Art Society of New York. II. Title. BIP

GAYLE, Margot. 721'.0447'1
Cast-iron architecture in New York : a photographic survey / text by Margot Gayle ; photos. by Edmund V. Gillon, Jr. New York : Dover Publications, 1974. xviii, 190 p. : ill. ; 26 cm. Includes indexes. [NA735.N5G39 1974] 74-78493 ISBN 0-486-22980-7 : 6.00
1. Architecture—New York (City) 2. Building, Iron and steel. 3. Cast-iron. I. Gillon, Edmund Vincent, illus. II. Title. BIP

HISTORIC American Buildings Survey. 720'.97471
New York city architecture. Washington, 1969. iv, 96 l. illus. 26 cm. (Its Selections, no. 7) Includes bibliographies. [NA705.A25 no. 7] 73-604028
1. Architecture—New York (City) 2. New York (City)—Historic houses, etc. I. Title. II. Series.

HUXTABLE, Ada Louise 720.97471
The architecture of New York; a history and guide [v.1] Garden City, N.Y., Doubleday [c.]1964. 142p. illus. 19cm. Contents.v.1. Classic New York: Georgian gentility to Greek elegance. (Anchor bks., A427d) Bibl. 64-22328 1.95 pap.,
1. Architecture—New York (City) 2. New York (City)—Buildings. 3. New York (City)—Descr.—Guide-books. I. Title.

HUXTABLE, Ada Louise. 720.973
Four walking tours of modern architecture in New York City. [New York] Museum of Modern Art; distributed by Doubleday, Garden City, N. Y. [c1961] 76p. illus. 18cm. [NA735.N5H8] 61-11270
1. Architecture—New York (City) 2. Architecture, Modern—i0th cent. New York. Museum of Modern Art. I. Title.

JACKSON, Huson. 720.97471
New York architecture, 1650-1952. Cover photo: J. Alex Langley. New York, Reinhold [1952] 72 p. illus. 22 cm. [NA735.N5J3] 52-3544
1. Architecture—New York (City) I. Title.

KOOLHAAS, Rem. 720'.9747'1
Delirious New York : a retroactive manifesto for Manhattan / Rem Koolhaas. New York : Oxford University Press, 1978. p. cm. [NA735.N5K66] 77-17418 ISBN 0-19-520035-7 : 20.00
1. Architecture—New York (City) I. Title.

Architecture—New York (City)—Guide-books.

AMERICAN Institute of Architects. New York Chapter. 917.47'1'044
AIA guide to New York City / Norval White, Elliot Willensky, [editors]. Rev. ed. New York : Macmillan, 1978. xv, 653 p. : ill. ; 26 cm. At head of title: New York Chapter, American Institute of Architects. Includes index. [NA735.N5A78 1978] 77-

Architecture—Outlines, syllabi, etc.

GLOAG, John, 1896- 720
Enjoying architecture. [Newcastle upon Tyne] Oriel Press [1965] 96p. illus., plans. 18cm. (Oriel guides) Bibl. [NA2530.G5] 66-5300 3.25
1. Architecture—Outlines, syllabi, etc. I. Title.
Available from Dufour in Chester Springs, Pa. BIP

MANSBRIDGE, John. 720'.9
Graphic history of architecture. New York, Viking Press [1967] 192 p. illus. 31 cm. (A Studio book) [N5305.M285 1967] 67-7827
1. Architecture—Outlines, syllabi, etc. I. Title.

Architecture—Oxfordshire, Eng.

SHERWOOD, Jennifer. 914.25'7'04857
Oxfordshire / by Jennifer Sherwood and Nikolaus Pevsner. Harmondsworth : Penguin, 1974. 936 p., [80] p. of plates : ill., maps ; 19 cm. (The Buildings of England) Includes index. [NA969.O9S44] 75-324606 ISBN 0-14-071045-0 : £5.00
1. Architecture—Oxfordshire, Eng. I. Pevsner, Nikolaus, Sir, 1902- joint author. II. Title.

Architecture—Palestine.

CANAAN, Gershon. 720
Rebuilding the land of Isreal. New York, Architectural Book Pub. Co., 1954. xv, 205p. illus., maps. 28cm. Bibliography: p. 199-201. [NA1477.C3] 54-8203
1. Architecture—Palestine. I. Title.

Architecture—Palm Beach, Fla.

HOFFSTOT, Barbara D. 720'.9759'32
Landmark architecture of Palm Beach / by Barbara D. Hoffstot ; with an introd. by Arthur P. Ziegler, Jr. Pittsburgh : Ober Park Associates, c1974. 227 p. : ill. ; 22 cm. [NA735.P35H64] 73-94010 10.00
1. Architecture—Palm Beach, Fla. I. Title.

Architecture—Paris—Exhibitions.

GUIMARD, Hector, 1867-1942. 720'.92'4
Hector Guimard : Architektur in Paris um 1900 : Museum Villa Stuck, Munchen, 27. Mai-17. August 1975 / [Ausstellung und Katalog, Yvonne Brunhammer, Klaus Bussmann, Roswitha Kock ; Ubersetzungen, Susanne Schmidt]. Munster : Landesmuseum fur Kunst und Kulturgeschichte, [1975?] 139 p., [7] leaves of plates : ill. ; 23 cm. Introductory essay by Yvonne Brunhammer in French and German. Bibliography: p. 122-128. [NA1053.G8B78] 75-521089
1. Guimard, Hector, 1867-1942. 2. Architecture—Paris—Exhibitions. 3. Decoration and ornament—Art nouveau—Exhibitions. I. Brunhammer, Yvonne. II. Bussmann, Klaus. III. Kock, Roswitha. IV. Stuck-Villa (Museum) V. Landesmuseum fur Kunst- und Kulturgeschichte Munster.

Architecture—Parkersburg, W. Va.

HERITAGE & horizons. 720'.9754'23
[Parkersburg, W. Va., Printed by Pappas Bros., c1972] 53 p. illus. (part col.) 28 cm. Cover title. Compilation of pictures and data selected from the exhibit which was arranged and sponsored by the Parkersburg Art Center and the West Virginia Arts and Humanities Council in 1971. [NA735.P37H47] 73-176018
1. Architecture—Parkersburg, W. Va. I. Parkersburg Art Center. II. West Virginia Arts and Humanities Council.

Architecture—Pennsylvania.

DICKSON, Harold Edward, 1900- 720.9748
A hundred Pennsylvania buildings. State College, Pa., Bald Eagle Press [1954] 1v. (unpaged) illus. 29cm. [NA730.P4D5] 54-12829
1. Architecture—Pennsylvania. I. Title.

RICHMAN, Irwin. 720'.9748
Pennsylvania's architecture. University Park, Pennsylvania Historical Association, 1969. iii, 63 p. illus. 23 cm. (Pennsylvania history studies, no. 10) [NA730.P4R5] 72-23534
1. Architecture—Pennsylvania. I. Title. II. Series.

STOTZ, Charles Morse 720.9748
The architectural heritage of early western Pennsylvania; a record of building before 1806. [Pittsburgh] Univ. of Pittsburgh Pr. [1966] xix, 293p. illus., map, plans. 35cm. Orig. pub. in 1936 under title: The early architecture of western Pennsylvania. Bibl. [NA730.P4S75 1966] 67-64 17.50
1. Architecture—Pennsylvania. I. Title.

Architecture—Pennsylvania—Huntingdon.

SHEDD, Nancy S. 720'.9748'73
An architectural study of the ancient Borough of Huntingdon / by Nancy S. Shedd. [s.l. : s.n.], c1976 (Huntingdon, Pa. : J. S. Rodgers Co.) 133 p. : ill. ; 29 cm. [NA730.P4S47] 77-357308
1. Architecture—Pennsylvania—Huntingdon. 2. Huntingdon, Pa.—History. I. Title.

Architecture—Pennsylvania—Lower Merion Township.

DOEBLEY, Carl. 720'.9748'12
Lower Merion, a portrait : from the Welsh tract to the present / by Carl E. Doebley ; edited by Phyllis C. Maier. 1st ed. [Lower Merion, Pa.] : Lower Merion Historical Society, 1976. 66 p., [4] leaves of plates : ill. ; 23 cm. Includes bibliographical references and index. [NA730.P42L683] 76-46768
1. Architecture—Pennsylvania—Lower Merion Township. I. Lower Merion Historical Society.

Architecture—Period.

GEORGIA. Institute of Technology, Atlanta. Dept. of Architecture. 720'.9773'11
Annual review. Atlanta. v. illus. 23 cm. Issued as Bulletin of the Georgia Institute of Technology. Issued 19 by the dept. under the institute's earlier name: Georgia School of Technology. [NA2300.G5] 51-39654
I. Title.

PERSPECTA; 720.5
the Yale architectural journal. [no.] 1-1952- New Haven. no.in v. illus. (part col.) diagrs. 30cm. Published by the students in the Schools of Architecture and Design, Yale University. [NA1.P46] 56-28005
1. Architecture—Period. I. Yale University. School of Architecture. II. Yale University. School of Design.

*SOCIETY of Architectural Historians 720.906
Journal; v.1-4 1941-1944. New York, Johnson Reprint, 1966. 4v. (various p.) 28cm. v.1-2, ea., pap., 15.00; v.3-4, ea., pap., 12.50
I. Title.

ZODIAC 5; 720.5
international magazine of contemporary architecture [New York, Wittenborn, 1960] 213p. [In French, English, Italian, German and Spanish] illus. (part col.) diagrs. 27cm. 58-1990 9.00 pap.,
1. Architecture—Period. I. Association pour la diffusion artistique et culturelle.

ZODIAC 6, 720.5
international magazine of contemporary architecture. [Bruxelles, Editions de la Connaissance; issued under the auspices of the A.D.A.C.; New York, G. Wittenborn, 1960] various pages illus., diagrs. 27cm. French, English, Italian, German. 58-1990 8.50 pap.,
1. Architecture—Period. I. Association pour la Diffusion Artistique et Culturelle.

ZODIAC 7. 709.94
International magazine of contemporary architecture. [New York, G. Wittenborn, 1961] 219p. Bibl. (part col.) 27cm. 9.00, pap., bxd.

Architecture—Period.—Catalogs.

COLUMBIA University. Libraries. Avery Architectural Library. 016.720'5
Avery index to architectural periodicals. Boston, G. K. Hall. 1963. 12 v. 37 cm. [Z5945.C649] 68-51892
1. Architecture—Period.—Catalogs. I. Title.

Architecture—Period.—Indexes.

THE Architectural index. 016.7205
[Denver] v. 23 cm. annual. Editor: 19 E. J. Bell. [Z5941.A66] 51-33537
1. Architecture—Period.—Indexes. I. Bell, Ervin J. ed.

COLUMBIA University. Libraries. Avery Architectural Library. 016.72
Avery index to architectural periodicals. 2d ed., rev. and enl. Boston, G. K. Hall, 1973- v. 37 cm. [Z5945.C653 1973] 74-152756 ISBN 0-8161-1070-0 1235.00 (15 vols.)
1. Architecture—Periodicals—Indexes. I. Title.

Architecture—Peru—History.

WETHEY, Harold Edwin. 720'.985
Colonial architecture and sculpture in Peru [by] Harold E. Wethey. Westport, Conn., Greenwood Press [1971, c1949] xvii, 330 p. 367 illus., map. 26 cm. Bibliography: p. 281-286. [N6713.W48 1971] 73-97337 ISBN 0-8371-4080-3
1. Architecture—Peru—History. 2. Sculpture—Peru—History. I. Title. BIP

Architecture—Philadelphia.

AMERICAN Institute of Architects. Philadelphia Chapter. 720.974811
Philadelphia architecture. New York, Reinhold Pub. Corp. [c.1961] 75p. illus. 14x22cm. 61-10817 2.00 pap.,
1. Architecture—Philadelphia. I. Title.

PHILADELPHIA Art Alliance. 720.9748
Philadelphia architecture in the nineteenth century [by] Theo B. White, editor, William P. Harbeson [and others] Philadelphia, Published for the Philadelphia Art Alliance by the University of Pennsylvania Press, 1953. 36, [86] p. (chiefly illus., plans) 32cm. 'A catalogue of the best examples of the exhibition held in the... galleries of the Art Alliance in May and June of 1953.' [NA735.P5P5] 53-7853
1. Architecture—Philadelphia. 2. Architecture—Exhibitions. I. White, Theophilus Ballou, 1902- ed. II. Title. BIP

Architecture—Philadelphia—Catalogs.

PHILADELPHIA Art Alliance. 720'.9748'11
Philadelphia architecture in the nineteenth century. Theo B. White, editor. [By] William P. Harbeson [and others] 2d rev. ed. Philadelphia, Art Alliance Press [1973] 36, [86] p. illus. 32 cm. A catalogue of the best examples of the exhibition held in the galleries of the Art Alliance in May and June of 1953. [NA735.P5P5 1973] 72-7854 ISBN 0-87982-005-5 10.00
1. Architecture—Philadelphia—Catalogs. 2. Architecture, Modern—19th century—Philadelphia. I. Harbeson, William Page, 1892- II. White, Theophilus Ballou, 1902- ed. III. Title.
Publisher's address: 251 South Eighteenth Street, Philadelphia, PA 19103.

Architecture—Philadelphia—Guide-books.

TEITELMAN, Edward. 917.48'11'044
Architecture in Philadelphia; a guide [by] Edward Teitelman [and] Richard W. Longstreth. Special consultant: George E. Thomas. Cambridge, Mass., MIT Press [1974] xviii, 284 p. illus. 19 x 21 cm. Bibliography: p. 256-263. [NA735.P5T44] 74-6070 ISBN 0-262-20028-7
1. Architecture—Philadelphia—Guide-books. I. Longstreth, Richard W., joint author. II. Title. BIP

Architecture—Philadelphia—Hist.

TATUM, George B. 720.974811
Penn's great town; 250 years of Philadelphia architecture illustrated in prints and drawings. Foreword by Theo. B. White. [Sponsors]: The Philadelphia Art Alliance and the College of Fellows of the American Institutes of Architects. Philadelphia, Univ. of Pennsylvania Press [c.1961] 352p. plates, map. 32cm. Bibl. 61-5546 12.50
1. Architecture—Philadelphia—Hist. 2. Philadelphia—Historic houses, etc. I. Title.

TATUM, George B 720.974811
Penn's great town;250 years of Philadelphia architecture illustrated in prints and drawings. Foreword by Theo. B. White. [Sponsors]: The Philadelphia Art Alliance and the College of Fellows of the American Institute of Architects. Philadelphia, University of Pennsylvania Press [1961] 352 p. plates, map. 32 cm. Bibliography: p. 337-340. [NA735.P5T3] 61-5546
1. Architecture — Philadelphia — Hist. 2. Philadelphia — Historic houses, etc. I. Title.

Architecture—Pictorial works.

MILLON, Henry A., ed. 720.9
Key monuments of the history of architecture. Text ed. Englewood Cliffs, N.J., Prentice-Hall [1964] 536 p. illus., maps, plans. 26 cm. Errata slip inserted. [NA202.M5] 64-10764
1. Architecture—Pictorial works. I. Title.

MILLON, Henry A., ed. 720.9
Key monuments of the history of architecture. Essays by Alfred Frazer. New York, Abrams [1965] 536, cxviii p. illus., maps, plans. 26cm. Essays, glossary, and a ser. of explanatory diagrams of basic structural systems are interspersed with separate paging [NA202.M5] 65-15146 17.50
1. Architecture—Pictorial works. 2. Architecture—Hist. I. Frazer, Alfred. II. Title.

REID, Richard. 720'.9
Picture panorama of world building / Richard Reid. London : Owlet Books, 1977. 264 p. : ill. ; 26 cm. Label mounted on t.p.: Transatlantic Arts, Inc., sole distributor for the U.S.A. [NA202.R44] 78-317487 ISBN 0-263-06307-0 : 15.00
1. Architecture—Pictorial works. I. Title. BIP

Architecture—Piedmont.

POMMER, Richard. 720'.9'451
Eighteenth-century architecture in Piedmont; the open structures of Juvarra, Alfieri & Vittone. New York, New York University Press, 1967. xvii, 300 p. illus., plans (1 fold.) 31 cm. Based on the author's thesis, New York University. Includes bibliographies. [NA1122.P6] 67-10331
1. Juvarra, Filippo, 1678-1736. 2. Alfieri, Benedetto, Conte, 1700-1767. 3. Vittone, Bernardo Antonio, 1702-1770. 4. Architecture—Piedmont. I. Title.

Architecture—Poland—History.

KNOX, Brian. 720'.9438
The architecture of Poland. New York, Praeger [1971] 161, [121] p. 216 illus., geneal. table, maps, plans. 26 cm. Bibliography: p. [152]-155. [NA1455.P6K55 1971] 76-107219 18.50
1. Architecture—Poland—History. I. Title.

Architecture—Port Townsend, Wash.

SIMPSON, Jerry, 1934- 720.979798
Victorian Port Townsend. Photos., drawings, text by Jerry Simpson. Port Townsend, Wash., c1961. 1 v. (unpaged) illus. 23 cm. [NA735.P6S5] 61-14068
1. Architecture—Port Townsend, Wash. I. Title.

Architecture, Renaissance—Rome (City)

PORTOGHESI, Paolo. 720'.945'632
Rome of the Renaissance; translated [from the Italian] by Pearl Sanders. London, Phaidon, 1972. 450 p. illus., facsims., plans. 29 cm. Translation of Roma del Rinascimento. Distributed in the USA by Praeger Publishers, New York, N.Y. Bibliography: p. 434-437. [NA1121.R6P613] 73-138246 ISBN 0-7148-1419-9
1. Architecture, Renaissance—Rome (City) 2. Architecture—Rome (City) I. Title.

Architecture, Renaissance—Spain.

PRENTICE, Andrew Noble. 720'.946
Renaissance architecture and ornament in Spain. Arquitectura y ornamentacion del Renacimiento en Espana. A series of examples selected from the purest works executed between the years 1500-1560, measured and drawn together with short descriptive text. New ed. with introd. and additional illus. by Harold W. Booton. [1st American ed.] New York, Transatlantic Arts, 1970. 63 p. illus., map, plates. 29 cm. Originally published in 1893. [NA565.P8 1970] 78-94643 ISBN 0-693-01144-0
1. Architecture, Renaissance—Spain. 2. Architecture—Spain. I. Booton, Harold W., ed. II. Title. III. Title: Arquitectura y ornamentacion del Renacimiento en Espana. BIP

Architecture, Renaissance—Venice.

HOWARD, Deborah. 720'.92'4
Jacopo Sansovino : architecture and patronage in Renaissance Venice / Deborah Howard. New Haven : Yale University Press, 1975. xi, 194 p. : ill. ; 26 cm. Includes index. Bibliography: p. 187-188. [NA1123.T3H68] 75-8441 ISBN 0-300-01891-6 : 18.50
1. Tatti, Jacopo, 1486-1570. 2. Architecture, Renaissance—Venice. 3. Art patronage—Venice.

Architecture—Rhode Island.

HITCHCOCK, Henry Russell, 1903- 720'.9745
Rhode Island architecture. With a new foreword by the author. New York, Da Capo Press, 1968. ix, 69 p., 81 plates. plans. 25 cm. (Da Capo Press series in architecture and decorative art, vol. 19) "Unabridged republication of the first edition published in 1939." [NA730.R5H5 1968] 68-27725 15.00
1. Architecture—Rhode Island. 2. Rhode Island—Historic houses, etc. I. Title. BIP

Architecture, Roman.

BOETHIUS, Axel 722.7
The golden house of Nero; some aspects of Roman architecture. Ann Arbor, University of Michigan Press [c.1960] 195p. (Jerome lectures, 5th ser.) (Bibl. footnotes) illus., plans 29cm. 57-9137 15.00
1. Architecture, Roman. 2. Cities and towns—Planning—Rome. 3. Cities and towns. Ancient. 4. Rome (City) Domus Aurea. I. Title. II. Series.

BOETHIUS, Axel, 1889- 722.7
The golden house of Nero; some aspects of Roman architecture. Ann Arbor, University of Michigan Press [1960] 195p. illus. 29cm. (Jerome lectures, 5th ser.) Bibliographical footnotes. [NA310.B6] 57-9137
1. Architecture, Roman. 2. Cities and towns—Planning—Rome. 3. Cities and towns, Ancient. 4. Rome (City) Domus Aurea. I. Title. II. Series.

BROWN, Frank Edward, 1908- 722.7
Roman architecture. New York, G. Braziller, 1961. 125 p. 100 illus. 26 cm. (The Great ages of world architecture) Bibliography: p. 113-117. [NA310.B75] 61-13688
1. Architecture, Roman. I. Title. II. Series. BIP

CHARLES-PICARD, Gilbert. 724'.22
Living architecture: Roman. Text by Gilbert Picard. Photos. by Yvan Butler. Pref. by Paolo Portoghesi. New York, Grosset & Dunlap [c1965] 192 p. illus., map, plans. 22 cm. (Living architecture) Cover title: Roman architecture. Translation of Empire romain. Bibliography: p. 180-190. [NA260.C513 1965] 66-25711
1. Architecture, Roman. I. Butler, Yvan. II. Title. III. Title: Roman architecture.

RIVOIRA, Giovanni Teresio, 1849-1919. 722'.7
Roman architecture and its principles of construction under the Empire, with an appendix on the evolution of the dome up to the XVIIth century. Translated from the Italian by G. McN. Rushforth. New York, Hacker Arts Books, 1972. xxvi, 310 p. illus. 31 cm. Reprint of the 1925 ed. Translation of Architettura romana. Includes bibliographical references. [NA310.R52 1972] 78-147038 ISBN 0-87817-095-2 50.00
1. Architecture, Roman. 2. Rome—Antiquities. 3. Domes—Rome. I. Title.

SMITH, Earl Baldwin, 1888-1956. 722.6 722.7
Architectural symbolism of imperial Rome and the Middle Ages. Princeton. Princeton University Press, 1956. ix, 219 p. 175 illus. 31 cm. (Princeton monographs in art and archaeology, 30) Bibliographical footnotes. [NA310.S6] 56-7636
1. Architecture, Roman. 2. Architecture, Medieval. 3. Symbolism in art. 4. Christian art and symbolism. I. Title. II. Series. BIP

SMITH, Earl Baldwin, 1888-1956. 725'.96'0937
Architectural symbolism of Imperial Rome and the Middle Ages / by E. Baldwin Smith. New York : Hacker Art Books, 1978, c1956. ix, 219 p., [8] leaves of plates : ill. ; 31 cm. Reprint of the ed. published by Princeton University Press, Princeton, which was issued as no. 30 of Princeton monographs in art and archaeology. Includes bibliographical references and index. [NA310.S6 1978] 76-27052 ISBN 0-87817-195-9 lib. bdg. : 40.00
1. Architecture—Rome. 2. Architecture, Roman. 3. Symbolism in architecture—Rome. 4. Architecture, Medieval. 5. Symbolism in architecture—Middle Ages. I. Title. II. Series: Princeton monographs in art and archaeology ; 30.

SWIFT, Emerson Howland, 1889- 723.1
Roman sources of Christian art. New York, Columbia University Press, 1951. xx, 248 p. illus., 48 plates. 31 cm. Bibliography: p. [227]-236. [NA360.S8] 51-11251
1. Architecture, Roman. 2. Architecture, Byzantine. 3. Church decoration and ornament. I. Title.

Architecture, Roman—Hist.

MACDONALD, William Lloyd 722.7
The architecture of the Roman Empire; v.1. New Haven, Conn., Yale [c.]1965 xxi, 211p. illus. (pt. fold.) plans. 29cm. (Yale pubns. in the hist. of art. 17) Contents.v.1. An introductory study. Bibl. [NA310.M2] 65-22333 17.50
1. Architecture, Roman—Hist. I. Title. II. Series.

Architecture, Roman—Leptis Magna, Tripoli.

BIANCHI Bandinelli, Ranuccio, 1900- ed. 913.39'74'03
The buried city; excavations at Leptis Magna. Introd. by Ranuccio Bianchi Bandinelli. Text by Ernesto Vergara Caffarelli and Giacomo Caputo. Photos. by Fabrizio Clerici. New York, F. A. Praeger [1966] 126 p. 256 illus. (part col.) 28 cm. Translation of Leptis Magna. Bibliography: p. 121-122. [NA335.L4B53] 66-12523
1. Architecture, Roman—Leptis Magna, Tripoli. 2. Art—Leptis Magna, Tripoli. I. Vergara Caffarelli, Ernesto, 1907-1961. II. Caputo, Giacomo. III. Clerici, Fabrizio, 1913- illus. IV. Title.

Architecture, Romanesque.

ALLSOPP, Bruce. 723'.4
Romanesque architecture; the Romanesque achievement. New York, John Day Co. [1971] 96 p. illus. (part col.), plans. 25 cm. (The World of architecture) Bibliography: p. 92. [NA390.A4] 76-113423 4.95
1. Architecture, Romanesque. 2. Church architecture. I. Title.

CURSEL, Raymond. 723'.4
Living architecture: Romanesque. Photos. by Jacques Rouiller. Pref. by Herman Baur. New York, Grosset & Dunlap [1967] 192 p. illus., map, plans. 22 cm. (Living architecture) Bibliography: p. 189-190. [NA390.O8 1967b] 67-20410
1. Architecture, Romanesque. I. Title.

KUBACH, Hans Erich, 1909- 723'.4
Romanesque architecture. Translated by Robert Erich Wolf. New York, Abrams [1974] p. cm. (History of world architecture) Translation of Architettura romanica. [NA390.K7913] 73-21549 ISBN 0-8109-1024-1 35.00
1. Architecture, Romanesque. I. Title. BIP

OURSEL, Raymond. 723'.4
Living architecture: Romanesque. Photos. by Jacques Rouiller. Pref. by Herman Baur. New York, Grosset & Dunlap [1967] Bibliography: p. 189-190. [NA390.O8] 67-20410
1. Architecture, Romanesque. I. Title.

Architecture, Romanesque—Great Britain.

STOLL, Robert Thomas, 1919- 723'.4
Architecture and sculpture in early Britain [by] Robert Stoll. With photos. by Jean Roubier. [Translated from the German by J. Maxwell Brownjohn] New York, Viking Press [1967] 356 p. map, plates. 32 cm. Translation of Britannia romanica. Bibliographical references included in "Acknowlegments" (p. 356) [NA963.S813 1967b] 67-7207
1. Architecture, Romanesque—Great Britain. 2. Architecture—Great Britain. I. Roubier, Jean, 1896- illus. II. Title.

Architecture, Romanesque—Spain.

WHITEHILL, Walter Muir, 1905- 720'.946
Spanish Romanesque architecture of the eleventh century. London, Oxford U.P., 1968. xxxiii, 307 p. illus. (part. fold.), 3 fold. maps, plates. 25 cm. Reprint of the Oxford 1941 ed. Bibliography: p. [285]-299. [NA1303.W5 1968] 73-419968 unpriced
1. Architecture, Romanesque—Spain. 2. Architecture, Spanish. I. Title. BIP

Architecture—Rome.

ANDERSON, William James, 1864-1900. 720'.9'376
The architecture of ancient Rome, an account of its historic development, being the second part of The architecture of Greece and Rome, by William J. Anderson and Richard Phene Spiers. Rev. and rewritten by Thomas Ashby. Freeport, N.Y., Books for Libraries Press [1971] xiii, 202 p. illus. 23 cm. Bibliography: p. [175]-179. [NA310.A6 1971] 71-37326 ISBN 0-8369-6675-9
1. Architecture—Rome. I. Spiers, Richard Phene, 1838-1916, joint author. II. Ashby, Thomas, 1874- III. Title.

SCHERER, Margaret Roseman. 722.6
Marvels of ancient Rome. Edited and with a foreword by Charles Rufus Morey. New York, Published by the Phaidon Press for the Metropolitan Museum of Art, 1955. ix, 430p. illus. 26cm. [NA31o.S4] [NA310.S4] 722.7 56-1344 56-1344
1. Architecture—Rome. 2. Rome (City)—Descr.—Views. I. Title.

Architecture—Rome (City)

ELLING, Christian, 1901-1974. 720'.945'632
Rome : the biography of her architecture from Bernini to Thorvaldsen / by Christian Elling. Boulder, Colo. : Westview Press, [1975] p. cm. Translation of Rom. Includes index. Bibliography: p. [NA1120.E5513] 75-23263 ISBN 0-89158-514-1
1. Architecture—Rome (City) I. Title.

HIBBARD, Howard, 1928- 720'.92'4
Carlo Maderno and Roman architecture, 1580-1630. London, Zwemmer, 1971. xvi, 404 p. illus., geneal. tables, plans. 31 cm. (Studies in architecture, v. 10) Sole distributor in the U.S.A.; Pennsylvania State University Press, University Park, Pa. English or Italian. "Catalogue": p. 107-234. Bibliography: p. 380-390. [NA1123.M3H5 1971] 72-195351 ISBN 0-302-02161-2
1. Maderno, Carlo, 1556-1629. 2. Architecture—Rome (City) I. Title.
39.50 BIP

NASH, Ernest 720.94563
Pictorial dictionary of ancient Rome; v.2. New York, Praeger [1962] 531p. illus. 30cm. Contents.v.2 [Lacus Iuturnae--Vocanal.] Bibl. 61-11329 37.50, bxd.
1. Architecture—Rome (City). 2. Architecture, Roman. 3. Art—Rome (City). 4. Art, Roman. 5. Rome (City)—Descr. I. Title.

NASH, Ernest 720.94563
Pictorial dictionary of ancient Rome v.1. New York, Praeger [1961] 544p. illus., plans. 30cm. Contents.v.1. Amphitheatrum Castrense--Lacus Curtius. Bibl. 61-11329 37.50, bxd.
1. Architecture—Rome (City) 2. Architecture, Roman. 3. Art—Rome (City) 4. Art, Roman. 5. Rome (City)—Descr. I. Title.

NASH, Ernest. 722'.7
Pictorial dictionary of ancient Rome. 2d ed., rev. New York, Praeger [1968, c1961] 2 v. illus., plans. 30 cm. Contents.Contents.—v. 1. Amphitheatrum Castrense-Lacus Curtius.—v. 2. Lacus Iuturnae-Volcanal. Includes bibliographies. [NA310.N28 1968] 68-17654
1. Architecture—Rome (City) 2. Architecture, Roman—Pictorial works. I. Title.

PORTOGHESI, Paolo. 720'.924
The Rome of Borromini; architecture as language. Translated by Barbara Luigia La Penta. New York, G. Braziller [1968] viii, 451 p. illus. 29 cm. Cover title: Borromini. Includes bibliographical references. [NA1123.B6P63] 68-25337 25.00
1. Borromini, Francesco, 1599-1667. 2. Architecture—Rome (City) I. Title.

ROMAN rococo 720'.92'2
architecture from Clement XI to Benedict XIV (1700-1758) / Nina A. Mallory. New York : Garland Pub., 1977. xiii, 184 p., [43] leaves of plates : ill. ; 32 cm. (Outstanding dissertations in the fine arts) Reprint of the author's thesis, Columbia University, 1965. Bibliography: p. 180-184. [NA1120.M34 1977] 76-23640 ISBN 0-8240-2710-8 : 32.50
1. Architecture—Rome (City) 2. Architecture, Rococo—Rome (City) I. Series. BIP

Architecture—Roxton, Eng.—Conservation and restoration.

BEDFORDSHIRE, Eng. County Planning Dept. 711'.4'0942565
Roxton conservation Area. Bedford, Bedfordshire County Council Planning Department, 1971. [3], 5 leaves (1 fold.). map. 30 cm. [NA109.G7B42] 72-190566 ISBN 0-901051-43-8
1. Architecture—Roxton, Eng.—Conservation and restoration. I. Title.

Architecture—Russia.

BUXTON, David Roden, 1910- 726'.5'0947
Russian mediaeval architecture : with an account of the Transcaucasian styles and their influence in the West / by David Roden Buxton. New York : Hacker Art Books, 1975. 112 p., [54] leaves of plates : ill., maps ; 27 cm. Reprint of the 1934 ed. published by the University Press, Cambridge, Eng.; with new pref. Includes index. Bibliography: p. 105-107. [NA1183.B8 1975] 73-81682 ISBN 0-87817-005-7 : 30.00
1. Architecture—Russia. 2. Architecture, Medieval—Russia. 3. Architecture—

Transcaucasia. 4. Architecture, Medieval—Transcaucasia. I. Title.

LISITSKII, Lazar' Markovich, 1890-1941. 720'.947
Russia: an architecture for world revolution. Translated by Eric Dluhosch. Cambridge, M.I.T. Press [1970] 239 p. illus., plans, port. 23 cm. Rev. translation of Russland; die Rekonstruktion der Architektur in der Sowjetunion. [NA1188.L513] 70-92782
1. Architecture—Russia. 2. Architecture, Modern—20th century—Russia. I. Title.

SENKEVITCH, Anatole. 720'.947
The evolution of the contemporary idiom; Soviet architecture. [Lubbock? Tex.] 1967. v, 97 l. 28 cm. Bibliography: leaves 95-97. [NA1188.S4] 68-443
1. Architecture—Russia. I. Title.

VOYCE, Arthur. 720'.947
Russian architecture; trends in nationalism and modernism. New York, Greenwood Press [1969, c1948] xxiv, 282 p. illus. 23 cm. Bibliography: p. [xxi] [NA1181.V69 1969] 79-90742
1. Architecture—Russia. I. Title.

Architecture—Russia—1917—

SENKEVITCH, Anatole. 720'.947
The evolution of the contemporary idiom; Soviet architecture. [Lubbock? Tex.] 1967. v. 97 l. 28 cm. Bibliography: leaves 95-97. [NA1188.S4] 68-443
1. Architecture—Russia—1917- I. Title.

Architecture—Russia—Bibliography—Catalogs.

SENKEVITCH, Anatole. 016.72'0947
Soviet architecture, 1917-1962; a bibliographical guide to source material. Charlottesville, University Press of Virginia [1974] xxxii, 284 p. 24 cm. [Z5944.R9S45] 73-75335 ISBN 0-8139-0415-3 13.50
1. Architecture—Russia—Bibliography—Catalogs. 2. Architecture, Modern—20th century—Russia—Catalogs. I. Title. BIP

Architecture—Russia—History.

RUSSIAN Orthodox Youth Committee. 947
Architecture of Russia from old to modern / [editor, Editorial College of the Committee ; photos provided by Committee members ; Russian and English texts composed by members of the Committee]. [New York] : Russian Orthodox Youth Committee, c1973-c1974. 2 v. : ill. (some col.) ; 31 cm. English and Russian. Contents.Contents.—v. 1. Churches and monasteries.—v. 2. Palaces, manors, and churches. Bibliography: v. 1, p. 293-294. [NA1181.R84 1973] 72-82216
1. Architecture—Russia—History. I. Title.

Architecture—Russia, Northern.

FEDOROV, Boris Nikolaevich. 720'.947'2
Architecture of the Russian North, 12th-19th centuries / [compiled and introduced by B. Fiodorov ; foreword by S. Vikulov ; photos. by V. Savik ; translated by N. Johnstone]. Leningrad : Aurora Art Publishers, c1976. 297, [1] p. : 212 col. ill. ; 27 cm. Translation of Zodchestvo russkogo Severa, dvenadtsatyi-deviatnadtsatyi vv. Bibliography: p. 297-[298] [NA1195.N57F413] 76-379032
1. Architecture—Russia, Northern. I. Title.

Architecture—Russian Republic—Moscow.

BERTON, Kathleen. 720'.947'31
Moscow : an architectural history / Kathleen Berton. New York : St. Martin's Press, 1978, c1977. 256 p. : ill. ; 25 cm. Includes index. Bibliography: p. 248-251. [NA1197.M6B42 1978] 77-81890 ISBN 0-312-54888-5 : 16.95
1. Architecture—Russian Republic—Moscow. I. Title. BIP

Architecture—St. Louis.

MCCUE, George 720.977866
The building art in St. Louis: two centuries; a guide to the architecture of the city and its environs Design by Peter Geist. Maps by Edgar Kulla [St. Louis] Sponsored, pub. by St. Louis Chapter, Amer. Inst. of Architects [1964] 96p. illus., maps. 22cm. 64-21898 2.00
1. Architecture—St. Louis. 2. St. Louis—Descr.—Guide-books. I. Title.

MCCUE, George. 720'.9778'66
The building art in St. Louis: two centuries; a guide to the architecture of the city and its environs. Design by Peter Geist. Maps by Edgar Kulla. [Rev. and enl. St. Louis] Sponsored and published by the St. Louis Chapter, American Institute of Architects [1967] 104 p. illus., maps. 22 cm. [NA735.S2M3 1967] 67-30078
1. Architecture—St. Louis. 2. St. Louis—Description—Guide-books. I. Title.

Architecture—San Francisco.

BAIRD, Joseph Armstrong. 720.973
Time's wondrous changes: San Francisco architecture, 1776-1915. With foreword by Susanna Bryant Dakin. San Francisco, California Historical Society, 1962. viii, 67p. illus., 2 maps. 27cm. ([California Historical Society] Special publication 36) Bibliography: p. 64-67. [NA735.S35B3] 62-21821
1. Architecture—San Francisco. I. Title. II. Series.

BRUCE, Curt. 720'.9794'61
The great houses of San Francisco. Photos. by Curt Bruce. Text by Thomas Aidala. [1st ed.] New York, Knopf, 1974. 200, iii p. illus. (part col.) 24 cm. [NA735.S35B78 1974] 73-7287 ISBN 0-394-48380-4 12.95
1. Architecture—San Francisco. 2. San Francisco—Buildings. 3. Decoration and ornament, Architectural—San Francisco. I. Aidala, Thomas. II. Title. BIP

OLMSTED, Roger R., 1928- 720'.9794'6
Here today; San Francisco's architectural heritage. Text by Roger Olmsted and T. H. Watkins. Photos by Morley Baer and others. San Francisco, Chronicle Books [1968] xi, 334 p. illus., maps. 32 cm. On cover: The Historic sites project of the Junior League of San Francisco, inc. Sponsored by the Historic Sites Committee of The Junior League of San Francisco. [NA735.S35O4] 68-57180 14.95
1. Architecture—San Francisco. 2. San Francisco—Buildings. I. Watkins, Tom H., joint author. II. Junior League of San Francisco. Historic Sites Committee. III. Title.

Architecture — San Francisco Bay region.

FREUDENHEIM, Leslie Mandelson, 1941- 720'.9794'6
Building with nature: roots of the San Francisco Bay Region tradition [by] Leslie Mandelson Freudenheim & Elisabeth Sussman. With photos. by Ambur Hiken. Santa Barbara, Calif., P. Smith, 1974. xii, 112 p. illus. 27 cm. Includes bibliographical references. [NA735.S35F73] 74-19328 ISBN 0-87905-021-7
1. Architecture—San Francisco Bay region. 2. Architecture and society—San Francisco Bay region. I. Sussman, Elisabeth Sacks, 1939- joint author. II. Title.

WOODBRIDGE, John Marshall, comp. 720.97946
Buildings of the bay area; a guide to the architecture of the San Francisco Bay region, compiled by John Marshall Woodbridge and Sally Byrne Woodbridge. Sketches by Rai Yukio Okamoto. Designed by Philip Thiel. New York, Grove Press [1960] 1 v. (unpaged) illus., maps. 21 cm. [NA735.S35W6] 60-9359
1. Architecture — San Francisco Bay region. 2. San Francisco Bay region — Descr. & trav. — Guide-books. I. Woodbridge, Sally Byrne, joint comp. II. Title.

Architecture—San Francisco—Guide-books.

A Guide to architecture in San Francisco & northern California [by] David Gebhard [and others] Designed by Marc Treib. Santa Barbara, Peregrine Smith, 1973. 557 p. illus. 26 x 12 cm. Bibliography: p. 544-549. [NA735.S35G83] 73-77784 ISBN 0-87905-010-1 6.95 917.94'04'5
1. Architecture—San Francisco—Guide-books. 2. Architecture—California—Guide-books. I. Gebhard, David. BIP

Architecture—Santa Barbara, Calif.—Guide-books.

ANDREE, Herb, 1942- 979.4'91
Santa Barbara architecture, from Spanish colonial to modern / text by Herb Andree and Noel Young ; photography by Wayne McCall ; foreword by David Gebhard. Santa Barbara, Ca. : Capra Press, 1975. p. cm. Includes index. [NA735.S42A52] 75-32571 ISBN 0-88496-053-6 : 30.00 pbk. : 12.50
1. Architecture—Santa Barbara, Calif.—Guide-books. I. Young, Noel, joint author. II. McCall, Wayne. III. Title.

Architecture—Santa Cruz, Calif.—Guide-books.

CHASE, John, 1953- 917.94'71
The sidewalk companion to Santa Cruz architecture / by John Chase. Santa Cruz, Calif. : Chase : distributed by the Santa Cruz Historical Society, [1975] xvi, 253 p. : ill. ; 22 cm. Includes index. Bibliography: p. 235-239. [NA735.S43C46] 75-308861 5.95
1. Architecture—Santa Cruz, Calif.—Guide-books. I. Title.

Architecture—Scandinavia—Hist.

PAULSSON, Thomas. 720.948
Scandinavian architecture; buildings and society in Denmark, Finland, Norway, and Sweden, from the iron age until today. [1st U. S. ed.] Newton, Mass., C. T. Branford Co. [1959] xvi, 256p. illus., maps. plans. 26cm. Bibliography: p.245-250. [NA1201.P3 1959] 59-6290
1. Architecture—Scandinavia—Hist. 2. Architecture —Finland—Hist. I. Title.

Architecture—Scotland—Hist.

DUNBAR, John G. 720.941
The historic architecture of Scotland [by] John G. Dunbar. London, Batsford, 1966. 268p. illus., maps. plans. 26cm. Bibl. [NA972.D8] 66-75490 25.00
1. Architecture— Scotland—Hist. I. Title. Available from Architectural Book Pub. Co., 151 E. 50th St., New York, N.Y. 10022.

WEST, T W 720'.941
A history of architecture in Scotland [by] T. W. West. New York, D. McKay Co. [1967] 208 p. illus. 23 cm. Bibliography: p. 198-201. [NA972.W4] 68-4021
1. Architecture—Scotland—Hist. I. Title. II. Title: Architecture in Scotland.

Architecture—Scotland—Outlines, syllabi, etc.

HAY, George. 720'.941
Architecture of Scotland. Newcastle upon Tyne, Oriel, 1969. 96 p. illus., maps, plans. 17 cm. (The Oriel guides) [NA972.H35 1969] 68-55975 16/-
1. Architecture—Scotland—Outlines, syllabi, etc. I. Title. BIP

Architecture—Seattle.

STEINBRUECK, Victor. 720
Seattle architecture, 1850-1953. New York, Reinhold [1953] 56 p. illus. 22 cm. [NA735.S45S8] 53-9168
1. Architecture—Seattle. I. Title.

Architecture—Serbia—History.

STEWART, Cecil. 720.94971
Serbian legacy. [1st American ed.] New York, Harcourt, Brace [1960, c1959] 135 p. illus. 25 cm. [NA1441.S7 1960] 59-12929
1. Architecture—Serbia—History. 2. Art—Serbia—History. I. Title.

Architecture, Shaker.

LASSITER, William Lawrence. 728'.09747
Shaker architecture; descriptions with photographs and drawings of Shaker buildings at Mount Lebanon, New York, Watervliet, New York [and] West Pittsfield, Massachusetts. Illustrated by Constantine Kermes. [1st ed.] New York, Vantage Press [1966] 127 p. illus., plans. 26 cm. Bibliography: p. 127. [NA730.N4L3] 66-23098
1. Architecture, Shaker. 2. Architecture—New York (State) 3. Architecture—Designs and plans.

Architecture, Shaker—Catalogs.

HISTORIC American Buildings Survey. 720'.974
Shaker built : a catalog of Shaker architectural records from the Historic American Buildings Survey / John Poppeliers, editor, with the assistance of Deborah Stephens. [Washington] : HABS, 1974. 87 p. : ill. ; 23 cm. Bibliography: p. 5. [NA710.H57 1974] 74-602720
1. Architecture, Shaker—Catalogs. I. Poppeliers, John C., ed. II. Stephens, Deborah, ed. III. Title.

Architecture—Shropshire, Eng.

PEVSNER, Nikolaus, 1902- 720.94245
Shropshire. [Harmondsworth, Middlesex; Baltimore] Penguin Books [1958] 368p. illus. 18cm. (His The buildings of England, 16) [NA969.S45P4] 58-4855
1. Architecture—Shropshire, Eng. I. Title.

Architecture—Sketch-books.

BENJAMIN, Asher, 1773-1845. 721
The American builder's companion; or, A system of architecture particularly adapted to the present style of building. New York, Dover Publications [1969] ix, 114 p. illus., plans. 28 cm. "An unabridged reprint of the 6th ed. [1827], with 70 plates and a new introduction by William Morgan." [NA2610.B4 1969] 68-58318 3.00
1. Architecture—Sketch-books. 2. Decoration and ornament, Architectural. I. Title. BIP

BENJAMIN, Asher, 1773-1845. 720'.28
The American builder's companion; or, A new system of architecture particularly adapted to the present style of building in the United States of America, by Asher Benjamin and Daniel Raynerd. New York, Da Capo Press, 1972. 70 p. 44 plates 27 cm. (The Works of Asher Benjamin, 2) (Da Capo Press series in architecture and decorative art, 14) Reprint of the 1806 ed. [NA2540.B35 1972] 68-18612 ISBN 0-306-71026-9 29.50
1. Architecture—Sketch-books. 2. Decoration and ornament, Architectural. I. Raynerd, Daniel, joint author. II. Title.

COULIN, Claudius. 741.9
Drawings by architects; from the ninth century to the present day. New York, Reinhold Pub. Corp. [1963, c1962] 144 p. (chiefly illus. plans) 33 cm. [NA2600.C6] 62-21998
1. Architecture—Sketch-books. I. Title.

KAHN, Louis I 1901- 741.973
Notebooks and drawings. [Edited and designed by Richard Saul Wurman and Eugene Feldman. 1st ed. Philadelphia, Falcon Press; distributed by Wittenborn, New York, 1962] [83] p. illus., port. 39 cm. [NA2610.K3] 62-22406
1. Architecture — Sketch — books. I. Title.

PILE, John, comp. 720'.223
Drawings of architectural interiors. [New York] Whitney Library of Design [1967] vi, 168 p. illus. (part col.) plans. 25 x 34 cm. [NA2605.P57] 67-25854
1. Architecture—Sketch-books. I. Title. BIP

Architecture—Societies.

LIVERPOOL Architectural Society. 720.6242
Liverpool Architectural Society (incorporated) [Council, list of committees, annual report, etc.] Liverpool. v. illus. 22 cm. [NA12.L84] 50-41297
1. Architecture—Societies. I. Title.

NATIONAL Association of Organizations of Students of Architecture. v. 12
Publication. [Washington?] v. illus., plans. 28cm. Includes 'work from ... schools of architecture ... reproduced in content, format and descriptive information as submitted by student representatives. [NA11.N42] 58-46290
1. Architecture—Societies, etc. I. Title.

SOCIETY of Architectural Historians. 720.9
Annual meeting. [Program] New York?] v. 28cm. [NA11.S574] 53-34196
I. Title.

Architecture—Socorro, N.M.—History.

NIEMAN, Charles L. 917.89'62'03 s
Spanish times and boom times; toward an architectural history of Socorro, New Mexico, by Charles L. Nieman. Edited by John DeWitt McKee and Spencer Wilson. Editorial assistant: Jeannette H. McKee. Figures redrawn by Mark Bolden. Socorro, N.M., Socorro County Historical Society, 1972. viii, 100 p. illus. 23 cm. (Socorro County Historical Society. Publications in history, v. 6) Bibliography: p. 98-100. [F802.S6S65 vol. 6] [NA730] 720'.9789'62 73-174255 3.00
1. Architecture—Socorro, N.M.—History. I. Title. II. Series.

Architecture—Sonora Desert—History.

PARACHEK, Ralph E. 720'.971
Desert architecture, by Ralph E. Parachek. Phoenix, Parr of Arizona [1967] 93 p. illus., maps. plans. 28 cm. Bibliography: p. 93. [NA725.P3] 67-25403
1. Architecture—Sonora Desert—History. I. Title. BIP

Architecture—South Carolina.

MARSH, Blanche 720.9757
Plantation heritage in upcountry, South Carolina. Photos. by Kenneth Frederick Marsh. Text by Blanche Marsh. [Asheville, N.C., Biltmore Pr., 1963] 189p. illus. 26cm. 63-914 apply
1. Architecture—South Carolina. 2. South Carolina—Historic houses, etc. I. Marsh, Kenneth Frederick. II. Title.

MARSH, Blanche. 720'.92'4
Robert Mills; architect in South Carolina. [Columbia, S.C.] R. L. Bryan Co., 1970. xi, 178 p. illus. 28 cm. Bibliography: p. 177-178. [NA737.M5M37] 72-125882
1. Mills, Robert, 1781-1855. 2. Architecture—South Carolina.

Architecture — Southern States.

ANDREWS, Wayne. 720'.975
Pride of the South : a social history of southern architecture / by Wayne Andrews. 1st ed. New York : Atheneum, c1979. p. cm. Includes index. Bibliography: p. [NA720.A5 1979] 78-3214 ISBN 0-689-10931-8 : 9.95
1. Architecture—Southern States. 2. Architecture and society—Southern States. I. Title. BIP

FORMAN, Henry Chandlee, 1904- 720'.975
The architecture of the Old South; the medieval style, 1585-1850. New York, Russell & Russell [1967, c1948] 203 p. illus., plans. 27 cm. Bibliography: p. [187]-191. [NA720.F6 1967] 66-27071
1. Architecture—Southern States. 2. Architecture, Colonial—Southern States. I. Title. BIP

WAUGH, Edward. 720.975
The South builds; new architecture in the Old South, by Edward Waugh and Elizabeth Waugh, with Henry L. Kamphoefner, advisor. Chapel Hill, University of North Carolina Press [1960] 173 p. illus., plans. 29 cm. [NA720.W3] 60-10825
1. Architecture — Southern States. I. Waugh, Elizabeth, joint author. II. Title.

Architecture — Southwest, New.

SANFORD, Trent Elwood, 1897- 720.979
The architecture of the Southwest; Indian, Spanish, American, [1st ed.] New York, Norton [1950] xii, 312 p. illus., maps. 24 cm. [NA720.S3] 50-10641
1. Architecture — Southwest, New. I. Title. BIP

SANFORD, Trent Elwood, 1897- 720'.979
The architecture of the Southwest; Indian, Spanish, American. Westport, Conn., Greenwood Press [1971, c1950] xii, 312 p. illus., maps. 24 cm. [NA720.S3 1971] 76-100242 ISBN 0-8371-4012-9
1. Architecture—Southwest, New. I. Title.

Architecture—Spain—Outlines, syllabi, etc.

BOOTON, Harold W. 720.946
Architecture of Spain, by Harold W. Booton. [Newcastle uponTyne] Oriel Pr. [1966] 96p. illus., maps, plans. 17cm. (Oriel guides) [NA1301.B57] 66-5329 3.25
1. Architecture—Spain—Outlines, syllabi, etc. I. Title. Now available from Dufour, Chester Springs, Pa. BIP

Architecture—Spanish America.

DAMAZ, Paul F. 720.98
Art in Latin American architecture. Pref. by Oscar Niemeyer. New York, Reinhold [c. 1963] 232p. illus. (pt. col.) 27cm. Bibl. 63-11424 15.00
1. Architecture—Spanish America. 2. Art, Spanish American. 3. Art, Modern—20th cent. I. Title.

HITCHCOCK, Henry Russell, 1903- 724.91
Latin American architecture since 1945. New York, Museum of Modern Art [1955] 208p. illus., plans. 25cm. Erratum slip inserted. 'Biographies of architects': p. 196-200. [NA702.H5] 55-12305
1. Architecture—Spanish America. 2. Architecture, Modern—20th cent. 3. Architecture—Designs and plans. I. New York. Museum of Modern Art. II. Title. BIP

Architecture—Spokane.

STAVE, Thomas, 1947- 720'.9797'37
Spokane sketchbook. Drawings and architectural observations by Roland Colliander [and others] Text by Thomas Stave. Seattle, University of Washington Press [1974] 96 p. illus. 23 cm. [NA735.S64S64] 73-22207 ISBN 0-295-95326-8 7.95
1. Architecture—Spokane. 2. Spokane—Description—Views. I. Colliander, Roland, 1939- illus. II. Title. BIP

Architecture—Springfield, Ill.

RUSSO, Edward J. 338.7'61'72
Helmle & Helmle, architects / Edward J. Russo. Srpingfield, Ill. : Sangamon County Historical Society, 1974. vii, 32 p. : ill. ; 22 cm. (Bicentennial studies in Sangamon history) Bibliography: p. 31-32. [NA737.H38R87] 75-305234 1.40
1. Helmle & Helmle. 2. Architecture—Springfield, Ill. I. Title. II. Series.

Architecture—Staffordshire, Eng.

PEVSNER, Nikolaus, Sir, 1902- 914.24'6'04857
Staffordshire / [by] Nikolaus Pevsner. Harmondsworth ; Baltimore [etc.] : Penguin, 1974. 376 p., [64] p. of plates : ill., map, plan ; 19 cm. (The Buildings of England) Includes indexes. [NA971.S72P48] 75-305581 ISBN 0-14-071046-9 : £3.50
1. Architecture—Staffordshire, Eng.

Architecture—Study and teaching.

AGUILAR, Rodolfo J. 720'.18
The mathematical formulation and optimization of architectural and planning functions, by Rodolfo J. Aguilar. Baton Rouge, Division of Engineering Research, Louisiana State University Agricultural and Mechanical College, 1967. 18 l. illus. 28 cm. (Louisiana State University, Agricultural and Mechanical College. Division of Engineering Research. Bulletin no. 93) Cover title. Bibliography: leaf 18. [TA7.L6 no. 93] 67-66181
1. Architecture—Study and teaching. 2. Electronic data processing—Architecture. I. Title. II. Series: Louisiana. State University and Agricultural and Mechanical College. Division of Engineering Research. Engineering research bulletin, no. 93.

DEGER, Stephen C. 720'.7'8
Computer assisted instruction applications to architecture. Prepared by Stephen C. Deger [and] David A. Spaeth. [Lexington? Ky., 1971?] 40, 61 l. 28 cm. "University of Kentucky Summer Teaching Improvement Fellowship; final report." Bibliography: leaves 37-38 (1st group) [NA2005.D43] 72-610887
1. Architecture—Study and teaching. 2. Computer-assisted instruction. I. Spaeth, David A., joint author. II. Title.

RITTER, Paul, 1925- 720.7
Educreation: education for creation. growth and change; the concept. general implications and specific applications to schools of architecture, environmental design of ekistics. [1st ed.] Oxford. New York, Pergamon [1966] xv, 380p. illus. 20cm. (Commonwealth & intl. lib.) Bibl. [NA2005.R5 1966] 66-18397 5.50 pap.,
1. Architecture—Study and teaching. 2. Creative thinking (Educations I. Title. BIP

RITTER, Paul, 1925- 370.1
Educreation : education for creation, growth, and change : the concept, general implications, and specific applications to schools of architecture, environmental design, or ekistics / by Paul Ritter. 2d ed. Oxford ; New York : Pergamon Press, 1978, c1977. p. cm. (Pergamon international library of science, technology, engineering, and social studies) Bibliography: p. [NA2005.R5 1978] 77-30753 ISBN 0-08-0116566 : 16.50
1. Architecture—Study and teaching. 2. Creative thinking (Education) I. Title.

Architecture—Study and teaching (Elementary)

TROGLER, George E. 372.5'044
Beginning experiences in architecture; a guide for the elementary school teacher [by] George E. Trogler. Photos. by Marjorie Pickens. New York, Van Nostrand Reinhold Co. [1972] 143 p. illus. 19 x 27 cm. Bibliography: p. 140-141. [NA2005.T7] 79-148263 8.95
1. Architecture—Study and teaching (Elementary) I. Title. BIP

Architecture—Study and teaching—Great Britain.

A Continuing experiment : learning and teaching at the Architectural Association / edited by James Gowan. London : Architectural Press, 1975. 175 p. : ill. ; 22 cm. Includes bibliographical references. [NA2310.G74A73] 75-311694 ISBN 0-85139-131-1 : 8.00 720'.7'1142142
1. Architectural Association, London. 2. Architecture—Study and teaching—Great Britain. I. Gowan, James. Distributed by Intl. Publication Service. Available from Northwestern Univ. School of Education. 2003 Sheridan Rd. Evanston, Ill. 60201

Architecture—Study and teaching—Texas.

ARCHITECTURAL education: 1990; a goals study for architectural education in Texas through 1990 [College Station] Texas A & M University, 1968. 117 p. illus. 28 cm. "Sponsors: Coordinating Board, Texas College and University System [and] Texas Engineering Experiment Station, Texas A & M University." Bibliography: p. 112-117. [NA2125.T4A8] 79-625414 720'.71'1764
1. Architecture—Study and teaching—Texas. I. Texas. Coordinating Board, Texas College and University System. II. Texas. A & M University, College Station. Engineering Experiment Station.

Architecture—Study and teaching—United States.

OBERMEYER, Thomas. 720'.7'1073
Architectural technology / Thomas Obermeyer. New York : Gregg Division, McGraw-Hill, c1976. 344 p. : ill. ; 28 cm. Includes index. [NA2108.O23] 75-42134 ISBN 0-07-047496-6 : 11.95
1. Architecture—Study and teaching—United States. 2. Architectural technicians—United States. I. Title. BIP

Architecture, Sukiya.

ITO, Teiji, 1922- 722'.1
The classic tradition in Japanese architecture; modern versions of the sukiya style. Text by Teiji Itoh. Photos. by Yukio Futagawa. Translated from the Japanese by Richard L. Gage. [1st ed.] New York, Weatherhill [1972] 279 p. illus. (part col.) 31 cm. Cover title in Sino-Japanese characters: Sukiya. Translation of Gendai no sukiya. [NA1555.I813 1972] 72-78596 ISBN 0-8348-1511-7 35.00
1. Architecture, Sukiya. 2. Architecture, Modern—20th century—Japan. 3. Architecture, Japanese. 4. Architecture—Designs and plans. I. Futagawa, Yukio, 1932- illus. II. Title. BIP

ITO, Teiji, 1922- 720'.9'52
The elegant Japanese house; traditional Sukiya architecture. Text by Teiji Itoh. Photos. by Yukio Futagawa. [1st ed.] New York, Walker/Weatherhill [1969] 218 p. illus. (part col.), plans (part col.) 37 cm. "A Weathermark edition." Translation of Sukiya (romanized form) [NA7451.I8613] 68-26952 25.00
1. Architecture, Sukiya. I. Futagawa, Yukio, 1932- II. Title. BIP

Architecture—Sweden.

SMITH, George Everard Kidder, 1913- 720.9485
Sweden builds. Extensively rev. [2d ed.] New York, Reinhold [1957] 270 p. illus. 29 cm. Includes bibliography. [NA1288.S6 1957] 56-11753
1. Architecture—Sweden. I. Title.

SMITH, George Everard Kidder, 1913- 720.9485
Sweden builds; its modern architecture and land policy; background, development and contribution. Photos. by the author. [1st ed.] London, Architectural Press; New York, A. Bonnier [1950] 279 p. illus. (part col.) maps, plans. 29 cm. "Swedish land policy [by] Sven Markelius": p. 23-32. Bibliography: p. 275-278. [NA1288.S6] 51-5024
1. Architecture—Sweden. I. Title.

SVENSKA ARKITEKTERS RIKSFORBUND 720.9485
Ny arkitektur i Sverige; 1950-talets svenska byggnadskonst. [Redaktionskommitte: Bengt Gate. et al. Redaktor: Marten J. Larsson. Dist. New York, Wiley, 1962] 341p. illus. 29cm. Added t. p.: New architecture in Sweden: a decade of Swedish building. 62-51029 14.50
1. Architecture—Sweden. 2. Architecture—Designs and plans. I.

Larson, Marten J., ed. II. Title. III. Title: New architecture in Sweden.

Architecture—Switzerland.

ALTHERR, Alfred, 1911- ed. 720.9494
Neue schweizer Architektur. New Swiss architecture [Eng. version: D. Q. Stephenson] New York, Architectural Bk. Pub. Co. [dist. Hastings, c.1965] vii, 212p. illus., plans. 26cm. English and German [NA1348.A65] 65-2298 16.50
1. Architecture—Switzerland. 2. Architecture—Designs and plans. 3. Architecture, Modern—20th cent. I. Title. II. Title: New Swiss architecture.

BACHMANN, Jul. 720'.9494
New directions in Swiss architecture [by] Jul Bachmann [and] Stanislaus von Moos. [Translated by Christian Casparis] New York, G. Braziller [1969] 128 p. illus., plans. 25 cm. (New directions in architecture) "Bibliographical note": p. 119-120. [NA1348.B313] 72-78052 5.95
1. Architecture—Switzerland. 2. Architecture, Modern—20th century—Switzerland. I. Moos, Stanislaus von, joint author. II. Title. BIP

SMITH, George Everard Kidder, 1913- 720.9494
Switzerland builds; its native and modern architecture. Photos. by the author. [1st ed.] London, Architectural Press; New York, A. Bonnier [1950] 234 p. illus. (part col.) plans. 29 cm. Bibliography: p. 233. [NA1348.S55] 50-58202
1. Architecture—Switzerland. 2. Architecture—Designs and plans. I. Title.

Architecture—Tasmania.

ROBERTSON, Edward Graeme. 919.4'6
Early buildings of southern Tasmania [by] E. Graeme Robertson. Melbourne, Georgian House [1970] 2 v. (418 p.) illus. 29 cm. Bibliography: p. 408-414. [NA1602.T2R6] 73-851336 ISBN 0-85585-470-7 42.50
1. Architecture—Tasmania. 2. Tasmania—Historic houses, etc. I. Title.

Architecture—Tempsford, Eng.—Conservation and restoration.

BEDFORDSHIRE, Eng., County Planning Dept. 711'.4'0942565
Tempsford Church End conservation area. Bedford, Bedfordshire County Council Planning Department, 1971. [3], 3 leaves (1 fold.). map. 30 cm. [NA109.G7B43] 72-190564 ISBN 0-901051-41-1
1. Architecture—Tempsford, Eng.—Conservation and restoration. I. Title.

Architecture—Tennessee—Clarksville—Guide-books.

†HALLIBURTON, John Howard, 1954- 720'.9768'45
Clarksville architecture / John Howard Halliburton ; pref. by Olen Bryant ; edited by Barbara Allen Smith. Nashville : Halliburton, c1977. 100 p. : ill. ; 26 cm. Bibliography: p. 99. [NA735.C57H34] 77-16338 15.95
1. Architecture—Tennessee—Clarksville—Guide-books. 2. Clarksville, Tenn.—Buildings. I. Title.
Publisher's address : 2217 Belmont Blvd., Apt. B, Nashville, TN 37212 BIP

Architecture—Tennessee, Middle.

BRUMBAUGH, Thomas B., 1921- 917.68'03'5
Architecture of Middle Tennessee: the Historic American Buildings Survey. Edited by Thomas B. Brumbaugh, Martha I. Strayhorn, and Gary G. Gore. Photos. by Jack E. Boucher. Nashville, Vanderbilt University Press, 1974. xvii, 170 p. illus. 29 cm. Based on an exhibit of photos. and drawings from the Historic American Buildings Survey presented at Vanderbilt University. Includes bibliographies. [NA730.T4B78] 72-2879 ISBN 0-8265-1184-8 18.50
1. Architecture—Tennessee, Middle. 2. Tennessee, Middle—Historic houses, etc. I. Strayhorn, Martha I., 1925- joint author. II. Gore, Gary G., 1932- joint author. III. Historic American Buildings Survey. IV. Title. BIP

Architecture—Terminology.

SUMMERSON, John Newenham, Sir, 1904- 721
The classical language of architecture [by] John Summerson. Cambridge, M.I.T. Press [1966, c1963] 56 p. 63 numbered illus. 19 x 24 cm. "Scripts of six talks, written for the B.B.C. and delivered in May-July 1963." Bibliography: p. 53-56. [NA31.S86 1966] 66-24572
1. Architecture—Terminology. 2. Architecture—Details. I. British Broadcasting Corporation. II. Title. BIP

ZEVI, Bruno, 1918- 720'.1'4
The modern language of architecture / by Bruno Zevi. Seattle : University of Washington Press, c1978. xiv, 241 p. : ill. ; 21 cm. Translated from the author's Il linguaggio moderno dell'architettura, and Architettura e storiografia. "The two parts formed the basis of two Walker-Ames lectures delivered at the University of Washington, Seattle, on January 27 and February 1, 1977." Includes index. [NA31.Z48213] 77-3829 ISBN 0-295-95568-6 : 14.95
1. Architecture—Terminology. 2. Architecture—Historiography. I. Zevi, Bruno, 1918- Architettura e storiografia. English. Selections. 1978. II. Title. BIP

Architecture—Texas.

JUTSON, Mary Carolyn Hollers. 720'.92'4
Alfred Giles: an English architect in Texas and Mexico. Photography by Joe S. Lawrie. San Antonio, Trinity University Press [1972] xviii, 178 p. illus. 29 cm. (San Antonio Conservation Society series, no. 1) Bibliography: p. 167-172. [NA997.G54J87] 72-75338 ISBN 0-911536-42-6
1. Giles, Alfred, 1853-1920. 2. Architecture—Texas. 3. Architecture—Mexico. I. Title. II. Series: San Antonio Conservation Society. San Antonio Conservation Society series, no. 1.

ROBINSON, Willard Bethurem, 1935- 720'.9764
Texas public buildings of the nineteenth century. Photos. by Todd Webb. Text by Willard B. Robinson. Foreword by Drury Blakeley Alexander. Austin, Published for the Amon Carter Museum of Western Art by University of Texas Press [1974] xiv, 290 p. illus. 28 cm. (The Texas architectural survey, publication no. 2) Bibliography: p. 273-282. [NA730.T5R62] 74-578 ISBN 0-292-78006-0 20.00
1. Architecture—Texas. 2. Architecture, Modern—19th century—Texas. 3. Texas—Public buildings. I. Webb, Todd, illus. II. Title. III. Series. BIP

Architecture—Texas—Pictorial works.

HEIMSATH, Clovis. 720'.9764
Pioneer Texas buildings; a geometry lesson. Photos. by Maryann Heimsath. Foreword by Louis Kahn. Austin, University of Texas Press [1968] 158 p. illus., col. map, plans. 26 cm. [NA730.T5H4] 68-25947 12.50
1. Architecture—Texas—Pictorial works. I. Heimsath, Maryann, illus. II. Title. BIP

Architecture—Toddington, Eng.—Conservation and restoration.

BEDFORDSHIRE, Eng., County Planning Dept. 711'.4'0942565
Toddington conservation area. Bedford, Bedfordshire County Council Planning Department, 1971. [3], 5 leaves (1 fold.). map. 30 cm. [NA109.G7B44] 72-190563 ISBN 0-901051-40-3
1. Architecture—Toddington, Eng.—Conservation and restoration. I. Title.

Architecture—Toledo—Guide-books.

JOHANNESEN, Eric. 917.71'13
Look again; landmark architecture in downtown Toledo and Old West End, by Eric Johannesen and Allen L. Dickes [with] Landmarks Committee of the Maumee Valley Historical Society. Pittsburgh, Ober Park Associates [1973] 228 p. illus. 26 cm. [NA735.T64J63] 73-85945
1. Architecture—Toledo—Guide-books. I. Dickes, Allen L., joint author. II. Maumee Valley Historical Society. Landmarks Committee. III. Title.

Architecture—Toronto—History.

ARTHUR, Eric Ross. 720'.9713'541
Toronto, no mean city [by] Eric Arthur. [Toronto] University of Toronto Press [1964] xvii, 280 p. illus., maps, plans, ports. 29 cm. Bibliography; p. 269-271. [NA747.T6A86] 65-3814
1. Architecture — Toronto — Hist. 2. Toronto — Hist. I. Title.

Architecture—Toronto—History.

ARTHUR, Eric Ross. 971.30713541
Toronto, no mean city [by] Eric Arthur. [Toronto], University of Toronto Press [1974, c1964]. xvii, 280 p. illus. 29 cm. Bibliography: p. 269-271. [NA747.T6A86] ISBN 0-8020-2139-5. 25.00
1. Architecture—Toronto—History. 2. Toronto—History. I. Title.
L.C. card number for original ed.: 65-3814.

Architecture, Tropical.

FRY, Edwin Maxwell, 1899- 720.9
Tropical architecture in the dry and humid zones [by] Maxwell Fry, Jane Drew. New York, Reinhold [c.1964] 264p. illus., maps, plans. 25cm. Bibl. 64-57413 17.50
1. Architecture, Tropical. 2. Architecture and climate. I. Fry, Jane Beverly (Drew) joint author. II. Title.

FRY, Edwin Maxwell, 1899- 721
Tropical architecture in the dry and humid zones / Maxwell Fry and Jane Drew. Huntington, N.Y. : R. E. Krieger Pub. Co., [1974] c1964. 264 p. : ill. ; 25 cm. Reprint of the ed. published by Reinhold, New York. Includes material from the authors' Tropical architecture in the humid zone. Includes bibliographical references and indexes. [NA2542.T7F79 1974] 74-22096 ISBN 0-88275-234-0 : 19.50
1. Architecture, Tropical. 2. Architecture and climate. I. Fry, Jane Beverly Drew, joint author. II. Title.

FRY, Edwin Maxwell, 1899- 724.9
Tropical architecture in the humid zone [by] Maxwell Fry and Jane Drew. New York, Reinhold [1956] 820p. illus., maps, charts, plans. 26cm. (Reinhold international library) [NA2540.F7] 56-5602
1. Architecture, Tropical. 2. Architecture and climate. I. Fry. Jane Beverly (Drew) joint author. II. Title.

SAINI, Balwant Singh. 720'.994
Architecture in tropical Australia. [1st ed.] New York, G. Wittenborn [1970] 67 p. illus., maps. 30 cm. (Architectural Association paper no. 6) Includes bibliographical references. [NA1600.S23] 74-145974 ISBN 0-8150-0007-3
1. Architecture, Tropical. 2. Architecture—Australia. I. Title. II. Series: Architectural Association, London. Paper no. 6 BIP

Architecture, Tropical—Bibliography.

†RIVERA de Figueroa, Carmen A. 720'.913
Architecture for the tropics : a bibliographical synthesis (from the beginnings to 1972) : con una version Castellana resumida (Arquitectura para el tropica) / Carmen A. Rivera de Figueroa. 1st ed. Rio Piedras, PR : University of Puerto Rico Press, 1977. p. cm. Spanish or English. Includes index. Bibliography: p. [Z5943.T75R58] [NA2542.T7] 77-26261 ISBN 0-8477-2107-8 pbk.: 15.00
1. Architecture, Tropical—Bibliography. I. Title. BIP

Architecture—Turkey.

VOGT, Ulya (Goknil) 720.9561
Living architecture: Ottoman. Text by Ulya Vogt-Goknil. Photos. by Eduard Widmer. Pref. by Jurgen Joedicke. New York, Grosset & Dunlap [1966] 192 p. illus., map, plans. 22 cm. (Living architecture) Bibliography: p. 183-184. [NA1364.V613 1966a] 66-9833
1. Architecture—Turkey. 2. Mosques—Turkey. I. Title.

Architecture—Ulster Co., N.Y.

JUNIOR League of Kingston. 974.7'34
Early architecture in Ulster County. New York : Junior League of Kingston, 1974. 222 p., [1] fold. leaf of plates : chiefly ill. ; 21 cm. Includes index. Bibliography: p. 10-11. [NA730.N42U474 1974] 75-300664
1. Architecture—Ulster Co., N.Y. 2. Ulster Co., N.Y.—Buildings. I. Title.

Architecture—United States.

AMERICAN Institute of Architects. 720.973
Mid-century architecture in America; honor awards of the American Institute of Architects, 1949-1961. Foreword by Philip Will, Jr. Ed., with introd. by Wolf Von Eckardt. Baltimore, Johns Hopkins [c.1961] 254p. illus. 29cm. 61-17081 12.50
1. Architecture—U.S. 2. Architecture, Modern—20th cent. I. Von Eckardt, Wolf, ed. II. Title.

AMERICAN Institute of Architects. 720.973
Mid-century architecture in America; honor awards of the American Institute of Architects, 1949-1961. Foreword by Philip Will, Jr. Edited and with an introd. by Wolf Von Eckardt. Baltimore, Johns Hopkins Press [1961] 254p. illus. 29cm. [NA712.A65] 61-17081
1. Architecture—U. S. 2. Architecture, Modern—20th cent. I. Von Eckardt, Wolf, ed. II. Title.

AMERICAN Institute of Architects. Commission for the Survey of Education and Registration. 720.973
The architect at mid-century; report. New York, Reinhold [1954] 2 v. illus. 26 cm. Contents.Contents.—v. 1. Evolution and achievement, edited by T. C. Bannister.—v. 2. Conversations across the Nation, edited by F. R. Bellamy. Includes bibliographical references. [NA712.A67] 54-9083
1. Architecture—U.S. I. Bannister, Turpin C., ed. II. Bellamy, Francis Rufus, 1886- ed. III. Title.

ANDREWS, Wayne. 720.973
Architecture, ambition and Americans; a history of American architecture, from the beginning to the present, telling the story of the outstanding buildings, the men who designed them and the people for whom they were built. New York, Harper [1955] 315 p. illus. 24 cm. [NA705.A5] 55-8014
1. Architecture—U.S. I. Title.

ANDREWS, Wayne. 720.973
Architecture in America; a photographic history from the colonial period to the present. Introd. by Russell Lynes. [1st ed.] New York, Atheneum Publishers, 1960. 179 p. illus. 30 cm. [NA705.A53] 60-7783
1. Architecture—U.S. I. Title. BIP

THE Architectural forum. 720.973
Building. U. S. A.; the men and methods that influence architecture in America today New York, McGraw-Hill [1957] 147p. illus. 22cm. [NA712.A827] 57-7994
1. Architecture—U. S. 2. Construction industry—U. S. 3. Real estate business—U. S. I. Title.

BLUMENSON, John J. G., 1942- 720'.973
Identifying American architecture : a pictorial guide to styles and terms, 1600-1945 / John J.-G. Blumenson ; foreword by Nikolaus Pevsner ; with photos. from the Historic American Buildings Survey. Nashville : American Association for State and Local History, c1977. viii, 118 p. : ill. ; 15 x 22 cm. Includes index. Bibliography:

p. 117-118. [NA705.B55] 76-30352 ISBN 0-910050-24-4 : 6.75
1. Architecture—United States. 2. Architecture—United States—Terminology. I. Title. BIP

CHERMAYEFF, Ivan. 720'.973
Observations on American architecture, by Ivan Chermayeff. With photos. by Elliott Erwitt. New York, Viking Press, 1972. 143 p. illus. (part col.) 29 cm. [NA705.C43] 72-81663 ISBN 0-670-52019-5 16.95
1. Architecture—United States. I. Erwitt, Elliott, illus. II. Title.

COLES, William A., ed. 720.973
Architecture in America; a battle of styles, ed. by William A. Coles, Henry Hope Reed, Jr. New York, Appleton-Century-Crofts [1961] 412p. illus. Bibl. 61-5653 2.40 pap.,
1. Architecture—U.S. 2. Architecture. I. Reed, Henry Hope, joint ed. II. Title.

CONDIT, Carl W. 725.232
The rise of the skyscraper. [Chicago] University of Chicago Press [1952] 239 p. illus. 25 cm. Bibliography: p. 249-250. [NA712.C65] 52-6468
1. Architecture—U.S. 2. Architecture, Modern—20th century. I. Title.

CONNELY, Willard, 1888- 720.973
Louis Sullivan as he lived; the shaping of American architecture, a biography. New York, Horizon Press, 1960. 322 p. illus. 25 cm. Includes bibliography. [NA737.S9C6] 60-8160
1. Sullivan, Louis Henry, 1856-1924. 2. Architecture—U.S.

DANA, Richard Henry, 730'.924
1879-1933.
Richard Henry Dana, 1879-1933, architect; illustrations of his work, selected by Richard H. Dana, Jr. With a foreword by Harmon H. Goldstone. New York, 1965. 1 v. (unpaged) 74 illus., port. 23 x 29 cm. 500 copies printed. [NA737.D3D3] 65-22926
I. Dana, Richard Henry, ed. II. Title.

EATON, Leonard K. 720'.973
American architecture comes of age; European reaction to H. H. Richardson and Louis Sullivan [by] Leonard K. Eaton. Cambridge, Mass., MIT Press [1972] xiii, 256 p. illus. 27 cm. Bibliography: p. [240]-242. [NA710.E24] 76-171556 ISBN 0-262-05010-2 14.95
1. Richardson, Henry Hobson, 1838-1886. 2. Sullivan, Louis Henri, 1856-1924. 3. Architecture—United States. 4. Architecture, Modern—19th century—United States. I. Title.

EDGELL, George Harold, 720'.973
1887-1954.
The American architecture of to-day. New York, AMS Press [1970] xxxi, 401 p. illus., plans. 24 cm. Reprint of the 1928 ed. Bibliography: p. 379-401. [NA705.E4 1970] 79-120562
1. Architecture—U.S. I. Title.

FERRISS, Hugh, 1889- 724.91
Power in buildings; an artist's view of contemporary architecture. Drawings and text by Hugh Ferriss. New York, Columbia University Press, 1953. 102 p. illus. 29 cm. [NA712.F47] 53-12306
1. Architecture—U.S. 2. Architecture, Modern—20th century.

FITCH, James Marston. 720.973
American building. 2d ed., rev. and enl. Boston, Houghton Mifflin, 1966- v. illus., maps, plans. 22 cm. Contents.Contents.—v. 1. The historical forces that shaped it. Bibliographical references included in "Notes" (v. 1, p. [321]-327) [NA705.F512] 65-10689
1. Architecture—U.S. 2. Building—U.S. I. Title. BIP

GILCHRIST, Agnes Eleanor 720.81
(Addison), 1907-
William Strickland, architect and engineer, 1788-1854. Philadelphia, University of Pennsylvania Press, 1950. xvii, 145 p. 51 plates (incl. ports., plans) 29 cm. Includes bibliographies. [NA737.S68G5] 51-515
1. Strickland, William, 1787-1854. 2. Architecture—U. S. I. Title.

GILCHRIST, Agnes Eleanor 720.81
(Addison) 1907-
William Strickland, architect and engineer, 1788-1854. Philadelphia, University of Pennsylvania Press, 1950. [n. p.] 1954. xvii, 145p. 51plates (incl. ports., plans) 29cm. 16p. illus. ports. 29cm. 'Documentary supplement, Journal of the Society of Architectural Historians, XIII, 3.' Includes bibliographies. [NA737.S68G5] 51-515
1. Strickland, William, 1787-1854. 2. Architecture—U. S. I. Society of Architectural Historians, Journal. Supplement. II. Title. III. Title: — Additions.

GILCHRIST, Agnes 720'.924 B
Eleanor (Addison) 1907-
William Strickland, architect and engineer, 1788-1854, by Agnes Addison Gilchrist. enl.ed. New York, Da Capo Press, 1969. 1 v. (various pagings) illus., plans, ports. 29 cm. (A Da Capo Press reprint edition) "An unabridged republication of the first edition, published in ... 1950 ... It includes as a supplement three articles about Strickland prepared by Mrs. Gilchrist [and first published in 1953-54]" Includes bibliographical references. [NA737.S68G5 1969] 69-13714 20.00
1. Strickland, William, 1787-1854. 2. Architecture—U.S. BIP

GUTHEIM, Frederick 720.973
Albert, 1908-
One hundred years of architecture in America, 1857-1957, celebrating the centennial of the American Institute of Architects. New York, Reinhold Pub. Corp. [1957] 96p. (chiefly illus. (part col.)) 24cm. [NA705.G8] 57-11223
1. Architecture—U. S. 2. Architecture—Exhibitions. 3. American Institute of Architects. I. Title.

GUTHEIM, Frederick 720.973
Albert, 1908-
One hundred years of architecture in America, 1857-1957, celebrating the centennial of the American Institute of Architects. New York, Reinhold Pub. Corp. [1957] 96 p. (chiefly illus. (part col.)) 24 cm. [NA705.G8] 57-11223
1. American Institute of Architects. 2. Architecture—U.S. 3. Architecture—Exhibitions. I. Title.

HISTORIC American 720'.973
Buildings Survey.
Documenting a legacy; 40 years of the Historic American Buildings Survey. [Washington, Library of Congress, 1973] 269-294 p. illus. 26 cm. Reprint from the Quarterly journal of the Library of Congress, Oct. 1973. Issued in conjunction with an exhibition held Nov. 1, 1973 to Jan. 31, 1974, in the Library of Congress. [NA705.H56 1973] 73-17422 ISBN 0-8444-0103-X
1. Historic American Buildings Survey. 2. Architecture—United States. 3. United States—Historic houses, etc. I. United States. Library of Congress. II. Title.

KIMBALL, Sidney Fiske, 720'.973
1888-1955.
American architecture. New York, AMS Press [1970] 262 p. illus. 23 cm. Reprint of the 1928 ed. Includes bibliographical references. [NA705.K5 1970] 77-108121 ISBN 0-404-03676-7
1. Architecture—United States. 2. Historic buildings—United States. I. Title.

KORNWOLF, James D. 720'.972
A history of American dwellings [by] James D. Kornwolf. Chicago, Rand McNally [1967] 64 p. illus., plans. 23 cm. (Rand McNally classroom library) Bibliography: p. 64. [NA705.K62] 68-243
1. Architecture—United States. I. Title.

KURTZ, Stephen A. 720'.973
Wasteland: building the American dream [by] Stephen A. Kurtz. Photos. by Laurence Fink. New York, Praeger [1973] 125 p. illus. 25 cm. Includes bibliographical references. [NA712.K87] 73-6972 7.95
1. Architecture—United States. 2. Architecture, Modern—20th century—United States. 3. Cities and towns—Planning—United States. I. Title.
pbk. 3.95.

LANCASTER, Clay. 709.73
The Japanese influence in America. With an introd. by Alan Priest. New York, W. H. Rawls; distributed by Twayne Publishers, 1963 xix, 292 p. illus. (part col.) port., plans. 32 cm. Bibliographical references included in "Notes" (p. 269-274) [NA705.L3] 63-18860
1. Architecture—United States. 2. Art—United States. 3. Architecture, Japanese. 4. Art, Japanese. 5. United States—Relations (general) with Japan. 6. Japan—Relations (general) with the U.S. I. Title.

MAASS, John, 1918- 720.973
The gingerbread age; a view of Victorian America. New York, Rinehart [1957] 212p. illus. 29cm. Includes bibliography. [NA710.M3] 57-7370
1. Architecture—U. 2. .—Hist. I. Title.

MCCALLUM, Ian Robert 720.973
More.
Architecture U. S. A. New York, Reinhold Pub. Corp. [1959] 216p. illus., ports., plans. 29cm. Bibliography: p.213-216. [NA712.M27] 59-16224
1. Architecture— U. S. 2. Architects, American. 3. Architecture, Modern—20th cent. I. Title.

MORRISON, Hugh Sinclair, 720.973
1905-
Early American architecture, from the first colonial settlements to the national period. New York, Oxford University Press, 1952. xiv, 619 p. illus., maps, plans. 24 cm. Includes bibliographies. [NA707.M63] 52-7831
1. Architecture — U.S. I. Title. BIP

MORRISON, Hugh 720'.924 B
Sinclair, 1905-
Louis Sullivan, prophet of modern architecture, by Hugh Morrison. Westport, Conn., Greenwood Press [1971, c1935] 391 p. illus. 23 cm. "Dankmar Adler, a biographical sketch": p. 283-293. Includes bibliographies. [NA737.S9M6 1971] 78-139141 ISBN 0-8371-5757-9
1. Sullivan, Louis Henri, 1856-1924. 2. Adler, Dankmar, 1844-1900. 3. Architecture—United States.

MUMFORD, Lewis, 1895- ed. 720.973
Roots of contemporary American architecture; a series of thirty-seven essays dating from the mid-nineteenth century to the present. Contains an introductory essay and biographies of the twenty-nine writers whose work appears herein. New York, Reinhold [1952] vii, 454 p. 24 cm. [NA710.M8] 52-10519
1. Architecture — U.S. 2. Architecture — Addresses, essays, lectures. I. Title. BIP

MUMFORD, Lewis, 1895- ed. 720.973
Roots of contemporary American architecture; a series of thirty-seven essays dating from the mid-nineteenth century to the present. Contains an introductory essay and biographies of the twenty-nine writers whose work appears herein. New York, Grove Press [1959] 454 p. 21 cm. (An Evergreen book, E-197) [NA710.M8 1959] 59-14138
1. Architecture—U.S. 2. Architecture—Addresses, essays, lectures. I. Title.

MUMFORD, Lewis, 1895- 720'.975
The South in architecture. New York, Da Capo Press, 1967. 147 p. 21 cm. (Da Capo Press series in architecture and decorative art, v. 6) (The Dancy lectures, 1941.) Reprint of the 1941 ed. Contents.Contents.—The basis for American form.—The universalism of Thomas Jefferson.—The regionalism of H. H. Richardson.—The social task of architecture. [NA705.M78 1967] 67-27462 6.50
1. Jefferson, Thomas, Pres. U.S., 1743-1826. 2. Richardson, Henry Hobson, 1838-1886. 3. Architecture—U.S. 4. Architecture—Southern States. I. Title. II. Series: Alabama College, Montevallo. Dancy lectures, 1941 BIP

MUMFORD, Lewis, 1895- 720.973
Sticks and stones; a study of American architecture and civilization. [2d rev. ed.] New York, Dover Publications [1955] 238 p. illus. 21 cm. [NA705.M8 1955] 55-14852
1. Architecture—United States. I. Title. BIP

NEW York (City). Museum 720'.973
of Modern Art.
Built in USA: 1932-1944, edited by Elizabeth Mock, foreword by Philip L. Goodwin; Post-war architecture, edited by Henry-Russell Hitchcock and Arthur Drexler. Reprint ed. New York, Published for the Museum of Modern Art by Arno Press, 1968. 127, 128 p. illus., plans. 27 cm. Built in USA: 1932-1944, first published in 1944; Built in USA: post-war architecture, first published in 1952. [NA712.N45 1968] 68-57299
1. Architecture—U.S. 2. Architecture, Modern—20th century—U.S. I. Kassler, Elizabeth (Bauer) 1911- ed. II. Hitchcock, Henry Russell, 1903- ed. III. Drexler, Arthur, ed. IV. New York (City). Museum of Modern Art. Built in USA: post-war architecture. V. Title. VI. Title: Built in USA: post-war architecture.

NEW York. Museum of Modern 724.91
Art.
Built in USA: post-war architecture, edited by Henry-Russell Hitchocock and Arthur Drexler. New York, Distributed by Simon & Schuster [1952] 128p. illus. 26cm. [NA712.N47] 53-568
1. Architecture—U. S. I. Hitchcock, Henry Russell, 1906- ed. II. Drexier, Arthur, ed. III. Title.

PURCELL, William Gray, 720'.924
1880-1965.
The Work of Purcell and Elmslie, architects. With a new introd. by David Gebhard. [Park Forest, Ill., Prairie School Press, c1965] 96 p. illus., plans, ports. 33 cm. Reproduced three issues of The Western architect: Jan. 1913, Jan. 1915, July 1915. Cover title: The architecture of Purcell and Elmaslie. [NA737.P8G4] 67-6747
1. Purcell & Elmslie. 2. Elmslie, George Grant, 1871-1952. 3. Architecture — U.S. I. The Western architect. II. Title. III. Title: The architecture of Purcell and Elmslie.

REED, Henry Hope. 720.973
The golden city. [1st ed.] Garden City, N. Y., Doubleday, 1959. 160p. illus. 27cm. Includes bibliography. [NA712.R43] 58-13295
1. Architecture—U. S. 2. Architecture, Modern—20th cent. I. Title. BIP

ROTH, Leland M. 720'.973
A concise history of American architecture / by Leland M. Roth. 1st ed. New York : Harper & Row, c1979. p. cm. (Icon editions) Includes index. Bibliography: p. [NA705.R67 1979] 78-2169 ISBN 0-06-438490-X : 22.50 ISBN 0-06-430086-2 pbk. : 8.95
1. Architecture—United States. I. Title. BIP

SCHUYLER, Montgomery, 720.973
1843-1914
American architecture, and other writings. Ed. by William H. Jordy. Ralph Coe. Abridged by William H. Jordy. New York. Atheneum, 1964[c.1961, 1963] 328p. 18cm. (A50) Bibl. 2.45 pap.,
*1. Architecture—U.S. I. Title. II. Series.*BIP

SCHUYLER, Montgomery, 720.973
1873-1914.
American architecture, and other writings. Edited by William H. Jordy and Ralph Coe. Cambridge, Belknap Press of Harvard University Press, 1961. 2v. (xvi, 664p.) illus., plans. 25cm. (The John Harvard Hbrary) Bibliography: p. [641]- 653. Bibliographical footnotes. [NA710.S42] 61-13743
1. Architecture—U. S. I. Title. II. Series.

SLOAN, Samuel, 1815- 720'.973
1884.
City and suburban architecture : containing numerous designs and details for public edifices, private residences, and mercantile buildings / by Samuel Sloan. Illustrated with one hundred and thirty-six engravings, accompanied by specifications and historical and explanatory text. New York : Da Capo Press, 1976 [c1859] 104 p., 136 [i.e. 73] leaves of plates : ill. ; 36 cm. (Da Capo Press series in architecture and decorative art) Reprint of the ed. published by Lippincott, Philadelphia. [NA705.S56 1976] 75-31711 50.00
1. Architecture—United States. 2. Architecture—Designs and plans. 3. Architecture—Details. I. Title.

STERN, Robert A. M. 720'.973
New directions in American architecture

24 cm. Vols. 3-4 by W. H. Jordy. Reprint of the ed. published by Doubleday, Garden City, N.Y. Contents.Contents.—v. 1. The colonial and neo-classical styles. v. 3. Progressive and academic ideals at the turn of the twentieth century.—v. 4. The impact of European modernism in the mid-twentieth century. Includes bibliographical references and indexes. [NA705.P5 1976] 76-369389 ISBN 0-385-06123-4 (v. 1) : 6.95
1. Architecture—United States—History. 2. Architects—United States. I. Jordy, William H. II. Title. BIP

SCULLY, Vincent Joseph, 1920- 720'.973
American architecture and urbanism [by] Vincent Scully. New York, Praeger [1969] 275 p. illus., maps, plans. 26 cm. "A note on method and bibliography": p. 257-262. [NA705.S36] 70-76793 18.50
1. Architecture—U.S.—History. 2. Cities and towns—Planning—U.S.—History. I. Title.

Architecture—U.S.—Juvenile literature.

DEVLIN, Harry. 720'.973
What kind of a house is that? New York, Parents' Magazine Press [1969] 48 p. illus. (part col.) 28 cm. Full-page color drawings accompany brief histories of various buildings, from fun house to outhouse, demonstrative of nineteenth-century American architecture and society. [NA705.D4] 78-77792 3.95
1. Architecture—U.S.—Juvenile literature. I. Title. BIP

Architecture—United States—Pictorial works.

ANDREWS, Wayne. 720'.973
Architecture in America : a photographic history from the colonial period to the present / by Wayne Andrews. Rev. ed. New York : Atheneum, 1977. 179, [6] p. : ill. ; 29 cm. Includes index. Bibliography: p. [1-2]. [NA705.A53 1977] 77-4273 ISBN 0-689-70549-2 : 8.95
1. Architecture—United States—Pictorial works. I. Title.

GILLON, Edmund Vincent. 720'.973
Early illustrations and views of American architecture [by] Edmund V. Gillon, Jr. New York, Dover [1971] vii, 295 p. (chiefly illus.) 31 cm. (Dover pictorial archive series) Bibliography: p. 287-288. [NA710.G53] 71-152420 ISBN 0-486-22750-2 6.95
1. Architecture—U.S.—Pictorial works. 2. Architecture, Modern—19th century—U.S. I. Title.

Architecture—Venezuela.

GASPARINI. GRAZIANO 720.987
La arquitectura colonial en Venezuela. Fotografias del autor Caracas Ediciones Armitano [New York, Wittenborn. 1966] 379p. illus. (pt. col.) plans. 28cm. El texto de la presente obra aparece publicado tambien por el Instituto de Geografia e Historia en la series dedicado a los monumentos de America. Bibl. [NA930.G3] 66-3308 30.00 bds.,
1. Architecture—Venezuela. 2. Architecture. Colonial. I. Title.

MOHOLY-NAGY, Dorothea Maria Pauline Alice Sibylle (Pietzsch) 720.987
Carlos Raul Villanueva and the architecture of Venezuela [Tr. into Spanish by Clara Diament de Sujo] New York, Praeger [1964] 179p. illus. (pt. col.) facsims., maps, port. 23x26cm. Bibl. 64-16683 12.50
1. Villanueva, Carlos Raul. 2. Architecture—Venezuela. 3. Architecture, Modern—20th cent. I. Title.

Architecture—Venice.

RUSKIN, John, 1819-1900. 720'.945'31
Ruskin's Venice / editor, Arnold Whittick ; pref. by Ashley Clarke. London : G. Godwin, 1976. xiii, 325 p. : ill. ; 24 cm. Consists of excerpts from the main work, index, and notes of Ruskin's The stones of Venice. Includes index. Bibliography: p. [307]-312. [NA1121.V4R72 1976] 76-380839 ISBN 0-7114-4802-7 : £7.50
1. Architecture—Venice. I. Whittick, Arnold, 1898- II. Title. III. Title: Venice.

RUSKIN, John, 1819-1900 720.94531
The stones of Venice, ed., abridged by J. G. Links. New York, Hill & Wang [1966, c.1960] 254p. illus. 21cm. [NA1121.V4] 64-24827 5.00 1.95 pap.,
1. Architecture—Venice. 2. Art—Venice. I. Links, J. G., ed. II. Title. BIP

RUSKIN, John, 1819-1900. 720'.945'31
The stones of Venice; introductory chapters and local indices (printed separately) for the use of travellers while staying in Venice and Verona. With an introd. by Charles Eliot Norton. Brantwood ed. New York, Merrill, 1891. St. Clair Shores, Mich., Scholarly Press, 1972. p. (The works of John Ruskin) [NA1121.V4R85 1972] 72-8218
1. Architecture—Venice. I. Title.

Architecture—Venice—Guide-books.

†RUSKIN, John, 1819-1900. 914.5'31
Ruskin's Venice / edited by Arnold Whittick ; pref. by Sir Ashley Clarke. New York : Whitney Library of Design, 1976. xiii, 325 p. : ill. ; 24 cm. Edited for the modern traveller from the author's The stones of Venice. Includes index. Bibliography: p. [307]-312. [NA1121.V4R47 1976] 76-12351 ISBN 0-8230-7445-5 : 12.95
1. Architecture—Venice—Guide-books. 2. Art, Venetian. 3. Venice—Description—Guide-books. I. Whittick, Arnold, 1898- II. Ruskin, John, 1819-1900. The stones of Venice. III. Title.

Architecture, Victorian.

*FEARNLEY, Charles, 1915- 720.942
Where have all the textures gone? Dunedin, John McIndoe, [1975] 88 p. ill. 21 cm. [NA967]
1. Architecture, Victorian. 2. Architecture—Details. I. Title.
Distributed by Int'l Publications Service for 7.00 (pbk.) BIP

SUMMERSON, John Newenham, Sir, 1904- 720'.942
Victorian architecture; four studies in evaluation, by John Summerson. New York, Columbia University Press, 1970. 131 p. illus., plans. 25 cm. (Bampton lectures in America, no. 19) Includes bibliographical references. [NA645.S9] 74-89565 7.50
1. Architecture, Victorian. I. Title. II. Series. BIP

Architecture, Victorian—Chicago.

LAUGHLIN, Clarence John. 770'.75
Photographs of Victorian Chicago. [New York, Printed by Clarke & Way, 1968] [12] p. illus. 26 cm. Cover title. Exhibition held Mar. 2-Apr. 14, 1968, in the Corcoran Gallery of Art, Washington. [TR6.L3] 68-24683
1. Architecture, Victorian—Chicago. 2. Chicago—Description—Views. 3. Photography—Exhibitions. I. Corcoran Gallery of Art, Washington, D.C. II. Title.

Architecture, Victorian—Colorado.

STOEHR, C. Eric. 978.8
Bonanza Victorian : architecture and society in Colorado mining towns / C. Eric Stoehr. 1st ed. Albuquerque : University of New Mexico Press, c1975. xiv, 173 p. : ill. ; 29 cm. Includes index. Bibliography: p. 168-169. [NA730.C6S86] 75-17370 ISBN 0-8263-0390-0 : 11.95
1. Architecture, Victorian—Colorado. 2. Architecture—Colorado. 3. Architecture and society—Colorado. 4. Mines and mineral resources—Colorado. I. Title. BIP

Architecture, Victorian—Great Britain.

CURL, James Stevens, 1937- 720'.942
Victorian architecture; its practical aspects. [Cranbury, N.J.] Fairleigh Dickinson University Press [1974] 128 p. illus. 25 cm. Bibliography: p. [120]-124. [NA967.C8 1974] 73-9291 ISBN 0-8386-1433-7 10.00
1. Architecture, Victorian—Great Britain. I. Title.

DIXON, Roger, 1935- 720'.941
Victorian architecture / Roger Dixon, Stefan Muthesius. New York : Oxford University Press, 1978. 288 p. : ill. ; 22 cm. ([The World of art]) Includes index. Bibliography: p. 250-251. [NA967.D59] 77-25059 ISBN 0-19-520048-9 : 12.95. ISBN 0-19-520049-7 pbk. : 6.95
1. Architecture, Victorian—Great Britain. 2. Architecture—Great Britain. I. Muthesius, Stefan, joint author. II. Title. III. Series.

JORDAN, Robert Furneaux. 720.942
Victorian architecture. Harmondsworth, Penguin, 1966. 278 p. illus. (incl. ports.) 20 cm. (Pelican book A836) Bibliography: p. 263-267. [NA967.J6 1966] 67-70591
1. Architecture, Victorian—Great Britain. I. Title.

MUTHESIUS, Stefan. 720'.942
The High Victorian movement in architecture, 1850-1870. London, Boston, Routledge and and K. Paul, 1972. xvii, 252 p. illus., plans. 26 cm. Bibliography: p. 243-246. [NA967.M83] 72-193291 ISBN 0-7100-7071-3 19.25
1. Architecture, Victorian—Great Britain. I. Title. BIP

Architecture, Victorian—Great Britain—Addresses, essays, lectures.

SEVEN Victorian architects / edited by Jane Fawcett ; introd. by Nikolaus Pevsner. University Park, Pa. : Pennsylvania State University Press, c1977. 160 p. : ill. ; 25 cm. Includes bibliographical references and index. [NA967.S48 1977] 76-42090 ISBN 0-271-00500-9 : 13.50 720'.92'2
1. Architecture, Victorian—Great Britain—Addresses, essays, lectures. 2. Architecture—Great Britain—Addresses, essays, lectures. 3. Architects—Great Britain. I. Fawcett, Jane.
Contents omitted

SEVEN Victorian architects / edited by Jane Fawcett ; introd. by Nikolaus Pevsner. London : Thames and Hudson, c1976. 160 p. : ill. ; 25 cm. Includes index. Contents.Contents.—Walker, D. William Burn.—Hobhouse. H. Philip and Philip Charles Hardwick.—Crook. J. M. Sydney Smirke.—Lloyd, D. John Loughborough Pearson.—Verey, D. George Frederick Bodley.—Smith, S. A. Alfred Waterhouse.—Gradidge, R. Edwin Lutyens. Bibliography: p. 137-148. [NA967.S48 1976] 77-357365 ISBN 0-500-34070-6 : £7.50 720'.92'2
1. Architecture, Victorian—Great Britain—Addresses, essays, lectures. 2. Architecture—Great Britain—Addresses, essays, lectures. 3. Architects—Great Britain. I. Fawcett, Jane. BIP

Architecture, Victorian—Hamilton, Ont.

MCKAY, Alexander Gordon, 1924- 720'.9713'52
Victorian architecture in Hamilton. [Text by Alexander G. McKay]. [Hamilton, Hamilton-Niagara Branch, Architectural Conservancy of Ontario, 1967] 28 p. illus., fold. map. 23 cm. Bibliography: p. 28. [NA747.H3M3] 70-437589 1.50
1. Architecture, Victorian—Hamilton, Ont. 2. Architecture—Hamilton, Ont. I. Architectural Conservancy of Ontario. Hamilton-Niagara Branch. II. Title.

Architecture, Victorian, in art.

LAZZARI, Mary Clifford. 759.13
Mary Clifford Lazzari paints Victorian Galveston / pref. by Peter Brink. Houston, Tex. : Oleander Enterprises, c1975- v. : ill. (some col.) ; 29 cm. [ND237.L37A54] 75-26389
1. Lazzari, Mary Clifford. 2. Architecture, Victorian, in art. 3. Architecture, Victorian—Galveston—Pictorial works. I. Title.

Architecture, Victorian—Iowa.

PLYMAT, William. 720'.9777
The Victorian architecture of Iowa / by Wm. Plymat, Jr. Des Moines : Elephant's Eye, c1976. 98 p. : chiefly ill. ; 24 x 28 cm. Includes bibliographical references. [NA730.I8P58] 76-373330
1. Architecture, Victorian—Iowa. 2. Architecture—Iowa. I. Title.

Architecture, Victorian—London.

METCALF, Priscilla. 720'.9421
Victorian London. New York, Praeger [1973, c1972] 190 p. illus. 24 cm. Bibliography: p. 183-184. [NA970.M47 1973] 72-76975 8.95
1. Architecture, Victorian—London. 2. Architecture—London—History. I. Title.

SUMMERSON, John Newenham, Sir, 1904- 720'.9421
The architecture of Victorian London / John Summerson. Charlottesville : University Press of Virginia, 1976. 109 p. : ill. ; 24 cm. (Page Barbour lectures, 1972) [NA970.S79] 75-16130 ISBN 0-8139-0592-3 : 10.00
1. Architecture, Victorian—London. 2. Architecture—London—History. I. Title. II. Series. BIP

SUMMERSON, John Newenham, 1904- 720'.9421
The London building world of the eighteen-sixties [by] John Summerson. London, Thames and Hudson [1973] 60 p. illus. 22 cm. (Walter Neurath memorial lectures, 5) Label mounted on t.p.: Transatlantic Arts, New York, sole distributor for the U.S.A. Includes bibliographical references. [NA970.S82] 74-157760 ISBN 0-500-55005-0 8.75
1. Architecture, Victorian—London. 2. Architecture—London. I. Title. II. Series.

Architecture, Victorian—Louisville, Ky.

THOMAS, Samuel W., 1938- 976.9'44
Old Louisville : the Victorian era / by Samuel W. Thomas and William Morgan. Louisville, Ky. : Published by Data Courier for the Courier-Journal, the Louisville Times, 1975. 152 p. : ill. ; 25 x 31 cm. [NA735.L6T46] 75-30382
1. Architecture, Victorian—Louisville, Ky. 2. Architecture—Louisville, Ky. I. Morgan, William, 1944- joint author. II. Title.

Architecture, Victorian—Portsmouth, Eng.

NASH, Andy. 720'.92'4
A. E. Cogswell, architect within a Victorian city / [by] Andy Nash. Portsmouth : School of Architecture, Portsmouth Polytechnic, 1975. [3], 115, viii, iii leaves : ill., map, plans ; 30 cm. Cover title. Bibliography: leaves i-iii. [NA997.C64N37] 76-359799 ISBN 0-905320-00-X : £3.50
1. Cogswell, Arthur Edward, 1858-1934. 2. Architecture, Victorian—Portsmouth, Eng. I. Title.

Architecture, Victorian—South Africa.

PICTON-SEYMOUR, Desiree. 720'.968
Victorian buildings in South Africa : including Edwardian and Transvaal Republican styles 1850-1910 / Desiree Picton-Seymour. Cape Town : Balkema (A.A.), 1977. xii, 412 p. : ill. ; 29 cm. "A survey of houses, churches, schools, public and commercial buildings with notes on the materials used, the architects concerned, the use of prefabricated ironmongery and the influence of European styles." Includes index. Bibliography: p. 403-405. [NA1592.P5] 78-302108 ISBN 0-86961-083-X : 46.00
1. Architecture, Victorian—South Africa. 2. Architecture—South Africa. 3. Architecture—Details. I. Title.
Distributed by International Scholarly Book Services Inc., P.O. Box 555 Forest Grove, OR 97116

Architecture, Victorian—The West.

FLORIN, Lambert.   720'.978
Victorian West / by Lambert Florin.
Seattle : Superior Pub. Co., [1978] p. cm.
Includes index. [NA725.F56] 78-23760
ISBN 0-87564-341-8 : 14.95
1. Architecture, Victorian—The West. 2.
Architecture—The West. I. Title.   **BIP**

Architecture, Victorian—U.S.

AMERICAN Victorian   720'.973
architecture : a survey of the 70's and 80's
in contemporary photographs / with a new
introd. by Arnold Lewis, and notes on the
plates by Keith Morgan. New York :
Dover Publications, c1975. viii, 152 p. : ill.
; 31 cm. Reproductions of the illustrations
from L'Architecture americaine published
by Andre, Paris, in 1886, with captions in
English. [NA710.A5 1975] 73-92261 ISBN
0-486-23177-1 pbk. : 6.00
1. Architecture, Victorian—United States.
I. Lewis, Arnold.

MAASS, John, 1918-   728.3
The Victorian home in America. New
York, Hawthorn Books [1972] xiv, 235 p.
illus. 29 cm. Bibliography: p. 219-223.
[NA710.M32 1972] 70-158019 19.95
1. Architecture, Victorian—United States.
2. Architecture, Domestic—United States.
I. Title.

SCHMIDT, Carl Frederick,   720'.973
1894-
The Victorian era in the United States, by
Carl F. Schmidt. [Scottsville, N.Y., 1971]
261 p. illus. 29 cm. "No. 140 of 300
copies." Bibliography: p. 257. [NA710.S33]
75-27803
1. Architecture, Victorian—U.S. I. Title.

VICTORIAN architecture   720.973
: two pattern books / by A. J.
Bicknell & William T. Comstock ; with a
new introd. by John Maass. 2d print. corr.
Watkins Glen, N.Y. : American Life
Foundation, 1976, c1975. 75, 80 p. :
chiefly ill. ; 36 cm. Reprint of the 1873 ed.
of Detail, cottage, and constructive
architecture, first published by A. J.
Bicknell, New York; and of the 1881 ed.
of Modern architectural designs and
details, first published by W. T. Comstock,
New York. [NA710.5.V5V52 1976] 75-
22530 ISBN 0-89257-001-6 : 15.00
1. Architecture, Victorian—United States.
2. Architecture—United States. 3.
Architecture—Details. 4. Architecture—
Designs and plans. I. Bicknell, Amos J.
Detail, cottage, and constructive
architecture. 1976. II. Comstock, William
T. Modern architectural designs and
details. 1976.

**Architecture—Virgin Islands of the
United States.**

GOSNER, Pamela W.   720'.97297'22
*Plantation and town, historic architecture
of the United States Virgin Islands,* a
guide, by Pamela W. Gosner. Durham,
N.C., Moore Pub. Co. [1971] 110 p. illus.
23 cm. Title on spine: Historic architecture
of the U.S. Virgin Islands. Bibliography: p.
101-104. [NA815.V5G6] 78-140952 ISBN
0-87716-026-0 4.95
1. Architecture—Virgin Islands of the
United States. I. Title. II. Title: Historic
architecture of the U.S. Virgin Islands.

Architecture—Virginia.

NICHOLS, Frederick   720.9755
Doveton.
Architecture in Virginia, 1776-1958: the
Old Dominion's twelve best buildings; a
survey made by Frederick D. Nichols and
William B. O'Neal. [Richmond] Virginia
Museum of Fine Arts [c1958] unpaged.
illus. 23x33cm. [NA730.V8N5] 58-14100
1. Architecture—Virginia. I. O'Neal,
William Bainter, joint author. II. Virginia
Museum of Fine Arts, Richmond. III.
Title.

O'NEAL, William   720.9'755
Bainter.
Architecture in Virginia; an official guide
to four centuries of building in the Old
Dominion, by William B. O'Neal. 1st ed.
New York, Pub. for the Virginia Mus. by

Walker, 1968. 192p. illus., facsims., maps.
23cm. Bibl. [NA730.V805] 67-13230 4.95
trade 2.95 pap.,
1. Architecture—Virginia. 2. Virginia—
Historic houses, etc. I. Virginia Museum of
Fine Arts, Richmond. II. Title.   **BIP**

Architecture—Virginia—Catalogs.

HISTORIC American   917.55
Buildings Survey.
*Historic American Buildings Survey:
Virginia catalog;* a list of measured
drawings, photographs, and written
documentation in the Survey. Compiled by
the Virginia Historic Landmarks
Commission and the Historic American
Buildings Survey. Charlottesville, Published
for the Historic American Buildings Survey
by the University Press of Virginia [1974]
p. cm. [NA730.V8H5 1974] 74-7402 ISBN
0-8139-0518-4
1. Architecture—Virginia—Catalogs. 2.
Virginia—Historic houses, etc. I. Virginia
Historic Landmarks Commission. II. Title:
Virginia catalog.   **BIP**

Architecture—Virginia—Danville.

CAHILL, Mary, 1918-   975.5'665
Victorian Danville : fifty-two landmarks :
their architecture & history / by Mary
Cahill and Gary Grant ; photos. and
architectural descriptions by Russell
Wright. [s.l. : s.n.], c1977 (Danville, Va. :
Womack Press) xi, 112 p. : ill. ; 29 cm.
Bibliography: p. 109-112.
[NA735.D25C33] 77-155987
1. Architecture—Virginia—Danville. 2.
Danville, Va.—Buildings. I. Grant, Gary,
joint author. II. Title.

Architecture—Vocational guidance.

PIPER, Robert J.   720'.23
Opportunities in an architecture career, by
Robert J. Piper. [Rev. ed.] New York,
Educational Books Division, Universal
Pub. and Distributing Corp. [1970] 126 p.
illus. 20 cm. (VGM career series, V160)
Published in 1975 under title:
Opportunities in architecture today.
Includes bibliographies. [NA1995.P5 1970]
77-112725 1.95
1. Architecture—Vocational guidance. I.
Title.

ROTH, Richard, 1904-   720'.23
Your future in architecture / Richard
Roth. Rev. ed. New York : R. Rosen
Press, 1979. p. cm. (Careers in depth ; 2)
Bibliography: p. [NA1995.R65 1979] 78-
24556 ISBN 0-8239-0478-4 lib.bdg : 4.98
1. Architecture—Vocational guidance. I.
Title.

**Architecture—Vocational guidance—
Addresses, essays, lectures.**

THE Architect :   720'.23
chapters in the history of the profession /
edited by Spiro Kostof. New York :
Oxford University Press, 1977]i.e. 1976[x,
371 p. : ill. ; 24 cm. Includes
bibliographical references and index.
[NA1995.A73]   75-46368   ISBN   0-19-
502067-7 : 19.50
1. Architecture—Vocational guidance—
Addresses, essays, lectures. I. Kostof, Spiro
K.

Architecture—Wales.

HILLING, John B.   720'.9429
The historic architecture of Wales : an
introduction / [by] John B. Hilling ; [maps,
plans and line drawings by John B. Hilling]
. Cardiff : University of Wales Press, 1976.
xiii, 234 p. : ill., maps, plans ; 21 cm.
Includes indexes. Bibliography: p. 218-222.
[NA992.H52] 77-364196 ISBN 0-7083-
0626-8 : £5.50
1. Architecture—Wales. 2. Historic
buildings—Wales. 3. Wales—Antiquities. I.
Title.   **BIP**

Architecture—Warren Co., Ohio.

PHILLIPS, Hazel   720'.9771'76
Spencer, 1896-
Traditional architecture, Warren County,

Ohio. [Lebanon? Ohio, c1969] xviii, 129 p.
illus. 24 cm. [NA730.O35P45] 70-12344
1. Architecture—Warren Co., Ohio. 2.
Warren Co., Ohio—Historic houses, etc. I.
Title.

PHILLIPS, Hazel   720'.9771'763
Spencer, 1896-
*Traditional architecture, Warren County,
Ohio.* [Lebanon, Ohio, 1973] xviii, 129 p.
illus. 24 cm. [NA730.O32W376 1973] 74-
160958
1. Architecture—Warren Co., Ohio. 2.
Warren Co., Ohio—Historic houses, etc. I.
Title.

Architecture—Warwickshire, Eng.

PEVSNER, Nikolaus,   720.94248
Sir, 1902-
Warwickshire, by Nikolaus Pevsner and
Alexandra Wedgwood. Harmondsworth,
Penguin, 1966. 531 p. front., illus., 64
plates, maps, diagrs. 19 cm. (His Buildings
of England, 31) [NA971.W3P4] 67-70684
1. Architecture—Warwickshire, Eng. 2.
Warwickshire, Eng.—Historic houses, etc.
I. Wedgwood, Alexandra (Gordon Clark)
1938- joint author.   II.   Title.

Architecture—Washington, D. C.

AMERICAN Institute of   750.9753
Architects. Washington-Metropolitan
Chapter.
Washington architecture. 1791-1957,
prepared by a committee of the
Washingom- Metropolitan Chapter,
American Institute of Architects. New
York, Reinhold [1957] 96p. illus. 22cm.
[NA735.Aw3A6] 57-10358
1. Architecture—Washington, D. C. I.
Title.

AMERICAN Institute of   720.9753
Architects. Washington-Metropolitan
Chapter.
Washington architecture, 1791-1957,
prepared by a committee of the
Washington-Metropolitan Chapter
American Institute of Architects. New
York, Reinhold [1957] 96p. illus. 22cm.
[NA735.W3A6] 57-10358
1. Architecture—Washington, D. C. I.
Title.

MADDEX, Diane.   720'.9753
Historic buildings of Washington, D.C.
With a foreword by Arthur Cotton Moore.
[1st ed.] Pittsburgh, Ober Park Associates
[1973] 191 p. illus. 29 cm. (Historic
buildings of America) "A selection from
the records of the Historic American
Buildings Survey, National Park Service,
U.S. Department of the Interior."
Bibliography: p. 182-187. [NA735.W3M32]
72-92006 17.50
1. Architecture—Washington, D. C. 2.
Washington, D.C.—Historic houses, etc. I.
Historic American Buildings Survey. II.
Title. III. Series: The Historic buildings of
America.

**Architecture—Washington, D.C.—
Bibliography.**

MEGLIS, Anne Llewellyn.   016.9753
A bibliographic tour of Washington, D.C. /
compiled by Anne Llewellyn Meglis.
Washington : D.C. Redevelopment Land
Agency, 1974. iv, 44 p. : ill. ; 23 cm.
[Z5944.U5M43] [NA735.W3] 75-622186
1. Architecture—Washington, D.C.—
Bibliography. I. District of Columbia
Redevelopment Land Agency. II. Title.

**Architecture—Washington, D.C.—
Catalogs.**

HISTORIC American   917.53'04'4
*Buildings Survey, District of Columbia
catalog, 1974* / compiled by Nancy B.
Schwartz. Charlottesville : Published for
the Columbia Historical Society by the
University Press of Virginia, 1975. p. cm.
Bibliography: p. [NA735.W3H57] 75-9696
ISBN 0-8139-0618-0
1. Architecture—Washington, D.C.—
Catalogs. 2. Historic buildings—
Washington, D.C.—Catalogs. 3.
Washington, D.C.—Buildings—Catalogs. I.
Schwartz, Nancy B. II. Historic American
Buildings Survey. III. Columbia Historical

Society, Washington, D.C. IV. Title:
District of Columbia catalog, 1974.

**Architecture—Washington, D.C.—
Guide-books.**

A Guide to the   917.53'04'4
architecture of Washington, D.C. Written
and edited by Warren J. Cox [and others]
for the Washington Metropolitan Chapter
of the American Institute of Architects.
[2d ed., rev. and expanded] New York,
McGraw-Hill [1974] 246 p. illus. 23 x 12
cm. First ed. is entered under Hugh
Newell Jacobsen. "[Includes] 20 walking
and motoring tours of Washington and the
vicinity." Includes bibliographical
references. [NA735.W3G84 1974] 74-1336
ISBN 0-07-013286-0 7.95
1. Architecture—Washington, D.C.—
Guide-books. 2. Washington, D.C.—
Buildings. I. Cox, Warren J. II. Jacobsen,
Hugh Newell, ed. A guide to the
architecture of Washington, D.C. III.
American Institute of Architects.
Washington-Metropolitan Chapter.
Pbk. 5.95, ISBN 0-07-13285-2   **BIP**

JACOBSEN, Hugh Newell,   917.5304
ed.
*A guide to the architecture of Washington,
D.C.* With an introd. by Francis Donald
Lethbridge. New York, Published for the
Washington Metropolitan Chapter,
American Institute of Architects by F. A.
Praeger [1965] 211 p. illus., col. maps (1
fold.) plans. 23 cm. [NA735.W3J3] 65-
22758
1. Architecture—Washington, D.C.—
Guide-books. 2. Washington, D.C.—
Description—1951- —Guide-books. 3.
Washington, D.C.—Buildings. I. American
Institute of Architects. Washington-
Metropolitan Chapter. II. Title. III. Title:
The architecture of Washington, D.C.

**Architecture—Washington, D.C.—
History.**

THE Architecture of   720'.9753
Washington, D.C. / Bates Lowry, editor.
Washington : Dunlap Society, 1977. p.
cm. [NA735.W3A72] 76-59742 185.00
1. Architecture—Washington, D.C.—
History. I. Lowry, Bates, 1923- II. Dunlap
Society.

**Architecture—Washington—Skagit
Co.—Guide-books.**

WILLIS, Margaret,   917.97'72'044
1899-
The buildings of Old Skagit County : ten
self-guided tours—1977 / Margaret Willis,
editor ; photos. by David Hall and
Margaret Willis in 1975, 1976 and 1977 ;
maps by Helen Barret and David Hall.
Mount Vernon, WA : Skagit County
Historical Society, 1977. 50 p. : ill. ; 28
cm. (Skagit County historical series ; no.
5) Text on p. [2] of cover.
[NA730.W22S537] 77-152849
1. Architecture—Washington—Skagit
Co.—Guide-books. I. Title.

**Architecture—West Indies, British—
Conservation and restoration.**

ACWORTH, Angus   720.9'729
Whiteford, 1898-
*Buildings of architectural or historic
interest in the British West Indies;* a report
with proposals as to the best means of
protecting them from damage or
destruction (otherwise than by acts of
God) Presented to His Majesty's Secretary
of State for the Colonies (The Right Hon.
Arthur Creech-Jones, M.P.) London, H.M.
Stationery Off., 1951. New York, Johnson
Reprint Corp., 1970. vi, 21 p. illus. 23 cm.
(Colonial research studies, no. 2) At head
of title: Colonial Office. [JV33.G7A48 no.
2, 1970] [NA109] 77-140791
1. Architecture—West Indies, British—
Conservation and restoration. I. Gt. Brit.
Colonial Office. II. Title. III. Series: Gt.
Brit. Dept. of Technical Co-operation.
Colonial research studies, no. 2   **BIP**

Architecture—Western Reserve.

CAMPEN, Richard N.   720'.9771'3
Architecture of the Western Reserve, 1800-1900 [by] Richard N. Campen. Cleveland, Press of Case Western Reserve University, 1971. xii, 260 p. illus. 32 cm. Bibliography: p.   255-258. [NA730.O32W43] 70-116382 ISBN 0-8295-0196-7 20.00
1. Architecture—Western Reserve. 2. Architecture, Modern—19th century—Western Reserve. I. Title.   **BIP**

Architecture—Westminster, Eng. St. Margaret's Parish.

FORREST, George Topham,   914.21'32
1872-1945.
The Parish of St. Margaret, Westminster. [Drawings, illustrations, and architectural descriptions by G. Topham Forrest] London, Published for the London County Council by B. T. Batsford, 1926- [New York, AMS Press, 1971- v. illus. 29 cm. (The Survey of London, v. 10), [DA685.W57F672] 70-138272 ISBN 0-404-51660-2 (v. 10)
1. Westminster, Eng. St. Margaret's Parish—Historic houses, etc. 2. Architecture—Westminster, Eng. St. Margaret's Parish. I. Title. II. Series: Joint Publishing Committee Representing the London County Council and the London Survey Committee. Survey of London, v. 10, etc.   **BIP**

Architecture—Wilmington, N.C.

NORTH Carolina.   711'.409'75627
Division of Community Planning.
Historic district development plan, Wilmington, North Carolina. [Raleigh; Available from Clearinghouse for Federal Scientific and Technical Information, Washington, 1968] 64 p. illus., col. maps. 28 x 32 cm. Prepared for the City of Wilmington. 1962 ed. issued under title: Wilmington, North Carolina, historic area. [NA735.W52A55 1968] 73-9026 2.00
1. Architecture—Wilmington, N.C. 2. Cities and towns—Planning—Wilmington, N.C. I. Title.

Architecture—Wisconsin—Hist.

PERRIN, Richard W E   720.9775
1909-
Historic Wisconsin buildings; a survey of pioneer architecture, 1835-1870. Photos by the author. [Milwaukee, Milwaukee Public Museum Press, 1962] 91p. illus. 23cm. (Milwaukee. Public Museum. Publications in history, no.4) This series of articles was originally published in Lore, the official magazine of the Milwaukee Public museum. [NA730.W5P4] 62-52989
1. Architecture—Wisconsin—Hist. I. Title.

Architecture—Yearbooks.

AMERICAN Institute of   720.6273
Architects. Long Island Society Chapter.
Year book. Hempstead. v. 23 cm. [NA11.A6L6] 51-19573
I.   Title.

ARCHITECTS' year book.   720.58
[v.]9. Ed.: Trevor Dannatt. [dist.] New York, Chemical Publishing Co. [c.]1960[ ] 227p. illus. 46-1647 10.00
1. Architecture—Yearbooks. 2. Building—Yearbooks.

ARCHITECTURE;   720.58
formes et function. 1962-1963 ed. Lausanne, Anthony Krafft [dist. New York, Wittenborn, 1963, c.1962] 287p. illus. (pt. col.) diagrs. (pt. col.) maps (pt. col.) 30cm. English, French or German. annual. 60-52081 7.50
1. Architecture—Yearbooks. 2. Cities and towns—Planning—Yearbooks.

ARCHITECTURE formes [et]   720.58
fonctions. Ed. 1960. [dist. New York, Wittenborn] c.1960. 266p. illus. 30cm. (Organe official du Jour Mondial de l'Urbanisme) (French text: summaries in English and German) Annual. 60-52081 7.50; 5.00 pap.,
1. Architecture—Yearbooks. 2. Cities and

towns—Planning—Yearbooks.   I. *Jour mondial de l'urbanisme.*

ARCHITECTURE; formes,   720.58
fonctions. Annual intl. review, 1967 ed. Lausanne, Eds. Anthony Krafft, 1967. v. illus. (pt. col.) diagrs. 21cm. French, German, English, or Spanish. annual. 60-52081 11.00
1. Architecture—Yearbooks. 2. Cities and towns —Planning—Yearbooks.
American distributor: Wittenborn, New York.

ARCHITECTURE in   720/.9495
*Gree*ce. 1- [i.e. et] fonctions. Lausanne, Switzerland, A. Krafft. v. illus. 31cm. annual. Official organ of the Jour mondial de l'urbanisme, [NA9.A47] 60-52081 12.00
1. Architecture—Yearbooks. 2. Cities and towns—Planning—Yearbooks. I. Jour mondial de l'urbanisme.
American distributor: Wittenborn, New York.

LOTUS;   720.58
architectural annual, 1964-1965. Ed. by Giulia Veronesi, Bruno Alfieri. Milan, Alfieri [New York, Wittenborn] c.1964. 223p. illus., plans. 25x25cm. English, French, German, Italian, or Spanish. 64-56568 15.00
1. Architecture—Yearbooks. 2. Cities and towns—Planning—Yearbooks. 3. Design, Industrial—Yearbooks.

LOTUS;   720.58
an international review of contemporary architecture. 1967-1968 [Venezia, Alfieri edizioni d'arte. Dist. New York, Wittenborn, 1967] v. illus., plans. 24x25cm. Ed.: no.1-Bruno Alfieri. English, Italian & French. [NA9.L6] 64-56568 15.00 bds.,
1. Architecture — Yearbooks. 2. Cities and towns — Planning — Yearbooks. 3. Design — Industrial — Yearbooks.

LOTUS;   720.58
architectural annual, annuario dell' 'architettura d'oggi, annuaire de l'architecture contemporaire v.2 1965-1966. Ed. by Giulia Veronesi, Bruno Alfieri, Milan. Alfieri [New York, Wittenborn, 1966[c.1964. 227p. illus., plans. 24x25cm. English, French, German, Italian or Spanish. [NA9.L6] 64-56568 15.00 bds.,
1. Architecture—Yearbooks. 2. Cities and towns—Planning—Yearbooks. 3. Design, Industrial—Yearbooks.

REPORT.   720'.9773'11
[New York] v. 27cm. annual. Reports for issued by the organization under its earlier name: Beaux-Arts Institute of Design. Issues for include also reports of the Society of Beaux-Arts Architects and the Societe des architectes diplomes par ie Gouvernment francals, Groupe americaine. [NA2300.N473]   44-17843
I. Society of Beaux-Arts Architects, New York. II. Societe des architectes diplomes par le Gouvernement. Groupe americaine.

Architecture—York, Eng.

PEVSNER, Nikolaus,   914.27'4'0485
Sir, 1902-
Yorkshire: York and the East Riding; with contributions from John Hutchinson. Harmondsworth, Penguin, 1972. 416, [64] p. illus., map, plan. 19 cm. (His The buildings of England) [NA971.Y7P48] 72-195678 ISBN 0-14-071043-4 £2.10
1.   Architecture—York, Eng. 2. Architecture—Yorkshire, Eng. East Riding. I. Title.

Architecture—Yorkshire, Eng. North Riding.

PEVSNER, Nikolaus,   720'.9427'4
1902-
Yorkshire: the North Riding. Harmondsworth, Penguin, 1966. 454 p. 2 fronts. (maps), illus., 62 plates, diagrs. 19 cm. (His The Buildings of England series) [NA969.Y6P37] 70-365905 30/-
1. Architecture—Yorkshire, Eng. North Riding. I. Title.

Architecture—Yorkshire, Eng. West Riding.

PEVSNER, Nikolaus,   720'.9427'4
1902-
Yorkshire: the West Riding. 2nd ed. revised by Enid Radcliffe. Harmondsworth, Penguin, 1967 [i.e. 1968] 652 p. 72 plates, illus., map. 19 cm. (His The Buildings of England, BE17) [NA969.Y6P4 1968] 75-356072 30/-
1. Architecture—Yorkshire, Eng. West Riding. I. Radcliffe, Enid. II. Title.

Archive buildings.

DUCHEIN, Michel.   725'.15
Archive buildings and equipment / Michel Duchein. Munchen : Verlag Dokumentation, 1977. 201 p. : ill. ; 24 cm. (ICA handbooks series ; v. 1) Includes index. Bibliography: p.   142-145. [CD981.D82] 78-311972 ISBN 3-7940-3780-4 : 14.00
1. Archive buildings. I. Title. II. Series: International Council on Archives. ICA handbooks series ; no. 1.
Distributed by UNIPUB.

Archives of American Art.

ARCHIVES of American   016.709'73
Art.
A checklist of the collection, spring 1975 / Archives of American Art ; compiled by Arthur J. Breton, Nancy H. Zembala, and Anne P. Nicastro. [Washington] : Smithsonian Institution, [1975] ca 150 p. ; 27 cm. [Z6616.A2A68 1975] [N6536] 76-600745
1. Archives of American Art. 2. Artists—United States—Archives. I. Breton, Arthur J. II. Zembala, Nancy H. III. Nicastro, Anne P.

Arcimboldi, Giuseppe, 1527?-1593.

KAUFMANN, Thomas   704'.35'11
DaCosta.
Variations on the Imperial theme : studies in ceremonial art and collecting in the age of Maximilian II and Rudolf II / Thomas Da Costa Kaufmann. New York : Garland Pub., [1978]   p.   cm. (Outstanding dissertations in the fine arts) Originally presented as the author's thesis, Harvard University, 1977. Bibliography: p. [ND623.A7K38 1978] 77-94699 ISBN 0-8240-3231-4 : lib.bdg. : 20.00
1. Arcimboldi, Giuseppe, 1527?-1593. 2. Maximilian II, Emperor of Germany, 1527-1576—Art patronage. 3. Allegories. 4. Festivals in art. 5. Festivals—Germany. I. Title. II. Series.   **BIP**

PIEYRE de Mandiargues,   759.5
Andre, 1909-
Arcimboldo the Marvelous / by Andre Pieyre de Mandiargues ; conception by Yasha David ; [editor, Patricia Egan ; translator, I. Mark Paris]. New York : Abrams, 1978, c1977. 128 p. : ill. (some col.) ; cm. Translation of Arcimboldo le merveilleux. [ND623.A7P5313] 77-25439 ISBN 0-8109-0689-9 : 28.50
1. Arcimboldi, Giuseppe, 1527?-1593. I. Arcimboldi, Giuseppe, 1527?-1593. II. Title.

Ardon, Mordekhai, 1896—

ARDON, Mordekhai, 1896-   759.95694
Mordecai Ardon [compiled by] Michele Vishny. New York, H. N. Abrams [1974] 240 p. (chiefly illus. (part col.)) 28 x 30 cm. Bibliography: p. [236]-[239] [ND979.A7V57] 73-22002 ISBN 0-8109-0171-4
1. Ardon, Mordekhai, 1896- I. Vishny, Michele, ed.

Argus camera.

COOPER, Joseph David,   771.31
1917-
Argus pocket companion. [New York] Universal Photo Bks.[dist. Amphoto, c.1962] 94p. illus. 15cm. (U-258) 62-14416 1.95, wire bdg.
1. Argus camera. 2. Photography—Handbooks, manuals, etc. I. Title.

DESCHIN, Jacob.   770.2
Picture making with the Argus, C3, C4, A4; a working manual. [1st ed.] San Francisco, Camera Craft Pub. Co. [1954] 128p. illus. 24cm. (Camera Craft plus value books) [TR263.A7D4] 54-12589
1. Argus camera. 2. Photography—Handbooks, manuals, etc. I. Title.

MURPHY, Burt.   771.31
Argus 35mm photography. [1st ed.] New York, Verlan Books [cu959] 128p. illus. 21cm. (A Universal photo book) [TR263.A7M8] 59-15881
1. Argus camera. 2. Photography—Handbooks, manuals, etc. I. Title.

TYDINGS, Kenneth S   770.2
The Argus 35mm guide and reference book. New York, Greenberg, c1952. 128 p. illus. 20 cm. (The Modern camera guide series) [TR263.A7T9] 52-8125
1. Argus camera. I. Title.

Ariosto, Lodovico, 1474-1533.

LEE, Rensselaer Wright, 1898-   760
Names on trees : Ariosto into art / by Rensselaer W. Lee. Princeton, N.J. : Princeton University Press, [1977], c1976. p. cm. (Princeton essays on the arts ; 3) Includes bibliographical references and index. [N66.L4 1977] 76-3270 ISBN 0-691-03914-3 : 14.50. ISBN 0-691-00311-4 pbk. : 5.95
1. Ariosto, Lodovico, 1474-1533. Orlando furioso—Illustrations. 2. Names carved on trees. 3. Ut pictura poesis (Aesthetics) I. Title.   **BIP**

Aristoteles. De caelo.

ASHLEY, Benedict M   v. 12
Aristotle's sluggish earth: the problematics of the De caelo. River Forest, Ill., Albertus Magnus Lyceum, 1958. viii, 73 p. 23 cm. (The Aquinas library) "Extracted from The New scholasticism, XXXII, 1, January, 1958, p. 1-31, and 2, April, 1958, p. 202-234."   Bibliographical   footnotes. Bibliography: p. 67-73. [NUC64-57666]
1. Aristoteles. De caelo. I. Title.

Arithmetic—Caricatures and cartoons.

HARDING, Lowry Waring.   741.5
Arithmetoons. Concepts and captions by Lowry W. Harding, designs and drawings by Michael Dooley. Dubuque, Iowa, W. C. Brown Co. [1956- v. illus. 22cm. [NC1429.H33D6] 56-10220
1. Arithmetic—Caricatures and cartoons. I. Dooley, Michael, illus. II. Title.

Arizona — Antiq.

WASLEY, William Warwick,   970.491
1919-
Salvage archaeology in Painted Rocks Reservoir, western Arizona [by] William W. Wasley and Alfred E. Johnson. With appendices by High C. Cutler [and] Mary Elizabeth King. Tucson, University of Arizona Press, 1965. xi, 123 p. illus., map. plans 27 cm. (University of Arizona.

Anthropological papers, no. 9) Bibliography: p. 115-123. [E78.A7W3] 64-63815
1. Arizona — Antiq. 2. Hobokam culture. 3. Excavations (Archaeology) — Arizona. 4. Painted Rocks Reservoir. I. Johnson, Alfred E. joint author. II. Title. III. Series: Arizona. University. Anthropological papers, no. 9 BIP

Arkansas—Antiq.—Yearbooks.

ARKANSAS 917.8963044
Archeological Society.
Arkansas archeology. 1962. Fayetteville, Arkansas Archeological Society. 109 p. illus., maps plans. 28 cm. annual. Absorbed by the Arkansas archeologist. [E78.A8A7] 64-6307
1. Arkansas—Antiq.—Yearbooks. 2. Indians of North America—Arkansas—Antiq.—Yearbooks. I. Title.

Arkansas—Description and travel—Views.

SMITH, Hubert, 1942- 779'.9'917670924
A world of beauty: Arkansas. Photography by Hubert Smith. Editors: Ralph W. Sanders [and others] 1st ed. Little Rock, Ark., Concept-Three [1972] 1 v. of illus. 31 cm. Consists of color photographs with captions on opposite pages. [F412.S63] 72-93659 19.95
1. Arkansas—Description and travel—Views. I. Sanders, Ralph W., 1945- ed. II. Title.

Arman, 1928-

ARMAN, 1928- 759.4
Arman : lyrical surfaces, December 3, 1975—January 5, 1976. New York : Andrew Crispo Gallery, 1975. [48] p. : ill. (some col.) ; 23 x 26 cm. Bibliography: p. [47] [ND1950.A74A84] 75-39556
1. Arman, 1928- 2. Musical instruments in art. I. Andrew Crispo Gallery.

Armand Marseille (Firm)

SMITH, Patricia R. 745.59'22'075
Armand Marseille dolls, 1865-1928 / by Patricia R. Smith ; edited by Dorothy Westbrook ; photo's by Dwight F. Smith. Paducah, Ky. : Collector Books, [1975] 144 p. : col. ill. ; 22 cm. Bibliography: p. 144. [TS2301.T7S58] 75-316885 7.95
1. Armand Marseille (Firm) 2. Dolls—Collectors and collecting. 3. Dolls—Catalogs. I. Title. BIP

Armina West site, Egypt.

TRIGGER, Bruce G. 932
The late Nubian settlement at Arminna West / by Bruce G. Trigger ; based on field work, notes, and plans by the author ... [et al.] ; Alexander H. Jeffries, Jr., architect ; James Delmege, photographer. New Haven : Peabody Museum of Natural History of Yale University, 1967. xx, 92 p., [20] leaves of plates (2 fold.) : ill., diagrs., plans, map (1 fold. in pocket) ; 35 cm. (Publications of the Pennsylvania-Yale Expedition to Egypt ; no. 2) Includes index. Bibliography: p. xiii-xv. [DT73.A812T75] 67-26193
1. Arminna West site, Egypt. I. Title. II. Series: Pennsylvania-Yale Expedition to Egypt, 1961-1962. Publications ; no. 2. BIP

WEEKS, Kent R. 913.32
The classic Christian townsite at Arminna West / by Kent R. Weeks ; based on field work, notes, and plans by the author and the director, and Peter Mayer ... [et al.]. New Haven : Peabody Museum of Natural History of Yale University, 1967. xv, 73 p., [9] leaves of plates (2 fold.) : ill. ; 35 cm. (Publications of the Pennsylvania-Yale Expedition to Egypt ; no. 3) Includes index. Bibliography: p. xi-xii. [DT73.A812W43] 67-26194
1. Armina West site, Egypt. I. Title. II. Series: Pennsylvania-Yale Expedition to Egypt, 1961-1962. Publications ; no. 3. BIP

Armitage, David, 1943—

ARMITAGE, David, 1943- 759.994
David Armitage : a survey exhibition ... organised by the Dunedin Public Art Gallery and ... sponsored and toured by the Queen Elizabeth II Arts Council of New Zealand. [Dunedin : Dunedin Public Art Gallery, 1974] ([Dunedin] : Dunedin Print) [40] p. : ill. (part col.), port. ; 20 x 24 cm. Cover title: Armitage. [ND1105.A75D86] 75-305609
1. Armitage, David, 1943- I. Dunedin Public Art Gallery. II. Queen Elizabeth the Second Arts Council of New Zealand.

Armory Show, New York, 1913.

ASSOCIATION of 709'.04'07401471
American Painters and Sculptors, New York.
The Armory Show; international exhibition of modern art, 1913. New York, Arno Press [1972] 3 v. illus. 23 cm. (v. 3: 29 cm.) (Arno series of contemporary art) Contents.Contents.—v. 1. Catalogues.—v. 2. Pamphlets.—v. 3. Contemporary and retrospective documents. Includes bibliographical references. [N6493 1913.A84] 72-165525 ISBN 0-405-00828-7
1. Armory Show, New York, 1913. 2. Art, Modern—20th century—Exhibitions. I. Title. BIP

MUNSON-WILLIAMS-PROCTOR 707.4
Institute, Utica, N.Y.
1913 Armory show; 50th anniversary exhibition, 1963. Organized by Munson-Williams-Proctor Institute. Sponsored by the Henry Street Settlement, New York. [Utica, 1963] 212 p. illus., plates (part col.) 28 cm. Reconstruction of the Armory show (International exhibition of modern art, organized by the Association of American Painters and Sculptors) to be exhibited at the institute Feb. 17-Mar. 31 and at the Armory of the 69th Regiment, New York, Apr. 6-28, 1963. [N5020.U8] 63-13993
1. Armory Show, New York, 1913. I. Henry Street Settlement, New York. II. Association of American Painters and Sculptors, New York. III. Title: Armory show. IV. Title: International exhibition of modern art.

Armour, Edward Jennings, 1937-

BROWN University. Dept. of 759.13
Art.
Four artists: Brown University 1963. [Faculty exhibition] Annmary Brown Memorial, 10 May through 10 June, 1963. [Providence, 1963] unpaged: illus. 24 cm. [ND237.A68B75] 63-17939
1. Armour, Edward Jennings, 1937- 2. Feldman, Walter, 1925- 3. Neuman, Robert S., 1926- 4. Townley, Hugh. I. Title.

Arms and armor.

CLEATOR, Philip 355.8'2'09
Ellaby, 1908-
Weapons of war [by] P. E. Cleator. Illustrated with photos. and drawings. New York, Crowell [1968, c1967] 224 p. illus., maps. 23 cm. Bibliography: p. 211-214. [U800.C57 1968] 68-20091
1. Arms and armor. 2. Ordnance. I. Title.

DILLON, Harold Arthur Lee- 739.7'5
Dillon, 17th Viscount, 1844-1932.
Armour: An Elizabethan armourer's album and Armour notes, by Viscount Dillon. York, Pa., G. Shumway [1968] 75 p. illus. 23 cm. "An Elizabethan armourer's album" is reprinted from v. 52 (2d ser., v. 2), 1895, and "Armour notes" is reprinted from v. 60 (2d ser., v. 10), 1903, of the Archaeological journal. [U810.D55] 71-218
1. Arms and armor. I. Title.

ELLACOTT, S E 355.8'2
Armour and blade [by] S. E. Ellacott. London, New York, Abelard-Schuman [1962] 191 p. illus. 22 cm. Bibliography: p. 185. [U800.E4] 67-2192
1. Arms and armor. I. Title.

FFOULKES, Charles John, 623.4'41
1868-1947.
Armour & weapons, by Charles Ffoulkes, with a preface by Viscount Dillon. [Wakefield, Eng.] EP Pub., 1973. 112 p. illus. 24 cm. Reprint of the 1909 ed. published by Clarendon Press, Oxford. [U800.F5 1973] 74-155332 ISBN 0-85409-898-4
1. Arms and armor. I. Title.
Distributed by Rowman and Littlefield, 7.50.

HALBRITTER, Kurt. 355.8'2'09
Halbritter's Arms through the ages : an introduction to the secret weapons of history. New York : Viking Press, [1979] p. cm. Translation of Waffenarsenal. Previous English ed. published under title: Halbritter's Armoury. "A Seaver book." Includes index. [U800.H2813 1979] 78-32104 ISBN 0-670-35908-4 : 12.95
1. Arms and armor. I. Arms through the ages. II. Title. BIP

KUNSTGEWERBLICHE 739.7
Werkstatten Ernst Schmidt.
Arms [and] armor from the atelier of Ernst Schmidt, Munich; [catalog, edited by] E. Andrew Mowbray. [Providence, Printed by the Mowbray Co., 1967] 168 p. illus., facsims., plates. 27 cm. [U810.K813] 67-31464
1. Arms and armor. I. Mowbray, E. Andrew, ed. II. Title.

WELLER, Jac. 356
Weapons and tactics; Hastings to Berlin. New York, St. Martin's Press [1966] 238 p. maps, plates, ports, 23 cm. Bibliography: p. 231-234 [U800.W4] 66-14030
1. Arms and armor. 2. Armed Forces. 3. Tactics. I. Title.

WELLER, Jac 356
Weapons and tactics: Hastings to Berlin. London, Vane [New York, St. Martin's, c.1966] 238p. plates (incl. facsims.) 9 maps, tables. 23cm. Bibl. [U800.W4] 66-70688 6.00
1. Arms and armor. 2. Armed Forces. 3. Tactics. I. Title.

WILKINSON, Frederick 355.8'2
John, 1922-
Edged weapons, by Frederick Wilkinson. Garden City, N.Y., Doubleday [1970] 256, xiv p. illus. (part col.) 25 cm. Bibliography: 6th prelim. page. [U800.W57 1970b] 72-113989 ISBN 0-85112-171-3 12.95
1. Arms and armor. I. Title.

WILKINSON, Henry. 355.8'2'09
Engines of war. [1st ed. reprinted]; new introduction by W. S. Curtis. Richmond, Richmond Publishing Co. Ltd, 1973. [2], v, viii, 269 p. 18 cm. Reprint of the 1841 ed. published by Longman, Orme, Brown, Green and Longmans, London. Includes bibliographical references. [U800.W6 1973] 74-154858 ISBN 0-85546-177-2 £3.40
1. Arms and armor. 2. Firearms. I. Title.

Arms and armor, African—Juvenile literature.

NICKEL, Helmut. 623.4'41'096
Arms and armor in Africa. [1st ed.] New York, Atheneum, 1971. 57 p. illus., map. 21 x 24 cm. Describes the weapons and tools found in Africa from prehistoric through modern times and discusses how they evince man's progression. [U800.N48] 75-115090 5.25
1. Arms and armor, African—Juvenile literature. I. Title.

Arms and armor, British.

FFOULKES, Charles 623.4'44'0942
John, 1868-1947.
Sword, lance & bayonet; a record of the arms of the British army & navy, by Charles Ffoulkes and E. C. Hopkinson. [2d ed.] New York, Arco [1967] xvi, 144 p. illus. 25 cm. Bibliography: p. 139-140. [U820.G7F4 1967b] 67-18415
1. Arms and armor, British. 2. Swords, British. 3. Great Britain—Army—Equipment. I. Hopkinson, Edward Campbell, joint author. II. Title.

WILKINSON-LATHAM, 739.7'2'0942
John.
British cut and thrust weapons. [1st ed.] Rutland, Vt., C. E. Tuttle Co. [1971] 112 p. illus. 26 cm. Bibliography: p. 109. [U820.G7W5 1971b] 72-182704 ISBN 0-8048-1023-0 7.50
1. Arms and armor, British. 2. Swords, British. I. Title. BIP

Arms and armor—California—Los Angeles—Catalogs.

LOS Angeles Co., Calif. 739.7
Museum of Natural History Los Angeles History Division.
A distinguished collection of arms and armor on permanent display. Edited by Russell E. Belous. Los Angeles, Ward Ritchie Press, 1969 [c1968] 128 p. illus. (part col.) 29 cm. (Its Bulletin no. 4) Cover title: Arms & armor. [NK6602.L74L63] 68-58975
1. Arms and armor—California—Los Angeles—Catalogs. I. Belous, Russell E., ed. II. Title. III. Title: Arms & armor. IV. Series.

Arms and armor—Catalogs.

JOHN Woodman Higgins 739.70838
Armory, Worcester, Mass.
Catalogue of armor: the JohnWoodman Higgins Armory, by Stephen V. Grancsay. Foreword by John Woodman Higgins. Worcester, 1961. 127p. illus. 27cm. [NK6602.W6J6] 61-19374
1. Arms and armor—Catalogs. I. Grancsay, Stephen Vincent, 1897- II. Title.

Arms and armor, Chinese.

GETTENS, Rutherford John. 739.7'2
Two early Chinese bronze weapons with meteoritic iron blades [by] Rutherford J. Gettens, Roy S. Clarke, Jr. [and] W. T. Chase. Washington, Freer Gallery of Art, 1971. xii, 77 p. illus., col. plate. 26 cm. (Freer Gallery of Art, Washington, D.C. Occasional papers, v. 4, no. 1) Bibliography: p. 73-77. [NK6683.A1G47] 73-170667
1. Arms and armor, Chinese. 2. Bronzes, Chinese. 3. Bronzes—Expertising. I. Clarke, Roy S., joint author. II. Chase, William Thomas, joint author. III. Title. BIP

KU kung po wu yuan, 739.72
Peking.
Chinese bronze age weapons; the Werner Jannings Collection in the Chinese National Palace Museum, Peking, by Max Loehr. Ann Arbor, University of Michigan Press [1956] xiii, 233p. illus., plates. 32cm. Title also in Chinese on t.p. Bibliography: p. [213]-224. [NK6683.P4] 56-7181
1. Arms and armor, Chinese. 2. Arms and armor—Collections. 3. China—Antiq. I. Loehr, Max. II. Jannings, Werner. III. Title.

PEKING. National Palace 739.72
Museum.
Chinese bronze are weapons; the Werner Jannings Collection in the Chinese National Palace Museum, Peking, by Max Loehr. Ann Arbor, University of Michigan Press [1956] xiii, 233p. illus., plates. 32cm. Title also in Chinese on t. p. Bibliography: p. [213]-224. [NK6683.P4] 56-7181
1. Arms and armor, Chinese. 2. Arms and armor—Collections. 3. China—Antiq. I. Loehr, Max. II. Jannings, Werner. III. Title.

Arms and armor, Cretan.

HOFFMANN, Herbert, 739.7'5'093918
1930-
Early Cretan armorers [by] Herbert Hoffmann, with the collaboration of A. E. Raubitschek. Cambridge, Mass., Fogg Art Museum, 1972. xv, 69 p., 57 p. of illus. (part col.) 31 cm. (Fogg Art Museum monographs in art and archaeology, 1) Bibliography: p. xiii-xv. [NK6651.A3C74 1972] 72-80736
1. Arms and armor, Cretan. I. Raubitschek, Antony Erich, 1912- II. Title. III. Series: Harvard University. William Hayes Fogg Art Museum. Monographs in art and archaeology, 1.

Arms and armor, European.

ASHDOWN, Charles Henry. 623.4
British & continental arms and armour. New York, Dover Publications [1970] x, 384 p. illus., plates. 22 cm. Reprint of the

1909 ed. published under title: British and foreign arms & armour. [U800.A8 1970] 74-113862 ISBN 0-486-22490-2
1. Arms and armor, European. 2. Arms and armor, English. I. Title. BIP

*LENK, Torsten 739.7
The flintlock, its origin and development. Tr. from Swedish by G. A. Urquhart, ed. by J. F. Hayward. Philadelphia, A. Saifer, Box 7791, 1965. xii, 188p. 134 plates. 24cm. 30.00
1. Arms and armor—European. 2. Flintlock pistol. I. Urquhart, G. A., tr. II. Title. BIP

THOMAS, Bruno, 1910-. 739.7
Arms and armour of the Western World [by] Bruno Thomas, Ortwin Gamber [and] Hans Schedelmann. [Translated from the German by Ilse Bloom and William Reid] New York, McGraw-Hill [1964] 251 p. illus. (part mounted col.) plates (part col.) 33 cm. "Notes and bibliographical references": p. [233]-239. [NK6642.T5] 64-22727
1. Arms and armor, European. I. Title.

WILKINSON, Frederick John, 1922- 739.7'094
Antique arms and armor [by] Frederick Wilkinson. New York, Drake Publishers [1972] 192 p. illus. 25 cm. Bibliography: p. 186-190. [U854.W55] 72-2515 ISBN 0-87749-252-2 9.95
1. Arms and armor, European. I. Title.

Arms and armor, European—History.

MARTIN, Paul, 1901- 355.8'2
Arms and armour, from the 9th to the 17th century. [Translated by Rene North. 1st U.S. ed. Rutland, Vt., C. E. Tuttle Co. [1968, c1967] 298 p. illus., 20 col. plates. 25 cm. Translation of Armes et armures de Charlemagne a Louis xiv. Bibliography: p. 289-292. [U800.A2M313] 67-28906 15.00
1. Arms and armor, European—History. I. Title.

Arms and armor—Germany, West—Catalogs.

DRESDEN. Historisches Museum. 739.7'074'0321
Fine arms and armor : treasures in the Dresden collection / by Johannes Schobel ; translated by M. O. A. Stanton ; photos. by Jurgen Karpinski ; pref. by Claude Blair. New York : Putnam, 1975. 255 p. : ill. (some col.) ; 31 cm. Translation of Prunkwaffen. Includes index. [NK6602.5.G35D73 1975] 73-94104 ISBN 0-399-11363-0 : 20.00
1. Dresden. Historisches Museum. 2. Arms and armor—Germany, West—Catalogs. I. Schobel, Johannes. II. Karpinski, Jurgen. III. Title.

Arms and Armor—History.

BLAIR, Claude 739.7
European & American arms. c.1100- 1850. New York, Crown [c.1962] x, 134p. illus. 31cm. Bibl. 62-11803 25.00
1. Arms and armor—Hist. 2. Arms and armor—Collectors and collecting. I. Title.

BRODIE, Bernard, 1910- 399
From crossbow to H-bomb, by Bernard and Fawn Brodie. [New York, Dell Pub. Co., 1962] 288p. illus. 17cm. (Laurel science series, LC167) Includes bibliography. [U800.B65] 62-3884
1. Arms and armor—Hist. 2. Tactics. I. Brodie, Fawn (McKay) 1915- joint author. II. Title. BIP

FFOULKES, Charles John, 1868-1947. 739.7'5
The armourer and his craft from the xith to the xvith century. New York, B. Blom [1967, c1912] xxii, 199 p. illus. 26 cm. Based on the author's thesis (B. Litt.), University of Oxford, 1911. [NK6606.F4 1967] 67-13328
1. Arms and armor — Hist. 2. Armorers. I. Title.

GRANCSAY, Stephen Vincent, 1897- 739.7
Arms and armor. New York, Odyssey [c.1964] 43p. illus. (pt. col.) 11x17cm. (Odyssey lib., 5) 64-13054 .95 bds.,
1. Arms and armor—Hist. I. Title. BIP

TUNIS, Edwain, 1897- 399
Weapons, a pictorial history. Written and illustrated by Edwin Tunis. Cleveland, World Pub. Co. [c1956] 151 p. illus. 31 cm. [U800.T8] 50-2249
1. Arms and armor — Hist. 2. Munitions — Hist. I. Title.

Arms and armor—History.

BUEHR, Walter. 399
Warriors' weapons. Illustrated by the author. New York, Crowell [1963] 186 p. illus. 21 cm. [U800.B8] 63-18412
1. Arms and armor—History. I. Title.

COWPER, Henry Swainson, 1865-1941. 623.4'41
The art of attack : being a study in the development of weapons and appliances of offence, from the earliest times to the age of gunpowder / by H. S. Cowper. Wakefield : EP Publishing, 1977,i.e.1978 xix, 312 p., plate : ill. ; 23 cm. Reprint of the 1906 ed. published by W. Holmes, Ulverston. Includes index. Bibliography: p. [299]-301. [U800.C7 1977] 78-311740 ISBN 0-7158-1212-2 : 16.00
1. Arms and armor—History. I. Title.
Distributed by Roman & Littlefield BIP

FFOULKES, Charles John, 1868-1947. 739.7'5
The armourer and his craft from the XIth to the XVIth century [by] Charles F. foulkes New York, F. Ungar Pub. Co. [1967] xx, 199 p. illus. 31 cm. Reissue of the 1912 ed. which was based on the author's thesis (B.Litt.) University of Oxford, 1911. Bibliography: p. xviii-xx. [NK6606.F4 1967b] 67-25838
1. Arms and armor—History. 2. Armorers. I. Title.

GROSE, Francis, 1731?-1791. 623.4'41
A treatise on ancient armour and weapons, by Francis Grose. Illustrated by plates taken from the original armour in the Tower of London and other arsenals, museums, and cabinets. Glendale, N.Y., Benchmark Pub. Co., 1970. vi, 118, xviii, 10 p. 62 plates. 27 cm. Reprint of the 1786 ed. with a 1789 supplement. [U800.G76 1970] 70-22764
1. Arms and armor—History. I. Title.

NICKEL, Helmut. 739.7
Warriors and worthies; arms and armor through the ages. Color photos. by Bruce Pendleton. [1st ed.] New York, Atheneum, 1969. 122 p. illus. (part col.) 25 x 27 cm. "Black and white photographs courtesy of the Metropolitan Museum of Art. All objects pictured are in the collections of the Metropolitan Museum of Art." Rev. ed. published 1971 under title: Arms and armour through the ages. [U800.N5 1969] 69-18965 10.00
1. Arms and armor—History. I. New York (City). Metropolitan Museum of Art. II. Title. BIP

NORMAN, A. Vesey B. 739.7
Arms and armor. New York, Putnam [1964] 128 p. illus. (part col.) ports. (part col.) 22 cm. (Pleasures and treasures) [U800.N6] 64-16766
1. Arms and armor—History. I. Title.

REID, William, 1926- 355.8'2'09
The lore of arms / [by] William Reid. London : Mitchell Beazley, 1976. 280 p. : ill. (some col.), col. coat of arms, facsims., plans (1 col.) ; 31 cm. Includes index. Bibliography: p. 269-270. [U800.R43] 77-354574 ISBN 0-85533-082-1 : £13.95
1. Arms and armor—History. 2. Military art and science—History. I. Title.

SAXTORPH, Niels M. 355.4'2
Warriors and weapons of early times, by Niels M. Saxtorph. Illustrated by Stig Bramsen. [1st American ed.] New York, Macmillan [1972] 260 p. illus. (part col.) 19 cm. Translation of Krigsfolk gennem tiden. Bibliography: p. 253-254. [U800.S2613] 72-85766 4.95
1. Arms and armor—History. I. Bramsen, Stig, illus. II. Title.

TUNIS, Edwin, 1897- 399
Weapons, a pictorial history, written and illustrated by Edwin Tunis. [1st ed.] Cleveland, World Pub. Co. [1954] 152 p. illus. 31 cm. [U800.T8] 54-5342
1. Arms and armor—History. 2. Munitions—History. BIP

Arms and armor—History—Juvenile literature.

TUNIS, Edwin, 1897-1973. 399
Weapons : a pictorial history / written and illustrated by Edwin Tunis. New York : Crowell, [1977], c1954. p. cm. Describes in text and pictures weapons used through the ages, from the stones of prehistoric man to the bombs of modern times. [U800.T8 1977] 76-29699 ISBN 0-690-01285-3 : 9.95
1. Arms and armor—History—Juvenile literature. 2. Munitions—History—Juvenile literature. I. Title.

Arms and armor, Indic.

EGERTON, Wilbraham Egerton, Earl, 1832-1909. 355.8'2
Indian and Oriental armour, by Lord Egerton of Tatton. Introd. by H. Russell Robinson. [Harrisburg, Pa.] Stackpole Books [1968] x, 178 p. illus. (part col.), col. map. 28 cm. First published in 1880 under title: An illustrated handbook of Indian arms. Rev. ed. published in 1896 under title: A description of Indian and Oriental armour. Reprint of the 1896 ed. [U821.I4E3 1968] 68-16504
1. Arms and armor, Indic. 2. Arms and armor, Oriental. I. Title.

Arms and armor, Indonesian.

DRAEGER, Donn F. 355.4'2
Weapons and fighting arts of the Indonesian archipelago [by] Donn F. Draeger. Rutland, Vt., C. E. Tuttle Co. [1972] 254 p. illus. 27 cm. Bibliography: p. 243-244. [U821.I5D7] 73-182060 ISBN 0-8048-0674-8 12.50
1. Arms and armor, Indonesian. 2. Fighting, Hand-to-hand. I. Title.

Arms and armor, Japanese.

ANDERSON, L. John. 739.7'5'0951
Japanese armour; an illustrated guide to the work of the Myochin and Saotome families from the 15th to the 20th century, by L. J. Anderson. [Harrisburg, Pa.] Stackpole Books [1968] 84 p. illus., geneal. table. 22 cm. (Stackpole arms and armour) Bibliography: p. 82. [U821.J3A65] 68-31180 4.95
1. Arms and armor, Japanese. I. Title.

JAPANESE arms & armor. 739.7'0952
Introd. by H. Russell Robinson. [New York] Crown Publishers [1969] 54 p., 112 illus., 29 col. plates. 32 cm. [NK6684.J33] 79-79521 14.95
1. Arms and armor, Japanese. I. Robinson, H. Russell.

Arms and armor—Juvenile literature.

GLUBOK, Shirley. 355.1'4
Knights in armor. Designed by Gerard Nook. New York, Harper & Row [1969] 48 p. illus. 33 cm. Depicts the customs and history of the era of knighthood and chivalry through descriptions of armor surviving as museum pieces and works of art. [U800.G55] 69-10208 4.79
1. Arms and armor—Juvenile literature. 2. Knights and knighthood—Juvenile literature. I. Title. BIP

MORRISON, Sean. j399
Armor. Illustrated by the author. New York, Crowell [1963] viii, 261 p. illus. 23 cm. [U800.M6] 63-15091
1. Arms and armor — Juvenile literature. I. Title. BIP

NICOLLE, Patrick. 739.7
A book of armour. [Harmondsworth, Middlesex; Baltimore, Penguin Books, 1960] unpaged. illus. 19x23cm. (Puffin picture book no. 97) [NK6606.N5] 60-4411
1. Arms and armor—Juvenile literature. I. Title.

OAKESHOTT, R Ewart. 399
A knight and his weapons. Illustrated by the author. Philadelphia, Dufour Editions, 1964. 95 p. illus. 21 cm. Bibliography: p. 91-92. [U800.034] 64-10264
1. Arms and armor — Juvenile literature. I. Title.

PETERSON, Harold Leslie, 1922- 739.7 (j)
A history of body armor [by] Harold L. Peterson. Illustrated by Daniel D. Feaser. New York, Scribner [1968] 64 p. illus. 27 cm. [U800.P47] 68-29367 3.50
1. Arms and armor—Juvenile literature. I. Feaser, Daniel D., illus. II. Title.

WILKINSON, Frederick John, 1922- 623.4'41
Arms and armor, by Frederick Wilkinson. Illustrated by John H. Batchelor and Arthur Gay. New York, Grossett & Dunlap [1971] 159 p. col. illus. 22 cm. (The Grossett all-color guide series, 39) Includes bibliographical references. Traces the history of armor and edged weapons in Europe from ancient times to World War II. Also includes sections on North America, Africa, and Asia. [U800.W56 1971] 75-154852 ISBN 0-448-00881-5 3.95
1. Arms and armor—Juvenile literature. I. Batchelor, John H., illus. II. Gay, Arthur, illus. III. Title.

Arms and armor, Oriental.

ROBINSON, H. Russell. 355.8'2
Oriental armour [by] H. Russell Robinson. New York, Walker [1967] x, 257 p. illus. 25 cm. (Arms and armour series) [U825.R6] 67-13231
1. Arms and armor, Oriental. I. Title. II. Series.

Arms and armor — Private collections.

KIENBUSCH, Carl Otto von, 1884- 739.7
The Kretzschmar von Kienbusch collection of armor and arms. [Princeton, N. J., Distributed by the Princeton University Library] 1963. 365 p. 165 plates. 31 cm. Cover title: Kretzschmar von Kienbusch collection. A catalogue prepared by various authors. Bibliography: p. 339-342. [NK6603.K5] 62-11957
1. Arms and armor — Private collections. I. Title.

Arms and armor, Roman.

ROBINSON, H. Russell. 739.7'5'0937
The armour of imperial Rome / by H. Russell Robinson. New York : Scribner, [1975] 200 p., [2] leaves of plates : ill. ; 36 cm. Errata slip inserted. Includes bibliographical references and index. [U805.R62] 74-11777 ISBN 0-684-13956-1 : 17.50
1. Arms and armor, Roman. I. Title. BIP

Arms and armor, Spanish.

BRINCKERHOFF, Sidney B., 1933- 355.8'2
Spanish military weapons in colonial America, 1700-1821, by Sidney B. Brinckerhoff and Pierce A. Chamberlain. [Harrisburg, Pa.] Stackpole Books [1972] 159 p. illus. 30 cm. Bibliography: p. [149]-153. [U820.S7B74] 76-179609 ISBN 0-8117-1584-1
1. Arms and armor, Spanish. I. Chamberlain, Pierce A., 1939- joint author. II. Title.

Arms and armor, Spanish—Exhibitions.

LONDON, Tower. 739.7
Exhibition of Spanish royal armour in H. M. Tower of London, April-25 September 1960. 1960[ ] 23p. illus. 22cm. 60-3240 .50 pap.,
1. Arms and armor, Spanish—Exhibitions. I. Title.

Arms and armor—Terminology—Juvenile literature.

LIMBURG, Peter R. 623.4'4'03
What's in the names of antique weapons, by Peter Limburg. Illustrated by W. K. Plummer. New York, Coward, McCann & Geoghegan [1973] 160 p. illus. 21 cm. (A What's-behind-the-word book) Traces the history, use, and name derivation of many different weapons from earliest times to the present. [U800.L54] 72-85619 ISBN 0-698-20233-3 4.49 (lib. bdg.)
1. Arms and armor—Terminology—Juvenile literature. I. Plummer, William K., illus. II. Title.

Armstrong, Jane B.

ARMSTRONG, Jane B. 730'.92'4
Discovery in stone / by Jane B. Armstrong. New York : East Woods Press, [1975] [44] p., [24] leaves of plates : ill. ; 21 cm. Autobiographical. [NB237.A75A42] 74-83472 ISBN 0-914788-01-9 : 9.95
1. Armstrong, Jane B. I. Title.

Arnett, William—Art collections.

HIGH Museum of Art. 709'.59'0740158231
*Beyond India : an exhibition of works of art from Southeast Asia in the William and Robert Arnett Collection, April 10-June 16, 1974. Atlanta : High Museum of Art, [1974?] [64] p. : ill. ; 29 cm. [N7311.H53 1974] 76-353910
1. Arnett, William—Art collections. 2. Arnett, Robert—Art collections. 3. Art, Southeast Asian—Exhibitions. I. Title.

Arnheim, Rudolf.

VISION and artifact / 701'.15
Mary Henle, editor ; foreword by Rudolf Arnheim. New York : Springer Pub. Co., c1976. xviii, 186 p. : ill. ; 24 cm. Contents.Contents.—Visual perception: Held, R. Single vision with doubled images. Metelli, F. What does "more transparent" mean? Kanizsa, G. and Gerbino, W. Convexity and symmetry in figure-ground organization. Kennedy, J. M. Attention, brightness, and the constructive eye. Jameson, D. and Hurvich, L. M. From contrast to assimilation. Wallach, H. The apparent rotation of pictorial scenes. Gibson, J. J., et al. The change from visible to invisible.—Visual thinking: Schaefer-Simmern, H. Basic structures in the earliest beginnings of artistic activity. Nash, E. Hidden visual patterns in Roman architecture and ruins. Gardner, H. Illuminating comparisons in the arts.—Artifact : Sekler, E. F. Le Corbusier's use of a "pictorial word" in his tapestry La femme et le moineau. Teuber, M. L. Blue night by Paul Klee. Zucker, W. M. The representation of the invisible. Hess, W.ary Henle, editor ; foreword by Rudolf Arnheim. New York : Springer Pub. Co., c1976. xviii, 186 p. : ill. ; 24 cm. Contents.Co
1. Arnheim, Rudolf. 2. Visual perception—Addresses, essays, lectures. 3. Optical illusions—Addresses, essays, lectures. 4. Art—Psychology—Addresses, essays, lectures. I. Henle, Mary, 1913- II. Arnheim, Rudolf. BIP

Arnold, Eve.

ARNOLD, Eve. 779'.9'9739
Flashback! : The 50's / Eve Arnold. 1st ed. New York : Knopf, 1978. 149 p. : ill. ; 27 cm. [E813.A83 1978] 78-54901 ISBN 0-394-50043-1 : 12.95
1. Arnold, Eve. 2. United States—History—1945-1953—Pictorial works. 3. United States—History—1953-1961—Pictorial works. I. Title. BIP

Arnold, Florence, 1900—

ARNOLD, Florence, 1900- 759.13
Florence Arnold: [catalog of] retrospective exhibition, September 16-October 31, 1973. [Fullerton? Calif., 1973] [18] p. illus. 22 cm. "Exhibit sponsored by: City of Fullerton Fine Arts Commission, Fullerton Library Board [and] Orange County Art Association." [ND237.A74C57] 73-87911
1. Arnold, Florence, 1900- I. City of Fullerton Fine Arts Commission. II. Fullerton Library Board. III. Orange County Art Association.

Arp-Hagenbach, Marguerite—Art collections.

ARP, Hans. 730'.92'4
Jean Arp, from the Collections of Mme. Marguerite Arp and Arthur and Madeleine Lejwa, at the Metropolitan Museum of Art. [New York, Metropolitan Museum of Art, 1972] [47] p. illus. (part col.) 25 cm. [NB553.A7N38] 72-77067
1. Arp-Hagenbach, Marguerite—Art collections. 2. Lejwa, Arthur—Art collections. 3. Lejwa, Madeleine—Art collections. I. New York (City). Metropolitan Museum of Art.

Arp, Hans.

ARP, Hans 730.943
Arp [by] Michel Seuphor [pseud.] New York, Universe Books [c.1961] [12] p. 32 plates (Universe sculpture series) Bibl. 60-14502 1.95 pap.,
I. Berckelaers, Ferdinand Louis, 1901- II. Title.

ARP, Hans. 735.43
Jean Arp [by] Carola Giedion-Welcker. Documentation: Marguerite Hagenbach. [Translation by Norbert Guterman] New York, H. N. Abrams [c1957] xiiii 122p. (p. 1-101 plates (part fold.)) illus. 30cm. [An Abrams art book] Bibliography: p. 113-122. [NB553.A7G5] [NB553.A7G5] 927.3 58-3464 58-3464
I. Gledion-Welcker, Carola. II. Title.

ARP, Hans. 730'.92'4
Jean Arp : sculpture, reliefs, works on paper : an exhibition organised by Madeleine Chalette Lejwa, 1975-1976 : [catalog]. New York : Chalette International, 1975. [78] p. : ill. (some col.) ; 24 cm. "Participating museums : Museum of Art, Carnegie Institute, Pittsburgh [and others]." Includes selected writings of Arp in translation. Includes bibliographical references. [NB553.A7L44] 74-25271
1. Arp, Hans. I. Lejwa, Madeleine. II. Pittsburgh. Carnegie Institute. Museum of Art.

ARP, Hans. 730'.924
Jean Arp: sculpture, his last ten years. Introd. by Eduard Trier. Bibliography by Marguerite Arp-Hagenbach. Catalogue of sculptures by Francois Arp. [Translated by Karen Philippson.] New York, N. N. Abrams [1968] xxii, 145 p. illus., port. 31 cm. Companion volume to Jean Arp, by Carola Giedon-Welcker, published in 1957. [NB553.A7A763 1968b] 68-28385
I. Title.

CATHELIN, Jean 730.944
Jean Arp. Translated from the French by Enid York. Color photos. by Luc Joubert. New York, Grove Press, 1960 [c.1959] 64p. Bibliography: p.62-64. illus. (part mounted col.) ports. 21cm. 59-14403 3.95
1. Arp, Hans. I. Title.

NEW York, Museum of Modern Art. 735.43
Arp. Edited with an introd. by James Thrall Soby. Articles by Jean Hans Arp [and others] Garden City, N. Y., Distributed by Doubleday [1958] 126p. illus. 25cm. [NB553.A7N4] 927.3 58-13761
1. Arp, Hans. I. Soby, James Thrall, 1906- ed. II. Title.

READ, Herbert Edward, Sir, 1893-1968. 709'.24
The art of Jean Arp. New York, H. N. Abrams [1968] 216 p. illus., ports. (both part col.) 21 cm. Bibliographical references included in "Text references" (p. 191-194) Bibliography: p. 195-199. [NB553.A7R4] 68-28388 3.95
1. Arp, Hans. I. Title.

Art.

AMERICAN Library Color Slide Company, inc., New York. 381'.45'7
Teachers manual for the study of art history and related courses. Derived from The American Library compendium and index of world art, and including all media-architecture, sculpture, painting, and the minor arts, from the paleolithic to the present. Compiled under the supervision of Nahum Tschacbasov. New York [1964] xiv, 513 p. 23 cm. On cover: American Library Color Slide catalpgue of world art. [N4040.A53] 64-2431
1. Art. I. Lantern slides — Catalogs. II. Tschacbasov, Nahum, 1899- III. American Library Color Slide Company, inc., New York. The American Library compendium and index of world art. IV. Title.

ART and education; 707
a collection of essays by John Dewey [and others] 3d ed., rev. and enl. Merion, Pa., Barnes Foundation Press [1954] xiii, 316 p. 21 cm. [N7425.A7 1954] 54-13256
1. Art. 2. Art—Study and teaching. 3. Aesthetics. 4. Barnes Foundation, Merion, Pa. I. Dewey, John, 1859-1952.

BALDINGER, Wallace Spencer, 1905- 704.91
The visual arts [by] Wallace S. Baldinger, in collaboration with Harry B. Green. New York, Holt, Rinehart and Winston [1960] 308 p. illus. 26 cm. Includes bibliography. [N7425.B25] 59-8691
1. Art. I. Title.

BEAM, Philip C 701.1
The language of art. New York, Ronald Press Co. [1958] 948p. illus. 24cm. Includes bibliography. [N7425.B35] 58-6055
1. Art. I. Title.

BROWN, Gerard Baldwin, 1849-1932. 701'.17
The fine arts; a manual. 4th ed. Freeport, N.Y., Books for Libraries Press [1973] p. Reprint of the 1916 ed. published by J. Murray, London. [N7425.B8 1973] 73-4570 ISBN 0-518-19022-6
1. Art. 2. Aesthetics. I. Title.

CANADAY, John Edwin, 1907- 701.18
Keys to art. Captions and commentary by Katherine H. Canaday. New York, Tudor Pub. Co. [1963] 182 p. illus. (part mounted col.) 30 cm. [N7435.C33] 63-25089
1. Art. 2. Criticism. 3. Aesthetics. I. Canaday, Katherine H. II. Title.

CAPERS, Roberta M. 701.18
Images and imagination; an introduction to art [by] Roberta M. Capers [and] Jerrold Maddox. New York, Ronald Press Co. [1965] x, 297 p. illus. (part col.) 26 cm. Includes bibliographical references. [N7435.C334] 65-11698
1. Art. 2. Art—Technique. I. Maddox, Jerrold, joint author. II. Title.

COLLINGWOOD, William Gershom, 1854-1932. 700
The art teaching of John Ruskin / by W. G. Collingwood. Folcroft, Pa. : Folcroft Library Editions, 1977. xvi, 376 p. ; 23 cm. Reprint of the 1891 ed. published by percival, London. Includes bibliographical references and index. [N7425.R95C7 1977] 77-17888 ISBN 0-8414-9975-6 lib. bdg. : 35.00
1. Art. I. Title. BIP

COOPER, Charles William, 1904- 701.1
The arts and humanity; a psychological introduction to the fine arts. [3d ed., rev.] New York, Philosophical Library [1952] 334 p. illus. 23 cm. [N70.C72 1952] 52-2663
1. Art. 2. Art and society. I. Title.

CRANE, Lucy, 1842-1882. 701
Art and the formation of taste / Lucy Crane. New York : Garland Pub., 1977. xiii, 292 p., [6] leaves of plates : ill. ; 19 cm. (The Aesthetic movement & the arts and crafts movement) Reprint of the 1882 ed. published by Macmillan, London. [N7425.C89 1977] 76-17755 ISBN 0-8240-2458-3 lib.bdg. : 35.00
1. Art. 2. Art, Decorative. 3. Aesthetics. I. Title. II. Series. BIP

DALI, Salvador, 1904- 709.04
Dali on modern art; the cuckolds of antiquated modern art. Translated by Haakon M. Chevalier. New York, Dial Press, 1957. 156 p. illus. 25 cm. English and French. [N69.D313] 57-14584
1. Art. I. Title. II. Title: The cuckolds of antiquated modern art.

DANIEL, Howard, 1911- 708
Adventures in art; a guide to gallery-going. New York, Abelard-Schuman [1961], c.1960] 323p. illus. Bibl. 60-72159 5.00
1. Art. 2. Art—Hist. 3. Art—Galleries and museums. I. Title.

DE SAUSMAREZ, Maurice, 1915- 745.4
Basic design; the dynamics of visual form [by] Maurice de Sausmarez. New York, Reinhold Pub. Corp. [1964] 96 p. illus. (part col.) 20 cm. (Reinhold paperbacks) Bibliography: p. 6. [N7425.D47 1964] 64-14629
1. Art. I. Title.

EDWARDS, Arthur Trystan, 1884- 701.17
The things which are seen; a philosophy of beauty. [2d ed.] London, J. Tiranti, 1947. xxi, 330p. illus. 19cm. [N7425.E4 1947] 48-2298 3.75
1. Art. 2. Esthetics. 3. Artists. I. Title.
Now available from Transatlantic Arts in Levittown, N.Y.

EITNER, Lorenz Edwin Alfred 707
Introduction to art, an illustrated topical manual. Minneapolis, Burgess [c.1961] 131p. illus. 28cm. 61-66550 2.75 pap.,
1. Art I. Title.

EPSTEIN, Jacob, Sir, 1880-1959. 709'.24
The sculptor speaks, Jacob Epstein to Arnold L. Haskell; a series of conversations on art. New York, B. Blom, 1971. xiii, 200 p. illus. 24 cm. Reprint of the 1932 ed. [N7445.2.E6 1971] 73-172922
1. Art. I. Haskell, Arnold Lionel, 1903- II. Title.

FAULKNER, Ray Nelson, 1906- 701
Art today, an introduction to the fine and functional arts [by] Ray Faulkner, Edwin Ziegfeld [and] Gerald Hill. 3d ed. New York, Holt [1956] 553 p. illus. 24 cm. [N7425.F3 1956] 56-6055
1. Art. 2. Art industries and trade. 3. Aesthetics. I. Title. BIP

FRIEDLANDER, Max J. 701.17
On art and connoisseurship. [Translated from the author's German manuscript by Tancred Borenius] Boston, Beacon Press [1960] 284p. 40 pl. (incl. front., ports.) 21cm. (Beacon paperback no. 99) 2.25 pap.,
1. Art. 2. Art—Philosophy. I. Borenius, Tancred, 1885-1948, tr. II. Title.

GETLEIN, Frank. 709
Art treasures of the world; 100 most precious masterpieces of all time in full color. With an introd. by John Walker. [1st ed.] New York, C. N. Potter [1968] 206 p. col. plates. 29 cm. [N5302.G45] 68-26882 12.50
1. Art. I. Title.

GIBSON, Katherine, 1893- 709.455'1
The goldsmith of Florence; a book of great craftsmen. Decorations by Kalman Kubinyi. Freeport, N.Y., Books for Libraries Press [1967] xv, 209 p. illus. 29 cm. (Essay index reprint series) Reprint of the 1929 ed. Contents.Contents.—Weavers of stories: tapestries.—Brothers of the guill; illuminated manuscripts.—Wood-carvers of lonng ago.—The armorer.—Ghiberti and the goblins.—Capping the Duomo: Brunelleschi.—Donatello's children.—The secret a bambino keeps: Della Robbia.—The goldsmith of Florence: Cellini.—Boston's handman: Paul Revere.—A wood-carver of today: I. Kirchmayer.—Master Smith: Frank Koralewsky.—Bibliography (p. 207-209) [N7438.G5 1967] 67-30215
1. Art. 2. Art—Florence. I. Title. BIP

GILL, Eric, 1882-1940. 701
Art. New York, Devin-Adair [1950] 148 p. 20 cm. First published in 1934 under title: Art and a changing civilization. Bibliography: p. [142] [N70.G48 1950] 51-6107
1. Art. 2. Aesthetics. I. Title.

GOLDSTEIN, Harriet Irene. 745
Art in everyday life [by] Harriet Goldstein [and] Vetta Goldstein. 4th ed. New York,

Macmillan 1954. 515 p. illus. 24 cm. [N7438.G6 1954] 54-2979
1. Art. 2. Interior decoration. 3. Clothing and dress. I. Goldstein, Vetta, joint author. II. Title. BIP

HOLMES, Charles John, Sir, 1868-1936. 701.8
A grammar of the arts. With an introd. by John C. Van Dyke. New York, AMS Press [1970] xlii, 242 p. illus. 23 cm. Reprint of the 1932 ed. Bibliography: p. 231-235. [N7425.H73 1970] 76-119652
1. Art. I. Title. BIP

HUYGHE, Rene. 709
Ideas and images in world art; dialogue with the visible. [Translated from the French by Norbert Guterman] New York, Abrams [1959] 447p. illus., col. plates. 23cm. Translation of Dialogue avec le visible. Bibliographical footnotes. [N7425.H883] 59-8097
1. Art. 2. Art—Hist. 3. Painting. I. Title.

KUH, Katharine. 701
Art has many faces; the nature of art presented visually. [1st ed. New York] Harper [1951] 185 p. illus. 29 cm. [N7433.K8] 51-13484
1. Art. 2. Art, Modern—20th century. I. Title. BIP

KUH, Katharine. 704
The artist's voice; talks with seventeen artists. [1st ed.] New York, Harper & Row [1962] 248 p. illus. (3 col.) 23 cm. [N7443.K8] 62-9893
1. Art. 2. Artists, American. I. Title. BIP

LINGSTROM, Freda. 701.17
The seeing eye; how to look at natural and man-made things with pleasure and understanding. New York, Macmillan [c1960] 81p. illus. 25cm. [N7435.L54 1960] 61-19872
1. Art. 2. Nature (Aesthetics) I. Title.

LOWRY, Bates, 1923- 701.18
The visual experience; an introduction to art. Englewood Cliffs, N.J., Prentice-Hall [1961?] 272 p. illus. 29 cm. [N7425.L88] 61-10977
1. Art. I. Title. BIP

MARVIN, Francis Sydney, 1863-1943, ed. 709
Art and civilization; essays arranged and edited by F. S. Marvin and A. F. Clutton-Brock. Freeport, N.Y., Books for Libraries Press [1967] 263 p. illus., plans, plates. 22 cm. (Essay index reprint series) (The Unity series, 8) Includes bibliographies. [N7443.M3 1967] 67-26762
1. Art. 2. Civilization. I. Clutton-Brock, Alan Francis, joint ed. II. Title.

METROPOLITAN seminars in art. Portfolio 1- 707.14 [New York] Metropolitan Museum of Art [1958- v. illus., plates (col. in pocket) [N7425.M5] 58-2318
1. Art. I. New York. Metropolitan Museum of Art.

MUNRO, Thomas, 1897- 700
The arts and their interrelations. [Rev. and enl. ed.] Cleveland, Press of Western Reserve University [1967] xvi, 587 p. illus. 24 cm. Bibliographical footnotes. [N7425.M9 1967] 67-11482
1. Art. 2. Aesthetics. I. Title.

MYERS, Bernard Samuel, 1908- 700
Understanding the arts. New York, Holt [1958] 469 p. illus. 25 cm. [N7425.M95] 58-6296
1. Art. I. Title.

MYERS, Bernard Samuel, 1908- 700
Understanding the arts. Rev. ed. New York, Holt, Rinehart and Winston [1963] 502 p. illus. 25 cm. [N7425.M95 1963] 63-7275
1. Art. I. Title.

NEWTON, Eric, 1893-1965. 709
The arts of man; an anthology and interpretation of great works of art. Greenwich, Conn., New York Graphic Society [1960] 314 p. illus. (part col.) 22 cm. [N7435.N45] 60-8920
1. Art. 2. Art—History. I. Title.

NIECE, Robert Clemens. 701.18
Art, an approach, written and designed by Robert C. Niece. 2d ed. [Dubuque, Iowa, W. C. Brown Co., 1963] 142 p. illus. 16 x 24 cm. [N66.N53] 63-11963
1. Art. I. Title.

NIECE, Robert Clemens 701.18
Art, an approach. Written and designed by Robert C. Niece. [Dubuque, Iowa, W. C. Brown Co., 1959] 123 p. illus., ports. 16 x 23 cm. Bibliography: p. 122. [N66.N53] 59=3194
1. Art. I. Title.

OZENFANT, Amedee, 1886- 701.17
Foundations of modern art. Translation by John Rodker. [New American ed., augm.] New York, Dover Publications [1952] xviii, 348 p. illus. 25 cm. Translation of Art. [N7438.O82 1952] 52-14596
1. Art. 2. Art — Hist. — 20th cent. I. Title.
Contents omitted. BIP

PACH, Walter, 1883-1958. 709.035
The classical tradition in modern art. New York, T. Yoseloff [1959] 57p. illus. 26cm. [N7428.P3] 59-7853
1. Art. 2. Art, Greek. 3. Art, Roman. I. Title.

PEPPER, Stephen Coburn, 1891- 701.18
The work of art. Bloomington, Indiana University Press, 1955. 183p. 22cm. [N70.P37] 55-6270
1. Art. 2. Art criticism. 3. Aethetics. I. Title.

READ, Herbert Edward, 1893- 704
The meaning of art. New York, Pitman Pub. Corp. [1951] 262 p. illus. 20 cm. Published in 1932 under title: The anatomy of art. [N7425.R4 1951] 51-12743
1. Art. 2. Art — Hist. 3. Aesthetica. I. Title. BIP

RICHARDSON, John Adkins. 701'.1
Art: the way it is. Englewood Cliffs, N.J., Prentice-Hall [1973] 348 p. illus. (part col.) 27 cm. Bibliography: p. [334]-[339] [N7425.R48 1973] 73-14637 ISBN 0-13-049221-3 7.95
1. Art. I. Title.

RICHARDSON, John Adkins. 701'.1
Art: the way it is. New York, H. N. Abrams [1974] 348 p. illus. (part col.) 28 cm. Bibliography: p. [334]-[339] [N7425.R48 1974] 73-14638 ISBN 0-8109-0544-2 15.00
1. Art. I. Title.

RODIN, Auguste, 1840-1917. 700
On art and artists. [Translated by Mrs. Romilly Fedden] With an introd. by Alfred Werner. New York, Philosophical Library [1957] 252p. 64 plates (incl. port.) 25cm. Translation of L'art, entretiens reunis par Paul Gsell. [N7445.R566] 57-59574
1. Art. 2. Sculpture. I. Gsell, Paul, 1870- II. Title.

RODIN, Auguste, 1840-1917. 701.1
Rodin on art. Translated from the French of Paul Gsell by Mrs. Romilly Fedden. Introductory essay by Richard Howard. New York, Horizon Press [1971] xiii, 259 p. illus. 24 cm. Translation of L'art. [N7445.3.R6313] 70-132323 ISBN 0-8180-0113-5 10.00
1. Art. I. Gsell, Paul, 1870- II. Title. BIP

ROWLAND, Benjamin, 1904- 709
Art in East and West; an introduction through comparisons. Boston, Beacon [1964, c.1954] 144p. illus. 21cm. (BP188) 1.95 pap.,
1. Art. I. Title. BIP

ROWLAND, Benjamin, 1904- 709
Art in East and West; an introduction through comparisons. Cambridge, Harvard University Press, 1954. xiii, 144p. 62 illus. 24cm. Bibliography: p. [141]-142. [N7428.R65] 54-9777
1. Art. I. Title.

RUSKIN, John, 1819-1900 704.94
The art criticism of John Ruskin. Selected, ed., introd. by Robert L. Herbert. [Gloucester, Mass., P. Smith, 1966,c.1964] xliii,430p. 19cm. (Anchor bk., A405 rebound) [N7445.R712] 3.50
1. Art. 2. Aesthetics. I. Herbert, Robert L., 1929- ed. II. Title.

RUSKIN, John, 1819-1900. 704.91
The art criticism of John Ruskin. Selected,edited, and with an introd. by Robert L. Herbert. Garden City, N. Y., Anchor Books, 1964. xiiii, 430 p. 19 cm. "A 405." [N7445.R712] 64-16241
1. Art. 2. Aesthetics. I. Herbert, Robert L., 1929- ed. II. Title.

RUSKIN, John, 1819-1900. 704.91
The lamp of beauty; writings on art. Selected and edited by Joan Evans. [London] Phaidon Publishers; distributed by Doubleday, Garden City, N. Y. [1959] 344p. 78 illus. (incl. port,; part mounted, part col.) 26cm. Half title: Ruskin's writings on art. [N7445.R835] 60-382
1. Art. I. Evans, Joan, 1893- ed. II. Title.

SCHINNELLER, James A. 701
Art; search and self-discovery. Scranton, Pa., Internatl. Textbks. Co. [c.1961] 322p. illus. 28cm. (Internatl. textbks. in art educ.) Bibl. 61-11879 8.75
1. Art. I. Title.

SCOTT, John Robert. 704
Dissertation on the progress of the fine arts. With an introd. by Roy Harvey Pearce. Los Angeles, William Andrews Clark Memorial Library, University of California, 1954. viii p., facsim.: vi, [125]-180p. 21cm. (Augustan Reprint Society. Publication no. 45) Original t. p. reads: Dissertations, essays, and parallels. London, Printed by T. Bensley and sold by J. Johnson and C. & R. Baldwin, 1804. Bibliographical references included in 'Notes' (p. vii-viii) [N7425.S42 1804a] 54-3669
1. Art. I. Title. II. Series.

SEDGWICK, John P 701.18
Art appreciation made simple. New York, Made Simple Books; distributed by Garden City Books, Garden City, N. Y. [1959] 224p. illus. 28cm. [N7435.S4] 59-1990
1. Art. 2. Art—Hist. I. Title. BIP

SEIBERLING, Frank. 701.17
Looking into art. New York, Holt [1959] 304 p. illus. 26 cm. Includes bibliography. [N7435.S44] 59-8692
1. Art. I. Title.

SHAFTESBURY, Anthony Ashley Cooper, 3d Earl of, 1671-1713. 701.17
Second characters; or, The language of forms. Edited by Benjamin Rand. New York, Greenwood Press [1969] xxviii, 182 p. illus., port. 23 cm. Reprint of the 1914 ed. [N62.S5 1969] 69-14078
1. Art. 2. Aesthetics. I. Rand, Benjamin, 1856-1934, ed. II. Title.

STABER, Karl. 741.9'0924
Art [by] K. Staber. [Ann Arbor?, Mich., 1966] iv, 57 p. (chiefly illus.) 28 cm. [NC1075.S72A43] 67-1776 201 A0002748STERNBERG, Harry, 1904-

STERNBERG, Harry, 1904- 709.04
Realistic abstract art. New York, Pitman Pub. Corp. [1959] unpaged, illus. 20 x 27 cm. (Pitman art series 29) [N7433.S7] 59-11225
1. Art. 2. Art, Abstract. 3. Drawing — Instruction. I. Title. BIP

STURT-PENROSE, Bourrie. 700
The art scene. London, New York, P. Hamlyn, [1969] 152 p. illus. (part col.), ports. (part col.) 29 cm. [N7425.S93] 77-481071
1. Art. I. Title.

*TAIT, Cornelia Damian. 701.'1
Art in its fourth dimension / by Cornelia Damian Tait. New York : Philosophical Library, c1976. 90p. : ill. ; 22 cm. Bibliography: pp. 89-90. [N7425] 76-4221 ISBN 0-8022-2182-3 : 7.95
1. Art. I. Title. BIP

TOLSTOI, Lev Nikolaevich, graf, 1828-1910 701.1
What is art? Tr. [from Russian] introd. by Alymer Maude. New York, Oxford, 1962. 339p. 21cm. (Hesperides bk., HS6) 1.75 pap.,
1. Art. 2. Art and morals. I. Title.

TOLSTOI, Lev Nikolaevich, graf, 1828-1910. 701.1
What is art? Translated from the Russian original by Aylmer Maude. With an introd. by Vincent Tomas. New York, Liberal Arts Press [1960] xviii, 213 p. 21 cm. (The Library of liberal arts, no. 51) Bibliography: p. xviii. Bibliographical footnotes. [N70.T72 1960] 60-9557
1. Art. 2. Art and morals. I. Title.

VERVE. 709
Moods and movements in art. New York, Reynal [1959] 153 p. illus. (part mounted, part col.) 37 cm. "This book [articles and lithographs] was originally published in France as a double number of Verve (27 & 28)" English translation by Serge Hughes (31 p.) in pocket. [N7521.V4] 59-65054
1. Art. 2. Art — Addresses, essays, lectures. I. Title.

WILSON, Morris Emett, 1894- 701.18
Be your own judge; an informal approach to the arts. London, New York, Abelard-Schuman [1959] Includes bibliography. [N7435.W5] 59-12313
1. Art. I. Title.

Art, Abelam (New Guinea tribe)—Exhibitions.

CALIFORNIA State University, Long Beach. Art Galleries. 709'.01'109955
Art of the Abelam : New Guinea : [exhibition], March 25-April 29, Galleries A&B, California State University, Long Beach / [introd. by Kristi Slayman Jones]. [Long Beach] : California State University, [1975?] 20 p. : ill. ; 22 x 28 cm. Cover title. Bibliography: p. 20. [N7411.N4C34 1975] 75-623121
1. Art, Abelam (New Guinea tribe)—Exhibitions. 2. Art, Primitive—New Guinea—Exhibitions. I. Jones, Kristi Slayman. II. Title.

Art—Aberdeen, Scot.—Catalogs.

ABERDEEN Art Gallery, Aberdeen, Scot. 759.2'074'0941235
Catalogue : oil paintings, water colours, drawings, sculpture / Aberdeen Art Gallery. 3d ed. [Aberdeen, Scot.] : The Gallery, 1950. 84 p. ; 21 cm. [N1185.A53 1950] 75-319377
1. Aberdeen Art Gallery, Aberdeen, Scot. 2. Art—Aberdeen, Scot.—Catalogs.

ABERDEEN Art Gallery, Aberdeen, Scot. 708.94125
Permanent collection catalogue: oil paintings, watercolours, drawings and sculpture [compiled by Charles Carter]. Aberdeen, Aberdeen Art Gallery, 1968. [12], 113 p., 33 plates. 47 illus. (1 col.), 3 plans. 25 cm. [N1185.A6] 76-461404
1. Art—Aberdeen, Scot.—Catalogs. I. Carter, Charles, 1903-

Art, Abstract.

AMERICAN Abstract Artists. 701.16
The world of abstract art. New York, G. Wittenborn [1957?] viii. 167p. illus. (part col.) 26cm. 'Artists from different parts of the world ... write on aspects of the movement in their respective countries.' [N6490.A64] 57-8548
1. Art. Abstract. 2. Art. Modern—20th cent. I. Title.

BERCKELAERS, Ferdinand Louis, 1901- 709.04
Abstract painting; fifty years of accomplishment, from Kandinsky to the present [by] Michel Seuphor [pseud. Translated from the French by Haakon Chevalier] New York, Abrams [1962] 320 p. illus. (part col.) 28 cm. Errata slip inserted. Bibliography: p. 320. [ND195.B45] 61-15924
1. Art, Abstract. 2. Painting, Modern—20th century.

BERCKELAERS, Ferdinando Louis, 1901- 709.04
Abstract painting; fifty years of accomplishment, from Kandinsky to the present. Text by Michel Seuphor [pseud. Tr. from French text, by Haakon Chevalier] New York, Dell, 1964] 192p. illus. (pt. col.) 17cm. (Laurel ed., 0012) Bibl. .95 pap.,
1. Art, Abstract. 2. Paintings. 3. Painting—Hist. I. Title.

CAPON, Robin. 741.2
Introducing abstract picture making. New York, Watson-Guptill Publications [1973]

128 p. illus. (part col.) 21 cm. Bibliography: p. 127. [N7433.C33] 72-7366 ISBN 0-8230-6097-7 7.95
1. Art, Abstract. 2. Art—Technique. 3. Art—Study and teaching. I. Title.

HALE, Nathan Cabot. 701'.8
Abstraction in art and nature; a program of study for artists, teachers, and students. New York, Watson-Guptill [1972] 301 p. illus. (part col.) 29 cm. Bibliography: p. [297] [N7432.5.A2H3] 70-180163 ISBN 0-8230-0049-4 17.50
1. Art, Abstract. 2. Nature (Aesthetics) 3. Natural history—Pictorial works. I. Title.

HILER, Hilaire, 1898- 709.04
Why abstract? [By] Hilaire Hiler, Henry Miller. Wm. Saroyan. New York, Wittenborn [1962, c.1946] unpaged. illus. 62-2027 2.50 pap.,
1. Art, Abstract. I. Title.
Contents omitted. **BIP**

KRUSKOPF, Erik. 080 s
Shaping the invisible : a study of the genesis of non-representational painting, 1908-1919 / Erik Kruskopf. Helsinki : Societas Scientiarum Fennica, [1976] 181 p. : ill. ; 25 cm. (Commentationes humanarum litterarum ; 55, 1976 ISSN 0069-6587s) A revision of the author's thesis, University of Helsinki, 1966. Includes index. Bibliography: p. 174-178. [P9.F5t.55 1976] [N6494.A2] 759.06 77-350963 ISBN 9-516-53052-4
1. Art, Abstract. 2. Art, Modern—20th century. 3. Art—Philosophy. I. Title. II. Series: Suomen Tiedeseura. Commentationes humanarum litterarum ; 55, 1976.

MCCAUGHEY, Patrick. 735'.29
Australian abstract art. Melbourne, New York, Oxford University Press [1969] 32 p. illus. 22 cm. (National Gallery booklets) Bibliography: p. 32. [N7400.M25] 77-558339 ISBN 0-19-550310-4
1. Art, Abstract. 2. Art, Australian. I. Title. II. Series: Victoria, Australia. National Gallery, Melbourne. Booklets

MALEVICH, Kazimir Severinovich, 1878-1935. 709'.04
The world as non-objectivity : unpublished writings 1922-25 / K. S. Malevich ; translated by Xenia Glowacki-Prus, Edmund T. Little ; edited by Troels Andersen. Copenhagen : Borgen, 1976- v. : ill. ; 18 cm. Issued as v. 3- of the author's Essays on art. [N6494.A2M3] 77-359359 ISBN 8-7418-6819-6 (v. 1)
1. Art, Abstract. 2. Art, Modern—20th century. I. Title. **BIP**

MOTHERWELL, Robert, ed. 709.73
Modern artists in America. 1st- New York, W. Schultz. 1949/50. v. illus. 26 cm. blennial. Editors: 1949/50- R. Motherwell and others [N6490.M57] 52-2111
1. Art, Abstract. 2. Art, Modern — 20th cent. Art — U.S. I. Title.

VALLIER, Dora. 709.04
Abstract art. Translated from the French by Jonathan Griffin. New York, Orion Press, 1970. viii, 342 p. illus. (part col.), ports. 22 cm. Bibliography: p. 322-330. [N6494.A2V313] 75-86121 ISBN 0-670-10117-6 12.95
1. Art, Abstract.

Art, Abstract—Exhibitions.

CLEVELAND Museum of Art. 707.4
Paths of abstract art [by] Edward B. Henning Cleveland ; Distributed by H. N. Abrams, New York, 1960. ix, 84p. illus., col. plates. 23cm. [N6490.C63] 60-16857
1. Art, Abstract—Exhibitions. I. Henning(Edward B. II. Title.

COLOR & form, 1909-1914; 759.06'074'019 the origin and evolution of abstract painting in futurism, orphism, rayonnism, synchromism, and the blue rider [by] Henry G. Gardiner [and others.] San Diego] Fine Arts Gallery of San Diego [1971] 103 p. col. illus. 27 cm. Issued in connection with the exhibition held Nov. 20, 1971-Jan. 2, 1972, in the Fine Arts Gallery of San Diego; Jan 25-Mar. 5, 1972, in the Oakland Museum, and Mar. 24-May 7, 1972, in the Seattle Art Museum. [ND196.A2C6] 75-172384
1. Art, Abstract—Exhibitions. 2. Painting, Modern—20th century. I. Gardiner, Henry G. II. San Diego, Calif. Fine Arts Gallery. III. Oakland Museum. IV. Seattle. Art Museum.

FRIENDS of the Whitney Museum of American Art. 759.06
Geometric abstraction in America [by] John Gordon. New York, Pub. for Whitney Mus. of Amer. Art by Praeger [c.1962] 66p. illus. 24cm. 62-14111 3.00
1. Art, Abstract—Exhibitions. 2. Art, American—Exhibitions. I. Gordon, John, 1912- II. Title.

NEW York (City). Museum of Modern Art. 709'.73
Abstract painting and sculpture in America, by Andrew Carnduff Ritchie. Reprint ed. [New York] Published for the Museum of Modern Art by Arno Press, 1969 [c1951] 159 p. illus. 27 cm. Catalogue of the exhibition held Jan. 23-Mar. 25, 1951, by Margaret Miller: p. 148-156. Bibliography, by Bernard Karpel: p. 156-159. [ND212.N395 1969] 70-86432
1. Art, Abstract—Exhibitions. 2. Art, Modern—20th century—U.S. I. Ritchie, Andrew Carnduff. II. Title.

SANTA Barbara, Calif. Museum of Art. 759.13
15 abstract artists, Los Angeles; [catalogue of] an exhibition organized by Ronald A Kuchta, with the assistance of Michael Walls, the Santa Barbara Museum of Art, January 19 through March 10, 1974. [Santa Barbara, 1974] [24] p. illus. 21 cm. "500 copies." [ND235.L6S26 1974] 74-76820
1. Art, Abstract—Exhibitions. 2. Art, Abstract—Los Angeles. 3. Painting, Modern—20th century—Los Angeles. I. Title.

A Selection of abstract art, 1917-1965. 760'.0922 [Chicago] Lillian H. Florsheim Foundation for Fine Arts [196-] [43] l. plates. 23 cm. On label on t.p.: Supplied by Worldwide Books, New York. Exhibition of works from the Lillian Florsheim Collection, held at Smith College Museum of Art, May 11-June 7, 1966, and at other museums. [N6494.A2S4] 68-30259
1. Art, Abstract—Exhibitions. I. Lillian H. Florsheim Foundation for Fine Arts. II. Smith College. Museum of Art.

STABER, Margit. 709'.04'07401471
Masters of early constructive abstract art. [Exhibition] October 1971. New York, Galerie Denise Rene [1971] 1 v. (unpaged) col. illus. 27 cm. Includes bibliographies. [ND196.A2S7] 72-198476
1. Art, Abstract—Exhibitions. 2. Painting, Modern—20th century. I. Galerie Denise Rene. II. Title.

VAN WAGNER, Judith K. 709'.04
Geometric abstraction; catalogue by Judith K. Van Wagner. Exhibition in cooperation with: Norman A. Geske, director, Sheldon Art Gallery, University of Nebraska-Lincoln. University of Nebraska-Omaha: April 12-May 2, 1974. University of Nebraska-Lincoln: May 14-June 16, 1974. Omaha, Klopp Print. & Lithographing Co. [1974] v, 76 p. illus. 28 cm. Bibliography: p. 65-76. [N6494.A2V35] 74-171067
1. Art, Abstract—Exhibitions. 2. Art, Modern—20th century. I. Nebraska. University. Sheldon Memorial Art Gallery. II. Nebraska. University at Omaha. III. Title.

Art, Abstract—United States.

JANIS, Sidney, 1897- 759.13
Abstract & surrealist art in America. New York, Arno Press [1969, c1944] 146 p. illus. 29 cm. (Arno series of contemporary art no. 26) Reprint of the ed. published by Reynal & Hitchcock, New York. [N6512.5.A2J36 1969] 70-91375
1. Art, Abstract—United States. 2. Surrealism—United States. 3. Art, Modern—20th century—United States. I. Title. **BIP**

Art—Abstracts.

GETTENS, Rutherford John, comp. 016.7
Abstracts of technical studies in art and archacology, 1943-1952, compiled by Rutherford J. Gettens and Bertha M. Usilton. Washington, 1955. viii, 408p. 24cm. (Freer Gallery of Art occasional papers, v. 2, no. 2) Smithsonian Institution. Publication 4176. [N7428.G44] 55-61312
1. Art—Abstracts. 2. Archaeology—Abstracts. I. Usilton, Bertha M., joint comp. II. Title. III. Series: Freer Gallery of Art, Washington, D. C. Coeasional papers, v.2, no. 2

Art—Addresses, essays, lectures.

ACKERMAN, James S. 701
Art and archaeology [by] James S. Ackerman [and] Rhys Carpenter. Englewood Cliffs, N.J., Prentice-Hall [1963] xi, 241 p. 22 cm. (The Princeton studies; humanistic scholarship in America) Bibliography: p. 230-231. [N7445.A26 1963] 63-12267
1. Art—Addresses, essays, lectures. 2. Archaeology—Addresses, essays, lectures. I. Carpenter, Rhys, 1889- II. Title. III. Series.

ALLSTON, Washington, 1779-1843. 818.209
Lectures on art and poems, 1850; and Monaldi, 1841. Facsim. reproductions including eight paintings, with an introd. by Nathalia Wright. Gainesville, Fla., Scholars' Facsimiles & Reprints, 1967. xi, 380, 253 p. illus., ports. 23 cm. Original t.p. of the first work reads: Lectures on art, and poems, by Washington Allston. Edited by Richard Henry Dana, Jr. New York, Baker and Scribner, 1850. Original t.p. of the second work reads: Monaldi, a tale. Boston, Little and Brown, 1841. [N7445.A52 1967] 67-10124
1. Art—Addresses, essays, lectures. I. Allston, Washington, 1779-1843. Monaldi. 1967. II. Title. III. Title: Monaldi.

ALLSTON, Washington, 1779-1843. 701.17
Lectures on art—poems. Edited by Richard Henry Dana, Jr. New York, Da Capo Press, 1972. xi, 380 p. 22 cm. (Library of American art) Reprint of 1850 ed. [N7445.2.A43 1972] 75-171379 ISBN 0-306-70414-5
1. Art—Addresses, essays, lectures. I. Title. **BIP**

ANSTRUTHER-THOMSON, Clementina, 1857-1921. 700
Art & man: essays & fragments. With twenty illus. and an introd. by Vernon Lee. Freeport, N.Y., Books for Libraries Press [1969] x, 371 p. illus., ports. 23 cm. (Essay index reprint series) Reprint of the 1924 ed. [N7445.A6 1969] 74-93314
1. Art—Addresses, essays, lectures. I. Title. **BIP**

APOLLINAIRE, Guillaume, 1880-1918. 709
Apollinaire on art: essays and reviews, 1902-1918. Edited by Leroy C. Breunig. Translated by Susan Suleiman. New York, Viking Press [1972] xxx, 546 p. illus. 22 cm. (The Documents of 20th-century art) Translation of Chroniques d'art. Bibliography: p. 525-531. [N7445.3.A63313 1972] 70-148266 ISBN 0-670-12960-7 17.50
1. Art—Addresses, essays, lectures. I. Breunig, LeRoy C., 1915- ed. II. Title. III. Series.

ART & artist. 704.92
Berkeley, University of California Press, 1956. 240p. illus. 21cm. Articles by contemporary artists working in various media. [N7443.A75] 56-8104
1. Art—Addresses, essays, lectures.

ART studies for an editor : 709
25 essays in memory of Milton S. Fox / edited by Frederick Hartt and Patricia Egan ; designed by Robin Fox. New York : H. N. Abrams, [1975] p. cm. [N7442.2.F692] 74-30303 ISBN 0-8109-0279-6 : 25.00
1. Fox, Milton S., 1904-1971. 2. Art—Addresses, essays, lectures. I. Fox, Milton S., 1904-1971. II. Hartt, Frederick, ed. III. Egan, Patricia, ed.

THE Art world : 700
a seventy-five-year treasury of ARTnews ; edited by Barbaralee Diamonstein ; foreword by Harold Rosenberg ; introd. by Richard F. Shepard. New York : ARTnews Books : distributed by Rizzoli International Publications, 1977. xix, 459 p. : ill. (some col.) ; 31 cm. Includes index. [N7443.2.A75] 77-79358 ISBN 0-8478-0142-X : 35.00
1. Art—Addresses, essays, lectures. I. Diamonstein, Barbaralee. II. Art news.

AYRTON, Michael, 1921- 704.92
The rudiments of paradise; various essays on various arts. New York, Weybright and Talley [1971] 319 p. illus. 25 cm. [N7443.2.A9] 76-22972 12.50
1. Art—Addresses, essays, lectures. I. Title.

BAUDELAIRE, Charles Pierre, 1821-1867 704.1
The painter of modern life, and other essays. Tr. [from French] ed. by Jonathan Mayne [London] Phaidon; dist. Greenwich, Conn., N.Y. Graphic [1965, c.1964] xx, 224p. plates. 26cm. Bibl. [N7445.B343] 65-633 6.95
1. Art—Addresses, essays, lectures. I. Mayne, Jonathan, ed. and tr. II. Title.

BAUDELAIRE, Charles Pierre, 1821-1867. 704.92
The painter of modern life, and other essays, by Charles Baudelaire. Translated and edited by Jonathan Mayne. London, New York, Phaidon [1970, c1965] xx, 224 p. illus., col. front., ports. 25 cm. (Phaidon paperback) Includes bibliographical references. [N7445.3.B3713 1970] 77-21813 3.95 (U.S.)
1. Art—Addresses, essays, lectures. I. Mayne, Jonathan, ed. II. Title.

BELL, Clive, 1881- 704
Art. New York, Capricorn Books [1958] 190 p. 19 cm. (A Putnam Capricorn book, CAP4) [N7445.B53 1958] 58-59755
1. Art—Addresses, essays, lectures. 2. Art—History. 3. Aesthetics. I. Title.

BELL, Clive, 1881- 709.04
Since Cezanne. Freeport, N.Y., Books for Libraries Press [1969] 229 p. illus. 22 cm. (Essay index reprint series) Reprint of the 1922 ed. Contents.—Since Cezanne.—The artistic problem.—The Douanier Rousseau.—Cezanne.—Renoir.—Tradition and movements.—Matisse and Picasso.—The place of art in art criticism.—Bonnard.—Duncan Grant.—Negro sculpture.—Order and authority (1 and 2)—Marquet.—Standards.—Criticism: First thoughts. Second thoughts. Last thoughts.—Othon Friesz.—Wilcoxism.—Art and politics.—The authority of M. Derain.—"Plus de jazz." [N7445.B54 1969] 68-22902
1. Art—Addresses, essays, lectures. 2. Post-impressionism (Art) I. Title. **BIP**

BENTON, Thomas Hart, 1889- 709
A Thomas Hart Benton miscellany; selections from his published opinions, 1916-1960. Edited by Matthew Baigell. Lawrence, University Press of Kansas [1971] 156 p. 23 cm. [N7454.B4A25] 74-129075 ISBN 0-7006-0071-X 6.75
1. Art—Addresses, essays, lectures.

BERENSON, Bernhard, 1865- 720
Essays in appreciation. New York, Macmillan [1958] x, 170p. 117 plates. 22cm. [N7445.B] A59
1. Art—Addresses, essays, lectures. I. Title.

BERENSON, Bernhard, 1865-1959. 701.1
Seeing and knowing. New York, Macmillan, 1953. 48 p. 88 plates. 22 cm. [N7445.B546 1953a] 54-2143
1. Art—Addresses,essays, lectures. I. Title.

BERENSON, Bernhard, 1865-1959. 701.1
Seeing and knowing. Greenwich, Conn., New York Graphic Society [1968] 89 p. illus. 22 cm. [N7445.B546 1968] 68-13052
1. Art—Addresses, essays, lectures. I. Title.

BERGER, John. 704.91
Toward reality; essays in seeing. Foreword by Harold Clurman. [1st American ed.] New York, Knopf, 1962. 233 p. 22 cm. [N7445.B548 1962] 61-18115
1. Art—Addresses, essays, lectures. I. Title.

BEYLE, Marie Henri, 1783-1842. 709
Stendhal and the arts. Selected & edited by David Wakefield. [New York] Phaidon;

[distributed by Praeger Publishers, 1973] x, 164 p. illus. 26 cm. Bibliography: p. 156-158. [N7445.3.B49] 72-86574 ISBN 0-7148-1554-3 12.50
1. Art—Addresses, essays, lectures. I. Title.

CANFIELD, Mary Cass. 700'.9
Grotesques and other reflections on art and the theatre. Port Washington, N.Y., Kennikat Press [1968, c1927] 237 p. illus. 19 cm. (Essay and general literature index reprint series) [PS3505.A56G7 1968] 68-16290
1. Art—Addresses, essays, lectures. 2. Literature—Addresses, essays, lectures. 3. Theater—Addresses, essays, lectures. I. Title.

CATHOLIC University of America. Workshop on Art as Language, 1956. 704.92
Art as language; the proceedings of the Workshop on Art as Language conducted at the Catholic University of America, June 15 to June 26, 1956. Edited by Sister M. Jeanne File. Washington, Catholic University of America Press, 1957. vii, 219p. illus. 22cm. Includes bibliographies. [N7443.C34 1956] 57-866
1. Art—Addresses, essays, lectures. I. File, Mary Jeanne, ed. II. Title.

CHARLOT, Jean, 1898- 709
Art from the Mayans to Disney. Freeport, N.Y., Books for Libraries Press [1969, c1939] 285 p. illus. 23 cm. (Essay index reprint series) Contents.Contents.—For people of good will.—Mayan art.—A twelfth century Mayan mural.—Mexico of the poor.—Aesthetics of Indian dances.—The Indian way I and II.—Pulqueria paintings.—On the completion of Rivera's first mural.—Postscript to a destruction of frescoes.—Mexican-printmakers I: Manila—Mexican-print makers II: Posada.—Martinez Pintao.—Jose Clemente Orozco.—Carlos Merida I and II.—The critic, the artist, and the problems of representation.—Art, quick and slow.—Pinning butterflies.—Louis M. Eilshemius.—Edward Weston.—Henrietta Shore.—Franklin C. Watkins.—Ben Shahn.—Cubism R.I.P.—Surrealism, or The reason for unreason.—From Altamira to Disney.—A Disquisition. "A list of periodicals and magazines in which [these articles] first appeared": p. 284-285. [N7445.C44 1969] 78-99623
1. Art—Addresses, essays, lectures. 2. Art, Mexican. 3. Mayas—Art. 4. Artists. I. Title. BIP

CHARLOT, Jean, 1898- 704.9'2
An artist on art; collected essays of Jean Charlot. Honolulu, University Press of Hawaii, 1972. 2 v. illus. 21 cm. Vol. 2 has also special title: Mexican art. [N7454.C45] 77-120323 ISBN 0-87022-118-3
1. Art—Addresses, essays, lectures. 2. Art, Mexican—Addresses, essays, lectures. I. Title. BIP

CLARK, Kenneth, Sir 1903- 704.943
Landscape into art. Boston, Beacon Press [1961] 147p. illus. (Beacon paperback BP117) 1.95
1. Art—Addresses, essays, lectures. 2. Art—Landscape in art. I. Title. BIP

CLAUDEL, Paul, 1868- 704.91
The eye listens; translated from the original French by Elsie Pell. New York, Philosophical Library [1950] ix, 293 p. illus. 23 cm. [N7445.C632] 50-6877
1. Art—Addresses, essays, lectures. I. Title. Contents Omitted. BIP

CLAUDEL, Paul, 1868-1955. 709'.4
The eye listens. Translated from the original French by Elsie Pell. Port Washington, N.Y., Kennikat Press [1969, c1950] ix, 293 p. illus. 23 cm. (Essay and general literature index reprint series) Translation of L'oeil ecoute. Contents.Contents.—Introduction to Dutch painting.—Post scriptum April in Holland.—Spanish painting.—Aegri somnia.—Stained glass windows of the cathedrals of France, twelfth and thirteenth centuries.—The road in art.—A few exegeses.—The cathedral of Strasbourg.—On music, to Arthur Honegger.—Arthur Honegger.—The Psalms and photography.—Old bones.—The mystical theology of precious stones.—The pearl.—A visit to the palace of the League of Nations. [N7445.C632 1969] 70-86003
1. Art—Addresses, essays, lectures. I. Title.

CLUTTON-BROCK, Arthur, 1868-1924. 700'.8
Essays on art. Freeport, N.Y., Books for Libraries Press [1968] xi, 143 p. 22 cm. (Essays index reprint series) "Reprinted from the Times literary supplement." "Reprint of the 1919 ed." Contents.Contents.—The adoration of the Magi.—Leonardo Da Vinci.—The Pompadour in art.—An unpopular master.—A defence of criticism.—The artist and his audience.—Wilfulness and wisdom.—The magic flute.—Process or person?—The artist and the tradesman.—Professionalism in art.—Waste or creation? [N7445.C68 1968] 68-22906
1. Art—Addresses, essays, lectures. I. Title. BIP

COOMARASWAMY, Ananda Kentish, 1877-1947. 704.91
Christian and Oriental philosophy of art. New York, Dover Publications [1956] 146 p. illus. 21 cm. First published in 1943 under title: Why exhibit works of art? [N7445] 57-3496
1. Art—Addresses, essays, lectures. I. Title. BIP

COOMARASWAMY, Ananda Kentish, 1877-1947. 704.9'2
Coomaraswamy / edited by Roger Lipsey. Princeton, N.J. : Princeton University Press, c1977- p. cm. (Bollingen series ; 89) Includes index. Contents.Contents.—v. 1. Selected papers, traditional art, and symbolism. [N7445.2.C68 1977] 76-41158 ISBN 0-691-09885-9 (v. 1) : 30.00
1. Art—Addresses, essays, lectures. I. Title. II. Series.

CORTISSOZ, Royal, 1869-1948. 709
Personalities in art. Freeport, N.Y., Books for Libraries Press [1968] viii, 444 p. illus., ports. 23 cm. (Essay index reprint series) Reprint of the 1925 ed. [N7445.C82 1968] 68-55844
1. Art—Addresses, essays, lectures. 2. Artists. I. Title. BIP

COX, Kenyon, 1856-1919. 709
Old masters and new; essays in art criticism. Freeport, N.Y., Books for Libraries Press [1969] 311 p. illus. 23 cm. (Essay index reprint series) Reprint of the 1905 ed. Contents.Contents.—Sculptors of the early Italian renaissance. Perugino. Michelangelo. The pictures of Venice. Veronese. Durer. Rubens. Frans Hals. Rembrandt. William Blake.—Painting in the nineteenth century. Ford Madox Brown and Preraphaelitism. Millais. Burne-Jones. Meissonier. Baudry. Puvis de Chavannes. Whistler. Sargent. The early work of Saint-Gaudens. Saint-Gaudens's "Sherman". [N7445.C85 1969] 74-90627
1. Art—Addresses, essays, lectures. 2. Artists. I. Title. BIP

COX, Kenyon, 1856-1919. 709'.22
Painters and sculptors; a second series of old masters and new. Freeport, N.Y., Books for Libraries Press [1970] xi, 187 p. illus., ports. 23 cm. (Essay index reprint series) Reprint of the 1907 ed. Contents.Contents.—The education of an artist.—The Pollaiuoli.—Painters of the mode.—Holbein.—The Rembrandt tercentenary.—Rodin.—Lord Leighton. [N7445.C87 1970] 70-105006
1. Art—Addresses, essays, lectures. I. Title. BIP

CRAM, Ralph Adams, 1863-1942. 709
The ministry of art. Freeport, N. Y., Books for Libraries Press [1967] xii, 245 p. 22 cm. (Essay index reprint series) Reprint of the 1914 ed. Contents.--Art the revealer.--The philosophy of the Gothic restoration.--The place of the fine arts in public education.--The artist and the world.--The craftsman and the architect.--American university architecture.--The ministry of art. [N7445.C9] 67-30203
1. Art—Addresses, essays, lectures. I. Title. BIP

CRANE, Walter, 1845-1915. 704.9'2
Ideals in art / Walter Crane. New York : Garland Pub., 1979. p. cm. (The Aesthetic movement & the arts and crafts movement ; 31) Reprint of the 1905 ed. published by B. Bell, London. Includes index. [N7445.C93 1979] 76-17775 ISBN 0-8240-2480-X : 35.00
1. Art—Addresses, essays, lectures. I. Title. Contents omitted. BIP

EGLINTON, Guy, 1896-1928. 700'.8
Reaching for art. Freeport, N.Y., Books for Libraries Press [1967] 152 p. illus., ports. 22 cm. (Essay index reprint series) Reprint of the 1931 ed. Contents.Contents.—An approach to painting.—An unpublished masterpiece by Courbet.—The theory of Seurat.—L'histoire d'un Fauve.—Elne.—The coronation of the Virgin at Villeneuve-Les-Avignon.—The Pieta of Villeneuve-Les-Avignon.—Dante and Blake.—Alfeo Faggi, sculptor.—Vincent Canade.—Towards a new museum. [N7445.E4 1967] 67-26738
1. Art—Addresses, essays, lectures. 2. Art criticism. I. Title. BIP

ESSAYS in honor of Walter Friedlaender. Edited by Marsyas. [New York] Institute of Fine Arts, New York University; distributed by J. J. Augustin, Locust Valley, N.Y., 1965. xiii, 194 p. 29 cm. (Marsyas; studies in the history of art. Supplement 2) Includes bibliographical references. [N7442.4.F74] 74-168035 709
1. Friedlaender, Walter F., 1873-1966. 2. Art—Addresses, essays, lectures. I. Friedlaender, Walter F., 1873-1966. II. New York University. Institute of Fine Arts. III. Title. IV. Series.

FESTSCHRIFT fur Peter Wilhelm Meister zum 65. [i.e. funfundsechzigsten] Geburtstag am 16. Mai 1974 / [hrsg. von Annaliese Ohm u. Horst Reber]. Hamburg : Hauswedell, [1975] 331 p. : ill., maps ; 30 cm. Includes three contributions in English. Bibliography of works by P. W. Meister: p. 327. [N7442.M442] 75-504057 DM240.00 069'.9'7
1. Meister, Peter Wilhelm. 2. Art—Addresses, essays, lectures. I. Meister, Peter Wilhelm. II. Ohm, Anneliese. III. Reber, Horst.

FRY, Roger Eliot, 1866-1934. 701.18
Last lectures. With an introd. by Kenneth Clark. Boston, Beacon Press [1962] xxix, 370 p. plates. 21 cm. (Beacon paperback, no. 131) [N7445.F73 1962] 63-6053
1. Art — Addresses, essays, lectures. 2. Art criticism. I. Title.

FRY, Roger, Eliot, 1866-1934. 704.91
Transformations; critical and speculative essays on art. Garden City, N. Y., Doubleday, 1956. xii, 306p. illus., plates. 18cm. (A Doubleday anchor book, A 77) [N7445] 56-8239
1. Art—Addresses, essays, lectures. I. Title.

FRY, Roger Eliot, 1866-1934. 700'.8
Transformations; critical and speculative essays on art. Freeport, N.Y., Books for Libraries Press [1968] viii, 230 p. illus. 29 cm. (Essay index reprint series) Reprint of the 1927 ed. Contents.Contents.—Some questions in esthetics.—Art and the state.—Culture and snobbism.—Some aspects of Chinese art.—Fra Bartolommeo.—The seicento.—J. S. Sargent.—London sculptors and sculptures.—Book illustration and a modern example.—Speculations in Languedoc.—Vincent van Gogh.—Seurat.—On some modern drawings.—Plastic colour. [N7445.F75 1968] 68-14904
1. Art—Addresses, essays, lectures. I. Title.

FRY, Roger Eliot, 1866-1934 704
Vision and design [Gloucester, Mass., Peter Smith, 1962] 302p. illus. 18cm. (Meridian bk., M33 rebound) 3.50
1. Art—Addresses, essays, lectures. I. Title. BIP

FRY, Roger Eliot, 1866-1934. 704
Vision and design. New York, Meridian Books, 1956. 392 p. illus. 19 cm. (Meridian books, M33) [N7445.F8 1956] 56-10013
1. Art—Addresses, essays, lectures. I. Title.

GABO, Naum, 1890- 704.9'2
Of divers arts. [New York] Pantheon Books [1962] xviii, 205 p. illus. (part col.) 26 cm. (Bollingen series, 35. The A. W. Mellon lectures in the fine arts, 8) [N7445.G19] 62-9369
1. Art—Addresses, essays, lectures. I. Title. II. Series: Bollingen series, 35. III. Series: The A. W. Mellon lectures in the fine arts, 8 BIP

GABO, Naum, 1890- 704.9'2
Of divers arts. [Princeton, N.J.] Princeton University Press [1971, c1962] xviii, 205 p. illus. (part col.) 26 cm. (Bollingen series, 35. The A. W. Mellon lectures in the fine arts, 8) Includes bibliographical references. [N7445.2.G3 1971] 74-162716 ISBN 0-691-01771-9
1. Art—Addresses, essays, lectures. I. Title. II. Series: Bollingen series, 35. III. Series: The A. W. Mellon lectures in the fine arts, 8.

GASSNER, John, 1903- ed. 704.92
The nature of art. Edited by John Gassner and Sidney Thomas. New York, Crown Publishers [1964] vii, 619 p. illus. 24 cm. Bibliographical footnotes. [N7443.G3] 63-21126
1. Art—Addresses, essays, lectures. I. Thomas, Sidney, 1915- joint ed. II. Title.

GATHERINGS in honor of Dorothy E. Miner. Edited by Ursula E. McCracken, Lilian M. C. Randall [and] Richard H. Randall, Jr. Baltimore, Walters Art Gallery [1974] xviii, 353 p. illus. 29 cm. [N7442.2.M563] 74-170951 36.00 700
1. Miner, Dorothy Eugenia. 2. Art—Addresses, essays, lectures. I. Miner, Dorothy Eugenia. II. McCracken, Ursula E., ed. III. Randall, Lilian M. C., ed. IV. Randall, Richard H., ed. V. Walters Art Gallery, Baltimore. BIP

GILL, Eric, 1882-1940. 701.17
Beauty looks after herself, essays. Freeport, N.Y., Books for Libraries Press [1966] 253 p. illus. 21 cm. (Essay index reprint series) "First published 1933." [N7445.G47 1966] 67-22095
1. Art—Addresses, essays, lectures. 2. Aesthetics. I. Title.

GOLDWATER, Robert John, 1907-1973, ed. and tr. 709
Artists on art, from the XIV to the XX century. Compiled and edited by Robert Goldwater and Marco Treves. [3d. ed.] New York, Pantheon Books [1974, c1945] xii, 499 p. illus. 21 cm. Bibliography: p. 480-488. [N7452.G64 1974] 74-176211 ISBN 0-394-70900-4 5.95
1. Art—Addresses, essays, lectures. I. Treves, Marco, joint ed. and tr. II. Title.

GOMBRICH, Ernst Hans Josef, 1909- 701
Art history and the social sciences / by E. H. Gombrich. Oxford [Eng.] : Clarendon Press, 1975. 60 p., [2] leaves of plates : ill. ; 22 cm. (The Romanes lecture ; 1973) Includes bibliographical references. [N7445.2.G57] 75-320983 ISBN 0-19-951297-3 pbk. : 2.50
1. Art—Addresses, essays, lectures. 2. Art—Philosophy—Addresses, essays, lectures. I. Title. II. Series.
Distributed by Oxford University Press, New York.

GOMBRICH, Ernst Hans Josef, 1909- 701
Mediations on a hobby horse, and others essays on the theory of art. With 140 illus. [London] Phaidon Publishers; distributed by New York Graphic Society Publishers, Greenwich, Conn. [1963] xi', 184 p. illus., ports., diagrs. 26 cm. Bibliographical references included in "Notes" (p. 163-173) [N7445.G63] 64-1059
1. Art — Addresses, essays, lectures. 2. Art-Philosophy. I. Title.

GOMBRICH, Ernst Hans Josef, 1909- 701
Meditations on a hobby horse and other essays on the theory of art, by E. H. Gombrich. 2nd ed. London, New York, Phaidon, 1971. xli, 252 p. illus. 23 cm. Includes bibliographical references. [N7445.G63 1971] 72-192259 ISBN 0-7148-1258-7 £3.50
1. Art—Addresses, essays, lectures. 2. Art—Philosophy. I. Title. BIP

GOMBRICH, Ernst Hans Josef, Sir, 1909- 701
Meditations on a hobby horse : and other essays on the theory of art / by E. H. Gombrich. 3d ed. London ; New York : Phaidon, 1978, c1963. x, 182 p., [32] leaves of plates : ill. ; 19 cm. Includes

bibliographical references and index. [N7445.2.G58 1978] 78-310735 ISBN 0-7148-1830-5 : 5.95
1. Art—Addresses, essays, lectures. 2. Art—Philosophy. I. Title.

GREENOUGH, Horatio, 1805-   701.17 1852.
Form and function: remarks on art, design, and architecture. Edited by Harold A. Small. With an introd. by Erle Loran. [1st paper-bound ed.] Berkeley, University of California Press, 1957. 136p. 19cm. [NB237] 57-13996
1. Art— Addresses, essays, lectures. I. Title.

GROSSER, Maurice Richard,   704 1903-
Critic's eye. Indianapolis, Bobbs-Merrill [1962] 232p. 22cm. [N7445.G69] 62-12979
1. Art—Addresses, essays, lectures. 2. Art, Modern—20th cent.—Addresses, essays, lectures.   I.   Title.

HAMERTON, Philip Gilbert,   814'.8 1834-1894.
Portfolio papers. Freeport, N.Y., Books for Libraries Press [1971] ix, 386 p. 23 cm. (Essay index reprint series) Reprint of the 1889 ed. Short biographies and essays reprinted from the Portfolio. Contents.Contents.—Notices of artists: Constable, 1873. Etty, 1875. Chintreuil, 1874. Adrien Guignet, 1874. Goya, 1879.—Notes on aesthetics, 1879, 1880.—Essays: Style, 1881. Soul and matter in the fine arts, 1884. The nature of the fine arts, 1885. Can science help art? 1870.—Conversations: Book illustration, 1888. [N7445.2.H3 1971] 77-37148 ISBN 0-8369-2504-1
1. Art—Addresses, essays, lectures. 2. Artists—Addresses, essays, lectures. I. Title.   BIP

HAMMER, Victor Karl, 1882-   720
Concern for the art of civilized man. Lexington, Ky., Stamperia del Santuccio, c1963. 49 p. 26 cm. "One hundred and nine copies." No. 100. [N7445.H32] 64-2601
1. Art—Addresses, essays, lectures. I. Title.

HAMMER, Victor Karl, 1882-   704.91
Memory and her nine daughters, the muses; a pretext for printing, cast into the mould of a dialogue in four chapters. [Lexington? Ky., 1956] iv, 90p. diagr. 29cm. Label on spine: Four dialogues. [N7445.H33] 57-30502
1. Art—Addresses, essays, lectures. I. Title.

HAMMER, Victor Karl, 1882-   704.91
Memory and her nine daughters, the Muses; a pretext for pruniting cast into the mould of a dialogue in four chapters. New York, G. Wittenborn, 1957. iv. 104p. illus, 26cm. 252 copies printed. No. 62. [N7445.H33 1957] 57-3494
1. Art—Addresses, essays, lectures. I. Title.

HAMMER, Victor Karl, 1882-   704.91
Memory and her nine daughters, the muses; a pretext for printing, cast into the mould of a dialogue in four chapters. [New York, G. Wittenborn, 1956] iv, 90p. diagr. 29cm. Label on spine: Four dialogues. [N7445.H33] 57-30502
1. Art— Addresses, essays, lectures. I. Title.

HAMMER, Victor Karl, 1882-   704.92
Some fragments for c.r.h. [by] Victor Hammer. [Lexington, Ky., Stamperia del Santuccio, 1967] 91 p. illus. 21 cm. 125 copies. No. 120. [N7445.H34] 720 68-130
1. Art—Addresses, essays, lectures. I. Title.

HARTLEY, Marsden, 1877-1943.   709
Adventures in the arts; informal chapters on painters, vaudeville and poets. New York, Hacker Art Books, 1972. xviii, 254 p. 23 cm. Reprint of the 1921 ed. [PS3515.A795A7 1972] 78-143351 ISBN 0-87817-071-5
1. Art—Addresses, essays, lectures. 2. Literature, Modern—Addresses, essays, lectures. 3. Vaudeville. I. Title.   BIP

HENRI, Robert, 1865-1929.   704.9
The art spirit; notes, articles, fragments of letters and talks to studnets, bearing on the concept and technique of picture making, the study of art generally, and on appreciation. Compiled by Margery Ryerson. Introd. by Forbes Watson.

Philadelphia, Lippincott, 1960 [c1958] 284p. 19cm. (Keystone books, KB18) [N7445.H56 1960] 61-1228
1. Art—Addresses, essays, lectures. I. Title.   BIP

HODIN, Josef Paul.   704.9
The dilemma of being modern; essays on art and literature. New York, Noonday Press [1959] 271p. illus. 22cm. (Noonday paperbacks, N154) [N7445.H66 1959] 59-15130
1. Art—Addresses, essays, lectures. 2. Literature—Addresses, essays, lectures. I. Title.

HOFMANN, Hans, 1880-1966.   700.8
Search for the real, and other essays. Ed. by Sara T. Weeks, Bartlett H. Hayes, Jr. [Rev. ed.] Cambridge, Mass., M.I.T. Pr. [1967] xiii, 72p. illus. (pt. col.) 21cm. Based on an exhibition, covering a half century of the art of Hans Hofmann, held at the Addison Gallery of American Art, Phillips Academy, Andover, January 2- February 22, 1948. [N7445.H76 1967] 67-15236 2.95 pap.,
1. Art—Addresses, essays, lectures. I. Weeks, Sarah T., 1926- ed. II. Hayes, Bartlett H., 1904- joint ed. III. Phillips Academy, Andover, Mass. Addison Gallery of American Art. IV. Title.

HOPPIN, James Mason, 1820-   709 1906.
The early Renaissance, and other essays on art subjects. Freeport, N.Y., Books for Libraries Press [1972] iv, 306 p. 22 cm. (Essay index reprint series) Reprint of the 1892 ed. Contents.Contents.—The early Renaissance.—Principles of art.—Tendencies of modern art.—French landscape-painting.—Murillo.—Art in education.—Art and religion.—Bourges Cathedral.—The Zeus-altar of Pergamon.—Critique of a Greek statue.—The masterpiece of Scopas.—Hellas. Includes bibliographical references. [N7445.2.H68 1972] 72-6827 ISBN 0-8369-7249-X
1. Art—Addresses, essays, lectures. 2. Art, Renaissance—Early Renaissance—Addresses, essays, lectures. I. Title.

HUNEKER, James Gibbons,   709.4 1857-1921.
Promenades of an impressionist. Freeport, N.Y., Books for Libraries Press [1970, c1910] 390 p. 23 cm. (Essay index reprint series)   Contents.Contents.—Paul Cezanne.—Rops the etcher.—Monticelli.—Rodin. Eugene Carriere.—Degas.—Botticelli.—Six Spaniards.—Chardin.—Black and white.—Impressionism.—A new study of Watteau.—Gauguin and Toulouse-Lautrec.—Literature and art.—Museum promenades.—Coda. [N7445.2.H85 1970] 73-134097 ISBN 0-8369-1959-9
1. Art—Addresses, essays, lectures. 2. Artists. I. Title.   BIP

HUXLEY, Aldous Leonard,   704.9 1894-
On art and artists. Edited and introduced by Morris Philipson. New York, Meridian Books [1960] 320p. 18cm. (Meridian books, M99) [N7445.H93 1960a] 60-12323
1. Art—Addresses, essays, lectures. 2. Literature—Addresses, essays, lectures. 3. Music—Addresses, essays, lectures. I. Title.

HUXLEY, Aldous Leonard,   704.9 1894-1963.
On art and artists. Edited and introduced by Morris Philipson. New York, Harper [1960] 320 p. 22 cm. [N7445.H93 1960] 60-10408
1. Art—Addresses, essays, lectures. 2. Literature—Addresses, essays, lectures. 3. Music—Addresses, essays, lectures. I. Title.

IN memoriam Otto J. Brendel   709
:   essays in archaeology and the humanities / ed. by Larissa Bonfante, Helga von Heintze ; with the collab. of Carla Lord. Mainz : von Zabern, 1976. xviii, 264, 62 p. : numerous ill. (some col.) ; 30 cm. "Bibliography of Otto J. Brendel": p. [xii]-xiv. [N7442.B73] 77-363280 ISBN 3-8053-0154-5 : DM135.00
1. Brendel, Otto, 1901-1973. 2. Art—Addresses, essays, lectures. I. Brendel, Otto, 1901-1973. II. Bonfante, Larissa. III. Heintze, Helga, Freifrau von. IV. Lord, Carla.

IYER, K. Bharatha, ed.   704
Art and thought, issued in honor of Dr. Ananda K Coomaraswamy on the occasion of his 70th birthday [Reissue] London, Luzae [dist. Mystic, Conn., Verry, 1965] xvi, 259p. illus. 26cm. Bibl. [N7443.C57] 49-4227 12.50
1. Coomaraswamy, Ananda Kentish, 1877-1947. 2. Art—Addresses, essays, lectures. 3. Philosophy—Addresses, essays, lectures. I. Title.

JAMES, Henry, 1843-1916.   720
The painter's eye; notes and essays on the pictorial arts. Selected and edited with an introd. by John L. Sweeney. Cambridge, Harvard University Press, 1956. 274p. port. 21cm. Includes bibliographies. [N7445.J] A58
1. Art—Addresses, essays, lectures. I. Title.

JANSON, Horst Woldemar,   704.9'2 1913-
16 studies, by H. W. Janson New York, H. A. Abrams [1974?] xi, 338 p. illus. 27 cm. "A collection of essays published in periodicals between 1937 and 1970." Contents.Contents.—The putto with the Death's head.—Titian's Laocoon caricature and the Vesalian-Galenist controversy.—The "image made by chance" in Renaissance thought.—Fuseli's Nightmare.—Nanni di Banco's Assumption of the virgin on the Porta della Mandorla.—Giovanni Chellini's Libro and Donatello.— The image of man in Renaissance art: from Donatello to Michelangelo.—Originality as a ground for judgment of excellence.—The equestrian monument from Cangrande della Scala to Peter the Great.—Observations on nudity in neoclassical art.—Ground plan and elevation in Masaccio's Trinity fresco.—Rodin and Carrier-Belleuse: the Vase des titans.—Donatello and the antique.—The right arm of Michelangelo's Moses.—The meaning of Giganti.—Criteria of periodization in the history of European art. Includes bibliographical references. [NO16 studies, by H. W. Janson New York,
1. Art—Addresses, essays, lectures. I. Title.

JARVES, James Jackson, 1818-   701 1888.
Art thoughts : the experiences and observations of an American amateur in Europe / by James Jackson Jarves ; edited with an introd. by H. Barbara Weinberg. New York : Garland Publ, 1976, c1869. p. cm. (The Art experience in late nineteenth-century America) Reprint of the ed. published by Hurd and Houghton, New York. [N7445.2.J37 1976] 75-28866 ISBN 0-8240-2226-2 lib.bdg. : 25.00
1. Art—Addresses, essays, lectures. I. Title. II. Series.

KAY, Hether, comp.   704.9
A new look at the arts. Illustrated by Kathleen Peyton. [London] Educational Productions [1961]; stamped: distributed by Sportshelf, New Rochelle, N. Y.] 64p. illus. 19cm. (New look series) Includes bibliography. [N7438.K3] 61-667
1. Art—Addresses, essays, lectures. 2. Theater—Addresses, essays, lectures. 3. Music—Addresses, essays, lectures. I. Title.

KEPES, Gyorgy, 1906- ed.   701
The nature and art of motion. New York, G. Braziller [1965] xi, 195 p. illus. 29 cm. (Vision+value series) Includes bibliographical references. [N7443.K4] 65-5600
1. Art—Addresses, essays, lectures. 2. Motion. I. Title.

KLEE, Paul, 1879-1940   759.3
Paul Klee: the thinking eye; the notebooks of Paul Klee. Ed. by Jurg Spiller [Tr. from German by Ralph Manheim, Charlotte Weidler, Joyce Wittenborn] New York, Wittenborn [1961] 541p. illus. (pt. col., pt mounted) Bibl. 60-15445 25.00 bds.,
1. Art—Addresses, essays, lectures. I. Spiller, Jurg, ed. II. Title. III. Title: The thinking eye. IV. Series. V. Documents of modern art, v. 15

KLEINBAUER, W. Eugene,   704.92 1937- comp.
Modern perspectives in Western art history; an anthology of 20th-century writings on the visual arts [by] W. Eugene Kleinbauer. New York, Holt, Rinehart and

Winston [1971] xiii, 528 p. illus., plans, ports. 24 cm. Includes bibliographical references.   [N7443.2.K57]   73-153955 ISBN 0-03-078220-1
1. Art—Addresses, essays, lectures. I. Title.   BIP

LETHABY, William Richard,   704.91 1857-1931.
Form in civilization; collected papers on art and labour. With a foreword by Lewis Mumford. 2d ed. London, New York, Oxford University Press, 1957. 196p. illus. 20cm. [N7445.L45 1957] 57-13661
1. Art—Addresses, essays, lectures. 2. Art, Municipal. 3. Architecture—Addresses, essays, lectures. 4. Aesthetics—Addresses, essays, lectures. I. Title.

LEWIS, Wyndham, 1882-1957.   701
Wyndham Lewis on art; collected writings 1913-1956. With introductions and notes by Walter Michel and C. J. Fox. New York, Funk & Wagnalls [1969] 480 p. facsims. 22 cm. Bibliography: p. [474]-475. [N7445.2.L38 1969] 77-87140 10.00
1. Art—Addresses, essays, lectures. I. Michel, Walter, 1922- II. Fox, Cyril James, 1931- III. Title.   BIP

LEWIS, Wyndham, 1886-1957.   759.2
Wyndham Lewis, the artist; from "Blast" to Burlington House. New York, Haskell House Publishers, 1971. 379 p. illus. 23 cm. Reprint of the 1939 ed. Contents.Contents.—Super-nature versus super-real.—The skeleton in the cupboard speaks.—Notes and vortices, I-III.—The Caliph's design.—Essay on the objective of art in our time.—The rejected portrait of T. S. Eliot. [N7445.2.L4 1971] 74-173843 ISBN 0-8383-1348-5
1. Art—Addresses, essays, lectures. I. Title: From "Blast" to Burlington House.   BIP

L'OEIL.   704.92
Modern art yesterday and tomorrow. The selective eye IV; an anthology of writings on modern art from L'Oeil, the European art magazine. Edited by Georges and Rosamond Bernier. Paris, G. & R. Bernier [dist.] New York, Reynal [1960] 181 p. illus., plates (part col.) ports., facsims. 32 cm. Title varies: v. 1-2, The Selective eye. Editors: G. Bernier, R. Bernier. Vol. 1. published by Random House. 55-11347 10.00 bds.,
1. Art—Addresses, essays, lectures. 2. Artists. I. Bernier, Georges, ed. II. Bernier, Rosamond, ed. III. Title. IV. Title: The selective eye.

L'OEIL.   704.92
The selective eye; an anthology of the best from L'Oeil, the European art magazine. Edited by Georges and Rosamond Bernier. With 48 pages in color. Paris, L OEil New and Rosamond Bernier. With 48 pages in color. Paris, L'Oeil NewYork Random House 1955 1939. illus., plates (part col.) ports., ports., facsims. 32cm. 'Selected from the first nine issues (January-September 1955) of L'Cell. The texts were originally printed in French, and are given here in English for the first time.' [N7443.O3] 55-11347
1. Art—Addresses, essays, lectures. I. Bernier, Georges, ed. II. Bernier, Rosamond, ed. III. Title.

MCBRIDE, Henry. 1867-   704.9'2 1962.
The flow of art : essays and criticisms of Henry McBride / selected, with an introd., by Daniel Catton Rich ; prefatory essay by Lincoln Kirstein. 1st ed. New York : Atheneum Publishers, c1975. ix, 462 p., [13] leaves of plates : ill. ; 24 cm. "A Chancellor Hall book." Includes index. [N7445.2.M3 1975] 75-13774 ISBN 0-689-10692-0 : 14.95
1. Art—Addresses, essays, lectures. I. Rich, Daniel Catton, 1904- II. Title.   BIP

MALEVICH, Kazimir   701'.09'04 Severinovich, 1878-1935.
Essays on art, 1915-1933 [by] K. S. Malevich. Translated by Xenia Glowacki-Prus [and] Arnold McMillin. Edited by Troels Andersen. [2d ed.] New York, G. Wittenborn [1971, c1968] 178 p. illus., facsim., ports. 19 cm. (The Documents of modern art, v. 16) Bibliography: p. 166-[170] [N7445.8.R9M313 1971] 71-152404 ISBN 0-8150-0419-2 18.00
1. Art—Addresses, essays, lectures. I. Title. II. Series.

MATISSE, Henri, 1869-1954. 701
Matisse on art. [Edited by] Jack D. Flam. [New York] Phaidon [1973] 199 p. illus. 26 cm. Bibliography: p. [177]-191. [ND553.M37F55] 72-79535 ISBN 0-7148-1518-7 12.50
1. Matisse, Henri, 1869-1954. 2. Art—Addresses, essays, lectures. I. Flam, Jack D., ed. II. Title. BIP

MUMFORD, Lewis, 1895- 701
Art and technics. London, Oxford University Press, 1952. 162p. 20cm. [N7445.M88 1952a] 53-24880
1. Art—Addresses, essays, lectures. 2. Art—Philosophy. I. Title.

MUMFORD, Lewis, 1895- 701
Art and technics. New York, Columbia University Press, 1952. 162 p. 21 cm. (Rampton lectures in America, no. 4) [N7445.M88] 52-1930
1. Art — Addresses, essays, lectures. 2. Art — Philosophy. I. Title. II. Series.

MUMFORD, Lewis, 1895- 701
Art and technics. New York, Columbia University Press [1960, c.1952] 162p. 'originally delivered as the fourth in the Bampton Lectures in America' series. (Columbia paperback 9) 1.25 pap.,
1. Art—Addresses, essays, lectures. 2. Art—Philosophy. I. Title. BIP

THE Necessity of art, 700
by A. Clutton Brock [and others] Freeport, N.Y., Books for Libraries Press [1969] vii, 181 p. 23 cm. (Essay index reprint series) Reprint of the 1924 ed. Contents.Contents.—Art and the escape from banality, by A. Clutton Brock.—Christianity and art, by P. Dearmer.—The art of movement, by A. S. Duncan-Jones.—The puritan objection to art, by M. Spencer.—The artist and the saint, by A. W. Pollard.—Literature and religion, by J. M. Murry.—The doctrine of values, by P. Dearmer. [N25.N4 1969] 78-93366
1. Art—Addresses, essays, lectures. 2. Art and religion. I. Clutton-Brock, Arthur, 1868-1924. BIP

NEW York University. 700
Institute of Fine Arts.
Essays in memory of Karl Lehmann. Edited by Lucy Freeman Sandler. [New York] Institute of Fine Arts, New York University; distributed by J. J. Augustin, Locust Valley, N.Y., 1964. xviii, 395 p. illus., facsims., maps, plans, mounted port. 29 cm. (Marsyas; studies in the history of art. Suppl. 1) "Bibliography of the writings of Karl Lehmann": p. xi-xv. Bibliographical references included in footnotes. [N7443.N44] 700 68-1101
1. Art—Addresses, essays, lectures. I. Lehmann, Karl, 1894-1960. II. Sandler, Lucy Freeman, ed. III. Title. IV. Series.

NEWTON, Eric, 1893-1965. 700'.8
In my view. Freeport, N.Y., Books for Libraries Press [1972] xii, 257 p. 22 cm. (Essay index reprint series) Essays. Reprint of the 1950 ed. [N7445.2.N48 1972] 72-1298 ISBN 0-8369-2882-2 11.00
1. Art—Addresses, essays, lectures. I. Title. BIP

OEIL. 704.92
Aspects of modern art. The selective eye; an anthology of writings on modern art from L'CEil. v. [1]- Paris, G. & R. Bernier; New York, Reynal [1955- v. illus., plates (part col.) ports., facsims. 32cm. Title varies: v. 1-2, The selective eye. Editors: G. Bernier, R. Bernier. Vol. 1 published by Random House. [N7443.O3] 55-11347
1. Art—Addresses, essays, lectures. 2. Artists. I. Bernier, Georges, ed. II. Bernier, Rosamond, ed. III. Title. IV. Title: The selective eye.

ON the future of art; 700
essays by Arnold J. Toynbee [and others] Introd. by Edward F. Fry. New York, Viking Press [1970] ix, 134 p. illus. 21 cm. "Sponsored by the Solomon R. Guggenheim Museum." Includes bibliographical references. [N7443.2.O5 1970] 73-104156 7.50
1. Art—Addresses, essays, lectures. I. Toynbee, Arnold Joseph, 1889- II. Solomon R. Guggenheim Museum, New York.

PANOFSKY, Erwin, 1892- 723.5
Gothic architecture and scholasticism. Latrobe, Pa., Archabbey Press, 1951. xviii, 156 p. illus. 20 cm. (Wimmer lecture, 1948) Bibliographical references included in "Notes" (p. [89]-108) [NA2563.P3] 51-14527
1. Art — Addresses, essays, lectures. 2. Architecture, Gothic. 3. Scholasticism. I. Title. II. Series.

PANOFSKY, Erwin, 1892- 704.9'2
1968.
Meaning in the visual arts : papers in and on art history / by Erwin Panofsky. Woodstock N.Y. : Overlook Press, 1974, c1955. xviii, 364 p., [16] leaves of plates : ill. ; 24 cm. Reprint of the ed. published by Doubleday, Garden City, N.Y. Includes index. Bibliography: p. vi-viii. [N7445.2.P35 1974] 74-78548 ISBN 0-87951-024-2 : 15.00
1. Art—Addresses, essays, lectures. I. Title. BIP

PANOFSKY, Erwin, 1892- 704.91
1968.
Meaning in the visual arts: papers in and on art history. [1st ed.] Garden City, N.Y., Doubleday, 1955. xviii, 362 p. illus. 18 cm. (Doubleday anchor books, A59) Bibliography: p. vi-x. Bibliographical footnotes. [N7445.P22] 55-9754
1. Art—Addresses, essays, lectures. I. Title.

PHILLIPS, Claude, Sir, 1848- 700
1924.
Emotion in art. Edited by Maurice W. Brockwell. Freeport, N.Y., Books for Libraries Press [1968] xxii, 282 p. illus. 22 cm. (Essay index reprint series) Reprint of 1925 ed. [N7445.P45 1968] 68-29238
1. Art—Addresses, essays, lectures. I. Title. BIP

PICASSO, Pablo, 1881- 701
Picasso on art: a selection of views. [Compiled by] Dore Ashton. New York, Viking Press [1972] xxvii, 187 p. illus. 22 cm. (The Documents of 20th-century art) Bibliography: p. [175]-183. [N7454.P52 1972] 73-184538 ISBN 0-670-55327-1 8.95
1. Art—Addresses, essays, lectures. I. Title. II. Series.
Pap. 3.50, ISBN 0-670-01943-7

PICASSO, Pablo, 1881-1973. 701
Picasso on art : a selection of views / [compiled by] Dore Ashton. New York : Penguin Books, 1977. xxvii, 187 p. : ill. ; 21 cm. (The Documents of 20th-century art) Bibliography: p. [175]-183. [N7454.P52 1977] 77-5626 ISBN 0-14-004528-7 pbk. : 4.50
1. Art—Addresses, essays, lectures. I. Title.

POOLE, Reginald Stuart, 1832- 708
1895.
Lectures on art, delivered in support of the Society for the Protection of Ancient Buildings, by Reginald Stuart Poole [and others] Freeport, N.Y., Books for Libraries Press [1972] x, 232 p. illus. 23 cm. (Essay index reprint series) Reprint of the 1882 ed. Contents.Contents.—The Egyptian tomb and the future state, by R. S. Poole.—Monumental painting, by W. B. Richmond.—Some remarks on ancient decorative art, by E. J. Poynter.—English parish churches, by J. T. Micklethwaite.—The history of pattern designing. The lesser arts of life. By W. Morris. [N7443.2.P65 1972] 78-39677 ISBN 0-8369-2781-8
1. Art—Addresses, essays, lectures. I. Society for the Protection of Ancient Buildings, London. II. Title.

PORTER, Fairfield. 704.9'2
Fairfield Porter : art in its own terms : selected criticism, 1935-1975 / edited by Rackstraw Downes. 1st ed. New York : Taplinger Pub. Co., 1978. p. cm. Includes index. [N7445.2.P67] 78-57598 ISBN 0-8008-2586-1 : 15.00. ISBN 0-8008-2587-X pbk. : 7.95
1. Art—Addresses, essays, lectures. I. Downes, Rackstraw.

POYNTER, Edward John, 704.9'2
Sir, bart., 1836-1919.
Ten lectures on art. Freeport, N.Y., Books for Libraries Press [1972] p. (Essays index reprint series) Reprint of the 1879 ed. [N7445.2.P68 1972] 72-8570 ISBN 0-8369-7325-9
1. Art—Addresses, essays, lectures. I. Title.

READ, Herbert Edward Sir 701.1
1893-
The grass roots of art; lectures on the social aspects of art in an industrial age. (Rev. and expanded] Cleveland, World Pub. Co. [1961, c.1946] 160p. illus. (Meridian bks., M108) Bibl. 1.25 pap.,
1. Art—Addresses, essays, lectures. 2. Art and society. I. Title. II. Series.

READ, Herbert Edward, Sir 701.1
1893-
The grass roots of art; lectures on the social aspects of art in an industrial age. [Rev. and expanded] New York, G. Wittenborn, 1955. 160p. illus. 22cm. (Problems of contemporary art, no. 2) Bibliographical footnotes. [N7445.R25 1955] 55-3860
1. Art—Addresses, essays, lectures. 2. Art and society. I. Title. II. Series.

READ, Herbert Edward, Sir 704
1893-
A letter to a young painter. [1st American ed.] New York, Horizon Press [1962] 277p. illus. 19cm. Essays. [N7445.R254 1962a] 62-17009
1. Art—Addresses, essays, lectures. 2. Artists. I. Title.

REYNOLDS, Joshua, Sir 704.94
1723-1792.
Discourses on art. Introd. by Robert R. Wark. New York, Collier Books [1966] 254 p. 18 cm. Bibliography: p. vii-viii. [N7445.R3 1966] 66-24893
1. Art—Addresses, essays, lectures. I. Title.

REYNOLDS, Joshua, Sir 704.91
1723-1792
Discourses on art. Introd. by Robert Lavine [Gloucester, Mass., Peter Smith, 1962, c.1961] 254p. 18cm. (Collier bks., art hist., AS3 rebound) 3.00
1. Art—Addresses, essays, lectures. I. Title.

REYNOLDS, Joshua, Sir 704.91
1723-1792.
Discourses on art. Introd. by Robert Lavine. New York, Collier Books [1961] 254p. 18cm. (Collier Books art history, AS3) [N7445.R3 1961] 61-17495
1. Art—Addresses, essays, lectures. I. Title.

REYNOLDS, Joshua, Sir, 704.9'4
1723-1792.
Discourses on art / Joshua Reynolds ; edited by Robert R. Wark. New Haven : Published for the Paul Mellon Centre for Studies in British Art (London) Ltd. by Yale University Press, 1975. xxxv, 349 p., [12] leaves of plates : ill. ; 26 cm. Text of the 1797 ed. of the author's Discourses. Includes index. Bibliography: p. 337-341. [N7445.R3 1975] 74-17647 ISBN 0-300-01823-1 : 20.00
1. Art—Addresses, essays, lectures. I. Paul Mellon Centre for Studies in British Art. II. Title.

REYNOLDS, Joshua, Sir 704.91
1723-1792.
Discourses on art. Edited by Robert R. Wark. San Marino, Calif., Huntington Library, 1959. xxxv, 321p. 24 plates. 27cm. (Huntington Library publications) 'The edition chosen as a base was that of 1797.' Bibliography: p. 309-313. [N7445.R3 1959] 59-10148
1. Art—Addresses, essays, lectures. I. Title. II. Series: Henry E. Huntington Library and Art Gallery, San Marino, Calif. Huntington Library publications

REYNOLDS, Joshua Sir 1723- 704.9
1792.
Discourses on art, with selections from The idler. Edited, with an introd., by Stephen O. Mitchell. Indianapolis, Bobbs-Merrill [1965] xxxviii, 252 p. illus., ports. 21 cm. (The Library of liberal arts, 204) Bibliography: p. xxxv-xxxvi. [N7445.R3] 65-26523
1. Art — Addresses, essays, lectures. I. Mitchell, Stephon O., ed. II. Title.

RICHMAN, Robert, ed. 709.04
The arts at mid-century. New York, Horizon Press, 1954. xi, 306 p. 24 cm. [N7443.R53] 54-7896
1. Art—Addresses, essays, lectures. I. Title.

ROSENFELD, Paul, 1890- 700'.8
1946.
By way of art; criticisms of music, literature, painting, sculpture, and the dance. Freeport, N. Y., Books for Libraries Press [1967] x, 309 p. 22 cm. (Essay index reprint series) Reprint of the 1928 edition. [PS3535.O714B8 1967] 67-30230
1. Art—Addresses, essays, lectures. 2. Music—Addresses, essays, lectures. 3. Literature—Addresses, essays, lectures. I. Title. BIP

RUSKIN, John, 1819-1900. 700
Lectures on art, delivered before the University of Oxford in Hilary term, 1870. With an introd. by Charles Eliot Norton. Brantwood ed. New York, Maynard, Merrill, 1893. St. Clair Shores, Mich., Scholarly Press, 1972 [c1890] p. (The works of John Ruskin) Contents.Contents.—Inaugural.—The relation of art to religion.—The relation of art to morals.—The relation of art to use.—Line.—Light.—Colour. [N7445.2.R79 1972] 72-8223 ISBN 0-403-02060-3
1. Art—Addresses, essays, lectures. I. Title.

RUSKIN, John, 1819-1900. 700'.8
Selected prose of John Ruskin. Edited, and with an introd., by Matthew Hodgart. New York, New American Library [1972] 351 p. 18 cm. (A Signet classic, CJ590) [N7445.2.R8 1972] 73-189542 1.95
1. Art—Addresses, essays, lectures. 2. Aesthetics—Addresses, essays, lectures. I. Title.

RUSKIN, John, 1819-1900. 700'.8
The two paths; being lectures on art and its application to decoration and manufacture, delivered in 1858-9. With an introd. by Charles Eliot Norton. Brantwood ed. New York, Maynard, Merrill, 1893. St. Clair Shores, Mich., Scholarly Press, 1972 [c1891] p. (The works of John Ruskin) Contents.Contents.—The deteriorative power of conventional art over nations.—The unity of art.—Modern manufacture and design.—The influence of imagination in architecture.—The work of iron in nature, art, and policy. [N7445.2.R82 1972] 72-8273 ISBN 0-403-02056-5
1. Art—Addresses, essays, lectures. I. Title.

SHAHN, Ben 704.91
The shape of content. New York. Vintage Books, 1960 [c.1957] 151p. illus. (part col.) 19cm. (V-108) (The Charles Eliot Norton lectures, 1956-1957) 1.10 pap.,
1. Art—Addresses, essays, lectures. I. Title. BIP

SHAHN, Ben, 1898-1969. 704.91
The shape of content. Cambridge, Harvard University Press, 1957. 131 p. illus. 24 cm. (The Charles Eliot Norton lectures, 1956-1957) [N7445.S516] 57-12968
1. Art—Addresses, essays, lectures. I. Title.

SIMONSON, Lee, 1888- 069'.9'7
Minor prophecies. Port Washington, N.Y., Kennikat Press [1973, c1927] 167 p. 19 cm. Contents.Contents.—Foreword.—The land of Sunday afternoon.—Prints and a frame of mind.—Historic impressionism.—Panic in art.—The painter's arc.—The war as art critic.—Minority report.—Curator: Moscow, 1926. [N7445.2.S55 1973] 72-85326 ISBN 0-8046-1745-7 8.50
1. Art—Addresses, essays, lectures. I. Title. BIP

SMITH, Bernard William. 704.9'2
The antipodean manifesto : essays in art and history / [by] Bernard Smith. Melbourne ; New York : Oxford University Press, 1976. vii, 222 p. ; 23 cm. Includes bibliographical references and index. [N7445.2S58] 76-377507 ISBN 0-19-550477-1 : 23.25
1. Art—Addresses, essays, lectures. 2. Art, Australian—Addresses, essays, lectures. 3. Art and history—Addresses, essays, lectures.

SMITHSON, Robert. 700
The writings of Robert Smithson : essays and illustrations / edited by Nancy Holt. New York : New York University Press, 1979. p. cm. Includes index. "Catalog of Robert Smithson's library": p. [N7445.2.S62] 78-15693 ISBN 0-8147-3394-8 : 19.50
1. Art—Addresses, essays, lectures. I. Holt, Nancy, 1938- II. Title. BIP

SOBY, James Thrall, 1906- 704.91
Modern art and the new past. With an

introd. by Paul J. Sachs. [1st ed.] Norman, University of Oklahoma Press [1957] 217 p. 23 cm. [N7445.S562] 57-5959
1. Art — Addresses, essays, lectures. 2. Art, Modern — 20th cent. — Addresses, essays, lectures. I. Title. **BIP**

STOKES, Adrian Durham, 1902- 704.9'2
The image in form: selected writings of Adrian Stokes; edited and introduced by Richard Wollheim. Harmondsworth, Penguin, 1972. 320, [12] p. illus. 19 cm. Includes bibliographical references. [N7445.2.S76 1972b] 73-162985 ISBN 0-14-021355-4 £0.60
1. Art—Addresses, essays, lectures. I. Wollheim, Richard, 1923- ed. II. Title.

STOKES, Adrian Durham, 1902- 701
Reflections on the nude [by] Adrian Stokes. London, New York, Tavistock Pubns., 1967. Dist. in the U.S.A. by Barnes & Noble. vii, 64p. 23cm. Bibl. [N7445.S75] 67-109329 3.25
1. Art—Addresses, essays, lectures. I. Title.

STUDIES in honor of 708.152'6 s
Gertrude Rosenthal. Baltimore, Baltimore Museum of Art, 1968- v. illus., music, ports. 27 cm. (The Baltimore Museum of Art. Annual 3-) Contents.Contents.—v. 1. The tenth muse in the Baltimore Museum of Art, by E. P. Spencer. The music in Van Dyck's Rinaldo and Armida, by S. Mathews and E. Van Schaack. Giandomenico Tiepolo e il tema di Rinaldo e Armida, by T. Pignatti. Marguerite Gerard and her stylistic significance, by G. Levitine. Charles Peale Polk: a Baltimore portraitist, by W. R. Johntson. Grenoble bridge by J. M. W. Turner, by D. F. Johnson. Transformations and imaginary views by Alfred Jacob Miller, by R. H. Randall, Jr. An undescribed Picasso print: Portrait of Fernande Olivier, by V. I. Carlson. Quality in sculpture, by W. C. Seitz. Includes bibliographical references. [N515.A18 no. 3, etc.] [N7442.2] 78-27434 4.00 per vol.
1. Art—Addresses, essays, lectures. I. Rosenthal, Gertrude, 1903- II. Title. III. Series. **BIP**

STUDIES in memory of David 709
Talbot Rice / editors, Giles Robertson, George Henderson. Edinburgh : Edinburgh University Press, [1975] 334 p., [48] leaves of plates : ill., maps ; 24 cm. Bibliography: p 317-325. [N7442.2.R527] 75-329001 ISBN 0-85224-253-0 : 30.00
1. Rice, David Talbot, 1903-1972. 2. Art—Addresses, essays, lectures. I. Rice, David Talbot, 1903-1972. II. Robertson, Giles. III. Henderson, George David Smith, 1931-
Distributed by Biblio distribution N.J.

TAUBES, Frederic, 1900- 704.91
New essays on art. New York, Watson-Guptill Publications [1955] 95p. illus. 24cm. 'Appeared on the Taubes page in American artist ... 1950-1954.' [N7445.T25] 55-14364
1. Art—Addresses, essays, lectures. I. Title.

TAUBES, Frederic, 1900- 759.13
Paintings & essays on art. New York Dodd, Mead, 1950. 176 p. illus. 32 cm. "Bibliography and data on work of Frederic Taubes in the United States": p. 176. [ND237.T37A47] 50-6912
1. Art — Addresses, essays, lectures. I. Title.

TODD, John Murray, ed. 704.92
The arts, artists, and thinkers, an inquiry into the place of the arts in human life; a symposium. London, New York, Longmans, Green [1958] ix, 345 p. plates. 23 cm. Bibliographical footnotes. [N7443.T6 1958] 59-1283
1. Art — Addresses, essays, lectures. I. Title.

WEBER, Max 704
Things; an essay and woodblock pring. Brooklyn, Pratt Adlib Press, 1960 [c.1916] [11]p. plate. 22cm. Three hundred copies . . . printed . . . No. 280. The essay. appeared originally in Essays on art, published in 1916. 60-50013 pap., not for sale
1. Art—Addresses, essays, lectures. I. Title.

WILLIAMS, William Carlos, 1883-1963. 704.9'2
A recognizable image : William Carlos William on art and artists / edited with an introd. and notes by Bram Dijkstra. New York : New Directions, c1978. p. cm. [N7445.W54 1978] 78-16919 ISBN 0-8112-0704-8 : 16.00
1. Art—Addresses, essays, lectures. I. Dijkstra, Bram. II. Title.

WIND, Edgar, 1900- 701.1
Art and anarchy. New York, Knopf, 1964[c.1963] 194p. illus., ports. 21cm. (Reith lect. 1960, rev., enl.) Bibl. 62-8687 6.95
1. Art—Addresses, essays, lectures. I. Title.

ZEKOWSKI, Arlene, 1892- 704.92
Cardinals & saints [by] Arlene Zekowski [and] Stanley Berne. Croton-on-Hudson, N.Y., Metier Editions [1958] 180 p. illus. 21 cm. [N7445.Z4] 58-11713
1. Art—Addresses, essays, lectures. 2. Literature—Addresses, essays, lectures. I. Berne, Stanley, 1923- joint author. II. Title.

Art, Afghan—Exhibitions.

ROWLAND, Benjamin, 1901- 709'.58'1
Ancient art from Afghanistan : treasures of the Kabul Museum / by Benjamin Rowland, Jr. New York : Arno Press, 1975, c1966. p. cm. (The Asia Society reprint collection) Catalogue of a traveling exhibition shown at the Asia House Gallery, New York, the Lytton Gallery, Los Angeles County Museum of Art, and the National Collection of Fine Arts, Smithsonian Institution, Washington, D.C., Jan. 13-Aug. 23, 1966. Reprint of the ed. published by the Asia Society, New York. [N7292.R68 1975] 75-6677 ISBN 0-405-06567-1 : 30.00 28.00
1. Art, Afghan—Exhibitions. 2. Afghanistan—Antiquities. I. Kabul, Afghanistan (City). Museum. II. Asia Society. III. Asia House Gallery, New York. IV. Los Angeles Co., Calif. Museum of Art, Los Angeles. V. Smithsonian Institution. National Collection of Fine Arts. VI. Title.

Art—Afghanistan—History.

AUBOYER, Jeannine. 709'.581
The art of Afghanistan; photographs by Dominique Darbois; translated [from the French] by Peter Kneebone. Feltham, Hamlyn, 1968. 75 p. 136 plates (2 fold.), illus. (some col.), map. 28 cm. Illus. on lining papers. Bibliography: p. 63-70. [N7292.A8513] 79-359016 50/-
1. Art—Afghanistan—History. I. Darbois, Dominique. II. Title.

Art—Africa.

GRIAULE, Marcel, 1898- 709.6
Folk art of black Africa. Photos. by Emmanuel Sougez. [Translated from the French by Michael Heron] Paris, Editions du Chene; New-York, Tudor Pub. Co. [1950] 126 p. illus. (part col.) 24 cm. (The World's art) Published also under title: Arts of the African native. [N7380.G714 1950] 51-4972
1. Art—Africa. 2. Art, Primitive. I. Title. II. Series.

Art—Africa, South.

SUID-AFRIKAANSE kuns van 759.968
die twintigste eeu. Twentieth century South African art. Kaapstad, Human & Rousseau, 1966. xvii, 133p. of illus. (pt. mounted col.) 37cm. Title on spine: S. A. kuns; S. A. art [N7392.S8] 67-37425 23.10
1. Art—Africa, South. 2. Artists, South African. I. Title: Twentieth century South African art.

Art—Africa, Sub-Saharan.

MOUNT, Marshall Ward. 709'.67
African art; the years since 1920. the years since 1920. Bloomington, Indiana University Press [1973] xviii, 236 p. illus. (part col.) 26 cm. Bibliography: p. 204-210. [N7391.65.M68 1973] 73-75401 ISBN 0-253-10056-9 12.50
1. Art—Africa, Sub-Saharan. 2. Negro art—Africa, Sub-Saharan. I. Title.

NEW York (City) Museum of Primitive Art. 709.6
Traditional art of the African nations. With an introd. by Robert Goldwater and photos. by Charles Uht. New York, Distributed by University Publishers, 1961. [72] p. (chiefly illus. (part col.) map) 29 cm. [N7380.N45] 61-4864
1. Art—Africa, Sub-Saharan. 2. Art, Primitive. I. Title.

Art—Africa, West.

BODROGI, Tibor. 709'.67
Art in Africa. New York, McGraw-Hill [1968] 131 p. illus. (part col.), maps, 191 plates. 26 cm. Translation of Afrika muveszete. Bibliographical footnotes. [N7397.W4B63] 68-12065
1. Art—Africa, West. 2. Negro art—Africa, West. I. Title.

BRAVMANN, Rene A. 732'.2'0967
Islam and tribal art in West Africa [by] Rene A. Bravmann. [London, New York] Cambridge University Press [1974] xii, 189 p. illus. 23 cm. (African studies series no. 11) Bibliography: p. 178-185. [N7398.B72] 73-77262 ISBN 0-521-20192-6 13.95
1. Art—Africa, West. 2. Art, Primitive—Africa, West. 3. Islam and art. I. Title. II. Series. **BIP**

DUERDEN, Dennis. 709'.01'1
African art. London, New York, Hamlyn, 1970. 39 p. 48 plates, illus. (chiefly col.). 27 cm. (The Colour library of art) (The Colour library of art paperbacks) Bibliography: p. 26. [N7398.D8 1970] 72-193448 ISBN 0-600-03743-6 £0.65
1. Art—Africa, West. 2. Art, Primitive—Africa, West. I. Title.

SADLER, Michael Ernest, Sir, 1861-1943, ed. 732'.2
Arts of West Africa (excluding music) Edited by Michael E. Sadler. With an introd. by Sir William Rothenstein. Freeport, N.Y., Books for Libraries Press, 1971. xi, 101 p. illus. 27 cm. (The Black heritage library collection) Reprint of the 1935 ed. [N7398.S2 1971] 77-173616 ISBN 0-8369-8908-2
1. Art—Africa, West. 2. Art, Primitive—Africa, West. I. Title. II. Series. **BIP**

TOMORROW and beyond : 758
masterpieces of science fiction art / edited by Ian Summers. New York : Workman Pub. Co., c1978. 158 p. : col. ill. ; 31 cm. Includes index. [ND1460.F35T65] 78-7119 ISBN 0-89480-062-0 : 19.95 ISBN 0-89480-055-8 pbk. : 9.95
1. Fantasy in art. 2. Science fiction—Illustrations. 3. Painting, Modern—20th century. **BIP**

TROWELL, Kathleen Margaret. 709'.66
African and Oceanic art. Texts by Margaret Trowell and Hans Nevermann. New York, H. N. Abrams [1968] 263 p. illus. (part col.), col. maps. 23 cm. (Panorama of world art) Contents.Contents.—Form and content of African art, by M. Trowell (p. 6-201)—The art of Oceania, by H. Nevermann, translated from the German by Robert E. Wolf (p. 204-258)—Bibliography (p. 259-260) [N7397.W4T7] 68-16798
1. Art—Africa, West. 2. Art—Oceanica. I. Nevermann, Hans, 1902- II. Title.

WASSING, Rene S. 700'.967
African art; its background and traditions. Text by Rene S. Wassing. Photos. by Hans Hinz. [Translated by Diana Imber] New York, H. N. Abrams [1968] xii, 285 p. illus., maps, col. plates. 30 cm. Bibliography: p. 274-275. [N7397.A3W33] 68-28387
1. Art—Africa, West. 2. Negro art. I. Title.

Art—Africa, West—Addresses, essays, lectures.

AFRICAN art & 709'.66
leadership. Edited by Douglas Fraser and Herbert M. Cole. Madison, University of Wisconsin Press [1972] xvii, 332 p. illus. 24 cm. Fourteen papers, 6 of which were presented at a symposium entitled The aristocratic traditions in African art, held at Columbia University, May 1965. Includes bibliographies. [N7398.A35] 72-157391 ISBN 0-299-05820-4
1. Art—Africa, West—Addresses, essays, lectures. 2. Art, Primitive—Africa, West—Addresses, essays, lectures. 3. Kings and rulers (in religion, folk-lore, etc.)—Addresses, essays, lectures. I. Fraser, Douglas, ed. II. Cole, Herbert M., ed.

Art—Africa, West—Catalogs.

EWING Museum of Nations. 732'.2'0966074017359
African art : permanent collection, Illinois State University Normal-Bloomington, the Ewing Museum of Nations, Illinois State University Foundation / [F. Louis Hoover, editor ; photography, Illinois State University Photographic Services]. [Normal] : Illinois State University, [1974?] [128] p. : chiefly ill. (some col.) ; 22 cm. Errata slip inserted. [N7398.E94 1974] 74-28644 3.00
1. Ewing Museum of Nations. 2. Art—Africa, West—Catalogs. 3. Art, Primitive—Africa, West—Catalogs. I. Hoover, Francis Louis, 1913- II. Title.

Art, African.

AFRICAN images; 709'.6
essays in African iconology. Edited by Daniel F. McCall [and] Edna G. Bay. New York, [Published by] Africana Pub. Co., for the African Studies Center, Boston University 1975] xiii, 326, [64] p. illus. 24 cm. (Boston University papers on Africa, v. 6) Includes bibliographical references. [DT1.B6 vol. 6] [N7398] 74-12204 ISBN 0-8419-0147-3
1. Art, African. 2. Art, Primitive—Africa, West. I. McCall, Daniel F., ed. II. Bay, Edna G., ed. III. Boston University. African Studies Center. IV. Series: Boston University. African Studies Center. Papers on Africa, v. 6.

BASCOM, William Russell, 1912- 709.66
Handbook of West African art, by William R. Bascom and Paul Gebauer. Assembled and edited by Robert E. Ritzenthaler. Published by order of the board of trustees. [Milwaukee, Bruce Pub. Co.] 1953 [i.e. 1954] 83p. 66 illus., maps. 19x21cm. ([Milwaukee. Public Museum] Popular science handbook series, no. 5) Bibliography: p. 44, 83. [N7397.W4B3] 54-1675
1. Art, African. I. Gebauer, Paul, 1900- II. Ritzenthaler, Robert Eugene, 1911- ed. III. Title. IV. Series.
Contents omitted.

BATTISS, Walter W. 709.6
The art of Africa, by Walter W. Battiss [others] Ed. arr. by J. W. Grossert, illus. drawn by the authors and Lucy Jacques-Rosset. Pietermaritzburg, Shuter & Shooter [Chester Springs, Pa., Dufour, 1966] 140p illus. 24cm. Bibl. [N7380.B35] 60-29684 5.00 bds.,
1. Art, African. I. Title.

CRANE, Louise, 1917- 709'.2'4 B
The antelope rises : Elimo Njau, East African artist / Louise Crane. Thompson, Conn. : InterCulture Associates, c1978. 60 p., [1] leaf of plates : ill. ; 21 cm. (The Africa sketches series) [N7397.6.T343N533] 77-94635 ISBN 0-89253-103-7 pbk. : 1.95
1. Njau, Elimo, 1932- 2. Artists—Tanzania—Biography. I. Title. II. Series. **BIP**

DELANGE, Jacqueline, 1923- 732'.2'0967
The art and peoples of Black Africa. Pref. by Michel Leiris. Translated by Carol F. Jopling with the assistance of Hannah Jopling Kaiser and Laura Schultz, and the additional aid of Vivian Cohen, Marcel Serraillier, and Willem Tissot. [1st ed.] New York, Dutton, 1974. xxvi, 354 p. illus. 22 cm. Translation of Arts et peuples de l'Afrique noire. Bibliography: p. 315-344. [N7380.D413 1974] 74-1179 ISBN 0-525-05853-2 10.95
1. Art, African. 2. Negro art—Africa. I. Title.
Pbk. 5.95; ISBN 0-525-47364-5. **BIP**

DUERDEN, Dennis. 709'.01'1096
African art : an introduction / Dennis Duerden. London ; New York : Hamlyn, 1974. 96 p. : ill. (some col.), map ; 29 cm. Includes index. Bibliography: p. 91. [N7380.D8] 76-356760 ISBN 0-600-34853-9 : £1.95
1. Art, African. I. Title.

GLUBOK, Shirley. 709.01
The art of Africa. Designed by Gerard Nook. Special photography by Alfred H. Tamarin. New York, Harper & Row [1965] 48 p. illus. (part col.) 26 cm. Examples of primitive African art, from many different tribes, with explanations of their use and meaning. Includes statues, masks, reliefs, headdresses, and household objects, made from ivory, gold, wood, bronze, and brass. [N7380.G55] AC 68
1. Art, African. 2. Art, Primitive. I. Title. BIP

GUILLAUME, Paul, 1891- 730'.967
Primitive Negro sculpture, by Paul Guillaume and Thomas Munro, with illustrations from the collection of the Barnes Foundation at Merion, Pennsylvania. New York, Hacker Art Books, 1968 [c1954] 134 p. illus., map. 27 cm. Bibliographical footnotes. [NB1080.G8 1968] 68-9003 15.00
1. Art, African. 2. Sculpture, Primitive—Africa. I. Munro, Thomas, 1897- joint author. II. Barnes Foundation, Merion, Pa. III. Title.

HERSKOVITS, Melville Jean, 1895-1963. 709'.6
The backgrounds of African art. New York, Biblo and Tannen, 1967. 64 p. illus., map. 28 cm. (Cooke-Daniels lecture series) "Limited to 500 copies." Three lectures presented at the Denver Art Museum in conjunction with an exhibition, January and February, 1945. Originally published 1945. Bibliography: p. 63-64. [N7380.H4 1967] 67-18433
1. Art, African. 2. Africa—Civilization. 3. Negroes in Africa. I. Denver. Art Museum. II. Title. III. Series.

LEIRIS, Michel, 1901- 732'.2
African art [by] Michel Leiris [and] Jacqueline Delange. Translated by Michael Ross. New York, Golden Press [1968] xi, 453 p. illus. (part col.) 29 cm. (The Arts of mankind) Translation of Afrique noire, la creation plastique. Bibliography: p. 385-[408]. [N7380.L3513 1968b] 68-22409 29.95
1. Art, African. 2. Masks (Sculpture)—Africa. 3. Negro art—Africa. 4. Decoration and ornament, African. I. Delange, Jacqueline, 1923- II. Title. III. Series.

ORNAMENT and sculpture in 709.011
primitive society; Africa, Oceania, Siberia. [Translated from the German by Peter Prochnik] New York, October House [1966] 13, [119]-138 p. 104 plates (part col.) 28 cm. "The collective work of scholars of the State Museum of Ethnology, Leipzig ... Dietrich Drost ... Hans Damm ... [and] Werner Hartwig." Translation of Ornament und Plastic fremder Volker. [N7380.O713 1966b] 66-26628
1. Art, African. 2. Art—Oceanica. 3. Art—Siberia. I. Drost, Dietrich. II. Leipzig. Museum fur Volkerkunde.

PHILADELPHIA. Commercial Museum. 709.6
A handbook of the African collections of the Commercial Museum, Philadelphia, by Harold D. Gunn. [Philadelphia, 1960?] 78 p. illus., fold. maps. 22 cm. Bibliography: p. 18-19. [N7380.P45] 66-58397
1. Art, African. I. Gunn, Harold D. II. Title.

SCHMALENBACH, Werner, 1917- 709.6
African art. [Translated from the German language by Glyn T. Hughes] New York, Macmillan [1954] 175p. illus. (part col.) map. 32cm. Bibliography: p.174. [N7380.S375] 55-1486
1. Art. African. 2. Sculpture, African. 3. Negroes in Africs.a 4. Art, Primitive. I. Title.

UNIVERSITY Prints, Boston. 732'.2
African art [edited under the direction of Paul S.] Wingert. Cambridge, Mass. [1970] [1] p., 150 plates. 14 x 22 cm. (Its The university prints series N: primitive art, section 1) Outline index of plates, 7 p., in pocket. [N7380.U5] 72-23392
1. Art, African. I. Wingert, Paul Stover, 1900- ed.

WILLETT, Frank. 709.01'1
African art, an introduction. [New York] Praeger [1971] 288 p. illus. (part col.), maps, plan. 22 cm. ([Praeger world of art series]) Bibliography: p. 275-279. [N7380.W5 1971b] 76-117394 8.50
1. Art, African. I. Title. BIP

Art, African—Catalogs.

DETROIT. Institute of Arts. 732'.2'0967074017434
A check list of African art in the permanent collection of the Detroit Institute of Arts. [Prepared by Michael E. Goodison and Richard A. Laprade] Detroit, 1971. 39 p. illus. 28 cm. "Includes objects acquired ... prior to May, 1971." [N7398.D47] 73-172051
1. Art, African—Catalogs. 2. Art, Primitive—Africa, West. 3. Art—Detroit—Catalogs. I. Goodison, Michael E., ed. II. Laprade, Richard A., ed. III. Title.

IMPERATO, Pascal James. 709'.01'1096
The cultural heritage of Africa. Chanute, Kan., Safari Museum Press [1974] ix, 47 p. illus. 28 cm. A catalog of part of the collection of the Martin and Osa Johnson Safari Museum. Bibliography: p. 44-47. [N7380.5.I46] 74-163545
1. Art, African—Catalogs. 2. Art, Primitive—Africa. I. Martin and Osa Johnson Safari Museum. II. Title.

Art, African—Exhibitions.

AFRICAN and 732'.2'0966074019461
ancient Mexican art : the Loran Collection [exhibited at the M. H. de Young Memorial Museum, October 12, 1974-January 12, 1975 : catalogue] / by Erle Loran ... [et al.]. [San Francisco] : Fine Arts Museums of San Francisco, c1974. 95 p., [3] leaves of plates : ill. (some col.) ; 28 cm. Bibliography: p. 92-95. [N7398.A34] 74-84681 ISBN 0-88401-004-X
1. Loran, Erle, 1905- —Art collections. 2. Art, African—Exhibitions. 3. Art, Primitive—Africa, West—Exhibitions. 4. Indians of Mexico—Art—Exhibitions. I. Loran, Erle, 1905- II. Fine Arts Museums of San Francisco. III. De Young Memorial Museum, San Francisco.

AFRICAN art 732'.2'0967074017758
from the Collection of Julian and Irma Brody : [exhibition] Des Moines Art Center, March 18-April 20, 1975. [Des Moines] : Des Moines Art Center, [1975] [44] p. : ill. (some col.) ; 25 cm. Catalog. Includes bibliography. [N7398.A353] 75-6023
1. Brody, Julian—Art collections. 2. Brody, Irma—Art collections. 3. Art, African—Exhibitions. 4. Art, Primitive—Africa, West. I. Des Moines Art Center.

AFRICAN arts of 709.01'1
transformation, an exhibition organized by Herbert M. Cole [and others] Nov. 24-Dec. 20, 1970, the Art Galleries, University of California, Santa Barbara. [Santa Barbara, University of California, c1970] 71 p. illus., map. 28 cm. [N7398.A36] 71-631887
1. Art, African—Exhibitions. 2. Art, Primitive—Africa, West. I. Cole, Herbert M. II. California. University, Santa Barbara. Art Galleries.

AFRICAN tribal art from 709'.6
the Jay C. Leff Collection. [Gainesville? Fla., 1967?] 1 v. (unpaged) illus., map. 23 cm. Cover title. Introduction by Jack D. Flam. Catalog of an exhibition at University Gallery, University of Florida, Gainesville, March 5-26, 1967 and Division of Fine Arts, University of South Florida, Tampa, April 11-May 10, 1967. Includes bibliography. [N7397.W4A65] 74-626339
1. Leff, Jay C.—Art collections. 2. Art, African—Exhibitions. 3. Art—Africa, West. I. Flam, Jack D. II. Florida. University, Gainesville. University Gallery. III. Florida. University of South Florida, Tampa. Division of Fine Arts.

BROOKLYN Institute of Arts and Sciences. Museum. 709.6
Masterpieces of African art. Exhibition dates: October 21, 1954--January 2, 1955. [Brooklyn] Brooklyn Museum [1954] 54p., [73] p. of illus. map. 25cm. Catalog': p. 37-53. [N7380.B67] 55-18270
1. Art, African—Exhibitions. I. Title.

BROOKLYN Institute of Arts and Sciences. Museum. 709'.6
Masterpieces of African art. Exhibition dates: October 21, 1954-January 2, 1955. Brooklyn Museum. [New York] Arno Press, 1974 [c1954] 54 p., [74] p. of illus. 25 cm. "Catalog": p. 37-53. [N7391.65.B76 1974] 73-114264 ISBN 0-405-00877-5 12.50
1. Art, African—Exhibitions. 2. Art, Primitive—Africa, Sub-Saharan. I. Title.

CONTEMPORARY African 709'.6
art; the catalogue of an exhibition of contemporary African art held at the Camden Arts Centre, London. London, New York, Studio International, 1969. 40 p. illus. (part col.), map, ports. 24 cm. Label mounted on t.p.: Supplied by Wittenborn and Co., New York. [N7380.C63] 70-461948
1. Art, African—Exhibitions. 2. Art, Modern—20th century—Africa. I. Camden Arts Centre. BIP

DALLAS. Museum of Fine Arts. 732'.2
African art from Dallas collections; [an exhibit at] Dallas Museum of Fine Arts, July 26 through September 4. [Dallas, 1972?] [80] p. illus. 26 cm. [N7380.D34] 72-193107 5.00
1. Art, African—Exhibitions. 2. Art—Africa, West. 3. Art—Zaire. 4. Art, African—Dallas. I. Title.

DETROIT. Institute of Arts. 730'.096'074017434
Detroit collects African art : exhibition, the Detroit Institute of Arts, April 21-May 29, 1977. Detroit : The Institute : distributed by Wayne State University Press, c1977. [104] p. : chiefly ill. ; 23 cm. [N7380.5.D47 1977] 77-151081
1. Art, African—Exhibitions. 2. Art, Primitive—Africa—Exhibitions. I. Title. BIP

FAGG, William Buller. 732
African sculpture from the Tara Collection. Exhibited by Mr. & Mrs. J. W. Gillon. Catalogue by William Fagg. [Notre Dame? Ind., 1971] 60 p. illus. (part col.) 29 cm. Erratum slip inserted. Held at Art Gallery, University of Notre Dame, March 28-May 23, 1971. Bibliography: p. 57-58. [N7398.F3] 72-198259
1. Gillon, Joseph Werner, 1905- —Art collections. 2. Art, African—Exhibitions. 3. Art, Primitive—Africa, West. I. Notre Dame, Ind. University. Art Gallery. II. Title.

FLORIDA. University, Gainesville. University Gallery. 709'.6
African art, from the collections of the American Museum of Natural History, the Field Museum of Natural History [and] the University Museum, University of Pennsylvania. November 29th thru December 20th, 1967, University Gallery. Gainesville, 1967. [16] p. (chiefly illus.) 23 cm. "A special loan exhibition marking the event of a Conference on Africa and Latin America." [N7380.F55] 78-650120
1. Art, African—Exhibitions. I. Title.

FRASER, Douglas. 199'.66
African art as philosophy / edited by Douglas Fraser. New York : Interbook, [1974] xii, 140 p. : ill. ; 23 cm. Catalog of a photographic exhibition organized by the Dept. of Art History and Archaeology, Columbia University, in conjunction with the 3d Triennial Symposium on African Art held in New York, April 1974. Bibliography: p. 127-140. [N7398.F72] 74-80783 ISBN 0-913456-22-5 pbk. : 8.00
1. Art, African—Exhibitions. 2. Art, Primitive—Africa, West. 3. Art—Philosophy. I. Columbia University. Dept. of Art History and Archaeology. II. Title.

HUDSON River Museum. 732'.2
African art in Westchester from private collections. [Yonkers, N.Y., 1971] [34] p. illus. 28 cm. Catalogue of exhibition held at the Hudson River Museum, Apr. 24-June 6, 1971. [N7398.H8] 79-27488
1. Art, African—Exhibitions. 2. Art, Primitive—Africa, West. 3. Art—Private collections—Westchester Co., N.Y. I. Title.

ISAAC Delgado Museum of Art, New Orleans. 709'.6
New Orleans collects African art. [New Orleans? 1968?] [39] p. illus. 26 cm. "First in a series of exhibitions in 1968 in conjunction with the celebration of the 250th anniversary of the founding of the City of New Orleans, February 2-March 31, 1968, Isaac Delgado Museum of Art." [N7380.177] 68-2287
1. Art, African—Exhibitions. I. Title.

MINNESOTA Museum of Art. 709'.01'1096
African heritage : traditional sculpture and crafts from the permanent collection of the Minnesota Museum of Art : [catalog of an exhibition] 16 April-1 August 1975, Permanent Collection Gallery ... Saint Paul, Minnesota. Saint Paul : The Museum, [1975] 36 p. : ill. (some col.) ; 24 cm. (Catalog - Minnesota Museum of Art ; 126) [N7380.5.M56 1975] 75-10774
1. Art, African—Exhibitions. 2. Art, Primitive—Africa—Exhibitions. I. Title. II. Series: Minnesota Museum of Art. Catalog ; 126.

ODITA, E. Okechukwu. 732'.2'0967074017157
Traditional African art, by E. Okechukwu Odita. Columbus, Ohio State University, Division of History of Art, 1971. 76 p. illus. 23 cm. A catalogue of an exhibition held Feb. 14-19 at Ohio State University. Errata slip inserted. Bibliography: p. 74-75. [N7380.O32] 72-611045
1. Art, African—Exhibitions. 2. Art, Primitive—Africa. I. Ohio. State University, Columbus. II. Title.

POST College, Brookville, N.Y. Fine Arts Center. 732'.2'09670747147245
African sculpture. [Exhibition: February, 1969. Brookville, N.Y., 1969] [16] p. illus. 21 x 28 cm. [N7398.P67] 73-172334
1. Art, African—Exhibitions. 2. Art, Primitive—Africa, West. I. Title.

Art, African—History.

RACHEWILTZ, Boris de 709.6
Introduction to African art, Tr. by Peter Whigham. [New York] New Amer. Lib. [1966] xx, 200p. plates (pt. col.) 23cm. Bibl. [N7380.R313] 66-18260 7.50
1. Art, African—Hist. I. Title.

Art, African—History.

LEUZINGER, Elsy. 709.67
Africa; the art of the Negro peoples. [Translated by Ann E. Keep] New York, McGraw-Hill [1960] 247 p. illus. (part mounted col.) 4 col. maps (3 on fold. 1) 24 cm. (Art of the world; the historical, sociological and religious backgrounds, Non-European cultures) Bibliography: p. 228-232. [N7380.L363] 60-13819
1. Art, African—History. 2. Negro art—History. I. Series: Art of the world; the historical, sociological and religious backgrounds.

Art, African—Juvenile literature.

GLUBOK, Shirley 709.011
The art of Africa, Designed by Gerard Nook. Special photography by Alfred H. Tamarin. New York, Harper [c.1965] 48p. illus. (pt. col.) 26cm. [N7380.G55] 65-21016 3.95; 3.99 lib. ed.,
1. Art, African—Juvenile literature. 2. Art, Primitive—Juvenile literature. I. Title.

MARSHALL, Anthony D. 709'.6
Africa's living arts, by Anthony D. Marshall. New York, F. Watts [1970] 96 p. illus., map, col. plates. 27 cm. Bibliography: p. 90-92. Describes the clothing, personal ornaments, household goods, religious and ceremonial objects, hunting implements, and other items of ancient and modern Africa which, though largely functional comprise the major portion of the continent's art. [N7380.M29] 72-100091 5.95
1. Art, African—Juvenile literature. I. Title.

Holcomb III, including correspondence and bibliography. With an introd. by William Morgan. [Syracuse, N.Y.] Castle Room Press, Syracuse University, 1971. 21 p. illus. 21 cm. 500 copies printed. No. 9. Bibliography: p. 19-21. [N6530.C2H6] 76-25619
1. Art, American. 2. Art, Modern—20th century—California. I. Title.

HOMER, William Innes. 709'.73
Stieglitz and the American avant-garde / William Innes Homer. 1st ed. Boston : New York Graphics Society, c1977. p. cm. Bibliography: p. [N5220.S858H65 1977] 76-50068 ISBN 0-8212-0676-1 : 17.50
1. Stieglitz, Alfred, 1864-1946—Art patronage. 2. Art, American. 3. Art, Modern—20th century—United States. 4. Photography, Artistic. 5. Artists—United States—Biography. I. Title.

HUDSON, William Norman. 338.4'3745'10973
Antiques at auction [by] Norman Hudson. South Brunswick, A. S. Barnes [1972] 403 p. illus. 32 cm. [N6507.H82] 76-111646 ISBN 0-498-07678-4 20.00
1. Art, American. 2. Art, Colonial—United States. 3. Art—Prices. 4. Art—Collectors and collecting. I. Title.

KRUSHENICK, Nicholas, 1929- 759.13
Nicholas Krushenick. An exhibition organized by Walker Art Center, January 24-February 25, 1968. Catalog by Dean Swanson. Minneapolis, Walker Art Center [1968] [20] p. illus. (part col.) 28 cm. [ND237.K75S9] 68-21569
I. Swanson, Dean. II. Walker Art Center, Minneapolis.

LIPMAN, Jean Herzberg, 1909- 759.13
Bright stars : American painting and sculpture since 1776 / Jean Lipman and Helen M. Franc ; introd. by John I. H. Baur. 1st ed. New York : Dutton, 1976. 208 p. : ill. (some col.) ; 31 cm. Includes index. Bibliography: p. 202-206. [N6505.L56] 76-25791 ISBN 0-525-07147-4 : 35.00
1. Art, American. 2. Art, Colonial—United States. 3. Art, Modern—19th century—United States. 4. Art, Modern—20th century—United States. I. Franc, Helen Margaret, 1908- joint author. II. Title.

LITTLE, Nina Fletcher, 1903- 745'.0973
Country arts in early American homes / Nina Fletcher Little ; foreword by Wendell Garrett. 1st ed. New York : Dutton, 1975. xv, 221 p., [8] leaves of plates : ill. (some col.) ; 22 cm. Includes bibliographical references and index. [N6507.L57 1975] 74-33139 ISBN 0-525-08680-3 : 11.95. ISBN 0-525-47392-0 pbk. : 6.95
1. Art, American. 2. Art, Modern—17th-18th centuries—United States. 3. Art, Modern—19th century—United States. I. Title. BIP

MARCKS, Gerhard. 741'.092'4
Gerhard Marcks; a retrospective exhibition organized by the UCLA Art Galleries with the participation of ... Portland Art Museum [and others] Los Angeles, University of California, 1969. 127 p. chiefly illus. 32 cm. Bibliography: p. 117-118. [N6888.M344C24] 77-104051
I. California. University. University at Los Angeles. Art Galleries.

MILLER, Richard E., 1875-1943. 759.13
Richard E. Miller, N.A.; an impression and appreciation. St. Louis, Longmire Fund [1968] [72] p. (chiefly col. illus., ports.) 25 x 23 cm. [ND237.M49L6] 67-14912 2.50 10.00 (deluxe ed.)
I. Longmire Fund.

MONTGOMERY, Walter, ed. 759.0573
American art and American art collections / edited by Walter Montgomery. New York : Garland Pub., 1977 [c1889] p. cm. (The Art experience in late nineteenth-century America) Reprint of the ed. published by E. W. Walker, Boston. [N6510.M6 1977] 75-28883 ISBN 0-8240-2241-6 lib.bdg. : 125.00 (set)
1. Art, American. 2. Art, Modern—19th century—United States. 3. Artists—United States—Biography. 4. Art—Private collections—United States. I. Title. II. Series. BIP

MUNRO, Eleanor C. 709'.2'2 B
Originals : American women artists / Eleanor Munro. New York : Simon & Schuster, c1979. p. cm. Includes index. Bibliography: p. [N6512.M78] 78-31814 ISBN 0-671-23109-X : 12.95
1. Art, American. 2. Art, Modern—20th century—United States. 3. Women artists—United States—Biography. I. Title. BIP

MURRAY, Richard D., 1921- 760'.0924
The rise and fall of the state, and other works, by Richard D. Murray. [1st ed.] New York, Book Explorers [196-] 1 v. (chiefly illus., part col.) 31 cm. [ND237.M924A58] 68-6415 10.00
I. Title.

MYRON, Robert. 709'.73
Modern art in America [by] Robert Myron [and] Abner Sundell. New York, Crowell-Collier Press [1971] 218 p. illus. 24 cm. Bibliography: p. [214] [N6512.M95] 76-153760
1. Art, American. 2. Art, Modern—20th century—U.S. I. Sundell, Abner, joint author. II. Title. BIP

O'CONNOR, Francis V., comp. 338.4'7'70973
Art for the millions; essays from the 1930s by artists and administrators of the WPA Federal Art Project, edited, and with an introd., by Francis V. O'Connor. Greenwich, Conn., New York Graphic Society [1973] 317 p. illus. 26 cm. Bibliography: p. 309. [N8838.O25] 78-181347 ISBN 0-8212-0439-4 22.50
1. Art, American. 2. Art, Modern—20th century—United States. 3. Federal aid to the arts—United States. I. Federal Art Project. II. Title. BIP

O'HARA, Frank. 709'.73
Art chronicles, 1954-1966 / Frank O'Hara. New York : G. Braziller, [1975] 165 p. : ill. ; 26 cm. "A Venture book." Bibliography: p. 165. [N6535.N5O37 1975] 74-77526 ISBN 0-8076-0755-X : 12.50.
1. Art, American. 2. Art, Modern—20th century—New York (City) I. Title. BIP

PARRY, Ellwood. 709'.73
The image of the Indian and the Black man in American art, 1590-1900. New York, G. Braziller [1974] xiv, 191 p. illus. 26 cm. Bibliography: p. 179-182. [N6505.P29 1974] 73-79606 ISBN 0-8076-0706-1 12.50
1. Art, American. 2. Indians of North America—Pictorial works. 3. Negroes in art. I. Title. BIP

PIRTLE, Caleb. 704.94'9'978
XIT, being a new and original exploration, in art and words, into the life and times of the American cowboy / by Caleb Pirtle and the Texas Cowboy Artists Association, Jack Bryant ... [et al.]. 1st ed. Birmingham, Ala. : Oxmoor House, 1975. 156 p. : ill. (some col.) ; 32 cm. Bibliography: p. 155-156. [N6530.T4P57] 75-18832 50.00
1. Art, American. 2. Art, Modern—20th century—Texas. 3. Cowboys in art. 4. Cowboys. I. Bryant, Jack, 1929- II. Texas Cowboy Artists Association. III. Title: XIT, being a new and original exploration, in art and words ... IV. Title: American cowboy.

PLAGENS, Peter. 709'.794
Sunshine muse; contemporary art on the west coast. New York, Praeger [1974] 200 p. illus. (part col.) 25 cm. Bibliography: p. 181-194. [N6530.C2P55] 72-86433 ISBN 0-275-46630-2 11.95
1. Art, American. 2. Art, Modern—20th century—California. I. Title.

PRICE, Melville, 1920-1970. 759.13
Melville Price: retrospective, 1920-1970. [Exhibition] Frame House Gallery and J. B. Speed Museum, Louisville, Ky., September 13 - October 10, 1970. [Catalog by T. E. Klitzke. Louisville, Ky., Frame House Gallery, 1970] [18] p. illus., port. 28 cm. [ND237.P89K56] 73-279631
I. Klitzke, T. E. II. Frame House Gallery. III. Speed Art Museum, Louisville, Ky. IV. Title.

RUBLOWSKY, John. 709.73
Pop art. Photography by Ken Heyman. Foreword by Samuel Adams Green. New York, Basic Books [1965] 174 p. illus. (part col.) ports. 28 cm. [N6512.R8] 65-16882
1. Art, American. 2. Pop art. I. Heyman, Ken, illus. II. Title.

SANDLER, Irving, 1925- 709'.747'1
The New York School : the painters and sculptors of the fifties / by Irving Sandler. 1st ed. New York : Harper & Row, c1978. xi, 366 p. : ill. ; 26 cm. (Icon editions) Includes index. Bibliography: p. [326]-344. [N6512.5.N4S26 1978] 77-82357 ISBN 0-06-438505-1 : 30.00
1. New York School. 2. Art, American. 3. Art, Modern—20th century—United States. I. Title. BIP

SMITH, Bradley. 704.94'9'973
The USA—a history in art / by Bradley Smith. New York : Crowell, c1975. 296 p. : col. ill. ; 33 cm. (A Gemini Smith Inc. book) Includes index. Bibliography: p. 294. [N6505.S54] 75-6016 ISBN 0-690-00966-6 : 30.00
1. Art, American. 2. United States in art. 3. United States—History—Pictorial works. I. Title.

SMITHSONIAN Institution. National Collection of Fine Arts. 709'.04'0740153
Highlights of the National Collection of Fine Arts. Washington, Published for the National Collection of Fine Arts by the Smithsonian Institution Press, 1968. 64 p. illus. (part col.) 23 cm. (Smithsonian publication 4737) Texts by David W. Scott, and others. [N857.A83] 68-60063
1. Art, American. 2. Art—Washington, D.C. I. Scott, David W., 1916- II. Title.

SOCIETY of Illustrators, New York. 709'.73
Illustration in the third dimension : the artist turned craftsman / Society of Illustrators. New York : Hastings House, c1977. p. cm. (Visual communication books) (Library of American illustration) [N6512.S63 1977] 77-7316 ISBN 0-8038-3399-7 : 15.00
1. Art, American. 2. Art, Modern—20th century—United States. 3. Artists—United States. I. Title. II. Series. BIP

SOYER, Moses, 1899- 759.13
Moses Soyer. Introd. by Charlotte Willard. Foreword by Philip Evergood. [1st ed.] Cleveland, World Pub. Co. [1962] 41 p. illus., plates (part col.) 32 cm. Errata slip inserted. [ND237.S635W5] 62-17154
I. Willard, Charlotte.

SOYER, Moses, 1899- 759.13
Moses Soyer. Introd. by Alfred Werner. Memoir by David Soyer. South Brunswick, A. S. Barnes [1970] 47 p. illus. 127 plates (part col.) 32 cm. [ND237.S635W4] 67-25169 ISBN 0-498-06461-1 12.50
I. Werner, Alfred, 1911- II. Soyer, David, 1928-

SOYER, Moses, 1899- 759.13
Moses Soyer: a human approach. New York, ACA Galleries [1972] 1 v. (chiefly illus., part col.) 30 cm. Catalog of the exhibition organized and circulated by ACA Galleries to various institutions from Jan. 9, 1972 to Feb. 15, 1973. Includes bibliography. [ND237.S635A62] 72-198108
I. A.C.A. Galleries.

SOYER, Moses, 1899- 741.9'73
Moses Soyer: drawings, watercolors. [New York, A.C.A. Galleries, 1972?] [48] p. illus. 28 cm. Catalog of an exhibition held at Loch Haven Art Center, Orlando, Fla., Jan. 9th to 23d, 1972; St. Lawrence University, Griffith Art Center, Canton, N.Y., Feb. 7th to 27th, 1972; and ACA Galleries, New York, Mar. 14th to Apr. 1st, 1972. "[Includes] quotations from Painting the human figure, by Moses Soyer." [NC139.S63L6] 72-198087
I. Loch Haven Art Center. II. Griffith Art Center. III. A.C.A. Galleries.

TAYLOR, Joshua Charles, 1917- 709'.73
America as art / Joshua C. Taylor ; with a contribution by John G. Cawelti. Washington : Published for the National Collection of Fine Arts by the Smithsonian Institution Press, 1976. p. cm. (Smithsonian Institution Press publication ; no. 6236) "Published in conjunction with an exhibition at the National Collection of Fine Arts, Smithsonian Institution, April 30-November 7, 1976." [N6505.T37] 76-4482
1. Art, American. 2. United States in art. I. Smithsonian Institution. National Collection of Fine Arts. II. Title. BIP

TAYLOR, Joshua Charles, 1917- 709'.73
To see is to think : looking at American art / Joshua C. Taylor. Washington : Smithsonian Institution Press, 1975. 117 p. : ill. (some col.) ; 24 cm. "The brief discussions are based for the most part on works to be seen in the galleries of the National Collection of Fine Arts in Washington, D.C." Includes bibliographies. [N6505.T38] 74-26647 ISBN 0-87474-176-9 7.50
1. Art, American. 2. Art—Psychology. I. Smithsonian Institution. National Collection of Fine Arts. II. Title.
Pbk. 3.95; ISBN 0-87474-177-9. Distributed by Braziller BIP

TIGHE, Mary Ann. 709'.73
Art America / Mary Ann Tighe, Elizabeth Ewing Lang. New York : McGraw-Hill, c1977. viii, 438 p. : ill. ; 24 cm. Companion volume to Art America: a resource manual by P. A. Cecchettini and D. Whittemore, for use with the video series Art America. Includes index. Bibliography: p. 419-427. [N6505.T54] 77-7125 ISBN 0-07-064601-5 : 17.25
1. Art America. 2. Art, American. 3. Art—Study and teaching—United States. I. Lang, Elizabeth Ewing, joint author. II. Cecchettini, Philip Alan. Art America. III. Title. BIP

TORR, Helen, 1886-1967. 759.13
Helen Torr, 1886-1967. [Exhibition] June 3-July 9, 1972, Heckscher Museum, Huntington, New York [and] July 17-August 18, 1972, Graham Gallery, New York, New York. [Huntington? N.Y., 1972] 12 p. illus. 29 cm. [ND237.T595H4] 72-84754
I. Heckscher Museum. II. Graham Gallery.

ULANOV, Barry. 709.73
The two worlds of American art, the private and the popular. New York, Macmillan [1965] 528 p. 22 cm. Bibliographical references included in "Notes" (p. 483-507) [E169.1.U5] 65-20170
1. Art, American. 2. American literature—20th century—History and criticism. 3. Performing arts—United States. 4. United States—Civilization—20th century. I. Title. BIP

VAUDECHAMP, Jean Joseph, 1790-1866. 759.4
Jean Joseph Vaudechamp, 1790-1866. [Lynne W. Farwell, catalogue] Exhibition presented by the Louisiana State Museum and the Friends of the Cabildo. November 13, 1967-January 7, 1968, the Presbytere, New Orleans, La. [New Orleans, Louisiana State Museum, 1968] [19] p. ports. 16 x 23 cm. [ND553.V37F3] 68-64772
I. Farwell, Lynne W. II. Louisiana State Museum, New Orleans. III. Friends of the Cabildo.

WHITNEY Museum of American Art, New York. 708.1471
American art of our century [by] Lloyd Goodrich, director [and] John I. H. Baur, associate director. New York, Praeger [1961] 309 p. illus. (part col.) 29 cm. (Books that matter) The illustrations are of works in the museum's collection. "Catalogue of the collection": p. 267-297. [N6512.W46] 61-15642
1. Art, American. 2. Art—New York (City)—Catalogs. 3. Art, Modern—20th century—United States. I. Goodrich, Lloyd, 1897- II. Baur, John Ireland Howe, 1909- III. Title.

WIENER, Isidor, 1886- 759.13
Grand Pa Wiener; a loan exhibition of works by a twentieth century folk artist, July-November 1970. [Cooperstown, N.Y., New York State Historical Association, 1970] ix, 41 p. illus., port. 14 x 22 cm. [ND237.W644A46] 78-22497
I. New York State Historical Association.

WASHINGTON Art 760'.0973'0740197 Consortium.
Works on paper : American art, 1945-1975. Seattle : Washington Art Consortium, 1977. 87 p. : ill. ; 27 cm. Text by R. Krauss. Includes bibliographical references. [N6512.W337 1977] 76-52834
1. Art, American—Catalogs. 2. Art, Modern—20th century—United States—Catalogs. 3. Art—Washington (State)—Seattle—Catalogs. I. Krauss, Rosalind E. II. Title.

THE West and 709'.73'074019173
Walter Bimson; paintings, watercolors, drawings, and sculpture collected by Mr. Walter Reed Bimson. Tucson, University of Arizona Museum of Art [1971] 223 p. (chiefly illus., part col.) 32 cm. [N6505.W4] 78-634896 15.00
1. Bimson, Walter Reed, 1892- —Art collections. 2. Art, American—Catalogs. 3. The West in art. I. Arizona. University. Museum of Art.

WHITNEY Museum 709'.73'07401471 of American Art, New York.
Catalogue of the collection / [catalogue of paintings, watercolors, drawings and sculpture by Margaret McKellar, catalogue of prints by Elke Morger Solomon and Mariann Nowack]. New York : Whitney Museum of American Art, 1975. 237 p. : ill. (some col.) ; 28 cm. Includes indexes. [N6512W532 1975a] 74-79170
1. Whitney Museum of American Art, New York. 2. Art, American—Catalogs. 3. Art, Modern—20th century—United States—Catalogs. 4. Art, Modern—20th century—Catalogs. 5. Art—New York (City)—Catalogs. I. McKellar, Margaret. II. Solomon, Elke Morger. III. Nowack, Mariann.

WHITNEY Museum 709'.73'07401471 of American Art, New York.
Selections from the permanent collection / Whitney Museum of American Art. Chicago : University of Chicago Press, 1977 p. cm. [N6512.W532 1977] 76-19074 ISBN 0-226-69818-1 12.50
1. Whitney Museum of American Art, New York. 2. Art, American—Catalogs. 3. Art, Modern—20th century—United States—Catalogs. 4. Art—New York (City)—Catalogs. I. Title. BIP

WILLIAMS, 760'.0973'0740155671 Mary Frances.
Catalogue of the collection of American art at Randolph-Macon Woman's College : a selection of paintings, drawings, and prints / Mary Frances Williams. 2d ed. Charlottesville : University Press of Virginia, 1977. p. cm. First ed. (1965) issued by Randolph-Macon Woman's College under title: Catalogue of the collection of American painting at Randolph-Macon Woman's College. Bibliography: p. [N6505.W53 1977] 76-51281 ISBN 0-8139-0591-5 : 15.00
1. Randolph-Macon Woman's College, Lynchburg, Va. 2. Art, American—Catalogs. 3. Art—Virginia—Lynchburg—Catalogs. I. Randolph-Macon Woman's College, Lynchburg, Va. II. Randolph-Macon Woman's College, Lynchburg, Va. Catalogue of the collection of American painting at Randolph-Macon Woman's College. III. Title. BIP

Art, American—Colorado—Exhibitions.

DENVER. Art 709'.788'074018883 Museum.
20 Colorado artists : [exhibition Denver Art Museum, September 9/ October 30, 1977. Denver : The Museum, c1977. [44] p. : ill. ; 31 cm. [N6530.C6D46 1977] 77-89063 ISBN 0-914738-12-7
1. Art, American—Colorado—Exhibitions. 2. Art, Modern—20th century—Colorado—Exhibitions. 3. Artists—Colorado—Biography. I. Title.

Art, American—Dictionaries.

THE Britannica 709'.73
encyclopedia of American art. Chicago, Encyclopaedia Britannica Educational Corp.; distribution by Simon and Schuster, New York [1973] 669 p. illus. (part col.) 29 cm. "A Chanticleer Press edition." Bibliography: p. 638-668. [N6505.B73] 73-6527 ISBN 0-671-21616-3 29.95
1. Art, American—Dictionaries. 2. Artists—United States—Biography—Dictionaries.

THE Britannica 709'.73
encyclopedia of American art : a special educational supplement to the Encyclopaedia Britannica. Chicago : Encyclopaedia Britannica Educational Corp. ; New York : distribution by Simon and Schuster, [1976?] 669 p. : ill. (some col.) ; 29 cm. "A Chanticleer Press edition." Bibliography: p. 638-668. [N6505.B73 1976] 73-80529 ISBN 0-87827-160-0 : write for information
1. Art, American—Dictionaries. 2. Artists—United States—Biography. BIP

Art, American—Exhibitions.

A.C.A. Galleries. 709'.73
Looking west. September 19-October 14, 1972. New York [1972] [52] p. (incl. cover) illus. (part col.) 28 cm. [N6530.C2A17 1972] 74-190872
1. Art, American—Exhibitions. 2. Art, Modern—20th century—California. I. Title.

AGEE, William C. 709'.73
The 1930's: painting & sculpture in America, by William Agee. New York, Whitney Museum of American Art, 1968. [90] p. illus. (part col.) 25 cm. Catalog of an exhibition held at the Whitney Museum of American Art, Oct. 15-Dec. 1, 1968. Bibliography: p. [88]-[90] [N6512.A564] 68-57216
1. Art, American—Exhibitions. 2. Art, Modern—20th century—U.S. I. Whitney Museum of American Art, New York. II. Title.

AKRON, Ohio. Art 709'.2'2 Institute.
Celebrate Ohio, September 27-November 7, 1971, Akron Art Institute, fiftieth anniversary exhibition. [Akron, Ohio, 1971] [76] p. illus. (part col.) 21 x 28 cm. [N6530.O3A75] 72-198347
1. Art, American—Exhibitions. 2. Art, Modern—20th century—Ohio. 3. Artists, American—Ohio. I. Title.

AKRON, Ohio. 709'.73'074017136 Art Institute.
Why is an object : an exhibition investigating motivation and purpose, the Akron Art Institute, Akron, Ohio, September 11-November 4, 1962. Akron : The Institute, 1962. [32] p. : ill. ; 17 x 26 cm. Cover title. [N6512.A5645 1962] 75-321242
1. Art, American—Exhibitions. 2. Art, Modern—20th century—United States—Exhibitions. 3. Art—Psychology. 4. Motivation (Psychology) I. Title.

ALDRICH Museum 709'.73'07401469 of Contemporary Art.
Second annual Contemporary Reflections, 1972-1973; [catalog of an] exhibition: April 22 through August 19, 1973. Ridgefield, Conn. [1973] [48] p. illus. 22 cm. [N6512.A565 1973] 75-313855
1. Art, American—Exhibitions. 2. Art, Modern—20th century—United States. I. Title. II. Title: Contemporary Reflections.

AMERICAN Academy of Arts 759.13 and Letters.
Exhibition of work by newly elected members and recipients of honors and awards. New York. v. 24 cm. annual. Title varies: 19 -57, Exhibition of work of newly elected members, recipients of honors, and Childe Hassam Fund purchases. Exhibitions for sponsored by the academy and National Institute of Arts and Letters. [N6512.A568] 68-7478
1. Art, American-Exhibitions. 2. Art, Modern—20th cent.—Exhibitions. I. National Institute of Arts and Letters. II. Title.

AMERICAN Academy 759.13'074'01471 of Arts and Letters.
Memorial exhibition: Lee Gatch, Hans Hofmann, Edward Hopper, Henry Schnakenberg [and] Charles Sheeler. [Held] March 4, 1971-April 10, 1971, in the museum. New York, 1971. [14] p., 5 plates. 26 cm. (Its Publication no. 268) [N6512.A569] 73-158125
1. Art, American—Exhibitions. 2. Art, Modern—20th century—United States. I. Title. II. Series.

AMERICAN art in 709'.73'0740147
upstate New York; drawings, watercolors, and small sculpture from public collections in Albany, Buffalo, Ithaca, Rochester, Syracuse and Utica. [Buffalo, N.Y., Buffalo Fine Arts Academy, 1974] 68 p. illus. 26 cm. Catalog of the exhibition held July 12-Aug. 25, 1974 at the Albright-Knox Art Gallery, Buffalo; Sept. 10-Oct. 13, 1974 at the Memorial Art Gallery, University of Rochester; Oct. 22-Nov. 24, 1974 at the Herbert F. Johnson Museum of Art, Cornell University, Ithaca; Dec. 5, 1974-Jan. 12, 1975 at the Everson Museum of Art, Syracuse; Jan. 26-Mar. 2, 1975 at the Munson-Williams-Proctor Institute, Utica; and Mar. 14-Apr. 27, 1975 at the Albany Institute of History and Art, Albany. [N6505.A57] 74-82546 ISBN 0-914782-00-2 3.00 (pbk.)
1. Art, American—Exhibitions. 2. Art, Colonial—United States. 3. Art, Modern—19th century—United States. 4. Art, Modern—20th century—United States. I. Albright-Knox Art Gallery.

AMERICAN Artists Congress. 759.13
Annual membership exhibition. [New York] v. illus. 24cm. [N6512.A58] 56-50907
1. Art. American—Exhibitions. I. Title.

AMERICAN Federation of 759.13'074 Arts.
Realism and surrealism in American art from the Sara Roby Foundation collection. [Edited by Catherine M. Perebinossoff] New York [1971] [16] p. illus. 21 cm. "AFA exhibition number 71-6." [N6512.5.R4A4] 79-169113
1. Art, American—Exhibitions. 2. Art, Modern—20th century—United States. 3. Realism in art—United States. 4. Surrealism—New York. I. Perebinossoff, Catherine M., ed. II. Sara Roby Foundation, New York. III. Title.

AMERICAN Institute of 760'.09'04 Graphic Arts.
Color : [catalogue] : an exhibition of original work of distinguished artists, designers, and photographers from the United States and abroad / sponsored by the American Institute of Graphic Arts. [Hamilton, Ohio] : Champion Papers, [1974] [7] p., [85] leaves of plates : chiefly ill. (some col.) ; 25 cm. [N6512.A615 1974] 75-310466
1. Art, American—Exhibitions. 2. Art, Modern—20th century—United States. 3. Color in art. I. Title.

ANGLO-AMERICAN Art 709'.73 Museum.
American folk art, 1730-1968; a loan exhibition, Anglo-American Art Museum, March 1--April 15, 1968. [Baton Rouge, La., 1968] 1 v. (chiefly illus.) 21 x 26 cm. Cover title. [N6505.A63] 68-65598
1. Art, American—Exhibitions. 2. Primitivism in art—United States. I. Title.

ARTISTS salute 709'.73'07401471
Skowhegan : [exhibition] December 8-21, 1977, Kennedy Galleries ... New York, New York. Skowhegan, Me. : Skowhegan School of Painting and Sculpture, c1977. [108] p. : chiefly ill. ; 21 cm. [N6512.A773] 77-89091
1. Art, American—Exhibitions. 2. Art, Modern—20th century—United States—Exhibitions. I. Skowhegan, Me. School of Painting and Sculpture. II. Kennedy Galleries, inc., New York.

AVANT-GARDE 730'.973'07401512
painting & sculpture in America, 1910-25 : [exhibition] Delaware Art Museum, April 4-May 18, 1975 / co-sponsored by the University of Delaware & Delaware Art Museum ; [William Innes Homer, general editor]. Wilmington, : Delaware Art Museum, [1975] 176 p. : ill. ; 28 cm. "Organized by the Department of Art History and Division of Museum Studies, University of Delaware, in cooperation with the Delaware Art Museum." Errata inserted. [N6512.A93] 75-361
1. Art, American—Exhibitions. 2. Art, Modern—20th century—United States—Exhibitions. 3. Avant-garde (Aesthetics) I. Homer, William Innes. II. Delaware. University, Newark. III. Delaware. University, Newark. Dept. of Art History. IV. Delaware. University, Newark. Division of Museum Studies. V. Delaware Art Museum.

†BARD, Joellen. 709'.73'0740147
Tenth Street days : the co-ops of the 50's : the galleries, Tanager, Hansa, James, Camino, March, Brata, Phoenix, Area : an artist-initiated exhibition, works from 1952-1962 / researched and organized by Joellen Bard, in co-operation with Pleiades Gallery and the Association of Artist-Run Galleries ; traveling exhibition circulated by the Gallery Association of New York State ; work selected for travel by Dore Ashton and Joellen Bard. New York : Education, Art & Service, inc., c1977. vii, 72 p. : ill. ; 21 x 28 cm. Held Dec. 20-Jan. 7, 1977 at Amos Eno Gallery et al. Bibliography: p. 72. [N6512.B27] 77-92798 Gratis
1. Art, American—Exhibitions. 2. Art, Modern—20th century—United States—Exhibitions. 3. Group work in art—United States—Exhibitions. I. Pleiades Gallery. II. Association of Artist-Run Galleries. III. Amos Eno Gallery.
Available from Pleiades Galleryk, 152 Wooster St., New York, NY 10012

BLASDEL, Gregg N. 759.13
Symbols and images; contemporary primitive artists. Selected by Gregg N. Blasdel. [Exhibition] circulated by the American Federation of Arts. [New York, 1970] 1 v. (unpaged) illus. 31 cm. "AFA Exhibition number 70-12. Circulated 1970-71." [N6512.5.P7B55] 70-134912
1. Art, American—Exhibitions. 2. Art, Modern—20th century—United States. 3. Primitivism in art—United States. I. American Federation of Arts. II. Title.

BOSTON. Institute 707.4'0144'61 of Contemporary Art.
Boston now. [Exhibition at] new City Hall, February 8-March 15, 1969. [Boston, 1969] [40] p. illus. 20 cm. "An exhibition organized by the Institute of Contemporary Art for Boston's new City Hall grand opening ceremonies." [N6535.B7B7] 76-77809
1. Art, American—Exhibitions. 2. Art, Modern—20th century—Boston. I. Title.

BOSTON. Institute of 709'.73 Contemporary Art.
A memorial exhibition; selections from the Nathaniel Saltonstall Collection. [Boston, 1969] [59] p. illus. (part col.) 23 cm. Catalog of the exhibition held Nov. 11-Dec. 14, 1969. [N6512.B58] 78-104038
1. Saltonstall, Nathaniel, 1903-1968—Art collections. 2. Art, American—Exhibitions. 3. Art, Modern—20th century—U.S. I. Title.

BOSTON. Museum 709'.73'074014461 of Fine Arts. Dept. of American Decorative Arts and Sculpture.
Paul Revere's Boston, 1735-1818 : [exhibition, April 18-October 12, 1975] / contributors to the catalogue, introd. by Walter Muir Whitehill : Jonathan C. Fairbanks ...[etal.]. Boston : Dept. of American Decorative Arts and Sculpture, Museum of Fine Arts : distributed by New York Graphic Society, 1975. 234 p. : ill. (some col.) ; 28 cm. Bibliography: p. 216-218. [N6535.B7B77 1975] 74-21766 ISBN 0-87846-088-8
1. Revere, Paul, 1735-1818. 2. Art, American—Exhibitions. 3. Art, Colonial—Boston—Exhibitions. I. Fairbanks, Jonathan L. II. Title. BIP

BOSTON University. 730'.74'014461 School of Fine and Applied Arts.
American artists of the nineteen sixties; Boston University School of Fine & Applied Arts centennial exhibition. [Boston? 1970] 60 p. illus. 27 cm. Catalog of an exhibition held on the occasion of Boston University's centennial celebration Feb. 6-Mar. 14, 1970, in the school's gallery. The exhibition was arranged and selected, and the introd. to the catalog written by H. H. Aranson. Includes bibliographical references. [N6512.B59] 70-18617
1. Art, American—Exhibitions. 2. Art, Modern—20th century—U.S. I. Aranson, H. Harvard. II. Title.

BRANDEIS University, 709.73
Waltham, Mass. Poses Institute of Fine Arts.
American art since 1950; a loan exhibition sponsored by the Poses Institute of Fine Arts, Brandeis University and the Institute of Contemporary Art, Boston, November 21,--December 23, 1962. [Waltham? Mass., 1962] 83 p. illus. 23 cm. "The exhibition ... was shown in the fine arts pavilion of the Seattle World's Fair this year from April through October." [N6512.B7] 63-35
1. Art. American — Exhibitions. I. Boston. Institute of Contemporary Art. II. Title.

BRANDYWINE 741.6'0973'074014814
River Museum.
Women artists in the Howard Pyle tradition : a catalogue presented in connection with the exhibition at the Brandywine River Museum of the Tri-County Conservancy of the Brandywine, Chadds Ford, Pennsylvania, September 6 through November 23, 1975. [Chadds Ford, Pa. : The Museum, 1975] 28 p. : ill. ; 20 cm. Includes bibliographical references. [N6512.B716 1975] 75-24692
1. Art, American—Exhibitions. 2. Art, Modern—20th century—United States—Exhibitions. 3. Women artists—United States. I. Title.

BRANDYWINE 760'.0973'07401512
tradition artists; featuring the works of Howard Pyle, Frank E. Schoonover, the Wyeth family, Charles Colombo, David Hanna. With introductory essay by Rowland Elzea. [Exhibition held] October 1971-October 1972. Exhibitors: International Art Gallery, Pittsburgh, Pennsylvania [and others. New York, Great American Editions, 1971] 54 p. illus. 22 x 29 cm. Cover title: An album of Brandywine tradition artists. [N6512.B72] 72-180989 3.50
1. Pyle, Howard, 1853-1911—Influence. 2. Art, American—Exhibitions. 3. Art, Modern—20th century—U.S. I. International Art Gallery. II. Title: An album of Brandywine tradition artists.

BRONX Museum 709'.73'0740147275
of the Arts.
The year of the woman : reprise : the Bronx Museum of the Arts, February 26-April 2, 1976 [exhibition]. Bronx, N.Y. : The Museum, c1976. 24 p. : ill. ; 22 cm. Text in English with part of text also in Spanish. [N6512.B74 1976] 76-361791
1. Art, American—Exhibitions. 2. Art, Modern—20th century—United States—Exhibitions. 3. Women artists—United States. I. Title.

BROOKLYN Institute of 708.14723
Arts and Sciences. Museum
Victoriana, an exhibition of the arts of the Victorian era in America, April 7-June 5, 1960. [Brooklyn New York] Brooklyn Museum, 1960 unpaged. illus. 23cm. 60-3084 1.25 pap.,
1. Art, American—Exhibitions. I. Title.

CARGILL, David, 1929- 730'.92'4
David Cargill. Dallas, Valley House Gallery, 1971 [c1968] [27] p. illus. 25 cm. Catalogue of an exhibition held October 1971 at Valley House Gallery, Dallas. [NB237.C38V3] 72-198081
I. Valley House Gallery.

CENTURY 709'.73'07401471
Association, New York.
Centurions associated with the Art Students League : [catalogue of] an exhibition at the Century Association in two parts : part one, The past, February 7-28, 1968, part two, The present, March 6-30, 1968 / [editing and planning of this catalogue by Lawrence Campbell]. New York : The Association, [1968] [28] p. : ill. ; 26 cm. [N6510.C45 1968] 75-307979
1. Art, American—Exhibitions. 2. Art, Modern—19th century—United States. 3. Art, Modern—20th century—United States. I. Campbell, Lawrence. II. New York (City). Art Students' League. III. Title.

CHAMBERS, 759.13'074'018883
Marlene.
American art since 1960 : the Virginia and Bagley Wright Collection : Denver Art Museum, February 1-March 16, 1975 / [text by Marlene Chambers Denver : Denver Art Museum, 1975. [23] p. : ill. (some col.) ; 23 x 28 cm. Bibliography: p. [23] [N6512.C45] 74-33089 ISBN 0-914738-08-9
1. Wright, Virginia—Art collections. 2. Wright, Bagley—Art collections. 3. Art, American—Exhibitions. 4. Art, Modern—20th century—United States. I. Denver. Art Museum. II. Title. III. Title: The Virginia and Bagley Wright collection.

CHEYENNE Centennial 709'.78
Committee.
150 years in Western art. [Exhibition] July 1 through August 15, 1967, Miller School, Cheyenne, Wyoming. one hundred and fifty years in western art [Cheyenne, 1967] 30 p. illus. (part col.) 28 cm. [N6525.C5] 67-26943
1. Art, American—Exhibitions. 2. The West in art. 3. Indians of North America—The West—Pictorial works. I. Title.

CINCINNATI. Art 759.194'61
Museum.
Artists of Cincinnati and vicinity. [Cincinnati] v. illus. 16-24 cm. annual. Title varies: Annual exhibition of the artists of Cincinnati and vicinity. [N6535.C55C5] 68-105
1. Art, American—Exhibitions. 2. Artists, American—Cincinnati. I. Cincinnati. Art Museum. Annual exhibition of the artists of Cincinnati and vicinity. II. Title.

CINCINNATI. Art Museum. 709'.73
Cincinnati invitational exhibition, November 21, 1972 through January 1, 1973: [catalog. Cincinnati, 1972?] [23] p. illus. 25 cm. [N6530.O32C56 1972] 74-185074
1. Art, American—Exhibitions. 2. Art, Modern—20th century—Cincinnati metropolitan area. I. Title.

CINCINNATI. ART MUSEUM. 759.13
Faculty exhibition: the Art Academy of Cincinnati. [Held at] the Cincinnati Art Museum, 1953. [Cincinnati, 1953] 1 v. (unpaged) illus. 26 cm. [N6512.C58] 66-89444
1. Art, American — Exhibitions. 2. Artists, American — Cincinnati. I. Cincinnati. Art Academy. II. Title.

COMMUNITY 704.94'36'0740147243
Arts Programs Association.
Contemporary landscape : image and idea : Burko, Feigenbaum, Hendricks, Resnick, Richards : an exhibition : April 13-May 12, 1977 ... Queensborough Community College, the City University of New York, Bayside, New York / organized by CAPA (Community Arts Programs Association). Bayside, N.Y. : CAPA, c1977. 28 p. : ill. ; 22 cm. Includes bibliographies. [N6512.C5814 1977] 77-152733
1. Art, American—Exhibitions. 2. Art, Modern—20th century—United States—Exhibitions. 3. Landscape in art—Exhibitions. I. Queensborough Community College. II. Title.

CONNECTICUT. University. 709'.73
Museum of Art.
Edith Halpert and the Downtown Gallery. [Exhibition. Storrs, Conn.] 1968. [41] p. 58 illus. 21 cm. [N6512.C5816] 68-65427
1. Halpert, Edith. 2. New York (City). Downtown Gallery. 3. Art, American—Exhibitions. I. Title.

CONTEMPORARY 709.04'6'074017252
Art Society, Indianapolis.
Painting & sculpture today. Indianapolis, 1970. v, 120 p. illus. 26 cm. Catalogue of the 1970 annual exhibition presented at the Indianapolis Museum of Art. [N6512.C59] 72-25547
1. Art, American—Exhibitions. 2. Art, Modern—20th century—U.S. I. Indianapolis Museum of Art. II. Title.

CONTEMPORARY 709'.04'7074017252
Art Society, Indianapolis.
Painting & sculpture today, 1976 : 9 June-18 July, 1976 / organized by the Contemporary Art Society of the Indianapolis Museum of Art. Indianapolis : The Museum, [1976] 57 p. : ill. ; 29 cm. Catalogue of the exhibition held at the Indianapolis Museum of Art. [N6512.C59 1976] 77-151476
1. Art, American—Exhibitions. 2. Art, Modern—20th century—United States—Exhibitions. I. Indianapolis Museum of Art. II. Title.

CONTEMPORARY 709'.73'07401641411
Arts Museum.
John Baldessari, Frances Barth, Richard Jackson, Barbara Munger, Gary Stephen; an exhibition organized by the Contemporary Arts Museum, Houston, Texas, September 8-November 16, 1972. [Houston, Tex., c1972] 31 p. illus. (part col.) 26 cm. Catalog of the exhibition. [N6512.C593] 72-93798
1. Art, American—Exhibitions. 2. Art, Modern—20th century—United States. I. Baldessari, John, 1931-

CORCORAN Gallery of Art, 709'.73
Washington, D.C.
Art and youth; creative works from D.C. senior high school students. [Washington, 1970] [16] p. illus. 28 cm. Exhibition held at the Corcoran Gallery of Art, Washington, D.C., June 2-July 19, 1970. [N6535.W3C58] 78-129198
1. Art, American—Exhibitions. 2. Youth as artists. 3. High school students—Washington, D.C. I. Title.

CREATIVE Artists Public 709'.747
Service Program.
Photographers, sculptors, painters, printmakers, 1972-73; [a catalog of New York State visual artists, selected for the Creative Artists Public Service Program. New York; distributed by the Gallery Association of New York State, Norwich, N.Y., 1973] [63] p. illus. 20 cm. "Prepared by CAPS and the Gallery Association of New York State." [N6530.N7C73] 73-79388
1. Art, American—Exhibitions. 2. Art, Modern—20th century—New York (State) 3. Artists—New York (State) I. Gallery Association of New York State. II. Title.

DE Saisset Art 709'.794'074019473
Gallery and Museum.
New Deal art, California. [Santa Clara, Calif.] : De Saisset Art Gallery and Museum, University of Santa Clara, c1976. 172 p. : ill. ; 22 cm. "Exhibition dates, January 17-June 15, 1976." Bibliography: p. 170-171. [N8838.D4 1976] 76-49434
1. Art, American—Exhibitions. 2. Art, Modern—20th century—California—Exhibitions. 3. Federal art project. I. Title.

THE Deluxe 709'.73'074016411
show. [Houston, Tex., 1971] 74 p. illus. (part col.) 24 x 26 cm. Catalogue of the art exhibition held at the former Deluxe Theatre in Houston, Tex., Aug. 15-Sept. 12, 1971. "Sponsored by the Menil Foundation." [N6512.D37] 75-177924
1. Art, American—Exhibitions. 2. Art, Modern—20th century—U.S.

DETROIT. Institute of 709.73
Arts.
Other ideas. 10 September-19 October, 1969, the Detroit Institute of Arts. Catalogue designed by Bill Butt. Detroit [1969] [43] p. illus. 23 x 31 cm. Cover title. [N6512.D4] 77-271764
1. Art, American—Exhibitions. 2. Art, Modern—20th century—U.S. I. Title.

DICKSON, Harold Edward, 709'.73
1900-
Arts of the young Republic; the age of William Dunlap, by Harold E. Dickson. Chapel Hill, University of North Carolina Press [1968] vi, 234 p. illus., ports. 29 cm. "This book was written, illustrated, and designed to celebrate the tenth anniversary in November, 1968, of the opening of the William Hayes Ackland Memorial Art Center in Chapel Hill, and to serve as a catalogue of the exhibition of early American art held at the Center on that occasion." [N6507.D5] 68-54950 10.00
1. Art, American—Exhibitions. 2. Art, Colonial—U.S. I. North Carolina. University. William Hayes Ackland Memorial Art Center. II. Title. III. Title: The age of William Dunlap.

DILLENBERGER, Jane.
The hand and the spirit; religious art in America, 1700-1900 [by] Jane Dillenberger and Joshua C. Taylor. [Exhibition: University Art Museum, Berkeley, June 28-August 27, 1972. Berkeley, University Art Museum, 1972] 192 p. illus. (part col.) 25 cm. "Exhibition sponsored by Graduate Theological Union, Berkeley, University Art Museum, Berkeley, National Collection of Fine Arts, Smithsonian Institution, Washington, D.C." [N7903.D5] 70-189052
1. Art, American—Exhibitions. 2. Art, Modern—United States. 3. Christian art and symbolism. I. Taylor, Joshua Charles, 1917- II. California. University. Art Museum. III. Title.

DUKE 709'.73'0740156563
University, Durham, N.C. Art Museum.
America the beautiful : a Bicentennial exhibition of American art from the Dalton Collection, the Duke University Museum of Art, July 1976. Durham, N.C. : The Museum, c1976. 63 p. : chiefly ill. (some col.) ; 22 cm. [N6505.D85 1976] 76-375221
1. Dalton, Harry L.—Art collections. 2. Dalton, Mary—Art collections. 3. Art, American—Exhibitions. I. Title.

A Family 707'.09747'43
collection; drawings, sculptures and oils by American artists, selected from the Collection of Lucille and Walter Fillin and their children. [Albany, Albany Institute of History and Art? 1962] 1 v. (chiefly illus.) 18 cm. An exhibit shown during 1962-1963 at the Albany Institute of History and Art, and other museums. [N6510.F35] 338.4'3745'10973 75-303517
1. Fillin family—Art collections. 2. Art, American—Exhibitions. 3. Art, Modern—19th century—United States. 4. Art, Modern—20th century—United States. I. Albany Institute of History and Art.

FARALLA, 1916- 730'.924
Faralla; an exhibition of the artist's work covering the years 1959 through 1965, San Francisco Museum of Art, August 20 to September 18, 1966. [San Francisco? 1966?] 1 v. (unpaged) illus. 18 cm. Cover title. [NB237.F34A43] 67-68163
I. San Francisco. Museum of Art.

FARMER, Jane M. 704.94'4'074013
The image of urban optimism / [by Jane M. Farmer]. Washington : Smithsonian Institution, Traveling Exhibition Service, [1977] p. cm. [N6512.F3] 77-13902
1. Art, American—Exhibitions. 2. Art, Modern—20th century—United States—Exhibitions. 3. Cities and towns in art—Exhibitions. 4. New York (City) in art—Exhibitions. I. Smithsonian Institution. Traveling Exhibition Service. II. Title.

FERBRACHE, 759.194'074'019466
Lewis.
The Dr. and Mrs. Bruce Friedman Collection. [San Francisco] California Historical Society [1969?] [31] p. illus. 28 cm. Loan exhibition held at the California Historical Society, Sept. 30-Nov. 15, 1969. [N6530.C2F4] 76-24094
1. Friedman, Bruce, 1924- —Art collections. 2. Friedman, Bruce Mrs.—Art collections. 3. Art, American—Exhibitions. 4. Art, American—California. I. California Historical Society. II. Title.

15 Los 709'.794'94074019493
Angeles artists. [Pasadena, Calif., Pasadena Art Museum, 1972] 40 p. illus. 26 cm. [N6535.L6F53] 73-152579
1. Art, American—Exhibitions. 2. Art, Modern—20th century—Los Angeles. I. Pasadena, Calif. Art Museum.

FIFTY years of 709'.73'074019454
Crocker-Kingsley : [fiftieth annual exhibition, work of northern California artists] April 5-May 4, 1975 / introd. by Ruth A. Holland and Susan J. Willoughby. Sacramento, Calif. : E. B. Crocker Art Gallery, 1975. ca. 130 p. : ill. ; 28 cm. Includes index. [N6512.F53] 75-7220
1. Art, American—Exhibitions. 2. Art, Modern—20th century—United States—Exhibitions. I. Crocker Art Gallery, Sacramento, Calif. II. Kingsley Art Club.

FRIENDS of the Whitney 708.1471
Museum of American Art.
Business buys American art. March 17-April 24, 1960; third loan exhibition by the Friends of the Whitney Museum of American Art. New York, Whitney Museum of American Art, 22 W. 54 St. [1960] 52p. illus. (part col.) 23 x 23cm. annual 58-2660 app., apply
1. Art,American—Exhibitions. I. Whitney Museum of American Art, New York. II. Title.

FRIENDS of the Whitney   708.1471
Museum of American Art
A decade of American drawings, 1955-1965. 8th exhibition sponsored by the Friends. April 28-June 6, 1965. New York. Whitney Mus. [1965] 51p. illus. 23cm. annual. Title varies. [N6512.F7] 58-2660 1.50 pap.
1. Art. American—Exhibitions. I. Whitney Museum of American Art, New York. II. Title.

GELDZAHLER, Henry.   708.1471
New York painting and sculpture: 1940-1970. Foreword by Thomas P. F. Hoving. [1st ed.] New York, Dutton [1969] 494 p. illus. (part col.) 23 cm. Catalog of an exhibition held at the New York Metropolitan Museum of Art, together with 5 related essays. Bibliography: p. [453]-483. [N6535.N5G4 1969] 71-87179 10.00
1. Art, American—Exhibitions. 2. Art, Modern—20th century—New York (City) I. New York (City). Metropolitan Museum of Art. II. Title.

GEORGE Goundie,   709'.73'074017595
sculpture—Joseph Friebert, paintings, professors emeritus, Department of Art : two retrospective exhibitions : with an exhibition of the work of their selected former students, University of Wisconsin-Milwaukee, Fine Arts Galleries, 7 March through 1 April 1977. [Milwaukee] : The Galleries, c1977. [28] p. : ill. ; 16 x 23 cm. [N6512.G36] 77-371307
1. Goundie, George, 1913- 2. Friebert, Joseph, 1908- 3. Art, American—Exhibitions. 4. Art, Modern—20th century—United States—Exhibitions. I. Goundie, George, 1913- II. Friebert, Joseph, 1908- III. Wisconsin. University—Milwaukee. School of Fine Arts. Galleries.

GERDTS, William H.   709'.73
Revealed masters : 19th century American art : [catalogue of] an exhibition organized by American Federation of Arts, New York / William H. Gerdts. New York : American Federation of Arts, [1974] 152 p. : ill. (some col.) ; 28 cm. "AFA exhibition number 74-1; circulated September 1974-September 1975." Bibliography: p. [130]-152. [N6510.G45] 74-16549
1. Art, American—Exhibitions. 2. Art, Modern—19th century—United States. I. American Federation of Arts. II. Title. **BIP**

GOOSSEN, E. C.   709'.73
The art of the real; USA, 1949-1968 by E. C. Goossen New York, Museum of Modern Art; distributed by New York Graphic Society, Greenwich Conn. [1968] 63, [1] p. illus. (part col.) 23 cm. Catalog of an exhibition, July 3-Sept. 8, 1968. Bibliography: p. 59-[64] [N6512.G64] 68-29837
1. Art, American—Exhibitions. 2. Realism in art. 3. Art, Modern—20th century—United States. I. New York (City). Museum of Modern Art. II. Title.

HADLER, Mona.   709'.73'07401471
Brooklyn College Art Department : past and present, 1942-1977 : September 13-October 8, 1977, Davis & Long Company ... Robert Schoelkopf Gallery ... / organized by Mona Hadler and Jerome Viola. [Brooklyn : The Dept., c1977. 112 p. : ill. ; 28 cm. Bibliography: p. 107-109. [N6512.H3] 77-84455
1. Art, American—Exhibitions. 2. Art, Modern—20th century—United States—Exhibitions. 3. College teachers as artists—New York (City)—Exhibitions. I. Viola, Jerome. II. Brooklyn College. Art Dept. III. Davis & Long Company. IV. Robert Schoelkopf Gallery.

HARVARD   709'.73'07401444
University. William Hayes Fogg Art Museum.
American art at Harvard. [Cambridge, Mass.] Fogg Art Museum, Harvard University [1972] 1 v. (unpaged) illus. 25 x 27 cm. Catalog of the exhibition held Apr. 19-June 18, 1972. Includes bibliographical references. [N6505.H34] 72-75437
1. Art, American—Exhibitions. I. Title.

HECKSCHER   759.147'25'074014725
Museum.
Artists of Suffolk County. Huntington, N.Y. [1970- v. illus., ports. 28 cm. Catalogs of exhibitions held during the

museum's 50th anniversary year, 1970, and later. Pt. 1 lacks special subtitle. Contents.Contents.—— —pt. 2. The abstract tradition.—pt. 3. Figurative tradition.—pt. 4. The new landscape.—pt. 5. New directions.—pt. 6. Contemporary prints.—pt. 7. Contemporary craftsmen.—pt. 8. Photographers.—pt. 9. Twenty women artists. [N6530.N72S84] 74-23450
1. Art, American—Exhibitions. 2. Art—Suffolk Co., N.Y. I. Title.

HOPPS, Walter.   709'.73'0740531
USA; XXXVI International Biennial Exhibition of Art/Venice, June 11-October 1, 1972: Diane Arbus, Ron Davis, Richard Estes, Sam Gilliam, James Nutt, Keith Sonnier. Director of the United States exhibition: Walter Hopps. [Washington, 1972] [16] p. illus. 22 x 28 cm. "Sponsored by: the National Collection of Fine Arts, Smithsonian Institution." [N6512.H66] 72-602400
1. Art, American—Exhibitions. 2. Art, Modern—20th century—United States. I. Venice. Biennale d'arte, II. 36th, 1972. III. Smithsonian Institution. National Collection of Fine Arts. IV. Title.

HUNTER, Sam,   709'.73'074014423
1923-
Critical perspectives in American art : an exhibition, Fine Arts Center Gallery, University of Massachusetts/Amherst, April 10, 1976-May 9, 1976 / selected by Sam Hunter, Rosalind Krauss and Marcia Tucker. Amherst : The Gallery, 1976. 66 p. : ill. (some col.) ; 24 cm. Includes bibliographical references. [N6512.H79] 76-8330
1. Art, American—Exhibitions. 2. Art, Modern—20th century—United States—Exhibitions. I. Krauss, Rosalind E., joint author. II. Tucker, Marcia, joint author. III. University of Massachusetts at Amherst. Fine Arts Center. Gallery. IV. Title.

HUNTINGTON,   709'.73'074017435
David C.
Art and the excited spirit: America in the romantic period. An exhibition organized by David Carew Huntington, assisted by Edward R. Molnar. Robert A. Yassin, editor. Ann Arbor, University of Michigan Museum of Art, 1972. ix, 93 p. illus. 26 cm. Includes bibliographical references. [N6510.5.R6H86] 73-158278
1. Art, American—Exhibitions. 2. Romanticism in art—United States. 3. Art, Modern—19th century—United States. I. Michigan. University. Museum of Art. II. Title.

IAKOVLEV, Aleksandr   741.9'73
Evgen'evich, 1887-1938.
Alexandre Iacovleff; an exhibition of fifty drawings & paintings. Cambridge, Mass., Gropper Art Gallery [1972] [47] p. illus. 26 cm. Catalog of an exhibition held at the Gropper Art Gallery, Cambridge, Mass., May and June, 1972. Bibliography: p. [45]-[46] [NC269.I17G7] 72-198249
I. Gropper Art Gallery.

ILLINOIS. Arts   759.13'074'0173
Council.
Painters and sculptors in Illinois, 1820-1945. Chicago [1971] [65] p. illus. 22 cm. Catalog of an exhibition held at the Illinois State Museum, Springfield, Oct. 30-Dec. 12, 1971, and others. [N6530.I4A42] 73-157518
1. Art, American—Exhibitions. 2. Art, Modern—19th century—Illinois. 3. Art, American—20th century—Illinois. I. Illinois. State Museum, Springfield. II. Title.

ILLINOIS. Dept. of   707.4'0173
Public Instruction.
Two hundred and fifty years of American art; the art resources traveler. [Springfield, 1968] [20] p. illus., ports. 15 x 23 cm. [N6505.I4] A 68
1. Art, American—Exhibitions. I. Title.

JARECKIE,   709'.74'07401443
Stephen B.
The early republic : consolidation of revolutionary goals : March 3-June 30, 1976 / Stephen B. Jareckie. Worcester, Mass. : Worcester Art Museum, c1976. 99 p. : ill. ; 23 cm. A catalogue of the Worcester Art Museum's second bicentennial exhibition. Includes

bibliographical references. [N6507.J37] 76-364188
1. Art, American—Exhibitions. 2. Art, Modern—19th century—United States—Exhibitions. 3. Decoration and ornament—Federal style—Exhibitions. 4. Neoclassicism (Art)—United States—Exhibitions. I. Worcester, Mass. Art Museum. II. Title.

JOHN and Mable Ringling   709'.73
Museum of Art, Sarasota, Fla.
Contemporary religious imagery in American art. [Catalog of an exhibition held] March 1-31, 1974, Ringling Museum of Art, Sarasota, Fla. [Sarasota, Friends Division of the Ringling Museums Members Council, 1974] 44 p. illus. (part col.) 31 cm. [N6512.J63 1974] 74-622367
1. Art, American—Exhibitions. 2. Art, Modern—20th century—United States. 3. Art and religion. I. Title.

JOHN and Mable Ringling   759.14
Museum of Art, Sarasota, Fla.
Young New England painters. [Exhibition] Ringling Museum of Art, Sarasota, Florida, March 10 through April 27, 1969; Portland Museum of Art, Portland, Maine, June 18 through July 20, 1969; Currier Gallery of Art, Manchester, New Hampshire, August 2 through August 31, 1969. Sarasota [Board of Trustees of the Ringling Museums, 1969] 32 p. illus. (part col.) 18 x 26 cm. [N6515.J6] 76-628312
1. Art, American—Exhibitions. 2. Artists, American—New England. I. Currier Gallery of Art, Manchester, N.H. II. Portland Museum of Art. III. Title.

JOHNSON, Floyd, 1932-   759.13
Floyd Johnson. [Syracuse, N.Y., Everson Museum of Art, 1972] [8] p. (chiefly illus.) 21 x 25 cm. Cover title. Catalog of the exhibition held May 20-June 25, 1972, at the Everson Museum of Art. [ND237.J715E9] 72-83793
I. Everson Museum of Art of Syracuse and Onondaga County.

KARP, Ivan C.   759.13
Nostalgia and the contemporary artist, selected by Ivan Karp, with the assistance of Edward Plunkett. [New York, 1969] [12] p. illus. 19 x 26 cm. Catalog of a loan exhibition organized and circulated 1968-69 by the American Federation of Arts. "Exhibition number 68-8." [N6512.K35] 75-75225
1. Art, American—Exhibitions. 2. Art, Modern—20th century—U.S. I. American Federation of Arts. II. Title.

KENNEDY   759.13'074'01471
Galleries, inc., New York.
American masters, 18th and 19th centuries. New York [1972] 64 p. illus. (part col.) 26 cm. Catalog of the exhibition held Mar. 22-Apr. 8, 1972. Includes bibliographical references. [N6507.K43] 72-196939
1. Art, American—Exhibitions. 2. Art, Modern—17th-18th centuries—United States. 3. Art, Modern—19th century—United States. I. Title.

KENNEDY   759.13'074'01471
Galleries, inc., New York.
American masters, 18th to 20th centuries; exhibition, March 10 through April 3, 1971, at Kennedy Galleries, inc. New York [1971] 47 p. illus., ports. 26 cm. [N6505.K33] 72-198110
1. Art, American—Exhibitions. I. Title.

KENNEDY   709'.73'07401471
Galleries, inc., New York.
Important American art, 1903-1972. New York [1972] [55] p. illus. (part col.) 28 cm. Catalog of the exhibition held Nov. 15-25, 1972. [N6512.K37] 73-152327
1. Art, American—Exhibitions. 2. Art, Modern—20th century—United States. I. Title.

KENNEDY   759.13'074'01471
Galleries, inc., New York.
Rare American masterpieces of the 18th, 19th, and 20th centuries : [catalogue]. N[ew] Y[ork] : Kennedy Galleries, [1974- v. : chiefly ill. (some col.) ; 28 cm. Includes index. [N6505.K33 1974] 74-195998
1. Art, American—Exhibitions. I. Title.

KENNEDY Galleries, inc.,   709'.73
New York.
A selection of twentieth century American masterpieces. On exhibition in our main galleries Nov. 7-Dec. 1, 1973. New York [1973] [63] p. illus. (part col.) 28 cm. [N6512.K39 1973] 73-180227
1. Art, American—Exhibitions. 2. Art, Modern—20th century—United States. I. Title.

KENNEDY   759.13'074'01471
Galleries, inc., New York.
Twentieth century American masters. New York [1971] [46] p. illus. (part col.) 28 cm. Catalogue of an exhibition held Oct. 12-NOv. 4, 1971. [N6512.K38] 76-31089
1. Art, American—Exhibitions. 2. Art, Modern—20th century—U.S. I. Title.

KRANNERT Art   759.13'074'017366
Museum.
American paintings and sculpture, 1948-1969 : an exhibition, March 7 through April 11, 1971. Champaign : Krannert Art Museum, College of Fine and Applied Arts, University of Illinois, [1971?] [84] p. : chiefly ill. ; 26 cm. Addendum slip inserted. [N6512.K72 1971] 74-622646
1. Art, American—Exhibitions. 2. Art, Modern—20th century—United States—Exhibitions. I. Title.

KRENTZIN, Earl, 1929-   730'.924
Earl Krentzin [silver sculpture, Kennedy Galleries, December 2-31, 1969] New York, Kennedy Galleries [1970] [16] p. (chiefly illus.) 28 cm. Label mounted on t.p.: Supplied by Worldwide Books, Boston. [NB237.K74A44] 78-18839
I. Kennedy Galleries, inc., New York.

LA Jolla Museum   709'.73'074019498
of Contemporary Art
University of California, Irvine, 1965-75 : an exhibition organized for the La Jolla Museum of Contemporary Art with the assistance of the University of California, Irvine, November 7-December 14, 1975. La Jolla, Calif. : The Museum, c1975. 95 p. : ill. ; 23 cm. Bibliography: p. 91-94. [N6530.C2L34 1975] 75-37097
1. Art, American—Exhibitions. 2. Art, Modern—20th century—California—Exhibitions. I. California. University, Irvine. II. Title.

LAKEVIEW Center for   704.94'9'9178
the Arts and Sciences.
Westward the artist. [Third anniversary exhibition of Lakeview Center, April 19-June 2, 1968. Peoria, Ill., 1968] [53] p. illus. 21 x 26 cm. Cover title. [N6510.L34 1968] 74-187162
1. Art, American—Exhibitions. 2. Art, Modern—19th century—United States. 3. The West in art. I. Title.

LEVINE, David,   759.13'074'014723
1926-
Paintings and drawings by David Levine and Aaron Shikler. Brooklyn Museum, April 24-May 23, 1971. [Brooklyn, N.Y., Brooklyn Museum, 1971] [136] p. illus. (part col.) 23 cm. [N6536.L62] 71-157112
1. Art, American—Exhibitions. 2. Art, Modern—20th century—U.S. I. Shikler, Aaron, 1922- II. Brooklyn Institute of Arts and Sciences. Museum. III. Title.

LIPMAN, Jean   709'.73'07401471
Herzberg, 1909-
Art about art / Jean Lipman and Richard Marshall ; introd. by Leo Steinberg. 1st ed. New York : Dutton, c1978. 159 p., [8] leaves of plates : ill. (some col.) ; 26 cm. "Published on the occasion of an exhibition held at the Whitney Museum of American Art, New York, July 19-September 24, 1978." Includes index. [N6512.L56] 77-93965 ISBN 0-525-47502-8 : 6.95
1. Art, American—Exhibitions. 2. Art, Modern—20th century—United States—Exhibitions. 3. Art—Reproduction—Exhibitions. 4. Art—Themes, motives—Influence—Exhibitions. I. Marshall, Richard, joint author. II. Whitney Museum of American Art, New York. III. Title. **BIP**

LITTLE, Nina Fletcher,   759.13
1903-
Land and seascape, as observed by the folk artist. [Williamsburg, Va., Colonial Williamsburg, 1969] 52 p. 103 illus. (part col.) 23 x 26 cm. Catalogue of an exhibition from the collection of Bertram K. and Nina Fletcher Little, held at the

Abby Aldrich Rockefeller Folk Art Collection, Williamsburg, Virginia, Jan. 13, 1969 to May 11, 1969. [ND207.L5] 75-2666
1. Art, American—Exhibitions. 2. Primitivism in art—United States. 3. Landscape painting, American. 4. Marine painting, American. I. Little, Bertram K., 1899- II. Abby Aldrich Rockefeller Folk Art Collection, Williamsburg, Va. III. Title.

LONG Beach, Calif. Museum of Art. 338.4'3745'10973
Arts of southern California; [exhibitions] prepared and circulated by Long Beach Museum of Art. Long Beach, 195 v. illus., map. 23cm. Contents.4. Prehistoric and indigenous Indian art. [N6530.C2L6] 59-30033
1. Art, American—Exhibitions. 2. Art—California. I. Title.

LOS Angeles Co., Calif. Museum of Art, Los Angeles. 760'.0973
Chosen works of American art, 1850-1924, from the Collection of Jo Ann and Julian Ganz, Jr. [1969] [32] p. illus. 19 x 22 cm. Catalog of a loan exhibition held in the Ahmanson Gallery of the museum Oct. 1-Nov. 16, 1969. [N6510.L67] 73-452642
1. Ganz, Jo Ann—Art collections. 2. Ganz, Julian—Art collections. 3. Art, American—Exhibitions. 4. Art, Modern—19th century—U.S. 5. Art, Modern—20th century—U.S. I. Title.

LOS Angeles Co., Calif. Otis Art Institute, Los Angeles. 709'.73
Otis Art Institute faculty exhibition, March 14 through April 28, 1968. Los Angeles [1968] [28] p. illus. 19 cm. [N6530.C2L63] 68-4064
1. Art, American—Exhibitions. 2. Artists, American—California. I. Title.

LOS Angeles County Museum, Los Angeles. 759.194'61
Annual exhibition, artists of Los Angeles and vicinity. Los Angeles. v. illus. 26cm. [N6535.L6L6] 56-26838
1. Art, American—Exhibitions. I. Title.

LOWE Art Museum. 709'.73'074015938
Less in more : the influence of the Bauhaus on American art / [exhibition] organized by the Lowe Art Museum, University of Miami, February 7-March 10, 1974 ; [catalog information prepared by Carol Hotchkiss]. Coral Gables, Fla. : The Museum, [1974] 47 p. : ill. ; 26 cm. Bibliography: p. 46. [N6512.L68 1974] 75-318272
1. Art, American—Exhibitions. 2. Art, Modern—20th century—United States—Exhibitions. 3. Art, European—Exhibitions. 4. Art, Modern—20th century—Europe—Exhibitions. 5. Bauhaus—Influence. I. Hotchkiss, Carol. II. Title.

MACAGY, Douglas, 1913- 709'.73'07401642812
One i at a time, by Douglas MacAgy. [Dallas, Tex., Division of Fine Arts, Southern Methodist University, 1971] 68 p. illus. 24 x 28 cm. "Pollock Galleries, Meadows School of the Arts, Southern Methodist University, Dallas, Texas, March 20-April 25, 1971." [N6512.M23] 72-198085
1. Art, American—Exhibitions. 2. Art, Modern—20th century—United States. I. Pollock Galleries. II. Title.

MACDONALD-WRIGHT, Stanton, 1890- 760'.0924
The art of Stanton Macdonald-Wright, introduced by David W. Scott. Washington, Published for the National Collection of Fine Arts by the Smithsonian Press, 1967. 100 p. illus. (part col.) 23 cm. (Smithsonian publication no. 4707) "A retrospective exhibition, May 4 through June 18, 1967, National Collection of Fine Arts, Smithsonian Institution." "A treatise on color [by] S. Macdonald Wright" Los Angeles, 1924: p. 65-100. [ND237.M19S3] 67-24900
I. Smithsonian Institution. National Collection of Fine Arts. II. Title.

MARLING, Karal Ann. 338.4'7'70977132
Federal art in Cleveland, 1933-1943 : an exhibition, September 16 to November 1, 1974, the Cleveland Public Library ... / organized by D. Michael Gormley, Karal Ann Marling ; essay and notes by Karal Ann Marling ; catalog by David R. Gregor ... [et al.]. [Cleveland : Cleveland Public Library, 1974] xi, 125 p. : ill. ; 26 cm. Includes bibliographical references. [N8838.M37] 74-11725
1. Art, American—Exhibitions. 2. Art, Modern—20th century—Cleveland. 3. Federal art project. I. Gormley, D. Michael. II. Gregor, David R. III. Cleveland. Public Library. IV. Title.

MICHIGAN. University. Museum of Art. 759.13
The face of the fifties; recent painting and sculpture from the collection of the Whitney Museum of American Art [selected by John I. H. Baur. Exhibition, April 12 through May 28, 1961. Ann Arbor, 1961] unpaged. illus. 16x23cm. [N6512.M5] 61-19011
1. Art. American— Exhibitions. I. Whitney Museum of American Art, New York. II. Title.

MILWAUKEE. Art Center. 709'.73'074017595
Eight artists: Lynda Benglis, Sam Gilliam, Ralph Goings, Hans Haacke, Duane Hanson, Sol LeWitt, DeWain Valentine, Richard Van Buren. [Exhibition] June 19 - August 8, 1971. [Milwaukee, 1971] [40] p. illus. 31 cm. (Directions 3) In portfolio. "Organized by the Milwaukee Art Center and sponsored by the Jos. Schlitz Brewing Company." Includes bibliographies. [N6512.M52] 77-174577
1. Art, American—Exhibitions. 2. Art, Modern—20th century—U.S. I. Schlitz (Jos.) Brewing Company. II. Title. III. Series.

MINNEAPOLIS. Institute of Arts. 338.4'3745'10973
Four centuries of American art; [exhibition held at] the Minneapolis Institute of Arts, 27 November 1963 -- 19 January 1964. [Catalogue. Editor: Forest Selvig. Minneapolis, 1963] 1 v. (unpaged) illus. 26 cm. [N6503.M5] 66-2970
1. Art, American — Exhibitions. I. Selvig, Forrest, ed. II. Title.

MINNESOTA State Agricultural Society. 759.13
Fine arts exhibition, Fine Art Galleries, Minnesota State Fair. [Catalog] [St. Paul] v. 23x11cm. annual. [N6512.M557] 55-34823
1. Art, American— Exhibitions. I. Title. II. Title: Minnesota State Fair.

MINNESOTA. University. Tweed Gallery. 709'.73
Twentieth anniversary exhibition, October 8 through November 8, 1970. Duluth [1970] 44 p. illus. (part col.) 28 cm. Exhibition catalog. [N6512.M57] 73-620689
1. Art, American—Exhibitions. 2. Art, Modern—20th century—United States. I. Title.

MORRIS, Edward. 709'.73'07402753
American artists in Europe, 1800-1900 : [catalogue of] an exhibition to celebrate the bicentenary of American independence [held at the] Walker Art Gallery, Liverpool, 14 November-2 January 1976-7 / [compiled by Edward Morris [Liverpool] : Merseyside County Council, [1976] 33 p., [34] p. of plates : ill., ports. ; 30 cm. Includes bibliographical references and index. [N6510.M65] 77-361418 ISBN 0-901534-43-9
1. Art, American—Exhibitions. 2. Art, Modern—19th century—United States—Exhibitions. 3. Artists—United States. 4. Artists—Europe. I. Liverpool. Public Libraries, Museums, and Art Gallery. Walker Art Gallery. II. Title.

NEBRASKA art today; 709'.782
a centennial invitational exhibition. [1st ed. Omaha, Joslyn Art Museum, 1967] 84 p. illus. 23 cm. Organized by the Nebraska Centennial Commission, Cultural Committee and the Nebraska Arts Council, with the cooperation of the Joslyn Art Museum and Sheldon Memorial Art Gallery. [N6530.N2N4] 75-113
1. Art, American—Exhibitions. 2. Artists, American—Nebraska. I. Nebraska Arts Council. II. Nebraska Centennial Commission. Cultural Committee.

THE Neuberger Collection: 708.13
an American collection; paintings, drawings, and sculpture. [Providence? 1968] 463 p. illus. (part col.) 28 cm. A combined catalog of 2 exhibitions of works selected from the collection of Roy R. Neuberger and held May 8-June 30, 1968, at the Museum of Art, Rhode Island School of Design, and Annmary Brown Memorial, Brown University. Most of the works were also shown at the National Collection of Fine Arts, Smithsonian Institution, Aug. 15-Sept. 25, 1968. [N6512.N34] 68-12325
1. Neuberger, Roy R.—Art collections. 2. Art, American—Exhibitions. I. Rhode Island School of Design, Providence. Museum of Art. II. Brown University. Annmary Brown Memorial. III. Smithsonian Institution. National Collection of Fine Arts. IV. Title: An American collection.

NEW Jersey. State Museum, Trenton. 709'.73
Geometric art: an exhibition of paintings and constructions by fourteen contemporary New Jersey artists. [Trenton, 1967] [3] p. illus. 22 cm. Exhibition held Sept. 30-Dec. 3, 1967. [N6530.N5A44] 68-63639
1. Art, American—Exhibitions. 2. Art, Modern—20th century—New Jersey. I. Title.

NEW Jersey. State Museum, Trenton. 760'.0922
Three artists view the human condition; an exhibition of paintings and graphics by Roosevelt artists; Jacob Landau, Stefan Martin [and] Gregorio Prestopino [held] June 22, 1968-September 15, 1968. Trenton [1968] [16] p. illus. 22 cm. [N6530.N5N4] 68-66934
1. Art, American—Exhibitions. 2. Artists, American—New Jersey. I. Title.

NEW York (City). Art Students' League. 709'.73'07401471
The Kennedy Galleries are host to the hundredth anniversary exhibition of paintings and sculptures by 100 artists associated with the Art Students League of New York, March 6-29, 1975. New York : Art Students League of New York, c1975. 284 p. : ill. ; 26 cm. [N6512.N344 1975] 75-331056
1. Art, American—Exhibitions. 2. Art, Modern—20th century—United States—Exhibitions. I. Kennedy Galleries, inc., New York.

NEW York (City). Metropolitan Museum of Art. 709'.73
19th-century America: paintings and sculpture; an exhibition in celebration of the hundredth anniversary of the Metropolitan Museum of Art, April 16 through September 7, 1970. Introd. by John K. Howat and John Wilmerding. Texts by John K. Howat Natalie Spassky and others. [New York] Distributed by New York Graphic Society [1970] 1 v. (unpaged) illus. (part col.), ports. (part col.) 27 cm. Bibliography: p. [187]-[188] [N6510.N48] 70-109966 14.95
1. Art, American—Exhibitions. 2. Art, Modern—19th century—U.S. I. Howat, John K. II. Spassky, Natalie. III. Title.

NEW York (City). Museum of Modern Art. 709'.73
American art of the 20's and 30's. Reprint ed. [New York] Published for the Museum of Modern Art by Arno Press, 1969. 87, [63], [62] p. illus. 27 cm. Comprised of reprints of catalogs originally published separately by the Museum of Modern Art under the titles: Paintings by nineteen living Americans [1930]; Painting and sculpture by living Americans [1930]; Murals by American painters and photographers [1932] [N6512.N38 1969] 76-86439
1. Art, American—Exhibitions. 2. Art, Modern—20th century—U.S. I. New York (City). Museum of Modern Art. Paintings by nineteen living Americans. 1969. II. New York (City). Museum of Modern Art. Painting and sculpture by living Americans. 1969. III. New York (City). Museum of Modern Art. Murals by American painters and photographers. 1969. IV. Title.

NEW York (City). Museum of Modern Art. 709'.73
American painting & sculpture, 1862-1932; October 31, 1932-1933, January 31. Reprint ed. New York, Published for the Museum of Modern Art by Arno Press, 1969 [c1932] 46, [80] p. plates. 26 cm. "American art, 1862-1932," by Holger Cahill: p. 9-22. [N6505.N45 1969] 79-86429
1. Art, American—Exhibitions. 2. Art, Modern—19th century—U.S. 3. Art, Modern—20th century—U.S. I. Cahill, Holger, 1893- II. Title.

NEW York (City). Museum of Modern Art. 760'.0973
American realists and magic realists. Edited by Dorothy C. Miller and Alfred H. Barr, Jr., with statements by the artists and an introd. by Lincoln Kirstein. [New York] Published for the Museum of Modern Art by Arno Press, 1969 [c1943] 67 p. illus. 27 cm. [N6512.N4 1969] 77-86431
1. Art, American—Exhibitions. 2. Realism in art—United States. 3. Surrealism—United States. I. Miller, Dorothy Canning, 1904- ed. II. Barr, Alfred Hamilton, 1902- joint ed. III. Title. **BIP**

NEW York (City). Museum of Modern Art. 709'.73
New horizons in American art; with an introd. by Holger Cahill. New York, Museum of Modern Art, 1936. Reprint ed. [New York] Published for the Museum of Modern Art by Arno Press, 1969. 171 p. illus. 27 cm. "Exhibition of work done under the Federal Art Project of the Works Progress Administration ... a documented survey of one year's activity." [N6512.N436 1970] 75-86428
1. Art, American—Exhibitions. 2. Art, Modern—20th century—U.S. I. Cahill, Holger, 1893-1960. II. Federal Art Project. III. Title. **BIP**

NEW York (City) Museum of Modern Art. 709.73
Sixteen Americans, edited by Dorothy C. Miller, with statements by the artists and others. New York, Distributed by Doubleday, Garden City, N.Y., 1959. 96 p. illus., ports. 24 cm. "Catalog of the exhibition, December 16, 1959 through February 14, 1960": p. 90-96. [N6512.N44] 59-15966
1. Art, American—Exhibitions. I. Miller, Dorothy Canning, 1904- ed. II. Title.

NEW York (City). Museum of Modern Art. 769'.973'07401471
Technics and creativity II. Gemini GEL. With an essay by Riva Castleman. [New York, 1971] 108 p. illus. (part fold., part col.), ports. 27 cm. Catalogue of an exhibition, May 5-July 6, 1971, works produced by Gemini. Issued in a case with an unfinished "multiple" (a 2-color offset lithograph with a collage of 3 wells of watercolor paint and a brush) by Jasper Johns, and a piece of white styrofoam. Bibliography: p. 104-105. [N6512.N447] 79-150085 ISBN 0-87070-615-2
1. Art, American—Exhibitions. 2. Art, Modern—20th century—U.S. I. Castleman, Riva. II. Gemini G.E.L. (Firm) III. Title.

NEW York (City). National Academy of Design. 709'.73'07401471
A century and a half of American art : [exhibition] commemorating the 150th anniversary of the founding of the National Academy of Design, October 10th through November 16th, 1975 / National Academy of Design. [New York] : The Academy, c1975. 262 p. : ill. ; 22 cm. [N6510.N49 1975] 75-29546
1. Art, American—Exhibitions. 2. Art, Modern—19th century—United States—Exhibitions. 3. Art, Modern—20th century—United States—Exhibitions. I. Title.

NEW York, Metropolitan Museum of Art. American Wing. 707.4
American art from American collections; decorative arts, paintings, and prints of the colonial and federal periods, from private collections, in an exhibition, March 6 to April 28, sponsored by the Friends of the American Wing. By James Biddle, associate curator in charge of the American Wing. New York, Metropolitan Mus. of Art, 1963. 114p. illus. 27cm. 63-10959 5.00; 2.95 pap.,

1. Art, American—Exhibitions. 2. Furniture, American—Exhibitions. I. Biddle, James. II. Title.

NEW York. Museum of Modern Art. 707.4
Americans 1963 Edited by Dorothy C. Miller, with statements by the artists and others Garden City, N.Y., Distributed by Doubleday [1963] 112 p. illus., ports. 24 cm. "Catalog of the exhibition, May 20 through August 18, 1963": p. 106-112. [N6512.N416] 63-17994
1. Art, American — Exhibitions. I. Miller, Dorothy Canning, 1904- ed. II. Title.

NEW York. Museum of Modern Art. 709.73
12 Americans, edited by Dorothy C. Miller, with statements by the artists and others. New York, Distributed by Simon and Schuster [1956] 95, [1]p. (chiefly illus. (part col.) ports.) 24cm. 'Catalog of the exhibition, May 29 through September 9, 1956': p. 92-[96] [N6512.N45] 56-3810
1. Art, American —Exhibitions. I. Miller, Dorothy Canning, 1904- ed. II. Title.

NEW York. Riverside Museum. 730'.74'01471
8 + 8. [Exhibition, the Riverside Museum] [New York, 1969?] [28] p. illus. 21 x 26 cm. Cover title. [N6512.N52] 72-20488
1. Art, American—Exhibitions. 2. Art, Modern—20th century—U.S. I. Title.

NEWARK Museum Association, Newark, N.J. 707.4
Classical America, 1815-1845; an exhibition at the Newark Museum, April twenty-sixth through September second, nineteen sixty-three. [Newark, 1963] 212 p. illus. 27 cm. Includes bibliographies. [N6510.N5] 63-24456
1. Art, American — Exhibitions. 2. Art industries and trade — U.S. 3. Art industries and trade — Exhibitions. I. Title.

NORTH Carolina Artists Exhibition. 709'.756'074015655
The 38th annual North Carolina Artists Exhibition : November 6 through December 14, 1975. Sponsored by the North Carolina Art Society. Raleigh : North Carolina Museum of Art, 1975. p. cm. "Catalogue": p. [N6530.N8N83 1975] 75-38621 ISBN 0-88259-081-2 : 1.00
1. Art, American—Exhibitions. 2. Art, Modern—20th century—North Carolina. 3. Art—Competitions. 4. Artists—North Carolina. I. North Carolina. Museum of Art, Raleigh. II. North Carolina Art Society.

NORTH Carolina. Museum of Art, Raleigh. 708.15'6
Acquisitions from North Carolina annuals, 1946-1966; exhibition, march 12-26, 1967. Raleigh [1967] 88 p. 43 illus. 26 cm. [N6530.N8N77] 67-65465
1. Art, American—Exhibitions. 2. Artists, American—North Carolina. I. Title.

OGUNQUIT, Me. Museum of Art. 709'.73
Paintings and drawings by Reginald Marsh. Paintings and sculpture by Americans of our times. Ogunquit, Me. [1970] [36] p. illus. 24 cm. Catalogue of an exhibition held July 4-Sept. 7, 1970. [N6512.O36] 73-171377 0.25
1. Marsh, Reginald, 1898-1954. 2. Art, American—Exhibitions. 3. Art, Modern—20th century—United States. I. Marsh, Reginald, 1898-1954. II. Title. III. Title: Paintings and drawings by Americans of our times.

OKLAHOMA Art Center. 709'.73
Past jurors invitational [exhibition] Oklahoma Art Center, Oklahoma City, September 14-November 2, 1969. [Oklahoma City? 1969?] 1 v. (unpaged) illus. 29 cm. [N6512.O39] 73-172030
1. Art, American—Exhibitions. 2. Art, Modern—20th century—United States. I. Title.

OREGON. University. Museum of Art. 759.13
A university collects: Oregon Pacific Northwest heritage; thirty-five paintings selected from the permanent collections, University of Oregon. Edited by Wallace S. Baldinger and Carol Ann Ivey Stewart. Layout by Barbara Lane. Photography by Harry Gross. Eugene, 1966. 49 p. illus. (part col.) 31 cm. "Catalogue of an exhibition. Exhibition circulated by the American Federation of Arts, 1967-1968." Bibliography: p. 46-49. [N6528.O7] 68-64674
1. Art, American—Exhibitions. 2. Art, Modern—20th century—Northwest, Pacific. I. Baldinger, Wallace Spencer, 1905- ed. II. Stewart, Carol Ann Ivey, ed. III. American Federation of Arts. IV. Title.

OTHER sources 709'.73'074019461
: an American essay : [exhibition] celebrating America's Bicentennial, San Francisco Art Institute, September 17-November 7, 1976. San Francisco : [San Francisco Art Institute], c1976. 128 p. : ill. ; 24 cm. [N6512.O84] 77-359440
1. Art, American—Exhibitions. 2. Art, Modern—20th century—United States—Exhibitions. 3. Minorities—United States. I. San Francisco Art Institute.

PASADENA, Calif. Art Museum. 709.73
United States of America: V Paris biennale. [Pasadena, c1967] 44 p. illus. (part col.), ports. 23 cm. Catalog of an exhibition organized by the Pasadena Art Museum and held Sept. 30 to Nov. 5, 1967, at the Musee d'art moderne de la ville de Paris and Nov. 28 to Dec. 31, 1967, at the Pasadena Art Museum. Includes bibliographies. [N6512.P33] 68-1691
1. Art, American—Exhibitions. 2. Art, Modern—20th century—United States. I. Paris. Musee d'art moderne de la ville de Paris. II. Title.

PENNSYLVANIA Academy of the Fine Arts, Philadelphia. 709.73
The one hundred and fiftieth anniversary exhibition, January 15, through March 13, 1955. Philadelphia [1955] 153p. illus. 26cm. [N6505.P4] 55-2532
1. Art, American—Exhibitions. I. Title.

PENNSYLVANIA Academy of the Fine Arts, Philadelphia. 759.148'11
Philadelphia painting and printing to 1776; an exhibition in conjunction with the seventeenth annual Winterthur Conference and with the cooperation of the Historical Society of Pennsylvania. Philadelphia [1971] 50 p. illus., ports. (part col.) 28 cm. Catalog of the exhibition held Mar. 26-Apr. 25, 1971. [N6535.P5P4] 71-156978
1. Art, American—Exhibitions. 2. Art, Modern—17th-18th centuries—Philadelphia. I. Winterthur Conference on Museum Operation and Connoisseurship, 17th, 1971. II. Pennsylvania. Historical Society. III. Title.

PENNSYLVANIA. University. Institute of Contemporary Art. 709'.73'074013
The highway : an exhibition / organized by Institute of Contemporary Art, University of Pennsylvania, Philadelphia, Pennsylvania, January 14 to February 25, 1970, in collaboration with Institute for the Arts, Rice University, Houston, Texas, March 12 to May 18, and the Akron Art Institute, Akron, Ohio, June 5 to July 26. Philadelphia : The Institute, c1970. 45 p. : ill. (some col.) ; 23 cm. [N6512.P46 1970] 75-313584
1. Art, American—Exhibitions. 2. Art, Modern—20th century—United States. 3. Roads in art. 4. Automobiles in art. I. Akron, Ohio. Art Institute. II. William Marsh Rice University, Houston, Tex. Institute for the Arts. III. Title.

ry Art.

PENNSYLVANIA. University. Institute of Contemporary Art.
Made in Philadelphia 2 : Charles Fahlen, Tom Hatten, Eleanor Hubbard, David Kettner, Gerald Nichols, Bill Richards, Warren Rohrer, Robert Younger: [catalogue of an exhibition] Institute of Contemporary Art, University of Pennsylvania, October 25 to December 14, 1974. Philadelphia : The Institute, c1974. [28] p. : ill. ; 21 cm. [N6535.P5P38 1974] 75-320306 ISBN 0-88454-014-6
1. Art, American—Exhibitions. 2. Art, Modern—20th century—Philadelphia—Exhibitions. 3. Artists—Pennsylvania—Philadelphia. I. Title.

PHOENIX, Ariz. Art Museum. 704.94'9'9178
Cowboy artists of America, 1973. Eighth annual exhibition, Sept. 14-Nov. 4, 1973. Flagstaff, Northland Press [1973] 80 p. illus. (part col.) 24 cm. [N6512.P48 1973] 74-153428 ISBN 0-87358-113-X 5.50
1. Art, American—Exhibitions. 2. Art, Modern—20th century—United States. 3. Cowboys in art. I. Title. BIP

PITTSBURGH. Carnegie Institute. Museum of Art. 709'.73'074014886
Forerunners of American abstraction; painters: Charles Demuth, Arthur G. Dove, John Marin, Georgia O'Keefe, Charles Sheeler, Joseph Stella; sculptors: John B. Flannagan, John Storrs. [Pittsburgh, 1971 or 2] 1 v. (unpaged) illus. (part col.) 22 cm. Catalog of an exhibition held Nov. 18, 1971-Jan. 9, 1972. Includes bibliography. [N6512.P5] 72-198012
1. Art, American—Exhibitions. 2. Art, Modern—20th century—United States. I. Title.

POMEROY, Ralph, 1926- 730'.973'074014966
Soft art. [Trenton, New Jersey State Museum, 1969] [39] p. illus. 22 cm. "[Catalog of a loan exhibition] organized by Ralph Pomeroy, March 1-April 27, 1969, New Jersey State Museum, Cultural Center, Trenton." [N6512.P6] 78-627609
1. Art, American—Exhibitions. 2. Art, Modern—20th century—U.S. I. New Jersey. State Museum, Trenton. II. Title.

PORTLAND, Or. Art Museum. 709'.79
The West Coast now; current work from the western seaboard. [Exhibition] Feb. 9 through Mar. 6, 1968. [Portland, 1968] 1 v. (unpaged) illus. 16 cm. [N6525.P67] 68-6382
1. Art, American—Exhibitions. 2. Art, American—The West. I. Title.

PRENDERGAST, Charles E., 1868-1948. 709'.24
The art of Charles Prendergast, By Richard J. Wattenmaker. [Exhibition: Museum of Fine Arts, Boston, October 2-November 3, 1968; Rutgers University Art Gallery, New Brunswick, New Jersey, November 17-December 22, 1968; The Phillips Collection, Washington, D.C., January 11-February 16, 1969. New Brunswick] Rutgers University Art Gallery, 1968. 118 p. illus. (part col.) 19 cm. (University Art Gallery bulletin, v. 2, no. 1) [N722.A3 vol. 2, no. 1] 68-9480
1. Wattenmaker, Richard J. II. Boston. Museum of Fine Arts. III. Phillips Collection, Washington, D.C. IV. Title. V. Series: Rutgers University, New Brunswick, N.J. University Art Gallery. Bulletin, v. 2, no. 1

QUEENS Museum. 759.3'0973'0740147243
Sons & others : women artists see men : [exhibition] March 15-April 27, 1975, the Queens Museum ... Flushing, N.Y. Flushing : The Museum, [1975] [24] p. : chiefly ill. ; 21 cm. Catalog. [N6512.Q43 1975] 75-313527
1. Art, American—Exhibitions. 2. Art, Modern—20th century—United States—Exhibitions. 3. Women artists—United States. 4. Men in art. I. Title.

RECENT works by 709'.794'91
Master of Fine Arts graduates of UCSB. Juror: Gerald Nordland. [Santa Barbara, Santa Barbara Museum of Art, 1974] [72] p. illus. 28 cm. Exhibition held May 11-June 9, 1974 at the Santa Barbara Museum of Art. [N6512.R38] 74-180240
1. California. University, Santa Barbara. Dept. of Art—Alumni. 2. Art, American—Exhibitions. 3. Art, Modern—20th century—United States. I. Nordland, Gerald. II. California. University, Santa Barbara. III. Santa Barbara, Calif. Museum of Art.

RHODE Island School of Design, Providence. Museum of Art. 759.13'074'01452
The Albert Pilavin Collection: twentieth-century American art. [Exhibition] Museum of Art, Rhode Island School of Design, October 7-November 23, 1969. [Providence, 1969] 58 p. illus. (part col.) 23 cm. Catalog. Includes bibliographies. [N6512.R44] 70-19905
1. Pilavin, Albert—Art collections. 2. Art, American—Exhibitions. 3. Art, Modern—20th century—U.S. I. Title. BIP

RHODE Island School of Design, Providence. Museum of Art. 709'.73
The George Waterman Collection. [Exhibition] October 22-November 23, 1969. [Providence, 1969] [55] p. illus. (part col.) 22 cm. Includes bibliographies. [N6512.R45] 78-105670
1. Waterman, George—Art collections. 2. Art, American—Exhibitions. 3. Art, Modern—20th century—U.S.

RIVER Edge Arts Commission. 708.14921
Snow brush '69. [River Edge, N.J., 1969] [32] p. illus. 19 x 19 cm. Cover title. Catalog of an exhibition held Feb. 17-21, 1969, at River Dell Senior High. [N6530.N6R5] 71-20485
1. Art, American—Exhibitions. 2. Artists, American—New Jersey. I. Title.

RYAN, Eric. 736'.4
Eric Ryan: recent works, 1966-1967. [Hamilton? N.Y., 1967] [8] p. (chiefly illus.) 25 cm. Catalogue of an exhibition held at the Charles A. Dana Creative Arts Center, Colgate University, Hamilton, N.Y., Sept. 29-Oct. 22, 1967. [NK9798.R9A46] 68-4699
I. Charles A. Dana Creative Arts Center.

SACRAMENTO 709'.73'0740194
sampler 1. [Sacramento, Calif., 1972] 36 p. illus. (part. col.) 28 cm. Exhibition at the E. B. Crocker Art Gallery, Sacramento, Calif., April 1 - May 7, 1972, and the Oakland Museum, Oakland, Calif., May 23 - July 2, 1972. [N6535.S27S23] 72-198393
1. Art, American—Exhibitions. 2. Art, Modern—20th century—Sacramento, Calif. I. Crocker Art Gallery, Sacramento, Calif. II. Oakland Musuem.

ST. Louis. City Art Museum. 709.77
Mississippi panorama; the life and landscape of the Father of Waters and its great tributary, the Missouri; v. ... 188 illustrations of paintings, drawings, prints, photographs, bank notes, river boat models, steamboat appurtenances and the Dickeson-Egan giant moving panorama of the Mississippi. Edited with an introd. by Perry T. Rathbone. [New and rev. ed.] St. Louis City Art Museum [distributed by the Caledonia Press, 1950] 288 p. illus., col. plates, map. 26 cm. Contents.. -- Staging "This gorgeous panorama." -- Character and history of the Mississippi, by C. van Ravenswaay. -- The art of the Mississippi, by P. T. Rathbone. -- Illustrations, notes and selected commentary (catalog of exhibition, p. 50-228) prepared by H. S. Leonard. [N5020.S325 1950] 50-13109
1. Art, American — Exhibitions. 2. Mississippi River — Descr. & trav. — Views. 3. Missouri River — Descr. & trave. — Views. I. Rathbone, Perry Townsend, 1911- ed. II. Title.

ST. Petersburg, Fla. Museum of Fine Arts. 709'.73
Transparent and translucent art; an exhibition presented at the Museum of Fine Arts, St. Petersburg, Fla., March 2 through March 28, 1971 and the Jacksonville Art Museum, Jacksonville, Fla., April 8 through May 2, 1971. [St. Petersburg? 1971] 1 v. (unpaged) illus. 28 cm. [N6512.S22] 75-198214
1. Art, American—Exhibitions. 2. Art, Modern—20th century—United States. 3. Light in art. I. Jacksonville Art Museum. II. Title.

SAN Francisco Art Institute. 709'.73'074019461
San Francisco Art Institute centennial exhibition, January 15-February 28, 1971; a juried exhibition of painting, photography, prints, and sculpture exhibited concurrently at: California Palace of the Legion of Honor [and others] [San Francisco, 1971] [35] p. illus. 23 cm. [N6530.C2S2] 73-156730
1. Art, American—Exhibitions. 2. Art, Modern—20th century—California. I. California Palace of the Legion of Honor, San Francisco.

SAN Francisco. Museum of Art. 704.948'2
Contemporary icons : [exhibition] San Francisco Museum of Art, December 10-

SUBJECT INDEX

ART, AMERICAN—EXHIBITIONS.

January 19, 1975 / David Best ... [et al.]. [San Francisco : The Museum, 1975] [16] p. : ill. ; 18 cm. Catalog. [N7904.S36 1975] 74-29129
1. Art, American—Exhibitions. 2. Art, Modern—20th century—United States—Exhibitions. 3. Christian art and symbolism. I. Best, David, 1945- II. Title.

SAN Francisco. Museum of Art. 709'.73
The Levi Strauss Collection. [San Francisco, c1974] [16] p. (chiefly illus.) 18 x 23 cm. Catalog of an exhibition held Mar. 15-Apr. 14, 1974. [N6487.S2S257 1974] 74-75999
1. Levi Strauss and Company—Art collections. 2. Art, American—Exhibitions. 3. Art, Modern—20th century—United States. I. Title.

SAN Francisco. Museum of Art. 709'.73'074019461
A third world painting/sculpture exhibition : San Francisco Museum of Art, June 8-July 28, 1974. San Francisco : The Museum, c1974. [12] p., [30] leaves of plates : chiefly ill. ; 22 cm. Issued in portfolio (denim pocket). [N6530.C2S16 1974] 74-80096
1. Art, American—Exhibitions. 2. Art, Modern—20th century—California—Exhibitions. I. Title.

SAN Francisco. Museum of Art. 709'.22
Untitled, 1968 [San Francisco, c1968] [60] p. illus. 26 cm. "[Catalog of] a national invitational exhibition selected by the Annuals Committee of the San Francisco Art Institute in collaboration with the San Francisco Museum of Art [and held at the] San Francisco Museum of Art, 9 November to 29 December 1968." [N6512.S254] 74-7032
1. Art, American—Exhibitions. 2. Art, Modern—20th century—U.S. I. San Francisco Art Institute. II. Title.

SANTA Barbara, Calif. Museum of Art. 709'.73'074019777
The Seattle show : [exhibition] Santa Barbara Museum of Art, May 9-June 22, 1975. Santa Barbara, Calif. : The Museum, [1975] [24] p. : chiefly ill. ; 21 cm. Five hundred copies printed. [N6512.S258 1975] 75-15255
1. Art, American—Exhibitions. 2. Art, Modern—20th century—United States—Exhibitions. 3. Art—Collectors and collecting—Seattle. I. Title.

SAO Paulo 9, United States of America: 709'.73 Edward Hopper and Environment U.S.A., 1957-1967. With essays by William C. Seitz and Lloyd Goodrich. Washington, Published for the National Collection of Fine Arts by the Smithsonian Institution Press [1967] xvi, 165 p. illus. (part col.), ports. 26 cm. English and Portuguese. Catalogs of the 2 parts of the U.S. exhibit shown at the 9th Bienal of the Museu de Arte Moderna, Sao Paulo, Sept 22, 1967-Jan. 8, 1968. Includes bibliographies. [N6512.S26] 67-29477
1. Art, American—Exhibitions. 2. Art, Modern—20th century—Exhibitions. I. Seitz, William Chapin. II. Goodrich, Lloyd, 1897- III. Smithsonian Institution. National Collection of Fine Arts. IV. Sao Paulo, Brazil (City) Museu de Arte Moderna. V. Title: Environment U.S.A., 1957-1967.

SEATTLE. Art Museum. 704.94'9'9780074018956
Annual exhibition of Northwest artists. [Seattle] v. illus. 23 cm. [N6525.S4] 68-422
1. Art, American—Exhibitions. 2. Artists, American—Northwestern States. I. Title.

SERGER, Frederick, 1889- 759.13
Frederick Serger: life & work. Text by George Stiles. Photography by O. E. Nelson. New York, Schoeman Galleries, 1962. 151 p. illus. (part col.) ports. 26 cm. [ND237.S439S7] 62-21417
I. Stiles, George Edward, 1914- II. Title.

7 artists : 709'.73'07401471 Dine, Fahlstrom, Kelly, Marisol, Oldenburg, Segal, Weselmann. [New York? 1969] 1 v. (unpaged) illus., ports. 28 cm. Catalog of the exhibition held at Sidney Janis Gallery, May 1-31, 1969. [N6512.S4] 71-198193
1. Art, American—Exhibitions. 2. Art, Modern—20th century—U.S. I. Sidney Janis Gallery.

SIX visions: Ronald Cohen, Ann McCoy, Richard Nonas, Katherine Porter, Douglas Sanderson, Pat Steir. 709'.73 [Philadelphia, Institute of Contemporary Art, University of Pennsylvania, 1973] [44] p. illus. 20 x 23 cm. Catalog of the exhibition shown at the Institute of Contemporary Art, University of Pennsylvania, Oct. 10-Nov. 25, 1973. [N6512.S59] 74-154473 ISBN 0-88454-012-X 4.00 (pbk.)
1. Art, American—Exhibitions. 2. Art, Modern—20th century—United States. 3. Visual perception. I. Pennsylvania. University. Institute of Contemporary Art.

SMITH, Andre, 1880-1959. 760'.0924
Andre Smith, 1880-1959; a retrospective exhibition, originated at the Andrew Dickson White Museum of Art, Cornell University 1968 [Winston-Salem, N.C., Printed by Hunter Pub. Co., 1968?] 47 p. illus. (part col.) 31 cm. Exhibition shown at the New Britain Museum of American Art, Nov. 22-Dec. 31, 1969. [N6537.S6A42] 74-253264
1. Cornell University. Andrew Dickson White Museum of Art. II. New Britain Museum of American Art. III. Title.

SOLOMON R. Guggenheim Museum, New York. 709'.73'07401471
10 independents: an artist-initiated exhibition. [New York, Solomon R. Guggenheim Foundation, 1972] [20] p. illus. 22 cm. "Exhibition 72/1." [N6512.S64] 76-186802
1. Art, American—Exhibitions. 2. Art, Modern—20th century—U.S. I. Title.

SOLOMON R. Guggenheim Museum, New York. 709'.73'07401471
Nine artists : Theodoron awards / The Solomon R. Guggenheim Museum. New York : Solomon R. Guggenheim Foundation, c1977. 36 p. : ill. ; 22 cm. "Exhibition 77/2." L.C. copy incomplete: insert (checklist) wanting. [N6512.S65 1977] 77-71597 ISBN 0-89207-008-0
1. Art, American—Exhibitions. 2. Art, Modern—20th century—United States—Exhibitions. 3. Art—Awards—Exhibitions. I. Theodoron (Foundation) II. Title. BIP

SOLOMON R. Guggenheim Museum, New York. 759.13'074'01471
Ten young artists: Theodoron awards. [Exhibition] the Solomon R. Guggenheim Museum, New York. [New York, Solomon R. Guggenheim Foundation, 1971] [24] p. illus. 22 cm. [N6512.S65] 77-178872
1. Art, American—Exhibitions. 2. Art, Modern—20th century—United States. 3. Art—Competitions. I. Theodoron (Foundation) II. Title.

SOLOMON R. Guggenheim Museum, New York. 709'.73'07401471
Twentieth-century American drawing : three avant-garde generations : [exhibition], Solomon R. Guggenheim Museum, New York. New York : Solomon R. Guggenheim Foundation, 1976. 127 p. : ill. (some col.) ; 26 cm. "Exhibition 76/1." Includes index. [N6512.S65 1976] 75-45506 ISBN 0-89207-001-3 pbk. : 6.50
1. Art, American—Exhibitions. 2. Art, Modern—20th century—United States—Exhibitions. I. Title. BIP

SOPHER, Aaron, 1905- 741.973
Aaron Sopher. Introd. by Wilbur Harvey Hunter, Jr. [1st ed.] New York, E. Weyhe [1960] unpaged (chiefly illus.) 20 cm. [NC1075.S7A43] 61-23237
I. Title.

SOUTH Dakota Memorial Art Center. 709'.73
South Dakota biennial exhibition, June 17th-August 26th, 1973. [Brookings, 1973] [16] p. illus. 17 x 21 cm. Catalog. [N6530.S68S68 1973] 74-185086
1. Art, American—Exhibitions. 2. Art, Modern—20th century—South Dakota. I. Title.

SOUTH Station studio show, Saturday and Sunday, October 27 and 28, 1973, 11:00 a.m.-7:00 p.m. 709'.73 [Boston, 1973] 46 p. illus. 18 cm. Catalog of exhibits shown at 655 Atlantic Ave., 90 South St., and 102 South St., Boston, in the studios of the artists. "Sponsored by the Institute of Contemporary Art [and others]" [N6535.B7S75] 73-89864
1. Art, American—Exhibitions. 2. Art, Modern—20th century—Boston. I. Boston. Institute of Contemporary Art.

SPRINGFIELD Art Association, Springfield, Ill. 709'.73
Images on paper. [Catalog of an exhibition] Springfield Art Association, February 9-March 10, 1974. [Springfield, 1974] [22] p. illus. 26 cm. [N6512.S66 1974] 74-76372
1. Art, American—Exhibitions. 2. Art, Modern—20th century—United States. 3. Grotesque in art. I. Title.

STILL life today. 758'.4 [New York, American Federation of Arts, 1970] folder ([8] p.) illus. 21 cm. Catalog of the 1970-71 exhibition circulated by the American Federation of Arts. [N6512.S67] 74-135038
1. Art, American—Exhibitions. 2. Art, Modern—20th century—U.S. 3. Still-life in art. I. American Federation of Arts.

SWEENEY, James Johnson, 1900- 759.13'074'0996931
Signals in the 'sixties. [Exhibition] Oct. 5-Nov. 10, 1968. James Johnson Sweeney, director of the exhibition. [Honolulu, Honolulu Academy of Arts, 1968?] 11, [41] p. illus. 22 cm. [N6512.S9] 70-282941
1. Art, American—Exhibitions. 2. Art, Modern—20th century—U.S. I. Honolulu Academy of Arts. II. Title.

TEXAS painting & sculpture: the 20th century. 709'.764'0740164 [Dallas, Printed by Brodnax Print. Co., 1971] 96 p. illus. 26 cm. Catalogue of an exhibition held at Pollock Galleries, Southern Methodist University, Dallas, Jan. 17-Mar. 7, 1971, and other museums. [N6530.T4T4] 76-198154
1. Art, American—Exhibitions. 2. Art, Modern—20th century—Texas. I. Pollock Galleries.

THREE young collections; 707.4'09794'91 selections from the collections of Donald and Lynn Factor, Dennis and Brooke Hopper, Andre and Dory Previn. [Exhibition] Santa Barbara Museum of Art, Jan. 15-Feb. 26, 1967. [Santa Barbara, Calif., 1967] [38] p. illus. (part col.), ports. 25 cm. [N6512.T45] 71-296467
1. Art, American—Exhibitions. 2. Art, Modern—20th century—United States. 3. Art—Private collections—Los Angeles. I. Santa Barbara, Calif. Museum of Art.

TWO aspects of illusion: Paul Gedeohn/Michael Mazur. 709'.73'07401471 Introd. and acknowledgment by Elayne H. Varian. [New York, c1971] [13] p. (incl. cover) illus. 28 cm. Catalogue of an exhibition held Nov. 19, 1970, to Jan. 15, 1971, in the Contemporary Wing of the Finch College Museum of Art. [N6512.T9] 74-184845
1. Art, American—Exhibitions. 2. Art, Modern—20th century—United States. 3. Optical illusions. I. Gedeohn, Paul. II. Mazur, Michael, 1935- III. Finch College, New York. Museum of Art. Contemporary Study Wing.

THE Tyler show : 759.13 working women artists from Tyler School of Art : an exhibition held by the Department of Special Collections, Samuel Paley Library, Temple University, April 1974 / with a new essay by Barrows Dunham. Philadelphia : Samuel Paley Library, [1974?] [72] p., [1] leaf of plates : ill. ; 33 cm. "Presented in conjunction with Philadelphia Focuses on Women in the Visual Arts." Compiled by Ann Bagnell. "Twenty-five works from 'The Tyler show' ... were selected for photographs in this catalog." "26 signed copies, lettered A to Z." T. [N6512.T95] 75-333209
1. Art, American—Exhibitions. 2. Art, Modern—20th century—United States—Exhibitions. 3. Women artists—United States. I. Dunham, Barrows, 1905- II. Bagnell, Ann. III. Tyler School of Art. IV. Samuel Paley Library. Dept. of Special Collections.

UNITED Bank of Denver. 704.94'9'917803
Western legacy; exhibition of western art, January 12-February 3, 1973. [Boulder, Colo., Peschel Publications, c1972] [36] p. illus. (part col.) 21 x 28 cm. "Presented by United Bank of Denver and Sandra Wilson Galleries—Santa Fe." [N6525.U54] 72-96947
1. Art, American—Exhibitions. 2. The West in art. 3. Artists, American—The West. I. Sandra Wilson Galleries. II. Title.

UNITED States. Bureau of Reclamation. 759.13
The American artist and water reclamation; a selection of paintings from the Collection of the Bureau of Reclamation. [Washington, U.S. Govt. Print. Off., 1973] 73 p. (chiefly illus.) 24 x 30 cm. Catalog of an exhibition circulated by the Traveling Exhibition Service, Smithsonian Institution. [N6512.U47 1973] 73-603115 1.75
1. United States. Bureau of Reclamation—Art collections. 2. Art, American—Exhibitions. 3. Art, Modern—20th century—United States. 4. Water reuse in art. I. Smithsonian Institution. Traveling Exhibition Service. II. Title.

U. S. Office of the United States Commissioner General, Brussels Universal and International Exhibition, 1958. 707.4
American art: four exhibitions. L'art americain: quatre expositions. Amerikaanse kunst: vier exposities. Brussels Universal and Intl. Exhibition, 1958, 17 April to October 18. [dist. New York, Citadel, 1963, c.1958] 177p. illus. 22cm. 63-24050 1.25 pap.,
1. Art, American—Exhibitions. I. Brussels, Exposition universelle et internationale, 1958. II. Title.

VAN DER MARCK, Jan, 1829- 709'.73
American art: third quarter century. Text by Jan Van der Marck. Seattle Art Museum Pavilion, August 22-October 14, 1973. [Seattle, Contemporary Art Council of the Seattle Art Museum, 1973] 138 p. illus. (part col.) 28 cm. Includes bibliographical references. [N6512.V36] 73-86482
1. Art, American—Exhibitions. 2. Art, Modern—20th century—Exhibitions. I. Seattle. Art Museum. II. Title.

VARIAN, Elayne H. 709'.73'07401471
Art in process IV. Prepared by Elayne H. Varian, with statements by the artists, Special photographic asistance, Dorothy Reskind. Exhibition December 11, 1969-January 26, 1970. New York [1969?] [32] p. illus., ports. 22 x 29 cm. [N6512.V37] 72-176346
1. Art, American—Exhibitions. 2. Art, Modern—20th century—United States. 3. Art—Philosophy. I. Finch College, New York. Museum of Art. Contemporary Study Wing. II. Beskind, Dorothy, illus. III. Title.

VIRGINIA Museum of Fine Arts, Richmond. 709'.73
Virginia artists, 1973. [Richmond, 1973] [22] p. illus. 18 cm. Cover title. Catalog of an exhibition held at the Virginia Museum of Fine Arts, May 7-June 3, 1973. [N6530.V8V55 1973] 74-185039
1. Art, American—Exhibitions. 2. Art, Modern—20th century—Virginia. I. Title.

VYTLACIL, Vaclav, 1893- 759.13
Vaclav Vytlacil : paintings & constructions from 1930, with Boris, Bourgeois, Boxer, Day, Garel, Hess, Krushenick, Leiber, Minewski, Moy, Ponce de Leon, Rauschenberg, Rosenquist, Smith, Stapleton, Stefanelli, Tania, Twombly : [exhibition] November 16, 1975, to January 25, 1976, Montclair Art Museum, Montclair, New Jersey. [Montclair, N.J. : Montclair Art Museum], c1975. 50 p. : ill. ; 26 cm. [ND237.V97M66] 76-351650
1. Vytlacil, Vaclav, 1893- 2. Art, American—Exhibitions. 3. Art, Modern—20th century—United States—Exhibitions. I. Montclair, N.J. Art Museum. II. Title.

WALKER Art Center, Minneapolis. 709.73
Biennial of paintings, prints and sculpture from the Upper Midwest. Minneapolis. v. illus. 27cm. Exhibition for 1956 includes the center's Six-state sculpture show. [N6512.W3] 57-24445
1. Art, American—Exhibitions. I. Title.

WALKER Art Center, Minneapolis. 709'.73
Invitation 1974: Joe Breidel, Larry Brown, Carole Fisher, Stuart Nielsen [and] Tom Rose; [catalogue of] an exhibition organized by Walker Art Center, 12 May-23 June, 1974. Essays by Dean Swanson. Biographical commentaries by Gwen Lerner. [Minneapolis, 1974] 1 portfolio (6 pieces) illus. 23 cm. [N6512.W32 1974] 74-80989
1. Art, American—Exhibitions. 2. Art, Modern—20th century—United States. I. Swanson, Dean. II. Lerner, Gwen. III. Title.

WALKER Art Center, Minneapolis. 759.13'074'0176579
Painting: new options: Bartlett, Benglis, Davis, Holland, LeWitt, Marden, Young. Introd. by Dean Swanson. Essays by Philip Larson. [Minneapolis, 1972] 26 p. illus. (part. col.) 28 cm. "An exhibition organized by Walker Art Center, Minneapolis, Minnesota, 23 April-4 June 1972." Includes bibliographies. [N6512.W315] 72-77488
1. Art, American—Exhibitions. 2. Art, Modern—20th century—United States. I. Larson, Philip. II. Title.

WALKER Art Center, Minneapolis. 735.73 927.3
Theodore Roszak [by] H. H. Arnason. Minneapolis, Walker Art Center in collaboration with the Whitney Museum of American Art, New York [1956] 54 p. illus. (part col.) port. 28 cm. "Catalogue of the exhibition": p. 48-50. Bibliography: p. 54. [N6537.R6W3] 57-925
1. Roszak, Theodore. 2. Art, American — Exhibitions. I. Arnason, H. H. II. Title.

WARD-NASSE Gallery. 709'.73
Salon, 1971-2 [New York, 1971] 1 v. (chiefly illus.) 29 cm. Cover title. Catalog of an exhibition. [N6512.W333 1971] 73-153170
1. Art, American—Exhibitions. 2. Art, Modern—20th century—United States. I. Title.

WARD-NASSE Gallery. 709'.73
Salon, 1972-73 [New York, 1972?] [126] p. (chiefly illus.) 29 cm. Cover title. [N6512.W333 1972] 74-156542
1. Art, American—Exhibitions. 2. Art, Modern—20th century—United States. I. Title.

WARD-NASSE Gallery. 709'.73
Salon, 1972-73 [New York, 1973?] 1 v. (chiefly illus.) 29 cm. Cover title. Catalogue of an exhibition. [N6512.W333 1973] 74-155961
1. Art, American—Exhibitions. 2. Art, Modern—20th century—United States. I. Title.

WASHINGTON, D.C. Gallery of Modern Art. 762'.0973
Art for embassies, selected from the Woodward Foundation Collection; an exhibition organized by the Washington Gallery of Modern Art, 30 September-5 November 1967. [Washington? c1967] [24] p. illus. (part col.) 31 x 14 cm. [N6512.W34] 67-29965
1. Art, American—Exhibitions. 2. Art, Modern—20th century—U.S. I. Woodward Foundation. II. Title.

WELLS, Cady, 1904-1954. 759.13
Cady Wells, a retrospective exhibition. [1st ed.] Albuquerque, University of New Mexico Art Museum, 1967. 23 p. illus. 26 cm. Held at University Art Museum, the University of New Mexico, September 10-October 15 and other institutions. Catalog by Kate C. Duncan is based on a master's thesis, University of New Mexico. Bibliography: p. 23. [ND237.W42D8] 67-65520
I. Duncan, Kate C. II. New Mexico. University. Art Museum. III. Title.

WEST Coast, 1945-1969. 709'.794
[Pasadena? 1969] 1 portfolio ([10] p., 25 plates, ports.) 26 cm. Catalog of a loan exhibition held at the Pasadena Art Museum, Nov. 24, 1969-Jan. 18, 1970, and at other art museums. Includes bibliographies. [N6530.C2W4] 70-98463
1. Art, American—Exhibitions. 2. Art, Modern—20th century—California. I. Pasadena, Calif. Art Museum.

WHITNEY Museum of American Art, New York. 709'.73
1975 biennial exhibition : [contemporary American art. [New York] : Whitney Museum of American Art, [1975] ca. 150 p. : ill. ; 21 cm. [N6512.W532 1975] 74-34505 pbk. : 5.00
1. Art, American—Exhibitions. 2. Art, Modern—20th century—United States. I. Title. II. Title: Contemporary American art.

WHITNEY Museum of American Art, New York. 709.73
Between the fairs; 25 years of American art, 1939-1964, by John I. H. Baur [associate director] With a foreword by Lloyd Goodrich. New York, Published for the Whitney Museum of American Art by F. A. Praeger [1964] 90 p. (chiefly illus. (part col.)) 27 cm. "The Whitney Museum's exhibition...and the present publication which grew out of it, are designed to present a survey of this vital and varied period, as represented by some of its leading figures." [N6512.W463] 64-23510
1. Art, American—Exhibitions. I. Bauer, John Ireland Howe, 1909- II. Title.

WHITNEY Museum of American Art, New York. 759.13
Contemporary American art; 1973 biennial exhibition. New York [1973] 83 p. illus. 21 cm. [N6512.W532 1973] 73-175526
1. Art, American—Exhibitions. 2. Art, Modern—20th century—United States. I. Title.

WHITNEY Museum of American Art, New York. 709.73
Forty artists under forty, from the collection of the Whitney Museum of American Art [by] Lloyd Goodrich and Edward Bryant. New York, Praeger [1962] [52] p. illus. (6 col.) 20 x 26 cm. (Books that matter) Based on an exhibition sponsored by the New York State Council on the Arts and circulated by the American Federation of Arts. [N6512.W468] 62-19111
1. Art, American — Exhibitions. 2. Artists, American. I. Goodrich, Lloyd, 1897- II. Bryant, Edward. III. New York (State) State Council on the Arts. IV. American Federation of Arts. V. Title.

WHITNEY Museum of American Art, New York. 759.13
Forty artists under forty, from the collection of the Whitney Museum of American Art. [Exhibition] July 23-Sept. 16, 1962. Sponsored by the New York State Council of the Arts. Circulated by the American Federation of Arts. [Biographical notes edited by Edward Bryant. New York, 1962] [52] p. illus. (part col.) 19 x 26 cm. Foreword by Lloyd Goodrich. [N6512.W4682] 62-51153
1. Art, American — Exhibitions. 2. Artists, American. I. Goodrich, Lloyd, 1897- II. Bryant, Edward. III. New York (State) State Council on the Arts. IV. American Federation of Arts. V. Title.

WHITNEY Museum of American Art, New York. 701.16
Nature in abstraction; the relation of abstract painting and sculpture to nature in twentieth-century American art. [Text by] John I. H. Baur [curator] [Artists' biographies by Rosalind Irvine, associate curator] New York, Macmillan, 1958. 85 p. illus. (part col.) 28 cm. "The result of an exhibition held at the Whitney Museum and elsewhere from January 1958 to February 1959." [N6512.W49] 58-14620
1. Art, American—Exhibitions. 2. Artists, American. 3. Art, Abstract. 4. Nature (Aesthetics) I. Baur, John Ireland Howe, 1909- ed. II. Title.

WHITNEY Museum of American Art, New York. 709'.73'07401471
Selections from the Lawrence H. Bloedel Bequest and related works from the permanent collection of the Whitney Museum of American Art ; [checklist / compiled by Jennifer Russell, assistant curator]. New York : The Museum, c1977. 55 p. : ill. ; 26 cm. Checklist of an exhibition held Apr. 5-June 19, 1977. [N6512.W532 1977b] 77-151746 ISBN 0-87427-023-5
1. Bloedel, Lawrence Hotchkiss, 1902-1976—Art collections. 2. Art, American—Exhibitions. 3. Art, Modern—20th century—United States—Exhibitions. I. Russell, Jennifer. II. Title: Selections from the Lawrence H. Bloedel bequest ...

WHITNEY Museum of American Art. New York. 709'.43'07401471
20th-century American art from Friends' collections. New York : Whitney Museum of American Art, [1977] [8] p. ; 20 cm. Cover title. Catalog of an exhibition, Whitney Museum of American art, July 27-Sept. 27, 1977. [N6512.W532 1977d] 77-374503
1. Art, American—Exhibitions. 2. Art, Modern—20th century—United States—Exhibitions. I. Friends of the Whitney Museum of American Art. II. Title.

WHITNEY Museum of American Art, New York. 759.13'074'01471
The Whitney Studio Club and American art, 1900-1932 : [exhibition, Whitney Museum of American Art, New York, May 23-September 3, 1975]. New York : The Museum, [1975] 23 p. : ill. ; 26 cm. Cover title. "Catalogue of the exhibition:" p. 22-23. [N6512.W532 1975b] 75-325749
1. Whitney Studio Club. 2. Art, American—Exhibitions. 3. Art, Modern—20th century—United States—Exhibitions. I. Title.

WIGHT, Frederick Stallknecht, 1902- 709'.22
Transparency, reflection, light, space: four artists. An exhibition arranged by Peter Alexander [and others. Los Angeles, UCLA Art Galleries, 1971] 140 p. illus., ports. 16 cm. Interviews of Frederick S. Wight with 4 artists: Peter Alexander, Larry Bell, Robert Irwin, and Craig Kauffman. "Presented by the UCLA Art Galleries, January 11-February 14, 1971." Includes bibliographies. [N6512.W56] 79-198215
1. Art, American—Exhibitions. 2. Art, Modern—20th century—U.S. 3. Art—Philosophy. I. Alexander, Peter, 1939- II. California. University. University at Los Angeles. Art Galleries. III. Title.

WYANT, Alexander Helwig, 1836-1892. 759.13
Alexander Helwig Wyant, 1836-1892 [Salt Lake City, Printed by Paragon Press, 1968] [38] p. illus., ports. 23 cm. Exhibition held Mar. 3-31, 1968, at the Utah Museum of Fine Arts, University of Utah. Bibliography: p. [18]. [ND237.W9U8] 68-63810
I. Utah Museum of Fine Arts.

Art, American—Exhibitions—Indexes.

NAYLOR, Maria. 709'.73
The National Academy of Design exhibition record, 1861-1900. New York, Kennedy Galleries, 1973. 2 v. (v, 1075 p.) 23 cm. On cover: Exhibition of the National Academy, 1861-1900. Continues the National Academy of Design exhibition record, 1826-1860, which is entered under New York (City). National Academy of Design. [N6510.N38] 73-174225 60.00
1. Art, American—Exhibitions—Indexes. 2. Art, Modern—19th century—United States—Indexes. 3. Artists—United States—Directories. I. New York (City). National Academy of Design. National Academy of Design exhibition record, 1826-1860.

Art, American—History.

BENJAMIN, Samuel Greene Wheeler, 1837-1914. 709'.73
Art in America : a critical and historical sketch / by S. G. W. Benjamin. New York : Garland Pub., 1976. p. cm. (The Art experience in late nineteenth-century America) Reprint of the 1880 ed. published by Harper, New York. [N6505.B5 1976] 75-28872 ISBN 0-8240-2232-7 lib.bdg. : 40.00
1. Art, American—History. 2. Art, Colonial—United States—History. 3. Art, Modern—19th century—United States—History. I. Title. II. Series.

BROWN, Milton Wolf, 1911- 709'.73
History of American art to 1900 : painting, sculpture, architecture / Milton W. Brown. New York : H. N. Abrams, [1975] p. cm. Includes index. Bibliography: p. [N6505.B76] 72-99241 ISBN 0-8109-0207-9
1. Art, American—History. 2. Art, Colonial—United States. 3. Art, Modern—19th century—United States. I. Title.

DORRA, Henri, 1924- 709.73
The American muse. Foreword by Hermann Warner Williams, Jr. New York, Viking Press [1961] 163 p. illus. (part col.) 29 cm. (A Studio book) Based on The American muse, parallel trends in literature and art, an exhibition held at the Corcoran Gallery of Art, April 4-May 17, 1959. [N6505.D65] 61-6664
1. Art, American—History. 2. American literature. 3. Art and literature. I. Corcoran Gallery of Art, Washington, D. C. II. Title.

DREPPERD, Carl William, 1898-1956. 709'.73
American pioneer arts & artists. With foreword by Rockwell Kent. Watkins Glen, N.Y., Century House [1972? c1942] 168 p. illus. 24 cm. (Basic books in American arts & crafts) Bibliography: p. 163-167. [N6510.5.P7D7 1972] 70-121195
1. Art, American—History. 2. Art, Modern—19th century—United States. 3. Primitivism in art. I. Title.

GOODRICH, Lloyd, 1897- 709.73
Pioneers of modern art in America; the decade of the Armory show, 1910-1920. New York, Pub. for Whitney Mus. of Amer. Art by Praeger [c.]1963. 94p. illus. (pt. col.) 24cm. 63-13597 6.00
1. Art, American—Hist. 2. Art. Modern—20th cent. I. Title. II. Title: The Armory show.

GREEN, Samuel M 709.73
American art, a historical survey [by] Samuel M. Green. New York, Ronald Press [1966] xi, 706 p. illus. 26 cm. Includes bibliographies. [N6505.G73] 66-16844
1. Art, American—Hist. 2. Architecture—U.S. I. Title.

HARRIS, Neil, 1938- 709.73
The artist in American society; the formative years, 1790-1860. New York, G. Braziller [1966] xvi, 432 p. illus., ports. 22 cm. Bibliography: p. 317-324. [N6507.H27] 66-25399
1. Art, American—History. 2. Artists—Psychology. 3. Art and society. I. Title. BIP

KRASNOFF, Robert Marshall, 1949-1970. 741.9'73
The art of Robert M. Krasnoff. [Compiled and edited by the family and friends of Robert M. Krasnoff. 1st ed. Kennett Square, Pa., Printed by KNA Press, 1972] 77 p. illus. 29 cm. [N6537.K72A42] 72-85608
I. Title.

LA FOLLETTE, Suzanne. 709'.73
Art in America. New York, Harper & Row [1968, c1929] xx, 361 p. illus. 22 cm. (J. & J. Harper editions) [N6505.L3 1968] 72-2187
1. Art, American—History. I. Title.

LYNES, Russell, 1910- 709'.73
The art-makers of nineteenth-century America. [1st ed.] New York, Atheneum, 1970. xii, 514 p. illus., ports. 27 cm. Bibliography: p. [493]-498. [N6510.L95 1970] 77-117338 22.50
1. Art, American—History. 2. Art, Modern—19th century—U.S. I. Title.

MCCOUBREY, John W., ed. 709.73
American art. 1700-1960: sources and documents. Englewood Cliffs, N.J., Prentice [c.1965] xi, 226p. facsim. 23cm. (Sources and documents in the hist. of art ser.) [N6505.M26] 65-23063 3.95 pap.,
1. Art. American—Hist.—Sources. I. Title. II. Series.

MCLANATHAN, Richard B. K. 709'.73
The American tradition in the arts [by] Richard McLanathan. [1st ed.] New York, Harcourt, Brace & World [1968] xv, 492 p. illus. 28 cm. Bibliography: p. 471-478. [N6505.M28] 65-21032 12.50
1. Art, American—History. 2. Art—Philosophy. I. Title. BIP

SUBJECT INDEX

ART, AMERICAN—YEARBOOKS.

MCLANATHAN, Richard B. K. 709'.73
Art in America; a brief history [by] Richard McLanathan. [1st American ed. New York] Harcourt Brace Jovanovich [1973] 216 p. 189 illus. (part col.) 21 cm. (The Harbrace history of art) Bibliography: p. 211-212. [N6505.M277 1973] 72-92358 ISBN 0-15-108470-X 6.95
1. Art, American—History. I. Title.
Pbk. 3.95; ISBN 0-15-503466-9. BIP

MELLQUIST, Jerome. 709'.73
The emergence of an American art. Port Washington, N.Y., Kennikat Press [1969, c1942] xvi, 421 p. illus. 24 cm. (Essay and general literature index reprint series) [N6512.M4 1969] 74-86571
1. Art, American—History. 2. Art, Modern—20th century—U.S. I. Title.

MENDELOWITZ, Daniel Marcus. 709.73
A history of American art [by] Daniel M. Mendelowitz. 2d ed. New York, Holt, Rinehart and Winston [1970] x, 522 p. 695 illus., col. plates. 29 cm. "Charles Pierre L'Enfant plan for Washington, D.C., c[irca] 1792" on lining papers. Bibliography: p. 510-512. [N6505.M4 1970] 71-111303
1. Art, American—History. I. Title.

MYRON, Robert. 709'.73
Art in America from colonial days through the nineteenth century [by] Robert Myron [and] Abner Sundell. [New York] Crowell-Collier Press [1969] 186 p. illus. 25 cm. Bibliography: p. [183] [N6505.M9 1969] 69-10347
1. Art, American—History. I. Sundell, Abner, joint author. II. Title.

PODOLINI-VOLKMAN, Arthur, 1891-1945. 759.36
The art of Arthur Podolini-Volkman. A foreword by Wallace S. Baldinger. Eugene, Or., 1962. unpaged (chiefly illus.) 28 cm. [ND538.P58A4] 63-617
I. Title.

ROSE, Barbara. 709'.73
American art since 1900; a critical history. New York, F. A. Praeger [1967] 320 p. illus. (part col.) 22 cm. Bibliography: p. 298-300. [N6512.R63] 67-20743
1. Art, American—History. I. Title.

ROSE, Barbara. 709'.73
American art since 1900. Rev. and expanded ed. New York, Praeger [1975] 320 p. illus. 21 cm. (Praeger world of art series) Bibliography: p. 289-292. [N6512.R63 1975] 72-83563 ISBN 0-275-43900-3 12.50; 6.95 (pbk.).
1. Art, American—History. 2. Art, Modern—20th century—United States. I. Title.

WILMERDING, John. 709'.73
American art / John Wilmerding. Harmondsworth, Eng. ; New York : Penguin Books, 1976. xxiii, 322 p., [97] leaves of plates : ill. (1 col.) ; 27 cm. (The Pelican history of art) Includes index. Bibliography: p. 269-302. [N6505.W54] 75-18755 ISBN 0-14-056040-8 : 40.00
1. Art, American—History. I. Title. II. Series.

Art, American—History—Addresses, essays, lectures.

ROSE, Barbara, comp. 709'.73
Readings in American art, 1900-1975 / edited by Barbara Rose. Rev. ed. New York : Praeger, 1975. p. cm. Published in 1968 under title: Readings in American art since 1900. Includes index. Bibliography: p. [N6512.R64 1975] 74-17891 ISBN 0-275-46710-4 : 12.50. ISBN 0-275-89120-8 pbk. : 5.95
1. Art, American—History—Addresses, essays, lectures. 2. Art, Modern—20th century—United States—Addresses, essays, lectures. I. Title.

ROSE, Barbara, comp. 709.73
Readings in American art since 1900; a documentary survey New York, F. A. Praeger [1968] xiv, 224 p. illus., ports. 22 cm. (Praeger world of art series) Bibliography: p. 209-224. [N6512.R64] 68-16421
1. Art, American—History—Addresses, essays, lectures. 2. Art, Modern—20th century—United States—Addresses, essays, lectures. I. Title. II. Title: American art since 1900.

Art, American—History—Juvenile literature.

BATTERBERRY, Ariane Ruskin. 709'.73
The Pantheon story of American art for young people / Ariane Ruskin Batterberry and Michael Batterberry ; introd. by Tom Armstrong. 1st ed. New York : Pantheon Books, c1976. 157 p. : ill. (some col.) ; 33 cm. A history of art in the United States which includes the contributions of the Indians and early settlers and discusses art movements and important individual artists in the eighteenth, nineteenth, and twentieth centuries. [N6505.B37 1976] 75-22249 ISBN 0-394-82842-9 : 14.95
1. Art, American—History—Juvenile literature. I. Batterberry, Michael, joint author. II. Title.

GLUBOK, Shirley. 709'.73
The art of America in the Gilded Age. Designed by Gerard Nook. New York, Macmillan [1974] 48 p. illus. 26 cm. Surveys the art, architecture, and crafts of the United States from the end of the Civil War to the beginning of the twentieth century. [N6510.G56] 73-6048 ISBN 0-02-736100-4 6.95
1. Art, American—History—Juvenile literature. I. Title. BIP

GLUBOK, Shirley. 709'.73
The art of the new American nation. Designed by Gerard Nook. New York, Macmillan [1972] 48 p. illus. 26 cm. Discusses how the paintings, architecture, furniture, sculpture, and other visual arts produced from 1776-1826 reflected the way of life in the new American nation. [N6507.G63] 76-160073 6.95
1. Art, American—History—Juvenile literature. I. Title. BIP

Art, American—Illinois—Chicago—Exhibitions.

CROCKER Art Gallery Association. 709'.773'11074019454
West coast '76, the Chicago connection : 1976 invitational exhibition / Crocker Art Gallery Association and E. B. Crocker Art Gallery; Susan Regan McKillop, editor. Sacramento, Calif. : The Gallery, c1976. 89 p. : ill. (some col.) ; 29 cm. Bibliography: p. 84-86. [N6535.C5C76 1976] 76-47748
1. Art, American—Illinois—Chicago—Exhibitions. 2. Art, Modern—20th century—Illinois—Chicago—Exhibitions. I. McKillop, Susan Regan. II. Crocker Art Gallery, Sacramento, Calif. III. Title. IV. Title: The Chicago connection.

Art, American—Indiana—Exhibitions.

MIRAGES of memory 709'.772'074017252
: 200 years of Indiana art : an exhibition ... Indianapolis Museum of Art, November 6, 1976-January 2, 1977, Art Gallery, University of Notre Dame, January 16-March 20, 1977. [s.l. : s.n.], c1977- (South Bend, Ind. : Osthimer) v. : ill. (some col.) ; 28 cm. Catalogue. Includes bibliographies. [N6530.I6M57] 77-153194
1. Art, American—Indiana—Exhibitions. 2. Art—Indiana—Exhibitions. 3. Artists—Indiana—Biography. I. Indianapolis Museum of Art. II. Notre Dame, Ind. University. Art Gallery.

Art, American—Juvenile literature.

GLUBOK, Shirley. 709'.73
The art of America in the early twentieth century. Designed by Gerard Nook. New York, Macmillan [1974] 48 p. illus. 26 cm. Traces the trends in American painting, sculpture, architecture, photography, and crafts from 1900 to the eve of World War II. [N6512.G57] 74-6329 6.95
1. Art, American—Juvenile literature. 2. Art, Modern—20th century—United States—Juvenile literature. I. Title. BIP

GLUBOK, Shirley. 709'.73
The art of America since World War II / by Shirley Glubok designed by Gerard Nook New York : Macmillan, c1976. 47 p. : ill. ; 26 x 26 cm. A survey of American art from 1940 to the present which includes "white writing," action painting, abstract expressionism, op art, pop art, stabiles, and kinetic sculpture. [N6512.G58] 75-34453 ISBN 0-02-736310-4 : 7.95
1. Art, American—Juvenile literature. 2. Art, Modern—20th century—United States—Juvenile literature. I. Title. BIP

Art, American—Minnesota—Catalogs.

COEN, Rena Neumann. 709'.776'0740176579
Painting and sculpture in Minnesota, 1820-1914 / Rena Nuemann Coen. Minneapolis : Published by the University of Minnesota Press for the University Gallery of the University of Minnesota, c1976. xiv, 146 p., [16] leaves of plates : ill. (some col.) ; 27 cm. Also serves as a catalogue for one of the components of the University Gallery's major Bicentennial exhibition, The art and architecture of Minnesota. Includes index. Bibliography: p. 138-139. [N6530.M6C63 1976] 75-27788 ISBN 0-8166-0771-0 : 19.50
1. Art, American—Minnesota—Catalogs. 2. Art, Modern—19th century—Minnesota—Catalogs. 3. Art, Modern—20th century—Minnesota—Catalogs. I. Minnesota. University. University Gallery. II. Title. BIP

Art, American—New England—Exhibitions.

DECORDOVA and Dana Museum and Park, Lincoln, Mass. 709'.74'07401444
By the people, for the people : New England, September 25-November 27, 1977, DeCordova Museum, Lincoln, Massachusetts. Lincoln, Mass. : The Museum, c1977. 92 p. : ill. ; 25 cm. "Catalog and exhibition." Includes bibliographical references. [N8838.D38 1977] 77-88006
1. Federal Art Project—Exhibitions. 2. Art, American—New England—Exhibitions. 3. Art, Modern—20th century—New England—Exhibitions. I. Title.

Art, American—New York (City)—Queens (Borough).

QUEENS Museum. 709'.747'2430740147243
Queens artists 76 : [exhibition] the Queens Museum, November 20, 1976 to January 2, 1977. Flushing, N.Y. : The Museum, c1976. [23] p. : ill. ; 18 x 28 cm. [N6530.N72Q436 1976] 76-151194
1. Art, American—New York (State)—Queens (Borough)—Exhibitions. 2. Art, Modern—20th century—New York (State)—Queens (Borough)—Exhibitions. 3. Artists—New York (State)—Queens (Borough) I. Title.

Art, American—North Carolina—Exhibitions.

NORTH Carolina. Museum of Art, Raleigh. 759.1756
Hobson Pittman: retrospective exhibition, his work since 1920, February 2-March 3, 1963. Raleigh, Author [1963] 96p. illus., ports. 26cm. Bibl. 63-63530 2.00 pap.,
I. Pittman, Hobson, 1900- II. Title.

TWO hundred 709'.756'074015656
years of the visual arts in North Carolina : [catalog of an exhibition] 12 September-24 October 1976. Raleigh : North Carolina Museum of Art, c1976. vi, 146 p. : ill. (some col.) ; 21 cm. Includes bibliographical references. [N6530.N8T93] 76-41365 ISBN 0-88259-083-9 pbk. : 9.50
1. Art, American—North Carolina—Exhibitions. 2. Art—North Carolina—Exhibitions. I. North Carolina. Museum of Art, Raleigh. BIP

Art, American—North Carolina—New Hanover Co.

HEWLETT, Crockette W. 975.6'27
Two centuries of art in New Hanover County / Crockette W. Hewlett ; foreword by Claude Howell. Durham, N.C. : Moore, Pub. Co., c1976. 329 p. : ill. ; 24 cm. Includes index. [N6530.N82N484] 76-12221 ISBN 0-87716-065-1 : 11.50
1. Art, American—North Carolina—New Hanover Co. 2. Art—North Carolina—New Hanover Co. 3. Artists—North Carolina—New Hanover Co.—Biography. 4. New Hanover Co., N.C.—History, Local. I. Title. BIP

Art, American—Philadelphia—Exhibitions.

PHILADELPHIA Museum of Art. 709'.73'074014811
Philadelphia, three centuries of American art : selections from the bicentennial exhibition held at the Philadelphia Museum of Art from April 11 to October 10, 1976. [Philadelphia] : The Museum, 1976. 160 p. : ill. (some col.) ; 27 cm. Includes index. [N6535.P5P5 1976a] 76-3171
1. Art, American—Philadelphia—Exhibitions. 2. Art—Philadelphia—Exhibitions. I. Title.

Art, American—The West—Exhibitions.

SANTA Fe 704.94'9'9780074018956
selects contemporary artists of the American West :Santa Fe Festival of the Arts, October 1977. Santa Fe, N.M. : [Santa Fe Chamber Foundation], c1977. [44] p. : col. ill. ; 28 cm. "Linda Monacelli ... wrote the cataloque." [N6525.S26] 77-154429
1. Art, American—The West—Exhibitions. 2. Art, Modern—20th century—The West—Exhibitions. 3. The West in art—Exhibitions. I. Monacelli, Linda.

Art, American—Washington, D.C.—Exhibitions.

ARTISTS Company. 709'.753'074013
Artists Company : exhibition of recent work / by nine from Washington, D.C., Marianne Bowles ... [et al.]. [Charlotte, N.C. : Mint Museum of Art], c1977. 32 p. : ill. ; 26 cm. Catalogue of an exhibition held at the Mint Museum of Art, Charlotte, N.C., Apr. 1-30, 1977; Art Associates, Lake Charles, La., May 8-27, 1977; The Art Center, Waco, Tex. June 1-30, 1977. [N6535.W3A67 1977] 77-73763
1. Art, American—Washington, D.C.—Exhibitions. 2. Art, Modern—20th century—Washington, D.C.—Exhibitions. 3. Artists—Washington, D.C. I. Bowles, Marianne. II. Mint Museum of Art. III. Art Associates. IV. Art Center, Waco, Tex. V. Nine from Washington, D.C.

CHAPMAN, Minerva J., 1858-1947. 759.13
Minerva J. Chapman; a retrospective exhibition, October 4 to November 15, 1971. Washington, D.C., Adams, Davidson Galleries [1971] 57 p. illus. (part col.) 26 cm. Bibliography: p. 57. [ND237.C463A64] 70-177265
I. Adams, Davidson Galleries. II. Title.

Art, American—Yearbooks.

AWARD-WINNING art; 707.9
bk. 6. Paintings, graphics, watercolors, sculpture. Ft. Lauderdale, Fla., Allied Pubns. [1966] 1v. (various p.) illus. (pt. col.) ports. 35cm. annual. Includes reprint of Prize-winning graphics, Prize-winning sculpture, Prize-winning water colors. Prize-winning paintings. Each sect. has t.p. and separate pagination. Comp.: 1965-66- Margaret Harold [N9.A87] 65-23508 9.95
1. Art—American—Yearbooks. 2. Art, Modern—20th cent.—Yearbooks. I. Harold, Margaret, comp.

PRIZE-WINNING art. 707'.9
bk. 7. Fort Lauderdale, Fla., Allied Pubns. v. illus. (pt. col.) ports. 35cm. annual. Orig. title: Award-winning art. Comp.: 1965- M. Harold. Includes reprint of Prize-winning graphics, Prize-winning sculpture, Prize-winning water colors, and Prize-winning paintings and assumes numbering of the last named. [N9.A87] 65-23508 12.00
1. Art, American—Yearbooks. 2. Art,

Modern—20th cent.—Yearbooks. I. Harold, Margaret, Comp.

Art, Amlash.

GABUS, Jean. 738'.0935
Amlash art [by] Jean Gabus and Roger-Louis Junod. Berne, Hallwag [1967] 9 p. illus., 19 col. plates. 19 cm. (Orbis pictus, 22) "Text by Roger-Louis Junod after an interview and notes by Jean Gabus." [N5899.A4G3] 67-99378
1. Art, Amlash. I. Junod, Roger Louis.

Art, Amlash — Exhibitions.

GALERIE Israel 738'.0935
The art of Amlash. From the collection of Galerie Israel, Limited. Tel-Aviv, Israel. National Antiques Show, Madison Square Garden. [New York, 1966] 1 v. (chiefly illus.) 26 cm. Catalog of an exhibition held Feb. 22-March 3, 1966 in New York. [N5899.A4G35] 67-7696
1. Art, Amlash — Exhibitions. I. National Antiques Show. II. Title.

NEWARK Museum 738'.0939'6
Association, Newark, N.J.
The art called Amlash; an art of ancient Iran as seen in its ceramics. A loan exhibition from collections in the New York-New Jersey metropolitan area, Newark Museum, Nov. 30, 1968-Mar. 30, 1969. [Newark, 1968] [16] p. illus., maps. 14 x 22 cm. [N5899.A4N4] 70-271067
1. Art, Amlash—Exhibitions. I. Title.

Art—Amsterdam.

AMSTERDAM. Stedelijk 708.9492
Museum.
Pioneers of modern art in the museum of the city of Amsterdam; [edited by] W. Sandberg and H. L. C. Jaffe Translation by Ian F. Finlay. New York, McGraw-Hill [1961] 1 v. (unpaged) illus. (part col.) 31cm. Translation of Kunst van heden in het Stedeliuk. List of works of modern art in the Municipal Museum of Amsterdam' ([14] p. plate) in pocket. [N2463.A583] 61-11654
1. Art—Amsterdam. 2. Art, Modern—20th cent. I. Sandberg, Willem Jacob Henri Bernard, 1897- ed. II. Jaffe, Hans Ludwig C., ed. III. Title.

Art—Amsterdam—Catalogs.

HAAK, B. 708.9492
Art treasures of the Rijksmuseum, Amsterdam. Foreword by A. F. E. van Schendel. Texts by B. Haak. [Translated by Elizabeth Willems-Treeman] New York, H. N. Abrams [1966?] [263] p. illus., plates (part fold., part col.) 33 cm. [N2460.H3 1966] 66-10326
1. Art—Amsterdam—Catalogs. I. Amsterdam. Rijks-Museum. II. Title.

HAAK, B 708.94923
Art treasures of the Rijksmuseum, Amsterdam; foreword by A. F. E. van Schendel, texts by B. Haak; translated [from the Dutch] by Elizabeth Willem-Treeman. London, Thames & Hudson, 1966. 263 p. illus. 42 col. plates. 33 cm. (Great galleries series) 8/8- (B66-11065) [N2460.H3 1966a] 66-73995
1. Art — Amsterdam — Catalogs. I. Amsterdam. Rijks-Museum. II. Title.

Art, Ancient.

BOARDMAN, John, 1927- 709'.38
Pre-classical: from Crete to Archaic Greece. Harmondsworth, Penguin, 1967. 186 p. 104 illus., map. 20 cm. (Style and civilization) Pelican book, A807. Bibliography: p. 183-184. [N5340.B6] 67-99818
1. Art, Ancient. I. Title.

FRANKFORT, Henriette 709.01
Antonia (Groenewegen) 1896-
The ancient world, by H. A. Groenewegen-Frankfort and Bernard Ashmole. New York, New American Library [1967] 304 p. illus. (part col.) 18 cm. (The Library of art history, v. 1) A Mentor book, MY731. Bibliography: p. 290-294. [N5340.F7] 67-15322
1. Art, Ancient. I. Ashmole, Bernard, 1894- II. Title. III. Series.

PAYNE, Pierre Stephen 709.01
Robert, 1911-
Lost treasures of the Mediterranean world. New York, Nelson [1962] 224 p. illus. 28 cm. [N5340.P3] 62-16354
1. Art, Ancient. 2. Art—Mediterranean region. 3. Mediterranean region—Antiquities. I. Title.

RADAN, George T 709
An introduction to ancient art and architecture, by George T. Radan & Lewis Greenberg [Villanova, Pa.] Villanova University Press [1966] xv. 237 p. (p. 236-237, blank for "notes") illus., maps. 23 cm. Bibliography: p. 224-228. [N5330.R2] 66-28228
1. Art, Ancient. 2. Architecture, Ancient. I. Greenberg, Lewis, joint author. II. Title.

SCRANTON, Robert Lorentz, 709.01
1912-
Aesthetic aspects of ancient art [by] Robert L. Scranton. Chicago. University of Chicago Press [1964] xvi, 381 p. illus., plans. 25 cm. Bibliography: p. 368-372. [N5330.S36] 64-24964
1. Art, Ancient. I. Title.

SMITH, Joseph Lindon, 1863- 709.3
1950.
Tombs, temples & ancient art. With paintings by the author. Edited by Corinna Lindon Smith. [1st ed.] Norman, University of Oklahoma Press [1956] 349 p. illus. 24 cm. [N5333.S5] 56-5999
1. Art, Ancient. 2. Tombs. 3. Temples. 4. Art, Egyptian. 5. Egypt—Antiquities. I. Title.

SMITH, William Stevenson. 709.3
Interconnections in the ancient Near-East; a study of the relationships between the arts of Egypt, the Aegean. and western Asia. New Haven, Conn., Yale [c.]1965. xxxii, 202p. 221 illus. (pt. fold.) maps (on lining papets) 29cm. Bibl. [N5345.S6] 65-22340 17.50
1. Art, Ancient. 2. Art—Near East. 3. Near East—Antiq. I. Title.

WEBSTER, James Carson, 1905- 709
The labors of the months in antique and mediaeval art to the end of the twelfth century. New York, AMS Press [1970, c1938] 185 p. 63 plates. 24 cm. (Northwestern University studies in the humanities, v. 4) Includes bibliographical references. [N7745.M6W4 1970] 75-128988 ISBN 0-404-50704-2
1. Art, Ancient. 2. Art, Medieval. 3. Months in art. I. Title. II. Series: Northwestern University studies. Humanities series, v. 4

WOLF, Walther, 1900- 709'.01
The origins of Western art: Egypt, Mesopotamia, the Aegean. New York, Universe Books [1971] 207 p. illus. (part col.) 23 cm. (Universe history of art) Translation of Fruhe Hochkulturen: Agypten, Mesopotamien, Agais. Bibliography: p. 202-203. [N5345.W613] 73-134760 ISBN 0-87663-146-4 6.95
1. Art, Ancient. 2. Art—Near East. I. Title.

Art, Ancient—Addresses, essays, lectures.

ANCIENT art: 709 s
pre-Greek and Greek art. New York : Garland Pub., 1976. 290 p. : ill. ; 29 cm. (The Garland library of the history of art ; v. 2) Includes bibliographical references. [N5300.G32 vol. 2] [N5330] 709'.38 76-14063 ISBN 0-8240-2412-5 lib.bdg. : 35.00
1. Art, Ancient—Addresses, essays, lectures. 2. Art, Greek—Addresses, essays, lectures. I. Series.

Art, Ancient—Catalogs.

HERBERT, Kevin 708.1419
Ancient art in Bowdoin College; a descriptive catalogue of the Warren and other collections. Cambridge, Mass., Harvard [c.1964] xv, 212p. 48 plates. 25cm. Bibl. 63-19138 6.95
1. Art, Ancient—Catalogs. 2. Bowdoin College. Museum of Fine Arts. I. Warren, Edward Perry, 1860-1928. II. Title.

VIRGINIA Museum of Fine 709'.01
Arts, Richmond.
Ancient art in the Virginia Museum. [Richmond, Va., 1973] 142 p. illus. (part col.) 25 cm. Includes bibliographical references. [N5335.R53A52] 73-78574 10.95
1. Virginia Museum of Fine Arts, Richmond. 2. Art, Ancient—Catalogs. 3. Art—Richmond—Catalogs. I. Title.

Art, Ancient—Cyprus.

NEW York 709'.393'707401471
(City). Metropolitan Museum of Art. Cesnola Collection.
Handbook of the Cesnola Collection of antiquities from Cyprus, by John L. Myres. New York, 1914. [New York] Arno Press, 1974. lv, 596 p. illus. 23 cm. Bibliography: p. xliii-lv. [N5430.N64 1974] 77-168425 ISBN 0-405-02263-8 38.00
1. New York (City). Metropolitan Museum of Art. Cesnola Collection. 2. Art, Ancient—Cyprus. 3. Cyprus—Antiquities. I. Myres, John Linton, Sir, 1869-1954. II. Title. BIP

Art, Ancient—Exhibitions.

BROOKLYN Institute of Arts 709.01
and Sciences. Museum.
The Pomerance collection of ancient art. [Catalog of an exhibition held at the Brooklyn Museum, June 14 to October 2, 1966. Brooklyn] Brooklyn Mus. [1966] 127p. illus. (pt. col.) map. 25cm. Exhibition of ancient art objects owned by Leon Pomerance and others. Bibl. [N5335.B72A6] 66-21097 4.50 pap.,
1. Art, Ancient—Exhibitions. 2. Art-Private collections. I. Pomerance, Leon. II. Title.
Contents omitted. BIP

NEW York. Metropolitan 709.01
Museum of Art.
Ancient art from New York private collections; catalogue of an exhibition held at the Metropolitan Museum of Art, December 17, 1959- February 28, 1960, by Dietrich von Bothmer. New York, 1961. 85p. 104 plates. 18x24cm. [N5335.N4N4] 61-10929
1. Art, Ancient—Exhibitions. 2. Art—Private collections. I. Von Bothmer, Dietrich, 1918- II. Title.

NEWARK Museum Association, 732
Newark, N.J.
Curator's choice from the ancient world. [Newark, 1968] [28] p. illus., map. 14 x 22 cm. Cover title. Catalog, by Dorothy Budd, of the exhibition held Jan. 31-June 16, 1968 at the Newark Museum. [N5335.N43N4] 78-266994
1. Art, Ancient—Exhibitions. 2. Near East—Antiquities. I. Budd, Dorothy M. II. Title.

QUEENS College, Flushing, 709.01
N. Y. Art Collection.
Man in the ancient world; an exhibition of pre-Christian objects from the regions of the Near East, Egypt, and the Mediterranean, February 10-March 7, 1958. Flushing, N. Y., 1958. 63p. illus. 24cm. 'Catalogue': p.13-24. Errata slip inserted. [N5334.Q4] 58-25440
1. Art, Ancient—Exhibitions. I. Title.

Art, Ancient—History.

POWELL, Ann. 709'.01
The origins of Western art. With 213 illus. [New York] Harcourt Brace Jovanovich [1973] 224 p. illus. 21 cm. (The Harbrace history of art) Bibliography: p. 219-220. [N5330.P64 1973] 74-183245 ISBN 0-15-170157-1 3.95 (pbk.)
1. Art, Ancient—History. I. Title.

WINCKELMANN, Johann 709.01
Joachim, 1717-1768.
History of ancient art. New York, F. Ungar Pub. Co. [1969, c1968] 4 v. in 2. illus. 26 cm. Translation of Geschichte der Kunst des Altertums. The text is that of the 1849-73 ed. "Winckelmann; a commemorative essay, by Johann Gottfried Herder": v. 1, p. vii-xvii. Bibliographical footnotes. [N5330.W743 1969] 68-8114 35.00
1. Art, Ancient—History. 2. Art, Greek—History. I. Title.

Art, Ancient—Nara, Japan—History.

HAYASHI, Ryoichi, 708'.952'18
1918-
The silk road and the Shoso-in / Ryoichi Hayashi; translated by Robert Ricketts New York : Weatherhill, 1975. p. cm. (The Heibonsha survey of Japanese art ; v. 6) Translation of Shiruku Rodo to Shosoin. [N3750.N36H3713] 75-23081 ISBN 0-8348-1022-0 : 12.50
1. Shosoin, Nara, Japan. 2. Silk Road. 3. Art, Ancient—Nara, Japan—History. 4. Art—Nara, Japan—History. I. Title. II. Series. BIP

Art, Ancient—Near East.

ROUGH, Robert H. 709'.01
The ancient Near East [by] Robert H. Rough. Dubuque, Iowa, W. C. Brown Co. [1969] vii, 107 p. illus. 23 cm. (Studies in art series) Bibliography: p. 103-104. [N5345.R59] 71-79617
1. Art, Ancient—Near East. 2. Near East—Antiquities. I. Title.

Art, Ancient—Palmyra, Syria.

COLLEDGE, Malcolm A. R. 709'.39'4
The art of Palmyra / Malcolm A. R. Colledge. Boulder, Colo. : Westview Press, 1976. 320 p. : ill. ; 25 cm. Includes index. Bibliography: p. 305-309. [N5460.C64 1976] 76-12473 ISBN 0-89158-617-2 : 35.00
1. Art, Ancient—Palmyra, Syria. 2. Art—Palmyra, Syria. 3. Palmyra, Syria—Antiquities. I. Title. BIP

COLLEDGE, Malcolm A. R. 709'.39'4
The art of Palmyra / [by] Malcolm A. R. Colledge. London : Thames and Hudson, 1976. 320 p. : ill., maps, plans ; 25 cm. (Studies in ancient art and archaeology) Includes index. Bibliography: p. 305-309. [N5460.C64 1976b] 76-382226 ISBN 0-500-69003-0 : 16.00
1. Art, Ancient—Palmyra, Syria. 2. Art—Palmyra, Syria. 3. Palmyra, Syria—Antiquities. I. Title. II. Series.

Art and literature.

ALLEN, Beverly Sprague, 701.17
1881-1935.
Tides in English taste (1619-1800); a background for the study of literature. New York, Pageant Books, 1958 [c1937] 2v. illus. 25cm. Includes bibliography. [N6766.A4 1958] 58-44144
1. Art and literature. 2. Aesthetics—Hist. 3. English literature—Early modern (to 1700)—Hist. & crit. 4. English literature—18th cent.—Hist. & crit. 5. Gt. Brit.—Civilization. I. Title. II. Title: English taste (1619-1800) BIP

CHEW, Samuel Claggett, 709.03
1888-1960
The pilgrimage of life. New Haven, Conn., Yale [c.]1962. xxv, 449p. illus. 27cm. Bibl. 62-8239 15.00
1. Art and literature. 2. Art, Renaissance. 3. Literature, Modern—15th and 16th cent.—Hist. & crit. I. Title. BIP

CHEW, Samuel 760'.09'024
Claggett, 1888-1960.
The pilgrimage of life. Port Washington, N.Y., Kennikat Press [1973, c1962] xxv, 449 p. illus. 24 cm. Includes bibliographical references. [NX450.5.C45 1973] 72-85277 ISBN 0-8046-1692-2
1. Art and literature. 2. The arts, Renaissance. I. Title.

LEE, Renssalaer Wright, 1898- 701
Ut pictura poesis; the humanistic theory of painting, by Rensselaer W. Lee. New York, Norton [1967] viii, 79, [33]p. 32 illus. 20cm. (Norton lib., N39) Bibl. [ND1263.L4] 67-15820 4.50
1. Art and literature. 2. Painting — Technique. 3. Composition (Art) I. Title. BIP

MOORE, Robert Etheridge, 759.2
1920-
Hogarth's literary relationships. New York,

Octagon Books, 1969 [c1948] viii, 202 p. illus. 24 cm. Bibliographical footnotes. [ND497.H7M6 1969] 70-76001
1. Hogarth, William, 1697-1764. 2. Fielding, Henry, 1707-1754. 3. Art and literature. 4. English literature—18th century—History and criticism. I. Title. **BIP**

PRAZ, Mario, 1896- 700
Mnemosyne: the parallel between literature and the visual arts. [Princeton, N.J.] Princeton University Press [1970] xv, 261 p. 121 illus. 27 cm. (Bollingen series, 35. The A. W. Mellon lectures in the fine arts, 16) Includes bibliographical references. [PN53.P7] 68-20876 15.00
1. Art and literature. I. Title. II. Series: Bollingen series, 35. III. Series: The A. W. Mellon lectures in the fine arts, 16

WEISMANN, Donald L. 700
Language and visual form; the personal record of a dual creative process [by] Donald L. Weismann. Austin, University of Texas Press [1968] 122 p. col. illus. 28 cm. Bibliographical footnotes. [NX175.W4] 65-27539 7.50
1. Art and literature. I. Title. **BIP**

Art and mental illness.

BILLIG, Otto. 701'.15
The painted message / Otto Billig and B. C. Burton-Bradley. Cambridge, Mass. : Schenkman Pub. Co. ; New York : distributed by Halsted Press, c1977. p. cm. [N71.B53] 77-3293 ISBN 0-470-99126-7 : 19.50
1. Art and mental illness. I. Burton-Bradley, B. G., joint author. II. Title. **BIP**

BROWN, Walter L. 701'.15
Introduction to psycho-iconography; the interpretation and use of schizophrenic art in psychotherapy [by] Walter L. Brown. [Bloomfield, N.J., Schering Corp., c1967] 67 p. (p. 64-67 advertisements) illus. 29 cm. Bibliography: p. 63. [N71.5.B76] 73-164612
1. Art and mental illness. 2. Psychoanalysis illness. I. Title.

CARDINAL, Roger. 709'.2'2
Outsider art. New York, Praeger Publishers [1972, i.e. 1973] 192 p. illus. (part col.) 26 cm. Bibliography: p. 181-187. [N71.5.C37 1973] 72-81584 15.00
1. Art and mental illness. I. Title.

PLOKKER. J. H. 704.096168982
Art from the mentally disturbed: the shattered vision of schizophrenics. [Tr. from Dutch by Ian Finlay] Boston. Little [1965. c.1962.1964] 224p. illus. (pt. col.) 27cm. Bibl. [N71.5.P513] 65-20009 15.00
1. Art and mental illness. I. Title.

PRINZHORN, Hans, 1886-1933. 701'.15
Artistry of the mentally ill; a contribution to the psychology and psychopathology of configuration. Translated by Eric von Brockdorff from the 2d German ed. With an introd. by James L. Foy. New York, Springer-Verlag, 1972. xxii, 274 p. illus. (part col.) 27 cm. Translation of Bildnerei der Geisteskranken. Bibliography: p. xv-xvi. [N71.5.P6813 1972] 70-162403 ISBN 0-387-05508-8 19.80
1. Art and mental illness. I. Title. **BIP**

Art and morals.

GREENBURG, Dan. 704.94'21
Porno-graphics: [the shame of our art museums] [New York] Random House [1969] [22] p. (on double leaves; chiefly col. plates) 20 cm. [N73.G7] 69-16410 2.95
1. Art and morals. 2. Nude in art. I. Title. **BIP**

LADD, Henry Andrews, 1895-1941. 701.17
The Victorian morality of art; an analysis of Ruskin's esthetic. New York, Octagon Books, 1968 [c1932] xi, 418 p. 22 cm. Includes bibliographical references. [N62.R8L3 1968] 68-22298
1. Ruskin, John, 1819-1900—Aesthetics. 2. Art and morals. I. Title. **BIP**

LAMOTTE, Charles. 759
An essay upon poetry and painting. New York, Garland Pub., 1970. 202 p. 22 cm. Facsim. of the Yale University Library copy, with imprint: London, F. Fayram, 1730. [N62.L3 1730a] 73-112172
1. Art and morals. 2. Realism in art. 3. Literature—History and criticism. I. Title.

MARITAIN, Jacques, 1882- 701.1
The responsibility of the artist. New York, Scribner [1960] 120p. 20cm. [N72.M29] 60-6331
1. Art and morals. 2. Art—Philosophy. 3. Literature and morals. I. Title. **BIP**

MARITAIN, Jacques, 1882- 701
The responsibility of the artist. New York, Gordian Press, 1972 [c1960] 120 p. 23 cm. Includes bibliographical references. [NX180.E8M3 1972] 70-150415 ISBN 0-87752-145-X
1. Art and morals. 2. Art—Philosophy. I. Title.

NISHIDA, Kitaro, 1870-1945. 111.8
Art and morality. Translated by David A. Dilworth [and] Valdo H. Viglielmo. Honolulu, University Press of Hawaii [1973] xi, 216 p. 24 cm. "An East-West Center book." Translation of Geijutsu to dotoku. Bibliography: p. [209]-211. [N72.E8N5713 1973] 72-92067 ISBN 0-8248-0256-X 8.00
1. Art and morals. I. Title. **BIP**

Art and moving-pictures.

LAWDER, Standish D. 791.43'0909'1
The Cubist cinema / Standish D. Lawder. New York : New York University Press, 1975. xvi, 265 p. : ill. ; 24 cm. (Anthology film archives series ; [1]) Includes bibliographical references and index. [N72.M6L38] 72-96466 ISBN 0-8147-4956-9 : 18.50 ISBN 0-8147-4957-7 pbk. : 11.75
1. Art and moving-pictures. 2. Cubism. I. Title. **BIP**

Art and music.

CLEAVER, Dale G. 700
Art and music : an introduction / Dale G. Cleaver, John M. Eddins. New York : Harcourt Brace Jovanovich, c1977. viii, 568 p., [16] leaves of plates : ill. (some col.) ; 24 cm. Includes bibliographies and index. [ML3849.C6] 77-72026 ISBN 0-15-503437-5 pbk. : 10.95
1. Art and music. 2. Music—History and criticism. I. Eddins, John M., joint author. II. Title. **BIP**

LOCKSPEISER, Edward, 1905- 780'.08
Music and painting; a study in comparative ideas from Turner to Schoenberg. [1st U.S. ed.] New York, Harper & Row [1973] 197 p. illus. 23 cm. (Icon editions) [ML3849.L62 1973] 73-7979 ISBN 0-06-435325-7 8.50
1. Art and music. I. Title.
Pbk. 4.95; ISBN 0-06-430040-4. **BIP**

Art and mythology—Dictionaries.

WATERS, Clara (Erskine) Clement, 1834-1916. 703
A handbook of legendary and mythological art. Enl. ed. Detroit, Gale Research Co., 1969 [c1881] xii, 575 p. illus. 23 cm. [N7760.W3 1969] 68-26616
1. Art and mythology—Dictionaries. 2. Christian art and symbolism—Dictionaries. I. Title. **BIP**

WATERS, Clara Erskine Clement, 1834-1916. 704.948
A handbook of legendary and mythological art / by Clara Erskine Clement. Boston : Longwood Press, 1977. x, 510 p. : ill. ; 22 cm. Reprint of the 1876 ed. published by Hurd and Houghton, New York. Includes index. [N7760.W3 1977] 76-27524 ISBN 0-89341-037-3 lib.bdg. : 50.00
1. Art and mythology—Dictionaries. 2. Christian art and symbolism—Dictionaries. I. Title.

WATERS, Clara Erskine Clement, 1834-1916. 704.94'6
A handbook of legendary and mythological art, by Clara Erskine Clement. With descriptive illustrations. [10th ed.] Boston, Milford House [1973] p. Reprint of the 1876 ed. published by Hurd and Houghton, New York. [N7760.W3 1973] 73-5551 ISBN 0-87821-128-4 40.00 (lib. bdg.)
1. Art and mythology—Dictionaries. 2. Christian art and symbolism—Dictionaries. I. Title. **BIP**

Art and photography.

NEW Mexico. University Art Museum. v. 12
The painter and the photograph; an exhibition, organized by the staff of the Art Gallery, the University of New Mexico. Van Deren Coke [director of the exhibition. 1st ed. Albuquerque] University of New Mexico Press [1964] 79 p. illus. 26 cm. "Shown during 1964 and 1965 at the following institutions: Rose Art Museum, Brandeis University, Waltham, Mass. [and others]" "Catalogue of the exhibition [and other illustrations]": p. 71-77. Bibliographical references included in "Notes" (p. 68-69) [N72P.5N48] 64-24357
1. Art and photography. 2. Paintings — Exhibitions. 3. Photography — Exhibitions. I. Coke, Van Deren, 1921- II. Brandeis University, Waltham, Mass. Rose Art Museum. III. Title.

Art and religion.

BAILEY, Albert Edward, 1871-1951. 701
The arts and religion, by Albert Edward Bailey, editor; Kenneth John Conant, Henry Augustine Smith [and] Fred Eastman. Freeport, N.Y., Books for Libraries Press [1972, c1944] xiv, 180 p. illus. 22 cm. (Essay index reprint series) Original ed. issued in series: The Ayer lectures of the Colgate-Rochester Divinity School, 1943. Includes bibliographies. [N72.R4B35 1972] 72-3349 ISBN 0-8369-2889-X
1. Art and religion. I. Conant, Kenneth John, 1894- II. Smith, Henry Augustine, 1874-1952. III. Eastman, Fred, 1886- IV. Title. V. Series: The Ayer lectures, 1943. **BIP**

BRANDON, Samuel George Frederick. 246
Man and God in art and ritual; a study of iconography, architecture and ritual action as primary evidence of religious belief and practice [by] S. G. F. Brandon. New York, Scribner [1974] p. Bibliography: p. [N72.R4B72] 73-1358 ISBN 0-684-13657-0 20.00
1. Art and religion. 2. Ritual. I. Title.

CATHOLIC University of America. Workshop on Art for Christian Living, 1957. 701.1
Art for Christian living; the proceedings of the Workshop on Art for Christian Living conducted at the Catholic University of America, June 14 to 25, 1957. Edited by Sister Mary Joanne Christie. Washington, Catholic University of America Press, 1958. x, 205p. illus., port., music. 22cm. Includes bibliographies. [N72.C44 1957] 58-1125
1. Art and religion. 2. Catholic Church. I. Christie, Joanne, ed. II. Title.

THE Church and the visual arts. 261.5
Andrew J. Buehner, editor. Saint Louis, Mo., Lutheran Academy for Scholarship [1968] 190 p. 21 cm. Papers presented at a conference in May 1968, sponsored by the Lutheran Academy for Scholarship. Includes bibliographies. [NX175.C5] 74-677
1. Art and religion. 2. The arts—Psychology. I. Buehner, Andrew J., ed. II. Lutheran Academy for Scholarship.

COULTON, George Gordon, 1858-1947. 709.02
Art and the Reformation. [2d ed.] Cambridge [Eng.] University Press, 1953. xxii, 622p. illus. 23cm. 'This volume has grown out of Lowell lectures delivered at Boston, Massachusetts, in the spring of 1923.' Bibliography: p. xix-xxii. [N5970.C6 1953] 53-11733
1. Art and religion. 2. Architecture, Medieval. 3. Architecture. Gothic. 4. Art, Medieval. 5. Church architecture—England. I. Title. **BIP**

COULTON, George Gordon, 1858-1947. 709'.42
Art and the Reformation. [Hamden, Conn.] Archon Books, 1969. xxii, 622 p. illus. 22 cm. Reprint of the 1928 ed. "This volume has grown out of Lowell lectures delivered in Boston, Massachusetts, in the spring of 1923." Bibliography: p. xix-xxii. Bibliographical footnotes. [N5970.C6 1969] 69-15789 ISBN 0-208-00738-5
1. Art and religion. 2. Architecture, Medieval—England. 3. Architecture, Gothic—England. 4. Art, Medieval—England. 5. Church architecture—England. I. Title.

DIXON, John W. 701
Art and the theological imagination / John W. Dixon, Jr. New York : Seabury Press, 1978. p. cm. "A Crossroad book." [N72.R4D48] 78-16249 ISBN 0-8164-0397-X : 10.95
1. Art and religion. 2. Man (Christian theology) I. Title. **BIP**

DIXON, John W., Jr. 704.9482
Nature and grace in art. Chapel Hill, Univ. of N.C. Pr. [c.1964] x, 220p. illus. 24cm. Bibl. 64-13549 7.50
1. Art and religion. 2. Art—Philosophy. 3. Christian art and symbolism. I. Title.

EGENTER, Richard, 1902- 704.948'2
The desecration of Christ. Translated by Edward Quinn. Edited by Nicolete Gray. Chicago, Franciscan Herald Press [1967] 154 p. illus. 21 cm. Abridged translation of Kitsch und Christenleben. [N72.R4E353 1967b] 68-2806
1. Art and religion. 2. Art—Psychology. 3. Kitsch. I. Title. **BIP**

EVERSOLE, Finley, ed. 704.92
Christian faith and the contemporary arts. New York, Abingdon Press [1962] 255 p. illus. 25 cm. [N72.E9] 62-16809
1. Art and religion. 2. Art, Modern—20th century—Addresses, essays, lectures. 3. Civilization, Christian—Addresses, essays, lectures. 4. Religion and music. I. Title.

HARNED, David Baily 701
Theology and the arts. Philadelphia, Westminster [1966] 204p.21cm. Bibl. [N72.R4H3] 66-15963 5.00
1. Art and religion. I. Title.

HAZELTON, Roger, 1909- 701
A theological approach to art. Nashville, Abingdon Press [1967] 158 p. 20 cm. Bibliographical footnotes. [N72.R4H38] 67-22165
1. Art and religion. 2. Art—Philosophy. I. Title.

HYGEN, Johan Bernitz, 1911- 701.1
Morality and the muses; Christian faith and art forms, by Johan B. Hygen. Translated by Harris E. Kaasa. Minneapolis, Augsburg Pub. House [1965] 113 p. 21 cm. Translation of Kunst, livssyn og moral. [N72.R4H93] 65-22836
1. Art and religion. 2. Art and morals. I. Title.

LEEUW, Gerardus van der, 1890-1950 701
Sacred and profane beauty; the holy in art. Pref. by Mircea Eliade. Tr. by David E. Green. [1st ed.] Nashville, Abingdon [1968, c.1963] xx, 357p. 23cm. (AC-295) Pub. in Germany under the title, Vom Heiligen in der Kunst. Bibl. [N72.L413] 2.95 pap.,
1. Art and religion. 2. Religion and literature. 3. Aesthetics. 4. Holiness. I. Title.

LEEUW, Gerardus van der, 1890-1950. 701
Sacred and profane beauty; the holy in art. Pref. by Mircea Eliade. Translated by David E. Green. [1st ed.] New York, Holt, Rinehart and Winston [1963] 357 p. 24 cm. "Published in Germany under the title, Vom Heiligen in der Kunst." Includes bibliography. [N72.L413] 63-11867
1. Art and religion. 2. Religion and literature. I. Title.

WADDELL, James, 1938- 700
Art and religion as communication, edited by James Waddell and F. W. Dillistone. Richmond, John Knox Press [1974, c1973] p. Bibliography: p. [N72.R4W32] 73-5353 ISBN 0-8042-1930-3 11.95

1. Art and religion. I. Dillistone, Frederick William, 1903- joint author. II. Title.

WEISS, Paul, 1901- 701
Religion and art. Milwaukee, Marquette University Press, 1963. 97 p. 19 cm. (The Aquinas lecture, 1963) Includes bibliography. [N72.W4] 63-13170
1. Art and religion. I. Title. BIP

WHITTLE, Donald Carey 704.948'2
Grenfell,
Christianity and the arts [by] Donald Whittle. Philadelphia, Fortress [1967, c. 1966] xiv, 157p. illus., plates. 18cm. (Fortress paperback orig.) Bibl. [BR115. A8W5 1967] 67-15024 1.50 pap.,
1. Art and religion. I. Title.

Art and religion—Addresses, essays, lectures.

FORSYTH, Peter Taylor, 704.948
1848-1921.
Religion in recent art; expository lectures on Rossetti, Burne Jones, Watts, Holman Hunt and Wagner. 3d ed. London, Hodder and Stoughton, 1905. [New York, AMS Press, 1972] xii, 316 p. illus. 23 cm. [NX650.R4F6 1972] 73-148780 ISBN 0-404-02515-3 15.00
1. Art and religion—Addresses, essays, lectures. 2. The arts—Addresses, essays, lectures. I. Title. BIP

Art and science.

DAVIS, Douglas M. 700
Art and the future; a history/prophecy of the collaboration between science, technology, and art [by] Douglas Davis. New York, Praeger [1973] 208 p. illus. 27 cm. Bibliography: p. 195-203. [N72.S3D38] 76-119522 20.00
1. Art and science. 2. Art and technology. 3. Art, Modern—20th century. I. Title.

HOMER, William Innes. 759.4
Seurat and the science of painting. Cambridge, Mass., M. I. T. Press [1964] xvi, 327 p. illus. (part col.) 24 cm. Bibliography: p. 305-317. [ND553.S5H63] 64-15751
1. Seurat, Georges Pierre, 1859-1891. 2. Art and science. I. Title.

HOMER, William Innes. 759.4
Seurat and the science of painting / by William Innes Homer. MA : MIT Press, 1978. 327p. : ill. ; 23 cm. Includes index. Bibliography: p. 305. [ND553.S5H63] ISBN 0-262-58036-5 pbk. : 8.95
1. Seurat, Georges Pierre, 1859-1891. 2. Art and science. I. Title.
L.C. card no. for 1964 MIT Press hardcover ed.: 64-15751. BIP

KEPES, Gyorgy, 1906- 701.1
The new landscape in art and science. Chicago, P. Theobald [c1956] 383p. illus. 29cm. [N72.K4] 57-576
1. Art and science. I. Title.

KEPES, Gyorgy, 1906- ed. 701
Structure in art and science. New York, G. Braziller [1965] vii, 189 p. illus. 29 cm. (Vision + value series) Includes bibliographical references. [N72.S3K4] 65-10807
1. Art and science. 2. Art—Addresses, essays, lectures. I. Title.

MUELLER, Robert E. 701.15
The science of art; the cybernetics of creative communication [by] Robert E. Mueller. With drawings by the author. New York, John Day Co. [1967] 352 p. illus. 22 cm. Bibliography: p. [327]-341. [N72.S3M8] 67-19392
1. Art and science. 2. Art—Psychology. I. Title.

RICHARDSON, John Adkins. 709.04
Modern art and scientific thought. Urbana, University of Illinois Press [1971] xix, 191 p. illus. 27 cm. Bibliography: p. 178-184. [N72.S3R5] 74-122914 ISBN 0-252-00125-7 10.00
1. Art and science. 2. Art, Modern—19th century. 3. Art, Modern—20th century. I. Title. BIP

ROWE, Albert 701.1
The basic theory of Mathartics; or the two-color shape calculus. Pittsfield, Mass., Author, 115 Pine Grove Drive, c.1961. 33p. illus. 2.00, pap plastic binding
I. Title.

Art and science—Addresses, essays, lectures.

JOHNSON, Martin Christopher, 700
1896-
Art and scientific thought; historical studies towards a modern revision of their antagonism, by Martin Johnson. With a foreword by Walter de la Mare. New York, AMS Press [1970, c1969] 200 p. illus. 23 cm. Bibliography: p. 194-196. [N72.S3J6 1970] 70-118944
1. Art and science—Addresses, essays, lectures. I. Title. BIP

RUSKIN, John, 1819-1900. 704
The eagle's nest; ten lectures on the relation of natural science to art, given before the University of Oxford in Lent term, 1872. With an introd. by Charles Eliot Norton. Brantwood ed. New York, Maynard, Merrill, 1893. St. Clair Shores, Mich., Scholarly Press, 1972 [c1891] p. (The works of John Ruskin) [N72.S3R85 1972] 72-8327 ISBN 0-403-02062-X
1. Art and science—Addresses, essays, lectures. I. Title.

Art and science—Exhibitions.

ALBANY Institute of 704.94'9'5
History and Art.
Art in science. [Albany, N.Y., Albany Institute of History and Art, 1965] [100] p. illus. (part col.) 18 x 22 cm. Cover title. Catalog of an exhibition. [N72.S3A42] 73-161617
1. Art and science—Exhibitions. 2. Art, Modern—20th century—Exhibitions. I. Title.

Art and society.

ALLSOPP, Bruce. 702'.3
The professional artist in a changing society: the inaugural address delivered as Master to the Art Workers Guild, in the Guild's Hall at 6 Queen Square, London, on January 9th 1970. Newcastle upon Tyne, Produced and published for The Art Workers Guild by Oriel, 1970. [2], 11 p. 22 cm. [N72.S6A4] 78-520009 5/-
1. Art and society. I. Art Workers Guild, London. II. Title.

BOWMAN, John F. 701.1
Issues in art; a survey of controversies on art in society [by] John F. Bowman. Dubuque, Iowa, W. C. Brown Book Co. [1965] xii, 68 p. 24 cm. Bibliography: p. 62-68. [N72.B65] 66-3156
1. Art and society. 2. Art — Philosophy. I. Title.

CANADAY, John Edwin, 1907- 701.18
Culture gulch; notes on art and its public in the 1960's [by] John Canaday. New York, Farrar, Straus and Giroux [1969] 212 p. illus. 21 cm. [N72.S6C27] 69-20375 5.95
1. Art and society. 2. Art, Modern—20th century. I. Title.

COUTTS-SMITH, Kenneth, 709'.046
1929-
The dream of Icarus. [1st American ed.] New York, G. Braziller [1970] 237 p. illus. 22 cm. Includes bibliographical references. [N72.S6C6 1970b] 74-104700 5.95
1. Art and society. I. Title.

DUNHAM, Barrows, 1905- 701
The artist in society. New York, Marzani & Munsel [1960] 125 p. 20 cm. [N72.D9] 61-3635
1. Title.

DUVIGNAUD, Jean. 700
The sociology of art. Translated from the French by Timothy Wilson. [1st U.S. ed.] New York, Harper & Row [1973, c1972] 159 p. 22 cm. (Icon editions, IN-35) Bibliography: p. 152-154. [N72.S6D813 1972b] 72-14012 ISBN 0-06-432010-3 7.50
1. Art and society. 2. Popular culture. I. Title.
Pbk. 3.95. BIP

GREENBERG, Clement, 1909- 704.91
Art and culture; critical essays. Boston, Beacon Press [1961] 278p. 21cm. [N72.G68] 61-7248
1. Art and society. 2. Artists. 3. Art—Addresses, essays, lectures. I. Title. BIP

GREENBERG, Clement. 1909- 704.91
Art and culture; critical essays. [Gloucester, Mass., P. Smith, 1965. c.1961] x, 278p. 21cm. (Beacon Pr. bk. rebound) [N72.G68] 4.25
1. Art and society. 2. Artists. 3. Art—Addresses, essays, lectures. I. Title.

GUYAU, Jean Marie, 1854- 700.1
1888.
L'art au point de vue sociologique / Marie Jean Guyau. New York : Arno Press, 1975, c1920. p. cm. (European sociology) Reprint of the ed. published by F. Alcan, Paris. [BH41.G88 1975] 74-25756 ISBN 0-405-06510-8
1. Art and society. 2. Literature—Philosophy. 3. Aesthetics. I. Title. II. Series.

HAUSER, Arnold, 1892- 701.1
The social history of art. [Translated in collaboration with the author by Stanley Godman] New York, Knopf, 1951. 2v. (1022p.) illus. 25cm. Bibliographical references included in 'Notes.' [N72.H353 1951a] 51-13993
1. Art and society. 2. Art—Hist. I. Title. BIP

HAUSER, Arnold, 1892- 701.1
The social history of art. [Translated in collaboration with the author by Stanley Godman. 1st Vintage ed.] New York, Vintage Books, 1957. 2v. 19cm. (A Vintage book, K-53A, K-53B) 'Comprises volume 1 of the complete work.' Translation of Socialgeschichte der Kunst und literatur, v. 1. [N72] 57-3952
1. Art and society. 2. Art—Hist. 3. Literature—Hist. & crit. I. Title.

HERBERT, Eugenia W. 701
The artist and social reform: France and Belgium, 1885-1898. New Haven, Conn., Yale Univ. Press [c.]1961. xvi, 236p. illus. 25cm. (Yale historical publications. Miscellany 74) Bibl. 61-6313 5.00
1. Art and society. 2. Art—France. 3. Art—Belgium. 4. France—Soc. condit. 5. Belgium—Soc. condit. I. Title. II. Series.

HERBERT, Eugenia W. 309.144'081
The artist and social reform; France and Belgium, 1885-1898, by Eugenia W. Herbert. Freeport, N.Y., Books for Libraries Press [1971, c1961] xvi, 236 p. illus. 24 cm. Bibliography: p. [214]-222. [N72.S6H4 1971] 75-164605 ISBN 0-8369-5889-6
1. Art and society. 2. Art—France. 3. Art—Belgium. I. Title. BIP

HOVEY, Walter Read, 1895- 701
The arts in changing societies: reflections inspired by works of art in the Frick Art Museum, Pittsburgh; five lectures by Walter Read Hovey delivered at the Frick Art Museum, Pittsburgh, Pennsylvania, 1970-1971. [Pittsburgh, Frick Art Museum, 1972] 41 p. 46 plates 26 cm. [N72.S6H68] 72-83949
1. Art and society. 2. Humanism in art. I. Frick Art Museum, Pittsburgh. II. Title.

KAVOLIS, Vytautas 701.15
Martynas, 1930-
Artistic expression; a sociological analysis [by] Vytautas Kavolis. Ithaca, N.Y., Cornell University Press [1968] viii, 272 p. 22 cm. Bibliographical references included in "Notes" (p. 211-263) [N72.S6K3] 68-14113
1. Art and society. 2. Art—Psychology. I. Title. BIP

KAVOLIS, Vytautas Martynas, 301.2
1930-
History on art's side; social dynamics in artistic efflorescences [by] Vytautas Kavolis. Ithaca [N.Y.] Cornell University Press [1972] vi, 222 p. 22 cm. Includes bibliographical references. [N72.S6K33] 70-38683 ISBN 0-8014-0715-X 8.50
1. Art and society. 2. Art—Psychology. I. Title. BIP

KEPES, Gyorgy, 1906- 701
Arts of the environment. Edited by Gyorgy Kepes. New York, G. Braziller [1972] 244 p. illus. 25 cm. (Vision + value series) Includes bibliographical references. [N72.S6K37] 72-161569 ISBN 0-8076-0620-0 12.50
1. Art and society. 2. Cities and towns—Planning—1945- 3. Human ecology. I. Title. BIP

LEITH, James A 301.1523
The idea of art as propaganda in France, 1750-1799; a study in the history of ideas [by] James A. Leith. [Toronto] University of Toronto Press [1965] ix, 184 p. plates. 24 cm. (University of Toronto romance series, no. 8) "An essay on sources": p. [161]-171. [N6846.L36] 65-1875
1. Art and society. 2. France — Hist. — Revolution — Propaganda. 3. France — Hist. — Revolution — Art. I. Title. II. Series: Toronto, University. University of Toronto romance series, no. 8 BIP

MUKERJEE, Radhakamal, 1889- 701.1
The social function of art. New York, Philosophical Library [1954] xxii, 280, xvp. illus. 26cm. [N72.M8 1954] 54-3247
1. Art and society. I. Title. BIP

MUKERJEE, Radhakamal, 1889- 701
The social function of art. Westport, Conn., Greenwood Press [1971] xxii, 280, xv p. illus. 24 cm. Reprint of the 1954 ed. Includes bibliographical references. [N72.S6M8 1971] 78-138597 ISBN 0-8371-5798-6
1. Art and society. I. Title.

PLEKHANOV, Georgii 709'.44
Valentinovich, 1856-1918.
Art and society & other papers in historical materialism / George V. Plekhanov. New York : Oriole Editions, [1974] 187 p. ; 23 cm. Contents.Contents.—Art and society.—Historical materialism and the arts.—Ibsen, petty bourgeois revolutionist.—French drama and painting of the 18th century. Includes bibliographical references. [N72.S6P5713] 74-79551 ISBN 0-88211-069-1 : 8.50
1. Ibsen, Henrik, 1828-1908. 2. Art and society. 3. Arts, French. I. Title.

PONENTE, Nello 709.034
The structures of the modern world, 1850-1900. [Tr. from Italian by James Emmons. Geneva] Skira [Cleveland, World 1966] 210p. illus. (pt. fold.) col. plates. 31cm. (Art ideas hist.) [N6450.P613] 65-24416 20.00
1. Art and society. 2. Art—Hist.—19th cent. I. Title. II. Series.

READ, Herbert Edward, 1893- 701.1
Art and society, [2d ed. New York] Pantheon Books [1950?] xv, 152 p. plates. 23 cm. Bibliographical footnotes. [N72.R28 1950] 50-9130
1. Art and society. 2. Art and religion. I. Title. BIP

READ, Herbert Edward, Sir, 701.1
1893-1968.
Art and society [by] Herbert Read. New York, Schocken Books [1966] xvii, 152 p. illus., ports. 21 cm. Bibliographical footnotes. [N72.S6R4 1966] 66-26728
1. Art and society. 2. Art and religion.

SMITH, Norris Kelly. 701
On art & architecture in the modern world; a collection of essays. [Watkins Glen, N.Y.] Published by the American Life Foundation for University of Victoria, Victoria, B.C., Canada, 1971. 95 p. illus. 29 cm. Contents.Contents.—Ideas about culture: Courbet and the arts & crafts.—Man's environment.—Millenary folly: the failure of an eschatology.—Appendix: The metaphor of the state. The Gothic cathedral. Includes bibliographical references. [N72.S6S55] 79-125613
1. Art and society. 2. Architecture and Society. 3. Aesthetics, Modern—19th century. 4. Aesthetics, Modern—20th century. I. Title.

VILAR, Sergio, 1936- ed. 701
Manifesto sobre arte y libertad; encuesta entre los intelectuales y artistas espanoles [New York] Las Americas [1964, c.]1963. 302p. 23cm. 64-3450 5.00
1. Art and society. I. Title.

Art and society—Hamburg—Exhibitions.

GARTEN, Landhauser und 943.423
Villen des hamburgischen Burgertums :

Kunst, Kultur und gesellschaftliches Leben in vier Jahrhunderten : Ausstellung 29. Mai-26. Oktober 1975, Museum fur Hamburgische Geschichte / [Katalogbearbeitung, Ulrich Bauche, Gisela Jaacks, Ute Scheurlen]. Hamburg : Museum fur Hamburgische Geschichte, 1975. 228 p. : ill. (some col.) ; 24 cm. (Aus den Schausammlungen des Museums fur Hamburgische Geschichte ; Heft 4) [DD901.H22H28 Heft 4] [N6886.H3] 760'.09174'924 76-450198
1. Art and society—Hamburg—Exhibitions. 2. Architecture and society—Hamburg—Exhibitions. 3. Middle classes—Germany, West—Hamburg—Exhibitions. I. Bauche, Ulrich. II. Jaacks, Gisela. III. Scheurlen, Ute. IV. Hamburg. Museum fur Hamburgische Geschichte. V. Series: Hamburg. Museum fur Hamburgische Geschichte. Aus den Schausammlungen ; Heft 4.

Art and society—United States.

GUERRILLA Art Action Group. 709'.747'1
GAAG, the Guerrilla Art Action Group, 1969-1976 : a selection / photos. by Jan van Raay ; designed by Pat Steir & Paula Greif ; additional photos. by Julie Abeles ... [et al.]. New York : Printed Matter, c1978. ca. 200 p. : ill. ; 22 cm. "The Guerrilla Art Action Group in basically Jon Hendricks and Jean Toche." [N6512.G78 1978] 76-48869 ISBN 0-89439-001-5 pbk. : 12.50
1. Guerrilla Art Action Group—Addresses, essays, lectures. 2. Dissident art—United States—Addresses, essays, lectures. I. Hendricks, Jon. II. Toche, Jean. III. Title.

SOMMER, Robert. 709'.73
Street art / Robert Sommer, New York : Links, [1975] x, 66 p., [42] leaves of plates : ill. (some col.) ; 21 cm. Bibliography: p. 65-66. [N72.S6S65] 74-78867 ISBN 0-8256-3044-4 pbk. : 7.95
1. Art and society—United States. 2. Art, Amateur—United States. 3. Street decoration—United States. I. Title. BIP

Art and state.

LEHMANN-HAUPT, Hellmut, 1903- 709.43
Art under a dictatorship. New York, Oxford University Press, 1954. xxii, 277 p. illus. ports. 24 cm. Bibliographical references included in 'Notes' (p. 249-308) [N8725.L4] 54-5292
1. Art and state. 2. Art—Germany. 3. Art—Russia. I. Title. BIP

LEHMANN-HAUPT, Hellmut, 1903- 709'.43
Art under a dictatorship. New York, Octagon Books, 1973 [c1954] xxii, 277 p. illus. 24 cm. Reprint of the ed. published by the Oxford University Press, New York. Includes bibliographical references. [N8725.L4 1973] 73-5521 ISBN 0-374-94896-8 11.00 (lib. bdg.)
1. Art and state. 2. Art—Germany. 3. Art—Russia. I. Title.

Art and state—Congresses.

SEMINAR on Preservation and Restoration, Williamsburg, va., 1963. 704
Historic preservation today. Charlottesville, Univ. Pr. of Va. [c.1966] x, 265p. 23cm. Essays presented to the Seminar on Preservation and Restoration, Williamsburg, Va., Sept. 8-11, 1963. Sponsored by the Natl. Trust for Historic Preservation and Colonial Williamsburg. Bibl. [N8720.S4] 66-4884 4.00 pap.,
1. Art and state—Congresses. 2. Monuments—Preservation—Congresses. I. National Trust for Historic Preservation in the United States. II. Colonial Williamsburg, inc. III. Title.

Art and state—Europe.

MOULIN, Raymonde. 338.4'7'7094
Public aid for creation in the plastic arts / by Raymonde Moulin. Oslo : Council of Europe, 1976. iv, 84 p. ; 21 cm. At head of title: Conference of Ministers with Responsiblity for Cultural Affairs. [N8846.E85M68] 77-373488
1. Art and state—Europe. I. Conference of Ministers with Responsiblity for Cultural Affairs, Oslo, 1976. II. Title.

Art and state—U.S.

HANKS, Nancy, 1927- 338.47'7
In support of freedom. [Tempe, Ariz.] Bureau of Educational Research and Services [1971] 20 p. 23 cm. (Grady Gammage memorial lecture, 10) [NX735.H3] 71-636394
1. Art and state—U.S. 2. The arts—U.S.—Finance. I. Title. II. Series.

O'CONNOR, Francis V. 350.854
Federal art patronage, 1933 to 1943, by Francis V. O'Connor. [College Park, Md., 1966] 60 p. illus., ports. 28 cm. "An exhibition, April 6 to May 13, 1966, University of Maryland Art Gallery, J. Millard Tawes Fine Arts Center, College Park, Maryland." "Catalog": p. 55-60. Bibliography: p. 41-54. [N8837.O25] 66-64996
1. Art and state—U.S. 2. Art, American—Exhibitions. 3. Art, Modern—20th century—U.S. I. Maryland. University. Art Gallery. II. Title.

O'CONNOR, Francis V. 338.4'7'7
Federal support for the visual arts: the New Deal and now; a report on the New Deal art projects in New York City and State with recommendations for present-day Federal support for the visual arts to the National Endowment for the Arts. By Francis V. O'Connor. Greenwich, Conn., New York Graphic Society, 1969. viii, 226 p. illus. 28 cm. Bibliography: p. 209-226. [N6512.O25] 76-109702
1. Federal Art Project. 2. Art and state—U.S. I. National Endowment for the Arts. II. Title.

PURCELL, Ralph, 1919- 706.9
Government and art, a study of American experience; with an introd. by Clarence Derwent. Washington, Public Affairs Press [1956] 129p. 24cm. [N6512.P8] 56-8543
1. Art and state—U. S. 2. State encouragement of science, literature and art. I. Title.

Art and state—United States—Directories.

WASHINGTON and the arts; 353.008'54'025753 a guide and directory to Federal programs and dollars for the arts. [Janet English Gracey and Sally Gardner, special editors. New York] Associated Councils of the Arts [1971] vi, 176 p. 23 cm. (ACA special) Published in 1975 under title: Cultural directory. [NX735.W3] 79-163014 6.50
1. Art and state—United States—Directories. 2. State encouragement of science, literature, and art—United States. I. Gracey, Janet English, ed. II. Gardner, Sally, ed. III. Associated Councils of the Arts.

Art and state—Yugoslavia.

MAJSTOROVIC, Stevan. 338.4'7'7
Cultural policy in Yugoslavia. Paris, Unesco, 1972. 81 p. illus. 24 cm. (Studies and documents on cultural policies) "SHC.70/XIV.12/A." [NX750.Y8M3] 75-187097 2.00 (pbk.)
1. Art and state—Yugoslavia. 2. The arts—Yugoslavia—Finance. I. Title. II. Series.
Distributed by Unipub, N.Y. BIP

Art and technology.

LOS Angeles Co., Calif. Museum of Art, Los Angeles. Art and Technology Program. 709.04'6
Art & technology; a report on the Art & Technology Program of the Los Angeles County Museum of Art, 1967-1971 [by] Maurice Tuchman. [Los Angeles] Los Angeles County Museum of Art; distributed by the Viking Press, New York [1971] 387 p. illus., map, plans. 29 cm. [N72.T4L6] 74-146884 ISBN 0-670-13372-8 12.50
1. Art and technology. I. Tuchman, Maurice. II. Title.

LOS Angeles Co., Calif. Museum of Art, Los Angeles. Art and Technology Program. 709'.046
A report on the Art and Technology Program of the Los Angeles County Museum of Art, 1967-1971 [by Maurice Tuchman. Los Angeles, Los Angeles County Museum of Art, 1971] 387 p. illus. 28 cm. Published also under title: Art & technology. [N72.T4L64] 73-29924 ISBN 0-87587-044-9
1. Art and technology. I. Tuchman, Maurice. II. Title.

Art and visual disorders.

TREVOR-ROPER, Patrick Dacre, 1916- 709
The world through blunted sight; an inquiry into the influence of defective vision on art and character [by] Patrick Trevor-Roper. [1st American ed.] Indianapolis, Bobbs-Merrill [1970] 191 p. illus. (part col.), ports. 26 cm. Bibliography: p. 172-181. [N71.8.T7 1970b] 73-123237 12.50
1. Art and visual disorders. I. Title.

Art, Anglo-Saxon.

JACKSON, Esther. 726.509
Art of the Anglo-Saxon age; an illustrated study of England's churches and Sculpture, A.D. 597-1066. Peterborough, N. H., R. R. Smith [1964] xiv, 176 p. illus., maps (on lining papers) 25 cm. Bibliography: p. 173-174. [N6763.J3] 63-17176
1. Art, Anglo-Saxon. I. Title. BIP

Art—Ann Arbor, Mich.

MICHIGAN. University. Museum of Art. v. 12
A handbook of the collections... Ann arbor, 1962. [93] p. (chiefly illus.) 27cm. [N513.A63] 62-63762
1. Art—Ann Arbor, Mich. I. Title.

Art appreciation.

ANAND, Mulk Raj, 1905- 701'.1
Seven little-known birds of the inner eye / Mulk Raj Anand. Rutland, Vt. : Charles E. Tuttle Co., 1978. 157 p. : ill. ; 24 cm. Includes index. Bibliography: p. 151-152. [N7477.A5] 77-72601 ISBN 0-8048-0936-4 : 17.50
1. Art appreciation. 2. Visual perception. I. Title.

ARNOLD, Nellie D., 1945- 700'.1
The interrelated arts in leisure : perceiving and creating / Nellie D. Arnold. Saint Louis : C. V. Mosby Co., 1976. ix, 188 p., [2] leaves of plates : ill. (some col.) ; 27 cm. Includes index. Bibliography: p. 183-185. [NX643.A76] 75-30965 ISBN 0-8016-0328-5 : 9.50
1. Art appreciation. 2. Arts—Psychology. I. Title. BIP

BAKER, Samm Sinclair. 709'.4
Introduction to art; a guide to the understanding and enjoyment of great masterpieces [by] Samm Sinclair Baker and Natalie Baker. New York, H. N. Abrams [1970] 221 p. illus., ports. 32 cm. Part of illustrative matter colored. [N7477.B35] 69-12482 ISBN 0-8109-0193-5
1. Art appreciation. 2. Art—Psychology. I. Baker, Natalie, joint author. II. Title.

DANIELS, Florence Margaret, 1921- 701'.18
Why art? / By Florence Margaret Daniels. Chicago : Nelson-Hall, [1978] p. cm. [N7477.D36] 77-28084 ISBN 0-88229-173-4 : 11.95 pbk. : 7.95
1. Art appreciation. I. Title. BIP

IMPROVING the teaching of art appreciation 701.18 [by a] research and development team for the improvement of teaching art appreciation in the secondary schools. David W. Ecker, project director. Columbus, Ohio State University Research Foundation, 1966. x, 340 p. 23 plates. 28 cm. Final report RF 2006. Cooperative research project no. V-006. Contract no. OE-5-10-308. School of Art, Ohio State University. Research reported was performed pursuant to a contract with the U.S. Office of Education. Includes bibliographical references. [N363.I43] 68-63120
1. Art appreciation. 2. Art—Study and teaching (Secondary) I. Ecker, Daniel W. II. Ohio. State University, Columbus. Research Foundation. III. Ohio. State University, Columbus. School of Art.

MARTIN, F. David, 1920- 700'.1
The humanities through the arts / F. David Martin, Lee A. Jacobus. 2d ed. New York : McGraw-Hill, c1978. xiii, 478 p. : ill. ; 24 cm. Includes bibliographies and indexes. [NX165.M37 1978] 78-6254 ISBN 0-07-040614-6 : 18.50 ISBN 0-07-040613-8 pbk. : 13.95
1. Arts—Psychology. 2. Art appreciation. I. Jacobus, Lee A., joint author. II. Title.

MOORE, Janet Gaylord. 701*.18
The many ways of seeing; an introduction to the pleasures of art. Cleveland, World Pub. Co. [1968] 141 p. illus. (part col.) 29 cm. Bibliography: p. 121-128. An introduction to art appreciation through a brief history of art, an explanation of various techniques and styles, and suggested exercises for the amateur. [N7435.M63] 67-23348 7.95
1. Art appreciation. I. Title. BIP

MORMAN, Jean Mary. 701'.18
Wonder under your feet; making the world of art your own, written and designed by Jean Mary Morman. [1st ed.] New York, Harper & Row [1973] 92 p. illus. (part col.) 23 cm. [N7477.M67 1973] 73-6329 ISBN 0-06-065974-2 7.95
1. Art appreciation. I. Title.
Pbk. 3.95; ISBN 0-06-065975-0.

PEPPER, Stephen Coburn, 1891- 701.18
Principles of art appreciation [by] Stephen C. Pepper. Westport, Conn., Greenwood Press [1970, c1949] vii, 326 p. illus., 20 plates. 23 cm. [N7477.P44 1970] 70-98238
1. Art appreciation. I. Title. BIP

READ, Herbert Edward, Sir, 1893-1968. 701'.17
The meaning of art. New York, Praeger [1972, c1971] 280 p. illus. 19 cm. (Praeger paperbacks, P-349) [N7477.R4 1972] 70-171237 2.95
1. Art appreciation. 2. Art—History. 3. Aesthetics. I. Title.

RIES, Estelle H. 701.18
Artists and artisans [by] Estelle H. Ries. South Brunswick [N.J.] A. S. Barnes [1968] 391 p. illus., maps, ports. 26 cm. [N7435.R5] 66-20485
1. Art appreciation. 2. Art industries and trade. 3. Art and society. I. Title.

RUSSELL, Stella Pandell. 701'.18
Art appreciation / Stella Pandell Russell. San Francisco : Rinehart Press, [1974] c1975. p. cm. Includes indexes. Bibliography: p. [N7477.R87] 74-23538 ISBN 0-03-011051-3
1. Art appreciation. I. Title.

SCHINNELLER, James A. 701'.1
Art : search & self discovery / James A. Schinneller. 3d ed. Worcester, Mass. : Davis Publications, c1975. viii, 375 p. : ill. (some col.) ; 23 cm. Includes bibliographies and indexes. [N7435.S33 1975] 75-322850 ISBN 0-87192-070-0 : 14.95 ISBN 0-87192-072-7 pbk. : 8.95
1. Art appreciation. I. Title: Art : search & self discovery.

SCHINNELLER, James A. 701
Art; search & self-discovery [by] James A. Schinneller. 2d ed. Scranton, Pa., International Textbook Co. [1968] xxii, 473 p. illus. (part col.), plans. 23 x 24 cm. (International textbooks in art and art education) Includes bibliographies. [N7435.S33 1968] 67-12110
1. Art appreciation. I. Title. BIP

Art appreciation—Juvenile literature.

HOLME, Bryan, 1913- 701'.1
Enchanted world : pictures to grow up with / Bryan Holme. New York : Oxford University Press, 1979. p. cm. Guides the reader through selected illustrations demonstrating how each particular artists achieves his special purpose. [N7477.H64] 78-11546 ISBN 0-19-520127-2 : 9.95

1. Art appreciation—Juvenile literature. I. Title. BIP

KAPP, Helen. 750'.11
Enjoying pictures / Helen Kapp. London : Routledge & Kegan Paul, 1975. vii, 80 p. : ill. ; 24 cm. (The Local search series) Bibliography: p. 78. [N7477.K33] 75-319169 ISBN 0-7100-8088-3 : 5.75
1. Art appreciation—Juvenile literature. I. Title.
Distributed by Routledge & Kegan Paul, Boston. BIP

Art appreciation—Study and teaching (Elementary)

HURWITZ, Al. 701'.18
The joyous vision : a source book for elementary art appreciation / al Hurwitz, Stanley S. Madeja. Englewood Cliffs, N.J. : Prentice-Hall, c1977. ix, 302 p. : ill. ; 24 cm. Bibliography: p. 292-294. [N350.H87] 76-30339 ISBN 0-13-511600-7 : 12.95
1. Art appreciation—Study and teaching (Elementary) 2. Art appreciation—Study and teaching (Secondary) I. Madeja, Stanley S., joint author. II. Title.

Art, Argentine.

MUJICA LAINEZ, Manuel, 1910- v. 12
Argentina. [English translation by William McLeod Rivera] Washington, Pan American Union, 1961. 74p. illus. 18cm. (Art in Latin America today) Bibliography: p. 72-74. [N6635.M8] PA61
1. Art, Argentine. I. Title. II. Series.

Art—Arnhem Land, Australia.

UNITED Nations Educational, Scientific and Cultural Organization. 759.994
Australia: aboriginal paintings, Arnhem Land. Introd. by Sir Herbert Read. [Greenwich, Conn.] New York Graphic Society [1954] 14 p. illus., 32 col. plates. 48 cm. (UNESCO world art series, 3) Material assembled by experts from UNESCO and the New York Graphic Society. [N7402.A7U5] 54-13494
1. Art—Arnhem Land, Australia. 2. Paintings, Australian (Aboriginal) I. Read, Herbert Edward, Sir, 1893-1968. II. New York Graphic Society. III. Title. IV. Series.

Art as a profession.

BERLYE, Milton K. 702'.3
Selling your art work: a marketing guide for fine and commercial artists, by Milton K. Berlye. South Brunswick, A. S. Barnes [1973] 272 p. illus. 22 cm. [N8353.B4] 72-37826 ISBN 0-498-01105-4 8.95
1. Art as a profession. 2. Commercial art as a profession. 3. Art dealers. I. Title. BIP

BRILL, Reginald 740
Art as a career. London, Batsford [New Rochelle, N.Y., SportShelf, 1965, c.1962] 124p. illus. 19cm. (Batsford career bks.) [N8350.B7] 65-907 4.00 bds.,
1. Art as a profession. I. Title.

BRILL, Reginald. 702'.3
Art as a career. London, Batsford [1962] Distributed by Sportshelf, New Rochelle, N.Y. 124 p. illus. 19 cm. (Batsford career books) Stamped on t. p. [N8350.B7] 65-907
1. Art as a profession. I. Title.

HARRIS, Kenneth, 1904- 750.69
How to make a living as a painter. [2d ed.] New York, Watson-Guptill [1964] 142 p. illus. 23 cm. [N8680.H35 1964] 64-24248
1. Art as a profession. I. Title. BIP

HARRIS, Kenneth, 1904- 750.69
How to make a living as a painter. Decorations by Doug Anderson; edited by Arthur L. Guptill. [1st ed.] New York, Watson-Guptill [1954] 114p. illus. 24cm. [N8680.H35] 54-12955
1. Art as a profession. I. Title.

HOLDEN, Donald. 706.9
Art career guide; a guidance handbook for art students, teachers, vocational counselors, and job hunters. New York, Watson-Guptill Publications, 1961. 275 p. 24 cm. [N8350.H6] 61-18280
1. Art as a profession. I. Title. BIP

HOLDEN, Donald. 702'.3
Art career guide; a guidance handbook for art students, teachers, vocational counselors, and job hunters. 2d ed., rev. and enl. [New York] Watson-Guptill Publications [1967, c1961] 258 p. 24 cm. [N8350.H6 1967] 67-9661
1. Art as a profession. I. Title.

HOLDEN, Donald. 702'.3
Art career guide; a guidance handbook for art students, teachers, vocational counselors, and job hunters. 3d ed., rev. and enl. [New York] Watson-Guptill Publications [1973] 303 p. 23 cm. [N8350.H6 1973] 72-10192 ISBN 0-8230-0251-9 7.95
1. Art as a profession. I. Title.

KELLY, Francis. 702'.3
The studio and the artist / Francis Kelly. New York : St. Martin's Press, 1975, c1974. 168 p. : ill. ; 25 cm. Includes index. Bibliography: p. 161-164. [N8350.K44 1975] 74-33166 8.95
1. Art as a profession. 2. Artists—Psychology. I. Title.

MCCAUSLAND, Elizabeth, 1899- 707.1173
Art professions in the United States, edited & compiled by Elizabeth McCausland, Royal Bailey Farnum and Dana P. Vaughan. New York, Cooper Union Art School, 1950. 111 p. 26 cm. [N7438.M3] 50-6768
1. Art as a profession. 2. Art—U. S. I. Cooper Union for the Advancement of Science and Art, New York. Art School. II. Title.

MCCAUSLAND, Elizabeth, 1899- 706.9
Careers in the arts: fine and applied. New York, J. Day Co. [1950] 278 p. 21 cm. [N7438.M3 1950a] 50-9439
1. Art as a profession. 2. Art—U. S. I. Title.

MILLS, John Fitz Maurice, 1917- 706.9
Careers through art. Foreword by Percy Horton. London, Museum Pr. [dist. New Rochelle, N.Y., Sport Shelf, 1964, c.1961] 138 p. illus. 23 cm. 62-379 bds., 4.25
1. Art as a profession. I. Title.

MILLS, John FitzMaurice, 1917- 702'.3
Career through art. Foreword by Percy Horton. London, Museum Press [1961] 138 p. illus. 23 cm. [N8350.M5] 62-379
1. Art as a profession. I. Title.

NEW York (City). School of Visual Arts. Alumni Society. Placement Office. 702'.3
Careers in the visual arts. [New York, Visual Arts Press, 1973] 80 p. 14 cm. Cover title. [N8350.N47 1973] 73-86659
1. Art as a profession. I. Title.

ROTH, Claire Jarett. 706.9
Art careers, by Claire Jarett Roth and Adelle Weiss. New York, H. Z. Walck, 1963. 116 p. illus., 21 cm. (Careers for tomorrow) Includes bibliography. [N8350.R6] 63-11113
1. Art as a profession. I. Weiss, Adelle, joint author. II. Title.

Art as a profession—Juvenile literature.

BERGER, Melvin. 700'.23
Jobs in fine arts and humanities. Consultants: Arthur J. Kerr [and] Carl M. Tausig. New York, Lothrop, Lee & Shepard [1974] 95 p. illus. 24 cm. (Exploring careers) Introduces the opportunities in and the requirements for a variety of careers in such fields as music, art, theatre, and dance. [NX163.B47] 73-17701 ISBN 0-688-75010-9 5.50
1. Art as a profession—Juvenile literature. I. Title. BIP

GRACZA, Margaret Young. 700'.23
Art [by] Margaret Gracza. Designed by Rick Lemons. Minneapolis, Dillon Press [1971] 90 p. illus. (part col.), ports. 24 cm. (Looking forward to a career) Discusses the opportunities in and qualifications for various careers in art including fashion design, architecture, print making, and museum work. [N8350.G7] 72-150279 ISBN 0-87518-028-0
1. Art as a profession—Juvenile literature. I. Title.

HORTON, Louise, 1916- 702'.3
Art careers / by Louise Horton ; illustrated by Mark Rubin. New York : F. Watts, 1975. 62 p. : ill. ; 24 cm. (A Career concise guide) Includes index. Bibliography: p. 58-59. Discusses careers in architecture, city planning, interior, industrial, and graphic design, fine art, illustrating, and photography. [N8350.H64] 75-12785 ISBN 0-531-02841-0
1. Art as a profession—Juvenile literature. I. Rubin, Mark, 1946- II. Title.

Art as an investment.

BLODGETT, Richard E. 332.6'78
How to make money in the art market / by Richard Blodgett. New York : P. H. Wyden, [1975] x, 267 p. ; 21 cm. Includes index. Bibliography: p. 251-252. [N8600.B56] 75-7648 ISBN 0-88326-093-X : 7.95
1. Art as an investment. 2. Art—Marketing. I. Title.

RUSH, Richard H. 707'.5
Investment you can live with and enjoy / by Richard H. Rush and the editors of U.S. News & World Report Books. Washington : U.S. News & World Report Books, [1974] 382 p. : ill. ; 24 cm. (U.S. news & world report money management library) Includes index. [N8600.R78] 74-81185 6.95
1. Art as an investment. 2. Art—Collectors and collecting. I. Title.

SHULMAN, Morton. 332.6'78
Anyone can make big money buying art / Morton Shulman. New York : Macmillan, c1977. 136 p., [8] leaves of plates : ill. ; 22 cm. Includes index. [N8600.S55] 77-834 ISBN 0-02-610560-8 8.95
1. Art as an investment. I. Title. BIP

Art—Asia.

RUBISSOW, Helen. 709.5
Art of Asia. New York, Philosophical Library [1954] xiii, 237p. illus., maps. 24cm. Includes bibliographical references. [N7260.R8] 54-12912
1. Art—Asia. I. Title.

Art—Asia, Central.

HRBAS, Milos 709.58
The art of Central Asia [by] Milos Hrbas, Edgar Knobloch; tr. by Roberta Finlayson-Samsour. London, Hamlyn [New York, Tudor, 1966, c.1965] 3-27, [10] p. front., illus., 136 plates (incl. 40 col.) 28cm. Bibl. [N7291.H713] 66-71049 7.95
1. Art—Asia, Central. 2. Art, Islamic. I. Knobloch, Edgar, joint author. II. Title.

Art—Asia, Central—History.

RICE, Tamara (Abelson) Talbot. 709.58
Ancient arts of Central Asia [by] Tamara Talbot Rice. New York, Praeger [1965] 288 p. illus. (part col.), maps. 22 cm. (Praeger world of art series) Bibliography: p. 263-264. [N7291.R5] 65-19586
1. Art—Asia, Central—History. 2. Asia, Central—Antiquities. I. Title. BIP

Art—Asia Minor—History.

PERROT, Georges, 1832-1914. 709'.392
History of art in Phrygia, Lydia, Caria, and Lycia / from the French of Georges Perrot and Charles Chipiez. Boston : Longwood Press, 1977. p.cm. Reprint of the 1892 ed. published by Chapman and Hall, London. Includes index. [N5480.P4 1977] 77-6971 ISBN 0-89341-213-9 lib.bdg. : 65.00
1. Art—Asia Minor—History. 2. Asia Minor—Antiquities. I. Title. BIP

Art—Asia, Southeastern.

RAWSON, Philip S. 709'.54
The art of Southeast Asia; Cambodia, Vietnam, Thailand, Laos, Burma, Java, Bali [by] Philip Rawson. New York, F. A. Praeger [1967] 288 p. illus. (part col.), maps, plans. 22 cm. (Praeger world of art series) Bibliography: p. 278-283. [N5877.A8R3 1967] 67-29399
1. Art—Asia, Southeastern. 2. Asia, Southeastern—Antiquities. I. Title. BIP

Art, Asian.

BINYON, Laurence, 1869-1943 709.5
The spirit of man in Asian art [Gloucester, Mass., P. Smith, 1966, c.1935, 1963] xv, 217p. 70 plates. 22cm. (Dover bk., T1435 rebound) Charles Eliot Norton lects. delivered in Harvard Univ., 1933-34 [N7260.B53] 4.00
1. Art, Asian. I. Title. II. Title: Asian art.

LA PLANTE, John D. 709'.5
Asian art [by] John D. La Plante. Dubuque, Iowa, W. C. Brown Co. [1968] xii, 185 p. illus., maps. 23 cm. (Art horizons series) Bibliography: p. 177. [N7260.L25] 68-14575
1. Art, Asian. BIP

Art, Asian—Catalogs.

LEE, Sherman E. 730'.095'07401471
Asian art; selections from the Collection of Mr. and Mrs. John D. Rockefeller 3rd [by] Sherman E. Lee. New York, Intercultural Arts Press [1970] [66] p. and slide set (29 col. slides. 2 x 2 in.) 30 cm. At head of title: Asia House Gallery. Lecture materials based on Asian art, the catalogue of an exhibition shown in the Asia House Gallery in the autumn of 1970. Includes bibliographical references. [N7262.L36] 77-25165 30.00
1. Rockefeller, John D., 1906- —Art collections. 2. Rockefeller, Blanchette Hooker, 1909- —Art collections. 3. Art, Asian—Catalogs. I. Asia House Gallery, New York. II. Title. BIP

WASHBURN, Gordon Bailey, 1904- 709'.5'07401471
Masterpieces of Asian art in American collections, II. New York, Intercultural Arts Press [1970] [68] p. and slide set (31 col. slides. 2 x 2 in.) 30 cm. At head of title: Asia House Gallery. Lecture materials based on Masterpieces of Asian art in American collections, II, the catalogue of an exhibition shown in the Asia House Gallery in the spring of 1970. Includes bibliographical references. [N7262.W3] 73-25172 30.00
1. Art, Asian—Catalogs. 2. Art, Asian—U.S. I. Asia House Gallery, New York. II. Title.

Art, Asian—Congresses.

THE Collector of Asian art and archaeology; 709'.5
problems of assembly, maintenance, and study. Doanda Randall, technical editor. [1st ed.] New York, Asian Conservation Laboratory [1966, c1965] 128 p. illus. 21 cm. (ACL symposium series, v. 2) "Proceedings of the symposium held March 28-29, 1963, sponsored and organized by the Asian Conservation Laboratory, inc., with the cooperation of Columbia University, Teacher's College, and the Donnell Library Center." Bibliographical references included in "Notes" (p. 115-122) [N7260.C63] 66-26598
1. Art, Asian—Congresses. 2. Art—Collectors and collecting—U.S.—Congresses. 3. Art objects—U.S.—Conservation and restoration—Congresses. I. Randall, Doanda, ed. II. Asian Conservation Laboratory. III. Title. IV. Series.

Art, Asian—Exhibitions.

ASIA Society. 709.5'074'013
Asian art; selections from the Collection of Mr. and Mrs. John D. Rockefeller 3rd. [New York]; distributed by New York Graphic Society [1970] 94 p. plates (part col.) 28 cm. "Catalogue of an exhibition ... shown in the Asia House Gallery in the

fall of 1970 as an activity of the Asia Society." [N7262.A8] 72-129577
1. Rockefeller, John D., 1906- —Art collections. 2. Rockefeller, Blanchette Hooker, 1909- —Art collections. 3. Art, Asian—Exhibitions. I. Asia House Gallery, New York. II. Title.

ASIA Society. 709.5
Masterpieces of Asian art in American collections II; an offering of treasures celebrating the tenth anniversary of Asia House Gallery. [New York]; Distributed by New York Graphic Society [1970] 150 p. illus., plates (part col.) 29 cm. "Catalogue of an exhibition shown in the Asia House Gallery in the spring of 1970." [N7262.A87] 71-19802
1. Art, Asian—Exhibitions. 2. Art, Asian—U.S. I. Asia House Gallery, New York. II. Title.

PARIS. Musee 709'.5'07401471
Guimet.
Rarities of the Musee Guimet : [exhibition] / introd. by Jeannine Auboyer. [New York] : Asia Society : distributed by New York Graphic Society, [1974] 121 p. : ill. (some col.) ; 28 cm. "An Asia House Gallery publication." "Catalogue of an exhibition shown in the Asia House Gallery in 1975 as an activity of The Asia Society." [N7262.P4 1974] 74-81967 ISBN 0-87848-043-9 : 19.50
1. Art, Asian—Exhibitions. I. Auboyer, Jeannine. II. Asia Society. III. Title. BIP

Art, Asiatic—Exhibitions.

ASIA Society. 709.5
Masterpieces of Asian art in American collections, [as shown in Asia House, New York City, January-February, 1960] Chosen by Committee under the direction of Laurence Sickman. New York, 1960. unpaged. illus. 21cm. [N7260.A8] 60-24379
1. Art, Asiatic—Exhibitions. 2. Art—U. S. I. Title.

Art Association of Indianapolis, Indiana. John Herron Art Institute.

ART Association of 750'.74'017252
Indianapolis, Indiana. John Herron Art Institute.
Complete list of European and American paintings in the permanent collection of the John Herron Art Museum, September 1958. [Indianapolis] : Art Association of Indianapolis, Indiana, [1958] [44] p. ; 23 cm. [N577.A55 1958] 75-318279
1. Art Association of Indianapolis, Indiana. John Herron Art Institute. 2. Paintings—Cincinnati—Catalogs. I. Title: Complete list of European and American paintings ...

Art, Assyro-Babylonian.

HARCOURTSMITH, Simon. 709'.35
Babylonian art / by Simon Harcourt-Smith. 1st AMS ed. New York : AMS Press, 1978. 50, 76 p. : ill. ; 23 cm. Reprint of the 1928 ed. published by E. Benn, London, in series: Kai Khosru monographs on eastern art. [N5370.H3 1978] 76-42704 ISBN 0-404-15360-7 : 20.00
1. Art, Assyro-Babylonian. I. Title. II. Series: Kai Khosru monographs on eastern art. BIP

PARROT, Andre, 1901- 709.35
The arts of Assyria. Tr. [from French] by Stuart Gilbert, James Emmons. New York, Golden Pr. [1961] xviii, 383p. illus. (pt. col.) maps. 29cm. (Arts of mankind, v.2) Bibl. 61-11170 25.00
1. Art, Assyro-Babylonian. 2. Art—Mesopatamia. I. Title. II. Series.

PIERPONT Morgan 730'.0935
Library, New York.
Ancient Mesopotamian art and selected texts : The Pierpont Morgan Library. New York : The Library, c1976. 42 p. : ill. ; 26 cm. Includes bibliographical references. [N5370.P53 1976] 76-45976 ISBN 0-87598-062-7
1. Pierpont Morgan Library, New York. 2. Art, Assyro-Babylonian. 3. Assyro-Babylonian language—Texts. 4. Iraq—Antiquities. I. Title. BIP

Art—Athens, Ga.—Catalogs.

GEORGIA Museum of Art. 759.13
A university collects: Georgia Museum of Art, the University of Georgia. Selected by Stuart P. Feld. [Athens?] 1969. 1 v. (unpaged) 44 plates. 28 cm. "Organized by the Georgia Museum of Art, Athens, Georgia, and the American Federation of Arts, New York. Circulated by A.F.A." [N514.A8A64] 76-90594
1. Art—Athens, Ga.—Catalogs. I. Feld, Stuart P. II. American Federation of Arts. III. Title. BIP

Art auctions.

ARNOLD Harvey 658'.91'7
Associates.
The anatomy of an art auction. Commack, N.Y. [1972] iii, 77 p. 21 cm. [N8602.A8] 75-185400 ISBN 0-913014-01-X
1. Art auctions. 2. Fund raising. I. Title. BIP

Art auctions—History.

PARKER, John, 1926- 380.1'45'7
Great art sales of the century / by John Parker. [New York] : Watson-Guptill Publications, [1975] p. cm. Includes index. [N8602.P37] 75-5852 ISBN 0-8230-2150-5 : 19.95
1. Art auctions—History. I. Title.

Art auctions—United States.

ROCKMORE, Cynthia. 745.1
The country auction antiques book / Cynthia and Julian Rockmore ; paintings and drawings by the authors. New York : Hawthorn Books, c1974. 160 p. : ill. (some col.) ; 29 cm. Includes index. [N8602.R62 1974] 74-2572 ISBN 0-8015-1780-X : 12.95
1. Art auctions—United States. 2. Art objects—Collectors and collecting—United States. I. Rockmore, Julian, joint author. II. Title.

Art—Audio-visual aids—Catalogs.

INTERNATIONAL 707.08460838
Institute of Films on Art
Le film sur l art repertoire general international du film sur l'art, 1953-1910, par Les soins de Pascuale Rocchetti et Cesare Molinari de l Institut international du film sur l'art Venezia N. Pozza. [dist. New York, Heinman, 1964] xiv, 524p. 22cm. (Raccolta pisana di saggi e studi, 12) Continues a first catalog pub. under title: Le film sur l'art: repetoire general international des film sur les arts, by the inst's. predecessor, the Intl. Comm. for the Cinema and the Figurative Arts (Roma, edizioni dell'Ateneo, 1953) The indexes of this vol. cover both catalogs. 64-56481 11.00 bds.,
1. Art—Audio-visual aids—Catalogs. 2. Moving-pictures—Catalogs. I. Rochetti, Pasquale, ed. II. Title. III. Title: Repertoire general international du film sur l'art, 1953-1960. IV. Series.

Art, Australian.

BERNDT, Ronald Murray, 709.94
1916- ed.
Australian aboriginal art. Edited by Ronald M. Berndt. With chapters by R. M. Berndt [and others] New York, Macmillan, 1964. xiii, 117 p. illus., maps, col. plates. 29 cm. Bibliography: p. 108-112. [N7401.B4 1964] 64-12214
1. Art, Australian. 2. Art, Primitive. I. Title.

KUPKA, Karel. 709.011
Dawn of art; painting and sculpture of Australian aborigines. With a foreword by A. P. Elkin and a pref. by Andre Breton. [Translated by John Ross] New York, Viking Press [1965] x, 180 p. illus. (part col.) map. 24 cm. (A Studio book) Translation of Un art a l'etat brut. Bibliography: p. 179-180 [N7401.K813] 65-21148
1. Art, Australian. 2. Art, Primitive. I. Title.

Art, Australian (Aboriginal)

AUSTRALIAN aboriginal 709'.01'1
art, primitive, traditional, decorative : authentic reproductions ready for framing. Melbourne : Newcraft Publicity, 1967- v. : chiefly col. ill. ; 49-79 cm. Cover title. Most vols. consist of 4 or 5 color plates with a leaf of text, The cave art & The bark paintings of Australia by C. P. Mountford. Vols. [21]-[22] have title: Central Australian aboriginal paintings, and consist of 13 plates with a foreword by W. Hilliard. [N7401.A92] 75-322549
1. Art, Australian (Aboriginal) I. Mountford, Charles Pearcy, 1890- II. Newcraft Publicity. III. Title: Central Australian aboriginal paintings.

Art, Australian (Aboriginal)—Congresses.

AUSTRALIAN 994'.004'991 s
Institute of Aboriginal Studies, Canberra.
Form in indigenous art : schematisation in the art of aboriginal Australia and prehistoric Europe / edited by Peter J. Ucko. Canberra : Australian Institute of Aboriginal Studies ; Atlantic Highlands, N.J. : Humanities Press, 1977. 486 p. : ill. (some col.) ; 27 cm. (Prehistory and material culture series ; no. 13) "Papers presented to a symposium at the 1974 meeting of the Australian Institute of Aboriginal Studies." Includes bibliographies and indexes. [DU120.A8 no. 13, 1977] [N7401] 709'.01'1 78-52020 ISBN 0-391-00864-1 : 49.00
1. Art, Australian (Aboriginal)—Congresses. 2. Art, Prehistoric—Europe—Congresses. I. Title. II. Series. BIP

Art, Australian (Aboriginal)—Exhibitions.

ALLEN, Louis A. 709'.01'1
Australian aboriginal art: Arnhem Land [by] Louis A. Allen. [Chicago] Printed by Field Museum Press, [1972] iii, 43 p. illus. 28 cm. Exhibition held at the Field Museum of Natural History, Chicago. Bibliography: p. 43. [N7401.A7] 71-175062
1. Art, Australian (Aboriginal)—Exhibitions. I. Field Museum of Natural History, Chicago. II. Title.

DAVIDSON, James A. 709.01'1
Australian aboriginal art; Louis A. Allen Collection. Text by James A. Davidson. [Exhibition] The Art Galleries, University of California, Santa Barbara, January 6 to February 1, 1970. [Santa Barbara, 1970] 21 p. illus., map. 22 x 23 cm. [N7401.D3] 71-629584
1. Allen, Louis A.—Art collections. 2. Art, Australian (Aboriginal)—Exhibitions. I. California. University, Santa Barbara. Art Gallery. II. Title.

ELSASSER, Albert B. 709.01'1
Australian aboriginal art; the Louis A. Allen collection. An exhibition at the Robert H. Lowie Museum of Anthropology of the University of California, Berkeley, January 17—August 25, 1969. Text by Albert B. Elsasser and Vivian Paul. [Berkeley, 1969?] 18 p. illus., map (on cover) 24 cm. Bibliography: p. 17. [N7401.E4] 79-632468
1. Allen, Louis A.—Art collections. 2. Art, Australian (Aboriginal)—Exhibitions. I. Paul, Vivian, joint author. II. California. University. Robert H. Lowie Museum of Anthropology. III. Title.

Art, Australian (Aboriginal)—Kimberley, Western Australia (Division)

CRAWFORD, Ian M., 1935- 759.994'1
The art of the Wandjina; aboriginal cave paintings in Kimberley, Western Australia [by] I. M. Crawford. Melbourne, New York [etc.] Oxford University Press [1968] 144 p. illus. (part col.), col. maps. 26 cm. Published in association with the Western Australian Museum. Bibliography: p. 140-141. [N7402.K5C7] 70-382538 6.00
1. Art, Australian (Aboriginal)—Kimberley, Western Australia (Division) I. Western Australian Museum. II. Title.

Art, Australian—Bibliography.

HANKS, Elizabeth Flinn, 016.70994
1937-
Bibliography of Australian art, 1901-1925 / [Elizabeth Hanks]. Melbourne : Library Council of Victoria, 1976. xii, 133 p. ; 26 cm. "Based on the holdings of the State Library of Victoria, supplemented by the collections in the Mitchell Library, Sydney and the Art Gallery of New South Wales." [Z5961.A85H35] [N7400] 77-362557 ISBN 0-909962-13-8
1. Art, Australian—Bibliography. I. Victoria, Australia. State Library, Melbourne. II. Library Council of Victoria. III. Title.

Art, Australian—Catalogs.

HELE, Ivor Henry Thomas, 759.994
1912-
The art of Ivor Hele. Preface by Sir Will Ashton. [Adelaide] Rigby [1966] 1v. (unpaged) illus. (pt. col.) ports. (pt. col.) 28cm. [ND1105.H43 A42] 65-19192 29.50
I. Title.

HEYSEN, Hans, Sir 1877- 759.994
The art of Hans Heysen. Text. Selection of pictures by David Dridan. Adelaide. Rigby [San Francisco, Tri-Ocean, c.1966] 1v. (unpaged) chiefly illus. (pt. col.) port.) 28x35cm. [ND1105H45D7] 66-10442 22.45
I. Dridan, David, 1932- ed. II. Title.

VICTORIA, 709'.94'07409945
Australia. National Gallery, Melbourne.
Freedom from prejudice : an introduction to the Australian Collection in the National Gallery of Victoria / [by] Brian Finemore ; selected and compiled by Jennifer Phipps ; consulting editor, Stephen Murray-Smith. Melbourne : National Gallery of Victoria, 1977. 144 p. : ill. (some col.) ; 25 cm. Includes index. Bibliography: p. 136-138. [N7400.V52 1977] 78-301525 ISBN 0-7241-0031-8
1. Victoria, Australia. National Gallery, Melbourne. 2. Art, Australian—Catalogs. 3. Art—Australia—Victoria—Catalogs. I. Finemore, Brian. II. Phipps, Jennifer. III. Title.

Art, Australian—Dictionaries.

MCCULLOCH, Alan. 709'.94
Encyclopedia of Australian art. New York, Praeger [1969, c1968] 668 p. illus. (part col.) 24 cm. [N7400.M27 1969] 69-17079 25.00
1. Art, Australian—Dictionaries. I. Title. BIP

Art, Australian—Exhibitions.

VICTORIA, 759.994'074'09945
Australia. National Gallery, Melbourne.
The field. [Melbourne? 1968?] 96 p. illus. (part col.) 30 cm. Exhibition, August 21 - September 28, 1968. [N7400.A58] 73-548672
1. Art, Australian—Exhibitions. 2. Art, Modern—20th century—Australia. I. Title.

VICTORIA, Australia. 709'.94
National Gallery, Melbourne.
Landfall; the Captain James Cook bicentenary exhibition of Australian art; National Gallery of Victoria, 7 April-30 June 1970. [Text by Ann Galbally. Photography: George Mehes. Melbourne, 1970] [40] p. illus. (part col.) col. plates. 30 cm. Caption title. Includes bibliographical references. [N7400.V52] 73-863177
1. Art, Australian—Exhibitions. I. Title.

Art, Australian—History.

EARLY artists of 759.994
Australia. London, Sydney, New York, Hamlyn [1971] 60 p. illus. (part col.) facsims. 29 cm. [N7400.E2] 72-193561 ISBN 0-600-07033-6 1.50 (Australia)
1. Art, Australian—History.

HUGHES, Robert, 1936- 759.994
The art of Australia. Revised ed. Harmondsworth, Penguin, 1970. 331 p., 8 plates. illus. (some col.). 20 cm.

Bibliography: p. 317-320. [N7400.H8 1970] 72-18946 21/-
1. Art, Australian—History. I. Title.

Art, Australian—Prices.

INGRAM, Terence. 709'.94'075
A matter of taste : investing in Australian art / Terry Ingram. Sydney : Collins, 1976. 152 p., [12] leaves of plates : ill. (some col.) ; 26 cm. Includes index. [N7400.I53] 76-377407 ISBN 0-00-211444-5
1. Art, Australian—Prices. 2. Art as an investment. 3. Art—Australia—Marketing. I. Title.

Art, Austrian.

GRIMSCHITZ, Bruno, 1892- 709.436
Ars Austriae [Tr. from German] [dist. New York, Lounz, 1961, c.1960] 60p. 244 plates (pt. col.) 35cm. A61 28.00
1. Art, Austrian. I. Title.

Art, Austrian—Exhibitions.

LA Boetie, inc. 760'.09436'07401471
Egon Schiele and his circle. New York [1971] [51] p. illus. (part col.), ports. 22 cm. Catalog of an exhibition held May-June 1971. [N6808.5.E9L3] 78-198239
1. Schiele, Egon. 1890-1918. 2. Art. Austrian—Exhibitions. 3. Expressionism (Art)—Austria. I. Title.

Art, Austrian—Hist.

SOTRIFFER, Kristian, 1932- 709.436
Modern Austrian art [Tr. from German by Alisa Jaffa] New York, Praeger [1965, c.1963] 140p. illus. (pt. mounted col.) plates. 24cm. [N6808.S613] 65-25389 9.95
1. Art, Austrian—Hist. I. Title.

Art—Baltimore—Catalogs.

BALTIMORE. Museum of Art. 708.152
200 objects in the Baltimore Museum of Art, a picture book Baltimore, 1955. 93 p. (chiefly illus.) 26 cm. 'Issued in lieu of the Baltimore Museum of Art News--vol. XVIII, no. 5, June, 1955.' --Sllp inserted. [N515.A55] 55-3538
1. Art—Baltimore—Catalogs. I. Baltimore. Museum of Art. News. II. Title.

Art, Baroque.

BAZIN, Germain. 709'.03'2
The baroque : principles, styles, modes, themes / Germain Bazin ; [translation by Pat Wardroper]. New York : Norton, [1978] c1968. p. cm. Reprint of the ed. published by New York Graphic Society, New York. Includes index. Bibliography: p. [N6415.B3B313 1978] 77-17416 pbk. : 10.95
1. Art, Baroque. I. Title.

BAZIN, Germain. 709.033
Baroque and rococo. [Translated from the French by Jonathan Griffin] New York, Praeger [1964] 288 p. illus. (part col.) 22 cm. (Praeger world of art series) Translation of Classique, baroque et rococo. Bibliography: p. 273-275. [N6410.B363] 64-22488
1. Art, Baroque. 2. Art, Rococo. I. Title.

HELD, Julius Samuel, 1905- 709'.03'2
17th and 18th century art; baroque painting, sculpture, architecture [by] Julius S. Held and Donald Posner. New York, H. N. Abrams [1971] 439 p. illus. (part col.) 30 cm. (Library of art history) Bibliography: p. 424-[427] [N6415.B3H4] 79-127417 ISBN 0-8109-0032-7
1. Art, Baroque. I. Posner, Donald. II. Title.

HUBALA, Erich, 1920- 709'.03'2
Baroque and Rococo art / Erich Hubala. New York : Universe Books, 1976. 196 p. : ill. (some col.) ; 23 cm. Translation of Barock und Rokoko. Includes index. Bibliography: p. 192-193. [N6415.B3H813 1976] 73-88459 ISBN 0-87663-195-2 : 7.95
1. Art, Baroque. 2. Art, Rococo. I. Title.
BIP

HUBALA, Erich, 1920- 709'.03'2
Baroque and Rococo art / [by] Erich Hubala ; [translated from the German]. London : Weidenfeld and Nicolson, 1976. 196 p. : ill. (some col.), plans, ports. (some col.) ; 23 cm. Translation of Barock und Rokoko. Includes index. Bibliography: p. 192-193. [N6415.B3H813 1976] 77-368325 ISBN 0-297-99444-1 : £4.25
1. Art, Baroque. 2. Art, Rococo. I. Title.

PHILLIPS, Michael. 709'.4
Baroque art. New York, Pitman Pub. Corp. [1968] 48 p. illus., plans, port. 20 x 26 cm. (Pitman art books, 61) [N6415.P5] 67-18154 1.00
1. Art, Baroque. BIP

SEWTER, A. C. 709'.03'2
Baroque and rococo [by] A. C. Sewter. [New York] Harcourt Brace Jovanovich [1972] 224 p. illus. 21 cm. (The Harbrace history of art) Bibliography: p. 218-221. [N6415.B3S4] 73-152765 ISBN 0-15-504890-2 (pbk) 3.95
1. Art, Baroque. 2. Art, Rococo. I. Title.
BIP

TAPIE, Victor Lucien, 1900- 709.033
The age of grandeur; Baroque art and architecture. Translated from the French by A. Ross Williamson. New York, Grove Press [1960] 305 p. plates (part col.) 27 cm. Translation of Baroque et classicisme. Bibliography: p. [285]-297. [N6410.T313 1960] 60-11100
1. Art, Baroque. 2. Architecture, Baroque. Full name: Victor Lucien Marie Joseph Tapie. I. Title.

TAPIE, Victor Lucien, 1900- 709.033
The age of grandeur: baroque art and architecture. Translated from the French by A. Ross Williamson. New York, Praeger [1961, c1960] 305 p. plates (part col.) 26 cm. (Books that matter) Translation of Baroque et classicisme. Bibliography: p. 285-297. [N6410.T313 1961] 61-17028
1. Art, Baroque. 2. Architecture, Baroque. I. Title.

Art, Baroque—Congresses.

INTERNATIONAL Congress of the History of Art, 20th, New York, 1961. 709'.03'2
Latin American art, and the baroque period in Europe. Princeton, N.J., Princeton University Press, 1963. x, 229 p., 72 plates. 24 cm. (Acts of the twentieth International Congress of the History of Art) (Its Studies in Western art, v. 3) Chiefly in English, some contributions in French or Spanish. Includes bibliographical references. [N21.I585 1961 vol. 3] [N6415.B3] 73-164483
1. Art, Baroque—Congresses. 2. Art, Baroque—Latin America—Congresses. 3. Art, Latin American—Congresses. I. Title. II. Series. III. Series: International Congress of the History of Art. Acts, 1961.

Art, Baroque—Europe, Southern.

SITWELL, Sacheverell, Sir, Bart., 1897- 709.03
Baroque and rococo. [1st American ed.] New York, Putnam [1967] xiii, 306 p. illus. (part col.) 26 cm. [N6410.S48 1967] 67-24868
1. Art, Baroque—Europe, Southern. 2. Art, Baroque—Latin America. 3. Art, Rococo—Europe, Southern. 4. Art, Rococo—Latin America. I. Title.

Art, Baroque—History.

HEMPEL, Eberhard, 1886- 709.43
Baroque art and architecture in central Europe Germany, Austria, Switzerland, Hungary, Czechoslovakia, Poland. Painting and sculpture: seventeenth and eighteenth centuries; architecture: sixteenth to eighteenth centuries. [Tr. from German by Elisabeth Hempel, Marguerite Kay] Baltimore. Penguin [1966] xxiii, 370p. illus., maps, plans, 200plates. 27cm. (Pelican hist. of art, Z22) [N6756.H413] 65-28970 20.00
1. Art, Baroque—Hist. 2. Architecture, Baroque—Hist. 3. Art, European—Hist. I. Title. II. Series.

KITSON, Michael. 709.4
The age of baroque. New York, McGraw-Hill [1966] 175 p. illus., maps (part col.) plans, col. plates. 30 cm. (Landmarks of the world's art) Bibliography: p. [172] [N6410.K57] 65-21591
1. Art, Baroque—History. I. Title.

MARTIN, John Rupert. 709'.03'2
Baroque / John Rupert Martin. 1st U.S. ed. New York : Harper & Row, c1977. 367 p. : ill. ; 25 cm. (Icon editions) "Catalogue of illustrations": p. [311]-357. Includes index. Bibliography: p. [305]-309. [N6415.B3M37 1977b] 77-156098 ISBN 0-06-435332-X : 23.50. ISBN 0-06-430077-3 pbk. : 12.50
1. Art, Baroque—History. I. Title. BIP

Art, Baroque—Jesuit influences—Addresses, essays, lectures.

BAROQUE art: 709'.03'2
the Jesuit contribution. Edited by Rudolf Wittkower & Irma B. Jaffe. New York, Fordham University Press, 1972. xvi, 139 p. 64 plates. 30 cm. Outgrowth of a symposium held at Fordham University, April 25-26, 1969. Includes bibliographical references. [N6415.B3B28] 75-119763 ISBN 0-8232-0900-8 20.00
1. Art, Baroque—Jesuit influences—Addresses, essays, lectures. I. Wittkower, Rudolf, ed. II. Jaffe, Irma B., ed. III. Fordham University, New York. BIP

Art, Baroque—Rome (City)

FOKKER, Timon Henricus, 1880- 709'.45'632
Roman baroque art; the history of a style, by T. H. Fokker. New York, Hacker Art Books, 1972. xxii, 368, xii, [194] p. 29 cm. Reprint of the 1938 ed. Contents.Contents.—Text.—Plates. Bibliography: v. 1, p. [xvii]-xxii. [N6920.F6 1972] 75-143345 ISBN 0-87817-065-0
1. Art, Baroque—Rome (City) 2. Art—Rome (City) I. Title. BIP

Art—Baton Rouge, La.—Catalogs.

ANGLO-AMERICAN Art Museum. 760'.074'016318
Catalog; paintings, prints, drawings. [Baton Rouge] Louisiana State University [1968?] [22] p., 26 p. of illus., ports. 23 cm. [N516.B5A53] 68-65466
1. Art—Baton Rouge, La.—Catalogs.

ANGLO-AMERICAN Art Museum. 760'.074'016318
Catalogue; paintings, prints, drawings. [Baton Rouge] Louisiana State University [1971] [40] p. plates. 19 x 26 cm. [N516.B5A53 1971] 70-636726
1. Art—Baton Rouge, La.—Catalogs.

Art—Belgrade—Galleries and museums.

BELGRADE. 708.9497'1
[Translated from the Serbo-Croatian by Celia Williams and rev. by D. Talbot Rice. Editor: Milica Baum. Photographer: Vladimir Popovic. 1st American ed.] South Brunswick, A. S. Barnes [1970] 59 p., [176] p. of illus. (part col.), facsims., ports. 35 cm. (Great centres of art) [N3690.Y8B397] 76-122325 ISBN 0-498-07741-1 20.00
1. Art—Belgrade—Galleries and museums. I. Baum, Milica, ed. II. Popovic, Vladimir, illus.

Art—Benin, Nigeria (Province)—Bibliography.

BEN-AMOS, Paula. 016.709'669'2
Bibliography of Benin art. New York, Library, Museum of Primitive Art, 1968. 17 p. 28 cm. (Primitive art bibliographies, no. 6) Cover title. [Z5961.N6B4] 68-6989
1. Art—Benin, Nigeria (Province)—Bibliography. I. Title. II. Title: Benin art. III. Series.

Art—Berlin.

BERLIN. STAATLICHE MUSEEN 708.3155
Art treasures of the Berlin State museums [Tr. from German] Introd. by John Russell. Text by the curatorial staff. New York, Abrams [1965, c.1962] 269p. plates (pt. col.) 35cm. [AM51.B4A552] 64-11573 20.00
1. Art—Berlin. I. Russell, John, 1919- II. Title.

Art — Berlin — Galleries and museums.

RUSSELL, John, 1919- 708.3155
Art treasures of the Berlin State Museums. Introd. by John Russell. Text by the curatorial staff. New York, H. N. Abrams [1965 c1962] 269 p. 1 mounted illus., plates (part col.) 35 cm. Translation with added introd., of Staatliche Museum au Berlin. Issued also under title: State Museums of Berlin. [N2220.S753] 64-11573
1. Art — Berlin — Galleries and museums. I. Berlin. Staaatliche Museum (East Berlin) II. Title.

Art, Bhutan—Exhibitions.

KNOBLOCK, John H. 709.549
Art of the Asian mountains; a group of paintings, sculptures, and objects from Bhutan, Nepal, Sikkim, and Tibet, lent by museums and private collections. Miami, Fla., Miami Art Center [1968?] 68 p. illus. (1 col.) 23 cm. Catalogue of an exhibition at the Miami Art Center, Dec. 17, 1968, through Jan. 24, 1969. Bibliography by Helen Ladd: p. 64. [N7330.H54K55] 70-23520
1. Art, Bhutan—Exhibitions. 2. Art, Nepali—Exhibitions. 3. Art, Sikkimese—Exhibitions. 4. Art, Tibetan—Exhibitions. 5. Art—Himalaya region. I. Miami Art Center. II. Title.

Art—Bibl.—Catalogs.

SURREALISM & its 016.75906
affinities; the Mary Reynolds collection, a bibliography compiled by Hugh Edwards. Chicago [1956] 131p. illus., facsims., group ports. 26cm. [Z5939.C52] [Z5939.C52] 016.759915 57-1550 57-1550
1. Art—Bibl.—Catalogs. 2. Surrealism—Bibl.—Catalogs. I. Chicago. Art Institute. II. Reynolds, Mary Louise. III. Edwards, Hugh L., comp.

SURREALISM & its 016.75906
afflinites; the Mary Renolds collection, a bibliography compiled by Hugh Edwards. Chicago [1956] 131p. illus., facsims., group ports. 26cm. [Z5939.C52] 016.759915 57-1550
1. Art—Bibl.— Catalogs. 2. Surrealism—Bibl.—Catalogs. I. Chicago. Art Institute. II. Reynolds, Mary Louise. III. Edwards, Hugh L., comp. IV. Title: Mary Reynolds collection.

Art—Bibliography.

CARRICK, Neville. 016.7
How to find out about the arts; a guide to sources of information. [1st ed.] Oxford, New York, Pergamon Press [1965] xi, 164 p. illus. 20 cm. (The Commonwealth and international library, 2250) [Z5931.C3 1965] 65-19834
1. Art—Bibliography. I. Title.

DOVE, Jack 016.7
Fine arts. London, Bingley, 1966. 88p. 23cm. (Readers guide ser.) [Z5931.D6] 66-76603 3.00 bds.,
1. Ar—Bibl. I. Title.
Guide to the literature on varied topics in the fine arts. Available from Shoe String, Hamden, Conn.

EHRESMANN, Donald L., 1937- 016.7
Fine arts : a bibliographic guide to basic reference works, histories, and handbooks / Donald L. Ehresmann ; appendix by

Julia M. Ehresmann. Littleton, Colo. : Libraries Unlimited, 1975. 283 p. ; 24 cm. Includes indexes. [Z5931.E47] [N7425] 74-32452 lib.bdg. : 13.50
1. Art—Bibliography. I. Title. BIP

LEDOUX Library. 016.76
Books of interest to the artist. Eunice [La.] 1970. [5] l. 28 cm. (Its Bibliography 1) [Z5931.L35] 70-633330
1. Art—Bibliography. I. Title. II. Series.

LUCAS, Edna Louise, 1899- 016.7
Art books; a basic bibliography on the fine arts [by] E. Louise Lucas. Greenwich, Conn., New York Graphic Society [1968] 245 p. 22 cm. "Based on the bibliographies previously prepared [by the author] under the title: The Harvard list of books on art." [Z5931.L92] 68-12364 4.50 2.50 (paper)
1. Art—Bibliography. I. Title.

NEW York. Metropolitan 016.7
Museum of Art.
Publications of the Metropolitan Museum of Art, 1870-1964, a bibliography. Compiled by Albert Ten Eyck Gardner, associate curator of American Paintings and sculpture [New York] 1965. vi. 72 p. 21 cm. [New York, Metropolitan Museum of Art -- Bibl. [Z5939.N538] 65-15284
1. Art — Bibl. I. Gardner, Albert TenEyck. II. Title.

PODSZUS, Carl O 016.7
Art, a selected annotated art bibliography. [New York? 1960?] 111p. 22cm. [Z5931.P6] 60-1621
1. Art— Bibl. I. Title.

QUEENSLAND. Public Library, 016.7
Brisbane. Country Extension Service.
Art: history and criticism [prepared by the] Country Extension Service, State Library of Queensland. Brisbane, Country Extension Service, State Library of Queensland, 1972. 92 p. 28 cm. Cover title. [Z5931.Q43 1972] 74-153160 ISBN 0-7242-0071-1 free
1. Art—Bibliography. 2. Artists—Indexes. 3. Authors—Indexes. I. Title.

STURGIS, Russell, 1836- 016.7
1909.
Annotated bibliography of fine art / painting, sculpture, architecture, arts of decoration, and illustration by Russell Sturgis, music by Henry Edward Krehbiel ; edited by George Iles. Boston : Longwood Press, 1976 p. cm. Reprint of the 1897 ed. published for the American Library Association Publishing Section by the Library Bureau, Boston, in series: American Library Association annotated lists. Includes index. [Z5931.S93 1977] [N7425] 76-27528 ISBN 0-89341-053-5 lib.bdg. : 12.50
1. Art—Bibliography. 2. Music—Bibliography. I. Krehbiel, Henry Edward, 1854-1923, joint author. II. Title. III. Series: American Library Association. Annotated lists. BIP

STURGIS, Russell, 1836- 016.17
1909.
Annotated bibliography of fine art: painting, sculpture, architecture, arts of decoration, and illustration by Russell Sturgis. Music by Henry Edward Krehbiel. Edited by George Iles. Boston, Milford House [1973] p. Reprint of the 1897 ed. published for the American Library Association Publishing Section by the Library Bureau, Boston, in series: American Library Association annotated lists. [Z5931.S93 1973] 73-12303 ISBN 0-87821-172-1 10.00
1. Art—Bibliography. 2. Music—Bibliography. I. Krehbiel, Henry Edward, 1854-1923. II. Title. III. Series: American Library Association. Annotated lists.

THOMPSON, Helen 016.7
(MacPherson) 1905-.
Manual arts and crafts, prepared by Helen M. Thompson. [San Francisco, Pacific Air Forces] 1965. viii, 188 p. 27 cm. (PACAF basic bibliographies) (U.S. Air Force. Pacific Air Forces. PACAF basic bibliographies) [Z5931.T5 1965] 66-62944
1. Art — Bibl. 2. Handicraft — Bibl. I. Title. II. Series.

Art—Bibliography—Catalogs.

CARLETON College, 016.700
Northfield, Minn. Library.
A catalogue of the Shedd Memorial art books presented to the Carleton College Library by the family of Willard Whitcomb Morse. Northfield, Printed by Colwell Press for Carleton College, 1962. x, 106 p. 23 cm. [Z5939.C3] 68-49908
1. Art—Bibliography—Catalogs. I. Morse, Willard Whitcomb. II. Title.

HARVARD University. Fine 016.7
Arts Library.
Catalogue of the Harvard University Fine Arts Library, the Fogg Art Museum. Boston, G. K. Hall, 1971. 15 v. 37 cm. Vol. 15: Catalogue of auction sales. [Z5939.H35] 72-179505 ISBN 0-8161-0919-2 (v. 1-14)
1. Art—Bibliography—Catalogs. I. Title. BIP

O'NEAL, William Bainter. 016.7
A fine arts library : Jefferson's selections for the University of Virginia together with his architectural books at Monticello : an exhibition sponsored by the Alderman Library & the Committee on the Bicentennial, February-May 1976 : catalogue / compiled by William B. O'Neal. Charlottesville : University of Virginia, 1976. 18 p., 38 leaves of plates : ill., facsims. ; 26 cm. [Z5939.O49] [N5300] 76-383681
1. Virginia. University. Library. 2. Jefferson, Thomas, Pres. United States., 1743-1826. 3. Art—Bibliography—Catalogs. 4. Architecture—Bibliography—Catalogs. I. Virginia. University. Library. II. Title.

O'NEAL, William Bainter. 016.7
Jefferson's fine arts library : his selections for the University of Virginia, together with his own architectural books / William Bainter O'Neal. Charlottesville : University Press of Virginia, 1976. xviii, 409 p. : ill. ; 26 cm. Based on the author's earlier ed. published under title: Jefferson's fine arts library for the University of Virginia, with additional notes on architectural volumes known to have been owned by Jefferson. Includes bibliographical references and index. [Z5939.O5] [N5300] 75-33229 ISBN 0-8139-0647-4 : 20.00
1. Virginia. University. Library. 2. Jefferson, Thomas, Pres. U.S., 1743-1826. 3. Art—Bibliography—Catalogs. 4. Architecture—Bibliography—Catalogs. I. Title. BIP

OTTAWA. National Gallery of 016.7
Canada. Library.
Catalogue of the Library of the National Gallery of Canada. Boston, G. K. Hall, 1973. 8 v. 37 cm. Added t.p. in French: Catalogue de la Bibliotheque de la Galerie nationale du Canada. [Z5939.O87 1973] 74-166203 ISBN 0-8161-1043-3
1. Ottawa. National Gallery of Canada. Library. 2. Art—Bibliography—Catalogs. I. Title. II. Title: Catalogue de la Bibliotheque de la Galerie nationale du Canada. BIP

SOUTH Kensington Museum, 016.700
London. National Art Library.
Universal catalogue of books on art. New York, B. Franklin [1964] 3 v. 26 cm. (Burt Franklin bibliography and reference series, #47) Edited by J. H. Pollen. Reprint of the 1870-77 ed., published under title: First proofs of the Universal catalogue of books on art. Contents.Contents.—v. 1. A to K.—v. 2. L to Z.—v. 3. Supplement. [Z5931.S722] 76-8725
1. Art—Bibliography—Catalogs. I. Pollen, John Hungerford, 1820-1902, ed. II. Title.

USES of Newer Media in Art 016.7
Education Project.
Reproductions and paperback books on art. Washington, National Art Education Association, 1967. 64 p. 24 cm. "No. 3 in a series of publications sponsored by the Uses of Newer Media Project of the National Art Education Association." [Z5939.U83 1967] 74-152062
1. Art—Bibliography—Catalogs. 2. Bibliography—Paperbacks—Catalogs. I. National Art Education Association. II. Title.

VICTORIA and Albert Museum, 016.7
South Kensington. National Art Library.
National Art Library catalogue, Victoria and Albert Museum, London, England. Boston, G. K. Hall, 1972- v. 37 cm. Contents.Contents.— —[2] Catalogue of exhibition catalogues. [Z5939.V64] 73-153208 ISBN 0-8161-1022-0 120.00
1. Art—Bibliography—Catalogs. I. Title.

Art—Biography.

INTERNATIONAL who's 709'.2'2 B
who in art and antiques / editorial director, Ernest Kay. 2d ed. Cambridge, Eng. : Melrose Press, 1976. xv, 525 p. ; 25 cm. [N40.I57 1976] 76-373141 ISBN 0-900332-37-9
1. Art—Biography. 2. Artists—Biography. I. Kay, Ernest, ed.

INTERNATIONAL who's 700'.92'2 B
who in art and antiques. Hon. General editor: Ernest Kay. Cambridge [Eng.] Melrose Press [1972] viii, 679 p. illus. 25 cm. [N40.I57] 79-189269 ISBN 0-900332-21-2 32.50
1. Art—Biography. 2. Artists—Biography. I. Kay, Ernest, ed.
Distributed by Rowman & Littlefield.

WHO'S who in art; 709.22
biographies of leading men and women in the world of art today--artists, designers, craftsmen, critics, writers, teachers, collectors and curators .... Havant, Hants. [Eng.] Art Trade Pr.
The 14th edition is now available from Intl. Pubns. Serv., New York, for $15.00. L.C. card order no.: 27-14051* BIP

Art—Boston.

BOSTON. Museum of Fine 709.744'61
Arts.
Back Bay Boston: the city as a work of art. With essays by Lewis Mumford & Walter Muir Whitehill. Boston [1969] 149 p. illus. (part col.), maps, plans, ports. 26 cm. Published on the occasion of the exhibition held Nov. 1, 1969-Jan. 11, 1970 at the Boston Museum of Fine Arts. [N6535.B7B75] 77-101356
1. Art—Boston. 2. Art—Exhibitions. I. Title.

Art—Boston—Catalogs.

BOSTON. Museum of 708'.144'61
Fine Arts.
The Rathbone years; masterpieces acquired for the Museum of Fine Arts, Boston, 1955-1972, and for the St. Louis Art Museum, 1940-1955. Boston, 1972. 203 p. illus. (part col) 25 cm. [N520.A718] 72-81916 ISBN 0-87846-067-5
1. Rathbone, Perry Townsend, 1911- 2. Art—Boston—Catalogs. 3. Art—St. Louis—Catalogs. I. St. Louis Art Museum. II. Title. BIP

Art, Brazilian.

RODMAN, Selden, 1909- 709'.2'2 B
Genius in the backlands : popular artists of Brazil / Selden Rodman ; photographs by Manu Sassoonian, William Negron, and Marilyn Bridges. Old Greenwich, Conn. : Devin-Adair Co., c1977. 148 p. : ill. (some col.) ; 24 cm. Includes bibliographical references. [N6655.5.P7R62] 76-46181 ISBN 0-8159-5616-9 : 10.00
1. Art, Brazilian. 2. Primitivism in art—Brazil. 3. Artists—Brazil—Biography. I. Title.

Art, Brazilian—Hist.

CASTEDO, Leopoldo 709.81
The baroque prevalence in Brazilian art. New York, C. Frank Pubns. [c.1964] 151p. illus. 26cm. Bibl. [N6650.C3] 64-25775 12.50
1. Art, Brazilian—Hist. 2. Art, Baroque. I. Title.

Art, British.

ART treasures in the 709'.42
British Isles; monuments, masterpieces, commissions, and collections. Introd. by Sir Philip Hendy. [General editors: Bernard S. Myers and Trewin Copplestone] New York, McGraw-Hill [1969] 176 p. illus. (part col.), col. maps (on lining papers), ports. (part col.) 29 cm. [N6761.A76] 76-76757
1. Art, British. 2. Art—Great Britain. I. Hendy, Philip, Sir, 1900- II. Myers, Bernard Samuel, 1908- ed. III. Copplestone, Trewin, ed.

FINCH, Christopher. 709'.22
Image as language: aspects of British art, 1950-1968. Harmondsworth, Penguin, 1969. 186 p. 64 plates. 19 cm. (Pelican books) Bibliography: p. [175]-179. [N6768.F5] 78-425861 10/-
1. Art, British. 2. Art, Modern—20th century—Gt. Brit. I. Title.

GEORGE, William. 941
British heritage : in colour / [by] William George. Poole : Blandford Press, 1976. 222 p. : ill. (some col.), col. coat of arms, facsims., (some col.), map, ports. (some col.) ; 20 cm. Ill. on lining paper. [N6761.G46] 77-361417 ISBN 0-7137-8519-5 : 9.95
1. Art, British. 2. Great Britain—Antiquities. I. Title.
Distributed by Standing Orders Inc. P. O. Box 183 Patterson N.Y.12563

NATIONAL Trust for Places 708'.2
of Historic Interest or Natural Beauty.
Treasures of the National Trust / edited by Robin Fedden ; associate editor, Rosemary Joekes. London : J. Cape, 1976. 208 p. : ill. (some col.) ; 26 cm. Includes index. Bibliography: p. [187]-188. [N6761.N37 1976] 76-376406 ISBN 0-224-01241-X : £5.95
1. National Trust for Places of Historic Interest or Natural Beauty. 2. Art, British. 3. Art—Great Britain. I. Fedden, Henry Romilly, 1908- II. Joekes, Rosemary. III. Title. BIP

READ, Herbert Edward, Sir 709.42
Contemporary British art [Reissue] Baltimore, Penguin [1965, c.1951, 1964] 61p. 70 plates (pt. col.) 18cm. (Pelican bks., A250) Bibl. [N6768.R37] 1.65 pap.,
1. Art, British. I. Title. BIP

READ, Herbert Edward, Sir 709.42
1893-
Contemporary British art [by] Herbert Read, [Rev. ed.] Baltimore, Penguin Books [1964] 61 p. 64 plates (part col.) 20 cm. (Pelican books, A250) Bibliographical references included in footnotes. [N6768.R37] 65-4675
1. Art, British. I. Title.

Art, British—Catalogs.

BRITISH painting : 760'.0942
paintings, drawings and prints : 116 illustrations / selected & introduced by Thomas Rawley. Oxford : Phaidon Press, 1977 [16] p., 96 p. of plates : ill. (some col.), ports. (some col.) ; 42 cm. [N6764.B77 1976] 76-26756 ISBN 0-7148-1759-7 pbk. : 7.95
1. Art, British—Catalogs. 2. Art, Modern—Great Britain—Catalogs. I. Rawley, Thomas.
Distributed by E.P. Dutton, N.Y.

CARLISLE, Eng. Museum 708'.28'5
and Art Gallery.
William Rothenstein; a unique collection. Rothenstein's purchases for Carlisle 1933-1942. [Carlisle, Eng., 1972?] 32 p. illus. 21 cm. Cover title. Bibliography: p. 32. [N6767.C27] 72-198132
1. Rothenstein, William, Sir, 1872-1945. 2. Art, British—Catalogs. 3. Art, Modern—19th century—Great Britain. 4. Art, Modern—20th century—Great Britain.

JOHNSON, Jane. 709'.2'2
Works exhibited at the Royal Society of British Artists, 1824-1893 : an Antique Collectors' Club research project / compiled by Jane Johnson. [Woodbridge? Eng.] : Antique Collectors' Club, c1975. 2 v. (617 p.) ; 30 cm. Cover title: The Royal Society of British Artists, 1824-1893. Contents.Contents.—v. 1. A-P.—v. 2. Q-Z and at the New English Art Club, 1888-1917. [N6767.J64] 76-350570 ISBN 0-902028-35-9 : £38.00
1. Art, British—Catalogs. 2. Art,

Modern—19th century—Great Britain—Catalogs. 3. Artists—Great Britain—Directories. I. Royal Society of British Artists, London. II. Antique Collectors' Club. III. New English Art Club. IV. Title.

Art, British—Exhibitions.

ARTS Council of Great Britain. 704.94'2'0941
The human clay : an exhibition / selected by R. B. Kitaj [for the] Arts Council of Great Britain. [London] : Arts Council of Great Britain, 1976. [64] p. : chiefly ill. ; 22 cm. [N6768.A864 1976] 77-361148 ISBN 0-7287-0101-4 : £1.20
1. Art, British—Exhibitions. 2. Art, Modern—20th century—Great Britain—Exhibitions. 3. Human figure in art—Exhibitions. I. Kitaj, R. B. II. Title.

CARLISLE, Eng. Museum and Art Gallery. 759.941'074'02789
The purchase scheme, 1933-1975 : [catalogue of an exhibition held at the] City Art Gallery Carlisle, 21 June-27 August 1975. [Carlisle] : [The Gallery], [1975] [1], 31 p. : ill., ports. ; 21 cm. Cover title. Includes index. [N6768.C34 1975] 76-352942 ISBN 0-9502457-5-5 : £0.10
1. Art, British—Exhibitions. 2. Art, Modern—20th century—Great Britain—Exhibitions. I. Title.

CARLISLE, Eng. Museum of Art Gallery. 709'.42
George Howard and his circle, 1843-1911. Carlisle, City Art Gallery, 1968. 32 p. illus., ports. 22 cm. Cover title. Catalogue compiled by W. Waters, Assistant Curator. [N6797.C33A44] 72-199351
1. Carlisle, George James Howard, 9th Earl of, 1843-1911. 2. Art, British—Exhibitions. 3. Art, Modern—19th century—Gt. Brit. I. Title.

DECORDOVA and Dana Museum and Park, Lincoln, Mass. 709'.41'07401444
The British are coming : contemporary British art : April 12-June 8, 1975, De Cordova Museum, Lincoln, Massachusetts. Lincoln : The Museum, 1975. 31, [5] p. : ill. ; 23 cm. Bibliography: p. [36] [N6768.D42 1975] 75-330362
1. Art, British—Exhibitions. 2. Art, Modern—20th century—Great Britain—Exhibitions. I. Title.

GILES, James, 1801-1870. 741.9'41
James Giles, R.S.A., 1801-1870. [an exhibition compiled and arranged to celebrate the centenary of the death of the Aberdeen artist James Giles R.S.A., Aberdeen Art Gallery, June 13-July 4, 1970]. Aberdeen, Aberdeen Art Gallery [1970]. [19] p., 12 plates. illus. 21 cm. Bibliography: p. 19. [N6797.G48A48] 78-536074 ISBN 0-900017-01-5 6/-
I. Aberdeen Art Gallery, Aberdeen, Scot.

MARLBOROUGH-GERSON Gallery. 709.42
The English eye. New York, 1965. 131 p. plates, ports. 23 cm. Catalog of the exhibition held Nov.-Dec., 1965 in the Marlborough-Gerson Gallery. [N6768.M33] 72-21974
1. Art, British—Exhibitions. 2. Art, Modern—20th century—Gt. Brit. I. Title.

Art, British—Exhibitions—Indexes.

LONDON. Royal Academy of Arts. 707'.4'02132
Royal Academy exhibitors, 1905-1970; a dictionary of artists and their work in the summer exhibitions of the Royal Academy of Arts Wakefield, EP Publishing [1974- v. 24 cm. Contents.Contents.—v. 1. A-CAR. [N6768.L64 1973a] 74-174238 ISBN 0-85409-987-5
1. Art, British—Exhibitions—Indexes. 2. Art, Modern—20th century—Great Britain. 3. Artists—Great Britain—Indexes. I. Title.
Distributed by British Book Center; 38.50 (vol. I) BIP

Art, British—Hist.

GARLICK, Kenneth, ed. 709.42
British and North American art to 1900 New York, Watts [1966, c.1965] 250p. illus., col. plates, 25cm. (Great art and artists of the world) Also pub. by Grolier, as a v. of its The Book of art. Bibl. [N6764.G3] 65-10268 12.95
1. Art, British—Hist. 2. Art, American—Hist. 3. Artists, British. 4. Artists, American. I. Title. II. Series.

ROTHENSTEIN, John Knewstub Maurice. Sir 1901- 709.42
British art since 1900; an anthology. Phaidon [dist.] Greenwich, Conn., N.Y. Graphic [c.1962] 181p. illus. (pt. mounted col.) 32cm. 62-52392 13.50
1. Art, British—Hist. I. Title.

ROTHENSTEIN, John Knewstub Maurice, Sir 1901- 709.42
British art since 1900; an anthology. [New York] Phaidon Publishers; distributed by New York Graphic Society, Greenwich, Conn. [1962] 181p. plates (part col.) 32cm. [N6768.R6 1962a] 62-52392
1. Art, British—Hist. I. Title.

WATERHOUSE, Ellis Kirkham, 1905- 709.42
Three decades of British art, 1740-1770. Philadelphia, American Philosophical Society, 1965. xii, 77 p. illus. 25 cm. (Jayne lectures, 1964) (Series. Series: American Philosophical Society, Philadelphia. Memoirs, v. 63) Memoirs of the American Philosophical Society, v. 63. Bibliographical footnotes. [N6766.W3] 65-23431
1. Art, British — Hist. I. Title. II. Series. BIP

WATERHOUSE, Ellis Kirkham, 1905- 709.42
Three decades of British art, 1740-1770 Philadelphia, Amer. Philosophical Soc. [c.] 1965. xii, 77p. illus. 25cm. (Jayne lects., 1964) Title, (Series. Series: American Philosophical Society, Philadelphia. Memoirs, v.63) Memoirs of the Amer. Philosophical Soc., v.63. Bibl. [N6766.W3] 65-23431 2.00
1. Art, British—Hist. I. Title. II. Series.

Art—Brooklyn.

BROOKLYN Society of Artists. 707.4
Exhibition. [Brooklyn] Brooklyn Institute of Arts and Sciences, Brooklyn Museum. v. illus. 22 cm. annual. [N11.B78] 50-1285
1. Art—Brooklyn. 2. Art—Exhibitions. I. Brooklyn Institute of Arts and Sciences. Museum. II. Title.

Art—Bruges.

CALI, Francois. 759.9493
Bruges, the cradle of Flemish painting. With photos. by Jean-Pierre Sudre. Translated by Dennis Chamberlin. Chicago, Rand McNally [1964] 96 p. 97 illus., col. map, plans, 4 col. plates. 24 cm. Bibliography: p. 82-83. [N6971.B8C313] 64-10807
1. Art—Bruges. 2. Bruges—Description. I. Sudre, Jean Pierre. II. Title.

Art brut.

THEVOZ, Michel. 709'.04
Art brut / text by Michel Thevoz ; foreword by Jean Dubuffet ; [translated from the French by James Emmons]. New York : Rizzoli, 1976. 179 p. : ill. (some col.) ; 31 cm. Translation of L'art brut. Includes index. Bibliography: p. 170-172. [N7432.5.A78T4713] 76-12314 ISBN 0-8478-0046-6 : 22.50
1. Art brut. 2. Art—Themes, motives. I. Title.

Art, Buddhist.

GRUNWEDEL, Albert, 1856-1935 709.54
Buddhist art in India. Tr. from German by A. C. Gibson. Rev., enl. by Jas. Burgess [Reissue] Santiago de Compostela, S. Gupta [dist. S. Pasadena, Calif., Hutchins, 1965] vii, 228p. illus., map. plan. 22cm. Bibl. [N7301.G8] 65-3064 7.50
1. Art, Buddhist. 2. India—Antiq. I. Title. BIP

MIYAZAKI, Enjun, 1906- 708.952
Nishi-Hongwanji, by Enjun Miyazaki, Yuzuru Okada, Tomohiko Horie. Photo Taikichi Irie, Sose Kuzunishi, Harumi Konishi [Dist. New York, Perkins Oriental, 1962] 274p. chiefly illus. col. front. 22cm. Japanese text; added t.p. in English. J62 3.50 bds.,
1. Nishi, Hongwanji, Kyoto. 2. Art, Buddhist. I. Irie, Taikichi, 1905- II. Title.

ROWLAND, Benjamin, 1904- 595.78
Religious art East and West. (in Smithsonian Institution. Annual report, 1963. Washington, 1964. 24 cm. p. 569-585. illus.) "Reprinted ... from Midway, no. 16, autumn 1963, and based on a longer and more detailed version in History of religions, vol. 2, no. 1, summer 1962." [Q11.S66] 65-6092
1. Art, Buddhist. 2. Christian art and symbolism. I. Title.

THAWAN Duchanee, 1939- 741.9'593
Forms of man : the Buddhist vision of Thawan Duchanee / commentary by Russell Marcus. Bangkok ; Ojai, Calif. : Books Marcus, 1974. 72 p. : chiefly ill. (some col.) ; 26 cm. [N7323.T46M37] 74-84663 18.00
1. Thawan Duchanee, 1939- 2. Art, Buddhist. 3. Symbolism in art. I. Marcus, Russell. II. Title. BIP

Art, Buddhist—Afghanistan.

GAULIER, Simone. 704.948'9'430958
Buddhism in Afghanistan and Central Asia / by Simone Gaulier, Robert Jera-Bezard and Monique Maillard. Leiden : Brill, 1976. 2 v. : ill. ; 26 cm. (Iconography of religions : Section 13, Indian religions ; fasc. 14) Contents.Contents.—pt. 1. Introduction, Buddha, Bodhisattva.—pt. 2. Minor divinities and assimilated divinities, monks and ascetics, mandalas. Bibliography: v. 1, p. [xi]-xii. [N8193.A7G38] 77-470670 ISBN 9-00-404744-1
1. Art, Buddhist—Afghanistan. 2. Art—Afghanistan. 3. Afghanistan—Antiquities. 4. Art, Buddhist—Asia, Central. 5. Art—Asia, Central. 6. Asia, Central—Antiquities. I. Jera-Bezard, Robert, joint author. II. Maillard, Monique, joint author. III. Title. IV. Series.

Art, Buddhist—History.

ASIA Society 709.59
The evolution of the Buddha image [by] Benjamin Rowland, Jr. [New York] Abrams [1963] 146p. illus. 25cm. (Asia House Gallery pubn.) 63-6099 7.00 bds.,
1. Art, Buddhist—Hist. I. Rowland, Benjamin, 1904- II. Asia House Gallery, New York. III. Title.

ASIA Society. 704.948'943
The evolution of the Buddha image / Benjamin Rowland, Jr. New York : Arno Press, 1975. p. cm. (The Asia Society reprint collection) Catalogue of an exhibition selected by B. Rowland, Jr., and shown in the galleries of Asia House as an activity of the Asia Society. Reprint of the 1963 ed. published by the Asia Society, New York. [N8193.A5A84 1975] 75-6676 ISBN 0-405-06568-X : 28.00
1. Art, Buddhist—History. I. Rowland, Benjamin, 1904- II. Asia House Gallery, New York. III. Title. IV. Series. BIP

SECKEL, Dietrich, 1910- 709.5
The art of Buddhism. [Translated by Ann E. Keep] New York, Crown Publishers [1964] 331 p. illus. (part mounted col.) maps. 24 cm. (Art of the world, non-European cultures; the historical, sociological and religious backgrounds) Bibliography: p. 313-318. [N8190.S413] 64-23800
1. Art, Buddhist—History. I. Title. II. Series: Art of the world; the historical, sociological and religious backgrounds

Art, Buddhist—Ikaruga, Japan.

MIZUNO, Seiichi, 1905-1971. 709'.52
Asuka Buddhist art: Horyu-ji. Translated by Richard L. Gage. [1st English ed.] New York, Weatherhill [1974] 172 p. illus. (part col.) 24 cm. (The Heibonsha survey of Japanese art, v. 4) Translation of Horyuji. [N8193.J3M5913] 73-88473 ISBN 0-8348-1020-4 12.50
1. Art, Buddhist—Ikaruga, Japan. 2. Art—Ikaruga, Japan. 3. Horyuji, Ikaruga, Japan. I. Title. II. Series.

Art, Buddhist—India.

FOUCHER, Alfred Charles Auguste, 1865-1952. 732'.4
The beginnings of Buddhist art and other essays in Indian and Central-Asian archaeology, by A. Foucher. Rev. by the author and translated by L. A. Thomas and F. W. Thomas, with a pref. by the latter. Varanasi, Indological Book House, 1972 [i.e. 1973] xvi, 316, [92] p. 50 p. of. illus. 24 cm. First published in 1917. Includes bibliographical references. [N7302.F68 1972] 72-905025
1. Art, Buddhist—India. 2. Art—India. 3. Art, Buddhist—Java. 4. Art—Java. I. Thomas, L. A., tr. II. Thomas, Frederick William, 1867-1956. tr. III. Title.
Distributed by International Publication Service; 17.50

Art, Buddhist—India—Ajanta.

WEINER, Sheila L. 726'.1'430954792
Ajanta : its place in Buddhist art / Sheila L. Weiner. Berkeley : University of California Press, c1977. xx, 138 p., [28] leaves of plates : ill. ; 25 cm. Includes index. Bibliography: p. 121-131. [N7308.A4W44] 74-22973 ISBN 0-520-02878-3 : 15.00
1. Art, Buddhist—India—Ajanta. 2. Art—India—Ajanta. 3. Cave temples, Buddhist—India—Ajanta. 4. Cave temples—India—Ajanta. I. Title.

Art, Buddhist—Japan.

ANESAKI, Masaharu, 1873-1949. 704.948'9'43920952
Buddhist art in its relation to Buddhist ideals : with special reference to Buddhism in Japan / by M. Anesaki. New York : Hacker Art Books, 1978. xv, 73, [49] leaves of plates : ill. ; 32 cm. Reprint of the 1923 ed. published by Houghton Mifflin, Boston. Includes index. Bibliography: p. [65]-67. [N8193.J3A53 1978] 78-39816 ISBN 0-87817-197-5 lib bdg : 50.00
1. Art, Buddhist—Japan. 2. Art, Japanese. 3. Buddhist art and symbolism—Japan. I. Title. BIP

Art, Buddhist—Pakistan.

NABI Khan, Ahmad. 704.948'9'43095491
Buddhist art and architecture in Pakistan / Ahmad Nabi Khan. Islamabad : Ministry of Information and Broadcasting. Directorate of Research, Reference and Publications, Government of Pakistan, [1976?] 81 p., [2] leaves of plates : ill. ; 28 cm. [N7310.7.N33] 77-370662 Rs.40
1. Art, Buddhist—Pakistan. 2. Art—Pakistan. I. Title.

Art, Bulgarian—Hist.

BOZHKOV, Atanas 759.94977
Bulgarian art. [Tr. by Gregor Pavlov. Ed.: Pauline Pirinska] Sofia, Foreign Languages Pr. [dist. New York, Vanous] 1964. 125p. illus. 25cm. Bibl. 64-56569 3.90 bds.,
1. Art, Bulgarian—Hist. I. Title.

Art, Burmese—History.

GRISWOLD, Alexander B. 709.51
The art of Burma, Korea, Tibet, by Alexander B. Griswold, Chewon Kim [and] Peter H. Pott. New York, Crown Publishers [1964] 277 p. illus. (part mounted col.), maps. 24 cm. (Art of the world, non-European cultures; the historical, sociological and religious backgrounds) Translation of Burma, Korea, Tibet. Bibliography: p. 255-263. [N7306.G7] 63-20855

1. Art, Burmese—History. 2. Art, Korean—History. 3. Art, Tibetan—History. I. Title. II. Series: Art of the world; the historical, sociological and religious backgrounds

Art, Byzantine.

AINALOV, Dmitrii Vlas'evich, 1862-1939. 709.02
The Hellenistic origins of Byzantine art. Translated from the Russian by Elizabeth Sobolevitch and Serge Sobolevitch. Edited by Cyril Mango. New Brunswick, N.J., Rutgers University Press [1961] xv, 322 p. illus., facsims. 25 cm. (Rutgers Byzantine series) "Published, for the first and only time, in 1900-1901 in the Bulletin of the Imperial Russian Archaeological Society." Bibliographical references included in "Notes" (p. 282-308) [N6250.A613 1961] 61-10252
1. Art, Byzantine. 2. Hellenism. I. Title.

BOYD, Susan A. 745'.09'02
Byzantine art / Susan A. Boyd. Chicago : University of Chicago Press, 1979. ix, 44 p. : ill. ; 22 cm. & microfiche (2 cards ; 10 x 15 in. (in pocket) (Chicago visual library) At head of title: Dumbarton Oaks collections, trustees of Harvard University. Bibliography: p. [43]-44. [NK715.B69] 78-12272 ISBN 0-226-68978-6 : 25.00
1. Dumbarton Oaks. 2. Art objects, Byzantine. 3. Illumination of books and manuscripts, Byzantine. I. Title.

DALTON, Ormonde Maddock, 1866-1945 709.02
Byzantine art and archeology. New York, Dover [1961] xix, 727p. illus. 25cm. (T776) Bibl. 61-19927 7.50
1. Art, Byzantine. 2. Christian antiquities. 3. Christian art and symbolism. I. Title.

DUMBARTON Oaks. 709.37
Handbook of the collection. Washington, 1946. 136 p.illus. 18 cm. Published by the Center under its earlier name: Dumbarton Oaks Research Library and Collection of Harvard University. [N858.H3A55] 55-35345
1. Art, Byzantine. I. Title.

KITZINGER, Ernst. 709'.02
Byzantine art in the making : main lines of stylistic development in Mediterranean art, 3rd-7th century / Ernst Kitzinger. Cambridge, Mass. : Harvard University Press, 1977. xii, 175 p., [68] leaves of plates : ill. (some col.) ; 26 cm. Includes bibliographical references and indexes. [N6250.K58] 77-73578 ISBN 0-674-08955-3 : 25.00
1. Art, Byzantine. I. Title. BIP

KITZINGER, Ernst, 1912- 709'.01'5
Byzantine art in the making : main lines of stylistic development in Mediterranean art, 3rd-7th century / Ernst Kitzinger. London : Faber and Faber, 1977. xii, 175 p., [68] leaves of plates : ill. (some col.) ; 26 cm. Includes bibliographical references and indexes. [N6250.K58 1977b] 78-301265 ISBN 0-571-11154-8 : 25.00
1. Art, Byzantine. I. Title.
Distributed by Harvard University Press, 79 Garden St., Cambridge, MA 02138

KONTOGLOUS, Photes, 1895- 704.9483
Byzantine sacred art: selected writings of the contemporary Greek icon painter Fotis Kontoglous on the sacred arts according to the tradition of Eastern Orthodox Christianity. Compiled, translated from the Greek, and edited with a pref., introd., notes. and illus. by Constantine Cavarnos. [1st ed.] New York, Vantage Press [1957] 111p. illus. 21cm. [N6250.K87] 56-12306
1. Art, Byzantine. 2. Christian art and symbolism. I. Cavarnos, Constantine, ed. and tr. II. Title.

MICHELES, Panagiotes Andreou. 1903- 709.495
An aesthetic approach to Byzantine art. Foreword by Sir Herbert Read. London. Batsford [Chester Springs, Pa., Dufour, 1966] xx, 284p. illus. 23cm. [N6250.M515] 55-4469 8.50
1. Art, Byzantine. I. Title. BIP

RICE, David Talbot 709.4961
The art of Byzantium; text and notes. Photos. by Max Hirmer. New York, Abrams [1959] 348p. illus., plates (part col.) plans. 31cm. 59-11864 25.00
1. Art, Byzantine. 2. Art—Istanbul. I. Hirmer, Max. II. Title.

RICE, David Talbot, 1903- 709'.02
The appreciation of Byzantine art. London, Oxford University Press [1972] 214 p. illus. 21 cm. (The Appreciation of the arts, 7) Bibliography: p. 207-212. [N6250.R45 1972] 73-155138 ISBN 0-19-211922-2 £4.50
1. Art, Byzantine. I. Title. BIP

RICE, David Talbot, 1903- 709.495
Byzantine art. [Reprinted with revisions] Baltimore, Penguin Books [1962] 272p. illus. 18cm. (Pelican books, A287) [N6250.R47 1962] 62-4507
1. Art, Byzantine. I. Title.

RICE, David Talbot, 1903- 709.02
Byzantine art. [Rev. ed.] Melbourne, Penguin Books [1954] 272p. illus., maps. 18cm. (Pelican books, A287) Bibliographical footnotes. [N6250.R] A 55
1. Art, Byzantine. I. Title.

RICE, David Talbot, 1903- 709.02
Byzantine art [by] D. Talbot Rice. Revised and expanded ed. Harmondsworth, Penguin, 1968. 580 p. 8 plates, illus. (some col.), 5 maps, plans. 21 cm. (Pelican book A287) Bibliography: p. 563-570. [N6250.R47 1968] 73-356968 45/-
1. Art, Byzantine.

RUNCIMAN, Steven, Sir, 1903- 709'.495
Byzantine style and civilization / [by] Steven Runciman. Harmondsworth Baltimore : Penguin, 1975. 238 p. : ill., plans, ports. ; 20 cm. (Style and civilization) Includes index. Bibliography: p. 227-229. [N6250.R86] 75-330373 ISBN 0-14-021827-0 pbk. : 5.95
1. Art, Byzantine. 2. Byzantine Empire—Civilization. I. Title. BIP

VICTORIA and Albert Museum, South Kensington 709.02
Late antique and Byzantine art. London, H.M.S.O. [dist. New York, British Info., 1964, c.1963] [6]p. 49 plates 22cm. (Its Illus. bklet no. 12) 64-1677 1.20 pap.,
1. Art, Byzantine. 2. Art, Ancient. I. Title. II. Series.

WEITZMANN, Kurt, 1904- 096.1
Greek mythology in Byzantine art. Princeton, Princeton University Press, 1951. xii, 218 p. 60 plates. 31 cm. (Studies in manuscript illumination, no. 4) Bibliographical footnotes. [N6250.W4] 51-2388
1. Art, Byzantine. 2. Decoration and ornament, Byzantine. 3. Mythology, Greek. 4. Art and mythology. I. Title. II. Series.

Art, Byzantine—Addresses, essays, lectures.

KITZINGER, Ernst, 1912- 709'.39'5
The art of Byzantium and the medieval West : selected studies / by Ernst Kitzinger ; edited by W. Eugene Kleinbauer. Bloomington : Indiana University Press, c1976. xvii, 419 p. : ill. ; 29 cm. "Ernst Kitzinger: bibliography": p. 397-400. [N6250.K57 1976] 75-34728 ISBN 0-253-31055-5 : 18.50
1. Art, Byzantine—Addresses, essays, lectures. 2. Art, Medieval—Byzantine influences—Addresses, essays, lectures. I. Title.
Contents omitted. BIP

Art, Byzantine—History.

BECKWITH, John, 1918- 709.02
The art of Constantinople; an introduction to Byzantine art, 330-1453. [New York] Phaidon Publishers; distributed by New York Graphic Society, Greenwich, Conn. [1961] 184p. illus. 26cm. [N6250.B4 1961] 61-18680
1. Art, Byzantine—Hist. 2. Art—Istanbul—Hist. I. Title.

GRABAR, Andre, 1896- 709.02
The art of the Byzantine Empire; Byzantine art in the Middle Ages. [Translated by Betty Forster] New York, Crown Publishers [1966] 216 p. illus., map, plates (part mounted col.) 24 cm. (Art of the world, non-European cultures; the historical, sociological, and religious backgrounds) Translation of Byzance. Bibliography: p. 209-210. [N6250.G6913] 66-21147
1. Art, Byzantine—History. I. Title. II. Series: Art of the world; the historical, sociological, and religious backgrounds

GRABAR, Andre, 1896- 709.02'1
The golden age of Justinian, from the death of Theodosius to the rise of Islam. Translated by Stuart Gilbert and James Emmons. New York, Odyssey Press [1967] 408 p. 392 illus. (part col.), col. maps, plans. (The Arts of mankind) Translation of L'age d'or de Justinien. Bibliography: p. [381]-[392] [N6250.G6713] 66-29363
1. Art, Byzantine—History. I. Title. II. Series.

MATHEW, Gervase, 1905- 709.02
Byzantine aesthetics. New York, Viking [1964, c.1963] xiii, 189p. 25 plates (pt. col.) 23cm. (Studio bk.) Bibl. 64-12098 6.50
1. Art, Byzantine—Hist. I. Title.

RICE, David Talbot, 1903- 709.02
Art of the Byzantine era. New York, Praeger [1963] 286 p. illus. (part col.) plans. 22 cm. Bibliography: p. 267-268. [N6250.R463 1963] 63-16444
1. Art, Byzantine—History. I. Title. BIP

Art, Byzantine—History—Sources.

MANGO, Cyril A., comp. 709'.02
The art of the Byzantine Empire, 312-1453; sources and documents [by] Cyril Mango. Englewood Cliffs, N.J., Prentice-Hall [1972] xvi, 272 p. front. 23 cm. (Sources and documents in the history of art series) Bibliography: p. 260. [N6250.M25] 72-380 ISBN 0-13-047027-9 4.50
1. Art, Byzantine—History—Sources. I. Title. II. Series. BIP

Art, Byzantine—Istanbul.

BECKWITH, John, 1918- 709'.561
The art of Constantinople: an introduction to Byzantine art 330-1453. 2nd ed. London, New York, Phaidon, 1968. viii, 184 p. 203 illus. 26 cm. (Phaidon paperback) Distributors in the United States: Frederick A. Praeger, New York. Bibliographical references included in "Notes" (p. 155-168) [N6250.B4 1968] 68-18908 ISBN 0-7148-1332-X 21/-
1. Art, Byzantine—Istanbul. 2. Art—Istanbul—History. I. Title.

Art, Byzantine—Italy.

CRENA de Iongh, Daniel, 1888- 709'.45
Byzantine aspects of Italy. [1st ed.] New York, W. W. Norton [1967] 194 p. illus., maps. 22 cm. Bibliography: p. 185-193. [N6913.C7 1967] 67-19211
1. Art, Byzantine—Italy. 2. Art—Italy. I. Title. BIP

Art—Calcutta—Galleries and museums.

CALCUTTA. 708'.954'14
[Edited by Heinz Mode] South Brunswick, A. S. Barnes [1973] 65, 167 p. illus. (part col.) 35 cm. (Great centres of art) [N3750.C27C34 1973] 72-9852 ISBN 0-498-01305-7 25.00
1. Art—Calcutta—Galleries and museums. 2. Calcutta—Museums. I. Mode, Heinz Adolph, 1913- ed.

Art calendars.

NEW York. Museum of Modern Art. Junior Council. v. 12
An appointment calendar with posters from the collection of the Museum of Modern Art. New York, N.D. v. illus. (part col.) 21 cm. Year of issue on cover. [[NC1800]] 64-9031
1. Art calendars. 2. Posters. I. Title.

WITTENBORN art calendar 1961. 741.68
[New York, Wittenborn, 1960] unpaged col. illus. 37x28cm. 2.50, pap., spiral binding

Art—California, Southern.

MOURE, Nancy Dustin Wall. 709'.2'2 B
Dictionary of art and artists in Southern California before 1930 / by Nancy Dustin Wall Moure, with research assistance by Lyn Wall Smith ; introd. by Carl Schaefer Dentzel. Glendale, Calif. : Dustin Publications, 1975. xxvi, 306 p. : ill. ; 28 cm. (Publications in Southern California art ; no. 3) "500 copies printed." Bibliography: p. 288-290. [N6530.S7M68] 75-329638
1. Art—California, Southern. 2. Artists—California, Southern—Biography. I. Smith, Lyn Wall, joint author. II. Title. III. Series.

Art—Cambridge, Mass.—Catalogs.

HARVARD University. William Hayes Fogg Art Museum. 708.1446
Acquisitions, 1959-1962. Cambridge, Mass., Harvard [1963] 143p. illus. 21cm. Bibl. 63-24087 price unreported
1. Art—Cambridge, Mass.—Catalogs. I. Title.

Art, Cameroon—Exhibitions.

GEBAUER, Paul, 1900- 730'.0967'11
A guide to Cameroon art from the Collection of Paul and Clara Gebauer. [Exhibition] Portland Art Museum, October 30 - December 1, 1968. [Portland, Or., 1968] [43] p. illus., maps, ports. 23 cm. [N7397] 76-5033
1. Gebauer, Clara—Art collections. 2. Art, Cameroon—Exhibitions. I. Portland, Or. Art Museum. II. Title.

*JANSEN, Gerard 709.011
Ancient art of the northern cameroons: Sao and Fali [by] Gerard Jansen and J. G. Gauthier Oosterhout, Netherlands, Anthropological Publications, 1973 [95 p.] illus. 25 cm. Bibliography: p. 35 [N5315]
I. Gauthier, J. G., joint author II. Title.
Distributed by Humanities Press, Atlantic Highlands, N.J. for 11.25.

Art, Canadian.

CANADIAN art today. 709'.71
Edited by William Townsend. London, New York, Studio International, 1970. 2-114, xii p. illus. (some col.), ports. 31 cm. English or French. Bibliography: p. 105-106. [N6545.C22 1970b] 72-181114 ISBN 0-902063-02-2 £2.125 ($5.00 U.S.)
1. Art, Canadian. 2. Art, Modern—20th century—Canada. I. Townsend, William, 1909- ed.

CANADIAN art today. 709'.71
Edited by William Townsend. Greenwich, Conn., New York Graphic Society [1970] 114 p. illus. (part col.), port. 32 cm. "A Studio international edition." English or French. Bibliography: p. 105-106. [N6545.C22 1970] 79-110663 10.00
1. Art, Canadian. 2. Art, Modern—20th century—Canada. I. Townsend, William, 1909- ed.

Art, Canadian—Catalogs.

ONTARIO. Art Gallery. 709.71'074'0113541
Art Gallery of Ontario; the Canadian collection. Toronto, New York, McGraw-Hill Co. of Canada [1970] xvi, 603 p. illus. (part col.) 26 cm. Bibliography: p. 560-582. [N6540.O57] 69-14868
1. Art, Canadian—Catalogs. I. Title. II. Title: The Canadian collection.

PICTURES from the Douglas M. Duncan Collection / selected and introduced by Frances Duncan Barwick. Toronto ; Buffalo : University of Toronto Press, [1975] 146 p. : ill. (some col.) ; 23 x 26 cm. [N6545.P52] 74-75587 ISBN 0-8020-3322-9 : 15.00 760'.0971
1. Duncan, Douglas Moerdyke, 1902-1968—Art collections. 2. Art, Canadian—Catalogs. 3. Art, Modern—20th century—

Canada. I. Barwick, Frances Duncan, 1909-

Art, Canadian—Exhibitions.

EDMONTON Art Gallery. 709'.71'074011
Changing visions : the Canadian landscape = Apercus divers : le paysage canadien : a travelling exhibition = esposition itinerante / organized by the Edmonton Art Gallery and the Art Gallery of Ontario. [Edmonton, Alta.] : Edmonton Art Gallery, c1976. 59 p. : ill. (some col.) ; 23 x 29 cm. English and French parallel text. Itinerary with list of artists and lenders inserted in pocket ([5] p.). Includes bibliographical references. [N6545.E35 1976] 77-351073 ISBN 0-919876-09-9
1. Art, Canadian—Exhibitions. 2. Art, Modern—20th century—Canada—Exhibitions. 3. Canada in art. I. Art Gallery of Ontario. II. Title. III. Title: Apercus divers.

49TH parallels: 709'.71'074013
new Canadian art. [Exhibition at the John and Mable Ringling Museum of Art, Sarasota, Fla., Feb. 14-Mar. 21, 1971 and Museum of Contemporary Art, Chicago, Ill., Apr. 3-May 16, 1971 Sarasota, Fla. [1971] [80] p. illus. 18 x 24 cm. [N6545.F66] 72-194163
1. Art, Canadian—Exhibitions. 2. Art, Modern—20th century—Canada. I. John and Mable Ringling Museum of Art, Sarasota, Fla. II. Museum of Contemporary Art, Chicago.

HAMILTON, Ont. Art Gallery. 709'.71'0740113
Nine out of ten, a survey of contemporary Canadian art : [Hamilton, Ont. : The Gallery, 1975?] [36] p. : chiefly ill. ; 21 x 23 cm. [N6545.H35 1975] 75-313016
1. Art, Canadian—Exhibitions. 2. Art, Modern—20th century—Canada. I. Kitchener Waterloo Art Gallery. II. Gallery Stratford. III. Title.

HUGHES, Edward John, 1913- 709'.71
E. J. Hughes: a retrospective exhibition organized by the Vancouver Art Gallery ... [Vancouver? 1968?] 1 v. (unpaged) illus., port. 22 cm. Label mounted on t.p.: Supplied by Worldwide Books, New York. Exhibition held at the Vancouver Art Gallery October 5-29, 1967, and at New York University, Toronto, November 13-December 8, 1967. [ND249.H8A42] 68-30058
I. Vancouver, B.C. Art Gallery. II. York University, Toronto.

IMAGES of 704.94'24'0971074011274
woman : the Winnipeg Art Gallery : November 14, 1975 to January 4th, 1976. [s.l. : s.n., 1976] 27 p. : ill. ; 22 x 28 cm. Catalog of an exhibition in support of International Women's Year. [N6544.I46] 77-373495 1.00
1. Art, Canadian—Exhibitions. 2. Art, Modern—19th century—Canada—Exhibitions. 3. Art, Modern—20th century—Canada—Exhibitions. 4. Women in art—Exhibitions. 5. Women in Canada—Exhibitions. I. Winnipeg Art Gallery.

LEMIEUX, Jean Paul, 1904- 759.11
Jean Paul Lemieux. [Montreal, Montreal Museum of Fine Arts, 1967] 80 p. illus. (part col.) 22 cm. Preface written by Luc d'Iberville-Moreau. Organised by the Montreal Museum of Fine Arts. Label mounted on p. [1]: Supplied by Worldwide Books, New York. Exhibition held at the Montreal Museum of Fine Arts Sept. 15-Oct. 11, 1967; the Musee du Quebec Oct. 18-Nov. 22, 1967; and the National Gallery of Canada Dec. 6, 1967-Jan. 7, 1968. French and English. Bibliography: p. 12. [ND249.L4A45] 68-30061
I. Iberville-Moreau, Luc d'. II. Montreal. Museum of Fine Arts. III. Quebec (City). Musee de la province de Quebec. IV. Ottawa. National Gallery of Canada.

NEWPORT Harbor Art Museum. 709.711'33'0740194
The new art of Vancouver. Catalogue by Thomas H. Garver [director. Balboa, Calif., c1969] 1 v. (unpaged) illus. 25 cm. Held at the Newport Harbor Art Museum, Balboa, Calif., Oct. 8-Nov. 9, 1969, and the Art Galleries, University of California, Santa Barbara, Nov. 16-Dec. 21, 1969. "The new art of Vancouver installations and projects, Newport Harbor Art Museum": [8] p. inserted. [N6547.V3N4] 73-23920
1. Art, Canadian—Exhibitions. 2. Art, Modern—20th century—Vancouver, B.C. I. Garver, Thomas H. II. California. University, Santa Barbara. Art Gallery. III. Title.

NORMAN Mackenzie Art Gallery. 708'.1124'4
Acquisitions to the permanent collection, 1973-1976 / Norman Mackenzie Art Gallery, University of Regina, Regina Saskatchewan [Regina, Sask. : The Gallery, 1976?] [35] p. : chiefly ill. ; 22 x 28 cm. Exhibition catalog. [N6545.N6 1977] 77-365847
1. Art, Canadian—Exhibitions. 2. Art, Modern—20th century—Canada—Exhibitions. 3. Art, Modern—20th century—Exhibitions. I. Title.

17 Canadian 709'.71'074011133
artists : a protean view, the Vancouver Art Gallery, May 31 through July 4, 1976. [s.l. : s.n., 1976] [64] p. : ill. (some col.) ; 25 x 26 cm. [N6545.S48] 76-378957
1. Art, Canadian—Exhibitions. 2. Art, Modern—20th century—Canada—Exhibitions. I. Vancouver Art Gallery.

SPECTRUM 709'.71'0740114281
Canada. [Montreal : Royal Canadian Academy of Arts, 1976] [104] p. : ill. (some col.) ; 22 cm. "The Royal Canadian Academy of Arts presents Spectrum Canada in conjunction with the Arts and Culture program of the Organizing Committee of the 1976 Olympic Games, July 5-31, 1976, Complexe Desjardins, Montreal, Quebec." English and French. [N6545.S68] 77-360354
1. Art, Canadian—Exhibitions. 2. Art, Modern—20th century—Canada—Exhibitions. I. Royal Canadian Academy of Arts.

Art, Canadian—Hist.

HUBBARD, Robert Hamilton, 1916- ed. 709.71
An anthology of Canadian art. Toronto, Oxford University Press, 1960. 187 p. illus. (part col.) 18 x 25 cm. "Bibliographical note": p. 167-169. [N6540.H8] 60-52066
1. Art, Canadian—Hist. I. Title.

Art, Canadian—Ontario—Exhibitions.

ART Gallery of Hamilton. 759.11
Ontario now : a survey of contemporary art : Kitchener-Waterloo Art Gallery, January 8 to February 1, 1976, Art Gallery of Hamilton, February 6 to February 29, 1976 / organized & circulated by the Art Gallery of Hamilton. [Hamilton, Ont. : The Gallery, 1976] [32] p. : chiefly ill. ; 21 x 24 cm. [N6545.A775 1976] 77-357060
1. Art, Canadian—Ontario—Exhibitions. 2. Art, Modern—20th century—Ontario—Exhibitions. I. Kitchener Waterloo Art Gallery. II. Title.

Art, Carlovingian.

HINKS, Roger Packman. 709.02
Carolingian art; a study of early medieval painting and sculpture in western Europe. [Ann Arbor] University of Michigan Press [1962] 226p. illus. 21cm. (Ann Arbor paperbacks, AA71) Includes bibliography. [N6245.H5 1962] 62-52487
1. Art, Carlovingian. I. Title. BIP

HUBERT, Jean. 709'.4
The Carolingian renaissance [by] J. Hubert, J. Porcher [and] W. F. Volbach. New York, G. Braziller [1970] xi, 380 p. illus. (part col.), col. maps (part fold.), plans (part col.) 25 cm. (The Arts of mankind) Translation of L'Empire carolingien. "Translated by James Emmons: parts one and four, Stuart Gilbert: part two, and Robert Allen: part three." Bibliography: p. 323-[338] [N6245.H813] 72-99513 30.00
1. Art, Carlovingian. 2. Architecture, Carlovingian. I. Porcher, Jean, joint author. II. Volbach, Wolfgang Friedrich, 1892- joint author. III. Title. IV. Series.

LASKO, Peter. 730'.094
Ars sacra, 800-1200. [Harmondsworth, Eng., Baltimore] Penguin Books [1972 i.e. 1973] xxix, 338 p. illus. 27 cm. (The Pelican history of art) Bibliography: p. 315-317. [N6245.L37] 73-162318 ISBN 0-14-056036-X 35.00 (U.S.)
1. Art, Carlovingian. 2. Art, Ottonian. 3. Art, Romanesque. I. Title. II. Series. BIP

Art, Catalan.

CERVERA, Joseph Phillip. 709'.46'7
Modernismo : the Catalan renaissance of the arts / Joseph Phillip Cervera. New York : Garland, 1976. viii, 462 p. : ill. ; 22 cm. (Outstanding dissertations in the fine arts) Originally presented as the author's thesis, University of California. Bibliography: p. 445-462. [N7109.C3C43 1976] 75-23787 ISBN 0-8240-1983-0 lib.bdg. : 32.50
1. Art, Catalan. 2. Art, Modern—19th century—Catalonia. I. Title. II. Series.

Art—Catalogs.

AGNES Etherington Art Centre. 759.11
Permanent collection, 1968. [Catalogue] Kingston [Ont., c1968] 1 v. (chiefly illus., part col.) 28 cm. [N910.K45A6] 76-439196 4.00

CLAPP, Jane. 708.1
Art reproductions. New York, Scarecrow Press, 1961. 350p. 22cm. 'List of art reproductions available from ninety-five museums in the United States and Canada.' [N4000.C5] 61-8714
1. Art—Catalogs. 2. Photographs—Catalogs. 3. Color prints—Catalogs. I. Title.

GAUNT, William, 1900- 760
Painters of fantasy : from Hieronymus Bosch to Salvador Dali : 104 reproductions / a selection introduced by William Gaunt. London : Phaidon, 1974. [16] p., [96] p. of plates : chiefly ill. (some col.) ; 42 cm. Distributed in the U.S. by Praeger, New York. [N8217.G8G38] 73-21451 ISBN 0-7148-1622-1 : pbk. : 8.95
1. Art—Catalogs. 2. Grotesque in art. 3. Surrealism. I. Title. BIP

HOUSE of El Dieff, inc. 708.1
Sixty-four; collections of British and American literature in the 20th century. French literature in the 19th and 20th centuries, the 'Broadway' theatre in the past 40 years, recorded music in the 19th and 20th centuries, William Faulkner, Ernest Hemingway, Thomas Wolfe, and individual offerings of manuscripts, literary and historical letters, drawings, sculptures, oils. New York, [1964] 1 v. (unpaged) illus., facsims., ports. 29 cm. On cover: Sixty four. Lew David Feldman. [N8650.H67] 66-8174
1. Art — Catalogs. I. Feldman, Lew David. II. Title.

PRANG (L.) and Company, Boston. v. 12
Illustrated catalogue. Boston. v. illus. 24cm. [N377.P84] 58-50807
1. Art—Catalogs. I. Title.

SCHAB, William, firm, New York 769.94
Catalogue 34, Rare books and manuscripts. Four centuries of fine illustrated books, literature and science in first editions. New York, Author [1963] 170p. illus. (pt col.) 29cm. 43-29955 4.00 pap.,
1. Art— Catalogs. 2. Art—Prices. I. Title.

SCHAB, William, firm, New York 769.94
Catalogue 33, a distinguished collection of old master engravings, drawings and woodcuts, modern master drawings and prints. New York, Author [1963] 195p. illus. (pt. col.) 29cm. 43-29955 4.00 pap.,
1. Art—Catalogs. 2. Art—Prices I. Title.

SCHAB, William, firm, New York, 769.94
Catalogue 32. Engravings and drawings, woodcuts and lithographs by old and modern masters. New York, Author, 48 E. 57 St. 151p. illus. (pt. col.) 29cm. 43-29955 4.00 pap.,
1. Art—Catalogs. 2. Art—Prices. I. Title.

SCHAB, William H., firm, New York 769.94
Catalog 45 New York [1968] 204p. illus. (pt. col.) 29cm. Each cat. has different title: Catalogue 45: Great master drawings & prints. from the 15th to 20th centuries. [N8650. S35] 43-29955 7.00; 4.00 pap.,
1. Art—Catalogs. 2. Art—Prices. I. Title.

SCHAB, William H., firm, New York. 769.94
French and Italian 18th century drawings and prints, exhibited and offered for sale. New York, 48 E. 57th St. William H. Schab, [1960] 121p. illus. (part col.) 29cm. (Its catalogue 28) pap., gratis
1. Art— Catalogs. 2. Art-Prices. I. Title.

SCHAB, William H. (gallery) firm, New York 769.94
Catalogue forty one; comprising. . .[items] offered for sale by the William H. Schab Gallery. New York [1966] illus. (pt. col.) 29cm. Cover title: Great books of art. science & music; early literary & illustrated editions. Each catalog has different title. 43-29955 4.00 pap.,
1. Art—Catalogs. 2. Art—Prices. I. Title.

SCHAB, William H. (Gallery) firm New York 769.94
Catalogue 38. New York, Author, 48 E. 57 St. [1964] 200p. illus. (col. front) 29cm. Each cat. has different title: Cat. 38.--Six centuries of graphic arts; prints and drawings of great masters exhibited and offered for sale by the William H. Schab Gallery. 43-29955 4.00 pap.,
1. Art—Catalogs. 2. Art—Prices. I. Title.

SCHAB, William H., New York 769.94
Catalogue 31. Early printed and illustrated books, illuminated manuscripts. New York, Author, 48 E. 57 St. 154p. illus. (pt. col.) 29cm. 43-29955 4.00 pap.,
1. Art—Catalogs. 2. Art—Prices I. Title.

SOTHEBY, firm, auctioneers, London 708.2
The ivory hammer; 2. The year at Sotheby's 220th season, 1963-1964. New York, Holt [1965, c.1963] xxii, 256p. illus. (pt. col. ports. (pt. col.) facsims. (incl. music) 28cm. [N8640.S58] 64-11566 12.50
1. Art—Catalogs. I. Title.

SOTHEBY, firm, auctioneers, London 708.2
The ivory hammer: the year at Sotheby's 219th season, 1962-1963. New York, Holt [1964, c.1963] xxxi, 254p. illus. (pt. col.) ports. (pt. col.) maps, facsims. (incl. music) 28cm. 'The property of a lady, by Ian Fleming.' 64-11566 12.50
1. Art—Catalogs. I. Title.

YAMANAKA and Company. 709.51
Illustrated catalogue of the rare and beautiful oriental art treasures of supreme quality, procured in China during the past year by the senior member of the well-known firm of Yamanaka & Company and their staff of experts. To be sold at unrestricted public sale. The sale will be conducted by Thomas E. Kirby and Otto Bernet, of the American Art Association, managers. New York, 1915. unpaged. illus. 23cm. [N8650.Y35] 52-57558
1. Art—Catalogs. 2. Art, Chinese. I. Title.

Art, Celtic.

FINLAY, Ian. 732'.6
Celtic art; an introduction. Park Ridge, N.J., Noyes Press [1973] 183 p. illus. (part col.) 26 cm. Bibliography: p. 174-175. [N5925.F56] 72-89198 ISBN 0-8155-5018-9 24.00
1. Art, Celtic.

JACOBSTHAL, Paul, 1880-1957. 709'.174'916
Early Celtic art. Oxford, Clarendon Press [1970] 2 v. illus. 32 cm. "First published 1944." Contents.Contents.—v. 1. Text.—v. 2. Plates. Includes bibliographical references. [N6240.J18 1970] 73-16002
1. Art, Celtic. 2. Celts—Antiquities. I. Title. BIP

MEGAW, J. V. S. 730'.094
Art of the European iron age; a study of the elusive image [by] J. V. S. Megaw. [1st

Korea and Vietnam. Translated from the French by Remy Inglis Hall. Edited by Charles McCurdy. Maps by Henri Jacquinet and Pierre Simonet. Drawings by Claude Abeille. Garden City, N.Y., Anchor Books [1967] x, 428 p. illus., maps. 19 cm. "Originally published as 'Extreme Orient' in Encyclopedie de la Pleiade, Histoire de l'art I." Bibliography: p. [333]-343. [N7340.B653] 67-10368
1. Art, Chinese. 2. Art, Japanese. I. Title.

BURLING, Judith. 709.51
Chinese art [by] Judith and Arthur Hart Burling. New York, Studio Publications, in association with Crowell [1953] 384 p. illus. (part col.) 26 cm. Bibliography: p. 364-374. [N7340.B69] 53-10705
1. Art, Chinese. I. Burling, Arthur Hart, joint author.

†BUSHELL, Stephen Wootton, 1844-1908. 709'.51
Chinese art / by Stephen W. Bushell. North Miami Beach, Fla. : Rare Reprints, 1977- v. : ill. ; 24 cm. At head of title: Board of Education, South Kensington, Victoria and Albert Museum. Reprint of the 1904- ed. printed for H.M. Stationery Office by Wyman, London; with new introd. Includes index. [N7340.B94 1977] 78-101410 ISBN 0-89592-030-1 : 37.50
1. Art, Chinese. 2. Art industries and trade—China. I. Victoria and Albert Museum, South Kensington. II. Title.

CAPON, Edmund. 709'.51
Art and archaeology in China / Edmund Capon. South Melbourne : Macmillan Co. of Australia ; Cambridge, Mass. : distributed by MIT Press, 1977. 180, [16] p. : chiefly col. ill. ; 26 cm. Includes index. Bibliography: p. [193] [N7343.C35] 77-369001 ISBN 0-333-22937-1 : 19.95 deluxe ed. : 50.00
1. Art, Chinese. 2. China—Antiquities. I. Title. BIP

CHINESE art; 709'.51
general editor Francesco Abbate; translated [from the Italian] by Pauline L. Phillips. London, New York, Octopus Books, 1972. 158 p. chiefly 101 col. illus. 20 cm. Translation of Arte della Cina. Bibliography: p. 154. [N7340.A71713] 72-171380 ISBN 0-7064-0027-5 £0.99
1. Art, Chinese. I. Abbate, Francesco, ed.

CHINESE art. 730.951
[1st American ed.] New York, Universe Books [1960- v. illus. (part mounted col.) 34 cm. ([The Universe library of antique art]) Vol. 1 is a translation of Les arts de la Chine, by Daisy Lion-Goldschmidt; translated by Diana Imber. Contents.Contents.—[v. 1] Bronze, jade, sculpture, ceramics, by D. G. Lion and J. C. Moreau-Gobard.—v. 2. The minor arts: gold, silver, bronze, cloisonne, Cantonese enamel, lacquer, furniture, wood, by R. S. Jenyns and W. Watson. Includes bibliographical references. [N7340.C483] 60-12415
1. Art, Chinese. I. Lion, Daisy Goldschmidt. Chinese art: bronze, jade, sculpture, ceramics. II. Moreau-Gobard, Jean Claude. III. Jenyns, Roger Soame, 1904- IV. Watson, William, 1917-

CHINESE arts 730.951
[v.4] New York, Universe Bks. [c.1965] 323p. illus. (pt. mounted col.) 34cm. (Universe lib. of antique art) Contents.v.4. The minor arts II; textiles: glass and painting on glass: carvings in ivory and rhinoceros horn: carvings in hardstones: snuff-bottles: inkcakes and inkstones. by R. Soame Jenyns. with the edit. assistance of William Watson. 60-12415 39.50
1. Art, Chinese. I. Jenyns, R. Soame. II. Watson, William, ed.

CH'U t'u wen wu chan lan kung tso tsu. 709.51
Wen hua ta ko ming ch'i chien ch'u tu wen wu. (Cultural relics unearthed during the period of the Great Cultural Revolution.) (Distributor: New York, China Books & Periodicals, 1972-) v. (chiefly illus. (part col.)) 26 cm. Vol. 1- : "(Explanation) in pocket. [N7340.C535] 72-837130 30.00 (v. 1)
1. Art, Chinese. 2. China—Antiquities. I. Title.
L.C. cataloging in Chinese.

COLUMBIA University. Dept. of Art History and Archaeology. 709'.9
Early Chinese art and the Pacific Basin; a photographic exhibition. [New York, 1968] xvi, 152 p. illus., map. 23 cm. "Organized by the Department of Art History and Archaeology, Columbia University, in conjunction with a symposium held in August 1967 ... The ... exhibition was designed and installed ... by Mr. Gene McCabe." Bibliography: p. 121-152. [N7343.C58] 68-28018 5.00
1. Art, Chinese. 2. Art, Oriental. I. Title. BIP

FEDDERSEN, Martin, 1888- 709.51
Chinese decorative art; a handbook for collectors and connoisseurs. Tr. [from German] by Arthur Lane. New York, T. Yoseloff [c.1961] 286p. illus. (part col.) map 25cm. Bibl. 61-9623 12.50
1. Art, Chinese. 2. Art objects, Chinese. 3. Art industries and trade, Chinese. I. Title.

FERGUSON, John Calvin, 1866-1945. 709'.51
Outlines of Chinese art. Freeport, N.Y., Books for Libraries Press [1972] xi, 263 p. illus. 23 cm. Reprint of the 1919 ed., issued in series: Scammon lectures. [N7340.F4 1972] 70-37879 ISBN 0-8369-6716-X
1. Art, Chinese. I. Title. II. Series: Scammon lectures. BIP

GARNER, Harry Mason, Sir, 1891- 709.51
Chinese art in three-dimensional colour, by Harry M. Garner and Margaret Medley. Photography by William B. Gruber and Rupert P. Leach. [New York] Published for the Gruber Foundation by the Asia Society [1969] 4 v. 29 cm. Vols. 1-3 each has 44 colored View-Master stereo reels in pockets; v. 4 has 48 in pockets. Contents.Contents.—v. 1. Neolithic period. Shang dynasty. Western Chou dynasty. Eastern Chou dynasty. Warring states period.—v. 2. Han dynasty. Six dynasties. Sui dynasty. T'ang dynasty.—v. 3. Five dynasties. Sung dynasty. Yuan dynasty.—v. 4. Ming dynasty. Ch'ing dynasty. Includes bibliographies. [N7340.G3] 69-11426
1. Art, Chinese. I. Medley, Margaret, joint author. II. Gruber, William B., 1903-1965, illus. III. Leach, Rupert P., illus. IV. Title.

LIN, Yutang, 1895- comp. 709.51
The Chinese theory of art; translations from the masters of Chinese art. New York, Putnam Sons [1967] xii, 244 p. illus., geneal. tables. 23 cm. [N7340.L49 1967] 67-21121
1. Art, Chinese. I. Title.

LION, Daisy (Goldschmidt) 730.951
Chinese art: bronze, jade, sculpture, ceramics, by Daisy Lion-Goldschmidt & Jean Claude Moreau-Gobard. Translated by Diana Imber with a foreword by George by George Savage. [1st American ed.] New York, Universe Books [1960] 425p. illus. (part mounted col.) 34cm. Translation of Arts de la Chine. Bibliography: p. 424-425. [N7340.L533] 60-12415
1. Art, Chinese. I. Moreau-Gobard, Jean Claude. II. Title.

MAUST, Don. 745.1'0951
Collectible Chinese art and antiques a collection of information on classic and common Chinese art objects that will teach one to recognize good Chinese art and antique collectables. Edited by Don. A. Maust. 1st ed. Uniontown, Pa., E. G. Warman, 1973. 159 p. illus. 28 cm. [N7340.M33] 73-159700 7.95
1. Art, Chinese. 2. Art—Collectors and collecting. 3. Art objects, Chinese. 4. Art objects—Collectors and collecting. I. Title.

MUNSTERBERG, Hugo, 1916- 709'.51
The arts of China. Rutland, Vt., C. E. Tuttle Co. [1972] 234 p. illus. (part col.) 25 cm. Bibliography: p. 221-223. [N7340.M817] 70-188012 ISBN 0-8048-0039-1 17.50
1. Art, Chinese. I. Title. BIP

SILCOCK, Arnold, 1889- 709'.51
Introduction to Chinese art and history. Westport, Conn., Greenwood Press [1972, c1948] p. Bibliography: p. [N7340.S5 1972] 76-170603 ISBN 0-8371-6254-8
1. Art, Chinese. 2. China—History. I. Title. BIP

SIREN, Osvald, 1879- 709'.51
A history of early Chinese art. New York, Hacker Art Books, 1970. 4 v. in 2. illus., plans, plates. 32 cm. Reprint of the 1929-30 ed.; each part has special t.p. Contents.Contents.—v. 1. The prehistoric and pre-Han periods. v. 2. The Han period.—v. 3. Sculpture. v. 4. Architecture. [N7343.S512] 74-78362
1. Art, Chinese. 2. Art—China—History. I. Title. BIP

SUGIMURA. YUZO, 1900- 709.51
Chinese sculpture, bronzes, and jades. in Japanese collections. English adaptation by Burton Watson. Honolulu, East-West Ctr. Pr. [1966] 1 v. (chiefly illus., col. plates) 31cm. [N7343.S85] 66-22477 17.50
1. Art, Chinese. 2. China—Antiq. I. Title.

SUGIMURA, Yuzo, 1900- 709.51
Chinese sculpture, bronzes, and jades in Japanese collections. English adaptation by Burton Watson. Honolulu, East-West Center Press [1966] 1 v. [chiefly illus., col. plates] 31 cm. [N7343.S85] 66-22477
1. Art, Chinese. 2. China — Antiq. I. Title. BIP

SULLIVAN, Michael, 1916- 709'.51
The arts of China / Michael Sullivan. Rev. ed. Berkeley : University of California Press, 1978,c1977. 287 p. : ill. (some col.) ; 27 cm. Includes index. Bibliography: p. 271-273. [N7340.S92 1977] 76-44639 ISBN 0-520-03366-3 : 20.00 pbk. : 7.95
1. Art, Chinese. I. Title. BIP

SULLIVAN, Michael, 1916- 709.51
An introduction to Chinese art. Berkeley, University of California Press, 1961 [c 1960] 223 p. illus., plates (part col.) maps. 26 cm. Errata slip inserted. Bibliography: p. 200-212. [N7340.S9] 61-3831
1. Art, Chinese. 2. Art—China—Hist. I. Title.

SULLIVAN, Michael [Donovan Michael Sullivan] 1916- 709.51
An introduction to Chinese art. Berkeley. Univ. of California Press, 1961 [c.1960] 223p. illus. (part col.) maps. 26cm. Bibl. 61-3831 8.00
1. Art, Chinese. 2. Art—China—Hist. I. Title.

TS'AO, Chao, 14thcent. 709'.51
Chinese connoisseurship: the Ko ku yao lun, the essential criteria of antiquities. A translation made and edited by Sir Percival David, with a facsimile of the Chinese text of 1388. New York, Praeger [1971] lxii, 351 p. illus., 3 col. plates. 29 cm. Translation of Ko ku yao lun. Includes bibliographical references. [N7343.5.T513 1971b] 78-134520 50.00
1. Art, Chinese. 2. Art—Expertising. 3. China—History—Ming dynasty, 1368-1644. I. David, Percival Victor, Sir, bart., 1892-1964, ed. and tr. II. Title. BIP

TSENG, Yu-ho, 1923- 709.51
Some contemporary elements in classical chinese art Honolulu, Univ. of Hawaii Pr. [c.]1963. viii, 72, [18]p. 49 illus. 21cm. Introd. matter, pictures, caption notes also in Chinese. 63-17008 2.25 pap.,
1. Art, Chinese. 2. Art, Modern—20th cent. I. Title. II. Title: Chung-kuo hua hsuan hsin yu. BIP

TUPPER, Emily Hartwell. 709.51
Birthplace: China; the life stories of some of the Chinese animals and birds in the Seattle Art Museum, gathered together by Emily Hartwell Tupper. Photos by Earl Fields; one by C. F. Todd. [Seattle?] [1950] unpaged. illus. 22 cm. [N7340.T8] 52-1931
1. Art, Chinese. 2. Animals in art. 3. Birds in art. I. Seattle. Art Museum. II. Title.

WATSON, William, 1917- 709'.51
Style in the arts of China / William Watson. New York : Universe Books, 1975, c1974. 126 p., [64] leaves of plates : ill. ; 23 cm. Bibliography: p. [121]-124. [N7340.W37 1975] 74-27246 ISBN 0-87663-216-9 : 12.50
1. Art, Chinese. I. Title. BIP

WATSON, William, 1917- 709'.51
Style in the arts of China / William Watson. Harmondsworth : Penguin, 1974. 126 p., [127] p. of plates : ill. ; 20 cm. (Pelican books) Errata slip inserted. Bibliography: p. [121]-124. [N7340.W37] 74-193821 ISBN 0-14-021863-7 pbk. : 4.25
1. Art, Chinese. I. Title.
Distributed by Penguin, Baltimore.

WILLETTS, William. 709.51
Chinese art. [Harmondsworth, Middlesex] Penguin Books [c1958] 2 v. (xxxiv, 802 p.) illus., maps (1 fold) 18 cm. Added t. p. in Chinese. Bibliographical footnotes. [[N7340]] 59-4112
1. Art — China — Illst. I. Title.

WILLIAM Rockhill Nelson Gallery of Art and Mary Atkins Museum of Fine Arts, Kansas City, Mo. 709'.51
The dragon's gate : exploring oriental art / William Rockhill Nelson Gallery of Art and Mary Atkins Museum of Fine Arts, Kansas City, Missouri, edited by Victoria R. Melcher and Dianne T. Deckert. 1st ed. Kansas City, Mo. : The Museum, 1976. 52 p. : ill. ; 22 x 28 cm. Includes index. Explores facets of Oriental art including sculpture, painting, and furniture. Includes suggestions for related activities. [N7340.W48 1976] 77-359560
1. William Rockhill Nelson Gallery of Art and Mary Atkins Museum of Fine Arts, Kansas City, Mo. 2. Art, Chinese. 3. Art appreciation. I. Melcher, Victoria R. II. Deckert, Dianne Turner. III. Title.

Art, Chinese—Addresses, essays, lectures.

CHINESE art. 709 s
New York : Garland Pub., 1976. 198 p., [1] leaf of plates : ill. ; 29 cm. (The Garland library of the history of art ; v. 14) Includes bibliographical references. [N5300.G32 vol. 14] [N7340] 709'.51 76-14077 ISBN 0-8240-2424-9 : 35.00
1. Art, Chinese—Addresses, essays, lectures. I. Series.
Contents omitted

EARLY Chinese art and its possible influence in the Pacific basin; 709'.01'1
a symposium arranged by the Department of Art History and Archaeology, Columbia University, New York City, August 21-25, 1967. Edited by Noel Barnard in collaboration with Douglas Fraser. New York, Intercultural Arts Press [1972] 3 v. (xlii, 896 p.) illus. 24 cm. Contents.Contents.—v. 1. Ch'u and the silk manuscript.—v. 2. Asia.—v. 3. Oceania and the Americas. Includes bibliographies. [N7429.E2] 79-92798
1. Art, Chinese—Addresses, essays, lectures. 2. Art, Prehistoric—Pacific area—Addresses, essays, lectures. 3. Art, Primitive—Pacific area—Addresses, essays, lectures. I. Barnard, Noel, ed. II. Columbia University. Dept. of Art History and Archaeology.

Art, Chinese—Bibliography.

YUAN, Tung Li, 1895-1965. 016.709'51
The T. L. Yuan bibliography of western writings on Chinese art and archaeology / Harrie A. Vanderstappen, editor ; Rachel E. McClellan, principal assistant ; Edward Schafer ... [et al.], assistants. London : Mansell, 1975. xlvii, 606 p. ; 29 cm. Label mounted on t.p.: Exclusive distributor in the U.S., ISBS, Beaverton, Ore. Includes indexes. Bibliography: p. xi-xxxv. [Z5961.C5Y9 1975] [N7340] 76-356246 ISBN 0-7201-0521-8 : 80.00
1. Art, Chinese—Bibliography. 2. China—Antiquities—Bibliography. I. Vanderstappen, Harrie A., 1921- II. Title. III. Title: Bibliography of western writings on Chinese art and archaeology. BIP

Art, Chinese—Catalogs.

FREER Gallery of Art, Washington, D.C. 709'.51'0740153
Masterpieces of Chinese and Japanese art : Freer Gallery of Art handbook. Washington : Smithsonian Institution, 1976. v, 142 p. : ill. (some col.) ; 23 cm. [N7336.F7 1976] 76-11656
1. Freer Gallery of Art, Washington, D.C. 2. Art, Chinese—Catalogs. 3. Art, Japanese—Catalogs. 4. Art—Washington, D.C.—Catalogs. I. Title. BIP

Art, Chinese—Exhibitions.

ALSDORF, Marilynn, 1926- 709'.51'074017311
Chinese art from the Collection of James W. and Marilynn Alsdorf. Chicago [1970] [32] p. illus. 26 cm. Cover title. Catalog by Marilynn Alsdorf of an exhibition held at the Arts Club of Chicago, Sept. 21-Nov. 13, 1970. [N7342.A75] 79-286239
1. Art, Chinese—Exhibitions. 2. Art—Private collections. I. Alsdorf, James William, 1913- II. Arts Club of Chicago. III. Title.

ASIA Society. 709.51
Relics of ancient China, from the collection of Dr. Paul Singer. By Max Loehr. [New York] Distributed by H. N. Abrams [1965] 170 p. illus. (part mounted col.) maps. 29 cm. "An Asia House Gallery publication." "Catalogue of an exhibition selected by Dr. Max Loehr ... and shown in the Asia House Gallery early in 1965 as an activity of the Asia Society." Includes bibliographical references. [N7343.A8] 65-12619
1. Art, Chinese — Exhibitions. 2. China — Antiq. I. Loehr, Max. II. Singer, Paul, 1904- III. Asia House Gallery, New York. IV. Title.

ASIA Society. 709'.51
Relics of ancient China, from the collection of Dr. Paul Singer / by Max Loehr. New York : Arno Press, 1975, c1965. p. cm. (The Asia Society reprint collection) "Catalogue of an exhibition ... shown in the Asia House Gallery early in 1965." Reprint of the ed. published by The Society, New York. Includes bibliographical references. [N7343.A82 1975] 75-6683 ISBN 0-405-06566-3 : 32.00
1. Art, Chinese—Exhibitions. 2. China—Antiquities. I. Singer, Paul, 1904- II. Loehr, Max. III. Asia House Gallery, New York. IV. Title.

CAHILL, James Francis, 1926- 709'.51
The art of Southern Sung China / James Cahill. New York : Arno Press, 1975. p. cm. (The Asia Society reprint collection) Catalog of an exhibition held at Asia House Gallery, New York. Reprint of the 1962 ed. published by the Asia Society, New York. [N7343.4.C34] 75-6750 ISBN 0-405-06560-4 : 40.00
1. Art, Chinese—Exhibitions. 2. Art, Chinese—Sung-Yuan dynasties, 960-1368. I. Asia House Gallery, New York. II. Title. III. Series. BIP

CALIFORNIA. University, Davis. Dept. of Art. 301.451'951'0794
China and California; the impact of nineteenth and twentieth century Chinese art and culture on California, an exhibition, prepared by students in Art 189, Museum Methods and Connoisseurship, Art Department, University of California, Davis Campus. [Davis, Calif., 1966] vii, 37 p. 21 cm. Held at University Library, University of California, Davis, California, May 15 to July 1, 1966. Includes bibliographies. [N7344.C3] 66-65181
1. Art, Chinese—Exhibitions. 2. Chinese Americans—California. I. Title.

CHUNG-HUA jen min kung ho kuo ch'u t'u wen wu chan lan kung tso wei yuan hui. 709'.51'0740153
The exhibition of archaeological finds of the People's Republic of China : [exhibition dates in the United States, National Gallery of Art, Washington, December 13, 1974-March 30, 1975, the Nelson Gallery-Atkins Museum, Kansas City, Missouri, April 20-June 8, 1975] / text provided by the Organization Committee of the Exhibition of Archaeological Finds of the People's Republic of China. [Washington : National Gallery of Art, 1974] 2 v. : ill. (some col.) ; 25 cm. Title also in Chinese: Chung-hua jen min kung ho kuo ch'u t'u wen wu chan lan. Vol. 2 has added t.p.: The Chinese exhibition; an illustrated handlist of the exhibition of archaeological finds of the People's Republic of China. [N7342.C48 1974] 75-300717 pbk. : 4.00
1. Art, Chinese—Exhibitions. 2. China—Antiquities—Exhibitions. I. United States. National Gallery of Art. II. William Rockhill Nelson Gallery of Art and Mary Atkins Museum of Fine Arts, Kansas City, Mo. III. Title. IV. Title: Chung-hua jen min kung ho kuo ch'u t'u wen wu chan lan. V. Title: The Chinese exhibition.

EVERSON Museum of Art of Syracuse and Onondaga County. 709'.51
Chinese art from the Cloud Wampler and other collections in the Everson Museum. Introd. by Max Loehr. Handbook of the collection by Celia Carrington Riely. [Syracuse, N.Y., c1968] xiii, 188 p. illus., map. 26 cm. Catalog of the exhibition held during October 1968. Bibliography: p. 185-188. [N7342.W35E9] 68-58832
1. Art, Chinese—Exhibitions. 2. Art—Private collections—United States. I. Wampler, Cloud. II. Riely, Celia Carrington. III. Title.

FONTEIN, Jan. 730'.0951
Unearthing China's past [by] Jan Fontein & Tung Wu. Boston, Museum of Fine Arts; distributed by New York Graphic Society, Greenwich, Conn. [1973] 239 p. illus. 26 cm. Catalogue of an exhibition held at the Boston Museum of Fine Arts. Bibliography: p. 238. [N7342.F66] 73-79825 ISBN 0-87846-076-4 20.00
1. Art, Chinese—Exhibitions. I. Wu, Tung, joint author. II. Boston. Museum of Fine Arts. III. Title. BIP

LEE, Sherman E. 709'.51
Chinese art under the Mongols: the Yuan dynasty, 1279-1368 [by] Sherman E. Lee [and] Wai-kam Ho. [Cleveland] Cleveland Museum of Art; [distributed by the Press of Case Western Reserve University, 1968] viii, 403 p. illus. (1 col.), maps. 27 cm. Based on an exhibition sponsored by the Cleveland Museum of Art. "Catalogue [of the exhibition]": p. [113]-[380] Bibliography: p. 381-387. [N7342.L37] 68-9276 15.00
1. Art, Chinese—Exhibitions. 2. China—History—Yuan dynasty, 1260-1368. I. Ho, Wai-kam. II. Cleveland Museum of Art. III. Title.

LEFEBVRE d'Argence, Rene Yvon. 709'.51
Chinese treasures from the Avery Brundage Collection. [New York] Asia Society; distributed by New York Graphic Society [1968] 151 p. illus. (part col.) 23 cm. "An Asia House Gallery publication." "Catalogue of an exhibition ... shown in the Asia House Gallery in the winter of 1968 as an activity of the Asia Society." Bibliography: p. 150-151. [N7342.A9L4] 68-12222
1. Brundage, Avery—Art collections. 2. Art, Chinese—Exhibitions. I. Asia House Gallery, New York. II. Asia Society. III. Title.

LOEHR, Max. 709'.51
Chinese art: symbols and images. [Wellesley, Mass., 1967] 63 p. illus. 26 cm. Catalogue of an exhibition held at Wellesley College, Jewett Arts Center. April 16-June 6, 1967, sponsored by the Mayling Soong Foundation. Includes bibliographical references. [N7342.L58] 67-22767
1. Art, Chinese—Exhibitions. I. Wellesley College. Jewett Arts Center. II. Wellesley College. Mayling Soong Foundation. III. Title.

LOEHR, Max. 709'.51
Chinese art: symbols and images. [Wellesley, Mass., 1967] 63 p. illus. 26 cm. Catalogue of an exhibition held at Wellesley College, Jewett Arts Center, April 16-June 6, 1967, sponsored by the Mayling Soong Foundation. Includes bibliographical references. [N7342.L58] 67-22767
1. Art, Chinese—Exhibitions. I. Wellesley College. Jewett Arts Center. II. Wellesley College. Mayling Soong Foundation. III. Title.

LOS Angeles Co., Calif. Museum, Los Angeles. 709.51
The art of the T'ang dynasty; a loan exhibition organized by the Los Angeles County Museum from collections in America, the Orient, and Europe, January 8-February 17, 1957. [Los Angeles, 1957] 133 p. illus. 27 cm. Errata slip inserted. Bibliography: p. 29-30. [N7343.L63] 58-4946
1. Art, Chinese — Exhibitions. 2. Art objects, Chinese — Exhibitions. 3. China — Hist. — T'ang dynasty, 618-907. I. Title.

LOS Angeles County Museum, Los Angeles. 709.51
The art of the T'ang dynasty; a loan exhibition organized by the Los Angeles County Museum from collections in America, the Orient, and Europe, January 8-February 17, 1957. [Los Angeles, 1957] 133p. illus. 27cm. Errata slip inserted. Bibliography: p. 29-30. [N7343.L63] 58-4946
1. Art, Chinese— Exhibitions. 2. Art objects, Chinese—Exhibitions. 3. China—Hist.—Tang dynasty, 618-907. I. Title.

SPELMAN, Ruth. 709'.51'0740147245
The arts of China : a retrospective, C. W. Post Art Gallery, School of the Arts, C. W. Post Center, Long Island University, Greenvale, L.I., N.Y., February 4-March 27, 1977 / by Ruth Spelman. Greenvale, N.Y. : C. W. Post Art Gallery, c1977. 96 p. : ill. ; 28 cm. Includes exhibition catalog. Bibliography: p. 95-96. [N7342.S67] 76-52608 10.00
1. Art, Chinese—Exhibitions. I. Post (C. W.) Art Gallery. II. Title.

Art, Chinese—History.

BEURDELEY, Michel 709.51
The Chinese collector through the centuries, from the Han to the 20th century. Tr. by. Diana Imber Rutland. Vt., Tuttle [1966] 286p. illus. (pt. col.) fold. col. map. 30cm. Tr. of L'amateur chinois, des Han au XXe siecle. Bibl. [N7340.B4313] 66-31992 22.50
1. Art, Chinese—Hist. 2. Art—Collectors and collecting. I. Title.

BEURDELEY, Michel. 709.51
The Chinese collector through the centuries, from the Han to the 20th century. [Translated by Diana Imber] Rutland, Vt., C. E. Tuttle Co. [1966] 286 p. illus. (part col.) fold. col. map. 30 cm. Translation of L'amateur chinois, des Han au XXe siecle. Bibliography: p. 263-267. [N7340.B4313] 66-31992
1. Art, Chinese—History. 2. Collectors and collecting—China. I. Title.

CARTER, Dagny (Olsen) 709'.51
China magnificent; five thousand years of Chinese art, by Dagny Carter. Westport, Conn., Greenwood Press [1972] xi, 225 p. illus. 23 cm. Reprint of the 1935 ed. Bibliography: p. 209-215. [N7340.C3 1972] 78-114493 ISBN 0-8371-4777-8 14.25
1. Art, Chinese—History. I. Title. BIP

FENOLLOSA, Ernest Francisco, 1853-1908 709.5
Epochs of Chinese & Japanese art, an outline history of East Asiatic design. v.1& 2. New rev. ed., copious notes by Professor Petrucci. New York, Dover [1963] 2v. (204; 235p.) illus. 21cm. Unabridged repub. of the 2d. (1913) ed. 63-5655 2.50 pap.,ea.,
1. Art, Chinese—Hist. 2. Art, Japanese—Hist. I. Title.

PRODAN, Mario. 709'.51
An introduction to Chinese art. [New ed.] London, Spring Books, 1966. 220 p. illus., 71 plates (incl. 7 col.) 20 1/2 cm. 18/- Originally published as Chinese art: an introduction. London,Hutchinson, 1958. (B66-18332) Bibliography: p. 209-213. [N7340.P75 1966] 67-77836
1. Art, Chinese—Hist. I. Title.

RIDLEY, Michael. 709'.51
Treasures of China / Michael Ridley. New York : Arco Pub. Co., 1974, c1973. 144 p. : ill. (some col.) ; 23 cm. Includes index. [N7340.R52 1974] 73-85998 ISBN 0-668-03377-0 : 8.95
1. Art, Chinese—History. I. Title.

SCOTT, Hugh Doggett, 1900- 709'.51
The golden age of Chinese art: the lively T'ang dynasty [by] Hugh Scott. Rutland, Vt., Tuttle [1967, c.1966] xii, 191p. 123 plates (pt. col.) 27cm. Bibl. [N7343.S37] 66-16264 15.00 bxd.,
1. Art, Chinese—Hist. 2. China—Hist.—T'ang dynasty, 618-907. I. Title.

SPEISER, Werner. 709.51
The art of China: spirit and society. [Translated by George Lawrence] New York, Crown Publishers [1961), c1960] 256 p. illus. (part mounted col.) maps. 24 cm. (Art of the world, non-European cultures; the historical, sociological, and religious backgrounds) Translation of China; Geist and Geselischaft. [N7340.S713] 61-10700
1. Art. Chinese — Hist. I. Title. II. Series: Art of the world; the historical, sociological, and religious backgrounds BIP

SULLIVAN, Michael, 1916- 709.51
Chinese and Japanese art. New York, Watts [1966, c.1965] 302p. illus. (pt. col.) 25cm. (Great art & artists of the world, 9) Also pub. by Grolier, Inc., as a v. in its Book of art. Bibl. [N7337.S8] 65-10271 12.95
1. Art Chinese—Hist. 2. Art, Japanese—Hist. I. Title. II. Series.

SULLIVAN, Michael, 1916- 709/.51
A short history of Chinese art. Berkeley, Univ. of Calif. [1967] 279p. illus., maps. 22cm. Bibl. [N7340.S92 1967b] 67-21260 6.95
1. Art, Chinese—Hist. I. Title.

SULLIVAN, Michael, 1916- 709'.51
The arts of China. Berkeley, University of California Press [1973] 256 p. illus. (part col.) 25 cm. "New and revised edition of A short history of Chinese art." Bibliography: p. 247-248. [N7340.S92 1973] 73-78421 ISBN 0-520-02496-6 14.50
1. Art, Chinese—History. I. Title.
Pbk. 5.95; ISBN 0-520-025948-2.

SWANN, Peter C. 709.5
Art of China, Korea, and Japan. New York, Praeger [c.1963] 285p. illus. (pt. col.) 22cm. Bibl. 63-18836 7.50; 3.95 pap.,
1. Art, Chinese—Hist. 2. Art, Korean—Hist. 3. Art, Japanese—Hist. I. Title.

SWANN, Peter C. 709.51
Chinese monumental art. [Tr. from French] Photos. by Claude Arthaud, Francois Herbert-Stevens. New York, Viking [1964, c.1963] 276p. illus. (pt. col.) maps, 29cm. (Studio bk.) Bibl. 63-20086 16.00
1. Art. Chinese—Hist. I. Arthaud, Claude, 1927- II. Herbert-Stevens, Francois, 1922- III. Title.

WILLETTS, William. 709.51
Foundations of Chinese art from Neolithic pottery to modern architecture. 322 illus. in colour and black and white, 91 maps, and line drawings. New York, McGraw-Hill [1965] 456 p. illus. (part col.) maps, plans. 29 cm. A revision and abridgment of the author's Chinese art, published in 1958. Bibliography: p. 437-441. [N7340.W474] 64-66127
1. Art, Chinese — Hist. I. Title.

Art, Chinese—History—Bibliography.

KAPLAN, Sidney M., 1912- 016.709'51
The art of China; systematic bibliography and reading assignments covering periods from earliest times through the Sung Dynasty [by] Prof. Kaplan. [Columbus? Ohio, 1967] [44] l. 29 cm. Cover title. [Z5961.C5K33] 70-9810
1. Art, Chinese—History—Bibliography. I. Title.

Art, Chinese—History—Juvenile literature.

GLUBOK, Shirley. 709'.51
The art of China. Designed by Gerard Nook. New York, Macmillan [1973] 48 p. illus. 26 cm. Surveys the art of China from prehistoric times to the present day, discussing it in terms of history and culture of each period. [N7340.G58] 72-81059 ISBN 0-02-736170-5 6.95 (Lib. Ed.)
1. Art, Chinese—History—Juvenile literature. I. Title.

Art—Chinese influences.

SULLIVAN, Michael, 1916- 709
The meeting of Eastern and Western art from the sixteenth century to the present

day. [Greenwich, Conn.] New York Graphic Society [1973] 296 p. illus. (part col.) 26 cm. Bibliography: p. 268-282. [N7429.S93 1973b] 73-77665 ISBN 0-8212-0543-9 16.50
1. Art—Chinese influences. 2. Art—Japanese influences. 3. Art, Chinese—Occidental influences. 4. Art, Japanese—Occidental influences. I. Title. BIP

Art, Chinese—Juvenile literature.

MOORE, Janet Gaylord. 709'.51
The Eastern Gate : an invitation to the arts of China and Japan / Janet Gaylord Moore. New York : Collins World, [1978] p. cm. Bibliography: p. An illustrated introduction to the sculpture, painting, and architecture of China and Japan. [N7337.M66] 78-59816 ISBN 0-529-05434-5 : 19.95
1. Art, Chinese—Juvenile literature. 2. Art, Japanese—Juvenile literature. I. Title. BIP

Art, Chinese—Terminology.

HANSFORD, S. Howard. 709.51
A glossary of Chinese art and archaeology, by S. Howard Hansford [2d ed., rev.] London, The China Soc., 1961 xi, 104p. illus. 23cm. (China Soc. Sinological ser. no. 4) Title also in Chinese at head of t.p. Glossary in Chinese characters and in Romanization, with definitions in English [N7340.H31961] 65-52348 5.25
1. Art, Chinese—Terminology. 2. China—Antiq.—Terminology. I. Title. II. Series: China Society, London. China Society Sinological series no. 4
American distributor: Intl. Pubns. Serv., New York.

MEDLEY, Margaret. 709.51
A handbook of Chinese art for collectors and students. [1st American ed.] New York, Horizon Press [1965, c1964] 142 p. illus., fold. map. 23 cm. Includes bibliographies. [N7340.M4 1965] 65-15366
1. Art, Chinese—Terminology. I. Title.

Art, Chinese—Three kingdoms, six dynasties-Sui dynasty, 220-618—Exhibitions.

JULIANO, 730'.0951'07401471
Annette L.
Art of the six dynasties : centuries of change and innovation : [exhibition] October 29, 1975 through February 1, 1976 / by Annette L. Juliano. New York : China House Gallery, [1975] 91 p. : ill. ; 24 cm. Bibliography: p. 89-90. [N7343.24.J84] 76-350141
1. Art, Chinese—Three kingdoms, six dynasties-Sui dynasty, 220-618—Exhibitions. 2. Art, Chinese—Exhibitions. I. China House Gallery. II. Title.

Art—Cincinnati—Catalogs.

CINCINNATI Institute of 708.171
Fine Arts. Taft Museum.
Catalogue. Cincinnati [1958] 205p. illus., ports., plans. 23cm. [N550.5A5 1958] A58
1. Art—Cincinnati—Catalogs. I. Title.

Art, Classical.

COOK, B. F. 709'.38'07402142
Greek and Roman art in the British Museum / B. F. Cook. London : British Museum Publications for the Trustees of the British Museum, c1976. 194 p. : ill. (1 col.) ; 25 cm. Includes index. Bibliography: p. 193. [N5604.G7L63] 77-353081 ISBN 0-7141-1249-6 : £4.95. pbk.
1. British Museum. 2. Art, Classical. 3. Art—England—London. I. British Museum. II. Title. BIP

RICHTER, Gisela Marie 709.38
Augusta, 1882-
Perspective in Greek and Roman art [by] Gisela M. A. Richter. London, New York, Phaidon [1970?] 142 p. illus. 28 cm. Distributed in the U.S.A. by Praeger. Bibliography: p. 129-130. [N5610.R5] 74-111064 ISBN 0-7148-1418-0 17.50 (U.S.)
1. Art, Classical. I. Title.

Art, Classical—Addresses, essays, lectures.

ESSAYS in honor of Dorothy FIC
Kent Hill. Baltimore : Trustees, 1977. xv, 135 p. : ill. ; 28 cm. (The journal of the Walters Art Gallery ; v. 36) Contents.Contents.—Randall, R. H., Jr. Dorothy Kent Hill.—Bibliography of Dorothy Kent Hill.—Ancient Near East: Porada, E. A cylinder seal with a camel in the Walters Art Gallery. Guterbock, H. G. The Hittite seals in the Walters Art Gallery.—Greece: Vitelli, K. D. Neolithic potter's marks from Lerna and the Franchthi Cave. Mitten, D. G. Man and ram. Harrison, E. B. Notes on Daedalic dress. Ridgway, B. S. The Peplos Kore, Akrolis 679. Pemberton, E. G. The name vase of the Peleus painter. Thompson, H. A. Dionysos among the nymphs in Athens and in Rome. Buitron, D. M. A bronze statuette of Hermes in the Metropolitan Museum of Art.—Etruria and Rome: Richardson, E. The wolf in the West. Jones, F. F. A terracotta head in Princeton. Matson, F. R. Technological comments on the Princeton terracotta head. Bonfante, L. The Corsini throne. McCann, A. M. Two fragments of sarcophagi inBaltimore : Trustees, 1977. xv, 135 p. : ill. ; 28 cm. (The journal of the Walters Art Gallery ; v. 36) Contents.Contents.—Randall, R. H., J
1. Art, Classical—Addresses, essays, lectures. 2. Art, Ancient—Addresses, essays, lectures. 3. Hill, Dorothy Kent. I. Hill, Dorothy Kent. II. Walters Art Gallery, Baltimore. III. Series: Walters Art Gallery, Baltimore. The journal of the Walters Art Gallery ; v. 36.

Art, Classical—Bibliography.

COULSON, William D. 016.709'38
E., 1942-
An annotated bibliography of Greek and Roman art, architecture, and archaeology / by William D. E. Coulson. New York : Garland Pub., 1975. p. cm. (Garland reference library of the humanities ; v. 28) [Z5932.3.C68] [N5610] 75-24081 ISBN 0-8240-9984-2 lib.bdg. : 14.00
1. Art, Classical—Bibliography. 2. Classical antiquities—Bibliography. I. Title. BIP

Art, Classical—Exhibitions.

CALIFORNIA. University. Art Museum.
Echoes from Olympus : reflections of divinity in small-scale classical art / Darrell A. Amyx, editor, Barbara A. Forbes, assistant editor. Berkeley : University Art Museum, 1974. 191 p. : ill. (some col.) ; 18 cm. Catalog of an exhibition held at the museum, Oct. 2-Nov. 17, 1974. Includes bibliographies. [N5613.C35 1974] 74-620069
1. Art, Classical—Exhibitions. 2. Gods in art—Exhibitions. I. Amyx, Darrell Arlynn, 1911- II. Forbes, Barbara A. III. Title.

Art, Classical—History—Outlines, syllabi, etc.

TRENDALL, Arthur Dale, 709'.38
1909-
Notes on Greek and Roman art, by A. D. Trendall. Melbourne, The Author, 1969. 86 p. illus. 26 cm. To accompany a course of lectures delivered in the Department of Fine Arts in the University of Melbourne, 1969. Includes bibliographies. [N5613.T7] 71-449347 unpriced
1. Art, Classical—History—Outlines, syllabi, etc. I. Melbourne. University. Dept. of Fine Arts. II. Title.

Art, Classical—Ionia, Asia Minor.

HANFMANN, George Maxim 709'.392
Anossov, 1911-
From Croesus to Constantine : the cities of western Asia Minor and their arts in Greek and Roman times / George M. A. Hanfmann. Ann Arbor : University of Michigan Press, [1975] xiii, 127 p., [31] leaves of plates : ill. ; 29 cm. (Jerome lectures ; 10th ser.) Includes index. Bibliography: p. 98-109. [N5865.A31564 1975] 73-80574 ISBN 0-472-08420-8 : 15.00
1. Art, Classical—Ionia, Asia Minor. 2. Art—Ionia, Asia Minor. 3. Ionia, Asia Minor—Antiquities. I. Title. II. Series. BIP

Art—Classification—Congresses.

MID-AMERICA College Art 709'.01'1
Association. Research Committee on Special Classification Systems for Visual Materials of the Third World Peoples.
Report of the Research Committee on Special Classification Systems for Visual Materials of the Third World Peoples, 1974-5 / Chester R. Cowen, editor. [Norman? Okla.] : Visual Resources Division of the Mid-America College Art Association, c1976- v. ; 29 cm. Bibliography: v. 1, p. 116-117. [N4000.M53 1976] 77-150799
1. Art—Classification—Congresses. 2. Art, Primitive—Classification—Congresses. 3. Ethnology—Classification—Congresses. I. Cowen, Chester R. II. Title.

Art—Cleveland.

CLEVELAND Museum of Art. 708.171
The Cleveland Museum of Art. Text by William M. Miliken, director. New York, H. N. Abrams [1958] 62p. illus. (part mounted col.) 39cm. (Great museums of the world) An Abrams art book. [N552.A5 1958] 58-8642
1. Art—Cleveland. I. Milliken, William Mathewson, 1889- II. Title.

CLEVELAND Museum of Art. 708.171
Handbook. [Cleveland] 1958. unpaged. illus. 23cm. [N 552.A6 1958] 58-35158
1. Art—Cleveland. I. Title.

CLEVELAND Museum of 708.171'32
Art.
Handbook. [Cleveland, Distributed by the Press of Western Reserve University] 1966. xv, 305 p. illus., plans. 23 cm. [N552.A6 1966] 66-21320
1. Art—Cleveland.

Art — Cleveland — Catalogs.

CLEVELAND Museum of 708.171'32
Art.
Selected works: Cleveland Museum of Art. [Cleveland, 1967?] ix. 240 p. (chiefly plates part col.) 30 cm. [N552.A73] 66-21226
1. Art — Cleveland — Catalogs. I. Title.

CLEVELAND Museum of 708.171'32
Art.
Selected works: Cleveland Museum of Art. [Cleveland, 1967?] ix, 240 p. (chiefly plates (part col.)) 30 cm. [N552.A73] 66-21226
1. Art—Cleveland—Catalogs. I. Title.

Art—Collected works.

REYNOLDS, Joshua, Sir, 759.2
1723-1792.
The works. Edited by Edmond Malone. (1797) Hildesheim, New York, G. Olms, 1971. 2 v. port. 25 cm. (Anglistica & Americana 129) Facsimile of the ed. published in London in 1797. [N7445.2.R48 1797a] 76-866761
1. Du Fresnoy, Charles Alphonse, 1611-1665. De arte graphica. 2. Art—Collected works. 3. Flanders—Description and travel. 4. Netherlands—Description and travel. 5. Painters. I. Malone, Edmond, 1741-1812. II. Title. III. Series.

STOKES, Adrian Durham, 704.9'2
1902-1972.
The critical writings of Adrian Stokes. [London] : Thames and Hudson, c1978. 3 v. : ill. ; 25 cm. Includes index. Contents.—v. 1. 1930-1937.—v. 2. 1937-1958.—v. 3. 1955-1967. Bibliography: v. 3, p. 356-360. [N7445.2.S75 1978] 78-310550 ISBN 0-500-01175-3 (v. 1) : 24.95 ISBN 0-500-01177-X (v.3) : 24.95 ISBN 0-500-01176-1 (v.2) : 24.95
1. Art—Collected works. I. Title.
Distributed by W. W. Norton, New York BIP

Art — Collections and collecting.

FARAH, Ted. 708.04
Art collecting for pleasure and profit. With an introd. by Huntington Hartford. New York, Cornerstone Library; [distributed by Affiliated Publishers, 1964] 192 p. illus., ports. 21 cm. "CN 91." Bibliography: p. 184-192. [N8380.F27] 64-7639
1. Art — Collections and collecting. 2. Art — Hist. I. Title.

TIMES, (the) London. 745.1075
From a collector; a selection of articles from the Saturday column in The Times. London, Weidenfeld & Nicolson [New York, Hillary House, c. 1965] viii, 125p. illus. 23cm. [AC5.T5] 66-1269 5.00
I. Title.

Art—Collectors and collecting.

BEHRMAN, Samuel 706'.5 B
Nathaniel, 1893-
Duveen [by] S. N. Behrman. Boston, Little, Brown [1972] 232 p. illus. (part. col.) 26 cm. [N8660.D8B4 1972] 78-183995 12.50
1. Duveen, Joseph Duveen, Baron, 1869-1939. 2. Art—Collectors and collecting.

BEHRMAN, Samuel Nathaniel, 927
1893-
Duveen. Illus. by Saul Steinberg. New York, Random House [1952] 302 p. illus. 22 cm. [N8386.D82B4] 52-5137
1. Duveen, Joseph Duveen, baron, 1869-1939. 2. Duveen brothers. 3. Art—Collectors and collecting. 4. Art dealers. 5. Collectors and collecting.

BEHRMAN, Samuel Nathaniel, 927
1893-
Duveen, Illus. by Saul Steinberg. [Gloucester, Mass., P. Smith, 1965, c.1951, 1952] 176p. illus. 19cm. (Vintage bk. rebound) [N8386.D82B4] 3.25
1. Duveen, Joseph Duveen, baron, 1869-1939. 2. Art—Collectors and collecting. 3. Art dealers. 4. Duveen brothers. 5. Collectors and collecting. I. Title.

BROUGH, James, 1918- 708
Auction! Indianapolis, Bobbs-Merrill [1963] 224 p. illus. 26 cm. [N8380.B83] 63-11637
1. Art—Collectors and collecting. 2. Art auctions. 3. Auctioneers. I. Title.

CABANNE, Pierre. 708.04
The great collectors. New York, Farrar, Straus [1963] xviii, 305 p. Lates. 22 cm. Translation of Le roman des grands collectionneurs. Errata slip inserted. Bibliographical footnotes. [N8380.C313] 63-22305
1. Art—Collectors and collecting. I. Title.

CONSTABLE, William George, 708.04
1887-
Art collecting in the United States of America; the outline of a history. New York, Nelson [c.1964] xi, 194p. plates. 26cm. Bibl. 63-24841 12.50
1. Art—Collectors and collecting. 2. Art—Private collections. 3. Art—U.S. I. Title.

CONSTABLE, William George, 708.04
1887-
Art collecting in the United States of America; an outline of a history [by] W. G. Constable. London, New York, Nelson [1964] xi, 210 p. 36 plates. 26 cm. Bibliographical footnotes. [N8383.C6 1964] 64-3638
1. Art—Collectors and collecting. 2. Art—Private collections. 3. Art—U.S. I. Title.

DREPPERD, Carl William, 708.051
1898-1956.
Handbook of tomorrow's antiques [by] Carl W. Drepperd and Marjorie Matthews Smith. New York, Crowell [1953] 212 p. illus. 24 cm. [NK1125.D66] 53-10706
1. Art—Collectors and collecting. 2. Art objects—Collectors and collecting. I. Smith, Marjorie Matthews, joint author. II. Title: Tomorrow's antiques.

DREPPERD, Carl William, 790.023'2
1898-1956.
Treasures in truck & trash, by Morgan Towne. Introd. by Carl W. Drepperd. Port Washington, N.Y., Kennikat Press [1969, c1949] xiv, 205 p. 22 cm. (Essay and general literature index reprint series) Includes bibliographies. [N8380.D7 1969] 78-86067
1. Art—Collectors and collecting. 2. Book collecting. I. Title. BIP

Art, Colonial—Mexico.

COLONIAL art of Mexico. 709'.72
An exhibition organized by the Programa National Fronterizo in cooperation with the University of New Mexico and shown at the following institutions: University Art Museum, the University of New Mexico, Albuquerque, Dec. 15 through Jan. 19, 1968-1969 [and others. With an introd. by Felipe Lacouture and an article on the paintings in the exhibition by Gonzalo Obregon. Albuquerque, University Art Museum, University of New Mexico, c1968] 36 p. illus. (part col.), ports. (part col.) 28 cm. Running title: Arte colonial de Mexico/Colonial art of Mexico. Text in English and Spanish. [N6553.C6] 68-66881
1. Art, Colonial—Mexico. 2. Art, Mexican—Exhibitions. I. Lacouture, Felipe. II. Obregon, Gonzalo. III. Programa National Fronterizo. IV. New Mexico. University. Art Museum. V. Title: Arte colonial de Mexico.

Art commissions—Handbooks, manuals, etc.

AMERICAN Council 338.4'7'700973
for the Arts.
Community arts agencies : a handbook and guide / [Ellen Stodolsky Daniels, editorial director, Robert Porter, editor]. [New York] : American Council for the Arts, c1978. iv, 408 p. ; 23 x 31 cm. [NX20.A46 1978] 78-107003 ISBN 0-915400-08-1 : 12.50
1. Art commissions—Handbooks, manuals, etc. I. Daniels, Ellen Stodolsky. II. Porter, Robert. III. Title.

Art commissions—United States.

AREY, June Batten. 353.9'3'854
State arts agencies in transition : purpose, program, and personnel / by June Batten Arey. Wayzata, Minn. : Spring Hill Conference Center, 1975. xi, 267 p. : ill. ; 24 cm. Derived from eight meetings held at Spring Hill Conference Center between December 1972 and December 1973. [NX22.A7] 75-14484 ISBN 0-89062-007-5 : 7.95
1. Art commissions—United States. 2. Federal aid to the arts—United States. I. Spring Hill Conference Center. II. Title.
BIP

SCUDDER, Michael. 338.4'7'700973
State arts agencies survey : an informal research survey of forty-three State arts agencies, abstracting their guidelines, priorities, criteria, and types and areas of assistance : an informational tool prepared for the Nebraska Arts Council / by Michael Scudder. [Omaha : Nebraska Arts Council], 1974. iii, 69 p. ; 28 cm. Cover title. [NX22.S35] 75-622656
1. Art commissions—United States. I. Nebraska Arts Council. II. Title.

Art—Congresses.

ASSOCIATED Councils of the 700
Arts.
The arts: planning for change; [proceedings of the] Twelfth National Conference, Associated Councils of the Arts, formerly Arts Councils of America, May 19-21, 1966, New York. [New York, 1966] xi, 131 p. 24 cm. [N21.A8 1966] 66-28347
1. Art—Congresses. I. Title.

CONFERENCE on the Fine 706.3747
Arts, State University Teachers College, New Paltz, N. Y., 1952.
Proceedings of Conference on the Fine Arts, State University teachers college, June 9-14, 1952. [New Paltz, New Paltz Press, 1952] 70p. illus., group ports. 28cm. [N21.C55 1952] 53-21513
1. Art—Congresses. I. Title.

INTERNATIONAL Congress of the 709
History of Art (20th)
Acts [v.1-4] Princeton, N.J., Princeton [c.] 1963. 4v. (various p.) illus. plates. 21cm. 1st congress held in 1873. 11th congress projected, not held, in its place the Congres d'histoire de l'art was held in Paris in 1921. Title varies: Actes, Atti, Kongressakten, or Rapports et communications. Some vols. have also distinctive titles. 1963: Studies in Western art. Chiefly in English, French, German or Italian. Confs. for 1963 sponsored by the Intl. Comm. of the Hist. of Art. Contents.v.1. Romanesque and Gothic art.--v.2. The Renaissance and mannerism.--v.3. Latin American art and the Baroque period in Europe.--v.4. Problems of the 19th and 20th centuries. 63-7158 30.00; 8.50 set, ea.,
1. Art—Congresses. I. International Congress of the History of Art. Atti. II. International Congress of the History of Art. Kongressakten. III. International Congress of the History of Art. Rapport et communications. IV. International Committee on the History of Art. V. Title.

INTERNATIONAL Congress of the 709
History of Art, 20th, New York, 1961.
Studies in Western art. Princeton, N.J., Princeton University Press, 1963. 4 v. plates. 24 cm. (Acts of the twentieth International Congress of the History of Art) Chiefly in English, some contributions in French, German, Italian, or Spanish. Includes bibliographical references. [N21.I585 1961] 73-164486
1. Art—Congresses. I. Title. II. Series: International Congress of the History of Art. Acts, 1961.

NEW directions for the 700'.6
arts; a symposium for artists, educators, and community and government leaders, April 19-21, 1967. Sponsored by the Georgia Center for Continuing Education and The Institute of Community and Area Development. Athens, University of Georgia [1967?] iv, 125 p. 28 cm. "Proceedings ... prepared by Editorial Services, Dept. of Conferences, the University of Georgia Center for Continuing Education, Athens." [N21.N43 1967] 68-64371
1. Art—Congresses. I. Georgia. University. Georgia Center for Continuing Education. II. Georgia. University. Institute of Community and Area Development. III. Title: A symposium for artists, educators, and community and government leaders.

NIAGARA Frontier 704.92
Convocation, University of Buffalo, 1951.
The future of the creative arts; a symposium. [Buffalo] Published by the University of Buffalo on the Roswell Park Publication Fund, 1952. [107]-128 p. 23 cm. (The University of Buffalo studies, v. 19, no. 4) [AS36.B95 N21.N5] 52-3247
1. Art — Congresses. 2. Art — Addresses, essays, lectures. 3. (Series: Buffalo. University. University of Buffalo studies, v. 19, no. 4) I. Title.

PENNSYLVANIA. University. 709
Bicentennial Conference.
Studies in the arts and architecture, by Carl W. Blegen [and others] Port Washington, N.Y., Kennikat Press [1969, c1941] 113 p. 25 cm. (Essay and general literature index reprint series) [N21.P4 1969] 68-26199
1. Art—Congresses. I. Blegen, Carl William, 1887- II. Title.
BIP

WOODSTOCK Art Conference, 708.1
Woodstock, N.Y., 1950.
The artist and the museum; the report of the Third Woodstock Art Conference, Spetember 1 and 2, 1950. Edited by John D. Morse. New York, American Artists Group [1951] 65 p. 24 cm. [N21.W6 1950a] 52-192
1. Art — Congresses. 2. Art — U.S. — Galleries and museums. I. Morse, John D., 1906- ed. II. Title.

Art—Connecticut.

FRENCH, Henry Willard, 709'.746
1854-
Art and artists in Connecticut, by H. W. French. New York, Kennedy Graphics, 1970. xvi, 176 p. illus., ports. 27 cm. (Library of American art) Reprint of the 1879 ed., issued in The pioneers of art in America series. [N6530.C8F8 1970] 70-87543
1. Art—Connecticut. 2. Artists, American—Connecticut. I. Title.
BIP

Art—Conservation and restoration—Bibliography.

RATH, Frederick L. 069
Guide to historic preservation, historical agencies, and museum practices: a selective bibliography. Compiled by Frederick L. Rath, Jr., and Merrilyn Rogers O'Connell. Cooperstown, New York State Historical Association [1970] xvi, 369 p. 21 cm. "A successor to ... NYSHA selective reference guide to historical preservation, which was published in 1966." [Z5940.R3] 76-138977
1. Art—Conservation and restoration—Bibliography. 2. Monuments—Preservation—Bibliography. 3. Museum techniques—Bibliography. I. O'Connell, Merrilyn Rogers, joint author. II. New York State Historical Association. III. New York State Historical Association. NYSHA selective reference guide to historic preservation. IV. Title.

Art—Conservation and restoration—Great Britain.

CANNON-BROOKES, P. 702'.8
After Gulbenkian : a study paper towards the training of conservators and curators of works of art / [by] Peter Cannon-Brookes ; foreword by Sir Norman Reid. Birmingham : The author, 1976. 28, [1] p. ; 21 cm. Includes bibliographical references. [N6761.C35] 77-369113 ISBN 0-9505214-0-X : £0.50
1. Art—Conservation and restoration—Great Britain. I. Title.

Art—Copenhagen.

COPENHAGEN. 708.89
Nationalmuseet.
The Danish collections; antiquity. Copehhagen, 1952. 115p. illus. 22cm. (Its Guides to the National Museum) [N1930.N3A54 1952] 54-25075
1. Art—Copenmagen—Catalogs. 2. Denmark—Antiq. I. Title.

COPENHAGEN. 708.89
NATIONALMUSEET.
The National Museum of Denmark. Editor: Age Rousell] Copenhagen, 1957. 326p. illus. (part col.) 30cm. [N1930.N3A57] 57-44873
1. Art—Copenhagen. I. Rousell, Age, 1901- ed. II. Title.

Art, Coptic.

BADAWY, Alexander. 704.948'2'0962
Coptic art and archaeology : the art of the Christian Egyptians from the late antique to the Middle Ages / Alexander Badawy. Cambridge, Mass. : MIT Press, c1977. p. cm. Includes index. Bibliography: p. [N7382.B3] 77-25101 ISBN 0-262-02025-4 : 45.00
1. Art, Coptic. 2. Christian antiquities—Egypt. I. Title.
BIP

DU BOURGUET, Pierre. 709'.32
The art of the Copts, by Pierre M. Du Bourguet. Translated by Caryll Hay-Shaw. New York, Crown Publishers [1971] 234 p. illus., map, plans, plates (part col.) 24 cm. (Art of the world) Translation of L'Art copte. Bibliography: p. 224-227. [N7382.D8313] 78-147350 6.95
1. Art, Coptic. I. Title. II. Series.

Art, Coptic—Hist.

WESSEL, Klaus 709.32
Coptic art. [Tr. from German by Jean Carroll, Sheila Hatton] New York, McGraw [c.1965] 247p. illus. (pt. mounted col., pt. col.) maps. 27cm. Bibl. [N7382.W413] 65-19075 17.50
1. Art, Coptic—Hist. I. Title.

Art, Cretan.

HIGGINS, Reynold 709'.39'1
Alleyne.
Minoan and Mycenaean art [by] Reynold Higgins. New York, Praeger [1967] 216 p. illus. (part col.), map, plans. 22 cm. (Praeger world of art series) Bibliography: p. 195. [N5660.H5] 67-27569
1. Art, Cretan. 2. Art, Mycenaean. I. Title.

MARINATOS, Spyridon 709.391
Crete and Mycenae. Photos. by Max Hirmer. New York, H. N. Abrams [1960] 177, [13]p. 'Bibl. notes': p.[180] illus. (part mounted col.) 236 plates, map, plans. 32cm. 60-8399 25.00
1. Art, Cretan. 2. Art, Mycenaean. 3. Crete—Antiq. 4. Mycenae. I. Hirmer, Max. II. Title.

Art—Crete.

HOEGLER, Rudolf G. 913.3918
Crete and its treasures. Text by Olivier Reverdin. Pref. by N. Platon. 88 colour photos. by Rudolf Hoegler, N. Platon, and N. Creutzburg. [New York] Viking Press [1961] 153 p. illus. (part mounted col.) col. plates, map. 33 cm. (A Studio book) "Translated from the French 'La Crete, berceau de la civilisation europeenne' by Eric and Mary Peters." First published in German under title: Kreta; Mutterland der Kultur Europas. [N5660.H613] 61-10335
1. Art—Crete. 2. Crete—Description and travel—Views. I. Beverdin, Olivier. II. Title.

Art criticism.

BEIGEL, Hugo G. 701
Wake up to art. New York, Stephen Daye Press [1950] 352 p. plates (part col.) 27 cm. "Portions of this book appear in ... Art appreciation, by the same author." Bibliography: p. 341-343. [N7435.B42] 50-8276
1. Art criticism. I. Title.

BERRY, Ana M. 701.1
Understanding art. Edited by Judith Wogan & Bride Scratton, in collaboration with Eleanor M. Elder.qiLondon, New York, Studio Publications [1952] 136p. illus. (part col.) 26cm. [N7435.B47] 53-8455
1. Art criticism. I. Title.

BESTERMAN, Theodore, 1904- 709
Voltaire on the arts; unity and paradox. Oxford, Clarendon Press, 1974. 24 p. 22 cm. (The Zaharoff lecture for 1973) Includes bibliographical references. [NX640.V64B47] 74-180229 ISBN 0-19-952240-5 £0.75
1. Voltaire, Francoise Marie Arouet de, 1694-1778. 2. Art criticism. I. Title. II. Series: The Zaharoff lecture, 1973.

BOAS, George, 1891- 701.18
The heaven of invention. Baltimore, Johns Hopkins Press, 1962. 394 p. illus. 22 cm. Includes bibliography. [N7435.B53] 63-8810
1. Art criticism. 2. Art — Philosophy. I. Title.
BIP

DIDEROT, Denis, 1713-1784 701.18
Salons; v. 3. Texte etabli et presente par Jean Seznec, Jean Adhemar. Oxford, Clarendon Pr. [dist. New York, Oxford, c.] 1963. 366p. plates. 30cm. Includes official catalog of each exhibition of the Academie Royale de Peinture et de sculpture covering the years 1759-81. Comments by Diderot, and added biog. and critical notes on the artists. Contents.v 3. 1767. A58 26.90
1. Art criticism. 2. Art—France. 3. Paris. Salon. I. Academie Royale de peinture et de sculpture, Paris. II. Title.
BIP

GIMPEL, Jean. 701.18
The cult of art; against art and artists. New York, Stein and Day [1969] 178 p. 22 cm. Translation of Contre l'art et les artistes, ou la naissance d'une religion. Bibliographical references included in "Notes" (p. [166]-178) [N7435.G513 1969] 70-87950 5.95
1. Art criticism. 2. Art and society. I. Title.

HEYL, Bernard Chapman, 701.18
1905-
New bearings in esthetics and art criticism; a study in semantics and evaluation, by Bernard C. Heyl. Westport, Conn., Greenwood Press [1971, c1943] xii, 172 p. illus. 23 cm. Bibliography: p. [159]-165. [N7475.H48 1971] 70-136069 ISBN 0-8371-5219-4
1. Art criticism. 2. Aesthetics. I. Title.
BIP

KADISH, Mortimer Raymond, 1916- 701.18
Reason and controversy in the arts [by] Mortimer R. Kadish. Cleveland, Press of Case Western Reserve University, 1968. xi, 282 p. 24 cm. Bibliographical footnotes. [N7435.K25] 67-27796
1. Art criticism. I. Title. BIP

MYERS, Bernard Samuel, 1908- 701.18
How to look at art. New York Watts [1966,c.1965] 239p. illus., col. plates. 25cm. (Great art and artists of the world) Also pub. by Grolier, inc., as a v. in its The Book of art. Bibl. [N7435.M9] 65-10272 12.95
1. Art criticism. 2. Art—Hist. I. Title. II. Series.

ROSENBERG, Jakob, 1893- 710.18
On quality in art; criteria of excellence, past and present. [Princeton, N.J.] Princeton University Press [1967] xxiv, 264 p. 168 illus. (part col.) 27 cm. (The A. W. Mellon lectures in the fine arts, 13) Bibliographical references included in "Notes" (p. 235-238) [NC715.R7] 67-22342
1. Art criticism. 2. Drawings. I. Title. II. Series. III. Bollingen series, 35.

SHAW, Theodore L. 701.18
Hypocrisy about art, and what you don't gain by it. Boston, Stuart Pubns., 719 Boyleston St. [c.1962] 153p. illus. (pt. col.) 29cm. 63-22807 4.95
1. Art criticism. 2. Art. I. Title.

STANILAND, Lancelot Norman, 1889- 701.1
Let's understand art; a book on art appreciation for all. [New York] Studio Publications [1951] 96 p. illus. 26 cm. [N7435.S8] 51-14725
1. Art criticism. I. Title.

STANILAND, Lancelot Norman, 1899- 701.1
Let's understand art; a book on art appreciation for all. [New York] Studio Publications [1951] 96p. illus. 26cm. [N7435.S8 1951] 51-14725
1. Art criticism. I. Title.

STOLNITZ, Jerome. 701.17
Aesthetics and philosophy of art criticism; a critical introduction. Boston, Houghton Mifflin [1960] 510 p. illus. 25 cm. [N7435.S83] 60-481
1. Art criticism. 2. Aesthetics. 3. Art — Philosophy. I. Title.

WALTON, Donald 750
Art is to enjoy; an introduction to art appreciation. Bloomfield Hills, Mich., Scott Pub. Co. [c.1965] 342p. illus., plates (pt. col.) 23cm. [N7435.W3] 65-13156 5.95
1. Art criticism. I. Title.

Art criticism—Addresses, essays, lectures.

ART criticism in the sixties; a symposium of the Poses Institute of Fine Arts, Brandeis University, Waltham, Massachusetts. Participants: Barbara Rose [and others] Moderator: William C. Seitz. [New York, October House, [1967] [31] p. ports. 23 cm. "Four papers delivered ... at Brandeis University on May 7, 1966." [N7435.A68] 68-1372 701.18
1. Art criticism—Addresses, essays, lectures. I. Rose, Barbara. II. Brandeis University, Waltham, Mass. Poses Institute of Fine Arts.

KUH, Katharine. 709
The open eye; in pursuit of art. [1st ed.] New York, Harper & Row [1971] xii, 272 p. illus. 22 cm. "Essays ... some of them briefly expanded, and, except for one, all selected from a monthly column in Saturday review." [N7475.K85 1971] 78-123947 8.50
1. Art criticism—Addresses, essays, lectures. I. Title.

LIPPARD, Lucy R. 709.04'6
Changing: essays in art criticism [by] Lucy R. Lippard. [1st ed.] New York, Dutton, 1971. 320 p. illus. 22 cm. (Documents in modern art criticism, 2) Includes bibliographical references. [N7476.L56 1971] 71-87187 ISBN 0-525-07942-4 8.95
1. Art criticism—Addresses, essays, lectures. 2. Art, Modern—20th century—Addresses, essays, lectures. I. Title.

ROSSETTI, William Michael, 1829-1919. 709.034
Fine art, chiefly contemporary: notices re-printed, with revisions. [1st AMS ed.] New York, AMS Press [1970] xx, 392 p. 19 cm. [N7476.R66 1970] 73-126701
1. Art criticism—Addresses, essays, lectures. I. Title.

SCHNEIDER, Pierre. 701*.18
Louvre dialogues. Translated from the French by Patricia Southgate. [1st ed.] New York, Atheneum, 1971. x, 243 p. illus. 25 cm. [N1476.S35 1971] 72-135572 10.00
1. Paris. Musee national du Louvre. 2. Art criticism—Addresses, essays, lectures. 3. Art—Psychology—Addresses, essays, lectures. I. Title. BIP

Art criticism—France.

BROOKNER, Anita. 701.18'0944
The genius of the future; studies in French art criticism: Diderot, Stendhal, Baudelaire, Zola, the brothers Goncourt, Huysmans. London, New York, Phaidon, 1971. viii, 172 p., 16 plates. illus., ports. 26 cm. Distributed in the U.S.A. by Praeger, New York. Includes bibliographical references. [N7482.B76 1971] 75-156471 ISBN 0-7148-1497-0 £3.50 ($8.95 U.S.)
1. Art criticism—France. I. Title.

Art criticism—Greece.

POLLITT, Jerry Jordan. 709'.38
The ancient view of Greek art: cricitism, history, and terminology [by] J. J. Pollitt. New Haven, Yale University Press, 1974. xiv, 464 p. 25 cm. (Yale publications in the history of art, 25) Includes bibliographical references. [N7476.P64] 73-86915 ISBN 0-300-01597-6 25.00
1. Art criticism—Greece. 2. Art criticism—Terminology. 3. Classical languages—Semantics. I. Title. II. Series.

Art criticism—Hist.

FISHMAN, Solomon 701.18
The interpretation of art; essays on the art criticism of John Ruskin, Walter Pater, Clive Bell, Roger Fry, Herbert Read. Berkeley, Univ. of Calif. Pr. [c.]1963. 195p. 23cm. Bibl. 63-16565 4.50
1. Art criticism—Hist. 2. Authors, English. I. Title.

VENTURI, Lionello, 1885- 701.18
History of art criticism; tr. from Italian by Charles Marriott. New, rev. ed. New York, Dutton, 1964 [c.1936, 1964] xvi, 398p. 19cm. (D123) Bibl. [N7435.V42] 36-30920 2.60 pap.,
1. Art criticism—Hist. I. Marriott, Charles, 1869- tr. II. Title. BIP

Art, Cycladic—Exhibitions.

KARLSRUHE. Badisches Landesmuseum. 730'.09391'5
Art and culture of the Cyclades in the third millennium B.C. / Jurgen Thimme, general editor ; Pat Getz-Preziosi, translator and editor of the English ed. ; Brinna Otto, assistant editor. Chicago : University of Chicago Press, 1978 616 p., [2] leaves of plates : ill. ; 29 cm. Translation of Kunst und Kultur der Kykladeninseln im 3. Jahrtausend v. Chr. Bibliography: p. 598-607. [N5899.C9K3713] 77-84340 ISBN 0-226-79499-7 : 80.00
1. Art, Cycladic—Exhibitions. 2. Greece—Antiquities—Exhibitions. I. Thimme, Jurgen. II. Getz-Preziosi, Pat. III. Title. BIP

Art, Cypriote.

SPETERES, Tones P. 708.9'5645
The art of Cyprus [by] Tony Spiteris. Translated from the French by Thomas Burton. New York, Reynal [1971, c1970] 207, [8] p. illus. (part col.) 33 cm. (A Forms and colors series book) Translation of L'art de Chypre. Bibliography: p. [215] [N5430.S613 1971] 75-128117 29.95
1. Art, Cypriote. I. Title. BIP

Art—Dallas—Catalogs.

MEADOWS Museum. 708'.164'2812
The Meadows Museum : a visitor's guide to the collection / by William B. Jordan. Dallas : Southern Methodist University, 1974. 137 p., [2] leaves of plates : ill. (some col.) ; 26 cm. Errata slip inserted. Includes bibliographical references. [N557.A86] 75-305020
1. Meadows Museum. 2. Art—Dallas—Catalogs. I. Jordan, William B., 1940-

Art, Danish.

POULSEN, Vagn, 1909-1970. 759.89
Danish painting and sculpture / by Vagn Poulsen ; [translated by Sigurd Mammen]. 2. ed. / rev. by H. E. Norregaard-Nielsen. Copenhagen : Det Danske Selskab, 1976. 234 p. : ill. ; 22 cm. (Denmark in print and pictures) Includes index. Bibliography: p. 228. [N7014.P68 1976] 77-374931 ISBN 8-7742-9023-1 : kr59.80
1. Art, Danish. 2. Art, Modern—Denmark.

Art, Danish—Exhibitions.

LANDSFORENINGEN DANSK KUNSTHAANDVAERK 709.489
The arts of Denmark: an exhibition organized by the Danish Society of Arts and Crafts and Industrial Design: United States of America, 1960-61. Copenhagen [dist.: New York, Metropolitan Museum of Art 1960] 132p. illus. (part col.) 25cm. 60-51930 2.00 pap.,
1. Art, Danish—Exhibitions. 2. Art industries and trade—Denmark. I. Title.

PHILADELPHIA Civic Center. Museum. 759.89'074'014811
Modern Danish art: Ebba Carstensen [and others. Exhibition] 27th October-3rd December 1967. [Philadelphia, 1968] [16] p. illus. 23 cm. [N7018.P45] 79-21965
1. Art, Danish—Exhibitions. 2. Art, Modern—20th century—Denmark. I. Title.

Art—Dayton, Ohio—Catalogs.

DAYTON Art Institute, Dayton, Ohio. 708.171'73
Fifty treasures of the Dayton Art Institute. Published to commemorate the fiftieth anniversary of the Dayton Art Institute, February 28, 1969. [Dayton, 1969] 146 p. illus. (part col.) 24 cm. [N559.D3A58] 78-12799
1. Art—Dayton, Ohio—Catalogs. I. Title.

Art dealers.

BAILEY, Emma. 817.54
Sold to the lady in the green hat. With illus. by Doug Anderson. New York, Dodd, Mead, 1962. 213p. illus. 21cm. [N8660.B25A3] 62-9212
1. Art dealers. 2. Collectors and collecting. I. Title.

BREMOND d'Ars, Yvonne de. 706.994
In the heart of Paris; the adventures of an antique dealer. Translated by Barbara Lucas. [1st American ed.] New York, Putnam, 1960 [c1959] 224 p. 22 cm. Translation of C'est arrive en plein Paris. [N8660.B7A313] 60-9119
1. Art dealers. 2. Art objects—Collectors and collecting. I. Title.

BREMOND D'ARS, Yvonne de. 706.994
The antique dealer's tale. Translated by Barbara Lucas. [1st American ed.] New York, Putnam [1962] 176 p. 22 cm. Translation of Le brocanteur du Marais. [N8660.B7A273] 62-7990
1. Art dealers. I. Title.

CLARK, Floyd Barzilia, 1886- v. 12
The marketing of works of art. Bryan, Tex, Wallace Print. Co. [1958 or 9] 1v. illus. 31cm. Includes bibliography. [N8620.C55] 60-23446
1. Art dealers. I. Title.

GIMPEL, Rene. 706.50924
Diary of an art dealer. Translated from the French by John Rosenberg. Introd. by Sir Herbert Read. New York, Farrar, Straus and Giroux [1966] xii, 465 p. illus., ports. 23 cm. [N8660.G5A313] 66-20172
1. Art dealers. 2. Art—Collectors and collecting. I. Title.

POUR Daniel-Henry Kahnweiler. [Ouvrage etablie sous la direction de Werner Spies] New York, Wittenborn [1966, c.1965] 311p. illus. (pt. mounted) facsims. (pt. mounted) 8 plates (7 col.) ports. 30cm. On spine: Pour Kahnweiler. Contributions, in French, German, English or Swedish, include poems, plays and 22 mounted facsims, of letters to Kahnweiler with their transcriptions. Bibl. [N8660.K3P6] 66-3307 27.50 759.3
1. Kahnweiler, Daniel Henry 1884- II. Spies, Werner, ed. III. Title: Pour Kahnweiler.

TAYLOR, John Russell. 706.5
The art dealers [by] John Russell Taylor and Brian Brooke. New York, Scribner [1969] 316 p. 22 cm. Bibliography: p. 309-310. [N8380.T33] 68-17336 6.95
1. Art dealers. 2. Art—Collectors and collecting. I. Brooke, Brian, joint author.

Art dealers—England—Biography.

LEFEVRE Gallery. 707'.4'02132
Alex Reid & Lefevre 1926-1976. [London] : Lefevre Gallery, c1976. 175 p. : chiefly ill. (some col.) ; 26 cm. [N8660.L43L43 1976] 77-368956 £11.00
1. Lefevre Gallery. 2. Art dealers—England—Biography. I. Title.

Art dealers—France—Biography.

VOLLARD, Ambroise, 1867-1939. 706'.5 B
Recollections of a picture dealer / Ambroise Vollard ; translated from the French by Violet M. Macdonald. New York : Dover Publications, 1978. 326 p., [18] leaves of plates : ill. ; 22 cm. Translation of Souvenirs d'un marchand de tableaux. Includes index. [N8660.V6A2 1978b] 77-88948 ISBN 0-486-23582-3 : 4.50
1. Vollard, Ambroise, 1867-1939. 2. Art dealers—France—Biography. I. Title. BIP

VOLLARD, Ambroise, 1867-1939. 706'.5 B
Recollections of a picture dealer / Ambroise Vollard ; with a new foreword by Una E. Johnson ; [translated from the French by Violet M. MacDonald]. New York : Hacker Art Books, 1978. xv, 326 p., [16] leaves of plates : ill. ; 25 cm. Translation of Souvenirs d'un marchand de tableaux. Includes index.. [N8660.V6A2 1978] 77-76778 ISBN 0-87817-218-1 : lib.bdg. : 30.00
1. Vollard, Ambroise, 1867-1939. 2. Art dealers—France—Biography. 3. Art—Collectors and collecting. 4. Art—Anecdotes, facetiae, satire, etc. I. Title.

Art dealers—France—Correspondence, reminiscences, etc.

KAHNWEILER, Daniel Henry, 1884- 706'.5 B
My galleries and painters, by Daniel-Henry Kahnweiler, with Francis Cremieux. Translated from the French by Helen Weaver, with an introd. by John Russell. New York, Viking Press [1971] 160 p. illus., ports. 22 cm. (The Documents of 20th-century art) Translation of Mes galeries et mes peintres. "Bibliography, by Bernard Karpel": p. 140-153. [N8660.K3A313 1971] 73-104164 ISBN 0-670-49960-9 8.50
1. Art dealers—France—Correspondence, reminiscences, etc. I. Cremieux, Francis, 1920- II. Title. III. Series.

Art dealers—Great Britain—Biography.

FOWLES, Edward. 706'.5 B
Memories of Duveen Brothers / [by] Edward Fowles ; introduction by Sir Ellis Waterhouse. London : Times Books, 1976 [7], 215 p., [16] p. of plates : ill., facsim., ports. ; 24 cm. "Abridged by Michael Glover." Includes index. [N8660.F67A25

1976] 77-359790 ISBN 0-7230-0155-3 : £7.95
1. Fowles, Edward. 2. Duveen Brothers. 3. Duveen, Joseph Duveen, Baron, 1869-1939. 4. Art dealers—Great Britain—Biography. I. Title.

Art dealers—Montreal—Correspondence, reminiscences, etc.

WATSON, William R., 1887-1973. 706'.5 B
Retrospective : recollections of a Montreal art dealer / William R. Watson. Toronto ; Buffalo : University of Toronto Press, [1974] 77 p., [8] leaves of plates : ill. ; 23 cm. Includes index. [N8660.W37A37] 74-75586 ISBN 0-8020-2148-4 : 8.50
1. Watson, William R., 1887-1973. 2. Art dealers—Montreal—Correspondence, reminiscences, etc. I. Title. BIP

Art dealers—United States—Correspondence, reminiscences, etc.

LEVY, Julien. 706'.5 B
Memoir of an art gallery / by Julien Levy. New York : Putnam, c1977. 320 p., [18] leaves of plates : ill. ; 22 cm. Includes index. [N8660.L47A53 1977] 76-24793 8.95
1. Levy, Julien. 2. Art dealers—United States—Correspondence, reminiscences, etc. I. Title. BIP

LUCAS, George A., 1824-1909. 706'.5 B
The diary of George A. Lucas, 1857-1909 / transcribed and with introd. by Lilian M.C. Randall Princeton, N.J. : Princeton University Press, c1979. p. cm. Includes bibliographical references and index. [N8660.L8A2 1979] 77-85561 ISBN 0-691-03933-X : 50.00
1. Lucas, George A., 1824-1909. 2. Art dealers—United States—Biography. I. Randall, Lilian M. C. II. Title.

Art dealers—U.S.—Directories.

EAGLE, Joanna. 706.5
Buying art on a budget; what to buy and where to buy it in the U.S.A. [1st ed.] New York, Hawthorn Books [1968] vi, 442 p. illus., ports. 24 cm. Includes bibliographical references. [N8630.E2] 67-24654 6.95
1. Art dealers—U.S.—Directories. I. Title.

Art dealers—Yearbooks.

ANNUAIRE international des galeries d'art, 1963-64. 706.994
Paris, Art et industrie [dist. New York, Wittenborn, 1964] 396p. illus. (pt. col.) 20cm. Compiler: 1963-64--M. Fourny. 64-3536 4.00
1. Art dealers—Yearbooks. 2. Art—Yearbooks. I. Fourny, Max, comp.

Art deco.

ART deco/ 709'.04
Victor Arwas. London : Academy Editions ; New York : St. Martin's Press, 1976. 88 p. : ill. (some col.) ; 20 cm. [N6494.A7A62 1976] 76-44579 ISBN 0-85670-224-2 pbk. : 3.95
1. Art deco. 2. Art, Modern—20th century. I. Arwas, Victor.

†ART deco : 760'.09'04
posters and graphics / [compiled by] Jean Delhaye. New York : Rizzoli, 1977. 96 p. : chiefly ill. (some col.) ; 30 cm. Includes index. [NC1845.A68A77 1977b] 77-74339 ISBN 0-8478-0111-X : 13.95 ISBN 0-8478-0110-1 pbk. : 7.95
1. Art deco. 2. Posters. 3. Graphic arts. I. Delhaye, Jean.

†ART deco interiors in color 747'.8'83
/ edited by Charles Rahn Fry. New York : Dover Publications, c1977. 46 p. : chiefly col. ill. ; 29 cm. "62 watercolor drawings from ... French design portfolios of the twenties." [NK1986.A78A77] 77-75887 ISBN 0-486-23527-0 pbk. : 4.00
1. Art deco. 2. Interior decoration—History—20th century. I. Fry, Charles Rahn.

†ART Deco internationale 709'.04
/ designed by Iris Weinstein ; text by Robert K. Brown. New York : Quick Fox, c1977. 93 p. : ill. ; 28 cm. Bibliography: p. 93. [N6494.A7A626] 77-78540 ISBN 0-8256-3070-3 pbk. : 7.95
1. Art deco. 2. Art, Modern—20th century. I. Weinstein, Iris. II. Brown, Robert K.

LOEB, Marcia. 745.4'44
Art deco designs & motifs; over 100 examples rendered by Marcia Loeb. New York, Dover Publications [1972] iv, 75 p. illus. 28 cm. (Dover pictorial archive series) Bibliography: p. iv. [NK1570.L56 1972] 70-188954 ISBN 0-486-22826-6 2.50
1. Art-deco. 2. Design, Decorative. I. Title. BIP

MCCLINTON, Katharine (Morrison) 709'.04
Art deco; a guide for collectors. [1st ed.] New York, C. N. Potter; distributed by Crown Publishers [1972] x, 278 p. illus. 26 cm. Bibliography: p. 271-272. [N6494.A7M32 1972] 76-187511 ISBN 0-517-50076-0 12.50
1. Art deco.

MENTEN, Theodore, comp. 709'.04
The Art Deco style in household objects, architecture, sculpture, graphics, jewelry; 468 authentic examples. New York, Dover Publications [1972] 182 p. illus. 29 cm. [N6494.A7M44] 72-78867 ISBN 0-486-22824-X 4.00
1. Art deco. I. Title.

ROWE, William, 1941- 745.4'49'24
Exotic alphabets and ornament. New York, Dover Publications [1974] 72 p. of illus. 29 cm. (Dover pictorial archive series) [NK1535.R68A45 1974] 73-93544 ISBN 0-486-22989-0 2.50 (pbk.)
1. Rowe, William, 1941- 2. Art deco. I. Title.

ROWE, William, 1941- 745.4'49'24
Original art deco designs eighty plates New York, Dover Publications [1973] 72 p. (chiefly illus., part col.) 29 cm. (Dover pictorial archive series) [NK1535.R68A52 1973] 73-75281 ISBN 0-486-22567-4 3.00 (pbk.)
1. Rowe, William, 1941- 2. Art deco. I. Title.

Art deco—California—Los Angeles.

PILDAS, Ave. 779'.4'09794940924
Art deco : Los Angeles : photographs / by Ave Pildas. 1st ed. New York : Harper & Row, c1977. 64 p. : chiefly col. ill. ; 21 cm. [N6535.L6P54 1977] 77-4581 ISBN 0-06-013338-4 pbk. : 4.95
1. Art deco—California—Los Angeles. 2. Art, Modern—20th century—California—Los Angeles. I. Title.

Art deco—Exhibitions.

APPLEGATE, Judith. 709.04
Art deco. Introd. by Elayne H. Varian. New York [Finch College Museum of Art; distributed by Wittenborn Art Books, 1970] [48] p. illus. 28 cm. Catalog of the exhibition held Oct. 14-Nov. 30, 1970, at Finch College Museum of Art, and Jan. 19-Feb. 28, 1971, at Galleries, Cranbrook Academy of Art. [N6494.A7A6] 73-138392
1. Art deco—Exhibitions. I. Finch College, New York. Museum of Art. II. Cranbrook Academy of Art, Bloomfield Hills, Mich. Galleries.

ART deco and the Cincinnati Union Terminal; 709'.04
an exhibition organized by the Art History Dept., University of Cincinnati, in cooperation with the Contemporary Arts Center, January 11 to February 10, 1973. Cincinnati, Ohio, Contemporary Arts Center [1973] 47, [1] p. illus. 31 cm. Bibliography: p. [48] [N6512.5.A7A87] 72-96930
1. Cincinnati. Union Terminal Station. 2. Art deco—Exhibitions. 3. Art deco—Cincinnati. I. Cincinnati. University. Dept. of Art History. II. Contemporary Arts Center, Cincinnati.

HECKSCHER Museum. 709'.04
Art deco and its origins : [catalogue of an exhibition] Heckscher Museum, Huntington, New York, September 22-November 3, 1974 / with essays by Priscilla de F. Williams, Donald Harris Dwyer. Huntington, N.Y. : The Museum, [1974] 20 p. : ill. ; 28 cm. [N6494.A7H42 1974] 74-19933
1. Art deco—Exhibitions. 2. Art, Modern—20th century. I. Williams, Priscilla de F. II. Dwyer, Donald Harris. III. Title.

MINNEAPOLIS. Institute of Arts. 709.04'2'0740176579
Art deco. [Minneapolis, 1971] 224 p. illus. (part col.) 25 cm. Catalogue of an exhibition organized by the Minneapolis Institute of Arts and held July 8-Sept. 5, 1971. Works of art selected by B. Hillier. Bibliography: p. 218-224. [N6494.A7M5] 75-152070
1. Art deco—Exhibitions. I. Hillier, Bevis, 1940-

MINNEAPOLIS. Institute of Arts. 709'.04
The world of art deco. Text by Bevis Hillier. An exhibition organized by the Minneapolis Institute of Arts July-September 1971. New York, Dutton, 1971. 224 p. illus. (part col.) 24 cm. Bibliography: p. 218-224. [N6494.A7M53 1971b] 73-166088 ISBN 0-525-47310-6 7.50
1. Art deco—Exhibitions. I. Hillier, Bevis, 1940- II. Title. BIP

1975 New York art deco exposition at Radio City Music Hall, January 28, 29, 30, 31, February 1 & 2 709'.04'07401471
: catalogue / [editor, Cara Greenberg.] New York : Big Apple Events, [1975] [64] p. : ill. ; 19 x 24 cm. Cover title: Art deco exposition, Radio City Music Hall, 75. [N6494.A7N56] 75-308117
1. Art deco—Exhibitions. 2. Art, Modern—20th century. I. Greenberg, Cara. II. Title: Art deco exposition, Radio City Music Hall, 75.

Art deco—France.

SCHNESSEL, S. Michael. 760'.092'4
Icart / by S. Michael Schnessel. 1st ed. New York : Potter : distributed by Crown, 1976. p. cm. Includes index. Bibliography: p. [N6853.I22S36 1976] 76-14478 ISBN 0-517-52498-8 : 19.95
1. Icart, Louis. 2. Art deco—France. BIP

Art deco—History.

LESIEUTRE, Alain, 1931- 709'.04
The spirit and splendour of art deco. [New York] Paddington Press [1974] 304 p. illus. (part col.) 29 cm. Bibliography: p. [303]-304. [N6494.A7L47] 73-20958 ISBN 0-8467-0029-8 19.95
1. Art deco—History. I. Title.

Art, Decorative.

DECORATIVE art and modern interiors, 1977 745.4'44
/ edited by Maria Schofield. New York : Van Nostrand Reinhold, [1977] p. cm. [NK1390.D4 1977] 76-29529 ISBN 0-442-27423-8 : 24.95
1. Art, Decorative. 2. Interior decoration. I. Schofield, Maria. BIP

HUNDLEY, Joyce Davies. 745.7'2
Decorative painting, folk art style; patterns and easy steps to creating unique furniture, toys [and] gifts, by Joyce Davies Hundley [and] Jeanne Davies Cole. [1st ed.] Garden City, N.Y., Doubleday, 1971. viii, 128, [2] p. illus. 26 cm. Bibliography: p. [130] [TT323.H85] 70-150928 3.95
1. Art, Decorative. 2. Furniture painting. I. Muller, Jeanne Davies, joint author. II. Title.

LICHTEN, Frances. 745.44
Decorative art of Victoria's era. New York, Scribner [1950] 274 p. illus. (part col.) 31 cm. Bibliography: p. [263]-270. [NK1380.L5] 50-9758
1. Art, Decorative. 2. Great Britain—Social life & customs—19th century. 3. United States—Social life & customs—19th century. I. Title.

PETRIE, William Matthew Flinders, Sir, 1853-1942. 745.4
Decorative patterns of the ancient world for craftsmen. New York, Dover Publications [1974] 16 p., lxxxviii p. of illus. 29 cm. Reprint of the 1930 ed. published by the British School of Archaeology in Egypt, London, under title: Decorative patterns of the ancient world. [NK1180.P4 1974] 73-79745 ISBN 0-486-22986-6 2.50 (pbk.).
I. Title. BIP

PLATH, Iona. 745.009485
The decorative arts of Sweden. New York, Dover Publications [1966] xxiii, 218 p. illus., map. 28 cm. Art industries and trade, Swedish. [NK995.P6] 65-20487
1. Art, Decorative. I. Title.

*SARI. 745.72
How I turn junk into fun & profit, as told to Uncle Milton. [No. Hollywood, Calif., Wilshire Book Co., 1974] 160 p illus. 21 cm. [ND1471] 74-79533 ISBN 0-87980-278-2 3.00 (pbk.)
1. Art, decorative. 2. Painting—Technique. I. Levine, Milton M. II. Title. BIP

Art, Decorative—Dictionaries.

THE Oxford companion to the decorative arts 745'.03
/ edited by Harold Osborne. Oxford : Clarendon Press, 1975. xiv, 865 p. : ill. ; 25 cm. Bibliography: p. 851-865. [NK30.O93] 75-331784 ISBN 0-19-866113-4 : 39.95 (U.S.)
1. Art, Decorative—Dictionaries. I. Osborne, Harold, 1905-
Distributed by Oxford University Press N.Y. N.Y.

Art, Decorative—Egypt.

PETRIE, William Matthew Flinders, Sir, 1853-1942. 745.4'49'32
Egyptian decorative art; a course of lectures delivered at the Royal Institution. New York, B. Blom, 1972. viii, 128 p. illus. 18 cm. Reprint of the 1895 ed. [NK1190.P5 1972] 72-83177 11.50
1. Art, Decorative—Egypt. I. Title. BIP

Art, Decorative—England.

CONWAY, Moncure Daniel, 1832-1907. 709'.42
Travels in South Kensington / Moncure Daniel Conway. New York : Garland Pub., 1977. 234 p. : ill. ; 23 cm. (The Aesthetic movement & the arts and crafts movement) Reprint of the 1882 ed. published by Trubner, London. [N1150.C7 1977] 76-17754 ISBN 0-8240-2457-5 lib.bdg. : 35.00
1. Victoria and Albert Museum, South Kensington. 2. Art, Decorative—England. 3. Architecture—England. 4. Suburban homes—England—Bedford Park. I. Title. II. Series. BIP

Art, Decorative—Exhibitions.

NEW York (City). Metropolitan Museum of Art. 745'.094'07401471
Highlights of the Untermyer Collection of English and continental decorative arts. New York : Metropolitan Museum of Art, c1977. 216 p. : ill. ; 28 cm. [NK613.N48M476 1977] 77-12235 ISBN 0-87099-169-8 : 12.50
1. Untermyer, Irwin—Art collections. 2. Art, Decorative—Exhibitions. I. Title. BIP

TISSOT, James Joseph Jacques, 1836-1902. 759.4
James Jacques Joseph Tissot, 1836-1902; a retrospective exhibition. Introductory essay and drawing entries, by Henri Zerner. Chronology and painting entries, by David S. Brooke. Print section, by Michael Wentworth. Museum of Art, Rhode Island School of Design, Providence, February 28-March 29, 1968. Art Gallery of Ontario, Toronto, April 6-May 5, 1968. [Providence, 1968] [35] p., 88 illus. 26 cm. Bibliography: p. 35. [ND553.T6Z4] 68-1324
1. Zerner, Henri. II. Brooke, David S. III. Wentworth, Michael. IV. Rhode Island School of Design, Providence. Museum of Art. V. Art Gallery of Ontario.

Clarendon P., 1970. xii, 1277 p., 2 plates. illus. (incl. 8 col.), plans. 25 cm. Bibliography: p. 1231-1277. [N33.O9] 71-526168 6/-/-
1. Art—Dictionaries. 2. Artists—Dictionaries. I. Osborne, Harold, 1905- ed.

PIERCE, James Smith. 703
From Abacus to Zeus : a handbook of art history / James Smith Pierce. Englewood Cliffs, N.J. : Prentice-Hall, c1977. viii, 131 p. : ill. ; 23 cm. Entries keyed to the reproductions in H. W. Janson's History of art, 2d ed. [N33.P5 1977] 77-6701 ISBN 0-13-330522-8 lib.bdg. : 4.95
1. Art—Dictionaries. I. Janson, Horst Woldemar, 1913- History of art. II. Title. BIP

PIERCE, James Smith. 703
From abacus to Zeus; a handbook of art history. Englewood Cliffs, N.J., Prentice-Hall [1968] viii, 131 p. illus., maps, plans. 23 cm. Entries keyed to the reproductions in H. W. Janson's History of art. [N33.P5] 68-12851
1. Art—Dictionaries. I. Janson, Horst Woldemar, 1913- History of art. II. Title. BIP

PRAEGER encyclopedia of art. 703
New York, Praeger Publishers [1971] 5 v. (2139 p.) illus. (part col.) 29 cm. This English-language ed. is an updated translation, with additional new material, of Dictionnaire universel de l'arte et des artistes. [N33.P68] 75-122093
1. Art—Dictionaries. 2. Artists—Dictionaries.

QUICK, John, 1931- 703
Artists' and illustrators' encyclopedia. New York, McGraw-Hill [1969] xi, 273 p. illus. 24 cm. Bibliography: p. 235-239. [N33.Q5] 69-12774
1. Art—Dictionaries. I. Title. BIP

QUICK, John, 1931- 703
Artists' and illustrators' encyclopedia / John Quick. 2d ed. New York : McGraw-Hill, c1977. viii, 327 p. : ill. ; 25 cm. Includes index. Bibliography: p. 295-299. [N33.Q5 1977] 77-6700 ISBN 0-07-051063-6 : 16.95
1. Art—Dictionaries. I. Title.

READ, Herbert Edward Sir 1893- ed. 703
Encyclopaedia of the arts. Consulting editor: Herbert Read. New York, Meredith Press [1966] 966 p. illus., 79 col. plates, ports. 29 cm. [N34.E54] 66-23883
1. Art — Dictionaries. 2. Artists — Dictionaries. I. Title.

SCHAFFRAN, Emerich, 1883- 703
Dictionary of European art. [Translated from the German by Kenneth Northcott] New York, Philosophical Library [1958] 283p. 19cm. Translation of Taschen-Lexikon der Kunst. [N33.S373] 58-2213
1. Art—Dictionaries. I. Title. BIP

A Visual dictionary of art. 703
[General editor: Ann Hill] Greenwich, Conn., New York Graphic Society [1974] 640 p. illus. (part col.) 27 cm. Bibliography: p. 633-636. [N33.V56 1974] 73-76181 ISBN 0-8212-0424-6 30.00
1. Art—Dictionaries. 2. Artists—Biography—Dictionaries. I. Hill, Ann, ed. BIP

WILSON, Jose. 703
Decorating defined; a dictionary of decoration and design, by Jose Wilson and Arthur Leaman. New York, Simon and Schuster [1970] 189, [2] p. illus. 29 cm. Bibliography: p. [191] [N33.W5] 70-101886 ISBN 0-671-20525-0 9.95
1. Art—Dictionaries. 2. Decoration and ornament—Dictionaries. I. Leaman, Arthur, joint author. II. Title. BIP

WOLF, Martin L 703
Dictionary of the arts; with an introd. by Eric Partridge. New York, Philosophical Library [1951] xiii, 797 p. 24 cm. [N33.W6] 51-13402
1. Art — Dictionaries. 2. Music — Dictionaries. 3. Literature — Dictionaries. 4. Theater — Dictionaries. I. Title.

Art, Dogon.

LAUDE, Jean. 732'.2'096623
African art of the Dogon; the myths of the cliff dwellers. [Translation by Joachim Neugroschel] Foreword by Lester Wunderman. New York, Brooklyn Museum in association with the Viking Press [1973] 60, [71] p. illus. (part col.) 25 cm. (A Studio book) Issued in connection with an exhibition of L. Wunderman's private collection of Dogon art, organized by the Brooklyn Museum in 1973. "The catalogue": p. [65]-[129] Bibliography: p. [130]-[131] [N7399.M3L3 1973] 72-12060 ISBN 0-670-10928-2 10.00
1. Wunderman, Lester—Art collections. 2. Art, Dogon. I. Brooklyn Institute of Arts and Sciences. Museum. II. Title.

Art, Dutch.

GELDER, Hendrik Enno van, 1876- 759.9492
Holland by Dutch artists, in paintings, drawings, woodcuts, engravings and etchings. [Dist. New York, Heinman, 1961, c.1959] 35p. illus., 200 plates (5 col.) 31cm. A60 20.00
1. Art, Dutch. 2. Netherlands— Descr. & trav.—Views. I. Title.

GLICENSTEIN, Henryk, 1870-1942. 730.9438
Glicenstein. [Translated by B. D.] New York, Crown Publishers [1958] 12, [8] o. plates. 29 cm. At head of title: Jean Cassou. Bibliography: p. [17] [NB237.G55C293] 58-12883
I. Cassou, Jean, 1897-

MASEREEL, Frans, 1889-1971. 769'.92'4
The city <Die Stadt>; 100 woodcuts. New York, Dover Publications [1972] [5] p., 100 p. of illus. 24 cm. "Unabridged republication of the work originally published ... in 1925 under the title Die Stadt." [NE1155.5.M3A56 1972] 71-182101 ISBN 0-486-22448-1 2.00
I. Title.

VERBEEK, Gustave 741.5
The incredible upside-downs of Gustave Verbeek. Summit, N.J., Rajah Pr., Box 23 [c.]1963. unpaged.illus. 24x32cm. 2.00 pap.,
I. Title.

Art, Dutch—Exhibitions.

MANDLE, Earl Roger. 741.9492
Dutch masterpieces from the eighteenth century: paintings & drawings 1700-1800. Essay by J. W. Niemeijer. [Minneapolis, Minneapolis Institute of Arts, 1971] 121, [107] p. illus., ports. 21 cm. "An exhibition organized by the Minneapolis Institute of Arts, the Toledo Museum of Art [and] the Philadelphia Museum of Art." Includes bibliographies. [N6936.M3] 75-168864
1. Art, Dutch—Exhibitions. 2. Art, Modern—17th-18th centuries—Netherlands. I. Minneapolis. Institute of Arts. II. Toledo. Museum of Art. III. Philadelphia Museum of Art. IV. Title.

REMBRANDT after three hundred years; 759.9492
an exhibition of Rembrandt and his followers. [Chicago] Art Institute of Chicago, 1969. 280 p. illus. (part col.) 26 cm. Held at the Art Institute of Chicago, the Minneapolis Institute of Arts, and the Detroit Institute of Arts. Contents.Contents.—Foreword, by C. C. Cunningham.—Introduction, by E. Haverkamp-Begemann.—Catalogue of paintings, by J. R. Judson.—Paintings, illustrations.—Catalogue of drawings, by E. Haverkamp-Begemann [and] A. M. Logan.—Drawings, illustrations. Includes bibliographical references. [N6946.R45] 76-96721
1. Rembrandt Harmenszoon van Rijn, 1606-1669. 2. Art, Dutch—Exhibitions. 3. Art, Modern—17th-18th centuries—Netherlands. I. Judson, Jay Richard. II. Haverkamp Begemann, Egbert. III. Chicago. Art Institute. IV. Minneapolis. Institute of Arts. V. Detroit. Institute of Arts.

SUTTON, Peter. 760'.09492'07401468
Dutch religious art of the seventeenth century / prepared by Peter Sutton and Otto Naumann. [New Haven] : Yale University Art Gallery, [1975] 21 p. ; 22 cm. Exhibition at the Yale University Art Gallery, Jan. 21-Mar. 16, 1975. Bibliography: p. 14-15. [N6946.S88] 76-350566
1. Bible—Pictures, illustrations, etc.—Exhibitions. 2. Art, Dutch—Exhibitions. 3. Art, Modern—17th-18th centuries—Netherlands—Exhibitions. I. Naumann, Otto, joint author. II. Yale University. Art Gallery. III. Title.

TUMPEL, Astrid. 709'.492
The Pre-Rembrandtists [exhibition] / introd. and catalogue by Astrid Tumpel; iconographic essay by Christian Tumpel; foreword by Wolfgang Stechow. Sacramento, Calif. : E. B. Crocker Art Gallery, 1974. 152 p. : ill. (some col.) ; 25 cm. "Essays and catalogue entries have been translated from the German by Beeke Sell Tower, Roger D. Clisby and Richard V. West." Includes bibliographical references. [N6946.T83] 74-24019
1. Art, Dutch—Exhibitions. 2. Art, Modern—17th-18th centuries—Netherlands. I. Crocker Art Gallery, Sacramento, Calif. II. Title.

Art, Early Christian.

BACKES, Magnus. 709.02'1
Art of the dark ages. Text by Magnus Backes and Regine Dolling. [Translated from the German by Francisca Garvie] New York, H. N. Abrams [1971? c1969] 263 p. illus. (part col.), col. facsims., col. maps, col. ports. 23 cm. (Panorama of world art) Translation of Die Geburt Europas. Bibliography: p. 258-259. [N5970.B2713] 70-90886 ISBN 0-8109-8023-1
1. Art, Early Christian. 2. Art, Carlovingian. 3. Art, Ottonian. I. Dolling, Regine, joint author. II. Title.

BECKWITH, John, 1918- 709.02
Early Christian and Byzantine art. Harmondsworth, Penguin, 1970. xxv, 211 p., 193 plates. illus. (incl. 1 col.), facsims., map. 27 cm. (The Pelican history of art) Bibliography: p. 191-192. [N7832.B3] 79-23592 ISBN 0-14-056033-5 £7/-/-
1. Art, Early Christian. 2. Art, Byzantine. I. Title. II. Series.

CHRISTIAN art of the 4th to 12th centuries; 709'.02
general editor Francesco Abbate; translated [from the Italian] by Pamela Swinglehurst. London, New York, Octopus Books, 1972. 158 p. chiefly 101 col. illus. 20 cm. Translation of Arte paleocristiana e Alto Medioevo. Bibliography: p. 153. [N7832.A7313] 72-171381 ISBN 0-7064-0063-1 2.95
1. Art, Early Christian. 2. Art, Byzantine. 3. Art, Medieval. I. Abbate, Francesco, ed. Publisher's Address: 375 Park Avenue New York.

DU BOURGUET, Pierre. 704.948'2
Early Christian art. Translated from the French by Thomas Burton. New York, Reynal [1971] 219 p. illus. 33 cm. (A Forms and colors series book) Bibliography: p. 216-217. [N7832.D7913] 77-151935 35.00
1. Art, Early Christian. I. Title.

DU BOURGUET, Pierre 759.02
Early Christian painting. Tr. by Simon Watson Taylor. New York, Viking [1966, c.1965] 54p. 176p. of illus. (pt. col.) 20cm. (Compass bks., CA3. Compass hist. of art) Bibl. [N7840.D813] 66-10721 2.25 pap.,
1. Art, Early Christian. 2. Mural painting and decoration. 3. Catacombs. I. Title.

GALLAGHER, Sharon. 709.02
Medieval art. Text and notes by Sharon Gallagher. New York, Tudor Pub. Co. [1969] 40 p., [94] p. of col. illus. 18 cm. ([Great painters series]) [N7832.G3] 68-30735 2.95
1. Art, Early Christian. 2. Art, Medieval.

GOUGH, Michael. 709'.01'5
The origins of Christian art. New York, Praeger [1974, c1973] 216 p. illus. (part col.) 22 cm. (Praeger world of art series) Bibliography: p. 203-204. [N7832.G62 1974] 73-8233 10.00, 5.95 (pbk.)
1. Art, Early Christian. 2. Art, Byzantine. I. Title.

GRABAR, Andre, 1896- 704.948'2
Early Christian art; from the rise of Christianity to the death of Theodosius. Translated by Stuart Gilbert and James Emmons. New York, Odyssey Press [1969] 325 p. illus., maps, plans. 28 cm. (The Arts of mankind, v. 9) Part of the illustrative matter is colored. Translation of Le Premier art chretien (200-395) Bibliography: p. 307-313. [N7832.G6813 1969] 68-10414
1. Art, Early Christian. I. Title. II. Series.

HUBERT, Jean. 709.01'5
Europe of the invasions [by] J. Hubert, J. Porcher [and] W. F. Volbach. [Translated by Stuart Gilbert and James Emmons] New York, G. Braziller [1969] xv, 387 p. illus. (part fold. col.), facsims. (part col.), col. maps (3 fold.), plans (part col.) 29 cm. (The Arts of mankind) Translation of L'Europe des invasions. Bibliography: p. 331-[345] [N7832.H813 1969] 75-81858 30.00
1. Art, Early Christian. 2. Art, Medieval. 3. Barbarian invasions. I. Porcher, Jean. II. Volbach, Wolfgang Friedrich, 1892- III. Title. IV. Series.

HUTTER, Irmgard. 709.02
Early Christian and Byzantine art. Foreword by Otto Demus. New York, Universe Books [1971] 191 p. illus. (part col.), plans. 23 cm. Translation of Fruhchristliche Kunst, byzantinische Kunst. Bibliography: p. 186-187. [N7832.H8713] 75-122018 ISBN 0-87663-132-4 6.95
1. Art, Early Christian. 2. Art, Byzantine. I. Title.

KRAUTHEIMER, Richard, 1897- 720'.94
Studies in early Christian, Medieval, and Renaissance art. [Translators: Alfred Frazer and others] New York, New York University Press, 1969. xxviii, 464 p. illus., plans. 27 cm. Collected essays. "Richard Krautheimer: Bibliography, 1925-1967": p. xi-xv. [N5940.K713] 68-29432
1. Art, Early Christian. 2. Art, Medieval. 3. Art, Renaissance. I. Title.

LASSUS, Jean. 709.02
The early Christian and Byzantine world. New York, McGraw-Hill [1967] 176 p. illus., col. map (on lining papers), plans 117 col. plates. 30 cm. (Landmarks of the world's art) Bibliography: p. [172] [N7832.L294] 67-11797
1. Art, Early Christian. 2. Art, Byzantine. 3. Church architecture. I. Title.

VERZONE, Paolo, 1902- 709'.4
The art of Europe: the Dark Ages from Theodoric to Charlemagne. Translated by Pamela Waley. New York, Crown Publishers [1968] 276 p. illus. (part col.), plans. 24 cm. (Art of the world, European cultures: the historical, sociological, and religious backgrounds) Translation of Da Bisanzio a Carlomagno. Bibliography: p. 259-260. [N7832.V413] 68-9069 6.95
1. Art, Early Christian. 2. Art, Byzantine. I. Title. II. Title: The Dark Ages from Theodoric to Charlemagne. III. Series: Art of the world.

VOLBACH, Wolfgang Friedrich, 1892- 709.02
Early Christian art. Photography by Max Hirmer. [Translated by Christopher Ligota] New York, Abrams [1962] 363 p. illus., 258 plates (part col.) plans. 32 cm. Bibliography: p. 305-307. [N7832.V63] 61-8333
1. Art, Early Christian. 2. Church architecture—Europe. I. Hirmer, Max, 1893- II. Title.

Art, Early Christian—Asturias.

BONET Correa, Antonio. 709'.46'19
Spanish pre-Romanesque art; the arts and architecture of the churches of Asturias [by] A. Bonet Correa. Greenwich, Conn., New York Graphic Society [1968, c1967] 267 p. illus. (part col.), col. map, plans. 28 cm. Translation of Arte pre-romanico Asturiano. Text and captions in Spanish, English, French, and German. Bibliography: p. 258-259. [N7962.B6513] 68-17555 30.00
1. Art, Early Christian—Asturias. 2. Art—Asturias. I. Title.

Art, Early Christian—Ireland.

STOKES, Margaret 709'.415
MacNair, 1832-1900.
Early Christian art in Ireland; handbook and guide to Irish antiquities collection. Rev. by G. N. Count Plunkett. Freeport, N.Y., Books for Libraries Press [1972] x, 189 p. illus. 23 cm. At head of title: National Museum of Science and Art. Reprint of the 1911 ed. Includes bibliographies. [N7946.S85 1972] 70-39211 ISBN 0-8369-6813-1
1. Art, Early Christian—Ireland. 2. Art—Ireland. I. Dublin. National Museum of Ireland. II. Title. BIP

Art, Early Christian—Italy—Rome (City)

BILLON, B. M. 704.948'2'09376
Early Christian art and symbolism / [by] B. M. Billon. Ilfracombe : Stockwell, 1976. 96 p. : ill., map. plan ; 19 cm. [N7840.B5 1976] 77-369506 ISBN 0-7223-0935-X : £2.00
1. Art, Early Christian—Italy—Rome (City) 2. Catacombs. 3. Christian art and symbolism—Italy—Rome (City) I. Title.

Art, Early Renaissance.

BATTERBERRY, Michael. 709.02'3
Art of the early Renaissance, adapted by Michael Batterberry. Foreword by Howard Conant. New York, McGraw-Hill [1970] 191 p. col. illus. 31 cm. (Discovering art series) "[Based] on the text of the magazine series Discovering art ... [with] adaptations from the Italian text of Capolavori nei secoli." [N6371.B36] 79-115138
1. Art, Early Renaissance. I. Title. BIP

Art—Early works to 1800.

FELIBIEN, Andre, Sieur des 700
Anaux et de Javercy, 1619-1965
Des principes del architecture, de la sculpture, de la peinture, et des autres arts qui en depedent. Farnborough (Hans.), Gregg Pr., 1966 [1.e.,1967] [26] 542p. illus., diagrs. 26cm. Facsim. of the 3rd ed., pub. in 1699. [N7420.F4 1699a] 67-79993 35.00
1. Art—Early works to 1800. 2. Art—Dictionaries— French. I. Title.
Available from Gregg Pr., Ridgewood, N.J.

HARRIS, James, 1709-1780. 131.3
Three treatises. New York, Garland Pub., 1970. 377 p. front. 21 cm. "Facsimile ... made from a copy in the Harvard University Library." Original t.p. reads: Three treatises; the first concerning art, the second concerning mvsic, painting and poetry, the third concerning happiness, by James Harris, Esq. The second edition, revised and corrected. London, printed for Iohn Novrse and Pavl Vaillant, MDCCLXV. [BH181.H2 1765a] 78-112141
1. Art—Early works to 1800. 2. Music. 3. Happiness. I. Title.

THEOPHILUS, called also 709.02
Rugerus
On divers arts; the treatise of Theophilus. Tr. from medieval Latin. Introd., notes by John G. Hawthorne, Cyril Stanley Smith. [Chicago] Univ. of Chic. Pr. [c.1963] xxxv, 216p. illus., plates, facsim. 25cm. Bibl. 63-11397 8.50
1. Art—Early works to 1800. 2. Christian art and symbolism. 3. Technology—Early works to 1800. I. Hawthorne, John G., ed. and tr. II. Smith, Cyril Stanley, 1903- ed. III. Title.

THEOPHILUS, called also 701.8
Rugerus
The various arts. Tr. from Latin with introd. and notes by C. R. Dodwell. New York, Nelson [c.1961] 1xxvii, 171, 171, 175-178p. (Medieval texts) Opposite pages numbered in duplicate. English and Latin: added t. p.: De diuersis artibus. Bibl. 61-66685 8.00
1. Art—Early works to 1800. 2. Christian artand symbolism. 3. Technology—Early works to 1800. I. Dodwell, Charles Reginald, ed. and tr. II. Title. III. Title: Dediuersis artibus. IV. Series: Medieval classics [London]

Art, East African.

*MILLER, Judith Von D. 709.'67
Art in East Africa: a guide to contemporary art [by] Judith Von D. Miller. [London] Frederick Miller [1976c1975] 125p. : ill,(part col.) ; 24 cm. Includes index. Bibliography: p.111-113. [N5290.x] ISBN 0-584-10154-6 : 17.50
1. Art, East African. I. Title.
Distributed by Africana Pub. BIP

Art—Easter Island—History.

HEYERDAHL, Thor. 730'.0996'18
The art of Easter Island / by Thor Heyerdahl ; foreword by Henri Lavachery. Garden City, N.Y. : Doubleday, 1975. 349 p., [168] leaves of plates : ill. (some col.) ; 29 cm. Includes index. Bibliography: p. 331-[335] [N6666.E18H48] 73-20829 ISBN 0-385-04716-9 : 35.00
1. Art—Easter Island—History. I. Title. BIP

Art—Egypt.

BOSTON. Museum of Fine 709.32
Arts.
Ancient Egypt as represented in the Museum of Fine Arts, by William Stevenson Smith, assistant curator of Egyptian art. 3d ed., fully rev. Boston, 1952. 187p. illus. 23cm. [N5350.B66 1952] 52-13864
1. Art—Egypt. 2. Egypt—Hist. 3. Art objects, Egyptian—Boston. I. Smith, William Stevenson. II. Title.

Art—Egypt—Hist.

LANGE, Kurt. 709'.32
Egypt: architecture. sculpture. painting in three thousand years, by K. Lange and M. Hirmer. New York, Phaidon Publishers: distributed by Garden City Books [1956] vii, 361. [1] p. [41]-[284] plates (part col.) plans. 31cm. 'Translated from the German by R. H. Boothroyd.' 'Short bibliography': p. 360- [362] [N5351.L] A57
1. Art—Egypt—Hist. I. Hirmer, Max, II. Title.

LANGE, Kurt. 709'.32
Egypt: architecture, sculpture, painting in three thousand years, by K. Lange and M. Hirmer. New York, Phaidon Publishers' distributed by Garden City Books [1956] vii, 361, [1] p. (p. [41]-[284] plates (part col.)) plans. 31cm. 'Translated from the German by R. H. Boothroyd. Short bibliography': p. 360-[362] [N5351.L] A57
1. Art—Egypt—Hist. I. Hirmer, Max, joint author. II. Title.

LANGE, Kurt. 709'.32
Egypt: architecture, sculpture, painting in three thousand years [by] Kurt Lange and Max Hirmer; with contributions by Eberhard Otto and Christiane Desroches-Noblecourt; translated by R. H. Boothroyd from the original German. 4th ed. revised and enlarged; with additional material in the fourth German ed. translated by Judith Filson and Barbara Taylor. London, New York, Phaidon, 1968. viii, 559 p. 60 plates, illus. (incl. 60 col.), plans. 31 cm. Translation of Aegypten: Architektur, Plastik, Malerei in drei Jahrtausenden. Bibliography: p. 548-549. [N5351.L313 1968] 68-12257 ISBN 0-7148-1349-4 L7/10/-
1. Art—Egypt—History. I. Hirmer, Max, joint author. II. Title.

Art, Egyptian.

BOSTON. Museum of Fine 709.32
Arts.
Ancient Egypt as represented in the Museum of Fine Arts, Boston, by William Stevenson Smith, curator of Egyptian art. [4th ed., fully rev.] [Boston] [1960] 215 p. illus. 24 cm. Includes bibliography. [N5350.B66 1960] 60-13944
1. Art, Egyptian. 2. Egypt—History—Ancient to 640 A. D. 3. Art—Boston. I. Smith, William Stevenson.

BROOKLYN Institute of Arts 709.32
and Sciences. Museum.
Egyptian art in the Brooklyn Museum collection. [Brooklyn? 1952] unpaged. illus. 24 cm. [N5350.B675] 52-14239
1. Art, Egyptian. I. Title.

CAPART, Jean, 1877-1947. 709'.62
Egyptian art; introductory studies. Translated from the French by Warren R. Dawson. Freeport, N.Y., Books for Libraries Press [1971] 179 p. illus. 26 cm. Reprint of the 1923 ed., which was a translation of the introductory chapters of the author's Lecons sur l'art egyptien. Includes bibliographies. [N5350.C22 1971] 78-179509 ISBN 0-8369-6638-4
1. Art, Egyptian. 2. Egypt—Antiquities.

EGYPTIAN art; 709'.32
general editor Francesco Abbate; translated [from the Italian] by H. S. Fields. London, New York, Octopus Books, 1972. 158 p. chiefly 103 col. illus. 20 cm. Translation of Arte egizia. Bibliography: p. 155. [N5350.A8213] 72-172102 ISBN 0-7064-0062-3 2.95
1. Art, Egyptian. I. Abbate, Francesco, ed.

MALY, Florence. 709.62
Egyptian art. New York, Pitman Pub. Corp. [1969] 48 p. illus., map. 20 x 27 cm. (Pitman art books, 64) [N5350.M27] 69-11191 1.00
1. Art, Egyptian.

PETRIE, William Matthew 709'.32
Flinders, Sir, 1853-1942.
Arts and crafts of ancient Egypt / by W. M. Flinders Petrie. New York : Attic Books, [1974?] xv, 157 p., [36] leaves of plates : ill. ; 19 cm. Reprint of the 1910 ed. Includes index. [N5350.P5 1974] 75-305238 ISBN 0-915018-05-5 : 8.00
1. Art, Egyptian. I. Title. BIP

POULSEN, Vagn, 1909- 709'.32
Egyptian art. [Translated from the German by Robin and Ursula Harrison] Greenwich, Conn., New York Graphic Society [1968] 183 p. illus. (part col.), map, plan. 27 cm. Translation of Agyptische Kunst. Contents.Contents.—Old and Middle Kingdoms.—New Kingdom and Late Period. Bibliography: p. 181. [N5350.P6513] 69-15492 8.95
1. Art, Egyptian.

RACHEWILTZ, Boris de. 709.62
Egyptian art, an introduction. Translated by R. H. Boothroyd. New York, Viking Press [1960] 255 p. illus. 20 cm. (A Studio book) Translation of Incontro con l'arte egiziana. Includes bibliography. [N5350.R253] 60-11232
1. Art, Egyptian.

RUSKIN, Ariane. 709'.01'1
Prehistoric art and ancient art of the Near East; adapted by Ariane Ruskin. Foreword by Howard Conant. New York, McGraw-Hill [1971] 192 p. col. illus. 31 cm. (Discovering art series) "[Based] on the text of the magazine series Discovering art ... [with] adaptations from the Italian text of Capolovori nei secoli." [N5350.R8] 72-154838 ISBN 0-07-054296-1 9.95
1. Art, Egyptian. 2. Art, Ancient—Near East. 3. Art, Prehistoric—Europe. I. Title. BIP

SCHAFER, Heinrich, 1868- 709'.32
1957.
Principles of Egyptian art / Heinrich Schafer ; edited, with an epilogue by Emma Brunner-Traut ; translated and edited, with an introd. by John Baines. Oxford [Eng.] : Clarendon Press, 1974. xxviii, 470 p., [72] leaves of plates : ill. ; 24 cm. Translation with revisions of Von agyptischer Kunst. Includes index. Bibliography: p. [392]-420. [N5350.S313] 75-300260 ISBN 0-19-817198-6 : 32.00
1. Art, Egyptian. I. Brunner-Traut, Emma, ed. II. Title.
Distributed by Oxford University Pr., N.Y.

WESTENDORF, Wolfhart. 709'.32
Painting, sculpture, and architecture of ancient Egypt. New York, H. N. Abrams [1969, c1968] 260 p. illus. (part col.), map. 24 cm. (Panorama of world art) Translation of Das alte Agypten. Bibliography: p. 255-256. [N5350.W4613] 68-28391
1. Art, Egyptian. I. Title.

YOYOTTE, Jean. 709'.32
Treasures of the pharaohs. The early period, the New Kingdom, the late period. Introd. by Christiane Desroches Noblecourt. Text by Jean Yoyotte. (Translated from the French by Robert Allen. Geneva,) Skira (1968) xii, 259 p. illus. 34 cm. (Treasures of the world, v. 7) "Distributed in the United States by the World Publishing Company, Cleveland, Ohio." Translation of Les tresors des pharaons. [N5350.Y613] 68-56859 132.00
1. Art, Egyptian.

Art, Egyptian—Addresses, essays, lectures.

†*ANCIENT Egypt in the* 709'.32
Metropolitan Museum journal, volumes 1-11 (1968-1976) : articles / by Cyril Aldred ... [et al.]. New York : Metropolitan Museum of Art, 1977. p. cm. Includes bibliographical references and index. [N5350.A68] 76-54181 ISBN 0-87099-159-0 : 10.00
1. Art, Egyptian—Addresses, essays, lectures. 2. Inscriptions, Hieroglyphic—Addresses, essays, lectures. I. Aldred, Cyril. II. New York (City). Metropolitan Museum of Art. Metropolitan Museum journal.

Art, Egyptian — Catalogs.

DENVER. Art Museum. 730'.093
Ancient Mediterranean art: the Denver Art Museum collection. [Catalogue compiled and designed by Cile M. Bach. Denver, 1968] 63 p. illus. 23 cm. Cover title: Ancient Mediterranean collection. [N5340.D36 1968] 74-154221
1. Art, Egyptian—Catalogs. 2. Art, Classical—Catalogs. 3. Art—Denver—Catalogs. I. Bach, Cile M. II. Title.

NEW York. Royal-Athena 301.15'43
Galleries.
A catalog of Egyptian and other Near Eastern antiquities, by Jerome M. Eisenberg, [director. New York, 1962] 48 p. (chiefly illus.) 23 cm. (Its Catalog no. 42) Cover title. [N5350.N44] 65-1290
1. Art, Egyptian — Catalogs. 2. Art — Near East — Catalogs. I. Eisenberg, Jerome M. II. Title.

Art, Egyptian—Exhibitions.

BROOKLYN Institute of Arts 709.62
and Sciences. Museum.
Five years of collecting Egyptian art, 1951-1956; catalogue of an exhibition held at the Brooklyn Museum, 11 December, 1956 to 17 March, 1957. Brooklyn, 1956. v, 63p. 97 plates. 28cm. Includes bibliographical references. [N7381.B68] 57-7253
1. Art, Egyptian—Exhibitions. I. Title.

BROOKLYN Institute of Arts 709.62
and Sciences. Museum.
Five years of collecting Egyptian art, 1951-1956; catalogue of an exhibition held at the Brooklyn Museum, 11 December, 1956 to 17 March, 1957. Brooklyn, 1956. v, 63p. 97 plates. 28cm. Includes bibliographical references. [N7381.B68] 57-7253
1. Art, Egyptian—Exhibitions. I. Title.

BROOKLYN Institute of 709'.62
Arts and Sciences. Museum.
Five years of collecting Egyptian art, 1951-1956. Brooklyn, Brooklyn Museum, 1956. [New York] Arno Press, 1969. v, 63 p. 97 plates. 29 cm. On spine: Collecting Egyptian art, 1951-1956. "Catalogue of an exhibition held at the Brooklyn Museum, 11 December, 1956 to 17 March, 1957." Includes bibliographical references. [N7381.B68 1969] 70-4392
1. Art, Egyptian—Exhibitions. I. Title. II. Title: Collecting Egyptian art, 1951-1956. BIP

BROOKLYN Institute of 709'.62
Arts and Sciences. Museum.
Pagan and Christian Egypt; Egyptian art from the first to the tenth century A.D. Exhibited at the Brooklyn Museum by the Department of Ancient Art, January 23-March 9, 1941. [Brooklyn] 1941. [New York] Reprinted by Arno Press, 1969. 86 p. 107 plates. 29 cm. Includes

bibliographical references. [N7381.B7 1969] 69-17449
1. Art, Egyptian—Exhibitions. 2. Art, Coptic—Exhibitions. 3. Textile industry and fabrics—Egypt. I. Title. BIP

TERRACE, Edward 732'.8'074096216
Lee Bockman.
Treasures of Egyptian art from the Cairo Museum; a centennial exhibition, 1970-71 [by] Edward L. B. Terrace and Henry G. Fischer. Boston, Museum of Fine Arts [1970] 188 p. illus. (part col.) 26 cm. Includes bibliographical references. [N5350.T47] 78-117507
1. Art, Egyptian—Exhibitions. I. Fischer, Henry George, joint author. II. Cairo. al-Mathaf al-Misri. III. Title. BIP

Art, Egyptian—Exhibitions—Public opinion.

NEFERTITI graffiti : 301.15'43
comments on an exhibition / analyzed and edited by Eleanor F. Wedge. Brooklyn : Brooklyn Museum, 1976 [c1977] 160 p. : ill. ; 28 cm. [N5350.N39] 76-54373 ISBN 0-913696-29-3 pbk. : 3.95
1. Amenhetep IV, King of Egypt, 1388-1358 B.C.—Art—Exhibitions. 2. Nefertiti, Queen of Egypt, 14th cent. B.C.—Art—Exhibitions. 3. Art, Egyptian—Exhibitions—Public opinion. 4. Public opinion—New York (City) I. Wedge, Eleanor F. II. Brooklyn Institute of Arts and Sciences. Museum. BIP

Art, Egyptian—History.

ALDRED, Cyril 709.32
New kingdom art in ancient Egypt during the eighteenth dynasty, 1570 to 1320 B. C. 2d ed. rev., enl. London, A. Tiranti [dist. Hollywood-by-the-Sea, Fla., Transatlantic, 1962] 93p. 175 illus., map. 19cm. [Chapters in art, v.19] Bibl. 62-51980 4.75
1. Art, Egyptian—Hist. I. Title.

MICHAIOWSKI, Kazimierz. 709'.32
Art of ancient Egypt. [Translated and adapted from the Polish and French by Norbert Guterman] New York, H. N. Abrams [1969] 600 p. illus., maps, plans, plates (part col.) 32 cm. Translation of the author's L'art de l'ancienne Egypte which was based on his Nie tylko piramidy. [N5350.M61423] 68-26865 40.00
1. Art, Egyptian—History. 2. Egypt—Civilization. I. Guterman, Norbert, 1900-tr. II. Michalowski, Kazimierz. Nie tylko piramidy. III. Title.

WOLDERING, Irmgard, 1919- 709.32
The art of Egypt; the time of the pharaohs. [Translated by Ann E. Keep] New York, Crown Publishers [1963, c1962] 260 p. illus. (part mounted col.) maps, plans. 24 cm. (Art of the world, non-European cultures; the historical, sociological and religious backgrounds) Translation of Agypten. Die Kunst der Pharaonen. Bibliography: p. 248-249. [N5350.W553] 62-20055
1. Art, Egyptian—History. I. Title. II. Series: Art of the world; the historical, sociological and religious backgrounds.

WOLDERING, Irmgard, 1919- 709'.32
Gods, men & pharaohs; the glory of Egyptian art. [Translated by Ann E. Keep] New York, H. N. Abrams [1967] xii, 275 p. 249 illus. (part col.), col. maps. 30 cm. Translation of Gotter und Pharaonen. Bibliography: p. 247-250. [N5350.W5613 1967b] 67-26468
1. Art, Egyptian—History. I. Title.

Art, Egyptian—Juvenile literature.

GLUBOK, Shirley 709.32
The art of ancient Egypt. Designed by Gerald Nook. New York, Atheneum [c.] 1962. 48p. illus. 26cm. 62-10249 3.95
1. Art, Egyptian—Juvenile literature. I. Title.

PRICE, Christine, 1928- 709'.32
Made in ancient Egypt. [1st ed.] New York, Dutton [1970] 160 p. illus. 25 cm. Bibliography: p. 160. Text and photographs recreate the life, art, and customs of the people who lived during Egypt's 1500 year peak civilization period. [N5350.P7 1970] 73-78946 ISBN 5-253-43083- 5.95
1. Art, Egyptian—Juvenile literature. I. Title.

Art—England.

BARRY, James, 1741-1806. 709'.42
An inquiry into the real and imaginary obstructions to the acquisition of the arts in England. New York, Garland Pub., 1972. vii, 227 p. 22 cm. Facsimile reprint. Original t.p. has imprint: London, Printed for T. Becket, Corner of the Adelphi, Strand, 1775. [N6761.B3 1775a] 70-112068
1. Art—England. 2. Art—Early works to 1800. I. Title.

SAUNDERS, O. Elfrida. 709'.42
A history of English art in the Middle Ages, by O. Elfrida Saunders. With a pref. by Tancred Borenius. Freeport, N.Y., Books for Libraries Press [1969] xxii, 272 p. illus. 23 cm. (Select bibliographies reprint series) Reprint of the 1932 ed. Bibliography: p. [260]-262. [N6763.S3 1969] 70-103658
1. Art—England. 2. Art, Medieval—England. I. Title. BIP

Art — England — Hist.

BROWN, Gerard Baldwin, 726.0942
1849-1932
The arts in early England [2vs. Reissue] London, J. Murray [dist. Mystic, Conn., Verry, 1965] 2v. (xxii, 383; xx, 318p. front. illus., plates, maps (pt. fold.) plans, tables (1 fold.) 23cm. st. ed. 1903: 2d. ed. 1926 [NA963.B9] 30-16973 10.00 ea.,
1. Art—England—Hist. 2. England—Antiq. 3. Architecture—England—Hist. 4. England—Soc. life & cust. I. Title.

THE Oxford history of 709.42
English art; edited by T. S. R. Boase. [Oxford, Clarendon Press, 19 v. illus., plates, maps, plans. 25cm. Half title: each vol. has also special t. p., with title: English art... Contents.v.2. 871-1100, by D. T. Rice.--v. 3. z1100-1216, by T. S. R. Boase.--v. 4. 1216-1307, by P. Brieger.--v. 5. 1307-1461, by J. Evans.--v. 8. 1625-1714, by M. Whinney and O. Millar. Includes bibliographies. [N6761.O9] 53-4155
1. Art—England—Hist. I. Boase, Thomas Sherrer Ross, 1898- ed.

RICE, David Talbot, 1903- 709.42
English art, 871-1100 Oxford, Clarendon Press, 1952. xix, 280 p. illus., 96 plates, maps. 25 cm. (The Oxford history of English art, v. 2) Bibliography: p. [256]-269. [N6763.R52] 52-10900
1. Art — England — Hist. I. Title. II. Series. BIP

Art—England—Leeds—Catalogs.

LEEDS City art 708'.28'19
galleries concise catalogue : paintings, sculpture, drawings, watercolours, prints / [compilation carried out by Miranda Strickland-Constable ... et al.]. [Leeds] : Leeds City Council Leisure Services Committee, 1976. [166] p. ; 21 cm. Catalogue of the holdings of the Leeds City Art Gallery, Temple Newsam House and Lotherton Hall. [N1403.L43] 77-364648 ISBN 0-901981-14-1 : £1.00
1. Art—England—Leeds—Catalogs. 2. Art museums—England—Leeds. 3. Leeds, Eng.—Museums. I. Strickland-Constable, Miranda. II. Leeds, Eng. Leisure Services Committee. III. Leeds, Eng. City Art Gallery. IV. Temple Newsam House, Leeds, Eng. V. Lotherton Hall.

Art—England—London.

TUESDAYS / 759.21
[editor, Kay Stout]. London : The Tuesday Group [of Art], [1976] [47] p. : of ill. ; 21 cm. [N6770.T83] 77-364487 ISBN 0-904936-06-6 : £1.50
1. The Tuesday Group of Art. 2. Art—England—London. I. Stout, Kay.

Art, English.

FRY, Roger Eliot, 1866- 709'.42
1934.
Georgian art (1760-1820) : an introductory review of English painting, architecture, sculpture, ceramics, glass, metalwork, furniture, textiles, and other arts during the reign of George III / by Roger Fry ... [et al.]. New York : AMS Press, [1979] p. cm. Reprint of the 1929 ed. published for the Burlington magazine by Batsford, London, which was issued as no. 3 of Burlington magazine monographs. Includes index. [N6766.F7 1979] 76-42713 ISBN 0-404-15359-3 : 34.50
1. Art, English. 2. Decoration and ornament—Georgian style. I. Burlington magazine for connoisseurs. II. Title. III. Series: Burlington magazine monographs ; 3. BIP

OWEN, William Harold, 759.2 B
1897-
Aftermath [by] Harold Owen. London, New York, Oxford U.P., 1970. xi, 199 p., 9 plates. illus. 23 cm. [CT788.O87A3 1970] 73-537524 ISBN 0-19-211195-7 55/-
I. Title. BIP

OWEN, William Harold, 759.2 B
1897-
Aftermath [by] Harold Owen. London, New York, Oxford U.P., 1970. xi, 199 p., 9 plates. illus. 23 cm. [CT788.O87A3 1970] 73-537524 ISBN 0-19-211195-7 55/-
I. Title. BIP

PAULSON, Ronald. 700'.942
Emblem and expression : meaning in English art of the eighteenth century / Ronald Paulson. Cambridge, Mass. : Harvard University Press, 1975. 256 p. : ill. ; 26 cm. Includes bibliographical references and index. [N6766.P38 1975b] 74-31988 ISBN 0-674-24778-7 : 25.00
1. Art, English. 2. Art, Modern—17th-18th centuries—England. 3. Allegories. 4. Emblems. I. Title. BIP

PEVSNER, Nikolaus, 1902- 709.42
The Englishness of English art; an expanded and annotated version of the Reith lectures broadcast in October and November 1955. New York, Praeger [1956] 208 p. plates, plans. 23 cm; (Books that matter) "Notes and references": p. 193-201. [N6764.P42] 56-8431
1. Art, English. I. The Reith lectures, 1955. II. Title.

POINTON, Marcia R. 760'.0942
Milton & English art [by] Marcia R. Pointon. [Toronto] University of Toronto Press [1970] xlii, 276 p. illus. 24 cm. Bibliography: p. [264]-269. [PR3588.P6 1970] 70-508609 14.50
1. Milton, John, 1608-1674—Influence. 2. Milton, John, 1608-1674—Illustrations. 3. Art, English. I. Title. BIP

SMITH, Matthew, 1879-1959 759.12
Matthew Smith. London, Allen & Unwin [dist. Hollywood-by-the-Sea, Fla., Transatlantic, 1963, c.1962] [22]p. 52 col. plates. 31cm. 62-51568 15.75
I. Title.

SMITH, Matthew, 1879-1959 759.12
Matthew Smith. London, Allen & Unwin [dist. Hollywood-by-the-Sea, Fla., Transatlantic, 1963, c.1962] [22]p. 52 col. plates. 31cm. 62-51568 15.75
I. Title.

WALKER, Stella A. 759.2
Sporting art, England 1700-1900 [by] Stella A. Walker. New York, C. N. Potter; distributed by Crown Publishers [1972] 200 p. illus. (part col.) 30 cm. Bibliography: p. 191-192. [N6764.W3] 70-187507 15.00
1. Sports in art. 2. Art, English. 3. Art, Modern—Great Britain. I. Title.

Art, English—England—Sheffield—Exhibitions.

SHEFFIELD, 709'.428'2107402821
Eng. City Art Galleries.
1850-1875, art & industry in Sheffield / Sheffield City Art Galleries. [Sheffield] : [Sheffield City Art Galleries], [1976] 36 p., [12] p. of plates : ill. (incl. 1 col.), port. ; 15 cm. Bibliography: p. [36] [N6771.S5S53 1976] 77-358287 ISBN 0-9500623-9-1 : £0.25
1. Art, English—England—Sheffield—Exhibitions. 2. Art, Modern—19th century—England—Sheffield—Exhibitions. 3. Art industries and trade—England—Sheffield—Exhibitions. I. Title. II. Title: Art and industry in Sheffield.

Art, English—Exhibitions.

READING, Eng. 709'.422'9307402293
Museum and Art Gallery.
Art and the University from 1860 : [catalogue of an exhibition held at Reading Museum and Art Gallery]. [Reading] : The Museum, [1976] [13] p., [4] p. of plates : ill., facsim., port. ; 30 x 11 cm. Cover title. "This exhibition using paintings, prints, drawings, sculpture, and documentary material offers a survey of the growth of the present Fine Art Department from its earliest beginnings. [N346.5.G72R47 1976] 77-355085 ISBN 0-9501247-5-3 : £0.30
1. Reading, Eng. University. Dept. of Fine Art. 2. Art, English—Exhibitions. 3. Art, Modern—19th century—England—Exhibitions. 4. Art, Modern—20th century—England—Exhibitions. I. Title.

WILLIAM Blake in the 760'.092'4
art of his time : [exhibition] : a faculty-graduate student project, University of California, Santa Barbara, organized by Corlette Rossiter Walker, University Art Galleries, University of California Santa Barbara, February 24-March 28, 1976. [Santa Barbara : The Galleries], c1976. 103 p. : ill. (some col.) ; 24 x 29 cm. Includes bibliographies. [N6797.B57W52] 75-620115
1. Blake, William, 1757-1827. 2. Art, English—Exhibitions. 3. Art, Modern—17th-18th centuries—England—Exhibitions. I. Blake, William, 1757-1827. II. Walker, Corlette Rossiter. III. California. University, Santa Barbara. Art Galleries.

YALE Center 760'.0942'07401468
for British Art.
The pursuit of happiness : a view of life in Georgian England : an exhibition selected from the Paul Mellon Collection, Yale Center for British Art, New Haven, April 19 to September 18, 1977 / J. H. Plumb ; catalogue entries by Edward J. Nygren and Nancy L. Pressly. [New Haven] : The Center, c1977. 139 p., [6] leaves of plates : ill. (some col.) ; 28 cm. Includes index. [N6766.Y34 1977] 77-71640
1. Mellon, Paul—Art collections. 2. Art, English—Exhibitions. 3. Art, Georgian—England—Exhibitions. I. Plumb, John Harold, 1911- II. Title.

Art, English—History.

BUXTON, John 709.42
Elizabethan taste. New York, St. Martin's, 1964 [c.1963] xiv, 370p. illus., ports. 23cm. Bibl. 64-12947 7.95
1. Art. English—Hist. 2. English literature—Early modern (to 1700)—Hist. &crit. 3. Music—England—Hist. & crit. I. Title.

IRWIN, David G 709.42
English neoclassical art; studies in inspiration and taste [by] David Irwin. Greenwich, Conn., New York Graphic Society [1966] 230 p. 158 illus. (1 col.) 26 cm. Based on thesis, University of London. Bibliography: p. 171-212. [N6766.I7] 66-18856
1. Art, English — Hist. 2. Classicism in art I. Title. BIP

Art, English—History.

FAWCETT, Trevor. 709'.42
The rise of English provincial art : artists, patrons, and institutions outside London, 1800-1830 / Trevor Fawcett. Oxford : Clarendon Press, 1974. xiii, 242 p., [8] leaves of plates : ill. ; 26 cm. (Oxford studies in the history of art and architecture) A revision of the author's thesis (M. Phil.), University of East Anglia. Includes index. Bibliography: p. [215]-231. [N6767.F38 1974] 74-195823 ISBN 0-19-817328-8 : £7.50
1. Art, English—History. 2. Art, Modern—

19th century—England. 3. Art patronage—England. 4. Art dealers—England. 5. Art—England—Galleries and museums. I. Title. II. Series. BIP

*PEVSNER, Nikolaus 709.42
The Englishness of English art; an expanded and annotated version of the Reith Lectures broadcast in Oct. and Nov., 1955 [Baltimore] Penguin [1964, c.1956] 229p. 20cm. (Peregrine bk. Y35) 1.95 pap.,
I. Title. BIP

PRIOR, Edward Schroder, 1852-1932. 726'.5'0942
A history of Gothic art in England / Edward S. Prior ; with illustrations by Gerald C. Horsley and many plans and diagrams. Wakefield : EP Publishing, 1974. xiv, 465 p. : ill., maps, plans ; 26 cm. Reprint of the 1900 ed. published by Bell, London. Includes bibliographical references and index. [N6763.P74 1974] 75-323087 ISBN 0-7158-1022-7 : £6.00
1. Art, English—History. 2. Art, Gothic—England—History. I. Title.

STEEGMAN, John, 1899-1966. 709'.42
The rule of taste; from George I to George IV. With an introd. by James Laver. New York, Russell & Russell [1968] xxviii, 202 p. illus. 23 cm. Reprint of the 1936 ed. Bibliography: p. 193-195. [N6766.S7 1968b] 68-20986
1. Art, English—History. 2. Aesthetics. 3. Eighteenth century. I. Title.

Art—Essex, Eng.

ESSEX, Eng. Record Office. 709'.426'7
The visual arts in Essex, 1066-1837. Chelmsford (Essex), Essex County Council, 1969. [28] p. of illus. (incl. 1 col.), facsims., maps, plans, port. 25 cm. (Essex Record Office. Publications, no. 50) [DA670.E7A17 no. 50] 70-461101 2/6
1. Art—Essex, Eng. I. Title. II. Series: Essex, Eng. Record Office. Publications, no. 50

Art, Etruscan.

BLOCH, Raymond, 1914- 709.375
Etruscan art. Greenwich, Conn., New York Graphic Society [1959] 47 p., 85 plates (part col.) illus. (part mounted col.) 39 cm. Bibliography: p. 46-47. [N5751.B55] 59-9330
1. Art, Etruscan.

BLOCH, Raymond, 1914- 709.375
Etruscan art. Text by Raymond Bloch. Greenwich, Con., N.Y. Graphic [1966, c. 1965] 103p. illus. (pt. col.) map. 28cm. (Pallas lib. of art, v.1) Bibl. [N5750.B52] 65-22674 10.00
1. Art, Etruscan. I. Title.

BLOCH, Raymond, 1914- 709.375
Etruscan art. Text by Raymond Bloch. Greenwich, Conn., New York Graphic Society [1966, c1965] 103 p. illus. (part col.) map. 28 cm. (The Pallas library of art, v. 1) Bibliography: p. 102-106. [N5750.B52] 65-22674
1. Art, Etruscan. I. Title.

BRENDEL, Otto, 1901-1973. 709'.37'5
Etruscan art / by Otto J. Brendel. New York : Penguin Books, [1977] p. cm. (The Pelican history of art) Includes index. Bibliography: p. [N5750.B67 1977] 77-22662 ISBN 0-14-056143-9 pbk. : 15.00
1. Art,Etruscan. I. Title. II. Series. BIP

BROWN, William Llewellyn, 1924-1958. 733.4
The Etruscan lion. [New York] Oxford, Univ. Press, 1960[ ] xxvi, 209p. 64 plates. port., map. 29cm. (Oxford monographs on classical archaeology) Bibl.: p.[xv]-xvi. Bibl. footnotes 60-50891 13.45
1. Art, Etruscan. 2. Lions in art. 3. Art, Greek. I. Title. II. Series.

GLUBOK, Shirley. 709.37 (j)
The art of the Etruscans. Designed by Gerard Nook. Special photography by Alfred H. Tamarin. New York, Harper & Row [1967] 40 p. illus. 26 cm. [N5750.G55] 67-14066
1. Art, Etruscan. I. Title. BIP

PALLOTTINO, Massimo. 709.375
Art of the Etruscans. 126 photos. by Walter Drayer and Martin Hurlimann. Text by Massimo Pallottino. Notes by H. and I. Jucker. New York, Vanguard Press [1955] 154 p. illus. (part col.) map. 31 cm. (A Thames and Hudson book) Bibliography: p. 29. [N5750.P313 1955a] 55-10480
1. Art, Etruscan. I. Drayer, Walter, 1911- II. Hurlimann, Martin, 1897- III. Title.

RIIS, Poul Jrgen, 1910- 709.375
An introduction to Etruscan art. New York, Philosophical Library [1954] 144p. 82 plates (incl. map. tables) 25cm. Translation of Den etruskiske kunst. Includes bibliographical references. [N5750] 55-57
1. Art, Etruscan. 2. Etruria—Antiq. I. Title.

Art, Etruscan—Exhibitions.

CAHN, Herbert Adolph, 1915- 730'.093
Art of the ancients: Greeks, Etruscans, and Romans; an exhibition organized in cooperation with Munzen and Medaillen AG, Basle, Switzerland. [Catalogue prepared by Herbert A. Cahn] New York, Andre Emmerich Gallery [1968] 52 p. illus. 23 cm. Catalog of the exhibition held Feb. 7-Mar. 13, 1968 at the Andre Emmerich Gallery in New York. [N5603.N4A53] 73-20421
1. Art, Etruscan—Exhibitions. 2. Art, Classical—Exhibitions. I. Munzen und Medaillen A.G. II. Andre Emmerich Gallery, New York. III. Title.

DEL CHIARO, Mario Aldo, 1925- 709'.37'5
Etruscan art from West Coast collections [by] Mario A. Del Chiaro. [Santa Barbara, 1967] 88 p. illus. (part col.) 26 cm. Catalog of an exhibition held at the Art Gallery, University of California, Santa Barbara, Feb. 7 - Mar. 15, 1967. Bibliography: p. 62-88. [N5750.D45] 67-63241
1. Art, Etruscan—Exhibitions. I. California. University, Santa Barbara. Art Gallery. II. Title.

TEITZ, Richard Stuart. 709.014
Masterpieces of Etruscan art; [exhibition at the] Worcester Art Museum, April 21 to June 4, 1967. [Worcester, Mass., Printed by the Davis Press, 1967] 206 p. illus., map. 24 cm. Bibliography: p. 204-206. [N5750.T4] 67-68039
1. Art, Etruscan—Exhibitions. I. Worcester, Mass. Art Museum. II. Title.

Art—Europe.

BRAIDER, Donald, 1923- 708
Putnam's guide to the art centers of Europe. New York, Putnam [c.1965] ix, 542p. 20cm. [N6750.B66] 64-18003 6.95
1. Art—Europe. 2. Europe—Descr. & trav.—Guidebooks. I. Title. II. Title: Guide to the art centers of Europe.

BROWN, Blanche R. 709.4
Five cities [art guides: 5v.] Garden City, N.Y., Doubleday [1966, c.1964] 5v. (various p.) maps. 18cm. (Anchor bks., A490a-A490e) Orig. pub. in 1964 by Doubleday in 1v. ed. Contents.1. Athens.--2.--Florence.--3.--Rome.--4.--Paris.--5. London. Bibl. [N6750.B76] .95 pap., ea.,
1. Art—Europe. 2. Europe—Descr. & trav.—Guidebooks I. Title. II. Title: An art guide to Athens. III. Title: An art guide to Rome. IV. Title: An art guide to Florence. V. Title: An art guide to Paris. VI. Title: An art guide to London.

MADSEN, Stephan Tschudi, 1923- 709.4
Sources of art nouveau. [English translation by Ragnar Christophersen] New York, G. Wittenborn [1956] 488p. 264 illus. 26cm. Bibliography: p. [451]-470. [N6757.M313] 56-12801
1. Art—Europe. 2. Art—Gt. Brit. I. Title.

NORMAN, Jane. 709.4
Traveler's guide to Europe's art, by Jane and Theodore Norman. Great Neck, N. Y., Channel Press [1959] 342p. illus. 21cm. [N1010.N6] 59-12036
1. Art—Europe. 2. Europe—Descr. & trav.— Guide-books. I. Norman, Theodore, joint author. II. Title.

NORMAN, Jane 709.4
Traveler's guide to Europe's art. by Jane and Theodore Norman [Rev., expanded ed.] Great Neck, N.Y., Channel [c.1959, 1963] 380p. illus. 21cm. 2.95 pap.,
1. Art.—Europe. 2. Europe—Descr. & trav.—Guidebooks. I. Norman, Theodore, joint author. II. Title.

NORMAN, Jane 709.4
Traveler's guide to Europe's art [by] Jane and Theodore Norman. Rev. ed. New York, Appleton-Century [dist. Meredith, 1959-1965] 426p. illus., maps. 21cm. [N1010.N6] 65-23426 6.95; 3.95 pap.,
1. Art—Europe. 2. Europe—Descr & trav.—Guide-books. I. Norman Theodore, joint author. II. Title.

SOYER, Raphael, 1899- 709.43
A painter's pilgrimage; an account of a journey with drawings by the author. New York, Crown Publishers [1962] 127 p. plates. 26 cm. [ND237.S636A2] 62-13782
1. Art — Europe. I. Title.

Art—Europe, Eastern.

RHODES, Anthony Richard Ewart. 709'.4
Art treasures of Eastern Europe [by] Anthony Rhodes. New York, Putnam [1972] 278 p. illus. (part col.), maps. 31 cm. Bibliography: p. 273. [N6750.R47] 75-186798 25.00
1. Art—Europe, Eastern. I. Title.

Art — Europe — Galleries and museums.

GUIDE to modern art in Europe. 708.0094
New York, Junior Council of the Museum of Modern Art; distributed by Doubleday, Garden City, N.Y. [1963] c120 p. illus. 21 cm. [N1010.L36] 63-15119
1. Art — Europe — Galleries and museums. 2. Art, Modern — 20th cent.

LAMANNA, Dolores B. ed. 708.0094
Guide to modern art in Europe. New York, Junior Council of the Museum of Modern Art; distributed by Doubleday, Garden City, N.Y. [1963] c120 p. illus. 21 cm. [N1010.L36] 63-15119
1. Art — Europe — Galleries and museums. 2. Art, Modern — 20th cent. I. Title.

LAMANNA, Dolores B ed. 708.0094
Guide to modern art in Europe [edited by Dolores B. Lamanna. 2d rev. ed.] New York, Published by the Junior Council of the Museum of Modern Art, with the cooperation of Pan American Airways; distributed by Doubleday, Garden City, N.Y. [1966] 120 p. illus. 21 cm. [N1010.L36 1966] 66-4800
1. Art — Europe — Galleries and museums. 2. Art, Modern — 20th cent. I. New York. Museum of Modern Art. Junior Council. II. Title.

Art, Europe—History.

MACINNES, M. J. 709.4
Nature to advantage dress'd; being a study of the sister arts of painting, poetry, & gardening, as practis'd in diverse countries of Europe during the years 1700 to 1800 with some remarks on architecture... Minneapolis, Printed for Ross and Haines, 1960. 168p. illus. 28cm. [N6756.M3] 60-51401
1. Art—Europe—Hist. 2. Poetry, Modern—Hist. & crit. 3. Landscape gardening—Europe. I. Title.

Art—Europe—History.

NOVOTNY, Fritz, 1902- 759.94
Painting and sculpture in Europe, 1780-1880. 2nd ed. Harmondsworth, Penguin, 1971. 479 p. illus. 21 cm. (The Pelican history of art PZ20) Bibliography: p. 431-450. [N6756.N68 1971] 73-156496 ISBN 0-14-056120-X £3.00
1. Art—Europe—History. 2. Neoclassicism (Art)—Europe. 3. Art, Modern—19th century—Europe. I. Title. II. Series.

NOVOTNY, Fritz, 1902- 759.94
Painting and sculpture in Europe, 1780 to 1880. Baltimore, Penguin Books [1960] xxii, 288 p. illus., 192 plates. 27 cm. (The Pelican history of art, Z20) Bibliography: p. 253-269. [N6750.N6] 60-51441
1. Art—Europe—History. I. Title. II. Series. BIP

WENTINCK, Charles. 709'.4
The art treasures of Europe / Charles Wentinck. New York : Simon and Schuster, [1974] 304 p. : 456 col. ill. ; 33 cm. Includes index. [N6750.W44] 74-7657 ISBN 0-671-21918-9 : 29.95
1. Art—Europe—History. I. Title. BIP

Art, European.

BENJAMIN, Samuel Greene Wheeler, 1837-1914. 709'.03'4
Contemporary art in Europe / by S. G. W. Benjamin. New York : Garland Pub., 1976, c1877. p. cm. (The Art experience in late nineteenth-century America) Originally published in Harper's monthly magazine. Reprint of the ed. published by Harper, New York. Includes index. [N6757.B46 1976] 75-28868 ISBN 0-8240-2228-9 lib.bdg. : 40.00
1. Art, European. 2. Art, Modern—19th century—Europe. I. Title. II. Series. BIP

HONOUR, Hugh. 704.94'9'973
The new golden land : European images of America from the discoveries to the present time / Hugh Honour. London : Allen Lane, 1976. vii, 301 p. : ill. (some col.), facsims., maps (chiefly col.), ports. (some col.) ; 29 cm. Includes bibliographical references and index. [N8214.5.U6H58 1976] 77-355328 ISBN 0-7139-0959-5 : £12.50
1. United States in art. 2. Art, European. I. Title.

SHINN, Earl, 1837-1886, ed. 709'.73
The art treasures of America / edited by Edward Strahan [i.e. E. Shinn]. New York : Garland, 1977, [c1879-1882] 3 v. : ill. ; 37 cm. (The Art experience in late nineteenth-century America) Reprint of the ed. published by G. Barrie, Philadelphia; with new introd. by H. B. Weinberg. Includes indexes. [N6750.S5 1977] 75-28871 ISBN 0-8240-2231-9 : 200.00
1. Art, European. 2. Art, European—United States. 3. Art patronage—United States. I. Title. II. Series. BIP

TAUBES, Frederic, 1900- 700.94
The illustrated guide to great art in Europe for amateur artists: travel, history, criticism [by] Frederic Taubes. New York, Reinhold Pub. Corp. [1966] xii, 307 p. illus., ports. 22 cm. [N6750.T3] 66-12167
1. Art, European. 2. Art—Europe—Galleries and museums. 3. Europe—Description and travel—1945- —Guide-books. I. Title.

Art, European — Catalogs.

MIAMI, University of, Coral Gables, Fla. Joe and Emily Lowe Art Gallery. 708.159381
The Samuel H. Kress collection; a catalog of European paintings and sculpture. Text and research by Fern Rusk Shapley; preliminary research by William E. Suida. [Coral Gables] 1961. 103 p. illus. (part col.) port. 31 cm. Bibliography: p. 99. Includes bibliographical references. [N6754-M5] 61-18466
1. Art, European — Catalogs. 2. Art — Coral Gables, Fla. — Catalogs. I. Shapely, Fern Rusk. II. Samuel H. Kress Foundation. III. Title.

Art, European—Chinese influences.

CALIFORNIA Palace of the Legion of Honor, San Francisco. 709'.01'1
Cathay invoked; chinoiserie, a celestial empire in the West. [San Francisco? 1966?] 1 v. (unpaged) illus. 26 cm. Catalog of an exhibition held June 10 to July 31, 1966, at the California Palace of the Legion of

Honor, San Francisco. [N7429.C3] 68-30101
1. Art, European—Chinese influences. 2. Art, Modern—17th-18th century—Exhibitions. I. Title. II. Title: Chinoiserie, a celestial empire in the West.

Art, European—Exhibitions.

MINNEAPOLIS. Institute of Arts. 709.4
European art today; 35 painters and sculptors. [A loan exhibition organized by the Minneapolis Institute of Arts in collaboration with the Los Angeles County Museum, and others] Edited with an introd. by Sam Hunter. Articles by Lawrence Alloway [and others. Minneapolis, 1959] 88p. illus., ports. 23x25cm. Exhibition to be held Sept. 23-Oct. 25, 1959. [N6758.M5] 60-51
1. Art, European—Exhibitions. I. Hunter, Sam, 1923- ed. II. Title.

SIDNEY Janis Gallery. 709.4'074'01471
20th century European art [New York, c1970] 1 v. (chiefly illus., part col.) 28 cm. Cover title. "Exhibition opening February 4 thru March 7, 1970 at Sidney Janis, N.Y." [N6758.S55] 70-198202
1. Art, European—Exhibitions. 2. Art, Modern—20th century—Europe. I. Title.

SMITH College. Museum of Art. 709.4
An exhibition of Chinoiserie, organized by the Smith College Museum of Art [May 10-June 7] Texts by Hugh Honour and Nelly Schargo Hoyt. Northampton, Mass., 1965. 1 v. (unpaged) plates. 23 cm. "Addenda" slip inserted. Includes bibliography. [N6754.S6] 76-214226
1. Art, European—Exhibitions. 2. Art, European—Chinese influences. I. Honour, Hugh. II. Hoyt, Nelly Noemie (Schargo) 1920- III. Title.

WADSWORTH Atheneum, Hartford. 759.94'074'01463
Selections from the Joseph L. Shulman Collection : [catalogue of] an exhibition, 5 March-13 April, 1975 / organized by the Wadsworth Atheneum, Hartford, Connecticut. Hartford, Conn. : The Atheneum, [1975] 47 p. : chiefly ill. (some col.) ; 28 cm. [N6758.W32 1975] 75-313874
1. Shulman, Joseph L.—Art collections. 2. Art, European—Exhibitions. 3. Art, Modern—20th century—Europe—Exhibitions.

WALTERS Art Gallery, Baltimore 707.4
The international style: the arts in Europe around 1400; [exhibition]: October 23-December 2, 1962, the Walters Art Gallery, Baltimore. [Baltimore], Author, c.1962. xv, 153p. 125 plates. col. front 28cm. Bibl. 62-52990 10.00 pap.,
1. Art, European—Exhibitions. 2. Art, Renaissance—Exhibitions. I. Title.

WALTERS Art Gallery, Baltimore. 707.4
The international style: the arts in Europe around 1400; [exhibition]: October 23-December 2, 1962, the Walters Art Gallery, Baltimore. [Baltimore, 1962] xv, 153 p. 125 plates. 28 cm. "Catalogue": p. 1-153. Includes bibliographies. [N6370.W3] 62-52990
1. Art, European — Exhibitions. 2. Art, Renaissance — Exhibitions. I. Title. BIP

Art, european—History.

HONOUR, Hugh, 709.4
Chinoiserie; the vision of Cathay. New York, Dutton [c.1961] viii, 294 p. illus., plates (4 col.) Bibl. 62-16001 12.50
1. Art, European—Hist. 2. Europe—Civilization—Chinese influences. 3. Art, Chinese. I. Title.

STADLER, Wolfgang, 1924- 709.4
European art; a traveller's guide. [New York] Herder and Herder [1960] 298 p. illus, (part col.) maps. 25 cm. "This translation is based on the original version of 'Fuhrer durch die europaische Kunst.'" [N6750.S753 1960a] 60-13250
1. Art. European — Hist. 2. Europe — Descr. & trav. — Guide-books. I. Title.

STADLER, Wolfgang, 1924- 709.4
European art; a traveller's guide. Freiburg, Herder [1960] 298 p. illus. (part col.) maps 25 cm. Translation of Fuhrer durch die europuische Kunst. [N6750.S753 1960] 60-13005
1. Art, European — Hist. 2. Europe — Descr. & trav. — Guide-books. I. Title.

VERMEULE, Cornelius Clarkson, 1925- 709.4
European art and the classical past [by] Cornelius Vermeule. Cambridge, Harvard University Press, 1964. xvi, 206 p. illus. 24 cm. Bibliographical references included in "Notes" (p. 179-192) [N6750.V44] 64-21248
1. Art, European — Hist. 2. Classicism in art. 3. Art, Greek. 4. Art, Roman. I. Title.

Art, European—History.

HAMILTON, George Heard. 759.94
Painting and sculpture in Europe, 1880-1940. [Rev. and corr.] Baltimore, Md.] Penguin Books [1972] 624 p. 307 illus. 22 cm. (The Pelican history of art, PZ29) Bibliography: p. [559]-591. [N6757.H3 1972] 71-128577 ISBN 0-14-056129-3 8.95
1. Art, European—History. 2. Art, Modern—19th century—Europe. 3. Art, Modern—20th century—Europe. I. Title. II. Series.

HONOUR, Hugh. 709.4
Chinoiserie; the vision of Cathay. New York, Harper & Row [1973, c1961] viii, 294 p. illus., plates. 24 cm. (Icon editions, IN-39) Bibliographical references included in "Notes": (p. 227-242) [N6754.H6] ISBN 0-06-430039-0 6.95 (pbk.)
1. Art, European—History. 2. Europe—Civilization—Chinese influences. 3. Art, Chinese. I. Title.
L.C. card no. for the hardbound edition: 62-16001.

NOVOTNY, Fritz, 1902- 759.94
Painting and sculpture in Europe, 1780-1880. 2d ed. Harmondsworth, Penguin [1972, c.1971] 479 p. illus. 21 cm. (Pelican history of art) Bibliography: p. [431]-450. [N6757.N6813 1971] 74-149800 ISBN 0-14-056120-X 11.95 (pbk)
1. Art, European—History. 2. Neoclassicism (Art). 3. Art, Modern—19th cent.—Europe. I. Title.
Available from the Baltimore office.

NOVOTNY, Fritz, 1902- 759.94
Painting and sculpture in Europe, 1780 to 1880. 2nd ed. Harmondsworth, Penguin, 1970. xxii, 290, 192 p., leaf. illus. (incl. 2 col.) 27 cm. (The Pelican history of art) Bibliography: p. 253-272. [N6757.N6813 1970] 74-149800 ISBN 0-14-056020-3 £5.75
1. Art, European—History. 2. Neoclassicism (Art)—Europe. 3. Art, Modern—19th century—Europe. I. Title. II. Series.

TOMORY, P. A., 1922- 709'.4
Foundations of European art [by] P. A. Tomory. New York, H. N. Abrams [1971? c1969] 288 p. illus. (part col.), plans, ports. (part col.) 22 cm. Bibliography: p. 264-267. [N6750.T6 1971] 78-105934 ISBN 0-8109-0125-0
1. Art, European—History. I. Title.

Art, European—Negro influences.

DIMENSIONS of Black. 709.1'74'96
[Exhibition] La Jolla Museum of Art, February 15-March 29, 1970. Jehanne Teilhet, editor. [San Diego? 1970] vi, 154 p. illus., map. 23 x 26 cm. The exhibition and this catalog result from a student project of the University of California, San Diego. Bibliography: p. 150-153. [N7428.5.D54] 72-630858
1. Art, European—Negro influences. 2. Negro art—Exhibitions. 3. Art—Africa, West. I. Teilhet, Jehanne, ed. II. La Jolla, Calif. Museum of Art. III. California. University, San Diego.

Art—Examinations, questions, etc.

ARCO Publishing Company, New York. 707
Teacher of fine arts: high school and junior high school, regular and substitute. New York, Author [1962] 27cm. (Arco teacher's license training text) 62-21612 3.50 pap.,
1. Art—Examinations, questions, etc. 2. Art—Study and teaching. I. Title.

ARCO Publishing Company, New York. 707.6
Teacher of fine arts: high school and junior high school. Edward C. Gruber, editor. New York [1966] 1 v. (various pagings) 27 cm. (Arco teacher license series) [N340.A72 1966] 66-28168
1. Art—Examinations, questions, etc. 2. Art—Study and teaching (Secondary) I. Gruber, Edward C., ed. II. Title.

ARCO Publishing Company, New York. 707'.6
Teacher of fine arts: high school and junior high school. Edward C. Gruber, editor. [New York, c1970] 1 v. (various pagings) 27 cm. (Arco teacher license series) "Arco catalog number: 1037." [N340.A72 1970] 71-24476 6.00
1. Art—Examinations, questions, etc. 2. Art—Study and teaching (Secondary) I. Gruber, Edward C., ed. II. Title.

COWLES Education Corporation. 707.6
How to pass NTE teaching area examination: art education. New York [1968] 1 v. (unpaged) 28 cm. [N340.C64] 67-26836
1. Art—Examinations, questions, etc. I. Title. II. Title: NTE teaching area examination: art education.

*RUDMAN, Jack. 707
Art education; examination section, questions and answers, selected background notes. Brooklyn, N.Y., Natl. Learning Corp., 1968. 1v. (unpaged) 28cm. (Passbk. ser. Passbks. for natl. teacher exams. Teaching area exam. no. 13) NT13. 3.95, pap., plastic bdg.
1. Art—Examinations, questions, etc. I. Title.

*RUDMAN, Jack. 707'.076
Fine arts: junior high school. Examination sect., questions & answers. Brooklyn, N.Y., Natl. Learning Corp., 1968. 1v. (various p.) 28cm. (Passbk. ser. Passbks. for teachers license exams., T18) 5.00, pap., plastic bdg.
1. Art—Examinations, questions, etc. I. Title.

*RUDMAN, Jack. 707'.076
Fine arts: senior high school. Examination sect., questions & answers. Brooklyn, N.Y., Natl. Learning Corp., 1968. 1v. (various p.) 28cm. (Passbk. ser. Passbks. for teachers license exams., T19) 5.00, pap., plastic bdg.
1. Art—Examinations, questions, etc. I. Title.

Art — Exhibitions.

ALASKO, Richard-Ryamond. 707'.4'017289
The change of perception, the perception of change. [Exhibition held at the] Art Gallery of the University of Notre Dame, 25 Aug. 27 Oct. 1968. Catalogue: Richard-Raymond Alasko. [Notre Dame? Ind., 1968?] [23] p. (incl. cover) illus. 22 x 28 cm. [N5020.N98N672] 74-151093
1. Art—Exhibitions. 2. Visual perception. I. Notre Dame, Ind. University. Art Gallery. II. Title.

THE Amherst sesquicentennial exhibition from the collections of Amherst College. 707'.4'01471
[Amherst? 1972] 71 p. illus. (part col.) 18 x 23 cm. Catalog of the exhibition held Mar. 22-Apr. 8, 1972, at the Hirschl & Adler Galleries, New York. [N5020.N7H52] 72-76252
1. Art—Exhibitions. I. Amherst College. II. Hirschl & Adler Galleries.

THE Armand Hammer Collection. 750'.74'019494
A loan exhibition for the benefit of the Smithsonian Institution, National Endowment for the Arts, American Association of Museums. Exhibited at the Smithsonian Institution [and elsewhere] Washington [1970] [136] p. col. illus. 28 cm. [N5220.H26A7] 72-22632
1. Hammer, Armand, 1897- —Art collections. 2. Art—Exhibitions. I. Smithsonian Institution.

THE Art of the director : 708'.147'25
Eva Gatling's fifteen years at the Heckscher Museum : a loan exhibition from the collection of the Heckscher Museum / organized by Ronald G. Pisano, July 16-September 5, 1977, The Museums at Stony Brook, Stony Brook, New York. Stony Brook : The Museums, c1977. [24] p. : ill. ; 21 cm. [N5020.N7H422] 77-371847
1. Gatling, Eva Ingersoll, 1912- 2. Art—Exhibitions. I. Pisano, Ronald G. II. Heckscher Museum. III. Museums at Stony Brook.

BACKLIN-LANDMAN, Hedy. 759.94'074'014967
European and American art from Princeton alumni collections. Edited by Hedy B. Landman. [Princeton, N.J.] Art Museum, Princeton University [1972] xvii, 170 p. illus. 28 cm. Catalogue of an exhibition held at the Princeton University Art Museum, May 7-June 11, 1972. Errata slip inserted. [N5215.B3] 74-188505 ISBN 0-691-03882-1 12.50
1. Art—Exhibitions. 2. Art—Private collections—United States. I. Princeton University. Art Museum. II. Title.

BALTIMORE. Museum of Art. 708'.152'6
Saidie A. May Collection. [Catalogue of an exhibition. Baltimore, 1972] 87 p. illus. (part col.) 26 cm. "An issue of the Baltimore Museum of Art Record, v. 3, no. 1, 1972." Includes bibliographical references. [N5220.M54B34 1972] 74-171020
1. May, Saidie Adler, 1879-1951—Art collections. 2. Art—Exhibitions. I. Baltimore. Museum of Art. Record, v. 3, no. 1. II. Title.

BAUDELAIRE, Charles Pierre, 1821-1867. 707.4'043'61
Art in Paris 1845-1862; salons and other exhibitions reviewed by Charles Baudelaire. Translated and edited by Jonathan Mayne. London, New York, Phaidon [1970, c1965] xiv, 241 p. illus., ports. 25 cm. (Phaidon paperback) Includes bibliographical references. [N5064.B313 1970] 71-21797 3.95 (U.S.)
1. Art—Exhibition. 2. Paris. Salon. 3. Art—France. I. Mayne, Jonathan, ed. II. Title.

BAUDELAIRE, Charles Pierre, 1821-1867. 707.4
Art in Paris, 1845-1862; salons and other exhibitions reviewed by Charles Baudelaire. Translated and edited by Jonathan Mayne [London] Phaidon Publishers; distributed by New York Graphic Society Publishers, Greenwich, Conn. [1965] xiv. 241 p. illus., facsim., ports. 26 cm. "Bibliographical note": p. xiii. Bibliographical references included in footnotes. [N5064.B313] 65-4692
1. Art — Exhibitions. 2. Paris. Salon. 3. Art — France. I. Mayne, Jonathan, ed. II. Title.

BOSTON. Institute of Contemporary Art. 759.06
The sources of modern painting. New York, Arno Press [1969] 107 p. illus. 27 cm. (Arno series of contemporary art, no. 31) Loan exhibition held at the Museum of Fine Arts, Boston, March 2-Apr. 9, 1939. Reprint of the 1939 ed. [N5020.B6M62 1969] 79-91372
1. Art—Exhibitions. I. Boston. Museum of Fine Arts. II. Title. BIP

BRAUER, Erich, 1929- 759.39
Brauer: oils, gouaches, watercolours, and etchings. [New York, Marlborough Gallery, 1971] 46 p. illus. (part col.) 30 cm. "Cat. no. 290." Exhibition held at Marlborough Gallery, New York, Sept. 1971. Errata slip inserted. [N6811.5.B7M3] 71-198394
I. Marlborough Gallery. II. Title.

BROOKLYN Institute of Arts and Sciences. Museum. 338.4'3745'10973
The Louis E. Stern collection; a special exhibition held at the Brooklyn Museum, from 25 September, 1962 through 10 March, 1963. Brooklyn, 1962] 24 p. illus., port. 23 cm. Cover title. [N5220.S79] 63-2412

1. Art — Exhibitions. 2. Art — Private collections. I. Stern, Louis E., 1886-1962. II. Title.

BROWN, Milton Wolf, 1911- 707.4
The story of the Armory show. Joseph H. Hirshhorn Foundation; dist. by New York Graphic Soc. [Greenwich, Conn., 1963] 320p. plates, ports., facsims. 24cm. Includes an account of the Intl. exhibition of modern art (1913) sponsored by the Assn. of Amer. Painters and Sculptors, and a catalogue raisonne. Bibl. 63-13496 5.50
1. Art—Exhibitions. I. Association of American Painters and Sculptors, New York. II. Title. III. Title: The Armory show. IV. Title: International exhibition of modern art. **BIP**

BROWN University. Dept. of Art. 708.145'1
Herbert and Nannette Rothschild collection. An exhibition in celebration of the seventy-fifth anniversary of the founding of Pembroke College in Brown University. October 7-November 6, 1966, Annmary Brown Memorial, Brown University; Museum of Art, Rhode Inland School of Design. Providence [1966] 1 v. (unpaged) illus. (part col.) 26 cm. Jointly sponsored by the Dept. of Art, Brown University, and the Museum of Art, Rhode Island School of Design. Catalogue by George Downing, and Daniel Robbins. [N5020.P676] 66-29131
1. Art—Exhibitions. 2. Art—Private collections. I. Rothschild, Herbert. II. Rothschild, Nannette. III. Robbins, Daniel. IV. Downing, George Elliot. V. Brown University. Annmary Brown Memorial. VI. Rhode Island School of Design, Providence. Museum of Art. VII. Brown University. Pembroke College. **BIP**

BUFFALO Fine Arts Academy. 709.04
Contemporary art--acquisitions. 1954/57- [Buffalo] v. illus. (part col.) 26cm. [N525.A52] 58-1641
1. Art—Exhibitions. I. Title.

BUFFALO Fine Arts Academy. 708.14'7
Paintings, sculpture, drawings, prints, collected by A. Conger Goodyear. [Exhibition] April 30-June 5, 1966, Albright-Knox Art Gallery, Buffalo, New York. [Buffalo, 1966] 20 p. illus. 25 cm. On cover: A. Conger Goodyear, 1877-1964. [N5020.B9734] 68-2339
1. Art—Exhibitions. 2. Art—Private collections. I. Goodyear, Anson Conger, 1877-1964. II. Title.

BUFFALO Fine Arts Academy. 707.4
Western New York exhibition. [Catalog] Buffalo, Buffalo Fine Arts Academy, Albright Art Gallery. v. illus. 26cm. annual. [N5020.B955] 54-24030
1. Art— Exhibitions. I. Title.

CALIFORNIA. University. Art Dept. 707.4
Art from Ingres to Pollock; painting and sculpture since neoclassicism: an exhibition inaugurating Alfred L. Kroeber Hall and the galleries of the Art Department of the University of California, Berkeley, March 6-April 3, 1960. [Berkeley, University of California, 1960] 59p. illus. (part col.) 28cm. [N5020.B29] 60-63949
1. Art—Exhibitions. I. Title.

CALIFORNIA. University, Irvine. Art Gallery. 769.9794
Bacon, Balthus, Dubuffet, Giacometti, Morandi; paintings and drawings. [Irvine, 1966] 36 p. illus. (part col.) 23 cm. Cover title: Five Europeans. Introduction signed: John Coplans. Exhibition held at the Art Gallery, University of California, Irvine, May 17th to June 12th, 1966. [N5020.I75] 67-63057
1. Art—Exhibitions. I. Coplans, John. II. Title.

CALIFORNIA. University, Santa Barbara. Art Galleries. 730'.9794
The Institute of Creative Arts: a traveling exhibition of painting and sculpture by members of the Institute of Creative Arts of the University of California. Organized by the Art Galleries, University of California, Santa Barbara. [Santa Barbara, c1969] [49] p. (chiefly illus. (part col.)) 22 x 23 cm. Catalogue. [N330.C25C3] 71-626050
1. California. University. Institute of Creative Arts. 2. Art—Exhibitions. I. Title.

CALIFORNIA. University, Santa Barbara. Art Galleries. 707.4
A selection of paintings, drawings, collages and sculpture from the Collection of Mr. and Mrs. Billy Wilder. [Santa Barbara? 1966] 38 p. illus. (part col.) 22 x 25 cm. Exhibition held at the Art Gallery, University of California, Santa Barbara, Oct. 11-Nov. 13, 1966, and sponsored by the Committee on Arts and Lectures. Introduction by H. J. Seldis. [N5220.W738C3] 67-65132
1. Wilder, Billy, 1906- —Art collections. 2. Wilder, Billy, Mrs.—Art collections. 3. Art—Exhibitions. I. California. University, Santa Barbara. Committee on Arts and Lectures. II. Title.

CALIFORNIA. University. University at Los Angeles. Art Galleries. 708.1794'94
From the Ludington Collection; an exhibition, sponsored by the UCLA Art Council in collaboration with the UCLA Art Galleries, Dickson Art Center, University of California, Los Angeles, March 16 to April 12, 1964. [Los Angeles, 1964] 43 p. illus. (part col.) 28 cm. [N5220.L77C3] 73-271763
1. Ludington, Wright S.—Art collections. 2. Art—Exhibitions. I. California. University. University at Los Angeles. Art Council. II. Dickson Art Center. III. Title.

CAPITOL Hill Community Council, Washington, D.C. 707.4
Community art show: organization guide and illustrated catalog. Based on the first annual open international fine art exhibition 'The Old Market Gallery Art Show,' held in Washington, D.C., May, 1961. Pub. in cooperation with Intl. Pubns. 1026 20 St., N. W. Washington, D.C., [c.1962] 111p. illus. 26cm. 62-15240 5.00, pap., plastic binding
1. Art—Exhibitions. I. Title. II. Title: The Old Market Gallery Art Show.

CHATTERTON, Clarence K., 1880- 759.13
The works of C. K. Chatterton. [New York, Chapellier Galleries, 1970] [51] p. illus., group port. 26 cm. Label on t.p.: Supplied by Worldwide Books, inc., Boston. Includes bibliographical references. [ND237.C485A58] 70-18625
I. Chapellier Galleries. II. Title.

CINCINNATI. Art Museum. 708.17177
The Lehman collection, New York. The Cincinnati Art Museum [exhibition] May 8 to July 5, 1959. [Cincinnati, 1959] 343 p. (p. [45]-[338] illus. (part col.)) 26 cm. "Catalog": p. [13]-43. [N5220.L39] 60-570
1. Lehman, Robert, 1892- —Art collections. 2. Art—Exhibitions. I. Title.

CINCINNATI Institute of Fine Arts. Taft Museum. 707'.4'017178
Best of 50. Cincinnati : Taft Museum, c1977. [87] p. : col. ill. ; 21 x 23 cm. Exhibition held at the Taft Museum Mar. 24-May 8, 1977 to commemorate its 50th anniversary. [N5020.C63C563] 77-70784
1. Art—Exhibitions. I. Title.

CLEVELAND Museum of Art. 708.171
In memoriam: Leonard C. Hanna, Jr. [Catalogue. Celveland] 1958. 1v. (unpaged, chiefly illus. (part col.)) 23cm. [N552.A63] 58-1662
1. Art—Exhibitions. 2. Art—Private collections. I. Hanna, Leonard Colton. II. Title.

CLEVELAND Museum of Art. 707.4
Some contemporary works of art. [Cleveland] 1958. 1v. (unpaged) illus. 26cm. Includes Catalog. [N5020.C734] 58-49039
1. Art—Exhibitions. I. Title.

COLLECTORS Club of Minnesota. 704.9489
Collectors Club exhibition, October 7-27, 1957. Sponsored by the Center Arts Council and the Walker Art Center. [Minneapolis] Center Arts Council [1957] unpaged. 26 cm. [N5020.M56] 63-2669
1. Art — Exhibitions. 2. Art — Private collections. I. Center Arts Council (Walker Art Center) II. Walker Art Center, Minneapolis. III. Title.

COLUMBUS Gallery of Fine Arts, Columbus, O. 750'.74'017157
From the Collection of Ferdinand Howald: 19th and 20th century paintings—School of Paris, Renaissance paintings, Italian and Middle Eastern ceramics; given to the Columbus Gallery of Fine Arts, 1931. [Columbus, 1969] [28] p. illus., port. 22 x 27 cm. Pref. signed: Mahonri Sharp Young. Catalogue of an exhibition held Oct. 10-Dec. 31, 1969. [N5220.H67] 70-277663
1. Howald, Ferdinand—Art collections. 2. Art—Exhibitions. I. Young, Mahonri Sharp, 1911- II. Title.

COPLANS, John. 707'.4'019
Serial imagery. [Pasadena, Calif.] Pasadena Art Museum [1968] 144 p. illus. (part col.), ports. 24 x 23 cm. Catalog of an exhibition sponsored by the Art Alliance to be held at the Pasadena Art Museum, Sept. 17-Oct. 27, 1968; Henry Art Gallery, University of Washington, Seattle, Nov. 17-Dec. 22, 1968; Santa Barbara Museum of Art, Jan. 25-Feb. 23, 1969. Bibliography: p. 138. [N5020.P34] 68-56613
1. Art—Exhibitions. 2. Composition (Art) I. Pasadena, Calif. Art Museum. Art Alliance. II. Henry Art Gallery. III. Santa Barbara, Calif. Museum of Art. IV. Title.

CORCORAN Gallery of Art, Washington, D. C. 708.153
Privately owned; a selection of works of art from collections in the Washington area, February tenth-March thirtieth, 1952. Washington [1952] 64 p. illus. 28 cm. [N5020.C77] 52-3172
1. Art—Exhibitions. 2. Art—Washington, D. C. I. Title.

COUNCIL of Europe. Cultural Affairs Division 707.4094
Record of European art exhibitions. [Strasbourg] iv. (various p.) 17cm. annual. English and French, the latter inverted with separate t.p. [N5050.C6] 66-6767 price unreported pap.,
1. Art—Exhibitions. I. Title.
Available from The World Wide Art Catalogue Ctr., 250 W. 57th St., New York, N.Y., 10019.

CROCKER Art Gallery, Sacramento, Calif. 707'.4'019454
The collecting muse : a selection from the Nathalie and Hugo Weisgall Collection. Sacramento, Calif. : E. B. Crocker Art Gallery, 1975. 68 p. : ill. ; 23 cm. Catalog of an exhibition held at the E. B. Crocker Art Gallery. [N5220.W58C76 1975] 75-25215
1. Weisgall, Nathalie—Art collections. 2. Weisgall, Hugo—Art collections. 3. Art—Exhibitions. I. Title.

DALLAS. Museum of Fine Arts. 759.13'074'01642812
The M. P. Potamkin Collection. [Dallas, 1970] [12] p. 24 plates. 26 cm. Catalogue of a loan exhibition, Jan. 28-Mar. 8, 1970. [N5220.P72D3] 70-25288
1. Potamkin, Meyer P., 1909- —Art collections. 2. Art—Exhibitions. I. Title.

DETROIT. Institute of Arts. 709.774
Annual exhibition for Michigan artists. [Detroit] v. illus. 24 cm. [N5020.D64] 50-16717
1. Art—Exhibitions. 2. Art—Michigan. I. Title.

DETROIT. Institute of Arts. 708.174
The French in America, 1520-1880; an exhibition organized by the Detroit Institute of Arts to commemorate the founding of Detroit by Antoine de Lamothe cadillac in the year 1701 Detroit] 1951. 207 p. illus., maps. 25 cm. Bibliography: p. 204-206. [N5020.D655] 51-8898
1. Cadillac, Antoine de la Mothe, 1656 (ca.)-1730. 2. Art—Exhibitions. 3. Art—Detroit—Catalogs. I. Title.

DETROIT. Institute of Arts. 708.174'34
The Robert Hudson Tannahill bequest to the Detroit Institute of Arts; a catalogue issued on the occasion of the exhibition "A collector's treasure: the Tannahill bequest", May 13-August 13, 1970. [Edited by Graham Hood. Detroit, 1970] 209 p. illus. (part col.) 29 cm. [N5220.T35] 71-122774
1. Tannahill, Robert Hudson—Art collections. 2. Art—Exhibitions. I. Hood, Graham, 1936- ed. **BIP**

THE Discerning eye : 708'.144'4
[catalogue] : Radcliffe collectors' exhibition, Fogg Art Museum [Oct. 9-Nov. 24, 1974]. [Cambridge, Mass.] : Fogg Art Museum, [1974] [124] p. : chiefly ill. ; 25 cm. Addendum slip inserted. [N5020.C24F632] 74-17603
1. Radcliffe College—Alumnae. 2. Art—Exhibitions. 3. Art—Private collections—United States. I. Harvard University. William Hayes Fogg Art Museum.

ETROG, Sorel, 1933- 730'.924
The painted constructions 1952-1960 of Sorel Etrog. By Theodore Allen Heinrich. Berne, Staempfli, 1968. 131 p. illus. 24 cm. [NB249.E8H4] 77-414938 42.00
I. Heinrich, Theodore Allen. II. Title.

FONSECA, Gonzalo, 1922- 730'.924
Gonzalo Fonseca: recent works. [Exhibition] Jewish Museum, New York City, Nov. 25 through Jan. 3, 1971. [New York, 1970] 36 p. (chiefly illus., port.) 26 cm. [N6729.F6A46] 70-145800
I. Jewish Theological Seminary of America. Jewish Museum. II. Title.

FREER Gallery of Art, Washington, D.C. 709'.5'0740153
Fiftieth anniversary exhibition. Washington, Smithsonian Institution, 1973- v. illus. (part col.) 31 cm. Contents.Contents.— —v. 2. Chinese figure painting.—v. 3. Ceramics from the world of Islam. Includes bibliographical references. [N5020.W52F733 1973] 73-176508
1. Art—Exhibitions. I. Title.

GRAVES, Algernon. 707'.4'02
A century of loan exhibitions, 1813-1912. New York, B. Franklin [196-?] 5 v. (2610 p.) 26 cm. (Burt Franklin bibliography and reference series, #69) Reprint of the 1913-15 ed. [N5051.G72] 70-6362
1. Art—Exhibitions. 2. Art—Gt. Brit. I. Title. **BIP**

THE Guennol 707'.4'01471
Collection : [exhibition] / edited by Ida Ely Rubin. New York : Metropolitan Museum of Art, c1975- v. : ill. ; 31 cm. Held at the Metropolitan Museum of Art in 1969. Includes bibliographical references. [N5220.M39G83] 75-33291 ISBN 0-87099-144-2 : 18.50
1. Martin, Alastair Bradley—Art collections. 2. Martin, Edith—Art collections. 3. Art—Exhibitions. I. Rubin, Ida Ely. II. New York (City). Metropolitan Museum of Art. **BIP**

HARVARD University. William Hayes Fogg Art Museum. 708.144'4
Genville L. Winthrop; retrospective for a collector, Fogg Museum of Art, Cambridge, Massachusetts, January 23-March 31, 1969. Cambridge [1969] xix, 261 p. illus., port. 22 cm. "This catalogue has been prepared as a Museum course project by Dorothy W. Gillerman, Gridley McKim, and Joan R. Mertens." "Grenville L. Winthrop and his bequest: a brief bibliography of publications": p. xviii-xix. [N5220.W782H3] 77-76429
1. Winthrop, Grenville Lindall, 1864-1943—Art collections. 2. Art—Exhibitions. I. Gillerman, Dorothy W. II. McKim, Gridley. III. Mertens, Joan R. IV. Title.

HARVARD University. William Hayes Fogg Art Museum. 707'.4'014461
Selections from the collections of Freddy and Regina T. Homburger; a loan exhibition. [Cambridge, Mass.] Harvard University, Fogg Art Museum [1971] ix, 190 p. illus. 22 cm. Held Apr, 2-24, 1971. [N5220.H63H3] 75-152744
1. Homburger, Freddy—Art collections. 2. Homburger, Regina T.—Art collections. 3. Art—Exhibitions. I. Title.

HECKSCHER Museum. 750'.74'014725
Salute to small museums. [Huntington, N.Y., 1970] 96 p. illus. (part col.) 28 cm. Catalog of an exhibition held May 9-June 21, 1970. [N5020.H8H47] 77-29243
1. Art—Exhibitions. 2. Art—United States—Galleries and museums. I. Title.

HORMATS, Bess. 709'.24
Retrospective for a critic: Duncan Phillips. "The critical writing of Duncan Phillips" and catalogue. Pref. [by] George Levitine. Introd. [by] William H. Gerdts. Foreword [by] J. William Fulbright. [College Park, University of Maryland, 1969] viii, 61 p. illus., port. 26 cm. An exhibition of paintings, sculpture, and watercolors from the Phillips Collection relating to the critical writing of Duncan Phillips, Feb. 12 through Mar. 16, 1969, University of Maryland Art Dept. and Art Gallery, J. Millard Tawes Fine Arts Center, College Park, Md. Includes bibliographical references. "The published writing of Duncan Phillips": p. 27-31. Bibliography: p. 32. [N5020.C7364] 79-625394
1. Phillips, Duncan, 1886-1966. 2. Art—Exhibitions. I. Phillips Collection, Washington, D.C. II. Maryland. University. Dept. of Art. III. Maryland. University. Art Gallery. IV. Title.

HOUSTON, Tex. University of St. Thomas. Art Dept. 707.4
Through the porthole. [Exhibition] July-October 1965. Houston [1965] 1 v. (unpaged) illus., plates. 23 cm. [N5020.H66] 68-38375
1. Art—Exhibitions. I. Title.

HUDSON River Museum. 750'.74'0147277
Art in Westchester from private collections. [Exhibition] September 28-November 2, 1969. [Yonkers, 1969?] [29] p. (chiefly illus.) 27 cm. [N5215.H8] 70-279676
1. Art—Exhibitions. 2. Art—Private collections—Westchester, N.Y. I. Title.

INDIANAPOLIS Museum of Art. 708'.172'52 s
Recent accessions, 1966-1972: New treasures, a six year retrospective. A bulletin/catalogue prepared for the exhibition, October 19 to December 10, 1972. [Indianapolis, 1972] 129 p. illus. 26 cm. (Its Bulletin/catalogue new ser. v. 1, no. 1-2) Includes bibliographical references. [N577.A4 n.s., vol. 1, no. 1-2] [N5020.I5] 708'.172'52 76-354030
1. Art—Exhibitions. I. Title. II. Series.

INDIANAPOLIS Museum of Art. 708.1471
Treasures from the Metropolitan; catalogue of the inaugural exhibition of the Indianapolis Museum of Art, October 25, 1970-January 3, 1971. [Indianapolis, 1970] 206 p. illus. 26 cm. [N5020.I5A63] 71-140929
1. Art—Exhibitions. I. New York (City). Metropolitan Museum of Art. II. Title.

IOWA. University. Museum of Art. 707'.4'0177655
An artist collects : selections from five continents : [exhibition] the University of Iowa Museum of Art, Iowa City, Iowa, March 23, 1975, through May 3, 1975 / [selected by] Ulfert Wilke. [Iowa City] : The Museum, [1975] 147 p. : ill. (some col.) ; 29 cm. Errata sheet inserted. [N5220.W739158 1975] 75-3924
1. Wilke, Ulfert, 1907- —Art collections. 2. Art—Exhibitions. I. Title.

*KRANNERT Art Museum, Champaign, Illinois. 708.9493
Contemporary American Painting and sculpture, 1974 Urbana, Univ. of Illinois Press, 1974. 135 p. illus. 26 cm. Catalogue of an exhibition held March 10-April 21, 1974. [N5020] A48 ISBN 0-252-00456-6 6.95 (pbk.)
1. Art—Exhibitions. I. Title.

LIGHT (R. M.) and Company. 381'.45'76
Venice Committee—Boston Chapter presents an exhibition of works of art donated to the Venice Committee to be sold for the restoration of the Scuola grande dei carmini; exhibition at the Fogg Art Museum, March 5th through 14th, 1971 ... catalogue. [Boston, 1971] 40 p. illus. 28 cm. "Offered for sale by R. M. Light & Co., Inc., acting as agent for the Venice Committee of the International Fund for Monuments." [N5020.B6F64 1971] 74-157559
1. Art—Exhibitions. I. International Fund for Monuments. Venice Committee. Boston Chapter.

LONG Beach, Calif. Museum of Art. 708'.9493
New acquisitions for the now and future museum. [Long Beach, Calif., 1973] [35] p. illus. 22 cm. Catalog of an exhibition held Feb. 18-Mar. 18, 1973. [N5020.L66L665] 73-76669
1. Art—Exhibitions. I. Title.

LOS Angeles Co., Calif. Museum, Los Angeles. 708.194
The Balch collection and Old masters from Los Angeles collections, assembled in memory of Mr. and Mrs. Allan C. Balch. Los Angeles County Museum. March 26 through April 30, 1944. [Los Angeles, 1944] [62] p. illus. 26 cm. "Catalogue prepared and edited by James Normile." -- p. [4] [N5020.L62] 45-4892
1. Art — Exhibitions. I. Balch, Allan Christopher, 1864-1943. II. Normile, James III. Title.

LOS Angeles Co., Calif. Museum of Art, Los Angeles. 730'.074'019494
Man came this way; objects from the Phil Berg Collection. Catalog and commentary by Phil Berg. [Los Angeles, 1971] 211 p. illus. (part col.), maps 22 x 28 cm. Catalog of the exhibition held Mar. 9-May 30, 1971 at the Los Angeles County Museum of Art. Bibliography: p. 209-211. [N5220.B43L6] 70-152278 ISBN 0-87587-043-0
1. Berg, Phil—Art collections. 2. Art—Exhibitions. I. Title.

LOS Angeles Co., Calif. Museum of Art, Los Angeles. 708'.194'94
X [i.e. Ten], a decade of collecting, 1965-1975 : [exhibition], Los Angeles County Museum of Art, April 8-June 29, 1975. Los Angeles : The Museum, [1975] 247 p. : ill. (some col.) ; 26 cm. Includes bibliographical references. [N5020.L68L67] 74-25968 ISBN 0-87587-064-3
1. Art—Exhibitions.

LOS Angeles Co., Calif. Otis Art Institute, Los Angeles. 707'.4'019493
The taste of angels; the artist in industry collects. [Exhibition] March 24 through May 8, 1966, The Otis Art Institute of Los Angeles County Galleries. [Los Angeles, 1966] [74] p. (chiefly illus.) 25 x 25 cm. [N5215.L67] 74-151086
1. Art—Exhibitions. 2. Art—Collectors and collecting—United States. I. Title.

MAINE State Museum. 707'.4'01416
Freddy and Regina T. Homburger Art Collection; [loan exhibition. Augusta, 1971] 1 v. (unpaged) illus. 21 x 27 cm. Cover title. [N5220.H63M34] 73-156895
1. Homburger, Freddy—Art collections. 2. Homburger, Regina T.—Art collections. 3. Art—Exhibitions. I. Title.

MASTERS of seven centuries: paintings and drawings from the 14th to 20th century; loan exhibition for the benefit of the Wellesley College Faculty Salary Advancement Fund, March 1 to 31, 1962. New York, Wildenstein [1962] 56 p. illus. 24 cm. [N5020.N7W54] 73-157733 759'.074'01471
1. Art—Exhibitions. I. Wellesley College Faculty Salary Advancement Fund. II. Wildenstein and Company, inc., New York.

MILWAUKEE. Art Center. 708.175'95
The Collection of Mrs. Harry Lynde Bradley. [Milwaukee, 1968] 186 p. illus. (part col.) 26 cm. Catalog of Mrs. Bradley's collection, most of which was included in an exhibition held at the Milwaukee Art Center Oct. 25, 1968, to Feb. 23, 1969. [N5220.B77] 70-2725
1. Bradley, Harry Lynde, Mrs.—Art collections. 2. Art—Exhibitions. I. Title.

MINNEAPOLIS. Institute of Arts. 708.176579
Fiftieth anniversary exhibition, 1915-1965. November 4, 1965--January 2, 1966 Minneapolis, 1966] 1 v. (unpaged) illus. 29 cm. [N5020.M62] 66-5968
1. Art — Exhibitions. 2. Art — Minneapolis. I. Title.

MINNEAPOLIS. Institute of Arts. 760'.074'0176579
The Jones Collection; the bequests of Herschel V. and Tessie Jones [exhibited at] the Minneapolis Institute of Arts, December 12, 1968-February 9, 1969. [Minneapolis, c1968] 1 v. (chiefly illus.) 28 cm. [N5220.J74M5] 68-59312
1. Jones, Herschel Vespasian, 1861-1928—Art collections. 2. Jones, Tessie—Art collections. 3. Art—Exhibitions. I. Title.

MINNEAPOLIS. Institute of Arts. 769'.074'0176579
The Minnich Collection: the Collection of Dwight and Helen Minnich. [Minneapolis, 1970] 1 v. (unpaged) illus. 24 cm. Catalog of the exhibition held Sept. 24-Nov. 8, 1970. Includes bibliography. [N5220.M9M5] 70-135309
1. Minnich, Dwight Elmer, 1890-1965—Art collections. 2. Minnich, Helen Benton—Art collections. 3. Art—Exhibitions. I. Title.

MINNESOTA. University. University Gallery. 708.1'76'579
The Hylton A. Thomas Collection; paintings, drawings, prints, furniture and decorative arts objects bequeathed to the University Gallery, University of Minnesota. [Prepared by Charles Helsell] Minneapolis [1971] 69 p. illus. 21 x 21 cm. Catalog of an exhibition held April 1 through May 16, 1971, University Gallery, University of Minnesota. Errata slip inserted. [N5220.T48M5] 74-198471
1. Thomas, Hylton, 1912-1969—Art collections. 2. Art—Exhibitions. I. Helsell, Charles. II. Title.

MINT Museum of Art. 750'.74'015676
North Carolinians collect. [Charlotte, N.C., 1971] 48 p. 32 plates (2 col.) 27 cm. Catalog of the exhibition held Sept. 12.-Nov. 7, 1971. [N5020.C47M56] 74-177905
1. Art—Exhibitions. 2. Art—Collectors and collecting—North Carolina. I. Title.

NEBRASKA. University. Sheldon Memorial Art Gallery. 708.178'411
The Howard S. Wilson memorial collection. [Catalogue of exhibition held Oct. 11 through Nov. 13, 1966. Lincoln, Printed by the F. Arnold Print. Co., 1966?] [48] p. illus. (1 col.), ports. 20 x 24 cm. Cover title. "First review in one place of all the paintings, drawings, and sculpture acquired [from 1959] to date." [N582.L5A57] 68-1052
1. Wilson, Howard Stebbins, 1894-1958—Art collections. 2. Art—Exhibitions. I. Wilson, Howard Stebbins, 1894-1958.

*NEOGY, Prithwish 709.1969
Nineteen painters and sculptors photographs by Francis Haar with an introduction by Jean Charlot. Honolulu, State Foundation on culture & the arts and the University Press of Hawaii [1974] xviii., 150 p. illus (part col.) 29 cm x 28 cm. (Artists of Hawaii, vol. 1) [N6530] 74-78861 ISBN 0-8248-0338-8 25.00
I. Title.

NEW Orleans Museum of Art. 707'.4'016335
New Orleans collects; a selection of works of art owned by New Orleanians. [New Orleans, 1971] [96] p. illus. 25 cm. Catalog of an exhibition held Nov. 14, 1971-Jan. 9, 1972. [N5215.N37] 79-183072
1. Art—Exhibitions. 2. Art—Collectors and collecting—New Orleans. I. Title.

NEW York (City). Metropolitan Museum of Art. 708.1471
Masterpieces of fifty centuries; [exhibition] Introd. by Kenneth Clark. [1st ed.] New York, Dutton [1970] 332, [4] p. illus. (part col.) 26 cm. Bibliography: p. [333]-[336] [N5020.N7A46 1970] 76-122794 12.50
1. Art—Exhibitions. I. Clark, Kenneth McKenzie, Baron Clark, 1903- II. Title.

NEW York (City). Metropolitan Museum of Art. 708'.147'1
Patterns of collecting : selected acquisitions, 1965-1975 : explanatory texts : an exhibition, December 6, 1975 through March 23, 1976, the Metropolitan Museum of Art. [New York] : The Museum, c1975. 50 p. : ill. ; 19 x 22 cm. [N5020.N43 1975] 76-354792
1. Art—Exhibitions. I. Title.

NEW York (City). Museum of Modern Art. 745.2
Machine art, March 6 to April 30, 1934. Reprint ed. New York, Published for the Museum of Modern Art by Arno Press, 1969 [c1934] [112] p. illus., plates. 27 cm. Bibliography: p. [18] [N8218.N4 1969] 77-86423
1. Art—Exhibitions. 2. Machinery—Exhibitions. 3. Art and industry. I. Title.

NEW York. Metropolitan Museum of Art. 708.147
The Lewisohn collection; a catalogue of the paintings, water colors and drawings, prints, and sculpture shown in a special exhibition, November 2 -- December 2, 1951, before the dispersal of bequests to various museums and galleries. New York [1951] 86 p. illus. 19 x 26 cm. [N5020.N432] 52-1035
1. Lewisohn, Sam Adolph, 1884- 2. Art — Exhibitions. I. Title.

NEW York. Museum of Modern Art. 707.4
The new decade; 22 European painters and sculptors. Edited by Andrew Carnduff Ritchie, with statements by the artists. The Museum of Modern Art, New York, in collaboration with the Minneapolis Institute of Arts [and others. New York, 1955] 111p. illus., ports. 25cm. 'Catalogue of the exhibition': p. 107-109. Bibilography:p. 110-111. [N5020.N44 1955] 55-2214
1. Art— Exhibitions. 2. Artists. I. Ritchie, Andrew Carnduff, ed. II. Title.

NORTH Carolina. Museum of Art, Raleigh. 707.4
Carolina Charter tercentenary exhibition, March 23-April 28, 1963. Raleigh, N.C. Author [1963] 146p. illus. 26cm. Bibl. 63-64063 1.00 pap.,
1. Art—Exhibitions. 2. Portraits—Exhibitions. 3. Art—North Carolina. I. Title. BIP

NORTH Carolina. Museum of Art, Raleigh. 707.4
Masterpieces of art; in memory of William R. Valentiner, 1880-1958, representing his achievements during fifty years of service in American museums. [Exhibition] North Carolina Museum of Art, Raleigh. April 6-May 17, 1959. [Raleigh, 1959] xxvi, 324p. illus., plates (part col.) port. 23x26cm. 'A bibliography of the writings of William R. Valentiner, by May Davis Hill': p.297-319. [N5020.R3] 59-63082
1. Valentiner, Wilheim Reinhold, 1880-1958. 2. Art—Exhibitions. I. Title.

NORTH Carolina. Museum of Art, Raleigh. 708.156
North Carolina collects. [Raleigh 1967?] [13] p., 274 illus. 26 cm. "[Catalogue of] a loan exhibition of North Carolina owned art objects, October 10-29, 1967." [N5020.R32] 68-63656
1. Art—Exhibitions. 2. Art—North Carolina. I. Title. BIP

NORTH Carolina. Museum of Art, Raleigh. 704'.361
Robert F. Phifer Collection; [exhibition] March 31-May 13, 1973. [Raleigh, 1973] 97 p. illus. 26 cm. [N5220.P48N67 1973] 73-622791 ISBN 0-88259-069-3 3.00 (pbk.)
1. Phifer, Robert Fulenwider, 1849-1928—Art collections. 2. Art—Exhibitions. BIP

NORTH Carolina. Museum of Art, Raleigh. 708.15'6
Selections from the collection of Mr. and Mrs. Harry L. Dalton, September 19-October 10, 1965, North Carolina Museum of Art, Raleigh. [Raleigh, 1966?] 1 v. (unpaged) illus. (part col.) 26 cm. Catalog of the exhibition. [N5020.R34] 66-64856
1. Dalton, Harry L. 2. Art—Exhibitions. I. Title. BIP

NORTHERN Arizona University. Art Gallery. 708.1
The colleges and universities collect. [Exhibition] May 1-25, 1966. [Flagstaff, Printed by Northland Press, 1966] 97 p. illus., ports. 23 cm. [N5020.N974] 67-65390
1. Art—Exhibitions. 2. Art patronage. 3. Art in universities and colleges. I. Title.

OAKLAND, Calif. Art Museum. 338.4'3745'10973
The art collection of Billy Pearson; a picture album of objects selected from the exhibition held March 6 through April 1, 1959. [Oakland, 1959] unpaged. illus. 23cm. [N5220.P4] 61-40768

1. Art—Exhibitions. 2. Art—Private collections. I. Pearson, Billy, 1920- II. Title.

OAKLAND Museum. 750'.74'019466
Art treasures in California; an exhibition of master paintings from museums and public collections in California, presented to open the great hall, November 29 through December 31, 1969. [Oakland, Calif., 1969?] [44] p. illus. 26 cm. [N5020.O15O32] 76-291543
1. Art—Exhibitions. 2. Art—California. I. Title.

PARKE-BERNET 380.1'45'7 s
Galleries, inc., New York.
Chinese porcelain, Italian majolica, European porcelain, Gothic & Renaissance sculpture, works of art, Italian Renaissance & French furniture, French 18th century decorations, old master paintings, oriental carpets and rugs, Gothic & 18th century tapestries and tapestry suites. Property of the Norton Simon Foundation, formerly in the inventory of Duveen Brothers, New York & old master drawings and paintings from the private Collection of Norton Simon. Public auction Friday and Saturday, May 7 and 8 at 2 p.m. New York, 1971. 217 p. illus. (part. col.) 28 cm. "Sale number 3204." Errata slip inserted. "Price list 3204, Simon works of art & furniture ..." ([3] p. 22 cm.) in pocket. [Z999.P23 no. 3204] [N5220] 707'.4'01471 72-195333
1. Simon, Norton—Art collections. 2. Art—Exhibitions. I. Norton Simon Foundation.

PEARLMAN, Henry, 1895- 707.4
A loan exhibition of paintings, watercolors, and sculpture from the collection of Mr. and Mrs. Henry Pearlman, for the benefit of Greenwich House (Greenwich House Music School) New York, January 27-February 21, 1959. New York, M. Knoedler [1959] 92p. illus. (part col.) 28cm. Includes bibliographical references. [N5020.N4165 1959] 59-7440
1. Art—Exhibitions. 2. Art, French—Exhibitions. 3. Art—Private collections. I. Pearlman, Rose (Freed) 1901- II. Greenwich House, New York. Music School. III. Title.

PETIT, Jacques, 1925- 759.4
J. Petit: recent works, December, 1971. Chicago, R. S. Johnson-International Gallery [1971] 16 p. illus. (part col.) 25 cm. [ND553.P443J6] 79-179682
I. Johnson (R. S.)-International Gallery.

PHILADELPHIA Museum 708'.148'11
of Art.
Gifts to mark a century : an exhibition celebrating the centennial of the Philadelphia Museum of Art, 18 February to 20 March, 1977, Philadelphia Museum of Art. Philadelphia : The Museum, c1977. [96] p. : chiefly ill. (some col.) ; 24 cm. [N5020.P45P456] 76-56646
1. Art—Exhibitions. I. Title.

PITTSBURGH. Carnegie 709.01
Institute. Dept. of Fine Arts.
Exotic art, from ancient and primitive civilizations; collection of Jay C. Leff. Dept. of Fine Arts, Carnegie Institute, Pittsburgh, Pa., 15 Oct. 1959 to 3 Jan. 1960. [Text by Walter A. Fairservis, Jr. Pittsburgh? 1959] 130p. illus., col. plate, fold, maps. 23cm. Catalog of exhibition of the Leff collection. [N5220.L37] 60-1234
1. Art—Exhibitions. 2. Art. Primitive — Exhibitions. 3. Art—Private collections. I. Leff, Jay C. II. Title.

PRIMITIVE to Picasso; 709
St. Paul's School alumni collect. Concord, N.H. [1968] 168 p. illus. (part col.) 28 cm. Half title: A benefit exhibition for the art program at St. Paul's School. Catalog of an exhibition of works loaned by alumni of St. Paul's School and held at the gallery of M. Knoedler and Company, New York, Dec. 2-21, 1968. Includes bibliographies. [N5215.P7] 72-2440
1. Art—Exhibitions. 2. Art—Private collections—U.S. I. St Paul's School, Concord, N.H. II. Knoedler (M.) and Company, inc.

RHODE Island School of 707.4
Design, Providence. Museum of Art.
Raid the icebox 1 with Andy Warhol; an exhibition selected from the vaults of the Museum of Art, Rhode Island School of Design. [Catalogue by Stephen E. Ostrow. Providence, R.I., 1969] 103 p. illus. (part col.) 23 cm. Catalog of the exhibition held Oct. 29, 1969-Jan. 4, 1970, at the Institute for the Arts, Rice University, Houston; Jan. 17-Feb. 15, 1970, at the Isaac Delgado Museum, New Orleans; and Apr. 23-June 30, 1970, at the Museum of Art, Rhode Island School of Design, Providence. [N5020.P77] 71-100013
1. Art—Exhibitions. I. Warhol, Andy, 1928- II. Ostrow, Stephen E. III. William Marsh Rice University, Houston, Tex. Institute for the Arts. IV. Isaac Delgado Museum of Art, New Orleans. V. Title.

RHODE Island School 760'.074'1452
of Design, Providence. Museum of Art.
Visions & revisions. [Exhibition] Oct. 18-Nov. 24, 1968. [Providence, 1968] 48, xxvi (i.e. lii) p. illus. 22 cm. Introductory text by Stephen E. Ostrow. Issued in folder form, Catalogue attached to front cover, Illustrations to back cover. Each part has special t.p. and separate paging. [N5020.P78] 68-56466
1. Art—Exhibitions. 2. Composition (Art) I. Ostrow, Stephen E. II. Title. BIP

ROSSETTI, William 759.2'074'02132
Michael, 1829-1919.
Notes on the Royal Academy exhibition, 1868. Part I. By Wm. Michael Rossetti. Part II. By Algernon C. Swinburne. London, J. C. Hotten. [New York, AMS Press, 1973] p. Reprint of the 1868 ed. [N5054.R47 1973] 75-144681 ISBN 0-404-05418-8 5.00
1. London. Royal Academy of Arts. 2. Art—Exhibitions. I. Swinburne, Algenon Charles, 1837-1909. II. Title.

RUDER, Celia. 701.8
Size. [Exhibition held at] the Junior Museum, Department of Museum Education, the Art Institute of Chicago. Exhibition by Lois Raasch assisted by Virginia Bath. Text by Celia Ruder. [Chicago, Junior Museum, Art Institute of Chicago, 1966] 21, [32] p. plates. 28 cm. [N5020.C6277] 75-523
1. Art—Exhibitions. 2. Proportion (Art) 3. Composition (Art) I. Raasch, Lois. II. Chicago. Art Institute. Junior Museum. III. Title.

SCHWEITZER Gallery. 750'.74'01471
40th anniversary exhibition; [catalog November, 1970.] New York [1970] 32 p. (chiefly illus. (part col.)) 28 cm. [N8655.N7S34] 76-25347
1. Art—Exhibitions.

SEATTLE. Century 21 707.4
Exposition, 1962.
Masterpieces of art, Fine Arts Pavilion, April 21 to September 4, 1962; catalogue. Seattle World's Fair, April 21 to October 21, 1962. [Seattle, 1962] 164p. illus. 23cm. [N4888 1962.A6] 62-6124
1. Art—Exhibitions. I. Title.

A Selection of nineteenth 709'.4
and twentieth century works from the Hunt Foods and Industries Museum of Art collection. [Irvine? Calif., 1967] 37 p. plates (part col.) 23 cm. Exhibition held at the University of California at Irvine, Davis, and Riverside, and at the Fine Arts Gallery of San Diego, Mar. 7-Oct. 1, 1967. Includes bibliographical references. [N5020.I76] 67-8063
1. Art—Exhibitions. I. Hunt Foods & Industries Museum of Art. II. California. University, Irvine. Art Gallery.

SMITH College. Museum 708.144'23
of Art.
An exhibition in honor of Henry-Russell Hitchcock: Smith College Museum of Art, April 11-April 28, 1968. [Northampton, Mass., 1968] 35 p. illus., port. 23 cm. [N5020.N95] 76-25170
1. Art—Exhibitions. I. Hitchcock, Henry Russell, 1903-

SOLOMON R. Guggenheim 708.17471
Museum, New York
Masterpieces of modern art. [New York, Author, 1965] 75p. illus. (pt. col.) facsims. 28cm. Cover title. Catalog of Exhibition 65/3, Apr.-Sept., 1965. Pub. on the occasion of the first showing of 19th and 20th century masterpieces arr. by courtesy of the Thannhauser Found. [N5020.N643] 65-20810 3.50
1. Art—Exhibitions. 2. Art, Modern—20th cent.—Exhibitions. I. Thannhauser Foundation, New York. II. Title.

THE Splendor of 707'.4'013
Dresden, five centuries of art collecting : an exhibition from the State Art Collections of Dresden, German Democratic Republic : the National Gallery of Art, Washington, June 1-September 4, 1978, the Metropolitan Museum of Art, New York, Oct. 21, 1978-January 13, 1979, the Fine Arts Museums of San Francisco, February 18-May 26, 1979. [New York] : Metropolitan Museum of Art, c1978. 279 p. : ill. (some col) ; 26 cm. Includes bibliographies. [N5020.W52N378] 78-6542 ISBN 0-87099-177-9 : 20.00
1. Dresden. Staatliche Kunstsammlungen—Exhibitions. 2. Art—Exhibitions. I. United States. National Gallery of Art. II. New York (City). Metropolitan Museum of Art. III. Fine Arts Museums of San Francisco.

U.S. National 760'.094'09753
Gallery of Art.
100 European paintings and drawings ; from the Collection of Mr. and Mrs. Leigh B. Block. [Washington? 1967] 1 v. (unpaged) illus. 26 cm. Exhibition held at the National Gallery of Art, May 4-June 11, 1967 and at the Los Angeles County Museum of Art, Sept. 21-Nov. 2, 1967. [N5220.B667U5] 79-605080
1. Block, Leigh B., 1905- —Art collections. 2. Block, Leigh B., Mrs., 1904-—Art collections. 3. Art—Exhibitions. I. Los Angeles Co., Calif. Museum of Art, Los Angeles. II. Title.

VIRGINIA Museum of Fine 707.4
Arts, Richmond.
A brief chronicle of the 25th birthday celebration and catalogue of the anniversary loan exhibition. Treasures in America, at the museum from January 13 to March 5 of 1961. [Richmond 1961] 105 p. illus. (1 mounted col.) plates. 26 cm. [N5020.R5] 61-8784
1. Art — Exhibitions. 2. Art — U.S. I. Title. II. Title: Treasures in America.

WADSWORTH 709'.746'307401463
Atheneum, Hartford.
Exhibition as process : Wadsworth Atheneum, Hartford, Connecticut, Lions Gallery of the Senses, September 14, 1977-January 8, 1977 [i.e. 1978] / participating artists, Andrew J. Coppola ... [et al.]. Hartford : The Museum, c1977. 36 p. : ill. ; 21 cm. [N4396.W3 1977] 77-154116
1. Art—Exhibitions. 2. Art exhibition audiences. 3. Art appreciation. 4. Visual perception. I. Title.

WILDERNESS, 760'.0973'0740153
presented by the National Endowment for the Arts, with the Corcoran Gallery of Art, October 9-November 14, 1971, Washington, D.C. [New York, Printed by Benson Litho; for sale by the Corcoran Gallery of Art, Washington, 1971?] [28] p. illus. 28 x 13 cm. [N8214.5.U6W5] 73-180650 0.50
1. Art—Exhibitions. 2. United States—Description and travel—Views. 3. Canada—Description and travel—Views. I. National Endowment for the Arts. II. Corcoran Gallery of Art, Washington, D.C.

WORCESTER, Mass. Art 707.4
Museum.
The Dial and the Dial collection. Worcester Art Museum, Worcester, Massachusetts, April 30 -- September 8, 1959. [Worcester] 1959] 110 p. illus. (1 mounted col.) 25 cm. Cover title [N5020.W86] 59-41852
1. Art — Exhibitions. 2. The Dial. I. Title.

Art—Exhibitions—Indexes.

MARLOR, Clark S., 708.147'23
1922-
A history of the Brooklyn Art Association with an index of exhibitions, by Clark S. Marlor. New York, J. F. Carr [1970] vii, 421 p. illus., ports. 29 cm. Photocopy of typescript. Includes bibliographical references. [N11.B783M3 1970] 74-125076
1. Brooklyn Art Association. 2. Art—Exhibitions—Indexes. I. Title.

Art—Expertising—Congresses.

APPLICATION of science in 702'.8
examination of works of art; proceedings of the seminar: June 15-19, 1970. Conducted by the Research Laboratory, Museum of Fine Arts, Boston, Mass. Editor: William J. Young. [Boston, Museum of Fine Arts, 1973] 271 p. illus. (part col.) 29 cm. Includes bibliographical references. [N8558.A67] 73-79826 ISBN 0-87846-071-3 25.00
1. Art—Expertising—Congresses. I. Young, William Jonathan, 1906- ed. II. Boston. Museum of Fine Arts. Research Laboratory.

Art, Fan (African people)—Exhibitions.

NEW York. Museum of 731.7'5'096
Primitive Art.
The Great Bieri; [exhibition] the Museum of Primitive Art, 1962. [New York, c1962] 1 v. (unpaged) illus. 28 cm. Cover title. [NB1097.F3N4] 68-713
1. Art, Fan (African people)—Exhibitions. 2. Sculpture, Primitive—Exhibitions. 3. Sculpture—Africa, West. I. Title.

Art, Far Eastern.

CHU, Arthur. 745.1'095
Oriental antiques and collectibles, a guide [by] Arthur and Grace Chu. New York, Crown Publishers [1973] v, 248 p. illus. (part col.) 24 cm. [N7337.C48 1973] 72-84289 ISBN 0-517-50098-1 7.95
1. Art, Far Eastern. 2. Art—Collectors and collecting. I. Chu, Grace, joint author. II. Title.

LEE, Sherman E. 709'.5
Tea taste in Japanese art / Sherman E. Lee. New York : Arno Press, 1975. p. cm. (The Asia Society reprint collection) Reprint of the 1963 ed. published by the Asia Society, New York. [N7337.L37 1975] 75-6589 ISBN 0-405-06565-5 : 26.00
1. Art, Far Eastern. 2. Japanese tea ceremony—Utensils. I. Title. II. Series. BIP

MUNSTERBERG, Hugo, 1916- 709'.5
Art of the Far East. New York, H. N. Abrams [1968] 264 p. illus. (part col.), col. map. 23 cm. (Panorama of world art) Bibliography: p. 260-262. [N7337.M85] 68-26866
1. Art, Far Eastern. I. Title.

RIDLEY, Michael. 709'.5
Far Eastern antiquities. Chicago, H. Regnery Co. [1972] 112 p. illus. (part col.) 31 cm. Bibliography: p. 108. [N7337.R52 1972b] 75-189801 10.95
1. Art, Far Eastern. I. Title.

Art, Far Eastern—Catalogs.

CHIBA, Keiko. 709'.5
Asian art treasures. [1st ed.] Rutland, Vt., Tuttle [1972] 104 p. col. illus. 45 cm. [N7336.C47] 75-170103 ISBN 0-8048-1017-6 21.50
1. Art, Far Eastern—Catalogs. I. Title.

RIDLEY, Michael. 709'.5
Oriental antiques in color / Michael Ridley. New York : Arco Pub. Co., 1978, c1977. 256 p. : ill. (some col.) ; 20 cm. (Arco color series) Includes index. [N7337.R53 1978] 77-26876 ISBN 0-668-04474-8 : 8.95. ISBN 0-668-04485-3 pbk. : 5.95
1. Art, Far Eastern—Catalogs. 2. Art objects, Far Eastern—Catalogs. I. Title.

YALE University. 709.5'074'01468
Art Gallery.
Selected Far Eastern art in the Yale University Art Gallery: a catalogue, by George J. Lee. New Haven, Yale University Press, 1970. xvi, 285 p. illus. 26 cm. Title on spine: Far Eastern art in the Yale Art Gallery. Bibliography: p. 269-273. [N7336.Y34] 71-118730 ISBN 0-300-01297-7 12.50
1. Art, Far Eastern—Catalogs. 2. Art—New Haven—Catalogs. I. Lee, George J., 1919- II. Title. III. Title: Far Eastern art in the Yale Art Gallery. BIP

Art, Far Eastern—Exhibitions.

YOUNG, Martie 709'.5'0740147
Wing.
Far Eastern art in upstate New York / organized by Martie W. Young. Ithaca, N.Y. : Office of University Publications, Cornell University, [1976] 140 p. : ill. ; 28 cm. Catalogue of an exhibition held at the Herbert F. Johnson Museum of Art and 5 other art museums, Sept. 15, 1976-Sept. 11, 1977. Bibliography: p. 136-139. [N7336.Y68] 76-27924
1. Art, Far Eastern—Exhibitions. 2. Art, Far Eastern—New York (State)—Exhibitions. I. Herbert F. Johnson Museum of Art. II. Title.

Art, Far Eastern—History.

LEE, Sherman E. 709'.5
A history of Far Eastern art, by Sherman E. Lee. Rev. ed. Englewood Cliffs, N.J., Prentice-Hall [1973] p. [N7337.L36 1973] 73-2951 ISBN 0-13-390088-6 14.95
1. Art, Far Eastern—History. I. Title.

LEE, Sherman E. 709.5
A history of Far Eastern art, by Sherman E. Lee. Englewood Cliffs, N.J., Prentice-Hall [1964] 527 p. illus. (part col.) 30 cm. Bibliography: p. 499-511. [N7260.L33] 64-11575
1. Art, Far Eastern—History. I. Title. BIP

LEE, Sherman E. 709'.5
A history of Far Eastern art, by Sherman E. Lee. Rev. ed. New York, H. N. Abrams [1973] 532 p. illus. 30 cm. Bibliography: p. 499-[516] [N7336.L43 1973] 73-2670 ISBN 0-8109-0113-7
1. Art, Far Eastern—History. I. Title.

Art, Far Eastern—United States.

CHISOLM, Lawrence W. 709'.2'4 B
Fenollosa : the Far East and American culture / by Lawrence W. Chisolm. Westport, Conn. : Greenwood Press, 1976. p. cm. Reprint of the 1963 ed. published by Yale University Press, New Haven, which was issued as 8 of Yale publications in American studies. Includes index. Bibliography: p. [N7483.F43C47 1976] 76-22680 ISBN 0-8371-8975-6 lib.bdg. : 19.75
1. Fenollosa, Ernest Francisco, 1853-1908. 2. Art, Far Eastern—United States. 3. East and West. I. Series: Yale publications in American studies ; 8.

Art—Farmington, Conn.

HILL-STEAD Museum, 708.1462
Farmington, Conn.
The Hill-Stead Museum, Farmington, Connecticut; a guide, with an introd. and notes on the principal paintings. Farmington, Trustees of the Hill-Stead Museum [1966] 1 v. (unpaged) illus. (1 mounted col.) plans, port. 16 x 21 cm. [N569.H5] 66-28688
1. Art—Farmington, Conn.

Art festivals—Planning.

CHAPMAN, Robert L., 658'.91'7
1946-
The arts festival planning guide / edited by Robert L. Chapman and Ardath Ann Goldstein. Raleigh : North Carolina Bicentennial, [1976] p. cm. [NX420.C43] 76-1861 2.00
1. Art festivals—Planning. I. Goldstein, Ardath Ann, 1949- joint author. II. Title.

Art—Film catalogs.

BOWIE, Theodore Robert. 704.94
Films on art; a critical guide. Bloomington, Indiana University Audio-Visual Center, 1956 [c1957] 73p. 23cm. Bibliography: p. 11. [N7428.B6] 57-62594
1. Art—Film catalogs. 2. Art in moving-pictures. I. Title.

CHAPMAN, William 704.94
McKissack, 1905- ed.
Films on art, 1952. [New York] American Federation of Arts in association with the Spaeth Foundation [1952] viii, 160p. illus. (1 col.) 24cm. [N7428.C47] 52-10966
1. Art—Film catalogs. 2. Art in moving-pictures. I. Title.

FILMS on art / 016.7
compiled and edited by the Canadian Centre for Films on Art for the American Federation of Arts. New York : Watson-Guptill, 1977. p. cm. Includes indexes. [N368.F54 1977] 77-21339 ISBN 0-8230-1780-X : 15.00
1. Art—Film catalogs. 2. Art in moving-pictures. I. Canadian Centre for Films on Art. II. American Federation of Arts. BIP

ILLINOIS. University. 704.976
Audio-Visual Aids Service.
Arts and crafts [catalog] 1958- [Urbana] v. 23cm. Title varies: 1958, Films on arts and crafts. Includes supplements. [N7428.I52] A 59
1. Art—Film catalogs. 2. Handicraft—Film catalogs. I. Title.

ILLINOIS. University. Visual 700
Aids Service.
Arts and crafts films catalog 1958 [Urbana] v. 23 cm. Title varies: 1958, Films on arts and crafts. Other slight variations in title. Vols. for 1958- issued by the service under a variant name: Audio-Visual Aids Service. Includes supplements. [N7428.I52] A 59
1. Art — Film catalogs. 2. Handicraft — Film catalogs. I. Illinois. University. Visual Aids Service. Films on arts and crafts. II. Title. III. Title: Films on arts and crafts.

THE Roland collection; 011
award winning films on art. Northfield, Ill. [1973?] 56 p. illus. 15 x 21 cm. [N369.R64R64] 73-179261
1. Roland, Anthony. 2. Art—Film catalogs. 3. Art in moving pictures.

Art, Finnish.

RACZ, Istvan, 1908- 709.471
Art treasures of medieval Finland. Photos. by Istvan Racz. Introd. and notes on the pictures by Riitta Pylkkanen. Translated from Finnish by Diana Tullberg and Judy Beesley. New York, F. A. Praeger [1967, c1961] 252 p. illus. (part col.) 32 cm. Translation of Suomen keskiajan taideaarteita. [N6993.R243 1967] 67-15670
1. Art, Finnish. 2. Art, Medieval—Finland. I. Title.

RACZ, Istvan, 1908- ed. 709.471
Early Finnish art, from prehistory to the Middle Ages. Photos. by Istvan Racz. Introd. by C. F Meinander and notes on the illus. by Pirkko-Liisa Lehtosalo. Tr. from Finnish by Diana Tullberg. New York, Praeger [1967, c1961] 176p. 159 illus. (pt. col.) 31 cm. Tr. Kivikirves ja hopearisti. [N6993.R2313] 67-15669 15.00
1. Art, Finnish. 2. Art, Primitive. 3. Finland—Antiq. I. Meinander, Carl Fredrik. II. Title.

Art, Flemish—Addresses, essays, lectures.

SEVENTEENTH century art in 709 s
Flanders and Holland. New York : Garland Pub., 1976. p. cm. (The Garland library of the history of art ; v. 9) Includes bibliographical references. [N5300.G32 vol. 9] [N6969.F5] 759.9492 76-14071 ISBN 0-8240-2419-2 lib. bdg. : 35.00
1. Art, Flemish—Addresses, essays, lectures. 2. Art, Modern—17th-18th centuries—Flanders—Addresses, essays, lectures. 3. Art, Dutch—Addresses, essays, lectures. 4. Art, Modern—17th-18th centuries—Netherlands—Addresses, essays, lectures. I. Series.
Contents omitted BIP

Art, Flemish—History.

HAMMACHER, Abraham Marie, 709.492
1897- ed.
Flemish and Dutch art. Ed., introd. by A. M. Hammacher. R. Hammacher Vandenbrande. New York, Watts [1966, c.1965] 316p. illus., col. plates, ports. 25cm. (Great art and artists of the world) Also pub. by Grolier, inc., as a v. of its The Book of art. Bibl. [N6925.H3] 64-23686 12.95
1. Art, Flemish—Hist. 2. Art, Dutch—Hist. 3. Artists, Flemish. 4. Artists. Dutch. I. Hammacher van de Brande, R., joint ed. II. Title. III. Series.

ROOSES, Max, 1839- 709'.493'1
1914.
Art in Flanders. New York, AMS Press [1970] viii, 341 p. illus., ports. 23 cm. (Ars una: species mille. General history of art) Reprint of the 1914 ed. [N6969.F5R6 1970] 79-100819 ISBN 4-04-053971-
1. Art, Flemish—History. 2. Art, Modern—Flanders. I. Title. II. Series. BIP

Art—Florence.

FATTORUSSO, Giuseppe. 914.5'51
Wonders of Florence : the churches, the palaces, the treasures of art : a handbook for students and travellers / by Joseph Fattorusso. Florence : Fattorusso, c1960. 253 p., [6] leaves of plates : ill. (some col.) ; 19 cm. (Italy for the tourist) (The Medici art series ; 2d ser., no. 3) Half title: Florence, the city of flowers. Running title: Wonders of Italy. Includes index. [N6921.F7F33] 75-325085
1. Art—Florence. 2. Art—Florence—Galleries and museums. I. Title. II. Title: Florence, the city of flowers. III. Series.

HUTTON, Edward, 1875- 709'.45'73
Florence. New York, D. McKay, 1952. xv, 284p. illus. 23cm. [N6921.F7H] A53
1. Art—Florence. I. Title.

MCCARTHY, Mary Therese, 709.4551
1912-
The stones of Florence. New York, Harcourt [1963] 230p. 19cm. (Harvest bk., HB60) 1.35 pap.,
1. Art—Florence. I. Title. BIP

MCCARTHY, Mary Therese, 709.4551
1912-
The stones of Florence. Photos. by Evelyn Hofer and others. New York, Harcourt, Brace [1959] 130p. illus. 29cm. [N6921.F7M28] 59-10257
1. Art— Florence. I. Title.

MOLAJOLI, Bruno, 1905- 709'.45'51
Florence. Special photography by Mario Carrieri. [1st ed.] New York, Holt, Rinehart and Winston [1972] 288 p. illus. 26 cm. (World cultural guides) [N6921.F7M6413 1972] 72-155539 ISBN 0-03-091932-0 9.95
1. Art—Florence. 2. Florence—Description.

RUSKIN, John, 1819-1900. 914.5'51
Mornings in Florence. Chicago, Homewood Pub. Co. St. Clair Shores, Mich., Scholarly Press, 1972. 208 p. 22 cm. First published 1875-77. Contents.—Santa Croce.—The Golden Gate.—Before the Soldan.—The vaulted book.—The Strait Gate.—The Shepherd's Tower. [N6921.F7R65 1972] 71-115266 ISBN 0-403-00306-7
1. Art—Florence. 2. Art, Italian—Florence. I. Title. BIP

Art—Florence—Catalogs.

FLORENCE. Galleria Degli 708.5'5
Uffizi
Masterpieces of the Uffizi. [Text by Margherita Lenzini and Emma Micheletti] Translated by Timothy Paterson. Firenze, Bonechi Editore [1973, c.1965] 64 p. col. plates. 18 cm.
1. Art—Florence—Catalogs. I. Lenzini, Margherita. II. Micheletti, Emma. III. Title.
Available from International Publications Service, New York, for 7.50. BIP

Art, Florentine.

ANTAL, Frederick. 709'.45'51
Florentine painting and its social background : the bourgeois republic before Cosimo de' Medici's advent to power, XIV and early XV centuries / Frederick Antal. New York : Harper & Row, [1975?] xxiii, 388 p., [80] leaves of plates : ill. ; 24 cm. (Icon editions ; IN-67) Reprint of the 1948 ed. published by Routledge and K. Paul, London. Includes bibliographical references and index. [N6921.F7A4 1975] 75-328162 ISBN 0-06-430067-6 : 8.95
1. Art, Florentine. 2. Art and society—Florence. 3. Florence—History—To 1421. I. Title. BIP

Art, Florentine—Exhibitions.

DETROIT. Institute of 709'.45'51
Arts.
The twilight of the Medici; late baroque art in Florence, 1670-1743. Detroit, the Detroit Institute of Arts, 27 March-2 June, 1974. Florence, Palazzo Pitti, 28 June-30 September, 1974. Exhibition sponsored by Founders Society, the Detroit Institute of Arts, and the City of Florence. [Florence] Centro Di; [distribution in U.S.: Wayne State University Press, Detroit, 1974] 507 p. illus. (part col.) 24 cm. (Centro Di catalog 43) Bibliography: p. 494-503. [N6921.F7D47 1974] 74-176274 15.00
1. Medici, House of—Art collections. 2. Art, Florentine—Exhibitions. 3. Art, Baroque—Florence. I. Founders Society. II. Florence. Palazzo Pitti. III. Title. BIP

NOTRE Dame, Ind. 709'.455'1074013
University. Art Gallery.
The age of Vasari; a loan exhibition under the high patronage of His Excellency, Egidio Ortona, the Ambassador of Italy to the United States [at] Art Gallery, University of Notre Dame, Notre Dame, Indiana, February 22-March 31, 1970 [and] University Art Gallery, State University of New York at Binghamton, April 12-May 10, 1970. [Notre Dame, Ind., 1970] 202 p. illus. (part col.), facsims. 26 cm. Includes bibliographical references. [N6921.N55N6] 77-632509
1. Vasari, Giorgio, 1511-1574. 2. Art, Florentine—Exhibitions. 3. Mannerism (Art)—Florence. I. New York (State). State University at Binghamton. University Art Gallery. II. Title.

PILLSBURY, Edmund P. 709'.4551
Florence and the arts; five centuries of patronage [by] Edmund P. Pillsbury. [Cleveland] Cleveland Museum of Art [1971] vi, 56 p. illus. 25 cm. At head of title: Florentine art in Cleveland collections. Catalog of an exhibition held at the Cleveland Museum of Art. [N6921.F7P54] 79-29178
1. Art, Florentine—Exhibitions. 2. Art—Collectors and collecting—Cleveland. I. Cleveland Museum of Art. II. Title. III. Title: Florentine art in Cleveland collections.

Art—Flushing, N. Y.—Catalogs.

QUEENS College, 709.01'1
Flushing, N. Y. Art Collection.
The Queens College Art Collection. Flushing [c1960] Flushing. 51p. illus. 26cm. v. illus. 26cm. -- --Supplement. 1st--spring 1961- [N620.Q4A3] 62-51003
1. Art—Flushing, N. Y.—Catalogs. I. Title.

Art for art's sake (Movement)

EGAN, Rose Frances. 111.8'5
The genesis of the theory of "art for art's sake" in Germany and in England / by Rose Frances Egan. Norwood, Pa. : Norwood Editions, 1976. p. cm. Reprint of the 1921 ed. published by Smith College, Northampton, Mass., which was issued as v. 2, no. 4 of Smith College studies in modern languages. Includes bibliographical references. [BH301.A7E36 1976] 76-13026 ISBN 0-8482-0653-3 lib. bdg. : 15.00
1. Art for art's sake (Movement) 2. Aesthetics, German. 3. Aesthetics, British. I. Title. II. Series: Smith College studies in modern languages ; v. 2, no. 4.

EGAN, Rose Frances. 700'.1
The genesis of the theory of "art for art's sake" in Germany and in England. [Folcroft, Pa.] Folcroft Library Editions, 1974. 61, ix, 33 p. 23 cm. Reprint of the 1921 ed. published by Smith College, Northampton, Mass., which was issued as v. 2, no. 4 of Smith College studies in modern languages. Includes bibliographical references. [BH301.A7E36 1974] 74-11067 ISBN 0-8414-3948-6 (lib. bdg.)
1. Art for art's sake (Movement) 2. Aesthetics, German. 3. Aesthetics, British.

I. Title. II. Series: Smith College studies in modern languages, v. 2, no. 4.

Art—Fort Worth, Tex.—Catalogs.

KIMBELL Art Museum. 708'.164'5315
Catalogue of the collection. [1st ed.] Fort Worth, Tex., Kimbell Art Foundation, 1972. v, 336 p. illus. (part col.) 22 x 29 cm. (Kimbell publication 1) Cover title: Kimbell Art Museum, Fort Worth Texas. Includes bibliographical references. [N570.8.A54] 73-177945 ISBN 0-912804-00-9 25.00
1. Art—Fort Worth, Tex.—Catalogs. I. Title. II. Series.

Art—France.

ART treasures in 709'.44
France: monuments, masterpieces, commissions, and collections. Introduced by Germain Bazin. [General editors: Bernard S. Myers and Trewin Copplestone] New York, McGraw-Hill [1969] 176 p. illus. (part col.), col. maps (on lining papers) 29 cm. [N6841.A974] 69-13326 6.95
1. Art—France. 2. Art patronage—France. I. Bazin, Germain. II. Myers, Bernard Samuel, 1908- ed. III. Copplestone, Trewin, ed.

BAUDELAIRE, Charles Pierre, 1821-1867. 704.91
The mirror of art, critical studies. Translated and edited with notes and illus. by Jonathan Mayne. Garden City, N. Y., Doubleday, 1956. xxi, [2], 370p. illus., plates. ports. 18cm. (Doubleday anchor books, A84) 'Bibliographical note': p. [xxiii] [N6847] 57-2188
1. Art—France. 2. Art criticism. I. Title.
BIP

BAUDELAIRE, Charles Pierre, 1821-1867. 704.91
The mirror of art, critical studies. Translated and edited with notes and illus. by Jonathan Mayne. New York, Phaidon Publishers; distributed by Garden City Books [1955] xix, [3], 361p. illus., plates, ports., facsim. 19cm. [Phaldon pocket series] 'Bibliographical note': p. [xxi] [N6847.B362 1955] 56-435
1. Art—France. 2. Art criticism. I. Title.

BLUNT, Anthony, Sir, 1907- 709.44
Art and architecture in France 1500 to 1700 London, Baltimore, Penguin Books [1953] xvii, 312 p. illus., plates, plans. 27 cm. (The Pelican history of art, Z4) Bibliography: p. 291-296. [N6844.B6] A 54
1. Art—France. 2. Art, Modern—France. 3. Architecture—France. 4. Architecture, Modern—France. I. Title. II. Series.
BIP

BLUNT, Anthony, Sir, 1907- 709'.44
Art and architecture in France, 1500 to 1700. [Harmondsworth, Eng.] Penguin Books [1973] 471 p. 193 plates. illus., plans. 21 cm. (The Pelican history of art, Z4) First paperback ed, based on second hardback ed. with revisions 1973. Bibliography: p. [441]-449. [N6844.B6 1973] 70-521859 ISBN 0-14-056104-8 9.95 (pbk.)
1. Art—France. 2. Architecture—France. 3. Art, Modern—France. 4. Architecture, Modern—France. I. Title. II. Series.
Available from Penguin Books, Baltimore, Md.

GUIDE to the art treasures 709.44
of France. [Prep. under the direction of Pierre Tisne, Laurent Tisne by Francoise Olivier-Michel, Claude Gisler. Tr. from French by Raymond Rudorff] New York, Dutton [c.1964.1966] 554p. illus., maps, col. plates. 25cm. [N6841.G7713] 66-4619 10.75
1. Art—France. 2. France—Descr. & trav.—Guide—books. I. Olivier-Michel, Francoise. II. Gisler, Claude.

OLIVIER-MICHEL, Francoise. 709.44
Guide to the art treasures of France. [Prepared under the direction of Pierre Tisne and Laurent Tisne by Francoise Olivier-Michel and Claude Gisler. Translated by Raymond Rudorff] New York, Dutton [1966] 554 p. illus., maps. col. plates. 25 cm. [N6841.O513] 66-4619
1. Art — France. 2. France — Descr. & trav. — Guide-books. I. Gisler, Claude, joint author. II. Title.

WHITE, Harrison C 759.4
Canvases and careers; institutional change in the French painting world [by] Harrison C. White and Cynthia A. White. New York, Wiley [1965] xii, 167 p. illus. 22 cm. Includes bibliographical references. [N6847.W5] 65-19469
1. Art — France. 2. Painters, French. 3. Art and society. 4. France — Intellectual life. I. White, Cynthia A., joint author. II. Title.

Art—France—Galleries and museums.

BABELON, Jean Pierre. 708.4
The museums of France. [Translated from the Italian by James Brockway] New York, Meredith Press [1968, c1965] 160 p. illus., plates (part col.) 28 cm. (Great galleries series) French ed. published under title: Musees de province. [N2010.B313] 70-4309 8.95
1. Art—France—Galleries and museums. I. Title.

Art—France—History.

GANTNER, Joseph, 1896- 709.44
The glory of Romanesque art [by] Joseph Gantner and Marcel Pobe. With a pref. by Marcel Aubert. 271 pictures in photogravure by Jean Roubier. [Translated from the German by Marie Heynemann] New York, Vanguard Press [1956] 80p. plates, maps. 31cm. Translation of Gallia Romanica. Bibliography: p. 78. [N6843.G313] 56-12036
1. Art—France—Hist. 2. Art, Romanesque. 3. Christian art and symbolism. I. Pobe, Marcel, 1907- II. Roubier, Jean, 1896-illus. III. Title.

Art—France—History.

MALE, Emile, 1862- 704.9482
The Gothic image; religious art in France of the thirteenth century. Translated by Dora Nussey. New York, Harper [1958] 414 p. illus. 21 cm. (Cathedral library) Harper torchbooks, TB44. Translation of L'art religieux du XIIIe siecle en France. Includes bibliography. [N7949.M313 1958] 58-10152
1. Art—France—History. 2. Art, Gothic—High Gothic—France. 3. Art, Medieval. I. Title.
BIP

SIMON, Matila. 709'.44
The battle of the Louvre; the struggle to save French art in World War II. New York, Hawthorn Books [1971] x, 214 p. illus., ports. 24 cm. Bibliography: p. 200-202. [N9165.F8S5 1971] 79-130709 8.95
1. Art—France—History. 2. World War, 1939-1945—Art and the war. 3. Art treasures in war. I. Title.

Art—France—Yearbooks.

ART de France. 709.44
no. 1. Editor: A. Chastel. Dist. New York, Wittenborn [c.1961] 435 p. Bibl. illus. (part col.) 33 cm. annual. 61-1279 12.50 pap.,
1. Art—France—Yearbooks. I. Chastel, Andre, 1912- ed.

Art, French.

*BLUNT, Anthony 780.08
French art and music since 1500 [by] Anthony Blunt and Edward Lockspeiser. [London] Methuen [1975 c1974] x, 101 p. ill. 21 cm. Includes index. Includes bibliographical references. [NX549] ISBN 0-416-81650-9
1. Art, French. 2. Music, French. I. Lockspeiser, Edward joint author II. Title.
Distributed by Harper & Row Publishers, Barnes &Noble Import Division for 4.75 (pbk.)

CHARCHOUNE, Serge, 1888- 759.4
Charehoune. [Chicago, William and Noma Copley Foundation, 1961?] 1 v. (unpaged) illus. (1 col.) port. 22 cm. Text by William N. Copley; previously published in Art news, March 1960. [ND553.C39C6] 66-39139
I. Copley, William N. II. William and Noma Copley Foundation, Chicago. III. Title.

EVANS, Joan, 1893- 704.948'2'0944
Monastic iconography in France from the Renaissance to the Revolution. Cambridge [Eng.] University Press, 1970. xv, 76 p. 117 plates. 28 cm. Bibliography: p. 57-59. [N7949.E9] 67-12317 ISBN 0-521-06960-2 19.50
1. Art, French. 2. Art, Renaissance—France. 3. Art, Modern—17th-18th centuries—France. 4. Christian art and symbolism. I. Title.
BIP

KALNEIN, Wend Graf, 1914- 709'.44
Art and architecture of the eighteenth century in France [by] Wend Graf Kalnein and Michael Levey. Translation of pt. 2 by J. R. Foster. [Harmondsworth, Eng.] Penguin Books [1972] xxv, 443 p. illus. 27 cm. (The Pelican history of art) Bibliography: p. 405-417. [N6846.K2613] 73-167862 ISBN 0-14-056037-8 35.00 (U.S.)
1. Art, French. 2. Art, Modern—17th-18th centuries—France. I. Levey, Michael, joint author. II. Title. III. Series.
Distributed by Penguin, Baltimore. BIP

MEISSONNIER, Juste Aurele. 709'.24
Ouvre de Juste Aurele Meissonnier. Introd. by Dorothea Nyberg. [New York] B. Blom, 1969. 43 p. illus., 74 plates (incl. plans; part fold.) 41 cm. "First published Paris ca. 1750." Includes bibliographical references. [N6853.M4N9 1969] 69-16909
I. Nyberg, Dorothea. II. Title.

SCHOFFER, Nicolas, 1912- 730.944
Nicolas Schoffer [space, light, time] Introd. by Jean Cassou. Texts by Guy Habasque, Jacques Menetrier [pseud.] Tr. from French by Haakon Chevalier. Neuchatel, Swizaland, Editions du Griffon [dist. New York, Wittenborn] c.1963. 149p. illus. (pt. col.) ports. 30cm. and phonodisc (2 s. 7 in. 45 rpm. in pocket) (Sculpture of the twentieth cent.) Bibl. 63-23706 22.50
I. Habasque, Guy. II. Giraud- Mours, Andre, 1908- III. Title.

Art, French—Exhibitions.

ALLENTOWN, Pa. Art Museum. 709'.44'074014827
French masterpieces of the 19th century from the Henry P. McIlhenny Collection : May 1 through September 18, 1977, Allentown Art Museum. [Allentown, Pa.] : The Museum, c1977. 100 p. : ill. (some col.) ; 28 cm. Includes bibliographies. [N6847.A44 1977] 77-74177
1. McIlhenny, Henry P.—Art collections—Exhibitions. 2. Art, French—Exhibitions. 3. Art, Modern—19th century—France—Exhibitions. I. Title.

BROWN University. Dept. of Art. 760'.0944
Rubenism : an exhibition by the Department of Art, Brown University, and the Museum of Art, Rhode Island School of Design, Bell Gallery, List Art Building, Brown University, Providence, Rhode Island, January 30 through February 23, 1975. [Providence, R.I.] : The Department, [1975] 278 p. : ill. ; 27 cm. "Catalogue number 3." Bibliography: p. 274-275. [N6846.B76 1975] 74-33245 12.00
1. Rubens, Peter Paul, Sir, 1577-1640—Influence. 2. Art, French—Exhibitions. 3. Art, Modern—17th-18th centuries—France—Exhibitions. 4. Romanticism in art—France—Exhibitions. 5. Art, English—Exhibitions. 6. Art, Modern—17th-18th centuries—England—Exhibitions. I. Rhode Island School of Design, Providence. Museum of Art. II. Title.

CUMMER Gallery of Art. 709'.44'074015912
The age of Louis xiii [Jacksonville, Fla., Printed by Convention Press, 1969?] [48] p. illus. (part col.), ports. 23 x 27 cm. Prepared for an exhibition at the Cummer Gallery of Art, Jacksonville, Fla., Oct. 29-Dec. 7, 1969, and the Museum of Fine Arts, St. Petersburg, Fla., Jan. 5-Feb. 8, 1970. "This catalogue was written and compiled by Mr. Dodge, Mrs. Parker and Mrs. Young of the Cummer Gallery of Art." [N6846.C8] 79-286385
1. Art, French—Exhibitions. 2. Art, Modern—17th-18th centuries—France. I. Dodge, Joseph Jeffers. II. St. Petersburg, Fla. Museum of Fine Arts. III. Title.

CUMMER Gallery of Art. 709'.44
French art of the sixteenth century, commemorating the Fort Caroline quadricentennial, June 27—September 30, 1964. Jacksonville, Fla., Cummer Gallery of Art, 1964. [32] p. illus. 28 cm. Cover title. [N6845.5.M3C85] 73-171389
1. Art, French—Exhibitions. 2. Mannerism (Art)—France. 3. Fort Caroline, Fla. I. Title.

DETROIT. Institute of Arts. 709.44
French taste in the eighteenth century. [Exhibition] the Detroit Institute of Arts, April 27 to June 3, 1956. [Detroit, 1956] 112p. illus. 26cm. Catalogue compiled by Paul L Grigaut. [N6846.D4] 57-270
1. Art, French—Exhibitions. I. Title.

JAPONISME : 709'.44'074013
Japanese influence on French art, 1854-1910 : [exhibition catalog] / Gabriel P. Weisberg ... [et al.]. Cleveland : Cleveland Museum of Art, [1975] xii, 220 p. : ill. (some col.) ; 27 cm. Catalog of an exhibition shown at the Cleveland Museum of Art, July 9-Aug. 31, 1975; the Rutgers University Art Gallery, Oct. 4-Nov. 16, 1975; and the Walters Art Gallery, Dec. 10, 1975-Jan. 26, 1976. Bibliography: p. 215-218. [N6847.J34] 75-16127 ISBN 0-910386-22-6 : 12.75 pbk. : 6.50
1. Art, French—Exhibitions. 2. Art, Japanese—Exhibitions. 3. Art, Modern—19th century—France—Exhibitions. 4. Art, French—Japanese influences. I. Weisberg, Gabriel P. II. Cleveland Museum of Art. III. Rutgers University, New Brunswick, N.J. University Art Gallery. IV. Walters Art Gallery, Baltimore.
Available from Kent State University Press, Kent, Ohio.

NORTH Carolina. Museum of Art, Raleigh. 709.44
Modern French art, Monet to Picasso; the Maurice Wertheim collection. [Exhibition] June 17-Setp. 4, 1960. [Raleigh, 1960] 78p. illus. 26cm. [N6847.N65] 60-63740
1. Art. French—Exhibitions. I. Wertheim, Maurice, 1886- II. Title.

NOTRE Dame, Ind. University. Art Gallery. 709'.44
Eighteenth century France; a study of its art and civilization. [Notre Dame, Ind., 1972] [56] p. illus. 28 cm. Catalogue of an exhibition held Mar. 12-May 15, 1972. [N6846.N67 1972] 73-299001
1. Art, French—Exhibitions. 2. Art, Modern—17th-18th centuries—France. 3. Art and society—France. I. Title.

PHILADELPHIA Museum of Art. 759.4
Toulouse-Lautrec; exhibition organized in collaboration with the Albi Museum. Philadelphia Museum of Art, October 29-December 11, 1955; the Art Institute of Chicago, January 2-February 15, 1956. [Philadelphia, 1955] 112p. (chiefly illus. (part col.)) 26c4. [N6853.T6P4] [N6853.T6P4] 927.5 56-1888 56-1888
1. Toulouse—Lautrec Monfa, Henri Marle Raymond de, 1864-1901. 2. Art, French—Exhibitions. I. Chicago. Art Institute. II. Title.

SCHRADER, J. L. 709'.4
The waning Middle Ages; an exhibition of French and Netherlandish art from 1350 to 1500, commemorating the fiftieth anniversary of the publication of The waning of the Middle Ages by Johan Huizinga. Catalogue by J. L. Schrader. [Lawrence, University of Kansas Museum of Art, 1969] 102 p. 76 plates, (1 col.) 26 cm. Exhibition shown at the University of Kansas Museum of Art, Nov. 1-Dec. 1, 1969. Includes bibliographies. [N6750.S39] 73-628610
1. Art, French—Exhibitions. 2. Art, Dutch—Exhibitions. 3. Art, Flemish—Exhibitions. 4. Art, Medieval—France. 5. Art, Medieval—Netherlands. I. Kansas. University. Museum of Art. II. Huizinga, Johan, 1872-1945. Herfsttij der Middeleeuwen. III. Title.

U.S. National Gallery of Art. 709.44
The splendid century; French art: 1600-1715.[Exhibition] the National Gallery of Art, Washington, the Toledo Museum of Art, the Metropolitan Museum of Art, 1960-1961. [Washington, 1960] xiv, 93 p. plates. 21 cm. Bibliography: p. 58-87 [N6846.U6] 60-532583
1. Art, French — Exhibitions. I. Title.

Art—French—History.

LACLOTTE, Michel, ed. 709.44
French art from 1350 to 1850. New York, Watts [1966,c.1965] 249p. illus., col. plates, ports. 25cm. (Great art and artists of the world) Also pub. by Grolier, inc., as a v. of its The Book of art. Bibl. [N6844.L25] 65-10267 12.95
1. Art, French—Hist. 2. Artists, French. I. Title. II. Series.

Art, French—History.

CALI, Francois. 914.4
The wonders of France. Introd. by Rene Huyghe. [Translated by Margaret Shenfield] New York, Viking Press [1961] 316 p. illus. 37 cm. (A Studio book) [N6841.C283] 61-10643
1. Art, French—History. 2. France—Description and travel—Views. I. Title.

JACOB, Max, 1876-1944. 709.04
Lettres, 1920-1941; edited by S. J. Collier. Oxford, Blackwell, 1966. vii, 159 p. front., 4 plates (incl. ports. facsim.) 18 1/2 cm. 32/6 (B66-13688) "Lettres a T. Briant et C. Valence." Bibliography: p. 155-159. [PQ2619.A17Z524] 66-74788
I. Collier, Stanley John, ed. II. Briant, Theophile. III. Moricand, Conrad. IV. Title.

Art—Galleries and museums.

ASSOCIATION of Art Museum Directors. Professional Practices Committee. 069'.97
Professional practices in art museums; report. [New York] 1971. 28 p. 24 cm. [N420.A8] 72-178748
1. Art—Galleries and museums. I. Title.

CAUMAN, Samuel. 708
The living museum, experiences of an art historian and museum director: Alexander Dorner. With an introd. by Walter Gropius. [New York] New York University Press, 1958. ix, 216p. illus. (part fold.) facsims., plans. 26cm. Bibliography: p. 211. [N8375.D6C3] 57-13239
1. Dorner, Alexander, 1893-1957. 2. Art—Galleries and museums. I. Title. BIP

**A Dore gallery.* 709.2
New York, Arco, [1974]. 304 p. illus. 31 cm. [N72.R4] 73-91686 ISBN 0-668-03444-0. 15.00
1. Dore, Gustave, 1832-1883. 2. Art—Galleries and museums.

DOSI-DELFINI, Luca. 709'.04
Le futur du musee d'art moderne. Analyse socio-s emiologique effectuee avec la participation de Francois Peraldi. Harlem, J. H. Gottmer [1974]. 198 p. plates. 24 cm. Bibliography: p. 197-198. [N430.D62] 74-185898 ISBN 9-02-570226-0 f135.00
1. Art—Galleries and museums. 2. Art, Modern—20th century. 3. Museum techniques. I. Peraldi, Francois, joint author. II. Title.

DUBLIN. National Gallery of Ireland. 708.9418'3
National Gallery of Ireland [by] James White. New York, Praeger [1968] 224 p. 223 illus. (32 col.) 29 cm. [N1250.A67] 68-8256 27.50
I. White, James, 1913-

HAMBURG. Kunsthalle. 708.3'515
Hamburger Kunsthalle; official guide [by] Alfred Hentzen; [English version by Edith Meyer-Ball]. English ed. Hamburg, 1967. 1 v. illus. (part col.), plans, 136 plates (part col.) 17 cm. Translation of Fuhrer durch die Hamburger Kunsthalle. [N2305.H3A433] 79-356597
I. Hentzen, Alfred, 1903- II. Title.

INDIANA. University. Museum of Art. v. 12
Handbook. Published on the occasion of the dedication of the Fine Arts Building and the opening of the inaugural exhibition in the Museum of Art, Oct. 21, 1962. [Bloomington, 1962] 95 p. illus. 26 cm. (Its Publication no. 1) [N518.B4A5] 62-64226
I. Title. II. Series.

SPRINGFIELD, Mass. Museum of Fine Arts. 708.14426
Handbook; a pictorial survey of additions to the collections of the museum acquired through purchase and gift within the last ten years ... [A 25th anniversary publication. 2d ed.] Springfield, 1958. 95 p. illus. (part col.) ports. 29 cm. 79 p. illus. (part col.) ports. 29 cm. N773.A6 1958 Suppl. Supplement; a pictorial survey of some important additions to the collections ... Springfield, 1963. [N773.A6 1958] 59-2834
I. Title.

SPRINGFIELD, Mass. Museum of Fine Arts. 708.14426
Handbook; a pictorial survey of additions to the collections of the museum acquired through purchase and gift within the last ten years... [A 25th Anniversary publication. 2d ed. Springfield, 1958. 95 p. illus. 29 cm. [N773.A6 1958] 59-2834
I. Title.

TIETZE, Hans, 1880- 708
Treasures of the great national galleries; an introduction to the paintings in the famous museums of the Western World. New York, Phaidon Publishers; distributed by Garden City Books [1954] vi, 424 p. illus., plates (part col.) 27 cm. [N410.T5] 54-13297
1. Art—Galleries and museums. I. Title.

Art—Galleries and museums—Addresses, essays, lectures.

ON understanding art museums. 069
Englewood Cliffs, N.J. : Prentice-Hall, [1975] vii, 212 p. ; 21 cm. (A Spectrum book) At head of title: the American Assembly, Columbia University. Background papers prepared for the 46th American Assembly, Arden House, Nov. 1974. Includes index. Bibliography: p. 203. [N410.O58] 74-34015 ISBN 0-13-936286-X : 9.95 ISBN 0-13-936278-9 pbk. : 4.95
1. Art—Galleries and museums—Addresses, essays, lectures. I. American Assembly.

Art—Galleries and museums—History.

BAZIN, Germain. 708.009
The museum age. Translated from the French by Jane van Nuis Cahill. [1st American ed.] New York, Universe Books [1967] 302 p. illus. (part col.), facsims., plans. 27 cm. [N410.B3513] 67-26914
1. Art—Galleries and museums—History. 2. Art—Collectors and collecting. 3. Art patronage. I. Title.

Art galleries, Commercial—United States.

TAMARIND Lithography Workshop. 658.2
Gallery facility planning for marketing original prints. Los Angeles [1967] 35 p. 28 cm. Cover title. [NE60.T35 1967] 75-319585
1. Art galleries, Commercial—United States. 2. Prints—United States—Marketing. I. Title.

Art Gallery of Windsor.

ART Gallery of Windsor. 708'.113'32
A checklist of the permanent collection to December 31, 1971. [Windsor, Ont., Art Gallery of Windsor, 1972] 55 p. illus. (part col.) 28 cm. [N910.W5A6] 74-168474 5.00
1. Art Gallery of Windsor. 2. Art—Windsor, Ont.—Catalogs. 3. Art, Canadian—Catalogs. I. Title.

Art—Gaul—Hist.

POBE, Marcel, 1907- 709.364
The art of Roman Gaul; a thousand years of Celtic art & culture. Photography by Jean Roubier. [Toronto] University of Toronto Press [1961] viii, 78p., 259illus. map (on lining papers) 31cm. [N5849.P613] 61-65525
1. Art—Gaul—Hist. 2. Art, Celtic. 3. Art, Roman. I. Roubier, Jean, 1896- II. Title.

Art, Genoese—Exhibitions.

FINCH College, New York. Museum of Art. 707.4*097471
Genoese painters: Cambiaso to Magnasco, 1550-1750; a loan exhibition of paintings and drawings. [Catalogue prepared by Robert L. Manning] New York [1964?] [60] p. illus. 23 cm. Catalog of the exhibition held Oct. 15, 1964-Feb. 1, 1965 at the Finch College Museum of Art, New York. [N6921.G4F5] 73-279422
1. Art, Genoese—Exhibitions. I. Manning, Robert L. II. Title.

Art, German.

ART treasures in Germany: 709'.43
monuments, masterpieces, commissions, and collections. Introd. by Stephan Waetzoldt. [General editors: Bernard S. Myers and Trewin Copplestone] New York, McGraw-Hill [1970] 176 p. illus. (part col.), col. maps (on lining papers) 29 cm. [N6861.A85] 73-76759 6.95
1. Art, German. 2. Art patronage—Germany. I. Waetzoldt, Stephan, 1920- II. Myers, Bernard Samuel, 1908- ed. III. Copplestone, Trewin, ed.

BENESCH, Otto, 1896-1964. 709'.43
German and Austrian art of the 15th and 16th centuries. Edited by Eva Benesch. London, Phaidon, 1972. xxi, 667 p. illus. 26 cm. (His Collected writings, v. 3) English or German. Includes index. Bibliography: p. xiv-xix. [N6865.B46 1972] 73-177463 ISBN 0-7148-1506-3
1. Art, German. 2. Art, Gothic—Germany. 3. Art, Renaissance—Germany. 4. Art, Austrian. 5. Art, Gothic—Austria. 6. Art, Renaissance—Austria. I. Title.
Distributed by Praeger; 25.00.

GIBSON, Charles Dana, 1867-1944. 741.973
The best of Charles Dana Gibson. Edited, with a biography and introd., by Woody Gelman. [New York] Bounty Books [1969] viii, 206 p. (chiefly illus.) 23 x 29 cm. [NC1429.G42G4 1969] 76-75094
I. Gelman, Woody, comp. II. Title.

KUHN, Charles Louis. 709'.43
German expressionism and abstract art: the Harvard collections. With an introductory essay by Jakob Rosenberg. Cambridge, Harvard University Press, 1957. xiv, 151 p. 219 illus. 28 cm. "Errata": slip laid in. A supplement to the 1957 catalogue of twentieth century German art at Harvard. Cambridge, Busch-Reisinger Museum; distributed by the Harvard University Press, 1967. [70] p. 57 illus. 26 cm. N6868.K83 Suppl. Bibliography: p. 125-127. Bibliographical references included in "Biographies" (p. 129-147) [N6868.K83] A57
1. Art, German. 2. Expressionism (Art) 3. Art, Abstract. I. Harvard University. II. Title. BIP

ROH, Franz, 1890-1965. 709'.43
German art in the 20th century. With additions by Juliane Roh. [Translated from the German by Catherine Hutter and edited by Julia Phelps] Greenwich, Conn., New York Graphic Society [1968] 516 p. illus. (part col.) 27 cm. Translation of Geschichte der deutschen Kunst von 1900 bis zur Gegenwart. [N6868.R623 1968b] 68-12367
1. Art, German. 2. Art, Modern—20th century—Germany. I. Roh, Juliane. II. Title.

WERKMAN, Hendrik Nicolaas, 1882-1945. 769'.924
H. N. Werkman. Herausgeber/Editor: Fridolin Muller. Einfuhrung/Introd: Peter F. Althaus. Biographie/Biography: Jan Martinet. New York, Hastings House [1967] 104 p. (chiefly illus. (part col.), port.) 25 cm. (Dokumente visueller Gestaltung, Bd. 2) Visual communication books. English, French, and German. [ND653.W43M8 1967b] 67-66203
I. Muller, Fridolin, ed.

Art, German—Exhibitions.

CORNELL University. Andrew Dickson White Museum of Art. 759.3'074'0147
Brucke. [Exhibition] Andrew Dickson White Museum of Art, Cornell University, Feb. 11 to Mar. 22, 1970 [and] Memorial Art Gallery, University of Rochester, Apr. 2 to May 10, 1970. [Ithaca, Cornell University, Office of University Publications, 1970] 29, [65] p. illus. (part col.) 26 cm. Label mounted on t.p.: Supplied by Worldwide Books, Boston. [N6868.5.E9C6] 77-112768
1. Die Brucke (Dresden) 2. Art, German—Exhibitions. I. Rochester, N.Y. University. Memorial Art Gallery.

NATIONALSOZIALISTISCHE Deutsche Arbeiter-Partei. Reichspropagandaleitung. Hauptkulturamt. 709'.43
Entartete "Kunst." [Redding, Conn., Silver Fox Press, 1972] 1 portfolio (30, 30 p.) illus. 21 cm. Title from portfolio. Portfolio consists of 2 booklets: facsim. of the original German guide (1936?) with title: Fuhrer durch die Ausstellung Entartete Kunst, and an English translation, by W. C. Bunce, with title: Degenerate "art"; exhibition guide, lacking illustrations. [N6868.N27 1972] 72-183107
1. Art, German—Exhibitions. 2. Art, Modern—20th century—Germany. I. Title.

NEW York (City). Museum of Modern Art. 730'.943'07401471
Modern German painting and sculpture. Introd. and notes by Alfred H. Barr, Jr. Reprint ed. [New York] Published for the Museum of Modern Art by Arno Press, 1972. 43 p. 50 illus. 27 cm. (Museum of Modern Art publications in reprint) Reprint of the 1931 ed. [N6868.N4 1972] 76-169296 ISBN 0-405-01556-9 13.00
1. Art, German—Exhibitions. 2. Art, Modern—20th century—Germany. 3. Artists, German. I. Barr, Alfred Hamilton, 1902- II. Title. BIP

VON Arseniew, Isenrath, Keusen, Kuhna, Scheel, Tadeusz, Ulrichs, Zellmann : 709'.43
Landesmuseum Munster 2.2.-2.3. 1975: Katalog. Munster : Institut fur Kunsterzieher, [1975?] 120 p. : chiefly ill. (some col.) ; 23 cm. [N6868.V64] 76-454921
1. Art, German—Exhibitions. 2. Art, Modern—20th century—Germany, West—Exhibitions. I. Landesmuseum fur Kunst und Kulturgeschichte Munster.

Art—German—History.

VEY, Horst, ed. 709.4
German and Spanish art to 1900, ed. by Hors Vey Xavier do Salas New York, Watts [1966,c.1965] 307p. illus., col. plates., 25cm. (Great art and artists of the world) Also pub. by Grolier, inc., as a v. of its The Book of art. Bibl. [N6864.V4] 64-23687 12.95
1. Art, German—Hist. 2. Art, Spanish—Hist. 3. Artists, Spanish. I. Salas, Xavier de ed. II. Title. III. Series.

Art, German—History.

LINDEMANN, Gottfried. 709'.43
History of German art; painting, sculpture, architecture [by] Gottfried Lindemann. Translated by Tessa Sayle. New York, Praeger [1973, c.1971] 228 p. illus. (part col.) 26 cm. (Praeger paperbacks, P372) Translation of Deutsche Kunst. [N6861.L513] 79-89605 5.95 (pbk.)
1. Art, German—History. I. Title.

OSTEN, Gert von der. 709'.4
Painting and sculpture in Germany and the Netherlands, 1500 to 1600 [by] Gertvonder Osten and Horst Vey. Baltimore, Md., Penguin Books [1969] xxii, 403 p. maps, plates. 27 cm. (The Pelican history of art, Z31) Bibliography: p. 375-378. [N6925.O813] 73-8246 25.00

SUBJECT INDEX ART—GT. BRIT.—YEARBOOKS.

1. Art, German—History. 2. Art, Flemish—History. 3. Art, Dutch—History. I. Vey, Horst. II. Title. III. Series.

OSTEN, Gert von der. 759.3
Painting and sculpture in Germany and the Netherlands, 1500 to 1600 [by] Gert vonder Osten & Horst Vey; [translated from the German MS. by Mary Hottinger] Harmondsworth, Penguin, 1969. xxii, 403 p., 193 plates. illus. (incl. 1 col.), 2 maps. 27 cm. (The Pelican history of art Z 31) Bibliography: p. 375-378. [N6925.O813 1969] 79-514834 7/7/-
1. Art, German—History. 2. Art, Flemish—History. 3. Art, Dutch—History. I. Vey, Horst. II. Title. III. Series.

SALOMON, Charlotte, 1917-1943. 759.3
Charlotte; a diary in pictures. Comment by Paul Tillich; biographical note by Emil Straus. [1st American ed.] New York, Harcourt, Brace & World [1963] 1 v. (unpaged, chiefly col. illus.) 28 cm. [ND588.S15A2] 63-14210
I. Title.

Art, German—Missouri.

VAN RAVENSWAAY, Charles. 709'.778
The art and architecture of German settlements in Missouri : a survey of a vanishing culture / Charles van Ravenswaay. Columbia, Mo. : University of Missouri Press, 1977. xvi, 533 p., [4] leaves of plates : ill. ; 29 cm. Includes index. Bibliography: p. [513]-518. [N6530.M73V36] 76-29635 ISBN 0-8262-0202-0 : 36.00
1. Art, German—Missouri. 2. Art—Missouri. 3. Architecture, German—Missouri. 4. Architecture—Missouri. 5. German Americans in Missouri. I. Title.

Art, Germanic.

HACHMANN, Rolf 913.0313
The germanic peoples translated from the German by James Hogarth Geneva, Nagel Pub., [1974 c1971] 208 p. illus (part. col.), maps (on lining papers) 24 cm. (Archaeologia Mundi Series) Bibliography: p. 177-190. [N5930.H3]
1. Art, Germanic. I. Title.
L.C. card no. for original edition: 75-863113 Distributed by Hippocrene Books, N.Y., for 19.50

Art—Germany—Hist.

NEW York. Museum of Modern Art. 709.43
German art of the twentieth century, by Werner Haftmann, Alfred Hentzen [and] William S. Lieberman. Edited by Andrew Carnduff Ritchie. New York, Museum of Modern Art, in collaboration with the City Art Museum of St. Louis, Missouri; distributed by Simon and Schuster [1957] 239p. illus. (part col.) 25cm. [N6868.N38] 57-11679
1. Art—Germany—Hist. 2. Art, German—Exhibitions. 3. St. Louis. City Art Museum. I. Haftmann, Werner. II. Ritchie, Andrew Carnduff, ed. III. Title.
Contents omitted. BIP

Art, Gothic.

DEUCHLER, Florens, 1931- 709'.02'2
Gothic art. [English translation by Vivienne Menkes] New York, Universe Books [1973] 184 p. illus. 23 cm. (Universe history of art) Translation of Gotik. Bibliography: p. 178-181. [N6310.D4813] 72-85081 ISBN 0-87663-172-3 6.95
1. Art, Gothic. BIP

DVORAK, Max, 1874-1921 709.02
Idealism and naturalism in Gothic art. Tr. with notes and bibl. by Randolph J. Klawiter. Pref. by Karl Maria Swoboda. [notre Dame, Ind.] Univ. of Notre Dame Pr., 1967. xxx, 252p. illus. (pt. col) 27cm. Tr. of Idealismus und Naturalismus in der gotschen Skulptur und Malerei. Bibl. [N6310.D813] 67-22143 22.50
1. Art, Gothic. 2. Sculpture, Gothic. 3. Idealism in art. 4. Naturalism in art. I. Title.

FRANCIS, Anne F., 1912- 759.69
Voyage of re-discovery : the Veneration of Saint Vincent / Anne F. Francis. 1st ed. Hicksville, N.Y. : Exposition Press, c1979. 158 p. : ill. (some col.) ; 24 cm. (An Exposition university book) Includes index. Bibliography: p. 149-154. [ND803.P343F7] 77-75877 ISBN 0-682-48429-6 : 15.00
1. Goncalves, Nuno, fl. 1450-1471. 2. Lisbon. Sao Vicente de Fora (Church) 3. Paineis de Sao Vicente de Fora (Panel painting) 4. Panel painting, Gothic—Portugal. 5. Panel painting—Attribution. I. Title.

HARVEY, John Hooper. 723.5
The Gothic world, 1100-1600; a survey of architecture and art London, New York, Batsford [1950] xii, 160 p. illus., maps. 27 cm. (The British art and building series) Bibliography: p. 133-136. [N6310.H3] 51-2293
1. Art, Gothic. 2. Architecture, Gothic. I. Title. II. Series.

HARVEY, John Hooper. 723'.5
The Gothic world, 1100-1600; a survey of architecture and art [by] John Harvey. New York, Harper & Row [1969] xv, 160 p. illus., maps. 21 cm. (Harper colophon books, CN137) Reprint of the 1950 ed. Bibliography: p. 133-136. [N6310.H3 1969] 69-12465 2.75
1. Art, Gothic. 2. Architecture, Gothic. I. Title.

HENDERSON, George David Smith, 1931- 709'.4
Gothic [by] George Henderson. Harmondsworth, Penguin, 1967. 223 p. 113 illus., plan, facsim. 20 cm. (Style and civilization) (B67-11607) Pelican book, A806. Bibliography: p. 217-219. [N6310.H4] 67-97913
1. Art, Gothic. I. Title. BIP

MARTINDALE, Andrew. 709.02'2
Gothic art from the twelfth to fifteenth centuries. New York, F. A. Praeger [1967] 287 p. illus. (part col.), facsims., plans. 22 cm. Bibliography: p. 272-273. [N6310.M3 1967b] 67-28194
1. Art, Gothic. I. Title.

SITWELL, Sacheverell, Sir, Bart., 1897- 709'.4
Gothic Europe. [1st ed.] New York, Holt, Rinehart and Winston [1969] xvi, 192 p. illus. (part col.) 26 cm. Bibliographical footnotes. [N6310.S5 1969b] 69-20055 11.95
1. Art, Gothic. I. Title.

WORRINGER, Wilhelm, 1881- 709.02
Form in Gothic. Authorized tr. [from German] ed. introd. by Sir Herbert Read. [Rev. ed.] Containing the original illus. New York, Schocken [1964] (Schocken paperbacks SB70) 63-22688 5.00; 1.95 pap.,
1. Art, Gothic. 2. Architecture, Gothic. 3. Aesthetic. I. Read, Herbert Edward, Sir 1893- ed. and tr. II. Title.

WORRINGER, Wilhelm, 1881- 709.02
Form in Gothic. Authorized translation edited with an introd. by Sir Herbert Read. Containing the original illus. New York, Schocken [1964, c1957] xv. 181 p. illus. 23 cm. Translation of Formprobleme der Gotik. [NG310.W6 1964a] 64-4440
1. Art, Gothic. 2. Architecture, Gothic. 3. Aesthetics. I. Read, Sir Herbert Edward, 1896- ed. and tr. II. Title.

Art, Gothic—Czechoslovak Republic.

KUTAL, Albert. 709'.437'1
Gothic art in Bohemia and Moravia; [translated from the Czech by Till Gottheiner]. London, New York, Hamlyn, 1972. 3-212 p. illus. (some col.), facsims. (some col.), maps, plans. 32 cm. Bibliography: p. 204-206. [N6826.K8913] 72-170063 ISBN 0-600-01658-7
1. Art, Gothic—Czechoslovak Republic. 2. Art, Czech. I. Title.
Distributed by Book Sales, 110 Enterprise Ave., Secaucus, N.J. 07094.

Art, Gothic—Czechoslovakia.

GOTHIC art in Bohemia 709'.437'1
: architecture, sculpture, and painting / Ferdinand Seibt ... [et al.] ; edited by Erich Bachmann ; [translated by Gerald Onn]. Abridged. New York : Praeger Publishers, 1977. 96 p., [78] leaves of plates : ill. (some col.) ; 29 cm. Translation of Gotik in Bohmen. Includes index. Bibliography: p. 90-92. [N6826.G67132] 77-111067 ISBN 0-275-36590-5 : 35.00
1. Art, Gothic—Czechoslovakia. 2. Art—Czechoslovakia. I. Seibt, Ferdinand. II. Bachmann, Erich, 1910-

Art, Gothic—Exhibitions.

AUSTRIA. Bundesministerium fur Unterricht. 709.02
L'art Europeen vers 1400 [i.e. mil quatre cent: huitieme exposition sous les auspices du Conseil de l Europe]Tr. francaise par Monique Aurenhammer ed al. Vienne, Kunsthistorisches Museum [1962] 470p. 160 plates. 21cm. Catalog. L'exposition 'L'art europeen vers 1400' est placee sous le haut patronage du Gouvernement federal autrichien et du Ministere de l'instruction publique. Elle est organisee . . . au Kunsthistorisches Museum de Vienne, 7 mai 1962-31 juillet 1962. [N6310.A8814] 66-9316 price unreported pap.,
1. Art, Gothic—Exhibitions. I. Council of Europe. II. Vienna. Kunsthistorisches Museum. III. Title.
Now available from World-Wide Bks., New York City.

BROWN University. Dept. of Art. 709'.02'207401452
Transformations of the court style : Gothic art in Europe, 1270 to 1330 : an exhibition by the Department of Art, Brown University at the Museum of Art, Rhode Island School of Design, Providence, Rhode Island, February 2 through February 27, 1977. [Providence, R.I.] : The Department, c1977. 163 p. : ill. ; 27 cm. Bibliography: p. 155-161. [N6310.B75 1977] 77-70260
1. Art, Gothic—Exhibitions. I. Rhode Island School of Design, Providence. Museum of Art. II. Title.

Art, Gothic—High Gothic.

AUBERT, Marcel, 1884-1962. 709.02
The art of the High Gothic era. By Marcel Aubert, with the collaboration of J. A. Schmoll gen. Eisenwerth and contributions by Hans H. Hofstatter. [Translated by Peter Gorge] New York, Crown Publishers [1965] 227 p. illus. (part mounted col.) maps, plans, plates. 24 cm. (Art of the world, non-European cultures; the historical, sociological, and religious backgrounds) Translation of Le Triomphe de l'art Gothique. Bibliography: p. 205-209. [N6310.A833] 64-24750
1. Art, Gothic—High Gothic. I. Schmoll gen. Eisenwerth, J. Adolph, 1915- II. Title. III. Series: Art of the world; the historical, sociological, and religious backgrounds

Art, Gothic—History—Sources.

FRISCH, Teresa Grace. 709.02'2
Gothic art 1140-c. 1450; sources and documents [by] Teresa G. Frisch. Englewood Cliffs, N.J., Prentice-Hall [1971] x, 181 p. front. 23 cm. (Sources and documents in the history of art series) Bibliography: p. 171-176. [N6310.F7] 77-135403 ISBN 0-13-360545-0
1. Art, Gothic—History—Sources. I. Title.

Art, Gothic—Late Gothic.

SWAAN, Wim. 709'.02'3
The late Middle Ages : art and architecture from 1350 to the advent of the Renaissance / Wim Swaan ; with photos. by the author. Ithaca, N.Y. : Cornell University Press, 1977. 232 p. : ill. (some col.) ; 32 cm. Includes index. Bibliography: p. [224]-227. [N6320.S92 1977b] 77-77552 ISBN 0-8014-1141-6 : 27.50
1. Art, Gothic—Late Gothic. I. Title.

Art, Gothic—Late Gothic—Addresses, essays, lectures.

FIFTEENTH century art and architecture. New York : Garland Pub., 1976. p. cm. (The Garland library of the history of art ; v. 6) Includes bibliographical references. [N5300.G32 vol. 6] [N6320] 709'.02'4 76-14068 ISBN 0-8240-2416-8 lib.bdg. : 35.00 709 s
1. Art, Gothic—Late Gothic—Addresses, essays, lectures. 2. Art, Renaissance—Addresses, essays, lectures. I. Series.
Contents omitted

Art, Gothic—Late Gothic—Exhibitions.

BROWN University. Dept. of Art. 704.948'2
Europe in torment: 1450-1550; [catalog of] an exhibition by the Department of Art, Brown University at the Museum of Art, Rhode Island School of Design, Providence, Rhode Island, March 6 through April 7, 1974. [Providence, 1974] 151 p. illus. 26 cm. Includes bibliographies. [N6320.B76 1974] 74-76417
1. Art, Gothic—Late Gothic—Exhibitions. 2. Art and religion. 3. Symbolism in art. I. Rhode Island School of Design, Providence. Museum of Art. II. Title.

Art—Graduate work.

STANFORD University. Dept. of Art. 707'.11
1972 graduate programs in painting, sculpture, lithography, and design [Menlo Park, Calif., Stanford University Press, 1972] [24] p. illus. 22 x 28 cm. Cover title. [N330.M432S73] 72-190323
1. Art—Graduate work. I. Title.

Art, Graeco-Roman.

DEISS, Joseph Jay. 913.37703
Herculaneum; Italy's buried treasure. New York, Crowell [1966] xv, 174 . illus., plans. 25 cm. Bibliography: p. 167-169. [N5775.D38] 66-26638
1. Art. Graeco-Roman. 2. Herculaneum. I. Title.

DEISS, Joseph Jay. 913.37'7
Herculaneum; Italy's buried treasure. New York, Crowell [1966] xv, 174 p. illus., plans. 25 cm. Bibliography: p. 167-169. [N5775.D38] 66-26638
1. Art, Graeco-Roman. 2. Herculaneum. I. Title.

Art — Gt. Brit.

TOYNBEE, Jocelyn M C 709.42
Art in Britain under the Romans, by J. M. C. Toynbee. Oxford, Clarendon Press, 1964. xxiv, 473, 99 p. illus., ports. 28 cm. bBibliographical footnotes. Bibliography: p. [444]-445. [N5843.T58] 64-56384
1. Art — Gt. Brit. 2. Art Roman. 3. Gt. Brit. — Antiquities, Roman. I. Title.

Art—Great Britain—Galleries and museums.

ABSE, Joan, 1926- 708'.941
The art galleries of Britain and Ireland : a guide to their collections / Joan Abse. 1st American ed. Rutherford, [N.J.] : Fairleigh Dickinson University Press, 1976, c1975. 248 p., [6] leaves of plates : ill. ; 24 cm. Includes index. [N1020.A27 1976] 75-24944 ISBN 0-8386-1850-2 : 12.00
1. Art—Great Britain—Galleries and museums. 2. Art—Northern Ireland—Galleries and museums. I. Title. BIP

Art—Gt. Brit.—Yearbooks.

ARTS Council of Great Britain 700.942
Report. 21st, 1965-66. Key year. [New York, British Info., 1967] 114p. illus. (pt. col.) 21cm. annual. Report year ends Mar. 31. Supersedes the council's Report on the work of C.E.M.A. [N9.A635] 66-4699 .70 pap.,
1. Art—Gt. Brit.—Yearbooks. I. Gt Brit. British Information Services. II. Title.

ARTS Council of Great Britian 700.942
Report. 20th. 1964.65. [New York, Brit. Info. 1966] 128p. illus., ports. 22cm. annual. Report year ends Mar. 31. Supersedes the council's Report on the

work of C.E.M.A. [N9.A635] 66-4699 .70 pap.,
1. Art—Gt. Brit.—Yearbooks. I. Gt. Brit. British Information Services. II. Title.

Art, Greco-Roman.

RICHTER, Gisela Marie Augusta, 1882- 709.37
Ancient Italy; a study of the interrelations of its peoples as shown in their arts. Ann Arbor, University of Michigan Press, 1955. xxiv, 137p. 305 illus. 29cm. (Jerome lectures, 4th ser.) Bibliographical footnotes. [N5760.R45] 55-10726
1. Art, Greco-Roman. 2. Art, Greek. 3. Art, Roman. 4. Art—Italy. I. Title. II. Series.

WEBSTER, Thomas Bertram Lonsdale, 1905- 709.01'4
The art of Greece; the age of Hellenism, by T. B. L. Webster. New York, Crown Publishers [1966] 243 p. illus. (part col., part mounted), maps. 24 cm. (Art of the world) Bibliography: p. 224-232. [N5613.W4] 66-26188
1. Art, Greco-Roman. I. Title. II. Series. BIP

Art, Greco-Roman—Pompeii.

KRAUS, Theodor, 1919- 913.37'7
Pompeii and Herculaneum : the living cities of the dead / text by Theodor Kraus ; photos. by Leonard von Matt ; translated from the German by Robert Erich Wolf. New York : H. N. Abrams, [1975] p. cm. Translation of Pompeji und Herculaneum. Includes bibliographical references and index. [N5769.K7213] 74-19453 ISBN 0-8109-0418-7 : 35.00
1. Art, Greco-Roman—Pompeii. 2. Art—Pompeii. 3. Art, Greco-Roman—Herculaneum. 4. Art—Herculaneum. I. Title. BIP

Art, Greek.

THE Art of classical Greece and the Etruscans; 709'.38
general editor Francesco Abbate; translated [from the Italian] by Enid Gordon. London, New York, Octopus Books, 1972. 158 p. chiefly 95 col. illus. 20 cm. Translation of Dalla Grecia classica all'Etruria. Bibliography: p. 155. [N5630.D313] 72-172040 ISBN 0-7064-0029-1
1. Art, Greek. 2. Art, Greco-Roman. 3. Art, Etruscan. I. Abbate, Francesco, ed.
Available from Books Sales 110 Enterprise Avenue Secaucus, N.Y. 07094; 2.95.

BECATTI, Giovanni, 1912- 709.01'4
The art of ancient Greece and Rome, from the rise of greece to the fall of Rome. New York, H.N. Abrams [1967] 441 p. 385 illus. (part col.) 32 cm. Bibliography: p. 401-423 [N5610.B32] 67-12684
1. Art. Greek. 2. Art, Roman I. Title.

BECATTI, Giovanni, 1912- 709'.38
The art of ancient Greece and Rome; from the rise of Greece to the fall of Rome. Englewood Cliffs, N.J., Prentice-Hall [1968] 440 p. illus. (part col.) 30 cm. Translation of L'eta classica. Bibliography: p. 401-423. [N5610.B3313 1968] 68-7276
1. Art, Greek. 2. Art, Roman. I. Title.

BECATTI, Giovanni, 1912- 709.01'4
The art of ancient Greece and Rome, from the rise of Greece to the fall of Rome. New York, H. N. Abrams [1967] 441 p. 385 illus. (part col.) 32 cm. Translation of L'eta classica. Bibliography: p. 401-423. [N5610.B32] 67-12684
1. Art, Greek. 2. Art, Roman. I. Title.

BOARDMAN, John, 1927- 709.38
Greek art. New York, Praeger [1964] 286 p. illus. (part col.) map. 22 cm. (Praeger world of art series) Bibliography: p. 271-272. [N5630.B58] 64-22936
1. Art, Greek. I. Title.

BOARDMAN, John, 1927- 709'.38
Greek art. Rev. ed. New York, Praeger [1973] 252 p. illus. (part col.) 21 cm. (Praeger world of art series) (Praeger world of art paperbacks, P-387) Bibliography: p. 238-241. [N5630.B58 1973] 72-90414 pap. 4.95
1. Art, Greek. I. Title.

BOARDMAN, John 1927- 709'.38
Greek art and architecture [by] John Boardman [and others] Photos. by Max Hirmer. New York, H. N. Abrams [1967] 600 p. illus. (part col.), map, plans. 30 cm. Translation of the Die Griechische Kunst. Bibliography: p. 587-588. [N5630.G713] 67-22850
1. Art, Greek. 2. Architecture, Greek. I. Hirmer, Max, A, II. Title.

BOHR, Russell LeRoi. 709.01/4
Classical art [by] R. L. Bohr. Dubuque, Iowa, W. C. Brown, 1967 [c.1968] xiii, 158p. illus., maps, plans. 23cm. (Art horizons ser.) Bibl. [N5610.B58] 67-21302 1.95 pap.,
1. Art, Greek. 2. Art, Greco-Roman. I. Title.

BOSTON. Museum of Fine Arts. 709.38
Greek, Etruscan, & Roman art; the classical collections. [Rev. with additions by Cornelius C. Vermeule III. Boston] 1963. 290 p. illus. (part col.) fold map, plans. 22 cm. Includes bibliographies. [N5634.B6] 63-15611
1. Art, Greek. 2. Art, Etruscan. 3. Art, Roman. I. Title. BIP

BRILLIANT, Richard. 709'.38
Arts of the ancient Greeks. New York, McGraw-Hill [1973] xxiii, 406 p. illus. (part col.) 30 cm. Includes bibliographies. [N5630.B74] 72-14098 ISBN 0-07-007850-5 16.95
1. Art, Greek. I. Title. BIP

CHAMOUX, Francois. 709.38
Greek art. Text by Francois Chamoux. [Translated from the French by Mary Ilford and Inge Sonn] Greenwich, Conn., New York Graphic Society [1966] 97, [7] p. illus. (part col.) maps, plans. 28 cm. (The Pallas library of art, v. 2) Bibliography: p. [101] [N5630.C453] 65-21746
1. Art, Greek. I. Title.

CHARBONNEAUX, Jean, 1895-1969. 709'.38
Classical Greek art (480-330 B.C.) [by] Jean Charbonneaux, Roland Martin [and] Francois Villard. Translated from the French by James Emmons] New York, G. Braziller [1972] xi, 422 p. illus. (part col.) 29 cm. (The Arts of mankind, v. 16) Translation of Grece classique (480-330 avant J.-C.) Bibliography: p. 367-376. [N5630.C4613 1972b] 72-80015 ISBN 0-8076-0627-8
1. Art, Greek. I. Martin, Roland, 1912- joint author. II. Villard, Francois, joint author. III. Title. IV. Series.

COOK, Robert Manuel. 709'.38
Greek art: its development, character, and influence [by] R. M. Cook. [1st American ed.] New York, Farrar, Straus, Giroux [1973, c1972] 277 p., 96 p. of illus. 23 cm. Bibliography: p. 261-266. [N5630.C73 1973] 72-84781 ISBN 0-374-16670-6 12.95
1. Art, Greek.

CRAVEN, Thomas, 1889- 709.38
The pocket book of Greek art. New York, Pocket Books [1950] 120 p. 32 plates. 17 cm. (Pocket book 677) Bibliography: p. 120. [N5630.C75] 50-3894
1. Art, Greek. I. Title.

FAIRBANKS, Arthur, 1864-1944 709.38
Greek art, the basis of later European art. New York, Cooper Sq., 1963. x, 136p. illus., ports. 19cm. (Our debt to Greece and Rome) Bibl. 63-10265 2.95
1. Art, Greek. I. Title. II. Series.

GARDNER, Ernest Arthur, 1862-1939. 709'.495
The art of Greece. New York, Cooper Square Publishers, 1975. viii, 54 p. 56 plates 24 cm. Reprint of the 1925 ed. published by The Studio Ltd, London. Bibliography: p. 53-54. [N5630.G2 1975] 74-84546 ISBN 0-8154-0503-0 7.50 (lib. bdg.)
1. Art, Greek. I. Title. BIP

GARDNER, Percy, 1846-1937. 733'.3
New chapters in Greek art. Oxford, Clarendon Press, 1926. [New York, AMS Press, 1971] xiv, 367 p. illus. 23 cm. Includes bibliographical references. [N5630.G33 1971] 73-149658 ISBN 0-404-02679-6
1. Art, Greek. 2. Sculpture, Greek. 3. Theater—Greece. I. Title. BIP

GLUBOK, Shirley. 709.38
The art of ancient Greece. Designed by Oscar Krauss. [1st ed.] New York, Atheneum, 1963. 48 p. illus. 26 cm. Presents various objects of Greek art—vases, statues, buildings, reliefs, friezes, and ornaments—and explains how they were made and used, and aspects of the culture which they present. [N5630.G56] AC 68
1. Art, Greek. I. Title.

HOFFMANN, Herbert, 1930- 709.38
Collecting Greek antiquities. Introd. by John D. Cooney. A chapter on coins by Herbert A. Cahn. [1st ed.] New York, C. N. Potter [1971] xii, 258 p. illus., map (on lining papers), col. plates. 24 cm. Includes bibliographies. [N5613.H64 1971] 69-13401 15.00
1. Art, Greek. 2. Art—Collectors and collecting. I. Title. BIP

HOMANN-WEDEKING, Ernst. 709'.38
The art of archaic Greece, by E. Homann-Wedeking. Translated by J. R. Foster. New York, Crown Publishers [1968] 224 p. illus. (part col.), map. 24 cm. (Art of the world; European cultures: the historical, sociological, and religious backgrounds) Translation of Das archaische Greichenland. Bibliographical references included in "Notes" (p. 209-211) [N5633.H7713] 68-16898
1. Art, Greek. I. Title. II. Series: Art of the world; the historical, sociological, and religious backgrounds

IVINS, William Mills, 1881-1961 742.09
Art & geometry; a study in space intuitions. New York, Dover [1964, c.1946] x, 113p. diagrs. 22cm. (T941) Bibl. 64-15511 1.00 pap.,
1. Art, Greek. 2. Space-perception. 3. Geometry—Hist. 4. Perspective. I. Title. BIP

LIBERMAN, Alexander, 1912- 704.948
Greece, gods, and art. Introd. by Robert Graves. Texts and commentaries on the photos. by Iris C. Love. New York, Viking Press [1968] 64 p., [158] p. of illus. (part col.) map. 34 cm. (A Studio book) [N5633.L5] 68-23205 22.50
1. Art, Greek. 2. Gods in art. I. Love, Iris C. II. Title.

MARKMAN, Sidney David, 1911- 709'.38
The horse in Greek art. New York, Biblo and Tannen, 1969 [c1943] xvii, 211 p. plates. 24 cm. A reprint of the author's thesis, Columbia, 1943. Bibliography: p. 197-206. [N5633.M36 1969] 72-88057
1. Art, Greek. 2. Horses in art. I. Title. BIP

NEW York. Metropolitan Museum of Art. 709.38
Handbook of the Greek collection, by Gisela M. A. Richter. Cambridge, Harvard University Press, 1953[i. e. 1954] viii, 322p. illus. 25cm. Bibliography: p. [315]-316. [N610.A674] 53-5059
1. Art, Greek. 2. Sculpture, Greek. I. Richter, Gisela Marie Augusta, 1882- II. Title.

POLLITT, Jerry Jordan. 709'.38
Art and experience in classical Greece [by] J. J. Pollitt. Cambridge [Eng.] Cambridge University Press, 1972. xiv, 205 p. illus. 25 cm. Bibliography: p. [199]-202. [N5630.P54 1972] 74-160094 ISBN 0-521-08065-7
1. Art, Greek. 2. Art—Psychology. I. Title. BIP

RICHTER, Gisela Mari Augusta, 1882- 709.38
A handbook of Greek art [4th ed., newly rev. London] Phaidon; dist. New York, Oxford [1965, c.1959] vi,424p. 508 illus., 4 col. plates. 26cm. Bibl. [N5630.R49] 66-1672 5.75
1. Art, Greek. I. Title.

RICHTER, Gisela Marie Augusta, 1882- 709.38
A handbook of Greek art. [2d ed., rev. Dist. New York, Oxford, 1962, c.1959] vi, 421p. 507 illus. (pt. col.) maps. 26cm. A62 5.75
1. Art, Greek. I. Title. BIP

RICHTER, Gisela Marie Augusta, 1882- 709'.38
A handbook of Greek art [by] Gisela M. A. Richter. [6th ed. redesigned] London, New York, Phaidon [1969] 431 p. illus., maps. 26 cm. Bibliography: p. 399-410. [N5630.R49 1969b] 68-18912 10.00
1. Art, Greek. I. Title.

RICHTER, Gisela Marie Augusta, 1882- 709.38
A handbook of Greek art, by Gisela M. A. Richter. [4th ed., newly rev. London] Phaidon; distributed by Oxford University Press, New York [1965] vi, 424 p. 508 illus., 4 col. plates. 26 cm. Bibliography: p. 389-401. [N5630.R49] 66-1672
1. Art, Greek. I. Title.

RIDDER, Andre Henri Pierre de, 1868-1921. 709'.38
Art in Greece, by A. de Ridder and W. Deonna. [Translated by V. C. C. Collum] New York, Barnes & Noble [1968] xxxii, 375 p. illus. 25 cm. (The History of civilization) Reprint of the 1927 ed. Bibliography: p. 355-363. [N5630.R52 1968b] 68-7275 9.00
1. Art, Greek. I. Deonna, Waldemar, 1880-1959, joint author. II. Title.

ROBERT, Carl, 1850-1922. 709'.38
Archaeologische Hermeneutik : Anleitung zur Deutung klassischer Bildwerke / von Carl Robert. New York : Arno Press, 1975. 432 p. : ill. ; 24 cm. (Ancient religion and mythology) Reprint of the 1919 ed. published by Weidmann, Berlin. Includes bibliographical references. [N5630.R62 1975] 75-10652 ISBN 0-405-07276-7
1. Art, Greek. 2. Greece—Antiquities. 3. Art and mythology. I. Title. II. Series. BIP

ROBERT, Carl, 1850-1922. 700'.938
Bild und Lied : archaologische Beitrage zur Geschichte der griechischen Heldensage / von Carl Robert. New York : Arno Press, 1975. 258 p. : ill. ; 23 cm. (Ancient religion and mythology) Reprint of the 1881 ed. published by Weidmann, Berlin, which was issued as Heft 5 of Philologische Untersuchungen. Includes bibliographical references and index. [N7760.R62 1975] 75-10653 ISBN 0-405-07277-5
1. Art, Greek. 2. Gods in art. 3. Mythology, Greek. I. Title. II. Series. III. Series: Philologische Untersuchungen ; Heft 5. BIP

SCHEFOLD, Karl. 709'.38
The art of classical Greece. [Tr. by J. R. Foster] New York, Crown [1966,c.1967] 294p. illus., 50 col. plates, map, plans. 24 cm. (Art of the world; European cultures, the hist., sociological, and religious backgrounds) Bibl. [N5630.S3313 1967] 67-17705 6.95
1. Art, Greek. I. Title. II. Series: Art of the world; the historical, sociological, and religious backgrounds

SCHODER, Raymond V., 1916- 709.38
Masterpieces of Greek art. Text and color photography by Raymond V. Schoder. Greenwich, Conn., New York, Graphic Society [1960] 15p. bBibl.: p.14-15. 96 col: plates, map (on lining papers) 26cm. 60-8922 12.50
1. Art, Greek. I. Title. BIP

SCHODER, Raymond V., 1916- 709'.38
Masterpieces of Greek art / text & photography by Raymond V. Schoder. 3d ed., rev. Chicago : Ares Publishers, 1975. 13, [15] p., 96 leaves of plates : col. ill. ; 23 cm. Commentary for each plate on verso of preceding plate. Bibliography: p. [5]-[10] (2d group) [N5630.S35 1975] 75-4410 ISBN 0-89005-071-6 : 15.00 pbk. : 6.00
1. Art, Greek. I. Title.

SCHUCHHARDT, Walter Herwig, 1900- 709'.38
Greek art. [Translated by Sabine MacCormack] New York, Universe Books [1972] 189 p. illus. 23 cm. Translation of Griechische Kunst. Bibliography: p. 186-187. [N5630.S3713] 70-175860 ISBN 0-87663-169-3 6.95

1. Art, Greek. BIP

SCHWEITZER, Bernhard, 1892-1966. 709'.38
Greek geometric art. [Edited by Ulrich Hausmann in co-operation with Jochen Briegleb. Translated by Peter and Cornelia Usborne. New York] Phaidon [1971] 352 p. illus., map (on lining paper), plans, ports. 26 cm. Translation of Die geometrische Kunst Griechenlands. Includes bibliographical references. [N5630.S3913 1971] 71-111066 ISBN 0-7148-1411-3 29.50
1. Art, Greek. I. Title. BIP

SELTMAN, Charles Theodore, 1886-1957. 709.38
Approach to Greek art. New York, Dutton, 1960. 132p. illus. (Dutton Everyman paperback, D52) 60-51408 1.65 pap.,
1. Art, Greek. I. Title.

WEGNER, Max, 1902- 709.38
Greek masterworks of art. Translated by Charlotte La Rue. New York, G. Braziller, 1961. 190, [2] p. 166 illus. (part col.) 31 cm. Bibliographical references: p. [191] [N5630.W453] 61-8475
1. Art, Greek. I. Title.

Art, Greek—Exhibitions.

CALIFORNIA. University, Santa Barbara. Art Gallery. v. 12
Greek art in private collections of southern California. [Santa Barbara, 1963] 8. [16]m 9-15 p. illus. 26 cm. "An exhibition [Nov. 19-Dec. 17, 1963]organized by the Art Gallery. University of California, Santa Barbara in cooperation with the Affiliates of Art." Introd. by M.A. Del Chiaro Bibliography: p. [3] (1st group) [N5635.C3] 66-63796
1. Art, Greek—Exhibitions. 2. Art—Private collections. I. Del Chiaro, Marlo Aldo, 1925- II. Title.

CALIFORNIA. University, Santa Barbara. Art Galleries. v. 12
Greek art in private collections of southern California; a loan exhibition at the Art Gallery, University of California, Santa Barbara [by] Mario A. Del Chiaro. Rev. and expanded ed. [Santa Barbara] 1966. 18 p. illus. 24 cm. Bibliography: p. 5. [N5635.C3 1966] 66-64410
1. Art, Greek—Exhibitions. 2. Art—Private collections—California, Southern. I. Del Chiaro, Mario Aldo, 1925- II. Title.

HOFFMANN, Herbert, 1930- 733'.074'0164
Ten centuries that shaped the West; Greek and Roman art in Texas collections, by Herbert Hoffmann. [Exhibition] Institute for the Arts, Rice University, Oct. 15, 1970-Jan. 3, 1971, Dallas Museum of Fine Arts, Feb. 3-Apr. 11, Witte Memorial Museum, San Antonio, May 16-July 11. [Houston? 1970] xxiii, 502 p. illus. (part col.) 23 cm. Organized and circulated by the Institute for the Arts, Rice University. Bibliography: p. 491-502. [N5603.H6W53] 71-131999
1. Art, Greek—Exhibitions. 2. Art, Roman—Exhibitions. 3. Art, Greek—Texas. 4. Art, Roman—Texas. I. William Marsh Rice University, Houston, Tex. Institute for the Arts. II. Dallas. Museum of Fine Arts. III. Witte Memorial Museum, San Antonio. IV. Title. BIP

Art—Greek—History.

CARPENTER, Rhys 709.38
The esthetic basis of Greek art of the fifth and fourth centuries B. C. [Rev. ed.] Bloomington, Indiana University Press [c.1959] 177p. (bibl.: p. 161-164 and bibl. notes: p. 167-171) illus. 21cm. 60-92 3.50
1. Art. Greek—Hist. 2. Aesthetics. I. Title.

CARPENTER, Rhys, 1889- 709.38
The esthetic basis of Greek art of the fifth and fourth centuries B. C. [Magnolia, Mass., P. Smith. 1966,c.1959] 177p. illus. 20cm. (Midland bk., MB19 rebound) [N5630.C3 1959] 3.75
1. Art, Greek—Hist. 2. Aesthetics. I. Title. BIP

CARPENTER, Rhys, 1889- 709.38
The esthetic basis of Greek art of the fifth and fourth centuries B. C. Bloomington, Indiana University Press [1959] 177p. illus. 20cm. (A Midland book, MB19) Includes bibliography. [N5630.C3 1959] 59-13530
1. Art, Greek—Hist. 2. Aesthetics. I. Title.

CARPENTER, Rhys, 1889- 709.38
Greek art; a study of the formal evolution of style. Philadelphia, Univ. of Pa. Pr. [1963, c.1962] 256p. illus. 26cm. 61-6619 12.50
1. Art, Greek—Hist. I. Title.

Art, Greek—History.

CHARBONNEAUX, Jean, 1895-1969. 709'.38
Archaic Greek art (620-480 B.C.) [by] Jean Charbonneaux, Roland Martin [and] Francois Villard. [Translated from the French by James Emmons [and] Robert Allen. New York, G. Braziller [1971] xi, 437 p. illus. (part. fold. col.), fold. col. maps. 29 cm. (The Arts of mankind, v. 14) Translation of Grece archaique. Bibliography: p. [383]-[396] [N5630.C45713] 78-136166 ISBN 0-8076-0587-5
1. Art, Greek—History. I. Martin, Roland, joint author. II. Villard, Francois, joint author. III. Title. IV. Series.

DEMARGNE, Pierre. 709.38
The birth of Greek art. Translated by Stuart Gilbert and James Emmons. New York, Golden Press [1964] 446 p. illus. (part col.) maps (part fold. col.) plans, plates (part col.) ports. 29 cm. (The Arts of mankind, v. 6) Bibliography: p. [419]-430. [N5630.D363] 64-21312
1. Art, Greek—History. 2. Greece—Antiquities. 3. Art, Primitive. I. Title. II. Series. BIP

FOWLER, Harold North, 1859-1955. 913.8'03
A handbook of Greek archaeology, by Harold North Fowler [and] James Rignall Wheeler. With the collaboration of Gorham Phillips Stevens. New York, AMS Press [1969] 559 p. illus. 23 cm. Reprint of the 1909 ed. Bibliography: p. 542-550. [N5630.F8 1969] 73-95403
1. Art, Greek—History. I. Wheeler, James Rignall, 1859-1918, joint author. II. Stevens, Gorham Phillips, 1876- joint author. III. Title. BIP

FOWLER, Harold North, 1859-1955. 709'.38
A handbook of Greek archaeology, by Harold North Fowler [and] James Rignall Wheeler with the collaboration of Gorham Phillips Stevens. New York, American Book Co. St. Clair Shores, Mich., Scholarly Press, 1974 [c1909] p. cm. Original ed. issued in series: Greek series for colleges and schools. Bibliography: p. [N5630.F8 1974] 74-3186 ISBN 0-403-03076-5
1. Art, Greek—History. I. Wheeler, James Rignall, 1859-1918, joint author. II. Stevens, Gorham Phillips, 1876- III. Title. IV. Series: Greek series for colleges and schools.

HOLLOWAY, R. Ross. 709'.38
A view of Greek art [by] R. Ross Holloway. New York, Harper & Row, 1974 [c 1973] xxii, 213 p. illus., 24 cm. (Icon editions) Includes bibliographical references. [N5630.H64] ISBN 0-06-430046-3 4.95 (pbk.)
1. Art, Greek—History. I. Title.
L.C. card no. for hardcover: 72-187947. BIP

HOLLOWAY, R. Ross, 1934- 709'.38
A view of Greek art [by] R. Ross Holloway. Providence, Brown University Press [1973] xxii, 213 p. illus. 26 cm. Includes bibliographical references. [N5630.H64] 72-187947 ISBN 0-87057-133-8 15.00
1. Art, Greek—History. I. Title.

KJELLBERG, Ernst, 1891-1938. 709'.38
Greek and Roman art; 3000 B.C. to A.D. 550 [by] Ernst Kjellberg & Gosta Saflund. New York, T. Y. Crowell Co. [1968] 250 p. illus., maps. 23 cm. Translation of Grekisk och romersk konst. Bibliography: p. 222-228. [N5610.K5513 1968b] 68-20758 7.95
1. Art, Greek—History. 2. Art, Roman—History. I. Saflund, Gosta, 1903- joint author. II. Title. BIP

MATZ, Friedrich, 1890- 709.3
The art of Crete and early Greece; the prelude to Greek art. [Translated by Ann E. Keep] New York, Crown Publishers [1962] 260 p. illus. (part mounted col.) maps, plans. 24 cm. (Art of the world, European cultures; the historical, sociological, and religious backgrounds.) Translation of Kreta und fruhes Griechenland. Bibliography: p. 248-250. [N5630.M313] 62-20056
1. Art, Greek—History. 2. Art, Cretan—History. 3. Art, Mycenaean—History. I. Title. II. Series: Art of the world; the historical, sociological, and religious backgrounds

ROBERTSON, Martin. 709'.38
A history of Greek art / Martin Robertson. London : Cambridge University Press, 1976 2 v. ([23], 835 p., [202] p. of plates) : ill., maps, plans ; 29 cm. Includes indexes. Bibliography: p. 740-759. [N5630.R63] 73-79317 ISBN 0-521-20277-9 : 75.00
1. Art, Greek—History. I. Title. BIP

STRONG, Donald Emrys. 709.38
The classical world [by] Donald E. Strong. New York, McGraw-Hill [1965] 166, [10] p. illus., col. plates, maps (on lining papers), plans. 30 cm. (Landmarks of the world's art) Bibliography: p. [169] [N5610.S83] 65-21594
1. Art, Greek—History. 2. Art, Roman—History. I. Title.

TARBELL, Frank Bigelow, 1853-1920. 709'.38
A history of Greek art, with an introductory chapter on art in Egypt and Mesopotamia. Westport, Conn., Greenwood Press [1971] 295 p. illus., plans. 23 cm. Reprint of the 1913 ed. Bibliography: p. 291-292. [N5630.T2 1971] 70-109860 ISBN 0-8371-4351-9
1. Art, Greek—History. I. Title. BIP

WALTERS, Henry Beauchamp, 1867-1944. 709'.38
The art of the Greeks. 3d ed., rev. Freeport, N.Y., Books for Libraries Press [1972] xvi, 284 p. illus. 27 cm. Reprint of the 1934 ed. Includes bibliographcial references. [N5630.W3 1972] 78-38373 ISBN 0-8369-6790-9
1. Art, Greek—History. I. Title. BIP

WEBSTER, Thomas Bertram Lonsdale, 1905- 700'.9495'12
Art and literature in fourth century Athens, by T. B. L. Webster. New York, Greenwood Press [1969] xvi, 159 p. 21 illus. 23 cm. Reprint of the 1956 ed. Bibliographical footnotes. [N5630.W4 1969] 69-14143
1. Art, Greek—History. 2. Greek literature—History and criticism. 3. Civilization, Greek. 4. Art and literature. I. Title. BIP

Art, Greek—History—Sources.

POLLITT, Jerry Jordan 709.38
The art of Greece, 1400-31 B. C.: sources and documents. Englewood Cliffs, N. J., Prentice [c.1965] xviii, 254p. 23cm. (Sources and docts. in the hist. of art ser.) Bibl. [N5630.P56] 65-23061 3.95 pap.,
1. Art, Greek—Hist.—Sources. I. Title. II. Series.

POLLITT, Jerry Jordan. 709.38
The art of Greece, 1400-31 B.C.: sources and documents [by] J. J. Pollitt Englewood Cliffs, N.J., Prentice-Hall [1965] xviii, 254 p. 23 cm. (Sources and documents in the history of art series) Bibliographical footnotes. [N5630.P56 1965] 65-23061
1. Art, Greek—History—Sources. I. Title. II. Series. BIP

Art, Greek — Juvenile literature.

GLUBOK, Shirley. j709.38
The art of ancient Greece. Designed by Oscar Krause. [1st ed.] New York, Atheneum, 1963. 48 p. illus. 26 cm. [N5630.G56] 63-16039
1. Art, Greek — Juvenile literature. I. Title.

Art — Greenville, S. C. — Guide-books.

BOB Jones University, Greenville, S. C. University Museum and Art Gallery. v. 12
Collection of religious art; xiv anniversary, 1951-1965. [Greenville, S. C.] Bob Jones University [1965] 1 v. (unpaged) illus., plates (part col.) 31 cm. Cover title. Published in connection with the opening of the Art Gallery and Museum building, Thanksgiving Day, 1965. [N571.B6] 66-89699
1. Art — Greenville, S. C. — Guide-books. 2. Bible — Pictures, illustrations, etc. I. Title.

Art, Guatemalan.

MENDEZ DAVILA, Lionel 709.7281
Guatemala. [english tr, by Ralph E. Dimmick] Washington, Pan Amer. Union, 1966. 110p. illus. 19cm. (Art in Latin Amer. today) Prepd. by the Div. of Visual Arts, Bibl. [N6576.M413] PA67 .75 pap.,
1. Art, Guatemalan. I. Pan American Union. Division of Visual Arts. II. Title. III. Series.

Art, Haitian.

RODMAN, Selden, 1909- 709'.7294
The miracle of Haitian art. [1st ed.] Garden City, N.Y., Doubleday [1974] 95 p. illus. (part col.) 25 cm. Includes bibliographical references. [N6606.R62] 73-81447 ISBN 0-385-07800-5 4.95
1. Art, Haitian. I. Title. BIP

Art, Haitian—Exhibitions.

CENTER for Inter-American Relations. Art Gallery. 709'.22
Art of Haiti and Jamaica; a loan exhibition, October 10-27, 1968. New York [1968] [33] p. illus. 17 cm. (Artists of the Western Hemisphere) Bibliography: p. [32]-[33] [N6606.C4] 77-3780
1. Art, Haitian—Exhibitions. 2. Art, Jamaican—Exhibitions. I. Title. II. Series.

RELIGION in the art of Haiti. 709'.7294
[New York? Printed by Maple Press, 1968?] [43] p. illus. 26 cm. Cover title. Catalogue, by L. Chalom, of an exhibition held Mar. 17-Apr. 10, 1968, Student Center Art Gallery, Seton Hall University, South Orange, N.J. [N6606.R44] 74-184192
1. Art, Haitian—Exhibitions. 2. Primitivism in art—Haiti. 3. Voodooism in art. I. Chalom, Leon. II. Seton Hall University, South Orange, N.J. Student Center Art Gallery.

Art, Haitian—History.

CHRISTENSEN, Eleanor Ingalls. 709'.7294
The art of Haiti. Philadelphia, Art Alliance Press [1975] 76 p., [48] p. of illus. (part col.) 32 cm. Bibliography: p. 73-74. [N6606.C54] 71-37807 ISBN 0-87982-006-3 12.50
1. Art, Haitian—History. 2. Primitivism in art—Haiti. I. Title. BIP

Art—Handbooks, manuals, etc.—Juvenile literature.

LALIBERTE, Norman. 702'.8
Reinhold book of art ideas / Norman Laliberte, Alex Mogelon. New York : Van Nostrand Reinhold, c1975. p. cm. Demonstrates uses of nine media, including woodcuts, collage, and ink, with a discussion of the history and development of each. [N7440.L34] 75-5150 ISBN 0-442-24611-0 pbk. : 8.95
1. Art—Handbooks, manuals, etc.—Juvenile literature. I. Mogelon, Alex, joint author. II. Title. III. Title: Book of art ideas. BIP

Art. — Hartford — Catalogs.

WADSWORTH Atheneum, Hartford. 708.146
Handbook. Hartford [1958] 103 p. (chiefly illus.) 23 cm. [N576.H3A32] 58-1211

1. Art. — Hartford — Catalogs. I. Title.

Art, Hausa—Catalogs.

HEATHCOTE, David. 745'.09669'5
The arts of the Hausa / David Heathcote. Chicago : University of Chicago Press, c1977. vii, 61 p. ; 23 cm. & microfiche (2 sheets : all col. ill. ; 11 x 16 cm.) in pocket. (A University of Chicago Press text-fiche) At head of title: The Commonwealth Institute. Based on the Arts of the Hausa exhibition held at the Commonwealth Institute, London, Apr.-June 1976. Bibliography: p. 55-61. [N7399.N5H38] 77-4274 ISBN 0-226-68899-2 : 22.50
1. Art, Hausa—Catalogs. 2. Art, Islamic—Nigeria—Catalogs. 3. Art, Primitive—Nigeria—Catalogs. I. Title. BIP

Art, Hausa—Exhibitions.

HEATHCOTE, David. 745'.09669'5
The arts of the Hausa : [catalogue of] a Commonwealth Institute exhibition : World of Islam Festival 1976 / [by] David Heathcote. [London] : World of Islam Festival Publishing Co. Ltd, 1976. 100 p., [8] p. of plates : ill. (some col.), facsims., 2 maps, ports. ; 25 cm. Exhibition held 6th Apr.-30th June, 1976. Bibliography: p. 87-95. [N7399.N5H4] 76-381420 ISBN 0-905035-05-4 : £2.50
1. Art, Hausa—Exhibitions. 2. Art, Islamic—Nigeria—Exhibitions. 3. Art, Primitive—Nigeria—Exhibitions. I. London. Commonwealth Institute. II. Title.

Art, Hellenistic.

CHARBONNEAUX, Jean, 1895- 709'.38 1969.
Hellenistic art (330-50 B.C.) [by] Jean Charbonneaux, Roland Martin [and] Francois Villard. [Translated from the French by Peter Green] New York, G. Braziller [1973] ix, 421 p. illus. (part col.) 28 cm. (The Arts of mankind, v. 18) Translation of Grece hellenistique. Bibliography: p. 371-382. [N5630.C46513 1973b] 72-89850 ISBN 0-8076-0666-9 35.00
1. Art, Hellenistic. I. Martin, Roland. II. Villard, Francois. III. Title. IV. Series.

HAVELOCK, Christine Mitchell. 709.38
Hellenistic art; the art of the classical world from the death of Alexander the Great to the Battle of Actium. Greenwich, Conn., New York Graphic Society [1970] 282 p. illus. (part col.), maps (on lining papers), plans, ports. 26 cm. Bibliography: p. 273-275. [N5630.H37] 79-85795 ISBN 0-8212-0364-9 17.50
1. Art, Hellenistic. I. Title.

Art, Hindu.

ANAND, Mulk Raj 709.54
The Hindu view of art. With an introductory essay on Art and reality by Eric Gill. [2nd ed.] Bombay, Asia Pub. House [dist. New York, Taplinger Pub. Co., 1960] xxiii, 128p. (bibl. footnotes) illus. 30cm. 60-17497 7.50
1. Art, Hindu. I. Gill, Eric, 1882-1940 II. Title.

MAURY, Curt. 709'.54
Folk origins of Indian art. New York, Columbia University Press, 1969. 245 p. illus. (part col.), map. 23 x 29 cm. Bibliography: p. 225-226. [N8195.A5M3] 75-94909 ISBN 0-231-03198-X 27.50
1. Art, Hindu. 2. Hindu symbolism. I. Title. BIP

RAMBACH, Pierre, 1925- 722'.4
The golden age of Indian art, vth-xiiith century [by] Pierre Rambach and Vitold de Golish. New York, Studio Publications in association with Crowell [1955] 180p. illus. (part col.) maps. 26cm. French ed. has title: L Inde, Images divines neuf siecles d art hindou meconnu vc-xiiic siecles. [N7302.R] A56
1. Art, Hindu. I. Gollsh, Vitold de, joint author. II. Title. BIP

Art — Hist.

BAZIN, Germain. 709
The loom of art. [Translated by Jonathan Griffin] New York, Simon and Schuster [1962] 328p. illus. (part col.) 32cm. [N5300.B413] 62-12408
1. Art—Hist. I. Title.

BIRO, Bela. 709
Handbook of art history; with 300 illus., by Bela Biro. Collaborators: Francis H. Brady [and] Annamaria Nagy. Dubuque, Iowa, W. C. Brown Book Co. [1963] 307 p. illus. 23 cm. [N5302.B5] 63-945
1. Art—Hist. I. Title.

BOWIE, Theodore Robert. 709
East-West in art; patterns of cultural & aesthetic relationships, by Theodore Bowie in collaboration with J. Leroy Davidson [and others] With an introd. by Rudolf Wittkower. Bloomington, Indiana University Press [1966] 191 p. illus., facsims., maps 26 cm. (Indiana University international studies) Includes bibliographies. [N6525.B6] 66-12723
1. Art — Hist. 2. East and West. 3. Intercultural communication. I. Title. II. Series: Indiana. University. International studies BIP

BRAUN, Julie (Vogelstein), 709 1883-
Art, the image of the West. [1st ed. New York] Pantheon [1952] xi, 245 p. 65 plates. 24 cm. [N5300.B813] 52-8962
1. Art—Hist. I. Title.

BROWN, Allison Travis. 709
Heritage: an illustrated history of Western culture, written and illustrated by Allison Travis Brown. New York, Coward-McCann [1956] 200p. illus., ports., maps. 31cm. Bibliography: p. 194. [N5301.B7] 56-11518
1. Art—Hist. 2. Civilization, Occidental. I. Title.

CHENEY, Sheldon, 1886- 709
A new World history of art. [Completely rev. ed., with additional text] New York, Viking Press, 1956. xxvi, 676p. illus. (part col.) maps (on lining papers) 26cm. First published in 1937 under title: A world history of art. Bibliography: p. 660-664. [N5300.C53 1956] 56-9221
1. Art—Hist. I. Title.

CHRISTENSEN, Edwin Ottomar, 709 1890-
A pictorial history of Western art [New York] New Amer. Lib. [1964] 479p. illus., facsims., plans, ports. 18cm. (Mentor bk., MQ564) Bibl. 64-19434 .95 pap.,
1. Art—Hist. I. Title.

ELSEN, Albert Edward, 1927- 709
Purposes of art. New York, Holt [c.1962] 341p. illus. 26cm. Bibl. 62-17343 6.50
1. Art—Hist. 2. Art. I. Title.

FLEMING, William Coleman, 709 1909-
Arts and ideas. Rev. ed. New York, Holt [c.1955, 1963] 788p. illus., map 24cm. 63-11722 9.50
1. Art—Hist. 2. Philosophy—Hist. I. Title. BIP

GARDNER, Helen. 709
Art through the ages. 4th ed., rev. under the editorship of Sumner M. Crosby by the Dept. of the History of Art, Yale University. New York, Harcourt, Brace [c.1926-1959] xiii, 840p. (bibls.) illus. (pt. col.), diagrs. 25cm. 59-5510 6.95
1. Art—Hist. I. Title. BIP

GOMBRICH, Erast Hans Josef. 709 1909-
The story of art [11th ed. rev., enl.] New York. Phaidon Pubs.: dist. Oxford [1966] vi. 488p. illus. (pt. col.) ports. (pt. col.) 25cm. (Phaidon coll. ed.) Bibl. [N5300] 64-9844 4.50 pap.,
1. Art—Hist. I. Title.

GOMBRICH, Ernst Hans Josef, 709 1909-
The story of art. [4th ed., rev.] New York, Phaidon Publishers; distributed by Garden City Books, 1952. 462 p. illus. 26 cm. [N5300.C643 1952] 52-3174
1. Art—Hist. I. Title.

GOMBRICH, Ernst Hans Josef, 709 1909-
The story of art. New York, Phaidon Publishers; distributed by Oxford University Press, 1950. vi, 462p. illus. (part col.) ports. 26cm. Bibliography:p. [447]-450. [N5300.G643] 50-7209
1. Art-Hist. I. Title. BIP

**JAHRBUCH der* 708.06 *kunsthistorischen sammlunger des allerhochsten Kaiserhauses;* v. 1-36. New York, Johnson Reprint, 1966. 36v. (various p.) illus., plates. First pub. in Vienna between 1883 and 1918. 3,160.00; 95.00 set, ea.,

JANSON, Horst Woldemar, 1913- 709 ed.
Key monuments of the history of art; a visual survey, edited by H. W. Janson, with Dora Jane Janson. Text ed. Englewood Cliffs, N. J., Prentice-Hall [1959] 1068p. plates. 26cm. [N5301.J3] 59-6934
1. Art—Hist. I. Title.

MARTIN, Michael Rheta, 1917- 709
The arts; a guide to painting, sculpture, architecture, music, and theater. Illus., with more than 600 drawings by Leo R. Summers. Indianapolis, Bobbs [c.1965] xxx, 423p. illus. 27cm. [N5300.M29] 64-15664 10.00 bds.,
1. Art—Hist. 2. Art—Dictionaries. I. Title.

ORIGINS of Western art. 709
General introd. by Sir Herbert Read. Text by Donald E. Strong[others] New York, Watts [1966, c.1965] 252p. illus., col. plates. 25cm. (Great art & artists of the world) Also pub. by Grolier, inc., as a vol. in its The Book of art. uContents omitted. [N5300.O67] 64-23542 12.95
1. Art Hist. I. Strong, Donald Emrys. II. Series.

ORPEN, William, Sir 1878- 709 1931, ed.
The outline of art. Rev. by Horace Shipp. [Rev. ed.] London, G.Newnes [dist. Transatlantic Arts, Hollywood-by-theSea, Fla. 1963, c.1929] xiv, 854p. illus. (pt. col.) 24cm. Bibl. 11.25
1. Art—Hist. I. Title.

PARS, H. H., pseud. 709
Pictures in peril. Translated from the German by Kathrine Talbot. New York, Oxford University Press, 1957. 240p. illus. 23cm. Translation of Noch leuchten die Bilder. [N5303.P312] 57-13817
1. Art—Hist. 2. Paintings. 3. Paintings—Conservation and restoration. 4. Art—Collectors and collecting. 5. Art treasures in war. I. Title.

PHILLIPPS, Lisle March, v. 12 1863-1917.
The works of man, with an introd. by Herbert Read. New York, Philosophical Library [1951] xxiv, 330 p. illus., plates. 22 cm. Also published under title: Art and enviroment. Bibliography: p. 329-330. [[N5300.P]] A52
1. Art — Hist. 2. Architecture — Hist. I. Title.

THE Praeger picture 703 *encyclopedia of art;* a comprehensive survey of painting, sculpture, architecture and crafts, their methods. styles and technical terms, from the earliest times to the present day. New York, F. A. Praeger [1958] 584p. 416 illus., 192 col. plates. 30cm. (Books that matter) 'Prepared ... with the assistance of James Cleugh ... [and others] under the supervision of Olive Cook and the editorial staff of Thames and Hudson, London ... Original German edition ... published by Georg Westermann Verlag, Brunswick, with contributions by Dr. Bert Bilzer ... Dr. Jurgen Eyssen ... and Dr. Otto Stelzer.' [N5300.P773] 58-11404
1. Art —Hist. 2. Art—Dictionaries. I. Praeger (Frederick A.) inc., New York.

RIFKIN, Benjamin. 709
Monarch review notes in art history. New York, Monarch Press [c1963] 127, [33] p. illus. 28 cm. (Monarch review notes and study guides, 11) Bibliography: p. [128] [[N5305]] 65-7183 CD
1. Art — Hist. 2. Art — Outlines, syllabi, etc. I. Title.

RILEY, Olive Lasette 709
Your art heritage. 2d ed. New York, McGraw [c.1952, 1963] 348p. illus. 25cm. Bibl. 63-13162 5.96
1. Art—Hist. I. Title.

ROBB, David Metheny, 1903- 709
Art in the Western World [by] David M. Robb [and] J. J. Garrison. 4th ed. New York, Harper & Row [1963] 782 p. illus. 27 cm. Includes bibliography. [N5300.R56] 63-7032
1. Art — Hist. I. Garrison, Jesse James, 1901- joint author. II. Title.

ROBB, David Metheny, 1903- 709
Art in the western world, by David M. Robb and J. J. Garrison. 3d ed. New York, Harper [1953] xxi, 1050p. illus., col. map (on lining paper) 24cm. Bibliography: p. 980-1008. [N5300.R56 1953] 52-10831
1. Art—Hist. 2. Architecture—Hist. 3. Sculpture—Hist. 4. Painting—Hist. I. Garrison, Jesse Janes, 1901- joint author. II. Title.

ROSENTHAL, Erwin 709
The changing concept of reality in art. New York, Wittenborn [1962] 99p. illus. 24cm. 62-16118 6.50
1. Art—Hist. 2. Realism in art. 3. Art, abstract. I. Title. BIP

SEDLMAYR, Hans, 1896- 301.1523
Art in crisis, the lost center. [Translation by Brian Battershaw] Chicago, H. Regnery Co., 1958. 266p. illus. 23cm. Translation of Veriust der Mitte. [N6450.S3813] 58-950
1. Art— Hist. 2. Civilization, Modern. I. Title.

SEWALL, John Ives. 709
A history of Western art. New York, Holt [1953] 927p. illus. 24cm. [N5300.S458] 52-13904
1. Art—Hist. I. Title.

SYPHER, Wylie ed. 709
Art history. an anthology of modern criticism. [Gloucester, Mass. P. Smith. 1965, c.1963] xiv, 428p. 19cm. (Vintage bk., V243 rebound) [N5303.S96] 4.50
1. Art—Hist. I. Title. BIP

SYPHER, Wylie, ed. 709
Art history, an anthology of modern criticism. New York, Vintage Books [1963] xiv, 428 p. 19 cm. "V243." Full name: Feltus Wylie Sypher. [N5303.S96] 63-15044
1. Art — Hist. I. Title.

SYPHER, Wylie. 709
Rococo to Cubism in art and literature. New York, Random House [1960] 353 p. illus. 24 cm. Includes bibliography. [N6350.S9] 60-8373
1. Art-Hist. 2. Literature. Modern — Hist. & crit. I. Title.

TAYLOR, Francis Henry 709
Fifty centuries of art. New York, Published for the Metropolitan Museum of Art by Harper [c.1954, 1960] xi, 183p. col. illus. 29cm. 60-9118 6.95 half cloth,
1. Art—Hist. I. Title.

UPJOHN, Everard Miller, 1903- 709
Highlights; an illustrated history of art [by] Everard M. Upiohn, John P. Sedgwick, Jr. New York, Holt [c.1963] vii, 333p. chiefly illus. 29cm. 63-7163 5.95
1. Art—Hist. I. Sedgwick, John P. II. Title.

UPJOHN, Everard Miller, 1903- 709
Highlights; an illustrated history of art [by] Everard M. Upjohn [and] John P. Sedgwick, Jr. New York, Holt, Rinehart and Winston [c1963] vii, 333 p. (chiefly illus.) 29 cm. [N5301.U6] 63-7163
1. Art — Hist. I. Sedgwick, John P. II. Title.

VINCENT, Jean Anne. 709
History of art. New York, Barnes & Noble [1955] 295p. 21cm. (College outline series, 95) [N5305.V5] 55-6770
1. Art—Hist. 2. Art—Outlines, syllabl, etc. I. Title. BIP

VINCENT, Jean Anne. 709
History of art. 2d ed. New York, Barnes & Noble [1967] xxv, 323p. illus. 21cm. (College outline ser., no. 95) Tabulated bibl. of standard textbks.: p. ix-x. [N5305.V5 1967] 66-12776 1.95 pap.,

City Books, 1954. vi, 462 p. illus. (part col.) ports. 26 cm. "A note on art books": p. [447]-450. [N5300.G643 1954] 54-13458
1. Art—History.

GOMBRICH, Ernst Hans Josef, 1909- 709
The story of art, by E. H. Gombrich. [11th ed., rev. and enl.] New York, Phaidon Publishers; distributed by Oxford University Press [1966] 488 p. 383 illus. (part col.) 25 cm. "A note on art books": p. [471]-475. [N5300.G643 1966] 66-542
1. Art—History. I. Title.

GOMBRICH, Ernst Hans Josef, 1909- 709
The story of art [by] E. H. Gombrich. [12th ed., enl. and redesigned. London] Phaidon [distributed by Praeger, New York, 1972] 498 p. illus. (part col.) 26 cm. "A note on art books": p. 491-494. [N5300.G643 1972] 72-186363 ISBN 0-7148-1522-5 15.00 (U.S.)
1. Art—History. I. Title.

GRIGSON, Geoffrey, 1905- 701.18
More shapes and stories; a book about pictures, by Geoffrey and Jane Grigson. New York, Vanguard Press [1967] 70 p. illus. (part col.) 30 cm. Presents thirty-seven examples from art history, from the eleventh through the twentieth centuries, with commentaries which include the stories behind the pictures, social customs of the times, facts about the artist, and brief quotations from relevant literature. [N7440.G65] AC 67
I. Grigson, Jane, joint author. II. Title. BIP

HARTT, Frederick. 709
Art : a history of painting, sculpture, and architecture / Frederick Hartt. New York : H. N. Abrams, 1976. 2 v. : ill. (some col.) ; 29 cm. Contents.Contents.—v. 1. Prehistory, the ancient world, the Middle Ages.—v. 2. The Renaissance, the Baroque, the modern world. Includes bibliographies and indexes. [N5300.H283] 75-33649 50.00
1. Art—History. I. Title.

HARTT, Frederick. 709
Art : a history of painting, sculpture, and architecture / Frederick Hartt. Englewood Cliffs, N.J. : Prentice-Hall, 1976. 2 v. : ill. (some col.) ; 28 cm. Contents.—v. 1. Prehistory, ancient world, Middle Ages.—v. 2. Renaissance, Baroque, modern world. Includes bibliographies and indexes. [N5300.H283 1976b] 75-37738 ISBN 0-13-046953-X(vol.1) pbk. : 9.95
1. Art—History. I. Title.

HARTT, Frederick. 709
History of art. New York, Abrams [1974] p. cm. [N5300.H284] 74-14894 ISBN 0-8109-0264-8
1. Art—History. I. Title.

HATJE, Ursula. 709
The styles of European art. Introd. by Sir Herbert Read. [Translated from the German by Wayne Dynes and Richard Waterhouse] New York, H. N. Abrams [1965] 468 p. 873 illus. 26 cm. Translation of Knaurs Stilkunde von der Antike bis zur Gegenwart. Bibliography: p. 452-457. [N5300.H28813 1965b] 67-14857
1. Art—History. I. Title.

HUYGHE, Rene, ed. 709.034
Larousse encyclopedia of modern art, from 1800 to the present day. New York, Prometheus dist. Putnam, c.1961, 1965] 444p. illus. (pt. col.) 30cm. At head of title: Art and mankind. English text prepared by Emily Evershed, Dennis Gilbert, Hugh Newbury, Ralph de Saram, Richard Waterhouse and Katherine Watson from the French original [N6450.H813] 65-19759 15.95 until 1/1/65,
1. Art—Hist. 2. Art, Modern—20th cent. I. Title. II. Title: Art and mankind.

JANSON, Horst Woldemar, 1813- 709
History of art : a survey of the major visual arts from the dawn of history to the present day / H. W. Janson, with Dora Jane Janson. 2d ed. Englewood Cliffs, N.J. : Prentice-Hall, [1977. 767 p. : ill. (some col.) ; 30 cm. Includes index. Bibliography: p. 751-755. [N5300.J3 1977] 76-27878 ISBN 0-13-389296-4 : 15.95
1. Art—History. I. Janson, Dora Jane, 1916- joint author. II. Title.

JANSON, Horst Woldemar, 1913- 709
A basic history of art [by] H. W. Janson, with Samuel Cauman. Englewood Cliffs, N.J., Prentice-Hall [1973, c1971] 412 p. illus. (part col.) 27 cm. Bibliography: p. [394]-399. [N5300.J29 1973] 73-8718 ISBN 0-13-389296-4 8.95 (pbk)
1. Art—History. I. Cauman, Samuel, joint author. II. Title. BIP

JANSON, Horst Woldemar, 1913- 709
History of art; a survey of the major visual arts from the dawn of history to the present day [by] H. W. Janson, with Dora Jane Janson. New York, Abrams [1962] 571 p. illus., 79 col. plates, plans. 30 cm. Bibliography: p. 554-560. [N5300.J3] 62-11620
1. Art—History.

JANSON, Horst Woldemar, 1913- 709
History of art : a survey of the major visual arts from the dawn of history to the present day / H. W. Janson, with Dora Jane Janson. 2d ed. New York : H. N. Abrams, 1977. 767 p. : ill. ; 30 cm. Includes index. Bibliography: p. 751-755. [N5300.J3 1976b] 76-27882 ISBN 0-8109-1052-7 : 28.50
1. Art—History. I. Janson, Dora Jane, 1916- joint author. II. Title.

JANSON, Horst Woldemar, 1913- 709
History of art; a survey of the major visual arts from the dawn of history to the present day [by] H. W. Janson, with Dora Jane Janson. [Rev. and enl.] Englewood Cliffs, N.J., Prentice-Hall [1969] 616 p. illus., maps (on lining papers), plans, col. plates. 30 cm. Bibliography: p. 594-603. [N5300.J3 1969] 73-91238
1. Art—History. I. Janson, Dora Jane, 1916- joint author. II. Title.

JANSON, Horst Woldemar, 1913- 700'.9
A history of art and music [by] H. W. Janson with Dora Jane Janson [and] Joseph Kerman. Englewood Cliffs, N.J., Prentice-Hall [1968] xxii, 318 p. illus. (part col.), maps. 26 cm. Bibliography: p. 302-305. [NX170.J35] 68-26864
1. Art—History. 2. Music—History and criticism. I. Kerman, Joseph, 1924- II. Title. BIP

JARVES, James Jackson, 1818-1888. 709.73
The art-idea. Edited by Benjamin Rowland, Jr. Cambridge, Mass., Belknap Press, 1960. 313p. 24cm. (The John Harvard library) [N7425.J428] 60-11559
1. Art—Hist. 2. Art—U. S. I. Title. BIP

KLIKA, Thom. 709'.2'4
Rainbows / Thom Klika. New York : St. Martin's Press, [1979] p. cm. [N6537.K57A4 1979] 78-21416 ISBN 0-312-66293-9 : 10.95. ISBN 0-312-66294-7 pbk. : 6.95
1. Klika, Thom. 2. Rainbow in art. I. Title.

LEVEY, Michael. 709'.4
A history of Western art. New York, Praeger [1968] 360 p. illus. (part col.) 22 cm. (Praeger world of art series) [N5300.L43] 68-54496 8.50
1. Art—History. I. Title.

MARTI Ibanez, Felix. 709
The adventure of art. Edited by Felix Marti-Ibanez. [1st ed.] New York, C. N. Potter; distributed by Crown [1970] 603 p. illus. (part col.), col. map. 29 cm. Bibliography: p. 581-590. [N5303.M28 1970] 69-13403 25.00
1. Art—History. I. Title. BIP

MUEHSAM, Alice, ed. 709.43
German readings II: A brief survey of art from the Middle Ages to the twentieth century, for students of German and fine arts. With vocabulary. New York, Distributed by Wittenborn [c1959] 91p. 26cm. German readings I, by Margarete Bieber, was published under the title: German readings in the history and theory of fine arts, I: Greek and Roman art. [N5940.M8] 60-2778
1. Art—Hist. 2. Art, German—Hist. I. Bieber, Margarete, 1879- ed. German readings in the history and theory of fine arts. II. Title. III. Title: A brief survey of art from the Middle Ages to the twentieth century.

MUNRO, Eleanor C. 703
The golden encyclopedia of art; painting, sculpture, architecture, and ornament, from prehistoric times to the twentieth century. With a glossary of artists and art terms. New York, Golden Press [1961] 300 p. illus. (part col.) 35 cm. [N5300.M865] 61-13297
1. Art—History. 2. Art—Dictionaries. I. Title.

MUNRO, Thomas, 1897- 709
Evolution in the arts, and other theories of culture history. [Cleveland] Cleveland Museum of Art, distributed by H. N. Abrams [1963?] 561 p. 26 cm. [N5303.M8] 63-12480
1. Art—History. 2. Art—Philosophy. 3. Civilization—History. I. Title.

MYERS, Bernard Samuel, 1908- 709
Art and civilization. New York, McGraw-Hill, 1957. 757 p. illus. 24 cm. Includes bibliography. [N5300.M94] 56-10328
1. Art—History. 2. Art and society. I. Title. BIP

MYERS, Bernard Samuel, 1908- 709
Art and civilization [by] Bernard S. Myers. [2d ed.] New York, McGraw-Hill [1967] 423 p. illus. (part col.) 30 cm. Bibliography: p. 413-419. [N5300.M94 1967] 66-23625
1. Art—History. 2. Art and society. I. Title.

OATES, Whitney Jennings, 1904- ed. 709.04
From Sophocles to Picasso: the present-day vitality of the classical tradition. Bloomington, Indiana University Press [1962] 208p. illus. 22cm. Cover title: The present-day vitality of the classical tradition. [N6490.O2] 62-7486
1. Art—Hist.—20th cent. 2. Classicism in art. I. Title. II. Title: The present-day vitality of the classical tradition. BIP

PAYNE, Pierre Stephen Robert, 1911- 709
The world of art [by] Robert Payne. [1st ed.] Garden City, N.Y., Doubleday, 1972. xiv, 534 p. illus. 25 cm. [N5300.P37] 73-157615 12.50
1. Art—History. I. Title.

PISCHEL-FRASCHINI, Gina. 709
A world history of art; painting, sculpture, architecture, decorative arts, by Gina Pischel. With an introd. by Luisa Becherucci. New York, Golden Press [1968] 718 p. illus. (part col.) 29 cm. Translation of Storia universale dell'arte; pittura, scultura, architettura, arti decorative. [N5300.P6513] 68-23216
1. Art—History. I. Title.

PISCHEL-FRASCHINI, Gina. 709
A world history of art : painting, sculpture, architecture, decorative arts / by Gina Pischel ; with an introd. by Luisa Becherucci. Rev. ed. New York : Simon and Schuster, c1975. 754 p. : col. ill. ; 29 cm. Includes index. Translation of Storia universale dell'arte. [N5300.P6513 1975] 74-29626 ISBN 0-671-22013-6 : 35.00
1. Art—History. I. Title.

PLINIUS SECUNDUS, C. 709'.38
The Elder Pliny's chapters on the history of art. Translated by K. Jex-Blake. With commentary and historical introd. by E. Sellers, and additional notes contributed by Heinrich Ludwig Urlichs. [1st American ed.] Chicago, Argonaut, 1968. [A]-Y, c, 252 p. facsim., geneal. tables. 20 cm. The text is a reprint of the 1896 ed. Translation of selected portions of Naturalis historia; Latin and English on facing pages. "Preface to the first American edition and select bibliography, 1896-1966, by Raymond V. Schoder": p. [A]-Y. Bibliography: p. xcv-c. [N5610.P6 1968] 66-19183
1. Art—History. 2. Art, Greco-Roman—History. I. Strong, Eugenie (Sellers) ed. BIP

ROOS, Frank John, 1903-1966. 709
An illustrated handbook of art history. Rev. ed. New York, Macmillan [1954] vi, 331 p. (p. 1-317 illus.) 25 cm. [N5301.R6 1954] 54-9647
1. Art—History. I. Title. BIP

ROOS, Frank John, 1903-1966. 709
An illustrated handbook of art history. 3d ed. [New York] Macmillan [1969, c1970] viii, 343 p. (chiefly illus.) 26 cm. [N5301.R6 1969] 74-84439
1. Art—History. I. Title.

RUSKIN, Ariane. 709
History in art. New York, F. Watts, 1974. xi, 307 p. illus. (part col.) 26 cm. Bibliography: p. [295]-[296] [N5303.R87] 73-5673 ISBN 0-531-01988-8 14.95
1. Art—History. 2. History in art.

SEWALL, John Ives. 709.4
A history of Western Art. With a chapter by John Canaday. Rev. New York, Holt, Rinehart and Winston [1961] 907 p. illus. 25 cm. [N5300.S458 1961] 61-14280
I. Title.

SPENCER, Harold, 1920- 709
The image-maker; man and his art. New York, Scribner [1975] xvi, 776 p. illus. 24 cm. Bibliography: p. 731-752. [N5303.S627] 74-13116 ISBN 0-684-14097-7 17.95; 9.95 (pbk.)
1. Art—History. 2. Imagery (Psychology) 3. Art and society. I. Title. BIP

THE story of modern art. 709.03
Rev. and enl. mid-century ed. New York, Viking Press [1958] 723p. illus. 25cm. [N6490.C52 1958] 709.04 58-7183
1. Art—Hist.—20th cent. 2. Modernism (Art) I. Cheney, Sheldon, 1886- BIP

SYMONDS, Maurice K. 709
The visual arts: a world survey from prehistoric times to the present, with special reference to Australia and New Zealand [by] Maurice K. Symonds, Coll Portley [and] Ralph E. Phillips. Milton, Queensland, Jacaranda, 1972. 182 p. illus. (part col.). 29 cm. Index. [N5300.S99] 73-167851 ISBN 0-7016-0337-2 4.50
1. Art—History. 2. Art, Australian. 3. Art, New Zealand. I. Portley, Coll, joint author. II. Phillips, Ralph E., joint author. III. Title.

TAYLOR, Francis Henry, 1903- 709
Fifty centuries of art. [1st ed.] New York, Published for the Metropolitan Museum of Art by Harper [1954] vii, 183 p. col. illus. 29 cm. [N5300.T35] 54-8996
1. Art—History. I. Title.

UPJOHN, Everard Miller, 1903- 709
History of world art [by] Everard M. Upjohn, Paul S. Wingert [and] Jane Gaston Mahler. 2d ed., rev. and enl. New York, Oxford University Press, 1958. xix, 876 p. 671 illus., 17 col. plates, maps (on lining papers) 24 cm. Bibliography: p. 841-850. [N5300.U6 1958] 57-10391
1. Art—History.

WIGHT, Frederick Stallknecht, 1902- 709
The potent image : art in the Western world from cave paintings to the 1970s / Frederick S. Wight. New York : Collier Books, 1976. 595 p. : ill. ; 24 cm. Includes index. Bibliography: p. [575]-583. [N5300.W615 1976b] 76-13199 pbk. : 19.95
1. Art—History. I. Title. BIP

WILENSKI, Reginald Howard, 1887- 709
A miniature history of art, by R. H. Wilenski. With a chapter on American art by Edward Alden Jewell. New York, Oxford University Press, 1930. St. Clair Shores, Mich., Scholarly Press, 1974. p. [N5302.W54 1974] 74-3194 ISBN 0-403-03077-3
1. Art—History. I. Jewell, Edward Alden, 1888-1947. II. Title.

Art—History—17th-18th century.

ARGAN, Giulio Carlo 709.033
The Europe of the capitals, 1600-1700. from Italian by Anthony Rhodes. Geneva] Skira [dist. Cleveland, World, 1965, c.1964] 222p. illus. (pt. fold., pt. mounted col.) ports.(pt. col.) 31cm. (Art ideas hist.) [N6410-A713] 64-23257 20.00 bds.,
1. Art—Hist.—17th—18th centuries. 2. Art, Baroque. 3. Art and society. I. Title. II. Series.

ROSENBLUM, Robert. 709.033
Transformations in late eighteenth century art. Princeton, N.J., Princeton University Press, 1967. xxvi, 203 p. illus. 25 cm.

Bibliographical footnotes. [N6410.R66] 66-21841
1. Art—History—17th-18th century. 2. Classicism in art. I. Title. BIP

STAROBINSKI, Jean 709.033
The invention of liberty, 1700-1789 [Tr. from French by Bernard C. Swift. Geneva] Skira [dist. Cleveland, World, 1965, c.1964] 222p. illus. (pt. mounted col.) ports. (pt. col.) 31cm. (Art ideas hist.) Bibl. [N6410.S813] 64-23258 20.00
1. Art—Hist.—17th-18th centuries. 2. Aesthetics. 3. Eighteenth century. I. Title. II. Series.

Art—History—19th century.

CASSOU, Jean, 1897- 709.035
Gateway to the twentieth century; art and culture in a changing world [by] Jean Cassou, Emil Langui, Nikolaus Pevsner. New York, Mcgraw [c.1962] 362 p. illus., col. plates. 35 cm. (Council of Europe ser.) Based on the exhibition held at the Musee d'art moderne in Paris, from November 9, 1960 to January 23, 1961, and called Les Sources du xxe siecle, les arts en Europe de 1884 a 1914. Bibl. 61-16868 25.00
1. Art—Hist.—19th cent. 2. Art—Hist.—20 cent. I. Paris, Musee national d'art moderne. II. Title.

CASSOU, Jean, 1897- 709.035
Gateway to the twentieth century; art and culture in a changing world [by] Jean Cassou, Emil Langui [and] Nikolaus Pevsner. New York, McGraw-Hill [1962] 362p. illus., col. plates. 35cm. Based on the exhibition held at the Musee d'art moderne in Paris, from November 9, 1960 to January 23, 1961, and called Les sources du xx siecle, les arts en Europe de 1884 a 1914. Bibliographical footnotes. [N6490.C268] 61-16868
1. Art—Hist.—19th cent. 2. Art—Hist.—20th cent. I. Paris. Musee national d'art moderne. II. Title.

CRAVEN, Thomas, 1889- 709.03
Modern art; the men, the movements, the meaning. [Rev. ed.] Garden City, N. Y., Halcyon House [1950, '1940] xxii, 387 p. 32 plates. 24 cm. [N6450.C7 1950] 50-14825
1. Art—Hist.—19th cent. 2. Art—Hist.—20th cent. 3. Artists. 4. Post-impressionism (Art) I. Title.

GLOAG, John Edward 1896- 709.42
Victorian comfort, a social history of design from 1830-1900. · New York, Macmillan [c.1961] xvi, 252p. (col. front.) illus. 26cm. Bibl. 61-3916 10.00
1. Art—Hist.—19th cent. 2. Design. 3. England—Soc. life and cust.—19th cent. I. Title.

HOLT, Elizabeth Basye 709.034
(Gilmore) ed.
From the classicists to the impressionists; a documentary history of art and architecture in the 19th century, selected and edited by Elizabeth Gilmore Holt. [New York] New York University Press [1966] xxi, 552 p. maps. 64 plates (incl. plans) 24 cm. Includes bibliographical references. [N6450.H6] 66-7011
1. Art — Hist. — 19th cent. — Sources. 2. Architecture — Hist. — Sources. 3. Art and society. I. Title.

KEYSER, Eugenie de 709.35
The romantic West, 1789-1850 [Tr. from French by Peter Price. Geneva] Skira [dist. Cleveland, World, c.1965] 210p. illus. (pt. mounted col.) 31cm. (Art ideas hist.) [N6450.K413] 65-16670 20.00 bds.,
1. Art—Hist.—19th cent. 2. Art and society. I. Title. II. Series.

KEYSER, Eugenie de. 709.35
The romantic West, 1789-1850. [Translated from the French by Peter Price] [Geneva] Skira [distributed in the U.S. by World Pub. Co., Cleveland] 1965. 210 p. illus. (part mounted col.) 31 cm. (Art ideas history) [N6450.K413] 65-16670
1. Art—History—19th century. 2. Art and society. I. Title. II. Series.

MCCURDY, Charles, ed. 709.03
Modern art, a pictorial anthology [by] A. L. Chanin [and others] Charlotte Trowbridge, designer. N[ew] Y[ork] Macmillan [1958] 489 p. illus. 28 cm. "The language of art: a bibliography, by Bernard Warpel": p. 431-464. [N6490.M284] 57-7115
1. Art—History—19th century. 2. Art—History—20th century. I. Chanin, A. L. II. Title.

SCHLENOFF, Norman 709.034
Art in the modern world. New York, Bantam [1966, c.1965] 255p. illus. (pt. col.) 18cm. (Bantam matrix eds., KM1030) [N6450.S29] 65-26247 1.35 pap.,
1. Art—Hist.—19th cent. 2. Art—Hist.—20th cent. I. Title.

WILENSKI, Reginald Howard, 709.04
1887-
The modern movement in art. [1st American ed.] New York, T. Yoseloff [1957] 216p. illus. 26cm. [N6450.W5 1957] 57-2946
1. Art—Hist.—19th cent. 2. Art—Hist.—20th cent. I. Title.

Art—History—Addresses, essays, lectures.

LONGAKER, Jon D. 709
Art, style & history; a selective survey of art [by] Jon D. Longaker. [Glenview, Ill.] Scott, Foresman [1970] xvii, 268 p. illus., plans, 16 col. plates. 24 cm. Includes bibliographical references. [N5303.L66] 70-90090
1. Art—History—Addresses, essays, lectures. I. Title. BIP

REINHARDT, Adolph Frederick. 709
Art as art : the selected writings of Ad Reinhardt / edited and with an introd. by Barbara Rose. New York : Viking Press, [1975] p. cm. (The Documents of 20th-century art) [N5303.R36] 75-19041 ISBN 0-670-13451-1 : 14.95
1. Art—History—Addresses, essays, lectures. I. Title. II. Series. BIP

SPENCER, Harold, 1920- comp. 709
Readings in art history. New York, Scribner [1969] 2 v. illus. 23 cm. Contents.Contents.—v. 1. Ancient Egypt through the Middle Ages. v. 2. The Renaissance to the present. Includes bibliographical references. [N5303.S63] 69-13587 4.95 per vol.
1. Art—History—Addresses, essays, lectures. I. Title. BIP

SPENCER, Harold, 1920- comp. 709
Readings in art history / edited by Harold Spencer. 2d ed. New York : Scribner, c1976. 2 v. : ill. ; 23 cm. Contents.Contents.—v. 1. Ancient Egypt through the Middle Ages. — v. 2. The Renaissance to the present. Includes bibliographical references and indexes. [N5303.S63 1976] 76-7404 ISBN 0-684-14617-7 pbk. : 6.95 (v. 1). 6.95 (v. 2)
1. Art—History—Addresses, essays, lectures. I. Title.

WHITWELL, W. L., comp. 709
Readings for introduction to art, compiled by W. L. Whitwell. Berkeley, Calif., McCutchan Pub. Corp. [1968] v, 107 p. 23 cm. [N5302.W4] 68-6488
1. Art—History—Addresses, essays, lectures. I. Title.

Art—History—Anecdotes, facetiae, satire, etc.

ARMOUR, Richard Willard, 709
1906-
It all started with nudes : an artful history of art / Richard Armour ; artistically illustrated by Campbell Grant. New York : McGraw-Hill, c1977. 155 p. : ill. ; 21 cm. [N5303.A74] 77-1437 ISBN 0-07-002271-2 : 7.95
1. Art—History—Anecdotes, facetiae, satire, etc. I. Title.

Art History-Bibliography.

STEWART, June 016.70994.
Bibliographical essays on art historical studies in Australia since 1958 by June M. Stewart. [Sidney] University Press for the Australian Academy of the Humanities [1975c1974] 36p. 23 cm. [Z5931.S88.] 75-311888 ISBN 0-424-07000-6 Distributed by International Scholarly Book Services for 2.60 (pbk.)
1. Art History-Bibliography. I. Title.

Art—History—Collections.

THE Garland library of the 709
history of art / editorial selection committee, James S. Ackerman ... [et al.] New York : Garland Pub., 1976- v. : ill. ; 29 cm. "One hundred and fifty-two articles in fourteen volumes." Includes bibliographical references. [N5300.G32] 76-21792 425.00 (14 vol. set)
1. Art—History—Collections. I. Ackerman, James S.

Art—History—Juvenile literature.

BATTERBERRY, Ariane Ruskin. 709
The Pantheon story of art for young people / Ariane Ruskin Batterberry. [Rev. ed.] New York : Pantheon Books, [1975] p. cm. Surveys the history of art in the western world from prehistoric cave paintings to modern abstracts emphasizing the major works and artists of each period. Includes a brief discussion of the art of Asia, Africa, and the South Seas. [N5302.B28 1975] 74-24717 ISBN 0-394-83107-1 : 12.95
1. Art—History—Juvenile literature. I. Title. II. Title: Story of art.

GEMMING, Elizabeth. 709
The world of art, by Elizabeth & Klaus Gemming. Barre, Mass., Barre [1968- v. illus. 25cm. Contents.v. 1. Learning through stamps. [N5300.G4] 68-17069 4.95
1. Art—Hist.—Juvenile literature. I. Gemming, Klaus. joint author. II. Title.

HILLYER, Virgil Mores, 709 (j)
1875-1931.
Fine art; 15,000 B.C. - 1,800 A.D. by V. M. Hillyer and E. G. Huey. New ed. designed and rev. by Children's Press, Chicago. Consultants: Ruth Esserman, Everett Saunders. New York, Meredith Press [1966] 127 p. illus., plates (part col.) 29 cm. (Young people's story of our heritage) Cover title: Young people's story of fine art, 15,000 B.C.-1,800 A.D. Originally published as a part of the author's A child's history of art. [N5302.H5 1966] 66-11323
1. Art—History—Juvenile literature. I. Huey, Edward Greene, 1899- joint author. II. Childrens Press, inc., Chicago. III. Title. IV. Title: Young people's story of fine art, 15,000 B.C.-1,800 A.D.

HILLYER, Virgil Mores, 709.034
1875-1931.
Fine art; [the last two hundred years] by V. M. Hillyer and E. G. Huey. New ed. designed and rev. by Childrens Press, Chicago. Consultants: Ruth Esserman [and] Everett Saunders. New York, Meredith Press [1966] 126 p. illus. (part col.) 29 cm. (Young people's story of our heritage) Cover title: Young people's story of fine art; the last two hundred years. Originally published as a part of the author's A child's history of art. [N5302.H52] 66-11324
1. Art—History—Juvenile literature. I. Huey, Edward Greene, 1899- joint author. II. Childrens Press, inc., Chicago. III. Title. IV. Title: Young people's story of fine art; the last two hundred years.

INTERNATIONAL Graphic 709
Society.
The arts of mankind: painting, architecture, music. Englewood Cliffs, N.J., [c1962] 192 p illus 25 cm. (The International pictorial treasury of knowledge [v. 5]) [N5302.I5] 63-1995
1. Art — Hist. — Juvenile literature. I. Title.

MACAGY, Douglas Guernsey, 759'.06
1913-
Going for a walk with a line; a step into the world of modern art, by Douglas & Elizabeth MacAgy. Garden City, N.Y., Doubleday [1973, c.1959] 1 v. (unpaged, chiefly/col. illus.) 24 cm. (Zephyr Book) [N6490.M28] 59-5899 pap., 1.25
1. Art, Modern—20th cent.—Juvenile literature. 2. Line (Art)—Juvenile literature. I. MacAgy, Elizabeth joint author. II. Title.

PAUL, Louis, 1901- j 709
The way art happens. New York, Washburn [1963] 205 p. illus. 23 cm. [N5302.P3] 63-10486
1. Art—Hist.—Juvenile literature. I. Title.

RUSKIN, Ariane. 709
The Pantheon story of art for young people. [New York] Pantheon Books [1964] 157 p. illus. (part col.) 33 cm. [N5302.R8] 64-18314
1. Art—History—Juvenile literature. I. Title. II. Title: Story of art.

WATERS, Clara Erskine 709'.2'2 B
Clement, 1834-1916.
Stories of art and artists, by Clara Erskine Clement. Boston, Ticknor, 1887. St. Clair Shores, Mich., Scholarly Press, 1972. p. A history of western art and artists from the ancient Greeks to the nineteenth century. [N5308.W37 1972] 72-11734 ISBN 0-403-02352-1
1. Art—History—Juvenile literature. 2. Artists—Juvenile literature. I. Title.

Art—History—Outlines, syllabi, etc.

HUTTER, Heribert. 709
Styles in art : an historical survey / Heribert Hutter, in collaboration with Irmgard Hutter. New York : Universe Books, 1978. 189 p. : ill. (some col.) ; 23 cm. Translation of Konfrontationen. Includes index. Bibliography: p. 186. [N5305.H8813 1978] 73-88460 ISBN 0-87663-205-3 : 8.95
1. Art—History—Outlines, syllabi, etc. I. Hutter, Irmgard, joint author. II. Title.

MYRON, Robert. 709
The Putnam collegiate guide to history of art, by Robert Myron and Ralph Fanning. New York, Putnam [1966- v. 22 cm. 1968 ed. published under title: Art history. [N5305.M96] 66-26057
1. Art—History—Outlines, syllabi, etc. I. Fanning, Ralph, 1889- joint author. II. Title.

WOLD, Milo Arlington. 709
An introduction to music and art in the Western World [by] Milo Wold [and] Edmund Cykler. 4th ed. Dubuque, Iowa, W. C. Brown Co. [1972] xiii, 318 p. illus. (part col.) 24 cm. (Music series) Includes bibliographies. [NX447.W6 1972] 72-76802 ISBN 0-697-03110-1
1. Art—History—Outlines, syllabi, etc. 2. Music—History and criticism—Outlines, syllabi, etc. 3. Civilization, Occidental—History. I. Cykler, Edmund, joint author. II. Title. III. Title: Music and art in the Western World.

WOLD, Milo Arlington. 709
An introduction to music and art in the Western World / Milo Wold, Edmund Cykler. 5th ed. Dubuque, Iowa : W. C. Brown Co., c1976. xiii, 354 p., [19] leaves of plates : ill. (some col.) ; 24 cm. Includes bibliographies and index. [NX447.W6 1976] 76-358066 ISBN 0-697-03113-6 : 7.95 study guide : 4.95
1. Art—History—Outlines, syllabi, etc. 2. Music—History and criticism—Outlines, syllabi, etc. 3. Civilization, Occidental—History. I. Cykler, Edmund, joint author. II. Title. III. Title: Music and art in the Western World.

Art—History—Pictorial works.

GOLDSCHEIDER, Ludwig, 1896- 709
Towards modern art; or, King Solomon's picture book; art of the new age and art of former ages shown side by side. London, Phaidon Press. St. Clair Shores, Mich., Scholarly Press, 1974 [c1951] p. [N5301.G6 1974] 74-4005 ISBN 0-403-03080-3
1. Art—History—Pictorial works. I. Title.

Art—History—Sources.

HOLT, Elizabeth Basye 709
(Gilmore) ed.
A documentary history of art. [2d ed.] Garden City, N.Y., Doubleday, 1957- v. illus. 19 cm. (Doubleday anchor books, A114a, 114b) Expansion and revision of the editor's Literary sources of art history, published in 1947. Contents.Contents.—v. 1. The Middle Ages and the

Renaissance.—v. 2. Michelangelo and the Mannerists, the baroque, and the eighteenth century. [N5303.H762] 57-10457
1. Art—History—Sources. I. Title.

HOLT, Elizabeth Basye 709.034
Gilmore, ed.
From the classicists to the impressionists; Art and Architecture in the 19th century. Selected and edited by Elizabeth Gilmore Holt. Garden City, N.Y., Anchor Books, 1966. 540 p. 18 cm. (Volume III of a Documentary History of Art) "A Doubleday Anchor Original, A114c." Includes bibliographical references. [N5303.H74] 65-20056
1. Art—History—Sources. 2. Architecture—History—Sources. 3. Art and society. 4. Nineteenth century. I. Title. BIP

HOLT, Elizabeth Basye 700'.94
(Gilmore), comp.
From the Classicists to the Impressionists; a documentary history of art and architecture in the 19th century; selected and edited by Elizabeth Gilmore Holt. London, University of London P.; New York, New York U. P. [1966] xxvii, 552 p. illus., 64 plates (incl. plans, facsims.). 23 1/2 cm. (B 67-9677) Includes bibliographical references. [N6450.H6 1966b] 67-109634
1. Art—Hist.—Sources. 2. Architecture—Hist.—Sources. 3. Art and society. 4. Nineteenth century. I. Title.

Art, Hittite—Hist.

AKURGAL, Ekrem 709.39
The art of the Hittites. Photos. by Max Hirmer. [Tr. by Constonce McNab] New York, Abrams [1962] 315p. illus. (pt. col.), map. 32cm. Bibl. 62-11624 25.00
1. Art, Hittite—Hist. I. Title.

Art—Honolulu—Catalogs.

HONOLULU Academy of 708.9969'31
Arts.
Academy album; a pictorial selection of works of art in the collections. Honolulu, Hawaii [1968] 145 p. illus. 26 cm. [N3990.H59] 68-8958
1. Art—Honolulu—Catalogs. I. Title.

Art, Hungarian.

BIAlOSTOCKI, Jan. 709'.43
The art of the Renaissance in Eastern Europe : Hungary, Bohemia, Poland / Jan Bialostocki. Ithaca, N.Y. : Cornell University Press, 1976. xxiv, 312 p., [3] leaves of plates : ill. (some col.) ; 28 cm. (The Wrightsman lectures ; v. 8) Includes index. Bibliography: p. [281]-306. [N6817.B52 1976] 75-38429 ISBN 0-8014-1008-8 : 25.00
1. Art, Hungarian. 2. Art, Renaissance—Hungary. 3. Art, Czech. 4. Art, Renaissance—Czechoslovak Republic. 5. Art, Polish. 6. Art, Renaissance—Poland. I. Title. II. Series. BIP

†PROFESSIONAL 709'.2'2 B
Hungarian artists outside of Hungary / edited by Ernest Gyimesy Kasas and Leslie L. Konnyu ; compiled by Leslie Konnyu. St. Louis : American Hungarian Review, c1977. 264 p. : ill. ; 22 cm. "English version of the Hungarian edition." Bibliography: p. 258-259. [N6820.P76] 77-94982 pbk. : 8.50
1. Art, Hungarian. 2. Art, Modern—20th century—Hungary. 3. Hungarians in foreign countries—Biography. 4. Artists—Hungary—Biography. I. Kasas, Ernest Gy. II. Konnyu, Leslie, 1914-

Art, Iberian.

NICOLINI, Gerard. 709'.395
The ancient Spaniards / Gerard Nicolini ; translated [from the French] by Jean Stewart. Farnborough, Hants. : Saxon House, [1975] xv, 232 p., viii p. of plates : ill. (some col.), maps, plans ; 24 cm. Translation of Les Iberes. Includes index. Bibliography: p. 219-226. [N5899.I2N5213] 74-9340 ISBN 0-347-00023-1 : 15.95
1. Art, Iberian. 2. Iberians. I. Title.

Distributed by Atheneum. BIP

TARRADELL i Mateu, 709'.46
Miquel, 1920-
Iberian art / M. Tarradell. New York : Rizzoli, 1978. 111 p. : ill. (some col.) ; 32 cm. Bibliography: p. 111. [N5899.I2T33] 77-39175 ISBN 0-8478-0163-2 : 18.50
1. Art, Iberian. I. Title. BIP

Art, Ibo—Exhibitions.

STARKWEATHER, Frank. 730.9*6
Traditional Igbo art, 1966; an exhibition of wood sculpture carved in 1965-66, from the Frank Starkheather Collection, August 15 through Octber 27, 1968. [Ann Arbor] University of Michigan [1968] [64] p. illus., col. map. 19 x 26 cm. Sponsored by the Dept. of Anthropology and the Museum of Art, University of Michigan. Bibliography: p. [60]-[64] [NB1255.N5S8] 68-66438
1. Starkweather, Frank—Art collections. 2. Art, Ibo—Exhibitions. I. Michigan. University. Dept. of Anthropology. II. Michigan. University. Museum of Art. III. Title.

Art—Iceland.

ELDJARN, Kristjan 1916- 709.491
Icelandic art. Tr. fro mGerman. New York, Abrams [1961, c.1957] 14p. plates (part col.) 29cm. 61-5785 8.50 bds.,
1. Art—Iceland. 2. Christian art and symbolism. I. Title.

Art—Illinois—Chicago—Directories.

THE Chicago art 702'.5'77311
review : [the complete source to art in Chicago] / [Leslie J. Krantz, editor ; contributors, Nancy Seeger ... et al. ; research, Marjorie Krantz ; photography, Jack McGovern]. Chicago : L. J. Krantz, c1977. 112 p. : ill. (some col.) ; 22 cm. Includes index. [N6535.C5C47] 77-179973 5.95
1. Art—Illinois—Chicago—Directories. 2. Chicago—Museums—Directories. 3. Art galleries, Commercial—Illinois—Chicago—Directories. I. Krantz, Leslie J. II. Seeger, Nancy.

Art—Illinois—History.

MADDEN, Betty I., 1915- 709'.773
Art, crafts, and architecture in early Illinois [by] Betty I. Madden. Urbana, University of Illinois Press [1974] xiii, 297 p. illus. 23 x 29 cm. "Published in cooperation with the Illinois State Museum." Bibliography: p. 269-279. [N6530.I4M32] 73-22468 ISBN 0-252-00391-8 22.50
1. Art—Illinois—History. 2. Architecture—Illinois—History. 3. Illinois—Industries—History. I. Illinois. State Museum, Springfield. II. Title. BIP

Art, Illyrian.

STIPCEVIC, Aleksandar. 709.389
The art of the Illyrians 90 illus., 2 maps [Tr. from Italian by Leslie van Rensselaer White] Milan, Edizioni del Milione [New York, Heinman, 1964] lviii, 75p. illus., 2 maps (1 fold.) plates. 24cm. (Dittamondo, 6) Bibl. 64-55160 7.50 pap.,
1. Art, Illyrian. I. Title. II. Series.

Art in Afro-American universities and colleges—Texas—Houston.

BIGGERS, John 707'.11'7641411
Thomas, 1924-
Black art in Houston : the Texas Southern University experience : presenting the art of Biggers, Simms and their students / by John Biggers and Carroll Sims, with John Edward Weems ; introd. by Donald Weismann. 1st ed. College Station : Texas A & M University Press, c1978. 106 p. : ill. (some col.) ; 29 cm. [N6538.N5B52] 77-99276 ISBN 0-89096-046-1 : 20.00
1. Biggers, John Thomas, 1924- 2. Simms, Carroll, 1924- 3. Texas. Southern University, Houston. School of Arts and Sciences. 4. Art in Afro-American universities and colleges—Texas—Houston. I. Simms, Carroll, 1924- joint author. II. Weems, John Edward, joint author. III. Title. BIP

Art in moving-pictures.

HUMPHRYS, Alfred W., comp. 016.7
Films on art. Introd. by Vincent Lanier. Washington, D.C. 20036, Natl. Art Educ. Assn., 1201 16th St., N.W., 1966. 60p. 23cm. No. 1 in a ser. of pubns. sponsored by the Uses of Newer Media Project of the Natl. Art Educ. Assn. [N7428.H8] 66-2918 1.50 pap.,
1. Art in moving-pictures. 2. Art — Film catalogs. I. National Art Education Association. II. Title.

Art in Negro universities and colleges.

ROUSE, Mary J. 707'.1'173
Art programs in Negro colleges [by] Mary J. Rouse. Bloomington, Indiana University, 1967. vi, 88, [80] l. 28 cm. The research was performed pursuant to a grant with the U.S. Office of Education, project no. 3159, contract no. OE-6-10-113. [N345.R6] 68-63903
1. Art in Negro universities and colleges. 2. Art—Study and teaching (Higher) I. Indiana. University. II. Title.

Art in universities and colleges.

BENSON, Emanuel Mervin, 707'.11
1904-
A pilot research study of art facilities in six colleges and universities: Cleveland Institute of Art, Massachusetts Institute of Technology, New York University, Pratt Institute, Sarah Lawrence College, University of Michigan. Emanuel M. Benson, chief investigator. Brooklyn, 1966. 53 l. illus. (on covers) 28 cm. Bibliography: leaves 50-53. [N330.A1B4] 67-62655
1. Cleveland. Institute of Art. 2. Massachusetts Institute of Technology. 3. New York University. 4. Pratt Institute, Brooklyn. 5. Sarah Lawrence College, Bronxville, N. Y. 6. Michigan. University. 7. Art in universities and colleges. I. Title.

Art in universities and colleges—United States.

FUNDABURK, Emma Lila, 709'.73
1922-
Art at educational institutions in the United States; a handbook of permanent, semi-permanent, and temporary works of art at elementary and secondary schools, colleges, and universities. Compiled by Emma Lila Fundaburk and Thomas G. Davenport. Metuchen, N.J., Scarecrow Press, 1974. xv, 670 p. illus. 29 cm. Bibliography: p. 523-565. [N510.F86] 74-3187 ISBN 0-8108-0715-7
1. Art in universities and colleges—United States. 2. School decoration—United States. 3. Art—United States—Galleries and museums. I. Davenport, Thomas G., joint author. II. Title. BIP

Art—Indexes

CLAPP, Jane. 016.7
Art in Life. New York, Scarecrow Press, 1959. 504 p. 23 cm. "This index . . . designed . . . to provide immediate reference to reproductions of paintings and graphic arts in Life, from its first issue, November 23, 1936, through 1956." New York, Scarecrow Press. v. 23 cm. First suppl. covers the years 1957-63. N7525.C552 [N7525.C55] 65-13552
1. Supplement. 1- 1965- 2. Art — Indexes. I. Life (Chicago) (Indexes) II. Title.

CLAPP, Jane. 016.7
Art in Life. New York, Scarecrow Press, 1959. 504 p. 23 cm. "This index . . . designed . . . to provide immediate reference to reproductions of paintings and graphic arts in Life, from its first issue, November 23, 1936, through 1956." New York, Scarecrow Press. v. 23 cm. First suppl. covers the years 1957-63. N7525.C552 [N7525.C55] 65-13552
1. Supplement. 1- 1965- 2. Art — Indexes. I. Life (Chicago) (Indexes) II. Title.

CLAPP, Jane. 016.7
Art in Life. New York, Scarecrow Press, 1959. 504 p. 23 cm. "This index . . . designed . . . to provide immediate reference to reproductions of paintings and graphic arts in Life, from its first issue, November 23, 1936, through 1956." New York, Scarecrow Press. v. 23 cm. First suppl. covers the years 1957-63. N7525.C552 [N7525.C55] 65-13552
1. Supplement. 1- 1965- 2. Art — Indexes. I. Life (Chicago) (Indexes) II. Title.

CLAPP, Jane 016.7
Art in Life. Supplement--1965. New York [c.]1965. Madison, Univ. of Wis. Pr. [c.] 1965. 379p. 23cyears gFirst suppl. covers the years 1957-63. xiv, 250p. 25cm. [N7525.C55] [Z5931.K5] 016.70115 65-13552 65-18877 8.50 6.50
1. Art—Indexes] 2. Art—Psychology—Bibl. 3. Psychiatry in art—Bibl. I. Life (Chicago) (Indexes) n3 II. Kiell, Norman III. Title. IV. Title: Psychiatry and psychology in the visual arts and aesthetics,

Art, India.

ELWIN, Verrier, 1902- 709.54
The tribal art of middle India; a personal record. [Bombay, New York] Indian Branch, Oxford University Press [1951] 213 p. illus. 25 cm. [N7301.E4] 52-7549
1. Art—India. 2. Art, Primitive. I. Title.

HAVELL, Ernest Binfield, 709.54
1861-1934
The art heritage of India, comprising: Indian sculpture and painting and Ideals of Indian art. Rev. ed., notes by Pramod Chandra. Bombay, D. B. Taraporevala Sons [New York, Tudor, 1965, c.1964] xii, 199p. illus., plates (pt. col.) 29cm. Each title orig. pub. separately [N7301.H24] SA65 22.50
1. Art, India. I. Chandra, Pramod. II. Title. III. Title: Indian sculpture and painting. IV. Title: Ideals of Indian art.

MOOKERJEE, Ajitcoomar 709.54
The arts of India from prehistoric to modern times [by] Ajit Mookerjee. Rev. & enl. Rutland, Vt., Tuttle [c.1966] 152p. 154 illus. (pt. col.) fold. map. 27cm. (Bks. to span the East & West) [N7301.M62] 66-17557 12.50
1. Art, India—Hist. I. Title. II. Series.

MUNSTERBERG, Hugo, 1916- 709'.54
Art of India and Southeast Asia. New York, H. N. Abrams [1970] 263 p. illus. (part. col.) 23 cm. (Panorama of world art) Bibliography: p. 260-261. [N7301.M83] 69-12487 ISBN 0-8109-8013-4
1. Art, India. 2. Art, Southeast Asian—India influences. I. Title.

Art, India—Exhibitions.

LOS Angeles County Museum, 709.54
Los Angeles.
The art of Greater India, 3000 B. C.-1800 A. D.; an exhibition of Indian art presented under the patronage of the Embassy of India functioning for the Government of India. Mar. 1 to Apr. 16, 1950. [Los Angeles, 1950] xxx, 128 p. 94 plates, map. 26 cm. Bibliography: p. xxvii-xxx. [N7301.L65] 51-2478
1. Art, India—Exhibitions. I. Title.

Art—India—History.

*CRAVEN, Roy C. 709'.54
A concise history of Indian art / Roy C. Craven. New York : Praeger Publishers, 1976. 252p. : ill. (some col.), maps ; 21 cm. Bibliography:p.246-248. [N7302] 75-37027 ISBN 0-275-22950-5 : 12.00 ISBN 0-275-85620-8 pbk. : 6.95
1. Art, India-History I. Title. BIP

GOETZ, Hermann, 1898- 709.54
India; five thousand years of Indian art. New York, McGraw-Hill [1959?] 275 p. mounted col. illus., maps. 24 cm. (Art of

New York : Collier Books, 1975, c1971. 208 p. : ill. ; 30 cm. Includes index. Bibliography: p. 204-205. [NK1390.B3 1975] 75-19411 ISBN 0-02-000210-6 pbk. : 7.95
1. Art industries and trade. 2. Decoration and ornament. I. Title.

COMINS, Harry Leon, 1901- 740
Arts-crafts for the Jewish school and center, by Harry L. Comins and Reuben Leaf. Rev. ed. New York, Union of American Hebrew Congregations, 1955 [c1956] 362p. illus. 22cm. (Union graded series) First published in 1934 under title: Arts-crafts for the Jewish club. [TT169.C6 1956] 57-15523
1. Art industries and trade. 2. Decoration and ornament, Jewish. I. Leaf, Reuben, joint author. II. Title.

DAVIDSON, Marion, 1942- 343'.73'078
Making it legal : a law primer for the craftmaker, visual artist, and writer / by Marion Davidson and Martha Blue. New York : McGraw-Hill, [1979] p. cm. Includes index. [KF390.A7D37] 78-23891 ISBN 0-07-015431-7 pbk. : 6.95
1. Law—United States. 2. Artists—United States—Handbooks, manuals, etc. 3. Artisans—United States—Handbooks, manuals, etc. 4. Authors—United States—Handbooks, manuals, etc. I. Blue, Martha, 1942- joint author. II. Title. BIP

HARRISON, Oval Stanley, 1903- 745.5
Industrial arts and handcraft activities. Minneapolis, Burgess Pub. Co. [1961, c1959] 132p. illus. 28cm. [NK70] 61-19873
1. Art industries and trade. 2. Handicraft. I. Title.

MITCHELL, Dorothy, 1904- 745
The studio workshops' handbook of decorative painting. [Wellesley Hills? Mass., 1953] 53p. illus. 29cm. [NK1130.M63] 54-27306
1. Art industries and trade. 2. Decoration and ornament. 3. Design, Decorative. I. Title.

MOSELEY, Spencer. 745.5
Crafts design, an illustrated guide [by] Spencer Moseley, Pauline Johnson [and] Hazel Koenig. Belmont, Calif., Wadsworth Pub. Co. [1962] 436 p. illus. 28 cm. Includes bibliography. [NK1130.M7] 61-13693
1. Art industries and trade. 2. Handicraft. I. Title. BIP

READ, Herbert Edward, Sir, 1893-1968. 745.2
Art and industry; the principles of industrial design. [1st American ed.] New York, Horizon Press, 1954 [c1953] 239 p. illus. 24 cm. "Revised edition." [NK1105.R4 1954] 54-78953
1. Art industries and trade. 2. Design, Industrial. I. Title.

*REED, Herbert Edward. Sir 1893- 745.2
Art and industry; the principles of industrial design [Gloucester, Mass., P. Smith, 1966,c.1953,1961] 239p. illus. 21cm. (Midland bk. rebound) [NK1105.R4 1954] 4.00
1. Art industries and trade. 2. Design, Industrial. I. Title. BIP

SLIVKA, Rose. 745
The crafts of the modern world, edited by Rose Slivka. With 405 illus. and texts by Aileen O. Webb, Rose Slivka [and] Margaret Merwin Patch. New York, Horizon Press [1968] 223 p. illus. (part col.) 32 cm. "In collaboration with the World Crafts Council." Includes glossary of craft terms in English, French, German, and Spanish (on end-papers) [NK780.S5] 68-8853 17.50
1. Art industries and trade. 2. Folk art. I. Webb, Aileen O. II. Patch, Margaret Merwin. III. World Crafts Council. IV. Title. BIP

Art industries and trade—Africa.

DICK-READ, Robert 745.096
Sanamu: adventures in search of African art. New York, Dutton [c.]1964. 271p. illus., 22cm. 64-23217 5.95
1. Art industries and trade—Africa. 2. Art, African. 3. Africa—Descr. & trav.—1951. I. Title.

Art industries and trade, American.

BENNETT, Ian. 745.1'0973
Book of American antiques. London, New York, Hamlyn, 1973. 96 p. illus. (some col.), facsims. 30 cm. Bibliography: p. 94. [NK805.B46] 74-150439 ISBN 0-600-30130-3 £2.50
1. Art industries and trade, American. I. Title.

COMSTOCK, Helen, ed. 745.10973
The concise encyclopedia of American antiques. New York, Hawthorn [1965] 848p. illus., facsims., maps, ports. 26cm. Bibl. [NK805.C65] 65-9391 12.50
1. Art industries and trade, American. 2. Art, American. 3. Art industries and trade—Dictionaries. 4. Collectors and collecting. I. Title. II. Title: Encyclopedia of American antiques.

COMSTOCK, Helen, ed. 708.051
The concise encyclopedia of American antiques. [1st ed.] New York, Hawthorn Books [1958] 2 v. (543 p.) illus., plates. 26 cm. Includes bibliographies. [NK805.C65] 58-5628
1. Art industries and trade, American. 2. Art, American. 3. Art industries and trade—Dictionaries. 4. Collectors and collecting. I. Title. II. Title: Encyclopedia of American antiques.

CONTEMPORARY crafts of the Americas / Nilda C. Fernandez Getty and Robert J. Forsyth. Chicago : H. Regnery Co., [1975] xlix, 172 p. : ill. (some col.) ; 24 cm. Catalog of an exhibition cosponsored by Colorado State University and the National Endowment for the Arts. Introductory text by N. C. F. Getty and others in English, French, Portuguese, and Spanish. Includes index. [NK801.C66 1975] 74-27806 ISBN 0-8092-8254-2 : 14.95 745'.09181'2
1. Art industries and trade—America—Exhibitions. I. Getty, Nilda C. Fernandez. II. Forsyth, Robert J. III. Colorado. State University, Fort Collins. IV. National Endowment fot the Arts.

CREEKMORE, Betsey Beeler. 745'.00973
Traditional American crafts, by Betsey B. Creekmore. [New York] Hearthside Press [1968] 191 p. illus. (part col.) 29 cm. Bibliography: p. 186-187. [NK805.C72] 68-8517 10.00
1. Art industries and trade, American. 2. Folk art—United States. I. Title. BIP

HORNUNG, Clarence Pearson. 745.4'0973
Treasury of American design; a pictorial survey of popular folk arts based upon watercolor renderings in the Index of American Design, at the National Gallery of Art, by Clarence P. Hornung. Foreword by J. Carter Brown. Introd. by Holger Cahill. New York, H. N. Abrams [1972] 2 v. (xxvii, 846 p.) illus. (part col.) 31 cm. [NK805.H67] 76-142742 ISBN 0-8109-0516-7 50.00
1. Art industries and trade, American. 2. Design, Decorative—United States. I. Index of American Design. II. Title. BIP

NORDNESS, Lee. 745'.0922
Objects: USA. New York, Viking Press [1970] 360 p. illus. (part col.), ports. 25 cm. (A Studio book) [NK808.N6 1970] 73-87253 12.95
1. Art industries and trade, American. I. Title.

Art industries and trade, American — Exhibitions.

BEASLEY, Ellen. 745.1'09768'074016855
Made in Tennessee; an exhibition of early arts and crafts. [Catalogue written and designed by Ellen Beasley and others. Exhibition held at] Tennessee Fine Arts Center at Cheekwood, Nashville, September 15-October 31, 1971. [Nashville? Printed by Williams Print. Co., 1971] 67 p. illus. 26 cm. Errata slip inserted. [NK835.T2B4] 73-157738
1. Art industries and trade, American—Exhibitions. 2. Art industries and trade, American—Tennessee. I. Tennessee Fine Arts Center. II. Title.

CLARK, Robert Judson. 745'.0973'074013
The arts and crafts movement in America, 1876-1916; an exhibition organized by the Art Museum, Princeton University and the Art Institute of Chicago. Edited by Robert Judson Clark. With texts by the editor and others. [Princeton, N.J.] distributed by Princeton University Press [1972] 190 p. illus. 35 cm. Catalog of an exhibition held at the Art Museum, Princeton University, Oct. 21-Dec. 17, 1972; the Art Institute of Chicago, Feb. 24-April 22, 1973; and the Renwick Gallery of the National Collection of Fine Arts, Smithsonian Institution, June 1-Sept. 10, 1973. Bibliography: p. 187-190. [NK1141.C55 1972] 72-77734 ISBN 0-691-03883-X 7.95 (pbk)
1. Art industries and trade, American—Exhibitions. 2. Arts and crafts movement. I. Princeton University. Art Museum. II. Chicago. Art Institute. III. Renwick Gallery. IV. Title. BIP

CROCKER Art Gallery, Sacramento, Calif. 745.5'09794'074019454
The Creative Arts League of Sacramento presents the ninth biennial crafts exhibition, February 8 through March 16, 1975 : [catalogue]. Sacramento, Calif. : E. B. Crocker Art Gallery, [1975] 78 p. : chiefly ill. ; 18 x 21 cm. Cover title: California crafts IX. [NK808.C76 1975] 75-308781
1. Art industries and trade, American—Exhibitions. 2. Handicraft—United States—Exhibitions. I. Creative Arts League of Sacramento. II. Title. III. Title: California crafts IX.

HENRY Art Gallery. 707.4
American craftsmen's invitational exhibition. [Catalog] Seattle. 1966. v. illus. 28 cm. biennial. Exhibitions for 1966- co-sponsored by the gallery (under a variant form of name: Henry Gallery) and the Friends of the Crafts, inc. [NK808.H4] 67-7279
1. Art industries and trade, American — Exhibitions. 2. Artists, American. I. Friends of the Crafts. II. Title.

ITHACA College, Ithaca, N.Y. Museum of Art. 708.147'71
New York crafts, 1700-1875, a historical survey. [Ithaca, N.Y., Printed by Cayuga Press, 1967] 56 p. illus. 18 cm. On label on t.p.: Supplied by Worldwide Books, New York. Exhibition held June 20-Aug. 19, 1967, at Ithaca College Museum of Art. Bibliography: p. 55-56. [NK835.N7I8] 68-30093
1. Art industries and trade, American—Exhibitions. 2. Art industries and trade—New York (State) I. Title. BIP

NEW York (City). Metropolitan Museum of Art. 745.2'0973
19th-century America: furniture and other decorative arts; an exhibition in celebration of the hundredth anniversary of the Metropolitan Museum of Art, April 16 through September 7, 1970. Introd. by Berry B Tracy. Furniture texts by Marilynn Johnson. Other decorative arts texts by Marvin D. Schwartz and Suzanne Boorsch [New York] Distributed by New York Graphic Society [1970] 1 v. (unpaged) illus. (part col.) 27 cm. Bibliography: p. [253]-[256] [NK807.N4] 77-109965 ISBN 8-7099-0047- 14.95
1. Art industries and trade, American—Exhibitions. I. Johnson, Marilynn. II. Schwartz, Marvin D. III. Boorsch, Suzanne. IV. Title.

NORTH Carolina. Museum of Art, Raleigh. 745.4'074'015655
Craftsmen: southeast 66 [Raleigh] 1966. 26 p. illus. 26 cm. Catalog of an exhibition held March 25-April 24, 1966. [NK814.N67] 66-65129
1. Art industries and trade, American—Exhibitions. 2. Art industries and trade—Southern States. I. Title.

NORTH Carolina. Museum of Art, Raleigh. 745.09'756'07455
North Carolina craftsmen 1971; an exhibition for North Carolina craftsmen sponsored by the North Carolina Arts Council and the North Carolina Museum of Art. September 12-October 10, 1971, North Carolina Museum of Art, Raleigh. [Raleigh, 1971] [19] p. illus. 26 cm. [NK835.N8N6] 79-198388
1. Art industries and trade, American—Exhibitions. 2. Art industries and trade, American—North Carolina. I. Title.

ST. Louis. City Art Museum. 745
The artist/craftsman; [catalogue of the exhibition held] April 11-30, 1972. Co-sponsored by The Craft Alliance and the St. Louis Art Museum. [St. Louis, 1972] [24] p. illus. 25 cm. [NK808.S24] 73-172185
1. Art industries and trade, American—Exhibitions. I. The Craft Alliance. II. Title.

TEXAS. University. Art Museum. 745'.0973
First survey of contemporary American crafts. Austin [1967 or 8] 63 p. illus. 22 cm. Exhibit held April 9-May 14, 1967. [NK808.T4] 68-66343
1. Art industries and trade, American—Exhibitions. I. Title.

Art industries and trade, American—History.

LAVINE, Sigmund A. 730
Handmade in America; the heritage of colonial craftsmen. New York, Dodd [c.1966] 148p. illus., facsims. 25cm. Bibl. [NK806.L35] 66-13347 4.50
1. Art industries and trade, American—Hist. 2. Handicraft—U.S. I. Title.

SMITH, Susan, 1885- 745.1'0973
Made in America. Drawings by Harrie Wood. New York, Knopf [c1929] Detroit, Singing Tree Press, 1971. 91 p. illus. 19 cm. [NK806.S5 1971] 71-145708
1. Art industries and trade, American—History. I. Title. BIP

Art industries and trade, American—Los Angeles—Directories.

WEINGARTEN, Lila, 1935- 338.4'7'745502579494
Selling your crafts and art in Los Angeles [by] Lila Weingarten [and] Kendall Taylor. Los Angeles, Wollstonecraft Inc. [1974] 143 p. illus. 21 cm. [NK838.L67W44] 74-218 ISBN 0-88381-007-7 3.95 (pbk.)
1. Art industries and trade, American—Los Angeles—Directories. 2. Art dealers—Los Angeles—Directories. I. Taylor, Kendall, 1941- joint author. II. Title.

Art industries and trade—Asia.

BOSSERT, Helmuth Theodor, 1889- ed. 745
Decorative art of Asia and Egypt; four hundred decorative motifs in color, forming a survey of the applied art of Egypt, China, Japan, Siam, Tibet, of the Lapps and Siberian and Islamic peoples. New York, Praeger [1956] 13 p. 40 col. plates. 35 cm. (Books that matter) [NK1037.B6] 56-9928
1. Art industries and trade—Asia. 2. Art industries and trade—Egypt. 3. Textile fabrics—Asia. 4. Textile fabrics—Egypt. 5. Decoration and ornament—Asia. 6. Decoration and ornament—Egypt. I. Title.

Art industries and trade—Bibliography.

EHRESMANN, Donald L., 1937- 016.745
Applied and decorative arts : a bibliographic guide to basic reference works, histories, and handbooks / Donald L. Ehresmann. Littleton, Colo. : Libraries Unlimited, 1977. 232 p. ; 24 cm. Includes indexes. [Z5956.A68E47] [NK1110] 76-55416 ISBN 0-87287-136-3 lib.bdg. : 15.00
1. Art industries and trade—Bibliography. I. Title. BIP

SUBJECT INDEX

ART INDUSTRIES AND

Art industries and trade, British.

PETER, Mary. 707.5
Collecting Victoriana. Drawings in the text by Jenefer Peter. New York, F. A. Praeger [1968, c1965] 189 p. illus. 23 cm. [NK928.P38 1968] 68-23167
1. Art industries and trade, British. 2. Art objects—Collectors and collecting. I. Peter, Jenefer, illus. II. Title.

Art industries and trade, British—History.

LAVINE, Sigmund A. 709'.42
Handmade in England; the tradition of British craftsmen, by Sigmund A. Lavine. New York, Dodd, Mead [1968] 148 p. illus. 25 cm. Bibliography: p. 135-137. [NK928.L35] 68-16179
1. Art industries and trade, British—History. 2. Handicraft—Great Britain. I. Title.

Art industries and trade, Canadian.

WEBSTER, Donald Blake. 745.1'0971
The book of Canadian antiques / edited by Donald Blake Webster. Toronto ; New York : McGraw-Hill Ryerson, [1974] 352 p. : ill. (some col.) ; 32 cm. Includes index. Bibliography: p. 343-346. [NK841.W42] 74-10381 ISBN 0-07-082140-2 pbk. : 5.95
1. Art industries and trade, Canadian. 2. Art objects—Collectors and collecting—Canada. I. Title.

Art industries and trade, Chinese.

JOURDAIN, Margaret. 745
Chinese export art in the eighteenth century, by Margaret Jourdain and R. Soame Jenyns. London, Country life; New York, Scribner, 1950. 152 p. (p. 73-144 illus.) col. front. 29 cm. Erratum slip inserted. Bibliographical footnotes. [NK1068.J6] 52-716
1. Art industries and trade, Chinese. 2. Art objects, Chinese. I. Jenyns, Roger Soame, 1904- joint author. II. Title.

Art industries and trade—Collectors and collecting.

MEBANE, John, 1909- 700'.75
The poor man's guide to trivia collecting / by John Mebane. 1st ed. Garden City, N.Y. : Doubleday, 1975. x, 193 p. : ill. ; 27 cm. Includes index. Bibliography: p. 182-185. [NK1125.M3595] 73-22805 ISBN 0-385-01947-5 : 8.95
1. Art industries and trade—Collectors and collecting. I. Title.

Art industries and trade—Denmark.

KARLSEN, Arne. 745.09489
Made in Denmark; a picture-book about modern Danish arts and crafts. By Arne Karlsen and Anker Tiedemann. [Translated by Eve M. Wendt] New York, Reinhold Pub. Corp. [1961? c1960] 175p. illus. 24cm. [NK983] CD62
1. Art industries and trade—Denmark. I. Tledemann, Anker, joint author. II. Title.

Art industries and trade—Dictionaries.

BOGER, Louise Ade. 703
The dictionary of antiques and the decorative arts; a book of reference for glass, furniture, ceramics, silver, periods, styles, technical terms, etc., compiled and edited by Louise Ade Boger and H. Batterson Boger. New York, Scribner [1967] ix, 662 p. illus. (part. col.) 28 cm. Bibliography: p. 661-662. [NK30.B57 1967] 67-18131
1. Art industries and trade—Dictionaries. 2. Art objects—Collectors and collecting. I. Boger, H. Batterson, joint author. II. Title.
BIP

BOGER, Louise Ade. 708.051
The dictionary of antiques and the decorative arts; a book of reference for glass, furniture, ceramics, silver, periods, styles, technical terms, etc. Compiled and edited by Louise Ade Boger and H. Batterson Boger. [Illus. by I. N. Steinberg and Associates] New York, Scribner [1957] ix, 566p. illus. 28cm. Bibliography: p. 559-566. [NK30.B57] 57-10768
1. Art industries and trade—Dictionaries. 2. Art objects—Collectors and collecting. I. Boger, H. Batterson, joint author. II. Title.

COWIE, Donald. 708.04
Antique collectors' dictionary [by] Donald Cowie and Keith Henshaw. New York, Arco Pub. Co. [1963, c1962] 208 p. illus. 21 cm. [NK30.C65] 62-21523
1. Art industries and trade—Dictionaries. 2. Art objects—Dictionaries. I. Henshaw, Keith, joint author. II. Title.
BIP

Art industries and trade, Early American—Collectors and collecting.

EBERLEIN, Harold Donaldson. 745.1'0973
The practical book of American antiques, exclusive of furniture / by Harold Donaldson Eberlein and Abbot McClure ; the chapter on early lace by Mabel Foster Bainbridge ; the chapter on Sandwich glass by Lenore Wheeler Williams ; with 257 illustration, the drawings by Abbot McClure. Rev. and with a new suppl. New York : Da Capo Press, 1977, c1927. iv, 390 p., [50] leaves of plates : ill. ; 22 cm. (A Da Capo paperback) First published in 1916 under title: The practical book of early American arts and crafts. Reprint of the ed. published by Lippincott, Philadelphia, issued in series: Lippincott practical books for the enrichment of home life. Includes index. Bibliography: p. [9] [NK806.E3 1977] 76-30449 ISBN 0-306-80062-4 pbk. : 7.95
1. Art industries and trade, Early American—Collectors and collecting. 2. Antiques—United States. I. McClure, Abbot, 1879- joint author. II. Title.

KIRK, John T. 745.1'0973
The impecunious collector's guide to American antiques / John T. Kirk. 1st ed. New York : Knopf : distributed by Random House, 1975. xvi, 178, vi p. : ill. ; 28 cm. Includes index. [NK806.K5 1975] 75-8224 ISBN 0-394-49620-5 : 12.50. ISBN 0-394-73096-8 pbk. : 5.95
1. Art industries and trade, Early American—Collectors and collecting. I. Title.
BIP

Art industries and trade, Early American—Congresses.

WINTERTHUR Conference, 20th, 1974. 745'.0974
Arts of the Anglo-American community in the seventeenth century : [twentieth annual Winterthur Conference, 1974] / edited by Ian M. G. Quimby. Charlottesville : Published for the Henry Francis du Pont Winterthur Museum [by] the University Press of Virginia, 1975. x, 299 p. : ill. ; 23 cm. (Winterthur Conference report ; 1974) Includes bibliographical references. [NK805.W53 1974] 74-22098 ISBN 0-8139-0612-1 pbk. : 4.50
1. Winterthur Conference, 20th, 1974. 2. Art industries and trade, Early American—Congresses. I. Quimby, Ian M. G., ed. II. Henry Francis du Pont Winterthur Museum. III. Title. IV. Series: Winterthur Conference. Report ; 1974.
BIP

Art industries and trade, Early American—Exhibitions.

DETROIT. Institute of Arts. 745'.0973
American decorative arts, from the pilgrims to the Revolution. An exhibition from Detroit area collections, organized by the Associates of the American Wing. Detroit, 1967. 48 p. illus. 28 cm. [NK806.D47 1967] 74-173447
1. Art industries and trade, Early American—Exhibitions. I. Founders Society. Associates of the American Wing. II. Title.

NEW Jersey. State Museum, Trenton. 709'.749'074014966
From Lenape Territory to Royal Province; New Jersey, 1600-1750. [Trenton, N.J., 1971] 88 p. illus. 22 cm. Catalog of an exhibition held April 30-September 12, 1971, at the New Jersey State Museum, Trenton. Bibliography: p. 84-85. [NK806.N4] 76-635173
1. Art industries and trade, Early American—Exhibitions. 2. Art industries and trade, Early American—New Jersey. I. Title.

Art industries and trade, Early American—History.

DYER, Walter Alden, 1878-1943. 745.5'0973
Early American craftsmen. New York, B. Franklin [1971] xv, 387 p. illus., ports. 19 cm. (Burt Franklin research and source works series, 693. American classics in history and social science, 183) Reprint of the 1915 ed. [NK806.D8 1971] 74-154640 ISBN 0-8337-0986-0
1. Art industries and trade, Early American—History. 2. United States—Biography. I. Title.
BIP

Art industries and trade, Early American—New York (State)—Long Island—Exhibitions.

FAILEY, Dean F. 745.5'074'014721
Long Island is my nation : the decorative arts & craftsmen, 1640-1830 : [exhibition] / Dean F. Failey, with the assistance of Robert J. Hefner & Susan E. Klaffky. Setauket, N.Y. : Society for the Preservation of Long Island Antiquities, c1976. 304 p. : ill. ; 28 cm. Bibliography: p. 215-217. [NK806.F34] 76-29485
1. Art industries and trade, Early American—New York (State)—Long Island—Exhibitions. 2. Decoration and ornament—New York (State)—Long Island—Exhibitions. I. Hefner, Robert J., joint author. II. Klaffky, Susan E., joint author. III. Society for the Preservation of Long Island Antiquities. IV. Title.

Art industries and trade, Early American—Williamsburg, Va.

COLONIAL Williamsburg Foundation. 917.55'4252'032
The Williamsburg collection of antique furnishings. Williamsburg, Va.; distributed by Holt, Rinehart and Winston, New York [1973] 120 p. col. illus. 29 cm. [NK838.W54C64 1973] 73-86811 ISBN 0-87935-018-0 6.95
1. Art industries and trade, Early American—Williamsburg, Va. 2. Art industries and trade, English—Williamsburg, Va. 3. Interior decoration—Williamsburg, Va. I. Title.
BIP

Art industries and trade—Europe.

BOSSERT, Helmuth Theodor, 1889- 745
Folk art of Europe. [Translation by Sybil Moholy Nagy] New York, F. A. Praeger [1953] 25 p. 88 plates (part col.) 34 cm. Translation of Ornamente der Volkskunst. [NK925.B653] 53-10344
1. Art industries and trade—Europe. 2. Textile fabrics—Europe. 3. Decoration and ornament—Europe. I. Title.
BIP

Art industries and trade—Exhibitions.

LONG Beach, Calif. Museum of Art. 745.209794
California designed, by Samuel Heavenrich [director of the exhibition] The Municipal Art Center, Long Beach, in collaboration with the Oakland Art Museum. [Long Beach, 1955?] unpaged. illus. 26cm. [NK835.C3L6] 59-43270
1. Art industries and trade—Exhibitions. 2. Art industries and trade—California. I. Heavenrich, Samuel. II. Title.

Art industries and trade—Finland.

SUOMEN Koristetaiteilijain Liitto Ornamo. 745.449471
The Ornamo book of Finnish design [Armi Ratia, ed.-in-chief Helsinki, Author; dist. New York, Heinman. 1964] 133p. illus. (pt. col.) ports. 31cm. 64-55183 10.00
1. Art industries and trade—Finland. 2. Design, Decorative—Finland. I. Title.

Art industries and trade—France.

COSTANTINO, Ruth T. 709.44
How to know French antiques. Illustrated by Helen Costantino. New York, C. N. Potter [1961] 240 p. illus. 32 cm. Bibliography: p. 232-233. [NK947.C64] 61-15111
1. Art industries and trade—France. 2. Furniture, French. 3. Art, French. I. Title.

Art industries and trade, Georgian.

FIELD, June. 745.5'075
Collecting Georgian and Victorian crafts. New York, Scribner [1973] 162 p. illus. 26 cm. Bibliography: p. 154-157. [NK770.F53] 72-11320 ISBN 0-684-13260-5 10.00
1. Art industries and trade, Georgian. 2. Art industries and trade, Victorian. 3. Art objects—Collectors and collecting. I. Title.

Art industries and trade—Germany.

CAMPBELL, Joan, 1929- 745'.06'243
The German Werkbund : the politics of reform in the applied arts / by Joan Campbell. Princeton, N.J. : Princeton University Press, 1977. p. cm. Includes index. Bibliography: p. [NK951.C35] 77-71974 ISBN 0-691-05250-6 : 20.00
1. Deutscher Werkbund. 2. Art industries and trade—Germany. I. Title.
BIP

Art industries and trade—Gt. Brit.

BEE, Alf. 745
From Gothic revival to functional form; a study in Victorian theories of design. Oslo, Oslo University Press; New York, Humanities Press, 1957. viii 183p. plates. 22cm. (Oslo studies in English. no. 6) 'Originally submitted in ... 1954 as a thesis for the degree of bachelor of letters in the University of Oxford.' Bibliography: p. 158-164. [NK928.B6 1957] 58-2530
1. Art industries and trade—Gt. Brit. 2. Design. I. Title. II. Series.

FARR, Michael. 745.43
Design in British industry, a mid-century survey. With a foreword andpostscript by Nikolaus Pevsner. Cambridge [Eng.] University Press, 1955. 332p. illus. 26cm. [NK928.F35] 55-14441
1. Art industries and trade—Gt. Brit. 2. Design, Industrial. I. Title.

GARRAD, Larch Sylvia. 745'.0941
A present from : holiday souvenirs of the British Isles / Larch S. Garrad. Newton Abbot ; North Pomfret, Vt. : David and Charles, 1976. 160 p. : ill. ; 23 cm. Includes index. Bibliography: p. 152-154. [NK928.G35] 75-43204 ISBN 0-7153-7080-4 : 13.95
1. Art industries and trade—Great Britain. 2. Souvenirs (Keepsakes)—Great Britain. I. Title.

SHULL, Thelma 745
Victorian antiques. Rutland, Vt., Tuttle [1963] xviii, 421p. illus. 22cm. Bibl. 63-14132 12.75
1. Art industries and trade—Gt. Brit. I. Title.

WOOD, Violet (Mackworth-Praed) 1898- 708.051
Victoriana, a collector's guide. New York, Macmillan, 1961[c.1960] 175p. illus. 61-65212 6.00
1. Art industries and trade—Gt. Brit. 2. Collectors and collecting. I. Title.

Art industries and trade—Hawaii—Catalogs.

STONE, Sarah. 709.01'1
Art and artifacts of the 18th century; objects in the Leverian Museum as painted by Sarah Stone. [Text] by Roland W. Force and Maryanne Force Honolulu, Hawaii, Bishop Museum Press, 1968. 232 p. illus. (part col.) 24 cm. "Published in observation of the 80th anniversary of the founding of Bishop Museum, 1889-1969." Bibliography: p. 231-232. [ND1942.S8A4] 79-6020
1. Art industries and trade—Hawaii—Catalogs. I. Force, Roland W. II. Force, Maryanne. III. Bernice Pauahi Bishop

Museum, Honolulu. IV. Leverian Museum, London. V. Title.

Art industries and trade—History.

BRUCE, Marjory. 600
The book of craftsmen; the story of man's handiwork through the ages. New York, Dodd, Mead. Detroit, Gale Research Co., 1974. 282 p. illus. 22 cm. Reprint of the 1937 ed. [NK600.B7 1974] 70-185352 ISBN 0-8103-3960-9 14.00
1. Art industries and trade—History. 2. Industrial arts—History. I. Title. BIP

Art industries and trade — India — Hist.

CHATTOPADHYAYA, Kamaladevi, 1903- 709'.54
Indian handicrafts. New Delhi, New York, Allied Publishers [1963] 95 p. illus. (part col.) 23 cm. Bibliography: p. 81-95. [NK1047.C48] 64-2679
1. Art industries and trade — India — Hist. I. Title.

Art industries and trade, Indic.

BUSSABARGER, Robert F. 709'.54
The everyday art of India, by Robert F. Bussabarger and Betty Dashew Robins. Andrew Tau, photographer. New York, Dover Publications [1968] xi, 205 p. illus. (part col.), maps. 28 cm. Bibliographical footnotes. [NK1047.B84] 68-20951 3.00
1. Art industries and trade, Indic. 2. Folk art—India. I. Robins, Betty Dashew, joint author. II. Title. BIP

Art industries and trade, Indic—History.

COOMARASWAMY, Ananda Kentish, 1877-1947. 709.54
The arts & crafts of India & Ceylon, by Ananda K. Coomaraswamy. Containing 225 illus. New York, Farrar, Straus [1964] xiii, 259 p. illus., ports. 21 cm. [N7301.C58 1964] 64-18969
1. Art industries and trade, Indic—History. 2. The arts, Indic—History. 3. The arts—Ceylon—History. 4. Art industries and trade—Ceylon—History. 5. Art—Ceylon—History. I. Title. BIP

Art industries and trade — Italy.

TOOR, Frances, 1890- 745
Made in Italy. With line decorations by Earle Goodenow and with photos. [1st ed.] New York, Knopf, 1957. 204 p. illus. 22 cm. (Borzol books for young people) [NK959.T57] 57-7081
1. Art industries and trade — Italy. 2. Folk art — Italy. I. Title.

Art Industries and trade—Japan.

GENDAI Kogei Bijutsuka Kyokai 745.0952
The 1st Japan's modern industrial art exhibition [dist. New York, Perkins Oriental, 1962] 64p. chiefly illus. 30cm. J62 7.00
1. Art Industries and trade—Japan. 2. Art Industries and trade exhibition. I. Title. II. Title: Nihon gendai kogei bijutsu ten. III. Title: The 1st Japan's modern industrial art exhibition. Daiikkai Nihon gendai kogei bijutsu ten.

Art industries and trade—Japan—Catalogs.

CHANDLER, Ceil. 338.4'3738'20952
Made in occupied Japan. Photography and art work by Edy J. Chandler. Houston, Chandler's Discriminating Junk [1972] 1 v. (unpaged) 43 illus. (part. col.) 22 cm. [NK1071.C45] 72-181450 7.50
1. Art industries and trade—Japan—Catalogs. I. Title.

Art industries and trade, Japanese.

IWAMIYA, Takeji, 1920- 745.0952
Design and craftsmanship of Japan: stone, metal, fibers and fabrics, bamboo. Photos. taken by Takeji Iwamiya. Introductory essay by Donald Richie. New York, H. N. Abrams [1965] xxviii p. 182 p. of illus. (part col.) 37 cm. [NK1071.I9] 64-22626
1. Art industries and trade, Japanese. 2. Decoration and ornament, Japanese. I. Title.

MURAOKA, Kageo, 1901- 745'.0952
Folk arts and crafts of Japan, by Kageo Muraoka and Kichiemon Okamura. Translated by Daphne D. Stegmaier. [1st English ed.] New York, Weatherhill [1973] 164 p. illus. (part col.) 23 cm. (The Heibonsha survey of Japanese art, v. 26) Translation of Mingei. [NK1071.M8713] 72-78600 ISBN 0-8348-1009-3 8.95
1. Art industries and trade, Japanese. 2. Folk art—Japan. I. Okamura, Kichiemon, 1916- joint author. II. Title. III. Series. BIP

Art industries and trade, Medieval—Juvenile literature.

PRICE, Christine, 1928- 709.02
Made in the Middle Ages. Written and illustrated by Christine Price. [1st ed.] New York, Dutton [1961] 118 p. illus. 21 cm. [NK700.P7] 61-12453
1. Art industries and trade, Medieval—Juvenile literature. I. Title.

Art industries and trade—Mexico.

ROSS, Patricia Fent, 1901- 745
Made in Mexico; the story of a country's arts and crafts. Illus. by Carlos Merida. [1st ed.] New York, Knopf, 1952. 329 p. illus. 22 cm. Includes bibliography. [NK844.R65] 51-11085
1. Art industries and trade—Mexico. 2. Folk art—Mexico. I. Title.

Art industries and trade—Netherlands—Leyden—History—Sources.

BANGS, Jeremy Dupertuis, 1946- 746.3'9492'3
Documentary studies in Leiden art and crafts, 1475-1575 / Jeremy Dupertuis Bangs. [1976] xx, 202 p. : ill. ; 21 cm. Thesis—Leiden. "Stellingen" (1 fold. sheet) and errata slip inserted. Includes bibliographical references. [NK969.L48B36] 77-362592
1. Art industries and trade—Netherlands—Leyden—History—Sources. I. Title.

Art industries and trade—New Hampshire.

WRITERS' Program. New Hampshire. 709'.742
Hands that built New Hampshire; the story of Granite State craftsmen, past & present. Brattleboro, Vt., Stephen Daye Press. [New York, AMS Press, 1973, c1940] p. At head of half title: Federal Writers' Project. "Sponsored by His Excellency, Francis P. Murphy, Governor of New Hampshire, and the honorable Council, sponsors of the New Hampshire Writers' Project." Bibliography: p. [NK835.N4W7 1973] 73-3635 ISBN 0-404-57935-3
1. Art industries and trade—New Hampshire. 2. Arts and crafts movement. 3. Handicraft—New Hampshire. 4. Artisans—New Hampshire. I. Federal Writers' Project. II. Title. BIP

Art industries and trade—New Mexico.

DICKEY, Roland F. 745
New Mexico village arts [by] Roland F. Dickey. Drawings by Lloyd Lozes Goff. [1970 ed.] Albuquerque, University of New Mexico Press [1970] xii, 264 p. illus. 21 cm. Bibliography: p. 254-258. [NK835.N5D5 1970] 71-107101
1. Art industries and trade—New Mexico. 2. Folk art—New Mexico. I. Title. BIP

Art industries and trade—New York (City)

GOTTESMAN, Rita Susswein, 1906- comp. 740.97471
The arts and crafts in New York; advertisements and news items from New York City newspapers. New York, Printed for the New York Historical Society, 1938- v. illus. 25. cm. (Collections of the New York Historical Society for the year 1936, 1948, 1949. Peyster publication fund series, 69, 81-82.) Contents.Contents. -- [v. 1] 1726-1776. -- [v. 2] 1777-1799. -- [v. 3] 1800-1894. [F116.N63 vol. 69, etc.] 38-18579
1. Art industries and trade — New York (City) I. Title. II. Series: New York Historical Society. Collections. The John Watts De Peyster publication fund series, 69 [etc.

GOTTESMAN, Rita Susswein, 1906- comp. 659.1'9'7455
The arts and crafts in New York, 1726-1776; advertisements and news items from New York City newspapers. Compiled by Rita S. Gottesman. New York, Da Capo Press, 1970. xviii, 450 p. 24 cm. (Da Capo Press series in architecture and decorative art, v. 35) Reprint of the 1938 ed. [NK838.N37G6] 70-127254
1. Art industries and trade—New York (City) I. Title. BIP

Art industries and trade—New York (State)—Utica—Exhibitions.

MUNSON-WILLIAMS-PROCTOR Institute, Utica, N.Y. Museum of Art. 680
Made in Utica : Museum of Art, Munson-Williams-Proctor Institute and Oneida Historical Society, April 11 through September 5, 1976. Utica, N.Y. : The Institute, c1976. 73 p. : ill. ; 28 cm. Bibliography: p. 72-73. [NK838.U86M86 1976] 76-377122
1. Art industries and trade—New York (State)—Utica—Exhibitions. 2. Handicraft—New York (State)—Utica—Exhibitions. I. Oneida Historical Society at Utica. II. Title.

Art industries and trade—Newport, R. I.

PRESERVATION Society of Newport County. 745
The arts and crafts of Newport, Rhode Island, 1640-1820, by Ralph E. Carpenter,Jr. Newport, 1954- v. illus. 29cm. 'Items illustrated in ... [v. 1] composed the loan exhibition held during the summer of 1953 at the Nichols-Wanton-Hunter House.' Bibliography: v. 1, p. 211. [NK838.N4P7] 54-9911
1. Art industries and trade—Newport, R. I. 2. Furniture—Newport. R. I. 3. Silversmithing—Rhode Island— Newport. I. Carpenter, Ralph E. II. Title.

Art industries and trade—North Carolina.

CRAIG, James Hicklin, 1937- 680.9756
The arts and crafts in North Carolina, 1699-1840, by James H. Craig. Winston-Salem, N.C., Museum of Early Southern Decorative Arts, Old Salem inc. 1965 [c1966] vii, 480 p. front, 25 cm. A compilation of newspaper advertisements, etc., of craftsmen. Bibliography: p. [379]-383. [NK835.N8C7] 66-18381
1. Art industries and trade—North Carolina. I. Winston-Salem, N. C. Museum of Early Southern Decorative Arts. II. Title.

Art industries and trade—Norway.

HOPSTOCK, Carsten Henrich, 1924- 745.449481
Norwegian design: from Viking age to industrial revolution. [New York, Taplinger, 1961] 210p. illus. (part col.) 26cm. 59-20547 15.00
1. Art industries and trade—Norway. 2. Decoration and ornament—Norway. I. Title.

Art industries and trade, Norwegian—Exhibitions.

CRAFTSMEN from Norway. 745'.00922 B
An exhibition under the patronage of H. E. Arne Gunneng, Ambassador of Norway to the United States. Circulated by the American Federation of Arts, New York. [New York? 1970] [42] p. illus. 22 cm. "Sponsored by the Cultural Department of the Royal Norwegian Ministry of Foreign Affairs, the Information Service of the Royal Norwegian Embassy, and the American Federation of Arts." "Selected for the Norwegian Association of Arts and Crafts by Tormod Alnaes." [NK991.C7] 75-103154
1. Art industries and trade, Norwegian—Exhibitions. I. Norway. Utenriksdepartementet. Kulturavdelingen. II. Norway. Ambassaden (U.S.). Informasjonskontoret. III. American Federation of Arts. IV. Landsforbundet norsk brukskunst.

Art industries and trade—Norwich, Conn.

SOCIETY of the Founders of Norwich, Conn. 709.7465
Craftsmen & artists of Norwich: furniture, paintings, clocks, silver, pewter, pottery. [Catalogue compiled by Jo Darmstadt. Stonington, Conn, Pequot Press, 1965] xii, 67 p. illus. 24 cm. Norwich Historical Exhibition, September 12 through October 3, 1965, at the Converse Art Gallery, Norwich, Conn. Presented by the Society of the Founders of Norwich and the Friends of the Slate Museum. [NK838.N6S6] 65-27719
1. Art industries and trade—Norwich, Conn. 2. Art industries and trade, American—Exhibitions. 3. Art—Norwich, Conn. 4. Art, American—Exhibitions. I. Darmstadt, Jo Raynes, comp. II. Friends of the Slater Memorial Museum, Norwich, Conn. III. Title. IV. Title: Norwich Historical Exhibition.

Art industries and trade — Pennsylvania.

STOUDT, John Joseph, 1911- 745.09748
Early Pennsylvania arts and crafts. With a foreword by S. K. Stevens. New York, A. S. Barnes [1964] 364 p. illus., facsims., col. plates, ports. 31 cm. [NK835.P4S72] 64-21360
1. Art industries and trade — Pennsylvania. 2. Art — Pennsylvania. I. Title.

Art industries and trade, Renaissance—Exhibitions.

THE Triumph of humanism : 745'.094
a visual survey of the decorative arts of the Renaissance / introd. by D. Graeme Keith ; with contributions by Charles Avery ... [et al.]. [San Francisco] : Fine Arts Museums of San Francisco, c1977. 95 p. : ill. (some col.) ; 28 cm. Catalogue of an exhibition held at the California Palace of the Legion of Honor, San Franciso, Oct. 22, 1977-Jan. 8, 1978. Bibliography: p. 95. [NK760.T74] 77-81221 ISBN 0-88401-030-9 pbk. : 4.95
1. Art industries and trade, Renaissance—Exhibitions. I. Keith, David Graeme, 1934- II. Avery, Charles. III. Fine Arts Museums of San Francisco. BIP

Art industries and trade, Renaissance—Juvenile literature.

PRICE, Christine, 1928- 745.443
Made in the Renaissance, arts and crafts of the age of exploration, written, illus. by Christine Price. New York, Dutton [c.1963] 120p. illus. (pt. col.) maps. 21cm. 63-7452 3.75
1. Art industries and trade, Renaissance—Juvenile literature. I. Title. BIP

PRICE, Christine, 1928- 745.443
Made in the Renaissance, arts and ccrafts of the age of exploration, written and illustrated by Christine Price. [1st ed.] New York, Dutton [1963] 120 p. illus. 21 cm. [NK760.P7] 63-7452
1. Art industries and trade. Renaissance—Juvenile literature. I. Title.

SUBJECT INDEX

ART INDUSTRIES AND

Art industries and trade—Russia—Catalogs.

LENINGRAD. 745'.0947'0740745
Gosudarstvennyi russkii muzei.
*Russian applied art : eighteenth to early twentieth century / Russian Museum, Leningrad ; [compiled and introd. by E. Ivanova ; edited by V. Pushkariov ; photos. by V. Stukalov ; translated by Yu. Nemetsky]. Leningrad : Aurora, 1976. 199 p. : chiefly col. ill. ; 29 cm. [NK975.L42 1976b] 77-364357 25.00
1. Leningrad. Gosudarstvennyi russkii muzei. 2. Art industries and trade—Russia—Catalogs. 3. Art industries and trade—Russia—Leningrad—Catalogs. I. Ivanova, Elena Aleksandrovna. II. Title.
Distributed by H.N. Abrams, New York

Art industries and trade—Scandinavia.

BEER, Eileene 745.4'4948
Harrison.
Scandinavian design : objects of a life style / Eileene Harrison Beer. New York : Farrar, Straus and Giroux, [1975] p. cm. Includes index. Bibliography: p. [NK979.B43] 75-25732 ISBN 0-374-25424-9 : 35.00
1. Art industries and trade—Scandinavia. 2. Design—Scandinavia. 3. Design, Industrial—Scandinavia. I. Title.

HARD AF SEGERSTAD, Ulf. 745.20948
Full name: Bror Ulf Jakob Hard af Segerstad.
Scandinavian design. [Tr. from Swedish by Nancy and Edward Mazel New York, Lyle Stuart [c.1961] 129p. illus. (part col.) 61-16138 4.00 bds.,
1. Art industries and trade—Scandinavia. I. Title. BIP

ZAHLE, Erik, 1898- ed. 745.0948
A treasury of Scandinavian design [Tr. from the Danish ed.] New York, Golden [1963, c.1961] 299p. illus. (pt. col.) ports. 29cm. 63-9343 14.95 bds.,
1. Art industries and trade—Scandinavia. 2. Art industries and trade—Finland. I. Title.

Art industries and trade, Shaker.

KLAMKIN, Marian. 745'.0974
Hands to work; Shaker folk art and industries. Illustrated with photos. by Charles Klamkin. New York, Dodd, Mead [1972] 212 p. illus. 25 cm. Bibliography: p. 207-208. [NK805.K57] 72-3922 ISBN 0-396-06647-X 8.95
1. Art industries and trade, Shaker. I. Title. BIP

Art industries and trade, Shaker—Connecticut—Enfield—Exhibitions.

UNITED Cerebral Palsy 749.2'14
Association of Greater Hartford. Women's Auxiliary.
The Shakers : an exhibition concerning their furniture, artifacts, and religion, with emphasis on Enfield, Connecticut, Hartford, Connecticut, November 7-11, 1975 / sponsored by the Women's Auxiliary of the United Cerebral Palsy Association of Greater Hartford. [Hartford] : The Auxiliary, c1975. [40] p. : ill. ; 28 cm. [NK838.E53U54 1975] 76-356045
1. Art industries and trade, Shaker—Connecticut—Enfield—Exhibitions. 2. Art industries and trade, Shaker—Exhibitions. 3. Shakers—Enfield, Conn. I. Title.

Art industries and trade—Shenandoah Valley.

SMITH, Elmer Lewis. 745'.09755'9
Arts and crafts of the Shenandoah Valley; [a pictorial presentation] compiled by Elmer L. Smith. Witmer, Pa., Published for Shenandoah Valley Folklore Society by Applied Arts [1968] 43 p. illus., facsims., music. 28 cm. ([American dollar publications]) [NK810.5.S6] 75-724 1.00
1. Art industries and trade—Shenandoah Valley. 2. Folk art—Shenandoah Valley. I. Shenandoah Valley Folklore Society. II. Title.

Art industries and trade—Southern States.

EATON, Allen 745'.0975
Hendershott, 1878-
Handicrafts of the Southern highlands [by] Allen H. Eaton. With a new pref. by Ralph Rinzler and a new introd. by Rayna Green. New York, Dover Publications [1973, c1937] xxi, 370 p. illus. 21 cm. Reprint of the ed. published by Russell Sage, New York. Bibliography: p. [347]-355. [NK814.E2 1973] 72-77661 ISBN 0-486-22211-X pap 5.00
1. Art industries and trade—Southern States. 2. Mountain whites (Southern States) 3. Arts and crafts movement. 4. Handicraft—Southern States. I. Title. BIP

Art industries and trade—Spain—History.

WILLIAMS, Leonard, 338.4'7'70946
1871-
The arts and crafts of older Spain. Freeport, N.Y., Books for Libraries Press [1972] p. Reprint of the 1907 ed., issued in series: The World of art series. Contents.Contents.—v. 1. Gold, silver, and jewel work. Iron-work. Bronzes. Arms.—v. 2. Furniture. Ivories. Pottery. Glass.—v. 3. Textile fabrics. Bibliography (p.) [NK999.W7 1972] 72-8450 ISBN 0-8369-6995-2
1. Art industries and trade—Spain—History. I. Title. II. Series: The World of art series.

Art industries and trade—Sweden—Yearbooks.

KONTUR, 745.209485
Swedish design annual [v.2.] Stockholm, Svenska slojdforeningen. [dist. Totowa, N.J., Bedminster. 1962] unpaged. illus. (pt. col.) ports. 27cm. In English (some vols. Swedish and English) 62-52991 2.00 pap.,
1. Art industries and trade—Sweden—Yearbooks. 2. Design. Decorative—Sweden—Yearbooks. I. Svenska slojdforeningen.

Art industries and trade, Swedish.

PLATH, Iona 745.009485
The decorative arts of Sweden. New York, Dover [c.1948,1966] xxiii, 218p. illus., map. 28cm. (T1478) [NK995.P6] 65-20487 2.50 pap.,
1. Art industries and trade, Swedish. 2. Art, Decorative. I. Title.

PLATH, Iona 745.0099485
The decorative arts of Sweden [Gloucester, Mass., P. Smith, c.1948,1966] xxiii, 218p. illus., map. 28cm. (Dover bk. T1478 rebound) First pub. by Scribners in 1948 [NK995.P6 1966] 5.00
1. Art industries and trade, Swedish. 2. Art, Decorative. I. Title. BIP

Art industries and trade — Texas.

DALLAS. Texas 745.1'09748'45
Crafts Exhibition.
Texas Crafts Exhibition; [catalog] [Dallas] v. illus. 26 cm. annual. Exhibitions sponsored by the Craft Guild of Dallas and the Dallas Museum of Fine Arts. [NK835.T4D3] 64-4169
1. Art industries and trade — Texas. 2. Art industries and trade — Exhibitions. I. Craft Guild of Dallas. II. Dallas. Museum of Fine Arts. III. Title.

Art industries and trade—Ukraine—Catalogs.

LVOV. 745.5'0947'7107407718
Ukrains'kyi derzhavnyi muzei etnografii ta khudozhn'oho promyslu.
State Museum of Ethnography and Crafts under the UKR.SSR Academy of Sciences = [Derzhavnyi muzei etnohrafii ta khudozhn'oho promyslu AN URSR (romanized form)] / [translated from the Ukrainian by Anatole Bilenko]. Kiev : Mistetstvo, 1976. ca. 250 p. : chiefly ill. (some col.) ; 25 cm. Catalogue of "articles of decorative and applied art" from the museum's collections. English and Ukranian. [NK976.U5L89 1976] 77-474693 6.07rub
1. Lvov. Ukrains'kyi derzhavnyi muzei etnografii ta khudozhn'oho promyslu. 2. Art industries and trade—Ukraine—Catalogs. I. Title. II. Title: Derzhavnyi muzei etnohrafii ta khudozhn'oho promyslu AN URSR.

Art industries and trade—United States.

*AMERICAN Crafts 745.5'025'73
Council
Contemporary crafts market place, compiled by American Crafts Council. 1975-1976 ed. New York, R. R. Bowker [1975] viii, 501 p. 23 cm. [NK805] 75-518 ISBN 0-8352-0806-0 13.95 (pbk.)
1. Art industries and trade—United States. I. Title.

BROOKLYN Institute of 745.50973
Arts and Sciences. Museum.
Masters of contemporary American crafts; a resume of the Masters of contemporary American crafts exhibition. [Brooklyn, 1961] unpaged. illus. 23cm. [NK808.B7] 61-3793
1. Art Industries and trade—U. S. 2. Art Industries and trade—Exhibitions. I. Title.

THE Craftsman : 700
an anthology / edited by Barry Sanders. Santa Barbara, Calif. : Peregrine Smith, 1978. xvi, 328 p. : ill. ; 28 cm. A collection of articles, photos, and drawings from the Craftsman. [NK1141.C7] 78-15909 ISBN 0-87905-029-2 pbk. : 9.95
1. TheCraftsman—Illustrations. 2. Art industries and trade—United States. 3. Arts and crafts movement. I. Sanders, Barry. II. The Craftsman. BIP

DREPPERD, Carl William, 749.211
1898-
New geography of American antiques, by Carl W. Drepperd, Lurelle Van Arsdale Guild. London, Tandem Bks.; New York, Award Bks. [1967, c.1948] 292p. illus. 18cm. (A245NK) Orig. pub. in 1927. [NK806.D685] .95 pap.,
1. Art industries and trade—U.S. 2. Furniture—U.S. 3. Art objects—U.S. I. Guild, Lurelle Van Arsdale, 1898- joint author. II. Title.

HORNUNG, Clarence 745.4'49'73
Pearson.
Treasury of American antiques : a pictorial survey of popular folk arts & crafts / Clarence P. Hornung. New York : H. N. Abrams, 1977. 175 p. : ill. (some col.) ; 30 cm. Concise ed. of the the author's Treasury of American design originally published in 2 v. in 1972. [NK805.H67 1977] 76-49914 ISBN 0-8109-1670-3. ISBN 0-8109-2060-3 pbk. : 8.75
1. Art industries and trade—United States. 2. Design, Decorative—United States. 3. Antiques—United States. I. Title. BIP

HUNT, Peter of Provincetown, 745
Mass.
How-to-do-it book. New York, Prentice-Hall [1952] 294 p. illus. 26 cm. [NK1141.H8] 52-10663
1. Art industries and trade—U.S. 2. Folk art—U.S. 3. Decoration and ornament. 4. Design, Decorative. I. Title.

KAUFFMAN, Henry J 1908- 739.51
Early American copper, tin, and brass. New York, McBride [1950] 112p. illus. 32cm. Bibliography: p.112. [NK806.K3] 50-11133
1. Art industries and trade—U. S. 2. Folk art—U. S. 3. Implements, utensils, etc.—U. S. I. Title.

LIFE (Chicago) 745
America's arts and skills, by the editors of Life. With an introd. by Charles F. Montgomery. New York, Dutton, 1957. 172p. illus. (part col.) 36cm. 'Appeared in Life at intervals of approximately six weeks from April 18, 1955 to May 21, 1956.' [NK805.L44] 57-8994
1. Art industries and trade—U. S. 2. U. S.—Civilization—Hist. I. Title.

WHITE, Margaret E 745.009749
The decorative arts of early New Jersey [by] Margaret E. White. Princeton, N.J., Van Nostrand, 1964. xiv, 137 p. illus., facsim., maps (on lining papers) 22 cm. (The New Jersey historical series, v. 25) "Bibliographical note": p. 124-128. [NK835.N45W5] 65-428
I. Art industries and trade — New Jersey. II. Title. III. Series.

Art industries and trade—U. S.—Congresses.

AMERICAN Craftsmen's v. 12
Council. National Conference.
Papers delivered. 1st 1957- New York [etc.] v. illus., ports. 28cm. Vols. for 1957-59 issued without series title. Issued by the conference under earlier names: 1957, conference of American Craftsmen 1958-59, Conference. Each vol. has also a distinctive title: 1957, Asilomar.--1958, Dimensions of design.--1959, The craftsman's world.--1961, Research in the crafts. [NK21.A53] 62-5440
1. Art industries and trade—U. S.—Congresses. I. Title.

Art industries and trade—Trade—U.S.—Directories.

GLAZER, Dorothy, 1914- 745.058
Where to sell handcrafts; a directory for marketing craft products with a list of sources for craft supplies. Boston, C. T. Branford Co. [1951] 72 p. 20 cm. [HD2346.U5G55] 51-11451
1. Art industries and trade—U. S.—Direct. I. Title.

Art industries and trade—U.S.—Directories.

AMERICAN Crafts 745.5'025'73
Council. Research & Education Dept.
Craft shops, galleries USA. [New York, American Crafts Council, c1970] 78 p. 11 x 23 cm. Cover title. [NK805.A1A65] 79-24581
1. Art industries and trade—U.S.—Directories. I. Title.

AMERICAN Crafts 745.5'025'73
Council. Research & Education Dept.
Craft shops, galleries, USA; a directory of shops, galleries & studios selling United States crafts. [4th ed. New York] American Crafts Council [1973] 214 p. 11 x 23 cm. [NK805.A67 1973] 73-175467 ISBN 0-88321-001-0
1. Art industries and trade—United States—Directories. I. Title.

Art industries and trade—United States—Exhibitions.

AMERICAN arts 709'.73'074017113
from Toledo collections, 1700-1840 : [exhibition at the Toledo Museum of Art, January 23, February 20, 1977 [Toledo] : The Museum, c1977. [52] p. : ill. ; 18 cm. Bibliography: p. [52] [NK805.A66] 76-55895
1. Art industries and trade—United States—Exhibitions. 2. Art industries and trade—Collectors and collecting—Ohio—Toledo—Exhibitions. I. Toledo. Museum of Art.

CROCKER Art 745.5'09794'074019454
Gallery, Sacramento, Calif.
Creative Arts League of Sacramento presents California crafts : tenth biennial exhibition of work by California craftsmen, March 12-April 10, 1977 : [catalogue]. Sacramento : E. B. Crocker Art Gallery, c1977. [80] p. : chiefly ill. ; 23 x 26 cm. Cover title: California crafts X. [NK808.C76 1977] 77-359571
1. Art industries and trade—United States—Exhibitions. 2. Handicraft—United States—Exhibitions. I. Creative Arts League of Sacramento. II. Title. III. Title: California crafts X.

HERBERT F. Johnson Museum of 680
Art.
The handwrought object, 1776-1976 : [exhibition], July 10-August 22, 1976, Herbert F. Johnson Museum of Art, Cornell University, Ithaca, New York / [edited by Holly M. Bailey]. Ithaca : The University, c1976. 55 p. : ill. ; 28 cm. Bibliography: p. 13. [NK805.H44 1976] 76-1614
1. Art industries and trade—United States—Exhibitions. 2. Handicraft—United

States—Exhibitions. I. Bailey, Holly M. II. Title.

OHIO Designer Craftsmen. 745.2'074'0171
Ohio Designer Craftsmen. [n.p., 1970?] [39] p. (chiefly illus.) 29 x 14 cm. Label mounted on t.p.: Supplied by Worldwide Books, inc., Boston. Catalog of a touring exhibition sponsored by the Ohio Arts Council. [NK835.O3O35] 79-19402
1. Art industries and trade—United States—Exhibitions. 2. Art industries and trade—Ohio. I. Ohio Arts Council.

Art industries and trade—U.S.—History.

CHRISTENSEN, Erwin Ottomar, 1890- 745.0973
American crafts and folk arts [by] Erwin O. Christensen. Washington, R. B. Luce [1964] 90 p. illus. 22 cm. (America today series, no. 4) Bibliography: p. 88-90. [NK805.C48] 64-19601
1. Art industries and trade—U.S.—History. 2. Folk art—U.S.—History. I. Title.

Art industries and trade—United States—History—20th century.

HALL, Julie. 709'.2'2
Tradition and change : the new American craftsman / by Julie Hall ; foreword by Rose Slivka. 1st ed. New York : Dutton, 1977. 192 p. : ill. (some col.) ; 29 cm. Includes index. Bibliography: p. 191. [NK808.H27 1977] 77-79798 ISBN 0-525-22195-6 : 25.00
1. Art industries and trade—United States—History—20th century. 2. Artisans—United States. I. Title. BIP

Art industries and trade—United States—History—20th century—Exhibitions.

YOUNG Americans 709'.73'07401471
: fiber, wood, plastic, leather : a national competition, the one in a series of three to focus on work by young Americans between the ages of eighteen and thirty years : June 7, 1977-July 15, 1977, the Southeastern Center for Contemporary Art, Winston-Salem, North Carolina, October 7, 1977-January 1, 1978, Museum of Contemporary Crafts of the American Crafts Council / sponsored by the American Crafts Council. [New York] : The Council, c1977. [48] p. : ill. (some col.) ; 22 cm. [NK808.Y68] 77-89424 ISBN 0-88321-020-7 pbk. : 4.85
1. Art industries and trade—United States—History—20th century—Exhibitions. 2. Handicraft—United States—Exhibitions. 3. Youth as artists—United States—Exhibitions. I. Southeastern Center for Contemporary Art. II. American Crafts Council. Museum of Contemporary Crafts. III. American Crafts Council.

Art industries and trade, Victorian.

GABRIEL, Juri. 749.2'04
Victorian furniture and furnishings. Illustrated by Peter Morter and Design Bureau. New York, Grosset & Dunlap [1971] 159 p. col. illus. 22 cm. (Grosset all-color guide series, 28) Bibliography: p. 156. Describes the furniture of the Victorian period and furnishings such as silver, pottery, glass, and metalwork. [NK775.G3] 74-134999 ISBN 0-448-00861-0 3.95
1. Art industries and trade, Victorian. I. Morter, Peter, illus. II. Design Bureau. III. Title.

Art industries and trade, Victorian—Great Britain.

BRIDGEMAN, Harriet. 745.1'09'034
The encyclopedia of Victoriana / edited by Harriet Bridgeman and Elizabeth Drury ; pref. by Marcus Linell. 1st American ed. New York : Macmillan, 1975. 368 p. : ill. (some col.) ; 29 cm. Includes bibliographies and index. [NK928.B66 1975] 75-10728 ISBN 0-02-533530-8 : 24.95
1. Art industries and trade, Victorian—Great Britain. 2. Art industries and trade, British. 3. Art industries and trade, Victorian—United States. 4. Art industries and trade, American. I. Drury, Elizabeth, joint author. II. Title. III. Title: Victoriana.

BRIDGEMAN, Harriet. 745.1'09'034
The encyclopedia of Victoriana / edited by Harriet Bridgeman and Elizabeth Drury ; pref. by Marcus Linell. London ; New York : Published for Country Life by Hamlyn Pub. Group, 1975. 368 p. : ill. (some col.) ; 29 cm. Includes bibliographies and index. [NK928.B66 1975b] 75-328918 ISBN 0-600-33123-7
1. Art industries and trade, Victorian—Great Britain. 2. Art industries and trade—Great Britain. 3. Art industries and trade, Victorian—United States. 4. Art industries and trade—United States. I. Drury, Elizabeth, joint author. II. Title. III. Title: Victoriana.

Art industries and trades—Dictionaries.

STOUTENBURGH, John Leeds, 1921- ed. 745.03
Dictionary of arts and crafts. New York, Philosophical Library [c1956] 259p. 22cm. (Midcentury reference library) [NK30.S8] 56-13756
1. Art industries and trades—Dictionaries. 2. Industrial arts—Dictionaries. I. Title.

STOUTENBURGH, John Leeds, 1924- ed. 745.03
Dictionary of arts and crafts. New York, Philosophical Library [1956] 259 p. 22 cm. (Midcentury reference library) [NK30.S8] 56-13756
1. Art industries and trades — Dictionaries. 2. Industrial arts — Dictionaries. I. Title. BIP

Art—Instruction.

D'AMICO, Victor Edmond, 1904- 707.14
Art for the family [by] Victor D'Amico, Frances Wilson [and] Moreen Maser. New York, Museum of Modern Art; distributed by Simon and Schuster [1954] 110 p. illus. 26 cm. [N85.D28] 54-13509
1. Art—Instruction. I. Title.

Art, Iranian.

BELLONI, Gianguido. 709'.55
Iranian art [by] Gian Guido Bellone [and] Liliana Fedi Dall'Asen. [Translated from the Italian by David Ross] New York, Praeger [1969] 29 p. 101 illus. (part col.) 30 cm. Bibliography: p. 29. [N7280.B413] 70-81992 18.50
1. Art, Iranian. I. Fedi Dall'Asen, Liliana, joint author. II. Title.

FREER Gallery of Art, Washington, D.C. 709'.55'0740153
Exhibition of 2500 years of Persian art, by Esin Atil. Washington, Smithsonian Institution, 1971. 24, [42] p. illus. 26 cm. Cover title: Persian exhibition. [N7280.F7] 72-192403
1. Art, Iramian—Exhibitions. I. Atil, Esin. II. Title. III. Title: Persian exhibition.

POPE, Arthur Upham, 1881-1969. 709'.55
An introduction to Persian art since the seventh century A.D. Westport, Conn., Greenwood Press [1972] xvi, 256, v p. illus. 23 cm. Reprint of the 1931 ed. Bibliography: p. 252-256. [N7280.P6 1972] 76-109824 ISBN 0-8371-4315-2 25.00
1. Art, Iranian. I. Title. BIP

POPE, Arthur Upham, 1881-1969. 709.55
Masterpieces of Persian art. Westport, Conn., Greenwood Press [1970, c1945] vi, 204 p. illus. 29 cm. [N7280.P62 1970] 76-97351
1. Art, Iranian. I. Title. BIP

Art, Iranian—Exhibitions.

COLUMBUS Gallery of Fine Arts, Columbus, O. 709'.35
The arts of old Persia: Columbus Gallery of Fine Arts, October 7 to November 11, 1951, Dayton Art Institute, November 18, 1951 to January 1, 1952 [and] John Herron Art Museum, January 13 to February 17, 1952. [Columbus? 1951?] 29 p. illus., map. 23 cm. [N7280.C6] 77-237439
1. Art, Iranian—Exhibitions. I. Dayton Art Institute, Dayton, Ohio. II. Art Association of Indianapolis, Indiana. John Herron Art Institute. III. Title.

SPEED Art Museum, Louisville, Ky. 730'.0955
Treasures of Persian art: March 1 through April 3, 1966, J. B. Speed Art Museum, Louisville, Kentucky. [Louisville, 1966] [28] p. illus. 28 cm. [N7283.S63] 75-17379
1. Art, Iranian—Exhibitions. I. Title.

TEXAS. University at Austin. Art Museum. 709'.55'07401643
Treasures of Persian art after Islam: the Mahboubian Collection. [New York, Printed by Plantin Press, c1970] 1 v. (unpaged) illus., map, plates. 23 x 28 cm. Catalog of an exhibition held at the University Art Museum of the University of Texas, at Austin. [N7280.T4] 79-198160
1. Mahboubian, Benyamin, 1868-1969—Art collections. 2. Art, Iranian—Exhibitions. I. Title.

WELCH, Anthony. 709'.55
Shah 'Abbas & the arts of Isfahan. [New York] The Asia Society; distributed by New York Graphic Society [Greenwich, Conn., 1973] 152 p. illus. (part col.) 29 cm. "An Asia House Gallery publication." Catalogue of an exhibition shown at Asia House Gallery, New York, Oct. 11-Dec. 2, 1973, and Fogg Art Museum, Harvard University, Jan. 19-Feb. 24, 1974. Bibliography: p. 150-151. [N7287.I83W44] 73-76938 ISBN 0-87848-041-2 19.95
1. 'Abbas I, the Great, Shah of Iran, 1571-1629—Art patronage. 2. Art, Iranian—Exhibitions. 3. Art, Islamic—Isfahan. I. Asia House Gallery, New York. II. Harvard University. William Hayes Fogg Art Museum. III. Title. BIP

Art, Iranian—History.

GODARD, Andre 709.55
Art Israel: 26 painters and sculptors. by William C. Seitz, assoc. curator. Exhibition organized by the Museum of Modern Art. New York, Praeger [c.1962, 1965] Dist., Garden City, N.Y., Doubleday [c.1964] 358p. illus., maps. plans, 6 col. plates. 24cm. Bibl. 88p. illus. 25cm. Includes Biog. of the artists and list of works of art. [N7280.G613] [N7277.N37] 709.5694 65-11169 64-8870 17.50 5.95
1. Art, Iranian—Hist. n3 2. Art, Israeli—Exhibitions. I. New York, Museum of modern Art II. Seitz, William Chapin. III. America-Israel Cultural Foundation. IV. Title.

Art, Iranian—History.

GHIRSHMAN, Roman. 709.35
The arts of ancient Iran from its origins to the time of Alexander the Great. Translated by Stuart Gilbert and James Emmons. New York, Golden Press [1964] xxi, 439 p. illus. (part col.) maps (part col. (1 fold.)) 28 cm. (The Arts of mankind) [N5390.G48] 64-13072
1. Art, Iranian—History. I. Title. II. Series.

GHIRSHMAN, Roman. 709.55
Persian art, Parthian and Sassanian dynasties, 249 B.C.-A.D. 651. Translated by Stuart Gilbert and James Emmons. New York, Golden Press [1962] 401 p. illus. (part col.) maps (1 fold.) 28 cm. (The Arts of mankind) Translation of Iran; Parthes et Sassanides. Bibliography: p. [367]-377. [N5390.G513] 62-19125
1. Art, Iranian—History. I. Title. II. Series.

GODARD, André. 709.55
The art of Iran. Translated from the French by Michael Heron. Edited by Michael Rogers. New York, Praeger [1965] 358 p. illus., maps, plans, 6 col. plates. 24 cm. Bibliography: p. [339]-345. [N7280.G613] 65-11169
1. Art, Iranian—History. I. Title.

PORADA, Edith, 1912- 709'.55
The art of ancient Iran; pre-Islamic cultures [by] Edith Porada with the collaboration of R. H. Dyson and contributions by C. K. Wilkinson. New York Crown Publishers [1965] 279 p. illus. (part mounted col.) map, plans. 24 cm. (Art of the world, non-European cultures; the historical, sociological, and religious backgrounds) Translation of Alt-Iran. Bibliography: p. 262-267. [N5390.P613] 65-15839
1. Art, Iranian—History. I. Title. II. Series: Art of the world; the historical, sociological, and religious backgrounds

Art, Iranian—Exhibitions.

MICHIGAN. University. Museum of Art. 709.55
Persian art before and after the Mongol conquest. [Exhibition] April 9-May 17, 1959, the University of Michigan, Museum of Art. Ann Arbor. [Ann Arbor [1959] 72p. illus. 28cm. 'Catalogue': p. [23]-45. [N7283.M5] 59-63226
1. Art, Iranist—Exhibitions. I. Title.

Art, Irish.

ARNOLD, Bruce. 709.415
A concise history of Irish art. New York, Praeger [1968] 213 p. illus. (part col.) 22 cm. (Praeger world of art series) Bibliography: p. 206-207. [N6782.A8] 68-54497 7.50
1. Art, Irish. I. Title. BIP

ARNOLD, Bruce. 709'.415
A concise history of Irish art / Bruce Arnold. Rev. ed. New York : Oxford University Press, 1977. 180 p. : ill. (some col.) ; 21 cm. (The World of art) Includes index. Bibliography: p. 175-176. [N6782.A8 1977b] 77-371291 ISBN 0-19-519966-9 : 6.95
1. Art, Irish. I. Title. II. Series.

ELLIOTT, Robert, fl.1902-1907. 709'.415
Art and Ireland. Pref. by Edward Martyn. Port Washington, N.Y., Kennikat Press [1970] xviii, 314 p. illus. 19 cm. (Kennikat series in Irish history and culture) "First published in 1902." [N6782.E4 1970] 74-102599
1. Art, Irish. I. Title. BIP

LUCAS, A. T. 709'.415
Treasures of Ireland; Irish pagan & early Christian art [by] A. T. Lucas. New York, Viking Press [1974, c1973] 200 p. illus. (part col.) 27 cm. (A Studio book) Bibliography: p. 187-189. [N6783.L82] 73-6063 ISBN 0-670-72652-4 14.95
1. Art, Irish. 2. Art, Ancient—Ireland. 3. Art, Early Christian—Ireland. I. Title.

MAHR, Adolf, 1887- ed. 709'.415
Christian art in ancient Ireland : selected objects illustrated and described / Adolf Mahr. New York : Hacker Art Books, 1976, i.e.1977 2 v. in 1 (xxii, 184 p., 65 leaves of plates) : ill. ; 32 cm. Vol. 2 edited by J. Raftery. Reprint of the 1932-1941 ed. published by Stationery Office of Saorstat Eireann, Dublin. Includes index. Bibliography: p. 169-176. [N6783.M3 1976] 75-11058 ISBN 0-87817-173-8 lib.bdg. : 50.00 (2 vols)
1. Art, Irish. 2. Christian art and symbolism—Ireland. 3. Art, Celtic—Ireland. 4. Christian antiquities—Ireland. I. Raftery, Joseph, 1913- II. Title. BIP

Art, Irish—Bibliography.

PARIS, Shirley. 016.709'415
A selected bibliography of ancient and medieval Irish art / Shirley Paris. [New York] : Paris, [1970?] ca. 150 leaves : ill. (some col.) ; 30 cm. Bibliography is accompanied by mounted postcards, pamphlets, folders, and related matter. [Z5961.I7P37] [N6782] 75-308318
1. Art, Irish—Bibliography. 2. Art, Ancient—Ireland—Bibliography. 3. Art, Medieval—Ireland—Bibliography. I. Title.

Art, Irish—Exhibitions.

IRISH art in the 19th century; 709'.415
an exhibition of Irish Victorian art at Crawford Municipal School of Art, 31st Oct. to 29th Dec. 1971. [Selector: Cyril Barrett. Dublin, Printed by Irish Printers];

Art, Italian.

BERENSON, Bernhard, 1865- 1959 709.45
Rudiments of connoisseurship: study and criticism of Italian art. New York, Schocken [1962] 152p. illus. 21cm. First pub. in 1902 under title: The study and criticism of Italian art. Second ser. 62-18157 4.50; 1.95 pap.,
1. Art, Italian. 2. Painting, Italian. I. Title.

BERENSON, Bernhard, 1865- 1959 709.54
The sense of quality; study and criticism of Italian art. New York, Schocken [1962] 152p. illus. 21cm. First pub. in 1901 under title: The study and criticism of Italian art. First ser. 62-19394 4.50; 1.95 pap.,
1. Art, Italian. 2. Painting, Italian. I. Title.

BUZZATI, Dino, 1906- 759.5
Dino Buzzati, pittore; con 'un equivoco' di Dino Buzzati e un testo critico di Bruno Alfieri. [Venezia] Alfieri. Stamped on t.p.: Amer. dist.: Wittenborn, 1967. New York. [48]p. (p. [13]-[46] illus., pt. col.) 53cm. [ND623.B96A45] 67-4299 8.00 pap.,
I. Alfieri, Bruno. II. Title.

DECKER, Heinrich, 1899- 709'.5
The Renaissance in Italy: architecture, sculpture, frescoes. New York, Viking Press [1969] 338 p. illus., plans, plates (part col.) 32 cm. (A Studio book) [N6915.D413] 68-23210 19.95
1. Art, Italian. 2. Art, Renaissance—Italy. I. Title.

ENGGASS, Robert, 1921- 709'.4
Italy and Spain, 1600-1750; sources and documents [by] Robert Enggass [and] Jonathan Brown. Englewood Cliffs, N.J., Prentice-Hall [1970] xi, 239 p. illus. 23 cm. (Sources and documents in the history of art series) Bibliographical footnotes. [N6916.E5] 70-102129 3.95
1. Art, Italian. 2. Art, Modern—17th-18th centuries—Italy. 3. Art, Spanish. 4. Art, Modern—17th-18th centuries—Spain. I. Brown, Jonathan, joint author. II. Title. III. Series. BIP

FORNARA, Carlo., 1871- 759.5
Fornara; divisionism--impressionism [by] Waldemar George [Tr. from Italian by Muriel Crawford] Novara, Instituto geografico de Agostini; New York, Reynal [1967] [76] p. illus. (pt. col.) 32cm. [ND623.F73A44] 68-1114 10.00
I. Waldemar-George, pseud. II. Title.

HARTT, Frederick. 709'.45
History of Italian Renaissance art: painting, sculpture, architecture. New York, H. N. Abrams [1969] 636 p. illus., 80 col. plates. 30 cm. Bibliography: p. 608-613. [N6915.H37] 74-95193
1. Art, Italian. 2. Art, Renaissance—Italy. I. Title. BIP

KELLER, Harald, 1903- 709'.45
The Renaissance in Italy: painting, sculpture, architecture. Translated by Robert E. Wolf. New York, H. N. Abrams [1974, c1969] 394 p. illus. (part col.) 32 cm. Translation of Il Rinascimento italiano. Bibliography: p. 375-379. [N6915.K4413] 69-12485 ISBN 0-8109-0205-2 25.00
1. Art, Italian. 2. Art, Renaissance—Italy. I. Title.

LEES-MILNE, James. 709.45
Baroque in Italy. New York, Macmillan, 1960 [c1959] 216p. illus. 23cm. Includes bibliography. [N6916.L4 1960] 60-1748
1. Art. Italian. 2. Art, Baroque. I. Title.

MURABITO, Rosario, 1907- 759.5
Murabito; text by Giampiero Giani. [dist. New York, Heinman, 1961] [15]p. illus. 1.22 plates (part col.) (front port.) Captions to the plates in Italian. 61-1961 5.00 bds.,
I. Giana, Giampiero, 1912- II. Title.

PINTORI, Giovanni, 1912- 741.9'45
Giovanni Pintori. Fotografie di Ugo Mulas. Testi di Libero Bigiaretti [e] Libero De Libero. [Milano] Bassoli fotoincisioni [1967] Stamped on p. [1]: American dist: Wittenborn, New York. 80p. illus. (pt. col.) 24cm. (Quaderni di imago, 6) Text. in Italian and English. [NC999.6.I 8P5] 68-1077 5.00 bds.,
I. Mulas, Ugo. illus. II. Bigiaretti, Libero. III. Libero, Libero de.' IV. Title.

ROMAGNONI, Giuseppe, 1930- 1964 759.5
Bepi Romagnoni, un giovane maestro della pittura contemporanea [di] Enrico Crispolti, Giorgio Kaisserlian [ed] Emilio Tadini. [Venezia], B. Alfieri. Stamped on t.p.: American dist.: wittenborn, N.Y. 1966. [143]p. (p. [53]-[139] plates, part col.) illus., ports. 33cm. Bibl. [NA623.R672C7] 67-4258 12.00 bds.,
I. Crispolti, Enrico. II. Kaisserlian, Giorgio. III. Tadini, Emilio. IV. Title.

SMART, Alastair, 1922- 709'.45
The Renaissance and mannerism in Italy. [New York] Harcourt Brace Jovanovich [1971] 252 p. illus. 21 cm. (The Harbrace history of art) Bibliography: p. 245-247. [N6915.S63 1971] 76-113711 ISBN 0-15-576595-7 (pbk)
1. Art, Italian. 2. Art, Renaissance—Italy. 3. Mannerism (Art)—Italy. I. Title. BIP

SYMONDS, John Addington, 1840-1893. 709.45
Renaissance in Italy: the fine arts. New York, Capricorn Books [1961] 394 p. illus. 19 cm. (A Capricorn book, CAP48) Includes bibliography. [DG533.S962] 61-2838
1. Art, Italian. I. Title.

SYMONDS, John Addington, 1840-1893 709.45
Renaissance in Italy: the fine arts [Gloucester, Mass., Peter Smith, 1961] 394p. illus. (Capricorn bk., CAP48 rebound) 'Third vol. of the author's 'Renaissance in Italy." bBibl. 3.75
1. Art, Italian. I. Title. BIP

WIND, Edgar, 1900- 704.947
Pagan mysteries in the Reaissance. Enlarged and revised ed. Harmondsworth, Penguin in association with Faber, 1967. xiii, 345 p. 64 plates (incl. facsims.) 20 cm. (Peregrine books) 25/- (B67-11608) Bibliography: p. 285-315. [N6915.W53 1967] 67-93547
1. Art, Italian. 2. Art, Renaissance — Italy. 3. Mysteries, Religious. I. Title.

WIND, Edgar, 1900- 709.45
Pagan mysteries in the Renaissance. New Haven, Yale University Press, 1958. 230 p. plates. 26 cm. Bibliographical footnotes. [N6915.W53] 58-59952
1. Art, Italian. 2. Art, Renaissance. 3. Mysteries, Religious. I. Title. BIP

WIND, Edgar, 1900- 704.947
Pagan mysteries in the Renaissance. New and enl. ed. New York, Barnes & Noble, 1968 [c1967] xiii, 345 p. illus. 26 cm. Includes bibliographical references. [N6915.W53 1968b] 79-1170
1. Art, Italian. 2. Art, Renaissance—Italy. 3. Mysteries, Religious. I. Title.

WIND, Edgar, 1900- 704.947
Pagan mysteries in the Renaissance. Rev. and enl. ed. New York, W. W. Norton [1969, c1968] xiii, 345 p. plates. 20 cm. (The Norton library of art and architecture) (The Norton library, N475.) Bibliographical footnotes. [N6915.W53 1969] 70-4048 2.85
1. Art, Italian. 2. Art, Renaissance—Italy. 3. Mysteries, Religious. I. Title.

Art, Italian—Addresses, essays, lectures.

SEVENTEENTH century art in Italy, France, and Spain. 709 s New York : Garland Pub., 1976. p. cm. (The Garland library of the history of art ; v. 8) Includes bibliographical references. [N5300.G32 vol. 8] [N7106] 709'.03'2 76-14070 ISBN 0-8240-2418-4 lib.bdg. : 35.00
1. Art, Italian—Addresses, essays, lectures. 2. Art, Modern—17th-18th centuries—Italy—Addresses, essays, lectures. 3. Art, French—Addresses, essays, lectures. 4. Art, Modern—17th-18th centuries—France—Addresses, essays, lectures. 5. Art, Spanish—Addresses, essays, lectures. 6. Art, Modern—17th-18th centuries—Spain—Addresses, essays, lectures. I. Series.
Contents omitted BIP

Art, Italian — Bibl.

AESCHLIMANN, Erardo, comp. 016.75945
Bibliografia del libro d'arte italiano; v.2, pts.1&2. Roma, C. Bestetti [New York, Heinman, 1965] 2v. (xxxix, 873p.) 20cm. Contents.v.2, pts.1&2. 1951-1962. [Z5961.18A4] A53 15.00 pap., set,
1. Art, Italian — Bibl. 2. Illustration of books — Italy — Bibl. I. Title.

Art, Italian — Bibl. — Catalogs.

FLORENCE, Kunsthistorisches Institut. 016.72'092'2
Katalog des Kunsthistorischen Instituts in Florenz. Boston, G. K. Hall, 1964. 9 v. 37 cm. Added t.p. and introd. in English. [Z5961.I8F55] 65-8839
1. Art, Italian — Bibl. — Catalogs. 2. Art — Bibl. — Catalogs. I. Title.

Art, Italian—Exhibitions.

ART in Italy, 1600-1700. 709.45
Organized by Frederick Cummings. Introd. by Rudolf Wittkower Commentaries by Robert Enggass and others Detroit] Detroit Inst. of Arts; dist. New York, Abrams [c.1965] 196p. illus. (pt. col.) map. 24cm. Bibl. [N6916.A7] 65-20153 7.50
1. Art, Italian—Exhibitions. I. Cummings, Frederick J. II. Detroit. Institute of Arts.

HEIM Gallery. 708'.21'32 s
Italian paintings & sculptures of the 17th and 18th centuries : tenth summer exhibition May 26-August 27, 1976. London : Heim Gallery, 1976. [80] p. : ill. ; 25 cm. (Heim exhibition catalogues ; no. 25) "Addendum": slip inserted. Includes bibliographical references. [N8640.H4 no. 25] [N6916] 730'.945'07402132 77-355612
1. Art, Italian—Exhibitions. 2. Art, Modern—17th-18th centuries—Italy—Exhibitions. I. Title. II. Series.

THE Italian heritage; 709'.4
an exhibition of works of art lent from American collections for the benefit of the Committee to Rescue Italian Art, May 17-August 29, 1967, Wildenstein. [Providence, 1967] 1 v. (unpaged) 74 illus. 26 cm. [N6911.I72] 67-24362
1. Art, Italian—Exhibitions. 2. Art—Exhibitions. 3. Art—United States. I. Committee to Rescue Italian Art. II. Wildenstein and Company, inc., New York.

JEWISH Theological Seminary of America. Jewish Museum. 709'.45
Recent Italian painting & sculpture. [New York? 1968] [52] p. illus., ports. 24 cm. "With the collaboration of the Istituto Italiano di Cultura of New York." Exhibition held May 24-Sept. 2, 1968 at the Jewish Museum, New York. Includes bibliographies. [N6918.J45] 68-31068
1. Art, Italian—Exhibitions. 2. Art, Modern—20th century—Italy. I. Italian Cultural Institute, New York. II. Title.

NEW York (City). Museum of Modern Art. 709'.45
Twentieth-century Italian art, by James Thrall Soby and Alfred H. Barr, Jr. [New York] Published for the Museum of Modern Art by Arno Press, 1972 [c1949] 144 p. illus. 27 cm. "Catalog of the exhibition": p. 125-135. "Bibliography by Bernard Karpel": p. 136-144. [N6918.N4 1972] 71-169320 ISBN 0-405-01578-X
1. Art, Italian—Exhibitions. 2. Art, Modern—20th century—Italy. I. Soby, James Thrall, 1906- II. Barr, Alfred Hamilton, 1902- III. Title. BIP

NEW York. Museum of Modern Art. 759.5
Modigliani; paintings, drawings, sculpture, with an introd. by James Thrall Soby. The Museum of Modern Art, New York, in collaboration with the Cleveland Museum of Art. [New York, 1951] 55 p. illus. (part col.) port. 26 cm. "Catalogue of the exhibition": p. 51-53. Bibliography, by H. B. Muller: p. 54-55. [ND623.M67N4] 51-10620
1. Modigliani, Amedeo, 1884-1920. 2. Art, Italian — Exhibitions. I. Cleveland Museum of Art. II. Soby, James Thrall, 1906- III. Title.

RHODE Island School of Design, Providence. Museum of Art. 709'.45
Seven centuries of Italian art. A benefit exhibition for CRIA to honor Rhode Island's Italian Festival, Museum of Art, Rhode Island School of Design, April 12 through May 21, 1967. [Providence? Printed by Foremost Lithograph Co., 1967] [16] p. illus. 22 cm. [N6911.R44] 67-8229
1. Art, Italian—Exhibitions. I. Committee to Rescue Italian Art. II. Title.

YOUNG Italians. 709'.45
Introd. by Alan Solomon. [Boston, Institute of Contemporary Art, 1968] [24] p. illus., ports. 24 cm. Exhibition shown Jan. 23-Mar. 23, 1968, at the Institute of Contemporary Art, Boston, and May 20-Sept. 2, 1968, at the Jewish Museum, New York. [N6918.Y64] 68-21497
1. Art, Italian—Exhibitions. 2. Art, Modern—20th century—Exhibitions. I. Solomon, Alan R. II. Boston. Institute of Contemporary Art. III. Jewish Theological Seminary of America. Jewish Museum.

Art, Italian—History.

CHASTEL, Andre, 1912- 709.45
Italian art. Translated by Peter and Linda Murray. [1st American ed.] New York, T. Yoseloff [1963] xv, 526 p. illus., plates (part col.) maps. 25 cm. Bibliography: p. 403-422. [N6911.C473 1963] 63-6134
1. Art, Italian — Hist. I. Title.

COOK, Olive 709.45
The wonders of Italy. Photos. by Edwin Smith. New York, Viking [c.1965] 255p. illus., map. 32cm. (Studio bk.) [N6911.C68] 65-24472 25.00
1. Art, Italian—Hist. 2. Architecture—Italy—Hist. 3. Italy—Descr. & trav.—Views. I. Title.

FANNING, Ralph, 1889- 759.45
Italian Renaissance [by] Ralph Fanning, Robert Myron. New York, Pitman [c.1965] 47p. illus. 20x26cm. (53) [N6915.F32] 65-12113 1.00 pap.,
1. Art, Italian—Hist. 2. Art, Renaissance—Hist. I. Myron, Robert, joint author. II. Title. BIP

MONTEVERDI, Mario, ed. 709.45
Italian art to 1850. New York. Watts [1966, c.1965] 433p. illus., col. plates. 25cm. (Great art and artists of the world) Also pub. 1965 by Grolier Incorporated under the title of The book of art. Bibl. [N6914.M6] 64-23685 12.95
1. Art, Italian—Hist. I. Title. II. Series.

SPLENDORS of Italy (The) 709.45
[Text by Jacqueline Bernard] Pref. by Guglielmo de Angelis d'Ossat. Tr. [from French] by Geoffrey Braithwaite. New York, Putnam [c.1960, 1964] 344p. illus. (pt. mounted col.) maps, plans. 32cm. At head of title: Realites. 64-23193 25.00; before Jan. 1, 20.00
1. Art Italian—Hist. I. Bernard, Jacqueline. II. Realites.

WHITE, John, 1924- 704.947
Art and architecture in Italy, 1250 to 1400. Baltimore, Penguin Books [1966] xxvi, 449 p. illus., map, plans, 193 plates. 27 cm. (The Pelican history of art, Z28) Issued in a case. Bibliography: p. 419-427. [N6915.W45] 67-5664
1. Art, Italian — Hist. 2. Architecture, Italian — Hist. I. Title. BIP

WOLFFLIN, Heinrich, 1864- 1945. 709.03
The art of the Italian Renaissance; a handbook for students and travellers. New York, Schocken Books [1963] 290 p. illus. 21 cm. (Schocken paperbacks, SB42) Translation of Die klassische Kunst. [N6915.W6] 63-13343
1. Art, Italian — Hist. 2. Art, Renaissance — Hist. I. Title. II. Title: Italian Renaissance.

WOLFFLIN, Heinrich, 1864- 1945. 704.947
Classic art; an introduction to the Italian Renaissance. [Translated by Peter and Linda Murray. 2d ed.] New York, Phaidon Publishers; distributed by Doubleday [1959] xviii, 206 p. illus., col. plates. 26 cm. Reprint of 1953 edition. [N6915.W] A62

1. Art, Italian — Hist. 2. Art, Renaissance — Hist. I. Title.

Art, Italian—History.

ARTE moderna in Italia, 709'.45
1915-1935. Firenze, Palazzo Strozzi, 26 febbraio-28 maggio 1967. Firenze, Marchi e Bertolli, 1967. Label mounted on t.p.: Supplied by Worldwide Bks, New York. lxvii, 424p. illus. 23cm. Bibl. [N6918.A8] 68-30041 8.95
1. Art, Modern—20th cent.—Italy. 2. Art, Italian—Exhibitions. I. Florence. Palazzo Strozzi.

CHASTEL, Andre, 1912- 709.45
The flowering of the Italian Renaissance. Translated by Jonathan Griffin. New York, Odyssey Press [1965] xi, 384 p. illus. (part fold., part col.), maps (part fold., part col.) 29 cm. (The Arts of mankind, v. 7) Bibliography: p. 359-366. [N6915.C463] 65-27309
1. Art, Italian—History. 2. Art, Renaissance—Italy—History. I. Title. II. Series. BIP

CHASTEL, Andre, 1912- 709'.45
Italian art. Translated from the French by Peter and Linda Murray. New York, Harper & Row [1972, c1963] xv, 526 p. illus., col. plates. 23 cm. (Icon editions, IN-7) Bibliography: p. 403-422. [N6911.C473 1972] 70-148424 ISBN 0-06-430007-2 5.95
1. Art, Italian—History.

CHASTEL, Andre, 1912- 709'.45
Studios and styles of the Italian Renaissance. Translated by Jonathan Griffin. New York, Odyssey [1966] xii, 417 p. 352 illus. (part col.), 6 col. maps. 28 cm. (The Arts of mankind v. 8) Translation of Le grand atelier d'Italie, 1460-1500. Bibliography: p. [387]-[399] [N6915.C46513 1966b] 66-18997
1. Art, Italian—History. 2. Art, Renaissance—Early Renaissance—Italy. I. Title. II. Series.

WITTKOWER, Rudolf. 709'.45
Art and architecture in Italy, 1600 to 1750. Baltimore, Penguin Books [1969, c1958] xxiv, 462 p. illus., plans, 193 plates (part col.) 27 cm. (The Pelican history of art, Z16) Bibliography: p. 405-430. [N6916.W5 1969] 70-12230 20.00
1. Art, Italian—History. 2. Art, Modern—17th-18th centuries—Italy. I. Title. II. Series.

WITTKOWER, Rudolf. 709'.45
Art and architecture in Italy, 1600 to 1750. [3d rev. ed. Harmondsworth, Eng., Baltimore, Md.] Penguin Books [1973, c1972] xxix, 485, 200 p. illus. (part col.) 27 cm. (The Pelican history of art) Bibliography: p. 415-452. [N6916.W5 1973] 75-128578 ISBN 0-14-056016-5 35.00 (U.S.)
1. Art, Italian—History. 2. Art, Modern—17th-18th centuries—Italy. I. Title. II. Series.

WITTKOWER, Rudolf. 709'.45
Art and architecture in Italy, 1600 to 1750. [Hammondsworth, Eng.] Penguin Books [1973] 664 p. illus. 21 cm. (The Pelican history of art, Z16) First paperback ed, based on third revised ed. 1973. Bibliography: p. [581]-620. [N6916.W5 1973] 75-128578 ISBN 0-14-056116-1 11.95 (pbk.)
1. Art, Italian—History. 2. Art, Modern—17-18th centuries—Italy. I. Title. II. Series. Available from Penguin, Baltimore.

Art, Italian—History—Sources.

KLEIN, Robert, 1918- 709.45
Italian art, 1500-1600; sources and documents [by] Robert Klein [and] Henri Zerner. Englewood Cliffs, N.J., Prentice-Hall [1966] xviii, 195 p. illus. 23 cm. (Sources and documents in the history of art series) Bibliography: p. xvii-xviii. [N6915.K55] 66-10953
1. Art, Italian—History—Sources. 2. Art, Renaissance—History—Sources. I. Zerner, Henri, joint author. II. Title. III. Series.

Art, Italian—Italy—Venice.

SHAW-KENNEDY, Ronald. 914.5'31
Venice rediscovered / Ronald Shaw-Kennedy. Philadelphia : Art Alliance Press, c1978. 136 p. : ill. ; 27 cm. First published in 1972 under title: Art & architecture in Venice. [N6921.V5S5 1978] 73-22608 ISBN 0-87982-020-9 : 15.00
1. Art, Italian—Italy—Venice. 2. Venice—Description—Guide-books. I. Title. BIP

Art—Italy.

ART treasures in Italy: 709'.45
monuments, masterpieces, commissions, and collections. Introduced by Giulio Carlo Argan. [General editors: Bernard S. Myers and Trewin Copplestone] New York, McGraw-Hill [1969] 176 p. illus. (part col.), col. maps (on lining papers) 29 cm. [N6911.A75] 72-76756 6.95
1. Art—Italy. I. Argan, Giulio Carlo. II. Myers, Bernard Samuel, 1908- ed. III. Copplestone, Trewin, ed.

BERENSON, Bernhard, 1865- 709.45
1959.
The passionate sightseer; from the diaries, 1947 to 1956. Pref. by Raymond Mortimer. New York, Simon and Schuster [1960] 200 p. illus., col. plates. 24 cm. [N8375.B46A29] 60-6799
1. Art—Italy. 2. Italy—Description and travel—1945- I. Title.

Art—Italy—Dictionaries.

DOGO, Giuliano. 709'.45
Treasures of Italy / by Giuliano Dogo ; [translated from the Italian by Daphne Newton]. 1st American ed. New York : Norton, 1976. 434 p. : ill. (some col.) ; 25 cm. Includes index. [N6911.D5713 1976] 76-373988 19.85
1. Art—Italy—Dictionaries. 2. Architecture—Italy—Dictionaries. I. Title. BIP

Art—Italy—History.

VENTURI, Adolfo, 1856- 709'.45
Storia dell'arte italiana Milano, U. Hoepli, 1901-1940. Nendeln, Liechtenstein, Kraus-Thomson Org., 1968. 11v. in 25. illus., plates. 25cm. [N6911.V5] 6-9698 1,485.00 set.,
1. Art—Italy—Hist. I. Title.
Order from Kraus-Thomson Org., 9491 Nendeln, Liechtenstein.

WOLFFLIN, Heinrich, 1864- 709.45
1945.
Classic art; an introduction to the Italian Renaissance. [Translated by Peter and Linda Murray] New York, Phaidon Publishers; distributed by Garden City Books, 1952. xviii, 296p. illus. (part col.) 26cm. [N6915.W5713] 52-11545
1. Art—Italy—Hist. 2. Art, Renaissance. I. Title.

Art—Italy—History.

DECKER, Heinrich, 1899- 720.945
Romanesque art in Italy [by] Hans [i. e. Heinrich] Decker. [Translated from the German by James Cleugh] New York, H. N. Abrams [1959] 82 p. 263 plates, maps. 32 cm. Translation of Italia Romanica. Bibliography: p. 82. [N6913.D413] 59-5999
1. Art—Italy—History. 2. Art, Romanesque. 3. Christian art and symbolism. I. Title.

MICHIEL, Marcantonio, 709'.45
1486?-1552.
The Anonimo; notes on pictures and works of art in Italy made by an anonymous writer in the sixteenth century. Translated by Paolo Mussi. Edited by George C. Williamson. New York, B. Blom [1969] xx, 143 p. illus. 20 cm. Reprint of the 1903 ed. Translated from a MS which was discovered by Abate Don Jacopo Morelli in 1800 in the Marciana manuscripts. The Italian ed., 1884, with notes by Dr. Frizzoni has been used as a basis of this ed. [N6915.M62 1969] 77-81557
1. Art—Italy—History. I. Williamson, George Charles, 1858-1942, ed. II. Morelli, Jacopo, 1745-1819. III. Title. BIP

WITTKOWER, Rudolf. 709.45
Art and architecture in Italy 1600 to 1750 [Harmondsworth, Middlesex; Baltimore] Penguin Books [1958] xxiii, 428 p. illus., 192 plates. 27 cm. (The Pelican history of art, Z16) Bibliography: 389-407. [N6916.W5] 59-1991
1. Art—Italy—History. 2. Architecture—Italy—History. I. Title. II. Series. BIP

Art—Italy—Siena.

SEYMOUR, Frederick H. 709'.45'58
A.
Siena and her artists / by Frederick Seymour. Boston : Longwood Press, 1977. p. cm. Reprint of the 1907 ed. published by Fisher Unwin, London. [N6921.S6S5 1977] 77-9436 ISBN 0-89341-201-5 lib.bdg. : 25.00
1. Art—Italy—Siena. 2. Architecture—Italy—Siena. 3. Painting, Italian—Italy—Siena. 4. Painting, Gothic—Italy—Siena. 5. Painting, Renaissance—Itlay—Siena. I. Title. BIP

Art, Jamaican—Exhibitions.

SPELMAN College of 709'.729'2
Atlanta University Center in association with the Contemporary Jamaican Artists' Association presents Jamaican art since the thirties. [Atlanta, Ga., Stein Printing Co., 1969] [32] p. illus. 22 cm. Cover title: Jamaican art since the thirties. Catalog of the exhibition held Nov. 9-Dec. 10, 1969 at Spelman College, Atlanta. Bibliography: p. [3] of cover. [N6609.S6] 75-8982
1. Art, Jamaican—Exhibitions. 2. Art, Modern—20th century—Exhibitions. I. Spelman College, Atlanta. II. Contemporary Jamaican Artists' Association. III. Title: Jamaican art since the thirties.

Art—Japan.

ANESAKI, Masaharu, 1873- 709'.52
1949.
Art, life, and nature in Japan. Westport, Conn., Greenwood Press [1971, c1933] xi, 178 p. illus. 23 cm. Originally published to commemorate the 25th anniversary of the Japan Society of New York. Includes bibliographical references. [N7350.A527 1971] 77-109705 ISBN 0-8371-4196-6
1. Art—Japan. 2. Japan—Social life and customs. 3. Nature (Aesthetics) I. Title.

ANESAKI, Masaharu, 1873- 709'.52
1949.
Art, life, and nature in Japan. With an introd. to the new ed. by Terence Barrow. Rutland, Vt., C. E. Tuttle Co. [1973] xviii, 178 p. illus. 19 cm. "Based on lectures presented by Professor Anesaki at the Fogg Museum of Art in Cambridge Massachusetts. In 1933 ... the Japan Society of New York published this book to commemorate their quarter century of existence." Includes bibliographical references. [N7350.A527 1973] 72-77520 ISBN 0-8048-1058-3 5.50
1. Art—Japan. 2. Japan—Social life and customs. 3. Nature (Aesthetics) I. Title. BIP

Art—Japan—History.

MUNSTERBERG, Hugo, 1916- 709.52
The arts of Japan, an illustrated history. [1st ed.' Tokyo, Rutland, Ct., C. E. Tuttle Co. [1957] xviii, 201p. illus. (part col.) 27cm. Bibliography: p. 187-190. [N7350.M94] 56-13414
1. Art—Japan—Hist. I. Title.

SWANN, Peter C 709.52
An introduction to the arts of Japan. New York, Praeger [1958] xi, 220 p. illus., map. 26 cm. (Books that matter) Bibliography: p. 216. [N7350.S85 1958] 58-12088
1. Art—Japan—Hist. I. Title. II. Title: The arts of Japan.

WARNER, Langdon, 1881- 709.52
The enduring art of Japan. Cambridge, Harvard University Press, 1952. xiii, 113 p. illus. 25 cm. Bibliography: p. [111]-113. [N7350.W3] 52-8220
1. Art — Japan — Hist. I. Title. BIP

WARNER, Langdon, 1881- 709.52
1955.
The enduring art of Japan. New York, Grove Press [1958? c1952] 113 p. illus. 21 cm. (Evergreen books, E-97) [N7350.W3 1958] 58-5966
1. Art — Japan — Hist. I. Title.

YASHIRO, Yukio. 709.52
2000 years of Japanese art. Edited by Peter C. Swann. with 135 photograveure plates and 42 plates in color. New York, H. N. Abrams [1958] 268 p. illus. (part mounted col.) 34 cm. [N7350.Y35] 58-13478
1. Art — Japan — Hist. I. Title.

Art—Japan—History.

MUNSTERBERG, Hugo, 1916- 709.52
The arts of Japan, an illustrated history. [1st ed.] Tokyo, Rutland, Vt., C. E. Tuttle Co. [1957] xviii, 201 p. illus. (part col.) 27 cm. Bibliography: p. 187-190. [N7350.M94] 56-13414
1. Art—Japan—History. I. Title. BIP

OKAKURA, Kakuzo, 1862- 709'.52
1913.
The ideals of the East, with special reference to the art of Japan. Rutland, Vt., C. E. Tuttle Co. [1970] xxiv, 244 p. port. 19 cm. First published in 1903. [N7350.O4 1970] 75-104214
1. Art—Japan—History. I. Title.

*PAINE, Robert Treat, 709'.52
1900
The art and architecture of Japan [by] Robert Treat Paine and Alexander Soper Rev. ed. Baltimore, Penguin Books, [1975] 495 p. illus., plates, maps, plans, tables 21 cm. (Pelican history of art) Bibliography, p. 453 [N7350.P3] 72-93371 ISBN 0-14-056108-0 12.50 (pbk.)
1. Art—Japan—History. 2. Architecture—Japan—History. I. Soper, Alexander, joint author II. Title. BIP

PAINE, Robert Treat, 1900- 709.52
The art and architecture of Japan [by] Robert Treat Paine [and] Alexander Soper. [Baltimore] Penguin Books [1955] xviii, 316 p. illus., plates, maps, plans, tables. 27 cm. (The Pelican history of art, Z8) Contents.Contents.—Painting and sculpture, by R. T. Paine.—Architecture, by A. Soper. Bibliography: p. 291-294. [N7350.P3] 55-12839
1. Art—Japan—History. 2. Architecture—Japan—History. I. Soper, Alexander Coburn, 1904- II. Title. III. Series.

Art, Japanese.

DRESSER, Christopher. 915.2'04'31
Japan : its architecture, art, and art manufactures / Christopher Dresser. New York : Garland Pub., 1977. p. cm. (The Aesthetic movement & the arts and crafts movement ; 5) Reprint of the 1882 ed. published by Longmans, Green, London. [N7350.D7 1977] 76-17752 ISBN 0-8240-2454-0 lib.bdg. : 35.00
1. Art, Japanese. 2. Architecture—Japan. 3. Art industries and trade—Japan. 4. Japan—Description and travel—Japan—1801-1900. I. Title. II. Series.

EATON, Allen Hendershott, 709.52
1878-
Beauty behind barbed wire; the arts of the Japanese in our war relocation camps. Foreword by Eleanor Roosevelt. New York, Harper [1952] xiv, 208 p. illus. (part col.) map (on lining papers) 24 cm. "Annotated selective bibliography on Japanese Americans": p. 197-203. [N7355.E2] 51-11905
1. Art, Japanese. 2. U. S. War Relocation Authority. 3. Concentration camps—U. S. 4. Japanese in the U. S. I. Title.

HASUMI, Toshimitsu 709.52
Zen in Japanese art, a way of spiritual experience. Tr. from German by John Petrie. New York, Philosophical [c.1960, 1962] 113p. illus. 19cm. Bibl. 62-5396 3.75
1. Art, Japanese. 2. Art, Buddhist. 3. Zen (Sect) I. Title.

HASUMI, Toshimitsu. 709.52
Zen in Japanese art, a way of spiritual experience. Translated from the German by John Petrie. New York, Philosophical

Library [1962] 113p. illus. 19cm. Includes bibliography. [N 350.H353] 62-5396
1. Art, Japanese. 2. Art, Buddhist. 3. Zen (Sect) I. Title.

JAPANESE art and Korean art; 709'.52 general editor Francesco Abbate; [translated from the Italian]. London, New York, Octopus Books, 1972. 158 p. chiefly 110 col. illus. 20 cm. Translation of Arte del Giappone e della Corea. Bibliography: p. 153. [N7350.A6913] 72-171382 ISBN 0-7064-0026-7 2.95
1. Art, Japanese. 2. Art, Korean. I. Abbate, Francesco, ed.

JAPANESE fine arts. 709.52 Introd., commentaries by Seiroku Noma. English tr. by Geotrge Saito. [dist. Los Angeles, Perkins Oriental Bks., 1961] [4] p. 1 mounted col. illus. 24 col. plates. 37cm. 61-65112 10.00, bds., in portfolio
1. Art, Japanese. I. Noma, Seiroku.

JARVES, James Jackson, 1818-1888. 700'.9'52
A glimpse at the art of Japan. Philadelphia, A. Saifer, 1970 [c1875] 216 p. 30 illus. 18 cm. [N7350.J38 1970] 72-17973
1. Art, Japanese. I. Title. BIP

JOLY, Henri L. 398.2'0952
Legend in Japanese art a description of historical episodes, legendary characters, folk-lore myths, religious symbolism, illustrated in the arts of old Japan, by Henri L. Joly. Rutland, Vt., Tuttle [1967] 623p. illus., 16 col. plates. 29cm. Reprint of the 1908 ed. Bibl. [N7350.J75 1967] 67-16411 25.00
1. Art, Japanese. 2. Legends—Japan. I. Title.

KANEKO, Shigetaka, 1914- 709.52
Guide to Japanese art. Rutland, Vt., Tuttle [c.1963] 227p. illus. 6 col. plates,fold. maps. 22cm. 63-14049 6.00
1. Art, Japanese. 2. Japan—Descr. &trav.—Guidebooks. I. Title.

KAWAKITA, Michiaki, 1914- 709'.52
Modern currents in Japanese art / by Michiaki Kawakita ; translated and adapted by Charles S. Terry. 1st English ed. New York : Weatherhill, 1974. 158 p. : ill. (some col.) ; 24 cm. (The Heibonsha survey of Japanese art ; v. 24) Translation of Kindai bijutsu no nagare. [N7354.5.K3713] 74-76106 ISBN 0-8348-1028-X : 12.50
1. Art, Japanese. 2. Art, Japanese—Occidental influences. 3. Art, Japanese—Meiji period, 1868-1912. 4. Art, Modern—20th century—Japan. I. Title. II. Series.

KIDDER, Jonathan Edward. 730.952
The birth of Japanese art, by J. Edward Kidder, Jr. Photos. by Kenishi Ozawa. New York, F. A. Praeger [1965] viii, 209 p. illus. (part mounted col.), maps. 29 cm. Translation of Japon: Naissance d'un art. Includes bibliographical references. Bibliography: p. 163-166. [N7353.K513] 65-16808
1. Art, Japanese. 2. Art, Primitive. I. Ozawa, Kenishi, illus. II. Title.

KIKUCHI, Sadao, 1924- 709.52
Japanese arts, what & where? [2d ed.] Tokyo, Japan Travel Bureau [dist. New York, Perkins, 1963, c.1962] 2v. (174, 162p.) illus. (pt. col.) maps. 18cm. Contents.v.1. Ancient times to the mid-19th century, comp. by Sadao Kikuchi.--v.2. Mid-19th century to the present, comp. by Tanio Nakamura. 62-21887 3.00 pap., ea.,
1. Art, Japanese, I. Nakamura, Tanio. II. Title.

KOBAYASHI, Kokei, 1883-1957. 759.952
Kobayashi Kokei; 1883-1957. Text by Michiaki Kawakita. English adaption by Roy Andrew Miller. [1st English ed.] Rutland, Vt., C. E. Tuttle Co. [1957] 1v. (unpaged) 47 plates (incl. cover, part fold., part col.) 18cm. e(Kodansha library of Japanese art, no. 11) Bibliography on last page. [ND1059.K6K3] 927.5 57-12495
I. Kawakita, Michiaki, 1914- II. Miller, Roy Andrew. III. Title.

MUNSTERBERG, Hugo, 1916- 709.52
Zen & oriental art. Rutland, Vt., C. E. Tuttle Co. [1965] 158 p. illus. 24 cm. Bibliographical references included in "Notes" (p. 149-150) [N7350.M944] 65-17589
1. Art, Japanese. 2. Art, Buddhist. 3. Zen Buddhism. I. Title.

MURASE, Miyeko. 709'.52
The arts of Japan / Miyeko Murase. New York : McGraw-Hill, c1977. 46 p. : ill. ; 19 cm. & slides (40 slides : col. ; 2 x 2 in.) in pockets. Bibliography: p. 45-46. [N7350.M947] 76-48069 ISBN 0-07-044053-0 : 14.95
1. Art, Japanese. I. Title. BIP

NOMA, Seiroku. 709'.52
The arts of Japan / by Seiroku Noma ; translated and adapted by John Rosenfield ; photos. by Takahashi Bin. Popular ed. Tokyo : Kodansha International ; New York : Kodansha International/USA ; distributors, U.S., Harper & Row, 1978. p. cm. Translation of Nihon bijutsu. Contents.Contents.—v. 1. Ancient and medieval.—v. 2. Late medieval to modern. Includes bibliographies and indexes. [N7350.N63913 1978] 78-18531 ISBN 0-87011-335-6 (v. 1) : 16.50. ISBN 0-87011-336-4 (v. 2) : 16.50
1. Art, Japanese. 2. Art—Japan. I. Takahashi, Bin. II. Title. BIP

SHAKAN, Asahi 709.52
The Japanese sense of beauty. Comp.: The Asahi Weekly. Text: Seiroku Noma. Photogs.: Zenkichi Kokubo [Tokyo] Asahi Shimbun Pub. Co. [dist. Rutland, Vt., Japan pubns., c.1963] iv, 143p. illus. col. plates. 27cm. 63-22033 7.95
1. Art, Japanese. I. Noma Seiroku. II. Kokubo, Zenkichi, illus. III. Title.

SMITH, Bradley. 915.2
Japan; a history in art. New York, Simon and Schuster, 1964. 295 p. col. illus., col. map, col. ports. 33 cm. (A Gemini book) Bibliography: p. 295. [N7350.S65] 64-21410
1. Art, Japanese. 2. Japan—History—Pictorial works. I. Title.

STERN, Harold P. 704.94'3'0952
Birds, beasts, blossoms, and bugs : the nature of Japan / Harold P. Stern. New York : H. N. Abrams, [1976] p. cm. Bibliography: p. [N7350.S73] 75-46630 ISBN 0-8109-0708-9. ISBN 0-8109-9020-2 pbk.
1. Art, Japanese. 2. Nature (Aesthetics) I. Title. BIP

SWANN, Peter C. 709.52
The art of Japan, from the Jomon to the Tokugawa period [by] Peter C. Swann. New York, Crown Publishers [1966] 238 p. illus. (part mounted col.) 24 cm. (Art of the world, non-European cultures; the historical, sociological, and religious backgrounds) Bibliography: p. [225]-228. [N7350.S846] 66-22128
1. Art, Japanese. I. Title. II. Series: Art of the world; the historical, sociological, and religious backgrounds

TAPIE, Michel. 398.2'0952
Avant-garde art in Japan Texts by Michel Tapie and Tore Haga. New York, H. N. Abrams [1962] 1 v. (unpaged) illus., plates (part col.) 28 x 31 cm. Full name: Michel Tapie de Celeyran. [N7355.T3] 62-12839
1. Art, Japanese. 2. Art, Modern—20th cent. I. Haga, Tore. joint author. II. Title.

†TERADA, Toru, 1915- 709'.52
Japanese art in world perspective / by Toru Terada ; translated by Thomas Guerin. 1st English ed. New York : Weatherhill, 1976. 161 p. : ill. (some col.) ; 24 cm. (The Heibonsha survey of Japanese art ; v. 25) Translation of Sekai no naka no Nihon bijutsu. [N7355.T4613] 75-41338 ISBN 0-8348-1007-7 : 15.00
1. Art, Japanese. 2. Art, Modern—20th century—Japan. 3. Art, Japanese—Occidental influences. I. Title. II. Series. BIP

TSUDA, Noritake, 1883- 709'.52
Handbook of Japanese art / by Noritake Tsuda. Rutland, Vt. : C. E. Tuttle Co., 1976. xxv, 525 p., [10] leaves of plates : ill. ; 19 cm. (Tut books : A) Includes index. Bibliography: p. [505]-508. [N7350.T73 1976] 74-78152 ISBN 0-8048-1139-3 : 5.50
1. Art, Japanese. I. Title. BIP

TURK, Frank A. 709.52
Japanese objets d'art. Revised & adapted by Judith Cohen. New York, Sterling Pub. Co. [1963] 156 p. illus. 21 cm. (Sterling collectors series) Includes bibliography. [N7350.T8 1963] 63-11584
1. Art, Japanese. I. Title.

Art, Japanese—1868-

MUNSTERBERG, Hugo, 1916- 709'.52
The art of modern Japan : from the Meiji restoration to the Meiji centennial, 1868-1968 / by Hugo Munsterberg. New York : Hacker Art Books, 1978. 159 p. : ill. ; 23 x 25 cm. Includes index. Bibliography: p. 153-154. [N7354.5.M86] 75-10873 ISBN 0-87817-187-8 : 18.50
1. Art, Japanese—1868- I. Title. BIP

Art, Japanese—Catalogs.

ART treasures from Japan. 709'.52 [1st ed.] Tokyo, Palo Alto, Calif., Kodansha International [1971] 196 p. illus., col. plates. 28 cm. Trade ed., with new introductory essay, of the 1966 exhibition catalog, Art treasures from Japan. [N7352.A88 1971] 79-162652 ISBN 0-87011-160-4 ($12.50 U.S.)
1. Art, Japanese—Catalogs.

HILLIER, Jack Ronald. 759.952'074
The Harari Collection of Japanese paintings and drawings. Catalogue compiled by J. Hillier. [1st ed.] Boston, Boston Book and Art [1970- v. illus., plates (part col.) 32 cm. Contents.Contents.—v. 1. Genre and Ukiyo-e school (excluding Hokusai and his school and Hiroshige)—v. 2. Hokusai and his school and Hiroshige. Bibliography: v. 2, p. 353-354. [N7352.H54] 73-120286
1. Harari, Michael—Art collections. 2. Art, Japanese—Catalogs. I. Title.

Art, Japanese—Exhibitions.

CONTEMPORARY Japanese art; 709.51 fifth Japan Art Festival exhibition. [Jointly presented by] the Solomon R. Guggenheim Museum, New York [and] Japan Art Festival Association, Tokyo. [New York, Solomon R. Guggenheim Foundation, 1970] 1 v. (unpaged) illus. (part col.) 22 x 26 cm. [N7355.C65] 75-145689
1. Art, Japanese—Exhibitions. 2. Art, Modern—20th century—Japan. I. Solomon R. Guggenheim Museum, New York. II. Japan Art Festival Association.

DALLAS. Museum of Fine Arts. 709'.52
Masterpieces of Japanese art; [catalogue of the exhibition] October 4 through November 30, 1969, Dallas Museum of Fine Arts. [Dallas, 1969?] 1 v. (chiefly illus.) 26 cm. [N7352.D33] 79-9187 4.00
1. Art, Japanese—Exhibitions. I. Title.

JAPAN. Bunkazei Hogo Iinkai. 759.952
Exhibition of Japanese painting and sculpture sponsored by the Government of Japan. National Gallery of Art, Washington; the Metropolitan Musuem of Art, New York; Museum of Fine Arts, Boston; the Art Institute of Chicago; Seattle Art Museum, Seattle. [Washington?] 1953. 207 p. illus. (part col.) 28 cm. "Assembled under the auspices of the Commission for the Protection of Cultural Properties." Errata slip inserted. [N7350.A277] 53-61152
1. Art, Japanese—Exhibitions. I. U.S. National Gallery of Art. II. Title.

LOS Angeles Co., Calif. 709'.52 Otis Art Institute, Los Angeles.
Japanese art: the Arthur Olaf Andersen Japanese Print Collection [and the] Mr. and Mrs. Maurice K. Grossman Japanese Ceramic Collection. Los Angeles [1966?] [28] p. illus. 23 cm. Catalog of an exhibition held Sept. 8 to Oct. 23, 1966, at the Otis Art Institute of Los Angeles County. [NE771.L6] 68-2638
1. Andersen, Arthur Olaf, 1880-1958—Art collections. 2. Grossman, Maurice K.—Art collections. 3. Grossman, Maurice K., Mrs.—Art collections. 4. Art, Japanese—Exhibitions. I. Title.

MOMOYAMA, Japanese art in the age of grandeur : 700'.952 [catalogue of] an exhibition at the Metropolitan Museum of Art organized in collaboration with the Agency for Cultural Affairs of the Japanese Government. [New York] : Metropolitan Museum of Art, [1975] xxii, 136 p., [8] leaves of plates : ill. (some col.) ; 27 cm. Bibliography: p. 134-136. [N7353.4.M65] 74-31186 ISBN 0-87099-125-6
1. Art, Japanese—Exhibitions. 2. Art, Japanese—Kamakura-Momoyama periods, 1185-1600. I. New York (City). Metropolitan Museum of Art. II. Japan. Bunkacho. III. Title.

MURASE, Miyeko. 709'.52'07401471
Japanese art : selections from the Mary and Jackson Burke Collection / Miyeko Murase. [New York] : Metropolitan Museum of Art, 1975. p. cm. Bibliography: p. [N7352.M86] 75-28053 ISBN 0-87099-136-1 : 50.00. ISBN 0-87099-138-8 pbk. : 14.95
1. Burke, Jackson, 1908-1975—Art collections. 2. Burke, Mary—Art collections. 3. Art, Japanese—Exhibitions. I. New York (City). Metropolitan Museum of Art. II. Title. BIP

ROSENFIELD, John M. 709'.52
Japanese arts of the Heian period, 794-1185 [by] John Rosenfield. Japanese arts of the Heian period seven ninety-four-eleven eighty-five [New York] Asia Society [1967] 135 p. illus. (part col.), map. 27 cm. "An Asia House Gallery publication." Catalog of an exhibition in the Asia House Gallery, New York City, Oct. 5-Dec. 17, 1967, as an activity of the Asia Society, and in the Fogg Art Museum, Harvard University, Cambridge, Mass., Jan. 17-Feb. 25, 1968. Bibliography: p. 135. [N7353.R6] 67-22187
1. Art, Japanese—Exhibitions. I. Asia Society. II. Asia House Gallery, New York. III. Harvard University. William Hayes Fogg Art Museum. IV. Title.

ROSENFIELD, John M. 709.52
Traditions of Japanese art; selections from the Kimiko and John Powers Collection [by] John M. Rosenfield [and] Shujiro Shimada. [Cambridge, Mass.] Fogg Art Museum, Harvard University, 1970. 393 p. illus. (part col.), facsims., maps. 29 cm. Exhibition catalog. Includes bibliographical references. [N7352.R67] 76-133788 ISBN 0-674-90125-8 25.00
1. Powers, Kimiko—Art collections. 2. Powers, John—Art collections. 3. Art, Japanese—Exhibitions. I. Shimada, Shujiro, 1907- joint author. II. Harvard University. William Hayes Fogg Art Museum. III. Title. BIP

STERN, Harold P. 709'.52
Rimpa, masterworks of the Japanese decorative school [by] Harold P. Stern. [New York] Japan Society [1971] 91 p. illus. (part col.) 21 x 22 cm. "Catalogue of the opening exhibition of Japan House Gallery shown in the fall of 1971 as an activity of the Japan Society, inc." Bibliography: p. 85-87. [N7353.5.S7] 75-164447
1. Art, Japanese—Exhibitions. 2. Decoration and ornament—Japan—United States. 3. Art, Japanese—United States. 4. Art, Japanese—Edo period, 1600-1868. I. Japan Society of New York. II. Title.

TOLEDO, Museum of Art. 740.952
A special exhibition of Japanese art; examples of screen painting, fan painting and lacquer-work from the collection of museums and private owners, shown in galleries fifteen, sixteen, seventeen, and nineteen during the month of January, nineteen hundred and thirty-eight. Toledo [1937] [52] p. illus. plates. 26 cm. [N7350.T57] 38-2099
1. Art. Japanese — Exhibitions. I. Title.

Art, Japanese—Heian period, 794-1185.

SAWA, Ryuken, 1911- 709'.52
Art in Japanese Esoteric Buddhism, by Takaaki Sawa. Translated by Richard L. Gage. [1st English ed.] Tokyo, New York, Weatherhill/Heibonsha [1972, c1971] 151 p. illus. (part col.) 24 cm. (The Heibonsha survey of Japanese art, 8) Translation of Mikkyo no bijutsu, v. 8 in the series,

Nihon no bijutsu. [N7353.3.S2713] 70-162682 ISBN 0-8348-1001-8 7.95
1. Art, Japanese—Heian period, 794-1185. 2. Art, Japanese. 3. Art, Buddhist—Japan. I. Title. II. Series. **BIP**

Art, Japanese—History.

BOGER, H. Batterson 709.52
The traditional arts of Japan, a complete illustrated guide. Garden City, N.Y., Doubleday, 1964. 351p. illus. (pt. col.) maps. 29cm. Bibl. 64-117267 17.50
1. Art, Japanese—Hist. I. Title.

LEE, Sherman, E. 709.52
Japanese decorative style. [Cleveland] Cleveland Mus. of Art; dist. by Abrams [New York, 1961] ix, 161p. illus. (part col.) 26cm. Bibl. 61-9910 7.50
1. Art, Japanese—Hist. 2. Decoration and ornament, Japanese. I. Cleveland Museum of Art. II. Title.

NEWMAN. ALEXANDER R. 709.52
Japanese art: a collector's guide [by] Alex R. Newman. Egerton Rverson. Drawings by Bon Dale. Cranbury, N.J. A. S. Barnes [1966. c.1964] 146p. illus., col. plates. 28cm. Bibl. [N7350.N45] 65-24841 12.50
1. Art. Japanese—Hist. 2. Art. Japanese—Diction-aries. I. Rverson. Egerton, joint author. II. Dale,Bon. illus. III. Title.

Art, Japanese—History.

HARTMANN, Sadakichi, 1867-1944. 709'.52
Japanese art. New York, Horizon Press [1971] 288 p. 22 cm. Reprint of the 1904 (?) ed. Bibliography: p. 279-281. [N7350.H33 1971] 77-170945 ISBN 0-8180-0119-4 8.95
1. Art, Japanese—History. I. Title.

KATO, Shuichi, 1919- 709'.52
Form, style, tradition; reflections on Japanese art and society. Translated from the Japanese by John Bester. Berkeley, University of California Press [1971] 216 p. illus., ports. 23 cm. Bibliography: p. [211] [N7350.K3513] 79-129612 ISBN 0-520-01809-5 10.00
1. Art, Japanese—History. 2. Art and society. I. Title. **BIP**

LEE, Sherman E. 709'.52
Japanese decorative style [by] Sherman E. Lee. New York, Harper & Row [1972] ix, 161 p. illus. 24 cm. (Icon editions, IN-17) Reprint of the 1961 ed. "A by-product of the exhibition ... organized by the Cleveland Museum of Art and co-sponsored by the Art Institute of Chicago." Bibliography: p. 155-[158] [N7350.L43 1972] 72-189842 ISBN 0-06-430017-X 3.95
1. Art, Japanese—History. 2. Decoration and ornament, Japanese. I. Cleveland Museum of Art. II. Title. **BIP**

NOMA, Seiroku. 709.52
The arts of Japan. Translated and adapted by John Rosenfield. Photos. by Takahashi Bin. [1st ed.] Tokyo, Kodansha International; [distributed outside Japan by Japan Publications Trading Co., Rutland, Vt., 1965, c1966-1967] 2 v. illus. (part mounted col.) maps. 38 cm. Contents.Contents.—v. 1. Ancient and medieval.—v. 2. Late medieval to modern. [N7353.N613 1965] 65-19186
1. Art, Japanese—History. I. Takahashi, Bin, illus. II. Title.

PAINE, Robert Treat, 1900-1965. 709'.52
The art and architecture of Japan / Robert Treat Paine and Alexander Soper. 1st paperback ed., fully rev. / [pt. 1 brought up to date by D. B. Waterhouse, pt. 2 brought up to date by Bunji Kobayashi] Harmondsworth, Eng. ; Baltimore : Penguin Books, 1975. 495 p. : ill. 21 cm. (The Pelican history of art) Includes index. Contents.Contents.—Paine, R. T. Painting and sculpture.—Soper, A. Architecture. Bibliography: p. [453]-464. [N7350.P3 1975] 75-309148 ISBN 0-14-056108-0 pbk. : 12.50
1. Art, Japanese—History. 2. Architecture—Japan—History. I. Soper, Alexander Coburn, 1904- II. Title. III. Series.

PAINE, Robert Treat, 1900-1965. 709'.52
The art and architecture of Japan / Robert Treat Paine, Alexander Soper. 2d ed. / pt. 1 brought up to date by D. B. Waterhouse ; pt. 2 brought up to date by Bunji Kobayashi. Harmondsworth, Eng. ; Baltimore : Penguin Books, 1974. xviii, 328 p., [87] leaves of plates : ill. (1 col.) ; 27 cm. (The Pelican history of art) Includes index. Contents.Contents.—Paine, R. T. Painting and sculpture.—Soper, A. Architecture. Bibliography: p. 293-306. [N7350.P3 1973] 74-186336 ISBN 0-14-056008-4 : 39.50 (U.S.)
1. Art, Japanese—History. 2. Architecture—Japan—History. I. Soper, Alexander Coburn, 1904- II. Title. III. Series.

TAMBURELLO, Adolfo. 709'.52
Japan. Text by Adolfo Tamburello. Foreword by Yasunari Kawabata. New York, Madison Square Press [1973] 192 p. illus. (part col.) 34 cm. (Monuments of civilization) Translation of Giappone. Bibliography: p. 190. [N7353.T2413 1973] 71-179262 ISBN 0-448-02022-X 19.95
1. Art, Japanese—History. I. Title. II. Series.

YOSHIKAWA, Itsuji. 709'.52
Major themes in Japanese art / by Itsuji Yoshikawa ; translated by Armins Nikovskis. 1st English ed. New York : Weatherhill, 1976. 166 p., [2] fold. leaves of plates : ill. (some col.) ; 24 cm. (The Heibonsha survey of Japanese art ; v. 1) Translation of Nihon Bijutsu nyumon. [N7350.Y6313] 75-22368 ISBN 0-8348-1003-4 : 12.50
1. Art, Japanese—History. I. Title. II. Series. **BIP**

Art, Japanese—Juvenile literature.

ALDEN, Carella. 709'.52
Sunrise island; a story of Japan and its arts. New York, Parent's Magazine Press [1971] 64 p. illus. (part col.), col. map. 24 cm. (Art tells a story series) Based on the author's This floating world, which was produced in the series Art entertainments at the Metropolitan Museum of Art. Explains the origins of the tea ceremony, the costumes and equipment of the samurai, and the gardens, scrolls, wood blocks, and other art forms associated with Japan. [N7350.A39] 71-152873 ISBN 0-8193-0523-5
1. Art, Japanese—Juvenile literature. I. Title. **BIP**

GLUBOK, Shirley. 709'.52
The art of Japan. Designed by Gerard Nook. Special photography by Alfred Tamarin. [New York] Macmillan [1970] 48 p. illus. (part col.) 24 x 26 cm. This introduction to Japanese art discusses the meaning of various symbols, the influence of religion on art, and makes art a part of every day life in Japan. [N7350.G55] 75-89584
1. Art, Japanese—Juvenile literature. I. Nook, Gerard. II. Title. **BIP**

Art—Jerusalem—Catalogs.

KATZ, Karl. 708.95694
From the beginning: archaeology and art in the Israel Museum, Jerusalem [by] Karl Katz, P. P. Kahane [and] Magen Broshi. Photos. by David Harris. Introd. by Philip Hendy. [Clifton, N. J.] Reynal [1968] 286 p. illus., facsims., ports. (all part col.) 26 cm. [N3750.J5K3] 68-23229 15.00 ($12.95 until 1/2/69)
1. Art—Jerusalem—Catalogs. I. Kahane, P. P., joint author. II. Broshi, Magen, joint author. III. Jerusalem. Israel Museum. IV. Title.

Art, Jewish.

NAMENYI, Ernest 709.5693
The essence of Jewish art. Tr. from French by Edouard Roditi. New York, T. Yoseloff [1961, c.1957 1960] 92p. illus. (Popular Jewish library) Bibl. 61-2822 2.95 bds.,
1. Art, Jewish. I. Title.

RABINO, Saul, 1892-1969. 769'.92'4
Eternal light collection. [Los Angeles] United Jewish Educational Art Foundation [1971?] 1 portfolio (16 plates) 32 cm. (Jewish symbolism, v. 1) Cover title. [NE2312.R3A44] 78-173828
I. Title. II. Series.

Art, Jewish—Exhibitions.

JEWISH Theological Seminary of America. Jewish Museum. 704.9489
Art of the Hebrew tradition; Jewish ceremonial objects for synagogue and home. An exhibit at the Metropolitan Museum of Art, New York City, commemorating the American Jewish tercentenary; arranged by the Jewish Museum of the Jewish Theological Seminary ofAmerica, January 20, 1955 to February 27, 1955. Stephen S. Kayser, editor; Guido Schoenberger, associate editor. Philadelphia, Jewish Publication Society of America, 1955. 168p. illus. 23cm. Issued also under title: Jewish ceremonial art. [N5020.N417 1955a] 55-1008
1. Art, Jewish—Exhibitions. I. Kayser, Stephen S., 1900- ed. II. Title.

JEWISH Theological Seminary of America. Jewish Museum. 704.94896
Jewish ceremonial art; a guide to the appreciation of the art objects used in synagogue and home, principally from thecollections of the Jewish Museum of the Jewish Theological Seminary of America. Stephen S. Kayser, editor; Guido Schoenberger, associate editor. [2d ed.] Philadelphia, Jewish Publication Society of America, 1959. 189p. illus. 24cm. [N5020.N417 1959] 59-3275
1. Art, Jewish—Exhibitions. I. Kayser, Stephen S., 1900- ed. II. Title.

JEWISH Theological Seminary of America. Jewish Museum. 704.9489
Jewish ceremonial art; a guide to the appreciation of the art objects used in synagogue and home, principally from the collections of the Jewish Museum of the Jewish Theological Seminary of America. Stephen S. Kayser, editor; Guido Schoenberger, associate editor. Philadelphia, Jewish Publication Society of America, 1955. 168p. illus. 24cm. Issued also under title: Art of the Hebrew tradition. [N5020.N417 1955] 55-7139
1. Art, Jewish—Exhibitions. I. Kayser, Stephen S., 1900- ed. II. Title.

SCHOENBERGER, Guido, 1891- 704.94896
The silver and Judaica collection of Mr. and Mrs. Michael M. Zagavski. Catalogue, by Guido Schoenberger, Tom L. Freudenheim. New York 28, Jewish Mus., 92md St. & 5th Ave., 1963. 1 v. (unpaged) illus. 25cm. 63-22378 3.00 pap.,
1. Art, Jewish—Exhibitions. 2. Art—Private collections. 3. Silversmithing, Jewish—Exhibitions. I. Freudenheim. Tom L., joint author. II. Zagayski, Michael M. III. Zagayski, Doris. IV. Title.

Art, Jewish—History.

ROTH, Cecil, 1899- ed. 704.94896
Jewish art: an illustrated history. New York, McGraw [c.1961] 971p. illus., col. plates, 28cm. 61-9776 14.95
1. Art, Jewish—Hist. I. Title. **BIP**

ROTH, Cecil, 1899- ed. 704.94896
Jewish art: an illustrated history. New York, McGraw-Hill [1961] 971p. illus., col. plates, ports., facsims., plans. 28cm. [N7415.R625 1961] 61-9776
1. Art, Jewish—Hist. I. Title.

Art, Jewish—History.

GUTFELD, Ludwig. 709'.176'6
Jewish art, from the Bible to Chagall. Translated from the German by William Wolf. New York, T. Yoseloff [1968] 128 p. illus. (part col.) 29 cm. Translation of Von der Bibel bis Chagall; Judentum und Kunst. Bibliography: p. 128. [N7415.G7813] 68-14821 8.50
1. Art, Jewish—History. I. Title.

LANDSBERGER, Franz, 1883-1964. 709
A history of Jewish art. Port Washington, N.Y., Kennikat Press [1973, c1946] 369 p. illus. 23 cm. Original ed. issued in series: Commission on Jewish Education of the Union of American Hebrew Congregations and the Central Conference of American Rabbis. Union adult series. Bibliography: p. 341-353. [N7415.L32 1973] 72-85324 ISBN 0-8046-1741-4 17.50
1. Landsberger, Franz, 1883-1964—Bibliography. 2. Art, Jewish—History. I. Title. II. Series: Commission on Jewish Education of the Union of American Hebrew Congregations and the Central Conference of American Rabbis. Union adult series.

ROTH, Cecil, 1899-1970, ed. 709
Jewish art: an illustrated history. [Edited by] Cecil Roth. Rev. [and enl.] ed. by Bezalel Narkiss. Greenwich, Conn., New York Graphic Society [1971] 332 p. illus. (part col.) 28 cm. [N7415.R625 1971] 70-148668 ISBN 0-8212-0391-6 20.00
1. Art, Jewish—History. I. Narkiss, Bezalel, ed. II. Title.

Art—Juvenile literature.

ABELES, Ehvn, 1909- 927.5
The man who painted the sun; the story of Vincent Van Gogh, by Kerwin Bowles [pseud.] Illustrated by Henry Kallem. New York, Stravon Publishers [1951] 31 p. illus. 22 x 28 cm. (A Child's book of great artists) [ND653.G7A6] 51-14728
1. Gogh, Vincent van, 1853-1890. 2. Art—Juvenile literature. I. Title.

ABELFS, Elivn, 1909- 759.9492
The magic painter; the story of Rembrandt, told by Kerwin Bowles [pseud.] Illustrated by Mitchell Foster. New York, Stravon Publishers [1951] 31 p. illus. 22 x 28 cm. (A Child's book of great artists) Stravon great artist series, 3. [ND653.R4A65] 927.5 51-8432
1. Rembrandt Hermanszoon van Rijn, 1606-1669. 2. Art—Juvenile literature. I. Title.

ABELES, Elivn, 1909- 927
Mike and the giant; the story of Michelangelo, told by Kerwin Bowles [pseud.] Illustrated by Mitchell Foster [pseud.] New York, Stravon Publishers [1951] 31 p. illus. 23 x 28 cm. (A Child's book of great artists) Stravon great artist series, 2. [N6923.B9A62] 51-13178
1. Buonarroti, Michel Angelo, 1475-1564. 2. Art—Juvenile literature. I. Title.

BORTEN, Helen. JUV
A picture has a special look. London, New York, Abelard-Schuman, c1961. unpaged. illus. 26cm. [PZ10.B4Pi] 741 61-15714
1. Art—Juvenile literature. 2. Drawing—Instruction—Juvenile literature. I. Title.

CHASE, Alice Elizabeth. 701.1
Looking at art. New York, Crowell [1966] 119 p. illus. (part col.) 26 cm. [N7440.C5] 66-11947
1. Art—Juvenile literature. I. Title.

COX, Beatrice, ed. 700
Exploring the arts. [London] Longacre Pr. [dist. Hollywood-by-the-Sea, Fla., Transatlantic, 1963, c.1961] 191p. illus., ports. 27cm. 63-25121 4.00
1. Art—Juvenile literature. 2. Music—Juvenile literature. 3. Performing arts—Juvenile literature. I. Title.

ERNEST, Brother, 1897- 927.5
Our Lady's portrait painter, a story of Raphael. Illus. reproductions from the works of Raphael. Notre Dame, Ind., Dujarie Press [1952] 94 p. illus. 24 cm. [ND623.R2E7] 52-3888
1. Raffaele Sanzio, 1483-1520. 2. Art—Juvenile literature. I. Title.

GETTINGS, Fred. 750
The meaning and wonder of art. New York, Golden Press [c1963] 91 p. illus. (part col.) ports. (part col.) 31 cm. [N7440.G4] 64-6952
1. Art — Juvenile literature. I. Title.

GRIGSON, Geoffrey, 1905- 709 (j)
More shapes and stories; a book about pictures, by Geoffrey and Jane Grigson. New York, Vanguard Press [1967] 70 p. illus. (part col.) 30 cm. [N7440.G65] 67-20942
1. Art—Juvenile literature. I. Grigson, Jane, joint author. II. Title.

GRIGSON, Geoffrey, 1905- 709
Shapes and people; a book about pictures. New York, Vanguard Press [1969] 72 p. illus. (part col.), ports. (part col.) 30 cm. Discusses how the works of artists from various periods and cultures captured the moods and activities of people. Examples of drawings and paintings are included. [N7440.G69] 76-11954 6.95
1. Art—Juvenile literature. I. Title. BIP

GRIGSON, Geoffrey, 1905- 701.18
Shapes and stories; a book about pictures, by Geoffrey and Jane Grigson. New York, Vanguard [1965. c.1964] 65p. illus. (pt. col.) 30cm. [N7440] 65-252 5.95
1. Art—Juvenile literature. I. Grigson, Jane, joint author. II. Title. BIP

HEYNE, Carl J. 372.5
Art for young America [by] Carl J. Heyne, with Florence W. Nicholas, Margaret M. Lee [and] Mabel B. Trilling. 6th ed. Peoria, Ill., C. A. Bennett Co. [1970] 256 p. illus. (part col.) 25 cm. First ed., 1946, by Florence W. Nicholas, Mabel B. Trilling, and Margaret Lee. Bibliography: p. 251-252. A textbook exploring the various areas of art and art appreciation. [N7440.H3 1970] 75-21980 ISBN 0-87002-056-0
1. Art—Juvenile literature. I. Nicholas, Florence (Williams) 1893- II. Title.

HEYNE, Carl J. 702'.4'0544
Art for young America / Carl J. Heyne, with Florence W. Nicholas, Margaret M. Lee, Mabel B. Trilling. 7th ed. / rev. by Paul Van Winkle. Peoria, Ill. : C. A. Bennett Co., [1975] 272 p. : ill. (some col.) ; 25 cm. First-2d ed. (1946-52) by F. W. Nicholas, M. B. Trilling, and M. Lee. Includes index. Bibliography: p. 266-267. A textbook exploring the various areas of art and art appreciation. [N7440.H3 1975] 74-83968 ISBN 0-87002-160-5
1. Art—Juvenile literature. I. Nicholas, Florence Williams, 1893- joint author. II. Van Winkle, Paul. III. Title.

HILLYER, Virgil Mores, 1875-1931. 709
A child's history of art, by V. M. Hillyer and E. G. Huey; illustrated with photos. Rev. and enl. New York, Appleton-Century-Crofts [1951] 465 p. illus. 24 cm. [N7440.H5 1951] 51-6216
1. Art—Juvenile literature. I. Title.

HOCHMAN, Shirley. 750'.118
Invitation to art. New York, Sterling Pub. Co. [1974] 40 p. illus. 32 cm. (Opening your eyes to art, 1) Discussions of eight famous paintings and their artists leading the reader into creative art activities suggested by the paintings. [N7440.H58 1974] 73-93593 ISBN 0-8069-5292-X 5.95
1. Art—Juvenile literature. 2. Art appreciation—Juvenile literature. I. Title. Lib. bdg. 5.69, ISBN 0-8069-5293-8.

YAUKEY, Grace (Sydenstricker) 1899- j700
How art and music speak to us [by] Cornelia Spencer [pseud.] New York, John Day Co. [1963] 95 p. illus. 22 cm. [N7440.Y3] 63-10234
1. Art — Juvenile literature. 2. Music — Juvenile literature. I. Title. BIP

Art—Kabul, Afghanistan (City)—Catalogs.

RICE, Frances Mortimer. 732'.9'6
Art in Afghanistan: objects from the Kabul Museum. Photos. by Frances Mortimer Rice. Introd. and text by Benjamin Rowland. Coral Gables, Fla., University of Miami Press [1971] 93 p. 214 plates. 29 cm. Bibliography: p. 64-66. [N3750.K3R5 1971b] 70-168548 ISBN 0-87024-225-3 29.50
1. Art—Kabul, Afghanistan (City)—Catalogs. I. Rowland, Benjamin, 1904- II. Kabul, Afghanistan (City). Muzah. III. Title.

Art—Kansas, Mo.—Catalogs.

WILLIAM ROCKHILL NELSON GALLERY OF ART AND MARY ATKINS MUSEUM OF FINE ARTS, Kansas City, Mo. 70S.1784111
Handbook of the collections in the William Rockhill Nelson Gallery of Art and Mary Atkins Museum of Fine Arts, Kansas City, Missouri. [Edited by Ross E. Taggart, associate curator] 4th ed. Kansas City, Mo., c1959. 270 p. illus. (part col.) port., plan. 28 cm. First published in 1933 under title: Handbook of the William Rockhill Nelson Gallery of Art. [N582.K3W5 1959] 59-616
1. Art — Kansas City, Mo. I. Title.

Art—Kansas, Mo.—Catalogs.

WILLIAM Rockhill Nelson Gallery of Art and Mary Atkins Museum of Fine Arts, Kansas City, Mo. 708'.178'411
Handbook of the collections in the William Rockhill Nelson Gallery of Art and Mary Atkins Museum of Fine Arts, Kansas City, Missouri. 5th ed. Kansas City, Mo., 1973. 2 v. illus. (part col.) 28 cm. Published in 1933 under title: Handbook of the William Rockhill Nelson Gallery of Art; in 1940 and 1949: The William Rockhill Nelson collection. Contents.Contents.—v. 1. Art of the Occident, edited by R. E. Taggart and G. L. McKenna.—v. 2. Art of the Orient, edited by R. E. Taggart, G. L. McKenna, and M. F. Wilson. [N582.K3A57 1973] 74-176114
1. William Rockhill Nelson Gallery of Art and Mary Atkins Museum of Fine Arts, Kansas City, Mo. 2. Art—Kansas, Mo.—Catalogs. I. Taggart, Ross E., ed. II. McKenna, George L., ed. III. Wilson, Marc F., ed. IV. Title.

Art—Kentucky.

COLEMAN, John Winston, 1898- 709'.2'2
Three Kentucky artists—Hart, Price, Troye / J. Winston Coleman, Jr. Lexington : University Press of Kentucky, [1974] 76 p., [4] leaves of plates : ill. ; 21 cm. (The Kentucky bicentennial bookshelf) "Partial list of portraits by Samuel Price": p. 44-[48] [N6530.K4C64] 74-7873 ISBN 0-8131-0202-2 pbk. : 3.95
1. Hart, Joel Tanner, 1810-1877. 2. Price, Samuel Woodson, 1828-1918. 3. Troye, Edward, 1808-1874. 4. Art—Kentucky. I. Title. II. Series.

Art, Khmer—Angkor, Cambodia.

MYRDAL, Jan. 726'.1'4309596
Angkor; an essay on art and imperialism [by] Jan Myrdal and Gun Kessle. Translated from the Swedish by Paul Britten Austin. [1st American ed.] New York, Pantheon Books [1970] 167 p. illus. 21 cm. Translation of Ansikte av sten. [N7315.2.A5M9513 1970] 74-90852 6.95
1. Art, Khmer—Angkor, Cambodia. 2. Art—Angkor, Cambodia. I. Kessle, Gun, illus.

Art, Korean—Exhibitions.

KOREA (Republic) Mungyobu. 709.519
Masterpices of Korean art; an exhibition under the auspices of the Government of the Republic of Korea. National Gallery of Art, Washington [and others. Washington, c1957] 182p. illus. (part col.) 24cm. Map on lining paper. [N7360.A53] 58-60241
1. Art, Korean—Exhibitions. I. U. S. National Gallery of Art. II. Title.

ROESIJADI, Widayati. 709'.519
The East Asian tradition, Korea : [catalogue of an exhibition], September 6, 1974 thru June 16, 1975 / Text by Widayati Roesijadi. Brockton, Mass. : Brockton Art Center—Fuller Memorial, [1974] 48 p. : ill. ; 22 cm. Bibliography: p. 47-48. [N7360.R63] 74-18013
1. Art, Korean—Exhibitions. I. Brockton Art Center—Fuller Memorial. II. Title.

Art, Korean—Hist.

MCCUNE, Evelyn 709.519
The arts of Korea; an illustrated history. Tokyo, Rutland, Vt., Tuttle [1961, c.1962] 452p. illus. (pt. col.) maps. 27cm. Bibl. 61-11122 17.50, bxd.
1. Art, Korean—Hist. I. Title.

Art, Kushan.

ROSENFIELD, John M. 709'.34
The dynastic arts of the Kushans [by] John M. Rosenfield. Berkeley, University of California Press, 1967. xliii, 377, [131] p. illus., maps, plans, plates. 29 cm. (California studies in the history of art, 6) Bibliography: p. [319]-349. [N5899.K8R6] 65-14981
1. Art, Kushan. 2. Yueh-chih. I. Title. II. Series. BIP

Art—Latin America.

WHYTE, Bertha Kitchell, 1890- 709.8
Seven treasure cities of Latin America. [1st ed.] New York, October House [1965, c1964] xiv, 286 p. illus., map. 29 cm. Bibliography: p. 277-281. [N6502.W45] 64-23112
1. Art—Latin America. 2. Latin America—History—To 1830. I. Title.

Art—Latin America—Bibliography.

SMITH, Robert Chester, 1912- ed. 016.709'8
A guide to the art of Latin America. Edited by Robert C. Smith and Elizabeth Wilder. New York, Arno Press, 1971. v, 480 p. 24 cm. Reprint of the 1948 ed. [Z5961.S72S5 1971] 74-151054 ISBN 0-405-03421-0
1. Art—Latin America—Bibliography. I. Weismann, Elizabeth (Wilder) 1908- joint ed. II. Title. BIP

Art, Latin American.

CHASE, Gilbert, 1906- 709'.8
Contemporary art in Latin America: painting, graphic art, sculpture, architecture. New York, Free Press [1970] viii, 292 p. illus. 22 cm. Bibliography: p. [275]-279. [N6502.C42] 70-78890
1. Art, Latin American. 2. Art, Modern—20th century—Latin America. I. Title. BIP

GOMEZ Sicre, Jose. 709.8
New names in Latin American art. Paintings, sculpture, drawings and prints selected by Jose Gomez-Sicre [and] circulated by the Smithsonian Institution Traveling Exhibition Service. Washington, Smithsonian Institution, 1966. [16] p. illus. 16 cm. (Smithsonian publication 4672) [N6620.G6] 66-61721
1. Art, Latin American. I. Smithsonian Institution. Traveling Exhibition Service. II. Title.

KELEMEN, Pal. 709'.8
Baroque and rococo in Latin America. 2d ed. New York, Dover Publications [1967- v. illus. 28 cm. "An unabridged and corrected republication of the work originally published in one volume ... in 1951." Contents.v. 1. Text. Bibliography (p. 273-288) [N6502.K42] 66-29056
1. Art, Latin American. 2. Art, Baroque — Latin America. I. Title. BIP

†KELEMEN, Pal. 709'.1'812
Vanishing art of the Americas / Pal Kelemen. New York : Walker, 1977. 232 p. : ill., maps (on lining papers) ; 26 cm. Includes bibliographical references and index. [N6502.K43 1977] 77-77886 ISBN 0-8027-0579-0 : 15.00
1. Art, Latin American. 2. Art, Colonial—Latin America. I. Title. BIP

Art, Latin American—Exhibitions.

CATLIN, Stanton Loomis. 709.8
Art of Latin America since independence, by Stanton Loomis Catlin, director of the exhibition, and Terence Grieder. [Rev. ed. New Haven, Conn., Yale University Press 1966] xiv, 246 p. illus. (part mounted, part col.) ports. 22 cm. Exhibition sponsored by Yale University and the University of Texas and various departments within the two universities. Held at the Yale University Art Gallery, Jan 27-Mar. 13, 1966; the University of Texas Art Museum, Apr. 17-May 15, 1966, and other museums of art. Bibliography: p. 205-207. [N6502.A76] 66-18340
1. Art, Latin American — Exhibitions. 2. Artists, Latin American. I. Grieder, Terence. II. Yale University. III. Texas University. IV. Title.

CATLIN, Stanton Loomis. 709.8
Art of Latin America since independence, by Stanton Loomis Catlin and Terence Grieder.[Rev. ed. New Haven, Conn., Yale University, 1966] xiv, 246 p. 118 plates (part col.) 22 x 23 cm. Exhibition sponsored by Yale University and the University of Texas and various departments within the two universities. Held at the Yale University Art Gallery, Jan. 27-Mar. 13, 1966: the University of Texas Art Museum, Apr. 17-May 15, 1966, and other museums of art. Bibliography: p. 205-207. [N6502.C33] 66-18340
1. Art, Latin American-Exhibitions. 2. Artists, Latin American. I. Grieder, Terence, joint author. II. Yale University. Art Gallery. III. Texas. University. Art Museum. IV. Title. BIP

CENTER for Inter-American Relations. Art Gallery. 759.98
Latin American paintings. From the collection of the Solomon R. Guggenheim Museum [Exhibition] July 2-September 14, 1969. New York [1969] 39 p. illus. (part col.) 21 cm. Includes bibliographies. [N6502.C37] 70-8316
1. Art, Latin American—Exhibitions. 2. Art, Modern—20th century—Latin America. I. Solomon R. Guggenheim Museum, New York. II. Title.

CENTER for Inter-American Relations. Art Gallery. 759.98'074'01471
Latin American paintings and drawings from the Collection of John and Barbara Duncan. New York [1970] 32 p. illus. (part col.) 22 cm. Exhibition held July 9-Aug. 30, 1970. [N6502.C38] 70-25033
1. Duncan, John, 1920- —Art collections. 2. Duncan, Barbara, 1921- —Art collections. 3. Art, Latin American—Exhibitions. I. Title. BIP

ISAAC Delgado Museum of Art, New Orleans. 709'.8
The art of ancient and modern Latin America; selections from public and private collections in the United States. New Orleans [1968] 1 v. (unpaged) illus., maps. 25 cm. Exhibition held May 10-June 16, 1968, at the Isaac Delgado Museum of Art, New Orleans. Includes bibliographies. [N6502.I8] 68-30688
1. Art, Latin American—Exhibitions. 2. Art, Latin American—United States. I. Title.

JOHN and Mable Ringling Museum of Art, Sarasota, Fla. 709'.8'0740159
Latin American horizons, 1976 / Ringling Museum of Art-Sarasota, Fla. [Sarasota] : The Museum, [1976] [36] p. : ill. ; 23 x 30 cm. Cover title. Catalogue of an exhibition held at Ringling Museum of Art, Sarasota, Apr. 8-May 16 et al. [N6502.J63 1976] 76-622616
1. Art, Latin American—Exhibitions. 2. Art, Modern—20th century—Latin America—Exhibitions. I. Title.

MASSACHUSETTS. University. Art Gallery. 709'.8'074014423
Tropic of Cancer, Tropic of Capricorn : contemporary Latin American art : [exhibition] February 21 to March 25, 1973, University Art Gallery, University of Massachusetts at Amherst. Amherst : The Gallery, [1973] [48] p. ; 16 cm. [N6502.M33 1973] 75-318271
1. Art, Latin American—Exhibitions. 2. Art, Modern—20th century—Latin America—Exhibitions. I. Title.

ORGANIZATION of American States. 709'.1'8120740153
Tribute to the arts of the Americas : [exhibition, March 15-April 7, 1974]. [Washington : General Secretariat, Organization of American States, 1974?] [60] p. : chiefly ill. ; 22 cm. Cover title: Art of the Americas in Washington private collections. [N6502.O73 1974] 75-304988
1. Art, Latin American—Exhibitions. 2. Art, Modern—20th century—Latin America. 3. Art—Private collections—Washington, D.C. I. Title. II. Title: Art of the Americas in Washington private collections.

Art, Latin American—History.

CASTEDO, Leopoldo. 709.8
A history of Latin American art and architecture from pre-Columbian times to the present. Translated and edited by Phyllis Freeman. New York, Praeger [1969] 320 p. illus. (part col.), maps, ports. 22 cm. (Praeger world of art series) Bibliography: p. 297-299. [N6502.C3213 1969b] 69-13421 8.95
1. Art, Latin American—History. I. Title.

Art, Latvian—Exhibitions.

AMERICAN Latvian 759.47'43
Association in the United States.
Latvian art on display: Cleveland, Toronto, Reading, New York. [Editors: Peteris Norvilis and Janis Silins. Washington, D.C.] 1967. 73 p. (chiefly plates) 18 x 24 cm. [N6995.L3A7] 73-265871
1. Art, Latvian—Exhibitions. I. Norvilis, Peteris, 1902- ed. II. Silins, Janis, 1896-1959, ed. III. Title.

NEW York, Latvian Art 759.47'43
Exhibition, 1963.
Latvju makslas izstades katalogs. Latvian art exhibition. 20-28 April, 1963, Barbizon Plaza Art Gallery, New York. Amerikas Latviesu apvienibas kulturas birojs. [Washington, 1963] 88 p. illus. 22 cm. Preface also in English. [N6995.L3N4] 66-53514
1. Art, Latvian — Exhibitions. I. American Latvian Association in the United States. II. Title. III. Title: Latvian art exhibition.

ROZENTALS, Janis, 1866- 759.743
1916.
Janis Rozentals, 1866-1916-1966 [by] August Annus, Arturs Ivanovs [and] Viktors Silmalis. [Compiled and edited by Ed. Dobelis] 3d, enl. ed. [Waverly, Iowa] Latvju gramata, 1972. 137 p. illus. (part col.) 28 cm. English or Latvian. [ND6.R678D6 1972] 73-156954 ISBN 0-87908-200-3
1. Annuss, Augusts, 1893- II. Ivanovs, Arturs. III. Silmalis, Viktors.

Art, Liberian—Exhibitions.

LIBERIA. Dept. of 709'.01'109662
Information and Cultural Affairs. Culture Bureau.
Plastic arts of Liberian hinterland; traditional, contemporary handicrafts. Arts plastiques de l'hinterland liberien; traditionnel, acien, sculptures de l'epoque contemporaine, arts artisanaux. Algiers, July-August 1969. Monrovia, 1969. 65 p. illus. 22 cm. Cover title. English and French. [N7399.L4L52 1969] 75-502360
1. Art, Liberian—Exhibitions. I. Title. II. Title: Arts plastiques de l'hinterland liberien.

Art libraries.

BROXIS, Peter F. 026'.7
Organising the arts [by] Peter F. Broxis. [Hamden, Conn.] Archon Books [1968] 132 p. illus. 23 cm. Includes bibliographies. [Z675.A85B7] 68-6567 ISBN 0-208-00855-1
1. Art libraries. I. Title.

HOFFBERG, Judith A. 026'.7'02573
Directory of art libraries and visual resource collections in North America / compiled for the Art Libraries Society of North America (ARLIS/NA) by Judith A. Hoffberg and Stanley W. Hess. New York : Neal-Schuman Publishers ; Santa Barbara, Calif. : distributed by ABC-Clio, c1978. xii, 298 p. ; 29 cm. Includes indexes. [Z675.A85H63] 78-61628 ISBN 0-918212-05-7 : 39.95
1. Art libraries—United States—Directories. 2. Art libraries—Canada—Directories. I. Hess, Stanley W., joint author. II. Arlis/North America. III. Title.
BIP

Art libraries—Handbooks, manuals, etc.

ART library manual : 026'.7
a guide to resources and practice / Philip Pacey. London ; New York : Bowker, 1977. xviii, 423 p. ; 23 cm. Includes bibliographies and index. [Z675.A85A79] 77-70290 ISBN 0-85935-054-1 : 22.50
1. Art libraries—Handbooks, manuals, etc. I. Pacey, Philip.

Art — Lincoln, Neb.

NEBRASKA. University. 70s.1784111
A selection of works from the art collections at the University of Nebraska. Published on the occasion of the inauguration of the Sheldon Memorial Art Gallery, May 1963. [Lincoln, 1963] 1 v. (unpaged) 105 illus. 26 cm. [N582.L5A54] 63-62925
1. Art — Lincoln, Neb. I. Nebraska. University. Sheldon Memorial Art Gallery. II. Title.

Art, Lithuanian—Exhibitions.

12 Lithuanian 709'.47'50973
artists in America : August 10-September 5, 1973, the Corcoran Gallery of Art, Washington, D C [Cleveland, Lithuanian World Community, 1973] 19 p. illus. 21 cm. "Exhibition committee: Dale Lukas, Algis Zemaitis ... and Vida Zubkus." Consists of biographical sketches of the artists and illustrations of their work. [N6995.L5T93] 73-85063
1. Art, Lithuanian—Exhibitions. 2. Artists—Lithuania. 3. Artists—United States. I. Corcoran Gallery of Art, Washington, D.C.

NEW York. Riverside 709.475
Museum.
Lithuanian international art exhibition 1st-, 1958- New York. v. illus. 21cm. [N6995.L5N4] 59-43046
1. Art, Lithuanian—Exhibitions. I. Title.

Art—Liverpool.

WILLETT, John. 709'.427'2
Art in a city. London, pub. for the Bluecoat Soc. of Arts by Methuen, 1967. xiv, 287p. illus. (incl. ports.), map, tables. 24cm. Map on endpapers. Bibl. [N6771.L55W5] 67-87307 12.50
1. Art—Liverpool. I. Bluecoat Society of Arts, Liverpool. II. Title.
American distributor: Hillary House, New York.

Art—London.

BROOKE, Brian 709.421
Art in London. New York, D. White [1966] 223p. illus. 19cm. [N6770.B7 1966] 66-23566 4.95 bds.
1. Art—London. I. Title.
60 East 55th St., New York, N.Y. 10022.

KING, Donald 708.2
Samplers. London, Her Majesty s Stationery Office [dist. New York 20, British Information Services, 45 Rockefeller Plaza] 1960 [i.e., 1961] 15p. plates (unpaged) illus., diagrs., Bibl.: p.11 and bibl. footnotes (Victoria and Albert Museum—large picture book no. 14) 25cm. 52-37670 2.40 (post paid) pap.,
1. Art—London. I. Title.

PIPER, David. 914.21'04'85
London. Special photography by Edwin Smith. [1st ed.] New York, Holt, Rinehart and Winston [1971] 288 p. illus. (part col.), col. map. 26 cm. (World cultural guides) [N6770.P5] 77-155540 9.95
1. Art—London. 2. London—Description—1951- —Guide-books. I. Smith, Edwin, 1912- illus.

VICTORIA and Albert Museum, 708.2
South Kensington.
Dolls. Small picture book. no. 50. London, H. M. Stationery Off. [dist. New York, British Information Services, 1960] unpaged (chiefly illus.) .50 pap.,
1. Art—London. I. Title.

VICTORIA and Albert 708.21
Museum, South Kensington
English chairs. Introd. by Ralph Edwards [2d ed.] London, H.M.S.O. [New York, Brit. Info., c.]1965. 26p. 120p. of plates. 25cm. (Large picture bk., no.10) [N1150.A752] 52-37670 2.70 pap.,
1. Art—London. I. Title.

VICTORIA and Albert 708.421
Museum, South Kensington.
Paintings at Apsley House, by C. M. Kauffman. London, H.M.S.O. [New York, Brit. Info., c.]1965. 1v. (unpaged, chiefly illus.) 25cm. At head of title: Wellington Museum (Large picture bk., no. 25) [N1150.A752] 52-37670 2.10 pap.,
1. Art—London. I. Kauffman, C. M. Paintings at Apsley House. II. Title.

VICTORIA and Albert 708.421
Museum, South Kensington, London.
The Duke of Wellington in caricature. London, H. M. S. O. [New York, Brit. Info., c.] 1965. 1 v. (various p.) illus. 22cm. (Large picture bk., No 19) [N1150.A752] 62 2.50 pap.,
1. Art—London. I. Title.

Art—London—Catalogs.

NICOLSON, Benedict. 709'.421
The treasures of the Foundling Hospital. With a catalogue raisonne based on a draft catalogue by John Kerslake. Oxford, Clarendon Press, 1972. xiv, 98 p. illus. 26 cm. (Studies in the history of art and architecture) p. [92]-95. [N5208.5.L6N5] 72-192246 ISBN 0-19-817186-2
1. London. Foundling Hospital. 2. Art—London—Catalogs. 3. Aesthetics, British. I. Kerslake, John F. II. London. Foundling Hospital. III. Title. IV. Series: Oxford studies in the history of art and architecture.
Available from Oxford University Press N.Y. 11.25.
BIP

ROTHENSTEIN, John Knewstub 708.2
Maurice, Sir, 1901-
The Tate Gallery. New York, H. N. Abrams [1958] 192 p. illus. (part mounted, part co.) 34 cm. Bibliography: p. 192. [N1080.R6] 58-13485
1. Tate Gallery, London. 2. Art—London—Catalogs.

Art—London—Catalogs—Bibliography.

VICTORIA and Albert Museum, 016.7
South Kensington. National Art Library.
Catalogue: author catalogue. Boston, G. K. Hall, 1972. 10 v. 37 cm. [Z5939.V63] 72-172479 ISBN 0-8161-0992-3
1. Art—London—Catalogs—Bibliography.

Art—London—Galleries and museums.

WHITTET, George Sorley, 708.21
1913-
Art centers of the world: London [by] G. S. Whittet. Cleveland, World Pub. Co. [1967] 192 p. illus. (part col.), map (on lining papers), ports. 21 cm. [N1030.W45 1967b] 66-23113
1. Art—London—Galleries and museums. I. Title.

Art—Los Angeles.

LOS Angeles Co., 70s.1784111
Calif. Museum, Los Angeles.
Illustrated handbook of the Los Angeles County Museum of Art. 1st ed. [Los Angeles] 1965. 184 p. illus. (part col.) 17 cm. [N582.L7A64] 67-5295
1. Art — Los Angeles. I. Title.

LOS Angeles Co., 70s.1784111
Calif. Museum of Art, Los Angeles.
Illustrated handbook of the Los Angeles County Museum of Art. 1st ed. [Los Angeles] 1965. 184 p. illus. (part col.) 17 cm. [N582.L7A64] 67-5295
1. Art—Los Angeles. I. Title.

Art — Lubbock, Tex.

WILBANKS, Elsie 709.7648
Montgomery.
Art on the Texas plains; the story of regional art and the South Plains Art Guild. [Golden anniversary 1st ed. Lubbock, Tex., South Plains Art Guild, 1959] 166 p. illus. 27 cm. [N6535.L8W5] 60-24376
1. Art — Lubbock, Tex. 2. Art — Texas. 3. South Plains Arts and Crafts Guild. I. Title.

Art — Lynchburg, Va.

LYNCHBURG, Va. Fine Arts 759.13
Center.
Image of an age; ante-bellum art and furnishings, the Lynchburg Fine Arts Center, April 7-May 3, 1963. Lynchburg, 1963. unpaged. illus. 28 cm. [N6512.L9] 63-3676
1. Art — Lynchburg, Va. 2. Art, American — Exhibitions. I. Title.

Art—Madrid—History.

CHUECA Goitia, 709'.46'41
Fernando.
Madrid & Toledo. Special photography by Mario Carrieri. [1st ed.] New York, Holt, Rinehart and Winston [1972] 288 p. illus. (part col.) 26 x 13 cm. (World cultural guides) [N7110.C4413] 78-175613 ISBN 0-03-091082-X 9.95
1. Art—Madrid—History. 2. Madrid—Description. 3. Art—Toledo, Spain—History. 4. Toledo, Spain—Description. I. Title.

Art—Magna Grecia.

MATT, Leonard von. 709.377
M Explanatory text by Umberto Zanotti-Bianco. Translated from the Italian by Herbert Hoffmann. [1st American ed.] New York, Universe Books [1962] 231p. plates (part col.) map. 29cm. [N5740.M433 1962] 61-14580
1. Art—Magna Grecia. 2. Art, Greek. I. Zanotti-Bianco, Umberto. II. Title.

Art—Maine—Hist.

MELLON, Gertrud A., ed. 709.741
Maine and its role in American art, 1740-1963. Gertrud A. Mellon, co-ordinating ed.; Elizabeth F. Wilder, ed. New York, Viking [c.1963] 178p. plates (pt. col.) map. 29cm. (Studio bk.) 63-12644 10.00
1. Art—Maine—Hist. I. Wilder, Elizabeth F., joint ed. II. Title.

MELLON, Gertrud A ed. 709.741
Maine and its role in American art, 1740-1963. Gertrude A. Mellon, co-ordinating editor: Elizabeth F. Wilder. New York, Viking Press [1963] 178 p. plates (part col.) map. 29 cm. (A Studio book) [N6530.M2M4] 63-12644
1. Art — Maine — Hist. I. Wilder, Elizabeth F. joint ed. II. Title.
BIP

Art, Maori.

BARROW, Terence. 709'.01'109931
Maori art of New Zealand / Terence Barrow. Paris : Unesco Press, 1978. xvi, 108 p. : ill. (some col.) ; 25 cm. Includes index. Bibliography: p. 102-103. [N7407.M36B37] 78-368496 ISBN 92-3-101319-X pbk. : 9.25
1. Art, Maori. 2. Art, Primitive—New Zealand. I. Title.
Distributed by Unipub, NYC
BIP

BARROW, Tui Terence, 745'.09931
1923-
The decorative arts of the New Zealand Maori, by T. Barrow. Rutland, Vt., C. E. Tuttle Co. [1973, c1972] 108, [4] p. illus. (part col.) 18 x 19 cm. Bibliography: p. [112] [N7406.B3 1973] 72-89740 ISBN 0-8048-1091-5 7.95
1. Art, Maori. I. Title.

POWNALL, Glen. 702'.8
New Zealand Maori arts and crafts / Glen Pownall. Wellington : Sevenseas Publishing, 1976. 159 p. : ill. (part col.) ; 29 cm. [N7406.P67] 77-482121 ISBN 0-85467-033-5 : 15.00
1. Art, Maori. 2. Art, Primitive—New Zealand. 3. New Zealand—Civilization. I. Title.
BIP

Art—Marketing.

BURNHAM, Bonnie. 338.4'7'7
The art crisis / Bonnie Burnham. New York : St. Martin's Press, [1975] 256 p. ; 22 cm. Includes bibliographical references and index. [N8600.B87] 75-9469 8.95
1. Art—Marketing. 2. Art as an investment. I. Title.

BURNHAM, Sophy. 338.4'7'7
The art crowd. New York, D. McKay Co. [1973] xiii, 395 p. illus. 22 cm. Bibliography: p. 371-373. [N8675.B87] 72-92643 8.95
1. Art—Marketing. 2. Art—Prices. 3. Art—Collectors and collecting. I. Title. BIP

CHAMBERLAIN, Betty. 658.8'09'7
The artist's guide to his market. New York, Watson-Guptill [1970] 128 p. 24 cm. [N8353.C45] 70-87323 5.95
1. Art—Marketing. I. Title. BIP

CHAMBERLAIN, Betty. 658.8'09'7
The artist's guide to his market / by Betty Chamberlain. 2d ed. New York : Watson-Guptill Publications, 1975. 176 p. ; 24 cm. Includes index. [N8600.C48 1975] 75-6896 ISBN 0-8230-0326-4 9.95
1. Art—Marketing. I. Title.

COCHRANE, Diane. 658'.91'7
This business of art / by Diane Cochrane. New York : Watson-Guptill Publications, 1978. 256 p. : ill. ; 24 cm. Includes index. Bibliography: p. 249. [N8600.C62] 77-26337 ISBN 0-8230-5360-1 : 12.50
1. Art—Marketing. I. Title. BIP

*CUMMINGS, Paul, ed. 700
Fine arts market place. New York : R.R. Bowker.
The third ed., 1977-1978, c1977 is available for 20.50 (pbk.) ISBN 0-8352-0918-0. L.C. card no.: 73-2497. BIP

GOODMAN, Calvin J. 658.8'09'7
Marketing art; a handbook for the artist and art dealer, by Calvin J. Goodman. Florence J. Goodman, editor. Los Angeles, Gee Tee Bee, c1972. xiv, 318 p. illus. 24 cm. [N8600.G66] 73-175450
1. Art—Marketing. I. Title.

HOLZ, Loretta. 381'.45'74550973
How to sell your art and crafts : a marketing guide for creative people / by Loretta Holz. New York : Scribner, [1976 p. cm. Includes index. Bibliography: p. [N8600.H65] 76-25904 ISBN 0-684-14806-4 : 12.50
1. Art—Marketing. 2. Handicraft—Marketing. I. Title.

KATCHEN, Carole, 1944- 658.89'7
Promoting & selling your art / by Carole Katchen. New York : Watson-Guptill Publications, 1978. 191 p. ; 24 cm. Includes index. Bibliography: p. [187] [N8600.K37] 77-28109 ISBN 0-8230-4422-X : 10.95
1. Art—Marketing. I. Title. BIP

Art—Marketing—Addresses, essays, lectures.

RUSKIN, John, 1819-1900. 658.8'09'7
"A joy for ever" (and its price in the market); being the substance (with additions) of two lectures on the political economy of art, delivered at Manchester, July 10th and 13th, 1857. With an introd. by Charles Eliot Norton. Brantwood ed. New York, C. E. Merrill, 1891. St. Clair Shores, Mich., Scholarly Press, 1972. p. (The works of John Ruskin) First published in 1852 under title: The political economy of art. Contents.Contents.—The discovery and application of art.—The accumulation and distribution of art.—Supplementary additional papers: Education in art. Art school notes. Social Policy. [N8600.R8 1972] 72-8222 ISBN 0-403-02063-8
1. Art—Marketing—Addresses, essays, lectures. I. Title.

Art—Massachusetts—Boston—Catalogs.

ISABELLA Stewart Gardner Museum, Boston. 708'.144'61
Guide to the collection / Isabella Stewart Gardner Museum. 2d ed. Boston : The Trustees, 1976. 116 p. : ill. ; 18 cm. First ed. published in 1959 under title: Selective guide to the collection. Includes index. [N521.I7A53 1976] 76-4176 ISBN 0-914660-02-0
1. Isabella Stewart Gardner Museum, Boston. 2. Art—Massachusetts—Boston—Catalogs. BIP

Art, Massim (Melanesian people)

NEWTON, Douglas, 1920- 732'.2'09953
Massim : art of the Massim area, New Guinea / Douglas Newton. New York : Museum of Primitive Art, 1975. 19 p., [13] leaves of plates : ill. ; 28 cm. "Based on an exhibition held at the Museum of Primitive Art, 1964." Bibliography: p. 18-19. [NK9796.A3N436] 72-97835 ISBN 0-912294-44-2
1. Art, Massim (Melanesian people) 2. Wood-carving, Primitive—Papua, New Guinea (Ter.) 3. Wood-carving—Papua, New Guinea (Ter.) I. New York (City). Museum of Primitive Art. II. Title.

Art—Mathematics—Addresses, essays, lectures.

VISUAL art, mathematics and computers : selections from the journal Leonardo / edited by Frank J. Malina. Oxford [Eng.] ; New York : Pergamon Press, c1977. p. cm. Includes index. [N72.M3V57 1977] 77-30656 ISBN 0-08-021854-7 : 25.00 pbk. : 18.00 701
1. Art—Mathematics—Addresses, essays, lectures. 2. Computer art—Addresses, essays, lectures. 3. Art and technology—Addresses, essays, lectures. I. Malina, Frank J. II. Leonardo (Oxford) BIP

Art, Maya.

PROSKOURIAKOFF, Tatiana Avenirovna, 1909- 972.015
A study of classic Maya sculpture. Washington, 1950. xi, 209 p. illus., maps (1 fold.) 29 cm. (Carnegie Institution of Washington. Publication 503) Bibliography: p. [207]-209. [F1435.3.A7P7] 51-7800
1. Art, Maya. 2. Mayas—Antiq. I. Title. II. Title: Classic Maya sculpture. III. Series. BIP

Art, Medieval.

BATTERBERRY, Michael. 709.02
Art of the Middle Ages, adapted by Michael Batterberry. Foreword by Howard Conant. New York, McGraw-Hill [1972] 157 p. col. illus. 31 cm. (Discovering art series) "[Based] on the text of the magazine series Discovering art ... [with] adaptations from the Italian text of Capolavori nei secoli." [N5970.B29] 72-38988 9.95
1. Art, Medieval. I. Title. BIP

BRITISH Museum. Dept. of British and Medieval Antiquities 709.02
Early medieval art in the British Museum, by Ernst Kitzinger. New preface by author. Bloomington, Ind. Univ. Pr. [c.1940, 1964] 114p. 48 plates. 20cm. (Midland bk. MB-65) 1.95 pap.,
1. Art, Medieval. I. Kitzinger, Ernest, 1912- II. Title.

CHRISTENSEN, Erwin Ottomar, 1890- 709.02
Objects of medieval art from the Widener Collection. Washington, National Gallery of Art, Smithsonian Institution, 1952. 32 p. illus. 23 cm. (National Gallery of Art handbook, 3) Bibliography: p. 31-32. [N5963.C53] 52-3889
1. Art, Medieval. 2. U. S. National Gallery of Art. Widener Collection. I. Title. II. Series: U. S. National Gallery of Art. National Gallery of Art handbook, 3

DUBY, Georges. 709.02
Foundations of a new humanism, 1280-1440. [Translated from the French by Peter Price. Geneva, Skira; [distributed in the U.S. by World Pub. Co., Cleveland, 1966] 222 p. illus. (part fold.) col. plates (part fold.) col. ports. 31 cm. (Art ideas history) [N5975.D813] 66-15283
1. Art, Medieval. 2. Art patronage. 3. Humanism. I. Title. II. Series.

DURANT, Gladys May 709.02
Discovering mediaeval art. London, G. Bell [dist. Chester Springs, Pa. Dufour, 1963, c.1960] 256p. illus. 20cm. Bibl. 60-4546 4.50 bds.,
1. Art, Medieval. I. Title.

EGBERT, Virginia Wylie. 709.02
The mediaeval artist at work. Princeton, N.J., Princeton University Press, 1967. 93 p. 54 illus. (incl. facsims) 29 cm. Bibliographical references included in "Notes" (p. 85-[87]) [N5975.E35] 67-12344
1. Art, Medieval. 2. Artists, Medieval. I. Title.

HENDERSON, George David Smith, 1931- 709'.4
Early medieval. Harmondsworth, Penguin, 1972. 272 p. illus., facsims., plan, ports. 20 cm. (Style and civilization) Bibliography: p. 265-268. [N5975.H35] 72-171390 ISBN 0-14-021420-8 £1.25 ($4.95 U.S.)
1. Art, Medieval. I. Title. BIP

HOFSTATTER, Hans Hellmut, 1928- 709'.4
Art of the late Middle Ages, by Hans H. Hofstatter. New York, H. N. Abrams [1968] 264 p. illus. (part col.) 23 cm. (Panorama of world art) Translation of Spates Mittelalter. Bibliography: p. 253. [N5970.H5713] 68-18131
1. Art, Medieval. I. Title.

HOLLANDER, Hans. 709'.02
Early medieval art. [English translation by Caroline Hillier] New York, Universe Books [1974] 192 p. illus. (part col.) 23 cm. Translation of Kunst des fruhen Mittelalters. Bibliography: p. 188-189. [N5975.H613] 72-91633 ISBN 0-87663-166-9 6.95
1. Art, Medieval. I. Title.

KIDSON, Peter. 709.4
The medieval world. New York, McGraw-Hill [1967] 176 p. illus. (part col.) maps, plans. 30 cm. (Landmarks of the world's art) Bibliography: p. [172] [N5970.K5] 67-11796
1. Art, Medieval. 2. Architecture, Medieval. I. Title.

KITZINGER, Ernst. 1912- 709.02
Early medieval art, with illustrations from the British Museum collection. [Gloucester. Mass., P. Smith. 1966, c.1940] 114p. illus. 20cm. (Midland bk. MB-65 rebound) First pub. in 1940 under title: Early medieval art in the British Museum [N5963.K5 1964] 4.00
1. Art, Medieval. I. British Museum. II. Title. BIP

LACROIX, Paul, 1806-1884. 709'.02
The arts in the Middle Ages and the Renaissance. New York, F. Ungar Pub. Co. [1964] xix, 520 p. illus. 27 cm. A reprinting of the 1870 ed. published under title: The arts in the Middle Ages and at the period of the Renaissance. [N5970.L32 1964] 64-25235
1. Art, Medieval. 2. Art, Renaissance. I. Title.

LEJEUNE-DEHOUSSE, Rita. 704.947
The legend of Roland in the Middle Ages [by] Rita Lejeune and Jacques Stiennon. [New York] Phaidon; [distributed by Praeger Publishers, 1971] 2 v. illus., map, col. plates. 31 cm. Translation of La legende de Roland dans l'art du moyen age. Includes bibliographical references. [N8210.L413 1971] 73-111061 ISBN 0-7148-1414-8 98.50
1. Chanson de Roland—Art. 2. Art, Medieval. I. Stiennon, Jacques, joint author. II. Title.

LETHABY, William Richard, 1857-1931. 709'.4
Medieval art, from the peace of the church to the eve of the Renaissance, 312-1350. Rev. by D. Talbot Rice. New York, Greenwood Press [1969] xiv, 223 p. illus., plans. 23 cm. Reprint of the 1950 ed. [N5970.L64 1969] 71-97315
1. Art, Medieval. I. Rice, David Talbot, 1903- ed. II. Title.

LETHABY, William Richard, 1857-1931. 709.02
Medieval art; from the peace of the Church to the eve of the Renaissance, 312-1350. Freeport, N.Y., Books for Libraries Press [1971] xviii, 315 p. illus., plans. 23 cm. Reprint of the 1904 ed. Includes bibliographical references. [N5970.L64 1971] 70-157345 ISBN 0-8369-5806-3
1. Art, Medieval.

LETHABY, William Richard, 1857-1931. 709.4
Medieval art from the peace of the church to the eve of the Renaissance, 312-1350. Rev. by D. Talbot Rice. New York, Philosophical Library [1950] xiv, 223 p. illus. 25 cm. [N5970.L64 1950] 50-9270
1. Art, Medieval. I. Title. BIP

MCLANATHAN, Richard B. K. 759.02
The pageant of medieval art and life, by Richard McLanathan. Philadelphia, Westminster Press [1966] 127 p. illus., facsims., plans. 31 cm. Bibliography: p. [117]-119. [N5970.M24] 66-15817
1. Art, Medieval. 2. Civilization, Medieval. I. Title.

MARTINDALE, Andrew. 709'.02
The rise of the artist in the Middle Ages and early Renaissance. New York, McGraw-Hill [1972] 144 p. illus. (part col.) 22 cm. (Library of medieval civilization) Bibliography: p. 130-135. [N5975.M37] 70-39289 ISBN 0-07-040649-9 5.95
1. Art, Medieval. 2. Art, Renaissance—Early Renaissance. 3. Artists. I. Title.

MEDIEVAL studies in memory of A. Kingsley Porter. Edited by Wilhelm R. W. Koehler. Freeport, N.Y., Books for Libraries Press [1969, c1939] 2 v. (xxiv, 728 p.) illus., plans, port. 29 cm. (Essay index reprint series) "Bibliography of the writings of A. Kingsley Porter": v. 1, p. [xvii]-xxiv. [N5975.M5 1969] 77-80391 709.02
1. Porter, Arthur Kingsley, 1883-1933. 2. Art, Medieval. 3. Archaeology, Medieval. I. Koehler, Wilhelm Reinhold Walter, 1884-1959, ed. BIP

NEW York (City). Metropolitan Museum of Art. The Cloisters. 708'.147'1
Medieval monuments at the Cloisters as they were and as they are. By James Rorimer. Rev. ed. by Katherine Serrell Rorimer. [New York, Metropolitan Museum of Art, 1972] 81 p. illus. 29 cm. [N611.C6 1972] 74-145765 ISBN 0-87099-026-8
1. Art, Medieval. 2. Art—New York (City) I. Rorimer, James Joseph, 1905-1966. II. Rorimer, Katherine Serrell. III. Title.

NEW York. Metropolitan Museum of Art. The Cloisters. 708.147
The Cloisters; the building and the collection of mediaeval art in Fort Tryon Park, by James J. Rorimer. [11th ed.] New York, 1951. 158 p. illus 22 cm. [N611.C6 1951] 51-6218
1. Art, Medieval. 2. Art — New York (City) I. Rorimer, James Joseph, 1905- II. Title. BIP

NEW York. Metropolitan Museum of Art. The Cloisters. 708.1471
The Cloisters, the building and the collection of medieval art in Fort Tryon Park, by James J. Rorimer. 3d ed. rev. in collaboration with Margaret B. Freeman and the staff on the Medieval Dept. and the Cloisters. New York, Metropolitan Museum of Art [c.]1963. 212p. illus. map (on lining pap.) 22cm. 62-20896 3.95; 2.00 pap.,
1. Art, Medieval. 2. Art—New York (City) I. Rorimer, James Joseph, 1905- II. Title.

SMITH, Norris Kelly. 709.02
Medieval art; an introduction to the art and architecture of Europe, A. D. 300-A. D. 1300. Dubuque, Iowa, W. C. Brown [1967] viii, 116 p. illus. 23 cm. (Art horizons series) Bibliography: p. 113-114. [N5970.S6] 67-22712
1. Art, Medieval. 2. Architecture, Medieval. I. Title.

WALTERS Art Gallery, Baltimore. 709.02
Arts of the migration period in the Walters Art Gallery, by Marvin Chauncey Ross. With an introd. and Historical survey by Philippe Verdier. Baltimore, 1961. 173 p. illus., fold. maps. 25 cm. Includes bibliographical references. [N5970.W3] 61-65213
1. Art, Medieval. 2. Europe—History—392-814. 3. Migrations of nations. I. Ross, Marvin Chauncey, 1904- II. Title.

Art, Medieval—Addresses, essays, lectures.

HORTUS imaginum : 709'.4
essays in Western art / edited by Robert Enggass & Marilyn Stokstad. Lawrence : University of Kansas, 1974. xiii, 211 p., [68] leaves of plates : ill. ; 25 cm. (Humanistic studies ; 45) (University of Kansas publications) Includes bibliographical references. [N5940.H67] 74-620191 12.00
1. Art, Medieval—Addresses, essays, lectures. 2. Art, Renaissance—Addresses, essays, lectures. 3. Art, Baroque—Addresses, essays, lectures. 4. Wethey, Harold Edwin—Bibliography. I. Enggass, Robert, 1921- II. Stokstad, Marilyn Jane, 1929- III. Series: Kansas. University. Humanistic studies ; 45.

MEDIEVAL art. 709'.02
New York : Garland Pub., [1976] p. cm. (Garland library of the history of art ; v. 5) Reprint of 7 articles published between 1932 and 1950 in various journals. [N5300.G32 Vol. 5] [N5970] 76-14067 ISBN 0-8240-2415-X : 35.00
1. Art, Medieval—Addresses, essays, lectures. I. Series.
Contents omitted. **BIP**

OAKESHOTT, Walter Fraser, 709.02
1903-
Classical inspiration in medieval art. New York, Praeger [1960] 146p. 143 plates. 29cm. (Rhind lectures, 1956) 60-13899 20.00 buck.,
1. Art, Medieval—Addresses, essays, lectures. 2. Art, Greek—Addresses, essays, lectures. 3. Art, Roman—Addresses, essays, lectures. I. Title. II. Series: The Rhind lectures in archaeology, 1956

Art, Medieval—Bibl.

SCHELLER, R W v. 12
A survey of medieval model books [by] R. W. Scheller. Haarlem, Erven F. Bohn, 1963 [i.e., 1964] xi, 215 p. illus. 24 cm. "Published by Teylers tweede genootschap." Includes bibliographical references. [Z5933.S23] 66-40175
1. Art, Medieval—Bibl. 2. Drawings—Bibl. I. Teyler's tweede genootschap, Haarlem. II. Title.

Art, Medieval—Byzantine influences.

DEMUS, Otto. 709.02
Byzantine art and the West. [New York] New York University Press [1970] xxi, 274 p. 264 illus., 8 col. plates. 28 cm. (The Wrightsman lectures, 3) Lectures delivered at the Metropolitan Museum of Art, New York, 1966. Bibliography: p. 253-266. [N5975.D4] 78-88132 ISBN 0-8147-0116-7 15.00
1. Art, Medieval—Byzantine influences. I. Title. II. Series. **BIP**

Art, Medieval—Catalogs.

BERKOWITZ, David Sandler, 016.096
1913-
In remembrance of creation; evolution of art and scholarship in the Medieval and Renaissance Bible. Waltham, Mass., Brandeis University Press [1968] xviii, 141, [160] p. illus., facsims. 29 cm. (Publications of the Society of Bibliophiles at Brandeis University, no. 3) "Catalogue of an exhibition to commemorate the twentieth anniversary of Brandeis University held at the Rapaporte Treasure Hall, Brandeis University Library, May 4th through June 11th, 1968." Includes bibliographies. [N8023.B4] 68-28658
1. Bible—Pictures, illustrations, etc. 2. Art, Medieval—Catalogs. 3. Art, Renaissance—Catalogs. I. Title. II. Series: Brandeis University, Waltham, Mass. Society of Bibliophiles. Publications, no. 3 **BIP**

Art, Medieval—Cumbria, Eng.—Exhibitions.

WHITWORTH Art 709'.02'07402733
Gallery.
Medieval and early Renaissance treasures in the North West : [exhibition] sponsored by the Greater Manchester Council, 15 January to 28 February 1976 / [Whitworth Art Gallery and University of Manchester, History of Art Department]. Manchester : The Gallery, [1976] 129 p., leaf of plate, 40 [i.e. 42] p. of plates : ill. (2 col.) ; 26 cm. [N6769.C92W45 1976] 76-377506 ISBN 0-903261-04-9 : £2.50
1. Art, Medieval—Cumbria, Eng.—Exhibitions. 2. Art, Renaissance—Cumbria, Eng.—Exhibitions. 3. Art—Cumbria, Eng.—Exhibitions. I. Victoria University of Manchester. History of Art Dept. II. Greater Manchester, Eng. Council. III. Title.

Art, Medieval—Exhibitions.

CALKINS, Robert G. 709'.4
A medieval treasury; an exhibition of medieval art from the third to the sixteenth century [by] Robert G. Calkins. [Ithaca, Office of University Publications, Cornell University, 1968] viii, 200 p. 114 plates (part col.) 26 cm. Catalog of exhibition held at Andrew Dickson White Museum of Art, Cornell University, Ithaca, N.Y., Oct. 8-Nov. 3, 1968 and at Munson-Williams-Proctor Institute, Utica, N.Y., Nov. 10,-Dec. 8, 1968. Bibliography: p. 189-199. [N5963.C3] 68-65401
1. Art, Medieval—Exhibitions. I. Cornell University. Andrew Dickson White Museum of Art. II. Munson-Williams-Proctor Institute, Utica, N.Y. Museum of Art. III. Title.

FOLDA, Jaroslav. 709'.02
A medieval treasury from Southeastern collections. Exhibited at the William Hayes Ackland Memorial Art Center, the University of North Carolina at Chapel Hill, April 4 - May 21, 1971. Exhibition organized and catalogue edited by Jaroslav Folda and John M. Schnorrenberg. [Chapel Hill, William Hayes Ackland Memorial Art Center, University of North Carolina, 1971] 77 p. illus. 27 cm. Includes bibliographical references. [N5963.C45F6] 70-198359
1. Art, Medieval—Exhibitions. 2. Art—Collectors and collecting—Southern States. I. Schnorrenberg, John M., 1931- joint author. II. North Carolina. University. William Hayes Ackland Memorial Art Center. III. Title.

MEDIEVAL art in 709'.02'074014765
upstate New York : [exhibition]. Syracuse, N.Y. : Everson Museum of Art of Syracuse and Onondaga County, c1974. 130 p. : ill. ; 24 cm. Includes bibliographical references. [N5963.S96E85] 74-82054
1. Art, Medieval—Exhibitions. I. Everson Museum of Art of Syracuse and Onondaga County.

NEW York (City). 709'.02
Metropolitan Museum of Art.
The secular spirit: life and art at the end of the Middle Ages, by the Metropolitan Museum of Art. New York, Dutton, 1974. p. cm. (A Dutton visual book) Catalog of an exhibition held at the Cloisters, Nov. 16, 1974-Jan. 12, 1975. Bibliography: p. [N5963.N4N46 1974] 74-7893 12.95
1. Art, Medieval—Exhibitions. 2. Art, Medieval—Themes, motives. I. New York (City). Metropolitan Museum of Art. The Cloisters. II. Title.

NEW York (City). 709'.4
Metropolitan Museum of Art. The Cloisters.
Medieval art from private collections; a special exhibition at The Cloisters, October 30, 1968 through January 5, 1969. Introd. and catalogue by Carmen Gomez-Moreno. [New York, 1968] 1 v. (chiefly illus.) 26 cm. [N5963.N43] 68-8865
1. Art, Medieval—Exhibitions. 2. Art—Private collections—United States. I. Gomez-Moreno, Carmen. II. Title. **BIP**

NEW York (City). 709'.4
Metropolitan Museum of Art. The Cloisters.
The Middle Ages; treasures from the Cloisters and the Metropolitan Museum of Art. Los Angeles County Museum of Art, January 18- March 29, 1970. The Art Institute of Chicago, May 16- July 5, 1970. [Los Angeles, Los Angeles County Museum of Art, c1969] 266 p. illus. (part col.) 27 cm. Text by Vera K. Ostoia. "Bibliography and notes": p. 251-262. [N5963.N4M45] 72-106813
1. Art, Medieval—Exhibitions. I. Ostoia, Vera K. II. New York (City). Metropolitan Museum of Art. III. Los Angeles Co., Calif. Museum of Art, Los Angeles. IV. Chicago. Art Institute. V. Title.

QUEENS College, Flushing, 709.02
N. Y. Art Collection.
The world as a symbol; an exhibition of medieval art, April 15-May 22, 1959. Flushing, Paul Klapper Library, Queens College, 1959. 54p. illus. 24cm. [N5963.Q4] 59-41998
1. Art, Medieval—Exhibitions. 2. Christian art and symbolism. I. Title.

Art, Medieval—France.

EVANS, Joan, 1893- 709'.44
Art in mediaeval France, 987-1948. 1st ed., 3rd impression (with additional bibliography). Oxford, Clarendon P., 1969. xxviii, 325 p. 280 plates (1 fold.), illus., maps, plans. 27 cm. "First published in 1948." Bibliography: p. [293]-310. [N6843.E8 1969] 70-430545 8/10/-
1. Art, Medieval—France. 2. Art—France. I. Title.

KRAUS, Henry, 1905- 709'.44
The living theatre of medieval art. Foreword by Harry Bober. Bloomington, Indiana University Press [1967] xxi, 248 p. illus., map. 26 cm. Bibliography: p. 223-237. [N6843.K7] 67-24004
1. Art, Medieval—France. 2. Art, French—History. 3. Art and society. I. Title.

WIXOM, William D. 709'.44
Treasures from medieval France, by William D. Wixom. [Cleveland] Cleveland Museum of Art [1967] xxi, 394 p. plates (part col.) 25 cm. Exhibition held at the Cleveland Museum of Art as part of the 1966-67 fiftieth anniversary celebrations. "Catalogue [of the exhibition]": p. 347-386. Includes bibliographical references. [N6843.W5] 66-21229
1. Art, Medieval—France. 2. Art, French—Exhibitions. I. Cleveland Museum of Art. II. Title.

Art, Medieval—History.

BECKWITH, John, 1918- 709.02
Early medieval art. New York, Praeger [1964] 270 p. illus. (part col.) map, plans. 22 cm. (Praeger world of art series) Bibliography: p. 264-265. [N5970.B4] 64-19953
1. Art, Medieval—History. I. Title.

HUYGHE, Rene, ed. 709.02
Larousse encyclopedia of Byzantine and medieval art. New York, Prometheus Press [1963] 416 p. illus., col. plates, ports., maps, plans. 30 cm. At head of title: Art and mankind. "Translated by Dennis Gilbert, Ilse Schreier and Wendela Schurmann from [v. 2 of] the French original: L'art et l'homme." [N5970.H813] 63-12755
1. Art, Medieval—History. 2. Art, Byzantine—History. 3. Art—History. I. Title. II. Title: Art and mankind.

ZARNECKI, George. 709'.02
Art of the medieval world : architecture, sculpture, painting, the sacred arts / George Zarnecki. Englewood Cliffs, N.J. : Prentice-Hall, 1975. 476 p. : ill. (some col.) ; 31 cm. (Library of art history) Includes index. Bibliography: p. [462]-467. [N9570.Z37 1975b] 75-25576 ISBN 0-8109-0361-X : 28.50
1. Art, Medieval—History. I. Title. **BIP**

ZARNECKI, George. 709'.02
Art of the medieval world, architecture, sculpture, painting, the sacred arts / George Zarnecki. New York : H. N. Abrams, [1975] p. cm. Includes index. Bibliography: p. [N5970.Z37] 75-6531 ISBN 0-13-047514-9 : 28.50
1. Art, Medieval—History. I. Title.

Art, Medieval—History—Sources.

DAVIS-WEYER, Caecilia, 709.02
comp.
Early medieval art, 300-1150; sources and documents [compiled by] Caecilia Davis-Weyer. Englewood Cliffs, N.J., Prentice-Hall [1971] x, 182 p. front. 23 cm. (Sources and documents in the history of art series) Includes bibliographical references. [N5975.D3] 70-135404 ISBN 0-13-222364-3
1. Art, Medieval—History—Sources. I. Title. II. Series.

Art, Medieval—Spain.

PALOL Salellas, Pedro de. 709.46
Early medieval art in Spain; text by Pedro de Palol and Max Hirmer. Photos. by Max Hirmer. New York, H. N. Abrams [1967] 500 p. illus. (part col.), geneal. tables, maps, plans. 32 cm. Translation of Spanien: Kunst des fruhen Mittelalters. Includes bibliographical references. [N7103.P2813 1967b] 66-26609
1. Art, Medieval—Spain. 2. Art, Spanish—History. I. Hirmer, Max, joint author. II. Title.

PALOL SALELLAS, Pedro de. 709.46
Early medieval art in Spain; text by Pedro de Palol and Max Hirmer. Photos. by Max Hirmer. New York, N. Abrams [1967] 500 p. illus. (part col.), geneal. tables, maps, plans. 32 cm. Translation of Spanlen: Kunst des fruhen Mittelalters. Includes bibliographical references. [N7103.P2813] 66-26609
1. Art, Medieval—Spain. 2. Art, Spanish—Hist. I. Hirmer, Max, joint author. II. Title.

Art, Medieval—Themes, motives.

PARKER, Elizabeth C. 700
The descent from the cross : its relation to the extra-liturgical "depositio" drama / Elizabeth C. Parker. New York : Garland Pub., 1978. p. cm. (Outstanding dissertations in the fine arts) Bibliography: p. [N8053.2.P37] 77-94713 ISBN 0-8240-3245-4 : lib.bdg. : 28.50
1. Jesus Christ—Art. 2. Art, Medieval—Themes, motives. 3. Drama, Medieval—History and criticism. 4. Liturgical drama. I. Title. II. Series.

Art, Melanesian—Exhibitions.

CALIFORNIA. University, 759.993
Irvine. Art Gallery.
Melanesian art. [Pasadena, Calif., Geddes Press, Printers, 1967?] 53 p. illus., maps (on lining papers) 24 cm. Stamped on t.p.: Worldwide Books, inc., New York. Catalog of an exhibition held Oct. 17 to Nov. 12, 1967, at the Art Gallery, University of California, Irvine, and Nov. 23, 1967 to Jan. 6, 1968, at the Art Gallery, University of California, Davis. Bibliography: p. 53. [N7411.M4C2] 68-63946
1. Art, Melanesian—Exhibitions. I. California. University, Davis. Art Gallery. II. Title. **BIP**

Art—Melbourne—Catalogs.

HOFF, Ursula. 708'.9945
The National Gallery of Victoria; with an introd. by Eric Westbrook. London, Thames and Hudson [1973, i.e.1974] 216 p. illus. 22 cm. [N3948.H62 1973] 73-180557 ISBN 0-500-18139-X
1. Victoria, Australia. National Gallery, Melbourne. 2. Art—Melbourne—Catalogs. I. Title.
Distributed by Transatlantic Arts, 11.00; 5.95 (pbk.)

Art, Mende—Exhibitions.

HOMMEL, William L. 732'.2
Art of the Mende. Catalogue by William L. Hommel. [College Park] University of Maryland Art Gallery [1974] [48] p. illus. 22 x 26 cm. Catalogue of an exhibition to be held at the University of Maryland Art Gallery and other galleries and museums, March-Oct. 1974. Bibliography: p. [44] [N7399.S5H64] 74-77367
1. Art, Mende—Exhibitions. I. Maryland. University. Art Gallery. II. Title.

Art—Mesopotamia.

MOORTGAT, Anton, 1897- 709'.35
The art of ancient Mesopotamia; the classical art of the Near East. [Translated

by Judith Filson] London, New York, Phaidon [1969] x, 356 p. illus., map, plans. 26 cm. Translation of Die Kunst des alten Mesopotamien. Bibliographical references included in "Notes" (p. [329]-340) [N5370.M6613] 69-12789 18.50
1. Art—Mesopotamia. I. Title.

Art—Mesopotamia—History.

GOFF, Beatrice Laura 709.35
Symbols of prehistoric Mesopotamia. New Haven, Conn., Yale [c.]1963. xliii, 276p. plates, fold. map. 29cm. Bibl. 62-8247 25.00
1. Art—Mesopotamia—Hist. 2. Symbolism in art. 3. Mesopotamia—Religion. I. Title.

Art—Mesopotamia—History.

MARGUERON, Jean Claude. 913.35
Mesopotamia. English translation by H. S. B. Harrison. Cleveland, World Pub. Co. [1965] 211 p. maps (on lining papers) 130 plates (part fold. col.) 24 cm. (Archaeologia mvndi) Bibliography: p. 203-204. [N5370.M373] 65-25783
1. Art—Mesopotamia—History. 2. Mesopotamia—Antiquities. I. Title. II. Series: Archaeologia mundi. [English ed.]

STROMMENGER, Eva. 709.35
5000 years of the art of Mesopotamia. Photos. by Max Hirmer. Translated by Christina Heglund. New York, H. N. Abrams [1964] 480 p. illus., maps (1 fold.) 44 col. plates. 32 cm. Translation of Funf Jahrtausende Mesopotamien. Bibliography: p. 465-469. [N5370.S713] 64-15231
1. Art—Mesopotamia—History. I. Hirmer, Max. II. Title. III. Title: Art of Mesopotamia.

Art metal-work.

BRAUN FELDWEG, Wilhelm 739
Metal; design and technique. New York, Van Nostrand Reinhold, [1975] 296 p., illus. 29 cm. Translation of Metall; Werkformen und Arbeitsweisen. Bibliography, p. 287-288. [NK6404.B7213] 74-14001 ISBN 0-442-21039-6 27.50
1. Art metal-work. I. Title. BIP

BRIDGE, Paul. 739
Designs in metal / Paul Bridge and Austin Crossland. New York : Scribner, [1975] c1966. 96 p. : ill. ; 21 cm. [NK6405.B7 1975] 74-10234 ISBN 0-684-14103-5 : 6.95
1. Art metal-work. I. Crossland, Austin, joint author. II. Title.

BRIDGE, Paul 739
Designs in metal. by Paul Bridge, Austin Crossland. London, Batsford. 1966. 83p. illus., diagrs. 22cm. Bibl. [NK6405.B7] 66-71880 8.00 bds.,
1. Art metalwork. I. Crossland, Austin, joint author. II. Title.
Available from SportShelf, New Rochelle, N.Y.

GEERLINGS, Gerald Kenneth, 739'.5
1897-
Metal crafts in architecture; bronze, brass, cast iron, copper, lead, lighting fixtures, tin, specifications [by] Gerald K. Geerlings. New York, Scribner [1971, c1929] vi, 202 p. illus. 31 cm. Subtitle varies slightly. Bibliography: p. 199. [NK6404.G4 1971] 73-31868
1. Art metal-work. 2. Architectural metal-work. 3. Decoration and ornament, Architectural. I. Title.

GLASS, Frederick James, 745.56
1881-1930.
Metal craft. London, University of London Press, 1928. [Kentfield, Calif., N. K. Gregg, 1971] viii, 70 p. illus. 19 cm. (Gregg series of reprints on crafts and hobbies) Original ed. issued in the author's series: The artistic, practical handicraft series. [TT205.G63 1971] 75-163529 ISBN 0-912318-05-8
1. Art metal-work. I. Title. BIP

GRUBER, Elmar. 739
Metal & wire sculpture. [Translated by Gangolf Geis] New York, Sterling Pub. Co. [1969] 48 p. illus. 20 x 20 cm. (Little craft book series) Translation of Arbeiten aus Buntmetall. [TT205.G813] 69-19489 ISBN 0-8069-5128-1 2.95
1. Art metal-work. 2. Metal-work—Amateurs' manuals. 3. Wire craft. I. Title. BIP

GRUBER, Elmar. 739
Metal & wire sculpture. New York, Sterling Pub. Co. [1973] 48 p. illus. 20 cm. (Little craft book series) Translation of Arbeiten aus Buntmetall. [TT205.G813 1973] 73-168399 ISBN 0-8069-5128-1 3.50
1. Art metal-work. 2. Metal-work—Amateurs' manuals. 3. Wire craft. I. Title.
Library binding, 3.29

HAWKINS, Leslie V. 739
Art metal and enameling [by] Leslie V. Hawkins. Peoria, Ill., C. A. Bennett Co. [1967] 234 p. illus. (part col.) 24 cm. Bibliography: p. 226. [TT205.H28] 67-10594
1. Art metal-work. 2. Enamel and enameling. I. Title. BIP

HAWKINS, Leslie V. 739'.1
Art metal and enameling [by] Leslie V. Hawkins. Rev. Peoria, Ill., C. A. Bennett [1974] 236 p. illus. (part col.) 24 cm. Bibliography: p. 227. [TT205.H28 1974] 74-164328 ISBN 0-87002-157-5 8.00
1. Art metal-work. 2. Enamel and enameling. I. Title.

KRONQUIST, Emil Fritjoff, 739
1882-
Metalwork for craftsmen; a step by step guide with 55 projects [by] Emil F. Kronquist. New York, Dover Publications [1972] ix, 202 p. illus. 22 cm. 1942 ed. published under title: Art metalwork. [TT205.K7 1972] 78-160856 ISBN 0-486-22789-8 2.50
1. Art metal-work. I. Title. BIP

LARKMAN, Brian 745.56
Contemporary design in metalwork [by] Brian Larkman, with S. H. Glenister. London, Murray [Holly-wood-by-the-Sea, Fla., Transatlantic, 1964, c.1963] vii, 119p. illus. 26cm. 64-3190 6.75 bds.,
1. Art metal-work. I. Title.

MARYON, Herbert. 739.2
Metalwork and enamelling; a practical treatise on gold and silversmiths' work and their allied crafts. 3d ed., rev. New York, Dover Publications, 1955. 331 p. illus. 23 cm. [TS725.M3 1955] 55-12632
1. Art metal-work. 2. Enamel and enamelling. 3. Goldsmithing. 4. Silversmithing. BIP

MARYON, Herbert. 739.2
Metalwork and enamelling; a practical treatise on gold and silversmiths' work and their allied crafts. Line drawings by Cyril Pearce. 5th rev. ed. New York, Dover Publications [1971] xii, 335 p. illus., plates. 22 cm. Bibliography: p. 318. [TS725.M3 1971] 76-130881 ISBN 0-486-22702-2 3.50
1. Art metal-work. 2. Enamel and enameling. 3. Goldsmithing. 4. Silversmithing. I. Title.

MILLER, John Guthrie, 745.56
1912-
Metal art crafts. 2d ed. Princeton, N.J., Van Nostrand [1962] 165p. illus. 22cm. 62-51743 4.95; 4.00 text ed.,
1. Art metal-work. I. Title.

*MORGENSTERN, Steven, 745.56
comp.
Metal crafting encyclopedia, compiled and edited by Steven Morgenstern. New York, Sterling, [1975] 208 p. ill. 26 cm. Includes index. [NK.6404] 75-14518 ISBN 0-8069-5336-5 12.95.
1. Art metal—Work. I. Title.
Lib. bdg. 11.29, ISBN 0-8069-5337-3. BIP

MUSEE Le Secq des 739'.4
Tournelles.
Decorative antique ironwork: a pictorial treasure, by Henry Rene d'Allemagne. Introd., bibliography, and translation of captions by Vera K. Ostoia. New York, Dover Publications [1968] x, 415 p. (chiefly illus.) 31 cm. (Dover pictorial archive series) "This Dover edition ... is a republication of all the plates in the two portfolios of Musee Le Secq des Tournelles a Rouen: Ferronnerie ancienne, originally published ... in 1924." "Other books by Henry Rene d'Allemagne": p. x. [NK6405.M813] 67-20193
1. Art metal-work. I. Allemagne, Henry Rene d', 1863-1950. II. Ostoia, Vera K. III. Title. IV. Series. BIP

SJOBERG, Jan. 739
Working with copper, silver, and enamel [by] Jan Sjoberg and Ove Sjoberg. New York, Van Nostrand Reinhold Co. [1974] (Reinhold craft paperbacks) Translation of Gor vackra ting av koppar, silver, emalj. [TT205.S5613] 73-16713 ISBN 0-442-30034-4 5.50
1. Art metal-work. 2. Jewelry making—Amateurs' manuals. 3. Enamel and enameling. I. Sjoberg, Ove, joint author. II. Title.
Pbk. 2.95; ISBN 0-442-30035-2.

ULLRICH, Heinz. 739
Creative metal design [by] Heinz Ullrich & Dieter Klante. New York, Reinhold Book Corp. [1968, c1967] 120 p. illus. 22 cm. (Creative play series, 8) Shows designs and projects made from metal wire, woven metal fabric, and metal foil. Many designs can be made by hand while other techniques include hammering, embossing, chasing, and soldering. [NK6535.U45] AC 68
1. Art metalwork. I. Klante, Dieter, joint author. II. Title.

UNTRACHT, Oppi. 739.15
Enameling on metal. Photos. by the author unless otherwise indicated. New York, Greenberg [1957] 191 p. illus. 27 cm. (Arts and crafts series) [NK6510.U5] 57-11904
1. Art metal-work. 2. Enamel and enameling. I. Title. BIP

UNTRACHT, Oppi. 739
Metal techniques for craftsmen; a basic manual for craftsmen on the methods of forming and decorating metals. [1st ed.] Garden City, N.Y., Doubleday [1968] xiv, 509 p. illus. 27 cm. Bibliography: p. 487-490. [TT205.U55] 65-16397
1. Art metal-work. I. Title. BIP

Art metal-work, American—Exhibitions.

FINCH College, New 739'.0973
York. Museum of Art.
Forms in metal : 275 years of metalsmithing in America, January 17-March 2, 1975 : 1700-1940's, Finch College Museum of Art, New York, N.Y., 1940's-1975, Museum of Contemporary Crafts of the American Crafts Council, New York, N.Y. New York : Museum of Contemporary Crafts of the American Crafts Council, 1975. 36 p. : ill. ; 22 cm. "This catalogue is co-sponsored by Cranbrook Academy of Art, Bloomfield Hills, Michigan where Forms in metal will be exhibited from March 16 through April 20, 1975." Bibliography: p. 34. [NK6412.F56 1975] 74-33197 ISBN 0-8150-0753-1 pbk. : 5.00
1. Art metal-work, American—Exhibitions. I. American Crafts Council. Museum of Contemporary Crafts. II. Cranbrook Academy of Art, Bloomfield Hills, Mich. III. Title.
Distributed by George Wittenborn.

Art metal-work, Anglo-Saxon—Catalogs.

OXFORD. 739.2'074'02572
University. Ashmolean Museum. Dept. of Antiquities.
A catalogue of the Anglo-Saxon ornamental metalwork, 700-1100 in the Department of Antiquities, Ashmolean Museum, by David A. Hinton. Oxford [Eng.] Clarendon Press, 1974. xii, 81 p. illus., 20 p. of plates. 28 cm. Bibliography: p. 71-76. [NK6408.O94 1974] 74-177284 ISBN 0-19-813187-9
1. Art metal-work, Anglo-Saxon—Catalogs. 2. Art metal-work—Oxford—Catalogs. I. Hinton, David Alban. II. Title.
Distributed by Oxford University Press, New York; 30.50. BIP

Art metal-work—Collectors and collecting.

PERRY, Evan. 739'.075
Collecting antique metalware. Garden City, N.Y., Doubleday [1974] 191 p. illus. (part col.) 27 cm. Bibliography: p. 187. [NK6404.P47] 73-19293 ISBN 0-385-05197-2 14.95
1. Art metal-work—Collectors and collecting. I. Title.

Art metal-work, English.

LINDSAY, John Seymour. 739.4742
Iron and brass implements of the English and American house [by] J. Seymour Lindsay. Illustrated by the author. With an introd. by Ralph Edwards. [Rev. and enl. ed.] Bass River, Mass., C. Jacobs [1964] vii, 88 p. 473 illus. 26 cm. Place of publication corrected in MS.: Deep River, Conn. First published in 1927. The English ed. had title: Iron & brass implements of the English house. The American ed. had title: Iron & brass implements of the English and American home. [NK6443.L5 1964] 64-4104
1. Art metal-work, English. 2. Art metal-work, American. 3. Implements, utensils, etc.—England. 4. Implements, utensils, etc.—U.S. I. Title. BIP

Art metal-work, Georgian.

AMIRANASHVILI, 739'.0947'95
Shalva IAsonovich, 1899-
Georgian metalwork, from antiquity to the 18th century; text by Shalva Amiranashvili [translated from the Russian MS. by Philippa Hentges] and photography by Karel Neubert. London, New York, Hamlyn, 1971. 175 p. (chiefly col. illus.). 29 cm. Bibliography: p. 173. [NK6475.7.G4A8] 72-179314 ISBN 0-600-10018-9 £4.00
1. Art metal-work, Georgian. 2. Icons, Georgian. I. Neubert, Karel. II. Title.

Art metal-work—History.

HAEDEKE, Hanns Ulrich. 739'.09
Metalwork. Translated by Vivienne Menkes. New York, Universe Books [1970, c1969] 227 p. plates (part col.) 24 cm. (The Universe social history of the decorative arts) Bibliography: p. 213-218. [NK6406.H313] 75-90382 17.50
1. Art metal-work—History. I. Title.

Art metal-work—Illinois—Chicago—History.

DARLING, Sharon S. 739.2'09773'11
Chicago metalsmiths : an illustrated history / by Sharon S. Darling, in association with Gail Farr Casterline ; photos. by Walter W. Krutz. Chicago : Chicago Historical Society, 1977. xvi, 141 p. : ill. ; 23 cm. Includes index. Bibliography: p. 137-138. [NK6412.D37] 77-76503 ISBN 0-913820-06-7 : 12.95
1. Art metal-work—Illinois—Chicago—History. 2. Art metal-workers—Illinois—Chicago. I. Casterline, Gail Farr, joint author. II. Title. BIP

Art metal-work—Iran—Exhibitions.

VICTORIA 739'.512'095507402134
and Albert Museum, South Kensington.
Islamic metalwork from Iranian lands (8th-18th centuries) / Victoria and Albert Museum, exhibition, April-May 1976 ; A. S. Melikian-Chirvani. [s.l.] : Crown, c1976. 19 p. : ill. ; 21 cm. Includes bibliographical references. [NK6474.A1V5 1976] 77-369605
1. Art metal-work—Iran—Exhibitions. 2. Art metal-work, Islamic—Iran—Exhibitions. I. Melikian-Chirvani, Assadullah Souren. II. Title.

Art metal-work, Islamic—Catalogs.

FEHERVARI, Geza.
Islamic metalwork of the eighth to the fifteenth century in the Keir Collection / Geza Fehervari ; with a foreword by Ralph Pinder-Wilson. London : Faber and Faber, 1976, i.e. 1977 143 p., [36] leaves of plates : ill. (some col.) ; 29 cm. (The Keir Collection) Bibliography: p. [19]-20. [NK6408.9.F44 1976] 76-376866 ISBN 0-571-09740-5 : 62.50
1. De Unger, Edmund—Art collections. 2.

SUBJECT INDEX ART, MODERN—19TH CENTURY.

Art metal-work, Islamic—Catalogs. I. Title. II. Series.
Distributed by Faber and Faber, Salem, NH

Art metal-work—Juvenile literature.

ULLRICH, Heinz. 739'.14
Creative metal design [by] Heinz Ullrich & Dieter Klante. New York, Reinhold Book Corp. [1968, c1967] 120 p. illus. 22 cm. ([Creative play series, 8]) [NK6535.U45] 68-20402
1. Art metal-work—Juvenile literature. I. Klante, Dieter, joint author. II. Title.

Art metal-work, Romanesque—Exhibitions.

A Medieval miscellany, 734'.24
Romanesque and early Gothic metalwork : an exhibition on the occasion of the 1974 annual meetings of the Medieval Association of the Pacific / a faculty-graduate student project ; sponsored by the Committee on Medieval Studies and the Art Galleries, University of California, Santa Barbara, 14-28 February 1974. Santa Barbara : Art Galleries, University of California, [1974] 39 p. : ill. ; 26 cm. Bibliography: p. 36-39. [NK6408.M42] 73-620252
1. Art metal-work, Romanesque—Exhibitions. 2. Art metal-work, Gothic—Exhibitions. I. Medieval Association of the Pacific. II. California. University, Santa Barbara. Committee on Medieval Studies.

Art metal work—Study and teaching.

BIZLEWICZ, George. 739
Industrial arts: art metal, teacher's guide. New Brunswick, N. J., Vocational Division, Curriculum Laboratory, 1960. 87 p. illus. 28 cm. Cover title: Industrial arts: guide to teaching art metal. Bibliography: p. 87. [NK6404.B58] A61
1. Art metal work—Study and teaching. I. New Jersey. Division of Vocational Education. Curriculum Laboratory, New Brunswick. II. Title. III. Title: Industrial arts: guide to teaching art metal.

Art—Meuse Valley.

COLLON-GEVAERT, Suzanne. 709'.02'1
A treasury of Romanesque art; metalwork, illuminations and sculpture from the valley of the Meuse [by] Suzanne Collon-Gevaert, Jean Lejeune [and] Jacques Stiennon. Foreword and introd. by Germaine Faider-Feytmans. Translated by Susan Waterston. [New York] Phaidon; [distributed by Praeger, 1972] 327 p. illus. (part col.) 31 cm. Translation of Art roman dans la vallee de la Meuse aux XIe, XIIe et XIIIe siecles. Bibliography: p. 309-316. [N6969.M4C59513] 76-161220 ISBN 0-7148-1421-0 50.00
1. Art—Meuse Valley. 2. Art, Romanesque—Meuse Valley. I. Lejeune, Jean, joint author. II. Stiennon, Jacques, joint author. III. Title.

Art, Mexican.

ROJAS Rodriguez, Pedro Mario. 709'.72
The art and architecture of Mexico: from 10,000 B.C. to the present day, by Pedro Rojas;translated from the Spanish manuscript by J. M. Cohen Feltham, Hamlyn, 1968. 3-71 p., 146 illus. (42 col.), 2 maps. 28 cm. Illus. on lining papers. [N6550.R6] 79-379618 50/-
1. Art, Mexican. 2. Architecture—Mexico. I. Title.

SCHMECKEBIER, Laurence Eli, 1906- 709'.72
Modern Mexican art [by] Laurence E. Schmeckebier. Westport, Conn., Greenwood Press [1971, c1939] xvii, 190 p. 216 plates. 27 cm. Bibliography: p. 181-183. [N6555.S3 1971] 70-141418 ISBN 0-8371-4692-5
1. Art, Mexican. 2. Art, Modern—20th century—Mexico. I. Title. BIP

SMITH, Bradley. 709'.72
Mexico a history of art New York, Harper & Row, 1968. 296 p. col. illus., maps. 33 cm. (A Gemini Smith book) Bibliography: p. 294-295. [N6550.S6] 68-28219 24.95
1. Art, Mexican. I. Title.

Art, Mexican American.

QUIRARTE, Jacinto, 1931- 709'.79
Mexican American artists. Austin, University of Texas Press [1973] xxv, 149 p. illus. 29 cm. (The John Fielding and Lois Lasater Maher series, no. 2) Bibliography: p. [139]-141. [N6538.M4Q57] 72-10925 ISBN 0-292-75006-4 12.50
1. Art, Mexican American. 2. Art, Modern—20th century—Southwest, New. 3. Artists, Mexican American. I. Title. II. Series. BIP

Art, Mexican— Exhibitions.

LOS Angeles Co., Calif. Museum of Art, Los Angeles. 709'.72
Masterworks of Mexican art, from pre-Columbian times to the present. [Los Angeles? c1963] xvii, 296 p. illus., maps. 24 cm. Catalogue of an exhibition, sponsored by Adolfo Lopez Mateos and John F. Kennedy, held at the Los Angeles County Museum of Art, Oct. 1963-Jan. 1964. Text by F. Gamboa, director of the exhibition. Bibliography: p. 292-296. [N6550.L6] 66-57727
1. Art, Mexican — Exhibitions. 2. Indians of Mexico — Art. 3. Mexico — Antiq. I. Gamboa, Fernando, 1909- II. Title.

MICHIGAN. University. 709.72
Mexican art; pre-Columbian to modern times; [exhibition held at] University of Michigan, Ann Arbor, State University of Iowa, Iowa City, Joslyn Art Museum, Omaha, Nebraska, Indiana University, Bloomington, The Columbus Gallery of Fine Arts, Columbus, Ohio, Syracuse University, Syracuse, New York, Dallas Museum of Fine Arts, Dallas, Texas, 1958-1959. [Ann Arbor] 1958. 55p. illus. 28cm. [N6550.M52] 58-63069
1. Art, Mexican— Exhibitions. I. Title.

NEW York (City). Museum of Modern Art. 709'.72'07401471
Twenty centuries of Mexican art. [New York] Published for the Museum of Modern Art by Arno Press, 1972 [c1940] 198 p. illus. 27 cm. Catalog of an exhibition at the Museum in 1940, held in collaboration with the Mexican Government. Added t.p. in Spanish: Veinte siglos de arte mexicano. Text in English and Spanish. Bibliography: p. 197-[199] [N6550.N4 1972] 79-169322 ISBN 0-405-01580-1 23.00
1. Art, Mexican—Exhibitions. 2. Art—Mexico. 3. Mexico—Antiquities. 4. Indians of Mexico—Art. 5. Artists, Mexican. I. Title. II. Title: Veinte siglos de arte mexicano. BIP

PHOENIX, Ariz. Art Museum. 709'.72
Contemporary Mexican artists. [Catalog of the exhibition, Dec. 12, 1964-Feb. 15, 1965. Phoenix, Printed by Lebeau Print., 1964?] 35 p. illus. 26 cm. [N6555.P53 1964] 74-175145
1. Art, Mexican—Exhibitions. 2. Art, Modern—20th century—Mexico. I. Title.

Art, Mexican—History.

CHARLOT, Jean, 1898- 709.72
Mexican art and the Academy of San Carlos, 1785-1915. Foreword by Elizabeth Wilder Weismann. Austin, University of Texas Press [1962] 177p. illus. 24cm. (The Texas Pan-American series) [N6554.C45] 61-13318
1. Art, Mexican- Hist. 2. Academia Naclonal de Sau Carlos, Mexico. I. Title. BIP

CHARLOT, Jean [Louis Henri Jean Charlot] 1898- 709.72
Mexican art and the Academy of San Carlos, 1785-1915. Foreword by Elizabeth Wilder Weismann. Austin, Univ. of Tex. Pr. [c.1962] 177p. illus. 24cm. (Tex. Pan-Amer. ser.) Bibl. 61-13318 4.50
1. Art, Mexican—Hist. 2. Academia Nacional de San Carlos, Mexico. I. Title.

TOUSSAINT, Manuel, 1895-1955. 709'.72
Colonial art in Mexico. Translated and edited by Elizabeth Wilder Weismann. Austin, University of Texas Press [1967] xxvi, 493 p. illus. (part col.), facsims., ports. 29 cm. (The Texas pan American series) Bibliography: p. 461-476. [N6553.T6813] 66-15696
1. Art, Mexican—Hist. I. Title.

Art, Mexican—History.

BURCHWOOD, Katharine Tyler, 1891- 709'.72
The origin and legacy of Mexican art. South Brunswick, A. S. Barnes [1972, c1971] 159 p. illus. 29 cm. Bibliography: p. 153-154. [N6550.B8] 71-146748 ISBN 0-498-07840-X 12.50
1. Art, Mexican—History. I. Title.

FERNANDEZ, Justino, 1904- 709.72
A guide to Mexican art, from its beginnings to the present. Translated by Joshua C. Taylor. Chicago, University of Chicago Press [1969] xvii, 398 p. 183 illus. 21 cm. Translated from Arte mexicano de sus origenes a nuestros dias, 2d ed., with additions by the author. Includes bibliographies. [N6550.F413] 69-16773
1. Art, Mexican—History. I. Title. BIP

Art—Mexico.

BRENNER, Anita, 1905- 709'.72
Idols behind altars. New York, Biblo and Tannen, 1967. 359 p. illus. 24 cm. Reprint of the 1929 ed. Bibliography: p. 353-354. [N6550.B7 1967] 67-19527
*1. Art—Mexico. 2. Mexico—Antiquities. 3. Indians of Mexico—Religion and mythology. 4. Artists, Mexican. I. Title.*BIP

Art — Minnesota — Hist.

TORBERT, Donald R 709.776
A century of art and architecture in Minnesota. Minneapolis, University of Minnesota Press [1958] 62 p. illus. 22 cm. (A History of the arts in Minnesota) [N6530.M6T6] 58-63623
1. Art — Minnesota — Hist. 2. Architecture — Minnesota — Hist. I. Title. II. Series.

Art, Modern.

*NEWMEYER, Sarah 709.035
Enjoying modern art [Reissue. New York] New Amer. Lib. [1965, c.1955] 240p. illus. 18cm. (Mentor bk., MP389) .60 pap.,
1. Art, Modern. I. Title.

PEVSNER, Nikolaus, 1902- 709.03
Studies in art, architecture, and design. New York, Walker [1968] 2 v. illus., plans. 30 cm. Contents.Contents.—v. 1. From mannerism to romanticism.—v. 2. Victorian and after. Includes bibliographical references. [N6350.P4 1968b] 68-27371 15.00 per vol.
1. Art, Modern. I. Title. BIP

RODMAN, Selden, 1909- 759.03
The eye of man; form and content in Western painting. New York, Devin-Adair, 1955. 181p. illus. 26cm. [N6350.R6] 750.903 55-10833
1. Art, Modern. 2. Painting. I. Title. BIP

SOLOMON, Frederick, 1899- 709.04
Critique of modern art. [Nashua, N.H.] Nathaniel Hawthorne College Press [1970] 222 p. illus. (part col.) 24 cm. [N6350.S6] 77-135052
1. Art, Modern. I. Title. BIP

Art, Modern—17th-18th centuries.

MOIR, Alfred. 760
Caravaggio and his copyists / by Alfred Moir. New York : New York University Press, 1976. p. cm. Bibliography: p. [N6407.M64] 75-27051 ISBN 0-8147-5408-2 : 22.50
1. Caravaggio, Michelangelo Merisi da, 1573-1610—Influence. 2. Art, Modern—17th-18th centuries. 3. Art, Modern—19th century. 4. Pictures—Copying. 5. Art—Attribution. I. Title. BIP

RUSKIN, Ariane. 709'.4
17th & 18th century art. Foreward by Howard Conant. New York, McGraw-Hill [1969] 191 p. col. illus. 31 cm. (Discovering art series) Bibliographical footnotes. [N6407.R87] 69-17190 8.95
1. Art, Modern—17th-18th centuries. I. Title.

STINSON, Robert E. 709'.4
Seventeenth-and eighteenth-century art; an introduction to baroque and rococo art in Europe from A. D. 1600 to A. D. 1800 [by] Robert E. Stinson. Dubuque, Iowa, W. C. Brown Co. [1969] viii, 149 p. illus. 23 cm. (Studies in art series) Bibliography: p. 143-144. [N6410.S83] 68-14580
1. Art, Modern—17th-18th centuries. I. Title.

Art, Modern—17th-18th centuries—Central Europe.

SOBOTIK, Kent. 709'.43'074015961
Central Europe, 1600-1800. Pref. by Curtis G. Coley. Introd. and catalog by Kent Sobotik. [Sarasota, Fla.] John & Mable Ringling Museum of Art, 1972. 80 p. illus. 26 cm. Catalog of an exhibition held Jan. 27-Feb. 27, 1972. [N6756.S6] 72-198147
1. Art, Modern—17th-18th centuries—Central Europe. 2. Art, European—Exhibitions. I. John and Mable Ringling Museum of Art, Sarasota, Fla. II. Title.

Art, Modern—17th-18th centuries—Exhibitions.

DEN Broeder, Frederick. 709'.45
The academy of Europe: Rome in the 18th century [catalogue of exhibition October 13-November 21, 1973. the William Benton Museum of Art, the University of Connecticut [Storrs, University of Connecticut Foundation, 1973] 168 p. illus. 23 cm. Includes bibliographical references. [N6920.D46] 73-89332
1. Art, Modern—17th-18th centuries—Exhibitions. 2. Art, Modern—17th-18th centuries—Rome (City) I. William Benton Museum of Art. II. Title. III. Title: Rome in the 18th century.

Art, Modern—19th century.

BOWNESS, Alan. 759.94
Modern European art. With 207 illus. [New York] Harcourt, Brace, Jovanovich [1972] 224 p. illus. (part col.) 21 cm. (The Harbrace history of art) Bibliography: p. 217-220. [N6447.B68 1972] 77-183243 ISBN 0-15-161000-2
1. Art, Modern—19th century. 2. Art, Modern—20th century. I. Title. BIP

CANADAY, John Edwin, 1907- 709.035
Mainstreams of modern art. New York, Holt [1959] xxiv, 576 p. 700 illus., 15 col. plates. 26 cm. [N6450.C33] 59-8693
1. Art, Modern—19th century. 2. Art, Modern—20th century. 3. Art—France—History. I. Title. BIP

CRAVEN, Thomas, 1889- 709'.04
Modern art; the men, the movements, the meaning. New York, Simon and Schuster, 1934. St. Clair Shores, Mich., Scholarly Press, 1974. p. cm. [N6447.C72 1974] 74-3183 ISBN 0-403-03081-1
1. Art, Modern—19th century. 2. Art, Modern—20th century. 3. Artists—Psychology. I. Title.

GALLOWAY, John Crozier. 709
Modern art: the nineteenth and twentieth centuries, by John Galloway. Dubuque, Iowa, W. C. Brown Co. [1967] viii, 149 p. illus. 23 cm. (Art horizons series) Bibliography: p. 131-139. [N6450.G26] 67-22713
1. Art, Modern—19th century. 2. Art, Modern—20th century. I. Title.

HAMILTON, George Heard. 709.04
19th and 20th century art: painting, sculpture, architecture New York, H. N. Abrams [1970] 483 p. illus. (part col.), ports. (part col.) 30 cm. (Library of art history) Bibliography: p. 459-[464] [N6450.H29] 70-100401
1. Art, Modern—19th century. 2. Art, Modern—20th century. I. Title.

HOLT, Elizabeth Basye Gilmore. 709'.034
The triumph of art for the public : the emerging role of exhibitions and critics / selected and edited by Elizabeth Gilmore Holt. 1st ed. Garden City, N.Y. : Anchor Press, 1979. xxviii, 530 p., [16] leaves of plates : ill. ; 18 cm. Includes index. Bibliography: p. [503]-505. [N6450.H62] 77-27708 ISBN 0-385-13511-4 : 5.95
1. Art, Modern—19th century. 2. Art—Exhibitions. 3. Art—Exhibition audiences. 4. Art criticism. I. Title. BIP

HUNTER, Sam, 1923- 709'.04
Modern art from post-impressionism to the present : painting, sculpture, architecture / Sam Hunter, John Jacobus. 1st ed. New York : H. N. Abrams, in association with Alexis Gregory, c1976. 351 p. : ill. (some col.) ; 33 cm. Includes index. Bibliography: p. 341-347. [N6447.H86] 76-14611 ISBN 0-8109-1616-9 : 40.00
1. Art, Modern—19th century. 2. Art, Modern—20th century. I. Jacobus, John M., joint author. II. Title.

HUYGHE, Rene. 709.034
Larousse encyclopedia of modern art from 1800 to the present day New York, Prometheus Press [1965] 444 p. illus. (part col.) 30 cm. At head of title: Art and mankind. "English text prepared by Emily Evershed, Dennis Gilbert, Hugh Newbury, Ralph de Saram, Richard Waterhouse and Katherine Watson from the French original L'art et l'homme." [N6450.H813] 65-19759
1. Art, Modern—19th century. 2. Art, Modern—20th century. I. Title. II. Title: Art and mankind.

JOHNSON, Ellen H. 709'.04
Modern art and the object : a century of changing attitudes / Ellen H. Johnson. London : Thames and Hudson, c1976. 240 p. : 109 ill. ; 25 cm. Includes bibliographical references and index. [N6447.J64] 77-357529 ISBN 0-500-23230-X : £9.50
1. Art, Modern—19th century. 2. Art, Modern—20th century. 3. Art—Psychology. 4. Attitude change. I. Title. BIP

†JOHNSON, Ellen H. 709'.04
Modern art and the object : a century of changing attitudes / Ellen H. Johnson. New York : Harper & Row, 1977, c1976 240 p. : 109 ill. ; 24 cm. (Icon editions) Includes bibliographical references and index. [N6447.J64 1976a] 76-20394 ISBN 0-06-430084-6 : 7.95
1. Art, Modern—19th century. 2. Art, Modern—20th century. 3. Art—Psychology. 4. Attitude change. I. Title.

KOZLOFF, Max. 709.04
Renderings; critical essays on a century of modern art. New York, Simon and Schuster [1969, c1968] 352 p. 23 plates. 22 cm. [N6450.K65] 68-28915 7.50
1. Art, Modern—19th century. 2. Art, Modern—20th century. 3. Art criticism. I. Title. BIP

KRAMER, Hilton. 709'.04
The age of the avant-garde; an art chronicle of 1956-1972. New York, Farrar, Straus and Giroux [1973] xviii, 565 p. illus. 24 cm. [N6447.K72 1973] 72-89885 ISBN 0-374-10238-4 15.00
1. Art, Modern—19th century. 2. Art, Modern—20th century. 3. Art—Philosophy. I. Title. BIP

PACH, Walter, 1883-1958. 709'.04
The masters of modern art. Freeport, N.Y., Books for Libraries Press [1972, c1924] 118 p. 36 plates. 22 cm. (Essay index reprint series) Bibliography: p. 116-118. [N6447.P3 1972] 72-5633 ISBN 0-8369-7295-3
1. Art, Modern—19th century. 2. Art, Modern—20th century. I. Title. BIP

PEVSNER, Nikolaus, Sir, 1902- 709.035
Pioneers of modern design, from William Morris to Walter Gropius. [Rev. ed. Harmondsworth, Middlesex] Penguin Books [1964, c1960] 253 p. illus. 20 cm. (Pelican books, A497) First published in 1936 under title: Pioneers of the modern movement, from William Morris to Walter Gropius. Bibliographical references included in "Notes" (p. 219-240) [N6450.P4 1964] 64-4000
1. Art, Modern—19th century. 2. Art, Modern—20th century. I. Title.

RUSSELL, John, 1919- 709'.04
The meanings of modern art / by John Russell. New York : Museum of Modern Art, c1974- v. : ill. (some col.) ; 26 x 27 cm. Contents.Contents.—v. 1. The secret revolution.—v. 2. The emancipation of color.—v. 3. History as nightmare. Includes bibliographies. [N6447.R87] 72-76416 ISBN 0-87070-477-X
1. Art, Modern—19th century. 2. Art, Modern—20th century. 3. Color in art. 4. Emotions in art. I. Title.

SCHAPIRO, Meyer, 1904- 709'.04
Modern art : 19th and 20th centuries / Meyer Schapiro. New York : G. Braziller, 1978. p. cm. (His Selected papers ; v. 2) Includes index. [N6447.S33] 78-6831 ISBN 0-8076-0899-8 : 24.95
1. Art, Modern—19th century. 2. Art, Modern—20th century. I. Title.
Contents omitted

VOGT, Adolf Max. 709'.03'4
Art of the nineteenth century. [English translation by A. F. Bance] New York, Universe Books [1973] 189 p. illus. (part col.) 23 cm. Translation of 19. [i.e. Neunzehntes] Jahrhundert. Bibliography: p. 184-186. [N6450.V5713] 72-85082 ISBN 0-87663-168-5 6.95
1. Art, Modern—19th century. I. Title.

WESTON, Neville, 1936- 709'.04
The reach of modern art; a concise history. [1st U.S. ed.] New York, Harper & Row [1969, c1968] 239 p. illus. 24 cm. Includes bibliographical references. [N6450.W42 1969] 69-15268 6.95
1. Art, Modern—19th century. 2. Art, Modern—20th century. I. Title.

Art, Modern—19th century—Catalogs.

CINCINNATI. Art Museum. 759.06'074'017178
The Mary E. Johnston Collection. [Cincinnati] 1972. 86 p. illus. (part col.) 26 cm. [N6447.C56 1972] 73-170354
1. Johnston, Mary Elizabeth, 1890-—Art collections. 2. Cincinnati. Art Museum. 3. Art, Modern—19th century—Catalogs. 4. Art, Modern—20th century—Catalogs. 5. Art—Cincinnati—Catalogs. I. Title.

GROPPER Art Gallery. 760'.074'01444
Recent acquisitions: important 19th & 20th century prints, plus master drawings & prints, sculpture & books; [catalogue] Cambridge, Mass. [1971] 1 v. (unpaged) illus. 28 cm. Cover title. Includes bibliography. [N6447.G7] 78-198535
1. Art, Modern—19th century—Catalogs. 2. Art, Modern—20th century—Catalogs. 3. Art—Cambridge, Mass.—Catalogs. I. Title. II. Title: Important 19th & 20th century prints, plus master drawings & prints, sculpture & books.

MILWAUKEE. Art Center. 769'.94'074017595
Personal selections from the Mrs. Harry Lynde Bradley Collection. New Orleans : Bradley Family Foundation, 1975. 107 leaves (3 fold.) : all col. ill. ; 29 cm. Cover title: Bradley. Includes index. [N6447.M5 1975] 74-14444
1. Bradley, Harry Lynde, Mrs.—Art collections. 2. Milwaukee. Art Center. 3. Art, Modern—19th century—Catalogs. 4. Art, Modern—20th century—Catalogs. 5. Art—Milwaukee—Catalogs. I. Title. II. Title: Bradley.

NEW York (City). Museum of Modern Art. 709'.04'07401471
Painting and sculpture in the Museum of Modern Art, with selected works on paper : catalog of the collection, January 1, 1977 / edited by Alicia Legg. New York : The Museum, c1977. 110 p. ; 28 cm. Bibliography: p. 100-102. [N6447.N4 1977] 77-81324 ISBN 0-87070-544-X pbk. : 3.95
1. New York (City). Museum of Modern Art. 2. Art, Modern—19th century—Catalogs. 3. Art, Modern—20th century—Catalogs. 4. Art—New York (City)—Catalogs. I. Legg, Alicia. II. Title. BIP

Art, Modern—19th century—Congresses.

INTERNATIONAL Congress of the History of Art, 20th, New York, 1961. 709'.03'4
Problems of the 19th & 20th centuries Princeton, N.J., Princeton University Press, 1963. xii, 211 p., 48 plates. 24 cm. (Acts of the twentieth International Congress of the History of Art) (Its Studies in Western art, v. 4) Chiefly in English, some contributions in French or Italian. Includes bibliographical references. [N21.I585 1961 vol. 4] [N6447] 73-164482
1. Art, Modern—19th century—Congresses. 2. Art, Modern—20th century—Congresses. I. Title. II. Series. III. Series: International Congress of the History of Art. Acts, 1961.

Art, Modern—19th century—Dictionaries.

CHARMET, Raymond. 709'.04
Concise encyclopedia of modern art / Raymond Charmet ; edited by Roger Brunyate ; translated from the French by William Hardie. English language ed. Chicago : Follett, 1974. 256 p. : ill. ; 22 cm. (A Follett-Larousse concise encyclopedia) Rev. translation of Dictionnaire de l'art contemporain. 73-91736
1. Art, Modern—19th century—Dictionaries. 2. Art, Modern—20th century—Dictionaries. I. Brunyate, Roger, ed. II. Title.

Art, Modern—19th century—Exhibitions.

BROOKLYN Institute of Arts and Sciences. Museum. 709'.03'4
An exhibition of paintings, watercolors, sculpture, and drawings from the Collection of Mr. and Mrs. Henry Pearlman, and Henry and Rose Pearlman Foundation, [May 22-Sept. 29, 1974 : catalog]. [New York] : The Museum, 1974. [8] p., [68] leaves of plates : ill. (some col.) ; 36 cm. Includes bibliographies. [N6447.B76 1974] 74-77468
1. Pearlman, Henry, 1895-—Art collections. 2. Art, Modern—19th century—Exhibitions. 3. Art, Modern—20th century—Exhibitions. I. Title.

*CAMDEN Arts Centre-London. 709'.04'0740147
The Aesthetic movement, 1869-1890; catalogue of an exhibition at the Camden Arts Centre, London, 15 August - 7 October 1973, edited by Charles Spencer. London, Academy Editions [1973] New York, St. Martin's Press [1973] 94 p. illus. 29 cm. Bibliography: p. 93-94. [NC6447] 4.95 (pbk.)
1. Art, Modern—19th century—Exhibitions. I. Spencer, Charles, comp. II. Title.

CHICAGO. Art Institute. 709'.04'074017311
The Grant J. Pick Collection; [exhibition] Art Institute of Chicago, June 20 through August 16, 1970. Chicago, 1970? 48 p. (chiefly illus., part col.) 26 cm. Catalog. [N6447.C52] 73-170356
1. Pick, Grant J., 1910-1963—Art collections. 2. Art, Modern—19th century—Exhibitions. 3. Art, Modern—20th century—Exhibitions. I. Title.

CHICAGO. Art Institute. 709'.03'4
Major works from the Collection of Nathan Cummings; [catalogue of the exhibition] the Art Institute of Chicago, October 20-December 9, 1973. [Chicago, 1973] 95 p. (chiefly illus. (part col.)) 26 cm. [N6867.C47 1973] 73-87962
1. Cummings, Nathan—Art collections. 2. Art, Modern—19th century—Exhibitions. 3. Art, Modern—20th century—Exhibitions. I. Title.

DENVER. Art Museum. 704.94'9'9178
Colorado collects historic Western art; the nostalgia of the vanishing West. [Exhibition] Jan. 13 through April 15, 1973. [Catalogue compiled and edited by Cile M. Bach and Marlene Chambers. Denver, 1973] 72 p. illus. (part col.) 21 cm. [N8214.5.W4D46] 73-159340
1. Art, Modern—19th century—Exhibitions. 2. Art, Modern—19th century—Colorado. 3. The West in art. 4. Indians of North America—Art. I. Bach, Cile M., ed. II. Chambers, Marlene, ed. III. Title.

ELVEHJEM Art Center. 709.03'4
19th & 20th century art from collections of alumni & friends; inaugural exhibition, September 11-November 8, 1970, Elvehjem Art Center. Madison, University of Wisconsin [1970] 141 p. illus. (part col.) 26 cm. Label on t.p.: Supplied by Worldwide Books, inc., Boston. [N6490.E55] 71-633987
1. Art, Modern—19th century—Exhibitions. 2. Art, Modern—20th century—Exhibitions. 3. Art—Private collections. I. Title.

FORT Lauderdale Museum of the Arts. 709'.03'4
Collections 1967. [An exhibition held Jan. 19 through Feb. 15, 1967 [Fort Lauderdale, 1967] 1 v. (unpaged) illus. 26 cm. "An exhibition organized by the Fort Lauderdale Museum of the Arts selected from many local private and public collections and sponsored by the Beaux Arts." [N6450.F66 1967] 73-171733
1. Art, Modern—19th century—Exhibitions. 2. Art, Modern—20th century—Exhibitions. 3. Art—Collectors and collecting—Fort Lauderdale. I. Title.

NEW York (City). Museum of Modern Art. 709'.04'07401471
Art in our time; an exhibition to celebrate the tenth anniversary of the Museum of Modern Art and the opening of its new building, held at the time of the New York World's Fair. Reprint ed. Museum of Modern Art, 1939. [New York] Published for the Museum of Modern Art by Arno Press, 1972. 384 p. illus. 27 cm. (Museum of Modern Art publications in reprint) [N6447.N4 1972] 79-169294 ISBN 0-405-01554-2 25.75
1. Art, Modern—19th century—Exhibitions. 2. Art, Modern—20th century—Exhibitions. I. Title. BIP

THE Protean century, 1870-1970; [catalogue of] a loan exhibition from the Dartmouth College Collection, alumni, and friends of the college. [Lunenberg, Vt., Designed & printed at the Stinehour Press, 1970] 1 v. (unpaged) illus. (part col.) 26 cm. Exhibition held Feb. 10-28, 1970, at the gallery of M. Knoedler & Co., New York, under the auspices of the Dartmouth Arts Council for the benefit of the acquisitions fund of the Hopkins Center Art Galleries, Dartmouth College. [N6447.P7] 79-112396 709.04
1. Art, Modern—19th century—Exhibitions. 2. Art, Modern—20th century—Exhibitions. I. Knoedler (M.) and Company, inc. II. Dartmouth Arts Council. III. Dartmouth College. Hopkins Center. Art Galleries.

SOLOMON R. Guggenheim Museum, New York. 709'.04'07401471
Masterpieces of modern art. [New and rev. ed. New York, Solomon R. Guggenheim Foundation, 1972] 83 p. illus. (part col.) 28 cm. Cover title. "A picture book of 19th and 20th century masterpieces from the Thannhauser Foundation." Catalogue of an exhibition celebrating J. K. Thannhauser's 80th birthday and the re-opening of the Justin K. Thannhauser Wing of the Guggenheim Museum. [N6447.S6 1972] 72-75939
1. Art, Modern—19th century—Exhibitions. 2. Art, Modern—20th century—Exhibitions. I. Thannhauser Foundation, New York. II. Title.

U.S. National Gallery of Art. 759.06'074'0153
Selections from the Nathan Cummings Collection. [Exhibition] National Gallery of Art, Washington, June 28-September 11, 1970; the Metropolitan Museum of Art, New York, July 1-September 7, 1971. [Catalogue notes by Carol Cutler. Photography by Malcolm Varon. Washington, 1970] 96 p. illus. (part col.) 27 cm. [N6867.U5] 71-606524
1. Cummings, Nathan—Art collections. 2. Art, Modern—19th century—Exhibitions. 3. Art, Modern—20th century—Exhibitions. I. New York (City). Metropolitan Museum of Art. II. Title.

Art, Modern—19th century—Exhibitions—History.

DUNLOP, Ian, 1940- 709'.04'074
The shock of the new; seven historic exhibitions of modern art. New York, American Heritage Press [1972] 272 p. illus. (part col.) 26 cm. Includes bibliographical references. [N6447.D86] 77-39481 ISBN 0-07-018267-1 14.95
1. Art, Modern—19th century—Exhibitions—History. 2. Art, Modern—20th century—Exhibitions—History. 3. Art and society. I. Title.

Art, Modern—19th century—History.

LYNTON, Norbert. 709.04
The modern world. New York, McGraw-Hill [1965] 175 p. illus. (part col.) 30 cm. (Landmarks of the world's art) Bibliography: p. [170]-171. [N6450.L9] 65-21593
1. Art, Modern—19th century—History. 2. Art, Modern—20th century—History. I. Title.

RICHARDSON, Edgar Preston, 1902- 709'.034
The way of western art, 1776-1914. New York, Cooper Square Publishers, 1969 [i.e. 1970, c1967] xxiii, 204 p. illus. 26 cm. Reprint of the 1939 ed. [N6450.R5 1970] 73-79604 10.00
1. Art, Modern—19th century—History. 2. Art, Modern—20th century—History. I. Title.

SYMONS, Arthur, 1865-1945. 709'.44
From Toulouse-Lautrec to Rodin; with some personal impressions. Freeport, N.Y., Books for Libraries Press [1968] vii, 242 p. facsims., port. 23 cm. (Essay index reprint series) Reprint of the 1929 ed. Contents.Contents.—Henri de Toulouse-Lautrec.—On the genius of Degas.—Constantin Guys.—Honore Daumier.—Jean Louis Forain.—The paintings of Henry de Groux.—Simeon Solomon.—Monticelli.—Gustave Moreau.—Odilon Redon.—Aubrey Beardsley.—Whistler and Manet.—Auguste Rodin. [N6450.S87 1968] 68-20342
1. Toulouse-Lautrec Monfa, Henri Marie Raymond de, 1864-1901. 2. Art, Modern—19th century—History. 3. Artists, French. I. Title.

WESTON, Neville, 1936- 709.04
Kaleidoscope of modern art. London, Toronto, Harrap, 1968. 240p. illus. 24cm. Bibl. [N6450.W4] 68-88051 7.50 bds.,
1. Art, Modern—19th cent.—Hist. 2. Art, Modern—20th cent.—Hist. I. Title.
Distributed by Verry, Mystic, Conn.

Art, Modern—19th century—History—Addresses, essays, lectures.

CHIPP, Herschel Browning, comp. 709.034
Theories of modern art; a source book by artists and critics [by] Herschel B. Chipp [with] contributions by Peter Selz and Joshua C. Taylor. Berkeley, University of California Press, 1968. xv, 664 p. illus., ports. 26 cm. (California studies in the history of art, 11) Bibliography: p. 627-651. [N6450.C62] 68-12038
1. Art, Modern—19th century—History—Addresses, essays, lectures. 2. Art, Modern—20th century—History—Addresses, essays, lectures. I. Title. II. Series. BIP

Art, Modern—19th century—Juvenile literature.

RUSKIN, Ariane. 709.034
Nineteenth century art, adapted by Ariane Ruskin. Foreword by Howard Conant. New York, McGraw-Hill [1968] 192 p. col. illus. 31 cm. (Discovering art series) "[Based] on the text of the magazine series Discovering art ... [with] adaptations from the Italian text of Capolavori nei secoli." A survey, illustrated by representative works, of prominent art movements during the nineteenth century with a discussion of the individual contributions of major artists. [N6450.R77] 68-55273 8.95
1. Art, Modern—19th century—Juvenile literature. I. Title. BIP

RUSKIN, Ariane. 709'.03'4
Nineteenth century art, adapted by Ariane Ruskin. Foreword by Howard Conant. New York, McGraw-Hill [1973] 254 p. col. illus. 22 cm. (McGraw-Hill paperbacks) (Discovering art series) Based on the text of the magazine series Discovering art, with adaptations from the Italian text of Capolavori nei secoli. A survey, illustrated by representative works, of prominent art movements during the nineteenth century with a discussion of the individual contributions of major artists. [N6450.R77 1973] 73-176513 ISBN 0-07-054293-7 4.95
1. Art, Modern—19th century—Juvenile literature. I. Title. II. Series.

Art, Modern—19th century—Washington, D.C.—Catalogs.

THE Hirshhorn 709'.04'0740153
Museum & Sculpture Garden, Smithsonian Institution. Foreword by S. Dillon Ripley. Edited and with an introd. by Abram Lerner. Essays by Linda Nochlin [and others] New York, H. N. Abrams [1974] 770 p. illus. (part col.) 30 cm. "Inaugural publication of the Hirshhorn Museum and Sculpture Garden." Includes bibliographies. [N857.6.H57] 74-5454 ISBN 0-8109-0165-X
1. Hirshhorn Museum and Sculpture Garden. 2. Art, Modern—19th century—Washington, D.C.—Catalogs. 3. Art, Modern—20th century—Washington, D.C.—Catalogs. I. Lerner, Abram, ed. II. Nochlin, Linda. III. Hirshhorn Museum and Sculpture Garden.

Art, Modern—19th century—Wichita, Kan.

WICHITA Art Museum. 709'.73'0740181423
Catalogue of the Roland P. Murdock Collection. [Text and notes: George P. Tomko. Wichita, Kan., 1972] 237 p. illus. (part col.) 24 cm. On spine: The Roland P. Murdock collection. Includes bibliographical references. [N6447.W52] 72-82939
1. Murdock, Roland P.—Art collections. 2. Art, Modern—19th century—Wichita, Kan. 3. Art, Modern—20th century—Wichita, Kan. 4. Art—Wichita, Kan.—Catalogs. I. Tomko, George P. II. Title. III. Title: The Roland P. Murdock Collection.

Art, Modern—20th century.

ALDER, William Fisher. 709.04
Peril on Parnassus. New York, Vantage Press [1954] 172p. illus. 22cm. [N6490.A55] 54-8338
1. Art, Modern—20th cent. 2. Modernism (Art) I. Title.

ALLEN, Clarence Canning, 1897- ed. 709.04
Are you fed up with modern art?... Tulsa, Rainbow Press [1953, 1952] 103p. illus. (part col) ports. 29cm. [N6490.A57] 53-25796
1. Art, Modern—20th cent. 2. Art—Addresses, essays, lectures. I. Title.

BIDDLE, George, 1885- 701.16
The yes and no of contemporary art, an artist's evaluation. Cambridge, Harvard University Press, 1957. 188p. illus. 25cm. [N6490.B48] 57-7606
1. Art, Modern—20th cent. 2. Modernism (Art.) 3. Art—Philosophy. I. Title.

BIEDERMAN, Charles Joseph, 1906- 709.04
Letters on the new art. [1st ed.] Red Wing, Minn., Art History [1951] 95 p. illus. 24 cm. [N6490.B5] 51-7425
1. Art. Modern—20th cent. I. Title.

CRIPPA, Roberto, 1921- 751.4
Crippa [Testo di] Alain Jouffroy. [Dist. New York, Wittenborn, c.1962] 52p. illus. (pt. col.) 29cm. Italian, French, and English. Bibl. 62-5590 17.50
I. Jouffroy, Alain, 1928- II. Title.

CRIPPA, Roberto, 1921- 709'.2'4
Crippa. [Catalogue. Paris, New York, Alexandre Tolas, 1971] [38] p. illus. (part col.) 23 cm. English, French, and Italian. Introductory article by A. Pieyre de Mandiargues. [N6923.C7P5] 74-198175
I. Pieyre de Mandiargues, Andre, 1909-

FIFTY years of modern art. 709.035
Introd. by Emile Langui. [Translated from the French by Geoffrey Sainsbury and James Oliver] 32 color plates, 305 monochrome illus.; 226 biographical notes. New York, Praeger [1960] 335p. illus. (part col.) 26cm. (PPG 1) 59-7300 2.95 pap.,
1. Art, Modern—20th cent. I. Langui, Emile, ed.

FLANAGAN, George Alexander. 709.04
How to understand modern art. [2d print., with revisions] New York, Studio Publications in association with T. Y. Crowell Co. [1954] 338p. illus. 25cm. [N6490.F55 1954] 54-4978
1. Art, Modern—20th cent. I. Title.

GAUNT, William, 1900- 709.04
The observer's book of modern art, from impressionism to the present day. London, New York, F. Warne [1964] xii, 148 p. illus., 14 col. plates. 15 cm. (The Observer's pocket series, 34) [N6490.G32] 64-13622
1. Art Modern — 20th cent. 2. Art — Hist. Title. I. Title. II. Series.

GIKOW, Ruth, 1915- 759.13
Ruth Gikow. Introd. by Matthew Josephson. New York, Maecenas Press [1970] [30] p., 131 plates (part col.) illus. 29 cm. [ND237.G44A57 1970] 71-127537 14.95

HARRIES, Karsten. 709.04
The meaning of modern art: a philosophical interpretation. Evanston [Ill.] Northwesten 1968. xiv, 166p. 24cm. (Northwestern Univ. studies in phenomenology & existential phil.) Bibl. footnotes. [N6490 H26] 68-17733 5.25
1. Art, Modern 20th cent. 2. Art—Philosophy. I. Title. II. Series. BIP

HUNTER, Sam, 1923- 709.09046
New art around the world; painting and sculpture [by] Sam Hunter and others. American ed. New York, H. N. Abrams, 1966] 509 p. illus. plates (part col.) 23 cm. [N6490.N36] 66-29665
1. Art, Modern — 20th cent. I. Title.

HUSAIN, Maqbul Fida. 759.954
Maqbool Fida Husain. Texts by Richard Bartholomew and Shiv S. Kapur. New York, H. N. Abrams [1972?] 60 p., 192 plates (part col.) 28 x 30 cm. [ND1010.H85B3] 79-125786 ISBN 0-8109-0189-7
I. Bartholomew, Richard. II. Kapur, Shiv S.

KENT, Corita, 1918- 769'.924
Sister Corita [by] Mary Corita Kent, Harvey Cox [and] Samuel A. Eisenstein. Philadelphia, Pilgrim Press [1968?] 80 p. illus., ports., 34 col. plates (part fold.) 37 cm. Issued in a case. Contents.Contents.—Art and beauty in the life of the sister, by Sister M. C. Kent.—Corita: celebration and creativity, by H. Cox.—Communications primer, by S. A. Eisenstein.—Catalog of prints.—Appendix: Permanent collections. Commissions. Partial list of exhibits. Galleries where prints are available. [NE539.K4C6] 68-54032
I. Cox, Harvey Gallagher. II. Eisenstein, Samuel A.

KRANZ, Kurt. 709.04
Art: the revealing experience. New York, Shorewood Publishers, 1964. 245 p. illus. (part col.) ports. (part col.) 27 cm. [N6490.K723] 64-22512
1. Art, Modern — 20th cent. I. Title.

KRANZ, Kurt 709.04
Art: the revealing experience. New York, Shorewood, 1964. 245p. illus. (pt. col.) ports. (pt. col.) 27cm. 64-22512 17.50
1. Art, Modern—20th cent. I. Title.

LEVI, Julian, 1900- v. 12
Modern art; an introduction. New York, Pitman Pub. Corp. [c1961] unpaged illus. 20x26cm. (Pitman art series, 36) [N6190.L45] 61-16643
1. Art. Modern—20th cent. 2. Paintings. I. Title.

LEWIS, Wyndham, 1886- 709.04
The demon of progres5 in the arts. Chicago, H. Regnery Co., 1955. 97p. illus. 22cm. [N6490] 55-4030
1. Art—Modern—20th cent. 2. Art—England. I. Title.

MACAGY, Douglas, 1913- 759.06
Going for a walk with a line; a step into the world of modern art, by Douglas and Elizabeth MacAgy. [1st ed.] Garden City, N. Y., Doubleday [1959] unpaged (chiefly illus.) 25cm. [N6490.M28] 59-5899
1. Art, Modern—20th cent. 2. Line (Art) I. MacAgy, Elizabeth (Tillett) joint author. II. Title. BIP

MALEVICH, Kazimir Severinovich, 1878-1935. 709.04
The non-objective world. [Translated from the German by Howard Dearstyne] Chicago, P. Theobald [c1959] 102p. illus. 28cm. [ND195.M333] 60-21761
1. Art, Modern—20th cent. 2. Painting. I. Title. BIP

READ, Herbert Edward, Sir 1893- ed. 709.04
The philosophy of modern art [essays] Greenwich, Conn., Fawcett [1967, c.1955] x, 288p. 18cm. (Premier bk., M345) [N6490.R43 1955] .95 pap.,
1. Art, Modern—20th cent. 2. Modernism (Art) 3. Artists. I. Title. BIP

READ, Herbert Edward, Sir 1893- 709.03
The philosophy of modern art. New York, Meridian Books, 1955. 309p. 18cm. (Meridian books, M7) [N6490.R43 1955] [N6490.R43 1955] 709.04 55-5935 55-5935
1. Art, Modern—20th cent. 2. Modernism (Art) 3. Artists. I. Title.

RODMAN, Selden 709.04
The insidersrejection and rediscovery of man in the arts of our time. [Baton Rouge] Louisiana State University Press [c.1960] viii, 130p. illus. 27cm. Bibl. footnotes. 60-15433 6.95
1. Art, Modern—20th cent. 2. Art—Philosophy. 3. Artists. I. Title.

RODMAN, Selden, 1909- 709.04
The insiders; rejection and rediscovery of man in the arts of our time. [Baton Rouge] Louisiana State University Press [1960] viii, 130p. illus. 27cm. Bibliographical footnotes. [N6490.R56] 60-15433
1. Art, Modern—20th cent. 2. Art—Philosophy. 3. Artists. I. Title. BIP

ROSENBERG, Harold. 709.04
The anxious object; art today and its audience. New York, Collier Books [1973, c.1966] 172 p. illus. 21 cm. [N6490.R59] pap., 2.94
1. Art, Modern—20th cent. I. Title. II. Title: Art today and its audience.
L.C. card no. for earlier edition: 64-24539.

SCHMIDT, Georg, 1896- ed. 709.04
Kunst und Naturform. Form in art and nature. Hrgg. von Georg Schmidt, Robert Schenk. Mit einer Einfuhrung von Adolf Portmann [Dist. New York, Heinman, 1962, c.1960] illus. (pt. col.) 29cm. A61 22.50, bxd.
1. Art, Modern—20th cent. 2. Nature (Aesthetics) I. Schenk, Robert, joint ed. II. Title. III. Title: Form in art and nature.

SCHMIDT, Georg, 1896-1965, ed. 709.04
Kunst and Naturform. Form in art and nature. Hrsg. von Georg Schmidt und Robert Schenk. Mit einer Einfuhrung von Addlf Portmann. 3d ed. New York, Universe Bks., 1967 [c.1960] 129p. plates (pt. col.) 29cm. Text in German, English, and French. Based on the exhibition Kunst und Naturform, held in 1958 in the Kunsthalle, Basel. [N6490.S29 1967] 67-5863 12.00
1. Art, Modern—20th cent. 2. Nature (Aesthetics) 3. Form (Aesthetics) I. Schenk, Robert, joint ed. II. Title. III. Title: Form in art and nature.

SEVERINI, Gino, 1883- 701.16
The artist and society. Translated by Bernard Wall. New York, Grove Press, 1952. viii, 94p. plates. 21cm. (The Changing world series, no. 1) Translation

of Arte Independente, arte borghese, arte sociale. [N6490.S] A 54
1. Art, Modern—20th cent. 2. Moderniam (Art) 3. Art and society. I. Title.

SNAITH, William, 1908- 701
The irresponsible arts. [1st ed.] New York, Atheneum, 1964. ix, 277 p. 22 cm. Bibliography: p. [265]-268. [N6490.S58] 64-18891
1. Art, Modern—20th cent. 2. Art and society. 3. Art—Philosophy. I. Title.

SYLVESTER, David, ed. 709.04
Modern art, from Fauvism to abstract expressionism. New York, Watts [1966, c.1965] 296p. illus., col. plates, ports. 25cm. (Great art and artists of the world) Also pub. by Grolier, inc., as a vol. in its The Book of art. Bibl. [N6490.S9] 65-10270 12.95
1. Art, Modern-20th cent. 2. Artists. I. Title. II. Series.

TAUBES, Frederic, 1900- 709.04
Abracadabra and modern art; nineteenth-twentieth-century critique and history. New York, Dodd, Mead [1963] x. 182 p. illus. 25 cm. [N6490.T348] 63-17077
1. Art, Modern—20th cent. 2. Art—Hist. 3. Art criticism. I. Title.

TAUBES, Frederic, 1900- 709.04
Modern art, sweet or sour. New York, Watson-Guptill Publications [1958] 143 p. illus. 24 cm. [N6490.T35] 58-8129
1. Art. Modern — 20th cent. 2. Art — Hist. I. Title.

VOLCK, Adalbert John, 1828-1912. 769'.924
The work of Adalbert Johann Volek, 1828-1912, who chose for his name the anagram V. Bada. Baltimore, Privately printed by G. M. Anderson, 1970. 222 p. illus., ports. 21 x 26 cm. [N6537.V6A67] 74-137860
I. Anderson, George McCullough, 1897- II. Title.

Art, Modern—20th century—Addresses, essays, lectures.

ART since mid-century; 709'.04
the new internationalism. With contributions by Werner Haftmann [and others] Foreword by Jean Leymarie. Greenwich, Conn., New York Graphic Society [1971] 2 v. illus. (part col.) 28 cm. Contents.Contents.—v. 1. Abstract art since 1945.—v. 2. Figurative art since 1945. [N6490.A719] 70-154332 ISBN 0-8212-0384-3
1. Art, Modern—20th century—Addresses, essays, lectures. I. Haftmann, Werner. II. Title: Abstract art since 1945. III. Title: Figurative art since 1945.

BATTCOCK, Gregory, 1937- ed. 709'.04
The new art; a critical anthology. New York, Dutton [1973, c.1966] 254 p. 18 cm. (Dutton paperback, D178) Includes bibliographical references [N6490.B35] 66-3422 ISBN 0-525-47178-2 1.75 (pbk.)
1. Art, Modern—20th cent.—Addresses, essays, lectures. 2. Art criticism. I. Title. BIP

CANADAY, John Edwin, 1907- 709.04
Embattled critic; views on modern art. New York, Farrar [c. 1959-1962] 238p. illus. 21cm. (Noonday, 226) 62-8827 2.45 pap.,
1. Art. Modern—20th cent.—Addresses, essays, lectures. I. Title. BIP

CANADAY, John Edwin, 1907- 709'.04
Embattled critic; views on modern art, by John Canaday. Freeport, N.Y., Books for Libraries Press [1972, c1962] p. (Essay index reprint series) [N6490.C24 1972] 72-8492 ISBN 0-8369-7309-7
1. Art, Modern—20th century—Addresses, essays, lectures. I. Title.

FLOCH, Joseph. 759.4
Joseph Floch. Introductory essays by Julius S. Held, Jean Cassou [and] Laurence Schmeckebier. New York, T. Yoseloff [1968] 143 p. (chiefly illus., part col.) 29 cm. [ND553.F54H4] 66-25029

FOUR essays on kinetic art 701.17
[by] Stephen Bann [others. St. Albans, Eng.] Motion Bks. Stamped on t. p.: Amer. dist.: Wittenborn. New York, 1966. 70p. illus. (pt. col.) 27cm. [N6490.I 67] 66-6557 3.00
1. Art, Modern—20th cent.—Addresses, essays, lectures. I. Bann. Stephen.

HARTFORD, Huntington, 1911- 709.04
Art or anarchy? How the extremists and exploiters have reduced the fine arts to chaos and commercialism. Garden City, N.Y., Doubleday, 1964[c. 1951-1964] x, 204p. illus. 22cm. 64-25389 4.95
1. Art, Modern—20th cent.—Addresses, essays, lectures. 2. Art—Philosophy. 3. Art criticism. I. Title.

HARTFORD, Huntington, 1911- 709.04
Art or anarchy? How the extremists and exploiters have reduced the fine arts to chaos and commercialism. [1st ed.] Garden City, N.Y., Doubleday, 1964. x, 204 p. illus. 22 cm. [N6490.H27] 64-25389
1. Art, Modern — 20th cent. — Addresses, essays, lectures. 2. Art — Philosophy. 3. Art criticism. I. Title.

HODIN, Josef Paul. 709'.04
Modern art and the modern mind [by] J. P. Hodin. Cleveland, Press of Case Western Reserve University, 1972. xvi, 365 p. illus. 24 cm. Includes bibliographical references. [N6490.H63] 75-81831 ISBN 0-8295-0170-3 12.95
1. Art, Modern—20th century—Addresses, essays, lectures. 2. Art—Philosophy—Addresses, essays, lectures. I. Title.

KANDINSKY, Wassily, 1866-1944, ed. 709'.04
The Blaue Reiter almanac. Edited by Wassily Kandinsky and Franz Marc. New documentary ed. Edited and with an introd. by Klaus Lankheit. New York, Viking Press [1974] 296 p. illus. 22 cm. (The Documents of 20th-century art) Translation of Der Blaue Reiter. Bibliography: p. 283-292. [N6490.K2913 1974] 75-170678 ISBN 0-670-17355-X 15.00
1. Blauer Reiter. 2. Art, Modern—20th century—Addresses, essays, lectures. I. Marc, Franz, 1880-1916, joint author. II. Lankheit, Klaus, joint ed. III. Title. BIP

KEPES, Gyorgy, 1906- ed. 709.04
The visual arts today. Middletown, Conn., Wesleyan University Press [c.1960] 272p. illus. 27cm. 60-13159 6.00 bds.,
1. Art, Modern—20th cent.—Addresses, essays, lectures. 2. Art—Philosophy. I. Title.

MAJOR European art movements, 1900-1945 709'.04
: a critical anthology / edited by Patricia Kaplan and Susan Manso. 1st ed. New York : Dutton, c1977. xii, 396 p. : ill. ; 21 cm. Includes bibliographical references. [N6490.M29145 1977] 77-71306 ISBN 0-525-47462-5 : 9.95
1. Art, Modern—20th century—Addresses, essays, lectures. I. Kaplan, Patricia. II. Manso, Susan. BIP

ROSENTHAL, Erwin, 1889- 709.04
Contemporary art in the light of history. New York, G. Wittenborn [1971] 94 p. 25 plates. 24 cm. Includes bibliographical references. [N6490.R597] 72-153830 ISBN 0-8150-0219-X 6.50
1. Art, Modern—20th century—Addresses, essays, lectures. 2. Art and history—Addresses, essays, lectures. I. Title. BIP

Art, Modern—20th century.

ADVENTURE in art; 709'.04
an international group of art collections in industrial environments. [Edited by H. J. Scheepmaker. Translated from the French by Gwenda Stephens and Leslie White] New York, H. N. Abrams [1969] 224 p. illus. (part col.) 31 cm. Contents.Contents.—Foreword, by Lord Robbins.—Introduction, by M. S. Fox.—Rodin and his contemporaries, by B. Champigneulle.—International sculpture, by D. Chevalier.—Scultura italiana, by A. M. Hammacher.—Art in the factory, by H. L. C. Jaffe.—Art of the space age, by W. C. Seitz.—Recent British painting, by B. Robertson.—Contemporary French tapestry, by D. Majorel. [N6490.A313] 73-84854 40.00
1. Art, Modern—20th century. I. Scheepmaker, H. J., ed.

ARNASON, H. Harvard. 709'.04
History of modern art : painting, sculpture, architecture / H. H. Arnason. 2d ed., rev. and enl. Englewood Cliffs, N.J. : Prentice-Hall, c1977. 740 p. : ill. (some col.) ; 31 cm. Includes index. Bibliography: p. 709-722. [N6490.A713 1977] 77-355840 ISBN 0-13-390351-6 : 16.95
1. Art, Modern—20th century. I. Title. BIP

ASHTON, Dore. 709.04
A reading of modern art. Rev. ed. New York, Harper & Row [1971] xiii, 238 p. illus. 22 cm. (Icon editions, IN-5) Includes bibliographical references. [N6490.A78 1971] 74-28248 2.95
1. Art, Modern—20th century. I. Title.

ASHTON, Dore. 709.04
A reading of modern art. Cleveland, Press of Case Western Reserve University, 1969. xii, 208 p. illus. (part col.) 24 cm. Bibliographical references included in "Notes" (p. 200-208) [N6490.A78] 68-19064 8.95
1. Art, Modern—20th century. I. Title.

ASHTON, Dore. 709.04
The unknown shore: a view of contemporary art. [1st ed.] Boston, Little, Brown [1962] 265 p. illus. 22 cm. [N6490.A8] 62-17954
1. Art, Modern—20th century. 2. Painting—History. I. Title.

BALLO, Guido, 1914- 701.17
The critical eye; a new approach to art appreciation. Translated by R. H. Boothroyd. [1st American ed.] New York, Putnam [1969] 291 p. illus. (part col.) 24 cm. Translation of Occhio critico. Bibliography: p. 281-282. [N6490.B2513] 69-11456 7.95
1. Art, Modern—20th century. I. Title.

BANN, Stephen. 701.15
Experimental painting; construction, abstraction, destruction, reduction. New York, Universe Books [1970] 144 p. illus. (part col.) 26 cm. Bibliography: p. [139]-142. [N6490.B254] 79-105961 ISBN 8-7663-1200- 7.95
1. Art, Modern—20th century. 2. Art—Psychology. I. Title.

BATTERBERRY, Michael. 709'.04
Twentieth century art. Foreword by Howard Conant. New York, McGraw-Hill [1969] 191 p. 244 col. illus. 31 cm. (Discovering art series) Based on the text of the magazine series Discovering art, and adapted from the Italian text of Capolavori nei secoli. [N6490.B353] 70-76821 8.95
1. Art, Modern—20th century. I. Title. BIP

BENTHALL, Jonathan. 701
Science and technology in art today. New York, Praeger [1972] 180 p. illus. 22 cm. (Praeger world of art series) Bibliography: p. 170-173. [N6490.B375 1972b] 78-183061 8.95
1. Art, Modern—20th century. 2. Art and science. 3. Art and technology. I. Title.

BESSET, Maurice. 709'.04
Art of the twentieth century / Maurice Besset. New York : Universe Books, 1976. 200 p. : ill. (some col.) ; 23 cm. Translation of 20. Jahrhundert. Includes index. Bibliography: p. 195-197. [N6490.B4513] 72-91630 ISBN 0-87663-186-3 : 7.95
1. Art, Modern—20th century. I. Title. BIP

BIHALJI-MERIN, Oto 1904- 709.04
Adventure of modern art; similarities and differences in art images, primitive, ancient, and modern. New York, H. N. Abrams [1966?] 368 p. 281 illus. 30 cm. Bibliography: p. [361]-362. [N6490.B518] 66-13270
1. Art, Modern—20th century. 2. Art criticism. I. Title.

CALAS, Nicolas. 708.5
The Peggy Guggenheim collection of modern art. Text by Nicolas Calas and Elena Calas. New York, H. N. Abrams [1966] 263 p. plates (part col.) 36 cm. [N5220.G889] 66-26654
1. Guggenheim, Marguerite, 1898- —Art collections. 2. Art, Modern—20th century. I. Calas, Elena, joint author. II. Title.

CARROLL, Donald. 709'.04
Movements in modern art [by] Donald Carroll and Edward Lucie-Smith. New York, Horizon Press [1973] 208 p. illus. 22 cm. [N6490.C264] 73-77640 ISBN 0-8180-0122-4 6.95
1. Art, Modern—20th century. I. Lucie-Smith, Edward, joint author. II. Title. BIP

CLAY, Jean. 709'.04
Modern art, 1890-1918 / Jean Clay. New York : Vendome Press : distributed by Viking Press, c1978. 320 p. : ill. (some col.) ; 32 cm. Translation of De l'impressionnisme a l'art moderne. Bibliography: p. 320. [N6490.C58913 1978] 78-9139 ISBN 0-670-48267-6 : 45.00
1. Art, Modern—20th century. 2. Color in art. 3. Art—Psychology. I. Title.

CONE, Michele. 709'.04
The roots & routes of art in the 20th century / Michele Cone. New York : Horizon Press, [1975] 252 p. : ill. ; 27 cm. Includes index. Bibliography: p. 236-248. [N6490.C6563] 74-28175 ISBN 0-8180-0123-2 : 15.00
1. Art, Modern—20th century. I. Title. BIP

FAULKNER, Ray Nelson, 1906- 701
Art today; an introduction to the fine and functional arts [by] Ray Faulkner, Edwin Ziegfeld [and] Gerald Hill. 4th ed. New York, Holt, Rinehart and Winston [1963] 567 p. illus. 26 cm. Includes bibliography. [N7425.F3 1963] 63-7502
1. Art, Modern—20th century. 2. Art industries and trade. 3. Aesthetics. I. Title.

FAULKNER, Ray Nelson, 1906- 701
Art today; an introduction to the visual arts [by] Ray Faulkner [and] Edwin Ziegfeld. 5th ed. New York, Holt, Rinehart and Winston [1969] x, 542 p. 647 illus., 64 col. plates. 29 cm. Bibliography: p. 525-531. [N6490.F33 1969] 69-19916
1. Art, Modern—20th century. 2. Art industries and trade. 3. Aesthetics. I. Ziegfeld, Edwin, 1905- joint author. II. Title.

FLANAGAN, George Alexander. 709.04
Understand and enjoy modern art. Rev. ed. New York, Crowell [1962] 344 p. illus. 26 cm. First published in 1961 under title: How to understand modern art. [N6490.F55 1962] 61-14528
1. Art, Modern—20th century. I. Title.

FRANKL, Paul Theodore, 1886- 709'.04
New dimensions : the decorative arts of today in words & pictures / by Paul T. Frankl. New York : Da Capo Press, 1975, c1928. 122 p. : ill. ; 31 cm. (Da Capo Press series in architecture and decorative art) Reprint of the ed. published by Payson & Clarke, New York. [N6490.F7 1975] 75-15851 ISBN 0-306-70741-1 lib.bdg. : 29.50
1. Art, Modern—20th century. 2. Decoration and ornament. 3. Art industries and trade. 4. Interior decoration. I. Title. BIP

GOTTLIEB, Carla. 709'.04
Beyond modern art / Carla Gottlieb. 1st ed. New York : Dutton, c1976. xiii, 434 p. : ill. ; 21 cm. Includes index. Bibliography: p. 405-409. [N6490.G636 1976] 76-359867 ISBN 0-525-47370-X pbk. : 8.95
1. Art, Modern—20th century. 2. Art—Philosophy. 3. Avant-garde (Aesthetics) I. Title. BIP

KAHMEN, Volker, 1939- 704.94'2
Erotic art today. [English translation by Peter Newmark] Greenwich, Conn., New York Graphic Society [1972] 282 p. illus. (part col.) 26 cm. Translation of Erotik in der Kunst. Bibliography: p. 281-282. [N6490.K2513 1972] 72-181340 ISBN 0-8212-0430-0 14.50
1. Art, Modern—20th century. 2. Erotic art. I. Title.

KUH, Katharine. 709.04
Break-up: the core of modern art. Greenwich, Conn., New York Graphic Society [1965] 136 p. illus. (part col.) 26 cm. [N6490.K78] 65-21745
1. Art, Modern—20th century. I. Title.

LISITSKII, Lazar' Markovich, 1890-1941. 709'.04
Die Kunstismen. Les ismes de l'art. The

26 cm. Distributed by Praeger Publishers, New York. Includes bibliographical references. [N6490.P46] 72-86572 ISBN 0-7148-1557-8 £5.50 ($15.00 U.S.)
1. Art, Modern—20th century—Dictionaries. 2. Artists—Biography—Dictionaries. I. Title: Dictionary of twentieth-century art.

Art, Modern—20th century—Europe—Exhibitions.

DES Moines Art Center. 709'.4'074017758
Art in Western Europe, the postwar years 1945-1955 : Des Moines Art Center, September 19-October 29, 1978 / introd. by Lawrence Alloway. [Des Moines] : The Center, 1978. 18, [20] p., [38] leaves of plates : ill. (some col.) ; 23 cm. Includes bibliographical references. [N6758.D39 1978] 78-66783 10.95
1. Art, Modern—20th century—Europe—Exhibitions. I. Title.
Publisher's address: Greenwood Park, Des Moines, IA 50312

Art, Modern—20th century—Exhibitions.

ALBRIGHT-KNOX Art Gallery. 709'.04'074014789
The Martha Jackson Collection at the Albright-Knox Art Gallery, November 22, 1975-January 4, 1976, [exhibition]. [Buffalo] : The Gallery, [1975] p. cm. Annotations by L. L. Cathcart. Bibliography: p. [N6490.B83A42 1975] 75-24230 ISBN 0-914782-04-5 : 5.00
1. Jackson, Martha, b. 1907- —Art collections. 2. Art, Modern—20th century—Exhibitions. I. Cathcart, Linda L. II. Title.

ALBRIGHT-KNOX Art Gallery. 709.04
Plus by minus: today's half-century. [Exhibition] March 3 through April 14, 1968, Albright-Knox Art Gallery, Buffalo, N.Y. [Buffalo, 1968] 1 v. (unpaged) illus. 31 cm. [N6490.A54] 68-30328
1. Art, Modern—20th century—Exhibitions. I. Title.

ALDRICH Museum of Contemporary Art. 709'.04
Art of the 60's : selections from the collection of Hanford Yang. [exhibition: September 29 through December 22, 1968.] Ridgefield, Conn., 1968] [39] p. illus. 20 cm. [N6487.R5A43 1968] 74-156512
1. Yang, Hanford—Art collections. 2. Art, Modern—20th century—Exhibitions. I. Title.

ALDRICH Museum of Contemporary Art. 709'.73
Cool art: 1967 [Ridgefield, Conn., 1968] [32] p. illus. 19 cm. On label on t.p.: Supplied by Worldwide Books, New York. Exhibition held Jan. 7-Mar. 17, 1968, at the Aldrich Museum of Contemporary Art, Ridgefield, Conn. [N6490.A567] 68-30100
1. Art, Modern—20th century—Exhibitions. I. Title.

AMERICAN Federation of Arts. 709'.4
Venice Biennale prize-winners, 1960; [exhibition] World House Galleries, New York, February 14-March 4, 1961. Organized and circulated by the American Federation of Arts. [New York, Printed by Clarke and Way at the Thistle Press, 1961] 23 p. illus. 21 cm. "Presented under the auspices of the Italian Cultural Institute, New York." [N6487.N4W67] 73-161535
1. Art, Modern—20th century—Exhibitions. 2. Art—Competitions. I. Venice. Biennale d'arte, II. 30th, 1960. III. World House Galleries, New York. IV. Title.

ANNELY Juda Fine Art. 709'.04'7074094134
Gallery choice : six artists from the Gallery : Christo, John Davies, Alan Green, Peter Kalkhof. Michaeledes, Wendy Taylor : [catalogue of] a Scottish Arts Council exhibition arranged by Annely Juda Fine Art ... January 24-February 22, 1976, Scottish Arts Council Gallery ... Edinburgh, March 23-April 11, 1976, the Third Eye Centre ... Glasgow. [Edinburgh] : [The Council], [1976]. [15] p. : ill., plan, port ; 18 cm. Cover title: Christo, John Davies, Alan Green, Peter Kalkhof, Michaeledes, Wendy Taylor. [N6488.G7E342 1976] 76-378549
1. Art, Modern—20th century—Exhibitions. I. Christo, 1935- II. Scottish Arts Council Gallery. III. Title. IV. Title: Christo, John Davies, Alan Green, Peter Kalkhof, Michaeledes, Wendy Taylor.

ASSOCIATION of American Painters and Sculptors, New York. 709'.04'07401471
The Armory Show; international exhibition of modern art, 1913. New York, Arno Press [1972] 3 v. illus. 23 cm. (v. 3: 29 cm.) (Arno series of contemporary art) Contents.Contents.—v. 1. Catalogues.—v. 2. Pamphlets.—v. 3. Contemporary and retrospective documents. Includes bibliographical references. [N6493 1913.A84] 72-165525 ISBN 0-405-00828-7
1. Armory Show, New York, 1913. 2. Art, Modern—20th century—Exhibitions. I. Title. BIP

BOSTON. Institute of Contemporary Art. 709.04'5
New directions in collecting. [Boston?] c1967- v. illus., ports. 31 cm. On label on t.p.: Supplied by Worldwide Books, New York. Exhibition organized by the Institute of Contemporary Art, Boston, and held Apr. 8-May 14, 1967, at the Institute of Contemporary Art and July 5-25, 1967, at the Berkshire Museum, Pittsfield. Contents.Contents.—pt. 1. Museum acquisitions. [N6490.B617] 68-30089
1. Art, Modern—20th century—Exhibitions. 2. Art—Collectors and collecting. I. Berkshire Museum, Pittsfield, Mass. II. Title.

BOSTON. Museum of Fine Arts. 709'.04'074014461
Earth, air, fire, water: elements of art. [Boston, 1971] 117 p. illus. 28 cm. Catalog of one in a series of exhibitions celebrating the 100th anniversary of the Museum. Illustrations (p. 74-117) issued separately. Bibliography: p. 63-65. [N6487.B6M84] 70-153512
1. Art, Modern—20th century—Exhibitions. I. Title.

BRAUNER, Victor, 1903- 759.4
Ses frontieres noires. [New York, A. Iolas, 1970] [56] p. (chiefly illus.) 26 cm. Cover title. Distributor named on label: Supplied by World-Wide Books, Boston. "Publie a l'occasion de l'exposition des tableaux de Victor Brauner a la Galerie Iolas, Paris." [ND553.B873A55] 70-19597
I. Galerie Alexandre Iolas, Paris. II. Title.

CALIFORNIA. University. Art Museum. 708.194'67
Selection 1968: recent accessions to the university art collections. Exhibition at the University art gallery, 6 Aug. 15 Sept. 1968 Berkeley, Calif. [1968] 191 p. illus. (part col.) 22 cm. [N6490.C217] 76-8993
1. Art, Modern—20th century—Exhibitions. 2. Art—Berkeley, Calif. I. Title.

CATHERINE Viviano Gallery. 759.06'074'01471
Paintings, sculpture, American and European. [Exhibition opening March 3rd through April 11th, 1970. New York, 1970] [2] p., 20 plates. 23 cm. Cover title. [N6490.C34] 78-23155
1. Art, Modern—20th century—Exhibitions. I. Title.

CLASSICS of contemporary art from the Maremont Collection. 709.04
Phoenix, 1968. [24] p. illus. 22 cm. Catalog, by H. T. Broadley, of an exhibition held at the Phoenix Art Museum, May-November, 1968. [N6490.C585] 68-7022
1. Maremont, Adele H., 1902- —Art collections. 2. Art, Modern—20th century—Exhibitions. I. Broadley, Hugh T. II. Phoenix, Ariz. Art Museum.

CORCORAN Gallery of Art, Washington, D.C. 707'.4'0153
The H. Marc Moyens Collection; a selection of paintings, drawings, and sculpture. [Washington, D.C., c1969] 35 p. illus. (1 col.) 25 cm. Catalog of the exhibition held at the Corcoran Gallery of Art, Dec. 12, 1969-Jan. 18, 1970. [N6490.C657] 79-111198
1. Moyens, H. Marc—Art collections. 2. Art, Modern—20th century—Exhibitions.

CROOKSHANK, Anne. 709'.04'074094183
Rosc '71: the poetry of vision; an international exhibition of modern art from outside Ireland and Viking Age art [Dublin, Printed by Cahill, 1971?] 231 p. illus. 25 cm. Addendum and errata slips inserted. Catalog of an exhibition held at the Royal Dublin Society, Oct. 24-Dec. 29, 1971. "The exhibition of Viking Age art [catalog by] D. M. Wilson": p. 121-203. Includes bibliographical references. [N6488.I77D83] 72-198167
1. Art, Modern—20th century—Exhibitions. 2. Art, Celtic—Exhibitions. I. Royal Dublin Society. II. Title.

CUCARO, Pascal, 1915- 759.13
Pascal Cucaro, by Robert E. Hopkins. New York, Sentinel Art Books, c1969. 63 p. (chiefly illus. (part col.)) 23 cm. English, Japanese, and French. [ND237.C846H6] 70-97895
I. Hopkins, Robert E., 1934-

DARTMOUTH College. Hopkins Center. 709'.73'074014461
Artists at Dartmouth; a retrospective of selected artists-in-residence at Dartmouth College since 1962. [Exhibition held at] New City Hall, Boston, Mass., Oct. 14-30, 1971. [Hanover, N.H., 1971?] [36] p. illus. 28 cm. Cover title. Sponsored by the Hopkins Center for the Creative & Performing Arts at Dartmouth College and the Mayor's Office of Cultural Affairs, Boston, Mass. [N6487.H3D33] 72-198180
1. Art, Modern—20th century—Exhibitions. I. Boston. Mayor's Office of Cultural Affairs. II. Title.

DAVID : 209.04'074'0147277
hommage a Michelangelo : Galerie Levy [Ausstellung vom 26. Mai - 26. Juli : Katalog / Text, Peter Grimm]. Hamburg : die Galerie, [1975?] [28] p. : chiefly ill. ; 21 x 30 cm. Limited ed. of 500 copies. [N6488.G3H283] 75-515163
1. Buonarroti, Michel Angelo, 1475-1564. David. 2. David, King of Israel—Art. 3. Art, Modern—20th century—Exhibitions. I. Grimm, Peter. II. Galerie Levy.

DOUBLE exposure. 709.04
Introd. by Ruth Bowman. New York [1969] [52] p. illus., ports. 26 cm. Catalog of an exhibition circulated 1969-70 by the American Federation of Arts. "Exhibition number 69-11." [N6490.D64] 74-91809
1. Art, Modern—20th century—Exhibitions. I. Bowman, Ruth. II. American Federation of Arts.

FINCH College, New York. Museum of Art. Contemporary Study Wing. 709.04'6
Destruction art; destroy to create. Introd. and acknowledgement by Elayne H. Varian. New York [1968] [16] p. illus. 28 cm. Exhibition held May 10-June 20, 1968 in the Contemporary Wing, Finch College Museum of Art. [N6490.F532] 68-30500
1. Art, Modern—20th century—Exhibitions. I. Varian, Elayne H. II. Title.

FINCH College, New York, Museum of Art. Contemporary Study Wing. 708.13
Jacques Kaplan's private collection. [Exhibition] February 12 through March 30, 1969. Foreword by Elayne H. Varian. New York [1969] [9] p. (incl. cover) illus. 28 cm. [N6487.N4F55] 71-75346
1. Kaplan, Jacques, 1924- —Art collections. 2. Art, Modern—20th century—Exhibitions. I. Varian, Elayne H. II. Title.

FORTH Worth Art Museum. 709'.04
Twentieth century art from Fort Worth Dallas collections : an exhibition organized by the Fort Worth Art Museum, Fort Worth, Texas, 8 September-15 October, 1974. Fort Worth, Tex. : The Museum, [1974] [40] p. : ill. (some col.) ; 27 cm. [N6487.F67F677 1974] 74-15494
1. Art, Modern—20th century—Exhibitions. 2. Art, Modern—20th century—Fort Worth, Tex. 3. Art, Modern—20th century—Dallas. I. Title.

GIMPEL Gallery. 735'.29'07401471
Gimpel Gallery, Gimpel & Weitzenhoffer Limited. New York, 1969. [46] p., chiefly illus. 19 x 24 cm. On p. [4] of cover: Collectors choice. Catalog of the Gimpel Gallery's opening exhibition. [N6487.N4G54] 73-150710
1. Art, Modern—20th century—Exhibitions. I. Title: Collectors choice.

GRIDS grids grids grids grids grids grids grids. 709'.04
[Exhibition] Jan. 27 to March 1, 1972, Institute of Contemporary Art, University of Pennsylvania, Philadelphia. [Philadelphia, 1972] [31] p. illus. 20 x 21 cm. Catalogue essay "Top to bottom, left to right," by L. R. Lippard (p. [5]-[14]) [N6487.P45P463] 74-160738
1. Art, Modern—20th century—Exhibitions. 2. Grids (Cartography) in art. I. Lippard, Lucy R. II. Pennsylvania. University. Institute of Contemporary Art.

GROUP zero. 709'.22
New York, Arno/Worldwide, 1968. [78] p. illus. 14 cm. Reprint of a catalog of an exhibition held at the Institute of Contemporary Art, University of Pennsylvania, Philadelphia, Oct. 30-Dec. 11, 1964. [N6758.G76] 68-20081
1. Art, Modern—20th century—Exhibitions. 2. Art, Modern—20th century—Europe. I. Pennsylvania. University. Institute of Contemporary Art. II. Title: Zero. BIP

HARVARD University. Busch-Reisinger Museum of Germanic Culture. 709.04'074'01444
Concepts of the Bauhaus: the Busch-Reisinger Museum Collection. Introd., exhibition catalogue, and handlist of the Bauhaus research collection, by John David Farmer and Geraldine Weiss. Introductory essays by Charles L. Kuhn [and others. Cambridge? 1971] 136 p. illus. 22 x 26 cm. An exhibition held at the Busch-Reisinger Museum, Apr. 30-Sept. 3, 1971. [N6487.C3H34] 74-198439
1. Art, Modern—20th century—Exhibitions. 2. Bauhaus. I. Farmer, John David, ed. II. Weiss, Geraldine, ed. III. Title.

INTERNATIONAL Play Group. 759.06
International Play Group and The Creche present: Young artists from around the world; exhibition and sale, May 6-June 6, 1969. [New York, 1969] 62 p. illus. 26 cm. (International Play Group. Exhibition, 69/1) Title on cover: Young artists from around the world. [N6487.N4I54] 78-87746
1. Art, Modern—20th century—Exhibitions. I. The Creche. II. Title. III. Title: Young artists from around the world. IV. Series.

JEWISH Theological Seminary of America. Jewish Museum. 709.04
The Harry N. Abrams family collection. [Exhibition] The Jewish Museum, New York, N.Y., June 29 through September 5, 1966. [Introd. by Sam Hunter, and an interview with Harry N. Abrams. New York, 1966] 1 v. (unpaged) 25 x 12 cm. Cover title. Issued in folder form, introd. and interview attached to front cover, list of paintings to back cover. [N6490.J49] 66-26094
1. Art, Modern—20th century—Exhibitions. 2. Art—Private collections. I. Abrams, Harry N. II. Title.

JOSLYN Art Museum. 707.4'09782'25
The thirties decade: American artists and their European contemporaries. [Omaha, 1971] 80 p. illus. 26 cm. Catalog of the exhibition held Oct. 10-Nov. 28, 1971. [N6493 1930.J6] 71-173356
1. Art, Modern—20th century—Exhibitions. I. Title.

KRAMER, Reuben, 1909- 730.973
The art of Reuben Kramer, by Theodore L. Low. Baltimore, Walters Art Gallery, Charles & Center, 1963. 112p. illus., plates. 29cm. 63-22459 7.50
I. Low, Theodore Lewis, 1915- II. Title. BIP

LE BROCQUY, Louis, 1916- 759.9415
Louis le Brocquy. 27 April to 15 May 1971, Gimpel & Weitzenhoffer, New York. [New York, 1971] [22] p. illus., port. 24 cm. [ND497.L45A49] 73-198156
I. Gimpel & Weitzenhoffer.

Includes index. [N6487.W3U548] 78-3715 15.95
1. Art, Modern—20th century—Exhibitions. I. Title.

Art, Modern—20th century—Exhibitions.

ANNIGONI, Pietro. 759.5
Pietro Annigoni; a retrospective exhibition. [Brooklyn] Brooklyn Museum [1969] 98 p. illus. (part col.) 23 cm. Catalog of a loan exhibition held at the Brooklyn Museum Apr. 27-June 22, 1969, and at the California Palace of the Legion of Honor, San Francisco, July 19-Aug. 31, 1969. Bibliography: p. 97-98. [ND623.A55A52] 79-81631
I. Brooklyn Institute of Arts and Sciences. Museum. II. California Palace of the Legion of Honor, San Francisco.

ANTONAKOS, Stephen, 1926- 746.9
"Pillows" (1962-1963) [Houston, Tex., Fidelity Print. Co., 1971] [30] p. (incl. cover) illus. 22 x 28 cm. Title from fabric cover. Catalogue of an exhibition held at the Meredith Long & Co., Houston Galleries, and organized by S. J. Adler. [N6537.A53A65] 78-159534
I. Adler, Sebastian J., 1936- II. Meredith Long Gallery. III. Title.

BAKKE, Larry, 1932- 759.11
Larry Bakke: drawings and paintings, 1957-1969, by Laurence Schmeckebier. Syracuse, N.Y., Syracuse University, School of Art [1969] 58 p. illus. 23 cm. "Introduction and catalog of an exhibition held in the galleries of the Joe and Emily Lowe Art Center, Syracuse University, February 1-28, 1969." [NC139.B32S3] 76-77474
I. Schmeckebier, Laurence Eli, 1906- II. Syracuse University. Joe and Emily Lowe Art Center.

BIEL-BIENNE, Eugene V., 1902- 759.1'3
A retrospective show of paintings and drawings by Biel. Nashville, Tennessee Fine Arts Center [1960] [56] p. illus. 21 cm. Cover title: E. Biel retrospective. French and English. Exhibition held Oct. 9-Nov. 13, 1960, at the Tennessee Fine Arts Center, Nashville. [N6537.B5A55] 741.9'73 75-284651
I. Tennessee Fine Arts Center. II. Title. III. Title: E. Biel retrospective.

BOGHOSIAN, Varujan. 730'.924
Varujan Boghosian, artist-in-residence, Hopkins Center, summer 1968. Hanover, N.H., Dartmouth College [1968] [16] p. (on double leaves) illus. 21 cm. Catalog of an exhibition held July 4-29, 1968, in the Jaffe-Friede Gallery, Hopkins Center, Dartmouth College; and Aug. 3-Sept. 2, 1968, in the Currier Gallery of Art. [NB237.B58A58] 68-66306
I. Dartmouth College. Hopkins Center. II. Currier Gallery of Art, Manchester, N.H.

CALIFORNIA. University. ArtMuseum. 701.16
Selection 1967; recent acquisitions in modern art. Exhibition at the University art gallery 20 June-10 Sept. 1967. Berkeley, Calif. [1967] 161 p. illus. (part col.) 22 cm. [N6490.C216] 67-63926
1. Art, Modern—20th cent.—Exhibitions. 2. Art—Berkeley, Calif. I. Title.

CALIFORNIA. University. University at Los Angeles. Art Council. 709.04
Years of ferment ; the birth of twentieth century art 1886-1914. An exhibition sponsored by the UCLA Art Council in collaboration with the UCLA Art Galleries. Presented at the following participating institutions: UCLA Art Galleries, San Francisco Museum of Art, Cleveland Museum of Art, 1965. [Los Angeles, 1965] 91 p. illus. 28 cm. Bibliography: p. 88-91. [N6490.C22] 65-16731
1. Art, Modern—20 cent.—Exhibitions. I. California. University. University at Los Angeles. Art Galleries II. San Francisco. Museum of Art. III. Cleveland Museum of Art. IV. Title.

CLEVELAND Museum of Art 709.04
Fifty years of modern art, 1916-1966 [by] Edward B. Henning. [Cleveland, 1966] vii, 209p. illus., col. plates (pt. fold.) 25cm. Catalog of an exhibition held at the Cleveland Mus. of Art in celebration of its fiftieth anniversary, Illus. 48a (1 leaf) inserted. Bibl. [N6490.C628] 66-21228 12.50
1. Art, Modern—20th cent.—Exhibitions. I. Henning, Edward B. II. Title.
Available from the Press of Western Reserve Univ., Cleveland.

CORNELL, Thomas. 741.9'73
Thomas Cornell drawings & prints. [Brunswick, Me.] Bowdoin College, Museum of Art, 1971. 1 v. (chiefly illus.) 29 cm. Catalogue of an exhibition held at Bowdoin College Museum of Art, Nov. 5-Dec. 19, 1971 and the Art Museum, Princeton University, Jan. 14-Feb. 13, 1972. [NC139.C65B68] 72-194220
I. Bowdoin College. Museum of Art. II. Princeton University. Art Museum. III. Title.

DICKINSON, Eleanor, 1931- 741.9'73
Revival! [Exhibition] September 25-November 1, 1970, the Corcoran Gallery of Art. [Washington, Printed by Georgetown Print. Co., 1970] [29] p. (incl. cover) illus. 26 cm. [NC139.D5A56] 77-139820
I. Corcoran Gallery of Art, Washington, D.C. II. Title.

DOWNING, Thomas, 1928- 759.13
Thomas Downing;paintings, 1962-1967 La Jolla? Calif., 1968?] [24] p. illus. (part col.), port. 24 cm. Exhibition held Jan. 18 to Feb. 25, 1968, at the La Jolla Museum of Art, and Apr. 2 to Apr. 28, 1968, at the Phoenix Art Museum. Bibliography: p. [23] . [ND237.D676L3] 68-2102
I. La Jolla, Calif. Museum of Art. II. Phoenix, Ariz. Art Museum.

DUNCANSON, Robert S., 1821-1872. 759.13
Robert S. Duncanson: a centennial exhibition. [Cincinnati, Cincinnati Art Museum, 1972] 42 p. illus. (part col.) 26 cm. Catalog of an exhibition held at the Cincinnati Art Museum, March 16-April 30, 1972. Bibliography: p. 16-17. [ND237.D77C5] 72-186854
I. Cincinnati. Art Museum.

FEELEY, Paul, 1910-1966. 709'.24
Paul Feeley, 1910-1966. A memorial exhibition: the Solomon R. Guggenheim Museum, New York. [New York, Solomon R. Guggenheim Foundation, 1968] 73 p. illus. (part col.), port. 26 cm. Catalog of "Exhibition 68/2, April-May 1968." Bibliographical references included in "Footnotes" (p. 19) [ND237.F3S6] 68-25521
I. Solomon R. Guggenheim Museum, New York.

FRAZIER, John Robinson, 1889-1966. 759.13
The late works. [Providence, Museum of Art, Rhode Island School of Design, 1969?] [42] p. illus. (part col.) 22 cm. Catalog of an exhibition held at the Museum of Art, Rhode Island School of Design, April 27-June 15, 1969, and at other galleries. Includes bibliographies. [ND237.F677A49] 70-7650
I. Rhode Island School of Design, Providence. Museum of Art.

GALERIE Louise Leiris, Paris. 759.4
Rouvre: peintures 1951-1961; Galerie Louise Leiris, 3 november-2 december 1961. [dist. New York, Witenborn, 1962] [9] p., 60 illus. (pt. col. 17cm. (Its Catalogue. Serie A, no 13) 62-819 2.00 pap.,
I. Title.

GATCH, Lee, 1902-1968. 759.13
Lee Gatch, 1902-1968, by Adelyn D. Breeskin. Washington, Published for the National Collection of Fine Arts by the Smithsonian Institution Press, 1971. 64 p. illus. (part col.) 26 cm. Catalog of an exhibition held at the National Collection of Fine Arts, Washington, D.C., Oct. 6-Nov. 14, 1971; Washington University Gallery of Art, St. Louis, Dec. 1, 1971-Jan. 15, 1972; and the Newark Museum, Newark, N.J., Feb. 2-Mar. 12, 1972. Bibliography: p. 59-63. [ND237.G29B7] 73-175636
I. Breeskin, Adelyn Dohme, 1896- II. Smithsonian Institution. National Collection of Fine Arts. III. Washington University, St. Louis. Gallery of Art. IV. Newark Museum Association, Newark, N.J.

GOTO, Joseph, 1920- 730'.924
Joseph Goto; [exhibition at] Museum of Art, Rhode Island School of Design, October 21-November 28, 1971. [Providence, Museum of Art, Rhode Island School of Design, 1971] 43 p. illus. 29 cm. [NB237.G64R45] 71-177398
I. Rhode Island School of Design, Providence. Museum of Art.

GRAU-GARRIGA, Josep, 1929- 709'.2'4
Josep Grau-Garriga; decade retrospective, 1960-1970. [Houston, Tex., Museum of Fine Arts, 1970] [115] p. illus. (part col.) 24 x 26 cm. Catalogue of an exhibition held at the Museum of Fine Arts, Houston, Tex., Jan. 21-Mar. 16, 1971. Erratum slip inserted. Bibliography: p. [24] -[27] [N7113.G7H6] 72-198202
I. Houston, Tex. Museum of Fine Arts.

HORIUCHI, Paul, 1906- 759.13
Paul Horiuchi: 50 years of painting. [Eugene? Or., 1969?] 45 p. illus. (part col.), port. 23 cm. Exhibition held at the Museum of Art, University of Oregon, Feb. 4 to Mar. 16, 1969 and the Seattle Art Museum, March 27 to May 4, 1969. Label mounted on t.p.: Supplied by Worldwide Books, Boston. Bibliography: p. 45. [ND1059.H75A56] 70-633756
I. Oregon. University. Museum of Art. II. Seattle. Art Museum.

HORIUCHI, Paul, 1906- 71019
Recent works by Paul Horiuchi. [Exhibition] March 21 to April 16, 1966 Los Angeles, Felix Landau Gallery [1966] 1 v. (chiefly illus., part col.) [68-51894]
I. Felix Landau Gallery. II. Title.

HOUSTON, Tex. University of St. Thomas. Art Dept. 760'.0922
Six painters: Mondrian, Guston, Kline, De Kooning, Pollock [and] Rothko. [Houston, 1968]C67 p. illus., part col. 23 cm. Exhibition held Feb.-April 1967. [N6490.H78] 67-30452
1. Art, Modern—20th cent.—Exhibitions. I. Title.

LARSEN, Jack Lenor. 745.4'4'924
Retrospective: Jack Lenor Larsen, an exhibition co-sponsored by the Designer/Craftsman Guild and the Fort Wayne Art Institute, July 12 through August 24, 1969. [Fort Wayne, Ind.] Fort Wayne Museum of Art [1969] [24] p. illus. (part col.) 21 x 22 cm. Bibliography: p. [22] [NK8998.L3A57] 72-90928
I. Designer/Craftsman Guild. II. Fort Wayne Museum of Art. III. Title.

MACCIO, Romulo, 1931- 759.982
Maccio: fictions. [New York, Center for Inter-American Relations, Art Gallery, 1969] [20] p. illus. 22 cm. Prepared for an exhibition held Feb. 6-Mar. 9, 1969, in the Art Gallery of the Center for Inter-American Relations, New York. [ND339.M25A5] 76-3560
I. Center for Inter-American Relations. Art Gallery. II. Title: Fictions.

MCWILLIAM, F. E., 1909- 730.9415
McWilliam. Introd. by Roland Penrose. London, A. Tiranti, 1964. 16p., [120]p. of illus., port. 26cm. English and French. [NB497.M3P4] 66-36234 13.50
I. Penrose, Roland. II. Title.
Available from Transatlantic, New York.

NESCH, Rolf, 1893- 709'.24
Rolf Nesch: graphics, material pictures, plastics. Introd. by Alfred Hentzen. Translated by Hans Rosenwald. New York, Universe Books [1969, c1960] 118 p. illus. (part col.) 35 cm. Translation of Graphik, Materialbilder, Plastik. [N6888.N4H413] 72-88589 22.50
I. Hentzen, Alfred, 1903- II. Title.

NUOVE tecniche d'immagine, San Marino, Palazzo dei congressi, 15 luglio-30 settembre 1967. [6. biennale d'arte Repubblica di S. Marino. Venezia] Alfieri [1967] Stamped on t.p.: American dist.: Wittenborn, New York. 160p. illus. (pt.col.),ports. 23x24cm. Italian, English, French and/or German. [N6490.N8] 67-9818 7.00 pap., 709.04
1. Art, Modern—20th cent.—Exhibitions. 2. Composition (Art)

PO-YONG. 709'.2'4
Po Yong: symmetrical development. [Fresno? Calif., Fresno Arts Center? 1971] [25] p. illus. (part col.) 25 cm. "Constructive art by Po-Yong, Fresno Arts Center, October 5-24, 1971": 1 leaf inserted. [N7349.P6F73] 73-156804
I. Fresno Arts Center. II. Title. III. Title: Constructive art by Po-Yong.

PORTLAND, Or. Art Museum. 701.16
Paintings, drawings, sculptures, from the collection of Caroline & Erwin Swann: "The pleasures of the eye"; an exhibition organized 1964 by the Portland Art Museum, Portland, Oregon. [Portland, 1964] 62 p. illus. (part col.) 24 cm. [N6490.P65] 66-3725
1. Art. Modern—20th cent.—Exhibitions 2. Art—Private collections. I. Swann, Caroline II. Swann, Erwin. III. Title. IV. Title: The pleasures of the eye.

PUBLIC Education Association of the City of New York. 709.04
Seven decades; 1895-1965; crosscurrents in modern art; exhibition April 26-May 21, 1966 text by Peter Selz. [New York, 1966] 192 p. illus. (part col.) 28 cm. [N6490.P77] 66-57731
1. Art, Modern—20th cent.—Exhibitions. I. Selz, Peter. II. Title.

SOBRINO, Francisco, 1932- 730'.924
Sobrino. New York, Galerie Denise Rene [1971] 1 v. (chiefly illus.) 27 cm. Catalog of an exhibition held November 1971. [NB813.S6G3] 70-198478
I. Galerie Denise Rene.

SOUNDERBORG, Kurt R. H., 1923. 759.3
Sounderborg [by] Otto Hahn. New York, Abrams [c.1964] 77p. illus. (pt. col.) 21x23cm. (Mod. artists) 64-18894 5.95
I. Hahn, Otto, German art critic. II. Title.

WOODVILLE, Richard Caton, 1825-1855. 759.13
Richard Caton Woodville, an early American genre painter. Washington, Corcoran Gallery of Art [1967] 1 v. (unpaged) illus., ports. 22 x 23 cm. Text by Francis S. Grubar. Exhibition at the Corcoran Gallery of Art, Washington, and at other museums, Apr. 21, 1967-Apr. 5, 1968. Bibliography: page at end. [ND237.W82G7] 67-68195
I. Grubar, Francis S. II. Corcoran Gallery of Art, Washington, D.C. III. Title.

Art, Modern—20th century—Germany.

NEW York (City). Museum of Modern Art. 709'.43
German art of the twentieth century, by Werner Haftmann, Alfred Hentzen [and] William S. Lieberman. Edited by Andrew Carnduff Ritchie. Reprint ed. [New York] Published for the Museum of Modern Art by Arno Press, 1972. 239 p. illus. 26 cm. (Museum of Modern Art publications in reprint) Reprint of the 1957 ed., which was issued to accompany an exhibition held at the Museum of Modern Art, New York, Oct. 1-Dec. 8, 1957, and at the City Art Museum of St. Louis, Jan. 8-Feb. 24, 1958. Bibliography, by N. Riegen: p. 227-235. [N6868.N38 1972] 78-169303 ISBN 0-405-01562-3 25.00
1. Art, Modern—20th century—Germany. 2. Art, German—Exhibitions. I. Haftmann, Werner. II. Hentzen, Alfred, 1903- III. Lieberman, William Slattery, 1924- IV. St. Louis. City Art Museum. V. Title.

Art, Modern—20th century—History.

ARNASON, H. Harvard. 709.04
History of modern art: painting, sculpture, architecture [by] H. H. Arnason. New York, H. N. Abrams [1968] 663 p. illus. (part. col.) 31 cm. Bibliography: p. 631-643. [N6490.A713] 68-26863 25.00
1. Art, Modern—20th century—History. I. Title.

BRUNHAMMER, Yvonne. 709.4
The nineteen twenties style [translated from the Italian by Raymond Rudorff] London, New York, Hamlyn, 1969. 159 p. col. illus. 20 cm. (Cameo) Translation of Lo stile 1925. [N6493 1925.B713] 76-546030 ISBN 0-600-01224-7 18/-
1. Art, Modern—20th century—History. 2. Art industries and trade—History. I. Title.

DELEVOY, Robert L. 709.04
Dimensions of the 20th century: 1900-1945[Tr. from french by Stuart Gilbert] Geneva] Skira [Cleveland, World, 1966,c.1965] 223p. illus. (pt. mounted col.) 31cm. (Art ideas hist.) Bibl. [N6490.D3813] 65-24417 20.00
1. Art, Modern—20th cent.—Hist. 2. Art and society. 3. Art—Psychology. I. Title. II. Series.

LUCIE-SMITH, Edward. 709'.04
Art now : from abstract expressionism to superrealism / Edward Lucie-Smith ; [introd., Gillo Dorfles ; brief biographies, Lara Vinca Masini ; editors, Mariella de Battisti, Marisa Melis]. New York : Morrow, 1977. 504 p. : col. ill. ; 29 cm. Originally published in 1976 under title: Arte oggi. Includes index. Bibliography: p. 501. [N6490.L77813 1977] 77-76724 ISBN 0-688-03201-X : 29.95
1. Art, Modern—20th century—History. 2. Art, Modern—20th century—Themes, motives. I. Title. BIP

ROOKMAAKER, Hendrik Roelof, 1922- 709
Modern art and the death of a culture [by] H. R. Rookmaaker. [1st ed. Downers Grove, Ill.] Inter-Varsity Press [1970] 256 p. illus. 20 cm. Bibliography: p. [253]-254. [N6490.R584 1970b] 73-130658 ISBN 0-87784-888-2
1. Art, Modern—20th century—History. 2. Art—Philosophy. 3. Art and society. I. Title. BIP

ROTERS, Eberhard. 759
Painters of the Bauhaus. [Translated from the German by Anna Rose Cooper.] New York, Praeger [1969, c1965] 215 p. illus. (part col.) 27 cm. Translation of Maler am Bauhaus. Bibliography: p. 207-209. [N332.B38R613] 69-15385 18.50
1. Bauhaus. 2. Art, Modern—20th century—History. I. Title.

VERONESI, Giulia. 709.04
Style and design, 1909-1929. New York, G. Braziller [1968] 367 p. illus. (part col.) 25 cm. Translation of Stile 1925. [N6493 1925.V4132] 68-20093 15.00
1. Art, Modern—20th century—History. 2. Art industries and trade—History. I. Title.

Art, Modern—20th century—Indexes.

PARRY, Pamela Jeffcott. 709'.04
Contemporary art and artists : an index to reproductions / compiled by Pamela Jeffcott Parry. Westpost, Conn. : Greenword Press, 1979 xlix, 327 p. ; 24 cm. "List of books indexed" p: [xiii]-xv. [N6490.P3234] 78-57763 ISBN 0-313-20544-2 lib. bdg. : 27.50
1. Art, Modern—20th century—Indexes. 2. Artists—Indexes. I. Title.

Art, Modern—20th century—Japan.

KUNG, David. 709.52
The contemporary artist in Japan. Honolulu, East-West Center Press [1966] 187 p. illus. (part col.) ports. 27 x 28 cm. [N7358.K8] 66-31499
1. Art, Modern—20th century—Japan. 2. Art, Modern I. Title. BIP

TAWARAYA, Sotatsu, d. 1643. 759.952
Sotatsu [by] Judith and Arthur Hart Burling. New York, Crown [1962] 17p. 23 plates (pt. col.) 18x19 cm. (Art of the East lib.) Bibl. 62-1653 1.45 bds.,
I. Burling, Judith. II. Burling, Arthur Hart. III. Title. IV. Series.

Art, Modern—20th century—San Francisco Bay region.

GLASSMAN, Joel, 1946- 709'.2'2
Joel Glassman, Carlos Gutierrez-Solana, Paul Kos; an exhibition organized by the La Jolla Museum of Contemporary Art, La Jolla, California, October 13-December 5, 1973. [La Jolla, Calif., c1973] 24 p. illus. 21 cm. Includes bibliographies. [N6530.C2G552] 73-92614
1. Glassman, Joel, 1946- 2. Gutierrez-Solana, Carlos, 1947- 3. Kos, Paul, 1942- 4. Art, Modern—20th century—San Francisco Bay region. I. Gutierrez-Solana, Carlos, 1947- II. Kos, Paul, 1942- III. La Jolla Museum of Contemporary Art.

Art, Modern—20th century—Scottsdale, Ariz.—Catalogs.

SCOTTSDALE Fine Arts Commission. 709'.73'074019173
The Scottsdale collection. [Scottsdale, Ariz., 1972] 48 p. illus. (part col.) 23 cm. A catalog. [N6535.S36S36] 72-169723 3.00
1. Art, Modern—20th century—Scottsdale, Ariz.—Catalogs. I. Title.

Art, Modern—20th century—Themes, motives.

BLOM, Dorothea (Johnson) 1911- 709'.04
Art and the changing world: uncommon sense in the 20th century, by Dorothea Blom. [Wallingford, Pa., Pendle Hill Publications, 1972] 35 p. illus. 20 cm. (Pendle Hill pamphlet 183) Bibliography: p. 35. [N6490.B54] 72-80094 ISBN 0-87574-183-5 0.70
1. Art, Modern—20th century—Themes, motives. 2. Art—Philosophy. I. Title.

LAVIN, Edward, comp. 709'.04
Discovery in art [compiled by] Edward Lavin [and] Terrence Manning. Paramus, N.J., Paulist Press [1969] 216 p. illus. (part col.) 21 cm. (Discovery series) [N6490.L33] 72-100008 4.95
1. Art, Modern—20th century—Themes, motives. 2. Art—Psychology. I. Manning, Terrence, joint comp. II. Title.

OSBORNE, Harold, 1905- 709'.04
Abstraction and artifice in twentieth-century art / Harold Osborne. Oxford : Clarendon Press ; New York : Oxford University Press, 1979. 193 p., [8] leaves of plates : ill. ; 22 cm. Includes bibliographical references and index. [N6490.O73] 78-40234 ISBN 0-19-817359-8 : 18.50
1. Art, Modern—20th century—Themes, motives. 2. Art, Abstract. 3. Conceptual art. I. Title. BIP

PRESENT projects / 709'.04
by George Brecht ... [et al.]. Malmo : Ed. Leger, [1976] 56 p. ill. ; 24 cm. Cover title. English, French, or Swedish. [N6490.P73] 77-353672 ISBN 9-18-547400-2 : kr20.00
1. Art, Modern—20th century—Themes, motives. 2. Avant-garde (Aesthetics) I. Brecht, George.

STUCKI, Margaret E. 709'.04
The revolutionary mission of modern art; or, Crud, and other essays on art [by] Margaret E. Stucki. Edited by Fred Karl Scheibe. [Cape Canaveral, Fla., Birds Meadow Pub. Co., 1973] 215 p. illus. 21 cm. Includes bibliographical references. [N6490.S83] 73-176523 3.50
1. Art, Modern—20th century—Themes, motives. 2. Aesthetics, Modern—20th century. 3. Politics in art. I. Title. II. Title: Crud, and other essays on art. BIP

Art, Modern—20th century—United States.

ATKINSON, J. Edward, comp. 709'.73
Black dimensions in contemporary American art. Compiled and edited by J. Edward Atkinson. New York, New American Library [1971] 126 p. col. illus. 21 cm. (A Plume book) [N6538.N5A8] 71-140263 3.95
1. Art, Modern—20th century—United States. 2. Negro artists—United States. I. Title. BIP

COWLES, Charles. 709'.73'07401469
Young artists, from the Collection of Charles Cowles. Exhibition: September 28 through December 14, 1969, [Aldrich Museum of Contemporary Art] [Ridgefield, Conn., 1969?] 1 v. (unpaged) illus. 20 cm. [N6512.C65] 70-288298
1. Art, Modern—20th century—U.S. 2. Art, American—Exhibitions. 3. Art—Private collections—U.S. I. Aldrich Museum of Contemporary Art. II. Title.

FINLAY, Virgil. 741.6'5'0924
Virgil Finlay. West Kingston, R.I., D. M. Grant, 1971. 153 p. illus. 27 cm. Contents.Contents.—Selected illustrations, by V. Finlay.—Virgil Finlay, an appreciation, by S. Moskowitz.—A Virgil Finlay checklist, by G. de la Ree. [NC975.5.F5M6] 75-30318 6.00
I. Moskowitz, Samuel. II. De la Ree, Gerry.

HUNTER, Sam, 1923- 709'.73
American art of the 20th century. New York, H. N. Abrams [1972] 487 p. illus. (part col.) 28 cm. Bibliography: p. [437]-470. [N6512.H78] 72-3634 ISBN 0-8109-0030-0 17.50
1. Art, Modern—20th century—United States. 2. Art, American. I. Title.

HUNTER, Sam, 1923- 709'.73
American art of the 20th century: painting, sculpture, architecture [by Sam Hunter. With sections on architecture by John Jacobus New York, H. N. Abrams [1973] 583 p. illus. (part col.) 27 cm. Bibliography: p. [525]-560. [N6512.H78 1973] 73-10211 ISBN 0-8109-0135-8
1. Art, Modern—20th century—United States. 2. Art, American. I. Jacobus, John M. II. Title.

HUNTER, Sam, 1923- 709'.73
American art of the 20th century; painting, sculpture, architecture [by] Sam Hunter. With sections on architecture by John Jacobus. Enl. ed. Englewood Cliffs, N.J., Prentice-Hall [1973] 583 p. illus. (part col.) 28 cm. Bibliography: p. [525]-560. [N6512.H78 1973b] 73-10210 13.95
1. Art, Modern—20th century—United States. 2. Art, American. I. Jacobus, John M. II. Title.

WADSWORTH Atheneum, Hartford. 709'.2'2
Gilliam / Edwards / Williams: extensions; [catalogue of an exhibition] Wadsworth Atheneum, Hartford, Connecticut, February 6-March 17, 1974. [Hartford, 1974] 39 p. illus. (part col.) 23 cm. Includes bibliographies. [N6512.W28 1974] 73-94026
1. Gilliam, Sam. 2. Edwards, Melvin E. 3. Williams, William T., 1942- 4. Art, Modern—20th century—United States. I. Title. II. Title: Extensions.

WALKER Art Center, Minneapolis. 709.'73'0740176579
Works for new spaces; an exhibition, 18 May-25 July, 1971. [Minneapolis, 1971] [36] p. illus., ports. 28 cm. [N6512.W32] 77-173466
1. Art, Modern—20th century—U.S. 2. Art, American—Exhibitions. I. Title.

WELLER, Allen Stuart, 1907- 709'.73
The joys and sorrows of recent American art, by Allen S. Weller. Urbana, University of Illinois Press, 1968. 185 p. illus. (part col.) 26 cm. (The De Young lectures in higher education at Illinois State University, 1966) (Illini books.) Bibliographical footnotes. [N6512.W4] 68-21666 ISBN 0-252-72689-8 7.95
1. Art, Modern—20th century—United States. 2. Art, American. I. Title. II. Series: The Marion De Young lectures in higher education, 1966 BIP

Art, Modern—20th century—United States—Exhibitions.

PROJECTS in nature : eleven environmental works executed at Merriewold West, Far Hills, New Jersey, September 22 through October 31, 1975 / with an introd. by Edward F. Fry. [Far Hills, N.J. : Merriewold West], 1975. [46] p. : ill. ; 28 cm. [N6512.P7] 75-21517 709'.73'074014944
1. Art, Modern—20th century—United States—Exhibitions. 2. Conceptual art—United States—Exhibitions. 3. Environment (Art)—United States—Exhibitions. 4. Technology in art. I. Merriewold West.

SEATTLE. Art Museum. 709'.73'074019777
Carpenter, Chihuly, Scanga : [catalogue]. [Seattle] : Seattle Art Museum, 1977. 1 portfolio ([3] fold. leaves) : ill. (some col.) ; 24 cm. Cover title. Exhibition sponsored by the Seattle Art Museum and the Pilchuck School. [N6512.S33 1977] 77-154285
1. Carpenter, James, 1949- —Exhibitions. 2. Chihuly, Dale, 1941- —Exhibitions. 3. Scanga, Italo, 1932- —Exhibitions. 4. Art, Modern—20th century—United States—Exhibitions. I. Pilchuck School. II. Title.

WARD, Velox. 759.13
Velox Ward; an essay and catalogue to accompany the retrospective exhibition of the works of Velox Ward. By Donald and Margaret Vogel. Fort Worth [Tex.] Amon Carter Museum [1972] 64 p. illus., col. plates. 25 cm. Exhibition presented at the Amon Carter Museum, Fort Worth, Tex., and others, from May 11, 1972 to July 29, 1973. [ND237.W352V6] 72-83074
I. Vogel, Donald. II. Vogel, Margaret. III. Amon Carter Museum of Western Art, Fort Worth, Tex. BIP

Art, Modern—20th century—Wales—Exhibitions.

FIFTY-SIX Group Wales. 709'.2'2
The artist and how to employ him / 56 Group Wales. [Cardiff : The Group], 1976. 64 p. : ill. (some col.), ports. ; 30 cm. [N6792.F53 1976] 76-381122 ISBN 0-9505005-0-X : £1.95
1. Fifty-six Group Wales. 2. Art, Modern—20th century—Wales—Exhibitions. I. Title.

Art, Modern—20the cent.—Exhibitions.

FLINT Institute of Arts. 709.04
The first Flint Invitational, November 4-December 31, 1966; an exhibition of contemporary painting ad sculpture. Flint, Mich., [196-] 1 v. (unpaged) illus. 27 cm. Cover title: Flint Invitational. On label on t.p.: Supplied by Worldwide Books, New York. [N6490.F56] 68-30092
1. Art, Modern—20the cent.—Exhibitions. I. Title. II. Title: Flint Invitational.

HARRIS, Ann Sutherland. 709'.03'074019494
Women artists, 1550-1950 / Ann Sutherland Harris, Linda Nochlin. 1st ed. Los Angeles : Los Angeles County Museum of Art ; New York : distributed by Random House, 1976. 367 p. : ill. (some col.) ; 27 cm. Exhibition catalog. Includes index. Bibliography: p. 362-365. [N6350.H35 1976] 76-39955 ISBN 0-87587-073-2 pbk. : 6.95
1. Art, Modern—Exhibitions. 2. Women artists. I. Nochlin, Linda, joint author. II. Los Angeles Co., Calif. Museum of Art, Los Angeles. III. Title. BIP

NORTON Simon, Inc. Museum of Art. 709'.4'074014967
Selections from the Norton Simon, Inc. Museum of Art. Edited by David W. Steadman. [Princeton, N.J.] Art Museum, Princeton University; distributed by Princeton University Press [1972] 263 p. illus. (part col.) 29 cm. Issued in conjunction with an exhibition held at the Princeton University Art Museum. Includes bibliographical references. [N6350.N67 1972] 72-77426 ISBN 0-691-03887-2 20.00
1. Art, Modern—Exhibitions. I. Steadman, David W., ed. II. Princeton University. Art Museum. III. Title.

Art, Modern—History.

HAGEN, Oskar Frank Leonard, 1888- 709
Art epochs and their leaders; a survey of the genesis of modern art, by Oscar Hagen. Freeport, N.Y., Books for Libraries Press [1971, c1927] xxi, 322 p. illus. 23 cm. [N6350.H3 1971] 75-165637 ISBN 0-8369-5946-9
1. Art, Modern—History. I. Title. BIP

MEIER-GRAEFE, Julius, 1867-1935 709.03
Modern art; being a contribution to a new system of aesthetics. From the German by Florence Simmonds and George W. Chrystal. Reprint ed. New York, Arno Press [1968] 2 v. illus. 29 cm. (Arno series of contemporary art, no. 16) Reprint of the 1908 ed. Translation of Entwicklungsgeschichte der modernen Kunst. Bibliographical footnotes. [N6350.M313 1968] 68-9239
1. Art, Modern—History. 2. Aesthetics. I. Title.

Art, Mogul—Exhibitions.

ASIA Society 709.54
The art of Mughal India: painting & precious objects. Introd., text, catalogue notes by Stuart C. Welch. New York, Abrams [1964] 179p. illus. (pt. mounted col.) map. 29cm. (Asia House Gallery Pubn.) Catalogue of an exhibition shown in the galleries of Asia House, during the winter of 1964, as an activi ty of theAsia Soc. Bibl. 64-1801 9.75
1. Art, Mogul—Exhibitions. I. Welch, Stuart Cary. II. Asia House Gallery, New York, III. Title.

ASIA Society. 709'.54
The art of Mughal India : painting & precious objects / with an introd., text, and catalogue notes by Stuart C. Welch. New York : Arno Press, 1975. p. cm. (The Asia Society reprint collection) Reprint of the 1963 ed. published by Asia Society, New York, which was issued as an Asia House Gallery publication. "Catalogue of an exhibition shown in the galleries of Asia House, during the winter of 1964, as an activity of the Asia Society." Bibliography: p. [N7302.A82 1975] 75-6678 ISBN 0-405-06569-8 : 32.00
1. Art, Mogul—Exhibitions. I. Welch, Stuart Cary. II. Asia House Gallery, New York. III. Title. IV. Series.

Art, Mohammedan.

HASSAN, Zaky Mohamed. 709.5
Moslem art in the Fouad I University Museum. Cairo, Fouad I University Press, 1950- v. plates. 24 cm. [N6260.H3] 52-37672
1. Art, Mohammedan. 2. Cairo. Fouad I University. Faculty of Arts. Museum of Moslem Art. I. Title.

NEW York. Metropolitan Museum of Art. 745
A handbook of Mohammedan art, by M. S. Dimand. 3d ed., rev. and enl. New York, 1958 [c1944] xi, 380p. illus., map (on lining papers) 23cm. First published in 1930 under title: A handbook of Mohammedan decorative arts. Bibliography: p. 332-348. [NK720.N4 1958] 58-2391
1. Art. Mohammedan. 2. Art, Decorative. 3. Decoration and ornament, Mohammedan. I. Dimand, Maurice Sven. II. Title.

Art—Mongolia.

OLSCHKI, Leonardo, 1885- 709'.24 B
Guillaume Boucher, a French artist at the court of the Khans. New York, Greenwood Press [1969, c1946] viii, 125 p. illus. 23 cm. Includes bibliographical references. [ND553.B7O4 1969] 69-14019
1. Boucher, Guillaume, 13th cent. 2. Art—Mongolia.

Art—Moscow.

DUNCAN, David Douglas. 709'.473'1
Great treasures of the Kremlin. [Rev. and enl. ed.] New York, H. N. Abrams [1968] 187 p. col. illus. 31 cm. 1960 ed. published under title: The Kremlin. Bibliography: p. 187. [N6997.M7D8 1968] 68-28379
1. Moscow. Kremlin. 2. Art—Moscow. 3. Russia—History. I. Title.

Art—Munich—Galleries and museums.

MUNICH. 708'.3'36
[By Theodor Muller and others. Translated from the German by Sylvia Furness and rev. by D. Talbot Rice. 1st American ed.] South Brunswick [N.J.] A. S. Barnes [1969, c1967] 59 p., 167 p. of illus. (part col.) 35 cm. (Great centres of art) [N2317.M813 1969] 73-86473
1. Art—Munich—Galleries and museums. I. Muller, Theodor, 1905-

Art, Municipal.

HEGEMANN, Werner, 1881-1936. 711'.4
The American Vitruvius: an architects' handbook of civic art, by Werner Hegemann and Elbert Peets. New York, B. Blom [1972] vi, 298 p. illus. 34 cm. Half title: Civic art. Reprint of the 1922 ed. published by the Architectural Book Pub. Co., New York. Bibliography: p. 294. [NA9030.H4 1972] 68-57189 37.50
1. Art, Municipal. 2. Cities and towns—Planning. I. Peets, Elbert, 1886-1968, joint author. II. Title. III. Title: Civic art. BIP

ROBINSON, Charles Mulford, 1869-1917. 711'.4
Modern civic art; or, The city made beautiful. New York, Arno Press, 1970 [c1918] xiii, 381 p. illus., maps, plan. 23 cm. (The Rise of urban America) [NA9030.R7 1970] 79-112570 ISBN 4-05-024738-
1. Art, Municipal. 2. Urban beautification. I. Title. II. Series. BIP

Art, Municipal—Addresses, essays, lectures.

ART and life and the building and decoration of cities / T. J. Cobden-Sanderson, et al. New York : Garland Pub., 1978. 260 p. ; 19 cm. (The Aesthetic movement & the arts and crafts movement) Reprint of the 1897 ed. published by Rivington, Percival, London. Contents.Contents.—Cobden-Sanderson, T. J. Of art and life.—Lethaby, W. R. Of beautiful cities.—Crane, W. Of the decoration of public buildings.—Blomfield, R. Of public spaces, parks, and gardens.—Ricardo, H. Of colour in the architecture of cities. [NA9040.A7 1978] 76-17778 ISBN 0-8240-2484-2 : lib.bdg. : 35.00 711'.4
1. Arts and Crafts Exhibition Society, London. 2. Art, Municipal—Addresses, essays, lectures. 3. Aesthetics—Addresses, essays, lectures. I. Cobden-Sanderson, Thomas James, 1840-1922. II. Title. III. Series.
Contents omitted

Art, Municipal—Baltimore.

PERLMAN, Bennard B. 338.4'7'70097526
1% art in civic architecture [by Bernard B. Perlman Baltimore, Printed by French/Bray, 1973] 48 p. illus. 28 cm. Cover title. "Prepared by RTKL Associates Inc." [N8844.P47 1973] 73-88938
1. Art, Municipal—Baltimore. 2. Baltimore—Public works. I. RTKL Associates Inc. II. Title.

Art, Municipal—United States.

PERLMAN, Bennard B. 338.4'7'720973
1% art in civic architecture. Prepared by RTKL Inc., architects and planners, William C. Boothe, associate-in-charge, and text by Bernard B. Perlman, author. [Baltimore? c1972] 48 p. illus. 28 cm. [N8844.P47 1972] 73-93518
1. Art, Municipal—United States. 2. Urban beautification—United States. I. RTKL Inc. II. Title.

Art museums—Educational aspects—Addresses, essays, lectures.

COUNCIL on Museums and Education in the Visual Arts. 658'.91'70813
The art museum as educator : a collection of studies as guides to practice and policy / Council on Museums and Education in the Visual Arts ; Barbara Y. Newsom and Adele Z. Silver, editors. Berkeley : University of California Press, c1978. 830 p. : ill. ; 28 cm. Includes indexes. [N430.C68 1978] 76-14301 ISBN 0-520-03248-9 : 30.00 ISBN 0-520-03249-7 pbk. : 14.95
1. Art museums—Educational aspects—Addresses, essays, lectures. I. Newsom, Barbara Y. II. Silver, Adele Z. III. Title. BIP

Art museums—Educational aspects—Case studies.

EDUCATIONAL alternatives in me-you-zeums : final report / Deborah Franklin, project director ; [photographer, Fred Meredith]. [Austin? Tex.] : Franklin, [1976?] iii, 304 p., [7] leaves of plates : ill. ; 29 cm. Cover title. Bibliography: p. 260-261. [N430.E34] 77-151267 708'.007
1. Art museums—Educational aspects—Case studies. I. Franklin, Deborah.

Art museums—Management.

ZELERMYER, Rebecca, 1919- 658'.91'708
Gallery management / Rebecca Zelermyer. 1st ed. New York : Syracuse University Press, 1976. 159 p. : ill. ; 20 cm. [N470.Z44] 76-24790 ISBN 0-8156-0127-1 : 8.95
1. Art museums—Management. I. Title. BIP

Art museums—Southern States.

LAWLESS, Jim. 708'.15
Southeastern art museums : a descriptive analysis / Jim Lawless, 2nd for Southern Federation of State Arts Agencies. Atlanta : [Southern Federation of State Arts Agencies], c1977. 32 p. ; 24 cm. Includes bibliographical references. [N510.5.S7L38] 77-153048
1. Art museums—Southern States. I. Southern Federation of State Arts Agencies. II. Title.

Art museums—United States.

COLORADO Springs. Fine Arts Center. 708.171
Report. Colorado Springs. v. illus. 23cm. annual. [N552.5.A3] 55-59500
I. Title.

COLUMBIA, S. C. Museum of Art. 708.157
Report. 1st- 1950- Columbia. v. illus. 23 cm. annual. Includes Report of the Columbia Museum of Art Commission. [N553.C64] 52-42297
I. Title.

HONOLULU Academy of Arts. 707.14
Report. [Honolulu] v. in illus. 22-28cm. (formerty News builetin and calendar) annual. Report for 1943, 1948- in the academy's Bulletin [N333.H6H618] 42-35239
I. Title.

MEYER, Karl Ernest. 069'.9'7
The art museum : power, money, and ethics : a Twentieth Century Fund report / by Karl E. Meyer. New York : Morrow, 1979. p. cm. Includes index. Bibliography: p. [N510.M47] 78-11780 ISBN 0-688-03390-3 : 15.00
1. Art museums—United States. I. Twentieth Century Fund. II. Title. BIP

PENNSYLVANIA ACADEMY OF THE FINE ARTS, Philadelphia. 708.148
Report. Philadelphia. v. in 23-25 cm. annual. Report year irregular. [N680.A3] 52-22247
I. Title.

ROCHESTER, N.Y. Museum of Arts and Sciences. 069.09747
Report of the director. Rochester. v. 28 cm. annual. [AM101.R5953] 51-35006
I. Title.

WASHINGTON County Museum of Fine Arts, Hagerstown, Md. v. 12
The twenty-fifth year; commemorating the twenty-fifth anniversary of the Washington County Museum of Fine Arts, 1931-1956. Written by Mrs. William T. Hamilton, Jr., president. [Hagerstown, 1956] 80 p. illus. 21 cm. [N573.H3W36] 57-45977
1. Hamilton, Mavin J. II. Title.

Art museums—Yugoslavia.

MUSEUMS of Yugoslavia 708'.9497
/ [text by Dragoslav Srejovic ; editor, Oto Bijalji-Merin]. New York : Newsweek, 1977, c1973. 171 p. : col. ill. ; 30 cm. (Great museums of the world) Translation of Muzeji Jugoslavije. Includes indexes. Bibliography: p. 168. [N3690.Y8A4513 1977] 76-56055 13.95
1. Art museums—Yugoslavia. I. Srejovic, Dragoslav. II. Bihalji-Merin, Oto, 1904- III. Series: Great museums of the world (New York, Newsweek) BIP

Art—Near East.

AKURGAL, Ekrem. 709'.35
The art of Greece; its origins in the Mediterranean and Near East. [Translated by Wayne Dynes] New York, Crown Publishers [1968] 258 p. illus. 24 cm. (Art of the world, non-European cultures; the historical sociological, and religious backgrounds) Translation of Orient und Okzident. Includes bibliographical references. [N5345.A6513 1968] 78-9056 6.95
1. Art—Near East. 2. Art, Greek. I. Title. II. Series: Art of the world; the historical, sociological, and religious backgrounds.

FRANKFORT, Henri, 1897-1954. 709.3
The art and architecture of the ancient Orient. [4th rev. impression] [Harmondsworth, Eng.] Penguin Books [1970] 456 p. illus., map. 21 cm. (The Pelican history of art PZ7) Bibliography: p. [415]-436. [N5345.F7 1970] 70-128007 ISBN 0-14-056107-2 8.45 (U.S.)
1. Art—Near East. 2. Architecture—Near East. I. Title. II. Series.

GARBINI, Giovanni. 709.39
The ancient world. New York, McGraw-Hill [1966] 176 p. illus. (part col.), maps. 30 cm. (Landmarks of the world's art) "Further reading": p. [172] [N5345.G3] 66-19270
1. Art—Near East. 2. Art, Ancient. I. Title.

GLUBOK, Shirley 709.56
The art of lands in the Bible. Designed by Gerard Nook. New York, Atheneum [c.] 1963. 48p. illus. (pt. col.) 26cm. 63-1547 3.79
1. Art—Near East. 2. Art, Ancient. 3. Bible—Pictures, illustrations, etc. I. Title.

Art—Near East—History.

WOOLLEY, Charles Leonard, Sir 1880-1960. 709.35
The art of the Middle East including Persia, Mesopotamia and Palestine. [Translated by Ann E. Keep] New York, Crown Publishers [1961] 259 p. illus., map, col. plates. 24 cm. (Art of the world, non-European cultures; the historical, sociological and religious backgrounds) [N5343.W613] 61-16972
1. Art — Near East — Hist. 2. Art, Ancient — Hist. 3. Art, Oriental — Hist. I. Title. II. Series: Art of the world; the historical, sociological and religious backgrounds

WOOLLEY, Charles Leonard, Sir 1880-1960 709.35
The art of the Middle East including Persia, Mesopotamia and Palestine. [Tr. by Ann E. Keep] New York, Crown [c.1961] 259p. illus., map, col. plates. (Art of the world lib.) Bibl. 61-16972 5.95
1. Art—Near East—Hist. 2. Art, Ancient—Hist. 3. Art, Oriental—Hist. I. Title. II. Series: Art of the world; the historical, sociological and religions backgrounds

Art—Near East—History.

LLOYD, Seton. 709.56
The art of the ancient Near East. New York, Praeger [1961] 303 p. illus. (part col.) map. 22 cm. (Books that matter) Bibliography: p. 283. [N5345.L55 1961a] 61-15605
1. Art—Near East—History. 2. Art, Ancient. 3. Art, Asian. I. Title. BIP

Art, Negro.

BROWN, Evelyn S 709.67
Africa's contemporary art and artists; a review of creative activities in painting, sculpture, ceramics, and crafts of more than 300 artists working in the modern industrialized society of some of the countries of sub-Saharan Africa, by Evelyn S. Brown. New York, Division of Social Research and Experimentation, Harmon Foundation, 1966. 136 p. illus. 28 cm. Cover title. Bibliographical references on p. [2] of cover. [N7397.S3B7] 66-8684
1. Art, Negro. 2. Art — Africa, Sub-Saharan. I. Harmon Foundation, inc. Division of Social Research and Experimentation. II. Title.

Art, Nepali—Exhibitions.

ASIA Society. 709.5496
The art of Nepal, by Stella Kramrisch. [New York] Distributed by H. N. Abrams [1964] 159 p. illus. (part counted col.) 25 cm. "An Asia House Gallery publication." "Catalogue of an exhibition selected by Dr. Stella Kramrisch and shown in the Asia House Gallery in the summer of 1964 as an activity of the Asia Society." Bibliography: p. 159. [N7307.N4A8] 64-16018
1. Art, Nepali—Exhibitions. I. Kramrisch, Stella, 1898- II. Asia House Gallery, New York. III. Title.

PAL, Pratapaditya. 732'.4
Nepal : where the gods are young / by Pratapaditya Pal. [New York] : Asia Society, [1975] 135, [1] p. : ill. (some col.) ; 26 cm. "Catalogue of an exhibition shown in Asia House Gallery in the fall of 1975"; shown in Seattle Art Museum Dec. 17, 1975-Jan. 25, 1976, and in Los Angeles County Museum of Art, Feb. 17-Apr. 4, 1976. "An Asia House Gallery publication." Bibliography: p. [136] [N7310.8.N4P35] 75-769 ISBN 0-87848-045-5 : 19.95
1. Art, Nepali—Exhibitions. 2. Art, Buddhist—Nepal. 3. Art, Hindu—Nepal. I. Pal, Pratapaditya. II. Asia House Gallery, New York. III. Seattle. Art Museum. IV. Los Angeles Co., Calif. Museum of Art, Los Angeles. V. Title. **BIP**

WALDSCHMIDT, Ernst, 1897- 709
Nepal: art treasures from the Himalayas [by] Ernst and Rose Leonore Waldschmidt. Translated by David Wilson. New York, Universe Books [1970, c1969] 160 p. plates (part col.) 25 cm. Translation of Nepal: Kunst aus dem Konigreich im Himalaja. Bibliography: p. 158. [N7307.N4W323 1970] .549'6 72-96964 ISBN 8-7663-1049- 10.00
1. Art, Nepali—Exhibitions. I. Waldschmidt, Rose Leonore, joint author. II. Title. **BIP**

Art—Netherlands—Galleries and museums.

LUTTERVELT, Remmet van. 759.492
Masterpieces from the great Dutch museums: Rijksmuseum, Mauritshuis, Boymans-Van Beuningen, Frans Hals Museum. New York, H. N. Abrams [1961] 318 p. plates (part col.) 21 cm. [N2450.L83] 61-6217
1. Art—Netherlands—Galleries and museums. 2. Paintings, Dutch. I. Title.

Art—New Brunswick, N.J.—Catalogs.

RUTGERS 750'.74'014942
University, New Brunswick, N.J. University Art Gallery.
The fine arts collection of Rutgers, the State University; a selection. [New Brunswick, N.J., Rutgers, the State University, c1966] 110 p. illus., ports. 19 cm. In commemoration of the Bicentennial Year of Rutgers, the works described in this catalog were exhibited at the State Museum, Trenton. [N588.A56] 66-28246
1. Art—New Brunswick, N.J.—Catalogs. I. New Jersey. State Museum, Trenton. II. Title.

Art — New Guinea.

FIRTH, Raymond 709'.01'10995
William, 1901-
Art and life in New Guinea / Raymond Firth. New York : AMS Press, [1977] p. cm. Reprint of the 1936 ed. published by The Studio, London and Studio Publications, New York. Bibliography: p. [N7411.N4F5 1977] 75-32815 ISBN 0-404-14119-6 : 18.50
1. Art—New Guinea. 2. Art, Primitive—New Guinea. 3. New Guinea—Social life and customs. I. Title. **BIP**

NEW York. Museum of 709.932
Primitive Art.
Three regions of Melanesian art, New Guinea and the New Hebrides. New York, Dist. University Publishers, [c.]1960. 24p. illus., map. 28cm. 'Prepared in conjunction with an exhibition [Sept. 21 to Nov. 13, 1960]' 60-51988 1.50 pap.,
1. Art—New Guinea. 2. Art—New Hebrides. I. Title.

NEWTON, Douglas, 1920- 709.01'1
New Guinea art in the collection of the Museum of Primitive Art. New York, Museum of Primitive Art; dist. by the N. Y. Graphic Soc., Greenwich, Conn., 1967.. 1 v. (unpaged) 132 illus., 2 maps. 21cm. (Mus. of Primitive Art handbks., 2) Bibl. [N620.M94A3 no. 2] 67-22358 6.50
1. Art—New Guinea. 2. Art, Primitive. I. Title. II. Series: New York. Museum of Primitive Art. Handbooks, no. 2

NEWTON, Douglas, 1920- 709.01'1
New Guinea art in the collection of the Museum of Primitive Art. New York, Museum of Primitive Art; distributed by the New York Graphic Society, Greenwich, Conn., 1967. 1 v. (unpaged) 132 illus., 2 maps. 21 cm. (Museum of Primitive Art handibooks, 2) Bibliography: p. [35]-[38] [N620.M94A3] 67-22358
1. Art — New Guinea. 2. Art, Primitive. I. Title. II. Series: New York. Museum of Primitive Art. Handbooks, no. 2

Art—New Haven—Catalogs.

YALE University. Art 708.146
Gallery.
Collection of the Societe Anonyme; Museum of Modern Art 1920 [presented to Yale University] New Haven, Yale University Art Gallery, published for the Associates in Fine Arts, 1950. xxiv, 223p. illus. 27cm. 'Catalogue, compiled and planned by Katherine S. Dreler and Marcel Duchamp.' [N590.A64] 51-3172
1. Art—New Haven—Catalogs. 2. Art, Modern—20th cent. I. Societe Anonyme. II. Dreler, Katherine Sophie, 1877- III. Title.

YALE University. 750'.74'01468
Art Gallery.
Selected paintings and sculpture from the Yale University Art Gallery. Introd.: Andrew Carnduff Ritchie. Commentaries: Katharine B. Neilson. New Haven, Published for the Yale University Art Gallery by Yale University Press, 1972. 1 v. (unpaged) illus. (part col.) 26 cm. [N590.A65] 76-179475 ISBN 0-300-01562-3 15.00
1. Art—New Haven—Catalogs. I. Neilson, Katharine Bishop. II. Title.

YALE University. Gallery 708.146
of Fine Arts.
Collection of the Societe Anonyme; Museum of Modern Art 1920 [presented to Yale University] New Haven, Yale University Art Gallery, published for the Associates in Fine Arts, 1950. xxiv, 223 p. illus. 27 cm. "Catalogue, compiled and planned by Katherine S. Dreler and Marcel Duchamp." [N590.A64] 51-3172
1. Art — New Haven — Catalogs. 2. Art, Modern — 20th cent. I. Societe Anonyme. II. Dreler, Katherine Sophie, 1877- III. Title.

Art—New Jersey—Directories.

GREEN, Jane Whipple. 700'.6'2749
Directory of art organizations in New Jersey. [Westfield? N.J.] Federated Art Associations of N.J. [1973] 30 p. illus. 21 cm. [NX24.N5G73] 73-175568 0.50
1. Art—New Jersey—Directories. I. Federated Art Associations of New Jersey. II. Title.

Art—New Jersey—Hist.

GERDTS, William H 709.749
Painting and sculpture in New Jersey [by] William H. Gerdts, Jr. Princeton, N.J., Van Nostrand, 1964. xix, 276 p. illus., col. maps (on lining papers) ports. 22 cm. (The New Jersey historical series, v. 24) Series number appears incorrectly at head of title as v. 21. "Bibliographical note": p. 253-262. [N6530.N5G4] 65-906
1. Art—New Jersey—Hist. I. Title. II. Series.

Art—New York (City)

ASHTON, Dore. 709'.747'1
New York. 150 illus. in colour and black and white. Special photography by Marie Carrieri. [1st ed.] New York, Holt, Rinehart and Winston [1972] 288 p. illus. 26 x 13 cm. (World cultural guides) Bibliography: p. 249. [N6535.N5A9] 70-155541 ISBN 0-03-088048-3 9.95
1. Art—New York (City) 2. New York (City)—Description. I. Title.

BAAL-TESHUVA, Jacob 708.1471
Art treasures of the United Nations. Foreword by Andrew W. Cordier. New York, Yoseloff [c.1964] 71p. illus., plates (pt. col.) ports. 29cm. 63-18238 7.50
1. Art—New York (City) 2. United Nations—Buildings. I. Title.

BAAL-TESHUVA, Jacob. 708.1471
Art treasures of the United States. With a foreword by Andrew W. Cordier. New York, T. Yoseloff [1964] 71 p. illus., plates (part col.) ports. 29 cm. [N620.U5B3] 63-18238
1. Art—New York (City) 2. United Nations—Buildings. I. Title.

MULAS, Ugo. 709.73
New York; the new art scene. Photograph [sic] by Ugo Mulas. Text by Alan Solomon. Design by Michele Provinciali. [1st ed. New York] Holt, Rinehart and Winston [1967] 337 p. (chiefly illus.) 34 cm. [N6535.N5M8] 67-11535
1. Art—New York (City) 2. Artists, American—New York (City) I. Solomon, Alan R. II. Title.

MYERS, Bernard Samuel, 709.747
1908-
Problems of the younger American artist: exhibiting and marketing in New York City, a pilot survey. New York, City College Press [1957] 83p. 23cm. (The City College. New York Area Research Council. Studies in the New York area, no.2) [N6535.N5M9] 57-4786
1. Art—New York (City) 2. Artists, American—New York (City) I. Title.

NEW York. Metropolitan 708.147
Museum of Art.
Art treasures of the Metropolitan; a selection from the European and Asiatic collections of the Metropolitan Museum of Art, presented by the curatorial staff. [1st ed.] New York, H. N. Abrams [1952] 240p. illus., plates (part col.) 33cm. rs. 53Library of great museums]) [N610.A615] 52-14388
1. Art—New York (City) I. Title.

SOLOMON R. 760'.074'01471
Guggenheim Museum, New York.
Acquisitions of the 1930's and 1940's; a selection of paintings, watercolors, and drawings in tribute to Baroness Hilla von Rebay, 1890-1967. [New York, 1968] 133 p. illus. (part col.), port. 26 cm. Catalog of "Exhibition 68/4, April 1968-May 1968." Includes bibliographical references. [N6490.S59] 68-25520
1. Art—New York (City) 2. Art, Modern—20th century—Exhibitions. I. Rebay, Hilla, 1890-1967. II. Title.

Art—New York (City)—Catalogs.

BROOKLYN Institute of 708.147'23
Arts and Sciences. Museum.
The Brooklyn Museum handbook. [1st ed.] Brooklyn [N.Y.] Brooklyn Museum, 1967. vii, 551 p. illus. (part col.), ports. 23 cm. [N620.B6A5] 67-23511
1. Art—New York (City)—Catalogs. I. Title.

NEW York (City). 708'.1471
Metropolitan Museum of Art.
The Metropolitan Museum of Art : notable acquisitions, 1965-1975. New York : The Museum, c1975. 300 p. : ill. ; 23 cm. [N610.A6745] 75-31761 ISBN 0-87099-141-8
1. New York (City). Metropolitan Museum of Art. 2. Art—New York (City)—Catalogs. **BIP**

NEW York. Metropolitan 708.1471
Museum of Art. H. O. Havemeyer Collection.
The H. O. Havemeyer collection; [catalogue] 2d ed. New York, 1958. x, 125p. plates. 25cm. [N611.H15 1958] 59-1158
1. Art— New York (City)—Catalogs. I. Title.

SOLOMON R. Guggenheim 708.1471
Museum, New York.
A handbook to the Solomon R. Guggenheim Museum collection. New York, [1959] 269 p. illus. 32 cm. "Printed ... on the occasion of the opening of the Solomon R. Guggenheim Museum building, designed by Frank Lloyd Wright." Includes bibliographical references. [N620.S63A55] 59-15750
1. Art — New York (City) — Catalogs. I. Title. II. Title: Guggenheim Museum collection.

Art—New York (City)—Galleries and museums.

CHANIN, A 708.1471
Art guide/New York [by] A. L. Chanin. New York, Horizon Press [1965] 320 p. illus., map. 23 cm. (World art guides, 1) [N600.C5] 65-15363
1. Art — New York (City) — Galleries and museums. I. Title.

CHANIN, A. L. 708.1471
Art guide/New York. New York, Horizon [c.1965] 320p. illus., map. 23cm. (World art guides, 1) [N600.C5] 65-15363 5.95
1. Art—New York (City)—Galleries and museums. I. Title.

HOWE, Winifred Eva, 708'.147'1
1876-
A history of the Metropolitan Museum of Art, with a chapter on the early institutions of art in New York, by Winifred E. Howe. New York, 1913. [New York] Arno Press, 1974. xvi, 361 p. illus. 23 cm. Reprint of v. 1 of the 2 v. work originally published, 1913-46, by the Metropolitan Museum of Art, New York. [N610.H76] 76-168422 ISBN 0-405-02260-3 27.00
1. New York (City). Metropolitan Museum of Art. 2. Art—New York (City)—Galleries and Museums. 3. New York (City)—Museums. I. Title. **BIP**

OSMAN, Randolph E., 708.1471
1940-
Art centers of the world: New York [by] Randolph E. Osman. Cleveland, World Pub. Co. [1968] 192 p. illus. (part col.), plans (on lining papers), ports. (part col.) 21 cm. [N600.O8] 68-26017 7.95
1. Art—New York (City)—Galleries and museums. I. Title.

POST, Nonnie. 708.1'471
On permanent view; a cross-referenced guide to the New York galleries exhibiting contemporary artists. [Compiled by N. Post & R. Harcourt] New York, P. Glenn Publications [1971] 95 p. illus. 21 cm. [N6535.N5P6] 73-30982 2.95
1. Art—New York—Galleries and museums. 2. Art, Modern—20th century—New York—Directories. I. Harcourt, Renee, joint author. II. Title.

Art—New York (City)—Galleries and museums—Directories.

FILSINGER, Cheryl. 702'.5'7471
Locus : a cross-referenced directory of New York galleries and art sources with their current stables of artists and art, the place to find everybody's work / [compiled by Cheryl Filsinger]. New York : Filsinger,

c1975. 192 p. (p. 184-192 blank for notes) ; 23 cm. [N6535.N5F54] 76-350143 10.00
1. Art—New York (City)—Galleries and museums—Directories. 2. Artists—New York (City)—Directories. 3. Art—New York (City)—Sources—Directories. I. Title. BIP

Art—New York metropolitan area—Directories.

SCOTT, Thomas J. 700'.25'747
Greater New York art directory. Edited by Thomas J. Scott. [New York, Center for Urban Education, 1968] 314 p. 24 cm. [N6535.N5S27] 68-56339 1.00
1. Art—New York metropolitan area—Directories. I. Center for Urban Education. II. Title.

Art—New York (State)

FAISON, Samson Lane, Jr., 1907- 708.147
Art tours & detours in New York State; a handbook to more than 75 outstanding museums & historic landmarks in the Empire State outside New York City [New York] Random [c.1964] xvi, 303p. illus., maps. 23cm. 64-17932 4.95
1. Art—New York (State) 2. New York (State)—Descr. & trav.—Guide-books. I. Title.

Art—New York (State)—Galleries and Museums.

CHAPMAN, Allan D. v. 12
Museum collections on Asia, Africa, Latin America, and the Soviet Union in New York State and their use in education. by Allan D. Chapman. Prelim. ed. Albany, University of the State of New York. State Education Dept. 1964. vi. 64 p. 28 cm. Bibliographical footnotes. [N511.N6C5] 66-65696
1. Art — New York (State) — Gallaries and museums. I. New York State University. II. Title.

Art—New Zealand.

SIMPSON, Edward C. 709.931
A survey of the arts in New Zealand. [Wellington, N. Z.] Wellington Chamber Music Soc. [dist. New York, Heinman, 1963] 180p. 22cm. 62-1509 5.00 bds.,
1. Art—New Zealand. 2. New Zealand—Intellectual life. 3. State encouragement of science, literature, and art. I. Title.

Art, New Zealand—Exhibitions.

EDGAR, James Douglas Charlton. 709'.931'0740993157
Otago School of Art centennial exhibition, 1870-1970. [compiled by Charlton Edgar and Oliver G. Cox] [Dunedin, Otago School of Art? 1970] 23 p. illus. (part col.) 24 cm. Cover title. Bibliography: p. 7. [N7406.E33] 73-167018 0.50 ($0.40 to libraries)
1. Otago School of Art. 2. Art, New Zealand—Exhibitions. I. Cox, Oliver Gordon, joint author. II. Title.

Art—Nigeria.

BEIER, Ulli 709.669
Art in Nigeria, 1960. [New York] Cambridge Univ. Press, [1961, c.]1960[ ] 24p. illus. 61-16002 3.75; 1.95 pap.,
1. Art—Nigeria. I. Title.

Art—North Carolina—Societies, etc.

NORTH Carolina Arts Council. 700'.9756
The arts in North Carolina, 1967 [Raleigh, 1967] 127 p. illus., maps, ports. 21 cm. [N11.N67] 67-65961
1. Art—North Carolina—Societies, etc. I. Title.

Art—Northwest, Pacific.

KINGSBURY, Martha, 1941- 709'.795
Art of the thirties; the Pacific Northwest. Seattle, Published for the Henry Art Gallery by the University of Washington Press [1972] 95 p. illus. 29 cm. (Index of art in the Pacfic Northwest, no. 4) Catalog for an exhibition held at the Henry Art Gallery, University of Washington, April 1972. Bibliography: p. 93-95. [N6528.K5] 72-1111 ISBN 0-295-95215-6
1. Art—Northwest, Pacific. 2. Art, Modern—20th century—Northwest, Pacific. I. Henry Art Gallery. II. Title. III. Series.

Art, Norwegian.

ELIASSEN, George Christen, 1880- v. 12
Arnstein Arneberg. Redaksjon: Georg Eliassen, Arne Pedersen [og] Olav Platou. Oslo, Gyldendal, 1952. 175p. illus. 27cm. (Kunst og kulturs serie)qArneberg, Arnstein Rynning. 1882- [NA1273.A7E4] 53-28782
I. Title.

HAUGLID, Roar 709.481
Old art and monumental buildings in Norway restored during the last fifty years. Introd. by Egil Smding-Larsen. Oslo. Dreyer [dist. New York, Vanous, 1963] xxii p., 163p. of illus. (pt. col.) col. front. 31cm. 63-3875 12.90
1. Art, Norwegian. 2. Architecture—Norway. 3. Architecture—Conservation and restoration. I. Title.

Art—Notre Dame, Ind.—Catalogs.

NOTRE Dame, Ind. University. Art Gallery. 708.172'89
Handbook of the collections. [Prepared and edited by the staff of the Art Gallery. Notre Dame, Ind.] University of Notre Dame Press [1967] xix, 186 p. illus. 28 cm. [N635.A66] 67-29997
1. Art—Notre Dame, Ind.—Catalogs. I. Title.

Art nouveau.

THE Anti-rationalists, 724.9
edited by J. M. Richards, Nikolcius Persner. Toronto, University of Toronto Press, 1973. 208 p. illus. 31 cm. "A number of the chapters in this book originally appeared in the Architectural review." Includes bibliographical references and index. [N6465.A7a57 1973b] 72-95812 ISBN 0-8020-1955-2 17.50
1. Art nouveau. I. Richards, James Maude, ed. II. Pevsner, Nikolaus, Sir, 1902-, ed.

ART nouveau: 709'.04
the style of the 1890s; general editor Francesco Abbate; translated [from the Italian] by Elizabeth Evans. London, New York, Octopus Books, 1972. 158 p., chiefly 92 col. illus. 20 cm. Translation of L'Ottocento in Europa. Le correnti di fine secolo. Bibliography: p. 154. [N6465.A7A7313] 73-151893 ISBN 0-7064-0026-7 2.98
1. Art nouveau. 2. Art, Modern—19th century. I. Abbate, Francesco, ed.

BARILLI, Renato. 709'.4
Art Nouveau; [translated from the Italian by Raymond Rudorff]. London, New York, Hamlyn, 1969. 3-157 p. 67 col. illus. 20 cm. (Cameo) Translation of Il liberty. [N6465.A7B2713] 76-437309 15/-
1. Art nouveau.

BATTERSBY, Martin. 709'.44
Art nouveau. Feltham, Hamlyn, 1969. 40 p. 48 plates, illus. (some col.) 28 cm. (The Colour library of art) [N6465.A7B3] 79-433805 ISBN 0-600-03798-3 17/6
1. Art nouveau.

BATTERSBY, Martin. 709.04
The world of art nouveau. New York, Funk & Wagnalls [1969, c1968] 183 p. illus., ports. 26 cm. Bibliography: p. [179]-180. [N6494.N6B33 1969] 69-14715 7.95
I. Title.

CHAMPIGNEULLE, Bernard, 1896- 709'.03'4
Art nouveau / by Bernard Champigneulle ; translated from the French by Benita Eisler. Woodbury, N.Y. : Barron's Educational Series, c1976. 287 p. : ill. (some col.) ; 23 cm. Includes index. [N6465.A7C5213] 76-8467 ISBN 0-8120-5111-4 : 13.95. ISBN 0-8120-0667-4 pbk. : 9.95
1. Art nouveau. 2. Art, Modern—19th century. I. Title.

CIRICI Pellicer, Alejandro. 709'.46'72
1900 in Barcelona: modern style, art nouveau, modernismo, jugendstil. [Text: A. Cirici Pellicer. Photos: Joaquim Gomis Selection and squence: J. Prats Valles. New York, G. Wittenborn, 1967] 55, lxxxviii p. illus. (part col.) 21 cm. Half title and cover title: 1900. Text in Spanish, French, English, and German. [N7111.B3C5] 67-9821
1. Art nouveau. 2. Art—Barcelona. I. Gomis, Joaquim, photographer. II. Title.

GANS, Louis, 1930- 709.04
Nieuwe kunst. De Nederlandse bijdrage tot de Art Nouveau. Dekoratieve kunst, kunstnijverheid en architektuur omstreeks 1900. [Door] L. Gans. Utrecht, A. Oosthoek, 1966 [1967] 136p., 160p. of photos. 27cm. [N6490.G28 1967] 67-92152 22.50
1. Art nouveau. 2. Art, Dutch. I. Title.
American distributor: Wittenborn, New York.

HUTTER, Heribert 709.04
Art noveau. Tr. by J. R. Foster. New York, Crown [1967] 56p. illus. (pt. col.) 19cm. (Movements in world art) Translation of Jugendstil. Bibl. [N6490.H873] 67-15641 .95 bds.,
1. Art noveau. 2. Indiana. I. Leary, Edward A., ed. II. Title.
Publisher s address: 3620 N. Mbridian St., Indianapolis, Ind.46208.

MADSEN, Stephan Tschudi, 1923- 709'.034
Art Nouveau [by] S. Tschudi Madsen. Translated from the Norwegian by R. I. Christopherson. New York, McGraw-Hill [1967] 256 p. illus. (part col.) 20 cm. (World university library) Bibliography: p. 247-248. [N6490.M2913 1967b] 66-24159
1. Art nouveau.

MADSEN, Stephan Tschudi, 1923- 709'.04
Sources of art nouveau / Stephan Tschudi Madsen ; [translated by Ragnar Christophersen]. New York : Da Capo Press, 1976, c1975. 488 p. : ill. ; 26 cm. (A Da Capo paperback) Reprint of the 1956 ed. published by H. Aschehoug, Oslo; with new pref. Includes index. Bibliography: p. [451]-470. [N6465.A7M33 1976] 75-26819 ISBN 0-306-70733-0 pbk. : 35.00
1. Art nouveau. I. Title.

MICHIGAN. University. Museum of Art. 701.16
Art nouveau sampler; [exhibition] December 15 through January 20, 1962-63. Ann Arbor [1962?] unpaged. illus. 26 cm. [N6490.M52] 63-63467
1. Art nouveau. 2. Art — Exhibitions. I. Title.

REVI, Albert Christian. 748.2'91
American art nouveau glass. [Camden, N. J.] Nelson [1968] 476 p. illus., facsims. 28 cm. Bibliography: p. 463-464. [NK5103.R4] 68-18778
1. Art nouveau. 2. Glassware, American—Catalogs. I. Title. BIP

RHEIMS, Maurice. 709.034
The flowering of art nouveau. [Translated from the French by Patrick Evans] New York, H. N. Abrams [1966] 450 p. illus. (part mounted col.) 32 cm. Translation of: L'art 1900. [N6490.R5343 1966a] 66-10988
1. Art nouveau. I. Title.

SCHMUTZLER, Robert 709.04
Art nouveau [tr. by Edouard Roditi] New York, Abrams [1964, c.1962] 322p. illus. (pt. mounted col.) 31cm. Bibl. 64-10765 25.00
1. Art nouveau. I. Title.

SCHMUTZLER, Robert. 709'.04
Art nouveau / Robert Schmutzler. New York : Abrams, 1978. 224 p. : ill. (some col.) ; 30 cm. Includes index. Bibliography: p. 216. [N6465.A7S3513 1978] 78-8781 ISBN 0-8109-0676-7 : 19.95 ISBN 0-8109-2177-4 pbk. : 9.95
1. Art nouveau. 2. Art, Modern—19th century. I. Title,

SELZ, Peter, ed. 709.04
Art nouveau; art and design at the turn of the century, edited by Peter Selz and Mildred Constantine, with articles by Greta Daniel [and others] New York, Museum of Modern Art: distributed by Doubleday. iGarden City [1960,c1959] 192p. illus. 25cm. 'Issued in conjunction with the art nouveau exhibition at the Museum of Modern Art [and others]' 'A bibliography of art nouveau, by James Grady':p. 152-161. [N6490.S37] 60-11987
1. Art nouveau. I. Constantine. Mildred. joint ed. II. Title.

SELZ, Peter Howard, 1919- ed. 709'.04
Art nouveau; art and design at the turn of the century. Edited by Peter Selz and Mildred Constantine, with articles by Greta Daniel [and others] Reprint ed. [New York] Published for the Museum of Modern Art by Arno Press, 1972 [c1959] 192 p. illus. 27 cm. "Issued in conjunction with the Art nouveau exhibition at the Museum of Modern Art [and others]." Bibliography: p. 152-161. [N6465.A7S4 1972] 72-169315 ISBN 0-405-01573-9 20.00
1. Art nouveau. I. Constantine, Mildred, joint author. II. New York (City). Museum of Modern Art.

SLOAN, John, 1871-1951 741.6'7
American art nouveau: the poster period of John Sloan; a selection of hitherto unpublished prints and autobiographical recollections by the artist, collected by Helen Farr Sloan. Lock Haven, Pa., Pub. privately by the Hammermill Paper Co., Lock Haven Div., 1967. [32] p., 12 col. plates. 24cm. [NC1850.S57S5] 67-29738 price unreported.
I. Sloan, Helen Farr, 1911- II. Title. III. Title: The poster period of John Sloan.

TAYLOR, John Russell 741.6'4
The art nouveau book in Britain. [Cambridge, Mass.] M.I.T. Pr. [1967, c.1966] 175p. illus. 25cm. Bibl. [N6490.T37 1967a] 67-13170 12.95 bds.,
1. Art nouveau. 2. Art, British. I. Title.

Art, nouveau—Belgium—Exhibitions.

†*ART nouveau,* 709'.44'07401641411
Belgium, France : catalogue of an exhibition organized by the Institute for the Arts, Rice University, and the Art Institute of Chicago : exhibition dates, Rice Museum, Houston, March 26, 1976, to June 27, 1976, the Art Institute of Chicago, August 28, 1976, to October 31, 1976 / Yvonne Brunhammer et al. Houston, Tex. : Institute for the Arts, Rice University, 1976. 512 p. : ill. (some col.) ; 23 cm. Includes index. Bibliography: p. 494-504. [N6967.5.A75A77] 76-1649 ISBN 0-914412-10-8 : 15.00
1. Art, nouveau—Belgium—Exhibitions. 2. Art, Modern—19th century—Belgium—Exhibitions. 3. Art nouveau—France—Exhibitions. 4. Art, Modern—19th century—France—Exhibitions. I. Brunhammer, Yvonne. II. William Marsh Rice University, Houston, Tex. Institute for the Arts. III. Chicago. Art Institute. IV. Houston, Tex. Rice Museum.

Art nouveau—Bibliography.

KEMPTON, Richard. 016.709'04
Art nouveau : an annotated bibliography / by Richard Kempton. Los Angeles : Hennessey & Ingalls, 1977- v. ; 22 cm. (Art & architecture bibliographies ; 4) Contents.Contents.—v. 1. General, Austria, Belgium & France. [Z5936.N6K45] [N6465.A7] 77-3689 ISBN 0-912158-59-X : 39.95
1. Art nouveau—Bibliography. I. Title. II. Series.

Art nouveau—Collectors and collecting.

MEBANE, John, 1909- 709.03'4
The complete book of collecting Art nouveau. New York, Coward-McCann [1970] 256 p. illus. 23 cm. Bibliography: p. 247-249. [N6465.A7M4] 76-132618 6.95
1. Art nouveau—Collectors and collecting. I. Title. II. Title: Collecting Art nouveau.

1. Art objects—Benin, Nigeria (Province) 2. Art, Primitive. I. Berlin. Staatliche Museen. II. Title.

Art objects—Catalogs.

MILLER, Robert William, 1922- 745.1
Wallace-Homestead price guide to antiques and pattern glass, compiled and edited by Robert W. Miller. 2d ed. Des Moines, Wallace-Homestead Book Co. [1974] 390 p. illus. 23 cm. [NK1125.M47 1974] 74-178258 6.95
1. Art objects—Catalogs. 2. Pattern glass—Catalogs. I. Title. II. Title: Price guide to antiques and pattern glass. BIP

Art objects, Chinese.

GUSTAV V I ADOLF King of Sweden, 1882. 709.51
Chinese art from the collection of H. M. King Gustaf VI Adolf of Sweden byBo Gyllensvard and John Alexander Pope. [New York] Asia Society; distributed by H. N. Abrams [1966] 147 p. illus., col. plates. 28 cm. ("An Asia House gallery publication") "Exhibition ... assembled by Bo Gyllensvard in cooperation with John A. Pope for a tour of American museums organized by the International Exhibitions Foundation, Washington, D.C." Bibliography: p. 147. [NK550.G8] 66-22367
1. Gustaf VI Adolf, King of Sweden, 1882- —Art collections. 2. Art objects, Chinese. I. Title.

Art objects, Chinese—Catalogs.

JAYNE, Horace Howard Furness, 1898- 730'.0951'074015932
A handbook of the Chinese collections in the Norton Gallery and School of Art, with descriptive notes by Horace H. F. Jayne. West Palm Beach, Fla., Palm Beach Art Institute, 1972. [103] p. illus. 23 cm. Half title: The Norton Chinese collections. [NK1068.J39] 72-97360
1. Art objects, Chinese—Catalogs. 2. Art objects—West Palm Beach, Fla.—Catalogs. I. Norton Gallery and School of Art, West Palm Beach, Fla. II. Title. III. Title: The Norton Chinese collections.

Art objects, Chinese—Exhibitions.

HARTMAN, Alan S. 738'.0951
Arts of the T'ang Dynasty; an exhibition organized by the Indianapolis Museum of Art and Rare Art, inc. Catalogue by Alan S. Hartman with an introd. by Paul A. J. Spheeris. [Indianapolis, Printed by Speedway Press, 1973] 62 p. illus. (part col.) 28 cm. Exhibition dates: Indianapolis Museum of Art, Oct. 2-Nov. 4, 1973; Rare Art, inc., New York, Nov. 12-Dec. 15, 1973. [NK1068.H37] 73-87279
1. Art objects, Chinese—Exhibitions. 2. Art objects, Chinese—T'ang-Five dynasties, 618-960. I. Indianapolis Museum of Art. II. Rare Art, inc. III. Title.

JULIANO, Annette L. 732'.7'074014733
Selections from the Asian collections of Vassar College, by Annette L. Juliano. [Poughkeepsie, Vassar College Art Gallery, 1972] 59 p. illus. 26 cm. Catalog of the exhibition held Apr. 4-30, 1972 at the Vassar College Art Gallery, Poughkeepsie. Bibliography: p. 57-59. [NK1065.J9] 72-77885
1. Art objects, Chinese—Exhibitions. 2. Art objects, Korean—Exhibitions. 3. Art objects, Japanese—Exhibitions. I. Vassar College. Art Gallery. II. Title.

Art objects, Classical—Catalogs.

HAMPE, Roland. 709.01'4
Aus der Sammlung des Archaologischen Institutes der Universitat Heidelberg [von] Roland Hampe [und] Hildegund Gropengiesser. Berlin, Heidelberg, New York, Springer-Verlag, 1967. 115p. 36 plates. 28cm. (Werke der Kunst in Heidelberg, 2) Bibl. [NK613.H3] 67-16137 6.00
1. Art objects, Classical—Catalogs. 2. Art objects—Heidelberg—Catalogs. I. Gropengiesser, Hildegund. joint author. II. Heidelberg. Universitat. Archaologisches Institut. III. Title. IV. Series.

Art objects—Collectors and collecting.

ANGUS, S. F. Ian. 745.1'0942
Collecting antiques / edited by S. F. Ian Angus. New York : Galahad Books, [1974] c1972. 128 p. : ill. ; 21 cm. Includes index. [NK1125.A58 1974] 74-184855 4.95
1. Art objects—Collectors and collectiong. I. Title.

WENHAM, Edward, 1884- 708.051
Antiques A to Z; a pocket handbook for collectors and dealers, with sections on weapons and armour by 'Segalas.' New York, Crowell [c1954] 159p. illus. 20cm. [NK1125.W45 1954a] 54-11028
1. Art. objects—Collections and Collecting. 2. Furniture—Collectors and collecting. I. Title.

Art objects—Collectors and collecting.

THE Antiquer's almanac & yearbook. 708.051
1953- Uniontown, Pa., Warman Pub. Co. v. illus. 20cm. Editor: 1963- E. G. Warman. [NK1125.A29] 53-33464
1. Art objects—Collectors and collecting. I. Warman, Edwin G., 1915- ed.

BAKER, Mary Gladys Steel, 1892- 707'.5
Small antiques for the small home [by] Sheila Stuart. South Brunswick [N.J.] A. S. Barnes [1969, c1968] 139 p. illus. 29 cm. Bibliography: p. 135. [NK1125.B35] 68-14418 10.00
1. Art objects—Collectors and collecting. I. Title.

BATES, Gloria M. 745.1
Antiques; beginners in the business, written and illustrated by Gloria M. Bates. [Minneapolis, Minn., Printed and distributed by Green Print. Co., 1969] 156 p. illus. (part col.), forms. 23 cm. [NK1125.B36] 77-111326 3.95
1. Art objects—Collectors and collecting. I. Title.

BEDFORD, John, 1907- 790.023'2
The collecting man. [1st American ed.] New York, D. McKay [1968] 256 p. illus., facsims., ports. 22 cm. Bibliography: p. 247-256. [NK1125.B38 1968b] 68-54167 5.95
1. Art objects—Collectors and collecting. I. Title.

BEDFORD, John, 1907- 708.04
Looking in junk shops. Illus. by Susan Holland. New York, McKay [1964, c1961] 251 p. illus. 18 cm. "Reading list": p. 243-251. [NK1125.B4 1964] 64-55937
1. Art objects—Collectors and collecting. 2. Collectors and collecting. I. Title.

BEDFORD, John, 1907- 708.04
More looking in junk shops. Illus. by Susan Holland. London, M. Parrish [dist. Chester Springs, Pa.,Dufour, 1963, c.1962] 248p. illus. 18cm. Bibl. 63-5454 2.95
1. Art objects—Collectors and collecting. 2. Collectors and collecting. I. Title.

BEDFORD, John, 1907- 745.1074
More looking in junk shops. Illustrated by Susan Holland. New York, D. McKay Co. [1965, c1962] 252 p. illus. 18 cm. Bibliography: p. 251-252. [NK1125.B42 1965] 65-16907
1. Art objects—Collectors and collecting. 2. Collectors and collecting. I. Title.

BLACK, Howard R., Jr. 708.04
Fell's collector's guide to valuable antiques. New York, Fell [1963] 328p. illus. 22cm. Bibl. 63-15067 5.95
1. Art objects—Collectors and collecting. 2. Collectors and collecting. I. Title.

BOS, Evelyn F. 745.1
Know about antiques. New Augusta, Ind., Editors & Engineers [c.1966] 96p. illus. 18cm. (Skillfact lib., 634) Bibl. [NK1125.B57] 66-20889 1.00 pap.,
1. Art objects—Collectors and collecting. I. Title.

BOWLES, Ella (Shannon) 1886- 745.1'0973
About antiques. Philadelphia, Lippincott, 1929. Detroit, Tower Books, 1971. 263 p. illus. 19 cm. "Books on early Americana": p. 259-263. [NK805.B6 1971] 70-174011
1. Art objects—Collectors and collecting. 2. Art objects, American. I. Title. BIP

BRESSIE, Wesley. 745.1'075
Relic trails to treasure; the Americana price guide, by Wes and Ruby Bressie. Salem, Or., Old Time Bottle Pub. Co. [1970] 192 p. illus. 22 cm. "Price guide 1970" inserted. [NK1125.B74] 70-113427 ISBN 0-911068-05-8 4.50
1. Art objects—Collectors and collecting. 2. Art objects—Prices. I. Bressie, Ruby, joint author. II. Title. BIP

BYRNS, John H. 381'.45'7451
Where the antiques are in Britain and Ireland; the complete guide to hundreds of antique shops and markets in more than 65 towns and villages, by John H. Byrns. [1st ed. East Meadow, N.Y., R. P. Long; trade distributor: Hastings House, New York, 1972] 128 p. illus. 21 cm. Pages 127-128, blank for "Notes." [NK1127.B9] 72-182244 2.95
1. Art objects—Collectors and collecting. 2. Art dealers—Great Britain—Directories. 3. Art dealers—Ireland—Directories. I. Title. BIP

CALLAHAN, Claire Wallis. 708.051
Antiques: how to identify, buy, sell, refinish, and care for them. Illustrated by Cynthia Rockmore. New York, D. McKay Co. [1957] 246p. illus. 22cm. Includes bibliography. [NK1125.C62] 57-11071
1. Art objects—Collectors and collecting. 2. Collectors and collecting. 3. Art industries and trade—U. S. I. Title.

CALLAHAN, Claire Wallis. 708.051
The beginning antique collector's handbook and guide to 1,000 items to' collect, by Ann Kilborn Cole [pseud.] New York, D. Mckay Co. [1959] 232p. illus. 22cm. [NK1125.C26] 59-12263
1. Art objects—Collectors and collecting. 2. Collectors and collectoing. I. Title.

CALLAHAN, Claire (Wallis) 745.1
How to collect new antiques; what they are, how to evaluate them, by Ann Kilborn Cole. New York, D. McKay Co. [1966] ix, 244 p. illus. 22 cm. Bibliography: p. 231-234. [NK1125.C262] 66-14586
1. Art objects—Collectors and collecting. 2. Collectors and collecting. I. Title.

[CALLAHAN, Claire (Wallis)] 745.1
How to collect the new antiques; what they are, how to evaluate them. by Ann Kilborn Cole [pseud.] New York, McKay [c.1966] ix, 244p. illus. 22cm. Bibl. [NK1125.C262] 66-14586 5.95
1. Art objects—Collectors and collecting. 2. Collectors and collecting. I. Title.

CALLAHAN, Claire (Wallis) 745.1
How to sell your antiques at a profit, by Ann Kilborn Cole. New York, D. McKay Co. [1969] vii, 181 p. 21 cm. [NK1125.C2623] 69-20210 4.50
1. Art objects—Collectors and collecting. 2. Art objects—Prices. I. Title.

COLE, Ann Kilborn 708.051
Antiques: how to identify, buy, sell, refinish, and care for them. Illus. by Cynthia Rockmore. New York, Collier [1962, c.1957] 287p. (BS60) Bibl. 1.50 pap.,
1. Art objects—Collectors and collecting. 2. Collectors and collecting. 3. Art industries and trade—U.S. I. Title.

COLE, Ann Kilborn. 708.051
Antiques: how to identify, buy, sell refnish, and care for them. Illustrated by cynthia Rockmore. New York, D. McKay Co. [1957] 246p. illus. 22cm. Includes bibliography. [NK1125.C62] 57-11071
1. Art objects—Collectors and collecting. 2. sCollectors and collecting. 3. Art industries and trade—U. S. I. Title.

COWIE, Donald. 745.1'075
Antiques: how to identify and collect them. South Brunswick, A. S. Barnes [1971, c1970] 201 p. col. illus., facsims. 29 cm. Includes bibliographical references. [NK1125.C65] 75-88256 ISBN 0-498-07368-8 12.50
1. Art objects—Collectors and collecting. I. Title.

COYSH, Arthur Wilfred. 745.1'075
Buying antiques; a beginner's guide to English antiques, by A. W. Coysh and J. King. New York, Praeger [1968, c1967] 224 p. illus. 23 cm. Bibliography: p. 157-160. [NK1125.C67 1968] 68-14155
1. Art objects—Collectors and collecting. I. King, J., joint author. II. Title.

COYSH, Arthur Wilfred. 745'.1'075
Buying antiques general guide; a beginner's guide to English antiques, by A. W. Coysh and J. King. New York, Praeger [1968] 180 p. illus. 23 cm. [NK1125.C66] 68-31672 6.95
1. Art objects—Collectors and collecting. I. King, J., joint author. II. Title.

*CURTIS, Tony. 745.1'.0973
Antiques on a budget. New York, Scribner [1974 c1973] 127 p. illus (part col.) 31 cm. [NK805] 74-3738 ISBN 0-684-13819-0 10.00
1. Art objects—Collectors and collecting. I. Title.

DE FORREST, Michael Jean, 1924- 745.1
Antiquing from A to Z : buying and selling antiques, collectibles, and other old things / Michael De Forrest. New York : Simon and Schuster, [1975] 285 p. ; 23 cm. Includes index. [NK2115.D44] 75-12860 ISBN 0-671-22075-6 : 7.95
1. Art objects—Collectors and collecting. I. Title. BIP

DORN, Sylvia O'Neill. 745.1'075
The insider's guide to antiques, art, and collectibles. [1st ed.] Garden City, N.Y., Doubleday, 1974. xxii, 334 p. 22 cm. Includes bibliographical references. [NK1125.D63] 73-11701 7.95
1. Art objects—Collectors and collecting. I. Title. BIP

DOUSSY, Michel. 745.1'028
Antiques: professional secrets for the amateur. Translated from the French by Patrick Evans. [New York] Quadrangle/New York Times Book Co. [1974, c1973] 373 p. illus. 24 cm. Translation of Guide des secrets de l'antiquaire. [NK1125.D6513 1973b] 73-79910 ISBN 0-8129-0380-3 10.00
1. Art objects—Collectors and collecting. 2. Art objects—Handbooks, manuals, etc. I. Title.

DU CANN, Charles Garefield Lott 1899- 745.1075
Adventures in antiques London F. Muller New Rochelle, N.Y. Sportshelf 1966, c.1965 204p. illus. 20cm. [NK1225.D75] 66-555 bds. 5.50
1. Art objects—collectors and collecting 2. Collectors and collecting I. Title.

DU CANN, Charles Garfield Lott, 1889- 745.1075
Adventures in antiques [by] C. G. L. Du Cann. London, F. Muller [1965] 204p. illus. 20cm. [NK1125.D75] 66-555 3.50
1. Art objects—Collectors and collecting. 2. Collectors and collecting. I. Title.
Distributed by Barnes & Noble, New York.

DU CANN, Charles Garfield Lott, 1889- 745.1'075
Antiques for amateurs, by C. G. L. Du Cann. London, F. Muller; New York, Barnes & Noble, 1968. 176p. illus. 21cm. (Barnes & Noble everyday handbks., no. 243) [NK1125.D76 1968] 68-30782 1.50 pap.,
1. Art objects—Collectors and collecting. I. Title.

EMMONS, Verna. 708.051
Briefs on antiques: know your antiques before you buy or sell. New York, Vantage Press [1953] 57p. 21cm. [NK1125.E5] 53-10290
1. Art objects—Collectors and collecting. I. Title.

FRY, Peter George Robin Somerset, 1931- 745.1'075
The world of antiques [by] Plantagenet Somerset Fry. Introduction by Ralph and Terry Kovel. London, New York, Hamlyn, 1970. 5-141 p. illus. (some col.), facsims. (1 col.). 29 cm. Illus. on lining papers. Bibliography: p. 137-138. [NK1125.F79] 70-597294 ISBN 0-600-39202-3 £1.50
1. Art objects—Collectors and collecting. I. Title.

SUBJECT INDEX

ART OBJECTS—COLLECTORS AND

GILBERT, Anne, 1927- 745.1'075
Antique hunting : a guide for freaks and fanciers / by Anne Gilbert ; photos by Anthony Hume. New York : Grosset & Dunlap, [1975] xvii, 237 p. : ill. ; 22 cm. [NK1125.G46] 74-856 ISBN 0-448-11637-5 : 8.95
1. Art objects—Collectors and collecting. I. Title.

GOHM, Douglas Charles. 745.1
Small antiques for the collector, by Douglas Gohm. New York, Arco [1970? c1968] 223 p. illus. (part col.), plates (part col.), port. 23 cm. Includes bibliographical references. [NK1125.G55 1970b] 71-116421 5.95
1. Art objects—Collectors and collecting. I. Title.

GROTZ, George. 745.1075
Antiques you can decorate with; a practical guide to what they are, where to find them, and how much to pay for them. With more than 400 drawings by the author. [1st ed.] Garden City, N.Y., Doubleday, 1966. xv, 296 p. illus. 22 cm. [NK1125.G76] 66-20923
1. Art objects—Collectors and collecting. I. Title.

GROTZ, George. 745.1
Antiques you can decorate with; a practical guide to what they are, where to find them, and how much to pay for them. With more than 400 drawings by the author. Rev. ed., with current price guide in back pages. Garden City, N.Y., Doubleday, 1971. xiii, 322 p. illus. 22 cm. [NK1125.G76 1971] 79-141246 6.95
1. Art objects—Collectors and collecting. I. Title.

HARDING, Arthur 708.04
Collecting English antiques. Line drawings by A. J. Turvey. London, W. & G. Foyle [dist. New Rochelle, N.Y., SportShelf 1965, c.1963] 92p. illus. 19cm. (Foyles handbks.) [NK1125.H325] 65-2596 1.50 bds.,
1. Art objects—Collectors and collecting. 2. Art objects, English. I. Title.

HERTZ, Louis Heilbroner. 745.1'075
Antique collecting for men / by Louis H. Hertz. New York : Galahad Books, [1975?] c1969. xv, 416 p., [4] leaves of plates : ill. ; 27 cm. Reprint of the ed. published by Hawthorn Books, New York. Includes index. [NK1125.H44 1975] 73-79806 ISBN 0-88365-045-2 : 15.00
1. Art objects—Collectors and collecting. 2. Men as collectors. I. Title.

HUGHES, George Bernard, 1896- 708.04
The antique collector's pocket book [by] G. Bernard Hughes. Illus. by Therle Hughes. [1st American ed.] New York, Hawthorn Books [1965, c1963] 351 p. illus. 16 cm. First published in London in 1963 under title: The Country Life collector's pocket book. [NK1125.H814 1965] 65-12897
1. Art objects—Collectors and collecting. I. Title.

HUGHES, George Bernard, 1896- 745.1'075
The Country Life collector's pocket book, by G. Bernard Hughes. Illus. by Therle Hughes. London, New York, Country Life [1972, c1963] 351 p. illus. 16 cm. Label mounted on t.p.: Transatlantic Arts, New York, sole distributors for the USA. [NK1125.H814 1972] 73-158280 ISBN 0-600-43055-3 4.95
1. Art objects—Collectors and collecting. I. Title. BIP

HUGHES, George Bernard, 1896- 708.051
Horse brasses and other small items for the collector. London. Country Life [dist. New York, Taplinger, 1964] 104p. illus. 26cm. 56-14665 8.50
1. Art objects—Collectors and collecting. I. Title.

HUGHES, George Bernard, 1896- 708.051
More about collecting antiques. London, Country Life: New York, Scribner [1952] 272p. illus. 25cm. Includes bibliography. [NK1125.H83] 53-1502
1. Art objects— Collectors and collecting. I. Title.

HUGHES, Therle 708.051
More small decorative antiques. New York, Macmillan, 1963[c.1962] 216p. illus (pt. col.) 23cm. 63-676 8.95
1. Art objects—Collectors and collecting. I. Title.

HUGHES, Therle 708.04
Small antiques for the collector. New York, Macmillan [1965, c.1964] 222p. plates (pt. col.) 23cm. [NK1125.H847] 65-12642 10.00
1. Art objects—Collectors and collecting. I. Title.

HUGHES, Therle 708.051
Small decorative antiques. New York, Macmillan [1960, c.1959] 223p. illus. 23cm. 60-9821 7.00
1. Art objects—Collectors and collecting. I. Title.

KLAMKIN, Marian. 709'.04
The collector's book of art nouveau. Illustrated with photos. by Charles Klamkin. New York, Dodd, Mead [1971] 112 p. illus. 25 cm. Bibliography: p. 109-110. [NK775.K55 1971] 74-154064 ISBN 0-396-06367-5 6.95
1. Art objects—Collectors and collecting. 2. Decoration and ornament—Art nouveau. I. Title.

KOBS, Betty, 1934- 658'.91'7451
Selling antiques & collectibles at your own flea market / Betty Kobs. Waukesha, Wis. : Country Beautiful Corp., [1975] p. cm. Bibliography: p. [NK1125.K595] 74-76833 ISBN 0-87294-058-6 : 19.95
1. Art objects—Collectors and collecting. 2. Art objects—Prices. I. Title. BIP

KOVEL, Ralph M. 745.1
Know your antiques; how to recognize and evaluate any antique, large or small, like an expert, by Ralph and Terry Kovel. New York, Crown Publishers [1967] x, 327 p. illus. 24 cm. Includes bibliographies. [NK1125.K65] 67-17713
1. Art objects—Collectors and collecting. I. Kovel, Terry H., joint author. II. Title. BIP

MCCLINTON, Katherine (Morrison) 745.1
Antiques, past and present. [1st ed.] New York, C. N. Potter; distributed by Crown [1971] 314 p. illus., facsims. 27 cm. [NK1125.M326 1971] 75-150695
1. Art objects—Collectors and collecting. I. Title.

*MACKAY, James. 745.1028
An encyclopedia of small antiques. New York, Harper & Row, [1975] 320 p. illus. (part col.), 26 cm. Bibliography: p. 314. [NK28] 75-4145 ISBN 0-06-012795-3 22.50
1. Art objects—Collectors and collecting. I. Title.

MACKAY, James Alexander. 745.1
Antiques of the future; a guide for collectors and investors [by] James A. Mackay. New York, Universe Books [1970] 208 p. illus. 25 cm. Bibliography: p. 206. [NK1125.M345 1970b] 73-106796 7.50
1. Art objects—Collectors and collecting. 2. Art objects as an investment. I. Title.

MACNAGHTEN, Patrick. 749.2'2
Beginner's guide to collecting antique furniture. [New York] Hippocrene Books [1973] 152 p. illus. 22 cm. [NK1125.M347 1973] 73-77020 ISBN 0-88254-049-1 5.95
1. Art objects—Collectors and collecting. I. Title.

MEBANE, John, 1909- 745.1'075
Collecting nostalgia; the first guide to the antiques of the 30s and 40s. New Rochelle, N.Y., Arlington House [1972] 367 p. illus. 25 cm. Bibliography: p. [353]-358. [NK1125.M352] 72-77644 ISBN 0-87000-173-6 11.95
1. Art objects—Collectors and collecting. I. Title.

MEBANE, John, 1909- 707.5
The coming collecting boom. South Brunswick [N. J.] A. S. Barnes [1968] 320 p. illus. 26 cm. Bibliography: p. 309-315. [NK1125.M353] 67-17074
1. Art objects—Collectors and collecting. I. Title.

MEBANE, John, 1909- 707.5
New horizons in collecting: Cinderella antiques. South Brunswick [N.J.] A. S. Barnes [1966] 280 p. illus. 26 cm. Bibliography: p. 267-275. [NK1125.M358] 66-18199
1. Art objects—Collectors and collecting. I. Title.

MEBANE, John, 1909- 707.5
New horizons in collecting: Cinderella antiques. South Brunswick [N.J.] A. S. Barnes [1966] 280 p. illus. 26 cm. Bibliography: p. 267-275. [NK1125.M358] 66-18199
1. Art objects—Collectors and collecting. I. Title.

MICHAEL, George, 1919- 745.1'075
The basic book of antiques / by George Michael. New York : Arco Pub. Co., [1974] viii, 293 p. : ill. ; 27 cm. Includes index. Bibliography: p. 281-284. [NK1125.M46] 74-77072 ISBN 0-668-03433-5 : 10.00
1. Art objects—Collectors and collecting. I. Title. BIP

MOBANE, John, 1909- 745.1'075
The poor man's guide to antique collecting. [1st ed.] Garden City, N.Y., Doubleday, 1969. ix, 209 p. illus. 27 cm. Bibliography: p. [191]-198. [NK1125.M359] 77-84382 7.50
1. Art objects—Collector's and collecting. I. Title.

NOLL, Bosco Cass. 745.1
Upstairs and downstairs with antiques. Garden City, N.Y., Doubleday [1970] 80 p. illus. (part col.) 24 cm. (The Doubleday home decorating program) Bibliography: p. 78. [NK1125.N64] 71-23452
1. Art objects—Collectors and collecting. I. Title.

PALMER, Mervyn. 745.1'075
Face to face with antiques. Dunedin, John McIndoe [1971] 78 p. illus. 22 cm. Bibliography: p. [75] [NK1125.P34] 72-192561
1. Art objects—Collectors and collecting. I. Title.

PATTERSON, Jerry E. 745.1'075
A collector's guide to relics & memorabilia / Jerry E. Patterson. New York : Crown Publishers, [1974] xiii, 178 p. : ill. ; 26 cm. Includes index. Bibliography: p. 169-170. [NK1125.P37 1974] 74-80301 ISBN 0-517-51606-3 : 7.95
1. Art objects—Collectors and collecting. I. Title.

PETERSON, Harold Leslie, 1922- 745.1
How do you know it's old? A practical handbook on the detection of fakes for the antique collector and curator, by Harold L. Peterson. New York, Scribner [1975] ix, 166 p. illus. 24 cm. Bibliography: p. 160-163. [NK1125.P435] 74-13118 ISBN 0-684-13981-2 8.95
1. Art objects—Collectors and collecting. 2. Collectors and collecting. I. Title. BIP

RAMSEY, L. G. G., comp. 749.2
Antique furniture; the guide for collectors, investors, and dealers, edited by L. G. G. Ramsey and Helen Comstock. New York, Hawthorn Books [1969] 362 p. illus. (part col.) 26 cm. Includes bibliographical references. [NK1125.R34] 76-91315 15.00
1. Art objects—Collectors and collecting. I. Comstock, Helen, joint comp. II. Title.

REIF, Rita. 749'.075
The antique collector's guide to styles and prices. New York, Hawthorn Books [1970] xii, 276 p. illus. (part col.) 26 cm. Bibliography: p. 253-254. [NK1125.R37] 75-102019 12.95
1. Art objects—Collectors and collecting. 2. Art objects—Prices. I. Title. II. Title: Guide to styles and prices.

REYNOLDS, Ernest Randolph, 1910- 708.051
Guide to European antiques. New York, A.S.Barnes [1964, c.1963] 183p. plates. 22cm. Published in 1963 under title: The plain man's guide to antique collecting. 64-2633 5.95
1. Art objects—Collectors and collecting. 2. Collectors and collecting. I. Title.

RHOADES, Orille (Bourassa) 709
The world of antique arts. 1st ed. Chicago, Lightner Pub. Corp., 1958. xviii, 301p. illus. 28cm. Bibliography: p. 293-298. [NK1125.R45] 58-13739
1. Art objects— Collectors and collecting. 2. Art industries and trade—Hist. I. Title.

ROE, Frederic Gordon, 1894- 745.1
Home furnishings with antiques [by] F. Gordon Roe. Illus. by Frances Maynard. New York, Hastings House [1965] 211 p. illus. 23 cm. Bibliographical references included in "Notes" (p. 201-204) [NK1125.R655 1965a] 65-9213
1. Art objects—Collectors and collecting. 2. Furniture—Collectors and collecting. I. Title.

ROE, Frederic Gordon, 1894- 709'.42
Victorian corners; the style and taste of an era, by F. Gordon Roe. With illus. by Frances Maynard and others. New York, Praeger [1969, c1968] 116 p. illus. 26 cm. Bibliographical footnotes. [NK928.R6 1969] 78-79072 6.95
1. Art objects—Collectors and collecting. 2. Design, Decorative—Gt. Brit. 3. Gt. Brit.—Social life and customs—19th century. I. Title.

RUSH, Richard H. 749
Antiques as an investment [by] Richard H. Rush. Drawings by Julia Rush. Englewood Cliffs, N.J., Prentice-Hall [1968] 536 p. illus. 26 cm. [NK1125.R86] 68-10170 14.95
1. Art objects—Collectors and collecting. 2. Art objects as an investment. I. Title.

SAVAGE, George, 1909- 745.1
The antique collector's handbook; drawings by Frederick Curl. New revised ed. Feltham, Spring Books, 1968. 304 p. 16 plates, illus., 23 cm. Bibliography: p. 276-287. [NK1125.S3 1968] 70-510278 25/-
1. Art objects—Collectors and collecting. I. Title. BIP

SAVAGE, George, 1909- 708.051
The antique collector's handbook. Drawings by Frederick Curl. London, *Barrie and Rockliff [1959]* 304p. illus. 22cm. Bibliography: p.276-287. [NK1125.S3] 60-1409
1. Art objects—Collectors and collecting. 2. Collectors and collecting. I. Title.

THOMAS, Gilbert 708.051
Antiques in your home; a book for the small collector of English antiques. [Rev.] New York, Sterling Pub. Co. [1959 i.e. 1960] 174p. illus. port., 23cm. 60-10375 2.95
1. Art objects—Collectors and collecting. 2. Collectors and collecting. 3. Art objects, English. I. Title.

THOMAS, Gilbert, 1903- 708.051
Antiques in your home; a book for the small collector of English antiques. [rev.] New York, Sterling Pub. Co. [c1959] 174 p. illus. 23 cm. [NK1125.T45 1959] 60-10375
1. Art objects — Collectors and collecting. 2. Collectors and collecting. 3. Art objects, English. I. Title.

WAY, Reginald Philip, 1893-1955. 708.051
Antique dealer. New York, Macmillan, 1956. 211 p. 22 cm. Autobiography. [NK1125.W3 1956a] 56-13241
1. Art objects—Collectors and collecting. I. Title.

WAY, Reginald Phillip, 1893-1955. 708.051
Antique dealer. New York, Macmillan, 1956. 211 p. 22 cm. Autobiography. [NK1125.W3 1956a] 56-13241
1. Art objects — Collectors and collecting. I. Title.

WILLS, Geoffrey. 708.04
Practical guide to antique collecting. Drawings by A. J. Turvey. New York, Arc Books [1963, c1961] 161 p. illus. 19 cm. [NK1125.W52] 62-20296
1. Art objects—Collectors and collecting. 2. Collectors and collecting. I. Title. II. Title: Antique collecting. BIP

WILSON, Peter Cecil, 1913- 745.1
Antiques international; collector's guide to current trends. General editor: Peter Wilson. [1st American ed.] New York, Putnam [1967, c1966] 360 p. illus. (part col.), maps, ports. 31 cm. "A Giniger book." Includes bibliographies. [NK1125.W525 1967] 67-23637
1. Art objects—Collectors and collecting. I. Title.

Art objects—Collectors and collecting—Dictionaries.

BEDFORD, John, 1907- 745.1'03
Still looking for junk. Illustrated by Susan Holland. [1st American ed.] New York, D. McKay Co. [1970, c1969] 228 p. illus. 18 cm. Bibliography: p. 227-228. [NK1125.B43 1970] 70-108575 3.95
1. Art objects—Collectors and collecting—Dictionaries. I. Title.

BOND, Harold Lewis. 745.1'03
An encyclopedia of antiques / by Harold Lewis Bond. Detroit : Gale Research Co., 1975, c1937. xiii, 389 p., [32] leaves of plates : ill. ; 22 cm. Reprint of the 1945 ed. published by Tudor Pub. Co., New York. Bibliography: p. 361-376. [NK30.B6 1975] 74-31297 ISBN 0-8103-4206-5 : 18.00
1. Art objects—Collectors and collecting—Dictionaries. I. Title.

MACKAY, James Alexander. 745.1
Turn-of-the-century antiques : an encyclopedia / James Mackay. New York : Dutton, 1974. 320 p. : ill. (some col.) ; 26 cm. (A Dutton Visual book) Bibliography: p. 314-319. [NK775.5.A7M32 1974] 74-3641 ISBN 0-525-49504-5 : 18.95
1. Art objects—Collectors and collecting—Dictionaries. 2. Decoration and ornament—Art nouveau—Dictionaries. I. Title.

THE Random House 745.1'075
encyclopedia of antiques. Introd. by John Pope-Hennessy. [1st American ed.] New York, Random House [1973] 400 p. illus. (part col.) 28 cm. Bibliography: p. [391]-398. [NK1125.R35 1973] 73-3997 ISBN 0-394-48811-3 25.00
1. Art objects—Collectors and collecting—Dictionaries. I. Title: Encyclopedia of antiques.

WHITTINGTON, Peter. 745.1
Undiscovered antiques, discovered by Peter Whittington. New York, Scribner [1973, c1972] 133 p. illus. 22 cm. [NK1125.W48 1973] 73-3004 ISBN 0-684-13404-7 5.95
1. Art objects—Collectors and collecting—Dictionaries. I. Title.

Art objects—Collectors and collecting—Handbooks, manuals, etc.

COHEN, Hal L. 745.1'075
Antiques, curios; the price to buy & sell ... by Hal L. Cohen. 4th ed. New York, House of Collectibles [1973] 222 p. illus. 14 cm. Second-3d editions published under title: Official guide to popular antiques, curios. [NK1125.C57 1973] 74-156774 ISBN 0-87637-325-2 2.00
1. Art objects—Collectors and collecting—Handbooks, manuals, etc. I. Title.

COHEN, Hal L. 745.1
Official guide to popular antiques, curios; the price to buy & sell. Rev. 4th ed. New York, House of Collectibles, 1973. 415 p. illus. col. plates. 18 cm. Cover title. Title on spine: Official guide to antiques. [NK2115.C57 1973] 68-31562 ISBN 0-87637-126-8 5.00 (pbk.)
1. Art objects—Collectors and collecting—Handbooks, manuals, etc. I. Title. II. Title: Official guide to antiques.
Publisher's address: 17 Park Ave., New York, NY 10016. The L.C. card no. was assigned to the 2d ed.

KELLEY, Austin P. 745.1'075
The anatomy of antiques : a collector's guide / Austin P. Kelley and the staff of Sotheby Parke Bernet. New York : Viking Press, 1974. 189 p., [8] leaves of plates : ill., (some col.) ; 29 cm. (A Studio book) Errata slip inserted. [NK1125.K44 1974] 73-6066 ISBN 0-670-12240-8 : 12.95
1. Art objects—Collectors and collecting—Handbooks, manuals, etc. I. Sotheby Parke Bernet Inc. II. Title.

Art objects—Collectors and collecting—Juvenile literature.

CALLAHAN, Claire Wallis. 708.04
Old things for young people; a guide to antiques, by Ann Kilborn Cole [pseud.] New York, McKay [1963] xii, 174 p. illus. 23 cm. Includes bibliographies. [NK1125.C263] 63-15885
1. Art objects—Collectors and collecting—Juvenile literature. I. Title.

PEEK, David T. 708
The book of antiques, for boys and girls, in four books: bk 2. Indianapolis 5, 3845 guilford ave., Author, [c.1962] 100 p. illus. Bibl. 3.50
1. Art objects—collectors and collecting—juvenile. I. Title.

PEEK, David T. 708.051
The book of antiques for boys and girls. Indianapolis. Author, 3845, Guilford, Ave. [1960] 91p. illus. Bibl. 60-38957 3.50
1. Art objects—Collectors and collecting—Juvenile literature. I. Title. II. Title: Antiques for boys and girls.

Art objects—Collectors and collecting—United States.

MEUGNIOT, Elinor. 745'.09776'31
Old Sleepy Eye. [1st ed. Tulsa, Okla., D. L. Hill, 1973] 46 p. illus. 22 cm. [NK808.M48] 73-173445 4.95
1. Sleepy Eye, Chief of the Lower Sisseton Sioux, d. 1859—Portraits, caricatures, etc. 2. Art objects—Collectors and collecting—United States. I. Title. BIP

Art objects—Conservation and restoration.

*BEEDELL, Suzanne. 745.1'028
Restoring junk [by] Suzanne Beedell, with the editorial assistance of Barbara Hargreaves. Foreword by John Bedford. New York, Lancer Books [1973, c.1970] 239 p. illus. 19 cm. (Larchmont Books) [NK1127.5] pap., 1.95
1. Art objects—Conservation and restoration. I. Hargreaves, Barbara, ed. II. Title.

BEEDELL, Suzanne. 745.1
Restoring junk / Suzanne Beedell;with the editorial assistance of Barbara Hargreaves ; foreword by John Bedford. New York : Berkley Pub. 1976c1970. 239p. : ill. ; 20 cm. (A Berkley Windhover book) Includes indices. [N8560] ISBN 0-425-03085-7 pbk. : 2.95
1. Art objects-Conversation and restoration. I. Title.
L.C. card no. for 1970 Mckay ed. 72-103147.

CROSBY, Jean Myers. 738.1
Two sisters guide to antique restoration & china repair; complete methods of restoring and repairing antiques and other articles, by Jean Myers Crosby & Judy Myers Denson. [Phoenix? Ariz., F. G. Crosby, 1973] 103 p. illus. (part col.) 29 cm. [NK1127.5.C76] 73-164613 16.95
1. Art objects—Conservation and restoration. 2. Pottery—Repairing. I. Denson, Judy Myers, joint author. II. Title.

FALL, Frieda Kay, 1913- 702
Art objects: their care and preservation; a reference for museums and collectors. [Washington, Museum Publications, 1967- v. illus. 22 cm. Includes bibliographies. [N8560.F3] 67-29319
1. Art objects—Conservation and restoration. I. Title. BIP

FALL, Frieda Kay, 1913- 702'.8
Art objects: their care and preservation; a handbook for museums and collectors. La Jolla, Calif., L. McGilvery, 1973. ix, 332 p. illus. 25 cm. Bibliography: p. 302-307. [N8560.F32] 72-148177 ISBN 0-910938-55-5 15.00
1. Art objects—Conservation and restoration. I. Title.

FREEMAN, Graydon La Verne, 749.2
1904-1963.
How to restore antiques. Watkins Glen, N.Y., Century House [1960] 96 p. illus. 22 cm. [N8560.F7] 60-13416
1. Art objects—Conservation and restoration. 2. Furniture—Repairing. I. Title. BIP

GULDBECK, Per Ernst. 702'.8
The care of historical collections; a conservation handbook for the nonspecialist [by] Per E. Guldbeck. Nashville, American Association for State and Local History, 1972. xvii, 160 p. illus. 23 cm. Includes bibliographies. [NK1127.5.G8] 72-76003 ISBN 0-910050-07-4
1. Art objects—Conservation and restoration. I. Title. BIP

KINARD, Epsie. 745.1
The care and keeping of antiques. Foreword by Marvin D. Schwartz. New York, Hawthorn Books [1972, c1971] 160 p. illus. 23 cm. Bibliography: p. 147-148. [NK1127.5.K5] 77-158029 6.95
1. Art objects—Conservation and restoration. I. Title.

MCGRATH, Lee Parr. 645
Housekeeping with antiques. New York, Dodd, Mead [1971] viii, 175 p. 24 cm. Bibliography: p. 165-166. [NK1127.5.M3] 70-165673 ISBN 0-396-06432-9 5.95
1. Art objects—Conservation and restoration. I. Title.

MILLS, John FitzMaurice, 069'.53
1917-
Treasure keepers. Garden City, N.Y., Doubleday [1973, i.e. 1974] 160 p. illus. (part col.) 28 cm. (Nature and science library) [N8555.M54 1973b] 73-82573 ISBN 0-385-04491-7 7.95
1. Art objects—Conservation and restoration. 2. Museum techniques. I. Title.

PLENDERLEITH, Harold 708.04
James, 1898-
The conservation of antiquities and works of art; treatment, repair, and restoration. London, New York, Oxford University Press, 1956. xv, 373p. illus., tables. 25cm. 'Errata' slip mounted on p. xii. Bibliographical footnotes. [N8560.P55] A57
1. Art objects—Conservation and restoration. 2. Antiquities—Conservation and restoration: I. Title. BIP

PLENDERLEITH, Harold 702'.8
James, 1898-
The conservation of antiquities and works of art: treatment, repair and restoration [by] H. J. Plenderleith and A. E. A. Werner. 2d ed. London, New York, Oxford University Press, 1971. xix, 394 p. illus. 25 cm. Includes bibliographical references. [N8560.P55 1971] 72-192419 ISBN 0-19-212960-0 £6.50
1. Art objects—Conservation and restoration. 2. Antiquities—Collection and preservation. I. Werner, Alfred Emil Anthony, 1911- joint author. II. Title.

PLENDERLEITH, Harold 708.04
James, 1908-
The conservation of antiquities and works of art; treatment, repair, and restoration. London, New York, Oxford University Press, 1956. xv, 373p. illus., tables. 25cm. 'Errata' slip mounted on p. xii. Bibliographical footnotes. [N8560.P55] A57
1. Art objects—Conservation and restoration. 2. Antiquities—Conservation and restoration. I. Title.

RATCLIFF, Rosemary. 745.1'028
Refurbishing antiques. Illustrated by Ted Western. Chicago, Regnery [1971] x, 209 p. illus. 22 cm. [NK1127.5.R3 1971b] 70-163269 5.95
1. Art objects—Conservation and restoration. I. Title.

RATCLIFF, Rosemary. 702'.8
Refurbishing antiques / Rosemary Ratcliff ; illustrated by Ted Western. New York : Galahad Books, [1974] c1971. x, 209 p. : ill. ; 22 cm. Includes index. [NK1127.5.R3 1974] 73-79815 ISBN 0-88365-034-7 : 5.95
1. Art objects—Conservation and restoration. I. Title.

REED, Jane M. 710.8
Art in the home; how to care for your valued possessions. Compiled by Jane M. Reed. St. Petersburg, Fla., Stuart Society for the Museum of Fine Arts, 1968. 30 p. illus. 28 cm. Bibliography: p. 30. [N8560.R37] 68-31765
1. Art objects—Conservation and restoration. I. St. Petersburg, Fla. Museum of Fine Arts. II. Stuart Society. III. Title.

SAVAGE, George, 1909- 708.04
The art and antique restorers' handbook; a dictionary of materials and processes used in the restoration & preservation of all kinds of works of art. New York, Philosophical Library [1954] 140 p. 23 cm. [N8560.S38 1954a] 54-3143
1. Art objects—Conservation and restoration. I. Title. BIP

SAVAGE, George, 1909- 708'.04'03
The art and antique restorers' handbook; a dictionary of materials and processes used in the restoration & preservation of all kinds of works of art. [Rev. ed.] New York, Praeger [1967] 142 p. 23 cm. Bibliography: p. 133. [N8560.S38 1967a] 67-17963
1. Art objects—Conservation and restoration. I. Title.

TAUBES, Frederic, 1900- 702'.8
Restoring and preserving antiques. New York, Watson-Guptill Publications [1969] 119 p. illus. (part col.) 27 cm. [N8560.T3] 69-12495 10.00
1. Art objects—Conservation and restoration. I. Title. BIP

WRIGHT, Veva Penick. 745.1
Pamper your possessions. Illus. by Grambs Miller. Barre, Mass., Barre Publishers, 1972. 130 p. illus. 24 cm. [NK1127.5.W7] 79-185322 ISBN 0-8271-7201-X 6.95
1. Art objects—Conservation and restoration. I. Title. BIP

YATES, Raymond Francis, 708.04
1895-
How to restore china, bric-a-brac, and small antiques. Photos. and drawings by the author. [1st ed.] New York, Harper [1953] 210 p. illus. 22 cm. [N8560.Y32] 53-11867
1. Art objects—Conservation and restoration. I. Title.

Art objects—Conservation and restoration—Bibliography.

NEW York State 016.7018
Historical Association.
NYSHA selective reference guide to historic preservation. Frederick L. Rath, Jr., general editor. Merrilyn Rogers, compiler. Cooperstown, N.Y. [Available from the Farmers' Museum Shop] 1966. viii, 133 p. 23 cm. [Z5940.N4] 68-1487
1. Art objects—Conservation and restoration—Bibliography. 2. Monuments—Preservation—Bibliography. I. Rath, Frederick L., ed. II. Rogers, Merrilyn, comp. III. Title. IV. Title: Selective reference guide to historic preservation.

Art objects—Conservation and restoration—Handbooks, manuals, etc.

ENCYCLOPEDIA of antique 745.1'03
restoration and maintenance / with an introd. by Dennis Young. 1st American ed. New York : C. N. Potter : distributed by Crown Publishers, 1974. 183, [4] p. : ill. ; 26 cm. "A Carter Nash Cameron book." Bibliography: p. [185]-[186] [NK1127.5.E52 1974] 73-90931 ISBN 0-517-51451-6 : 12.50
1. Art objects—Conservation and restoration—Handbooks, manuals, etc. I. Young, Dennis.

Art objects—Dictionaries.

BERNASCONI, John R. 700.3
The collectors' glossary of antiques and fine arts, by J. R. Bernasconi. Over 100 illus., including reproductions from the books of Chippendale, Sheraton and Hepplewhite. [Rev. ed.] London, Estates Gazette, Ltd. [1963] xvi, 587p. illus., facsims. 18cm. [NK30.B4 1963] 66-48284 11.50
1. Art objects—Dictionaries. 2. Art industries and trade—Dictionaries. I. Title.
Available from Transatlantic in New York.

BIP

CLARK, Maryjane. 745.1
An illustrated glossary of decorated antiques from the late 17th century to the early 20th century. [1st ed.] Rutland, Vt., C. E. Tuttle Co. [1972] 400 p. illus. 24 cm. "A publication of the Historical Society of Early American Decoration." Bibliography: p. 310-316. [NK30.C43] 74-138080 ISBN 0-8048-0953-4 8.75
1. Art objects—Dictionaries. 2. Art industries and trade—Dictionaries. 3. Decoration and ornament—Dictionaries. I. Historical Society of Early American Decoration. II. Title.

THE Connoisseur. 708.051
The concise encyclopaedia of antiques. Editor: L. G. G. Ramsey. London & New York, 1954. 288p. illus. 25cm. Includes bibliographies. [NK30.C6] A54
1. Art objects—Dictionaries. 2. Furniture—Dictionaries. 3. Art industries and trade—Dictionaries. 4. Collectors and collecting. I. Ramsey, L. G. G., ed. II. Title.

CONNOISSEUR (The) 708.051
The concise encyclopedia of antiques. v. 5. Ed.: L. G. G. Ramsey. New York, Hawthorn Books [c.1961] 272p. illus. Bibl. 25cm. 12.50
1. Art objects—Dictionaries 2. Furniture—Dictionaries. 3. Art industries and trade—Dictionaries. 4. Collector and collecting. I. Ramsey, L. G. G., ed. II. Title.

DURANT, Mary B. 745.1'03
The American heritage guide to antiques, by Mary Durant. New York, American Heritage Press [1970] 1 v. (unpaged) illus. 23 cm. Includes bibliography. [NK30.D87] 72-111653 6.95
1. Art objects—Dictionaries. 2. Art objects—Handbooks, manuals, etc. I. Title.
BIP

GOODWIN, Michael, 1916- 745'.03
Pocket dictionary of collector's terms. Illus. by C. Dampier Freeman. [New York] Philosophical Library [1967] 317 p. illus. 16 cm. London ed. (Country Life) has title: The Country Life pocket dictionary of collector's terms. Bibliography: p. 316-317. [NK30.G6 1967b] 68-31927
1. Art objects—Dictionaries. I. Title. II. Title: Dictionary of collector's terms.

HAYWARD, Helena, ed. 703
The Connoisseur's handbook of antique collecting; a dictionary of furniture, silver, ceramics, glass, fine art, etc. With an introd. by L. G. G. Ramsey. New York, Hawthorn Books [1960] 320 p. illus. 22 cm. Bibliography: p. 317-320. [NK30.H45] 60-8797
1. Art objects—Dictionaries. 2. Art industries and trade—Dictionaries. 3. Antiques. I. Title. II. Title: Antique collecting.

PHILLIPS, Phoebe. 745.1
The collectors' encyclopedia of antiques. Edited by Phoebe Phillips. Associate editors: David Coombs [and] Joseph Butler. Drawings by Christopher Evans. New York, Crown Publishers [1973] 703 p. illus. (part col.) 29 cm. [NK28.P494 1973] 73-76934 ISBN 0-517-50451-0 20.00
1. Art objects—Dictionaries. 2. Art objects—Collectors and collecting. I. Title.
BIP

THE Random House 745.1
collector's encyclopedia, Victoriana to Art Deco. Introd. by Roy Strong. [1st American ed.] New York, Random House [1974] 302 p. illus. 28 cm. Bibliography: p. 297-302. [NK775.R36 1974] 74-5380 ISBN 0-394-49450-4
1. Art objects—Dictionaries. 2. Decoration and ornament—Victorian style. 3. Decoration and ornament—Art nouveau. 4. Art deco. I. Title: Collector's encyclopedia.

SAVAGE, George, 1909- 745.1'03
Dictionary of antiques. New York, Praeger [1970] ix, 534 p. illus. (part col.) 27 cm. Bibliography: p. 504-534. [NK30.S27 1970] 75-107216 14.95
1. Art objects—Dictionaries. I. Title. BIP

Art objects, Egyptian—Exhibitions.

EDWARDS, Iorwerth Eiddon 709'.32
Stephen.
Tutankhamun, his tomb and its treasures / I. E. S. Edwards ; black and white photos. by Harry Burton, color photos. by Lee Boltin. 1st ed. New York : Metropolitan Museum of Art : distributed by Random House, c1976. ca. 250 p. : ill. (some col.) ; 29 cm. "Published on the occasion of the exhibition Treasures of Tutankhamun at the National Gallery of Art, Washington, D.C., Field Museum of Natural History and the Oriental Institute of the University of Chicago, New Orleans Museum of Art, Los Angeles County Museum of Art, Seattle Art Museum, and the Metropolitan Museum of Art, 1976-1979." [DT87.5.E347 1976] 76-49330 ISBN 0-394-41170-6 : 35.00
1. Tutankhamen, King of Egypt—Tomb. 2. Art objects, Egyptian—Exhibitions. 3. Egypt—Antiquities—Exhibitions. I. Burton, Harry, 1879-1940. II. Boltin, Lee. III. New York (City). Metropolitan Museum of Art. IV. Title.

Art objects—Europe.

STEINGRABER, Erich. 708.9'4
Royal treasures, edited by Erich Steingraber. Translated by Stefan de Haan. Photos. by Claus and Liselotte Hansmann. [1st American ed.] New York, Macmillan [1968] 100 p., [160] p. of illus. (part col.) 32 cm. Translation of Weltliche Schatzkammern. Bibliography: p. 96-98. [NK475.S713 1968] 68-26433 25.00
1. Art objects—Europe. 2. Royal houses—Art collections. I. Title.

Art objects, European—Catalogs.

WALTERS Art Gallery, 709'.4
Baltimore.
Treasures & rarities; Renaissance, mannerist, and baroque [by] Ann Gabhart. Baltimore [1971] 39 p. illus. 28 cm. (A Walters Art Gallery picture book) [NK925.W34] 72-198355
1. Art objects, European—Catalogs. 2. Art objects—Baltimore—Catalogs. I. Gabhart, Ann. II. Title. III. Series.

Art objects—Exhibitions.

CRANBROOK 746.1'4'074017438
Academy of Art, Bloomfield Hills, Mich. Museum.
Historic fiberworks/Cranbrook; objects in fiber from the third to the twentieth century. [Exhibition, Cranbrook Academy of Art/Museum, March 26-October 6, 1974. Catalogue edited by Rosalyn Chat. Bloomfield Hills, Mich., 1974] [19] p. illus. 26 cm. "Volume 1, number 4." [NK8801.B57C722 1974] 74-77266
1. Art objects—Exhibitions. 2. Fibers. 3. Textile industry and fabrics. I. Chat, Rosayln, ed. II. Title.

A La Vieille Russie, 739.27'074
inc.
The art of the goldsmith & the jeweler; a loan exhibition for the benefit of the Young Women's Christian Association of the City of New York, November 6-November 23, 1968. New York [1968] 139 p. illus. (part col.) 28 cm. [NK7101.N4A64] 68-58939
1. Art objects—Exhibitions. 2. Goldsmiths. 3. Jewelers. I. Title.

Art objects, French-Canadian.

LESSARD, Michel. 745.1'09714
Complete guide to French-Canadian antiques / text by Michel Lessard ; illustrated by Huguette Marquis ; translated by Elisabeth Abbott. New York : Hart Pub. Co., [1974] 255 p. : ill. ; 29 cm. Includes index. Bibliography: p. 248-251. [NK842.Q4L38] 74-188209 ISBN 0-8055-1116-4 : 27.50
1. Art objects, French-Canadian. 2. Art objects—Collectors and collecting—Quebec (Province) I. Marquis, Huguette, ill. II. Title.

Art objects—Gt. Brit.—Directories.

COYSH, Arthur Wilfred. 745.1
Guide to buying antiques in Britain; price lists, museums, &c. Compiled by A. W. Coysh. Auction room prices contributed by J. King. New York, Drake Publishers [1972] 344 p. illus. 23 cm. Bibliography: p. 117-186. [NK928.C67] 76-178084 ISBN 0-87749-163-1 7.95
1. Art objects—Gt. Brit.—Directories. 2. Art objects—Collectors and collecting—Directories. I. Title.

Art objects—History.

LISTER, Raymond. 700
Great works of craftsmanship. [1st American ed.] South Brunswick [N.J.] A. S. Barnes [1968, c1967] 206 p. illus. 22 cm. Bibliography: p. [192]-197. [NK600.L5 1968] 68-14406
1. Art objects—History. I. Title.

Art objects, Islamic.

KUHNEL, Ernst, 1882- 709'.176'71
1964.
The minor arts of Islam. Translated from the German by Katherine Watson. Ithaca, N.Y., Cornell University Press [1971, c1970] viii, 255 p. illus. (part col.), facsims. (part col.) 24 cm. Translation of Islamische Kleinkunst. Includes bibliographical references. [NK1674.K813 1971] 75-110331 ISBN 0-8014-0563-7 15.00
1. Art objects, Islamic. I. Title. BIP

Art objects, Japanese—Catalogs.

JOSEPH, Marie A. 738'.0952
Occupied Japan collectibles [by] Marie A. Joseph. [Whitesboro, N.Y., 1972] 48 p. col. illus. 23 cm. [NK1071.J67] 73-161330 5.95
1. Art objects, Japanese—Catalogs. 2. Art objects—Collectors and collecting. I. Title.

Art objects, Korean.

KIM, Chewon, 1909- 709.519
Treasures of Korean art; 2000 years of ceramics, sculpture, and jeweled arts. Text by Chewon Kim and Won-Yong Kim. New York, H. N. Abrams [1966] xv, 283 p. illus. (part mounted col.) maps. 30 cm. Bibliography: p. 261-263. [NK1073.5.K52] 66-23402
1. Art objects, Korean. 2. Pottery—Korea. 3. Art, Buddhist—Korea. I. Kim, Wonyong, 1922- joint author. II. Title.

Art objects—Limited editions—Collectors and collecting.

KOVEL, Ralph M. 745.1'075
The Kovels' collector's guide to limited editions / by Ralph M. and Terry H. Kovel. New York : Crown Publishers, [1974] 250 p., [12] leaves of plates : ill. ; 28 cm. [NK1125.K66 1974] 74-84027 ISBN 0-517-51508-3 pbk. : 6.95
1. Art objects—Limited editions—Collectors and collecting. I. Kovel, Terry H., joint author. II. Title. III. Title: Collector's guide to limited editions.

Art objects—Limited editions—Collectors and collecting—Handbooks, manuals, etc.

HOTCHKISS, John F. 745.1
Limited edition collectibles; a handbook with prices [by] John F. Hotchkiss. New York, Hawthorn Books [1974] ix, 182 p. illus. 24 cm. Bibliography: p. 181. [NK1125.H67 1974] 73-353 5.95
1. Art objects—Limited editions—Collectors and collecting—Handbooks, manuals, etc. I. Title.

Art objects—New England.

MICHAEL, George, 1919- 745.1'0974
The treasury of New England antiques. New York, Hawthorn Books [1969] x, 210 p. illus. 27 cm. [NK810.M5 1969] 77-85442 10.00
1. Art objects—New England. 2. Art objects—Collectors and collecting. I. Title.

Art objects—New York (City)—Catalogs.

NEW York (City). 745.1
Metropolitan Museum of Art.
Decorative art from the Samuel H. Kress Collection at the Metropolitan Museum of Art: the tapestry room from Croome Court, furniture, textiles, Sevres porcelains, and other objects. [By James Parker, Edith Appleton Standen, and Carl Christian Dauterman. London] Published by the Phaidon Press for the Samuel H. Kress Foundation; [distributed by New York Graphic Society, Greenwich, Conn., 1964] 303 p. illus. (part col.), plan, ports. 31 cm. (Complete catalogue of the Samuel H. Kress collection) Bibliography: p. 285-289. [NK460.N45A47] 77-9812
1. Art objects—New York (City)—Catalogs. I. Parker, James, 1924- II. Standen, Edith Appleton. III. Dauterman, Carl Christian, 1908- IV. Samuel H. Kress Foundation. V. Title. VI. Series.

Art objects—Nigeria—Benin City—Catalogs.

PITT-RIVERS, Augustus 730'.09669
Henry Lane-Fox 1827-1900.
Antique works of art from Benin / by Augustus Pitt-Rivers ; with a new introd. by Bernard Fagg. New York : Dover Publications, 1976. vi, 100 p. : ill. ; 31 cm. Reprint of the 1900 ed. printed privately, London. [NK1087.6.N52B46 1976] 76-3246 ISBN 0-486-23323-5 : 5.00
1. Art objects—Nigeria—Benin City—Catalogs. I. Title. BIP

Art objects—Oceanica—Catalogs.

FORCE, Roland W. 709'.9
The Fuller Collection of Pacific artifacts [by] Roland W. Force and Maryanne Force. New York, Praeger [1971] xvi, 360 p. illus. 32 cm. Bibliography: p. 352-356. [NK1093.A1F6 1971b] 75-131354 35.00
1. Fuller, Alfred Walter Francis, 1882-1961—Art collections. 2. Art objects—Oceanica—Catalogs. I. Force, Maryanne, joint author. II. Title.

Art objects, Oriental—Catalogs.

MILLER, Robert William, 709'.5
1922-
Wallace-Homestead oriental primer, by Robert W. Miller. Des Moines, Wallace-Homestead Book Co. [1974] 135 p. illus. (part col.) 29 cm. On spine: Oriental primer. [NK1037.M47] 74-175878 9.95
1. Art objects, Oriental—Catalogs. 2. Art industries and trade, Oriental—Catalogs. I. Title. II. Title: Oriental primer.

Art objects—Packing.

KECK, Caroline (Kohn) 069'.53
Safeguarding your collection in travel [by] Caroline K. Keck. Nashville, American Association for State and Local History, 1970. 78 p. illus. 21 cm. [N8585.K43] 73-138325
1. Art objects—Packing. BIP

Art objects—Prices.

ANTIQUES and their current 709.45
prices; a checklist and price guide for antique dealers. 8th. Uniontown, Pa., 1966. v. illus. 18cm. First issued without subtitle. Comp.: 1st-8th E. G. Warman. 8th ed. t.p. reads Warman's eigth antiques and their current prices; a check list and guide of comparative prices for antique dealers and collectors. On spine: Eighth antiques and current price. [N8675.A5] 56-2031 9.95
1. Art objects—Prices. 2. Art objects—Collectors and collecting. I. Warman, Edwin G., 1915- comp.
Distributed by Hobby House Pr., Washington, D.C.

FARWELL, William 338.4'7'7451
Henry, 1898-
What is it worth? Advice on buying & selling antiques, by William & Georgie Farwell. Rutland, Vt., C. E. Tuttle Co. [1973] 135 p. 19 cm. (Tut books) [NK1125.F37] 73-75282 ISBN 0-8048-0980-1

1. Art objects—Prices. 2. Art objects—Collectors and collecting. I. Farwell, Georgie, joint author. II. Title. III. Title: Advice on buying and selling antiques. BIP

KOVEL, Ralph M. 745.1
The complete antiques price list; a guide to the 1969 market for professionals, dealers, and collectors, by Ralph M. and Terry H. Kovel. New York, Crown Publishers [1968] 436 p. 21 cm. [NK1125.K64] 68-9064
1. Art objects—Prices. 2. Art objects—Collectors and collecting. I. Kovel, Terry H., joint author. II. Title.

KOVEL, Ralph M. 338.4'37451
The complete antiques price list; a guide to the 1971 market for professionals, dealers, and collectors, by Ralph M. and Terry H. Kovel. 3d ed. New York, Crown Publishers [1970] 616 p. illus. (part col.) 24 cm. [NK1125.K64 1970] 79-21772
1. Art objects—Prices. 2. Art objects—Collectors and collecting. I. Kovel, Terry H., joint author. II. Title.

WARMAN, Edwin G., 1915- 659.1'9'663620973
Antiques and their current prices; a check list and price guide for antique dealers and collectors. Uniontown, Pa., E. G. Warman Pub. Co. [1960] 365 p. illus. 17 cm. [NK1125.W28 1960] 60-1629
1. Art objects — Prices. 2. Art objects — Collectors and collecting. I. Title.

WARMAN, Edwin G., 1915- 704.95
The fourth Antiques and their current prices; a check list and price guide for antique dealers and collectors. Uniontown, Pa., E. G. Warman Pub. Co. [1956] 281 p. illus. 18 cm. [N8675.W3 1956] 56-2031
1. Art objects — Prices. 2. Art objects — Collectors and collecting. I. Title. II. Title: Antiques and their current prices.

WARMAN, Edwin G., 1915- 704.95
The second Antiques and their current prices; a check list and price guide for antiques dealers and collectors. New Ed. Uniontown, Pa. [1950] 293 p. illus. 18 cm. [N8675.W3] 50-2758
1. Art objects — Prices. 2. Art objects — Collectors and collecting. I. Title. II. Title: Antiques and their current prices.

WARMAN, Edwin G., 1915- 704.95
The second Antiques and their current prices; a check list and price guide for antiques dealers and collectors. 2d ed., rev. and corr. Uniontown, Pa. [1951] 293p. illus.18cm. [N8675.W3 1951] 61-6307
1. Art objects—Prices. 2. Art objects—Collectors and collecting. I. Title. II. Title: Antiques and their current prices.

WARMAN, Edwin G., 1915- 704.95
The third Antiques and their current prices; a check list and price guide for antique dealers and collectors. New ed. Uniontown, Pa., Warman Pub. Co. [1953] 293p. illus. 17cm. [N8675.W3 1953] 54-398
1. Art objects—Prices. 2. Art objects—Collectors and collecting. I. Title. II. Title: Antiques and their current prices.

Art objects—United States.

BUTLER, Joseph T. 745
American antiques, 1800-1900; a collector's history and guide, by Joseph T. Butler. New York, Odyssey Press [1965] 203 p. illus., col. plates. 27 cm. Erratum slip inserted. Bibliography: p. 187-195. [NK1125.B85] 65-3478
1. Art objects—United States. 2. Art objects—Collectors and collecting. I. Title.

Art objects, Victorian.

HOWE, Bea. 745.1'0942
Antiques from the Victorian home. New York, Scribner [1973] 232 p. illus. 26 cm. Bibliography: p. 225. [NK775.H68 1973b] 72-7974 ISBN 0-684-13212-5 14.95
1. Art objects, Victorian. I. Title.

Art objects, Victorian—Dictionaries.

WOODHOUSE, Charles Platten. 745.1'0942
The Victoriana collector's handbook. New York, St. Martin's Press [1972, c1970] xiv, 238 p. illus. 26 cm. [NK775.W6 1972] 70-156345 11.95
1. Art objects, Victorian—Dictionaries. I. Title. BIP

Art objects, Victorian—Great Britain.

NORBURY, James, 1904- 745.1'0942
The world of Victoriana: illustrating the progress of furniture and the decorative arts in Britain and America from 1837 to 1901. London, New York, Hamlyn, 1972. 128 p. illus. (some col.). 30 cm. [NK928.N58] 72-169722 ISBN 0-600-39121-3 £1.75
1. Art objects, Victorian—Great Britain. 2. Art objects, Victorian—United States. I. Title.

Art objects, Victorian—Handbooks, manuals, etc.

D'IMPERIO, Dan. 745.1'0942
The ABCs of Victorian antiques / by Dan D'Imperio ; illustrated by Edgar Blakeney. New York : Dodd, Mead, [1974] 250 p. : ill. ; 25 cm. [NK775.D55] 73-21163 ISBN 0-396-06925-8 : 9.95
1. Art objects, Victorian—Handbooks, manuals, etc. I. Title.

Art—Oceanica.

BLANDING, M 730.99
Listing of the M. Blanding collection of South Seas primitives, with The birth of art, a commentary by Andre V. Simeon. 23 illus. by Clement E. Inskeep, except nos. 2, 5, 6 and 7 by Glen Chang. [Altadena? Calif., c1958] unpaged. illus. 25cm. [N7410.B6] 59-32875
1. Art—Oceanica. 2. Art, Primitive. I. Simeon, Andre V. The birth of art. II. Title. III. Title: The birth of art.

Art—Oceanica.

AMBESI, Alberto Cesare. 709.01'1
Oceanic art; [translated from the Italian by Rachel Montgomery] Feltham, Hamlyn, 1970. 159 p. col. illus., col. map. 20 cm. (Cameo) Translation of Arte dell 'Oceania. [N7410.A6613] 78-563041 ISBN 0-600-36702-9 18/-
1. Art—Oceanica. 2. Art, Primitive—Oceanica. I. Title.

BUHLER, Alfred, 1900- 709.99
The art of the South Sea Islands, including Australia and New Zealand, by Alfred Buehler, Terry Barrow [and] Charles P. Mountford. New York, Crown Publishers [1962] 249p. illus. (part mounted col.) maps. 24cm. (Art of the world, non-European cultures; the historical, sociological and religious backgrounds) Bibliography: p. 235-[240] [N7410.B8] 62-11806
1. Art—Oceanica. 2. Art, Primitive. I. Title. II. Series: Art of the world; the historical, sociological and religious backgrounds

BUHLER, Alfred, 1900- 709.99
The art of the South Sea Islands, including Australia and New Zealand, by Alfred Buehler, Terry Barrow [and] Charles P. Mountford. New York, Crown Publishers [1962] 249 p. illus. (part mounted col.), maps. 24 cm. (Art of the world, non-European cultures; the historical, sociological and religious backgrounds) Bibliography: p. 235-[240] [N7410.B8] 62-11806
1. Art—Oceanica. 2. Art, Primitive. I. Title. II. Series: Art of the world; the historical, sociological and religious backgrounds.

EXPLORING the visual art of Oceania : Australia, Melanesia, Micronesia, and Polynesia / edited by Sidney M. Mead. Honolulu : University Press of Hawaii, c1979. p. cm. Includes bibliographical references and index. [N7410.E95] 79-12707 ISBN 0-8248-0598-4 : 25.00 709'.01'1099
1. Art—Oceania. 2. Art, Primitive—Oceania. I. Mead, Sidney, M. BIP

GUIART, Jean. 709.9
The arts of the South Pacific. Translated by Anthony Christie. New York, Golden Press [1963] 461 p. illus. (part col.) col. maps (part fold.) 28 cm. (The Arts of mankind, v. 4) Bibliography: p. [419]-438. [N7410.G813] 63-7331
1. Art—Oceanica. 2. Art, Primitive. 3. Ethnology—Oceanica. I. Title. II. Series. BIP

LINTON, Ralph, 1893-1953. 709'.01'1
Arts of the South Seas, by Ralph Linton and Paul S. Wingert, in collaboration with Rene d'Harnoncourt. Color illus. by Miguel Covarrubias. [New York] Published for the Museum of Modern Art by Arno Press, 1972 [c1946] 199 p. illus. 27 cm. (Museum of Modern Art publications in reprint) Based on an exhibition at the Museum of Modern Art. Bibliography: p. 196-199. [N7410.L5 1972] 76-169308 ISBN 0-405-01567-4 24.00
1. Art—Oceanica. 2. Art, Primitive—Oceanica. 3. Ethnology—Oceanica. I. Wingert, Paul Stover, 1900- joint author. II. New York (City). Museum of Modern Art. III. Title. BIP

SCHMITZ, Carl August. 730'.099
Oceanic art; myth, man, and image in the South Seas. [Translated from German by Norbert Guterman] New York, H. N. Abrams [1971] 405 p. 337 illus. (50 col.) 28 x 30 cm. Bibliography: p. 402-405. [N7410.S313] 69-12797 ISBN 0-8109-0351-2 35.00
1. Art—Oceanica. I. Title.

SMITH, Bernard [William] 709.9
European vision and the South Pacific, 1768-1850; a study in the history of art and ideas. [New York, Cxford Univ. Press, 1960] xviii, 287p. (bibl. notes: p. 258-274) plates. 28cm. 60-2082 13.45
1. Art—Oceanica. 2. Art—Australia. 3. Art, European. 4. Art and science. 5. Oceanica—Descr. & trav.—Views. I. Title.

SMITH, Bernard William. 709.9
European vision and the South Pacific, 1768-1850; a study in the history of art and ideas. Oxford, Clarendon Press, 1960. xviii, 287 p. plates. 28 cm. "Bibliography and graphic sources": p. [258]-274. [N7410.S6] 60-2082
1. Art — Oceanica. 2. Art — Australia. 3. Art, European. 4. Art and science. 5. Oceanica — Descr. & trav. — Views. I. Title.

TISCHNER, Herbert. 709.9
Oceanic art. 96 photos. by Friedrich Hewicker. [New York] Pantheon Books [1954] 32p. 96plates. 31cm. [N7410.T5] 54-11740
1. Art—Oceanica. 2. Art, Primitive. 3. Ethnology—Oceanica. I. Hewicker, Friedrich, illus. II. Title.

WINGERT, Paul Stover, 1900- 709.9
Art of the South Pacific islands. New York, Beechhurst Press [1953] 64p. illus., maps. 27cm. First appeared as a catalogue of the 1953 loan exhibition of the art of the South Pacific islands held at the M. H. de Young Memorial Museum, San Francisco. Bibliography: p. 46. [N74 10.W48 1953a] 55-444
1. Art—Oceanica. 2. Art, Primitive. I. De Young Memorial Museum, San Francisco. II. Title.

Art—Oceanica—Exhibitions.

PARSONS, Lee Allen, 1932- 730'.099
Ritual arts of the South Seas : the Morton D. May Collection : the St. Louis Art Museum, 22 August-19 October, 1975 / catalogue by Lee A. Parsons ; photos. by Jack Savage. [St. Louis : The Museum], c1975. 204, [3] p., [2] leaves of plates : 250 ill. (some col.), 3 maps ; 25 cm. Bibliography: p. [207] [N7410.P37] 75-24647
1. May, Morton D., 1914- —Art collections. 2. Art—Oceanica—Exhibitions. 3. Art, Primitive—Oceanica—Exhibitions. I. Savage, Jack. II. St. Louis Art Museum. III. Title.

Art—Ohio.

CLARK, Edna Maria. 709'.771
Ohio art and artists. Richmond, Garrett and Massie. Detroit, Gale Research, 1975 [c1932] xiii, 509 p. illus. 22 cm. [N6530.O3C6 1975] 74-13860 ISBN 0-8103-4058-5 24.00
*1. Art—Ohio. 2. Artists—Ohio. I. Title.*BIP

Art—Oregon.

PORTLAND, Oregon. Art Museum 338.4'3745'10973
All-Oregon exhibition. Portland. v. 23cm. Bagan publication in 1940. [N6530.O7P6] 55-34821
1. Art—Oregon. 2. Art, American—Exhibitions. I. Title.

Art, Oriental.

AUBOYER, Jeannine. 709.5
The Oriental world: India and South-East Asia [by] Jeannine Auboyer. New York, McGraw-Hill [1967] 176 p. illus., maps (on lining papers), col. plates. 30 cm. (Landmarks of the world's art) Bibliography: p. [171]-172. [N7260.A82] 67-1795
1. Art, Oriental. I. Goepper, Roger. II. Title. III. Title: China, Korea, and Japan

AUBOYER, Jeannine. 709.5
The Oriental world: India and South-East Asia [by] Jeannine Auboyer. China, Korea, and Japan [by] Roger Goepper. New York, McGraw-Hill [1967] 176 p. illus., maps (on lining papers), col. plates. 30 cm. (Landmarks of the world's art) Bibliography: p. [171]-172. [N7260.A82] 67-11795
1. Art, Oriental. I. Goepper, Roger. II. Title.

BABELON, Ernest Charles Francois, 1854-1924. 913.3
Oriental antiquities. Translated and enl. by B. T. A. Evetts. San Diego, Calif., Malter-Westerfield Pub. Co. [1969?] xix, 312 p. illus., plans. 21 cm. "Library series." Translation of Manuel d'archeologie orientale. Reprint of the 1889 ed. which was published under title: Manual of Oriental antiquities. Bibliographical footnotes. [N5345.B2513 1969] 68-59306
1. Art, Oriental. 2. Oriental antiquities. I. Evetts, Basil Thomas Alfred, 1858- ed. and tr. II. Title.

BALL, Katherine M., 1859- 709'.5
Decorative motives of Oriental art. New York, Hacker Art Books, 1969. xxvi, 286 p. illus. 31 cm. Reprint of the 1927 ed. Bibliography: p. [273]-281. [N7260.B3 1969] 68-9001
1. Art, Oriental. 2. Decoration and ornament, Oriental. 3. Design, Decorative. I. Title. BIP

BELTRAN, Orlando Alfredo, 1906- 704.948
Symbolism of Oriental religious art. Foreword by Manly Palmer Hall. 1st ed. Photography by George H. Lark. Los Angeles, Philosophical Research Society [1953] 122p. illus. (part col.) 24cm. [N7301.B43] 54-33
1. Art, Oriental. 2. Symbolism in art. I. Title.

FRANKFORT, Henri, 1897-1954. 709.3
The art and architecture of the ancient Orient. [Harmondsworth, Middlesex] Penguin Books [1954] xxvi, 279p. illus., 192 plates, fold. map. 27cm. (The Pelican history of art, Z7) Erratum slip mounted on p. xix. Bibliography: p. 269-270. [N7265.F7] 55-12563
1. Art, Oriental. 2. Architecture, Oriental. I. Title. II. Series. BIP

ORIENTAL art in Rumania. 709.5
Introd. text by George Oprescu. Bucharest, Meridiane Pub. House [dist. New York, Vancus, 1964] [10]p., 138 plates (pt. col.) 29cm. 64-4915 price unreported
1. Art, Oriental. 2. Art—Rumania. I. Oprescu. George, 1881- II. Bucharest. Muzeul de Arta al Republicii Populare Romine.

TAKAHASHI, Sohei, 1803-1834 741.4
Oriental art motifs; a sketchbook for artists and connoisseurs. Tokyo, Rutland, Vt., C. E. Tuttle Co. [1957] 79 p. (Chiefly illus.) 26 cm. [NC1235.T3A5] 57-12846

SUBJECT INDEX
ART—PAGAN, BURMA.

1. Art, Oriental. 2. Drawing — Instruction. I. Title.

Art, Oriental—Catalogs.

BOSTON. Museum of Fine Arts. 709'.5
Museum of Fine Arts, Boston: oriental art [by] Jan Fontein [and] Pratapaditya Pal. Boston; Distributed by New York Graphic Society, Greenwich, Conn. [1969] 195 p. 137 illus. (part col.) 37 cm. "Catalogue": p. 165-193. Bibliography: p. 195. [N7262.B6] 73-93137
1. Art, Oriental—Catalogs. I. Fontein, Jan. II. Pal, Pratapaditya. III. Title.

GULBENKIAN Museum of Oriental Art and Archaeology. 709'.5'0740281
Gulbenkian Museum of Oriental Art and Archaeology. [Durham] Gulbenkian Museum of Oriental Art and Archaeology [1972] [2], 21, [8] p. illus., map. 22 cm. Cover title. At head of title: University of Durham. [N7262.G84] 73-156219 ISBN 0-900926-10-4

ISABELLA Stewart Gardner Museum, Boston. 709'.5'074014461
Oriental and Islamic art in the Isabella Stewart Gardner Museum / Yasuko Horioka, Marylin Rhie, Walter B. Denny. Boston : Trustees of the Museum, 1974. p. cm. Bibliography: p. [N7262.I82] 74-22427 ISBN 0-914660-01-2 pbk. : 3.50.
1. Isabella Stewart Gardner Museum, Boston. 2. Art, Oriental—Catalogs. 3. Art, Islamic—Catalogs. 4. Art—Boston—Catalogs. I. Horioka, Yasuko. II. Rhie, Marylin. III. Denny, Walter B. IV. Title. BIP

SEATTLE. Art Museum. 709'.5'074019777
Asiatic art in the Seattle Art Museum : a selection and catalogue / by Henry Trubner, William Jay Rathbun, Catherine A. Kaputa ; photography by Paul Macapia. Seattle : The Museum, 1973. 300 p. : ill. (some col.) ; 27 cm. Includes bibliographies and index. [N7262.S4 1973] 73-88583
1. Seattle. Art Museum. 2. Art, Oriental—Catalogs. 3. Art—Seattle—Catalogs. I. Trubner, Henry. II. Rathbun, William Jay. III. Kaputa, Catherine A. IV. Title.

Art, Oriental — Exhibitions.

EAST meets West. 709
[Huntington, N.Y., Heckscher Museum, 1973] 14 p. illus. 28 cm. Catalog of an exhibition held at the Museum Mar. 2-Apr. 15, 1973. [N7429.E23] 73-77876
1. Art, Oriental—Exhibitions. 2. Art, Oriental—Indic influences. 3. Art, European—Exhibitions. 4. Art, European—Oriental influences. I. Heckscher Museum.

MICHIGAN. University. Museum of Art. 704.9432
James Marshall Plumer memorial collection. [Exhibition] December 6, 1964-January 10, 1965. [Catalogue] Ann Arbor [1965] 1 v. (unpaged) illus. 26 cm. Includes bibliographies. [N7260.M5] 66-63086
1. Art, Oriental — Exhibitions. I. Plumer, James Marshall. II. Title.

YOUNG, Martie Wing. 709'.5'074014771
Asian art: a collector's selection [by] Martie W. Young. [Ithaca, N.Y., Office of University Publications, Cornell University, 1973] 231 p. illus. 27 cm. Catalog of an exhibition held at the Herbert F. Johnson Museum of Art, Cornell University, Ithaca, N.Y., Oct. 17-Nov. 25, 1973, and at Munson-Williams-Proctor Institute, Utica, N.Y., Dec. 16, 1973-Jan 13, 1974. Bibliography: p. 227-231. [N7262.Y68] 73-13447
1. Art, Oriental—Exhibitions. 2. Art—Private collections. I. Herbert F. Johnson Museum of Art. II. Munson-Williams-Proctor Institute, Utica, N.Y. III. Title.

Art, Oriental—Hist.

JAIRAZBHOY, Rafique Ali, 1925- 709.5
Oriental influences in Western art [by] R. A. Jairazbhoy. New York, Asia Pub. House [c1965] vii, 340 p. illus., plates. 23 cm. Bibliographical footnotes. [N7260.J3 1965] 65-16029
1. Art, Oriental—Hist. 2. Art—Europe. I. Title. BIP

VJAIRAZBHOY, Rafique Ali, 1925- 709.5
Oriental influences in Western art. New York, Asia Pub. [dist. Taplinger, 1966, c.1965] vii,340p. illus., plates. 23cm. Bibl. [N7260.J3] 65-16029 17.50
1. Art, Oriental—Hist. 2. Art—Europe. I. Title.

Art—Oriental—Outlines, syllabi, etc.

ROWLAND, Benjamin, 1904- 709.5
The Harvard outline and reading lists for Oriental art. Cambridge, Harvard University Press, 1952. 64 p. 22 cm. Previous editions published under title: Outline and bibliographies of Oriental art. [N7260.R6 1952] 52-5040
1. Art, Oriental — Outline, syllabi, etc. 2. Art, Oriental — Bibl. I. Title.

Art, Oriental—Outlines, syllabi, etc.

ROWLAND, Benjamin, 1904- 709.5
The Harvard outline and reading lists for Oriental art. 3d ed. Cambridge, Harvard University Press, 1967. 77 p. 21 cm. First published in 1938 under title: Outline and bibliographies of Oriental art. [N7260.R6 1967] 67-22872
1. Art, Oriental—Outlines, syllabi, etc. 2. Art, Oriental—Bibliography. I. Title.

ROWLAND, Benjamin, 1904- 709.5
The Harvard outline and reading lists for Oriental art. Rev. ed. Cambridge, Harvard University Press, 1958. 74p. 21cm. First published in 1938 under title: Outline and bibliographies of Oriental art. [N7260.R6 1958] 58-13770
1. Art, Oriental—Outlines, syllabi, etc. 2. Art, Oriental—Bibl. I. Title.

Art, Oriental—Period.

ARTIBUS Asiae 708.95'05
. . . 1925/26-1958. v. 1-21. Hellerau-Dresden, Avalunverlag [1925-1958] New York, Johnson Reprint, 1968 v. illus. (pt. col., pt. mounted) 30cm. Two nos. (no. 1-2) issued in 1925; 2 nos. (no. 3-4) in 1926; 4 nos. a year, 1927-Eds.: 1925- Carl Hentze, Alfred Salmony. Includes section Bibliographia. [N8.A75] 28-30403 585.00 set,; 525.00 set, pap.,; 25.00 ea., pap.,
1. Art, Oriental—Period. I. Hentze, Carl. ed. II. Salmony,Alfred. ed.

Art—Orissa, India—History.

FABRI, Charles Louis, 1899-1968. 709'.54'13
History of the art of Orissa / Charles Louis Fabri. Bombay : Orient Longman, 1974 [i.e.1975] xxiv, 220 p., [61] leaf of plates : ill. (some col.) ; 25 cm. Includes index. Bibliography: p. [209]-210. [N7307.O74F32 1974] 75-902061 ISBN 0-88386-575-0 : 17.50
1. Art—Orissa, India—History. I. Title. Distributed by S. Asia Books. BIP

Art—Ottawa—Catalogs.

OTTAWA. National Gallery of Canada. 708.11381
Catalogue of paintings and sculpture. Ottawa. Published for the Trustees of the National Gallery of Canada by the University of Toronto Press. 1957- v. illus. 26 cm. Vol. 4 has title: The National Gallery of Canada catalogue. Vols. 1-3 edited by R. H. Hubbard: v. 4 edited by A. E. Popham and K. M. Fenwick. Contents.v. 1. Older schools. -- v. 2. Modern European schools. -- v. 3. Canadian school. -- v. 4. European drawings. [N910.O7A55] 58-44304
1. Art — Ottawa — Catalogs. I. Hubbard, Robert Hamilton, 1916- ed. II. Popham, Arthur Ewart, 1889- ed. III. Fenwick, Kathleen M., ed. IV. Title.

OTTAWA. National Gallery of Canada 708.113
European drawings, and two Asian drawings, in the collection of the National Gallery of Canada. Toronto, Pub. for the Trustees of the Natl. Gallery of Canada by Toronto Univ. Pr. [c.]1965. x, 233p. plates. 26cm. [N910.07A19] 17-2066 13.50
1. Art—Ottawa—Catalogs. I. Title.

Art—Otterlo, Netherlands.

JOOSTEN, Ellen 708.94923
The Kroller-Muller Museum, Otterlo, Holland. New York, Shorewood [c.1965] 206p. illus., col. plates, port. 25cm. (Museums discovered) [N2500.J6] 65-23713 7.95
1. Art—Otterlo, Netherlands. I. Otterlo, Netherlands. Rijksmuseum Kroller-Muller. II. Title. III. Series.

JOOSTEN, Ellen. 708.94923
The Kroller-Muller Museum, Otterlo, Holland. New York, Shorewood Publishers [1965] 206 p. illus., col. plates, port. 25 cm. (Museums discovered) [N2500.J6] 65-23713
1. Art—Otterlo, Netherlands. I. Otterlo, Netherlands. Rijksmuseum Kroller-Muller. II. Title. III. Series.

Art — Outlines, syllabi, etc.

CHRISTIE, Mary Joanne. 702
The picture story of art. Toledo, Gregorian Institute Press [1963] xiii, 174 p. illus. (part col.) 26 cm. (Art appreciation series, book 2) Bibliography: p. 167-169. [N5305.C54] 63-4681
1. Art — Outlines, syllabi, etc. 2. Art. I. Title.

CLEAVER, Dale G. 709
Art : an introduction / Dale G. Cleaver. 3d ed. New York : Harcourt Brace Jovanovich, c1977. viii, 440 p., [16] leaves of plates : ill. (some col.) ; 24 cm. Includes bibliographies and index. [N5305.C56 1977] 76-16436 ISBN 0-15-503432-4 : 8.95
1. Art—Outlines, syllabi, etc. I. Title.

CLEAVER, Dale G. 709
Art; an introduction [by] Dale G. Cleaver. 2d ed. New York, Harcourt Brace Jovanovich [1972] viii, 375 p. illus. (part col.) 24 cm. Includes bibliographies. [N5305.C56 1972] 74-182343 ISBN 0-15-503431-6
1. Art—Outlines, syllabi, etc. I. Title.

FINGESTEN, Peter 709
Basic facts of art history. General ed.: John E. Flaherty. New York, Collier [c.1963] 64p. 18cm. (AS107) Bibl. 63-13021 .95 pap.,
1. Art—Outlines, syllabi, etc. I. Title.

ILLUSTRATED survey of Western Art, (An) (audio-visual series); fifteen coordinated lectures on architecture, sculpture, painting, and the minor arts, from the Stone Age through the 18th century. New York, Amer. Archives of World Art [1967] 284p. illus. 29cm. Issued previously, as individual lectures, by the Amer Lib. Color Slide Co. [N5305.I4] 67-18358 25.00 709
1. Art—Outlines, syllabi, etc. I. American Library Color Slide Company, inc., New York.

KAINZ, Luise C., 1902- 709
Understanding art; people, things, and ideas from ancient Egypt to Chagall & Picasso [by] Luise C. Kainz [and] Olive L. Riley. New York, H. N. Abrams [1966] 135 p. illus. (part col.) 27 cm. [N5305.K3] 66-11012
1. Art—Outlines, syllabi, etc. 2. Art criticism. I. Riley, Olive Lasette, joint author. II. Title.

MICHIGAN. State University, East Lansing. Dept. of Literature and Fine Arts. 702
Students syllabus for literature & fine arts, 1947-48. 4th ed. revision East Lansing, Michigan State College, 1947. vi, 149 p. illus. 28 cm. "Music"; p. [77]-135. [N5305.M38] 50-35764
1. Art — Outlines, syllabi, etc. 2. Literature — Outlines, syllabi, etc. 3. Music — Hist. & crit. — Outlines, syllabi, etc. I. Title.

SHOREWOOD Publishers, inc., New York. 759
The Shorewood art reference guide. Prepared [by Matila Simon] under the direction of the editors of Shorewood Publishers, inc. New York, Shorewood Reproductions [1966] xv, 256 p. illus. 24 cm. [N5305.S5] 65-27895
1. Art—Outlines, syllabi, etc. 2. Art—Study and teaching. I. Simon, Matila. II. Title.

SHOREWOOD Publishers, inc., New York. 759
The Shorewood art reference guide. Written by Matila Simon. Prepared under the direction of the editors of Shorewood Publishers, inc. Rev. and enl. 3d ed. New York, Shorewood Reproductions [1970] xviii, 600 p. illus. 24 cm. Bibliography: p. 579-586. [N5305.S5 1970] 70-110685
1. Art—Outlines, syllabi, etc. 2. Art—Study and teaching. I. Simon, Matila. II. Title.

TAYLOR, Joshua Charles, 1917- 702
Learning to look; a handbook for the visual arts. Prepared with the Humanities staff of the College at the University of Chicago. [Chicago] University of Chicago Press [1957] 152 p. illus. 25 cm. "[A revision of the Humanities 1 handbook used in] the art portion of the initial humanities course at the University of Chicago." [N5305.T3] 57-11213
1. Art — Outlines, syllabi, etc. I. Chicago, University. College. II. Title. BIP

WICKISER, Ralph Lewanda, 1909- 702'.02
An introduction to art activities [by] Ralph L. Wickiser. New York, Greenwood Press [1969, c1947] vii, 275 p. illus. 24 cm. [N87.W5 1969] 74-94598
1. Art—Outlines, syllabi, etc. I. Title. II. Title: Art activities. BIP

Art—Outlines, syllabi, etc.

CLEAVER, Dale G 709
Art; an introduction [by] Dale G. Cleaver. New York, Harcourt, Brace & World [1966] xii, 291 p. illus., plans, plates (part col.) 22 cm. Includes bibliographies. [N5305.C56] 66-17347
1. Art — Outlines, syllabl, etc. I. Title.

WILSON, Robert Curtis, 1926- 745.4
An alphabet of visual experience; an examination of the basic principles of design, by Robert C. Wilson. Scranton, International Textbook co. [1966] xi, 228 p. illus. (part col.) 19 cm. (International textbooks in art and art education) [N87.W55] 65-18386
1. Art — Outlines, syllabl, etc. 2. Design. I. Title.

Art—Oxford—History.

†PIPER, David. 708'.25'74
The Oxford collections : art in Oxford / David Piper. New York : Paddington Press, c1976. p. cm. Includes index. Bibliography: p. [N6771.O9P56] 76-1375 ISBN 0-8467-0128-6 : 12.95
1. Art—Oxford—History. I. Title.

Art — Pacific States.

AMON Carter Museum of Western Art, Fort Worth, Tex. 709'.795
The artist's environment: west coast. An exhibition presented by the Amon Carter Museum of Western Art, Fort Worth, Texas, in collaboration with the UCLA Art Galleries and the Oakland Art Museum, 1962-1963. [Los Angeles, 1962] 132 p. illus. 26 cm. "Exhibition ... organized from within the University of California." "Bibliography": p. 119-129. [N6528.A4] 62-20199
1. Art — Pacific States. 2. Art, American — Exhibitions. I. California. University. University at Los Angeles. II. Title.

Art—Pagan, Burma.

LUCE, Gordon Hannington, 1889- 709'.591
Old Burma—Early Pagan, by Gordon H. Luce. Assisted by Bo-hmu Ba Shin, U Tin

Co, the staff of the Burma Historical Commission, the Burma Archaeological Dept. and many other friends. Locust Valley, N.Y., Published for Artibus Asiae and the Institute of Fine Arts, New York University [by] J. J. Augustin, 1969-70. 3 v. illus (part col.), maps (part col.; 2 fold. in pocket), plans. 32 cm. (Artibus Asiae. Supplementum 25) Contents.Contents.—v. 1 Text.—v. 2. Catalogue of plates. Indexes.—v. 3. Plates. Bibliography: v. 2, p. [215]-230. [N7312.2.P3L8] 68-56006
1. Art—Pagan, Burma. 2. Pagan, Burma—History. I. Title. II. Series.

Art—Papua.

NEWTON, Douglas. 709.95
Art styles of the Papuan Gulf. New York, Museum of Primitive Art; distributed by University Publishers, 1961. 100p. illus., maps (1 fold.) 29cm. 'Prepared in conjunction with an exhibition at the Museum of Primitive Art.' Bibliography: p. 98. [N7411.N4N43] 61-16108
1. Art—Papua. 2. Art, Primitive. I. Title.

NEWTON, Douglas, 1920- 709.95
Art styles of the Papuan Gulf. New York, Museum of Primitive Art; distributed by University Publishers, 1961. 100 p. illus., maps (1 fold.) 29 cm. "Prepared in conjunction with an exhibition at the Museum of Primitive Art." Bibliography: p. 98. [N7411.N4N43] 61-16108
1. Art—Papua. 2. Art, Primitive. I. Title.

Art, Paraguayan.

FERNANDEZ, Miguel Angel, 1938- 709'.892
Paraguay. [English translation by Ralph E. Dimmick] Washington, General Secretariat of the Organization of American States, 1969. 18 p. 62 plates. 19 cm. (Art in Latin America today) "Prepared by the Division of Visual Arts, Department of Cultural Affairs, Pan American Union." [N6705.F3713] 74-180965
1. Art, Paraguayan. 2. Art, Modern—20th century—Paraguay. I. Pan American Union. Division of Visual Arts. II. Title. III. Series.

Art—Paris.

HUYGHE, Rene. 708.4
Art treasures of the Louvre. Text adapted from the French of Rene Huyghe. Commentary by Mme. Rene Huyghe. With a brief history of the Louvre by Milton S. Fox. New York, H. N. Abrams [1960] 211 p. illus. (part mounted col.), plates (part col.) 33 cm. [N2030.H8 1960] 60-8496
1. Paris. Musee national du Louvre. 2. Art—Paris. I. Title.

HUYGHE, Rene. 708.4
Art treasures of the Louvre; text translated and adapted from the French of Rene Huyhge. Commentary by Mme. Rene Huyghe, with a brief history of the Louvre by Milton S. Fox. [1st ed.] New York, H. N. Abrams [1951] 178 p. illus., col. plates. 33 cm. ([The Library of great museums]) [N2030.H8] 52-6134
1. Paris. Musee national du Louvre. 2. Art—Paris. I. Title.

Art—Paris—Galleries and museums.

CHARMET, Raymond. 708.4'3'6
The museums of Paris. [Translated from the Italian by James Brockway] New York, Meredith Press [1967, c1965] 152 p. illus. (part col.) 28 cm. (Great galleries series) [N2020.C4613] 68-31929
1. Art—Paris—Galleries and museums. I. Title.

WATT, Alexander, 1909- 708.43'6
Art centers of the world: Paris. Cleveland, World Pub. Co. [1967] 192 p. illus. (part col.), map (on lining papers), ports. 21 cm. [N2020.W3 1967] 67-13619
1. Art—Paris—Galleries and museums. I. Title.

Art—Paris—History.

CHASTEL, Andre, 1912- 709'.443'6
Paris. Special photography by Mario Carrieri. [Translated from the French by Emily Lane, Barbara Thompson, and David Britt. 1st ed.] New York, Holt, Rinehart and Winston [1971] 288 p. illus. (part col.), col. maps, plans. 26 cm. (World cultural guides) Translation of Paris. [N6850.C45513 1971] 72-138897 ISBN 0-03-085987-5 9.95
1. Art—Paris—History. 2. Paris—Description.

Art, Parthian.

COLLEDGE, Malcolm A. R. 709'.35
Parthian art / Malcolm A. R. Colledge. Ithaca, N.Y. : Cornell University Press, 1977. xvi, 200 p., [16] leaves of plates : ill. ; 25 cm. Includes index. Bibliography: p. [172]-192. [N5899.P36C64 1977] 77-74919 ISBN 0-8014-1111-4 : 23.50
1. Art, Parthian. 2. Parthia. I. Title. BIP

Art patronage.

ARTIST and advocate; 704
an essay on corporate patronage. [Ed. by Nina Kaiden, Bartlett Hayes. New York, Renaissance Eds., 1967] 93p. illus. (pt. col.) 28cm. [N8410.A7] 67-24916 7.50
1. Art patronage. I. Kaiden, Nina N. ed. II. Mead Corporation.
Contents Omitted.

CHAMBERS, David Sanderson, comp. 331.7'61'7
Patrons and artists in the Italian Renaissance [by] D. S. Chambers. Columbia, University of South Carolina Press [1971] xxxv, 219 p. illus. 23 cm. (History in depth) Bibliography: p. 209-214. [N6915.C4413 1971] 78-145530 ISBN 0-87249-220-6 7.95
1. Art partonage—Italy—History—Sources. 2. Art, Renaissance—Italy. 3. Artists, Italian. I. Title.

FOX, Daniel M. 706.992
Engines of culture: philanthropy and art museums. Madison, State Hist. Soc. of Wis. for the Dept. of Hist., Univ. of Wis. [c.]1963. 90p. 23cm. (Logmark eds.) 63-63372 2.00 pap.,
1. Art patronage. 2. State encouragement of science, literature, and art. 3. Art—U.S.—Galleries and Museums. I. Title.

HARVARD Tercentenary Conference of Arts and Sciences, Cambridge, Mass., 1936. 081
Independence, convergence, and borrowing in institutions, thought, and art. New York, Russell & Russell [1970, c1964] x, 272 p. illus. 23 cm. (Harvard tercentenary publications) Includes bibliographical references. [AS36.H25 1936dc] 76-83847
I. Title. II. Series.

HASKELL, Francis, 1928- 706.992
Patrons and painters; a study in the relations between Italian art and society in the age of the Baroque. New York, Knopf, 1963. xix, 454 p. 64 plates. 26 cm. Bibliography: p. [396]-421. [N8410.H3 1963a] 63-20833
1. Art patronage. 2. Art and society. 3. Art, Italian. 4. Art, Baroque. I. Title.

LEES-MILNE, James. 706.992
Earls of creation; five great patrons of eighteenth-century art. New York, London, House & Maxwell [1963, c1962] 285 p. illus., ports., plan. 26 cm. Bibliography: p. 265-271. [N8410.L4] 63-21751
1. Art patronage. 2. Art — England. I. Title.

Art patronage—Addresses, essays, lectures.

THE Community and the arts. 704'.36
Edited by William Howard Adams. [Columbia] University of Missouri [1964?] 53 p. front. 32 cm. Cover title: Papers on the community and the arts. "A miscellany of papers presented at a conference on the campus of the University of Missouri, November 17th and 18th, 1963; sponsored by the University of Missouri and the Governor's Committee on the Arts." Includes bibliographical references. [NX700.C6] 66-64778
1. Art patronage—Addresses, essays, lectures. I. Adams, William Howard, ed. II. Missouri. University. III. Missouri. Governor's Committee on the Arts. IV. Title: Papers on the community and the arts.

Art patronage—Chicago.

JONES (John Price) Company, inc., New York. 338.4'7'700977311
A program for the arts in Chicago. [Chicago] Mayor's Committee for Economic and Cultural Development, 1966. vi, 180 p. 28 cm. "A report for the Mayor's Committee for Economic and Cultural Development." [NX705.5.U62C454 1966] 74-187196
1. Art patronage—Chicago. 2. Arts—Chicago—Finance. I. Chicago. Mayor's Committee for Economic and Cultural Development. II. Title.

Art patronage—England.

FOSS, Michael. 709'.42
The age of patronage; the arts in England, 1660-1750. Ithaca, N.Y., Cornell University Press [1972, c1971] ix, 234 p. illus. 24 cm. Includes bibliographical references. [NX705.5.G7F6] 74-172507 ISBN 0-8014-0684-6 8.50
1. Art patronage—England. I. Title. BIP

Art patronage—Great Britain.

HASKELL, Francis, 1928- 704'.7
Rediscoveries in art : some aspects of taste, fashion, and collecting in England and France / Francis Haskell. Ithaca, N.Y. : Cornell University Press, 1976. x, 246 p. : ill. ; 28 cm. (The Wrightsman lectures ; 7th) Includes index. Bibliography: p. [231]-242. [N5208.G7H37] 75-21656 ISBN 0-8014-0995-0 : 19.50
1. Art patronage—Great Britain. 2. Aesthetics, British. 3. Art patronage—France. 4. Aesthetics, French. I. Title. II. Series. BIP

Art patronage—Illinois—Chicago.

HOROWITZ, Helen Lefkowitz. 700'.9773'11
Culture & the city : cultural philanthropy in Chicago from the 1880's to 1917 / Helen Lefkowitz Horowitz. Lexington : University Press of Kentucky, c1976. xv, 288 p. ; 23 cm. Includes bibliographical references and index. [NX711.U5H67] 75-3546 ISBN 0-8131-1344-X : 14.75
1. Art patronage—Illinois—Chicago. 2. Chicago—Popular culture. I. Title. BIP

Art patronage—Massachusetts.

THE arts: 338.4'7'7009744
a priority for investment; the report of the Governor's task forces on the arts & humanities. [Boston] 1973. ix, 42, 61 p. map. 29 cm. "A study of the economics of non-profit arts and humanities organizations in the Commonwealth of Massachusetts, by Becker Research Corporation": p. 1-61. [NX711.U5A77] 73-623140 0.50
1. Art patronage—Massachusetts. 2. Arts—Massachusetts. I. Becker Research Corporation. A study of the economics of non-profit arts and humanities organizations in the Commonwealth of Massachusetts. 1973.

Art patronage—North Carolina.

MERCER, Charles V. 704'.361
Business and the arts in North Carolina, by Charles V. Mercer. Raleigh, Agricultural Experiment Station, North Carolina State University, 1969. 46 l. map. 28 cm. (Dept. of Sociology & Anthropology. Progress report Soc. 53, 1969) "[Prepared] under the sponsorship of the North Carolina Arts Council." Bibliography: leaves [38]-39. [NX711.U5M4] 72-610318
1. Art patronage—North Carolina. I. North Carolina Arts Council. II. Title. III. Series: North Carolina. State University, Raleigh. Dept. of Sociology and Anthropology. Progress report Soc. 53, 1969.

Art patronage—United States.

**THE foundation grants index* : 001.4'4
a cumulative listing of foundation grants. New York : Published by The Foundation Center.
The 1978 ed. is available from Columbia University Press, for 20.00. ISBN 0-87954-020-6 ; L.C. card no.: 72-76018. BIP

HEDRICK, Wally, 1928- 759.13
Wally Hedrick, Sam Tchakalian. Presented by the Fine Arts Patrons of Newport Harbor. [San Diego, Neyenesch Printers, 1967?] [24] p. illus. (part col.), ports. 29 x 36 cm. Includes catalog of the exhibition held at Balboa Pavilion Gallery, May 3-June 11, 1967. Includes bibliographies. [ND237.H42T35] 76-9197
I. Tchakalian, Sam, 1929- II. Fine Arts Patrons of Newport Beach. III. Balboa, Calif. Pavilion Gallery. IV. Title.

ILLINOIS. Arts Council. 338.4'7'7
Illinois Arts Council. Chicago, 1970. 49 l. 28 cm. Caption title. [NX24.I3A7] 70-636190

LEVINE, Faye. 338.4'7'700973
The culture barons / by Faye Levine. New York : Crowell, c1976. 312 p. : ill. ; 24 cm. Includes index. [NX711.U5L48 1976] 75-43877 ISBN 0-690-01098-2 : 10.95
1. Art patronage—United States. 2. Arts—United States—Management. I. Title.

REISS, Alvin H. 338.4'7'7
Culture & company, by Alvin H. Reiss. New York, Twayne Publishers [1972] xiv, 309 p. 22 cm. Bibliography: p. 287-298. [NX711.U5R45] 72-728 8.95
1. Art patronage—United States. I. Title.

Art patronage—U.S.—Addresses, essays, lectures.

THE State of the arts and corporate support. 338.4'7'7
Gideon Chagy, editor. The contributors: Robert O. Anderson [and others] New York, P. S. Eriksson [1971] 184 p. illus., ports. 32 cm. "A Business Committee for the Arts publication." Contents.Contents.—Foreword, by G. Chagy.—The businessman and the artist, by R. O. Anderson.—Corporate patronage: signs and portents, by G. A. McLellan.—The state of the arts, by G. Meader.—Symphony orchestras in the seventies, by D. L. Engle.—How corporations support the arts, by G. Chagy.—Who should be an arts administrator? By H. Faine.—Confessions of a public relations man, by W. Ruder.—The corporate donor: the arts view, by G. Stewart. Bibliography: p. 73-75. [NX711.U5S7 1971] 75-131240 ISBN 0-8397-1226-X 10.00
1. Art patronage—U.S.—Addresses, essays, lectures. 2. The arts—U.S.—Finance—Addresses, essays, lectures. I. Chagy, Gideon, ed. II. Anderson, Robert O., 1917- III. Business Committee for the Arts.

Art patronage—United States—History.

CHAGY, Gideon. 338.4'7'7
The New patrons of the arts. New York, H. N. Abrams [1973] 128 p. illus. (part col.) 30 cm. [NX711.U5C45] 72-13107 ISBN 0-8109-0357-1 10.00
1. Art patronage—United States—History. I. Title.

Art patrons—England.

GEAR, Josephine. 759.2 B
Masters or servants? : A study of selected English painters and their patrons of the late eighteenth and early nineteenth centuries / Josephine Gear. New York : Garland Pub., 1977. xx, 381, 88 p. : ill. ; 21 cm. (Outstanding dissertations in the fine arts) Originally presented as the author's thesis, New York University, 1976. Bibliography: p. [374]-381. [N5245.G36 1977] 76-23619 ISBN 0-8240-2690-X : 40.00
1. Art patrons—England. 2. Painters—England. 3. Painting—Psychology. 4. Art and society—England. I. Title. II. Series. BIP

1. Art—Period.—Indexes. I. Title. BIP

Art, Peru.

UBBELOHDE-DOERING, Heinrich, 1889- 709.85
The art of ancient Peru. New York, F. A. Praeger [1952] 55 p. illus., 244 plates (part col.) map. 28 cm. (Books that matter) Bibliography: p. 53-55. [N6713.U23] 52-7489
1. Art, Peru. I. Title.

Art—Peshawar (District)

HALLADE, Madeleine. 709'.34
Grandharan art of North India and the Graeco-Buddhist tradition in India, Persia, and Central Asia. Photos. by Hans Hinz. [Translated by Diana Imber] New York, H. N. Abrams [1968] xvi, 266 p. illus. (part col.), col. maps. 30 cm. Includes bibliographies. [N7307.P4H313] 68-18130
1. Art—Peshawar (District) 2. Art, Buddhist—Asia. I. Title.

MARSHALL, John Hubert Sir 732.4
The Buddhist art of Gandhara: the story of the early school. its birth, growth, and decline. Cambridge [Eng.] Published for the Dept. of Archaeology in Pakistan at the University Press [dist. New York, Cambridge, Univ. Press] 1960 xvii, 117p. (Bibl. footnotes.) 111 plates. 26cm. (Memoirs of the Dept of Archaeology in Pakistan, v. 1) 60-16225 8.50
1. Art—Peshawar (District) 2. Art, Buddhist. I. Title. II. Series: Pakistan. Dept. of Archaeology. Memoirs, v. 1

Art—Peshawar (District).

LYONS, Islay, 1922- 709.54
Gandharan art in Pakistan; with 577 illustrations photographed by Islay Lyons, and 77 pictures from other sources. Introd. and descriptive catalogue by Harald Ingholt. [New York] Pantheon Books [c1957] 203p. illus., maps. 31cm. Bibliographical references included in 'Notes' (p. 41-45) [N7307.P3L9] 57-10237
1. Art— Peshawar, India (District) 2. Art, Buddhist. I. Ingholt, Harald, 1896- II. Title.

Art—Philadelphia.

PRIME, Alfred Coxe, 1883-1926, comp. 709'.73
The arts & crafts in Philadelphia, Maryland, and South Carolina; gleanings from newspapers. New York, Da Capo Press, 1969. 2 v. illus. 24 cm. (Da Capo Press series in architecture and decorative art, v. 31) Reprint of the 1929 ed. [N6507.P72] 79-75356
1. Art—Philadelphia. 2. Art—Maryland. 3. Art—South Carolina. 4. Art industries and trade—Philadelphia. 5. Art industries and trade—Maryland. 6. Art industries and trade—South Carolina. I. Title. BIP

Art—Philadelphia—Catalogs.

PENNSYLVANIA Academy of the Fine Arts, Philadelphia. 708.148'11
Check list: paintings, sculptures, miniatures from the permanent collection. Philadelphia, 1969. 105 p. 28 cm. [N680.A62] 70-11241
1. Art—Philadelphia—Catalogs.

PHILADELPHIA Museum of Art. 708.148
The Louise and Walter Arensberg Collection. [Philadelphia] 1954. 2 v. illus. (part col.) ports. 27cm. Contents.1. 20th century section. [Catalogue, compiled by Marianne Winter Martin]--2. Pre-Columbian sculpture. [Catalogue] classified and annotated by George Kubler. [N685.A6] 54-14691
1. Art—Philadelphia—Catalogs. 2. Art, Moern—20th cent. 3. Indians of Mexico—Antiq. 4. Indians of Central America—Antiq. I. Arensberg, Louise. II. Arensberg, Walter Conrad, 1878-1954. III. Title.

PHILADELPHIA Museum of Art. 708'.148'11
Treasures of the Philadelphia Museum of Art and the John G. Johnson Collection. [Editor: George H. Marcus] Philadelphia, 1973. 111 p. illus. (part col.) 29 cm. [N685.A67] 74-160937 4.95
1. Philadelphia Museum of Art. 2. John G. Johnson Collection, Philadelphia. 3. Art—Philadelphia—Catalogs. I. Marcus, George H., ed. II. Title.

Art—Philadelphia—Catalogs—Bibl.

RUTLEDGE, Anna Wells, ed. 709.748
Cumulative record of exhibition catalogues: the Pennsylvania Academy of the Fine Arts, 1807-1870; the Society of Artists, 1800-1814: the Artists' Fund society, 1835-1845. Philadelphia, American Philosophical Society, 1955. v. 450p. 31cm. (Memoirs of the American Philosophical Society, v. 38) [N680.A63] 55-6795
1. Art—Philadelphia—Catalogs—Bibl. I. Pennsylvania Academy of the Fine Arts, Philadelphia. II. Columbian Society of Artists, Philadelphia. III. Artists' Fund Society of Philadelphia. IV. Title. V. Series: American Philosophical Society, Philadelphia. Memoirs, v. 38

Art, Philippine.

ZOBEL, Fernando 709.914
Philippine religious imagery [by] Fernando Zobel de Ayala. Photos. by Nap C. Jamir [Quezon, Philippines] Ateneo de Manila [dist., Detroit Mich., Cellar Bk. Shop, 1964, c.1963] 154p. illus. 23x31cm. Expanded rev. version of the author's Philippine colonial structure which appeared in Philippine studies, v.6, no. 3, Aug. 1958. Bibl. [N7327.Z6] 63-15860 12.50 bds.,
1. Art, Philippine. 2. Christian art and symbolism. I. Jamir, Napoleon C. II. Title. BIP

Art—Philosophy.

ALBERS, Josef. 760'.092'4
Formulation, articulation / Josef Albers. New York : H. N. Abrams, c1972. 2 portfolios ([14] p., [113] leaves of plates : 127 col. ill. ; 52 x 40 cm. [ND588.A34A45] 72-2150 ISBN 0-8109-4752-8
1. Albers, Josef. 2. Art—Philosophy. I. Title.

ALDRICH, Virgil C. 701
Philosophy of art. Englewood Cliffs, N. J., Prentice [1967, c.1963] xi, 116p. illus. 24cm. (Founds. of phil. ser.) Bibl. [N66.A4] 63-01528 4.95
1. Art—Philosophy. 2. Aesthetics. I. Title.

ALDRICH, Virgil C. 701
Philosophy of art. Englewood Cliffs, N.J., Prentice-Hall [1963] 116 p. illus. 23 cm. (Prentice-Hall foundations of philosophy series) Includes bibliography. [N66.A4] 63-10526
1. Art—Philosophy. 2. Aesthetics.

ALEXANDER, Samuel, 1859-1938. 701
Art and instinct. [Folcroft, Pa.] Folcroft Library Editions, 1973. 23 p. 26 cm. Reprint of the 1927 ed. published by Clarendon Press, Oxford, which was issued as the Herbert Spencer lecture at Oxford, May 23, 1927. Includes bibliographical references. [N70.A49 1973] 73-16256 ISBN 0-8414-2929-4 (lib. bdg.)
1. Art—Philosophy. 2. Aesthetics. I. Title. II. Series: Herbert Spencer lecture, 1927. BIP

BALJEU, Joost. 100
Attempt at a theory of synthesist plastic expression. London, A Tiranti, 1963. 26 p. illus. (part col.) diagrs, plans. 25 cm. Stamped on 1 p.: American distributor: Wittenborn, New York. [N66.B25] 64-1613
1. Art—Philosophy. I. Title.

BARKAN, Manuel. 707
Viktor Lowenfeld: his impact on art education. Washington, National Art Education Association, 1966. iii, 24 p. 23 cm. (Research monograph 2) "Delivered as a Viktor Lowenfeld memorial lecture at the 1965 National Art Education Association Conference." "Response to Barkan's paper [by] W. Lambert Brittain": p. [20]-24. Includes bibliographical references. [N70.B24] 79-265878
1. Lowenfeld, Viktor. 2. Art—Philosophy. I. Brittain, W. Lambert. II. Series: National Art Education Association. Research monograph 2

BEITTEL, Kenneth R. 701'.9
Alternatives for art education research; inquiry into the making of art [by] Kenneth R. Beittel. Dubuque, Iowa, W. C. Brown Co. [1973] viii, 141 p. illus. 28 cm. (Trends in art education) Includes bibliographical references. [N71.B39] 72-88899 ISBN 0-697-03293-0 3.95 (pbk.)
1. Art—Philosophy. 2. Art—Psychology. 3. Art—Technique. I. Title.

BERNHEIMER, Richard. 701.17
The nature of representation; a phenomenological inquiry. Edited by H. W. Janson. New York, New York University Press [c1961] 249p. 22cm. [N66.B46] 61-8057
1. Art—Philosophy. I. Title.

BRONSTEIN, Leo. 701
Fragments of life, metaphysics, and art. New York, B. Wheelwright Co., 1953. xii, 218p. 68 illus. 28cm. Bibliographical references included in 'Notes' (p. 213-214) [N66.B75] 53-6237
1. Art—Philosophy. I. Title.

BURNHAM, Jack, 1931- 701
Great western salt works; essays on the meaning of post-formalist art. New York, G. Braziller [1974] 165 p. illus. 23 cm. Includes bibliographical references. [N70.B835] 73-92677 ISBN 0-8076-0740-1 12.50
1. Art—Philosophy. 2. Symbolism of numbers. 3. Signs and symbols. I. Title. BIP

CAMPBELL, Hugh H 811.54
Knock vigorously to be heard; reflections of a yoga-trained artist, by Hugh H. Campbell. New York, Philosophical Library [1966] xiv, 196 p. 21 cm. "Verses and essays." [PS3553.A46K6] 65-26184
I. Title. BIP

CHARPIER, Jacques, ed. 750.82
The art of painting, edited by Pierre Seghers in collaboration with Jacques Charpier. Excerpts translated by Sally T. Abeles. [1st American ed.] New York, Hawthorn Books [1964-65] 3 v. col. illus. 26 cm. In the original French ed. Charpier's name appeared first on the title page. Contents.Contents.—1. From prehistory through the Renaissance.—2. From the baroque through postimpressionism.—[3] In the twentieth century. Includes bibliographies. [ND1135.C463] 64-19203
1. Art—Philosophy. 2. Painting—Technique. I. Seghers, Pierre, joint ed. II. Title.

CHIARI, Joseph. 701
Art and knowledge / Joseph Chiari. New York : Gordian Press, 1977. ix, 132 p. ; 23 cm. Includes index. Bibliography: p. 125-127. [N70.C53] 76-57236 ISBN 0-87752-208-1 : 10.00
1. Art—Philosophy. I. Title. BIP

CLEMENTS, Robert John, 1912- 701
Michelangelo's theory of art. [New York] New York University Press, 1961. xxxiii, 471p. 20 plates, port. 27cm. Bibliographical references included in 'Notes' (p.421-457) 'Bibliographical note': p.458. [N6923.B9C55 1961a] 60-14318
1. Buonarroti, Michel Angelo, 1475-1564. 2. Art—Philosophy. 3. Art, Renalssance. I. Title. BIP

COLLIER, Graham. 701'.15
Art and the creative consciousness. Introd. by Rene Huyghe. Englewood Cliffs, N.J., Prentice-Hall [1972] xii, 212 p. illus. (part col.) 24 cm. Includes bibliographical references. [N70.C597] 72-5634 ISBN 0-13-046755-3
1. Art—Philosophy. 2. Art—Psychology. I. Title. BIP

DANZ, Louis. 101
Dynamic dissonance in nature and the arts. [New York, Farrar, Straus and Young, 1952] 261 p. illus. (part col.) 25 cm. [N70.D28] 701.17 52-14185
1. Art—Philosophy. 2. Aesthetics. I. Title.

DAVIS, James Joachim. 706.9
Art for everyman; a discussion of art, artists, and the layman's attitudes. [1st ed.] New York, Vantage Press [1956] 62p. illus. 21cm. [N70.D35] 56-9031
1. Art—Philosophy. I. Title.

DUCASSE, Curt John, 1881- 701.17
The philosophy of art. [Rev. and enl. version] New York, Dover Publications [1966] xx, 345 p. 22 cm. [N70.D83 1966] 66-14554
1. Art — Philosophy. 2. Aesthetics. I. Title.

DUCASSE. CURT JOHN. 1881- 701.17
The philosophy of art [Rev., enl. version. Gloucester. Mass., P. Smith. c.1966] xx, 345p. 22cm. First pub. by Dial Pr. in 1929 (Cover bk., T1549 rebound) [N70D83 1966] 4.00
1. Art—Philosophy. 2. Aesthetics. I. Title.

DUCHAMP, Marcel, 1887-1968. 759.4
Salt seller; the writings of Marcel Duchamp. Marchand du sel. Edited by Michel Sanouillet and Elmer Peterson. New York, Oxford University Press, 1973. xii, 196 p. illus. 24 cm. Bibliography: p. 196. [N6853.D8A57] 73-87343 ISBN 0-19-519749-6 10.95
1. Duchamp, Marcel, 1887-1968. 2. Art—Philosophy. I. Title.

EDDINGTON, Thomas. 700'.1
Contemporary art & the metaphysics of the art expression / Thomas Eddington. [Albuquerque, N.M.] : Gloucester Art Press, [1978] 23 leaves ; 28 cm. Cover title. [N70.E18] 78-2726 ISBN 0-930582-02-0 : 32.50
1. Art—Philosophy. 2. Art—Psychology. 3. Art, Modern—20th century. I. Title. BIP

FALLICO, Arturo B. 701
Art & existentialism. Englewood Cliffs, N.J., Prentice-Hall [1962] 175 p. 21 cm. (A Spectrum book, S-42) [N72.F3] 62-13725
1. Art—Philosophy. 2. Aesthetics. 3. Existentialism. I. Title.

FEIBLEMAN, James Kern, 1904- 701
The quiet rebellion; the making and meaning of the arts [by] James K. Feibleman. New York, Horizon Press [1972] 240 p. 25 cm. Includes bibliographical references. [N70.F38] 76-188192 ISBN 0-8180-1314-1 7.95
1. Art—Philosophy. 2. Art—Psychology. I. Title. BIP

FIEDLER, Konrad, 1841-1895. 704
Three fragments from the postumous [sic] papers of Conrad Fiedler, MDCCCXLI-MDCCCXCV, translated from the German by Thornton Sinclair together with Victor Hammer who also has contributed an introduction. Lexington, Ky., Printed under the auspices of Transylvania University at the Stamperia del Santuccio, 1951. 180 p. 21 cm. "One hundred and fifty-two copies ... printed on the hand press." First published in v. 2 of the author's Schriften uber Kunst under title: Wirklichkelt und Kunst. [N68.F45] 52-24832
1. Art—Philosophy. 2. Aesthetics. I. Title.

FINCH, Margaret, 1932- 701
Style in art history; an introduction to theories of style and sequence. Metuchen, N.J., Scarecrow Press, 1974. viii, 170 p. illus. 22 cm. Bibliography: p. 161-165. [N71.F56] 73-14705 ISBN 0-8108-0679-7
1. Art—Philosophy. 2. Aesthetics. 3. Art—Psychology. I. Title.

FINKELSTEIN, Sidney Walter, 1909- 701
Realism in art. New York, International Publishers [1954] 190p. 21cm. [N70.F54] 54-12924
1. Art —Philosophy. I. Title.

FISCHER, Ernst, 1899- 701
The necessity of art, a Marxist approach. Translated by Anna Bostock. Baltimore, Penguin Books [1963] 233 p. 18 cm. (Pelican books, A632) [N68.F553] 64-909
1. Art — Philosophy. I. Title. BIP

GABLIK, Suzi. 701
Progress in art / Suzi Gablik. London : Thames & Hudson, c1976. 192 p. : 162 ill. ; 25 cm. Includes index. Bibliography: p.

180-182. [N70.G32] 76-382247 ISBN 0-500-23220-2 : £8.50
1. Art—Philosophy. 2. Visual perception. 3. Cognition. I. Title.

GABLIK, Suzi. 701
Progress in art / Suzi Gablik. New York : Rizzoli, 1977, c1976. 192 p. : 162 ill. ; 25 cm. Includes index. Bibliography: p. 180-182. [N70.G32 1977] 76-62549 ISBN 0-8478-0082-2 : 15.00
1. Art—Philosophy. 2. Visual perception. 3. Cognition. I. Title. BIP

GENTILE, Giovanni, 1875-1944. 701
The philosophy of art. Translated, and with an introd. by Giovanni Gullace. Ithaca, Cornell University Press [1972] c, 292 p. port. 23 cm. Translation of La filosofia dell'arte. Includes bibliographical references. [BH204.G413 1972] 75-162548 ISBN 0-8014-0664-1 15.00
1. Art—Philosophy. I. Gullace, Giovanni, ed. II. Title.

GOMBRICH, Ernst Hans Josef, 1909- 701
The ideas of progress and their impact on art [by] E. H. Gombrich. [New York] Cooper Union School of Art and Architecture [1971] 89 p. illus. 29 cm. The inaugural Mary Duke Biddle lecture, Cooper Union School of Art and Architecture, 1971. Includes bibliographical references. [N70.G6155] 73-171379
1. Art—Philosophy. 2. Progress. I. Title.

GOTSHALK, Dilman Walter, 1901- 701
Art and social order. 2d ed. New York, Dover Publications [1962] 255 p. 22 cm. (Dover books, T294) [N72.G6 1962] 63-678
1. Art — Philosophy. 2. Art and society. I. Title.

GOTSHALK, Dilman Walter, 1901- 701
Art and the social order. 2d ed. [Gloucester, Mass., P. Smith, 1963, c.1947, c.1962] 255p. 22cm. (Dover bk., T294 rebound) 3.50
1. Art—Philosophy. 2. Art and society. I. Title.

GUGGENHEIMER, Richard Henry 701
Creative vision for art and for life. Rev. ed. New York, Harper [c.1960] xii, 175p. (Bibl. footnotes) 22cm. First published in 1950 under title: Creative vision in artist and audience. 60-11496 3.50 half cloth,
1. Art—Philosophy. 2. Aesthetics. I. Title.

GUGGENHEIMER, Richard Henry, 1906- 701
Creative vision for art and for life. Rev. ed. New York, Harper [1960] 175p. 22cm. First published in 1950 under title: Creative vision in artist and audience. [N66.G817 1960] 60-11496
1. Art—Philosophy. 2. Aesthetics. I. Title.

GUGGENHEIMER, Richard Henry, 1906- 701
Creative vision in artist and audience. New York, Harper [1950] x, 173 p. 21 cm. Sequel to Sight and insight. [N66.G817] 50-9522
1. Art—Philosophy. 2. Aesthetics. I. Title.

GUGGENHEIMER, Richard Henry, 1906- 701
Sight and insight; a prediction of new perceptions in art [by] Richard Guggenheimer. Port Washington, N.Y., Kennikat Press [1968, c1945] ix, 246 p. plates. 22 cm. (Essay and general literature index series) [N66.G82 1968] 68-15827
1. Art—Philosophy. 2. Aesthetics. I. Title. BIP

HAYES, Bartlett H 1904- 701.1
The naked truth and personal vision; a discussion about the length of the artistic road. Andover, Mass., Addison Gallery of American Art, Phillips Academy, 1955. 112p. illus. 28cm. [N66.H3] 55-14229
1. Art—Philosophy. I. Title.

HOSPERS, John, 1918- 701
Meaning and truth in the arts. Hamden, Conn., Archon [dist. Shoe String] 1964[c.1946] viii, 252p. 22cm. Bibl. 64-18539 7.00
1. Art—Philosophy. 2. Aesthetics. I. Title. BIP

HOSPERS, John, 1918- 701.1
Meaning and truth in the arts, by John Hospers. Chapel Hill, Univ. of N.C. Pr., [1967,c.1946] viii p., 2 1., 3-252p. 21cm. (Chb8) Issued also as thesis (PH.D.) Columbia Univ. Bibl. [N70.H74 1947] 47-2307 1.95 pap.,
1. Art — Philososphy. 2. Esthetics. I. Title.

HUYGHE, Rene 701
Art and the spirit of man. [Tr. from French by Norbert Guterman] New York, Abrams [1962] 526p. illus. (pt. col.) 23cm. 62-11622 15.00
1. Art—Philosophy. 2. Art—Hist. 3. Soul. I. Title.

JARRETT, James L. 701.17
The quest for beauty. Englewood Cliffs, N.J., Prentice-Hall, 1957. 318 p. illus. 24 cm. Includes bibliography. [N66.J3] 57-7846
1. Art—Philosophy. 2. Aesthetics. I. Title.

JARRETT, James Louis, 1917- 701.17
The quest for beauty. Englewood Cliffs, N. J., Prentice-Hall, 1957. 318p. illus. 24cm. Includes bibliography. [N66.J3] 57-7846
1. Art—Philosophy. 2. Aesthetics. I. Title.

JENKINS, Iredell. 701
Art and human enterprise. Cambridge, Harvard University Press, 1958. 318p. 22cm. [N70.J4] 58-7502
1. Art— Philosophy. 2. Aesthetics. I. Title.

JENKINS, Iredell. 701
Art and the human enterprise. [Unaltered and unabridged ed. Hamden, Conn.] Archon Books, 1969 [c1958] ix, 318 p. 22 cm. Bibliographical footnotes. [N70.J4 1969] 69-15793
1. Art—Philosophy. 2. Aesthetics. I. Title.

KARSHAN, Donald H., comp. 701.1
Conceptual art and conceptual aspects. Exhibition organized and catalogue compiled by Donald Karshan. New York, New York Cultural Center [1970] 100 p. 28 cm. Exhibition held Apr. 10-Aug. 25, 1970. "The seventies: post-object art": 2 p. inserted. Includes bibliographies. [N70.K37] 70-122334
1. Art—Philosophy. 2. Art—Exhibitions. I. New York Cultural Center. II. Title.

KUBLER, George, 1912- 701.17
The shape of time; remarks on the history of things. New Haven, Yale University Press, 1962. 136p. 23cm. [N66.K8] 62-8250
1. Art—Philosophy. 2. Aesthetics. I. Title.

KUBLER, George Alexander, 1912- 701.17
The shape of time; remarks on the history of things. New Haven, Conn., Yale [c.] 1962. 136p. 62-8250 3.75
1. Art—Philosophy. 2. Aesthetics. I. Title. BIP

LANGER, Susanne Katherina (Knauth) 1895- 701
Problems of art; ten philosophical lectures. New York, Scribners [1961, c.1957] 184p. (Scribners library, SL35) 1.25 pap.,
1. Art—Philosophy. 2. Aesthetics—Addresses, essays, lectures. I. Title.

LANGER, Susanne Katherina (Knauth) 1895- ed. 701.17
Reflections on art: a source book of writings by artists, critics and philosophers. Baltimore. Johns Hopkins Press [1959, c1958] 364p. illus. 24cm. [N79.L2] 58-59767
1. Art—Philosophy. 2. Aesthetics—Addresses, essays,;) lectures. 3. Music—Philosophy and aesthetics. I. Title.

LEGER, Fernand, 1881-1955. 701
Functions of painting, by Fernand Leger. Translated by Alexandra Anderson. Edited and introduced by Edward F. Fry. With a pref. by George L. K. Morris. New York, Viking Press [1973] xxxiv, 221 p. illus. 22 cm. (The Documents of 20th-century art) Translation of Fonctions de la peinture. Bibliography: p. [193]-215. [N70.L45213 1973] 71-184540 ISBN 0-670-33221-6 10.00
1. Art—Philosophy. 2. Aesthetics. 3. Art and society. I. Title. II. Series. BIP

LIPMAN, Matthew. 701
What happens in art. New York, Appleton-Century-Crofts [1966, c1967] vii, 177 p. 21 cm. (The Century philosophy series) Bibliography: p. 161-172. [N70.L465] 66-27473
1. Art—Philosophy. 2. Visual discrimination. I. Title. BIP

LOEWENBERG, Jacob. 701
Dialogues from Delphi. Freeport, N.Y., Books for Libraries Press [1970, c1949] x, 304 p. 23 cm. (Essay index reprint series) [N70.L475 1970] 77-121485
1. Art—Philosophy. 2. Aesthetics. I. Title. BIP

MALRAUX, Andre, 1901- 701.1
The metamorphosis of the gods. Translated by Stuart Gilbert. [1st ed. in English] Garden City, N.Y., Doubleday, 1960- v. illus. (part col.) 24 cm. [N72.M2643] 60-10395
1. Art—Philosophy. 2. Art and religion. I. Title. BIP

MARGOLIS, Joseph Zalman, 1924- 701
Art and philosophy / Joseph Margolis. Nyborg, [Denmark] : F. Lokkes ; Atlantic Highlands, N.J. : Humanities Press, 1976, i.e.1977 p. cm. (Eclipse books) Includes bibliographical references and index. [N70.M34 1976] 76-19063 ISBN 0-391-00645-2 pbk. : 3.00
1. Art—Philosophy. I. Title. BIP

MUNDT, Ernest. 701.17
Art, form, and civilization. Berkeley, University of California Press, 1952. vii, 246 p. illus. 24 cm. [N66.M8] 52-14575
1. Art — Philosophy. 2. Aesthetics. I. Title.

NEUTRA, Richard Joseph, 1892- 720'.1
Survival through design. London, New York, Oxford University Press [1969] xvi, 384 p. illus., ports. 21 cm. (A Galaxy book, GB285) [N66.N38 1969] 76-94526 2.95
1. Art—Philosophy. I. Title.

NEUTRA, Richard Joseph, 1892-1970. 720.1
Survival through design. New York, Oxford University Press, 1954. 384 p. 22 cm. [N66.N38] 53-9190
1. Art—Philosophy. I. Title. BIP

NEW York University Institute of Philosophy. 7th, 1964 700.1
Art and philosophy; [proceedings of] a symp., ed. by Sidney Hook [New York] N.Y.U. [c.]1966. x,346p. 21cm. Bibl. [N70.N395] 66-13841 6.50 bds.,
1. Art—Philosophy. I. Hook, Sidney. 1902- ed. II. New York. University. III. Title.

NEW York University Institute of Philosophy. 7th, 1964. 700.1
Art and philosophy; [proceedings of] a symposium, edited by Sidney Hook. [New York] New York University Press. 1966. x, 346 p. 21 cm. Includes bibliographical references. [N70.N395 1964] 66-13841
1. Art — Philosophy. I. Hook, Sidney, 1902- ed. II. New York. University. III. Title.

NEWTON, Eric, 1893- 701.17
The meaning of beauty. [Baltimore] Penguin [1963] 212p. illus. 18cm. (Pelican bk., A580) 1.25 pap.,
1. Art—Philosophy. 2. Aesthetics. I. Title.

NEWTON, Eric, 1893- 701.17
The meaning of beauty. London, New York, Longmans, Green [1950] 205 p. illus. 23 cm. [N66.N4] 51-923
1. Art — Philosophy. 2. Aesthetics. I. Title.

NEWTON, Eric, 1893- 701.17
The meaning of beauty. New York, Whittlesey House [1950] 205 p. illus. 23 cm. [N66.N4 1950a] 50-10495
1. Art—Philosophy. 2. Aesthetics. I. Title.

ORBAN, Desiderius, 1884- 701
What is art all about? / Desiderius Orban. New York : Van Nostrand Reinhold Co., [1978] p. cm. Includes index. Bibliography: p. [N71.O72] 78-9670 ISBN 0-442-26283-3 : 7.95
1. Art—Philosophy. 2. Art—Psychology. I. Title. BIP

ORTEGA y Gasset, Jose, 1883-1955. 759.6
Velazquez, Goya and the dehumanization of art. Translated by Alexis Brown. With an introd. by Philip Troutman. New York, W. W. Norton [1972] 142 p. illus. 26 cm. Bibliography: p. 137. [ND813.V4O69413 1972] 74-177440 ISBN 0-393-04358-4 17.50
1. Velazquez, Diego Rodriguez de Silva y, 1599-1660. 2. Goya y Lucientes, Francisco Jose de, 1746-1828. 3. Art—Philosophy. I. Title.

PAINTERLY painting. 750.18
Edited by Thomas B. Hess and John Ashbery. New York [Newsweek; distributed by] Macmillan [1971] 162 p. (p. 149-162 advertisements) illus. (part col.) 31 cm. (Art news annual 37) Includes bibliographical references. [N1.A613 vol. 37] [N71] 79-30465 7.95
1. Art—Philosophy. 2. Art—Psychology. I. Hess, Thomas B., ed. II. Ashbery, John, ed. III. Title. IV. Series.

PASTO, Tarmo 701.18
The space-frame experience in art. New York, A. S. Barnes [1964] 440p. illus. 29cm. Bibl. 64-14733 15.00
1. Art—Philosophy. 2. Art—Psychology. 3. Art criticism. I. Title.

PECKHAM, Morse 701
Man's rage for chaos; biology, behavior, and the arts. New York, Schocken [1967,c.1965] xv, 339p. plates. 21cm. (SB142) Bibl. [N66.P4] 2.95 pap.,
1. Art—Philosophy. 2. Literature—Philosophy. 3. Performing arts. 4. Aesthetics. I. Title. BIP

PECKHAM, Morse. 701
Man's rage for chaos; biology, behavior, and the arts. [1st ed.] Philadelphia, Chilton Books [1965] xv, 339 p. plates. 25 cm. Bibliography: p. 325-328. [N66.P4] 65-22544
1. Art—Philosophy. 2. Literature—Philosophy. 3. Performing arts. 4. Aesthetics. I. Title.

PHILIPSON, Morris H., 1926- ed. 701.17
Aesthetics today; reading selected, ed., introd. by Morris Philipson. Cleveland, World Pub. Co. [1961] 475p. illus. (Meridian books, M112) Bibl. 61-11473 1.65 pap.,
1. Art—Philosophy. 2. Aesthetics. I. Title.

PHILIPSON, Morris H., 1926- ed. 701.17
Aesthetics today; readings selected, ed., introd. by Morris Philipson [Gloucester, Mass., P. Smith, 1964, c.1961] 475p. illus. 19cm. (Meridian bks., M112 rebound) Bibl. 4.00
1. Art—Philosophy. 2. Aesthetics. I. Title. BIP

PIPER, Raymond Frank. 701.17
The hungry eye; an introduction to cosmic art. Los Angeles, De Vorss [1956] 145p. illus. 22cm. [N70.P48] 57-28087
1. Art—Philosophy. 2. Christian art and symbolism. I. Title.

PODRO, Michael. 111.8'5
The manifold in perception: theories of art from Kant to Hildebrand. Oxford, Clarendon Press, 1972. xv, 129, [8] p. illus. 25 cm. (Oxford-Warburg studies) Bibliography: p. [xiii]-xv. [N66.P62] 72-169546 ISBN 0-19-920034-3
1. Art—Philosophy. 2. Visual perception. I. Title.
Distributed by Oxford In New York 11.00

READ, Herbert Edward, Sir 1893- 701
Icon and idea; the function of art in the development of human consciousness [New pref. by the author] New York, Schocken [c.1965] 161p. illus. 21cm. (SB105) Orig. pub. in 1954. Bibl. [N66.R4] 65-25410 2.45 pap.,
1. Art—Philosophy. 2. Aesthetics. I. Title.

READ, Herbert Edward, Sir 1893- 701
The origins of form in art [by] Herbert Read. [1st American ed.] New York, Horizon Press [1965] 207 p. illus. 23 cm. Bibliography: p. [189]-197. [N70.R353] 65-21703

1. Art — Philosophy. 2. Aesthetics. I. Title.

READ, Herbert Edward, Sir, 1893-1968. 701
The origins of form in art [by] Herbert Read. [1st American ed.] New York, Horizon Press [1965] 207 p. illus. 23 cm. Bibliography: p. [189]-197. [N70.R353] 65-21703
1. Art—Philosophy. 2. Aesthetics. I. Title.

READ, Herbert Edward, Sir, 1893-1968. 709.04
The philosophy of modern art; collected essays. Freeport, N.Y., Books for Libraries Press [1971, c1953] 278 p. illus. 23 cm. (Essay index reprint series) Includes bibliographical references. [N6490.R43 1971] 70-128294 ISBN 0-8369-2023-6
1. Art—Philosophy. 2. Art, Modern—20th century. I. Title.

ROTHSCHILD, Lincoln, 1902- 701.1
Style in art; the dynamics of art as cultural expression. New York, T. Yoseloff [1960] 175p. 47plates. 25cm. [N74.R6] 60-13622
1. Art—Philosophy. I. Title.

ROTHSCHILD, Lincoln 1902- 701.1
Style in art; the dynamics of art as cultural expression. New York, T. Yoseloff [c.1960] 175p. 47 plates. 25cm. 60-13622 6.00
1. Art—Philosophy. I. Title.

SAARINEN, Eliel, 1873-1950. 701.8
Search for form; a fundamental approach to art. Port Washington, Kennikat Press [1969, c1948] xxi, 354 p. illus. 23 cm. [N70.S27 1969] 70-91052
1. Art—Philosophy. I. Title.

SARTRE, Jean Paul, 1905- 701.17
Essays in aesthetics. Selected, tr. [from French] by Wade Baskin. New York, Citadel [c.1963] 94p. 21cm. (C-126) 1.75 pap.,
1. Art-Philosophy. 2. Artists. I. Title.

SARTRE, Jean Paul, 1905- 701.17
Essays in aesthetics. Selected and translated by Wade Baskin. New York, Philosophical Library [1963] 94 p. 22 cm. [N67.S243] 63-11486
1. Art—Philosophy. 2. Artists. I. Title. BIP

SIRCELLO, Guy. 701
Mind & art: an essay on the varieties of expression. [Princeton, N.J.] Princeton University Press [1972] xiii, 349 p. 23 cm. Bibliography: p. 340-342. [N70.S57] 70-166390 ISBN 0-691-07184-5 13.50
1. Art—Philosophy. 2. Art—Psychology. I. Title.

STOKES, Adrian Durham, 1902- 701
The invitation in art. Pref. by Richard Wollheim. New York, Chilmark [dist. Random. 1966,c.1965] xxxiii,67p. 23cm. Bibl. [N66.S79] 66-13329 3.95
1. Art—Philosophy. 2. Aesthetics. I. Title.

SYLVESTER, David. 759.9415
Francis Bacon / interviewed by David Sylvester. 1st American ed. New York : Pantheon Books, [1975] 128 p. : ill. ; 29 cm. [ND497.B16S9 1975] 74-26206 ISBN 0-394-49763-5 : 12.95. ISBN 0-394-73062-3 pbk. : 5.95
1. Bacon, Francis, 1909- 2. Art—Philosophy. I. Bacon, Francis, 1909-

TAYLOR, Harold, 1914- 701
Art and the intellect. Moral values and the experience of art. New York, Published for the National Committee on Art Education by the Museum of Modern Art; distributed by Doubleday, Garden City, N.Y. [1960] 62 p. 19 cm. [N72.T32] 60-53180
1. Art — Philosophy. 2. Art and morals. I. Title. II. Title: Moral values and the experience of art.

TAYLOR, John Francis Adams 701.8
Design and expression in the visual arts. New York, Dover [c:1964] x, 245p. illus. (pt. col.) 22cm. (T1195) Bibl. 63-19502 1.75 pap.,
1. Art—Philosophy. I. Title.

TAYLOR, John Francis Adams 701.8
Design and expression in the visual arts [Gloucester, Mass., P. Smith, 1965, c.1964] x, 245p. illus. (pt. col.) 22cm. (Dover bk., T1195 rebound) Bibl. [N70.T47] 3.75
1. Art—Philosophy. I. Title. BIP

TEJERA, Victorino. 701
Art and human intelligence. New York, Appleton-Century-Crofts [1965] xii, 237 p. illus. (part col.) 25 cm. Bibliography: p. 217-227. [N70.T48] 65-15781
1. Art—Philosophy. 2. Aesthetics. I. Title. BIP

THOMAS, Brian, 1912- 751.4
Vision and technique in European painting. London, New York, Longmans, Green [1952] 172p. illus. 23cm. [N70.T5] 52-12599
1. Art—Philosophy. I. Title.

USHENKO, Andrew Paul, 1901- 701.17
Dynamics of art; with a foreword by Stephen C. Pepper. Bloomington, Indiana University Press, 1953. xiii, 257p. illus. (1 col.) 24cm. (Indian University publications. Humanities series, no. 28) Bibliographical references included in 'Notes' (p. 249-251) [AS36.I385 no.28] 53-9836
1. Art—Philosophy. 2. Aeathetics. I. Title. II. Series: Indiana. University. Indiana University publications. Humanities series, no. 28 BIP

WARBEKE, John Martyn, 1879-1950. 701
The power of art. New York, Philosophical Library [1951] 493 p. 23 cm. [N66.W28] 51-14699
1. Art — Philosophy. 2. Aesthetics. I. Title. BIP

WEISS, Paul, 1901- 701
Nine basic arts. Carbondale, Southern Illinois University Press [1961] 238 p. 23 cm. [N66.W32] 61-7164
1. Art — Philosophy. 2. Literature — Philosophy. 3. Aesthetics. I. Title. BIP

WEISS, Paul, 1901- 701.17
The world of art. Carbondale, Southern Illinois University Press [1961] 193 p. 22 cm. [N66.W34] 61-5168
1. Art — Philosophy. 2. Aesthetics. I. Title. BIP

WEISS, Paul, 1901- 701.17
The world of art. Carbondale, Southern Ill. Univ. Pr. [1964, c.1961] 193p. 21cm. (Arcturus bk. AB10) 61-5168 1.95 pap.,
1. Art—Philosophy. 2. Aesthetics. I. Title.

WEITZ, Morris 701.17
Philosophy of the arts. New York, Russell & Russell, 1964 [c.1950] xi, 239p. 23cm. Bibl. 64-10395 6.50
1. Art—Philosophy. I. Title. BIP

WEITZ, Morris. 701.17
Philosophy of the arts. Cambridge, Harvard University Press, 1950. xi, 230 p. 22 cm. Bibliography: p. [210]-226. [N66.W37] 50-10351
1. Art — Philosophy. I. Title.

WERHANE, Patricia Hogue. 701
Art and nonart / Patricia Hogue Werhane. Washington : University Press of America, c1978. vi, 195 p. : ill. ; 22 cm. Includes bibliographical references and indexes. [N71.W447] 78-100408 ISBN 0-8191-0404-3 pbk. : 9.50
1. Art—Philosophy. I. Title. BIP

WULF, Maurice Marie Charles Joseph de, 1867-1947. 701
Art and beauty; translated by Sister Mary Gonzaga Udell St. Louis, Herder, 1950. ix, 213 p. 22 cm. [N67.W814] 51-1663
1. Art — Philosophy. I. Title.

Art—Philosophy—Addresses, essays, lectures.

ART: a Bryn Mawr symposium, 701
by Richard Bernheimer [and others] New York, Oriole Editions, 1972. xii, 350 p. 22 cm. Reprint of the 1940 ed., which was issued as no. 9 of Bryn Mawr notes and monographs. Includes bibliographical references. [N70.A77 1972] 72-84808 ISBN 0-88211-031-4 9.00
1. Art—Philosophy—Addresses, essays, lectures. I. Bernheimer, Richard. II. Bryn Mawr College. III. Series: Bryn Mawr notes and monographs, 9.

HOSPERS, John, 1918- comp. 700'.1
Artistic expression. New York, Appleton-Century-Crofts [1971] vi, 333 p. music. 25 cm. (The Century philosophy series) Contents.Contents.—Art as communication, by L. Tolstoi.—Art, intuition, and expression, by B. Groce.—Art as expression, by R. G. Collingwood.—The Groce-Collingwood theory of art, by J. Hospers.—The act of expression, by J. Dewey.—Art and the language of the emotions, by C. J. Ducasse.—Music as impressive and music as expressive, by E. Gurney.—Expression, by G. Santayana.—The expressiveness of colors, by W. Kadinsky.—Expression and association, by C. Hartshorne.—Expressiveness, by R. Arnheim.—The expression theory of art, by O, K. Bouwsma.—The concept of expression in art, by V. Tomas, D. Morgan and M. Beardsley.—Musical expression, by M. Beardsley.—Expressive predicates of art, by G. Sircello. Includes bibliographies. [N70.H739] 71-142225 ISBN 0-390-46187-3
1. Art—Philosophy—Addresses, essays, lectures. 2. Music—Philosophy and aesthetics—Addresses, essays, lectures. I. Title. BIP

TAINE, Hippolyte Adolphe, 1828-1893. 701
Lectures on art. Translated by John Durand. New York, Holt. [New York, AMS Press, 1971] 2 v. 19 cm. Reprint of the 1875 ed. Contents.Contents.—1st ser. The philosophy of art. The ideal in art.—2d ser. The philosophy of art in Itlay. The philosophy of art in the Netherlands. The philosophy of art in Greece. [N70.T18 1971] 75-137295 ISBN 0-404-06334-9 (v. 1)
1. Art—Philosophy—Addresses, essays, lectures. I. Title. BIP

WOLLHEIM, Richard, 1923- 701
On art and the mind. Cambridge, Mass., Harvard University Press, 1974. 338 p. illus. 25 cm. Includes bibliographical references. [N71.W64 1974] 73-94137 ISBN 0-674-63405-5 15.00
1. Art—Philosophy—Addresses, essays, lectures. 2. Art—Psychology—Addresses, essays, lectures. I. Title.

Art—Philosophy—Bibliography.

KAPRELIAN, Mary H. 016.7'001
Aesthetics for dancers : a selected annotated bibliography / compiled and annotated by Mary H. Kaprelian. Washington : [National Dance Association] , c1976. vii, 87 p. ; 28 cm. (AAHPER publications) Includes indexes. [Z5931.K34] [N70] 76-360816
1. Art—Philosophy—Bibliography. 2. Dancing—Philosophy—Bibliography. I. Title. II. Series: American Alliance for Health, Physical Education, and Recreation. AAHPER publications. BIP

Art—Philosophy—History.

MARITAIN, Jacques, 1882- 701
Art and scholasticism, and The frontiers of poetry. Translated by Joseph W. Evans. New York, Scribner [1962] 234p. 22cm. [N61.M3 1962] 62-9652
1. Art—Philosophy—Hist. 2. Scholasticism. 3. Poetry. I. Title. II. Title: The frontiers of poetry. BIP

Art—Philosophy—History.

MCMAHON, Amos Philip, 1890-1947. 701
Preface to an American philosophy of art. Port Washington, N.Y., Kennikat Press [1968, c1945] vi, 194 p. 22 cm. Bibliographical references included in "Notes" (p. 180-190) [N61.M27 1968] 68-15830
1. Art—Philosophy—History. 2. Art, American. 3. Aesthetics, American. I. Title. BIP

MARITAIN, Jacques, 1882- 701.17
Art and scholasticism, with other essays. Translated by J. F. Scanlan. Freeport, N.Y., Books for Libraries Press [1971] ix, 177 p. 23 cm. (Essay index reprint series) "First published 1930." Translation of Art et scolastique. Includes bibliographical references. [N61.M3 1971] 70-152196 ISBN 0-8369-2241-7
1. Art—Philosophy—History. 2. Scholasticism. I. Title. BIP

MARITAIN, Jacques, 1882-1973. 701
Art and scholasticism and The frontiers of poetry. Translated by Joseph W. Evans. Notre Dame [Ind.] University of Notre Dame Press [1974, c1962] vi, 234 p. 22 cm. Translation of the author's Art et scolastique and his Frontieres de la poesie. Reprint of the ed. published by Scribner, New York. Includes bibliographical references. [N61.M3 1974] 74-13601 ISBN 0-268-00556-7 9.95
1. Art—Philosophy—History. 2. Scholasticism. 3. Poetry. I. Maritain, Jacques, 1882-1973. Frontieres de la poesie. English. 1974. II. Title.
Pbk. 3.25; ISBN 0-268-00557-5

Art—Pittsburgh.

FRICK Art Museum, Pittsburgh. 708'.14'886
Treasures of the Frick Art Museum / text by Walter Read Hovey. Pittsburgh : The Museum, 1975. p. cm. Includes index. [N710.5.A87] 75-26681
1. Frick Art Museum, Pittsburgh. 2. Art—Pittsburgh. I. Hovey, Walter Read, 1895- II. Title.

Art, Polish.

PIOTROWSKA, Irena (Glebocka) 1904- 709'.438
The art of Poland, by Irena Piotrowska. Freeport, N.Y., Books for Libraries Press [1971, c1947] xiv, 238 p. illus. 29 cm. (Biography index reprint series) Bibliography: p. 227-228. [N7255.P6P5 1971] 75-179736 ISBN 0-8369-8104-9
1. Art, Polish. I. Title.

Art, Polish—Exhibitions.

CHICAGO. Art Institute. 709'.438
Treasures from Poland: a loan exhibition from the State Art Collection of Wawel Castle; Cracow; the Treasury of Wawel Cathedral; the National Museum of Cracow; and the National Museum of Warsaw. [Chicago? 1966] 1 v. (unpaged) illus., ports. 19 x 26 cm. At head of title: The Art Institute of Chicago, Philadelphia Museum of Art, the National Gallery of Canada, 1966-1967. "Stanislaw Lorentz...[compiled] the catalogue of the exhibition." [N6991.C47] 68-16271
1. Art, Polish—Exhibitions. I. Philadelphia Museum of Art. II. Ottawa. National Gallery of Canada. III. Lorentz, Stanislaw. IV. Title.

CHICAGO. Art Institute. 709'.438
Treasures from Poland: a loan exhibition from the State Art Collection of Wawel Castle; Cracow; the Treasury of Wawel Cathedral; the National Museum of Cracow; and the National Museum of Warsaw. [Chicago? 1966] 1 v. (unpaged) illus., ports. 19 x 26 cm. At head of title: The Art Institute of Chicago, Philadelphia Museum of Art, the National Gallery of Canada, 1966-1967. "Stanislaw Lorentz ... [compiled] the catalogue of the exhibition." [N6991.C47] 68-1627
1. Art, Polish—Exhibitions. I. Philadelphia Museum of Art. II. Ottawa. National Gallery of Canada. III. Lorentz, Stanislaw. IV. Title.

SANTA Barbara, Calif. Museum of Art. 709'.438
Three Polish artists: Anna Guntner, Zbigniew Makowski [and] Josef Twirbutt. From the Collection of Eva Pape at the Santa Barbara Museum of Art, March 30-April 28, 1974; [catalogue. Santa Barbara, 1974] [16] p. illus. 20 x 26 cm. [N7255.P6S27 1974] 74-79200
1. Pape, Eva—Art collections. 2. Art, Polish—Exhibitions. 3. Art, Modern—20th century—Poland. I. Guntner, Anna, 1933- II. Makowski, Zbigniew, 1930- III. Twirbutt, Josef, 1930- IV. Title.

Art, Polynesian.

DODD, Edward Howard, 1905- 709/.96
A pictorial peregrination through the shapely and harmonious, often enigmatical, sometimes shocking realms of Polynesian art. Introductory and captional commentary, by Edward Dodd. New York,

Dodd, 1967. 368p. illus. 32cm. (His The ring of fire, v. 1) On spine: Polynesian art. [N7410.D6] 67-16863 25.00
1. Art, Polynesian. I. Title.

Art, Portuguese.

SMITH, Robert Chester, 1912- 709'.469
The art of Portugal, 1500-1800 [by] Robert C. Smith New York, Meredith Press [1968] 320 p. illus. (part col.), plans. 29 cm. "Notes and bibliographies": p. 313-316. [N7124.S6 1968b] 68-31684 24.95
1. Art, Portuguese. 2. Architecture—Portugal. I. Title.

Art—Poughkeepsie, N.Y.—Catalogs.

VASSAR College. Art Gallery. 708.147'33
Selections from the permanent collection. Poughkeepsie, N. Y. [1967] xvi, 179 p. illus. (part col.) 26 cm. [N713.A55] 67-31281
1. Art—Poughkeepsie, N. Y.—Catalogs. I. Title.

Art, Prehistoric.

GRANDE, Paul Marie, 1914- 709.011
Prehistoric art; Paleolithic painting and sculpture. Text by P. M. Grande. Greenwich, Conn., New York Graphic Society [1967] 103 p. illus. (part col.), maps. 28 cm. (The Pallas library of art, v. 3) Bibliography: p. 101. [N5310.G65] 67-28690
1. Art, Prehistoric. I. Title.

LEROI-GOURHAN, Andre, 1911- 709.01
Treasures of prehistoric art. New York, H. N. Abrams [1967?] 543 p. illus. (part col.), plans. 32 cm. Translation of Prehistoire de l'art occidental. Bibliography: p. [525]-537. [N5310.L5313] 67-22851
1. Art, Prehistoric. 2. Cave-drawings. I. Title.

LOMMEL, Andreas. 709.01
Prehistoric and primitive man. New York, McGraw-Hill [1966] 176 p. illus. (part col.) maps. 30 cm. (Landmarks of the world's art) Bibliography: p. [171]-172. [N5310.L683] 66-15836
1. Art, Prehistoric. I. Title.

PERICOT, Garcia, Luis, 1899- 709.01'1
Prehistoric and primitive art [by] Luis Pericot-Garcia, John Galloway [and] Andreas Lommel. [Prehistoric art translated from Spanish and The art of Oceania translated from German by Henry Mins] New York, H. N. Abrams [1968] 340 p. illus., maps, plates (part col.) 32 cm. Originally published under title: La preistoria e i primitivi attuali. [N5310.P4813 1968] 68-26867
1. Art, Prehistoric. 2. Art, Primitive. I. Galloway, John Crozier. II. Lommel, Andreas. III. Title.

POWELL, Thomas George Eyre, 1916- 709.01
Prehistoric art [by] T. G. E. Powell. New York, Praeger [1966] 284 p. illus. (part col.), map. 22 cm. (Praeger world of art series) Bibliography: p. 263-264. [N5310.P63 1966a] 66-12991
1. Art, Prehistoric.

WAAGE, Frederick Oswin, 1906- 709.01'1
Prehistoric art [by] Frederick O. Waage. Dubuque, Iowa, W. C. Brown [1967] xv, 113 p. illus. 23 cm. (Art horizons series) Bibliography: p. 109-110. [N5310.W28] 67-22709
1. Art, Prehistoric. I. Title.

Art, Prehistoric—Africa, Southern.

LEE, D. Neil. 759.01'1'0968
Art on the rocks of Southern Africa [by] D. N. Lee and H. C. Woodhouse. Drawings by Marion Didcott. New York, Scribner [1974, c1970] 165 p. illus. (part col.) 30 cm. Bibliography: p. 164-165. [N5310.5.S6L4 1974] 73-18801 ISBN 0-684-13742-9 15.00
1. Art, Prehistoric—Africa, Southern. I. Woodhouse, H. C., 1919- joint author. II. Title.

Art, Prehistoric—Australia.

STUBBS, Dacre. 709'.01'10994
Prehistoric art of Australia / Dacre Stubbs. New York : Scribner, [1975] c1974. 112 p. : ill. (some col.) ; 30 cm. Includes index. Bibliography: p. 107-108. [N5310.5.A83S85] 74-14154 ISBN 0-684-14123-X : 17.50
1. Art, Prehistoric—Australia. 2. Australia—Antiquities. I. Title.

Art, Prehistoric—Dictionaries.

HUYGHE, Rene, ed. 709.01
Larousse encyclopedia of prehistoric and ancient art; art and mankind. New York, Prometheus Press [1962] 414 p. illus., col. plates, maps. 30 cm. "Translated by Michael Heron, Corinne Lambert and Wendela Schurmann from [v. 1 of] the French original: L'art et l'homme." [N5300.H953] 62-7998
1. Art, Prehistoric—Dictionaries. 2. Art, Ancient. I. Title. II. Title: Art and mankind.

Art, Prehistoric—Europe.

SANDARS, Nancy K. 709'.3
Prehistoric art in Europe [by] N. K. Sandars. Harmondsworth, Penguin, 1968. xlix, 350 p. 189 plates, illus. (incl. 1 col.), maps. 27 cm. (Pelican history of art, Z30) In slip case. Bibliography: p. 329-332. [N5310.S32] 79-352957 6/6/-
1. Art, Prehistoric—Europe. 2. Europe—Antiquities. I. Title. II. Series.

TORBRUGGE, Walter. 709'.01'1
Prehistoric European art. [Translated from the German by Norbert Guterman] New York, H. N. Abrams [1968] 260 p. illus. (part. col.) 23 cm. (Panorama of world art) Translation of Europaische Vorzeit. Bibliography: p. 255-256. [N5310.5.E8T613] 68-28390
1. Art, Prehistoric—Europe. 2. Art—Europe. I. Title.

Art, Prehistoric—Exhibitions.

GEBHARD, David. 709.01'1
The rock art of Dinwoody, Wyoming; an exhibition [at] the Art Galleries, University of California, Santa Barbara, California, September 30 to November 6, 1969. Organized by David Gebhard. [Santa Barbara, c1969] 40, [40] p. illus., map. 22 cm. Bibliography: p. 31-38. [N5310.5.D5G4] 70-627997
1. Art, Prehistoric—Exhibitions. 2. Art, Prehistoric—Dinwoody Valley. I. California. University, Santa Barbara. Art Gallery. II. Title.

Art, Prehistoric—Greece, Modern.

HOOD, Sinclair. 709'.38
The arts in prehistoric Greece / Sinclair Hood. Harmondsworth, Eng. ; New York : Penguin Books, 1977. p. cm. (The Pelican history of art) Includes index. Bibliography: p. [N5310.5.G8H66] 77-28512 ISBN 0-14-056142-0 pbk. : 12.95
1. Art, Prehistoric—Greece, Modern. 2. Greece, Modern—Antiquities. I. Title. II. Series. BIP

Art, Prehistoric—History.

MOULIN, Raoul Jean. 709.01'2
Prehistoric painting. Translated by Anthony Rhodes. New York, Funk & Wagnalls [1969, c1965] 207 p. illus. (part col.), maps. 28 cm. (History of painting) Translation of Sources de la peinture. Bibliography: p. 204. [N5310.M6413 1969] 68-27363 7.95
1. Art, Prehistoric—History. 2. Art—Dictionaries. 3. Painting, Prehistoric. I. Title.

Art, Prehistoric—Juvenile literature.

SAMACHSON, Dorothy. 709.01'1
The first artists, by Dorothy and Joseph Samachson. [1st ed.] Garden City, N.Y., Doubleday [1970] x, 147 p. illus. (part col.) 25 cm. Discusses reasons for cave paintings, the choice of subjects, the tools and pigments used, and what these works of art reveal about the prehistoric cultures that produced them. [N5310.S317] 77-116251 4.95
1. Art, Prehistoric—Juvenile literature. I. Samachson, Joseph, joint author. II. Title.

Art—Prices.

ART Reference Gallery. Art Appraisal Information Division. 709'.2'4
Price profile on all works by John Singer Sargent. Montclair, N.J. [1973] vi, 20 p. 22 cm. [N6537.S32A77] 73-158797 12.00
1. Sargent, John Singer, 1856-1925. 2. Art—Prices. I. Title.

ART Reference Gallery. Art Appraisal Information Division. 760'.092'4
Price profile on oils, drawings, watercolors, and pastels by James Abbott McNeill Whistler. Montclair, N.J. [1973] v, 13 p. 22 cm. [N6537.W4A89] 73-163959 8.00
1. Whistler, James Abbott McNeill, 1834-1903. 2. Art—Prices. I. Title.

BERARD, Michele. 338.4'3'7
Encyclopedia of modern art auction prices. New York, Arco Pub. Co. [1971] x, 417 p. 32 cm. Bibliography: p. 417. [N6447.B47] 79-161210 ISBN 0-668-02493-3 45.00
1. Art—Prices. 2. Art, Modern—19th century—Catalogs. 3. Art, Modern—20th century—Catalogs. I. Title.

JACOBSEN, Anita. 700'.75
Jacobsen's painting price guide. Staten Island, N.Y., Manor Pub. Co., 1973. 173 p. 18 cm. "A comprehensive list of prices realized at auction from 1967 to 1972 for more than 6000 paintings, graphic arts, and bronzes by more than 2350 American and European artists." [N8675.J26] 73-82656
1. Art—Prices. 2. Art auctions. I. Title.

KEEN, Geraldine, 1940- 338.4'3'76
Money and art; a study based on the Times-Sotheby Index. [1st Amer. ed.] New York, Putnam [1971] 286 p. illus. (part col.) 26 cm. Bibliography: p. 272. [N8675.K4 1971] 77-135261 20.00
1. Times-Sotheby Index of Fine Art Prices. 2. Art—Prices. I. Title.

REITLINGER, Gerald, 1900- 708.051
The economics of taste. [1st ed.] New York, Holt Rinehart and Winston [1964-65, c1961-63] 2 v. illus. 22 cm. Contents.Contents.—[1] The rise and fall of the picture market, 1760-1960.—[2] The rise and fall of the objets d'art market since 1750. Includes bibliographies. [N8675.R45] 64-21929
1. Art—Prices. 2. Art—Collectors and collecting. I. Title. BIP

Art—Prices—Yearbooks.

INTERNATIONAL art sales, 704.95
v.2, 1962 New York, Crown [1962] illus. (pt. col.) 29cm. annual. Ed.: 1962-G. Savage. 62-11811 7.95
1. Art—Prices—Yearbooks. 2. Art—Yearbook. 3. Collectors and collecting—Yearbooks. I. Savage, George, 1909— ed.

Art, Primitive.

ADAM, Leonhard, 1891-1960 709.011
Primitive art. London, Cassell [dist. New York, Barnes & Noble, 1964, c.1940-1963] 250p. illus. 22cm. (Belle sauvage lib.) Bibl. 64-6042 5.00
1. Art. Primitive. I. Title.

ANDERSON, Richard L., 1944- 709'.01'1
Art in primitive societies / Richard L. Anderson. Englewood Cliffs, N.J. : Prentice-Hall, [1978] p. cm. Includes index. Bibliography: p. [N5311.A52] 78-15512 ISBN 0-13-048108-4 pbk. : 7.95
1. Art, Primitive. I. Title. BIP

THE Art of the stone age; 571.7
forty thousand years of rock art [by] Hans-Georg Bandi [and others] [translated by Ann E. Keep] New York, Crown Publishers [1961] 249 p. illus. (part mounted col.) maps. 24 cm. (Art of the world, non-European cultures; the historical, sociological, and religious backgrounds) Translation of Die Steinzelt. Bibliography: p. 234-237. [N5310.S683] 61-10701
1. Art, Primitive. 2. Cave-drawings. I. Bandi, Hans Georg. II. Series: Art of the world; the historical, sociological, and religious backgrounds

ATTENBOROUGH, David, 1926- 709'.01'1
The tribal eye / David Attenborough. New York : Norton, c1976. 144 p., [12] leaves of plates : ill. (some col.) ; 27 cm. Includes index. Bibliography: p. 142. [N5311.A87 1976] 77-150030 ISBN 0-393-04466-1 : 14.95
1. The Tribal eye. 2. Art, Primitive. 3. Ethnology. I. Title.

BANDI, Hans Georg. 709.01
Art in the ice age, Spanish Levant art, Arctic art [by] Johannes Maringer and Hans-Georg Bandi in execution of a plan by Hugo Obermeier. [Translated by Robert Allen] New York, Praeger [1953] 167 p. illus. (part col.) 32 cm. (Books that matter) Authors' names in reverse order on t.p. of German ed. Bibliography: p. 164-165. [N5310.B3513] 52-13999
1. Art, Primitive. I. Maringer, John. II. Title.

BATTERBERRY, Michael. 709'.01'1
Primitive art, adapted by Michael Batterberry and Ariane Ruskin. Foreword by Howard Conant. New York, McGraw-Hill [1972 i.e. 1973] 192 p. col. illus. 31 cm. (Discovering art series) [N5311.B3] 72-2295 ISBN 0-07-004073-7 9.95
1. Art, Primitive. I. Ruskin, Ariane, joint author. II. Title. III. Series.

BOAS, Franz, 1858-1942 709.01
Primitive art. [New ed., Gloucester, Mass., Peter Smith, 1962, c.1955] 372p. illus. (Dover bk. rebound) Bibl. 4.00
1. Art, Primitive. 2. Literature, Primitive. I. Title.

CELEBONOVIC, Stevan. 571.7
Old stone age [photos.] by Stevan Celebonovic. With a commentary by Geoffrey Grigson. New York, Philosophical Library [1957] 92p. illus., plates. 33cm. (His Art and nature, a series) [GN799.S4C4] 57-59502
1. Art, Primitive. 2. Stone age. I. Grigson, Geoffrey, 1905- II. Title.

CHRISTENSEN, Erwin Ottomar, 1890- 709.01
Primitive art. New York, Crowell [1955] 384 p. illus. (part col.) maps. 29 cm. (A Studio publication) Bibliography: p. 367-376. [N5310.C54] 55-11109
1. Art, Primitive.

DWYER, Jane Powell. 709'.01'1
Traditional art of Africa, Oceania, and the Americas [by] Jane Powell Dwyer and Edward Bridgman Dwyer. San Francisco, Fine Arts Museums [1973] 1 v. (various pagings) illus. (part col.) 26 cm. Includes a bibliography. [N5310.D95] 73-75844
1. Art, Primitive. I. Dwyer, Edward Bridgman, joint author. II. Title. BIP

FRASER, Douglas. 709.011
Primitive art. Garden City, N.Y., Doubleday [1962] 320 p. illus. (part col.) maps. 22 cm. (The Arts of man series) Bibliography: p. 313-316. [N5310.F7] 62-13342
1. Art, Primitive. I. Series.

GIEDION, Sigfried, 1888- 709.011
The eternal present. A contribution on constancy and change. [New York, Bollingen Foundation; distributed by] Pantheon Books [1962-64] 2 v. illus., col. plates, col. maps (part fold.), plans. 27 cm. (Bollingen series, 35.6.1- The A. W. Mellon lectures in the fine arts, 1957) Contents.Contents.—1. The beginnings of art.—The beginnings of architecture. Includes bibliographies. [N5310.G48] 62-7942
1. Art, Primitive. 2. Architecture, Ancient. 3. Art—Psychology. I. Title. II. Series: Bollingen series, 35. III. Series: The A. W. Mellon lectures in the fine arts, 6, pt. 1-2

GRAND, Paule Marie, 1914- 709.011
Prehistoric art; Paleolithic painting and sculpture. Text by P.M. Grand. Greenwich,

Conn., New York Graphic Society [1967] 103 p. illus. (part col.), maps, 28 cm. (The Palias library of art, v. 3) Bibliography: p. 101. [N5310.G65] 67-28690
1. Art, Primitive. I. Title.

GRAZIOSI, Paolo, 1907- 571.7
Palaeolithic art. New York, McGraw-Hill, 1960. xi, 278 p. illus., 306 plates (part col.) maps (part fold.) 35 cm. Translation of L'arte dell'antica eta della pietra, Bibliography: p. [221]-236. [N5310.G663] 59-13435
1. Art, Primitive. I. Title.

HOOPER, James T 709.01
The art of primitive peoples, by J. T. Hooper and C. A. Burland. With 116 photos. of specimens from the Hooper collection by R. H. Bomback. New York, Philosophical Library [1954] 168p. illus., maps. 23cm. Pt. 1 by C. A. Burland; pt. 2 by J. T. Hooper. Bibliography: p.71-72. [N5310] 54-13272
1. Art, Primitive. I. Burland, Cottle Arthur, 1905- II. Title.

LIPS, Julius Ernst, 709.01'1
1895-1950.
The savage hits back, by Julius E. Lips. With an introd. by Bronislaw Malinowski. [Translated from the German by Vincent Benson] New Hyde Park, N.Y., University Books [1966] xxxi, 254 p. illus., ports. 23 cm. "First published in 1937." Bibliography: p. 239-244. [N5310.L62 1966] 66-24909
1. Art, Primitive. I. Title.

MASTERPIECES of 709'.01'107401471
primitive art / photographs by Lee Boltin ; text by Douglas Newton ; foreword by Andre Malaraux ; introduction by Nelson A. Rockefeller. New York : Knopf, 1978. p. cm. (The Nelson A. Rockefeller collection) Bibliography: p. [N5310.M286] 78-54888 ISBN 0-394-50057-1 : 30.00
1. Rockefeller, Nelson Aldrich, 1908- — Art collections. 2. Art, Primitive. I. Boltin, Lee. II. Newton, Douglas, 1920- III. Title. IV. Series.

MOVIUS, Hallam Leonard, 571.7
1907-
Three regions of primitive art [by] Hallam L. Movius, Jr., S. Kooijman [and] George Kubler. New York, Museum of Primitive Art; distributed by University Publishers, 1961. 75p. illus., plates. 23cm. ([New York] Museum of Primitive Art. Lecture series, no. 2) Includes bibliographical references. [N5310.M65] 61-12117
1. Art, Primitive. I. Title. II. Series.
Contents omitted.

MYRON, Robert. 709.01
Prehistoric art. Drawings by John Hopkins. New York, Pitman Pub. Corp. [1965, c1964] 92 p. illus. 23 cm. [N5310.M9] 65-6620
1. Art, Primitive 2. Europe — Antiq. I. Title. **BIP**

MYRON, Robert. 759.01
Prehistoric art. Drawings by John Hopkins. New York, Pitman Pub. Corp. [1964] 46 p. illus., port. 20 x 26 cm. (Pitman $1.00 art books, 52) [N5310.M9] 64-22767
1. Art, Primitive. 2. Europe—Antiquities. I. Title.

NEW York. Museum 709.01107401471
of Primitive Art
Masterpieces in the Museum of Primitive Art: Africa, Oceania, North America, Mexico, Central to South America, Peru. [New York, Author] 1965. 134 (i.e. 159)p. (chiefly maps, plates) 21cm. [N5310.N48] 65-23544 4.95
1. Art, Primitive. 2. Art—New York (City) I. Title.

NEW York. Museum of 709.011
Primitive Art.
Selected works from the collection no. 1 - spring 1957- New York. no. illus. 28cm. [N5310.N5] 57-59142
1. Art, Primitive. 2. Sculpture, Primitive. I. Title.

PIERCE, James Smith. 759.9494
Paul Klee and primitive art / James Smith Pierce. New York : Garland Pub., 1976. 192 p. ; 21 cm. (Outstanding dissertations in the fine arts) Originally presented as the author's thesis, New York University. Bibliography: p. 189-192. [ND588.K5P53 1976] 75-23807 ISBN 0-8240-2001-4 lib.bdg. : 20.00
1. Klee, Paul, 1879-1940. 2. Art, Primitive. I. Title. II. Series. **BIP**

ROY, Claude, 1915- 709.011
The art of the savages. [Translated by Eh. S. Seldon] New York, Arts, inc. [c1958] 105p. illus. (part col.) maps. 19x22cm. (Golden griffin books. Essential encyclopedia, 2) [N5310.R613] 58-13504
1. Art, Primitive. I. Title.

SANDARS, Nancy K. 709'.3
Prehistoric art in europe [by] N. K. Sandars Baltimore, Harmondsworth, Penguin [1975 c1968] xlix, 350 p. 189 plates ill. (incl. 1 col.) maps 27 cm. (Pelican history of art, Z30) Includes index Bibliography: p. 329-332 [N5310.S32] 50.00.
1. Art primative. 2. Europe—Antiq. I. Title.
In slip case. L.C. card no. for original edition: 79-352957 **BIP**

SIEVEKING, Ann. 709.01
The caves of France and northern Spain, a guide, by Ann & Gale Sieveking. Philadelphia, Dufour, 1966 [c1962] 269 p. illus., maps. 23 cm. Bibliography: p. 265. [N5310.S48 1966] 66-12952
1. Art, Primitive. 2. Cave-drawings. 3. France—Antiquities. 4. Spain—Antiquities. I. Sieveking, Gale, joint author. II. Title.

SYMPOSIUM on the Artist 709.011
in Tribal Society, London, 1957.
The artist in tribal society; proceedings of a symposium held at the Royal Anthropological Institute. Edited by Marian W. Smith. New York, Free Press of Glencoe [1961] xiii, 150 p. illus. 23 cm. Bibliography: p. 137-146. [N5310.S96 1957] 62-11760
1. Art, Primitive. 2. Artists. 3. Art — Congresses. I. Smith, Marian Wesley, 1907-1961, ed. II. Title.

WARTENSTEIN Symposium on 759.011
Rock Art of Western Mediterranean and Sahara, Wartenstein Castles, 1960
Prehistoric art of the Western Mediterranean and the Sahara. Ed. by Luis Pericot Garcia, Eduardo Ripoll Perello. Chicago, Aldine [1965, c.1964] xiv, 262p. illus. 26cm. (Viking Fund pubns. in anthropology. n0.39) Various languages. Bibl. [N5310.W3] 65-28748 6.75
1. Art, Primitive. 2. Cave-drawings. 3. Art—Western Mediterranean. 4. Westen Mediterranean—Antiq. 5. Art—Sahara. 6. Sahara—Antiq. I. Perico Garcia, Luis, 1899- ed. II. Ripoll Perello, Eduardo, ed. III. Title. IV. Series.

WINGERT, Paul Stover, 709.011
1900-
Primitive art: its traditions and styles. Cleveland, World [1965, c.1962] 421p. 21cm. (Meridian bks., M185) [N5310.W766] 3.45 pap.,
1. Art, Primitive. I. Title.

WINGERT, Paul Stover, 709.011
1900-
Primitive art: its traditions and styles. New York, Oxford University Press, 1962. 421 p. illus. 22 cm. Includes bibliography. [N5310.W766] 62-20161
1. Art, Primitive. I. Title. **BIP**

Art, Primitive—Addresses, essays, lectures.

ETHNIC and tourist arts 709'.01'1
: cultural expressions from the fourth world / Nelson H. H. Graburn, editor. Berkeley : University of California Press, c1976. xv, 412 p., [4] leaves of plates : ill. (some col.) ; 23 cm. Some of the papers were presented at the Symposium on the Arts of Acculturation at the annual meeting of the American Anthropological Association in San Diego, Calif., Nov. 1970. Includes index. Bibliography: p.[371]-393. [N5311.E73] 74-30521 ISBN 0-520-02949-6 : 19.95
1. Art, Primitive—Addresses, essays, lectures. I. Graburn, Nelson H. H.

FRASER, Douglas, comp. 709.011
The many faces of primitive art; a critical anthology. Englewood Cliffs, N.J., Prentice-Hall [1966] xi, 300 p. illus. 23 cm. Includes bibliographies. [N5310.F68] 66-15402
1. Art, Primitive—Addresses, essays, lectures. I. Title.

GRABURN, Nelson H.H. 709'.01'1
Ethnic and tourist arts : cultural expressions from the fourth world / Nelson H.H. Graburn, Editor. Berkeley : University of California Press, 1979, c1976. xv, 412p., [4] leaves of plates : ill.(col.) ; 22 cm. Includes index. Bibliography: p. [371]-393. [N5311.E73] ISBN 0-520-03842-8 pbk. : 10.95
1. Art. Primitive—Addresses, essays, lectures. I. Title.
L.C. card no. for 1976 hardcover ed.: 74-30521. **BIP**

JOPLING, Carol F., comp. 709.01'1
Art and aesthetics in primitive societies; a critical anthology. Edited by Carol F. Jopling. [1. ed.] New York, E. P. Dutton, 1971. xx, 426 p. illus. 21 cm. Bibliography: p. [425]-426. [N5311.J66 1971] 73-87202 ISBN 0-525-05783-8 9.95
1. Art, Primitive—Addresses, essays, lectures. 2. Aesthetics—Addresses, essays, lectures. I. Title. **BIP**

MEAD, Margaret, 1901- 709.011
Technique & personality [by] Margaret Mead, Junius B. Bird, Hans Himmelheber. New York, Mus. of Primitive Art; dist. N. Y. Graphic, 1963. 110p. illus. (pt. col.) 22cm. (New York Muse. of Primitive Art. Lecture ser., no. 38 Bibl. 63-19321 3.95
1. Art, Primitive—Addresses, essays, lectures. I. Title.
Contents omitted.

OTTEN, Charlotte M., 709.01'1
1915- comp.
Anthropology and art; readings in cross-cultural aesthetics. Edited by Charlotte M. Otten. [1st ed.] Garden City, N.Y., Published for the American Museum of Natural History [by] the Natural History Press, 1971. xvi, 440 p. illus. 22 cm. (American Museum sourcebooks in anthropology) [N5311.O75] 74-103770 8.95
1. Art, Primitive—Addresses, essays, lectures. I. American Museum of Natural History, New York. II. Title. III. Series.

OTTEN, Charlotte M., 709'.01'1
1915- comp.
Anthropology and art : readings in cross-cultural aesthetics / edited by Charlotte M. Otten. Austin : University of Texas Press, [1976], c1971. p. cm. (Texas Press sourcebooks in anthropology ; 10) Reprint of the ed. published for The American Museum of Natural History by the National History Press, Garden City, N.Y., in series: American Museum sourcebooks in anthropology. Includes index. Bibliography: p. [N5311.O75 1976] 75-43853 ISBN 0-292-70313-9 pbk. : 6.95
1. Art, Primitive—Addresses, essays, lectures. I. Title. II. Series. III. Series: American Museum sourcebooks in anthropology.

REDFIELD, Robert 709.011
Aspects of primitive art [by] Robert Redfield, Melville J. Herskovits [and] Gordon F. Ekholm. New York, Museum of Primitive Art; distributed by University Publishers, [c.]1959. 100p. (bibl. notes) illus. 23cm. ([New York] 59-15780 2.75
1. Art, Primitive—Addresses, essays, lectures. I. Title. II. Series.

REDFIELD, Robert, 1897- 709.011
Aspects of primitive art [by] Robert Redfield, Melville J. Herskovits [and] Gordon F. Ekholm. New York, Museum of Primitive Art; distributed by University Publishers, 1959. 100p. illus. 23cm. ([New York] Museum of Primitive Art. Lecture series, no. 1) Includes bibliographies. [N5310.R38] 59-15780
1. Art, Primitive—Addresses, essays, lectures. I. Title. II. Series.
Contentsomitted.

TRADITION and creativity 709.01'1
in tribal art, edited and with an introduction by Daniel P. Biekuyck. Berkeley, University of California [1974, c1969] 236 p. illus. 23 cm. gBased on a lecture series and symposium entitled Individual creativity and tribal norms in non-Western arts, given at the University of California, Los Angeles, December 1965-May 1966. Bibliography: p. 215-224. [N5311.T7] 69-12457 ISBN 0-520-02487-7 4.95 (pbk.)
1. Art, Primitive—Addresses, essays, lectures. I. Biebuyck, Daniel P., 1925- ed. **BIP**

Art, Primitive—Africa.

AFRICAN art and 732'.2'0967
Oceanic art; general editor Francesco Abbate; [translated from the Italian] London, New York, Octopus Books, 1972. 158 p. chiefly 92 col. illus. 20 cm. Translation of Arte dell'Africa e dell'Oceania. Bibliography: p. 154. [N7380.A7813] 72-172111 ISBN 0-7064-0064-X £0.99
1. Art, Primitive—Africa. 2. Art, Primitive—Oceanica. 3. Art—Africa. 4. Art—Oceanica. I. Abbate, Francesco, ed.

Art, Primitive—Africa, West.

LAUDE, Jean. 730'.0967
The arts of Black Africa. Translated by Jean Decock. Berkeley, Univ. of California Pr. [1973 c.1971] xv, 290 p. illus. 21 cm. Translation of Les arts de l'Afrique noire. Bibliography: p. [279]-284. [N7398.L313] 71-125165 ISBN 0-520-02358-7 pap., 3.45
1. Art, Primitive—Africa, West. 2. Negro art—Africa, West. I. Title. **BIP**

LEUZINGER, Elsy. 732'.2'0966
The art of Black Africa. [Translated by R. A. Wilson] Greenwich, Conn., New York Graphic Society [1972] 378 p. illus. (part. col.) 23 cm. Translation of Die Kunst von Schwarz-Afrika. Bibliography: p. 363-369. [N7398.L413 1972b] 70-186806 ISBN 0-8212-0468-8 16.50
1. Art, Primitive—Africa, West. 2. Art—Africa, West. I. Title. **BIP**

LEUZINGER, Elsy. 732'.2'0966
The art of Black Africa / Elsy Leuzinger ; photos. by Isabelle Wettstein & Brigitte Kauf ; [translated by Ann Keep]. New York : Rizzoli, 1977, c1976. 244 p. : ill. (some col.) ; 21 cm. Translation of Die Kunst von Schwarz-Afrika. Includes index. [N7398.L413 1977] 76-62892 ISBN 0-8478-0077-6 : 29.50
1. Art, Primitive—Africa, West. 2. Art—Africa, West. I. Wettstein, Isabelle. II. Kauf, Brigitte. III. Title.

NAYLOR, Penelope, 732'.2'0966
comp.
Black images; the art of West Africa, by Penelope Naylor, with photos. by Lisa Little. [1st ed.] Garden City, N.Y., Doubleday [1973] 95, [1] p. illus. 29 cm. Bibliography: p. [96] [N7398.N38 1973] 72-92233 ISBN 0-385-06025-4 6.95
1. Art, Primitive—Africa, West. 2. Art—Africa, West. I. Little, Lisa, illus. II. Title. **BIP**

Art, Primitive—Africa, West—Exhibitions.

TOPEKA, Kan. 732'.2'0966074018163
Public Library. Gallery of Fine Arts.
Africa! : Creative expression in rural West Africa : [exhibition] presented by the Gallery of Fine Arts, Topeka Public Library. Topeka, Kan. : The Library, 1976. 12 p. : ill. ; 28 cm. Bibliography: p. 11-12. [N7398.T66 1976] 76-375111
1. Art, Primitive—Africa, West—Exhibitions. 2. Art—Africa, West—Exhibitions. 3. Art and religion—Africa, West—Exhibitions. I. Title.

Art, Primitive—America.

PRIMITIVE art : 709'.01'1
pre-Columbian, North American Indian, African, Oceanic / texts by Ferdinand Anton ... [et al.]. New York : H. N. Abrams, 1978. p. cm. Includes index. Contents.—Anton, A. and Dockstader, F. J. Pre-Columbian art and later Indian tribal arts.—Trowell, K. M. and Nevermann, H. African and Oceanic art. Bibliography: p. [N6501.P7 1978] 78-12164 ISBN 0-8109-1459-X : 30.00
1. Art, Primitive—America. 2. America—Antiquities. 3. Art, Primitive—North America. 4. Indians of North America—

Art. 5. Art, Primitive—Africa, West. 6. Art—Africa, West. 7. Art, Primitive—Oceanica. 8. Art—Oceanica. I. Anton, Ferdinand. Pre-Columbian art and later Indian tribal arts. 1978. II. Trowell, Kathleen Margaret. African and Oceanic art. 1978.

Art, Primitive—Benin, Nigeria (Province)

DARK, Philip John Crosskey. 709'.01'1096693
An introduction to Benin art and technology, by Philip J. C. Dark. Oxford, Clarendon Press, 1973. 114, 80 p. illus. 29 cm. Bibliography: p. [83]-85. [N7399.N5D37] 74-158081 ISBN 0-19-817191-9 £8.50
1. Art, Primitive—Benin, Nigeria (Province) 2. Art—Benin, Nigeria (Province) I. Title. BIP

Art, Primitive—Catalogs.

CHICAGO. Art Institute 709.01107417311
Primitive art in the collections of the Art Institute of Chicago [Chicago, Author, Michigan Ave. at Adams St., c.1965] 52p. (chiefly illus., pt. col.) 26cm. Bibl. [N5310.C52] 65-18942 2.50 pap.,
1. Art, Primitive—Catalogs. I. Title.

CHICAGO. Art Institute. 709.01107417311
Primitive art in the collections of the Art Institute of Chicago. [Chicago, 1965] [52] p. (chiefly illus. (part col.)) 26 cm. Bibliography: p. [52] [N5310.C52] 65-18942
1. Art, Primitive — Catalogs. I. Title.

Art, Primitive—Congresses.

PRIMITIVE art & society, edited by Anthony Forge. London, New York, Oxford University Press, for Wenner-Gren Foundation for Anthropological Research, 1973; [i.e. 1974] xxii, 286 p. illus. (part col.) 26 cm. Papers delivered at a symposium sponsored by the Wenner-Gren Foundation for Anthropological Research, held in Burg Wartenstein from 27 June to 5 July 1967. Includes bibliographies. [N5312.P74] 74-165271 ISBN 0-19-212953-8 21.00 709'.01'1
1. Art, Primitive—Congresses. 2. Art and society—Congresses. I. Forge, Anthony, ed. II. Wenner-Gren Foundation for Anthropological Research, New York.

Art, Primitive—Exhibitions.

CALIFORNIA. University. University at Los Angeles. Museum and Laboratories of Ethnic Arts and Technology. 709.01'1
Art of New Guinea: Sepik, Maprik, and highlands; an exhibition arr. by the Museum and Laboratories of Ethnic Arts and Technology, UCLA, and the Ethnic Arts Council. Los Angeles, 1967. 75 p. illus. 28 cm. The exhibition was held at the Ethnic Art Galleries, University of California, Los Angeles, Nov.-Dec. 1967. Bibliography: p. 74-75. [N7410.C3] 78-270960
1. Art, Primitive—Exhibitions. 2. Art, Primitive—New Guinea. I. California. University. University at Los Angeles. Ethnic Art Galleries. II. California. University. University at Los Angeles. Ethnic Arts Council. III. Title.

CALIFORNIA. University. University at Los Angeles. Museum and Laboratories of Ethnic Arts and Technology. 709.01'1
The George G. Frelinghuysen collection at UCLA; objects from Africa, Indonesia, the South Seas, and Asia. [Los Angeles? 1968?] 35 p. illus. 29 cm. Catalog of the collection, part of which was exhibited May 5-June 30, 1968, in the Ethnic Art Galleries, University of California, Los Angeles. [N5311.C25] 68-66150
1. Frelinghuysen, George G.—Art collections. 2. Art, Primitive—Exhibitions. I. Title.

CALIFORNIA. University. University at Los Angeles. Museum and Laboratories of Ethnic Arts and Technology. 730'.074'019494
Ralph C. Altman memorial exhibition. [Los Angeles, 1968] 35 p. illus. 29 cm. Catalog of the exhibition held April 8-June 30, 1968, in the Ethnic Art Galleries, University of California, Los Angeles. "List of articles, exhibition catalogues, and book reviews by Ralph C. Altman": p. 35. [N5311.C3] 68-66149
1. Art, Primitive—Exhibitions. I. Altman, Ralph C. II. Title.

DALLAS. Museum of Fine Arts. 732'.2
Arts of Oceania. [Dallas, 1970?] [63] p. illus., maps. 26 cm. Catalog of the exhibition held Oct. 10-Nov. 29, 1970, at the Dallas Museum of Fine Arts. Bibliography: p. [62] [N7410.D28] 71-18951
1. Art, Primitive—Exhibitions. 2. Art, Primitive—Oceanica. I. Title.

ELSASSER, Albert B. 708.194'67
Treasures of the Lowie Museum. An exhibition of the Robert H. Lowie Museum of Anthropology, University of California, Berkeley, January 2-October 27, 1968. Catalogue text by Albert B. Elsasser. [Berkeley, University of California, 1968] 95 p. illus. (part col.) 24 cm. "University of California centennial year, 1968." [GN37.C283E35] 68-63029
I. California. University. Robert H. Lowie Museum of Anthropology. II. Title.

LOS Angeles Co., Calif. Otis Art Institute, Los Angeles. 709.01'1
Contemporary New Guinea art. Los Angeles [1971] [31] p. illus. 23 cm. Catalogue of an exhibition held Jan. 16-Feb. 28, 1971, with an introductory essay by U. Beier. [N7411.N4L6] 79-198128
1. Art, Primitive—Exhibitions. 2. Art—New Guinea. I. Beier, Ulli. II. Title.

NEW York (City). Museum of Primitive Art. 709.01'1
Art of Oceania, Africa, and the Americas, from the Museum of Primitive Art; an exhibition at the Metropolitan Museum of Art, May 10-August 17, 1969. [New York] Metropolitan Museum of Art [1970?] 1 v. (unpaged) illus. (part col.), maps. 23 cm. [N5311.N4] 73-77259
1. Art, Primitive—Exhibitions. I. New York (City). Metropolitan Museum of Art. II. Title.

NEW York (City). Museum of Primitive Art. 709.01'1'07401471
The Robert and Lisa Sainsbury Collection. [New York]; Distributed by the New York Graphic Society [Greenwich, Conn.] 1963. [40] p. (chiefly illus.) 28 cm. Catalogue of an exhibition held at the museum May 15-Sept. 8, 1963. [N5310.N45] 71-19112
1. Sainsbury, Robert J.—Art collections. 2. Sainsbury, Lisa—Art collections. 3. Art, Primitive—Exhibitions. I. Title.

NEW York. Museum of Primitive Art. 709.011
The John and Dominique deMenil collection. New York Distributed by University Publishers, 1962. [64] p. illus. 29 cm. "A representative selection from the objects in the exhibition." [N5310.N46] 63-2038
1. Art, Primitive — Exhibitions. 2. Art — Private collections. I. DeMenil, John. II. Title.

WARDWELL, Allen. 732'.2'09955
The art of the Sepik River. Catalogue by Allen Wardwell. [Chicago, Art Institute of Chicago, 1971] 100 p. illus. (part col.) 26 cm. Exhibition held Oct. 16-Nov. 28, 1971, at the Art Institute of Chicago. Bibliography: p. 98-99. [N7411.S4W37] 73-176329
1. Art, Primitive—Exhibitions. 2. Art, Primitive—Sepik Valley. 3. Art—Sepik Valley. I. Chicago. Art Institute. II. Title.

Art, Primitive—New Ireland (Island)

LEWIS, Phillip Harold, 1922- 709'.01'1
The social context of art in northern New Ireland [by] Phillip H. Lewis. [Chicago] Field Museum of Natural History, 1969. iv, 186 p. illus., maps. 24 cm. (Field Museum of Natural History. Publication 1069.) (Fieldiana: anthropology, v. 58) Based on the author's thesis published in 1966, University of Chicago. Bibliography: p. 177-182. [GN2.F4 vol. 58] 71-83764
1. Art, Primitive—New Ireland (Island) 2. Art—New Ireland (Island) 3. Ethnology—New Ireland (Island) I. Title. II. Series. III. Series: Field Museum of Natural History Chicago. Publication 1069.

Art, Primitive—Oceanica.

WINGERT, Paul Stover, 1900- 709.01'1
An outline of Oceanic art, by Paul S. Wingert. Cambridge, Mass., University Prints [1970] 39 p. maps (on cover) 19 cm. "A supplement to University Prints series N, section II, Oceanic art (125 plates)" In part based on the author's Art of the South Pacific islands. [N7410.W52] 70-19842 1.00 (pbk.)
1. Art, Primitive—Oceanica. 2. Art—Oceanica. I. University Prints, Boston. The University Prints series N. Section II: Oceanic art. II. Title.

Art, Primitive—Papua-New Guinea (Ter.)

SERRA Guell, Eudaldo, 1911- 709'.01'109953
The art of Papua and New Guinea / Eudald Serra & Alberto Folch. New York : Rizzoli, [1977, c1976] 214 p. : ill. (some col.) ; 21 cm. Translation of Arte de Papua y Nueva Guinea. [N7411.P3S4713 1977] 76-62890 ISBN 0-8478-0076-8 : 29.50
1. Art, Primitive—Papua-New Guinea (Ter.) 2. Art—Papua-New Guinea (Ter.) I. Folch Rusinol, Alberto, joint author. II. Title. BIP

Art, Primitive—Sepik Valley.

MAKSIC, Sava. 730'.09955
Primitive art of New Guinea, Sepik River Basin [by] Sava Maksic and Paul Meskil. Worcester, Mass., Davis Publications [1973] 95 p. illus. 24 cm. [N7411.S4M34] 73-87241 ISBN 0-87192-054-9 8.95
1. Art, Primitive—Sepik Valley. 2. Art—Sepik Valley. I. Meskil, Paul, 1923- joint author. II. Title.

Art—Private collections.

**ARTHUR B. Davies; essays on his art* [Edited by Martin S. and Diane L. Ackerman]. New York, Arco, 1974. 1v. (unpaged) illus 31 cm. (Arco collectors' series) Essays by Dwight Williams [and others] [N5210] 74-76369 ISBN 0-668-03489-0 8.95 (pbk.). 741.9
1. Davies, Arthur B. 2. Art—Private collections. 3. Art criticism. I. Ackerman, Martin S. ed. II. Ackerman, Diane L. joint ed. III. Williams, Dwight

BEHRENS, Walter Lionel. 708.1
W. L. Behrens collection; catalogue, by Henri L. Joly. New York. Paragon Book Reprint Corp., 1966. 4 v. illus. 32 cm. "An unaltered and unabridged reprint of the original edition published in 1912." Contents.-- pt. 1. Netsuke -- pt. 2. Lacquer and Inro. -- pt. 3. Swordfittings, tsuba metal, tsuba and swords. -- pt. 4. Buddhistic section, Chinese antiques, Chinese and Japanese miscellanea. [N5220.B39] 66-289910
1. Art — Private collections. 2. Art, Oriental. I. Joly, Henri L. II. Title.

BOSTON. Institute of Contemporary Art. 708.1446
Selections from the Dana collection; a memorial exhibition, Lester H. Dana, 1901-1962. Boston [1962] [54]p. illus. 19cm. (Its Exhibition catalog 1/1962) Exhibition to be held Oct. 17 to Nov. 11, 1962. [N5020.B6127 1/1962] 62-52589
1. Art—Private collections. 2. Art—Exhibitions. 3. Art, Modern—20th cent. I. Dana, Lester H., 1901-1962. II. Title. III. Title: The Dana collection. IV. Series: Boston. Institute of Contemporary Art. Exhibition 1/1962

CALIFORNIA Palace of the Legion of Honor, San Francisco. 709.04
The collection of Mr. & Mrs. William Goetz, California Palace of the Legion of Honor, Lincoln Park, San Francisco, April 18-May 31, 1959. [San Francisco, Author, 1959] [70]p. 68 illus. 28cm. 59-4599 2.00 pap.,
1. Art—Private collections. 2. Art, French—Exhibitions. I. Goetz, William. II. Title.

COLIN, Ralph F. 708.13
The Colin collection; paintings, watercolors, drawings and sculpture collected by Mr. & Mrs. Ralph F. Colin, Pamela T. Colin & Ralph F. Colin, Jr. New York 22 M. Knoedler & Co., Inc., 14 E. 57 St. [1960] 1 v. (unpaged, chiefly illus. (part col.)) 28cm. Catalog prepared by Ralph F. Colin. 'Exhibited at the Knoedler Gallery in New York from April 12 to May 14, 1960.' 60-9553 10.00
1. Art—Private collections. 2. Art—Exhibitions. I. Title.

COOPER, Douglas, 1911- ed. 708
Great family collections. Edited and with an introd. by Douglas Cooper. New York, Macmillan [1965] 304 p. illus. (part col.) 33 cm. [N5240.C6 1965] 65-10731
1. Art—Private collections. 2. Art—Collectors and collecting. 3. Art—Europe. I. Title.

COOPER, Douglas, 1911- ed. 708
Great private collections. Introd. by Kenneth Clark. New York, Macmillan [1963] 302p. illus. (pt. col.) ports. (pt. col.) facsims. 33cm. 63-12758 19.95; after Dec. 31, 25.00
1. Art—Private collections. 2. Art—Collectors and collecting. I. Title.

CORNELL University. Andrew Dickson White Museum of Art. 338.4'3745'10973
The Dr. and Mrs. Milton Lurie Kramer collection, on extended loan from Mrs. Helen Kroll Kramer, December 1966, Andrew Dickson White Museum of Art, Cornell University. [Ithaca, Office of University Publications, Cornell University, c1966] 44 p. illus. 22 x 23 cm. [N5220.K67] 66-30565
1. Art—Private collections. 2. Art—Exhibitions. I. Kramer, Milton Lurie, 1906-1965. II. Kramer, Helen Kroll. III. Title: Kramer collection.

DETROIT. Institute of Arts 708.17434
The W. Hawkins Ferry collection. [Detroit] 1966. 1 v (unpaged) illus. (pt. col.) 25cm. [N5220.F44] 66-27963 1.00 pap.,
1. Art—Private collections. I. Ferry, W. Hawkins. II. Title.

GOVERNOR Rockefeller's collection from the Albany mansion; [exhibition at] Wollman Hall, New School Art Center, New York City, May 4th-31st, 1967. [New York, New School Art Center, 1967] 41 p. illus. 21 x 26 cm. (American private collections.) [N5020.A37] 67-68035 708'.147'43
1. Art—Private collections. 2. Art—Exhibitions. I. Rockefeller, Nelson Aldrich, 1908- II. New York. New School for Social Research. New School Art Center.

HANLEY, T. Edward. 708.17471
Selections from the collection of Dr. and Mrs. T. Edward Hanley. [Exhibition], Gallery of Modern Art Including the Huntington Hartford Collection, 3 January-12 March, 1967, Philadelphia Museum of Art, 6 April-28 May, 1967. [New York, Gallery for Modern Art Including the Huntington Hartford Collection, Foundation for Modern Art, 1967] 69 p. illus. (part col.) 24 cm. [N5220.H282] 67-1052
1. Art—Private collections. I. New York. Gallery of Modern Art Including the Huntington Hartford Collection. II. Philadelphia Museum of Art. III. Title.

HERRINGTON, Arthur William Sidney, 1891- 750.74
The collection of Mr. and Mrs. A. W. S. Herrington of Indianapolis, Indiana: European and American paintings and graphic art; European, American, and Oriental decorative arts; an exhibition, Sept. 27 through Oct. 25, 1964, Krannert Art Mus., Coll. of Fine and Applied Arts, Univ. of Ill., Champaign [Champaign, Krannert Art Mus., Coll. of Fine and

Applied Arts. Univ. of Ill., c.1964] 1v. (unpaged) illus. 24cm. [N5220.H514] 64-8499 1.00 pap.,
1. Art—Private collections. 2. Art—Exhibitions. I. Herrington, Nell Ray (Clarke) II. Illinois. University. Krannert Art Museum. III. Title.

HERRINGTON, Arthur William Sidney, 1891- 750.74
The collection of Mr. and Mrs. A. W. S. Herrington of Indianapolis, Indiana: European and American paintings and graphic art; European, American, and Oriental decorative arts; an exhibition, September 27 through October 25, 1964, Krannert Art Museum, College of Fine and Applied Arts, University of Illinois, Champaign. [Champaign] Krannert Art Museum, College of Fine and Applied Arts, University of Illinois, 1964] 1 v. (unpaged) illus. 24 cm. [N5220.H514] 64-8499
1. Art — Private collections. 2. Art — Exhibitions. I. Herrington, Nell Ray (Clarke) II. Illinois. University. Krannert Art Museum. III. Title.

KNOEDLER (M.) and Company, inc. 708.147
Modern painting, drawing & sculpture, collected by Louise and Joseph Pulitzer, Jr. An exhibition: Knoedler and Company. New York, April 9 to May 4; Fogg Art Museum, Cambridge. May 16 to September 15, 1957. [Catalogue by Charles Scott Chetham. New York, 1957] 101p. 64 plates. 28cm. Includes bibliographical references. [N5220.K57] 58-12923
1. Art—Private collections. 2. Art—Exhibitions. I. Pulitzer, Louise (Vauclain) II. Chetham, Charles Scott. III. Harvard University. William Hayes Fogg Art Museum. IV. Title.

NEW York. Museum of Modern Art. 708.1471
The James Thrall Soby collection of works of art pledged or given to the Museum of Modern Art. Exhibited for the benefit of the museum's library at M. Knoedler and Company, Inc., New York, Feb. 1 to Feb. 25, 1961, as a contribution to the museum's 30th anniversary fund. Garden City, N. Y., Dist., Doubleday [c.1961] 68p. illus., col. plates. Bibl. 25cm. 61-9658 1.50 pap.,
1. Art—Private collections. 2. Art—Exhibitions. I. Soby, James Thrall, 1906- II. Knoedler (M.) and Company, inc. III. Title.

PULITZER, Louise (Vauclain) 708.17866
Modern painting, drawing & sculpture, collected by Louise and Joseph Pulitzer, Jr. [Catalogue by Charles Scott Chetham. Cambridge, Mass., Fogg Art Museum, 1958] 2v. (327p.) 128 plates. 28cm. Vol. 1 is a second printing of the catalogue which accompanied an exhibition of the collection at Knoedler and Company, New York, Apr. 9 to May 4 and Fogg Art Museum, Cambridge, May 16 to Sept. 15, 1957: v. 2, catalogue describing other items in the collection. by C. S. Chetham, with contributions by Agnes Mongan, and others. Includes bibliographical references. [N5220.P744] 59-2336
1. Art—Private collections. 2. Art—Exhibitions. I. Pulitzer, Joseph, 1913- II. Chetham, Charles Scott. III. Knoedler (M.) and Company, inc. IV. Title.

ST. Louis. City Art Museum. 709.034
Works of art of the nineteenth and twentieth centuries, collected by Louise and Joseph Pulitzer, Jr. [St. Louis? 1968] [27] p. illus. 28 cm. Catalog of an exhibition held Jan. 23 to Mar. 24, 1968, at the City Art Museum of St. Louis. [N5220.P745] 68-21068
1. Art—Private collections. 2. Art, Modern—19th century—Exhibitions. 3. Art, Modern—2oth century—Exhibitions. I. Pulitzer, Louise (Vauclain) II. Pulitzer, Joseph, 1913- III. Title.

SCHUMACHER, Frederick W 708.171
The Frederick W. Schumacher collection, catalogued by William R. Valentiner with the assistance of Paul Wescher. Columbus, Ohio, 1955. xx, 188p. illus., port. 30cm. Includes bibliographical references. [N5220.S28] 56-3164
1. Art—Private collections. 2. Paintings—Private collections. I. Valentiner, Wilheim Reinhold, 1880- ed. II. Title.

SHINN, Earl, 1837-1886. 338.4'3745'10973
Mr. Vanerbilt's house and collection. DescribedbyEdward Strahan [pseud.] Japan ed. Boston, G. Barrie [c1883-84] 4v. illus., plates (part col.) 65cm. 'Five hundred copies . . . have been printed . . . No. 35.; [N5220.S54] 54-48277
1. Vanderbilt, William Henry, 2. Art—Private collections. 3. Art—New York (City) I. Title.

U.S. National Gallery of Art. 707.4
Exhibition of the Marie and Averell Harriman collection, April 15 -- May 14, 1961. [Catalogue] Washington [1961] 63 p. (chiefly illus.) 26 cm. Erratum slip inserted. [N5220.H29] 61-61252
1. Art — Private collections. 2. Art — Exhibitions. I. Harriman, Marie. II. Harriman, William Averell 1891- III. Title.

WALKER Art Center, Minneapolis. 708.176579
John and Dorothy Rood collection. John Rood sculpture collection at the University of Minnesota. [Huldah Curl, editor of the catalogue, and director of the exhibition held at] Walker Art Center, January 10-February 7, 1960, University Gallery, University of Minnesota, February 11-March 21, 1960. [Minneapolis, 1959] unpaged. illus. 24 cm. Lists some paintings not in this exhibition. [N5220.R6] 61-20255
1. Art — Private collections. 2. Art — Exhibitions. I. Minnesota. University. University Gallery. II. Rood, John, 1902- III. Rood, Dorothy (Bridgman) 1890- IV. Title.

WRIGHTSMAN, Charles B. 708'.147'1
The Wrightsman collection, by F. J. B. Watson. [New York] Metropolitan Museum of Art; distributed by New York Graphic Society, Greenwich, Conn. [1966- v. illus., col. plates. 29 cm. "Catalogue of the collection of Mr. and Mrs. Charles B. Wrightsman." Contents.Contents.—v. 1. Furniture.—v. 2. Furniture. Gilt bronze and mounted porcelain. Carpets.—v. 3. Furniture, gold boxes, by F. J. B. Watson. Porcelain boxes, by C. C. Dauterman.—v. 4. Porcelain, by C. C. Dauterman. Bibliography: v. 2, p. 596-635. [N5220.W88] 66-10181 ISBN 0-87099-008-X (set, v. 1-5)
1. Art—Private collections. 2. Art, French—Catalogs. I. Wrightsman, Jayne. II. Watson, Francis John Bagott, 1907- III. Dauterman, Carl Christian, 1908- IV. Title.

YALE University. Art Gallery. 707.4
Two modern collectors: Susan Morse Hilles, Richard Brown Baker; a loan exhibition, May 23-September 1, 1963, Yale Art Gallery. [New Haven, Conn., Author, 1963] 63p. illus. 20cm. 63-4927 apply
1. Art—Private collections. 2. Art—Exhibitions. I. Hilles, Susan Morse. II. Baker, Richard Brown. III. Title.

Art—Private collections—Great Britain.

LLOYD, Reginald J., 1926- 760'.092'4
Paintings, drawings and monotypes in private collections / [by] R. J. Lloyd ; [compiled by Louise MacMillan]. [Barnstaple] : [Porcupines], [1976] [105] p. : of ill., ports. ; 30 cm. [N6797.L58M3] 77-364177 ISBN 0-85531-010-3 : £2.50
1. Lloyd, Reginald J., 1926- 2. Art—Private collections—Great Britain. I. MacMillan, Louise. II. Title.

Art—Private collections—New York (City)

NEW York (City). New School for Social Research. New School Art Center. 707'.4
Museum leaders collect; selections from the private collections of ten New York museum directors and curators. [Exhibition] April 24-May 27, 1970. New York [1970] 43 p. illus., ports. 26 cm. [N5215.N4] 79-22205
1. Art—Private collections—New York (City) 2. Art—Exhibitions. I. Title.

Art—Protection.

MASON, Donald L. 069'.54
The fine art of art security / by Donald L. Mason. New York : Van Nostrand Reinhold Co., [1979] p. cm. Includes index. [N463.M37] 78-14894 ISBN 0-442-25118-1 : 15.00
1. Art—Protection. 2. Art museums—Security measures. 3. Art galleries, Commercial—Security measures. I. Title.

Art—Providence.

RHODE Island School of Design, Providence. Museum. 708.145
Treasures in the Museum of Art, Rhode Island School Design. Providence, 1956. unpaged (chiefly illus.) 23cm. [N714.P7R53] 57-19183
1. Art—Providence. I. Title.

RHODE Island School of Design, Providence. Museum of Art. 708.145
Treasures in the Museum of Art, Rhode Island School of Design. Providence, 1956. unpaged (chiefly illus.) 23 cm. [N714.P7 53] 57-19185
1. Art—Providence. I. Title.

Art — Psychology.

ARNHEIM, Rudolf. 701'.15
Art and visual perception : a psychology of the creative eye / Rudolf Arnheim. New version, expanded and rev. ed. Berkeley : University of California Press, [1974] x, 508 p., [2] leaves of plates : ill. ; 23 cm. Includes index. Bibliography: p. [487]-501. [N71.A67 1974] 73-87587 ISBN 0-520-02327-7 : 14.95 ISBN 0-520-02613-6 pbk. : 5.95
1. Art—Psychology. 2. Visual perception. I. Title.

ARNHEIM, Rudolf. 701.15
Toward a psychology of art; collected essays. Berkeley, University of California Press, 1966. viii, 369 p. illus. (part col.) 27 cm. Includes bibliographies. [N70.A69] 66-10692
1. Art—Psychology. 2. Perception. I. Title. **BIP**

BERLYNE, D. E. 701'.17
Studies in the new experimental aesthetics: steps toward an objective psychology of aesthetic appreciation, edited by D. E. Berlyne. Washington, Hemisphere Pub. Corp., 1974. viii, 340 p. illus. 24 cm. "A Halsted Press book." Includes bibliographies. [N71.B42] 74-13600 ISBN 0-470-07039-0 14.95
1. Art—Psychology. 2. Aesthetics. I. Title.

BLOM, Dorothea (Johnson) 1911- 701.15
The prophetic element in modern art [by] Dorothea Blom. [Wallingford, Pa.] Pendle Hill Publications [1966] 32 p. 19 cm. (Pendle Hill pamphlet 148) Bibliography: p. 32. [N71.B55] 66-28100
1. Art—Psychology. 2. Art and society. I. Title.

BRADLEY, William, 1934- 701
Art: magic, impulse, and control; a guide to viewing. Englewood Cliffs, N.J., Prentice-Hall [1973] x, 182 p. illus. 22 cm. Includes bibliographical references. [N71.B69] 72-8963 ISBN 0-13-046664-6 8.95
1. Art—Psychology. 2. Visual perception. I. Title.
pap 4.95.

BURNHAM, Jack, 1931- 701.15
The structure of art, by Jack Burnham. Assisted by Charles Harper and Judith Benjamin Burnham. New York, G. Braziller [1971] xii, 195 p. illus., facsims. 25 cm. Bibliography: p. 183-189. [N71.B86 1971] 75-143195 ISBN 0-8076-0596-4 8.95
1. Art—Psychology. 2. Form (Aesthetics) I. Harper, Charles, joint author. II. Burnham, Judith Benjamin, joint author. III. Title. **BIP**

CARPENTER, Patrick. 701'.1
Art and ideas; an approach to art appreciation [by] Patrick Carpenter & William Graham. London, Mills & Boon, 1971. viii, 220 p. 12 plates, illus. (some col.) 25 cm. [N71.C3 1971] 72-178941 ISBN 0-263-51524-9
1. Art—Psychology. 2. Art—Philosophy. I. Graham, William, 1923- joint author. II. Title.
Distributed by Transatlantic Arts, Levittown, N.Y., for 15.00.

CHILD, Irvin Long, 1915- 152.1'4
A study of esthetic judgment. [New Haven? Conn.] 1962. 126 l. 29 cm. "Cooperative research project no. 669 ... supported by the Cooperative Research Program of the Office of Education." Includes bibliographies. [N71.C5] 64-60400
1. Art — Psychology. I. Title.

CLIFFORD, Derek Plint. 701.1
Art and understanding; towards a humanist aesthetic [by] Derek Clifford. Greenwich, Conn., New York Graphic Society [1968] xv, 168 p. illus., 8 col. plates. 25 cm. [N71.C58] 69-12308 11.50
1. Art—Psychology. 2. Art criticism. I. Title.

DALI, Salvador, 1904- 701.15
Open letter to Salvador Dali. [Translated from the French by Harold J. Salemson. New York, J. H. Heineman, 1968, c1967] 155 p. 20 cm. (Open letter series) (A Heineman paperback, H11.) Translation of Lettre ouverte a Salvador Dali. [N71.D313] 68-10243
1. Art—Psychology. I. Title. **BIP**

DUBUFFET, Jean, 1901- 709'.24
Dubuffet and the anticulture. [Edited by Richard L. Feigen] New York, R. L. Feigen & Co. [1969] 79 p. (chiefly illus.) 26 cm. "Jean Dubuffet: Anticultural positions, facsimile of the artist's manuscript notes for a lecture at the Arts Club of Chicago on December 20, 1951." (22 leaves inserted) "[Exhibition] November 25, 1969-January 3, 1970, for the benefit of the Harlem Preparatory School." [N6490.D78] 75-110252
1. Art—Psychology. 2. Art, Modern—20th century—Exhibitions. I. Feigen, Richard L., ed. II. Title.

EHRENZWEIG, Anton, 1908-1966. 701.15
The hidden order of art; a study in the psychology of artistic imagination. Berkeley, University of California Press, 1967. xiv, 306 p. illus. 23 cm. Bibliography: p. [297]-299. [N71.E5 1967] 67-20443
1. Art—Psychology. 2. Imagination. I. Title. **BIP**

EHRENZWEIG, Anton, 1908-1966. 701.15
The hidden order of art : a study in the psychology of artistic imagination / Anton Ehrenzweig. Berkeley : University of California Press 1976c1967. xiv, 306p. : ill. ; 23 cm. (California library reprint series) Includes index. Bibliography: p. [297]-299. [N71E5] 16.50
1. Art-Psychology. 2. Imagination. I. Title.
L. C. card no. for original ed. 67-20443.

FELDMAN, Edmund Burke. 701
Art as image and idea. Englewood Cliffs, N.J., Prentice-Hall [1967] 511 p. illus. (part col.) 25 cm. Rev. ed. published in 1972 under title: Varieties of visual experience. Bibliography: p. [499]-501. [N71.F4] 67-10232
1. Art—Psychology. 2. Composition (Art) I. Title.

FELDMAN, Edmund Burke. 701
Varieties of visual experience. Basic ed. New York, H. N. Abrams [1973] 504 p. illus. (part col.) 27 cm. Abridged ed. of the work published in 1967 under title: Art as image and idea. Bibliography: p. 487-489. [N71.F42 1973] 72-12661 ISBN 0-8109-0535-3
1. Art—Psychology. 2. Composition (Art) I. Title. **BIP**

FELDMAN, Edmund Burke. 701
Varieties of visual experience. Basic ed. Englewood Cliffs, N.J., Prentice-Hall [1973] 504 p. illus. (part col.) 27 cm. Abridged ed. of the work published in 1967 under title: Art as image and idea.

Bibliography: p. 487-489. [N71.F42 1973b] 72-12663 ISBN 0-13-940593-3 8.95
1. Art—Psychology. 2. Composition (Art) I. Title.

FRY, Edwin Maxwell, 1899- 746.3'9'24
Tapestry and architecture: an address given at the opening of an exhibition of tapestries by Miriam Sacks at the Ben Uri Gallery October 22, 1969 by Maxwell Fry. Richmond, Keepsake P., 1970. [8] p. illus. 25 cm. [N71.F68] 75-529877
1. Art—Psychology. I. Title.

GOMBRICH, Ernst Hans Josef, 1909- 701.15
Art and illusion; a study in the psychology of pictorial representation. [New York] Pantheon Books [1960] xxxi, 466 p. illus. (part col.) 26 cm. (Bollingen series, 35. The A. W. Mellon lectures in the fine arts, 5) Bibliographical references included in "Notes" (p. [397]-439) [N70.G615 1960] 59-13517
1. Art—Psychology. I. Title. II. Series: The Bollingen series, 35. III. Series: The A. W. Mellon lectures in the fine arts, 5. BIP

GOMBRICH, Ernst Hans Josef, 1909- 701.15
Art and illusion; a study in the psychology of pictorial representation [by] E. H. Gombrich. [2d ed., 3d print. Princeton, N.J.] Princeton University Press [1969] xxxi, 466 p. illus. (part col.) 26 cm. (Bollingen series, 35. The A. W. Mellon lectures in the fine arts, 5) Includes bibliographical references. [N70.G615 1969] 71-12016
1. Art—Psychology. I. Title. II. Series: Bollingen series, 35. III. Series: The A. W. Mellon lectures in the fine arts, 5

GOMBRICH, Ernst Hans Josef, 1909- 701'.15
Art and illusion; a study in the psychology of pictorial representation [by] E. H. Gombrich. [2d ed., rev. New York, Bollingen Foundation, distributed by] Patheon Books [1961] xxxi, 466 p. illus. (part col.) 27 cm. (Bollingen series, 35. A. W. Mellon lectures in the fine arts, 5) Bibliography: p. [440]-441. [N71.G63 1961] 74-160497
1. Art—Psychology. I. Title. II. Series: Bollingen series, 35. III. Series: The A. W. Mellon lectures in the fine arts, 5.

GOMBRICH, Ernst Hans Josef, 1909- 701'.17
Art, perception and reality [by] E. H. Gombrich, Julian Hochberg [and] Max Black. Baltimore, Johns Hopkins University Press [1972] x, 132 p. illus. 24 cm. (The Alvin and Fanny Blaustein Thalheimer lectures, 1970) Includes bibliographies. [N71.G64] 76-186514 ISBN 0-8018-1354-9 7.50
1. Art—Psychology. 2. Visual perception. I. Hochberg, Julian E. II. Black, Max, 1909- III. Title. IV. Series. BIP

HASTIE, W. Reid. 709
Encounter with art [by] Reid Hastie [and] Christian Schmidt. New York, McGraw-Hill [1969] xiii, 463 p. illus. (part col.) 26 cm. Bibliography: p. 447-452. [N7430.H36] 69-13608
1. Art—Psychology. 2. Art—Technique. 3. Art appreciation. I. Schmidt, Christian, 1927- joint author. II. Title.

KHATCHADOURIAN, Haig. 701.1
The concept of art. New York, New York University Press, 1971. xi, 289 p. 24 cm. Includes bibliographical references. [N71.K48] 70-145512 ISBN 0-8147-4553-9
1. Art—Psychology. 2. Art—Philosophy. I. Title. BIP

KRIS, Ernst, 1900- 701.1
Psychoanalytic explorations in art. New York, International Universities Press [1952] 358 p. plates. 24 cm. Bibliography: p. 321-341. [N70.K84] 52-10509
1. Art—Psychology. 2. Psychoanalysis. I. Title. BIP

KRIS, Ernst, 1900- 701.15
Psychoanalytic explorations in art. New York, Schocken Books [1964, c1952] 358 p. illus., ports. 21 cm. (Schocken paperbacks) "SB76." Bibliography:p. [319]-343. [N70.K84] 64-16947
1. Art — Psychology. 2. Psychoanalysis. I. Title.

LINDERMAN, Earl W. 704.94
Invitation to vision; ideas and imaginations for art [by] Earl W. Linderman. Dubuque, Iowa, W. C. Brown Co. [1967] xii, 264 p. illus. 22 x 28 cm. (Brown art series) Bibliography: p. 259-261. [N71.L59] 66-30355
1. Art—Psychology. 2. Imagination. 3. Perception. I. Title.

MALRAUX, Andre, 1901- 701.15
The voices of silence [New ed.] Tr. by Stuart Gilbert. Garden City, N.Y., Doubleday [1963] 661p. illus. (pt. col.) 23cm. Based on the author's Psychologie de l'art. 15.00
1. Art—Psychology. 2. Art—Philosophy. I. Malraux, Andre, 1901- Psychology de l'art. II. Title.

MALRAUX, Andre, 1901- 701.15
The voices of silence. Tr. from French by Stuart Gilbert, Francis Price. [1st ed. in the U.S.] Garden City, N.Y., Doubleday, 1967- v. illus. 17cm. Tr. of Les Voix du silence. Contents.[1] Museum without walls [N70M3362] 67-15679 4.95
1. Art—Psychology. 2. Art—Philosophy, I. Title. BIP

MALRAUX, Andre, 1901-1976. 701.15
The voices of silence. Translated by Stuart Gilbert. Garden City, N. Y., Doubleday, 1953. 661 p. illus. (part col.) 23 cm. Based on the author's Psychologie de l'art. [N70.M336] 53-9134
1. Art—Psychology. 2. Art—Philosophy. I. Malraux, Andre, 1901-1976. Psychologie de l'art. II. Title.

MANDEL, David. 701
Changing art, changing man. New York, Horizon Press [1967] 162 p. 24 cm. Bibliography: p. 161-162. [N71.M26] 67-27909
1. Art—Psychology. 2. Art and society. I. Title.

MASTERS, Robert E. L. 701.15
Psychedelic art [by] Robert E. L. Masters, Jean Houston. With contributions by Barry N. Schwartz, Stanley Krippner. Ed., designed & prod. by Marshall Lee. New York, Grove [1968] 190p. illus. 29cm. (Balance House bk.) Bibl. [N71.M728] 67-31583 15.00
1. Art—Psychology. 2. Hallucinogenic drugs. I. Houston, Jean. joint author. II. Title.

MEIER, Norman Charles, 1893- ed. 701'.15
Studies in the psychology of art, edited by Norman C. Meier. Vol. III. New York, Arno Press, 1973. viii, 158 p. illus. 23 cm. (Classics in psychology) Originally published in 1939 as part of a 3 volume work. Vol. 3 of that ed. was published by American Psychological Association, Columbus, Ohio, and was issued as Psychological monographs, v. 51, no. 5, whole no. 231, and as University of Iowa studies in psychology, no. 23. Includes bibliographies. [N71.M42 1973] 73-2977 ISBN 0-405-05149-2 9.00
1. Art—Psychology. I. Title. II. Series. III. Series: Iowa. University. University of Iowa studies in psychology, no. 23. IV. Series: Psychological monographs: general and applied, v. 51, no. 5; whole no. 231. BIP

PICKFORD, Ralph William, 1903- 701'.15
Psychology and visual aesthetics [by] R. W. Pickford. London, Hutchinson Educational, 1972. xviii, 270, [11] p. illus. (some col.). 23 cm. Includes bibliographies. [N71.P42] 72-193824 ISBN 0-09-110820-9
1. Art—Psychology. I. Title. Available from Crane-Russak, 16.25, 0-8448-0014-7. BIP

RAPHAEL, Max, 1889-1952. 701
The demands of art. With an appendix, Toward an empirical theory of art. Translation by Norbert Guterman. [Princeton, N.J., Published for Bollingen Foundation by] Princeton University Press [1968] xxiii, 258 p. illus. (part col.) 32 cm. (Bollingen series, 78) Translation of two unpublished manuscripts, Wie ein Kunstwerk gesehen sein will, and Empirische Kunstwissenschaft. Includes bibliographical references. [N71.R34] 65-10431
1. Art—Psychology. 2. Art—Philosophy. 3. Art criticism. I. Title. II. Series. BIP

RYDZEWSKI, Pamela 709
Art and human experience. [1st ed.] Oxford, New York, Pergamon [1967] xiv, 208p. illus. 20cm. (Commonwealth & intl. lib. Liberal studies div.) Bibl. [N71.R89 1967] 66-29603 4.00 pap.,
1. Art—Psychology. 2. Art—Hist. I. Title. BIP

SWEENEY, James Johnson, 1900- 701
Vision and image; a way of seeing. New York, Simon and Schuster [1968] 188 p. 21 cm. (Credo perspectives) Bibliographical footnotes. [N71.S9 1968] 68-11018 4.95
1. Art—Psychology. 2. Composition (Art) I. Title.

WAELDER, Robert. 701.15
Psychoanalytic avenues to art. New York, Intl. Univs. Pr. [c.1965] 122p. illus. 21cm. (Freud anniversary lect. sers., 1963) Bibl. [N70.W28] 65-14735 4.00
1. Art—Psychology. 2. Psychoanalysis. I. Title. II. Series. BIP

WAELDER, Robert. 701.15
Psychoanalytic avenues to art. New York, International Universities Press [1965] 122 p. illus. 21 cm. (The Freud anniversary lecture series, 1963) "Expanded version of the lecture given at the New York Academy of Medicine on May 21, 1963." Bibliography: p. 105-107. [N70.W28] 65-14735
1. Art—Psychology. 2. Psychoanalysis. I. Title. II. Series.

WEBER, Jean Paul. 701.15
The psychology of art. Translated from the French by Julius A. Elias. [New York] Delacorte Press [1969] 187 p. 21 cm. Translation of La psychologie de l'art. Bibliography: p. 185-187. [N71.W413] 68-15591 6.00
1. Art—Psychology. I. Title.

WEINER, Egon. 701'.15
Art and human emotions. Springfield, Ill., Thomas [1974, c1975] x, 90 p. illus. 24 cm. [N71.W425] 74-16414 ISBN 0-398-03265-3 6.75
1. Art—Psychology. I. Title. BIP

WEISMANN, Donald L. 701.15
The visual arts as human experience [by] Donald L. Weismann. Englewood Cliffs, N.J., Prentice-Hall [1970] viii, 313 p. illus. (part col.) 29 cm. Bibliography: p. 311-313. [N71.W43] 74-90765
1. Art—Psychology. 2. Composition (Art) I. Title.

WHEELER, Joseph F. 741'.019
Why draw? : A conversation about art with Donald L. Weismann / conducted by Joseph F. Wheeler. San Francisco : Chandler & Sharp Publishers, [1974] viii, 40 p. : ill. ; 23 cm. (The National Humanities Faculty why series) Bibliography: p. 39-40. [N71.W465] 74-14125 ISBN 0-88316-512-0 pbk. : 1.75
1. Art—Psychology. I. Weismann, Donald L., joint author. II. Title. III. Series: National Humanities Faculty. The National Humanities Faculty why series. BIP

WILSON, Frank Avray 701.1
Art into life; an interpretation of contemporary trends in painting. [New York, Corinth Bks., dist., Citadel Press, 1961, c.1958] 230p. illus., plates (part col.) 59-25976 6.95 buck.,
1. Art—Psychology. 2. Creaton (Literary, artistic, etc.) 3. Painting. 4. Art, Modern—20th cent. I. Title. BIP

Art—Psychology—Addresses, essays, lectures.

BEYOND aesthetics : 701'.15
investigations into the nature of visual art / general editor, Don Brothwell ; with a preface by C. H. Waddington. London : Thames and Hudson, c1976. 212 p., [18] leaves of plates : ill. ; 25 cm. Errata slip inserted. Includes indexes. Bibliography: p. 198-207. [N71.B45] 76-372343 ISBN 0-500-01147-8 : 25.00
1. Art—Psychology—Addresses, essays, lectures. 2. Visual perception—Addresses, essays, lectures. 3. Art and society—Addresses, essays, lectures. I. Brothwell, Don.
Distributed by Transatlantic BIP

HOGG, James, comp. 701.15
Psychology and the visual arts: selected readings. Harmondsworth, Penguin, 1969. 415 p., 28 plates. illus. 18 cm. (Penguin modern psychology readings) (Penguin education, UPS13.) Bibliography: p. 389-393. [N71.H6] 70-457936 10/-
1. Art—Psychology—Addresses, essays, lectures. I. Title.

Art — Psychology — Bibl.

KIELL, Norman. 016.70115
Psychiatry and psychology in the visual arts and aesthetics, a bibliography. Madison, University of Wisconsin Press, 1965. xiv, 250 p. 25 cm. [Z5931.K5] 65-18877
1. Art — Psychology — Bibl. 2. Psychiatry in art — Bibl. I. Title. BIP

Art, Puerto Rican.

KAIDEN, Nina N ed. 700.97295
Puerto Rico: la nueva vida; the new life, edited by Nina Kaiden, Pedro Juan Soto and Andrew Vladimir. [1st ed.] New York, Renaissance Editions [1966] 1 v. (unpaged) illus., col. plates. 26 cm. [N6612.K3] 65-29178
1. Art. Puerto Rican. 2. Puerto Rican literature (Selections: Extracts, etc.) I. Soto, Pedro Juan, joint ed. II. Vladimir, Andrew N., joint author. III. Title.

KAIDEN, Nina N., ed. 700.97295
Puerto Rico: la nueva vida; the life. ed. by Nina Kaiden, Pedro Juan Soto, Andrew Vladimir. New York. 10022, [33 E. 63th St., Renaissance c.1966 1 v. (unpaged) illus., col. plates. 26cm. [N6612.K3] 65-29178 5.00
1. Art, Puerto Rican. 2. Puerto Rican literature (Selections: Extracts, etc.) I. Soto, Pedro Juan, joint ed. II. Vladimir, Andrew N., joint author. III. Title.

Art, Puerto Rican—Exhibitions.

CATALOGUE commemorating 709'.7295
the exhibition: the art heritage of Puerto Rico, pre-Columbian to present. Catalogo conmemorando la exposicion: la herencia artistica de Puerto Rico, epoca pre-Colombina al presente. [New York] Metropolitan Museum of Art [1974] 120 p. illus. (part col.) 25 cm. Exhibition held Apr. 30-July 1 at El Museo del Barrio, New York, and July 25-Sept. 16, 1973, at the Metropolitan Museum of Art, New York. Bibliography: p. 118-120. [N6612.C37] 74-8168 ISBN 0-87099-093-4 Gratis
1. Art, Puerto Rican—Exhibitions. I. Museo del Barrio. II. New York (City). Metropolitan Museum of Art.

Art—Purchase, N.Y.—Catalogs.

NEUBERGER Museum. 708'.147'277
The making of a museum: 1. Neuberger Museum, State University of New York, College at Purchase: May 1974. [Purchase, N.Y., 1974] [116] p. 77 illus. 16 x 23 cm. "Catalog for the inaugural installation and opening of the Neuberger Museum." [N714.P8N48 1974] 74-181593
1. Neuberger Museum. 2. Art—Purchase, N.Y.—Catalogs. I. Title.

Art—Quotations, maxims, etc.

GALLATIN, Albert Eugene, 1881- ed. 704.922
Of art: Plato to Picasso-= aphorisms and observations, ed. with contributions by A. E. Gallatin. New York, Wittenborn [1963] 62p. illus. 17cm. 2.00 pap.,
1. Art—Quotations, maxims, etc. I. Title.

Art—Ravenna.

BOVINI, Giuseppe. 709'.45'47
Ravenna. Text by Giuseppe Bovini. Photos. by Leonard von Matt. Translated from the Italian by Robert Erich Wolf. New York, Abrams [1973, c1971] 214 p.

illus. (part col.) 33 cm. Bibliography: p. 212-214. [N6921.R3B62] 72-4832 ISBN 0-8109-0431-4 45.00
1. Art—Ravenna. I. Matt, Leonard von, illus. II. Title.

Art, Renaissance.

SIMPSON, Lucie. 709.03
The Greek spirit in Renaissance art. [New York] Philosophical Library, 53. 207p. illus. 22cm. [N6370.S5] 53-11125
1. Art, Renaissance. I. Title.

Art, Renaissance.

BENESCH, Otto, 1896- 709.4
The art of the Renaissance in northern Europe, its relation to the contemporary spiritual and intellectual movements. [Hamden, Conn.] Archon [dist. Shoe String] 1964[c.1945] xiv, 174p. illus. 23cm. Bibl. 64-13171 7.50
1. Art, Renaissance. 2. Art, European. 3. Renaissance. I. Title.

BENESCH, Otto, 1896-1964. 709.4
The art of the Renaissance in northern Europe; its relation to the contemporary spiritual and intellectual movements. [Rev. ed. London] Phaidon Publishers; distributed by New York Graphic Society, Greenwich, Conn. [1965] ix, 195 p. illus., port. 26 cm. Bibliographical references included in "Notes" (p. [167]-185) [N6370.B37 1965] 66-177
1. Art, Renaissance. 2. Art, European. 3. Renaissance. I. Title.

CHASTEL, Andre, 1912- 709'.4
The crisis of the Renaissance, 1520-1600. (Translated from the French by Peter Price.) Geneva) Skira, (1968). 220 p. illus., col. plates. 31 cm. (Art ideas history) Distributed in the U.S.A. by The World Publishing Company, Cleveland, Ohio. [N6370.C413] 68-20498 100.00
1. Art, Renaissance. 2. Sixteenth century. I. Title. II. Series.

GOMBRICH, Ernst Hans Josef, 1909- 709'.02'4
The heritage of Apelles / by E. H. Gombrich. Ithaca, N.Y. : Cornell University Press, 1976. viii, 250 p., [3] leaves of plates : ill. (some col.) : 26 cm. Includes bibliographical references and index. [N6370.G57] 76-3080 ISBN 0-8014-1012-6 : 22.50
1. Art, Renaissance. 2. Art—Technique. 3. Composition (Art) 4. Apelles. I. Title. BIP

GOMBRICH, Ernst Hans Josef, Sir, 1909- 704.94'6
Symbolic images : studies in the art of the Renaissance / by E. H. Gombrich. 2d [small format] ed. Oxford : Phaidon, 1978. viii, 247 p., [48] leaves of plates : ill. ; 19 cm. (Phaidon paperback) (His Studies in the art of the Renaissance ; 2) Includes index. Bibliography: p. 236. [N6370.G58 1978] 77-84371 ISBN 0-7148-1831-3 pbk. : 5.95
1. Art, Renaissance. 2. Symbolism in art. I. Title. II. Series. BIP

MURRAY, Peter. 709.03
The art of the Renaissance [by] Peter and Linda Murray. New York, Praeger [1963] 286 p. illus. (part col.), ports. (part col.) 22 cm. [N6370.M97] 63-18834
1. Art, Renaissance. I. Murray, Linda, joint author. II. Title. BIP

PANOFSKY, Erwin, 1892- 709.03
Studies in iconology; humanistic themes in the art of the Renaissance [Gloucester, Mass., Peter Smith, c.1939, 1962] 262p. illus. 21cm. (Harper torchbks., Academy lib., TB1077 rebound) Bibl. 4.25
1. Art, Renaissance. 2. Humanism. I. Title. II. Title: Iconology, Studies in.

PANOFSKY, Erwin, 1892- 709.03
Studies in iconology; humanistic themes in the art of the Renaissance. New York, Harper & Row [1962] xiiii, 262p. illus., 93 plates, 21cm. (Harper torchbooks, TB1077. The Academy library) Bibliography: p. 235-250. [N6370.P3 1962] 62-6203
1. Art, Renaissance. 2. Humanism. I. Title. II. Title: Iconology.

PANOFSKY, Erwin, 1892-1968. 709'.4
Renaissance and renascences in Western art. New York, Harper & Row [1969, c1960] xx, 242 p., [119] p. of illus. 21 cm. (Harper torchbooks, TB1447) Bibliography: p. 211-230. [N6370.P28 1969] 75-5834 2.95
1. Art, Renaissance. I. Title. BIP

SMART, Alastair, 1922- 709'.02'4
The Renaissance and mannerism in northern Europe and Spain. [New York] Harcourt Brace Jovanovich [1972] 224 p. illus. (part col.) 21 cm. (The Harbrace history of art) Bibliography: p. 218-220. [N6370.S55] 70-165326 ISBN 0-15-176826-9 3.95
1. Art, Renaissance. 2. Mannerism (Art) I. Title. BIP

STUDIES in 709.02/4/08
Renaissance & Baroque art presented to Anthony Blunt on his 60th birthday. London, New York. Phaidon, 1967. xi. 268p. illus., plate (port.), maps, plans. facsims. 32cm. Contributions in English. French and German. The writings of Anthony Blunt. comp. by Elsa Scheerer: p. 257-268. Bibl. [N6370.S72] 67-114194 17.50
1. Art, Renaissance, 2. Art, Baroque. I. Blunt. Anthony, Sir 1907-
Distributed by Praeger.

SYPHER, Wilie 709.03
Four stages of Renaissance style; transformations in art and literature, 1400-1700. [Gloucester, Mass., P. Smith, 1965, c.1955] 312p. illus. 18cm. (Anchor bk., A45 rebound) [N6370.S95] 3.50
1. Art, Renaissance. 2. Renaissance. I. Title. BIP

SYPHER, Wylie. 709.03
Four stages of Renaissance style; transformations in art and literature, 1400-1700. [1st ed.] Garden City, N.Y., Doubleday, 1955. 312 p. illus. 18 cm. (A Doubleday anchor original A45) [N6370.S95] 55-6749
1. Art, Renaissance. 2. Renaissance. I. Title.

WOLF, Robert Erich. 709'.4
Renaissance and mannerist art. Text by Robert Erich Wolf and Ronald Millen. New York, Abrams [1968] 263 p. illus. (part col.) 23 cm. (Panorama of world art) Translation of Geburt der Neuzeit. Bibliography: p. 258-[260] [N6370.W63] 68-18132
1. Art, Renaissance. 2. Mannerism (Art) I. Millen, Ronald, joint author. II. Title.

WOLFFLIN, Heinrich, 1864-1945. 709.03
The sense of form in art; a comparative psycological study. Translated from the German by Alice Muehsam and Norma A. Shatan. New York, Chelsea Pub. Co. [1958] 230 p. illus. 25 cm. Translation of Die Kunst der Renaissance; Italien und das deutsche Formgefuhl. [N6370.W553] 57-12877
1. Art, Renaissance. 2. Art, German. 3. Art, Italian. 4. Art — Psychology. I. Title. BIP

WUNDRAM, Manfred. 709'.02'4
Art of the Renaissance. [English translation by Francisca Garvie] New York, Universe Books [1972] 196 p. illus. 23 cm. Translation of Renaissance. Bibliography: p. 190-192. [N6370.W8513] 73-175861 ISBN 0-87663-170-7 6.95
1. Art, Renaissance. I. Title. BIP

Art, Renaissance—Addresses, essays, lectures.

GILBERT, Creighton, comp. 709'.4
Renaissance art. New York, Harper & Row [1970] xxi, 247 p. illus. 21 cm. (The Contemporary essays series) (Harper torchbooks TB 1465.) Contents.Contents.—Introduction, by C. Gilbert.—Jan van Eyck's Arnolfini portrait, by E. Panofsky.—Muscipula Diaboli: The symbolism of the Merode altarpiece, by M. Schapiro.—Light as form and symbol in some fifteenth-century paintings, by M. Meiss.—The painter Niccolo Pizzolo, by E. Rigoni.—The hall of the Great Council of Florence, by J. Wilde.—The architectural theory of Francesco di Giorgio, by H. Millon.—Architectural practice in the Italian Renaissance, by J. S. Ackerman.—The importance of Sammicheli in the formation of Palladio, by G. C. Argan.—Maniera as an aesthetic ideal, by J. Shearman.—Jacopo Bassano: 1568-69, by W. R. Rearick. Includes bibliographical references. [N6370.G46] 70-92848 3.25
1. Art, Renaissance—Addresses, essays, lectures. BIP

SIXTEENTH century art and architecture. 709 s
New York : Garland Pub., 1976. p. cm. (The Garland library of the history of art ; v. 7) Includes bibliographical references. [N5300.G32 vol. 7] [N6374] 709'.03'1 76-14069 lib.bdg. : lib.bdg. : 35.00
1. Art, Renaissance—Addresses, essays, lectures. 2. Classicism in art—Addresses, essays, lectures. I. Series.
Contents omitted. Contents omitted BIP

Art, Renaissance—Austria.

TREVOR-ROPER, Hugh. 709'.03'1
Princes and artists : patronage and ideology at four Habsburg courts, 1517-1633 / Hugh Trevor-Roper. With 123 ill. London : Thames and Hudson, c1976. 176 p. : ill. ; 25 cm. "Lectures ... delivered at the State University of New York, College at Purchase, New York, in October 1974, being the first of the annual Yaseen Lectures." Includes index. Bibliography: p. 165-167. [N6805.T73] 77-362465 ISBN 0-500-23232-6 : £6.50
1. Habsburg, House of—Art patronage. 2. Art, Renaissance—Austria. 3. Art, Modern—17th-18th centuries—Austria. 4. Art—Austria. I. Title. BIP

Art, Renaissance—Catalogs.

MOLLISON, James Allan. 708.994
Renaissance art [by] James Mollison. Melbourne, New York [etc.] Oxford University Press [1968] 32 p. illus. 22 cm. (National Gallery booklets) Bibliography: p. 32. [N6370.M6] 79-364641 0.70
1. Art, Renaissance—Catalogs. 2. Art—Victoria, Australia—Catalogs. I. Title. II. Series: Victoria, Australia. National Gallery, Melbourne. Booklets

Art, Renaissance—Congresses.

INTERNATIONAL Congress of the History of Art, 20th, New York, 1961. 709'.02'4
The Renaissance and mannerism. Princeton, N.J., Princeton University Press, 1963. x, 261 p., 56 plates. 24 cm. (Acts of the twentieth International Congress of the History of Art) (Its Studies in Western art, v. 2) Chiefly in English, some contributions in French, German, or Italian. Includes bibliographical references. [N21.I585 1961 vol. 2] [N6370] 73-164481
1. Art, Renaissance—Congresses. 2. Mannerism (Art)—Congresses. I. Title. II. Series. III. Series: International Congress of the History of Art. Acts, 1961.

Art, Renaissance—Early Renaissance.

LEVEY, Michael. 709.02'4
Early Renaissance. Harmondsworth, Penguin, 1967. 224 p. 112 illus. 20 cm. (Style and civilization) (Pelican book, A 914.) Bibliography: p. 217-219. [N6370.L4] 68-88043 12/6
1. Art, Renaissance—Early Renaissance. I. Title. BIP

Art, Renaissance—Early Renaissance—Italy.

LENGYEL, Alfonz. 709'.45
The Quattrocento; a study of the principles of art and a chronological biography of the Italian 1400's. Dubuque, Iowa, Kendall/Hunt Pub. Co. [1971] xii, 208 p. 23 cm. Bibliography: p. 177-204. [N6915.L4] 79-167841 ISBN 0-8403-0470-6
1. Art, Renaissance—Early Renaissance—Italy. 2. Artists, Italian—Bio-bibliography. I. Title.

Art, Renaissance—Europe.

STOKSTAD, Marilyn Jane, 1929- 709.02'4
Renaissance art outside Italy [by] Marilyn Stokstad. Dubuque, Iowa, W. C. Brown Co. [1968] viii, 113 p. illus. 23 cm. (Art horizons series) [N6750.S78] 68-14577
1. Art, Renaissance—Europe. I. Title.

Art, Renaissance—Europe, Northern.

FARMER, John David. 709'.4
The virtuoso craftsman; Northern European design in the sixteenth century. [Worcester, Mass., Worcester Art Museum, 1969] 202, [8] p. illus. 23 cm. Catalogue of the loan exhibition held at the Worcester Art Museum March 27-May 25, 1969. Bibliography: p. [206]-[210]. [N6750.F3] 73-7005
1. Art, Renaissance—Europe, Northern. 2. Art, Renaissance—Exhibitions. 3. Mannerism (Art)—Europe, Northern. 4. Mannerism (Art)—Exhibitions. I. Worcester, Mass. Art Museum. II. Title.

Art, Renaissance—Exhibitions.

THE Fortuna of 709'.02'4074019454
Michelangelo : prints, drawings and small sculpture from California collections : the E. B. Crocker Art Gallery, Sacramento, the University of California, Davis, October 21-December 14, 1975 / edited by L. Price Amerson, Jr. Sacramento : The Gallery, c1975. 47 p. : ill. ; 28 cm. Catalogue of the exhibition. Includes bibliographical references. [N6374.F67] 76-355013
1. Buonarroti, Michel Angelo, 1475-1564—Influence. 2. Art, Renaissance—Exhibitions. 3. Art—Atribution. I. Amerson, Price. II. Crocker Art Gallery, Sacramento, Calif. III. California. University, Davis. Dept. of Art.

HOUSTON, Tex. University of St. Thomas. Art Dept. 709.03
Builders and humanists: the Renaissance Popes as Patrons of the arts; exhibition March-May 1966 Houston [1966] 363p. illus., facsims., plans, fold, plate, ports. 23cm. Cover title: The Popes as builders and humanist. from Nicholas V. 1447 through Clement IX, 1669 . . . Bibl. [N6370.H59] 66-7845 8.00 pap.,
1. Art, Renaissance—Exhibitions. 2. Art patronage. 3. Popes. I. Title. II. Title: The Popes as builders and humanists.
Available from Univ. of St. Thomas, 3812 Montrose Blvd., Houston, Tex. 77006

Art, Renaissance—Finland.

RACZ, Istvan, 1908- 709'.471
Treasures of Finnish renaissance and baroque art. Photos by Istvan Racz. Introd. and notes on the illustrations by Nils Cleve. Translated from Finnish by Diana Tullberg. New York, Praeger [1969, c1967] 229 p. (chiefly illus. (part col.), ports. (part col.)) 32 cm. Translation of Suomen renessanssin ja barokin taideaarteita. [N6993.R2513] 71-84859 15.00
1. Art, Renaissance—Finland. 2. Art, Baroque—Finland. 3. Art—Finland. I. Cleve, Nils, 1905- II. Title.

Art, Renaissance—High Renaissance.

MURRAY, Linda. 709'.03'1
The High Renaissance and mannerism : Italy, the north, and Spain, 1500-1600 / Linda Murray. New York : Oxford University Press, c1977. p. cm. (World of art) Published in 1967 under 2 separate titles: The late Renaissance and mannerism and The High Renaissance. Includes index. Bibliography: p. [N6374.M87] 77-79636 ISBN 0-19-519990-1 pbk. : 7.95
1. Art, Renaissance—High Renaissance. 2. Mannerism (Art) I. Murray, Linda. The late Renaissance and mannerism. II. Title. III. Series. BIP

RUSKIN, Ariane. 709.02'4
Art of the High Renaissance, adapted by Ariane Ruskin. Foreword by Howard Conant. New York, McGraw-Hill [1970?] 189 p. col. illus. 31 cm. (Discovering art series) "[Based] on the text of the magazine series Discovering art ... [with]

adaptations from the Italian text of Capolavori nei secoli." [N6374.R86] 76-110961
1. Art, Renaissance—High Renaissance. I. Title. BIP

Art, Renaissance—High Renaissance—History.

LEVEY, Michael. 709'.03'1
High Renaissance / Michael Levey. Harmondsworth ; Baltimore [etc.] : Penguin, 1975. 320 p. : ill., facsims. ; 20 cm. (Style and civilization) (Pelican books) Includes index. Bibliography: p. 307-309. [N6374.L48] 75-316482 ISBN 0-14-021823-8 pbk. : 5.95
1. Art, Renaissance—High Renaissance—History. I. Title.

Art, Renaissance—High Renaissance—Italy.

MURRAY, Linda. 709.03
The late Renaissance and Mannerism. New York, F. A. Praeger [1967] 215 p. illus. (part col.), plans. 22 cm. (Praeger world of art series) Bibliography: p. 200-202. [N6915.M98 1967] 67-25566
1. Art, Renaissance—High Renaissance—Italy. 2. Mannerism (Art) I. Title.

Art, Renaissance—History.

CLARK, Kenneth McKenzie, Sir 1903- 759.9492
Rembrandt and the Italian Renaissance. New York, Norton [1968,c.1966] [xv,] 225p. 181 plates. 20cm. (Wrightsman lects., 1964. Norton lib., N424) Bibl. [ND653.R4C5] 1.95 pap.,
1. Rembrandt, Hermanszoon van Rijn, 1606-1667. 2. Art, Rennaissance—Hist. I. Title. BIP

HUYGHE, Rene. 709.03
Larousse encyclopedia of Renaissance and Baroque art. New York, Prometheus Press [1964] 444 p. illus. (part col.) maps, ports. (part col.) 30 cm. At head of title: Art and mankind. "English text prepared by Emily Evershed, Hugh Newbury, Ralph de Seram and Katherine Watson from [v. 3 of] the French original, L'art et l'homme. [N6350.H813] 64-13787
1. Art, Renaissance — Hist. 2. Art, Baroque — Hist. I. Title. II. Title: Art and mankind.

Art, Renaissance—History.

BENESCH, Otto, 1896-1964. 759
Collected writings. Edited by Eva Benesch. [New York] Phaidon [1970- v. illus., ports. 26 cm. Contents.Contents.—v. 1. Rembrandt.—v. 2. Netherlandish art of the 15th and 16th centuries. Flemish and Dutch art of the 17th century. Italian art. French art. Includes bibliographies. [N7483.B43A22] 709.24 79-13232 ISBN 0-7148-1365-6 (v. 1) 15.00 (v. 1) varies

GILBERT, Creighton. 709'.02'4
History of Renaissance art: painting, sculpture, architecture throughout Europe. Englewood Cliffs, N.J., Prentice-Hall [1973?] 460 p. illus. (part col.) 31 cm. (Library of art history) Bibliography: p. 423-436. [N6370.G45 1973b] 72-10180 ISBN 0-13-392100-X
1. Art, Renaissance—History. I. Title.

GILBERT, Creighton. 709'.02'4
History of Renaissance art: painting, sculpture, architecture throughout Europe. New York, H. N. Abrams [1973] 460 p. illus. (part col.) 30 cm. (The Library of art history) Bibliography: p. 423-436. [N6370.G45] 72-4791 ISBN 0-8109-0169-2 18.50
1. Art, Renaissance—History. I. Title.

MARTINDALE, Andrew. 709'.4
Man and the Renaissance. New York, McGraw-Hill [1966] 176 p. illus. (part col.) maps. 30 cm. (Landmarks of the world's art) Bibliography: p. [167] [N6370.M3] 66-15837
1. Art, Renaissance—History. I. Title.

Art, Renaissance—History—Sources.

STECHOW, Wolfgang, 1896- ed. 709.024
Northern Renaissance art, 1400-1600; sources and documents Englewood Cliffs, N.J., Prentice-Hall [1966] x, 187 p. port. 23 cm. (Sources and documents in the history of art series) [N6370.S66] 66-16399
1. Art, Renaissance—History—Sources. I. Title. II. Series.

Art, Renaissance—Italy.

EGLINSKI, Edmund. 709'.45
The art of the Italian Renaissance. Dubuque, Iowa, W. C. Brown Co. [1968] vii, 104 p. illus. 23 cm. (Art horizons) Includes bibliographical references. [N6915.E35] 68-14576
1. Art, Renaissance—Italy. 2. Art, Italian. I. Title.

KELDER, Diane. 759.5
Pageant of the Renaissance. New York, F. A. Praeger [1969, c1966] 192 p. illus., plates (part col.) 31 cm. [N6915.K4] 68-30941 6.95
1. Art, Renaissance—Italy. 2. Art, Italian. I. Title.

MURRAY, Linda 709'.45
The High Renaissance. New York, Praeger [1967] 213p. illus. (pt. col.) 22cm. (Praeger world of art ser.) Bibl. [N6915.M97 1967b] 67-18404 7.50
1. Art, Renaissance—Italy. I. Title.

PAATZ, Walter, 1902- 709'.45
The arts of the Italian Renaissance: painting, sculpture, architecture. New York, H. N. Abrams [1974] p. cm. [N6915.P15 1974] 69-12488 ISBN 0-8109-0029-7 25.00
1. Art, Renaissance—Italy. 2. Art, Italian. I. Title.

PAATZ, Walter, 1902- 709'.45
The arts of the Italian Renaissance: painting, sculpture, architecture. Englewood Cliffs, N.J., Prentice-Hall [1974] 277 p. illus. (part col.) 26 cm. Bibliography: p. [257]-263. [N6915.P15 1974b] 73-21965 9.95
1. Art, Renaissance—Italy. 2. Art, Italian. I. Title.

PAGET, Violet, 1856-1935. 709'.45
Renaissance fancies and studies / Vernon Lee [i.e. V. Paget]. New York : Garland Pub., 1977. p. cm. (The Decadent consciousness) Reprint of the 1895 ed. published by Smith, Elder, London. Contents.Contents.—The love of the saints.—The imaginative art of the Renaissance.—Tuscan sculpture.—A seeker of pagan perfection, being the life of Domenico Neroni, pictor sacrilegus.—Valedictory. [N6915.P2 1977] 76-20099 ISBN 0-8240-2767-1 lib.bdg. : 26.00
1. Art, Renaissance—Italy. 2. Art, Italian. I. Title. II. Series. BIP

Art, Renaissance—Italy—Addresses, essays, lectures.

COLLABORATION in Italian Renaissance art / edited by Wendy Stedman Sheard and John T. Paoletti. New Haven : Yale University Press, 1978. p. cm. Includes index. [N6915.C64] 77-91068 ISBN 0-300-02175-5 : 20.00 709'.45
1. Art, Renaissance—Italy—Addresses, essays, lectures. 2. Art, Italian—Addresses, essays, lectures. 3. Group work in art—Italy—Addresses, essays, lectures. I. Sheard, Wendy Stedman. II. Paoletti, John T. BIP

DAVIS, Phil. 770
Photography / Phil Davis. 3d. ed. Dubuque, Iowa : W. C. Brown Co., c1979. ix, 336 p. : ill. ; 22 x 28 cm. Includes index. Bibliography: p. 329-332. [TR145.D33 1979] 78-58252 ISBN 0-697-03217-5 : 13.95
1. Photography. I. Title.

Art, Renaissance—Italy—Florence.

STEINBERG, Ronald M. 709'.45'51
Fra Girolamo Savonarola, Florentine art, and Renaissance historiography / Ronald M. Steinberg. Athens : Ohio University Press, c1977. 151 p. : ill. ; 25 cm. Includes index. Bibliography: p. 142-148. [N6921.F7S377] 76-8304 ISBN 0-8214-0202-1 lib.bdg. : 11.00
1. Savonarola, Girolamo Maria Francesco Matteo, 1452-1498. 2. Art, Renaissance—Italy—Florence. 3. Art, Italian—Italy—Florence. 4. Humanism in art. I. Title.

Art, Renaissance—Italy—History.

CLARK, Kenneth McKenzie, Sir, Baron Clark, 1903- 759.9492
Rembrandt and the Italian Renaissance. [New York] New York University Press [1966] xv, 225 p. 181 plates, port. 28 cm. (The Wrightsman lectures, no. 1) Includes bibliographical references. [ND653.R4C5] 66-13550
1. Rembrandt Harmenszoon van Rijn, 1606-1667. 2. Art, Renaissance—Italy—History. I. Title. II. Series.

Art—Research.

JONES, Lois Swan. 707'.2
Art research methods and resources : a guide to finding art information / Lois Swan Jones. Dubuque, Iowa : Kendall/Hunt Pub. Co., c1978. ix, 243 p. : facsims. ; 28 cm. Includes bibliographies and index. [N85.J64] 77-93281 ISBN 0-8403-1846-4 : 12.95
1. Art—Research. I. Title. BIP

Art—Richmond—Catalogs.

VIRGINIA Museum of Fine Arts, Richmond 708.155451
European art in the Virginia Museum of Fine Arts; a catalogue. Richmond [1966] 149p. illus. (pt. col.) 26cm. [N716.V45A64] 66-63300 4.00
1. Art—Richmond—Catalogs. I. Title.

VIRGINIA Museum of Fine Arts, Richmond. 708'.155'451
Treasures in the Virginia Museum / [Pinkney L. Near, curator and author]. Richmond : Virginia Museum, [1974] 124 p. : col. ill. ; 31 cm. [N716.M8A7] 74-80700 ISBN 0-8139-0600-8 : 13.95
1. Virginia Museum of Fine Arts, Richmond. 2. Art—Richmond—Catalogs. I. Near, Pinkney L. II. Title.

Art—Rifle, Colo.

CHRISTO, 1935- 709'.2'4
Christo: Valley Curtain, Rifle, Colorado, 1970-72. Photos.: Harry Shunk. [1st ed.] New York, H. N. Abrams [1973] 1 v. (chiefly illus., part col.) 31 cm. [N7193.C5A43] 73-173891 ISBN 0-8109-0050-5 35.00
1. Christo, 1935- 2. Art—Rifle, Colo. I. Title. II. Title: Valley Curtain, Rifle, Colorado, 1970-72.

Art—Rochester, N. Y.

ROCHESTER, N. Y. University. Memorial Art Gallery. 708.1474789
Handbook. Rochester [c1961] 120p. (chiefly illus. (part col.)) 23cm. [N719.A55 1961] 62-3746
1. Art—Rochester, N. Y. I. Title.

Art—Rocky Mountain region—History.

MUSICK, Archie Leroy, 1902- 709'.78
Musick medley; intimate memories of a Rocky Mountain art colony, by Archie Musick. [Colorado Springs, 1971] 121 p. illus. 22 x 11 cm. [N6522.M87] 73-156766 2.95
1. Art—Rocky Mountain region—History. I. Title.

Art, Rococo.

BALTIMORE, Museum of Art. 709.033
Age of elegance the rocro and its effect; an exhibition presented by the Baltimore Museum of Art april 25 to june 14, 1959 [Baltimore, 1959] 91p. illus. 26cm. 'Catalogue of the exhibition': p. [27]-91. [N6410.B3] 59-2334
1. Art, Rococo. I. Title.

SCHONBERGER, Arno 709.033
The rococo age; art and civilization of the 18th century [by] Arno Schonberger and Halldor Soehner, with the collaboration of Theodor Muller. [Translated from the German by Daphne Woodward] New York, McGraw-Hill [1960] 393p. illus., plates (part col.) 35cm. 60-11310 23.50
1. Art, Rococo. 2. Eighteenth century. 3. Europe—Civilization. I. Soehner, Halldor, joint author. II. Title.

SCHONBERGER, Arno, 1915- 709.033
The rococo age; art and civilization of the 18th century [by] Arno Schonberger and Halldor Soehner, with the collaboration of Theodor Muller. [Translated from the German by Daphne Woodward] New York, McGraw-Hill [1960] 393p. illus., plates (part col.) 35cm. Translation of Die Welt des Rokoko. [N6410.S313] 60-11310
1. Art, Rococo. 2. Eighteenth century. 3. Europe—Civilization. I. Soehner, Halldor, joint author. II. Title.

SCHWARZ, Michael. 759.04
The age of the Rococo. Translated by Gerald Onn. New York, Praeger [1971] 194 p. illus. (part col.) 31 cm. Translation of Das Zeitalter der galanten Malerei. [N6425.R6S3613] 73-147093 9.95
1. Art, Rococo. I. Title.

Art, Rococo—France.

DUNCAN, Carol. 759.4
The pursuit of pleasure : the rococo revival in French romantic art / Carol Duncan. New York : Garland Pub., 1976. vii, 157 p. : ill. ; 21 cm. (Outstanding dissertations in the fine arts) An edited version of the author's dissertation, Columbia, 1969, issued under title: The persistence and re-emergence of the rococo in French romantic painting. Bibliography: p. 116-127. [N6846.5.R6D86 1976] 75-23789 ISBN 0-8240-1985-7 lib.bdg. : 20.00
1. Art, Rococo—France. 2. Romanticism in art—France. I. Title. II. Series.

GONZALEZ-PALACIOS, Alvar. 709'.44
The age of Louis XV; [translated from the Italian by Henry Vidon London, New York, Hamlyn, 1969. 3-156 p. port., 69 col. illus. 20 cm. (Cameo) Originally published as Il Luigi XV. Milano, Fabbri, 1966. [N6846.G6213] 77-452619 15/-
1. Art, Rococo—France. 2. Art, French. 3. Decoration and ornament—Louis XV style. I. Title.

Art, Roman.

ANDREAE, Bernard. 709'.37
The art of ancient Rome / Bernard Andreae ; translated from the German by Robert Erich Wolf. New York : H. N. Abrams, 1976,i.e. 1977 p. cm. Translation of Romische Kunst. Includes index. Bibliography: p. [N5760.A4813] 75-8855 ISBN 0-8109-0626-0 : 75.00
1. Art, Roman. I. Title.

BERTMAN, Stephen. 709'.37
Art and the Romans : a study of Roman art as a dynamic expression of Roman character / by Stephen Bertman. Lawrence, Kan. : Coronado Press, 1975. xi, 83 p., 43 leaves of plates : ill. ; 22 cm. Includes index. Bibliography: p. 75-81. [N5760.B47] 75-328268 ISBN 0-87291-070-9 : 10.00
I. Title. BIP

BIANCHI Bandinelli, Ranuccio, 1900- 709'.37
Rome, the center of power, 500 B.C. to A.D. 200. Translated by Peter Green. New York, G. Braziller [1970] xii, 437 p. illus. (part col.), col. plans. 29 cm. (The Arts of mankind, v. 15) Translation of Rome, le centre du pouvoir. Bibliography: p. [389]-396. [N5760.B513] 70-116985 30.00
1. Art, Roman. 2. Rome—Antiquities. I. Title. II. Series.

BIANCHI Bandinelli, Ranuccio, 1900- 709'.37
Rome, the late Empire; Roman art, A.D. 200-400. Translated by Peter Green. New York, G. Braziller [1971] x, 463 p. illus. (part col.), col. maps (part fold.) 29 cm.

(Arts of mankind series, v. 17) Translation of Rome, la fin de l'art antique. Bibliography: p. 411-420. [N5763.B513 1971] 71-136167 ISBN 0-8076-0593-X 30.00
1. Art, Roman. 2. Art, Early Christian. I. Title. II. Series.

BRENDEL, Otto, 1901-1973. 709'.37
Prolegomena to the study of Roman art / Otto J. Brendel. New Haven : Yale University Press, 1979. p. cm. Includes bibliographical references and index. [N5760.B73 1979] 78-24455 ISBN 0-300-02268-9 : 16.00 ISBN 0-300-02372-3 pbk. : 4.95
1. Art, Roman. 2. Art, Greco-Roman. I. Title. BIP

BURN, Robert, 1829-1904. 709'.37
Roman literature in relation to Roman art. Port Washington, N.Y., Kennikat Press [1969] x, 315 p. illus. 21 cm. (Kennikat classics series) Reprint of the 1888 ed. Bibliographical footnotes. [N5763.B9 1969] 70-101034
1. Art, Roman. 2. Art, Greco-Roman. 3. Latin literature—History and criticism. I. Title.

GLUBOK, Shirley. 709.37
The art of ancient Rome. Designed by Oscar Krauss. New York, Harper & Row [1965] 40 p. illus. 26 cm. Presents objects of Roman art—columns, statues, mosaics, portraits, reliefs, buildings, and murals—and explains how and why they were created. [N5760.G55] AC 68
1. Art, Roman. I. Title.

HANFMANN, George Maxim 709'.37
Anossov, 1911-
Roman art : a modern survey of the art of imperial Rome / by George M. A. Hanfmann. New York : Norton, [1975] 328 p. : ill. ; 19 cm. Bibliography: p. 53-58. [N5740.H3 1975] 74-30063 ISBN 0-393-09222-4 pbk. : 6.25
1. Art, Roman. I. Title.

HANFMANN, George Maxim 709.37
Anossov, 1911-
Roman art; a modern survey of the art of imperial Rome, by George M. A. Hanfmann. Greenwich, Conn., New York Graphic Society [1964] 224 p. 145 illus., 52 col. plates, maps (on lining papers) 26 cm. Bibliography: p. 53-55. Each illus. accompanied by a commentary and a bibliography. [N5740.H3] 64-21814
1. Art, Roman.

ROMAN art; 709'.37
general editor Francesco Abbate; translated [from the Italian], by A. J. Sutton. London, New York, Octopus Books, 1972. 158 p. chiefly 114 col. illus. 20 cm. Translation of Arte romana dalla Repubblica al Tardo Impero. Bibliography: p. 154. [N5760.A7613] 72-172341 ISBN 0-7064-0059-3 2.95
1. Art, Roman. 2. Art, Early Christian. I. Abbate, Francesco, ed.

STRONG, Eugenie (Sellers) 709.37
Art in ancient Rome. Westport, Conn., Greenwood Press [1970] xiv, 199, viii, 220 p. illus., plans, ports. 23 cm. (Ars una: species mille. General history of art) Reprint of the 1928 ed. Contents.Contents.—From the earliest times to the principate of Nero.—From the Flavian dynasty to Justinian, with chapters on painting and the minor arts in the first century, A.D. Bibliography: p. xii (1st group) [N5760.S7 1970] 72-109858
1. Art, Roman. I. Title. II. Series.

WHEELER, Robert Eric 709.37
Mortimer, Sir, 1890-
Roman art and architecture [by] Sir Mortimer Wheeler. New York, F. A. Praeger [1964] 250 p. illus. (part col.) plans. 22 cm. Bibliography: p. 237. [N5760.W5] 64-22933
1. Art, Roman. I. Title. BIP

Art, Roman—Addresses, essays, lectures.

ANCIENT art : 709 s
Roman art and architecture. New York : Garland Pub., 1976. 279 p. : ill. ; 29 cm. (The Garland library of the history of art ; v. 3) Includes bibliographical references. [N5300.G32 vol. 3] [N5760] 709'.37 76-14064 ISBN 0-8240-2413-3 lib.bdg. 35.00
1. Art, Roman—Addresses, essays, lectures. 2. Architecture—Rome—Addresses, essays, lectures. I. Series. Contents omitted

Art, Roman—Exhibitions.

BRANDEIS University, 709'.37
Waltham, Mass. Poses Institute of Fine Arts.
Art of the late antique from American collections; a loan exhibition of the Poses Institute of Fine Arts [held at] Rose Art Museum, Brandeis University, December 18, 1968-February 16, 1969. [Waltham, 1968] 62 p. illus. 26 cm. Catalogue of the exhibition: p. [45]-60. [N5740.B7] 68-59518
1. Art, Roman—Exhibitions. 2. Art, Early Christian—Exhibitions. I. Brandeis University, Waltham, Mass. Rose Art Museum. II. Title.

DEL CHIARO, Mario 709'.37'0740194
Aldo, 1925-
Roman art in West Coast collections [by] Mario A. Del Chiaro. [Santa Barbara, University of California, 1973] 98 p. illus. (part col.). 26 cm. Catalog of a loan exhibition held at the Art Galleries, University of California, Santa Barbara, Jan. 10-Feb. 11, 1973 and at the University Art Museum, University of California, Berkeley, Mar. 28-May 13, 1973. Bibliography: p. 56-57. [N5760.D44] 72-619650
1. Art, Roman—Exhibitions. 2. Art, Roman—California. I. California. University, Santa Barbara. Art Galleries. II. California. University. Art Museum. III. Title.

Art, Roman—Greece.

VERMEULE, Cornelius 709.01'4
Clarkson, 1925-
Roman imperial art in Greece and Asia Minor [by] Cornelius C. Vermeule. Cambridge, Mass., Belknap Press of Harvard University Press, 1968. xxiv, 548 p. illus., maps. 29 cm. Bibliographical references included in "Notes" (p. 505-517) [N5851.V4] 67-20886
1. Art, Roman—Greece. 2. Art, Roman—Asia Minor. I. Title. BIP

Art, Roman—History.

L'ORANGE, Hans Peter, 709.37
1903-
Art forms and civic life in the late Roman Empire, by H. P. L'Orange. [Translated from the Norwegian by Dr. and Mrs. Knut Berg] Princeton, N.J., Princeton University Press, 1965. 131 p. illus. 23 cm. Translation of Fra principat til dominat. Bibliographical footnotes. [N5760.L613] 65-10831
1. Art, Roman — Hist. 2. Discletianus, Emperor of Rome, 245-313. I. Title. BIP

TOYNBEE. JOCELVN M. C. 709.37
The art of the Romans. New York, Praeger [c.1965] 271p. illus. 21cm. (Ancient peoples and places. v. 43) Bibl. [N5760.T58] 65-20080 7.50
1. Art. Roman—Hist. I. Title.

Art, Roman—History.

CHARLES-PICARD, Gilbert. 709.37
Roman painting. Text by Gilbert Picard. Greenwich, Conn., New York Graphic Society [1970, c1968] 104, [1] p. illus. (part col.) 28 cm. (The Pallas library of art, v. 4) Translation of Art romain. Bibliography: p. [105] [N5760.C5213] 70-86263 12.50
1. Art, Roman—History. I. Title.

KAHLER, Heinz. 709.37
The art of Rome and her empire. [Translated by J. R. Foster] New York, Crown Publishers [1963, c1962] 262 p. illus. (part mounted col.), fold. map, plans. 24 cm. (Art of the world, European cultures; the historical, sociological and religious backgrounds) Bibliography: p. 216-224. [N5760.K313] 63-14558
1. Art, Roman—History. I. Title. II. Series: Art of the world; the historical, sociological and religious backgrounds

STRONG, Donald Emrys. 709'.37
Roman art / Donald Strong ; prepared for press by J. M. C. Toynbee. Harmondsworth ; Baltimore [etc.] : Penguin, 1976. xxvii, 197 p., [81] leaves of plates : ill. (some col.) ; 27 cm. (The Pelican history of art) Includes index. Bibliography: p. 175-184. [N5760.S68] 76-380183 ISBN 0-14-056039-4 : 40.00
1. Art, Roman—History. I. Toynbee, Jocelyn M. C. II. Title. III. Series. BIP

Art, Roman—History—Chronology.

LENGYEL, Alfonz. 709'.37
A chronological survey of Roman art from the beginning to Constantine I. Granville, Ohio, Denison University [1968] 128 p. 29 cm. At head of title: Consortium in art history supported by the Samuel H. Kress Foundation. Includes bibliographies. [N5763.L4] 68-5857
1. Art, Roman—History—Chronology. I. Title.

Art, Roman—History—Sources.

POLLITT, Jerry Jordan. 709.37
The art of Rome, c. 753 B.C.-337 A.D.; sources and documents [by] J. J. Pollitt Englewood Cliffs, N.J., Prentice-Hall [1966] xx, 252 p. illus., map. 23 cm. (Sources and documents in the history of art series) Bibliographical footnotes. [N5760.P57] 66-18490
1. Art, Roman—History—Sources. I. Title. II. Series.

Art, Roman—Juvenile literature.

GLUBOK, Shirley 709.38
The art of ancient Rome. Designed by Oscar Krauss. New York, Harper [c.1965] 40p. illus. 26cm. [N5760.G55] 65-11449 3.95; 3.99 lib. ed.,
1. Art, Roman—Juvenile literature. I. Title.

Art, Romanesque.

BUSCH, Harald, 1904- ed. 709.02
Pre-Romanesque art. With an introd. by Louis Grodecki. Edited by Harold Busch and Bernd Lohse. With commentaries on the illus. by Eva-Maria Wagner. New York, Macmillan, 1966. xlii p. illus., plans, 217 plates (1 col.) 27 cm. ([Buildings and sculpture of Europe]) Legends to the plates in German and English. Translation of Vorromanische Kunst und ihre Wurzeln. [N6280.B813 1966a] 66-16924
1. Art, Romanesque. 2. Architecture, Romanesque. I. Lohse, Bernd, joint ed. II. Title. BIP

EVANS, Joan, 1893- 709.44
Cluniac art of the Romanesque period. Cambridge [Eng.] University Press, 1950. xxxv, 134 p. 210 plates, 29 cm. Bibliography: p. [xxxi]-xxxv. [N6280.E8] 51-2070
1. Art, Romanesque. 2. Art, Cluniac. 3. Cluniacs. I. Title.

FOCILLON, Henri, 1881- 709'.4
1943.
The art of the West in the Middle Ages; edited and introduced by Jean Bony; [translated from the French by Donald King]. 2d ed. London, New York, Phaidon, 1969. 2 v. illus. 26 cm. (Phaidon paperback, PH 58, 59) Translation of Art d'Occident, le moyen age, roman et gothique. Contents.Contents.—v. 1. Romanesque art.—v. 2. Gothic art. Includes bibliographies. [N6280.F613 1969] 71-444367 27/6 per vol. (pbk) ($4.50 (v. 1) 4.95 (v. 2))
1. Art, Romanesque. 2. Art, Gothic. I. Title.

FOCILLON, Henri Joseph, 709.02
1881-1943
The art of the West in the Middle Ages, [2v.] Ed., introd. by Jean Bony. Tr. from French by Donald King; glossary by P. Kidson. Phaidon Pubs. dist. N. Y. Graphic, Greenwich, Conn. [1963] 2 v. (310 381p.) plates. 26cm. Contents.v. 1. Romanesque art.--v. 2. Gothic art. Bibl. 63-4333 7.95 ea.,
1. Art, Romanesque. 2. Art, Gothic. I. Title.

*KOVACS, Eva 739.227'022'09439
Romanesque goldsmiths' art in Hungary. Corvina, Corvina Press, [1975 c1974] 58 p. 48 p. of plates ill. (part col) 19 cm. [NK7108]
1. Art, Romanesque. 2. Goldwork. 3. Art, Hungarian. I. Title.
Distributed by Int'l Publications Service for 5.00. BIP

KUNSTLER, Gustav, 709'.02'1
comp.
Romanesque art in Europe; architecture and sculpture. Edited by Gustav Kunstler. New York, Norton [1973, c1968] 327 p. illus. 24 cm. (The Norton library) [N6280.K8 1973] 72-13235 ISBN 0-393-00687-5 4.95
1. Art, Romanesque. I. Title. BIP

NEBOLSINE, George A. 709'.4
Journey into Romanesque; a traveller's guide to Romanesque monuments in Europe [by] George Nebolsine. Edited by Robyn Cooper. [1st ed.] New York, Putnam [1969] 272 p. illus. 26 cm. [N6280.N4] 79-77551 8.95
1. Art, Romanesque. 2. Europe—Description and travel—Guide-books. I. Title.

SOUCHAL, Francois. 709'.4
Art of the early Middle Ages. [Text translated from the French by Ronald Millen] With an introd. by Hans H. Hofstatter. [Introd. translated from the German by Robert Erich Wolf] New York, Abrams [1968] 263 p. illus. (part col.) 23 cm. (Panorama of world art) Bibliography: p. 258-259. [N6280.S613] 68-27428
1. Art, Romanesque. I. Title.

SWARZENSKI, Hanns, 1903- 709.02
Monuments of Romanesque art; the art of church treasures in north-western Europe. Chicago, University of Chicago Press [1954] 1v. (chiefly illus.) 32cm. Bibliographies included in 'Notes on the plates' (p. 37-85) [N6280.S9] 55-937
1. Art, Romanesque. 2. Christian art and symbolism. 3. Art objects, Romanesque. I. Title. BIP

TIMMERS, J. J. M., 1907- 709'.4
A handbook of Romanesque art, by J. J. M. Timmers. [Translated by Marian Powell. 1st American ed. New York] Macmillan [1969] 240 p. illus. (part col.), maps (part col.), plans. 22 cm. Translation of Atlas van het Romaans. Bibliography: p. 234-235. [N6280.T513 1969b] 79-80800 6.95
1. Art, Romanesque. I. Title. BIP

ZARNECKI, George. 709.021
Romanesque art. New York, Universe Books [1971] 196 p. illus. (part col.), plans. 23 cm. Bibliography: p. 190-193. [N6280.Z36] 75-122322 ISBN 0-87663-132-4 6.95
1. Art, Romanesque.

Art, Romanesque—Congresses.

INTERNATIONAL Congress 709'.02'1
of the History of Art, 20th, New York, 1961.
Romanesque and Gothic art. Princeton, N.J., Princeton University Press, 1963. xii, 231 p., 80 plates. 24 cm. (Acts of the twentieth International Congress of the History of Art) (Studies in Western art, v. 1) Chiefly in English, some contributions in French or Italian. Includes bibliographical references. [N21.I585 1961 vol. 1] [N6280] 73-164485
1. Art, Romanesque—Congresses. 2. Art, Gothic—Congresses. I. Title. II. Series. III. Series: International Congress of the History of Art. Acts, 1961.

Art, Romanesque—Exhibitions.

SCHER, Stephen K. 709'.4
The renaissance of the twelfth century. An exhibition organized by Stephen K. Scher, May 8-June 22. Providence, Museum of Art, Rhode Island School of Design, 1969. xii, 197 p. illus. 28 cm. Includes bibliographical references. [N6280.S3] 68-56467
1. Art, Romanesque—Exhibitions. I. Rhode

Island School of Design, Providence. Museum of Art. II. Title. BIP

SPAIN. Direccion General de Relaciones Culturales. 708.46
L'art roman; exposition organisee par le gouvernement espagnol sous les auspices du conseil de l'Europe, Catalogue. Barcelona, 1961. Lxxviii, 666p. 96 plates. 22cm. Bibl. [N6280.S67] price unreported pap.,
1. Art, Romanesque—Exhibitions. I. Title. Available from World-Wide Bks., New York.

THE year 1200. 709.02'1
[New York] Metropolitan Museum of Art; distributed by New York Graphic Society [1970] 2 v. illus. (part col.), facsims., plans. 26 cm. (The Cloisters studies in medieval art, 1-2) Contents.Contents.—1. A centennial exhibition at the Metropolitan Museum of Art, February 12 through May 10, 1970; catalogue, written and edited by K. Hoffmann.—2. A background survey, published in conjunction with the centennial exhibition at the Metropolitan Museum of Art, February 12 through May 10, 1970. Compiled and edited by F. Deuchler. Bibliography: v. 1, p. 337-354. [N6280.Y4] 73-109964 ISBN 0-87099-000-4 (v. 1) 12.95 per vol.
1. Art, Romanesque—Exhibitions. 2. Art, Gothic—Exhibitions. I. Hoffmann, Konrad, 1938- II. Deuchler, Florens, 1931- ed. III. New York (City). Metropolitan Museum of Art. IV. Title. V. Series.

Art, Romanesque—Spain.

BONET, Blas, 1926- 709'.46
El movimiento romanico en Espana. The Romanesque movement in Spain. Le mouvement roman en Espagne. Die romanische Bewegung in Spanien. [Por] Blai Bonet. Barcelona, Edicones Poligrafa [1967] Stamped on t. p.: American dist. Wittenborn, New York. 307p. 58 col. plates. 23 cm. [N7103.B65] 68-74678 15.00
1. Art, Romanesque—Spain. 2. Art, Spanish—Hist. I. Title.

Art—Rome (City)

CURTIUS, Ludwig, 1874- 709.456
Rome, an illustrated selective guide to all important art treasures in Rome and its environs. [New York] Pantheon [1950] 185 p. illus., map (fold. col. in pocket) 18 cm. [N6920.C8] 50-6243
1. Art—Rome (City) I. Title.

LABANDE, Yvonne. 914.56
Rome [by] Y. et E.-R. Labande. Translated and adapted by Janet Hamilton. New York, McGraw-Hill Book Co. [1952] 249 p. illus. 23 cm. [N6920.L273] 52-8959
1. Art—Rome (City) 2. Rome (City)—Descr. I. Title.

LABANDE, Yvonne. 914.56
Rome [by] Y. and E. R. Labande; translated and adapted by George Millard. Cover painting by Yves Brayer; 203 illus. in heliogravure. Fair Lawn, N. J., Essential Books [1956] 269p. illus., maps. 23cm. [N6920.L273 1956] 56-59163
1. Art—Rome (City) 2. Rome (City)—Descr. I. Labande, Edmond Rene, 1908- joint author. II. Title.

MATT, Leonard Von 704.9482
Early Christian art in Rome. Commentary by Enrico Josi. New York, Universe [1962, c.1961] xvi p. illus. 29cm. (His The Roma ser.) 61-14581 4.75
1. Art—Rome (City) 2. Christian art and symbolism—Hist. I. Josi, Enrico. II. Title.

MATT, Leonard von 709.4563
Renaissance art in Rome. Commentary by Valerio Mariani. New York, Universe Bks. [c.1961] xvi, p., 48p. of illus. 29cm. (Roma ser.) 61-14583 4.75
1. Art—Rome (City) 2. Art, Renaissance. I. Mariani, Valerio, 1899- II. Title.

VATICAN museums: 708.56'34
Rome. [Texts by Gigetta Dalli Regoli and others] New York, Newsweek [1968] 171 p. col. illus., plans. 30 cm. (Great museums of the world) Bibliography: p. [168] [N2940.V4] 68-20026
1. Art—Rome (City) 2. Art—Vatican City. I. Dalli Regoli, Gigetta. II. Series: Great museums of the world (New York, Newsweek)

Art—Rome (City)—Galleries and museums.

BOTTRALL, Ronald, 1906- 708.5'63
Art centers of the world: Rome. Cleveland, World Pub. Co. [1968] 192 p. illus., map (on lining papers), plates (part col.), ports. (part col.) 21 cm. [N2810.B6] 68-26016 7.95
1. Art—Rome (City)—Galleries and museums. I. Title.

TRAVELER'S guide to 708'.5'632
art in Rome. New York, Scribner [1972] 126 p. col. illus. 28 cm. Translation of L'Arte a Roma. [N2810.A8513] 79-38944 ISBN 0-684-12884-5 9.95
1. Art—Rome (City)—Galleries and museums. I. Title: Art in Rome.

Art—Rome (City)—History.

CARANDENTE, Giovanni. 709'.456'32
Rome. Special photography by Mario Carrieri. [Translated from the Italian by Muriel Grindrod and Geoffrey Webb. 1st ed.] New York, Holt, Rinehart and Winston [1971] 288 p. illus. (part col.), col. maps, plans. 26 cm. (World cultural guides) [N6920.C2713] 70-138899 ISBN 0-03-085984-0 9.95
1. Art—Rome (City)—History. 2. Rome (City)—Description.

Art, Rumanian.

ZDERCIUC, Boris 745.4494976
Folk art in Rumania; text by Boris Zderciuc, Paul Petrescu [and] Tancred Banateanu. Bucharest, Meridiane Pub. [dist. New York, Vanous, 1964] 133, [44] p. illus. (pt. col.) 27cm. [N7221.Z35] 65-1339 7.50
1. Art, Rumanian. 2. Folk Art—Rumania. I. Petrescu, Paul, joint author. II. Banateanu, Tancred, joint author. III. Title.

Art—Russia—Hist.

ALPATOV, Mikhail Vladimirovich, 1903- 709.47
Russian impact on art, edited and with a preface by Martin L. Wolf; translated from the Russian, by Ivy Litvinov. New York, Philosophical Library [1950] xx, 352 p. illus., ports. 24 cm. [N6981.A54] 50-83023
1. Art—Russia—Hist. 2. Russia—Civilization—Hist. I. Title.

Art, Russian.

ALPATOV, Mikhail Vladimirovich, 1903- 709'.47
Art treasures of Russia. Text by M. W. Alpatov. Commentaries by Olga Dacenko. [Translated by Norbert Guterman] New York, H. N. Abrams [1967 or 8] 178 p. 104 col. plates. 33 cm. French translation published in 1966 under title: Tresors de lart russe. [N6981.A5613] 67-12683
1. Art, Russian. 2. Architecture—Russia. I. Title.

ART treasures in 709'.47
Russia; monuments, masterpieces, commissions, and collections. Introd. by Dimitri Obolensky. [General editors: Bernard S. Myers and Trewin Copplestone] New York, McGraw-Hill [1970] 174 p. illus., col. plates. 29 cm. [N6981.A75] 71-101167 6.95
1. Art, Russian. 2. Art—Russia—Galleries and museums. 3. Art patronage—Russia. I. Obolensky, Dimitri, 1918- II. Myers, Bernard Samuel, 1908- ed. III. Copplestone, Trewin, ed.

NEW art from the Soviet 709'.47
Union : the known and the unknown / [prepared by] Norton Dodge, Alison Hilton. Washington : Acropolis Books, [1977] p. cm. Bibliography: p. [N6988.N47] 77-13442 ISBN 0-87491-209-1 : 14.50
1. Art, Russian. 2. Dissident art—Russia. 3. Art, Modern—20th century—Russia. I. Dodge, Norton T. II. Hilton, Alison. BIP

Art, Russian—20th century.

SJEKLOCHA, Paul. 709.47
Unofficial art in the Soviet Union, by Paul Sjeklocha and Igor Mead. Berkeley, University of California Press, 1967. xv, 213 p. illus. (part col.), ports. 27 cm. Bibliography: p. 205-213. [N6998.S52] 67-28461
1. Art, Russian—20th century. I. Mead, Igor, joint author. II. Title. BIP

Art, Russian—Catalogs.

SELECTED works of Russian 709'.47
art : architecture, sculpture, painting, graphic art : 11th-early 20th century / edited by Natalia Sokolova. Leningrad : Aurora Art Publishers, c1976. ca. 200 p. : 150 ill. (some col.) ; 27 cm. [N6981.S44] 77-350647
1. Art, Russian—Catalogs. I. Sokolova, Natal'ia Ivanovna.

Art, Russian—Exhibitions.

LEONARD Hutton Galleries. 760'.0947'074014771
[Russkii avangard (romanized form)] 1908-1922. Russian avant-garde, 1908-1922 New York [1971] 102 p. illus. (part col.), ports. 31 cm. Exhibition held Oct. 16-Dec. 18, 1971. [N6988.L47] 72-198008
1. Art, Russian—Exhibitions. 2. Art, Modern—20th century—Russia. I. Title. II. Title: Russian avant-garde, 1908-1922.

NAKOV, Andrei B. 709'.47'07402142
Russian pioneers : at the origins of non-objective art == Precurseurs russes : aux sources de l'art nonobjectif / Andrei B. Nakov. London : Annely Juda Fine Art, c1976. 95 p. : ill. (some col.) ; 19 x 24 cm. Translation of Precurseurs russes. Parallel French and English text. Catalog of an exhibition held May 27-September 18, 1976. Includes bibliographical references. [N6988.5.A24N34] 77-478623 £4.00
1. Art, Russian—Exhibitions. 2. Art, Abstract—Russia—Exhibitions. 3. Art, Modern—20th century—Russia—Exhibitions. I. Title.

RISSELADA, Max. 709'.47'07401471
Art & architecture, USSR, 1917-32; exhibit, June 3-18, 1971, at the Institute for Architecture and Urban Studies, New York. [Catalogue prepared by Max Risselada, with the assistance of Kenneth Frampton] New York, G. Wittenborn [1971?] 24 p. illus. 28 cm. Bibliography: p. 22-24. [N6988.R5] 72-198266
1. Art, Russian—Exhibitions. 2. Art, Modern—20th century—Russia. I. Institute for Architecture and Urban Studies. II. Title.

RUSSIAN 709'.47'07402132
Suprematist and Constructivist art, 1910-1930 : [catalogue of an exhibition held at Fischer Fine Art Limited London March-April, 1976] London : Fischer Fine Art Ltd, [1976] 40 p. (2 fold) : ill. (some col.) ; 17 cm. [N6988.5.S9R87] 77-364171 ISBN 0-904867-07-2 : £1.50
1. Art, Russian—Exhibitions. 2. Suprematism in art—Exhibitions. 3. Constructivism (Art)—Russia—Exhibitions. 4. Art, Modern—20th century—Russia—Exhibitions. I. Fischer Fine Art Limited.

Art, Russian—History.

CHAMOT, Mary, 1900- 759.7
Russian painting and sculpture. Oxford, Pergamon Press; New York, Macmillan [1963] xii, 55 p. illus. (part col.) 20 cm. (The Commonwealth and international library of science, technology, engineering, and liberal studies. Pergamon Oxford Russian series. Background books, 2) "147." Bibliography: p. 50-51. [N6981.C5 1963] 63-19242
1. Art, Russian — Hist. I. Title. II. Series.

GRAY, Camilla 709.47
The great experiment: Russian art, 1863-1922. New York, Abrams [1962] 326p. mounted col. illus. 28cm. Bibl. 62-14462 25.00
1. Art, Russian—Hist. I. Title.

HARE, Richard 709.47
The art and artists of Russia. Greenwich, Conn., N. Y., Graphic [1966, c.1965] 294p. illus. (pt. col.) 26cm. Bibl. [N6981.H37] 66-16279 17.50
1. Art, Russian—Hist. 2. Artists, Russia. I. Title.

Art, Russian—History.

ALPATOV, Mikhail Vladimirovich, 1903- 709'.47
Russian impact on art [by] Mikhail Alpatov. Edited and with a pref. by Martin L. Wolf. Translated from the Russian by Ivy Litvinov. New York, Greenwood Press [1969, c1950] xx, 352 p. illus., ports. 23 cm. [N6981.A5413 1969] 75-90461
1. Art, Russian—History. 2. Russia—Civilization—History. I. Title. BIP

GRAY, Camilla. 709.47
The Russian experiment in art 1863-1922 New York, H. N. Abrams [1971, c1962] 296 p. illus. (part col.) 22 cm. First published under title: The great experiment: Russian art, 1863-1922. Bibliography: p. 280-282. [N6988.G7 1971b] 79-106516 ISBN 0-8109-0465-9
1. Art, Russian—History. I. Title.

HAMILTON, George Heard. 709'.47
The art and architecture of Russia / George Heard Hamilton. 2d ed. Harmondsworth [Eng.] ; Baltimore : Penguin Books, 1975[i.e.1976] xxiv, 342 p., [91] leaves of plates : ill. ; 27 cm. (The Pelican history of art) Includes index. Bibliography: p. 317-322. [N6981.H34 1975] 77-352526 ISBN 0-14-056006-8 : 29.50
1. Art, Russian—History. 2. Architecture—Russia—History. I. Title. II. Series. BIP

KORNILOVICH, Kira Viktorovna. 709'.47
Arts of Russia. Translated from the Russian by James Hogarth. Cleveland, World Pub. Co. [1967-68] 2 v. illus. (part col.) 35 cm. Contents.Contents.—v. 1. From the origins to the end of the 16th century by K. Kornilovich.—v. 2. 17th and 18th centuries, by A. L. Kaganovich. [N6981.K573] 67-24469 29.95 (v. 2)
1. Art, Russian—History. 2. Architecture—Russia—History. I. Kaganovich, A. L., joint author. II. Title.

RICE, Tamara (Abelson) Talbot. 709.47
A concise history of Russian art. New York, Praeger [1963] 288 p. illus. (part col.) ports., map, plans. 22 cm. Bibliography: p. 272-273. [N6981.R52 1963] 63-16653
1. Art, Russian—History. I. Title.

VOYCE, Arthur. 709'.47
The art and architecture of medieval Russia. [1st ed.] Norman, University of Oklahoma Press [1967] xii, 432 p. illus., maps (1 fold.), ports. 23 cm. Bibliography: p. 405-416. [N6983.V6] 66-13433
1. Art, Russian—History. 2. Architecture—Russia—History. 3. Civilization, Medieval. I. Title. BIP

Art, Russian—History—Collected works.

RUSSIAN art of the avant- 709'.47
garde : theory and criticism, 1902-1934 / edited and translated by John E. Bowlt. New York : Viking Press, [1976] xl, 360 p. : ill. ; 22 cm. (The Documents of 20th-century art) Includes index. Bibliography: p. 309-348. [N6988.R84 1976] 73-17687 ISBN 0-670-61257-X : 20.00
1. Art, Russian—History—Collected works. 2. Art, Modern—20th century—Russia—Collected works. I. Bowlt, John E. II. Series. BIP

Art—San Diego, Calif.—Catalogs.

SAN Diego, Calif. Fine Arts Gallery. 708.19498
Catalogue; a selective listing of all the collections of the Fine Arts Society. [1st ed. San Diego, 1960] 141p. illus. 31cm. [N737.A52] 60-41577
1. Art—San Diego, Calif.—Catalogs. I. Fine Arts Society of San Diego. II. Title.

SAN Diego, Calif. Fine Arts Gallery. 708.194'98
Master works from the collection of the Fine Arts Gallery of San Diego. [Edited by Martin E. Petersen. San Diego, Calif., 1968] [69] p. illus. (part col.) 29 cm. [N737.A55] 69-13265
1. Art—San Diego, Calif.—Catalogs. I. Petersen, Martin E., ed. II. Title.

Art—San Francisco.

CALIFORNIA Palace of the Legion of Honor, San Francisco. 708.19461
Handbook of the collections. [4th ed.] San Francisco [1960] 109p. (chiefly illus. (part mounted col.)) 28cm. First ed. published in 1942 under title: Illustrated handbook of the collections. [N739.A45 1960] 60-37827
1. Art—San Francisco. I. Title.

SNIPPER, Martin, 1914- 709.794
A survey of art work in the City and County of San Francisco, prepared by Martin Snipper for the Art Commission, City and County of San Francisco. [San Francisco] Art Commission, City and County. of San Francisco, c1953. unpaged. 28cm. [N6535.S3S3] 53-36911
1. Art—San Francisco. I. San Francisco. Art Commission. II. Title.

Art—San Francisco Bay region.

REGIONAL Arts Council of the San Francisco Bay Area 709.79461
The arts in the San Francisco Bay area; an inventory of private organizations and their activities. By Mel Scott, executive director [dist. Berkeley, Calif., Inst. of Govt, Studies, Univ. of Calif., 348 Library Annex] 1965. iii, 80p. 23cm. [N6530.C2R4] 65-64289 1.00 pap.,
1. Art—San Francisco Bay region. 2. Performing arts—San Francisco Bay region. I. Scott, Mellier Goodin, 1906- II. Title.

SCOTT, Mellier Goodin, 1906- 700
Partnership in the arts; public and private support of cultural activities in the San Francisco Bay area. Berkeley, Institute of Governmental Studies, University of California, 1963. 55 p. 24 cm. (The 1963 Franklin K. Lane project) [N6530.C2S3] 63-63548
1. Art—San Francisco Bay region. 2. San Francisco Bay region—Intellectual life. I. Title.

Art — San Francisco — Catalogs.

DE Young Memorial Museum, San Francisco 709'.4
European works of art in the M. H. de Young Memorial Museum. [Berkeley, Calif.] Pub. by Diablo Pr. for De Young Mus: Soc. [c.1966] 221p. illus. (pt. col.), ports. (pt. col.) 26cm. [N739.5.A42] 66-29482 3.50 pap.,
1. Art — San Francisco — Catalogs. 2. Art, European — Catalogs. I. Title.

DEYOUNG Memorial Museum. San Francisco. 709.'4
European works of art in the M. H. de Young Memorial Museum. [Berkeley, Calif.] Published by Diable Press for De Young Museum Society [c1966] 221 p. illus. (part col.), ports. (part col.) 26 cm. 66-29482
1. Art — San Francisco — Catalog. 2. Art, European — Catalogs. I. Title. BIP

SIMPSON, David, 1928- 759.13
David Simpson, 1957-1967. San Francisco Museum of Art, March 15-April 23. [San Francisco, 1967] 31 p. 17 illus. (part col.) 22 cm. "Organized by the San Francisco Museum of Art." [ND237.S554A5] 68-6112
I. San Francisco. Museum of Art.

Art—San Francisco—Galleries and museums.

FLOATING Seminar, 2d, San Francisco, 1975. 709'.794'61
A survey of alternative art spaces : Floating Seminar #2 : a revised transcription of the meeting held October 2, 1975 at The Farm, San Francisco / edited, with an introd. by Paul Kagawa. San Francisco : The Seminar, 1975. 80 p. ; 21 cm. [N6535.S3F56 1975] 75-43082 3.00
1. Floating Seminar, 2d, San Francisco, 1975. 2. Art—San Francisco—Galleries and museums. 3. Art societies—California—San Francisco. 4. Art—Periodicals. I. Kagawa, Paul. II. Title.

HOOVER, F. Herbert. 917.94'61
Hoover's guide to galleries: San Francisco, by F. Herbert Hoover. Introd. by Alfred Frankenstein. Sketches by Barry Brenner. [1974-75 ed.] Los Angeles, Camaro Pub. Co. [1974] 189 p. illus. 21 cm. [N738.H66 1974] 74-16348 ISBN 0-913290-09-2 2.95
1. Art—San Francisco—Galleries and museums. 2. San Francisco—Museums. I. Title. II. Title: Guide to galleries: San Francisco.

Art—San Marino, Calif.—Catalogs.

HENRY E. Huntington Library and Art Gallery, San Marino, Calif. 708.194
Handbook of the art collections. [Prepared by Maurice Block. 4th ed.] San Marino, 1951 ['1941] xv, 107 p. illus., port. 25 cm. Cover title: The Huntington art collections. [N741.A5 1951] 52-4476
1. Art—San Marino, Calif.—Catalogs. I. Block, Maurice, 1890- II. Title.

Art — Santa Fe, N.M.

ARTISTS of Santa Fe; 709.78956
their works and words. Santa Fe, N.M., C. R. Wenzell Publications [1965] 51 p. illus., ports. 22 cm. [N6535.S33A7] 65-3262
1. Art — Santa Fe, N.M. 2. Artists, American — Santa Fe, N.M.

Art—Santa Fe, N.M.—Catalogs.

SANTA Fe, N.M. Museum of New Mexico. Museum of Fine Arts. 708'.189'56
Handbook of the collections, 1917-1974, Museum of Fine Arts. [Santa Fe] : Museum of New Mexico, [1974] 192 p. : ill. (some col.) ; 26 cm. [N742.S3A55] 74-84236
1. Santa Fe, N.M. Museum of New Mexico. Museum of Fine Arts. 2. Art—Santa Fe, N.M.—Catalogs.

Art — Scandinavia.

WILSON, David, McKenzie. 709.48
Viking art, by David M. Wilson and Ole Klindt-Jensen. Ithaca, N.Y., Cornell University Press [1966] 173 p. illus., plates (1 col.) 26 cm. Bibliography: p. 162-166. [N7003.W5 1966] 66-13813
1. Art — Scandinavia. 2. Art, Medieval. 3. Vikings. I. Klindt-Jensen, Ole, joint author. II. Title.

Art, Scandinavian.

ANKER, Peter. 709'.48
The art of Scandinavia. With a contribution by Aron Andersson. London, New York, P. Hamlyn [1970] 2 v. illus., maps, plates (part col.) 23 cm. French translation originally published in 1968-69 under title: L'Art scandinave. Vol. 2 by Aron Andersson. Includes bibliographical references. [N7001.A68] 79-21555 ISBN 0-600-10006-5 (v. 1)
1. Art, Scandinavian. I. Andersson, Aron, 1919- II. Title.

SCANDINAVIAN art 709'.48
[by] Carl Laurin, Emil Hannover [and] Jens Thiis. With an introd. by Christian Brinton. New York, B. Blom, 1968. 662 p. illus. 26 cm. (Scandinavian monographs, v. 5) Reprint of the 1922 ed. Contents.Contents.—A survey of Swedish art, by C. G. Laurin.—Danish art in the nineteenth century, by E. Hannover.—Modern Norwegian art, by J. Thiis. [N7001.S3 1968] 69-13242
1. Art, Scandinavian. I. Laurin, Carl Gustaf Johannes, 1868-1940. II. Hannover, Emil, 1864-1923. III. Thiis, Jens Peter, 1870-1942. IV. Title. V. Series. BIP

Art—Scholarships, fellowships, etc.

INSTITUTE of International Education. 707.9
Directory of international scholarships in the arts. New York, 1958. 120p. 14x22cm. [N347.I5] 59-38191
1. Art—Scholarships, fellowships, etc. I. Title. II. Title: International scholarships in the arts.

Art—Scholarships, fellowships, etc.—Directories.

VARGAS, Lois. 338.4'7'700973
A guide to grants and funding for the visual artist / Lois Vargas, Barbara Sahli. [s.l. : s.n.], c1976. 166 p. ; 22 cm. Includes bibliographical references. [N347.V37] 76-150252
1. Art—Scholarships, fellowships, etc.—Directories. I. Sahli, Barbara, joint author. II. Title.

Art schools.

BELL, Quentin 707
The schools of design. London, Routledge & K. Paul [dist. New York, Hillary House. 1964, c.1963] x, 290p. illus., ports., facsims. 23cm. Bibl. 64-1630 8.00
1. Art schools. 2. Art—Study and teaching—Gt. Brit. I. Title.

GEORGIA. University. Dept. of Art. 707'.1'175818
The University of Georgia Department of Art. [Athens, 1968?] 22 p. illus. 26 cm. [N386.G4A56] 76-626578
I. Title.

PEVSNER, Nikolaus, Sir, 1902- 707'.11
Academies of art, past and present. New pref. by the author. New York, Da Capo Press, 1973. x, xiv, 323 p. illus. 23 cm. Reprint of the 1940 ed. Bibliography: p. 305-309. [N325.P4 1973] 78-87379 ISBN 0-306-71603-8 15.00
1. Art schools. 2. Art—Study and teaching. I. Title. BIP

Art schools—Direct.

THE Art school directory. 707
1961- [New York, Watson-Guptill] v. 22cm. [N325.A75] 62-1557
1. Art schools—Direct.

Art, Scottish—Exhibitions.

THE Royal Scottish Academy 150th anniversary exhibition, 1826-1976 / 709'.04'074094134
[catalogue compiled by Elizabeth Blackadder et al.]. [Edinburgh] : Royal Scottish Academy], [1976] 3-96 p. : ill. (some col.), plans, ports. (1 col.) ; 22 x 25 cm. Includes index. [N6778.R69] 77-361080 ISBN 0-905783-00-X : £1.50
1. Art, Scottish—Exhibitions. 2. Art, Modern—19th century—Scotland—Exhibitions. 3. Art, Modern—20th century—Scotland—Exhibitions. I. Blackadder, Elizabeth. II. Edinburgh. Royal Scottish Academy of Painting, Sculpture, and Architecture.

Art, Scythian.

ARTAMONOV, Mikhail Illarionovich, 1898- 739
The splendor of Scythian art; treasures from Scythian tombs [by] M. I. Artamonov. With an introd. by Tamara Talbot Rice. Photos. by Werner Forman. [Translated from the Russian by V. R. Kupriyanova] New York, F. A. Praeger [1969] 296 p. illus., maps, plates (part col.) 31 cm. Translation of Sokrovishcha skifskikh kurganov v sobranii Gosudarstvennogo Ermitazha (romanized form) London ed. (Thames & Hudson) has title: Treasures from Scythian tombs in the Hermitage Museum, Leningrad. Bibliography: p. 273. [N5899.S3A813 1969] 68-31440 20.00
1. Art, Scythian. 2. Art—Leningrad. I. Forman, Werner, illus. II. Leningrad. Ermitazh. III. Title.

BOROVKA, Grigorii Iosifovich 709.39'51
Scythian art, by Gregory Borovka. Tr. from German by V. G. Childe. New York, Paragon, 1967. 111. 74p. illus. 23cm. Reprint of the 1928 ed. Bibl. [N5899.S3B6 1967] 67-22932 7.50
1. Art, Scythian. I. Title.

BOROVKA, Grigorii Iosifovich 709.3951
Scythian art, by Gregory Borovka. Tr. from German by V. G. childe. New York, Paragon Bk. Gallery [1962] 74p. (Kai Khosu monographs on eastern art) Bibl. 7.50 pap.,
1. Art, Scythian. 2. Scythia. I. Childe Vere Gordon, 1892- tr. II. Title.

BOROVKA, Grigoril Iosifovich. 709.39'51
Scythian art. by Gregory Borovka. Translated from the German by V. G. Childe. New York, Paragon Book Reprint Corp. 1967. 111, 74 p. illus. 23 cm. Reprint of the 1928 ed. Bibliography: p. 11-[14]. Bibliographical references included in "Description of plates" (p. 91-111) [N5899.S3B6] 67-22932
1. Art, Scythian. I. Title.

JETTMAR, Karl. 709.39'51
Art of the Steppes. [Translated by Ann E. Keep.] New York, Crown Publishers [1967] 272 p. illus., maps, col. plates. 24 cm. (Art of the world: European cultures: the historical, sociological, and religious backgrounds) Translation of Die fruhen Steppenvolker. Bibliography: p. 242-258. [N5899.S3J43] 67-17700
1. Art, Scythian. 2. Animals in art. I. Title. II. Series: Art of the world; the historical, sociological, and religious backgrounds

Art, Scythian—Exhibitions.

FROM the lands of the Scythians : 739'.0939'51
ancient treasures from the museums of the U.S.S.R., 3000 B.C.-100 B.C. : the Metropolitan Museum of Art, the Los Angeles County Museum of Art. [New York] : Metropolitan Museum of Art : distributed by New York Graphic Society, [1975, i.e.1976] 160 p. : ill. (33 col.) ; 29 cm. Exhibition held in 1975. [N5899.S3F7] 76-5965 ISBN 0-87099-143-4 : 17.50
1. Art, Scythian—Exhibitions. I. New York (City). Metropolitan Museum of Art. II. Los Angeles Co., Calif. Museum of Art, Los Angeles.

Art— Sentani Lake area.

NEW York. Museum of Primitive Art. 709.951
The art of Lake Sentani. [Text by S. Kooijman. Translation by Mrs. G. E. van Baaren-Pape] New York, 1959. 63p. illus., maps. 29cm. Catalogue of the exhibition': p. 62-63. Bibliography: p. 25. [N7326.N453] 60-3863
1. Art— Sentani Lake area. 2. Art, Primitive. I. Kooijman, S. II. Title.

Art—Sepik Valley.

THE Garrick introduction to Sepik art, 709'.01'109955
edited by Gloria Stewart. Melbourne, Garrick, 1972. 52 p. col. illus., map. 25 cm. [N7411.S4G34] 73-168048 ISBN 0-86931-000-3 1.50
1. Art—Sepik Valley. 2. Art, Primitive—Sepik Valley. I. Stewart, Gloria, ed.

GUIART, Jean. 731.7'5'0995
Oceanic art; the Sepik area of New Guinea. New York, New American Library [1968] 24 p. map, 32 col. plates. 17 cm. (A Mentor-Unesco art book) Translation of Art de l'Oceanie. Includes bibliography. [N7411.S4G833] 74-3644 1.25
1. Art—Sepik Valley. 2. Art, Primitive. I. Title.

Art—Sepik Valley—Bibl.

NEWTON, Douglas, 1920- comp. 016.72'092'2
Bibliography of Sepik District art annotated for illustrations. [New York, Library, Museum of Primitive Art] 1965-

v. 28 cm. (Primitive art bibliographies, no. 4) Cover title. [Z5961.N54N4] 65-4723
1. Art—Sepik Valley—Bibl. 2. Art—New Guinea—Bibl. 3. Art, Primitive—Bibl. I. Title. II. Series.

Art, Shaker—Addresses, essays, lectures.

A Shaker reader   704.94'9'264098 / edited by Milton C. and Emily Mason Rose. 1st ed. New York : Universe Books, 1977,c1975. 125 p. : ill. ; 29 cm. (Antiques magazine library) A collection of articles which originally appeared in Antiques. "A Main Street Press book." Includes index. [N6510.S5] 77-70773 ISBN 0-87663-297-5 : 12.95 ISBN 0-87663-969-4 pbk. : 6.95
1. Art, Shaker—Addresses, essays, lectures. I. Rose, Milton C. II. Rose, Emily Mason. III. Antiques.   BIP

Art—Shelburne, Vt.—Catalogs.

SHELBURNE, Vt.   759.13'074'014317 Museum.
Paintings and drawings at the Shelburne Museum / Nancy C. Muller. Shelburne, Vt. : Shelburne Museum, 1976. 200 p. : ill. (some col.) ; 29 cm. (Forge ahead ; no. 2) Includes index. [N749.A62] 76-367506
1. Shelburne, Vt. Museum. 2. Art—Shelburne, Vt.—Catalogs. 3. Art, American—Catalogs. I. Muller, Nancy C. II. Title. III. Series: The Forge ahead series ; no. 2.   BIP

Art, Shinto.

GUTH, Christine.   704.948'9'9561
The arts of Shinto, by Haruki Kageyama. Translated and adapted with an introd. by Christine Guth. [1st ed.] New York, Weatherhill [1973] 143 p. illus. (part col.) 23 cm. (Arts of Japan, 4) Adapted from Shinto bijutsu. Bibliography: p. [139]-140. [N8194.G8713 1973] 73-9640 ISBN 0-8348-2706-9 7.95
1. Art, Shinto. I. Kageyama, Haruki, 1916- Shinto bijutsu. II. Title.
Pbk. 4.95; ISBN 0-8348-2707-7   BIP

Art, Sinhalese—Addresses, essays, lectures.

SOUVENIR on the   700'.9549'3
occasion of the 5th Non-Aligned Summit Conference held in Colombo, Sri Lanka, 9-20 August 1976 in conjunction with an exhibition of paintings and sculpture of Sri Lanka at the Colombo Art Gallery ... / [edited and compiled by L. P. Goonetilleke]. [Colombo] : Issued by the Dept. of Cultural Affairs in collaboration with the Cultural Council of Sri Lanka Panel on Painting and Sculpture, [1976] viii, 127 p., [2] leaves of plates : ill., map ; 20 cm. Cover title: Viskam: Creativity. English or Sinhalese. [N7310.6.S66] 77-900482 Rs25.00
1. Art, Sinhalese—Addresses, essays, lectures. 2. Art, Buddhist—Sri Lanka—Addresses, essays, lectures. I. Goonetilleke, Lionel Perere, 1914- II. Conference of Heads of State or Government of Non-aligned Countries, Colombo, 1976. III. Title: Viskam: creativity.

Art—Slides.

SKALE, Patricia E.   381'.45'7
Rosenthal art slides / edited by Patricia E. Skale. Chicago : J. W. Rosenthal, [1974] vi, 173 p. ; 23 cm. [N4040.R67S58] 74-84118
1. Art—Slides. I. Title.

Art—Slides—Catalogs.

DELAURIER,   380.1'45'0015534025
Nancy.
Slide buyer's guide. [Edited by] Nancy DeLaurier. [Rev. ed. Kansas City; distributed by Nancy DeLaurier, Dept. of Art & Art History, University of Missouri-Kansas City, 1974] 105 p. 28 cm. "Published for the College Art Association of America." Limited to 500 copies. [N4040.C643D44 1974] 74-75721

1. Art—Slides—Catalogs. I. College Art Association of America. II. Title.

GARRARD, Mary D.   709'.2'2
Slides of works by women artists, a source book. Compiled by Mary D. Garrard for the College Art Association Women's Caucus. [Washington] 1974. iii, 94 p. 21 cm. [N4040.C646G37] 74-163529
1. Art—Slides—Catalogs. 2. Women artists. I. College Art Association Women's Caucus. II. Title.

NATIONAL Gallery of   708'.113'84
Canada.
Slide catalogue / The National Gallery of Canada. Ottawa : National Gallery of Canada, 1976. 73 p. ; 22 x 10 cm. Added t.p.: Repertoire des diapositives. Text in English and French; French text on inverted pages. Bibliography: p. [2] of cover. [N910.O7A7] 77-369226 ISBN 0-88884-319-4 : 5.00
1. National Gallery of Canada. 2. Art—Slides—Catalogs. I. Title. II. Title: Repertoire des diapositives.

PETRINI, Sharon.   380.1'45'069134
A handlist of museum sources for slides and photographs [by] Sharon Petrini [and] Troy-Jjohn Bromberger. [Santa Barbara, Slide Library, Art Dept., University of California, 1972] ii, 147 p. 29 cm. [N4000.P47] 72-169110
1. Art—Slides—Catalogs. 2. Photographs—Catalogs. 3. Art—Galleries and museums—Catalogs. I. Bromberger, Troy-Jjohn, joint author. II. Title.

Art societies—California—Los Angeles—Directories.

MOURE, Nancy Dustin   706'.0794'9
Wall.
Artists' clubs and exhibitions in Los Angeles before 1930 / by Nancy Dustin Wall Moure ; index by Phyllis Moure. [Los Angeles? : s. n.], 1974. ca. 150 p. ; 28 cm. (Publications in Southern California art ; no. 2) Label mounted on cover: Index of Southern California artists' clubs and their exhibitions. "Privately printed; edition of 300." [N6535.L6M68] 74-187947
1. Art societies—California—Los Angeles—Directories. 2. Art—Exhibitions—Indexes. I. Moure, Phyllis. II. Title. III. Title: Index of Southern California artists' clubs and their exhibitions. IV. Series.

Art—Societies, etc.

AMERICAN Academy of Arts   061.3
and Letters.
[Report on activities] New York. v. 28cm. annual. [AS36.A474] 59-45668
I. Title.

ARTS and Crafts   338.6'42
Conference, Fairbanks, Alaska, 1970.
Arts & Crafts Conference. Fairbanks, Dept. of Economic Development [1971?] 70 l. ports. 23 x 36 cm. Cover title. [NK21.A78 1970] 75-636230

ROERICH Society.   v. 12
Report. New York. v. 21cm. annual. [N10.R6] 56-25246
1. Art—Societies, etc. I. Title.

TORONTO. Art Gallery.   708'.113'32
Report to members. [Toronto] v. illus. 28cm. annual. Report year ends June 30. [N910.T6A35] 56-25245
I. Title.

Art societies — U.S.

WHITE, Leslie C. ed.   706.273
Survey of arts councils. Editors: Leslie C. White [and] Helen M. Thompson. Charleston, W.Va., American Symphony Orchestra League [c1959] 115 p. 23 cm. [N11.A725] 60-23443
1. Art societies — U.S. I. Thompson, Helen Mulford, 1908- joint ed. II. Title. III. Title: Arts councils.

Art societies—United States—Directories.

†SHLIEN, Helen.   706'.073
Artists associations in the U.S.A. : a descriptive directory / compiled by Helen Shlien. Boston : Boston Visual Artists Union, c1977. iv, 307 p. ; 21 cm. Errata slip inserted. [N51.S5] 77-155714 pbk. : 4.20
1. Art societies—United States—Directories. 2. Art commissions—United States—Directories. I. Title.
Publisher's address: 77 N. Washington St., Boston, MA 02114

Art—Sources.

MUEHSAM, Gerd, 1913-   700'.7
Guide to basic information sources in the visual arts / by Gerd Muehsam. Santa Barbara, Calif. : J. Norton Publishers/ABC-Clio, [1977] p. cm. Includes index. Bibliography: p. [N7425.M88] 77-17430 ISBN 0-87436-278-4 : 14.95
1. Art—Sources. I. Title.   BIP

Art, Southeast Asian—Catalogs.

BRAKE, Brian.   709.5'9
The house on the klong; the Bangkok home and Asian art collection of James Thompson. Photos.: Brian Brake. Text: William Warren. New York, Walker/Weatherhill [1969, c1968] 87 p. (chiefly illus. (part col.), plan, ports.) 27 cm. "A Weathermark edition." [N7311.B7 1969] 68-20640 7.50
1. Thompson, James Harrison Wilson, b. 1906—Art collections. 2. Art, Southeast Asian—Catalogs. 3. Bangkok, Thailand. House on the Klong. I. Warren, William, 1930- II. Title.

Art, Southeast Asian—Exhibitions.

HIGH Museum of   709'.59'0740158231
Art.
Beyond India : an exhibition of works of art from Southeast Asia in the William and Robert Arnett Collection, April 10-June 16, 1974. Atlanta : High Museum of Art, [1974?] [64] p. : ill. ; 29 cm. [N7311.H53 1974] 76-353910
1. Arnett, William—Art collections. 2. Arnett, Robert—Art collections. 3. Art, Southeast Asian—Exhibitions. I. Title.

Art—Spain—Hist.

KUBLER, George, 1912-   709.46
Art and architecture in Spain and Portugal and their American dominions, 1500 to 1800 [by] George Kubler [and] Martin Soria. [Harmondsworth, Middlesex] Penguin Books [1959] xxviii, 445p. illus., 192 plates, maps, plans. 27cm. (The Pelican history of art, Z17) Bibliographical references included in 'Notes' (p. 351-401) Bibliography: p. 403-416. [N7104.K8 1959a] 60-666
1. Art—Spain—Hist. 2. Architecture—Spain—Hist. 3. Art—Portugal—Hist. 4. Architecture—Portugal—Hist. 5. Art—Spanish America—Hist. 6. Architecture—Spanish America—Hist. I. Soria, Martin Sebastian. II. Title. III. Series.

PITA ANDRADE, Jose   709/.46
Manuel.
Treasures of Spain, from Altamira to the Catholic kings. Text by J. M. Pita Andrade. Introd. by F. J. Sanchez Canton. [Geneva] Skira; [Dist. in the U. S. by World, Cleveland, 1967] 248p. illus. (pt. col.) map. 34cm. [N7101.P543] 67-25118 29.50
1. Art—Spain—Hist. 2. Architecture—Spain—Hist. I. Title.

Art, Spanish.

LEES-MILNE, James.   709.033
Baroque in Spain and Portugal, and its antecedents. [dist. New York, Macmillan, 1961, c1960] 224p. illus. Bibl. 61-1109 7.00
1. Art, Spanish. 2. Art, Portuguese. 3. Art, Baroque. I. Title.

Art, Spanish—Addresses, essays, lectures.

CONTEMPORARY Spanish art   709'.46 / edited by William Dyckes. New York : Art Digest, c1975. 159 p. : ill. (some col.) ; 32 cm. Includes index. [N7108.C58] 75-10244 22.50
1. Art, Spanish—Addresses, essays, lectures. 2. Art, Modern—20th century—Spain—Addresses, essays, lectures. I. Dyckes, William.

Art — Spanish America.

PAN American Union.   709.8
Art in Latin America [essays] Washington [1950] 91 p. illus. 27 cm. (Club and study fine art series) Cover title. "Art publications of the Pan American Union": p. 85. bibliography: p. 86-91. [N6502.P28] 51-60367
1. Art — Spanish America. I. Title. II. Series.

Art, Spanish-American.

KELEMEN, Pal.   709.8
Baroque and rococo in Latin America. New York, Macmillan, 1951. xii, 302 p. 192 plates, map (on lining papers) 29 cm. Bibliography: p. 279-294. [N6502.K4] 51-4124
1. Art, Spanish-American. 2. Art, Baroque. I. Title.

Art, Spanish American—Colorado.

ADAMS, Robert Hickman,   709'.788
1937-
The architecture and art of early Hispanic Colorado. Written and photographed by Robert Adams. [Boulder] Colorado Associated University Press [1974] vi, 234 p. illus. 23 cm. [N6530.C6A32] 73-92503 ISBN 0-87081-059-6 10.00
1. Art, Spanish American—Colorado. 2. Art—Colorado. I. Title.   BIP

Art, Spanish-American—History.

CALI, Francois.   709.8
The Spanish arts of Latin America. Photos. by Claude Arthaud and Francois Hebert-Stevens. [Translated by Bryan Rhys] New York, Viking Press [1961] 300 p. illus., plates (part col.) maps. 25 cm. (A Studio book) Translation of L'art des conquistadors. "Bibliographical notes": p. 295-296. [N6502.C253 1961] 61-8357
1. Art, Spanish-American—History. I. Arthaud, Claude, 1927- II. Hebert-Stevens, Francois, 1922- III. Title.

Art, Spanish American—Juvenile literature.

GLUBOK, Shirley.   709'.73
The art of the Spanish in the United States and Puerto Rico. Designed by Gerard Nook. Photos. by Alfred Tamarin. New York, Macmillan [1972] 48 p. illus. 25 x 26 cm. Text and photographs examine the Spanish influence in the art and architecture of the United States and Puerto Rico. [N6538.S6G55] 75-185218 6.95
1. Art, Spanish American—Juvenile literature. 2. Folk art—United States—Juvenile literature. I. Tamarin, Alfred H., illus. II. Title.   BIP

Art, Spanish American—The West—Exhibitions.

THE Cross & the sword =   709'.78
La cruz y la espada : an exhibition at the Fine Arts Gallery of San Diego, April 3 to May 16, 1976 / edited by Jean Stern ; articles by Carl S. Dentzel ... [et al.]. San Diego, Calif. : [Fine Arts Society of San Diego], 1976. 106, E38 p. : ill. ; 28 cm. "Catalogue": p. 100-106. Bibliography: p. 42-43. [N6538.S6C76] 76-9415
1. Art, Spanish American—The West—Exhibitions. 2. Folk art—The West—Exhibitions. I. Stern, Jean, 1946- II. San Diego, Calif. Fine Arts Gallery. III. Title: La cruz y la espada.

Art, Spanish—Bibliography.

SMITH, Virginia Carlson.   759.6
Juan de Borgona and his school: a bibliography, by Virginia Smith. Los

Angeles, Hennessey & Ingalls, 1973. vi, 41 p. port. 23 cm. (Art & architecture bibliographies, no. 2) [Z8109.37.S62] 72-96390 ISBN 0-912158-40-9 4.95
1. Borgona, Juan de, d. 1533—Bibliography. 2. Art, Spanish—Bibliography. I. Title. II. Series.

Art, Spanish—Exhibitions.

BIRMINGHAM, Ala. Museum of Art. 709.46
Art of Spain [Catalog compiled by Edward F. Weeks. Birmingham, 1971?] 35 p. (chiefly plates) 21 x 23 cm. Cover title. Exhibition held Mar. 19-Apr. 4, 1971? [N7104.B5] 70-198332
1. Art, Spanish—Exhibitions. I. Weeks, Edward F. II. Title.

Art, Spanish—History.

CIRICI PELLICER, Aleiandro 709.46
Treasures of Spain from Charles V to Goya. Introd. byF. J. Sanchez Canton. Text by Alexandre Cirici Pellicer Tr. from Spanish by Robin Kemball, Gladys Ronkin. Catherine Moran. Geneva] Skira [Cleveland. World. 1966. c.1965] xxiv. 236p. mounted illus. (pt. col.) map. 34cm. (Treasures of the world) [N7104.C513] 65-24418 29.50
1. Art. Spanish—Hist. I. Title.

GUDIOL i Ricart, Josep. 709.46
The arts of Spain, by Jose Gudiol. Garden City, N.Y., Doubleday [1964] 318 p. illus. (part col.) 22 cm. (The Arts of man series) "A Chanticleer Press edition." [N7101.G78] 64-15731
1. Art, Spanish — Hist. I. Title. II. Series.

Art, Spanish—History.

CIRICI Pellicer, Alejandro. 709.46
Treasures of Spain from Charles V to Goya. Introd. by F.J. Sanchez Canton. Text by Alexandre Cirici-Pellicer. Translated from the Spanish by Robin Kemball, Gladys Ronkin, and Catherine Moran Geneva] Skira; [distributed in the U.S. by World Pub. Co., Cleveland, 1965] xxiv, 236 p. mounted illus. (part col.) map. 34 cm. (Treasures of the world) Translation of Los tesoros de Espana desde Carlos Quinto hasta Goya. [N7104.C513] 65-24418
1. Art, Spanish—History. I. Title.

Art—Springfield, Mass.—Catalogs.

SPRINGFIELD, Mass. Museum of Fine Arts. 708'.144'26
Handbook. [A fortieth anniversary publication. 4th ed.] Springfield [1973] 71 p. illus. (part col.) 28 cm. "The 1973 handbook is the fourth pictorial survey of the Museum of Fine Arts collections acquired by purchase and gift since 1963." [N773.A6 1973] 74-160799
1. Springfield, Mass. Museum of Fine Arts. 2. Art—Springfield, Mass.—Catalogs. I. Title.

Art—Stockholm—Catalogs.

STOCKHOLM. Nationalmuseum 707.4
Nationalmusei utstallningskataloger, 1966. Stockholm, Author. [New York, N.Y., 10019, 250W. 57th St.] World Wide Bks., 1966. 592p. 96p. of plates. 21cm. Eleventh exhibition of the Council of Europe, held at the Nationalmuseum, Stockholm, arranged by The Royal Library, others, 1966. Title: Christina, Queen of Sweden, a personality of European civilization. Suppls. accompany some numbers [N3540.A27] 48-33888 price unreported pap.,
1. Art—Stockholm—Catalogs. I. Title.

Art—Stockholm—Galleries and museums.

STOCKHOLM. 708.87
[English translation by Sylvia Furness and revision by D. Talbot Rice. 1st American ed.] South Brunswick, A. S. Barnes [1969] 63 p., 167 p. of illus. (part col.), ports. 35 cm. (Great centres of art) "The joint work of the professional staff of the Stockholm museums under the direction of Professor Carl Nordenfalk." [N3538.S813 1969] 77-86474 20.00
1. Art—Stockholm—Galleries and museums. I. Rice, David Talbot, 1903- ed. II. Nordenfalk, Carl Adam Johan, 1907- ed.

Art — Study and teaching.

ABISCH, Roz. 372.5
Art is for you, by Roz Abisch & Boche Kaplan. [New York] D. McKay Co. [1967] 48 p. col. illus. 22 cm. Art instructions in brief rhymes for beginners of all ages and creative levels. Directions for making a collage, a mobile, papier-mache, and woodcuts are included. [N361.A25] AC 67
1. Art—Study and teaching. 2. Handicraft. I. Kaplan, Boche, illus. II. Title.

ALKEMA, Chester Jay. 707
Alkema's complete guide to creative art for young people. Photos. by the author. New York, Sterling Pub. Co. [1971] 192 p. illus. (part col.) 22 x 25 cm. [N85.A46] 70-167654 ISBN 0-8069-5188-5
1. Art—Study and teaching. 2. Imagination. I. Title. BIP

ART appreciation course. 701.18
[New York] 1953- v. illus. 26cm. At head of title: Art treasure of the world. Contents.1. The pleasures of painting, by H. W. Janson.--2. On truth to nature, by H. W. Janson.--3.Expression in art, by H. Bober.--4. How to 'read' a picture, by W. Stechow.--5. Form and design, by S. Silve.--6. Style and styles, by H. W. Janson.--7. Abstraction in art, by R. Goldwater.--8. What pictures are made of, by W. S. Hechschel.--9. What makes a masterpiece by W. M. Ivins, Jr. [N7435.A7] 53-2445
1. Art—Study and teaching. 2. Art criticism. I. Title: Art treasures of the world.

ART Treasures of the world art appreciation course. 701.18 [New York, 1953- v. illus. 26cm. Vol. 9 has subtitle: How to appreciate art; v. 10-subtitle. Vols. 10-each with special t.p., have general title on p. 4 of cover. [N7435.A7] 53-2445
1. Art—Study and teaching. 2. Art criticism.

ASHBEE, Charles Robert, 1863-1942. 707
Should we stop teaching art / C. R. Ashbee. New York : Garland Pub., 1978. 122 p. ; 19 cm. (The Aesthetic movement & the arts and crafts movement) Reprint of the 1911 ed. published by B. T. Batsford, London. [N85.A7 1978] 76-17774 ISBN 0-8240-2478-8 : lib.bdg. : 35.00
1. Art—Study and teaching. I. Title. II. Series. BIP

BARKAN, Manuel. 372.5
A foundation for art education: New York, Ronald Press Co. [c1955] 235 p. 21cm. [N85.B36] 55-6077
1. Art—Study and teaching. I. Title.

BARKAN, Manuel. 372.5
Through art to creativity; art in the elementary school program. Boston, Allyn and Bacon, 1960. 365p. illus. 26cm. Includes bibliography. [N350.B3] 60-9679
1. Art—Study and teaching. 2. Children as artists. I. Title.

BASSETT, Richard, comp. 707
The open eye in learning: the role of art in general education, edited by Richard Bassett. [Cambridge, Mass., MIT Press, 1974 c1969] 216 p. illus. 23 cm. Undertaken as the report of a Special Committee on the Study of Art. Bibliography: [p.205]-209. [N85.B37] 69-10530 ISBN 0-262-52032-X. 2.95 (pbk.)
1. Art—Study and teaching. 2. Art and society. I. Special committee on the Study of Art. II. Title. BIP

BEITTEL, Kenneth R. 700'.7
Effect of self-reflective training in art on the capacity for creative action, by Kenneth R. Beittel. Washington, National Art Education Association, 1968. [16] p. 23 cm. (NAEA occasional paper no. 2) Abstract of the work first published in 1964. Bibliography: p. [16] [N87.B382] 76-24429 0.50
1. Art—Study and teaching. 2. Creation (Literary, artistic, etc.) 3. Learning, Psychology of. I. Title. II. Series: National Art Education Association. NAEA occasional paper no. 2

BEITTEL, Kenneth R 702
Effect of self-reflective training in art on the capacity for creative action [by] Kenneth R. Beittel. University Park, Pennsylvania State University, 1964. xx, 242 p. illus. 29 cm. "Cooperative research project no. 1874." "Research ... supported by the Cooperative Research Program of the [U.S.] Office of Education." Bibliography: p. 123-128. [N87.B38] 66-63263
1. Art — Study and teaching. 2. Creation (Literary, artistic, etc.) 3. Learning, Psychology of. I. Pennsylvania. State University. II. Title.

BOYLAN, Marie A. 707
Art experiences for all ages; a discussion of the values of the art experience in the school of today. New York, American Pr. [1964] 64p. illus. 21cm. [N350.B7] 64-210820 2.50
1. Art—Study and teaching. I. Title.

BURGART, Herbert J 350.p25
Creative art: the child and the school [by] Herbert J. Bergart. Rev. ed. Athens, Ga., University of Georgia Print Dept. [1964] 139 p. illus. 22 cm. [N357.B87] 64-7958
1. Art — Study and teaching. 2. Creative activities and seat work. 3. Child study. I. Title.

BURKHART, Robert Christopher, 1928- 707
Spontaneous and deliberate ways of learning. Scranton, International Textbook Co. [1962] 260p. illus. (part col.) 24cm. (International textbooks in art education) Bibliography: p. 229-231. [N87.B8] 62-12777
1. Art—Study and teaching. 2. Learning, Psychology of. 3. Orestion (Literary, artistic, etc.) I. Title.

CATHOLIC University of America. Workshop on Art in Catholic Secondary Schools, 1952. 707.12
Art in Catholic secondary schools; the proceedings of the Workshop on Art in Catholic Secondary Schools, conducted at the Catholic University of America from June 13th to June 24th, 1952. Edited by Sister Augusta Zimmer. Washingon, Cathlic University of America Press, 1953: vi, 189p. illus. 22cm. Bibliography at end of some of the chapters. [N363.C3 1952] A53
1. Art—Study and teaching. I. Zimmer, Augusta, Sister, ed. II. Title.

CLEVELAND Museum of Art. 708.171
Educational work at the Cleveland Museum of Art, by Thomas Munro and Jane Grimes. Rev., 2d ed. Cleveland, 1952. 89p. illus. 26cm. [N552.A453 1952] 53-274
1. Art—Study and teaching. I. Munro, Thomas, 1897- II. Title.

CONANT, Howard 707
Art in education [by] Howard Conant, Arne Randall. Peoria, Ill., C. A. Bennett [1963] 345p. illus. 26cm. Bibl. 63-39461 6.00
1. Art—Study and teaching. I. Randall, Arne W., joint author. II. Title.

CONRAD, George 1916- ed. 701'.18
Art and education. Edited by George Conrad. [Glassboro, N.J.] Dept of Art, Glassboro State College, 1965. vl. 93 l. col. illus. 28 cm. Bibliographical footnotes. [N350.A83] 67-63972
1. Art — Study and teaching. I. Title.

D'AMICO, Victor Edmond, 1904- 707
Art for the family [by] Victor D'Amico, Frances Wilson [and] Moreen Maser. New York, Museum of Modern Art; distributed by Doubleday [1965, c1954] 110 p. illus. 26 cm. 66-2957
1. Art — Study and teaching. I. Wilson, Frances, joint author. II. Maser, Moreen, joint author. III. Title.

DEAN, Joan. 372.5
Arts and crafts in the elementary school. New York, Philosophical Library [1964] 184 p. illus. 23 cm. Running title: Art and craft in the primary school. [N350.D43 1964] 64-5426
1. Art — Study and teaching. 2. Art — Technique. 3. Handicraft. I. Title.

DELONG, Patrick D. 701.18
Art and music in the humanities [by] Patrick D. DeLong, Robert Thomas [and] Robert E. Egner. Englewood Cliffs, N.J., Prentice-Hall [1966] xii, 244 p. illus., music 24 cm. Music: p. [147]-228. 1970 edition published under title: Art in the humanities. [N87.D4 1966] 66-28179
1. Art—Study and teaching. 2. Music—Analysis, appreciation. I. Thomas, Robert, 1930- joint author. II. Egner, Robert Edward, 1924- joint author. III. Title.

DELONG, Patrick D. 701.18
Art in the humanities [by] Patrick D. Delong. Englewood Cliffs, N.J., Prentice-Hall [1970] 150 p. illus. 23 cm. 1965-1966 editions published under title: Art and music in the humanities. [N87.D4 1970] 78-115833
1. Art—Study and teaching. I. Title. BIP

EISNER, Elliot W. 707
Educating artistic vision [by] Elliot W. Eisner. New York, Macmillan [1972] vi, 306 p. illus. (part col.) 24 cm. Includes bibliographical references. [N85.E48] 76-155268 8.95
1. Art—Study and teaching. I. Title.

ELLSWORTH, Maud. 707.12
Art for the high school. Syracuse [N.Y.] L. W. Singer Co. [1957] 96p. illus. 28cm. (Growing with art) Includes bibliography. [N350.E4] 57-31362
1. Art—Study and teaching. I. Title.

ELLSWORTH, Maud. 372.5
Growing with art, Maud Ellsworth and Michael F. Andrews. Chicago, B. H. Sanborn [1950-51] 8 v. illus. (part col.) 28 cm. --The teacher's book, books one through eight [by] Maud Ellsworth [and] Michael F. Andrews. Chicago, B. H. Sanborn, '1951. 16 p. 23 cm. Contents.book 1. Fun to begin.--book 2. Learning to talk a new way.--book 3. Seeing and doing.--book 4. Discovering surprises.--book 5. Exploring and making.--book 6. Art where we live.--book 7. Adventure at your elbow.--book 8. Everybody's business. [N362.E4] 51-6182
1. Art—Study and teaching. I. Andrews, Michael F. joint author. II. Title.

ERDT, Margaret Hamilton. 372.5
Teaching art in the elementary school; child growth through art experiences. New York, Rinehart, 1954. 284 p. illus. 27 cm. [N353.E7] 54-7609
1. Art—Study and teaching. I. Title.

FELDMAN, Edmund Burke. 707'.1
Becoming human through art; aesthetic experience in the school. Englewood Cliffs, N.J., Prentice-Hall [1970] x, 389 p. illus. (part col.), ports. 24 cm. Bibliography: p. 384-385. [N85.F37] 76-98454 9.95
1. Art—Study and teaching. 2. Aesthetics—Study and teaching. I. Title. BIP

FINE arts and the university (The) [by] A Whitney Griswold [others] Toronto. Macmillan: New York. St. Martin's [c.]1965. xii.89p. 23cm. (Frank Gerstein lects., 1965: York Univ. invitation ser.) Bibl. [N345.F5] 65-27623 2.95 700 711
1. Art—Study and teaching. 2. Performing arts—Study and teaching. I. Griswold. Alfred Whitney. 1906-1963. II. Series. III. Series: York University, Toronto. Invitation lecture series. 1965

GAITSKELL, Charles D 707.12
Art education during adolescence [by] Charles D. Gaitskell [and] Margaret R. Gaitskell. New York, Harcourt, Brace [c1954] 116p. illus. 24cm. [N350.G3] 56-160
1. Art—Study and teaching. I. Gaitskell, Margaret R., joint author. II. Title.

GOLDMAN, Freda H 707.1173
The arts in higher adult education; a second review of programs [by] Freda H. Goldman. [Brookline, Mass.] Center for the Study of Liberal Education for Adults at Boston University [1966] iii, 75 p. 23 cm. (CSLEA reports) [N345.G58] 66-31230
1. Art — Study and teaching. 2. Adult

SUBJECT INDEX

ART — STUDY

education — U.S. I. Title. II. Series: Center for the Study of Liberal Education for Adults. CSLEA reports

GREEN, Arthur S 372.5
Creative arts and crafts activities. Illus. by the author. Minneapolis, T.S. Denison [1960] 96p. illus. 29cm. [N350.G7] 60-9801
1. Art—Study and teaching. 2. Handicraft. I. Title.

GREENBERG, Pearl, 1927- 702.8
Art and ideas for young people. Photos. by Murray Greenberg. New York, Van Nostrand Reinhold Co. [1970] 151 p. illus. (part col.) 21 cm. Bibliography: p. 149. Discusses various techniques in several art forms including drawing and painting, glass, photography, graphics and textiles, yarns, and sculpture. [N350.G73] 70-90303
1. Art—Study and teaching. 2. Children as artists. I. Greenberg, Murray, illus. II. Title. BIP

HARLAN, Calvin. 707
Vision and invention; a course in art fundamentals. Englewood Cliffs, N.J., Prentice-Hall [1970] xiii, 203 p. illus. (part col.), port. 24 cm. Includes bibliographical references. [N87.H28] 69-10224
1. Art—Study and teaching. 2. Art—Technique. I. Title. BIP

HARRISON, Elizabeth, 1907- 372.5
Self-expression through art; an introduction to teaching and appreciation. Foreword by C. D. Gaitskell. Toronto, W. J. Gage [1951; label: Peoria, Ill., C. A. Beenett Co.] 112 p. illus 25 cm. [N350.H28] 52-8589
1. Art — Study and teaching. I. Title.

HART, Florence M 372.5
What shall we do in art? Practical ideas for elementary schools. Foreword by C. D. Gaitskell. Maplewood, N. J., C. S. Hammond [1960] 160p. illus. 22cm. [N350.H29 1960] 60-1509
1. Art—Study and teaching. I. Title.

HENKES, Robert. 700
Insights in art and education / by Robert Henkes. New York : Gordon Press, 1978. p. cm. (Gordon Press art series) [N85.H39] 78-2560 ISBN 0-8490-1371-2 lib.bdg. : 44.45
1. Art—Study and teaching. 2. Children as artists. 3. Creation (Literary, artistic, etc.) I. Title.

HOOVER, Francis Louis, 1913- 707
Art activities for the very young, from 3 to 6 years. Worcester, Mass., Davis Publications [1961] 77 p. illus. 28 cm. [N361.H6] 61-11263
1. Art—Study and teaching. I. Title. BIP

HORN, George F. 707
Art for today's schools [by] George F. Horn. Worcester, Mass., Davis Pubns. [1967] 272p. illus. 26cm. Bibl. [N350.H58] 67-17976 14.50
1. Art—Study and teaching. 2. Teachers—Handbooks, manuals, etc. I. Title. BIP

HORN, George F. 707
Art for today's schools [by] George F. Horn. [Text ed.] Worcester, Mass., Davis Publications [1969] 264 p. illus. 26 cm. Includes bibliographies. [N350.H58 1969] 72-1419
1. Art—Study and teaching. 2. Teachers—Handbooks, manuals, etc. I. Title.

HORNE, Joicey M. 372.5
Young artists, a handbook for teachers and parents. Illustrated by Joicey Horne and Martin Stringer. [1st ed.] Toronto, Longmans, Green [1961] 274 p. illus. 26 cm. [N352.H67] 61-3644
1. Art—Study and teaching. 2. Children as artists. I. Title.

AN Introduction to literature 709
& the fine arts. [East Lansing] Michigan State College Press, 1950. xiv, 418 p. illus., music. 28 cm. "The execution ... has been the charge of a committee in the Department of Literature and Fine Arts of the Basic College at Michigan State College." Includes bibliographies. [N85.I 5] 50-62757
1. Art—Study and teaching. 2. Music—Instruction and study. 3. Literature—Study and teaching. I. Michigan. State College of Agriculture and Applied Science, East Lansing. Basic College. Dept. of Literature and Fine Arts.

INTRODUCTION to the visual 707
arts [by] Monique Baque [and others] Under the patronage of Jean Sauboa. American editor: S. Ralph Maurello. New York, Tudor Pub. Co. [1968] 192 p. illus. (part col.) 19 x 25 cm. "Planned and written by a number of French art teachers of all ages and art disciplines at the behest and under the supervision of Jean Sauboa, inspector general of public education, France." [N85.I52] 74-2079 4.95
1. Art—Study and teaching. I. Baque, Monique. II. Sauboa, Jean. III. Maurello, S. Ralph, 1911- ed.

JEFFERSON, Blanche. 372.5
Teaching art to children; the values of creative expression. Boston, Allyn and Bacon, 1959. 294 p. illus. 24 cm. Includes bibliography. [N350.J4] 59-14282
1. Art—Study and teaching. 2. Children as artists. I. Title.

JEFFERSON, Blanche. 372.5
Teaching art to children; the values of creative expression. [2d ed.] Boston, Allyn and Bacon, 1963. 286 p. illus. 24 cm. Includes bibliography. [N350.J4 1963] 63-16654
1. Art—Study and teaching. 2. Children as artists. I. Title.

KAGAN, Pauline Wright. 372.5
From adventure to experience through art. Illustration layouts by David A. Russo. San Francisco, H. Chandler [c1959] 76p. illus. 28cm. [N350.K28] 61-1412
1. Art—Study and teaching. I. Title.

KAUFMAN, Irving. 707
Art and education in contemporary culture. New York, Macmillan [1966] xi, 531 p. illus. 26 cm. Bibliographical footnotes. [N87.K38] 66-22531
1. Art—Study and teaching. 2. Art and society. I. Title.

KEILER, Manfred L 1908- 707
The art in teaching art. Lincoln, University of Nebraska Press, 1961. 247p. illus. 29cm. [N350.K38] 61-5497
1. Art—Study and teaching. I. Title. BIP

KEILER, Manfred L, 1908- 372.5
Art in the schoolroom. Lincoln, University of Nebraska Press [1951] 214 p. illus. 25 cm. (The Small school in action series) [N350.K36] 51-12230
1. Art—Study and teaching. I. Title.

KEILER, Manfred L 1908- 372.5
Art in the schoolroom. [2d ed.] Lincoln, University of Nebraska Press [1955] 230p. illus. 25cm. (The Small school in action series) [N350.K36 1955] 55-2951
1. Art—Study and teaching. I. Title.

KNUDSEN, Estelle Hagen. 372.5
Children's art education [by] Knudsen & Christensn. Pooria, Ill., C. A. Bennett Co., c1957. 206p. illus. 26cm. [N350.K58] 57-5429
1. Art—Study and teaching. I. Christensen, Ethel Madill, joint author. II. Title.

LANDIS, Mildred M, 1898- 372.5
Meaningful art education. Peoria, Ill., C. A. Bennett Co. [1951] 185 p. illus. (part col.) 23 cm. Bibliography: p. 179-182. [N85.L28] 51-3517
1. Art—Study and teaching. I. Title.

LANSING, Kenneth Melvin, 372.5'2
1925-
Art, artists, and art education [by] Kenneth M. Lansing. New York, McGraw-Hill [1969?] x, 650 p. illus. (part col.) 25 cm. Includes bibliographies. [N85.L36] 71-77229
1. Art—Study and teaching. 2. Children as artists. I. Title. BIP

LAWLEY, Leslie William 707
A basic course in art [1st Amer. ed.] Boston, Boston Bk. & Art Shop [1965, c.1962] x, 85p. illus. (pt. col.) 25cm. Bibl. [N353.L3] 64-8586 5.95
1. Art—Study and teaching. I. Title.

LEE, Carvel. 707
Art guide. Illus. by the author. Minneapolis, T. S. Denison [1959] 111p. illus. 29cm. [N350.L38] 59-14409
1. Art—Study and teaching. I. Title.

LIDSTONE, John. 707
Reinhold visuals; aids for art teaching [by] Lidstone, Lewis [and] Brody. New York, Reinhold Book Corp. [1968- portfolios of illus. (part col.) 62 cm. Cover title. Each portfolio contains 24 posters, each with descriptive text on back, and a 15 p. descriptive pamphlet. Contents.—1. Line.—2. Mass.—3. Organization.—4. Surface. [N4035.L5] 68-16037
1. Art—Study and teaching. 2. Art—Audio-visual aids—Catalogs. I. Lewis, Stanley T., joint author. II. Brody, Sheldon, joint author. III. Title.

LINDERMAN, Earl W 372.5
Developing artistic and perceptual awareness art practice in the elementary classroom [by] Earl W. Linderman and Donald W. Herberholz. Dubuque, Iowa, W. C. Brown [c1964] xii, 102 p. illus. 22 x 28 cm. (Brown art series) Includes bibliographies. [N350.L46] 64-16394
1. Art — Study and teaching. I. Herberholz, Donald W., joint author. II. Title.

LISSIM, Simon, 1900- 706.9
How to be an artist. New York, W. Funk [1952] 212 p. illus. 24 cm. [N85.L58] 52-9790
1. Art—Study and teaching. I. Title.

LONG Island Art Teachers 372.5
Association.
Art education in modern elementary schools. Fred Schwartz, editor. Preface by Howard Conant. [n. p.] O. Schmidt, 1957. 102p. illus. 28cm. Includes bibliography. [N357.L6] 57-44773
1. Art—Study and teaching. I. Schwartz, Fred, ed. II. Title.

LONGMAN, Lester Duncan, 1905- 707
History and appreciation of art, the State University of Iowa, Iowa City, Iowa. Dubuque, W. C. Brown Co. [1950,1949] 601 28 cm. [N386.I6L6] 51-61921
1. Art—Study and teaching. I. Iowa. University. II. Title.

LORD, Lois. 372.5
Collage and construction in elementary and junior high schools. Worcester, Mass., Davis Publications [1958] 111 p. illus. 27 cm. [N350.L56] 58-9168
1. Art—Study and teaching. 2. Handicraft. I. Title.

LOUGHRAN, Bernice B. 707
Art experiences; an experimental approach. New York, Harcourt [1963] 154p. illus. 28cm. 62-22022 3.45
1. Art—Study and teaching. 2. Art—Technique. I. Title.

LOWENFELD, Viktor. 707
Creative and mental growth. 3d ed. New York, Macmillan [1957] 541p. illus. 24cm. [N85.L6 1957] 57-6356
1. Art—Study and teaching. 2. Creation (Literary, artistic, etc.) 3. Children as artists. 4. Art—Psychology. I. Title.

LOWENFELD, Viktor. 707
Creative and mental growth. Rev. ed. New York, Macmillan [1952] 408 p. illus. 25 cm. [N85.L6 1952] 52-8529
1. Art—Study and teaching. 2. Creation (Literary, artistic, etc.) 3. Children as artists. 4. Art—Psychology. I. Title. BIP

LOWENFELD, Viktor. 707
Creative and mental growth [by] Viktor Lowenfeld [and] W. Lambert Brittain. 4th ed. New York, Macmillan [1964] xv, 412 p. illus. (part col.) 25 cm. Includes bibliographical references. [N85.L6 1964] 64-12531
1. Art—Study and teaching. 2. Creation (Literary, artistic, etc.) 3. Children as artists. 4. Artists—Psychology. I. Brittain, W. Lambert. II. Title.

LOWENFELD, Viktor. 707
Creative and mental growth / Viktor Lowenfeld and W. Lambert Brittain. 6th ed. New York : Macmillan, [1975] xi, 430 p. : ill. ; 24 cm. Includes index. Bibliography: p. 415-423. [N350.L62 1975] 74-5721 ISBN 0-02-372090-5 : 9.95
1. Art—Study and teaching. 2. Creation (Literary, artistic, etc.) 3. Children as artists. 4. Artists—Psychology. I. Brittain, W. Lambert, joint author. II. Title.

MCFEE, June King. 707
Art, culture, and environment : a catalyst for teaching / June King McFee, Rogena M. Degge. Belmont, Calif. : Wadsworth Pub. Co., c1977. xviii, 398 p. : ill. ; 25 cm. Includes indexes. Bibliography: p. 381-386. [N85.M24] 76-42286 ISBN 0-534-00472-5 : 12.95
1. Art—Study and teaching. I. Degge, Rogena M., joint author. II. Title. BIP

MCFEE, June King. 372.5
Preparation for art. 2d ed. Belmont, Calif., Wadsworth Pub. Co. [1970] 409 p. illus. 21 cm. Includes bibliographies. [N350.M23 1970] 70-118325
1. Art—Study and teaching. I. Title.

MCFEE, June King. 372.5
Preparation for art. Illustrated by Jean Ray Laury. San Francisco, Wadsworth Pub. Co. [1961] 341 p. illus. 23 cm. Includes bibliography. [N350.M23] 61-5915
1. Art—Study and teaching. I. Title.

MCILVAIN, Dorothy S 372.5
Art for primary grades. New York, Putnam [1961] 297p. illus. 26cm. Includes bibliography. [N350.M24] 61-13155
1. Art—Study and teaching. I. Title.

MACLEISH, Archibald, 1892- 707
Art education and the creative process. New York, Published for the Committee on Art Education by the Museum of Modern Art [c1954] 11p. 26cm. [N87.M23] 55-1772
1. Art—Study and teaching. I. Title.

MANZELLA, David 707
Educationists and the evisceration of the visual arts. Scranton, Pa., Intl. Textbk. [c.1963] 97p. 17cm. (Intl. textbks. in art educ.) 63-13869 1.75 pap.,
1. Art—Study and teaching. I. Title.

MARSHALL, Sybil. 707
An experiment in education. Cambridge [Eng.] University Press, 1963. 222 p. illus. 23 cm. Autobiographical. [N350.M266] 63-22812
1. Art—Study and teaching. 2. Teachers—Correspondence, reminiscences, etc. I. Title. BIP

MERRITT, Helen. 707
Guiding free expression in children's art. New York, Holt, Rinehart and Winston [1964] viii, 88 p. 22 cm. [N350.M45] 64-21407
1. Art—Study and teaching. 2. Creation (Literary, artistic, etc.) I. Title.

MICHAEL, John Arthur, 1921- 707
A handbook for art instructors and students based upon concepts and behaviors [by] John A. Michael. [1st ed.] New York, Vantage Press [1970] 223 p. illus., ports. 21 cm. Bibliography: p. 221-223. [N85.M5] 78-18358 4.95
1. Art—Study and teaching. I. Title.

MILLS, John FitzMaurice 751
Instructions to young artists. London, Museum Press [1960; stamped: distributed by Sportshelf, New Rochelle, N. Y.] 116p. illus., diagrs. 23cm. (The Brompton library) 60-4180 3.75 bds.,
1. Art—Study and teaching. I. Title.

MILLS, John FitzMaurice, 751
1917-
Instructions to young artists. [2d ed.] London, Museum Pr. [dist. New Rochelle, N.Y., SportShelf, 1965, c.1960, 1964] 111p. illus. 23cm. (Brompton lib.) [ND1262.M5] 65-1874 4.25 bds.,
1. Art—Study and teaching. I. Title.

MORMAN, Jean Mary. 707
Art: of wonder & a world. Editorial consultants: Olive L. Riley, Mary Cole Emerson [and] Albert W. Porter. Design consultant: Norman Laliberte. Blauvelt, N.Y., Art Education [1967] 111 p. illus. (part col.) 26 cm. [N87.M6] 67-29873
1. Art—Study and teaching. 2. Aesthetics. I. Title.

MUNRO, Thomas, 1897- 707
Art education, its philosophy and psychology; selected essays. New York, Liberal Arts Press, 1956. 387 p. 25 cm. [N85.M83] 56-58510
1. Art—Study and teaching. 2. Art—Philosophy. 3. Art—Psychology. I. Title.

NEW York. Museum of Modern Art. Dept. of Education. 707
Experiments in creative art teaching; a progress report on the Dept. of Education, 1937-1960 [by] Victor D'Amico [director. New York, Museum of Modern Art]; distributed by Doubleday, Garden City, N. Y. [1960] 64p. illus. 60-7938 2.50 pap.,
1. Art—Study and teaching. 2. Children as artists. I. D'Amico, Victor Edmond, 1904- II. Title.

NICHOLAS, Florence (Williams) 1893- 707.12
Art for young America, by Florence W. Nicholas, Mabel B. Trilling, and Margaret Lee, in collaboration with Elmer A. Stephan. Edited by William G. Whitford. [2d rev. ed.] Peoria, Ill., C. Bennett Co. [1952] 292 p. illus. 23 cm. Full name: Florence Elizabeth (Williams) Nicholas. [N350.N52] 52-14452
1. Art — Study and teaching. I. Title. **BIP**

NICHOLAS, Florence (Williams) 1893- 707.12
Art for young America [by] Carl J. Heyne, Jr., Florence W. Nicholas, Margaret M. Lee [and] Mabel B. Trilling. [3d rev. ed.] Peoria, Ill., C. A. Bennett Co. [1960] 286p. illus. 23cm. Earlier editions by Florence W. Nicholas, Mabel B. Trilling, and Margaret Lee, in collaboration with Elmer A. Stephan. [N350.N52 1960] 60-6617
1. Art—Study and teaching. I. Heyne, Carl J., joint author. II. Title.

NICHOLAS, Florence (Williams) 1893- 707.1273
Art for young America [by] Carl J. Heyne, Jr., Florence W. Nicholas, Margaret M. Lee [and] Mabel B. Trilling. [1th rev. ed.] Peoria, Ill., C. A. Bennett Co. [1962] 286p. illus. 23cm. First ed., 1946, by Florence W. Nicholas, Mabel B. Trilling and margaret Lee, in collaboration with Elmer A. Stephan. [N350.N52 1962] 62-5548
1. Art—Study and teaching. I. Heyne, Carl J., joint author. II. Title.

NICHOLAS, Florence (Williams) 1893- 707.1'273
Art for young America [by] Carl J. Heyne, with Florence W. Nicholas, Margaret M. Lee [and] Mabel B. Trilling. 5th ed. Peoria, Ill., C. A. Bennett Co. [1967] 256 p. illus. (part col.) 25 cm. First ed. 1946, by Florence W. Nicholas, Mabel B. Trilling, and Margaret Lee, in collaboration with Elmer A. Stephan. Bibliography: p. 251-252. [N350.N52] 67-7715
1. Art — Study and teaching. I. Heyne, Carl J., joint author. II. Title.

OKLAHOMA. Agricultural and Mechanical College, Stillwater. School of Arts and Sciences. 707.11766
Fine arts activities. Programs. [Stillwater?] v. 26 cm. [N386.O564] 50-15182
I. Title.

OKLAHOMA. State University of Agriculture and Applied Science, Stillwater. School of Arts and Sciences. 707.11766
Fine arts activities. Programs. [Stillwater?] v. 26cm. Vols. for issued by the school under an earlier name of the university: Agricultural and Mechanical College. [N386.O55A6] 50-15182
I. Title.

PAINE, Irma Littler. 372.5
Art aids for elementary teaching, a handbook. [Rev. ed.] Tacoma [1953] 88 p. illus. 28 cm. Previous editions published under title: Art aids for primary teaching. [N350.P25 1953] 54-1615
1. Art—Study and teaching. I. Title.

PAINE, Irma Littler. 372.5
Art aids for elementary teaching, a handbook. Rev. ed. Minneapolis, Burgess Pub. Co. [1959] 135 p. illus. 28 cm. First published in 1949 under title: Art aids for primary teaching. [N350.P25 1959] 59-15151
1. Art—Study and teaching. I. Title.

PAINE, Irma Littler. 372.5
Art aids for elementary teaching, a handbook. 5th ed. Minneapolis, Burgess Pub. Co. [1965] viii, 168 p. illus. (part col.) 28 cm. First published in 1949 under title: Art aids for primary teaching. "Annotated film list": p. 161-168. Bibliography: p. 157-159. [N350.P25] 65-16574
1. Art — Study and teaching. I. Title.

PEARSON, Ralph M., 1883- 707
The new art education; foreword by Eduard C. Lindeman. Rev ed. New York, Harper [1953] 272 p. illus. 24 cm. [N85.P4 1953] 52-12046
1. Art—Study and teaching. I. Title.

PERRY, Kenneth Frederick, 1902- 707
An experiment with a diversified art program. New York, Bureau of Publications, Teachers College, Columbia University, 1943. [New York, AMS Press, 1972, i.e. 1973 ix, 163 p. illus. 22 cm. On spine: A diversified art program. Reprint of the 1943 ed., issued in series: Teachers College, Columbia University. Contributions to education, no. 863. Originally presented as the author's thesis, Columbia. Bibliography: p. 161-163. [N350.P4 1972] 79-177148 ISBN 0-404-55863-1 10.00
1. Art—Study and teaching. I. Title. II. Title: A diversified art program. III. Series: Columbia University. Teachers College. Contributions to education, no. 863. **BIP**

PRICE, Charles Matlack. 707
Art school self-taught, by Matlack Price and A. Thornton Bishop. New York, Greenberg [1952] 439 p. illus. 28 cm. Includes bibliography. [N87.P75] 52-9968
1. Art—Study and teaching. I. Bishop, Albert Thornton, joint author. II. Title.

READ, Herbert Edward, Sir, 1893-1968. 707
Education through art. [3d rev. ed.] New York, Pantheon Books [1974] xxii, 328 p. illus., 64 plates. 22 cm. Bibliography: p. 309-321. [N85.R42 1974] 74-163504 ISBN 0-394-49178-5 10.00
1. Art—Study and teaching. 2. Art—Psychology. 3. Education—Philosophy. I. Title.
Pbk., 4.95, ISBN 0-394-70640-4.

REED, Carl. 745.5
Art from scrap. The authors: Carl Reed [and] Joseph Orze. [Worcester, Mass., Davis Publications, 1960] 89 p. illus. 28 cm. [N350.R4] 60-9507
1. Art—Study and teaching. 2. Found objects (Art) I. Orze, Joseph, joint author. II. Title. **BIP**

REED, Carl. 745.5
Art from scrap [by] Carl Reed [and] Joseph Orze. [Rev. and expanded ed.] Worcester, Mass., Davis Publications [1974] 111 p. illus. 28 cm. [N350.R4 1974] 73-87725 ISBN 0-87192-055-7 6.25 (pbk.)
1. Art—Study and teaching. 2. Found objects (Art) I. Orze, Joseph, joint author. II. Title.

REED, Carl. 707.12
Early adolescent art education. Peoria, Ill., C. A. Bennett Co. [1957] 205p. illus. 26cm. [N363.R4] 57-5430
1. Art— Study and teaching. I. Title.

RICE, David Talbot, 1903- 707
Teach yourself to study art. New York, Roy Publishers [1955?] 164p. illus. 18cm. (The Teach yourself books) Includes bibliographies. [N87] 55-9316
1. Art—Study and teaching. I. Title.

ROBERTSON, Seonaid Mairi. 707
Rosegarden and labyrinth; a study in art education. Foreword by Herbert Read. New York, Barnes & Noble [1963] 216 p. illus. 23 cm. Includes bibliography. [N87.R6 1963] 63-3317
1. Art—Study and teaching. 2. Art—Philosophy. 3. Creation (Literary, artistic, etc.) I. Title. **BIP**

ROTTGER, Ernst. 745
Surfaces in creative drawing [by] Ernst Rottger, Dieter Klante, and Friedrich Salzmann. New York, Van Nostrand Reinhold Co. [1970, c1969] 119 p. illus. (part col.) 21 cm. ([Creative play series]) Translation of Die Flache. [N85.R6213 1970b] 75-119597 5.95
1. Art—Study and teaching. I. Klante, Dieter, joint author. II. Salzmann, Friedrich, joint author. III. Title.

ROUKES, Nicholas. 701'.18
Classroom craft manual. San Francisco, Fearon Publishers, c1960. 64 p. illus. 28 cm. [N350.R6] 63-39459
1. Art — Study and teaching. 2. Handicraft. I. Title. **BIP**

SCHNEIDER, Dawn E 372.5
Correlated art. Scranton, International Textbook Co., 1951. xi, 196 p. illus. (part col.) 26 cm. (International textbooks in art education) [N362.S35] 51-11386
1. Art — Study and teaching. 2. Drawing — Instruction. I. Title.

SCHULTZ, Larry T. 707'.1073
Studio art; a resource for artist-teachers [by] Larry T. Schultz. New York, Van Nostrand Reinhold [1973] 103 p. illus. 21 cm. [N350.S55 1973] 75-155588 ISBN 0-442-27433-5 4.50
1. Art—Study and teaching. 2. Project method in teaching. 3. Artists as teachers. I. Title. **BIP**

SCHWARTZ, Fred R. 707
Structure and potential in art education [by] Fred R. Schwartz. Waltham, Mass., Ginn-Blaisdell [1970] xv, 414 p. illus. 26 cm. Bibliography: p. 397-405. [N87.S3] 75-96335
1. Art—Study and teaching. 2. Art teachers. I. Title.

SIMPSON, Martha. 707
Art is for everyone. New York, McGraw-Hill [1951] x, 173 p. plates. 21 cm. [N7435.S5] 51-10790
1. Art—Study and teaching. I. Title.

SLOAN, John, 1871-1951. 760'.028
Gist of art : principles and practise expounded in the classroom and studio / John Sloan ; recorded with the assistance of Helen Farr Sloan. [3d rev. ed.] New York : Dover Publications, 1977. li, 200 p. : ill. ; 22 cm. (Dover art instruction and reference books) "Revised republication of the work originally published by American Artists Group, inc., New York." Includes index. [N85.S55 1977] 76-27459 ISBN 0-486-23435-5 pbk. : 3.50
1. Art—Study and teaching. 2. Art—Philosophy. I. Sloan, Helen Farr, 1911- II. Title. **BIP**

SMITH, Ralph Alexander, ed. 707
Aesthetics and criticism in art education; problems in defining, explaining, and evaluating art. Edited by Ralph A. Smith. Chicago, Rand McNally [1966] xix, 513 p. 23 cm. (Rand McNally education series) Bibliography: p. 493-501. [N87.S52] 66-13452
1. Art—Study and teaching. 2. Aesthetics. 3. Art criticism. I. Title.

SPROUL, Adelaide. 372.5'044
Teaching art: sources & resources. Photos. by John Urban. New York, Van Nostrand-Reinhold Co. [1971] 88 p. illus. 29 cm. Bibliography: p. 87. [N87.S65] 70-149263
1. Art—Study and teaching. 2. Nature (Aesthetics) 3. Learning by discovery. I. Title.

STAFFORD, Cora Elder, 1897- 372.5
Art for living [by] Cora Eldder Stafford, Ivan E. Johnson, and Viola McElhiney. Chicago, Laidlaw Bros., c1947-[50] 8 v. illus. (part col.) 26 cm. [N353.S72] 51-1418
1. Art — Study and teaching. I. Title.

STAFFORD, Cora Elder, 1897- 372.5
Art for living [by] Cora Elder Stafford, Ivan E. Johnson, and Viola McElhiney. Teachers' ed. Chicago, Laidlaw Bros., c1947-50. 8 v. illus. (part col.) 26 cm. Each vol. includes a "pupils' books" with special t.p. [N353.S7] 51-1419
1. Art — Study and teaching. I. Title.

STEVENI, Michael. 707
Art & education. New York, Atherton Press [1969, c1968] 239 p. illus. 23 cm. Bibliography: p. [233]-235. [N85.S74 1969] 68-57348
1. Art—Study and teaching. I. Title.

STEVENS, Harold. 707
Ways with art; 50 techniques for teaching children. New York, Reinhold [1963] 224 p. illus. (part col.) 22 cm. [N350.S83] 63-11423
1. Art—Study and teaching. 2. Art—Technique. I. Title.

TOLCES, Toska. 707
Creative disciplines; explorations in awareness. Portland, Me., B. Wheelwright Co. [1956] 115p. 21cm. [N87.T6] 56-13470
1. Art—Study and teaching. 2. Creation (Literary, artistic, etc.) I. Title. II. Title: Awareness.

TRITTEN, Gottfried. 372.52
Art techniques for children. New York, Reinhold Pub. Corp. [1964] 174 p. illus. (part col.) 25 cm. Translation of Gestaltende Kinderhande. [N350.T733] 64-13641
1. Art—Study and teaching. 2. Art—Technique. I. Title.

TRITTEN, Gottfried. 707'.1
Teaching color and form. New York, Van Nostrand Reinhold [1971- v. illus. 31 cm. Translation of Erziehung durch Farbe und Form. [N87.T7313] 78-90313
1. Art—Study and teaching. 2. Color—Study and teaching. I. Title.

UNITED Nations Educational, Scientific and Cultural Organization. 707
Art education: an international survey. Paris, Unesco, 1972. 109 p. illus. (part col.) 22 cm. (Its [Document] no. SHC.70/D.60/A) [AS4.U8A15 SHC.70/D.60/A] [N85] 73-150169 9.00
1. Art—Study and teaching. I. Title. II. Series: United Nations Educational, Scientific and Cultural Organization. Document no. SHC.70/D.60/A.
Distributed by Unipub, 6.50 (pbk.)

USES of Newer Media in Art Education Project. 707
Final report. [Washington] National Art Education Association, 1966. 94 p. illus. 23 cm. "NDEA project no. 5-16-027, sponsored by the National Art Education Association and the U.S. Office of Education; Vincent Lanier, project director." Includes bibliographies. [N87.U8] 67-61271
1. Art—Study and teaching. 2. Teaching—Aids and devices. I. Lanier, Sidney. II. National Art Education Association.

WHITE, Eugene, 1908- 372.5
Art for the child; for the development of an adequate teacher background. Los Angeles, Pepperdine College, 1952. 153 l. illus. 27 cm. [N350.W46] 52-40980
1. Art—Study and teaching. I. Title.

WICKISER, Ralph Lewanda, 1909- 707
An introduction to art education. Yonkers-on-Hudson, N.Y., World Book Co. [1957] 342 p. illus. 24 cm. [N85.W47] 57-11697
1. Art — Study and teaching. I. Title.

WOLFF, Robert Jay, 1905- 707
Essays on art and learning. [Los Angeles?] Manas Pub. Co. [1970] x, 100 p. 22 cm. [N85.W6] 70-17896
1. Art—Study and teaching. I. Title.

WOLFF, Robert Jay, 1905- 707
Essays on art and learning [by] Robert Jay Wolff. New York, Grossman, 1971 [c1970] x, 100 p. 23 cm. [N85.W6 1971] 79-143539 ISBN 0-670-52414-X 7.95
1. Art—Study and teaching. I. Title.

WORFOLK, Helen S. 707
Fundamentals of art; [a clear-guide text by Helen S. Worfolk, Carlton E. Naugle, and Carleton F. Worfolk. Las Vegas, Nev., Vowco, inc., 1965] 7 pts. in 1 v. illus. (part col.) 30 cm. Cover title. "Programmed study guide" (96 p.) and 7 fold. col. plates, in pockets. [N85.W63] 65-28636
1. Art—Study and teaching. I. Naugle, Carlton Elwood, 1921- joint author. II. Worfolk, Carleton F., joint author. III. Title.

YOCHIM, Louise Dunn, 1909- 707
Building human relationships through art. Chicago, L. M. Stein [1954] 157p. illus. 24cm. [N85.Y62] 55-1089
1. Art—Study and teaching. I. Title.

YOCHIM, Louise Dunn, 1909- 707
Perceptual growth in creativity. Scranton, Intl. Textbk. [1967] xiii, 265p. illus. 24cm. Bibl. [N87.Y6] 66-16245 7.50
1. Art—Study and teaching. 2. Creative ability. 3. Perception. I. Title.

ZIEGFELD, Edwin, 1905- ed. 707
Education and art; a symposium. Freeport, N.Y., Books for Libraries Press [1973, c1953] p. (Essay index reprint series)

Bibliography: p. [N85.Z5 1973] 73-1246 ISBN 0-518-10072-3
1. Art—Study and teaching. I. Title. **BIP**

ZIEGFELD, Ernest. 707.11
Art in the college program of general education. New York, Bureau of Publications, Teachers College, Columbia University, 1953. 239p. 24cm. (Teachers College studies in education) [N345.Z53] 53-8328
1. Art—Study and teaching. 2. Education, Higher. I. Title.

Art—Study and teaching—Addresses, essays, lectures.

ALBERS, Josef. 707'.1
Search versus re-search; three lectures by Josef Albers at Trintiy College, April 1965. Hartford, Conn., Trinity College Press, 1969. 85 p. illus. (part col.) 27 cm. [N87.A37] 68-31182
1. Art—Study and teaching—Addresses, essays, lectures. I. Title.

BATTCOCK, Gregory, 1937- 707
New ideas in art education; a critical anthology. [1st ed.] New York, E. P. Dutton, 1973. xiii, 289 p. illus. 19 cm. Includes bibliographical references. [N85.B393 1973] 73-166189 ISBN 0-525-47345-9 2.95
1. Art—Study and teaching—Addresses, essays, lectures. I. Title. **BIP**

BRITTAIN, W. Lambert, 707'.08
comp.
Creativity and art education. Edited by W. Lambert Brittain. Washington, National Art Education Association [1964] 146 p. illus. 23 cm. "Articles for this publication were selected from issues of Studies in art education." [N87.B7] 702 75-24844
1. Art—Study and teaching—Addresses, essays, lectures. 2. Creative ability—Addresses, essays, lectures. I. Title.

BUTLER, Reginald Cotterell, 701
1913-
Creative development. New York, Horizon [1963, c.1962] 88p. 22cm. 63-21571 2.75 bds.,
1. Art—Study and teaching—Addresses, essays, lectures. 2. Creation (Literary, artistic, etc.) I. Title.

CHALLENGE and change in art 707
education / Guy A. Hubbard, guest editor. Bloomington : School of Education, Indiana University, 1976. v, 101 p. : ill. ; 23 cm. (Viewpoints ; v. 52, no. 3 ISSN 0019-6835s) Includes bibliographies and index. [N85.C43] 76-373078 2.00
1. Art—Study and teaching—Addresses, essays, lectures. I. Hubbard, Guy. II. Series: Viewpoints (Bloomington, Ind.) ; v. 52, no. 3.

EISNER, Elliott W., ed. 707
Readings in art education [by] Elliot W. Eisner, David W. Ecker Waltham, Mass., Blaisdell [c.1966] xii, 468p. illus. 26cm. (Blaisdell bk. in the humanities) Bibl. [N85.E5] 65-14578 8.50
1. Art—Study and teaching—Addresses, essays, lectures. I. Ecker. David W., joint ed. II. Title.

FIELD, Dick. 707'.1
The study of education and art, edited by Dick Field and John Newick. London, Boston, Routledge & Kegan Paul [1973] ix, 244 p. 22 cm. Includes bibliographies. [N85.F53 1973] 73-83074 ISBN 0-7100-7648-7 12.75
1. Art—Study and teaching—Addresses, essays, lectures. I. Newick, John, joint author. II. Title.
Pbk. 5.95, ISBN 0-7100-7775-0 **BIP**

LANIER, Vincent. 707
Essays in art education : the development of one point of view / by Vincent Lanier. 2d ed. New York : MSS Information Corp., c1976. 149 p. ; 21 cm. Bibliography: p. 146-149. [N85.L33 1976] 75-17822 ISBN 0-8422-0516-0 pbk. : 3.75
1. Art—Study and teaching—Addresses, essays, lectures. I. Title.
Contents omitted

LOWENFELD, Viktor. 707
Viktor Lowenfeld speaks on art and creativity. Edited by W. Lambert Brittain. [Washington, National Art Education Association, 1968] 64 p. 23 cm. Selections edited from tape recordings of Lowenfeld's speeches. [N87.L64] 71-30254
1. Art—Study and teaching—Addresses, essays, lectures. 2. Creation (Literary, artistic, etc.)—Addresses, essays, lectures. I. Title. **BIP**

NATIONAL Society for the 707
Study of Education. Committee on Art Education.
Art education, by the yearbook committee and associated contributors. Edited by W. Reid Hastie. Editor for the society, Herman G. Richey. Chicago, NSSE; distributed by the University of Chicago Press, 1965. xi, 357, cxi p. 24 cm. (Yearbook of the National Society for the Study of Education [new ser.] 64th, pt. 2) Bibliographical footnotes. [LB5.N25] 65-4791
1. Art — Study and teaching — Addresses, essays, lectures. I. Hastie, W. Reid, ed. II. Title. III. Series: National Society for the Study of Education. Yearbook, new ser., 64th, pt. 2

NEW directions in art 707'.1
education; report of the international symposium, Belgrade, Yugoslavia — July 27-29, 1966. Manuel Barkan, editor. Washington, National Art Education Association, 1967. 110 p. 23 cm. At head of title: Final report, Project no. 6-1840-24, Contract no. OEC 2-6-061840-1247. "Research ... performed pursuant to a contract with the Office of Education, U.S. Department of Health, Education, and Welfare." [N85.N38] 71-20170
1. Art—Study and teaching—Addresses, essays, lectures. I. Barkan, Manuel, ed. II. National Art Education Association.

PAPPAS, George, 1929- comp. 707
Concepts in art and education; an anthology of current issues. [New York] Macmillan [1970] xiii, 273 p. illus. 24 cm. Includes bibliographical references. [N85.P36] 75-87894
1. Art—Study and teaching—Addresses, essays, lectures. I. Title. **BIP**

STODDARD, Geroge Dinsmore, 701
1897-
Art: as the measure of man, by George D. Stoddard; as education, by Irwin Edman; a personal vision, by Bruno Bettelheim. New York, [Published by] the Museum of Modern Art for the National Committee on Art Education; distributed by Doubleday, Garden City, N.y. [c1964] 64 p. 18 cm. Lectures, delivered at annual conferences of the National Committee on Art Education, for the years, 1963, 1950, and 1962 respectively. [N85.A65] 64-15286
1. Art — Study and teaching — Addresses, essays, lectures. 2. Art — Philosophy — Addresses, essays, lectures. I. Edman, Irwin, 1896-1954. II. Bettelheim, Bruno, III. National Committee on Art Education. IV. Title.

Art—Study and teaching—Australia.

DIMMACK, Max. 707
Art techniques for students. [Melbourne] Macmillan of Australia, 1969. 180 p. illus., diagrs. 25 cm. [N365.A9D5] 71-405820 4.00
1. Art—Study and teaching—Australia. 2. Art—Technique. 3. Artists' materials. I. Title.

Art—Study and teaching—Bibliography.

BUNCH, Clarence. 016.707
Art education : a guide to information sources / Clarence Bunch. Detroit : Gale Research Co., [1977] p. cm. (Art and architecture information guide series ; v. 6) Includes indexes. [Z5818.A8B85] [N85] 73-17518 ISBN 0-8103-1272-7 : 18.00
1. Art—Study and teaching—Bibliography. I. Title.

Art—Study and teaching—Boulder, Colo.

TRUCKSESS, Fran, 1898- 372.5
Creative art; guide for teachers, elementary grades, Boulder Public Schools, Boulder, Colorado, October 1954. [Boulder, Colo.] c1955. 105p. illus. 22 x 28cm. [N355.B6T7] 56-29037
1. Art—Study and teaching—Boulder, Colo. I. Boulder, Colo. Public schools. II. Title.

Art — Study and teaching — Congresses.

THE Arts in education; 707
papers presented at Seminar '72. Topic: order and discipline in art as models for effective human behavior. Lancaster, Mass., Doctor Franklin Perkins School [1973] 1 v. (various pagings) illus. 28 cm. (International seminar series, 1972-1980) Includes bibliographical references. [N82.A77] 73-168168
1. Art—Study and teaching—Congresses. I. Perkins School, Lancaster, Mass. II. Title. III. Series.
Publisher's Address: 971 Main St., Lancaster, Mass. 01523

CONFERENCE on Curriculum and 707
Instruction Development in Art Education, Washington, D.C., 1966.
A project report. Alice A. D. Baumgarner, director. Washington, National Art Education Association [1967] 129 p. illus. 23 cm. "Funded by United States Office of Education grant contract OE-C 2-6-061772-0804." [N350.C63 1966] 79-296434
1. Art—Study and teaching—Congresses. I. Baumgarner, Alice A. D.

INSEA World Congress, 20th, 707
Conventry, Eng., 1970.
Art in a rapidly changing world. Report of the XXth INSEA World Congress, 1970. L'art dans un monde qui se transforme rapidement. Rapport du XXieme Congres Mondial de l'INSEA, 1970. Die Kunste in der Welt des schnellen Wandels. Bericht uber den XX Welt Kongress der INSEA 1970. [General editor: Mary Hobbs] Coventry, Eng., UK Committee for INSEA '70 [1971] 83 p. illus. 30 cm. Summary in French and German. [N82.I17 1970] 73-162431
1. Art—Study and teaching—Congresses. I. Hobbs, Mary, ed. II. International Society for Education Through Art. III. Title. IV. Title: L'art dans un monde qui se transforme rapidement. V. Title: Die Kunste in der Welt des schnellen Wandels.

NATIONAL Conference on the 707
Arts in Education.
Proceedings, 1st- [New Haven] 1962 v. 28 cm. Conferences for 1962- sponsored by the National Council of the Arts in Education. [N81.N28] 64-8140
1. Art — Study and teaching — Congresses. 2. Art and society. I. National Council of the Arts in Education. II. Title.

SEMINAR in Art Education for 707
Research and Curriculum Development, Pennsylvania State University, 1965.
A Seminar in Art Education for Research and Curriculum Development; [papers] Edward L. Mattil, project director. University Park, Pennsylvania State University, 1966. 433 p. illus., ports. 28 cm. Cooperative research project V-002, with the U. S. Office of Education. Includes bibliographies. [N81.S4 1965] 66-64540
1. Art—Study and teaching—Congresses. I. Mattil, Edward L. II. Pennsylvania. State University. III. Title.

SEMINAR on Elementary and 707
Secondary School Education in the Visual Arts, New York University, 1964.
Seminar on Elementary and Secondary School Education in the Visual Arts; [report. Edited by] Howard Conant. New York, New York University, 1965. xii, 234 p. illus., ports. 28 cm. "Cooperative research project no. V-003...supported by the Cooperative Research Program of the Office of Education." Bibliography: p. 216-220. [N81.S45 1964] 67-370
1. Art—Study and teaching—Congresses. I. Conant, Howard, ed. II. New York University. III. U. S. Office of Education. IV. Title.

SYRACUSE University. 707
Symposium Conference on Creative Arts Education.
Aesthetic form and education, edited by Michael F. Andrews. [Syracuse] Syracuse University Press, 1958. ix, 105 p. illus., ports. 23 cm. "The combined lectures of the first two symposia [held in 1957 and 1958]" "A bibliography on the nature of creativity and aesthetic form [by] Michael F. Andrews": p. 97-105. [N81.S87 1958] 58-11799
1. Art — Study and teaching — Congresses. 2. Creation [Literary, artistic, etc.] I. Andrews, Michael, ed. II. Title.

VOCATIONAL alternatives 707'.1073
in art education : fall conference, Cuny Graduate Center, New York City, November 15-16, 1975 / William Mahoney, conference coordinator ; compiled and edited by Robert J. Saunders. [Union, N.J.] : Institute for the Study of Art in Education, 1975. 36 p. ; 22 cm. (ISAE abstracts ; v. 1, no. 1) Limited ed. of 300 copies. [N82.V62] 76-358475 1.00
1. Art—Study and teaching—Congresses. I. Mahoney, William, 1921- II. Saunders, Robert J., 1926- III. Institute for the Study of Art in Education. IV. Series: Institute for the Study of Art in Education. ISAE abstracts ; v. 1, no. 1.

Art — Study and teaching — Connecticut.

CHILD, Irvin Long, 372.5'09764
1915-.
Development of sensitivity to esthetic values [by] Irvin L. Child. New Haven, Conn., Yale University, 1964. v. 130 l. 28 cm. Cooperative research project no. 1748. Research supported by U.S. Office Bibliography: l. 51. [N354.C62C5] 66-62354
1. Art — Study and teaching — Connecticut. 2. Aesthetics — Study and teaching. I. Yales University. II. Title.

Art — Study and teaching (Elementary)

ANDERSON, Warren H 372.52
Art learning situations for elementary education [by] Warren Anderson. Belmont. Calif., Wadsworth Pub. Co. [1965] 181 p. 28 cm. Bibliography: p. 178-181. [N350.A53] 65-22642
1. Art — Study and teaching (Elementary) I. Title.

ART education in the 372.5
elementary school, edited by Mary M. Packwood. Washington, National Art Education Association, 1967. 111 p. 23 cm. Bibliography: p. 87-97. [N361.A6] 67-9644
1. Art—Study and teaching (Elementary) I. Packwood, Mary M., ed. II. National Art Education Association.

BERGTHOLDT, Susan 702'.8
MacDonald.
Easy art for children / by Susan MacDonald Bergtholdt. Minneapolis : T. S. Denison, c1978. 32 p. : ill. ; 28 cm. [LB1591.B4] 77-85468 ISBN 0-513-01616-3 pbk. : 1.95
1. Art—Study and teaching (Elementary) 2. Creative activities and seat work. I. Title.

BOEVE, Edgar. 372.5
Children's art and the Christian teacher. St. Louis, Concordia [c.1966] xi, 200p. illus. (pt. col.) 26cm. Bibl. [N350.B64] 66-12667 5.95
1. Art—Study and teaching (Elementary) I. Title.

CARSON, Janet. 372.5'044
It's art time : a handbook of art awareness activities for teachers / Janet Carson. Columbus, Ohio : Merrill, [1975] xii, 242 p. : ill. ; 23 cm. Includes bibliographies. [N350.C38] 74-31821 ISBN 0-675-08702-3 : 5.95
1. Art—Study and teaching (Elementary) 2. Perceptual learning. I. Title.

CHURCHILL, Angiola R. 372.5
Art for preadolescents [by] Angiola R. Churchill. New York, McGraw-Hill [1971] xvi, 455 p. illus. 23 cm. Bibliography: p. 425-436. [N350.C45] 70-144767
1. Art—Study and teaching (Elementary) I. Title.

†COHEN, Elaine Pear. 372.5'044
Art, another language for learning / Elaine Pear Cohen and Ruth Straus Gainer. New York : Citation Press, 1976. xiv, 254 p. : ill. ; 26 cm. Includes index. Bibliography: p. 243-251. [N350.C54] 76-24826 ISBN 0-590-09405-X : 7.95
1. Art—Study and teaching (Elementary) 2. Perceptual learning. 3. Children as artists. I. Gainer, Ruth Straus, joint author. II. Title. BIP

CONRAD, George, 1916- 372.5
The process of art education in the elementary school. Englewood Cliffs, N.J., Prentice-Hall [1964] xvii, 296 p. illus. (part col.) 28 cm. Bibliography: p. 281-282. [N350.C65] 64-15648
1. Art—Study and teaching (Elementary) I. Title.

CRAIG, Jennie E. 372.5
Creative art activities; a handbook for the elementary teacher [by] Jennie E. Craig. Scranton, Pa., International Textbook Co. [1967]. xvi, 302 p. illus. (part col.) 26 cm. Includes bibliographies. [N361.C7] 67-12109
1. Art—Study and teaching (Elementary) 2. Elementary school teachers—Handbooks, manuals, etc. I. Title.

CRESSE, Else Bartlett. 372.5
Creative crafts with elementary children. Designed by Richard D. Roberts. Dansville, N.Y., F. A. Owen Pub. Co. [1963] 79 p. illus. 33 cm. (The Instructor activity guide series) [N350.C73] 63-4239
1. Art—Study and teaching (Elementary) 2. Handicraft—Study and teaching. I. Title.

D'AMICO, Victor Edmond, 1904- 707'.1
Assemblage: a new dimension in creative teaching in action [by] Victor D'Amico and Arlette Buchman. New York, Museum of Modern Art; distributed by New York Graphic Society, Greenwich, Conn. [1972] 228 p. illus. 22 x 26 cm. [N350.D26 1972b] 76-86412 ISBN 0-87070-223-8 10.95
1. Art—Study and teaching (Elementary) 2. Assemblage (Art) I. Buchman, Arlette, joint author. II. Title.

DAVIS, James Joachim. 350.p25
Art adventures week by week [by] James J. Davis. Sketches by the author. Grade one -- [six] Darien, Conn., Teachers Pub. Corp. [1964] 6 v. col. illus. 28 cm. [N361.D3] 64-15325
1. Art — Study and teaching (Elementary) 2. Creative activities and seat work. I. Title.

DIMONDSTEIN, Geraldine. 372.5'044
Exploring the arts with children. New York, Macmillan [1974] xi, 320 p. illus. 25 cm. Bibliography: p. 315-318. [N350.D55] 73-8488 ISBN 0-02-329910-X 9.95
1. Art—Study and teaching (Elementary) 2. Perceptual learning. I. Title. BIP

EBEN, Lois Ellen, 1922- 372.5'044
129 art lessons in 26 media / by Lois Ellen Eben Englewood Cliffs, N.J. : Parker Pub. Co., [1977] p. cm. Includes index. Bibliography: p. [N350.E18] 77-4983 ISBN 0-13-634782-7 : 12.95
1. Art—Study and teaching (Elementary) I. Title.

ERDT, Margaret Hamilton. 372.5
Teaching art in the elementary school; child growth through art experiences. Rev. ed. New York, Holt, Rinehart and Winston [1962] 367 p. illus. 26 cm. [N353.E7 1962] 62-9525
1. Art—Study and teaching (Elementary) I. Title.

ESCOBAR, Alice, 1931- 372.5'044
167 new art lessons for a single class period / Alice Escobar Englewood Cliffs, N.J. : Parker Pub. Co., [1978] p. cm. Includes index. [N350.E82] 78-7979 12.95
1. Art—Study and teaching (Elementary) I. Title.

GAILER, Lionel. 372.5'044
Living with art: an environmental approach to understanding and teaching art [by] Lionel Gailer [and] Jim Porter. Sydney, New York, McGraw-Hill, 1973. 163 p. ill. 25 cm. Includes index. Bibliography: p. [157] [N350.G26] 73-181435 ISBN 0-07-093154-2 4.95
1. Art—Study and teaching (Elementary) 2. Learning by discovery. 3. Man—Influence on environment. I. Porter, John James, joint author. II. Title.

GAITSKELL, Charles D. 372.3
Children and their art; methods for the elementary school [by] Charles D. Gaitskell, under the general editorship of Willard B. Spalding. [New York] Harcourt, Brace [1958] 446 p. illus. 22 cm. Includes bibliography. [N350.G32] 58-8943
1. Art—Study and teaching (Elementary) 2. Children as artists. I. Title. BIP

GAITSKELL, Charles D. 372.5'044
Children and their art : methods for the elementary school / Charles D. Gaitskell, Al Hurwitz. 3d ed. New York : Harcourt Brace Jovanovich, 1975. xii, 547 p. : ill. (some col.) ; 24 cm. Includes index. Bibliography: p. 517-530. [N350.G32 1975] 74-12519 ISBN 0-15-507298-6 : 12.95
1. Art—Study and teaching (Elementary) 2. Children as artists. I. Hurwitz, Al, joint author. II. Title.

GAITSKELL, Charles D. 372.5
Children and their art; methods for the elementary school [by] Charles D. Gaitskell [and] Al Hurwitz. 2d ed. New York, Harcourt, Brace & World [1970] x, 507 p. illus. (part col.) 25 cm. Bibliography: p. 485-496. [N350.G32 1970] 70-111316 ISBN 1-550-72978-
1. Art—Study and teaching (Elementary) 2. Children as artists. I. Hurwitz, Al, joint author. II. Title.

GLASS, Fredrica 745.5
Calendar capers [by] Frederica Glass, Lela Gross. Illus by Robert V. Poppert. Milwaukee, Bruce [c.1965] 96p. illus. 24cm. [N350.G55] 65-25656 3.50 bds.,
1. Art—Study and teaching (Elementary) 2. Handicraft. I. Gross, Lela, joint author. II. Title.

HERBERHOLZ, Donald W. 372.5'2
A child's pursuit of art; 110 motivations for drawing, painting, and modeling [by] Donald W. Herberholz, Barbara J. Herberholz. Dubuque, Iowa, W. C. Brown [1967] 206p. illus. 22x28cm. (Brown art series) [N362.H4] 67-21308 price unreported pap.,
1. Art—Study and teaching (Elementary) 2. Motivation (Psychology) I. Herberholz, Barbara J., joint author. II. Title.

HILL, Bessie May. 372.5'2
Picture memory contest bulletin, for use in the picture memory contest for grades four and five. Austin, Bureau of Public School Service, Division of Extension, University of Texas, 1967. 37 p. 23 cm. (University of Texas publication no. 6714) Cover title. Prepared for the University Interscholastic League for its 1967/68 and 1968/69 contest. [N347.H5] 68-63202 0.30
1. Art—Study and teaching (Elementary) I. University Interscholastic League. II. Title.

HORN, George F. 372.5
Experiencing art in the elementary school [by] George F. Horn and Grace Sands Smith. Dallas, Hendrick-Long Pub. Co. [1970, c1971] 240 p. illus. 27 cm. Bibliography: p. 234-239. [N350.H584] 70-135743 ISBN 0-87192-036-0
1. Art—Study and teaching (Elementary) I. Smith, Grace Sands, joint author. II. Title.

HORN, George F. 372.5'044
Experiencing art in the elementary school [by] George F. Horn and Grace Sands Smith. Worcester, Mass., Davis Publications [1971] 240 p. illus. (part col.) 27 cm. Bibliography: p. 234-239. [N350.H584 1971b] 73-31998
1. Art—Study and teaching (Elementary) I. Smith, Grace Sands, joint author. II. Title.

JAMESON, Kenneth. 372.5
Primary school art. New York, Van Nostrand Reinhold [1971] 144 p. illus. (part col.) 26 cm. Includes bibliographical references. [N350.J3 1971] 72-149620
1. Art—Study and teaching (Elementary) I. Title.

JEFFERSON, Blanche. 372.5
Teaching art to children; content & viewpoint. 3d ed. Boston, Allyn and Bacon [1969] xii, 256 p. illus. (part col.) 26 cm. Bibliography: p. 247-250. [N350.J4 1969] 68-23563
1. Art—Study and teaching (Elementary) 2. Children as artists. I. Title.

KLAGER, Max. 745.6'1
Letters, type, and pictures : teaching alphabets through art / Max Klager. New York : Van Nostrand Reinhold, [1975] 88 p. : ill. ; 21 cm. Translation of Bild und Buchstaben. Bibliography: p. 88. [N350.K5313 1975] 72-9724 ISBN 0-442-24482-7 : 9.95 ISBN 0-442-24481-9 pbk. : 5.95
1. Art—Study and teaching (Elementary) 2. Letters in art. 3. Alphabets. I. Title.

KLONSKY, Ruth L., 1929- 372.5'044
Art lessons that mirror the child's world / Ruth L. Klonsky. West Nyack, N.Y. : Parker Pub. Co., [1975] 270 p. : ill. ; 26 cm. Includes index. Bibliography: p. 259-260. [N350.K565] 75-1477 ISBN 0-13-047423-1
1. Art—Study and teaching (Elementary) I. Title. BIP

KNUDSEN, Estelle Hagen. 372.5
Children's art education [by] Knudsen & Christensen. Peoria, Ill., C. A. Bennett Co., 1971. 208 p. illus. (part col.) 26 cm. [N350.K58 1971] 70-22602 ISBN 0-87002-060-9
1. Art—Study and teaching (Elementary) I. Christensen, Ethel Madill, joint author. II. Title. BIP

KRANZ, Stewart. 372.5
The fourth "R": art for the urban school [by] Stewart Kranz [and] Joseph Deley. With an essay by Colin Greer. Photographic studies by William Briggs, Eugene Bizzel, and Clarence Jacobs. Consulting editor, Karen Soderquist. New York, Van Nostrand [1970] 116 p. illus. (part col.), ports. 22 cm. Includes bibliographies. [N350.K67] 78-90305
1. Art—Study and teaching (Elementary) I. Deley, Joseph, joint author. II. Title.

KRINSKY, Norman. 372.5'2
Art for city children. New York, Van Nostrand Reinhold [1970] 96 p. illus. 22 x 27 cm. [N350.K7] 69-16383
1. Art—Study and teaching (Elementary) I. Title.

LIDSTONE, John. 372.5
Self expression in classroom art, material, process, idea. Photos. [by] Roger Kerkham. Worcester Mass., Davis Pub. [c1967] 96p. illus. 19 x 22cm. [N361.L5] 67-31613 6.25 bds.,
1. Art—Study and teaching (Elementary) 2. Creative activities and seat work. 3. Children as artists. I. Title.

LINDERMAN, Earl W. 372.5
Developing artistic and perceptual awareness; art practice in the elementary classroom [by] Earl W. Linderman [and] Donald W. Herberholz. 2d ed. Dubuque, Iowa, W. C. Brown Co. [1969] xv, 146 p. illus. 22 x 29 cm. (Art series) Includes bibliographies. [N350.L46 1969] 76-75437
1. Art—Study and teaching (Elementary) I. Herberholz, Donald W., joint author. II. Title.

LINDERMAN, Earl W. 372.5'044
Developing artistic and perceptual awareness; art practice in the elementary classroom [by] Earl W. Linderman [and] Donald W. Herberholz. 3d ed. [Dubuque, Iowa, W. C. Brown Co., 1974] xvii, 166 p. illus. 22 x 28 cm. Includes bibliographies. [N350.L46 1974] 74-75039 ISBN 0-697-03296-5 4.50 (pbk.).
1. Art—Study and teaching (Elementary) I. Herberholz, Donald W., joint author. II. Title.

LINDERMAN, Marlene M. 372.5'2
Art in the elementary school; drawing, painting, and creating for the classroom [by] Marlene M. Linderman. Dubuque, Iowa, W. C. Brown Co. [1974] xiii, 200 p. illus. 28 cm. (Trends in art education) Bibliography: p. 195-196. [N350.L467] 72-92849 ISBN 0-697-03294-9 4.50 (pbk.).
1. Art—Study and teaching (Elementary) I. Title. BIP

LUCA, Mark. 372.5
Art education: strategies of teaching. by Mark Luca and Robert Kent. Englewood Cliffs, N. J., Prentice [c.1968] viii, 99p. illus. 24cm. (Modern elem. methods ser.) Bibl. [N361.L8] 68-20766 4.95; 2.50 pap.,
1. Art—Study and teaching (Elementary) 2. Artists' materials. I. Kent, Robert. joint author. II. Title.

MONTGOMERY, Chandler. 372.5
Art for teachers of children; foundations of aesthetic experience. Columbus, Ohio, Merrill [1968] xi, 209 p. illus. 24 cm. (Merrill's international series in education) Bibliography: p. 201-205. [N361.M58] 68-10088
1. Art—Study and teaching (Elementary) 2. Creative activities and seat work. I. Title.

PATTEMORE, Arnel W. 372.5'044
Art and environment; an art resource for teachers [by] Arnel W. Pattemore. New York, Van Nostrand Reinhold Co. [1974] 143 p. illus. (part col.) 21 cm. Bibliography: p. 141. [N350.P28] 72-9708 ISBN 0-442-26513-1
1. Art—Study and teaching (Elementary) 2. Activity projects in education. 3. Learning by discovery. 4. Man—Influence of environment. I. Title. BIP

PECK, Ruth L. 372.5'2
Art lessons on a shoestring; new ideas for practical art lessons in the elementary school, by Ruth L. Peck and Robert S. Aniello. Three dimensional photos. by Thomas Austin Cramer. West Nyack, N.Y., Parker Pub. Co. [1968] x, 239 p. illus. 26 cm. [N361.P4] 68-25940 8.95
1. Art—Study and teaching (Elementary) I. Aniello, Robert S., joint author. II. Title. BIP

PECK, Ruth L. 372.5
Art lessons that teach children about their natural environment [by] Ruth L. Peck. West Nyack, N.Y., Parker Pub. Co. [1973] 282 p. illus. 25 cm. [N350.P37] 73-741 ISBN 0-13-047415-0 9.95
1. Art—Study and teaching (Elementary) 2. Human ecology. I. Title.

PECK, Ruth L. 372.5
What can I do for an art lesson? A practical guide for the elementary classroom teacher, by Ruth L. Peck and Robert S. Aniello. West Nyack, N.Y., Parker Pub. Co. [1966] xiii, 224 p. illus. 26 cm. [N362.P4] 66-12751
1. Art—Study and teaching (Elementary) I. Aniello, Robert S., joint author. II. Title. BIP

PEIRSON, Lorna Noel. 372.5'044
Art in the classroom / Lorna Peirson. Alberton : Varia Books, [1976] 123 p., [4] col. plates : ill. ; 19 x 25 cm. Includes index. Bibliography: p. 120-121. [N350.P39] 77-365401 ISBN 0-7990-0128-7 : R4.25
1. Art—Study and teaching (Elementary) I. Title.

PENN, Elizabeth Hall, 1917- 372.5'044
Individualized arts and crafts lessons for the elementary school / Elizabeth Hall Penn ; drawings by Anne Marie Nelsen. West Nyack, N.Y. : Parker Pub. Co., [1975] p. cm. [N351.P35] 75-14112 ISBN 0-13-457184-3 : 10.95
1. Art—Study and teaching (Elementary) 2. Individualized instruction. 3. Children as artists. I. Nelsen, Anne Marie. II. Title.

PLUCKROSE, Henry Arthur. 372.5'044
Art [by] Henry Pluckrose. New York, Citation Press, 1972. 45 p. illus. (part col.) 19 cm. (Informal schools in Britain today) Bibliography: p. 42-43. [N350.P54] 77-168886 ISBN 0-590-09524-2 1.95
1. Art—Study and teaching (Elementary) 2. Project method in teaching. I. Title. II. Series.

PLUMMER, Gordon S. 372.5'044
Children's art judgment; a curriculum for elementary art appreciation [by] Gordon S. Plummer. Dubuque, Iowa, W. C. Brown Co. Publishers [1974] xii, 137 p. illus. 28 cm. (Trends in art education) Bibliography: p. 117-132. [N350.P56] 73-86173 ISBN 0-697-03240-X 4.50 (pbk.)
1. Art—Study and teaching (Elementary) 2. Art appreciation. I. Title. BIP

ROBBINS, Ireene. 372.5'044
Arts and crafts media ideas for the

elementary teacher. West Nyack, N.Y., Parker Pub. Co. [1973] 236 p. illus. 26 cm. [N350.R54] 73-8803 ISBN 0-13-047050-3 8.95
1. Art—Study and teaching (Elementary) I. Title. BIP

ROWLAND, Kurt F. 707
Visual education and beyond / Kurt Rowland. London : Looking and Seeing, 1976. 148 p. : ill. ; 26 cm. Includes index. [N350.R63] 77-365198 ISBN 0-903923-06-8 : £4.50. ISBN 0-903923-05-X pbk.
1. Art—Study and teaching (Elementary) 2. Perceptual learning. I. Title.

RUESCHHOFF, Phil H. 372.5
Teaching art in the elementary school; enhancing visual perception [by] Phil H. Rueschhoff [and] M. Evelyn Swartz. New York, Ronald Press [1969] vi, 339 p. illus. (part col.) 26 cm. Includes bibliographies. [N350.R83] 78-75641
1. Art—Study and teaching (Elementary) 2. Visual perception. I. Swartz, M. Evelyn, joint author. II. Title. BIP

SANDERSON, Gretchen S. 372.5'044
Elementary teacher's art ideas desk book [by] Gretchen S. Sanderson. West Nyack, N.Y., Parker Pub. Co. [1974] 270 p. illus. 25 cm. [N350.S27] 73-19864 ISBN 0-13-260679-8 9.95
1. Art—Study and teaching (Elementary) 2. Creative activities and seat work. I. Title.

SAWYER, John R. 372.5
Elementary school art for classroom teachers [by] John R. Sawyer and Italo L. deFrancesco. New York, Harper & Row [1971] xvi, 239 p. illus., col. plates. 24 cm. Bibliography: p. 225-228. [N350.S37] 75-127337
1. Art—Study and teaching (Elementary) I. De Francesco, Italo Luther, 1901- joint author. II. Title.

THEMAL, Joachim. 372.5'044
A contemporary approach to art teaching / Joachim Themal. New York : Van Nostrand Reinhold, 1977. 64 p., [4] leaves of plates : ill. ; 21 cm. Includes index. [N350.T46] 77-3327 ISBN 0-442-28450-0 pbk. : 5.95
1. Art—Study and teaching (Elementary) 2. Activity programs in education. 3. Learning by discovery. I. Title. BIP

TUCH, Barbara, 1932- 372.5'044
How to teach children to draw, paint, and use color / Barbara Tuch and Harriet Judy. West Nyack, N.Y. : Parker Pub. Co., [1975] p. cm. [N350.T82] 75-8606 ISBN 0-13-435362-5 : 10.95
1. Art—Study and teaching (Elementary) I. Judy, Harriet, 1928- joint author. II. Title.

WACHOWIAK, Frank. 372.5'44
Emphasis, art : a qualitative art program for the elementary school / Frank Wachowiak. 3d ed. New York : Crowell, c1977. x, 252 p. : ill. (some col.) ; 23 x 26 cm. Includes index. [N350.W26 1977] 76-40321 ISBN 0-690-00868-6 : 12.00
1. Art—Study and teaching (Elementary) I. Title. BIP

WACHOWIAK, Frank. 372.5
Emphasis: art; a qualitative program for the elementary school [by] Frank Wachowiak, in collaboration with Theodore Ramsay. Scranton, Pa., International Textbook Co. [1965] ix, 180 p. illus. (part col.) 28 x 26 cm. (International textbooks in art and art education) Bibliography: p. 154-160. [N350.W26] 64-23782
1. Art—Study and teaching (Elementary) I. Ramsay, Theodore K., joint author. II. Title.

WACHOWIAK, Frank. 372.5
Emphasis: art; a qualitative art program for the elementary school [by] Frank Wachowiak [and] Theodore Ramsay. 2d ed. Scranton, Intext Educational Publishers [1971] xiii, 255 p. illus. (part col.) 23 x 26 cm. (An Intext textbook in art and art education) Bibliography: p. 228-237. [N350.W26 1971] 71-152648
1. Art—Study and teaching (Elementary) I. Ramsay Theodore K., joint author. II. Title.

***WHITMAN** *creative art books.* 707 Racine, Wis., Whitman Pub. Co., 1967. 2v. (unpaged) col. illus. 30cm. (Whitman creative art bk., 1 & 3) Contents.1. Constructing.--3. Painting. 1.00 bds., ed.,
1. Art—Study and teaching (Elementary)

Art—Study and teaching (Elementary)—Arkansas.

ARKANSAS. Dept. of Education. 372.5'09767
A guide to art education in the elementary schools of Arkansas. [Little Rock, Division of Instructional Services, State Dept. of Education, 1967] 86 p. illus. 22 x 28 cm. [N362.A7] 67-66029
1. Art—Study and teaching (Elementary)—Arkansas. I. Title.

Art—Study and teaching (Elementary)—Canada.

MACGREGOR, Ronald Norman, 1932- 372.5'044
Art plus / Ronald N. MacGregor. Toronto ; New York : McGraw-Hill Ryerson, 1978 x, 109 p. : ill. ; 23 cm. [N365.C2M32] 77-365578 ISBN 0-07-082450-9 pbk. : 5.95
1. Art—Study and teaching (Elementary)—Canada. I. Title. BIP

Art—Study and teaching (Elementary)—Great Britain.

WOOFF, Terence. 707'.1041
Developments in art teaching / [by] Terence Wooff. London : Open Books, 1976. xii, 117 p. : ill., plans ; 21 cm. (The Changing classroom) Includes index. Bibliography: p. 112-113. [N365.G7W64] 77-361003 ISBN 0-7291-0039-1 : £3.90. ISBN 0-7291-0034-0 pbk.
1. Art—Study and teaching (Elementary)—Great Britain. 2. Art—Study and teaching (Secondary)—Great Britain. 3. Educational innovations—Great Britain. I. Title. BIP

Art—Study and teaching (Elementary)—Handbooks, manuals, etc.

PECK, Ruth L. 372.5'044
Best of Teacher's arts and crafts workshop [by] Ruth L. Peck. West Nyack, N.Y., Parker Pub. Co. [1974] 255 p. illus. 24 cm. [N350.P38] 74-2437 ISBN 0-13-073668-6 9.95
1. Art—Study and teaching (Elementary)—Handbooks, manuals, etc. 2. Creative activities and seat work—Handbooks, manuals, etc. I. Title. II. Title: Teacher's arts and crafts workshop. BIP

Art—Study and teaching (Elementary)—New York (State)

NEW York (State) Bureau of Elementary Curriculum Development. 372.5'09747
Art appreciation for elementary schools. [Albany, 1968] v, 62 p. illus. 22 cm. Bibliography: p. 36-51. [N362.N4] 68-66802
1. Art—Study and teaching (Elementary)—New York (State) 2. Art appreciation. I. Title.

Art—Study and teaching (Elementary)—Texas.

TEXAS. Education Agency. 372.5'09764
Education through art: [elementary school. Austin, 1969] viii, 110 p. illus. 22 x 28 cm. "TEA-21." Bibliography: p. 83-110. [N354.T45A43] 70-630466
1. Art—Study and teaching (Elementary)—Texas. I. Title.

Art—Study and teaching (Elementary)—U.S.

CHAPMAN, Laura H. 372.5'044
Approaches to art in education / Laura H. Chapman. New York : Harcourt Brace Jovanovich, c1978. xi, 444 p., [4] leaves of plates : ill. (some col.) ; 24 cm. Includes index. Bibliography: p. 425-432. [N362.C45] 77-90208 ISBN 0-15-502896-0 : 14.95
1. Art—Study and teaching (Elementary)—United States. I. Title. BIP

EISNER, Elliot W. 372.5'2
Stanford University Kettering Project curriculum in the visual arts productive for elementary school children [by] Elliot W. Eisner. Honolulu, Office of Instructional Services, Dept. of Education, State of Hawaii, 1972, c1969. 211 p. illus. 28 cm. [N362.E38] 73-172251
1. Art—Study and teaching (Elementary)—United States. I. Stanford University. Kettering Project. II. Title.

HUBBARD, Guy. 372.5'045
Art: meaning, method, and media [by] Guy Hubbard [and] Mary J. Rouse. Westchester, Ill., Benefic Press [1972] 6 v. illus. (part col.) 29 cm. [N362.H8] 77-169528 4.96 (v. 1) varies
1. Art—Study and teaching (Elementary)—United States. I. Rouse, Mary J., joint author. II. Title.

LIDSTONE, John. 372.5'044
Design activities for the classroom / John Lidstone ; photos. by Roger Kerkham. Worcester, Mass. : Davis Publications, c1977. vii, 104 p. : ill. ; 27 cm. First published in 1964 under title: Design activities for the elementary classroom. Bibliography: p. 104. [N353.L53 1977] 76-54608 ISBN 0-87192-091-3 : 8.95
1. Art—Study and teaching (Elementary)—United States. 2. Art—Study and teaching (Secondary)—United States. 3. Design—Study and teaching (Elementary)—United States. 4. Design—Study and teaching (Secondary)—United States. I. Title. BIP

MARTIN, Anne, 1931- 372.5'044
Portfolio of low expense art lessons : featuring 43 novel display techniques / Anne Martin. West Nyack, N.Y. : Parker Pub. Co., c1977. 224 p. : ill. ; 25 cm. Includes index. [N362.M37] 76-44007 ISBN 0-13-686469-4 : 12.95
1. Art—Study and teaching (Elementary)—United States. 2. Project method of teaching. 3. Displays in education. I. Title. BIP

PHILLIPS, Billie. 372.5'044
The new "discovery" technique for art instruction : an innovative handbook for the elementary teacher / Billie M. Phillips & Virginia S. Brown. West Nyack, N.Y. : Parker Pub. Co., [1976] p. cm. Includes index. [N353.P44] 76-6912 ISBN 0-13-612507-7 : 9.95
1. Art—Study and teaching (Elementary)—United States. 2. Learning by discovery. I. Brown, Virginia, joint author. II. Title. BIP

RITSON, John E., 1919- 372.5'044
Creative teaching of art in the elementary school / John E. Ritson, James A. Smith. Boston : Allyn and Bacon, [1975] xii, 371 p. : ill. ; 22 cm. (The Allyn and Bacon series in creative teaching in the elementary school) Includes bibliographies and index. [N362.R57] 74-23192 10.95
1. Art—Study and teaching (Elementary)—United States. I. Smith, James A., joint author. II. Title. BIP

STRAATVEIT, Tyyne. 372.5'044
Easy art lessons, K-6 [by] Tyyne Straatveit and Carolyn K. Corl. West Nyack, N.Y., Parker Pub. Co. [1971] 154 p. illus. 28 cm. [N362.S8] 70-137449 ISBN 0-13-222372-4
1. Art—Study and teaching (Elementary)—U.S. I. Corl, Carolyn K., joint author. II. Title.

STUBBS, Charles B., 1930- 372.5'044
Art is elementary : a guide for teaching elementary art / Charles B. Stubbs, Nathan B. Winters, Ivan E. Cornia. Provo, Utah : Brigham Young University Press, [1977- p. cm. [N353.S75] 76-28241 ISBN 0-8425-1517-8 : 15.95
1. Art—Study and teaching (Elementary)—United States. I. Winters, Nathan B., 1937- joint author. II. Cornia, Ivan E., 1929- joint author. III. Title. BIP

Art—Study and teaching—England.

WORKING Party on Foundation Course Validation. 707'.11'42
Report of the Working Party on Foundation Course Validation. [London?] : National Standing Conference for Foundation Education in Art and Design, 1976. [61] leaves : col. map ; 30 cm. Cover title. [N185.W67 1976] 77-364486 £1.00
1. Art—Study and teaching—England. 2. Design—Study and teaching—England. I. Title.

Art—Study and teaching—Germany.

ITTEN, Johannes, 1888-1967. 707
Design and form; the basic course at the Bauhaus. Translated by John Maass. New York, Reinhold Pub. Corp. [1964] 190 p. illus. 29 cm. Translation of Mein Vorkurs am Bauhaus; Gestaltungs- und Formenlehre. [N332.B38I83] 63-19225
1. Art—Study and teaching—Germany. 2. Art—Technique. I. Bauhaus. II. Title. BIP

ITTEN, Johannes, 1888-1967. 707
Design and form : the basic course at the Bauhaus / Johannes Itten ; [translated from the German by Bradley]. Rev. ed. New York : Van Nostrand Reinhold, [1975] p. cm. Translation of Gestaltungs- und Formenlehre; Vorkurs am Bauhaus und spater, first published in 1964 under title: Mein Vorkurs am Bauhaus; Gestaltungs- und Formenlehre. [N332.G33B44613 1975] 75-12905 ISBN 0-442-24044-9 : 9.95 ISBN 0-442-24039-2 pbk. : 6.95
1. Art—Study and teaching—Germany. 2. Art—Technique. I. Bauhaus. II. Title.

Art—Study and teaching—Gt. Brit.

ALEXANDER, Eugenie, 1919- 707.1242
Art for young people, by Eugenie Alexander and Bernard Carter. London, Mills & Boon stamped: distributed by SportShelf. New Rochelle, N. Y.] 1958; 83p. illus. 26cm. Includes bibliography. [N365.G7A7] 58-4533
1. Art—Study and teaching—Gt. Brit. I. Carter, Bernard, 1920- joint author. II. Title.

CROSS, Jack. 707'.12'41
For art's sake? : a strategic approach to teaching art in schools / Jack Cross. London ; Boston : Allen & Unwin, 1977. 116 p. : ill. ; 23 cm. (Classroom close-ups ; 6) Bibliography: p. [114]-116. [N185.C7] 78-305314 ISBN 0-04-371051-4 : 12.50 ISBN 0-04-371052-2 pbk. : 5.75
1. Art—Study and teaching—Great Britain. I. Title.

SUTTON, Gordon 707.1
Artisan or artist? A history of the teaching of art and crafts in English schools. [1st ed.] Oxford, New York, Pergamon [1967] xi, 328p. illus., ports. 23cm. Revision of thesis, Univ. of Leicester. Bibl. [N185.S9 1967] 67-19822 9.50
1. Art—Study and teaching—Gt. Brit. 2. Handicraft —Gt. Brit. I. Title.

Art—Study and teaching (Higher)—Great Britain.

THE Hornsey affair 378.42'188
[by] students and staff of Hornsey College of Art. Harmondsworth, Penguin, 1969. 220 p. illus. 19 cm. (Penguin education special) [N346.5.G72H66] 72-170210 ISBN 0-14-080096-4 £0.30
1. Hornsey, Eng. (Middlesex). College of Art—Riot, 1968 (May-July) 2. Art—Study and teaching (Higher)—Great Britain.

Art—Study and teaching (Higher)—United States.

WEIL, Dorothy. 709'.2'4 B
Continuing education / by Dorothy Weil. New York : Rawson, Wade, c1979. p. cm. [N346.A1W44 1979] 78-72895 ISBN 0-89256-096-7 : 8.95
1. Art—Study and teaching (Higher)—United States. 2. Professional education—United States. I. Title. BIP

Art—Study and teaching—History.

MACDONALD, Stuart. 707
The history and philosophy of art education. New York, American Elsevier Pub. Co., 1970. 400 p. illus., plan, ports.

25 cm. Includes bibliographical references. [N90.M3 1970b] 79-116703 15.50
1. Art—Study and teaching—History. I. Title.

Art—Study and teaching—London.

BERGER, Margareta (Hamerschlag) 1905- 707.14
Journey into a fog. New York, Sheed and Ward, 1956. 254p. illus. 21cm. [N365.G7B4 1956] 56-6123
1. Art—Study and teaching—London. 2. Social settlements. 3. London—Soc. condit. I. Title.

Art — Study and teaching — Missouri.

MISSOURI. Dept. of Education. 372.5
Art for the elementary schools of Missouri, grades one-six. 1956 ed. [Jefferson City, 1956] 164p. illus. 28cm. (Its Missouri's elementary curriculum guide) Publication no. 102G. [N354.M5A52 1956] 57-62925
1. Art—Study and teaching—Missouri. I. Title. II. Series.

WULFEKAMMER, Verna M 372.5
My picture study book; ten masterpieces selected for study during the school year, 1951-1952, and listed on page 533 of the Course of study for elementary schools, with changes in the list, made by the Course of Study Committee on the Fine Arts. Missouri ed. Champaign, Ill., Randolph School Supply Co., c1951. 3 v. illus. 28 cm. [N354.M5W8] 51-39003
1. Art — Study and teaching — Missouri. I. Title.

Art—Study and teaching—New York (State)

NEW York (State) Bureau of Secondary Curriculum Development. 701'.18
Films and filmstrips for art education K-12. Albany, University of the State of New York, State Education Dept., Curriculum Development Center, 1965. v, 34 p. 28 cm. "Prepared ... with the cooperation of the Bureau of Elementary Curriculum Development." [N350.N45] A 66
1. Art—Study and teaching—New York (State) 2. Art—Film catalogs. I. New York (State). Bureau of Elementary Curriculum Development. II. New York (State) Curriculum Development Center. III. Title.

Art — Study and teaching — Period.

I. Wisconsin, University. University Extension Division. 707
Arts in society. v. [1]- Jan. 1958- [Madison, University of Wisconsin Extension Division] v, illus. 26 cm. Frequency varies. Suspended during 1961. INDEXES: Vols. 1-3; Jan. 1958-summer 1966, in v. 3, no 4. [N81] [A893] 67-115032
1. Art — Study and teaching — Period. I. Title.

WALTERS Art Gallery, Baltimore. 708.01
Circular on museum education. no. -13; Jan. 1958. Baltimore. no. in v. 29 cm. semiannual (irregular) No more published? [N81.W3] 59-2262
1. Art — Study and teaching — Period. I. Title.

Art—Study and teaching (Primary)

ELLIS, Mary Jackson. 372.5
Creative art ideas: third and fourth grades, by Mary Jackson Ellis and Gene Watson. Illus. by Carvel Lee. Minneapolis, T. S. Denison [1959] 26 p. illus. 29 cm. [N361.E4] 59-14414
1. Art—Study and teaching (Primary) I. Watson, Gene, joint author. II. Title.

HOOVER, Francis Louis, 1913- 707
Art activities for the very young, from 3 to 6 years Worcester, Mass., Davis Publications [1961] 77 p. illus. 28 cm. [N361.H6] 61-11263
1. Art—Study and teaching (Primary) I. Title.

JAMESON, Kenneth. 372.5'2
Art and the young child. Foreword by George Kaye. New York, Viking Press [1968] 155 p. illus. (part col.) 26 cm. (A Studio book) Bibliography: p. 154. [N361.J3 1968] 69-10629 ISBN 0-670-13389-2 6.95
1. Art—Study and teaching (Primary) 2. Art—Psychology. I. Title.

MELZI, Kay. 372.5
Art in the primary school; with 136 photographs by William Palmer. Oxford, Blackwell, [1967]. xii, 291p. illus., plates (136 illus.). 23cm. Bibl. [N361.M45] 67-87918 10.50
1. Art—Study and teaching (Primary) I. Title. BIP

PLUCKROSE, Henry Arthur. 372.5'044
Let's make pictures; a handbook of picturemaking techniques for teachers in primary and middle schools [by] Henry Pluckrose. Photographs by G. W. Hales. [Rev. ed.] London, Mills & Boon [1972] 128 p. illus. 22 cm. Label mounted on t.p.: Transatlantic Arts, Levittown, New York, sole distributor for the U.S.A. Bibliography: p. 127-128. [N361.P57 1972] 73-174799 ISBN 0-263-05161-7 6.50
1. Art—Study and teaching (Primary) 2. Art—Study and teaching (Elementary) 3. Art teachers—Handbooks, manuals, etc. I. Title.

PLUCKROSE, Jenry Arthur 372.5'2
Let'8s make pictures; a handbook of picture-making techniques for Teachers [by] H. Pluckrose. London, Mills & Boon New York, Taplinger [1967, c.1965] 119p. illus. 23cm. Bibl. [N361.P57 1967] 67-12489 3.95
1. Art—Study and teaching (Primary) 2. Teachers—Handbooks, manuals, etc. I. Title.

Art—Study and teaching (Primary)—U.S.

HERBERHOLZ, Barbara J. 372.5'044
Early childhood art [by] Barbara Herberholz. Dubuque, Iowa, W. C. Brown [1974] xi, 174 p. illus. 29 cm. (Trends in art education) Bibliography: p. 165-169. [N361.H47] 73-91058 ISBN 0-697-03241-8 4.50 (pbk.)
1. Art—Study and teaching (Primary)—United States. I. Title. BIP

SEVILLE, Renee. 372.5'044
Beginning arts and crafts. New York, Drake Publishers [1971] 95 p. illus. 22 cm. [N361.S48] 70-26723 ISBN 0-87749-063-5 3.95
1. Art—Study and teaching (Primary)—U.S. I. Title.

Art — Study and teaching (Secondary)

FRANKSTON, Leon. 707'.12
Effects of two programs and two methods of teaching upon the quality of art products or [sic] adolescents. University Park, Pa., Pennsylvania State University, 1965. viii, 144 l. illus. 28 cm. "Cooperative research project no. S-055." "Research ... supported by the Cooperative Research Program of the Office of Education, U.S. Department of Health, Education, and Welfare." Bibliography: leaves 98-100. [NX280] 74-650040
1. Art—Study and teaching (Secondary) I. Title: Effects of two programs and two methods of teaching upon the quality of art products of adolescents.

HUBBARD, Guy 707.1'273
Art in the high school. Belmont, Calif., Wadsworth [1967] xi, 307p. illus. 24cm. Bibl. [N363.H8] 67-13665 7.95
1. Art—Study and teaching Secondary). I. Title.

LINDERMAN, Earl W. 707'.1'2
Teaching secondary school art; discovering art objectives, art skills, art history, art ideas [by] Earl W. Linderman. Dubuque, Iowa, W. C. Brown Co. [1971] xiv, 243 p. illus. 22 x 28 cm. (Art series) "Building a secondary school art library": p. 239-243. [N350.L465] 79-148038 ISBN 0-697-03283-3
1. Art—Study and teaching (Secondary) I. Title. BIP

PALMER, Frederick, 1936- 707.1'2
Art and the young adolescent. [1st ed.] Oxford, New York, Pergamon Press [1970] xii, 136 p. illus. (part col.) 23 cm. (The Commonwealth and international library. Painting, sculpture and fine art) [N350.P26 1970] 78-112046
1. Art—Study and teaching (Secondary) I. Title.

PORTCHMOUTH, John. 707
Secondary school art. New York, Van Nostrand Reinhold [1971] 144 p. illus. (part col.) 26 cm. Includes bibliographical references. [N350.P6 1971] 76-149621
1. Art—Study and teaching (Secondary) I. Title.

VAN HOMRIGH, C M B 701.8
Introduction to art and craft, by C. M. B. Van Homrich. [Sydney] Angus and Robertson; San Francisco, Tri-Ocean Books [1965] 119 p. illus., col. plates. 25 cm. Bibliography: p. 115. [N350.V3] 66-1551
1. Art — Study and teaching (Secondary) 2. Art — Technique. I. Title.

Art—Study and teaching (Secondary)—Texas.

TEXAS. Education Agency. 707.1'2'764
Education through art: secondary school. Austin, 1970. vi, 86 p. illus. 22 x 28 cm. (Its Bulletin 697) Bibliography: p. 76-86. [N354.T45A44] 79-634316 2.00
1. Art—Study and teaching (Secondary)—Texas. I. Title. II. Series.

Art—Study and teaching (Secondary)—U.S.

A High school curriculum in the fine arts for able students. Norman L. Rice, project supervisor. Orville M. Winsand, project director. Pittsburgh, Carnegie Institute of Technology, 1966. 178 l. illus. 28 cm. Cooperative research project no. 5-0236 ... supported by the Cooperative Research Program of the U.S. Office of Education. Includes bibliographies. [N363.H5] 75-7709 707'.1'274886
1. Art—Study and teaching (Secondary)—U.S. I. Rice, Norman L. II. Winsand, Orville M. III. Carnegie Institute of Technology, Pittsburgh.

LIDSTONE, John. 707'.12'73
Working big : a teacher's guide to environmental sculpture / by John Lidstone, Clarence Bunch. New York : Van Nostrand Reinhold, [1975] 96 p. : ill. ; 24 cm. Bibliography: p. 94. Discusses the child's natural inclination to "work big" and suggests large-scale art activities including some in the new air art. [N363.L5] 74-15716 ISBN 0-442-24795-8
1. Art—Study and teaching (Secondary)—United States. 2. Air art. I. Bunch, Clarence, joint author. II. Title. BIP

NATIONAL Art Education Association. 707'.1'273
College & university acceptance of high school art credits for admission. [Washington, 1968] [16] p. 28 x 11 cm. Cover title. [N363.N3] 73-21977 0.40
1. Art—Study and teaching (Secondary)—U.S. 2. School credits. 3. Universities and colleges—U.S.—Directories. I. Title. BIP

WACHOWIAK, Frank. 707
Art in depth; a qualitative program for the young adolescent [by] Frank Wachowiak [and] David Hodge. Scranton, Pa., International Textbook Co. [1970] ix, 180 p. illus. (part col.) 23 x 26 cm. (An International textbook in art and art education) "Supplemental visual resources" (bibliographical): p. 151-163. [N362.W3] 77-105075 8.45
1. Art—Study and teaching (Secondary)—U.S. I. Hodge, David, joint author. II. Title.

Art — Study and teaching — Societies, etc.

CHICAGO, Art Institute 708.1
Museum studies. 2. Chicago, 1967 v. illus. 25cm. annual. Eds.: no. 2, John Maxon, Harold Joachim, Fredreck A. Sweet [N81.C45] 66-20632 5.00 pap.,
1. Art— Study and teaching—Societies, etc. I. Title.

CHICAGO. Art Institute. 707
Museum studies 1- Chicago, 1966- v. illus. 25 cm. annual. [N81.C45] 66-20632
1. Art — Study and teaching — Societies, etc. I. Title.

Art—Study and teaching. Teachers—Correspondence, reminiscences, etc.

MARSHALL, Sybil 372.924
An experiment in education. Cambridge, Cambridge Univ. Pr. 1966. vii, 222 p. illus., 36 plates [incl. facsims., 4 col.] 22 cm. [Cam 372] [N450.M266] 66-7786 pap., 1.95
1. Art—Study and teaching. Teachers—Correspondence, reminiscences, etc. I. Title.
Available from publisher' New York office.

Art—Study and teaching—U.S.

CATHOLIC University of America. Workshop on Art in Christian Education, 1955. 707
Art in Christian education; the proceedings of a Workshop on Art in Christian Education conducted at the Catholic University of America, June 10 to 21, 1955. Edited by Sister Mary Jeanne File. Washington, Catholic University of America Press, 1956. vi, 221p. illus. 22cm. Includes bibliographies. [N108.C35 1955] 56-1263
1. Art—Study and teaching—U. S. 2. Catholic Church—Education. I. File, Mary Jeanne, ed. II. Title.

CATHOLIC University of America. Workshop on Art in Christian Education, 1955. 707
art in Christian education;the proceedings of a Workshop on Art in Christian Education conducted at the Catholic University of America, June 10 to 21, 1955. Edited by Sister Mary Jeanne File. Washington, Catholic University of America Press, 1956. vi, 221p. illus. 22cm. Includes bibliographies. [N108.C35 1955] 56-1263
1. Art—Study and teaching—U. S. 2. Catholic Church—Education. I. File, Mary Jeanne, ed. II. Title.

CATHOLIC University of America. Workshop on New Trends in Catholic Art Education, 1958. 707.15
Catholic art education: the new trends; the proceedings of the Workshop on New Trends in Catholic Art Education, conducted at the Catholic University of America, June 13 to June 24, 1958. Edited by Esther Newport. Washington, Catholic University of America Press, 1959. vii, 214p. illus. 22cm. Includes bibliographies. [N108.C36 1958] 59-2497
1. Art—Study and teaching—U. S. 2. Catholic Church—Education. I. Newport, Esther, ed. II. Title.

CATHOLIC University of America. Workshop on Re-evaluating Art in Education, 1959. 707
Re-evaluating art in education; the proceedings of the Workshop on Re-evaluating Art in Education, conducted at the Catholic University of America, June 12 to June 3, 1959. Edited by Esther Newport Washington, Catholic University of America Press, 1960. viii, 221p. 22cm. Includes bibliographies. [N108.C37 1959] 60-3536
1. Art—Study and teaching—U. S. 2. Catholic Church—Education. I. Newport., Esther, ed. II. Title.

CONANT, Howard. 707
Art education. Washington, Center for Applied Research in Education [c1964] xi, 116 p. 24 cm. (The Library of education) Bibliography: p. 109-112. [N108.C6] 64-11019
1. Art — Study and teaching — U.S. I. Title.

CONFERENCE on Art for the Academically Talented, Washington, D.C., 1959. 707.12
Art for the academically talented student

MEYERS, Hans. 701.8
150 techniques in art New York, Reinhold [1963, c1961] 93 p. illus. 23 cm. [N7433.M4] 62-19481
1. Art—Technique. I. Title.

MEYERS, Hans. 707
150 themes in art. New York, Reinhold Pub. Corp. [1965, c1964]. 196 p. illus. (part col.) 23 cm. "Companion volume to [the author's] 150 techniques in art." -- Dust jacket. [N7433.M42] 65-19675
1. Art — Technique. I. Title.

MILLS, John FitzMaurice, 1917- 701.8
Studio and art-room techniques. New York, Pitman Pub. Corp. [1965] ix, 86 p. illus., plates (part col.) 26 cm. [N7430.M54] 66-2274
1. Art — Technique. I. Title.

MURPHY. BURT. 770.24
Teenagres guide to Photography. New York, Verlan Books, [1960] 128p. illus. 21cm. (A Universal photo book) [TR146.M85] 60-7950
1. Photopgraphy—Handbooks, manuals, etc. I. Title.

OCVIRK, Otto G. 701'.8
Art fundamentals : theory and practice / by Otto G. Ocvirk ... [et al.]. 3d ed. Dubuque, Iowa : W. C. Brown Co., [1975] xv, 194 p., [30] leaves of plates : ill. (some col.) ; 28 cm. Includes index. Bibliography: p. 187. [N7430.O3 1975] 75-313378 ISBN 0-697-03231-0 pbk. : 8.95
1. Art—Technique. 2. Art. I. Title. BIP

OCVIRK, Otto G. 701.8
Art fundamentals; theory and practice [by] Otto G. Ocvirk [others] Dubuque, Iowa, Brown [c.1960, 1962] 169p. illus. 28cm. Bibl. 60-15498 5.75 pap., plastic bdg.
1. Art—Technique 2. Art. I. Title.

OCVIRK, Otto G. 701.8
Art fundamentals; theory and practice [by] Otto G. Ocvirk [and others] 2d ed. Dubuque, Iowa, W. C. Brown Co. [1968] xvi, 170 p. illus. (part col.) 29 cm. Bibliography: p. 165. [N7430.O3 1968] 68-28171
1. Art—Technique. 2. Art. I. Title.

PEEBLES, Dorothy. 702'.8
The artless artist's guide to artistic achievement / by Dorothy Peebles ; ill. by Dorothy Peebles and Carl Moreus. Norwalk, Conn. : C. R. Gibson Co., [1975] 48 p. : ill. ; 22 cm. [N7433.P43] 74-76215 ISBN 0-8378-3005-2 : 2.00
1. Art—Technique. 2. Artists' materials. I. Title. II. Title: Artistic achievement.

PETRINA, John, 1893- 701.8
Art work: how produced, how reproduced; the making and the reproduction of drawings, water colors, oil paintings, monotypes, block prints, lithographs, etchings, etc. Explained and illustrated by John Petrina. Freeport, N.Y., Books for Libraries Press [1970] 121 p. illus. (part col.), port. 26 cm. (Essay index reprint series) "First published 1934." [N7430.P45 1970] 70-107733
1. Art—Technique. 2. Engraving—Technique. 3. Photoengraving—Halftone process. I. Title.

PROHASKA, Ray. 702'.8
A basic course in design ... introduction to drawing and painting. Designed by Howard Munce. [Westport, Conn., Fletcher Art Services; distributed by Van Nostrand Reinhold, New York, 1971] 95 p. illus. (part col.) 34 cm. [N7430.P73] 74-128611 17.95
1. Art—Technique. I. Title.

ROBBINS, Vesta O. 702'.8
Basics in art, by Vesta O. Robbins. Philadelphia, Dorrance [1971] 57 p. illus. 22 cm. [N7433.R6] 73-155854 2.95
1. Art—Technique. I. Title.

SCHORR, Justin, 1928- 701
Aspects of art. South Brunswick [N. J.] Barnes [1967] 162 p. illus. 22 cm. Bibliography: p. [156]-160. [N7430.S3] 67-11728
1. Art—Technique. 2. Art—Psychology. I. Title.

SNEUM, Gunnar. 701.8
Teaching design and form. New York, Reinhold Pub. Corp. [1965] 125 p. illus. (part col.) 23 cm. Translation of Tegn og form. [N7430.S613] 65-13366
1. Art—Technique. I. Title.

SPERRY, Vicci. 701.8
The art experience. Andre Sauret, editeur. Boston, Boston Book and Art Shop [1969] 92 p. 4 col. plates. 29 cm. [N7430.S68] 68-26914
1. Art—Technique. 2. Composition (Art) I. Title. BIP

TONEY, Anthony. 702'.8
Painting and drawing : discovering your own visual language / Anthony Toney. Englewood Cliffs, N.J. : Prentice-Hall, c1978. xi, 163 p., [6] leaves of plates : ill. (some col.) ; 29 cm. (A Spectrum book) Includes index. [N7430.T66] 77-11873 ISBN 0-13-648113-2 : 17.95 pbk. : 8.95
1. Art—Technique. 2. Composition (Art) I. Title. BIP

TUTHILL, Marge. 702'.8
In the image of God : art projects with kids 8 years old and up / written and illustrated by Marge Tuthill. N[ew] Y[ork] : Paulist Press, c1976. 101 p. : ill. ; 23 cm. [N7433.T88] 75-42050 ISBN 0-8091-1926-9 pbk. : 2.95
1. Art—Technique. I. Title. BIP

WARNER, Esther Sietmann, 1910- 744.4
Art: an everyday experience. New York, Harper & Row [1963] 225 p. illus. 25 cm. [N7430.W34] 63-7668
1. Art—Technique. 2. Art. I. Title.

ZAIDENBERG, Arthur, 1903- 701.8
Anyone can paint! Practical instruction in the various media of art: oil painting, watercolor, mural painting, tempera, woodcut, etching, pencil, pen and ink, pastel, linoleum block, lithography, etc. New techniques such as roller, spray, and chemical painting. Introd. by Burton Jones. Special articles by Chris Ritter, Nathaniel Dirk, Aaron Berkman. Rev. ed. New York. Crown [1965] 296p. illus., 16 col. plates. 28cm. [N7430Z3] 64-17844 4.95
1. Art—Technique. 2. Painting—Technique. I. Title.

Art—Technique—Handbooks, manuals, etc.

BAKER, Leslie A. 702'.8
The art teacher's desk top resource book / Leslie A. Baker. Reston, Va. : Reston Pub. Co., c1979. p. cm. Includes index. [N7430.B26] 78-12617 ISBN 0-87909-022-7 : 14.95
1. Art—Technique—Handbooks, manuals, etc. 2. Artists' materials—Handbooks, manuals, etc. 3. Artists' tools—Handbooks, manuals, etc. 4. Art—Study and teaching (Elementary)—Handbooks, manuals, etc. I. Title.

Art Technique—Juvenile literature.

DAVIES, Rita. 751.4'93
Let's make a picture. New York, Van Nostrand Reinhold [1972] c1971. 32 p. illus. (part col.) 21 cm. (Starting points) Instructions for creating pictures from a variety of materials including newspapers, straws, fabrics, tissue paper, and others. [N7440.D38] 77-188483 Pap. 1.45
1. Art—Technique—Juvenile literature. I. Title.

KEIGHTLEY, Moy. 702'.8
Investigating art : a practical guide for young people / Moy Keightley. London : Elek, 1976. 160 p., [4] p. of plates : ill. (some col.) ; 23 cm. Label mounted on t.p.: P. Elek Inc., Salem, N.H. Includes index. [N7430.5.K39] 77-353110 ISBN 0-236-31143-3 : 14.95
1. Art—Technique—Juvenile literature. 2. Visual perception—Juvenile literature. I. Title.
Distributed by Technical Impex BIP

KENNY, Maxine. 702'.8
Getting to know you through art / by Maxine Kenny. Minneapolis : T. S. Denison, c1977. 92 p. : ill. ; 29 cm. Presents a variety of art projects focusing on the individuality of the reader. [N7430.K46] 77-89443 ISBN 0-513-01573-6 : 8.95
1. Art—Technique—Juvenile literature. 2. Learning by discovery—Juvenile literature. 3. Art—Psychology—Juvenile literature. I. Title.

LESSIN, Andrew. j 701
Here is your hobby; art. New York, Putnam [1963] 128 p. illus. 23 cm. (Here is your hobby series) Includes bibliography. [N7433.L4] 63-9684
1. Art — Technique — Juvenile literature. 2. Painting — Technique — Juvenile literature. I. Title.

LESSIN, Andrew 701
Here is your hobby: art. New York, Putnam [c.1963] 128p. illus. 23cm. (Here is your hobbv ser.) Bibl. 63-9684 2.95; 2.86 lib. ed.,
1. Art Technique—Juvenile literature. 2. Painting—Technique—Juvenile literature. I. Title.

MARGRIE, Janet. 702'.8
Pictures and patterns / words by Janet Margrie ; ill. by Janet Seaward, Janet Margrie. Milwaukee : Macdonald-Raintree, c1977. p. cm. Includes index. Easy-to-follow instructions for making pictures and patterns in various media. [N7433.M29] 77-8005 ISBN 0-8393-0117-0 lib. bdg. : 7.99
1. Art—Technique—Juvenile literature. I. Seaward, Janet. II. Title.
Publisher's address:205West Highland Ave.,Milwaukee Wi.53203 BIP

STACY, Don, 1925- 702'.8
Experiments in art / Donald L. Stacy. New York : Four Winds Press, [1975] 88 p. : ill. ; 23 cm. An introduction to the techniques of collage, printmaking, and drawing with suggestions for projects. [N7430.S82] 75-9551 ISBN 0-590-07332-X : 6.95
1. Art—Technique—Juvenile literature. I. Title.

Art—Terminology.

EHRESMANN, Julia M. 703
The pocket dictionary of art terms, edited by Julia M. Ehresmann. [Rev., expanded and illustrated] Greenwich, Conn., New York Graphic Society [1971] 1 v. (unpaged) illus. 18 cm. Revised version of the original ed., first published in 1961, compiled by Mervyn Levy. Includes bibliography. [N33.E45 1971] 74-143464 ISBN 0-8212-1115-3 1.25
1. Art—Terminology. I. Levy, Mervyn. The pocket dictionary of art terms. II. Title. III. Title: Art terms.

LEVY, Mervyn, ed. 703
The pocket dictionary of art terms. Greenwich, Conn., New York Graphic Society [1961] 121 p. 15 cm. [N33.L4 1961] 61-3651
1. Art—Terminology. I. Title. II. Title: Art terms. BIP

O'DWYER, John. 701.14
A glossary of art terms, by John O'Dwyer and Raymond Le Mage, with a foreword by Ruskin Spear. London, New York, P. Nevill [1950] 148 p. 20 cm. [N33.O3] 51-9175
1. Art—Terminology. I. Le Mage, Raymond, joint author. II. Title.

O'DWYER, John 703
Glossary of modern art, by John O'Dwyer, Raymond Le Mage. Foreword by Ruskin Spear. New York, Philosophical [1962] 148p. 19cm. (Wisdom Lib., WL99) 1.45 pap.,
1. Art—Terminology. I. Le Mage, Raymond, joint author. II. Title. BIP

ROUSE, Mary J 701'.4
The development of a descriptive scale for art products, by Mary J. Rouse. Bloomington, School of Education, Indiana University, c1967. iii, 42 p. 23 cm. (Indiana. University. Bulletin of the School of Education, v. 44, no. 1) Research was supported by the Cooperative Research Program of the U.S. Office of Education, project S-077, 1965. Bibliography: p. 39-40. [N340.R6] 68-63968
1. Art—Terminology. 2. Multiple-choice examinations. I. Indiana. University. School of Education. II. Title.

WALKER, John Albert, 1938- 701'.4
Glossary of art, architecture, and design since 1945. Terms and labels describing movements, styles, and groups derived from the vocabulary of artists and critics [by] John A. Walker. [Hamden, Conn.] Linnet Books [1973] 240 p. 23 cm. Bibliography: p. 213-215. [N34.W34] 73-3339 ISBN 0-208-01194-3 10.50
1. Art—Terminology. I. Title. BIP

WALKER, John Albert, 1938- 709'.04
Glossary of art, architecture, and design since 1945 : terms and labels describing movements styles and groups derived from the vocabulary of artists and critics / by John A Walker. 2d rev. ed. London : Bingley ; Hamden, Ct. : Linnet Books, 1977. 352 p. ; 23 cm. Includes bibliographical references and index. [N34.W34 1977] 77-3201 ISBN 0-208-01543-4 : 15.00
1. Art—Terminology. I. Title.

Art, Terminology.

LEVY, Mervyn. 700'.3
The pocket dictionary of art terms. [3d ed.] Greenwich, Conn. New York Graphic Society [1964, c1961] 126 p. 18 cm. [N33.L4 1964] 64-21818
1. Art — Termionolgy. I. Title. II. Title: Art terms.

Art, Thai—Exhibitions.

INDIANA. University. 709'.593
The arts of Thailand : a handbook of the architecture, sculpture, and painting of Thailand (Siam), and a catalogue of the exhibition in the United States in 1960-61-62 [at Indiana University and other museums / editor, Theodore Bowie ; contributors, Alexander B. Griswold, M. C. Subhadradis Diskul, Elizabeth Lyons]. Westport, Conn. : Greenwood Press, 1975, c1960. 219 p. : ill. ; 23 cm. Reprint of the ed. published by Indiana University Press, Bloomington. Includes index. Bibliography: p. 215-216. [N7321.I5 1975] 74-31411 ISBN 0-8371-7884-3 : 20.50
1. Art, Thai—Exhibitions. I. Bowie, Theodore Robert, ed. II. Griswold, Alexander B. III. Title.

ITHACA 730'.9593'074014771
College, Ithaca, N.Y. Museum of Art.
Art of Thailand. [Ithaca, N.Y., 1971] [32] p. illus., map (on p. [3] of cover) 22 cm. Catalog of the exhibition held summer, 1971 at the Ithaca College Museum of art. Bibliography: p. [32] [N7321.I85] 74-28055
1. Art, Thai—Exhibitions. I. Title.

Art, Thai—Hist.

LE MAY, Reginald Stuart, 1885- 709.593
A concise history of Buddhist art in Siam. [2d ed.] Rutland, Vt., Tuttle [1963, c.1962] xxiii, 169p. plates, fold. maps. 28cm. Complete photographic reprint of the orig. 1938 with minor rev. Bibl. 62-18359 10.00
1. Art, Thai—Hist. 2. Art, Buddhist—Hist. I. Title. II. Title: Buddhist art in Siam. BIP

Art, Thailand.

BOWIE, Theodore Robert, ed. 709.593
The arts of Thailand; a handbook of the architecture, sculpture, and painting of Thailand (Siam) Bloomington, Indiana University Press [1961, c.1960] 219p. illus., map. 23cm. Bibl. 61-62831 8.95
1. Art—Thailand. I. Title.

INDIANA. University. 709.593
The arts of Thailand; a handbook of the architecture, sculpture, and painting of Thailand (Siam) Bloomington, Indiana University Press [c1960] 219p. illus., map. 23cm. Includes a 'catalogue of the exhibition' circulating in 1960-1962. Bibliography: p. [215]-216. [N7321.B6] 61-62831
1. Art—Thailand. I. Title. BIP

INDIANA. University. 709.593
The arts of Thailand; a handbook of the architecture, sculpture and painting of Thailand (Siam) [Editor:Theodore Bowie.

Contributors: Alexander B. Griswold, M. C. Subhadradis Diskul, Elizabeth Lyons] Bloomington, Indiana University Press [1961, c1960] 219 p. illus., map. 23 cm. Includes a catalogue of the exhibition held at Indiana University and other places, from 1960 to 1962. Bibliography: p. [215]-216. [N7321.I 5] 61-62831
1. Art, Thai — Exhibitions. I. Bowie, Theodore Robert, ed. II. Griswold, Alexander B. III. Title.

Art—The West.

EWERS, John Canfield. 759.18
Artists of the Old West, by John C. Ewers. Garden City, N. Y., Doubleday [1965] 240 p. illus. (part col.) ports. (part col.) 29 cm. Bibliography: p. 237-240. [N6525.E9] 65-20054
1. Art—The West. 2. Artists, American—The West. 3. Indians of North America—Pictures, illustrations, etc. I. Title. BIP

Art. — The West. — Galleries and museums.

DAVENPORT, William. 709.78
Art treasures in the West, by William Davenport and the Sunset editors. Supervising editor: Jack McDowell. Book design and layout: William Gibson. Architectural renderings: Jim M'Guinness. Regional art consultants: Robert Wark [and others] Menlo Park, Calif., Lane Magazine & Book Co. [1966] 320 p. illus. (part col.) 29 cm. (A Sunset book) [N6525.D3] 66-24883
1. Art. — The West. — Galleries and museums. I. Sunset. II. Title.

Art thefts.

ESTEROW. MILTON 704.341
The art stealers. New York, Macmillan [c.1966] viii, 246p. 22cm. [N8380.E8] 66-17873 5.95
1. Art thefts. I. Title.

ESTEROW, Milton. 364.1'62
The art stealers. Rev. ed. New York, Macmillan [1973] viii, 255 p. 22 cm. [N8795.E87 1973] 73-7680 6.95
1. Art thefts. 2. Antiquities—Thefts. I. Title. BIP

MEYER, Karl Ernest. 382'.45'7
The plundered past [by] Karl E. Meyer. [1st ed.] New York, Atheneum, 1973. xxv, 353 p. illus. 25 cm. Bibliography: p. 315-337. [N8795.M49 1973] 73-80753 ISBN 0-689-10522-3 12.95
1. Art thefts. 2. Antiquities—Thefts. I. Title.

MEYER, Karl Ernest. 382'.45'7
The plundered past / Karl E. Meyer. New York : Atheneum, 1977,c1973. 353p. : ill. ; 21 cm. Includes index. Bibliography:p.315-337. [N8795.M49 1973] ISBN 0-689-70551-4 pbk. : 5.95
1. Art thefts. 2. Antiquities-Thefts. I. Title. L.C. card no. for 1973 atheneum hardcover ed.:73-80753. BIP

MIDDLEMAS, Robert Keith, 1935- 364.1'62
The double market : art theft and art thieves / Keith Middlemas. Farnborough, Eng. : Saxon House, c1975. vii, 237 p., [8] leaves of plates : ill. ; 24 cm. Includes bibliographical references and index. [N8795.M5] 74-24313 ISBN 0-347-00037-1 : 15.95
1. Art thefts. 2. Art thieves. I. Title.
Distributed by Atheneum Publishers, N.Y. BIP

Art thefts—France.

LEITCH, David. 364.16'2
The discriminating thief. With a foreword by Milton Esterow. [1st ed.] New York, Holt, Rinehart and Winston [1969, c1968] 182 p. illus. 24 cm. [N8387.L4 1969] 69-10231 5.95
1. Richier, Xavier, 1922- 2. Art thefts—France. I. Title.

Art thefts—New York (City)

ADAMS, Laurie. 364.1'62
Art cop Robert Volpe, art crime detective / by Laurie Adams. New York : Dodd, Mead, [1974] xi, 240 p., [4] leaves of plates : ill. ; 24 cm. Includes index. [N8795.5.V64A32] 74-15238 ISBN 0-396-07027-2 : 8.95
1. Volpe, Robert, 1942- 2. Art thefts—New York (City) I. Title.

Art—Themes, motives.

ROTHSCHILD, Lincoln, 1902- 709
Forms and their meaning in Western art / by Lincoln Rothschild. South Brunswick : A.S. Barnes and Co., c1976. p. cm. Includes index. Bibliography: p. [N7565.R67] 74-9298 ISBN 0-498-01608-0 : 15.00
1. Symbolism in art. 2. Art—Themes, motives. 3. Form (Aesthetics) 4. Art—Philosophy. I. Title. BIP

TODD, Alden. 704.94
Favorite subjects in Western art, by A. L. Todd and Dorothy B. Weisbord. Foreword by John Walker. [1st ed.] New York, Dutton, 1968. 224 p. illus. 19 cm. [N7430.T6] 68-55032
1. Art—Themes, motives. I. Weisbord, Dorothy B., joint author. II. Title.

Art—Themes, motives—Addresses, essays, lectures.

SAXL, Fritz, 1890-1948. 709.02'4
A heritage of images: a selection of lectures; edited by Hugh Honour & John Fleming; with an introduction by E. H. Gombrich. Harmondsworth, Penguin, 1970. 154 p., 128 plates. illus., facsims. 20 cm. (Peregrine books) Selection from Lectures, London, Warburg Institute, 1957. Bibliography: p. 141-145. [N7560.S28 1970] 77-19502 ISBN 0-14-055088-7 20/- ($4.95 U.S.)
1. Art—Themes, motives—Addresses, essays, lectures. I. Honour, Hugh, ed. II. Fleming, John, 1919- ed. III. Title.

Art—Themes, motives—Dictionaries.

HALL, James, 1917- 704.94'094
Dictionary of subjects and symbols in art / James Hall ; introd. by Kenneth Clark. 1st U.S. ed. New York : Harper & Row, c1974. xxix, 345 p. : ill. ; 23 cm. (Icon editions) Bibliography: p. [xxv]-xxix. [N7560.H34 1974b] 74-6578 ISBN 0-06-433315-9 : 12.50
1. Art—Themes, motives—Dictionaries. 2. Symbolism in art—Dictionaries. I. Title.

HALL, James, 1918- 704.94'094
Dictionary of subjects and symbols in art. Introduction by Kenneth Clark. New York, Harper & Row [1974] xxlx, 345 p. 22 cm. (Icon editions) Bibliography: [p. xxv]-xxlx [N7560.H34] 74-6578 ISBN 0-06-433315-9 12.50
1. Art—Themes, motives—Dictionaries. 2. Symbolism in art—Dictionaries. I. Title. II. Title: Hall's dictionary of subjects and symbols in art. BIP

Art—Themes, motives—Sources.

THE Picture reference file 704.94
/ under the general editorship of Harold H. Hart. New York : Hart Pub. Co., c1976- v. : chiefly ill. ; 32 cm. Includes index. Contents.Contents.—v. 1. A compendium. Bibliography: v. 1, p. 379-381. [N7560.P5] 75-31405 ISBN 0-8055-1160-1 (v. 1) : 60.00
1. Art—Themes, motives—Sources. 2. Pictures—Sources. I. Hart, Harold H., 1903-

Art, Thracian—Exhibitions.

BRITISH Museum. 739'.0939'8
Thracian treasures from Bulgaria : a special exhibition held at the British Museum, January-March 1976. London : Published for the Trustees of the British Museum by British Museum Publications, 1976. 96 p. : ill. (some col.) ; 24 cm. Text written by I. Venedikov. [N5899.T5B74 1976] 76-361174 ISBN 0-7141-1257-7. ISBN 0-7141-1256-9 pbk.
1. Art, Thracian—Exhibitions. I. Venedikov, Ivan. II. Title.

Art, Tibetan.

GORDON, Antoinette K. 704.948943
Tibetan religious art. 2d ed. Introd. by Thubten Jigme Norbu. New York, Paragon Bk. Reprint [1964, c.]1963. 104p. illus. (pt. col.) ports. 27cm. Bibl. 63-22617 13.75
1. Art, Tibetan. 2. Lamaism. 3. Idols and images. 4. Art, Buddhist. I. Title.

LAUF, Detlef Ingo. 704.948'9'4392309515
Tibetan sacred art : the heritage of Tantra / by Detlef Ingo Lauf ; [translated into English by Ewald Osers]. Berkeley, Calif. : Shambhala : [New York] : distributed by Random House, 1976. 228 p. : ill. (some col.) ; 31 cm. Translation of Das Erbe Tibets. Includes index. Bibliography: p. 215-221. [N8193.3.T35L3813] 76-14204 ISBN 0-394-40935-3 : 37.50
1. Art, Tibetan. 2. Art, Tantric-Buddhist—Tibet. I. Title.

VICTORIA and Albert Museum, South Kensington. 709'.51'5
Tibetan art [by] John Lowry. London, H.M. Stationery Off.; [Distributed in the U.S.A. by Pendragon House, Redwood City, Calif.] 1973. 111 p. illus. 22 cm. [N7346.T5V5] 73-167077 ISBN 0-11-290109-3
1. Art, Tibetan. I. Lowry, John.

Art, Tibetan—Catalogs.

PAL, Pratapaditya. 709'.515
The art of Tibet. New York, Intercultural Arts Press [1970] [90] p. map. and slide set (39 col. slides. 2 x 2 in.) 30 cm. At head of title: Asia House Gallery. Lecture materials based on The art of Tibet, the catalogue of an exhibition shown in the Asia House Gallery in the spring of 1969. Bibliography: p. [83]-[82] [N7346.T5P28] 78-25168 35.00
1. Art, Tibetan—Catalogs. I. Asia House Gallery, New York. II. Title.

PAL, Pratapaditya. 709'.515
Lamaist art: the aesthetics of harmony [by] Pratapaditya Pal [and] Hsien-Chi Tseng. Boston, Museum of Fine Arts; distributed by New York Graphic Society, Greenwich, Conn. [1969?] 56 p. 76 plates (4 col.) 27 cm. "Catalogue": p. 34-56. Bibliography: p. 32-33. [N7346.T5P33] 75-93140 10.00
1. Art, Tibetan—Catalogs. I. Tseng, Hsien-Chi, joint author. II. Boston. Museum of Fine Arts. III. Title.

Art, Tibetan—Exhibitions.

DRAGHI, Paul Alexander. 709'.51'50740172255
Tibert, sacred and secular : [exhibition] Indiana University Museum of Fine Arts, September 9-20, 1975 / by Paul Alexander Draghi. Bloomington, Ind. : Business Services, [1975] [43] p. : 15 ill. ; 24 cm. "Sponsored by the Tibet Society, Inc., Bloomington, Indiana." Bibliography: p. [43] [N7346.T5D7] 76-358223
1. Art, Tibetan—Exhibitions. I. Indiana. University. Museum of Art. II. Tibet Society. III. Title.

PAL, Pratapaditya. 709'.515
The art of Tibet. With an essay by Eleanor Olson. [New York] Asia Society; distributed by New York Graphic Society [Greenwich, Conn., 1969] 163 p. illus. (part col.), map. 28 cm. "An Asia House Gallery publication." Prepared for an exhibition held Apr. 10-June 8, 1969, at Asia House Gallery, New York; July 3-Sept. 1, 1969, at National Collection of Fine Arts, Washington, D.C.; and Oct. 2-Nov. 16, 1969, at the Seattle Museum, Seattle. Bibliography: p. 161-163. [N7346.T5P3] 69-19422
1. Art, Tibetan—Exhibitions. I. Olson, Eleanor. II. Asia House Gallery, New York. III. Smithsonian Institution. National Collection of Fine Arts. IV. Seattle. Art Museum. V. Title.

Art—Torres Strait Islands—Bibliography.

FRASER, Douglas. 016.70901
Bibliography of Torres Straits art. New York, Library, Museum of Primitive Art, 1963. 6 p. 28 cm. (Primitive art bibliographies, no. 1) [Z5961.T6F7] 016.72'092'2 68-329
1. Art—Torres Strait Islands—Bibliography. 2. Art, Primitive—Bibliography. I. Title. II. Series.

Art treasures in war.

GRANT, Judith. 733'.3
A pillage of art. New York, Roy Publishers [1968, c1966] 224 p. illus. 22 cm. Bibliography: p. 216-218. [N8750.G65 1968] 68-12417
1. Art treasures in war. 2. Sculpture, Greek. I. Title.

TREUE, Wilhelm, 1909- 709
Art plunder; the fate of works of art in war and unrest. Translated from the German by Basil Creighton. [1st American ed.] New York, John Day Co. [1961, c1960] 264 p. illus. 23 cm. [N8750.T713] 61-11465
1. Art treasures in war. I. Title.

Art—Tucson. Ariz.—Catalogs.

ARIZONA. University. Art Gallery. 759.0838
The Edward Joseph Gallagher III memorial collection at the University of Arizona. Tucson [1958] 52p. (chiefly illus., port.) 28cm. Collection presented to the university by Edward J. Gallagher, Jr., as a memorial to his son, Edward Joseph Gallagher III. [N830.A53] 59-63943
1. Art—Tucson. Ariz.—Catalogs. I. Gallagher, Edward Joseph. II. Title.

Art—Turkey—Catalogs.

SMITHSONIAN Institution. 709'.561
Art treasures of Turkey. Circulated by the Smithsonian Institution, 1966-1968. Washington, 1966. 120 p. illus. (part col.) map (on lining papers) 25 cm. (Smithsonian publication 4663) Includes bibliographies. [N7161.S6] 66-61710
1. Art—Turkey—Catalogs. I. Title.

Art, Turkish.

ASLANAPA, Oktay. 720'.561
Turkish art and architecture. New York, Praeger Publishers [1971] 422 p. illus. (part col.) 29 cm. Bibliography: p. 355-399. [N7161.A87 1971b] 72-144222 50.00
1. Art, Turkish. 2. Art, Islamic. I. Title. BIP

LEVEY, Michael. 709'.561
The world of Ottoman art / Michael Levey. New York : Scribner, 1977c1975 152 p. : ill. (some col.) ; 25 cm. Includes index. Bibliography: p. 149. [N7164.L48 1975b] 76-40383 ISBN 0-684-14850-1 : 10.95
1. Art, Turkish. 2. Art, Islamic—Turkey. I. Title.

Art, Tuscan—Addresses, essays, lectures.

RUSKIN, John, 1819-1900. 709'.45'5
Val d'Arno; ten lectures on the Tuscan art directly antecedent to the Florentine year of victories, given before the University of Oxford in Michaelmas term, 1873. With an introd. by Charles Eliot Norton. Brantwood ed. New York, C. E. Merrill, 1891. St. Clair Shores, Mich., Scholarly Press, 1972. p. (The works of John Ruskin) Contents.Contents.—Nicholas the Pisan.—John the Pisan.—Shield and apron.—Parted per pale.—Pax vobiscum.—Marble couchant.—Marble rampant. Franchise.—The Tyrrhene sea.—Fleur de lys. [N6919.T9R9 1972] 72-8231 ISBN 0-403-02051-4
1. Art, Tuscan—Addresses, essays, lectures. I. Title.

Art—Ukraine—Mutilation, defacement, etc.

SICHYNSKI, Volodymyr, 1894- 709.477'1
Destruction of Ukrainian monuments of art and culture under the Soviet Russian Administration between 1917-1957, by Volodymyr Sichynsky. New York, Ukrainian Congress Committee of America, 1958. 22 p. illus. 23 cm. [N9012.U4S5] 71-270630
1. Art—Ukraine—Mutilation, defacement, etc. 2. Art treasures in war. 3. Vandalism. I. Title.

Art, Ukrainian.

DMYTRIW, Olya, 1922- comp. 709.477
Ukrainian arts; edited by Anne Mitz. [1st ed.] New York, Ukrainian Youth's League of North America, 1952. 212p. illus. 21cm. [N6995.U5D55] 52-14078
1. Art, Ukrainian. I. Ukrainian Youth's League of North America. II. Title.

DMYTRIW, Olya, 1922- comp. 709.477
Ukrainian arts. Edited by Anne Mitz. [Rev. ed.] New York, Ukrainian Youth's League of North America, 1955. 217p. illus. 21cm. [N6995.U5D55 1955] 55-24571
1. Art, Ukrainian. I. Ukrainian Youth's League of North America. II. Title.

Art, Ukrainian — Exhibitions.

UKRANIAN Artists Association in U.S.A. 709.4771
Catalogue of the annual exhibition: painting, graphic arts, sculpture. 1st- [New York] 1952- v. illus. 21 cm. Title varies slightly. First exhibition held by the society under its earlier name: Association of Ukrainian Artists in New York. Ukrainian and English; v. 1- have added title pages in Ukrainian. [N6995.U5U5] 53-34868
1. Art, Ukrainian — Exhibitions. I. Title.

Art—U. S.

ART in the environment in the United States : a book of 600 photographs of art in architectural, natural, historic, and modern settings across the nation / compiled by Emma Lila Fundaburk and Mary Douglass Foreman. Luverne, Ala. : Fundaburk, c1975. 223 p. : chiefly ill. ; 28 cm. Includes index. [N6505.A73] 75-24620 ISBN 0-910642-02-8 709'.73
1. Fundaburk, Emma Lila, 1922- 2. Art—United States. 3. Art—United States—Galleries and museums. I. Foreman, Mary Douglass Fundaburk, 1922-

BAUR, John Ireland Howe, 1909- v. 12
Revolution and tradition in modern American art. Cambridge, Harvard University Press, 1966 [1951] x, 170 p. plates 25 cm. (The Library of Congress series in American civilization) Bibliographical references included in "Notes" (p. 157-160) [NUC68-27995]
1. Art—U. S. 2. Art, Modern—20th cent. I. Title. II. Series.

BAUR, John Ireland Howe, 1909- 709'.73
Revolution and tradition in modern American art [by] John I. H. Baur. New York, F. A. Praeger [1967] xxii, 170 p. illus. 24 cm. (Praeger paperbacks, p-228) Bibliographical references included in "notes" (p. 157-160) [N6512.B3 1967] 67-27417
1. Art—United States. 2. Art, Modern—20th century—United States. I. Title.

GRAHAM, Robert, 1938- 730'.92'4
Robert Graham. [Exhibition] Dallas Museum of Fine Arts, May 24 through June 25, 1972. [Dallas? 1972] [16] p. illus. 22 cm. Bibliography: p. [16] [ND237.G72D3] 72-189141 2.00
I. Dallas. Museum of Fine Arts.

HANOVER bank, New York. 709.73
The fine arts in philanthropy. New York, Department of philanthropic information, Central Hanover bank and trust company [1937] 61p. 24cm. [N6505.H27] 37-9348
1. Art—U. S. 2. Endowments—U. S. 3. Gifts—U. S. I. Title.

INTERNATIONAL Association of Art. 709.73
Profile: art and artists in the U.S.A., on the occasion of the Fourth Congress, International Association of Plastic Arts, New York City, October 1963. [New York] United States Committee of the International Association of Plastics Arts [1963] 119 p. illus., port. 25 cm. Cover title: Art and artists. "Planned, selected, and edited by the Congress Book Committee." English and French. [N6512.I48] 66-6487
1. Art — U.S. I. Title. II. Title: Art and artists.

TAYLOR, Joshua Charles, 1917- 709'.73
The fine arts in America / Joshua C. Taylor. Chicago : University of Chicago Press, c1979. p. cm. (The Chicago history of American civilization) Includes index. Bibliography: p. [N6505.T373] 78-23643 ISBN 0-226-79150-5 : 15.00
1. Art—United States. 2. Art, American. I. Title. II. Series. BIP

Art—United States—Directories.

AMERICAN Art Directory. 705.8
v.43 New York, Bowker, 1967. illus., ports. 26cm. At head of title: American Federation of Arts. Title varies. Ed.: D. B. Gilbert The biographical material formerly included in the directory is issued separately as Who's who in American art. [N50.A54] 99-1016 22.50
1. Art—U.S.— Direct. 2. Art—Canada—Direct. 3. Art—Spanish—Direct. I. Gilbert, Dorothy G., ed. II. American Federation of Arts.

AMERICAN art directory. 705.8
v.42 [1964] New York. Bowker [c.]1964. 461p. illus. ports. 26cm. At head of title, v.42: American Federation of Arts. Title varies. v.42: ed. by Dorothy B. Gilbert. The biographical material formerly included in the directory is issue separately as Who's who in American art. [N50.A54] 99-1016 22.50
1. Art—U.S.—Direct. 2. Art—Canada—Direct. 3. Art—Spanish—America—Direct. I. Gilbert, Dorothy B., ed. II. American Federation of Arts.

†FOREMAN, Mary Douglass Fundaburk, 1925- 702'.5'73
Pocket guide to the location of art in the United States / originated by Mary Douglass Foreman ; compiled by Emma Lila Fundaburk. Luverne, Ala. : Fundaburk, c1977. 314 p. ; 24 cm. [N51.F67] 77-83294 ISBN 0-910642-04-4 : 10.75 pbk. : 5.50
1. Art—United States—Directories. I. Fundaburk, Emma Lila, 1922- II. Title.
Publisher's address : P.O.Box 231, Laverne, Ala. 36049

NORMAN, Jane. 702'.5'73
Traveler's guide to America's art [by] Jane and Theodore Norman. [1st ed.] New York, Meredith Press [1968] x, 436 p. 24 cm. [N6505.N6] 68-10621
1. Art—United States—Directories. 2. Architecture—United States—Directories. I. Norman, Theodore, joint author. II. Title.

Art—United States—Exhibitions.

ARNHOLM, Ronald. 759.13
Ronald Arnholm. [Exhibition] Georgia Museum of Art, University of Georgia. Athens, Ga., 1969. 56 p. (chiefly illus.) 23 cm. [N6537.A7A57] 72-632442
I. Georgia Museum of Art.

CURTIS, Philip C. 759.13
Philip C. Curtis [catalogue] Comments by John Russell and Claire Boothe Luce. Schedule of exhibitions 1970: March - Arizona State University, Tempe, Arizona [and others. Flagstaff, Ariz., Printed by Northland Press, 1970] 72 p. illus. (part col.), port. 26 cm. Bibliography: p. 70-71. [ND237.C884R8] 77-115794
I. Russell, John, 1919- II. Luce, Claire (Boothe) 1903- III. Arizona. State University, Tempe.

INDIANA, Robert, 1928- 769'.924
Robert Indiana; graphics. An introd. by Richard-Raymond Alasko. Poem by Michael Patrick O'Connor with commentary by the artist. An exhibition organized by the Department of Art of Saint Mary's College, Notre Dame, Indiana. June 12 to July 6, 1969. [Notre Dame, Ind., 1969] 47 p. illus. (part col.), port. 23 x 24 cm. Half title: The prints and posters of Robert Indiana, 1961-1969. [NE2237.5.I5A54] 75-92206
I. Saint Mary's College, Notre Dame, Ind. Dept. of Art.

INDIANA, Robert, 1928- 760'.0924
Robert Indiana. With statements by the artist [and] an introd. by John W. McCoubrey. [Philadelphia, Printed by the Falcon Press, 1968] 63 p. illus. (part col.) 23 x 24 cm. Cover title: Love. Catalog of an exhibition of the author's works organized by the Institute of Contemporary Art of the University of Pennsylvania, Philadelphia (April 17-May 27, 1968) in collaboration with the Marion Koogler McNay Art Institute, San Antonio (July 1-August 15, 1968) and the Herron Museum of Art, Indianapolis (Sept. 1-29, 1968) Bibliography: p. 60-61. [ND237.I47P4] 71-104
I. Pennsylvania. University. Institute of Contemporary Art. II. Marion Koogler McNay Art Institute, San Antonio. III. Art Association of Indianapolis, Indiana. John Herron Art Institute. IV. Title: Love.

LAURENT, Robert, 1890-1970. 730'.92'4
The Robert Laurent memorial exhibition, 1972-1973, University of New Hampshire, Durham, New Hampshire. Catalogue prepared by Peter V. Moak. Including an essay "Robert Laurent at Indiana University" by Henry R. Hope. [Durham, University of New Hampshire, 1972] 33 p., 63 p. of illus. 28 cm. Bibliography: p. 32. [NB237.L277M6] 72-193001
I. Moak, Peter V. II. New Hampshire. University. III. Title.

MCCABE, Cynthia Jaffee. 709'.73'0740153
The golden door : artist-immigrants of America, 1876-1976 / text by Cynthia Jaffee McCabe ; introd. by Daniel J. Boorstin. Washington : Published by the Smithsonian Institution Press for the Hirshhorn Museum and Sculpture Garden, Smithsonian Institution, 1976. p. cm. Catalogue of an exhibition, Hirshhorn Museum and Sculpture Garden, May 20-Oct. 20, 1976. Includes index. Bibliography: p. [N6510.M32] 76-8827
1. Art—United States—Exhibitions. 2. Art, Modern—19th century—United States—Exhibitions. 3. Artists—United States. 4. United States—Foreign population. I. Hirshhorn Museum and Sculpture Garden. II. Title. BIP

MCHUGH, Joseph 709'.73
A power set apart / by Joseph McHugh and Latif Harris. Millbrae, Calif. : Celestial Arts, 1976. p. cm. [PS3563.A31162P6] 75-28759 ISBN 0-89087-164-7 pbk. : 4.50
I. Harris, Latif, joint author. II. Title.

PEARLSTEIN, Philip, 1924- 760'.0924
Philip Pearlstein. [Athens, Ga., Georgia Museum of Art, 1970] 1 v. (unpaged) illus., ports. 22 x 25 cm. Catalog of the exhibition held Sept. 20-Nov. 8, 1970, at the Georgia Museum of Art, University of Georgia; Jan. 2-Feb. 10, 1971, at the Wichita Art Museum; Feb. 24-Apr. 18, 1971, at the Vassar College Art Gallery. Includes bibliography. [ND237.P33A54] 74-198246
I. Georgia Museum of Art. II. Wichita Art Museum. III. Vassar College. Art Gallery.

SCRIVER, Robert MacFie, 1914- 730'.92'4
Scriver. [Edited by Vivian A. Paladin. Helena, Montana Historical Society, 1972] v, 25 p. (chiefly illus.) 21 x 23 cm. Cover title. [NB237.S39P3] 72-611440
I. Paladin, Vivian A., ed. II. Montana Historical Society.

ULFERT Wilke: recent works. 759.13
[Des Moines, Print: Wright Lithographing and Print. Co., 1970] xxx p. illus. (part col.), port. 19 x 26 cm. Catalog of the exhibition held at the Des Moines Art Center, Nov. 2-Dec. 4, 1970, and elsewhere. Bibliography: p. xxviii-[xxix] [N6537.W5U4] 74-198191
I. Wilke, Ulfert, 1907- II. Des Moines Art Center.

UPTON, Richard. 760'.0924
Richard Upton: prints, drawings, paintings from the collection of Syracuse University; a retrospective exhibition, 1962-1970, in the galleries of the Joe and Emily Lowe Art Center, April-May, 1970. Introd. by Laurence Schmeckebier. Syracuse, N.Y., Syracuse University, School of Art [1970] [24] p. illus. 23 cm. Catalog. [NE539.U6A54] 79-121673
I. Syracuse University. Joe and Emily Lowe Art Center. II. Syracuse University. School of Art. III. Title.

Art—U. S.—Galleries and museums.

CANAJOHARIE Library and Art Gallery. 759.13
Catalogue of the permanent collection of the Canajoharie Library and Art Gallery. Canajoharie, N.Y. [1969] 1 v. (unpaged) illus. (part col.) 28 cm. [N529.C15A53] 70-14894
I. Title.

CARTWRIGHT, W Aubrey. 708.1
Guide to art museums in the United States. [1st ed.] New York, Duell, Sloan and Pearce [1958- v. illus., map (on lining papers) 18cm. Contents.[1] East coast: Washington to Miami. [N510.C3] 58-6767
1. Art—U. S.—Galleries and museums. I. Title.

CHRISTENSEN, Erwin Ottomar, 1890- 708.13
A guide to art museums in the United States [by] Erwin O. Christensen. New York, Dodd, Mead [1968] xiii, 303 p. illus. 23 cm. "Museum directories and regional guides to art museums": p. 289. [N510.C5] 67-26838
1. Art—United States—Galleries and museums. I. Title. II. Title: Art museums in the United States.

LOW, Theodore Lewis, 1915- 708'.13
The educational philosophy and practice of art museums in the United States. New York, Bureau of Publications, Teachers College, Columbia University, 1948. [New York, AMS Press, 1972, i.e. 1973] viii, 245 p. 22 cm. Reprint of the 1948 ed., issued in series: Columbia University. Teachers College. Contributions to education, no. 942. Originally presented as the author's thesis, Columbia. Bibliography: p. 217-228. [N510.L6 1972] 77-177012 ISBN 0-404-55942-5 12.50
1. Art—United States—Galleries and museums. I. Title. II. Series: Columbia University. Teachers College. Contributions to education, no. 942. BIP

NORTH Carolina. University. William Hayes Ackland Memorial Art Center. 708.1'56'565
Catalogue of the collection. Chapel Hill, 1971- v. 1- illus. 25 cm. Contents.Contents.—v. 1. Paintings and selected sculpture, by G. M. Hertzman. [N529.C2A52] 75-151179 ISBN 0-8078-1169-6
I. Title.

SPAETH, Eloise. 708.13
American art museums; an introduction to looking. Rev. ed. New York, McGraw-Hill [1969] xiii, 321 p. illus., ports. 21 cm. Bibliography: p. [293]-295. [N510.S6 1969] 68-55274
1. Art—U.S.—Galleries and museums. 2. Art dealers—U.S.—Directories. I. Title. BIP

SPAETH, Eloise. 708'.13
American art museums : an introduction to looking / Eloise Spaeth. 3d ed., expanded. New York : Harper & Row, [1975] xxiii, 483 p. : ill. ; 22 cm. Includes index. Bibliography: p. 445-446. [N510.S6 1975] 74-1857 ISBN 0-06-013978-1 : 15.00
1. Art—United States—Galleries and museums. 2. Art dealers—United States—Directories. I. Title.

1. Art, Victorian—History. 2. Great Britain—Social life and customs. I. Title.

Art, Vietnamese.

HEJZLAR, Josef. 709.597
The art of Vietnam [by] J. Hejzlar, with photographs by W. and B. Forman. [Translated from the Czech ms. by Till Gottheiner] London, New York, Hamlyn, 1973. 3-263 p. illus. (some col.) 28 cm. Bibliography: p. [254]. [N7314.H4313] 74-165651 ISBN 0-600-39125-6 £5.00
1. Art, Vietnamese. I. Forman, Werner, illus. II. Forman, Bedrich, illus. III. Title.

Art, Vietnamese — Exhibitions.

SMITHSONIAN Institution. 709.597
National Collection of Fine Arts.
Art and archeology of Viet Nam; Asian crossroad of cultures. A traveling exhibition circulated by the National Collection of Fine Arts. Washington, Smithsonian Institution, 1961. 63 p. plates, maps. 26 cm. (Smithsonian publication 4430) Bibliography: p. 61. [N7314.S6] 61-60775
1. Art, Vietnamese — Exhibitions. 2. Vietnam — Antiq. I. Title.

Art, Viking—Juvenile literature.

GLUBOK, Shirley. 709'.02
The art of the Vikings / Shirley Glubok ; designed by Gerard Nook. New York : Macmillan, c1978. 48 p. : ill. ; 26 cm. A survey of the art and culture of the Norsemen from approsimately 800 A.D. to approximately 1100 A.D. [N6275.G58 1978] 78-6849 ISBN 0-02-736460-7 : 8.95
1. Art, Viking—Juvenile literature. I. Nook, Gerard. II. Title. BIP

Art—Vocational guidance.

HAWES, Carolyn. 700'.23
Your career in art and design / by Carolyn Hawes, Margaret Johnson, Judith Nylen. New York : Arco Pub. Co., c1977. 159 p. : ill. ; 21 cm. (Arco's career guidance series) Includes index. Bibliography: p. 154-155. [N8350.H38] 76-41912 ISBN 0-668-04133-1 : 4.95. ISBN 0-668-04141-2 pbk. : 1.95
1. Art—Vocational guidance. I. Johnson, Margaret, 1923- joint author. II. Nylen, Judith, joint author. III. Title. BIP

Art—Vocational guidance—Juvenile literature.

GRACZA, Margaret Young. 700'.23
Art / by Margaret Gracza ; designed by Rick Lemons. Minneapolis : Dillon Press, c1976. p. cm. (Looking forward to a career) Includes index. Discusses the opportunities in and qualifications for various careers in art including fashion design, architecture, printmaking, and musum work. [N8350.G7 1976] 76-4925 ISBN 0-87518-130-9
1. Art—Vocational guidance—Juvenile literature. I. Title.

Art—Washington, D. C.—Catalogs.

ADVENTURE in art : 750'.74'0153
the National Gallery, Washington, D.C. / [compiled by Marian King]. New York : H. N. Abrams, [1978] p. cm. Includes index. Bibliography: p. [N856.A513] 77-20926 ISBN 0-8109-1769-6 : 14.95 ISBN 0-8109-2167-7 pbk. : 7.95
1. United States. National Gallery of Art. 2. Art—Washington, D.C. I. King, Marian. II. United States. National Gallery of Art.

DUMBARTON Oaks. 709.37
Catalogue of Greek and Roman antiquities in the Dumbarton Oaks collection, by Gisela M. A Richter. Cambridge, Harvard University Press, 1956. 77 p. 27 plates. 30 cm. (Dumbarton Oaks catalogues) [N858.D8A56] 56-10351
1. Art—Washingon, D. C.—Catalogs. 2. Art, Greek—Catalogs. 3. Art, Roman—Catalogs. I. Richter, Gisela Marie Augusta, 1882- II. Title. III. Title: Greek and Roman antiquities in the Dumbarton Oaks collection. BIP

DUMBARTON Oaks. 708.153
The Dumbarton Oaks Collection, Harvard University; handbook. Washington, 1955. 164 p. illus. 23 cm. Published by the Center under its earlier name: Dumbarton Oaks Research Library and Collection of Harvard University. [N858.H3A54] 55-11604
1. Art — Washington, D.C. — Catalogs. 2. Christian art and symbolism. 3. Art, Byzantine. I. Title.

DUMBARTON Oaks. 708.153
Handbook of the Byzantine collection. Washington, 1967. xv, 125, [95] p. illus., maps (on lining papers) 23 cm. [N858.D8A6] 68-608
1. Art—Washington, D.C.—Catalogs. 2. Art, Byzantine—Catalogs. I. Title.

HARVARD University. 709.37
Dumbarton Oaks Research Library and Collection, Washington, D.C.
Catalogue of Greek and Roman antiquities in the Dumbarton Oaks collection, by Gisela M.A. Richter. Cambridge, Harvard University Press, 1956. 77p. 27plates. 30cm. (Dumbarton Oaks catalogues) [N858.H3A53] 56-10351
1. Art—Washington, D.C.—Catalogs. 2. Art, Greek. 3. Art, Roman. I. Richter, Gisela Marie Augusta, 1882- II. Title. III. Title: Greek and Roman antiquities in the Dumbarton Oaks collection. IV. Series.

HARVARD University. 708.153
Dumbarton Oaks Research Library and Collection, Washington, D. C.
The Dumbarton Oaks Collection, Harvard University; handbook. Washington, 1955. 164p. illus. 23cm. [N858.H3A54] 55-11604
1. Art—Washington, D. C.—Catalogs. I. Title.

HARVARD University. 709.37
Dumbarton Oaks Research Library and Collection, Washington, D. C.
Handbook of the collection. Washington, 1946. 136p. illus. 18cm. [N858.H3A55] 55-35345
1. Art—Washington, D. C.— Catalogs. 2. Christian art and symbolism. 3. Art, Byzantine. I. Title.

PHILLIPS Collection, 750'.74'0153
Washington, D.C.
A collection in the making : works from the Phillips Collection / compiled by Kevin Grogan ; with a foreword by Milton W. Brown. Chicago : University of Chicago Press, c1976. ix, 60 p. ; 24 cm. & 5 sheets (11x15 cm.) in pocket. (A University of Chicago Press text/fiche) The sheets are microfiche. Includes 2 essays by D. Phillips: A collection in the making (1926) and A collection still in the making (1931) [N858.P4A53] 76-10817 ISBN 0-226-69538-7 : 27.50
1. Phillips Collection, Washington, D.C. 2. Art—Washington, D.C.—Catalogs. I. Grogan, Kevin. II. Phillips, Duncan, 1886-1966. A collection in the making. 1976. III. Title. BIP

UNITED States. Architect 708'.153
of the Capitol.
Art in the United States Capitol / prepared by the Architect of the Capitol under the direction of the Joint Committee on the Library. Washington : U.S. Govt. Print. Off., 1976. xi, 453 p. : ill. (some col.) ; 27 cm. (House document - 91st Congress, 2d session ; no. 91-368) Includes index. [N6535.W3U54 1976] 72-600081 12.55
1. Art—Washington, D.C.—Catalogs. 2. United States in art. 3. Washington, D.C. Capitol. I. Title. II. Series: United States. 91st Congress, 2d session, 1970. House. Document ; no. 91-368.

U.S. National 069'.9'70924
Gallery of Art
Portfolio. Washington [n.d.] v, col. plates. 36 cm. [N856.A682] 56-23748
1. Art — Washington,D.C. I. Title.

U.S. National 750'.74'0153
Gallery of Art.
European paintings and sculpture: illustrations. Washington, 1968. 171 p. (chiefly illus.) 23 cm. "Companion to the Summary catalogue of European paintings and sculpture, published in 1965." [N856.A54] 70-600202
1. Art—Washington. D.C.—Catalogs. I. Title.

Art—Weimar.

SCHEIDIG, Walther. 707.1'5
Crafts of the Weimar Bauhaus, 1919-1924; an early experiment in industrial design. Photos. by Klaus G. Beyer. [Translated from the German by Ruth Michaelis-Jena with the collaboration of Patrick Murray] New York, Reinhold Pub. Corp. [1967] 150 p. illus. (part col.) 28 cm. Translation of Bauhaus Weimar, 1919-1924. Bibliography: p. [147]-148. [N332.B38S283 1967] 66-25545
1. Bauhaus. 2. Art—Weimar. I. Beyer, Klaus G., 1922- illus. II. Title.

Art — Wellesley, Mass. — Catalogs.

WELLESLEY College. 708.1447
Jewett Arts Center.
Catalogue of European and American Sculpture, paintings, and drawings at Wellesley College, by Curtis H. Shell & John McAndrew. [Wellesley, Mass., Wellesley College, 1958] 110 p. illus. 21 cm. [N860.A3] 59-20689
1. Art — Wellesley, Mass. — Catalogs. I. Shell, Curtis H. II. Title.

Art—Windsor, Ont.—Catalogs.

ART Gallery of 708'.113'32
Windsor.
A checklist of the permanent collection to December 31, 1971. [Windsor, Ont., Art Gallery of Windsor, 1972] 55 p. illus. (part col.) 28 cm. [N910.W5A6] 74-168474 5.00
1. Art Gallery of Windsor. 2. Art—Windsor, Ont.—Catalogs. 3. Art, Canadian—Catalogs. I. Title.

Art—Worcester, Mass.—Catalogs.

WORCESTER, Mass. Art 708'.144'3
Museum.
A handbook to the Worcester Art Museum. Worcester, Mass. : The Museum, [1973] 222 p. : ill. ; 21 cm. [N870.A76] 75-320885
1. Worcester, Mass. Art Museum. 2. Art—Worcester, Mass.—Catalogs. I. Title.

Art—Yearbooks.

HARVARD University. 707.11744
Committee on the Visual Arts at Harvard.
Report. Cambridge, Harvard University, 1956. xviii, 155p. illus. 25cm. [N330.C36A57] 56-2985
I. Title.

JAHRBUCH der 705
kunsthistorischen sammlungen in Wien. bd. 1-36. Wien, A. Schroll & co.; 1883-19-; New York, Johnson Reprint [1967] v. illus., plates (pt. mounted) ports., facsims. 37-40cm. Pt of the illustrative material is colored, part folded. Vs. 1-5, 7, 11-34 each in two parts: 1. th. Abbhandlungen. 2. th. Quellen zur gaschichte der kaiserlichen haussammlungen und der kunstbestrebungen des allerdurchlauchtigsten erzhauses. Vol. 9 consists of Abhandlungen, v. 10, of Quellen zur Geschichte . . . Titles varies: 1883-1918, Jarbuch der kunsthistorischen sammlungen des Allerhochsten kaiserhauses. 1919- Jahrbuch der kunsthistorischen sammlungen in Wien. Vls. 1-34 herausgegeben unter leitung des oberstkammerers Seiner Kaiserlichen und Koniglichen apostolischen Majestat . . . vom Oberst-kammerer-amte (varies slightly); new ser., v. 1- 'herausgegeben vom letter des Kunsthistorischen museums' (varies slightly) Triumph des kaisers Maximilian I. Wien, A. Holzhausen, 1883-84. 1 p. 1., 137pl. 46-59cm. Supplement to v. 1-2 of Jahrbuch der kbd. 1-36. Wien, A. Schroll & co.; 1883-19-; New York, Johnson Reprint [1967] v. illus., plates (pt. mounted) ports., facsims. 37-40cm. Pt of the illustrative material is colored, part folded. Vs. 1-5, 7, 11-34 each in two parts: 1. th. Abbhandlungen. 2. th. Quellen zur gaschichte der kaiserlichen haussammlungen und der kunstbestrebungen des allerdurchlauchtigsten erzhauses. Vol. 9 consists of Abhandlungen, v. 10, of Quellen zur Geschichte . . . Titles varies: 1883-1918, Jarbuch der kunsthistorischen sammlungen des Allerhochsten kaiserhauses. 1919- Jahrbuch der kunsthistorischen sammlun
1. Art—Year-books. 2. Art— Austria. I. Austro-Hungarian monarchy. Oberstkammereramt. II. Austro- Hungarian monarchy. Kunsthistorische sammlungen des Allerhochsten kaiserhauses. III. Vienna. Kunsthistorisches museum.

MARSYAS 707.9
studies in the history of art. New York. v. illus. 28cm. 'A publication by the students of the Institute of Fine Arts, New York University.' [N9.M34] 54-30868
1. Art—Yearbooks. I. New York University. Institute of Fine Arts.

MARSYAS; 705.8
studies in the history of art, v.9, 1960-1961. Inst. of Fine Arts, New York Univ., dist. Locust Valley, N. Y., J. J. Augustin, 1961[ ] 77p. illus. Bibl. 54-30868 5.00 pap.,
1. Art—Yearbooks. I. New York University. Institute of Fine Arts.

MARSYAS; 705.8
studies in the history of art. v. 8, 1957-1959. Dist. by J. J. Augustin, Locust Valley, N.Y. 1959[ ] v, 90p. (bibl. footnotes) illus. 28cm. 'A publication by the students of the Institute of Fine Arts, New York University' 54 5.00 pap.,
1. Art—Yearbooks. I. New York University. Institute of Fine Arts.

MARSYAS; studies in the 705.8
history of art; v.11, 1962-1964. Locust Valley, N.Y., J. J. Augustin [1965] 84p. illus. 28cm. Pub. by the students of the Inst. of Fine Arts, N.Y.U. Bibl. [N9.M34] 54-30868 5.00 pap.,
1. Art—Yearbooks. I. New York University. Institute of Fine Arts.

MARSYAS; studies in the 705.8
history of art; v. 12. 1964-1965 Locust Valley, N.Y., 11560. J.J. Augustin, 1966 72p. illus. 28cm. Pubn. by the students of the Inst. of Fine Arts, New York Univ. [N9.M34] 54-30868 5.00 pap.,
1. Art—Yearbooks. I. New York University. Institute of Fine Arts.

MONTCLAIR Art 706.2749
Association.
Year book. Montclair, N.J. v. 21 cm. [N11.M613] 51-36344
1. Art — Yearbooks. I. Title.

MUNSON-WILLIAMS-PROCTOR 707.152
INSTITUTE, Utica, N.Y.
Yearbook. Utica. v. illus., ports. 20-26 cm. [N330.U82] 50-30460
I. Title.

ROCHESTER Museum 914.22'5
Association.
A year at the Rochester Museum. [Rochester] v. illus. 26 cm. [AM101.R59577] 51-36338
I. Title.

ROSENTHAL, George S. ed. 705.8
Portfolio; the annual of the graphic arts. winter 1950- [Cincinnati, Zebra Press] v. illus. (part col.) 34 cm. Quarterly 1950; annual, 1951- Issues for 1950 called v. 1, no. 1-2. Subtitle varies: 1950, A magazine for the graphic arts. Editors: 1950- G. S. Rosenthal, F. Zachary. [N9.P6] 51-10415
1. Art — Yearbooks. I. Title.

STRUCTURIST (The) 709.04
no.4, 1964 [Dist. New York, Wittenborn, 1964] 64p. illus. (pt. col.) 28cm. annual. Ed.: Eli Bornstein, Special issue on art and music. 61-912 2.50 pap.,
1. Art—Yearbooks. 2. Art, Modern—20th cent.—Yearbooks. I. Bornstein, Eli, ed.

STRUCTURIST (The) no. 2, 709.4
1961-62. Special issue Art in architectures

[dist. New York, Wittenborn, 1962] 51 p. illus. (pt. col.) 28 cm. annual. Ed.: Eli Bornstein. 61-912 pap., 2.50
1. Art—Yearbooks. 2. Art, Modern— 0th cent.—Yearbooks. I. Bornstein, Eli, ed.

WINTERTHUR portfolio. 700'.5
3. 1967. Winterthur, Del., The Henry Francis Du Pont Winterthur Mus. v. maps (pt. col.) ports. 29cm. Ed.: 3d. Milo M. Naeva [N9.] [52] 64-7642 9.75
1. Art—Yearbooks. I. Henry Francis Du Pont Winterthur Museum.

WINTERTHUR portfolio, II- 1965. 700.5
Winterthur, Del., Henry Francis du Pont Winterthur Mus. c.1965.*216p. illus. maps (pt. col.) plans, ports. 29cm. annual [N9.W52] 64-7642 9.50 bds.,
1. Art—Yearbooks. I. Henry Francis du Pont Winterthur Museum.

Art, Yoruba.

CARROLL, Kevin, 1920- 736'.09668
.
Yoruba religious carving; pagan & Christian sculpture in Nigeria & Dahomey. Foreword by William Gaff. [1st ed.] New York, Praeger [1967, c1966] xi. 172 p. illus. (part col.), map (on lining papers), ports. 29 cm. Bibliography: p. 169. [NB1097.N5C3] 67-13951
I. Title.

THOMPSON, Robert Farris. 732'.2
Black gods and kings / by Robert Farris Thompson. Bloomington : Indiana University Press, [1975] c1971. p. cm. Bibliography: p. [N7399.N52Y66 1975] 75-10719 ISBN 0-253-31204-3 : 18.50
1. Art, Yoruba. I. Title.

THOMPSON, Robert Farris. 732'.2
Black gods and kings; Yoruba art at UCLA. Los Angeles, University of California, Museum and Laboratories of Ethnic Arts and Technology, 1971. 1 v. (various pagings) illus. (part col.), maps. 28 cm. (Occasional papers of the Museum and Laboratories of Ethnic Arts and Technology, University of California, Los Angeles, no. 2) Includes bibliography. [N7399.N52Y66] 72-634175
1. Art, Yoruba. I. California. University. University at Los Angeles. Museum and Laboratories of Ethnic Arts and Technology. II. Title. III. Title: Yoruba art at UCLA. IV. Series: California. University. University at Los Angeles. Museum and Laboratories of Ethnic Arts and Technology. Occasional papers, no. 2
BIP

Art, Yoruba—Exhibitions.

ARNESON, 709'.01'109669074019454
Jeanette Jensen.
Tradition and change in Yoruba art. [Sacramento, Calif.] E. B. Crocker Art Gallery, 1974. 79 p. illus. 28 cm. Exhibition held Mar. 9-Apr. 14, 1974. [N7399.N5A73] 74-75073
1. Art, Yoruba—Exhibitions. I. Crocker Art Gallery, Sacramento, Calif. II. Title.

Art, Yugoslav—Exhibitions.

CAMDEN Arts 709'.497'07402142
Centre.
Naive art in Yugoslavia : [catalogue of an exhibition held at] Camden Arts Centre, 7th July-22nd August 1976. London : Sterling and Silver International Ltd, [1976] 26 p. : ill. ; 20 cm. Cover title. "Presented by the London Borough of Camden and Arkwright Arts Trust in association with the Government of the Socialist Federal Republic of Yugoslavia." Errata slip, 1 leaf, inserted. Bibliography: p. 25. [N7248.5.P7C35 1976] 77-355106 ISBN 0-901389-24-2 : £0.30
1. Art, Yugoslav—Exhibitions. 2. Primitivism in art—Yugoslavia—Exhibitions. 3. Art, Modern—20th century—Yugoslavia—Exhibitions. I. Camden, Eng. II. Arkwright Arts Trust. III. Yugoslavia. IV. Title.

Art—Yugoslavia—Addresses, essays, lectures.

BIHALJI-MERIN, Oto 1904- 709'.497
Art treasures of Yugoslavia. Texts by Milutin Garasanin [and others] Edited by Oto Bihalji-Merin. New York, H. N. Abrams [1972, c1969] 445 p. illus. (part col.) 33 cm. Translation of Umetnicko blago Jugoslavije. Bibliography: p. [425]-434. [N7241.B4713 1972] 72-5237 ISBN 0-8109-0548-5
1. Art—Yugoslavia—Addresses, essays, lectures. 2. Art, Yugoslav—Addresses, essays, lectures. I. Garasanin, Milutin V. II. Title.
BIP

Arthurs, Stanley, 1877-1950.

ARTHURS, Stanley, 1877- 759.13
1950.
Stanley Arthurs. [Wilmington, Wilmington Society of the Fine Arts, 1974] 47 p. illus. 28 cm. Exhibition held at the Delaware Art Museum, May 3-June 16, 1974. Includes bibliographical references. [ND237.A75D44] 74-80485
1. Arthurs, Stanley, 1877-1950. I. Delaware Art Museum.

Artificial flowers.

CONROY, Norma M. 745.59'43
Making shell flowers, by Norma M. Conroy. Photos. by James Wallhermfechtel. New York, Sterling Pub. Co. [1972] 48 p. illus. 20 cm. (Little craft book series) Directions for making many realistic flowers by gluing shells and adding paint and stems. [TT890.C55] 72-78587
1. Artificial flowers. 2. Shellcraft. I. Title.

FARLIE, Barbara L. 745.59'43
Flowercraft / by Barbara L. Farlie and Vivian Abell. Indianapolis : Bobbs-Merrill Co., [1978]i.e. 1979. p. cm. Includes index. [TT890.F37] 78-55664 ISBN 0-672-52150-4 : 14.95
1. Artificial flowers. I. Abell, Vivian, joint author. II. Title.
BIP

HORNBERGER, Helen. 745.59'43
The art of making tole flowers and ornaments. Drawings by Eileen Pillar. Great Neck, N.Y., Hearthside Press [1972] 223 p. illus. 25 cm. [TT890.H63] 72-79083 ISBN 0-8208-0347-2 10.00
1. Artificial flowers. 2. Art metal-work. I. Title.

IIDA, Miyuki, 1903- 745.59'43
The art of handmade flowers [by] Miyuki and Tomoko Iida. Photos. by Akira Tsukui. Tokyo, Palo Alto, Calif., Kodansha International [1971] 124 p. illus. (part col.) 25 x 27 cm. Translation of Zoka. [TT890.I3513] 77-128687 ISBN 0-87011-136-1 8.95 (U.S.)
1. Artificial flowers. I. Iida, Tomoko, joint author. II. Title.
BIP

KEBBELL, Clara. 745
Flower making. London, New York, Studio Publications [1951] 64 p. illus. 17 cm. (A Make it yourself book) [TT890.K4] 51-14905
1. Artificial flowers. I. Title.

LEEMING, Joseph, 1897- 745.59
Fun with artificial flowers. Illustrated by Jessie Robinson. [1st ed.] Philadelphia, Lippincott [1959] 95p. illus. 24cm. [TT890.L4] 59-9220
1. Artificial flowers. I. Title.

LOBLEY, Priscilla. 745.59
Flower making. [1st American ed.] New York, Taplinger Pub. Co. [1969, c1968] 91 p. illus. (part col.) 26 cm. [TT890.L6 1969] 69-11682 5.50
1. Artificial flowers. I. Title.
BIP

NATHANSON, Virginia. 745.59
The art of making bead flowers and bouquets. New York, Hearthside Press [1967] 192 p. illus. (part col.) 24 cm. [TT890.N3] 67-27169
1. Artificial flowers. 2. Beadwork. I. Title.

WILKINSON, Jean. 745.59'43
Flower fabrications : forty hand fashioned flowers to create, including silk tulips, organdy roses, gingham cornflowers and crepe paper daisies / Jean Wilkinson, with Katharyn Duff. New York : Butterick Pub., c1977. 206 p. : ill. (some col.) ; 26 cm. Includes index. [TT890.W56] 76-26364 ISBN 0-88421-025-1 : 12.95
1. Artificial flowers. I. Duff, Katharyn, joint author. II. Title.
BIP

YATES, Marguerite W. 635.9663
The complete flower hobby book. [1st ed.] New York, Longmans, Green, 1955. 152 p. illus. 21 cm. [TT890.Y3] 54-9209
1. Artificial flowers. 2. Floral decoration. I. Title.

Artinian, Artine, 1907-—Art collections.

BOWDOIN College. Museum of 743'.4
Art.
The French visage; a century and a half of portraiture and caricature from the Artine Artinian Collection. [Brunswick, Me.] 1969. [20] p. illus., ports. 23 cm. Catalogue of an exhibition held at Bowdoin College Museum of art. [ND1301.6.A78B68] 72-194226
1. Artinian, Artine, 1907-—Art collections. 2. Portraits—Exhibitions. 3. Caricatures and cartoons—Exhibitions. I. Title.

Artisans — Appalachian Mountains, Southern.

DUPUY, Edward L. 745.5'0975
Artisans of the Appalachians. Photos, and original material by Edward L. DuPuy. Text by Emma Weaver. Asheville, N.C., Miller Print. Co. [1967] xi, 123 p. illus., ports. 30 cm. [HD2346.U52A64] 67-28477
1. Artisans — Appalachian Mountains, Southern. I. Weaver, Emma. II. Title.

Artisans in art.

TACHIBANA, Minko, fl.1751- 745.5
1771
Traditional crafts of Japan, illus. with the eighteenth-century artisan prints of Tachibana Minko, by Charles A. Pomeroy. New York, Walker [1968,c.1967] vii, 119p. col. illus. 27cm. Weathermark ed. Title romanized: Saiga shokunin burui. [NE1310.T27 1968] J 68 8.95 bds.,
1. Artisans in art. 2. Color prints, Japanese. I. Pomeroy, Charles A. ed. II. Title. III. Title: Traditionl crafts of Japan.

Artisans—Japan—Pictorial works.

SUGIMURA, Tsune, 1926- 745.5
The enduring crafts of Japan; 33 living national treasures. Photos. by Tsune Sugimura. Text by Masataka Ogawa. Introd. by Tsuneari Fukuda. Foreword by Gordon B. Washburn. [1st ed.] New York, Walker/Weatherhill [1968] xxi, 229 p. illus. (part col.), ports. 27 cm. "A Weathermark edition." Translation of Ningen kokuho, dento kogei. [NK1071.S813] 68-15702 13.50
1. Artisans—Japan—Pictorial works. 2. Art objects, Japanese—Pictorial works. I. Ogawa, Masataka, 1925- II. Title.

Artist—Correspondence, reminiscences, etc.

GOGH, Vincent van, 1835- 759.9492
1890.
Van Gogh: a self-portrait; letters revealing his life as a painter(selected by W. H. Auden. New York, Dutton, 1963. 398p. illus. 21cm. (Dutton paperback D116) 2.75 pap.,
1. Artist—Correspondence, reminiscences, etc. I. Auden, Wystan Hugh, 1907- II. Title.

GREENMAN, Frances Cranmer. 927.5
Higher than the sky. Illustrated by the author. [1st ed.] New York, Harper [1954] 305 p. illus. 22 cm. Autobiography. [ND237.G62A2] 54-8953
I. Title.

Artists.

CHANDLER, Anna Curtis. 927
Story-lives of master artists. With 23 reproductions from paintings. 1953 revision. Philadelphia, Lippincott [1953] 255 p. illus. 21 cm. Twenty biographies from the author's Story-lives of master artists, first and second series. Cf. Dust jacket. [N40.C52] 53-5426
1. Artists. I. Title.
BIP

CLARK, Kenneth McKenzie, 709'.2'2
Baron Clark, 1903-
The artist grows old [by] Kenneth Clark. London, Cambridge University Press, 1972. [1], 30, [4] p. illus. 19 cm. (The Rede lecture 1970) [NX163.C57] 72-89808 ISBN 0-521-20038-5
1. Artists. 2. Creation (Literary, artistic, etc.) 3. Ability, Influence of age on. I. Title. II. Series.
Distributed by Cambridge U. Press, N.Y., 1.65.

FRASNAY, Daniel. 709'.22
The artist's world. Text and photos. by Daniel Frasnay. Pref. by Rene Huyghe. New York, Viking Press [1969] 369 p. illus. (part col.), facsims., ports. 31 cm. (A Studio book) Translation of peintres et sculpteurs, leur monde. [N40.F7613 1969] 69-10630 27.50
1. Artists. I. Title.

INSTITUTE of International 700
Education.
International arts program. [New York] v. 23cm. [N7438.I6] 56-25250
1. Artists. 2. Exchange of persons programs, American. I. Title.

KALES, David. 920
Masters of art, by David and Emily Kales. Illustrated by Earl Mayan. New York, Grosset & Dunlap [1967] 128 p. illus., ports. 28 cm. Forty profiles in picture and prose explain the formation and development of the styles of the world's master artists. [N42.K3] AC 67
1. Artists. I. Mayan, Earl, illus. II. Title.

LIBERMAN, Alexander, 1912- 709.04
The artist in his studio; text and photos. by Alexander Liberman, with a foreword by James Thrall Soby. New York, Viking [1968, c.1960] 142p. plates ports. 21cm. (Studio bk., S1) 60-13244 3.50 pap.,
1. Artists. 2. Art—Paris. 3. Art. Modern—20th cent. I. Title.

LIBERMAN, Alexander, 1912- 709.04
The artist in his studio; text and photos. by Alexander Liberman, with a foreword by James Thrall Soby. New York, Viking Press [1960] 72 p. plates (part col.) ports. (part col.) 34 cm. (A Studio book) [N6850.L5] 60-13244
1. Artists. 2. Art—Paris. 3. Art, Modern—20th century—Paris. I. Title.

RANK, Otto, 1884-1939. 701.15
Art and artist; creative urge and personality development. With a pref. by Ludwig Lewisohn. Translated from the German by Charles Francis Atkinson. New York, Agathon Press, 1968 [c1932] xlix, 431, xii p. illus. 22 cm. Bibliographical footnotes. [N71.R33 1968] 68-16358
1. Artists. 2. Artists—Psychology. I. Title.
BIP

SIMA, Michel. 709.04
Faces of modern art. Translated by Gloria Levy. New York, Tudor Pub. Co. [1960, c1959] 24, 157 p. (chiefly illus. (part col.) ports. (part col.) facsims.) 29 cm. Translation of 21 visages d'artistes. [N6490.S513] 60-51612
1. Artists. 2. Art, Modern — 20th century. I. Title.

VAN RENSSELAER, Mariana 709'.2'2
(Griswold) 1851-1934.
Six portraits: Della Robbia, Correggio, Blake, Corot, George Fuller, Winslow Homer, by Mrs. Schuyler Van Rensselaer. Freeport, N.Y., Books for Libraries Press [1973] p. (Essay index reprint series) Reprint of the 1889 ed. [N8351.V36 1973] 72-14101 ISBN 0-518-10029-4
1. Artists. 2. Art—Psychology.

Artists, American.

AMERICAN Contemporary Art 759.13
Gallery, New York.
31 American contemporary artists: David Burliok and others New York [1959] unpaged. illus. 27cm. [N6512.A59] 59-1381
1. Artists, American. I. Title.

BIRCHMAN, Willis. 760'.0922
Faces & facts by and about 26 contemporary artists. With an introd. by James Montgomery Flagg & biographies by Willis Birchman. Freeport, N.Y., Books for Libraries Press [1968] 1 v. (unpaged) illus., ports. 24 cm. (Essay index reprint series) Reprint of the 1937 ed. [N6536.B5 1968] 68-25600
1. Artists, American. 2. Caricatures and cartoons—United States. I. Title.

CORTISSOZ, Royal, 1869-1948. 709'.22
American artists. New York, AMS Press [1970] viii, 363 p. illus. 23 cm. Reprint of the 1923 ed. [N6536.C6 1970b] 70-121282
1. Artists, American. 2. Art, American. I. Title. BIP

CORTISSOZ, Royal, 1869-1948. 759.13 B
American artists. New York, Scribner, 1923. Freeport, N.Y., Books for Libraries Press [1970] viii, 363 p. illus. 23 cm. (Essay index reprint series) [N6536.C6 1970] 74-128228
1. Artists, American. 2. Art, American. I. Title.

DUNLAP. WILLIAM, 1766-1839 709.22
History of the rise and progress of the arts of design in the United States. Introd. by William P. Campbell. Newly ed. by Alexander Wyckoff, incorporating the notes and additions comp. by Frank W. Bayley. Charles Goodspeed. [New ed., rev., enl. New York] Blom [1966] 3v. 26cm. Running title: History of the arts of design. Bibl. [N6505.D9] 65-16236 57.50 set,
1. Artists, American. 2. Art, American—Hist. I. Wyckoff, Alexander, ed. II. Title. III. Title: History of the arts of design. IV. Title: The arts of design.

DUNLAP, William, 1766-1839. 709'.73
A history of the rise and progress of the arts of design in the United States. A reprint of the original 1834 ed. with a new introd. by James Thomas Flexner. Newly edited by Rita Weiss. New York, Dover Publications [1969] 2 v. in 3. illus. 24 cm. Title on spine: History of the arts of design in the United States. Includes bibliographical references. [N6505.D9 1969] 69-16810 4.50 per vol.
1. Artists, American. 2. Art, American—History. I. Weiss, Rita, ed. II. Title. III. Title: History of the arts of design in the United States. IV. Title: The arts of design. BIP

FREEDGOOD, Lillian. 927
Great artists of America. New York, Crowell [1963] xvii, 253 p. col. plates. 26 cm. "Recommended reading list": p. 237-238. Bibliography: p. 239-245. [N6505.F7] 63-15086
1. Artists, American. I. Title.

GUITAR, Mary Anne. 759.13
22 famous painters and illustrators tell how they work; invaluable advice from the guiding faculty of Famous Artists Schools, Westport, Connecticut. New York, D. McKay Co. [1964] ix, 240 p. illus., ports. 22 cm. Interviews. [N6512.G8] 63-19334
1. Artists, American. 2. Painting. 3. Drawing. 4. Creation (Literary, artistic, etc.) I. Famous Artists Schools, Westport, Conn. II. Title.

KELBY, William, 1841-1898, comp. 709.22
Notes on American artists, 1754-1820, copied from advertisements appearing in the newspapers of the day. To which is added a list of portraits and sculpture in the possession of the New-York Historical Society. New York, B. Franklin [1970] 80 p. ports. 23 cm. (American classics in history and social science, 159) (Burt Franklin research and source works series, 601) Originally published as the John Divine Jones Fund series, 5. Reprint of the 1922 ed. The collection was originally published in Quarterly bulletin of the New-York Historical Society, Oct. 1918-Jan. 1922. [N6507.K4 1970] 77-140984 ISBN 0-8337-1906-8
1. Artists, American. 2. Art, Modern—U.S. I. Title. BIP

LESTER, Charles Edwards, 1815-1890. 759.13 B
The artists of America; a series of biographical sketches of American artists. New York, Kennedy Galleries, 1970. vi, 257 p. ports. 24 cm. (Library of American art) Reprint of the 1846 ed. Contents.Contents.—Washington Allston.—Henry Inman.—Benjamin West.—Gilbert Charles Stuart.—John Trumbull.—James DeVeaux.—Rembrandt Peale.—Thomas Crawford. [N6536.L6 1970] 68-8689
1. Artists, American. I. Title. BIP

MULLER, Gregoire. 709'.04
The new avant-garde; issues for the art of the seventies. Text by Gregoire Muller. Photos. by Gianfranco Gorgoni. New York, Praeger [1972] 177 p. illus. 24 cm. [N6512.M75] 72-166514 9.95
1. Artists, American. 2. Art, Modern—20th century—United States. 3. Art—Philosophy. I. Gorgoni, Gianfranco, illus. II. Title.

THE New Mexico quarterly review. 709.789
New Mexico artists: John Sloan, Ernest L. Blumenschein, Gustave Baumann, Kenneth M. Adams, Adja Yunkers, Raymond Jonson, Peter Hurd, Howard Cook. Albuquerque, University of New Mexico Press, 1952. xii, 124 p. illus. 25 cm. (New Mexico artist series, no. 3) "Guest artist series from the New Mexico quarterly, spring 1949, through winter 1950-51." [N6530.N6N4] 52-8536
1. Artists, American. 2. Art — New Mexico. I. Title. II. Series.

PARIS, William Francklyn, 1871-1954. 709'.22
Personalities in American art. Freeport, N.Y., Books for Libraries Press [1970- v. ports. 23 cm. (Essay index reprint series) Vols. 2-10 have title: The Hall of American Artists. Reprint of the 1930-ed. [N6536.P32] 72-107731
1. New York University. Hall of American Artists. 2. Artists, American. I. Title. II. Title: The Hall of American Artists. BIP

PEARSON, Ralph M 1883- 709.73
The modern renaissance in American art, presenting the work and philosophy of 54 distinguished artists. New York, Harper [1954] xxv, 300p. illus. 26cm. 'Much of the material here presented in revised and amplified form was first privately printed by the Design Workshop as (the author's) Critical appreciation course II.' [N6536.P5] 53-11856
1. Artists, American. 2. Art, Modern—20th cent. I. Title. BIP

PEARSON, Ralph M., 1883- 709'.73
The modern renaissance in American art; presenting the work and philosophy of 54 distinguished artists [by] Ralph M. Pearson. Freeport, N.Y., Books for Libraries Press [1968, c1954] xxv, 300 p. illus. 26 cm. (Essay index reprint series) "Much of the material here presented in revised and amplified form was first privately printed by the Design Workshop as [the author's] Critical appreciation course II." [N6536.P5 1968] 68-20329
1. Artists, American. 2. Art, Modern—20th century—United States. I. Title.

PERKINS, Michael. 760'.0924
Renie Perkins; the life and work of a young artist who died by her own hand at the age of twenty-five. Text by Michael Perkins. [1st ed.] New York, Croton Press; distributed by Small Publisher's Co., 1969. 57 p. illus., ports. 21 cm. [N6537.P4P4] 70-91411 1.50
I. Perkins, Renie, 1942-1968.

RODMAN, Selden, 1909- 709.73
Conversations with artists. Introd. by Alexander Eliot. [New York] Devin-Adair Co., 1957. 234 p. illus. 22 cm. [N6536.R6] 57-5945
1. Artists, American. 2. Artists—Correspondence, reminiscences, etc. 3. Art, American. I. Title.

RODMAN, Selden, 1909- 709.73
Conversations with artists. Introd. by Alexander Eliot. New York [Putnam] 1961 [c.1957] 234p. illus. (Capricorn Bks., CAP giant 208) 1.45 pap.,
1. Artists, American. 2. Artists—Correspondence, reminiscences, etc. 3. Art, American. I. Title.

ROSENBERG, Bernard, 1923- . 702.3
The vanguard artist, portrait and self-portrait, by Bernard Rosenberg and Norris Fliegel. Chicago, Quadrangle Books, 1965. xi, 366 p. 25 cm. Bibliographical references included in "Notes" (p. 355-360) [N6512.R67] 65-18244
1. Artists, American. 2. Art — New York (City) 3. Art and society. 4. Artists — Psychology. I. Fliegel, Norris, joint author. II. Title.

SMITH, Ralph Clifton, 1898- 016.709'73
A biographical index of American artists. Charleston, S.C., Garnier [1967] x, 102 p. 24 cm. "Unabridged and unaltered reproduction of the work originally published ... in 1930." [N6536.S6 1967] 67-30446
1. Artists, American. I. Title. BIP

SMITH, Ralph Clifton, 1898- 705.8
A biographical index of American artists, by Ralph Clifton Smith, Charlston, S. C., Garnier Co. [1967, c.1930] x, 102p. 24cm. Unabridged, unaltered repunb. of the work orig. pub. by Williams & Wilkins in 1930. [N6536.S6] 7.50
1. Artists, American. I. Title.
Publisher's address: 192 King St., Charleston, S.C.

TAFT, Robert, 1894-1955. 709.78
Artists and illustrators of the Old West, 1850-1900. New York, Scribner, 1953. xvii, 400 p. plates, maps (on lining papers) 26 cm. "Sources and notes": p. 249-381. [N6510.T27] 53-7577
1. Artists, American. 2. Illustrators, American. 3. Paintings, American. 4. Drawing, American. 5. The West—History. 6. History in art. I. Title.

TUCKERMAN, Henry Theodore, 1813-1871. 709.22
Book of the artists: American artist life comprising biographical and critical sketches of American artists, preceded by an historical account of the rise & progress of art in America. [2d ed.] New York, J. F. Carr, 1966. 639p. 24cm. First pub. 1867. [N6536.T9] 65-28493 17.50
1. Artists, American. 2. Art, American—Hist. I. Title.

WHO'S who in American art 1966 709.22
New York Bowker [c.]1966. 600p. 27cm. Biennial. 1936-37--1940-41: irregular 1940-47--1966. Vs. for 1936-37--1940-47 called v. 1-4. Vols. Vols. 1-4 pub. by the Amer. Federation of Arts. Formerly pub. in the American art annual (later American art directory); v.4 issued as pt.2 of v.36 of the annual (NA50.A54) Ed., 1966, Dorothy B. Gilbert [N6536.W5] 36-27014 22.50
1. Artists, American. I. American Federation of Arts.

Artists, American—Biography.

THE Art and poetry of Pearl and Geneva Highfill / Samuel J. Underwood, editor ; Marjorie Pearl Highfill, Geneva Highfill. Charlotte, N.C. : Delmar, c1974. 159 p. : ill. (some col.) ; 23 cm. [PS3558.I364A7] 74-16761 759.13
I. Underwood, Samuel J. II. Highfill, Marjorie Pearl. III. Highfill, Geneva.

MICHIGAN. State Library, Lansing. 709'.2'2
Biographical sketches of American artists. Compiled by Helen L. Earle. 5th ed., rev. and enl. Charleston, S.C., Garnier [1972] 370 p. 24 cm. Reprint of the 1924 ed. Bibliography: p. [349]-356. [N6536.M6 1972] 73-155552
1. Artists, American—Biography. I. Earle, Helen L., d. 1925, comp. II. Title.

RHYS, Hedley Howell 759.13
Maurice Prendergast, 1859-1924. Boston [dist.] Cambridge, Mass., Harvard Univ. Press, 1960. 156p. illus. (part col.) 60-16756 7.50
I. Prendergast Maurice Brazil, 1859-1924. II. Title.

RHYS, Hedley Howell 759.13
Maurice Prendergast, 1859-1924. Boston [dist.] Cambridge, Mass., Harvard Univ. Press, 1960. 156p. illus. (part col.) 60-16756 7.50
I. Prendergast Maurice Brazil, 1859-1924. II. Title.

STERNE, Maurice, 1878-1957. 759.13
Shadow and light: the life, friends and opinions of Maurice Sterne. Edited by Charlotte Leon Mayerson. Introd. by George Biddle. [1st ed.] New York, Harcourt, Brace & World [1965] xxxii, 266 p. illus., col. plates, ports. 25 cm. [ND237.S69M3] 64-22099
I. Mayerson, Charlotte Leon, 3d. II. Title.

Artists, American—Brandywine Valley.

PITZ, Henry Clarence, 1895- 760'.09748'13
The Brandywine tradition [by] Henry C. Pitz. Illustrated with 16 color and 32 black and white plates. Boston, Houghton Mifflin, 1969 [c1968] xv, 252 p. illus. (part col.), map, ports. 27 cm. Bibliography: p. [243]-246. [N6517.P5] 68-28457 12.95
1. Pyle, Howard, 1853-1911—Influence. 2. Artists, American—Brandywine Valley. I. Title.

Artists, American—Correspondence, reminiscences, etc.

ARTZYBASHEFF, Boris, 1899- 741.5
As I see. Notes to folios by the artist. New York, Dodd, Mead, 1954. [100] p. (chiefly illus. (2 col.) 30cm. [NC1075.A77A42] 54-14456
I. Title.

BEMELMANS, Ludwig, 1898- 750.69
My life in art. New York, Harper [1958] 63p. illus., col. plates. 33cm. [ND237.B456A2] 58-8821
I. Title.

BIBERMAN, Edward, 1904- 759.13
Time and circumstance; forty years of painting. Los Angeles, Ward Ritchie Press [1968] 118 p. (chiefly illus.) 29 cm. [ND237.B55A57] 68-22788
I. Title.

CHAMBERLAIN, Samuel, 1895- 760'.0924
Etched in sunlight; fifty years in the graphic arts. [Boston] Boston Public Library, 1968. x, 227 p. illus., facsims., ports. 32 cm. Autobiographical. [N6537.C45A2] 68-29421 20.00
1. Artists, American—Correspondence, reminiscences, etc. I. Title. BIP

THE color of life. 759.13
Boston, Houghton Mifflin, 1957. 203p. 21cm. Autobiographical. [ND237.W87A25] 927.5 57-12076
I. Wright, Catharine (Morris) 1899-

FEELINGS, Tom. 741'.092'4 B
Black pilgrimage. New York, Lothrop, Lee & Shepard Co. [1972] 72 p. illus. 29 cm. A black artist describes his life, from his birthplace in Brooklyn to his adopted home, Ghana, and how various experiences helped him develop new aspects of his talent. [NC139.F36A2] 92 70-177328 5.95
I. Title. BIP

FORTRESS, Karl E. 709'.22
The preparation of a library of taped interviews with American artists, on problems of professional concern, as resource material for faculty and students of art on the level of higher education [by] Karl E. Fortress. [Washington] U.S. Dept. of Health, Education, and Welfare, Office of Education, Bureau of Research, 1968 [cover 1967] iii, 18 l. 28 cm. Final report, contract no. OEC-1-6-058441-0599, Bureau of Research, U.S. Office of Education. [N6536.F6] 68-66572
1. Artists, American—Correspondence, reminiscences, etc. 2. Art as a profession. 3. Phonotapes. I. Title.

FUERTES, Louis Agassiz, 1874-1927. 759.13
Louis Agassiz Fuertes: his life briefly told and his correspondence edited by Mary Fuerles Boynton. New York, Oxford University Press, 1956. 317p. illus. 24cm.

[ND237.F78A3] [ND237.F78A3] 927.5
56-5705 56-5705
I. Boynton, Mary (Fuertes) 1906- ed. II. Title.

GRUEN, John. 700'.92'2 B
The party's over now; reminiscences of the fifties—New York's artists, writers, musicians, and their friends. New York, Viking Press [1972] 282 p. illus. 22 cm. [NX511.N4G7 1972] 78-170676 ISBN 0-670-54129-X 8.95
I. Artists, American—Correspondence, reminiscences, etc. 2. Artists, American—New York (City) I. Title.

JAMES, Marquis, 1891-1955. 709.24
The Cherokee strip; a tale of an Oklahoma boyhood. New York, Viking Press [1965] xvi, 298 p. map. 20 cm. (Compass books, c178) [E175.5.J3A3 1965] 65-5531
I. Title.

MACNICOL, Roy, 1889- 759.13
Paintbrush ambassador. [1st ed.] New York, Vantage Press [c1957] 255p. illus. 21cm. Autobiography. [ND237.M217A3] 927.5 56-1272
I. Title.

PAVAL, Philip, 1899- 759.13 B
Paval; autobiography of a Hollywood artist. Hollywood, Calif., Gunther Press, 1968. 247 p. illus., ports. 23 cm. [N6537.P3A2] 68-57212 4.95
I. Artists, American—Correspondence, reminiscences, etc.

SIMON, Howard, 1903- 709'.24
Cabin on a ridge. Chicago, Follett [1970] 159 p. illus. 24 cm. Autobiographical. [NC139.S54A2 1970] 69-10267 4.95
I. Artists, American—Correspondence, reminiscences, etc. I. Title.

WRIGHT, Catharine [759.13] 927.5
(Morris) 1899-
The color of life. Boston, Houghton Mifflin, 1957. 203 p ; 21 cm. Autobiographical. [ND237.W87A25] 57-12076
I. Title.

YOUNG-HUNTER, John, 1874- 927.5
1955.
Reviewing the years. New York, Crown Publishers, [1963] 173 p. illus. 24 cm. Autobiographical. [ND497.Y6A2] 63-14861
I. Title.

Artists, American—Dictionaries.

CUMMINGS, Paul 709.22
A dictionary of contemporary American artists. New York, St. Martin's [c.1966] xx, 331p. illus. 25cm. Bibl. [N6536.C8] 65-20815 17.50
I. Artists, American—Dictionaries. I. Title. **BIP**

CUMMINGS, Paul. 709'.22
A dictionary of contemporary American artists. 2d ed. New York, St. Martin's Press [1971] xv, 368 p. illus. 24 cm. Bibliography: p. [343]-368. [N6536.C8 1971] 76-31377 25.00
I. Artists, American—Dictionaries. I. Title.

FIELDING, Mantle, 1865- 709'.22
1941.
Dictionary of American painters, engravers, and sculptors. Stratford, Conn., J. Edwards, 1971. vi, 423 p. 24 cm. 1926, 1945, and 1965 editions have title: Dictionary of American painters, sculptors, and engravers. [N6536.F5 1971] 75-31236 15.00
I. Artists, American—Dictionaries. I. Title. **BIP**

FIELDING, Mantle, 1865- 709.22
1941.
Dictionary of American painters, sculptors, and engravers. With an addendum containing corrections and additional material on the original entries, compiled by James F. Carr. New York, J. F. Carr, 1965. vi, 529 p. 27 cm. 1971 ed. has title: Dictionary of American painters, engravers, and sculptors. Bibliography: p. 528-529. [N6536.F5 1965] 65-27268
I. Artists, American—Dictionaries. I. Carr, James F. II. Title. **BIP**

NEW YORK Historical 927.5
Society.
Dictionary of artists in America, 1564-1860, by George C. Groce and David H. Wallace Dictionary of artists in America fifteen sixty-four eighteen sixty New Haven, Yale University Press, 1957. xxvii, 759p. 25cm. Bibliography: p. 713-759. [N6536.N4] 57-6338
I. Artists, American—Dictionaries. I. Groce, George Outhbert, 1899- II. Wallace, David H. III. Title.

YOUNG, William, 1929- 709'.73
A dictionary of American artists, sculptors and engravers: from the beginnings through the turn of the twentieth century. Edited and compiled by William Young. Research editor: Philip Baker, Jr.; associate editors: Janet M. Conn and Dorothy M. Young. Cambridge, Mass., W. Young [1968] 515 p. 24 cm. [N6536.Y7] 68-3733
I. Artists, American—Dictionaries. I. Title.

Artists, American—Direct.

CHAIET, Harold. 702'.5'73
1968 register of United States living artists, written; comp. by Harold & Margaret Szego Chaiet. [Canoga Park, Calif., Szego & Chaiet, 1968] 296p. 22cm. [N6536.C45] 67-29179 price unreported
I. Artists, American—Direct. I. Chaiet, Margaret Szego. joint author. II. Title. III. Title: Register of United States living artists.

Artists, American—Hudson Valley.

SEARS, Clara Endicott 759.1'47'3
1863-
Highlights among the Hudson River artists. Port Washington, N.Y., Kennikat Press [1968, c1947] xvii, 216 p. illus. 26 cm. Bibliography: p. 215-216. [ND236.S4 1968] 67-27644
I. Artists, American—Hudson Valley. I. Title. II. Title: Hudson River artists. **BIP**

Artists, American—Indexes.

THE Index of twentieth 709.73
century artists v. 1-4, no. 7; Oct. 1933-Apr. 1937. New York, Arno Press [1970] 4 v. in 1. 29 cm. Reprint of a serial published monthly (except Dec.) in New York by the College Art Association (1933-Feb. 1934 by the association's Research Institute) and edited by F. M. Pollack, 1933-Jan. 1937, and G. A. Cornell, Feb.-Apr. 1937. Includes index. [N6536.I52] 70-114606
I. Artists, American—Indexes. 2. Art, American—Indexes. 3. Art, Modern—20th century—U. S.—Indexes. I. College, Art Association of America. II. Pollack, Frances M., ed. III. Cornell, Greta A., ed.

Artists, American—Juvenile literature.

IRWIN, Grace, 1894- 709.22 B
Trail-blazers of American art. Port Washington, N.Y., Kennikat Press [1971, c1930] 228 p. illus., ports. 22 cm. (Essay and general literature index reprint series) Contents.Contents.—Gilbert Stuart.—George Inness.—Winslow Homer.—John Quincy Adams Ward.—James McNeill Whistler.—Edwin Austin Abbey.—Augustus Saint Gaudens.—Joseph Pennell.—Joseph Singer Sargent.—Thomas Nast.—Howard Pyle, and some others. Bibliography: p. 227-228. [N6505.I7 1971] 920 73-122875 ISBN 8-04-613362-
I. Artists, American—Juvenile literature. I. Title.

SMARIDGE, Norah. 700'.922 B
Trailblazers in American arts. Illustrated by Paul Frame. New York, J. Messner [1971] 96 p. illus. 22 cm. Contents.Contents.—Henry Wadsworth Longfellow—Stephen Foster.—Mark Twain.—Winslow Homer.—Marian Anderson. [NX503.A1S6 1971] 920 72-146487 ISBN 0-671-32397-0 4.50
I. Artists, American—Juvenile literature. I. Frame, Paul, illus. II. Title.

Artists, American—Los Angeles.

COPLANS, John. 709'.22
Los Angeles 6; an exhibition organized for the Vancouver Art Gallery by John Coplans, March 31-May 5, 1968 [Vancouver, 1968] 42 p. illus. (part col.), ports. 24 cm. Includes bibliographies. [N6535.L6C6] 68-59571 unpriced
I. Artists, American—Los Angeles. 2. Art, American—Exhibitions. I. Vancouver, B.C. Art Gallery. II. Title.

Artists, American—Montana.

CROWELL, Dave. 759.186
Montana's own. Pen and ink sketches by Ron and Bill Bailey. [Missoula, Mont., 1970] vii, 64 p. illus. (part col.), ports. 28 cm. [N6530.M75C7] 74-23426
I. Artists, American—Montana. 2. Art—Montana. I. Title.

Artists, American—New York (City)

MCDARRAH, Fred W 1926- 709.7471
The artist's world in pictures Introd. by Thomas B. Hess; commentary by Gloria Schoffel McDarrah. [1st ed.] New York, Dutton, 1961. 191p. illus. 21cm. (A Dutton paperback original, D84) [N6535.N5M3] 62-377
I. Artists, American—New York (City) 2. Art—New York (City) I. McDarrah, Gloria Schoffel. II. Title.

Artists, American—North Dakota.

BARR, Paul Everett, 1892- 709.784
1953.
North Dakota artists. [Grand Forks, N. D.] The Library, 1954. . Title. ii, 64 p. illus., ports. 23 cm. (University of North Dakota Library studies, no.1) [N6530.N9B3] 54-63075
I. Artists, American—North Dakota. I. Title. II. Series: North Dakota. University. Library. Studies, no.1

Artists, American—Northwestern States.

ARCHITECTURAL craftsmen 705.8795
of the Northwest, illustrated directory, 1961. [Seattle] [1960- 1 v. (loose-leaf) illus. 28 cm. Cover title. "Developed with the help of the American Craftsmen's Council." [N6528.A7] 61-37678
I. Artists, American—Northwestern States.

Artists, American—San Francisco Bay region.

CALIFORNIA. University. 730/.0922
Art Museum
Funk, by Peter Selz. [Berkeley, Calif., 1967] 59p. illus. (pt. col.), facsim., ports. 22x25cm. Exhibition held April 18 to May 29, 1967 at the Univ. Art Museum, Univ. of Calif., Berkeley. [N6530.C2C2] 67-64028 3.95 pap.,
I. Artists, American—San Francisco Bay region. 2. Pop art—Exhibitions. I. Selz, Peter. II. Title.

Artists, American—Utah.

KAYSVILLE Art Club. 709.22 B
Pioneers of Utah art. Editors: Elsie S. Heaton, Alice B. Rampton [and] Clover B. Sanders. [Logan, Utah, Educational Printing Service, c1968] xiii, 137 p. ports. 29 cm. [N6530.U8K3] 77-20552
I. Artists, American—Utah. I. Heaton, Elsie S., ed. II. Rampton, Alice B., ed. III. Sanders, Clover B., ed. IV. Title.

Artists, American—Washington, D.C.

ARTISTS Equity 709.7'53
Association. D.C.Chapter.
Washington artists today; a directory. [Designed by Kurt Wiener] Washington, Distributed by AcropolisBooks [1967] 79 p. illus. 29 cm. [N6535.W3A7] 68-7643
I. Artists, American—Washington, D.C. 2. Artists—Direct. I. Title.

ARTISTS Equity 709.7'53
Association. D.C. Chapter.
Washington artists today; a directory. [Designed by Kurt Wiener] Washington, Distributed by Acropolis Books [1967] 79 p. illus. 29 cm. [N6535.W3A7] 67-29368
I. Artists, American—Washington, D.C. 2. Artists—Directories. I. Title.

Artists, American—Washington, D.C.—Directories.

ARTISTS Equity 709'.2'2
Association. D.C. Chapter.
Washington artists; a directory. [Washington, 1972] 123 p. 22 cm. [N6535.W3A68] 72-189977
I. Artists, American—Washington, D.C.—Directories. I. Title.

Artists and community—Great Britain.

BRADEN, Su. 709'.41
Artists and people / Su Braden. London ; Boston : Routledge and K. Paul, 1978. xviii, 199 p., [8] leaves of plates : ill. ; 22 cm. (Gulbenkian studies) Includes bibliographical references and index. [NX180.A77B7] 78-40108 ISBN 0-7100-8920-1 : 7.50
I. Artists and community—Great Britain. 2. Art and society—Great Britain. I. Title. II. Series: Fundacao Calouste Gulbenkian. Gulbenkian studies.

Artists—Anecdotes, facetiae, satire, etc.

HOOVER, F. Herbert. 709'.22
Brushstrokes; laugh lines by and about famous artists [by] F. Herbert Hoover. Drawings by Michael von Meyer. San Francisco, Hess Reproductions [1971] 71 p. illus. 21 cm. [N7460.H64] 75-179480
I. Artists—Anecdotes, facetiae, satire, etc. I. Title.

Artists as teachers.

RISENHOOVER, Morris, 700'.92'2
1940-
Artists as professors : conversations with musicians, painters, sculptors / Morris Risenhoover and Robert T. Blackburn. Urbana : University of Illinois Press, c1976. x, 217 p. ; 21 cm. Bibliography: p. 214-217. [NX304.R57] 75-38681 ISBN 0-252-00574-0 : 9.95
I. Artists as teachers. 2. Artists—United States—Interviews. 3. Art—Study and teaching (Higher)—United States. 4. College teachers as artists. I. Blackburn, Robert T., joint author. II. Title. **BIP**

Artists as teachers—United States.

AQUINO, John. 700'.7'1073
Artists as teachers / by John T. Aquino. Bloomington, Ind. : Phi Delta Kappa Educational Foundation, c1978. 34 p. : ill. ; 18 cm. (Fastback ; 113) Bibliography: p. 32-34. [NX396.5.A67] 78-61316 ISBN 0-87367-113-9 pbk. : 0.75
I. Artists as teachers—United States. 2. Arts—Study and teaching—United States. I. Title. II. Series: Phi Delta Kappa. Educational Foundation. Fastback ; 113. **BIP**

Artists—Australia—Biography.

DUTTON, Ninette. 738.4'092'4 B
Portrait of a year / Ninette Dutton. Melbourne : Nelson, 1976. viii, 176 p. ; 24 cm. [N7405.D87A56] 77-373787 ISBN 0-17-005089-0
I. Dutton, Ninette. 2. Artists—Australia—Biography. I. Title.

THIELE, Colin. 760'.092'4
Heysen's early Hahndorf / [Text by] Colin Thiele ; illustrated with early works by Sir Hans Heysen, including drawings from his sketchbooks selected by David Heysen. Adelaide : Rigby, 1976. 63 p : ill. (some col.) ; 24 cm. [N7405.H4T45] 76-379632 ISBN 0-7270-0066-7
I. Heysen, Hans, Sir, 1877-1968. 2. Artists—Australia—Biography. 3. Hahndorf, Australia, in art. I. Title.

Artists—Bermuda—Biography.

SMITH, Lois, 1941- 709'.2'4 B
The life and works of Charles Lloyd Tucker / by Lois Smith. [Hamilton?], Bermuda : Smith, [1976?]. 44 p., [2] leaves of plates : ill. (some col.) ; 23 cm. [N6615.B4T827] 77-358582
1. Tucker, Charles Lloyd, 1913-1971. 2. Artists—Bermuda—Biography. I. Title.

Artists—Biography.

**WHO'S who in art;* 709.22
biographies of leading men and women in the world of art today; artists, designers, craftmen, critics, writers, teachers, collectors and curators, with an appendix of signatures. 13th ed. Havant [Eng.] Art trade Pr. [New York, Intl. Pubns. Serv. 1966, c.1962] xix, 699p. facsims. 20cm. Subtitle varies [N40.W6] 27-14051 15.00
1. Artists—Biog.

Artists—Biography.

KALTENBACH, Gustav Emile. 709'.2'2
Dictionary of pronunciation of artists' names, with their schools and dates for American readers and students / by G. E. Kaltenbach. 2d ed. Detroit : Gale Research Co., 1976 [i.e.1975] c1938. p. cm. Reprint of the ed. published by the Art Institute of Chicago. [N40.K3 1976] 73-167017 ISBN 0-8103-4190-5 : 9.00
1. Artists—Biography. 2. Names—Pronunciation. 3. Names—Dictionaries. I. Title: Dictionary of pronunciation of artist's names ...

MALLETT, Daniel Trowbridge, 1862-1944. 709'.2'2 B
Mallett's index of artists, international-biographical : including painters, sculptors, illustrators, engravers, and etchers of the past and present / by Daniel Trowbridge Mallett. Detroit : Gale Research Co., [1975] c1935. p. cm. Reprint of the 1948 ed. published by P. Smith, New York. Bibliography: p. [N40.M3 1975] 79-185365 ISBN 0-8103-4246-4
1. Artists—Biography. I. Title. II. Title: Index of artists, international—biographical.

*NORDLAND, Gerald. 730.92
Gaston Lanchaise; the man and his work. New York, George Braziller, [1974] viii, 184 p. illus. 26 cm. Bibliography: p. 183-184 [NA549] 74-80661 ISBN 0-8076-0761-4 15.00
1. Lanchaise, Gaston, 1882- 2. Artists—Biography. 3. Sculptors—Biography. I. Title.

WILLARD, Charlotte. 759.06
Famous modern artists; from Cezanne to pop art. New York, Platt & Munk [1971] 119 p. illus. (part col.), ports. 29 cm. "A Chanticleer Press edition." [N40.W64] 72-151241 6.95
1. Artists—Biography. 2. Art, Modern—19th century. 3. Art, Modern—20th century. I. Title.

Artists—Biography and works.

*EVANS, Hilary. 709.2
John Kay of Edinburgh; barber, miniaturist and soccial commentator 1742-1826, [by] Hilary and Mary Evans. Aberdeen, Impulse, 1973. 53 p. illus. 26 cm. [N44]
1. Kay, John, 1742-1826. 2. Artists—Biography and works. I. Evans, Mary, joint author. II. Title.
Distributed by International Publications Service, N.Y., for 22.50.

LISITSKII, Lazar' Markovich, 1890-1941. 709'.47
El Lissitzky; life, letters, texts [edited by] Sophie Lissitzky-Kuppers. Introd. by Herbert Read. Translated from the German by Helene Aldwinckle and Mary Whittall Greenwich, Conn., New York Graphic Society [1968] 407 p. illus. (part col.), ports. 28 cm. Includes bibliographical references. [N6999.L5K813] 68-12366 30.00
I. Kuppers-Lissitzky, Sophie, 1891- ed.

Artists—Biography—Directories.

HARDMAN, Sammy J. 703
Hardman's Dictionary of artists & estimates. [Atlanta, Ga. : Hardman, 1974] xviii, 258 p. ; 14 cm. Cover title. [N40.H37 1974] 74-189408
1. Artists—Biography—Directories. 2. Art—Prices. I. Title.

HARDMAN, Sammy J. 709'.2'2
Supplement to Hardman's Dictionary : with revised price list / compiled by Sammy J. Hardman. Decatur, Ga. : Hardman, c1976- v. ; 14 cm. [N40.H37 1974 suppl.] 76-151051
1. Artists—Biography—Directories. 2. Art—Prices. I. Hardman, Sammy J. Dictionary of artists & estimates. II. Title.

Artists—Biography—Indexes.

HAVLICE, Patricia Pate. 709'.2'2
Index to artistic biography. Metuchen, N.J., Scarecrow Press, 1973. 2 v. (viii, 1362 p.) 22 cm. Bibliography: p. v-viii. [N40.H38] 72-6412 ISBN 0-8108-0540-5
1. Artists—Biography—Indexes. I. Title. BIP

Artists books.

GREGORY, Albert. 709.04
Overlap. Cambridge, Mass.; distributed by G. Wittenborn, New York, 1967. 89 p. (chiefly illus.) 18 cm. Includes 6 plastic "movable pages", in pocket, to be used with p. 79-89. [N6537.G7A55] 67-8267
I. Title.

HATCH, Denison. 704.98
Status of limitations; intimate views of life among the marbles. New York, Coward-McCann [1961] unpaged (chiefly illus.) 23cm. [NC1429.H3335A58] 61-16723
I. Title.

HIGGINS, Richard Carter. 709.04
Postface, by Dick Higgins. New York, Something Else Press [1964] 90 p. illus. 21 cm. Bound with the author's Jefferson's birthday. New York [1964] Bibliographical references included in "Footnotes" (p. 89) [PS3558.I36J4] 65-706
I. Title.

LAVIGNE, Harold. 769'.924
Persons. San Francisco, 1966. 1 portfolio ([1] l., 19 plates) 29 cm. (A Running elk publication) "[Number] 41 of 100 copies," (in MS. on t.p.) signed by the artist. [NE1215.L37A56] 72-228734
I. Title.

LEE, Ian. 709'.2'4
*The third wor*d war* / Ian Lee. New York : A & W Visual Library, 1978. 127 p. : chiefly ill. ; 28 cm. "*Apostrophe theory." [N7433.4.L43A4 1978] 78-55111 ISBN 0-89104-115-X pbk. : 4.95
1. Lee, Ian. 2. Artists' books—England. I. Title.

Artists, British.

GRAVES, Algernon. 709'.42'07402132
The Royal Academy of Arts; a complete dictionary of contributors and their work from its foundation in 1769 to 1904. New York, B. Franklin [1972- v. ports. 23 cm. (Burt Franklin bibliography & reference series, 320. Art history & art reference, 27) Reprint of the 1905-06 ed. [N5054.G72] 76-118750 ISBN 0-8337-1425-2 189.50 (8 vols.)
1. London. Royal Academy of Arts. 2. Artists, British. BIP

ROTHENSTEIN, John Knewstub Maurice, Sir, 1901- 759.2 B
A pot of paint; the artists of the 1890's, by John K. M. Rothenstein. Freeport, N.Y., Books for Libraries Press [1970] 215 p. 7 illus. 23 cm. (Essay index reprint series) Reprint of the 1929 New York ed. First ed., 1928, has title: The artists of the 1890's. Contents.Contents.—The artist and the industrial world.—Qui nous delivrera des Grecs et des Romains?—Whistler.—Greaves.—Steer.—Sickert.—Conder.—Beardsley.—Ricketts and Shannon.—Rothenstein.—Max. Includes bibliographical references. [N6767.R55 1970] 70-128303 ISBN 8-369-18479-
1. Artists, British. I. Title.

WHITLEY, William Thomas, 1858-1942. 709'.22
Artists and their friends in England, 1700-1799. New York, B. Blom [1968] 2v. illus. 23 cm. Reprint of the 1928 ed. [N6766.W5 1968] 68-56471
1. Artists, British. I. Title. BIP

Artists, British—Correspondence, reminiscences, etc.

HENDERSON, Keith, 1883- 759.2
Till 21. London, New York, Regency Press, 1970. 187 p. illus., ports. 23 cm. [N6797.H4A2] 79-569151 ISBN 0-7212-0092-3 £1.80
1. Artists, British—Correspondence, reminiscences, etc. I. Title.

Artists, British—Indexes.

GRAVES, Algernon. 708.21
Dictionary of artists who have exhibited works in the principal London exhibitions from 1760 to 1893. 3d ed., with additions and corrections. New York, B. Franklin [1970] xiv, 314 p. 27 cm. (Burt Franklin bibliography and reference series, 372. Art history and art reference, 26) Reprint of the 1901 ed. [N5053.G75 1970] 72-132538 ISBN 0-8337-1415-5
1. Artists, British—Indexes. 2. Art—Exhibitions. 3. Art—London. I. Title. BIP

Artists, British—Newcastle-upon-Tyne.

WILKES, Lyall. 700'.92'2
Tyneside portraits: studies in art and life. Newcastle upon Tyne, Graham, 1971. xi, 164 p. illus., facsim., ports. 23 cm. [NX544.N4W5] 72-192304 ISBN 0-902833-93-6 £2.50
1. Artists, British—Newcastle-upon-Tyne. I. Title.

Artists—Canada—Biography.

THEBERGE, Pierre. 759.11 B
Guido Molinari : [exposition : catalogue] / par Pierre Theberge. Ottawa : Galerie nationale du Canada, 1976. vii, 160 p. : ill. (some col.) ; 26 cm. English and French. Bibliography: p. 153-159. [N6549.M6T48] 77-457773 ISBN 0-88884-307-0
1. Molinari, Guido, 1933- 2. Artists—Canada—Biography. I. Molinari, Guido, 1933- II. National Gallery of Canada.

Artists—Canada—Dictionaries.

CREATIVE Canada; 790'.971
a biographical dictionary of twentieth-century creative and performing artists. Compiled by Reference Division, McPherson Library, University of Victoria. [Toronto] Published in association with McPherson Library, University of Victoria, by University of Toronto Press [1971- v. 26 cm. [NX513.A1C7] 71-151387 ISBN 0-8020-3262-1 (v. 1) 15.00 (v. 1)
1. Artists—Canada—Dictionaries. I. British Columbia. University of Victoria. McPherson Library. Reference Division. BIP

Artists—Correspondence, reminiscences, etc.

ARDIZZONE, Edward, 1900- 741'.0924 B
The young Ardizzone; an autobiographical fragment. [1st American ed. New York] Macmillan [1970] 144 p. illus. (part col.) 26 cm. Reminiscences of the English author/artist's childhood. [NC978.5.A7A3 1970b] 92 71-125295 7.95
I. Title. BIP

BENTON, Thomas Hart, 1889- 759.13 B
An American in art; a professional and technical autobiography. Lawrence, University Press of Kansas [1969] 197 p. illus. 26 cm. Contents.Contents.—An American in art.—Selected paintings by Thomas Hart Benton (p. [79]-144)—American regionalism; a personal history of the movement. [ND237.B47A28] 69-16060 10.00
1. Artists—Correspondence, reminiscences, etc. I. Title.

BENTON, Thomas Hart, 1889- 759.13 B
An artist in America. 3d [rev. ed.] Columbia, University of Missouri Press [1968] xxii, 369 p. illus. 24 cm. [ND237.B47A3 1968] 68-20096
1. Artists—Correspondence, reminiscences, etc. 2. United States—Description and travel—1920-1940. I. Title.

BENTON, Thomas Hart, 1889- 927.5
An artist in America. New and rev. ed. with 79 illus. New York, University of Kansas City Press-Twayne Publishers ['1951] 324 p. illus. 25 cm. [ND237.B47A3 1951] 52-6288
1. Artists—Correspondence, reminiscences, etc. 2. U. S.—Descr. & trav.—1920-1940. I. Title.

CARRINGTON, Dora de Houghton, 1893-1932. 759.2
Carrington: letters and extracts from her diaries. Chosen and with an introd. by David Garnett. With a bibliographical note by Noel Carrington. New York, Ballantine Books [1974, c1970] xvii, 650 p. illus., geneal. tables, ports. 18 cm. Bibliography: p. 640. [ND497.C375G3 1974] ISBN 0-345-24262-9 2.25 (pbk.)
I. Title.
L.C. card no. for original ed.: 79-137332.

CELLINI, Benvenuto, 1500-1571. 927.3
Autobiography; translated by John Addington Symonds, with an introd. by David B. Guralnik. Cleveland, Fine Editions Press [1952] 435 p. 21 cm. [NB623.C3S45 1952] 52-4477
I. Title.

CHASE, Joseph Cummings, 1878- 927.5
My friends look better than ever. [1st ed.] New York, Longmans, Green [1950] xv, 300 p. ports. 22 cm. [ND237.C47A49] 50-10901
1. Artists—Correspondence, reminiscences, etc. I. Title.

DAVIDSON, Jo, 1883- 927.3
Between sittings, an informal autobiography. New York, Dial Press, 1951. 369 p. illus. 24 cm. [NB237.D3A2] 51-14393
1. Artists—Correspondence, reminiscences, etc. I. Title.

DEANS, Alister Austen. 709'.9'31
Pictures, by Austen Deans. Wellington, Auckland, Reed [1967] 64p. illus., 20 col. plates (incl. 2 ports.) 33cm. [ND2092.D4A2] 68-96342 12.50
1. Artists—Correspondence, reminiscences, etc. I. Title.
Distributed by Tri-Ocean, San Francisco.

EPSTEIN, Jacob, 1880- 927.3
Epstein, an autobiography. [Rev. and extended ed.] New York, Dutton [1955] x, 294 p. plates, ports. 24 cm. First published in 1940 under title: Let there be sculpture. [NB497] 55-4439
1. Artists—Correspondence, reminiscences, etc. 2. Sculpture. I. Title.

EVANS, Joan, 1893- 925.72
Prelude & fugue, an autobiography. London, Museum Pr. [New Rochelle, N. Y., SportShelf, 1965, c.]1964. 167p. illus., ports. 23cm. Bibl. [N8375.E9A2] 65-2191 5.75
I. Title.

FRIEDENTHAL, Richard, 1896- ed. 927
Letters of the great artists. New York, Random House [1963] 2 v. illus. (part col.) ports. (part col.) facsims. 24 cm. Contents.-- 1. From Ghiberti to Gainsborough. -- 2. From Blake to Pollock. [N40.F8 1963a] 63-14981
1. Artists — Correspondence, reminiscences, etc. I. Title.

GREENOUGH, Horatio, 1805-1852. 927.3
The travels, observations, and experience of a Yankee stonecutter (1852) A facsimile reproduction with an introd. by Nathalia Wright. Gainesville, Fla., Scholars'

Facsimiles & Reprints, 1958. xvi p., facsim.: 222p. illus. 23cm. 'Reproduced from a copy in the Library of Congress.' [NB237.G8A3 1958] 58-5421
1. Artists— Correspondence, reminiscences, etc. I. Title.

HARVEY, Eli, 1860- 730.924
The autobiography of Eli Harvey, Quaker sculptor from Ohio. Edited by Dorothy Z. Bicker, Jane Z. Vail [and] Vernon G. Wills. Wilmington, Ohio, Clinton County Historical Society [1966] 100 p. illus., ports. 24 cm. [NB237.H34A2] 66-26139
1. Artists—Correspondence, reminiscences, etc. I. Title.

HOYLAND, Francis. 759.2
Alive to paint. London, New York,[etc.] Oxford U.P., 1967. 108 p. front., illus. 20 1/2 cm. (Oxford paperbacks, handbooks for artists.2) [ND497.H855A2] 68-71039
1. Artists—Correspondence, reminiscences, etc. I. Title.

HOYLAND, Francis. 759.2
A painter's diary; with a foreword by Edward Blishen. Reading (Berks.), Educational Explorers, 1967. 110 p. illus., 4 plates (incl. 2 col.). 21 1/2 cm. (My life and my work series) 21/- [ND497.H855A15] 67-91666
I. Title.

JACKSON, Thomas Graham, 927.2
Sir bart., 1835-1924.
Recollections. Arranged and edited by Basil H. Jackson. London, New York, Oxford University Press, 1950. xiv, 283 p. illus., ports. 22 cm. [NA997.J3A3] 50-10153
1. Artists—Correspondence, reminiscences, etc. I. Title.

JACOBS, Michel, 1877- 759.13
Epigramus of an ignoramus; the life of Michel Jacobs by himself. [1st ed. Rumson, N. J., Primatic Art Co., c1953] 241p. illus. 22cm. [ND237.J2A3] 927.5 53-10883
1. Artists—Correspondence, reminiscences, etc. I. Title.

KENT, Adaline, 1900-1957. 730.973
Autobiography from the notebooks and sculpture of Adaline Kent. [Houston? Tex., c1958] 87p. illus., ports. 25cm. [NB237.K38A2] 61-19938
I. Title.

KENT, Rockwell, 1882- 927
It's me, O Lord; the autobiography of Rockwell Kent. New York, Dodd, Mead [1955] x, 617 p. illus. (part col.) 25 cm. [NC139.K4A3] 55-6470
1. Artists—Correspondence, reminiscences, etc. I. Title. BIP

KIESLER, Frederick. 720.924
Inside the endless house; art, people, and architecture: a journal. New York, Simon and Schuster [1966] 573 p. illus. 27 cm. [NA737.K5A3] 64-18655
1. Artists — Correspondence, reminiscences, etc. I. Title.

KLEE, Paul, 1879-1940 927.5
The diaries of Paul Klee, 1898-1918. Ed., introd., by Felix Klee. Berkeley, Univ. of Calif. Pr., 1968. [c.1964] xx, 434p. illus., facsims., ports. 25cm. (Cal 158) First complete English-language version based upon the text of the German hardcover ed., pub. in 1957. [ND588.K5A252] 64-20993 3.45 pap.,
1. Artists—Correspondance, reminiscences, etc. I. Klee, Felix, 1907- ed. II. Title.

KLEE, Paul, 1879-1940. 709'.494
The diaries of Paul Klee, 1898-1918. Edited, with an introd. by Felix Klee. Berkeley, University of California Press, 1968 [c1964] xx, 434 p. illus. 21 cm. "First California paper-bound printing." Translation of Tagebucher. [ND588.K5A252 1968] 68-6958 3.45
1. Artists—Correspondence, reminiscences, etc. I. Klee, Felix, 1907- ed. BIP

KLEE, Paul, 1879-1940. 927.5
The diaries of Paul Klee, 1898-1918. Edited, with an introd., by Felix Klee. Berkeley, University of California Press, 1964. xx, 424 p. illus., facsims., ports. 25 cm. "First complete English-language version ... based upon the text of the German hardcover edition, published ... in 1957." [ND588.K5A252] 64-20993
1. Artists — Correspondence, reminiscences, etc. I. Klee, Felix, 1907- ed. II. Title.

KOLLWITZ, Kathe (Schmidt) 927.4
1867-1945.
Diary and letters edited by Hans Kollwitz. translated by Richard and Clara Winston Chicago, H. Regnery Co., 1955. vi, 200p. illus., 48plates. 26cm. [NC251.K6A312] 55-9336
1. Artists—Correspondence, reminiscences, etc. I. Title.

LINDSAY, Lionel Arthur, 579.9/94
Sir 1874-1961
Comedy of life; an autobiography by Sir Lionel Lindsay. Foreword by Peter Lindsay. [Sydney] Angus & Robertson [1967] xvii, 272p. illus., ports. 23cm. [N7405.L5A3] 67-110632 6.95
1. Artists—Correspondence, reminiscences, etc. I. Title.
American distributor: Tri-Ocean, San Francisco.

MCINTYRE, Florence Makin, 706.9
1878-
Art and life. Memphis, S. C. Toof, printers [1952] 198 p. 21 cm. [ND237.M213A2] 52-28655
1. Artists—Correspondence, reminiscences, ets. 2. Art—Memphis. I. Title.

MORISOT, Berthe, 1841-1895. 927.5
The correspondence of Berthe Morisot with her family and her friends: Manet, Puvis de Chavannes, Degas, Monet, Renoir, and Mallarme. Compiled and edited by Denis Rouart; translated by Betty W. Hubbard. [1st ed.] New York, G. Wittenborn [1957] 187 p. illus. (part mounted, part col.) facsims. 29 cm. [ND553.M88A313] 759.4 57-9529
1. Artists—Correspondence, reminiscences, etc.

MOSES, Anna Mary 927.5
(Robertson) 1860-1961.
Grandma Moses: my life's history. Edited by Otto Kallir. [1st ed. New York] Harper [1952] xi, 140 p. plates (part col.) ports., facsims. 25 cm. [ND237.M78A22] 51-11940
1. Artists—Correspondence, reminiscences, etc.

NEUHAUS, Eugen, 1879-1963. 927.5
Drawn from memory, a self portrait. Palo Alto, Calif., Pacific Books [1964] 208 p. illus., ports. 22 cm. [ND237.N45A2] 64-23486
1. Artists — Correspondence, reminiscences, etc. I. Title.

OLIVIER, Fernande 759.6
Picasso and his friends. Tr. [from French] by Jane Miller [1st Amer. ed.] New York, Appleton-Century [dist. Meredith, 1965, c.1933-1964] 186p. illus., ports. 21cm. [ND553.P5O413] 65-25447 3.95
1. Picasso, Pablo, 1881- 2. Artists—Correspondence, reminiscences, etc. I. Title.

OROZCO, Jose Clemente, 927.5
1883-1949.
An autobiography. Translated by Robert C. Stephenson. Introd. by John Palmer Leeper. Austin, University of Texas Press [1962] 171 p. illus. 21 cm. (The Texas Pan-American series) [ND259.O7A213] 62-9790
1. Artists—Correspondence, reminiscences, etc.

PORTRAIT of Manet by 759.4
himself and his contemporaries. Ed. by Pierre Courthion, Pierre Cailler. Tr. by Michael Ross. New York, Roy [1962, c.1953-1960] 238p. illus. 22cm. Bibl. 62-10706 6.50
1. Artists—Correspondence, reminiscences. etc. I. Manet(Edouard, 1832-1883. II. Courthion, Pierre, ed.

PRICE, Al, 1927- 741.6'092'4 B
Haunted by a paintbrush; a true story. Prepared under the direction of Margaret Friskey. Chicago, Childrens Press [1972, c1968] 30 p. illus. 21 cm. A successful Negro commercial artist writes briefly of his childhood, education, and the events leading to his decision to become an artist. [ND237.P86F7 1972] 92 72-181838 ISBN 0-516-04834-1 3.00
I. Friskey, Margaret, 1901- II. Title.

ROSENBERG, James Naumburg, 759.13
1874-
Painter's self-portrait. Edited with an introd. by Milton S. Fox. New York, Crown Publishers, 1958. 203p. illus. (part mounted: part col.) ports. 32cm. [ND237.R72F6] 58-11411
I. Title.

ROSSETTI, Dante Gabriel, 759.2 B
1828-1882.
Dante Gabriel Rossetti: his family-letters. With a memoir by William Michael Rossetti. [1st AMS ed.] New York, AMS Press [1970] 2 v. facsim., ports. 23 cm. Reprint of the 1895 ed. [PR5246.A43 1970] 70-130231 ISBN 0-404-05434-X
1. Rossetti, Dante Gabriel, 1828-1882. 2. Rossetti family. 3. Artists—Correspondence, reminiscences, etc. I. Rossetti, William Michael, 1829-1919, ed.

SELIGMANN, Herbert 779.0924
Jacob, 1891-
Alfred Stieglitz talking; notes on some of his conversations, 1925-1931. Foreword by Herbert J. Seligmann. New Haven [Conn.] Yale University Library, [c.]1966. ix, 149p. 24cm. [TR140.S7S4] 66-21942 7.50
1. Stieglitz, Alfred, 1864-1946. 2. Artists—Correspondence, reminiscences, etc. I. Stieglitz, Alfred, 1864-1946. II. Title.

SHEN, Fu, 1763-ca.1808 759.951
Chapters from a floating life; the autobiography of a Chinese artist. Translated from the Chinese by Shirley M. Black. Poems by Tu Fu and Li Po, translated by S. M. B. London, New York, Oxford University Press, 1960[ ] 108p. 8 ptes. 60-4904 3.75
I. Title.

SHEPARD, Ernest Howard, 927.41
1879-
Drawn from life. New York, Dutton [1962, c1961] 217 p. illus. 22 cm. Autobiography. [NC242.S47A28 1962] 63-1603
I. Title.

SHEPARD, Ernest Howard, 927.41
1879-
Drawn from memory. Philadelphia, Lippincott [1957] 190 p. illus. 22 cm. Autobiographical. [NC242.S47A3] 57-13370
I. Title.

SHIELDS, Frederic James, 759.2
1833-1911.
The life and letters of Frederic Shields. Edited by Ernestine Mills. London, New York, Longmans, Green, 1912. [New York, AMS Press, 1972] xiv, 368 p. illus. 23 cm. [N6797.S5A3 1972] 76-148281 ISBN 0-404-04344-5
I. Mills, Ernestine (Bell) ed. II. Title. BIP

SOYER, Raphael, 1899- 709.43
Homage to Thomas Eakins, etc. Ed. by Rebecca L. Soyer. New York, Yoseloff [c.1966] 183p. illus., col. plates, ports. 29cm. [ND237.S636A23] 65-24829 10.00
1. Artists—Correspondence, reminiscences, etc. 2. Art—Europe. I. Title.

SPRATLING, William 709'.73
Philip, 1900-1967.
File on Spratling; an autobiography. With drawings by the author. Introd. by Budd Schulberg. [1st ed.] Boston, Little, Brown [1967] xiv, 235 p. illus., ports. (1 col.) 20 cm. [N6537.S65A2] 67-21097
1. Artists—Correspondence, reminiscences, etc. I. Title.

STRUGGLING with paint. 759.2
New York, Roy Publishers [1957] 127p. illus. 22cm. [ND497.D8A25] [ND497.D8A25] 927.5 57-6200 57-6200
1. Artists—Correspondence, reminiscences, etc. 2. Painting. I. Dunlop, Ronald Ossory, 1894-

TAMARIN, Alfred H. 730'.924 B
The autobiography of Benvenuto Cellini, edited by Alfred Tamarin. Abridged and adapted from the translation by John Addington Symonds. [New York] Macmillan [1969] x, 164 p. illus. 26 cm. [NB623.C3S45 1969] 69-11591
I. Symonds, John Addington, 1840-1893, tr. II. Cellini, Benvenuto, 1500-1571. The autobiography.

VLAMINCK, Maurice de, 1876- 759.4
1958.
Dangerous corner. Translated by Michael Ross. Introd. by Denys Sutton. New York, Abelard-Schuman [1967, c1961] 171 p. illus. 22 cm. Autobiographical. [ND553.V6A2313 1967] 66-25005
1. Artists—Correspondence, reminiscences, etc. I. Title.

WAUGH, Alfred S d.1856. 927
Travels in search of the elephant; the wanderings of Alfred S. Waugh, artist, in Louisiana, Missouri, and Santa Fe, in 1845-1846. Edited and annotated by John Francis McDermott. St. Louis, Missouri Historical Society, 1951. xxi, 153 p. 24 cm. Bibliography: p. [145]-148. [N6537.W3A3] 51-13469
1. Artists — Correspondence, reminiscences, etc. 2. U.S. — Descr. & trav. — 1783-1848. I. McDermott, John Francis, 1902- ed. II. Missouri Historical Society, St. Louis. III. Title.

WILLS, Royal Barry, 1895- 927.2
Houses have funny bones; with drawings by the author. New York, B. Wheelwright Co., 1951. 179 p. illus. 24 cm. [NA737.W53A3] 51-14060
1. Artists—Correspondence, reminiscences, etc. I. Title.

ZORACH, William, 1887- 730'.924
1966.
Art is my life; the autobiography of William Zorach. Cleveland, World Pub. Co. [1967] ix, 205 p. illus., ports. 26 cm. [NB237.Z6A2] 67-12900
1. Artists—Correspondence, reminiscences, etc. 2. Art—United States. I. Title.

Artists—Dictionaries.

ATLANTIC brief 700.922 [B]
lives: a biographical companion to the arts. Edited by Louis Kronenberger. Assoc. ed.: Emily Morrison Beck. Boston, Little, Brown [1975, c1971] xxii, 900 p. 21 cm. "An Atlantic Monthly Press Book" Includes bibliographical references. [NX90.A73 1975] 73-154960 4.95 (pbk.)
1. Artists—D I. Kronenberger, Louis-1904- ed. II. Title: Brief lives.

BRADLEY, John William, 1830- 703
1916.
A dictionary of miniaturists, illuminators, calligraphers, and copyists, with references to their works, and notices of their patrons, from the establishment of Christianity to the eighteenth century. New York, B. Franklin [1958] 3v. 25cm. (Burt Franklin bibliographical series, 8) [ND2890.B83] 61-35160
1. Artists—Dictionaries. 2. Illumination of books and manuscripts. 3. Caligraphers. 4. Copyists. I. Title.

COYSH, Arthur Wilfred. 745.1'03
The antique buyer's dictionary of names [by] A. W. Coysh. New York, Praeger [1970] 278 p. illus. 23 cm. Includes bibliographical references. [N40.C67 1970] 70-125355
1. Artists—Dictionaries. I. Title.

PHAIDON encyclopedia of art 703
and artists. Oxford : Phaidon, 1978. 704 p., [60] p. of plates : ill. (some col.), ports. (some col.) ; 28 cm. "Adapted from the Pall Mall encyclopedia of art." [N31.P48] 77-89312 ISBN 0-7148-1513-6 : 35.00
1. Art—Dictionaries. 2. Artists—Biography. I. Pall Mall encyclopedia of art. Distributed by Dutton, New York
Distributed by Dutton, N.Y.

WATERS, Clara (Erskine) 709.22 B
Clement, 1834-1916.
Artists of the nineteenth century and their works [by] Clara Erskine Clement Waters and Laurence Hutton. [7th ed., rev.] New York, Arno Press, 1969 [c1884] 2 v. in 1. 23 cm. Bibliography: v. 1, p. [ix]-x. [N40.W28 1969] 70-88820
1. Artists—Dictionaries. I. Hutton, Laurence, 1843-1904, joint author. II. Title.

Artists — Direct.

DIRECTOR'S Art Institute, 760.58
New York.
Who's who in commercial art and

photography; a guide to artists, photographers, agents, studios, representatives and buyers of art in the graphics field. New York, 176 e. 75 St. Author, [c.1960] 168p. illus. 25cm. 60-50460 15.00
1. Artists—Direct. 2. Photographers—Direct. 3. Commercial art— Direct. 4. Graphic arts—Direct. I. Title.

DIRECTOR'S ART INSTITUTE, New York. 655.3
Who's who in commercial art and photography; a guide to artists, photographers, agents and studios in the graphics field. Edited by Julia W. Philip. [2d ed.] New York, 1964. 192 p. illus. 25 cm. [NC997.D5 1964] 66-235
1. Artists — Direct. 2. Photographers — Direct. 3. Commercial art — Direct. 4. Graphic arts — Direct. I. Phillip, Julia W., ed. II. Title.

Artists—England—Biography.

DOYLE, Charles Altamont. 741'.092'4 B
The Doyle diary : the last great Conan Doyle mystery : with a Holmesian investigation into the strange and curious case of Charles Altamont Doyle / by Michael Baker. New York : Paddington Press, c1978. xxix, 91 p. : ill. ; 18 x 25 cm. Facsim. of the author's diary-sketchbook, with an additional introd., and a page transcription of the words of Charles Doyle as they appear in the diary. [N6797.D68A2 1978] 78-6356 ISBN 0-448-22068-7 : 12.95
1. Doyle, Charles Altamont. 2. Artists—England—Biography. I. Baker, Michael, 1948- II. Title. **BIP**

FARINGTON, Joseph, 1747-1821. 759.2 B
The diary of Joseph Farington / edited by Kenneth Garlick and Angus Macintyre. New Haven : Published for the Paul Mellon Centre for Studies in British Art by Yale University Press, 1978- p. cm. (Studies in British art) Contents.Contents.—v. 1. July 1793-December 1794.—v. 2. January 1795-August 1796. [N6797.F37A2 1978] 78-7056 ISBN 0-300-02294-8 : 60.00 set
1. Farington, Joseph, 1747-1821. 2. London. Royal Academy of Art. 3. Artists—England—Biography. 4. Arts, English. 5. England—Civilization—18th century. 6. England—Civilization—19th century. I. Garlick, Kenneth, 1916- II. Macintyre, Angus D. III. Paul Mellon Centre for Studies in British Art. IV. Title. V. Series.

Artists, English—Cumberland.

CARLISLE, Eng. Museum and Art Gallery. 709'.22
Cumberland artists, 1700-1900; summer exhibition. [Carlisle, Eng.] Carlisle City Art Gallery, 1971. 44 p. illus. 21 cm. Cover title. Label mounted on p. [1] of cover: Supplied by Worldwide Books, Boston. Bibliography: p. 44. [N6769.C9C3] 70-198321
1. Artists, English—Cumberland. I. Title.

Artists—Europe—Correspondence, reminiscences, etc.

SHAPIRO, Theda. 759.06
Painters and politics : the European avant-garde and society, 1900-1925 / Theda Shapiro. New York : American Elsevier Pub. Co., [1976] p. cm. Includes index. Bibliography: p. [N6758.S49 1976] 75-20954 ISBN 0-444-99012-7
1. Artists—Europe—Correspondence, reminiscences, etc. 2. Art, Modern—20th century—Europe. 3. Art and society—Europe. 4. Art and revolutions—Europe. 5. Avant-garde (Aesthetics) I. Title.

Artists, European.

BOLTON, Sarah Knowles, 1841-1916. 709'.22
Famous European artists. Freeport, N.Y., Books for Libraries Press [1972] 423 p. ports. 23 cm. (Essay index reprint series) Reprint of the 1890 ed. Contents.Contents.—Michael Angelo.—Leonardo da Vinci.—Raphael of Urbino.—Titian.—Murillo.—Rubens.—Rembrandt.—Sir Joshua Reynolds.—Sir Edwin Landseer.—Turner. [N40.B64 1972] 74-39676 ISBN 0-8369-2750-8
1. Artists, European. I. Title. **BIP**

Artists—France—Biography.

HARGROVE, June Ellen. 730'.92'4 B
The life and work of Albert Ernest Carrier-Belleuse / June Ellen Hargrove. New York : Garland Pub., 1977. p. cm. (Outstanding dissertations in the fine arts) Thesis—New York University, 1975. Bibliography: p. [N6853.C278H37] 76-23625 ISBN 0-8240-2695-0 lib.bdg. : 50.00
1. Carrier-Belleuse, Albert Ernest, 1824-1887. 2. Artists—France—Biography. I. Carrier-Belleuse, Albert Ernest, 1824-1887. II. Title. III. Series.

Artists, French.

BERNHEIM DE VILLERS, Gaston, 1870- 750.88
Little tales of great artists; translated and edited by Denys Sutton. Paris, Quatre Chemins-Editart; New York, E. Weyhe [1950] 105 p. plates (1 col.) ports., mounted facsim. 29 cm. An abridgment of the author's Petites histoires sur de grands artistes, with the addition of notes. [N6852.B53] 50-3548
1. Artists, French. I. Title.

MAYWALD, Wilhelm 709.44
Portraitatelier: photos. [Brattleboro, Vt., Stephen] Greene [1960] 1 v. (unpaged) illus., ports., facsims. 25cm. English, German, and French. 60-10050 4.95
1. Artists, French. 2. Artists. I. Title.

Artists—Great Britain—Biography.

HOCKNEY, David. 759.2 B
David Hockney / by David Hockney ; edited by Nikos Stangos ; introductory essay by Henry Geldzahler. New York : H. N. Abrams, 1977, c1976. 312 p. : ill. (some col.) ; 28 cm. Includes index. [N6797.H57A42 1977] 76-11721 ISBN 0-8109-1058-6 : 35.00
1. Hockney, David. 2. Artists—Great Britain—Biography. **BIP**

HOCKNEY, David. 759.2 B
David Hockney / by David Hockney ; edited by Nikos Stangos ; introductory essay by Henry Geldzahler. London : Thames & Hudson, c1976. 312 p. : with 414 ill. ; 27 cm. Includes index. [N6797.H57S7 1976] 77-354409 ISBN 0-500-09108-0 : £10.00
1. Hockney, David. 2. Artists—Great Britain—Biography. I. Stangos, Nikos.

JOHNSON, Jane. 709'.2'2 B
The dictionary of British artists, 1880-1940 : an Antique Collectors' Club research project listing 41,000 artists / compiled by J. Johnson and A. Greutzner. [Suffolk, Eng.] : Antique Collectors' Club, c1976. 567 p. ; 29 cm. Bibliography: p. 6. [N6767.J63] 77-357303 ISBN 0-902028-36-7 : £17.50
1. Artists—Great Britain—Biography. 2. Art, Modern—19th century—Great Britain. 3. Art, Modern—20th century—Great Britain. I. Greutzner, A., joint author. II. Antique Collectors' Club. III. Title.

Artists—Hawaii—Biography.

ARTISTS of Hawaii / 709'.2'2
photos. by Francis Haar ; interviews by Prithwish Neogy ; with an introd. by Jean Charlot. Honolulu : State Foundation on Culture & the Arts, [1974- v. : ill. (some col.) ; 26 x 28 cm. Contents.Contents.—v. 1. Nineteen painters and sculptors. [N6530.H3A77] 74-78861 ISBN 0-8248-0338-8 : 25.00
1. Artists—Hawaii—Biography. I. Haar, Francis, ill. II. Neogy, Prithwish.

Artists—Interviews.

COTT, Jonathan. 700'.92'2 B
Forever young / by Jonathan Cott. [1st ed.] New York : Random House, [1978] xiii, 219 p. : ill. ; 23 cm. "A Random House/Rolling Stone Press book." Contents.Contents.—Oriana Fallaci.—Glenn Gould.—Stephane Grappelli.—Werner Herzog.—Walter Lowenfels.—Henry Miller.—Harry Partch.—Maurice Sendak. [NX165.C67] 77-5963 ISBN 0-394-41655-4 : 12.50. ISBN 0-394-73398-3 pbk. : 5.95
1. Artists—Interviews. 2. Arts—Psychology. I. Title. **BIP**

Artists—Ireland—Dictionaries.

STRICKLAND, Walter G., 1850-1928. 709'.22
A dictionary of Irish artists. Introd. by Theo J. Snoddy. New York, Hacker Art Books [1969, c1968] 2 v. illus., ports. 26 cm. Reprint of the 1913 ed. [N6782.S7 1969] 79-94898
1. Artists—Ireland—Dictionaries. I. Title. II. Title: Irish artists. **BIP**

Artists, Italian.

VASARI, Giorgio, 1511-1574 709.45
The lives of the artists; a selection, tr. [from Italian] by George Bull. Baltimore, Penguin [1966, c.1965] 478, [1] p. 18cm. (Penguin classics, L164) Bibl. [N6922.V4915] 66-1653 1.95 pap.,
1. Artists, Italian. 2. Art, Renaissance—Hist. I. Title. **BIP**

VASARI, Giorgio, 1511-1574. 709'.45
Lives of the most eminent painters. Selected, edited, and introduced by Marilyn Aronberg Lavin. [Translated by Mrs. Jonathan Foster] New York, Heritage Press [1967] 2 v. illus. (part col.), ports. 29 cm. Translations from Le vite de' piu eccellenti pittori, scultori, et architettori. [N6922.V474] 67-7982
1. Artists, Italian. 2. Art, Italian—History. I. Lavin, Marilyn Aronberg, ed. II. Foster, Jonathan, Mrs., tr. III. Title.

VASARI, Giorgio, 1511-1574. 759.5 B
Lives of the most eminent painters. Selected, edited, and introduced by Marilyn Aronberg Lavin. [Translated by Mrs. Jonathan Foster] Verona, Printed for the members of the Limited Editions Club at the Stamperia Valdonega, 1966. 2 v. illus. (part col.), ports. 30 cm. Translations from Le vite de' piu eccellenti pittori, scultori, et architettori. [N6922.V473] 72-185270
1. Artists, Italian. 2. Art, Italian—History. I. Lavin, Marilyn Aronberg, ed. II. Foster, Jonathan, Mrs., tr. III. Limited Editions Club, inc., New York. IV. Title.

WETHEY, Harold Edwin. 759.6
El Greco and his school. Princeton, N.J., Princeton University Press, 1962. 2 v. plates. 29 cm. Contents.1. Text and plates. -- 2. Catalogue raisonne. Includes bibliographical references. [ND813.T4W4] 61-7427
1. Theotocopuli, Dominico, called El Greco, d. 1614. 2. Artists, Italian. I. Title.

Artists, Italian—Lombardy.

BERTOLOTTI, Antonino, 1836-1893. 709'.45'2
Artisti lombardi a Roma nei secoli XV, XVI, XVII; studi e ricerche negli archivi romani. New York, B. Franklin [1973] 2 v. 22 cm. (Burt Franklin research & source works series. Art history & reference series, 37) Reprint of the 1881 ed. [N6920.B547 1973] 77-146239 ISBN 0-8337-0266-1 35.00
1. Artists, Italian—Lombardy. 2. Art—Rome (City) I. Title. **BIP**

Artists, Italian—Rome (City)

BERTOLOTTI, Antonino, 1836-1893. 709'.45
Artisti bolognesi, ferraresi ed alcuni altri del gia Stato pontificio in Roma nei secoli XV, XVI e XVII; studi e ricerche tratte dagli archivi romani. New York, B. Franklin [1972] xi, 295 p. 21 cm. (Burt Franklin research & source works series. Art history & reference series, 38) Reprint of the 1885 ed. [N6920.B545 1972] 79-136047 ISBN 0-8337-0263-7 19.50
1. Artists, Italian—Rome (City) 2. Art—Rome (City) I. Title.

Artists—Italy—Biography.

HIBBARD, Howard, 1928- 700'.92'4 B
Michelangelo : painter, sculptor, architect / Howard Hibbard. New York : Vendome Press : distributed by Viking Press, [1978] 213 p. : ill. (some col.) ; 32 cm. "An Alexis Gregory book." Includes index. Bibliography: p. 209-212. [N6923.B9H493 1978] 78-7748 ISBN 0-670-47397-9 : 40.00
1. Buonarroti, Michel Angelo, 1475-1564. 2. Artists—Italy—Biography.

VASARI, Giorgio, 1511-1574. 709'.2'2 B
Lives of the most eminent painters, sculptors & architects / by Giorgio Vasari ; newly translated by Gaston du C. de Vere. With five hundred ill. New York : AMS Press, [1976] p. cm. Translation of Le vite de' piu eccellenti pittori. Reprint of the 1912-15 ed. published by Macmillan and the Medici Society, London. Includes indexes. [N6922.V213 1976] 71-153610 ISBN 0-404-09730-8 lib.bdg. : 425.00(set) 42.50 ea.
1. Artists—Italy—Biography. 2. Art, Italian—History. I. De Vere, Gaston du C. II. Title. **BIP**

Artists—Italy—Rome (City)—Biography.

ANDREWS, Keith. 760'.092'4
Adam Elsheimer : paintings, drawings, prints / Keith Andrews. New York : Rizzoli, 1977. 178 p. : ill. (some col.) ; 29 cm. Includes indexes. Bibliography: p. 171. [N6888.E63A5] 77-73365 ISBN 0-8478-0089-X : 60.00
1. Elsheimer, Adam, 1578-1610. 2. Artists—Italy—Rome (City)—Biography. 3. Artists—Germany—Biography. I. Elsheimer, Adam, 1578-1610.

Artists—Japan—Autographs.

LAZARNICK, George, 1913- 736'.68'0922
The signature book of netsuke, inro, and ojime artists in photographs / George Lazarnick ; [foreword by Neil K. Davey]. Honolulu : Reed Publishers, [1976] p. cm. Bibliography: p. [NK6050.L38] 76-9504 ISBN 0-917064-01-1 : 85.00
1. Artists—Japan—Autographs. 2. Netsukes. 3. Inro. 4. Ojime. I. Title. **BIP**

Artists—Japan—Biography.

ROBERTS, Laurance P. 709'.2'2 B
A dictionary of Japanese artists : painting, sculpture, ceramics, prints, lacquer / Laurance P. Roberts ; with a foreword by John M. Rosenfield. 1st ed. Tokyo ; New York : Weatherhill, 1976. xi, 299 p. ; 27 cm. Title on spine: Japanese artists. Includes indexes. Bibliography: p. 223-232. [N7358.R6] 76-885 ISBN 0-8348-0113-2 : 22.50
1. Artists—Japan—Biography. I. Title. **BIP**

Artists, Japanese

NEW York. Museum of Modern Art 709.52
The new Japanese painting and sculpture: an exhibition selected by Dorothy C. Miller, William S. Lieberman. Essay by William S. Lieberman. Garden City, N. Y., Dist. Doubleday [1966] 116p. illus. (pt. col.) ports. 25cm. Catalog of an exhibition presented by the Mus. of Modern Art, New York, in collaboration with the San Francisco Mus. of Art. shown there & at seven other museums, Apr. 29, 1965-May 14. 1967. Circulated under the auspices of the Intl. Council of the Mus. [N7358.N4] 65-25726 5.95, .95 pap.,
1. Artists, Japanese 2. Art, Modern—20th cent.—Exhibitions. I. Miller, Dorothy Canning. 1904- II. Lieberman. William Slattery, 1924- III. San Francisco. Museum of Art. IV. International Council of the

Museum of Modern Art, New York. V. Title.

Artists, Jewish.

LEWBIN, Hyman. 709'.2'2
Rebirth of Jewish art : the unfolding of Jewish art in the nineteenth century / by Hyman Lewbin. New York ; Shengold Publishers, [1974] 128 p., [8] leaves of plates : ill. ; 25 cm. Includes index. [N7418.L48] 74-76483 ISBN 0-88400-006-0 : 6.95
1. Artists, Jewish. 2. Art, Modern—19th century. I. Title. BIP

SCHWARZ, Karl, 1885- 709.03
Jewish artists of the 19th and 20th centuries. Freeport, N.Y., Books for Libraries Press [1970, c1949] xiii, 273 p. illus., ports. 23 cm. (Biography index reprint series) [N7417.S28 1970] 75-117332
1. Artists, Jewish. 2. Art, Modern—19th century—History. 3. Art, Modern—20th century—History. I. Title.

Artists, Jewish—U. S.

GROSSMAN, Emery, 1905- 709.73
Art and tradition. New York, T. Yoseloff, [1968, c1967] 176 p. illus. (part col.), ports. 29 cm. Contents.--Samuel Adler.--David Aronson.--Ben-Zion.--Adolph Gottlieb.--Chaim Gross.--Ibram Lassaw.--Jack Levine.--Jacques Lipchitz.--Seymour Lipton.--Herman Maril.--Sigmund Menkes.--Bernard Reder.--Larry Rivers.--George Segal.--Ben Shahn.--Moses Soyer.--William Zorach. [N6538.J4G7] 67-173842
1. Artists, Jewish—U. S. 2. Art, American. I. Title.

RASHELL, Jacob. 709'.73
Jewish artists in America. [1st ed.] New York, Vantage Press [1967] 197 p. illus. 21 cm. Bibliography: p. 197. [N6538.J4R3] 66-29963
1. Artists, Jewish—United States. 2. Art—United States. I. Title.

Artists — Juvenile literature.

KALES, David 759'.0922
Masters of art, by David & Emily Kales. Illus. by Earl Mayan. New York, Grosset [1967] 128p. illus., ports. 28cm. [N42K3] 67-14758 3.95
1. Artists—Juvenile literature. I. Title. II. Title: From Giotto to Picasso. Young readers.

WICKER, Ireene (Seaton) 701.15
1905-
Young master artists; boyhoods of famous artists. Indianapolis, Bobbs-Merrill [1962] 256 p. illus. 22 cm. [N42.W5] 62-10025
1. Artists — Juvenile literature. I. Title.

Artists—Maine—Directories.

MAINE artists, 1850- 709'.2'2 B
1899. [Augusta] : Maine State Museum, [1976] [28] p. ; 23 cm. (Maine State Museum checklist series) Cover title. [N6530.M2M3] 77-620992
1. Artists—Maine—Directories. 2. Art, American—Maine—Directories. 3. Art, Modern—19th century—Maine—Directories. I. Maine State Museum. II. Series: Maine State Museum. Maine State Museum checklist series.

Artists' marks.

HASLAM, Malcolm. 702'.78
Marks and monograms of the Modern Movement, 1875-1930 : a guide to the marks of artists, designers, retailers, and manufacturers, from the period of the Aesthetic Movement to Art Deco and Style Moderne / Malcolm Haslam. New York : Scribner, 1977. 192 p. : ill. ; 26 cm. Includes index. [N45.H37 1977b] 76-26189 ISBN 0-684-14828-5 : 12.50
1. Artists' marks. 2. Monograms. 3. Modernism (Art) I. Title. BIP

UNITT, Doris Joyce. 745.1'02'78
Book of marks : antiques and collectables / compiled and edited by Doris and Peter Unitt. Rev. Peterborough, Ont. : Clock House Publications, 1973. 208 p. : ill. ; 22 cm. Cover title: Unitt's book of marks. Includes index. Bibliography: p. 201-203. [N45.U54 1973] 75-325204 8.95
1. Artists' marks. 2. Antiques. I. Unitt, Peter, 1914- joint author. II. Title. III. Title: Unitt's book of marks.

Artists' marks—Directories.

CAPLAN, H. H. 760'.092'2
The classified directory of artists signatures, symbols & monograms / [compiled by] H. H. Caplan. London : Prior, 1976. [5], viii, 738 [i.e. 744] p. : chiefly facsims. ; 31 cm. English text; English, French, German, Spanish, and Italian introd. [N45.C36] 77-356200 ISBN 0-86043-004-9 : £29.50
1. Artists' marks—Directories. 2. Monograms—Directories. I. Title. BIP

Artists' materials.

CHAVATEL, George. 751.2
Exploring with polymer; a guide to new media for young adults. New York, Reinhold [1966] 104 p. illus. (part col.) 21 cm. [ND1620.C45] 66-11935
1. Artists' materials. 2. Polymers and polymerization. I. Title.

GETTENS, Rutherford John. 751
Painting materials; a short encyclopaedia, by Rutherford J. Gettens and George L. Stout. New York, Dover Publications [1966] x, 333 p. illus. 22 cm. "Corrected republication of the work originally published ... in 1942." Includes bibliographies. [ND1500.G4 1966] 65-26655
1. Artists' materials. 2. Pigments. I. Stout, George Leslie, joint author. II. Title. BIP

HILER, Hilaire, 1898-1966. 751.4
The painter's pocket-book of methods and materials. Edited by Jan Gordon and rev. by Colin Hayes. [3d ed.] New York, Watson-Guptill Publications [1970] 266 p. illus. 21 cm. [ND1500.H52 1970] 70-101417 4.95
1. Artists' materials. 2. Painting—Technique. I. Title. BIP

JENSEN, Lawrence N 751.2
Synthetic painting media. Englewood Cliffs, N.J., Prentice-Hall [1964] v. 138 p. illus. 22 cm. Bibliography: p. 128. [ND1500.J4] 64-14538
1. Artists' materials. 2. Painting — Technique. I. Title.

KAY, Reed. 751
The painter's companion, a basic guide to studio methods and materials. Cambridge [Mass.] Webb Books [1961] 264 p. illus. 21 cm. (A Webb art book, W-2) Includes bibliography. [ND1500.K3] 61-10546
1. Artists' materials. 2. Painting—Technique. I. Title.

KAY, Reed. 751
The painter's guide to studio methods and materials. Rev. ed. Garden City, N.Y., Doubleday, 1972. 265 p. illus. 22 cm. First published in 1961 under title: The painter's companion, a basic guide to studio methods and materials. Bibliography: p. [254]-258. [ND1500.K3 1972] 79-175387 6.95
1. Artists' materials. 2. Painting—Technique. I. Title.

LAMB, Lynton. 751
Materials and methods of painting. London, New York, Oxford U.P., 1970. 112 p. illus. 21 cm. (Oxford paperbacks, Handbooks for artists, 8) Bibliography: p. [109] [ND1500.L35] 78-507201 16/-
1. Artists' materials. 2. Painting—Technique. I. Title. BIP

MEILACH, Dona Z. 701
Creating art from anything : ideas, materials, techniques / Dona Z. Meilach. New York : Galahad Books, [1974] c1968. v, 119 p., [2] leaves of plates : ill. ; 29 cm. [N7433.7.M44 1974] 73-92081 ISBN 0-88365-076-2 : 7.95
1. Artists' materials. 2. Assemblage (Art) 3. Art—Technique. I. Title.

MEILACH, Dona Z. 701
Creating art from anything; ideas, materials, techniques [by] Dona Z. Meilach. Chicago, Reilly & Lee [1968] v, 119 p. illus. (part col.) 29 cm. [N7430.M4] 68-18480
1. Artists' materials. 2. Assemblage (Art) 3. Art—Technique. I. Title.

MILLS, John FitzMaurice, 701
1917-
The painter and his materials. London, New York, Artist Pub. Co. [1960] 55 p. 19 cm. (The Artist's handbooks, no. 11) [ND1500.M53] 62-5708
1. Artists' materials. 2. Painting — Technique. I. Title. II. Series.

TAUBES, Frederic, 1900- 751.45
Oil & tempera painting; 500 questions and answers. [New York] Watson-Guptill Publications [1957] 144 p. 21 cm. [ND1500.T3] 57-7806
1. Artists' materials. 2. Painting—Technique. 3. Tempera painting. I. Title.

TAUBES, Frederic, 1900- 751
Painting materials & techniques. [New York] Watson-Guptill Publications [1964] 162 p. 21 cm. [ND1260.T273] 64-14766
1. Artists' materials. 2. Painting—Technique. I. Title.

TIMMONS, Virginia 702'.8
Gayheart.
Art materials, techniques, ideas: a resource book for teachers. Worcester, Mass., Davis Publications [1974] 167 p. illus. 27 cm. Bibliography: p. 162-163. [N7433.T55] 73-89254 ISBN 0-87192-057-3 10.95
1. Artists' materials. 2. Art—Technique. I. Title. BIP

TORCHE, Judith. 751.4'26
Acrylic and other water-base paints for the artist. [Rev. ed.] New York, Sterling Pub. Co. [1969, c1967] 80 p. illus. (part col.) 29 cm. Bibliography: p. 77-78. [ND1535.T6 1969] 75-23776 ISBN 0-8069-5082-X
1. Artists' materials. 2. Polymer painting. I. Title.

WEHLTE, Kurt. 751
The materials and techniques of painting / Kurt Wehlte ; translated by Ursus Dix. New York : Van Nostrand Reinhold, [1975] 678 p., [48] leaves of plates : ill. ; 25 cm. Translation of Werkstoffe und Techniken der Malerei. Includes index. Bibliography: p. 649. [ND1500.W413] 79-155589 ISBN 0-442-29253-8 : 27.50
1. Artists' materials. 2. Painting—Technique. I. Title.

WOODY, Russell O., Jr. 751
Painting with synthetic media. Technical appendix by Henry W. Levison. New York, Reinhold [c.1965] 160p. illus. (pt. col.) 29cm. [ND1260.W66] 15.00
1. Artist's materials. 2. Painting—Technique. I. Title.

Artists' materials—Dictionaries.

TAUBES, Frederic, 1900- 703
The painter's dictionary of materials and methods. New York, Watson-Guptill Publications [1971] 253 p. illus. 22 cm. [ND1505.T38] 71-155142 ISBN 0-8230-1335-9 6.95
1. Artists' materials—Dictionaries. 2. Painting—Technique—Dictionaries. I. Title. BIP

Artists' materials—Direct.

AMERICAN artist. 702'.9
Artists' guide. [New York, American artist. v. illus. (part col.) 30 cm. annual. Began in 1968. Supersedes Art materials buyer's guide. [ND1500.A7] 68-7643
1. Artists' materials—Direct. I. Title.

Artists' materials—Formulae, tables, etc.

MASSEY, Robert. 751.2
Formulas for painters. New York, Watson-Guptill Publications [1967] 224 p. 24 cm. Bibliography: p. 219-220. [ND1540.M3] 67-21790
1. Artists' materials—Formulae, tables, etc. I. Title. BIP

Artists, Mentally handicapped—England—Cornwall—Biography.

JONES, Ruth. 759.2 B
The path of the son : a biography of Bryan Pearce / by Ruth Jones. Sheviock : Sheviock Gallery Publications, 1976. 104 p., [20] p. of plates : ill. (some col.), ports. ; 22 cm. [N6797.P34J65] 76-380640 ISBN 0-9504904-0-7 : £3.95
1. Pearce, Bryan. 2. Artists, Mentally handicapped—England—Cornwall—Biography. I. Title.

Artists, Mexican.

MERIDA, Carlos, 1893- 760'.0922
Modern Mexican artists; critical notes. Freeport, N. Y., Books for Libraries Press [1968] 202 p. illus. 23 cm. (Essay index reprint series) Reprint of the 1937 ed. [N6555.M4 1968] 68-22931
1. Artists, Mexican. 2. Paintings, Mexican. I. Title. BIP

STEWART, Virginia, 1909- 709.72
45 contemporary Mexican artists; a twentieth-century renaissance. Stanford, Calif., Stanford University Press [1951] xix, 167 p. illus., ports. 29 cm. (Stanford art series) Bibliography: p. [161]-167. [N6558.S8] 51-14200
1. Artists, Mexican. I. Title. II. Series.

VELAZQUEZ CHAVEZ, 759.972
Agustin.
Contemporary Mexican artists. Freeport, N.Y., Books for Libraries Press [1969] 304 p. illus. 23 cm. (Essay index reprint series) Reprint of the 1937 ed. Bibliography: p. 285-304. [ND255.V38 1969] 77-88034
1. Artists, Mexican. 2. Art, Mexican. I. Title. BIP

Artists—Michigan—Biography.

GIBSON, Arthur Hopkin. 709'.2'2 B
Artists of early Michigan : a biographical dictionary of artists native to or active in Michigan, 1701-1900 / compiled by Arthur Hopkin Gibson ; research assistants, Beverly Bassett and Jean Spang. Detroit : Wayne State University Press, 1975. 249 p. : ill. ; 24 cm. Bibliography: p. 19-31. [N6530.M5G52] 74-32480 ISBN 0-8143-1528-3 : 9.95
1. Artists—Michigan—Biography. I. Bassett, Beverly. II. Spang, Jean. III. Title. BIP

Artists—Netherlands—Biography.

BAILEY, Anthony. 759.9492 B
Rembrandt's house / Anthony Bailey. Boston : Houghton Mifflin, 1978. 246 p. : ill. ; 24 cm. Includes index. Bibliography: p. 237-240. [N6953.R4B25] 77-26987 ISBN 0-395-25706-9 : 15.00
1. Rembrandt Harmenszoon van Rijn, 1606-1669. 2. Artists—Netherlands—Biography. 3. Rembrandthuis. 4. Amsterdam—Social life and customs. I. Title. BIP

CLARK, Kenneth 759.9492 B
McKenzie, Baron Clark, 1903-
An introduction to Rembrandt / Kenneth Clark. 1st U.S. ed. New York : Harper & Row, c1978. 153 p. : ill. ; 25 cm. (Icon editions) "Based on a series of television programmes ... made for the Ashwood Trust." Includes index. [N6953.R4C55 1978] 77-3745 ISBN 0-06-430860-X : 12.95
1. Rembrandt Harmenszoon van Rijn, 1606-1669. 2. Artists—Netherlands—Biography. I. Title.

DAVIES, Alice I., 760'.092'4
1943-
Allart van Everdingen / Alice I. Davies. New York : Garland Pub., 1979 p. cm. (Outstanding dissertations in the fine arts) Originally presented as the author's thesis, Harvard, 1973. Bibliography: p. [N6953.E93D38 1978] 77-94692 ISBN 0-8240-3223-3 lib bdg : 52.50
1. Everdingen, Allart van, 1621-1675. 2. Artists—Netherlands—Biography. I. Everdingen, Allart van, 1621-1675. II. Title. III. Series. BIP

Artists—New England—Biography.

ROBINSON, Frank Torrey, 1845-1898. 759.14 B
Living New England artists / Frank T. Robinson. New York : Garland Pub., 1977 [c1888] 200 p., 27 leaves of plates : ill. ; 24 cm. (The Art experience in late nineteenth-century America) Reprint of the ed. published by S. E. Cassino, Boston. [N6515.R6 1977] 75-28880 ISBN 0-8240-2238-6 lib.bdg. : 30.00
1. Artists—New England—Biography. 2. Art, American—New England. 3. Art, Modern—19th century—New England. I. Title. II. Title: New England artists. III. Series. BIP

Artists—Northumberland, Eng.—Biography—Dictionaries.

HALL, Marshall. 760'.092'2 B
The artists of Northumbria: a dictionary of Northumberland and Durham painters, draughtsmen and engravers, born 1647-1900. Newcastle upon Tyne, Marshall Hall Associates, 1973. 72, 32 p. illus., ports. (on lining papers) 29 cm. (Artists of the regions series [1]) Bibliography: p. 72. [N6769.N79H34] 73-178417 ISBN 0-903858-00-2 £3.00
1. Artists—Northumberland, Eng.—Biography—Dictionaries. 2. Artists—Durham, Eng. (County)—Biography—Dictionaries. I. Title.

Artists—Portraits.

BASKIN, Leonard, 1922- 769'.924
Laus pictorum; portraits of nineteenth century artists invented and engraved by Leonard Baskin. Northampton [Mass.] Gehenna Press [1969] [9] p., 15 plates (1 col.) (in portfolio) 38 cm. "One hundred copies have a double set of the portraits ... numbered I to C: seventy-five copies have in addition ... an extra suite of the portraits and are numbered CI to CLXXV: one hundred & seventy-five copies have a single set of matted portraits and are numbered 1 to 175. A group of artist's sets are lettered A to ZZ." No. 175. "Notes on the artists": p. [3-8] [NE539.B3A48] 77-20674
1. Artists—Portraits. I. Title.

BOUCHE, Rene, 1905-1963. 759.37
Rene Bouche: portraits of figures in the arts. Foreword and acknowledgement by Elayne H. Varian. [Exhibition at the] Contemporary Wing, Finch College Museum of Art, opening October 4, 1967. [New York, 1967] [16] p. ports. 28 cm. [ND237.B735V3] 67-30695
I. Varian, Elayne H. II. Finch College, New York. Museum of Art. Contemporary Study Wing. III. Title: Portraits of figures in the arts.

KNOPF, Alfred A., 1892- 779'.2'0924
Sixty photographs : to celebrate the sixtieth anniversary of Alfred A. Knopf, publisher / Alfred A. Knopf. 1st ed. New York : Knopf, 1975. 61 p. : ports. ; 23 cm. [NX90.K56 1975] 75-8235 ISBN 0-394-49892-5 : 10.00. ISBN 0-394-73097-6 pbk. : 5.95
1. Artists—Portraits. I. Title. BIP

Artists' preparatory studies.

ESHERICK, Wharton. 741.9'73
Drawings by Wharton Esherick / compiled, edited, and with an introd. by Gene Rochberg. New York : Van Nostrand Reinhold, c1978. [112] p. : chiefly ill. ; 29 cm. [NC139.E83A4 1978] 77-70383 ISBN 0-442-26967-6 : 15.00
1. Esherick, Wharton. 2. Artists' preparatory studies. I. Rochberg, Gene. II. Title. BIP

O'GORMAN, James F. 720'.92'4
H. H. Richardson and his office, a centennial of his move to Boston, 1874 : selected drawings : [exhibition organized by the Department of Printing and Graphic Arts, Harvard College Library, Fogg Art Museum, Harvard University, October 23-December 8, 1974, Albany Institute of History and Art, January 7-February 23, 1975, Renwick Gallery, Washington, D.C., The National Collection of Fine Arts, Smithsonian Institution, March 21-June 22, 1975 : catalogue] / [James F. O'Gorman]. [Cambridge, Mass.] : Dept. of Printing and Graphic Arts, Harvard College Library, 1974. xii, 220 p., [8] leaves of plates : ill. (some col.) ; 22 x 28 cm. Includes bibliographical references and index. [NA737.R5O35] 74-80839 ISBN 0-914630-00-8
1. Richardson, Henry Hobson, 1836-1886. 2. Artists' preparatory studies. I. Richardson, Henry Hobson, 1838-1886. II. Harvard University. Library. Dept. of Printing and Graphic Arts. III. Harvard University. William Hayes Fogg Art Museum. IV. Albany Institute of History and Art. V. Renwick Gallery. VI. Title.

Artists' preparatory studies—England—Exhibitions.

LIVERPOOL. Public Libraries, Museums, and Art Gallery. Walker Art Gallery. 726'.595
Ceri Richards and the Metropolitan Cathedral of Christ the King : [catalogue of an exhibition held at the] Walker Art Gallery, Liverpool, 1975-6. [Liverpool] : [Walker Art Gallery], [1976] 15 p. : ill. ; 25 cm. [NC242.R52L58 1976] 77-355315 ISBN 0-901534-34-X : £0.50
1. Richards, Ceri, 1903-1971. 2. Liverpool. Metropolitan Cathedral of Christ the King. 3. Artists' preparatory studies—England—Exhibitions. I. Richards, Ceri, 1903-1971. II. Title.

Artists' preparatory studies—Exhibitions.

GINSBURG, Susan. 730'.973
3d into 2d: drawing for sculpture; an exhibition organized by Susan Ginsburg, January 19-March 11, 1973, New York Cultural Center, in association with the Fairleigh Dickinson University. [New York, New York Cultural Center, 1973] 32 p. illus. 23 cm. [N7433.5.G56] 73-75017
1. Artists' preparatory studies—Exhibitions. 2. Artists' preparatory studies—United States. I. New York Cultural Center. II. Title.

PERRY, Meira K. 741.9'074'01447
The finished study and its object; catalogue and exhibition by Meira K. Perry. [Boston, Printed by Two-Penny Press, 1972] 27 p. illus. 18 cm. "250 copies." An exhibition organized as the equivalent of the author's master's thesis, Wellesley College; held at the Wellesley College Art Museum, Jewett Arts Center, Sept. 10-Oct. 10, 1972. Includes bibliographical references. [N7433.5.P47] 72-89379
1. Artists' preparatory studies—Exhibitions. 2. Art—Exhibitions. I. Wellesley College. Jewett Arts Center. II. Title.

UNITED States. National Gallery of Art. 769'.92'4
Jacques Callot prints & related drawings / H. Diane Russell, Jeffrey Blanchard, theater section ; John Krill, technical appendix. Washington : National Gallery of Art, 1975. xxiv, 351 p. : ill. ; 22 x 29 cm. "Exhibition dates at the National Gallery of Art: June 29-September 14, 1975." Includes index. Bibliography: p. 342-344. [NE650.C3U52 1975] 75-14429
1. Callot, Jacques, 1592-1635. 2. Artists' preparatory studies—Exhibitions. I. Russell, Helen Diane. II. Blanchard, Jeffrey. III. Title.

Artists' preparatory studies—France.

COLTON, Judith, 1943- 709'.2'4
The Parnasse francois : Titon du Tillet and the origins of the monument to genius / Judith Colton. New Haven : Yale University Press, 1979. p. cm. (Yale publications in the history of the art ; 27) Includes index. [N6853.T48C64] 78-9878 ISBN 0-300-02270-0 : 25.00
1. Titon du Tillet, Evrard, 1677-1762. Parnasse francois. 2. Artists' preparatory studies—France. I. Title. II. Series. BIP

EIDELBERG, Martin P. 760'.092'4
Watteau's drawings : their use and significance / Martin P. Eidelberg. New York : Garland Pub., 1977. vi, xiv, 277 p., [52] leaves of plates : ill. ; 21 cm. (Outstanding dissertations in the fine arts) Thesis—Princeton. Bibliography : p. [271]-277. [NC248.W3E36] 76-23616 ISBN 0-8240-2687-X lib.bdg. : 40.00
1. Watteau, Jean Antoine, 1684-1721. 2. Artists' preparatory studies—France. I. Title. II. Series. BIP

Artists' preparatory studies—Great Britain.

BIRMINGHAM Museums and Art Gallery. 741.9'42
Pre-Raphaelite drawings : Dante Gabriel Rossetti / Andrea Rose. Chicago : University of Chicago Press, 1977. 72 p. ; 23 cm. & microfiche (3 sheets : all ill. ; 11 x 15 cm.) in pocket. (A University of Chicago Press text-fiche) At head of title: Birmingham Museums and Art Gallery. [NC242.R646B57 1977] 77-24058 ISBN 0-226-68840-2 : 23.00
1. Rossetti, Dante Gabriel, 1828-1882. 2. Artists' preparatory studies—Great Britain. 3. Preraphaelitism—Great Britain. I. Rose, Andrea. II. Title.

Artists' preparatory studies—United States.

GROSS, Chaim, 1904- 730'.92'4
Chaim Gross: sculpture and drawings. Washington, Published for National Collection of Fine Arts by Smithsonian Institution Press; [for sale by the Supt. of Docs., U.S. Govt. Print Off.] 1974. 47 p. illus. 26 cm. ([Smithsonian Institution Press publication, no. 5243]) Text by J. Flint. Catalog of an exhibition held Sept. 13-Nov.24, 1974, at the National Collection of Fine Arts Smithsonian Institution. Bibliography: p. 43-45. [NB237.G85F55] 74-18237
1. Gross, Chaim, 1904- 2. Artists' preparatory studies—United States. I. Flint, Janet A. II. Smithsonian Institution. National Collection of Fine Arts. III. Title.

MORRIS, Robert, 1931- 741.9'73
Robert Morris/projects. [Catalogue of an exhibition] Institute of Contemporary Art, University of Pennsylvania, Philadelphia, March 23 to April 27, 1974. [Philadelphia, Institute of Contemporary Art, University of Pennsylvania, 1974] [24] p. illus. 22 x 28 cm. Bibliography: p. [23] [NC139.M66P46] 74-176094 ISBN 0-88454-013-8
1. Morris, Robert, 1931- 2. Artists' preparatory studies—United States. I. Pennsylvania. University. Institute of Contemporary Art. II. Title.

Artists' preparatory studies—United States—Exhibitions.

JOE and Emily Lowe Art Gallery. 760'.092'4
The mural art of Ben Shahn : original cartoons, drawings, prints, and dated paintings, September 28-October 30, 1977 : a loan exhibition / organized by the Joe and Emily Lowe Art Gallery, Sims Hall, College of Visual and Performing Arts, Syracuse University. Syracuse, N.Y. : The Gallery, c1977. [24] p. : ill. ; 28 cm. Bibliography: p. [20] [N6537.S5A4 1977] 78-100275
1. Shahn, Ben, 1898-1969—Exhibitions. 2. Artists' preparatory studies—United States—Exhibitions. I. Shahn, Ben, 1898-1969. II. Title.

Artists—Psychology.

ARNHEIM, Rudolf. 701.15
Art and visual perception: a psychology of the creative eye. Berkeley, University of California Press, 1954. x, 408 p. illus. (part col.) 29 cm. Bibliography: p. [395]-401. [N70.A68] 54-6467
1. Artists—Psychology. I. Title. BIP

BARRON, Frank X., 1922- 707
Artists in the making [by] Frank Barron. With the collaboration or assistance in particular chapters of: Wallace B. Hall [and others] New York, Seminar Press, 1972. xix, 237 p. 24 cm. Bibliography: p. [229]-232. [NX165.B3] 72-77220 ISBN 0-12-806850-7
1. Artists—Psychology. 2. The arts—Study and teaching. I. Title. BIP

GETZELS, Jacob W. 701'.15
Problem finding and creativity : a longitudinal study of artists / Jacob W. Getzels and Mihaly Csikszentmihalyi. New York : Wiley, c1976. p. cm. "A Wiley-Interscience publication." Includes index. Bibliography: p. [N71.G4] 76-16862 ISBN 0-471-01486-9
1. Artists—Psychology. 2. Self-perception. 3. Creation (Literary, artistic, etc.) I. Csikszentmihalyi, Mihaly, joint author. II. Title.

HAMMER, Emanuel Frederick 706.907
Creativity; an exploratory investigation of the personalities of gifted adolescent artists. New York, Random House [c.1961] 150p. illus. (Studies in psychology, PP20) Bibl. 61-8789 1.25 pap.,
1. Artists—Psychology. 2. Children as artists. 3. Gifted children. 4. Creation (Literary, artistic, etc.) I. Title.

THE Looney tunes poster book / introd. by Mel Blanc. New York : Harmony Books, c1979. p. cm. [PN1997.5.L6] 78-24549 ISBN 0-517-53680-3. : 7.95 769'.5
1. Looney tunes cartoon (Motion picture)—Posters. 2. Moving-picture cartoons—Posters. I. Blanc, Mel.

OERI, Georgine. 701.15
Man and his images; a way of seeing. New York, Viking Press [1968] 155 p. illus. (part col.) 25 cm. (A Studio-book) [N71.O32 1968] 68-23208 8.95
1. Artists—Psychology. 2. Imagination. I. Title.

READ, Herbert Edward, Sir, 1893-1968. 701.15
Art and alienation; the role of the artist in society [by] Herbert Read. [1st American ed.] New York, Horizon Press [1967] 176 p. illus. 25 cm. "Text references": p. [166]-169. [N71.R4 1967b] 67-25449
1. Artists—Psychology. 2. Art and society. I. Title.

WITTKOWER, Rudolf. 706.972
Born under Saturn; the character and conduct of artists: a documented history from antiquity to the French Revolution [by] Rudolf and Margot Wittkower. New York, Random House [1963] 344 p. illus. 25 cm. Includes bibliography. [N71.W54] 63-7128
1. Artists — Psychology. 2. Artists. I. Wittkower, Margot, joint author. II. Title. BIP

Artists — San Francisco Bay region.

THIEL, Yvonne Greer. 927
Artists and people. New York, Philsophical Library [1960, c1959] 327 p. illus. 22 cm. [N6535.S3T45] 60-247
1. Artists — San Francisco Bay region. 2. Artists — Psychology. I. Title.

Artists—South Africa—Biography.

SCHOLTZ, Johannes Du Plessis. 730'.92'4 B
Moses Kottler : his Cape years / J. du P. Scholtz. 1st ed. Cape Town : Tafelberg, 1976. 134 p. : ill. ; 29 cm. Includes catalogue illustrations and catalogue of paintings and sculptures. Includes bibliographical references and index. [N7396.K67S36] 77-355339 ISBN 0-624-00956-4
1. Kottler, Moses, 1896- 2. Artists—South Africa—Biography. I. Kottler, Moses, 1896-

Artists—South Dakota—Directories.

SOUTH Dakota Memorial Art Center. 709'.2'2
Index of South Dakota artists / Joseph Stuart, editor ; compiled and edited by the staff of the South Dakota Memorial Art Center of South Dakota State University in Brookings, 1972-74. Brookings : The Center, [1974] 1 v. ; 28 cm. Loose-leaf for updating. Includes bibliography. [N6530.S68S68 1974] 74-8832
1. Artists—South Dakota—Directories. I. Stuart, Joseph, 1932- ed. II. Title.

SUBJECT INDEX

ARTISTS—UNITED STATES—CORRESPONDENCE, REMINISCENCES

Artists—Spain—Biography.

TAPIES Puig, Antonio, 1923- 709'.2'4 B
Tapies / Roland Penrose. New York : Rizzoli, 1978. 278 p. : ill. (some col.) ; 25 cm. Bibliography: p. 263-270. [N7113.T3A4 1978] 77-88715 ISBN 0-8478-0155-1 : 25.00
1. Tapies Puig, Antonio, 1923- 2. Artists—Spain—Biography. I. Penrose, Roland, Sir.

Artists—Spain—Interviews

PORCEL, Baltasar. 709'.2'2
La palabra del arte / Baltasar Porcel. Madrid : Ediciones Rayuela, 1976. 222 p. : ill. ; 20 cm. (Coleccion Maniluvios ; 4) [N7108.P67] 77-451598 ISBN 8-485-25307-8
1. Artists—Spain—Interviews 2. Art, Modern—20th century—Spain. I. Title.

Artists' studios—Italy—Venice.

SCHULZ, Anne Markham, 1938- 730'.92'2
The sculpture of Giovanni and Bartolomeo Bon and their workshop / Anne Markham Schulz. Philadelphia : American Philosophical Society, 1978. 81 p. : ill. ; 29 cm. (Transactions of the American Philosophical Society ; v. 68. pt. 3 ISSN 0065-9746s) Includes bibliographical references and index.I[NB623.B718S38] 78-50190 ISBN 0-87169-683-5 : 6.00
1. Bon, Giovanni, ca. 1360-1443. 2. Bon, Bartolomeo, ca. 1407-1467. 3. Artists' studios—Italy—Venice. 4. Sculpture, Gothic—Italy—Venice. I. Title. II. Series: American Philosophical Society, Philadelphia. Transactions ; v. 68, pt. 3.

Artists—Texas—Biography.

MCGUIRE, James Patrick. 760'.092'4 B
Iwonski in Texas : painter and citizen / James Patrick McGuire. [San Antonio] : San Antonio Museum Association, c1976. 96 p. : ill. (some col.) ; 24 cm. "Published in conjunction with an exhibition, Iwonski in Texas: painter and citizen, held at the Witte Memorial Museum, Brackenridge Park, San Antonio, Texas, August 1, 1976, to September 30, 1976, in cooperation with the University of Texas at San Antonio Institute of Texan Cultures." Includes index. Bibliography: p. 90-92. [N6537.I75M3] 76-12295
1. Iwonski, Carl G. von, 1830-1922. 2. Artists—Texas—Biography. I. Witte Memorial Museum, San Antonio. II. Title.

Artists' tools—Handbooks, manuals, etc.

STUDLEY, Vance. 702'.8
Making artist's tools / Vance Studley. New York : Van Nostrand Reinhold, 1978. p. cm. Includes index. Bibliography: p. [N8543.S88] 78-18233 ISBN 0-442-27903-5 : 14.00
1. Artists' tools—Handbooks, manuals, etc. I. Title. BIP

Artists—United States.

JOHNSTON, Randolph Wardell, 1904- 730'.92'4 B
Artist on his island : a study in self-reliance / by Randolph W. Johnston ; with notes by Denny Johnston. Park Ridge, N.J. : Noyes Press, [1976] c1975. 186 p. : ill. ; 23 cm. [N6537.J66A22] 75-34929 ISBN 0-8155-5042-1 : 8.95
1. Johnston, Randolph Wardell, 1904- 2. Artists—United States. 3. Artists—Bahamas—Great Abaco Island. I. Title.

*KYSAR, Flossie. 745.5
Young artists, bks. 7 & 8. Columbus, C. E. Merrill [1968] JHS price unreported
I. Title.

Artists—United States—Archives.

ARCHIVES of American Art. 016.709'73
A checklist of the collection, spring 1975 / Archives of American Art ; compiled by Arthur J. Breton, Nancy H. Zembala, and Anne P. Nicastro. [Washington] : Smithsonian Institution, [1975] ca 150 p. ; 27 cm. [Z6616.A2A68 1975] [N6536] 76-600745
1. Archives of American Art. 2. Artists—United States—Archives. I. Breton, Arthur J. II. Zembala, Nancy H. III. Nicastro, Anne P.

Artists—United States—Archives—Exhibitions.

ARCHIVES of American Art. 709'.2'2
From reliable sources : an exhibition of letters, photographs, and other documents from the collections of the Archives of American Art, Smithsonian Institution, commemorating the 20th anniversary of the founding of the Archives, Gallery of the Archives of American Art. Washington : The Archives, c1974. [64] p. : ill. ; 26 cm. [Z6616.A2A68 1974] [N6536] 74-19501
1. Artists—United States—Archives—Exhibitions. I. Title.

Artists—United States—Biography.

AULT, Louise. 759.13 B
Artist in Woodstock : George Ault, the independent years / by Louise Ault. Philadelphia : Dorrance, c1978. 176 p., [1] leaf of plates : ill. ; 22 cm. [N6537.A9A9] 78-57264 ISBN 0-8059-2550-3 : 7.95
1. Ault, George, 1891-1948. 2. Ault, Louise. 3. Artists—United States—Biography. 4. Wives—United States—Biography. I. Title.

CHAMPNEY, Benjamin, 1817-1907. 704'.7 B
Sixty years' memories of art and artists. by Benjamin Champney ; [edited with an introduction by H. Barbara Weinberg]. [New York : Garland Pub., 1977] c1899. 178 p., [13] leaves of plates : ill. ; 19 cm. (The Art experience in late nineteenth-century America) Title page preceded by introd. (13 p.). Reprint of the 1900 ed. published by The News Print., Wallace & Andrews, Woburn, Mass. [N6537.C46A25 1977] 75-28887 ISBN 0-8240-2244-0 lib.bdg. : 25.00
1. Champney, Benjamin, 1817-1907. 2. Artists—United States—Biography. 3. Art, American—History. 4. Art, Modern—19th century—United States—History. I. Title. II. Series. BIP

CRICHTON, Michael, 1942- 709'.2'4
Jasper Johns / by Michael Crichton. New York : Abrams, 1977. p. cm. Bibliography: p. [N6537.J6C74] 77-78150 ISBN 0-8109-1161-2 : 28.50
1. Johns, Jasper, 1930- 2. Artists—United States—Biography. I. Johns, Jasper, 1930-

CUMMINGS, Paul. 709'.22
Dictionary of contemporary American artists / Paul Cummings. 3d ed. New York : St. Martin's Press, 1976. p. cm. Includes index. Bibliography: p. [N6536.C8 1976] 76-10548 35.00
1. Artists—United States—Biography. I. Title.

DAWDY, Doris Ostrander. 709'.2'2
Artists of the American West : a biographical dictionary / Doris Ostrander Dawdy. 1st ed. Chicago : Sage Books, [1974] viii, 275 p. ; 24 cm. Bibliography: p. 261-275. [N6536.D38] 72-91919 ISBN 0-8040-0607-5 : 12.50
1. Artists—United States—Biography. 2. Artists—Biography. 3. The West in art. I. Title. BIP

DUBOIS, June, 1927- 709'.2'4 B
William R. Leigh, artist of frontiers / by June DuBois. Kansas City, Mo. : Lowell Press, [1977] p. cm. [N6537.L423D8] 77-15343 ISBN 0-913504-42-4 : 40.00
1. Leigh, William Robinson, 1866-1955. 2. Artists—United States—Biography. 3. The West in the art. I. Title.

FINNEY, Ben, 1900- 917.3'03'910924 B
Feet first. Foreword by John O'Hara. With five decades of personal photographs. New York, Crown [1971] 255 p. illus., ports. 22 cm. [CT275.F5544A3 1971] 78-151020 5.95
I. Title.

KIMBROUGH, Sara Dodge. 709'.2'2 B
Drawn from life : the story of four American artists whose friendship & work began in Paris during the 1880s / by Sara Dodge Kimbrough. Jackson : University Press of Mississippi, 1976. 177 p., [16] leaves of plates : ill. ; 24 cm. Includes index. [N6536.K55] 76-5682 ISBN 0-87805-073-6 : 12.00
1. Artists—United States—Biography. 2. Artists—Paris—Biography. 3. Art, Modern—19th century—Paris. 4. Art—Paris. I. Title.

LAMB, Thomas G. 709'.2'4 B
Eight Bears : a biography of E. W. Deming, 1860-1942 / by Thomas G. Lamb. Oklahoma City : Griffin Books, c1978. xiv, 145 p. : ill. (some col.) ; 28 cm. Includes index. Bibliography: p. 133-138. [N6537.D44L35] 78-59986 15.95
1. Deming, Edwin Willard, 1860-1942. 2. Artists—United States—Biography. 3. Indians of North America—Pictorial works. I. Title.

LEWIS, Anne Suydam. 709'.2'4 B
Lockwood de Forest, painter, importer, decorator / foreword by Eva Ingersoll Gatling ; essay by Anne Suydam Lewis. Huntington, N.Y. : Heckscher Museum, 1976. 52 p. : ill. ; 28 cm. & catalog in pocket. Errata sheet inserted. Bibliography: p. 42-43. [N6537.D36L48] 76-53309
1. DeForest, Lockwood, 1850-1932. 2. Artists—United States—Biography. I. DeForest, Lockwood, 1850-1932. II. Heckscher Museum. III. Title.

QUIGLEY, Ed, 1895- 759.13
Ed Quigley, western artist, by Carl Gohs. [Portland, Or., G. H. Quigley, 1971] 168 p. (chiefly illus., part col.) 32 cm. [ND237.Q53G6] 75-174275 18.00
I. Gohs, Carl.

ROSENBERG, Harold. 709'.2'4
Barnett Newman / by Harold Rosenberg. New York : Abrams, [1978] p. cm. (Contemporary artists series) Includes index. Bibliography: p. [N6537.N48R67] 77-25433 ISBN 0-8109-1360-7 : 45.00
1. Newman, Barnett, 1905-1970. 2. Artists—United States—Biography. I. Title. II. Series. BIP

SCHWAB, Arnold T. 709'.2'2 B
A matter of life and death : vital biographical facts about selected American artists / Arnold T. Schwab in cooperation with the Art Libraries Society of North America. New York : Garland Pub., 1977. p. cm. (Garland reference library of the humanities ; v. 90) Includes bibliographical references. [N6536.S35] 76-52694 ISBN 0-8240-9883-8 lib.bdg. : 9.50
1. Artists—United States—Biography. I. Arlis/North America. II. Title.

VANDERBILT, Gloria, 1924- 700'.92'4 B
Woman to woman / by Gloria Vanderbilt. 1st ed. Garden City, N.Y. : Doubleday, 1979. p. cm. [N6537.V33A2 1979] 77-25612 ISBN 0-385-13645-5 : 14.95
1. Vanderbilt, Gloria, 1924- 2. Artists—United States—Biography. I. Title. BIP

VORPAHL, Ben Merchant. 709'.2'4 B
Frederic Remington and the West : with the eye of the mind / by Ben Merchant Vorpahl. Austin : University of Texas Press, c1978. p. cm. Includes bibliographical references and index. [N6537.R4V67] 77-25953 ISBN 0-292-78703-0 : 15.95
1. Remington, Frederic, 1861-1909. 2. Artists—United States—Biography. 3. The West in art. I. Title.

WHO was who in American history, arts and letters. 700.922B 76 bicentennial ed. Chicago : Marquis Who's Who, c1975. xiii, 604 p. ; 27 cm. [NX503.Z8W48] 75-29617 47.50
1. Artists—United States—Biography. 2. Arts, American. I. Marquis-Who's Who, inc. BIP

Artists—United States—Biography—Dictionaries.

FIELDING, Mantle, 1865-1941. 709'.2'2
Dictionary of American painters, sculptors and engravers / by Mantle Fielding. Enl. ed. with over 2,500 new listings of seventeenth, eighteenth, and nineteenth century American artists / edited by Genevieve C. Doran. Greens Farms, Conn. : Modern Books and Crafts, [1974] vi, 455 p. ; 24 cm. Edition of 1971 published under title: Dictionary of American painters, engravers, and sculptors. [N6536.F5 1974] 74-192539 17.50
1. Artists—United States—Biography—Dictionaries. I. Doran, Genevieve C., ed. II. Title.

Artists—United States—Biography—Indexes.

SMITH, Ralph Clifton, 1898- 709'.2'2 B
A biographical index of American artists / by Ralph Clifton Smith. Detroit : Gale Research Co., [1975] c1930. p. cm. Reprint of the ed. published by Williams & Wilkins, Baltimore. [N6536.S6 1975] 79-167186 ISBN 0-8103-4251-0 : 11.00 11.00
1. Artists—United States—Biography—Indexes. I. Title.

Artists—United States—Biography—Juvenile literature.

SIGNIFICANT American artists and architects. 709'.2'2 B Chicago : Childrens Press, [1976] p. cm. Includes index. Brief biographies of 166 American artists and architects arranged alphabetically within broad chronological periods of American history. [N6536.S48] 920 75-20688 ISBN 0-516-05303-5 lib. bdg. : 9.25
1. Artists—United States—Biography—Juvenile literature. 2. Architects—United States—Biography—Juvenile literature. I. Title: Artists and architects. BIP

Artists—United States—Correspondence—Exhibitions.

JOHNSON, Raymond Edward, 1927- 700'.92'4
Correspondence : an exhibition of the letters of Ray Johnson : North Carolina Museum of Art, 31 October-5 December, 1976. [Raleigh] : The Museum, [1976?] 1 portfolio (84 leaves : ill.) ; 30 cm. Title from portfolio. [N6537.J63A33] 77-360309 ISBN 0-88259-085-5 pbk. : 5.00
1. Johnson, Raymond Edward, 1927- 2. Artists—United States—Correspondence—Exhibitions. I. North Carolina. Museum of Art, Raleigh. BIP

Artists—United States—Correspondence, reminiscences, etc.

ANDERSON, Alexander, 1775-1870. 759.13
Autobiography of an early American wood engraver. New York, Traders Press, 1968. [48] p. illus. 63 mm. "Limited to 500 copies ... no. 79." "Alexander Anderson ... a short bibliography": p. [44]-[47] [NE1215.A5A2] 68-5976
I. Title.

LOW, David, 1891- 927.415
Autobiography. New York, Simon and Schuster, 1957 [c1956] 387p. illus. 24cm. [NC1479. 65A2 1957] 57-7304
I. Title.

O'KEEFFE, Georgia, 1887- 741.9'73
Some memories of drawings / Georgia O'Keeffe. New York : Atlantis Editions, 1974. 1 case ([97] p., 21 leaves of plates : 21 ill. (some col.)) ; 23 cm. "One hundred and twenty copies ..." No. T. [NC139.O45A45] 74-14986
1. O'Keeffe, Georgia, 1887- 2. Artists—United States—Correspondence, reminiscences, etc. I. Title. BIP

VEDDER, Elihu, 1836-1923. 759.5 B
The digressions of V. With a new introd. by Robert Lee White. New York, Johnson Reprint Corp., 1970 [c1910] xxiv, xxvi, 521 p. illus., facsim., geneal. table, ports.

24 cm. (Series in American studies) Includes bibliographical references. [ND237.V3A44 1970] 74-108604
1. Title. II. Series.

WHITTREDGE, Worthington, 1820-1910. 759.13
The autobiography of Worthington Whittredge, 1820-1910. Edited by John I. H. Baur. New York, Arno Press, 1969 [c1942] 68 p. illus., port. 27 cm. Originally published in 1942 in the Journal of the Brooklyn Museum. [ND237.W624A3] 74-85661 10.00

Artists—United States—Directories.

CENTER for Contemporary Celebration. 700'.25'73
Directory of artists and religious communities / edited by the Center for Contemporary Celebration. West Lafayette, Ind. : The Center, [1975] iii, 145 p. ; 23 cm. [NX110.C46 1975] 75-318304
1. Artists—United States—Directories. 2. Arts—United States—Directories. 3. Art and religion. 4. Christian art and symbolism. I. Title.

Artists, Women.

KIRKLAND, Winifred Margaretta, 1872-1943. 709.73
First who became artists, by Winifred and Frances Kirkland. Freeport, N. Y., Books for Libraries Press [1967] 115 p. 22 cm.. (Essay index reprint series) Reprint of the 1934 ed. [N43.K5 1967] 67-26753
1. Artists, Women. I. Kirkland, Frances, joint author. II. Title.
Contents omitted.

KIRKLAND, Winifred Margaretta, 1872-1943. 709.73
Girls who became artists, by Winifred and Frances Kirkland. Freeport, N.Y., Books for Libraries Press [1967] 115 p. 22 cm. (Essay index reprint series) Reprint of the 1934 ed. Contents.Contents.—Wanda Gag, who followed her own way.—Pamela Bianco, famous since she was twelve.—Marguerite Kirmse, etcher of dogs.—Margaret Bourke-White, photographer of steel.—Meta Warrick Fuller, leading sculptor of her race.—Cecilia Beaux, painter behind the portraits.—Madame le Brun, playmate of Marie Antoinette.—Angelica Kauffmann, the picture-worker.—Janet Scudder, a girl who made her own name.—Anna Hyatt Huntington, who loved horses.—Malvina Hoffman, sculptor of types. [N43.K5 1967] 67-26753
1. Artists, Women. I. Kirkland, Frances, joint author. II. Title. BIP

The arts.

THE Arts and man; 700
a world view of the role and functions of the arts in society. [1st American ed.] Englewood Cliffs, N.J., Prentice-Hall, 1969. 171 p. illus. (part col.), ports. 32 cm. [NX60.A7 1969] 75-87973 12.95
1. The arts.

DUDLEY, Louise, 1884- 700'.1
The humanities / Louise Dudley, Austin Faricy. 6th ed. / rev. by James G. Rice. New York : McGraw-Hill, c1978. vii, 536 p., [24] leaves of plates : ill. (some col.) ; 24 cm. Includes index. Bibliography: p. 500-519. [NX440.D82 1978] 77-22110 ISBN 0-07-017971-9 : 14.95
1. Arts. I. Faricy, Austin, joint author. II. Rice, James G. III. Title.

DUDLEY, Louise, 1884- 700'.1
The humanities [by] Louise Dudley and Austin Faricy. rev. and expanded by the editorial staff of McGraw-Hill. 5th ed., rev. and expanded by the editorial staff of McGraw-Hill. New York, McGraw-Hill [1973] xix, 439 p. illus. (part col.) 25 cm. Bibliography: p. 418-424. [NX440.D82 1973] 72-12766 ISBN 0-07-017970-0 10.95
1. The arts. I. Faricy, Austin. II. McGraw-Hill Book Company. III. Title.

DUDLEY, Louise, 1884- 700.1
The humanities; applied aesthetics [by] Louise Dudley [and] Austin Faricy. 4th ed. New York, McGraw-Hill [1967] xxi, 436 p. illus., music. 23 cm. Includes bibliographical references. [N7425.D8 1967] 67-12622
1. The arts. I. Faricy, Austin. II. Title.

GREENE, Theodore Meyer, 1897- 700'.1
The arts and the art of criticism. New York, Gordian Press, 1973 [c1940] xxxii, 690 p. illus. 25 cm. Includes music. Reprint of the 1952 ed. published by Princeton University Press, Princeton. Includes bibliographical references. [NX640.G73 1973] 73-16391 ISBN 0-87752-162-X 22.50
1. Arts. 2. Art criticism. I. Title. BIP

JULLIAN, Philippe. 759.05
Dreamers of decadence; symbolist painters of the 1890s. [Translated by Robert Baldick] New York, Praeger [1971] 272 p. illus. (part col.) 26 cm. Translation of Esthetes et magiciens. [NX454.J813] 77-147094 12.50
1. The arts. 2. Art nouveau. I. Title.

KAREL, Leon C. 700
Avenues to the arts; a general arts textbook, by Leon C. Karel. [2d ed.] Kirksville, Mo. [Printed by Simpson Pub. Co., 1969] 333 p. illus. (part col.), music. 23 cm. [NX620.K36 1969] 68-8836
1. The arts. I. Title.

MALVERN, Marjorie M. 704.948'6
Venus in sackcloth : the Magdalen's origins and metamorphoses / by Marjorie M. Malvern. Carbondale : Southern Illinois University Press, [1975] xiii, 219 p. : ill. ; 25 cm. Includes index. Bibliography: p. 207-212. [NX652.M27M34] 75-6197 ISBN 0-8093-0707-3 : 8.95
1. Mary Magdalene, Saint—Art. 2. Mary Magdalene, Saint. 3. Arts. I. Title.

SPORRE, Dennis J. 700'.1
Perceiving the arts : an introduction / Dennis J. Sporre. Dubuque, Iowa : Kendall/Hunt Pub. Co., c1978. v, 166 p. : ill. ; 24 cm. [NX620.S68] 78-56646 ISBN 0-8403-1884-7 : 7.75
1. Arts. 2. Perception. 3. Visual perception. I. Title.

VAN DE BOGAT, Doris 700'.9
Introduction to the humanities; painting, sculpture, architecture, music, and literature. New York, Barnes & Noble [1968] xviii, 422 p. illus. 22 cm. Bibliography: p. 357-371. [NX440.V3] 67-29656
1. The arts. I. Title. BIP

VYVERBERG, Henry. 700'.9
The living tradition : art, music, and ideas in the Western World / Henry Vyverberg. New York : Harcourt Brace Jovanovich, c1978. xii, 385 p., [16] leaves of plates : ill. (some col.) ; 26 cm. Includes index. [NX440.V95] 77-86480 ISBN 0-15-551125-4 : 12.95
1. Arts. I. Title. BIP

WALLIS, Mieczyslaw. 700'.9
Arts and signs / Mieczyslaw Wallis. Bloomington : Indiana University, 1976, c1975 ix, 102 p. ; 23 cm. (Indiana University publications) (Studies in semiotics ; v. 2) Includes bibliographical references. [NX445.W34] 75-18437 ISBN 0-87750-188-2 : 6.00
1. Arts. 2. Semiotics. I. Title. II. Series. BIP

Arts—Addresses, essays, lectures.

ART and changing civilization 301.16'1 s
/ edited by Peter Davidson, Rolf Meyersohn, Edward Shils. Cambridge : Chadwyck-Healey ; Teaneck, N.J. : Somerset House, c1978. x, 291 p. ; 25 cm. (Literary taste, culture, and mass communication ; v. 4) Contents.Contents.—Davison, P. Introduction.—Bahr, H. Expressionism.—Lewis, W. Editorial to The enemy.—Gill, E. Art and changing civilization.—Forster, E. M. Art for art's sake. Bibliography: p. [281]. [AC1.L79 vol. 4] [NX60] 700'.9'04 77-90612 ISBN 0-914146-47-5 lib.bdg. : 35.00
1. Arts—Addresses, essays, lectures. 2. Arts, Modern—20th century—Addresses, essays, lectures. I. Title. II. Series.
Contents omitted

ART and confrontation; 700
the arts in an age of change. [Translated from the French by Nigel Foxell] Greenwich, Conn., New York Graphic Society [1970] 201 p. illus. 22 cm. Essays by J. Cassou and others. Includes bibliographical references. [NX60.A6813] 70-86266 7.50
1. The arts—Addresses, essays, lectures. I. Cassou, Jean, 1897-

BACHELARD, Gaston, 1884-1962. 701
The right to dream. Translated from the French by J. A. Underwood. New York, Grossman, 1971. viii, 215 p. 22 cm. (An Orion Press book) Translation of Le droit de rever. Bibliography: p. 214-215. [NX65.B313 1971] 70-159567 ISBN 0-670-59847-X 7.95
1. The arts—Addresses, essays, lectures. I. Title.

BAUDELAIRE, Charles Pierre, 1821-1867. 700'.9
Selected writings on art and artists [of] [Baudelaire,] translated [from the French] with an introduction by P. E. Charvet. Harmondsworth, Penguin, [1972 i.e. 1973] 460 p. 19 cm. (Penguin classics) [NX65.B3813] 73-160489 ISBN 0-14-044276-6 3.95
1. Arts—Addresses, essays, lectures. I. Charvet, Patrick Edward. II. Title.

BERENSON, Bernhard, 1865-1959. 700'.8
Conversations with Berenson / Umberto Morra ; translated from the Italian by Florence Hammond. Westport, Conn. : Greenwood Press, 1975, c1965. x, 305 p. ; 22 cm. Translation of Colloqui con Berenson. Reprint of the 1st American ed. published by Houghton Mifflin, Boston. Includes index. [NX65.B4713 1975] 73-15311 ISBN 0-8371-7181-4 lib.bdg. 14.75
1. Arts—Addresses, essays, lectures. I. Morra, Umberto. II. Title.

BRONOWSKI, Jacob, 1908-1974. 700
The visionary eye : essays in the arts, literature, and science / J. Bronowski ; selected and edited by Piero E. Ariotti in collaboration with Rita Bronowski. Cambridge, Mass. : MIT Press, c1978. x, 185 p. : ill. ; 24 cm. Includes index. [NX65.B696 1978] 78-18163 ISBN 0-262-02129-3 : 14.95
1. Arts—Addresses, essays, lectures. 2. Science and the arts—Addresses, essays, lectures. 3. Imagination—Addresses, essays, lectures. I. Ariotti, Piero E. II. Bronowski, Rita. III. Title. BIP

BROWNELL, Baker, 1887-1965. 700
Art is action; a discussion of nine arts in a modern world. Port Washington, N.Y., Kennikat Press [1972, c1939] vi, 231 p. 23 cm. (Essay and general literature index reprint series) Includes bibliographical references. [NX65.B7 1972] 72-183136 ISBN 0-8046-1690-6
1. The arts—Addresses, essays, lectures. I. Title.

BROWNELL, Baker, 1887-1965. 700
Art is action; a discussion of nine arts in a modern world. Freeport, N.Y., Books for Libraries Press [1969] vi, 231 p. 23 cm. (Essay index reprint series) Reprint of the 1939 ed. Contents.Contents.—The point of view.—Muscular conditions of life and culture.—Art.—Dancing.—Music.—Cooking.—Poetry.—The drama, the novel, the movie.—Architecture.—Painting.—Sculpture.—Costume.—Modern tendencies in the arts.—Arts and symbols.—Art and religion. Bibliographical footnotes. [NX65.B7 1969] 73-90616
1. The arts—Addresses, essays, lectures. I. Title. BIP

CHERRINGTON, Leon G., comp. 947.7'6'06
Aesthetic man: his contemporary values. Edited by Leon G. Cherrington and Richard W. Massa. Berkeley, McCutchan Pub. Corp. [1969] vii, 178 p. 23 cm. Bibliographical footnotes. [NX210.C45] 76-93703 ISBN 8-211-02125-
1. The arts—Addresses, essays, lectures. 2. Aesthetics—Addresses, essays, lectures. I. Massa, Richard W., joint comp. II. Title.

COTT, Jonathan. 700'.8
He dreams what is going on inside his head. [San Francisco, Calif., Straight Arrow Books; distributed by Quick Fox, New York, 1973] 349 p. illus. 21 cm. [NX65.C67] 73-79839 ISBN 0-87932-065-6 5.95
1. Arts—Addresses, essays, lectures. I. Title.

DIDEROT, Denis, 1713-1784. 704.92
Diderot's thoughts on art and style; with some of his shorter essays, selected and translated by Beatrix L. Tollemache. New York, B. Franklin [1971] 291 p. 19 cm. (Burt Franklin research & source works series, 791) (Philosophy monograph series, 72) Reprint of the 1893 ed. [NX65.D513 1971] 77-168922 ISBN 0-8337-4077-6
1. The arts—Addresses, essays, lectures. I. Title. BIP

ENCOUNTERS: 700'.1
essays on literature and the visual arts. Edited by John Dixon Hunt. New York, Norton [1971] 176 p. illus. 26 cm. Includes bibliographical references. [NX620.E5] 79-31288 ISBN 0-289-70026-4 10.00
1. The arts—Addresses, essays, lectures. I. Hunt, John Dixon, ed.

FIEDLER, Leslie A. 809
Cross the border—close the gap [by] Leslie A. Fiedler. New York, Stein and Day [1972, c1971] 148 p. 21 cm. Includes bibliographical references. [NX65.F53 1972] 72-81822 ISBN 0-8128-1479-7 2.95
1. Arts—Addresses, essays, lectures. I. Title.

GREENOUGH, Horatio, 1805-1852. 701
The miscellaneous writings of Horatio Greenough / edited and with an introd. by Nathalia Wright. Delmar, N.Y. : Scholars' Facsimiles & Reprints, 1975. 68 p. ; 22 cm. Contents.Contents.—Review of Poems by Richard H. Dana.—Memorial of Horatio Greenough.—Etchings with a chisel.—When we speak of man.—Burke on the beautiful.—Criticism in search of beauty.—Fashion.—Dress.—A sketch.—The Chinese make a plaything. [NX65.G7 1975] 75-1118 ISBN 0-8201-1152-X
1. Arts—Addresses, essays, lectures. I. Title. BIP

GRIGSON, Geoffrey, 1905- ed. 700'.9'04
The arts to-day, edited, with an introd., by Geoffrey Grigson. Port Washington, N.Y., Kennikat Press [1970] xiv, 301 p. illus., plates, plan. 22 cm. (Essay and general literature index reprint series) Reprint of the 1935 ed. Contents.Contents.—Psychology and art, by W. H. Auden.—Poetry, by L. MacNeice.—Painting and sculpture, by G. Grigson.—Fiction, by A. Calder-Marshall.—Music, by E. Crankshaw.—The theatre, by H. Jennings.—The cinema, by J. Grierson.—Architecture, by J. Summerson. Includes bibliographical references. [NX60.G7 1970] 78-111310
1. The arts—Addresses, essays, lectures. I. Title.

HIGGINS, Ian. 700'.34
Literature and the plastic arts, 1880-1930; seven essays, edited by I. Higgins. New York, Barnes & Noble [1973] x, 120 p. illus. 25 cm. Includes bibliographical references. [NX454.H53] 74-157762 ISBN 0-06-492870-5 7.50
1. Arts—Addresses, essays, lectures. 2. Modernism (Art)—Addresses, essays, lectures. I. Title.

THE Humanities in the schools; 700
a contemporary symposium. Edited by Harold Taylor. New York, Citation Press, 1968. 176 p. ports. 20 cm. Papers presented at a symposium held at and under the auspices of the University of Kentucky in Dec., 1968. Contents.Contents.—The arts and the humanities, by H. Taylor.—Where to begin, by H. Rosenberg.—Language as communication, by S. Spender—Films and the future, by S. Kaufmann.—The conservative arts, by R. Shaw.—A teaching credential for Philoctetes? By E. Z. Friedenberg.—Some ideas for action, by H. Taylor. [NX175.H8] 68-29402 2.65
1. The arts—Addresses, essays, lectures. 2. Humanities—Addresses, essays, lectures. I. Taylor, Harold, 1914- ed. II. Kentucky. University.

JACOB, Hildebrand, 1693-1739. 700
Of the sister arts; an essay. New York,

c1977. x, 501 p. ; 22 cm. Includes bibliographical references. [NX504.H3 1977] 76-51134 ISBN 0-15-570742-6 pbk. : 6.95
1. Arts, American—Addresses, essays, lectures. 2. United States—Popular culture—Addresses, essays, lectures. I. Title.

Arts, American—Exhibitions.

ASSOCIATED Artists of Pittsburgh. 704.94'9'30136
Our environment; 59th annual exhibition, March 7, 1969 to April 10, 1969, Museum of Art, Carnegie Institute, Pittsburgh, Pennsylvania. [Pittsburgh? 1969?] 101 p. illus. 21 x 23 cm. [NX511.P5A8] 72-198354
1. The arts, American—Exhibitions. 2. The arts, American—Pittsburgh. 3. The arts and society—Pittsburgh. I. Pittsburgh. Carnegie Institute. Museum of Art. II. Title.

DALLAS. Museum of Fine Arts. 709'.73
Poets of the cities of New York and San Francisco, 1950-1965 / organized by the Dallas Museum of Fine Arts and Southern Methodist University under the direction of Neil A. Chassman. [New York] : E. P. Dutton, 1974. 175 p. : ill. (some col.) ; 22 x 26 cm. Catalogue of the exhibition held Nov. 20-Dec. 29, 1974 in the Dallas Museum of Fine Arts and the Pollock Galleries, Southern Methodist University, Jan. 31-Mar. 23, 1975 in the San Francisco Museum of Art, and Apr. 23-June 1, 1975 in the Wadsworth Atheneum, Hartford. Bibliography: p. 171-173. [NX511.N4D34 1974] 75-300674 ISBN 0-525-47388-2 pbk. : 9.95
1. Arts, American—Exhibitions. 2. Arts, Modern—20th century—New York (City) 3. Arts, Modern—20th century—San Francisco. I. Chassman, Neil A. II. Dallas. Southern Methodist University. III. Title.

SEVEN decades of MacDowell artists : 700'.9742'8 an exhibition to honor Nancy Hanks, chairman of the National Endowment for the Arts and the National Council on the Arts, at the James Yu Gallery, 393 West Broadway, New York City, New York, October 24 to 28, 1976. New York : MacDowell Colony, c1976. [94] p. : ill. ; 25 cm. [NX504.S48] 76-46769
1. Arts, American—Exhibitions. 2. Arts, Modern—20th century—United States—Exhibitions. I. Hanks, Nancy, 1927- II. James Yu Gallery. III. MacDowell Colony.

WORD, image, number : 700'.973 Sarah Lawrence Gallery, Bronxville, New York, September 23-October 19, 1975. [Bronxville, N.Y.] : Sarah Lawrence College], c1975. [72] p. : ill. ; 21 cm. [NX504.W67] 75-332177 3.00
1. Arts, American—Exhibitions. 2. Arts, Modern—20th century—United States—Exhibitions. 3. Words in art. 4. Numerals in art. 5. Symbolism in art. I. Sarah Lawrence Gallery.

Arts, American—History.

SILVERMAN, Kenneth. 700'.973
A cultural history of the American Revolution : painting, music, literature, and the theatre in the Colonies and the United States from the Treaty of Paris to the Inauguration of George Washington, 1763-1789 / Kenneth Silverman. New York : T. Y. Crowell, c1976. xvii, 699 p. : ill. ; 24 cm. Includes bibliographical references and index. [NX503.5.S54 1976] 75-35947 ISBN 0-690-01079-6 : 17.50
1. Arts, American—History. 2. United States—History—Colonial period, ca. 1600-1775—Miscellanea. 3. United States—History—Revolution, 1775-1783—Miscellanea. 4. United States—History—Confederation, 1783-1789—Miscellanea. I. Title. BIP

Arts, American—New England.

TILT : 700'.974
an anthology of New England women's writing and art. Lebanon, N.H. : New Victoria Publishers, c1978. v, 85 p. : ill. ; 22 x 29 cm. [NX505.T54] 77-84053 pbk. : 5.00
1. Arts, American—New England. 2. Women artists—New England. 3. Feminism and the arts—New England. 4. American literature—Women authors. I. New Victoria Publishers.
Publisher's address: 7 Bank St., Lebanon, NH 03766 BIP

Arts, American—North Carolina.

FOUSHEE, Ola Maie, 1905- 709'.756
Art in North Carolina; episodes and developments, 1585-1970. Chapel Hill, N.C. [1972] xvi, 238 p. illus. 23 cm. [NX510.N8F68] 72-95223 12.85
1. Arts, American—North Carolina. 2. Arts—North Carolina. I. Title.

Arts and children—Washington metropolitan area—Directories.

NAIMON, Judith Sandberg. 700'.7
A guide to cultural arts resources in the Washington area for young people. [Kensington, Md.] Cultural Arts Committee of the Montgomery County Council of Parent-Teacher Associations [1973] vii, 45 p. 28 cm. Bibliography: p. 43-44. [NX505.5.A3W376] 74-166375
1. Arts and children—Washington metropolitan area—Directories. 2. Arts and youth—Washington metropolitan area—Directories. I. National Congress of Parents and Teachers. Maryland Branch. Montgomery County Council. Cultural Arts Committee. II. Title.

Arts and Crafts Exhibition Society, London.

ART and life and the building and decoration of cities 711'.4 / T. J. Cobden-Sanderson, et al. New York : Garland Pub., 1978. 260 p. ; 19 cm. (The Aesthetic movement & the arts and crafts movement) Reprint of the 1897 ed. published by Rivington, Percival, London. Contents.Contents.—Cobden-Sanderson, T. J. Of art and life.—Lethaby, W. R. Of beautiful cities.—Crane, W. Of the decoration of public buildings.—Blomfield, R. Of public spaces, parks, and gardens.—Ricardo, H. Of colour in the architecture of cities. [NA9040.A7 1978] 76-17778 ISBN 0-8240-2484-2 : lib.bdg. : 35.00
1. Arts and Crafts Exhibition Society, London. 2. Art, Municipal—Addresses, essays, lectures. 3. Aesthetics—Addresses, essays, lectures. I. Cobden-Sanderson, Thomas James, 1840-1922. II. Title. III. Series.
Contents omitted

Arts and crafts movement.

ANSCOMBE, Isabelle. 745'.0941
Arts & crafts in Britain and America / Isabelle Anscombe & Charlotte Gere. New York : Rizzoli, 1978. 232 p. : ill. (some col.) ; 26 cm. Includes index. Bibliography: p. 226-229. [NK1142.A5 1978] 78-58700 ISBN 0-8478-0184-5 : 20.00
1. Arts and crafts movement. 2. Art industries and trade—Great Britain—History—19th century. 3. Art industries and trade—Great Britain—History—20th century. 4. Art industries and trade—United States—History—19th century. 5. Art industries and trade—United States—History—20th century. I. Gere, Charlotte, joint author. II. Title. BIP

ASHBEE, Charles Robert, 1863-1942. 338.6'32'0942
Craftmanship in competitive industry / C. R. Ashbee. New York : Garland Pub., 1977, i.e.1978 258 p. : ill. ; 24 cm. (The Aesthetic movement & the arts and crafts movement) Reprint of the 1908 ed. published by Essex House Press, Campden, England. [NK1149.G8A8 1977] 76-17772 ISBN 0-8240-2477-X lib.bdg. : 35.00
1. Guild of handicraft, London. 2. Arts and crafts movement. I. Title. II. Series.

ASHBEE, Charles Robert, 1863-1942. 745.4'49'42
An endeavour towards the teaching of John Ruskin and William Morris. [Folcroft, Pa.] Folcroft Library Editions, 1973. 52 p. 23 cm. Reprint of the 1901 ed. published by E. Arnold, London. [NK1142.A7 1973] 73-7761 10.00
1. Ruskin, John, 1819-1900. 2. Morris, William, 1834-1896. 3. Guild of Handicraft, London. 4. Essex House Press, London. 5. Arts and crafts movement. I. Title.

JACKSON, Holbrook, 1874-1948. 745.4'49'24
William Morris & the arts & crafts. [Folcroft, Pa.] Folcroft Library Editions, 1974. 17 p. 23 cm. Reprint of the 1934 ed. published by the Oriole Press, Berkeley Heights, N.J. [NK1148.J32 1974] 74-18287 ISBN 0-8414-5318-7 (lib. bdg.)
1. Morris, William, 1834-1896. 2. Arts and crafts movement. I. Title. BIP

TRIGGS, Oscar Lovell, 1865-1930. 709
Chapters in the history of the arts and crafts movement. New York, B. Blom, 1971. 198 p. ports. 21 cm. Reprint of the 1902 ed. [NK1140.T8 1971] 73-173126
1. Arts and crafts movement. I. Title. BIP

Arts and crafts movement—Addresses, essays, lectures.

ARTS and Crafts Exhibition Society, London. 745
Arts and crafts essays / [by members of the Arts and Crafts Exhibition Society] ; pref. by William Morris. New York : Garland Pub., 1977. xvii, 420 p. : ill. ; 19 cm. (The Aesthetic movement & the arts and crafts movement) Reprint of the 1893 ed. published by Scribner, New York. [NK1147.A8 1977] 76-17783 ISBN 0-8240-2483-4 lib.bdg. : 35.00
1. Arts and crafts movement—Addresses, essays, lectures. 2. Art industries and trade—Addresses, essays, lectures. I. Title. II. Series. BIP

CRANE, Walter, 1845-1915. 704.9'2
William Morris to Whistler : papers and addresses on art and craft and the commonweal / by Walter Crane ; with ill. from drawings by the author & other sources. Norwood, Pa. : Norwood Editions, 1976. x, 277 p. : ill. ; 23 cm. Reprint of the 1911 ed. published by G. Bell, London. Includes index. Contents.Contents.—William Morris and his work.—The English revival in decorative art.—The socialist ideal as a new inspiration in art.—On the study and practice of art.—On some of the arts and crafts allied to architecture.—Notes on colour embroidery and its treatment.—Notes on early Italian gesso work.—Notes on the treatment of animals in art.—Modern aspects of life and the sense of beauty.—A short survey of the art of the nineteenth century.—Art and the commonweal.—The apotheosis of "The Butterfly". [NK1147.C7 1976] 76-1986 ISBN 0-88305-334-9 lib. bdg. : 22.50
1. Arts and crafts movement—Addresses, essays, lectures. 2. Art—Addresses, essays, lectures. I. Title.

CRANE, Walter, 1845-1915. 704.9'2
William Morris to Whistler; papers and addresses on art and craft and the commonweal. With illus. from drawings by the author & other sources. [Folcroft, Pa.] Folcroft Library Editions, 1973. x, 277 p. illus. 24 cm. Reprint of the 1911 ed. published by G. Bell, London. Contents.Contents.—William Morris and his work.—The English revival in decorative art.—The socialist ideal as a new inspiration in art.—On the study and practice of art.—On some of the arts and crafts allied to architecture.—Notes on colour embroidery and its treatment.—Notes on early Italian gesso work.—Notes on the treatment of animals in art.—Modern aspects of life and the sense of beauty.—A short survey of the art of the nineteenth century, chiefly in England, with some notes on recent developments.—Art and the commonweal.—The apotheosis of "The Butterfly." [NK1147.C7 1973] 73-19972 25.00
1. Arts and crafts movement—Addresses, essays, lectures. 2. Art—Addresses, essays, lectures. I. Title.
Contents omitted. BIP

Arts and crafts movement—Exhibitions.

ARTS and crafts in Detroit 1906-1976 : 707'.4'017434 the movement, the society, the school : the Detroit Institute of Arts, November 26, 1976-January 16, 1977 : exhibition / sponsored by Founders Society Detroit Institute of Arts and the Center for Creative Studies—College of Art and Design. Detroit : The Institute, c1976. 296 p. : ill. (some col.) ; 26 cm. Bibliography: p. 265-293. [NK1137.A77] 77-358697
1. Society of Arts and Crafts, Detroit. 2. Society of Arts and Crafts, Detroit. Art School. 3. Arts and crafts movement—Exhibitions. I. Detroit. Institute of Arts.

Arts and crafts movement—History.

ASLIN, Elizabeth. 709'.03
The aesthetic movement; prelude to Art nouveau. New York, Praeger [1969] 192 p. illus. (part col.), ports. 29 cm. Bibliography: p. 190. [NK1175.A8] 76-84860 15.00
1. Arts and crafts movement—History. I. Title.

The arts and morals—Addresses, essays, lectures.

GIRVETZ, Harry K., 1910- comp. 700
Literature and the arts: the moral issues [by] Harry Girvetz [and] Ralph Ross. Belmont, Calif., Wadsworth Pub. Co. [1971] vi, 297 p. illus. 24 cm. Includes bibliographical references. [NX180.E8G5] 71-150363 ISBN 0-534-00060-6
1. The arts and morals—Addresses, essays, lectures. I. Ross, Ralph Gilbert, 1911- joint comp. II. Title.

Arts and religion.

ROBERTSON, Alec. 700
Contrasts: the arts & religion. [Folcroft, Pa.] Folcroft Library Editions, 1973. p. Reprint of the 1947 ed. published by S.C.M. Press, London. [NX180.R4R62 1973] 73-3418 ISBN 0-8414-2564-7
1. Arts and religion. I. Title.

SCHAEFFER, Edith. 153.3'5
Hidden art. Illustrated by Deirdre Ducker. Wheaton, Ill., Tyndale House [1972, c1971] 213 p. illus. 22 cm. [NX180.R4S32 1972] 70-123287 ISBN 0-8423-1420-2 3.95
1. Arts and religion. 2. Creation (Literary, artistic, etc.) I. Title. BIP

Arts and religion—North Carolina.

THE Arts in the churches and synagogues of North Carolina : 700'.9756 a renaissance / Jean McLaughlin, editor. [Raleigh] : Division of the Arts, North Carolina Dept. of Cultural Resources, 1976. 118 p. : ill. ; 23 cm. "Handbook evolved as a result of a conference held for religious leaders on June 24-25, 1975, at the Quail Roost Conference Center." Includes bibliographies. [NX180.R4A78] 76-375585 1.00
1. Arts and religion—North Carolina. I. McLaughlin, Jean.

Arts and society.

ABERCROMBIE, Nigel. 700
Artists and their public / by Nigel Abercrombie. Paris : Unesco Press, c1975. 123 p. ; 21 cm. Includes bibliographical references. [NX180.S6A2] 76-359209 ISBN 92-3-101252-5 pbk. : 4.95
1. Arts and society. I. Title.
Distributed by UNIPUB. BIP

BAYNES, Ken. 700
Art in society / by Ken Baynes, with contributions by Kate Baynes, and Alan Robinson ; pref. by Milton Glaser. 1st ed. Woodstock, N.Y. : Overlook Press, 1975. 288 p. : ill. (some col.) ; 27 cm. Includes bibliographical references. [NX180.S6B39] 74-21587 ISBN 0-87951-027-7 : 35.00
1. Arts and society. I. Baynes, Kate, joint author. II. Robinson, Alan, joint author. III. Title.

SUBJECT INDEX

THE ARTS—BOSTON.

FAUROT, Albert 709'.599
Culture currents of the world Quezon City, Republic of the Philippines, New Day Publishers [1974] vii, 196 p. ill (some col.) 23 cm. Includes index. Bibliography: p. 189-190. [NX180.S6F38] 74-79586
1. Arts and society. I. Title.
Distributed the Cellar Book Shop for 7.50 (pbk.)

HALL, James B., comp. 701.1
Modern culture and the arts [edited by] James B. Hall [and] Barry Ulanov. New York, McGraw-Hill [1967] xi, 560 p. illus., ports. 22 cm. [N72.S6H3] 67-19148
1. The arts and society. 2. Popular culture. I. Ulanov, Barry, joint comp. II. Title. BIP

HALL, James B., comp. 700'.1
Modern culture and the arts. [Edited by] James B. Hall [and] Barry Ulanov. 2d ed. New York, McGraw-Hill [1972] xvi, 574 p. illus. 22 cm. [NX180.S6H3 1972] 79-177373
1. The arts and society. 2. Popular culture. I. Ulanov, Barry, joint comp. II. Title.

WILSON, Robert Neal, 1924- ed. 701
The arts in society. Englewood Cliffs, N. J., Prentice [1964] xii, 372p. 22cm. Bibl. 64-15597 9.00
I. Title. BIP

The arts and society—Addresses, essays, lectures.

ALBRECHT, Milton C., 1904- comp. 700
The sociology of art and literature; a reader. Edited by Milton C. Albrecht, James H. Barnett, & Mason Griff. New York, Praeger [1970] xiv, 752 p. 25 cm. Includes bibliographies. [NX650.S6A4 1970] 70-76785 15.00
1. The arts and society—Addresses, essays, lectures. I. Barnett, James Harwood, 1906- joint comp. II. Griff, Mason, 1924- joint comp. III. Title.

BARZUN, Jacques, 1907- 700
The use and abuse of art. [Princeton, N.J.] Princeton University Press [1974] 150 p. 27 cm. (Bollingen series, 35. The A. W. Mellon lectures in the fine arts, 22) [NX456.B38] 73-16780 ISBN 0-691-09903-0 6.95
1. Arts and society—Addresses, essays, lectures. 2. Arts, Modern—20th century—Addresses, essays, lectures. 3. Arts and religion—Addresses, essays, lectures. I. Title. II. Series: Bollingen series, 35. III. Series: The A. W. Mellon lectures in the fine arts, 22. BIP

CREEDY, Jean. 700
The social context of art, edited by Jean Creedy. London, New York, Tavistock Publications [1970] 217 p. 23 cm. "Distributed in the USA by Barnes & Noble." Includes bibliographies. [NX650.S6C7] 70-511629 42/-
1. The arts and society—Addresses, essays, lectures. I. Title.

GRANA, Cesar. 301.5'7
Fact and symbol; essays in the sociology of art and literature. New York, Oxford University Press, 1971. ix, 212 p. 22 cm. Includes bibliographical references. [NX180.S6G7] 77-127174 ISBN 0-19-501285-2 7.50
1. The arts and society—Addresses, essays, lectures. I. Title. BIP

THE Sociology of the arts / 700
editors, Mildred Weil and Duncan Hartley. Danville, Ill. : Interstate Printers & Publishers, c1975. xxiii, 179 p. ; 23 cm. Includes bibliographies and index. [NX180.S6S62] 75-7162 pbk. : 4.40
1. Arts and society—Addresses, essays, lectures. I. Weil, Mildred W. II. Hartley, Duncan. BIP

Arts and society—France.

ROBERTS, Warren E. 700'.944
Morality and social class in eighteenth-century French literature and painting / Warren Roberts. Toronto ; Buffalo : University of Toronto Press, [1974] xvi, 188 p., 20 leaves of plates : ill. ; 24 cm. (University of Toronto romance series ; 25) Includes index. Bibliography: p. [165]-180. [NX549.A1R62] 74-187951 ISBN 0-8020-5250-9 : 15.00
1. Arts and society—France. 2. Erotica. 3. Aesthetics, Modern—18th century. I. Title. II. Series: Toronto. University. University of Toronto romance series ; 25. BIP

Arts and society—United States.

ADLER, Judith E., 1944- 301.5'7
Artists in offices : an ethnography of an academic art scene / Judith E. Adler. New Brunswick, N.J. : Transaction Books, c1978. Includes index. Bibliography: p. [NX180.S6A27] 78-55941 ISBN 0-87855-281-2 : 16.95
1. California Institute of the Arts. 2. Arts and society—United States. 3. Arts—Study and teaching (Higher)—United States. 4. Arts, Modern—20th century—United States. I. Title.

BURNS, Joan Simpson. 301.2
The awkward embrace : the creative artist and the institution in America : an inquiry based on interviews with nine men who have, through their organizations, worked to influence American culture / by Joan Simpson Burns. 1st ed. New York : Knopf : distributed by Random House, 1975. xxv, 512 p. : ill. ; 25 cm. Includes index. Bibliography: p. 507-511. [NX180.S6B87 1975] 74-21303 ISBN 0-394-49563-2 : 15.00
1. Arts and society—United States. 2. Arts, Modern—20th century—United States. I. Title.

Arts and society—United States—Addresses, essays, lectures.

IMAGES of the American city 700
in the arts / [compiled by] Joel C. Mickelson. Dubuque, Iowa : Kendall/Hunt Pub. Co., c1978. ix, 160 p. ; 24 cm. Includes bibliographical references and index. [NX180.S6I45] 78-50370 ISBN 0-8403-1858-8 : 7.95
1. Arts and society—United States—Addresses, essays, lectures. 2. Cities and towns in art—Addresses, essays, lectures. 3. Cities and towns—United States—Addresses, essays, lectures. I. Mickelson, Joel C.

Arts—Arkansas—Directories.

ARKANSAS. Office of 700'.25'767
Arkansas State Arts and Humanities.
Arkansas arts : an inventory of cultural programs, organizations, and facilities of Arkansas. Little Rock : Dept. of Planning, Office of Arkansas State Arts and Humanities, 1973. ix, 87 p. : maps ; 28 cm. Includes index. [NX510.A8A74 1973] 75-318405
1. Arts—Arkansas—Directories. I. Title.

Arts as a profession—Addresses, essays, lectures.

AN Artist's guide to 700'.23
professional security / edited by Barry Nickelsberg ; foreword by Robert D. Ray. 1st ed. Des Moines : Iowa State Arts Council, 1975. viii leaves, 154 p. ; 28 cm. Edited proceedings of a conference held Mar. 21-23, 1975, by the Iowa State Arts Council. [NX163.A77] 75-18590 4.25
1. Arts as a profession—Addresses, essays, lectures. I. Nickelsberg, Barry. II. Iowa State Arts Council.

Arts—Asia—Management—Congresses.

SEMINAR on Cultural 658'.91'70095
Planning in Asia, 1st, Teheran, 1976.
Seminar on Cultural Planning in Asia, 23-27 February, 1976, Tehran : final report. Tehran : Asian Cultural Documentation Centre for UNESCO, 1976. ii, 97 p. ; 22 cm. English or French. [NX770.A78S45 1976] 77-558555
1. Arts—Asia—Management—Congresses. I. Asian Cultural Documentation Centre for Unesco.

Arts — Atlanta — Galleries and museums.

ATLANTA Art Association v. 12
Galleries.
Masterpieces in the High Museum of Art; a group of works of art from the museum's collection [prepared as a catalogue for the exhibition, November 13, 1965 to January 9, 1956] Atlanta, 1965. 53 p. illus. 22 x 28 cm. [NUC67-79943]
1. Arts — Atlanta — Galleries and museums. I. Title.

The arts, Australian.

IN the making 701.15
[by] Craig McGregor [and others. Melbourne, Thomas Nelson (Australia) 1969] 265 p. illus. (part col.) 34 cm. Spine title. [NX590.I5] 75-463481
1. The arts, Australian. 2. The arts—Psychology. I. McGregor, Craig.

THOMAS, Laurie. 709'.94
The most noble art of them all : the selected writings of Laurie Thomas / introduced by Charles Blackman, John Olsen. St. Lucia, Australia : University of Queensland Press ; Hemel Hempstead, Eng. : distributed by Prentice-Hall International, 1977,c1976. vi, 321 p. ; 25 cm. [NX590.A1T48] 77-368356 ISBN 0-7022-1370-5 : 15.75
1. Arts, Australian. 2. Artists—Australia—Biography. I. Title.
Distributed by Technical Impex. BIP

Arts, Australian—History.

SERLE, Geoffrey. 700'.994
From deserts the prophets come: the creative spirit in Australia 1788-1972 [by] Geoffrey Serle. Melbourne, Heinemann, 1973. xii, 274 p. 23 cm. Index. Bibliography: p. 237-260. [NX590.A1S47] 72-97325 ISBN 0-85561-029-8 8.50
1. Arts, Australian—History. I. Title.

Arts, Baroque.

JENSEN, H. James. 700'.9'032
The muses' concord : literature, music, and the visual arts in the baroque age / H. James Jensen. Bloomington : Indiana University Press, c1976. p. cm. Includes bibliographical references and index. [NX451.5.B3J46 1976] 76-11940 ISBN 0-253-33945-6 : 12.95
1. Arts, Baroque. I. Title. BIP

Arts, Baroque—England.

HOOK, Judith. 700.942
The Baroque Age in England / Judith Hook. London : Thames and Hudson, c1976. 207 p. : ill. ; 24 cm. Includes index. Bibliography: p. 196-198. [NX543.H66] 76-366606 ISBN 0-500-23229-6 : 19.50
1. Arts, Baroque—England. 2. Arts, English. I. Title.
Distributed by Transatlantic Arts. BIP

The arts, Baroque—Germany—Addresses, essays, lectures.

THE German baroque; 709'.43
literature, music, art. Edited by George Schulz-Behrend. Austin, Published for the Dept. of Germanic Languages of the University of Texas at Austin, by the University of Texas Press [1972] 166 p. illus. 23 cm. "Four of the five papers presented here were read on November 13-15, 1967, at a symposium sponsored by the Department of Germanic Languages of the University of Texas at Austin." Includes bibliographical references. [NX550.A1G4] 70-38923 ISBN 0-292-70703-7 7.50
1. The arts, Baroque—Germany—Addresses, essays, lectures. 2. The arts, German—Addresses, essays, lectures. I. Schulz-Behrend, George, 1913- ed. II. Texas. University at Austin. Dept. of Germanic Languages.

The arts, Baroque—Italy.

SITWELL, Sacheverell, 709'.03'2
Sir, bart., 1897-
Southern baroque art; a study of painting, architecture and music in Italy and Spain of the 17th & 18th centuries. Freeport, N.Y., Books for Libraries Press [1971] 319 p. illus. 23 cm. Reprint of the 1924 ed. Contents.Contents.—The serenade at Caserta.—"Les Indes galantes."—The king and the nightingale: Philip V and Farinelli.—Mexico.—Biographical index and bibliography (p. 279-319) [NX552.A1S5 1971] 70-179539 ISBN 0-8369-6668-6
1. Farinelli, Carlo Broschi, called, 1705-1782. 2. The arts, Baroque—Italy. 3. The arts, Baroque—Spain. 4. The arts, Baroque—Mexico. BIP

Arts—Berkshire Hills, Mass.

THE Second Berkshire 700'.9744'1
anthology / editors, Mark Canner & Dana Collins. Lenox, Mass. : Bookstore Press, [1975] 185 p. : ill. ; 23 cm. [NX510.M4S42] 74-78475 ISBN 0-912846-10-0 pbk. : 4.95
1. Arts—Berkshire Hills, Mass. 2. Artists—Berkshire Hills, Mass. I. Canner, Mark. II. Collins, Dana. III. Title: The Berkshire anthology.

Arts—Bibliography.

MODERN Language Association 016.7
of America. General Topics 9. Bibliography Committee.
Literature and the other arts; a select bibliography, 1952-1958. Collected by the Bibliography Committee of the Modern Language Association's discussion group: Literature and the Other Arts (General Topics 9) Calvin S. Brown [and others] Compiled by Alfred R. Neumann, and edited by David V. Erdman. [Norwood, Pa.] Norwood Editions, 1974. p. cm. Reprint of the 1959 ed. published by New York Public Library, New York. [Z5931.M53 1974] 74-9588 5.50
1. Arts—Bibliography. I. Neumann, Alfred Robert, 1921- comp. II. Title.

Arts—Bibliography—Catalogs.

HOUSE of El Dieff, 380.1'45'7
inc.
Sixty five : manuscripts and correspondence, paintings and sculptures, drawings and graphics, books and periodicals ... / [Lew David Feldman]. New York : House of El Dieff, c1965. ca. 150 p. : ill. ; 29 cm. [Z5939.H68 1965] [NX620] 75-321246
1. Arts—Bibliography—Catalogs. I. Feldman, Lew David. II. Title.

NEW York (City). 016.709'04
Museum of Modern Art. Library.
Catalog of the Library of the Museum of Modern Art, New York City. Boston, Mass. : G. K. Hall, 1976. 14 v. ; 37 cm. [Z5939.N557 1976] [N5300] 76-383620 ISBN 0-8161-0015-2 lib.bdg. : 1140.00
1. New York (City). Museum of Modern Art. Library. 2. Arts—Bibliography—Catalogs. I. Title.

Arts—Bibliography—Periodicals.

ART Research Libraries 016.7'005
of Ohio.
Union list of periodicals and serials in art research libraries / by Art Research Libraries of Ohio (ARLO) ; Stephen G. Matyi, editor. [Columbus] : Ohio State University Libraries, Office of Educational Services, 1974 [i.e.1975] vii, 646 p. ; 28 cm. [Z5937.A792 1974] [NX1.A1] 74-620198 ISBN 0-88215-040-5 : 22.50
1. Arts—Bibliography—Periodicals. I. Matyi, Stephen G. II. Title.

The arts—Boston.

TAPER, Bernard. 709.744'61
The arts in Boston. Cambridge, Mass., Harvard University Press, 1970. 170 p. illus., plans. 22 cm. (A publication of the Joint Center for Urban Studies of the Massachusetts Institute of Technology and

Harvard University) Includes bibliographical references. [NX511.B6T3 1970] 76-113186 6.00
1. The arts—Boston. I. Title. II. Series: Joint Center for Urban Studies. Publications **BIP**

The arts, Brazilian.

BARDI, Pietro Maria, 1900- 709'.81
New Brazilian art. New York, Praeger [1970] 160 p. illus. (part col.), maps (part col.), plans, ports. 30 cm. [NX533.B3] 73-106816 20.00
1. The arts, Brazilian. I. Title.

Arts—Cameroon—Management.

BAHOKEN, J. C. 354'.67'110085
Cultural policy in the United Republic of Cameroon / J. C. Bahoken and Engelbert Atangana. Paris : The Unesco Press, 1976. 91 p., [2] leaves of plates : ill. ; 24 cm. (Studies and documents on cultural policies) Includes bibliographical references. [NX770.C17B33] 76-381338 ISBN 9-231-01316-5 pbk. : 4.00
1. Arts—Cameroon—Management. 2. Art and state—Cameroon. I. Atangana, Engelbert, joint author. II. Title. III. Series.
Distributed by Unipub.

Arts, Canadian.

CREAN, Susan May, 1945- 301.5
Who's afraid of Canadian culture? / S. M. Crean. Don Mills, Ont. : General Pub. Co., c1976. 296 p. ; 22 cm. Includes index. Bibliography: p. 279-286. [NX513.A1C68] 77-354563 ISBN 0-7736-0044-2 : 12.95. ISBN 0-7736-1019-7 pbk.
1. Arts, Canadian. 2. Canada—Culture. 3. Art patronage—Canada. I. Title.

Arts—Censorship—Great Britain.

GRIFFITHS, Richard. 344'.41'097
Censorship and the arts / by Richard Griffiths. Bramcote : Grove Books, 1976. 24 p. ; 22 cm. (Grove booklets on ethics ; no. 11 ISSN 0305-4241s) Bibliography: p. 21. [NX180.C44G74] 77-358286 ISBN 0-901710-92-X : £0.30
1. Arts—Censorship—Great Britain. I. Title.

Arts—Ceylon—Management.

BANDARA, H. H. 338.4'7'70095493
Cultural policy in Sri Lanka, by H. H. Bandara. Paris, Unesco, 1972. 70 p. illus. 25 cm. (Studies and documents on cultural policies) Includes bibliographical references. [NX770.C4B36] 72-95233 ISBN 9-231-01004-2 2.00 (pbk.)
1. Arts—Ceylon—Management. I. Title. II. Series.
Distributed by Unipub, N.Y. **BIP**

Arts—Colombia—Management.

RUIZ, Jorge Eliecer. 354'.861'0085
Cultural policy in Columbia / prepared by Jorge Eliecer Ruiz ; with the assistance of Valentina Marulanda. Paris : Unesco, 1978. 93 p., [2] leaves of plates : ill. ; 24 cm. (Studies and documents on cultural policies) Bibliography: p. 30-31. [NX770.C7R84] 78-306946 ISBN 92-3-101417-X pbk. : 5.75
1. Arts—Colombia—Management. I. Marulanda, Valentina, joint author. II. Title. III. Series.
Distributed by Unipub in New York City.
Distributed by Unipub, NYC

The arts—Colorado.

COLORADO Council on the Arts and Humanities. 700'.9788
Report and recommendations on the cultural resources of Colorado. [Denver] 1967. 50 p. 22 x 36 cm. Cover title. [NX510.C6A45] 68-66921
1. The arts—Colorado. 2. Colorado—Intellectual life. I. Title.

Arts—Costa Rica—Management.

ROVINSKI, Samuel. 354'.7286'0085
Cultural policy in Costa Rica / Samuel Rovinski. Paris : Unesco, 1978. 61 p., [2] leaves of plates : ill. ; 24 cm. (Studies and documents on cultural policies) Includes bibliographical references. [NX770.C8R68] 78-374165 ISBN 92-3-101400-5 pbk. : 3.25
1. Arts—Costa Rica—Management. I. Title. II. Series.
Distributed by Unipub, NYC **BIP**

The arts—Data processing—Addresses, essays, lectures.

REICHARDT, Jasia, comp. 001.53
Cybernetics, art, and ideas. Greenwich, Conn., New York Graphic Society [1971] 207 p. illus. 26 cm. [NX458.R42] 79-153639 ISBN 0-8212-0431-9 13.50
1. The arts—Data processing—Addresses, essays, lectures. 2. Computers and civilization—Addresses, essays, lectures. I. Title.

Arts—Dictionaries.

THE Lincoln library of the arts. 700'.3
[1st ed.] Columbus, Ohio, Frontier Press Co. [1973] 2 v. (846 p.) illus. 29 cm. Contents.Contents.—v. 1. History. Literature.—v. 2. The arts. Biography. Includes bibliographies. [NX70.L54] 73-78393
1. Arts—Dictionaries. I. Title.

THE Lincoln library of the arts. 700'.3
2d ed. Columbus, Ohio : Frontier Press Co., 1978. 2 v. (846 p., [48] leaves of plates) : ill. ; 28 cm. Contents.Contents.—v. 1. History. Literature. Fine arts.—v. 2. Biography. Includes bibliographies and indexes. [NX70.L54 1978] 78-113448 ISBN 0-912168-051 lib. bdg. : 52.95
1. Arts—Dictionaries.

SCHWARZ, Ira P. 702
A brief source book for the humanities and related arts [by] Ira P. Schwarz. Dubuque, Iowa, Kendall/Hunt Pub. Co. [1972] vii, 136 p. 23 cm. Bibliography: p. 126-137. [NX80.S3] 77-184240 ISBN 0-8403-0565-6
1. The arts—Dictionaries. I. Title.

The arts—Directories.

*CUMMINGS, Paul, ed. 700
Fine arts Market place 73-74 New York, R. R. Bowker, 1973. 258 p. 28 cm. [NX620] 73-2497 ISBN 0-8352-0626-2. 16.50
1. The arts—Directories. I. Title.

*POLKING, Kirk, comp. 700
Artist's market. Edited by Kirk Polking. Cincinnati, Ohio Writer's Digest [1974] 480 p., illus., 23 cm. [NX620] 8.95
1. The arts—Directories. I. Title.

The arts—Endowments.

GINGRICH, Arnold. 658.4
Business & the arts; an answer to tomorrow. Foreword by David Rockefeller. New York, P. S. Eriksson [1969] xiii, 141 p. illus. 25 cm. "A Business Committee for the Arts publication." Bibliography: p. 133-134. [NX710.G5] 69-16864 4.95
1. The arts—Endowments. I. Business Committee for the Arts. II. Title.

TAFT, J. Richard. 700'.6'073
Report to the National Endowment for the Arts; foundation giving to the arts, by J. Richard Taft. [Washington?] 1967. 37 p. 27 cm. Cover title. "Report on Part I of the study: Analysis of potential cooperation between private foundations, local agencies, and the Federal government in the arts." [NX705.T3] 68-61131
1. The arts—Endowments. I. National Endowment for the Arts. II. Title. III. Title: Foundation giving to the arts.

The arts—England.

LIPKING, Lawrence I., 1934- 709'.42
The ordering of the arts in eighteenth-century England. Princeton, N.J., Princeton University Press, 1970. xiv, 503 p. illus., ports. 25 cm. Includes bibliographical references. [NX543.L56] 76-90953 ISBN 0-691-06177-7 12.50
1. The arts—England. I. Title. **BIP**

Arts, English—Exhibitions.

ENGLISH art today, 1960-76 : 709'.42
[exhibition]. New York : Rizzoli, c1976. 2 v. (468 p.) : ill. (some col.) ; 25 cm. English and Italian. Jointly produced by the Comune of Milan and the British Council. Includes bibliographies and filmographies. [NX543.A1E5] 76-19195 ISBN 0-8478-0060-1 : 30.00
1. Arts, English—Exhibitions. 2. Arts, Modern—20th century—England—Exhibitions. 3. Avant-garde (Aesthetics) I. Milan. II. Great Britain. British Council.

Arts—Eton, Eng.

TREASURES of Eton / 700'.74'02296
editor, James McConnell ; technical editor, Jeremy M. Potter ; art editor, William Winter. London : Chatto & Windus, 1976. 180 p., [16] leaves of plates : ill. ; 29 cm. Includes index. Bibliography: p. 171-172. [NX544.E86T73] 76-376871 ISBN 0-7011-2162-9 : £8.50
1. Eton College. 2. Arts—Eton, Eng. I. McConnell, James Douglas Rutherford, 1915- **BIP**

Arts, European—Turkish influences.

ST. Clair, Alexandrine N. 700'.94
The image of the Turk in Europe [by] Alexandrine N. St. Clair. New York, Metropolitan Museum of Art [1973] 72 p. illus. 22 cm. Partial catalog of the Art of Imperial Turkey and its European Echoes, an exhibition presented at the Metropolitan Museum of Art beginning Nov. 17, 1973. Bibliography: p. 71-72. [NX542.S24] 73-18358 3.50
1. Arts, European—Turkish influences. 2. Europe—Civilization—Turkish influences. I. New York (City). Metropolitan Museum of Art. II. Title. **BIP**

The arts—Exhibitions.

INFORMATION. 707'.4'01471
Edited by Kynaston L. McShine. [New York, Museum of Modern Art, 1970] 207 p. illus. 28 cm. Exhibition held at the Museum of Modern Art, New York, July 2 - Sept. 20, 1970, under the auspices of the International Council of the Museum of Modern Art. Bibliography: p. 200-205. [NX427.N715] 71-100683
1. The arts—Exhibitions. I. McShine, Kynaston, ed. II. New York (City). Museum of Modern Art. III. International Council of the Museum of Modern Art, New York.

Arts—Expertising—Congresses.

APPLICATION of science in examination of works of art : 702'.8
proceedings of the seminar at the Museum of Fine Arts, Boston, September 15-18, 1958 / [conducted by the Research Laboratory, Museum of Fine Arts, Boston]. New York : Arno Press, [197-?- c1959] xiii, 198 p. : ill. ; 29 cm. Reprint of the ed. published by the Museum of Fine Arts, Boston. Includes bibliographical references. [N8558.A66 1970z] 78-99280
1. Arts—Expertising—Congresses. I. Boston. Museum of Fine Arts. Research Laboratory.

The arts—Florida—Directories.

FLORIDA. Division of Cultural Affairs. 702'.5'759
Florida arts directory. [Tallahassee, 1971?] 45 p. 28 cm. [NX110.F55] 72-611129
1. The arts—Florida—Directories. I. Title.

The arts, French.

FRENCH news. 270.3
no. 1-Nov./Dec. 1957- New York, Cultural Services of the French Embassy no. in v. illus., ports. 28 cm. Some no. issued in 2 parts: Books, and Theater and arts. Includes a special issue, dated Feb./Mar. 1961, in honor of La Comedie-Francaise. [DC33.7.F73] 65-66222

PARIS, William Francklyn, 1871-1954. 700'.944
French arts & letters, and other essays, by W. Francklyn Paris. Port Washington, N.Y., Kennikat Press [1968] xvii, 182 p. illus., ports. 22 cm. (Essay and general literature index reprint series) Reprint of the 1937 ed. [NX549.P3 1968] 68-26235
1. The arts, French. I. Title.

PINCUS-WITTEN, Robert. 700'.944
Occult symbolism in France : Josephin Peladan and the Salons de la Rose-Croix / Robert Pincus-Witten. New York : Garland Pub., 1976. ix, 291 p. : ill. ; 21 cm. (Outstanding dissertations in fine arts) Originally presented as the author's thesis, University of Chicago, 1968, under the title: Josephin Peladan and the Salons de la Rose-Croix. Bibliography: p. 225-240. [NX549.A1P56 1976] 75-23809 ISBN 0-8240-2003-0 lib.bdg. : 27.50
1. Peladan, Josephin, 1859-1918. 2. Arts, French. 3. Symbolism in art—France. 4. Paris. Salons de la Rose-Croix. 5. Rosicrucians. I. Title. II. Series. **BIP**

Arts, French—Catalogs.

LAKE, Carlton. 016.7'00944
Baudelaire to Beckett : a century of French art & literature : a catalogue of books, manuscripts, and related material drawn from the collections of the Humanities Research Center / selected and described by Carlton Lake. [Austin] : Humanities Research Center, University of Texas at Austin, c1976. 204 p. : ill. ; 26 cm. Includes index. Bibliography: p. [188] [NX549.A1L34] 76-365682 ISBN 0-87959-019-X 20.00 ISBN 0-87959-020-3 pbk. : 10.00
1. Texas. University at Austin. Humanities Research Center. 2. Arts, French—Catalogs. 3. Arts, French—Bibliography—Catalogs. I. Texas. University at Austin. Humanities Research Center. II. Title. **BIP**

The arts, French—Exhibitions.

PRE-IMPRESSIONISM, 1860-1869, a formative decade in French art and culture. 709.44
[Exhibitions: May 5- June 14, 1969, Memorial Union Art gallery, Art Department Gallery Main Library [Davis] University of California at Davis, 1969. 118 p. illus. 25 cm. Edited by Joseph Armstrong Baird, Jr. "Footnotes and bibliographies": p. [103]-118. [NX549.P73] 76-271047
1. The arts, French—Exhibitions. 2. Decoration and ornament—Second Empire style. 3. France—History—Second Empire, 1852-1870. I. Baird, Joseph Armstrong, ed. II. California. University, Davis. Art Gallery. III. California. University, Davis. Dept. of Art.

Arts—Germany, East—Management.

KOCH, Hans, 1927- 354'.43'10085
Cultural policy in the German Democratic Republic / Hans Koch. Paris : Unesco Press, 1975[i.e.1976] 62 p., [2] leaves of plates : ill. ; 25 cm. (Studies and documents on cultural policies) [NX770.G35K62] 76-350283 ISBN 92-31-01291-6 pbk. : 3.30
1. Arts—Germany, East—Management. 2. Art and state—Germany, East. 3. Germany, East—Intellectual life I. Title. II. Series.
Distributed by Unipub, New York **BIP**

Arts—Ghana—Management.

GHANA. Ministry of Education and Culture. Cultural Division. 354'.667'0085
Cultural policy in Ghana / a study prepared by the Cultural Division of the Ministry of Education and Culture. Paris : Unesco Press, 1975,i.e.1976 50 p., [2] leaves of plates ; 25 cm. (Studies and documents on cultural policies) "[B.6] SHC. 75/XIX-37/A" [NX770.G4G46 1976] 76-350488 ISBN 92-31-01328-9 pbk. : 2.00

1. Arts—Ghana—Management. I. Title. II. Series.
Distributed by Unipub

The arts, Gothic—Italy.

LARNER, John, 1930- 914.5'03'4
Culture and society in Italy, 1290-1420. New York, Scribner [1971] xi, 399 p. illus., facsim., geneal. tables. 24 cm. (Studies in cultural history) Bibliography: p. [357]-384. [NX552.A1L3 1971b] 72-110680 ISBN 0-684-12367-3 14.95
1. The arts, Gothic—Italy. 2. Italy—Civilization. 3. Art and society. I. Title.

The arts—Gt. Brit.

HARRIS, John S. 354.42'008'5
Government patronage of the arts in Great Britain [by] John S. Harris. Chicago, University of Chicago Press [1970] x, 341 p. illus. 24 cm. Includes bibliographical references. [NX750.G7H3] 72-120007 ISBN 0-226-31743-9
1. The arts—Gt. Brit. 2. Art and state—Gt. Brit. I. Title. BIP

LANE, John, 1930- 700'.941
Arts centres : every town should have one / [by] John Lane with contributions by Robert Atkins ... [et al.]. London ; Salem, N.H. : P. Elek, 1978. xii, 160 p., [4] p. of plates : ill. ; 23 cm. Bibliography: p. 145-146. [NA6813.G7L36] 79-304657 ISBN 0-236-40069-X : 13.95
1. Art centers—Great Britain—Addresses, essays, lectures. I. Atkins, Robert, joint author. II. Title.
Distributed by Merrimack Book Service

TODD, Ruthven, 1914- 760
Tracks in the snow : studies in English science and art / Ruthven Todd. Folcroft, Pa. : Folcroft Library Editions, 1975. 133 p., [23] leaves of plates : ill. ; 26 cm. Reprint of the 1946 ed. published by Grey Walls Press, London. Contents.Contents.—Tracks in the snow.—William Blake and the eighteenth-century mythologists.—The reputation and prejudices of Henry Fuseli.—The imagination of John Martin. Includes bibliographical references and index. [PR6039.O26T7 1975] 75-40220 ISBN 0-8414-8546-1 lib. bdg. : 22.50
I. Title.

The arts—Gt. Brit.—Societies, etc.

AITCHISON, Raymond. 706'.2
Notes of guidance on the formation of a Regional Arts Association; prepared by Raymond Aitchison, Alexander Dunbar and Eric White. Newcastle upon Tyne, Northern Arts Association, [1968] [16] p. 22 cm. [NX28.G7A65] 72-437288 1/6
1. The arts—Gt. Brit.—Societies, etc. I. Dunbar, Alexander, joint author. II. White, Eric Walter, 1905- joint author. III. Northern Arts Association. IV. Title.

Arts, Greek.

BOARDMAN, John, 1927- 700'.938
Eros in Greece / text by John Boardman and Eugenio La Rocca ; photos. by Antonia Mulas. New York : Erotic Art Book Society, 1978, c1975. 175 p. : col. ill. ; 30 cm. Includes indexes. Bibliography: p. 169. [NX551.A1B62] 77-94381 ISBN 0-913568-25-2 : 25.00
1. Arts, Greek. 2. Erotica. I. La Rocca, Eugenio, joint author. II. Mulas, Antonia, 1939- III. Title.
Publisher's address : 251 W. 57th St., New York, NY 10019 BIP

Arts—Guyana—Management.

SEYMOUR, Arthur J. 354'.88'10085
Cultural policy in Guyana / A. J. Seymour. Paris : Unesco, 1978. 68 p., [2] leaves of plates : ill. ; 24 cm. (Studies and documents on cultural policies) [NX770.G8S49] 78-306897 ISBN 9-231-01511-7 pbk. : 4.75
1. Arts—Guyana—Management. I. Title. II. Series.
Distributed by Unipub, NYC BIP

Arts—History.

ARTZ, Frederick Binkerd, 1894- 901.93
From the Renaissance to romanticism; trends in style in art, literature, and music, 1300-1830. [Chicago] University of Chicago Press [1962] 311 p. 24 cm. Includes bibliography. [N6350.A7] 62-20021
1. The arts—History. I. Title. BIP

DAVIS, Beverly Jeanne. 709
Chant of the centuries; a history of the humanities: the visual arts and their parallels in music and literature. Austin, Tex., W. S. Benson [1969] 200 p. illus. (part col.) 27 cm. [NX440.D39] 71-2586
1. The arts—History. I. Title. BIP

FLEMING, William, 1909- 709
Art, music & ideas. New York, Holt, Rinehart and Winston [1970] viii, 366 p. 314 illus. (incl. music, ports.), 32 col. plates. 26 cm. Based on the author's Arts & ideas, 3d ed., 1968. [NX440.F55] 75-111304 ISBN 0-308-28651-
1. The arts—History. I. Title.

FLEMING, William, 1909- 709
Arts & ideas / William Fleming. New and brief ed. New York : Holt, Rinehart and Winston, [1974] viii, 454 p. : ill. (some col.) ; 26 cm. Includes index. [NX440.F56 1974] 74-5920 ISBN 0-03-089434-4 : 9.95
1. Arts—History. I. Title.

POGGIOLI, Renato, 1907-1963. 709.04
The theory of the avant-garde. Translated from the Italian by Gerald Fitzgerald. Cambridge, Mass., Belknap Press of Harvard University Press, 1968. xvii, 250 p. 21 cm. Translation of Teoria dell'arte d'avanguardia. Bibliography: p. 233-240. [NX456.P613] 68-17630
1. The arts—History. I. Title. II. Title: The avant-garde. BIP

SEDGWICK, John P. 709
Rhythms of western art, by John P. Sedgwick, Jr. Metuchen, N.J., Scarecrow Press, 1972. 334 p. illus. 22 cm. Includes bibliographical references. [NX440.S4] 73-170648 ISBN 0-8108-0449-2
1. The arts—History. 2. The arts—Psychology. I. Title. BIP

VAN LOON, Hendrik Willem, 1882-1944. 709
The arts, written and illustrated by Hendrik Willem Van Loon. A new, updated version. New York, Liveright, 1974. xxv, 681 p. illus. 22 cm. [NX440.V33 1974] 73-93130 ISBN 0-87140-579-2 9.95
1. Arts—History. I. Title. BIP

Arts—History—Juvenile literature.

**THE artist and his studio* 709
New York, St. Martin's Press [1974] 60 p. illus. (some col.) 25 cm. [ND1146] 74-83590 4.95
1. Arts—History—Juvenile literature.

Arts—Honduras—Management.

ALONSO de Quesada, Alba. 354'.866'0085
Towards a cultural policy for Honduras / Alba Alonso de Quesada. Paris : Unesco, c1978. 73 p., [2] leaves of plates : ill. ; 24 cm. (Studies and documents on cultural policies) Includes bibliographical references. [NX770.H8A46] 79-301804 ISBN 92-3-101520-6 pbk. : 4.75
1. Arts—Honduras—Management. I. Title. II. Series.
Dist. by Unipub, NYC. BIP

The arts—Illinois.

ILLINOIS. Arts Council. 700'.9773
Illinois Arts Council survey of the arts 1966-1967. [Springfield] 1969. 62 p. maps. 28 cm. [NX510.I3A45] 72-633080
1. The arts—Illinois. I. Title.

The arts—Illinois—Finance.

ILLINOIS. Advisory Commission on Financing the Arts in Illinois. 338.4'7'7
Report. [Chicago] 1971. xvii, 127 p. 23 cm. [NX742.I3A42] 70-178941
1. The arts—Illinois—Finance.

Arts in General Education Project.

MADEJA, Stanley S. 707
All the arts for every child; final report on the Arts in General Education Project in the School District of University City, Mo., by Stanley S. Madeja. Foreword by Kathryn Bloom. [New York, JDR 3rd Fund, 1973] 111 p. illus. 23 cm. Includes bibliographical references. [NX511.U53M32] 74-173133
1. Arts in General Education Project. 2. School District of University City, Mo. I. Title.

Arts—India—Management.

VATSYAYAN, Kapila Malik. 338.4'7'700954
Some aspects of cultural policies in India. Paris, Unesco, 1972. 105 p. illus. 24 cm. (Studies and documents on cultural policies) "SHC.71/XIX.13/A" [NX770.I4V37] 72-77399 2.00 (pbk.)
1. Arts—India—Management. I. Title. II. Series.
Distributed by Unipub, N.Y. BIP

Arts—Indonesia—Management.

INDONESIA. Departemen Pendidikan dan Kebudayaan. 338.4'7'7009598
Cultural policy in Indonesia; a study prepared by the staff of the Directorate-General of Culture, Ministry of Education and Culture of the Republic of Indonesia. Paris, Unesco, 1973, [i.e.1974] 46 p. illus. 24 cm. (Studies and documents on cultural policies) Issued also in French. [NX750.I5I52 1973] 74-175530 ISBN 9-231-01128-6
1. Arts—Indonesia—Management. 2. Art and state—Indonesia. I. Title. II. Series.
Distributed by Unipub; 2.75 (pbk.). BIP

Arts—Iran—Management.

BAHNAM, Jamshid. 338.4'7'700955
Cultural policy in Iran [by] Djamchid Behnam. Paris, Unesco, 1973. 46 p. illus. 24 cm. (Studies and documents on cultural policies) Includes bibliographical references. [NX770.I7B34] 73-174818 ISBN 9-231-01002-6
1. Arts—Iran—Management. I. Title. II. Series.
Distributed by Unipub, 2.00 (pbk.) BIP

Arts, Iranian.

NASR, Seyyed Hossein. 700'.955
Sacred art in Persian culture / [by] S. H. Nasr. Ipswich : Golgonooza Press, 1976. 23 p. : 1 ill. ; 24 cm. [NX574.A1N37] 77-363444 ISBN 0-903880-09-1 : £0.90
1. Arts, Iranian. 2. Arts, Islamic—Iran. 3. Islamic art and symbolism—Iran. I. Title.

Arts—Ireland.

RICHARDS, James Maude, Sir. 338.4'7'7009417
Provision for the arts : report of an inquiry carried out during 1974-75 throughout the twenty-six counties of the Republic of Ireland / chairman, J. M. Richards ; director, Millicent Bowerman. Dublin : The Arts Council, 1976. 159 p. ; 25 cm. "The Inquiry was set up, in the summer of 1974, by An Chomhairle Ealaion (the Arts Council) and the Calouste Gulbenkian Foundation." "Summary of principal recommendations" as insert ([4] p.). Erratum slip inserted. [NX546.A1R52] 76-371502 ISBN 0-903319-05-5 : £1.50
1. Arts—Ireland. I. Arts Council of Ireland. II. Fundacao Calouste Gulbenkian. III. Title.

The arts—Jamaica.

BAXTER, Ivy. 709'.7292
The arts of an island: the development of the culture and of the folk and creative arts in Jamaica, 1494-1962 (Independence). Metuchen, N.J., Scarecrow Press, 1970. 407 p. 22 cm. Bibliography: p. 368-386. [NX527.B38] 71-14849
1. The arts—Jamaica. I. Title.

Arts—Jamaica—Management.

CULTURAL policy in Jamaica : a study / prepared by the Institute of Jamaica. Paris : Unesco, 1978. 53 p., [2] leaves of plates : ill. ; 24 cm. (Studies and documents on cultural policies) Includes bibliographical references. [NX770.J29C84] 78-306899 ISBN 9-231-01521-4 pbk. : 3.25 354'.7292'0085
1. Arts—Jamaica—Management. I. Institute of Jamaica, Kingston. II. Title. III. Series.
Distributed by Unipub NYC BIP

Arts, Japanese.

ROSENFIELD, John M. 709'.52'07401444
The courtly tradition in Japanese art and literature: selections from Hofer and Hyde collections [by] John M. Rosenfield, Fumiko E. Cranston [and] Edwin A. Cranston. [Cambridge] Fogg Art Museum, Harvard University, 1973. 316 p. illus. (part col.) 22 x 28 cm. [NX584.A1R67] 73-85473
1. Hofer, Philip, 1898- —Art collections. 2. Hyde, Donald Frizell, 1909-1966—Art collections. 3. Hyde, Mary Morley Crapo—Art collections. 4. Arts, Japanese. I. Cranston, Fumiko E., joint author. II. Cranston, Edwin A., joint author. III. Harvard University. William Hayes Fogg Art Museum. IV. Title.

Arts—Juvenile literature.

LOGAN, Frederick M. 700'.9
The world of the arts, by Fred Logan, Marcella O'Leary [and] Paul Gauger. Anne Neigoff, managing ed., illus. by Katherine Grace [and others] Special advisor: Virgil Herrick. Chicago, Standard Education Corp., 1974. 193, [7] p. illus. (part col.) 26 cm. (The Child's world) Bibliography: p. [194]-[195] [NX633.L63] 74-12311
1. Arts—Juvenile literature. I. O'Leary, Marcella, joint author. II. Gauger, Paul, 1914- joint author. III. Grace, Katherine, illus. IV. Title. V. Series.

Arts—Kenya.

PARROTT, Fred J. 700'.967
Introduction to African arts of Kenya, Zaire, and Nigeria, by Fred J. Parrott. Illus. by Naomichi Kimura. New York, Arco Pub. Co. [1972] xv, 188 p. illus. 24 cm. Bibliography: p. 177-182. [NX588.9.K4P37] 72-3332 2.95
1. Arts—Kenya. 2. Arts—Zaire. 3. Arts—Nigeria. I. Title.

Arts—Kenya—Management.

NDETI, Kivuto. 354'.676'20085
Cultural policy in Kenya / Kivuto Ndeti. Paris : Unesco Press, 1975. 70 p., [2] leaves of plates : ill. ; 24 cm. (Studies and documents on cultural policies) [NX770.K4N38] 75-320705 ISBN 92-3-101202-9 pbk. : 3.30
1. Arts—Kenya—Management. I. Title. II. Series.
Distributed by Unipub. BIP

Arts—Korea—Management.

KIM, Yersu, 1936- 354'.519'50085
Cultural policy in the Republic of Korea / by Kim Yersu. Paris : Unesco, 1976. 59 p., [2] leaves of plates : ill. ; 25 cm. (Studies and documents on cultural policies) Includes bibliographical references. [NX770.K8K55] 77-467612 ISBN 9-231-01384-X pbk. : 2.65
1. Arts—Korea—Management. 2. Art and state—Korea. 3. Korea—Intellectual life. I. Title. II. Series.

Distributed by Unipub BIP

The arts—Latin America—Congresses.

TEXAS. University. College of Fine Arts. 709'.8
Proceedings of the conference on Latin-American fine arts June 14-17, 1951. Westport, Conn., Greenwood Press [1970, c1952] xi, 127 p. illus., ports. 23 cm. (Latin-American studies, 13) "Cosponsored by the College of Fine Arts and the Institute of Latin-American Studies, the University of Texas." Includes bibliographical references. [NX501.A1T4] 75-144117 ISBN 0-8371-5032-9
1. The arts—Latin America—Congresses. I. Texas. University. Institute of Latin-American Studies. II. Series: Texas. University. Institute of Latin-American Studies. Latin-American studies, 13

Arts—Liberia—Management.

BEST, Kenneth Y. 338.4'7'7
Cultural policy in Liberia / Kenneth Y. Best. Paris : Unesco Press, 1974. 59 p., [2] leaves of plates : ill. ; 25 cm. (Studies and documents on cultural policies) Bibliography: p. 51. [NX770.L7B47] 74-183242 ISBN 9-231-01160-X pbk. : 2.65.
1. Arts—Liberia—Management. I. Title. II. Series.
Distributed by Unipub. BIP

Arts, Liberian.

LIBERIA. Dept. of Information and Cultural Affairs. 709'.01'1096662
Liberia: arts and crafts. [Monrovia, 1971] 48 p. illus. 27 cm. Cover title. [NX589.6.L5A5] 73-172088
1. Arts, Liberian. I. Title.

Arts, Malay.

SHEPPARD, Mubin, 1905- 700'.9595'1
Taman indera: a royal pleasure ground: Malay decorative arts and pastimes. London, New York, Oxford University Press, 1972 [i.e. 1973] xviii, 207 p. illus. (some col.) col. maps. 29 cm. Includes bibliographical references and index. [NX579.A3M397 1972] 73-175394 ISBN 0-19-638144-4 23.00
1. Arts, Malay. I. Title. BIP

Arts—Management.

FISCHER, Joseph O. 658'.91'7
Concepts for the development of local arts councils and other art groups; a handbook for basic orientation to matters dealing with the administration of arts programs and projects for the practical solution of routine problems and for reference in times of crisis or concern, by Joseph O. Fischer. 2d ed. St. Louis, 1972. iv, 95 p. 29 cm. "Presented by the Missouri State Council on the Arts." Bibliography: p. 95. [NX760.F57 1972] 72-612267
1. Arts—Management. I. Missouri State Council on the Arts. II. Title.

NELSON, Charles A. 658.1'954
Financial management for the arts : a guidebook for arts organizations / by Charles A. Nelson and Frederick J. Turk. New York : Associated Councils of the Arts, c1975. 52 p. : ill. ; 22 x 29 cm. [NX760.N44] 75-43360 ISBN 0-915400-01-4 : 4.50
1. Arts—Management. 2. Arts—Finance. I. Turk, Frederick J., joint author. II. Title.

TRANSFORMATION; 769'.973
arts, communication, environment. v. 1, no. 1-3; 1950-52. [New York, Wittenborn, Schultz] 176p. illus. 22x29cm. Edited by H. Holtzman. No more published? [AP2.T723] 56-23902
I. Holtzman, Harry, ed.

WEHLE, Mary M. 658'.91'7
Financial management for arts organizations / Mary M. Wehle. Cambridge, Mass. : Arts Administration Research Institute, c1975. xi, 163 p. : graphs ; 28 cm. [NX760.W44] 75-321713 ISBN 0-915440-01-6
1. Arts—Management. 2. Arts—Finance. I. Title.

Arts—Management—Addresses, essays, lectures.

GREYSER, Stephen A., comp. 338.4'7'7
Cultural policy and arts administration. Stephen A. Greyser, editor. [Cambridge, Mass.] Harvard Summer School Institute in Arts Administration; [distributed by the Harvard University Press, 1973] xi, 173 p. 18 cm. Papers delivered at international colloquiums of the Harvard Summer School Institute in Arts Administration, 1970-1972. Includes bibliographical references. [NX760.G73] 78-188975 ISBN 0-674-17980-3 5.95 (pbk.).
1. Arts—Management—Addresses, essays, lectures. I. Harvard Summer School Institute in Arts Administration. II. Title.
Contents omitted. BIP

Arts—Management—Bibliography.

GEORGI, Charlotte. 658'.91'7
The arts and the world of business; a selected bibliography. Metuchen, N.J., Scarecrow Press, 1973. 123 p. 22 cm. [Z5956.A7G46] 73-3380 ISBN 0-8108-0611-8 5.00
1. Arts—Management—Bibliography. I. Title.

Arts—Management—United States—Directories.

EDUCATIONAL Facilities Laboratories. 338.4'7'002573
Technical assistance for arts facilities : a sourcebook : a report from Educational Facilities Laboratories and the National Endowment for the Arts. New York : EFL, 1977. 30 p. ; 23 cm. Cover title. Includes index. [NX765.E34 1977] 76-53139
1. Arts—Management—United States—Directories. I. National Endowment for the Arts. II. Title.

Arts—Mangagement—Bibliography.

GEORGI, Charlotte. 016.658'91'7
The arts and the world of business / by Charlotte Georgi. 2d ed. Metuchen, N.J. : Scarecrow Press, 1979. p. cm. Includes index. A rev. and updated bibliography, superseding all previous versions. [Z5956.A7G46 1978] [NX760] 78-12103 ISBN 0-8108-1174-X : 7.00
1. Arts—Mangagement—Bibliography. I. Title. BIP

Arts—Massachusetts—Finance.

BECKER Research Corporation. 338.7'61'7009744
A study of the economics of non-profit arts and humanities organizations in the Commonwealth of Massachusetts for the Commonwealth of Massachusetts Council on the Arts and Humanities / [prepared by Becker Research Corporation]. Boston : The Corporation, 1973. 221 p. in various pagings ; 28 cm. [NX705.5.U62M43 1973] 74-620559 1.60
1. Arts—Massachusetts—Finance. 2. Art patronage—Massachusetts. I. Massachusetts Council on the Arts and Humanities. II. Title.

Arts—Mathematics.

LINN, Charles F. 700'.1'51
The golden mean; mathematics and the fine arts [by] Charles F. Linn. [1st ed.] Garden City, N.Y., Doubleday [1974] xvii, 131 p. illus. 25 cm. Bibliography: p. [121]-123. [NX180.M33L56] 73-15480 ISBN 0-385-04110-1 4.95
1. Arts—Mathematics. I. Title.
Library binding 5.70. BIP

Arts, Medieval.

PEARSALL, Derek Albert. 758'.1'094
Landscapes and seasons of the medieval world [by] Derek Pearsall and Elizabeth Salter. [Toronto] University of Toronto Press [1973] xv, 252 p. illus. 26 cm. Includes bibliographical references. [NX449.P42] 73-85089 ISBN 0-8020-2110-7 25.00
1. Arts, Medieval. 2. Landscape in art. 3. Seasons in art. I. Salter, Elizabeth, joint author. II. Title. BIP

Arts—Michigan.

MICHIGAN. Legislature. Joint Legislative Committee on the Arts. 353.9'774'00854
The status of the arts in Michigan : report of the Joint Legislative Committee on the Arts. [Grand Rapids : The Committee, 1974?] viii, 216 p. : ill. ; 23 cm. [NX510.M5M52 1974] 75-621813
1. Arts—Michigan. I. Title.

Arts, Modern—19th century.

GAUNT, William, 1900- 700'.9'04
The march of the moderns / by William Gaunt. Westport, Conn. : Hyperion Press, [1979] p. cm. Reprint of the 1949 ed. published by J. Cape, London. Includes index. Bibliography: p. [NX454.G38 1979] 78-13860 23.50
1. Arts, Modern—19th century. 2. Arts, Modern—20th century. I. Title. BIP

Arts, Modern—20th century.

CALAS, Nicolas. 700'.9'04
Art in the age of risk, and other essays. [1st ed.] New York, Dutton, 1968. xvii, 238 p. illus. 19 cm. (Documents in modern art criticism) [NX456.C34] 68-28885 5.00
1. The arts, Modern—20th century. I. Title.

COMMON sense addressed to the inhabitants of America. 811'.5'4
[1st ed. Amherst, Mass., Paz Press, 1973] 138 p. illus. 23 cm. Contents.Contents.—English, B. The fire of being, poems.—Common sense is an odyssey in search of love [a collection of] art and photography arranged by M. A. Cohen. [NX456.C65] 73-174200
1. Arts, Modern—20th century. I. Cohen, Michael A. II. English, Bill. The fire of being. 1973.

DAVIS, Douglas M. 700'.9'04
Artculture : essays on the post-modern / by Douglas Davis. 1st ed. New York : Harper & Row, c1977. p. cm. (Icon editions) Includes index. Contents.Contents.—Artpolitics.—The size of non-size.—What is content?—Photography as culture.—Filmgoing/videogoing.—The decline and fall of pop.—The idea of a twenty-first century museum.—Utopia.—Post-modern form. [NX458.D38] 76-27504 ISBN 0-06-431000-0 : 8.95
1. Arts, Modern—20th century. 2. Avant-garde (Aesthetics) I. Title. BIP

HIGGINS, Richard Carter. 700'.9'046
Towards the 1970's, by Dick Higgins. [Somerville, Mass.] Abyss Publications, 1969. 6 p. 22 cm. Cover title. [NX458.H53] 79-129087
1. The arts, Modern—20th century. I. Title.

KULTERMANN, Udo. 709.04'6
Art and life. Translated by John William Gabriel. New York, Praeger Publishers [1971] 210 p. illus. 24 cm. Translation of Leben und Kunst. [NX458.K8413] 76-145535 12.50
1. The arts, Modern—20th century. I. Title.

NEWPORT, John P., 1917- 704.948'2'0904
Theology and contemporary art forms [by] John P. Newport. Waco, Tex., Word Books [1971] 131 p. 23 cm. Includes bibliographical references. [NX650.C5N4] 75-134940 3.95
1. Arts, Modern—20th century. 2. Christian art and symbolism. I. Title.

ROSENBERG, Harold. 700'.9'04
Discovering the present : three decades in art, culture, and politics / Harold Rosenberg. Chicago : University of Chicago Press, 1973. xii, 336 p. ; 23 cm. Includes bibliographical references and index. [NX456.R63] 72-92852 ISBN 0-226-72680-0
1. Arts, Modern—20th century. 2. Arts and society. 3. Politics in art. I. Title. BIP

ROTHSCHILD, Edward Francis. 709'.04
The meaning of unintelligibility in modern art [by] Edward F. Rothschild. New York, Oriole Editions [1973] xi, 102 p. illus. 21 cm. First published in 1934 by the University of Chicago Press, in series: Studies of meaning in art. [NX456.R64 1973] 72-91188 ISBN 0-88211-041-1 8.00
1. Arts, Modern—20th century. 2. Arts—Psychology. I. Title. II. Series: Studies of meaning in art. BIP

SCHORR, Justin, 1928- 701'.1
Toward the transformation of art. Rutherford, Fairleigh Dickinson University Press [1974] 118 p. 22 cm. Bibliography: p. 114-116. [NX458.S36] 73-8298 ISBN 0-8386-1382-9 6.50
1. Arts, Modern—20th century. 2. Aesthetics, Modern—20th century. 3. Arts and society. I. Title. BIP

SMITH, John, 1924- 700'.9'04
The arts betrayed / John Smith. New York : Universe Books, 1978. 256 p. : ill. ; 25 cm. Includes bibliographical references and index. [NX456.S55 1978] 78-56385 ISBN 0-87663-322-X : 13.50
1. Arts, Modern—20th century. 2. Artists—Psychology. I. Title. BIP

WOODS, Gerald, comp. 709'.2'2
Art without boundaries. Edited by Gerald Woods, Philip Thompson [and] John Williams. New York, Praeger [1974, c1972] 215 p. illus. (part col.) 22 cm. (Praeger world of art series) Published in 1972 under title: Art without boundaries, 1950-70. [NX458.W66 1974] 73-7821 8.50
1. Arts, Modern—20th century. I. Thompson, Philip, joint comp. II. Williams, John, joint comp. III. Title.

The arts, Modern—20th century—Exhibitions.

AGAINST order; 709.04'074'014811
chance and art. [Exhibition] November 14 to December 22, 1970, Institute of Contemporary Art, University of Pennsylvania. [Philadelphia, 1970] [28] p. illus. 22 cm. Catalogue essay "Against order: poetical sources of chance art" by Robert Pincus-Witten (p. [5]-[18]) Includes bibliographical references. [NX456.A37] 70-25285
1. The arts, Modern—20th century—Exhibitions. 2. The arts—Psychology. I. Pincus-Witten, Robert. II. Pennsylvania. University. Institute of Contemporary Art.

The arts, Modern—20th century—History.

MCMULLEN, Roy. 700'.9'04
Art, affluence, and alienation; the fine arts today. New York, Praeger [1968] vii, 272 p. 25 cm. (Britannica perspective) Bibliographical footnotes. [NX456.M2] 68-19508 5.95
1. The arts, Modern—20th century—History. I. Title.

Arts Modern—20th century—Miscellanea.

THREE places in New Inkland 700'.9'04
: three works in word and image / edited by Lynn and Paul Zelevansky. New York : Zartscorp, 1977. 35, 5 p., [18] leaves of plates : ill. ; 28 cm. Contents.Contents.—Cole, D. New Inkland.—Kostelanetz, R. Constructivist fictions.—Shipley, B. The object of an art object and the work of an artwork. [NX458.T49] 77-72826
1. Arts Modern—20th century—Miscellanea. I. Zelevansky, Lynn. II. Zelevansky, Paul. III. Cole, David, 1939- New Inkland. 1977. IV. Kostelanetz, Richard. Constructivist fictions. 1977. V. Shipley, Bill. The object of an art object and the work of an artwork. 1977. BIP

Arts, Modern—20th century—United States.

ASHTON, Dore. 700'.9747'1
The New York school; a cultural reckoning. New York, Viking Press [1973, c1972] x, 246 p. illus. 22 cm. Published in 1972 under title: The life and times of the New York school. Includes bibliographical references. [NX504.A87 1973] 72-80897 ISBN 0-670-50912-4 10.00
1. New York School. 2. Arts, Modern—20th century—United States. I. Title.
Pbk. 4.95; ISBN 0-670-00368-9.

Arts, Modern—20th century—Vienna.

VERGO, Peter. 709'.436'13
Art in Vienna 1898-1918 : Klimt, Kokoschka, Schiele and their contemporaries / Peter Vergo. London : Phaidon, 1975. 256 p. : ill. (some col.) ; 29 cm. Distributed in the U.S.A. by Praeger Publishers, Inc., New York. Includes index. Bibliography: p. 250-251. [NX600.W53V47 1975] 75-722 ISBN 0-7148-1600-0 : 27.50
1. Vereinigung Bildender Künstler "Wiener Secession." 2. Arts, Modern—20th century—Vienna.

Arts—Montana—Addresses, essays, lectures.

THE Arts in Montana / 700'.8
collected and edited by H. G. Merriam. Missoula, Mont. : Mountain Press Pub. Co., c1977. xvi, 238 p. : ill. ; 24 cm. Material originally published in the magazine Montana arts. [NX510.M9A77] 76-58521 8.95
1. Arts—Montana—Addresses, essays, lectures. I. Merriam, Harold Guy, 1883- II. Montana arts.

Arts, Mormon.

MORMON 700'.9792'074019224
Festival of Arts, 1st-3d, Brigham Young University, 1969-1972.
Mormon arts; featuring articles and art work by Mormon artists and authors. Presented by the College of Fine Arts and Communications, Brigham Young University. Lorin F. Wheelwright, general editor. Lael J. Woodbury, associate editor. Provo, Utah, Brigham Young University Press [1972- v. illus. (part col.) and phonodisc s. 12 in. 33 1/3 rpm. stereophonic) in pocket. 33 cm. Includes bibliographical references. [NX427.P76M67 1971] 72-93467 ISBN 0-8425-0094-4 13.95 (v. 1)
1. Arts, Mormon. I. Wheelwright, Lorin Farrar, 1909- ed. II. Woodbury, Lael Jay, 1927- ed. III. Brigham Young University, Provo, Utah. College of Fine Arts and Communications. IV. Title.

Arts—Nebraska.

ARTS Development 338.4'7'7009782
Associates.
A report on Dialogue on the arts : a public planning project of the Nebraska Arts Council. Minneapolis : Arts Development Associates, 1976. 141 p. in various pagings ; 28 cm. [NX510.N2A77 1976] 77-622395
1. Arts—Nebraska. I. Nebraska Arts Council. II. Title. III. Title: Dialogue on the arts.

The arts—New Jersey.

NEW Jersey. Commission 700'.9749
to Study the Arts in New Jersey.
The arts and New Jersey; report. Trenton, 1966. 188 p. illus. 25 cm. [NX510.N4A43] 67-63646
1. The arts—New Jersey. I. Title.

Arts—New Jersey—Directories.

THE Arts catalogue of 700'.25'749
New Jersey / compiled and edited by Pamela Pipines & Terence Ripmaster. Wayne, N.J. : Avery Pub. Group, c1978. ix, 249 p. : ill. ; 26 cm. [NX110.A78] 78-67411 ISBN 0-89529-064-2 : 7.95
1. Arts—New Jersey—Directories. I. Pipines, Pamela. II. Ripmaster, Terence.

The arts—New Mexico.

GILBERT, Jim. 709'.789
A survey of the arts in New Mexico. Santa Fe, State Planning Office, 1966- v. illus., maps. 28 cm. Contents.Contents.—v. 1. State resources development plan. Includes bibliographical references. [NX510.N43G5] 72-627846
1. The arts—New Mexico. I. Title. II. Title: The arts in New Mexico.

NEW Mexico Arts 700'.9789
Commission.
A report on the cultural and arts survey of New Mexico. [Santa Fe, 1966] 80 p. illus. 28 cm. [NX510.N43A42] 74-627529
1. The arts—New Mexico. 2. New Mexico—Intellectual life. I. Title.

Arts—New York (City)

WERTHEIM, Arthur 700'.9747'1
Frank, 1935-
The New York Little Renaissance : iconoclasm, modernism, and nationalism in American culture, 1908-1917 / by Arthur Frank Wertheim. New York : New York University Press, 1976. xiii, 276 p. : ill. ; 26 cm. Includes index. Bibliography: p. 247-260. [NX511.N4W47] 75-21805 ISBN 0-8147-9164-6 : 15.00
1. Arts—New York (City) 2. Arts, Modern—20th century—New York (City) I. Title. BIP

Arts—New York (City)—Directories.

NEW York (City). 338.4'7'70097471
Cultural Council.
New York City resources for the arts and artists; a listing of services and support available through the agencies and institutions of New York City. [New York, 1973] 95 p. 21 cm. [NX110.N48 1973] 73-91956 2.00
1. Arts—New York (City)—Directories. I. Title. BIP

Arts—New York (State)—Management.

CENTER for Arts 338.4'7'70025747
Information.
Directory for the arts : services, programs, and funds for arts organizations, local sponsors, and artists in New York State. New York : Center for Arts Information, 1978. xxi, 83 p. ; 28 cm. Includes indexes. [NX767.N7C46 1978] 78-18486 ISBN 0-89062-061-X : 6.00
1. Arts—New York (State)—Management—Directories. 2. Arts—New York (State)—Finance—Directories. 3. Arts—Information services—New York (State)—Directories. I. Title. BIP

Arts—New York (State)—Management—Statistics.

NATIONAL Research 338.4'7'7009747
Center of the Arts.
A study of the non-profit arts and cultural industry of New York State. [New York] 1972. v, 194 p. map. 28 cm. "Conducted for the Performing Arts Association of New York State, Inc., in cooperation with the New York State Association of Museums, Inc." "Study no. A002." [NX767.N7N37 1972] 73-170989
1. Arts—New York (State)—Management—Statistics. I. Performing Arts Association of New York State. II. Title. BIP

Arts—New Zealand.

SMYTH, Bernard 338.4'7'70099311
W.
The role of culture in leisure time in New Zealand [by] Bernard W. Smyth. Paris, Unesco, 1973. 88 p. illus. 26 cm. (Studies and documents on cultural policies) Bibliography: p. 87-88. [NX593.A1S58] 73-83403 ISBN 9-231-01041-7
1. Arts—New Zealand. I. Title. II. Series. Distributed by Unipub, 3.00 (pbk.). BIP

Arts—Nigeria—Management.

FASUYI, T. A. 338.4'7'7
Cultural policy in Nigeria, by T. A. Fasuyi. Paris, Unesco, 1973. 63 p. illus. 24 cm. (Studies and documents on cultural policies) Includes bibliographical references. [NX770.N55F37] 72-95232 ISBN 9-231-01029-8 pap. 2.00
1. Arts—Nigeria—Management. I. Title. II. Series.
Distributed by Unipub, New York. BIP

Arts—Norway—Management.

WILHELMSEN, Leif 354'.481'0085
Jarmann, 1910-
Cultural policy in Norway / by Leif J. Wilhelmsen. [Oslo : s.n., 1976] 21 leaves ; 30 cm. [NX770.N8W54] 77-352660
1. Arts—Norway—Management. 2. Art and state—Norway. I. Title.

Arts objects, Byzantine—Catalogs.

DUMBARTON Oaks. 709.02
Catalogue of the Byzantine and early mediaeval antiquities in the Dumbarton Oaks collection [by] Marvin C. Ross] Washington, Dumbarton Oaks Research Library and Collection, Trustees for Harvard University; [distributed by J.J. Augustin, Locust Valley, N.Y., 1962-1965) 2 v. col. illus., plates (part col.) 30 cm. (Dumbarton Oaks catalogues) Vol. 2 has imprint: Dumbarton Oaks Center for Byzantine Studies Trustees for Harvard University, Title on spine: Byzantine and early mediaeval antiquities in the Dumbarton Oaks collection. Contents.—v. 1. Metalwork, ceramics, glass, glyptics, painting.—v. 2. Jewelry, enamels, and art of the migration period. Bibliography: v. 1, p. 113-115; v. 2, p. 141-144. [NK715.D8] 68-25
1. Arts objects, Byzantine—Catalogs. 2. Art objects, Early Christian—Catalogs. I. Ross, Marvin Chauncey, 1904- II. Title. III. Title: Byzantine and early mediaeval antiquities in the Dumbarton Oaks collection. BIP

Arts—Ontario—Directories.

ONTARIO. 338.4'7'70025713
Ministry of Culture and Recreation.
Cultural resources in Ontario. [Toronto] : Ontario Ministry of Culture and Recreation : available from the Govt. Book Store, [1976?] 51 p. ; 23 cm. Cover title. [NX120.C2O57 1976] 77-358122 1.00
1. Arts—Ontario—Directories. I. Title.

The arts—Oregon.

OREGON. Governor's 338.4'7'709795
Planning Council on the Arts and Humanities.
Survey of the arts in Oregon, 1967. [Eugene, 1967] ii, 92, iii-iv p. illus. 23 cm. Cover title. [NX510.O7A44] 74-632882 1.00
1. The arts—Oregon. I. Title.

The arts—Paris.

GONCOURT, Edmond Louis 709'.4436
Antoine Huot de, 1822-1896.
Paris and the arts, 1851-1896; from the Goncourt Journal. Edited and translated by George J. Becker and Edith Philips. With an afterword on Japanese art and influence by Hedley H. Rhys. Ithaca [N.Y.] Cornell University Press [1971] vi, 374 p. illus., ports. 22 cm. Translation of selections from Journal des Goncourt. "Writings of the Goncourts": p. 337-338.

[NX549.P3A2513 1971] 72-161309 ISBN 0-8014-0655-2 12.50
1. The arts—Paris. I. Goncourt, Jules Alfred Huot de, 1830-1870, joint author. II. Becker, George Joseph, ed. III. Philips, Edith, ed. IV. Title. BIP

The arts—Pennsylvania.

PENNSYLVANIA. Council 700'.9748
on the Arts.
Pennsylvania culture: the arts, the artists, the audience. Editor-in-chief: Vincent R. Artz. [Harrisburg? 1969- v. illus. 31 x 32 cm. [NX510.P4A45] 73-76732
1. The arts—Pennsylvania. I. Artz, Vincent R., ed. II. Title.

Arts—Periodicals.

AMERICAN Craftsmen's 746.7'5'08
Council.
Report. [New York] v. 15cm. annual. [NK11.A54] 56-56395
I. Title.

ARTS yearbook, 4. 705.8
Ed.: Hilton Kramer; assoc. eds.: Francis Kloeppel, James R. Mellow. [Pub. by Art Digest, Inc.] New York [dist.] Horizon, c.1961. 199p. illus. (part col.) 32cm. annual. 57-11409 5.95 bds.,

GUMMES grinning : 700'.979
[poems, stories, and graphic materials]. [Moorpark, Calif. : Moorpark College, 1974] 56 p. : ill. ; 21 cm. (Pacific journal of the arts in two year colleges) Cover title. [NX1.G85] 74-195936
1. Arts—Periodicals. I. Title. II. Series.

Arts—Periodicals—Bibliography.

BRITISH periodicals in 016.7'005
the creative arts : an index to the microfilm collection / edited by Jean Hoornstra and Trudy Heath. Ann Arbor, Mich. : University Microfilms International, 1979. p. cm. [Z5937.B75] [N1] 79-4226 ISBN 0-8357-0371-1 : 10.00
1. Arts—Periodicals—Bibliography. 2. English periodicals—Bibliography. 3. Periodicals on microfilm—Bibliography. I. Hoornstra, Jean. II. Heath, Trudy. III. University Microfilms International.

BRITISH periodicals in 016.7'005
the creative arts : an index to the microfilm collection / edited by Jean Hoornstra and Trudy Heath. Ann Arbor, Mich. : University Microfilms International, 1979. p. cm. [Z5937.B75] [N1] 79-4226 ISBN 0-8357-0371-1 : 10.00
1. Arts—Periodicals—Bibliography. 2. English periodicals—Bibliography. 3. Periodicals on microfilm—Bibliography. I. Hoornstra, Jean. II. Heath, Trudy. III. University Microfilms International.

Arts—Peru—Management.

INSTITUTO Nacional 354'.85'0085
de Cultura (Peru).
Cultural policy in Peru / prepared by the National Institute of Culture. Paris : Unesco, 1978. 70 p., [2] leaves of plates : ill. ; 24 cm. (Studies and documents on cultural policies) [NX770.P4I56 1977] 78-306896 ISBN 9-231-01470-6 pbk. : 4.75
1. Arts—Peru—Management. I. United Nations Educational, Scientific and Cultural Organization. II. Title. III. Series.
Distributed by Unipub, NYC BIP

Arts—Philadelphia—Miscellanea.

DELMONTE, Diana. 700'.9748'11
Dynamics in the arts. New York, R. Speller [1974] 67 p. 24 cm. Based on columns printed in the Philadelphia welcomat from Nov. 1972 to Nov. 1973. [NX511.P35D44] 74-565 ISBN 0-8315-0144-8 3.50
1. Arts—Philadelphia—Miscellanea. 2. Philadelphia—Intellectual life—Miscellanea. I. Title. BIP

Arts—Philippine Islands—Management.

CULTURAL policy in the Philippines; a study prepared under the auspices of the Unesco National Commission of the Philippines. Paris, Unesco, 1973. 40 p. 24 cm. (Studies and documents on cultural policies) "SAC.73/XIX-27/A." [NX750.P6C84] 74-175648 ISBN 92-3-101133-2 338.4'7'7009599
1. Arts—Philippine Islands—Management. 2. Art and state—Philippine Islands. I. Philippines (Republic). United Nations Educational, Scientific and Cultural Organization National Commission.
Distributed by Unipub, 2.25 (pbk.).

Arts—Psychological aspects.

ARMSTRONG, Robert Plant. 700'.1
Wellspring : on the myth and source of culture / Robert Plant Armstrong. Berkeley : University of California Press, c1975. xiv, 153 p., [14] leaves of plates : 24 ill. (1 col.) ; 23 cm. Includes bibliographical references and index. [NX165.A75] 73-85781 ISBN 0-520-02571-7 : 10.00
1. Arts—Psychological aspects. 2. Art and mythology. I. Title. BIP

The arts—Psychology.

BERNDTSON, Arthur, 1913- 701.1
Art, expression, and beauty. New York, Holt, Rinehart and Winston [1969] xi, 305 p. illus. 24 cm. Bibliography: p. 287-293. [NX165.B39] 69-14249
1. The arts—Psychology. 2. Aesthetics. I. Title. BIP

BERNDTSON, Arthur, 1913- 701'.1
Art, expression, and beauty. Huntington, N.Y., R. E. Krieger Pub. Co., 1975 [c1969] xi, 305 p. illus. 23 cm. Reprint of the ed. published by Holt, Rinehart and Winston, New York. Bibliography: p. 287-293. [NX165.B39 1975] 74-13933 ISBN 0-88275-217-0 12.50
1. Arts—Psychology. 2. Aesthetics. I. Title.

CARY, Joyce, 1888-1957. 701.15
Art and reality: ways of the creative process. Freeport, N.Y., Books for Libraries Press [1970, c1958] xiv, 174 p. 23 cm. (Essay index reprint series) [NX165.C36 1970] 77-128218 ISBN 0-8369-1906-8
1. The arts—Psychology. I. Title.

GARDNER, Howard. 701'.15
The arts and human development; a psychological study of the artistic process. New York, Wiley [1973] xix, 395 p. illus. 23 cm. "A Wiley-Interscience publication." Bibliography: p. 351-382. [NX165.G37] 72-13404 ISBN 0-471-29145-5 12.95
1. The arts—Psychology. 2. Aesthetics. I. Title. BIP

JENCKS, Charles. 701'.15
Adhocism; the case for improvisation [by] Charles Jencks [and] Nathan Silver. [1st ed.] New York, Doubleday, 1972. 216 p. illus. 27 cm. [NX165.J46] 72-76174 ISBN 0-385-01617-4 10.00
1. The arts—Psychology. I. Silver, Nathan. II. Title.
Pbk. 4.95, ISBN 0-385-01711-1

KREITLER, Hans. 700'.1'9
Psychology of the arts [by] Hans Kreitler and Shulamith Kreitler. Durham, N.C., Duke University Press, 1972. xiv, 514 p. illus. 25 cm. Bibliography: p. 394-453. [NX165.K68] 70-185466 ISBN 0-8223-0269-1 13.75
1. The arts—Psychology. I. Kreitler, Shulamith, joint author. II. Title. BIP

*A Letter to His Excellency Count *** on poetry, painting, and sculpture.* Anonymous. New York, Garland Pub., 1973. 33 (i.e. 57) p. 21 cm. Facsimile reprint of the 1768 ed. printed for T. Becket and P. A. De Hondt, London. [NX165.L43 1768a] 74-112175 700'.1'9
1. Arts—Psychology.
Sold only as part of a series. Sold only as part of the 208 title series, English literary criticism of the 18th century, for 3900.00.

MARTIN, F. David, 1920- 701'.15
The humanities through the arts [by] F. David Martin [and] Lee A. Jacobus. New York, McGraw-Hill [1974, c1975] ix, 394 p. illus. 24 cm. Includes bibliographical references. [NX165.M37] 74-6347 ISBN 0-07-040612-X 7.95 (pbk.).
1. Arts—Psychology. 2. Art appreciation. I. Jacobus, Lee A., joint author. II. Title. BIP

RUSK, William Sener, 1892- 701.15
Art in its environment. [1st ed.] New York, Vantage Press [1969] 111 p. 21 cm. Includes bibliographies. [NX165.R8] 70-10402
1. The arts—Psychology. I. Title.

SCHOEN, Max, 1888- ed. 700'.1
The enjoyment of the arts. Freeport, N.Y., Books for Libraries Press [1971, c1944] 336 p. illus., ports. 23 cm. (Essay index reprint series) [NX165.S3 1971] 74-90678 ISBN 0-8369-2173-9
1. The arts—Psychology. 2. Art appreciation. I. Title. BIP

STEIN, George Philip, 1917- 701.15
The ways of meaning in the arts [by] George P. Stein. New York, Humanities Press [1970] 167 p. 23 cm. Bibliography: p. 165-167. [NX165.S7 1970] 70-116445 5.00
1. The arts—Psychology. I. Title.

VYGOTSKII, Lev Semenovich, 1896-1934. 701.15
The psychology of art [by] Lev Semenovich Vygotsky. Introd. by A. N. Leontiev. Commentary by V. V. Ivanov. [Translated from the Russian by Scripta Technica] Cambridge, Mass., M.I.T. Press [1971] xi, 305 p. 24 cm. Translation of Psikhologiia iskusstva. Includes bibliographical references. [NX165.V913] 74-103904 ISBN 0-262-22013-X 12.50
1. The arts—Psychology. I. Title.

Arts—Psychology—Addresses, essays, lectures.

THE Arts and cognition / edited by David Perkins and Barbara Leondar. Baltimore : Johns Hopkins University Press, c1977. viii, 341 p. : ill. ; 24 cm. Includes bibliographical references and index. [NX165.A79] 76-17237 ISBN 0-8018-1843-5 : 16.50 700'.1
1. Arts—Psychology—Addresses, essays, lectures. 2. Cognition—Psychology—Addresses, essays, lectures. I. Perkins, David. II. Leondar, Barbara.

Arts—Psychology—Bibliography.

ROTHENBERG, Albert, 1930- 016.700'92'2
The index of scientific writings on creativity: creative men and women [by] Albert Rothenberg and Bette Greenberg. [Hamden, Conn.] Archon Books [1974] ix, 117 p. 25 cm. [Z5931.R65] 74-14823 ISBN 0-208-01429-2
1. Arts—Psychology—Bibliography. 2. Artists—Psychology—Bibliography. I. Greenberg, Bette, 1937- joint author. II. Title.

Arts—Public opinion—New York (State)

NATIONAL Research Center of the Arts. 301.15'43'709747
Arts and the people; a survey of public attitudes and participation in the arts and culture in New York State. [New York; available from Cranford Wood, inc., c1973] x, 101, A124 p. 28 cm. "Conducted for the American Council for the Arts in Education, inc., with support from the New York State Council on the Arts." [NX510.N46N37 1973] 74-621236 5.00
1. Arts—Public opinion—New York (State) I. American Council for the Arts in Education. II. Title. BIP

The arts—Public opinion—United States.

AMERICAN Institute of Public Opinion. 301.15'43'7
Attitudes of college students toward the arts; a public opinion study, December-January 1972. [Princeton? N.J., 1972] [36] l. 29 cm. [NX165.A47] 72-194298
1. The arts—Public opinion—United States. 2. College students—United States—Attitudes. I. Title.

Arts, Renaissance.

LLOYD, Joan Barclay. 704.94'32
African animals in Renaissance literature and art. Oxford, Clarendon Press, 1971. xi, 145 p. illus. 26 cm. (Oxford studies in the history of art and architecture) Based on the author's thesis, University of London. Bibliography: p. 137-140. [NX450.5.L5] 72-170261 ISBN 0-19-817180-3
1. The arts, Renaissance. 2. Animals in art. 3. Zoology—Africa—Pictorial works. I. Title. II. Series.
Distributed by Oxford University Press, N.Y. 15.25.

PATER, Walter Horatio, 1839-1894. 700'.9'024
The Renaissance : studies in art and poetry / by Walter Pater. Folcroft, Pa. : Folcroft Library Editions, 1977. p. cm. Reprint of the 1917 ed. published by Macmillan, London. [NX450.5.P37 1977b] 77-14040 ISBN 0-8414-6846-X lib. bdg. : 20.00
1. Arts, Renaissance. I. Title. BIP

Arts, Renaissance—Addresses, essays, lectures.

GORDON, Donald James. 700'.9'24
The Renaissance imagination : essays and lectures / by D. J. Gordon ; collected and edited by Stephen Orgel. Berkeley : University of California Press, [1976] c1975. xi, 327 p. : ill. ; 26 cm. Includes bibliographical references and index. [NX450.5.G67] 74-81432 ISBN 0-520-02817-1 : 22.50
1. Arts, Renaissance—Addresses, essays, lectures. I. Title. BIP

Arts—Romania—Management.

BALAN, Ion Dodu, 1929- 354'.498'0085
Cultural policy in Romania / Ion Dodu Balan ; with the co-operation of the Directorates of the Council of Socialist Culture and Education. Paris : Unesco Press, 1975. 70 p., [4] leaves of plates : ill. ; 25 cm. (Studies and documents on cultural policies) "[B.10] SHC.74/XIX.29/A." Includes bibliographical references. [NX770.R6B35] 75-308807 ISBN 92-3-101188-X pbk. : 3.30
1. Arts—Romania—Management. I. Title. II. Series. BIP

Arts, Russian.

DE ROPP, S. 700'.947
Changing patterns of Russian arts & letters, by S. de Ropp. [Syracuse?] 1968. xviii, 645 p. illus. 24 cm. "Russian texts of literary fragments quoted": p. [243]-363. Bibliography: p. 591-629. [NX556.D4] 79-697
1. The arts, Russian. I. Title.

LONDON, Kurt, 1899- 709'.47
The seven Soviet arts. [Translated by Eric S. Bensinger] Westport, Conn., Greenwood Press [1970] xi, 381 p. illus., ports. 23 cm. Reprint of the 1937 ed. [NX556.A1L613 1970] 70-109773 ISBN 0-8371-4263-6
1. The arts, Russian. I. Title. BIP

WILLIAMS, Robert Chadwell, 1938- 700'.947
Artists in revolution : portraits of the Russian avant-garde, 1905-1925 / Robert C. Williams. Bloomington : Indiana University Press, c1977. p. cm. Includes index. Bibliography: p. [NX556.A1W54 1977] 76-26428 ISBN 0-253-31077-6 : 17.50
1. Arts, Russian. 2. Arts, Modern—20th century—Russia. 3. Arts and revolutions—Russia. 4. Avant-garde (Aesthetics) I. Title. BIP

The arts, Russian—History.

FRANKEL, Tobia. 700'.947
The Russian artist; the creative person in Russian culture. New York, Macmillan [1972] 198 p. illus. 24 cm. (Russia old and new series) Bibliography: p. 187-189. [NX556.A1F72] 72-78617 5.95
1. The arts, Russian—History. 2. Artists, Russian. I. Title. II. Series. BIP

Arts—St. Lawrence Valley.

ASSOCIATED Colleges of the St. Lawrence Valley. 700'.9747'5
Cultural resources of the Black River-St. Lawrence region / Associated Colleges of the St. Lawrence Valley, Arts and Humanities Council of the St. Lawrence Valley, inc. Canton, N.Y. : Black River-St. Lawrence Regional Planning Board, 1973. iii, 191 p. ; 28 cm. (Comprehensive planning series ; rept. no. 3) Cover title. Bibliography: p. 189. [NX510.N462S242 1973] 76-351614 9.65
1. Arts—St. Lawrence Valley. 2. St. Lawrence Valley—Intellectual life. I. Arts and Humanities Council of the St. Lawrence Valley. II. Black River-St. Lawrence Regional Planning Board. III. Title. IV. Series: Comprehensive planning series (Canton) ; rept. no. 3.

Arts—Scholarships, fellowships, etc.—New York (State)

CREATIVE Artists Public Service Program. 658'.91'70079
Caps in capsule : a fellowship program for individual artists. [New York : Creative Artists Public Service Program, c1975] 67 p. : ill. ; 26 cm. Cover title. [NX742.N7C73 1975] 75-24028
1. Creative Artists Public Service Program. 2. Arts—Scholarships, fellowships, etc.—New York (State) I. Title.

NEW York (State). State University. Washington Office. 338.4'7'7009747
Support for the arts; a survey of possible sources for State University of New York. [Susan G. Sorrels, editor] Washington] 1973. 164 p. 24 cm. Bibliography: p. 161-164. [NX705.5.U62N77 1973] 73-176026 2.00
1. New York (State). State University. 2. Arts—Scholarships, fellowships, etc.—New York (State) 3. Federal aid to the arts—New York (State) I. Sorrels, Susan G., ed. II. Title.

The arts—Scholarships, fellowships, etc.—U.S.—Directories.

INSTITUTE of International Education. 707'.9
International awards in the arts; for graduate and professional study. [New York, 1969] 105 p. map. 23 cm. Bibliography: p. 101. [NX398.I5] 68-57352
1. The arts—Scholarships, fellowships, etc.—U.S.—Directories. I. Title.

Arts—Senegal—Management.

M'BENGUE, Mamadou Seyni. 658'.91'709663
Cultural policy in Senegal. Paris, Unesco, 1973 [i.e. 1974] 61 p. illus. 24 cm. (Studies and documents on cultural policies) [NX770.S44M23] 74-162520 ISBN 9-231-01118-9
1. Arts—Senegal—Management. I. Title. II. Series.
Distributed by Unipub, 2.25 (pbk.). BIP

The arts—Spain—Addresses, essays, lectures.

ILIE, Paul, 1932- comp. 700'.946
Documents of the Spanish vanguard. Chapel Hill, University of North Carolina Press [1969] 451 p. 23 cm. (University of North Carolina. Studies in the Romance languages and literatures, no. 78) Documents in Spanish or Catalan. [PC13.N67 no. 78] 73-628708
1. The arts—Spain—Addresses, essays, lectures. I. Title. II. Series: North Carolina. University. Studies in the Romance languages and literatures, no. 78

The arts—Study and teaching.

THE Arts in higher education. Edited by Lawrence E. Dennis & Renate M. Jacob. Foreword by Harry 707

Ransom. [1st ed.] San Francisco, Jossey-Bass, 1968. xvi, 157 p. 22 cm. (The Jossey-Bass series in higher education) "A publication of the American Association for Higher Education." Report of the AAHE arts study project. Includes bibliographies. [NX280.A7] 68-57442 5.50
1. The arts—Study and teaching. I. Dennis, Lawrence Edward, 1920- ed. II. Jacob, Renate M., ed. III. American Association for Higher Education.

EDUCATIONAL Policies Commission. 700
The role of the fine arts in education. [Washington, 1968] 17 p. 24 cm. [NX280.E3] 68-54315 1.25
1. The arts—Study and teaching. I. Title.

EVALUATING the arts in 707'.1
education : a responsive approach / edited by Robert Stake with assistance from the JDR 3rd Fund. Columbus, Ohio : Merrill, c1975. vi, 122 p. : ill. ; 24 cm. Bibliography: p. [77]-122. [NX282.E9] 75-6076 ISBN 0-675-08700-7 : 6.95
1. Arts—Study and teaching. 2. Educational accountability. I. Stake, Robert E. II. JDR 3rd Fund.

The arts—Study and teaching—Addresses, essays, lectures.

EDUCATION and the 370.11'2
popular arts: the proceedings of a conference held at Magee University College, Friday and Saturday, 16th and 17th May 1969; edited by Edwin Rhodes. Londonderry, Magee University College (Extra Mural Studies) [1970] [5], 67 p. 26 cm. [NX282.E3] 74-558357 ISBN 0-901049-02-6
1. The arts—Study and teaching—Addresses, essays, lectures. 2. The arts and society—Addresses, essays, lectures. I. Rhodes, Edwin, ed. II. Magee University College, Londonderry, Ire. Extra-Mural Studies.

THE Fourth 'R; 707
a commentary on youth, education, and the arts. [New York] Associated Councils of the Arts [1972] 56 p. 23 cm. (ACA special) At head of title: RRRR. "The genesis of this book was a conference sponsored by Associated Councils of the Arts in St. Louis in May 1970." [NX280.F68] 72-83012 4.00
1. The arts—Study and teaching—Addresses, essays, lectures. I. Associated Councils of the Arts. II. Series: Associated Councils of the Arts. ACA special.

The arts—Study and teaching (Elementary)

MONTGOMERY, Chandler. 372.5'044
Art for teachers of children; foundations of aesthetic experience. 2d ed. Columbus, Ohio, Merrill [1973] xi, 235 p. illus. 24 cm. Bibliography: p. 221-226. [NX282.M66 1973] 72-97008 ISBN 0-675-08962-X 8.95
1. Arts—Study and teaching (Elementary) 2. Aesthetics. I. Title.

MONTGOMERY, Chandler. 372.5
Art for teachers of children; foundations of aesthetic experience. Columbus, Ohio, Merrill [1968] xi, 209 p. illus. 24 cm. (Merrill's international series in education) Bibliography: p. 201-205. [N361.M58] 68-10088
1. Arts—Study and teaching (Elementary) 2. Aesthetics. I. Title.

SPEER, Robert Kenneth, 1898-1959. 372.5
Measurement of appreciation in poetry, prose, and art, and studies in appreciation. New York, Bureau of Publications, Teachers College, Columbia University, 1929. [New York, AMS Press, 1973, c1972] viii, 77 p. 22 cm. Reprint of the 1929 ed., issued in series: Teachers College, Columbia University. Contributions to education, no. 362. Originally presented as the author's thesis, Columbia. [NX282.S6 1972] 78-177756 ISBN 0-404-55362-1 10.00
1. The arts—Study and teaching (Elementary) 2. Art appreciation—Testing. I. Title. II. Series: Columbia University. Teachers College. Contributions to education, no. 362.

Arts—Study and teaching—Great Britain.

WITKIN, Robert Winston. 700'.7'1
The intelligence of feeling / [by] Robert W. Witkin. London : Heinemann Educational, 1974. xiv, 198 p. : ill. ; 23 cm. Bibliography: p. 190-198. [NX343.W57] 74-188984 ISBN 0-435-80937-7 : 11.25
1. Arts—Study and teaching—Great Britain. 2. Arts—Psychology. I. Title.
Distributed by Humanities Press.

The arts—Study and teaching (Higher)

THE Arts on campus: 707'.1'173
the necessity for change, by James Ackerman [and others] Edited by Margaret Mahoney with the assistance of Isabel Moore. Greenwich, Conn., New York Graphic Society [1970] 143 p. illus. 22 cm. Bibliography: p. 142-143. [NX280.A73] 72-110664 ISBN 0-8212-0392-4
1. The arts—Study and teaching (Higher) I. Ackerman, James S. II. Mahoney, Margaret, 1924- ed.

The arts—Study and teaching (Higher)—Addresses, essays, lectures.

THE Arts and education; a new 707
beginning in higher education [by] Samuel B. Gould [and others. New York, Special Studies Project, Rockefeller Brothers Fund, 1968] 31 p. 22 cm. Papers presented at a series of meetings held in New York City in the fall of 1967 sponsored by the Mary Reynolds Babcock Foundation, the Rockefeller Brothers Fund, the Twentieth Century Fund, and the New York State Council on the Arts. [NX280A69] 68-59387
1. The arts—Study and teaching (Higher)—Addresses, essays, lectures. 2. Education, Humanistic—Addresses, essays, lectures. I. Gould, Samuel B. II. Rockefeller Brothers Fund.

Arts—Study and teaching (Higher)—New Jersey.

NEW Jersey. Phase III 707'.11'749
Fine Arts Committee.
The fine arts in New Jersey colleges and universities; report and proposal. [Trenton] Dept. of Higher Education, 1973. ii, 79 p. 28 cm. Cover title. [NX310.N3N36 1973] 74-621901
1. Arts—Study and teaching (Higher)—New Jersey. I. Title.

The arts—Study and teaching—New York (City)—Directories.

TARSHIS, Barry. 700'.7'107471
The creative New Yorker; a participant's guide to arts, crafts, music, and theater in New York. New York, Simon and Schuster [1972] 192 p. 19 cm. (A Fireside book) [NX311.N4T37] 72-83924 ISBN 0-671-21374-1 2.95
1. The arts—Study and teaching—New York (City)—Directories. I. Title. BIP

Arts—Study and teaching—New York (State)

NEW York (State). 375'.7'009747
Commission on Cultural Resources.
Arts and the schools: patterns for better education; report. [Albany] 1972. x, 100 p. 23 cm. [NX310.N4N43 1972] 72-619576
1. Arts—Study and teaching—New York (State) I. Title.

Arts—Study and teaching—New Zealand—Addresses, essays, lectures.

THE Creative arts / 372.1'9
[editors: Danny A. Knudson, Moira E. Fleming, Reg. Jarratt]. Wellington : New Zealand Educational Institute, 1976. 208 p. : ill. (part col.) ; 21 cm. (Yearbook of education ; no. 5) Includes bibliographies. [NX393.A1C73] 77-365480 10.74
1. Arts—Study and teaching—New Zealand—Addresses, essays, lectures. 2. Creative thinking (Education)—Addresses, essays, lectures. I. Knudson, Danny Alan. II. Fleming, Moira Ellen. III. Jarratt, Reginald Horatio.

Arts—Study and teaching (Secondary)—United States.

NEW York (City). 375'.009747'1 s
Board of Education. Division of Educational Planning and Suppot.
Art for the middle school. New York : Board of Education of the City of New York, Division of Educational Planning and Suppot, c1977. iv, 127 p. : ill. ; 28 cm. (Curriculum bulletin ; 1977-78 ser., no. 3) Includes bibliographies. [LB1563.N57 1977-78, ser. no. 3] [NX304] 700'.28 78-300107 ISBN 0-88315-430-7 : 6.00
1. Arts—Study and teaching (Secondary)—United States. 2. Learning by discovery. 3. Project method in teaching. I. Title. II. Series: New York (City). Board of Education. Curriculum bulletin ; 1977-78 ser., no. 3.

Arts—Study and teaching—United States.

AMERICAN Council for 700'.7'1073
the Arts in Education. Arts, Education and Americans Panel.
Coming to our senses : the significance of the arts for American education : a panel report / Arts, Education and Americans Panel. New York : McGraw-Hill, c1977. xiii, 334 p. : ill. ; 23 cm. Includes index. Bibliography: p. 312-323. [NX503.A52 1977] 77-6401 ISBN 0-07-002360-3 : 9.95. ISBN 0-07-002361-1 pbk. : 5.95
1. Arts—Study and teaching—United States. I. Title. BIP

ARTS in education 700'.7'1073
partners : schools and their communities / jointly sponsored by the Junior League of Oklahoma City ... [et al.]. ; edited by Nancy Shuker. New York : [Associated Councils of the Arts], c1977. 125, [2] p. : ill. ; 28 cm. Based on the Arts in Education Symposium held Nov. 30-Dec. 3, 1976 in Oklahoma City. Bibliography: p. [127] [NX303.A77] 77-72944
1. Arts—Study and teaching—United States. 2. Arts—United States—Finance. I. Shuker, Nancy. II. Junior League of Oklahoma City. III. Arts in Education Symposium, Oklahoma City, 1976.

PENNSYLVANIA. State 709'.73
University. Arts Impact Evaluation Team.
IMPACT: Interdisciplinary Model Programs in the Arts for Children and Teachers; a summary report. Submitted to the Arts and Humanities Program, Office of Education, the U.S. Dept. of Health, Education, and Welfare. University Park, 1973. 47 p. 28 cm. Cover title: Arts impact: curriculum for change. [NX304.P46 1973] 74-185053
1. Interdisciplinary Model Programs in the Arts for Children and Teachers (Project) 2. Arts—Study and teaching—United States. 3. Curriculum enrichment. I. United States. Office of Education. Arts and Humanities Program. II. Title: Arts impact: curriculum for change.

Arts—Tanzania—Management.

MBUGHUNI, L. A. 301.5
The cultural policy of the United Republic of Tanzania / L. A. Mbughuni. Paris : Unesco Press, 1974. 72 p., [2] leaves of plates : ill. ; 25 cm. (Studies and documents on cultural policies) Bibliography: p. 63-64. [NX750.T34M28] 75-305243 ISBN 9-231-01179-0 pbk. : 3.30
1. Arts—Tanzania—Management. I. Title. II. Series.
Distributed by Unipub. BIP

Arts—Togo—Management.

AITHNARD, K. M. 354'.66'810085
Some aspects of cultural policy in Togo / by K. M. Aithnard. Paris : Unesco Press, 1976. 101 p., [2] leaves of plates : ill. ; 24 cm. (Studies and documents on cultural policies) [NX770.T63A48] 76-372510 ISBN 9-231-01315-7 pbk. : 4.00
1. Arts—Togo—Management. 2. Art and state—Togo. I. Title. II. Series.
Distributed by Unipub. BIP

Arts, Ukrainian.

INVINCIBLE spirit : 746.4'4
art and poetry of Ukrainian women political prisoners in the U.S.S.R. / album design by Taras B. Horalewskyj ; color photography by Taras B. Horalewskyj ; poetry and text translated by Bohdan Yasen ; Ukrainian text by Bohdan Arey. Baltimore : Smoloskyp Publishers, 1977. 136 p. : ill. (some col.) ; 32 cm. Added t.p.: Nezdolannyi dukh. English and Ukrainian. [NX556.A3U52] 76-39675 ISBN 0-914834-09-6 : 25.00
1. Arts, Ukrainian. 2. Women prisoners—Ukraine. 3. Prisoners as artists—Ukraine. 4. Political prisoners—Ukraine. I. Horalewskyj, Taras B. II. Yasen, Bohdan. III. Arey, Bohdan. IV. Title: Nezdolannyi dukh.

The arts—U.S.

BUSINESS in the arts 338.4'7'7
'70. Gideon Chagy, editor. New York, P. S. Eriksson [1970] xi, 176 p. illus., ports. 32 cm. "A Business Committee for the Arts publication." [NX711.U5B8] 77-93233 6.95
1. The arts—U.S. 2. Art patronage—U.S. 3. Endowments—U.S. I. Chagy, Gideon, ed. II. Business Committee for the Arts.

CARTER, Jimmy, 1924- 700
Carter on the arts / introd. by Joan Mondale. New York : ACA, 1977. 74 p. ; 23 cm. [E873.2.C37] 77-151706 ISBN 0-915400-03-0 pbk. : 2.50
1. Carter, Jimmy, 1924-—Views on the arts. 2. Arts—United States. I. Title.
Publisher's address: Associated Council of the Arts, 1564 Broadway Rm. 820 N. Y. N. Y.10036 BIP

DUFFUS, Robert Luther, 700'.973
1888-
The American renaissance [by] R. L. Duffus. New York, AMS Press [1969] 321 p. 23 cm. Reprint of the 1928 ed. "The inquiries reported in this volume were carried out as part of the fine arts program of the Carnegie Corporation of New York City." [N6505.D8 1969] 70-105679
1. The arts—U.S. I. Carnegie Corporation of New York. II. Title. BIP

KOUWENHOVEN, John Atlee, 709'.73
1909-
Made in America : the arts in modern civilization / John A. Kouwenhoven ; introd. by Mark Van Doren. New York : Octagon Books, 1975, c1948. p. cm. Reprint of the ed. published by Doubleday, New York. Originally presented as the author's thesis, Columbia, 1948. [NX503.K68 1975] 75-29371 ISBN 0-374-94626-4 lib.bdg. : 13.00
1. Arts—United States. 2. American literature—History and criticism. 3. United States—Civilization. I. Title. BIP

LEVY, Alan. 700'.973
The culture vultures; or, Whatever became of the emperor's new clothes? New York, Putnam [1968] 380 p. 22 cm. [NX503.L48] 68-15513 6.95
1. The arts—United States. 2. United States—Popular culture. I. Title. II. Title: Whatever became of the emperor's new clothes?

MCDONALD, William 700'.973
Francis, 1898-
Federal relief administration and the arts; the origins and administrative history of the arts projects of the Works Progress Administration [by] William F. McDonald. [Columbus] Ohio State University Press [1969] xiv, 869 p. 25 cm. Includes bibliographies. [NX735.M3] 68-31422 17.50
1. U.S. Work Projects Administration—History. 2. The arts—U.S. I. Title. BIP

Arts—United States—Finance.

THE Economics of the 338.4'7'7
arts / edited by Mark Blaug ; pref. by William J. Baumol. Boulder, Colo. : Westview Press, [1976] p. cm. Includes bibliographical references.

[NX705.5.U6E27] 76-5889 ISBN 0-89158-613-X : 20.00
1. Arts—United States—Finance. 2. Arts—Great Britain—Finance. I. Blaug, Mark. BIP

Arts—United States—History.

NEIL, J. Meredith, 1937-   700'.973
Toward a national taste : America's quest for aesthetic independence / J. Meredith Neil. Honolulu : University Press of Hawaii, [1975] xiii, 402 p. ; 23 cm. Includes index. Bibliography: p. [359]-389. [NX503.N44] 75-6873 ISBN 0-8248-0340-X : 12.00
1. Arts—United States—History. I. Title. BIP

Arts—United States—Management.

NATIONAL Committee   338.4'7'700973
for Cultural Resources.
National report on the arts : a research report on the economic and social importance of arts organizations and their activities in the United States, with recommendations for a national policy of public and private support / by the National Committee for Cultural Resources. [New York] : The Committee, [1975] 36 p. : graphs ; 22 cm. Bibliography: p. 33-35. [NX765.N37 1975] 75-34838
1. Arts—United States—Management. I. Title.

Arts—United States—Management—Case studies.

CASES in arts   658'.91'70073
administration / [edited by] Thomas C. Raymond, Stephen A. Greyser, Douglas Schwalbe. Rev. ed. Cambridge [sic] Mass. : Arts Administration Research Institute, 1975. xv, 389 p. : ill. ; 28 cm. Includes bibliographical references. [NX765.C37 1975] 75-321290 ISBN 0-915440-00-8
1. Arts—United States—Management—Case studies. I. Raymond, Thomas Cicchino. II. Greyser, Stephen A. III. Schwalbe, Douglas.

Arts—United States—Societies, etc.

NATIONAL Research   338.4'7'70973
Center of the Arts.
State arts councils. [Special editors: Janet English Gracey and Sally Gardner. New York] Associated Councils of the Arts [1972] ix, 80 p. illus. 28 cm. (ACA special) [NX22.N35 1972] 74-180244 5.00
1. Arts—United States—Societies, etc. 2. Arts—United States—Finance. I. Gracey, Janet English, ed. II. Gardner, Sally, ed. III. Title. IV. Series: Associated Councils of the Arts. ACA special.

The arts—U.S.—Societies, etc.—Directories.

ASSOCIATED Councils of   700'.6'073
the Arts.
ACA arts yellow pages / [prepared by Margot Honig, with the assistance of Raymond Baron]. New York : Associated Councils of the Arts, c1977. vii, 127 p. ; 23 cm. [NX22.A823 1977] 76-58748 ISBN 0-915400-02-2 : 7.50
1. Arts—United States—Societies, etc.—Directories. I. Honig, Margot. II. Baron, Raymond. III. Title.

ASSOCIATED Councils of   700'.25'73
the Arts.
Directory of national arts organizations. [New York] 1969. 76 p. 22 cm. Pages 74-76, blank for "Notes". [NX22.A823] 75-77987 2.00 (pbk)
1. The arts—U.S.—Societies, etc.—Directories. I. Title.

The arts—Utah.

REPORT on the fine arts   709.792
in Utah, 1968. Study conducted by Bureau of Economic and Business Research, University of Utah; directed by Utah State Institute of Fine Arts. [Salt Lake City] 1968. xiv, 133 p. illus., forms, maps, ports. 22 cm. Includes reports from individuals,

professionals,   and   educators. [NX510.U8R4] 68-66409
1. The arts—Utah. I. Utah. University. Bureau of Economic and Business Research. II. Utah. State Institute of Fine Arts, Salt Lake City. III. Title: The arts in Utah.

Arts, Victorian—England—Addresses, essays, lectures.

THE Mind and art of   700'.942
Victorian England / edited by Josef L. Altholz. Minneapolis : University of Minnesota Press, c1976. vii, 206 p., [18] leaves of plates : ill. (some col.) ; 24 cm. Includes index. Bibliography: p. 195-197. [NX543.A1M55 1976] 75-22686 ISBN 0-8166-0772-9 : 15.00
1. Arts, Victorian—England—Addresses, essays, lectures. 2. Arts, English—Addresses, essays, lectures. I. Altholz, Josef Lewis, 1933-
Contents omitted.   BIP

Arts—Vienna.

POWELL, Nicolas.   709'.436'13
The sacred spring : the arts in Vienna, 1898-1918 / by Nicolas Powell ; with an introd. to the cultural background by Adolf Opel. Greenwich, Conn. : New York Graphic Society, 1974. 224 p. : ill. (some col.) ; 29 cm. Includes bibliographical references and index. [NX600.W53P68 1974] 74-78460 ISBN 0-8212-0619-2 : 25.00
1. Vereinigung Bildender Kunstler "Wiener Secession." 2. Arts—Vienna. I. Title.

Arts—Vocational guidance.

FIXMAN, Adeline.   700'.23
Your future in a creative career / by Adeline Fixman. 1st ed. New York : Richards Rosen Press, 1978. xi, 115 p. : ill. ; 22 cm. (Careers in depth) Bibliography: p. 111-115. [NX163.F59] 77-24560 ISBN 0-8239-0402-4 lib.bdg. : 4.98
1. Arts—Vocational guidance. I. Title.

The arts—Washington (State)—Directories.

*ALLIED Arts of   703'.9797
Seattle, Inc.
Puget Sound's lively arts; a directory of arts organizations and their activities, with a tour guide to art in public places. [Seattle, 1972- v. 22 cm.
1. The arts—Washington (State)—Directories.
Vol. 2, 1973, is available from Allied Arts, 107 South Main, Seattle, WA 98104

Arts—Woodstock, N.Y.—Directories.

WOODSTOCK resources   974.7'34
catalog : a guide to the artists, musicians, craftspeople, shops & community services of Woodstock, New York. [s.l. : s.n.], 1976 (s.l. : KTB Associates) iv, 124 p. : ill. ; 29 cm. Cover title. Includes index. [NX110.W66] 76-374560 2.50
1. Arts—Woodstock, N.Y.—Directories.

The arts, Yoruba.

ARMSTRONG, Robert Plant.   709.01'1
The affecting presence; an essay in humanistic anthropology. Urbana, University of Illinois Press [1971] xxii, 213 p. illus. 24 cm. Bibliography: p. 205-206. [NX589.6.N5A7] 75-107090 ISBN 0-252-00104-4 6.95
1. The arts, Yoruba. 2. The arts, Javanese. 3. The arts—Psychology. 4. The arts and society. I. Title. II. Title: Humanistic anthropology.   BIP

Arts—Zaire—Management.

CULTURAL policy in   354'.675'10085
the Republic of Zaire : a study / prepared under the direction of Bokonga Ekanga Botombele. Paris : Unesco Press, 1976. 119 p., [4] leaves of plates : ill. ; 24 cm. (Studies and documents on cultural policies) Includes bibliographical

references.   [NX770.Z28C84]   77-357403
ISBN 9-231-01317-3 pbk. : 4.65
1. Arts—Management. 2. Art and state—Zaire. 3. Zaire—Popular culture. I. Botombele, Bokonga Ekanga. II. Series. Distributed by Unipub   BIP

Aruba—Descr. & trav.—Views.

HANNAU, Hans W., 1904-   917.298/6
Aruba [by] Hans W. Hannau. Munich, W. Andermann]; dist. Doubleday, Garden City, N. Y. [1968] 60p. col. illus., map. 17cm. (Panorama-bks.) Captions in English and Dutch. [F2038.H3] 68-11378 3.25
1. Aruba—Descr. & trav.—Views. I. Title.

Asawa, Ruth.

SAN Francisco. Museum   730'.92'4
of Art.
Ruth Asawa : a retrospective view ; [exhibition] organized by the San Francisco Museum of Art, June 29 - August 19, 1973. [San Francisco] : San Francisco Museum of Art, c1973. [28] p. : ill. ; 26 cm. Text by Gerald Nordland. Bibliography: p. [26] [NB237.A82S36 1973] 75-314491
1. Asawa, Ruth. I. Asawa, Ruth. II. Nordland, Gerald. III. Title.

Ashbourne, Eng.—Descr.—Guide-books.

COME-TO-DERBYSHIRE   914.251
Association.
Ashbourne, Dovedale, and the Manifold Valley. Designed and produced by the Come-to-Derbyshire Association in collaboration with the Ashbourne Urban District Council. Derby, [1950?] 72 p. (p. 58-72 advertisements) illus., maps (1 fold.) 22 cm. [DA690.A797C6] 51-22932
1. Ashbourne, Eng.—Descr.—Guide-books. 2. Dove Dale, Eng.—Descr. & trav.—Guidebooks. 3. Manifold Valley, Eng.—Descr. & trav.—Guide-books. I. Title.

Ashby-de-la-Zouch.

HEXTALL'S Ashby-de-la-   914.25'48
Zouch. London ; New York : White Lion Publishers, 1974. [2], viii, 166 p. : plate, ill. ; 19 cm. Reprint of the 1852 ed. published by W. & J. Hextall, Ashby-de-la-Zouch, Eng., under title: The history and description of Ashby-de-la-Zouch. [DA690.A8H48 1974] 75-324734 ISBN 0-85617-857-8 : £2.00
1. Ashby-de-la-Zouch.

Ashcan School.

REICH,   760'.0973'074019225
Sheldon.
Graphic styles of the American Eight : [exhibition and catalogue], Utah Museum of Fine Arts, University of Utah, Salt Lake City, Utah, 29 February-11 April, 1976 / by Sheldon Reich. Salt Lake City : Utah Museum of Fine Arts, c1976. 118 p. : ill. ; 22 x 27 cm. Bibliography: p. 102-116. [NC108.R44] 76-5654
1. Ashcan School. 2. Drawings, American—Exhibitions. 3. Water-colors, American—Exhibitions. 4. Prints, American—Exhibitions. I. Utah Museum of Fine Arts. II. Title.

Asia—Bibliography.

HUGO-BRUNT, Michael.   016.3092 s
Architecture and planning in China, Mongolia, and Korea / M. Hugo-Brunt. Monticello, Ill. : Council of Planning Librarians, 1976. 79 p. ; 28 cm. (Exchange bibliography ; 1055-1056) Cover title. [Z5942.C68 no. 1055-1056] [Z3001] [DS5] 016.951 76-379258 pbk. : 8.00
1. Asia—Bibliography. 2. Architecture, Chinese—Bibliography. I. Title. II. Series: Council of Planning Librarians. Exchange bibliography ; 1055-1056.   BIP

Asia, Peru.

ENGEL, Frederic.   595.78
A preceramic settlement on the central coast of Peru: Asia. unit l. Philadelphia,

American Philosophical Society, 1963. 139 p. illus., maps, plan, profiles, tables, 30 cm. (Transactions of the American Philosophical Society, new ser., v. 53. pt. 3) Bibliography: p. 138-139. [Q11.Py n.s. vol. 53.pt. 3] 62-21774
1. Asia, Peru. 2. Peru. 3. Indians of South America — Peru.excavations (Archaeology) — Peru — Asia. I. Title. II. Series. III. Series: American Philosophical Society, Philadelphia. Transactions, new ser., v. 53. pt. 3   BIP

Asolo Theater, Sarasota, Fla.

JOHN and Mable Ringling   725.82
Museum of Art, Sarasota, Fla.
The Asolo Theater. [Text by Creighton Gilbert] Sarasota [1959] unpaged. illus. 23cm. [NA6835.S3J6] 59-65231
1. Asolo Theater, Sarasota, Fla. I. Gilbert, Creighton. II. Title.

Assemblage (Art)

SEITZ, William Chapin.   709.04
The art of assemblage. New York, Museum of Modern Art; distributed by Doubleday, Garden City, N.Y. [1961] 176 p. illus. (part col.) 25 cm. Includes bibliographies. [N6490.S35] 61-17803
1. Assemblage (Art) 2. Art—Exhibitions. I. Title.

Assemblage (Art)—Exhibitions.

ASSEMBLAGE in   730'.922
California, works from the late 50's and early 60's. [Exhibition] Art Gallery, University of California, Irvine, Oct. 15 to Nov. 24, 1968. [Alhambra, Calif., Printed by Cunningham Press, 1968] 58 p. illus. (part col.) 23 cm. Includes bibliographical references. [N6530.C2A75] 68-66853
1. Assemblage (Art)—Exhibitions. 2. Assemblage (Art)—California. I. California. University, Irvine. Art Gallery.

Assisi— Descr.

HUTTON, Edward, 1875-   913.4575
Assisi and Umbria revisited. New York, McKay [1953] xi, 247p. illus. 22cm. [DG975.A] A56
1. Assisi— Descr. 2. Umbria—Descr. & trav. I. Title.

HUTTON, Edward, 1875-   914.56
Assisi and Umbria revisitied. London, Hollis & Carter, [Chester Springs, Pa., Dufour, 1966] xi, 247p. illus. 23cm. First pub. in 1953. [DG975.A8H8] 54-19588 6.00 bds.,
1. Assisi—Descr. 2. Umbria—Descr. & trav. I. Title.

Assisi. San Francesco (Church)

MEISS, Millard [Lazare]   759.5
Giotto and Assisi. [New York] New York University Press, [c.]1960   28p. Bibliography: p. 26-28. (Walter W. S. Cook alumni lecture, 1959) 60-9443 lates. 25cm. 5.00
1. Giotto di Bondone, 1266?-1337. 2. Assisi. San Francesco (Church) I. Title. II. Series.

Astronomy in art.

ERNST, Max, 1891-   709'.2'4
Maximiliana : the illegal practice of astronomy : hommage a Dorothea Tanning / Max Ernst ; Peter Schamoni [editor]. Boston : New York Graphic Society, [1975] c1974. 89 p. : chiefly ill. (some col.) ; 25 cm. Issued also under title: Max Ernst, Maximiliana: die widerrechtliche Ausubung der Astronomie. Text in English, French, and German. [N6888.E7S248] 74-24832 ISBN 0-8212-0655-9 : 17.50
1. Ernst, Max, 1891- 2. Astronomy in art. I. Schamoni, Peter. II. Title.

Astronomy, Prehistoric.

†BROWN, Peter Lancaster,   936
1927-
Megaliths,   myths,   and   men   :   an

: ill. (some col.) ; 27 cm. [NC139.F47F54] 76-360965 15.00
1. Finlay, Virgil. 2. Atrology in art. I. Finlay, Beverly C.

Auburn, Mass.—Description—Views.

TOWN of Auburn : 974.4'3
glimpses of the past / [compiled and edited by Raymond Twarowski and Ralph Rothera] ; presented by Auburn Historical Society. Auburn, Mass. : Auburn Historical Society, 1975. [24] p. : chiefly ill. ; 22 cm. Cover title. [F74.A9T68] 75-324271
1. Auburn, Mass.—Description—Views. 2. Auburn, Mass.—Buildings—Pictorial works. I. Twarowski, Raymond. II. Rothera, Ralph. III. Auburn Historical Society.

Audio-visual education—Great Britain.

STEWART, James Henderson. 711'.07'8
The role of audio-visual self teaching packages : a pilot study of the acceptability of audio-visual self teaching packages in a Town and Country Planning School ... / [by] James H. Stewart. Newcastle upon Tyne : [University of Newcastle upon Tyne, Department of Town and Country Planning], 1976. [3], 20, [8] leaves, plate : 1 ill. ; 30 cm. Bibliography: leaf 20. [LB1043.2.G7S7] 77-362652 ISBN 0-905770-00-5 : £1.00
1. Audio-visual education—Great Britain. I. Title.

Auditorium.

LITTLE (Arthur D.) inc. 725.83
Report to the county of Los Angeles on a new auditorium and music center. Cambridge, Mass. [1956] 96, 5p. illus., maps, plans, tables. 29cm. Part of illustrative matter is colored. Ruler in pocket. [NA6815.L5] 56-39734
1. Audioriums. 2. Music-halls. 3. Cities and towns—Planning—Los Angeles. I. Los Angeles Co., Calif. II. Title.

Auditoriums.

DUNCAN, Cyril John, ed. 727
Modern lecture theatres; ed. by C. J. Duncan Newcastle upon. Tyne, Oriel Pr. [1966] 301, A40 p. illus., plans, diagrs. 31cm. (Oriel academic pubns.) Largely paps. presented at a conf. convened by the Univ. of Manchester Sch. of Educ. [NA6602.A8D8] 67-72587 14.50
1. Auditoriums. 2. Architecture—Designs and plans. I. Victoria University of Manchester. School of Education. II. Title. III. Series.

INTERNATIONAL Association of Auditorium Managers. Publications Committee. 725
Auditoriums and arenas; facts from a survey by the International Association of Auditorium Managers. Prepared under direction of the I. A. A. M. Publications Committee by Francis R. Deering, Don Jewell [and] Lindsley C. Lueddeke, chairman. Chicago, Public Administration Service [1961] 86 p. illus. 28 cm. [NA6815.I5] 61-8219
1. Auditoriums. I. Deering, Francis R. II. Title.

JEWELL, Don, 1921- 725'.8
Public assembly facilities : planning and management / Don Jewell. New York : Wiley, c1978. x, 195 p. : ill. ; 24 cm. "A Wiley-Interscience publication." Includes index. [NA6815.J45] 77-16524 ISBN 0-471-02437-6 : 15.00
1. Auditoriums. 2. Theaters. 3. Stadia. 4. Convention facilities. 5. Exhibition buildings. I. Title. BIP

SYMONS, Farrell George Hardy. 352.5
Municipal auditoriums. Chicago, Public Administration Service [1950] 78 p. tables. 22 x 28 cm. [NA6815.S9] 50-14318
1. Auditoriums. 2. Municipal buildings — U.S. I. Public Administration Service, Chicago; II. Title.

TAYLOR, Jeremy Reginald Buckley. 727'.38
The science lecture room: a planning study to examine the principles of location and design of lecture rooms in the development of university science areas: prepared with the support of the Nuffield Foundation at the School of Architecture, Cambridge [by] Jeremy Taylor. Cambridge, U.P., 1967. viii, 119 p. illus., plans. tables, diagrs. 30 1/2 cm. (B 67-23660) [NA6602.S3T3] 67-24941
1. Auditoriums. 2. Science—Study and teaching. 3. Universities and colleges—Buildings. I. Title. BIP

U.S. District of Columbia Auditorium Commission. 725.83
Plans for a national civic auditorium and cultural center for the citizens of the United States, submitted to the President of the United States and the Congress, January 31, 1957. [Washington, 1957] 95 p. illus., maps, plans. 23 x 31 cm. Cover title. [NA6815.U53] 57-63497
1. Auditoriums. 2. Civic centers — Washington, D.C. I. Title. II. Title: National civic auditorium and cultural center

Audubon, John James, 1785-1851.

ADAMS, Alexander B. 598.20924
John James Audubon; a biography. New York, Putnam [c.1966] 510p. illus., facsims., ports. 22cm. Bibl. [QL31.A9A6] 66-15573 7.95
1. Audubon, John James, 1785-1851. I. Title.

ADAMS, Alexander B 598.20924 (B)
John James Audubon; a biography, by Alexander B. Adams. New York, Putnam [1966] 510 p. illus., facsims., ports. 22 cm. Bibliography: p. 475-486. [QL31.A9A6] 66-15573
1. Audubon, John James, 1785-1851. I. Title.

AUDUBON, John James, 1785-1851. 598.2'0924 B
Audubon in Louisiana. New Orleans, Louisiana State Museum; Friends of the Cabildo, 1966. [40] p. col. illus. 23 x 31 cm. Label mounted on t.p.: Supplied by Worldwide Books, Boston, Mass. [QL31.A9A225] 71-21616
1. Audubon, John James, 1785-1851. 2. Birds—Pictorial works. 3. Birds—Louisiana. I. Louisiana State Museum, New Orleans. II. Friends of the Cabildo. III. Title.

AUDUBON, John James, 1785-1851. 598.209'24
The 1826 journal of John James Audubon. Transcribed with an introd. and notes by Alice Ford from the original in the collection of Henry Bradley Martin. [1st ed.] Norman, University of Oklahoma Press [1967] xii, 409 p. facsims., ports., plates. 24 cm. [QL31.A9A24] 66-22713
I. Ford, Alice Elizabeth, 1906- II. Title.

AUDUBON the naturalist; 598.2'0924
a history of his life and time [Magnolia, Mass., Peter Smith, 1968] 2v. illus., facsims., ports. 22cm. (Dover bk. rebound) Orig. documents, v. 2, p. [313]-379. Bibl. [QL31.A9H4 1968] (B) 11.00 set,
1. Audubon, John James, 1785-1851. I. Herrick, Francis Hobart, 1858-1940

CHANCELLOR, John. 598.2'092'4 B
Audubon : a biography / by John Chancellor. New York : Viking Press, 1978. 224 p. : ill. ; 26 cm. (A Studio book) Includes index. Bibliography: p. 219. [QL31.A9C43] 78-8465 ISBN 0-670-14053-8 : 16.95
1. Audubon, John James, 1785-1851. 2. Ornithologists—United States—Biography. BIP

CLEMENT, Roland C. 598.2'974
The living world of Audubon / by Roland C. Clement ; photographers, Fred J. Alsop III ... [et al.] ; designed by Albert Squillace. New York : Grosset & Dunlap, 1974. 272 p. : col. ill. ; 32 cm. "A Ridge Press book." Includes index. [QL674.C53] 74-81535 ISBN 0-448-11831-9 : 25.00
1. Audubon, John James, 1785-1851. 2. Birds—Pictorial works. I. Title.

FORD, Alice Elizabeth, 1906- 925.9
John James Audubon, by Alice Ford. [1st ed.] Norman, University of Oklahoma Press [1964] xiv, 488 p. illus. (part col.) ports. 25 cm. Bibliography: p. 451-469. [QL31.A9F6] 64-20757
1. Audubon, John James, 1785-1851. BIP

FRIES, Waldemar H., 1889- 598.2'973
The double elephant folio: the story of Audubon's Birds of America [by] Waldemar H. Fries. Chicago, American Library Association, 1973 [i.e. 1974] xxii, 501 p. illus. 27 cm. Includes bibliographical references. [QL674.A953F74] 73-12101 ISBN 0-8389-0103-4 3.50 (pbk.)
1. Audubon, John James, 1785-1851. The birds of America. 2. Audubon, John James, 1785-1851. I. Title. BIP

GORDON, Patricia, 1904- 925.9
The story of John J. Audubon, by Joan Howard [pseud.] Illustrated by Federico Castellon. New York, Grosset & Dunlap [1954] 181p. illus. 22cm. (Signature books, 27cm. [QL31.A9G66] 54-5859
1. Audubon, John James, 1785-1851. I. Title.

HERRICK, Francis Hobart, 1858-1940. 598.2'0924 B
Audubon the naturalist; a history of his life and time. New York, Dover Publications [1968] 2 v. illus., facsims., ports. 22 cm. "Original documents": v. 2, p. [313]-379. Bibliography: v. 2, p. 401-461. [QL31.A9H4 1968] 68-14996
1. Audubon, John James, 1785-1851.

HOGEBOOM, Amy, 1891- 925.9
Audubon and his sons; illustrated with prints by John James Audubon, John Woodhouse Audubon, and others. Supplemented with drawings by Paul Galdone. New York, Lothrop, Lee & Shepard Co. [1956] 210p. illus. 22cm. [QL31.A9H6] 53-6740
1. Audubon, John James, 1785-1851. 2. Audubon, John Woodhouse, 1812-1862. I. Title.

KEATING, Louis Clark, 1907- 598.2'092'4 B
Audubon : the Kentucky years / L. Clark Keating. Lexington : University Press of Kentucky, c1976. viii, 92 p. : port. ; 21 cm. (The Kentucky bicentennial bookshelf) [QL31.A9K4] 75-38216 ISBN 0-8131-0215-4 : 3.95
1. Audubon, John James, 1785-1851. I. Title. II. Series. BIP

KNAGGS, Nelson S. 769'.924
The rediscovery of John J. Audubon's white wolf, by Nelson S. Knaggs. [Cincinnati? 1970] 30 p. illus., ports. 22 cm. [QL31.A9K55] 75-13739
1. Audubon, John James, 1785-1851. 2. Animal painting and illustration. 3. Lithographs. I. Title.

MUSCHAMP, Edward A. 598.2'092'4 B
Audacious Audubon; the story of a great pioneer, artist, naturalist & man. Freeport, N.Y., Books for Libraries Press [1973] p. Reprint of the 1929 ed. published by Brentano's, New York. [QL31.A9M85 1973] 73-5962 ISBN 0-518-19063-3
1. Audubon, John James, 1785-1851. I. Title.

PEARE, Catherine Owens. 925.9
John James Audubon, his life; illustrated by Margaret Ayer. [1st ed.] New York, Holt [1953] 89p. illus. 21cm. [QL31.A9P36] 52-13070
1. Audubon, John James, 1785-1851. I. Title.

Audubon, John James, 1785-1851 — Juvenile literature.

AYARS, James Sterling. j92
John James Audubon: bird artist. Illustrated by George I. Parrish. Campaign, Ill., Garrard Pub. Co. [1966] 80 p. col. illus. 23 cm. (A Discovery book) [QL31.A9A9] 66-10013
1. Audubon, John James, 1785-1851 — Juvenile literature. I. Title.

STEVENSON, Janet. 925.9
John James Audubon, painting America's wildlife. Illustrated by Robert Boehmer. Chicago, Kingston House; distributed in association with Lippincott, Philadelphia [1961] 191 p. illus. 22 cm. (Bookshelf for young Americans) [QL31.A9S75] 61-13229
1. Audubon, John James, 1785-1851 — Juvenile literature. I. Title.

Audubon, John Woodhouse, 1812-1862.

HOGEBOOM, Amy, 1891- 925.9
Audubon and his sons; illustrated with prints by John James Audubon, John Woodhouse Audubon, and others. Supplemented with drawings by Paul Galdone. New York, Lothrop, Lee & Shepard Co. [1956] 210p. illus. 22cm. [QL31.A9H6] 53-6740
1. Audubon, John James, 1785-1851. 2. Audubon, John Woodhouse, 1812-1862. I. Title.

Augustincic, Antun, 1900—

AUGUSTINCIC, Antun, 1900- 730'.92'4
Augustincic / [editors, Boris Kukoc, Igor Prizmic ; photos, Toso Dabac ... [et al.]. Zagreb : Priredni vjesnik, 1976. [168] p. : chiefly ill. (some col.) ; 34 cm. "Published in Croatian or Serbian, English, Russian, and German." [NB953.A8K84] 77-365848
1. Augustincic, Antun, 1900- I. Kukoc, Boris. II. Prizmic, Igor.

Ault, George, 1891-1948.

AULT, Louise. 759.13 B
Artist in Woodstock : George Ault, the independent years / by Louise Ault. Philadelphia : Dorrance, c1978. 176 p., [1] leaf of plates : ill. ; 22 cm. [N6537.A9A9] 78-57264 ISBN 0-8059-2550-3 : 7.95
1. Ault, George, 1891-1948. 2. Ault, Louise. 3. Artists—United States—Biography. 4. Wives—United States—Biography. I. Title.

Aurelius Antoninus, Marcus, Emperor of Rome, 121-180.

RYBERG, Inez (Scott) 731.5'4
Panel reliefs of Marcus Aurelius. New York, Archaeological Institute of America, 1967. xii, 102 p., 63 plates. 31 cm. (Monographs on archaeology and the fine arts 14) On label: Stechert-Hafner Service Agency, New York. Bibliographical footnotes. [NB165.A85R9] 67-8802
1. Aurelius Antoninus, Marcus, Emperor of Rome, 121-180. 2. Relief (Sculpture) I. Title. II. Series.

Austen, Alice, 1866-1952.

NOVOTNY, Ann. 770'.92'4 B
Alice's world : the life and photography of an American original, Alice Austen, 1866-1952 / by Ann Novotny ; pref. by Oliver Jensen. Old Greenwich, Conn. : Chatham Press, c1976. 221 p. : ill. ; 31 cm. [TR140.A83N67] 76-18489 ISBN 0-85699-128-7 : 22.50
1. Austen, Alice, 1866-1952. 2. Photographers—United States—Biography. I. Austen, Alice, 1866-1952. II. Title. BIP

Austen, Jane, 1775-1817.

GARNETT, Christopher Browne, 1906- 111.8'5
Taste; an essay in critical imagination [by] Christopher Browne Garnett, Jr. [1st ed.] New York, Exposition Press [1968] 88 p. 21 cm. (An Exposition-university book) Bibliography: p. [87]-88. [BH39.G34] 68-27310
1. Austen, Jane, 1775-1817. 2. Aesthetics. 3. Taste. I. Title.

Austin, Arthur Everett, 1900-1957.

JOHN and Mable Ringling Museum of Art. Sarasota, Fla. 708.159
A. Everett Austin, Jr.; a director's taste and achievement. [Hartford? 1958] 92p. illus. 26cm. '[Exhibition held at the] John and Mable Ringling Museum of Art, Sarasota, Florida, February 23 to March

30, 1958 [and at the] Wadsworth Atheneum, Hartford, Connecticut, April 23 to June 1, 1958.' [N8384.A78J6] 58-34776
1. Austin, Arthur Everett, 1900-1957. 2. Paintings—Exhibitions. I. Wadsworth Atheneum, Hartford. II. Title.

Australia—Biography—Portraits.

GRAHAM, Anne, 1925- 741.9'94
Australian outlines : drawings / by Anne Graham ; introd. by Bruce Petty. Melbourne : Lansdowne, 1976. [115] p. : chiefly ill. ; 21 x 27 cm. [NC371.G7A58] 76-370346 ISBN 0-7018-0520-X
1. Graham, Anne, 1925- 2. Australia—Biography—Portraits. I. Title.

Australia in art.

LOOBY, Keith Ronald, 1940- 741.9'94
The history of Australia / drawings by Keith Looby, songs and poems by David Campbell. Sydney : Macleay Museum, University of Sydney, 1976. [57] leaves : chiefly ill. ; 24 x 31 cm. [NC371.L66C35] 77-363175 ISBN 0-909635-06-4
1. Looby, Keith Ronald, 1940- 2. Australia in art. I. Campbell, David Watt Ian. II. Title.

Australian aborigines—New South Wales—Antiquities.

MCCARTHY, Frederick David, 1905- 994'.004'991 s
Rock art of the Cobar Pediplain in central western New South Wales / F. D. McCarthy. Canberra : Australian Institute of Aboriginal Studies, 1976. viii, 163 p. : ill. ; 30 cm. (Australian aboriginal studies) Bibliography: p. 159-163. [DU120.R45 no. 7] [GN667.N5] 732'.2 77-357526 ISBN 0-85575-049-9
1. Australian aborigines—New South Wales—Antiquities. 2. Rock paintings—Australia—New South Wales. 3. New South Wales—Antiquities. I. Title. II. Series. III. Regional and research studies ; no. 7 BIP

Australian wit and humor, Pictorial.

LINDESAY, Vane, 1920- 741.5994
The inked-in image; a survey of Australian comic art. Melbourne, Heinemann [1970] 298 p. (chiefly illus.) 28 cm. [NC1750.L55] 77-95167 7.50
1. Australian wit and humor, Pictorial. I. Title.

Authors, American—20th century—Portraits.

CHARTERS, Ann, comp. 810.9'005'4
Scenes along the road; photographs of the desolation angels, 1944-1960. With three poems and comments by Allen Ginsberg. [New York] Portents/Gotham Book Mart [1970] 56 p. illus. 26 cm. Contents.Contents.—New York, 1944-1954.—On the road, 1947-1956.—San Francisco and Berkeley, 1954-1959.—Mexico and abroad, 1951-1960.—Three poems by A. Ginsberg: Neal's ashes. Memory gardens. In a car. [PS137.C5] 76-21660
1. Authors, American—20th century—Portraits. I. Title.

TEXAS. University at Austin. Humanities Research Center. 704.942
The faces of authorship; an exhibition of twentieth century literary portraits from the Humanities Research Center collections, the University of Texas at Austin. [Austin, 1969?] [44] p. illus. 21 x 22 cm. Catalog of an exhibition held at the Art Museum of the University of Texas at Austin, Nov. 24, 1968-Jan. 4, 1969. [PS137.T4] 72-628433
1. Authors, American—20th century—Portraits. 2. Authors, English—20th century—Portraits. 3. Art, Modern—20th century—Exhibitions. I. Texas. University at Austin. Art Museum. II. Title.

Authors, American—Autographs—Facsimiles.

CAHOON, Herbert, 1918- 929.9
American literary autographs, from Washington Irving to Henry James / Herbert Cahoon, Thomas V. Lange, Charles Ryskamp. New York : Dover Publications, 1977. x p., p. 200-208, 98 leaves of plates : facsims. ; 31 cm. Includes index. [Z42.3.A9C34] 77-89415 ISBN 0-486-23548-3 : 7.95
1. Authors, American—Autographs—Facsimiles. I. Lange, Thomas V., joint author. II. Ryskamp, Charles, joint author. III. Title.

Authors, American—Caricatures and cartoons.

MARKEY, Gene, 1895- 741.5'973
Literary lights; a book of caricatures. New York, Knopf, 1923. Detroit, Gale Research, 1974. p. cm. [NC1429.M4A53 1974] 74-13934 ISBN 0-8103-4066-6
1. Authors, American—Caricatures and cartoons. 2. American wit and humor, Pictorial. I. Title.

Authors as artists—United States—Biography—Juvenile literature.

SMARIDGE, Norah. 920
Famous author-illustrators for young people. New York, Dodd, Mead [1973] 159 p. ports. 22 cm. (Famous biographies for young people) Brief biographies of nineteen author-illustrators include Roger Duvoisin, Dr. Seuss, Kate Greenaway, Lois Lenski, and Tomi Ungerer. [NC975.S57] 73-6033 ISBN 0-396-06831-6 3.95
1. Authors as artists—United States—Biography—Juvenile literature. I. Title.

Authors—Caricatures and cartoons.

BEERBOHM, Max, Sir, 1872-1956. 741.5'942
Beerbohm's literary caricatures : from Homer to Huxley / selected, introduced, and annotated by J. G. Riewald. Hamden, Conn. : Archon Books, 1977. 295 p. : ill. ; 24 cm. Includes index. Bibliography: p. 287-291. [NC1479.B37R53 1977] 77-3974 ISBN 0-208-01632-5 : 15.00
1. Authors—Caricatures and cartoons. 2. English wit and humor, Pictorial. I. Riewald, Jacobus Gerhardus. II. Title. III. Title: Literary caricatures. BIP

LEVINE, David, 1926- 741.9'73
Pens and needles; literary caricatures. New York, Liveright [1973] 1 v. (chiefly illus.) 21 cm. [NC1429.L47A53 1973] 74-161800 ISBN 0-87140-089-8 2.95 (pbk.)
1. Authors—Caricatures and cartoons. 2. American wit and humor, Pictorial. I. Title.

LEVINE, David, 1926- 809
Pens and needles; literary caricatures by David Levine. Selected and introduced by John Updike. Boston, Gambit, 1969. viii, 150 p. (chiefly illus.) 26 cm. [NC1429.L47A53] 70-98143 6.95
1. Authors—Caricatures and cartoons. 2. American wit and humor, Pictorial. I. Title. BIP

Authors, English—19th century—Biography.

MASEFIELD, John, 1878-1967. 828'.8'09 B
John Ruskin / by John Masefield. Folcroft, Pa. : Folcroft Library Editions, 1977. p. cm. "Originally delivered by Mr. Masefield as a lecture at the Ruskin Centenary Exhibition held at the Royal Academy in the autumn of 1919." Reprint of the 1920 ed. printed by H. Whitehouse and E. Daws at the Yellowsands Press, Bembridge, Eng. [PR5263.M28 1977] 77-24663 ISBN 0-8414-6213-5 lib. bdg. : 10.00
1. Ruskin, John, 1819-1900—Biography. 2. Authors, English—19th century—Biography. I. Title.

VALLANCE, Aymer, 1862-1943. 709'.24
William Morris, his art, his writings, and his public life : a record / by Aymer Vallance. Boston : Longwood Press, 1977. p. cm. Reprint of the 1898 ed. published by G. Bell, London. Includes index. "Chronological list of the printed works of William Morris": p. [PR5083.V3 1977] 77-6968 ISBN 0-89341-208-2 lib.bdg. : 50.00
1. Morris, William, 1834-1896. 2. Authors, English—19th century—Biography. 3. Artists—England—Biography.

WILENSKI, Reginald Howard, 1887- 828'.8'09 B
John Ruskin : an introduction to further study of his life and work / by R. H. Wilenski. New York : AMS Press, [1978] p. cm. Reprint of the 1933 ed. published by Faber & Faber, London. Includes index. [PR5263.W476 1978] 75-30042 ISBN 0-404-14046-7 : 28.50
1. Ruskin, John, 1819-1900. 2. Authors, English—19th century—Biography.

Authors, English—20th century—Biography.

LESLIE, Anita. 730'.92'4 B
Clare Sheridan / Anita Leslie. 1st ed. Garden City, N.Y. : Doubleday, 1977. xv, 318 p., [8] leaves of plates : ill. ; 22 cm. Includes index. [PR6037.H465Z7 1977] 76-23773 ISBN 0-385-06745-3 : 10.00
1. Sheridan, Clare Consuelo Frewen, 1885-1970—Biography. 2. Authors, English—20th century—Biography. 3. Artists—Great Britain—Biography. BIP

WATNEY, John Basil, 1915- 741'.092'4 B
Mervyn Peake / John Watney. New York : St. Martin's Press, 1976. 255 p. : ill. ; 25 cm. Includes index. Bibliography: p. 246-249. [PR6031.E183Z95 1976] 76-17422 10.95
1. Peake, Mervyn Laurence, 1911-1968—Biography. 2. Authors, English—20th century—Biography. 3. Painters—England—Biography. BIP

Authors, English—Autographs.

TEXAS. University 016.0915
A creative century; selections from the twentieth century collections at the University of Texas. An exhibition held in Nov. 1964 at the Academic Center & Undergraduate Lib., the Univ. of Texas. [Austin] Author [c.1964] 71p. facsims. 23cm. [Z42.T34] 65-63269 price unreported pap.,
1. Authors, English—Autographs. 2. Authors, American—Autographs. 3. Autographs—Texas—Collections. I. Title. BIP

Authors, French — Portraits.

NEW York. State University College, New Paltz. Art Gallery. 704.942
From Victor Hugo to Jean Cocteau; portraits of 19th and 20th century French writers from the Artinian collection. Catalogue by P. J. Bohan and A. Arinian. A loan exhibition, May 28-August 6, 1965, the Art Gallery, State University College, New Paltz, New York. [New Paltz, 1965] viii, 68 p. illus., ports. 22 cm. [N7604.N45] 65-27073
1. Authors, French — Portraits. 2. Portraits, French — Exhibitions. 3. Portraits — Private collections. I. Bohan, Peter J. II. Artinian, Artine, 1907- III. Title.

Authors—Iconography—Exhibitions.

PARKIN Gallery. 760'.074'02132
Artists & writers : an exhibition of watercolours, drawings, and etchings / Parkin Gallery. London : the Gallery, 1976. [33] p. : ill. ; 24 cm. Cover title. Catalog of the exhibition held at the Parkin Gallery, Oct. 8-Nov. 7, 1976. [PN452.P3 1976] 77-369011
1. Authors—Iconography—Exhibitions. 2. Art—Exhibitions. I. Title.

Authors—Self-portraits.

SELF-PORTRAITS : 741.9'24
book people picture themselves / collected by Burt Britton. 1st ed. New York : Random House, c1976. p. cm. [PN453.S46] 75-10271 ISBN 0-394-49648-5 : 12.50 ISBN 0-394-73104-2 pbk. : 4.95
1. Authors—Self-portraits. 2. Drawings. I. Britton, Burt, 1933-

Autograph albums—Juvenile literature.

AUTOGRAPH fun. 818.02
Illustrated by John Huehnergarth. New York, Grosset & Dunlap [1969] [64] p. col. illus. 21 cm. (Easy-to-do-book) Includes verses and rhymes to sign as autographs. Also provides blank pages for personal use. [Z41.A9] 70-75343 1.00
1. Autograph albums—Juvenile literature. I. Huehnergarth, John, illus.

Autographs.

HAMILTON, Charles, 1913- 098'.3
Scribblers & scoundrels. Introd. by Diane Hamilton. New York, Eriksson [1968] vii, 282p illus. 22cm. [Z41.H36] 67-27017 6.95
1. Autographs. 2. Literary forgeries and mystifications. I. Title.
Distributed by Hill & Wang.

Autographs—Collections.

JERVIS Library. 929.8
The Thomas C. Bright autograph collection and the Huntington autograph collection. Rome, N.Y., 1970. [22] l. 29 cm. Caption title. [Z42.J535] 76-30684
1. Bright, Thomas C. 2. Autographs—Collections. I. Title. II. Title: Huntington autograph collection.

KENNETH W. Rendell, inc. 929.8
Autograph letters, manuscripts, documents. [Newton, Mass., 1974] 65 p. illus. 22 cm. (Its Catalogue 95) Cover title. [Z42.K417 1974] 74-181601
1. Autographs—Collections. 2. Autographs—Prices. 3. Manuscripts—Catalogs. 4. Manuscripts—Prices. I. Title. II. Series.

KENNETH W. Rendell, inc. 929.8
Autographs and manuscripts: the American Revolution. [Newton, Mass., 1974] 64 p. 22 cm. (Its Catalogue 92) Cover title. [Z42.K42 1974] 74-162967
1. Kenneth W. Rendell, inc. 2. Autographs—Collections. 3. United States—History—Revolution, 1775-1783—Manuscripts—Catalogs. I. Title. II. Series.

KENNETH W. Rendell, inc. 929.8
Autographs and manuscripts: the American Civil War. [Newton, Mass., 1974] 104 p. ports. 22 cm. (Its Catalogue no. 96) Cover title. [Z42.K43] 74-181594
1. Kenneth W. Rendell, inc. 2. Autographs—Collections. 3. United States—History—Civil War, 1861-1865—Sources—Bibliography—Catalogs. I. Title. II. Series.

SZLADITS, Lola L. 016.098'3
Documents: famous & infamous; selected from the Henry W. and Albert A. Berg Collection of English and American Literature, by Lola L. Szladits. [New York] New York Public Library, 1972. 34 p. illus. 26 cm. [Z42.S95] 73-153602 ISBN 0-87104-240-1
1. New York (City). Public Library. Berg Collection. 2. Autographs—Collections. 3. Literary forgeries and mystifications—Bibliography—Catalogs. I. New York (City). Public Library. Berg Collection. II. Title. BIP

Autographs — Collectors and collecting.

AUTOGRAPHS and manuscripts, 929.8
a collector's manual / Edmund Berkeley, Jr., editor, Herbert E. Klingelhofer and Kenneth W. Rendell, coeditors ; sponsored by the Manuscript Society. Chichester : Ellis Horwood ; New York : Halsted Press, 1978. 274 p. : ill. ; 24 cm. (Mathematics & its applications) Includes index. Includes bibliographies and index. [Z41.A92] 78-8177 ISBN 0-684-15622-9 : 24.95
1. Autographs—Collectors and collecting. 2. Manuscripts—Collectors and collecting. I. Klingelhofer, Herbert E. II. Rendell, Kenneth W. III. Manuscript Society.

BENJAMIN, Mary A 091.5
Autographs: a key to collecting. Corr. and rev., with a new pref. and a selected list of reference works. New York, W. R. Benjamin Autographs, 1963. 313 p. illus. 23 cm. [Z41.R4 1963] 63-10776
1. Autographs — Collectors and collecting. I. Title.

HAMILTON, Charles, 1913- 929.8
The book of autographs : an introduction to the joys and techniques of autograph collecting by the world's foremost authority / by Charles Hamilton. New York : Simon and Schuster, c1978. p. cm. [Z41.H334] 78-14570 ISBN 0-671-24258-X : 12.95
1. Autographs—Collectors and collecting. I. Title. BIP

HAMILTON, Charles, 1913- 091.5 ed.
Collecting autographs and manuscripts. Illustrated with more than 800 facsims. and other reproductions. [1st ed.] Norman, University of Oklahoma Press [1961] xviii, 269 p. illus., ports., facsims. 27 cm. "The best books about autographs": p. 250-251. [Z41.H34] 61-9007
1. Autographs—Collectors and collecting. 2. Manuscripts—Collectors and collecting. I. Title. BIP

MADIGAN, Thomas F., 1891- 929.8 1936.
Word shadows of the great; the lure of autograph collecting. Detroit, Gale Research Co., 1971. xiv, 300 p. illus., facsims. 22 cm. Reprint of the 1930 ed. [Z41.M19 1971] 70-145705
1. Autographs—Collectors and collecting. I. Title. BIP

PATTERSON, Jerry E. 929.8
Autographs: a collector's guide [by] Jerry E. Patterson. New York, Crown Publishers [1973] vii, 248 p. illus. facsims. 24 cm. Bibliography: p. [238]-239. [Z41.P36 1973] 73-82935 ISBN 0-517-50588-6 6.95
1. Autographs—Collectors and collecting. I. Title.

PELTON, Robert W., 652'.1'075 1934-
The autograph collector; a new guide, by Robert Notlep. New York, Crown [1968] 240 p. illus., facsims., ports. 22 cm. [Z41.P45] 68-20470
1. Autographs—Collectors and collecting. I. Title.

SULLIVAN, George, 1927- 929.8
The complete book of autograph collecting. New York, Dodd, Mead [1971] 154 p. illus. 24 cm. Bibliography: p. 150. [Z41.S93] 70-153891 ISBN 0-396-06385-3 4.95
1. Autographs—Collectors and collecting. I. Title.

SULLIVAN, George, 1927- 929.8
Making money in autographs / by George Sullivan. New York : Coward, McCann & Geoghegan, c1976. p. cm. Includes index. Bibliography: p. [Z41.S94 1976] 76-21275 ISBN 0-698-10747-0 : 8.95
1. Autographs—Collectors and collecting. I. Title. BIP

WILLIAMS, Robert, 1892- 091.5
Adventures of an autograph collector; an introduction to collecting, with suggestions for beginners. [1st ed.] New York, Exposition Press [1952] 99 p. illus. 23 cm. [Z41.W5] 52-5693
1. Autographs—Collectors and collecting. I. Title.

Autographs—Collectors and collecting—Juvenile literature.

HAMILTON, Charles, 1913- 929.8
Big name hunting; a beginner's guide to autograph collecting, by Charles Hamilton with Diane Hamilton. New York, Simon and Schuster [1973] 95 p. illus. 23 cm. Bibliography: p. 95. An introduction to autograph collecting with instructions on building and organizing a collection. [Z41.H33] 72-92158 4.95
1. Autographs—Collectors and collecting—Juvenile literature. I. Hamilton, Diane, 1938- joint author. II. Title. BIP

Autographs—Facsimiles.

HENRY E. Huntington Library 929.8 and Art Gallery, San Marino, Calif.
Letters in manuscript. Selected and introduced by James Thorpe. [San Marino, Calif., 1971] 48 p. facsims. 28 cm. "A facsimile reproduction of original manuscripts in the Huntington Library, San Marino, Calif." [Z42.H55] 73-31659
1. Autographs—Facsimiles. I. Thorpe, James Ernest, 1915- II. Title.

Autographs—Gt. Brit.

RAWLINS, Ray, 1917- 929.8
Four hundred years of British autographs; a collector's guide. Austin [Tex.] Jenkins Pub. Co., 1970. 188 p. facsims. 26 cm. Bibliography: p. [175]-[177] [Z42.R285 1970b] 75-27199 9.50
1. Autographs—Gt. Brit. 2. Autographs—Collectors and collecting. I. Title. BIP

Autographs—Gt. Brit.—Facsimiles.

GREG, Walter Wilson, 1875- 652.1 ed.
English literary autographs, 1550-1650, selected for reproduction and ed. by W.W. Greg with J.P. Gilson, Hilary Jenkinson, R.B. McKerrow, A.W. Pollard London, Printed at the Oxford Univ. Pr., 1932. Nendeln. Liechtenstein, Kraus-Thomson, 1968. [278]p. facsims. on cx pl. 36cm. Issued in 3pts. & suppl., each with special t.p., 1925-32. A general t.p. with pref., list of plates addenda and corrogenda, and index was issued with pt. 3. The text consists of biog. notes on the author, with description and transcription of the facsims. The issue was limited to 250 sets. Contents.pt. I. Dramatists.--pt. II. Poets--Pt. III. Prose writers & appendix.--Supplement: Scholars & archaeologists [Z42.G82] 27-2650 49.50
1. Autographs—Gt. Brit.—Facsimiles. I. Title.
Order from Kraus-Thomson Org., 9491 Nendeln, Liechtenstein.

Automobile parking.

KANAFANI, Adib K. 711'.73
The location of parking facilities in town centers [by] Adib K. Kanafani. Berkeley, Institute of Transportation and Traffic Engineering, University of California, 1969. x, 150 l. illus. 28 cm. (University of California. Institute of Transportation and Traffic Engineering. Dissertation series) Thesis—University of California, Berkeley. Bibliography: leaves 148-150. [HE370.K34] 72-632292
1. Automobile parking. 2. Cities and towns—Planning. I. Title. II. Series: California. University. Institute of Transportation and Traffic Engineering. Dissertation series

Automobiles in art.

GURR, Henry, 1933- 741.6396292
How to draw cars of tomorrow. Text and illus. by Henry Gurr. Arcadia, Calif., D. Post Publications [1952] 62p. illus. 22cm. [NC825.A8G87] 53-23538
1. Automobiles in art. I. Title.

JENKS, Bill 743.896292
You can draw cars. Illus. by Stu Denker. New York, Sports Car Press [dist. Arco, 1961, c.1960] 126p. 14x21cm. (Modern sports car series) 60-16541 2.75
1. Automobiles in art. 2. Drawing—Instruction. I. Title. BIP

RAYNES, John, 1929- 743.962922
Cars. [1st American ed.] [New York] [Watson-Guptill Publications] [1964] 55 p. illus. 18 x 20 cm. (Watson-Guptill drawing books) Cover title: Drawing cars. [NC825.A8R3 1964] 65-2801
1. Automobiles in art. 2. Drawing—Instruction. I. Title: Drawing cars.

Automotive drafting.

SOCIETY of Automotive 744.4'22'29 Engineers.
SAE drawing standards. [2d ed.] New York [1969- 1 v. (loose-leaf) illus. 30 cm. First ed. published in 1963 under title: Aerospace-automotive drawing standards. [TL253.S65] 77-11949
1. Automotive drafting. 2. Aircraft drafting. I. Title.

Autun, France. SaintLazare (Cathedral)

GRIVOT, Denis 730.944
Gislebertus sculptor of Autun, by Denis Grivot, George Zarnecki. Introd. by T. S. R. Boase. [New York] Orion Pr. with Trianon Pr. [c.1961] 180p. illus., maps. 32cm. Bibl. 61-14186 13.50
1. Gislebertus, 12th cent. 2. Autun, France. SaintLazare (Cathedral) I. Zarnecki, Jerzy, joint author. II. Title.

Avant-garde (Aesthetics)

ADAMS, Hugh. 709'.04'6
Art of the sixties / [by] Hugh Adams. Oxford : Phaidon, 1978. 80 p. : ill. (some col.) ; 29 cm. Bibliography: p. 6. [N6490.A27] 78-56662 ISBN 0-7148-1824-0 : 14.95
1. Art, Modern—20th century. 2. Avant-garde (Aesthetics) I. Title.
Distributed by Dutton, N.Y. BIP

GREEN, Christopher, 1943- 759.4
Leger and the avant-garde / Christopher Green. New Haven : Yale University Press, 1976. xv, 350 p. : ill. (some col.) ; 26 cm. Includes index. Bibliography: p. 316. [ND553.L58G7] 75-11499 ISBN 0-300-01800-2 : 35.00
1. Leger, Fernand, 1881-1955. 2. Avant-garde (Aesthetics) 3. Arts, Modern—20th century. I. Leger, Fernand, 1881-1955. II. Title. BIP

Avedon, Richard.

AVEDON, Richard. 779'.9'39100924
Avedon—photographs, 1974-1977. 1st ed. [New York] : Farrar, Straus, & Giroux, 1978. ca. 250 p. : all ill. ; 27 cm. [TR679.A93] 78-50653 ISBN 0-374-23200-8 : 50.00
1. Avedon, Richard. 2. Fashion photography. I. Title. II. Title: Photographs, 1947-1977. BIP

Avery, Milton.

AMERICAN Federation of 759.13 Arts.
Milton Avery. by Adelyn Breeskin. New York Author [1083 Fifth Ave.] [c.1960] 26p. (Bibl.: p.16-23) plates (part col.) ports. 18cm. 60-2194 2.00; .50 pap.,
1. Avery, Milton. I. Breeskin, Adelyn Dohme. II. Title.

Avery, Milton, 1893-1965.

AVERY, Milton, 1893- 759.13
Paintings, 1930-1960. Introductory text by Hilton Kramer. New York, T. Yoseloff [1962] 30 p. illus., 112 plates (part col.) 32 cm. [ND237.A85K7] 61-15261
I. Kramer, Hilton.

AVERY, Milton, 1893-1965. 759.13
Milton Avery. Washington, Lunn Gallery/Graphics International [1974] [17] p. illus. (part col.) 16 x 23 cm. Catalogue of the exhibition held at the Lunn Gallery, Washington, May 4-June 18, 1974. [ND237.A85L86] 74-79441
1. Avery, Milton, 1893-1965. I. Lunn Gallery. II. Title.

AVERY, Milton, 1893-1965. 759.13
Milton Avery. Introd. by Adelyn D. Breeskin. [Washington] National Collection of Fine Arts, Smithsonian Institution; distributed by the New York Graphic Society, Greenwich, Conn., 1969. [96] p. plates (part col.), ports. (part col.) 26 cm. Catalog of the exhibition held Dec. 12, 1969-Jan. 25, 1970, at the National Collection of Fine Arts; Feb. 17-Mar. 29, 1970, at the Brooklyn Museum, Brooklyn, N.Y.; and Apr. 24-May 31, 1970, at the Columbus Gallery of Fine Arts, Columbus, Ohio. Bibliography: p. [95]-[96] [ND237.A85B7] 78-91440
I. Breeskin, Adelyn Dohme, 1896- II. Smithsonian Institution. National Collection of Fine Arts. III. Brooklyn Institute of Arts and Sciences. Museum. IV. Columbus Gallery of Fine Arts, Columbus, O.

AVERY, Milton, 1893- 769'.92'4 1965.
Milton Avery: prints, 1933-1955. Compiled and edited by Harry H. Lunn, Jr. Washington, Graphics International [1973] [95] p. illus. (part col.) 22 x 28 cm. Bibliography: p. [93] [NE539.A93L86] 72-13980
1. Avery, Milton, 1893-1965. I. Lunn, Harry Hyatt, 1933- ed.

BROOKLYN Institute of 769.924 Arts and Sciences. Museum
Milton Avery: prints and drawings. 1930-1964.[Text by Una E. Johnson. curator of prints and drawings. Commemorative essay, by Mark Rothko. Dist. by Shorewood. New York, 1966] 68p. illus. (pt. col.) port. 24cm. (Amer. graphic artists of the twentieth cent. Monograph no. 4) [NE2225.B7A9] 65-23719 2.75
1. Avery, Milton, 1893-1965. I. Johnson, Una E. II. Rothko, Mark, 1903- III. Title. IV. Series.

Avnet, Lester—Art collections.

OLD master drawings from 741.9'23 *the Collection of Mr. & Mrs. Lester Francis Avnet.* [New York? c1968] [179] p. illus. (part col.) 23 cm. "Circulated by the American Federation of Arts, New York." [NC30.O4] 72-76721
1. Avnet, Lester—Art collections. 2. Avnet, Joan—Art collections. 3. Drawings—Catalogs. I. American Federation of Arts.

Avon Products, inc.

SCHNEIDER, Dee. 748.8
Avon's bottles : by any other name / Dee Schneider. Glendale, Ca. : Avons Research, [1974] 56 p. : ill. ; 22 cm. Includes index. [NK5440.B6S43] 74-30220 ISBN 0-913772-04-6 : 5.50
1. Avon Products, inc. 2. Bottles, American. 3. Bottles—Collectors and collecting—United States. I. Title. BIP

Avon Products, inc.—Catalogs.

TOMASCHEFSKY, Herbert D. 748.8
Herb's guide to Avon test bottle collecting / by Herbert D. Tomaschefsky. [Cudahy, Wis.] : Avon Club of Cudahy, c1977. 139 p. : ill. ; 22 cm. Includes index. [NK5440.B8T58] 78-102595 6.95
1. Avon Products, inc.—Catalogs. 2. Bottles—United States—Collectors and collecting—Catalogs. I. Title.

Awatovi, Ariz.

SMITH, Watson, 1897- 970.3
Painted ceramics of the western mound at Awatovi. With a note on technology by Anna O. Shepard. Cambridge, Mass., The Museum, 1971. xxii, 630 p. illus. (part col.), maps. 27 cm. (Reports of the Awatovi Expedition. Report no. 8) (Papers of the Peabody Museum of Archaeology and Ethnology, Harvard University, v. 38) "Munsell chart for identification of ceramic color designations referred to in this volume" inserted in pocket. Bibliography: p. [615]-619. [E51.H337 vol. 38] 79-102785
1. Awatovi, Ariz. 2. Indians of North America—Arizona—Pottery. 3. Pueblo Indians—Antiquities. I. Title. II. Series: Harvard University. Peabody Museum of Archaeology and Ethnology. Awatovi Expedition. Report no. 8 III. Series: Harvard University. Peabody Museum of Archaeology and Ethnology. Papers, v. 38 BIP

Ayrton, Michael, 1921—

AYRTON, Michael, 1921- 709.42
Drawings and sculpture. Foreword by C. P. Snow. [London] Cory, Adams Mackay dist. Hollywood-by-the-Sea, Fla., Transatlantic, 1963, c.1962] 23p. 96p. of illus. 25cm. 63-6367 10.50
I. Title.

AYRTON, Michael, 1921- 730'.92'4
Michael Ayrton, recent sculpture & drawings, 1972-1975. Chicago : R. S. Johnson-International Gallery, 1975. 47 p. : ill. ; 25 cm. Bibliography: p. 43-44. [NB497.A9J62] 75-18561
1. Ayrton, Michael, 1921- I. Johnson (R. S.)-International Gallery. II. Title.

AYRTON, Michael, 1921- 730'.92'4
Michael Ayrton: the maze; bronzes, drawings, etchings, 1962-1972. Chicago, R. S. Johnson-International Gallery, 1972. 64 p. illus. 25 cm. Catalog of a retrospective exhibition of 76 works held at the R. S. Johnson-International Gallery, Chicago, winter 1972. Bibliography: p. 59-60. [NB497.A9J63] 72-91131
1. Ayrton, Michael, 1921- I. Johnson (R. S.)-International Gallery. II. Title.

Aztalan, Wis.

BARRETT, Samuel Alfred, 1879-1965. 917.75'64
Ancient Aztalan. Introd. to the Greenwood reprint by Robert E. Ritzenthaler. Westport, Conn., Greenwood Press [1970] 602 p. illus., maps, plates. 23 cm. Reprint of the 1933 ed., originally published as v. 13 of the Bulletin of the Public Museum of the City of Milwaukee, Apr. 24, 1933. Bibliography: p. 389-396. [E78.W8B3 1970] 70-111394
1. Aztalan, Wis. 2. Wisconsin—Antiquities. 3. Jefferson Co., Wis.—Antiquities. 4. Earthworks (Archaeology)—Wisconsin. I. Title. BIP

Aztecs.

CAINE, Ralph Lawrence, 1903- 732.2
Historic Aztlan and the Laguna de Ora. Los Angeles, c1962. unpaged. illus. 23cm. [F1219.C25] 62-41035
1. Aztecs. 2. Indians—Origin. I. Title.

NARRATIVE of some things of New Spain, and of the great city of Temestitan, Mexico, 917.2'03'2 written by the anonymous conqueror, a companion of Hernan Cortes. Translated into English and annotated by Marshall H. Saville. Boston, Milford House [1972] 93 p. illus. 22 cm. Reprint of the 1917 ed., issued in series: Documents and narratives concerning the discovery and conquest of Latin America. Translation of Relacion de algunas cosas de la Nueva Espana, which was a translation of Relatione di alcune cose della Nuova Spagna. The original Spanish text has been lost. [F1219.R41413 1972] 73-134866 ISBN 0-87821-084-9
1. Aztecs. 2. Mexico—Description and travel. 3. America—Early accounts to 1600. I. Saville, Marshall Howard, 1867-1935, ed. II. The anonymous conqueror. BIP

NARRATIVE of some things of New Spain and of the great city of Temestitan, Mexico 972 / written by the anonymous conqueror, a companion of Hernan Cortes ; translated into English and annotated by Marshall H. Saville. Boston : Longwood Press, 1977. p. cm. Translation of Relacion de algunas cosas de la Nueva Espana, which was a translation of Relatione di alcune cose della Nueva Spagna. The original Spanish text has been lost. Reprint of the 1917 ed. published by Cortes Society, New York, in series: Documents and narratives concerning the discovery and conquest of Latin America. [F1219.R41413 1977] 77-88569 ISBN 0-89341-276-7 lib.bdg. : 10.00
1. Aztecs. 2. Mexico—Description and travel. 3. America—Early accounts to 1600. I. The annonymous conqueror. II. Saville, Marshall Howard, 1867-1935. III. Series: Documents and narratives concerning the discovery and conquest of Latin America.

Aztecs—Art.

NICHOLSON, Henry B. 704.948'9'7
Two Aztec wood idols: iconographic and chronologic analysis, by H. B. Nicholson and Rainer Berger. Washington, Dumbarton Oaks, Trustees for Harvard University, 1968. 28 p. illus. 27 cm. (Studies in pre-Columbian art and archaeology, no. 5) Bibliography: p. 26-28. [E51.S85 no. 5] 68-58701 2.00
1. Aztecs—Art. I. Berger, Rainer, 1930- joint author. II. Title. III. Series. BIP

Aztecs—Papermaking.

VON HAGEN, Victor Wolfgang, 1908- 676.2'0972
The Aztec and Maya papermakers / by Victor Wolfgang Von Hagen ; with an introd. by Dard Hunter. New York : Hacker Art Books, 1977. 120 p., [23] leaves of plates : ill. ; 23 cm. Reissue of the 1944 ed. Includes index. Bibliography: p. 111-115. [F1219.3.P3V66 1977] 76-6317 ISBN 0-87817-206-8 : 25.00
1. Aztecs—Papermaking. 2. Mayas—Papermaking. 3. Indians of Mexico—Papermaking. 4. Indians of Central America—Papermaking. I. Title.
Publisher's address : 54 W. 57th St., New York, N.Y. 10019 BIP

Bacigalupa, Andrea, 1923—

BACIGALUPA, Andrea, 1923- 759.13 B
Journal of an itinerant artist / Drew Bacigalupa. Huntington, Ind. : Our Sunday Visitor, inc., c1977. 176 p., [4] leaf of plates : ill. ; 24 cm. [BX4705.B10195A34] 77-78739 ISBN 0-87973-887-1 : 9.95
1. Bacigalupa, Andrea, 1923- 2. Catholics—New Mexico—Santa Fe—Biography. 3. Art dealers—New Mexico—Santa Fe—Biography. 4. Santa Fe, N.M.—Biography. I. Title. BIP

Bacon, Francis, 1909-

ALLEY, Ronald. 759.2
Francis Bacon. Introd. by John Rothenstein. Catalogue Raisonne and documentation by Ronald Alley. New York, Viking Press [1964] 292 p. illus. (part mounted col.) ports. 29 cm. (A Studio book) Bibliography: p. 281-288. [ND497.B16A65] 64-15492
1. Bacon, Francis, 1909- I. Title.

BACON, Francis, 1909- 759.9415
Francis Bacon / [text by] Lorenza Trucchi ; translated [from the Italian] by John Shepley. London : Thames and Hudson, 1976. [4], 41 p., [170] p. of plates, [22] leaves of plates (10 fold.) : chiefly ill. (some col.) ; 32 cm. Bibliography: p. 22-35. [ND497.B16T7813 1976] 77-353997 ISBN 0-500-09109-9 : £16.00
1. Bacon, Francis, 1909- I. Trucchi, Lorenza.

BACON, Francis, 1909 759.9415
Francis Bacon, Recent paintings, 1968-1974: March 20-May 31, 1975, The Metropolitan Museum of Art, New York catalog New York, Metropolitan Museum of Art, [1975] p. cm. Bibliography: p. [CND497.B16N48] 75-1250 ISBN 0-87099-130-2 pbk. : 5.95
1. Bacon, Francis, 1909 I. New York (City). Metropolitan Museum of Art II. Title.

SOLOMON R. Guggenheim Museum, New York. 759.2
Francis Bacon [exhibition 63/6, October 1963-January 1964] The Solomon R. Guggenheim Museum, New York, in collaboration with the Art Institute of Chicago. [New York, Solomon R. Guggenheim Foundation, 1963.] 77 p. illus. (part col.) 28 cm. Addendum slip inserted. Bibliography: p.25: p. [74]-77. [ND497.B16S6] 63-21154
1. Bacon, Francis, 1909- I. Chicago, Art Institute. II. Title.

SYLVESTER, David. 759.9415
Francis Bacon / interviewed by David Sylvester. 1st American ed. New York : Pantheon Books, [1975] 128 p. : ill. ; 29 cm. [ND497.B16S9 1975] 74-26206 ISBN 0-394-49763-5 : 12.95. ISBN 0-394-73062-3 pbk. : 5.95
1. Bacon, Francis, 1909- 2. Art—Philosophy. I. Bacon, Francis, 1909-

TRUCCHI, Lorenza. 759.9415
Francis Bacon / Lorenza Trucchi ; translated by John Shepley. New York : H. N. Abrams, [1975] p. cm. Includes index. Bibliography: p. [ND497.B16T7813] 75-6819 ISBN 0-8109-0234-6 : 37.50
1. Bacon, Francis, 1909- BIP

Bader, Alfred, 1924- —Art collections.

SELECTIONS from the Bader Collection. 759.9492 With an introd. by Wolfgang Stechow. Milwaukee, 1974. [71] p. illus. 29 cm. Includes bibliographies. [ND636.S38] 74-79521
1. Bader, Alfred, 1924- —Art collections. 2. Paintings, Dutch—Catalogs. 3. Painting, Modern—17th-18th centuries—Netherlands. 4. Paintings, Flemish—Catalogs. 5. Painting, Modern—17th-18th centuries—Flanders.

Badii, Libero, 1916—

ARGENTINE works of art in the John F. Kennedy Center for the Performing Arts. 730'.92'4 Washington, 1972. [17] p. illus. 26 cm. Cover title. "Presentation" also in Spanish. [NB339.B25A83] 72-602958
1. Badii, Libero, 1916- Phoenix. 2. Forner, Raquel, 1902- Combat of the Astrobeings. I. United States. John F. Kennedy Center for the Performing Arts.

Baeder, John.

BAEDER, John. 759.13
Diners / by John Baeder. New York : H. N. Abrams, [1978] p. cm. [ND237.B215A44] 77-13203 ISBN 0-8109-2078-6 pbk. : 7.95
1. Baeder, John. 2. Diners (Restaurants) in art. I. Title. BIP

Baer, Jo, 1929—

BAER, Jo, 1929- 759.13
Jo Baer : [exhibition, Whitney Museum of American Art, New York, May 1-July 13, 1975] / Barbara Haskell. New York : The Museum, [1975] [40] p. : ill. (some col.) ; 25 cm. Bibliography: p. [38] [ND237.B218H37] 75-8353
1. Baer, Jo, 1929- I. Haskell, Barbara. II. Whitney Museum of American Art, New York. BIP

Baertling, Olie, 1911-

BRUNIUS, Teddy, 1922- 759.85
Baertling. Discoverer of open form. Stockholm, A Nyblom; New York, Rose Fried Gallery, 1965. 42, (1) p. illus. 24 cm. unpriced (S 66-21) Bibliography: p. 39-42. [ND793.B3B7] 67-74384
1. Baertling, Olie, 1911- I. Title.

Bailey, Ben P.

BAILEY, Ben P. 741.9'73
Border lands sketchbook = Libro de bosquejos fronterizos / Ben P. Bailey, Jr. ; translated by Channing Horner and Louise Bailey Horner. [Waco? Tex.] : Bailey, c1976. v, 170 p. : ill. (some col.) ; 29 cm. English and Spanish. Includes bibliographical references. [NC139.B28A42] 76-39665
1. Bailey, Ben P. 2. Historic buildings—Texas—Rio Grande Valley—Pictorial works. 3. Buildings in art. I. Title. II. Title: Libro de bosquejos fronterizos.

Baileys Harbor, Wis. Chapel.

BOYNTON, Winifred Case, 1887- 726.41
Faith builds a chapel; the story of an adventure in craftsmanship. [New York] Reinhold, 1953. 135p. illus. (part mounted col.) 32cm. [NA5235.B3B6] 53-9170
1. Baileys Harbor, Wis. Chapel. I. Title.

Bainbridge Island, Wash.—Biography.

COMBS, Ann, 1935- 979.7'76 B
Helter shelter / Ann Combs. 1st ed. Philadelphia : Lippincott, 1979. p. cm. [CT275.C73A36] 78-26921 ISBN 0-397-01334-5 : 8.95
1. Combs, Ann, 1935- 2. Bainbridge Island, Wash.—Biography. I. Title. BIP

Baja California in art.

SCOTT, Annette. 759.13
Cruising and sketching Baja. [1st ed.] Flagstaff, Northland Press [1974] x, 116 p. illus. 19 x 25 cm. [ND1839.S38A43] 73-93994 ISBN 0-87358-123-7 12.50
1. Scott, Annette. 2. Baja California in art. 3. Baja California—Description and travel. I. Title.

TAYLOR, Edgar Dorsey, 1904- 760'.0924
Baja California woodcuts; with notes by the artist. Introd. by Robert Hilton Simmons. Los Angeles, Plantin Press, 1969. xvi, 50 (i.e. 100) p. illus. 20 x 23 cm. [NE1215.T3A42] 78-84109
1. Baja California in art. I. Title.

Bak, Samuel.

BAK, Samuel. 759.95694
Bak : paintings of the last decade. Artistic development ; The metaphysical works / Paul T. Nagano. Conversation with the artist / A. Kaufman. 2d ed. New York : Aberbach Fine Art, 1976. 156, [5] p. : ill. (some col.) ; 29 cm. Bibliography: p. [157]-[158] [ND979.B27A23] 77-358850
1. Bak, Samuel. 2. Painters—Israel—Interviews.

Baker, Herbert, 1924- —Art collections.

NEW York (City). Museum of Primitive Art. 732'.2
The Herbert Baker Collection. [Exhibition. New York] Distributed by New York Graphic Society, Greenwich, Conn., 1969. 44 p. illus. (part col.) 28 cm. [NB62.N42] 78-105741
1. Baker, Herbert, 1924- —Art collections. 2. Sculpture, Primitive—Exhibitions. I. Title.

Baker, Herbert, Sir, 1862-1946.

GREIG, Doreen E. 720'.92'4
Herbert Baker in South Africa [by] Doreen E. Greig. Cape Town, New York, Purnell [1970] xvi, 276 p. illus., port. 28 cm. Bibliography: p. 273-274. [NA997.B25G7] 73-558409 ISBN 0-360-00103-3 R15.00
1. Baker, Herbert, Sir, 1862-1946. I. Title.

Baker, Richard Brown—Art collections.

MARANDEL, J. Patrice. 709'.73
Small works: selections from the Richard Brown Baker Collection of contemporary act. [Providence, Museum of Art, Rhode Island School of Design, 1973] 123 p. illus. 21 x 26 cm. Catalog of an exhibition held at the Museum of Art, Rhode Island School of Design, April 5-May 6, 1973, prepared by J. P. Marandel. Errata sheet inserted. [N6487.P7R465] 73-174120
1. Baker, Richard Brown—Art collections. 2. Art, Modern—20th century—Exhibitions. I. Rhode Island School of Design, Providence. Museum of Art. II. Title.

RICHARD Brown Baker collects! 709'.04'07401468 : A selection of contemporary art from the Richard Brown Baker Collection : [exhibition], April 24-June 22, 1975, Yale University Art Gallery, New Haven, Connecticut. New Haven : The Gallery, 1975. 132 p. : ill. (some col.) ; 22 x 28 cm. The exhibition and the catalog are the result of a course taken in the fall of 1974 by twelve Yale students. The students selected the objects to be exhibited and wrote the essays. Includes bibliographical references. [N6487.N34Y346] 76-360425
1. Baker, Richard Brown—Art collections. 2. Art, Modern—20th century—Exhibitions. 3. Art, American—Exhibitions. I. Yale University. Art Gallery.

SAN Francisco. Museum of Art. 759.06'074'019461
A selection of American and European paintings from the Richard Brown Baker Collection : [exhibition], September 14-November 11, 1973, San Francisco Museum of Art, December 7, 1973-January 27, 1974, Institute of

Contemporary Art, University of Pennsylvania, Philadelphia / organized by San Francisco Museum of Art. [San Francisco] : The Museum, c1973. [32] p. : ill. ; 26 cm. [ND195.S22 1973] 75-316853
1. Baker, Richard Brown—Art collections. 2. Paintings, Modern—20th century—Exhibitions. I. Pennsylvania. University. Institute of Contemporary Art. II. Title.

Bakst, Lev Samoilovich, 1866-1924.

ALEXANDRE, Arsene, 1859-   759.47
The decorative art of Leon Bakst. Appreciation by Arsene Alexandre. Notes on the ballets by Jean Cocteau. Translated from the French by Harry Melvill. New York, B. Blom, 1971. 9 p. illus., 78 plates (part col.), port. 26 cm. "First published 1913." [ND699.B3A613 1971] 68-57183
1. Bakst, Lev Samoilovich, 1866-1924. 2. Ballet. I. Title.

ALEXANDRE, Arsene, 1859-   759.47
The decorative art of Leon Bakst. Appreciation by Arsene Alexandre. Notes on the ballets by Jean Cocteau. Translated from the French by Harry Melvill. New York, Dover Publications [1972] x, 52 p., 77 plates (part col.) 31 cm. "A republication [with minor changes] of the work originally published by the Fine Art Society, London, in 1913." [ND699.B3A613 1972] 73-187844 ISBN 0-486-22871-1 pap. 5.00
1. Bakst, Lev Samoilovich, 1866-1924. I. Title.   BIP

BAKST, Lev   792.8'025'0924
Samoilovich, 1866-1924.
Bakst. New York : Rizzoli, 1977. [103] p. : chiefly ill. (some col.) ; 24 cm. [ND699.B3A43] 76-51470 ISBN 0-8478-0072-5 pbk. : 4.95
1. Bakst, Lev Samoilovich, 1866-1924. BIP

LEVINSON, Andrei   759.47
IAkovlevich, 1887-1933.
Bakst, the story of the artist's life. New York, B. Blom, 1971. 240 p. illus., 68 plates, ports. 27 cm. "First published 1923." [ND699.B3L36 1971] 68-57182
1. Bakst, Lev Samoilovich, 1866-1924.

Bald eagle in art.

HORNUNG, Clarence   745.4'49'73
Pearson.
The American eagle in art and design : 321 examples / selected and edited by Clarence P. Hornung. New York : Dover Publications, 1978. x, [1], 113 p. : chiefly ill. ; 29 cm. (Dover pictorial archives series) Bibliography: p. [xi] [N6505.H67] 77-15711 ISBN 0-486-23604-8 pbk. : 5.00
1. Bald eagle in art. 2. Art, American. 3. Design, Decorative—United States. I. Title.   BIP

Bald Mountains, N.C. and Tenn., in art.

HOLYFIELD, Frank.   741.9'73
The southern mountains; a collection of drawings. Chapel Hill, University of North Carolina Press [1973] 1 portfolio ([1] l., 9 plates) 51 cm. Title from portfolio. [NC139.H58A55] 73-8001 ISBN 0-8078-1215-3 17.50
1. Holyfield, Frank. 2. Bald Mountains, N.C. and Tenn., in art. I. Title.

Baldaccini, Cesar, 1921—

RESTANY, Pierre.   730'.92'4
Cesar / text by Pierre Restany ; translated by John Shepley. New York : H. N. Abrams, [1975] p. cm. Includes index. Bibliography: p. [NB553.B22R4713] 74-30064 ISBN 0-8109-0358-X : 45.00
1. Baldaccini, Cesar, 1921- I. Title.   BIP

Baldwin, Billy.

BALDWIN, Billy.   747'.213
Billy Baldwin decorates. [1st ed.] New York, Holt, Rinehart and Winston [1972] 219 p. illus. (part col.) 30 cm. "A House & Garden book." [NK2135.B34A42 1972] 74-161814 ISBN 0-03-001021-7 15.00
1. Baldwin, Billy. 2. Interior decoration—United States. I. Title.

BALDWIN, Billy.   747'.21'3
Billy Baldwin remembers. New York, Harcourt Brace Jovanovich [1974] 232 p. illus. 29 cm. [NK2004.3.B34A22] 74-8712 ISBN 0-15-112070-6 19.95
1. Baldwin, Billy. 2. Interior decorators—United States—Correspondence, reminiscences, etc. I. Title.

Ball Corporation.

BRANTLEY, William F.   666'.19
A collector's guide to Ball jars / by William F. Brantley ; foreword by Edmund F. Ball ; color photography by David A. Harris. Muncie, Ind. : R. H. Martin, 1975. xix, 100 p. : ill. (some col.) ; 20 cm. Includes bibliographical references and index. [TP866.B72] 75-7881
1. Ball Corporation. 2. Glass fruit jars—Collectors and collecting. I. Title.

Ball, Thomas, 1819-1911.

BALL, Thomas, 1819-   730'.92'4 B
1911.
My threescore years and ten : an authobiography / by Thomas Ball. 2d ed. New York : Garland Pub., 1977, c1891. 13, xi, 379 p., [5] leaves of plates ; ill. ; 19 cm. (The Art experience in late nineteenth-century America) Reprint of the 1892 ed. published by Roberts Bros., Boston; with new introd. [NB237.B3A25 1977] 75-28884 ISBN 0-8240-2242-4 : 25.00
1. Ball, Thomas, 1819-1911. 2. Sculptors—United States—Biography. I. Title. II. Series.   BIP

Balla, Giacomo, 1871-1958.

DORAZIO, Virginia Dortch.   759.5
Giacomo Balla; an album of his life and work. Introd. by Giuseppe Ungaretti. New York, Wittenborn [1969?] 1 v. (unpaged) illus., facsims., ports. 23 x 25 cm. [N6923.B27D6] 70-140146 ISBN 0-8150-0405-2
1. Balla, Giacomo, 1871-1958.

Ballarat, Australia.

REICHL, Phyllis.   711'.4'09945
Ballarat, a study of a city. [Melbourne] Nelson [(Australia) 1968] [vi], 28 p. illus., diagrs., maps (part col.) 25 cm. (Place, time and people field studies series, 3) Bibliography: p. [iv] [DU230.B3R4] 79-417316 0.75
1. Ballarat, Australia. I. Title.

Ballet.

ALEXANDRE, Arsene, 1859-   759.47
The decorative art of Leon Bakst. Appreciation by Arsene Alexandre. Notes on the ballets by Jean Cocteau. Translated from the French by Harry Melvill. New York, B. Blom, 1971. 51 p. illus., 78 plates (part col.), port. 26 cm. "First published 1913." [ND699.B3A613 1971] 68-57183
1. Bakst, Lev Samoilovich, 1866-1924. 2. Ballet. I. Title.

CLARKE, Mary, 1923-   704.94'9'7928
Ballet art : from the Renaissance to the present / by Mary Clarke and Clement Crisp. New York : C. N. Potter : distributed by Crown Publishers, c1978. 144 p. : ill. (some col.) ; 28 cm. Includes index. [N8217.B35C55 1978] 78-7195 ISBN 0-517-53454-1 : 14.95 ISBN 0-517-53455-X pbk. : 6.95
1. Ballet in art. 2. Art. I. Crisp, Clement, joint author. II. Title.   BIP

Ballet in art—Exhibitions.

†ERAS of the dance :   760
the George Verdak Collection, Montgomery Museum of Fine Arts, December 10, 1976, through January 13, 1977, Huntsville Museum of Art, April 11, 1976, through May 22, 1976 [Montgomery, Ala] : Montgomery Museum of Fine Arts, c1976. 90 p. : ill. ; 24 cm. On spine: The George Verdak Collection. Exhibition catalog. [N8217.B35E73] 76-52823 ISBN 0-89280-004-6 pbk. : 6.50

1. Verdak, George—Art collections. 2. Ballet in art—Exhibitions. 3. Art—Exhibitions. I. Montgomery Museum of Fine Arts. II. Huntsville Museum of Art. III. Title: The George Verdak Collection.

Ballet—Pictorial works.

HAMILTON, David.   779'.2'0924
La danse [by] David Hamilton. Text [by] Charles Murland. New York, Morrow [1974] 95 p. illus. 30 cm. Text in English. [GV1787.H23713] 73-18486 ISBN 0-688-00248-X 16.95
1. Ballet—Pictorial works. I. Murland, Charles. II. Title.   BIP

Balloons in art.

GIBBS-SMITH, Charles   769.49623
Harvard, 1909-
Balloons and ships, introd. by Charles H. Gibbs-Smith, Oliver Warner. Princeton. N.J., Van Nostrand [1966] 10p. 20 col. plates. 25cm. (Golden Ariels, no. 6) [19th cent. transport prints. v. 1] [NE962.B3G5 1965a] 67-529 3.95 bds.
1. Balloons in art. 2. Naval prints. I. Warner, Oliver, 1903- II. Title.

Balsa wood.

LIDSTONE, John.   745.51
Building with balsa wood. Photography by Roger Kerkham. Princeton, N.J. Van Nostrand [1965] 61 p. illus. (part col.) 23 x 26 cm. [TT200.L48] 65-9599
1. Balsa wood. 2. Handicraft. I. Title. BIP

Balsa wood craft.

WARRING, Ronald Horace.   745.59'28
Balsa wood modeling, by Ron Warring. New York, Sterling Pub. Co. [1973] 47 p. illus. 20 cm. (Little craft book series) Describes the tools and techniques used in working with balsa wood and gives instructions for making a periscope, kite, model ship, and other objects from this soft, light wood. [TT189.W37 1973] 72-95192 2.95
1. Balsa wood craft. 2. Models and modelmaking. I. Title.

Balsa wood craft—Juvenile literature.

WEISS, Peter, 1945-   745.51
Balsa wood craft. Written and illustrated by Peter Weiss. New York, Lothrop, Lee & Shepard Co., 1972. 96 p. illus. 24 cm. Instructions for working with balsa wood to create doll furniture, toys, party ornaments, and other items. [TT189.W44] 72-1105 ISBN 0-688-40007-8 3.95
1. Balsa wood craft—Juvenile literature. I. Title.   BIP

Baltimore—Buildings.

BALTIMORE. Museum of   728.3'0924
Art.
Robert Mills' Waterloo Row—Baltimore 1816. [Baltimore, 1971] 24 p. illus., plans. 26 cm. Written by William Voss Elder, III, curator of decorative arts. Includes bibliographical references. [NA735.B3B3] 72-257509
1. Mills, Robert, 1781-1855. 2. Baltimore. Museum of Art. 3. Baltimore—Buildings. I. Elder, William Voss. II. Title.

Baltimore—City planning.

BALTIMORE. Dept. of   711'.4'097526
Planning.
Baltimore's development program : an overview / Baltimore City Planning Commission, Department of Planning. [Baltimore] : The Dept., 1977. 52 p. : ill. ; 28 cm. [HT168.B35B34 1977a] 77-82566
1. Baltimore—City planning. 2. City planning—Maryland. 3. Urban renewal—Maryland—Baltimore. 4. Capital budget—Maryland—Baltimore. I. Title.

Baltimore. Museum of Art.

BALTIMORE.   739.2'3'775207401526
Museum of Art.
Eighteenth and nineteenth century Maryland silver in the collection of the Baltimore Museum of Art / text by Jennifer Faulds Goldsborough ; edited by Ann Boyce Harper. Baltimore : The Museum, 1975. ix, 204 p. : ill. ; 26 cm. "A project supported by the Stieff Company, Baltimore." Bibliography: p. 201-204. [NK7112.B26 1975] 75-15344
1. Baltimore. Museum of Art. 2. Silverwork—Maryland—Catalogs. I. Goldsborough, Jennifer F. II. Title: Eighteenth and nineteenth century Maryland silver ... III. Title: Maryland silver.   BIP

GREENFIELD, Kent   708.152'6
Roberts, 1893-1967.
The museum; its first half century. Baltimore, 1966. 103 p. illus. 27 cm. (Baltimore. Museum of Art. Annual 1) [N515.A18 no. 1] 70-4727 4.00
1. Baltimore. Museum of Art. I. Title. II. Series.

Baltimore—Public works.

BALTIMORE. Planning   711'.4'097526
Commission.
Baltimore's development program, 1973, 1974, 1975, 1976, 1977, 1978, as approved and adopted by the Board of Estimates, November 1, 1972. Baltimore [1973] 255 p. illus. 29 cm. Part of illustrative matter in pocket. [HD4606.B2B34 1973] 74-184732
1. Baltimore—Public works. I. Title.

Bama, James.

BAMA, James.   759.13
Western paintings : [exhibitions] / James Bama. New York : Coe Kerr Gallery, c1977. [44] p. : ill. (some col.) ; 28 cm. Held at the Coe Kerr Gallery, New York, March 15-April 16, 1977 and at the Buffalo Bill Historical Center, Cody, Wyoming, June 1-July 18, 1977. [ND237.B235C63] 77-151080
1. Bama, James. 2. The West in art. I. Coe Kerr Gallery. II. Buffalo Bill Historical Center. III. Title.

*BAMBA, James   759.13
The western art of James Bamba introduction by Ian Ballantine New York, Charles Scribner's Sons [1975] [6] p. [45] leaves of plates 45 col. ill. 29 cm. [ND1839] 10.00.
1. Bama, James. 2. The west in art. I. Title. L.C. card no. for original edition: 75-7782.

Bambara tribe—Rites and ceremonies.

MCNAUGHTON, Patrick   732'.2'096623
R.
Secret sculptures of Komo : art and power in Bamana (Bambara) initiation associations / Patrick R. McNaughton. Philadelphia : Institute for the Study of Human Issues, c1979. p. cm. (Working papers in the traditional arts ; 4) Bibliography: p. [DT551.42.M3] 79-12169 ISBN 0-89727-004-5 pbk. : 3.95
1. Bambara tribe—Rites and ceremonies. 2. Komo (Secret order) 3. Sculpture, Bambara. I. Title. II. Series.   BIP

Bamberg. Dom.

VALENTINER, Wilhelm   734.43
Reinhold, 1880-
The Bamberg rider; studies of mediaeval German sculpture. Los Angeles, Zeitlin & Ver Brugge, 1956. ix, 166p. illus. 27cm. 'Limited edition of 500 copies.'--Dust jacket. Bibliographical references included in 'Notes' (p. 150-157) Bibliography: p. 158-159. [NA5586.B3V3] 56-58361
1. Friedrich II, Emperor of Germany, 1194-1250. 2. Bamberg. Dom. 3. Sculpture, German. 4. Sculpture, Medieval. I. Title.

Bamboo.

AUSTIN, Robert.   745
Bamboo, by Robert Austin and Koichiro Ueda. Photos. by Dana Levy. [1st ed.]

New York, Walker/Weatherhill [1970] 215 p. illus. (part col.) 31 cm. Bibliography: p. 213. [TT190.A95] 70-96051 15.00
1. Bamboo. I. Ueda, Koichiro, 1898- joint author. II. Levy, Dana, illus. **BIP**

Bank-notes.

STEN, George J. 769'.55
Banknotes of the world, 1368-1966; handbook-catalog in four volumes [by] George J. Sten. Menlo Park, Calif., Shirjieh Publishers [1967- v. illus., facsims., map. 28 cm. [HG353.S68] 67-7759
1. Bank-notes. I. Title.

Bank-notes—China.

SMITH, Ward D. 769'.559'51
Chinese banknotes. [By] Ward D. Smith and Brian Matravers. Menlo Park, Calif., Shirjieh Publishers, 1970. 225 p. illus. 29 cm. [HG1227.S6] 73-23064
1. Bank-notes—China. I. Matravers, Brian, joint author. II. Title. **BIP**

Bank-notes—Mexico.

SHLIEKER, Ed. 769'.55972
The un peso of the Bank of Mexico (BDM-I) [by] Ed Shlieker, Samuel M. Paonessa [and] William L. Spencer. 1st ed. El Paso, Tex., 1973. 56 p. illus. 21 cm. Introduction and "Paper money grading guide" in English and Spanish. Includes bibliographical references. [HG667.S55] 73-86539 3.00
1. Bank-notes—Mexico. 2. Paper money—Mexico. 3. Paper money—Catalogs. I. Paonessa, Samuel M., joint author. II. Spencer, William L., joint author. III. Title.

Bank-notes—Nebraska.

MCKEE, James L. 769'.55
The wildcat bank notes, scrip and currencies of Nebraska prior to 1900, by James L. Mckee [Lincoln? Neb., 1970] 60 p. facsims. 30 cm. Includes bibliographical references. [HG627.N2M3] 78-117401
1. Bank-notes—Nebraska. 2. Paper money—Nebraska. I. Title.

Bank-notes—New England.

WISMER, David Cassel, 1857- 769'.55974
The obsolete bank notes of New England. Boston, Quarterman Publications [1972] 311 p. illus. 24 cm. (Gleanings from the Numismatist, v. 2) "Originally published serially (although not consecutively) between August 1922 and July 1935 in the Numismatist under the title: Descriptive list of obsolete paper money." [HG627.N45W58] 72-85119 ISBN 0-88000-006-6 15.00
1. Bank-notes—New England. I. Title. II. Series. **BIP**

Bank-notes—Texas.

MEDLAR, Bob. 769'.559'764
Texas obsolete notes and scrip. [1st ed. Anderson, S.C.] Society of Paper Money Collectors; distributed by R. A. Glascock, San Antonio [1968] xi, 204 p. facsims. 29 cm. Bibliography: p. 203. [HG627.T4M4] 68-57685
1. Bank-notes—Texas. 2. Paper money—Texas. I. Society of Paper Money Collectors. II. Title.

Bank of the United States (1816-1836)—Buildings.

MORRISON, Andrew 725'.24'0974811
Craig.
The interior of the Second Bank of the United States. Denver, Colo., Denver Service Center, National Park Service, 1973. xi, 160 p. illus. 27 cm. (Historic structure report) On cover: Independence National Historical Park, Pennsylvania. Issued as a supplement to The interior of the Second Bank of the United States, by N. Souder, published in 1970. [NA6243.P5B34] 73-602846
1. Bank of the United States (1816-

1836)—Buildings. 2. Philadelphia—Historic houses, etc.—Conservation and restoration. I. Souder, Norman M. The interior of the Second Bank of the United States. II. Title. III. Title: Independence National Historical Park, Pennsylvania. IV. Series: Historic structures report.

SOUDER, Norman M. 332.1'1'0973
The interior of the Second Bank of the United States, by Norman M. Souder. Washington, Office of History and Historic Architecture, Eastern Service Center, 1970. 64d (i.e. 218) p. illus. 27 cm. At head of title: Independence National Historical Park, Philadelphia, Pennsylvania. "Historic structures report, architectural data report section." [NA6243.P5B36] 75-614497
1. Bank of the United States (1816-1836)—Buildings. I. Title. II. Title: Independence National Historic Park, Philadelphia, Pennsylvania.

Bannard, Walter Darby, 1934—

BANNARD, Walter Darby, 759.13
1934-
Walter Darby Bannard. Introd. and an interview with the artist by Jane Harrison Cone. [Baltimore] Baltimore Museum of Art [1973] 72 p. illus. (part col.) 27 cm. Catalog of an exhibition held at the Baltimore Museum of Art, Oct. 2-Nov. 11, 1973; the High Museum of Art, Atlanta, Feb. 24-Mar. 31, 1974; and the Museum of Fine Arts, Houston, May 30-July 28, 1974. Bibliography: p. 68-72. [ND237.B24A57] 73-87987
1. Bannard, Walter Darby, 1934- I. Cone, Jane Harrison. II. Baltimore. Museum of Art. III. High Museum of Art. IV. Houston, Tex. Museum of Fine Arts. **BIP**

Bannerman, Jane Campbell.

BANNERMAN, Jane Campbell. 759.13
Bermuda, as seen by Jane Campbell Bannerman. [s.l. : s.n., 1976?] [30] leaves of plates : all col. ill. ; 16 x 24 cm. Cover title. [ND1839.B23A42] 77-354153 11.50
1. Bannerman, Jane Campbell. 2. Bermuda Islands in art.

Banvard, John, 1815-1891.

AGLE, Nan Hayden. 759.13
The ingenious John Banvard, by Nan Hayden Agle and Frances Atchinson Bacan. Illustrated by Joseph Papin. New York, Seabury Press [1966] 128 p. illus. 24 cm. [ND237.B26A65] 66-11214
1. Banvard, John, 1815-1891. I. Bacon, Frances Elizabeth (Atchinson) 1903- joint author. II. Papin, Joseph, illus. III. Title.

Barber and McMurry.

BARBER and McMurry. 720'.6'576685
The architecture of Barber and McMurry, 1915-1940 : an exhibition of photographs and drawings, September 20-October 15, 1976, Dulin Gallery of Art, Knoxville, Tennessee / exhibition organization and catalog text, W. R. McNabb ; design by Ronald Childress. Knoxville : Dulin Gallery of Art, c1976. 92 p. : ill. ; 19 x 27 cm. Includes bibliographical references. [NA737.B25M32] 76-150412
1. Barber and McMurry. 2. Architecture, Modern—20th century—United States—Exhibitions. I. McNabb, W. R. II. Dulin Gallery of Art. III. Title.

Barber bottles—Catalogs.

NAMIAT, Robert. 748.8
Barber bottles : with prices / by Robert Namiat ; [photography by John O'Donnell] . Des Moines : Wallace-Homestead Book Co., c1977. [46] p. : col. ill. ; 23 cm. Bibliography: p. [46] [NK5440.B6N35] 76-58064 ISBN 0-87069-199-6 : 7.95
1. Barber bottles—Catalogs. 2. Bottles—United States—Catalogs. I. Title.

Barber, John Warner, 1798-1885.

BARBER, John Warner, 769'.92'4
1798-1885.
Early woodcut views of New York and New Jersey : 304 illustrations from the "Historical collections" / by John W. Barber and Henry Howe. New York : Dover Publications, 1975. 118 p. : chiefly ill. ; 29 cm. (Dover pictorial archive series) Includes index. [NE1112.B37H68] 75-3823 ISBN 0-486-23196-8 : 3.50
1. Barber, John Warner, 1798-1885. 2. Howe, Henry, 1816-1893. 3. New York (State) in art. 4. New Jersey in art. I. Howe, Henry, 1816-1893, joint author. II. Barber, John Warner, 1798-1885. Historical collections of the State of New York. III. Barber, John Warner, 1798-1885. Historical collections of the State of New Jersey. IV. Title. **BIP**

Barber, Philip, 1946—

BARBER, Philip, 1946- 741.9'71
The road home : sketches of rural Canada / Philip Barber ; text by Brian Swarbrick. Scarborough, Ont. : Prentice-Hall of Canada, c1976. [32] p., [62] leaves of plates : chiefly ill. ; 24 x 27 cm. [NC1112.B37S93] 77-357606 ISBN 0-13-781559-X : 19.95
1. Barber, Philip, 1946- 2. Canada in art. I. Swarbrick, Brian, 1929- II. Title. Distributed by Prentice-Hall, Englewood Cliffs, N.J. **BIP**

Barbier, George.

BARBIER, George. 759.4
The illustrations of George Barbier in full color / edited by Francois Meyer and Frederica T. Harlow. New York : Dover Publications, 1977. 47 p. : col. ill. ; 29 cm. [NC980.5.B37A46] 76-42589 ISBN 0-486-23476-2 : 5.00
1. Barbier, George. I. Title. **BIP**

Barbizon school.

HERBERT, Robert L 1929- 759.4
Barbizon revisited, essay and catalogue. New York, Clarke & Way [c1962] 208 p. illus. (part col.) 23 cm. Exhibition to be held at the California Palace of the Legion of Honor and other places, from Sept. 1962 to Apr. 1963. Bibliography: p. 71-73. [ND547.H53] 62-21297
1. Barbizon school. 2. Paintings, French—Exhibitions. I. California Palace of the Legion of Honor, San Francisco. II. Title.

HOEBER, Arthur, 1854-1915. 759.4
The Barbizon painters; being the story of the Men of Thirty. New York, Books for Libraries Press [1969] xxiv, 296 p. illus. 23 cm. (Essay index reprint series) Reprint of the 1915 ed. Bibliography: p. 291-292. [ND547.H6 1969] 76-84312
1. Barbizon school. I. Title. **BIP**

TOMSON, Arthur. 759.4
Jean-Francois Millet and the Barbizon school. Freeport, N.Y., Books for Libraries Press [1973] p. Reprint of the 1903 ed. published by G. Bell, New York. Bibliography: p. [NC547.5.B3T65] 73-6507 ISBN 0-518-19070-6
1. Millet, Jean Francois, 1814-1875. 2. Barbizon school. 3. Painting, Modern—19th century—France. I. Title.

Barchus, Eliza Rosanna, 1857-1959.

BARCHUS, Agnes, 1893- 759.13
Eliza R. Barchus, the Oregon artist, 1857-1959 / by Agnes Barchus. 1st ed. Portland, Or. : Binford & Mort, c1974. ix, 166 p., [4] leaves of plates : ill. (some col.) ; 24 cm. [ND237.B2615A46] 74-24495 ISBN 0-8323-0245-7 : 8.95
1. Barchus, Eliza Rosanna, 1857-1959.

Barfreston, Church.

BONNER, Stephen. 726'.5'094223
Early Norman secular musicians on the church of Barfreston in Kent; drawings by Roy Bishop. Cambridge, Bois de Boulogne, 1969. [14] p. 5 illus. (1 col.). 22 cm. "This first edition is limited to sixty copies only,

of which this is no. 28." Bibliography: p. [14] [ML85.B635] 72-463152 20/-
1. Barfreston, Church. 2. Musical instruments—Pictorial works. 3. Music in art. I. Title.

Bark.

MILLARD, Nancy. 745.925
Pictures from bark. New York, Crescent Books [1970] 64 p. illus. (part col.) 26 cm. 73-76079 ISBN 0-517-11292-2
1. Bark. 2. Handicraft. I. Title.

Barker, Alfred Charles, 1819-1873.

BURDON, Cotsford 770'.92'4 B
Carlton.
Dr. A. C. Barker, 1819-1873, photographer, farmer, physician [by] C. C. Burdon. Dunedin, McIndoe [1972] 88 p., 24 p. of illus. illus., geneal. table, ports. 23 cm. Bibliography: p. 88. [TR140.B27B87] 73-174677 4.50
1. Barker, Alfred Charles, 1819-1873.

Barlach, Ernst, 1870-1938.

CARLS, Carl Dietrich, 730'.924
1905-
Ernst Barlach. [New, expanded, rev. ed.] New York, Praeger [1969] 216 p. plates. 29 cm. [NB588.B35C313 1969] 78-89602 17.50
1. Barlach, Ernst, 1870-1938.

WERNER, Alfred, 1911- 709.43
Ernst Barlach. New York, McGraw-Hill [1966] 176 p. illus. 25 cm. [NB588.B35W4] 66-16774
1. Barlach, Ernst, 1870-1938. I. Title.

Barlow, Francis, 1626?-1702.

HODNETT, Edward, 1901- 741'.092'4
Francis Barlow : first master of English book illustration / Edward Hodnett. [Berkeley] : University of California Press, 1978. 237 p. : ill. ; 26 cm. Includes index. Bibliography: p. 223-226. [NC978.5.B37H63] 76-55570 ISBN 0-520-03409-0 : 35.00
1. Barlow, Francis, 1626?-1702. **BIP**

Barnabe, Duilio, 1914-1961.

BARNABE, Duilio, 1914- 759.5
1961.
Barnabe, 1914-1961; twenty-five paintings from a private Swiss collection; [catalog] Chicago, International Galleries, 1969. 31 p. illus. (part col.) 25 cm. An exhibition shown at the International Galleries, Chicago, Spring 1969. Bibliography: p. 28. [ND623.B24A43] 77-284011
1. International Galleries.

BARNABE, Duilio, 1914- 759.5
1961.
Homage to Barnabe, 1914-1961 : [exhibition]. Chicago : R. S. Johnson International Gallery, 1976. p. : ill. (some col.) ; 25 cm. Held in Chicago at the R. S. Johnson International Gallery, 1976. Bibliography: p. 12. [ND623.B24J63] 76-5952
1. Barnabe, Duilio, 1914-1961. I. Johnson (R. S.)-International Gallery. II. Title.

Barnes, Albert Coombs, 1872-1951.

HART, Henry, 1903- 069'.97
Dr. Barnes of Merion, an appreciation. New York, Farrar, Straus [1963] 252 p. illus. 22 cm. [N8375.B28H3] 63-9069
1. Barnes, Albert Coombs, 1872-1951. I. Title.

SCHACK, William. 926.1
Art and argyrol; the life and career of Dr. Albert C. Barnes. New York, T. Yoseloff [1960] 412p. illus. 22cm. [CT275.B446S3] 60-6835
1. Barnes, Albert Combs, 1872-1951. I. Title.

Barnes, Burt, 1872-1947.

DOWNEY, Cleta H. 759.13
Burt Barnes / by Cleta H. Downey ; notes

by Mildred and Marjorie Barnes. Albuquerque : University Art Museum, [1974] 24 p. : ill. ; 21 x 24 cm. Catalogue of the exhibition held at the University of New Mexico Art Museum. [ND1839.B26D68] 74-77151
1. Barnes, Burt, 1872-1947. I. Barnes, Mildred, 1912- II. Barnes, Marjorie, 1913- III. New Mexico. University. Art Museum.

Barnes Foundation, Merion, Pa.

CANTOR, Gilbert M. 706.274812
The Barnes Foundation; reality vs. myth. [1st ed.] Philadelphia, Chilton Books [1963] 219 p. 21 cm. [N81.B326C3] 63-14149
1. Barnes Foundation, Merion, Pa.

Barnet, Will, 1911-

BARNET, Will, 1911- 759.13
Paintings; a selection of 36 paintings completed during the decade 1939-1949 and reproduced in black and white, with an introd. by James T. Farrell. New York, Press Eight, 1950. 1 v. (unpaged) 36 plates. 27 cm. [ND237.B264F3] 51-6106
I. Title.

BARNET, Will, 1911- 769'.92'4
Will Barnet: etchings, lithographs, woodcuts, serigraphs, 1932-1972; catalogue raisonne. Compiled and edited by Sylvan Cole, Jr. With a foreword by Robert Doty. New York, Associated American Artists Gallery, 1972. [94] p. illus. 24 cm. Catalogue of the exhibition held at Associated American Artists Galleries, New York, 1972. Includes bibliographical references. [NE539.B27C64] 72-91760
I. Cole, Sylvan, comp. II. Associated American Artists. III. Title.

BOSTON. Institute of Contemporary Art. 759.13
Will Barnet. Boston [1961] unpaged. illus. 19cm. (Its Exhibition 5/1961) Catalogue of an exhibition held Aug. 19-Sept. 17, 1961. [N5020.B6127 5/1961] 61-19769
1. Barnet, Will, 1911- I. Title.

BROOKLYN Institute of Arts and Sciences. Museum. 769.924
Will Barnet; prints, 1932-1964. [Text by Una E. Johnson, curator of prints and drawings. Research by Jo Miller, assistant curator of prints and drawings. Brooklyn, Brooklyn Museum; distributed by Shorewood Publishers, New York, c1965] 66 p. illus. (part col.) port. 24 cm. (American graphic artists of the twentieth century, monograph no. 3) Bibliography: p. 64-66. [NE539.B27B7] 66-1081
1. Barnet, Will, 1911- I. Johnson, Una E. II. Title. III. Series.

BROOKLYN Institute of Arts and Sciences Museum. 769.924
Will Barnet; prints, 1932-1964. [Text by Una E. Johnson, curator of prints and drawings. Research by Jo Miller, assistant curator of prints and drawings. Brooklyn, Brooklyn Museum; dist. by Shorewood, New York, c1965] 66p. illus. (pt. col.) port. 24cm. (Amer.graphic artists of the twentieth cent., monograph no.3) Bibl. [NE539.B27B7] 66-1081 2.75
1. Barnet, Will, I. Johnson, Una E. II. Title. III. Series.

Barns.

SLOANE, Eric. 728.9
An age of barns. New York, Funk & Wagnalls [1966?] 95 p. illus. (part col.) 27 x 32 cm. Bibliography: p. 94. [NA8230.S57] 66-26946
1. Barns. 2. Farm buildings — U.S. I. Title. BIP

Barns—California—Pictorial works.

THOLLANDER, Earl. 741.9'73
Barns of California : a collection / by Earl Thollander. 1st ed. San Francisco : California Historical Society, [1974] ca. 150 p. : ill. ; 32 cm. [NC139.T47A42] 74-78099 15.95
1. Thollander, Earl. 2. Barns—California—Pictorial works. 3. Barns in art. I. Title. BIP

Barns—Designs and plans.

RADFORD, William A., 1865- 728'.9
Practical plans for barns, carriage houses, stables & other country buildings / William Radford ; David and Joan Loveless. Stockbridge, Mass. : Berkshire Traveller Press, c1978. 206 p. : ill. ; 25 cm. "William Radford's Practical barn plans originally printed in 1908 in ... Radford's combined house and barn plan book." [NA8230.R3 1978] 78-60318 ISBN 0-912944-50-1 : 8.95
1. Barns—Designs and plans. 2. Farm buildings—Designs and plans. 3. Barns—Remodeling for other use—Designs and plans. I. Loveless, David. II. Loveless, Joan. III. Title.

Barns—England—Norfolk (County)

EBBAGE, Sheridan. 728'.9
Barns and granaries in Norfolk / Sheridan Ebbage. Ipswich : Boydell Press, c1976. 48 p. : ill., 21 cm. (Bygones) Based on an Anglia Television program. Bibliography: p. 48. [NA8230.E2] 77-370573 ISBN 0-85115-079-9 : £0.80
1. Barns—England—Norfolk (County) 2. Granaries—England—Norfolk (County) I. Title.

Barns—Massachusetts—Martha's Vineyard.

JOSEPHS, Peter Colt, 1939- 728.9
The remarkable brick barns of Martha's Vineyard. Drawings by Donald A. Voltz. Photos. by Roswell Colt Josephs and the author. [1st ed.] Chilmark, Mass., Brick Barn Press [1974] xi, 23 p. illus. 23 cm. Bibliography: p. 23. [NA8230.J67] 74-83461
1. Barns—Massachusetts—Martha's Vineyard. 2. Building, Brick. I. Title.

Barns—Northeastern States.

ARTHUR, Eric Ross. 728'.9
The barn : a vanishing landmark in North America / Eric Arthur and Dudley Witney. New York A & W Visual Library, [1975], c1972 256 p. : ill. ; 29 cm. Includes index. Bibliography: p. 249-250. [NA8230.A77 1972c] 74-33776 ISBN 0-89104-004-8 pbk. : 9.95
1. Barns—Northeastern States. 2. Barns—Canada. I. Witney, Dudley, joint author. II. Title. BIP

Barns—Pennsylvania—Chester Co.

BALL, Berenice M., 1903- 917.48'13
Barns of Chester County, Pennsylvania / by Berenice M. Ball. 1st ed. West Chester, Pa. : Chester County Day Committee of the Women's Auxiliary, Chester County Hospital, 1974. xii, 241 p. : ill. (some col.) ; 27 cm. Includes index. Bibliography: p. 239. [NA8230.B26] 74-82632
1. Barns—Pennsylvania—Chester Co. I. Title.

Barns—United States.

SLOANE, Eric. 728.95
American barns and covered bridges. New York, W. Funk [1954] 112 p. illus. 26 cm. [NA8201.S6] 54-12510
1. Barns—United States. 2. Covered bridges. I. Title.

Barnsley, Ernest, 1863-1926.

CHELTENHAM Art Gallery and Museum. 749.2'2
Good citizen's furniture : the work of Ernest and Sidney Barnsley : [catalogue of an exhibition held at Cheltenham Art Gallery & Museum 5th November 1976-15th January 1977]. [Cheltenham] : [The Art Gallery and Museum], [1976] [49] p. : ill., ports. ; 15 x 21 cm. Cover title. Errata slip inserted. [TS882.G73C483] 77-364064 ISBN 0-905157-01-X : £0.75
1. Barnsley, Ernest, 1863-1926. 2. Barnsley, Sidney, 1865-1926. 3. Furniture—England—Exhibitions. I. Barnsley, Ernest, 1863-1926. II. Barnsley, Sidney, 1865-1926. III. Title.

Barra, Didier.

SLUYS, Felix, 1885- 759.4
Didier Barra et Francois de Nome, dits Monsu Desiderio [Dist. New York, Wittenborn, 1962, c.1961] 143p. illus. (pt. mounted col.) 26cm. (Le Cabinet fantastique, v. 2) Bibl. 62-1914 12.50
1. Barra, Didier. 2. Nome, Francois de. I. Title.

Bartarian invasions of Rome.

LEVI, Annalina Calo. 737.4
Barbarians on Roman imperial coins and sculpture. New York, American Numismatic Society, 1952. xi, 56, xviip. illus. 23cm. (Numismatic notes and monographs, no. 123) Bibliographical footnotes. [D135.L48] 52-10117
1. Bartarian invasions of Rome. 2. Germanic tribes. 3. Coins, Roman. 4. Sculpture, Roman. I. Title. II. Series.

Bartholdi, Frederic Auguste, 1834-1904.

GSCHAEDLER, Andre. 730.924
True light on the Statue of Liberty and its creator. [1st ed.] Narberth, Pa., Livingston Pub. Co. [1966] xiii, 186 p. illus., ports. 23 cm. "Sources": p. 171-173. [NB553.B3G8] 65-28279
1. Bartholdi, Frederic Auguste, 1834-1904. 2. Statue of Liberty, New York. I. Title.

LUDMANN, Oscar Henry, 1900- 730.924
Quand? Or, Liberty nee Bartholdi, by Oscar H. Ludmann. [1st ed.] New York, Vantage Press [1965] 251 p. ports. 21 cm. [NB553.B3LS] 65-20120
1. Bartholdi, Frederic Auguste, 1834-1904. 2. State of Liberty, New York. I. Title. II. Title: Liberty nee Bartholdi.

PRICE, Willadene. 730.944
Bartholdi and the Statue of Liberty. Chicago, Rand McNally [1959] 188 p. illus. 22 cm. [NB553.B3P7] 59-10473
1. Bartholdi, Frederic Auguste, 1834-1904. 2. Statue of Liberty, New York.

TRACHTENBERG, Marvin. 730'.92'4
The Statue of Liberty. New York, Viking Press, 1976. 224 p. illus. 23 cm. Includes bibliographical references. [NB553.B3T72] 74-19306 ISBN 0-670-66854-0 : 10.95
1. Bartholdi, Frederic Auguste, 1834-1904. 2. Statue of Liberty, New York. I. Title. BIP

TRACHTENBERG, Marvin. 730'.92'4
The Statue of Liberty / Marvin Trachtenberg. New York : Penguin Books, 1977. 224 p. : ill. ; 23 cm. Includes bibliographical references and index. [NB553.B3T72 1977] 77-5624 ISBN 0-14-004513-9 pbk. : 5.95
1. Bartholdi, Frederic Auguste, 1834-1904. 2. Statue of Liberty, New York. I. Title.

Bartiesville, Okla. Price Tower.

WRIGHT, Frank Lloyd, 1869- 725.232
The story of the Tower; the tree that escaped the crowded forest. New York, Horizon Press, 1956. 130p. illus. (part col.) ports., plans. 29cm. [NA6233.B3P7] 56-7826
1. Bartiesville, Okla. Price Tower. I. Title.

Bartlett, John Russell, 1805-1886.

HINE, Robert V., 1921- 760'.09791
Bartlett's West; drawing the Mexican boundary [by] Robert V. Hine. New Haven, Published for the Amon Carter Museum, Fort Worth [by] Yale University Press, 1968. xv, 155 p. illus. (part col.), map, col. port. 19 x 26 cm. (Yale Western Americana series, 19) The illustrations are chiefly from the John Russell Bartlett papers in the John Carter Brown Library, Brown University. Bibliography: p. 95-96. [ND1839.B3H5] 68-13910
1. Bartlett, John Russell, 1805-1886. 2. Southwest, New—Description and travel—Views. I. Amon Carter Museum of Western Art, Fort Worth, Tex. II. Brown University. John Carter Brown Library. III. Title. IV. Series. BIP

Bartlett, William Henry, 1809-1854.

ROSS, Alexander M. 760'.092'4
William Henry Bartlett; artist, author and traveller [by] Alexander M. Ross. Containing a reprint of Dr. William Beattie's Brief memoir of the late William Henry Bartlett. [Toronto, Buffalo] University of Toronto Press [1973] ix, 164 p. illus. 29 cm. Bibliography: p. 151-154. [NX547.6.B37R67] 72-97783 ISBN 0-8020-1986-2 15.00
1. Bartlett, William Henry, 1809-1854. I. Beattie, William, 1793-1875. Brief memoir of the late William Henry Bartlett. 1973. BIP

Bartram, William, 1739-1823—Juvenile literature.

SANGER, Marjory (Bartlett) 574'.092'4 B
Billy Bartram and his green world; an interpretative biography. [1st ed.] New York, Farrar, Straus & Giroux [1972] 207 p. plates. 24 cm. Bibliogaphy: p. [197]-202. A biography of the eighteenth-century man who devoted his life to studying and drawing birds, animals, and plants in America's wilderness. [QL31.B33S35 1972] 92 78-175822 ISBN 0-374-30707-5 6.50
1. Bartram, William, 1739-1823—Juvenile literature. 2. Ornithologists—United States—Juvenile literature. I. Title. BIP

Barye, Antoine Louis, 1796-1875.

DEKAY, Charles, 1848-1935. 730'.92'4
Barye: life and works of Antoine Louis Bayre, sculptor; with eighty-six wood-cuts, artotypes, and prints, in memory of an exhibition of his bronzes, paintings, and water-colors, held at New York in aid of the fund for his monument at Paris. New York, Barye Monument Association, 1889. [New York, AMS Press, 1974] xi, 158 p. illus. 23 cm. [NB553.B4D3 1974] 73-163696 ISBN 0-404-02068-2
1. Barye, Antoine Louis, 1796-1875.

Bas-relief.

WINLOCK, Herbert Eustis, 1884-1950. 732'.8'0932
The temple of Rames[s]es I at Abydos. [New York] Arno Press, 1973. 54, 20 p. illus., 16 plates. 29 cm. Reprint of the 1921 ed. of Bas-reliefs from the temple of Rameses I at Abydos, published by the Metropolitan Museum of Art, New York, and issued as v. 1, pt. of the Papers of the Metropolitan Museum of Art; and of the 1937 ed. of The temple of Ramesses I at Abydos, published by the Metropolitan Museum of Art, New York, and issued as no. 5 of the Papers of the Metropolitan Museum of Art. Includes bibliographical references. [NB75.W53 1973] 75-168411 ISBN 0-405-02247-6 35.00
1. Abydos, Egypt. Temple of Rameses I. 2. Bas-relief. 3. Sculpture, Egyptian. I. Winlock, Herbert Eustis, 1884-1950. Bas-reliefs from the temple of Rameses I at Abydos. 1973. II. Title. III. Series: New York (City). Metropolitan Museum of Art. Papers v. 1, pt. 1 [etc.]

Baseball cards.

BOYD, Brendan C. 769'.4'2
The great American baseball card flipping, trading and bubble gum book / Brendan C. Boyd and Fred C. Harris. New York : Warner Paperback Library, 1975, c1973. 271 p. : col. ill. ; 18 cm. [GV875.2.B69 1975] 75-312013 pbk. : 2.25
1. Baseball cards. I. Harris, Fred C., 1943- joint author. II. Title.

BOYD, Brendan C. 769'.4'2
The great American baseball card flipping, trading, and bubble gum book [by] Brendan C. Boyd and Fred C. Harris. [1st ed.] Boston, Little, Brown [1973] 151 p. col. illus. 22 cm. "A Sports illustrated

Industries. I. Seeler, Edgar, joint author. II. Title. BIP

Baskets, Glass—United States.

MILLER, Robert William, 1922- 748.8
The art glass basket / by Robert W. Miller ; [photography by Marshall Thurman]. Des Moines, Iowa : Wallace-Homestead Book Co., [1972] [6] p., 16 leaves of plates : col. ill. ; 23 cm. [NK5112.M55] 75-322688
1. Baskets, Glass—United States. 2. Glassware—United States. 3. Decoration and ornament—Art nouveau. I. Thurman, Marshall. II. Title.

Basketwork—Analysis.

ADOVASIO, J. M. 746.4'1
Basketry technology : a guide to identification and analysis / J. M. Adovasio ; drawings by Edward Schumacher and Rhonda Andrews. Chicago : Aldine Pub. Co., 1977. x, 182 p. : ill. ; 29 cm. (Aldine manuals on archeology) Includes index. Bibliography: p. [173]-176. [CC79.5.B37A36] 77-70388 ISBN 0-202-33035-4 : 12.50
1. Basketwork—Analysis. I. Title. BIP

Basketwork—Collectors and collecting.

THOMPSON, Frances, 1920- 746.4'1
Antique baskets and basketry / Frances Thompson. Cranbury, N.J. : A. S. Barnes, c1976. p. cm. Includes index. [TS913.T48] 75-38443 ISBN 0-498-01873-3 : 9.95
1. Basketwork—Collectors and collecting. I. Title.

Basketwork—United States—Collectors and collecting.

KETCHUM, William C., 1931- 746.4'1
American basketry and woodenware, a collector's guide [by] William C. Ketchum, Jr. New York, Macmillan [1974] ix, 228 p. illus. 21 cm. Bibliography: p. 215-219. [TS913.K47] 73-6486 ISBN 0-02-562970-0 6.95
1. Basketwork—United States—Collectors and collecting. 2. Treenware—United States—Collectors and collecting. I. Title. BIP

Baskin, Leonard, 1922-

BASKIN, Leonard, 1922- 741.9'73
Ars anatomica : a medical fantasia, thirteen drawings / Leonard Baskin. New York : Medicina Rara, c1972. [7] p., 13 leaves of plates in portfolio : ill. ; 56 cm. [NC139.B37A47] 75-315752
1. Baskin, Leonard, 1922- 2. Anatomy, Artistic. I. Title.

BASKIN, Leonard, 1922- 709.24
Baskin: sculpture, drawings & prints. New York, G. Braziller, 1970. 170 p. (incl. 136 plates, part col.) 29 cm. Bibliography: p. 167-170. [N6537.B23A43 1970] 73-132198 15.00
I. Title.

BASKIN, Leonard, 1922- 730.924
Figures of dead men. Pref. by Archibald MacLeish. Photos. by Hyman Edelstein. [Amherst?] University of Massachusetts Press, 1968. 1 v. chiefly illus. 26 cm. [NB237.B38A45] 68-19668
I. Title. BIP

BASKIN, Leonard, 1922- 769'.924
The graphic work, 1950-1970. New York, Far Gallery, 1970. [103] p. illus., ports. 28 cm. [NE539.B3A46] 77-24890
I. Far Gallery. II. Title.

BASKIN, Leonard, 1922- 730'.92'4
Leonard Baskin; an exhibition of recent work, November 30-December 31, 1971. New York, Kennedy Galleries, 1972. 1 v. (chiefly illus.) 28 cm. [NB237.B38K4] 72-198262
I. Kennedy Galleries, inc., New York.

BASKIN, Leonard, 1922- 709'.2'4
Leonard Baskin : sculpture & watercolors, June 9-July 9, 1976, Kennedy Galleries, N.Y. [New York] : Kennedy Galleries, 1976. [32] p. : chiefly ill. ; 28 cm. Catalog. [N6537.B23K46] 76-370399
1. Baskin, Leonard, 1922- I. Kennedy Galleries, inc., New York.

BASKIN, Leonard, 1922- 709'.24
Leonard Baskin. Essay by Alan Fern, annotated by Leonard Baskin. Washington, Published for the National Collection of Fine Arts by the Smithsonian Institution Press, 1970. 76 p. (chiefly illus.) 27 cm. Catalog of the exhibition held June 12-July 26, 1970, at the National Collection of Fine Arts of the Smithsonian Institution, Washington. Bibliography: p. 72-76. [N6537.B23F4] 78-606653
I. Fern, Alan Maxwell, 1930- II. Smithsonian Institution. National Collection of Fine Arts.

BASKIN, Leonard, 1922- 760'.092'4
Leonard Baskin—recent watercolors and lithographs : [catalogue of the exhibition], May 15-June 1, 1974, Kennedy Galleries. [New York] : Kennedy Galleries, [1974] [12] p. : chiefly ill. ; 28 cm. [ND1837.B37K46] 74-187909
1. Baskin, Leonard, 1922- I. Kennedy Galleries, inc., New York.

BASKIN, Leonard, 1922- 730'.92'4
Sculpture and drawings. New York, Kennedy Galleries, c1973. [41] p. illus. 28 cm. Catalogue of the exhibition held at the Kennedy Galleries, New York, May 9-June 1, 1973. [NB237.B38K42] 74-184376
1. Baskin, Leonard, 1922- I. Kennedy Galleries, inc., New York.

BOWDOIN College. Museum of Fine Arts. 707.4
Leonard Baskin [exhibition. Brunswick, Me.] 1962. 1 v. (unpaged) illus., ports., facsims. 25 cm. Includes bibliography. [N6537.B3B6] 63-3376
1. Baskin, Leonard, 1922- I. Title.

Baston, Eng. Tinker's Urn.

MAYES, Philip. 942.5'38
An Anglo-Saxon cemetery at Baston, Lincolnshire / [by] P. Mayes and the late M. J. Dean ; with a report on the pottery by J. N. L. Myres. Sleaford : Society for Lincolnshire History and Archaeology, 1976. 63 p. : ill., maps, plans ; 30 cm. (Occasional papers in Lincolnshire history and archaeology ; 3 ISSN 0307-2797s) Includes bibliographical references..[DA690.B296M38] 77-372997 ISBN 0-904680-05-3 : £1.40
1. Baston, Eng. Tinker's Urn. 2. Anglo-Saxons. 3. Baston, Eng.—Antiquities, Saxon. 4. England—Antiquities, Saxon. I. Dean, M. J., joint author. II. Myres, John Nowell Linton. III. Title. IV. Series: Occasional papers in Lincolnshire history and archaeology ; 3.

Bateman, Hester (Needham) 1709-1794.

SHURE, David S. 739.2374219
Hester Bateman, queen of English silversmiths. Garden City, N.Y., Doubleday [1960, c.1959] 31p. plates, geneal. table. 29cm. 59-11609 7.95
1. Bateman, Hester (Needham) 1709-1794. I. Title.

Bathrooms.

AMERICAN builder. 747.78
Book of modern bathrooms, compiled from the pages of American builder magazine. New York, Simmons- Boardman Pub. Corp., 1958. 112p. illus. 29cm. [NK2117.A5] 58-10982
1. Bathrooms. I. Title.

GILLIATT, Mary. 747'.78
Bathrooms. Photos. by Brian Morris [and others] New York, Viking Press [1971] 120 p. illus. 24 x 25 cm. (A Studio book) [NK2117.B33G5] 70-162663 ISBN 0-670-14898-9 12.95
1. Bathrooms.

HOLMES, David. 747'.78
Planning your bathroom for beauty and efficiency. Garden City, N.Y., N. Doubleday [1968] 68 p. illus. (part col.) 24 cm. (The Doubleday home decorating program) [NK2117.H6] 76-680
1. Bathrooms. 2. Interior decoration. I. Title.

KIRA, Alexander. 747'.76
The bathroom / Alexander Kira. New and expanded ed. New York : Viking Press, [1975] p. cm. Includes index. [TH6488.K5 1975] 75-19052 ISBN 0-670-14897-0 : 15.00
1. Bathrooms. 2. Plumbing—Equipment and supplies. 3. Human engineering. I. Title. BIP

†KIRA, Alexander. 747'.78
The bathroom / Alexander Kira. New and expanded ed. New York : Penguin Books, 1976. p. cm. Includes index. [TH6488.K5 1976b] 76-28447 ISBN 0-14-004371-3 pbk. : 7.95
1. Bathrooms. 2. Plumbing—Equipment and supplies. 3. Human engineering. I. Title.

SNOW, Anthony. 747'.78
Planning your bathroom / [by] Anthony Snow and Graham Hopewell. London : Design Council, 1976. 71 p. : ill. (some col.) ; 21 x 22 cm. (A Design Centre book) [TH6485.S66] 77-370385 ISBN 0-85072-027-3 : £3.25. ISBN 0-85072-026-5 pbk.
1. Bathrooms. I. Hopewell, Graham, joint author. II. Title. BIP

Batik.

ADASKO, Laura. 746.6
Batik in many forms [by] Laura Adasko & Alice Huberman. Photography by Frank Conaway. New York, Morrow [1975] 159 p. illus. 26 cm. Bibliography: p. 155-156. [TT852.5.A3] 74-16376 ISBN 0-688-00340-0 12.95
1. Batik. I. Huberman, Alice, joint author. II. Title. BIP

BELFER, Nancy. 746.6
Designing in batik and tie dye / Nancy Belfer. Rev. paper ed. Englewood Cliffs, N.J. : Prentice-Hall, c1977. xii, 145 p., [4] leaves of plates : ill. ; 24 cm. (The Creative handicrafts series) (A Spectrum book) Bibliography: p. 141-142. [TT852.5.B44 1977] 76-58911 ISBN 0-13-201996-5 pbk. : 6.95
1. Batik. 2. Tie-dyeing. I. Title. BIP

BYSTRM, Ellen. 746.6
Creating with batik / Ellen Bystrm ; [translated from the Danish by Christine James]. New York : Van Nostrand Reinhold Co., c1974. 87 p. : ill. ; 23 cm. Translation of Batik, teknik og ideer. Includes index. [TT852.5.B913] 72-9720 ISBN 0-442-29974-5 : 4.95
1. Batik. I. Title.

DEYRUP, Astrith. 746.6
Getting started in batik. New York, Bruce Pub. Co. [1971] xi, 79 p. illus. (part col.) 28 cm. (Getting started series) Bibliography: p. 75-76. [TP930.D48] 74-152295 2.95
1. Batik. I. Title. BIP

GIBBS, Joanifer, 1947- 746.6
Batik unlimited. Photos. by Tom B. Burgher II. New York, Watson-Guptill Publications [1974] 151 p. illus. 29 cm. Bibliography: p. 147. [TP930.G52 1974] 73-21552 ISBN 0-8230-0460-0 11.95
1. Batik. I. Title. BIP

HERSK, Bernadette. 746.6
The ABC's of batik / Bernadette Hersk. 1st ed. Radnor, Pa. : Chilton Book Co., c1975. xiii, 155 p., [6] leaves of plates : ill. (some col.) ; 27 cm. (Chilton's creative crafts series) Includes index. [TT852.5.H47 1975] 75-28095 ISBN 0-8019-6134-3 : 12.50 ISBN 0-8019-6135-1 pbk. : 6.95
1. Batik. I. Title. II. Title: Batik. BIP

HOUSTON, John. 746.6
Batik with Noel Dyrenforth / John Houston. Indianapolis : Bobbs-Merrill, 1976c1975 80 p. : col. ill. ; 31 cm. Bibliography: p. 80. [TT852.5.H68] 75-13836 ISBN 0-672-52179-2 : 9.95
1. Batik. I. Dyrenforth, Noel. II. Title.

KELLER, Ila 746.6
Batik; the art and craft. Rutland, Vt., Tuttle [c.1966] 75p. illus. (pt. col.) 21x22cm. [NK9503.K4] 66-16267 5.00 bds.,
1. Batik. I. Title. BIP

KREVITSKY, Nik. 746.6
Batik art and craft. New York, Reinhold Pub. Corp. [1964] 68 p. illus. (part col.) 21 cm. (An Art horizons book) [NK9503.K7] 64-13647
1. Batik. I. Title.

KREVITSKY, Nik. 746.6
Batik art and craft. [Enl. ed.] New York, Van Nostrand Reinhold Co. [1973] 92 p. illus. (part col.) 21 cm. (An Art horizons book) [NK9503.K7 1973] 73-178274 ISBN 0-442-24539-4 3.95
1. Batik. I. Title.

MARTIN, Beryl. 746.6
Batik for beginners. New York, Scribner [1972, c1971] 34 p. illus. 24 cm. Describes the necessary materials and techniques for creating various batik designs and suggests how they may be applied to a variety of objects. [TP930.M37 1972] 72-39725 ISBN 0-684-12897-7 4.95
1. Batik. I. Title.

MEILACH, Dona Z. 746.6
Contemporary batik and tie-dye; methods, inspiration, dyes, by Dona Z. Meilach. New York, Crown Publishers [1973] vi, 280 p. illus. 27 cm. (Crown's arts and crafts series) Bibliography: p. 271-273. [TP930.M45 1973] 72-84320 ISBN 0-517-50088-4 8.95
1. Batik. 2. Tie-dyeing. I. Title. BIP

MUHLING, Ernst. 746.6
The book of batik. New York, Taplinger Pub. Co. [1967] 72 p. illus. (part col.) 22 cm. Translation of Das Batik-Buch. [TP930.M813] 67-11515
1. Batik. 2. Textile printing. I. Title. BIP

SHAW, Robin. 746.6
Batik; new look at an ancient art [by] Robin and Jennifer Shaw. [1st ed.] Garden City, N.Y., Doubleday, 1974. 96 p. illus. (part col.) 26 cm. Bibliography: p. 96. [NK9503.S46] 72-89677 ISBN 0-385-01946-7 3.95
1. Batik. I. Shaw, Jennifer, joint author. II. Title.

STEIN, Vivian. 746.6
Batik, as a hobby. New York, Sterling Pub. Co. [1969] 80 p. illus. (part col.) 22 cm. [TP930.S88] 69-19491
1. Batik. I. Title. BIP

Batik—Juvenile literature.

HOWE, Emmy. 746.6
Rennie the fish; illustrated and with instructions for batiking by Emmy Howe. New York, Van Nostrand Reinhold [1972] [32] p. illus. 22 x 27 cm. A chronicle of Rennie the Fish's adventures in the New York sewers, illustrated with batiks, accompanies instructions for creating batik designs. [TP930.H68] 72-1858 ISBN 0-442-23555-0 4.50
1. Batik—Juvenile literature. I. Title.

REIS, Mary. 746.6
Batik. Pictures by George Overlie. Minneapolis, Lerner Publications Co. [1973] 32 p. illus. 21 cm. (An Early craft book) Explains the ancient craft of batik and gives instructions for creating a variety of designs. [TP930.R44] 72-13334 ISBN 0-8225-0852-4 3.95
1. Batik—Juvenile literature. I. Overlie, George, illus. II. Title. BIP

YERIAN, Cameron John. 746.6
Batik & tie dyeing. Cameron and Margaret Yerian, editors. Chicago, Childrens Press [1974] 44 p. col. illus. 25 cm. "Fun time." Introduces basic techniques of tie dyeing, batik, and dollmaking and suggests simple projects using these techniques. [TT852.5.Y47] 74-8440 ISBN 0-516-01303-3
1. Batik—Juvenile literature. 2. Tie-dyeing—Juvenile literature. 3. Dollmaking—Juvenile literature. I. Yerian, Margaret, joint author. II. Title. BIP

Batista y Zaldivar, Fulgencio, Pres. Cuba, 1901-1973—Art collections.

MUSEUM of Arts an Sciences. 759.97291
Cuban paintings from the Collection of General Fulgencio Batista / with an introd. by Gary Russell Libby. Daytona Beach, Fla. : Museum of Arts and Sciences, c1977. 48 p. : chiefly ill. (some col.) ; 21 cm. [ND303.M87 1977] 77-152462
1. Batista y Zaldivar, Fulgencio, Pres. Cuba, 1901-1973—Art collections. 2. Museum of Arts and Sciences. 3. Painting, Cuban—Catalogs. I. Title.

Batman (Comic strip)

BATMAN from the 30s to the 70s. 741.5'9
Introd. by E. Nelson Bridwell. New York, Crown Publishers [1972, c1971] 388 p. 28 cm. Comics based on the character created by B. Kane, written and drawn by Kane and others. Bibliography: p. 385-386. [NC1426.3.B3B3 1971] 73-168329 10.00
1. Batman (Comic strip) I. Bridwell, E. Nelson. II. Kane, Bob.

Baton Rouge, La. State Capitol.

KUBLY, Vincent F. 725'.11'0976318
The Louisiana capitol : its art and architecture / by Vincent F. Kubly ; foreword by Solis Seiferth. Gretna, La. : Pelican Pub. Co., 1976. p. cm. Includes index. [NA4413.B36K8] 76-49889 ISBN 0-88289-082-4 : 15.00
1. Baton Rouge, La. State Capitol. I. Title. BIP

Battiss, Walter, 1906—

BATTISS, Walter, 1906- 760'.092'4
Walter Battiss / [text] by Murray Schoonraad. Cape Town : Struik (C.), 1976. 66 p. : chiefly ill. (some col.) ; 25 x 28 cm. (South African art library) Includes index. Bibliography: p. 63. [N7396.B28S36] 77-368762 ISBN 0-86977-071-3 : R9.75
1. Battiss, Walter, 1906- I. Schoonraad, Murray. II. Title. III. Series.

Batty, Bob H.—Art collections.

BATTY, Bob H. 748.2'913
A complete guide to pressed glass / by Bob H. Batty ; drawings by John T. Hendricks. Gretna [La.] : Pelican Pub. Co., 1978. p. cm. Bibliography: p. [NK5203.B37] 77-19211 ISBN 0-88289-057-3 : 19.95
1. Batty, Bob H.—Art collections. 2. Pressed glass—United States. 3. Pattern glass—United States. 4. Glassware—United States—History—19th century. I. Title. BIP

Baudelaire, Charles Pierre, 1821-1867.

INDIANA. University. Dept. of Fine Arts. 769
Baudelaire and the graphic arts, by Theodore Bowie. [Catalogue prepapred in connection with an exhibition, Oct. 25 through Nov. 19, 1957, jointly presented by the Departments of Fine Arts and of French and Italian] Bloomington, Indiana University, 1957. unpaged. illus. 23cm. [N8375.B33I5] 57-63902
1. Baudelaire, Charles Pierre, 1821-1867. 2. Engravings— Exhibitions. 3. Drawings—Exhibitions. I. Bowie, Theodore. II. Indiana. University. Dept. of French and Italian. III. Title.

Bauer, John Albert, 1882-1918—Juvenile literature.

BAUER, John Albert, 1882-1918. 759.85
In the troll wood / ill. by John Bauer ; text by Olive Jones. Toronto ; New York : Methuen, [1978] p. cm. Fifteen full-page illustrations of the strange haunting world of the trolls accompanied by a simple descriptive text. [ND793.B33A4 1978] 77-18419 ISBN 0-458-93240-X : 8.95
1. Bauer, John Albert, 1882-1918—Juvenile literature. 2. Trolls in art—Juvenile literature. I. Jones, Olive. II. Title. BIP

Bauer, Marius Alexander Jacques, 1864-1932.

HENNUS, M F 372.5
Marcius Bauer. Amsterdam, H. J. W. Becht [1947] 60p. illus. 27cm. (Palet serie; een reeks monografleen over Hollandsche en Vlaamsche schilders. Negentiende en twintigste eeuw) Bibliography: p. 60. [ND653.B38H4] 56-41533
1. Bauer, Marius Alexander Jacques, 1864-1932. I. Title. II. Series.

Bauer, Rudolf, 1889-1953.

RUDOLF Bauer, 1889-1953; 759.3
a retrospective exhibition of non-objective paintings New York, Hutton-Hutschnecker Gallery [1970] 28 p. illus. (part col.), port. 28 cm. Catalog of the exhibition held Oct. 23d-Dec. 19th, 1970. Label mounted on t.p.: Boston, Supplied by Worldwide Books. [ND588.B346R6] 76-199904
1. Bauer, Rudolf, 1889-1953. I. Hutton-Hutschnecker Gallery.

Bauhaus.

BAYER, Herbert, 1900- ed. 707'.11'43155
Bauhaus, 1919-1928. Edited by Herbert Bayer, Walter Gropius, [and] Ise Gropius. New York, Museum of Modern Art, 1938. [New York] Published for the Museum of Modern Art by Arno Press, 1972. 224 p. illus. 26 cm. "Bibliography of Bauhaus publications": p. 222-224. [N332.G33B435 1972] 77-169299 ISBN 0-405-01559-3 25.00
1. Bauhaus. I. Gropius, Walter, ed. II. Gropius, Ise (Frank) ed.

FRANCISCONO, Marcel. 707'.1
Walter Gropius and the creation of the Bauhaus in Weimar: the ideals and artistic theories of its founding years. Urbana, University of Illinois Press [1971] xvi, 336 p. illus. 24 cm. Bibliography: p. 298-322. [N70.F69] 73-126519 ISBN 0-252-00128-1 11.95
1. Gropius, Walter, 1883-1969. 2. Bauhaus. 3. Art—Philosophy. I. Title.

GROPIUS, Walter, 1883-1969. 724.9
The new architecture and the Bauhaus. Translated from the German by P. Morton Shand, with an introd. by Frank Pick. Cambridge, Mass., M.I.T. Press [1965] 112 p. illus. 21 cm. (The M.I.T. paperback series, MIT21) [NA680.G7 1965] 65-10279
1. Bauhaus. 2. Architecture, Modern—20th century. 3. Industrial arts—Study and teaching—Germany. I. Title. BIP

NAYLOR, Gillian. 707'.1'5
The Bauhaus, London, Studio Vista, 1968. 159p. (Chiefly illus., facsims.). 19cm. (Studio vista/Dutton pictureback) Bibl. [N332.B38N3 1968] 68-111683 1.95 pap.,
1. Bauhaus. I. Title.
Available from Dutton, New York.

NEUMANN, Eckhard. 709.04
Bauhaus and Bauhaus people; personal opinions and recollections of former Bauhaus members and their contemporaries. Edited by Eckhard Neumann. [Translation by Eva Richter and Alba Lorman] New York, Van Nostrand Reinhold [1970] 256 p. illus., ports. 25 cm. "Texts in the original catalog of the exhibition [The Bauhaus—idea, form, purpose, time, at Goppinger Gallerie, 1964] were partly revised ... and ... augmented by many contributions written by new authors." Photoreproduction of "Programm des Staatlichen Bauhauses in Weimar [April, 1919]" (folder [4] p. 25 cm.) inserted between p. 8-9; translation: p. 9-10. [N332.G33B45] 66-22690
1. Bauhaus. I. Title.

POLING, Clark V. 709'.04'074013
Bauhaus color : an exhibition organized by the High Museum of Art and supported by a grant from the National Endowment for the Arts / by Clark V. Poling. Atlanta : High Museum of Art, [1975] 71 p. : ill. (some col.) ; 24 cm. Exhibition to be held Jan. 31-Mar. 14, 1976 at the High Museum of Art, Atlanta, Apr. 8-May 30, 1976 at the Museum of Fine Arts, Houston, and Aug. 1-Sept. 21, 1976 at the Fine Arts Gallery of San Diego. Bibliography: p. 71. [N332.G33B475] 75-39143
1. Bauhaus. 2. Color in art—Exhibitions. 3. Art, Modern—20th century—Exhibition. I. High Museum of Art. II. Title.

ROTERS, Eberhard. 759
Painters of the Bauhaus. [Translated from the German by Anna Rose Cooper.] New York, Praeger [1969, c1965] 215 p. illus. (part col.) 27 cm. Translation of Maler am Bauhaus. Bibliography: p. 207-209. [N332.B38R613] 69-15385 18.50
1. Bauhaus. 2. Art, Modern—20th century—History. I. Title.

SCHEIDIG, Walther. 707.1'5
Crafts of the Weimar Bauhaus, 1919-1924; an early experiment in industrial design. Photos. by Klaus G. Beyer. [Translated from the German by Ruth Michaelis-Jena with the collaboration of Patrick Murray] New York, Reinhold Pub. Corp. [1967] 150 p. illus. (part col.) 28 cm. Translation of Bauhaus Weimar, 1919-1924. Bibliography: p. [147]-148. [N332.B38S283 1967] 66-25545
1. Bauhaus. 2. Art—Weimar. I. Beyer, Klaus G., 1922- illus. II. Title.

WINGLER, Hans Maria. 707'.1'5
The Bauhaus: Weimar, Dessau, Berlin, Chicago [by] Hans M. Wingler. [Translated by Wolfgang Jabs and Basil Gilbert. Edited by Joseph Stein. Cambridge, Mass., MIT Press, 1969] xv, 653 p. illus., facsims., maps, plans, 24 col. plates, ports. 37 cm. "[Translation of] second, revised edition published in 1968 ... and includes extensive supplementary material." Bibliography: p. 627-647. [N332.B38W513] 68-20052
1. Bauhaus. I. Stein, Joseph, 1917- ed. II. Title. BIP

Baumeister, Will, 1889-1955.

GROHMANN, Will, 1887- 759.3
Willi Baumeister: life and work. [Tr. from German by Robert Allen] New York, Abrams [1966] 360p. illus., facsims., plates (pt. col.) ports. 30cm. Bibl. [ND588.B35G763] 65-20322 35.00
1. Baumeister, Will, 1889-1955. I. Title.

Baxter, George, 1804-1867.

BALL, Abraham, 1908- 769'.92'4
The price guide to Baxter prints / [text] by A. Ball and M. Martin. Woodbridge : Antique Collectors' Club, 1974. [8], 275 p. : chiefly ill. (some col.), port., 28 cm. Includes index. [NE1860.B2B35] 75-310254 ISBN 0-902028-23-5 : £8.75
1. Baxter, George, 1804-1867. 2. Color prints—Catalogs. I. Martin, Michael, 1935- joint author. II. Baxter, George, 1804-1867. III. Title. IV. Title: Baxter prints.

LEWIS, Charles Thomas Courtney. 769'.92'4
George Baxter—his life and work, by C. T. Courtney Lewis. [1st ed., reprinted with a new foreword by Helen Courtney Lewis. Wakefield, E.P. Publishing, 1972. vi, xviii, 276 p., 31 leaves. illus., ports. 20 cm. Bibliography: p. 236-254. [NE1860.B2L7 1972] 73-167780 ISBN 0-85409-918-2 £3.15
1. Baxter, George, 1804-1867.

MITZMAN, Max E. 769'.92'4 B
George Baxter and the Baxter prints / Max E. Mitzman. Newton Abbot [Eng.] ; North Pomfret, Vt. : David and Charles, c1978. 176 p. : ill. (Chiefly col.) ; 24 cm. Includes indexes. Bibliography: p. [169] [NE1860.B2M57] 78-52165 ISBN 0-7153-7629-2 : 17.95
1. Baxter, George, 1804-1867. 2. Printmakers—England—Biography. 3. Color prints, English. I. Baxter, George, 1804-1867. II. Title. BIP

Bayer, Herbert, 1900—

BAYER, Herbert, 1900- 709'.2'4
Herbert Bayer: a total concept. Exhibition; Denver Art Museum, Nov. 11 - Dec. 23, 1973. [Denver, Denver Art Museum, c1973] 70 p. illus. (part col.) 23 cm. Bibliography: p. 10. [N6537.B34D46] 74-170339
1. Bayer, Herbert, 1900- I. Denver. Art Museum. II. Title.

BAYER, Herbert, 1900- 709.73
Herbert Bayer: painter, designer, architect. New York, Reinhold [1967] 211 p. illus. (part col.), plans. 29 cm. Bibliography: p. 207-211. [N6537.B24A44 1967] 66-11934
I. Title.

BLACK, Carl, 1938- 759.3
Two visions of space: Herbert Bayer [and] Ingeborg Ten Haeff. [Yonkers, N.Y., 1969] [40] p. illus., ports. 22 cm. Cover title. Exhibition held Nov. 9-Dec. 7, 1969 at the Hudson River Museum. [N6494.S7B55] 73-22757
1. Bayer, Herbert, 1900- 2. Ten Haeff, Ingeborg. 3. Spatialism (Art)—Exhibitions. I. Hudson River Museum at Yonkers, Yonkers, N.Y. II. Title.

Bayeux tapestry.

FOWKE, Frank Rede. 746.3
The Bayeux tapestry: a history and description. London, G. Bell, 1913. St. Clair Shores, Mich., Scholarly Press, 1971. ix, lxxix, 139 p. illus. 21 cm. (Bohn's antiquarian library) Original ed. issued as part of Ex-libris series. [NK3049.B3F7 1971] 75-131705 ISBN 0-403-00592-2
1. Bayeux tapestry. I. Series: Ex-libris series.

STENTON, Sir Frank Merry, 1880- ed. 746.3
The Bayeux tapestry, a comprehensive survey, by Frank Stenton, general editor, Simone Bertrand [and others] New York, Phaidon Publishers; distributed by Garden City Books [1957] 182 p. illus. (part mounted, part col.) map. 31 cm. Includes bibliographical references. [NK3049.B3S73] 58-2214
1. Bayeux tapestry. I. Title.

Bayeux tapestry—Juvenile literature.

DENNY, Norman George, 1901- 746.3942
The Bayeux tapestry; the story of the Norman Conquest: 1066 [by] Norman Denny & Josephine Filmer-Sankey. [1st U.S.A. ed.] New York, Atheneum, 1966. 1 v. (unpaged) col. illus. 22 x 26 cm. [NK3049.B3D4 1966] 66-12846
1. Bayeux tapestry—Juvenile literature. I. Filmer-Sankey, Josephine, joint author. II. Title.

Beacon Hill, Boston.

MCINTYRE, Alex McVoy 917.44'61
Beacon Hill : a walking tour / A. McVoy McIntyre photos. by William Clift, line drawings by Robert Polomski. 1st ed. Boston : Little, Brown, [1975] p. cm. [F73.68.B4M32] 75-16449 ISBN 0-316-55600-9 pbk. : 3.95
1. Beacon Hill, Boston. 2. Boston—Description—1951- —Tours. I. Title. BIP

Beads.

BECK, Horace C. 745.59'4
Classification and nomenclature of beads and pendants, by Horace C. Beck. York, Pa., Liberty Cap Books [1973] 76 p. illus. 28 cm. "Read before the Society of Antiquaries of London on 19 October 1926, and ... [published] in volume LXXVII [1928] of Archaeologia." [GN34.B42] 73-163348 ISBN 0-87387-061-1 8.00 (pbk.)
1. Beads. 2. Pendants (Jewelry) I. Title.
Liberty Cap Books is a division of George Shumway. BIP

SLEEN, Wicher Gosen Nicholaas van der, 1886- 745.1
A handbook of beads [by] W. G. N. van der Sleen. York, Pa., Liberty Cap Books [1973] 128 p. illus. 23 cm. Reprint of the 1967 ed. published by Musee du verre, Liege, in series: Publication de Journees internationales du verre. Bibliography: p. [120]-[124] [NK3650.S56 1973] 73-163415 5.00 (pbk.)

1. Beads. I. Title. II. Series: Journees internationales du verre. Publication. Division of George Shumway.

SLEEN, Wicher Gosen 745.1
Nicholaas van der, 1886-
A handbook on beads [by] W. G. N. van der Sleen. York, Pa., Liberty Cap Books [1973] 128 p. illus. 23 cm. Reprint of the 1967 ed. published by Musee du verre, Liege, in series: Publication de Journees internationales du verre. Bibliography: p. [120]-[124] [NK3650.S56 1973] 73-163415
1. Beads. I. Title. II. Series: Journees internationales du verre. Publication.

Beads and beadwork—History.

*VAN DER SLEEN, W. G. N. 746.5
A handbook on beads.* York, Pa., Liberty Cap Books [1973] 128 p. illus. 23 cm. "First published in 1967 by the Journees Internationales du Verre, at the Museum of Glass, Liege, Belgium." Bibliography: p. [120-124] ISBN 0-87387-060-3 pap., 5.00
1. Beads and beadwork—History. I. Title. II. Title: Journee Internationales de Verre. Available from George Shumway Pubs., R.D. 7, York, PA 17402. **BIP**

Beads (in religion, folk-lore, etc.)

ERIKSON, Joan Mowat. 391'.7
The universal bead. Drawings by Mary Austin. [1st ed.] New York, Norton [1969] 191 p. illus. (part col.) 24 cm. [GT2250.E7] 68-20819 10.00
1. Beads (in religion, folk-lore, etc.) I. Title. **BIP**

Beadwork.

CROIX, Grethe la. 746.5
Beads plus macrame; applying knotting techniques to beadcraft. [Translated by Eric Greweldinger] New York, Sterling Pub. Co. [1971] 48 p. illus. (part col.) 20 cm. (Little craft book series) Translation of Draad en kralen. Instructions in beadwork, embroidery, and macrame technique for making and decorating jewelry, handbags, belts, and other objects. [TT860.C75213 1971] 78-151710 ISBN 0-8069-5168-0
1. Beadwork. 2. Macrame. I. Title. **BIP**

CROIX, Grethe la. 746.5
Creating with beads. [Translated by Eric Greweldinger] New York, Sterling Pub. Co. [1969] 48 p. illus. (part col.) 19 cm. (Little craft book series) Translation of Kralen. [TT860.C7513] 69-19487 ISBN 8-06-951249-
1. Beadwork. 2. Jewelry making—Amateurs' manuals. I. Title.

EDWARDS, Joan, designer. 746.5
Bead embroidery, written and illustrated by Joan Edwards. New York, Taplinger [1967, c1966] 200 p. illus. 26 cm. [TT860.E3 1967] 67-19282
1. Beadwork. I. Title. **BIP**

ERLANDSEN, Ida Merete. 745.5
The bead book, by Ida-Merete Erlandsen and Hetty Mooi. New York, Van Nostrand Reinhold Co. [1974] p. cm. Combined translation of Sy og vav med perler, by I. - M. Erlandsen, and Kralen weven & weven met kralen, by H. Mooi. [TT860.E7313] 74-3582 ISBN 0-442-30052-2 5.95
1. Beadwork. I. Mooi, Hetty, joint author. II. Erlandsen, Ida Merete. Sy og vaaev med perler. III. Mooi, Hetty. Kralen weven & weven met kralen. IV. Title. Pbk. 3.50, ISBN 0-442-30053-0. **BIP**

FARLIE, Barbara L. 746.5
Beading: basic and boutique [by] Barbara L. Farlie. [Des Moines] Creative Home Library [1971] 149 p. illus. (part col.) 27 cm. [TT860.F37] 76-168465 7.95
1. Beadwork. I. Title.

GILL, Ann E. 746.5
Beadwork : the technique of stringing, threading, and weaving / Ann E. Gill. New York : Watson-Guptill Publications, 1977. 184 p., [2] leaves of plates : ill. ; 26 cm. p. cm. Includes index. Bibliography: p. 186. [TT860.G53 1977] 76-26528 ISBN 0-8230-0480-5 : 12.95
1. Beadwork. I. Title. **BIP**

GLASSMAN, Judith. 746.5
Step-by-step beadcraft. New York, Golden Press [1974] 64 p. illus. 29 cm. (The Golden Press step-by-step craft series) Bibliography: p. 64. [TT860.G58] 73-88437 2.95 (pbk.)
1. Beadwork. I. Title. II. Title: Beadcraft.

HOFSINDE, Robert. 746.5
Indian beadwork, written and illustrated by Robert Hofsinde (Gray-Wolf) New York, Morrow, 1958. 122 p. illus. 21 cm. [TT860Costume and adornment.] 58-5251
1. Beadwork. 2. Indians of North America—Costume and adornment. I. Title. **BIP**

HUNT, Walter Bernard, 970.67465
1888-1970.
American Indian beadwork, by W. Ben Hunt and J. F. "Buck" Burshears. Milwaukee, Bruce [1951] 63 p. illus. 14 col. plates, ports. 32 cm. [E98.C8H8] 51-2514
1. Beadwork. 2. Indians of North America—Costume and adornment. I. Burshears, J.F. **BIP**

LEEMING, Joseph, 1897-1968. 746.5
Fun with beads, illustrated by Jessie Robinson. [1st ed.] Philadelphia, Lippincott [1954] 96 p. illus. 26 cm. [TT860.L4] 54-5585
1. Beadwork. I. Title.

MURPHY, Marjorie, 1937- 745.5
Beadwork from American Indian designs. New York, Watson-Guptill Publications [1974] 95 p. illus. 21 cm. [TT860.M86 1974] 73-20420 ISBN 0-8230-6010-1 8.95
1. Beadwork. 2. Indians of North America—Costume and adornment. I. Title.

MURPHY, Marjorie, 1937- 746.5
Beadwork; modern and American Indian design. Radnor, Pa., Chilton Book Co. [1974] p. "A comprehensive introduction to a North American Indian craft, outlining both hand-worked and loom-woven techniques." [TT860.M87] 73-18352 ISBN 0-8019-6066-5
1. Beadwork. 2. Indians of North America—Costume and adornment. I. Title.

OSTERLAND, Virginia. 745.92
Bouquets from beads. New York, Scribner [1971] 222 p. illus. 27 cm. [TT860.O87] 78-143938 ISBN 0-684-12343-6 12.50
1. Beadwork. 2. Artificial flowers. I. Title.

WASLEY, Ruth. 746.5
Bead design; a comprehensive course for beginner and experienced craftsman, by Ruth Wasley and Edith Harris. New York, Crown Publishers [1970] 216 p. illus. (part col.) 27 cm. [TT860.W34 1970] 74-93401
1. Beadwork. I. Harris, Edith, joint author. II. Title. **BIP**

WHITE, Mary, 1869- 746.5
How to do beadwork. Illustrated by the author. New York, Dover Publications [1972] 142 p. illus. 21 cm. Reprint of the 1904 ed. [TT860.W58 1972] 76-183981 ISBN 0-486-20697-1
1. Beadwork. I. Title. **BIP**

WILDSCHUT, William. 970.67465
Crow Indian beadwork; a descriptive and historical study, by William Wildschut [and] John C. Ewers. New York, Museum of the American Indian, Heye Foundation, 1959. vii, 55 p. illus. (part col.) ports. 26 cm. (Contributions from the Museum of the American Indian, Heye Foundation, v. 16) Bibliography: p. 53-55. [E51.N42 vol. 16] 59-3744
1. Beadwork. 2. Indians of North America — Costume and adornment. 3. Crow Indians. I. Ewers, John Canfield. II. Title. III. Series: New York. Museum of the American Indian, Heye Foundation. Contributions, v. 16 **BIP**

Beadwork—Juvenile literature.

DIERINGER, Beverly. 745.5
The paper bead book / Beverly Dieringer, with Marjorie Morton. New York : D. McKay Co., c1976. p. cm. Instructions for making and decorating paper beads for necklaces, with advice on equipment, stringing the beads, and using other materials in combination with the paper beads. [TT860.D53] 76-13251 ISBN 0-679-20319-2 : 8.95 ISBN 0-679-20378-8 pbk. :
1. Beadwork—Juvenile literature. I. Morton, Marjorie, joint author. II. Title. **BIP**

DONNA, Natalie. 746.5
Bead craft, written and illustrated by Natalie Donna. New York, Lothrop, Lee & Shepard [1972] 128 p. illus. 25 cm. Includes bibliographies. Instructions for making useful and decorative items from commercial beads or beads made at home from straws, spools, flip-top cans, and other materials. [TT860.D66] 72-1101 ISBN 0-688-40013-2 4.95
1. Beadwork—Juvenile literature. I. Title. **BIP**

Beal, Jack, 1931—

BEAL, Jack, 1931- 759.13
Jack Beal; [catalog of] a loan exhibition of paintings by Jack Beal, organized by John Arthur, on display at the Virginia Museum from 19 November to 23 December 1973 [and] Boston University, School of Fine and Applied Arts, Art Gallery from 18 January to 17 February 1974. Richmond, Virginia Museum [1973] 16 p. illus. (part col.) 21 x 24 cm. Bibliography: p. 16. [ND237.B3A88] 73-90582
1. Beal, Jack, 1931- I. Arthur, John, 1939- II. Virginia Museum of Fine Arts, Richmond. III. Boston University. Art Gallery.

Beals, Jessie Tarbox.

ALLAND, Alexander. 770'.92'4 B
Jessie Tarbox Beals, first woman news photographer / Alexander Alland, Sir. New York : Camera/Graphic Press, [1978] p. cm. Includes index. [TR140.B38A65] 78-4406 ISBN 0-918696-08-9 : 25.00
1. Beals, Jessie Tarbox. 2. News photographers—United States—Biography. I. Title. **BIP**

Bearden, Romare, 1914—

BEARDEN, Romare, 1914- 759.13
The art of Romare Bearden; the prevalence of ritual. Text by M. Bunch Washington, with an introd. by John A. Williams. New York, Abrams [1973] 230 p. illus. (part col.) 35 cm. Bibliography: p. 227-230. [N6537.B4W37] 72-4399 ISBN 0-8109-0033-5 35.00
1. Bearden, Romare, 1914- I. Washington, M. Bunch.

BEARDEN, Romare, 1914- 759.13
Paintings and projections [exhibition], the Art Gallery, State University of New York at Albany, November 25 through December 22, 1968. Introd. by Ralph Ellison. [Albany, N.Y., 1968?] [24] p. illus. 24 cm. [N6537.B4E4] 76-634874
1. Ellison, Ralph. II. New York (State). State University, Albany. Art Gallery. III. Title.

NEW YORK (City). Museum of 759.13
Modern Art.
Romare Bearden: the prevalence of ritual. Introductory essay by Carroll Greene. New York [1971] 24 p. illus. (part col.) 21 x 27 cm. Catalogue of an exhibition to be held at the Museum of Modern Art, New York, Mar. 25-June 7, 1971, and at four other museums, July 16, 1971-Apr. 9, 1972. "Bibliography, by Judy Goldman": p. 19-24. [N6537.B4N4] 78-150082 ISBN 0-87070-251-3
1. Bearden, Romare, 1914- I. Greene, Carroll. II. Title.

Beardsley, Aubrey Vincent, 1872-1898.

BEARDSLEY, Aubrey 741.9'42
Vincent, 1872-1898.
Aubrey Beardsley; selected drawings. New York, Grove Press,[1967] 1 v. (unpaged) 120 illus. 29 cm. Translation of Aubrey Beardsley: Zeichnungen. [NC1115.B31443] 67-21210
I. Title.

BEARDSLEY, Aubrey 760'.0924
Vincent, 1872-1898.
Aubrey Beardsley [by] Brian Reade. Introd. by John Rothenstein. New York, Viking Press [1967] 372 p. 502 illus., port. 31 cm. (A Studio book) [NC1115.B314 1967] 67-9578
I. Reade, Brian.

BEARDSLEY, Aubrey 741.9'42
Vincent, 1872-1898.
Beardsley / [text by] Simon Wilson. Oxford : Phaidon ; New York : E. P. Dutton, 1976,i.e.1977 16 p., [48] p. of plates : chiefly ill. (some col.), facsims. (1 col.) ; 31 cm. [NC242.B3W5] 76-1533 ISBN 0-7148-1742-2 : 6.95
1. Beardsley, Aubrey Vincent, 1872-1898. I. Wilson, Simon, fl. 1974-

BEARDSLEY, Aubrey 741'.092'4
Vincent, 1872-1898.
The best of Aubrey Beardsley / [compiled and with text] by Kenneth Clark. New York : Abbeville Press, [1978] Includes index. Bibliography: p. [NC242.B3A4 1978] 78-7061 65.00
1. Beardsley, Aubrey Vincent, 1872-1898. I. Clark, Kenneth McKenzie, Baron Clark, 1903- II. Title. **BIP**

BEARDSLEY, Aubrey 741.942
Vincent, 1872-1898.
The collected drawings of Aubrey Beardsley. With an appreciation by Arthur Symons. Edited by Bruce S. Harris. New York, Crescent Books [1967] xii, 212 p. (chiefly illus.) 29 cm. [NC1115.B319] 67-26201
I. Harris, Bruce S., ed. II. Symons, Arthur, 1865-1945. **BIP**

BEARDSLEY, Aubrey 741.6'0924
Vincent, 1872-1898.
Drawings [by] Aubrey Beardsley. New York, United Book Guild, 1967. 151 p. (chiefly illus., port.) 29 cm. [NC139.B4A44] 67-4068
I. Title.

BEARDSLEY, Aubrey 741.9'0924
Vincent, 1872-1898
The early work of Aubrey Beardsley. New York, Da Capo, 1967. 18p., 157 plates (incl. ports.) 29cm. Text by H. C. Marillier. Da Capo reprint ed. [NC1115.B32 1967] 67-17516 12.50
I. Marillier. Henry Currie, 1865-1951. II. Title. Available from Plenum.

BEARDSLEY, Aubrey 741.9'0924
Vincent, 1872-1898.
The early work of Aubrey Beardsley. Prefatory note by H. C. Marillier [Magnolia, Mass., P. Smith. 1967] 15p., 157 plates (incl. ports.) 28cm. (Dover bk. rebound) Unabridged repubn. of the rev. 1920 ed. [NC1115.B32 1967a] 6.00
I. Martillier, Henry Currie, 1865-1951. II. Title. **BIP**

BEARDSLEY, Aubrey 741.9'0924
Vincent, 1872-1898.
The early work of Aubrey Beardsley. With prefatory note by H. C. Marillier. [New York] Dover Publications [1967] 15 p., 157 plates (incl. ports.) 28 cm. "An unabridged republication of the revised 1920 edition." [NC1115.B32 1967a] 67-21705
I. Marillier, Henry Currie, 1865-1951. II. Title.

BEARDSLEY, Aubrey 760'.092'4
Vincent, 1872-1898.
Last letters of Aubrey Beardsley. With an introductory note by the Rev. John Gray. [Folcroft, Pa.] Folcroft Library Editions, 1973, [i.e.1974] p. Reprint of the 1904 ed. published by Longmans, Green, London. [NC242.B3A2 1973] 73-12999 20.00
1. Beardsley, Aubrey Vincent, 1872-1898. I. Gray, John, 1866-1934. II. Title. **BIP**

BEARDSLEY, Aubrey 741.9'0924
Vincent, 1872-1898
The later work of Aubrey Beardsley. New York, Da Capo, 1967. [16]p., 174 plates (incl. ports.) 29cm. A Da Capo reprint ed. [NC1115.B35 1967] 67-17517 12.50
I. Title. Available from Plenum. **BIP**

BEARDSLEY, Aubrey 741.9'0924
Vincent, 1872-1898.
The later work of Aubrey Beardsley

[Magnolia, Mass., P. Smith, 1967] [10] p., 174 plates (incl. ports.) 28cm. (Dover bk. rebound) Unabridged repubn. of the rev. 1930 ed. [NC1115.B35 1967a] 6.00
I. Title.

BEARDSLEY, Aubrey Vincent, 1872-1898. 741.9'0924
The later work of Aubrey Beardsley. [New York] Dover Publications [1967] [10] p., 174 plates (incl. ports.) 28 cm. "An unabridged republication of the revised 1930 edition." [NC1115.B35 1967a] 67-21706
I. Title.

BEARDSLEY, Aubrey Vincent, 1872-1898. 741'.0924
The letters of Aubrey Beardsley, edited by Henry Maas, J. L. Duncan and W. G. Good. Rutherford, Fairleigh Dickinson University Press [1970] 472 p. illus., facsims., ports. 27 cm. [NC242.B3M28] 68-11571 ISBN 8-386-68844- 20.00
I. Maas, Henry, ed. II. Duncan, John, 1937- ed. III. Good, W. G., 1909- ed. **BIP**

BEARDSLEY, Aubrey Vincent, 1872-1898. v. 12
Unter dem Hugel, Eine romantische Erzahlung [von] Aubrey Beardsley. Mit funf Illustrationen des Autors. Ubertragen von Rudolf Alexander Schroder. [Frankfurt a. M.] Insel-Verlag [1965] 50 p. 5 plates. 19 cm. [Insel-Bucherei, Nr. 844.) [NUC68-40421]
I. Title.

BROPHY, Brigid, 1929- 741'.092'4 B
Beardsley and his world / by Brigid Brophy. New York : Harmony Books, 1976. p. cm. [NC242.B3B68 1976] 76-5969 ISBN 0-517-52628-X
1. Beardsley, Aubrey Vincent, 1872-1898. I. Title.

BROPHY, Brigid, 1929- 741'.092'4 B
Beardsley and his world / Brigid Brophy. London : Thames and Hudson, c1976. 128 p. : ill. ; 24 cm. Includes index. Bibliography: p. 118. [NC242.B3B68 1976b] 76-366635 ISBN 0-500-13057-4 : £3.50
1. Beardsley, Aubrey Vincent, 1872-1898. I. Title.

BROPHY, Brigid, 1929- 741'.0924 B
Black and white; a portrait of Aubrey Beardsley. New York, Stein and Day [1969, c1968] 95 p. 44 illus. 24 cm. Bibliography: p. 95. [NC242.B3B7 1969] 69-15906 4.95
1. Beardsley, Aubrey Vincent, 1872-1898. I. Title.

EASTON, Malcolm. 741'.092'4
Aubrey and the dying lady: a Beardsley riddle. [Boston] D. R. Godine [1972] xxxii, 272 p. illus. 25 cm. Includes bibliographical references. [NC242.B3E27 1972b] 73-75834 ISBN 0-87923-068-1 12.50
1. Beardsley, Aubrey Vincent, 1872-1898. 2. Beardsley, Mable, 1871-1916. I. Title.

MACFALL, Haldane, 1860-1928. 741.0924 B
Aubrey Beardsley, the man and his work. Freeport, N.Y., Books for Libraries Press [1972] xiv, 109 p. illus. 29 cm. Reprint of the 1928 ed. [NC242.B3M32 1972] 73-39472 ISBN 0-8369-9918-5
1. Beardsley, Aubrey Vincent, 1872-1898. I. Title.

MACFALL, Haldane, 1860-1928. 741'.092'4 B
Aubrey Beardsley, the man and his work / by Haldane Macfall. Norwood, Pa. : Norwood Editions, 1975. xiv, 109 p., [11] leaves of plates : ill. ; 28 cm. Reprint of the 1928 ed. published by John Lane, London. [NC242.B3M32 1975] 75-33095 ISBN 0-88305-443-4 : 30.00
1. Beardsley, Aubrey Vincent, 1872-1898.

READE, Brian 769'.924
Aubrey Beardsley. London, H.M.S.O., 1966. [4], 18p. illus., 50 plates, 25cm. (Large picture bk., no. 32) [N1150.A752no.32] 67-74986 2.50 pap.,
1. Beardsley, Aubrey Vincent, 1872-1898. I. Title. II. Series: Victoria and Albert Museum, South Kensington. Large picture books, no. 32
Available from British Info. New York.

ROSS, Robert Baldwin, 1869-1918. 741'.092'4
Aubrey Beardsley. With sixteen full-page illustrations and a revised iconography by Aymer Vallance. [Folcroft, Pa.] Folcroft Library Editions, 1973. 120 p. illus. 23 cm. Reprint of the 1909 ed. published by J. Lane, London and New York. "List of drawings by Aubrey Beardsley, comp. by Aymer Vallance": p. [57]-112. [NC242.B3R8 1973] 73-13523 30.00
1. Beardsley, Aubrey Vincent, 1872-1898. I. Vallance, Aymer, 1862-1943.

SYMONS, Arthur, 1865-1945 741.0924
Aubrey Beardsley. [New ed.] London, Baker, 1966. 63p. front. illus. 23cm. [NC242.B3S8 1966] 66-69121 2.95
1. Beardsley, Aubrey Vincent, 1872-1898. II. Title.
American distributor: Dufour, Chester Springs, Pa.

WEINTRAUB, Stanley, 1929- 741'.092'4 B
Aubrey Beardsley, imp of the perverse / Stanley Weintraub. University Park, Pa. : Pennsylvania State University Press, [1976] p. cm. Includes index. Bibliography: p. [NC242.B3W39] 75-27231 ISBN 0-271-01215-3 : 15.00 ISBN 0-271-01216-1 pbk. :
1. Beardsley, Aubrey Vincent, 1872-1898. I. Title.

WEINTRAUB, Stanley, 1929- 741'.0924 B
Beardsley; a biography. New York, G. Braziller [1967] xv, 285 p. 16 illus., port. 22 cm. Bibliographical references included in "Notes" (p. 265-279) [NC242.B4W4] 67-19874
1. Beardsley, Aubrey Vincent, 1872-1898.

WEINTRAUB, Stanley, 1929- 741'.092'4 B
Beardsley. Revised ed. Harmondsworth, Penguin, 1972. 287, 16 p. illus. 18 cm. (Pelican biographies) Includes bibliographical references. [NC242.B3W4 1972] 73-161896 ISBN 0-14-021555-7 £0.50
1. Beardsley, Aubrey Vincent, 1872-1898.

Beardsley Limner.

SCHLOSS, Christine Skeeles. 757'.9'0973074013
The Beardsley Limner and some contemporaries; postrevolutionary portraiture in New England, 1785-1805. [Williamsburg, Va., Colonial Williamsburg Foundation, 1972] 47 p. illus. (part col.) 24 cm. Exhibition organized by Abby Aldrich Rockefeller Folk Art Collection, Oct. 15-Dec. 3, 1972; Montclair Art Museum, Dec. 17, 1972-Jan. 28, 1973; and New Haven Colony Historical Society, Feb. 11-Mar. 25, 1973. Includes bibliographical references. [ND1329.B38S34] 72-91465 ISBN 0-87935-005-9
1. Beardsley Limner. 2. Portraits, American—Exhibitions. 3. Portrait painting, American—New England. I. Abby Aldrich Rockefeller Folk Art Collection, Williamsburg, Va. II. Montclair, N.J. Art Museum. III. New Haven Colony Historical Society, New Haven. IV. Title. **BIP**

Beaton, Cecil Walter Hardy, Sir, 1904—

BEATON, Cecil Walter Hardy, 1904- 779'.092'4 B
Cecil Beaton: memoirs of the 40's, by Cecil Beaton. New York, McGraw-Hill Book Co. [1972] 310 p. illus. 24 cm. London ed. (Weidenfeld & Nicolson) has title: The happy years. [TR140.B4A28 1972b] 72-5857 ISBN 0-07-004225-X 10.00
I. Title. II. Title: Memoirs of the 40's.

BEATON, Cecil Walter Hardy, Sir, 1904- 770'.92'4 B
The restless years : diaries, 1955-63 / Cecil Beaton. London : Weidenfeld and Nicolson, c1976. 190 p., [6] leaves of plates : ill. ; 23 cm. [TR140.B4A32] 76-377856 ISBN 0-297-77155-8 : £4.95
1. Beaton, Cecil Walter Hardy, Sir, 1904- 2. Photographers—England—Biography. I. Title.

BEATON, Cecil Walter Hardy, 1904- 927.7
The wandering years; diaries, 1922-1939. Boston, Little, Brown [1962, c1961] 387 p. illus. 23 cm. [TR140.B4A34 1962] 62-8059
I. Title.

Beaudin, Andre, 1895—

BEAUDIN, Andre, 1895- 709'.2'4
Andre Beaudin / text by Georges Limbour ; [translated by Stuart Gilbert]. New York : Harcourt, Brace and World, [1961] ca. 150 p., [20] leaves of plates : chiefly ill. (some col.) ; 30 cm. "Planned and produced by Editions Verve." Includes bibliography. [ND553.B46L513] 75-303482
1. Beaudin, Andre, 1895- I. Limbour, Georges, 1902-1970.

BEAUDIN, Andre, 1895- 709'.2'4
Andre Beaudin: drawings, watercolors, sculpture, spring 1973. Chicago, R. S. Johnson-International Gallery, 1973. 30 p. illus. 25 cm. Catalog of an exhibition, spring 1973. [N6853.B37J63] 73-77875
1. Beaudin, Andre, 1895- I. Johnson (R. S.)-International Gallery.

Beaufort, S. C.—Historic houses, etc.

GRAYDON, Nell S. 728.0975799
Tales of Beaufort. Photos. by Eugene B. Sloan. Beaufort, S.C., Beaufort Bk. Shop, 808 Day St. [c.1963] xii, 156p. illus. 24cm. 63-22685 5.95
1. Beaufort, S. C.—Historic houses, etc. I. Title. **BIP**

Beauly Priory.

HORN, Walter Williams, 1908- 728.9
The barns of the Abbey of Beaulieu at its granges of Great Coxwell & Beaulieu-St. Leonards, by Walter Horn, Ernest Born. Berkeley, Univ. of Calif. Pr. [c.]1965. xviii, 74p. illus. (pt. col.) maps (1 col.) plans. 36cm. Bibl. [NA5471.B4H6] 64-19011 10.00
1. Beauly Priory. 2. Barns. 3. Framing (Building) I. Born, Ernest, 1898- joint author. II. Title.

Beaumount. S. George Howland 1753-1827.

GREAVES. MARGARET 704.360924
Regency Patron: Sir George Beaumont. London Methuen, 1966. 3-163p. front. 14 plates (incl. ports) 23cm. Bibl. [CT788.B353G7] 66-76165 6.50 bds.,
1. Beaumount. S. George Howland 1753-1827. I. Title.
Available from Barnes & Noble.

Beauty culture.

MILADY Publishing Corporation, New York. 646.7
Standard textbook of cosmetology; a practical course on the scientific fundamentals of beauty culture for students and practicing cosmetologists, by Constance V. Kibbe. Completely rev. Illus. by Warren Meek. Bronx, N.Y., 1965. xvi, 494 p. illus. (part col.) 25 cm. Bibliography: p. 494. [TT957.M55] 66-2325
1. Beauty culture. I. Title. **BIP**

TREMBLAY, Suzanne, 1932- 646.7'26
The professional skin care manual / Suzanne Tremblay. Englewood Cliffs, N.J. : Prentice-Hall, c1978. xvii, 231 p. : ill. ; 24 cm. Includes index. Bibliography: p. [215]-219. [TT958.T73] 78-4167 ISBN 0-13-725358-3 : 12.95
1. Beauty culture. 2. Skin—Care and hygiene. I. Title. **BIP**

Beauty culture — Hist.

WYCKES-JOYCE, Max. 391
Cosmetics and adornment: ancient and contemporary usage. [New York] Philosophical Library [1961] 190 p. illus. 22 cm. Includes bibliography. [GT2340.W9] 61-16286
1. Beauty culture — Hist. 2. Cosmetics — Hist. I. Title.

Beauty culture—Vocational guidance.

GELB, Lawrence M. 646.7'2'023
Your future in beauty culture [by] Lawrence M. Gelb. [Rev. ed.] New York, B. Rosen Press [1970] 190 p. illus. 22 cm. (Careers in depth, 11) First ed. by Richard L. Gelb published in 1964. Bibliography: p. [126]-128. Discusses the requirements, advantages, and drawbacks of a beauty culture career as a hairdresser or salon owner. [TT958.G39 1970] 77-101522 ISBN 0-8239-0201-3
1. Beauty culture—Vocational guidance. I. Gelb, Richard L. Your future in beauty culture. II. Title. **BIP**

Beauty operators.

PORTER, Gladys L 646.720922
Three Negro pioneers in beauty culture, by Gladys L. Porter. [1st ed.] New York, Vantage Press [1966] 48 p. ports. 21 cm. Bibliography: p. 48. [TT955.A1P6] 65-28002
1. Beauty operators. I. Title.

Beaux, Cecilia, 1863-1942.

CECILIA Beaux : 759.13
portrait of an artist : an exhibition organized by the Pennsylvania Academy of the Fine Arts in cooperation with Museum of the Philadelphia Civic Center, Philadelphia, Pennsylvania, Indianapolis Museum of Art, Indianapolis, Indiana, 1974-1975. Philadelphia : Pennsylvania Academy of the Fine Arts, c1974. 126 p. : ill. (some col.) ; 28 cm. Exhibition held Sept. 6-Oct. 20, 1974 at the Museum of the Philadelphia Civic Center and Jan. 21-March 2, 1975 at the Indianapolis Museum of Art. Includes index. Bibliography: p. 125. [ND237.B33C4] 74-84248
1. Beaux, Cecilia, 1863-1942. I. Beaux, Cecilia, 1863-1942. II. Pennsylvania Academy of the Fine Arts, Philadelphia. III. Philadelphia Civic Center. Museum. IV. Indianapolis Museum of Art.

Becca, R. G.

BECCA, R. G. 741.9'73
Suffolk County family album of art / R. G. Becca. Huntington, N.Y. : R. E. Krieger Pub. Co., 1977. p. cm. [NC139.B416A55] 77-8645 ISBN 0-88275-574-9 pbk. : 4.95
1. Becca, R. G. 2. Suffolk Co., N.Y., in art. I. Title.

Bechtle, Robert, 1932—

BECHTLE, Robert, 1932- 759.13
Robert Bechtle: a retrospective exhibition. [Sacramento, Calif., Joint Board of Trustees, E. B. Crocker Art Gallery, 1973] [48] p. illus. (part col.) 26 cm. Catalog of the exhibition held Sept. 15-Oct. 14, 1973 at the E. B. Crocker Art Gallery, Sacramento, Calif., and Dec. 8, 1973-Jan. 20, 1974 at the Fine Arts Gallery of San Diego, San Diego, Calif. Bibliography: p. [46] [ND237.B35C76] 73-82551
1. Bechtle, Robert, 1932- I. Crocker Art Gallery, Sacramento, Calif. II. San Diego, Calif. Fine Arts Gallery. III. Title.

Beck, George, 1748 or 9-1812.

PLEASANTS, Jacob Hall, 1873-1957. 759.1
Four late eighteenth century Anglo-American landscape painters. Freeport, N.Y., Books for Libraries Press [1970] 146 p. illus. 24 cm. (Essay index reprint series) "Proceedings of the American Antiquarian Society for October, 1942." Reprint of the 1943 ed. Includes bibliographical references. [ND1351.4.P55 1970] 78-128288
1. Beck, George, 1748 or 9-1812. 2. Groombridge, William, 1748-1811. 3. Guy, Francis, 1760-1820. 4. Winstanley, William, fl. 1793-1806. 5. Landscape painting, American. I. Title. **BIP**

Beck, John A., 1916-1973—Art collections.

HOUSTON, Tex. Museum of Fine Arts. 759.05
The Collection of John A. and Audrey Jones Beck: Impressionist and post-Impressionist paintings; a catalogue issued on the occasion of the first public exhibition of the Beck Collection, the Jesse H. Jones Galleries. Houston, 1974. 101 p. col. illus. 25 cm. [ND192.I4H68 1974] 73-91194
1. Beck, John A., 1916-1973—Art collections. 2. Impressionism (Art)—Exhibitions. 3. Painting, Modern—19th century. 4. Post-impressionism (Art)—Exhibitions. 5. Painting, Modern—20th century. 6. Beck, Audrey Jones—Art collections. I. Title.

Beck, Rosemarie.

DUKE University, Durham, N.C. Art Museum. 730'.74'0156563
Paintings by Rosemarie Beck. Sculpture by Richard A. Miller. Durham, Duke University Museum of Art [1971] 48 p. illus., facsims. 22 cm. On cover: The human form in contemporary art. Catalog of the exhibition held Mar. 21-Apr. 23, 1971. Bibliography: p. 22-29. [N6536.D8] 71-27486
1. Beck, Rosemarie. 2. Miller, Richard A., 1922- 3. Human figure in art. I. Title. II. Title: Sculpture by Richard A. Miller. III. Title: The human form in contemporary art.

Beckmann, Max, 1884-1950.

BECKMANN, Max, 1884-1950. 709'.2'4
A catalogue of paintings, sculptures, drawings & water colors. [New York, C. Viviano, 1973] 1 v. (unpaged) illus. 23 cm. [N6888.B4A43] 74-152471
1. Beckmann, Max, 1884-1950.

BECKMANN, Max, 1884-1950. 760'.092'4
Max Beckmann graphics. Selected from the Ernest and Lilly Jacobson Collection. Introd. by Richard A. Vogler. Essay by Stephan E. Lackner. Exhibition organized by Jason D. Wong. Tucson, Ariz., Tucson Art Center [1973] 80 p. illus. 28 cm. "Participating institutions: Fine Arts Gallery, California State University, Northridge ... [and others]" Bibliography: p. 79. [NE654.B37W66] 72-93456
1. Beckmann, Max, 1884-1950. I. Wong, Jason D. II. Tucson Art Center. III. California State University, Northridge. Fine Arts Gallery.
Publishers Address: 325 W. Franklin Ave., Tucson, Arizona 85705

BECKMANN, Max, 1884-1950. 759.3
Max Beckmann in America. [New York, Catherine Viviano Gallery, 1969] [31] p. illus. (1 fold.) 23 cm. "An exhibition of paintings, 1947-1950, opening November 11, through December 6, 1969." [ND588.B37A52] 71-24906
I. Catherine Viviano Gallery. II. Title.

BECKMANN, Max, 1884-1950. 759.3
Max Beckmann in America. [New York, Catherine Viviano Gallery, 1969] [31] p. illus. (1 fold.) 23 cm. "An exhibition of paintings, 1947-1950, opening November 11, through December 6, 1969." [ND588.B37A52] 71-24906
I. Catherine Viviano Gallery. II. Title.

FISCHER, Friedhelm Wilhelm. 759.3
Max Beckmann [by] Friedhelm W. Fischer. Translated by P. S. Falla [London] Phaidon [distributed in U.S.A. by Praeger Publishers, Inc., 1973] 96 p. illus. (part col.) 30 cm. Translation of Der Maler Max Beckmann. Bibliography: p. 96. [ND588.B37F49513 1973] 72-83182 ISBN 0-7148-1577-2 25.00 (U.S.)
1. Beckmann, Max, 1884-1950.

KESSLER, Charles S. 759.3
Max Beckmann's triptychs [by] Charles S. Kessler. Cambridge, Belknap Press of Harvard University Press, 1970. 173 p. illus. (part col.), port. 21 cm. Includes bibliographical references. [ND588.B37K4] 78-88806 ISBN 0-674-55640-2 15.00
1. Beckmann, Max, 1884-1950. I. Title. BIP

LACKNER, Stephan. 759.3
Max Beckmann; memories of a friendship. Coral Gables, Fla., University of Miami Press [1969] 126 p. illus. (part col.) 23 cm. Translation of Ich erinnere mich gut an Max Beckmann. [ND588.B37L293] 75-81622 7.95
1. Beckmann, Max, 1884-1950. I. Title. BIP

LACKNER, Stephan. 759.3
Max Beckmann / text by Stephan Lackner. New York : H. N. Abrams, 1977. 175 p. : ill. (some col.) ; 34 cm. (The Library of great painters) Includes index. Bibliography: p. 169-170. [ND588.B37L297] 74-22446 ISBN 0-8109-0269-9 : 22.50
1. Beckmann, Max, 1884-1950. 2. Painters—Germany, West—Biography.

SELZ, Peter Howard, 1919- 759.3
Max Beckmann. With contributions by Harold Joachim and Perry T. Rathbone. New York, Museum of Modern Art, Distributed by Doubleday, Garden City, N.Y. [1964] 160 p. illus. (part col.) 24 cm. "Catalogue of the exhibition, prepared by Alicia Legg": p. 150-154. "Bibliography, by Inga Forslund": p. 137-149. [ND588.B37S4] 64-18334
1. Beckmann, Max, 1884-1950.

ZIMMERMANN, Frederick, 1906?-1967. 759.3
Beckmann in America; the address delivered before the Max Beckmann Gesellschaft at Murnau on July 15, 1962. [New York, Marchbanks Press] 1967. 17 p. 24 cm. "Five hundred numbered copies ... Number [16]" [ND588.B37Z5] 68-6423
1. Beckmann, Max, 1884-1950. I. Title.

Bedford, Clay P., 1903- —Art collections.

†GUSLER, Wallace B. 739.7'4
Decorated firearms, 1540-1870, from the Collection of Clay P. Bedford / by Wallace B. Gusler and James D. Lavin. Williamsburg, Va. : Colonial Williamsburg Foundation ; Charlottesville : distributed by the University Press of Virginia, c1977. xi, 242 p. : ill. ; 24 x 28 cm. Includes index. Bibliography: p. 239. [NK6903.B4G87] 76-53750 ISBN 0-87935-041-5 : 25.00
1. Bedford, Clay P., 1903- —Art collections. 2. Firearms—Catalogs. 3. Art metal-work—Catalogs. I. Lavin, James D., joint author. II. Title. BIP

Bedroom furniture.

LEAVY, Herbert T. 643'.53
Designing and building beds, lofts, and sleeping areas / by Herbert T. Leavy. New York : Drake Publishers, [1977] p. cm. [TT197.5.B4L4] 76-58842 ISBN 0-8473-1289-5 : 8.95. ISBN 0-8473-1168-6 pbk. : 4.95
1. Bedroom furniture. 2. Beds and bedsteads. 3. Lofts. 4. Interior decoration—Amateurs' manuals. I. Title.

Bedrooms.

BRANDT, Mary L. 747.77
How to plan your bedroom. New York, Greenberg, c1955. 96 p. illus. 21 cm. (Room-by-room decorating series) [NK2117.B65] 55-10659
1. Bedrooms. 2. Interior decoration. I. Title.

CONRAN, Terence. 747'.77
The bed and bath book / by Terence Conran. New York : Crown Publishers, 1978. p. cm. Includes index. [NK2117.B4C66 1978] 77-28086 ISBN 0-517-53399-5 : 30.00
1. Bedrooms. 2. Bathrooms. 3. Interior decoration. I. Title. BIP

HAUTZIG, Esther (Rudomin) 747
Redecorating your room for practically nothing, by Esther Hautzig. Illustrated by Sidonie Coryn. New York, Crowell [1967] 203 p. illus. 23 cm. Easy directions for making and modifying furniture, window treatments, bed accessories, closets and bureaus, and miscellaneous items for your bedroom. [NK2117.H37] AC 67
1. Bedrooms. 2. Interior decoration. I. Coryn, Sidonie, illus. II. Title.

SUNSET. 747.79
Children's rooms and play yards, by the editorial staffs of Sunset books & Sunset magazine. Menlo Park, Calif., Lane Book Co. [1960] 96 p. illus. 28 cm. (A Sunset book) [NK2117.S8] 60-11801
1. Bedrooms. 2. Recreation rooms. 3. Interior decoration 4. Patios. I. Title.

Beeler, Joe.

BEELER, Joe. 741.9'73
The Joe Beeler sketch book / by Joe Beeler ; with a foreword by Frederic G. Renner. 1st ed. [Flagstaff, Ariz.] : Northland Press, [1974] x, 141 p. : ill. ; 28 cm. [NC139.B42A48] 72-79075 ISBN 0-87358-099-0 : 12.50
1. Beeler, Joe. 2. The West in art. I. Title. BIP

Beer bottles—Catalogs.

MARTIN, Byron, 1928- 663'.42
Here's to beers; blob top beer bottles, 1880-1910, by Byron & Vicky Martin. Northridge, Calif., Achin Back Saloon [1973] 64 p. illus. 28 cm. [NK5440.B6M35] 73-166405
1. Beer bottles—Catalogs. 2. Beer trays—Catalogs. I. Martin, Vicky, 1928- II. Title.

Beer cans—Collectors and collecting.

DOLPHIN, Richard R. 663'.42'028
Collecting beer cans : a world guide / Richard R. Dolphin. New York : Bounty Books, [1977] 120 p. : ill. (some col.) ; 26 cm. Includes index. [NK8459.B36D64 1977] 76-49700 ISBN 0-517-21564-0 : 4.95
1. Beer cans—Collectors and collecting. I. Title. BIP

Beer cans—United States.

BEER Can Collectors of America. 663'.42'028
Guide to United States beer cans / prepared & presented by the Beer Can Collectors of America. 1st ed. St. Louis : The Collectors, 1975. viii, 182 p. : chiefly ill. ; 28 cm. [NK8459.B36B43 1975] 75-328738 10.00
1. Beer cans—United States. 2. Beer cans—Collectors and collecting. I. Title. BIP

CADY, Lew. 681'.7664
Beer can collecting : America's fastest growing hobby / by Lew Cady. New York : Tempo Books, c1976. 209 p. : ill. ; 18 cm. [NK8459.B36C3] 76-13375 lib. bdg. ISBN 0-448-12535-8 pbk. : 1.95
1. Beer cans—United States. 2. Beer cans—Collectors and collecting—United States. I. Title.

Beer cans—United States—Collectors and collecting.

MARTELLS, Jack. 671
The beer can collector's bible / by Jack Martells. Matteson, Ill. : Greatlakes Living Press, 1977, c1976 124 p. : ill. (some col) ; 30 cm. [NK8459.B36M37] 75-41639 ISBN 0-915498-16-2 : 19.95
1. Beer cans—United States—Collectors and collecting. I. Title. BIP

Beer—Posters—Catalogs.

ANDERSON, Will, 1940- 769'.5
The beer poster book / Will Anderson. [Harrisburg, Pa.] : Cameron House ; [New York : for distribution in the U.S. by Two Continents Pub. Group, c1977] [4] p., [22] leaves of plates : ill. ; 41 cm. [HF6161.B75A53 1977] 77-76772 ISBN 0-8117-2074-8 pbk. : 8.95
1. Beer—Posters—Catalogs. 2. Advertising—Brewing industry. I. Title.

Beerbohm, Max, Sir, 1872-1956.

HART-DAVIS, Rupert, Sir. 016.7415'942
A catalogue of the caricatures of Max Beerbohm. Cambridge, Mass., Harvard University Press, 1972. 258 p. illus. 26 cm. Includes bibliographical references. [NC1479.B37H37 1972b] 72-75409 ISBN 0-674-10075-1
1. Beerbohm, Max, Sir, 1872-1956. I. Title. BIP

Bell, Clive, 1881-1964.

BYWATER, William G., 1940- 701'.17
Clive Bell's eye / William G. Bywater, Jr. Detroit : Wayne State University Press, 1975. 249 p. : ill. ; 24 cm. Includes index. "A checklist of the published writings of Clive Bell, by Donald A. Laing": p. [211]-242. [N7445.2.B44B9] 74-23853 ISBN 0-8143-1534-8
1. Bell, Clive, 1881-1964. 2. Form (Aesthetics) 3. Art—Philosophy. I. Title. BIP

Bell, Larry, 1939—

BELL, Larry, 1939- 730'.92'4
Larry Bell. An exhibition organized by Barbara Haskell, Pasadena Art Museum, April 11 to June 11, 1972. [Pasadena, Calif., Pasadena Art Museum, 1972] [38] p. illus. 21 x 26 cm. Bibliography: p. [34]-[37] [NB237.B42P37] 73-152496
1. Bell, Larry, 1939- I. Pasadena, Calif. Art Museum. BIP

Bell, Vanessa Stephen, 1874-1961.

SHONE, Richard. 759.21'42
Bloomsbury portraits : Vanessa Bell, Duncan Grant, and their circle / Richard Shone. Oxford : Phaidon ; New York : E. P. Dutton, 1976. 272 p., [4] leaves of plates : ill. (some col.) ; 26 cm. Includes index. Bibliography: p. 266-269. [ND497.B44S56] 76-5354 ISBN 0-7148-1628-0 : 18.95
1. Bell, Vanessa Stephen, 1874-1961. 2. Grant, Duncan James Corrowr, 1885- 3. Painters—England—Biography. 4. Bloomsbury group. I. Title.

Bella, Stefano della, 1610-1664.

BAUDI di Vesme, Alessandro, conte, 1854-1923 769'.924
Stefano della Bella; catalogue raisonne [by] Alexandre De Vesme. With introd. and additions by Phyllis Dearborn Massar. [New York] Collectors Editions [1971] 2 v. illus., facsims. 32 cm. Errata slip inserted. "The De Vesme catalogue is an unaltered reprint of the chapter on Della Bella appearing in Alexandre de Vesme, Le peintre-graveur italien, Milan, 1906, pp. 66-332." Contents.Contents.—[1] Text.—[2] Plates. Bibliography: [v. 1] p. 220-225. [NE2052.5.B4B3 1971] 78-110443 ISBN 0-87681-042-3
1. Bella, Stefano della, 1610-1664. I. Massar, Phyllis Dearborn.

Bellange, Jacques, 1594-1683.

WORTHEN, Amy N. 769'.92'4
The etchings of Jacques Bellange : [exhibition], Des Moines Art Center, October 7-November 16, 1975, Museum of Fine Arts, Boston, December 12, 1975-February 15, 1976, The Metropolitan Museum of Art, March 23-May 2, 1976 / Amy N. Worthen and Sue Welsh Reed. Des Moines : The Center, c1975. 86 p. : ill. ; 29 cm. Errata slip inserted. [NE2049.5.B4W67] 75-27177 ISBN 0-87846-094-2
1. Bellange, Jacques, 1594-1683. I. Reed, Sue Welsh, joint author. II. Bellange, Jacques, 1594-1683. III. Des Moines Art Center. IV. Boston. Museum of Fine Arts. V. New York (City). Metropolitan Museum of Art. VI. Title. BIP

Bellingrath Gardens.

MACLEOD, Katherine. 712.64
Bellingrath and other famous gardens. [1st ed. New York] Comet Press Books [1955] unpaged. illus. 22cm. [SB465.M25] 55-11744
1. Bellingrath Gardens. 2. Gardens. I. Title.

xviii, 265 p. 44 plates (part col.) 24 cm. Reprint of the 1926 ed. published by Houghton Mifflin, Boston. Includes bibliographical references. [NK4027.B4S6 1972] 72-80878 ISBN 0-486-22876-2 3.50
1. Bennington pottery. 2. Potters—Bennington, Vt. I. Title.

Benson, John Howard, 1901-1956.

HOFER, Philip, 1898- 927.456
John Howard Benson & his work, 1901-1956. With a pref. by Lawrence C. Wroth and an introd. by Rudolph Ruzicka. New York, The Typophiles, 1957. x, 56p. illus., port. 19cm. (Typophile chap book no. 31) Bibliography: p. 49-51. [NK3648.B4H6] 57-4173
1. Benson, John Howard, 1901-1956. I. Title. II. Series: The Typophiles, New York. Typophile chap books, no. 31

Bentley, Fred D.—Art collections.

CUMMER Gallery of Art. 759.13'074'0159121
American paintings from the Collection of Mr. and Mrs. Fred D. Bentley, Sr., and Mr. and Mrs. J. Alan Sellars : [catalog of an exhibition], the Cummer Gallery of Art, Jacksonville, Florida, March 12-April 27, 1975. [Jacksonville, Fla.] : The Gallery, 1975. 96 p. : ill. (some col.) ; 21 cm. On cover: Bentley-Sellars Collection. Errata slip inserted. Includes index. [ND210.C78 1975] 75-314877
1. Bentley, Fred D.—Art collections. 2. Sellars, J. Alan—Art collections. 3. Paintings, American—Exhibitions. 4. Painting, Modern—19th century—United States—Exhibitions. 5. Painting, Modern—20th century—Exhibitions. I. Title: American paintings ...

Benton, Suzanne.

BENTON, Suzanne. 731.4
The art of welded sculpture / Suzanne Benton ; with sculptural pieces, drawings, and photos. by the author. New York : Van Nostrand Reinhold, [1975] 148 p. : ill. (some col.) ; 25 cm. Includes index. Bibliography: p. 145-146. [NB1220.B46] 74-22513 ISBN 0-442-20692-5 : 12.95
1. Benton, Suzanne. 2. Welded sculpture. I. Title. BIP

Benton, Thomas Hart, 1889—

BENTON, Thomas Hart, 1889- 741.9'73
Benton drawings; a collection of drawings. Columbia, University of Missouri Press [1968] 135 p. (chiefly illus.) 31 cm. [NC1075.B522A45] 68-20095
I. Title.

BENTON, Thomas Hart, 1889- 769'.924
The lithographs of Thomas Hart Benton. Compiled and edited by Creekmore Fath. Austin, University of Texas Press [1969] xii, 195 p. illus., facsims., port. 24 x 32 cm. "Chronology and bibliography": p. [183]-193. [NE2415.B417F3] 69-15946 12.50
I. Fath, Creekmore, ed. II. Title. BIP

BENTON, Thomas Hart, 1889- 759.13
Thomas Hart Benton, [by] Matthew Baigell. New York, Abrams [1974] 278 p. illus. (part col.) 31 x 34 cm. Bibliography: p. 269-[273] [ND237.B47B3] 73-6789 ISBN 0-8109-0132-3
1. Benton, Thomas Hart, 1889- I. Baigell, Matthew. BIP

BENTON, Thomas Hart, 1889- 708'.178'411 s
Thomas Hart Benton : an artist's selection, 1908-1974 : [exhibition at the] William Rockhill Nelson Gallery of Art, Mary Atkins Museum of Fine Arts, Kansas City, Missouri, October 12, 1974-November 10, 1974, Brooks Memorial Art Gallery, Memphis, Tennessee, December 1, 1974-January 7, 1975. Kansas City, Mo. : Nelson Gallery and Atkins Museum, [1974] [31] p. : ill. (some col.) ; 25 cm. (The Nelson Gallery and Atkins Museum bulletin ; v. 5, no. 2) [N582.K3A25a vol. 5, no. 2] [ND237.B47] 759.13 74-196850
1. Benton, Thomas Hart, 1889- I. William Rockhill Nelson Gallery of Art and Mary Atkins Museum of Fine Arts, Kansas City, Mo. II. Brooks Memorial Art Gallery, Memphis, Tenn. III. Series: William Rockhill Nelson Gallery of Art and Mary Atkins Museum of Fine Arts, Kansas City, Mo. Bulletin ; v. 5, no. 2.

BENTON, Thomas Hart, 1889- 759.13
Thomas Hart Benton: a personal commemorative; a retrospective exhibition of his works, 1907-1972, Spiva Art Center, Missouri Southern State College, Joplin, Missouri, March 24 through April 27, 1973. [Kansas City, Mo., Burd & Fletcher, 1973] 119 p. illus. (part col.) 31 cm. "In honor of the Joplin centennial." [ND237.B47S64] 72-97358
1. Benton, Thomas Hart, 1889- I. Spiva Art Center. II. Title.

KANSAS. University. Museum of Art. 759.13
Thomas Hart Benton; a retrospective exhibition of the works of the noted Missouri artist presented under the patronage of Harry S. Truman and Mrs. Truman of Independence, Missouri, April 12 to May 18, 1958, the University of Kansas Museum of Art. Lawrence [1958] unpaged. illus. 23cm. [ND237.B47K3] 927.5 58-63062
1. Benton, Thomas Hart, 1889- I. Title.

RUTGERS University, New Brunswick, N.J. Art Gallery. 759.13
Thomas Hart Benton: a retrospective of his early years, 1907-1929. New Brunswick, N.J. [1972] [24] p. plates (part col.) 23 cm. Errata slip stapled to t.p. Catalog of the exhibition held Nov. 19-Dec. 30, 1972. Bibliography: p. [11] [ND237.B47R87] 72-619618
1. Benton, Thomas Hart, 1889-

Benton, Thomas Hart, 1889-1975.

BENTON, Thomas Hart, 1889-1975. 769'.92'4
The lithographs of Thomas Hart Benton / compiled and edited by Creekmore Fath. New ed. Austin : University of Texas Press, c1979. xxii, 223 p. : ill. ; 24 x 32 cm. Includes index. "Chronology and bibliography": p. [209]-222. [NE2312.B48A4 1979] 78-70912 ISBN 0-292-74621-0 : 24.95
1. Benton, Thomas Hart, 1889-1975—Catalogs. I. Fath, Creekmore. II. Title.

BENTON, Thomas Hart, 1889-1975. 759.13
Thomas Hart Benton / text by Matthew Baigell. New concise NAL ed. New York : H. N. Abrams : distributed by New American Library, 1976,c1975 159 p. : ill. (some col.) ; 29 cm. [ND237.B47B3 1975] 75-27668 limited ed. : 150.00 ISBN 0-8109-0132-3 : 40.00
1. Benton, Thomas Hart, 1889-1975. I. Baigell, Matthew.

EDELMAN, Nancy. 759.13
The Thomas Hart Benton murals in the Missouri State Capitol : a social history of the State of Missouri / Nancy Edelman. [Jefferson City] : Missouri State Council on the Arts, 1975. v, 46 p. : ill. (some col.) ; 22 x 28 cm. Bibliography: p. 42-46. [ND237.B47E33] 75-331413
1. Benton, Thomas Hart, 1889-1975. Missouri mural. 2. Jefferson City, Mo. State Capitol. I. Title.

SHANE, Frederick, 1906- 741.973
Drawings. Introductory essay by Thomas Hart Benton. Biographical sketch by Sidney Larson. Columbia, University of Missouri Press [1964] 116 p. illus., ports. 32 cm. [NC139.S5B4] 64-12584
I. Benton, Thomas Hart, 1889- II. Title.

YEO, Wilma. 759.13 B
Maverick with a paintbrush : Thomas Hart Benton / by Wilma Yeo & Helen K. Cook. 1st ed. Garden City, N.Y. : Doubleday, 1977. 125 p., [4] leaves of plates : ill. ; 25 cm. [ND237.B47Y46] 73-11639 ISBN 0-385-00421-4 : 6.95. ISBN 0-385-08017-4 lib.bdg. : 7.90
1. Benton, Thomas Hart, 1889-1975. 2. Painters—United States—Biography. I. Cook, Helen K., joint author. II. Title. BIP

Benvenuto di Giovanni, 1436-ca. 1518.

FREDERICKSEN, Burton B. 759.5
Benvenuto di Giovanni, Girolamo di Benvenuto: their altarpieces in the J. Paul Getty Museum. And a summary catalogue of their paintings in America, by Burton B. Fredericksen and Darrell D. Davisson. [Malibu, Calif.] 1966. 35, [27] p. map, plates. 23 cm. (Getty (J. Paul) Museum. Publication no. 2) Includes bibliographical references. [ND622.G4 no. 2] 71-557
1. Benvenuto di Giovanni, 1436-ca. 1518. 2. Girolamo di Benvenuto, 1470-1524. I. Davisson, Darrell D. II. Getty (J. Paul) Museum. III. Title. IV. Series.

Benziger, August, 1867-1955.

BENZIGER, Marieli G 927.5
August Benziger, portrait painter, by Marieli Benziger, with the assistance of Rita Benziger. Glendale, Calif., A. H. Clark Co., 1958. 485p. illus., ports., facsims. 27cm. Bibliography: p. p.[471]-474. [ND853.B4B4] 58-11787
1. Benziger, August, 1867-1955. I. Title. BIP

Berard, Christian, 1902-1949.

HASTINGS, Baird. 759.4
Christian Berard, painter, decorator, designer. With an introd. by Louis Jouvet. [New York, Published by Chanticleer Press for] Institute of Contemporary Art, Boston [1950] 62 p. illus. 25 cm. [ND553.B519H3] 52-1071
1. Berard, Christian, 1902-1949. 2. Paintings, French—Exhibitions. I. Title.

Berber, Mersad.

BERBER, Mersad. v. 12
Mersad Berber. Hamburg : Galerien, Grafische Editionen H. Hoeppner, c1975. [69] p. : chiefly ill. (chiefly col.) ; 24 cm. Published on the occasion of exhibitions held at the Galerien Hans Hoeppner, Hamburg and Munich. Includes bibliography. [N7253.B37G34] 75-522123
1. Berber, Mersad. I. Galerie Hans Hoeppner.

Berenson, Bernhard, 1865-1959.

BERENSON, Bernhard, 1865- 927
Sketch for a self-portrait. Bloomington, Indiana University Press [1958, c1949] 184p. illus. 20cm. (A Midland book, MB11) [N8370] 58-12203
I. Title.

BERENSON, Bernhard, 1865-1959. 927
The Bernard Berenson treasury; a selection from the works, unpublished writings, letters, diaries, and journals of the most celebrated humanist and art historian of our times, 1887-1958. Selected and edited by Hanna Kiel. Introd. by John Walker. Pref. by Nicky Mariano. New York, Simon and Schuster, 1962. 414p. illus. 22cm. [N8375.B46A15] 62-14273
I. Title. BIP

BERENSON, Bernhard, 1865-1959. 700.8
Conversations with Berenson [by] Umberto Morra. Translated from the Italian by Florence Hammond. [1st American ed.] Boston, Houghton Mifflin, 1965. x, 305 p. 22 cm. [N8375.B46A53] 65-18489
I. Morra, Umberto. II. Hammond, Florence, tr. III. Title. BIP

BERENSON, Bernhard, 1865-1959. 927
Sunset and twilight; from the diaries of 1947-1958. Edited, and with an epilogue by Nicky Mariano. Introd. by Iris Origo. [1st ed.] New York, Harcourt, Brace & World [1963] xxv, 547 p. illus., ports. 24 cm. [N8375.B46A33] 63-15313
I. Title.

MARIANO, Nicky. 709.24
Forty years with Berenson. With an introd. by Sir Kenneth Clark. [1st American ed.] New York, Knopf, 1966. xvi, 352 xiv p. illus., ports. 22 cm. [N8375.B46M3 1966a] 66-19387
1. Berenson, Bernhard, 1865-1959. I. Title.

SPRIGGE, Sylvia (Saunders) 927
Berenson; a biography. Boston, Houghton Mifflin, 1960. 287 p. illus. 25 cm. [N8375.B46S65] 60-7386
1. Berenson, Bernhard, 1865-1959. I. Title.

Berg, Phil—Art collections.

LOS Angeles Co., Calif. Museum of Art, Los Angeles. 730'.074'019494
Man came this way; objects from the Phil Berg Collection. Catalog and commentary by Phil Berg. [Los Angeles, 1971] 211 p. illus. (part col.), maps 22 x 28 cm. Catalog of the exhibition held Mar. 9-May 30, 1971 at the Los Angeles County Museum of Art. Bibliography: p. 209-211. [N5220.B43L6] 70-152278 ISBN 0-87587-043-0
1. Berg, Phil—Art collections. 2. Art—Exhibitions. I. Title.

Bergdorf Goodman, New York.

HERNDON, Booton. 687.12065
Bergdorf's on the Plaza; the story of Bergdorf Goodman and a half-century of American fashion.[1st ed.] New York, Knopf, 1956. 244p. illus. 22cm. [TT505.B4H4] 55-9286
1. Bergdorf Goodman, New York. I. Title.

Bergenfield, N.J. South Presbyterian Church.

LEIBY, Adrian Coulter. 726'.58'5174921
The buildings of the South Church, Bergenfield, New Jersey [by] Adrian C. Leiby. Drawings by Richard G. Belcher. [New York, Printed by Sorg Print. Co.] 1968 [c1969] vii, 70 p. illus., facsim., map, plans. 24 cm. [NA5235.B43L4] 72-79419
1. Bergenfield, N.J. South Presbyterian Church. I. Title.

Berkeley, Calif.—Historic houses, etc.

BERNHARDI, Robert. 720'.9'79467
The buildings of Berkeley. Photography and text by Robert Bernhardi. [Berkeley, Calif., Printed by Lederer, Street & Zeus Co., 1971] vii, 116 p. illus. 28 cm. Includes bibliographical references. [NA735.B38B4] 72-175190 8.50
1. Berkeley, Calif.—Historic houses, etc. 2. Architecture—Berkeley, Calif. I. Title.

Berkowitz, Leon, 1919—

BERKOWITZ, Leon, 1919- 759.13
An exhibition of current painting by Leon Berkowitz: the sound of light. Transparent air poems by Ida Fox. Sound by Carlus Dyer. Edited by Judson Rosebush. Corcoran Gallery of Art, Sept. 14 through Oct. 21, 1973. Everson Museum of Art, Feb. 21 through Mar. 21, 1974. Syracuse, N.Y., Everson Museum of Art [1973] [17] p. illus. (part col.) 31 cm. Cover title: The sound of light. Catalog of the exhibition. Bibliography: p. [15] [ND237.B5R67] 73-88664
1. Berkowitz, Leon, 1919- I. Rosebush, Judson, ed. II. Corcoran Gallery of Art, Washington, D.C. III. Everson Museum of Art, Syracuse, N.Y. IV. Title. V. Title: The sound of light.

Berkshire Hills, Mass., in art.

FILMUS, Michael, 1943- 741.9'73
Green River : Berkshire scenes / by Michael Filmus ; with text by Berkshire authors. Lenox, Mass. : Bookstore Press, [1975] [32] p. : ill. ; 16 x 23 cm. [NC139.F453A45] 75-320690
1. Filmus, Michael, 1943- 2. Berkshire Hills, Mass., in art. I. Title.

Berlant, Anthony—Art collections.

ARIZONA. University. Museum of Art. 746.9'7
Navajo blankets, from the collection of Anthony Berlant; [exhibition] Text by Joseph Ben Wheat. [Tucson, 1974] [15] p. 36 p. of illus. (part col.) 32 cm.

SUBJECT INDEX BEVAN, ROBERT, 1865-1925.

Bibliography: p. [53]-[54] [E99.N3A79 1974] 74-76013
1. Berlant, Anthony—Art collections. 2. Navajo Indians—Textile industry and fabrics. 3. Indians of North America—Southwest, New—Textile industry and fabrics. I. Wheat, Joe Ben. II. Title.

Berlin. Gemaldegalerie (West Berlin)

KLESSMANN, Rudiger. 759.4'074'013155
The Berlin Museum; paintings in the Picture Gallery, Dahlem-West Berlin. [Translated from the German D. J. S. Thomson] New York, H. N. Abrams [1972, c1971] 308 p. illus., 90 col. plates. 22 cm. 1971 ed. published under title: The Berlin Gallery. [N2230.K5513 1972] 78-153494 ISBN 0-8109-0037-8 7.50
1. Berlin. Gemaldegalerie (West Berlin) 2. Berlin. Museum Dahlem. I. Title.

Berman, Eugene, 1899-1972.

BERMAN, Eugene, 1899- 760'.0924
The graphic work of Eugene Berman. [1st ed.] New York, C. N. Potter; distributed by Crown Publishers [1971] xviii, 332 p. (chiefly illus.) 32 cm. [NC139.B46A44 1971] 73-118298 15.00
I. Title.

TEXAS. University at Austin. Art Museum. 759.13
Eugene Berman in perspective : an exhibition formed around selections from the Robert L. B. Tobin Collection, April 27-June 29, 1975, Michener Galleries, Upper Level, Harry Ransom Center, University Art Museum, University of Texas at Austin. Austin : The Museum, [1975]. 20 p. ; 23 cm. [ND1839.B47T48 1975] 75-323581
1. Berman, Eugene, 1899-1972. 2. Tobin, Robert L. B.—Art collections. I. Title.

TEXAS. University. Humanities Research Center. 792.025
An exhibition of designs for the theatre by Eugene Berman. [Austin] Research Center, University of Texas, 1960. unpaged. illus. 25 cm. [ND2885.T4] 60-63789
1. Berman, Eugene, 1899- 2. Theaters — Stage-setting and scenery. I. Title.

Bermuda Islands in art.

BANNERMAN, Jane Campbell. 759.13
Bermuda, as seen by Jane Campbell Bannerman. [s.l. : s.n., 1976?] [30] leaves of plates : all col. ill. ; 16 x 24 cm. Cover title. [ND1839.B23A42] 77-354153 11.50
1. Bannerman, Jane Campbell. 2. Bermuda Islands in art.

Bernaldo, Allan T., 1900—

BERNALDO, Allan T., 1900- 759.994 B
A lifetime with water colours : recollections / by Allan T. Bernaldo. Frankston, Australia : Heritage Book Publications, 1976. 59 p. : ill. (chiefly col.) ; 27 cm. Includes index. [ND2091.B47A25] 77-368972
1. Bernaldo, Allan T., 1900- 2. Water-colorists—Australia—Biography. I. Title.

Bernini, Giovanni Lorenzo, 1598-1680.

BALDINUCCI, Filippo, 1624?-1696. 730.924
The life of Bernini. Translated from the Italian by Catherine Enggass. Forword by Robert Enggass. University Park, Pennsylvania State University Press, 1966. xviii, 117 p. illus., port. 23 cm. Translation of Vita del cavaliere Glo. Lorenzo Bernino. [N6923.B5B33] 65-26094
1. Bernini, Giovanni Lorenzo, 1598-1680. I. Title.

BERNINI, Giovanni Lorenzo, 1598-1680. 741.9'45
Selected drawings of Gian Lorenzo Bernini / edited by Ann Sutherland Harris. New York : Dover Publications, 1977. xxiv p., [50] leaves of plates : ill. ; 31 cm. [NC257.B42H37] 77-70028 ISBN 0-486-23525-4 : 5.00
1. Bernini, Giovanni Lorenzo, 1598-1680. I. Title. BIP

BERNINI in perspective 730'.92'4
/ edited by George C. Bauer. Englewood Cliffs, N.J. : Prentice-Hall, c1976. viii, 140 p., [6] leaves of plates : ill. ; 23 cm. (The Artists in perspective series) (A Spectrum book ; S-379) Bibliography: p. 133-138. [N6923.B5B47] 75-31546 ISBN 0-13-074500-6 : 9.95 ISBN 0-13-074492-1 pbk. :
1. Bernini, Giovanni Lorenzo, 1598-1680. I. Bauer, George C.

CHANTELOU, Paul Freart de, ca.1605-ca.1694. 730'.924
Journal du voyage en France du cavalier Bernin. Pref de G. Charensol. New York, B. Franklin [1973 c.1972] 300 p. 22 cm. (Burt Franklin research & source works series. Art history, 35) Reprint of the 1930 ed., which was issued as v. 2 of Collection Ateliers. [N6923.B5C5 1972] 72-86907 ISBN 0-8337-0531-8 16.50
1. Bernini, Giovanni Lorenzo, 1598-1680. I. Title. II. Series: Collection "Ateliers," 2. BIP

HIBBARD, Howard, 1928- 730.924
Bernini. [Baltimore] Penguin [1966, c.1965] 255p. illus., plans, ports. 20cm. (Pelican bk. A701) Bibl. [NB623.B5H5] 66-3256 2.45 pap.,
1. Bernini, Giovanni Lorenzo, 1598-1680. I. Title.

HIBBARD, Howard, 1928- 730.924
Bernini [Magnolia, Mass., P. Smith, 1967, c.1965] 255p. illus., plans, ports. 20cm. (Pelican bk. A701 rebound) Bibl. [NB623.B5H5] 4.50
1. Bernini, Giovanni Lorenzo, 1598-1680. I. Title. BIP

HIBBARD, Howard, 1928- 730.924
Bernini. Baltimore, Penguin Books, [1974] 255 p. illus., plans, ports. 20 cm. (Pelican book, A701) Includes index Includes bibliographical references [NB623.B5H5] ISBN 0-14-020701-5 3.95 (pbk.)
1. Bernini, Giovanni Lorenzo, 1598-1680. I. Title.
L.C. card no. for original: 66-3256

KITAO, Timothy K. 720'.92'4
Circle and oval in the Square of Saint Peter's : Bernini's art of planning / Timothy K. Kitao. New York : Published by New York University Press for the College Art Association of America, 1974. xiv, 156 p., [16] leaves of plates : ill. ; 29 cm. (Monographs on archaeology and the fine arts ; 29) A revision of the author's thesis, Harvard, 1966. Includes index. Bibliography: p. 139-148. [NA1123.B28K57 1974] 73-14849 ISBN 0-8147-4557-1
1. Bernini, Giovanni Lorenzo, 1598-1680. 2. Rome (City)—Plazas—Piazza di San Pietro. I. Title. II. Series. BIP

LAVIN, Irving, 1927- 730'.924
Bernini and the crossing of Saint Peter's. New York, Published for the College Art Association of America, by New York University Press, 1968. vii, 94 p. illus., plans. 28 cm. (Monographs on archaeology and the fine arts, 17) Includes bibliographical references. [NA1123.B5L3] 68-22570
1. Bernini, Giovanni Lorenzo, 1598-1680. 2. Vatican City. San Pietro in Vaticano (Basilica) I. The College Art Association of America. II. Title. III. Series.

WITTKOWER, Rudolf. 730'.92'4
Gian Lorenzo Bernini, the sculptor of the Roman Baroque. New York, Phaidon Publishers; distributed by Garden City Books [1955] x, 255p. illus., 122 plates, port. 31cm. Bibliography: p. [169]-171. [NB623.B] A57
1. Bernini, Giovanni Lorenzo, 1598-1680. I. Title.

Bernini, Givovanni Lorenzo, 1598-1680.

WITTKOWER, Rudolf 730.924
Gian Lorenzo Bernini: the sculptor of the Roman baroque. 2nd ed. London, Phaidon Pr., 1966. xi, 286p. front., 254 illus., 9 plates. tables. 32cm. Bibl. [NB623.B5W55 1966] 66-69911 17.50
1. Bernini, Givovanni Lorenzo, 1598-1680. I. Title.
American distributor: N.Y. Graphic, Greenwich, Conn.

Berry, Burton Yost—Art collections.

BERRY, Burton Yost. 704'.7 B
Out of the past : the Istanbul Grand Bazaar / by Burton Y. Berry ; illustrated by Azzedine El-Aaji. New York : Arco Pub. Co., c1976. p. cm. [N5220.B46A52] 74-29791 ISBN 0-668-03778-4 : 12.50
1. Berry, Burton Yost—Art collections. 2. Istanbul. Kapalicarsi. 3. Diplomats—United States—Correspondence, reminiscences, etc. I. Title. BIP

Berry, Burton Yost—Coin collections.

AMERICAN Numismatic Society. 737.4'9'38
The Burton Y. Berry Collection. New York, 1961-62. 2 v. plates. 40 cm. (Its Sylloge nummorum Graecorum) Contents.Contents.—pt. 1. Macedonia to Attica.—pt. 2. Megaris to Egypt. [CJ309.A4 vol. 1] 73-176717
1. Berry, Burton Yost—Coin collections. 2. Coins, Greek.

Berry, Jean de France, duc de, 1340-1416.

MEISS, Millard. 096'.1'0944
French painting in the time of Jean De Berry; the late Fourteenth century and the patronage of the Duke. London, Phaidon, 1967. U. S. dist.: Praeger, New York. 2v. illus., plates (1 col.) 31cm. (Natl. Gallery of Art: Kress Found. studies in the hist. of European art no. 2) Bibl. [ND3147.M37 1967] 67-29885 30.00 set,
1. Berry, Jean de France, duc de, 1340-1416. 2. Illumination of books and manuscripts, Medieval—France. 3. Miniature painting, French. I. Title. II. Series: Kress Foundation studies in the history of European art, no. 2 BIP

Berthon, Paul, 1872-1909.

ARWAS, Victor. 709'.2'2
Berthon & Grasset / Victor Arwas. New York : Rizzoli, 1978. 144 p. : ill. (some col.) ; 30 cm. Includes index. Bibliography: p. 141-143. [N6853.B42A78 1978] 77-73366 ISBN 0-8478-0103-9 : 29.50
1. Berthon, Paul, 1872-1909. 2. Grasset, Eugene, 1850-1917. 3. Art nouveau—France. I. Title. BIP

Bertini, Aldo.

BOTTICELLI, Sandro, 1447?-1510. 741.9'45
Drawings by Botticelli, by Aldo Bertini. Translated by Florence H. Phillips. New York, Dover Publications [1968] 11 p., 32 plates. 28 cm. (The Great masters of drawing) Translation of Botticelli. [NC1055.B7B43 1968] 67-27876 1.50
1. Bertini, Aldo. I. Title.

Bertini, Gianni, 1922-

RESTANY, Pierre 759.5
Bertini. [dist. New York, Efron, 1962] 68p. illus. (pt. mounted col.) 19cm. (Le Musee depoche) 62-4283 1.50 pap.,
1. Bertini, Gianni, 1922- I. Title.

Bertoia, Harry.

NELSON, June Kompass. 730'.924
Harry Bertoia: sculptor. Detroit, Wayne State University Press, 1970. 137 p. illus., port. 26 cm. Bibliography: p. 129-133. [NB237.B44N4 1970] 70-78546 11.50
1. Bertoia, Harry. I. Title. BIP

Bertram, Master, of Minden, d. ca. 1415.

PORTMANN, Paul Ferdinand 759.3
The Nativity: Master Betram. New York, Taplinger [c.1961] [48]p. 19col. illus. (Orbis pictus ser., 6) 61-65204 2.00 bds.,
1. Bertram, Master, of Minden, d. ca. 1415. 2. Jesus Christ—Art. I. Title.

Bertrand, Raymond.

BERTRAND, Raymond. 741.9'44
The drawings of Raymond Bertrand / with an introd. by Emmanuelle Arsan. [New York] : Grove Press : distributed by Random House, [1974] [126] p. : chiefly ill. (some col.) ; 32 cm. Translation of Dessins erotiques de Bertrand. [NC248.B43A7713] 73-21034 ISBN 0-8021-0040-6 : 20.00
1. Bertrand, Raymond. 2. Erotic art. I. Arsan, Emmanuelle. II. Title.

Bertrand (Steamboat)

PETSCHE, Jerome E. 913'.031'08 s
The steamboat Bertrand: history, excavation, and architecture, by Jerome E. Petsche. Washington, National Park Service, 1974. p. cm. (Publications in archeology, 11) Bibliography: p. [E51.U75 no. 11] [VM461.5.B47] 917.82'2 72-600352
1. Bertrand (Steamboat) 2. Shipwrecks—Missouri River. I. Title. II. Series.

Berwick-upon-Tweed, Eng.—Description—Guide-books.

GRAHAM, Frank, 1913- 914.28'2
Berwick: a short history and guide. Newcastle upon Tyne, Graham, 1972. 45 p. illus., 2 maps. 22 cm. (Northern history booklets, no. 25) [DA690.B5G73] 73-152432 ISBN 0-902833-26-X £0.40
1. Berwick-upon-Tweed, Eng.—Description—Guide-books. I. Title.

Beseler Topcon camera.

WOOLLEY, Al E. 771.3'1
Beseler Topcon Unirex/Auto 100 manual [by] A. E. Woolley. New York, Amphoto [1972] 159 p. illus. 24 cm. [TR263.B47W6] 78-153478 ISBN 0-8174-0522-4
1. Beseler Topcon camera. 2. Photography—Handbooks, manuals, etc. I. Title.

Beth-El Synagogue, New Rochelle, N.Y.

BATKIN, Stanley I., 1914- 726'.3'0947277
Let them make me a sanctuary : a contemporary American synagogue inspired by the art of ancient Israel / by Stanley Irving Batkin. New York : Behrman House, 1979, c1978. p. cm. Includes index. [NA5235.N583B37] 78-16933 ISBN 0-87441-316-8 : 29.95
1. Beth-El Synagogue, New Rochelle, N.Y. 2. Jews in New Rochelle, N.Y. I. Title.

BATKIN, Stanley I., 1914- 726'.3'0947277
Let them make me a sanctuary : a contemporary American synagogue inspired by the art of ancient Israel / by Stanley Irving Batkin. New York : Behrman House, 1979, c1978. p. cm. Includes index. [NA5235.N583B37] 78-16933 ISBN 0-87441-316-8 : 29.95
1. Beth-El Synagogue, New Rochelle, N.Y. 2. Jews in New Rochelle, N.Y. I. Title. BIP

Betrothal—Caricatures and cartoons.

BOLTINOFF, Henry. 301.41'4'0207
So you're getting married. New York, ARC Books [1969] [80] p. (chiefly illus.) 19 cm. [NC1429.B659A57] 72-77607 0.95
1. Betrothal—Caricatures and cartoons. I. Title.

Bevan, Robert, 1865-1925.

BEVAN, Robert Alexander 759.2
Robert Bevan, 1865-1925: a memoir by his son [R. A. Bevan] London, Studio Vista [1966] 28p., 88p. of illus. (pt. col.) 33cm. Bibl. [ND497.B48B48] 67-6557 12.00
1. Bevan, Robert, 1865-1925. I. Title.

Bewick, Thomas, 1753-1828.

BEWICK, Thomas, 1753-1828. 769'.92'4 B
A memoir of Thomas Bewick / written by himself. Newcastle upon Tyne : Graham, 1974. [4], ii-xix, 344 p. : ill. ; 24 cm. Reprint of 1st ed. Newcastle upon Tyne, J. Bewick, 1862. [NE1147.6.B47A25 1974] 74-193399 ISBN 0-85983-065-9 : £3.50
1. Bewick, Thomas, 1753-1828. I. Title. BIP

BEWICK, Thomas, 1753-1828. 769'.92'4 B
A memoir of Thomas Bewick / written by himself ; edited with an introd. by Iain Bain. London ; New York : Oxford University Press, 1975. xliv, 258 p., [4] leaves of plates : ill. ; 25 cm. (Oxford English memoirs and travels) Includes index. Bibliography: p. xl-xli. [NE1147.6.B47A25 1975] 75-326114 ISBN 0-19-255413-1 : 21.00
1. Bewick, Thomas, 1753-1828. I. Title. II. Series.

BEWICK, Thomas, 1753-1828. 769'.924
A portfolio of Thomas Bewick wood engravings. One hundred prints made from the original blocks engraved by Thomas Bewick, with an introd. by James M. Wells. [Chicago] Published by the Newberry Library for the Cherryburn Press, 1970. 18 p. and 2 portfolios (100 plates) in a case. 27 cm. The engravings were printed by R. Hunter Middleton, who selected the blocks from a collection at the Newberry Library. "Limited to 150 copies, of which 125 are for sale."—Prospectus. [NE1143.5.B4A53] 70-26687
I. Wells, James M. II. Middleton, Robert Hunter, 1899- III. Title.

BEWICK, Thomas, 1753-1828. 769'.9'24
Select fables; impressions from 84 blocks [Northampton, Mass.] Gehenna Press [1968] 1 v. (84 plates) 19 cm. "These blocks were engraved by Thomas Bewick, his brother John and by several pupils in the shop. They were used in editions of Select fables printed in 1776 and 1784. They are printed here with the kind permission of Philip Hofer who owns them." "Thirty five copies printed." [NE1147.6.B47A5] 72-194871
I. Bewick, John, 1760-1795. II. Title.

BEWICK, Thomas, 1753-1828. 769'.92'4
Thomas Bewick: ten working drawing reproductions shown with impressions of the corresponding engravings. Chicago, Cherryburn Press, 1972. [10] p., 20 plates, port. (in case) 17 x 20 cm. Pairs of plates mounted in 10 numbered folders in a portfolio within the case. The reproductions are from an album containing 29 pencil drawings in the Cherryburn Press Bewick Collection. "Acknowledgements" signed: R. Hunter Middleton. [NC242.B48M52 1972] 73-168118
1. Bewick, Thomas, 1753-1828. I. Middleton, Robert Hunter, 1899- II. Title.

DOBSON, Austin, 1840-1921. 769'.924 B
Thomas Bewick and his pupils. London, Chatto and Windus, 1884; Detroit, Singing Tree Press, 1968. xviii, 232 p. illus., ports. 20 cm. [NE1212.B5D64 1968] 69-17340
1. Bewick, Thomas, 1753-1828. 2. Wood-engravers, English. I. Title. BIP

HUGO, Thomas, 1820-1876. 016.769'922
The Bewick collector; a descriptive catalogue of the works of Thomas and John Bewick. New York, B. Franklin [1970] xxiii, 562 p. illus. 23 cm. (Burt Franklin bibliography & reference series, 314) (Art history & art reference, 33.) Reprint of the 1866 ed. [NE1112.B48H8 1970] 70-128113
1. Bewick, Thomas, 1753-1828. 2. Bewick, John, 1760-1795. 3. Wood-engravings—Catalogs. 4. Engravings—Private collections. I. Title. BIP

ROBINSON, Robert, 769'.92'4 bookseller, fl.1887-1892.
Thomas Bewick: his life and times. Newcastle upon Tyne, Graham, 1972. xxxviii, 328, [30] p. illus., facsims., ports. 25 cm. Facsimile of 1st ed., Newcastle, R. Robinson, 1887. Bibliography: p. 274-305. [NE1147.6.B47R62 1887a] 72-171487 £4.00
1. Bewick, Thomas, 1753-1828. I. Title.

WEEKLEY, Montague. 927.6
Thomas Bewick. London, New York, Oxford University Press, 1953. x, 224p. illus. 23cm. 'Bewickiana: a supplementary note on manuscripts. personal relics. etc.':p. [218]-219. [NE1217.B4W4] 53-2758
I. Bewick, Thomas, 1753-1828. II. Title. BIP

Bexhill, Eng. De La Warr Pavillion.

WHITE, Ralph Barton 725'.8
Qualitative studies of buildings: the De La Warr Pavilion, Bexhill-on-Sea and the Gilbey Building. Oval Road, London, N. W. 1, by R. ,b. White. London H.M.S.O., 1966. .v60p. illus., 16 plates, plans, diagrs. 30cm. (Natl. bldg. studies. Special report, 39) At head of title: Ministry of Technology Building Research Station. Bibl. [TH7.N37 no. 39] 67-80300 5.50 pap.,
1. Bexhill, Eng. De La Warr Pavillion. 2. London, Gilbey Building. 3. Building research. I. Garston. Eng. Building Research Station. II. Title. III. Series.
Distributed by British Info., New York City.

Beyer, Richard S., 1925—

BEYER, Richard S., 1925- 761'.2
George Washington and the wolves / woodblock prints by Richard S. Beyer ; text by Jerome Hellmuth. Seattle : Madrona Publishers, [1977] p. cm. [NE1112.B49H44] 77-20798 ISBN 0-914842-23-4 pbk. : 3.95
1. Beyer, Richard S., 1925- 2. Wolves in art. 3. Wolves—United States. 4. United States—Social life and customs—Colonial period, ca. 1600-1775. I. Hellmuth, Jerome. II. Title.

Bianco, Yvonne, 1930-1976.

BIANCO, Yvonne, 1930-1976. 745.6'1'0924
Every dawn is first, Yvonne Bianco, 1930-1976 : [catalogue] / [edited by Callum MacColl]. [s.l. : s.n.], c1976 ([Portland?] : J. Y. Hollingsworth Co.) [32] p. : chiefly ill. (some col.) : 29 cm. Cover title: Yvonne. [NK3631.B47A45] 76-151852
1. Bianco, Yvonne, 1930-1976. 2. Lettering. I. Title. II. Title: Yvonne.

Bianconi, Piero, 1899-

FRANCESCHI, Pietro di Benedetto dei, 1416?-1492. 759.5
All the paintings of Piero della Francesca, Text by Piero Bianconi. Tr. by Paul Colacicchi. New York, Hawthorn [1962] 81p. illus., 180 plates (pt. col.) 19cm. (Complete lib. of world art, v.5) Bibl. 62-10519 3.95
1. Bianconi, Piero, 1899- I. Title. II. Series.

LOTTO, Lorenzo, 1480?-1556? 759.5
All the paintings of Lorenzo Lotto. [2v.] By Piero Bianconi. Tr. from Italian by Paul Colacicchi. New York, Hawthorn [1964, c.1963] 2v. (113p.) 216 plates, 8 col. plates. 18cm. (Complete lib. of world art, v.16-17) Bibl. 63-12214 3.95 ea.,
1. Bianconi, Piero, 1899- I. Title. II. Series.

Bible crafts.

GRAMELSBACH, Helen W. 745.59'2
30 Bible story projects to make / by Helen W. gramelsbach ; illustrated by Allison Mehta Cincinnati : Standard Pub., [1975] 63 p. : ill. ; 29 cm. [BS613.G72] 74-82559 ISBN 0-87239-038-1 pbk. : 2.25
1. Bible crafts. I. Title.

STUART, Monica. 745.5
Come, hear, and see : creative activities for use with Bible stories / [by] Monica Stuart and Gill Soper ; with drawings by Juliet Renny. London : Faber, 1976. 96 p. : ill. ; 19 x 25 cm. (Faber paperbacks) Imprint label mounted on t.p.: Faber & Faber, Salem, N.H. [BS613.S73] 77-357112 ISBN 0-571-10935-7 : 6.95
1. Bible crafts. I. Soper, Gill, joint author. II. Title. BIP

Bible crafts—Juvenile literature.

HUTCHINGS, Margaret. 745.59'2
Making New Testament toys / Margaret Hutchings, with ill. by the author. New York : Hawthorn Books, c1972. 96 p. : ill. (some col.) ; 24 cm. Instructions for making a variety of toy and craft representations of characters and scenes from New Testament stories. [BS613.H765] 74-21169 ISBN 0-8015-4802-0 : 3.95 ($4.50 Can)
1. Bible crafts—Juvenile literature. 2. Toy making—Juvenile literature. I. Title. BIP

HUTCHINGS, Margaret. 745.59'2
Making Old Testament toys / Margaret Hutchings ; with ill. by the author. New York : Hawthorn Books, [1975] c1972. 95 p. : ill. (some col.) ; 24 cm. Instructions for making a variety of toy and craft representations of characters and scenes from Old Testament stories. [BS613.H77 1975] 74-21167 ISBN 0-8015-4804-7 : 3.95
1. Bible crafts—Juvenile literature. 2. Toy making—Juvenile literature. I. Title. BIP

Bible. Latin. ca.1454-55. Mainz. Gutenberg (42 lines)

THORPE, James Ernest, 1915- 220'.47
The Gutenberg Bible, landmark in learning / by James Thorpe. San Marino, Calif. : Huntington Library, 1975. 23 p. : facsims. ; 24 cm. [Z241.B58T47] 75-324777
1. Gutenberg, Johann, 1397?-1468. 2. Bible. Latin. ca.1454-55. Mainz. Gutenberg (42 lines) I. Title.

Bible. Latin. ca. 1454-55. Mainz. Gutenberg (42 lines)—Bibl.

NORMAN, Don Cleveland. 220.47
The 500th anniversary pictorial census of the Gutenberg Bible. With introd. on the life and work of Johannes Gutenberg by Aloys Ruppel. Chicago, Coverdale Press, 1961. xvi, 263p. illus. (part col.) ports. (part col.) col. maps, facsims. 43cm. Issued in a case. [Z241.B58N6] 60-53456
1. Bible. Latin. ca. 1454-55. Mainz. Gutenberg (42 lines)—Bibl. I. Ruppel, Aloys Leonhard, 1882- II. Title.

Bible. Latin. Stavelot Bible—Illustrations.

DYNES, Wayne. 745.6'7'094934
The illuminations of the Stavelot Bible / Wayne Dynes. New York : Garland, 1979 p. cm. (Outstanding dissertations in the fine arts) Bibliography: p. [ND3355.D96] 77-94693 ISBN 0-8240-3225-X lib bdg : 30.00
1. Bible. Latin. Stavelot Bible—Illustrations. 2. Illumination of books and manuscripts, Romanesque—Belgium—Meuse Valley. 3. Illumination of books and manuscripts—Belgium—Meuse Valley. I. Title. II. Series. BIP

Bible. Manuscripts, Latin. Lambeth Bible.

DODWELL, Charles Reginald. 755.4
The great Lambeth Bible. With introd. and notes by C. R. Dodwell. New York, T. Yoseloff [1959] 38 p. mounted col. illus. 29 cm. [The Library of illuminated manuscripts] Bibliographical references included in "Notes" (p. 37-38) [ND3355.L3] 59-16875
1. Bible. Manuscripts, Latin. Lambeth Bible. 2. Illumination of books and manuscripts—Canterbury, Eng. 3. Miniature painting—Canterbury, Eng. I. Title. II. Series.

Bible. Manuscripts, Latin. N. T. Gospela. Codex aureus Epternacensis.

METZ, Peter, 1901- 096.1
The Golden Gospels of Echternach, Codex aureus Epternacensis. Text based on the German by Peter Metz. [Rendered into English by Ilse Schrier and Peter Gorge] New York, Praeger [1957] 96p. mounted illus, 106 facsims. (12 col.) 34cm. Translation of Das Goldene Evangelienbuch von Echternach in Germanischen National- Museum su Nurnberg. Bibliography: p. 94-96. [ND3359.E6M413] 57-5327
1. Bible. Manuscripts, Latin. N. T. Gospela. Codex aureus Epternacensis. 2. Illumination of books and Specimens, reproductions, etc. I. Title.

Bible. Manuscripts, Latin. N. T. Gospels. Book of Kells.

SULLIVAN, Edward, Bart., Sir 1852-1928. 096.1
The Book of Kells, described by Sir Edward Sullivan, bart. With 24 colour reproductions from the original pages. Foreword by J. H. Holden. [5th ed.] London, New York, Studio Publications [1952] 111p. col. plates. 30cm. [ND3359.B7S8 1952] 53-1608
1. Bible. Manuscripts, Latin. N. T. Gospels. Book of Kells. 2. Decoration and ornament, Celtic. 3. Illumination of books and manuscripts—Specimens, reproductions, etc. I. Title. BIP

Bible. Manuscripts, Latin. N.T. Gospels. Book of Kells—Illustrations.

THE Book of Kells 745.6'7'0941822
: reproductions from the manuscript in Trinity College, Dublin / with a study of the manuscript by Francoise Henry. 1st American ed. New York : Knopf, 1974. 226 p. : ill. ; 35 cm. "126 colour plates, 75 monochrome illustrations." Issued in a slipcase. Includes bibliographical references. [ND3359.B7B65] 74-194761 ISBN 0-394-49475-X : 65.00
1. Bible. Manuscripts, Latin. N.T. Gospels. Book of Kells—Illustrations. 2. Illumination of books and manuscripts, Celtic. I. Henry, Francoise.

Bible. Manuscripts, Latin. N. T. Gospels. Codex aureus Epternacensis.

METZ, Peter, 1901- 096.1
The Golden Gospels of Echternach, Codex aureus Epternacensis. Text based on the German by Peter Metz. [Rendered into English by Ilse Schrier and Peter Gorge] New York, Praeger [1957] 96p. mounted illus., 106 facsims. (12 col.) 34cm. Translation of Das Goldene Evangelienbuch von Echternach im Germanischen National-Museum zu Nurnberg. Bibliography: p. 94-96. [ND3359.E6M413] 57-5327
1. Bible. Manuscripts, Latin. N. T. Gospels. Codex aureus Epternacensis. 2. Illumination of books and manuscripts—Specimens, reproductions, etc. I. Title.

Bible. N.T. Gospels—Pictures, illustrations, etc.

AUCLAIR, Marcelle, 1899- 704.9485
Christ's image. Translated from the French by Lionel Izod. Illus. selected by Michel Deon. Book design by Sonja Knapp. New York, Tudor Pub. Co. [1961] 139 p. illus. (part mounted col.) 22 cm. [N8050.A683] 61-15511
1. Jesus Christ—Art. 2. Bible. N.T. Gospels—Pictures, illustrations, etc. I. Title.

BAILEY, Albert Edward, 1871-1951. 704.948'2
The Gospel in art / Albert Edward Bailey. Detroit : Gale Research Co., 1975 [c1944] p. cm. Reprint of the ed. published in 1946 by the Pilgrim Press, Boston. Includes index. [N8030.B15 1975] 75-26559 ISBN 0-8103-4165-4 : 20.00
1. Jesus Christ—Art. 2. Bible. N.T. Gospels—Pictures, illustrations, etc. I. Title.

BIBLE. N. T. Gospels. 704.9485 English. Selections. 1957. Authorized.
The life of Christ in masterpieces of art and the words of the New Testament.

Selection of masterworks, with an introd. by Marvin Ross. New York, Harper [1957] 125p. mounted col. illus. 33cm. [N8050.B55] 57-8167
1. Jesus Christ—Art. 2. Bible. N. T. Gospels—Pictures, Illustrations, etc. I. Ross, Marvin Chauncey, ed. II. Title.

DANA, Ethel Nathalie (Smith) 1878- 704.9485
The story of Jesus; Pictures from paintings by Giotto, Fra Angelico, Duccio, Ghirlandaio and Barnja da Siena; descriptive text from the New Testament, selected and arranged by Ethel Nathalie Dana. Boston, Marshall Jones company, 1920. [92] p. XL col. pl. 24 x 31 1/2 cm. [N8050.D3] 20-26575
1. Jesus Christ — Art. 2. Bible. N. T. Gospels — Pictures, illustrations, etc. 3. Paintings, Italian. I. Bible. N. T. Gospels. English. Selections. 1920. II. Title.

PATRICK, Sam. 741.6384
Jesus loved them, by Sam Patrick and Oman Garrison. Englewood Cliffs, N. J., Prentice-Hall [1957] 133p. illus. 28cm. [NC1075.P29G3] 57-12421
1. Bible. N. T. Gospels— Pictures, illustrations, etc. 2. Bible. N. T. Gospels—History of Biblical events. I. Garrison, Omar. II. Title.

Bible. N. T. — Pictures, illustrations, etc.

STRAND, Kenneth Albert, 1927- 225.52
Reformation Bible pictures; woodcuts from early Lutheran and Emserian New Testaments. Compilation and commentary by Kenneth A. Strand. [Rev. and enl.] Ann Arbor, Mich., Ann Arbor Publishers [1963] 104 p. 58 illus. (incl. facsims.) 23 cm. Woodcuts by Cranach and Lemberger. Published in 1962 under title: Woodcuts from the earliest Lutheran and Emserian New Testaments. [NE1205.S8A54 1963] 63-14417
1. Bible. N. T. — Pictures, illustrations, etc. 2. Bible. N. T. German, 1522. Luther. 3. Bible. N. T. Low German. 1527. Emser. I. Cranach, Lucas, 1472-1553. II. Lemberger, Georg, 1495?-1540? III. Title.

STRAND, Kenneth Albert, 1927- 769.943
Woodcuts from the earliest Lutheran and Emserian New Testaments. Compilation and commentary by Kenneth A. Strand. Ann Arbor, Mich., Ann Arbor Publishers [1962] 80 p. 33 illus. (incl. facsims.) 23 cm. Woodcuts by Cranach and Lemberger. [NE1205.C7S8] 62-21954
1. Bible. N. T. Pictures, illustrations, etc. 2. Bible. N. T. German. 1522. Luther. 3. Bible. N. T. Low German. 1527. Emser. I. Cranach, Lucas, 1472-1553. II. Lemberger, Georg, 1495?-1540? III. Title.

Bible. N.T.—Pictures, illustrations, etc.—Exhibitions.

NEW Testament 741.9'4'074019454
narratives in master drawings : selected from the collections of the E. B. Crocker Art Gallery : an exhibition and catalogue / cosponsored by the Department of Art, University of California at Davis and the E. B. Crocker Art Gallery of Sacramento ; edited by Seymour Howard. Sacramento : The Gallery, 1976. 47 p. : ill. ; 28 cm. "Largely the work of graduate students in the history of art at the University of California, Davis—the product of a seminar dealing with problems of iconology and connoisseurship in master drawings." [NC15.S3C766] 76-47754
1. Bible. N.T.—Pictures, illustrations, etc.—Exhibitions. 2. Drawing—Exhibitions. I. Howard, Seymour, 1928- II. Crocker Art Gallery, Sacramento, Calif. III. California. University, Davis. Dept. of Art.

Bible. N.T.—Pictures, illustrations, etc.—Juvenile literature.

SHISSLER, Barbara Johnson. 704.948'4
The New Testament in art. Designed by Patricia Koskey. Minneapolis, Lerner Publication Co., 1970. 67 p. illus. (part col.) 27 cm. (Fine art books for young people) Traces the life of Christ from birth to death in famous works of art. [N8030.S5 1970] 70-84411
1. Bible. N.T.—Pictures, illustrations, etc.—Juvenile literature. I. Title. BIP

Bible. N.T. Revelation—Pictures, illustrations, etc.

STRAND, Kenneth Albert, 1927- comp. 769
Woodcuts to the Apocalypse from the early 16th century; pictures from seven sets produced during the 1520s. Compilation and introductions by Kenneth A. Strand. [Ann Arbor, Mich.] Ann Arbor Publishers, 1969. 40 p. (chiefly illus.) 29 cm. Companion vol. to the author's Woodcuts to the Apocalypse in Durer's time. Contents.Contents.—Woodcuts of Lemberger and the 1530 Lufft New Testament (woodcuts 1-47).—Sample woodcuts from Holbein and several other artists (woodcuts 48-67).—Heinrich Vogtherr's woodcuts to the Apocalypse (woodcuts 68-74). [NE1253.S7] 78-11558
1. Bible. N.T. Revelation—Pictures, illustrations, etc. I. Title.

STRAND, Kenneth Albert, 1927- comp. 769'.924
Woodcuts to the Apocalypse in Durer's time; Albrecht Durer's woodcuts plus five other sets from the 15th and 16th centuries. Compilation and introductions by Kenneth A. Strand. [Ann Arbor, Mich.] Ann Arbor Publishers, 1968. 86 p. (chiefly illus.) 29 cm. [NE1205.D9S7] 73-3625 10.00
1. Durer, Albrecht, 1471-1528. Apocalypse. 2. Bible. N.T. Revelation—Pictures, illustrations, etc. I. Title.

Bible—Natural history.

CAMERON, Josephine. 769
Birds of prophecy. Text from the Old Testament. [Portland, Or., Lithographed by Graphic Arts Center, 1970] 1 portfolio (28 col. plates) 27 x 33 cm. Title from portfolio. Each plate has a quotation from the Old Testament. [NE1215.C3] 71-10519 10.00
1. Bible—Natural history. I. Title.

Bible, new Testament-Study and teaching.

KRAAY, Colin M 737.49495
Greek coins, by Colin M. Kraay. Photos. by Max Hirmer. New York, H. N. Abrams [1966] 396 p. maps, plates (part mounted col.) 31 cm. Includes bibliographies. [CJ335.K7] 66-13272 66-90092
1. Bible, new Testament-Study and teaching. I. Hirmer, Max. II. Title.

Bible—Numismatics.

AKERMAN, John Yonge, 1806-1873. 225.87374
Numismatic illustrations of the narrative portions of the New Testament. Chicago, Argonaut, 1966. vii, 62 p. illus. 22 cm. (Argonaut library of antiquities) Bibliographical footnotes. [CJ255.A5 1966] 66-19185
1. Bible—Numismatics. I. Title.

BANKS, Florence (Aiken) 737.4
Coins of Bible days. New York, Macmillan, 1955. 178p. illus. 25cm. [GJ255.B3] 55-13740
1. Bible —Numismatics. I. Title.

MADDEN, Frederic William. 737.49'33
History of Jewish coinage, and of money in the Old and New Testament. Prolegomenon by Michael Avi-Yonah. With 254 woodcuts and a plate of alphabets, by F. W. Fairholt. New York, Ktav Pub. House [1967] lvii, 350 p. illus. 24 cm. (Library of Biblical studies) Includes bibliographical references. [CJ1375.M2 1967b] 66-26486
1. Bible—Numismatics. I. Title. II. Series.

MADDEN, Frederic William. 737.49'33
History of Jewish coinage, and of money in the Old and New Testament, by Frederic W. Madden. With 254 woodcuts, and a plate of alphabets, by F. W. Fairholt. San Diego, Calif., Pegasus Pub. Co. [1967] xii, xi, 350 p. illus. 24 cm. Originally published in 1864, New ed., with Hebrew inscriptions and Reifenberg Ancient Jewish coinage numbers added to illustrations. Bibliographical footnotes. [CJ1375.M2 1967] 67-30146
1. Bible—Numismatics. I. Title.

YEOMAN, Richard S 737.4093
Moneys of the Bible; an illustrated digest of the coinage of Biblical times with Scriptural references. Racine, Wis., Whitman Pub. Co., c1961. 61 p. illus. 20 cm. Includes bibliography. [CJ255.Y4] 61-3238
1. Bible — Numismatics. I. Title.

Bible—Numismatics—Juvenile literature.

CURRIER, Richard L. 737.4'09
Coins of the ancient world / by Ya'akov Meshorer ; retold for young readers by Richard L. Currier. Minneapolis : Lerner Publications Co., 1975, c1974. 94 p. : ill. ; 21 cm. (The Lerner archaeology series) (Digging up the past) Includes index. Discusses the many different kinds of coins found in the Holy Land explaining how they were made and stamped with designs indicating their value and origin. [CJ255.C87 1975] 72-10795 ISBN 0-8225-0835-4 lib.bdg. : 6.95
1. Bible—Numismatics—Juvenile literature. 2. Coins, Ancient—Juvenile literature. I. Meshorer, Ya'akov, 1935- II. Title. BIP

Bible. O. T. Job—Pictures. illustrations. etc.

BLAKE, William, 1757-1827 769.924
Blake's Job; William Blake's Illustrations from the book of Job. Introd. commentary by S. Foster Damon Providence, R.I., Brown Univ. Pr. [c.]1966. ix, 66p. 22 illus. 29cm. The illus. are reprod. from the proof state set in the Harvard Coll. Lib. [NC1115.B72D34] 66-13155 6.00
1. Bible. O. T. Job—Pictures. illustrations. etc. I. Damon, Samuel Foster, 1893- II. Title. III. Title: Illustrations of the book of Job.

BLAKE, William, 1757-1827. 769.924
Blake's Job; William Blake's Illustrations of the book of Job. With an intord. and commentary by S. Foster Damon. Providence, Brown University Press, 1966. ix, 66 p. 22 illus. 29 cm. The illustrations are reproduced from the proof state set in the Harvard College Library. [NC1115.B72D34] 66-13155
1. Bible. O. T. Job — Pictures, illustrations, etc. I. Damon, Samuel Foster, 1893- II. Title. III. Title: Illustrations of the book of Job. BIP

Bible. O.T.—Pictures, illustrations, etc.

CHAGALL, Marc, 1887- 759.7
The Biblical message of Marc Chagall. Pref. by Jean Chatelain. New York, Tudor Pub. Co. [1973] 199 p. illus. (part col.) 33 cm. [ND699.C5A5513] 73-4832 ISBN 0-8148-0568-X 60.00
1. Bible. O.T.—Pictures, illustrations, etc. 2. Bible—Influence. I. Title.

CHAGALL, Marc, 1887- 769.944
Drawings for the Bible. Text by Gaston Bachelard. [Translated from the French by Stuart Gilbert] New York, Harcourt, Brace [1960] unpaged. (96 numbered) plates, (24 unnumbered) col. plates. (Added t.p. in French) 37 cm. 'This double number of Verve contains the drawings made by Chagall in 1958 and 1959 on Biblical themes which in general be [i.e. he] had not dealt wich [i.e. with] in his Illustrations for the Bible reproduced in Verve 33/34. 60-51657 30.00 bds.,
1. Bible. O.T.—Pictures. illustrations. etc. I. Bachelard, Gaston, 1884- II. Title.

HOLBEIN, Hans, the Younger, 1497-1543. 769'.92'4
Images from the Old Testament = Historiarum Veteris Testamenti icones / by Hans Holbein (the Younger). New York : Paddington Press, c1976. p. cm. (Masterpieces of the illustrated book) Reprint of the 1543 ed. published by Trechsel and Frellon, Lyons; with new introd. French and Latin. [NE1150.5.H64A4714 1976] 76-3813 ISBN 0-8467-0147-2 pbk. : 4.95
1. Holbein, Hans, the Younger, 1497-1543. 2. Bible. O.T.—Pictures, illustrations, etc. I. Title. II. Title: Historiarum Veteris Testamenti icones. BIP

JEWISH Theological Seminary of America. Jewish Museum. 704.9484
The Hebrew Bible in Christian, Jewish and Muslim art. [Exhibition] organized by Arthur A. Cohen. Feb. 18 to Mar. 24, 1963. [New York] Jewish Mus. [1963] [52] p. illus. 25cm. Catalog of the exhibition comp. by Ruth Gurin: p. [39]-[50] 63-13092 1.75 pap.,
1. Bible. O. T.—Pictures, illustrations, etc. 2. Christian art and symbolism—Exhibitions. 3. Art, Jewish—Exhibitions. 4. Art, Mohammedan—Exhibitions. I. Cohen, Arthur A. II. Title.

KAYSER, Stephen S 1900- ed. 755.2
The Book of Books in art, a selection of Biblical paintings and sculptures; five centures of Western civilization. New York, Shengold Publishers, 1956. 172p. 70illus. (part col.) 29cm. [N8020.K3] 56-3228
1. Bible. O. T.—Pictures, illustrations, etc. I. Title.

KAYSER, Stephen S 1900- ed. 755.2
The Books of Books in art, a selection of Biblical paintings and sculptures; five centuries of Western civilization. New York, Shengold Publishers, 1956. 172p. 70 illus. (part col.) 29cm. [N8020.K3] 56-3228
1. Bible. O. T.—Pictures, illustrations, etc. I. Title.

LEVEEN, Jacob, 1891- 096'.1
The Hebrew Bible in art / by Jacob Leveen. New York : Hermon Press, [1974] xx, 140 p., [21] leaves of plates : ill. ; 24 cm. Reprint, with a new pref. and addenda and corrigenda by the author, of the 1944 ed. published for the British Academy by H. Milford, Oxford University Press, London, in series: The Schweich lectures of the British Academy, 1939. Includes index. Bibliography: p. [129]-135. [N8023.L47 1974] 74-78239 ISBN 0-87203-045-8 : 12.50
1. Bible. O.T.—Pictures, illustrations, etc. 2. Mural painting and decoration, Jewish. 3. Illumination of books and manuscripts, Jewish. I. Title. II. Series: The Schweich lectures ; 1939. BIP

OLD Testament 755'.4
miniatures: a medieval picture book with 283 paintings from the Creation to the story of David. Introd. and legends by Sydney C. Cockerell. Pref. by John Plummer. New York, G. Braziller [1969] 208 p. col. illus. 40 cm. Reproduction of 46 leaves of an imperfect manuscript of Old Testament illustrations now in the Morgan Library, with additional reproductions of 2 leaves in the Bibliotheque nationale, Paris, and another now in the possession of Dr. and Mrs. Peter Ludwig, Aachen, Germany. Previously published in 1927 for the Roxburghe Club under the title: A Book of Old Testament illustrations of the middle of the thirteenth century. The descriptive pages have been inserted between the plates and pertinent Biblical passages have been supplied. Bibliography: p. 4. [ND3356.B6 1969] 75-82000 50.00
1. Bible. O.T.—Pictures, illustrations, etc. 2. Illumination of books and manuscripts. I. Cockerell, Sydney Carlyle, Sir, 1867-1962. II. Plummer, John. III. Bible. O.T. English, Douai. Selections. 1969.

SHRAMCHENKO, Mykola. 741.973
In the beginning... an interpretation of the Old Testament in art. New York, I. Obolensky [c1962] 95 p. illus. 22 x 29 cm. [NC1075.S55 1 5] 62-18788
1. Bible. O. T.—Pictures, illustrations, etc. I. Title.

Bible O.T.—Pictures, illustrations, etc.—Juvenile literature.

COEN, Rena Neumann. 704.948'4
The Old Testament in art. Designed by Patricia Koskey. Minneapolis, Lerner Publications Co., 1970. 71 p. illus. (part col.) 27 cm. (Fine art books for young

people) Critical descriptions accompany photographic reproductions of paintings and sculpture depicting stories of the Old Testament. [N8020.C57 1970] 77-84410
1. Bible O.T.—Pictures, illustrations, etc.—Juvenile literature. I. Title. BIP

Bible—Pictorial illustrations.

DORE, Gustave, 1832-1883. 741.64
The Bible, illustrated. New York, Pilsbury Publishers [1951] 1 v. (unpaged, chiefly illus.) 31 cm. [N8027.D69] 51-11460
1. Bible—Pictorial illustrations. I. Title.

UNDERWOOD, Paul Atkins, 1902- 745.67
The Fountain of life in manuscripts of the Gospels. Cambridge, Mass., 1950. 30 cm. no. 5. p. [41]-138. illus.) (In Dumharton Oaks papers. Bibliographical footnotes. [N5970.D8] 51-4858
1. Bible — Pictorial illustrations. 2. Ilumination of books and manuscripts. I. Title. II. Series: Dumbarton Oaks papers, no. 5, p. [41]-138

Bible—Pictures, illustrations, etc.

BERKOWITZ, David Sandler, 1913- 016.096
In remembrance of creation; evolution of art and scholarship in the Medieval and Renaissance Bible. Waltham, Mass., Brandeis University Press [1968] xviii, 141, [160] p. illus., facsims. 29 cm. (Publications of the Society of Bibliophiles at Brandeis University, no. 3) "Catalogue of an exhibition to commemorate the twentieth anniversary of Brandeis University held at the Rapaporte Treasure Hall, Brandeis University Library, May 4th through June 11th, 1968." Includes bibliographies. [N8023.B4] 68-28658
1. Bible—Pictures, illustrations, etc. 2. Art, Medieval—Catalogs. 3. Art, Renaissance—Catalogs. I. Title. II. Series: Brandeis University, Waltham, Mass. Society of Bibliophiles. Publications, no. 3 BIP

BIBLE. English. Selections. 1959. Authorized. 755.4
Treasury of Bible masterpieces. Cincinnati, Standard Pub. Co. [1959] 160p. illus. 32cm. [N8020.B48] 59-9857
1. Bible—Pictures, illustrations, etc. I. Title.

BLOM, Dorothea Johnson, 1911- 755'.4
Art responds to the Bible / Dorothea Blom. [Wallingford, Pa.] : Pendle Hill Publications, 1974. 30 p. : ill. ; 19 cm. (Pendle Hill pamphlet ; 197) [N8020.B54] 74-24006 ISBN 0-87574-197-5 : 0.95
1. Bible—Pictures, illustrations, etc. I. Title. BIP

DILLENBERGER, John. 759.13
Benjamin West : the context of his life's work, with particular attention to paintings with religious subject matter, including a correlated version of early nineteenth-century lists of West's paintings, exhibitions, and sales records of his works, and also a current checklist of his major religious works / by John Dillenberger. San Antonio : Trinity University Press, c1977. xvii, 238 p. : ill. ; 29 cm. Includes indexes. Bibliography: p. 217-224. [ND237.W45D54] 76-42004 ISBN 0-911536-65-5 : 25.00
1. West, Benjamin, 1738-1820. 2. Bible—Pictures, illustrations, etc.

DORE, Gustave, 1832-1883. 769'.92'4
The Dore Bible illustrations. With a new introd. by Millicent Rose. New York, Dover Publications [1974] xiii p., 241 p. of illus. 31 cm. [N8027.D82 1974] 73-87048 ISBN 0-486-23079-1. 5.00
1. Dore, Gustave, 1832-1883. 2. Bible—Pictures, illustrations, etc. I. Title. BIP

GUTMANN, Joseph, comp. 704.948
No graven images: studies in art and the Hebrew Bible. New York, Ktav Pub. House [1971] lxiii 599 p. illus. 23 cm. English, German, or French. Includes bibliographical references. [N7416.G8] 70-107000
1. Bible—Pictures, illustrations, etc. 2. Jewish art and symbolism. I. Title.

ISSER'T HOOFT, Willein Adolph, 1900- 755.5
Rembrandt and the Gospel. Philadelphia, Westminster Press [1958?] 192 p. plates. 23 cm. "Translated by K. Gregor Smith from the German, Rembrandt's Weg zum Evangelium [a translation of Rembrandt et la Bible] ... and revised by the author." [ND653.R4V5713] 58-5487
1. Rembrandt Hermanszoon van Rijn, 1606-1669. 2. Bible — Pictures, illustrations, etc. I. Title. BIP

KESSLER, Herbert L., 1941- 745.6'7
The illustrated Bibles from Tours / by Herbert L. Kessler. Princeton, N.J. : Princeton University Press, c1977. p. cm. (Studies in manuscript illumination ; no. 7) Based on the author's thesis, Princeton, 1965. Includes bibliographical references and index. [ND3355.K47] 76-45902 ISBN 0-691-03923-2 : 42.50
1. Bible—Pictures, illustrations, etc. 2. Illumination of books and manuscripts, Carlovingian—France—Tours. 3. Illumination of books and manuscripts—France—Tours. I. Title. II. Series.

KRAUS, Johann Ulrich, 1645-1719. 769'.924
Baroque cartouches for designers and artists; 136 plates from the "Historische Bilder-Bibel" designed and engraved by Johann Ulrich Krauss. With an introd. by Edward A. Maser. New York, Dover Publications [1969] xv p., 136 plates (incl. maps) 21 x 24 cm. (Dover pictorial archive series) The author's Historische Bilder-Bibel was originally published in Augsburg between 1698-1700. Includes bibliographical references. [N8025.K8 1969] 69-16808 ISBN 0-486-22222-5 3.00
1. Bible—Pictures, illustrations, etc. I. Maser, Edward Andrew, 1923- II. Title. BIP

KUP, Karl, 1903- 745.6'7
The Christmas story in medieval and Renaissance manuscripts from the Spencer Collection. [New York] New York Public Library, 1969. [121] p. 55 facsims. 26 cm. (Spencer Publication Fund publication no. 1) [ND3355.K8] 70-98680
1. Bible—Pictures, illustrations, etc. 2. Illumination of books and manuscripts, Medieval—Catalogs. 3. Illumination of books and manuscripts, Renaissance—Catalogs. I. New York (City). Public Library. Spencer Collection. II. Title. III. Series.

LUZWICK, Dierdre. 741.9'73
The surrealist's Bible : a collection of charcoal drawings / by Dierdre Luzwick. Middle Village, N.Y. : Jonathan David, c1976. 118 p. : ill. ; 29 cm. [NC139.L89A58] 75-44001 ISBN 0-8246-0206-4 : 12.95
1. Luzwick, Dierdre. 2. Bible—Pictures, illustrations, etc. 3. Surrealism. I. Title. BIP

MASTERPIECES of Biblical art. 755'.4
St. Paul, Catholic Digest Edition, College of St. Thomas, 1973. xvi, 95 plates of col. illus. 29 cm. [ND1430.M33 1973] 74-176212 ISBN 0-8326-1802-0 14.95
1. Bible—Pictures, illustrations, etc. 2. Paintings—Catalogs.

PICTURES from a mediaeval Bible. 769.484
Commentary by James Strachan. Boston, Beacon [1961,c.1959] 127p. col. illus. 61-10568 3.50 bds.,
1. Bible—Pictures, illustrations, etc. 2. Wood-engravings, German—Cologne. I. Strachan, James, retired inspector of schools.

RAPHAEL, 1483-1520. 759.5
The Raphael Bible [compiled by] Rumer Godden. New York, Viking Press [1970] 248 p. illus. (part col.), geneal. tables, maps, ports. 17 x 25 cm. (A Studio book) Bible passages taken from the Knox translation. Includes bibliographical references. [ND623.R2G58] 70-101783 ISBN 0-670-58943-8 8.95
1. Vatican. Loggie. 2. Bible—Pictures, illustrations, etc. I. Godden, Rumer, 1907- II. Title.

REMBRANDT Harmenszoon van Rijn, 1606-1669. 759.9492
Bible paintings. Text by Seymour Slive. New York, H. N. Abrams [1971] 24 p. illus. (part col.) 33 cm. (The Library of great painters. Portfolio ed.) [ND653.R4S64 1971] 71-130293 ISBN 0-8109-3053-6
1. Bible—Pictures, illustrations, etc. I. Slive, Seymour, 1920- II. Title.

REMBRANDT Harmenszoon van Rijn, 1606-1669. 760'.0924
Rembrandt's drawings and etchings for the Bible [by] Hans-Martin Rotermund. Translated by Shierry M. Weber. Philadelphia, Pilgrim Press [1969] 315 p. illus. 32 cm. Translation of Handzeichnungen und Radierungen zur Bibel. "About the list of plates and the Rembrandt literature": p. 309-310. [NC1055.R4R613] 69-15869 22.50
1. Bible—Pictures, illustrations, etc. I. Rotermund, Hans Martin, ed. II. Title. III. Title: Drawings and etchings for the Bible.

SCHAPIRO, Meyer, 1904- 704.948'4
Words and pictures. On the literal and the symbolic in the illustration of a text. The Hague, Mouton, 1973. 74 p. , 34 p. of photos. 23 cm. (Approaches to semiotics. Paperback series, 11) "The substance of this book was presented at a symposium, 'Language, Symbol, Reality', held at St. Mary's College, Notre Dame, Indiana, on November 7, 1969." Includes bibliographical references. [N8020.S32] 73-176481
1. Bible—Pictures, illustrations, etc. 2. Christian art and symbolism. 3. Artists—Psychology. I. Title. II. Series.
Distributed by Humanities Press, 8.25 (pbk.) BIP

SCHLOSS, Ezekiel 755.4
Scenes from the Bible. Introd. by Alfred Werner. [New York] Ktav [c.1966] [11]p., illus., 25 col. plates (in portfolio) 38cm. [ND237.S432W4] 67-4004 25.00
1. Bible—Pictures, illustrations, etc. I. Werner, Alfred, 1911- II. Title.

STRACHAN, James, retired inspector of schools. 704.9484
Early Bible illustrations; a short study based on some fifteenth and early sixteenth century printed texts. Cambridge [Eng.] University Press, 1957. viii, 169 p. 126 illus. 23 cm. Bibliography: p. 160-161. [N8023.S8] A58
1. Bible — Pictures, illustrations, etc. 2. Illustrated books — 15th and 16th cent. 3. Wood-engravings. I. Title.

VISSER 'T HOOFT, Willem Adolph, 1900- 755
Rembrandt and the Gospel. Translated by K. Gregor Smith from the German text, revised by the author. New York, Meridian Books [1960] 192p. Bibl. notes: p.117-128. illus. 19cm. (Living Age Books, LA30) 1.25 pap.,
1. Rembrandt Hermanszoon van Rijn, 1606-1669. 2. Bibl—Pictures, illustrations, etc. I. Title.

VISSER'T HOOFT, Willem Adolph 1900- 755.5
Rembrandt and the Gospel. [Magnolia, Mass., P. Smith, 1967] 192p. plates. 19cm. (Meridian living age bk. rebound) Tr. by K. Gregor Smith from the German, Rembrandt's Weg zum Evangelium [a tr. of Rembrandt et la Bible] rev. by the author. [ND653.R4V5713] 3.50
1. Rembranot Hermanszoon van Rijn, 1606-1669. 2. Bible—Pictures, illustrations, etc. I. Title.

Bible—Pictures, illustrations, etc.—Exhibitions.

SUTTON, Peter. 760'.09492'07401468
Dutch religious art of the seventeenth century / prepared by Peter Sutton and Otto Naumann. [New Haven] : Yale University Art Gallery, [1975] 21 p. ; 22 cm. Exhibition at the Yale University Art Gallery, Jan. 21-Mar. 16, 1975. Bibliography: p. 14-15. [N6946.S88] 76-350566
1. Bible—Pictures, illustrations, etc.—Exhibitions. 2. Art, Dutch—Exhibitions. 3. Art, Modern—17th-18th centuries—Netherlands—Exhibitions. I. Naumann, Otto, joint author. II. Yale University. Art Gallery. III. Title.

Bible—Pictures, illustrations, etc.—O. T.

CHAGALL, Marc, 1887- 769.2
Illustrations for the Bible. Text by Jean Wahl, with an appreciation by Meyer Schapiro. New York, Harcourt, Brace [1956] 1v. (unpaged) illus. (part col.) 37cm. 'The artist specially composed for the present work 16 lithographs in colors and 12 in black as well as the cover and title page. This book constitutes a double number (33-34) of Verve in the French edition.' [ND699.C5W3] 57-3683
1. Bible—Pictures, illustrations, etc.—O. T. I. Wahl, Jean Andre, 1888- II. Title.

Bible stories, English.

MEYER, Carolyn. 746.4
The needlework book of Bible stories / by Carolyn Meyer ; illustrated by Janet McCaffery. 1st ed. New York : Harcourt Brace Jovanovich, [1975] p. cm. Retells nine familiar Bible stories accompanied by instructions for making relevant projects such as wall hangings, pillows, and stuffed toys. [BS551.2.M39] 75-10135 ISBN 0-15-256793-3 : 6.95
1. Bible stories, English. 2. Bible crafts—Juvenile literature. I. McCaffery, Janet. II. Title. BIP

Bible-Study and teaching.

ADAMS, Alice Dana, 1864- ed. v. 12
4000 questions and answers on the Bible. Philadelphia, Pa., Holman [1963?] 99 p. 17 cm. [NUC64-44915]
1. Bible-Study and teaching. I. Title.

Bibliographical exhibitions.

BLUMENTHAL, Joseph, 1897- 338.7'65'557074
The Spiral Press; an exhibition of selected books and ephemera designed and printed at the Spiral Press in New York from 1926 to 1968. With an introductory commentary by Joseph Blumenthal. [New York, 1968] 38, [31] p. illus. 28 cm. "Shown at the Royal Library of Belgium in Brussels, May-June 1968, and at the Meermanno-Westreenianum Museum in The Hague, September-October 1968." [Z232.S75B55] 68-20133
1. Spiral Press inc., New York. 2. Bibliographical exhibitions. I. Spiral Press, inc., New York. II. Brussels. Bibliotheque royale de Belgique. III. Hague. Museum Meermanno-Westreenianum.

CHICAGO. University. Library. 011
One hundred books and manuscripts recently acquired by the University of Chicago Library : a catalogue of an exhibition held at the Joseph Regenstein Library, spring 1975. [s.l. : s.n., 1975] 100 p. ; 22 cm. [Z121.C54 1975] 75-13963
1. Chicago. University. Library. 2. Bibliographical exhibitions. 3. Manuscripts—Exhibitions. I. Joseph Regenstein Library. II. Title: One hundred books and manuscripts ....

COLUMBIA University. Libraries. 655.1074
Quality in book-production; an exhibition of fine books of all periods selected from the Columbia University Libraries, with special emphasis on the typographic collection. For the Friends of the Columbia Libraries and their guests, Mar. 27, 1952. [New York] Low Memorial Library [1952] 63 p. facsims. 22 cm. "This exhibition was selected and the catalog prepared by Roland Baughman, head of special collections." [Z121.N47 1952] 52-3143
1. Bibliographical exhibitions. I. Title.

GUILD of Book Workers. 655.72074
An exhibition of hand bookbinding, casemaking, restoration, calligraphy & illumination, and hand-decorated papers. 1959- [New York] v. illus. 24cm. [Z121.G8] 59-65252
1. Bibliographical exhibitions. I. Title.

HENRY E. Huntington Library and Art Gallery, San Marino, Calif. 655.125
Great books in great editions, selected and

described by Roland Baughman and Robert O. Schad. San Marino, Calif., 1954. 65p. illus., facsims. 25cm. Based on the library's exhibition catalog published in 1940 under the same title. [Z121.H55] 54-3578
1. Bibliographical exhibitions. I. Baughman, Robland Orvil, 1902- II. Schad, Robert Oliver, 1900- III. Title.

HINDMAN, Sandra, 1944- 091'.074'015251
Pen to press : manuscripts and printed books in the first century of printing / by Sandra Hindman and James Douglas Farquhar. [College Park] : Art Dept., University of Maryland, 1977. p. cm. "An exhibition at the University of Maryland, Art Department Gallery, College Park, Maryland, September 15-October 23, 1977." Sponsored jointly by the Art Dept., University of Maryland and the Dept. of the History of Art, Johns Hopkins University. Includes index. Bibliography: p. [Z121.H6] 77-15026
1. College Park, Md.—Exhibitions. 2. Manuscripts—Exhibitions. 3. Bibliographical exhibitions. 4. Illumination of books and manuscripts—Exhibitions. I. Farquhar, James Douglas, 1941- joint author. II. Maryland. University. Dept. of Art. III. Johns Hopkins University. Dept. of the History of Art. IV. Maryland. University. Art Gallery. V. Title.

INDIANA. University. Lilly Library. 016.09
Printing and the mind of man; an exhibition of the world's most influential books, January 1-April 1, 1964. [Bloomington 1964] folder (6 p.) 1 illus. 28 cm. [Z121.I 45] 65-64262
1. Bibliographical exhibitions. I. Title.

JOHN and Mable Ringling Museum of Art, Sarasota, Fla. Library. 016.7599'4
Rare books of the 16th, 17th and 18th centuries from the Library of the Ringling Museum of Art, Sarasota, Florida. An exhibition prepared by Valentine L. Schmidt and presented by the Ringling Museum November 3-23, 1969. [Sarasota, Fla., 1969] 32 p. illus. 26 cm. [Z121.R54] 75-633858
1. Bibliographical exhibitions. I. Schmidt Valentine Lucille. II. Title.

NEEDHAM, Paul, 1943- 686.2'092'4 B
William Morris and the art of the book : with essays on William Morris, as book collector by Paul Needham, as calligrapher by Joseph Dunlap, and as typographer by John Dreyfus. New York : Pierpont Morgan Library, c1976. 140, cxiv p. : ill. (some col.) ; 30 cm. Includes bibliographical references. [Z232.M87N4] 76-29207 55.00 pbk. : 27.50
1. Morris, William, 1834-1896—Addresses, essays, lectures. 2. Bibliographical exhibitions. I. Dunlap, Joseph Riggs, 1913- joint author. II. Dreyfus, John, joint author. III. Pierpont Morgan Library, New York. IV. Title. BIP

PIERPONT Morgan Library, New York. 686.2'2'07401471
Art of the printed book, 1455-1955; masterpieces of typography through five centuries from the collections of the Pierpont Morgan Library. With an essay by Joseph Blumenthal. New York, 1973. xiv, 192 p. 125 plates. 31 cm. Catalog of an exhibition held at the Pierpont Morgan Library, Sept. 11-Dec. 2, 1973. Bibliography: p. 181-183. [Z121.P58 1973] 73-82830 ISBN 0-87598-041-4
1. Pierpont Morgan Library, New York. 2. Bibliographical exhibitions. I. Blumenthal, Joseph, 1897- II. Title.

SZLADITS, Lola L. 016.09
Owen D. Young, book collector / by Lola L. Szladits ; with an introd. by Josephine Young Case. [New York] : New York Public Library : distributed by Readex Books, 1974. 47 p. : ill. ; 23 cm. Five hundred copies printed. [Z121.S93] 74-83044 ISBN 0-87104-253-3 pbk. : 5.00
1. Young, Owen D., 1874- 2. Bibliographic exhibitions. 3. Manuscripts—Exhibitions. BIP

U.S. Library of Congress. 016.09
Author, artist, and publisher: the creation of notable books. [New Haven] Printed for the American Book Publishers Council at the Printing Office of the Yale University Press [1965] 1 v. (unpaged) illus., facsims. 21 cm. "Catalog of an exhibition at the Library of Congress on the occasion of the Seventeenth Congress of the International Publishers Association to be held in Washington, D.C., May 30 through June 5, 1965." [Z121.U56] 65-60051
1. Bibliographical exhibitions. I. International Publishers Association. II. Title.

WASHINGTON, D.C. Cathedral of St. Peter and St. Paul. Rare book Library. 016.22
In the beginning was the word. Washington, 1965. 71 p. illus., facsims., ports. 28 cm. "Opening exhibition of written and printed Biblical and liturgical texts from the eighth century to the present, May sixteenth to October fifteenth, nineteen hundred and sixty-five." [Z121.W3] 65-24006
1. Bibliographical exhibitions. 2. Bible — Bibl. — Catalogs. I. Title.

Bibliography—Best books—Art.

GOLDMAN, Bernard, 1922- 016.7
Reading and writing in the arts: a handbook. Detroit, Wayne State University Press, 1972. 163 p. 22 cm. [Z5931.G6] 73-165938 ISBN 0-8143-1456-2 4.50
1. Bibliography—Best books—Art. 2. Art—Bibliography. I. Title.

GOLDMAN, Bernard, 1922- 016.7
Reading and writing in the arts : a handbook / Bernard Goldman. Rev. ed. Detroit : Wayne State University Press, 1978. 191 p. ; 23 cm. (Wayne books ; WB45) Includes index. [Z5931.G6 1978] [N7425] 77-27856 ISBN 0-8143-1604-2 : 10.95
1. Bibliography—Best books—Art. 2. Art—Bibliography. I. Title.

Bibliography—Bibliography—Art.

BESTERMAN, Theodore, 1904- 016.0167
Art and architecture; a bibliography of bibliographies. Totowa, N.J., Rowman and Littlefield, 1971. 216 p. 20 cm. (His The Besterman world bibliographies) [Z5931.B45 1971] 74-29568 ISBN 0-87471-045-6 10.00
1. Bibliography—Bibliography—Art. I. Title.

Bibliography—Bibliography—Book industries and trade.

BESTERMAN, Theodore, 1904- 016.011
Printing, book collecting, and illustrated books; a bibliography of bibliographies. Totowa, N.J., Rowman and Littlefield, 1971. 2 v. (609 p.) 20 cm. (His The Besterman world bibliographies) [Z117.B54 1971] 70-29686 ISBN 0-87471-042-1 30.00
1. Bibliography—Bibliography—Book industries and trade. I. Title.

Bibliography—Bibliography—Incunabula.

BERKOWITZ, David Sandler, 1913- 016.016093
Bibliotheca bibliographica incunabula; a manual of bibliographical guides to inventories of printing, of holdings, and of reference aids. With an appendix of useful information on place-names and dating, collected and classified for the use of researchers in incunabulistics. Waltham, Mass., 1967. vi, 336 l. 29 cm. [Z240.A1B4] 68-1209
1. Bibliography—Bibliography—Incunabula. I. Title.

PEDDIE, Robert Alexander, 1869-1951. 016.016'.093
Fifteenth-century books: a guide to their identification. With a list of the Latin names of towns and an extensive bibliography of the subject. New York, B. Franklin [1969] 89 p. 20 cm. (Burt Franklin bibliography and reference series, 294) "Originally published: 1913." [Z240.A1P4 1969] 73-101990
1. Bibliography—Bibliography—Incunabula. 2. Printing—History—Bibliography. I. Title. BIP

Bibliography—Bibliography—U.S.

TANSELLE, George Thomas, 1934- 016.015'73
Guide to the study of United States imprints [by] G. Thomas Tanselle. Cambridge, Mass., Belknap Press of Harvard University Press, 1971. 2 v. (lxiv, 1050 p.) front. 26 cm. "Appendix: A basic collection of two hundred and fifty titles on United States printing and publishing": p. 897-906. [Z1215.A2T35] 79-143232 ISBN 0-674-36761-8
1. Bibliography—Bibliography—U.S. I. Title.

Bibliography—Microscopic and miniature editions—Specimens.

THE Babees book, 099
being a concatenation of the ABC's of Aristotle & the drawings of Kate Greenaway, with a sampling of types from the Rob Run Press, Okemos, Michigan. [Okemos, Rob Run Press, 1971] [35] p. illus. 50 mm. Issued in a portfolio (13 x 17 cm.) Caption title: The ABC of Aristotle. Text selected from F. J. Furnivall's The babees book, 1868. "About one hundred copies printed & bound by hand." [Z116.A4B17] 73-29313
1. Bibliography—Microscopic and miniature editions—Specimens. I. Greenaway, Kate, 1846-1901, illus. II. Title: The ABC of Aristotle.

COMBS, Tram, 1924- 811'.5'4
Briefs; poems. With illus. by D. Clark. Franklin, N.H., Hillside Press, 1966. 80 p. illus. 60 mm. "425 copies ... number 72." [PS3553. 48B7] 67-4139
1. Bibliography—Microscopic and miniature editions—Specimens. I. Title.

LINCOLN, Abraham, Pres. U.S., 1809-1865. 973'.074'016971
Maxims, observations and comments. Chronologically arranged. Chicago, Black Cat Press [196-?] 62 p. port. 63 mm. [E457.99.L52] 68-3696
1. Bibliography—Microscopic and miniature editions—Specimens. I. Title.

Bibliography, National—American.

ROGERS, Joseph William, 1906- 015.73
U.S. national bibliography and the copyright law; an historical study. Foreword by Verner W. Clapp. New York, Bowker, 1960. xii, 115 p. 23 cm. Bibliographical references included in "Notes" (p. 97-107) [Z1216.R6] 60-15545
1. U.S. Copyright Office. Catalog of copyright entries. 2. Bibliography, National—American. I. Title.

Bibliography—Rare books—Exhibitions.

NEW York (City). Public Library. Rare Book Division. 016.09
The imprint catalog in the Rare Book Division. Boston : G. K. Hall, 1979. 10 v. ; 36 cm. At head of title: The New York Public Library, the Research Libraries. [Z1029.N48 1979] 79-101770 ISBN 0-8161-0092-6(21 volumes.). : 1848.00
1. Bibliography—Rare books—Catalogs. 2. Catalogs, Imprint. I. New York (City). Public Library. Research Libraries. II. Title.

UKRAINIAN incunabula, 016.91477'1
manuscripts, early printed and rare books. [Cambridge] Houghton Library, 1970. [8] p., 39 p. of facsims. 24 cm. [Z2514.U5U366] 79-31639
1. Bibliography—Rare books—Exhibitions. 2. Incunabula—Exhibitions. 3. Manuscripts, Ukrainian—Exhibitions. I. Harvard University. Library. Houghton Library.

Bick, Esther S.—Art collections.

DARTMOUTH College. Hopkins Center. Art Galleries. 741.9'45
Italian drawings; selections from the Collection of Esther and Malcolm W. Bick; [exhibition. Edited by Franklin W. Robinson and John T. Paoletti] Hanover, N.H., 1971. 1 v. (unpaged) illus. 25 cm. Includes bibliographies. [NC255.D28 1971] 74-157102
1. Bick, Esther S.—Art collections. 2. Bick, Malcolm W.—Art collections. 3. Drawings, Italian—Exhibitions. I. Robinson, Franklin Westcott, ed. II. Paoletti, John T., ed. III. Title.

Bick, Malcolm W.—Art collections.

JOHN and Mable Ringling Museum of Art, Sarasota, Fla. 741.9'45'074015961
The Bick Collection of Italian religious drawings. [Exhibition] John & Mable Ringling Museum of Art. [Sarasota] 1970. 1 v. (unpaged) illus. 23 cm. [NC255.J6] 72-635854
1. Bick, Malcolm W.—Art collections. 2. Drawings, Italian—Exhibitions. I. Title.

Bickford, George P.—Art collections.

CZUMA, Stanislaw. 709'.54'074017132
Indian art from the George P. Bickford Collection : catalog / by Stanislaw Czuma ; introd. by W. G. Archer. Cleveland : Cleveland Museum of Art, [1975] ix, 125 p. : ill. (some col.) ; 24 cm. Exhibition held Jan. 14-Feb. 16, 1975 at the Cleveland Museum of Art and through Feb. 13, 1977 at various other museums. [N7301.C98] 74-29377
1. Bickford, George P.—Art collections. 2. Art, Indic—Exhibitions. I. Cleveland Museum of Art. II. Title.

Bicycles and tricycles in art.

GOREY, Edward St. John. 741.9'73
The broken spoke / Edward Gorey. New York : Dodd, Mead, c1976. [30] leaves of plates : chiefly ill. ; 14 x 20 cm. [NC1879.G67A43] 76-13327 ISBN 0-396-07375-1 : 6.95
1. Gorey, Edward St. John. 2. Bicycles and tricycles in art. I. Title. BIP

Bicycles and tricycles—Posters.

RENNERT, Jack. 769'.4'96292272
100 years of bicycle posters. [1st ed.] New York, Harper & Row [1973] 112 p. illus. (part col.) 41 cm. "A Darien House book." [HF6161.B5R46 1973] 73-4118 ISBN 0-06-013533-6 6.95
1. Bicycles and tricycles—Posters. 2. Advertising—Bicycle industry. I. Title. II. Title: Bicycle posters.

Bidwell, Raymond Austin, 1876-1954—Art collections.

SPRINGFIELD, Mass. Museum of Fine Arts. 739*.5*12
The Raymond A. Bidwell Collection of Chinese bronzes and ceramics. Springfield, Mass., Published by the Raymond A. and Bertha U. Bidwell Fund for the Museum of Fine Arts, 1965. 85 p. illus. 29 cm. [NK7983.A1S67] 72-196643
1. Bidwell, Raymond Austin, 1876-1954—Art collections. 2. Bronzes, Chinese—Catalogs. 3. Pottery, Chinese—Catalogs. 4. Porcelain, Chinese—Catalogs. I. Title.

Biehn, Betty.

RIDGE Press, inc., New York. 778.921
The model; a portrait of beauty by ten master photographers. [Prepared and produced by the Ridge Press. New York, Distributed by Pocket Books, 1959, c1958] 112p. illus. 28cm. [TR675.R5] 58-14477
1. Biehn, Betty. 2. Photography of the nude. I. Title.

Bierstadt, Albert, 1830-1902.

BIERSTADT, Albert, 1830-1902 759.13
Albert Bierstadt, 1830-1902 : [exhibition], September 15-October 10, 1972 / Gordon Hendricks New York : M. Knoedler, [1972] 26 p. : ill. (some col.) ; 22 cm.

Includes index. [ND237.B585H415] 75-316284
1. Bierstadt, Albert, 1830-1902. 2. Landscape in art. I. Hendricks, Gordon. II. Knoedler (M.) and Company, inc.

HENDRICKS, Gordon. 759.13
ABierstadt; an essay and catalogue to accompany a retrospective exhibition of the work of Albert Bierstadt. Fort Worth, Amon Carter Museum [1972] 48 p. illus. (part col.) 22 cm. Exhibition presented at Amon Carter Museum, Fort Worth, Texas, Jan. 27-Mar. 19, 1972, and elsewhere. Includes bibliographical references. [ND237.B585H4] 70-184170
1. Bierstadt, Albert, 1830-1902. 2. Landscape in art. I. Amon Carter Museum of Western Art, Fort Worth, Tex.

HENDRICKS, Gordon. 759.13
Albert Bierstadt: painter of the American West. [Text by] Gordon Hendricks. New York, H. N. Abrams [1974] 360 p. illus. (part col.) 28 cm. Published in association with the Amon Carter Museum of Western Art. Bibliography: p. 353-354. [ND237.B585H42] 73-14954 ISBN 0-8109-0151-X
1. Bierstadt, Albert, 1830-1902. 2. United States in art. 3. Landscape in art. I. Amon Carter Museum of Western Art, Fort Worth, Tex.

Bietry-Salinger, Jehanne.

CASCELLA, Michele, 1892- 759.5
Michele Cascella. Text by Jehanne Salinger. New York, Ungar [1966, c.1965] 56, [68]p. illus. (pt. mounted col.) port. 34cm. Bibl. [ND623.C439B5] 65-19173 25.00
1. Bietry-Salinger, Jehanne. I. Title.

Big Bean site, Ill.

DENNY, Sidney G. 081 s
Rend Lake archaeology, 1967 and 1968 seasons, by Sidney G. Denny. Carbondale, University Museum, Southern Illinois University [1970] iv, 83 l. illus. 28 cm. (Research records of the University Museum. Southern Illinois studies, no. 4) "Carried out under the auspices of the U.S. Department of Interior, National Park Service, Northeast Region, contract numbers 14-10-5-950-4 and 14-10-950-18." Bibliography: leaves 82-83. [HC107.I3S64 no. 4] [E78.I3] 917.73'993 77-633364
1. Big Bean site, Ill. 2. Brown Swamp site, Ill. 3. Rend Lake—Antiquities. I. Title. II. Series: Southern Illinois studies, no. 4.

Big Horn Basin—Antiquities.

HUSTED, Wilfred M. 970.4'87'33
Bighorn Canyon archeology, by Wilfred M. Husted. Lincoln, Neb., 1969. v, 138 p. illus., maps. 25 cm. (River Basin Surveys. Publications in salvage archeology, no. 12) Bibliography: p. 101-104. [F737.B5H8] 75-601738
1. Big Horn Basin—Antiquities. I. Title. II. Series.

Big Horn Co., Mont.—Antiquities.

FREDLUND, Lynn B. 917.86'38
[Missoula, University of Montana Statewide Archaeological Survey] 1974. ix, 55 p. illus. 28 cm. "Special report from the University of Montana Statewide Archaeological Survey." "Submitted to Westmoreland Resources." Bibliography: p. 45-48. [F737.B5F73] 74-159879
1. Big Horn Co., Mont.—Antiquities. 2. Excavations (Archaeology)—Montana—Big Horn Co. I. Fredlund, Dale E., joint author. II. Westmoreland Resources (Firm) III. Montana. University, Missoula. Statewide Archaeological Survey. IV. Title.

Big Thicket, Tex.—Description and travel—Views.

FRARY, Michael, 1918- 917.64'14
Impressions of the Big Thicket. Paintings by Michael Frary. Text by William A. Owens. Foreword by John Palmer Leeper. Austin, University of Texas Press [1973] 112 p. illus. (part col.) 31 cm. (Blaffer series of southwestern art, no. 4) [ND1839.F69O83] 73-1674 ISBN 0-292-70706-1 17.50
1. Big Thicket, Tex.—Description and travel—Views. I. Owens, William A., 1905- II. Title. III. Series. BIP

Biggers, John Thomas, 1924—

BIGGERS, John Thomas, 1924- 707'.11'7641411
Black art in Houston : the Texas Southern University experience : presenting the art of Biggers, Simms and their students / by John Biggers and Carroll Sims, with John Edward Weems ; introd. by Donald Weismann. 1st ed. College Station : Texas A & M University Press, c1978. 106 p. : ill. (some col.) ; 29 cm. [N6538.N5B52] 77-99276 ISBN 0-89096-046-1 : 20.00
1. Biggers, John Thomas, 1924- 2. Simms, Carroll, 1924- 3. Texas. Southern University, Houston. School of Arts and Sciences. 4. Art in Afro-American universities and colleges—Texas—Houston. I. Simms, Carroll, 1924- joint author. II. Weems, John Edward, joint author. III. Title. BIP

Bill, Max, 1908—

BILL, Max, 1908- 709'.2'4
Max Bill / [contribution by] Eduard Huttinger. New York : Rizzoli, 1978. 225 p. : ill. (some col.) ; 29 cm. Translation of Max Bill. "Based on the catalogue of the travelling exhibition mounted in the United States by the Albright-Knox Art Gallery." Bibliography: p. 215-222. [N7153.B5A413 1978] 77-88612 ISBN 0-8478-0153-5 : 35.00
1. Bill, Max, 1908- I. Huttinger, Eduard. II. Albright-Knox Art Gallery.

BILL, Max, 1908- 709'.2'4
Max Bill : [catalogue / compiled and edited by Max Bill and James N. Wood]. Buffalo, N.Y. : Buffalo Fine Arts Academy, [1974] 198 p. : ill. (some col.) ; 28 cm. Issued in conjunction with the exhibition held Sept. 28-Nov. 17, 1974 at the Albright-Knox Art Gallery, Buffalo, N.Y., Dec. 17, 1974 to Feb. 16, 1975 at the Los Angeles County Museum of Art, and Mar. 4-Apr. 20, 1975 at the San Francisco Museum of Art. Bibliography: p. 191-193. [N7153.B5W66] 74-81593 ISBN 0-914782-01-0 pbk. : 10.00
1. Bill, Max, 1908- I. Wood, James N. II. Albright-Knox Art Gallery. III. Los Angeles Co., Calif. Museum of Art, Los Angeles. IV. San Francisco. Museum of Art.

Billboards—United States.

BLAKE, Peter, 1920- 711
God's own junkyard; the planned deterioration of America's landscape. [1st ed.] New York, Holt, Rinehart and Winston [1964] 143 p. illus. 27 cm. [HF5843.5.B55] 63-22178
1. Billboards—United States. 2. Natural monuments—United States. I. Title. BIP

Billingsley, William, 1758-1828.

JOHN, William David, 1898- 738.2'0924
William Billingsley (1758-1828): his outstanding achievements as an artist and porcelain maker, by W.D. John assisted by Anne Simcox and Jacqueline Simcox; an illustrated appendix by Sir Leslie Joseph on the identification of William Billingsley's painting on Swansea porcelain Newport, Ceramic Book Co., 1968. xvi, 97 p. 74 plates, 180 illus. (40 col.), map. 32 cm. [NK4210.B47J6] 72-400311 12/12-
1. Billingsley, William, 1758-1828. I. Simcox, Anne. II. Simcox, Jacqueline.

Bimson, Walter Reed, 1892- —Art collections.

THE West and 709'.73'074019173
Walter Bimson; paintings, watercolors, drawings, and sculpture collected by Mr. Walter Reed Bimson. Tucson, University of Arizona Museum of Art [1971] 223 p. (chiefly illus., part col.) 32 cm. [N6505.W4] 78-634896 15.00
1. Bimson, Walter Reed, 1892- —Art collections. 2. Art, American—Catalogs. 3. The West in art. I. Arizona. University. Museum of Art.

Binder, Joseph, 1898-1972.

BINDER, Joseph, 1898-1972. 760'.092'4 B
Joseph Binder : an artist and a lifestyle : from the Joseph Binder Collection of posters, graphic and fine art, notes, and records / [compiled by Carla Binder]. 1st ed. Vienna : A. Schroll, 1976. 143 p. : ill. (some col.) ; 25 cm. [NC1850.B48B558] 77-366012 ISBN 3-7031-0437-6. ISBN 3-7031-0436-8 pbk.
1. Binder, Joseph, 1898-1972. I. Binder, Carla. II. Title.

Bing, Ilse.

BING, Ilse. 741.9'43
Numbers in images : illuminations of numerical meanings / by Ilse Bing. 1st ed. New York : Ilkon Press, 1976. [171] p. : ill. ; 24 x 32 cm. [NC251.B53A52] 76-5739 ISBN 0-916832-00-7 : 9.95
*1. Bing, Ilse. 2. Numbers in art. I. Title.*BIP

BING, Ilse. 741.9'43
Words as visions; logograms. Worte als Visionen. Mots comme visions. [1st ed.] New York, Drigh-Graph, inc. [1974] 1 v. (chiefly illus.) 22 x 28 cm. [NC251.B53A57] 73-90744 8.95
1. Bing, Ilse. 2. Words in art. I. Title.
Publisher's address: 75 E., 55 St., N.Y. 10019. BIP

Bingham, George Caleb, 1811-1879.

BINGHAM, George Caleb, 1811-1879. 759.13
Bingham's Missouri. [Saint Louis : Bingham Sketches, inc., c1975] [56] p. : ill. (some col.) ; 23 x 27 cm. Cover title. Catalogue and text by George McCue. Catalogue of an exhibition held Sept. 26, 1975-Apr. 11, 1976, in Kansas City, Mo., at the Nelson Gallery—Atkins Museum and other museums. Bibliography: p. [56] [ND237.B587M32] 75-332334
1. Bingham, George Caleb, 1811-1879. 2. Missouri in art. I. McCue, George. II. William Rockhill Nelson Gallery and Mary Atkins Museum of Fine Arts, Kansas City, Mo. III. Title.

BLOCH, E. Maurice. 759.13
The drawings of George Caleb Bingham, with a catalogue raisonne / E. Maurice Bloch. Columbia : University of Missouri Press, [1975] p. cm. Includes index. Bibliography: p. [ND237.B59B38] 75-15613 ISBN 0-8262-0180-6 : 45.00
1. Bingham, George Caleb, 1811-1879. I. Bingham, George Caleb, 1811-1879. II. Title.

BLOCH, E. Maurice. 759.13
George Caleb Bingham, by E. Maurice Bloch. Berkeley, Univ. of Calif. Pr., 1967. 2v. illus. (pt. col.), ports. (pt. col.) 28cm. (Calif. studies in the hist. of art, 7) Bibl. [ND237.B59B4] 65-10714 45.00 set,
I. Bingham, George Caleb, 1811-1879. II. Title. III. Series.

BLOCH, E. Maurice. 759.13
George Caleb Bingham, 1811-1879. Washington, Published for the National Collection of Fine Arts by Smithsonian Institution Press [1967] v, 99 p. illus. 22 cm. (Smithsonian publication 4725) Catalog of the exhibition held in the National Collection of Fine Arts, Smithsonian Institution, Oct. 19, 1967-Jan. 1, 1968, in the Cleveland Museum of Art, Jan. 24-Mar. 10, 1968, and in the Art Galleries, University of California at Los Angeles, Apr. 7-May 19, 1968. "The catalog of paintings and drawings and the chronology ... are derived from the ... books by E. Maurice Bloch: George Caleb Bingham: The evolution of an artist, and ... Catalogue raisonne." Bibliography: p. 97-99. [ND237.B59B43] 67-62923
1. Bingham, George Caleb, 1811-1879. I. Smithsonian Institution. National Collection of Fine Arts. II. Cleveland Museum of Art. III. California. University. University at Los Angeles. Art Galleries.

CHRIST-JANER, Albert, 1910- 759.13
George Caleb Bingham; frontier painter of Missouri. New York, H. N. Abrams [1975] 180 p. illus. (part col.) 28 x 30 cm. Bibliography: p. 175-[177] [ND237.B59C49] 74-2303 ISBN 0-8109-0220-6
1. Bingham, George Caleb, 1811-1879. BIP

CONSTANT, Alberta Wilson. 759.13
Paintbox on the frontier: the life and times of George Caleb Bingham. New York, Crowell [1974] x, 193 p. illus. (part col.) 26 cm. Bibliography: p. [185]-186. [ND237.B59C66] 73-6954 ISBN 0-690-60844-6 7.50
1. Bingham, George Caleb, 1811-1879. I. Title. BIP

FOUR American 759.13'074'01471
painters: George Caleb Bingham, with texts by Meyric C. Rogers, James B. Musick, and Arthur Pope. Winslow Homer, Albert P. Ryder, Thomas Eakins, with texts by Frank Jewett Mather, Jr., Bryson Burroughs, and Lloyd Goodrich. Reprint ed. [New York] Published for the Museum of Modern Art by Arno Press, 1969. 20, 31, [43] p. of illus. 28 cm. The two exhibition catalogs were originally published separately, 1930-1935. [ND236.F6] 72-86438
1. Bingham, George Caleb, 1811-1879. 2. Homer, Winslow, 1836-1910. 3. Ryder, Albert Pinkham, 1847-1917. 4. Eakins, Thomas, 1844-1916. I. New York (City). Museum of Modern Art. George Caleb Bingham, the Missouri artist, 1811-1879. 1969. II. New York (City). Museum of Modern Art. Winslow Homer, Albert P. Ryder, Thomas Eakins. 1969.

LARKIN, Lew, 1918- 759.13
Bingham: fighting artist; the story of Missouri's immortal painter, patriot, soldier, and statesman. Point Lookout, Mo., S of O Press, Book Division [1971] 358 p. illus., ports. 21 cm. [ND237.B59L3 1971] 77-29322
1. Bingham, George Caleb, 1811-1879. I. Title.

LARKIN, Lew, 1918- 927.5
Bingham: fighting artist; the story of Missourl's immortal painter, patriot, soldier, and statesman. Illus. from photos. of the original paintings. Kansas City, Mo., Burton Pub. Co. [1954] 358p. illus. 22cm. [ND237.B59L3] 55-19715
1. Bingham, George Caleb, 1811-1879. I. Title.

MCDERMOTT, John Francis, 1902- 759.13
George Caleb Bingham, river portraitist. Norman, University of Oklahoma Press [1959] xxviii, 454p. illus. 27cm. Bibliography: p. 438-446. [ND237.B59M3] 59-13474
1. Bingham, George Caleb, 1811-1879. I. Title.

Binghamton Commission on Architecture and Urban Design.

MALO, Paul. 352'.96'0974776
The Binghamton Commission on Architecture and Urban Design; the first three years: 1964-1967. Prepared for the Commission by Paul Malo. Binghamton, N.Y., 1968. 84 p. 28 cm. Bibliographical references included in "Footnotes" (p. 57-60) [NA9000.B53M3] 68-64328
1. Binghamton Commission on Architecture and Urban Design.

Binney, Edwin—Art collections.

BINNEY, Edwin. 759.954
Indian miniature painting from the Collection of Edwin Binney, 3rd. An exhibition at the Portland Art Museum, Dec. 2, 1973—Jan. 20, 1974. Catalogue and text by Edwin Binney, 3rd. Portland, Or., Portland Art Museum [1974- c1973 v. illus. 20 x 22 cm. Contents.Contents.—1. The Mughal and Deccani schools. Bibliography: v. 1, p. 198-202. [ND1337.I5B56] 74-170338
1. Binney, Edwin—Art collections. 2. Miniature painting, Indic—Exhibitions. 3. Illumination of books and manuscripts, Indic—Exhibitions. I. Portland, Or. Art Museum. II. Title.

BINNEY, Edwin. 745.6'7'0954s
Indian miniature painting from the Collection of Edwin Binney 3rd : an exhibition at the Portland Art Museum, December 2, 1973-January 20, 1974 : catalogue and text / by Edwin Binney 3rd. Portland, Or. : The Museum, 1974-c1973- v. : ill. (some col.) ; 20 x 22 cm. Contents.Contents.—1. The Mughal and Deccani schools with some related Sultanate material. Bibliography: v. 1, p. 198-202. [ND3247.B5] 75-322917
1. Binney, Edwin—Art collections. 2. Illumination of books and manuscripts, Indic—Exhibitions. 3. Miniature painting, Indic—Exhibitions. I. Portland, Or. Art Museum. II. Title.

BINNEY, Edwin. 016.091
Persian and Indian miniatures: from the Collection of Edwin Binney, 3rd. [Text and catalog by Edwin Binney, 3rd.] Exhibited at the Portland Art Museum Sept. 28-Nov. 29, 1962. [Portland, Ore., Portland Art Association, 1962] 47 p. illus. (part. col.) 20 cm. [ND3241.B49] 74-159780
1. Binney, Edwin—Art collections. 2. Illumination of books and manuscripts, Iranian—Exhibitions. 3. Illumination of books and manuscripts, Indic—Exhibitions. 4. Miniature painting, Iranian—Exhibitions. 5. Miniature painting, Indic—Exhibitions. I. Portland, Or. Art Museum. II. Title.

BINNEY, Edwin. 745.6'7'09561
Turkish miniature paintings and manuscripts from the collection of Edwin Binney, 3rd, by Edwin Binney, 3rd. [New York] The Metropolitan Museum of Art [1973] 139 p. illus. 22 cm. Catalog of an exhibition held in the Metropolitan Museum of Art, New York and the Los Angeles County Museum of Art. Bibliography: p. 135-137. [ND3211.B56] 73-11016 ISBN 0-87099-077-2 4.95 (pbk.).
1. Binney, Edwin—Art collections. 2. Illumination of books and manuscripts, Turkish—Exhibitions. 3. Miniature painting, Turkish—Exhibitions. I. New York (City). Metropolitan Museum of Art. II. Los Angeles Co., Calif. Museum of Art, Los Angeles. III. Title.

SMITHSONIAN 709'.17'671
Institution. Traveling Exhibition Service.
Islamic art from the Collection of Edwin Binney 3rd. Circulated by the Smithsonian Institute Traveling Exhibition Service, 1966-1968 [Washington, 1966. 1 v. (unpaged) illus. (part col.) 23 cm. (Smithsonian publication 4682) Includes bibliography. [N6263.W3S58] 72-178981
1. Binney, Edwin—Art collections. 2. Art, Islamic—Exhibitions. I. Title.

Biography—19th century—Caricatures and cartoons—Catalogs.

LONDON. 741.5'942'07402132
National Portrait Gallery.
Catalogue of original Vanity fair cartoons in the National Portrait Gallery / by Richard Ormond. London : The Gallery, 1976. 20 p. ; 21 cm. Cover title: Original Vanity fair cartoons in the National Portrait Gallery. Published to coincide with the Vanity fair exhibition, held at the National Portrait Gallery, July to Aug., 1976. Includes index. [NC1478.V36L66 1976] 77-369105 ISBN 0-904017-09-5 : £0.10
1. Vanity fair. 2. Biography—19th century—Caricatures and cartoons—Catalogs. I. Ormond, Richard. II. Title. III. Title: Original Vanity fair cartoons in the National Portrait Gallery.

Biography—19th century—Portraits—Caricatures and cartoons.

SAVORY, Jerold. 741.5'942
The Vanity fair gallery : a collector's guide to the caricatures / Jerold J. Savory, with Michael Broome ... [et al.]. South Brunswick, [N.J.] : A. S. Barnes, c1978. p. cm. Bibliography: p. [NC1478.V36S38] 78-353 ISBN 0-498-02240-4 : 30.00
1. Biography—19th century—Portraits—Caricatures and cartoons. 2. English wit and humor, Pictorial. 3. Caricatures and cartoons—Collectors and collecting. I. Vanity fair (London) II. Title. **BIP**

Biography—Caricatures and cartoons.

HEINONEN, Kai. 741.5'9471
Let's face it: Kai Heinonen's world. [1st ed.] New York, Phaedra [1971] 216 p. illus. 26 cm. [NC1670.H4A5] 70-156218 12.50
1. Biography—Caricatures and cartoons. I. Title.

Biological illustration.

BETHKE, Emil G. 744.4'2
Basic drawing for biology students, by Emil G. Bethke. Springfield, Ill., Thomas [1969] xii, 86 p. illus. 26 cm. (American lecture series, publication no. 746. A monograph in American lectures in medical illustration) [QH318.B4] 69-12978
1. Biological illustration. 2. Drawing—Scientific applications. I. Title. **BIP**

ZWEIFEL, Frances W 744.42
A handbook of biological illustration. [Chicago] University of Chicago Press [1961] xv, 131 p. illus., diagrs. 21 cm. (Phoenix science series, PSS510) Includes bibliographical references. [QH318.Z97] 61-19734
1. Biological illustration. 2. Photography—Scientific applications. I. Title. **BIP**

Biological specimens—Collection and preservation.

KNUDSEN, Jens W. 579
Biological techniques; collecting, preserving, and illustrating plants and animals [by] Jens W. Knudsen. New York, Harper & Row [1966] xi, 525 p. illus. 24 cm. Includes bibliographies. [QH318.5.K6] 66-10839
1. Biological specimens—Collection and preservation. I. Title.

Biology in art.

RITTERBUSH, Philip C. 701.8
The art of organic forms [by] Philip C. Ritterbush. Washington, Smithsonian Institution Press [1968] v, 149 p. illus. (part col.) 27 cm. (Smithsonian publication 4740) Published in conjunction with an exhibition held at the Museum of Natural History, Washington, June 15-July 31, 1968. "A catalogue of the exhibit, prepared by Diana Hamilton": p. [95]-[131] Bibliography: p. [133]-139. [N72.B5R5] 68-31365 10.00
1. Biology in art. 2. Form (Aesthetics) 3. Art, Modern—20th century—Exhibitions. I. United States. Museum of Natural History. II. Title. **BIP**

Biology-laboratory manuals.

BEAVER, William Carl, 1896- v. 12
Workbook and laboratory manual in general biology. By William C. Beaver and George B. Noland. St. Louis, Mosby [1966] 1 v. [NUC68-48990]
1. Biology-laboratory manuals. I. Noland, George B. II. Title.

Bird-houses.

BRANN, Donald R. 690'.8'9
How to build birdhouses and a bird feeder, by Donald R. Brann. Briarcliff Manor, N.Y., Directions Simplified [1968] c1967. 49 p. illus., plans. 23 cm. (Easi-bild simplified directions, 669) Published in 1975 under title: How to build birdhouses and bird feeders. [QL676.5.B7] 67-14311 1.00
1. Bird-houses. 2. Bird feeders. I. Title. II. Title: Birdhouses and a bird feeder.

BRANN, Donald R. 639'.97'82
How to build birdhouses and bird feeders / by Donald R. Brann. Rev. ed. Briarcliff Manor, N.Y. : Directions Simplified, 1975. 66 p. : ill. ; 23 cm. (Easi-bild ; 669) Published in 1967 under title : How to build birdhouses and a bird feeder. [QL676.5.B7 1975] 75-323068 1.50
1. Bird-houses. 2. Bird feeders. I. Title.

PERRY, L. Day, 1887- 598.2
Bird houses, by L. Day Perry and Frank Slepicka. Peoria, Ill., C. A. Bennett Co.

[1955] 96 p. illus. 25 cm. [QL676.5.P46] 55-586
1. Bird-houses. I. Slepicka, Frank, 1907- joint author.

RUSSO, Monica. 690'.8'9
The complete book of birdhouses & feeders / by Monica Russo & Robert Dewire. New York : Drake Publishers, 1976. 128 p. : ill. ; 28 cm. Bibliography: p. 124-125. [QL676.5.R87] 75-36155 ISBN 0-8473-1156-2 pbk. : 4.95
1. Bird-houses. 2. Bird feeders. 3. Birds—United States. I. Dewire, Robert, joint author. II. Title. **BIP**

SCHUTZ, Walter E. 598.2
How to build birdhouses and feeders, and how to attract birds to your garden. Milwaukee, Bruce [1955] 134 p. illus. 24 cm. [QL676.5.S35] 55-8805
1. Bird-houses. I. Title.

SIBLEY, Hi, 1883- 598.2
72 new bird houses, feeders you can make. Chicago, Goodheart-Willcox co. [1957] 80p. (chiefly illus.) 29cm. [QL676.5.S47] 57-4411
1. Bird-houses. I. Title.

Bird-houses—Design and construction.

MCNEIL, Don. 690'.8'9
The birdhouse book : building houses, feeders, and baths / by Don McNeil. Seattle : Pacific Search Press, c1979. p. cm. Bibliography: p. [QL676.5.M332] 79-254 ISBN 0-914718-36-3 pbk. : 6.95
1. Bird-houses—Design and construction. 2. Bird feeders—Design and construction. 3. Birdbaths—Design and construction. I. Title. **BIP**

SIBLEY, Hi, 1883- 690'.8'9
102 bird houses, feeders you can make / Hi Sibley. South Holland, Ill. : Goodheart-Willcox Co., c1976. 96 p. : chiefly ill. ; 28 cm. [QL676.5.S46] 77-359921 ISBN 0-87006-220-4 pbk. : 4.00
1. Bird-houses—Design and construction. 2. Bird feeders—Design and construction. I. Title. II. Title: Bird houses, feeders you can make.

Bird-houses—Juvenile literature.

CREATIVE Educational 690'.8'9
Society, Mankato, Minn.
How to have fun making birdhouses and birdfeeders, by the editors of Creative. Illustrated by Nancy Inderieden. [Mankato, Minn., Creative Education; distributed by Childrens Press, Chicago, 1973, c1974] 31 p. illus. (part col.) 25 cm. (Creative craft book) Lists the necessary tools and materials and gives instructions for constructing bird feeders and birdhouses for a variety of birds. [QL676.5.C7] 73-10463 ISBN 0-87191-271-6
1. Bird-houses—Juvenile literature. 2. Bird feeders—Juvenile literature. I. Inderieden, Nancy, illus. II. Title.

Birds.

AUDUBON, John 598.2'092'4 B
James, 1785-1851.
Audubon and his journals, by Maria R. Audubon. With zoological and other notes by Elliot Coues. Freeport, N.Y., Books for Libraries Press [1972] 2 v. illus. 23 cm. Reprint of the 1897 ed. [QL31.A9A2 1972] 75-38340 ISBN 0-8369-6660-0
1. Birds. I. Audubon, Maria Rebecca, 1843-1925. II. Title.

AUDUBON, John James, 1785- 925.9
1851.
Audubon and his journals, by Maria R. Audubon. With zoological and other notes by Elliott Coues. New York, Dover Publications [1960] 2 v. illus., ports. 21 cm. "An unabridged and unaltered republication of the first edition originally published ... in 1897." [QL31.A9A2 1960] 60-51778
1. Birds. I. Audubon, Maria Rebecca, 1843- II. Title.

EVERITT, Charles, 1906- 598.2
Birds of the Edward Marshall Boehm aviaries; major portion devoted to softbills. [Trenton, N.J., E. M. Boehm, 1973] 297 p.

illus. 32 cm. Bibliography: p. 285. [QL676.E93] 73-76875
1. Boehm, Edward Marshall, 1913-1969. 2. Birds. 3. Aviaries—New Jersey—Trenton. I. Boehm, Edward Marshall, 1913-1969. II. Title.

FISHER, James, 1912- 598.2
James Fisher and Roger Tory Peterson's World of birds / bird paintings by Roger Tory Peterson. New and rev. ed. [New York] : Crescent Books, [1977?] 191 p. : ill. (some col.) ; 28 cm. Includes index. Bibliography: p. [184]-185. [QL676.F55 1977] 77-149490 5.98
1. Birds. I. Peterson, Roger Tory, 1908- II. World of birds. III. Title.

FISHER, James, 1912- 598.2
The world of birds, [by] James Fisher and Roger Tory Peterson. Bird paintings by Roger Tory Peterson. Garden City, N.Y., Doubleday [1964] 288 p. illus. (part col.) facsims., maps (part col.) ports. 33 cm. Bibliography: p. 274-281. [QL676.F55] 64-17398
1. Birds. I. Peterson, Roger Tory, 1908- illus. II. Title.

PETERSON, Roger Tory, 1908- 598.2
The birds. By Roger Tory Peterson and the editors of Time-Life Books. New York, Time-Life Books [1968] 192 p. illus. (part col.) 28 cm. (Life nature library) Bibliography: p. 187. Traces the evolution of birds from prehistory to the present. Lists the twenty-seven orders and describes their characteristics, habits, and adaptation to man. [QL676.P444 1968] AC 68
1. Birds. I. Time-Life Books. II. Title. **BIP**

Birds—Addresses, essays, lectures.

PETERSON, Roger Tory, 598.2082
1908- ed.
The bird watcher's anthology. [1st ed.] New York, Harcourt, Brace [1957] 401 p. illus. 26 cm. [QL676.5.P49] 57-10067
1. Birds—Addresses, essays, lectures. I. Title.

Birds—Caricatures and cartoons.

LIFTON, Robert Jay, 741.5'973
1926-
Psychobirds / words and birds by Robert Jay Lifton. Taftsville, Vt. : Countryman Press, c1978. 64 leaves : ill. ; 14 x 20 cm. [NC1429.L537A4 1978] 78-13463 ISBN 0-914378-42-2 : 6.95 ISBN 0-914378-41-4 pbk. : 3.95
1. Birds—Caricatures and cartoons. 2. American wit and humor, Pictorial. I. Title. **BIP**

Birds—Dictionaries.

BRUUN, Bertel. 598.2'03
The Dell encyclopedia of birds. Illustrated by Paul Singer. [New York, Dell Pub. Co., 1974] 240 p. col. illus. 18 cm. "A Vineyard book." Bibliography: p. 239-240. [QL676.B895] 74-165209 2.45 (pbk.)
1. Birds—Dictionaries. I. Title. **BIP**

Birds—Habits and behavior.

PETERSON, Roger Tory, 1908- 598.2
The birds [by] Roger Tory Peterson and the editors of Time-Life Books. Young readers ed. New York, Time, inc. [1967] 128 p. illus. (part col.), col. maps. 26 cm. (Life nature library) An illustrated survey of bird life, describing evolution, physiology, migration and flight patterns, wing and body communication, nesting, feeding, and family life. [QL676.P445] AC 68
1. Birds—Habits and behavior. I. Time-Life Books.

Birds in art.

ARIZONA. University. Art 704.9432
Gallery.
The bird in art; [exhibition] November 7, 1964, through January 3, 1965, the University of Arizona Art Gallery, Tucson, Arizona. [Tuscon, 1964] 118 p. illus. (part col.) 22 x 26 cm. [N7665.A7] 64-64759
1. Birds in art. 2. Art — Exhibitions. I. Title.

BRONSON, Clark. 759.13
Portfolio of bird paintings. Chicago, Rand McNally [1968] [5] p., 17 col. illus. 36 cm. [ND1380.B7] 68-25837 3.95
1. Birds in art. 2. Paintings. I. Title.

GRACZA, Margaret Young. 704.9432
The bird in art. Designed by Wendell Carroll. Minneapolis, Lerner Publications Co. [1966] 72 p. illus. (part col.) 27 cm. (Fine art books for young people) [N7665.G7] 65-29035
1. Birds in art. I. Title. **BIP**

THE Illustrated bird 704.94'32
/ edited by Maggie Oster ; designed by Sonja Douglas. Garden City, N.Y. : Dolphin Books, 1978. 80 p. : ill. (some col.) ; 31 cm. "A Tree Communications edition." [N7665.I38] 78-61182 ISBN 0-385-14576-4 : 6.95
1. Birds in art. 2. Art. I. Oster, Maggie.

KELLY, Richard Barrett 758.3982
Talbot, 1896-
Bird life and the painter. London, New York, Studio Publications [1955] 160p. illus. 23cm. [ND1380.K4] 56-1403
1. Birds in art. 2. Painting—Technique. I. Title.

MAASS, David. 759.13
A gallery of waterfowl and upland birds / paintings by David Maass ; stories by Gene Hill. Los Angeles : Petersen Pub. Co., c1978. 120 p. : ill. (some col.) ; 30 x 32 cm. [ND237.M12A4 1978] 78-61769 39.95
1. Maass, David. 2. Waterfowl in art. 3. Upland game birds in art. I. Hill, Gene. II. Title. **BIP**

POSTLE, Joy. 743.682
Drawing birds. New York, Pitman Pub. Corp. [1953] unpaged. illus. 20 x 27 cm. (Pitman drawing series) [NC782.P6] 53-13161
1. Birds in art. I. Title.

SHEPPARD, Raymond. 743.682
More birds to draw. London, New York, Studio Publications [1956] 64 p. illus. 18 cm. (How to draw. [39]) [(NC782)] 56-14368
1. Birds in art. 2. Drawing-Instruction. I. Title.

SWENEY, Fredric. 743.682
Course in drawing and painting birds. New York, Reinhold Pub. Corp., c1961. 61 p. illus. 27 cm. [NC782.S9] 61-10719
1. Birds in art. 2. Animal painting and illustration. I. Title.

TRIMM, Wayne. 759.13
The beauty of birds. With original paintings by Wayne Trimm. Poetry selected by J. W. Dunn. Norwalk, Conn., C. R. Gibson Co. [1974] 39 p. col. illus. 28 cm. [ND1839.T73D86] 73-88088 ISBN 0-8378-1864-8 5.95
1. Trimm, Wayne. 2. Birds in art. 3. English poetry (Selections: Extracts, etc.) 4. American poetry (Selections: Extracts, etc.) I. Dunn, J. W., comp. II. Title.

Birds—Juvenile literature.

PETERSON, Roger Tory, 1908- 598.2
The birds. By Roger Tory Peterson and the editors of Time-Life Books. New York, Time-Life Books [1968] 192 p. illus. (part col.) 28 cm. (Life nature library) Bibliography: p. 187. [QL676.P444 1968] 68-5876
1. Birds—Juvenile literature. I. Time-Life Books. II. Title. III. Series.

PETERSON, Roger Tory, 1908- 598.2
The birds [by] Roger Tory Peterson and the editors of Time-Life Books. Young readers ed. New York, Time, inc. [1967] 128 p. illus. (part col.), col. maps. 26 cm. (Life nature library) [QL676.P445] 67-26096
1. Birds—Juvenile literature. I. Time-Life Books.

TAGGART, George H. 598.2
The wonderful world of birds. Paintings by Joe Maniscalco. Text by George H. Taggart. Washington, Review and Herald Pub. Association [1970] 63 p. col. illus. 24 cm. Profiles of thirty-one familiar North American birds. Includes the Canada Goose, Golden Eagle, Snowy Owl, Great Horned Owl, and Common Puffin. [QL676.T24] 71-120098
1. Birds—Juvenile literature. I. Maniscalco, Joseph, illus. II. Title.

Birds—North America.

AUDUBON, John James, 598.297
1785-1851.
Bird biographies. Selected and edited by Alice Ford. New York, Macmillan, 1957. xv, 282 p. col. plates. 26 cm. Selections from the author's Ornithological biography, the text to his folio, The birds of America. Bibliography: p. 281-282. [QL674.A94] 56-7286
1. Birds—North America. I. Title.

AUDUBON, John James, 598.2973
1785-1851.
Birds of America. Introd. and descriptive captions by Ludlow Griscom. Popular ed. New York, Macmillan, 1950. 320 p. col. illus. 21 cm. [QL674.A9 1950] 50-6931
1. Birds—North America. 2. Birds—Pictorial works. I. Griscom, Ludlow, 1890- II. Title.

AUDUBON, John James, 598.2973
1785-1851.
The birds of America. With a new introd. by Dean Amadon [and new indexes by John Bull] New York, Dover Publications [1967] 7 v. illus. 22 cm. "Unabridged republication of the work first published ... in 1840-1844." [QL674.A9 1967] 66-21183
1. Birds—North America. 2. Birds—Pictorial works. I. Amadon, Dean. II. Bull, John L. III. Title. **BIP**

AUDUBON, John James, 598.297
1785-1851.
Favorite birds of America; engravings by John J. Audubon. Text by Kenneth D. Morrison. New York, Grosset & Dunlap [1951] unpaged. illus. 34 cm. Engravings selected from Audubon's The birds of America. [QL674.A945] 51-12470
1. Birds—North America. 2. Birds—Pictorial works. I. Morrison. Kenneth Douglas, 1918- II. Title.

AUDUBON, John James, 598.297
1785-1851.
The original water-color paintings by John James Audubon for The birds of America, reproduced in color for the first time from the collection at the New-York Historical Society. Introd. by Marshall B. Davidson. [Original ed.] New York, American Heritage Pub. Co.; distributed to booksellers by Houghton Mifflin Co., Boston, 1966. 2 v. illus. (part col.) facsim., 431 col. plates (part fold.) ports. (1 col.) 35 cm. M. B. Davidson edited the descriptive captions, which include many quotations from Audubon's Ornithological biography. [QL674.A9 1966] 66-17926
1. Birds—North America. 2. Birds—Pictorial works. I. Davidson, Marshall B., ed. II. Title.

Birds—North America—Exhibitions.

A Selection from The 769'.92'4
birds of America by John James Audubon : an exhibition, 26 September-10 October 1976, North Carolina Museum of Art, Raleigh. Raleigh : North Carolina Museum of Art, [1976] p. cm. [QL674.S48] 76-46336 ISBN 0-88259-084-7 : 4.00
1. Birds—North America—Exhibitions. 2. Birds—Pictorial works—Exhibitions. I. North Carolina. Museum of Art, Raleigh. II. Audubon, John James, 1785-1851. The birds of America. Selections. 1976.

Birds—Pictorial works.

AUDUBON, John James, 598.2973
1785-1851.
The Audubon folio. Text by George Dock, Jr. New York. N. Abrams [1964] 32 p. illus. 36 cm. and portfolio (30 col. plates) 44 cm. [QL674.A87] 64-11580
1. Birds — Pictorial works. I. Dock, George. II. Title.

AUDUBON, John James, 598.2'0924 B
1785-1851.
Audubon in Louisiana. New Orleans, Louisiana State Museum; Friends of the Cabildo, 1966. [40] p. col. illus. 23 x 31 cm. Label mounted on t.p.: Supplied by Worldwide Books, Boston, Mass. [QL31.A9A225] 71-21616
1. Audubon, John James, 1785-1851. 2. Birds—Pictorial works. 3. Birds—Louisiana. I. Louisiana State Museum, New Orleans. II. Friends of the Cabildo. III. Title.

CLEMENT, Roland C. 598.2'974
The living world of Audubon / by Roland C. Clement ; photographers, Fred J. Alsop III ... [et al.] ; designed by Albert Squillace. New York : Grosset & Dunlap, 1974. 272 p. : col. ill. ; 32 cm. "A Ridge Press book." Includes index. [QL674.C53] 74-81535 ISBN 0-448-11831-9 : 25.00
1. Audubon, John James, 1785-1851. 2. Birds—Pictorial works. I. Title.

DU BOIS, Alexander Dawes, 598.2'5
1875-1966
Glimpses of bird life. Minneapolis, T. S. Denison [1974] 100 p. illus. 29 cm. [QL674.D8 1974] 73-84573 ISBN 0-513-01343-1 5.95
1. Birds—Pictorial works. 2. Birds—Behavior. I. Title.

FUERTES, Louis 598.2'0924 B
Agassiz, 1874-1927.
Louis Agassiz Fuertes & the singular beauty of birds: paintings, drawings, letters. Assembled and edited by Frederick George Marcham. Foreword by Dean Amadon. Introd. by Roger Tory Peterson. [1st ed.] New York, Harper & Row [1971] xi, 220 p. illus., 60 col. plates. 37 cm. Bibliography: p. 213-214. [QL674.F8 1971] 76-156537 ISBN 0-06-012775-9 35.00
1. Birds—Pictorial works. I. Marcham, Frederick George, 1898- ed. **BIP**

HANZAK, Jan. 598.2'0222
The pictorial encyclopedia of birds [by] J. Hanzak. Edited by Bruce Campbell. American consultant: Ned R. Boyajian. New York, Crown Publishers [1967] 581 p. illus. (part col.) 23 cm. [QL674.H23] 68-11449
1. Birds—Pictorial works. I. Title. **BIP**

HARGREAVES, Harry, 1922- 741.5942
The birds, and others. New York, Norton [1962] unpaged (chiefly illus.) 26 cm. [NC1429.H332A43] 62-14350
I. Title.

HARPER, Charles. 598.2'022'2
Charles Harper's Birds & words. [Louisville, Ky.] : Frame House Gallery, [1974] 151 p. : col. ill. ; 17 x 22 cm. Includes index. [QL674.H28] 74-24857 30.00
1. Birds—Pictorial works. 2. Birds—Anecdotes, facetiae, etc. 3. Birds in art. I. Title: Birds & words.

LEVENSON, Donald W. 598.2
Birds : north, east, south, and west / by Donald W. Levenson. Natick, Mass. : Bio-photo Service, [1976?]. 175 p. : ill. ; 22 cm. Includes index. [QL674.L48] 77-371416
1. Birds—Pictorial works. I. Title.

LIFTON, Robert Jay, 741.5973
1926-
Birds, words and birds. By Robert Jay Lifton. New York, Random House [1969] [95] p. illus. 15 x 22 cm. [NC1429.L537A42] 75-89698 2.95
I. Title.

LINE, Les. 598.2
The Audubon Society book of wild birds / by Les Line and Franklin Russell. New York : H. N. Abrams, [1976] p. cm. [QL674.L54] 76-17094 ISBN 0-8109-0661-9 : 35.00
1. Birds—Pictorial works. I. Russell, Franklin, 1922- joint author. II. National Audubon Society. III. Title. **BIP**

LIVINGSTON, John A. 598.2971
Birds of the northern forest [by] J. F. Landowne John A. Livingston. Boston, Houghton, 1966. 247p. illus. (pt. col.) 35cm. Bibl. [QL674.L7] 66-8365 20.00
1. Birds—Pictorial works. 2. Birds—Canada. I. Lansdowne, James Fenwick, illus. II. Title. **BIP**

NEWBERRY, Cyril William. 598.2084
The beauty of birds. Garden City, N. Y., Hanover House, 1958, c1954. 102 p. (chiefly illus., part col.) 28 cm. [QL674.N45] 59-98
1. Birds—Pictorial works. 2. Birds—Behavior I. Title.

NORTHSHIELD, Robert, 598.2'022'2
1922-
The people's birds. Foreword by David Brinkley. New York, Scribner [1972] 310 p. illus. 24 x 31 cm. [QL674.N67] 72-1221 ISBN 0-684-12909-4 20.00
1. Birds—Pictorial works. I. Title.

POPE, William, 500.9'713'360924 B
1811-1902.
The 19th-century journals & paintings of William Pope / Harry B. Barrett; introd. and commentary by J. Fenwick Landsdowne Toronto : M. F. Feheley, c1976. 175 p. : col. ill. ; 32 cm. Includes index. [QL674.P83 1976] 77-360540 ISBN 0-919880-00-2 : 28.00
1. Birds—Pictorial works. 2. Natural history—Canada. 3. Canada—Description and travel. I. Barrett, Harry B. II. Lansdowne, James Fenwick. III. Title.

SAUER, Gordon C. 769'.92
John Gould bird print reproductions / Gordon C. Sauer. 1st ed. Kansas City, Mo. : Distributed by Richland Enterprises, 1977. v, 76 p. : ill. ; 24 cm. [QL674.S23] 77-367544
1. Gould, John, 1804-1881. 2. Birds—Pictorial works. I. Gould, John, 1804-1881. II. Title.

3000 pictures of 598.2084
birds. [Label:354 New York, Research Book Co., 1953] unpaged. illus. 28cm. [QL674.T5] 53-38541
1. Birds—Pictorial works.

WOOD, Peter, 1930- 598.2
Birds of field & forest : based on the television series Wild, wild world of animals / author, Peter Wood. [New York] : Time-Life Films, c1977. 128 p. : col. ill. ; 28 cm. (Wild, wild world of animals) "A Time-Life Television book." Includes index. Bibliography: p. 126. [QL674.W66] 77-5596 ISBN 0-913948-13-6 : 7.95
1. Birds—Pictorial works. I. Time-Life Television. II. Title. III. Series. **BIP**

Birds—Pictorial works—Juvenile literature.

PARNALL, Peter. 598.2
A dog's book of birds / by Peter Parnall. New York : Scribner, c1977. [48] p. : ill. ; 16 x 21 cm. Illustrates a dog's self-sought encounters with a variety of birds including a blue heron, albatross, loon, and eagle. [QL676.2.P37] 77-7194 ISBN 0-684-15181-2 : 5.95
1. Birds—Pictorial works—Juvenile literature. I. Title. **BIP**

Birds—Pictures, illustrations, etc.

WILSON, Maurice Charles 743'.68'2
John, 1914-
Birds [by] Maurice Wilson. [1st American ed. New York, Watson-Guptill Publications, 1965] 56 p. illus. 18 x 20 cm. (Watson-Guptill drawing books) Cover title: Drawing birds. [NC782.W5 1965] 65-18999
1. Birds—Pictures, illustrations, etc. 2. Animal painting and illustration. I. Title. II. Title: Drawing birds.

Birds—Tropics—Pictorial works.

DUNNING, John Stewart, 598.298
1906-
Portraits of tropical birds, by John S. Dunning. Wynnewood, Pa., Livingston Pub. Co., 1970. xx, 153 p. col. illus. 29 cm. Bibliography: p. 153. [QL674.D85] 71-134304 ISBN 0-87098-033-5 20.00
1. Birds—Tropics—Pictorial works. 2. Birds—Latin America—Pictorial works. 3. Photography of birds. I. Title.

Bireline, George, 1923—

BIRELINE, George, 1923- 759.13
Original Bireline : a retrospective of the work of George Bireline, March 7-April 11, 1976, North Carolina Museum of Art, Raleigh. Raleigh : The Museum, c1976.

104 p. : ill. (some col.) ; 23 cm. Includes bibliographical references. [ND237.B5935N67] 76-6072 ISBN 0-88259-082-0 pbk. : 4.50
1. Bireline, George, 1923- I. North Carolina. Museum of Art, Raleigh. II. Title.

Birger, Boris.

BIRGER, Boris. 759.7
Boris Birger : a catalogue / edited by Shirley Glade & Ellendea Proffer ; preface by Heinrich Boll. Ann Arbor [Mich.] : Ardis, c1975. [31] p. : ill. (some col.) ; 22 x 28 cm. Includes a list of the artist's works in English and Russian. [ND699.B545G55] 76-353741
1. Birger, Boris. I. Glade, Shirley. II. Proffer, Ellendea. BIP

Birmingham, Ala. Birmingham-Jefferson Civic Center (Proposed)

BIRMINGHAM-JEFFERSON Civic Center Authority. 725'.8
Birmingham-Jefferson Civic Center national architectural competition. [Editor: Les Adams. Birmingham] 1969. vi, 314 p. illus., plans. 25 x 34 cm. [NA2340.B5] 68-9481
1. Birmingham, Ala. Birmingham-Jefferson Civic Center (Proposed) 2. Architecture—Competitions. I. Adams, Les, ed. II. Title.

Birmingham, Ala.—Description—Views.

HELDMAN, Max. 917.61'781'036
Max Heldman's Birmingham; a collection of drawings depicting important events in the early history of Birmingham. Introd. and pictorial commentary, Virginia Pounds Brown. [Birmingham, Ala., Distributed by the Book-Keepers, 1971] 79 p. illus. 29 x 38 cm. [NC139.H4B7] 70-173929 20.00
1. Birmingham, Ala.—Description—Views. I. Brown, Virginia (Pounds) II. Title. III. Title: Birmingham.

Birmingham, Eng.—Description—Views.

PRICE, Stephen Jonathan. 942.4'96'080222
Birmingham old and new / [compiled by] Stephen J. Price. [Wakefield] : EP Publishing, 1976. [5], 99 p. : of ill. ; 19 x 25 cm. [DA690.B6P74] 76-376235 ISBN 0-7158-1098-7 : £1.95
1. Birmingham, Eng.—Description—Views. 2. Birmingham, Eng.—Buildings—Pictorial works. 3. Historic buildings—England—Birmingham—Pictorial works. I. Title.

Birmingham, Eng.—Industries.

GOODISON, Nicholas. 739.2
Ormolu: the work of Matthew Boulton. [London] Phaidon, [distributed by Praeger Publishers, New York, 1974] xii, 398 p. illus. 29 cm. Bibliography: p. 207-212. [TS140.B68G66] 78-165860 ISBN 0-7148-1589-6 35.00
1. Boulton, Matthew, 1728-1809. 2. Birmingham, Eng.—Industries. 3. Art metal-work—Birmingham, Eng. 4. Gilding. I. Title.

Birthdays — Caricatures and cartoons.

SETTEL, Irving. 741.5973
Congratulations, it's your birthday! By Irving Settel & Bill Adler. Illustrated by Fred Schwab. New York, Citadel Press [1959] Unpaged (chiefly illus.) 21 cm. [NC1429.S439S4] 59-13060
1. Birthdays — Caricatures and cartoons. I. Adler, Bill, joint author. II. Schwab, Fred, illus. III. Title.

Bischof, Werner Adalbert, 1916-1954.

BISCHOF, Werner Adalbert, 1916-1954. 770'.92'4 B
Werner Bischof, 1916-1954 / [editors, Rosellina Bischof Burri, Rene Burri]. New York : Grossman Publishers, 1974. 93, [2] p. : ill. ; 23 cm. (ICP library of photographers ; v. 2) Bibliography: p. [95] [TR140.B5A33 1974] 73-14141 ISBN 0-670-75717-9 : 10.00. ISBN 0-670-75718-7 pbk : 5.95
1. Bischof, Werner Adalbert, 1916-1954. 2. Photography, Artistic. I. Series: International Fund for Concerned Photography. ICP library of photographers ; v. 2.

BISCHOF, Werner Adalbert, 1916-1954. 779'.092'4
Werner Bischof : [photos. and drawings / text by] Niklaus Flueler ; [English translation, Maureen Oberli-Turner]. Garden City, N.Y. : AMPHOTO, c1976. 92 p. : ill. ; 27 cm. (Photography, men and movements) Includes bibliographical references and index. [TR820.5.B5713 1976] 75-34606 ISBN 0-8174-0318-3 : 5.95
1. Bischoff, Werner Adalbert, 1916-1954. 2. Photography, Documentary. I. Flueler, Niklaus, 1934- BIP

Bishop, Bernice Pauahi, 1831-1884—Portraits, etc.

KENT, Harold Winfield. 779'.2
An album of likenesses; Princess Bernice Pauahi Bishop, benefactress of the Kamehameha schools and Charles Reed Bishop, man of Hawaii. [Rev. ed.] Honolulu, Hawaii, Bernice Pauahi Bishop Museum, 1972. 1 v. (chiefly ports.) 29 cm. [DU627.17.B4K4 1972] 73-123994
1. Bishop, Bernice Pauahi, 1831-1884—Portraits, etc. 2. Bishop, Charles Reed, 1822-1915—Portraits, etc. I. Title.

Bishop, Isabel, 1902—

BISHOP, Isabel, 1902- 759.13 B
Isabel Bishop [by] Karl Lunde. New York, Abrams [1975] 181 p. illus. (part col.) 28 x 30 cm. Bibliography: p. 176-179. [ND237.B594L86] 73-17122 ISBN 0-8109-0150-1 37.50
1. Bishop, Isabel, 1902- I. Lunde, Karl.

BISHOP, Isabel, 1902- 760'.092'4
Isabel Bishop : [first retrospective exhibition]. Tucson : University of Arizona Museum of Art, 1974. 221 p. : ill. (some col.) ; 25 cm. Bibliography: p. 220-221. [N6537.B55A74] 74-19882
1. Bishop, Isabel, 1902- I. Arizona. University. Museum of Art.

BROOKLYN Institute of Arts and Sciences. Museum. 769.973
Isabel Bishop: prints and drawings, 1925-1964. [Text by Una E. Johnson, curator of prints and drawings. Res. by Jo Miller, assist. curator of prints and drawings. Brooklyn, N.Y., Author, 1965] 63p. illus. (part col.) port. 24cm. (Amer. graphic artists of 20th cent. Monograph no.2) Bibl. [NE2210.B46B7] 65-2054 2.75
1. Bishop, Isabel, 1902- I. Johnson, Una E. II. Title. III. Series.

NEW Jersey. State Museum, Trenton. 730'.924
Paintings by Isabel Bishop. Sculpture by Dorothea Greenbaum. [Exhibition] May 2-July 5, 1970. Trenton [1970] [12] p. illus., ports. 22 cm. Includes bibliographies. [N6536.N37] 71-632876
1. Bishop, Isabel, 1902- 2. Greenbaum, Dorothea, 1893- I. Title. II. Title: Sculpture by Dorothea Greenbaum.

Bison, American, in art—Exhibitions.

BARSNESS, Larry. 704.94'32
The bison in art : a graphic chronicle of the American bison / by Larry Barsness ; foreword by Barbara Tyler. 1st ed. Flagstaff, Ariz. : Northland Press, c1977. viii, 142 p. : ill. (some col.) ; 24 x 28 cm. Catalog of an exhibition held at the Amon Carter Museum of Western Art. Includes index. [N8214.5.U6B37] 76-52543 ISBN 0-87358-158-X : 14.50
1. Bison, American, in art—Exhibitions. 2. The West in art—Exhibitions. 3. Art, American—Exhibitions. I. Amon Carter Museum of Western Art, Fort Worth, Tex. II. Title. BIP

Bissier, Julius, 1893-1965.

MESSER, Thomas M. 760'.0924
Julius Bissier, 1893-1965; a retrospective exhibition. [New York, Printed by Sterlip Press, 1968] 62 p. illus. (part col.) 26 cm. Participating institutions: San Francisco Museum of Art and the Solomon R. Guggenheim Museum, New York, and others. Bibliography: p. 60-61. [ND588.B53M4] 68-57008
1. Bissier, Julius, 1893-1965. I. San Francisco. Museum of Art. II. Solomon R. Guggenheim Museum, New York.

SCHMALENBACH, Werner, 1917- 759.3
Bissier. New York, Abrams [1964, c.1963] 73p. illus. (pt. col.) 21x23cm. Bibl. 64-17628 5.95
1. Bissier, Julius, 1893- I. Title.

Bitters bottles.

WATSON, Richard, 1932- 748.8
Bitters bottles. New York T. Nelson 1965 304 p. illus., facsims. 24 cm. Bibliography: p. 284. [NK5440.B6W3] 65-20598
1. Bitters bottles. I. Title. BIP

Bitters bottles—Catalogs.

BARTHOLOMEW, Ed Ellsworth. 748'.8
1001 bitters bottles, by Ed Bartholomew. [Limited ed.] Fort Davis, Tex., Bartholomew House, 1970. 176 p. illus. 23 cm. [NK5440.B6B38] 75-10150
1. Bitters bottles—Catalogs. I. Title.

WILSON, Bill, 1926- 748'.8
Western bitters, by Bill & Betty Wilson. [Santa Rosa, Calif., B & B Enterprises, 1969] 95 .p. illus. 26 cm. Bibliography: p. 87-88. [NK5440.B6W53] 73-89625
1. Bitters bottles—Catalogs. I. Wilson, Betty, 1932- joint author. II. Title.

Bitters, Stan.

†BITTERS, Stan. 738
Environmental ceramics / Stan Bitters ; Micha Langer, photographer. New York : Van Nostrand Reinhold Co., 1976. 144 p. : ill. ; 28 cm. Includes index. Bibliography: p. 141. [NK4235.B57] 75-44615 ISBN 0-442-20781-6 : 15.00
1. Bitters, Stan. 2. Ceramic sculpture—Technique. I. Title. BIP

Black Canyon of the Gunnison National Monument, Colo.

WALKER, Dexter B. 779'.36'0978819
Fifty photographs taken by Dexter B. Walker at the time the survey was made in the bottom of the Black Canyon National Monument. [Montrose?,] Colo., 1967. 1 v. (chiefly illus.) 23 x 32 cm. Photo album with mounted snapshots. [F782.B5W3] 68-2592
1. Black Canyon of the Gunnison National Monument, Colo. I. Title.

Black in art.

RICHARDSON, Brenda. 759.13
Frank Stella : the black paintings : [exhibition, November 23, 1976-January 23, 1977] / by Brenda Richardson, with assistance from Mary Martha Ward. Baltimore : Baltimore Museum of Art, c1976. xiv, 90 p. : ill. ; 28 cm. Bibliography: p. 85-87. [ND237.S683R47] 76-48793 10.00
1. Stella, Frank. 2. Black in art. I. Stella, Frank. II. Ward, Mary Martha, joint author. III. Baltimore. Museum of Art.

Black Partizan site.

CALDWELL, Warren Wendell. 970.4'83'58
The Black Partizan site, by Warren W. Caldwell. Lincoln, Neb., River Basin Surveys, 1966. iii, 145 p. illus., maps. 26 cm. (River Basin Surveys. Publications in salvage archeology, no. 2) Includes bibliographical references. [E78.S63C3] 67-60629
1. Black Partizan site. I. Title. II. Series.

Blackboard drawing.

PRINGLE, Bert 741.23
Chalk illustration; a manual for technical teachers. by B. Pringle [1st ed.] Oxford, New York, Pergamon [1966] vii, 65p. illus. 29cm. (Commonwealth and intl. lib., 1723) [T361.P7 1966] 64-18837 3.95
1. Blackboard drawing. 2. Mechanical drawing. I. Title.

SWEETING, George, 1924- 741.7
How to be a chalk artist. Grand Rapids, Zondervan Pub. House [1953] 63p. illus. 26cm. [NC865.S9] 53-37395
1. Blackboard drawing. I. Title. BIP

Blackman, Charles Raymond. 1928-

SHAPCOTT, Thomas W. 759.994'3
Focus on Charles Blackman [by] Thomas Shapcott. [St. Lucia. Brisbane] Univ. of Queensland Pr. [1967] 75p. illus. (pt. col.) port. 24cm. (Artists in Queensland) Bibl. [ND1105.B55S5] 68-80698 8.95
1. Blackman, Charles Raymond. 1928- I. Title.
Distributed by Tri-Ocean, San Francisco. BIP

Blacks in art—Addresses, essays, lectures.

THE Image of 704.94'9'30145196
the Black in Western art / foreword by Amadou-Mahtar M'Bow. [Fribourg] : Office du livre, [1976- v. : ill. (some col.) ; 29 cm. Contents.Contents.—v. 1. Vercoutter, J. ... et al. From the pharaohs to the fall of the Rome Empire. Includes bibliographical references and index. [N8232.I46] 76-25772 ISBN 0-688-03086-6 (v. 1) : 160.00F (v. 1)
1. Blacks in art—Addresses, essays, lectures. 2. Art—Addresses, essays, lectures. I. Vercoutter, Jean, 1910-

Blacksmithing.

ANDREWS, Jack. 682
Edge of the anvil : a resource book for the blacksmith / written and illustrated by Jack Andrews. Emmaus, PA : Rodale Press, c1977. p. cm. Includes index. Bibliography: p. [TT220.A53] 77-15115 ISBN 0-87857-186-8 : 10.95. ISBN 0-87857-195-7 pbk. : 6.95
1. Blacksmithing. I. Title. BIP

BEALER, Alex W. 682
The art of blacksmithing [by] Alex W. Bealer. New York, Funk & Wagnalls [1969] 425 p. illus. 22 cm. Bibliography: p. 419-420. [TT220.B35] 68-56455 10.00
1. Blacksmithing. I. Title. BIP

BEALER, Alex W. 682
The art of blacksmithing / Alex W. Bealer. Rev. ed. New York : Funk & Wagnalls, 1976. 438 p. : ill. ; 21 cm. Includes index. Bibliography: p. 431-432. [TT220.B35 1976] 76-4546 ISBN 0-308-10254-1 ; 11.95
1. Blacksmithing. I. Title.

HOLMSTROM, John Gustaf. 682
Drake's modern blacksmithing and horseshoeing, by J. G. Holmstrom. New York, Drake Publishers [1971] 111 p. illus. 22 cm. First published in 1941 under title: Modern blacksmithing and horseshoeing. [TT220.H69 1971] 73-24471
1. Blacksmithing. 2. Horseshoeing. I. Title. II. Title: Modern blacksmithing and horseshoeing.

WATSON, Aldren Auld, 1917- 682'.0974
The village blacksmith / by Aldren A. Watson ; ill. by the author. New expanded ed. New York : Crowell, c1977. 171 p. : ill. ; 26 cm. Includes index. Bibliography: p. 165-167. [TT220.W3 1977] 77-4766 ISBN 0-690-01449-X : 10.95
1. Blacksmithing. I. Title.

WATSON, Aldren Auld, 1917- 682
The village blacksmith, by Aldren A. Watson. Illus. by the author. New York,

Crowell [1968] ix, 125 p. illus. 26 cm. Bibliography: p. 119-121. Describes the work of a blacksmith, including the development of techniques for working iron, the tools used, and the objects made on the forge. Also discusses the decline of this profession with the expansion of large scale industry. [TT220.W3] AC 68
1. Blacksmithing. I. Title. BIP

WEYGERS, Alexander G. 682'.4
The modern blacksmith [by] Alexander G. Weygers. Illustrated by the author. New York, Van Nostrand Reinhold Co. [1974] 96 p. illus. 28 cm. [TT220.W48] 73-14101 ISBN 0-442-29362-3 8.95
1. Blacksmithing. I. Title.
Pbk 4.95; ISBN 0-442-29363-1 BIP

Blacksmithing—History.

WEBBER, Ronald. 682
The village blacksmith. [1st American ed.] South Brunswick, Great Albion Books [1972, c1971] 160 p. illus. 23 cm. Bibliography: p. [154]-[156] [TT220.W42 1972] 73-170289 ISBN 0-8453-1059-3 5.95
1. Blacksmithing—History. 2. Blacksmiths. I. Title.

Blacksmithing—United States—History—Juvenile literature.

FISHER, Leonard Everett. 338.4'7'682
The blacksmiths / written & illustrated by Leonard Everett Fisher. New York : F. Watts, 1976. 47 p. : ill. ; 23 cm. (Colonial American craftsmen) Includes index. Introduces the history of blacksmithing and discusses the techniques, products, well-known blacksmiths, and commercial importance of this trade in colonial America. [TT220.F57] 75-26684 ISBN 0-531-02901-8 : 3.90
1. Blacksmithing—United States—History—Juvenile literature. 2. Blacksmiths—United States—Juvenile literature. 3. United States—History—Colonial period, ca. 1600-1775—Juvenile literature. I. Title. BIP

Blackwork embroidery.

DRYSDALE, Rosemary. 746.4'4
The art of blackwork embroidery / Rosemary Drysdale. New York : Scribner, [1975] 159 p., 8 leaves of plates : ill. ; 28 cm. [TT778.B5D79] 75-6990 ISBN 0-684-14330-5 : 9.95
1. Blackwork embroidery. I. Title. BIP

GOSTELOW, Mary. 746.4'4
Blackwork / Mary Gostelow. New York : Van Nostrand Reinhold, 1977. 160 p. : ill. ; 26 cm. Includes index. Bibliography: p. [151] [TT778.B5G67 1977] 76-25967 ISBN 0-442-22792-2 : 12.95
1. Blackwork embroidery. I. Title. BIP

Blackwork embroidery—Patterns.

GEDDES, Elisabeth. 746.4'4
Blackwork embroidery / Elisabeth Geddes and Moyra McNeill. New York : Dover Publications, 1976, c1965. 113 p., [1] leaf of plates : ill. ; 26 cm. Reprint of the ed. published by Mills & Boon, London. [TT778.B5G4 1975] 75-31285 ISBN 0-486-23245-X pbk. : 3.00
1. Blackwork embroidery—Patterns. I. McNeill, Moyra, joint author. II. Title. BIP

SCHEUER, Nikki. 746.4'4
Designs for Holbein embroidery : 110 new geometric patterns / by Nikki Scheuer. 1st ed. Garden City, N.Y. : Doubleday, 1976. 136 p. : ill. ; 21 x 27 cm. Bibliography: p. 136. [TT778.B5S33] 75-40743 ISBN 0-385-11001-4 : 9.95
1. Blackwork embroidery—Patterns. I. Title.

Blain site.

PRUFER, Olaf H. 917.71'82'03
Blain Village and the Fort Ancient tradition in Ohio, by Olaf H. Prufer and Orrin C. Shane, III. Contributors: Olaf H. Prufer [and others. 1st ed. Kent, Ohio] Kent State University Press [1970] viii, 287 p. illus., plans. 24 cm. (Kent studies in anthropology and archaeology, 1) Bibliography: p. 269-275. [E78.O3P7] 79-99082 10.00
1. Blain site. I. Shane, Orrin C., 1939- joint author. II. Title. III. Series. BIP

Blaine, Nell, 1922—

NELL Blaine; 759.13
a loan exhibition of works by Nell Blaine, organized by Frederick R. Brandt, on display at the Virginia Museum, from 19 November to 23 December 1973. Richmond, Virginia Museum [1973] 20 p. illus. (part col.) 21 x 24 cm. Bibliography: p. 20. [ND237.B597N44] 73-90583
1. Blaine, Nell, 1922- I. Blaine, Nell, 1922- II. Virginia Museum of Fine Arts, Richmond.

Blair, Robert, 1699-1746—Illustrations.

BLAKE, William, 1757-1827. 096
Blake's Grave; a prophetic book, being William Blake's illustrations for Robert Blair's The grave, arranged as Blake directed. With a commentary by S. Foster Damon. Providence, Brown University Press, 1963. [45] p. illus., port. 36 cm. (Brown University bicentennial publications: studies in the fields of general scholarship) [NC1115.B72D3] 62-21991
1. Blair, Robert, 1699-1746—Illustrations. I. Damon, Samuel Foster, 1893- II. Title. III. The grave.

Blake, William, 1757-1827.

BA HAN, Maung, 1890- 760'.092'4
William Blake, his mysticism. [Folcroft, Pa.] Folcroft library editions, 1973. x, 269 p. 26 cm. Originally presented as the author's thesis, Universite de Bordeaux, 1924. Bibliography: p. [263]-269. [PB4148.M8B3 1973] 72-13650 ISBN 0-8414-1234-0
1. Blake, William, 1757-1827. I. Title.

BENTLEY, Gerald Eades, 1930- 700'.924
Blake records [by] G. E. Bentley. Oxford, Clarendon P., 1969. xxviii, 678 p., 62 plates. illus., facsims., plans, ports. 23 cm. Includes bibliographical references. [PR4146.B37] 71-457241 ISBN 0-19-811639-X 8/10/-
1. Blake, William, 1757-1827. I. Title. BIP

BINDMAN, David. 760'.092'4
Blake as an artist / David Bindman. Oxford [Eng.] : Phaidon ; New York : E. P. Dutton, 1977. 256 p., [36] leaves of plates : ill. (some col.) ; 26 cm. A revision of the author's thesis, Courtauld Institute. Includes bibliographical references and indexes. [N6797.B57B56 1977] 77-71183 ISBN 0-7148-1637-X : 18.95
1. Blake, William, 1757-1827. I. Title. BIP

BLAKE, William, 1757-1827. 760'.92'4
The apocalyptic vision. Pref. and catalogue by Harvey Stahl. Introd. by Bruce Daryl Barone. [An exhibition at Reid Hall, Manhattanville College, April 21 to May 13, 1974] Purchase, N.Y., Manhattanville College [1974] [74] p. illus. 23 cm. Bibliography: p. [73]-[74] [N6797.B57S82] 74-175885
1. Blake, William, 1757-1827. 2. Apocalyptic art. I. Stahl, Harvey. II. Manhattanville College of the Sacred Heart, Purchase, N.Y. III. Title.

BLAKE, William, 1757-1827. 821'.7
The book of Los. [Boissia, Clairvaux : Trianon Press for the William Blake Trust, London : distributed by B. Quaritch, London, 1976] [5] leaves of plates, [8] p. : col. ill. ; 30 cm. Facsim. of the unique British Museum copy, with imprint: Lambeth, Printed by Wm. Blake, 1795. "The edition consists of 538 copies ... 32 copies numbered I-XXXII ... each containing a set of plates shewing the progressive stages of the collotype and hand-stencil process, and a guide sheet and stencil. 480 copies numbered 1 to 480 ... 26 copies numbered A to Z, reserved for the trustees of the William Blake Trust and the publishers." No. I of the 1st group. "Commentary and bibliographical history" (p. [3-7]) signed: Geoffrey Keynes. [PR4144.B57 1795a Rosenwald Coll] 77-357163
I. Title.

BLAKE, William, 1757-1827. 769'.924
The book of Thel; a facsimile and a critical text. Edited by Nancy Bogen. Providence, Brown University Press [1971] xiv, 82 p. illus. 29 cm. Includes col. facsim. reproduction of the 1789 ed. in the possession of the New York Public Library. Bibliography: p. 75-79. [NE642.B5B6] 74-155857 ISBN 0-87057-127-3 10.00
I. Bogen, Nancy, 1932- ed. II. Title. BIP

BLAKE, William, 1757-1827. 741.9'42
Drawings of William Blake; 92 pencil studies. Selection, introd. and commentary, by Sir Geoffrey Keynes. New York, Dover Publications [1970] xiv p. 92 plates. 28 cm. Text on versos of plates. [NC242.B55K38] 71-100545 ISBN 4-86223-035- 3.50
I. Keynes, Geoffrey Langdon, Sir, 1887- ed. II. Title. BIP

BLAKE, William, 1757-1827. 760'.092'4
The illuminated Blake / annotated by David V. Erdman. London : Oxford University Press, 1975. 416 p. : ill., facsims. ; 21 x 27 cm. Includes index. [NE642.B5E72 1975] 76-353563 ISBN 0-19-211848-X : £10.00. ISBN 0-19-281182-7 pbk.
1. Blake, William, 1757-1827. I. Erdman, David V. II. Title.

BLAKE, William, 1757-1827. 769'.92'4
The illuminated Blake : all of William Blake's illuminated works with a plate-by-plate commentary / annotated by David V. Erdman. 1st ed. Garden City, N.Y. : Anchor Press/Doubleday, 1974. 416 p. : ill. ; 22 x 28 cm. Includes index. [NE642.B5E72] 74-3702 ISBN 0-385-07821-8 : 25.00
1. Blake, William, 1757-1827. I. Erdman, David V. II. Title.

BLAKE, William, 1757-1827. 821'.7
The marriage of heaven and hell / [William Blake] ; [with an introduction and commentary by Sir Geoffrey Keynes]. London ; New York : Oxford University Press, 1975. xxviii, [54] p. : ill. (some col.) ; 22 cm. [PR4144.M3 1975] 75-4495 ISBN 0-19-212588-5 pbk. : £7.50
I. Keynes, Geoffrey Langdon, Sir, 1887- II. Title. BIP

BLAKE, William, 1757-1827. 821'.7
The marriage of heaven and hell / [William Blake] ; [with an introduction and commentary by Sir Geoffrey Keynes]. London ; New York : Oxford University Press, 1975. xxviii, [54] p. : ill. (some col.) ; 22 cm. [PR4144.M3 1975] 75-4495 ISBN 0-19-212588-5 pbk. : £7.50
I. Keynes, Geoffrey Langdon, Sir, 1887- II. Title. BIP

BLAKE, William, 1757-1827. 821.7
The marriage of Heaven and Hell. With an introd. by Clark Emery. [Coral Gables, Fla., University of Miami Press, 1963] 104 p. facsim.: 27 l. illus. 21 cm. (University of Miami. Critical studies, no. 1) "A song of liberty": leaves 25-27. "Photographed from Max Plowman's facsimile reproduction of 'an original copy of the work printed and illuminated by the author between the years 1825-1827 and now in the Fitzwilliam Museum, Cambridge.'" Bibliography: p. 104. [PR4144.M3 1825c] 63-19483
I. Emery, Clark Mixon, 1909- ed. II. Title. III. Title: A song of liberty. IV. Series: Miami, University of, Coral Gables, Fla. Critical studies, no. 1

BLAKE, William, 1757-1827. 821.7
The marriage of Heaven and Hell. With an introd. by Clark Emery. [Coral Gables, Fla., University of Miami Press, 1963] 104 p. facsim.: 27 l. illus. 21 cm. (University of Miami. Critical studies, no. 1) "A song of liberty": leaves 25-27. "Photographed from Max Plowman's facsimile reproduction of 'an original copy of the work printed and illuminated by the author between the years 1825-1827 and now in the Fitzwilliam Museum, Cambridge.'" Bibliography: p. 104. [PR4144.M3 1825c] 63-19483
I. Emery, Clark Mixon, 1909- ed. II. Title. III. Title: A song of liberty. IV. Series: Miami, University of, Coral Gables, Fla. Critical studies, no. 1

BLAKE, William, 1757-1827. 821.7
Songs of innocence. With decorations by Harold Jones. New York, Barnes [1961] 1 v. (unpaged) illus. (part col.) 22 cm. (A Wonderful world book) [PR4144.S6 1961] 60-10198
I. Title.

BLAKE, William, 1757-1827. 821.7
Songs of innocence. Illus. by Ellen Raskin. [1st ed.] Garden City, N. Y., Doubleday [1966] 48 p. col. illus. 21 x 27 cm. [PR4144.S6 1966] 66-11658
I. Raskin, Ellen, illus. II. Title. BIP

BLAKE, William, 1757-1827. 769'.924
Songs of innocence. New York, Dover Publications [1971] [vi], 55 p. col. plates. 18 cm. Facsim. of the 1789 ed. (being 31 plates, each containing hand-col. illus. and hand-lettered text) made from the copy in the Rosenwald collection in the Library of Congress, with an added introd., table of contents, and text of the poems in letterpress. [NE642.B5A55 1789ab] 70-165396 ISBN 0-486-21395-1 (clothbound) 2.00
I. Title.

BLAKE, William, 1757-1827. 821'.7
Songs of innocence & of experience. [Folcroft, Pa.] Folcroft Press [1969] 54 p. illus. 23 cm. [PR4144.S6 1969] 72-194985
I. Title. BIP

BLAKE, William, 1757-1827. 821'.7
Songs of innocence and of experience, shewing the two contrary states of the human soul, 1789-1794. [With an introd. and commentary by Geoffrey Keynes] [New York] [Orion Press] [1967] 1 v. (unpaged) 55 plates (part col.) 23 cm. [PR4144.S6 1967] 67-21229
I. Keynes, Geoffrey Langdon, Sir, 1887- II. Title.

BLAKE, William, 1757-1827. 821'.7
Songs of innocence and of experience : shewing the two contrary states of the human soul 1789-1794 / W. Blake ; [with an introd. and commentary by Geoffrey Keynes. London ; New York : Oxford University Press, 1977. 155 p. : col. facsims. ; 21 cm. [PR4144.S6 1977] 78-300013 ISBN 0-19-519977-4 (New York) : 18.95
I. Keynes, Geoffrey Langdon, Sir, 1887- II. Title.

BLAKE, William, 1757-1827 759.2
William Blake / William Vaughan. New York : St. Martin's Press, 1978, c1977. [88] p. : chiefly col. ill. ; 28 cm. [N6797.B57A4 1978] 77-9208 ISBN 0-312-88023-5 pbk. : 5.95
1. Blake, William, 1757-1827. I. Vaughn, William, 1943-

BLAKE, William, 1757-1827. 760'.092'4
The works of William Blake: poetic, symbolic, and critical. Edited with lithographs of the illustrated "Prophetic books," and a memoir and interpretation by Edwin John Ellis and William Butler Yeats. London, B. Quaritch, 1893. [New York, AMS Press, 1973] 3 v. illus. 23 cm. Contents.Contents.—v. 1. Memoir. Literary period. The symbolic system.—v. 2. Interpretation and paraphrased commentary. Blake the artist. Some references.—v. 3. Poems. [ND497.B6E4 1973] 75-151964 ISBN 0-404-08960-7 35.00 ea.
1. Blake, William, 1757-1827. I. Ellis, Edwin John, ed. II. Yeats, William Butler, 1865-1939, ed.
Set 100.00. BIP

BLUNT, Anthony, Sir 1907- 759.2
The art of William Blake. New York, Columbia University Press, 1959. ix, 122p. 64 plates (incl. facsims.) 24cm. (Bampton lectures in America, no. 12) Bibliography: p. [115]- 118. [ND497.B6B42] 59-12399
1. Blake, William, 1757-1827. I. Title. II. Series. BIP

SUBJECT INDEX BLAKE, WILLIAM, 1757-1827.

BLUNT, Anthony, Sir, 1907- 759.2
The art of William Blake. New York, Harper & Row [1974, c1959] 122 p. illus. 23 cm. (Harper icon editions) Bibliography: p. 115-118. [ND497.B6B42] ISBN 0-06-430045-5. 5.95 (pbk.)
1. Blake, William, 1757-1827 I. Title.
L.C. card number for original ed.: 59-12399.

BRONOWSKI, Jacob, 1908- 828'.7'09
William Blake, 1757-1827; a man without a mask, by J. Bronowski New York, Haskell House Publishers, 1967. 153 p. port. 24 cm. Half title: A man without a mask. Bibliographical references included in "Notes" (p. [146]-149) [PR4146.B67 1967] 67-30809
1. Blake, William, 1757-1827. I. Title: A man without a mask.

BRUCE, Harold Lawton, 1887-1934. 760'.092'4
William Blake in this world. [Folcroft, Pa.] Folcroft Library Editions, 1973 [c1925] v, 234 p. illus. 24 cm. Bibliography: p. 220-227. [PR4146.B7 1973] 73-3184 ISBN 0-8414-1779-2 4.95
1. Blake, William, 1757-1827. I. Title. BIP

BUTTERWORTH, Adeline M. 769'.92'4
William Blake, mystic; a study, by Adeline M. Butterworth. Together with Young's Night thoughts: nights I & II, with illus. by William Blake, and frontispiece Death's door, from Blair's "The grave." [Folcroft, Pa.] Folcroft Library Editions, 1974. 14, 2, 42 p. illus. 29 cm. Reprint of the 1911 ed. published by Liverpool Booksellers Co., Liverpool. [NE642.B5B87 1974] 74-8017 ISBN 0-8414-3186-8 (lib. bdg.)
1. Blake, William, 1757-1827. 2. Young, Edward, 1683-1765. Night thoughts—Illustrations. I. Young, Edward, 1683-1765. Night thoughts. Selections. 1974. II. Title.

CAMBRIDGE. University. Fitzwilliam Museum. 760'.0924
William Blake: catalogue of the collection in the Fitzwilliam Museum, Cambridge; edited by David Bindman. Cambridge, Heffer, 1970. vii, 88 p., 44 plates. illus. (incl. 1 col.), facsims., ports. 23 x 26 cm. Bibliography: p. 3-4. [N6797.B57C3] 71-587450 ISBN 0-85270-053-9 £3.00
1. Blake, William, 1757-1827. I. Bindman, David, ed.

CHESTERTON, Gilbert Keith, 1874-1936. 760'.092'4
William Blake / by G. K. Chesterton. Folcroft, Pa. : Folcroft Library Editions, 1976. viii, 210 p. : ill. ; 23 cm. Reprint of the 1910 ed. published by Duckworth, London, and Dutton, New York, in series: The Popular library of art. [ND497.B6C5 1976] 76-7995 ISBN 0-8414-3383-6 lib. bdg. : 17.50
1. Blake, William, 1757-1827. I. Series: The Popular library of art.

CLUTTON-BROCK, Alan Francis. 760'.0924 B
Blake, by Alan Clutton-Brock. New York, Haskell House, 1970. 140 p. 23 cm. (Great lives [14]) Reprint of the 1933 ed. Bibliography: p. 139-140. [PR4146.C6 1970] 77-119438
1. Blake, William, 1757-1827. I. Title. II. Series. BIP

CLUTTON-BROCK, Alan Francis. 760'.092'4 B
Blake, by Alan Clutton-Brock. [Folcroft, Pa.] Folcroft Library Editions, 1973. p. Reprint of the 1933 ed. published by Duckworth, London, which was issued as no. 14 of Great lives. Bibliography: [PR4146.C6 1973] 73-4597 ISBN 0-8414-3353-4 (lib. bdg.)
1. Blake, William, 1757-1827. BIP

DE SELINCOURT, Basil, 1876- 700'.924
William Blake. New York, Cooper Square Publishers, 1971. xi, 298 p. illus. 22 cm. Reprint of the 1909 ed. [ND497.B6D4 1971] 72-162018 ISBN 0-8154-0389-5
1. Blake, William, 1757-1827.

DE SELINCOURT, Basil, 1876- 760'.0924 B
William Blake, by Basil De Selincourt. Port Washington, N.Y., Kennikat Press [1972] xi, 298 p. illus. 21 cm. Reprint of the 1909 ed. [ND497.B6D4 1972] 75-160752 ISBN 0-8046-1568-3
1. Blake, William, 1757-1827.

EASSON, Roger R. 769'.92'4
William Blake: book illustrator; a bibliography and catalogue of the commercial engravings, by Roger R. Easson and Robert N. Essick. Normal, American Blake Foundation at Illinois State University, 1972- v. plates. 28 cm. Contents.Contents.—v. 1. Plates designed and engraved by Blake. [NE642.B5E2] 72-82993 ISBN 0-913130-01-X
1. Blake, William, 1757-1827. 2. Illustration of books—Bibliography—Catalogs. I. Essick, Robert N., joint author. II. Blake, William, 1757-1827. III. Title.

ELLIS, Edwin John. 700.924 B
The real Blake; a portrait biography, by Edwin J. Ellis. New York, Haskell House Publishers, 1970. xix, 443 p. 13 illus., facsims. 23 cm. Reprint of the 1906 ed. [PR4146.E4 1970] 75-117994 ISBN 0-8383-1049-4
1. Blake, William, 1757-1827. I. Title. BIP

*ERDMAN, David V. 760.092'4
The illuminated Blake, annotated by David V. Erdman Garden City, New York, Doubleday 1974 416 illus., 21 cm. x 27 cm. [ND497] ISBN 0-385-06053-X 7.95 (pbk.)
1. Blake, William, 1757-1827 I. Title. BIP

*ESSICK, Robert N., comp. 760'.0924
The visionary hand; essays for the study of William Blake's art and aesthetics, edited and with an introduction by Robert N. Essick. Los Angeles, Hennessey & Ingalls, 1973. 558 p. 23 cm. Includes bibliographical references [ND497] 72-96392 ISBN 0-912158-22-0. 7.95 (pbk.)
1. Blake, William, 1757-1827. I. Title. BIP

GARDNER, Charles, 1874- 760'.092'4
Vision & vesture; a study of William Blake in modern thought. [Folcroft, Pa.] Folcroft Library Editions, 1973. xi, 226 p. 23 cm. Reprint of the 1929 rev. ed. published by E. P. Dutton, New York. [PR4147.G32 1973] 73-15646 ISBN 0-8414-4470-6 (lib. bdg.)
1. Blake, William, 1757-1827. 2. Religion in poetry. 3. Literature, Modern—19th century—History and criticism. I. Title. BIP

GARDNER, Charles, 1874- 760'.092'4
William Blake, the man. London, Dent; New York, Dutton, 1919. [New York, AMS Press, 1973] 202 p. illus. 23 cm. [PR4146.G3 1973] 79-153324 ISBN 0-404-07906-7 9.00
1. Blake, William, 1757-1827.

GARNETT, Richard, 1835-1906. 700'.924
William Blake; painter and poet. New York, Haskell House, 1971. 80 p. illus., port. 23 cm. Reprint of the 1895 ed. [ND497.B6G3 1971] 77-115857 ISBN 0-8383-1074-5
1. Blake, William, 1757-1827. I. Title.

GARNETT, Richard, 1835-1906. 759.2
William Blake, painter and poet. [Folcroft, Pa.] Folcroft Library Editions, 1973. 80 p. illus. 33 cm. Reprint of the 1895 ed. published by Seeley, London, which was issued as no. 22 of Portfolio; artistic monographs. [ND497.B6G3 1973] 73-3347 ISBN 0-8414-2012-2
1. Blake, William, 1757-1827. I. Title. II. Series: Portfolio; monographs on artistic subjects, no. 22.

GARNETT, Richard, 1835-1906. 759.2
William Blake, painter and poet / by Richard Garnett. Norwood, Pa. : Norwood Editions, 1976. 80 p., [7] leaves of plates : ill. ; 34 cm. Reprint of the 1895 ed. published by Seeley, London, which was issued as no. 22 of Portfolio; artistic monographs. Includes index. [ND497.B6G3 1976] 76-6107 ISBN 0-8482-0860-9 : 12.50
1. Blake, William, 1757-1827. I. Title. II. Series: Portfolio; monographs on artistic subjects ; no. 22.

GILCHRIST, Alexander, 1828-1861. 760'.092'4 B
Life of William Blake, with selections from his poems and other writings. A new and enl. ed. illustrated from Blake's own works, with additional letters and a memoir of the author. New introd. by W. A. G. Doyle-Davidson. Totowa, N.J., Rowman and Littlefield, 1973. xxi, 431 p. illus. 24 cm. Reprint of v. 1 of the 1880 ed. published by Macmillan, London. [PR4146.G5 1973] 73-166130 ISBN 0-87471-170-3 16.50
1. Blake, William, 1757-1827. BIP

HENRY E. Huntington Library and Art Gallery, San Marino, Calif. 741
Catalogue of William Blake's drawings in the Huntington Library, by C. H. Collins Baker. [2d ed.] San Marino, 1957. vii, 55p. 38plates. 24cm. nl. and rev. by R. R. Wark. (Huntington Library publications) Includes bibliographical references [ND497.B6H4 1957] 57-12881
1. Blake, William, 1757-1827. I. Baker, Charles Henry Collins, 1880- II. Title. III. Series: Henry E. Huntington Library and Art Gallery, San Marino, Calif. Huntington Library publications

JAMES, Laura DeWitt. 821.79
William Blake: the finger on the furnace. [1st ed.] New York, Vantage Press [c1956] 126p. illus. 21cm. [PR4147.J3] 55-10867
1. Blake, William, 1757-1827. I. Title.

JENKINS, Herbert George, 1876-1923. 760'.092'4 B
William Blake; studies of his life and personality. Edited with an introd. by C. E. Lawrence. [Folcroft, Pa.] Folcroft Library Editions, 1974. 110 p. illus. 24 cm. Reprint of the 1925 ed. published by H. Jenkins, London. [PR4146.J4 1974] 73-3386 ISBN 0-8414-2153-6 15.00
1. Blake, William, 1757-1827. I. Lawrence, Charles Edward, 1870-1940, ed. II. Title.

KEYNES, Geoffrey Langdon, Sir, 1887- 700'.924
Blake studies: notes on his life and works in seventeen chapters, by Geoffrey Keynes. New York, Haskell House Publishers, 1971. xiii, 208, 47 p. illus., facsims. 23 cm. "First published in 1949." Bibliography: p. [191]-199. [PR4146.K4 1971] 79-117995 ISBN 0-8383-1050-8
1. Blake, William, 1757-1827. I. Title. BIP

KEYNES, Geoffrey Langdon, Sir, 1887- 759.2
A study of the illuminated books of William Blake, poet, printer, prophet, by Geoffrey Keynes. New York, Orion Press [1964] 89 p. col. plates. 32 cm. Published in part, earlier in 1964, under title: An exhibition of the illuminated books of William Blake ... a commemorative handbook. [NE642.B5K44 1964b] 64-24236
1. Blake, William, 1757-1827. I. Title.

KINGSBURY, Pamela D. 769'.92'4
Imagination and vision; prints and drawings of William Blake. [Exhibition at] the Art Gallery, Illinois State University, Oct. 17 to Nov. 7, 1971 [and] the University of Kansas Museum of Art, Nov. 28 to Dec. 18, 1971. [Lawrence, Kan., 1971?] [30] p. illus. 23 cm. (Miscellaneous publications of the Museum of Art, no. 84) Bibliography: p. [29]-[30] [NE642.B5K5] 71-637001
1. Blake, William, 1757-1827. I. Illinois. State University, Normal. Art Gallery. II. Kansas. University. Museum of Art. III. Series: Kansas. University. Museum of Art. Miscellaneous publications, no. 84.

KLONSKY, Milton. 760'.092'4
William Blake, the seer and his visions / by Milton Klonsky. New York : Harmony Books, 1977. p. cm. [N6797.B57K55 1977] 77-3979 ISBN 0-517-52939-4 : 12.00 ISBN 0-517-52940-8 pbk. : 6.95
1. Blake, William, 1757-1827. I. Title. BIP

LISTER, Raymond. 760'.0924 B
William Blake; an introduction to the man and to his work. With a foreword by G. E. Bentley, Jr. [1st American ed.] New York, Ungar [1970, c1968] xi, 200 p. illus. (part col.) 23 cm. Bibliography: p. [191]-193. [PR4146.L5 1970] 70-99289 7.50
1. Blake, William, 1757-1827.

MACDONALD, Greville, 1856-1944. 821'.7
The sanity of William Blake / by Greville MacDonald ; with six ill. of Blake's drawings. Folcroft, Pa. : Folcroft Library Editions, 1975. 59 p., [4] leaves of plates : ill. ; 24 cm. Reprint of the 1920 ed. published by G. Allen and Unwin, London. [PR4146.M28 1975] 75-22389 ISBN 0-8414-6156-2 : 5.50
1. Blake, William, 1757-1827. I. Title.

MACDONALD, Greville, 1856-1944. 760'.092'4 B
The sanity of William Blake / by Greville MacDonald ; with six ill. of Blake's drawings. Norwood, Pa. : Norwood Editions, 1975. 59 p., [4] leaves of plates : ill. ; 23 cm. Reprint of the 1920 ed. published by Allen and Unwin, London. [PR4146.M28 1975b] 75-35576 ISBN 0-88305-914-2 : 8.50
1. Blake, William, 1757-1827. I. Title. BIP

OSTRIKER, Alicia 821.7
Vision and verse in William Blake. Madison, Univ. of Wisc. Pr. [c.]1965. x, 224p. 22cm. Bibl. [PR4147.O8] 65-16363 6.00
1. Blake, William, 1757-1827. I. Title. BIP

PERCIVAL, Milton Oswin, 1883- 821.7
William Blake's circle of destiny [by] Milton O. Percival. New York, Octagon Books, 1964 [c1938] viii, 334 p. illus. 24 cm. Bibliographical references included in "Notes" (p. [293]-329) [PR4147.P4 1964] 64-24854
1. Blake, William, 1757-1827. I. Title. BIP

PRESTON, Kerrison. 700'.92'2
Blake and Rosetti / by Kerrison Preston. Folcroft, Pa. : Folcroft Library Editions, 1976. p. cm. Reprint of the 1944 ed. published by A. Moring, London. [PR4146.P7 1976] 76-29028 ISBN 0-8414-6782-X lib. bdg. : 17.50
1. Blake, William, 1757-1827. 2. Rossetti, Dante Gabriel, 1828-1882. 3. Poets, English—19th century—Biography. 4. Painters—England—Biography. I. Title.

PRESTON, Kerrison. 700'.922
Blake and Rossetti. New York, Haskell House Publishers, 1971. 111 p. illus., ports. 29 cm. Reprint of the 1944 ed. [PR4146.P7 1971] 73-117999 ISBN 0-8383-1054-0
1. Blake, William, 1757-1827. 2. Rossetti, Dante Gabriel, 1828-1882. BIP

RAINE, Kathleen J 759.2
William Blake. London, New York, Published for the British Council by Longmans, Green [1951] 40 p. illus., port. 22 cm. (Bibliographical series of supplements to 'British book news') "William Blake, a select bibliography": p. 33-40. [ND497.B6R3] 52-2173
1. Blake, William, 1757-1827. I. Title. II. Series.

ROE, Albert S. 741.9'42
Blake's illustrations to the Divine comedy / by Albert S. Roe. Westport, Conn. : Greenwood Press, 1977, c1953. xiii, 219 p., [103] leaves of plates : ill. ; 27 cm. Reprint of the ed. published by Princeton University Press, Princeton, N.J. A revision of the author's thesis, Harvard. Includes index. Bibliography: p. 207-210. [NC978.5.B55R63 1977] 77-4443 ISBN 0-8371-9595-0 lib.bdg. : 38.00
1. Blake, William, 1757-1827. Illustrations to the Divine Comedy of Dante. 2. Dante Alighieri, 1265-1421—Illustrations. I. Title.

RUSSELL, Archibald George Blomefield, 1879-1955. 769'.924
The engravings of William Blake. New York, B. Blom [1968] 220p. illus. 24cm. Reprint of the 1912 ed. [NE642.B5R8 1968] 67-13339 17.50
1. Blake, William. 1757-1827. 2. Blake, William, 1757-1827—Bibl. I. Title.

RYSKAMP, Charles. 769'.924
William Blake; engraver. A descriptive catalogue of an exhibition [Dec. 1969 through Feb. 1970] by Charles Ryskamp. With an introductory essay by Geoffrey Keynes. Princeton, N.J., Princeton University Library, 1969. x, 61 p. illus. 24 cm. [NE642.B5R86] 72-108006
1. Blake, William, 1757-1827. I. Princeton University. Library. BIP

SHORT, Ernest Henry, 1875-1959. 760'.0924
Blake. New York, Haskell House, 1970. vi,

167 p. plates. 23 cm. (British artists) Reprint of the 1926 ed. Bibliography: p. 166-167. [ND497.B6S5 1970] 70-118002
1. Blake, William, 1757-1827.

STORY, Alfred Thomas, 1842-1934. 700'.924 B
William Blake: his life, character, and genius. New York, Haskell House, 1970. 160 p. port. 23 cm. Reprint of the 1893 ed. [PR4146.S7 1970] 77-115183
1. Blake, William, 1757-1827. I. Title.

STORY, Alfred Thomas, 1842-1934. 759.2 B
William Blake: his life, character, and genius. [Folcroft, Pa.] Folcroft Library Editions, 1973. p. Reprint of the 1893 ed. published by S. Sonnenschein, London. [ND497.B6S7 1973] 73-4498 ISBN 0-8414-7537-7
1. Blake, William, 1757-1827.

SWINBURNE, Algernon Charles, 1837-1909. 821'.7
William Blake; a critical essay. With illus. from Blake's designs in facsim. New York, B. Blom [1967] iv, 304 p. facsims. 24 cm. Reprint of the 1868 ed. [PR4146.S77 1967] 67-12468
1. Blake, William, 1757-1827.

SYMONS, Arthur, 1865-1945. 760'.0924
William Blake. New York, Cooper Square Publishers, 1970. [14], 433 p. 23 cm. Reprint of the 1907 ed. "Records from contemporary sources": p. [249]-433. [PR4146.S8 1970] 79-115694
1. Blake, William, 1757-1827. BIP

TAYLER, Irene. 745.6'7
Blake's illustrations to the poems of Gray. Princeton, N.J., Princeton University Press, 1971. 169 p. 114 plates (1 col.) 28 cm. Bibliography: p. 163-165. [NC242.B55T38] 73-90963 ISBN 0-691-06182-3 25.00
1. Blake, William, 1757-1827. 2. Gray, Thomas, 1716-1771—Illustrations. I. Title. BIP

TODD, Ruthven, 1914- 760
Tracks in the snow : studies in English science and art / Ruthven Todd. Norwood, Pa. : Norwood Editions, 1976. p. cm. Reprint of the 1946 ed. published by the Grey Walls Press, London. Contents.Contents.—Tracks in the snow.—William Blake and the eighteenth-century mythologists.—The reputation and prejudices of Henry Fuseli.—The imagination of John Martin. Includes bibliographical references and index. [PR6039.O26T7 1976] 76-9070 ISBN 0-8482-2600-3 : 20.00
1. Blake, William, 1757-1827. 2. Fuseli, Henry, 1741-1825. 3. Martin, John, 1789-1854. 4. Literature and science. I. Title.

TOULOUSE-LAUTREC Monfa, Henri Marie Raymond de, 1864-1901. 708 s
A bestiary by Toulouse-Lautrec. Cambridge, Mass., Fogg Art Museum, 1954. 46 p. illus., port. 20 cm. (Fogg Museum picture book, no. 3) Prepared by the Dept. of Printing and Graphic Arts, Harvard Library. "Seventeen of the twenty-two lithographic illustrations by Toulouse-Lautrec in Jules Renard's Histoires naturelles ... The text has been translated, and considerably shortened ... for this publication." Bibliography: p. [13] [N527.A55 no. 3] 79-14394
I. Renard, Jules, 1864-1910. Histoires naturelles. II. Harvard University. Library. Dept. of Printing and Graphic Arts. III. Title. IV. Series: Fogg picture book, no. 3

WHITE, Hal Saunders, 1893- 821.79
A primer of Blake. Ames, Iowa, Littlefield, Adams [1951] 94 p. 22 cm. [PR4146.W45] 51-13695
1. Blake, William, 1757-1827. I. Title.

WICKSTEED, Joseph Hartley, 1870- 821'.7
Blake's Innocence and Experience; a study of the songs and manuscripts "shewing the two contrary states of the human soul," by Joseph H. Wicksteed. London & Toronto, Dent; New York, Dutton, 1928. [Folcroft, Pa.] Folcroft Library Editions, 1973. p. Includes facsimile texts of Blake's Songs of innocence and of his Songs of experience, 3 pages from the MS "An island in the moon," and 17 pages from his sketch book known as the Rossetti MS. [PR4144.S63W5 1973] 73-4392 ISBN 0-8414-9350-2 (lib. bdg.)
1. Blake, William, 1757-1827. Songs of innocence. 2. Blake, William, 1757-1827. Songs of experience. I. Title. BIP

WICKSTEED, Joseph Hartley, 1870- 821'.7
Blake's Innocence and Experience; a study of the songs and manuscripts "shewing the two contrary states of the human soul," by Joseph H. Wicksteed. London, J. M. Dent; New York, E. P. Dutton, 1928. St. Clair Shores, Mich., Scholarly Press, 1972. p. Includes facsimile texts of Blake's Songs of innocence and of his Songs of experience, 3 pages from the MS "An island in the moon," and 17 pages from his sketch book known as the Rossetti MS. [PR4144.S63W5 1972] 70-145370 ISBN 0-403-01275-9
1. Blake, William, 1757-1827. Songs of innocence. 2. Blake, William, 1757-1827. Songs of experience. I. Title. BIP

WILKIE, Brian. 821'.7
Blake's Four zoas : the design of a dream / Brian Wilkie and Mary Lynn Johnson. Cambridge : Harvard University Press, 1978. xiv, 302 p. : 24 cm. Includes index. Bibliography: p. 277-279. [PR4144.V33W5] 77-26738 15.00
1. Blake, William, 1757-1827. Vala. I. Johnson, Mary Lynn, 1937- joint author. II. Title. BIP

WILLIAM Blake : 760'.092'4
the critical heritage / edited by G. E. Bentley, Jr. London ; Boston : Routledge & K. Paul, 1975. xix, 294 p., [8] leaves of plates : ill. ; 23 cm. (The Critical heritage series) Includes index. Bibliography: p. 270. [PR4146.W47] 75-331134 ISBN 0-7100-8234-7 : 24.00
1. Blake, William, 1757-1827. I. Bentley, Gerald Eades, 1930-

WILLIAM Blake in the art of his time : 760'.092'4
[exhibition] : a faculty-graduate student project, University of California, Santa Barbara, organized by Corlette Rossiter Walker, University Art Galleries, University of California Santa Barbara, February 24-March 28, 1976. [Santa Barbara : The Galleries], c1976. 103 p. : ill. (some col.) ; 24 x 29 cm. Includes bibliographies. [N6797.B57W52] 75-620115
1. Blake, William, 1757-1827. 2. Art, English—Exhibitions. 3. Art, Modern—17th-18th centuries—England—Exhibitions. I. Blake, William, 1757-1827. II. Walker, Corlette Rossiter. III. California. University, Santa Barbara. Art Galleries.

WINGFIELD-DIGBY, George Frederick 1911- 769.2
Symbol and image in William Blake. Oxford, Clarendon Press, 1957. xx, 143 p. 77 illus. 25 cm. "Based on The gates of Paradise [by William Blake] and the newly found picture at Arlington Court, with reference to nearly sixty other designs and paintings by him, all of which are reproduced here." Bibliographical references included in "Notes" (p. 128-129) Bibliography: p. 130-133. [NE642.B5W5] 58-298
1. Blake, William, 1757-1827. 2. Blake, William, 1757-1827. For the sexes: The gates of Paradise. 3. Symbolism in art. I. Title.

WITTREICH, Joseph Anthony, comp. 700'.924
Nineteenth century accounts of William Blake, by Benjamin Heath Malkin [and others] Facsim. reproductions, edited, with introd. and headnotes, by Joseph Anthony Wittreich, Jr. Gainesville, Fla., Scholars' Facsimiles & Reprints, 1970. ix, 289 p. 23 cm. [PR4147.W54 1970] 78-133330
1. Blake, William, 1757-1827. I. Malkin, Benjamin Heath, 1769-1842. II. Title.

WRIGHT, Thomas, 1859-1936. 760'.092'4 B
The life of William Blake. New York, B. Franklin [1969] 2 v. in 1. illus. (part col.), facsims., maps, ports. 27 cm. (Burt Franklin research and source works series, 303.) (Selected papers in literature and criticism, 16) Reprint of the 1929 ed. [PR4146.W7 1969] 68-57922
1. Blake, William, 1757-1827. I. Blake, William, 1757-1827. II. Title. III. Series.

Blake, William, 1757-1827—Addresses, essays, lectures.

THE Visionary hand : 760'.092'4
essays for the study of William Blake's art and aesthetics / edited and with an introd. by Robert N. Essick. Los Angeles : Hennessey & Ingalls, 1973. xviii, 558 p. : ill. ; 24 cm. Includes bibliographical references and index. [N6797.B57V57] 72-96392 ISBN 0-912158-22-0
1. Blake, William, 1757-1827—Addresses, essays, lectures. I. Essick, Robert N.

WILLIAM Blake; 760'.09'24
essays in honour of Sir Geoffrey Keynes, edited by Morton D. Paley and Michael Phillips. Oxford, Clarendon Press, 1973. xiv, 390 p. illus. 26 cm. "A Checklist of writings on Blake by Geoffrey Keynes, 1910-72: p. 356-376." Contents.Contents.—Phillips, M. Blake's early poetry.—Bindman, D. Blake's Gothicised imagination and the history of England.—Essick, R. N. The altering eye: Blake's vision in the Tiriel designs.—Leavis, F. R. Justifying one's valuation of Blake.—Miles, J. Blake's frame of language.—Tolley, M. J. Blake's songs of spring.—Hagstrum, J. H. Christ's body.—Knight, G. W. The chapel of gold.—Erdman, D. V., Dargan, T. and Deverell-Van Meter, M. Reading the illuminations of Blake's Marriage of heaven and hell.—Warner, J. Blake's figures of despair: Man in his spectre's power.—Eaves, M. The title-page of The book of Urizen.—Beer, J. Blake, Coleridge, and Wordsworth: some cross-currents and parallels, 1789-1805.—Paley, M. D. William Blake, The prince of the Hebrews, and ssays in honour of Sir Geoffrey Keynes, edited by Morton D. Paley and Michael Phillips. Oxford, Clarendon Press, 1973. xiv, 390 p. illus. 26 cm. "A Checklist of writings on Blake by Geoffrey Keynes, 1910-72: p. 356-376." Contents.Contents.—Phillips, M. Blake's early poetry.—Bindman, D. Blake's Gothicised imagination and the history of England.—Essick, R. N. The altering eye: Blake's vision in the Tiriel designs.—Leavis, F. R. Justifying one's valuation of Blak
1. Blake, William, 1757-1827—Addresses, essays, lectures. 2. Keynes, Geoffrey Langdon, Sir, 1887- I. Paley, Morton D., ed. II. Phillips, Michael Curtis, ed.

Blake, William, 1757-1827—Bibliography.

BENTLEY, Gerald Eades, 1930- 012
Blake books : annotated catalogues of William Blake's writings in illuminated printing, in conventional typography and in manuscript, and reprints thereof, reproductions of his designs, books with his engravings, catalogues, books he owned, and scholarly and critical works about him / G. E. Bentley. Rev. ed. Oxford : Clarendon Press, 1977. xii, 1079 p., [1] leaf of plates : port. ; 24 cm. Includes index. First ed. published in 1964 under title: A Blake bibliography. [Z8103.B4 1977] [PR4146] 77-363108 ISBN 0-19-818151-5 : 88.00
1. Blake, William, 1757-1827—Bibliography. I. Title.
Distributed by Oxford University Press, New York. BIP

RUSSELL, Archibald George Blomefield, 1879-1955. 769'.924
The engravings of William Blake. New York, B. Blom [1968] 220p. illus. 24cm. Reprint of the 1912 ed. [NE642.B5R8 1968] 67-13339 17.50
1. Blake, William. 1757-1827. 2. Blake, William, 1757-1827—Bibl. I. Title.

Blake, William, 1757-1827—Biography.

BURDETT, Osbert, 1885-1936. 760'.092'4 B
William Blake. [Folcroft, Pa.] Folcroft Library Editions, 1974. viii, 198 p. 24 cm. Reprint of the 1926 ed. published by Macmillan, London, in series: English men of letters. Includes bibliographical references. [PR4146.B8 1974b] 74-3371 ISBN 0-8414-3132-9 20.00 (lib bdg)
1. Blake, William, 1757-1827—Biography.

BURDETT, Osbert, 1885-1936. 760'.092'4 B
William Blake / by Gilbert Burdett. Norwood, Pa. : Norwood Editions, 1976. p. cm. Reprint of the 1926 ed. published by Macmillan, London, in series: English men of letters. Includes bibliographical references. [PR4146.B8 1976] 76-15161 ISBN 0-8482-0159-0 : 15.00
1. Blake, William, 1757-1827—Biography. BIP

DAVIS, Michael. 760'.092'4 B
William Blake : a new kind of man / Michael Davis. Berkeley : University of California Press, 1977. 181 p., [20] leaves of plates : ill. (some col.) ; 25 cm. Includes index. Bibliography: p. 165-170. [PR4146.D34 1977] 77-71059 ISBN 0-520-03443-0 : 12.95
1. Blake, William, 1757-1827—Biography. 2. Poets, English—19th century—Biography. 3. Artists—England—Biography.

GARDNER, Charles, 1874- 700'.924 B
William Blake, the man. New York, Haskell House, 1970. 202 p. illus. 23 cm. Reprint of the 1919 ed. [PR4146.G3 1970] 76-118001 ISBN1 0-8383-1056-7
1. Blake, William, 1757-1827—Biography. I. Title.

GILCHRIST, Alexander, 1828-1861. 760'.092'4 B
Life of William Blake, with selections from his poems and other writings. A new and enl. ed., illustrated from Blake's own works, with additional letters and a memoir of the author. New York, Phaeton Press, 1969. 2 v. illus., ports. 24 cm. Reprint of the 1880 ed. "Annotated lists of Blake's paintings, drawings, and engravings": v. 2, p. [207]-307. [PR4146.G5 1969] 72-90368
1. Blake, William, 1757-1827—Biography. I. Title.

JENKINS, Herbert George, 1876-1923. 760'.092'4 B
William Blake : studies of his life and personality / by Herbert Jenkins ; edited with an introd. by C. E. Lawrence. Norwood, Pa. : Norwood Editions, 1975. 110 p., [1] leaf of plates : ill. ; 22 cm. Reprint of the 1925 ed. published by H. Jenkins, ltd., London. [PR4146.J4 1975] 75-31936 ISBN 0-88305-312-8 : 20.00
1. Blake, William, 1757-1827—Biography.

WILSON, Mona, 1872- 700'.924 B
The life of William Blake. 3rd ed.; edited by Geoffrey Keynes. London, New York, Oxford University Press, 1971. xiv, 415 p., plate; 1 illus., facsim., port. 21 cm. Bibliography: p. [389]-390. [PR4146.W5 1971] 78-853448 ISBN 0-19-211707-6 £3.25
1. Blake, William, 1757-1827—Biography. I. Title.

WILSON, Mona, 1872- 700'.924 B
The life of William Blake. New York, Cooper Square Publishers, 1969 [i.e. 1970] xv, 397 p. illus., ports. 27 cm. "This edition has been reproduced from the limited Nonesuch Press edition of 1927, with the last revisions of the 1949 edition." Includes bibliographical references. [PR4146.W5 1970] 68-57020 12.50
1. Blake, William, 1757-1827—Biography. I. Title. BIP

Blake, William, 1757-1827—Biography—Character.

WITCUTT, William Purcell. 760'.092'4 B
Blake : a psychological study / by W. P. Witcutt. [Folcroft, Pa.] : Folcroft Library Editions, 1974. 127 p. ; 24 cm. Reprint of the 1946 ed. published by Hollis & Carter, London. Includes bibliographical references. [PR4148.P8W5 1974] 74-20909 ISBN 0-8414-9574-2 lib. bdg.
1. Blake, William, 1757-1827—Biography—Character. 2. Blake, William, 1757-1827—Criticism and interpretation. I. Title. BIP

WITCUTT, William Purcell. 760'.092'4 B
Blake, a psychological study / by W. P. Witcutt. Norwood, Pa. : Norwood Editions, 1976. p. cm. Reprint of the 1946 ed. published by Hollis & Carter, London. Includes bibliographical references. [PR4148.P8W5 1976] 76-15401 ISBN 0-8482-2858-8 lib. bdg. : 15.00
1. Blake, William, 1757-1827—Biography—Character. 2. Blake, William, 1757-1827—Criticism and interpretation. I. Title.

Blake, William, 1757-1827—Catalogs.

BLAKE, William, 1757-1827. 769'.92'4
The complete graphic works of William Blake / David Bindman, assisted by Deirdre Toomey. New York : Putnam, c1978. 494 p. : 765 ill. ; 34 cm. [NE642.B5A4 1978b] 77-92146 ISBN 0-399-12152-8 : 45.00
1. Blake, William, 1757-1827—Catalogs. I. Bindman, David. II. Toomey, Deirdre. III. Title.

BLAKE, William, 1757-1827. 769'.92'4
Engravings. Edited with an introd. by Geoffrey Keynes. New York, Cooper Square Publishers, 1972. 30 p., 118 p. of plates. 26 cm. Reprint of the 1950 ed. [NE642.B5K4 1972] 72-76491 ISBN 0-8154-0417-4
I. Keynes, Geoffrey Langdon, Sir, 1887- ed.

Blake, William, 1757-1827—Congresses.

BLAKE in his time / 760'.092'4
edited by Robert N. Essick and Donald Pearce. Bloomington : Indiana University Press, c1978. p. cm. Revised papers presented at a conference sponsored by the English and Arts departments of the University of California, Santa Barbara, held March 1976. Includes bibliographical references and index. [N6797.B57B58 1978] 77-15759 ISBN 0-253-31207-8 : 17.50
1. Blake, William, 1757-1827—Congresses. I. Essick, Robert N., 1942- II. Pearce, Donald Ross, 1917- III. California. University, Santa Barbara. Dept. of English. IV. California. University, Santa Barbara. Dept. of Art. BIP

Blake, William, 1757-1827—Criticism and interpretation.

BLAKE, William, 1757-1827. 821.7
Jerusalem. A simplified version prepared and edited, with commentary and notes, by William R. Hughes. New York, Barnes & Noble [1964] 235 p. illus. 23 cm. Poems [PR4144.J4] 64-56593
I. Title.

ERDMAN, David V. 700'.924
Blake's visionary forms dramatic, edited by David V. Erdman and John E. Grant. Princeton, N.J., Princeton University Press, 1970. xxiv, 476 p. illus., 121 plates (part col.) 25 cm. Includes bibliographical references. [PR4147.E73] 79-112999 ISBN 0-691-06189-0 20.00
1. Blake, William, 1757-1827—Criticism and interpretation. I. Grant, John Ernest, joint author. II. Title.

GAUNT, William, 1900- 760'.092'4
Arrows of desire : a study of William Blake and his romantic world / by William Gaunt. Folcroft, Pa. : Folcroft Library Editions, 1978. 200 p., [9] leaves of plates : ill. ; 26 cm. Reprint of the 1956 ed. published by Museum Press, London. Includes index. Bibliography: p. 196. [PR4147.G38 1978] 78-5530 ISBN 0-8414-4484-6 lib. bdg. : 25.00
1. Blake, William, 1757-1827—Criticism and interpretation. I. Title. BIP

HAGSTRUM, Jean H. 821.7
William Blake, poet and painter: an introduction to the illuminated verse, by Jean H. Hagstrum. Chicago, University of Chicago Press [1964] xi, 156 p. 80 plates (incl. facsims., map) 25 cm. Bibliographical footnotes. [PR4147.H25] 64-13950
1. Blake, William, 1757-1827—Criticism and interpretation. BIP

MELLOR, Anne Kostelanetz. 760'.092'4
Blake's human form divine. Berkeley, University of California Press [1974] xxiii, 354 p. illus. 25 cm. Includes bibliographical references. [PR4147.M4] 72-161995 ISBN 0-520-02065-0 15.00
1. Blake, William, 1757-1827—Criticism and interpretation. I. Title. BIP

MITCHELL, W. J. Thomas, 1942- 821'.7
Blake's composite art : a study of the illuminated poetry / W. J. T. Mitchell. Princeton, N.J. : Princeton University Press c1978. xix, 230 p., [27] leaves of plates : ill. ; 25 cm. Includes bibliographical references and index. [PR4147..M5] 77-7116 16.50
1. Blake, William, 1757-1827—Criticism and interpretation. 2. Blake, William, 1757-1827—Aesthetics. 3. Illumination of books and manuscripts, English. I. Title. BIP

MURRY, John Middleton, 1889-1957. 760'.0924
William Blake. New York, Haskell House Publishers, 1971. 380 p. 23 cm. Reprint of the 1933 ed. [PR4147.M8 1971] 71-173845 ISBN 0-8383-1344-2
1. Blake, William, 1757-1827—Criticism and interpretation.

MURRY, John Middleton, 1889-1957. 760'.092'4
William Blake. [Folcroft, Pa.] Folcroft Library Editions, 1974. p. Reprint of the 1936 ed. published by J. Cape, London, which was issued as no. 76 of the Life and letters series. [PR4147.M8 1974] 74-9888 ISBN 0-8414-6142-2 (lib. bdg.)
1. Blake, William, 1757-1827—Criticism and interpretation. I. Series: The Life and letters series (London), no. 76.

PALEY, Morton D. 760'.0924
Energy and the imagination: a study of the development of Blake's thought, by Morton D. Paley. Oxford, Clarendon P., 1970. xiii, 272 p., 8 plates. 23 cm. Includes bibliographical references. [PR4147.P3] 74-489414 ISBN 0-19-811682-9 50/-
1. Blake, William, 1757-1827—Criticism and interpretation. I. Title. BIP

PINTO, Vivian de Sola, 1895- ed. 700'.924
The divine vision; studies in the poetry and art of William Blake, born November 28th, 1757, by Kathleen Raine [and others] and with an introductory poem by Walter de la Mare. Collected and edited by Vivian de Sola Pinto for the William Blake Bicentenary Committee. New York, Haskell House Publishers, 1968. 216 p. illus. 23 cm. Reprint of the 1957 ed. [PR4147.P5 1968] 68-24905
1. Blake, William, 1757-1827—Criticism and interpretation. I. Raine, Kathleen Jessie, 1908- II. William Blake Bicentenary Committee. III. Title. BIP

RAINE, Kathleen Jessie, 1908- 700'.924
Blake and England. Cambridge, W. Heffer [1960] 27 p. 19 cm. (Founders' memorial lecture, Girton College, 1960) [PR4146.R3] 68-35968
1. Blake, William, 1757-1827—Criticism and interpretation. I. Title. II. Series: Cambridge. University. Girton College. Founders' memorial lecture, 1960 BIP

RAINE, Kathleen Jessie, 1908- 760'.092'4
Blake and England, by Kathleen Raine. [Folcroft, Pa.] Folcroft Library Editions, 1973 [c1960] p. cm. Reprint of the ed. published by W. Heffer, Cambridge, Eng., in series: Founders' memorial lecture, Girton College, 1960. [PR4146.R3 1973] 73-20088 ISBN 0-8414-7285-8 (lib. bdg.)
1. Blake, William, 1757-1827—Criticism and interpretation. I. Title. II. Series: Cambridge. University. Girton College. Founders' memorial lecture, 1960.

RAINE, Kathleen Jessie, 1908- 769'.924
William Blake [by] Kathleen Raine. New York, Praeger [1971, c1970] 216 p. illus. (part col.), ports. 22 cm. (Praeger world of art series) Includes bibliographical references. [PR4146.R32 1971] 70-121081 8.50
1. Blake, William, 1757-1827—Criticism and interpretation.

WILLIAM Blake; essays 760'.0924
for S. Foster Damon. Edited by Alvin H. Rosenfeld. Providence, Brown University Press, 1969. xlvi, 498 p. 31 plates. 24 cm. On cover: Essays for S. Foster Damon. On spine: William Blake. Contents.Contents.—S. Foster Damon, the New England voice, by M. Cowley.—S. Foster Damon; a bibliography, by E. D. Costa and E. C. Wescott.—Blake and the postmodern, by H. Adams.—The visionary cinema of romantic poetry, by H. Bloom.—Blake's Miltonic moment, by H. Fisch.—Blake and the progress of poesy, by G. H. Hartman.—Blake and Shelley; beyond the uroboros, by D. Hughes.—William Blake and D. H. Lawrence, by V. de Sola Pinto.—The evolution of Blake's large color prints of 1795, by M. Butlin.—Blake's 1795 color prints; an interpretation, by A. T. Kostelanetz.—Blake's Night thoughts; an exploration of the fallen world, by M. D. Paley.—The thunder of Egypt, by A. S. Roe.—Blake and the kabbalah, by A. A. Ansari.—Blake's reading of the book of Job, by N. Frye.—The divine tetrad in Blake's Jerusalem, by G. M. Harper.—Edited by Alvin H. Rosenfeld. Providence, Brown University Press, 1969. xlvi, 498 p. 31 plates. 24 cm. On cover: Essays for S. Foster Damon. On spine: William Blake. Contents.Contents.—S. Foster Damon, the New England voice, by M. Cowley.—S. Foster Damon; a bibliography, by E. D. Costa and E. C. Wescott.—Blake and the postmodern, by H. Adams.—The visionary cinema of romantic poetry, by H. Bloom.—Blake's Miltonic moment, by H. Fisch.—Blake and the progress of poesy, by G. H. Hartman.—Blake and Shelley; beyond the ur
1. Blake, William, 1757-1827—Criticism and interpretation. I. Bosenfeld, Alvin Hirsch, ed. II. Damon, Samuel Foster, 1893- III. Title: Essays for S. Foster Damon.

Blake, William, 1757-1827—Dictionaries, indexes, etc.

DAMON, Samuel Foster, 1893- 821.7
A Blake dictionary; the ideas and symbols of William Blake. Providence, R. I., Brown Univ. Pr. [c.]1965. xii, 460p. illus., maps. 29cm. (Brown Univ. bicentennial pubns.: studies in the fields of gen. scholarship) [PR4146.A24] 65-18187 15.00
1. Blake, William, 1757-1827—Dictionaries, indexes, etc. I. Title. BIP

DAMON, Samuel Foster, 1893-1971. 821'.7
A Blake dictionary, the ideas and symbols of William Blake / S. Foster Damon ; with a new index by Morris Eaves. Boulder, Colo. : Shambhala, 1979, c1965. p. cm. Reprint of the ed. published by Brown University Press, Providence, in series: Brown University bicentennial publications: studies in the fields of general scholarship. [PR4146.A24 1979] 78-65433 ISBN 0-394-73688-5 pbk. : 8.95
1. Blake, William, 1757-1827—Dictionaries, indexes, etc. I. Title.

Blake, William, 1757-1827—Exhibitions.

BENTLEY, Gerald Eades, 1930- 760'.092'4
The Blake collection of Mrs. Landon K. Thorne. Catalogue by G. E. Bentley, Jr. Introd. by Charles Ryskamp. New York, Pierpont Morgan Library, 1971. 65 p. 30 plates. 28 cm. Catalog of the exhibition held at the Pierpont Morgan Library in New York, Nov. 19, 1971- Jan. 22, 1972. Includes bibliographical references. [PR4146.B36] 71-179936 ISBN 0-87598-034-1
1. Blake, William, 1757-1827—Exhibitions. I. Blake, William, 1757-1827. II. Thorne, Landon K., Mrs. III. Pierpont Morgan Library, New York. IV. Title. BIP

Blake, William, 1757-1827. Illustrations to the Divine comedy of Dante.

ROE, Albert S 741.91
Blake's illustrations to the Divine comedy. Princeton, Princeton University Press, 1953. xiii, 219p. plates, ports. 31cm. 'A revision and condensation of a study undertaken originally as a doctoral dissertation at Harvard University.; Includes reproductions of all the plates in the portfolio published in 1922 by the National Art-Collections Fund. London, under the title Illustrations to the Divine comedy of Dante by William Blake. Bibliography: p. 207-210. [NC233.B5R6] 52-13167
1. Blake, William, 1757-1827. Illustrations to the Divine comedy of Dante. 2. Dante—Illustrations. I. Title. BIP

Blake, William, 1757-1827—Manuscripts—Facsimiles.

BLAKE, William, 1757-1827. 535.2
Vala: or. The four zoas. A facsimile of the manuscript, a transcript of the poem, and a study of its growth and significance, by G. F. Bentley, Jr. Oxford, Clarendon Press, 1963. xviii, 220 p., facsim.: 145 (i.e. 142) p. illus. 47 cm. Pages 141-145 of the facsimile are reproduced on two pages. The poem, illustrated by Blake, is reproduced from the original in the British Museum (Add. Mss. 39764) [PR4144.V3] 63-5204
I. Bentley, Gerald Eades, 1930- II. Title.

BLAKE, William, 1757-1827. 821.79
Jerusalem. Foreword by Geoffrey Keynes. New York, Beechhurst Press [1955] 115p., facsim. (100p. illus.) front. 26cm. 'A facsimile in heliogravure of the Linnell-Rinder copy ... together with a typographical reprint of the text of the poem.' Original title page reads: Jerusalem, the emanation of the giant Albion. Printed by W. Blake, 1804. Errata slip inserted. [PR4144.J4 1955a] 56-46904
I. Title.

BLAKE, William, 1757-1827. 821'.7
The Pickering manuscript. Introd. by Charles Ryskamp. New York, Pierpont Morgan Library, 1972. [8] p., 22 p. of facsims. 22 cm. Poems. Contents.—The smile.—The golden net.—The mental traveller.—The land of dreams.—Mary.—The crystal cabinet.—The grey monk.—Auguries of innocence.—Long John Brown and Little Mary Bell.—William Bond. [PR4144.P5 1972] 72-89974 ISBN 0-87598-036-8
1. Blake, William, 1757-1827—Manuscripts—Facsimiles. I. Pierpont Morgan Library, New York. II. Title. BIP

BLAKE, William, 1757-1827 821/.7
Tiriel: facsimile and transcript of the manuscript, reproduction of the drawings and a commentary on the poem by G. E. Bentley, Jr. Oxford, Clarendon Pr., 1967. [9], 94p. 25 illus., 2 tables, 2 diagrs. 26cm. 60/- The poem is reproduced from the original in the British Museum. Bibl. [PR4144.T53 1967] 67-111038 9.60
I. Bentley, Gerald Eades, 1930- II. Title.
American distributor: Oxford Univ. Pr., New York.

Blake, William, 1757-1827 — Religion and ethics.

ALTIZER, Thomas J. J. 821'.7
The new apocalypse: the radical Christian vision of William Blake, by Thomas J. J. Altizer. [East Lansing] Michigan State University Press, 1967. xxi. 226 p. port. 24 cm. Bibliographical references included in "Notes" (p. 219-224) [PR4147.A7] 67-15436
1. Blake, William, 1757-1827 — Religion and ethics. I. Title. BIP

Blake, William, 1757-1827—Sources.

BLAKE, William, 1757-1827. 760'.092'4 B
Letters from William Blake to Thomas Butts, 1800-1803. Printed in facsim. with an introductory note by Geoffrey Keynes. Folcroft, Pa., Folcroft Press [1969] [77] p. 34 cm. Reprint of the 1926 ed. Includes

the text of a letter of Butts. [PR4146.A55 1969] 72-194986
1. Keynes, Geoffrey Langdon, Sir, 1887-, ed. BIP

RAINE, Kathleen Jessie, 1908- 821'.7
Blake and antiquity / Kathleen Raine. Princeton, N.J. : Princeton University Press, c1977. xv, 116 p., [24] leaves of plates : ill. ; 24 cm. (The A. W. Mellon lectures in the fine arts ; 1962) (Princeton/Bollingen paperbacks) (Bollingen series) "A shorter version of Blake and tradition." "Published as Blake's debt to antiquity in the Sewanee review, LXXX: 3 (summer 1963)" Bibliography: p. [105]-116. [PR4147.R332 1977] 74-5640 ISBN 0-691-01802-2 pbk. : 5.95
1. Blake, William, 1757-1827—Sources. 2. Blake, William, 1757-1827—Allegory and symbolism. I. Title. II. Series. III. Series: The A. W. Mellon lectures in the fine arts ; 11. BIP

Blakelock, Ralph Albert, 1847-1919.

BLAKELOCK, Ralph Albert, 1847-1919. 759.13
Ralph Albert Blakelock, 1847-1919 : [exhibition] January 14-February 9, 1975, Sheldon Memorial Art Gallery, University of Nebraska, Lincoln, Nebraska [and] May 4-June 7, 1975, New Jersey State Museum, Trenton, New Jersey. [Lincoln : Nebraska Art Association], c1974. 100 p. : ill. (some col.) ; 22 x 23 cm. Includes bibliographical references. [ND237.B6N42] 74-33118
1. Blakelock, Ralph Albert, 1847-1919. I. Sheldon Memorial Art Gallery. II. New Jersey. State Museum, Trenton. III. Nebraska Art Association.

KNOEDLER (M.) and Company, inc. 759.13
Ralph Albert Blakelock, 1849-1919 : [exhibition] March 3-March 31, 1973. New York : M. Knoedler, [1973] 34 p. : ill. (some col.) ; 22 cm. [ND237.B6K56 1973] 75-314181
1. Blakelock, Ralph Albert, 1849-1919. I. Blakelock, Ralph Albert, 1847-1919.

Blaue Reiter.

KANDINSKY, Wassily, 1866-1944, ed. 709'.04
The Blaue Reiter almanac. Edited by Wassily Kandinsky and Franz Marc. New documentary ed. Edited and with an introd. by Klaus Lankheit. New York, Viking Press [1974] 296 p. illus. 22 cm. (The Documents of 20th-century art) Translation of Der Blaue Reiter. Bibliography: p. 283-292. [N6490.K2913 1974] 75-170678 ISBN 0-670-17355-X 15.00
1. Blauer Reiter. 2. Art, Modern—20th century—Addresses, essays, lectures. I. Marc, Franz, 1880-1916, joint author. II. Lankheit, Klaus, joint ed. III. Title. BIP

MUNICH. Stadtische Galerie. 759.3'074'0336
The Blue Rider, with a catalog of the works by Kandinsky, Klee, Macke, Marc, and other Blue Rider artists in the Municipal Gallery, Munich [by] Hans K. Roethel. New York, Praeger Publishers [1971] 174 p. illus. (part col.) 29 cm. Translation of Der blaue Reiter. Includes bibliographical references. [ND568.5.E9M813] 75-148140 17.50
1. Blauer Reiter. 2. Painting, Modern—20th century—Germany. 3. Paintings, Modern—20th century—Exhibitions. I. Roethal, Hans Konrad, 1909-

VERGO, Peter. 759.3'36
The Blue Rider / Peter Vergo. Oxford : Phaidon Press, 1977. 16 p., [24] leaves of plates : col. ill. ; 31 cm. Bibliography: p. 14. [ND568.5.E9V47] 77-75307 ISBN 0-7148-1749-X : 6.95
1. Blaue Reiter. 2. Expressionism (Art)—Germany. 3. Painting, Modern—20th century—Germany. I. Title.
Distributed by E.P. Dutton, New York

Blaue Vier (Group of artists)

ALLENTOWN, Pa. Art Museum. 709'.43
The Blue Four and German expressionism, March 10-April 21, 1974; a fiftieth anniversary exhibition commemorating the group's founding in Weimar during 1924, plus work by other artists active in Germany between 1905 and 1930. [Catalogue. Allentown, 1974] 42 p. illus. (part col.) 28 cm. Bibliography: p. 38. [N6868.5.E9A44 1974] 74-75202
1. Blaue Vier (Group of artists) 2. Expressionism (Art)—Exhibitions. 3. Expressionism (Art)—Germany. 4. Art, Modern—20th century—Germany. I. Title.

Blaue Vier (Group of artists)—Catalogs.

NORTON Simon Museum of Art at Pasadena. 709'.04
The Blue Four Galka Scheyer Collection, Norton Simon Museum of Art at Pasadena : Feininger, Jawlensky, Kandinsky, Klee / edited by Sara Campbell. Pasadena, Calif. : The Museum, [1976] p. cm. [N6868.5.E9N67 1976] 76-13890 ISBN 0-915776-01-4 pbk.
1. Scheyer, Galka E.—Art collections. 2. Norton Simon Museum of Art at Pasadena. 3. Blaue Vier (Group of artists)—Catalogs. 4. Expressionism (Art)—Germany—Catalogs. 5. Art, Modern—20th century—Germany—Catalogs. 6. Art—Pasadena, Calif.—Catalogs. I. Campbell, Sara, 1941- II. Title.

Blegvad, Erik.

BLEGVAD, Erik. 741'.092'4 B
Self-portrait—Erik Blegvad / written and illustrated by Erik Blegvad. Reading, Mass. : Addison-Wesley, c1979. p. cm. A well-known illustrator discourses on himself, his life, and his work. [NC975.5.B55A2 1979] 92 78-23765 ISBN 0-201-00498-4 lib.bdg. : 7.95
1. Blegvad, Erik. 2. Illustrators—United States—Biography. I. Title.

Blessing, Charles A.

BLESSING, Charles A. 741.9'73
The form of cities in perspective; the Graeco-Roman world—500 B.C. to A.D. 200. An exhibition of drawings, March, 1973; a guide, by Charles A. Blessing. Ann Arbor, Center for Coordination of Ancient and Modern Studies, University of Michigan [1973] iv, 39 p. illus. 28 cm. Exhibition held at the University of Michigan Art Museum. [NC139.B53M52] 73-161629
1. Blessing, Charles A. 2. Architecture, Greco-Roman—Exhibitions. I. Michigan. University. Center for Coordination of Ancient and Modern Studies. II. Michigan. University. Museum of Art. III. Title.

Bliss, Robert Woods, 1875-1962—Art collections.

HARVARD University. Robert Woods Bliss Collection of Pre-Columbian Art, Washington, D.C. 709'.01'1
Pre-Columbian art / edited by Elizabeth P. Benson. Chicago : University of Chicago Press, c1976. p. cm. (A University of Chicago Press text/fiche) At head of title: Dumbarton Oaks collections. [E59.A7H34 1976] 76-8176 ISBN 0-226-68981-6
1. Bliss, Robert Woods, 1875-1962—Art collections. 2. Indians—Art—Catalogs. 3. Indians—Antiquities—Catalogs. 4. America—Antiquities—Catalogs. I. Benson, Elizabeth P. II. Title. III. Title: Dumbarton Oaks collections.

Block books—Facsmiles.

TOKURIKI, Tomikichiro 769.952
Ko suribotoke shu, Tokuriki Tomikichiro cho. Kyoto, Matsukyu, Showa [dist. Los Angeles, Perkins Oriental Books 1959, i.e., 1960] *10]1., 50 mounted illus. (in portfolio) 39cm. Plates engraved by the author after Buddhist prints of the Kamakura period. Publisher's announcement ([2]1.) in English, inserted, with title: A collection of old Japanese Buddhist wood-block prints. 25.00 bds.,
1. Block books—Facsmiles. 2. Wood-engravings, Japanese. I. Title.

Block, Leigh B., 1905- —Art collections.

U.S. National Gallery of Art. 760'.094'09753
100 European paintings and drawings ; from the Collection of Mr. and Mrs. Leigh B. Block. [Washington? 1967] 1 v. (unpaged) illus. 26 cm. Exhibition held at the National Gallery of Art, May 4-June 11, 1967 and at the Los Angeles County Museum of Art, Sept. 21-Nov. 2, 1967. [N5220.B667U5] 79-605080
1. Block, Leigh B., 1905- —Art collections. 2. Block, Leigh B., Mrs., 1904-—Art collections. 3. Art—Exhibitions. I. Los Angeles Co., Calif. Museum of Art, Los Angeles. II. Title.

Bloedel, Lawrence Hotchkiss, 1902-1976—Art collections.

WHITNEY Museum of American Art, New York. 709'.73'07401471
Selections from the Lawrence H. Bloedel Bequest and related works from the permanent collection of the Whitney Museum of American Art ; [checklist / compiled by Jennifer Russell, assistant curator]. New York : The Museum, c1977. 55 p. : ill. ; 26 cm. Checklist of an exhibition held Apr. 5-June 19, 1977. [N6512.W532 1977b] 77-151746 ISBN 0-87427-023-5
1. Bloedel, Lawrence Hotchkiss, 1902-1976—Art collections. 2. Art, American—Exhibitions. 3. Art, Modern—20th century—United States—Exhibitions. I. Russell, Jennifer. II. Title: Selections from the Lawrence H. Bloedel bequest ...

Bloom, Hyman, 1913—

BLOOM, Hyman, 1913- 741.9'73
The drawings of Hyman Bloom; an exhibition organized by the University of Connecticut Museum of Art, 1968. [Storrs, Conn., 1968] 1 v. (chiefly illus.) 28 cm. [NC139.B55A43] 68-6757
I. Connecticut. University. Museum of Art. II. Title.

BLOOM, Hyman, 1913- 759.13
Hyman Bloom : recent paintings : [exhibition] April 1-April 26, 1975. New York : Terry Dintenfass, [1975?] [20] p. : ill. ; 14 x 21 cm. Text by A. Werner. [ND237.B64W47] 76-350628
1. Bloom, Hyman, 1913- I. Werner, Alfred, 1911- II. Terry Dintenfass, inc.

Blount family.

BOND, Brian. 914.25'7
Mapledurham House, the historic home of the Blount family: official guide; history and description of contents by Brian Bond. Derby, English Life Publications, 1968. 20 p. illus., coat of arms, geneal. table, map. 14 x 21 cm. Illus. on lining papers. [DA690.M4097B6] 78-453197 unpriced
1. Blount family. 2. Mapledurham, Eng. I. Title.

Blue.

WOLFF, Robert Jay, 1905- 701.8
Feeling blue. New York, Scribner [1968] [32] p. col. illus. 21 cm. Blue is a shy color; it can be cold or warm, or sad or cheerful; and bright blue always fights with red but dark blue and green are friendly colors. [ND1283.W56 1968] AC 68
1. Blue. 2. Color. I. Title.

Blue and white transfer ware.

COYSH, Arthur Wilfred. 738.3'0942
Blue and white transfer ware, 1780-1840 [by] A. W. Coysh. [1st ed.] Rutland, Vt., C. E. Tuttle Co. [1971] 112 p. illus. (part col.) 25 cm. Includes bibliographical references. [NK4277.C6 1971] 76-146524 ISBN 0-8048-0975-5 6.50
1. Blue and white transfer ware. I. Title. BIP

GARNER, Harry Mason, Sir, 1891- 738.2'095
Oriental blue and white. By Sir Harry Garner. New York, Praeger Publishers [1970] xxx, 86 p. illus. (part col.) 26 cm. Bibliography: p. 83-84. [NK4563.A1G36 1970] 76-121080 18.50
1. Blue and white transfer ware. 2. Porcelain, Oriental. I. Title. BIP

WILLIAMS, Petra. 738.2'8
Flow blue china; an aid to identification. Jeffersontown, Ky., Fountain House East [1971- v. illus. 23 cm. Bibliography: v. 1, p. [211]; v. 2, p. 282. [NK4277.W54] 77-171985
1. Blue and white transfer ware. I. Title. BIP

WILLIAMS, Petra. 738.3
Flow blue china and mulberry ware : similarity and value guide / Petra Williams ; layout and photographic ill. for the text by Marguerite R. Weber. Jeffersontown, Ky. : Fountain House East, [1975] v, 198 p. : ill. ; 23 cm. Includes index. [NK4277.W55] 74-24029 ISBN 0-914736-03-5 : 8.95
1. Blue and white transfer ware. I. Title. BIP

Blue-printing.

HALLETT, Ellen Kathleen 772.2
Blue print and dyeline for schools. London, Faber & Faber. [dist. Hollywood-by-the-Sea, Fla., Transatlantic, 1964, c.1963] 61p. illus. 22cm. [TR921.H3] 64-57980 4.50 bds.,
1. Blue-printing. 2. Diazotype. I. Title.

Blue-prints.

BELLIS, Herbert F. 744.5
Blueprint reading for the construction trades [by] Herbert F. Bellis [and] Walter A. Schmidt. New York, McGraw-Hill [1968] ix, 147 p. illus. 28 cm. Bibliography: p. 135. [T379.B365] 68-13622
1. Blue-prints. I. Schmidt, Walter A., 1918- joint author. II. Title. BIP

BERGEN, Jay H. 744.5
Elements of print reading, by Jay H. Bergen. [Ed. 2] Scranton, Pa., International Correspondence Schools, 1968. 76, 4 p. illus. 23 cm. "Serial 6719-2." [T379.B39 1968] 68-3022
1. Blue-prints. I. International Correspondence Schools, Scranton, Pa. II. Title. III. Title: Print-reading.

BERGEN, Jay H. 744.5
Reading shop prints, by Jay H. Bergen. Serial 6720A-3-[B-3. Ed. 2] Scranton, International Correspondence Schools [1968] 2 v. illus. 23 cm. [T379.B394 1968] 68-3702
1. Blue-prints. I. International Correspondence Schools, Scranton, Pa. II. Title.

CONNECTICUT. Curriculum Committee for Blueprint Reading for the Building Trades. 744.532
Blueprint reading and sketching: carpentry trades, residential [by] Leo P. McDonnell. [1st ed.] Albany, N. Y., Delmar Publishers [1957] 200p. illus. 26cm. [TH5611.C6] 56-10376
1. Blue-prints. 2. Architectural drawing. I. McDonnell, Leo P. II. Title.

GRAHAM, Frank Duncan, 1875- 744.532076
Audels answers on blue print reading for mechanics and builders. New York, Audel [1956] 394p. illus. 17cm. [T379.G7 1956] 56-1693
1. Blue-prints. I. Title. II. Title: Blue print reading for mechanics and builders.

HORNUNG, William J. 744.5
Blueprint reading: interpretation of architectural working drawings. Englewood Cliffs, N. J., Prentice-Hall, 1961. 129 p. illus. 29 cm. [T379.H58] 61-7819
1. Blue-prints. I. Title.

HORNUNG, William J. 744.5
Blueprint reading: interpretation of mechanical working drawings [by] William J. Hornung. Englewood Cliffs, N.J., Prentice-Hall [1969] ix, 166 p. illus. 29 cm. [T379.H582] 69-14805 8.95
1. Blue-prints. I. Title.

JONES, David Thomas. 604.25
Reading architects' blueprints. Serial 1842A-5. [Ed. 4] Scranton, International

SUBJECT INDEX
BOEHM, EDWARD MARSHALL

Correspondence Schools, 1961- v. illus. 19cm. [T379.J62] 61-30033
1. Blue-prints. 2. Architectural drawing. I. International Correspondence Schools, Scranton, Pa. II. Title.

KENNEY, Joseph E. 744.532
Blueprint reading for the building trades. 2d ed. New York, McGraw-Hill, 1955. 120 p. illus. 32 cm. [T379.K4 1955] 54-9697
1. Blue-prints. 2. Architectural drawing.

LIGHTLE, R Paul. 744.532
Blueprint reading and sketching. Bloomington, Ill., McKnight & McKnight ['1950] 71 p. illus. 26 cm. "Answer key" (15 p.) inserted. [T379.L46] 51-3948
1. Blue-prints. I. Title. BIP

NICHOLSON, Frederick Samuel, 1902- 744.5
Blueprint reading; understanding shop practices [by] Fred Nicholson, Fred Jones [and] Cavins Baughman. 2d ed. Princeton, N.J., Van Nostrand [1959] 143 p. illus. 26 cm. [T379.N5 1959] 59-10113
1. Blue-prints. BIP

PALMQUIST, Roland E. 744.42
Audels answers on blue print reading, by Roland E. Palmquist. [2d ed.] Indianapolis, T. Audel [1966] 405 p. illus. 18 cm. [T379.P24 1966] 66-23336
1. Blue-prints. I. Title. II. Title: Answers on blue print reading.

ROGERS, William W. 1912- 744.532
Blueprint reading at work; a text to assist workers in metal trades to understand blueprints and incrase their trade knowledge [by] William W. Rogers [and] Paul L. Welton. New York, Silver Burdett Co. [1951] 136 p. illus. 28 cm. [T379.R6 1951] 51-8240
1. Blue-prints. I. Title.

WRIGHT, William N 744.532
A simple guide to blueprint reading, with applications to aircraft. [Rev. ed.] New York, McGraw-Hill, 1956. 120 p. illus. 29 cm. [T379.W7 1956] 55-8297
1. Blue-prints. I. Title.

Bluemner, Oscar, 1867-1938.

BLUEMNER, Oscar, 1867-1938. 759.13
Oscar Bluemner: paintings, drawings. [Exhibition] December 16, 1969-March 8, 1970, New York Cultural Center, New York, in association with Fairleigh Dickinson University. [New York? 1970?] [80] p. (chiefly illus. (part col.), port.) 27 cm. Label mounted on t.p.: Supplied by Worldwide Books, Boston. [ND237.B65A54] 77-18836
I. New York Cultural Center. II. Fairleigh Dickinson University.

OSCAR Bluemner; 760'.0924
American colorist. [Cambridge? Mass., 1967?] [79] p. illus. 21 x 23 cm. On label on t.p.: Supplied by Worldwide Books, New York. Exhibition organized by students and held Oct. 11-Nov. 15, 1967, at the Fogg Art Museum, Harvard University. Bibliography: p. [37]-[48] [ND1839.B57O7] 68-30090
1. Bluemner, Oscar, 1867-1938. I. Harvard University. William Hayes Fogg Art Museum.

Blueprints.

CONNECTICUT. Curriculum Committee for Blueprint Reading for the Building Trades. 744.532
Building trades blueprint reading and sketching, basic course. Albany, Delmar Publishers [1952] 193 p. illus. 27 cm. [TH431.C6 1952] 52-29180
1. Blueprints. 2. Architectural drawings. I. Title.

COOVER, Shriver L. 744.5
Programmed blueprint reading [5v. by] Shriver L. Coover, Jay D. Helsel. New York, McGraw [c.1963] 5v. (various p.) illus. (pt. col.) 22x28cm. Contents.[v.1] Introduction to blueprint reading.--[v.2] Applied blueprint reading.--[v.3] Dimensioning.--[v.4] Orthographic interpretation.-- *v.5] Sectioning and fasteners. (13051-13055) 4.80 pap., set,
1. Blueprints. 2. Machinery drawing. I. Helsel, Jay D., joint author. II. Title. BIP

Bluhm, Norman, 1920—

BLUHM, Norman, 1920- 759.13
Norman Bluhm at the Everson Museum of Art, 31 March-30 April, 1973. [Syracuse, N.Y., Everson Museum of Art, 1973] 15 p., 16-30 l. illus. 24 x 32 cm. Bibliography: p. 12. [ND237.B66E93] 73-80290
1. Bluhm, Norman, 1920- I. Everson Museum of Art of Syracuse and Onondaga County.

CORCORAN Gallery of Art, Washington, D.C. 759.13
Norman Bluhm : exhibition, June 4-July 17, 1977, the Corcoran Gallery of Art, Washington, D.C. Washington : The Gallery, [1977] [16] p. : ill. (some col.) ; 21 cm. Bibliography: p. [13]-[14] [N6537.B57C67] 77-77613
1. Bluhm, Norman, 1920- I. Bluhm, Norman, 1920- II. Title.

Blythe, David Gilmour,

MILLER, Dorothy, 1915- 927.5
The life and work of David G. Blythe. [Pittsburgh] University of Pittsburgh Press [1950] 142 p. illus., ports. 24 cm. Bibliography: p. 135-138. [ND237.B72M5] 50-4228
1. Blythe, David Gilmour, 1815-1865. I. Title.

Boats and boating.

*ALLYN, Rube 728.7
How to build a houseboat for $900. Illus. by the author. St. Petersburg, Fla., Great Outdoors [c.1964] 82p. illus., diagrs. 22cm. Cover title: How to build a houseboat; complete bill of materials, working plans, and specifications. 1.00 pap.,
I. Title.

HOGEBOOM, Amy, 1891- 741.6396238
Boats, and how to draw them. New York, Vanguard Press [1950] 39 p. illus. 22 cm. [NC825.B6H6 1950] 50-7738
1. Boats and boating. 2. Drawing—Instruction. BIP

Boats and boating—Nevada.

MITCHELL J. Serven and Associates. 711'.558
Boating in Nevada. [Reno, Nev., 1968] 61 p. illus., maps. 28 x 44 cm. Cover title. Bibliography: p. 61. [GV835.2.N73M5] 68-66770
1. Boats and boating—Nevada. 2. Lakes—Nevada. I. Title.

Boats in art—Juvenile literature.

AMES, Lee J. 743'.8'93805
Draw 50 boats, ships, trucks & trains / Lee J. Ames Garden City, N.Y. : Doubleday, 1975. p. cm. Step-by-step instructions for drawing fifty different ships, boats, trucks, and trains. [NC825.S5A43] 75-19011 ISBN 0-385-08903-1 : 5.95
1. Boats in art—Juvenile literature. 2. Ships in art—Juvenile literature. 3. Motor-trucks in art—Juvenile literature. 4. Railroads in art—Juvenile literature. 5. Drawing—Instruction—Juvenile literature. I. Title.

Bobbin lace.

BOBBIN lace, first series. 746.2'2
An English translation by Mary McPeek. Detroit, Gale Research Co., 1974. p. cm. (Dollfus-Mieg & Co. Library) Translation of: Les Dentelles aux fuseaux, Ire serie. Also has imprint of original French ed.: Mulhouse, France, T. de Dillmont. [TT805.D4613] 73-18374 15.00
1. Bobbin lace. I. McPeek, Mary, tr. II. Series: Dollfus-Mieg et cie. Library. BIP

DAWSON, Amy. 746.2'2
Bobbin lacemaking for beginners / [by] Amy Dawson. Poole : Blandford Press, 1977. 88 p. : ill. ; 23 cm. Includes index. Bibliography: p. 83. [TT805.D38] 77-375617 ISBN 0-7137-0817-4 : 3.95
1. Bobbin lace. I. Title.
Distributed by Sterling Publishers, New York, NY 10016 BIP

FUHRMANN, Brigita. 746.2'2
Bobbin Lace / by Brigita Fuhrmann. New York : Watson-Guptill Publications, 1976. p. cm. Includes index. Bibliography: p. [TT805.F83 1976] 76-21855 ISBN 0-8230-0520-8 : 12.95
1. Bobbin lace. I. Title. BIP

JOHANSON, Sally. 746.2'2
Traditional lace making. New York, Van Nostrand Reinhold [1974] p. Translation of Knyppling. [TT805.J6313] 73-16709 ISBN 0-442-30037-9 6.50
1. Bobbin lace. I. Title.

KLIOT, Kaethe. 746.2'2
Bobbin lace: form by the twisting of cords; a new look at a traditional textile art [by] Kaethe and Jules Kliot. New York, Crown Publishers [1973] ix, 245 p. illus. 27 cm. Bibliography: p. 237-238. [TT805.K56 1973] 73-82937 ISBN 0-517-50592-4 8.95
1. Bobbin lace. I. Kliot, Jules, joint author.

LES Dentelles aux fuseaux, Ire serie = Bobbin lace / With an English translation by Mary McPeek. 746.2'2
Detroit : Gale Research Co., 1974. 18 p., [58] leaves of plates : ill. (52 in pocket) ; 24 cm. Patterns and English translation of the text in pocket. French text is a reprint of the 1909 ed. published by T. de Dillmont, Mulhouse, France, in series: Bibliotheque D.M.C. [TT805.D4613] 73-18373
1. Bobbin lace. I. McPeek, Mary. II. Series: Dollfus-Mieg et cie. Bibliotheque.

NOTTINGHAM, Pamela. 746.2'2
Complete book of English bobbin lace / Pamela Nottingham. New York : Van Nostrand Reinhold, 1977, c1976. 222 p. : ill. ; 26 cm. Includes index. [TT805.N67] 76-26621 ISBN 0-442-26063-6 : 13.95
1. Bobbin lace. I. Title. BIP

SOUTHARD, Doris. 746.2'2
Bobbin lacemaking / by Doris Southard. New York : Scribner, [1977] p. cm. [TT805.S68] 77-2240 ISBN 0-684-15032-8 : 14.95
1. Bobbin lace. I. Title. BIP

Bobbin lace—Patterns.

MALMBERG, Kristina, 1932- 746.2'2
New designs in lacemaking [by] Kristina Malmberg [and] Naime Thorlin. [Translated from the Swedish by Lotta Juhlin] New York, Van Nostrand Reinhold Co. [1974] p. cm. (Reinhold craft paperback) Translation of Knyppla. Ideer och modeller inya och kanda material. [TT805.M3413] 74-5941 ISBN 0-442-30050-6 5.95
1. Bobbin lace—Patterns. I. Thorlin, Naime, joint author. II. Title.
Pbk., 3.50, ISBN 0-442-30051-4.

Boccioni, Umberto, 1882-1916.

GOLDING, John. 730'.92'4
Boccioni's Unique forms of continuity in space. [Newcastle upon Tyne] University of Newcastle upon Tyne, 1972. 32 p. illus. 25 cm. (Charlton lecture 54) Includes bibliographical references. [NB623.B65G64] 73-168650 £1.00
1. Boccioni, Umberto, 1882-1916. 2. Space (Art) I. Title. II. Series.

TAYLOR, Joshua Charles, 1917- 655.3
The graphic work of Umberto Boccioni. New York, Museum of Modern Art; distributed by Doubleday, Garden City, N.Y. [c1961] unpaged. illus. 26 cm. [NC1155.B56T3] 61-16521
1. Boccioni, Umberto, 1882-1916. I. Title.

Bochner, Mel, 1940—

RICHARDSON, Brenda. 741.9'73
Mel Bochner : number and shape / Brenda Richardson. Baltimore : Baltimore Museum of Art, c1976. x, 68 p. : ill. (some col.) ; 24 x 26 cm. Issued in connection with the exhibition held at the Baltimore Museum of Art, Oct. 5-Nov. 28, 1976. "Catalogue of the exhibition": p. 59-62. Bibliography: p. 65-66. [NC139.B625R52] 76-27589 8.50
1. Bochner, Mel, 1940- I. Bochner, Mel, 1940- II. Baltimore. Museum of Art. III. Title: Number and shape.

Bodine, A. Aubrey, 1907-1970.

WILLIAMS, Harold A., 1916- 779
Bodine; a legend in his time, by Harold A. Williams. [1st ed.] Baltimore, Bodine, 1971. 82 p., [77] p. of illus. 27 cm. "The photography of A. Aubrey Bodine, 1924-1970": p. [1]-[75] (2d group) [TR140.B55W5] 70-169537 ISBN 0-910254-70-2 12.50
1. Bodine, A. Aubrey, 1907-1970. 2. Photography, Artistic. I. Bodine, A. Aubrey, 1907-1970. II. Title.

Bodoni, Giovanni Battista, 1740-1813.

MARDERSTEIG, Hans, 1892- 655.1'45'0924
On G. B. Bodoni's type faces [by] Giovanni Mardersteig. Verona [Printed at the Officina Bodoni] 1968. [33] p. 26 cm. "200 copies." "Printed ... as a keepsake for Gallery 303 to remember a lecture given at New York by G. Mardersteig at the Morgan Library 25 November 1968." [Z232.B66M36] 73-528701
1. Bodoni, Giovanni Battista, 1740-1813. I. Title.

Body art—Exhibitions.

MUSEUM of Contemporary Art, Chicago. 709'.04
Bodyworks : [exhibition] : March 8 to April 27, 1975, Museum of Contemporary Art, Chicago, Illinois. Chicago : The Museum, c1975. [20] p. : ill. ; 23 cm. Filmography: p. [19] [N6494.B63M87 1975] 76-359031
1. Body art—Exhibitions. 2. Art, Modern—20th century—Exhibitions. I. Title.

N. E. Thing Company. 704.94'2'074011372
Celebration of the body : Agnes Etherington Art Centre, Kingston, Ontario, 19 June—31 June, 1976 / N. E. Thing Co. Ltd. [Vancouver] : N. E. Thing Co., [1976] 1 portfolio ([38] p., [68] leaves of plates : ill.) ; 32 cm. Cover title. [N6494.B63N2 1976] 77-375433
1. Body art—Exhibitions. 2. Art, Modern—20th century—Exhibitions. I. Agnes Etherington Art Centre. II. Title.

Boege, Uli.

BOEGE, Uli. 759.13
Elsewhere : collages / by Uli Boege. New York : Links Books : distributed by Quick Fox, [1974] [60] p. : all ill. (some col.) ; 31 cm. [N6537.B58A45] 74-77395 ISBN 0-8256-3037-1 : 6.95
1. Boege, Uli. I. Title.

Boehm, Edward Marshall, 1912-

COSENTINO, Frank J. 738.27
Boehm's birds; the porcelain art of Edward Marshall Boehm. Appreciation by John D. Morse. New York, Fell [1966, c.1960] 202p. plates (pt. col.) ports. 28cm. Bibl. [NK4210.B6C6] 60-13256 15.00
1. Boehm, Edward Marshall, 1912- I. Title.

COSENTINO, Frank J. 738'.0924
Edward Marshall Boehm, 1913-1969, by Frank J. Cosentino. [Chicago, Printed by The Lakeside Press, 1970] 264 p. illus. (part col.), ports. (part col.) 32 cm. Bibliography: p. 264. [NK4210.B6C63] 75-130889
1. Boehm, Edward Marshall, 1913-1969.

EVERITT, Charles, 1906- 598.2
Birds of the Edward Marshall Boehm aviaries; major portion devoted to softbills. [Trenton, N.J., E. M. Boehm, 1973] 297 p. illus. 32 cm. Bibliography: p. 285. [QL676.E93] 73-76875
1. Boehm, Edward Marshall, 1913-1969. 2. Birds. 3. Aviaries—New Jersey—Trenton.

I. Boehm, Edward Marshall, 1913-1969. II. Title.

†PALLEY, Reese. 738.2'092'4
The porcelain art of Edward Marshall Boehm / by Reese Palley. New York : H. N. Abrams, [1976] p. cm. Includes index. [NK4210.B6P34] 76-20690 ISBN 0-8109-0701-1 : 35.00
1. Boehm, Edward Marshall, 1913-1969. 2. Porcelain, American. I. Title.

Boer, Saskia de, 1945—

BOER, Saskia de, 1945- 730'.92'4
Celebrated images, sculptures of film stars, pin-ups & famous paintings / [by] Saskia de Boer. London : Whitechapel Art Gallery, 1976. Folder ([4] p.) : chiefly ill., ports. ; 30 cm. Catalogue of an exhibition held at the Whitechapel Art Gallery, Ideas Gallery, 2nd June-4th July 1976. Bibliography: p. [2] [NB653.B63W47] 76-380626 ISBN 0-85488-032-1 : £0.22
1. Boer, Saskia de, 1945- I. Whitechapel Art Gallery, London. II. Title.

Bognor Regis, Eng. Hotham Park House.

ALLAM, David P. 942.2'67
A brief history of Hotham Park House, Bognor Regis / written and compiled by David P. Allam and Ronald Iden. [Bognor Regis] : [The author], [1976] [4], 12, [4] p., fold. plate : ill., map, plans, port. ; 21 cm. [DA690.B646A43] 77-366981 ISBN 0-9505465-0-X : £0.50
1. Bognor Regis, Eng. Hotham Park House. I. Iden, Ronald, joint author. II. Title.

Bohemianism—Caricatures and cartoons.

JOANS, Ted 741.5973
The hipsters. [New York, Corinth Bks., dist. Citadel Pr. c.1961] unpaged (chiefly illus.) 61-15877 1.50 pap.,
1. Bohemianism—Caricatures and cartoons. I. Title.

Bohen, Mildred M.—Art collections—Exhibitions.

SELECTIONS from 759.94'074'017796
the Collection of Mrs. Fred Bohen : [exhibition], November 13, 1977-January 1, 1978, Des Moines Art Center. [Des Moines] : The Center, c1977. [10] p., [10] leaves of plates : ill. (some col.) ; 23 cm. [ND189.S44] 77-92746
1. Bohen, Mildred M.—Art collections—Exhibitions. 2. Painting, Modern—19th century—Exhibitions. 3. Painting, Modern—20th century—Exhibitions. I. Des Moines Art Center.

Bohrod, Aaron.

WISCONSIN sketches. 741.9'73
Drawings by Aaron Bohrod. Words by Robert E. Gard. Edited by Mark E. Lefebvre. [1st ed. Madison, Wisconsin House, 1973] 1 v. (unpaged) illus. 23 x 27 cm. [NC139.B63W57] 73-89027 ISBN 0-88361-026-4 12.95
1. Bohrod, Aaron. 2. Wisconsin in art. 3. Wisconsin—Poetry. I. Bohrod, Aaron. II. Gard, Robert Edward. III. Lefebvre, Mark E., ed. BIP

Bok, Hannes, 1914-1964.

PETAJA, Emil, 1915- comp. 741.64'092'2
The Hannes Bok memorial showcase of fantasy art. Compiled & edited by Emil Petaja. San Francisco, SISU Publishers [1974] 166 p. illus. (part col.) 28 cm. [NC960.P467] 73-92462 10.00
1. Bok, Hannes, 1914-1964. 2. Grotesque in art. 3. Illustration of books. I. Bok, Hannes, 1914-1964. II. Title. III. Title: Showcase of fantasy art.

Bollinger, James Wills, 1867-

IOWA. University. Library. 923.173
The Bollinger Lincoln lectures; addresses given at the dedication of the Lincoln Library, collected by James W. Bollinger, November 19, 1951. Edited by Clyde C. Walton, Jr. [curator of rare books] With a pref. by Virgil M. Hancher. [Iowa City] State University of Iowa Libraries, Bollinger Lincoln Foundation, 1953. 80p. port. 25cm. 'Three hundred and fifty copies... have been printed... Number 40.' Includes bibliographies. [E457.65.I6] 57-36852
1. Bollinger, James Wills, 1867- 2. Lincoln, Abraham, Pres. U. S.—Museums, relics, etc. 3. Lincoln, Abraham, Pres. U. S.—Law practice. I. Walton, Clyde G., ed. II. Title.
Contents omitted.

Bologne, Jean de, 1524-1608.

HOLDERBAUM, James. 730'.92'4
The sculptor Giovanni Bologna / James Holderbaum. New York : Garland Pub., 1977. p. cm. (Outstanding dissertations in the fine arts) Originally presented as the author's thesis, Harvard, 1959. Bibliography: p. [NB623.B7H64 1977] 76-23626 ISBN 0-8240-2696-9 lib.bdg. : 46.00
1. Bologne, Jean de, 1524-1608. 2. Sculptors—Italy—Biography. I. Title. II. Series. BIP

Bolotowsky, Ilya, 1907—

BOLOTOWSKY, Ilya, 1907- 759.13
Ilya Bolotowsky : the Solomon R. Guggenheim Museum, New York. New York : Solomon R. Guggenheim Foundation, 1974. 133 p. : ill. (some col.) ; 26 cm. "Exhibition 74/5." Bibliography: p. 132-133. [ND237.B725S64] 74-14271 pbk. : 6.95
1. Bolotowsky, Ilya, 1907- I. Solomon R. Guggenheim Museum, New York.

BOLOTOWSKY, Ilya, 1907- 759.13
Ilya Bolotowsky; paintings & columns. An exhibition organized by the staff of the University Art Museum, the University of New Mexico, and shown at the following institutions: Newport Harbor Art Museum, Balboa, California [and others. Albuquerque, University Art Museum, University of New Mexico, 1970] 24 p. illus., port. 25 cm. [ND237.B725A47] 72-631331
I. New Mexico. University. Art Museum. II. Newport Harbor Art Museum.

Bolzano (Province)—Descr. & trav.—Views.

RIEDL, Franz Hieronymus. 914.5383
Southern Tyrol. Introd. by Franz H. Riedl. Translated by G. A. Colville. Garden City, N. Y., Distributed by Doubleday [1965] 61 p. (p. [17]-[46] col. plates) 17 x 18 cm. (Panorama-books) Translation of Sildtirol. Captions in German, English, and French. [DG975.B68R513] 65-5542
1. Bolzano (Province)—Descr. & trav.—Views. I. Title.

Bon, Giovanni, ca. 1360-1443.

SCHULZ, Anne Markham, 1938- 730'.92'2
The sculpture of Giovanni and Bartolomeo Bon and their workshop / Anne Markham Schulz. Philadelphia : American Philosophical Society, 1978. 81 p. : ill. ; 29 cm. (Transactions of the American Philosophical Society ; v. 68. pt. 3 ISSN 0065-9746s) Includes bibliographical references and index.I[NB623.B718S38] 78-50190 ISBN 0-87169-683-5 : 6.00
1. Bon, Giovanni, ca. 1360-1443. 2. Bon, Bartolomeo, ca. 1407-1467. 3. Artists' studios—Italy—Venice. 4. Sculpture, Gothic—Italy—Venice. I. Title. II. Series: American Philosophical Society, Philadelphia. Transactions ; v. 68, pt. 3.

Bond, Frederick Bligh, 1864-1945.

KENAWELL, William W. 726.7094238
The quest at Glastonbury, a biographical study of Frederick Bligh Bond. New York, Helix [dist. Taplinger, 1965] xi, 318p. illus., facsims., plans, ports. 24cm. Bibl. [DA690.G45K4] 65-18997 8.50
1. Bond, Frederick Bligh, 1864-1945. 2. Glastonbury Abbey. I. Bond, Frederick Bligh, 1864-1945. II. Title. BIP

Bone carving.

RITCHIE, Carson I. A. 736'.6
Bone and horn carving : a pictorial history / Carson I. A. Ritchie. South Brunswick : A. S. Barnes, [1975] 166 p. : ill. ; 28 cm. Includes bibliographical references and index. [NK6020.R52] 73-22601 ISBN 0-498-01404-5 : 12.00
1. Bone carving. 2. Horn carving. I. Title.

Bonfire Shelter site, Texas.

DIBBLE, David S. 970.4'64'881
Bonfire shelter: a stratified bison kill site, Val Verde County, Texas, by David S. Dibble [and] Dessamae Lorrain. With appendix by Ruben Frank. [Austin, University of Texas, Texas Memorial Museum, 1968] 138 p. illus. 29 cm. (A Publication of the Texas Memorial Museum. Miscellaneous papers, no. 1) Originally issued in August, 1965, as a report to the National Park Service by the Texas Archeological Salvage Project (Miscellaneous papers, no. 5), University of Texas. Contents.Contents.—Part 1: The archeology, by D. S. Dibble.—Part 2: Analysis of the bison bones, by D. Lorrain.—Bibliography (p. 135-138) [E78.T4D5] 68-65623
1. Bonfire Shelter site, Texas. 2. Paleo-Indians—Texas—Val Verde County. I. Lorrain, Dessamae, joint author. II. Title. III. Series: Texas. Memorial Museum, Austin. Miscellaneous papers, no. 1

Bonheur, Rosa, 1822-1899.

PEARE, Catherine Owens. 759.4
Rosa Bonheur, her life. Illustrated by Margaret Ayer. [1st ed.] New York, Holt [1956] 126p. illus. 21cm. [Holt books for young people] [ND553.B6P35] [ND553.B6P35] 927.5 56-10035 56-10035
1. Bonheur, Rosa, 1822-1899. I. Title.

STANTON, Theodore, 1851-1925, ed. 759.4 B
Reminiscences of Rosa Bonheur / edited by Theodore Stanton. New York : Hacker Art Books, 1976. xvii, 413 p., [23] leaves of plates : ill. ; 25 cm. Reprint of the 1910 ed. published by D. Appleton, New York. Includes indexes. [ND553.B6S8 1976] 74-147039 ISBN 0-87817-096-0 : 30.00
1. Bonheur, Rosa, 1822-1899. 2. Painters—France—Biography. I. Title. BIP

Bonheur, Rosa, 1822-1899—Juvenile literature.

PRICE, Olive M. 759.4
Rosa Bonheur, painter of animals, by Olive Price. Illustrated by Cary. Champaign, Ill., Garrard Pub. Co. [1972] 144 p. illus. 22 cm. A biography of a nineteenth-century French artist acclaimed internationally during her lifetime for her realistic animal paintings. [ND553.B6P74] 92 71-190739 ISBN 0-8116-4515-0
1. Bonheur, Rosa, 1822-1899—Juvenile literature. I. Cary, Louis F., 1915- illus. II. Title.

Bonkei.

HIROTA, Jozan, 1896- 745.92
Bonkei: tray landscapes. Photos. by Yoshikazu Ezaki. [1st ed.] Tokyo, Palo Alto, Calif., Kodansha International [1970] 128 p. illus. (part col.) 19 x 27 cm. [SB447.5.H57] 79-117384 6.95
1. Bonkei. BIP

Bonnard, Pierre, 1867-1947.

BONNARD, Pierre, 1867-1947. 759.4
Bonnard, by Raymond Cogniat. [Translated from the French by Anne Ross] New York, Crown Publishers [1968] 94 p. illus. (part col.), col. plates. 29 cm. Bibliography: p. 94. [ND553.B65C543] 68-31977 3.50
I. Cogniat, Raymond, 1896- BIP

BONNARD, Pierre, 1867-1947. 741.944
Drawings from 1893-1946. New York, American Federation of Arts [1972] 1 v. (chiefly illus.) 23 cm. Catalog of the exhibition held at various museums. [NC248.B58A84] 72-87024
I. American Federation of Arts.

BONNARD, Pierre, 1867-1947. 759.4
Pierre Bonnard. Text by Andre Fermigier. [1st ed.] New York, H. N. Abrams [1969] 160 p. illus., 49 col. plates. 34 cm. (The Library of great painters) Bibliography: p. 160. [ND553.B65F413] 69-12442
I. Fermigier, Andre. II. Title.

BONNARD, Pierre, 1867-1947. 759.4
Pierre Bonnard, 1867-1947 [catalogue of an exhibition, May-October, 1971] Melbourne, National Gallery of Victoria, 1971. 24, [80] p. 40 plates. 25 cm. Exhibition to be held at the National Gallery of Victoria, Art Gallery of South Australia, Art Gallery of New South Wales and the Western Australian Art Gallery. [ND553.B65V5] 77-198429
I. Victoria, Australia. National Gallery, Melbourne.

BONNARD, Pierre, 1867-1947. 759.4
Pierre Bonnard; exhibition, Nov. 9-Dec. 11, 1965 New York, Acquavella Galleries [1965] [46] p. col. illus. 24 cm. [ND553.B65A62] 72-170821
I. Acquavella Galleries.

BOURET, Jean. 759.4
Bonnard; the magic ring. New York, French & European Publications [1967] 58, [2] p. col. illus. 21 cm. (Rhythm and colour, 2d ser., v. 1) Translation of Bonnard; seductions. Bibliography: p. [60]. [ND553.B65B613] 68-1749
1. Bonnard, Pierre, 1867-1947. I. Title: The magic ring.

NEW York. Museum of Modern Art. 759.4
Bonnard and his environment, Texts by James Thrall Soby, James Elliott, and Monroe Wheeler. Garden City, N.Y. Doubleday [1964] 116 p. illus. (part col.) port. 25 cm. Includes the "catalogue of the exhibition: the Museum of Modern Art, New York, October 7-November 29, 1964, the Art Institute of Chicago, January 8-February 28, 1965 [and the] Los Angeles County Museum of Art, March 31-May 30, 1965" Bibliography: p. 111-116. [ND553.B65N4] 64-7643
1. Bonnard, Pierre, 1867-1947. I. Soby, James Thrall, 1906- II. Title.

TERRASSE, Antoine. 759.4
Bonnard; biographical and critical study. Translated from the French by Stuart Gilbert. [Geneva] Skira; [distributed in the U.S. by the World Pub. Co., Cleveland, 1964] 115 p. mounted col. illus. 19 cm. (The Taste of our time, v. 42) Bibliography: p. 103-105. [ND553.B65T423] 64-23256
1. Bonnard, Pierre, 1867-1947. I. Title.

VAILLANT, Annette 759.4
Bonnard; with a dialogue between Jean Cassou and Raymond Cogniat; commentaries by Hans R. Hahnloser. [Tr. from French by David Britt] Greenwich, Conn., N.Y. Graphic [1966, c.1965] 229p. illus. (pt. mounted col.) plates. ports. 29cm. Bibl. [ND553.B65V33 1966a] 66-15809 27.50
1. Bonnard, Pierre, 1867-1947. I. Cassou, Jean, 1897- II. Cogniat, Raymond, 1896- III. Hahnloser, Hans Robert, 1899- IV. Title.

Bonnin and Morris.

HOOD, Graham, 1936- 738.2'09748'11
Bonnin and Morris of Philadelphia; the first American porcelain factory, 1770-1772. Chapel Hill, Published for the Institute of Early American History and Culture at Williamsburg, Va., by the University of North Carolina Press [1972] xiii, 78 p. illus. 24 cm. (An Institute book on the arts and material culture in early America) Includes bibliographical

League, 7 Albemarle Street, London W.1, Saturday 16th to Thursday 28th October 1976. [London] : [Private Libraries' Association], 1976. [50] p., [4] p. of plates : ill. ; 26 cm. Cover title. Includes index. [Z994.E5B66 1976] 77-360162 ISBN 0-900002-43-3 : £0.65
1. Book-plates, English—Exhibitions. 2. London—Exhibitions. I. Title.

Book-plates, Jewish.

GOODMAN, Philip, 1911- 769'.5
Illustrated essays on Jewish bookplates. New York, Ktav Pub. House, 1971. 196 p. illus. 24 cm. Bibliography: p. 181-196. [Z993.G65] 78-139464 ISBN 0-87068-142-7
1. Book-plates, Jewish. I. Title.

Bookbinding.

BARROW (W. J.) Research Laboratory, Richmond. 655.7
Permanence/durability of the book -- IV; polyvinyl acetate (PVA) adhesives for use in library bookbinding. Richmond, 1965. 66 p. 23 cm. (Its Publication no. 4) Bibliography: p. 65. [Z247.B3] 65-8459
1. Bookbinding. 2. Adhesives. 3. Vinyl acetate. I. Title. II. Title: Polyvinyl acetate (PVA) adhesives for use in library bookbinding. III. Series.

Bookmarks—Collectors and collecting.

COYSH, Arthur Wilfred. 741.6
Collecting bookmarkers / A. W. Coysh. New York : Drake, c1974. 96 p. : 159 ill. ; 25 cm. Includes index. Bibliography: p. 9. [Z987.C66 1974b] 74-13577 ISBN 0-87749-730-3 : 8.95
1. Bookmarks—Collectors and collecting. I. Title.

Books.

BOOK Manufacturers' Institute. 655.5
Helpful aids in book production. New York, 1953. 184p. illus. 29cm. [Z244.B687] 53-33710
1. Books. 2. Printing, Practical. I. Title.

CARR, Jess. 658.8'09'070573
How a book is born : how a book is written, edited, published, printed, distributed, and sold / by Jess Carr. Durham, N.C. : Moore Pub. Co., c1978. x, 103 p. : ill. ; 27 cm. [Z116.A2C37] 78-59112 ISBN 0-87716-088-0 : 10.95
1. Books. 2. Book industries and trade. 3. Authorship. I. Title. BIP

JENNETT, Sean. 655
The making of books. 4th ed. rev. New York, Praeger [1967] 512p. illus. (pt. col.). facsims., col. port. 23cm. Bibl. [Z116.A2J47 1967b] 67-15898 15.00
1. Books. I. Title. BIP

Books—Addresses, essays, lectures.

WHITE, Lewis Felix, 1895- 655
The art of the book, a talk given under the auspices of the Type Directors Club of New York City. New York, L.F. White Co., 1951. unpaged, illus. 19 cm. (Typophiles monographs, 31) [Z246.W6] 52-467
1. Books—Addresses, essays, lectures. I. Title. II. Series: The Typophiles, New York. Typophile monographs, 31

Books and reading.

BENNETT, James O'Donnell, 1870-1940. v. 12
Much loved books; a key to 35 best sellers of the ages; novels, poetry, drama. Introduction by John K. Hutchens. Greenwich, Conn., Fawcett Publications [1959] 256 p. 18 cm. [A Premier book, d81] These essays first appeared in the Chicago tribune. "First Premier printing, September 1959." [NUC64-3473]
1. Books and reading. I. Title. BIP

BERENSON, Bernhard, 1865-1959. 927
One year's reading for fun, 1942. [1st ed.] Introd. by John Walker. New York, Knopf, 1960. 166, xiip. illus. 25cm. [N8375.B46A28] 59-153161
1. Books and reading. I. Title.

Books and reading—Great Britain—History.

KNIGHT, Charles, 1791-1873. 686.2'092'4
The old printer and the modern press. London, J. Murray, 1854. [New York, AMS Press, 1974] ix, 314 p. illus. 19 cm. Includes bibliographical references. [Z232.C38K67 1974] 71-148340 ISBN 0-404-08838-4 14.50
1. Caxton, William, 1422 (ca.)-1491. 2. Books and reading—Great Britain—History. I. Title. BIP

Books—Dictionaries.

GLAISTER, Geoffrey Ashall. 655.03
An encyclopedia of the book; terms used in paper-making, printing, bookbinding and publishing. With notes on illuminated manuscripts, bibliophiles, private presses, and printing societies. Incl. illus. and translated extracts from Grafisk Uppslagsbok, Esselte, Stockholm. [1st ed.] Cleveland, World Pub. Co. [1960] 484 p. illus. (part col., part mounted) 26 cm. Bibliography: p. 477-484. [Z118.G55] 60-6660
1. Books—Dictionaries. I. Title.

Books—Format.

FREIMAN, Ray. ed. 655.53
The author looks at format, comments by Van Wyck Brooks [and others. New York] A[merican] I[nstitute of G[raphic] A[rts, 1951] 58 p. 17 cm. [Z246.F865] 52-465
1. Books—Format. I. Brooks, Van Wyck, 1886- II. Title.

RICE, Stanley. 686.2'25
Book design : text format models / Stanley Rice. New York : R. R. Bowker Co., c1978. xiv, 215 p. ; 24 cm. [Z245.R5] 77-26908 ISBN 0-8352-1045-6 : 17.50
1. Books—Format. I. Title. BIP

Books — Hist. — 400-1400.

ALMU'IZZ IBN BADIS Emir of Ifriqiyah, 1008-1062 002.0902
Mediaeval Arabic bookmaking and its relation to early chemistry and pharmacology [by] Martin Levey. Philadelphia, American Philosophical Society, 1962. 79 p. 30 cm. (Transactions of the American Philosophical Society, new ser., v. 52, pt. 4) Appendix (p. 51-55): Translation of Abu'l-'Abbas Ahmed ibn Muhammed al Sufyani: Sina'at tasfir al-kutub wa-hill al-dhahab (Art of bookbinding and of gilding) from the Arabic text published by P. Ricard, 1925. Bibliography: p. 56-57. Bibliographical footnotes. [Q11.P6] [Z115.1.M8] 62-15117
1. Books — Hist. — 400-1400. 2. Paleography, Arabic. 3. Chemistry, Technical. I. Levey, Martin. II. Title. III. Series: American Philosophical Society, Philadelphia. Transactions, new ser., v. 52 pt. 4
BIP

Books—Hist.—Antiquity and Middle Ages.

THE hand-produced book. 655.4
New York, Philosophical Library [1953] 603p. illus., facsims. 24cm. A companion vol. to the author's The alphabet; a key to the history of mankind. Includes bibliographies. [Z112] [Z112] 002 53-7899 53-7899
1. Books—Hist.—Antiquity and Middle Ages. I. Diringen, David, 1900-

THE hand-produced book. 655.4
London, New York, Hutchinson's Scientific and Technical Publications [1953] 603p. illus., facsims. 24cm. A companion vol. to the author's The alphabet; a key to the history of mankind. Includes bibliographies. [Z112.D57] [Z112.D57] 002 54-840 54-840
1. Books—Hist.—Antiquity and Middle Ages. I. Diringer, David, 1900-

KENYON, Frederic George, Sir 1863- 655.4
Books and readers in ancient Greece and Rome. 2d ed. Oxford, Clarendon Press, 1951. vii, 136 p. illus., facsims. 19 cm. [Z112.K] A52
1. Books—Hist.—Antiquity and Middle Ages. 2. Books and reading. 3. Manuscripts (Papyri) 4. Parchment. I. Title. BIP

Books—Juvenile literature.

GREENFIELD, Howard. 808'.02
Books : from writer to reader / Howard Greenfeld. New York : Crown, c1976. 211 p. : ill. ; 24 cm. Includes index. Bibliography: p. 205-206. Follows a book through the various stages of publishing, printing, and marketing. [Z116.A2G74 1976] 76-15991 ISBN 0-517-52620-4 : 8.95
1. Books—Juvenile literature. 2. Book industries and trade—Juvenile literature. I. Title. BIP

SPECTOR, Marjorie. 686
Pencil to press : how this book came to be / Marjorie Spector. New York : Lothrop, Lee & Shepard Co., [1975] 95 p. : ill. ; 24 cm. Includes index. A step-by-step explanation of how this book came into being, from conception to its arrival in the reader's hands. [Z116.A2S63] 75-14356 ISBN 0-688-41713-2 : 5.50 ISBN 0-688-51713-7 lib.bdg. : 4.81
1. Books—Juvenile literature. I. Title. BIP

Books on microfilm.

HAWKINS, Reginald 778.315
Production of micro-forms. New Brunswick, N.J., Graduate School of Library Service, Rutgers, the State University; distributed by Rutgers University Press, 1960. v. 208 p. 'References': p. 167-194. 23cm. (The state of the Library art v.5, pt. 1) 60-7277 5.00
1. Books on microfilm. 2. Microphotography. I. Title. II. Title: Microforms. III. Series. BIP

Books—Owners' marks—Catalogs.

LEE, Brian North. 769'.5
Early printed book labels : a catalogue of dated personal labels and gift labels printed in Britain to the year 1760. Pinner, [Eng.] : Private Libraries Association, 1976. xxii, 185 p. : ill. ; 26 cm. Includes indexes. Bibliography: p. 176. [Z994.G74L43] 76-361058 ISBN 0-900002-72-7
1. Books—Owners' marks—Catalogs. 2. Book collectors—Great Britain. 3. Bibliography—Early printed books—Catalogs. I. Title.

Books—Prices.

HAZEN, Allen Tracy, 1904- 094
A bibliography of the Strawberry Hill Press; with a record of the prices at which copies have been sold, including a new supplement, by A. T. Hazen; together with a bibliography and census of the detached pieces, by A. T. Hazen and J. P. Kirby. [New ed.] Folkestone [Eng.] Dawsons of Pall Mall, 1973. xxxiv, 300 p. illus. 25 cm. The bibliography is based in large part on the Walpolian collection of W. S. Lewis, who has written the preface. [Z232.S9H25 1973] 74-155393 ISBN 0-7129-0571-5 £7.50
1. Strawberry Hill Press. 2. Books—Prices. I. Kirby, John Pendy. II. Lewis, Wilmarth Sheldon, 1895- III. Title.
Distributed by Barnes and Noble, 25.00 BIP

Boonzaier, Gregoire, 1909-

SCOTT, F P 1915- 759.968
Gregoire Boonzaier [by] F. P. Scott. Cape Town, Tafelberg-Uitg., 1964. 149, [2] p. illus. (part col.) port. 21 cm. Text in English and Afrikaans. Bibliography: p. [151] [ND1096.B6S3] 65-67855
1. Boonzaier, Gregoire, 1909- I. Title.

Booth, Franklin, 1874-1948.

BOOTH, Franklin, 1874-1948. 741.9'73
The art of Franklin Booth : sixty reproductions from original drawings / with an appreciation by Ernest Calkins ; and an introd. by Meredith Nicholson. New York : Nostalgia Press, c1976. [71] p. : chiefly ill. ; 30 cm. Reprint of the 1925 ed. published by R. Frank, New York. [NC139.B637A42 1976] 76-373081 8.95
1. Booth, Franklin, 1874-1948. I. Title.

Boots and shoes.

CLARK, Christine Lewis. 646.4
The make-it-yourself shoe book / Christine Lewis Clark. 1st ed. New York : Knopf, 1977. 100. p. : ill. ; 28 cm. Includes index. [TT678.5.C58 1977] 76-47933 ISBN 0-394-41057-2 : 10.00
1. Boots and shoes. I. Title. BIP

EVRARD, Gwen. 646.4
Twinkletoes : footgear to make and wear / by Gwen Evrard. New York : Scribner, c1976. 144 p. : ill. ; 24 cm. "A Gladstone book." [TT678.5.E95] 75-41523 ISBN 0-684-14606-1 : 9.95
1. Boots and shoes. 2. Handicraft. I. Title.

KATZ, Ruth J. 746.9'2
Footwear / Ruth Katz. New York : Van Nostrand Reinhold, [1979] p. cm. Includes index. [TT678.5.K37] 78-14043 ISBN 0-442-26144-6 : 13.95
1. Boots and shoes. 2. Needlework. I. Title. BIP

LOOMIS, Mary Wales. 646.4'8
Custom-make your own shoes and handbags : a simplified method of making women's shoes and handbags at home / by Mary Wales Loomis. New York : Crown Publishers, c1978. ix, 118 p., [2] leaves of plates : ill. ; 27 cm. Includes index. [TT678.5.L66 1978] 77-13699 ISBN 0-517-53138-0 : 10.00 ISBN 0-517-53139-9 pbk. : 5.95
1. Boots and shoes. 2. Handbags. I. Title. BIP

The Borden Limner.

BISHOP, Robert Charles. 759.13
The Borden Limner and his contemporaries : an exhibition, The University of Michigan Museum of Art, November 14, 1976-January 16, 1977 / organized by Robert C. H. Bishop. [Detroit : Michigan Council for the Arts], [1977] c1975. x, 90 p. : ill. (some col.) ; 21 x 26 cm. Includes bibliographical references. [ND1329.B64B57] 77-621415
1. The Borden Limner. 2. Portraits, American—Exhibitions. 3. Portrait painting, American—New England—Exhibitions. 4. Portrait painting—19th century—New England—Exhibitions. 5. Primitivism in art—New England—Exhibitions. I. Michigan. University. Museum of Art. II. Title.

Borduas, Paul Emile.

BORDUAS, Paul Emile. 759.11
Paul-Emile Borduas / Francois-Marc Gagnon. Toronto : National Gallery of Canada, 1976. 93 p. : ill. (some col.) ; 24 cm. (Canadian artists series ; no. 3) Bibliography: p. 93-95. [ND249.B6G33] 77-360042 ISBN 0-88884-271-6
1. Borduas, Paul Emile. 2. Painters—Canada—Biography. I. Gagnon, Francois. II. Title. III. Series.

BORDUAS, Paul Emile. 759.11
Paul-Emile Borduas, 1905-1960: a loan exhibition [at the Currier Gallery of Art, Manchester, N.H., Jan. 6-29, 1967, and the Jaffe-Friede Gallery, Hopkins Center, Dartmouth College, Feb. 3-Mar. 5, 1967] Hanover, N.H., Hopkins Center Art Galleries, Dartmouth College, 1967. 1 v. (unpaged) illus., port. 25 cm. Introductory essay by Evan H. Turner. [ND249.B6T8] 67-68013
I. Turner, Evan H. II. Currier Gallery of Art, Manchester, N.H. III. Dartmouth College. Hopkins Center. IV. Title.

Borein, Edward, 1872-1945.

BOREIN, Edward, 1872- 741.9'73 1945.
Drawings & paintings of the Old West [by] Edward Borein. Compiled with an introd. by Nicholas Woloshuk, Jr. Foreword by Harold McCracken. [1st ed.] Flagstaff, Ariz., Northland Press, 1968- v. chiefly illus. 31 cm. Contents.Contents.—v. 1. The Indians. [NC139.B64W64] 68-22584
1. Borein, Edward, 1872-1945. 2. The West in art. I. Woloshuk, Nicholas, 1924- II. Title.

BOREIN, Edward, 1872- 741.9'73 1945.
Edward Borein: the Katherine H. Haley Collection. [Phoenix, Ariz., Phoenix Art Museum, 1974] 23 p. illus. 26 cm. Catalog of an exhibition held at the Phoenix Art Museum, Apr. 5-May 21, 1974. [NC139.B64P58] 74-175064
1. Borein, Edward, 1872-1945. 2. Haley, Katherine H.—Art collections. I. Phoenix, Ariz. Art Museum. II. Title.

BOREIN, Edward, 1872- 769'.92'4 1945.
The etchings of Edward Borein. A catalogue of his work by John Galvin. Complied with the assistance of Warren R. Howell, in collaboration with Harold G. Davidson. San Francisco, J. Howell—Books, 1971. 1 v. (unpaged) illus. 32 cm. [NE2012.B6G3] 76-174984
1. Borein, Edward, 1872-1945. 2. The West in art. I. Galvin, John, ed.

DAVIDSON, Harold G., 769'.92'4 B 1912-
Edward Borein, cowboy artist; the life and works of John Edward Borein, 1872 [sic]-1945 [by] Harold G. Davidson. [1st ed.] Garden City, N.Y., Doubleday, 1974. 189 p. illus. (part col.) 32 cm. Includes bibliographical references. [N6537.B63D38 1974] 74-2063 ISBN 0-385-09607-0 25.00
1. Borein, Edward, 1873-1945. 2. The West in art. I. Borein, Edward, 1873-1945. II. Title.

Boren, James.

KRAKEL, Dean Fenton, 1923- 759.13
James Boren; a study in discipline, by Dean Krakel. Flagstaff, Ariz., Northland Press [1968] xii, 59 p. illus. (part col.) 27 cm. [ND237.B726K7] 68-56218 8.50
1. Boren, James.

CASEY, Robert Joseph, 1890- 927.3
Give the man room; the story of Gutzon Borglum, by Robert J. Casey and Mary Borglum. [1st ed.] Indianapolis, Bobbs-Merrill [1952] 326 p. illus. 23 cm. [NB237.B6C3] 52-5804
1. Borglum, John Gutson de la Mothe, 1867-1941. I. Title.

Borglum, John Gutzon de la Mothe, 1867-1941.

FITE, Gilbert Courtland, 978.3 1918-
Mount Rushmore. [1st ed.] Norman, University of Oklahoma Press [1952] xiv, 272 p. illus., ports., maps. 22 cm. Bibliography: p. 255-260. [NB237.B6F5] 52-7919
1. Borglum, John Gutzon de la Mothe, 1867-1941. 2. Mount Rushmore National Memorial. I. Title. BIP

PRICE, Willadene. 730.973
Gutzon Borglum, artist and patriot. Chicago, Rand McNally [1961] 224p. illus. 22cm. [NB237.B6P7] 61-13983
1. Borglum, John Gutzon de la Mothe, 1867-1941. I. Title. BIP

Borglum, Solon Hannibal, 1868-1922.

DAVIES, Alfred 730'.92'4 B Mervyn.
Solon H. Borglum, "a man who stands alone"; a biography, by A. Mervyn Davies. [1st ed.] Chester, Conn., Pequot Press [1974] xxi, 285 p. illus. 26 cm. Bibliography: p. [257]-265. [NB237.B62D38] 74-181506 ISBN 0-87106-140-6 18.50
1. Borglum, Solon Hannibal, 1868-1922.

Borgona, Juan de, d. 1533—Bibliography.

SMITH, Virginia Carlson. 759.6
Juan de Borgona and his school: a bibliography, by Virginia Smith. Los Angeles, Hennessey & Ingalls, 1973. vi, 41 p. port. 23 cm. (Art & architecture bibliographies, no. 2) [Z8109.37.S62] 72-96390 ISBN 0-912158-40-9 4.95
1. Borgona, Juan de, d. 1533—Bibliography. 2. Art, Spanish—Bibliography. I. Title. II. Series.

Borobudur, Indonesia.

SOEKMONO, R. 726'.1'43095982
Chandi Borobudur : a monument of mankind / by Dr. Soekmono. Assen : Van Gorcum ; Paris : The Unesco Press, 1976. 53 p., [8] leaves of plates : ill. ; 24 cm. Bibliography: p. 52-53. [NA6026.6.B6S57 1976] 77-361411 ISBN 9-02-321356-4 : 7.30
1. Borobudur, Indonesia. 2. Temples, Buddhist—Indonesia, Borobudur. 3. Temples—Conservation and restoration—Indonesia—Borobudur. I. Title.
Distributed by Unipub BIP

Borowsky, Peter.

BOROWSKY, Peter. 709'.2'4
Peter Borowsky : [exhibition] February 7 to 29, 1976. London [Ont.] : London Art Gallery, [1976] [24] p. : ill. ; 26 x 33 cm. Cover title. [N6549.B66L65] 76-379635
1. Borowsky, Peter. I. London Public Library and Art Museum (Ont.)

Borromini, Francesco, 1599-1667.

BLUNT, Anthony, Sir, 720'.92'4 1907-
Borromini / by Anthony Blunt. Cambridge, Mass. : Harvard University Press, [1979] p. cm. Includes index. Bibliography: p. [NA1123.B6B56] 78-11320 ISBN 0-674-07925-6 : 15.00
1. Borromini, Francesco, 1599-1667. 2. Architects—Italy—Biography. 3. Architecture, Baroque—italy.

BLUNT, Anthony, Sir, 720'.92'4 1907-
Borromini / by Anthony Blunt. Cambridge, Mass. : Harvard University Press, [1979] p. cm. Includes index. Bibliography: p. [NA1123.B6B56] 78-11320 ISBN 0-674-07925-6 : 15.00
1. Borromini, Francesco, 1599-1667. 2. Architects—Italy—Biography. 3. Architecture, Baroque—italy. BIP

PORTOGHESI, Paolo. 720'.924
The Rome of Borromini; architecture as language. Translated by Barbara Luigia La Penta. New York, G. Braziller [1968] viii, 451 p. illus. 29 cm. Cover title: Borromini. Includes bibliographical references. [NA1123.B6P63] 68-25337 25.00
1. Borromini, Francesco, 1599-1667. 2. Architecture—Rome (City) I. Title.

STEINBERG, Leo, 726'.5'0945632 1920-
Borromini's San Carlo alle Quattro Fontane : a study in multiple forms and architectural symbolism / Leo Steinberg. New York : Garland Pub., 1977. p. cm. (Outstanding dissertations in the fine arts) Originally presented as the author's thesis, New York University. Includes index. Bibliography: p. [NA5620.C32S73 1977] 75-23815 lib.bdg. : 27.50
1. Borromini, Francesco, 1599-1667. 2. San Carlo alle Quattro Fontane, Rome. 3. Symbolism in architecture—Italy—Rome (City) I. Title. BIP

Bosch, Hieronymous van Aken, known as, d.1516.

BALDASS, Ludwig von, 759.9492 1887-
Hieronymus Bosch. [Translated from the German] New York, H. N. Abrams [1960] 242p. Bibl.: p.241-242. mounted col. illus., plates (part col. &part fold-out) port. 34cm. 59-12876 18.50
1. Bosch, Hieronymus van Aken, known as. d. 1516. I. Title.

BOSCH, Hieronymus van 759.9492 Aken, known as, d.1516.
Bosch / text by Joseph-Emile Muller. Bourne End, Bucks. : Spurbooks, [1976] [41] p., [94] p. of plates : chiefly ill. (chiefly col.), ports. (chiefly col.) ; 18 cm. [ND653.B65M84] 77-352091 ISBN 0-904978-16-8 : £2.50
1. Bosch, Hieronymus van Aken, known as, d. 1516. I. Muller, Joseph Emile.

BOSCH, Hieronymus van 759.9492 Aken, known as, d.1516.
The complete paintings of Bosch. Introd. by Gregory Martin. Notes and catalogue by Mia Cinotti. New York, H. N. Abrams [1971, c1966] 118 p. illus., col. plates. 32 cm. (Classics of the world's great art) First published in 1967 under title: L'opera completa di Bosch. Bibliography: p. 11-15. [ND653.B65C513 1971] 69-16896 5.95
I. Cinotti, Mia. II. Title.

BOSCH, Hieronymus van 759.9492 Aken, known as, d.1516.
Hieronymus Bosch. Text by Lotte Brand Philip. New York, H. N. Abrams [1970] 40 p. illus. (part col.) 33 cm. (Great art of the ages) [ND653.B65P42 1970] 69-19703 ISBN 0-8109-5100-2
I. Philip, Lotte Brand.

BOSMAN, Anthony 759.9492
Hieronymus Bosch. [Tr.: Albert J. Fransella] New York, Barnes & Noble [1963, c.1962] 90p. illus. (pt. col.) 18cm. (Barnes & Noble art ser. 610) 63-5388 .75 pap.,
1.) I. Title.

BUSSAGLI, Mario. 759.9492
Bosch. [Translated from the Italian by Claire Pace. 1st American ed.] New York, Grosset & Dunlap [1967] 39, [80] p. illus. (part col.) 18 cm. (The New Grosset art library, 3) On cover: Bosch; the life and work of the artist. [ND653.B65B83 1967] 67-24230
1. Bosch, Hieronymus van Aken, known as, 1516, d.

DELEVOY, Robert L. 759.9492
Bosch: biographical and critical study. Translated by Stuart Gilbert. [Lausanne] Skira; [distributed in the U. S. by World Pub. Co., Cleveland, 1960] 141p. mounted col. illus. (The Taste of our time, v. 34) Bibl.: 60-15595 .125-[134] 5.75
1. Bosch, Hieronymus van Aken, known as, d.1516. I. Title.

DE TOLNAY, Charles, 760'.0924 1899-
Hieronymus Bosch. New York, Reynal [1966, c1965] 451 p. illus. (part col.) 33 cm. "Catalogue Raisoune": p. [331]-377. Includes bibliographical references. [ND653.B65D413 1966a] 66-23355
1. Bosch, Hieronymus van Aken, known as, d. 1516. I. Title.

FRAENGER, Wilhelm, [759.9492] 1890-
The Millennium of Hieronymus Bosch; outlines of a new interpretation. Translated by Eithne Wilkins & Ernst Kaiser. Chicago, University of Chicago Press [1951] xiii, 164 p. illus. 27 plates (part col.) 28 cm. [ND653.B65F713 1951] 927.5 52-11051
1. Bosch, Hieronymus van Aken, known as, d. 1516. I. Title.

†FRANGER, Wilhelm, 759.9492 1890-1964.
The Millennium of Hieronymus Bosch : outlines of a new interpretation / by Wilhelm Franger ; translated by Eithne Wilkins & Ernst Kaiser. New York : Hacker Art Books, 1976. xi, 164 p., [14] leaves of plates : ill. ; 29 cm. Translation of Hieronymus Bosch, Das tausendjahrige Reich; Grundzuge einer Auslegung. Includes index. [ND653.B65F713 1976] 75-11062 ISBN 0-87817-172-X lib.bdg. : 20.00
1. Bosch, Hieronymus van Aken, known as, d. 1516. I. Title.

GIBSON, Walter S. 759.9492
Hieronymus Bosch [by] Walter S. Gibson. New York, Praeger [1973] 180 p., 151 illus. (26 in color) 22 cm. Bibliography: p. 175-176. [ND653.B65G52] 73-6495 10.00
1. Bosch, Hieronymus van aken, known as, d. 1516.

JEROME Bosch. 759.9492
Paris, P. Tisne; New York, Universe Books [1957] 103p. illus., 140 plates (part col.) 29cm. Bibliography: p.99-[100] [ND653.B65C613] [ND653.B65C613] 927.5 57-12103 57-12103
1. Bosch, Hieronymus van Aken, known as, d. 1516. I. Combe, Jacques.

LINFERT, Carl, 1900- 759.9492
Hieronymus Bosch. Text by Carl Linfert. [Translated from the German by Robert Erich Wolf. 1st ed.] New York, Abrams [1971] 134, [2] p. illus., col. plates. 34 cm. (The Library of great painters) Bibliography: p. [136] [ND653.B65L513] 71-149853 ISBN 0-8109-0043-2
1. Bosch, Hieronymus van Aken, known as, d. 1516.

SNYDER, James, comp. 759.9492
Bosch in perspective. Englewood Cliffs, N.J., Prentice-Hall [1973] x, 178 p. illus. 21 cm. (The Artists in perspective series) (A Spectrum book) Bibliography: p. 169-175. [ND653.B65S58 1973] 73-16063 ISBN 0-13-080416-9 6.95
1. Bosch, Hieronymus van Aken, known as, d. 1516. I. Title.
Pbk. 2.45; ISBN 0-13-08040-8. BIP

Bosch, Hieronymus van Aken, Known as, d. 1516—Catalogs.

HIERONYMUS Bosch / 759.9492
Gregory Martin. New York : St. Martin's Press, [1979] p. cm. [ND653.B65A4 1979] 78-19811 ISBN 0-312-09306-3 pbk. : 5.95
1. Bosch, Hieronymus van Aken, Known as, d. 1516—Catalogs. I. Martin, Gregory.

Boston.

FROST, John Edward. 917.4461
Boston, America's home port; a sketch book. [Boston, Hawthorne Press, 1955] 92p. illus. 26cm. [F73.3.F7] 56-17889
1. Boston. I. Title.

TAYLOR, Alice. 301.43'15'0974461
Boston. [Prepared with the cooperation of the American Geographical Society] Garden City, N.Y., Doubleday [1962] 63 p. illus. 21 cm. (Know your America Program) [F73.3.T3 1962] 62-51136
1. Boston. I. Title.

TAYLOR, Alice. 917.44'6'1
Boston. [Prepared with the cooperation of the American Geographical Society] Garden City, N.Y., N. Doubleday [1967] 64 p. illus. (part col.) maps. 21 cm. (Know your America program) [F73.3.T3 1967] 67-6047
1. Boston. I. American Geographical Society of New York.

Boston—Buildings—Juvenile literature.

HALL, Elvajean. 917.44'61'044
Today in old Boston / text by ElvaJean Hall ; sketches by Joanna Adamska-Koperska. Chicago : Childrens Press, [1975] p. cm. Explains the historical significance of Boston's most important historic buildings and sights. [F73.33.H34] 75-1035 ISBN 0-516-03803-6 lib.bdg. : 4.95
1. Boston—Buildings—Juvenile literature. 2. Historic buildings—Massachusetts—Boston—Juvenile literature. 3. Boston—History—Juvenile literature. I. Adamska-Koperska, Joanna, ill. II. Title. BIP

Boston Celtics (Basketball team)—History.

POWERS, John, 1948- 769.32'364'0974461
The short season : a Boston Celtics diary, 1977-1978 / by John Powers. 1st ed. New York : Harper & Row, c1979. p. cm. [GV885.52.B67P68 1979] 78-2158 ISBN 0-06-013451-8 : 10.00
1. Boston Celtics (Basketball team)—History. I. Title. BIP

Boston—Descr.—1951—

CHIANG, I, 1903- 917.446
The silent traveller in Boston. Written and illustrated by Chiang Yee. [1st ed.] New York, W. W. Norton [1959] xii, 275p. illus. (part col.) 22cm. Includes Chinese poems by the author with English translations. [F73.52.C48] 59-10935
1. Boston—Descr.—1951- I. Title. BIP

Boston — Descr. — Views.

BUSSE, Fritz 741.943
Boston, cradle of liberty. Text by Edward Weeks. Sketches by Fritz Busse, New York, Arts, Inc., 667 Madison Ave. [1965] 64p. (chiefly illus., pt. col.) 18x21cm. [NC1075.B9W4] 65-16857 3.95
1. Boston—Descr.—Views. I. Weeks, Edward, 1898- II. Title.

LAWLOR, David F 301.43'15'0974461
A Boston image; 100 photos by Dave Lawlor. [Boston, 1962] unpaged. illus. 28 cm. [F73.37.L3] 63-27392
1. Boston — Descr. — Views. I. Title.

SIRKIS, Nancy 917.4461
Boston. Introd. by Edward M. Kennedy. New York, Viking [c.1965, 1966] 154p. (chiefly illus. (1 col.) ports.) 29cm. (A Stdido bk.) [F73.37.S55] 66-16069 10.00
1. Boston—Descr.—Views. 2. Boston—Biog.—Portraits. I. Title.

WAINWRIGHT, Wainwright Johnson, 1917- 917.4461
Boston in picture and story. Cotuit, Mass., Picture Book Press [1954] 64p. illus. 22cm. [F73.5.w3] 54-3893
1. Boston—Descr.—Views. I. Title.

WHITEHILL, Walter Muir, 1905- 917.446
Boston: portrait of a city. Photographs by Katharine Knowles. Barre, Mass., Barre Publishers, 1964. 112 p. illus. 23 cm. [F73.37.W63] 64-14908
1. Boston — Descr. — Views. I. Knowles, Katharine, illus. II. Title. BIP

Boston—Description.

DRAKE, Samuel Adams, 1833-1905. 917.44'61
Old landmarks and historic personages of Boston. New and rev. ed. Detroit, Singing Tree Press, 1970. xviii, 484 p. illus., ports. 22 cm. Reprint of the 1900 ed. [F73.37.D79] 76-99068
1. Boston—Description. 2. Boston—Historic houses, etc. I. Title. BIP

DRAKE, Samuel Adams, 1833-1905. 917.44'61'03
Old landmarks and historic personages of Boston. Rev. ed. Rutland, Vt., C. E. Tuttle [1971] xxi, 484 p. illus. 19 cm. (Tut books. H.) "Revised edition published 1906." [F73.37.D792] 70-157258 ISBN 0-8048-0993-3 2.95
1. Boston—Description. 2. Boston—Dwellings. I. Title.

Boston—Description—1951-

BERCHEN, William. 779'.9'974461
Aspects of Boston / William Berchen. Boston : Houghton Mifflin, 1975. p. cm. [F73.52.B47] 74-32403 ISBN 0-395-19418-0 : 19.95 ISBN 0-395-20549-2 pbk : 9.95
1. Boston—Description—1951- I. Title.

MCBRIDE, Stewart Dill. 974.4'61'04
Boston in color : a collection of color photographs / by Peter H. Dreyer ; with an introductory text and notes on the ill. by Stewart Dill McBride. New York : Hastings House, 1976. p. cm. (Profiles of America) [F73.52.M32 1976] 76-44540 ISBN 0-8038-0775-9 : 5.95
1. Boston—Description—1951- 2. Boston—Description—1951- —Views. I. Title. BIP

Boston—Description—1951- —Views.

MATSUBARA, Naoko. 769'.924
Boston impressions. Woodcuts by Naoko Matsubara. Text by Sinclair Hitchings. Barre, Mass., Barre Publishers, 1970. 63 p. illus. (part col.) 24 cm. [NE1184.5.M37H5] 79-111104 ISBN 0-8271-7004-1 10.00
1. Boston—Description—1951- —Views. I. Hitchings, Sinclair H. II. Title.

WESTMAN, Barbara. 759.1
The bean & the scene; drawings of Boston and Cambridge. Introd. by Herbert A. Kenny. Barre, Mass., Barre Publishers, 1969. 34 p. col. illus. 23 x 28 cm. [F73.7.W4] 74-87004 ISBN 0-8271-6919-1 5.95
1. Boston—Description—1951- —Views. 2. Cambridge, Mass.—Description—Views. 3. Drawings, American. I. Title. BIP

WESTMAN, Barbara. 917.44'61'0440222
A Boston picture book [by] Barbara Westman and Herbert A. Kenny. Boston, Houghton Mifflin, 1974. 45 p. 23 cm. [F73.37.W47] 74-3079 ISBN 0-395-19336-2 6.95
1. Boston—Description—1951- —Views. I. Kenny, Herbert A., joint author. II. Title. BIP

Boston—Description—Views.

HAWES, Josiah Johnson, 1808-1901. 917.44'61'030222
The legacy of Josiah Johnson Hawes; 19th century photographs of Boston. Edited, with an introd., by Rachel Johnston Homer. Barre, Mass., Barre Publishers, 1972. 131 p. (chiefly illus.) 29 cm. Bibliography: p. 131. [F73.37.H37 1972] 72-83295 ISBN 0-8271-7223-0 12.50
1. Boston—Description—Views. 2. Boston—Dwellings—Pictorial works. I. Homer, Rachel Johnston, ed. II. Title.

KNOWLES, Katharine. 917.44'4
Boston & Cambridge; portrait of two cities. Photos. by Katharine Knowles. Text by Walter Muir Whitehill. Barre, Mass., Barre Publishers [1972] 222 p. illus. 22 cm. [F73.52.K58] 72-83360 7.95
1. Boston—Description—Views. 2. Cambridge, Mass.—Description—Views. I. Whitehill, Walter Muir, 1905- II. Title.

Boston—Exhibitions.

BOSTON artifacts 974.4'61'0074
: objects collected for Where's Boston? : A bicentennial exhibition designed and produced by Cambridge Seven Associates, Inc., sponsored by the Prudential Insurance Company of America / Cambridge Seven Associates, Inc. & Fred Kresse ; photos. of the collection by Stephen Rosenthal. Cambridge, Mass. : The Associates, 1975. 94 p. : ill. (some col.) ; 27 cm. Exhibition at the Bicentennial Pavilion in the Prudential Center, Boston. [F73.15.B67] 75-16060
1. Boston—Exhibitions. I. Cambridge Seven Associates. II. Kresse, Fred. III. Rosenthal, Stephen.

Boston metropolitan area—Transit systems.

MASSACHUSETTS Bay Transportation Authority. 711'.75'0974461
Program for mass transportation; a program for improving mass transportation facilities in the area constituting the authority. [Boston] 1966. 1 v. (various pagings) maps (1 fold. col.) 28 cm. [HE4491.B75M36] 73-6016
1. Boston metropolitan area—Transit systems. I. Title.

MASSACHUSETTS Bay Transportation Authority. 711'.75'0974461
Report on alternative programs for suburban commuter service. [Boston] 1969. 3, 78 p. illus., maps (part col.) 29 cm. [HE4491.B75M38] 75-630462
1. Boston metropolitan area—Transit systems. I. Title.

Boston. Museum of Fine Arts.

BOSTON. Museum of Fine Arts. 737.4'9'38
Catalogue of Greek coins / by Agnes Baldwin Brett, honorary curator of classical coins, Museum of Fine Arts, Boston ; with a new introd. by Mary B. Comstock and Cornelius C. Vermeule, Jr. New York : Attic Books, 1974. xvii, 340 p., [58] leaves of plates : ill. ; 29 cm. Reprint of the 1955 ed. published by the museum. Includes bibliographies and indexes. [CJ315.U52B673 1974] 75-305887 ISBN 0-915018-04-7
1. Boston. Museum of Fine Arts. 2. Coins, Greek. I. Brett, Agnes Baldwin, 1876-1955. II. Title.

BOSTON. Museum of Fine Arts. 733
Greek & Roman portraits, 470 BC - AD 500. Boston, 1972. [82] p. illus. 22 cm. Includes bibliographical references. [N7585.B66 1972] 72-77975
1. Boston. Museum of Fine Arts. 2. Portraits, Greek—Catalogs. 3. Portraits, Roman—Catalogs. 4. Portraits—Boston—Catalogs. I. Title.

BOSTON. Museum of Fine Arts. 708.144
Illustrated handbook. Boston, 1964. xvi, 389 p. illus. (part col.) 23 cm. [N520.A56] 65-3479
I. Title.

BOSTON. 739'.533'0974074014461
Museum of Fine Arts. Dept. of American Decorative Arts and Sculpture.
American pewter in the Museum of Fine Arts, Boston, Department of American Decorative Arts and Sculpture. Photos. by Daniel Farber. Boston, Museum of Fine Arts; distributed by New York Graphic Society, Greenwich, Conn. [1974] xiii, 119 p. illus. 28 cm. Bibliography: p. 119. [NK8412.B67 1974] 74-78551 ISBN 0-87846-080-2 12.50
1. Boston. Museum of Fine Arts. 2. Pewter, American—Catalogs. 3. Pewter—Boston—Catalogs. 4. Hall-marks. I. Title. BIP

MUSEUM of Fine Arts, 708.144'61
Boston. [Texts by Adolph S. Cavallo and others] New York, Newsweek [1969] 171 p. col. illus., plans. 30 cm. (Great museums of the world) Bibliography: p. 168. [N520.A76] 69-19065
1. Boston. Museum of Fine Arts. I. Cavallo, Adolph S. II. Series: Great museums of the world (New York, Newsweek)

WHITEHILL, Walter Muir, 1905- 708.144'61
Museum of Fine Arts, Boston; a centennial history. Cambridge, Mass., Belknap Press, 1970. 2 v. (888 p.) illus. 25 cm. Includes bibliographical references. [N520.W5] 70-102674 25.00
1. Boston. Museum of Fine Arts. BIP

Boston—Statues.

WHITEHILL, Walter Muir, 1905- 914.4'61'03
Boston, statues. With photos. by Katharine Knowles. Barre, Mass., Barre Publishers, 1970. 120 p. illus., ports. 27 cm. [F73.64.A1W45] 72-128387 ISBN 0-8271-7015-7 10.00
1. Boston—Statues. I. Knowles, Katharine, illus. II. Title.

Boston University. Marsh Chapel.

MARSH, Daniel Lash, 1880- 726.41
The charm of the chapel. Boston. Boston University Press, 1950. 207 p. illus. 24 cm. [NA5235.B76M3] 51-2057
1. Boston University. Marsh Chapel. I. Title.

Boswell, James, 1906-1971.

NOTTINGHAM, Eng. University. Art Gallery. 760'.092'4
James Boswell, 1906-71 : drawings, illustrations and paintings / [Nottingham University Art Gallery. [Nottingham] : The Gallery, 1976. 32 p. : ill., port. ; 25 cm. Catalogue of an exhibition held 22 Nov.-16 Dec., 1976. Bibliography: p. 32. [N7408.B67N67 1976] 77-363162 ISBN 0-9504622-1-7 : £0.50
1. Boswell, James, 1906-1971.

Botanical illustration.

HUNT Botanical Library. 759.4
A catalogue of Redouteana exhibited at the Hunt Botanical Library 21 April to 1 August 1963. Pittsburgh, 1963. vii, 117 p. plates (part col.) 26 cm. Catalogue of 203 items in the Hunt Botanical Library. Includes bibliographies. [QK31.R4H8] 70-229937
1. Redoute, Pierre Joseph, 1759-1840. 2. Botanical illustration. I. Title.

Botanical illustration—Exhibitions.

HUNT Botanical Library. 760'.092'2
Catalogue: a selection of 20th century botanical art & illustration; presented at XI International Botanical Congress, August 1969. Compiled by George H. M. Lawrence. Pittsburgh, 1969. 168 p. illus. 23 cm. Title on cover: 20th century botanical art & illustration. Title on spine: Botanical art & illustration. Errata sheet inserted. "A selection of works of botanical art from the 2d International Exhibition of 20th century botanical art and illustration that opened at the Hunt Botanical Library, Pittsburgh, Pa., on 20 October 1968." [QK98.2.H79] 73-155882
1. Botanical illustration—Exhibitions. 2. Illustrators. 3. Plants in art—Exhibitions. I. Lawrence, George Hill Mathewson, 1910- II. Title: 20th century botanical art & illustration. III. Title: Botanical art & illustration.

HUNT Botanical Library. 760'.0922
Catalogue, 2nd International Exhibition of Botanical Art & Illustration, 20 October 1968 to 15 April 1969. Compiled by George H. M. Lawrence. Pittsburgh, 1968. 267 p. illus., ports. 24 cm. Cover title: 20th century botanical art & illustration, 1968-1969. Title on spine: Botanical art & illustration, 1968/69. [QK98.2.H8] 68-58544
1. Botanical illustration—Exhibitions. 2. Illustrators. 3. Plants in art—Exhibitions. I. Lawrence, George Hill Mathewson, 1910- II. Title: International Exhibition of Botanical Art & Illustration. III. Title: 20th century botanical art & illustration, 1968/69. IV. Title: Botanical art & illustration.

Botany—Pictorial works.

BELVIANES, Marcel, 1893- 580.84
Exotic plants of the world. Translated and adapted from Marcel Belvianes' "Beautes de la flore exotique" by Anthony J. Huxley. Garden City, N. Y., Hanover House, 1957 [c1955] 93 p. illus. 28 cm. [QK98.B413] 57-14006
1. Botany—Pictorial works. I. Title.

BRUEHL, Anton, 1900- 779'.34
Tropic patterns. Hollywood, Fla., Dukane Press [1970] [4] p., 24 col. plates. 37 cm. [QK98.B83] 78-105524 ISBN 0-87800-113-1 10.95
1. Botany—Pictorial works. I. Title.

HARLOW, William Morehouse, 1900- 581.0222
Patterns of life; the unseen world of plants [by] William M. Harlow. Prologue by Paul B. Sears. [1st ed.] New York, Harper & Row [1966] 128 p. illus. 26 cm. [QK98.H3] 66-13918
1. Botany—Pictorial works. I. Title.

MILNE, Lorus Johnson, 1910- 581'.022'2
Living plants of the world [by] Lorus and Margery Milne. Photos. by Josef Muench [and others] New York, Random House [1967] 336 p. illus. (part col.) 29 cm. "A

the author. Photography by Malcolm Kurtz. [Placerville, Calif., Printed by Pioneer Press, 1968] 56 p. illus. 26 cm. Bibliography: p. 56. [NK5440.B6R6] 68-22314
1. Bottles. 2. Flower arrangement. I. Title. BIP

TIBBITTS, John C. 748.8
1200 bottles priced; a bottle price guide, catalogue, and classification system, by John C. Tibbitts. Photos, by Don Alverson Sacramento, Calif., Little Glass Shack [1964] 164 p. illus. 14 x 23 cm. [NK5440.B6T53] 64-21303
1. Bottles. 2. Glassware—Prices. 3. Glassware—Collectors and collecting. I. Title.

WATSON, Richard, 1932- 748.8
Bitters bottles. Supplement. [New York] T. Nelson [1968] 160 p. illus., facsims. 24 cm. Bibliography: p. 154. [NK5440.B6W3 Suppl.]
1. Bottles. 2. Bitters. I. Title.

WATSON, Richard., 1932- 748.8
Supplement to Bitter bottles. [New York] Nelson [1968] 160p. illus. facsims. 24cm. [NK5440.B6W3] 6.50 bds.,
1. Bottles. 2. Bitters. I. Title.

WEARIN, Otha Donner, 1903- 738
Statues that pour; the story of character bottles [by] Otha D. Wearin. Denver, Sage Books [1965] 202 p. illus. 23 cm. Bibliography: p. 192-196. [NK5440.B6W4] 64-25349
1. Bottles. 2. Glassware—Collectors and collecting. I. Title.

Bottles, American.

ABBOTT, Allan L. 666'.19
Old bottles; how and where to find them, by A. L. Abbott. Anaheim, Calif., Abbott & Abbott [1970] 74 p. illus. 23 cm. [NK5440.B6A2] 79-127930 2.95
1. Bottles, American. 2. Bottles—Collectors and collecting. I. Title. BIP

BEARE, Nikki 748.8
Bottle bonanza; a handbook for glass collectors. [Miami, Fla., Hurricane House. 1965] 108p. illus., map. 23cm. Bibl. [NK5440.B6B4] 65-23040 6.50; 4.00 pap.,
1. Bottles, American. I. Title.

BLUMENSTEIN, Lynn. 748.8
Old time bottles found in the ghost towns. [Rev. ed.] Salem, Or., Old Time Bottle Pub. Co. [1971] 79 p. illus. 22 cm. [NK5440.B6B55 1971]
1. Bottles, American. 2. Ghost towns—The West. I. Title. BIP

BLUMENSTEIN, Lynn. 748.8
Old time bottles found in the ghost towns. [Rev.] Salem, Or., Old Time Bottle Pub. Co. [1966] 80 p. illus. 22 cm. "Pictures and prices of over 300 bottles in the 50 to over 100 year class that are to be found in the Ghost Towns of the West." [NK5440.B6B55] 66-31782
1. Bottles, American. 2. Cities and towns, Ruined, extinct, etc — The West. I. Title.

BLUMENSTEIN, Lynn. 748.8
Redigging the West for old time bottles. Rev. ed. Salem, Or., Old Time Bottle Pub. Co. [1966] 199 p. (p. 196-199 blank) illus. 22 cm. [NK5440.B6B56 1966] 66-4894
1. Bottles, American. I. Title.

BLUMENSTEIN, Lynn 748.8
Redigging the West for old time bottles Rev. ed. Salem, Ore., Old Time Bottle [1966] 199p. (p. 196-199 blank) illus. 22cm. [NK5440.B6B56 1966] 66-4894 4.25
1. Bottles, American. I. Title.
3915 Rivercrest Drive, Salem, Ore., 97303 BIP

COLCLEASER, Donald E. 748.8
Bottles of bygone days; a guide book of modern bottles, eighteen-fifty to date Illustrated by Donald E. Colcleaser 1st ed. [Klamath Falls, Or.] [1965] 92 p. illus. 22 cm. [NK5440.B6C6] 66-1218
1. Bottles, American. I. Title. BIP

EASTIN, June. 748.8
Bottles West. [Joshua Tree? Calif., 1965- v. illus. 22 cm. [NK5440.B6E2] 66-4858
1. Bottles, American. I. Title.

HORST, Melvin. 748'.8
Bottles ... sampler of the collectibles. Photography by Mel Horst. Compiled and edited by Elmer L. Smith. Lebanon, Pa., Applied Arts Publishers [1971] 31 p. illus. 28 cm. [NK5440.B6H66] 71-30498 1.25
1. Bottles, American. 2. Bottles—Collectors and collecting—U.S. I. Smith, Elmer Lewis. II. Title.

KAUFFMAN, Donald M 748'.8
Dig those crazy bottles; [a handbook of pioneer bottles] by Don and June Kauffman. Cheyenne, Wyo. [1966] 64 p. (chiefly illus.) 22 cm. [NK5440.B6K3] 67-2510
1. Bottles, American. I. Kauffman, June, joint author. II. Title.

KENDRICK, Grace. 748.8
The antique bottle collector; secrets revealed to date and evaluate old bottles. Laura Mills, photographer. [3d ed. Sparks, Nev., Western Print. and Pub. Co., 1966] 92 p. illus. 22 cm. Bibliography: p. 91-92. [NK5440.B6K4 1966] 67-7763
1. Bottles, American. 2. Glassware — Collectors and collecting. I. Title. BIP

KETCHUM, William C., 1931- 748.8
A treasury of American bottles / by William C. Ketchum, Jr. ; photos. by John Garetti. Indianapolis : Bobbs-Merrill, c1975. 224 p. : ill. (some col.) ; 27 cm. "A Rutledge book." Includes index. [NK5440.B6K42] 74-17594 ISBN 0-672-51962-3 : 16.95
1. Bottles, American. 2. Bottles—Collectors and collecting—United States. I. Garetti, John. II. Title. III. Title: American bottles.

KINCADE, Steve. 748.8
Early American bottles and glass. Clovis, Calif., Printed by Clovis Print, Co., 1964. 68 p. illus. 22 cm. [NK5440.B6K5] 66-3972
1. Bottles, American. 2. Glassware, American. 3. Glassware — Collectors and collecting. I. Title.

REED, Adele. 748.8
Old bottles and ghost towns. Illus. by May Jones. Bishop, Calif., Chalfant Press, 1965, c1961. [3], 55 p. illus. 28 cm. Bibliographical references included in "Foreword" (p. [3]) [NK5440.B6R4] 66-816
1. Bottles, American. 2. Cities and towns, Ruined, extinct, etc. — The West. I. Title.

SCHNEIDER, Dee. 748.8
Avon's bottles : by any other name / Dee Schneider. Glendale, Ca. : Avons Research, [1974] 56 p. : ill. ; 22 cm. Includes index. [NK5440.B6S43] 74-30220 ISBN 0-913772-04-6 : 5.50
1. Avon Products, inc. 2. Bottles, American. 3. Bottles—Collectors and collecting—United States. I. Title. BIP

THOMAS, John L., 1931- 666'.19
Picnics, coffins, shoo-flies, by John L. Thomas. [Weaverville, Calif., 1974] ix, 92, 6, 2 p. illus. 28 cm. Cover title. [NK5440.B6T49] 74-167317
1. Bottles, American. 2. Bottles—Collectors and collecting—United States. I. Title.

UMBERGER, Arthur L. 666'.19
Corralling the corkers, by Art and Jewel Umberger. Tyler, Tex., Corker Book Co. [196 v. illus., facsims. 28 cm. [NK5440.B6U35] 78-17212 3.00
1. Bottles, American. I. Umberger, Jewel, joint author. II. Title.

VAN RENSSELAER, Stephen, 1871?-1945. 748'.8
Check list of early American bottles and flasks. Southampton, N.Y., Cracker Barrell Press [1969? c1921] 109 p. illus. 20 cm. [NK5440.B6V3 1969] 77-3756 3.00
1. Bottles, American. 2. Glassware—U.S. I. Title.

VAN RENSSELAER, Stephen, 1871?-1945. 748'.8
Early American bottles and flasks. Rev. ed., edited by J. Edmund Edwards. New introd. by Charles B. Gardner. Stratford, Conn., J. E. Edwards, 1969. xi, 320 p. illus. 24 cm. Reprint of the rev. ed., published 1929. Pages 314-320 and other scattered pages are blank for memoranda. [NK5440.B6V32 1969] 76-6905
1. Bottles, American. I. Title.

VINCENT, Pal. 748'.8
The Moses bottle. [1st ed.] Poland Spring, Me., Palabra Shop, 1969. 58 p. illus., facsims., group port. 23 cm. Bibliography: p. 58. [NK5440.B6V5] 79-11534
1. Ricker, Hiram, & Sons, Inc. 2. Bottles, American. I. Title.

Bottles, American—Catalogs.

BARTHOLOMEW, Ed Ellsworth. 615'.1'028
1200 old medicine bottles, with prices current, by Ed Bartholomew. Fort Davis, Tex., Frontier Book Co., 1970. 120 p. illus., facsims., port. 22 cm. [NK5440.B6B353] 79-23927
1. Bottles, American—Catalogs. 2. Bottles—Prices. I. Title.

BLUMENSTEIN, Lynn. 748.8
Bottle rush U.S.A.; the story of our historic past through old time bottles. Salem, Or., Old Time Bottle Pub. Co. [1966] 184 p. illus. 22 cm. "Bottle rush U. S. A. pricing" ([8] p.) inserted. [NK5440.B6B54] 66-28187
1. Bottles, American—Catalogs. I. Title. BIP

BRAZEAL, Frances. 748.8
Old bottles sketched and catalogued. Clovis, Calif., Printed by Clovis Print. Co. [1964] 1 v. (chiefly illus.) 28 cm. Cover title: Old bottles price and reference book. [NK5440.B6B68] 66-3962
1. Bottles, American — Catalogs. 2. Glassware, American — Catalogs. I. Title. II. Title: Old bottles price and reference book.

BRESSIE, Wesley. 338.4'3748'8
Ghost town bottle price guide; average market price guide for antique bottle collectors, with an expanded section on Oriental relics, by Wes and Ruby Bressie. Illus. by Jeanne Bressie. Photos by Terry Skibby. 8th ed., rev. and enl. Caldwell [Idaho] Caxton Printers, 1972. 124 p. illus. 22 cm. Bibliography: p. [111]-[112] [NK5440.B6B7 1972] 79-151058 ISBN 0-87004-225-4 2.95
1. Bottles, American—Catalogs. 2. Bottles—Collectors and collecting. I. Bressie, Ruby, joint author. II. Title.

BUD Hastin's Avon Collector Guide, Inc. 666'.19
Avon collectables. Kansas City, Mo., 1969- 1 v. (loose-leaf) illus. 23 cm. [NK5440.B6B9] 77-13848 5.00
1. Bottles, American—Catalogs. I. Avon Products, inc. II. Title.

CEMBURA, Al. 738.2'8
Beam bottles: identification and price guide, by Al Cembura and Constance Avery. Photos. by Leslie Avery. [Berkeley? Calif., 1967] 158 p. illus. 22 cm. At head of title: Jim Beam. [NK5440.B6C4] 67-6780
1. Bottles, American — Catalogs. 2. Bottles — Prices. I. Avery, Constance, joint author. II. Title.

CEMBURA, Al. 738.2'8
Beam bottles; 1968 identification and price guide, by Al Cembura and Constance Avery. Photos. by Leslie Avery. [Berkeley, Calif., Wagner Print. Co., 1968] 202 p. illus. (part col.), port. 22 cm. At head of title: Jim Beam. Price supplement ([4] p.) inserted. [NK5440.B6C4 1968] 68-4297
1. Bottles, American—Catalogs. 2. Bottles—Prices. I. Avery, Constance, joint author. II. Title.

CEMBURA, Al 738.2'8
Beam bottles: identification and price guide, by Al Cembura. Constance Averv. Photos. by Leslie Avery. [Berkeley? Calif., 1967] 158p. illus. 22cm. At head of title: Jim Beam. [NK5440.B6C4] 67-6780 3.00 pap.,
1. Bottles, American—Catalogs. 2. Bottles—Prices. I. Avery, Constance, joint author II. Title.

COHEN, Hal L. 748.8
Official guide to bottles old & new / by Hal L. Cohen. 2d ed. Florence, Ala. : House of Collectibles, [1975] 397 p. : ill. (some col.) ; 18 cm. Bibliography: p. 12-14. [NK5440.B6C59 1975] 73-93246 ISBN 0-87637-330-9 : 5.00
1. Bottles, American—Catalogs. I. Title. BIP

COLCLEASER, Donald E. 748'.8
Bottles: yesterday's trash, today's treasures, by Donald E. Colcleaser. [Napa? Calif.] [1967] 114 p. illus. 28 cm. [NK5440.B6C64] 67-8403
1. Bottles, American—Catalogs. I. Title.

EDWARDS, Jack M. 666'.19
A collectors guide to the whiskeys that were, by Jack M. Edwards. King City, Calif., 1967. 80 p. illus. 22 cm. Bibliography: p. 75. [NK5440.B6E3] 74-15844
1. Bottles, American—Catalogs. I. Title.

FOUNTAIN, John C. 748'.8
Dictionary of soda & mineral water bottles. Co-authors: John C. Fountain [and] Donald E. Colcleaser. Photography by, Alzura H. Pearson. Amador City, Calif., Ole Empty Bottle House Pub. Co. [1968] 95 p. illus. 28 cm. [NK5440.B6F63] 68-6379
1. Bottles, American—Catalogs. I. Colcleaser, Donald E., joint author. II. Title. BIP

GARDNER, Charles B. 666'.19
Collector's price guide to historical bottles & flasks. Compiled by Charles B. Gardner & J. Edmund Edwards. Stratford, Conn., J. Edwards [1970] 170 p. illus. 12 x 16 cm. [NK5440.B6G3] 77-15361 6.00
1. Bottles, American—Catalogs. 2. Bottles—Prices. I. Edwards, J. Edmund, joint author. II. Title.

GOODELL, Donald. 666'.19
The American bottle collector's price guide to historical flasks, pontils, bitters, mineral waters, inks & sodas. With photos. by Dugway Photography, Chatham, N.Y. [1st ed.] Rutland, Vt., C. E. Tuttle Co. [1973] 144 p. illus. 20 cm. Bibliography: p. 141. [NK5440.B6G6] 72-89738 6.00
1. Bottles, American—Catalogs. 2. Bottles—Collectors and collecting—United States. I. Title.

HARRISON, Elmer J. 748'.8
Modern bottle collector's catalog, by Elmer J. Harrison. 1970-71 ed. Cheyenne, Wyo., Distributed by Beamorama [1970?] 80 p. (p. 72-80 advertisements) illus. 23 cm. [NK5440.B6H3] 76-28026 2.95
1. Bottles, American—Catalogs. 2. Bottles—Prices. I. Title.

HASTIN, Bud, 1939- 748.8
Avon bottle encyclopedia, written & produced by Bud Hastin. 1972 ed. Kansas City, Mo., B. Hastin Enterprises [1972] 24, 208 p. illus. 28 cm. Cover title: Bud Hastin's Avon bottle encyclopedia. [NK5440.B6H33] 72-193161 9.95
1. Bottles, American—Catalogs. I. Bud Hastin Enterprises. II. Avon Products, inc. III. Title.

HOLT, Don, 1940- 666'.19
Avon bottles: identification and price guide, by Don Holt and Beverly Craig. Photos. by Modern Studio. [Hudson, N.H., 1969] 43 p. illus. 22 cm. "Avon bottle collection owned by Mr. & Mrs. Roland Houvling." [NK5440.B6H6] 76-21829 2.00
1. Houvling, Ronald—Art collections. 2. Houvling, Ronald Mrs.,—Art collections. 3. Bottles, American—Catalogs. I. Craig, Beverly, joint author. II. Avon Products, inc. III. Title.

JONES, John Lemuel, 1907- 663'.62'028
Soda and mineral water bottles, by J. L. Jones. Greer, S.C., Palmetto Enterprises [1972] 163 p. illus. 28 cm. At head of title: Over 2,000 varieties. [NK5440.B6J63] 73-175237 8.00
1. Bottles, American—Catalogs. I. Title.

KOVEL, Ralph M. 666'.19
The Kovels' official bottle price list / by Ralph M. and Terry H. Kovel. 3d ed. New York : Crown Publishers, [1975] xxxvi, 220 p. : ill. ; 21 cm. First-2d ed. published under title: The official bottle price list. Bibliography: p. xii-xxii. [NK5440.B6K6 1975] 75-12542 ISBN 0-517-52189-X pbk. : 6.95
1. Bottles, American—Catalogs. I. Kovel, Terry H., joint author. II. Title. III. Title: Official bottle price list. BIP

Bottles—Collectors and collecting—United States.

AUSTEN, Ferol.   748.8
Poor man's guide to bottle collecting. Garden City, N.Y., Doubleday, 1971. 161 p. illus. 27 cm. Bibliography: p. 6. [NK5440.B6A89] 74-150877 7.95
1. *Bottles—Collectors and collecting—U.S.* I. Title.

NEAL, Nelson D.   666'.19
Common bottles for the average collector / by Nelson D. Neal, Marna D. Neal. [Wolfe City? Tex.] : N. D. Neal, [1975] 112 p. : ill. ; 23 cm. Includes index. Bibliography: p. 112. [NK5440.B6N42] 75-147
1. *Bottles—Collectors and collecting—United States.* I. Neal, Marna D., joint author. II. Title.

Bottles—Colorado.

SEAMANS, Berna Mackey.   666'.19
Colorado bottle history: when and where? By Berna Mackey Seamans and Mertie Mackey Robb. [Denver, R & S Publication] 1969. 71 p. illus., maps. 23 cm. [NK5440.B6S46] 75-14192 4.95
1. *Bottles—Colorado.* I. Robb, Mertie Mackey, joint author. II. Title.

Bottles—Columbia, S.C.

JETER, Paul.   666'.19
Columbia's past in glass / by Paul Jeter & Harvey S. Teal. [s.l. : s.n.], c1976. 58 p. : ill. ; 22 cm. "Pricing guide for Columbia, S.C. bottles, March, 1976," 7 p. inserted. [NK5440.B6J46] 76-366970
1. *Bottles—Columbia, S.C.* 2. *Bottles—Collectors and collecting—United States.* I. Teal, Harvey S., joint author. II. Title.

Bottles—Conservation and restoration.

WAGONER, George E.   748'.8
Restoring antique bottles. Rev. [i.e. 2d] ed. West Sacramento, Calif., Printed by Gorman's Stationery [1967] 69 p. illus. 22 cm. Bibliography: p. [72] [NK5440.B6W26 1967] 67-9588
1. *Bottles—Conservation and restoration.* I. Title.   BIP

Bottles—Florida Keys—Catalogs.

MONROE, Loretta.   748'.8
Old bottles found along the Florida Keys. Warren F. Buxton, special editor. [1st ed. Coral Gables, Fla.] Wake-Brook House [1967] 216 p. illus., map (on lining papers) 22 cm. [NK5440.B6M6] 65-26590
1. *Bottles—Florida Keys—Catalogs.* 2. *Bottles—Collectors and collecting.* I. Title.

Bottles—Great Britain.

DAVIS, Derek C.   748.8
English bottles and decanters 1650-1900 [by] Derek C. Davis. [1st American ed.] New York, World Pub. Co. [1972] 80 p. illus. 22 cm. (on box) p. 80. [NK5440.B6D3 1972b] 79-161612 5.95
1. *Bottles—Great Britain.* 2. *Decanters—Great Britain.* I. Title.

Bottles, Hawaiian.

ELLIOTT, Rex R.   666'.19
Hawaiian bottles of long ago, by Rex R. Elliott. [Honolulu, Hawaiian Service, 1971] iv, 93 p. illus., facsims., map (on cover) 23 cm. Bibliography: p. 91. [NK5440.B6E4] 78-134504
1. *Bottles, Hawaiian.* I. Title.   BIP

Bottles—Long Island—Catalogs.

WEINHARDT, Donald H.   666'.19
100 years of Long Island bottles / editor-compiler, Donald H. Weinhardt. Melville, N.Y. : Suffolk County Antique Bottle Association of Long Island, c1976-v. ; 29 cm. Includes index. Contents.Contents.—v. 1. Ale, beer, porter, cider, mineral water, and soda bottles, 1850-1950. Bibliography: v. 1, p. 176-178. [NK5440.B6W44] 76-378707

1. *Bottles—Long Island—Catalogs.* 2. *Bottles—Collectors and collecting.* I. Suffolk County Antique Bottle Association of Long Island. II. Title.

Bottles—Marks.

TOULOUSE, Julian   666'.19
Harrisson, 1899-
Bottle makers and their marks. New York, T. Nelson [1971] 624 p. illus. 23 cm. [NK5440.B6T6] 76-147915 ISBN 0-8407-4318-1
1. *Bottles—Marks.* 2. *Bottles, American.* I. Title.

Bottles—New England.

BATES, Virginia T.   748'.8
Antique bottle finds in New England [by] Virginia T. Bates [and] Beverly Chamberlain. Peterborough, N.H., Noone House [1968] 80 p. illus. 18 cm. Bibliography: p. 80. [NK5440.B6B36] 68-9146 ISBN 0-87233-002-8 3.95
1. *Bottles—New England.* 2. *Bottles—Collectors and collecting.* I. Chamberlain, Beverly, joint author. II. Title.

Bottles—New England—Catalogs.

ADAMS, John Phillip, 1932-   748'.8
Bottle collecting in New England; a guide to digging, identification, and pricing, by John P. Adams. Somersworth, New Hampshire Pub. Co., 1969. 120 p. illus., ports. 26 cm. [NK5440.B6A3] 71-97516 3.95
1. *Bottles—New England—Catalogs.* 2. *Bottles—Collectors and collecting.* I. Title.

LINCOLN, Gerald David.   666'.19
Antique blob top bottles, central and southern New England. [Marlboro, Mass., 1970] 128 p. illus., facsims., map. 28 cm. [NK5440.B6L5] 77-278505 3.25
1. *Bottles—New England—Catalogs.* I. Title.

Bottles—Orange Co., N.Y.—Catalogs.

ROSENBLUM, Beatrice.   666.19
Beatrice Rosenblum's Handbook guide to Orange County bottles / photos. by Mike Carey ; ill. by Edward J. McLaughlin III. 1st ed. Middletown, N.Y. : T. E. Henderson, 1974. 228 p. : ill. ; 23 cm. Includes index. [NK5440.B6R63] 73-86871
1. *Bottles—Orange Co., N.Y.—Catalogs.* I. Title. II. Title: Handbook guide to Orange County bottles.

Bottles—Prices.

CLEVELAND, Hugh.   666'.19
Bottle pricing guide. [Rev. ed. San Angelo, Tex., 1972] 319 p. illus. 22 cm. Bibliography: p. 319. [NK5440.B6C55 1972] 73-153863 5.95
1. *Bottles—Prices.* I. Title.

DAVIS, Marvin.   748'.8
Antique bottles [by Marvin and Helen Davis] Pictures and prices of over 225 bottles, many in full color. Bottle photography by Terry Skibby. Medford, Or., Printed by Gandee Printing Center [1967] 62 p. illus. (part col.), ports. 22 cm. [NK5440.B6D35] 67-8994
1. *Bottles—Prices.* 2. *Bottles—Collectors and collecting.* I. Davis, Helen, joint author. II. Skibby, Terry. III. Title.

SELLARI, Carlo.   666'.19
Eastern bottles price guide. Compiled by Carlo and Dot Sellari. Dunedin, Fla., Area Print. Co., 1970- v. illus. 22 cm. [NK5440.B6S48] 73-19185 4.50 (v. 1)
1. *Bottles—Prices.* I. Sellari, Dot, joint author. II. Title.

UMBERGER, Arthur L.   748'.8
It's a corker! Bottle price guide, by Art and Jewel Umberger. Rev. ed. Tyler, Tex., Corker Book Co. [1968] 60 p. illus. 21 cm. Pages 58-60, blank for "Notes." [NK5440.B6U4 1968] 68-2354
1. *Bottles—Prices.* 2. *Bottles—Collectors and collecting.* I. Umberger, Jewel, joint author. II. Title.

Bottles—Private collections—United States.

FLOWERS, Bryant.   666'.19
The Flowers Collection [by Bryant Flowers and Devonne Wilson. Pampa, Tex., 1970] 62 p. (chiefly illus.) 21 x 25 cm. On cover: The Flowers Collection: Avon guide. [NK5440.B6F55] 71-22203
1. *Bottles—Private collections—United States.* 2. *Bottles, American—Catalogs.* I. Wilson, Devonne, joint author. II. Avon Products, inc. III. Title. IV. Title: Avon guide.

Bottles—South Carolina.

FRASER, Robert B.   666'.19
The South Carolina dispensary bottle, by Robert B. Fraser. [n.p., 1969] 8 l. illus. 29 cm. Caption title. [NK5440.B6F68] 79-19429
1. *Bottles—South Carolina.* I. Title.

Bottles—The West—Catalogs.

WILSON, Bill, 1926-   748.8
Spirits bottles of the Old West, by Bill and Betty Wilson. All photography by Bill Wilson. [Santa Rosa, Calif.] [1968] 180, [1] p. illus. 29 cm. Bibliography: p. [181] [NK5440.B6W5] 68-20257
1. *Bottles—The West—Catalogs.* 2. *Bottles—Collectors and collecting.* I. Wilson, Betty, 1932- joint author. II. Title.

Bottles—United States.

MCKEARIN, Helen.   666'.19
American bottles & flasks and their ancestry / by Helen McKearin and Kenneth M. Wilson. New York : Crown Publishers, c1978. p. cm. Includes index. Bibliography: p. [NK5440.B6M29] 78-18520 ISBN 0-517-53147-X : 29.95
1. *Bottles—United States.* I. Wilson, Kenneth M., joint author. II. Title.   BIP

Bottles—United States—Catalogs.

KOVEL, Ralph M.   666'.19
The Kovel's complete bottle price list / by Ralph M. and Terry H. Kovel. 4th ed. New York : Crown Publishers, c1977. xxxiv, 220 p., [12] leaves of plates : ill. (some col.) ; 20 cm. First-2d ed. published under title: The official bottle price list; 3d ed. published in 1975 under title: The Kovel's official bottle price list. Bibliography: p. xxv-xxx. [NK5440.B6K6 1977] 77-4267 ISBN 0-517-53013-9 pbk. : 7.95
1. *Bottles—United States—Catalogs.* I. Kovel, Terry H., joint author. II. Title. III. Title: Complete bottle price list.

Bottles—United States—Collectors and collecting—Catalogs.

EASTIN, June   748.8
Bottles West; v.1. [Joshua Tree, Calif., 92252, Author, P. O. Box 703, 1966] c.1965. 63p. illus. 22cm. [NK5440.B6E2] 66-4858 3.00 pap.,
I. Title.

TOMASCHEFSKY, Herbert D.   748.8
Herb's guide to Avon test bottle collecting / by Herbert D. Tomaschefsky. [Cudahy, Wis.] : Avon Club of Cudahy, c1977. 139 p. : ill. ; 22 cm. Includes index. [NK5440.B8T58] 78-102595 6.95
1. *Avon Products, inc.—Catalogs.* 2. *Bottles—United States—Collectors and collecting—Catalogs.* I. Title.

Boubat, Edouard, 1923—

BOUBAT, Edouard,   779'.2'0924
1923-
Edouard Boubat [by] Bernard George. [English translation by Maureen Oberli-Turner] New York, Macmillan [1973] 18 p., 59 plates. 28 cm. (Photography: men and movements, v. 3) [TR820.5.B6813] 73-7351 10.95
1. *Boubat, Edouard, 1923-* 2. *Photography, Documentary.* I. George, Bernard.

Boucher, Francois, 1703-1770.

BOUCHER, Francois,   741.9'44
1703-1770.
Francois Boucher in North American collections: 100 drawings. [Text by] Regina Shoolman Slatkin. [Washington, National Gallery of Art, 1973] xxv, 130 p. illus. 22 x 29 cm. Catalog of an exhibition to be held at National Gallery of Art, Dec. 23, 1973-Mar. 17, 1974, and the Art Institute of Chicago, Apr. 4-May 12, 1974. Bibliography: p. xxiii-xxiv. [NC248.B587S55] 73-89398 11.95
1. *Boucher, Francois, 1703-1770.* 2. *Drawings, French—United States.* 3. *Drawings, French—Canada.* I. Slatkin, Regina Shoolman, 1909- II. United States. National Gallery of Art. III. Chicago. Art Institute. IV. Title.
Pbk. 4.95

Boucher, Guillaume, 13th cent.

OLSCHKI, Leonardo,   709'.24 B
1885-
Guillaume Boucher, a French artist at the court of the Khans. New York, Greenwood Press [c1946] viii, 125 p. illus. 23 cm. Includes bibliographical references. [ND553.B7O4 1969] 69-14019
1. *Boucher, Guillaume, 13th cent.* 2. *Art—Mongolia.*

Bouguereau, William Adolphe, 1825-1905.

BOUGUEREAU, William   759.4
Adolphe, 1825-1905.
William Adolphe Bouguereau : ... exhibition ... organized by Mario Amaya, the New York Cultural Center, in association with Fairleigh Dickinson University, 13 December 1974 to 2 February 1975 : catalogue and selection / by Robert Isaacson. [New York] : The Center, [1975?] 51 p. : ill. ; 26 cm. Bibliography: p. 51. [ND553.B8I82] 75-327401
1. *Bouguereau, William Adolphe, 1825-1905.* I. Isaacson, Robert. II. Amaya, Mario. III. New York Cultural Center. IV. Fairleigh Dickinson University.

Boullee, Etienne Louis, 1728-1799.

LEMAGNY, J. C.   720'.922
Visionary architects: Boullee, Ledoux, Lequeu. [Houston, Tex., Printed by Gulf Print. Co., 1968] 240 p. illus. 23 cm. Catalogue of an exhibition held at the University of St. Thomas, Houston, Tex., Oct. 19, 1967-Jan. 3, 1968, and at four other American museums, Jan. 22-Oct. 29, 1968. Bibliography: p. 235-240. [NA1052.L4] 68-24454
1. *Boulee, Etienne Louis, 1728-1799.* 2. *Ledoux, Claude Nicolas, 1736-1806.* 3. *Lequeu, Jean Jacques, 1757-ca. 1825.* I. Houston, Tex. University of St. Thomas. II. Title.

PEROUSE de Montclos,   720'.92'4
Jean Marie.
Etienne-Louis Boullee (1728-1799); theoretician of revolutionary architecture. [Translated from the French by James Emmons.] New York, Braziller [1974] 128 p. illus. 25 cm. Bibliography: p. 119-121. [NA1053.B69P413 1974] 72-92833 ISBN 0-8076-0672-3 6.95
1. *Boullee, Etienne Louis, 1728-1799.*

Boulton, Matthew, 1728-1809.

DELIEB, Eric.   739.3'72'4
Matthew Boulton: master silversmith, 1760-1790. Research collaboration by Michael Roberts; distributed by Crown Publishers [1971] 144 p. illus. 26 cm. Bibliography: p. 139. [NK7198.B66D4 1971] 71-176094 10.95
1. *Boulton, Matthew, 1728-1809.*

GOODISON, Nicholas.   739.2
Ormolu: the work of Matthew Boulton. [London] Phaidon, [distributed by Praeger Publishers, New York, 1974] xii, 398 p. illus. 29 cm. Bibliography: p. 207-212. [TS140.B68G66] 78-165860 ISBN 0-7148-1589-6 35.00
1. *Boulton, Matthew, 1728-1809.* 2.

Birmingham, Eng.—Industries. 3. Art metal-work—Birmingham, Eng. 4. Gilding. I. Title.

Bourdelle, Emile Antoine, 1861-1929.

JIANU, Ionel 730.924
Bourdelle [by] Ionel Jianou. Michel Dufet. [Tr. by KathleenMuston, Bryan Richardson] Paris, Arted, Editions d'Art [New York, Tudor 1966, c.] 1965 215p. 105 illus., port. 28cm. Bibl. [NB553.B6J53] 66-4925 15.00
1. Bourdelle, Emile Antoine, 1861-1929. I. Dufet, Michel. joint author. II. Title.

OTTAWA. National Gallery 730.944
of Canada.
Antoine Bourdelle, 1861-1929. Introd. by Philip Rhys Adams. Bourdelle as sculptor, by Jean Casson. Boundelle and modern sculpture, by Jean Charbonneaux New York, C. E. Slatkin Galleries [1961?] 95 p. 79 illus. 29 cm. An exhibition of sculptures and drawings held at the National Gallery of Canada and at other museums. Articles by Cassou and Charbonneaux in English and French. Bibliography: p. 95. [NB553.B6O8] 61-18141
1. Bourdell, Emile Antoine, 1861-1929. I. Adams, Philip Rhys, 1908- II. Title.

Bourges. Saint-Etienne (Cathedral)

BAYARD, Tania. 726'.591
Bourges Cathedral : the west portals / Tania Bayard. New York : Garland, 1976. vii, 437 p. : ill. ; 21 cm. (Outstanding dissertations in the fine arts) Originally presented as the author's thesis, Columbia, 1968. Bibliography: p. 431-437. [NB551.B7B38 1976] 75-23780 ISBN 0-8240-1977-6 lib.bdg. : 30.00
1. Bourges. Saint-Etienne (Cathedral) 2. Sculpture—Bourges. 3. Sculpture, Gothic—Bourges. 4. Facades—Bourges. 5. Doorways—Bourges. I. Title. II. Series.

BRANNER, Robert 726.60944552
La cathedrale de Bourges et sa place dans l'architecture gothique in French Tr. from English by Anne Paillard. Paris, Tardy [dist. New York,,, Wittenborn, 1963, c.1962] xvi, 205p. illus., plans. (pt. of illus. in pocket) 28cm. Bibl. 63-5591 10.00
1. Bourges, Saint-Etienne (Cathedral) I. Title.

Bourke-White, margaret, 1906-1971.

BROWN, Theodore M. 779'.092'4
Margaret Bourke-White, photojournalist [by] Theodore M. Brown. [Ithaca, N.Y.] Andrew Dickson White Museum of Art, Cornell University, 1972. 136 p. illus. 29 cm. "Catalog of the exhibition, Andrew Dickson White Museum of Art, Cornell University, March 15-April 23, 1972:" (p. [127]-131) Bibliography: p. [109]-119. [TR140.B6B76] 76-188882
1. Bourke-White, Margaret, 1905-1971. 2. Photography, Journalistic—Exhibitions. I. Cornell University. Andrew Dickson White Museum of Art. II. Title.

BOURKE-WHITE, Mararet, 779'.092'4
1906-1971.
The photographs of Margaret Bourke-White. Edited by Sean Callahan. Introd. by Theodore M. Brown. Foreword by Carl Mydans. [Greenwich, Conn.] New York Graphic Society, 1972. 208 p. illus. 32 cm. Bibliography: p. 203-208. [TR140.B6A29 1972] 72-80415 ISBN 0-8212-0462-9 15.00
1. Bourke-White, Margaret, 1906-1971. 2. Photography, Artistic. 3. Photography, Journalistic. I. Callahan, Sean. II. Title.

BOURKE-WHITE, Margaret, 927.7
1906-1971.
Portrait of myself. New York, Simon and Schuster, 1963. 383 p. illus. 24 cm. [TR140.B6A3] 63-11141
I. Title.

BOURKE-WHITE, Margaret, 1906- 779
1971.
The photographs of Margaret Bourke-White, introduction by Theodore M. Brown, foreword by Carl Mydans. Boston, New York Graphic Society, 1975 c1972 208 p. ill. 30 cm. Bibliography: p. 203-208. [TR650] ISBN 0-8212-0656-7 7.50 (pbk.)
1. Bourke-White, Margaret, 1906-1971. 2. Photography, artistic. 3. Photography, journalistic. I. Callahan, Sean, comp. II. Title.
L.C. card number for original edition: 72-80415. **BIP**

DUNHAM, Montrew. 770'.92'4 B
Margaret Bourke-White, young photographer / by Montrew Dunham ; illustrated by Robert Doremus. Indianapolis : Bobbs-Merrill, c1977. 192 p. : ill. ; 20 cm. (Childhood of famous Americans) A biography of the photographer and writer who was one of the original staff photographers for Life magazine and the first accredited woman war correspondent to be sent overseas during World War II. [TR140.B6D86] 92 75-34512 ISBN 0-672-52225-X : 3.95 ISBN 0-672-71413-2 lib.bdg. : 3.73
1. Bourke-White, Margaret, 1906-1971. 2. Photographers—United States—Biography—Juvenile literature. I. Doremus, Robert. II. Title.

Bourke-White, Margaret, 1906-1971—Juvenile literature.

NOBLE, Iris. 770'.92'4 B
Cameras and courage: Margaret Bourke-White. New York, J. Messner [1973] 191 p. 21 cm. Bibliography: p. 183. Biography of a woman renowned for her photographic interpretations of war, revolution, and poverty and for her personal battle against Parkinsonism. [TR140.B6N6] 92 72-11927 ISBN 0-671-32577-9 4.95
1. Bourke-White, Margaret, 1906-1971—Juvenile literature. I. Title.
Library ed. 4.29.

Bow and arrow.

*POPE, Saxton T. 739.73
Bows and arrows, by Saxton T. Pope. Foreword by Robert F. Heizer. Berkeley, University of California Press [1974] 83 p. illus. 20 cm. (California library reprint series, no. 52.) "Originally published in 1923 as a study of bows and arrows, University of California Publications in American Archaeology and Ethnology, volume 13, number 9." [GN498.B78] ISBN 0-520-02641-1 9.25
1. Bow and arrow. I. Title.
Pbk. 1.50, ISBN 0-520-01022-1. **BIP**

Bowdoin College. Museum of Art.

BOWDOIN 759.13'074'014191
College. Museum of Art.
Nineteenth century American paintings at Bowdoin College : [catalog]. [Brunswick, Me.] : The Museum, 1974. [77] p. : chiefly ill. ; 24 cm. [ND210.B74 1974] 75-322572
1. Bowdoin College. Museum of Art. 2. Paintings, American—Catalogs. 3. Paintings, Modern—19th century—United States—Catalogs. 4. Paintings—Brunswick, Me.—Catalogs. I. Title.

Bowen site, Ind.

DORWIN, John T. 970.4'72'52
The Bowen Site: an archaeological study of culture process in the late prehistory of central Indiana, by John T. Dorwin. Indianapolis, Indiana Historical Society, 1971. 195-411 p. illus. 26 cm. (Prehistory research series, v. 4, no. 4) Bibliography: p. 407-411. [E78.I53D6] 72-187706
1. Bowen site, Ind. 2. Culture diffusion. I. Title. II. Series: Indiana Historical Society. Prehistory research series, v. 4, no. 4.

Bowser, William D., 1912- —Art collections.

OAKLAND Museum. 759.13'074'019466
The California Collection of William and Zelma Bowser; an exhibition of paintings in the great hall of the Oakland Museum, Oakland, California, May 26 through September 27, 1970. [Oakland, 1970] 42 p. illus. (part col.) 26 cm. [ND230.C3O15] 72-21075
1. Bowser, William D., 1912- —Art collections. 2. Bowser, Zelma—Art collections. 3. Paintings, American—Exhibitions. 4. Painting, American—California. I. Title.

Bowyer, William, 1699-1777.

NICHOLS, John, 1745- 686.2'092'2
1826.
Biographical and literary anecdotes of William Bowyer. With two memoirs of John Nichols. New York, Garland Pub., 1974. p. cm. (The English book trade, 1660-1853.) Reprint of Biographical and literary anecdotes of William Bowyer, printer, F.S.A., and of many of his learned friends, by J. Nichols, printed in 1782 by and for the author, London; of Brief memoirs of John Nichols, printed in 1804 by Nichols and Son, London; and of Memoir of John Nichols, Esq., F.S.A., by A. Chalmers, from the Gentleman's magazine for December 1826. [Z232.B79N498 1974] 74-16185 ISBN 0-8240-0971-1 22.00
1. Bowyer, William, 1699-1777. 2. Nichols, John, 1745-1826. 3. Printing—History—Great Britain. I. Brief memoirs of John Nichols. 1974. II. Title. III. Series.

Boxes.

BEDFORD, John, 1907- 745.1
All kinds of small boxes. New York, Walker [1965, c1964] 68 p. illus., col. plates. 19 cm. (His Collectors' pieces, 4) [NK9990.B6B4 1965] 65-22127
1. Boxes. 2. Snuff boxes and bottles. 3. Art objects—Collectors and collecting. I. Title.

HEADLEY, George W. 736.22
The Headley treasure of bibelots and boxes. Foreword, notes by George W. Headley. Introd. by Marvin C. Ross. New York, October House [1966, c.1965] 92p. illus., 32 col. plates, col. port. 27cm. [NK7198.H4A45] 65-29280 25.00 bxd.
I. Title.

MEILACH, Dona Z. 745.5
Box art : assemblage and construction / by Dona Z. Meilach. New York : Crown Publishers, [1975] 96 p., [4] leaves of plates : ill. (some col.) ; 29 cm. Includes index. Bibliography: p. 95. [NK3665.M44 1975] 74-20513 ISBN 0-517-51620-9 : 5.95 ISBN 0-517-51621-7 pbk. : 3.95 3.95
1. Boxes. 2. Boxes in art. I. Title.

Boxes—Collectors and collecting.

KLAMKIN, Marian. 745.5
The collector's book of boxes. Illustrated with photos. by Charles Klamkin. New York, Dodd, Mead [1970] vii, 145 p. illus. 25 cm. Bibliography: p. 139-142. [NK3665.K55] 72-111909 5.95
1. Boxes—Collectors and collecting. I. Title.

Boxes in art.

MOGELON, Alex. 709'.04
Art in boxes [by] Alex Mogelon [and] Norman Laliberte. New York, Van Nostrand Reinhold [1974] 240 p. illus. (part col.) 36 cm. [N6490.M585] 74-5947 ISBN 0-442-24607-2 45.00
1. Boxes in art. 2. Art, Modern—20th century. I. Laliberte, Norman, joint author. II. Title.

Boy Scouts in art.

HILLCOURT, William, 1900- 759.13
Norman Rockwell's world of scouting / by William Hillcourt. New York : H. N. Abrams, [1977] p. cm. Includes index. [ND237.R68H54] 77-8491 ISBN 0-8109-1582-0 : 14.95
1. Rockwell, Norman, 1894- 2. Boy Scouts of America—History. 3. Boy Scouts in art. I. Rockwell, Norman, 1894- II. Title. **BIP**

Boyana, Bulgaria. Boianska tsurkva.

MIIATEV, Krustiu, 751.73094977
1892-
The Boyana murals [by] Krustyu Miyatev. Dresden, Veb Verlag der Kunst; Sofia, Bulgarski Houdozhnik Pub. House [dist. New York, Vanous, 1962] 93p. illus. (pt. col.) 35cm. Bibl. 62-51948 10.80
1. Boyana, Bulgaria. Boianska tsurkva. 2. Mural painting and decoration—Boyana, Bulgaria. I. Title.

Boyce, John.

BOYCE, John. 741.9'73
Aphrodisiac : erotic drawings / by John Boyce for selected passages from the works of Anais Nin. New York : Crown Publishers, c1976. p. cm. [NC139.B68A74 1976] 76-15163 ISBN 0-517-52678-6 : 7.95 ISBN 0-517-52679-4 pbk. :
1. Boyce, John. 2. Erotic art. I. Nin, Anais, 1903- II. Title. **BIP**

Boyceau de la Baraudiere, Jacques.

HAZLEHURST, Franklin 712.0944
Hamilton.
Jacques Boyceau and the French formal garden. Athens, University of Georgia Press [1966] xiii, 137 p. illus., plans. 25 cm. Bibliography: p. 132-134. [SB470.B6H3] 66-12954
1. Boyceau de la Baraudiere, Jacques. 2. Gardens — France. I. Title.

Boyd, Guy Martin a Beckett, 1923—

VON BERTOUCH, Ann. 730'.92'4 B
Guy Boyd / [by] Ann von Bertouch [and] Patrick Hutchings. Melbourne : Lansdowne Press, 1976. 136 p. : ill. ; 38 cm. Includes bibliographical references and index. [NB1105.B7V66] 77-350246 ISBN 0-7018-0079-8
1. Boyd, Guy Martin a Beckett, 1923- 2. Sculptors—Australia—Biography. I. Hutchings, Patrick A., joint author. II. Boyd, Guy Martin a Beckett, 1923-

Boydell, John, 1719-1804.

FRIEDMAN, Winifred 759.2'074'0212
H.
Boydell's Shakespeare gallery / Winifred H. Friedman. New York : Garland Pub., 1976. 266 p., [103] leaves of plates : ill. ; 21 cm. (Outstanding dissertations in the fine arts) Originally presented as the author's thesis, Harvard, 1974. Bibliography: p. 246-256. [PR2883.B553F7 1976] 75-23791 ISBN 0-8240-1987-3 lib.bdg. : 30.00
1. Boydell, John, 1719-1804. The gallery of illustrations for Shakespeare's dramatic works. 2. Shakespeare, William, 1564-1616—Illustrations. 3. Paintings, English. 4. Paintings, Modern—17th-18th centuries—England I. Title. II. Series. **BIP**

Boynton, Ray, 1883-1951.

FABILLI, Mary. 741.9'73
Ray Boynton and the Mother Lode : the depression years : [exhibition], May 4 through August 15, 1976, the Oakland Museum, History Special Gallery / compiled by Mary Fabilli. [Oakland, Calif.] : History Dept., the Oakland Museum, c1976. 62 p. : ill. ; 21 x 31 cm. Bibliography: p. 18. [NC139.B69F3] 76-13276
1. Boynton, Ray, 1883-1951. 2. Mother Lode (The phrase) 3. California in art. 4. Gold mines and mining—California—Pictorial works. I. Boynton, Ray, 1883-1951. II. Oakland Museum. III. Title.

Boys—Portraits.

NELSON, Ronald C., joint 779.25
ed.
The boy; a photographic essay. Edited by Georges St. Martin and Ronald C. Nelson. New York, Book Horizons, 1964. 232 p. (chiefly illus., part col.) 32 cm. [TR680.S14] 65-7
1. Boys—Portraits. I. Title.

ST. Martin, Georges, ed. 779.25
The boy; a photographic essay. Ed. by Georges St. Martin, Ronald C. Nelson. New York, Book Horzons, 550 Fifth Ave [c.1964] 232p. (chiefly illus., pt. col.) 32cm. [TR680.S14] 65-7 25.00; 19.95 before Jan. 30, 1965,
1. Boys—Portraits. I. Title.

ST. Martin, Georges, ed. 779.25
Boys will be boys! Edited by Georges St. Martin and Ronald C. Nelson. New York, Book Adventures, 1966. 256 p. (chiefly illus.) 84 cm. [TR680.S15] 66-1965
1. Boys—Portraits. I. Title.

Bracelets.

BOLLINGER, Joseph Walter, 1897- 739.27
Simple bracelets. Milwaukee, Bruce [1951] 77 p. illus. 24 cm. [TS741.B6] 52-1
1. Bracelets. I. Title.

Brach, Paul, 1924—

GARVER, Thomas H. 759.13
Paul Brach & Miriam Schapiro; paintings and graphic works. Essays by Thomas H. Garver. [Balboa, Calif., Newport Harbor Art Museum, 1969] 31 p. plates (part col.), group port. 23 cm. Issued in connection with the exhibition held Jan. 22-Feb. 23, 1969, in the Newport Harbor Art Museum and Mar. 2-30, 1969, in the La Jolla Museum of Art. [ND236.G3] 76-199939
1. Brach, Paul, 1924- 2. Schapiro, Miriam, 1923- I. Newport Harbor Art Museum. II. La Jolla, Calif. Museum of Art. III. Title.

Brackman, Robert, 1898—

BATES, Kenneth, 1895- 759.13
Brackman: his art and teaching. [Rev. enl. ed.] [Madison, Conn.] Madison Art Gallery Pub. Co., in cooperation with Mr. Robert Brackman [1973] p. cm. "The first one hundred copies of this edition are numbered and signed by Robert Brackman." [ND237.B77B3 1973] 73-19805 12.50
1. Brackman, Robert, 1898- I. Title.
Publisher's address: Signal Hill Road, Madison, Conn. 06443.

Bradford, Eng. (Yorkshire)—Description—Views.

AYERS, Jane. 942.8'17'080222
Bradford old and new / [compiled by] Jane & John Ayers. Wakefield : EP Publishing, 1976. [5], 98 p. : of ill. ; 18 x 24 cm. [DA690.B7A9] 76-370747 ISBN 0-7158-1191-6 : £1.95
1. Bradford, Eng. (Yorkshire)—Description—Views. I. Ayers, John, 1930- joint author. II. Title.

Bradley, Harry Lynde, Mrs.—Art collections.

MILWAUKEE. Art Center. 708.175'95
The Collection of Mrs. Harry Lynde Bradley. [Milwaukee, 1968] 186 p. illus. (part col.) 26 cm. Catalog of Mrs. Bradley's collection, most of which was included in an exhibition held at the Milwaukee Art Center Oct. 25, 1968, to Feb. 23, 1969. [N5220.B77] 70-2725
1. Bradley, Harry Lynde, Mrs.—Art collections. 2. Art—Exhibitions. I. Title.

MILWAUKEE. Art Center. 769'.94'074017595
Personal selections from the Mrs. Harry Lynde Bradley Collection. New Orleans : Bradley Family Foundation, 1975. 107 leaves (3 fold.) : all col. ill. ; 29 cm. Cover title: Bradley. Includes index. [N6447.M5 1975] 74-14444
1. Bradley, Harry Lynde, Mrs.—Art collections. 2. Milwaukee. Art Center. 3. Art, Modern—19th century—Catalogs. 4. Art, Modern—20th century—Catalogs. 5. Art—Milwaukee—Catalogs. I. Title. II. Title: Bradley.

Bradley, Will H., 1868-1962.

BRADLEY, Will, 1868- 926.55
Will Bradley, his chap book; an account, in the words of the dean of American typographers, of his graphic arts adventures: as a boy printer in Ishpeming, art student in Chicago, designer, printer, and publisher at the Wayside Press, the years as art director in periodical publishing, and the interludes of stage, cinema, and authorship. New York, The Typophiles, 1955. vii, 104p. 19cm. (Typophile chap books, 30) [Z232.B812A3] 55-4441
I. Title. BIP

BRADLEY, Will H. 1868- 926.55
Will Bradley, his chap book; an account, in the words of the dean of American typographers, of his graphic arts adventures: as a boy printer in Ishpeming, art student in Chicago, designer, printer, and publisher at the Wayside Press, the years as art director in periodical publishing, and the interludes of stage, cinema, and authorship. New York, The Typophiles, 1955. vii, 104 p. 19 cm. (Typophile chap books, 30) [Z232.B812A3] 55-4441
I. Title. II. Series: The Typophiles, New York. Typophile chap books, 30

BRADLEY, Will H., 1868-1962. 769'.92'4
Will Bradley: his graphic art; a collection of his posters, illustrations, typographic designs & decorations. Edited by Clarence P. Hornung. New York, Dover Publications [1974] xxxvi p., 89 [i.e. 97] p. of illus. 31 cm. [NC139.B7H67] 73-87711 ISBN 0-486-22120-2 4.00 (pbk.)
1. Bradley, Will H., 1868-1962. I. Hornung, Clarence Pearson, ed.

Brady, James, 1928—

BRADY, James, 1928- 746.9'2'0924 B
Superchic. [1st ed.] Boston, Little, Brown [1974] 266 p. 22 cm. Autobiographical. [TT505.B7A34] 74-13303 ISBN 0-316-10593-7 6.95
1. Brady, James, 1928- I. Title.

Brady, Mathew B., 1823 (ca.)-1896.

BRADY, Mathew B., 1823(ca.)-1896. 779'.2'0973
Mathew Brady's Great Americans : prints from the original glass negatives in the Meserve collection / produced in collaboration with Time-Life Books. [Alexandria, Va.] : Time-Life Books, [1977,c1976] 1 case : ports. ; 30 cm. Title from case. Contains text (6 p.), by P. B. Kunhardt, Jr., 1 photoprint (9 x 11 in.), and 10 contact prints (3 x 4 in.), each mounted on a folder with accompanying descriptive text. [TR681.F3B7 1976] 77-150942 19.95
1. Brady, Mathew B., 1823 (ca.)-1896. 2. Photography—Portraits. 3. United States—Biography—Portraits. I. Time-Life Books. II. Title: Great Americans.

HORAN, James David, 1914- 927.7
Mathew Brady, historian with a camera. Picture collation by Gertrude Horan. New York, Crown Publishers [1955] xix, 244 p. illus., ports., map. 32 cm. "A picture album": p. [91]-[228] "A pictorial bibliography of Brady pictures": p. 235-238. Includes bibliographies. [TR140.B7H6] 55-10171
1. Brady, Mathew B., 1823 (ca.)-1896. 2. United States—Biography—Portraits. 3. United States—History—Pictorial works. 4. Photography—History—United States.

KUNHARDT, Dorothy Meserve, 1901- 770'.92'4 B
Mathew Brady and his world : produced by Time-Life Books from pictures in the Meserve collection / by Dorothy Meserve Kunhardt and Philip B. Kunhardt, Jr., and the editors of Time-Life Books. Alexandria, Va. : Time-Life Books ; Morristown, N.J. : school and library distribution by Silver Burdett Co., c1977. 303 p. : ill. ; 30 cm. [TR140.B7K8] 77-73043 ISBN 0-8094-1775-8 : 25.00
1. Brady, Mathew B., 1823 (ca.)-1896. 2. Meserve, Frederick Hill, 1865-1962—Photograph collections. 3. Photographers—United States—Biography. I. Kunhardt, Philip B., joint author. II. Time-Life Books. III. Title.

MEREDITH, Roy, 1908- 770'.92'4 B
Mr. Lincoln's camera man, Mathew B. Brady / Roy Meredith. 2d rev. ed New York : Dover Publications, [1974] xiii, 368 p. : ill. ; 29 cm. An unabridged and corrected republication of the work originally published in 1946 by Scribner, New York, with a new index of negative numbers. Bibliography: p. 365-368. [TR140.B7M4 1974] 73-92262 ISBN 0-486-23087-2 : 12.50 ISBN 0-486-23021-X : 6.95
1. Brady, Mathew B., 1823 (ca.)-1896. 2. Photography, Artistic. 3. United States—History—Civil war, 1861-1865—Pictorial works. I. Title.

Brady, Mathew B., 1823 (ca.)-1896—Juvenile literature.

HOOBLER, Dorothy. 770'.92'4 B
Photographing history : the career of Mathew Brady / by Dorothy and Thomas Hoobler. New York : Putnam, c1977. 143 p. : ill. ; 24 cm. Includes index. A biography of the photographer of famous men and women of his time who left his studio at the zenith of his career to travel with Union troops photographing the Civil War. [TR140.B7H59 1977] 92 77-3009 ISBN 0-399-20602-7 : 8.95.
1. Brady, Mathew B., 1823 (ca.)-1896—Juvenile literature. 2. Photographers—United States—Biography—Juvenile literature. I. Hoobler, Thomas, joint author. II. Title.

KOMROFF, Manuel, 1890- j92
Photographing history; Mathew Brady. Photos. from the Ansco Historical Collection, the Chicago Historical Society. and Kean Archives, Philadelphia. Chicago, Encyclopaedia Britannica Press [1964? c1962] 192 p. illus. 22 cm. (Britannica bookshelf: Great lives series) Title on spine: Mathew Brady. [[TR140.B7]] 64-57459
1. Brady, Mathew B., 1823 (ca)-1896 — Juvenile literature. I. Title.

Braid.

BARKER, June. 746
Decorative braiding and weaving. [Newton Centre, Mass.] C. T. Branford Co. [1973] 112 p. illus. (part col.) 21 cm. Bibliography: p. 111. [TT880.B3] 72-10627 7.50
1. Braid. 2. Hand weaving. I. Title. BIP

BELASH, Constantine A 748.2
Braiding and knotting for amateurs. Boston, C. T. Branford, 1952. viii, 133p. illus. 20cm. (Branford handicraft series) [TT880.B] A53
1. Braid. 2. Knots and splices. I. Title. II. Title: Knotting for amateurs.

BELASH, Constantine A. 746.4
Braiding and knotting: techniques and projects, by Constantine A. Belash. Illus. by Charles E. White, Jr. New York, Dover Publications [1974] iv, 126 p. illus. 21 cm. Reprint, without foreword and pref., of the 1936 ed. published by Beacon Press, Boston, under title: Braiding and knotting for amateurs. [TT880.B4 1974] 74-75266 ISBN 0-486-23059-7 1.50 (pbk.)
1. Braid. 2. Knots and splices. I. Title.

Bramante, Donato, 1444?-1514.

BRAMANTE, Donato, 1444?-1514 720.945
Donato Bramante, 1444-1514 [by Gino Chierici. [Translated from the Italian by Peter Simmons.] New York, Universe Books [1960] [31]p. illus., 64 plates, plans. 17cm. (Universe architecture series) Bibl.: p.[27]-[28] 60-12422 1.50 pap.,
I. Chierici, Gino. II. Title.

MURRAY, Peter. 726'.5'0924
Bramante's Tempietto. [Newcastle upon Tyne] University of Newcastle upon Tyne, 1972. 21 p. illus. 24 cm. (Charlton lecture, 53) Includes bibliographical references. [NA1123.B7M82] 73-161098
1. Bramante, Donato, 1444?-1514. 2. Rome (City). Tempietto. I. Title. II. Series.

Brancusi, Constantin, 1876-1957.

BRANCUSI, Constantin, 1876-1957 730.924
Brancusi. Designed, photographed by Nicolae Sandulescu. Bucharest, Meridiane Pub. House, 1965. [76] p. (chiefly illus.) 31 x 31 cm. Text by Geo. Bogza. [NB553.B73B6] 66-9313 7.50
I. Sandulescu, Nicolae. II. Bogza, Ged. III. Title.
Available from Vanous in New York.

BRANCUSI, Constantin, 1876-1957. 730'.92'4
Brancusi : 1876-1976 / text, anthology, and chronology, Mircea Deac. Bucharest : Litera Pub. House, 1976. [36] p. : ill. ; 32 x 33 cm. "Main events: retrospective—one-man shows, books, films, etc. after the artist had died": p. [35]-[36] [NB933.B7D4] 76-372766
1. Brancusi, Constantin, 1876-1957. I. Deac, Mircea.

BRANCUSI, Constantin, 1876-1957. 730.9498
Constantin Brancusi, [by] Carola Giedion-Welcker. Translated by Maria Jolas and Anne Leroy. New York, G. Braziller, 1959. 240 p. (p. 45-192 plates (part col)) illus., ports. 31 cm. "Bibliography, by Hans Bolliger": p. 225-234. [NB553.B73G513] 59-9867
I. Giedion-Welcker, Carola, ed.

BRANCUSI, Constantin, 1876-1957. 730'.924
Constantin Brancusi, 1876-1957; a retrospective exhibition, by Sidney Geist. [New York, Solomon R. Guggenheim Foundation, 1969] 157 p. illus. (part col.), ports. 28 cm. "The Solomon R. Guggenheim Museum New York, in collaboration with Philadelphia Museum of Art [and] the Art Institute of Chicago." Bibliography: p. 156-157. [NB933.B7G42] 76-95574
I. Geist, Sidney. II. Solomon R. Guggenheim Museum, New York. III. Philadelphia Museum of Art. IV. Chicago. Art Institute.

BREZEANU, Barbu, 1909- 730'.924
Brancusi in Romania / Barbu Brezianu ; [translated by Delia Razdolescu and Ilie Marcu]. Bucuresti : Editura Academiei Republicii Socialist Romania, 1976. 316 p. : ill. ; 24 x 25 cm. At head of title: Institute of History of the Arts. "Revised and updated version of Opera lui Constantin Brancusi in Romania, published in 1974." Bibliography: p. 247-268. [NB933.B7B7313] 77-483316 lei57.00
1. Brancusi, Constantin, 1876-1957. I. Title.

CONSTANTIN Brancusi. 735.44
New York, Wittenborn, 1957 [i.e. 1958] vi, 50p. 65 plates. 20cm. Bibliography: p. 48-50. [NB553.B73L4] 927.3 58-2232
1. Brancusi, Constantin, 1876-1957. I. Lewis, David, writer on art.

GEIST, Sidney. 730'.924
Brancusi; a study of the sculpture. New York, Grossman, 1968 [c1967] viii, 247 p. illus., port. 23 cm. Bibliography: p. 233-236. [NB933.B7G4] 66-26540
1. Brancusi, Constantin, 1876-1957.

GEIST, Sidney. 730'.92'4
Brancusi: the sculpture and drawings. New York, H. N. Abrams, [1975] 200 p. illus. (part col.) 28 x 30 cm. "Catalogue of the sculpture": p. [171]-193. Bibliography: p. 169-[170] [NB933.B7G43] 74-17450 ISBN 0-8109-0124-2
1. Brancusi, Constantin, 1876-1957. I. Brancusi, Constantin, 1876-1957.

GEIST, Sidney. 730'.92'4
Brancusi/The kiss / by Sidney Geist. 1st ed. New York : Harper & Row, c1977. (Icon editions) Includes bibliographical references and index. [NB933B7G39 1977] 76-27502 ISBN 0-06-433257-8 : 10.00. ISBN 0-06-430081-1 pbk. : 5.95
1. Brancusi, Constantin, 1876-1957. The kiss. I. Title. BIP

JIANU, Ionel 730.9498
Brancusi. New York, Tudor [c.]1963. 223p. illus., ports. 28cm. Bibl. 63-5890 12.50
1. Brancusi, Constantin, 1876-1957. I. Title. BIP

SUBJECT INDEX

BRASSES—GREAT BRITAIN—CATALOGS.

LEWIS, David Neville, 1922- 735.44
Constantin Brancusi. New York, Wittenborn, 1957 [i.e. 1958] vi, 50 p. 65 plates. 20 cm. Bibliography: p. 48-50. [NB553.B73L4] 58-2232
1. Brancusi, Constantin, 1876-1957. II. Title.

SPEAR, Athena Tacha. 730'.924
Brancusi's birds [by] Athena T. Spear. New York, New York University Press for the College Art Association of America, 1969. 152 p. illus. 29 cm. (Monographs on archaeology and the fine arts, 21) Part of illustrative matter in pocket. "Catalogue raisonne": p. [51]-[114] Bibliography: p. [139]-152. [NB933.B7S68] 69-18287
1. Brancusi, Constantin, 1876-1957. I. Title. II. Series. BIP

Brandegee, Robert Bolling, 1849-1922.

NEW Britain Museum of American Art. 759.13
An exhibition of the work of Robert Bolling Brandegee, A.N.A., 1849-1922. New Britain, Conn. [1971?] 28 p. illus., ports. 26 cm. Catalog of a retrospective exhibition held March 18 through April 25, 1971, at the New Britain Museum of American Art, New Britain, Conn. Bibliography: p. 27. [ND237.B79N4] 78-293910
1. Brandegee, Robert Bolling, 1849-1922. I. Title.

Brandeis University, Waltham, Mass. Rose Art Museum.

TWO hundred 726'.3'097307401444
years of American synagogue architecture : [exhibition], the Rose Art Museum, Brandeis University, Waltham, Massachusetts, [March 30 to May 2, 1976] . Waltham, Mass. : American Jewish Historical Society, c1976. 63 p. : ill. ; 25 cm. Bibliography: p. 55-63. [NA4690.T86] 76-15469
1. Brandeis University, Waltham, Mass. Rose Art Museum. 2. Synagogue architecture—United States—Exhibitions. 3. United States—Religious life and customs—Exhibitions. I. Brandeis University, Waltham, Mass. Rose Art Museum. II. American Jewish Historical Society. BIP

Brandon, Man.—City planning.

MANITOBA. Municipal Planning Branch. 711'.4'0971273
Background studies, Brandon development plan / prepared by Municipal Planning Branch, Department of Municipal Affairs, Province of Manitoba, in co-operation with the Council of the City of Brandon. [s.l. : s.n.], 1976. 115 p. in various pagings, [42] leaves of plates (some fold.) : ill., maps (some fold. col.) ; 28 x 44 cm. [HT169.C32B75] 77-369952
1. Brandon, Man.—City planning. 2. City planning—Manitoba. 3. Brandon, Man.—City planning—Maps. I. Title.

Braque, Georges, 1882-1963.

BRAQUE, Georges, 1882- 759.4
Georges Braque (born in 1882) Text by Joan Cassou. New York, H.N. Abrams [1957] [74]p. 31 illus. (incl. port., part col.) 17cm. (The Pocket library of great art, A31) Bibliography: p. [74] [ND553.B86C3] 59-4561
I. Cassou, Jean, 1897- II. Title.

BRAQUE, Georges, 1882-1963. 759.4
G. Braque [by] Francis Ponge, Pierre Descargues [and] Andre Malraux. Texts translated by Richard Howard. Biography and captions translated by Lane Dunlop. New York, H. N. Abrams [1971] 261, [7] p. illus. (part col.) 31 cm. "To the memory of Georges Braque, funeral oration by A. Malraux": p. [263]-[264] [ND553.B86P6313] 78-160123 ISBN 0-8109-0044-0
I. Ponge, Francis. II. Descargues, Pierre.

BRAQUE, Georges, 1882-1963. 759.4
Georges Braque: his graphic work. Introd. by Werner Hofmann. New York, H. N. Abrams [1961] xxxiii, 86 p. (chiefly plates (part col.) ports.) 33 cm. Bibliography: p. xxviii-xxx. [NE650.B58H6] 61-15293
I. Hofmann, Werner, 1928-

BRAQUE, Georges, 1882-1963. 741.9'44
Illustrated notebooks, 1917-1955. Translated by Stanley Appelbaum. New York, Dover Publications [1971] 117 p. illus. 29 cm. Original text, with English translation, of Cahier de Georges Braque. [NC248.B68A47 1971] 76-137003 ISBN 0-486-20232-1 3.00
I. Title. BIP

BRION, Marcel, 1895- 759.4
Braque. [Tr. from French by A. H. N. Molesworth] New York, Abrams [1962] 87p. illus. (pt. col.) (Student's ser. of great artists) 60-11165 1.95
1. Braque, Georges, 1882- I. Title.

COGNIAT, Raymond, 1896- 709'.24
Braque. [Translated from the French by Eileen B. Hennessy] New York, Crown Publishers [1970] 96 p. illus. (part col.) 29 cm. ([The Q.L.P. art series]) Includes bibliographical references. [N6853.B7C613] 78-125042 3.95
1. Braque, Georges, 1882-1963.

COOPER, Douglas, 1911- 759.4
Braque: the great years. [Chicago] Art Institute of Chicago [1972?] 116 p. illus. 26 cm. Catalog of an exhibition held at the Art Institute of Chicago, Oct. 7-Dec. 3, 1972. Bibliography: p. 115-116. [ND553.B86C57] 72-82731
1. Braque, Georges, 1882-1963. I. Chicago. Art Institute. II. Title.

DAMASE, Jacques. 759.4
Georges Braque. [Translation: Tony White] New York, Barnes & Noble [1963] 90 p. illus. (part col.) port. 18 cm. (Barnes & Noble art series) "No. 611." [ND553.B86D313] 63-5389
1. Braque, Georges, 1882- I. Title.

GIEURE, Maurice. 759.4
G. Braque. Paris, Editions P. Tisne; New York, Universe Books [1956] 108p. illus., 148 plates (part col.) 29cm. Text in English; picture captions in French. Bibliography: p. 105-107. [ND553.B86G5] 927.5 56-58864
1. Braque, Georges, 1831- I. Title.

LEYMARIE, Jean. 759.4
Braque. Translated by James Emmons. [New York] Skira; [distributed by World Pub. Co., Cleveland, 1961] 133 p. mounted col. illus. 19 cm. (The Taste of our time, v. 35) Bibliography: p. 119-122. [ND553.B86L45] 61-10170
1. Braque, Georges, 1882-1963.

MULLINS, Edwin B. 759.4
The art of Georges Braque [by] Edwin Mullins. New York, H. N. Abrams [1968] 216 p. illus. (part col.), port. 22 cm. London ed. (Thames & Hudson) has title: Braque. Bibliography: p. 206. [ND553.B86M8 1968b] 68-28389
1. Braque, Georges, 1882-1963. I. Title.

RICHARDSON, John Patrick, 1924- 759.4
G. Braque. Greenwich, Conn., New York Graphic Society [c.1961] 32p. illus., 68 plates (part col.) 36cm. Bibl. 61-8631 12.50
1. Braque, Georges, 1882- I. Title.

WALLY F. Galleries. 739.27'092'4
The prestigious collection, Bijoux de Braque, executed by Heger de Lowenfeld. New York [1963] [24] p. illus. (part col.) 26 cm. Catalog of an exhibition. [NK7398.B7W34 1963] 74-152197
1. Braque, Georges, 1882-1963. 2. Jewelry, French. I. Braque, Georges, 1882-1963. II. Heger de Lowenfeld, Henri Michel. III. Title.

Brasher, Rex, 1869-1960.

BRASHER, Milton E. 927.5
Rex Brasher: painter of birds, a biography. New York, Rowman and Littlefield [1962] 345 p. illus. 24 cm. [QL31.B684B7] 61-18827
1. Brasher, Rex, 1869-1960. BIP

Brass rubbing.

MCGEER, William J. A. 760
Reproducing relief surfaces; a complete handbook of rubbing, dabbing, casting, and daubing, by William J. A. McGeer. [Concord, Mass., Minuteman Press, 1972] 40 p. illus. 21 cm. Bibliography: p. 39. [NC915.R8M3] 72-186587
1. Brass rubbing. I. Title.

WOOD, Emma. 760
Brass and other rubbings / Emma Wood. Newton Abbot [Eng.] ; North Pomfret, Vt. : David and Charles, 1978. 128 p. : ill. ; 22 cm. (Leisure and travel series) Includes index. Bibliography: 91-92. [NB1840.W6] 77-91731 ISBN 0-7153-7500-8 : 6.95
1. Brass rubbing. 2. Rubbing. I. Title. BIP

Brass rubbing—England.

LEWIS, Betsey, 1924- 914.2'04'857
Through England on my knees / Betsey Lewis. South Brunswick, N.J. : A. S. Barnes, c1977. 241 p. : ill. ; 25 cm. Includes index. Bibliography: p. 220. [NB1842.L48] 76-10880 ISBN 0-498-01864-4 : 12.00
1. Brass rubbing—England. 2. Brasses—England. 3. England—Description and travel—1970- —Guide-books. I. Title. BIP

NEWCASTLE upon Tyne. University. Library. 760
The Charlton Collection of brass rubbings. [Newcastle upon Tyne] 1967. 21 p. 31 cm. Cover title. [NB1842.N38] 73-171350
1. Charlton, Oswin J., 1871-1941—Art collections. 2. Brass rubbing—England. 3. Brass rubbing—Newcastle upon Tyne—Catalogs. I. Title.

Brasses.

BURGESS, Frederick William, 1855- 739.51
Chats on old copper and brass. Edited and rev. by C. G. E. Bunt. New York, A. A. Wyn, 1955. 183p. illus. 20cm. [The Chats series] [NK7804.B8 1955] 55-544
1. Brasses. 2. Coper. 3. Metal-work—Collectors and collecting. I. Title.

BURGESS, Frederick William, 1855-1945. 739'.51
Chats on old copper and brass, by F. W. Burgess. Revised ed. Edited and revised by C. G. E. Bunt. Wakefield, E.P. Publishing, 1973. 184 p., [47] p. of plates. illus. 20 cm. Reprint of the 1954 ed. [NK7804.B8 1973] 74-173988 ISBN 0-85409-830-5 £2.75
1. Brasses. 2. Copper articles. 3. Metal-work—Collectors and collecting. I. Bunt, Cyril George Edward, 1882- ed. II. Title.

MACKLIN, Herbert Walter, 1866?-1917. 739'.52
Monumental brasses. Rev. by John Page-Phillips. New York, Praeger [1969] 188 p. illus., map. 22 cm. Bibliography: p. 117-124. [NB1840.M3 1969] 74-84096 7.50
1. Brasses. I. Page-Phillips, John, ed. II. Title.

MACKLIN, Herbert Walter. 1866?-1917 739.52
Monumental brasses, together with a selected bibliography and county lists of brasses remaining in the churches of the United Kingdom. New pref., rev. by Charles Oman. [7th rev. ed.] London. Allen & Unwin [Mystic. Conn., Verry, 1966] 196p. illus. 21cm. [NB1840.M3] 53-29231 4.00 bds.,
1. Brasses. 2. Brasses—Gt. Brit. I. Title.

NORRIS. MALCOLM 739.52
Brass rubbing. London, Studio Vista [New York, Dover, 1966, c.1965] 112p. illus. 26cm. Bibl. [NK7804.N6] 66-22479 5.00 bds.,
1. Brasses. I. Title.

Brasses—England.

BERTRAM, Jerome. 739'.52'0942
Brasses and brass rubbing in England. [1st American ed.] South Brunswick, Great Albion Books [1972, c1971] 206 p. illus. 22 cm. Bibliography: p. [163] [NB1842.B4 1972] 77-164434 ISBN 0-8453-1013-5 8.50
1. Brasses—England. 2. Brass rubbing—England. I. Title.

BERTRAM, Jerome. 739'.52'0941
Lost brasses / Jerome Bertram. Newton Abbot ; North Pomfret, Vt. : David and Charles, 1976. 196 p. : ill., facsims., maps, ports. ; 23 cm. Includes index. Bibliography: p. 190-193. [NB1842.B43] 75-43208 ISBN 0-7153-7141-X : 13.95
1. Brasses—England. 2. Brasses—England—Indents. I. Title.

SUFFLING, Ernest Richard. 739'.52
English church brasses from the 13th to the 17th century, by Ernest R. Suffling. Baltimore, Genealogical Pub. Co., 1970. xii, 456 p. illus. 23 cm. "Originally published ... 1910." Includes bibliographical references. [NB1842.S8 1970] 73-126133 ISBN 0-8063-0437-5
1. Brasses—England. 2. Sepulchral monuments—England. I. Title.

TRIVICK, Henry H. 739'.52'0942
The picture book of brasses in gilt [by] Henry Trivick. With 242 illus. in gilt and black. New York, Scribner [1973 c1971] 33 p. illus., plates. 29 cm. [NB1842.T75 1972] 72-3240 ISBN 0-684-13099-8 15.00
1. Brasses—England. I. Title.

Brasses—England—Cambridgeshire.

CAMBRIDGE, Eng. City Libraries. 739'.52'094259
Monumental brasses in Cambridgeshire and the Isle of Ely. 3rd ed. Cambridge, Cambridge City Libraries, 1968. [2], 29 p. 26 cm. Includes bibliographies. [NB1842.C3 1968] 79-439561 2/6
1. Brasses—England—Cambridgeshire. 2. Brasses—England—Isle of Ely. I. Title.

CAMBRIDGE, Eng. City Libraries. 739'.52'094259
Monumental brasses in Cambridgeshire and the Isle of Ely. 4th ed. (completely revised). Cambridge, Cambridge City Libraries, 1970. [2], 29 p. 26 cm. Bibliography: p. 27-29. [NB1842.C3 1970] 77-871939 ISBN 0-903027-00-3 £0.15
1. Brasses—England—Cambridgeshire. 2. Brasses—England—Isle of Ely. I. Title.

Brasses—England—History.

GENTLE, Rupert. 739'.52'0942
English domestic brass, 1680-1810, and the history of its origins / Rupert Gentle & Rachael Feild ; foreword by Graham Woods. New York : Dutton, 1975. 204 p., [1] leaf of plates : ill. ; 29 cm. Includes index. Bibliography: p. 87. [NK7843.G45 1975] 75-327278 ISBN 0-525-09835-6 : 32.50
1. Brasses—England—History. I. Feild, Rachael, joint author. II. Title.

Brasses—England—Indents.

SADLER, Arthur George. 739'.52'09422
The indents of lost monumental brasses in Southern England / by A. G. Sadler Ferring-on-Sea : The author, [1976] 40 p. : ill. ; 21 cm. Bibliography: p. 15. [NB1842.S15] 76-363202 ISBN 0-9500405-9-2 : £0.85
1. Brasses—England—Indents. I. Title.

Brasses—Europe.

BOUQUET, Alan Coates, 1884- 739'.52
European brasses, with an introd. and notes by A. C. Bouquet. In collaboration with Michael Waring. New York, F. A. Praeger [1967] 78 p. illus. 53 cm. [NB1846.B6 1967b] 67-28527
1. Brasses—Europe. 2. Sepulchral monuments—Europe. I. Waring, Michael J. II. Title.

Brasses—Great Britain—Catalogs.

LE STRANGE, Richard 739'.52'0942
A complete descriptive guide to British monumental brasses. London, Thames and Hudson, 1972. 150 p. 22 cm. On spine:

British monumental brasses. Bibliography: p. 149-150. [NB1842.L47] 72-193327 ISBN 0-500-01076-5
1. Brasses—Great Britain—Catalogs. I. Title. II. Title: British monumental brasses.
Available from Transatlantic, 10.00. BIP

Brasses—United States.

KAUFFMAN, Henry J., 1908- 739'.51'0973
American copper & brass [by] Henry J. Kauffman. [Camden, N.J.] T. Nelson [1968] 288 p. illus., facsims. 26 cm. Bibliography: p. 282-283. [NK7803.K3] 68-13938
1. Brasses—United States. 2. Implements, utensils, etc.—Collectors and collecting. I. Title.

Braynard, Frank Osborn, 1916—

BRAYNARD, Frank Osborn, 1916- 741.9'73
The tall ships : official OpSail '76 portfolio / Frank Braynard. New York : Sabine Press, c1976. 1 portfolio ([4] leaves, [20] leaves of plates : 20 ill.) ; 38 cm. [NC139.B73A56] 76-369981
1. Braynard, Frank Osborn, 1916- 2. Ships in art. 3. Operation Sail, '76. I. Operation Sail 1976. II. Title. BIP

Brazing.

ALUMINUM Company of America. 673.7226
Brazing Alcoa aluminum. Pittsburgh [c1955] 134p. illus. 22cm. [TT267.A4] 56-986
1. Brazing. 2. Aluminum. I. Title.

AMERICAN Welding Society. Committee on Brazing and Soldering. 671.56
Brazing manual. New York, Reinhold Pub. Corp., 1955. 193p. illus. 24cm. [TT267.A53] 55-9167
1. Brazing. I. Title. BIP

AMERICAN Welding Society. Committee on Brazing and Soldering. 671.5'6
Brazing manual / prepared by AWS Committee on Brazing and Soldering under the direction of AWS Technical Activities Committee. 3d ed., rev. Miami : American Welding Society, 1976. ix, 309 p. : ill. ; 25 cm. Includes bibliographies and index. [TT267.A55 1976a] 76-9440 8.50
1. Brazing. I. Title.

AMERICAN Welding Society. Committee on Brazing and Soldering. 671.56
Brazing manual. Prepared by AWS Committee on Brazing and Soldering under the direction of AWS Technical Activities Committee. Edward A. Fenton, technical secretary. [2d ed.] New York, American Welding Society; trade distributor: Reinhold Pub. Corp. [1963] 290 p. illus. 24 cm. [TT267.A53] 63-17712
1. Brazing. I. Title.

AMERICAN Welding Society. Committee on Filler Metal. 671.5'6
Specification for brazing filler metal / prepared by AWS Committee on Filler Metal ; under the direction of AWS Technical Activities Committee. Miami, FL : AWS, c1976. vi, 30 p. ; 28 cm. "AWS A5.8-76." [TT267.A55 1976] 75-36866 ISBN 0-87171-127-3 pbk. : 3.50
1. Brazing. 2. Filler metal—Specifications. I. American Welding Society. Technical Activities Committee. II. Title.

Bread dough craft.

GARDNER, Pat. 745.5
Dough creations : food to folk art / Pat Gardner, Kay Gleason. Radnor, Pa. : Chilton Book Co., c1977. p. cm. (Chilton's creative crafts series) [TT880.G37] 77-4588 ISBN 0-8019-6376-1 : 12.50. ISBN 0-8019-6377-X pbk. : 6.95
1. Bread dough craft. 2. Dough. I. Gleason, Kay, joint author. II. Title.

KERN, Marna Elyea. 745.5
An introduction to breadcraft / by Marna Elyea Kern ; photos. by Ray H. Harrison. Boston : Houghton Mifflin, 1978. 108 p. : ill. ; 24 cm. [TT880.K47] 77-24981 ISBN 0-395-25770-0 : 8.95
1. Bread dough craft. I. Title. BIP

MEILACH, Dona Z. 745.5
Creating art with bread dough / by Dona Z. Meilach ; photos. by Mel and Dona Meilach. New York : Crown Publishers, c1976. 120 p. : ill. (some col.) : 29 cm. Includes index. [TT880.M43 1976] 76-8944 ISBN 0-517-52590-9 pbk. : 4.95
1. Bread dough craft. I. Meilach, Mel. II. Title. BIP

MERGELER, Karen. 731
Too good to eat! The art of dough sculpture. Photography by Magda R. White. Introd. by Gerard Marquis Du Corday. Santa Ana, Calif., Folk Art Publications [1972] 80 p. illus. (part col.) 21 cm. Instructions for making decorative items from bread dough with a brief history of this ancient art form. [TT880.M47] 72-95386 5.95
1. Bread dough craft. I. White, Magda R., illus. II. Title. BIP

NICKELL, Molli. 731.4'2
This is baker's clay; a new sculpture/craft medium. Illus. by Marlo Johansen. Photography by Molli Nickell. New York, Drake Publishers [1973?] 149 p. illus. 27 cm. [TT880.N52] 73-5550 ISBN 0-87749-525-4
1. Bread dough craft. I. Title. BIP

WILLIAMSON, Ethie. 745.5
Baker's clay : cutouts, sculptures, and projects with flour, salt, and water / Ethie Williamson. New York : Van Nostrand Reinhold Co., 1976. 96 p. [4] leaves of plates : ill. ; 28 cm. Includes index. [TT880.W54 1976] 76-4449 ISBN 0-442-29487-5 : 10.95. ISBN 0-442-29486-7 pbk. : 6.95
1. Bread dough craft. I. Title. BIP

Bread dough craft—Juvenile literature.

CHERNOFF, Goldie Taub. 745.5
Clay-dough, play-dough. Clay-dough creations and drawings by Margaret A. Hartelius. New York, Walker [1974] [24] p. col. illus. 20 x 24 cm. Gives instructions for making jewelry, baskets, monsters, Easter eggs, mobiles, and a variety of other objects from dough. [TT880.C43 1974] 73-92449 ISBN 0-8027-6178-X 3.50
1. Bread dough craft—Juvenile literature. I. Hartelius, Margaret A., illus. II. Title. BIP

SOMMER, Elyse. 745.5
The bread dough craft book. Illustrated by Giulio Maestro. New York, Lothrop, Lee and Shepard [1972] 128 p. illus. 24 cm. Instructions for making jewelry, decorations, mobiles, sculpture, and other items from a mixture of bread dough and glue. [TT880.S65] 79-177330 4.50
1. Bread dough craft—Juvenile literature. I. Maestro, Giulio, illus. II. Title. BIP

Bread flowers.

HITOMI, Junco. 745.59'43
Luna flora: sculpture in bread. San Francisco, Japan Publications [1974] 79 p. illus. (part col.) 27 cm. Translation of Pan no hana. [TT890.3.H5713] 73-90496 ISBN 0-87040-255-2 6.95
1. Bread flowers. I. Title.

Breast in art.

LEVY, Mervyn 704.9424
The moons of paradise; some reflections on the appearance of the female breast in art. [1st Amer. ed.] New York, Citadel [1965, c.1962] 145p. illus. 25cm. [N8217.B75L4] 64-18241 5.95 bds.,
1. Breast in art. I. Title.

Breechcloths.

OSBORNE, Carolyn M 970.6677
Shaped breechcloths from Peru. [Berkeley, University of California Press, 1950] iii, 157-184 p. illus., map. 28 cm. (Anthropological records, v. 13, no. 2) Bibliography: p. 181. [E51.A58 vol. 13, no. 2] A 50
1. Breechcloths. 2. Indians of South America—Peru. 3. Indians of South America—Textile industry and fabrics. I. Title. II. Series.

Brehat—Description and travel.

KLEINHOLZ, Frank, 1901- 941.4'1'0482
Ile de Brehat: the flowering rock. Text and illus. by Frank Kleinholz. Coral Gables, Fla., University of Miami Press [1971] 95 p. illus. 23 x 29 cm. [NC139.K57A46] 74-171455 ISBN 0-87024-220-2 10.00
1. Brehat—Description and travel. 2. Brehat—Description and travel—Views. I. Title. II. Title: The flowering rock.

Bremo.

HODSON, Peter. 728.8'3
The design and building of Bremo: 1815-1820 [Birmingham, Ala., Priv. print. by Hayes International Corp., 1968, c1967] 70, [3] p. illus., facsims., plans. 27 cm. Thesis—University of Virginia. Bibliography: p. [71]-[73] [NA730.V8H6] 72-1731
1. Bremo. I. Title.

Brendel, Otto, 1901-1973.

IN memoriam Otto J. Brendel 709
: essays in archaeology and the humanities / ed. by Larissa Bonfante, Helga von Heintze ; with the collab. of Carla Lord. Mainz : von Zabern, 1976. xviii, 264, 62 p. : numerous ill. (some col.) ; 30 cm. "Bibliography of Otto J. Brendel": p. [xii]-xiv. [N7442.B73] 77-363280 ISBN 3-8053-0154-5 : DM135.00
1. Brendel, Otto, 1901-1973. 2. Art—Addresses, essays, lectures. I. Brendel, Otto, 1901-1973. II. Bonfante, Larissa. III. Heintze, Helga, Freifrau von. IV. Lord, Carla.

Breton, Andre, 1896-1966.

CARROUGES, Michel, 1910- 759.06
Andre Breton and the basic concepts of surrealism / by Michel Carrouges ; translated by Maura Prendergast. University : University of Alabama Press, [1974] 294 p. ; 22 cm. (Studies in the humanities : Philosophy) Translation of Andre Breton et les donnees fondamentales du surrealisme. Includes index. Bibliography: p. 284-289. [NX600.S9C3313] 73-21060 ISBN 0-8173-7316-0 : 10.00
1. Breton, Andre, 1896-1966. 2. Surrealism. I. Title. II. Series: Studies in the humanities (University, Ala.) : Philosophy. BIP

OMAGGIO a/Hommage a/ 759.4
Homage to Andre Breton. Sotto l'egida del Centro francese di studi, Milano, del Centro culturale francese. Roma, e con la collaborazione di Arturo Schwarz. 17 gennaio--4 febbraio 1967: Prime edizioni, documenti, manifesti, Centro francese di studi, Milano; 17 gennaio--11 febbraio 1967: Alcuni degli artisti che Breton amava. Galleria Schwarz, Milano; Febbraio 1967: Centro culturale francese, Roma. Milano, Edizioni della Galleria Schwarz. Stamped on t.p.: Amer. dist.: Wittenborn, New York, [1967] 61p. illus., facsims., ports. 24cm. [PQ2603.R35Z88] 67-3868 2.50 pap.,
1. Breton, Andre, 1896-1966. I. Schwarz, Arturo, 1924- II. Parinaud, Andre, 1924- III. Centre francais d'etudes et d'information. IV. Centre culturel francais. V. Title.
Contents omitted.

Breton, Andre 1896-1966—Art collections.

GUILLAUME, Paul, 1891- comp. 732'.2
Sculptures negres; 24 photographies precedees d'un avertissement de Guillaume Apollinaire et d'un expose de Paul Guillaume. Collection Andre Breton et Paul Eluard: Sculptures d'Afrique, d'Amerique, d'Oceanie; Me Alph. Bellier, commissaire-priseur ... New York, Hacker Art Books, 1972 [i.e. 1973] [12] p., 24 plates, 50 p., 24 plates. map. 34 cm. "Sculptures negres first published in Paris by Paul Guillaume, 1917. Sculptures d'Afrique, d'Amerique, d'Oceanie first published in Paris, 1931. Reprinted 1973." [NB1098.G84] 71-143336 ISBN 0-87817-056-1
1. Breton, Andre 1896-1966—Art collections. 2. Eluard, Paul, 1895-1952—Art collections. 3. Negro art—Catalogs. 4. Sculpture—Africa, West—Catalogs. 5. Sculpture, Primitive—Catalogs. I. Apollinaire, Guillaume, 1880-1918. II. Bellier, Alphonse. III. Sculptures d'Afrique, d'Amerique, d'Oceanie. 1973. IV. Title. V. Title: Collection Andre Breton et Paul Eluard. BIP

Breviaries.

MEISS, Millard. 091
The Master of the Breviary of Jean Sans Peur and the Limbourgs. London, Oxford University Press for the British Academy, 1971. [2], 19 p., 17 plates; illus. (some col.) 25 cm. (Lecture on aspects of art, Henriette Hertz Trust of the British Academy, 1970) Includes bibliographical references. [ND3365.A1M4] 70-867616 ISBN 0-19-725658-9 £0.50
1. Jean sans Peur, Duke of Burgundy, 1371-1419. 2. Limbourg, Pol de, ca. 1385-ca. 1416. 3. Breviaries. 4. Illumination of books and manuscripts, French. I. Title. II. Series: British Academy, London (Founded 1901). Annual lecture on aspects of art, Henriette Hertz trust, 1970.

Brevoort, James Renwick, 1832-1918.

MCCOLLEY, Sutherland. 759.13
The works of James Renwick Brevoort, 1832-1918, American landscape painter; a catalogue, compiled with an introd. by Sutherland McColley [Yonkers, N.Y., Hudson River Museum, 1972] xviii, 67 p. illus. 28 cm. Catalogue of an exhibition held at the Hudson River Museum, Mar. 12-Apr. 30, 1972. Bibliography: p. 63-64. [ND1839.B73M3] 74-182824
1. Brevoort, James Renwick, 1832-1918. I. Hudson River Museum. II. Title.

Brewster, Mass.—Description—Views.

BREWSTER Historical Society. 974.4'92
Brewster : a Cape Cod town remembered. [Brewster, Mass. : Brewster Historical Society], c1976. [76] p. : chiefly ill. ; 21 cm. Cover title. [F74.B64B58 1976] 76-373319
1. Brewster, Mass.—Description—Views.

Bricher, Alfred Thompson, 1837-1908.

BROWN, Jeffrey R. 759.13
Alfred Thompson Bricher, 1837-1908, by Jeffrey R. Brown, assisted by Ellen W. Lee [Indianapolis] Indianapolis Museum of Art, 1974 [c1973] 103 p. illus. (part col.) 26 cm. Catalogue of an exhibition held at the Indianapolis Museum of Art, Sept. 12-Oct. 28, 1973; George Walter Vincent Smith Art Museum, Nov. 25, 1973-Jan. 13, 1974. Includes bibliographical references. [ND237.B864B76] 73-86756
1. Bricher, Alfred Thompson, 1837-1908. I. Bricher, Alfred Thompson, 1837-1908. II. Indianapolis Museum of Art. III. George Walter Vincent Smith Art Museum, Springfield, Mass.

Bricklaying.

HANDISYDE, Cecil C. 721'.0442'1
Bricks and brickwork / [by] C. C. Handisyde, B. A. Haseltine. London : Brick Development Association, [1976] [1], 142 p. : ill. (chiefly col.), form, plans (some col.) ; 31 cm. Col. ill. on lining papers. Includes index. Bibliography: p. 128-129. [TH5501.H32] 76-362580 ISBN 0-900191-03-1
1. Bricklaying. 2. Bricks. 3. Building, Brick. I. Haseltine, Barry A., joint author. II. Title.

Bridges, Charles, 1670-1747.

HOOD, Graham, 1936- 759.155
Charles Bridges and William Dering : two Virginia painters, 1735-1750 / by Graham Hood. Williamsburg, Va. : Colonial Williamsburg Foundation ; Charlottesville : distributed by University Press of Virginia,

SUBJECT INDEX

BRITT, PETER, 1819-1905.

c1978. xvi, 125 p., [5] leaves of plates : chiefly ill. ; 27 cm. Includes bibliographical references and index. [ND1329.B75H66] 77-13772 ISBN 0-87935-047-4 : 15.00
1. Bridges, Charles, 1670-1747. 2. Dering, William. 3. Portraits—Virginia—Catalogs. I. Title.

Bridges — Design — Addresses, essays, lectures.

NATIONAL Research Council. Highway Research Board. 725.98
Bridges and structures; 8 reports, presented at the 44th annual meeting, January 11-15, 1965. Washington, D.C., 1965. 113 p. illus. 25 cm. (Highway research record, no. 106) national Research Council. Publication 1320. [TE7.H5] 66-60066
1. Bridges — Design — Addresses, essays, lectures. I. Title. II. Series. III. Series: National Research Council. Publication 1320

Bridges—Gt. Brit.

CASSON. HUGH MAXWELL. Sir 1910- ed. 725.98
Bridges. London Pub. by Chatto & Windus for the Natl. Benzole Co. [New York. Taplinger. 1966, c.1965] 124p. illus. (pt. col.) 2 col. maps. 19cm. (Natl. Benzole bks. Gold leaf Brit. landmarks ser.) Res., design, illus. by Paul Sharp. Writing by E. M. Hatt. [TG57.C5] 66-2728 1.50 pap.,
1. Bridges—Gt. Brit. I. Sharp, Paul. II. Hatt, E. M. III. Title.

Bridges—Hist.

SILVERBERG, Robert 725.98
Bridges. Philadelphia, Macrae [1966] 189p. illus. 24cm. Bibl. [IG15.S4] 66-17880 4.50
1. Bridges—Hist. I. Title.

TRACHTENBERG, Alan. 624.5'5'097471
Brooklyn Bridge : fact and symbol / Alan Trachtenberg. Phoenix ed. Chicago : University of Chicago Press, 1979. p. cm. Includes bibliographical references and index. [TG25.N53T7 1979] 78-68548 ISBN 0-226-81115-8 : 6.95
1. New York (City)—Bridges—Brooklyn Bridge. I. Title. BIP

Bridlington, Eng. (Yorkshire). St. Mary the Virgin (Church)

EARNSHAW, John R. 726'.7'0942839
A reconstruction of Bridlington Priory / by J. R. Earnshaw. Bridlington : North Wolds Borough Council, [1976] 38 p. (4 fold.) : ill., plans ; 26 cm. Caption title. Bibliography: p. 37. [NA5471.B75E27] 77-358290 ISBN 0-905614-00-3 : £0.50
1. Bridlington, Eng. (Yorkshire). St. Mary the Virgin (Church) I. Title.

Bright, Thomas C.

JERVIS Library. 929.8
The Thomas C. Bright autograph collection and the Huntington autograph collection. Rome, N.Y., 1970. [22] l. 29 cm. Caption title. [Z42.J535] 76-30684
1. Bright, Thomas C. 2. Autographs—Collections. I. Title. II. Title: Huntington autograph collection.

Brighton, Eng.—Description—Views.

DALE, Antony. 942.25'6'080222
Brighton old and new / [compiled by] Antony Dale and James S. Gray. Wakefield : EP Publishing, 1976. [5], 98 p. : chiefly ill. ; 18 x 24 cm. [DA690.B78D29] 76-379229 ISBN 0-7158-1188-6 : £1.95
1. Brighton, Eng.—Description—Views. 2. Brighton, Eng.—Buildings—Pictorial works. 3. Historic buildings—England—Brighton—Pictorial works. I. Gray, James S., joint author. II. Title. BIP

Brighton, Eng.—History.

DALE, Antony. 942.2'5
Fashionable Brighton, 1820-1860. 2nd ed. Newcastle- upon-Tyne, Oriel P., 1967. 192 p. 56 plates, illus., ports. 26 cm. 63/- (B68-01238) (SBN 85326 028 8) Bibliography: p. 181-183. [DA690.B78D3 1967] 68-76838
1. Brighton, Eng.—Hist. 2. Brighton, Eng.—Descr. 3. Architecture—Brighton, Eng. I. Title. BIP

DALE, Antony. 914.22'52
The history and architecture of Brighton. [1st ed., reprinted]; with a new foreword by the author. Wakefield, S.R. Publishers, 1972. viii, 96, [17] p. illus., map, plan, ports. 23 cm. [DA690.B78D32 1972] 72-189780 ISBN 0-85409-740-6 £1.50
1. Brighton, Eng.—History. 2. Architecture—Brighton, Eng. I. Title.

Brighton, Eng. Pavilion.

GOFF, Martyn. 942.2'56
The Royal Pavilion, Brighton / [by] Martyn Goff. London : Joseph, 1976. 32 p., [16] p. of plates : ill. (chiefly col.), port. ; 19 cm. (Folio miniatures) Ill. on lining papers. Bibliography: p. 3. [NA7746.B8G63 1976] 76-379882 ISBN 0-7181-1477-9 : £1.75
1. Brighton, Eng. Pavilion. I. Title.

Brighton, N. Y. (Township, Monroe Co.) — Orringh Stone Tavern.

HAYES, Charles F 917.4788033
The Orringh Stone Tavern and three Seneca sites of the late historic period, by Charles F. Hayes III. Rochester, N. Y., Rochester Museum Association, 1965. vi, 82 p. illus., maps, 26 cm. (Research records of the Rochester Museum of Arts and Science, no. 12) Bibliography: p. 47-51. [E78.N7H37] 66-8124
1. Brighton, N. Y. (Township, Monroe Co.) — Orringh Stone Tavern. 2. New York (State) — Antiq. 3. Seneca Indians — Antiq. 4. Excavations (Archaeology) — New York (State) — Brighton (Township, Monroe Co.) I. Title. II. Series: Rochester, N. Y. Museum of arts and sciences. Research records, no. 12

Brigman, Anne.

HEYMAN, Therese Thau. 770'.92'4
Anne Brigman : pictorial photographer, pagan, member of the photo-secession : [an exhibition] The Oakland Museum, Oakes Gallery, September 17 through November 17, 1974 / by Therese Thau Heyman. [Oakland, Calif.] : Oakland Museum, Art Dept., [1974] 18 p. : ill. ; 28 cm. Bibliography: p. 15. [TR140.B77H48] 74-195232
1. Brigman, Anne. 2. Photography, Artistic—Exhibitions. I. Oakland Museum.

Bristol, Eng.—Description.

BRACE, Keith, 1928- 942.3'93'0857
Portrait of Bristol / [by] Keith Brace. New ed. London : Hale, 1976. 208 p., [24] p. of plates : ill., maps ; 23 cm. (The Portrait series) Includes index. Bibliography: p. 11-12. [DA690.B8B75 1976] 76-377045 ISBN 0-7091-5435-6 : £3.90
1. Bristol, Eng.—Description. 2. Bristol, Eng.—History. I. Title. BIP

Bristol, Eng.—Description—Views.

BRISTOL old and new / 942.3'93
[compiled by] Reece Winstone ; [new photographs by Charles Thorn]. Wakefield : E. P. Publishing, 1974. [5], 99 p. : of ill. ; 18 x 24 cm. [DA690.B8B83] 75-311273 ISBN 0-8277-3354-2 : 8.50
1. Bristol, Eng.—Description—Views. I. Winstone, Reece. II. Thorn, Charles.
Distributed by British Book Center, N.Y. BIP

BRISTOL past & present : 942.3'93'080222
a pictorial record of the ancient City of Bristol / [compiled by] Reece Winstone. Oxford : Oxford Illustrated Press, 1976. [63] p. : of ill., port. ; 28 cm. [DA690.B8B85] 77-356818 ISBN 0-902280-35-X : £3.25
1. Bristol, Eng.—Description—Views. 2. Bristol, Eng.—Social life and customs—Pictorial works. I. Winstone, Reece.

British Columbia—Description and travel—Views.

BRITISH Columbia 779'.9'91711044
/ featuring Birtish Columbia photographers ; text by Ted Wrinkle. 1st ed. Portland, Or. : Beautiful West Pub. Co., c1977. 72 p. : col. ill. ; 29 cm. [F1087.8.B73] 78-102334 ISBN 0-915796-44-9 : 12.95. ISBN 0-915796-43-0 pbk. : 5.95
1. British Columbia—Description and travel—Views. I. Wrinkle, Ted. BIP

BRITISH Columbia, 779'.9'9171044
our land / words by Paul St. Pierre ; photos. by some of the people who live in the land. Saanichton, B.C. ; Seattle : Hancock House, c1977. 160 p. : chiefly col. ill. ; 36 cm. [F1087.8.B76] 78-305706 ISBN 0-919654-96-7 : 35.00
1. British Columbia—Description and travel—Views. I. St. Pierre, Paul H., 1923-

British Guiana—Antiquities.

EVANS, Clifford, 1920- 913.881
Archeological investigations in British Guiana, by Clifford Evans and Betty J. Meggers. Washington, U. S. Govt. Print. Off., 1960. xxi, 418 p. illus., 68 plates, maps (4 fold.) diagrs., profiles, tables. 24 cm. ([U.S.] Bureau of American Ethnology Bulletin 177) Bibliography: p. 348-351. [E51.U6 no. 177] [F2379.E8] 60-62223
1. British Guiana—Antiquities. 2. Indians of South America—British Guiana. I. Meggers, Betty Jane, joint author. II. Title. III. Series.

British Library.

BRITISH Library. 016.091'0942
Catalogue of the manuscripts in the Spanish language in the British Library / Don Pascual de Gayangos. London : British Museum Publications for the British Library, 1976. 4 v. ; 26 cm. Reprint of the 1875 ed. published by the British Museum, Department of Manuscripts, London. [Z6621.B86S7 1976] 77-356349 ISBN 0-7141-0491-4 : £60.00
1. British Library. 2. Manuscripts, Spanish—England—London—Catalogs. I. Gayangos y Arce, Pascual de, 1809-1897. II. British Museum. Dept. of Manuscripts. Catalogue of manuscripts in the Spanish language in the British Museum. III. Title.

British Library. Dept. of Manuscripts.

BRITISH Library. Dept. of Manuscripts. 010.8 s
Register of microfilms and other photocopies in the Department of Manuscripts, British Library. London : Swift, 1976. [2], 239 p. ; 33 cm. (Special series - List and Index Society ; v. 9) Includes index. [CD1042.A2L56 Vol. 9] [Z6621.B837] 011 77-354423 ISBN 0-902573-53-5 : £5.00
1. British Library. Dept. of Manuscripts. 2. Manuscripts on microfilm—Catalogs. 3. Manuscripts—Facsimiles—Catalogs. I. Title. II. Series: List and Index Society. Special series ; v. 9.

British Museum.

BRITISH Museum. 739.27'074'02142
Jewellery through 7000 years / British Museum. London : British Museum Publications, c1976. 276 p. : ill. (some col.) ; 25 cm. Includes index. Bibliography: p. 267-271. [NK7302.5.G7L63 1976] 77-353071 ISBN 0-7141-0054-4 : £5.50. ISBN 0-7141-0055-2 pbk.
1. British Museum. 2. Jewelry—England—London—Catalogs. I. Title. BIP

BRITISH Museum, 708.21'2
London. [Texts by Antonino Caleca [others] New York, Newsweek [c.1967] 171p. illus. (pt. col.) 30cm. (Great museums of the world) Bibl. [N1040.B7] 68-200232 6.95; 8.95 deluxe ed.,
1. British Museum. I. Caleca, Antonino. II. Series.

COOK, B. F. 709'.38'07402142
Greek and Roman art in the British Museum / B. F. Cook. London : British Museum Publications for the Trustees of the British Museum, c1976. 194 p. : ill. (1 col.) ; 25 cm. Includes index. Bibliography: p. 193. [N5604.G7L63] 77-353081 ISBN 0-7141-1249-6 : £4.95. pbk.
1. British Museum. 2. Art, Classical. 3. Art—England—London. I. British Museum. II. Title. BIP

CROOK, Joseph Mordaunt. 069'.09421'42
The British Museum [by] J. Mordaunt Crook. New York, Praeger Publishers [1972] 251 p. illus. 23 cm. Errata slip inserted. Bibliography: p. 235-239. [N1040.C7] 74-183060 12.50
1. British Museum.

CROOK, Joseph Mordaunt. 069'.2'0942142
The British Museum, [by] J. Mordaunt Crook. London, Allen Lane, 1972. 251 p. illus., plans, ports. 23 cm. (The Architect and society) Bibliography: p. 235-239. [N1040.C7 1972] 72-195096 ISBN 0-7139-0254-X
1. British Museum.
Available from Praeger, 12.50.

FRANCIS, Frank Chalton, 1901- 069'.9421'42
Treasures of the British Museum / edited and introduced by Frank Francis. Rev. ed. London : Thames and Hudson, c1975. 360 p. : ill. (some col.) ; 21 cm. (The World of art library) Includes index. [AM101.B87F7 1975] 75-320625 ISBN 0-500-20119-6 pbk. : 8.75
1. British Museum. I. Title.
Distributed by Transatlantic Arts. BIP

British Museum. Dept. of Manuscripts.

BRITISH Museum. Dept. of Manuscripts. 016.091
Catalogue of the Stowe manuscripts in the British Museum. Reprograf. Nachdr. d. Ausg., London, 1895-96. Hildesheim, New York, Olms, 1973. 2 v. 20 cm. Contents.Contents.—v. 1. Text.—v. 2. Index. [Z6621.B85S83 1973] [DA26] 74-185865 ISBN 3-487-04783-7 DM198.00
1. British Museum. Dept. of Manuscripts. 2. Manuscripts—England—London—Catalogs. 3. Great Britain—History—Sources—Bibliography—Catalogs. I. British Museum. Mss. (Stowe). 1973. II. Title.

British Museum. Mss. (Cottonian)

BRITISH Museum. Dept. of Manuscripts. 016.091
A catalogue of the manuscripts in the Cottonian Library deposited in the British Museum. Hildesheim, New York, G. Olms, 1974. xv, 618, [75] p. 26 cm. Reprint of the ed. published in London in 1802. [Z6621.B85C8 1974] 74-177966 ISBN 3-487-05018-8
1. British Museum. Mss. (Cottonian) 2. Manuscripts—Great Britain—Catalogs. 3. Great Britain—History—Sources—Bibliography. I. British Museum. Mss. (Cottonian) II. Title.

British Museum. Mss. (Lansdowne)

BRITISH Museum. MSS. (Lansdowne) 016.091
A catalogue of the Lansdowne manuscripts in the British Museum. With indexes of persons, places, and matters. Hildesheim, New York, G. Olms, 1974. 1 v. (various pagings) 29 cm. Reprint of the ed. published in London in 1819. [Z6621.B85L3 1974] 74-177997 ISBN 3-487-05184-2
1. British Museum. Mss. (Lansdowne) 2. Manuscripts—Great Britain—Catalogs. 3. Great Britain—History—Sources—Bibliography. I. Title.

Britt, Peter, 1819-1905.

MILLER, Alan Clark. 770'.92'4 B
Photographer of a frontier : the photographs of Peter Britt / by Alan Clark Miller. Eureka : Interface California Corp., c1976. 107 p. : ill. ; 27 cm. (Interface monographs on photography)

[TR140.B78M54] 76-48832 ISBN 0-915580-05-5 : 20.95
1. Britt, Peter, 1819-1905. 2. Jacksonville, Or.—Description—Views. 3. Photographers—Oregon—Biography. I. Britt, Peter, 1819-1905. II. Title. III. Series. BIP

Brocade.

TIDBALL, Harriet. 746.1
Brocade. Lansing, Mich., Shuttle Craft Guild; dist. by Craft & Hobby Bk. Serv., Big Sur, Calif., 1967, c1968. 50p. illus. 27cm. (Shuttle Craft Guild. Monograph 22) [TT848.T52] 68-5499 5.00 pap.,
1. Brocade. 2. Hand weaving. I. Title. II. Series. BIP

Brock, 1912-

BROCK, 1912- 759.2
Brock: paintings, drawings, watercolors [by] Daniel L. Cusick. [Albany? N.Y., Cusick Associates, c1972] 97 p. illus. (part col.) 29 cm. [ND237.B868C87] 73-76296 20.00
1. Brock, 1912- I. Cusick, Daniel L. II. Title.

Broderson, Morris, 1928—

MORRIS Broderson. 759.13
Tucson : University of Arizona Museum of Art, c1975. 65 p. : col. ill. ; 32 cm. "Limited edition, 500 printed." [N6537.B73M67] 75-27404
1. Broderson, Morris, 1928- I. Arizona. University. Museum of Art.

Brodie, Agnes Hahn—Exhibitions.

BRODIE, Agnes Hahn. 709'.2'4
Arches and columns by Agnes Hahn Brodie at the Mather Gallery, Case Western Reserve U., Cleveland, Ohio, Nov. 1977. [Arlington? Va.] : Brodie, c1977. 15 p. : chiefly ill. ; 23 cm. Bibliography: p. [14] [N6537.B74M37] 77-85187
1. Brodie, Agnes Hahn—Exhibitions. I. Mather Gallery. II. Title.

Brody, Julian—Art collections.

AFRICAN art 732'.2'0967074017758
from the Collection of Julian and Irma Brody : [exhibition] Des Moines Art Center, March 18-April 20, 1975. [Des Moines] : Des Moines Art Center, [1975] [44] p. : ill. (some col.) ; 25 cm. Catalog. Includes bibliography. [N7398.A353] 75-6023
1. Brody, Julian—Art collections. 2. Brody, Irma—Art collections. 3. Art, African—Exhibitions. 4. Art, Primitive—Africa, West. I. Des Moines Art Center.

Bromley, London. (Parish)—Historic houses, etc.

THE Survey of London: 914.21'78
being the first volume of the register of the Committee for the Survey of the Memorials of Greater London, containing the Parish of Bromley-by-Bow. Edited by C. R. Ashbee, from the material collected by members of the Survey Committee. London, P. S. King, 1900. [New York, AMS Press, 1971] xxxv, 53 p., 36 l. illus., fold. map. 29 cm. Includes bibliographical references. [DA685.B843P37 1971] 73-138270 ISBN 0-404-51651-3
1. Bromley, London. (Parish)—Historic houses, etc. 2. Architecture—Bromley, London (Parish) I. Ashbee, Charles Robert, 1863-1942, ed. II. Series: Joint Publishing Committee Representing the London County Council and the London Survey Committee. Survey of London, v. 1.

Bronze.

ROAST, Harold J 673.32
Cast bronze. Foreword by Howard F. Taylor. Cleveland, American Society for Metals, 1953. 458p. illus. 24cm. [TS570.R6] 53-1539
1. Bronze. 2. Founding. I. Title.

Bronze age.

BASS, George Fletcher. 913.3'5'03
Cape Gelidonya: a bronze age shipwreck [by] George F. Bass. With the collaboration of Peter Throckmorton [and others] Philadelphia, American Philosophical Society, 1967. 177 p. illus., maps. 30 cm. (Transactions of the American Philosophical Society, new ser., v. 57, pt. 8) Bibliography: p. 7-13. [Q11.P6 n.s., vol. 57, pt. 8] 67-28643
1. Bronze age. 2. Underwater archaeology. I. Title. II. Series: American Philosophical Society, Philadelphia. Transactions, new ser., v. 57, pt. 8.

Bronze age—Aegean Sea region.

BRANIGAN, Keith. 739'.09391
Aegean metalwork of the Early and Middle Bronze Age / [by] Keith Branigan. Oxford : Clarendon Press, 1974. xv, 216 p., 44 p. of plates : ill., maps ; 28 cm. (Oxford monographs on classical archaeology) Includes bibliographical references and indexes. [GN778.22.A35B72] 75-305007 ISBN 0-19-813213-1 : 54.00
1. Bronze age—Aegean Sea region. 2. Metal-work—Aegean Sea region. 3. Aegean Sea region—Antiquities. I. Title. II. Series.
Distributed by Oxford University Press, New York. BIP

Bronze age—England.

LANGMAID, Nancy G. 739'.512'09362
Bronze Age metalwork in England and Wales / [by] Nancy G. Langmaid. Aylesbury : Shire Publications, 1976. 64 p. : ill. ; 21 cm. (Shire archaeology) Includes index. Bibliography: p. 25-26. [GN778.22.G7L36] 74-83356 ISBN 0-85263-266-5 : £1.00
1. Bronze age—England. 2. Bronze age—Wales. 3. England—Antiquities. 4. Wales—Antiquities. I. Title.

Bronze founding.

MILLS, John W. 731.4'56
Studio bronze casting: lost wax method [by] John W. Mills and Michael Gillespie. New York, Praeger [1970, c1969] 90 p. illus. 26 cm. [TS570.M55 1970] 78-96806 12.50
1. Bronze founding. 2. Sculpture—Technique. I. Gillespie, Michael, joint author. II. Title.

Bronzes.

BERMAN, Harold, 1933- 731'.82
Bronzes; sculptors & founders, 1800-1930. [1st ed.] Chicago, Abage [1974] 224 p. illus. 29 cm. [NK7909.8.B47] 74-78612 30.00
1. Bronzes. I. Title.

SAVAGE, George, 1909- 731
A concise history of bronzes. New York, Praeger [1969, c1968] 264 p. 209 illus. (part col.) 22 cm. Bibliography: p. 250-252. [NB1230.S2] 69-19617 7.50
1. Bronzes. 2. Sculpture—History. I. Title.

Bronzes—Africa, West.

UNDERWOOD, Leon, 739'52'0966
1890-
Bronzes of West Africa. 2nd rev. ed. London, Tiranti, 1968. 40p. illus., maps. 64 plates. 19cm. Bibl. [NK7987.U55 1968] 68-124336 3.50
1. Bronzes—Africa, West. I. Title.
Distributed by Transatlantic, Levittown, N.Y. BIP

Bronzes, Ancient.

KASTELIC, Joze 739.512
Situla art; ceremonial bronzes of ancient Europe. With contributions by Karl Kromer, Guido Mansuelli. New York, McGraw, 1965. xxxvi, 80p. (chiefly illus. (pt. col.) map) 32cm. Photos. by Mladen Grcevic. Bibl. [NK7907.K3513] 65-19076 9.95
1. Bronzes, Ancient. I. Grcevic, Mladen, illus. II. Title.

Bronzes, Ancient—Exhibitions.

PITTSBURGH. Carnegie Institute. Museum of Art.
Ancient bronzes; a selection from the Heckett Collection, Heckmeres Highlands, Valencia, Pennsylvania. Pittsburgh, 1964. [84] p. illus. 23 cm. Catalog of the exhibition held Nov. 5, 1964-Jan. 10, 1965. [NK7907.P5] 73-172084
1. Heckett, Eric H, Mrs.—Art collections. 2. Bronzes, Ancient—Exhibitions. I. Title.

Bronzes — Asia.

GROSZ, Joy. 704.9432
Oriental treasures; an illustrated color presentation of oriental art series, by Joy and Walter Grosz. Vancouver, Wash., 1964. 2 v. 262 col. slides 30 cm. Slides issued in 66 pockets, inserted in portfolio at end of each vol. Vol. 1 includes slides of the Thailand exhibit of sculpture, which was exhibited throughout the United States. Contents.CONTENTS. -- 1. Bronze. -- 2. Painting. [N7260.G7] 65-4472
1. Bronzes — Asia. 2. Idols and images. 3. Paintings, Japanese. 4. Screens. Lantern slides. I. Gross, Walter, joint author. Title. II. Title.

Bronzes—China.

BULLING, Anneliese. 741'.512'0951
Chinese bronze mirrors. Notes prepared by Anneliese Bulling. New York, Intercultural Arts Press [1969] 3 v. 75 col. slides (film, 2 x 2 in.) 30 cm. (The Sackler collections, ser. 8, lecture 1-3) The slides are in pockets in 6 transparent leaves. Contents.Contents.—lecture 1. Late Chou-early Han.—lecture 2. Han and Six Dynasties.—lecture 3. Sui/Tang and later. Bibliography (leaves [27]-[30]). [NK7983.B8] 68-29051
1. Bronzes—China. 2. Mirrors, Chinese. I. Title. II. Series.

Bronzes—China—To 221 B.C.—Exhibitions.

KUWAYAMA, 739'.512'0951074019494
George.
Ancient ritual bronzes of China / George Kuwayama. Los Angeles : Far Eastern Council of the Los Angeles County Museum of Art, c1976. 80 p. : ill. ; 28 cm. Catalog of an exhibition held at Los Angeles County Museum of Art, Feb. 3-April 26, 1976. Bibliography: p. 77-78. [NK7983.22.K88] 75-43865 ISBN 0-87587-068-6
1. Bronzes—China—To 221 B.C.—Exhibitions. 2. Rites and ceremonies—China. I. Los Angeles Co., Calif. Museum of Art, Los Angeles. II. Title. BIP

Bronzes, Chinese.

KOOP, Albert James, 1877- 732'.7
1945.
Early Chinese bronzes. New York, Hacker Art Books, 1971. viii, 84 p. 110 plates. 30 cm. Reprint of the 1924 ed. Includes bibliographical references. [NK7983.K6 1971] 77-116357 ISBN 0-87817-047-2
1. Bronzes, Chinese. I. Title. BIP

LEFEBVRE 739'.512'0951
d'Argence, Rene Yvon.
Ancient Chinese bronzes in the Avery Brundage Collection; a selection of vessels, weapons, bells, belthooks, mirrors, and various artifacts from the Shang to the T'ang dynasty, including a group of gold and silver wares. [Berkeley, Calif.] Published by Diablo Press for the De Young Museum Society [1967, c1966] 132 p. illus. (part col.), map. 23 cm. On cover: Avery Brundage Collection; the ancient Chinese bronzes. M. H. de Young Memorial Museum, San Francisco, California. Bibliography: p. 132. [NK7983.L4 1967] 68-2529
1. Bronzes, Chinese. 2. Avery Brundage Collection. I. Young Memorial Museum, San Francisco. II. Title.

LEFEBVRE D'ARGENCE, 739'.512'0951
Rene Yvon.
Ancient chinese bronzes in the Avery Brundage Collection; a selection of vessels, weapons, bells, belthooks, mirrors, and various artifacts from the Shang to the Tang dynasty, including a group of gold and silver wares. [Berkeley, Calif.] Published by Diablo Press for the De Young Museum Society [1967, c1966] 132 p. illus. (part col.), map. 23 cm. On cover: Avery Brundage Collection; the ancient Chinese bronzes. M. H. de Young Memorial Museum, San Francisco, California. Bibliography: p. 132. [NK7983.L4] 68-2529
1. Bronzes, Chinese. 2. Avery Brundage Collection. I. De Young Memorial Museum, San Francisco. II. Title.

MUNSTERBERG, 731.8'89'43'0951
Hugo, 1916-
Chinese Buddhist bronzes. Rutland, Vt., Tuttle [1967] 192p. illus. 31cm. Bibl. [NK7983.M8] 67-26308 17.50
1. Bronzes, Chinese. 2. Art, Buddhist. I. Title.

POOR, Robert. 739'.512'0951
Bronze ritual vessels of ancient China. Notes prepared by Robert Poor. [Photos. by Otto E. Nelson] New York, Intercultural Arts Press [1969] 9 v. 225 col. slides (film, 2 x 2 in.) 30 cm. (The Sackler collections, ser. 1, lecture 1-9) The slides are in pockets in 18 transparent leaves. Contents.Contents.—lecture 1. Shang 1.—lecture 2. Shang 2.—lecture 3. Shang 3.—lecture 4. Chou 1. lecture 5. Chou 2.—lecture 6. Chou 3.—lecture 7. Chou 4.—lecture 8. Chou 5.—lecture 9. Han. [NK7983.P6] 68-28017
1. Bronzes, Chinese. I. Nelson, Otto E., illus. II. Title. III. Series.

WATSON, William, 1917- 739.512
Ancient Chinese bronzes. Rutland, Vt. Tuttle [c.1962] 117p. illus., 107 plates (pt. col.) 26cm. (Arts of the East) Bibl. 62-6451 10.00
1. Bronzes, Chinese. I. Title. II. Series. BIP

WEBER, George W. 739'.512'0951
The ornaments of late Chou bronzes; a method of analysis [by] George W. Weber, Jr. New Brunswick, N.J., Rutgers University Press [1973] xxi, 631 p. illus. 29 cm. Bibliography: p. 625-631. [NK7983.A1W42] 72-163965 ISBN 0-8135-0701-4 75.00
1. Bronzes, Chinese. 2. Decoration and ornament, Chinese. 3. Bronzes—Expertising. I. Title. BIP

WHITE, William Charles, 571.3
Bp., 1873-
Bronze culture of ancient China; an archaeological study of bronze objects from northern Honan, dating from about 1400 B.C. -- 771 B.C. [Toronto] University of Toronto Press, 1956. xviii, 219 p. illus., plates (part col.) maps 29 cm. (Royal Ontario Museum, Division of Archaeology. Museum studies, no. 5) 500 copies. No. 81. Bibliographical footnotes. [NK7983.W45] 57-4556
1. Bronzes, Chinese. 2. Honan, China. (Province) — Antiq. I. Title. II. Series: Toronto. Royal Ontario Museum of Archaeology. Museum studies, no. 5

WHITE, William Charles, 571.3
Bp., 1873-
Bronze culture of ancient China; an archaeological study of bronze objects from northern Honan, dating from about 1400 b. c.--771 b. c. [Toronto] University of Toronto Press, 1956. xviii, 219p. illus., plates (part col.) maps. 29cm. (Royal Ontario Museum, Division of Archaeology. Museum studies, no. 5) 500 copies. No. 81. *biliographical footnotes. [NK7983.W45] 57-4556
1. Bronzes, Chinese. 2. Honan, China (Province)—Antiq. I. Title. II. Series: Toronto. Royal Ontario Museum of Archaeology. Museum studies, no. 5

Bronzes, Chinese—Catalogs.

BUSSAGLI, Mario. 739'.512'0951
Chinese bronzes; translated by Pamela Swinglehurst from the Italian. London, New York, Hamlyn, 1969. 3-158 p. col. illus. 20 cm. (Cameo) Translation of

SUBJECT INDEX BROOKS, JAMES, 1906

Bronzi Cinesi. [NK7983.B8413] 79-473121 15/-
1. Bronzes, Chinese—Catalogs. I. Title.

FREER Gallery of Art, Washington, D.C. 739'.512'0951
The Freer Chinese bronzes, by John Alexander Pope [and others] Washington, Smithsonian Institution, 1967- v. illus., maps. 31 cm. (Its Oriental studies, no. 7) Smithsonian publication 4706. Contents.-- v. 1. Catalogue.-- Bibliography: v. 1, p. 621-629; [NK7983.F73] 68-61307
1. Bronzes, Chinese—Catalogs. I. Pope, John Alexander, 1906- II. Title. III. Series. BIP

MINNEAPOLIS. Institute of Arts. 739.512
A catalogue of the Chinese bronzes in the Alfred F. Pillsbury collection, by Bernhard Karlgren. Minneapolis, Published for the Minneapolis Institute of Arts by the University of Minnesota Press [1952] [16], 228 p. illus., 114 plates. port. 32 cm. On spine: The Pillsbury collection of Chinese bronzes. Bibliography: 10th-11th prelim. pages. [NK7983.M53] 52-5320
1. Bronzes, Chinese — Catalogs. 2. Bronzes — Minneapolis — Catalogs. I. Karlgren, Bernhard, 1889- II. Pillsbury, Alfred F. III. Title.

SPRINGFIELD, Mass. Museum of Fine Arts. 739*.5*12
The Raymond A. Bidwell Collection of Chinese bronzes and ceramics. Springfield, Mass., Published by the Raymond A. and Bertha U. Bidwell Fund for the Museum of Fine Arts, 1965. 85 p. illus. 29 cm. [NK7983.A1S67] 72-196643
1. Bidwell, Raymond Austin, 1876-1954—Art collections. 2. Bronzes, Chinese—Catalogs. 3. Pottery, Chinese—Catalogs. 4. Porcelain, Chinese—Catalogs. I. Title.

Bronzes, Chinese—Exhibitions.

LOEHR, Max. 739'.512'0951
Ritual vessels of bronze age China. [New York] Asia Society; distributed by New York Graphic Society [Greenwich, Conn., 1968] 183 p. illus. (part col.), map. 28 cm. "An Asia House Gallery publication." "Catalogue of an exhibition selected by Dr. Max Loehr ... and shown in the Asia House Gallery in the fall of 1968 as an activity of the Asia Society." Bibliography: p. 181-183. [NK7983.L57] 68-30798
1. Bronzes, Chinese—Exhibitions. 2. Implements, utensils, etc.—China. I. Asia Society. II. Asia House Gallery, New York. III. Title. BIP

Bronzes, Chinese—To 221 B.C.

WATSON, William, 1917- 739'.512'0931
Ancient Chinese bronzes / by William Watson. 2d ed. London : Faber and Faber, 1977. 128 p., [56] leaves of plates (some col.) : ill. ; 26 cm. (The Arts of the East) Includes index. Bibliography: p. 112-116. [NK7983.22.W37 1977] 77-379502 ISBN 0-571-04917-6 : 19.95
1. Bronzes, Chinese—To 221 B.C. 2. Bronzes, Chinese—Chi'in-Han dynasties, 221 B.C.-220 A.D. I. Title. II. Series. Distributed by Faber and Faber, Salem, NH

Bronzes—Collectors and collecting.

CURTIS, Tony. 730
Bronzes / compiled by Tony Curtis. [Galashiels] : [Lyle Publications], [1976] 3-124 p. : ill. ; 16 cm. (Antiques and their values) Includes index. [NK7905.C87] 77-352380 ISBN 0-902921-40-1 : £1.50
1. Bronzes—Collectors and collecting. 2. Bronzes—Prices. I. Title.

Bronzes, Greek.

ART and technology; 739'.512'0938 a symposium on classical bronzes. Edited by Suzannah Doeringer, David Gordon Mitten [and] Arthur Steinberg. Cambridge, Published for the Fogg Art Museum, Harvard University and the Dept. of Humanities, M.I.T. by M.I.T. Press [1970] xvi, 290 p. illus. (part col.) 29 cm. Includes bibliographical references. [NB135.A75] 70-113372
1. Bronzes, Greek. 2. Bronzes, Roman. 3. Bronzes, Etruscan. I. Doeringer, Suzannah F., ed. II. Mitten, David Gordon, ed. III. Steinberg, Arthur, 1937- ed. IV. Harvard University. William Hayes Fogg Art Museum. V. Massachusetts Institute of Technology. Dept. of Humanities.

CHARBONNEAUX, Jean, 1895- 733.3
Greek bronzes. Translated by Katherine Watson. New York, Viking Press, 1962. 163 p. illus. 22 cm. (A Studio book) Includes bibliography. [NB140.C413] 61-5482
1. Bronzes, Greek. I. Title.

CHARBONNEAUX, Jean, 1895- 1969. 733.3
Greek bronzes. Translated by Katherine Watson. New York, Viking Press, 1962. 163 p. illus. 22 cm. (A Studio book) Includes bibliography. [NB140.C413] 61-5482
1. Bronzes, Greek.

LAMB, Winifred. 739'.512
Ancient Greek and Roman bronzes. Enl. ed. with a foreword and reference bibliography by Lenore Keene Congdon. Chicago, Argonaut, 1969. xliii, 261, [97] p. illus., plates. 24 cm. Reprint, with additions, of the 1929 ed., published under title: Greek and Roman bronzes. Bibliography: p. xxiii-xliii. [NB135.L3 1969] 67-17575
1. Bronzes, Greek. 2. Bronzes, Roman. I. Title.

Bronzes, Greek—Catalogs.

BOSTON. Museum of Fine Arts. 733
Greek, Etruscan, & Roman bronzes in the Museum of Fine Arts, Boston, by Mary Comstock & Cornelius Vermeule. [Boston]; distributed by New York Graphic Society, Greenwich, Conn. [1971] xxvi, 511 p. illus. 24 cm. Bibliography: p. xi-xviii. [NK7907.3.B6] 75-166291 ISBN 0-87846-060-8 35.00
1. Bronzes, Greek—Catalogs. 2. Bronzes, Etruscan—Catalogs. 3. Bronzes, Roman—Catalogs. 4. Bronzes—Boston—Catalogs. I. Comstock, Mary, 1934- II. Vermeule, Cornelius Clarkson, 1925- III. Title.

Bronzes—Hist.

MONTAGU, Jennifer 739.512
Bronzes. New York, Putnam [1963] 128p. illus. (pt. col.) 22cm. (Pleasures and treasures) 63-15529 4.95
1. Bronzes—Hist. I. Title.

Bronzes—India.

THAPAR, Daya Ram, 1894- 739.512
Icons in bronze, an introduction to Indian metal images. New York [dist. Taplinger, c.1961] 171p. illus. map. 25cm. 61-3436 9.25
1. Bronzes—India. 2. Idols and images. 3. Gods, Hindu. I. Title.

Bronzes, Indic.

PAL, Pratapaditya. 732'.4
Krishna: the cowherd king. With a technical report by Ben B. Johnson. [Los Angeles, Los Angeles County Museum of Art, c1972] xii, 62 p. illus. (part col.) 28 cm. (Los Angeles County Museum of Art. Monograph series, no. 1) Includes bibliographical references. [NK7976.A1P34] 70-185825 ISBN 0-87587-048-1
1. Bronzes, Indic. 2. Krishna—Art. I. Los Angeles Co., Calif. Museum of Art, Los Angeles. II. Title. III. Series: Los Angeles Co., Calif. Museum of Art, Los Angeles. Monograph series, no. 1.

Bronzes, Iranian—Catalogs.

OXFORD. University. Ashmolean Museum. 739'.512'0935
Catalogue of the ancient Persian bronzes in the Ashmolean Museum, by P. R. S. Moorey. Oxford, Clarendon Press, 1971. xxiv, 343 p., 85 p. illus. 29 cm. Bibliography: p. 320-327. [NK7974.A1O9] 76-593764 ISBN 0-19-813160-7 £13.00
1. Bronzes, Iranian—Catalogs. 2. Bronzes—Oxford—Catalogs. I. Moorey, Peter Roger Stuart. II. Title. BIP

Bronzes—Kashmir.

PAL, Pratapaditya. 732'.4
Bronzes of Kashmir / Pratapaditya Pal. New York : Hacker Art Books, c1975. 255 p. : 120 ill. ; 26 x 28 cm. Bibliography: p. 253-255. [NK7976.A3K376] 75-902 ISBN 0-87817-158-4 lib.bdg. : 35.00
1. Bronzes—Kashmir. 2. Gods, Hindu, in art. 3. Gods, Buddhist, in art. I. Title. BIP

Bronzes—Private collections.

ISTITUTO Italiano per il Medio ed. Estremo Oriente, Rome. 739.5120951
Chinese, Korean, and Japanese bronzes; a catalogue of the Auriti collection donated to ISMEO and preserved in MUSEO nazionale d'arte orientale in Rome by Alexander C. Soper Roma, Label mounted on t. p.: Sole dist. in the USA: Paragon New York 1966. xii, 79p. illus., port. 25cm. (Serie orientale Roma, 35) Bibl. [NK7982.I78] 66-9178 13.00 pap.,
1. Bronzes—Private collections. 2. Bronzes, Asiatic. I. Auriti, Giacinto, 1883- II. Soper, Alexander Coburn, 1904- III. Rome (City) Museo nazionale d'arte orientale. IV. Title. V. Title: Auriti collection. VI. Series.

UNTERMYER, Irwin 739.512
Bronzes, other metalwork and sculpture in the Irwin Untermyer collection. Introd. by Yvonne Hackenbroch. New York, Metropolitan Mus. of Art [1962] lxv, 64p. illus. 31cm. (Irwin Untermyer collection, 5) Bibl. 62-51105 25.00
1. Bronzes—Private collections. 2. Art metal-work—Private collections. 3. Sculpture—Private collections. I. Hackenbroch, Yvonne. II. Title. III. Series.

Bronzes, Renaissance—Exhibitions.

WIXOM, William D. 730'.094
Renaissance bronzes from Ohio collections : [exhibition] / William D. Wixom. Cleveland : Cleveland Museum of Art, [1975] p. cm. Bibliography: p. [NK7909.3.W58] 75-30966 ISBN 0-910386-24-2
1. Bronzes, Renaissance—Exhibitions. 2. Bronzes—Private collections—Ohio. I. Cleveland Museum of Art. II. Title.

Bronzes, Renaissance—History.

MONTAGU, Jennifer. 739'.512
Bronzes. London, Octopus Books Ltd, 1972. 96 p. illus. (some col.). 25 cm. [NK7909.3.M66 1972] 73-150218 ISBN 0-7064-0037-2 2.95
1. Bronzes, Renaissance—History. I. Title. Available from Octopus Books, N.Y.

Bronzes, Thai.

CHAND, Emcee 730.9593
Thai monumental bronzes. by Emcee Chand and Khien Yimsiri. Pref. by Silp Birasri. [dist. S. Pasadena, Cal., Hutchins Oriental Bks.] 96p. plates. 22cm. 5.50 bds.,
1. Bronzes, Thai. 2. Sculpture—Thailand. 3. Art, Buddhist. I. Yimsiri, Khien, joint author. II. Title.

Bronzes—The West.

BRODER, Patricia Janis. 739'.512'0978
Bronzes of the American West. Introd. by Harold McCracken. New York, H. N. Abrams [1974] 431 p. illus. (part col.) 28 x 30 cm. Includes bibliographical references. [NK7912.B76] 73-8848 ISBN 0-8109-0133-1
1. Bronzes—The West. 2. Sculptors, American. I. Title. BIP

Bronzino, Angelo, 1502-1572.

SMYTH, Craig Hugh. 741'.092'4
Bronzino as draughtsman; an introduction, with notes on his portraiture and tapestries. Locust Valley, N.Y., J. J. Augustin [1971] x, 104, [38] p. illus. 26 cm. Bibliography: p. 102-103. [NC257.B7S6] 74-178089
1. Bronzino, Angelo, 1502-1572. I. Title. BIP

Brooklyn Art Association.

MARLOR, Clark S., 1922- 708.147'23
A history of the Brooklyn Art Association with an index of exhibitions, by Clark S. Marlor. New York, J. F. Carr [1970] vii, 421 p. illus., ports. 29 cm. Photocopy of typescript. Includes bibliographical references. [N11.B783M3 1970] 74-125076
1. Brooklyn Art Association. 2. Art—Exhibitions—Indexes. I. Title.

Brooklyn Institute of Arts and Sciences. Children's Museum.

BROOKLYN Institute of Arts and Sciences. Children's Museum. 069.016
Brooklyn Children's Museum; what we do and how we do it, by Margaret De Wolf Tullock, director. [Rev. ed.] Brooklyn, 1953. 23p. illus. 23cm. [AM101.B8983 1953] 53-33163
I. Tullock, Margaret De. Wolf 1910- II. Title.

BROOKLYN Institute of Arts and Sciences. Museum. 069
Accessions to the collections. Brooklyn. v. 22 cm. Issues for include Brooklyn Children's Museum accessions. [N522.B7A3] 51-20857
1. Brooklyn Institute of Arts and Sciences. Children's Museum. I. Title.

Brooklyn Institute of Arts and Sciences. Museum. Frieda Schiff Warburg Memorial Sculpture Garden.

BROOKLYN Institute of Arts and Sciences. Museum. 730.74014723
The Frieda Schiff Warburg Memorial Sculpture Garden. [Brooklyn] Brooklyn Museum [1966] 31 p. illus. 23 cm. The essay Fragmentary landmarks is signed: Frederick Fried. Bibliography: p. [21] [NA3503.A1B7] 66-22570
1. Brooklyn Institute of Arts and Sciences. Museum. Frieda Schiff Warburg Memorial Sculpture Garden. I. Fried, Frederick. II. Title.

Brooks, James, 1906-

BROOKS, James, 1906- 759.13
James Brooks. Dallas, Museum of Fine Arts [1972] 1 v. (unpaged) illus. (part col.) 26 cm. Catalog of the exhibition held May 10-June 25, 1972, at the Dallas Museum of Fine Arts. Includes bibliography. [ND237.B8717D3] 72-189142
I. Dallas. Museum of Fine Arts.

BROOKS, James, 1906- 759.13
James Brooks : paintings 1952-1975, works on paper 1950-1975 : [catalogue of the] exhibitions, FInch College Museum of Art, New York, New York ... April 30-June 8, 1975, Martha Jackson Gallery, New York, New York ... April 30-May 24, 1975 / introd. by Elayne H. Varian. New York : Martha Jackson Gallery : distributed by Wittenborn Art Books, 1975. 48 p. : ill. (some col.) ; 22 x 27 cm. Bibliography: p. 48. [ND237.B8717V37] 75-877 ISBN 0-8150-0726-4 (Wittenborn)
1. Brooks, James, 1906- I. Varian, Elayne H. II. Finch College, New York. Museum of Art. III. Martha Jackson Gallery.

HUNTER, Sam, 1923- 759.13
James Brooks. Foreword by John I. H. Baur. New York, Pub. for the Whitney Mus. of Amer. Art by Praeger [c.]1963. 55p. illus. (4 col.) port. 24cm. Pub. on the occasion of the exhibition held at the Whitney Mus. of American Art and the Rose Art Mus. of Brandeis Univ., spring, 1963. Bibl. 63-9455 3.50
1. Brooks, James, 1906- I. Whitney Museum of American Art, New York. II. Title.

Brooks, Romaine.

BROOKS, Romaine. 759.13
Portraits, tableaux, dessins / Romaine Brooks. New York : Arno Press, 1975 [c1952] 52 p. : chiefly ill. ; 23 cm. (Homosexuality) Reprint of the ed. published in Paris. [ND237.B872A53 1975] 75-12306 ISBN 0-405-07396-8
1. Brooks, Romaine. I. Title. II. Series. BIP

SECREST, Meryle. 759.13 B
Between me and life; a biography of Romaine Brooks. [1st ed.] Garden City, N.Y., Doubleday, 1974. xviii, 432 p. illus. 24 cm. Bibliography: p. [417]-422. [ND237.B872S42] 74-6991 ISBN 0-385-03469-5
1. Brooks, Romaine. I. Title.

Brosse, Salomon de, 1571?-1626.

COOPE, Rosalys. 720'.92'4
Salomon de Brosse and the development of the classical style in French architecture from 1565 to 1630. University Park, Pennsylvania State University [1972] xxii, 295, [119] p. illus. 26 cm. (Studies in architecture, v. 11) Bibliography: p. 287. [NA1053.B73C66] 70-127381 ISBN 0-271-00140-2 32.00
1. Brosse, Salomon de, 1571?-1626. I. Title. BIP

Brouwer, Adriaen, d. 1638.

KNUTTEL, Gerhardus, 1889- 759.9492
Adriaen Brouwer, the master and his work. Tr. from Dutch by J. G. Talma- Schilthuis, Robert Wheaton. The Hague, L. J. C. Boucher [dist. New York, Heinman, 1963] 195p. illus., 13 col. plates, ports. 34cm. Bibl. 63-3090 20.00
1. Brouwer, Adriaen, d. 1638. I. Title.

Brown, Ford Madox, 1821-1893.

FORD, Ford Madox, 1873-1939. 759.2
Ford Madox Brown; a record of his life and work. London, New York, Longmans, Green, 1896. [New York, AMS Press, 1972] xx, 459 p. illus. 23 cm. "A list of Madox Brown's more important works" p. [ND497.B73F6 1972] 76-144609 ISBN 0-404-02459-9 25.00
1. Brown, Ford Madox, 1821-1893.

RABIN, Lucy Feiden. 759.2 B
Ford Madox Brown and the pre-Raphaelite history-picture / Lucy Rabin. New York : Garland Pub., 1979 p. cm. (Outstanding dissertations in the fine arts) Originally presented as the author's thesis, Bryn Mawr College, 1973. Bibliography: p. [ND497.B73R3 1978] 77-94725 ISBN 0-8240-3246-2 : 25.00
1. Brown, Ford Madox, 1821-1893. 2. Painters—England—Biography. 3. Preraphaelitism—Europe. I. Title. II. Series. BIP

Brown, Joan, 1938—

RICHARDSON, Brenda. 759.13
Joan Brown; [exhibition. Prepared by] Brenda Richardson. Berkeley [Calif.] University Art Museum, 1974. 48 p. illus. (part col.) 20 cm. Held at the University Art Museum, Mar. 6-Apr. 21, 1974. [ND237.B874R52] 74-75326
1. Brown, Joan, 1938- I. Brown, Joan, 1938-

Brown, Lancelot, 1716-1783.

HYAMS, Edward S. 712'.0922 B
Capability Brown and Humphry Repton, by Edward Hyams. New York, Scribner [1971] vii, 248 p. illus., facsims., port. 26 cm. Bibliography: p. 238-239. [SB470.B7H9 1971b] 71-123850 ISBN 0-684-10273-0 7.95
1. Brown, Lancelot, 1716-1783. 2. Repton, Humphry, 1752-1818. 3. Landscape architecture—Gt. Brit.—History. I. Title. BIP

STROUD, Dorothy. 712'.092'4 B
Capability Brown / Dorothy Stroud ; with an introd. by Christopher Hussey. New ed. London : Faber, 1975. 262 p. : ill. ; 26 cm. Includes index. Bibliography: p. 248-250. [SB470.B7S7 1975] 75-318594 ISBN 0-571-10267-0 : 24.95
1. Brown, Lancelot, 1716-1783. I. Title.
Distributed by Faber and Faber; Salem, N. H. BIP

Brown, Oliver Madox, 1855-1874.

INGRAM, John Henry, 1842-1916. 759.2 B
Oliver Madox Brown; a biographical sketch, 1855-1874, by John H. Ingram. London, E. Stock, 1883. [New York, AMS Press, 1972] x, 238 p. illus. 19 cm. [ND497.B7515 1972] 70-148798 ISBN 0-404-03503-5 10.00
1. Brown, Oliver Madox, 1855-1874. BIP

Browne, Hablot Knight, 1815-1882.

BROWNE, Edgar Athelstane, 1841-1917. 759.2 B
Phiz and Dickens as they appeared to Edgar Browne. With original illus. by Hablot K. Browne. New York, Haskell House Publishers, 1972. xiv, 320 p. illus. 23 cm. Reprint of the 1914 ed. [NC978.5.B7B7 1972] 72-39035 ISBN 0-8383-1391-4
1. Browne, Hablot Knight, 1815-1882. 2. Dickens, Charles, 1812-1870—Illustrations. I. Title.

KITTON, Frederic George, 1856-1904. 741.9'42
"Phiz" (Hablot Knight Browne); a memoir, including a selection from his correspondence and notes on his principal works. New York, Haskell House, 1974. 32 p. illus. 20 cm. Reprint of the 1882 ed. published by W. Satchell, London. [NC978.5.B7K57 1974] 73-20467 ISBN 0-8383-1817-7 8.95
1. Browne, Hablot Knight, 1815-1882.

Brownie camera.

TYDINGS, Kenneth S 771.31
Guide to Kodak Brownie Star camera, including "20" and automatic 35 mm models. Philadelphia, Chilton Co., Book Division, c1962. 128 p. illus. 20 cm. (Modern camera guide series. 833) [TR263.B7T9] 62-15228
1. Brownie camera. 2. Photography — Handbooks, manuals, etc. I. Title.

TYDINGS, Kenneth S. 771.31
Guide to Kodak Brownie Star cameras, including '20' and automatic 35mm models. Philadelphia, Chilton, c.1962. 128p. illus. 20cm. (Modern camera guide ser., 833) 62-15228 1.95 pap.,
1. Brownie camera. 2. Photography—Handbooks, manuals, etc. I. Title.

Browning, Colleen.

BROWNING, Colleen. 759.13
Colleen Browning : recent paintings : March 18-April 3, 1976. New York : Kennedy Galleries, c1976. [24] p. : ill. (some col.) ; 28 cm. [ND237.B875K45] 76-363097
1. Browning, Colleen. I. Kennedy Galleries, inc., New York.

BROWNING, Colleen. 759.13
Colleen Browning; [exhibition] March 5-29, 1969, Kennedy Galleries. [New York, Kennedy Galleries, c1969] [28] p. 17 illus. 28 cm. [ND237.B875A43] 72-284026
I. Kennedy Galleries, inc., New York.

BROWNING, Colleen. 759.13
The recent paintings of Colleen Browning. Exhibition to be shown at Kennedy Galleries, New York City, Jan. 5-22, 1972; the Columbus Museum of Arts and Crafts, Columbus, Ga., Feb. 13-Mar. 5, 1972; Columbia Museum of Art, Columbia, S.C., Mar. 19-Apr. 23, 1972; the Florence Museum, Florence, S.C., Apr. 30-May 28, 1972. New York, Kennedy Galleries [1971] c1972. [16] p. (chiefly illus. (part col.)) 28 cm. [ND237.B875K46] 73-155857
I. Kennedy Galleries, inc., New York.

BROWNING, Colleen. 759.13
The recent paintings of Colleen Browning. New York, Kennedy Galleries [1972] [16] p. (chiefly illus., part col.) 28 cm. Catalog of the exhibition held at the Kennedy Galleries, New York, Jan. 5-22, 1972; at the Columbus Museum of Arts and Crafts, Columbus, Ga., Feb. 13-Mar. 5, 1972; at the Columbia Museum of Art, Columbia, S.C., Mar. 19-Apr. 23, 1972; and at the Florence Museum, Florence, S.C., Apr. 30-May 28, 1972. [ND497.B77K4] 72-177923
I. Kennedy Galleries, Inc., New York. II. Title.

Browning firearms.

WEST, Bill. 683'.4
Browning arms & history. [1st ed. Azusa, Calif., c1972] 1 v. (various pagings) illus. 24 cm. (West arms library) [TS533.2.W45] 72-81300
1. Browning firearms. I. Title.

Browning, Russell.

BROWNING, Norma Lee. 770'.92'4 B
He saw a hummingbird / Norma Lee Browning and Russell Ogg. 1st ed. New York : Dutton, c1978. xi, 143 p., [4] leaves of plates : ill. ; 21 cm. [TR140.B785B76] 78-2559 8.95
1. Browning, Russell. 2. Photographers—United States—Biography. 3. Diabetic rutinopathy—Biography. I. Ogg, Russell, joint author. II. Title. BIP

Browse, Lillian.

NICHOLSON, William Newzam Prior Sir 759.2
William Nicholson [by] Lillian Browse. London R. Hart-Davis Chester Springs Pa. Dufour, 1966 144 p. 54 plates (pt.col) 25 cm. Catalogue raisonne of oil paintings. Bibl. [ND497.N6B7] 56-58962 bds., 10.00
1. Browse, Lillian. I. Title. BIP

Bruce, Ailsa Mellon—Art collections—Exhibitions.

UNITED States. National Gallery of Art. 759.4'074'0153
Small French paintings from the bequest of Ailsa Mellon Bruce : [catalogue / written by David E. Rust]. Washington : National Gallery of Art, 1978. xvii, 121 p. : ill. (some col.) ; 27 cm. Includes bibliographies and index. [ND547.5.I4U6 1978a] 78-606019 7.00
1. Bruce, Ailsa Mellon—Art collections—Exhibitions. 2. Painting, French—Exhibitions. 3. Impressionism (Art)—France—Exhibitions. 4. Post-impressionism (Art)—France—Exhibitions. 5. Painting, Modern—19th century—France—Exhibitions. I. Rust, David E. II. Title.

Bruegel, Jan, 1568-1625.

WINKELMANN-RHEIN, Gertraude. 760'.0924
The paintings and drawings of Jan 'Flower' Bruegel. New York, H. N. Abrams [1969, c1968] 88 p. illus. (part col.). 30 cm. Title on spine: Jan 'Flower' Bruegel. Translation of Brueghel. Bibliography:p. 86-87. [ND653.B75W513] 69-12479
1. Bruegel, Jan, 1568-1625. I. Title.

Bruegel, Pieter, the Elder, d. 1569.

ALEXANDRIAN, Sarane. 759.9'493
Pieter Brueghel, the elder. Translated from the French by Anne Ross. New York, Crown Publishers [1969] 45 p. illus. (part col.) 19 cm. (Basic art library) [ND673.B73A713] 70-87937 1.00
1. Bruegel, Pieter, the Elder, d. 1569.

BRUEGEL, Pieter, the Elder, d.1569. 759.9493
Bruegel / text by Jacques Dopagne. Bourne End, Bucks. : Spurbooks, [1976] [41] p., [95] p. of plates : chiefly col. ill. ; 18 cm. [ND673.B73D66] 77-354821 ISBN 0-904978-18-4 : £2.50
1. Bruegel, Pieter, the Elder, d. 1569. I. Dopagne, Jacques.

BRUEGEL, Pieter, the Elder, d.1569. 759.9493
Bruegel [Photos. and picture research by] M. Seidel. [Text, catalog, and notes by] R. H. Marijnissen. [1st American ed.] New York, Putnam [1971] 351 p. illus. (part col.) 31 cm. Bibliography: p. 344-348. [ND673.B73S413 1971] 77-150587 50.00
1. Bruegel, Pieter, the Elder, d. 1569. I. Seidel, Max, 1904- II. Marijnissen, Roger H.

BRUEGEL, Pieter, the elder, d.1569. 759.9493
The complete paintings of Bruegel. Introd. by Robert Hughes. Notes and catalogue by Piero Bianconi. New York, H. N. Abrams [1970] 120 p. illus., geneal. table, 64 col. plates, ports. 32 cm. (Classics of the world's great art) Translation of L'opera completa di Bruegel. Bibliography: p. 82. [ND673.B73B533] 78-84184
I. Bianconi, Piero, 1899-

BRUEGEL, Pieter, the elder, d.1569. 759.9493
The complete paintings of Bruegel. Introd. by Robert Hughes. Notes and catalogue by Piero Bianconi. New York, H. N. Abrams [1970] 120 p. illus., geneal. table, 64 col. plates, ports. 32 cm. (Classics of the world's great art) Translation of L'opera completa di Bruegel. Bibliography: p. 82. [ND673.B73B533] 78-84184
I. Bianconi, Piero, 1899-

BRUEGEL, Pieter, the Elder, d.1569. 741.9493
The drawings. [Text] by Ludwig Munz. [Translated from the German ms. by Luke Herrmann] Complete ed. [New York] Phaidon; [distributed by Praeger, 1968, c1961] 247 p. illus. 31 cm. Bibliography: p. [206] [NC266.B78M813 1968] 68-18907 ISBN 0-7148-1237-4 13.50
I. Munz, Ludwig, 1889-1957.

BRUEGEL, Pieter, theelder,d.1569. 759.9493
Pieter Bruegel. Text by E. R. Meijer. Greenwich, Conn., Fawcett Publications [1962] 9 p., 32 illus. (part col.) 18 cm. (Premier art library, v. 1) Bibliography: p. 9. [ND673.B73M4] 62-14884
I. Meijer, Emil R., ed. II. Title.

BRUEGEL, Pieter, the Elder, d.1569. 759.9493
Pieter Bruegel: complete edition of the paintings [by] F. Grossmann. [3d ed., rev. New York] Phaidon; [distributed by Praeger, 1973] v. illus. part col. 32 cm. First-2d eds. published under title: Bruegel, the paintings. Bibliography: v. 1, p. 51-56. [ND673.B73G713 1973] 75-177242 ISBN 0-7148-1511-X 22.50
1. Bruegel, Pieter, the Elder, d. 1569. I. Grossmann, Fritz.

BRUEGEL, Pieter, the elder, d.1569. 759.9493
Pieter Bruegel, the elder. Text by Wolfgang Stechow. New York, H. N. Abrams [1969] 40 p. illus. (part col.) 33 cm. (Great art of the ages) [ND673.B73S672 1969] 69-19704 ISBN 0-8109-5103-7
I. Stechow, Wolfgang, 1896-

BRUEGEL, Pieter,the Elder, 1569 759.492
Brueghel, by M. Ledivelec. New York, Crown [1965] 36p. (chiefly illus. (pt. col.)) 18cm. (Little bks. on great artists) [ND673.B73L4] 65-5028 .69 bds.,
I. Ledivelec, Madeleine. II. Title.

BRUEGEL, Pieter, the elder d1569 741.9492
The drawings. [Text] by Ludwig Munz. [Translated from the German ms. by Luke Hermann] Complete ed. Greenwich, Conn., Phaidon Publishers; distributed by New York Graphic Society [1961] 247p. illus., plates. 31cm. Bibliography: p. [206] [NC1055.B85M83 1961] 61-19495
I. Munz, Ludwig, 1889-1937. II. Title.

BRUEGEL, Pieter, the elder, d. 1569. 759.9492
All the painting of Pieter Brugel. Ed. by Valentin Denis. Tr. from Italian by Paul Colacicchi. New York, Hawthorn [c.1961] 56p. 164 plates (4 col.) (Complete lib. of world art, v.1) Bibl. 61-18846 3.95
I. Denis, Valentin. II. Title. III. Series.

SUBJECT INDEX

BUCKINGHAM, CLARENCE.

BRUEGEL, Pieter, the elder, d. 1569. 759.9493
Pieter Bruegel, the elder (about 1525-1569) Text by Wolfgang Stechow. New York, H. N. Abrams [1954] [74] p. 48 illus. (part col.) 18cm. (The Pocket library of great art, A21) Bibliography: p.]74] [ND673.B73S67] [ND673.B73S67] 927.5 55-590 55-590
I. Stechow, Wolfgang, 1896- II. Title.

BRUEGHEL, Peeter, the elder, d. 1569. 759.9493
Peter Brueghel, the elder, by Gustav Gluck. New York, G. Braziller [c1936] 53p. 87 plates (part col.) 30 x 36cm. Bibliography: p. 51-52. [ND673.B73G52] 927.5 56-3355
I. Gluck, Gustav, 1871- II. Title.

BRUEGHEL, Peeter, the elder, d. 1569. 759.9493
Pieter Bruegel, the elder (about 1525-1569) Text by Wolfgang Stechow. New York, H. N. Abrams in association with Pocket Books [1954] [74]p. 48 illus. (part col.) 18cm. (The Pocket library of great art, A21) An Abrams art book. Bibliography: p. [74] [ND673.B73S67] 927.5 55-590
I. Stechow, Wolfgang, 1896— II. Title.

FOOTE, Timothy. 759.9'492
The world of Bruegel, c. 1525-1569, by Timothy Foote and the editors of Time-Life Books New York, Time-Life Books [1968] 192 p. illus. (part col.), geneal. table, maps. 32 cm. (Time-Life library of art) Bibliography: p. 187. [ND673.B73F6] 68-31677
1. Bruegel, Pieter, the Elder, d. 1569. I. Time-Life Books. II. Title.

GIBSON, Walter S. 760'.092'4
Bruegel / Walter S. Gibson. New York : Oxford University Press, 1977. 216 p. : ill. (some col.) ; 21 cm. (The World of art) Includes index. Bibliography: p. 207-209. [ND673.B73G47 1977b] 76-56922 ISBN 0-19-519953-7 pbk. : 6.95 ISBN 0-19-519952-9 : 10.95
1. Bruegel, Pieter, the Elder, d. 1569. I. Title. II. Series.

KAY, Marguerite. 759.9493
Bruegel. London, New York, Hamlyn, 1969. 40 p. 48 plates, illus., port. 28 cm. (The Colour library of art) Bibliography: p. 29. [ND673.B73K3] 77-438849 17/6
1. Bruegel, Pieter, the Elder, d. 1569.

KLEIN, H. Arthur 769.9493
Graphic worlds of Peter Breugel the elder, reproducing 64 engravings and a woodcut after designs by Peter Breugel the elder [Selec., ed., commentary] by H. Arthur Klein [Gloucester, Mass., P. Smith, 1965, c.1963] xviii, 288p. plates. 21x29cm. (Dover bk. T1132 rebound) Bibl. [NE674.B7K55] 5.50
1. Breugel, Pieter, the elder, d. 1569. I. Title.

KLEIN, H. Arthur 769.9493
Graphic worlds of Peter Bruegel the elder, reproducing 64 engravings and a woodcut after designs by Peter Bruegel, the elder. Selected, ed. commentary by H. Arthur Klein. New York, Dover [1964, c. 1963] xviii, 288p. plates. 21x29cm. Bibl. 63-17907 3.00 pap.,
1. Bruegel, Pieter, the elder, d. 1569. I. Title. BIP

LOS Angeles Co., Calif. Museum, Los Angeles. 769'.92'4
Prints & drawings of Pieter Bruegel the elder; exhibition 22 March-7 May 1961. [Los Angeles, 1961] 67 p. illus. 21 x 29 cm. [NE674.B7L65] 62-3487
1. Bruegel, Pieter, the elder, d. 1569. I. Title.

LOS Angeles County Museum, Los Angeles. 769'.92'4
Prints & drawings of Piete Brugel, the elder;exhibition, 22 March-7 May 1961. [Los Angeles, 1961] 67p. illus. 21x29cm. [NE674.B7L65] 62-3487
1. Bruegel, Pieter, the elder, d. 1569. I. Title.

ZUPNICK, Irving L., 1920- 759.9493
Bruegel [by] Irving L. Zupnick. New York, McGraw-Hill [1970] 48 p. illus., 20 col. slides (2 x 2 in. (in pocket)) 29 cm. Bibliography: p. 48. [ND673.B73Z8] 72-118784
1. Bruegel, Pieter, the elder, d. 1569.

Bruegel, Pieter, the Elder, d. 1569—Catalogs.

BRUEGEL, Pieter, the Elder, d.1569. 759.9493
Bruegel / Gregory Martin. New York : St. Martin's Press, 1978. [88] p. : 40 col. ill. ; 28 cm. [ND673.B73A4 1978] 77-95301 ISBN 0-312-10676-9 pbk. : 5.95
1. Bruegel, Pieter, the Elder, d. 1569—Catalogs. I. Martin, Gregory. II. Title.

DE TOLNAY, Charles, 1899- 741.9'45
The drawings of Pieter Bruegel the elder, with a critical catalogue. [Translated by Charles R. Sleeth from the German] New York, Twin Editions [1953] 92, xcvip. illus. 31cm. Bibliography: p. [54] [NC1055.B85D] A53
1. Brueghel, Peeter, the elder, d. 1569. I. Title.

Bruegel, Pieter, the Elder, d. 1569—Juvenile literature.

KLEIN, H. Arthur. 760'.0924
Peter Bruegel the Elder, artist of abundance; an illustrated portrait of his life, era, and art, by H. Arthur Klein & Mina C. Klein. New York, Macmillan [1968] xix, 188 p. illus. (part col.) 26 cm. [ND673.B73K42] 68-20616
1. Bruegel, Pieter, the Elder, d. 1569—Juvenile literature. I. Klein, Mina C., joint author.

Bruegel, Pieter, the Younger, 1564-1637 or 8.

CRAFT, Ruth. 759.9493
Pieter Brueghel's The fair / story by Ruth Craft. 1st American ed. Philadelphia : Lippincott, 1976, c1975 [32] p. : col. ill. ; 27 cm. On spine: The fair. Interprets in rhyme some of the many details to be found in Brueghel's large painting, "The Village Fair." [ND673.B74C7 1975] 76-10256 ISBN 0-397-31698-4 7.50
1. Bruegel, Pieter, the Younger, 1564-1637 or 8. Fair—Juvenile literature. I. Bruegel, Pieter, the Younger, 1564-1637 or 8. II. Title. III. Title: The fair. BIP

Bruguiere, Francis.

ENYEART, James. 770'.92'4 B
Bruguiere, his photographs and his life / by James Enyeart. New York : Knopf, [1977] p. cm. Bibliography: p. [TR140.B79E58] 77-75355 ISBN 0-394-40852-7 : 17.50 ISBN 0-394-73385-1 pbk. : 9.95
1. Bruguiere, Francis. 2. Photography, Artistic. 3. Photographers—United States—Biography. I. Title.

Brumidi, Constantine, 1805-1880.

MURDOCK, Myrtle M (Cheney) [759.13]927.5
Constantino Brumidi, Michelangelo of the United States Capitol. Washington, Monumental Press, 1950. xvi, 111 p. illus. (part col.) ports. (part col.) 33 cm. Bibliography: p. 103-104. [ND237.B877M8] 51-72
1. Brumidi, Constantine, 1805-1880. I. Title.

U.S. 90th Congress, 2d session, 1968. 709'.24
Dedication of the bust of Constantino Brumidi, Michelangelo of the United States Capitol [in the] rotunda, United States Capitol, Tuesday, April 30, 1968. Washington, U.S. Govt. Print. Off., 1968. xii, 32 p. illus. 24 cm. (Ninetieth Congress, second session. House of Representatives. House document no. 321) [NB623.B78U54] 68-67044
1. Brumidi, Constantine, 1805-1880. I. Title. II. Series: U.S. 90th Congress, 2d session, 1968. House. Document no. 321

Brun Charles Frederic, d. 1871

GIONO JEAN, 1895- 759.4
It Disertone, testo di Jean Giono. traduzione dal francese di Patrizio Bocconi] Parma, F.M. Ricci; Stamped on t.p.: Amer. dist. Wittenborn,New York. Parma, F.M. Ricci; Stamped on t.p.: Amer. dist. Wittenborn,New York. 165p. facsims., map, col. plates. 36cm. (1 Segni dell'uomo) [NK950 B7G516] 67-4114 35.00
1. Brun Charles Frederic, d. 1871 I. Title.

Brundage, Avery—Art collections.

LEFEBVRE d'Argence, Rene Yvon. 709'.51
Chinese treasures from the Avery Brundage Collection. [New York] Asia Society; distributed by New York Graphic Society [1968] 151 p. illus. (part col.) 23 cm. "An Asia House Gallery publication." "Catalogue of an exhibition ... shown in the Asia House Gallery in the winter of 1968 as an activity of the Asia Society." Bibliography: p. 150-151. [N7342.A9L4] 68-12222
1. Brundage, Avery—Art collections. 2. Art, Chinese—Exhibitions. I. Asia House Gallery, New York. II. Asia Society. III. Title.

LEFEBVRE d'Argence, Rene Yvon. 730'.959
Indian and South-east Asian stone sculptures from the Avery Brundage Collection [by] Rene-Yvon Lefebvre d'Argence and Terese Tse. [Pasadena, Calif., Pasadena Art Museum, 1969] 116 p. illus. (part col.), map. 23 cm. Catalogue of an exhibition shown at Pasadena Art Museum, Nov. 22, 1969-Feb. 1, 1970 and at four other museums, Feb. 26-Dec. 31, 1970. Bibliography: p. 115-116. [NB1000.L4] 70-93704
1. Brundage, Avery—Art collections. 2. Sculpture, Indic—Exhibitions. 3. Sculpture—Asia, Southeastern—Exhibitions. I. Tse, Terese, joint author. II. Pasadena, Calif. Art Museum. III. Title.

LEFEBVRE D'ARGENCE, Rene Yvon. 709'.51
Chinese treasures from the Avery Brundage Collection. [New York] Asia Society; distributed by New York Graphic Society [1968] 151 p. illus. (part col.) 23 cm. "An Asia House Gallery publication." "Catalogue of an exhibition ... shown in the Asia House Gallery in the winter of 1968 as an activity of the Asia Society." Bibliography: p. 150-151. [N7342.A9L4] 68-12222
1. Brundage, Avery—Art collections. 2. Art, Chinese—Exhibitions. I. Asia House Gallery, New York. II. Asia Society. III. Title.

Brunelleschi, Filippo, 1377-1446.

HYMAN, Isabelle, comp. 720'.92'4
Brunelleschi in perspective. Englewood Cliffs, N.J., Prentice-Hall [1974] xii, 171 p. illus. 21 cm. (Artists in perspective series) (A Spectrum book) Bibliography: p. 169-170. [NA1123.B8H95 1974] 73-12583 ISBN 0-13-084897-2
1. Brunelleschi, Filippo, 1377-1446. I. Title.

MANETTI, Antonio, 1423-1497. 720'.924 B
The life of Brunelleschi, by Antonio di Tuccio Manetti. Introd., notes, and critical text ed. by Howard Saalman. English translation of the Italian text by Catherine Enggass. University Park, Pennsylvania State University Press [1970] vii, 176 p. illus., facsims. 24 cm. English and Italian. Translation of Vita di Filippo di Ser Brunelleschi. [NA1123.B8M33] 68-8183 12.50
1. Brunelleschi, Filippo, 1377-1446. BIP

PRAGER, Frank D. 720'.924
Brunelleschi: studies of his technology and inventions [by] Frank D. Prager and Gustina Scaglia. Cambridge, Mass., MIT Press [1970] xiii, 152 p. illus. 24 cm. Includes bibliographical references. [NA1123.B8P7] 73-103901
1. Brunelleschi, Filippo, 1377-1446. I. Scaglia, Gustina, joint author.

Brunner, Frank.

BRUNNER, Frank. 741.9'73
The Brunner mystique. [s.l. : s.n.], c1976. [32] p. : ill. ; 28 cm. (Artist index series ; v. 1) Cover title. Prepared by S. R. Johnson and H. Sharples. [NC975.5.B75J63] 76-380451 4.00
1. Brunner, Frank. I. Johnson, Steven R. II. Sharples, Hendrik. III. Title. IV. Series.

Brush drawing.

BROOKS, Leonard, 1911- 751.422
Course in wash drawing. New York, Reinhold Pub. Corp. [1961] 61 p. illus. 27 cm. [ND2460.B7] 61-10717
1. Brush drawing. 2. Pen drawing. I. Title.

Brush, George de Forest, 1855-1941.

BOWDITCH, Nancy Douglas. 759.13 B
George de Forest Brush; recollections of a joyous painter. Peterborough, N.H., Noone House [1970] xxi, 257 p. illus., plates, ports. 25 cm. Bibliography: p. 243-245. [ND237.B88B68] 72-88207 8.50
1. Brush, George de Forest, 1855-1941. BIP

Brushwork.

GRUPPE, Emile A., 1896- 751.4
Brushwork : a guide to expressive brushwork for oil painting / by Emile A. Gruppe ; edited by Charles Movalli. New York : Watson-Guptill Publications, 1977. 151 p. : ill. (some col.) ; 29 cm. Includes index. Bibliography: p. 149. [ND1505.G78] 76-30892 ISBN 0-8230-0525-9 : 16.95
1. Brushwork. 2. Painting—Technique. I. Title. BIP

Brussels. Musees royaux d'art et d'histoire.

HULST, Roger Adolf d'. 759.9'493
The Royal Museum, Brussels. Text by Roger A. d'Hulst. [Translated from the Italian by James Brockway] New York, Meredith Press [1967, c1965] 158 p. illus. (part col.) 28 cm. (Great galleries series) Translation of Musei reali di Bruxelles. [N1835.H813 1967b] 67-66208
1. Brussels. Musees royaux d'art et d'histoire. I. Title.

Bruton, Eng.

SOMERSET, Eng. Planning Dept. 711'.4'094238
Bruton conservation area. Taunton, Somerset County Council, 1969. 8 p. illus., col. map. 30 cm. Cover title. [DA690.B885S65] 78-518593 4/-
1. Bruton, Eng. I. Title.

Bryant, Harold, 1894-1950.

LOOK, Al, 1893- 759.13
Harold Bryant; Colorado's maverick with a paint brush. Denver, Golden Bell Pr. [c.1962] 115p. illus. (pt. col.) ports. 32cm. 62-52590 12.50 bds.,
1. Bryant, Harold, 1894-1950. I. Title.

Bryce, David, 1803-1876.

DAVID Bryce, 1803-1876 720'.92'4
: [catalogue of] an exhibition to mark the centenary of Scotland's great Victorian architect / [compiled by] Valerie Fiddes & Alistair Rowan. Edinburgh : University of Edinburgh, 1976. 132 p., leaf of plate, [40] p. of plates : ill., plans, ports. ; 24 cm. [NA997.B74D38] 77-361137 ISBN 0-902511-19-X : £1.80
1. Bryce, David, 1803-1876. I. Fiddes, Valerie. II. Rowan, Alistair John.

Buckingham, Clarence.

CHICAGO. Art Institute. 745.5
The Clarence Buckingham collection of Japanese prints. Catalogue by Helen C. Gunsaulus. [Chicago, 1955- v. illus., col. plates. 40cm. 'This edition is limited to 500 numbered catalogues ... [Vol. 1] Number 20.' Contents.[1] The primitives.

Bibliography: v. 1, p. 278. [NE1310.C43] A55
1. Buckingham, Clarence. 2. Color printeseJapanses. I. Gunsaulus, Helen Cowen, ed. II. Title. III. Title: The primitives.

Buckingham Palace.

HARRIS, John, 1931- 708.21
Buckingham Palace and its treasures [by] John Harris, Geoffrey de Bellaigue [and] Oliver Millar. Introd. by John Russell. Photography by Lionel Bell, Kerry Dundas [and] Sidney Newbury. New York, Viking Press [1968] 320 p. 297 illus. (79 col.), plans, ports. 34 cm. (A Studio book) Includes bibliographical references. [N1025.H27] 68-23206 25.00
1. Buckingham Palace. I. De Bellaigue, Geoffrey. II. Millar, Oliver Nicholas, 1923-

Buckland, William, 1734-1774

WILLIAM Buckland, 720.9752 1734-1774; architect of Virginia and Maryland, by Rosamond Randall Beirne and John Henry Scarff. Baltimore, Maryland Historical Society, 1958. xiii, 175p. plates (incl. ports., map) plans. 26cm. (Studies in Maryland history, no. 4) Bibliography included in 'Notes' (p. 157-165) [NA737.B76B4] [NA737.B76B4] 720.81 58-13073 58-13073
1. Buckland, William, 1734-1774 I. Beirne, Rosamond Randall. II. Scarff, John Henry, 1887- joint author. III. Series: Maryland Historical Society. Studies in Maryland history, no. 4

Budapest—Hungarian National Gallery.

*TELEPY, Katalin. 704.9436'439
Landscapes in the Hungarian National Gallery [Budapest] Corvina Press [1973] 34 p. 36 col. plates 24 cm. [N3690]
1. Budapest—Hungarian National Gallery. 2. Landscape painting—Hungary. I. Title.
Distributed by International Publications Service, N.Y. for 9.00 BIP

Buddhist shrines—Borobudur, Indonesia.

BERNET Kempers, 726'.1'43095982 August Johan, 1906-
Ageless Borobudur : Buddhist mystery in stone, decay and restoration, Mendut and Pawon, folklife in ancient Java / A. J. Bernet Kempers. Wassenaar : Servire, [1976] 288 p. : ill. ; 28 cm. Rev. translation of Borobudur. Includes index. Bibliography: p. 280-284. [NA6026.6.B6B47 1976] 77-465019 ISBN 9-06-077553-8 : fl 49.00
1. Buddhist shrines—Borobudur, Indonesia. 2. Shrines—Conservation and restoration—Indonesia—Borobudur. I. Title. BIP

Buell, Abel, 1742-1822.

WROTH, Lawrence Counselman, 927.6 1884-
Abel Buell of Connecticut, silversmith, typefounder & engraver. [2d ed. rev.] Middletown, Wesleyan University Press, 1958. xiv, 102 p. illus., facsims. 24 cm. Bibliographical references included in "Notes" (p. 86-96) [NK7198.B8W7 1958] 58-13601
1. Buell, Abel, 1742-1822.

Bufano, Beniamino, 1898-1970.

FALK, Randolph, 1939- 730'.92'4
Bufano / Randolph Falk. Millbrae, Calif. : Celestial Arts, 1975. viii, 135 p. : ill. ; 28 cm. [NB237.B76F34] 75-9069 ISBN 0-89087-175-2 : 12.95. ISBN 0-89087-061-6 pbk.
1. Bufano, Beniamino, 1898-1970. BIP

RATHER, Lois, 1905- 730'.92'4 B
Bufano and the U.S.A. / Lois Rather. Oakland, CA : Rather Press, 1975. 125 p. : ill. ; 24 cm. "An edition of one hundred fifty copies. This is number 13." Includes bibliographical references and index. [NB237.B76R37] 75-322851
1. Bufano, Beniamino, 1898-1970. I. Title.

WILKENING, Howard. 730'.92'4 B
Bufano: an intimate biography, by H. Wilkening and Sonia Brown. Berkeley, Calif., Howell-North Books [1972] 232 p. illus. 24 cm. [NB237.B76W5] 72-79789 ISBN 0-8310-7089-7 6.50
1. Bufano, Beniamino, 1898-1970. I. Brown, Sonia, joint author. II. Title. BIP

Buffalo. Ansley Wilcox House.

SHELGRIN, William 728.8'3'0974797 O.
Ansley Wilcox House N.H.S., by William O. Shelgrin and Walter S. Dunn, Jr. Edited by Norman M. Souder. [Washington] U.S. Office of Archeology and Historic Preservation, 1969. 26, 35, [22] l. illus., plans. 28 cm. (Historic structures report) Includes bibliographical references. [NA7238.Z9B87] 79-608835
1. Buffalo. Ansley Wilcox House. I. Dunn, Walter S., joint author. II. Title. III. Series.

Buffalo—Blizzard, 1977—Pictorial works.

BUFFALO buried : 779'.9'974797 the blizzard of '77 / [compiled by] Katy Kline & Carol Nash. [s.l. : s.n.], c1977 (Buffalo : Thorner-Sidney Press) 63 p. : chiefly ill. ; 20 x 22 cm. [F129.B8143B83] 78-300382
1. Buffalo—Blizzard, 1977—Pictorial works. I. Kline, Katy. II. Nash, Carol.

Buffalo China, inc.

ALTMAN, Violet. 738.2
The book of Buffalo Pottery, by Violet and Seymour Altman. New York, Crown [1969] 192 p. illus. (part col.) 29 cm. Bibliography: p. 187. [NK4210.B76A67 1969] 70-75071 7.50
1. Buffalo China, inc. 2. Pottery—Private collections—U.S. I. Altman, Seymour, joint author. II. Title. BIP

ALTMAN, Violet. 738.2'7
Price guide to Buffalo pottery, by Vi and Si Altman. [Amherst, N.Y., Vi and Si's Antiques, 1969] 13 p. 22 cm. Cover title. [NK4210.B76A68] 71-21833 1.50
1. Buffalo China, Inc. 2. Pottery—Prices. I. Altman, Seymour, joint author. II. Title.

Buffalo Fine Arts Academy.

STILL, Clyfford, 1904- 759.13
Clyfford Still: thirty-three paintings in the Albright-Knox Art Gallery Buffalo, N.Y., 14222 Buffalo Fine Arts Acad., 1966. 87p. col. plates, port. 33cm. [ND237.S78A44] 66-15942 15.00
1. Buffalo Fine Arts Academy. I. Title.

TOWNSEND, James 708.14797 Benjamin, 1918-
100 : The Buffalo Fine Arts Academy, 1862-1962, Albright-Knox Art Gallery. Comp. and written by J Benjamin Townsend, assigned by Ruth M. Peyton. Buffalo 22, Buffalo Fine Arts Academy, dist. Albright-Knox Art Gallery, 1285 Elmwood Ave., 1963, c.1962] 144p. (chiefly illus., pt. col.) 26cm. 63-1625 4.00
1. Buffalo Fine Arts Academy. I. Title.

Buffalo site, W. Va.

BROYLES, Bettye J. 975.4'35
A late archaic component at the Buffalo Site, Putnam County, West Virginia / by Bettye J. Broyles. Morgantown : West Virginia Geological and Economic Survey, 1976. v, 28 leaves : ill. ; 28 cm. (Report of archeological investigations ; no. 6) Bibliography: leaf 28. [E78.W6B68] 77-622029
1. Buffalosite, W. Va. I. Title. II. Series.

HANSON, Lee H. 975.4'35
The Buffalo Site : a late 17th century Indian village site (46 Pu 31) in Putnam County, West Virginia / by Lee H. Hanson, Jr. Morgantown : West Virginia Geological and Economic Survey, 1975. vii, 110 p. : ill. ; 29 cm. (Report of archeological investigations ; no. 5) Bibliography: p. 103-104. [E78.W6H33] 76-620773
1. Buffalo site, W. Va. 2. Fort Ancient culture. I. Title. II. Series.

Buffet, Bernard, 1928-

BUFFET, Bernard, 1928- 769'.924
Bernard Buffet: lithographs, 1952-1966. Pref. by Georges Simenon. Catalogue compiled by Fernand Mourlot. New York, Tudor Pub. Co. [1968] 177 p. illus. (part col.) 32 cm. Translation of Bernard Buffet, ouvre grave. [NE650.B93M613] 70-184 37.50
I. Mourlot, Fernand.

DRUON, Maurice, 1918- 759.4
Bernard Buffet. Text. Maurice Druon [tr. from French by Humphrey Hare] Photos.: Luc Fournol. Captions: Annabel Buffet. Design: Jean Widmer. [New York] October House [1966, c.1964] 1v. (unpaged) illus. (pt. col.) facsims., ports. (pt. col.) 30cm. [ND553.B98D73] 66-14713 17.50
1. Buffet, Benard, 1928- I. Fournol, Luc. II. Title.

Buglioni, Benedetto, 1459?-1520.

MARQUAND, Allan, 1853- 730'.92'4 1924.
Benedetto and Santi Buglioni. New York, Hacker Art Books, 1972 [i.e. 1973] xlvi, 223 p. illus. 27 cm. Reprint of the 1921 ed. published by Princeton University Press, which was issued as v. 9 of Princeton monographs in art and archaeology. Bound with the author's The brothers of Giovanni della Robbia. New York, 1972. Bibliography: p. 219-221. [NB623.B8M3 1972] 70-173999 ISBN 0-87817-111-8
1. Buglioni, Benedetto, 1459?-1520. 2. Buglioni, Santi, 1494-1576. I. Title. II. Series: Princeton monographs in art and archaeology, 9.
Set of 8 vols. bound in four selling for 250.00.

Buhen, Sudan.

EXCAVATIONS at Buhen. 932
London : Egypt Exploration Society, 1976- v. : ill. ; 32 cm. (Excavation memoir ; 48) ISSN 0307-5109) [DT73.B84E9] 77-366368
1. Buhen, Sudan. I. Egypt Exploration Society. II. Title. III. Series.

SMITH, Harry Sidney. 932 s
The fortress of Buhen : the inscriptions / by H. S. Smith ; with assistance from W. B. Emery ... [et al.]. London : Egypt Exploration Society, 1976. xii, 255 p., [40] leaves of plates : ill. ; 32 cm. (Excavations at Buhen ; 2) Exclusive distributor: ISBS, Forest Grove, Or. Includes bibliographical references and indexes. [DT73.B84E9 vol. 1] 932 77-366369 75.00
1. Buhen, Sudan. 2. Inscriptions—Sudan—Buhen. I. Title. II. Series. III. Excavation memoir ; 48 BIP

Building.

BARR, Donald. 720.9
The how and why wonder book of building. Illustrated by Robert Doremus. Editorial production: Donald D. Wolf. [Deluxe ed] New York, Grosset & Dunlap [1964] 48 p. illus. (part col.) ports. 29 cm. A survey of building showing the solutions man has found to the problems of stress and tension in construction and how he has utilized his discoveries in walls, buildings, and bridges. [PZ10.B26Hp] AC 68
1. Building. I. Doremus, Robert, illus. II. Title.

EMMERSON, Henry Russell. 728.6
It's fun to build a house. Minneapolis, T. S. Denison [1962] 160 p. illus. 29 cm. [TH4811.E5] 62-14152
1. Building. 2. Dwellings. I. Title.

MAINSTONE, Rowland J., 1923- 721
Developments in structural form / Rowland Mainstone. 1st American ed. Cambridge, Mass. : M.I.T. Press, 1975. 350 p. : ill. ; 31 cm. Includes index. Bibliography: p. 327-[328] [TH145.M2796 1975b] 74-3472 ISBN 0-262-13111-0 : 25.00
1. Building. 2. Structural engineering. 3. Architecture. I. Title. BIP

PATTERSON, Donald, 1897- 721.3
How to design pole-type buildings. Chicago, American Wood Preservers Institute, c1957. 67p. illus. 23cm. Includes bibliography. [TH2252.P3] 59-4446
1. Building. 2. Columns, Wooden. I. Title. II. Title: Pole-type buildings.

Building, Adobe.

GIFFEN, Helen Smith, 1893- 728.63
Casas & courtyards; historic adobe houses of California. Foreword by W. W. Robinson; photos. by Guy J. Giffen. [1st California ed.] Oakland, Calif., Biobooks, 1955. 153p. illus. 27cm. (California relations, no. 40) [NA7165.G5] 55-3048
1. Building, Adobe. 2. Architecture, Domstic—California. 3. California—Historic houses, etc. I. Title. BIP

STEDMAN, Myrtle. 728.6'4
Adobe architecture, by Myrtle & Wilfred Stedman. [1st ed.] Santa Fe, N.M., Sunstone Press, 1973. 42 p. illus. 28 cm. [TH4818.A3S74] 73-77322 ISBN 0-913270-12-1 3.95 (pbk.)
1. Building, Adobe. 2. Architecture, Domestic—Designs and plans. I. Stedman, Wilfred Henry, 1892-1950, joint author. II. Title.
Publisher's Address: P.O. Box 2321 Santa Fe, N.M. 07501. BIP

Building—Bibliography.

GREAT Britain. Property 016.69 Services Agency. Library.
Building design and construction : an annotated list / [Property Services Agency Library Service] ; [compiled by Mavis Parry and Henry Field ; edited by Nola Pressey]. Croydon : The Service, [1976] v, 66 p. ; 30 cm. (PSA publications ; 1976) Includes index. [Z7914.B9G73 1976] [TH145] 77-366046 ISBN 0-7184-0023-2
1. Building—Bibliography. I. Parry, Mavis. II. Field, Henry, 1923- III. Title. IV. Series: Great Britain. Property Services Agency. PSA publications ; 1976.

PHILLIPS, Margaret, 1939- 016.721
Guide to architectural information. Lansdale, Pa., Design Data Center [1971] vi, 89 p. 24 cm. [Z7914.B9P47] 74-27031
1. Building—Bibliography. 2. Architecture—Bibliography. 3. Building—Information services. I. Title.

Building, Brick.

HANDISYDE, Cecil C. 712
Hard landscape in brick / Cecil C. Handisyde. London : Architectural Press, 1976. 74 p. : ill. ; 30 cm. Includes index. Bibliography: p. 73. [TA679.H35] 77-359753 ISBN 0-85139-283-0 : £3.25
1. Building, Brick. 2. Landscape architecture. I. Title. BIP

Building, Brick—History.

WIGHT, Jane A. 721'.0442'10942
Brick building in England from the Middle Ages to 1550, [by] Jane A. Wight. London, J. Baker, 1972. 439, [48] p. illus., maps. 24 cm. Bibliography: p. [400]-406. [TH1301.W48] 72-170280 ISBN 0-212-98400-4
1. Building, Brick—History. 2. Building—England—History. 3. Architecture, Medieval. I. Title.
Distributed by Fernhill, 13.50. BIP

Building—Details.

BALL, John E. 694'.69
Exterior and interior trim / John E. Ball. Albany : Delmar Publishers, c1975. 192 p. : ill. ; 26 cm. Includes index. [TH153.B34] 75-6060 ISBN 0-8273-1120-6 pbk. : 6.60
1. Building—Details. 2. Carpentry. I. Title. BIP

SUBJECT INDEX BUILDINGS IN ART.

Building—Details—Drawings.

RAMSEY, Charles George, 1884- 692.2
Architectural graphic standards for architects, engineers, decorators, builders, draftsmen, and students [by] Charles George Ramsey [and] Harold Reeve Sleeper. 5th ed. New York, Wiley [1956] x, 758 p. (chiefly illus.) 30 cm. [TH2031.R35 1956] 56-14178
1. Building—Details—Drawings. I. Sleeper, Harold Reeve, 1893- joint author. II. Title.

RAMSEY, Charles George, 1884- 692.2
Architectural graphic standards for architects, engineers, decorators, builders, and draftsmen [by] Charles George Ramsey [and] Harold Reeve Sleeper. 4th ed. New York, Wiley [1951] xv, 614 p. (chiefly illus., plans) 30 cm. [TH2031.435 1951] 51-11243
1. Building — Details — Drawings. I. Sleeper, Harold Reeve, 1803- joint author. II. Title.

RAMSEY, Charles George, 1884-1963. 692'.2
Architectural graphic standards [by] Charles G. Ramsey and Harold R. Sleeper. Chairman: Editorial Advisory Committee, Harold D. Hauf. Editor: Joseph N. Boaz. 6th ed. New York, J. Wiley [1970] 695 p. illus. 30 cm. At head of title: The American Institute of Architects. [TH2031.R35 1970] 79-136970
1. Building—Details—Drawings. I. Sleeper, Harold Reeve, 1893-1960, joint author. II. American Institute of Architects. III. Title. BIP

Building—Dictionaries.

PUTNAM, R. E. 721'.03
Architectural and building trades dictionary [by] R. E. Putnam [and] G. E. Carlson. 3d ed. Chicago, American Technical Society [1974] 510 p. illus. 24 cm. Previous editions by A. E. Burke. [TH9.P82 1974] 74-75483 ISBN 0-8269-0402-5 9.25
1. Building—Dictionaries. 2. Architecture—Dictionaries. I. Carlson, G. E., joint author. II. Burke, Arthur Edward, 1909- Architectural and building trades dictionary. III. Title. BIP

Building—Egypt—History.

CLARKE, Somers, 1841-1926. 690'.0932
Ancient Egyptian masonry; the building craft, by Somers Clarke and R. Engelbach. [Boston] Milford House [1974] p. cm. Reprint of the 1930 ed. published by Oxford University Press, London. Bibliography: p. [TH16.C6 1974] 74-2041 ISBN 0-87821-267-1
1. Building—Egypt—History. 2. Masonry—History. 3. Egypt—Antiquities. I. Engelbach, Reginald, 1888-1946, joint author. II. Title.

Building—Estimates.

HARTKOPF, Volker. 728.3'1
The cost of flexibility in low-cost housing / by Volker Hartkopf. [Pittsburgh] : Carnegie-Mellon University, Institute of Physical Planning, 1974. 20, [1] leaves : ill. ; 28 cm. (Research report - Institute of Physical Planning, Carnegie-Mellon University ; no. 51) Bibliography: leaf [21]. [TH437.H3] 76-353521
1. Building—Estimates. 2. Housing. 3. Apartment houses. 4. Cost effectiveness. I. Title. II. Series: Carnegie-Mellon University. Institute of Physical Planning. Research report — Institute of Physical Planning, Carnegie-Mellon University ; no. 51.

Building—Handbooks, manuals, etc.

NEUFERT, Ernst. 690'.02'02
Architects' data. Edited and rev. by Rudolf Herz. From translations from the German by G. H. Berger [and others. 1st English ed.] Hamden, Conn., Archon Books, 1970. xiv, 354 p. illus., plans. 31 cm. Translation of Bau-Entwurfslehre. Bibliography: p. 339-350. [TH151.N513 1970b] 74-19799
1. Building—Handbooks, manuals, etc. I. Title.

ULREY, Harry F 690.02
Audels architects and builders guide, by Harry F. Ulrey. [1st ed.] Indianapolis, T. Audel [1964] 374 p. illus. 18 cm. [TH151.U4] 64-23152
1. Building — Handbooks, manuals, etc. 2. Architecture — Handbooks, manuals, etc. I. Title. II. Title: Architects and builders guide.

ULREY, Harry F. 690
Building construction and design (revision of Architects and builders guide) by Harry F. Ulrey. [2d ed.] Indianapolis, T. Audel [1970] 390 p. illus., plans. 22 cm. First ed. published in 1964 under title: Audels architects and builders guide. [TH151.U4 1970] 79-128020 5.95
1. Building—Handbooks, manuals, etc. 2. Architecture—Handbooks, manuals, etc. I. Title.

Building—History.

BOWYER, Jack. 690'.09
History of building. St. Albans, Crosby Lockwood Staples, 1973. vi, 275 p. illus., plans. 23 cm. [TH15.B68 1973] 74-183047 ISBN 0-258-96861-3 £2.25 (pbk.)
1. Building—History. I. Title.

COWAN, Henry J. 690'.09
The master builders : a history of structural and environmental design from ancient Egypt to the nineteenth century / Henry J. Cowan. New York : Wiley, [1977] p. cm. Bibliography: p. [TH15.C62] 77-5125 ISBN 0-471-02740-5 : 19.95
1. Building—History. 2. Architecture—History. I. Title.

COWAN, Henry J. 721'.09'034
Science and building : structural and environmental design in the nineteenth and twentieth centuries / Henry J. Cowan. New York : Wiley, [1977] p. cm. "A Wiley-Interscience publication." Includes bibliographical references and index. [TH15.C63] 77-7297 ISBN 0-471-02738-3 : 15.00
1. Building—History. 2. Structural engineering—History. I. Title. BIP

KLEIN, H. Arthur. 721'.09
Great structures of the world, by H. Arthur Klein and Mina C. Klein. [1st ed.] Cleveland, World Pub. Co. [1968] 288 p. illus. 26 cm. Includes bibliographies. [TH15.K56] 68-14699 4.95
1. Building—History. 2. Civil engineering—History. I. Klein, Mina C., joint author. II. Title.

Building, Iron and steel.

BRYAN, Eric Reginald, 1927- 721'.044'7142
The stressed skin design of steel buildings [by] E. R. Bryan. New York, Wiley [1973] xii, 159 p. illus. 25 cm. (Constrado monographs) "A Halsted Press book." Bibliography: p. 131-136. [TA684.B8448] 73-1278 ISBN 0-470-11455-X 13.50
1. Building, Iron and steel. 2. Plates, Iron and steel. 3. Structural frames. I. Title.

GRINTER, Linton Elias, 1902- 624.182
Design of modern steel structures. 2d ed. New York, Macmillan [1960] 491p. illus. 24cm. [TH1611.G752 1960] 60-5086
1. Building. Iron and steel. I. Title.

THE Origins of cast iron architecture in America. 721'.0447'14 New introd. by W. Knight Sturges. New York, Da Capo Press, 1970. xii, 35, v, 16 p., 102 plates. illus. 36 cm. (Da Capo Press series in architecture and decorative art, v. 13) On spine: Cast iron architecture in America. Comprised of reprints of the 1865 ed. of Illustrations of iron architecture made by the Architectural Iron Works of the city of New York, by D. D. Badger, and of the 1856 ed. of Cast iron buildings: their construction and advantages, by James Bogardus, who attributes authorship to J. W. Thomson. Bibliography: p. [xi]-xii. [TH1610.O75] 68-25760 ISBN 0-306-71039-0 37.50
1. Building, Iron and steel. 2. Architecture—U.S. I. Bogardus, James, 1800-1874. II. Badger, Daniel D. Illustrations of iron architecture made by the Architectural Iron Works of the city of New York. 1970. III. Thomson, John W. Cast iron buildings: their construction and advantages. 1970. IV. Title: Cast iron architecture in America. BIP

PARKER, Harry, 1887- 624.182
Simplified design of structural steel. 3d ed. New York, Wiley [c.1945-1965] xvi, 307p. illus. 21cm. [TH1611.P3] 65-16420 7.75
1. Building, Iron and steel. 2. Steel, Structural. I. Title. BIP

PARKER, Harry, 1887- 624.177
Simplified design of structural steel. 2d ed. New York, Wiley [c1955] 244p. illus. 20cm. [TH1611.P3 1955] [TH1611.P3 1955] 691.7 55-6378 55-6378
1. Building, Iron and steel. 2. Steel, Structural. 3. Strength of materials. I. Title.

Building materials.

HICKS, Clifford B 691.1
Popular mechanics do-it-yourself materials guide. [Chicago, 1955] 160p. illus. 24cm. [TT155.H5] 55-13877
1. Building materials. 2. Handicraft. I. Title. II. Title: Do-it-yourself materials guide. III. Title: Materials guide.

Building—Repair and reconstruction.

[POPULAR homecraft] 643.7
450 questions and answers on home repairs and workshop methods. [Edited by Perry S. Graffam] Chicago, General Pub. Co., 1950] 95 p. illus. 23 cm. (The Home workshop library) Hobby books. Reprints of articles from Popular-homecraft magazine. [TT151.P6] 50-11204
1. Building — Repair and reconstruction. 2. Workshop receipts. I. Graffam, Perry S., 1890- ed. II. Title.

Building sites.

DE CHIARA, Joseph, 1929- 721
Site planning standards / Joseph De Chiara, Lee E. Koppelman. New York : McGraw-Hill, c1978. ix, 351 p. : ill. ; 23 x 29 cm. Includes bibliographical references and index. [NA2540.5.D4] 77-9440 ISBN 0-07-016216-6 : 24.50
1. Building sites. I. Koppelman, Lee, joint author. II. Title.

Building—Tables, calculations, etc.

ARCHITECTURAL record. 690.2
Time-saver standards, a manual of essential architectural data for architects, engineers, draftsmen, builders, and other technicians. Ed. no. 2, new enl. ed. New York, F. W. Dodge Corp. [1950] 884 p. illus. 29 cm. "An Architectural record book." [TH151.A72 1950] 51-1937
1. Building—Tables, calculations, etc. 2. Building—Handbooks, manuals, etc. I. Title.

Building—Tropics.

MANUAL of tropical housing and building 721'.0913 [by] O. H. Koenigsberger [and others. London] Longman [1974- c1973] v. illus. 25 cm. Vol. 1 has protractor in pocket. Contents.Contents.—pt. 1. Climatic design. Includes bibliographies. [TH153.M35] 74-165187
1. Building—Tropics. 2. Dwellings—Tropics. I. Koenigsberger, Otto H.
Distributed by Longman, New York, 15.00.

Building, Wooden.

HANSEN, Hans Jurgen, 1921- 721'.0448'09
Architecture in wood; a history of wood building and its techniques in Europe and North America. Edited by Hans Jurgen Hansen. Translated by Janet Seligman. With contributions by Arne Berg [and others] New York, Viking Press [1971] 288 p. illus. (part col.) 31 cm. (A Studio book) Translation of Holzbaukunst; eine Geschichte der abendlandischen Holzarchitektur und ihrer Konstruktionselemente. [TH1101.H2913] 71-101786 ISBN 0-670-13148-2 40.00
1. Building, Wooden. 2. Woodwork. I. Berg, Arne, 1917- II. Title. BIP

HOFFMANN, Kurt, 1923- 721
Building with wood; form, structural design, and preservation [by] Kurt Hoffmann and Helga Griese. With contributions by Johannes Wetzel and Hellmut R. W. Kuhne. New York, Praeger [1969, c1966] 169 p. illus. 30 cm. Translation of Bauen mit Holz. [NA4110.H613] 68-15930 15.00
1. Building, Wooden. 2. Architecture—Designs and plans. I. Griese, Helga, joint author. II. Title.

REMPEL, John I. 720'.9713
Building with wood and other aspects of nineteenth-century building in Ontario [by] John I. Rempel. [Toronto] University of Toronto Press [1967] ix, 287 p. illus., maps, plans. 29 cm. Bibliography: p. 279-283. [NA744.R4] 68-71816 17.50
1. Building, Wooden. 2. Architecture—Ontario—History. I. Title. BIP

Building, Wooden—British Columbia.

CLEMSON, Donovan. 971.1
Old wooden buildings / Donovan Clemson. Saanichton, B.C. ; Seattle : Hancock House, c1978. 95 p. : ill. ; 28 cm. [NA746.B8C55] 77-27836 ISBN 0-919654-90-8 pbk. : 4.95
1. Building, Wooden—British Columbia. 2. Architecture—British Columbia—Guide-books. I. Title.
Distributed by Hancock House Pubs., 12008 First Ave., S. Seattle, WA 98168 BIP

Buildings—Energy conservation.

ENERGY conservation through building design 721 / edited by Donald Watson. New York : McGraw-Hill, [1978] c1979. p. cm. "An Architectural record book." Includes bibliographical references and index. [TJ163.5.B84E54] 78-6189 16.50 ISBN 0-07-068460-X : 16.50
1. Buildings—Energy conservation. 2. Architecture and energy conservation. I. Watson, Donald, 1937- BIP

Buildings—Energy conservation—Bibliography.

BARTHOLOMEW, Robert. 016.3092'08 s
Energy conservation in building design / Robert Bartholomew. Monticello, Ill. : Council of Planning Librarians, 1977. 12 p. ; 28 cm. (Exchange bibliography - Council of Planning Librarians ; 1223) Cover title. [Z5942.C68 no. 1223] [Z7914.B9] [TJ163.B84] 016.697 77-360790 pbk. : 1.50
1. Buildings—Energy conservation—Bibliography. 2. Architecture and energy conservation—Bibliography. I. Title. II. Series: Council of Planning Librarians. Exchange bibliography ; 1223.

Buildings—Energy conservation—Case studies.

LEE, Kaiman. 729
Encyclopedia of energy-efficient building design : 391 practical case studies / by Kaiman Lee. Boston : [Environmental Design and Research Center], c1977. 2 v. (1023 p.) : ill. ; 27 cm. Includes bibliographical references and indexes. [TJ163.5.B84L43] 77-150686 ISBN 0-915250-18-7 : 150.00 (set)
1. Buildings—Energy conservation—Case studies. I. Title. BIP

Buildings in art.

BARBOUR, Arthur J., 1926- 751.4'22
Painting buildings in watercolor, by Arthur J. Barbour. New York, Watson-Guptill Publications [1973] 143 p. illus. 29 cm. Bibliography: p. 141. [ND2310.B37] 72-12765 ISBN 0-8230-3583-2 15.95
1. Buildings in art. 2. Water-color painting—Technique. I. Title. BIP

CADY, Lanore. 759.13
Houses & letters : a heritage in architecture & calligraphy / by Lanore Cady. Freeport, Me. : Bond Wheelwright Co., c1977. 1 portfolio ([32] leaves : col. ill.) in case ; 27 x 38 cm. [ND1839.C26A4 1977] 77-77370 ISBN 0-87027-183-0 : 27.50
1. Cady, Lanore. 2. Buildings in art. 3. Humboldt Co., Calif.—Buildings—Pictorial works. I. Title. BIP

WELLING, Richard, 1926- 743'.8'4
The technique of drawing buildings. New York, Watson-Guptill Publications [1971] 157 p. illus. (part col.) 29 cm. [NC825.B8W4 1971] 78-157103 ISBN 0-8230-5088-2 10.95
1. Buildings in art. 2. Drawing—Instruction. I. Title.

ZAIDENBERG, Arthur, 1903- 743'.8'4
How to draw houses. London, New York, Abelard-Schuman [1968] 64 p. illus. 27 cm. [NC825.B8Z3] 68-13240 3.50
1. Buildings in art. 2. Drawing—Instruction. I. Title.

Buildings, Octagonal.

SCHMIDT, Carl Frederick, 1894- 720.973
The octagon fad. [Scottsville, N. Y.], 1958. 207p. illus., plans. 22cm. Bibliography: p. 144. [NA4160.S3] 58-46956
1. Buildings, Octagonal. 2. Architecture—U. S. I. Title.

Buildings, Prefabricated.

CHERNER, Norman. 728.6
Fabricating houses from component parts; how to build a house for $6000. New York, Reinhold Pub. Corp. [1957] 208 p. illus. 27 cm. Published also under title: How to build a house for $6,000; fabricating houses from component parts. [NA8480.C5 1957] 57-6539
1. Buildings, Prefabricated. 2. Architecture, Domestic—Designs and plans. 3. Building. I. Title.

CHERNER, Norman. 728.6
How to build a house for (6,000; fabricating houses from component parts New York, Reinhold Pub. Corp. [1957] 208p. illus. 27cm. Published also under title: Fabricating houses from component parts; how to build a house for (6,000. [NA8480.C5 1957a] 57-2846
1. Buildings, Prefabricated. 2. Architecture, Domestic— Designs and plans. 3. Building. I. Title.

Buildings—Repair and reconstruction.

KERTH, A. L. 725'.2
A new life for the abandoned service station / A. L. Kerth. Massapequa Park, N.Y. : Kerth, [1974] 83 p. : ill. ; 29 cm. [TH3411.K43] 74-194778
1. Buildings—Repair and reconstruction. 2. Automobiles—Service stations. I. Title. BIP

Buildings—United States—Remodeling for other use.

DIAMONSTEIN, Barbaralee. 720'.28
Buildings reborn : new uses, old places / Barbaralee Diamonstein ; pref. by John Brademas. 1st ed. New York : Harper & Row, c1978. 255 p. : ill. ; 29 cm. Includes index. Bibliography: p. 245-246. [NA2793.D5] 78-2134 ISBN 0-06-011068-6 : 25.00
1. Buildings—United States—Remodeling for other use. I. Title. BIP

FRACCHIA, Charles A., 1937- 725
So this is where you work! : A guide to unconventional working environments / text by Charles A. Fracchia ; photos. by Mark Kauffman. New York : Viking Press, [1978] p. cm. (A Studio book) [NA2793.F7] 78-27664 ISBN 0-670-65491-4 : 17.95
1. Buildings—United States—Remodeling for other use. I. Kauffman, Mark. II. Title. BIP

Buildings, Wooden.

WILLS, Royal Barry, 1895- 690
Tree houses, With illus. by the author and Charles H. Crombie. Boston, Houghton Mifflin, 1957. 67 p. illus. 23 x 26 cm. [TH153.W5] 57-8902
1. Buildings, Wooden. 2. Architecture, Domestic. 3. Dwellings. I. Title.

Built-in furniture.

BAKER, Bill. 684.2
How to make your own built-ins and space savers. Editor: William Sill. Cover and display photos. by Art Braker; all other photos. by the author. Illustrations by Marion Sweetman. New York, Popular Science Pub. Co. [1958] 159p. illus. 28cm. At head of title: Popular science. [TT197.5.B8B3] 57-12885
1. Built-in furniture. I. Popular science monthly. II. Title. III. Title: Space savers.

BLANDFORD, Percy W. 684.1'6
How to make your own built-in furniture / by Percy Blandford. 1st ed. Blue Ridge Summit, Pa. : G/L Tab Books, c1976. 336 p. : ill. ; 22 cm. Includes index. [TT197.5.B8B53] 76-45057 ISBN 0-8306-6910-8 : 9.95 ISBN 0-8306-5910-2 pbk. : 5.95
1. Built-in furniture. I. Title. BIP

COLLANI, Arthur. 643.7
Built-in cabinets and storage walls. New York, Home Craftsman Pub. Corp. [1956] 96p. illus. 29cm. (The Home craftsman series of woodworking manuals) [TT197.5.B8C6] 56-8647
1. Built-in furniture. I. Title.

DAL Fabbro, Mario, 1913- 684.1
How to make built-in furniture. New York, F. W. Dodge Corp. [1955] 262 p. illus. 26 cm. [TT197.5.B4D3] 55-11033
1. Built-in furniture. I. Title.

DAL Fabbro, Mario, 1913- 684.1'6
How to make built-in furniture. 2d ed. New York, McGraw-Hill [1974] vii, 263 p. illus. 25 cm. [TT197.5.B8D34 1974] 74-6265 ISBN 0-07-015181-4 8.50
1. Built-in furniture. I. Title.

THE Family handyman. 684.1
Built-ins you can make, by the editors of the Family handyman magazine. [New York, Universal Pub. & Distributing Corp., 1956] 118p. illus. 23cm. (Its How-to book, 104) [TT197.5.B8F3 1956a] 56-59165
1. Built-in furniture. I. Title.

FRANKEL, Virginia. 684.1'6
The incredible, wonderful, flexible world of built-ins / by Virginia Frankel ; rooms designed by Virginia Frankel ; floor plans and sketches executed by Augusto Rojas. New York : Scribner, c1977. x, 196 p. : ill. ; 28 cm. [TT197.5.B8F7] 76-51754 ISBN 0-684-14874-9 : 12.50
1. Built-in furniture. 2. Interior decoration. I. Title. BIP

HEDDEN, Jay W. 684.1'6
Successful shelves & built-ins / Jay Hedden. Farmington, Mich. : Structures Pub. Co., 1979, c1978. p. cm. Includes index. [TT197.5.B8H42 1979] 78-27234 ISBN 0-912336-77-3 : 12.00 ISBN 0-912336-78-1 pbk. : 5.95
1. Built-in furniture. 2. Cabinet-work. 3. Storage in the home. I. Title. BIP

HENNESSEY, William James, 1901- 684
The complete book of built-ins. Technical drawings by Sigman-Ward, design sketches by the author. New York, Harper [1950] x, 182 p. illus. 26 cm. [TT197.5.B8H4] 50-10025
1. Built-in furniture.

JORDAN, Robert Oakes, 1920- 684
Built-ins for home improvement. Illus. by Wally Bieger. Wilmette, Ill., F. J. Drake [1955] 137 p. illus. 22 cm. (How-to-do-it) [TT197.5.B8J6] 55-14207
1. Built-in furniture. I. Title.

NUNN, Richard V. 684.1'6
Home storage / by Richard V. Nunn. [Birmingham, Ala. : Oxmoor House], 1975. 96 p. : ill. ; 28 cm. (Family guidebook series) Includes index. [TT197.5.B8N86] 75-12122 pbk. : 1.95
1. Built-in furniture. 2. Storage in the home. I. Title. BIP

ROHDE, Peggy Ann. 684
Making built-in furniture. New York, McBride [1950] 114 p. illus. 18 cm. Bibliography: p. 113-114. [TT197.5.B8R6] 50-9658
1. Built-in furniture.

SCHARFF, Robert. 684.1
Improve your home with built-ins. New York, McGraw-Hill [1954] 241 p. illus. 26 cm. [TT197.5.B8S3] 53-9892
1. Built-in furniture. I. Title.

SIEGELE, Herman Hugo, 1883- 694.7
Cabinets and built-ins; an up-to-date treatment of cabinets and built-ins for kitchens, bathrooms, utility rooms, and closets. Chicago, F. J. Drake [1961] 100 p. illus., diagrs., plans. 21 cm. (How-to-do-it series) [TT197.5.B8S5] 62-536
1. Built-in furniture. I. Title.

SUNSET ideas for storage 684.1'6
/ by the editors of Sunset books and Sunset magazine. 3d ed. Menlo Park, Calif. : Lane Pub. Co., [1975] 96 p. : ill. ; 28 cm. (Sunset building, remodeling & home design books) First ed. published in 1958 under title: Sunset ideas for storage in your home. Includes index. [TT197.5.B8S8 1975] 74-20021 ISBN 0-376-01553-5 pbk. : 2.45
1. Built-in furniture. 2. Storage in the home. I. Sunset.

WILLIAMS, Henry Lionel. 684.2
The practical book of built-in furniture. Boston, R. C. Dresser, 1959. 124 p. illus. 24 cm. [TT197.5.B8W5] 59-10379
1. Built-in furniture. I. Title.

Bulfinch, Charles, 1763-1844.

BULFINCH, Charles, 1763-1844. 720'.92'4 B
The life and letters of Charles Bulfinch, architect, with other family papers, edited by his granddaughter, Ellen Susan Bulfinch. With an introd. by Charles A. Cummings. New York, B. Franklin [1973] xiv, 323 p. illus. 23 cm. (Burt Franklin research & source works series. Art history & reference series, 45) Reprint of the 1896 ed. published by Houghton Mifflin, Boston. [NA737.B8A3 1973] 78-166963 ISBN 0-8337-0417-6 19.50
1. Bulfinch, Charles, 1763-1844. I. Bulfinch, Ellen Susan, ed.

KIRKER, Harold. 720'.924
The architecture of Charles Bulfinch. Cambridge, Harvard University Press, 1969. xxiii, 398 p. 174 illus., port. 25 cm. "Charles Bulfinch's architectural library": p. 387-388. Includes bibliographical references. [NA737.B8K5] 70-78519 11.95
1. Bulfinch, Charles, 1763-1844. I. Title. BIP

PLACE, Charles Alpheus, 1866- 720'.924 B
Charles Bulfinch, architect and citizen, by Charles A. Place. New York, Da Capo Press, 1968 [c1925] xiv, 294 p. illus., maps, plans, ports. 26 cm. (Da Capo Press series in architecture and decorative art, v. 16) (A Da Capo Press reprint edition.) [NA737.B8P5 1968] 68-27717
1. Bulfinch, Charles, 1763-1844.

Bull-fights in art.

DEGRAZIA, Ted Ettore, 1909- 704.94'7918'2
Ah ha, Toro, text & illus. by Ted De Grazia. Flagstaff, Ariz., Northland Press, 1967. 1 v. (unpaged) illus. (part col.) 32 cm. [ND237.D3337A42] 67-28199
1. Bull-fights in art. I. Title.

PICASSO, Pablo, 1881- 769.946
Picasso: toreros, with four original lithographs. [Text by] Jaime Sabartes. [Tr. from French by Patrick Gregory] New York, Braziller [1961] 153p. 103 illus. (pt. col.) 4 plates (1 col.) 26x33cm. 61-16860 17.50
1. Bull- fights in art. I. Sabartes, Jaime, 1881- II. Title.

PICASSO, Pablo, 1881- 741.946
Toros y toreros. Texte de Luis Miguel Dominguin, et une etude de Georges Boudaille. [Translation by Edouard Roditi. New York] H. N. Abrams [1961] 1v. (chiefly illus. (part col.)) 38cm. English and Spanish. [NC1135.P5D63] 61-15294
1. Bull-fights in art. I. Dominguin, Luis Miguel. II. Title.

SABARTES, Jaime, 1881- 769.946
Picasso; toreros; with four original lithographs. [Text by] Jamie Sabartes. [Translated from the French by Patrick Gregory] New York, G. Braziller [1961] 153 p. 103 illus. (part col.) 4 plates (1 col.) 26 x 33 cm. [NC1135.P5S33] 61-16860
1. Bull-fights in art. I. Picasso, Pablo, 1881- II. Title.

Bullock, Wynn.

BULLOCK, Wynn. 779'.092'4
Wynn Bullock photography: a way of life. Edited by Liliane De Cock. Text by Barbara Bullock-Wilson. [Dobbs Ferry, N.Y., Morgan & Morgan, 1973] 160 p. illus. 28 cm. [TR650.B82] 73-77663 ISBN 0-87100-034-2 12.00
1. Bullock, Wynn. 2. Photography, Artistic. I. Bullock-Wilson, Barbara. II. Title.

Bulls in art.

MARRERO SUAREZ, Vicente, 1922- 759.6
Picasso and the bull. Translated by Anthony Kerrigan. Chicago, H. Regnery Co., 1956. 132p. illus. 22cm. [ND553.P5M372] [ND553.P5M372] 927.5 56-11852 56-11852
1. Picasso, Pablo, 1881- 2. Bulls in art. 3. Bull (in religion. folk-lore, etc.) I. Title.

Bungalows.

THE Book of economical homes. 728.6084
[St. Paul] Home Plan Book Co. v. illus. 28 cm. [NA7571.B6] 51-28912
1. Bungalows. 2. Architecture, Domestic—Designs and plans. I. Home Plan Book Company, St. Paul.

THE Book of medium homes. 728.6084
[St. Paul] Home Plan Book Co. v. illus. 28 cm. [NA7571.B62] 51-28911
1. Bungalows. 2. Architecture, Domestic—Designs and plans. I. Home Plan Book Company, St. Paul.

Bunker, Dennis Miller, 1861-1890.

GAMMELL, Robert Hale Ives, 1893- 759.13
Dennis Miller Bunker. New York, Coward-McCann [1953] xii, 81p. illus., ports. 22cm. [ND237.B885G3] [ND237.B885G3] 927.5 53-7057 53-7057
1. Bunker, Dennis Miller, 1861-1890. I. Title.

Bunny, Rupert Charles Wulsten, 1864-1947.

THOMAS, David Emlyn Liddon. 759.9'94
Rupert Bunny, 1864-1947 [by David Thomas] [Melbourne] Lansdowne [1970] 113, [14] p. illus. (part col.) 32 cm. (Australian art library) Bibliography: p. [13]-[14] (2d group) [ND1105.B85T5] 71-862592 ISBN 0-7018-0380-0 10.00
1. Bunny, Rupert Charles Wulsten, 1864-1947.

Buonarroti, Michel Angelo, 1475-1564.

ABELES, Elivn, 1909- 927
Mike and the giant; the story of Michelangelo, told by Kerwin Bowles [pseud.] Illustrated by Mitchell Foster [pseud.] New York, Stravon Publishers [1951] 31 p. illus. 23 x 28 cm. (A Child's book of great artists) Stravon great artist series, 2. [N6923.B9A62] 51-13178
1. Buonarroti, Michel Angelo, 1475-1564. 2. Art—Juvenile literature. I. Title.

ACKERMAN, James S. 720.945
The architecture of Michelangelo. New York, Viking [1961] xxxv, 156p. illus., 26cm. (Studio bk.) Bibl. 61-7886 12.50

GOLDSCHEIDER, Ludwig, 1896- 730.945
A survey of Michelangelo's models in wax and clay. London, Phaidon Pr. [dist. Greenwich, Conn., N.Y., Graphic, 1963, c.1962] unpaged. illus. 31cm. Bibl. 63-3273 6.00
1. Buonarroti, Michel Angelo, 1475-1564. I. Title. II. Title: Michelangelo's models in wax and clay.

HARTT, Frederick. 730'.924
Michelangelo the complete sculpture New York, H. N. Abrams [1968?] 310 p. illus. (part col.) 33 cm. Bibliography: p. 309-310. [NB623.B9H3] 68-24045
1. Buonarroti, Michel Angelo, 1475-1564.

HIBBARD, Howard, 1928- 700'.92'4 B
Michelangelo / Howard Hibbard. 1st U.S. ed. New York : Harper & Row, c1974. 347 p. : ill. ; 23 cm. (Icon editions) Includes index. Bibliography: p. 321-325. [N6923.B9H49 1974] 74-6576 ISBN 0-06-433323-X 12.50
1. Buonarroti, Michel Angelo, 1475-1564.

HIBBARD, Howard, 1928- 700'.92'4 B
Michelangelo : painter, sculptor, architect / Howard Hibbard. New York : Vendome Press : distributed by Viking Press, [1978] 213 p. : ill. (some col.) ; 32 cm. "An Alexis Gregory book." Includes index. Bibliography: p. 209-212. [N6923.B9H493 1978] 78-7748 ISBN 0-670-47397-9 : 40.00
1. Buonarroti, Michel Angelo, 1475-1564. 2. Artists—Italy—Biography.

KUHN, Rudolf Edwin. 759.5
Michelangelo, die sixtinische Decke : Beitr. uber ihre Quellen u. zu ihrer Auslegung / von Rudolf Kuhn. Berlin ; New York : de Gruyter, 1975. xiii, 173 p. : 1 fold. ill (in pocket) ; 27 cm. (Beitrage zur Kunstgeschichte ; Bd. 10) Includes index. Bibliography: p. 166-168. [ND623.B92K83] 73-93163 ISBN 3-11-004497-8 : DM76.00
1. Buonarroti, Michel Angelo, 1473-1564. 2. Vatican. Cappella sistina. I. Title.

LA FARGE, John, 1835-1910. 709'.2
Great masters. Freeport, N.Y., Books for Libraries Press [1968] xiv, 249 p. illus., ports. 26 cm. (Essay index reprint series) Reprint of the 1903 ed. Contents.Contents.—Michelangelo.—Raphael.—Rembrandt.—Rubens.—Velasquez.—Durer.—Hokusai. [N40.L3 1968] 68-16945
1. Buonarroti, Michel Angelo, 1475-1564. 2. Raphael, 1483-1520. 3. Rembrandt Harmenszoon van Rijn, 1606-1669. 4. Rubens, Peter Paul, Sir, 1572-1640. 5. Velasquez, Diego Rodriguez de Silva y, 1599-1660. 6. Durer, Albrecht, 1471-1528. 7. Katsushika, Hokusai, 1760-1849. I. Title. BIP

LOMBARDO, Josef Vincent 730.945
Michelangelo: the Pieta and other masterpieces. New York, Pocket Bks. [c.] 1965. 64p. plates (pt. col.) 24cm. (Pocket bk special) Bibl. [NB623.B9L6] 65-15362 4.95; 1.95 pap.,
1. Buonarroti, Michel Angelo, 1475-1564. I. Title.

LOMBARDO, Josef Vincent. 730'.92'4
Michelangelo—new discoveries / Josef Vincent Lombardo. [s. l. : s. n.], c1976. 49, 49, 50-134 p. : ill. ; 28 cm. Pages 1-49 numbered in duplicate on opposite pages. English and Italian. Lecture delivered at the University of Cambridge, Apr. 1976. Includes bibliographical references. [NB623.B9L59] 76-13262
1. Buonarroti, Michel Angelo, 1475-1564. Saint John. 2. Sculpture—Attribution. I. Title.

MAFFEI, Fernanda de' 730.945
Michelangelo's lost St. John, the story of a discovery. Pref. by Henry A. LaFarge [Tr. by Lee H. B. Malone] New York, Reynal [dist. Morrow, 1964] 40 p. illus. (1 mounted col.) plates. 39 cm. Bibl. 62-7041 15.00
1. Buonarroti, Michel Angelo. 1475-1564. I. Title.

MORGAN, Charles Hill 709.45
The life of Michelangelo. New York, Reynal [c.1960] 253p. (bibl. p.245-246) illus. 22cm. 60-9228 6.00
1. Buonarroti, Michel Angelo, 1475-1564 I. Title.

PAPINI, Giovanni, 1881- 927
Michelangelo, his life and his era; translated from the Italian by Loretta Murnane. [1st ed.] New York, Dutton, 1952. 542 p. illus. 24 cm. [N6923.B9P313] 52-10425
1. Buonarroti, Michel Angelo, 1475-1564. I. Title.

PATER, Walter Horatio, 1839-1894. 709*.2*4
Michelangelo, by Walter Pater. [1st ed.] Tokyo, Palo Alto, Calif., Kodansha International Ltd. [1968] [138] p. col. illus. 20 cm. (This beautiful world, v. 6) [ND623.B9p3] 70-563957
1. Buonarroti, Michel Angelo, 1475-1564. I. Title.

REDIG de Campos, Deoclecio. 759.5
Michelangelo the Last Judgment / [by Deoclecio Redig de Campos ; translation by Serge Hughes]. Garden City, N.Y. : Doubleday, 1978. 106 p., [64] leaves of plates : ill. (some col.) ; 37 cm. Translation of Il Giudizio universale di Michelangelo. "Limited edition of 475." Includes bibliography and index. [ND623.B9A69 1978] 76-39674 ISBN 0-385-12299-3 : 100.00
1. Buonarroti, Michel Angelo, 1475-1564. Last Judgment. I. Title.

RIPLEY, Elizabeth, 1906- 927
Michelangelo, a biography. With drawings, paintings, and sculpture by Michelangelo. New York, Oxford University Press, 1953. 68 p. illus. 26 cm. (Oxford books for boys and girls) [N6923.B9R53] 53-3955
1. Buonarroti, Michel Angelo, 1475-1564.

RUSSOLI, Franco. 730.945
All the sculpture of Michelangelo. Translated from the Italian by Paul Colacicchi. New York, Hawthorn Books [1963] 77 p. illus., 132 plates (part col.) 19 cm. (The Complete library of world art, v. 11) "Bibliographical note": p. 76-77. [NB623.B9R853] 62-19555
1. Buonarroti, Michel Angelo, 1475-1564. I. Series.

SAPANARO, Michele, 1885- 927
Michelangelo. Translated from the Italian by C. J. Richards. New York, Pellegrini & Cudahy [1950] vii, 201 p. plates, ports. 25 cm. [N6923.B9S254 1950] 50-14841
1. Buonarroti, Michel Angelo, 1475-1564. I. Title.

SCHOTT, Rudolf, 1891- 709.24
Michelangelo [by] Rolf Schott. [Tr., adapted from German by Constance McNab] New York, Abrams [1965, c.1962] 254p. illus. (pt col.) ports. (pt col.) 21cm. [N6923,B9S343] 65-23846 3.95 pap.,
1. Buonarroti, Michel Angelo, 1475-1564. I. Title.

SCHOTT, Rudolf, 1891- 709.45
Michelangelo [by] Rolf Schott. [Translated and adapted from the German by Constance McNab] New York, Tudor Pub. Co. [1963] 254 p. illus. (part col.) ports. (part col.) 22 cm. "Text references": p. 248. [N6923.B9S343] 64-554537
1. Buonarroti, Michel Angelo, 1475-1564. I. Title.

SEYMOUR, Charles, 1912- comp. 759.5
Michelangelo, the Sistine Chapel ceiling: illustrations, introductory essays, backgrounds and sources, critical essays. [1st ed.] New York, Norton [1972] xxi, 243 p. illus. 21 cm. (A Norton critical study in art history) Bibliography: p. 239-243. [ND623.B92S42] 74-90982 ISBN 0-393-04319-3
1. Buonarroti, Michel Angelo, 1475-1564. 2. Vatican. Cappella sistina. I. Title.

SEYMOUR, Charles, 1912- 730'.924
Michelangelo's David; a search for identity. [Pittsburgh] University of Pittsburgh Press [1967] xxi, 194 p. illus. 21 cm. (A. W. Mellon studies in the humanities) Includes bibliographical references. [ND623.B92S43] 67-22277
1. Buonarroti, Michel Angelo, 1475-1564. I. Title. II. Series. BIP

SEYMOUR, Charles, 1912- 730'.92'4
Michelangelo's David; a search for identity. New York, Norton [1974, c1967] xxi, 194 p. illus. 20 cm. Reprint of the ed. published by University of Pittsburgh Press, Pittsburgh, in series: A. W. Mellon studies in the humanities. Includes bibliographical references. [NB623.B9S49 1974] 74-10608 ISBN 0-393-00735-9
1. Buonarroti, Michel Angelo, 1475-1564. David. I. Title. II. Series: A. W. Mellon studies in the humanities.

STONE, Irving, 1903- 730.945
The story of Michelangelo's Pieta. [1st ed.] Garden City, N.Y., Doubleday, 1964. 60 p. 22 cm. "Official edition, Vatican Pavilion, New York World's Fair, inc." [NB623.B9S75] 64-11376
1. Buonarroti, Michel Angelo, 1475-1564. I. Title.

WEINBERGER, Martin. 730'.924
Michelangelo, the sculptor. London, Routledge & K. Paul; New York, Columbia U.P., 1967. 2 v. illus., 144 plates (incl. facsims.), plans. 29 cm. 12/12/- (B67-15971) Contents.CONTENTS. -- v. 1. Text. -- v. 2. Plates, indexes. Bibliography: p. v. 1. ix-x. [NB623.B9W4] 65-22158
1. Buonarroti, Michel Angelo, 1475-1564. I. Title.

WEINBERGER, Martin 730'.924
Michelangelo, the sculptor. London, Routledge & K. Paul; New York, Columbia, 1967. 2v. illus., 144 plates (incl. facsims.), plans. 29cm. Contents.v. 1. Text.--v.2. Plates. indexes. Bibl.: p. v. 1. ix-x. [NB623.B9W4] 65-22158 42.50 set, bxd.
1. Buonarroti, Michel Angelo, 1475-1564. I. Title.

WILDE, Johannes. 709'.2'4
Michelangelo : six lectures / by Johannes Wilde ; [editors, John Shearman and Michael Hirst]. Oxford [Eng.] ; New York : Clarendon Press, 1978. p. cm. (Oxford studies in the history of art and architecture) Includes bibliographical references and index. [N6923.B9W66] 77-30203 ISBN 0-19-817346-6 : 21.00 ISBN 0-19-817316-4 pbk. : 10.50
1. Buonarroti, Michel Angelo, 1475-1564—Collected works. I. Title. II. Series.
Contents omitted. BIP

Buonarroti, Michel Angelo, 1475-1564—Biography.

BUONARROTI, Michel Angelo, 1475-1564. 730.945
I, Michelangelo, sculptor; an autobiography through letters. edited by Irving and Jean Stone. From the translation by Charles Speroni. [1st ed.] Garden City, N. Y., Doubleday, 1962. 283 p. plates, facsim. 24 cm. [NB623.B9A253] 62-11312
I. Stone, Irving, 1903- ed. II. Stone, Jean, ed. III. Title.

GRIMM, Herman Friedrich, 1828-1901. 709'.24 B
Life of Michael Angelo. Translated with the author's sanction by Fanny Elizabeth Bunnett. Boston, Little, Brown, 1865. St. Clair, Mich., Scholarly Press, 1970- v. 22 cm. Translation of Leben Michelangelos. [ND623.B9G7213] 70-115244 ISBN 0-403-00399-7
1. Buonarroti, Michel Angelo, 1475-1564—Biography. I. Title. BIP

Buonarroti, Michel Angelo, 1475-1564—Influence.

THE Fortuna of Michelangelo : prints, drawings and small sculpture from California collections : the E. B. Crocker Art Gallery, Sacramento, the University of California, Davis, October 21-December 14, 1975 / edited by L. Price Amerson, Jr. Sacramento : The Gallery, c1975. 47 p. : ill. ; 28 cm. Catalogue of the exhibition. Includes bibliographical references. [N6374.F67] 76-355013 709'.02'4074019454
1. Buonarroti, Michel Angelo, 1475-1564—Influence. 2. Art, Renaissance—Exhibitions. 3. Art—Atribution. I. Amerson, Price. II. Crocker Art Gallery, Sacramento, Calif. III. California. University, Davis. Dept. of Art.

Buonarroti, Michel Angelo, 1475-1564—Juvenile literature.

ABELES, Elvin, 1909- 927
Mike and the giant; the story of Michelangelo, told by Kerwin Bowles. Illustrated by Mitchell Foster. New York, Stravon Publishers [1951] 31 p. illus. 23 x 28 cm. (A Child's book of great artists) Stravon great artist series, 2. [N6923.B9A62] 51-13178
1. Buonarroti, Michel Angelo, 1475-1564 — Juvenile literature. I. Title.

PECK, Anne Merriman, 1884- 92
Wings of an eagle; the story of Michelangelo, by Anne Merriman Peck with Frank and Dorothy Getlein. Illustrated by Lili Rethi. New York, Hawthorn Books [1963] 186 p. illus. 22 cm. (Credo books) [N6923.B9P4] 63-8785
1. Buonarroti, Michel Angelo, 1475-1564—Juvenile literature. I. Title.

RABOFF, Ernest Lloyd. 709'.24
Michelangelo Buonarroti, by Ernest Raboff. Garden City, N.Y., Doubleday [1971] [31] p. illus. (part col.), ports. 29 cm. (Art for children) (A Gemini Smith book) Discusses the life and art of the Renaissance sculptor, poet, and painter. Includes color and black and white reproductions of many of his works. [ND623.B9R3] 71-139055 3.95
1. Buonarroti, Michel Angelo, 1475-1564—Juvenile literature. I. Title.

STEARNS, Monroe. 730'.924 B
Michelangelo. New York, F. Watts [1970] x, 246 p. illus., port. 25 cm. (Immortals of art) Bibliography: p. [237]-239. The life of the Renaissance sculptor, painter, architect, and poet. [ND623.B9S7] 92 78-95640 5.95
1. Buonarroti, Michel Angelo, 1475-1564—Juvenile literature. I. Title.

Buonarroti, Michel Angelo, 1475-1564.

BUONARROTI, Michel Angelo, 1568-1646. 730'.92'4
Michelangelo : a lesson in anatomy / James Beck. New York : Viking Press, 1975. 31 p., [32] leaves of plates : ill. ; 31 cm. (A Studio book) [NB623.B9B34 1975] 74-29472 ISBN 0-670-47396-0 : 12.95
1. Buonarroti, Michel Angelo, 1568-1646. 2. Anatomy, Artistic. 3. Artists' preparatory studies. I. Beck, James H. II. Title.

DE TOLNAY, Charles, 1899- 731.76
The tomb of Julius II. Princeton, Princeton University Press, 1954. viii, 200p. plates. 31cm. (His Michelangelo, 4) Bibliography: p. 163-166. [NB623.B9D4] 58-6582
1. Buonarrott, Michel Angelo, 1475-1564. 2. Julius II, Pope, 1443-1513. 3. Rome (City)—Sepulchral monuments. I. Title.

MORGAN, Charles Hill, 1902- 709.45
The life of Michelangelo. New York, Reynal [1960] 253p. illus. 22cm. Includes bibliography. [N6923.B9M59] 60-9228
1. Buonarrotl, Michel Angelo, 1475-1564. I. Title.

Burchfield, Charles Ephraim, 1893-1967.

AMERICAN Academy of Arts and Letters. 759.13
Charles Burchfield memorial exhibition; paintings and drawings March 1, 1968-April 21, 1968, in the Museum, the American Academy of Arts and Letters, New York City. [New York, Spiral Press, 1968?] [23] p. 8 plates. 26 cm. (Its Publication no. 246) [ND1839.B8A7] 70-20822
I. Burchfield, Charles Ephraim, 1893-1967. II. Title. III. Series.

ARIZONA. University. Art Gallery. 759.13
CB: his golden year; a retrospective exhibition of watercolors, oils, and graphics by Charles E. Burchfield, November 14, 1965 -- January 9, 1966. Designed and edited by the University of Arizona Art Gallery. Tuscon, University of Arizona Press [1965] 127 p. illus. (part col.) ports. 27 cm. Includes an article by the artist which sums up his fifty years as a painter.

SUBJECT INDEX

BUTLER, HOWARD RUSSELL

"Catalogue"6 p. 90-101. Bibliography: p. 124-126. [ND1839.B8A9] 65-28066
I. Burchfield, Charles Ephraim, 1893- II. Title.

BAIGELL, Matthew. 759.13
Charles Burchfield / by Matthew Baigell. New York : Watson-Guptill Publications, 1976. p. cm. Includes index. [ND237.B89B24] 76-15169 ISBN 0-8230-0533-X : 35.00
1. Burchfield, Charles Ephraim, 1893-1967. BIP

BAUR, John Ireland Howe, 1909- 927.5
Charles Burchfield. [Research by Rosalind Irvine] New York, Published for the Whitney Museum of American Art by Macmillan, 1956. 86 p. 75 illus. (part col.) port. 27 cm. "This book grew out of a retrospective exhibition of Charles Burchfield's paintings and drawings, held at the Whitney Museum of American Art in January and February, 1956." Bibliography: p. [82]-85. [ND237.B89B3] 759.13 56-322
1. Burchfield, Charles Ephraim, 1893-1967. I. Whitney Museum of American Art, New York.

BURCHFIELD, Charles Ephraim, 1893-1967. 759.13
Charles Burchfield, watercolors and drawings, 1915-1966 : October 15-November 1, 1975. New York : Kennedy Galleries, c1975. [40] p. : chiefly ill. (some col.) ; 28 cm. [ND1839.B8K45] 76-353732
1. Burchfield, Charles Ephraim, 1893-1967. I. Kennedy Galleries, inc., New York.

BURCHFIELD, Charles Ephraim, 1893-1967. 759.13
Charles E. Burchfield: watercolors. New York, Kennedy Galleries [1974] [32] p. illus. (part col.) 28 cm. "In our main galleries, March 27-April 20, 1974." [ND1839.B8K46] 74-177319
1. Burchfield, Charles Ephraim, 1893-1967. I. Kennedy Galleries, inc., New York.

BURCHFIELD, Charles Ephraim, 1893-1967. 759.13
Charles E. Burchfield watercolors : visual music, October 13-November 13, 1976. New York : Kennedy Galleries, 1976. [64] p. : chiefly ill. (some col.) ; 29 cm. Includes index. [ND1839.B8K47] 77-374938
1. Burchfield, Charles Ephraim, 1893-1967. I. Kennedy Galleries, inc., New York.

BURCHFIELD, Charles Ephraim, 1893-1967. 741.9'73
The drawings of Charles Burchfield. With text by Charles Burchfield. Edited by Edith H. Jones. New York, Praeger [1968] 15, [110] p. 57 illus. 29 x 32 cm. "Published in association with the Drawing Society." [NC1075.B88J6] 69-10514 12.50
I. Drawing Society. II. Title.

THREE American romantic painters: Charles Burchfield, with an introd. by Alfred H. Barr, Jr. Florine Stettheimer, by Henry McBride. Franklin C. Watkins, by Andrew Carnduff Ritchie. Reprint ed. New York, Published for the Museum of Modern Art by Arno Press, 1969. [24], 55, 48 p. illus. 29 cm. On cover: Burchfield, Stettheimer, Watkins. The three exhibition catalogs were originally published separately, 1930-1950. Includes bibliographies. [ND236.T442 1969] 74-86441 759.13'074'01471
1. Burchfield, Charles Ephraim, 1893-1967. 2. Stettheimer, Florine, 1871-1944. 3. Watkins, Franklin Chenault, 1894- I. New York (City). Museum of Modern Art. II. New York (City). Museum of Modern Art. Charles Burchfield, early water colors. 1970. III. McBride, Henry, 1867-1962. Florine Stettheimer. 1970. IV. New York (City). Museum of Modern Art. Franklin C. Watkins. 1970. V. Title: Burchfield, Stettheimer, Watkins. BIP

Burden, Chris.

BURDEN, Chris. 779'.2
Chris Burden, 71-73. [Los Angeles, 1974] 84 p. (chiefly illus.) 27 cm. Cover title. [N6537.B87A43] 74-178224
1. Burden, Chris. I. Title.

Burford, Byron, 1920—

FUMAGALLI, Orazio. 759.13
Byron Burford. Duluth, Tweed Gallery, University of Minnesota, 1964. 27 p. illus. 23 cm. [ND237.B894F8] 68-40558
1. Burford, Byron, 1920-

Burford, Eng. (Oxfordshire) St. John Baptist (Church)

THE Church of Saint John Baptist, Burford. 7th ed. Gloucester, British Publishing Co., 1966. 49 p. illus., plan. 19 cm. 21- (B66-8509) [NA5471.B895C5 1966] 2 67-73783 728.9
1. Burford, Eng. (Oxfordshire) St. John Baptist (Church)

Burke, Jackson, 1908-1975—Art collections.

MURASE, Miyeko. 709'.52'07401471
Japanese art : selections from the Mary and Jackson Burke Collection / Miyeko Murase. [New York] : Metropolitan Museum of Art, 1975. p. cm. Bibliography: p. [N7352.M86] 75-28053 ISBN 0-87099-136-1 : 50.00. ISBN 0-87099-138-8 pbk. : 14.95
1. Burke, Jackson, 1908-1975—Art collections. 2. Burke, Mary—Art collections. 3. Art, Japanese—Exhibitions. I. New York (City). Metropolitan Museum of Art. II. Title. BIP

Burlap craft.

FRESSARD, M. J. 746.4
Creating with burlap: decorating, painting, embroidering, by M. J. Fressard. Translated by Rhea Rollin. New York, Sterling Pub. Co. [1970] 48 p. illus. 20 cm. (Little craft book series) Translation of Avec de la toile de jute. Describes the use of burlap to create lamp shades, picture frames, tapestries, draperies, and paintings. [TT880.F7313 1970] 72-90806 ISBN 0-8069-5144-3
1. Burlap craft. 2. Needlework. 3. Handicraft. I. Title. II. Series.

HUTCHINGS, Margaret. 746.4
Sculpting in burlap / Margaret Hutchings. New York : Taplinger Pub. Co., 1975. 112 p. : ill. ; 26 cm. [TT880.H87] 74-19853 ISBN 0-8008-7011-5 : 9.95
1. Burlap craft. 2. Soft sculpture. I. Title.

Burlap craft—Juvenile literature.

SOMMER, Elyse. 746'.04'13
Make it with burlap. Illustrated by Giulio Maestro. New York, Lothrop, Lee & Shepard Co. [1973] 96 p. illus. 25 cm. Step-by-step instructions for making a variety of objects from burlap including sculptures, flowers, games, and others. [TT880.S66] 73-4954 ISBN 0-688-41559-8 4.50
1. Burlap craft—Juvenile literature. I. Maestro, Giulio, illus. II. Title.
Library edition 4.14; ISBN 0-688-51559-2. BIP

Burne-Jones, Edward Coley, Sir, bart., 1833-1898.

BELL, Malcolm. 759.2
Sir Edward Burne-Jones; a record and review. London, G. Bell, 1898. [New York, AMS Press, 1972] xii, 151 p. illus. 23 cm. First published in 1893 under title: Edward Burne-Jones. Reprint of the 1898 ed. [ND497.B8B4 1972] 73-148748 ISBN 0-404-00733-3
1. Burne-Jones, Edward Coley, Sir, bart., 1833-1898. BIP

[BURNE-JONES, Georgiana (Macdonald), Lady] 1840-1920. 759.2
Memorials of Edward Burne-Jones, by G B-J. New York, B. Blom, 1970. xii, 309, 372 p. illus. 21 cm. Reprint of the 1904 ed. [ND497.B8B85 1970] 71-174396
1. Burne-Jones, Edward Coley, Sir, bart., 1833-1898. I. Title. BIP

SPALDING, Frances. 759.2
Magnificent dreams : Burne-Jones and the late Victorians / Frances Spalding. New York : Dutton, 1978. 80 p. : ill. (some col.) ; 29 cm. Bibliography: p. 6. [ND497.B8S83 1978] 78-55004 ISBN 0-7148-1827-5 : 12.95. ISBN 0-7148-1909-3 pbk. : 6.95
1. Burne-Jones, Edward Coley, Sir, bart., 1833-1898. 2. Preraphaelitism—Influence. 3. Symbolism (Art movement)—England. 4. Painting, Victorian—England. I. Title. BIP

WATERS, William. 759.2
Sir Edward Coley Burne-Jones, Bart. 1833-1898; Laus Veneris. Newcastle upon Tyne, Laing Art Gallery, 1973. [16] p. illus. 24 cm. BibliographY: p. [9] [ND497.B8W37] 74-188073
1. Burne-Jones, Edward Coley, Sir, Bart., 1833-1898. Laus Veneris. I. Laing Art Gallery, Newcastle-upon-Tyne. II. Title: Laus Veneris.

Burnham, Daniel Hudson, 1846-1912.

HINES, Thomas S. 720'.92'4 B
Burnham of Chicago, architect and planner / Thomas S. Hines. New York : Oxford University Press, 1974. xxiii, 445 p. : ill. ; 24 cm. Includes index. Bibliography: p. 387-400. [NA737.B85H56] 74-79625 ISBN 0-19-501836-2 : 19.50
1. Burnham, Daniel Hudson, 1846-1912. I. Title.

MOORE, Charles, 1855-1942. 720'.924 B
Daniel H. Burnham; architect, planner of cities. New York, Da Capo Press, 1968. 2 v. in 1. illus. 26 cm. (Da Capo Press series in architecture and decorative art, v. 17) (A Da Capo Press reprint edition.) Reprint of the 1921 ed. Each vol. has also special t.p. Bibliographical footnotes. [NA737.B85M6 1968] 68-27726
1. Burnham, Daniel Hudson, 1846-1912.

SPENCE, Robert, 1925- 330.9'73 s
Daniel H. Burnham and the "Renaissance" in American architecture. (In Wisconsin Academy of Sciences, Arts and Letters. Transactions. Madison. 23 cm. v. 29 (1960) p. 295-809) Bibliographical footnotes. [[AS36.W7 vol. 49]] A 62
1. Burnham, Daniel Hudson, 1846-1912. 2. Architecture, American. I. Title.

Burnley, Eng.—Description—Views.

DOUGLAS, Arthur. 942.7'642'00222
Burnley once upon a time / [compiled by Arthur Douglas. Nelson : Hendon Publishing Co., 1976. [46] p. : chiefly ill., facsims., map, ports. ; 21 x 29 cm. [DA690.B953D68] 76-375277 ISBN 0-902907-91-3 : £1.30
1. Burnley, Eng.—Description—Views. I. Title.

Burns, William, 1921-1972.

ABERDEEN Art Gallery, Aberdeen, Scot. 759.941
William Burns [catalogue of a] memorial exhibition [held at the] Aberdeen Art Gallery [20th October-10th November 1973] Aberdeen, Aberdeen Art Gallery, 1973. [23] p. illus. (some col.), port. 30 cm. Bibliography: p. [14]. [ND497.B83A23 1973] 74-165620 ISBN 0-900017-05-8 £0.66
1. Burns, William, 1921-1972. I. Burns, William, 1921-1972.

Burr, George Elbert, 1859-1939.

SEEBER, Louise Combes. 760'.0924 B
George Elbert Burr, 1859-1939; catalogue raisonne and guide to the etched works with biographical and critical notes. Flagstaff, Ariz., Northland Press, 1971. xii, 179 p. illus. (part col.) 32 cm. Bibliography: p. 177-179. [NE2012.B8S4] 78-150685 ISBN 0-87358-067-2 15.00
1. Burr, George Elbert, 1859-1939.

Burri, Alberto, 1915—

BRANDI, Cesare 759.5
Burri [Tr. from Italian by Martha Leeb Hadzi] Roma, Editali [dist. NewYork, Wittenborn, 1964. c.1963] 234p. (p. [49]-220 illus., 48 col. plates) 33cm. (Maestri del xx secolo) Bibl. 64-2677 40.00. bxd.
1. Burri, Alberto, 1915- I. Title.

BURRI, Alberto, 1915- 709'.2'4
Alberto Burri [by] Maurizio Calvesi. Translated from the Italian by Robert Erich Wolf. New York, Abrams [1974, i.e.1975] p. cm. Bibliography: p. [N6923.B92C313] 74-5412 ISBN 0-8109-0232-X 37.50
1. Burri, Alberto, 1915- I. Calvesi, Maurizio.

Burroughs, Edgar Rice, 1875-1950—Illustrations.

THE Edgar Rice Burroughs library of illustration / [conceived, designed, and edited by Russ Cochran] Limited Centennial ed. West Plains, Mo. : Cochran, 1976- v. : ill. (some col.) ; 32 cm. Most of the ill. by J. A. St. John. [NC975.E24] 77-150518 741.64'0973
1. Burroughs, Edgar Rice, 1875-1950—Illustrations. 2. Illustration of books—United States. I. Burroughs, Edgar Rice, 1875-1950. II. Cochran, Russ. III. St. John, James Allen, 1872-1957.

Bush-Brown, Harold.

BUSH-BROWN, Harold Bushbrown harold 720'.92'4 B
Beaux arts to Bauhaus and beyond : an architect's perspective / by Harold Bush-Brown. New York : Whitney Library of Design, 1976. 128 p. : ill. ; 26 cm. Includes bibliographical references and index. [NA737.B87A22] 76-17005 ISBN 0-8230-7067-0 : 12.95
1. Bush-Brown, Harold. 2. Architects—United States—Correspondence, reminiscenses, etc. 3. Architecture, Modern—20th century. I. Title. BIP

Bushey Urban District, Eng.—History.

LONGMAN, Grant. 707'.11'425895
The Herkomer Art School, 1883-1900 / [by] Grant Longman. Bushey : The author, 1976. 16 p. : ill. ; 30 x 11 cm. (Bushey reference paper ; no. 1) Bibliography: p. 16. [N332.G75B874] 77-359296 ISBN 0-901957-04-6 : £1.00
1. Herkomer Art School. 2. Bushey Urban District, Eng.—History. I. Title. II. Series.

Busts.

SCHUYLER, Jane. 731'.82'094551
Florentine busts : sculpted portraiture in the fifteenth century / Jane Schuyler. New York : Garland Pub., 1976. xii, 315 p. : ill. ; 21 cm. (Outstanding dissertations in the fine arts) Originally presented as the author's thesis, Columbia, 1972. Bibliography: p. 245-269. [NB1309.S38 1976] 75-23814 ISBN 0-8240-2007-3 lib.bdg. : 27.50
1. Busts. 2. Portrait sculpture, Florentine. 3. Sculpture, Renaissance—Florence. I. Title. II. Series.

Busts—Exhibitions.

THE Portrait bust; Renaissance to Enlightenment. [Providence? 1969?] [64] p. illus. 23 cm. Catalog of an exhibition prepared by students in the Dept. of Art, Brown University, and held at the Museum of Art, Rhode Island School of Design, Mar. 5-30, 1969. Includes bibliographical references. [NB1309.P6] 70-3627 731.7'4
1. Busts—Exhibitions. 2. Europe—Biography—Portraits. I. Brown University. Dept. of Art. II. Rhode Island School of Design, Providence. Museum of Art.

Butler, Howard Russell, 1856-1934.

BUTLER, Howard Russell, 1856-1934. 759.13
E. R. Squibb and Sons, Inc. presents Howard Russell Butler : an exhibition of his oils, pastels, & drawings. [Princeton, N.J.] : E. R. Squibb & Sons, c1977. 35 p. : 25 ill. ; 21 cm. Bibliography: p. 35. [N6537.B88S65] 77-362423
1. Butler, Howard Russell, 1856-1934. I. Squibb (E. R.) and Sons. II. Title.

Butler, Maude Kimball, 1880—

BUTLER, Maude Kimball, 1880- 759.13
Cathlamet pioneer; the paintings of Maude Kimball Butler. With descriptive notes by Julia Butler Hansen. Tacoma, Washington State Historical Society, 1973. 39 p. illus. 26 cm. Exhibition to be held at Washington State Historical Society Museum in Aug. 1973. [ND237.B97H36] 73-80884
1. Butler, Maude Kimball, 1880- 2. Cathlamet, Wash., in art. I. Hansen, Julia Butler. II. Washington State Historical Society. Museum. III. Title. BIP

Butter molds.

SMITH, Elmer Lewis. 736'.4
Early American butter prints; [a collection of rural folk art, designs illustrated from hand carved wooden butter molds and prints] Compiled and edited by Elmer L. Smith. Photos. by Mel Horst. Witmer, Pa., Applied Arts [1968] 42 p. (chiefly illus.) 28 cm. (Americana dollar publications) [NK8490.S6] 71-1763 1.00
1. Butter molds. 2. Wood-engravings, American. I. Title. BIP

TRICE, James E. 736'.4
Butter molds; a primitive art form, by James E. Trice. Des Moines, Wallace-Homestead Book Co. [1973] 100 p. illus. 23 cm. [NK8490.T74] 73-163421 3.95
1. Butter molds. 2. Art, Primitive.

Buttersworth, James Edward, 1817-1894.

SCHAEFER, Rudolph J. 759.13
J. E. Buttersworth : 19th-century marine painter / by Rudolph J. Schaefer. Mystic, Conn. : Mystic Seaport, 1975. xxvi, 276 p., [24] leaves of plates : ill. (some col.) ; 31 cm. Errata slip inserted. Includes index. Bibliography: p. 227-231. [ND237.B98S32] 74-82666 ISBN 0-913372-12-9 : 75.00
1. Buttersworth, James Edward, 1817-1894. 2. Ships in art. 3. Schaefer, Rudolph J.—Art collections. I. Title.

Button craft—Juvenile literature.

NEWSOME, Arden J. 745.5
Button collecting and crafting / written and illustrated by Arden J. Newsome. New York : Lothrop, Lee and Shepard, c1976. 96 p. : ill. ; 24 cm. Includes index. Bibliography: p. 91-92. A guide to collecting, displaying, and making buttons and using them to decorate toys, jewelry, clothing, and other items. [TT880.N47] 76-969 ISBN 0-688-41742-6 : 5.95 lib.bdg. : 5.21
1. Button craft—Juvenile literature. 2. Buttons—Collectors and collecting—Juvenile literature. I. Title. BIP

Buttonhooks—Collectors and collecting.

BETENSLEY, Bertha. 688
Antique buttonhooks for shoes, gloves, and clothing / by Bertha Betensley. Westville, Ind. : Educator's Press, c1975. 117 p. : ill. ; 23 cm. [NK4890.B8B47] 75-14753
1. Buttonhooks—Collectors and collecting. I. Title.

Buttons, American.

ALBERT, Alphaeus Homer, 1891- 391'.45'0973
Record of American uniform and historical buttons, with supplement ... 1775-1973 [by] Alphaeus H. Albert. [Boyertown, Pa., Boyertown Pub. Co.] 1973. 448, 28 p. illus. 22 cm. "First edition, with supplement." First ed. published in 1969 under title: Record of American uniform and historical buttons ... 1775-1968. Bibliography: p. 448. [NK3670.A48 1973] 73-78488
1. Buttons, American. 2. Buttons—Collectors and collecting. I. Title.

ALBERT, Alphaeus Homer, 1891- 391'.45'075
Record of American uniform and historical buttons ... 1775-1968 [by] Alphaeus H. Albert. [1st ed. Boyertown, Pa., Printed by Boyertown Pub. Co. 1969. 448 p. illus. 23 cm. Published in 1973 under title: Record of American uniform and historical buttons, with supplement, ... 1775-1973. Bibliography: p. 448. [NK3670.A48] 71-76867
1. Buttons, American. 2. Buttons—Collectors and collecting. I. Title.

JENKINS, Dan L. 355.1'4
Military buttons of the gulf coast, 1711-1830 / by Dan Jenkins. Mobile, Ala. : Museum of the City of Mobile, 1973. viii, 44 p. : ill. ; 19 cm. (Museum publication - Museum of the City of Mobile ; no. 2) Includes index. Bibliography: p. 43. [NK3670.J46] 74-185504 2.00
1. Buttons, American. 2. Military paraphernalia—Gulf States. I. Title. II. Series: Museum of the City of Mobile. Museum publication — Museum of the City of Mobile ; no. 2.

Buttons—Collectors and collecting.

ALBERT, Alphaeus Homer, 1891- 737'.2
Political campaign and commemorative buttons; an illustrated catalog with descriptions of the buttons used during the various political campaigns including the Washington inaugural buttons and other commemorative and patriotic buttons, by Alphaeus H. Albert. [1st ed. Hightstown, N.J.] 1966. xi, 76 p. illus. 22 cm. Bibliography: p. 76. [NK3670.A47] 66-30678
1. Buttons—Collectors and collecting. 2. Campaign insignia. I. Title.

ALBERT, Lillian Smith. 391.4
The button sampler, by Lillian Smith Albert and Jane Ford Adams. New York, M. Barrows [1951] 185 p. illus. 15 cm. (Collectors' little-book library) [NK3670.A525] 51-9881
1. Buttons—Collectors and collecting. I. Adams, Jane Ford, joint author. II. Title.

ALBERT, Lillian Smith. 391'.45
The complete button book, by Lillian Smith Albert and Kathryn Kent. With a foreword by Carl W. Drepperd. Stratford, Conn., J. Edwards [1971, c1949] xix, 409 p. illus. 24 cm. [NK3670.A53 1971] 73-30059 15.00
1. Buttons—Collectors and collecting. I. Schwerke, Kathryn, joint author. II. Title.

CHAMBERLIN, Erwina. 391'.45'075
Button heritage, by Erwina Chamberlin and Minerva Miner. Sherburne, N. Y. F. E. Faulkner Print. Co. [1967] 247 p. illus. (part col.) 30 cm. Bibliographical references included in "foreword" (p. 5) [NK3670.C45] 67-66389
1. Buttons—Collectors and collecting. I. Miner, Minerva, joint author. II. Title.

COUSE, Laura Erwina (Blanchard) 1902- 391'.45'075
Yesterday's button classics, by L. Erwina Couse and Marguerite Maple. Watkins Glen, N.Y., Century House [1970] 255 p. illus., col. plates. 24 cm. First ed. published in 1941 under title: Button classics. [NK3670.C63] 77-121197
1. Buttons—Collectors and collecting. I. Maple, Marguerite, joint author. II. Title.

EPSTEIN, Diana. 391'.45'075
Buttons. New York, Walker [1968] 84 p. illus., 2 col. plates. 22 cm. (Collectors' blue books) [NK3670.E6] 68-16101 3.50
1. Buttons—Collectors and collecting. I. Title.

GUIDELINES for collecting china buttons, by Ruth Lamm [and others] 738.2'8
Drawings by Charles Lamm and Lester Lorah. Photos. by Alphaeus H. Albert. [Hightstown, N.J.?] National Button Society of America, 1970. xi, 151 p. illus. 23 cm. [NK3670.G8] 73-12902
1. Buttons—Collectors and collecting. I. Lamm, Ruth.

LUSCOMB, Sally. 391.4
The old button box, by Sally Luscomb and Ethel Cassidy. Southerington, Conn., 1951. 180 p. illus. 21 cm. [NK3670.L8] 52-211
1. Buttons—Collectors and collecting. I. Title.

LUSCOMB, Sally C. 737
The collector's encyclopedia of buttons. New York, Crown Publishers [1967] xii, 242 p. illus. (part col.) 26 cm. [NK3670.L79] 67-27049
1. Buttons—Collectors and collecting. I. Title.

PEACOCK, Primrose. 687'.8
Antique buttons; their history and how to collect them. New York, Drake Publishers [1972] 128 p. illus. (part col.) 26 cm. First published under title: Buttons for the collector. Bibliography: p. 127-128. [NK3670.P4 1972b] 70-188796 ISBN 0-87749-235-2 7.95
1. Buttons—Collectors and collecting. I. Title.

ROBERTS, Catherine Christopher, 1905- 391.45
Who's got the button? Old and new angles to button collecting. Illustrated by the author, and with photos. New York, McKay [1962] 97 p. illus. 21 cm. [NK3670.R6] 62-18709
1. Buttons—Collectors and collecting. I. Title.

WEARIN, Otha Donner, 1903- 737'.2
Political campaign buttons in color, with prices, by Otha D. Wearin. Leon, Iowa, Published and distributed by Mid-America Book Co. [1969] 50 p. col. illus. 23 cm. [NK3670.W4] 74-21369 4.95
1. Buttons—Collectors and collecting. 2. Elections—U.S. I. Title.

Buttons—Europe—Collectors and collecting—Dictionaries.

HOUART, Victor. 739.27'8
Buttons : a collector's guide / by Victor Houart. New York : Scribner, c1977. 128 p. : ill. ; 22 cm. [NK3670.H63 1977] 77-79904 ISBN 0-684-15334-3 : 9.95
1. Buttons—Europe—Collectors and collecting—Dictionaries. I. Title.

Buttons—United States.

ALBERT, Alphaeus Homer, 1891- 391'.45'0973
Record of American uniform and historical buttons ... 1775-1976 / Alphaeus H. Albert. Bicentennial ed. Hightstown, N.J. : Albert, 1976, c1977. 487 p. : ill. ; 23 cm. Bibliography: p. 482. [NK3670.A48 1977] 76-58596
1. Buttons—United States. 2. Buttons—Collectors and collecting. I. Title.

Bye, Ranulph, 1916—

BYE, Ranulph, 1916- 759.13
The vanishing depot. Wynnewood, Pa., Livingston Pub. Co. [1973] xiii, 113 p. illus. (part col.) 29 cm. [ND1839.B93A57] 73-16229 ISBN 0-87098-058-0 20.00
1. Bye, Ranulph, 1916- 2. Railroads—United States—Stations—Pictorial works. I. Title.

Cabinet-work.

ALBERS, Vernon Martin, 1902- 684.1'6
Amateur cabinet making [by] Vernon M. Albers. New York, Barnes & Noble [1973, c.1972] 110 p. illus. 21 cm. (Everyday handbooks, EH346) [TT197.A43] ISBN 0-06-463346-2 1.50 (pbk.)
1. Cabinet-work. I. Title.
L.C. card no. for hardbound ed.: 70-37801.

ALBERS, Vernon Martin, 1902- 684.1'6
Amateur cabinetmaking [by] Vernon M. Albers. South Brunswick, A. S. Barnes [1972] 110 p. illus. 22 cm. [TT197.A43] 70-37801 ISBN 0-498-01012-0
1. Cabinet-work. I. Title. BIP

BRANN, Donald R. 684.1'6
How to build a colonial tavern bar cabinet, by Donald R. Brann. Briarcliff Manor, N.Y., Directions Simplified [1967] c1966. 49 p. illus., plans. 23 cm. (Easi-bild simplified directions, 662) (Easi-bild home improvement library.) [TT197.B76] 66-21082 1.00
1. Cabinet-work. I. Title.

BRANN, Donald R. 684.1'6
How to build a home workshop, radiator enclosure, bird feeder, by Donald R. Brann. Rev. ed. Briarcliff Manor, N.Y., Directions Simplified, 1973. 82 p. illus. 23 cm. (Easi-bild, 677) Published 1965-72 under title: How to plan and build a home workshop. [TT197.B762 1973] 73-180261 1.50 (pbk.)
1. Cabinet-work. 2. Workshops. I. Title.

BRANN, Donald R. 684.1'6
How to build and install a hi-fi music wall, by Donald R. Brann. Briarcliff Manor, N.Y., Directions Simplified, [1967] 50 p. (p. 47-50 advertisements) illus., plans. 23 cm. (Easi-bild simplified directions, no. 612) Published in 1973 under title: Wall to wall cabinets; in 1975, Stereo installation simplified. [TT197.B763 1967] 66-28495 0.75
1. Cabinet-work. I. Title.

BRANN, Donald R. 645'.4
How to build gun cabinet & racks, by Donald R. Brann. Briarcliff Manor, N.Y., Directions Simplified, c1967. 66 p. illus., plans. 23 cm. (Easi-bild simplified directions, 630) Page 55, blank for "Notes." [TT197.B764] 67-14312 1.00
1. Cabinet-work. I. Title.

BRANN, Donald R. 684.1'6
How to build sportsman's revolving storage cabinet : archery, gun, fishing rod, cabinets-racks / by Donald R. Brann. Rev. ed. Briarcliff Manor, N.Y. : Directions Simplified, 1974, c1967. 98 p. : ill. ; 23 cm. (Easi-bild home improvement library ; 630) (Easi-bild simplified directions) On spine: Sportsman's revolving cabinet. "A Business of your own book." [TT197.B766 1974] 74-187897 pbk. : 2.00
1. Cabinet-work. I. Title. II. Title: Sportsman's revolving cabinet.

BRANN, Donald R. 684.1'6
How to plan and build a home workshop, by Donald R. Brann. Briarcliff Manor, N.Y., Directions Simplified [1967] c1965. 50 p. illus., plans. 23 cm. (Easi-bild simplified directions, 677) Page 36, blank for "Notes." Published in 1973 under title: How to build a home workshop, radiator enclosure, bird feeder. [TT197.B767] 65-19667 1.00
1. Cabinet-work. 2. Workshops. I. Title. II. Title: Home workshop.

DAHL, Alf A., 1893-- 684.2
Cabinetmaking and millwork: tools, materials, layout [by] Alf A. Dahl [and] J. Douglas Wilson. Chicago, American Technical Society, 1953. 235p. illus. 22cm. (Books of the building trade series) [TT197.D25] 53-11586
1. Cabinet-work. 2. Woodworking machinery. I. Wilson, John Douglas. 1888- joint author. II. Title.

DAHL, Alf A., 1893- 684.2
Cabinetmaking and millwork: tools, materials, construction, layout [by] Alf Dahl [and] J. Douglas Wilson. [2d ed., rev.] Chicago, American Technical Society, 1956. 352 p. illus. 22 cm. [TT197.D25 1956] 56-11194
1. Cabinet-work. 2. Woodworking machinery. I. Wilson, John Douglas, 1888- joint author. II. Title.

DUNCAN, S. Blackwell. 684.1'6
The build-it book of cabinets and built-ins / S. Blackwell Duncan. Blue Ridge Summit, Pa. : Tab Books, 1979. p. cm. Includes index. [TT197.D85] 78-11248 ISBN 0-8306-9854-X : 12.95. ISBN 0-8306-1002-2 pbk. : 7.95
1. Cabinet-work. 2. Built-in furniture. I. Title. BIP

FEIRER, John Louis. 684.1'04
Cabinetmaking and millwork [by] John L. Feirer. Peoria, Ill., C. A. Bennett Co. [1967] 928 p. illus. (part col.) 25 cm. [TT197.F4] 67-10060
1. Cabinet-work. 2. Millwork (Woodwork) I. Title. BIP

FEIRER, John Louis. 684.1'04
Cabinetmaking and millwork [by] John L. Feirer. Peoria, Ill., C. A. Bennett Co. [1970] 928 p. illus. (part col.) 24 cm. [TT197.F4 1970] 77-16823 ISBN 0-87002-075-7
1. Cabinet-work. 2. Millwork (Woodwork) I. Title.

selected and edited by Elizabeth T. Billington ; with an appreciation by Maurice Sendak. New York : F. Warne, c1978. 288 p. : ill. (some col.) ; 25 x 27 cm. Includes index. Bibliography: p. 285-286. [NC978.5.C3A4 1978] 76-45308 ISBN 0-7232-6139-3 : 30.00
1. Caldecott, Randolph, 1846-1886. I. Billington, Elizabeth T. II. Title. BIP

CALDECOTT, Randolph, 1846-1886. 741'.092'4 B
Yours pictorially : illustrated letters of Randolph Caldecott / edited by Michael Hutchins. London : F. Warne, 1976, i.e.1977 x, 284 p., [8] p. of plates : ill., facsims. (some col.), port. ; 24 cm. Includes index. [NC978.5.C3A347 1976] 76-2923 ISBN 0-7232-1981-8 : 15.00
1. Caldecott, Randolph, 1846-1886. 2. Illustrators—Great Britain—Correspondence. I. Hutchins, Michael. II. Title.

Calder, Alexander, 1898-1976.

ARNASON, H. H. 730.924
Calder, text by H. H. Arnason. Photogs. by Pedro E. Guerrero. [Princeton, N.J.] Van Nostrand [1966] xi, 192p. illus. (pt. col.) ports. (pt. col.) 29cm. Bibl. [NB237.C28A8] 66-31776 15.00
I. Calder, Alexander, 1898- II. Title.

ARNASON, H H 730'.924
Calder; text by H.H.Arnason, photographs by Pedro E. Guerrero. London, Studio Vista; New York, Van Nostrand, 1967. xii, 192 p. front., illus. (incl.ports.). 28 1/3 cm. (B67-16966) Illus. on endpapers. Bibliography: p. 184-185. [NB237.C28A8 1967] 67-107434
1. Calder, Alexander, 1898- I. Title.

CALDER, Alexander, 1898- 746.3'92'4
Aubusson tapestries, with a selection of mobiles. [Chicago] 1972?] [9] p. (chiefly col. illus.) 21 cm. Cover title. Catalog of an exhibition held at the Arts Club of Chicago, Nov. 15-Dec. 30, 1972. [NK3012.A3C32] 73-171211
1. Calder, Alexander, 1898- 2. Tapestry, American. I. Arts Club of Chicago. II. Title.

CALDER, Alexander, 1898- 730'.924
Calder. Photos. and design by Ugo Mulas. Introd. by H. Harvard Arnason. With comments by Alexander Calder. New York, Viking Press [1971] 216 p. illus., ports. 32 cm. (A Studio book) Bibliography: p. 207-214. [NB237.C28M8 1971] 71-125244 ISBN 0-670-11219-4 22.50
I. Mulas, Ugo. II. Arnason, H. Harvard. BIP

CALDER, Alexander, 1898- 730.924
Calder; an autobiography with pictures. New York, Pantheon Books [1966] 285 p. illus. (part col.) ports. 28 cm. [NB237.C28A2] 66-23203
1. Calder, Alexander, 1898- 2. Sculptors—United States—Correspondence, reminiscences, etc. I. Title.

CALDER, Alexander, 1898- 759.13
Calder gouaches; the art of Alexander Calder. [Exhibition] organized by the Long Beach Museum of Art. Long Beach Museum of Art, January 11-February 8, 1970; Fine Arts Gallery of San Diego, February 27-March 29, 1970; Phoenix Art Museum, May 1-May 31, 1970. [Long Beach, Calif., Long Beach Museum of Art, 1970] [28] p. illus. (part col.) 27 cm. [ND1839.C3A43] 70-114081
I. Long Beach, Calif. Museum of Art. II. Phoenix, Ariz. Art Museum. III. San Diego, Calif. Fine Arts Gallery. IV. Title.

CALDER, Alexander, 1898- 730'.924
Calder; mobiles and stabiles. Text by Giovanni Carandente. New York, New American Library [1968] 24 p. illus., 32 col. plates, port. 18 cm. (A Mentor-Unesco art book) Includes bibliography. [NB237.C28C3] 74-3226 1.25
I. Carandente, Giovanni. II. Title.

CALDER, Alexander, 1898- 730'.92'4
Calder's circus. Edited by Jean Lipman, with Nancy Foote. Circus figures photographed by Marvin Schwartz. Designed by Ellen Hsiao. [1st ed.] New York, Dutton [1972] 171 p. illus. (part col.) 25 cm. Bibliography: p. 170-171. [NB237.C28A45] 72-75014 ISBN 0-525-07305-1 15.00
I. Title. BIP

CALDER, Alexander, 1898- 709'.2'4 B
Calder's universe / Jean Lipman ; Ruth Wolfe, editorial director. New York : Viking Press in cooperation with the Whitney Museum of American Art, [1976] p. cm. (A Studio book) An exhibition based on this book is scheduled to be held at the Whitney Museum of American Art, Oct. 14, 1976 to May 1, 1977, and at other museums at later dates. Includes index. Bibliography: p. [N6537.C33L56] 76-28232 ISBN 0-670-19966-4 : 28.50
1. Calder, Alexander, 1898- I. Lipman, Jean Herzberg, 1909- II. Whitney Museum of American Art, New York. III. Title. BIP

CALDER, Alexander, 1898- 730'.924
A salute to Alexander Calder; sculpture, watercolors and drawings, prints, illustrated books, and jewelry in the collection of the Museum of Modern Art. Introductory essay by Bernice Rose. New York, Museum of Modern Art [1969] 31 p. illus. 22 cm. Catalog of the exhibition held Dec. 22, 1969-Feb. 15, 1970, at the Museum of Modern Art, New York. [NB237.C28R6] 72-110987
I. Rose, Bernice. II. New York. Museum of Modern Art. III. Title.

CALDER, Alexander, 1898-1976. 709'.2'4 B
Calder : an autobiography with pictures / with a new introd. by Jean Davidson. New York : Pantheon Books, 1977,c1966 288 p., [6] leaves of plates : ill. ; 27 cm. [NB237.C28A2 1966b] 77-5300 ISBN 0-394-42142-6 : 15.95. ISBN 0-394-73408-4 pbk. : 7.95
1. Calder, Alexander, 1898-1976. 2. Sculptors—United States—Biography. I. Title.

FIVE American 730.922
sculptors. Reprint ed. New York, Published for the Museum of Modern Art by Arno Press, 1969. 1 v. (various pagings) illus. 27 cm. Reprint of 5 exhibition catalogs, previously published separately between 1935 and 1954 of the sculptors' works exhibited at the Museum of Modern Art. Contents.—Alexander Calder, by J. J. Sweeney.—The sculpture of John B. Flannagan, edited by D. C. Miller.—Gaston Lachaise, by L. Kirstein.—The sculpture of Elie Nadelman, by L. Kirstein.—The sculpture of Jacques Lipchitz, by H. R. Hope. Includes bibliographies. [NB236.F5 1969] 71-86443
1. Calder, Alexander, 1898- 2. Flannagan, John Bernard, 1895?-1942. 3. Lachaise, Gaston, 1882-1935. 4. Nadelman, Elie, 1882-1946. 5. Lipchitz, Jacques, 1891- I. New York (City). Museum of Modern Art. II. Sweeney, James Johnson, 1900- Alexander Calder. 1969. III. New York (City). Museum of Modern Art. The sculpture of John B. Flannagan. 1969. IV. New York (City). Museum of Modern Art. Gaston Lachaise. 1969. V. Kirstein, Lincoln, 1907- The sculpture of Elie Nadelman. 1969. VI. Hope, Henry Radford, 1905- The sculpture of Jacques Lipchitz. 1969. BIP

MANCEWICZ, Bernice Winslow. 730'.924
Alexander Calder, a pictorial essay. Grand Rapids, Eerdmans [1969] 64 p. illus., ports. 23 cm. [NB237.C28M3] 79-80878 3.95
1. Calder, Alexander, 1898- I. Title.

MUSEUM of Contemporary Art, Chicago. 730'.92'4
Alexander Calder, a retrospective exhibition, work from 1925 to 1974, October 26 to December 8, 1974. Chicago : Museum of Contemporary Art, c1974. [32] p. : ill. (some col.) ; 28 cm. Includes a catalog. Includes bibliographical references. [NB237.C28M85 1974] 76-351859
1. Calder, Alexander, 1898- I. Calder, Alexander, 1898-

SOLOMON R. Guggenheim Museum, New York. 730.973
Alexander Calder: a retrospective exhibition [by] the Solomon R. Guggenheim Museum, New York [and] Musee national d'art moderne, Paris. [New York, 1964] 87 p. illus. (part col.) 28 cm. Exhibition 64/7, November 1964-January 1965 at the Solomon R. Guggenheim Museum, New York: also shown at Musee national d'art moderne, Paris, Milwaukee Art Center, and the Washington University Gallery of Art, St. Louis. Catalog of works in the exhibition ([12]) p. laid in. [NB237.C28S6] 64-66058
1. Calder, Alexander, 1898- I. Paris, Musee national de'art moderne. II. Title.

SWEENEY, James Johnson, 1900- 731.27
Alexander Calder. New York, Museum of Modern Art [1951] 80 p. illus., ports. 26 cm. "Bibliography, by Bernard Karpel": p. 77-80. [NB237.C28S9 1951] 51-8022
1. Calder, Alexander, 1898- I. New York (City) Museum of Modern Art.

Calder, Alexander Milne, 1846-1923.

HAYES, Margaret Calder, 1896- 709'.2'2 B
Three Alexander Calders : a family memoir / by Margaret Calder Hayes ; introd. by Malcolm Cowley. Middlebury, Vt. : P. S. Eriksson, c1977. xix, 300 p. : ill. ; 24 cm. Includes index. [NB237.C29H39 1977] 77-79244 ISBN 0-8397-8017-6 : 15.00
1. Calder, Alexander Milne, 1846-1923. 2. Calder, Alexander Stirling, 1870-1945. 3. Calder, Alexander, 1898-1976. 4. Hayes, Margaret Calder, 1896- 5. Sculptors—United States—Biography. 6. United States—Biography. I. Title. BIP

Caldwell Village.

AMBLER, J Richard, 71019
Caldwell Village, With appendices by Erik K. Reed[and others.*alt Lake City] 1966. 118 p. illus., map. (Utah. University. Dept. of Anthropology. Anthropological papers, no. 84) [68-28353]
1. Caldwell Village. 2. Utah—Antiq. I. Title. BIP

Caley, George L.—Art collections.

CALEY, George L. 769'.5
Post cards of yesteryear: 1893-1926; Delaware and elsewhere, by George L. Caley. Smyrna, Del., Printed by Shane Quality Press [1973] 92 p. illus. 27 cm. [NC1875.U6C34] 73-85391
1. Caley, George L.—Art collections. 2. Postal cards. I. Title.

California. Arts Commission.

SCOTT, Mellier Goodin, 1906- 700'.61
The states and the arts; the California Arts Commission and the emerging federal-state partnership, by Mel Scott. Berkeley, Institute of Governmental Studies, University of California, 1971. xiv, 129 p. 23 cm. Bibliography: p. 127-129. [NX26.C33S3] 70-633156 ISBN 0-87772-075-4 3.00
1. California. Arts Commission. 2. State encouragement of science, literature, and art—U.S. I. Title.

California—Description and travel—Views.

BAIRD, Joseph Armstrong. 769.9
California's pictorial letter sheets, 1849-1869 San Francisco, D. Magee, 1967. 171 p. facsims. (part fold., 1 in pocket) 36 cm. A catalog of "all currently known letter sheets." "475 copies printed ... MCMLXVI." Bibliography: p. [161]-162. [NE215.U5B3] 67-5531
1. California—Description and travel—Views. 2. Engravings, American—Catalogs. I. Title.

BAIRD, Joseph Armstrong. 760'.0973'074019467
Catalogue of original paintings, drawings, and watercolors in the Robert B. Honeyman, Jr. Collection [Bancroft Library, University of California, Berkeley] Compiled by Joseph Armstrong Baird, Jr. Berkeley, The Friends of the Bancroft Library, University of California, 1968. vii, 196 p. 28 cm. Bibliography: p. vii. [N5220.H64B3] 70-25367
1. Honeyman, Robert B.—Art collections. 2. California—Description and travel—Views. I. California. University. Bancroft Library. II. Title.

ERICSON, Augustus William, 1848-1927. 779'.9'9794
Fine California views : the photographs of A. W. Ericson / by Peter E. Palmquist. Eureka : Interface California Corp., c1975. 111 p. : ill. ; 27 cm. [TR140.E73A33 1975] 75-7846 ISBN 0-915580-02-0 : 20.95
1. Ericson, Augustus William, 1848-1927. 2. California—Description and travel—Views. I. Palmquist, Peter E. II. Title.
Publisher's address: 1806 E. St., Suite B., Eureka, Ca. 95501. BIP

California Institute of the Arts.

ADLER, Judith E., 1944- 301.5'7
Artists in offices : an ethnography of an academic art scene / Judith E. Adler. New Brunswick, N.J. : Transaction Books, c1978. Includes index. Bibliography: p. [NX180.S6A27] 78-55941 ISBN 0-87855-281-2 : 16.95
1. California Institute of the Arts. 2. Arts and society—United States. 3. Arts—Study and teaching (Higher)—United States. 4. Arts, Modern—20th century—United States. I. Title.

California. University. Bancroft Library.

CALIFORNIA. University. Bancroft Library. 091'.0973
A guide to the manuscript collections, edited by Dale L. Morgan and George P. Hammond. Berkeley, Published for the Bancroft Library by the University of California Press, 1963- v. 27 cm. (Bancroft Library publications. Bibliographical series) Vol. 2- edited by G. P. Hammond. Contents.Contents.—v. 1. Pacific and Western manuscripts (except California)—v. 2. Manuscripts relating chiefly to Mexico and Central America. [Z6621.C159] 63-16986 ISBN 0-520-01991-1 (v. 2) 20.00 (v. 2)
1. California. University. Bancroft Library. 2. Manuscripts—California—Berkeley—Catalogs. 3. America—History—Sources—Bibliography—Catalogs. I. Morgan, Dale Lowell, 1914- ed. II. Hammond, George Peter, 1896- ed. III. Title. IV. Series: California. University. Bancroft Library. Bancroft Library publications. Bibliographical series

California. University. Institute of Creative Arts.

CALIFORNIA. University, Santa Barbara. Art Galleries. 730'.9794
The Institute of Creative Arts: a traveling exhibition of painting and sculpture by members of the Institute of Creative Arts of the University of California. Organized by the Art Galleries, University of California, Santa Barbara. [Santa Barbara, c1969] [49] p. (chiefly illus. (part col.)) 22 x 23 cm. Catalogue. [N330.C25C3] 71-626050
1. California. University. Institute of Creative Arts. 2. Art—Exhibitions. I. Title.

California. University. Press.

GOUDY, Frederic William, 1865-1947. 686.2'24
Typologia : studies in type design & type making, with comments on the invention of typography, the first types, legibility, and fine printing / Frederic W. Goudy. Berkeley : University of California Press, 1977. xviii, 170 p. : ill. ; 24 cm. Reprint of the 1940 ed. published by University of California, Berkeley. [Z250.A2G6 1977] 78-305196 ISBN 0-520-03308-6 : 15.00
1. California. University. Press. 2. Type and type-founding—History. 3. Printing—History. 4. Printing—Specimens. I. Title. BIP

California. University, Santa Barbara. Art Gallery.

PIERSON, Conway, 1927- 730'.924
Conway Pierson; an exhibition of recent

SUBJECT INDEX CALLIGRAPHY — EXHIBITIONS.

work in ceramics and bronze, October 5 to November 5, 1967, the Art Gallery, University of California, Santa Barbara. [Santa Barbara, Calif., 1967] 1 v. (chiefly illus., part col., port.) 26 cm. [NK4210.P52A43] 67-65564
1. California. University, Santa Barbara. Art Gallery. I. Title.

California. University, Santa Barbara. Dept. of Art—Alumni.

RECENT works by 709'.794'91
Master of Fine Arts graduates of UCSB. Juror: Gerald Nordland. [Santa Barbara, Santa Barbara Museum of Art, 1974] [72] p. illus. 28 cm. Exhibition held May 11-June 9, 1974 at the Santa Barbara Museum of Art. [N6512.R38] 74-180240
1. California. University, Santa Barbara. Dept. of Art—Alumni. 2. Art, American—Exhibitions. 3. Art, Modern—20th century—United States. I. Nordland, Gerald. II. California. University, Santa Barbara. III. Santa Barbara, Calif. Museum of Art.

California, University. University at Los Angeles. Art Galleries.

ARCHIPENKO, Alexander, 1887-1964 709'.73
Alexander Archipenko [Los Angeles] Ritchie [1967] 80p. illus. (pt. col.) ports. 23x29cm. Catalogue of a memorial exhibition, org. by the UCLA Art Galleries, traveling to 11 museums across the country, 1967-1969. Bibl. [NB237.A7A42] 67-17777 9.75
1. California, University. University at Los Angeles. Art Galleries. I. Title.
Distributed by Lane, Menlo Park, Calif.

California Watercolor Society.

MOURE, Nancy Dustin Wall. 759.13
The California Water Color Society: prize winners 1931-1954, index to exhibitions 1921-1954. Los Angeles, 1973. [78] p. 28 cm. (Publications in Southern California art, no. 1) Includes bibliographies. [ND1808.M68] 73-174909
1. California Watercolor Society. 2. Watercolors, American—Exhibitions—Indexes. 3. Painters, American—Directories. I. Title. II. Series.

Callahan, Harry M.

CALLAHAN, Harry M. 779'.092'4
Callahan / edited with an introduction by John Szarkowski. Millerton, N.Y. : Aperture, c1976. 201 p. : chiefly ill. ; 32 cm. Exhibition of photos. held at the Museum of Modern Art, New York, Dec. 2, 1976-Feb. 8, 1977. Bibliography: p. 197-199. [TR654.C3 1976] 76-42104 ISBN 0-912334-75-4 : 30.00
1. Callahan, Harry M. 2. Photography, Artistic. 3. Photographers—United States—Biography. I. Szarkowski, John. II. New York (City). Museum of Modern Art. **BIP**

Callahan, Kenneth, 1905—

CALLAHAN, Kenneth, 1905- 759.13
Kenneth Callahan: universal voyage. Edited by Michael R. Johnson. Introd. by James Harithas. Seattle, Published for the Henry Art Gallery by the University of Washington Press [1973] 79, [1] p. illus. (part col.) 29 cm. (Index of art in the Pacific Northwest, no. 6) Bibliography: p. [80] [ND237.C19J63 1973] 73-96 ISBN 0-295-95270-9 11.95
1. Callahan, Kenneth, 1905- I. Johnson, Michael R., ed. II. Title. III. Series.

MILES, Emily Winthrop. 759.13
An exhibition of paintings and drawings by Kenneth Callahan. from the collection of Emily Winthrop Miles and lent by her for an extended tour of American museums, 1961-1964. [New York, c1960] unpaged (chiefly illus.) 26cm. [ND237.C19M4] 61-1414
1. Caliahan, Kenneth, 1906- I. Title.

Callaway Gardens.

PIRTLE, Caleb. 917.58'466
Callaway Gardens: the unending season. Photos. by Gerald Crawford. [Birmingham, Ala., Southern Living Books [1973] 88 p. illus. 29 cm. [SB466.U7C36] 73-80502 5.95
1. Callaway Gardens. I. Title.

Callender, Bessie (Stough) 1889-1951.

CALLENDER, Harold, 1892- 927.3
Fun tomorrow, the story of an artist and of a way life. New York, Priv. print., 1953. 164p. illus. 24cm. [NB237.C33C3] 53-10157
1. Callender, Bessie (Stough) 1889-1951. I. Title.

Calligraphers, Chinese.

CH'EN, Chih-mai, 1908- 741.0951
Chinese calligraphers and their art. Melbourne, Univ. Pr.; iLondon, New York, Cambridge Uni. Pr. [1966. i.e. 1967] xx, 286p. illus. 28cm. [Z44.C4623] 65-22861 22.50
1. Calligraphers, Chinese. 2. Calligraphy, Chinese. I. Title. **BIP**

Calligraphers—Great Britain—Biography.

JOHNSTON, Priscilla, 1910- 745.6'1'0924 B
Edward Johnston / by Priscilla Johnston. 2nd ed. London : Barrie and Jenkins, 1976. 316 p., [20] p. of plates : ill., facsims., ports. ; 23 cm. Text on lining papers. Includes index. Bibliography: p. [14] [NK3631.J63J63 1976] 76-377127 ISBN 0-214-20253-4 : £5.25. ISBN 0-214-20295-X pbk.
1. Johnston, Edward, 1872-1944. 2. Calligraphers—Great Britain—Biography. **BIP**

Calligraphy.

ANDERSON, Donald M. 741
The art of written forms; the theory and practice of calligraphy [by] Donald M. Anderson. New York, Holt, Rinehart and Winston [1969] ix, 358 p. illus., facsims., maps. 28 cm. "Notes and bibliography": p. 329-344. [Z40.A5] 68-21782 ISBN 0-306-86253- 10.95
1. Calligraphy. I. Title.

ANGEL, Marie. 745.6'197
The art of calligraphy : a practical guide / Marie Angel. New York : Scribner, c1977. 120 p. : ill. ; 24 cm. Bibliography: p. 119-120. [NK3600.A68] 77-5782 ISBN 0-684-15068-9 : 9.95
1. Calligraphy. I. Title. **BIP**

BAKER, Arthur. 745.6'1
Calligraphic alphabets / by Arthur Baker. New York : Dover Publications, 1974. 153 p. : all ill. ; 29 cm. (Dover pictorial archive series) [Z43.B16] 74-82203 ISBN 0-486-21045-6 pbk. : 3.50
1. Calligraphy. 2. Alphabets. I. Title. **BIP**

BAKER, Arthur. 745.6'1
Calligraphy. New York, Dover Publications [1973] 155 p. illus. 21 x 29 cm. (Dover pictorial archive series) [Z43.B17] 72-93759 ISBN 0-486-22895-9 3.50 (pbk.)
1. Calligraphy.

CARTNER, William Carruthers. 741
The young calligrapher; a how-it-is done book of penmanship, by William C. Cartner. New York, F. Warne [1969] 57 p. illus. (part col.), facsims. 29 cm. [Z43.C3 1969b] 70-79874 3.95
1. Calligraphy. I. Title.

DROGIN, Marc. 745.6'197
Medieval calligraphy, its history & techniques / Marc Drogin. Montclair, N.J. : Allanheld & Schram, [1978] p. cm. Includes indexes. Bibliography: p. [Z43.A3D76] 77-25436 ISBN 0-8390-0211-4 : 25.00
1. Calligraphy. I. Title.

*EAGER, Fred 741.07
Guide to italic handwriting. Rev. ed. Caledonia, N. Y., Italimuse [1967] 80p. illus. 28cm. 3.95 pap.,
1. Calligraphy. 2. Handwriting, Italic. I. Title.

GILLON, Edmund Vincent, comp. 745.6'1
Pictorial calligraphy and ornamentation; 86 plates selected by Edmund V. Gillon, Jr. from the work of Pedro Diaz Morante, Isiuliano Sellari, and Leopardo Antonozzi. [Magnolia, Mass.] [Peter Smith] [1973, c1972] vi, 86 p. illus. 22 x 29 cm. (Dover paperback rebound) (Dover pictorial archive ser.) [NK3630.G5] 73-188809 ISBN 0-486-22788-X 5.00
1. Calligraphy. 2. Lettering. 3. Decoration and ornament. I. Diaz, Morante, Pedro. II. Sellari, Isiuliano. III. Antonozzi, Leopardo. IV. Title. **BIP**

GOINES, David Lance. 745.6'1
An introduction to the elements of calligraphy [by] Goines. 2d ed. [Berkeley, Calif., Saint Heironymous Press, 1970] [28] p. illus. 45 cm. Bibliography: p. [28] [Z43.A2G6 1970] 78-20433
1. Calligraphy. I. Title. **BIP**

†GOLDSTEIN, Sanford. 811'.5'4
This tanka world / Sanford Goldstein ; calligraphy, Akiko Minami. West Lafayette, Ind. : Distributed by Sparrow Press, c1977. ii, 53 p. ; 22 cm. "A Purdue Poets Cooperative book." [PS3557.O424T5] 77-365512 pbk. : 2.95
I. Title.
Publisher's address: 103 Waldron St., West Lafayette, Ind. 47906

GOURDIE, Tom. 745.6'197
Calligraphic styles / Tom Gourdie. New York : Taplinger Pub. Co., c1979. 106 p. : ill. ; 25 cm. "A Pentalic book." [Z43.G66] 79-52316 ISBN 0-8008-1181-X pbk. : 6.95
1. Calligraphy. I. Title. **BIP**

JEFFARES, Katherine. 745.6'197
Calligraphy : the art of beautiful writing / by Katherine Jeffares. No. Hollywood, Calif. : Wilshire Book Co., c1978. 73 p. : ill. ; 28 cm. [Z43.J485] 78-52137 ISBN 0-87980-356-8 pbk. : 5.00
1. Calligraphy. I. Title.

JOHNSTON, Edward, 1872-1944. 745.6'1
Formal penmanship and other papers. Edited by Heather Child. [1st ed.] New York, Hastings House [1971] 156 p. illus. 29 cm. (Visual communication books) [Z43.J776] 75-159047 ISBN 0-8038-2282-0 17.50
1. Calligraphy. I. Title.

SHEPHERD, Margaret. 745.6'1
Learning calligraphy : a book of lettering, design and history / Margaret Shepherd. New York : Collier Books, 1978, c1977. vi, 121 p. : ill. ; 28 cm. [Z43.S544 1978] 78-18419 ISBN 0-02-015550-6 : 7.95
1. Calligraphy. 2. Lettering. I. Title. **BIP**

STUDLEY, Vance. 745.6'1
Calligraphy : appreciation and form / Vance Studley. Dubuque, Iowa : Kendall/Hunt Pub. Co., c1976. vii, 97 p. : ill. ; 22 x 28 cm. Bibliography: p. 96-97. [Z43.S9] 75-30447 ISBN 0-8403-1309-8 : 5.95
1. Calligraphy. I. Title.

SVAREN, Jacqueline. 745.6'197
Written letters : 22 alphabets for calligraphers / written out by Jacqueline Svaren. Freeport, Me. : Bond Wheelwright Co., [1975] vi, 55 p. ; 33 cm. Bibliography: p. 54-55. [NK3600.S95] 75-312673 ISBN 0-87027-161-X pbk. : 8.95
1. Calligraphy. 2. Alphabets. I. Title. **BIP**

Calligraphy—America—Exhibitions.

DOYLE, Gerald P. 745.6'1'0740164145
Calligraphy on the Spanish borderlands : an exhibition organized by the Beaumont Art Museum and made possible through the generous assistance of the Mobil Foundation, Inc., and the Texas Commission on the Arts and Humanities and the National Endowment for the Arts, a Federal agency, Beaumont Art Museum, January 9-February 15, 1976, San Jacinto Museum of History, March 2-April 30, 1976 / Gerald P. Doyle. Beaumont, Tex. : The Museum, c1976. 48 p. : ill. ; 31 cm. Bibliography: p. 46. [Z43.D69] 76-1263
1. Calligraphy—America—Exhibitions. 2. Calligraphy—Southwest, New—Exhibitions. 3. Calligraphy—Spain—Exhibitions. I. Beaumont Art Museum. II. San Jacinto Museum of History, San Jacinto Monument, Tex. III. Title.

Calligraphy, Chinese.

CHIANG, Yee, 1903- 745.6'199'51
Chinese calligraphy; an introduction to its aesthetic and technique. With a foreword by Sir Herbert Read. 3d ed. rev. and enl. Cambridge, Mass., Harvard University Press, 1973. xx, 250 p. illus. 26 cm. Half title in Chinese. Bibliography: p. 240-241. [NK3634.A2C465 1973] 72-75400 ISBN 0-674-12225-9 12.00
1. Calligraphy, Chinese.

ECKE Tseng, Yu-ho, 1923- 745.6'19'951
Chinese calligraphy. Co-published by the Philadelphia Museum of Art and Boston Book & Art, Publisher. [Philadelphia] 1971. 1 v. (unpaged) illus. 31 cm. Catalogue of an exhibition, Philadelphia Museum of Art. [NK3634.A2E25] 75-161453 15.00
1. Calligraphy, Chinese. I. Philadelphia Museum of Art. II. Title.

LAI, T'ien-ch'ang. 745.6'199'51
Chinese calligraphy : an introduction / T. C. Lai ; introd. by Jiu-fong L. Chang. Seattle : University of Washington Press, 1975, c1973. xvii, 252 p. : ill. ; 23 cm. Bibliography: p. xvii. [NK3634.A2L34 1975] 74-31264 ISBN 0-295-95340-3 : 10.00. ISBN 0-295-95381-0 pbk. : 4.95
1. Calligraphy, Chinese. I. Title. **BIP**

LEDDERHOSE, Lothar. 745.6'199'51
Mi Fu and the classical tradition of Chinese calligraphy / Lothar Ledderose. Princeton, N.J. : Princeton University Press, c1978. p. cm. Portions of this work originally presented as the author's Habilitationsschrift, Cologne University. Includes index. Bibliography: p. [NK3634.A2L43] 78-51177 ISBN 0-691-03937-2 : 25.00
1. Mi, Fu, 1051-1107—Influence. 2. Calligraphy, Chinese. I. Title. **BIP**

WANG, Chi-yuan, 1895- 745.6'199'51
Essentials of Chinese calligraphy / Wang Chi-Yuan, with Ruth Martin. New York : Pitman, c1974. 48 p. : ill. ; 20 x 26 cm. (The Pitman art series ; 75) [NK3634.A2W26] 73-92321
1. Calligraphy, Chinese. I. Martin, Ruth. II. Title.

Calligraphy — Exhibitions.

BALTIMORE, Museum of Art. 741
2,000 years of calligraphy; a three-part exhibition organized by the Baltimore Museum of Art, the Peabody Institute Library and the Walters Art Gallery, June 6- July 18, 1965. A comprehensive catalog. Comp. by Dorothy E. Miner, Victor I. Carlson, P. W. Filby Baltimore [Walters Art Gallery, c.]1965. 201p. illus., facsims. 28cm. [Z43.A2B3] 65-22689 13.00; 9.00 bds., pap.,
1. Calligraphy—Exhibitions. I. Miner, Dorothy Eugenia, comp. II. Carlson, Victor I., comp. III. Filby, P. W., comp. IV. Peabody Institute, Baltimore. Library. V. Walters Art Gallery, Baltimore. VI. Title.

BROWN University. Annmary Brown Memorial. 411
The working calligrapher and lettering artist; an international exhibition of contemporary design. [Providence?] 1961. 1 v. (unpaged) facsims. 28 cm. Cover title. [Z43.A2B75] 66-40191
1. Calligraphy — Exhibitions. 2. Writing in art. I. Title.

MARYLAND Institute, College of Art. 745.6'1
Modern calligraphy: American & British; [exhibition] January 22-February 10, 1973, Maryland Institute, College of Art, Mt. Royal Gallery. Baltimore [1973] 10 p. 29 cm. Cover title. Catalog. [Z43.M36 1973] 74-191276

1. Caligraphy—Exhibitions. I. Title.

Calligraphy—History.

CHILD, Heather. 745.6'1'0904
Calligraphy today / [by] Heather Child. Revised ed. London : Studio Vista, 1976. 112 p. : chiefly facsims., map, plan ; 29 cm. Includes index. Bibliography: p. 109-111. [Z43.C55 1976] 77-355585 ISBN 0-289-70736-6 : £4.50
1. Calligraphy—History. I. Title. BIP

Calligraphy, Islamic.

ISLAMIC 745.6'199'27
calligraphics. London : Merrion Press, 1976. [16] p. : chiefly facsims ; 17 cm. [NK3636.5.A2185] 77-355555 ISBN 0-903560-14-3 : £1.20
1. Calligraphy, Islamic.

KHATIBI, Abdelkabir, 745.6'199'27
1938-
The splendour of Islamic calligraphy / Abdelkebir Khatibi, Mohammed Sijelmassi. London : Thames and Hudson, c1976. 254 p. : ill. (some col.) ; 31 cm. Translation of L'art calligraphique arabe. Bibliography: p. 250-251. [NK3636.5.A2K4613] 77-354237 ISBN 0-500-23252-0 : £18.00
1. Calligraphy, Islamic. I. Sijelmassi, Mohamed, joint author. II. Title.

KHATIBI, Abdelkebir, 745.6'199'27
1938-
The splendour of Islamic calligraphy / Abdelkebir Khatibi, Mohammed Sijelmassi ; [translated from the French by James Hughes]. New York : Rizzoli, 1977, c1976. 254 p. : 174 ill. (54 col.) ; 31 cm. Translation of L'art calligraphique arabe. Errata slip inserted. Bibliography: p. 250-251. [NK3636.5.A2K4613 1976b] 76-28285 ISBN 0-8478-0066-0 : 45.00
1. Calligraphy, Islamic. I. Sijelmassi, Mohamed, joint author. II. Title.

Calligraphy, Islamic—Exhibitions.

LINGS, 745.6'0917'67107402142
Martin.
The Qur'an : catalogue of an exhibition of Qur'an manuscripts at the British Library, 3 April-15 August 1976 / [by] Martin Lings, Yasin Hamid Safadi. [London] : World of Islam Publishing Co. Ltd for the British Library, 1976. 98 p., xxiv p. of plates : facsims. (some col.), map ; 26 cm. Includes index. Bibliography: p. 95-96. [ND1457.I82L64] 76-378960 ISBN 0-905035-20-8. ISBN 0-905035-21-6 pbk.
1. Koran—Illustrations. 2. Calligraphy, Islamic—Exhibitions. 3. Illumination of books and manuscripts—Exhibitions. I. Safadi, Yasin Hamid, joint author. II. British Library. III. Title.

WELCH, Anthony. 745.6'199'27
Calligraphy in the arts of the Muslim world / by Anthony Welch. Austin : University of Texas Press, c1979. p. cm. "Catalogue of an exhibition shown in Asia House Gallery in the winter of 1979 as activity of the Asia Society." Bibliography: p. [NK3636.5.A2W44] 78-11796 ISBN 0-292-73818-8 : 25.00
1. Calligraphy, Islamic—Exhibitions. I. Asia House Gallery, New York. II. Asia Society. III. Title. BIP

Calligraphy, Japanese.

NAKATA, Yujiro, 745.6'199'52
1905-
The art of Japanese calligraphy. Translated by Alan Woodhull in collaboration with Armins. Nikovskis. [1st English ed.] New York, Weatherhill [1973] 172 p. illus. (part col.) 24 cm. (The Heibonsha survey of Japanese art) Translation of Sho. [NK3637.A2N3213 1973] 72-92096 ISBN 0-8348-1013-1 8.95
1. Calligraphy, Japanese. I. Title. II. Series. BIP

Callot, Jacques, 1592?-1635.

AVERILL, Esther Holden. 769'.924
Eyes on the world; the story & work of Jacques Callot: his gypsies, beggars, festivals, "Miseries of war", and other famous etchings and engravings, together with an account of his days, by Esther Averill. New York, Funk & Wagnalls [1969] x, 166 p. illus., port. 31 cm. Bibliography: p. 163. [NE650.C3A94 1969] 68-13077 6.95
1. Callot, Jacques, 1592-1635. I. Title.

BROWN University. Dept. 769'.924
of Art.
Jacques Callot, 1592-1635. [Exhibition held] at the Museum of Art, Rhode Island School of Design, Providence, Rhode Island, Mar. 5 through Apr. 11, 1970. [Providence, 1970] 1 v. (unpaged) illus. 21 x 22 cm. Includes bibliographical references. [NE650.C3B75] 76-566770
1. Callot, Jacques, 1592-1635. 2. Prints—Exhibitions. I. Rhode Island School of Design, Providence. Museum of Art.

CALLOT, Jacques, 1592- 769'.92'4
1635.
Callot's etchings / edited by Howard Daniel. New York : Dover Publications, 1974. xxxvi, [137] p. : 338 ill. ; 32 cm. Bibliography: p. xxiv-xxv. [NE2049.5.C3D36] 73-81506 ISBN 0-486-23081-3 : 12.00 ISBN 0-486-23073-2 pbk. : 6.50
1. Callot, Jacques, 1592-1635. I. Daniel, Howard, 1911- ed. II. Title. BIP

DUNBAR, John Raine, 1911- 769.92
The combat at the barrier; an account by John R. Dunbar. With reproductions of Callot's etchings. Pasadena, Calif., G. Dahlstrom, 1967. 36 p. illus. 33 cm. 300 copies printed. Bibliography: p. 36. [NE2165.C3D8] 67-3783
1. Callot, Jacques, 1592-1635. I. Title. BIP

FAITHORNE, William, 1616- 760
1691.
The art of graveing and etching. New introd. by Jacob Kainen. New York, Da Capo Press, 1970. 1 v. (unpaged) illus., facsim. 19 cm. (Da Capo Press series in graphic art, v. 9) Reprint of the 1662 ed. [NE1760.F3 1970] 68-54841 ISBN 0-306-71049-8
1. Callot, Jacques, 1592?-1635. 2. Bosse, Abraham, 1602-1676. 3. Engraving—Early works to 1800. 4. Engraving—Technique. 5. Etching—Technique. I. Title. BIP

KAHAN, Gerald. 769'.92'4
Jacques Callot : artist of the theatre / Gerald Kahan. Athens : University of Georgia Press, c1976. xiii, 118 p. : ill. ; 22 x 29 cm. Bibliography: p. 117-118. [NE2049.5.C3K33] 73-76787 ISBN 0-8203-0345-3 : 15.00
1. Callot, Jacques, 1592-1635. 2. Theater in art. BIP

UNITED States. National 769'.92'4
Gallery of Art.
Jacques Callot prints & related drawings / H. Diane Russell, Jeffrey Blanchard, theater section ; John Krill, technical appendix. Washington : National Gallery of Art, 1975. xxiv, 351 p. : ill. ; 22 x 29 cm. "Exhibition dates at the National Gallery of Art: June 29-September 14, 1975." Includes index. Bibliography: p. 342-344. [NE650.C3U52 1975] 75-14429
1. Callot, Jacques, 1592-1635. 2. Artists' preparatory studies—Exhibitions. I. Russell, Helen Diane. II. Blanchard, Jeffrey. III. Title.

Calvert, Edward, 1799-1883.

LISTER, Raymond George 759.42
Edward Calvert. London, G. Bell [Chester Springs, Pa., Dufour, 1965, c.1962] 116p. illus. 23cm. Bibl. [N6797.C3L5] 62-53442 6.95
1. Calvert, Edward, 1799-1883. I. Title.

Cambiaso, Luca, known as Luchetto da Genova, 1527-1585.

CAMBIASO, Luca, known 741.9'45
as Luchetto da Genova, 1527-1585.
The Genoese Renaissance, grace and geometry: paintings and drawings by Luca Cambiaso from the Suida-Manning Collection, by Bertina Suida Manning and Robert L. Manning. [Houston, Museum of Fine Arts, 1974] 77 p. 52 illus. 25 cm. Catalog of the exhibition held Jan. 14-Mar. 10, 1974 at the Museum of Fine Arts, Houston, Tex. Includes bibliographical references. [NC257.C264H68] 73-94302
1. Cambiaso, Luca, known as Luchetto da Genova, 1527-1585. 2. Manning, Robert L.—Art collections. 3. Suida Manning, Bertina—Art collections. I. Houston, Tex. Museum of Fine Arts. II. Title.

Cambridge Drawing Society.

CLAY, Anne C. 741'.06'24259
A picture of the Cambridge Drawing Society. Cambridge, Cambridge Drawing Society, 1969. 8 p. illus. 25 cm. [NC1.C353C55] 74-174262 ISBN 0-9501324-0-3 £0.235
1. Cambridge Drawing Society. I. Title.

Cambridge, Eng.—City planning.

CAMBRIDGE, Eng. 711'.59'0942659
Environment Committee.
St Matthews general improvement area declaration report / [Cambridge City Council Environment Committee. [Cambridge] : [The Committee], 1976. [2], 16 [i.e. 24] p. : ill., maps, plans ; 21 x 30 cm. Cover title. [HT169.G72C2933] 77-369054 ISBN 0-902696-05-X : £0.30
1. Cambridge, Eng.—City planning. 2. City planning—England. 3. Architecture—England—Cambridge—Restoration and conservation. I. Title.

Cambridge, Eng.—Description—Guide-books.

BRITTAIN, Frederick. 914.25'9
Illustrated guide to Cambridge: based on the guide by Frank Rutter first published in 1922. 15th ed. fully revised. Cambridge, Heffer, [1967] 93 p. illus., col. plates (map). 18 1/2 cm. [DA690.C2B7 1967] 67-91842
1. Cambridge. University—Description. 2. Cambridge, Eng.—Description—Guide-books. I. Rutter, Frank Vane Phipson, 1876-1937. Guide to Cambridge. II. Title.

Cambridge Glass Company, Cambridge, Ohio.

CAMBRIDGE Glass 748.2'9171'92
Company, Cambridge, Ohio.
Catalogue of table glassware, lamps, barware, and novelties manufactured by the Cambridge Glass Company. [1st ed.]. [Cambridge, Ohio : H. Bennett, 1976] 106 p. : chiefly ill. ; 22 x 29 cm. Cover title: 1903 catalog of pressed and blown glass ware manufactured by the Cambridge Glass Co., Cambridge, O. Reprint of the 1903 ed. published by the Cambridge Glass Co., Cambridge, Ohio. Includes index. [NK5198.C28A43 1976] 76-362976
1. Cambridge Glass Company, Cambridge, Ohio. 2. Glassware—Ohio—Catalogs. I. Title: Catalogue of table glassware, lamps, barware, and novelties ... II. Title: 1903 catalog of pressed and blown glass ware ...

WELKER, Mary. 748.2'9171'92
Cambridge, Ohio, glass in color, by Mary and Lyle Welker and son Lynn. New Concord, Ohio [1969] [32] p. col. illus. 23 cm. [NK5112.W43] 75-8016 4.95
1. Cambridge Glass Company, Cambridge, O. 2. Glass, Colored. I. Welker, Lyle, joint author. II. Welker, Lynn, joint author. III. Title.

Cambridge, Mass. — Descr. — Views.

O'HARA, Tom. 917.444
Cambridge: candids and comments. Candids by Tom O'Hara: comments grave and gay by Newell Keyes. Watertown, Mass., N. Keyes [1966] 100 p. illus. 21 cm. [F74.C1O4] 66-7732
1. Cambridge, Mass. — Descr. — Views. I. Keyes, Newell. II. Title.

WHITEHILL, Walter 917.444034
Muir, 1905-
Cambridge. Photos. by Katherine [sic] Knowles. [Barre, Mass., Barre, c.1965] 1v. (unpaged) illus. 23cm. [F74.C1W55] 65-16657 5.00 bds.,
1. Cambridge, Mass.—Descr.—Views. I. Knowles, Katherine, illus. II. Title.

Cambridge, Mass.—Description—Views.

WESTMAN, Barbara 917.444
The beard and the braid; drawings of Cambridge. [New York, Crown Pubs., 1975, c1970] [36 p.] illus. (part col.) 23 x 27 cm. (A Barre Book) [F74.C1W47] 76-128388 ISBN 0-517-52112-1 2.50 (pbk.)
1. Cambridge, Mass.—Description—Views. I. Title.

WESTMAN, Barbara. 917.44'4
The beard and the braid; drawings of Cambridge, by Barbara Westman, with her own observations. Barre, Mass., Barre Publishers [1970] 35 p. illus. (part col.) 23 x 28 cm. [F74.C1W47] 76-128388 ISBN 0-8271-7014-9 6.95
1. Cambridge, Mass.—Description—Views. I. Title.

Cambridge. University. Corpus Christi College.

CAMBRIDGE. 737.4'938 s
University. Corpus Christi College.
The Lewis Collection in Corpus Christi College, Cambridge. London, Oxford University Press for the British Academy, 1972- v. illus. 39 cm. (Sylloge nummorum graecorum, v. 6) Includes index. Contents.Contents.—pt. 1. The Greek and Hellenistic coins (with Britain and Parthia) [CJ314.B7 vol. 6] [CJ315.G672] 737.4'938'0740259 74-174825 ISBN 0-19-725924-3 (v. 1) £8.00 (v. 1)
1. Cambridge. University. Corpus Christi College. 2. Lewis, Samuel Savage, 1836-1891—Coin collections. 3. Coins, Greek. I. Title. II. Series: British Academy, London (Founded 1901) Sylloge nummorum graecorum, v. 6

Cambridge. University—Description.

BRITTAIN, Frederick. 914.25'9
Illustrated guide to Cambridge: based on the guide by Frank Rutter first published in 1922. 15th ed. fully revised. Cambridge, Heffer, [1967] 93 p. illus., col. plates (map). 18 1/2 cm. [DA690.C2B7 1967] 67-91842
1. Cambridge. University—Description. 2. Cambridge, Eng.—Description—Guide-books. I. Rutter, Frank Vane Phipson, 1876-1937. Guide to Cambridge. II. Title.

Cambridge. University. Fitzwilliam Museum.

CAMBRIDGE. University. 708'.259
Fitzwilliam Museum.
Handbook to the Fitzwilliam Museum, Cambridge. (Revised ed.) Cambridge, Fitzwilliam Museum, 1971. vii, 87, xvi, (1) p. illus., facsim., plans, ports. 23 cm. [N1217.A63 1971] 73-156128 ISBN 0-85601-001-4 £0.25
I. Title.

EUROPEAN drawings 741.9'4'074013
from the Fitzwilliam : lent by the syndics of the Fitzwilliam Museum, University of Cambridge : organized and circulated by the International Exhibitions Foundation, 1976-1977 / introduction by Michael Jaffe. [Washington : International Exhibitions Foundation], c1976. xiv, 84 p., [61] leaves of plates : ill. ; 26 cm. "Participating museums: The Pierpont Morgan Library, New York, New York, Kimbell Art Museum, Fort Worth, Texas, The Baltimore Museum of Art, Baltimore, Maryland, The Minneapolis Institute of Arts, Minneapolis, Minnesota, Philadelphia Museum of Art, Philadelphia, Pennsylvania." Draft entries for the catalog prepared by M. Cormack and D. Robinson and edited by A. M. Jaffe. Includes index. [NC225.E97] 76-25622
1. Cambridge. University. Fitzwilliam Museum. 2. Drawing, European—Exhibitions. I. Jaffe, Andrew Michael. II. Cormack, Malcolm. III. Robinson, Duncan. IV. International Exhibitions Foundation. V. Pierpont Morgan Library, New York. BIP

1. Campaign insignia. I. Title.

BRISTOW, Dick. 737'.2
Presidential campaign items, 1789-1892. [Santa Cruz, California Political Items Co., 1973] 103 p. (chiefly illus.) 27 cm. [NK3669.B76] 73-88493 4.00
1. Campaign insignia. I. Title.

FORD, Marian A. 737'.2
Project '68; the presidential election of 1968 as seen through campaign pins, by Marian A. Ford. [Burbank, Calif., North Hollywood Print. Co., 1971] 1 v. (chiefly illus.) 28 cm. [NK3669.F67] 78-30655
1. Campaign insignia. 2. Presidents—U.S.—Election—1968. I. Title.

Campaign insignia—History.

WAGNER, Dale E., 1941- 737'.2
A concise history of American campaign graphics, 1789-1972 [by] Dale E. Wagner. Washington, Public Policy Research Associates [1972] 123 p. illus. 22 cm. Includes bibliographical references. [NK3669.W29] 72-169610
1. Campaign insignia—History. I. Title.

Campaign paraphernalia—United States.

KAHLER, James G. 745
Hail to the Chief; an illustrated guide to political Americana, by James G. Kahler. [1st ed.] Princeton, Pyne Press; [distributed by Scribner, New York] 1972. 143 p. illus. 24 cm. [NK3669.K33] 72-76869 ISBN 0-87861-018-9 8.95
1. Campaign paraphernalia—United States. I. Title.

WAGNER, Dale E., 1941- 737'.2
Presidential campaign memorabilia; a concise history, 1789-1972 [by] Dale E. Wagner. Washington, Public Policy Research Associates [1972] 223 p. illus. 21 cm. Bibliography: p. 198. [NK3669.W3] 72-183091
1. Campaign paraphernalia—United States. I. Title.

Campbell, Colin, d. 1729.

STUTCHBURY, Howard Edward. 720'.924
The architecture of Colen Campbell [by] Howard E. Stutchbury. Cambridge, Harvard University Press, 1967. xvi, 186 p. illus., facsims., plans. 26 cm. Bibliography: p. [170]-173. [NA997] 68-1443
1. Campbell, Colin, d. 1729. I. Title.

STUTCHBURY, Howard Edward. 720'.924
The architecture of Colen Campbell [by] Howard E. Stutchbury. Manchester, Manchester U. P., [196754. xvi, 186 p. front., 59 plates (incl. plans, facsims.). 251/2 cm. Bibliography: p. [170]-173. [NA997.C32S8] 67-114400
1. Campbell, Colin I. Title.

Campin, Robert, d. 1444.

FRINTA, Mojmir Svatopluk. 759.9493/1
The genius of Robert Campin [by] Mojmir S. Frinta. The Hague, Mouton, 1966. 123p. 73 illus. 26cm. (Studies in art, v. 1) Bibl. [ND673.C274F7] 65-24785 11.00
1. Campin, Robert, d. 1444. I. Title. II. Series.
American distributor: Humanities, New York. BIP

Camping.

MASON, Bernard Sterling, 1896-1953. 796.54 s
Camping crafts. Illus. by Frederic H. Kock. South Brunswick, A. S. Barnes [1973] 190 p. illus. 22 cm. (His Woodcrafts library, pt. 1) First published in 1939 as pt. 1 (p. 3-186) of the author's Woodcraft. Includes bibliographical references. [TT7.M37 pt. 1] [TT145] 796.54 72-9065 ISBN 0-498-01295-6 5.95
1. Camping. 2. Handicraft. I. Title. II. Series.

Campion, Edmund, 1540-1581.

FRENCH, Leonard, 1928- 704.947
The Campion paintings. Introd. and annotation of plates by Vincent Buckley. Melbourne, Grayflower Publications, [1962] 103 p. 35 col. plates. 29 cm. "Catalogue [of French's paintings] 1948-1962": p. 97-102. [ND1105.F67B8] 68-7985
1. Campion, Edmund, 1540-1581. I. Buckley, Vincent, ed. II. Title.

Camps.

WHITE, Charles Danville, 1875- 728.7
Camps and cottages: how to build them; with plans and diagrs. by the author. [Rev. ed.] New York, Crowell [1953] 280p. illus. 25cm. '3rd enlarged edition.'--Dust jacket. [NA8470.W5 1953] 53-7526
1. Camps. 2. Cottages. I. Title.

YOUNG Men's Christian Associations. National Commission on YMCA Camp Layouts, Buildings, and Facilities. 728.7
Developing camp sites and facilities. New York, Association Press [c.1960] 63p. illus., diagrs. 28cm. 60-6556 3.50 pap.,
1. Camps. 2. Log cabins. 3. Architecture—Designs and plans. I. Title.

Campus planning—India.

KANVINDE, Achyut, 1916- 711'.59
Campus design in India; experience of a developing nation [by] Achyut Kanvinde and H. James Miller. Topeka, Kan., Printed by Jostens/American Yearbook Co. [1969] 160 p. illus., maps, plans. 22 x 28 cm. "Sponsored by United States Agency for International Development contract AID/nesa 146 with Kansas State University, Manhattan." Bibliography: p. 159. [LB3223.K35] 75-629865 10.00
1. Campus planning—India. I. Miller, H. James, joint author. II. Title.

Campus planning—Texas.

WOOLF, J. R., 1924- 378.764 s
Space factors and space utilization values for use in meeting the facilities needs of Texas colleges and universities [by] J. R. Woolf. [Austin, Coordinating Board, Texas College and University System, 1971] 49 p. 29 cm. (Texas College and University System. Coordinating Board. CB study paper 12) Bibliography: p. 20. [LB2300.T48 no. 12] [LB3223.4.T4] 727'.3'09764 77-636784
1. Campus planning—Texas. 2. Classroom utilization. I. Title. II. Series: Texas. Coordinating Board, Texas College and University System. CB study paper 12

Canada in art.

BARBER, Philip, 1946- 741.9'71
The road home : sketches of rural Canada / Philip Barber ; text by Brian Swarbrick. Scarborough, Ont. : Prentice-Hall of Canada, c1976. [32] p., [62] leaves of plates : chiefly ill. ; 24 x 27 cm. [NC143.B37S93] 77-357606 ISBN 0-13-781559-X : 19.95
1. Barber, Philip, 1946- 2. Canada in art. I. Swarbrick, Brian, 1929- II. Title.
Distributed by Prentice-Hall, Englewood Cliffs, N.J. BIP

BELL, Michael, comp. 758
Painters in a new land. [Greenwich, Conn.] New York Graphic Society [1973] 224 p. illus. 32 cm. Bibliography: p. 220. [ND1841.B44 1973] 73-79998 ISBN 0-8212-0581-1 22.50
1. Canada in art. 2. Water-colors, Canadian. 3. Drawings, Canadian. I. Title.

HARPER, J. Russell. 759.11
William G. R. Hind / J. Russell Harper. Ottawa : National Gallery of Canada, 1976. 91 p. : chiefly ill. (some col.) ; 24 cm. (Canadian artists series ; no. 2) Bibliography: p. 91. [ND1843.H56H37] 77-366096 ISBN 0-88884-273-2
1. Hind, William George Richardson, 1833-1888. 2. Canada in art. I. Hind, William George Richardson, 1833-1888. II. Title. III. Series.

KURELEK, William, 1927- 759.11
Kurelek country / William Kurelek. Boston : Houghton Mifflin, 1975. p. cm. [ND249.K85A49 1975] 75-17697 ISBN 0-395-21971-X : 20.00
1. Kurelek, William, 1927- 2. Canada in art. I. Title.

Canada, Northern, in art.

SCHOONOVER, Frank Earle, 1877-1972. 760'.092'4
The edge of the wilderness : a portrait of the Canadian North / Frank E. Schoonover ; edited by Cortlandt Schoonover. 1st U.S. ed. Secausus [i.e. Secaucus] N.J. : Derbibooks, 1974. 166 p. : ill. (some col.) ; 32 cm. Contents.Contents.—From the day book of the winter expedition of 1903-1904.—From the day book of the summer expedition of 1911.—The Canadian stories: The edge of the wilderness. Breaking trail. The fur harvesters. Bringing the outdoors in. The snow baby.—The Canadian illustrations. [ND237.S4338S36 1974b] 75-312671 ISBN 0-89009-026-2 : 25.00
1. Schoonover, Frank Earle, 1877-1972. 2. Canada, Northern, in art. 3. Indians of North America—Canada, Northern—Pictorial works. 4. Canada, Northern—Description and travel. I. Title.

Canaday, Molly Morpeth, 1903-1971.

CANADAY, Frank H., 1896-1976. 759.9931
Triumph in color : the life and art of Molly Morpeth Canaday / Frank H. Canaday ; with art commentary by Janet Paul. Canaan, N.H. : Phoenix Pub., c1977. vii, 152 p. : ill. (some col.) ; 29 cm. Includes index. [ND1108.C36C36] 76-30866 ISBN 0-914016-38-5 : 20.00
1. Canaday, Molly Morpeth, 1903-1971. 2. Canaday, Molly Morpeth, 1903-1971. 3. Painters—New Zealand—Biography. I. Title. BIP

Canadian wit and humor, Pictorial.

MACPHERSON, Duncan Ian, 1924- 741.5'971
Macpherson editorial cartoons, 1976. Toronto : Star Reader Service, 1976. [130] p. : all ill. ; 24 cm. Cover title. [NC1449.M3A52] 77-374600
1. Macpherson, Duncan Ian, 1924- 2. Canadian wit and humor, Pictorial. I. Title.

Canal, Antonio, called Canaletto, 1697-1768.

BARCHAM, William L. 759.5
The imaginary view scenes of Antonio Canaletto / William L. Barcham. New York : Garland Pub., 1977. xxix, 345, xiv p. : ill. ; 21 cm. (Outstanding dissertations in the fine arts) Originally presented as the author's thesis, New York University, 1974. Bibliography: p. i-xiv (3d group). [ND623.C2B37 1977] 76-23603 ISBN 0-8240-2677-2 lib.bdg. : 45.00
1. Canal, Antonio, called Canaletto, 1697-1768. 2. Landscape in art. 3. Venice in art. I. Title. II. Series. BIP

CANAL, Antonio, called Canaletto, 1697-1768. 760'.0924
Canaletto: paintings, drawings, and etchings selected and introduced by Gregory Martin. Boston, Newbury Books, 1970. [14] p., 62 plates (part col.) port. 22 x 30 cm. [ND623.C2M3 1970] 72-125858
I. Martin, Gregory.

CANAL, Antonio, called Canaletto, 1697-1768. 741.945
Canaletto; selected drawings annotated by Terisio Pignatti. [Translated from the Italian by Stella Rudolph] University Park, Pennsylvania State University Press [1970] 19, [21] p., 65 plates (part fold., part col.) 44 cm. Bibliography: p. [19] (2d group) [NC257.C27P4913] 74-104778
I. Pignatti, Terisio, 1920-

CANAL, Antonio, called Canaletto, 1697-1768. 741.945
Drawings by Canaletto, by Vittorio Moschini. New York, Dover Publications [1969, c1963] 21, [65] p. 72 illus. 28 cm. (The Great masters of drawing) "Unabridged and slightly altered republication of the English language edition of the work first published ... 1963." Bibliography: p. 15. [NC1155.C23M613] 68-20572 1.75
I. Moschini, Vittorio. II. Title. BIP

CANAL, Antonio, called Canaletto, 1697-1768. 769'.924
The etchings of Canaletto, by Jacob Kainen. Washington, Smithsonian Press, 1967. 1 v. (unpaged), 30 illus. 20 x 25 cm. (Smithsonian publication 4676) Includes bibliography. [NE2180.C3K3] 67-19731
I. Kainen, Jacob.

CANAL, Antonio, called Canaletto, 1697-1768. 759.5
Canaletto, by F. J. B. Watson. London, P. Elek [dist. Chester Springs, Pa., Dufour, 1964] 21p. illus., 31 plates (14 col.) 39cm. (Master painters, 1) Bibl. A50 12.50
I. Watson, F. J. B. II. Title. III. Series.

THE Circle of Canaletto: 759.5
a special exhibition, sponsored by GAC Corporation and its Allentown units, GAC Finance Inc. and Stuyvesant Insurance Group, February 21-March 21, 1971, Allentown Art Museum. [Allentown? Pa., 1971] [52] p. illus. 15 x 26 cm. [ND621.V5C54] 72-198130
1. Canal, Antonio, called Canaletto, 1697-1768. 2. Paintings, Venetian—Exhibitions. 3. Venice in art. I. Allentown, Pa. Art Museum.

CONSTABLE, William George, 1887- 759.5
Canaletto: Giovanni Antonio Canal, 1697-1768; 2v. [New York] Oxford [c.]1962[ ] 2v. (xiv, 663p.) 184 plates (incl. facsim.) 26cm. Bibl. 62-1558 32.60 set,
I. Canal, Antonio, called Canaletto, 1697-1768. II. Title.

CONSTABLE, William George, 1887- 759.5
Canaletto : Giovanni Antonio Canal 1697-1768 / by W. G. Constable. 2d ed. / rev. by J. G. Links. Oxford [Eng.] ; New York : Clarendon Press, 1976. 2 v. (x, 723 p., [117] leaves of plates) : ill. ; 26 cm. Vol. 2: Catalogue raisonne. Includes indexes. Bibliography: v. 1, p. 180-186. [ND623.C2C6 1976] 77-359771 ISBN 0-19-817324-5 : 88.00
1. Canal, Antonio, called Canaletto, 1697-1768. I. Links, J. G. II. Title.
Dist. by Oxford University Press, NY NY

PILO, Giuseppe Maria 759.5
Canaletto. New York, Barnes & Noble [1962, c.1961] 90p. illus. (pt. col.) 18cm. (Barnes &noble art ser.) 62-52813 .75 pap.,
I. Title.

Cancellations (Philately)

LOSO, Foster William, 1902- 383.22
20th century United States fancy cancelations [by] Foster W. Loso [and] Heyliger de Windt. Thunderbolt Elizabeth? N.J. 1952] 162 p. illus. 27 cm. [HE6183.L58] 52-27086
1. Cancellations [Philately] 2. Postage-stamps—U. S. I. Title.

LUFF, Moe, 1911- 383.22
Catalog of United States postal slogan cancels. New York, 1953. 96p. illus. 22cm. Published in 1950 under title: United States postal slogan cancels. [HE6183.L8 1953] 53-2080
1. Cancellations (Philately) 2. Postmarks—U. S. I. Title.

LUFF, Moe, 1911- 383.22
United States postal slogan cancels. New York, Call Business Service, 1950. 54p. illus. 22cm. [HE6183.L8] 52-18175
1. Cancellations (Philately) 2. Postmarks—U. S. I. Title.

STRITE, Richard K 383.22
Catalogue of United Nations first flight covers. Williston Park, N.Y. [c1961] 58 p. illus. 23 cm. [HE6183.S815] 62-3596
1. Cancellations (Philately) 2. Air mail stamps — Catalogs. I. Title. II. Title: United Nations first flight covers.

TROUT, Horace Q., ed. 383.22973
Specialists' guide to bureau print precancels. 2d ed. Listings complete

through March 6, 1965. Horace Q. Trout, editor. Winter Park, Fla., G. W. Nobel, 1965. 324 p. illus. 25 cm. Pages 323-324 blank for "interleaving sheets." [HE6183.S6 1965] 65-3050
1. Cancellations (Philately) 2. Postmarks — U.S. I. Bureau Issues Association. II. Title. III. Title: Bureau print precancels.

UNITED States postal 383.22
slogan cancel catalog. Rev. and enl. ed. Spring Valley, N.Y., 1963. 127 p. illus. 22 cm. First published in 1950 under title: United States postal slogan cancels. [HE6183.L8 1963] 63-25170
1. Cancellations (Philately) 2. Postmarks — U.S.

ZARESKI, Michel. 383.22
Fancy cancellations on 19th century United States postage stamps. 2d ed., rev. Edited and published by Herman Herst, Jr. Shrub Oak, N.Y., c1951. 287 p. illus. 26 cm. On cover: 19th century United States fancy cancellations [by] Herst-Zareski. First ed. Published in France in 1947 under title: Obliterations & marques postales des etata-Unis du 19c aiecle. [HE6183.Z3 1951] 51-22445
1. Cancellations (Philately) 2. Postage-stamps — U.S. I. Herst, Herman. II. Title. III. Title: 19th century United States fancy cancellations.

Cancellations (Philately)—Australia—New South Wales.

FRANKENSTEIN, Victor. 769'.569944
Handstamps of the travelling post offices of New South Wales / by V. Frankenstein. London : Lowe, [1976] 7 p. : facsims., map ; 25 cm. [HE6184.C3F72] 77-353885 ISBN 0-85397-051-3 : £1.00
1. Cancellations (Philately)—Australia—New South Wales. I. Title.

Cancellations (Philately) — Mexico.

YAG, Otto. 769.5690972
The pre-stamp postal markings of Mexico, by Otto Yag and John K. Bash. Elmhurst, Ill., Elmhurst Philatelic Society [1965] viii, 153 p. illus. 29 cm. "A limited edition of 300 copies." [HE6185.M52Y3] 65-4947
1. Cancellations (Philately) — Mexico. I. Bash, John K., joint author. II. Elmhurst Philatelic Society, Elmhurst, Ill. III. Title.

Cancellations (Philately)—Solomon Islands.

VERNON, D. H. 769'.56993'5
Cancellation study of the British Solomon Island Protectorate / compiled by D. H. Vernon. [Worthing] : Pacific Islands Study Circle of Great Britain, 1976. 19, [3] p. : facsims., map ; 30 cm. Cover title. [HE6184.C3V47] 77-356576 ISBN 0-9505320-0-2 : £1.50
1. Cancellations (Philately)—Solomon Islands. I. Pacific Islands Study Circle of Great Britain. II. Title.

Cancellations (Philately)—South Africa—Orange Free State—Catalogs.

BATTEN, Archibald 769'.56968'5
George Mount.
The Orange Free State, its post offices and their markings, 1868-1910 / by A. G. M. Batten. Woking : The author, 1976. 2 v. ([7], 347 p., fold. plate) : facsims., 2 maps ; 26 cm. First published in 1972 under title: The postmarks of the Orange Free State and the Orange River Colony, 1868-1910. [HE6184.C3B32 1976] 77-354813 ISBN 0-9502176-4-6 : £7.00
1. Cancellations (Philately)—South Africa—Orange Free State—Catalogs. I. Title.

Cancellations (Philately) — U.S.

LANGFORD, Frederick, 1916- 383
Standard flag cancel encyclopedia; a classifying research work. Compiled from original sources, including official records no longer existing. 2d, completely rev. ed. Pasadena, Calif. [1965] 80 p. illus. 26 cm. Cover title: Flag cancel encyclopedia. Errata leaf and Revised standard flag cancel type chart (1 leaf) in pocket. [HE6183.L28] 66-219
1. Cancellations (Philately) — U.S. I. Title. II. Title: Flag cancel encyclopedia.

LUFF, Moe, 1911- 383.22
United States postal slogan cancel catalog. New York, c1956. 128p. illus. 22cm. First published in 1950 under title: United States postal slogan cancels. [HE6183.L8 1956] 56-41651
1. Cancellations (Philately)—U. S. 2. Postmarks—U. S. I. Title.

LUFF, Moe, 1911- 769'.56'0973
United States postal slogan cancel catalog. Rev. and enl. ed. Spring Valley, N.Y., 1968. 128 p. illus. 22 cm. First published in 1950 under title: United States postal slogan cancels. [HE6183.L8 1968] 68-2266
1. Cancellations (Philately)—United States. 2. Postmarks—United States. I. Title.

NATHAN, Mel C. 769'.56
Franks of Western expresses, by M. C. Nathan. [Chicago?, 1973] xii, 281 p. illus. 27 cm. [HE6184.C3N38] 73-163385
1. Cancellations (Philately)—United States. 2. Express service—United States. I. Title.

STRATTON, Frank B. 769'.56
Descriptive catalog of the Leavitt machine cancellations / by Frank B. Stratton. [Bloomington, Ill.] : United Postal Stationery Society, 1976. 48 p. : ill. ; 23 cm. "An official publication of the United Postal Stationery Society." Bibliography: p. 47-48. [HE6184.C3S77 1976] 76-150510
1. Cancellations (Philately)—United States. I. United Postal Stationery Society. II. Title.

Candedo, Eulogio, 1924—

ZAMAN, Karen M. 759.13
A short biographical sketch of Eulogio Candedo / by Karen M. Zaman. 1st ed. Raleigh, N.C. : Art Collectors, c1975. 36 p. : col. ill. ; 15 cm. Cover title: Candedo, life is a carnival. [ND237.C23Z35] 75-21789
1. Candedo, Eulogio, 1924- I. Title. II. Title: Candedo, life is a carnival.

Candela, Felix.

FABER, Colin. 720.971
Candela, the shell builder. With a foreword by Ove Arup. New York, Reinhold Pub. Corp. [1963] 240 p. illus., ports., diagrs., plans. 27 cm. Bibliography: p. 235-240. [NA759.C3F23 1963] 62-14294
1. Candela, Felix.

Candilis-Josic-Woods.

WOODS, Shadrach, 1923- 720'.922
Candilis-Josic-Woods; building for people. Introd. by Jurgen Joedicke. New York, F. A. Praeger [1968] 226 p. illus. (part col.), maps, plans. 28 cm. English, German, and French. [NA1053.C33W66] 67-29465
1. Candilis-Josic-Woods. I. Title: Building for people.

Candlemaking.

CAREY, Mary. 745.59'3
Step-by-step candlemaking. New York, Golden Press [1972] 64 p. illus. (part col.) 29 cm. [TT896.5.C37] 72-82941 2.50
1. Candlemaking. I. Title.

COLLINS, Paul. 745.59'3
Introducing candlemaking / Paul Collins. New York : Taplinger Pub. Co., 1972. 96 p., [2] leaves of plates : ill. (some col.) ; 21 cm. Introduces the craft of making candles at home using jars, bottles, cartons, and cans. [TT896.5.C64 1972b] 72-563 ISBN 0-8008-4199-9 : 6.95
1. Candlemaking. I. Title. BIP

DIVALENTIN, Maria 745.59'3
Messuri, 1911-
Candle making / Maria and Louis di Valentin. Buchanan, N.Y. : Emerson Books, 1974. 127 p. : ill. ; 21 cm. [TT896.5.D58] 74-79898 ISBN 0-87523-186-1 : 5.95
1. Candlemaking. I. DiValentin, Louis, joint author. II. Title.

FEDER, Carol. 745.59'3
The candlemaking design book. Illus. by Emmett McConnell. Photos. by Alan Breslaw. New York, F. Watts, 1974. 122 p. illus. (part col.) 28 cm. [TT896.5.F4] 72-9781 ISBN 0-531-02668-X 5.95
1. Candlemaking. I. Title.
Pbk; 3.95, ISBN 0-531-02414-8.

GUY, Gary V. 745.59'3
Tall book of candle crafting, by Gary V. Guy, with photos. by Dave Pedegana. New York, Sterling Pub. Co. [1974] 108 p. illus. 29 x 15 cm. (Little craft book series) Directions for making block, sand-cast, moulded, hand-formed, tapes, and applique candles. [TT896.5.G89] 73-83458 ISBN 0-8069-5268-7 7.95
1. Candlemaking. I. Title.

HELLER, Beatrice. 745.59'3
Introduction to candle making; a step-by-step guide. Illus. by Ann Bruce Chamberlain. Los Angeles, Nash Pub. [1972] 118 p. illus. 21 cm. [TT896.5.H45] 72-81854 ISBN 0-8402-8053-X 2.45
1. Candlemaking. I. Title.

HIRST-SMITH, Ann. 745.59'3
The complete candlemaker. Photos. and drawings by Peter Hirst-Smith. New York, Van Nostrand Reinhold Co. [1974] 128 p. illus. 25 cm. Bibliography: p. 124. [TT896.5.H57] 74-7823 ISBN 0-442-23414-7
1. Candlemaking. I. Title.

KOEPPEL, Gary, 1938- 745.59'3
Sculptured sandcast candles. [1st ed.] Philadelphia, Chilton Book Co. [1972] xiii, 124 p. illus. (part col.) 26 cm. [TT896.5.K64] 72-8484 ISBN 0-8019-5748-6 9.95
1. Candlemaking. 2. Sand sculpture. I. Title. BIP

LEINWOLL, Stanley. 745.59'3
Candles and candlecrafting. New York, Scribner [1973] 139 p. illus. (part col.) 28 cm. [TT896.5.L45] 72-6556 ISBN 0-684-13187-0 8.95
1. Candlemaking. I. Title.
pap. 4.95. BIP

MCLAUGHLIN, Terence. 745.59'3
Candle making. New York, Drake Publishers [1974, c1973] 93 p. illus. 26 cm. (Pelham craft books) [TT896.5.M34 1974] 73-10903 ISBN 0-87749-561-0 6.95
1. Candlemaking. I. Title.

MONROE, Ruth. 745.59
Kitchen candlecrafting. South Brunswick, A. S. Barnes [1970] 172 p. illus. 26 cm. [TT896.5.M65] 72-85193 ISBN 0-498-06853-6 6.95
1. Candlemaking. I. Title.

NEWMAN, Thelma R. 745.59'33
Creative candlemaking, by Thelma R. Newman. New York, Crown Publishers [1972] 212 p. illus. (part col.) 27 cm. Bibliography: p. 204. [TT896.5.N48 1972] 77-185071 7.95
1. Candlemaking. I. Title. BIP

NUSSLE, William, 1912- 665'.19
Candle crafting, from an art to a science. South Brunswick, A. S. Barnes [1971] 202 p. illus. 27 cm. Bibliography: p. 199-200. [TT896.5.N88] 70-146769 ISBN 0-498-07863-9 7.95
1. Candlemaking. I. Title.

OLSEN, Don. 745.59'33
Nature's candles / Don Olsen. South Brunswick : A. S. Barnes, [1975] p. cm. Includes index. [TT896.5.O39 1975] 74-30730 ISBN 0-498-01669-2 : 9.95
1. Candlemaking. 2. Nature craft. I. Title. BIP

SCHUTZ, Walter E. 745.59'3
Getting started in candlemaking [by] Walter E. Schutz. New York, Collier Books [1972] 96 p. illus. (part col.) 28 cm. (Getting started series) Discusses the materials, equipment, and techniques needed for making and decorating a variety of candles. [TT896.5.S38] 70-183410 2.95
1. Candlemaking. I. Title. BIP

UNGER, Joan Ann. 745.59'3
Creative candlecraft. New York, Grosset & Dunlap [1972] 94 p. illus. 21 cm. [TT896.5.U53] 72-194369 ISBN 0-448-01556-0 1.95
1. Candlemaking. I. Title.

WEBSTER, William Earl, 745.59'3
1937-
Contemporary candlemaking [by] William E. Webster, with Claire McMullen. Garden City, N.Y., Doubleday, 1972. 79 p. illus. (part col.) 27 cm. [TT896.5.W4] 72-84974 ISBN 0-385-00775-2
1. Candlemaking. I. Title.

Candlemaking—Juvenile literature.

GILBREATH, Alice 745.59'3
Thompson.
Candles for beginners to make, by Alice Gilbreath. Illustrated by Jenni Oliver. New York, Morrow, 1975. 64 p. illus. 24 cm. Detailed instructions for making many different kinds of candles. [TT896.5.G54] 74-14968 ISBN 0-688-22010-X 4.95
1. Candlemaking—Juvenile literature. I. Oliver, Jenni, illus. II. Title.
Lib. bdg. 4.59, ISBN 0-688-32010-4. BIP

WELS, Byron G. 745.59'33
Here is your hobby, candlemaking / by Byron G. Wels ; ill. by Harriet Sherman. New York : Putnam, c1977. 64 p. : ill. ; 24 cm. (Here is your hobby) Includes index. An introduction to candlemaking including discussions of equipment, materials, and different types of candles. [TT896.5.W44 1977] 76-41791 ISBN 0-399-20570-5 : 4.99. ISBN 0-399-61059-6 lib. bdg. : 4.69
1. Candlemaking—Juvenile literature. I. Sherman, Harriet. II. Title.

Candles.

BOURN, Eugenia. 745.59'3
Candlemaking for profit [by] Eugenia (Deannie) Bourn. South Brunswick, A. S. Barnes [1973] 99 p. illus. 26 cm. Bibliography: p. 98. [TT896.5.B68] 72-9062 ISBN 0-498-01282-4 6.95
1. Candles. 2. Self-employed. I. Title.

CHISHOLM, K. Lomneth. 745.59'3
The candlemaker's primer, by K. Lomneth Chisholm. [1st ed.] New York, Dutton, 1973. 130 p. illus. 24 cm. [TT896.5.C48 1973] 72-82712 ISBN 0-525-07308-6 7.95
1. Candles. I. Title. BIP

MONROE, Ruth. 745.59'3
Candle decorating. South Brunswick, A. S. Barnes [1973] 151 p. illus. 26 cm. [TT896.5.M64] 73-3171 ISBN 0-498-01281-6 8.95
1. Candles. I. Title.

SHAW, Ray. 745.59'3
Candle art; a gallery of candle designs & how to make them. With 16 color plates and 115 photos. by the author. New York, Morrow, 1973. 160 p. illus. (part col.) 26 cm. [TT896.5.S48] 73-5324 ISBN 0-688-00172-6 8.95
1. Candles. I. Title. BIP

STROSE, Susanne. 745.59
Candle-making, by Susanne Strose. New York, Sterling Pub. Co. [1968] 48 p. illus. 20 cm. (Little craft book series) Translation of Kerzen. [TP993.S713] 68-8759
1. Candles. I. Title. BIP

WEAKLEY, Tom. 745.59'3
How to make candles. Illustrated by Barbara Weakley. [Arlington, Vt., Highland Publications, 1971] 56 p. illus. 22 cm. Includes bibliographical references. [TT896.5.W38] 73-154528 1.95
1. Candles. I. Title. BIP

WEBSTER, William Earl, 745.59'3
1937-
The complete book of candle-making; an expanded version of Contemporary candlemaking, by William E. Webster with Claire McMullen. Garden City, N.Y., Doubleday, 1973. 160 p. illus. (part col.) 27 cm. [TT896.5.W39] 73-77847 ISBN 0-385-01930-0 8.95
1. Candles. I. Title. II. Title: Candlemaking.

Candlesticks.

ROWFANT CLUB, Cleveland 745.59
The Rowfant candlesticks, by John Calder Pearson [chairman of the Candlestick Book Committee] Cleveland, 1959. xxxi, 355p. (chiefly illus.) facsim. 29cm. 60-734 25.00; 15.00 to members lim. ed.,
1. Candlesticks. I. Pearson, John Calder. II. Title.

WILLS, Geoffrey. 738.8
Candlesticks. [1st American ed.] New York, C. N. Potter; distributed by Crown Publishers [1974] 120 p. illus. (part col.) 29 cm. Bibliography: p. 119. [NK3685.W54 1974] 73-88646 ISBN 0-517-51414-1 6.95
1. Candlesticks.

Candlesticks—Collectors and collecting.

BUTLER, Joseph T. 745.59
Candleholders in America, 1650-1900; a comprehensive collection of American and European candle fixtures used in America [by] Joseph T. Butler New York, Crown Publishers [1967] xiv, 178 p. illus. (part col.) 27 cm. Bibliography: p. 170-172. [NK9990.C2B8] 67-15986
1. Candlesticks—Collectors and collecting. 2. Art objects—U.S. I. Title.

Canon camera.

CRAWLEY, Geoffrey. 771.3'1
Canon F-1 system. Critically reviewed by Geoffrey Crawley. Garden City, N.Y., Amphoto [1974, c1973] 87 p. illus. 22 cm. [TR263.C3C7 1974] 73-86190 ISBN 0-8174-0921-1 5.95
1. Canon camera. 2. Photography—Handbooks, manuals, etc. I. Title.

DESCHIN, Jacob. 770.2
Canon photography; a working manual of 35 mm photography with the Canon v and ivS2. [1st ed.] San Francisco, Camera Craft Pub. Co. [1957] 192p. illus. 25cm. [TR263.C3D4] 57-6547
1. Canon camera. 2. Photography—Handbooks, manuals, etc. I. Title.

EMANUEL, Walter Daniel, 1908- 771.3'1
Canon reflex guide: how to use the Canon QLFT, Pellix, Canon FX, FP, EE EX, by W. D. Emanuel. London, New York, Focal P., 1970. 72, 14 p. illus. 17 cm. (The Camera guide) [TR263.C3E44] 72-193265 ISBN 0-240-50659-6 15/-
1. Canon camera. 2. Photography—Handbooks, manuals, etc. I. Title.

JONAS, Paul. 771.31
The Canon, Canonet, Canonflex manual. New York, Universal Photo Books [1961] 128p. illus. 24cm. [TR263.C3J6] 61-8112
1. Canon camera. 2. Photography—Handbooks, manuals, etc. I. Title.

JONAS, Paul. 771.3'1
The Canon manual. Garden City, N.Y., Amphoto [1973] 160 p. illus. 24 cm. [TR263.C3J62] 72-77137 ISBN 0-8174-0486-4 8.95
1. Canon camera. 2. Photography—Handbooks, manuals, etc. I. Title. BIP

JONAS, Paul. 771.3'1
The Canon manual / Paul Jonas. Rev. ed. Garden City, N.Y. : Amphoto, c1976. 158 p., [2] leaves of plates : ill. (some col.) ; 24 cm. Includes index. [TR263.C3J62 1976] 76-354383 ISBN 0-8174-1486-X : 10.95
1. Canon camera. 2. Photography—Handbooks, manuals, etc. I. Title.

LONDON, Barbara, 1936- 771.3'1
A short course in Canon photography / Barbara London. New York : Van Nostrand Reinhold Co., [1979] p. cm. Includes index. Bibliography: p. [TR263.C3L66] 78-23913 ISBN 0-442-26617-0 : 14.95
1. Canon camera. 2. Photography—Handbooks, manuals, etc. I. Title. BIP

SHIPMAN, Carl. 771.3'1
How to select and use Canon SLR cameras / by Carl Shipman. Tucson, AZ : HP Books, c1977. 192 p. : ill. ; 28 cm. Caption title. Includes index. [TR263.C3S54] 76-50430 ISBN 0-912656-56-5 pbk. : 5.95
1. Canon camera. 2. Photography—Handbooks, manuals, etc. I. Title.

TYDINGS, Kenneth S 770.2
The Canon guide to 35mm photography. New York, Greenberg, c1954. 128p. illus. 20cm. (The Modern camera guide series) [TR263.C3T9] 53-12274
1. Canon camera. 2. Photography—Handbooks, manuals, etc. I. Title.

Canter, David V.—Bibliography.

HIGGINBOTTOM, Nick. 016.3092'08 s
David Canter's architectural psychology : an overview and bibliography / Nick Higginbottom. Monticello, Ill. : Council of Planning Librarians, 1974. 22 p. ; 28 cm. (Exchange bibliography - Council of Planning Librarians ; 679) Cover title. [Z5942.C68 no. 679] [NA2540] 720'.1'9 75-314184 2.00
1. Canter, David V.—Bibliography. 2. Architecture—Psychological aspects. I. Title. II. Series: Council of Planning Librarians. Exchange bibliography ; 679.

Canterbury Cathedral.

CAVINESS, Madeline Harrison, 1938- 748.5'922'34
The early stained glass of Canterbury Cathedral, circa 1175-1220 / Madeline Harrison Caviness. Princeton, N.J. : Princeton University Press, c1977. p. cm. Includes index. Bibliography: p. [NK5344.C3C38] 77-10419 ISBN 0-691-03927-5 : 35.00
1. Canterbury Cathedral. 2. Glass painting and staining, Romanesque—England—Canterbury. 3. Glass painting and staining, Gothic—England—Canterbury. 4. Glass painting and staining—England—Canterbury. I. Title.

Cantor, B. Gerald, 1916- —Art collections.

RODIN, Auguste, 1840-1917. 730'.924
Homage to Rodin. Collection of B. Gerald Cantor. [Los Angeles] Los Angeles County Museum of Art, 1967. 108 p. illus. 31 cm. Exhibition shown at the Los Angeles County Museum of Art, Nov. 14, 1967 to Jan. 7, 1968, and other museums. Bibliography: p. 106-107. [NB553.R7C3] 67-31131
1. Cantor, B. Gerald, 1916- —Art collections. I. Los Angeles Co., Calif. Museum of Arts, Los Angeles. II. Title.

RODIN, Auguste, 1840-1917. 730'.924
Rodin bronzes, from the Collection of B. Gerald Cantor. Introd. by Ellen Landis. New York [1969] [85] p. illus., ports. 26 cm. "Exhibition number 69-8, circulated 1969-1970 ... by the American Federation of Arts." Bibliography: p. [34]-[35] [NB553.C28R6] 79-98172
1. Cantor, B. Gerald, 1916- —Art collections. I. American Federation of Arts. II. Title.

Canvas embroidery.

AGNEW, Patience. 746.4'4
Needlepoint for churches. New York, Scribner [1972] 127 p. illus. 28 cm. Bibliography: p. 117. [TT778.C3A46] 72-327 ISBN 0-684-12927-2 8.95
1. Canvas embroidery. 2. Ecclesiastical embroidery.

AIKEN, Joyce. 746.4'4
The portable needlepoint boutique / Joyce Aiken. 1st ed. New York : Taplinger Pub. Co., 1977. p. cm. [TT778.C3A47 1977] 76-53870 ISBN 0-8008-6416-6 : 10.95
1. Canvas embroidery. I. Title. BIP

AMBUTER, Carolyn. 746.4'4
Complete book of needlepoint. Illustrated by Patti Baker Russell. Photos. by Fred Samperi. New York, World Pub. [1972] 147 p. illus. 22 x 30 cm. Bibliography: p. 139. [TT778.C3A48 1972] 70-178814 6.95 (pbk)
1. Canvas embroidery. I. Title. BIP

AMLICK, Barbara H. 746.4'4
Designs for needlepoint, by Barbara H. Amlick. New York, Drake Publishers [1973] p. [TT778.C3A5] 73-4344 ISBN 0-87749-513-0 7.95
1. Canvas embroidery. I. Title.

ARCHER, Katherine B. 746.4'4
Perfect needlepoint projects from start to finish / by Katherine B. Archer, Patricia Falk Feeley ; illustrated by Sidonie Coryn. New York : St. Martin's Press, [1977] p. cm. Includes index. Bibliography: p. [TT778.C3A73] 75-40786 ISBN 0-312-60070-4 : 10.00
1. Canvas embroidery. I. Feeley, Patricia Falk, joint author. II. Title. BIP

BAKER, Muriel L. 746.4'4
The A B C's of canvas embroidery, by Muriel L. Baker. Sturbridge, Mass., Old Sturbridge Village [1968] 64 p. illus. 22 cm. (Old Sturbridge Village booklet series, 26) [NK9204.B3] 70-136
1. Canvas embroidery. I. Title. II. Series.

BAKER, Muriel L. 746.4'4
The XYZ's of canvas embroidery, by Muriel L. Baker. Sturbridge, Mass., Old Sturbridge Village [1971] 72 p. illus., facsim. 22 cm. (Old Sturbridge Village booklet series) [TT778.C3B3] 74-24423
1. Canvas embroidery. I. Title. II. Series.

BARNES, Charles. 746.4'4
Bargello and related stitchery, by Charles Barnes and David P. Blake. Great Neck, N.Y., Hearthside Press [1971] 245 p. illus. (part col.) 25 cm. [TT778.C3B35] 71-151458 ISBN 0-8208-0337-5 8.95
1. Canvas embroidery. I. Blake, David P., joint author. II. Title.

BEINECKE, Mary Ann. 746.4'4
Basic needlery stitches on mesh fabrics. New York, Dover Publications [1973] 1 v. (unpaged) illus. 28 cm. "Sponsored by the Nantucket Historical Trust." [TT778.C3B44 1973] 73-77444 ISBN 0-486-21713-2 2.00 (pbk.)
1. Canvas embroidery. I. Title. BIP

BETTER homes and gardens needlepoint. 746.4'4 1st ed. Des Moines : Meredith Corp., c1978. 96 p. : ill. ; 27 cm. (Better homes and gardens books) [TT778.C3B47] 78-56632 ISBN 0-696-00475-5 : 3.95
1. Canvas embroidery. I. Better homes and gardens. II. Title: Needlepoint. BIP

BOYLES, Margaret. 746.4'4
Needlepoint stitchery. New York, Macmillan [1973] 158 p. illus. (part col.) 27 cm. [TT778.C3B68] 72-77274 12.95
1. Canvas embroidery. I. Title.

BUCHER, Jo. 746.4'4
Complete guide to creative needlepoint. [New York] Creative Home Library [1973] x, 324 p. illus. (part. col.) 27 cm. [TT778.C3B8] 72-6674 ISBN 0-696-34300-2 8.95
1. Canvas embroidery. I. Title. II. Title: Creative needlepoint.

BURCHETTE, Dorothy. 746.4'4
Needlework: blocking and finishing. New York, Scribner [1974] 136 p. illus. 24 cm. Bibliography: p. 125. [TT778.C3B87] 73-1096 7.95
1. Canvas embroidery. I. Title.

CHRISTENSEN, Jo Ippolito. 746.4'4
Bargello stitchery; vertical needle-point, by Jo Ippolito Christensen and Sonie Shapiro Ashner. New York, Sterling Pub. Co. [1972] 48 p. illus. 20 cm. (Little craft book series) Directions for using vertical needlepoint stitches to make pillows, eyeglass cases, picture frames, key cases, and other useful accessories. [TT778.C3C47] 70-180459
1. Canvas embroidery. I. Ashner, Sonie Shapiro, joint author. II. Title.

CHRISTENSEN, Jo Ippolito. 746.4'4
Cross stitchery; needlepointing with yarns in a variety of decorative stitches, by Jo Ippolito Christensen and Sonie Shapiro Ashner. New York, Sterling Pub. Co. [1973] 48 p. illus. (part col.) 20 cm. (Little craft book series) Instructions for needlepoint designs for use on purses, tennis racket covers, pillows, paintings, key cases, and other items. [TT778.C3C473] 72-95196 ISBN 0-8069-5260-1 2.95
1. Canvas embroidery. I. Ashner, Sonie Shapiro, joint author. II. Title.
Library binding 2.69; ISBN 0-8069-5261-X.

CHRISTENSEN, Jo Ippolito. 746.4'4
The needlepoint book : 303 stitches with patterns and projects / Jo Ippolito Christensen ; drawings by Lynn Lucas Jones, photos. by James T. Long. Englewood Cliffs, N.J. : Prentice-Hall, c1976. xvi, 384 p., [8] leaves of plates : ill. (some col.) ; 24 cm. (The Creative handcrafts series) (A Spectrum book) Includes indexes. Bibliography: p. 371-374. [TT778.C3C478] 76-182 ISBN 0-13-610980-2 : 17.95. ISBN 0-13-610972-1 pbk. : 9.95
1. Canvas embroidery. I. Title. BIP

CHRISTENSEN, Jo Ippolito. 746.4'4
Needlepoint simplified, by Jo Ippolito Christensen and Sonie Shapiro Ashner. Photos. by Mike E. Bergen. New York, Sterling Pub. Co. [1971] 48 p. illus. (part col.) 20 cm. (Little craft book series) Describes the stitches best suited for creating a number of effects on pillows, footstools, wall hangings, and other articles made of canvas. [TT778.C3C48 1971] 75-167666
1. Canvas embroidery. I. Ashner, Sonie Shapiro, joint author. II. Bergen, Mike E., illus. III. Title. BIP

CHRISTENSEN, Jo Ippolito. 746.4'4
Teach yourself needlepoint / Jo Ippolito Christensen ; drawings by Lynn Lucas Jones ; designs by Cindy Pendleton ; photos. by Richard D. Moats, James T. Long, Paul Hagerty. Englewood Cliffs, N.J. : Prentice-Hall, c1978. xv, 333 p. : ill. ; 28 cmm. (The Creative handcrafts series) (A Spectrum book) Includes indexes. [TT778.C3C483] 78-838 ISBN 0-13-888024-7 : 17.95 ISBN 0-13-888016-6 pbk. : 9.95
1. Canvas embroidery. I. Title.

COATS Sewing Group. 746.4'4
50 needlepoint stitches / Coats Sewing Group. New York : Scribner, 1977 128 p. : ill. ; 15 cm. (The Scribner library : Emblem editions) Cover title. British ed. published in 1975 under title: 50 canvas embroidery stitches. Includes index. [TT778.C3C6 1975] 77-80339 ISBN 0-684-14786-6 pbk. : 1.75
1. Canvas embroidery. I. Title.

COLLINS, Carol Huebner. 746.4'4
Needlepoint : a basic manual / Carol Huebner Collins. 1st ed. Boston : Little, Brown, c1976. xvii, 172 p. : ill. ; 22 cm. (The Craft series) Bibliography: p. 169. [TT778.C3C64] 76-2695 ISBN 0-316-15225-0 : 4.95
1. Canvas embroidery. I. Title.

COOK, Inman. 746.4'4
Pleasures of needlepoint; a how-to book of beautiful new designs everyone can make, by Inman Cook and Daren Pierce. New York, Universal Pub.; distributed by Scribner [1972] 136 p. illus. 27 cm. (The Betty Crocker home library) [TT778.C3C66] 70-179428 ISBN 0-684-12866-7
1. Canvas embroidery. I. Pierce, Daren, joint author. II. Title.

COSENTINO, Geraldine. 746.4'4
Step-by-step bargello. New York, Golden Press [1974] 64 p. illus. 29 cm. (The Golden Press step-by-step craft series) Bibliography: p. 64. [TT778.C3C67] 73-88436 2.95
1. Canvas embroidery. I. Title. II. Title: Bargello.

CROWELL, Muriel B. 746.4'4
The fine art of needlepoint [by] Muriel B. Crowell. New York, Crowell [1973] 128 p. illus. (part col.) 27 cm. [TT778.C3C76 1973] 73-9564 ISBN 0-690-29799-8 10.00
1. Canvas embroidery. I. Title.

DENITTO, Elizabeth Brenner. 746.4'4
Needlepoint on plastic canvas / Elizabeth Brenner DeNitto. New York : Scribner, [1978] 127 p., [4] leaves of plates : ill. ; 24 cm. [TT778.C3D46] 78-705 ISBN 0-684-15534-6 : 14.95 ISBN 0-684-15577-X pbk. : 6.95
1. Canvas embroidery. I. Title. II. Title: Plastic canvas. BIP

and Marjorie Sablow. [Des Moines] : Meredith Corp., c1975. 192 p. : ill. (some col.) ; 26 cm. [TT778.C3S357] 75-18983 ISBN 0-696-34600-1 : 9.95
1. Canvas embroidery. I. Sablow, Marjorie, joint author. II. Title.

SCOBEY, Joan. 746.4'4
Do-it-all-yourself needlepoint, by Joan Scobey and Lee Parr McGrath. Original designs by Marjorie Sablow. Photos. by Eugene Sablow. New York, Essandess Special Editions [1971] vii, 184 p. illus. 23 cm. [TT778.C3S36] 72-29956 ISBN 0-671-10617-1 6.95
1. Canvas embroidery. I. McGrath, Lee Parr, joint author. II. Title.

SCOBEY, Joan. 746.4'4
The first easy-to-see needlepoint workbook / Joan Scobey and Marjorie Sablow. 1st ed. New York : Rawson Associates Publishers, c1977. xii, 193 p., [2] leaves of plates : ill. ; 31 cm. Includes index. [TT778.C3S37 1977] 76-43425 ISBN 0-89256-005-3 : 14.95
1. Canvas embroidery. I. Sablow, Marjorie, joint author. II. Title. BIP

SIDNEY, Sylvia. 746.4'4
Sylvia Sidney needlepoint book [by] Sylvia Sidney with Alfred Allen Lewis. New York, Reinhold Book Corp. [1968] 120 p. illus. (part col.) 29 cm. [TT771.S55] 68-22738
1. Canvas embroidery. I. Lewis, Alfred Allan, joint author.

SIDNEY, Sylvia. 746.4'4
Sylvia Sidney needlepoint book / Sylvia Sidney with Alfred Allan Lewis. New York : Galahad Books, [1974] c1968. 120 p. : ill. (some col.) ; 29 cm. Reprint of the ed. published by Reinhold, New York. Includes index. Bibliography: p. 119. [TT778.C3S52 1974] 74-79062 ISBN 0-88365-255-2 : 10.95
1. Canvas embroidery. I. Lewis, Alfred Allan, joint author. II. Title.

SILVERSTEIN, Mira. 746.4'4
Bargello plus. Photos. by Salvatore D. Lopes. Diagrs. by Roberta Frauwirth. New York, Scribner [1973] 90 p. illus. (part col.) 28 cm. [TT778.C3S53] 73-1108 ISBN 0-684-13412-8 9.95
1. Canvas embroidery. I. Title. BIP

SILVERSTEIN, Mira. 746.4'4
Mira Silverstein's Guide to combination stitches : exciting needlework projects, patterns, and designs anyone can make / artwork by Roberta Frauwirth ; photos. by Sandy L. Studios. New York : D. McKay Co., c1977. p. cm. [TT778.C3S542 1977] 77-10919 ISBN 0-679-50820-1 : 9.95. ISBN 0-679-50786-8 pbk. : 3.95
1. Canvas embroidery. I. Title. II. Title: Guide to combination stitches. BIP

SILVERSTEIN, Mira. 746.4'4
Mira Silverstein's Guide to slanted stitches : exciting needlework projects, patterns, and designs anyone can make / artwork by Roberta Frauwirth ; photos. by Sandy L. Studios. New York : D. McKay Co., c1977. 128 p., [2] leaves of plates : ill. ; 24 cm. [TT778.C3S543 1977] 77-10839 ISBN 0-679-50819-8 : 9.95. ISBN 0-679-50783-3 pbk. : 3.95
1. Canvas embroidery. I. Title. II. Title: Guide to slanted stitches. BIP

SILVERSTEIN, Mira. 746.4'4
Mira Silverstein's Guide to upright stitches : exciting needlework projects, patterns, and designs anyone can make / artwork by Roberta Frauwirth ; photos. by Sandy L. Studios. New York : D. McKay Co., c1977. p. cm. [TT778.C3S544 1977] 77-10913 ISBN 0-679-50818-X : 9.95. ISBN 0-679-50784-1 pbk. : 3.95
1. Canvas embroidery. I. Title. II. Title: Guide to upright stitches. BIP

SILVERSTEIN, Mira. 746.4'4
Needlepoint on a shoestring. Photos. by Salvatore D. Lopes. Diagrs. by Roberta Frauwirth. New York, Funk & Wagnalls [1973] 101 p. illus. (part col.) 24 cm. [TT778.C3S55] 73-9575 ISBN 0-308-10082-4 4.95
1. Canvas embroidery. 2. Embroidery. I. Title.

SLATER, Elaine. 746.4'4
Elaine Slater's Book of needlepoint projects / ill. by Lisa Levitt. 1st ed. New York : Holt, Rinehart and Winston, c1978. p. cm. [TT778.C3S57] 78-2597 13.95
1. Canvas embroidery. I. Title. II. Title: Book of needlepoint projects. BIP

SNOOK, Barbara. 746.4'4
The craft of Florentine embroidery. New York, Scribner [1971] 96 p. illus. 28 cm. (The Scribner library. Emblem editions) "Abridged from [the author's] Florentine embroidery." [TT778.C3S66] 75-165164 ISBN 0-684-12502-1 2.95
1. Canvas embroidery. I. Title.

STEVENS, Gigs. 746.4'4
Free-form bargello / by Gigs Stevens. New York : Scribner, c1977. 106 p., [8] leaves of plates : ill. (some col.) ; 29 cm. [TT778.C3S73] 77-5784 ISBN 0-684-15024-7 : 7.50 ISBN 0-684-15055-7 pbk. : 7.95
1. Canvas embroidery. I. Title. BIP

WALL, Maggie. 746.4'4
Creative needlepoint borders / Maggie Wall ; drawings by Barbara Eyre ; photography by Harold Pratt. New York : Scribner, c1977. 107 p. : ill. ; 28 cm. Includes index. [TT778.C3W33] 76-46366 ISBN 0-684-14854-4 : 9.95
1. Canvas embroidery. I. Eyre, Barbara. II. Pratt, Harold, 1912- III. Title. BIP

WALZER, Mary Meister. 746.4'4
Handbook of needlepoint stitches. New York, Van Nostrand Reinhold Co. [1971] 99 p. illus. 16 x 23 cm. [TT778.C3W35] 70-153457
1. Canvas embroidery. I. Title. BIP

WEAL, Michele. 746.4'4
Texture and color in needlepoint / Michele Weal. 1st ed. New York : Harper & Row, [1975] xix, 183 p. : ill. ; 27 cm. Includes index. Bibliography: p. 173-174. [TT778.C3W4 1975] 74-1871 ISBN 0-06-014522-6 : 12.50
1. Canvas embroidery. I. Title. BIP

WILLIAMS, Elsa S. 746.4'4
Bargello; Florentine canvas work [by] Elsa S. Williams. New York, Van Nostrand Reinhold [1967] 64 p. illus. (part col.) 21 x 26 cm. [TT778.C3W54] 67-24705
1. Canvas embroidery. I. Title. BIP

WILLIAMS, Elsa S. 746.44
Creative canvas work [by] Elsa S. Williams. New York, Van Nostrand Reinhold [1975] 64 p. illus (part col) 20 cm. x 25 cm. [TT778] 74-141443 4.95 (pbk.)
1. Canvas embroidery. I. Title. BIP

WOLFMAN, Peri. 746.4'4
Bargello is easy / by Peri Wolfman. New York : Grossett & Dunlap, [1974] c1973. 86 p. : ill. ; 21 cm. [TT778.C3W64] 75-301317 ISBN 0-448-02433-0 pbk. : 1.95
1. Canvas embroidery. I. Title.

Canvas embroidery—Juvenile literature.

CREATIVE Educational Society, Mankato, Minn. 746.4'4
How to have fun with needlepoint, by editors of Creative [Educational Society] Illustrated by Nan Brooks. Mankato, Minn.; [distributed by Childrens Press, Chicago, 1973, c1974] 31 p. illus. (part col.) 25 cm. (Creative craft book) On spine: Needle point. Introduces basic needlepoint stitches and simple projects such as a hot mat and patches for jeans. [TT778.C3C73 1973] 73-18226 ISBN 0-87191-296-1
1. Canvas embroidery—Juvenile literature. I. Brooks, Nan, illus. II. Title. III. Title: Needlepoint. BIP

HARAYDA, Marel. 746.4'4
Needlework magic with two basic stitches : young ideas for canvas and yarn / Marel Harayda ; diagrs. by Marie and Nils Ostberg. New York : D. McKay Co., c1978. xi, 114 p. : ill. ; 24 cm. Includes index. Presents instructions for two basic needlework stitches and their variations. Also offers project designs for woven and plastic canvas. [TT778.C3H38] 77-12494 ISBN 0-679-20423-7 : 7.95
1. Canvas embroidery—Juvenile literature. I. Title.

HODGSON, Mary Anne. 746.4'4
Fast and easy needlepoint / Mary Anne Hodgson and Josephine Ruth Paine ; photos. by Michael Pitts and Richard Fowlkes. 1st ed. Garden City, N.Y. : Doubleday, c1977. p. cm. Includes index. Uses a series of learning designs to teach the basic needlepoint stiches, then guides the reader into original designs for a belt, pillow, guitar strap, and other objects. [TT778.C3H63] 76-56302 ISBN 0-385-12431-7 : 5.95.
1. Paine, Josephine Ruth, joint author. 2. Canvas embroidery—Juvenile literature. I. Pitts, Michael. II. Fowlkes, Richard. III. Title. BIP

LIGHTBODY, Donna M. 746.4'4
Introducing needlepoint, by Donna M. Lightbody. Illustrated with photos. and charts. New York, Lothrop, Lee & Shepard Co. [1973] 157 p. illus. 25 cm. Bibliography: p. 152. Describes in text and illustrations the tools, techniques, and embroidery stitches for creating and decorating a variety of objects. [TT778.C3L5] 73-4946 ISBN 0-688-41550-4 4.95
1. Canvas embroidery—Juvenile literature. I. Title.
Library binding; 4.59, ISBN 0-688-51550-9. BIP

PARKER, Xenia Ley. 746.4'4
A beginner's book of needlepoint and embroidery / Xenia Ley Parker ; illustrated with drawings and photos. by the author. New York : Dodd, Mead, [1975] 160 p. : ill. ; 25 cm. Includes index. Discusses the history, materials, tools, patterns, procedures, and stitches of embroidery and needlepoint. [TT778.C3P37] 74-25511 ISBN 0-396-07066-3 : 5.95
1. Canvas embroidery—Juvenile literature. 2. Needlework—Juvenile literature. I. Title. BIP

YOUNG, Eleanor R. 746.4'4
Needlepoint, by Eleanor R. Young. New York, F. Watts, 1976 59 p. illus. 25 cm. (A Concise guide) Includes index. Introduces the materials and various stitches used in canvas embroidery and gives suggestions for projects. [TT778.C3Y68] 74-12046 ISBN 0-531-02779-1
1. Canvas embroidery—Juvenile literature. I. Title.

Canvas embroidery—Patterns.

AMBUTER, Carolyn. 746.4'4
Carolyn Ambuter's needlepoint celebrations / ill. by Patti Baker Russell ; photos. by Jerry Darvin. New York : Workman Pub. Co., c1976. 221, [1] p. : chiefly ill. ; 27 cm. Bibliography: p. [222] [TT778.C3A49] 75-8305 ISBN 0-8129-0583-0 : 14.95
1. Canvas embroidery—Patterns. I. Title. II. Title: Needlepoint celebrations.

ARNOLD, Dennis M. 746.4'4
The needlepoint pattern book, by Dennis M. Arnold. Photography by Rica Molofsky. New York, Morrow [1974] 183 p. illus. 26 cm. Bibliography: p. 183. [TT778.C3A76] 73-22143 ISBN 0-688-00241-2 12.95
1. Canvas embroidery—Patterns. I. Molofsky, Rica, illus. II. Title. BIP

BARNES, Charles. 746.4'4
120 needlepoint design projects / Charles Barnes, David Blake, in collaboration with William Baker. New York : Crown Publishers, [1974] 202 p., [4] leaves of plates : ill. ; 27 cm. Includes index. [TT778.C3B36 1974] 73-91517 ISBN 0-517-51473-7 : 4.95
1. Canvas embroidery—Patterns. I. Blake, David P., joint author. II. Baker, William, 1934- joint author. III. Title.

BODI, Jack. 746.4'4
A gardener's book of needlepoint / by Jack Bodi, Meg Merrill, Catherine di Montezemolo ; introd. by C. Z. Guest ; photos. by Joe Leombruno and Gianni Lami. New York : Simon and Schuster, c1978. p. cm. Includes index. Bibliography: p. [TT778.C3B6] 78-13116 ISBN 0-671-23015-8 : 9.95
1. Canvas embroidery—Patterns. 2. Design, Decorative—Plant forms. I. Merrill, Meg, joint author. II. Di Montezemolo, Catherine, joint author. III. Title. IV. Title: Book of needlepoint.

BORSSUCK, B. 746.4'4
97 needlepoint alphabets / B. Borssuck New York : Arco, c1975. 144 p. : chiefly ill. ; 28 cm. [TT778.C3B64] 74-19792 ISBN 0-668-03723-7 lib.bdg. : 6.95 ISBN 0-668-03655-9 pbk. : 4.95.
1. Canvas embroidery—Patterns. 2. Alphabets. I. Title.

BORSSUCK, B. 746.4'4
1001 designs for needlepoint and cross stitch / B. Brossuck. New York : Arco Pub. Co., c1977. p. cm. Bibliography: p. [TT778.C3B65] 77-1701 ISBN 0-668-04214-1 : 12.95.
1. Canvas embroidery—Patterns. 2. Cross-stich—Patterns. I. Title.

BOYLES, Margaret. 746.4'4
American Indian needlepoint workbook / Margaret Boyles. New York : Collier Books, 1975 [i.e.1976] p. cm. "Based on material by W. Ben Hunt and Buck Burshears." Includes index. [TT778.C3B66 1975] 75-20417 pbk. : 7.95
1. Canvas embroidery—Patterns. 2. Indians of North America—Textile industry and fabrics. I. Title. BIP

BOYLES, Margaret. 746.4'4
Bargello: an explosion in color. New York, Macmillan [1974] 149 p. col. illus. 29 cm. [TT778.C3B67] 73-2753 12.95
1. Canvas embroidery—Patterns. I. Title.

BOYLES, Margaret. 746.4'4
The Margaret Boyles bargello workbook : a collection of original designs / Margaret Boyles. New York : Macmillan, 1976. p. cm. [TT778.C3B678] 76-6991 ISBN 0-02-514330-1
1. Canvas embroidery—Patterns. I. Title. BIP

BRAGDON, Bill. 746.4'4
Pillow people : needlepoint designs for 40 unusual doll pillows / Bill Bragdon and Jeanne Harrison. New York : Hawthorn Books, c1976. viii, 116 p. : ill. ; 28 cm. [TT778.C3B7 1976] 75-28697 ISBN 0-8015-5875-1 : 5.95
1. Canvas embroidery—Patterns. 2. Pillows. 3. Dollmaking. I. Harrison, Jeanne, joint author. II. Title.

BRENT, Eva. 746.4'4
Nature in needlepoint / designs by Eva Brent ; text by Meg Merrill. New York : Simon and Schuster, [1975] 127 p., [4] leaves of plates : ill. (some col.) ; 29 cm. Bibliography: p. 125-126. [TT778.C3B73] 75-16129 ISBN 0-671-22081-0 : 9.95
1. Canvas embroidery—Patterns. 2. Design, Decorative—Animal forms. I. Merrill, Meg. II. Title. BIP

CAMMANN, Nora. 746.4'4
Needlepoint designs from American Indian art. Photos. and illus. by Rolf Siljander. New York, Scribner [1973] 84 p. illus. 29 cm. Bibliography: p. 84. [TT778.C3C35] 72-11136 ISBN 0-684-13298-2 9.95
1. Canvas embroidery—Patterns. 2. Indians of North America—Art. I. Title.

CHARTED monograms for needlepoint and cross-stitch / edited by Rita Weiss. New York : Dover Publications, 1977. 36 p. : chiefly ill. ; 28 cm. (Dover needlework series) "Contains all of the charted designs from the sixth printing of 'Album der Monogramme fur Kreuzstich' as published by the Verlag der 'Wiener Mode' in Vienna, circa 1900." [TT778.C3C45 1977] 77-77047 ISBN 0-486-23555-6 pbk. : 1.50 ($1.75 Can) 746.4'4
1. Canvas embroidery—Patterns. 2. Cross-stitch—Patterns. 3. Monograms. I. Weiss, Rita. II. Album der Mongramme fur Kreuzstich. BIP

COSTABEL-DEUTSCH, Eva. 746.4'4
Full-color floral needlepoint designs : charted for easy use / Eva Costabel-Deutsch. New York : Dover Publications, c1976. 32 p. : all ill. ; 28 cm. (Dover needlework series) [TT778.C3C68 1976] 76-15691 ISBN 0-486-23387-1 : 2.00
1. Canvas embroidery—Patterns. 2. Design, Decorative—Plant forms. I. Title. II. Title: Floral needlepoint designs. BIP

DACOSTA, Morton, 1914- 746.4'4
Book of needlepoint. Designs developed in

collaboration with Arne Besser. New York, Simon and Schuster [1974] 127 p. illus. (12 fold. in pocket) 31 cm. [TT778.C3D3] 74-11020 ISBN 0-671-21846-8
1. Canvas embroidery—Patterns. I. Besser, Arne, illus. II. Title.

DAVIS, Mary Kay. 746.4'4
More needlepoint from America's great quilt designs / Mary Kay Davis and Helen Giammattei ; illustrated by Elizabeth Meyer, photographed by Mason Pawlak. New York : Workman Pub., c1977. 208 p. : ill. ; 28 cm. Bibliography: p. 207-208. [TT778.C3D39 1977] 77-5305 ISBN 0-89480-005-1 : 12.50 ISBN 0-89480-006-X pbk. : 6.95
1. Canvas embroidery—Patterns. 2. Coverlets, American. I. Giammattei, Helen, joint author. II. Title. BIP

DAVIS, Mary Kay. 746.4'4
Needlepoint from America's great quilt designs / written and stitched by Mary Kay Davis and Helen Giammattei ; illustrated by Elizabeth Meyer ; photographed by Mason Pawlak. New York : Workman Pub. Co., 1974. 170 p. : ill. (some col.) ; 28 cm. Bibliography: p. 169-170. [TT778.C3D38] 75-8815 ISBN 0-911104-42-9 : 10.95 ISBN 0-911104-41-0 pbk. : 5.95
1. Canvas embroidery—Patterns. 2. Coverlets, American. I. Giammattei, Helen, joint author. II. Title. BIP

EDMONDS, Mary Jane. 746.4'4
Geometric designs in needlepoint / Mary Jaene Edmonds. New York : Van Nostrand Reinhold, 1976. 131 p. : ill. ; 29 cm. Includes index. Bibliography: p. 129. [TT778.C3E35] 75-3860 ISBN 0-442-22238-6 : 12.50
1. Canvas embroidery—Patterns. I. Title. BIP

EPSTEIN, Roslyn. 746.4'4
American Indian needlepoint designs for pillows, belts, handbags & other projects. New York, Dover Publications [1973] vii, 37 p. illus. 28 cm. [TT778.C3E67 1973] 73-82422 ISBN 0-486-22973-4 1.50 (pbk.)
1. Canvas embroidery—Patterns. I. Title. BIP

FARLIE, Barbara L. 746.4'4
Your house in needlepoint / Barbara L. Farlie and Constance C. Sloan. Indianapolis : Bobbs-Merrill, [1976] p. cm. Includes index. [TT778.C3F37] 75-511 ISBN 0-672-52055-9 : 12.95
1. Canvas embroidery—Patterns. I. Sloan, Constance C., joint author. II. Title. BIP

FELCHER, Cecelia. 746.4'4
The needlepoint workbook of traditional designs. Diagrs. and graphs by Jerome Felcher. Photos. by Salvatore Lopes. New York, Hawthorn Books [1973] xi, 233 p. illus. 27 cm. Bibliography: p. 225-226. [TT778.C3F44 1973] 72-7781 12.00
1. Canvas embroidery—Patterns. I. Title.

FIELDS, Barbara. 746.4'4
Instant needlepoint designs, by Barbara Fields and Lorelle Phillips. Illustrated by Carol Nicklaus. New York, Grosset & Dunlap [1973] 93 p. illus. (part col.) 36 cm. [TT778.C3F53 1973] 72-90853 ISBN 0-448-01312-6 12.95
1. Canvas embroidery—Patterns. I. Phillips, Lorelle, joint author. II. Nicklaus, Carol, illus. III. Title.
Pbk. 6.95.

FISCHER, Pauline. 746.4'4
Egyptian designs in modern stitchery / Pauline Fischer ; text by Mary Lou Smith. 1st ed. New York : Dutton, c1979. p. cm. Includes index. Bibliography: p. [TT778.C3F574 1979] 78-11162 ISBN 0-87690-316-2 : 12.50
1. Canvas embroidery—Patterns. 2. Design, Decorative—Egypt. I. Smith, Mary Lou. II. Title. BIP

FONTANA, Frank. 746.4'4
Patchwork quilt designs for needlepoint : charted for easy use / Frank Fontana. New York : Dover Publications, 1976. v, 41 p. : chiefly ill. ; 28 cm. (Dover needlework series) [TT778.C3F66] 75-31281 ISBN 0-486-23300-6 pbk. : 1.50
1. Canvas embroidery—Patterns. 2. Patchwork—Patterns. I. Title. BIP

GRAFTON, Carol Belanger. 746.4'4
Geometric needlepoint designs : charted for easy use / Carol Belanger Grafton. New York : Dover Publications, 1975. v, 40 p. : chiefly ill. ; 28 cm. (Dover needlework series) [TT778.C3G67 1975] 74-21225 ISBN 0-486-23160-7 pbk. : 1.50
1. Canvas embroidery—Patterns. I. Title. BIP

GROSS, Judith. 746.9'5
Needlepoint designs for chair covers / Judith Gross. New York : Van Nostrand Reinhold, [1979] p. cm. Includes index. [TT778.C3G75] 78-25761 ISBN 0-442-22882-1 : 14.95
1. Canvas embroidery—Patterns. 2. Chairs. I. Title. BIP

HALPERN, Frieda. 746.4'4
Full-color Russian folk needlepoint designs : charted for easy use / Frieda Halpern. Don Mills, Ont. : General Pub. Co., c1976. 31 p. : chiefly col. ill. ; 28 cm. (Dover needlework series) Cover title. [TT778.C3H34 1976b] 77-372813 ISBN 0-486-23451-7 : 2.60 ($2.25 U.S.)
1. Canvas embroidery—Patterns. 2. Folk art—Russia. 3. Design, Decorative—Russia. I. Title.

HALPERN, Frieda. 746.4'4
Full-color Russian folk needlepoint designs charted for easy use / Frieda Halpern. New York : Dover Publications, 1976. 31 p. : all col. ill. ; 28 cm. (Dover needlework series) Cover title. [TT778.C3H34 1976] 76-44988 ISBN 0-486-23451-7 pbk. : 2.25
1. Canvas embroidery—Patterns. 2. Folk art—Russia. 3. Design, Decorative—Russia. I. Title. BIP

HAMMOND, Natalie Hays, 1905- 746.4'4
New adventures in needlepoint design. New York, Simon and Schuster [1973] 128 p. illus. 29 cm. Bibliography: p. 127-128. [TT778.C3H35] 73-10927 ISBN 0-671-21575-2 8.95
1. Canvas embroidery—Patterns. I. Title. BIP

HANLEY, Hope. 746.9'5
Needlepoint styles for period furniture / Hope Hanley ; drawings by James A. Stygar ; diagrs. by Trudy Nicholson ; cartoons by Mary Beth Hawn ; photos. (unless otherwise noted) by Philip L. Coltrain. New York : Scribner, c1978. 176 p., [8] leaves of plates : ill. ; 24 cm. Includes index. Bibliography: p. 167-171. [TT778.C3H373] 78-3496 ISBN 0-684-15582-6 : 14.95
1. Canvas embroidery—Patterns. 2. Furniture—History—17th century. 3. Furniture—History—18th century. 4. Furniture—History—19th century. I. Title.

IREYS, Katharine. 746.4'4
The encyclopedia of canvas embroidery stitch patterns. New York, Crowell [1972] xv, 160 p. illus. 29 cm. [TT778.C3I73] 72-78267 ISBN 0-690-26336-8 6.95
1. Canvas embroidery—Patterns. I. Title. BIP

IREYS, Katharine. 746.4'4
The encyclopedia of canvas embroidery stitch patterns / Katharine Ireys. Rev. ed. New York : Crowell, [1977] p. cm. Includes index. Bibliography: p. [TT778.C3I73 1977] 77-1524 ISBN 0-690-01516-X : 12.95 ISBN 0-690-01517-8 pbk. : 6.95
1. Canvas embroidery—Patterns. I. Title.

KAESTNER, Dorothy. 746.4'4
Needlepoint bargello. Photos. by George F. Kaestner. New York, Scribner [1974] 136 p. illus. (part col.) 28 cm. Bibliography: p. 136. [TT778.C3K34] 75-24259 ISBN 0-684-13646-5 12.50
1. Canvas embroidery—Patterns. I. Title. BIP

KATZENBERG, Gloria. 746.4'4
Needlepoint and pattern: themes and variations. New York, Macmillan [1974] ix, 148 p. illus. 26 cm. Bibliography: p. 143. [TT778.C3K37] 72-92450 ISBN 0-02-560810-X 12.95
1. Canvas embroidery—Patterns. I. Title.

KLUGER, Phyllis. 746.4'4
Patterns from the past / by Phyllis Kluger. New York : Knopf, 1975. p. cm. Includes index. [TT778.C3K59] 75-8234 15.00
1. Canvas embroidery—Patterns. I. Title.

LANDSMAN, Anne Cheek, 1948- 746.4'4
Needlework designs from the American Indian tribes of the Southeastern United States / by Anne Cheek Landsman. Cranbury, N.J. : A. S. Barnes, c1977. p. cm. Includes index. [TT778.C3L27] 76-10871 ISBN 0-498-01804-0 : 15.00
1. Canvas embroidery—Patterns. 2. Indians of North America—Southern States—Textile industry and fabrics. I. Title.

LANE, Maggie. 746.9'7
Maggie Lane's needlepoint pillows. New York : Scribner, [1976] p. cm. [TT778.C3L32] 76-24824 ISBN 0-684-14760-2 : 12.50. ISBN 0-684-14724-6 pbk. : 6.95
1. Canvas embroidery—Patterns. 2. Pillows. 3. Design, Decorative—China. I. Title. II. Title: Needlepoint pillows. BIP

LANTZ, Sherlee. 746.4'4
A pageant of pattern for needlepoint canvas; centuries of design, textures, stitches, a new exploration. With diagrs. by Maggie Lane. [1st ed.] New York, Atheneum, 1973. xvii, 509 p. illus. (part col.) 29 cm. Bibliography: p. 503-505. [TT778.C3L33 1973] 73-80751 ISBN 0-689-10571-1 25.00
1. Canvas embroidery—Patterns. I. Lane, Maggie. II. Title.

LANTZ, Sherlee. 746.4'4
A pageant of pattern for needlepoint canvas : centuries of design, textures, stitches : a new exploration / by Sherlee Lantz ; with diagrs. by Maggie Lane. New York : Grosset & Dunlap, 1975, c1973. xvii, 509 p., [9] leaves of plates : ill. (some col.) ; 29 cm. Includes index. Bibliography: p. 503-505. [TT778.C3L33 1975] 75-331087 ISBN 0-448-12034-8 : 15.95
1. Canvas embroidery—Patterns. I. Lane, Maggie. II. Title.

LANTZ, Sherlee. 746.4'4
Trianglepoint / Sherlee antz. 1st ed. New York : Viking Press, 1976. 334 p. : ill. ; 23 cm. (History of science : Selections from Isis) Includes bibliographical references. [TT778.C3L35 1976] 76-3550 ISBN 0-670-73030-0 : 8.95
1. Canvas embroidery—Patterns. I. Title. BIP

LOEB, Marcia. 746.4'4
Pennsylvania Dutch needlepoint designs : charted for easy use / Marcia Loeb. New York : Dover Publications, 1976. v, 37 p. : chiefly ill. ; 28 cm. (Dover needlework series) [TT778.C3L63 1976] 75-31282 ISBN 0-486-23299-9 pbk. : 1.50
1. Canvas embroidery—Patterns. 2. Design, Decorative—Pennsylvania. I. Title. BIP

MARKRICH, Lilo. 746.4'4
Victorian fancywork: nineteenth century needlepoint patterns and designs [by] Lilo Markrich and Heinz Edgar Kiewe. Chicago, Regnery [1974] 172 p. illus. 24 cm. Bibliography: p. 171-172. [TT778.C3M37] 74-6901 ISBN 0-8092-8348-4 10.95
1. Canvas embroidery—Patterns. 2. Decoration and ornament—Victorian style. I. Kiewe, Heinz Edgar, joint author. II. Title.

MARTON, Sheila Nassberg. 746.4'4
Patterned backgrounds for needlepoint / Sheila Nassberg Marton, Muriel Brandwein Selick. New York : Van Nostrand Reinhold, [1977] p. cm. Includes index. [T778.C3m44] 77-3147 ISBN 0-442-27480-7 : 15.00
1. Canvas embroidery—Patterns. I. Selick, Muriel Brandwein, joint author. II. Title. BIP

NICOLETTI, Sally. 746.4'4
Weaving designs for needlepoint / by Sally Nicoletti ; photos. by John McKee, William Froelich, and Joseph Nicoletti, graphs by D. Andrew Eddy and Sally Nicoletti, diagrs. by Mary Hoffman Treworgy. 1st ed. New York : Morrow, c1978. 182 p. : ill. ; 29 cm. Bibliography: p. 179. [TT778.C3N52] 78-5878 ISBN 0-688-03330-X : 17.95
1. Canvas embroidery—Patterns. 2. Weaving—Patterns. I. Title. BIP

ORMOND, Brande. 746.4'4
American primitives in needlepoint / by Brande Ormond. Boston : Houghton Mifflin, 1977. 139 p., [4] leaves of plates : ill. ; 29 cm. [TT778.C3O74] 77-8277 ISBN 0-395-25485-X : 15.00
1. Canvas embroidery—Patterns. 2. Primitivism in art—United States. I. Title. BIP

PAKULA, Marion Broome. 746.4'4
Needlepoint patterns for signs and sayings / by Marion Broome Pakula and Rhoda Ochser Goldberg. New York : Crown Publishers, c1977. p. cm. [TT778.C3P33] 76-30717 ISBN 0-517-52859-2 pbk. : 4.95
1. Canvas embroidery—Patterns. 2. Aphorisms and apothegms. 3. Signs and sign-boards. I. Goldberg, Rhoda Ochser, joint author. II. Title. BIP

PAKULA, Marion Broome. 746.4'4
Needlepoint plaids / Marion Broome Pakula. New York : Crown Publishers, [1975] 96 p. : ill. (some col.) ; 29 cm. [TT778.C3P34 1975] 75-4520 ISBN 0-517-52041-9 : 5.95 ISBN 0-517-52042-7 pbk. : 3.95
1. Canvas embroidery—Patterns. 2. Tartans. 3. Plaid. I. Title. BIP

PAKULA, Marion Broome. 746.4'4
New ideas for needlepointers / Marion Broome Pakula. New York : Crown Publishers, c1976. 95 p. : ill. ; 29 cm. Includes index. [TT778.C3P345 1976] 75-37799 7.95
1. Canvas embroidery—Patterns. I. Title.

PARKER, Elinor Milnor, 1906- 746.4'4
Letters and numbers for needlepoint / E. M. Parker. New York : Scribner, c1978. 93 p. : chiefly ill. ; 28 cm. [TT778.C3P36] 77-16711 ISBN 0-684-15527-3 pbk. : 4.95
1. Canvas embroidery—Patterns. 2. Alphabets. 3. Numerals. I. Title.

PARKER, Xenia Ley. 746.4'4
Mosaics in needlepoint / by Xenia Ley Parker. New York : Scribner, [1977] p. cm. Includes index. Bibliography: p. [TT778.C3P38] 77-5045 ISBN 0-684-15035-2 : 12.95. ISBN 0-684-15036-0 pbk. : 5.95
1. Canvas embroidery—Patterns. 2. Mosaics. I. Title. BIP

PERRONE, Lisbeth. 746.4'4
Lisbeth Perrone's book of folk art embroidery / Lisbeth Perrone. 1st ed. New York : Random House, c1978. p. cm. [TT778.C3P44 1978] 78-3710 ISBN 0-394-42401-8 : 9.95
1. Canvas embroidery—Patterns. 2. Cross-stitch—Patterns. 3. Folk art. 4. Design, Decorative. I. Title. II. Title: Book of folk art embroidery.

PERRONE, Lisbeth. 746.4'4
Needlepoint workbook. [1st ed.] [New York, Random House, 1973] 48 p. illus. (part col.) 36 cm. Cover title. [TT778.C3P46] 73-5023 ISBN 0-394-47268-3 6.95
1. Canvas embroidery—Patterns. I. Title.

PERRONE, Lisbeth. 746.4'4
The Walt Disney characters needlepoint book : embroideries and needlepoint instruction / by Lisbeth Perrone. 1st ed. New York : Random House, c1976. 95 p. : ill. (some col.) ; 29 cm. [TT778.C3P48] 76-10360 ISBN 0-394-49910-7 : 9.95
1. Canvas embroidery—Patterns. I. Title.

PROJANSKY, Ella. 746.4'4
Sculptured needlepoint stitchery / Ella Projansky. New York : Scribner, c1978. vii, 132 p., [2] leaves of plates : ill. (some col.) ; 29 cm. Includes index. [TT778.C3P76] 77-15969 ISBN 0-684-15371-8 : 14.95
1. Canvas embroidery—Patterns. I. Title. BIP

ROGERS, Gay Ann. 746.4'4
Tribal designs for needlepoint : 30 original designs adapted from Eskimo, Polynesian, and Indian art / Gay Ann Rogers. 1st ed. Garden City, N.Y. : Doubleday, 1977. 159 p., [6] leaves of plates : ill. (some col.) ; 26

cm. [TT778.C3R6] 76-2814 ISBN 0-385-09967-3 pbk. : 3.95
1. Canvas embroidery—Patterns. 2. Indians of North America—Art. 3. Art, Polynesian. 4. Design, Decorative—Themes, motives. I. Title. BIP

ROME, Carol Cheney. 746.4'4
Needlepoint letters and numbers / Carol Cheney Rome and Donna Reidy Orr. 1st ed. New York : Doubleday, c1976. p. cm. Includes index. Bibliography: p. [TT778.C3R63] 75-36609 ISBN 0-385-09980-0 : 10.00
1. Canvas embroidery—Patterns. 2. Alphabets. 3. Numerals. I. Orr, Donna Reidy, joint author. II. Title. BIP

ROSS, Robert Horace. 746.4'4
Treasures of Tutankhamun in needlepoint / by Robert Horace Ross ; photos. by Edward L. Wintringham. 1st ed. New York : Morrow, c1978. 86 p. : ill. ; 29 cm. [TT778.C3R67] 78-10342 ISBN 0-688-03430-6 : 15.00 ISBN 0-688-08430-3 pbk. : 8.95 pbk.
1. Tutankhamen, King of Egypt. 2. Canvas embroidery—Patterns. I. Title. II. Title: Tutankhamun in needlepoint.

SCHEUER, Nikki. 746.4'4
Designs for bargello; 62 original patterns inspired by or adapted from a range of historical and cultural sources. Photographed by Jerry Rosen. [1st ed.] Garden City, N.Y., Doubleday, 1973. 144 p. illus. 21 x 28 cm. [TT778.C3S3] 72-97259 ISBN 0-385-00066-9 9.95
1. Canvas embroidery—Patterns. I. Title. BIP

SCHOENFELD, Susan. 746.4'4
Pattern design for needlepoint & patchwork, by Susan Schoenfeld, with Winifred Bendiner. New York, Van Nostrand Reinhold Co. [1973] 199 p. illus. (part col.) 25 cm. Part of illustrative matter in pocket. [TT778.C3S33] 72-9709 ISBN 0-442-27417-3 11.50
1. Canvas embroidery—Patterns. 2. Quilting—Patterns. I. Title.

TURNER, Diana Oliver. 746.4'4
African needlepoint designs : charted for easy use / Diana Oliver Turner. New York : Dover Publications, 1976. v, 41 p. : ill. ; 28 cm. (Dover needlework series) [TT778.C3T87 1976] 75-21352 ISBN 0-486-23244-1 pbk. : 2.00
1. Canvas embroidery—Patterns. 2. Design, Decorative—Africa. I. Title. BIP

WEISS, Rita. 746.4'4
Christmas needlepoint designs / Rita Weiss. New York : Dover Publications, 1975. 19 p. : ill. (some col.) ; 28 cm. (Dover needlework series) [TT778.C3W44 1975] 74-21224 ISBN 0-486-23161-5 : 1.50
1. Canvas embroidery—Patterns. 2. Christmas decorations. I. Title. BIP

WEISS, Rita. 746.4'4
The needlepoint alphabet sampler book : 26 full-color designs with easy-to-follow instructions for working and using 32 stitches / Rita Weiss and Carol Belanger Grafton. New York : Dover Publications, 1977. 48 p. : ill. ; 29 cm. (Dover needlepoint series) Includes index. [TT778.C3W45 1977] 76-47810 ISBN 0-486-23472-X pbk. : 2.75
1. Canvas embroidery—Patterns. 2. Alphabets. I. Grafton, Carol Belanger, joint author. II. Title.

Canyon de Chelly National Monument.

STEEN, Charlie R. 970.4'91'37
Tse-ta'a; excavations at Tse-ta'a, Canyon de Chelly National Monument, Arizona, by Charlie R. Steen. Washington, U.S. National Park Service, 1966. vii, 160 p. illus. 29 cm. (Archeological research series 9) Includes bibliographies. [E51.U75 no. 9] 66-62000 1.75 (pbk)
1. Canyon de Chelly National Monument. I. Title. II. Series: U.S. National Park Service. Archeological series 9

Capa, Robert, 1913-1954.

CAPA, Robert, 1913-1954. 770'.92'4
Robert Capa, 1913-1954 / [editors, Cornell Capa, Bhupendra Karia]. New York : Grossman Publishers, 1974. 127 p. : ill. ; 23 cm. (ICP library of photographers ; v. 1) [TR140.C28A32 1974] 72-11005 ISBN 0-670-60095-4 : 12.50. ISBN 0-670-60096-2 pbk. : 6.95
1. Capa, Robert, 1913-1954. 2. Photography, Journalistic. I. Series: International Fund for Concerned Photography. ICP library of photographers ; v. 1.

ROBERT Capa. 779'.9'9047
Text by John Hersey [and others] New York, Paragraphic Books [1969] 106 p. illus., ports. 18 cm. [TR140.C28R6] 67-21240 2.95
1. Capa, Robert, 1913-1954. I. Hersey, John Richard, 1914-

Caparn, Rhys, 1909—

CAPARN, Rhys, 1909- 730'.92'4
Rhys Caparn, by Robert Beverly Hale. Danbury, Conn., Retrospective Press [1972] [25] p., 87 [i.e. 88] plates. port. 30 cm. [NB237.C37H34] 73-152063 15.00
1. Caparn, Rhys, 1909- I. Hale, Robert Beverly, 1901-

Cape Town—Descr.—Views.

DIXON, Leng, 1916- 741.91
Malay and Cape sketches. [With an introd. by Ruth Prowse. Cape Town, Maskew Miller, 1952] unpaged (chiefly illus.) 26cm. [NC1260.D5] 56-56066
1. Cape Town—Descr.—Views. I. Title.

Cape Town in art.

GROGAN, Tony. 759.968
Tony Grogan's vanishing Cape Town / text by Brian Barrow. Cape Town : D. Nelson, 1976. [39] p. : ill. (some col.) ; 25 x 33 cm. [NC368.6.S63G76] 77-357819 ISBN 0-909238-21-9
1. Grogan, Tony. 2. Cape Town in art. 3. Cape Town—Description. I. Barrow, Brian. II. Title. III. Title: Vanishing Cape Town.

Capitols—United States—History.

HITCHCOCK, Henry-Russell, 1903- 973
Temples of democracy : the state capitols of the U.S.A. / Henry-Russell Hitchcock and William Seale. New York : Harcourt Brace Jovanovich, c1976. p. cm. Includes index. Bibliography: p. [NA4411.H57] 75-35973 ISBN 0-15-188536-2 : 25.00
1. Capitols—United States—History. 2. Architecture—United States—History. I. Seale, William, joint author. II. Title. BIP

Capp, Al, 1909-

BERGER, Arthur Asa, 1933- 741.5973
Li'l Abner: a study in American satire. New York, Twayne [1970] 191 p. illus. 21 cm. Bibliography: p. 178-185. [NC1429.C295B4] 68-24281
1. Capp, Al, 1909- Li'l Abner. I. Title.

CAPP, Al, 1909- 741.5'973
The best of Li'l Abner / Al Capp. 1st ed. New York : Holt, Rinehart, and Winston, c1978. 190 p. : chiefly ill. (some col.) ; 29 cm. Cartoons. Cartoonist Al Capp presents 26 of his favorite sequences from his cartoon strip. [PN6728.L5C28] 78-53782 ISBN 0-03-044071-8 : 14.95. ISBN 0-03-045516-2 pbk. : 12.95
I. Title.

Caravaggio, Michelangelo Merisi da, 1569?-1609.

BOTTARI, Stefano. 759.5
Caravaggio. [Translated from the Italian by Diane Goldrei. 1st American ed.] New York, Grossett & Dunlap [1971] 38 p. illus., 79 col. plates. 18 cm. (The New Grosset art library, 34) Bibliography: p. 11. [ND623.C26B613 1971] 77-110101
1. Caravaggio, Michelangelo Merisi da, 1573-1610.

FRIEDLAENDER, Walter F 1873- 759.5
Caravaggio studies. Princeton, Princeton University Press, 1955. xxviii, 320p. illus., plates, port. 31cm. Includes bibliographical references. [ND623.C26F7] [ND623.C26F7] 927.5 53-6385 53-6385
1. Caravaggio, Michelangelo Merisi da, 1569?-1000. I. Title.
Contents omitted. BIP

FRIEDLAENDER, Walter F., 1873-1966. 759.5 B
Caravaggio studies. New York, Schocken Books [1969, c1955] xxviii, 320 p. illus., plates, port. 24 cm. Contents.Contents.—Caravaggio studies.—Catalogue raisonne.—Biographies and documents. Includes bibliographical references. [ND623.C26F7 1969] 72-86848 5.95
1. Caravaggio, Michelangelo Merisi da, 1573-1610. I. Title. BIP

HINKS, Roger Packman. 759.5
Caravaggio's Death of the Virgin. London, New York, Oxford University Press, 1953. 15p. illus. 17cm. (Charlton lecture, 35) Bibliographical footnotes. [ND623.C26H47] 54-1858
1. Caravaggio, Michelangelo Merisi da, 1569?-1609. I. Title. II. Title: Death of the Virgin. III. Series.

HINKS, Roger Packman. 927.5
Michelangelo Merisi da Caravaggio: his life, his legend, his works. London, Faber and Faber [1953] 126p. 97plates (1 col.) 26cm. 'Bibliographical note':p. 121-122. [ND623.C26H5 1953] A54
1. Caravaggio, Michelangelo Merisi da, 1569?-1609. I. Title.

Caravaggio, Michelangelo Merisi da, 1569?-1609—Influence.

CARAVAGGIO, Michelangelo Merisi da, 1573-1610. 759.5
All the paintings of Caravaggio. Edited by Costantino Baroni. Translated by Anthony Firmin O'Sullivan. New York, Hawthorn Books [1962] 38 p. 100 plates (4 col.) 19 cm. (The Complete library of world art, v. 7) "Bibliographical note": p. 35. [ND623.C26B283] 62-10521
I. Baroni, Costantino, ed. II. Title. III. Series.

COHEN (B.) and Sons Trafalgar Galleries. 759.04
In the light of Caravaggio : [catalogue of an exhibition]. London : Trafalgar Galleries, 1976. 61 p. : ill. (some col.) ; 31 cm. Errata slip: [1] leaf inserted. Bibliography: p. 53-61. [ND172.M3C64 1976] 77-359600 £4.00
1. Caravaggio, Michelangelo Merisi da, 1573-1610—Influence. 2. Mannerism (Art)—Exhibitions. 3. Painting, Renaissance—Exhibitions. I. Title.

MOIR, Alfred. 760
Caravaggio and his copyists / by Alfred Moir. New York : New York University Press, 1976. p. cm. Bibliography: p. [N6407.M64] 75-27051 ISBN 0-8147-5408-2 : 22.50
1. Caravaggio, Michelangelo Merisi da, 1573-1610—Influence. 2. Art, Modern—17th-18th centuries. 3. Art, Modern—19th century. 4. Pictures—Copying. 5. Art—Attribution. I. Title. BIP

MOIR, Alfred. 759.5
The Italian followers of Caravaggio. Cambridge, Harvard University Press, 1967. 2 v. 403 illus. 27 cm. Bibliography: v. 1, p. 319-345. [ND623.C26M6] 66-10315
1. Caravaggio, Michelangelo Merisi da, 1573-1610—Influence. 2. Painters, Italian. 3. Painting, Italian—History. I. Title. BIP

SPEAR, Richard E., 1940- 759.94
Caravaggio and his followers / by Richard E. Spear. Rev. ed. New York : Harper & Row, c1975. x, 244 p. : ill. ; 24 cm. (Icon editions ; IN-34) Bibliography: p. 231-242. [ND182.B3S65 1975] 75-328941 ISBN 0-06-430034-X : 5.95
1. Caravaggio, Michelangelo Merisi da, 1573-1610—Influence. 2. Paintings, Baroque—Exhibitions. I. Title.

SPEAR, Richard E., 1940- 759.94
Caravaggio and his followers, by Richard E. Spear. [Cleveland] Cleveland Museum of Art [1971] x, 214 p. illus. (part col.) 26 cm. Exhibition catalog. Bibliography: p. 203-211. [ND182.B3S65] 76-169620 ISBN 0-910386-17-X 15.00
1. Caravaggio, Michelangelo Merisi da, 1573-1610—Influence. 2. Paintings, Baroque—Exhibitions. I. Title. BIP

Caravaggio, michelangelo Merisi da, 1569?-1609.

CARAVAGGIO, 759.5
his incongruity and his fame. New York, Macmillan, 1953. 122p. 88plates. 22cm. [ND623.C26B45] [ND623.C26B45] 927.5 54-812 54-812
1. Caravaggio, Michelangelo Merisl da, 1569?-1609. I. Berenson, Bernhard, 1865-

Card weaving.

BIRD, Eileen. 746.1'4
Introducing tablet weaving / by Eileen Bird. New York : Pitman, [1974] 64 p., [2] leaves of plates : ill. (some col.) ; 26 cm. [TT848.B48] 74-79268 ISBN 0-273-07076-2 : 8.95
1. Card weaving. I. Title.

CROCKETT, Candace, 1945- 746.1'4
Card weaving. Illus. by Lawrence Duke. New York, Watson-Guptill Publications [1973] 143 p. illus. (part col.) 26 cm. Bibliography: p. 138-139. [TT848.C67 1973] 73-6913 ISBN 0-8230-0562-3 10.50
1. Card weaving. BIP

KATZ, Ruth J. 746.1'4
Card weaving / Ruth J. Katz. New York : Van Nostrand Reinhold Co., 1977. 152 p. : ill. ; 22 x 24 cm. Includes index. Bibliography: p. 145-146. [TT848.K33] 73-16712 ISBN 0-442-24261-1 : 13.50
1. Card weaving. I. Title. BIP

SNOW, Marjorie. 746.1'4
Step-by-step tablet weaving, by Marjorie and William Snow. New York, Golden Press [1973] 80 p. illus. (part col.) 29 cm. Bibliography: p. 79. [TT848.S62] 73-76937 2.50
1. Card weaving. I. Snow, William, 1947- joint author. II. Title.

SPECHT, Sally. 746.1'4
Creating with card weaving; a simple, non-loom technique [by] Sally Specht and Sandra Rawlings. New York, Crown Publishers [1973] 95 p. illus. 29 cm. Bibliography: p. 93. [TT848.S67 1973] 72-96647 ISBN 0-517-50348-4 4.95
1. Card weaving. I. Rawlings, Sandra, joint author. II. Title.
Pbk. 2.50; ISBN 0-517-50379-4 BIP

SUTTON, Ann. 746.1'4
Tablet weaving [by] Ann Sutton and Pat Holtom. Newton Centre, Mass., C. T. Branford Co. [1975] 103 p. illus. 21 cm. Bibliography: p. 102. [TT848.S9 1975] 74-18323 ISBN 0-8231-5045-3 10.50
1. Card weaving. I. Holtom, Pat, joint author. II. Title. BIP

Carder, Frederick.

GARDNER, Paul Vickers, 1908- 748.2'913
The glass of Frederick Carder, by Paul V. Gardner. Introd. by Paul N. Perrot. New York, Crown Publishers [1971] vi, 373 p. illus., 32 col. plates. 29 cm. Bibliography: p. 363-364. [NK5198.C3G3] 74-168313 20.00
1. Carder, Frederick. 2. Steuben Glass, inc. I. Title. BIP

HOTCHKISS, John F. 748.2913085
Steuben glass. Rochester, N.Y., Author, 89 Sagamore Dr. [c.1964] 103p. illus. (pt. col.) facsim., port. 23cm. Vol. 1 includes a reduced size copy of the 1932 catalogue, Steuben hand-blown glassware, pub. by Steuben Div., Corning Glass Works, with price code letters added to show 1964 price ranges [NK5198.C3H6] 65-1047 5.00 pap.,
1. Carder, Frederick. 2. teuben glass; index & price guide 3. Steuben Glass, Inc. 4. Glassware, American—Catalogs. I. Steuben

Glass, Inc. Steuben hand-blown glassware. II. Title.

Cardew, Michael, 1901—

CLARK, Garth. 738.3'092'4 B
Michael Cardew : a portrait / by Garth Clark. 1st ed. Tokyo ; New York : Kodansha International ; New York : distributed by Harper & Row, 1976. 228 p. : ill. (some col.) ; 26 cm. Includes index. Bibliography: p. 225-226. [NK4210.C29C55] 76-9358 ISBN 0-87011-277-5 : 25.00
1. Cardew, Michael, 1901- 2. Potters—Great Britain—Biography. BIP

Cardew, Michael, 1901- —Addresses, essays, lectures.

MICHAEL Cardew : 738.3'092'4 B
a collection of essays / with an introd. by Bernard Leach ; and contributions by Michael Cardew ... [et al.]. London : Crafts Advisory Council ; New York : distributed in the United States of America and Canada by Watson-Guptill, c1976. 80 p. : ill. ; 21 x 22 cm. Includes index. Contents.Contents.—Leach, B. Introduction.—Houston, J. The early years.—Finch, R. Working at Winchcombe in 1936.—Bouverie, K. P. A personal account.—Houston, J. Africa and Cornwall.—Cardew, M. Slipware and stoneware.—Chronology.—Pottery marks. Bibliography: p. 77-79. [NK4210.C29M5] 76-381211 ISBN 0-903798-07-7 : 9.95.
1. Cardew, Michael, 1901- —Addresses, essays, lectures. 2. Potters—Great Britain—Biography—Addresses, essays, lectures. I. Cardew, Michael, 1901-

Cards.

WAYLAND, Virginia. 795.4'09
The Winstanley geographical cards. Pasadena, Calif., V. & H. Wayland [1967] 75 p. facsims. 25 cm. (The Wayland playing card monographs, no. 1) Bibliography: p. 75. [GV1235.W3] 68-2737
1. Winstanley, Henry, d. 1703. 2. Cards. 3. Geography—Early works. I. Title.

Cards—Art.

HICKLIN, Frances. 769'.4'9688754
Playing cards / Frances Hicklin. London : H.M. Stationery Office, 1976. [12] p. : col. ill. ; 16 x 13 cm. (Small colour book ; 12) Bibliography: p. [3] [GV1235.H47] 77-361022 £0.35
1. Cards—Art. I. Title. II. Series: Victoria and Albert Museum, South Kensington. Small colour book ; 12.

Cards—Collectors and collecting.

CLARK, Freida, 1909- 791.4
Playing card collectors handbook; description and check lists: English royalty and cards issued by Worshipful Company of Makers of Playing Cards. [Chicago?] c1954. 64p. illus. 18cm. [NC1280.C55] 55-25980
1. Cards—Collectors and collecting. I. Title.

MANN, Sylvia. 688.754075
Collecting playing cards. New York, Crown Publishers [1966] 215 p. illus. 22 cm. Bibliography: p. 202-207. [GV1235.M3 1966a] 66-26164
1. Cards—Collectors and collecting. I. Title.

Cards—Collectors and collecting—Directories.

LERNER, Irving W., 1936- 769'.5
Who's who in card collecting. 1st ed. Philadelphia, 1970. 106 p. 28 cm. [NC1877.L4] 76-12899
1. Cards—Collectors and collecting—Directories. I. Title.

Carducci, Vincenzio, 1578-1638.

VOLK, Mary Crawford. 759.6 B
Vicencio Carducho and seventeenth century Castilian painting / Mary Crawford Volk. New York : Garland Pub., 1977, i.e.1978 428 p., [76] leaves of plates : ill. ; 22 cm. (Outstanding dissertations in the fine arts) Reprint of the author's thesis, Yale, 1973. Bibliography: p. 415-428. [ND813.C287V64 1977] 76-23650 ISBN 0-8240-2734-5 lib.bdg. : 45.00
1. Carducci, Vincenzio, 1578-1638. 2. Painters—Spain—Castile—Biography. I. Title. II. Series.

Caribbean area—Descr. & trav.—Views.

PASCIN, Jules, 1885-1930. 741.973
Jules Pascin's Caribbean sketchbook. Introd. by John Palmer Leeper. Austin, Published for the Marion Koogler McNay Art Institute, San Antonio, by the University of Texas Press [1964] x, 106 p. (chiefly illus. (part col.)) 26 cm. [NC1075.P2864] 64-22385
1. Caribbean area—Descr. & trav.—Views. I. Leeper, John Palmer. II. Marion Koogler McNay Art Institute, San Antonio. III. Title. IV. Title: Caribbean sketchbook.

Caribbean area in art.

HOMER, Winslow, 1836-1910. 759.13
Winslow Homer's sub-tropical America. Coral Gables, Fla., Lowe Art Museum [1968?] 40 p. illus. 31 cm. Catalog of an exhibition held at the Lowe Art Museum, Coral Gables, Fla. which opened on Aug. 4, 1968. Includes bibliographical references. [ND1839.H6L68] 74-158943
1. Homer, Winslow, 1836-1910. 2. Caribbean area in art. I. Lowe Art Museum. II. Title.

Caricature.

BERGER, Oscar, 1901- 741.5
My victims; how to caricature. New York, Harper [1952] 128 p. illus. 28 cm. [NC1429.B36A52] 51-11885
1. Caricature. I. Title.

BLAFER Publishing Company, New York. 741.5
Cartooning; new easy method of drawing cartoons that sell. New York [1952] 84 p. illus. 26 cm. [NC1320.B6] 52-3510
1. Caricature. 2. Drawing—Instruction. I. Title.

DARVAS, Lou. 741.5
You can draw cartoons. [1st ed.] Garden City, N. Y., Doubleday, 1960. 152 p. illus. 29 cm. [NC1320.D35] 60-9426
1. Caricature. 2. Drawing—Instruction. I. Title.

FRAYDAS, Stan 741.5
Graphic humor. New York, Reinhold [c.1961] 128p. illus. 27cm. 61-13196 7.50
1. Caricature. 2. Drawing—Instruction. I. Title.

FRAYDAS, Stan. 741.5
Professional cartooning; a complete course in graphic humor. [1st ed. Huntington, N.Y.] R. E. Krieger Pub. Co. [1972] 160 p. illus. 28 cm. Based on the author's Graphic humor, published in 1961. [NC1320.F74] 72-81126 ISBN 0-88275-064-X 12.50
1. Caricature. 2. Drawing—Instruction. I. Title.
pap. 5.95. BIP

HAMM, Jack. 741.5'028
Cartooning the head & figure. New York, Grosset & Dunlap [1967] 120 p. illus. 28 cm. [NC1320.H25] 67-14755
1. Caricature. 2. Head in art. 3. Figure drawing. I. Title. BIP

HOFF, Sydney, 1912- 741.5'973
The art of cartooning [by] Syd Hoff. New York, Stravon Educational Press [1973] 224 p. illus. 27 cm. [NC1320.H53] 72-12659 ISBN 0-87396-072-6 7.95
1. Caricature. I. Title. BIP

HOFF, Sydney, 1912- 741.5
It's fun learning cartooning. New York, Stravon Publishers, 1952. 127 p. illus. 29 cm. [NC1320.H54] 52-13851
1. Caricature. 2. Drawing—Instruction. I. Title.

HOFF, Sydney, 1912- 741.5
Learning to cartoon [New York, N.Y., 10023,] 43 W. 61 St. Stravon Educational Pr. [c.1966] 191p. illus., port. 28cm. [NC1320.H56] 65-28844 4.95
1. Caricature. 2. Drawing—Instruction. I. Title.

HOFMANN, Werner, 1928- 741.5
Caricature from Leonardo to Picasso. [Translated by M. H. L.] New York, Crown Publishers [1957] 150p. illus., plates. 29cm. Bibliography: p. 142-144. [NC1340.H63] 57-12829
1. Caricature. 2. Caricatures and cartoons. I. Title.

LARIAR, Lawrence, 1908- 741.5069
Careers in cartooning; illustrated with over 100 cartoons. New York, Dodd, Mead, 1949 ['1950] 182 p. illus. 25 cm. [NC1320.L28] 50-5167
1. Caricature. I. Title.

MARKOW, Jack, 1905- 741.5
Drawing and selling cartoons. [New York] [Pitman] [1956] 63 p. illus. 20 x 26 cm. (Pitman drawing series) [NC1320.M28] 55-12072
1. Caricature. 2. Drawing—Instruction. I. Title. BIP

MARKOW, Jack, 1905- 741.5
Drawing and selling cartoons. Rev. ed. New York, Pitman Pub. Corp. [1964] 48 p. illus., port. 20 x 26 cm. (Pitman $1.00 art books, 4) [NC1320.M28 1964] 64-20009
1. Caricature. 2. Drawing—Instruction. I. Title.

MARKOW, Jack, 1905- 741.5
Drawing funny pictures. New York, Pitman Pub. Corp. [1969] 48 p. (chiefly illus., port.) 20 x 26 cm. [NC1320.M285] 70-84845 1.00
1. Caricature. I. Title. BIP

NELSON, Roy Paul. 741.5
Cartooning / Roy Paul Nelson. Chicago : H. Regnery, [1975] p. cm. Includes index. Bibliography: p. [NC1320.N38 1975] 75-13236 ISBN 0-8092-8212-7 : 14.95 ISBN 0-8092-8211-9 pbk. : 5.95
1. Caricature. I. Title. BIP

NELSON, Roy Paul. 741.5
Fell's guide to the art of cartooning. New York, Fell [1962] 112 p. illus. 29 cm. [NC1320.N4] 62-14346
1. Caricature. 2. Drawing — instruction. I. Title. BIP

NORTON, Clarence Clifford. 741.5
The art of caricature. [Spartanburg, S.C., 1951] 68 p. illus. 21 cm. [NC1320.N63] 51-37082
1. Caricature. I. Title.

WHITMAN, Bert. 817'.5'4
Here's how ... About the newspaper editorial cartoon. Words and pictures by Bert Whitman. Lodi, Calif., Lodi Pub. Co. [1968] 96 p. illus. 22 x 28 cm. [NC1429.W48A48] 68-1620
I. Title.

WRIGHT, Grant. 741.5
The art of caricature. New York, Baker Taylor Co. Detroit, Gale Research Co., 1974 [c1904] p. cm. [NC1320.W83 1974] 74-17184 ISBN 0-8103-4073-9
1. Caricature. I. Title.

ZAIDENBERG, Arthur 741.5
How to draw cartoons! A beginner's book for boys and girls. New York, Vanguard Press [c.1959] 61p. illus. 28cm. 59-13011 3.00 bds.,
1. Caricature. 2. Drawing—Instruction. I. Title.

Caricature and cartoons.

*ARMSTRONG, William 741.5973
Franciscan cartoons by Wm. Armstrong. Seattle, Seattle University, 1974. 1 v. (unpaged), illus. 22 cm. [NC1320] ISBN 0-913452-24-6. 1.00 (pbk.)
1. Caricature and cartoons. 2. Franciscans—Juvenile literature. I. Title. BIP

*CHAPMAN, Bernard F. 741.59
Caricature in rime & line. Lebanon, N.H., Author, Hardy Hill. [c.1963] 62p. chiefly illus. 18cm. 1.25 pap.,
I. Title.

CURRIE, Gordon. 741.5994
The caricatures of Gordon Currie. Introd. by Art Linkletter. [1st ed.] Alhambra, Calif., Borden Pub. Co. [1967] [48] p. (chiefly illus.) 31 cm. (Master draughtsman series) [NC1429.C88A46] 67-30961
I. Title.

*HAMILTON, William. 741.59
William Hamilton's anti-social register. San Francisco, Chronicle Books, [1974] (192 p.) illus. 19 cm. [NC1320] 74-10401 ISBN 0-87701-048-X 6.95
1. Caricature and cartoons. I. Title. BIP

Caricature and cartoons—Social aspects.

ROGERS, William Garland, 1896- 741.5
Mightier than the sword; cartoon, caricature, social comment [by] W. G. Rogers. [1st ed.] New York, Harcourt, Brace & World [1969] 287 p. illus. 21 cm. Bibliography: p. 267-273. [NC1340.R6] 71-82637 5.25
1. Caricature and cartoons—Social aspects. I. Title. BIP

Caricature—Great Britain.

BEERBOHM, Max, Sir, 1872-1956. 741.5942
Observations. New York, Haskell House Publishers, 1971. viii p., 51 plates. 29 cm. "A book of caricatures." Reprint of the 1925 ed. [NC1479.B37A55 1971] 71-163891 ISBN 0-8383-1249-7
I. Title. BIP

EVERITT, Graham. 741.5'9'42
English caricaturists and graphic humourists of the nineteenth century; how they illustrated and interpreted their times. Freeport, N.Y., Books for Libraries Press [1972] xix, 427 p. illus. 24 cm. (Essay index reprint series) Reprint of the 1885 ed. Appendices (p. 401-416):—1. Some illustrative work of Isaac Robert Cruikshank.—2. Some miscellaneous work of Robert Seymour executed between 1822 and 1836.—3. Some of the illustrated work of John Leech.—4. Some miscellaneous work of Alfred Henry Forrester (Alfred Crowquill)—5. Some works illustrated by Hablot Knight Browne. [NC1475.E8 1972] 77-37523 ISBN 0-8369-2547-5
1. Caricature—Great Britain. 2. Illustration of books—Great Britain. I. Title. BIP

Caricature—Gt. Brit.—Hist.

GEORGE, Mary Dorothy (Gordon) 741.50942
English political caricature; a study of opinion and propaganda. New York, Oxford University Press, 1959[ ] 2v. various pages illus. 24cm. Contents.1. To 1792.--2. 1793-1832. 60-1102 11.20 ea.,
1. Caricature—Gt. Brit.—Hist. I. Title.

Caricature—History.

GEIPEL, John, 1937- 741.5'09
The cartoon; a short history of graphic comedy and satire. [1st American ed.] South Brunswick, A. S. Barnes [1972] 185 p. illus. 22 cm. Bibliography: p. [177]-179. [NC1325.G44 1972b] 71-38804 ISBN 0-498-01149-6 8.95
1. Caricature—History. I. Title.

LYNCH, John Gilbert Bohun, 1884- 741.5'909
A history of caricature, by Bohun Lynch. Boston, Little, Brown, 1927. Detroit, Gale Research Co., 1974. xiv, 126 p. illus. 23 cm. Bibliography: p. 121-123. [NC1325.L9 1974] 74-6414 ISBN 0-8103-4044-5 10.00
1. Caricature—History. 2. Caricature—Great Britain—History. I. Title. BIP

PARTON, James, 1822-1891. 741.5'09
Caricature and other comic art in all times and many lands. New York, Harper & Row [1969] 340 p. illus., facsims., maps, ports. 22 cm. (J. & J. Harper editions) Reprint of the 1877 ed. "A large portion of ... [the] contents appeared in Harper's monthly magazine during the year 1875." [NC1325.P3 1969] 70-81862

1. Caricature—History. I. Title.

SHIKES, Ralph E. 769'.922
The indignant eye; the artist as social critic in prints and drawings from the fifteenth century to Picasso, by Ralph E. Shikes. Boston, Beacon Press [1969] xxviii, 439 p. illus. 26 cm. "Notes and bibliography": p. 407-430. [NC1340.S5] 69-14604 12.50
1. Caricature—History. I. Title. BIP

WRIGHT, Thomas, 1810-1877. 741.5
A history of caricature and grotesque in literature and art. Introd. and index by Frances K. Barasch. New York, F. Ungar Pub. Co. [1968] lxxiv, 508 p. illus. 24 cm. "Reprinted from the London edition of 1865 from a copy in the collections of the New York Public Library Astor, Lenox and Tilden Foundations." [NC1325.W83 1968] 67-23513
1. Caricature—History. I. Title. II. Title: Caricature and grotesque in literature and art. BIP

Caricatures and cartoons.

BERGER, Oscar, 1901- 741.5
Famous faces; caricaturist's scrapbook. London, New York, Hutchinson ['1950] 97 p. illus. 26 cm. [NC1489.B45A45] 51-29461
1. Caricatures and cartoons. I. Title.

BYRNES, Eugene. 741.5
A complete guide to professional cartooning. Drexel Hill, Pa., Bell Pub. Co., c1950. 254 p. illus. 32 cm. "With the cooperation of 157...cartoonists and artists." [NC1320.B96] 51-22921
1. Caricatures and cartoons. 2. Drawing—Instruction.

COLE, William, 1919- ed. 741.59
The classic cartoons, edited by William Cole and Mike Thaler. Cleveland, World Pub. Co. [1966] 336 p. (chiefly illus.) 29 cm. [NC1320.C56] 66-21125
1. Caricatures and cartoons. I. Thaler, Mike, 1936- joint ed. II. Title.

HOLME, Geoffrey, 1887- ed. 741.5'9
Caricature of to-day. With an introd. by Randall Davies. New York, A. & C. Boni, 1928. Detroit, Gale Research Co., 1974. xi, 16 p. 136 plates. 28 cm. [NC1355.H6 1974] 73-20081 14.00
1. Caricatures and cartoons. I. Title.

MOTHER Goose. 398.8
The Chas. Addams Mother Goose. [Harper crest library ed. New York] Windmill Books; distributed by Harper & Row [1967] 1 v. (unpaged) illus. (part col.) 32 cm. [NC1429.A25A42] 67-24372
I. Addams, Charles, 1912- illus. II. Title. BIP

SUTPHEN, Richard, comp. 769
Uncensored situations; copyright free old engravings and illustrations [compiled by] Dick Sutphen. [Minneapolis, D. Sutphen Studio, 1966] 191 p. (chiefly illus.) 29 cm. [NC1428.S9] 66-28211
1. Caricatures and cartoons. I. Title.

Caricatures and cartoons—England—Exhibitions.

ORMOND, Richard. 741.5'942'07402132
Vanity Fair : an exhibition of original cartoons / introduction by Eileen Harris ; catalogue by Richard Ormond. London : National Portrait Gallery, 1976. 2-31 p. : ill., ports. ; 30 cm. "Published for the exhibition held at the National Portrait Gallery from 9 July to 30 August 1976." [NC1478.V36O75] 77-359299 ISBN 0-904017-06-0 : £1.00
1. Vanity fair. 2. Caricatures and cartoons—England—Exhibitions. I. London. National Portrait Gallery. II. Title.

Caricatures and cartoons—Exhibitions.

AMERICAN Federation of Arts. 769
The indignant eye. [Exhibition, catalog. New York, c1971] [16] p. illus. 29 cm. Exhibition "... based upon the book, The indignant eye: the artist as social critic in prints and drawings from the fifteenth century to Picasso, by Ralph E. Shikes." "Circulated 1971-1972." [NC1310.N4A8] 71-185599
1. Caricatures and cartoons—Exhibitions. I. Shikes, Ralph E. The indignant eye. II. Title.

BARTON, Ralph, 1891-1931. 741.5
The jazz age, as seen through the eyes of Ralph Barton, Miguel Covarrubias, and John Held, Jr. [Providence, 1968] [59] p. (incl. cover) illus., map, ports. 22 cm. A catalog of an exhibition of the jazz age in caricature arranged by Richard Merkin and held at the Museum of Art, Rhode Island School of Design, Sept. 25-Nov. 10, 1968, and at the Art Gallery, State University of New York College at Potsdam, Nov. 15-Dec. 18, 1968. [NC1427.P74B3] 68-56465
1. Caricatures and cartoons—Exhibitions. I. Covarrubias, Miguel, 1904-1957. II. Held, John, 1899-1958. III. Merkin, Richard. IV. Rhode Island School of Design, Providence. Museum of Art. V. New York. State University College, Potsdam. Art Museum. VI. Title. BIP

BROWN University. Dept. of Art. 760'.074'01451
Caricature and its role in graphic satire; an exhibition by the Department of Art, Brown University. Providence, R.I. [1971] 120 p. illus. 28 cm. Held at the Museum of Art, Rhode Island School of Design, Apr. 7-May 9, 1971. Includes bibliographical references. [NC1310.P7R472] 75-31402
1. Caricatures and cartoons—Exhibitions. I. Rhode Island School of Design, Providence. Museum of Art. II. Title. BIP

LOWE Art Museum. 741.9'42
Drolls, or, English wit as expressed in common prints of the 18th and 19th centuries. Prepared completely from the fine collection of the Lowe Art Museum, University of Miami, and on exhibit September 20 through October 7, 1973. [Coral Gables, Fla., 1973] 16 p. illus. 18 x 23 cm. [NC1473.L68 1973] 74-162827
1. Caricatures and cartoons—Exhibitions. 2. English wit and humor, Pictorial. I. Title.

Caricatures and cartoons—Gt. Brit.

PUNCH (London) 741.5
A century of Punch cartoons. Edited by R. E. Williams. With a foreword by Malcolm Muggeridge. New York, Simon and Schuster, 1955. 340p. illus. 29cm. [NC1478.P83] 55-10054
1. Caricatures and cartoons—Gt. Brit. I. William, Roo E., ed.s8 II. Title. BIP

Caricatures and cartoons—Handbooks, manuals, etc.

MARKOW, Jack, 1905- 741.5'02'02
Cartoonist's and gag writer's handbook. Cincinnati, Writer's Digest [1967] 157 p. illus. 27 cm. [NC1320.M27] 67-18846
1. Caricatures and cartoons—Handbooks, manuals, etc. I. Title. BIP

Caricatures and cartoons—Israel.

GARDOSH, Kariel 741.595694
To Israel with love. by Dosh [pseud.] Foreword by Abba Eban. New York, T. Yoseloff [c.1960] 127p. illus. 26cm. 60-8417 4.95
1. Caricatures and cartoons—Israel. 2. World politics—Humor, caricatures, etc. I. Title.

Caricatures and cartoons—Marketing.

BREGER, David, 1908- 741.5
How to draw and sell cartoons. New York, Putnam [1966] 311 p. illus. 25 cm. [NC1320.B75] 66-15577
1. Caricatures and cartoons—Marketing. 2. Drawing—Instruction. I. Title.

Caricatures and cartoons—New Orleans.

SPRATLING, William Philip, 1900-1967. 741.5973
Sherwood Anderson and other famous creoles [by] William Spratling and William Faulkner. Austin, Published for the Humanities Research Center of the University of Texas by the University of Texas Press [1967, c1966] 80 p. illus. 26 cm. A facsimile of the 2d issue, Jan. 1927, published by the Pelican Bookshop Press, New Orleans, with the "Chronicle of friendship: William Faulkner in New Orleans," by William Spratling, and "William Spratling's Mexican world," by R. D. Duncan, which are reprinted from the Texas quarterly. [F379.N5S884 1967] 67-30911
1. Caricatures and cartoons—New Orleans. 2. New Orleans—Biography—Portraits. I. Faulkner, William, 1897-1962, joint author. II. Texas. University. Humanities Research Center. III. Title.

Caricatures and cartoons—Period.

CARTOON annual; 791.5058
a selection from the cream of the year's best cartoons. New York, A. A. Wyn. v. 28cm. Editor: R. E. Shikes. [NC1300.C33] 53-3648
1. Caricatures and cartoons—Period. 2. Caricatures and cartoons—U. S. I. Shikes, Ralph E., ed.

Caricatures and cartoons — Russia.

MILENKOVITCH, Michael M 741.5947
The view from Red Square; a critique of cartoons from Pravda and Izvestia, 1947-1964, by Michael M. Milenkovitch. New York, Hobbs, Dorman [1966] 152 p. illus. 28 cm. Bibliography: p. 137-138. [NC1576.M5] 65-15684
1. Caricatures and cartoons — Russia. I. Title.

Caricatures and cartoons — U.S.

THE Art in cartooning 741.5'973
: seventy-five years of American magazine cartoons / edited by Edwin Fisher, Mort Gerberg, and Ron Wolin for the Cartoonists Guild. New York : Scribner, c1975. 224 p., [8] leaves of plates : chiefly ill. (some col.) ; 29 cm. Includes index. [NC1426.A78] 75-6035 ISBN 0-684-14329-1 : 14.95
1. Caricatures and cartoons—United States. 2. American wit and humor, Pictorial. I. Fisher, Edwin Zaalmon. II. Gerberg, Mort. III. Wolin, Ron. IV. Cartoonists Guild.

CHASE, John Churcill. 741.5973
Today's cartoon, by John Chase and 139 other editorial cartoonists who draw'them damn pictures'! With a foreword by Ralph McGiol. New Orleans, Hauser Press [1962] unpaged: illus. 29cm. [NC1426.C5] 62-18654
1. Caricatures and cartoons—U. S. I. Title.

HIRSCHFELD, Albert. 741.5973
The world of Hirschfeld [by] Al Hirschfeld. Introd. by Lloyd Goodrich. New York, H. N. Abrams [1970?] 233 p. illus. (part col.) 28 x 30 cm. [NC1429.H527A57] 70-82875 ISBN 0-8109-0177-3
I. Title.

**THE image of America* 741.590973
in caricature and cartoon. Fort Worth, Tex., Amon Carter Museum of Western Art [1975] vii, 192 p. ill. 24 cm. Includes bibliographical references. [NC1420] 75-22592 ISBN 0-88360-023-4 6.00 (pbk.)
1. Caricatures and cartoons—United States.

SCHEEL, Theodor, 1905- 741.5
The face is familiar. New York, Beechhurst Press [c1951] 64 p. illus. 29 cm. [NC1429.S36A45] 52-7781
1. Caricatures and cartoons — U.S. I. Title.

SOKOL, Erich. 741.5973
American natives; [drawings] Introd. by Steve Allen. New York, Harper [1960] unpaged (chiefly illus.) 31 cm. [NC1489.S6A45] 60-10417
1. Caricatures and cartoons — U.S. I. Title.

SPENCER, Richard, 1921- 741.5
Pulitzer prize cartoons; the men and their masterpieces. Ames, Iowa State College Press [1951] 125 p. illus. 27 cm. [NC1428.S7] 51-11716
1. Caricatures and cartoons — U.S. I. Title.

SPENCER, Richard, 1921- 741.5
Pulitzer prize cartoons: the men and their masterpieces. 2d ed. Ames, Iowa State College Press [1953] 135p. illus. 27cm. [NC1428.S7 1953] 53-5492
1. Caricatures and cartoons—U. S. I. Title.

Carles, Arthur B., 1882-1952.

GARDINER, Henry G. 708'.148'11 s
Arthur B. Carles: a critical and biographical study [by Henry G. Gardiner] Philadelphia, Philadelphia Museum of Art, 1970. 139-185, [7] p. illus. (part col.) 24 cm. (Philadelphia Museum of Art. Bulletin v. 64, no. 302-303) "Catalogue of works by Arthur B. Carles in the Philadelphia Museum of Art": p. [186]-[189] Includes bibliographical references. [N685.A45 vol. 64, no. 302-303] [ND237.C27] 759.13 72-186965
1. Carles, Arthur B., 1882-1952. I. Title. II. Series.

Carlisle, Eng.—Description—Exhibitions.

CARLISLE, Eng. Museum and Art Gallery. 914.28'5
Nineteenth century Carlisle: [catalogue of paintings, drawings and photographs]. [Carlisle] Carlisle City Art Gallery [1972] [1], 35 p. illus. 21 cm. Catalogue compiled by D. R. Perriam. Cover title. [DA690.C335C33] 73-157850 ISBN 0-9502457-1-2 £0.10
1. Carlisle, Eng.—Description—Exhibitions. 2. Carlisle, Eng.—History—Exhibitions. I. Perriam, D. R. II. Title.

Carlisle, George James Howard, 9th Earl of, 1843-1911.

CARLISLE, Eng. Museum of Art Gallery. 709'.42
George Howard and his circle, 1843-1911. Carlisle, City Art Gallery, 1968. 32 p. illus., ports. 22 cm. Cover title. Catalogue compiled by W. Waters, Assistant Curator. [N6797.C33A44] 72-199351
1. Carlisle, George James Howard, 9th Earl of, 1843-1911. 2. Art, British—Exhibitions. 3. Art, Modern—19th century—Gt. Brit. I. Title.

Carlson, George, 1940—

CARLSON, George, 1940- 730'.92'4
George Carlson bronzes, October 27 through November 20, 1976. New York : Kennedy Galleries, 1976. 40 p. : chiefly ill. (some col.) ; 27 cm. [NK7998.C28K46] 77-360240
1. Carlson, George, 1940- 2. Tarahumare Indians—Pictorial works—Exhibitions. 3. Bronzes—United States—Exhibitions. I. Kennedy Galleries, inc., New York. II. Title.

Carmean, Harry, 1922—

CARMEAN, Harry, 1922- 759.13
Carmean, by June Harwood. [Los Angeles, Calif., 1974] 143 p. (chiefly col. illus.) 29 cm. [ND237.C28H37] 74-77101
1. Carmean, Harry, 1922- I. Harwood, June. BIP

Carnival glass.

COSENTINO, Geraldine. 748.2'913
Carnival glass / Geraldine Cosentino, Regina Stewart. New York : Golden Press, 1977, c1976 128 p. : ill. ; 21 cm. (A Golden handbook of collectibles) Includes index. Bibliography: p. 124. [NK5439.C35C67] 76-406 ISBN 0-307-43175-4 pbk. : 3.95
1. Carnival glass. 2. Glassware—Collectors and collecting. 3. Glass, Colored. I. Stewart, Regina, joint author. II. Title.

EDWARDS, Bill. 748.2'9171'64
Millersburg, the queen of carnival glass / by Bill Edwards. Paducah, Ky. : Collector Books, c1975. 134 p. : col. ill. ; 22 cm.

[NK5198.M54E38] 76-350543 ISBN 0-89145-002-5 : 8.95
1. Millersburg Glass Company. 2. Carnival glass. 3. Glassware—United States. I. Title.

HAND, Sherman. 748'.8
Colors in carnival glass. [Rochester, N.Y., 1967.- v. col. illus. 23 cm. Cover title.
[NK5103.H3] 68-1971
1. Carnival glass. 2. Glassware, American. 3. Color. I. Title.

KLAMKIN, Marian. 748.2'913
The collector's guide to carnival glass / Marian Klamkin ; photos. by Charles Klamkin. New York : Hawthorn Books, c1976. 204 p., [4] leaves of plates : ill. (32 col.) ; 29 cm. Includes index. Bibliography: p. 195-196. [NK5112.K54 1976] 75-221 ISBN 0-8015-1396-0 : 19.95
1. Carnival glass. 2. Glassware—United States—Collectors and collecting. I. Klamkin, Charles. II. Title. **BIP**

MOORE, Donald E. 748.2'913
The shape of things in carnival glass / by Donald E. Moore. Alameda, Calif. : Moore, [1975] iv, 117 p. : col. ill. ; 23 cm. Includes index. [NK5112.M66] 75-316982 9.95
1. Carnival glass. 2. Glassware, American. I. Title.

PRESZNICK, Rose M. 748.8
Carnival & iridescent glass: price guide. Pen and ink drawings made by Rose M. Presznick. 1st ed. Wadsworth? Ohio, 1962-? 4 v. illus. 21 cm. [NK5112.P7] 63-2413
1. Carnival glass. 2. Glassware—Prices. I. Title.

PRESZNICK, Rose M. 748.2913
Carnival & iridescent glass, price guide, by Rose M. Presznick. Pen and ink drawings made by Rose M. Presznick. Rev. ed. Wadsworth? Ohio, 1965- v. illus. 22 cm. [NK5112.P72] 65-2695
1. Carnival glass. 2. Glassware—Prices. I. Title.

UMBRACO, Kitty. 748.2'9154
Iridescent stretch glass, by Kitty & Russell Umbraco. Photography by Leslie Avery. [Berkeley, Calif., Cembura and Avery Publishers, 1972] 62 p. illus. (part col.) 23 cm. Bibliography: p. 62. [NK5112.U42] 72-169318 5.95
1. Carnival glass. I. Umbraco, Russell, joint author. II. Title. **BIP**

Carnival glass—Catalogs.

OWENS, Richard E. 748.8
Carnival glass tumblers. Author/photographer: Richard E. Owens. [La Habra, Calif., 1973] 128 p. illus. (part col.) 23 cm. [NK5112.O93] 73-176020 7.95
1. Carnival glass—Catalogs. 2. Stemware, American—Catalogs. I. Title.

REICHEL, Lloyd. 748.2'913
Modern carnival glass collectors. [Marceline, Mo.] Walsworth Pub. Co., 1971-74. 2 v. illus. 22 cm. [NK5105.R4] 78-27091 4.00 (v. 1) 4.95 (v. 2)
1. Carnival glass—Catalogs. 2. Glassware—Collectors and collecting. I. Title.

WIGGINS, Berry. 748.2'913
Stretch in color. [Orange, Va. 1972, c1971-v. illus. 24 cm. Cover title. Page [4] of cover: Stretch glass in color. [NK5104.W49] 72-195231 7.95 (pbk)
1. Carnival glass—Catalogs. 2. Glass, Colored. I. Title. II. Title: Stretch glass in color.

Carnival glass—Collectors and collecting.

HAND, Sherman. 748.2'913
The collector's encyclopedia of carnival glass / by Sherman Hand. Paducah, Ky. : Collector Books, c1978. 256 p. : col. ill. ; 29 cm. On spine: Carnival glass. Includes index. [NK5439.C35H35] 78-103766 ISBN 0-89145-071-8 : 19.95
1. Carnival glass—Collectors and collecting. 2. Glassware—United States—Collectors and collecting. II. Title. Carnival glass. **BIP**

HARTUNG, Marion T. 748.2'9'13
Carnival glass in color; a collector's reference book, by Marion T. Hartung. [Emporia, Kan., 1967] 1 v. (unpaged) illus., col. plates. 28 cm.
1. Carnival glass—Collectors and collecting. I. Title. **BIP**

OLSON, O. Joe. 748.2'913
The carnival glass scene in the mid-1970's / by O. Joe Olson ; drawings by Joan Kilbourne. Kansas City, Mo. : Olson, c1975. v, 74 p. : ill. ; 29 cm. "Feature articles, research monographs and news items ... from two national carnival newsletters conducted by the author." [NK5112.O47] 75-332700 5.65
1. Carnival glass—Collectors and collecting. 2. Glassware—United States. I. Title.

Carnival glass—Collectors and collecting—Catalogs.

EDWARDS, Bill. 748.2'913
Rarities in carnival glass / by Bill Edwards. Paducah, Ky. : Collector Books, c1978. 104 p. : col. ill. ; 22 cm. [NK5439.C35E36] 78-113423 ISBN 0-89145-075-0 : 8.95
1. Carnival glass—Collectors and collecting—Catalogs. I. Title. **BIP**

KLAMKIN, Marian. 748.2'913
The Carnival glass collector's price guide / Marian Klamkin ; photos. by Charles Klamkin. New York : Hawthorn Books, c1978. 95 p. : ill. ; 23 cm. [NK5439.C35K56 1978] 77-92365 ISBN 0-8015-1094-5 : 4.95
1. Carnival glass—Collectors and collecting—Catalogs. I. Title. **BIP**

Caro, Anthony, 1924—

WHELAN, Richard. 730'.92'4
Anthony Caro / [by] Richard Whelan ; with additional texts by Clement Greenberg ... [et al.]. Harmondsworth ; New York : Penguin, 1974. 134 p. : ill. ; 20 cm. Bibliography: p. 83-84. [NB497.C35W46] 74-193694 ISBN 0-14-021797-5 : £1.10
1. Caro, Anthony, 1924-

WHELAN, Richard. 730'.92'4
Anthony Caro [by] Richard Whelan; with additional texts by Clement Greenberg...[et al.] New York, E. P. Dutton, [1975 c1974] 131 [3] p. 63 ill. 21 cm. Bibliography: p. 83-84 [NB497.C35W46] ISBN 0-525-47400-5 3.50 (pbk).
1. Caro, Anthony, 1924- I. Title.
L.C. no. for original edition: 74-193694

Caroff, Joseph.

CAROFF, Joseph. 741.9'73
Graphic design : works & words / Joseph Caroff. [New York : J. Caroff Associates, c1974] [40] p. : chiefly ill. ; 21 cm. [NC999.4.C37A43] 75-309853
1. Caroff, Joseph. I. Title.

Carpaccio, Vittore, 1455?-1525?

CARPACCIO: 759.5
biographical and critical study. Translated from the Italian by James Emmons. [New York] Skira [1958] 119p. mounted col. illus. 18cm. (The Taste of our time, 24) Bibliography: p.[111] [ND623.C3P53] 927.5 58-12919
1. Carpaccio, Vittore, 1455?-1525? I. Pignatti, Terisio, 1920-

CARPACCIO, Vittore, 1455?-1525?. 709.45
Paintings and drawings. Complete ed. by Jan Lauts. [Translated from the German by Erica Millman (introductory text) and Marguerite Kay (catalogue) New York] Phaidon Publishers; distributed by New York Graphic Society, Greenwich, Conn. [1962] 309 p. plates (part col.) 31 cm. Bibliography: p. 305-307. [ND623.C3L33] 63-341
1. Lauts, Jan. 1908-   . II. Title.

Carpenter, James, 1949- —Exhibitions.

SEATTLE. Art 709'.73'074019777 Museum.
Carpenter, Chihuly, Scanga : [catalogue]. [Seattle] : Seattle Art Museum, 1977. 1 portfolio ([3] fold. leaves) : ill. (some col.) ; 24 cm. Cover title. Exhibition sponsored by the Seattle Art Museum and the Pilchuck School. [N6512.S33 1977] 77-154285
1. Carpenter, James, 1949- —Exhibitions. 2. Chihuly, Dale, 1941- —Exhibitions. 3. Scanga, Italo, 1932- —Exhibitions. 4. Art, Modern—20th century—United States—Exhibitions. I. Pilchuck School. II. Title.

Carpentry.

MATTHEW, William Percival. 694
Modern carpentry; a complete guide for the amateur, by W.P. Matthew and F.H. Titmuss. London, New York, W. Foulsham [1953?] 127p. illus. 19cm. (The Know how books) [TT197.M39] 53-31924
1. Carpentry. I. Titmuss, F.H., joint author. II. Title.

Carpets.

HOPF, Albrecht 746.75
Oriental carpets and rugs. [Tr. from German by Daphne Woodward] New York, Viking [c.1961, 1962] 140p. 62 col. plates. 28cm. (Studio bk.) 62-11771 22.50
1. Rugs, Oriental. 2. Carpets. I. Title.

KENDRICK, Albert Frank, 746.7'5 1872-
Hand-woven carpets, Oriental & European, by A. F. Kendrick and C. E. C. Tattersall. New York, Dover Publications [1973] xvii, 388 p. illus. 24 cm. Reprint of the 1922 ed. published in 2 v. by Benn, London. Bibliography: p. 193-194. [NK2795.K4 1973] 73-77381 ISBN 0-486-20385-9 6.00 (pbk.)
1. Carpets. I. Tattersall, Creassey Edward Cecil, 1877-1957, joint author. II. Title. **BIP**

VON Rosenstiel, Helene. 746.7'973
American rugs and carpets from the seventeenth century to modern times / Helene Von Rosenstiel. New York : Morrow, c1978. 192 p. : ill. ; 29 cm. Includes index. Bibliography: p. [184]-187. [NK2812.V66] 78-50700 ISBN 0-688-03325-3 : 25.00
1. Rugs—United States. 2. Carpets—United States. I. Title.

Carracci, Agostino, 1557-1602.

BELLORI, Giovanni Pietro, 759.5 1615?-1696
The lives of Annibale & Agostino Carracci. Tr. from Italian by Catherine Enggass. Foreword by Robert Enggass. University Park, Penn. State Univ. Pr., 1968. xix, 122p. illus., ports. 23cm. On spine: Annibale & Agostino Carracci. Essays tr. from Vite de'pittori, scultori et architetti moderni. [ND622.B413] 67-16194 5.00 bds.
1. Carracci, Agostino, 1557-1602. 2. Carracci, Annibale, 1560-1609. I. Bellori, Giovanni Pietro, 1615?-1696. II. Title. III. Title: Vite de'pittori, scultori et architetti moderni. **BIP**

Carrey, Jacques, 1646-1726.

BOWIE, Theodore Robert. 741.9'44
The Carrey drawings of the Parthenon sculptures, edited by Theodore Bowie and Diether Thimme. Bloomington, Indiana University Press [1971] xii, 98 p. illus. (part col.) 39 x 43 cm. Bibliography: p. 97-98. [NC248.C32B6] 77-155287 ISBN 0-253-31320-1
1. Carrey, Jacques, 1646-1726. 2. Athens. Parthenon. 3. Athens. Acropolis. I. Thimme, Diether, joint author. II. Title. **BIP**

Carriages and carts—Bibl.

RITTENHOUSE, Jack 016.6847 DeVere, 1912-
Carriage hundred; a bibliography on horse-drawn transportation. Houston, Stagecoach Press, 1961. 49p. facsim. 16cm. 450 copies printed. [Z7914.C32R5] 61-9110

1. Carriages and carts—Bibl. I. Title.

Carriages and carts in art.

CADFRYN-ROBERTS, John, 388.341 ed.
Coaches and trains, ed., introd. by John Cadfryn-Roberts. Princeton, N.J., Van Nostrand [1965] 12p., [20] col. plates. 25cm. (Golden Ariels, no. 7) [19th cent. transport prints, v.2] [NE962.C3C3] 66-31821 3.95
1. Carriages and carts in art. 2. Railroads in art. I. Title.

Carrier-Belleuse, Albert Ernest, 1824-1887.

HARGROVE, June Ellen. 730'.92'4 B
The life and work of Albert Ernest Carrier-Belleuse / June Ellen Hargrove. New York : Garland Pub., 1977. p. cm. (Outstanding dissertations in the fine arts) Thesis—New York University, 1975. Bibliography: p. [N6853.C278H37] 76-23625 ISBN 0-8240-2695-0 lib.bdg. : 50.00
1. Carrier-Belleuse, Albert Ernest, 1824-1887. 2. Artists—France—Biography. I. Carrier-Belleuse, Albert Ernest, 1824-1887. II. Title. III. Series.

Carriere, Eugene, 1849-1906.

EUGENE Carriere, 1849- 759.4 1906, seer of the real. A loan exhibition organized by the Allentown Art Museum [Allentown? Pa., 1968?] 78 p. illus. 26 cm. For presentation in 5 American museums, from Nov. 2, 1968-April 5, 1970. Bibliography: p. [77]-78. [N6853.C28E8] 77-274076
1. Carriere, Eugene, 1849-1906. I. Allentown, Pa. Art Museum.

Carrousel of the sea (Art object)

STEUBEN Glass, inc. 748'.8
The Carrousel of the sea. Designed by George Thompson. Engraving design by Alexander Seidel. Engraving executed by Ladislav Havlik. [New York, 1970] 18 p. illus. (part col.) 25 cm. [NK5198.S7A43] 75-125190
1. Carrousel of the sea (Art object) I. Title.

Carte de visite photographs.

ALLAND, Alexander. 779'.2'0924
Heinrich Tonnies, cartes-de-visite photographer extraordinaire : det 19. arhundredes "fotograf extraordinaire" / Alexander Alland, Sr. ; pref. by Bjorn Ochsner. New York : Camera/Graphic Press, [1978] p. cm. English and Danish. [TR680.A45] 77-18650 ISBN 0-918696-06-2 pbk : 9.95
1. Carte de visite photographs. I. Tonnies, Heinrich, 1825-1903. II. Title.

Carter, Jimmy, 1924—

ALLEN, 779'.9'9739260924 B Frederick.
Jimmy Carter, a photobiography / written by Frederick Allen. Houston, Tex. : EFP Pub. Co., c1976. 80 p. : ill. ; 28 cm. [F291.3.C37A76] 76-150399 2.95
1. Carter, Jimmy, 1924- 2. Georgia—Governors—Biography. I. Title.

Carter, Jimmy, 1924- —Cartoons, satire, etc.

SZEP, Paul Michael. 741.5'973
"...them damned pictures" / editorial cartoons / by Szep. Boston : Boston globe, 1977. [112] p. : all ill. ; 23 x 29 cm. Cartoons originally published in the Boston globe, Jan. 3, 1975-Sept. 14, 1977. [E865.S93] 77-154785 2.95
1. Carter, Jimmy, 1924- —Cartoons, satire, etc. 2. United States—Politics and government—1974-1977—Caricatures and cartoons. 3. United States—Politics and government—1977—Caricatures and cartoons. 4. World politics—1975-1985—Caricatures and cartoons. 5. American wit and humor, Pictorial. I. Title.

Carter, Jimmy, 1924—Views on the arts.

CARTER, Jimmy, 1924- 700
Carter on the arts / introd. by Joan Mondale. New York : ACA, 1977. 74 p. ; 23 cm. [E873.2.C37] 77-151706 ISBN 0-915400-03-0 pbk. : 2.50
1. Carter, Jimmy, 1924—Views on the arts. 2. Arts—United States. I. Title.
Publisher's address: Associated Council of the Arts, 1564 Broadway Rm. 820 N. Y. N. Y.10036 BIP

Cartier, Edd, 1914—

†CARTIER, Edd, 1914- 741.9'73
The known and the unknown / Edd Cartier ; edited by Dean Cartier. Saddle River, N.J. : G. de la Ree, 1977. 128 p. : chiefly ill. ; 29 cm. [NC975.5.C37C38] 77-153004 15.00
1. Cartier, Edd, 1914- I. Cartier, Dean, 1953- II. Title.
Publisher's address : 7 Cedarwood Lane, Saddle River, NJ 07458

Cartography—Bibliography.

INTERNATIONAL 016.5268
Cartographic Association. Commission V, Communication in Geography.
Bibliography of works on cartographic communication = Bibliographie des ouvres sur la communication cartographique / International Cartographic Association, Commission V, Communication in Cartography ; edited by Christopher Board. Provisional ed. London : [International Cartographic Association], 1976. xiv, 147 p. ; 21 cm. Errata slip inserted. English text, English and French introd. Includes index. [Z6021.I594 1976] [GA105.3] 77-371653 ISBN 0-85328-052-5
1. Cartography—Bibliography. I. Board, Christopher. II. Title. III. Title: Bibliographie des ouvres sur la communication cartographique.

Cartography—Bibliography—Catalogs.

UNITED States. Library of 016.526
Congress. Geography and Map Division.
The bibliography of cartography. Boston, G. K. Hall, 1973. 5 v. 37 cm. A reproduction of a card bibliography in the Geography and Map Division, which contains an estimated 90,000 entries for works published from the early 19th century through 1971. [Z6028.U49 1973] 73-12977 ISBN 0-8161-1008-5 490.00
1. United States. Library of Congress. Geography and Map Division. 2. Cartography—Bibliography—Catalogs. I. Title. BIP

Cartography—Congresses.

SYMPOSIUM on Experimental 726.8
Cartography, Oxford, 1963.
Experimental cartography: report on the Oxford symposium, October 1963. [New York] Oxford 1964. 93p. illus. 26cm. Bibl. 64-55423 4.00, pap., plastic bdg.
1. Cartography—Congresses. I. Royal Society of London. II. Title.

Cartography — Exhibitions.

ROYAL Institution of 526.8074
Chartered Surveyors.
Five centuries of maps & map-making; an exhibition at 12 Great George Street, Westminister [10th June -- 4th July 1953. London] 1953. 127 p. 25 cm. [GA190.L65R6] 62-45834
1. Cartography — Exhibitions. I. Title.

Cartography—History.

BALTIMORE. Museum of Art 526.8074
The world encompassed; an exhibition of the history of maps held at the Baltimore Museum of Art October 7 to November 23, 1952. Organized by the Peabody Institute Library, the Walters Art Galley [and] the John Work Garrett Library of the Johns Hopkins University in cooperation with the Baltimore Museum of Art.---baltiore, Trustees of the Walters Art Gallery, 1952. xiv, [125] p. 60 plates (incl. maps) 31 cm. 'Addenda and Corrigenda' slip inserted. Includes bibliographies. [GA190.B2B2] A53
1. Cartography—Hist. 2. Cartography—Exhibitions. I. Walters Art Gallery, Baltimore. II. Title.

SKELTON, Raleigh Ashlin. 910.9
Explorers' maps; chapters in the cartographic record of geographical discovery. New York, Praeger [1958] xi, 337 p. illus., maps, charts. 26 cm. A reprint, with revisions, of a series of 14 articles published in the Geographical magazine (London) between July 1953 and Aug. 1956. Includes bibliographical references. [GA203.S55] 58-8182
1. Cartography—History. 2. Discoveries (in geography) I. Title.

SKELTON, Raleigh Ashlin. 910.9
Explorers' maps: chapters in the cartographic record of geographical discovery, by R. A. Skelton. [New ed.] Feltham, New York, Spring Books, 1970. xi, 337 p., plate. illus. (1 col.), charts, maps, plans. 29 cm. A reprint, with revisions, of a series of 14 articles published in the Geographical magazine (London) between July 1953 and Aug. 1956. Bibliography: p. 328. [GA203.S55 1970] 74-572632 ISBN 0-600-01195-X 35/-
1. Cartography—History. 2. Discoveries (in geography) I. Title.

Cartography—U.S.—Bibliography.

WHEAT, James Clements. 016.5268
Maps and charts published in America before 1800; a bibliography, by James Clements Wheat and Christian F. Brun. New Haven, Yale University Press, 1969. xxii, 215 p. maps. 27 cm. Bibliography: p. 187-207. [Z6027.A5W68] 69-15464 30.00
1. Cartography—U.S.—Bibliography. I. Brun, Christian, joint author. II. Title. BIP

Cartooning.

LOW, David, 1891- 741.5
Low's cartoon history, 1945-1953. New York, Simon Schuster, 1953. 159p. illus. 27cm. [NC1479.L65A3477] 53-9695
I. Title.

NELSON, Roy Paul. 741.5
Comic art and caricature / Roy Paul Nelson. Chicago : Contemporary Books, c1978. p. cm. Bibliography: p. [NC1320.N383 1978] 78-9132 ISBN 0-8092-7848-0 : 10.00. pbk. : 5.95
1. Cartooning. 2. Wit and humor, Pictorial. I. Title. BIP

RICHARDSON, John Adkins. 741.5
The complete book of cartooning / John Adkins Richardson. Englewood Cliffs, N.J. : Prentice-Hall, 1976c1977 p. cm. (Creative handicrafts series) (A Spectrum book) Includes index. Bibliography: p. [NC1320.R5] 76-28407 ISBN 0-13-157594-5 : 13.95. ISBN 0-13-157586-4 pbk. : 5.95
1. Cartooning. 2. Caricature. I. Title. BIP

ROTH, Abraham, 1911- 741.5
Cartooning fundamentals / Al Ross [i.e. A. Roth]. New York : Stravon Educational Press, c1977. 192 p. : ill. ; 28 cm. Includes index. [NC1320.R67] 77-1201 ISBN 0-873961-080-7 : 9.75
1. Cartooning. I. Title. BIP

WARSHAW, Jerry. 741.5
The funny drawing book / by Jerry Warshaw ; with photos by Dick Masek. Chicago : A. Whitman, [1977] p. cm. [NC1320.W38] 77-14389 ISBN 0-8075-2681-9 : 4.50
1. Cartooning. I. Masek, Dick. II. Title. BIP

Cartooning—Technique.

LANGHOLTZ, Esther. 741.5
Pick-up book of cartoon-style illustrations / cartoon ill., Dave Ubinas ; text, Esther Langholtz. New York : Arco Pub. Co., [1978] p. cm. Includes index. [NC1320.L24] 78-19183 ISBN 0-668-04665-1 : 12.95. ISBN 0-668-04505-1 pbk. : 9.95
1. Cartooning—Technique. I. Ubinas, Dave. II. Title. BIP

Cartooning—Vocational guidance.

FIXMAN, Adeline. 741.5'023
Aim for a job in cartooning / by Adeline Fixman. 1st ed. New York : R. Rosen Press, 1976. p. cm. (Aim high vocational series) Bibliography: p. Discusses cartooning careers for such areas as comic strips, greeting cards, magazines, and editorials. Lists schools offering training courses. [NC1320.F53] 76-2727 ISBN 0-8239-0355-9 lib.bdg. : 4.80
1. Cartooning—Vocational guidance. I. Title. BIP

Cartoonists—England—Biography.

EVANS, Hilary, 1929- 760'.092'4 B
The life & art of George Cruikshank, 1792-1878 : the man who drew The Drunkard's daughter / Hilary and Mary Evans. New York : S. G. Phillips, 1978. p. cm. [NC1479.C9E82] 77-19166 ISBN 0-87599-227-7 : 35.00
1. Cruikshank, George, 1792-1878. 2. Cartoonists—England—Biography. I. Evans, Mary, 1890- joint autor. II. Title. BIP

Cartoonists—United States.

FITZGERALD, Richard. 741.5'973
Art and politics; cartoonists of the Masses and Liberator. Westport, Conn., Greenwood Press [1973] xiv, 254 p. illus. 24 cm. (Contributions in American studies, no. 8) Contents.Contents.—The Masses and the Liberator.—Art Young.—Robert Minor.—John Sloan.—K. R. Chamberlain.—Maurice Becker.—Bibliography (p. 235-241) [NC1305.F57] 72-609 ISBN 0-8371-6006-5 14.50
1. The Masses. 2. The Liberator. 3. Cartoonists—United States. 4. American wit and humor, Pictorial. I. Title. BIP

Cartoonists—United States—Biography.

LENDT, David L. 741'.092'4 B
Ding : the life of Jay Norwood Darling / David L. Lendt. 1st ed. Ames : Iowa State University Press, 1978. p. cm. Includes index. Bibliography: p. [NC1429.D237L46] 78-10321 ISBN 0-8138-0010-2 : 7.95
1. Darling, Jay Norwood, 1876-1962. 2. Cartoonists—United States—Biography. I. Title. BIP

ROBINSON, Jerry. 741.5'973 B
Skippy and Percy Crosby / Jerry Robinson ; with the art of Percy Crosby. 1st ed. New York : Holt, Rinehart and Winston, c1978. x, 155 p. : ill. (some col.) ; 29 cm. [NC1429.C76R62] 78-53777 ISBN 0-03-018491-6 : 16.95
1. Crosby, Percy Leo, 1891-1964. 2. Cartoonists—United States—Biography. I. Crosby, Percy Leo, 1891-1964. II. Title.

Cartoonists—United States—Juvenile literature.

DEUR, Lynne. 741.5'973
Political cartoonists. Minneapolis, Lerner Publications [1972] 87 p. illus. 22 cm. (A Pull ahead book) A brief discussion of the techniques and functions of political cartoons accompanies capsule biographies of sixteen political cartoonists from Ben Franklin to Tom Darcy. [NC1305.D4] 72-128809 ISBN 0-8225-0463-4
1. Cartoonists—United States—Juvenile literature. 2. United States—Politics and government—Caricatures and cartoons—Juvenile literature. I. Title.

Cartoons and children.

SHAFFER, Laurence Frederic, 372.6
1903-
Children's interpretations of cartoons; a study of the nature and development of the ability to interpret symbolic drawings, by Laurance F. Shaffer. New York, Bureau of Publications, Teachers College, Columbia University, 1930. [New York, AMS Press, 1972, ie 1973] vi, 73 p. illus. 22 cm. Reprint of the 1930 ed., issued in series: Teachers College, Columbia University. Contributions to education, no. 429. Originally presented as the author's thesis, Columbia. Bibliography: p. 72-73. [LB1139.H8S5 1972] 70-177794 ISBN 0-404-55429-6 10.00
1. Cartoons and children. 2. Caricatures and cartoons—Psychological aspects. I. Title. II. Series: Columbia University. Teachers College. Contributions to education, no. 429.

Carvalho, Solomon Nunes, 1815-1897.

STURHAHN, Joan, 1930- 770'.92'4 B
Carvalho, artist-photographer-adventurer-patriot : portrait of a forgotten American / by Joan Sturhahn. [Merrick, N.Y. : Richwood Pub. Co., 1975] p. cm. Bibliography: p. [TR140.C29S88] 75-22386 ISBN 0-915172-01-1 : 18.50
1. Carvalho, Solomon Nunes, 1815-1897. I. Title.

Carver, Humphrey.

CARVER, Humphrey. 712'.092'4 B
Compassionate landscape / Humphrey Carver. Toronto ; Buffalo : University of Toronto Press, [1975] viii, 251 p. : ill. ; 24 cm. Includes index. [HT166.C32A33] 75-22280 ISBN 0-8020-2186-7 : 15.00. ISBN 0-8020-6269-5 pbk. : 6.00
1. Carver, Humphrey. I. Title. BIP

Carving (Art industries)

DAWSON, Robert, 1921- 731.4'6
Practical carving in wood, stone, plastics, and other materials. New York, Watson-Guptill [1972] 95 p. illus. 25 cm. Bibliography: p. 94. [NB1170.D37] 79-187891 ISBN 0-8230-4369-X 8.95
1. Carving (Art industries) 2. Sculpture—Technique. I. Title.

MEILACH, Dona Z. 731
Creative carving: materials, techniques, appreciation [by] Dona Z. Meilach. Chicago, Reilly & Lee [1969] 120 p. illus. (part col.) 29 cm. [NK5500.M4] 69-17430 6.95
1. Carving (Art industries) I. Title. BIP

WALTNER, Elma. 731.832
Carving animal caricatures. Bloomington, Ill., McKnight & McKnight Pub. Co. [1951] 104 p. illus. 26 cm. [NK9705.W3] 51-13779
1. Carving (Art industries) I. Title. BIP

Casas Grandes, site, Mexico.

DI PESO, Charles 972'.1
Corradino, 1920-
Casas Grandes : a fallen trading center of the Gran Chichimeca / by Charles C. Di Peso ; edited by Gloria J. Fenner ; illustrated by Allice Wesche. 1st ed. Dragoon [Ariz.] : Amerind Foundation, [1974] 3 v. (1104 p.) : ill. ; 31 cm. (Amerind Foundation, inc., series ; no. 9) Includes index. Contents.Contents.—v. 1. Preceramic-viejo periods.—v. 2. Medio period.—v. 3. Tardio and espanoles periods. Bibliography: v. 3, p. 1021-1076. [F1219.1.C3D56] 74-82018 ISBN 0-87358-056-7
1. Casas Grandes, site, Mexico. 2. Mexico—Antiquities. 3. Southwest, New—Antiquities. I. Title. II. Series: Amerind Foundation. Amerind Foundation, inc., series ; no. 9. BIP

Cascade range—Antiquities.

RICE, David G. 917.97'5
Archaeological reconnaissance south-central Cascades, Washington, by David G. Rice. Seattle, Washington Archaeological Society, 1969. vi, 41 p. illus., map, plans. 28 cm. (Washington Archaeological Society. Occasional paper, no. 2) Bibliography: p. 17-19. [E78.W3R5] 73-277069
1. Cascade range—Antiquities. 2. Indians of North America—Cascade range. 3. Excavations (Archaeology)—Washington (State)—Cascade range. I. Title. II. Series.

Casein painting.

BROOKS, Leonard, 1911- 751.4
Course in casein painting. New York, Reinhold Pub. Corp. [1961] 60 p. illus. 27 cm. [ND2490.B7] 61-10718
1. Casein painting.

Casper site, Wyo.

FRISON, George C. 978.7'93
The Casper site : a Hell Gap bison kill on the high plains / edited by George C. Frison. New York : Academic Press, [1974] xviii, 266 p. : ill. ; 25 cm. (Studies in archeology) Includes indexes. Bibliography: p. [251]-259. [E78.W95F74] 74-21592 ISBN 0-12-268550-4 : 14.50
1. Casper site, Wyo. 2. Bison, Fossil. 3. Indians of North America—Wyoming—Hunting. I. Title. BIP

Cassatt, Mary, 1844-1926.

BREESKIN, Adelyn Dohme, 1896- 759.13
Mary Cassatt; a catalogue raisonne of the oils, pastels, watercolors, and drawings. Washington, Smithsonian Institution Press, 1970. vi, 322 p. illus. (part col.), ports. 34 cm. Bibliography: p. 307-309. [ND237.C3B68] 73-104775 ISBN 0-87474-100-9 29.95
1. Cassatt, Mary, 1844-1926.

BROOKLYN Institute of Arts and Sciences. Museum. 759.13
Leaders of American impressionism: Mary Cassatt, Childe Hassam, John H. Twatchman [and] J. Alden Weir. New York, Arno Press, 1974. 43 p. illus. 22 cm. Reprint of the 1937 ed. published by the Brooklyn Museum, Brooklyn, N.Y. Catalog of an exhibition. [ND210.5.I4B76 1974] 75-128385 ISBN 0-405-00876-7 6.50
1. Cassatt, Mary, 1844-1926. 2. Hassam, Childe, 1859-1935. 3. Twachtman, John Henry, 1853-1902. 4. Weir, Julian Alden, 1852-1919. 5. Impressionism (Art)—United States. 6. Paintings, American—Exhibitions. I. Title.

BULLARD, Edgar John, 1942- 759.13
Mary Cassatt: oils and pastels, by E. John Bullard. New York, Watson-Guptill Publications [1972] 87 p. col. illus. 29 cm. Bibliography: p. 8. [ND237.C3B8] 70-190524 ISBN 0-8230-0569-0 17.50
1. Cassatt, Mary, 1844-1926. BIP

CASSATT, Mary, 1844-1926. 760'.0924
The graphic art of Mary Cassett. Introd. by Adelyn D. Breeskin. Foreword by Donald H. Karshan. [New York] Museum of Graphic Art [1967] 111 p. illus. 26 cm. Exhibition organized by the Museum of Graphic Art, New York. "Participating museums: Cincinnati Art Museum [and others]" [NE539.C3A44 1967] 67-30432
I. Museum of Graphic Art. II. Cincinnati. Art Museum. III. Title.

CASSATT, Mary, 1844-1926. 759.13
Mary Cassatt, 1844-1926, retrospective exhibition. Introductory notes by Frederick A. Sweet. International Galleries, Chicago, November-December 1965. [Chicago] International Galleries, 1965. 1 v. (unpaged) illus. (part col.), ports. 25 cm. Includes bibliography. [NE539.C3A49] 769'.924 75-222503
I. International Galleries.

CASSATT, Mary, 1844-1926. 759.13
Mary Cassatt, 1844-1926, retrospective exhibition. Introductory notes by Frederick A. Sweet. International Galleries, Chicago, November-December 1965. [Chicago] International Galleries, 1965. 1 v. (unpaged) illus. (part col.), ports. 25 cm. Includes bibliography. [NE539.C3A49] 769'.924 75-222503
I. International Galleries.

CASSATT, Mary, 1844-1926. 759.13
Mary Cassatt, 1844-1926. [Exhibition, National Gallery of Art, September 27, 1970 through November 8, 1970] Washington, National Gallery of Art, 1970. 119 p. (chiefly illus. (part col.), ports. (part col.)) 29 cm. Introd. and catalogue notes by A. D. Breeskin. Bibliography: p. 119. [ND237.C3B685] 71-133323
I. Breeskin, Adelyn Dohme, 1896- II. U.S. National Gallery of Art.

CASSATT, Mary, 1844-1926. 759.13
Mary Cassatt, 1844-1926. [Exhibition, National Gallery of Art, September 27, 1970 through November 8, 1970] Washington, National Gallery of Art, 1970. 119 p. (chiefly illus. (part col.), ports. (part col.)) 29 cm. Introd. and catalogue notes by A. D. Breeskin. Bibliography: p. 119. [ND237.C3B685] 71-133323
I. Breeskin, Adelyn Dohme, 1896- II. U.S. National Gallery of Art.

HALE, Nancy, 1908- 759.13 B
Mary Cassatt / by Nancy Hale. 1st ed. Garden City, N.Y. : Doubleday, 1975. xxvii, 333 p., [16] leaves of plates : ill. ; 25 cm. Includes index. Bibliography: p. [293]-315. [ND237.C3H3] 74-18805 ISBN 0-385-00486-9 : 10.00
1. Cassatt, Mary, 1844-1926. BIP

JOSLYN Art Museum. 760'.0944
Mary Cassatt among the impressionists. Omaha [1969] 80 p. illus. (part col.) 25 cm. Exhibition held April 10 through June 1, 1969. [ND237.C3J6] 70-292994
1. Cassatt, Mary, 1844-1926. I. Title.

MCKOWN, Robin. 759.13 B
The world of Mary Cassatt. Illustrated with photos. New York, Crowell [1972] xiii, 253 p. illus. 21 cm. (Women of America) Bibliography: p. 239-241. [ND237.C3M3] 77-139106 ISBN 0-690-90274-3 4.50
1. Cassatt, Mary, 1844-1926. I. Title. BIP

SWEET, Frederick Arnold, 1903- 759.1
Miss Mary Cassatt, impressionist from Pennsylvania, by Frederick A. Sweet. Norman, Univ. of Okla. Pr. [1966] xx, 242p. illus. (pt. col.) 23cm. Bibl. [ND237.C3S9] 66-13423 7.95
1. Cassatt, Mary, 1845-1926. I. Title.

Cassatt, Mary, 1844-1926—Juvenile literature.

CARSON, Julia Margaret (Hicks) 1899- 759.1 B
Mary Cassatt, by Julia M. H. Carson. Illustrated with photos. from paintings and color prints by Mary Cassatt. New York, D. McKay Co., 1966. xi, 193 p. illus. 21 cm. Bibliography: p. 177-178. [ND237.C3C3] 66-9532
1. Cassatt, Mary, 1844-1926—Juvenile literature.

MYERS, Elisabeth P. 759.13 B
Mary Cassatt: a portrait, by Elisabeth P. Myers. Chicago, Reilly & Lee Books [1971] 138 p. illus., port. 24 cm. Bibliography: p. [137]-138. A biography of the American artist who spent most of her life in Europe because she felt her homeland restricted women in certain areas of artistic study. [ND237.C3M9] 92 75-143869 5.95
1. Cassatt, Mary, 1844-1926—Juvenile literature. I. Title.

SCHEADER, Catherine. 759.13 B
Mary Cassatt / by Catherine Scheader. Chicago : Childrens Press, [1977] p. cm. (They found a way) A biography of an American artist whose many paintings of women and children reveal the influence of French Impressionism. [ND237.C3S3] 92 77-7359 ISBN 0-516-01852-3 lib.bdg. : 6.60
1. Cassatt, Mary, 1844-1926—Juvenile literature. 2. Painters—United States—Biography—Juvenile literature. I. Title. II. Series. BIP

WILSON, Ellen Janet (Cameron) 759.13 B
American painter in Paris; a life of Mary Cassatt, by Ellen Wilson. New York, Farrar, Straus & Giroux [1971] xii, 205 p. illus., ports. (part col.) 24 cm. (An Ariel book) Bibliography: p. 198-201. The biography of the nineteenth-century Pennsylvania woman who became one of America's best known artists. [ND237.C3W53 1971] 92 70-149223 ISBN 0-374-30270-7 4.95
1. Cassatt, Mary, 1844-1926—Juvenile literature. I. Title. BIP

Casson, Alfred Joseph, 1898—

GRAY, Margaret Blair. 759.11 B
A. J. Casson / Margaret Gray, Margaret Rand, Lois Steen. Agincourt, Ont. : Gage Pub., c1976. 58 p. : ill. (some col.) ; 24 cm. (Canadian art series ; 1) Bibliography: p. 58. [ND249.C33G7] 77-359767 ISBN 0-7715-9962-5 : 14.95
1. Casson, Alfred Joseph, 1898- 2. Painters—Canada—Biography. I. Rand, Margaret, 1918- joint author. II. Steen, Lois, joint author.

Castaic Lake, Calif.—Recreational use.

CALIFORNIA. Dept. of Water Resources. 711'.558'0979493
Castaic Lake area recreation development plan. [Sacramento] 1970. 15 p. map. 28 cm. (Its Bulletin no. 117-9) [GV54.C22C33] 76-632810 1.00
1. Castaic Lake, Calif.—Recreational use. I. Title. II. Series.

Castelfranco, Giorgio, 1896—

LEONARDO da Vinci, 1452-1519. 741.9'45
Drawings by Leonardo da Vinci, by Giorgio Castelfranco. Translated by Florence H. Phillips. New York, Dover Publications [1968] 11 p., 32 plates. 28 cm. (The Great masters of drawing) Translation of Leonardo. [NC1055.L5C383] 67-25595 1.50
1. Castelfranco, Giorgio, 1896- I. Title.

Castelseprio, Italy. Santa Maria (Church)

WEITZMANN, Kurt, 1904- 751.73
The fresco cycle of S. Maria di Castelseprio. Princeton, Princeton University Press, 1951. vi, 101, xxxii p. illus. 31 cm. (Princeton monographs in art and archaeology, 26) [NA5621.C3W4] 51-11255
1. Castelseprio, Italy. Santa Maria (Church) 2. Church decoration and ornament. 3. Christian art and symbolism. I. Title. II. Series.

Castiglione, Giovanni Benedetto, called Il Grechetto, 1610?-1670?

PERCY, Ann. 741'.092'4
Giovanni Benedetto Castiglione, master draughtsman of the Italian Baroque. Foreword by Sir Anthony Blunt. Introd. and catalogue by Ann Percy. [Philadelphia? c1971] 161 p. illus. 31 cm. Exhibition held at the Philadelphia Museum of Art Sept. 17-Nov. 28, 1971. Includes bibliographical references. [NC257.C36P4] 70-163131
1. Castiglione, Giovanni Benedetto, called Il Grechetto, 1610?-1670? I. Philadelphia Museum of Art.

Castiglione, Giuseppe, 1688-1796.

BEURDELEY, Cecile. 759.5
Giuseppe Castiglione, a Jesuit painter at the court of the Chinese emporers, by Cecile and Michel Beurdeley. Translated by Michael Bullock. Rutland, Vt., C. E. Tuttle Co. [1972] 204 p. illus. 26 x 29 cm. Bibliography: p. 199-201. [ND623.C485B413] 77-157257 ISBN 0-8048-0987-9 25.00
1. Castiglione, Giuseppe, 1688-1796. I. Beurdeley, Michel, joint author. BIP

Castle, Wendell, 1932—

WICHITA Art Museum. 749.213
The furniture of Wendell Castle. Organized by the Wichita Art Museum. [Wichita, Kan., 1969] [15] p. illus. 23 x 31 cm. Label mounted on t.p.: Supplied by Worldwide Books, Boston. Catalogue of an exhibition held at the Wichita Art Museum, Wichita, Kan., May 6-June 24, 1969, and at the University of Kansas Museum of Art, Lawrence, Kan., July 11-Aug. 24, 1969. [NK2439.C3W5] 75-23725
1. Castle, Wendell, 1932- I. Kansas. University. Museum of Art. II. Title.

Castleden, George Frederick, 1861-1945.

CASTELDEN, Louise Decatur. 927.5
George Frederick Castleden, etcher-painter; a brief biography, Wth a foreword by Elihu Root, Jr. [1st ed.] New York, Exposition Press [1954, c1953] 72p. illus. 21cm. [ND497.C38C3] 53-12070
1. Castleden, George Frederick, 1861-1945. I. Title.

Castles.

CONTI, Flavio, 1943- 909
Homes of kings / Flavio Conti ; translated by Patrick Creagh. Boston : HBJ Press, c1978. 168 p. : ill. ; 31 cm. (His The grand tour) [NA7710.C6613] 77-88245 ISBN 0-15-003724-4 : 14.95
1. Castles. 2. Palaces. 3. Towers. I. Title. II. Series. BIP

CONTI, Flavio, 1943- 720'.9
Shrines of power / Flavio Conti ; translated by Patrick Creagh. Boston : HBJ Press, c1978. 168 p. : ill. ; 31 cm. (His The grand tour) Translation of I templi del potere. [NA7710.C6713] 77-90863 ISBN 0-15-003725-2 : 11.95
1. Castles. 2. Churches. 3. Temples. I. Title. II. Series. BIP

WARWICK, Alan Ross. 728.8
Let's look at castles [by] Alan R. Warwick. Illustrated by E. Cumberland Owen. Chicago, A. Whitman [1967, c1965] 63 p. illus. 21 cm. (Let's look series) A history of the castles devised and built by Europeans in the Middle Ages for protection and shelter. [NA7710] AC 67
1. Castles. 2. Fortification. I. Owen, E. Cumberland, illus. II. Title. BIP

Castles—England.

BROWN, Reginald Allen, 1924- 942
English castles / R. Allen Brown. 3rd revised ed. London : Batsford, 1976. 240 p. : ill., facsims., maps, plans ; 26 cm. Distributed in the United States by Hippocrene Books. First ed. published in 1954 under title: English medieval castles. Includes bibliographical references and index. [DA660.B85 1976] 77-366863 ISBN 0-7134-3119-9 : 17.50
1. Castles—England. 2. Castles—Wales. 3. Great Britain—History—Medieval period, 1066-1485. I. Title.

BROWN, Reginald Allen, 1924- 942
English medieval castles. [1st American ed.] New York, Simmons-Boardman Pub. Corp. [1961] 208 p. illus., map, plans. 23 cm. Erratum slip mounted on p. 9. [DA660.B85] 63-1159
1. Castles — England. 2. Castles — Wales. 3. Gt. Brit. — Hist. — Medieval period, 1066-1485. I. Title.

HOGG, Garry. 623'.1
Castles of England. New York, Arco, 1969. 112 p. illus. 26 cm. [DA660.H66 1969] 79-93744 5.95
1. Castles—England. I. Title.

SIMPSON, William Douglas, 1896- 914.2'03
Castles in England and Wales [by] W. Douglas Simpson. New York, Hastings House [1969] ix, 174 p. illus. 23 cm. Includes bibliographical references. [NA7745.S523 1969b] 70-87054 ISBN 0-8038-1136-5 7.95
1. Castles—England. 2. Castles—Wales. I. Title.

SORRELL, Alan. 914.2'03
British castles. New York, Hastings House Publishers [1973] 80 p. illus. 23 x 30 cm. Bibliography: p. [4] [DA660.S65] 73-10468 ISBN 0-8038-0751-1 7.95
1. Castles—England. I. Title.

Castles—England—Guide-books.

WARNER, Philip. 914.1'04'857
A guide to castles in Britain : where to find them and what to look for / [by] Philip Warner. London : New English Library, 1976. 166 p., [16] p. of plates : ill., plans ; 22 cm. [DA660.W325 1976] 77-353745 ISBN 0-450-03062-8 : £4.50
1. Castles—England—Guide-books. 2. Great Britain—History, Local. I. Title.

Castles—Europe.

ARTHAUD, Claude, 1927- 914'.03
Enchanted visions; fantastic houses and their treasures. [1st American ed.] New York, Putnam [1972] 355 p. illus. 32 cm. Translation of Les palais du reve. [NA7710.A7513 1972] 76-147284 ISBN 0-399-10988-9 30.00
1. Castles—Europe. I. Title.

Castles — France — Hist.

GEBELIN, Francois, 1884- 728.82
The chateaux of France. Translated by H. Eaton Hart. New York, Putnam [1964] 192 p. illus. (part col.) plans. 21 cm. Bibliography: p. 185-186. [NA7735.G373] 64-13024
1. Castles — France — Hist. I. Title.

Castles—Great Britain.

BIRD, Paul C. 942
A guide book to the castles of Great Britain [by Paul C. Bird] Gooding, Idaho [1971] 179 p. illus. 22 cm. Bibliography: p. 11. [DA660.B5] 71-26584
1. Castles—Gt. Brit. I. Title.

CASSON, Hugh Maxwell, 914.20485
Sir 1910- ed.
Castles [by] Paul Sharp. E M. Hatt [1st Amer. ed. New York] Taplinger [1966, c.1965] 128p. illus. (part col.) 19cm. (Gold leaf Brit. landmarks ser.) Res. by Paul Sharp, E. M. Hatt; text by E. M. Hatt; design. illus. by Paul Sharp [DA660.C27] 66-2322 1.50 pap.,
1. Castles—Gt. Brit. I. Sharp, Paul. II. Hart, E. M. III. Title.

CASSON, Hugh Maxwell 914.20485
Sir 1910- ed.
Monuments [1st Amer. ed. New York] Taplinger [1966, c.1965] 128p. illus. (pt. col.) 2 col. maps. 19cm. (Gold leaf Brit. landmarks ser.) Res., design, and illus. by Paul Sharp. Writing by E. M. Hatt [DA655.C3] 66-2321 1.50 pap.,
1. Castles—Gt. Brit. I. Sharp, Paul. II. Hatt. E. M. III. Title.

**CASTLES of* 728.8'1'0941
Britain 1st ed. Huntingdon, England, Balfour Books [1973] 96 p. col. illus. 25 cm. [NA7745]
1. Castles—Great Britain.
Distributed by Transatlantic Arts Levittown, N.Y. for 5.95

FRY, Peter George Robin 914.2'03
Somerset, 1931-
British medieval castles / Plantagenet Somerset Fry [i.e. P.G.R.S. Fry]. Newton Abbot ; North Pomfret, Vt. : David & Charles, [1974]. 176 p. : ill. ; 22 cm. Includes index. Bibliography: p. 173-174. [DA660.F79 1974] 74-193875 ISBN 0-7153-6304-2 : £3.95
1. Castles—Great Britain. 2. Great Britain—History. I. Title.

GASCOIGNE, Christina, 941
1938or9-
Castles of Britain / photos. and descriptive text by Christina Gascoigne ; introd. by Bamber Gascoigne. New York : Putnam, c1975. 224 p. : ill. ; 27 cm. Includes index. [DA660.G26] 75-18597 ISBN 0-399-11676-1 : 15.95
1. Castles—Great Britain. 2. Great Britain—History. I. Gascoigne, Bamber. II. Title.

HAMMOND, Muriel 728.810942
Castles of Britain [London] Ian Allan [dist. New Rochelle, N.Y., SportShelf, 1964, c.1963] 64p. illus. 19cm. Contents.1. England. 64-6043 1.75 bds.,
1. Castles— Gt. Brit. I. Title.

HAMMOND, Muriel 728.810942
Castles of Britain, v.3 [London] I. Allan [dist. New Rochelle, N. Y., SportShelf, 1965, c.1964] 55p. illus. 19cm. [NA7745.H3] 64-6043 1.75 bds.,
1. Castles—Gt. Brit. I. Title.
Contents omitted.

SIMPSON, William 728.810942
Douglas, 1896-
Castles in Britain [by] W. Douglas Simpson; drawings by Peter Fraser. London, Batsford, 1966. 95p. illus., plans. 23cm. Bibl. [NA7745.S52] 66-2617 3.75 bds.,
1. Castles—Gt. Brit. I. Title.
Available from Hastings House in New York.

*WILKINSON, 728.8'1'0941
Frederick
The castles of England London, George Philip, [1973] 191 p. illus. 23 cm. [NA7745] ISBN 0-540-07050-5
1. Castles—Great Britain. 2. Great Britain—Description and travel—Guidebooks. I. Title.
Distributed by International Publications Service, N.Y., for 12.50. BIP

Castles—Great Britain—History.

CLEATOR, Philip 728.810942
Ellaby, 1908-
Castles and kings. Diagrs., maps by the author. London, R. Hale [dist. Chester Springs, Pa., Dufour, 1964, c.1963] 224p. illus., maps, plans. 23cm. t. Brit.-- Kings and rulers. Bibl. 64-5769 4.50
1. Castles—Gt. Brit.—Hist. I. Title.

Castles—Great Britain—History.

JOHNSON, Paul, 1928- 942
The National Trust book of British castles / Paul Johnson. New York : Putnam, c1978. 288 p. : ill. ; 29 cm. Includes index. Bibliography: p. 281-282. [DA660.J64] 77-10261 ISBN 0-399-12091-2 : 20.00
1. Castles—Great Britain—History. 2. Great Britain—History. I. Title. II. Title: British castles. BIP

KEMP, Anthony. 941
Castles in color / Anthony Kemp. New York : Arco, 1978, c1977. 208 p. : ill. (some col.) ; 19 cm. Includes index. Bibliography: p. 205-206. [DA660.K35 1978] 77-20984 ISBN 0-668-04469-1 : 8.95. ISBN 0-668-04480-2 pbk. : 6.95
1. Castles—Great Britain—History. 2. Castles—Europe—History. 3. Great Britain—History, Military. 4. Europe—History, Military. I. Title. BIP

Castles — Gt. Brit. — Juvenile literature.

TREECE, Henry, 1911- 728.810942
The true book about castles. Illustrated by G. H. Channing. London, F. Muller [1960] c1959; New Rochelle, N.Y.] stamped; distributed by Sportshelf, 144 p. illus. 20 cm. [NA7745.T75] 61-16
1. Castles — Gt. Brit. — Juvenile literature. I. Title.

UNSTEAD, R. J. 942
British castles [by] R. J. Unstead. New York, Crowell [1970] 92 p. illus., map, plans, ports. 26 cm. "Originally published in Great Britain under the title: Castles." Describes the purpose and construction of castles in Great Britain from the early Norman period through the seventeenth century. Illustrated with photographs. [DA660.U55 1970] 74-94224 3.50
1. Castles—Gt. Brit.—Juvenile literature. I. Title. BIP

Castles—Ireland.

LEASK, Harold Graham 728.8109415
Irish castles and castellated houses [Rev.] Dundalk [Ire.] Dundalgan Pr. [dist. Chester Springs, Pa., Dufour, 1964] 170p. illus., map (on lining paper) plans. 23cm. 64-9808 3.50
1. Castles—Ireland. 2. Architecture, Domestic—Ireland. I. Title.

Castles—Japan.

HIRAI, Kiyoshi, 728.8'1'0952
1929-
Feudal architecture of Japan. Translated by Hiroaki Sato and Jeannine Ciliotta. [1st English ed.] New York, Weatherhill [1973] 166 p. illus. (part col.) 24 cm. (The Heibonsha survey of Japanese art, v. 13) Translation of Shiro to shoin. [NA7451.H4813] 73-3354 ISBN 0-8348-1015-8 8.95
1. Castles—Japan. 2. Architecture, Shoin. I. Title. II. Series. BIP

*SCHMORLEITZ, Morton 728.810952
S.
Castles in Japan by Morton S. Schmorleitz Rutland, Vermont, Charles E. Tuttle, [1974] 188 p. illus. 24 cm. Bibliography: p. 181-182. [NA7451] 72-91553 ISBN 0-8048-1102-4 15.00
1. Castles—Japan. I. Title. BIP

Castles—Juvenile literature.

BERENSTAIN, Michael. 940.1
The castle book / Michael Berenstain. New York : D. McKay Co., c1977. p. cm. Briefly describes the purpose and construction of European castles built during the Middle Ages. [NA7710.B47] 77-263 ISBN 0-679-20403-2 : 6.95
1. Castles—Juvenile literature. I. Title. BIP

BOARDMAN, Fon Wyman, 1911- 728.81
Castles. New York, H. Z. Walck, 1957. 104 p. illus. [NA7710.B603]
1. Castles—Juvenile literature. 2. Feudalism—Juvenile literature. BIP

Castles—Latin Orient.

BOASE, Thomas Sherrer 726'.095694
Ross, 1898-
Castles and churches of the crusading kingdom; by T. S. R. Boase; with colour photographs by Richard Cleave. London, New York [etc.] Oxford U.P., 1967] xiv, 121 p. illus., 24 col. plates, maps, plans. 30 cm. Bibliography: p. 114. [NA1460.B6 1967] 67-99184
1. Castles—Latin Orient. 2. Churches—Latin Orient. I. Title.

MULLER-WIENER, Wolfgang. 725.18
Castles of the crusaders. Photos. by A. F. Kersting. [Translated from the German by J. Maxwell Brownjohn] New York, McGraw-Hill [1966] 111 p. mounted col. illus., fold. map, plans, 160 plates. 28 cm. Includes bibliographies. [NA1460.M813 1966a] 66-24887
1. Castles—Latin Orient. I. Title.

Castles—Loire Valley.

ROWE, Vivian. 728.82
Chateaux of the Loire. New York, Norton [1958] 243p. illus. 23cm. [NA7735.R69 1958] 58-7392
1. Castles—Loire Valley. I. Title.

Castles—Netherlands.

REYEN, Paul E. van. v. 12
Middeleeuwse kastelen in Nederland / Paul E. van Reijen. 3., geheel herziene druk. Haarlem : Fibula-Van Dishoeck, c1976. 184 p. : ill. ; 25 cm. Includes index. Bibliography: p. 175-178. [NA7750.R48 1976] 77-461942 ISBN 9-02-283009-8
1. Castles—Netherlands. 2. Architecture, Medieval—Netherlands. I. Title.

Castles—Spain.

WEISSMULLER, Alberto A. 725'.18
Castles from the heart of Spain [by] Alberto A. Weissmuller. Photos. by the author. New York, C. N. Potter [1967] 228 p. illus. (part col.), facsim., maps, plans. 25 cm. Bibliography: p. 227-228. [NA7775.W4 1967b] 67-24607
1. Castles—Spain. I. Title.

Castles—United States.

CAVALIER, Julian, 1931- 917.3'03
American castles. South Brunswick, A. S. Barnes [1973] 243 p. illus. 29 cm. [NA705.C39] 72-6394 ISBN 0-498-01254-9 15.00
1. Castles—United States. I. Title.

Castles—Wales.

*REID, Alan 728'.810941
The castles of Wales: castellu cymru. London, George Philip, [1974] 140 p. col. illus. 23 cm. [NA7745] ISBN 0-540-07052-1 10.50
1. Castles—Wales. I. Title.
Distributed by International Publications Service. BIP

Cataloging of art.

NEW York (City). 025'.02
Metropolitan Museum of Art. Library.
Exhibition catalogue manual in use in the Library of the Metropolitan Museum of Art : procedures for processing, cataloguing, and classification of exhibition catalogues, based on a system devised by Elizabeth R. Usher / compiled by Lucy Chao Ho ; rev. and enl. by Dobrila-Donya Schimansky and the Library staff. New York : Metropolitan Museum of Art, 1974. p. cm. Includes index. [N440.N48 1974] 74-22245 ISBN 0-87099-099-3 pbk. : 2.50
1. New York (City). Metropolitan Museum of Art. Library. 2. Cataloging of art. 3. Art—Exhibitions—Catalogs. I. Ho, Lucy Chao. II. Schimansky, Dobrila-Donya. III. Title. BIP

PINK, Marilyn. 025.3'4'71
How to catalogue works of art; a guide for the private collector. [1st ed. Los Angeles, Museum Systems, 1972] 53 p. illus. 23 cm. Bibliography: p. 44-50. [N440.P55] 72-86380
1. Cataloging of art. I. Title. BIP

Catalogue of an exhibition held at University Art Gallery, Berkeley, March 18-May 1, 1966 and at Santa Barbara Museum of Art, June 5-July 10, 1966.

CALIFORNIA. University. 735'.29
Art Museum.
Directions in kinetic sculpture [an exhibition prepared by] Peter Selz. Presented by the University Art Museum [and] the Committee for Arts and Lectures, University of California, Berkeley. With and introd. by George Rickey and statements by the artists. [Berkeley, 1966] 78 p. illus., ports. 28 cm. Bibliography: p. 77-78. [NB1272.C3] 66-63482
1. Catalogue of an exhibition held at University Art Gallery, Berkeley, March 18-May 1, 1966 and at Santa Barbara Museum of Art, June 5-July 10, 1966. 2. Kinetic sculpture—Exhibitions. I. Selz, Peter. II. California. University. Committee for Arts and Lectures. III. Santa Barbara, Calif. Museum of Art. IV. Title.

Catharina, Saint, of Alexandria—Art.

SCHRODER, Anneliese 704.9486
Catherine [by] Anneliese Schroder. Text of story and legend by Leonard [i.e. Leonhard]Kuppers. [Tr. from German by Hans Hermann Rosenwald] Recklinghausen [Ger.] A. Bongers. dist. by Taplinger [New York, c.1965] 73p. col. illus. 18cm. (Saints in legend art, v.17) [N8080.S3613] 67-4497 2.50 bds.,
1. Catharina, Saint, of Alexandria—Art. I. Kuppers, Leonhard. 1903- II. Title.

Cathedrals.

*CHEAM, Frederick. 726.6
Great cathedrals. [New York] Golden Press [1974] 80 p. illus. (part. col.) 30 cm. (Golden highlights library.) [BV634] 73-87968 ISBN 0-307-43120-7 2.95
1. Cathedrals. I. Title.

COWEN, Painton. 748.5'9
Rose windows / Painton Cowen. San Francisco : Chronicle Books, c1979. p. cm. (Art and imagination) "A Prism edition." Includes index. Bibliography: p. [NK5308.C64] 78-23286 22.50
1. Cathedrals. 2. Rose windows. 3.

Christian art and symbolism. 4. Glass painting and staining, Medieval. I. Title.

GRUNENFELDER, Josef. 726'.6'094
Cathedrals of Europe / text by Josef Grunenfelder ; photos. by Michael Wolgensinger ; translated by David Lawrence Grambs. New York : Crowell, [1976] p. cm. [NA4830.G78] 76-8897 ISBN 0-690-01172-5
1. Cathedrals. I. Wolgensinger, Michael. II. Title.

MACAULAY, David. 726'.6
Cathedral: the story of its construction. Boston, Houghton Mifflin, 1973. 77 p. illus. 31 cm. [NA4830.M32] 73-6634 ISBN 0-395-17513-5 6.95
1. Cathedrals. 2. Architecture, Gothic. I. Title.

SIMSON, Otto Georg von, 1912- 726.64
The Gothic cathedral; origins of Gothic architecture and the medieval concept of order, [2d ed.] New York, Harper & Row [1964] xx, 275 p. illus., 44 plates (incl. facsims.) 21 cm. (Harper torchbooks. The Bollingen library) "TB2018." Bibliography: p. [242]-261. [NA4830.S5 1964] 64-3673
1. Cathedrals. 2. Architecture, Gothic. 3. Chartres, France. Notre Dame (Cathedral) I. Title.

SIMSON, Otto Georg von, 1912- 726.6
The Gothic cathedral; origins of Gothic architecture and the medieval concept of order. [2d ed., rev. with additions] [New York] Pantheon Books [1962] xxiii, 278 p. illus., plates (part col.) plans. 26 cm. (Bollingen series, 48) Bibliography: p. [245]-264. [NA4830.S5 1962] 63-2039
1. Cathedrals. 2. Architecture, Gothic. 3. Chartres, France. Notre-Dame (Cathedral) I. Title. II. Series.

SIMSON, Otto Georg von, 1912- 726
The Gothic cathedral origins of Gothic architecture and the medieval concept of order. With an appendix on the proportions of the south tower of Chartres Cathedral, by Ernst Levy. [New York] Pantheon Books [1956] xxiii, 307 p. illus. (part mounted col., 1 fold. col. in pocket) 26 cm. (Bollingen series, 48) Bibliography: p. [267]-289. [NA4830.S5] 55-11599
1. Cathedrals. 2. Architecture, Gothic. 3. Chartres, France. Notre-Dame (Cathedral I. Title. II. Series.

SIMSON, Otto Georg von, 1912- 726
The Gothic cathedral: origins of Gothic architecture and the medieval concept of order. With an appendix on the proportions of the south tower of Chartres Cathedral, by Ernst Levy. [New York] Pantheon Books [1956] xxiii, 307 p. illus. (part mounted col., 1 fold. col. in pocket) 26 cm. (Bollingen series, 48) Bibliography: p. [267]-289. [NA4830.S5] 55-11599
1. Chartres, France. Notre-Dame (Cathedral) 2. Cathedrals. 3. Architecture, Gothic—France. I. Title. II. Series.

Cathedrals—England.

BATSFORD, Harry 726.60942
The cathedrals of England [by] Harry Batsford, Charles Fry. Rev. by Bryan Little. [10th ed.] [dist. New York, Macmillan, 1960] 224p. illus. 61-680 3.75 bds.,
1. Cathedrals—England. 2. Church architecture—England. I. Fry, Charles, 1903- joint author. II. Title.

CLIFTON-TAYLOR, Alec. 726'.6'0942
The cathedrals of England. Photos. by Martin Hurlimann and others. [1st American ed.] New York, Association Press [1970, c1967] 288 p. illus. (part col.), map, plans. 22 cm. Includes bibliographical references. [NA5461.C486 1970] 77-98142 7.95
1. Cathedrals—England. I. Title.

COOK, George Henry 726.6
The English cathedral through the centuries. London, Phoenix House [dist. Mystic, Conn., Verry, 1965] 384p. plates, diagrs., plans. 23cm. Bibl. [NA5641.C72] 10.00
1. Cathedrals—England. 2. Church architecture—England. I. Title.

FELTON, Herbert 726.0942
A portrait of English cathedrals, a selection of photos. by Herbert Felton, text by John Harvey. [New York, Norton, 1961] 96p. illus. 31cm. 5.95
1. Cathedrals—England. I. Harvey, John Hooper. II. Title.

HARVEY, John Hooper. 726'.6'0942
Cathedrals of England and Wales [by] John Harvey. [2d ed.] New York, Hastings House [1974] 272 p. illus. 26 cm. Bibliography: p. [254]-259. [NA5461.H29 1974] 74-5158 ISBN 0-8038-1195-0
1. Cathedrals—England. 2. Cathedrals—Wales. I. Title. BIP

HARVEY, John Hooper 726.60942
English cathedrals. [Rev. ed. dist. New York, Norton, 1962, c.1961] 188p. illus. (Batsford paperbacks, 2) 62-2186 1.50 pap.,
1. Cathedrals—England. I. Title.

HARVEY, John Hooper. 726.6
The English cathedrals, photographed by Herbert Felton and with a text by John Harvey. London, New York, Batsford [1950] xii, 99 p. illus. 23 cm. (The British art and building series) Bibliography: p. 92. [NA5461.H3] 50-9434
1. Cathedrals—England. I. Felton, Herbert. illus. II. Title. III. Series.

HURLIMANN, Martin, 1897- 726.60942
English cathedrals. Foreword by Geoffrey Grigson. Introd. by Martin Hurlimann. Descriptive text by Peter Meyer. 169 photogravure plates, 3 in colour. [Rev. ed.] New York, Viking [1962] 47p. 31cm. (Studio bk.) 62-2878 12.00
1. Cathedrals—England. 2. Church architecture—England. I. Meyer, Peter, 1894- II. Title.

LINNELL, Charles Lawrence Scruton. 726.650942
English cathedrals in colour a collection of colour photographs, by A. F. Kersting; with an introductory text and notes on the illus. by C. L. S. Linnell. London, Batsford [dist. New York, Hastings House, 1960] 94p. illus. 25cm. 60-50036 3.95
1. Cathedrals—England. 2. Church architecture—England. I. Kersting, A. F., illus. II. Title.

PRIOR, Edward Schroder, 1852-1932. 726'.6'0942
The cathedral builders in England / by Edward S. Prior. Boston : Longwood Press, 1978. p. cm. Reprint of the 1905 ed. published by Seeley, London, which was issued as no. 46 of Portfolio; artistic monographs. Includes index. [NA5461.P8 1978] 77-94613 ISBN 0-89341-247-3 lib.bdg. : 15.00
1. Cathedrals—England. 2. Architects—England. I. Title. II. Series: The Portfolio : monographs on artistic subjects ; no. 46.

WATSON, Percy. 726'.6'0942
Building the medieval cathedrals / Percy Watson ; [illustrations by David Harris ; maps and diagrams by Leslie Marshall and Oxford Illustrators Ltd]. Cambridge ; New York : Cambridge University Press, 1976. 48 p. : ill., maps, plans ; 21 x 22 cm. (Cambridge introduction to the history of mankind : Topic book) [NA5463.W37] 77-355431 pbk. : 2.45
1. Cathedrals—England. 2. Architecture, Medieval—England. 3. Building—England. I. Title.

WATSON, Percy. 726'.6'0942
Building the medieval cathedrals / Percy Watson ; [ill. by David Harris ; maps and diagrams by Leslie Marshall and Oxford Illustrators Ltd.]. Minneapolis : Lerner Publications Co., 1978, c1976. p. cm. (A Cambridge topic book) (The Cambridge history library) Includes index. Discusses the materials and methods used in building the great English cathedrals, the craftsmen who built them, and the styles in which they were built. [NA5463.W37 1978] 78-56794 ISBN 0-8225-1213-0 lib. bdg. : 4.94
1. Cathedrals—England. 2. Architecture, Medieval—England. 3. Building—England. I. Harris, David, fl. 1967- II. Title. III. Series. BIP

Cathedrals—Europe.

SWAAN, Wim. 726'.6'094
The Gothic cathedral. With an historical introd.: The cathedral in medieval society [by] Christopher Brooke. Garden City, N.Y., Doubleday [1969] 328 p. illus. (part col.), plans, ports. 32 cm. Bibliography: p. 324-326. [NA5453.S95] 75-85498 30.00
1. Cathedrals—Europe. 2. Architecture, Gothic—Europe. I. Title. BIP

Cathedrals—France.

HOWGRAVE-GRAHAM, Robert Pickersgill, 1880- 726.640944
The cathedrals of France. With photos. by the author and others. New York, Hastings House [1959] 280p. illus. 23cm. [NA5541.H65] 59-16419
1. Cathedrals—France. 2. Church architecture—France. I. Title.

HURLIMANN, Martin, 1897- 726.6
French cathedrals. [Text by] Jean Bony. Photos. by Martin Hurlimann. Descriptive notes by Peter Meyer. Boston, Houghton Mifflin, 1951. 47 p. 160 plates. 31 cm. [NQ5543.H8] 51-14430
1. Cathedrals—France. 2. Architecture, Gothic. I. Bony, Jean. II. Title.

HURLIMANN, Martin, 1897- 726.60944
French cathedrals. [Text by] Jean Bony. 199 photos. by Martin Hurlimann. Descriptive notes by Peter Meyer. [Rev. ed.] New York, Viking Press [1961] 311p. plates (part col.) 32cm. (A Studio book) [NA5543.H8 1961] 61-8827
1. Cathedrals—France. 2. Architecture, Gothic. I. Title.

HURLIMANN, Martin, 1897- 726'.6'0944
French cathedrals [by] Martin Hurlimann [and] Jean Bony. Descriptive notes by Peter Meyer. [New rev. ed.] New York, Viking Press [1967] 229 p. map, plans, 189 plates (part col.) 31 cm. (A Studio book) Photos. by M. Hurlimann; introductory text by J. Bony. [NA5543.H8 1967a] 67-5209
1. Cathedrals—France. 2. Architecture, Gothic—France. I. Bony, Jean. II. Meyer, Peter, 1894- III. Title.

RODIN, Auguste. 1840-1917 726.640944
Cathedrals of France. Tr. by Elisabeth Chase Geissbuhler. Pref. by Herbert Read. Boston. Beacon [1965] xvii. 278p. illus. 24cm. [NA5541.R613] 65-20784 17.50
1. Cathedrals—France. I. Title.

Cathedrals—Germany.

BAUM, Julius, 1882- 726.5
German cathedrals. Photos. by Helga Schmidt-Glassner. New York, Vanguard Press [1956] 63p. plates. 31cm. Bibliography: p. 57-59. [NA5563.B3 1956] [NA5563.B3 1956] 726.6 57-2247 57-2247
1. Cathedrals—Germany. 2. Church architecture—Germany. I. Schmidt-Glassner, Helga. II. Title.

Cathedrals—Great Britain.

*ABBEYS, *Priories and Cathedrals* 1st ed. Huntingdon, England, Balfour Books [1973] 96 p. col. illus 25 cm. [NA5461] ISBN 0-85944-004-4 726.60941
1. Cathedrals—Great Britain.
Distributed by Transatlantic Arts, Levittown, N.Y. for 5.95

ANDERSON, William Francis Desnaux, 1935- 941
Cathedrals in Britain and Ireland : from early times to the reign of Henry VIII / William Anderson, Clive Hicks. 1st American ed. New York : Scribner, 1978. 184 p. : ill. ; 25 cm. Includes index. Bibliography: p. 182. [NA5463.A53 1978] 77-92814 ISBN 0-684-15657-1 : 17.50
1. Cathedrals—Great Britain. 2. Architecture, Medieval—Great Britain. 3. Cathedrals—Ireland. 4. Architecture, Medieval—Ireland. I. Hicks, Clive, joint author. II. Title. BIP

HAMMOND, Muriel 726.60942
Cathedrals of Britain. London, I. Allan [dist. New Rochelle, N.Y., SportShelf, 1964, c.1963] 96p. illus. 19cm. 64-5653 2.00 bds.,
1. Cathedrals—Gt. Brit. I. Title.

*HOUGHTON, Leighton. 726'60941
A guide to the British Cathedrals. London, John Baker, [1973] 148 p. illus. 20 cm. [NA5461] ISBN 0-212-97007-0
1. Cathedrals—Great Britain. I. Title.
Distributed by Transatlantic Arts, N.Y. for 8.75 BIP

Cathedrals—Italy.

BAXTER, Lucy E. Barnes, 1837-1902. 726'.6'0945
The cathedral builders : the story of a great Masonic guild / by Leader Scott [i.e. L. E. B. Baxter]. Boston : Longwood Press, 1978. p. cm. Reprint of the 1899 ed. published by Scribner, New York. Includes index. Bibliography: p. [NA5613.B3 1978] 78-58191 ISBN 0-89341-354-2 : 50.00
1. Comacine Masters (Builders) 2. Freemasons. Italy. 3. Cathedrals—Italy. 4. Architecture, Medieval—Italy. I. Title.

FRANKLIN, J. W. 726.60945
The cathedrals of Italy. With photos. by A. F. Kersting and others. New York, Hastings House [1958] 280 p. illus. 23 cm. Includes bibliography. [NA5611.F7 1958a] 59-1538
1. Cathedrals—Italy. 2. Church architecture—Italy.

Cathedrals—Juvenile literature.

GRANT, Neil. 726'.6
Cathedrals. Illustrated with photos. New York, Watts, 1972. 90 p. illus. 23 cm. (A First book) Describes the design and building of various cathedrals throughout the world from the early Middle Ages to the present day. [NA4830.G73] 79-183939 ISBN 0-531-00755-3
1. Cathedrals—Juvenile literature. I. Title. BIP

Cathedrals—Spain.

HARVEY, John Hooper. 726.5
The cathedrals of Spain. New York, Hastings House [c1957] 279p. illus. 23cm. Includes bibliography. [NA5801] 726.6 58-14631
1. Cathedrals—Spain. 2. Church architecture—Spain—Hist. I. Title.

Catherwood, Frederick.

VON HAGEN, Victor Wolfgang, 1908- 720.9'24
F. Catherwood, architect-explorer of two worlds. Introd. by Aldous Huxley. Barre, Mass., Barre, 1968 [c1967] xv, 60p. illus. 24cm. Bibl. [NA997.C33V57] 67-25571 6.95
I. Catherwood, Frederick. II. Title.

VON HAGEN, Victor Wolfgang, 1908- 927.2
Frederick Catherwood, arch. Introd. by Aldous Huxley. New York, Oxford University Press, 1950. xix, 177 p. illus., maps. 24 cm. Bibliography: p. 165-169. [NA997.C33V6] 49-50430
1. Catherwood, Frederick.

Cathlamet, Wash., in art.

BUTLER, Maude Kimball, 1880- 759.13
Cathlamet pioneer; the paintings of Maude Kimball Butler. With descriptive notes by Julia Butler Hansen. Tacoma, Washington State Historical Society, 1973. 39 p. illus. 26 cm. Exhibition to be held at Washington State Historical Society Museum in Aug. 1973. [ND237.B97H36] 73-80884
1. Butler, Maude Kimball, 1880- 2. Cathlamet, Wash., in art. I. Hansen, Julia Butler. II. Washington State Historical Society. Museum. III. Title. BIP

Catholic Church. Liturgy and ritual. Evangeliary (Cuthbert's Gospel)

CINCIK, Joseph G 745.67
Anglo-Saxon and Slovak-Avar patterns of Cuthbert's Gospel; a study in Slovak art of the early Carolingian era [Cleveland, Slovak Institute] 1958 [c1956] 123p. illus. (part col.) maps, facsims. 24cm. (Series Cyrilomethodiana, v. 1) Bibliography: p.105-119. [ND3359.C88S4 vol.1] 57-12719
1. Catholic Church. Liturgy and ritual. Evangeliary (Cuthbert's Gospel) 2. Evangeliaries. 3. Illumination of books and manuscripts—Slovakia. 4. Art, Slovak. 5. Art, Anglo-Saxon. 6. Art, Carlovingian. 7. Avars. I. Title. II. Series.

Catholic institutions—Buildings.

THE Portfolio of 726'.5'0973
Catholic institutional design. Edward L. Spencer, editor. George E. O'Halloran, publisher. 3d ed. [Duluth, Catholic property administration] 1962. 1 portfolio ([2] 1., 150 plates) 32 x 40 cm. Title on portfolio: Third portfolio of Catholic institutional designs. Includes photos., floor plans, and detailed descriptions of 150 structures selected by the editors of the Catholic property administration. [NA5212.P6 1962] 73-10731
1. Catholic institutions—Buildings. 2. Architecture, Modern—20th century—U.S. 3. Church architecture—Designs and plans. 4. Churches, Catholic. I. Spencer, Edward L., ed. II. O'Halloran, George E. III. Catholic property administration. IV. Title: Third portfolio of Catholic institutional designs.

Catholics—New Mexico—Santa Fe—Biography.

BACIGALUPA, Andrea, 1923- 759.13 B
Journal of an itinerant artist / Drew Bacigalupa. Huntington, Ind. : Our Sunday Visitor, inc., c1977. 176 p., [4] leaf of plates : ill. ; 24 cm. [BX4705.B10195A34] 77-78739 ISBN 0-87973-887-1 : 9.95
1. Bacigalupa, Andrea, 1923- 2. Catholics—New Mexico—Santa Fe—Biography. 3. Art dealers—New Mexico—Santa Fe—Biography. 4. Santa Fe, N.M.—Biography. I. Title. BIP

Catlin, George, 1796-1872.

CATLIN, George, 1796-1872. 759.13
George Catlin : painter of the Indians of the Americas : opening exhibition, Sordoni Art Gallery, Wilkes College, Wilkes-Barre, Pennsylvania / introd. and catalogue by Vivian Varney Guyler. [Wilkes-Barre, Pa. : Sordoni Art Gallery?, 1973] [28] p. : ill. (some col.) ; 26 cm. [ND237.C35G89] 75-315758
1. Catlin, George, 1796-1872. 2. Indians of North America—Pictorial works. I. Guyler, Vivian Varney. II. Sordoni Art Gallery.

CATLIN, George, 1796-1872. 759.13
George Catlin book of American Indians / Royal Hassrick. New York : Watson-Guptill, 1977. p. cm. Includes index. Bibliography: p. [ND237.C35H36] 77-7930 ISBN 0-8230-2111-4 : 25.00
1. Catlin, George, 1796-1872. 2. Indians of North America—Pictorial works. I. Hassrick, Royal B. BIP

HAVERSTOCK, Mary Sayre. 759.13 B
Indian gallery; the story of George Catlin. New York, Four Winds Press [1973] xx, 229 p. illus. 26 cm. Bibliography: p. 221-222. [ND237.C35H38] 72-87075 7.88 (reinforced bdg.)
1. Catlin, George, 1796-1872. 2. Indians of North America—The West. I. Catlin, George, 1796-1872. II. Title. BIP

MCCRACKEN, Harold, 1894- 759.13
George Catlin and the old frontier. New York, Dial Press, 1959. 216 p. illus. (part col.), ports. (part col.) 32 cm. Bibliography: p. [212]-214. [ND237.C35M3 1959] 59-9434
1. Catlin, George, 1796-1872. 2. Indians of North America—The West—Pictorial works.

MILLICHAP, Joseph R. 759.13
George Catlin / by Joseph R. Millichap. Boise, Idaho : Boise State University, c1977. 48 p. ; 21 cm. (Boise State University Western writers series ; no. 27) Bibliography: p. 47-48. [ND237.C35M54] 77-76200 ISBN 0-88430-051-X : 2.00
1. Catlin, George, 1796-1872. 2. Indians of North America—Pictorial works. I. Title. II. Series: Boise State University. Boise State University Western writers series ; no. 27. BIP

PLATE, Robert. 927.5
Palette and tomahawk; the story of George Catlin, July 27, 1796--December 23, 1872. Illus. from drawings by George Catlin. New York, D. McKay Co., 1962. 248p. illus. 22cm. Includes bibliography. [ND237.C35P6] 62-18967
1. Catlin, George, 1796-1872. I. Title.

ROEHM, Marjorie (Catlin) ed. 759.13
The letters of George Catlin and his family; a chronicle of the American West. Berkeley, University of California Press, 1966. xxi, 463 p. illus., geneal. table, ports. 25 cm. Includes the diary of Francis Catlin, written Oct. 31-Dec. 30, 1868. and many letters addressed to him. Bibliographical footnotes. [ND237.C35R6] 66-13090
1. Catlin, George, 1796-1872. 2. Indians of North America—The West. I. Catlin, George, 1796-1872. II. Catlin, Francis Putnam. 1815-1900. III. Title. BIP

TRUETTNER, William H. 759.13 B
The natural man observed : a study of Catlin's Indian gallery / William H. Truettner. 1st ed. Washington : Smithsonian Institution Press, [1978] p. cm. Includes indexes. Bibliography: p. [ND237.C35T78] 78-15152 ISBN 0-87474-918-2 : 35.00
1. Catlin, George, 1796-1872. 2. Painters—United States—Biography. 3. Indians of North America—Pictorial works. 4. The West in art. I. Title. BIP

Catlin, George, 1796-1872—Juvenile literature.

ROCKWELL, Anne F. 759.13
Paintbrush & peacepipe: the story of George Catlin, by Anne Rockwell. [1st ed.] New York, Atheneum, 1971. 86 p. illus. 25 cm. A biography of the nineteenth-century artist who traveled in the West painting the Indians and their way of life. [ND237.C35R57 1971] 92 74-154762 5.25
1. Catlin, George, 1796-1872—Juvenile literature. I. Title.

Cats.

SPIES, Joseph R. 779.32
Cats, and how I photograph them. New York, Studio Publications, [1958] 96 p. illus. 24 cm. [SF442.S7] 58-6785
1. Cats. 2. Cats — Pictures, Illustrations, etc. 3. Photography of animals. I. Title.

Cats in art.

LYS, Claudia de. 704.94'32
Centuries of cats, in art and the written word, by Claudia de Lys and Frances Rhudy. [1st American ed.] Norwalk, Silvermine Publishers [1971] 93 p. illus. 27 cm. Bibliography: p. 88-91. [NX650.C3L9] 78-120176 6.95
1. Cats in art. I. Rhudy, Frances, joint author. II. Title.

MCCLINTON, Katherine (Morrison) 704.94'32
Antique cats for collectors. New York, Scribner [1973] 180, [1] p. illus. 27 cm. Bibliography: p. [181] [NK1125.M315 1973] 73-1104 ISBN 0-684-13381-4 10.00
1. Cats in art. 2. Art objects—Collectors and collecting. I. Title.

NEWBERRY, Clare (Turlay) 1903- 743.6974428
Cats & kittens; a portfolio of drawings. New York, Harper [1956] unpaged. illus. 36cm. [N7660.N39] 56-9668
1. Cats in art. I. Title.

STIRNWEIS, Shannon. 751.4'5
The art of painting cats / paintings by Shannon Stirnweis ; art instruction method created by Lester Rossin. New York : M. Grumbacher, c1977. 30 p. : col. ill. ; 32 cm. (The Grumbacher library ; B432) [ND1380.S74] 77-155434 1.95
1. Cats in art. 2. Painting—Technique. I. Rossin, Lester. II. Title.

SUARES, Jean-Claude. 769'.4'32
The illustrated cat : a poster book / by Jean-Claude Suares and Seymour Chwast. New York : Harmony Books, c1976. p. cm. [NC1810.S82 1976] 76-22694 ISBN 0-517-52644-1 : 10.95 ISBN 0-517-52643-3 pbk. :
1. Cats in art. 2. Posters. I. Chwast, Seymour, joint author. II. Title. BIP

SUARES, Jean-Claude. 760
The illustrated cat / compiled by Jean-Claude Suares ; designed by Seymour Chwast ; edited by William E. Maloney. London : Omnibus Press, 1976. 72 p. : chiefly ill. (some col.), facsims. (some col.) ; 33 cm. "A Push Pin Press/Omnibus Press Book." [NC1810.S82 1976b] 77-372954 ISBN 0-86001-295-6 : £3.95
1. Cats in art. 2. Posters. I. Chwast, Seymour. II. Title.

Cats in art—Juvenile literature.

FISH, Enrica. 704.94'32
The cat in art. Designed by Linda Stewart. Minneapolis, Lerner Publications Co., 1970. 71 p. illus. (part col.) 27 cm. (Fine art books for young people) Photographic reproductions of sculpture and paintings trace the appearance of symbolic, domestic, and wild cats in art from ancient to modern times. [N7660.F5 1970] 71-84406
1. Cats in art—Juvenile literature. I. Title. BIP

Cats—Pictorial works.

HAYWARD, Bill, 1942- 779'.2'0924
Cat people / Bill Hayward ; with an introd. by Rogers E. M. Whitaker. 1st ed. Garden City, N.Y. : Dolphin Books, 1978. p. cm. Includes index. [SF446.H38 1978b] 78-6040 ISBN 0-385-13472-X pbk. : 5.95 ISBN 0-385-14313-3-3 : 12.95
1. Cats—Pictorial works. I. Title. BIP

KUHN, Robert. 636.8'7
Cats themselves: a portfolio in duotone color. Descriptive text by Faire Edwards. Brattleboro, Vt., S. Greene Press [1967] [2] p., [11] plates (in portfolio) 43 cm. [SF446.K8] 67-7481
1. Cats—Pictorial works. I. Edwards, Faire. II. Title.

SAYER, Angela. 636.8
Portrait of cats / [by] Angela Sayer. London ; New York : Hamlyn, 1975. 3-126 p. : chiefly ill. (some col.) ; 29 cm. Col. ill on lining papers. [SF446.S28] 76-355293 ISBN 0-600-37105-0 : £1.99
1. Cats—Pictorial works. 2. Cat breeds. I. Title.

STYCHZYNSKI, Jan 779.32
Cats. Photos by Jan Styczynski, others. Text by Eugen Skasa-Weiss. New York, Hill & Wang [1962, c.1961] 14p. 66 illus. 24cm. 62-15220 3.50 bds.,
1. Cats—Pictorial works. I. Skasa-Weiss, Eugen, 1905- II. Title.

Cats—Pictures, illustrations, etc.

BRYAN, Christopher. 779.32
Kittens. New York, Studio Publications [1955] unpaged. illus. 22 cm. [SF446.B7] 55-7328
1. Cats—Pictures, illustrations, etc. I. Title.

CHANDOHA, Walter. 636.87
Book of kittens and cats. [1st ed.] New York, Citadel Press [1963] 256 p. plates. 29 cm. [SF446.C48] 63-21198
1. Cats—Pictures, illustrations, etc. 2. Photography of animals. I. Title.

CHURCHILL, De. 636.87
On all fours. Photos. by De Churchill. [1st ed.] New York, Vantage Press [1956] 60p. illus. 21cm. [SF446.C5] 56-10548
1. Cats—Pictures, illustrations, etc. I. Title.

COOK, Gladys Emerson, 1899- 636.87
The big book of cats, text by Gladys Emerson Cook and Felix Sutton. New York, Grossett & Dunlap, c1954. unpaged. illus. 34cm. (Big treasure books) [SF446.C6] 54-8543
1. Cats—Pictures, illustrations, etc. I. Sutton, Felix, joint author. II. Title. BIP

COOK, Gladys Emerson, 1899- 743.6974428
Drawing cats; breeds, structure, anatomy, poses, and behavior. New York, Pitman Pub. Corp. [1955] unpaged. illus. 20x26cm. (Pitman drawing series) [NC780.C6 1955] 55-12074
1. Cats—Pictures, Illustrations, etc. I. Title. BIP

HOLME, Bryan, 1913- ed. 636.87
Cats and kittens. Introd. by Alleine E. Dodge. New York, Studio Publications, in association with Crowell [1950] 98 p. (chiefly illus.) 28 cm. [SF446.H6] 50-9553
1. Cats—Pictures, illustrations, etc. 2. Cats (in religion, folk-lore, etc.)

HOUSE, Brant, pseud., ed. 636.87
The big book of cats and kittens. Combining The book of cats and The book of kittens. New York, Hill and Wang [1958] unpaged (chiefly illus.) 32cm. [SF446.H66] 58-4346
1. Cats—Pictures, illustrations, etc. I. Title.

HOUSE, Brant, pseud. 636.87
The book of cats. New York, Wyn, 1950. [5] p., [81] p. of illus. 31 cm. [SF446.H67] 50-9910
1. Cats—Pictures, illustrations, etc. I. Title.

HOUSE, Brant, pseud. 636.87
The book of kittens. New York, Wyn [1951] unpaged. illus. 31 cm. [SF446.H68] 51-7496
1. Cats—Pictures, illustrations, etc. I. Title.

IRWIN, Peggy Louise. 636.87
The curious kittens; story and pictures by Peggy Louise Irwin. New York, A. A. Wyn [1955] unpaged. illus. 29 cm. [SF446.I7] 55-7640
1. Cats—Pictures, illustrations, etc. I. Title.

NORDIN, Gosta, illus. 636.87
My own little cat. Photos. by Gosta Nordin. Story by Marianne Gerland-Ekeroth. New York, Coward-McCann [1963] 57 p. (chiefly illus.) 26 cm. [SF446.N64] 63-155533
1. Cats — Pictures, illustrations, etc. I. Gerland-Ekeroth, Marianne. II. Title.

SPILLMAN, Ronald. 636.87
Cat's whiskers. With words by Paul Dehn. [Garden City, N.Y.] Doubleday [1963] [64] (chiefly illus.] 24 cm. [SF446.S615 1963a] 63-19844
1. Cats — Pictures, illustrations, etc. I. Dehn, Paul II. Title.

WHITE, Jeanne 778.932
Cats in pictures; how to photograph your favorite feline. New York, Amphoto [1965] 128p. illus. 24cm. [TR673.W5] 65-6581 3.95
1. Cats—Pictures, illustrations, etc. 2. Photography of animals. I. Title.

WHITE, Jeanne. 778.932
Cats in pictures; how to photograph your favorite feline. Philadelphia, Chilton Books [1965] 128 p. illus. 24 cm. [TR673.W5 1965] 65-17112
1. Cats—Pictures, illustrations, etc. 2. Photography of animals. I. Title.

Caudill, Rowlett, Scott.

CAUDILL, William Wayne. 720'.28
Architecture by team; a new concept for the practice of architecture. New York, Van Nostrand Reinhold [1971] xvi, 346 p. illus., ports. 16 x 24 cm. [NA737.C3C3] 75-157696
1. Caudill, Rowlett, Scott. 2. Group work in architecture. I. Title.

Caughley porcelain.

GODDEN, Geoffrey A. 738.2'7
Caughley and Worcester porcelains, 1775-1800 [by] Geoffrey A. Godden. New York, Praeger [1969] xxi, 166 p. illus. (part col.)

Caxton, William, 1422 (ca.)-1491—Addresses, essays, lectures.

CAXTON : 686.2'092'4 B an American contribution to the quincentenary celebration / edited by Susan Otis Thompson. New York : The Typophiles, 1976. xvi, 54 p., [3] leaves of plates : ill. ; 19 cm. (Typophile chap book ; 52) Contents.Contents.—Blumenthal, J. Introduction.—Dunlap, J. R. From Westminster to Hammersmith vis Chiswick.—Lawton, J. Caxton's autograph?—Griffith, R. R. The early years of William Caxton. Includes bibliographical references. [Z232.C38C37] 76-29112
1. Caxton, William, 1422 (ca.)-1491—Addresses, essays, lectures. 2. Printing—History—England—Addresses, essay, lectures. I. Thompson, Susan Otis. II. The Typophiles, New York. III. Series: The Typophiles, New York. Typophile chap books ; 52.

DREYFUS, John. 070.5'092'4 B
William Caxton and his quincentenary / by John Dreyfus. New York : Typophiles, 1976. 54 p. : ill. ; 19 cm. (Typophile chap book ; 51) [Z232.C38D66] 77-351420
1. Caxton, William, 1422 (ca.)-1491—Addresses, essays, lectures. I. Title. II. Series: The Typophiles, New York. Typophile chap books ; 51.

Caxton, William, 1422 (ca.)-1491—Bibliography.

ST. Bride Printing Library. 686.2'092'4
Caxtoniana : or, The progress of Caxton studies from the earliest times to 1976 : [catalogue of] an exhibition at the St Bride Printing Library ... 20 September-29 October 1976 .... London : The Library, 1976. 16 p. : ill. ; 25 cm. Selected and with an introd. by Robin Myers. [Z232.C38S24 1976] 77-361465 ISBN 0-9504161-2-6 : £0.75
1. Caxton, William, 1422 (ca.)-1491—Bibliography. 2. Printing—England—History—Bibliography. 3. Bibliographical exhibitions. I. Myers, Robin, fl. 1967- II. Title. III. Title: The progress of Caxton studies from the earliest times to 1976.

Cecchi. Emilio, 1884—

GIOTTO DI BONDONE, 1266?-1337 759.5
Giotto. Text by Emilio Cecchi. [Tr. by Elizabeth Andrews] 60 plates in colour, 37 plates in monochrome. New York, McGraw [1961, c.1960] 33p. illus. (pt. counted col.) 39cm. (Silvana collection) Bibl. 61-14993 25.00, bxd.
1. Cecchi. Emilio, 1884- I. Title.

Ceilings.

ROTHERY, Guy Cadogan, 1863-1940. 747'.3
Ceilings and their decoration : art and archaeology / by Guy Cadogan Rothery. Boston : Longwood Press, 1978. p. cm. Reprint of the 1911 ed. published by F. A. Stokes, New York, in series: The house decoration series. Includes index. Bibliography: p. [NK2119.R7 1978] 78-15910 ISBN 0-89341-357-7 : 30.00
1. Ceilings. 2. Decoration and ornament. I. Title. II. Series: The House decoration series.

Cement sculpture.

OLSON, Lynn. 731.4'52
Sculpting with cement / by Lynn Olson. New York : Drake Publishers, [1975] p. cm. [NB1215.O47] 75-1381 ISBN 0-87749-843-1 : 14.95
1. Cement sculpture. I. Title.

Cemeteries.

EATON, Hubert, 1881- 718
The comemoral; the cemetery of the future. Los Angeles, Interment Association of California [1954] 58p. 23cm. [GT3320.E2] 55-37956
1. Cemeteries. I. Title.

Cent.

MERRILL, Willard S. 737.4'9'73
"Penny facts"; historical and statistical facts about the Lincoln head cent [by Willard S. Merrill] Limited 1st ed. [North Bergen, N.J.] 1972. 15 p. 22 cm. [CJ1836.M47] 74-173219 1.00
1. Cent. I. Title. II. Title: Lincoln head cent.

MONOGRAPHS on 737.4'9'73 *varieties of United States large cents, 1793-1794* / edited by John W. Adams. Lawrence, Mass. : Quarterman Publications, 1977c1976 xv, 205 p. : ill. ; 29 cm. [CJ1836.M67] 75-28712 ISBN 0-88000-071-6 : 30.00
1. Cent. 2. Numismatics—United States. I. Adams, John Weston, 1936- II. Title: Varieties of United States large cents, 1793-1794.

MONOGRAPHS on 737.4'9'73 *varieties of United States large cents, 1795-1803* / edited by Denis W. Loring. Lawrence, Mass. : Quarterman Publications, c1976. ix, 233 p. : ill. ; 29 cm. Reprint of the 1947 ed. of The United States cents of the years 1795, 1796, 1797 and 1800, by G. H. Clapp and H. R. Newcomb; of the 1931 ed. of The United States cents of the years 1798-1799, by G. H. Clapp; and of the 1925 ed. of The United States cents of the years 1801-1802-1803, by H. R. Newcomb. [CJ1836.M66] 75-39497
1. Cent. I. Loring, Denis W. II. Clapp, George Hubbard, 1858-1949. The United States cents of the years 1795, 1796, 1797 and 1800. 1976. III. Clapp, George Hubbard, 1858-1949. The United States cents of the years 1798-1799. 1976. IV. Newcomb, Howard Rounds, d. 1945. The United States cents of the years 1801-1802-1803. 1976. BIP

NEWCOMB, Howard Rounds, d.1945. 737.42
United copper cents eighteen sixteen-eighteen fifty-seven [New York? c1956] 284p. illus. 11 plates. 29cm. [CJ1836.N4 1956] 56-44911
1. Cent. I. Title.

SHELDON, William Herbert, 1899- 737.4'9'73
Penny whimsy : a revision of early American cents, 1793-1814 : an exercise in descriptive classification with tables of rarity and value / William H. Sheldon, with the collaboration of Dorothy I. Paschal and Walter Breen. Lawrence, Mass. : Quarterman Publications, c1976. xii, 340 p., [26] leaves of plates : ill. ; 24 cm. Bibliography: p. 26-27. [CJ1836.S5 1976] 76-19190 ISBN 0-88000-087-2 : 25.00
1. Cent. I. Paschal, Dorothy I., joint author. II. Breen, Walter H., joint author. III. Title. BIP

SHELDON, William Herbert, 1899- 737.4
Penny whimsy, a revision of Early American cents, 1793-1814; an exercise in descriptive classification with tables of rarity and value. By William H. Sheldon, with the collaboration of Dorothy I, Paschal and Walter Breen. New York, Harper [1958] xii, 340 p. illus. 24 cm. (The John J. Ford, Jr. numisco series) Bibliography: p. 26-27. [CJ1836.S5 1958] 57-10570
1. Cent. I. Title.

Cent—Errors.

COHEN, Jean, 1930- 737.4
The classification and value of errors on the Lincoln cent; the encyclopedia of fidology. Written, compiled, and illustrated by Jean Cohen. Lincoln cent imprint by Margood. Photography by Ganar Brown. [1st ed.] Bonita Springs, Fla. [1969] 600 p. illus. 29 cm. [CJ1836.C58] 76-91934
1. Cent—Errors. I. Title.

HARDY, Howard O. 737.4'973
BIE handbook, edited by Howard O. Hardy. [Fort Lauderdale, Fla., BIE Mint Oddity Collector's Guild, 1972] ix, 42, cix p. illus. 28 cm. Appendix (p. ii-cix, 3d group): The Gedko catalogue. [CJ1832.H37] 72-193669
1. Cent—Errors. I. Title.

Central America—Antiq.

BOTSFORD, Ward. 972.801
Archaeology: Middle America. [Prepared with the cooperation of Science Service] Garden City, N. Y., N. Doubleday [1961] 64p. illus. 21cm. (Science Service science program) [F1434.B6] 61-3119
1. Central America—Antiq. 2. Mexico—Antiq. 3. Indians of Central America—Antiq. 4. Indians of Mexico—Antiq. I. Title.

Central business districts—Addresses, essays, lectures.

SCHRETTER, Howard A., comp. 711'.45
Downtown revitalization; a collection of selected writings from professional journals. Compiled by Howard A. Schretter. [Athens] [Institute of Community & Area Development, University of Georgia] 1967. v, 118 l. illus. 28 cm. [HF5429.S355] 68-63221
1. Central business districts—Addresses, essays, lectures. 2. Retail trade—Addresses, essays, lectures. 3. Automobile parking—Addresses, essays, lectures. I. Title.

Central business districts—Bibliography.

SCHRETTER, Howard A. 711'.552
Downtown revitalization; an annotated listing of selected articles from professional journals, prepared by Howard A. Schretter, assisted by Ronald J. Shaw [and] George C. Wischmann. [Athens, Institute of Community & Area Development, University of Georgia, 1967?] iii, 21 l. 28 cm. [Z5942.S35] 70-631786 1.00
1. Central business districts—Bibliography. 2. Cities and towns—Planning—1945- —Bibliography. I. Shaw, Ronald J., joint author. II. Wischmann, George C., joint author. III. Title.

Central business districts—Grants Pass, Or.

OREGON. University. Bureau of Municipal Research and Service. 711'.552
Planning for the central business district, Grants Pass, Oregon. [Eugene] 1966. 44 l. illus. (part col.) 28 cm. [HF5429.O78] 67-64204
1. Central business districts—Grants Pass, Or. 2. Cities and towns—Planning—Grants Pass, Or. I. Title.

Central business districts—North Las Vegas, Nev.

NORTH Las Vegas, Nev. Planning Dept. 711'.4'0979313
Central business district study: City of North Las Vegas, Nevada. [North Las Vegas, Nev.] 1971. ii, 80 l. illus. 22 x 38 cm. Part of illustrative matter in pocket. Bibliography: leaf 79. [HT168.N617N67 1971] 74-151592
1. Central business districts—North Las Vegas, Nev. 2. Cities and towns—Planning—North Las Vegas, Nev. I. Title.

Central Business Districts—San Diego, Calif.

SAN Diego, Calif. City Planning Commission. 711.40979498
Centre city, 75; a development plan for centre city San Diego. San Diego, 1965. 52 p. illus., maps [[KFX2343]]
1. Central Business Districts—San Diego, Calif. 2. Cities and towns—Planning. I. San Diego, Calif. City Planning Department. II. Title.

Central business districts—Seattle.

WASHINGTON (State). University. College of Architecture and Urban Planning. 711'.4'0979777
People and downtown; use, attitudes, settings [by] Arthur L. Grey [and others] Seattle, 1970. xx, 150 p. illus., maps, plans. 28 cm. Bibliography: p. 145-150. [HF5429.5.S4W35] 70-635118
1. Central business districts—Seattle. 2. Central business districts—Portland, Or. I. Grey, Arthur L. II. Title.

Central places—Baltimore metropolitan area.

REGIONAL Planning Council, Baltimore. 711'.3'08 s
Multi-purpose centers for the Baltimore region; summary report. Baltimore, 1965. vi, 84 p. illus. 28 cm. (Its Publication, 4) [HT394.B3R4 no. 4] 711'.3'097526 73-172670
1. Central places—Baltimore metropolitan area. 2. Regional planning—Baltimore metropolitan area. I. Title. II. Series.

Centre Georges Pompidou.

CENTRE Pompidou. 725.8
New York : Rizzoli International Publications, 1977. [64] p. : ill. (some col.) ; 28 cm. Cover title. English, French, German or Italian. [NA6813.F82P373] 77-72743 ISBN 0-8478-0102-0 pbk. : 4.95
1. Centre Georges Pompidou. I. Centre Georges Pompidou.

Ceramic materials.

LAWRENCE, Willis Grant, 1916- 666
Ceramic science for the potter [by] W. G. Lawrence. [1st ed.] Philadelphia, Chilton Book Co. [1972] xiii, 239 p. illus. 24 cm. Includes bibliographies. [TP810.5.L38] 72-4811 ISBN 0-8019-5728-1 10.00
1. Ceramic materials. 2. Pottery. I. Title. BIP

Ceramic sculpture—Technique.

†BITTERS, Stan. 738
Environmental ceramics / Stan Bitters ; Micha Langer, photographer. New York : Van Nostrand Reinhold Co., 1976. 144 p. : ill. ; 28 cm. Includes index. Bibliography: p. 141. [NK4235.B57] 75-44615 ISBN 0-442-20781-6 : 15.00
1. Bitters, Stan. 2. Ceramic sculpture—Technique. I. Title. BIP

WINTER, Thelma Frazier. 738.1
The art and craft of ceramic sculpture. New York, Wiley [1974, c1973] xxii, 269 p. illus. (part col.) 26 cm. "A Halsted Press book." Bibliography: p. 244. [NK4235.W56] 73-20150 ISBN 0-470-95475-2 18.75
1. Ceramic sculpture—Technique. I. Title. BIP

Ceramic sculpture—United States.

MASON, John, 1927- 730'.92'4
John Mason ceramic sculpture, Pasadena Museum of Modern Art, May 7-June 23, 1974. An exhibition organized by Barbara Haskell. [Pasadena, Pasadena Museum of Modern Art, 1974] 32 p. illus. 25 cm. Bibliography: p. 27-30. [NK4210.M29H37] 74-176122
1. Mason, John, 1927- 2. Ceramic sculpture—United States. I. Haskell, Barbara. II. Pasadena Museum of Modern Art. III. Title.

Ceramic sculpture—United States—Exhibitions.

CALIFORNIA State University, Fullerton. Art Gallery. 730'.973'074019496
Richard Shaw, Ed Blackburn, Tony Costanzo, Redd Ekks, John Roloff : [exhibition] : California State University, Fullerton, November 12-December 16, 1976. Fullerton : [Art Gallery, California State University], c1976. 52 p. : ill. (some col.) ; 22 cm. Includes bibliographies. [NK4008.C34 1976] 77-350794
1. Ceramic sculpture—United States—Exhibitions. I. Title.

HUGHTO, Margie, 1944- 730'.973'074014766
New works in clay by contemporary painters and sculptors : [exhibition] : Everson Museum of Art of Syracuse and Onondaga County, January 23-April 4, 1976 / [prepared by Margie Hughto]. 1st ed. [s.l.] : Visual Artis Publications, c1976.

95 p. : ill. (some col.) ; 26 cm. [NB212.H83] 76-12141
1. Ceramic sculpture—United States—Exhibitions. 2. Sculpture, Modern—20th century—United States—Exhibitons. I. Everson Museum of Art of Syracuse and Onondaga County. II. Title.

Ceramics.

CERAMICS MONTHLY. 738.1082
Ceramic projects; a selection of projects for classroom, home, and studio, originally published in the form of articles in Ceramics monthly magazine. [1st ed.] Columbus, Ohio, Professional Publications [1963] 64 p. illus. 28 cm. (A CM handbook) [[TP808]] 64-9765
1. Ceramics I. Title. BIP

ENGEL, Gertrude 738
Getting started in ceramics. New York, Cornerstone [1966] 128p. illus. 20cm. CN 105. [TP808.E53] 65-22092 1.00
1. Ceramics. I. Title.

ENGEL, Gertrude. 738
How to make ceramics. New York, Arco Pub. Co. [1957] 144 p. illus. 25 cm. (The Do-it-yourself series) [TP808.E55] 57-12452
1. Ceramics. I. Title.

KENNY, John B. 738.1
Ceramic design [by] John B. Kenny. Drawings by Carla Kenny. London, Pitman [1964, c1963] xiv, 321 p. illus., ports. 26 cm. [[TP807]] 64-7397
1. Ceramics. I. Title. BIP

KENNY, John B. 738.1
Ceramic design. Drawings by Carla Kenny. [1st ed.] Philadelphia, Chilton Books [1963] xiv, 321 p. illus. (part col.) ports. 27 cm. [TP807.K36] 63-10419
1. Ceramics.

NELSON, Glenn C 738.3
Ceramic reference manual. Minneapolis, Burgess Pub. Co. [1957] 125p. illus. 28cm. Includes bibliography. [TP807.N36] 57-1533
1. Ceramics. I. Title.

NELSON, Glenn C. 738.14
Ceramics. New York, Holt, Rinehart and Winston [c.1960] xvi, 236p. Bibl.: p.216-217. illus. 26cm. 60-8740 5.95
1. Ceramics. I. Title.

NELSON, Glenn C. 738.14
Ceramics; a potter's handbook [by] Glenn C. Nelson. 2d ed. New York, Holt, Rinehart and Winston [1966] xviii, 331 p. illus. (part col.) 25 cm. Includes bibliographies. [TP807.N363 1966] 66-188801
1. Ceramics.

NELSON, Glenn C. 738.1'4
Ceramics : a potter's handbook / Glenn C. Nelson. 4th ed. New York : Holt, Rinehart and Winston, c1978. x, 339 p. : ill. ; 27 cm. Includes index. Bibliography: p. 326-328. [TP807.N363 1978] 77-24224 ISBN 0-03-022725-9 : 19.95
1. Ceramics. I. Title.

NELSON, Glenn C. 738.1'4
Ceramics; a potter's handbook [by] Glenn C. Nelson. 3d ed. New York, Holt, Rinehart and Winston [1971] x, 348 p. illus. (part col.) 26 cm. Bibliography: p. 329-332. [TP807.N363 1971] 70-145911 ISBN 0-03-086000-8
1. Ceramics.

ROY, Vincent A 738.14
Geramics, an illustrated guide to creating and enjoying pottery. New York, McGraw-Hill [1959] 278p. illus. 26cm. Includes bibliography. [TP807.R68] 58-14361
1. Ceramics. I. Title.

SEELEY, Vernon D. 738.14
Activities in ceramics [by] Vernon D. Seeley [and] Robert L. Thompson. Bloomington, Ill., McKnight & McKnight Pub. Co. [1956] 82 p. illus. 27 cm. [TP807.S43] 56-4534
1. Ceramics. I. Thompson, Robert Long, 1908- joint author. II. Title.

ZARCHY, Harry. 738.3
Ceramics, written and illustrated by Harry Zarchy. [1st ed.] New York, Knopf [1954] 171 p. illus. 22 cm. [TP808.Z3] 52-6398
1. Ceramics.

Ceramics—Addresses, essays, lectures.

CURRENT development in the whiteware industry. 620.1'4
George A. Kirkendale, editor. Alfred, N.Y., State University of New York, College of Ceramics at Alfred University, 1966. iv, 189 p. illus. 23 cm. "A summary of the information presented at a Continuing Education Symposium at SUNY College of Ceramics at Alfred University in June, 1966." Includes bibliographies. [TP815.C8] 68-54
1. Ceramics—Addresses, essays, lectures. I. Kirkendale, George Alderson, 1907- ed. II. State University of New York College of Ceramics.

Ceramics—Drying.

FORD, R. W. 666'.12
Drying, by R. W. Ford. London, Maclaren [1964] vi, 62p. illus. 22cm. (Inst. of Ceramics. Textbk. ser., 3) Label mounted on t. p.: Sole dist. for U. S. A., Transatlantic New York. [TP815.F6] 67-8832 2.50 pap.,
1. Ceramics—Drying. I. Title. II. Series: Stoke-on-Trent, Eng. Institute of Ceramics. Textbook series, 3
Order from the distributor's Levittown, N.Y. office.

Ceramics—Formulae, tables, etc.

CONRAD, John W. 666'.021'2
Ceramic formulas: the complete compendium; a guide to clay, glaze, enamel, glass, and their colors. New York, Macmillan [1973] x, 309 p. illus. 22 cm. [TP809.C66] 72-90282 10.95
1. Ceramics—Formulae, tables, etc. I. Title. BIP

Ceramics—Study and teaching.

NEW York (State). Bureau of Industrial Arts Education. 738'.028
Ceramics, project ideas for industrial arts. Albany, University of the State of New York, Bureau of Secondary Curriculum Development, 1968. x, 176 p. illus. 28 cm. "Developed during the summer session of 1958 at the State University College at Oswego, in a curriculum construction workshop." Bibliography: p. 171-173. [TP808.N39 1968] 68-66247
1. Ceramics—Study and teaching. 2. Pottery—Study and teaching. I. New York (State). Bureau of Secondary Curriculum Development. II. New York. State University College, Oswego. III. Title.

Cervantes Saavedra, Miguel de. Don Quixote — Illustrations.

SMIRKE, Robert, 1752-1845. 535.2
Don Quixote. [n.p., n.d.] 74 plates. 39 cm. Title from spine. In MS. on fly leaf: Plates by Smirke. [NE642.S53A44] 65-272
1. Cervantes Saavedra, Miguel de. Don Quixote — Illustrations. I. Title. BIP

Cesnola, Luigi Palma di, 1832-1904.

MCFADDEN, Elizabeth. 708'.00924 B
The glitter & the gold; a spirited account of the Metropolitan Museum of Art's first director, the audacious and high-handed Luigi Palma di Cesnola. New York, Dial Press, 1971. ix, 277 p. illus. 22 cm. Bibliography: p. [263]-267. [N406.C46M3] 78-131178 7.95
1. Cesnola, Luigi Palma di, 1832-1904. I. Title.

Cezanne, Paul, 1839-1906.

ANDERSEN, Wayne V. 741'.0924
Cezanne's portrait drawings [by] Wayne Andersen. Cambridge, MIT Press [1970] x, 247 p. illus. 30 cm. Bibliography: p. 243-245. [NC1135.C45A7] 69-10529
1. Cezanne, Paul, 1839-1906. I. Title.

BADT, Kurt, 1890- 759.4
The art of Cezanne. Translated by Sheila Ann Ogilvia. Berkeley, University of California Press, 1965. 345 p. illus., ports. 25 cm. Includes bibliographical references. [ND553.C33B233] 65-21266
1. 1. Cezanne, Paul, 1839-1906. I. Title.

BARNES, Albert Coombs, 1872-1951. 759.4
The art of Cezanne, by Albert C. Barnes and Violette de Mazia. [1st ed.] Merion Pa., Barnes Foundation Press [1962? c1939] xviii, 456 p. plates, ports. 24 cm. "Catalogue data": p. 401-435 Bibliographical footnotes. [ND553.C33B3] 62-13133
1. Cezanne, Paul, 1839-1906. I. De Mazia, Violette, 1899- joint author. II. Title.

BELZ, Carl. 759.4
Paul Cezanne. New York, McGraw-Hill [1974, i.e.1975] p. cm. (Color slide program of the great masters) [ND553.C33B38] 74-16088 ISBN 0-07-004417-1 10.95
1. Cezanne, Paul, 1839-1906. 2. Paintings—Slides. I. Title. II. Series.

BEUCKEN, Jean de, 1905- 927.5
Cezanne, a pictorial biography. Translated and adapted by Lothian Small. New York, Viking Press [1962] 143p. illus. (part col.) ports. 24cm. (A Studio book) Translation of Cezanne, eine Bildblographie. The original french ed. has title: Un portrait de Cezanne. [ND553.C33B453] 61-8824
1. Cezanne, Paul, 1839-1906. I. Title.

BRION, Marcel, 1895- 759.4
Cezanne. [1st U.S. ed.] Garden City, N.Y., Doubleday [1974, c1973] 95 p. illus. (part col.) 34 cm. (The Great impressionists) Includes bibliographical references. [ND553.C33B6713 1974] 73-11045 ISBN 0-385-09546-5 9.95
1. Cezanne, Paul, 1839-1906.
Library binding 10.70; ISBN 0-385-08371-8.

CEZANNE, Paul, 1839-1906. 759.4
Cezanne. Text and notes by Keith Roberts. New York, Tudor Pub. Co. [1967] 36 p., 92 col. plates. 18 cm. Bibliography: p. 15. [ND553.C33R59] 67-19840
I. Roberts, Keith, 1937- II. Title.

CEZANNE, Paul, 1839-1906. 759.4
Cezanne, by F. Novotny. With 50 plates in full colour. [New York] Phaidon Publishers; distributed by New York Graphic Society, Greenwich, Conn. [1961] 16, [8] p. col. plates, port. 32 cm. Bibliography: p. [17] [ND553.C33N615] 61-66003
I. Novotny, Fritz, 1902-

CEZANNE, Paul, 1839-1906. 759.4
Cezanne/Gauguin, by Parker Tyler. [Garden City, N.Y., Doubleday, 1969] 139 p. illus. (part col.), 75 col. plates, ports. 25 cm. (World art series) [ND552.C4] 68-23389 7.95
I. Gauguin, Paul, 1848-1903. II. Tyler, Parker.

CEZANNE, Paul, 1839-1906 759.4
Cezanne watercolors, by John Coplans. Los Angeles, Pasadena Art Mus. [c.1967] 60p. illus. (pt. col.), ports. 26cm. Catalog of an exhibition sponsored by the Art Alliance of the Pasadena Art Mus. and held Nov. 10 to Dec. 10, 1967, at the Pasadena Art Mus. Bibl. [ND1950.C4C64] 68-16778 5.00 pap.,
I. Coplans, John. II. Pasadena, Calif. Art Museum. Art Alliance. III. Pasadena, Calif. Art Mustum. IV. Title.

CEZANNE, Paul, 1839-1906. 704.94'7918'2
Drawings. Introd. by Stephen Longstreet. [1st ed.] Los Angeles, Borden Pub. Co. [1964] (chiefly illus.) 31 cm. (Master draughtsman series) [NC1135.C45L6] 64-57144
I. Longstreet, Stephen, 1907- II. Title.

CEZANNE, Paul, 1839-1906. 741.91
Drawings. New York, T. Yoseloff [1958] 63 p., [86] p. of illus. 29 cm. (A Bittner art book) At head of title: Alfred Neumeyer. "Catalogue": p. 35-63. Bibliography: p. 33. [NC1135.C45N4] 58-6713
I. Neumeyer, Alfred, 1901-

CEZANNE, Paul, 1839-1906. 741.9'44
The drawings of Paul Cezanne; a catalogue raisonne by Adrien Chappuis. [Translated from the French] Greenwich, Conn., New York Graphic Society [1973] 2 v. illus. 32 cm. Translation of Album de Paul Cezanne. Contents.—v. 1. Introduction and catalogue.—v. 2. Plates. [NC248.C37C4513] 72-187143 ISBN 0-8212-0427-0 125.00 (boxed set)
1. Cezanne, Paul, 1839-1906. I. Chappuis, Adrien. II. Title. BIP

CEZANNE, Paul, 1839-1906. 759.4
Paul Cezanne. Text by Meyer Schapiro. New York, H. N. Abrams [197-] 126 p. illus. (part col.) 34 cm. (The Library of great painters) [ND553.C33S38 1970z] 72-191938
I. Schapiro, Meyer, 1904-

CEZANNE, Paul, 1839-1906. 759.4
Paul Cezanne. Text by Meyer Schapiro. New York, H. N. Abrams [1969] 40 p. illus., col. plates. 33 cm. (Great art of the ages) [ND553.C33S38 1969] 69-19705 ISBN 0-8109-5106-1
I. Schapiro, Meyer, 1904-

CEZANNE, Paul, 1839-1906. 759.4
Paul Cezanne. Text by Meyer Schapiro. [1st ed.] New York, H. N. Abrams [1952] 126p. illus., col. plates, ports. 34cm. (The Library of great painters) An Abrams art book. [ND553.C33S38] 53-2104
I. Schapiro, Meyer, 1904- II. Title.

CEZANNE, Paul, 1839-1906. 759.4
Paul Cezanne, Text by Meyer Schapiro. [2d ed., with corrections] New York, Abrams [1962, c1952] 126 p. illus. (part mounted col.) ports. 33 cm. (The Library of great painters) [ND553.C33S38] 63-5318
I. Schapiro, Meyer, 1904- II. Title.

CEZANNE, Paul, 1839-1906. 759.4
Paul Cezanne (1839-1906) Text by Theodore Rousseau, Jr. New York, H. N. Abrams in association with Pocket Books [1953] [74] p. 39 illus. (part col.) 18cm. (The Pocket library of great art, A4) An Abrams art book. Bibliography: p. [74] [ND553.C33R65] 54-15089
I. Rousseau, Theodore, 1912- II. Title.

CEZANNE, Paul, 1839-1906. 759.4
Paul Cezanne, 1839-1906. [Documentation: Erika Neubauer. Catalogue entries: Klaus Demus. Catalogue translation: David Hermges. Eng. ed. Vienna [Printed by Steyremuhl, 1961] 38 p. 52 plates (part col.) 22 cm. Catalog of an exhibition presented by the Kulturamt der Stadt Wien and held Apr. 14-June 18, 1961, at the Osterreichische Galerie, Oberes Belvedere, Vienna. [ND553.C33A54 1961] 74-237753
I. Vienna. Kulturamt. II. Vienna. Osterreichische Galerie. III. Title.

CEZANNE, Paul, 1839-1906. 759.4 B
Paul Cezanne, letters / edited by John Rewald ; [translated from the French by Marguerite Kay]. 4th ed. rev. and enl. Oxford [Eng.] : B. Cassirer, 1976. 374 p. ; 22 cm. "The letters of Zola represent nearly one-third of the whole correspondence." Includes index. [ND553.C33A212 1976] 77-359768 ISBN 0-85181-061-6 : £6.50
1. Cezanne, Paul, 1839-1906. 2. Painters—France—Correspondence. I. Rewald, John, 1912- ed. II. Zola, Emile, 1840-1902. III. Kay, Marguerite, tr.

CHICAGO. Art Institute. 759.4
Cezanne: paintings, watereolors & drawings; a loan exhibition, the Art Institute of Chicago, the Metropolitan Museum of Art. [Chicago, 1952] 100 p. illus. 26 cm. [ND553.C33C47] 52-1163
1. Cezanne, Paul, 1839-1906. 2. Paintings, French—Exhibitions. 3. Drawings, French—Exhibitions. I. New York. Metropolitan Museum of Art. II. Title.

COLUMBIA University. Dept. of Art History and Archaeology. 759.5
Cezanne watercolors; an exhibition at M. Knoedler & Co., 14 E. 57th St., New York City, 2 April to 20 April, 1963. [Catalogue ed.: Theodore Reff] New York, dist. Wittenborn [1963] 61p. 69 plates (4 col.) 23cm. Exhibition sponsored by the Advisory Council of the Dept. of Art Hist.

& Archaeology, Columbia Univ. Additions to the Cezanne watercolors exhibition: [2] l. inserted. Bibl. 63-3517 3.75 pap.,
1. Cezanne, Paul, 1839-1906. I. Reff, Theodore, ed. II. Knoedler (M.) and Company, inc. III. Title.

DOWNER, Marion. 927.5
Paul Cezanne. Illustrated with half-tones. New York, Lothrop, Lee & Shepard [1951] 117 p. illus. 21 cm. [ND553.C33D63] 51-8762
1. Cezanne, Paul, 1839-1906. I. Title.

ELGAR, Frank. 759.4 B
Cezanne. New York, N.N. Abrams [196-] 287 p. illus. (part col.) 22 cm. Bibliography: p. 273-274. [ND553.C33E483 1960z] 75-76013
1. Cezanne, Paul, 1839-1906. I. Title.

ELGAR, Frank. 759.4 B
Cezanne / Frank Elgar. New York : Praeger Publishers, 1975. 287 p. : ill. (some col.) ; 21 cm. (Praeger world of art paperbacks) (A Praeger world of art profile) Translated from the French. Includes index. Bibliography: p. 273-274. [ND553.C33E483 1975] 75-24042 ISBN 0-275-71700-3 pbk. : 5.95
1. Cezanne, Paul, 1839-1906. I. Title.

FRY, Roger Eliot, 1866-1934. 759.4
Cezanne; a study of his development. New York, Macmillan [1952] 88 p. 40 plates. 26 cm. 2d ed. [ND553.C33F7 1952] 52-14645
1. Cezanne, Paul, 1839-1906. I. Title.

HANSON, Lawrence. 759.4
Mortal victory; a biography of Paul Cezanne. [1st ed.] New York, Holt, Rinehart and Winston [1960] 245 p. illus. 22 cm. Includes bibliographies. [ND553.C33H3] 60-9054
1. cezanne, Paul, 1839-1906. I. Title.

HIND, Charles Lewis, 1862-1927. 759.4
The post impressionists. Freeport, N.Y., Books for Libraries Press [1969] vii, 93 p. illus., ports. 24 cm. (Select bibliographies reprint series) Reprint of the 1911 ed. [ND547.H56 1969] 75-102244 ISBN 0-8369-5129-8
1. Cezanne, Paul, 1839-1906. 2. Gauguin, Paul, 1848-1903. 3. Gogh, Vincent van, 1853-1890. 4. Post-impressionism (Art)—France. I. Title. BIP

HUYGHE, Rene 759.4
Cezanne. [Tr. from French by Kenneth Martin Leake] New York, Abrams [1963] 87p. illus. 19cm. 62-15678 1.95
1. Cezanne, Paul, 1839-1906. I. Title.

LINDSAY, Jack, 1900- 759.4 B
Cezanne; his life and art. [Greenwich, Conn.] New York Graphic Society [1969] viii, 360 p. illus. (part col.), ports. 25 cm. Title on spine: Cezanne; life and art. Bibliography: p. 354-358. [ND553.C33L5 1969b] 76-77230 12.50
1. Cezanne, Paul, 1839-1906.

LORAN, Erle, 1905- 759.4
Cezanne's composition: analysis of his form, with diagrams and photographs of his motifs. [3d ed.] Berkeley, Univ. of Calif. Pr., 1963 [c.1943] 143p. illus. (pt. col.) ports., diagrs. 32cm. Bibl. 64-2459 8.00
1. Cezanne, Paul, 1839-1906. 2. Composition (Art) I. Title. BIP

MACK, Gerstle, 1894- 759.4 B
Paul Cezanne / Gerstle Mack. New York : Octagon Books, 1976, c1935. xiv, 437, xxiv p., [24] leaves of plates : ill. ; 24 cm. Reprint of the ed. published by Knopf, New York. Includes index. Bibliography: p. 435-437. [ND553.C33M3 1976] 76-7909 ISBN 0-374-95241-8 : 20.00
1. Cezanne, Paul, 1839-1906.

MCLEAVE, Hugh. 759.4 B
A man and his mountain : a biography of Paul Cezanne / by Hugh McLeave. New York : Macmillan, 1977. p. cm. [ND553.C33M33] 77-9511 ISBN 0-02-583670-6 : 9.95
1. Cezanne, Paul, 1839-1906. 2. Painters—France—Biography. I. Title. BIP

MICHELI, Mario de. 759.4
Cezanne. [1st American ed. Translated from the Italian by Pearl Sanders] New York, Grosset & Dunlap [1967, c1968] 39, [80] p. col. illus. 18 cm. (The New Grosset art library, 10) On cover: Cezanne; the life and work of the artist. Bibliography: p. 29-31. [ND553.C33M513 1968] 68-12744
1. Cezanne, Paul, 1839-1906.

MURPHY, Richard W. 759.4
The world of Cezanne, 1839-1906, by Richard W. Murphy and the editors of Time-Life Books New York, Time-Life Books [1968] 192 p. illus. (part col.), ports. 31 cm. (Time-Life library of art) Bibliography: p. 187. [ND553.C33M8] 68-17688
1. Cezanne, Paul, 1839-1906. I. Time-Life Books. II. Title. BIP

THE new Cezanne; 759.4
from Monet to Mondriaan. In commemoration of the 50th anniversary of Paul Cezanne's death. Red Wing, Minn., Art History [1958] 111p. illus. 25cm. [ND553.C33B5] [ND553.C33B5] 927.5 58-10644 58-10644
1. Cezanne, Paul, 1839-1906. 2. Painting, French. I. Biederman, Charles Joseph, 1906- BIP

NEW York (City). Museum of Modern Art. 759.4
First loan exhibition: New York, November, 1929; Cezanne, Gauguin, Seurat, Van Gogh. Reprint ed. [New York] Published for the Museum of Modern Art by Arno Press, 1972. 52 p. 98 plates. 29 cm. (Museum of Modern Art publications in reprint) On spine: Cezanne, Gauguin, Seurat, Van Gogh: first loan exhibition. Foreword signed: A. H. B., jr. [i.e. Alfred Hamilton Barr, jr.] [ND547.5.I4N4 1972] 72-169295 ISBN 0-405-01555-0
1. Cezanne, Paul, 1839-1906. 2. Gauguin, Paul, 1848-1903. 3. Seurat, Georges Pierre, 1859-1891. 4. Gogh, Vincent van, 1853-1890. 5. Impressionism (Art)—Exhibitions. I. Barr, Alfred Hamilton, 1902-

PERRUCHOT, Henri, 1917- 927.5
Cezanne. Translated by Humphrey Hare. [1st ed.] Cleveland, World Pub. Co. [1962, c1961] 348 p. illus. 23 cm. (His Art and destiny, 2) Translation of La vie de Cezanne. Includes bibliography. [ND553.C33P43] 62-7476
1. Cezanne, Paul, 1839-1906.

REWALD, John, 1912- 759.4
Paul Cezanne; a biography. [Translated by Margaret H. Liebman] New York, Schocken Books [1968, c1967] xvii, 235 p. illus., ports. 21 cm. "First published in 1936 in Paris as a Sorbonne thesis under the title Cezanne et Zola." Bibliography: p. 223-230. [ND553.C33R42 1968] 67-26992
1. Cezanne, Paul, 1839-1906. 2. Zola, Emile, 1840-1902.

ROBERTS, Jane, 1929- 759.4
The world view of Paul Cezanne : a psychic interpretation / by Jane Roberts ; introd. by Seth. Englewood Cliffs, N.J. : Prentice-Hall, c1977. xviii, 246 p. ; 22 cm. Includes index. [ND553.C33R587] 77-8079 ISBN 0-13-968859-5 : 7.95
1. Cezanne, Paul, 1839-1906. 2. Psychical research. I. Title. BIP

TAILLANDIER, Yvon. 759.4
P. Cezanne. [Translated from the French by Graham Snell] New York, Crown Publishers, 1961. 90, [6] p. illus. (part col., part mounted) ports. 29 cm. Bibliography: p. [93] [ND553.C33T33] 61-66408
1. Cezanne, Paul, 1839-1906.

TAYLOR, Basil. 759.4
Cezanne. Revised ed. Feltham, Hamlyn, 1968. 39 p. 48 plates. 54 illus. (48 col.). 28 cm. (The Colour library of art) Bibliography: p. 30. [ND553.C33T38 1968] 79-499550 17/6
1. Cezanne, Paul, 1839-1906.

VENTURI, Lionello, 1885-1961. 759.4
Cezanne / Lionello Venturi ; pref. by Giulio Carlo Argan. New York : Rizzoli, 1978. 175 p. : ill. (some col.) ; 35 cm. (Discovering the nineteenth century) Includes index. Bibliography: p. 168-169. [ND553.C33V39] 78-58702 ISBN 0-8478-0187-X : 55.00
1. Cezanne, Paul, 1839-1906. I. Cezanne, Paul, 1839-1906. II. Title. III. Series. BIP

WECHSLER, Judith, 1940- comp. 759.4
Cezanne in perspective. Englewood Cliffs, N.J., Prentice-Hall [1975] x, 169 p. illus. 23 cm. (The Artists in perspective series) (A Spectrum book) Bibliography: p. 168-169. [ND553.C33W42] 74-13479 ISBN 0-13-123356-4
1. Cezanne, Paul, 1839-1906. I. Title. BIP

Cezanne, Paul, 1839-1906—Addresses, essays, lectures.

CEZANNE : 759.4
the latework : essays / by Theodore Reff ... [et al.] ; edited by William Rubin. New York : Museum of Modern Art ; Boston : distributed by New York Graphic Society, c1977. 416 p. : ill. (some col.) ; 29 cm. "Published on the occasion of the exhibition ... organized by the Museum of Modern Art, New York, and the Reunion des musees nationaux, France, and shown also at the Museum of Fine Arts, Houston." Includes bibliographical references. [ND553.C33A35 1977] 77-77287 ISBN 0-87070-278-5 : 40.00.
1. Cezanne, Paul, 1839-1906—Addresses, essays, lectures. I. Cezanne, Paul, 1839-1906. II. Reff, Theodore. III. Rubin, William Stanley. IV. New York (City). Museum of Modern Art. V. Reunion des musees nationaux, Paris. VI. Houston, Tex. Museum of Fine Arts.

Ch'i, Pai-shih, 1861-1957.

CH'I, Pai-shih, 1861-1957. 759.951
Ch'i Pai-shih, the versatile genius = I yuan ch'i ying / introd. by C. C. Wang. 1st ed. Fort Thomas, Ky. : Pine Studios, 1976. [16] p., 50 leaves of plates : col. ill. ; 31 cm. Introd. in English and Chinese. [ND2070.C45A43] 75-17069 40.00
1. Ch'i, Pai-shih, 1861-1957. I. Title. II. Title: I yuan ch'i ying.

LAI, Tien-chang, comp. 759.951
Ch'i Pai Shih, by T. C. Lai. Kowloon, Swindon Book Co. [1973] xi, 209 p. illus. 23 cm. Consists of an abridged translation by the compiler of Ch'i Pai-shih's autobiography published in 1962 under title: Pai-shi lao jen tzu chuan; articles and anecdotes by various writers about Ch'i; and poems and other inscriptions on paintings by Ch'i, some (p. [121]-150) translated by the compiler. Bibliography in Chinese: p. 185. [ND1049.C5L33] 73-76338 12.50
1. Ch'i, Pai-shih, 1861-1957. I. Ch'i, Pai-shih, 1861-1957. Pai-shih lao jen tzu chuan. English. 1973 BIP

Chagall, Marc, 1887—

ALEXANDER, Sidney, 1912- 759.7 B
Marc Chagall : the artist with seven fingers / by Sidney Alexander. New York : Putnam, c1978. p. cm. Includes index. [ND699.C5A67 1978] 77-16526 15.00
1. Chagall, Marc, 1887- 2. Painters—Russian Republic—Biography.

AMISHAI, Ziva, 1939- 915.694'8
Tapestries and mosaics of Marc Chagall at the Knesset. New York, Tudor Pub. Co. [1973] p. [NK3056.A3C452] 73-12270 ISBN 0-8148-0567-1 12.50
1. Chagall, Marc, 1887- 2. Israel. Keneset. I. Chagall, Marc, 1887- II. Israel. Keneset. III. Title. BIP

BIDERMANAS, Izis. 709'.24
The world of Marc Chagall. Photographed by Izis Bidermanas. Text by Roy McMullen. Garden City, N.Y., Doubleday [1968] 267 p. illus. (part col.) 34 cm. At head of title: Izis. Bibliography: p. 264. [ND699.C5B5] 68-20454 25.00
1. Chagall, Marc, 1887- I. McMullen, Roy.

BRION, Marcel, 1895- 759.4
Chagall [Tr. from French by A. H. N. Molesworth] New York, Abrams [1962] 85p. col. illus. (Student's ser. of great artists) 60-11164 1.95
1. Chagal, Marc, 1887- I. Title.

BUCCI, Mario. 759.7
Chagall; [translated from the Italian]. London, New York, Hamlyn, 1971. 94 p. chiefly illus. (some col.), ports. 32 cm. (Twentieth-century masters) Distributed in the U.S.A. by Crown Publishers Inc. Bibliography: p. 93-94. [ND699.C5B813] 72-177405 ISBN 0-600-31617-3 £2.25
1. Chagall, Marc, 1887-

CASSOU, Jean, 1897- 759.7
Chagall. [Translated from the French by Alisa Jaffa] New York, Praeger [1966, c1965] 286 p. illus. (part col.) 22 cm. (Praeger world of art profiles) Bibliography: p. 269-271. [ND699.C5C33] 65-20071
1. Chagall, Marc, 1887-

CHAGALL at the Met. 759.7
Text by Emily Genauer. New York, Metropolitan Opera Association; distributed by Tudor Pub. Co. [1971] 149 p. col. illus. 37 cm. Includes illus. of Chagall's murals at the Metropolitan Opera House, Lincoln Center, and of the sets and costumes he designed for Mozart's Die Zauberflote. Contents.—Introduction, by Sir R. Bing.—Chagall at the Met, by E. Genauer.—The Magic flute.—Plot outline of Die Zauberflote, by I. Kolodin.—Dedication speech, by M. Chagall. [ND699.C5C45] 75-169707 ISBN 0-8148-0046-7
1. Chagall, Marc, 1887- II. Genauer, Emily, 1910- III. Mozart, Johann Chrysostom Wolfgang Amadeus, 1756-1791. Die Zauberflote. IV. New York (City). Metropolitan Opera. BIP

CHAGALL, Marc, 1887- 759.7
Chagall. Text and notes by Alfred Werner. New York, Tudor Pub. Co. [1967] 36, [96] p. illus. (part col.), col. ports. 18 cm. Bibliography: p. 15. [ND699.C5W44] 67-19835
I. Werner, Alfred, 1911-

CHAGALL, Marc, 1887- 759.7
Chagall. Text by Werner Schmalenbach. Tr. from German by M. Ledivelec. New York, Crown [1965] 26p. illus. (10 mounted col.) 30cm. (Folio art bks.) [ND699.C5S273] 65-5032 price unreported pap.,
I. Schmalenbach, Werner, 1917- II. Title.

CHAGALL, Marc, 1887- 741.9'47
Chagall: unpublished drawings. Text by Jacques Lassaigne. [Geneva] Skira [1968] 95 p. illus. (part col.) 19 cm. (The Taste of our time) "Distributed in the United States by The World Publishing Company ... Cleveland, Ohio." [NC269.C42L3] 68-31877
I. Lassaigne, Jacques, 1910-

CHAGALL, Marc, 1887- 769'.92'4
Chagall's posters : a catalogue raisonne / edited by Charles Sorlier ; pref. by Jean Adhemar. New York : Crown, c1975. 146, [13] p. : ill. (some col.) ; 33 cm. [NC1850.C45S67] 75-329617 ISBN 0-517-52441-4 : 60.00
1. Chagall, Marc, 1887- I. Sorlier, Charles. II. Title.

CHAGALL, Marc, 1887- 748.5'97
The Jerusalem windows / Marc Chagall ; text and notes by Jean Leymarie ; [translated from the French by Elaine Desautels]. 2d ed. New York : G. Braziller, 1975. xix, 89 p. : ill. (some col.) ; 27 cm. Translation of Vitraux pour Jerusalem. [NK5398.C5L433 1975] 75-326569 ISBN 0-8076-0807-6 : 15.00 ISBN 0-8076-0807-6 pbk. : 6.95
1. Chagall, Marc, 1887- 2. Hadassah-University Medical Center, Jerusalem. Synagogue. 3. Glass painting and staining—Israel. I. Leymarie, Jean. II. Title.

CHAGALL, Marc, 1887- 769.944
Lithographs. [Pref. by] Julien Cain. Introd. by Marc Chagall. Notes and catalogue by Fernand Mourlot. [Translated from the French by Maria Jolas] New York, G. Braziller [1960] 220p. illus. (part col.) plates (part col.) 33cm. 60-15726 25.00
I. Mourlot, Fernand. II. Title.

CHAGALL, Marc, 1887- 769.924
Marc Chagall: posters and personality, by Joseph K. Foster. New York, Reynal [1966] 16p. 26 col. plates. 37cm. [NC1850.C45F6] 66-23354 10.00 bds.,
I. Foster, Joseph K., ed. II. Title.

CHAGALL, Marc, 1887- 759.7
Marc Chagall : work on paper : selected

masterpieces / organized by the International Exhibitions Foundation ; introd. by Jean Leymarie ; pref. by Thomas M. Messer. Washington : The Foundation, 1975. 78 p. : ill. (some col.) ; 29 x 27 cm. Exhibition held at the Solomon R. Guggenheim Museum, New York, June 8-Sept. 28, 1975. [ND1978.C5S64] 75-15204
1. Chagall, Marc, 1887- I. Solomon R. Guggenheim Museum, New York. II. International Exhibitions Foundation.

CHAGALL, Marc, 1887- 760'.0924
Marc Chagall: drawings and water colors for the ballet. [Text by] Jacques Lassiagne. [Translated from the French by Joyce Reeves] New York, Tudor Pub. Co. [1969] 155 p. illus. (part col.) 36 cm. Cover title: Marc Chagall: the ballet. Contents.Contents.—Aleko.—The firebird.—Daphnis and Chloe. [NC269.C42L3213] 75-9119
I. Lassaigne, Jacques, 1910- II. Title. III. Title: Marc Chagall: the ballet.

CHAGALL, Marc, 1887- 927.5
My life. Translated from the French by Elisabeth Abbott. New York, Orion Press [1960] 173p. illus. 22cm. [ND699.C5A233] 60-8361
I. Title.

COGNIAT, Raymond, 1896- 759.7
Chagall, by Raymond Cogniat. [Translated from the French by Anne Ross] New York, Crown Publisher [1965] 95 p. illus. (part col.) plates (part mounted col.) 29 cm. Bibliography: p. 95. [ND699.C5C63] 65-8841
1. Chagall, Marc, 1887-

CRESPELLE, Jean Paul. 759.7
Chagall. Translated from the French by Benita Eisler. [1st American ed.] New York, Coward-McCann [1970] 287 p. illus., ports. 22 cm. Translation of Chagall, l'amour, le reve, et la vie. Bibliography: p. 275-276. [ND699.C5C713 1970] 76-104686 7.95
1. Chagall, Marc, 1887-

DAMASE, Jacques 759.7
Marc Chagall. New York, Barnes & Noble [c.1963] 90p. illus. (pt. col.) ports. 18cm. (Barnes & Noble art ser. 612) 63-5390 .75 pap.,
1. Chagall, Marc, 1887- I. Title.

ERBEN, Walter 759.7
Marc Chagall [Tr. by Michael Bullock] Rev. ed. New York, Praeger [1966] 166p. illus. (pt. mounted col.) ports. 26cm. [ND699.C5E713 1966] 66-21776 10.00
1. Chagall, Marc, 1887- I. Title.

FREUND, Miriam Kottler, 1906- 748.5995694
Jewels for a crown; the story of the Chagall windows. Foreword by Rene d'Harnoncourt. New York, McGraw-Hill [1963] 64 p. illus. (part col.) 26 cm. [NK5398.C5F7] 63-19440
1. Chagall, Marc, 1887- 2. Hadassa-University Medical Center, Jerusalem. Synagogue. 3. Glass painting and staining—Jerusalem. I. Title.

GREENFELD, Howard. 92
Marc Chagall. With reproductions of the artist's work in color and black and white. Chicago, Follett Pub. Co. [1967] 192 p. illus. (part col.), ports. 25 cm. Bibliography: p. 189. A biography of the Russian-born painter famous for his dream-like paintings, use of brilliant colors, and his creation of the stained glass Jerusalem Windows for a synagogue. [ND699.C5G7] AC 67
1. Chagall, Marc, 1887-

HAFTMANN, Werner. 759.7
Marc Chagall. Translated by Heinrich Baumann and Alexis Brown. New York, H. N. Abrams [1973] 162 p. illus., 48 col. plates. 34 cm. (The Library of great painters) Bibliography: p. 162. [ND699.C5H3313] 73-7657 ISBN 0-8109-0074-2
1. Chagall, Marc, 1887- I. Chagall, Marc, 1887-

LASSAIGNE, Jacques, 1910- 759.7
Marc Chagall: the ceiling of the Paris Opera; sketches, drawings, and paintings. Translated by Brenda Gilchrist. New York, Praeger [1966] 83 p. illus. (part col.) 34 cm. [ND699.C5L323] 66-12324
1. Chagall, Marc, 1887- 2. Paris. Opera. I. Title. II. Title: The ceiling of the Paris Opera.

LASSAIGNE, Jacques, 1910- 759.7
Marc Chagall: the ceiling of the Paris Opera; sketches, drawings, and paintings. Tr. [from French] by Brenda Gilchrist. New York, Praeger [c.1966] 86p. illus. (pt. col.) 34cm. [ND699.C5L323] 66-12524 27.50
1. Chagall, Marc, 1887- 2. Paris. Opera. I. Title. II. Title: The ceiling of the Paris Opera.

LEYMARIE, Jean 759.7
Marc Chagall: monotypes. 1961-1965. Catalouge etablipah Geral Cramer. Geneva, G. Cramers. New York dist. in the U.S.A. by Wittenborn. 1966. 131p. illus. (pt. mounted col.) 28cm. [ND699.C5L48 1966] 66-6595 42.50
1. Chagall, Marc, 1887- I. Cramer, Gerald. II. Title.

MARC Chagall. 759.7
[Translated by Michael Bullock from the German ed.] New York, Praeger [1957] 158 p. illus. (part mounted col.) port. 26 cm. [ND699.C5E7] [ND699.C5E7] 927.5 57-12449 57-12449
1. Chagall, Marc, 1887- I. Erben, Walter.

MARTEAU, Robert. 748.5'97
The stained-glass windows of Chagall 1957-1970. With an afterword by Charles Marq. New York, Tudor Pub. Co. [1973] 159 p. illus. (part col.) 37 cm. Translation of Les Vitraux de Chagall. [NK5398.C5M3713] 73-3119 ISBN 0-8148-0565-5
1. Chagall, Marc, 1887- 2. Glass painting and staining. I. Chagall, Marc, 1887- II. Title.

MEYER, Franz, writer on art. 759.7
Marc Chagall. [Translated from the German by Robert Allen] New York, H. N. Abrams [1964] 775 p. illus. (part mounted col.) ports., facsims. 31 cm. Bibliography, by Hans Bolliger: p. 711-731. [ND699.C5M43] 63-19571
1. Chagall, Marc, 1887-

RABOFF, Ernest Lloyd. 760
Marc Chagall, by Ernest Raboff. Garden City, N.Y., Doubleday, 1968. [31] p. illus. (part col.) 29 cm. (Art for children) A Gemini-Smith book. A brief biography of this twentieth-century artist and an explanation of his philosophy of art are followed by analyses of twelve of his paintings. Includes color reproductions of the paintings. [ND699.C5R3] AC 68
1. Chagall, Marc, 1887- I. Title.

*SORLIER, Charles. 709.04
The lithographs of Chagall, [vol. 4], 1969-1973. Notes and catalogue by Charles Sorlier [and] Fernand Mourlot. New York, Crown Publishers [1974] 180 p. col. illus. 32 cm. [NE2298] 60.00
1. Chagall, Marc, 1887- 2. Lithography. I. Title.

SWEENEY, James Johnson, 1900- 709'.24
Marc Chagall. In collaboration with the Art Institute of Chicago. New York, Museum of Modern Art. Reprint ed. [New York] Published for the Museum of Modern Art by Arno Press, 1969 [c1946] 102 p. illus. 27 cm. Bibliography, by Hannah B. Muller: p. 93-101. [ND699.C5S85 1969] 74-86433
1. Chagall, Marc, 1887- I. Chicago. Art Institute. II. New York (City). Museum of Modern Art. BIP

VENTURI, Lionello, 1885-1961. 927.5
Chagall: [biographical and critical study. Translated by S. J. C. Harrison and James Emmons. New York] Skira [1956] 122 p. mounted col. illus. 19 cm. (The Taste of our time, v. 18) Bibliography: p. 108-[113] [ND699.C5V42] 759.7 56-10713
1. Chagall, Marc, 1887-

WERNER, Alfred, 1911- 759.4
Chagall. New York, McGraw-Hill [1969] 48 p. illus., plates. 29 cm. (Color slide program of the great masters) Half title: Marc Chagall. Twenty col. slides (2 x 2 in.) of Chagall's works in pockets inside front cover. Bibliography: p. 48. [ND553.C355W4] 70-92726
1. Chagall, Marc, 1887- I. Title. II. Series. BIP

WERNER, Alfred, 1911- 759.7
Chagall: watercolors and gouaches. [Edited by Heather Meredith] New York, Watson-Guptill [1970] 87 p. 32 col. illus. 29 cm. Bibliography: p. 11. [ND1978.C5W4] 70-128389 17.50
1. Chagall, Marc, 1887- I. Title.

Chagall, Marc, 1887- —Juvenile literature.

GREENFELD, Howard. 759.7 B
Marc Chagall. With reproductions of the artist's work in color and black and white. Chicago, Follett Pub. Co. [1967] 192 p. illus. (part col.), ports. 25 cm. Bibliography: p. 189. [ND699.C5G7] 68-10479
1. Chagall, Marc, 1887- —Juvenile literature.

RABOFF, Ernest Lloyd. 760'.0924 (j)
Marc Chagall, by Ernest Raboff. Garden City, N.Y., Doubleday, 1968. 1 v. (unpaged) illus. (part col.) 29 cm. (Art for children) (A Gemini-Smith book.) [ND699.C5R3] 68-26549 3.95
1. Chagall, Marc, 1887- —Juvenile literature.

Chaikovskii, Petr Il'ich, 1840-1893.

BAKST, Lev Samoilovich, 1866-1924. 792.84
The designs of Leon Bakst for the Sleeping princess, a ballet in five acts after Perrault. Music by Tchaikovsky. Pref. by Andre Levinson. New York, B. Blom, 1971. 18 p. illus., 55 plates (part col.), ports. 26 cm. "First published 1922." [ND2888.B3A43] 68-56514
1. Chaikovskii, Petr Il'ich, 1840-1893. The sleeping beauty—Illustrations. I. Title. II. Title: The sleeping princess, a ballet in five acts after Perrault.

Chairs.

BLANCHARD, Roberta Ray. 749.31
How to restore and decorate chairs. Drawings by the author. New York, Avenel Books [1952] 128 p. illus. 28 cm. [NK2715.B57] 52-11241
1. Hitchcock, Lambert, 1795-1852. 2. Chairs. 3. Stencil work. I. Title.

FITZGERALD, Charles Patrick, 1902- 749.3
Barbarian beds; the origin of the chair in China [by] C. P. Fitzgerald. South Brunswick [N.J.] A. S. Barnes [1966, c1965] xvii, 85 p. illus. 30 cm. Bibliographical references included in "Notes" (p. 75-82) [NK2715] 66-9562
1. Chairs. 2. China—Civilization. I. Title.

FREY, Gilbert, 1937- 749'.3
The modern chair: 1850 to today. Le siege moderne de 1850 a aujourd'hui. Das moderne Sitzmobel von 1850 bis heute. New York, Architectural Book Pub. Co. [1970] 187 p. illus. 22 x 26 cm. Bibliography: p. 186-187. [NK2715.F7 1970b] 78-136107
1. Chairs. I. Title. II. Title: Le siege moderne de 1850 a aujourd'hui. III. Title: Das moderne Sitzmobel von 1850 bis heute.

GLOAG, John, 1896- 749'.3
The chair, its origins, design and social history. [1st American ed.] South Brunswick [N.J.] A. S. Barnes [1967, c1964] 221 p. illus., ports. 28 cm. First published in 1964 under title: The Englishman's chair. Bibliography: p. 201-204. [NK2715.G55 1967b] 67-13174
1. Chairs. 2. Furniture, English. I. Title.

IVERSON, Marion Day. 749.31
The American chair, 1630-1890. Illustrated by Ernest Donnelly. New York, Hastings House [c1957] 241p. illus. 27cm. [NK2715.I85] 57-11664
1. Chaira. 2. Furniture, American. I. Title.

LEA, Zilla Rider, ed. 749.3
The ornamented chair: its development in America, 1700-1890. [1st ed.] Rutland, Vt., C. E. Tuttle Co. [1960] 173 p. illus. (part col.) 28 cm. "Publication of the Esther Stevens Brazer Guild of the Historical Society of Early American Decoration, inc." Bibliography: p. [165]-167. [NK2715.L4] 60-8158
1. Chairs. 2. Furniture, American. 3. Decoration and ornament, American. I. Title.

NELSON, George, 1908- ed. 749.31
Chairs. [New York, Whitney Publication, 1953] 174 p. (chiefly illus.) 32 cm. (Interiors library, 2) [NK2715.N4] 53-3012
1. Chairs. I. Title.

NUTTING, Wallace, 1861-1941. 749'.3
A Windsor handbook; comprising illustrations & descriptions of Windsor furniture of all periods. Southampton, N.Y., Cracker Barrel Press [1969? c1917] 192 p. illus. 20 cm. On cover: American Windsors. [NK2715.N8 1969] 70-3749 3.75
1. Chairs. I. Title. II. Title: American Windsors. BIP

NUTTING, Wallace, 1861-1941. 749'.3
A Windsor handbook; comprising illustrations & descriptions of Windsor furniture of all periods, including side chairs, arm chairs, comb-backs, writing-arm Windsors, babies' high backs, babies' low chairs, child's chairs, also settees, love seats, stools & tables. Rutland, Vt., C. E. Tuttle [1973] 192 p. illus. 19 cm. (Tut books. C) Reprint of the 1917 ed. published by Old America Co., Framingham, Mass. [NK2715.N8 1973] 73-77579 ISBN 0-8048-1105-9 3.25
1. Chairs. I. Title.

ORMSBEE, Thomas Hamilton, 1890- 749.3
The Windsor chair. New York, Deerfield Books distributed by Hearthside Press [1962] 223p. illus. 24cm. [NK2715.O7] 62-10516
1. Chairs. 2. Furniture, American. I. Title.

ROE, Frederic Gordon, 1894- 749.31
Windsor chairs. New York, Pitman Pub. Corp. [1953] 96p. illus. 23cm. [NK2715] 53-13021
1. Chairs. I. Title.

*SPARKES, Ivan G. 749'3
The English country chair an illustrated history of chairs and chairmaking [by] Ivan G. Sparkes. Buckinghamshire, Spurbooks, [1974 c1973] 160 p. illus. 23 cm. Bibliography: p. 155-158. [NK2715] ISBN 0-902875-36-1
1. Chairs. I. Title.
Distributed by Transatlantic Arts, Levittown, N.Y. for 9.50 BIP

Chairs—Addresses, essays, lectures.

CHAIR : 749'.3
the current state of the art, with the who, the why, and the what of it / produced by Peter Bradford ; edited by Barbara Prete. New York : Crowell, c1978. 137 p. : ill. ; 32 cm. Based on a lecture series sponsored by the Cooper-Hewitt Museum, New York, 1976. [TS886.5.C45C43] 78-60172 ISBN 0-690-01783-9 : 19.95
1. Chairs—Addresses, essays, lectures. I. Bradford, Peter, 1936- II. Prete, Barbara. III. Cooper-Hewitt Museum of Decorative Arts and Design. BIP

Chairs—Exhibitions.

THE American chair; 749'.3
[catalogue of an exhibition by the Connoisseurship, Research, and Gallery Course, Mary Washington College, in 1972. Fredericksburg? Va., 1972] 93 p. illus. 28 cm. Cover title. Bibliography: p. 86-90. [NK2715.A45] 73-170453
1. Chairs—Exhibitions. 2. Chairs—United States. I. Mary Washington College, Fredericksburg, Va.

BUCHWALD, Hans H. 749'.3
Form from process—the Thonet chair; an exhibition of historic bentwood furniture from the collection of John Sailer, Vienna. Carpenter Center for the Visual Arts,

Harvard University, Cambridge, Mass., fall and winter 1967. Catalogue and research by Hans H. Buchwald. Design and graphic by Toshihiro Katayama. [Cambridge? 1967] 64 p. illus., port. 23 cm. Bibliography: p. [61]-64. [NK2546.T5B8] 68-1205
1. Thonet, Michael, 1796-1871. 2. Chairs—Exhibitions. 3. Chairs—Private collections. I. Sailer, John. II. Harvard University. Carpenter Center for the Visual Arts. III. Title.

STOWE-DAY Foundation. 749'.3
A selection of nineteenth century American chairs. Organized by Joseph S. Van Why & Anne S. MacFarland. Hartford, Conn. [1973] 107, [8] p. illus. 26 cm. Catalogue of an exhibition held at Nook Farm Visitors' Center, Dec. 4, 1973-Mar. 1974. Bibliography: p. [115] [NK2715.S85 1973] 74-154244
1. Chairs—Exhibitions. 2. Chairs—United States. I. Van Why, Joseph S. II. MacFarland, Anne S. III. Nook Farm Visitors' Center. IV. Title.

VICTORIA and Albert 749'.3
Museum, South Kensington. Circulation Dept.
Modern chairs, 1918-1970. Boston, Boston Book and Art [1971, c1970] 28, 120, 29-32 p. illus., ports. 25 cm. "Catalogue ... for the exhibition held at the Whitechapel Art Gallery, London, from 22 July - 30 August 1970 ... arranged by the Circulation Department, Victoria and Albert Museum." [NK2715.V53 1971] 76-148178 ISBN 0-8435-1008-0 12.50
1. Chairs—Exhibitions. I. Whitechapel Art Gallery, London. II. Title.

Chairs—History.

SCHWARTZ, Marvin D. 749'.3
Please be seated; the evolution of the chair, 2000 BC-2000AD [by] Marvin D. Schwartz. [New York] American Federation of Arts [1968] 61 p. illus. 26 cm. Catalog of an educational exhibition organized and circulated by the Decorative Arts Program of the American Federation of Arts in collaboration with the Cooper-Hewitt Museum of Design, Smithsonian Institution. Bibliography: p. 57. [NK2715.S3] 68-58410
1. Chairs—History. I. American Federation of Arts. Decorative Arts Exhibition Program. II. Cooper-Hewitt Museum of Design. III. Title.

Chairs—Juvenile literature.

CHECROUN, Natalie 749
Pull up a chair. Written and illus. by Natalie Checroun. Minneapolis, Lerner [1967] 46p. illus. 24cm. [NK271.C44] 67-15704 2.95
1. Chairs—Juvenile literature. I. Title. BIP

Chairs—United States.

BISHOP, Robert Charles. 749'.3
Centuries and styles of the American chair, 1640-1970, by Robert Bishop. Foreword by Charles F. Hummel. [1st ed.] New York, Dutton, 1972. 516 p. illus. 29 cm. Bibliography: p. 508-510. [NK2715.B55] 72-82702 ISBN 0-525-07826-6 27.50
1. Chairs—United States. I. Title. II. Title: The American chair.

KIRK, John T. 749.3
American chairs: Queen Anne and Chippendale, by John T. Kirk. [1st ed.] New York, Knopf, 1972. 208 p. illus. 32 cm. Includes bibliographical references. [NK2715.K5] 72-2239 ISBN 0-394-47328-0 17.50
1. Chairs—United States. 2. Decoration and ornament—Queen Anne style. 3. Decoration and ornament—Chippendale style. I. Title.

Chairs—United States—Exhibitions.

MORRIS Museum of Arts and 749'.3
Sciences.
Chairs made for American children. Morristown, N.J. : Morris Museum of Arts and Sciences, c1975. [16] p. : ill. ; 28 cm. Exhibition held Dec. 13, 1975-May 16, 1976. [NK2715.M63 1975] 75-42533
1. Chairs—United States—Exhibitions. 2. Children's paraphernalia—United States—Exhibitions. I. Title.

Chaix, Yves.

CHAIX, Yves. 769'.92'4
Presences. Dessins et texte d'Yves Chaix. Adaptation anglaise de Tom Costner. [New York, Murray Hill, 1973] 78 p. illus. 32 cm. French and English. Poems. [NC248.C39C67] 74-169229
1. Chaix, Yves. I. Costner, Tom, 1933- II. Title.

Chalchuapa, Salvador—Antiquities.

†THE Prehistory of 972.84
Chalchuapa, El Salvador / Robert J. Sharer, general editor. Philadelphia : University of Pennsylvania Press, 1977. 3 v. : ill. ; 28 cm. (Museum monographs - University Museum, University of Pennsylvania) Part of illustrative matter fold. in pocket of v. 1. Bibliography: v. 3, p. [218]-226. [F1435.1.C45P73] 74-031606 ISBN 0-8122-7689-2 (v.1) pbk. : 17.00 ISBN 0-8122-7690-6 (v.2) pbk. : 17.00 ISBN 0-8122-7692-2 (set) pbk. : 45.00 ISBN 0-8122-7691-4 (v.3) pbk. : 17.00
1. Chalchuapa, Salvador—Antiquities. 2. Mayas—Antiquities. 3. Salvador—Antiquities. 4. Excavations (Archaeology)—Salvador. I. Sharer, Robert J. II. Sheets, Payson D. III. Series: Pennsylvania. University. University Museum. Museum monographs.
Contents omitted

Chalk-talks.

LEHNUS, Opal Hull. 741.2'3
Something new in chalk talks. Illustrated by the author. Anderson, Ind., Warner Press [1972] 64 p. illus. 28 cm. [NC865.L4] 70-169963 ISBN 0-87162-124-X
1. Chalk-talks. I. Title. BIP

SMITH, Robert Leonard. 741.2'3
Successful chalk talking; a complete guide. Grand Rapids, Mich., Baker Book House [1972] 103 p. illus. 28 cm. [NC865.S53] 72-77660 ISBN 0-8010-7948-9
1. Chalk-talks. I. Title.

TARBELL, Harlan E., 1890- 741.23
1960.
The chalk talk manual, a complete presentation of the theory and practice of this fascinating form of entertainment. Minneapolis, T. S. Denison [1962] 278 p. illus. 22 cm. [NC865.T23] 62-18865
1. Chalk-talks. I. Title.

Chambord, Chateau de.

GASCAR, Pierre, 1916- 728.82
Chambord. Tr. from French by Richard Howard. Photos. by Andre Martin. New York, Macmillan [1964, c.1962] 115p. illus. (pt. col.) plans. 24cm. Bibl. 64-12213 9.95
1. Chambord, Chateau de. I. Title.

Champney, Benjamin, 1817-1907.

CHAMPNEY, Benjamin, 704'.7 B
1817-1907.
Sixty years' memories of art and artists. by Benjamin Champney ; [edited with an introduction by H. Barbara Weinberg]. [New York : Garland Pub., 1977] c1899. 178 p., [13] leaves of plates : ill. ; 19 cm. (The Art experience in late nineteenth-century America) Title page preceded by introd. (13 p.). Reprint of the 1900 ed. published by The News Print., Wallace & Andrews, Woburn, Mass. [N6537.C46A25 1977] 75-28887 ISBN 0-8240-2244-0 lib.bdg. : 25.00
1. Champney, Benjamin, 1817-1907. 2. Artists—United States—Biography. 3. Art, American—History. 4. Art, Modern—19th century—United States—History. I. Title. II. Series. BIP

Chanel, Coco, 1883-1971.

BAILLEN, Claude. 746.9'2'0924 B
Chanel solitaire / by Claude Baillen ; translated from the French by Barbara Bray. New York : Quadrangle/New York Times Book Co., 1974, c1973. 192 p. : ill. ; 25 cm. [TT505.C45B313 1974] 74-78651 ISBN 0-8129-0474-5 : 7.95
1. Chanel, Coco, 1883-1971. I. Title.

CHARLES-ROUX, 746.9'2'0924 B
Edmonde
Chanel : her life, her world, and the woman behind the legend she herself created / by Edmonde Charles-Houx. 1st ed. New York : Knopf, 1975. p. cm. Translation of L'irreguliere. Includes index. [TT505.C45C4613] 75-8254 ISBN 0-394-47613-1 : 15.00
1. Chanel, Coco, 1883-1971. BIP

GALANTE, Pierre. 746.9'2'0924 B
Mademoiselle Chanel. Translated by Eileen Geist and Jessie Wood. Chicago, H. Regnery Co. [1973] 298 p. 23 cm. [TT505.C45G35] 72-11173 8.95
1. Chanel, Coco, 1883-1971. I. Title.

HAEDRICH, Marcel, 746.9'2'0924 B
pseud.
Coco Chanel; her life, her secrets. Translated from the French by Charles Lam Markmann. [1st English language ed.] Boston, Little, Brown [1972] 277 p. illus. 25 cm. Translation of Coco Chanel secrete. [TT505.C45H313] 79-187788 8.95
1. Chanel, Coco, 1883-1971.

Chang, Ta-ch'ien, 1899—

LAI, T'ien-ch'ang. 759.951
Three contemporary Chinese painters : Chang Da-chien, Ting Yin-yung, Ch'eng Shih-fa / [T. C. Lai]. Seattle : University of Washington Press, c1975. 128 p. : ill. (some col.) ; 23 cm. Includes bibliographical references (Chinese and English). [ND1045.L34] 75-327590 10.00
1. Chang, Ta-ch'ien, 1899- 2. Ting, Yin Yung, 1902- 3. Ch'eng, Shih-fa. 4. Painting, Chinese—20th century. I. Title. BIP

Channon, Howard.

CHANNON, Howard. 942.7'53
Portrait of Liverpool / [by] Howard Channon. 3rd ed. London : Hale, 1976. 231 p., [24] p. of plates : ill., map ; 23 cm. Includes index. [DA690.L8C48 1976] 76-382112 ISBN 0-7091-5575-1 : £4.00
1. Channon, Howard. 2. Liverpool—Description. I. Title.

Chanson de Roland—Art.

LEJEUNE-DEHOUSSE, Rita. 704.947
The legend of Roland in the Middle Ages [by] Rita Lejeune and Jacques Stiennon. [New York] Phaidon; [distributed by Praeger Publishers, 1971] 2 v. illus., map, col. plates. 31 cm. Translation of La legende de Roland dans l'art du moyen age. Includes bibliographical references. [N8210.L413 1971] 73-111061 ISBN 0-7148-1414-8 98.50
1. Chanson de Roland—Art. 2. Art, Medieval. I. Stiennon, Jacques, joint author. II. Title.

Chantries.

COOK, George Henry 726.5
Mediaeval chantries and chantry chapels [Rev. ed.] London, Phoenix House [dist. Mystic, Conn., Verry 1965, c.1963] xii, 244p. illus., 59 plates. 23cm. Bibl. [NA5463.C66] 9.50
1. Chantries. 2. Chapels—England. 3. Church architecture—England. I. Title.

Chao, Wu-chi.

ROY, Claude 759.951
Zao Wou-ki. Translated from the French by Rita Barisse. New York, Grove Press 1960 [c.1959] 68p. illus. (part mounted col.) 21cm. (Evergreen gallery bk. no. 7) 59-12072 3.95; 1.95 pap.,
1. Chao, Wu-chi. I. Title.

Chapel Hill, N.C.—History.

STOLPEN, Steven, 779'.9'9756565
1951-
Chapel Hill : a pictorial history / by Steven Stolpen design by Fischbach & Edenton. Norfolk, Va. : Donning Co., c1978. 156 p. : ill. ; 28 cm. [F264.C38S85] 77-28580 ISBN 0-915442-34-5 : 16.95
1. Chapel Hill, N.C.—History. 2. Chapel Hill, N.C.—Description—Views. I. Title. BIP

Chapman, Conrad Wise, 1842-1910.

VALENTINE Museum, 759.13
Richmond, Va.
Conrad Wise Chapman, 1842-1910; an exhibition of his works in the Valentine Museum. Richmond, 1962. 98 p. illus., col. plates, 26 cm. "Journal and sketchbook of Conrad Wise Chapman": p. 49-63. Bibliography: p. 71-72. [ND237.C458V3] 63-6312
1. Chapman, Conrad Wise, 1842-1910. I. Chapman, Conrad Wise, 1842-1910. II. Title.

Character steins—Germany—Catalogs.

MANUSOV, Eugene. 738'.0943
Encyclopedia of character steins / by Eugene Manusov. Des Moines : Wallace-Homestead Book Co., c1976. 208 p., [4] leaves of plates : ill. (some col.) ; 29 cm. [NK4695.C52M35] 75-21330 ISBN 0-87069-122-8 : 15.95 pbk. : 12.95
1. Character steins—Germany—Catalogs. I. Title.

Charcoal-drawing.

GRAVES, Douglas R. 743'.4
Life drawing in charcoal, by Douglas R. Graves. [Edited by Diane Hines] New York, Watson-Guptill Publications [1971] 159 p. illus. 29 cm. [NC850.G7] 70-141059 ISBN 0-8230-2765-1 10.00
1. Charcoal-drawing. 2. Anatomy, Artistic. I. Title. BIP

PITZ, Henry Clarence, 741.2'2
1895-
Charcoal drawing, by Henry C. Pitz. New York, Watson-Guptill Publications [1971] 159 p. illus. 26 cm. Bibliography: p. 158. [NC850.P5] 73-133980 ISBN 0-8230-0615-8 8.95
1. Charcoal-drawing. I. Title. BIP

Chardin, Jean Baptiste Simeon, 1699-1779.

ROSENBERG, Pierre. 759.4
Chardin. [Biographical and critical study; translated from the French by Helga Harrison. Lausanne] Skira [distributed in the U.S. by World Pub. Co., Cleveland, 1963] 126 p. mounted col. illus. 19 cm. (The Taste of our time, v. 40) Bibliography: p. 113-[118] [ND553.C4R583] 63-20241
1. Chardin, Jean Baptiste Simeon, 1699-1779. I. Title.

WILDENSTEIN, Georges. 759.4
Chardin. [Translated from the French by Stuart Gilbert. Rev. and enl. ed. by Daniel Wildenstein] Greenwich, Conn., New York Graphic Society [1969, c1963] 276 p. illus. (part col.) 34 cm. Bibliography:p. 249-261. [ND553.C4W4913 1969] 74-81847 ISBN 8-212-03584-
1. Chardin, Jean Baptiste Simeon, 1699-1779. I. Wildenstein, Daniel, 1917-

Charles, Prince of Wales, 1948-

JONES, Iona Trevor. 745.92'6
Pilgrimage of flowers. Chester (1 Bank Close, Chester, CH2 1PB), J. L. Pearce, 1970. 191 p. illus. (some col.), coats of arms, facsims., map, ports. (some col.) 25 cm. [SB449.5.C4J65] 76-884679 ISBN 0-9501938-0-1 £3.00
1. Charles, Prince of Wales, 1948- 2. Flower arrangement in churches. 3. Churches—Wales. I. Title.

collection. Text by Yvonne Hackenbroch. Cambridge, Published for the Metropolitan Museum of Art by Harvard University Press, 1957. xxx, 286p. 146 plates (part col.) 31cm. Bibliography: p. 275-283. [NK4399.C5U55] 57-1429
1. Chelsea porcelain. 2. Porcelain, English. 3. Porcelain—Private collections. I. Hackenbroch, Yvonne. II. Title.

Chelsea porcelain—Catalogs.

†COLONIAL Williamsburg Foundation. 738.2'7
Chelsea porcelain at Williamsburg / by John C. Austin. Williamsburg, Va. : Colonial Williamsburg Foundation ; Charlottesville : distributed by the University Press of Virginia, c1977. xii, 227 p. : ill. (some col.) ; 29 cm. (The Williamsburg decorative art series) Includes index. Bibliography: p. xi-xii. [NK4399.C5C64 1977] 76-49537 ISBN 0-87935-023-7 : 30.00
1. Colonial Williamsburg, inc. Dept. of Collections. 2. Chelsea porcelain—Catalogs. 3. Porcelain—Williamsburg, Va.—Catalogs. I. Austin, John Cecil, 1931- II. Title. III. Series. BIP

Cheltenham, Eng.—Description—Views.

CHELTENHAM as it was / 942.4'16081'0222 [compiled by] Roger Beacham. Nelson : Hendon Publishing Co., 1976. [38] p. : chiefly ill., ports. ; 21 x 29 cm. [DA690.C48C48] 76-375275 ISBN 0-902907-89-1 : £1.30
1. Cheltenham, Eng.—Description—Views. 2. Cheltenham, Eng.—Social life and customs—Pictorial works. I. Beacham, Roger.

Chen, Chi, 1912—

CHEN, Chi, 1912- 741.9'51
China from the sketchbooks of Chen Chi. [New York, Chen Chi Studio, 1974] 1 v. (chiefly illus., part col.) 25 cm. [NC350.C47A43 1974] 73-92748
1. Chen, Chi, 1912- 2. China in art. I. Title.

Chenavard, Paul Marc Joseph, 1807-1895.

SLOANE, Joseph C 759.4
Paul Marc Joseph Chenavard, artist of 1848. Chapel Hill, University of North Carolina Press [1962] 214 p. illus. 24 cm. Includes bibliography. [ND553.C48S55] 62-3624
1. Chenavard, Paul Marc Joseph, 1807-1895. 2. Paris. Pantheon. 3. France — Intellectual life. I. Title. II. Title: Artist of 1848.

Cheney Cowles Memorial Museum.

CHENEY Cowles Memorial Museum. 746.4'1
Cornhusk bags of the Plateau Indians / Cheney Cowles Memorial Museum of the Eastern Washington State Historical Society. Chicago : University of Chicago Press, c1976. p. cm. (A University of Chicago Press text/fiche) Bibliography: p. [E78.W3C45 1976] 76-9025 ISBN 0-226-68987-5
1. Cheney Cowles Memorial Museum. 2. Indians of North America—Washington (State)—Basket making. 3. Indians of North America—Great Basin—Basket making. 4. Cornhust craft. I. Title. BIP

Cheops, King of Egypt.

SEISS, Joseph Augustus, 1823-1904. 913.32
The Great Pyramid: a miracle in stone. New introd. by Paul M. Allen. Blauvelt, N.Y., R. Steiner Publications [1973] 250 p. 18 cm. Reprint of the 1877 ed. published by Porter & Coates, Philadelphia, under title: A miracle in stone; or, The Great Pyramid of Egypt. Includes bibliographical references. [DT63.S462] 72-81590 1.95
1. Cheops, King of Egypt. I. Title. BIP

Cherokee Indians—Industries.

LEFTWICH, Rodney L. 745.5'09701
Arts and crafts of the Cherokee [by] Rodney L. Leftwich. Cullowhee, N.C., Land-of-the-Sky Press [1970] xiii, 160 p. illus. 24 cm. Bibliography: p. [155]-160. [E99.C5L37] 75-21207
1. Cherokee Indians—Industries. I. Title.

Chesapeake Bay region—Descr. & trav. —Views.

LEWIS, Jack, 1912- 759.13
The Chesapeake Bay scene. [Federalsburg? Md., c1953] 1v. (unpaged) illus. (part mounted col.) 31cm. [ND1839.L45A445] 54-21990
1. Chesapeake Bay region—Descr. & trav. —Views. I. Title.

Chesney, Lee, 1920- —Exhibitions.

CHESNEY, Lee, 1920- 769'.92'4
Lee Chesney—25 years of printmaking / Wayne A. Miyamoto ; with a foreword by Kenneth A. Kerslake. Orlando : University Presses of Florida, c1978. p. cm. Catalog of a touring retrospective exhibition of prints which opened in Orlando at the Florida Technological University in Nov. 1977. "A Florida Technological University book." [NE539.C53A4 1978] 78-13555 ISBN 0-8130-0615-5 : 7.50
1. Chesney, Lee, 1920- —Exhibitions. I. Miyamoto, Wayne A., joint author. II. Florida Technological University. III. Title.

Chesrow, Frank W., 1903- —Art collections.

PHILBROOK Art Center, Tulsa, Okla. 759.03'074'016686
Masterpieces of Renaissance and Baroque painting from the Collection of Colonel Frank W. Chesrow. [Tulsa, 1970?] 44 p. illus. (part col.) 28 cm. Exhibition held at the Philbrook Art Center, Oct. 5-28, 1970 and the Oklahoma Art Center, Nov. 8-Dec. 6, 1970. [ND170.P47] 73-172401
1. Chesrow, Frank W., 1903- —Art collections. 2. Paintings, Renaissance—Exhibitions. 3. Paintings, Baroque—Exhibitions. I. Oklahoma Art Center. II. Title.

Chessmen.

MACKETT-BEESON, Alfred Ernest James. 731.8'9'79414
Chessmen [by] A. E. J. Mackett-Beeson. New York, Putnam [1968] 119 p. illus. (part col.), map. 22 cm. (Pleasures and treasures) [NK9990.C4M3 1968] 68-12221 5.95
1. Chessmen.

WICHMANN, Hans, 1925- 736
Chess, the story of chesspieces from antiquity to modern times [by] Hans and Siegfried Wichmann. [Translated by Cornelia Brookfield and Claudia Rosoux] New York, Crown Publishers [1964] 328 p. illus. (part col.) facsims., plates (part col.) 31 cm. Bibliography: p. 324-328. [NK9990.C4W53] 64-23808
1. Chessmen. 2. Chess — Pictorial works. 3. Chess — Hist. I. Wichmann, Siegfried, 1921- joint author. II. Title.

Chessmen—Juvenile literature.

CARROLL, David, 1942- 731'.89'7941
Make your own chess set. Englewood Cliffs, N.J., Prentice-Hall [1974] 151 p. illus. 17 x 24 cm. Introduces the history of chess and chess pieces and gives instructions for making twenty-five different chess sets out of easily available materials. [TT896.55.C37] 74-8224 ISBN 0-13-547802-2
1. Chessmen—Juvenile literature. 2. Handicraft—Juvenile literature. 3. Chess—History—Juvenile literature. I. Title. BIP

Chester County Historical Society, West Chester, Pa.

CHESTER County Historical Society, West Chester, Pa. 746.9'7
Coverlets in the collection of the Chester County Historical Society : from an exhibition, June 6th to October 2nd, 1976, 225 North High Street, West Chester, Pennsylvania / [editor, Ruth K. Hagy ; consultants, Jane A. Bolster ... et al. ; photography, Dan Coxe]. [West Chester, Pa.] : The Society, c1976. 28 p. : chiefly ill. ; 26 cm. [NK9112.C45 1976] 76-371684
1. Chester County Historical Society, West Chester, Pa. 2. Coverlets—Pennsylvania—West Chester—Catalogs. I. Hagy, Ruth K. II. Title.

Chesterfield, Eng. St. Mary and All Saints (Church)

EDMUNDS, W. Hawksley. 942.5'12
The crooked spire of Chesterfield : how it was saved from destruction by fire : historical and other notes / by W. Hawksley Edmunds. Rev. ed., brought up to date / by the publishers. Chesterfield, [Eng.] : W. Edmunds, ltd., 1963. 40 p. : ill. ; 22 cm. [NA5471.C55E4 1963] 75-318290
1. Chesterfield, Eng. St. Mary and All Saints (Church) I. Title.

Chests—Juvenile literature.

RECORD, Nancy A. 749'.3
Coffers and cabinets, written and illustrated by Nancy A. Record. Minneapolis, Lerner Publications [1968] 55 p. illus. 24 cm. Describes various "things to put things in"—coffers, cabinets, caskets, chests, commodes, casapancas, cassoni, and closets—used throughout history from ancient Egypt to the twentieth century. [NK2725.R39] 68-56700
1. Chests—Juvenile literature. I. Title. BIP

Chests—Pennsylvania.

FABIAN, Monroe H. 974.8'004'31 s
The Pennsylvania-German decorated chest / Monroe H. Fabian ; foreword by Frederick S. Weiser. 1st ed. New York : Universe Books, c1978. 230 p. : ill. (some col.) ; 26 cm. ([Publications of the Pennsylvania German Society] ; v. 12) "A Main Street Press book." Includes index. Bibliography: p. 222-225. [GR110.P4A372 vol. 12] [NK2435.P4] 749'.3 77-91892 ISBN 0-87663-310-6 : 25.00
1. Chests—Pennsylvania. 2. Painted country furniture, Pennsylvania German. I. Title. II. Series: Pennsylvania-German Society. Publications ; 12. BIP

Cheyenne Indians—Art.

POWELL, Peter J., 1928- 741'.092'2
Montana, past and present : papers read at a Clark Library seminar, April 5, 1975 / by Peter J. Powell, Michael P. Malone. Los Angeles : William Andrews Clark Memorial Library, University of California, 1976. vi, 84 p. : ill. ; 23 cm. (William Andrews Clark Memorial Library seminar papers) Contents.Contents.—Powell, P. J. They drew from power.—Malone, M. P. Montana as a corporate bailiwick. Includes bibliographical references. [E99.C53P58] 77-621076
1. Anaconda Company—History. 2. Cheyenne Indians—Art. 3. Cheyenne Indians—Wars. 4. Indians of North America—Great Plains—Art. I. Malone, Michael P., joint author. II. California. University. University at Los Angeles. William Andrews Clark Memorial Library. III. Title. IV. Series.

Chicago. Art Institute.

CEZANNE, Paul, 1839-1906. 741.91
Paul Cezanne sketch book, owned by the Art Institute of Chicago. New York, C. Valentin, 1951. 2 v. illus. 15 x 23 cm. Contents.1. Introductory text, by C. O. Schniewind. Contents of the sketchbook.--2. Plates. [NC248.C37 A47] 52-1411
1. Chicago. Art Institute. I. Title.

CHICAGO. Art Institute. 746.9'7
Coverlets; a handbook on the collection of woven coverlets in the Art Institute of Chicago, by Mildred Davison and Christa C. Mayer-Thurman. [Chicago] 1973. 228 p. illus. (part col.) 26 cm. Bibliography: p. 227-228. [NK9112.C48] 73-82570 7.50 (pbk.)
1. Chicago. Art Institute. 2. Coverlets, American—Catalogs. 3. Coverlets—Chicago—Catalogs. I. Davison, Mildred. II. Mayer-Thurman, Christa C. III. Title.

CHICAGO. Art Institute. 741.9'44'074017311
French drawings and sketchbooks of the eighteenth century / Harold Joachim ; compiled by Sandra Haller Olsen ; Art Institute of Chicago. Chicago : University of Chicago Press, 1977. vii, 112 p. ; 23 cm. & microfiche (4 sheets : ill. (some col.) ; 11 x 15 cm.) in pocket (A University of Chicago Press text/fiche) Bibliography: p. 109-112. [NC246.C45 1977b] 77-20132 ISBN 0-226-68795-3 : 45.00
1. Chicago. Art Institute. 2. Drawing, French—Catalogs. 3. Drawing—18th century—France—Catalogs. I. Joachim, Harold. II. Olsen, Sandra Haller. III. Title. BIP

CHICAGO. Art Institute. 741.9'44'074017311
French drawings of the sixteenth and seventeenth centuries / Harold Joachim ; compiled by Sandra Haller Olsen. Chicago : University of Chicago Press, 1977. vii, 32 p. ; 23 cm. & microfiche (1 sheet : col. ill. ; 11 x 15 cm.) in pocket. (A University of Chicago Press text/fiche) Bibliography: p. 31-32. [NC246.C45 1977a] 77-9417 ISBN 0-226-68794-5 : 45.00
1. Chicago. Art Institute. 2. Drawing, French—Catalogs. 3. Drawing—16th century—France—Catalogs. 4. Drawing—17th century—France—Catalogs. 5. Drawing—Illinois—Chicago—Catalogs. I. Joachim, Harold. II. Olsen, Sandra Haller. III. Title. BIP

PICASSO, Pablo, 1881- 709'.46
Picasso in Chicago: paintings, drawings, and prints from Chicago collections. [Exhibition at] the Art Institute of Chicago, February 3-March 31, 1968. [Chicago, Art Institute of Chicago, 1968] 120 p. illus. 26 cm. [ND553.P5C486] 68-21275
1. Chicago. Art Institute. I. Title.

Chicago. Art Institute—Catalogs.

CHICAGO. Art Institute. 750'.74'017311
The Art Institute of Chicago : 100 masterpieces / [editor and coordinator, Janice J. Feldstein, co-editor, Maureen Smith]. Chicago : The Institute : distributed by Rand McNally, c1978. 159 p. : ill. (some col.) ; 36 cm. Includes indexes. [N530.A534] 78-56322 35.00
1. Chicago. Art Institute—Catalogs. 2. Painting—Illinois—Chicago—Catalogs. I. Feldstein, Janice J. II. Smith, Maureen, 1945-

Chicago, Burlington, and Quincy Railroad Company.

RAPP, William F. 725'.31'09782
Nebraska C.B.& Q. depots, by William F. Rapp. Crete, Neb., J-B Pub. Co. [1970] 46 p. illus., plans. 28 cm. [TF300.R37] 78-253249
1. Chicago, Burlington, and Quincy Railroad Company. 2. Railroads—Nebraska—Stations. I. Title.

Chicago, Clurllonio carde galerija.

LITHUANIAN American Art Club, Chicago. 708.177311
Art gallery of 'Ciurlionis.' [Chicago, 1958?] unpaged. illus. 30cm. [N531.C5L53] 60-32708
1. Chicago, Clurllonio carde galerija. I. Title.

Chicago. First National Bank—Art collections.

CHICAGO. First National Bank. 708'.173'11
The Art Collection of the First National Bank of Chicago. Chicago : The Bank, 1974. 274 p. : ill. (some col.) ; 25 cm. [N5220.C45C44 1974] 74-15702
1. Chicago. First National Bank—Art collections. I. Title.

Chicago. Frederick C. Robie House.

WRIGHT, Frank Lloyd, 1867-1959. 728.8'3'0223
The Robie House. [Palos Park, Ill., Prairie School Press, 1968] 14 l. of plans. 29 x 39 cm. Recorded by the U.S. National Park Service, Historic American Buildings Survey. [NA7238.Z9C59] 79-22465
1. Chicago. Frederick C. Robie House. I. Historic American Buildings Survey. II. Title.

Chicago. George Washington-Robert Morris-Haym Salomon Monument.

BARNARD, Harry, 1906- 731.7'6
"This great triumvirate of patriots"; the inspiring story behind Lorado Taft's Chicago monument to George Washington, Robert Morris, and Haym Salomon. Chicago, Follett [1971] 105 p. illus. 22 cm. [F548.64.G4B3] 72-162791 ISBN 0-695-80272-0 5.95
1. Salomon, Haym, 1740-1785. 2. Washington, George, Pres. U.S., 1732-1799. 3. Morris, Robert, 1734-1806. 4. Chicago. George Washington-Robert Morris-Haym Salomon Monument. I. Title.

Chicago, Judy, 1939—

CHICAGO, Judy, 1939- 759.13
Through the flower : my struggle as a woman artist / by Judy Chicago ; with an introd. by Anais Nin. 1st ed. Garden City, N.Y. : Doubleday, 1975. xi, 226 p., [24] leaves of plates : ill. ; 22 cm. Autobiographical. Includes bibliographical references and index. [ND237.C492A28] 74-12680 ISBN 0-385-09782-4: 8.95
1. Chicago, Judy, 1939- I. Title. BIP

Chicago metropolitan area—Historic houses, etc.

HISTORIC American Buildings Survey 720.977311
Historic American buildings survey: Chicago and nearby Illinois areas; list of measured drawings. photographs. and written documentation in the survey. 1966. Comp., ed. by Historic Amer. Buildings Survey. Eastern Off.: Design and Construction, Natl. Park Serv., Dept. of the Interior. J. William Rudd. comp. Park Forest. Hill. 60466. Prairie Sch. Pr., 117 Fir St. [1966] 52p. illus., plans. 23cm. [NA735.C4H5] 66-2882 1.50 pap.,
1. Chicago metropolitan area—Historic houses, etc. 2. Architecture—Chicago metropolitan area. 3. Architecture—Conservation and restoration. I. Rudd, J. William. comp. II. Title.

Chicago—Museums.

CHICAGO'S museums are in trouble. 069'.09773'11 [Chicago, 1969?] 28 p. illus., map. 26 cm. Caption title. A booklet jointly prepared by the Art Institute of Chicago, Chicago Academy of Sciences, Chicago Historical Society, Field Museum of Natural History, John G. Shedd Aquarium, and Museum of Science and Industry, to acquaint legislators of the Illinois General Assembly with their financial crisis. [AM13.C5C5] 74-289060
1. Chicago—Museums. I. Chicago. Art Institute.

Chicago School of Architecture.

COHEN, Stuart E., 1942- 720.977
Chicago architects : documenting the exhibition of the same name organized by Laurence Booth, Stuart E. Cohen, Stanley Tigerman, and Benjamin Weese / by Stuart E. Cohen ; with an introd. by Stanley Tigerman. Chicago : Swallow Press, c1976. 120 p. : ill. ; 24 x 31 cm. Includes bibliographical references. [NA722.C63] 76-2194 ISBN 0-8040-0731-4 pbk. : 6.95
1. Chicago School (Architecture) 2. Architects—Illinois—Chicago. I. Title. BIP

MILLER, Hugh C. 720'.9773'11
The Chicago School of Architecture; a plan for preserving a significant remnant of America's architectural heritage, by Hugh C. Miller. [Washington, U.S. National Park Service, 1972?] v, 36, [2] p. illus. 27 cm. "Study was prepared by the Office of Archeology and Historic Preservation, National Park Service, Department of the Interior." Bibliography: p. [38] [NA2300.C4M54] 73-601208
1. Chicago School of Architecture. 2. Architecture—Chicago—Conservation and restoration. I. United States. Office of Archeology and Historic Preservation.

Chicago. University. Library.

CHICAGO. University. Library. 016.091
The Latin manuscript book; an exhibition held on the occasion of the seminars in Latin palaeography sponsored by the Division of the Humanities of the University of Chicago and the Medieval Academy of America, summer MCMLXXIII, selected from the collections of the University of Chicago Library. The Joseph Regenstein Library, July through September, 1973. [Chicago, 1973] [55] p. illus. 26 cm. Catalog. [Z114.C53 1973] 73-173470 1.50 (pbk.)
1. Chicago. University. Library. 2. Manuscripts, Latin—Chicago—Exhibitions. 3. Paleography, Latin—Exhibitions. I. Joseph Regenstein Library. II. Title.

CHICAGO. University. Library. 011
One hundred books and manuscripts recently acquired by the University of Chicago Library : a catalogue of an exhibition held at the Joseph Regenstein Library, spring 1975. [s.l. : s.n., 1975] 100 p ; 22 cm. [Z121.C54 1975] 75-13963
1. Chicago. University. Library. 2. Bibliographical exhibitions. 3. Manuscripts—Exhibitions. I. Joseph Regenstein Library. II. Title: One hundred books and manuscripts ....

Chicago. World's Colombian Exposition, 1893.

ROSSEN, Howard M., 1936- 745.1'075
Columbian World's Fair collectibles, Chicago (1892-1893) / by Howard M. Rossen and John M. Kaduck. 1st ed. Des Moines : Wallace-Homestead Book Co., c1976. xi, 149 p. : ill. ; 29 cm. Includes index. Bibliography: p. 148. [NK1125.R69] 77-360322 ISBN 0-87069-157-0 : 9.95
1. Chicago. World's Colombian Exposition, 1893. 2. United States—Centennial celebrations, etc.—Collectibles. I. Kaduck, John M., joint author. II. Title.

Chichen Itza, Mexico.

BOLLES, John S. 722'.91
Las Monjas : a major pre-Mexican architectural complex at Chichen Itza / adapted and edited from the field notes and drawings by John S. Bolles, with new contributions by J. Eric S. Thompson and Ian Graham. Norman : University of Oklahoma Press, [1976] p. cm. (Civilization of the American Indian series ; 139) Includes indix. Bibliography: p. [F1435.1.C5B64] 75-16295 ISBN 0-8061-1282-4 : 35.00
1. Chichen Itza, Mexico. 2. Mayas—Architecture. 3. Indians of Mexico—Architecture. I. Title. II. Series.

COHODAS, Marvin. 972'.6
The Great Ball Court of Chichen Itza, Yucatan, Mexico / Marvin Cohodas. New York : Garland Pub., [1978] p. cm. (Outstanding dissertations in the fine arts) Originally presented as the author's thesis, Columbia University, 1974. Bibliography: p. [F1435.1.C5C63 1978] 77-94690 ISBN 0-8240-3221-7 lib.bdg. : 40.00
1. Chichen Itza, Mexico. I. Title. II. Series. BIP

EDIGER, Donald. 917.2'6
The well of sacrifice. [1st ed.] Garden City, N.Y., Doubleday, 1971. 288 p. illus. (part col.), ports. 24 cm. [F1435.1.C5E3] 68-14216 10.00
1. Chichen Itza, Mexico. 2. Mayas—Antiquities. I. Title.

Chidabaram, India. Temple.

HARLE, James C 726.145
Temple gateways in south India; the architecture and iconography of the Cidambaram gopuras [by] James C. Harle. Oxford, B. Cassirer [1963] xxiii, 179 p. 181 illus. 26 cm. Bibliography: p. 175-179. [NA6008.C5H3] 64-563577
1. Chidabaram, India. Temple. 2. Temples — India. 3. Sculpture — India. I. Title.

Chiesa della Madonna dell'Orto di Venezia.

THE Church of the Madonna dell'Orto 726'.5'094531 : restoring Venice / edited by Ashley Clarke and Philip Rylands ; with contributions by Francesco Valcanover ... [et al.]. London : Elek, 1977. 98 p., [2] leaves of plates : ill. (some col.) ; 25 cm. (Restoring Venice) Includes index. Bibliography: p. 93. [NA5621.V434C48] 77-366434 ISBN 0-236-40080-0 : 14.95
1. Chiesa della Madonna dell'Orto di Venezia. 2. Church architecture—Italy—Venice—Conservation and restoration. I. Clarke, Ashley, Sir, 1903- II. Rylands, Philip. III. Valcanover, Francesco. IV. Series.

Chihuahua, Mexico— (State)—Antiq.

LISTER, Robert Hill, 1915- 972.1
Archaeological excavations in the northern Sierra Madre Occidental, Chihuahua, and Sonora, Mexico, with reports by Paul C. Mangelsdorf and Kate Peck Kent. Boulder, University of Colorado Press, 1958. vii, 121p. illus., maps. tables. 26cm. (University of Colorado studies. Seriesin anthropology, no. 7) Bibliography: p. 120-121. [F1219.L68] 913.72 58-63188
1. Chihuahua, Mexico— (State)—Antiq. 2. Sonora, Mexico—Antiq. 3. Indians of Mexico— Antiq. 4. Excavations (Archaeology)—Mexico. I. Title. II. Series: Colorado. University University of Colorado studies. Series in anthropology, no. 7

Child psychology.

ALSCHULER, Rose (Haas) 1887- 155.4
Painting and personality: a study of young children [by] Rose H. Alschuler & La Berta Weiss Hattwick. Rev., abridged ed. Chicago, University of Chicago Press [1969] xviii, 205 p. illus. (part col.) 25 cm. Bibliography: p. 197-200. [LB1139.P3A42] 75-75966
1. Child psychology. 2. Children as artists. I. Hattwick, La Berta Weiss, 1909- joint author. II. Title.

Children.

LYMAN, Julie Ann 779.25
As the twig is bent. Photos. by Julie Ann Lyman: text by Diane David. Indianapolis, Bobbs [c.1965] 118p. (chiefly illus.) 26cm. [HQ781.L9] 65-21400 4.00
1. Children. 2. Children—Portraits. I. David, Diane. II. Title.

Children as artists.

BANNON, Laura. 372.5
Mind your child's art; a guide for parents and teachers. New York, Pellegrini & Cudahy [1952] 62 p. illus. 26 cm. [N352.B35] 52-8453
1. Children as artists. 2. Art—Study and teaching. I. Title.

BLAND, Jane Cooper. 706.9
Art of the young child: 3 to 5 years. New York, Museum of Modern Art; distributed by Simon and Schuster [1957] 47 p. illus. (part col.) 26 cm. [N352.B55] 57-4940
1. Children as artists. 2. Art—Study and teaching. I. Title.

BLAND, Jane Cooper. 372.5
Art of the young child; understanding and encouraging creative growth in children three to five. [3d ed., rev.] New York, Museum of Modern Art; distributed by New York Graphic Society, Greenwich, Conn. [1968] 57 p. illus. (part col.) 23 cm. Published in 1957 and 1960 under title: Art of the young child, 3 to 5 years. [N352.B55 1968] 68-20399 3.95
1. Children as artists. 2. Art—Study and teaching (Primary) I. Title.

CHILDREN from many lands illustrate Grimm's fairy tales. 760 Sponsored by the Follett Pub. Co. Circulated by the American Federation of Arts. [New York, 1968] 30 p. illus. (part col.) 21 cm. "Catalog ... prepared by the American Federation of Arts for the Follett Publishing Company." [N352.C53] 68-21567
1. Grimm, Jakob Ludwig Karl, 1785-1863. Kinder- und Hausmarchen. 2. Children as artists. 3. Fairy tales—Illustrations—Catalogs. I. American Federation of Arts. II. Follett Publishing Company, Chicago.

EISNER, Elliot W. 372.5'2
A comparison of the developmental drawing characteristics of culturally advantaged and culturally disadvantaged children [by] Elliot W. Eisner. Stanford, Calif., Stanford University, 1967. viii, 129 p. 28 cm. Research reported was performed pursuant to a contract with the U.S. Office of Education under project no. 3086, contract no. OE-6-10-027. Final report: School of Education, Stanford University. Bibliography: p. 83-89. [LB1139.D7E3] 68-60425
1. Children as artists. 2. Child study. I. Stanford University. School of Education. II. Title.

GETTINGS, Fred. 702'.8
Your child is an artist: simple art methods for children and bright adults. Reading, Osprey, 1971. 127 p. illus. (some col.) 28 cm. [N351.G4] 72-181691 ISBN 0-85045-035-7 £2.50
1. Children as artists. 2. Art—Technique. I. Title.

GEZARI, Temima (Nimtzowitz) 706.9
Footprints and new worlds; experiences in art with child and adult. [New York] Reconstructionist Press [1957] 168p. illus. 26cm. [N352.G43] 57-7329
1. Children as artists. 2. Art—Study and teaching. I. Title.

GROZINGER, Wolfgang, 1902- 706.9
Scribbling, drawing, painting; the early forms of the child's pictorial creativeness. Translated by Ernst Kaiser and Eithne Wilkins. New York, Praeger [1955] 142p. illus. 22cm. (Books that matter) Translation of Kinder kritzein, zeichnen, malen. [N352.G752] 55-8109
1. Children as artists. I. Title.

HOLMES, Kenneth, 1902- 372.5
Child art grows up [by] Kenneth Holmes and Hugh Collinson. London, New York, Studio Publications [1952] 95p. illus. 26cm. [N352.H63] 52-14609
1. Children as artists. 2. Art—Study and teaching. I. Collinson, Hugh, joint author. II. Title.

HORNE, Lois Thomasson. 372.5'2
Painting for children; a collection of paintings done in the classroom by children from five to twelve. New York, Reinhold Book Corp. [1968] 104 p. illus. (part col.) 19 x 26 cm. [N352.H68] 68-16027
1. Children as artists. 2. Art—Study and teaching (Elementary) I. Title.

HOROVITZ, Betty (Lark) 1894- 372.5
Understanding children's art for better teaching [by] Betty Lark-Horovitz, Hilda Lewis [and] Mark Luca. Columbus, Ohio, C. E. Merrill Books [1967] xi, 259 p. illus. (part col.) 26 cm. Includes bibliographies. [N352.H69] 66-14404
1. Children as artists. 2. Child study. I. Lewis, Hilda, joint author. II. Luca, Mark, joint author. III. Title.

HOROVITZ, Betty (Lark) 1894- 372.5
Understanding children's art for better teaching [by] Betty Lark-Horovitz, Hilda

Lewis [and] Mark Luca. 2d ed. Columbus, Ohio, C. E. Merrill [1973] x, 357 p. illus. (part col.) 26 cm. Includes bibliographies. [N352.H69 1973] 73-81970 ISBN 0-675-08927-1
1. Children as artists. I. Lewis, Hilda, joint author. II. Luca, Mark, joint author. III. Title.

KELLOGG, Rhoda, 1898- 704'.073
Analyzing children's art. Palo Alto, Calif., National Press Books [1969] 308 p. illus. 21 cm. Bibliography: p. 291-298. [N351.K4] 67-29530 8.95
1. Children as artists. I. Title. BIP

KELLOGG, Rhoda, 1898- 704'.073
The psychology of children's art, by Rhoda Kellogg with Scott O'Dell. [San Diego, Calif.] CRM; distributed by Random House, New York [1967] 109 p. col. illus. 29 cm. (A Psychology today book) [N352.K4] 67-31968
1. Children as artists. 2. Art—Psychology. I. O'Dell, Scott, 1903- joint author. II. Title.

LINDSAY, Zaidee. 371.92
Art is for all; arts and crafts for less able children. New York, Taplinger Pub. Co. [1968, c1967] 111 p. illus. 22 cm. [NK70.L48 1968] 68-14773
1. Children as artists. 2. Slow learning children. 3. Creative activities and seat work. I. Title.

LINDSTROM, Miriam. 706.9
Children's art; a study of normal development in children's modes of visualization. Berkeley, University of California Press, 1957. 100p. illus. 19cm. Includes bibliography. [N352.L5] 57-10499
1. Children as artists. I. Title. BIP

LOWENFELD, Viktor. 706.9
Your child and his art; a guide for parents. New York, Macmillan, 1954. 186 p. illus. 24 cm. [N352.L65] 54-9226
1. Children as artists. 2. Drawing. 3. Child study. I. Title. BIP

MENDELOWITZ, Daniel Marcus. 706.907
Children are artists; an introduction to children's art for teachers and parents. 2d ed. Stanford, Calif., Stanford University Press, 1963. ix, 158 p. illus. (part col.) 24 cm. Includes bibliographies. [N352.M44 1963] 63-10734
1. Children as artists. I. Title. BIP

MENDELOWITZ, Daniel Marcus. 706.9
Children are artists; an introduction to children's art for teachers and parents. Stanford, Calif., Stanford University Press [1953] 140 p. illus. 24 cm. (Stanford University publications. University series. Education and psychology, 3) [LB1051.A2L4 vol. 3] [AS36.L525 vol. 3] 53-9963
1. Children as artists. I. Title.

RANDALL, Arne W. 372.5
Murals for schools; sharing creative experiences. Illustrated by author. Worcester, Mass., Davis Press, c1956. 100 p. illus. 28 cm. [N352.R3] 56-8266
1. Children as artists. 2. Painting—Study and teaching. 3. Mural painting and decoration—United States. I. Title.

SPROUL, Adelaide. 372.5
With a free hand: painting, drawing, graphics, ceramics, and sculpture for children. New York, Reinhold Book Corp. [1968] 144 p. illus. 22 cm. Bibliography: p. 141. [N361.S65] 68-15902
1. Children as artists. 2. Art—Study and teaching (Elementary) I. Title.

VIOLA, Wilhelm 707
Child art. 2d ed. [London] Univ. of London Pr. [dist. Mystic, Conn., Verry, 1965] 206p. illus. 24cm. Reprint of 2d ed. of 1944. [N352.V48] 5.00 bds.,
1. Cizek, Franz, 1865- 2. Children as artists. 3. Art—Study and teaching. I. Title.

WHITNEY, Charlotte 709.73
Children's art. Photography: Ted Carland. Printing: Bill Suggitt. [Olivet, Mich.] Olivet Coll. Pr. [1965] 1v. (unpaged) illus. 22 x 28cm. [N352.W5] 64-20772 3.95; 2.95 pap., plastic bdg.
1. Children as artists. 2. Art—Michigan. I. Title.

Children—Clothing—Juvenile literature.

BARWELL, Eve. 792'.026
Disguises you can make / by Eve Barwell ; illustrated by Richard Rosenblum. New York : Lothrop, Lee & Shepard Co., c1977. 111 p. : ill. ; 25 cm. Includes index. Step-by-step instructions for twenty-four basic disguises plus variations using common craft materials and makeup. [TT649.B37] 77-24998 ISBN 0-688-41810-4 : 6.95 5.95 ISBN 0-688-41810-4 lib.bdg. : 6.43
1. Children—Clothing—Juvenile literature. 2. Costume—Juvenile literature. 3. Make-up, Theatrical—Juvenile literature. I. Rosenblum, Richard. II. Title. BIP

Children—Costume.

GREENHOWE, Jean. 646.4'7
Stage costumes for girls / by Jean Greenhowe. 1st American ed. Boston : Plays, inc., 1976, c1975. 95 p. : ill. ; 21 cm. [TT562.G7] 75-23205 ISBN 0-8238-0196-9 : 8.95
1. Children—Costume. 2. Sewing. I. Title. BIP

Children—Costume—Juvenile literature.

GREENHOWE, Jean. 792'.026
Costumes for nursery tale characters / by Jean Greenhowe ; photography by A. P. S. Aberdeen. 1st American ed. Boston : Plays, 1976, c1975. 87 p. : ill. ; 21 cm. British ed. (1975) published under title: Fancy dress from nursery tales. Instructions with pictures and diagrams for making costumes for fairy tale characters such as Robin Hood, Cinderella, Aladdin, and Puss in Boots. [TT560.G74 1976] 75-23444 ISBN 0-8238-0199-3 : 8.95
1. Children—Costume—Juvenile literature. 2. Sewing—Juvenile literature. I. Aberdeen, A. P. S. II. Title. BIP

Children in art.

CHILDREN : 769'.4'250942
a pictorial archive from nineteenth-century sources : 240 copyright-free illustrations for artists and designers / selected by Carol Belanger Grafton. New York : Dover Publications, 1978. v, 119 p. : chiefly ill. ; 29 cm. (Dover pictorial archive series) Engravings originally published in 1884-99 in The Chatterbox and in 1874 in the British workwoman. [NE962.C47C47 1978] 78-59321 ISBN 0-486-23694-3 : 3.50
1. Children in art. 2. Wood-engraving, English. 3. Wood-engraving—19th century—England. I. Grafton, Carol Belanger.

DOMBROWSKI, Ernst, Ritter von, 1896- 741.9'43
Children : sketches, stories, and thoughts about children / Ernst von Dombrowski ; translated from the German by Norma and Garold Davis. Provo, Utah : Brigham Young University Press, c1976. 91 p. : chiefly ill. ; 29 cm. Translation of Kinder. [NC251.D65A4813] 75-43798 14.95
1. Dombrowski, Ernst, Ritter von, 1896- 2. Children in art. I. Title. BIP

GARLAND, Madge 757.5
The changing face of childhood. New York, October House [1965, c.1963] 208p. illus. (pt. col.) 24cm. [N7640] 65-12912 7.95
1. Children in art. 2. Paintings. I. Title. BIP

GODFREY, Frederick M. 757.5
Child portraiture from Bellini to Cezanne. London, New York, Studio Publications [1956] 144p. 96plates. 30cm. [N7640.G6] 57-13666
1. Children in art. 2. Paintings. I. Title.

GODFREY, Frederick M 757.5
Child portraiture from Bellini to Cezanne. London, New York, Studio Publications [1956] 144 p. 96 plates. 30 cm. [N7640.G6] 57-13666
1. Children in art. 2. Paintings. I. Title.

KAY, Helen, pseud. 709.46
Picasso's world of children. Introd. by Daniel-Henry Kahnweiler. Garden City, N. Y., Doubleday [1965] 241p. illus. (pt. col.) 33cm. Chanticleer pr. ed. [ND553.P5K3] 65-15754 25.00; 22.50 pre-Christmas,
1. Picasso, Pablo, 1881- 2. Children in art. I. Title.

KEANE, Walter Stanley, 1920- 759.13
Walter Keane. [Redwood City, Calif., Johnson Meyers Pub. Co., 1964] 1. v. (chiefly illus., part mounted, part col.) port. 33 cm. (Tomorrow's masters series) A selection of 48 paintings and drawings done between 1945 and 1963, with comments by the artist. Foreword by Eric Schneider. [ND237.K395S3] 66-45456
1. Children in art. I. Schneider, Eric, ed. II. Title.

KING, Marian 757.5
A gallery of children; portraits from the National Gallery of Art. Washington, Acropolis Bks. [1967] 112p. illus. (pt. col.) 16 x 23cm. Bibl. [N7640.K54 1967] 67-17589 5.95
1. Children in art. 2. Paintings—Washington, D.C. I. U.S. National Gallery of Art. II. Title.

LONGSTREET, Stephen, 1907-. 704.9425
The Child in art. Introd. by Stephen Longstreet. [1st ed.] Alhambra, Calif., Borden Pub. Co. [1966] 1 v. (chiefly illus.) 31 cm. (Master draughtsman series) [NC1005.C5] 66-5102
1. Children in art. 2. Drawings. I. Title.

SALINGER, Margaretta, 1907- 757.5
Great paintings of children. [New York, H. N. Abrams, 1956] 5p. illus., 16 col. plates (incl. cover) 39cm. (An Abrams art book) In portfolio. [N7642.S3] 57-587
1. Children in art. I. Title.

SEEMANN, Margarete, 1893-1949 *741.943
The Hummel-book by the late Berta Hummel. Poems and pref. by the late Margarete Seemann. Tr. [from German] by Lola Ch. Eytel. [7th ed.] New York, W. S. Heinman [1960] 64p. illus. (part col.: p4.50 61-2064
1. Children in art. 2. Children's poetry. I. Hummel, Innocentia, Sister, 1909-1946, illus. II. Title.

SEEMANN, Margarete, 1893-1949 831.912
The Hummel-book, by the late Berta Hummel. Poems, pref. by the late Margarete Seemann. Tr. by Lola Ch. Eytel. 10th ed. Stuttgart, E. Fink-Verlag, On label mounted on t.p.: W. S. Heinman, New York. 1966[c.1962] 64p. illus. (pt. col.) 24cm. [NC1145] 66-9681 5.50
1. Children in art. 2. Children's poetry. I. Hummel, Innocentia, Sister, 1909-1946, illus. II. Title.

Children in art—Juvenile literature.

BEHRENS, June. 701'.1
Looking at children / by June Behrens ; illustrated with art reproductions ; pictures collected by Bernard Sharpiro. Chicago : Childrens Press, c1977. 30 p. : col. ill. ; 22 x 27 cm. (Adventures in art series) "A Golden Gate junior book." Discusses the subjects and artistic techniques of fourteen sculptures and paintings from the fifth century B.C. to the present day. [N7642.B4] 76-48157 ISBN 0-516-08825-4 lib.bdg. : 6.60
1. Children in art—Juvenile literature. 2. Art appreciation—Juvenile literature. I. Title. BIP

DOWNER, Marion. 704.94'25
Children in the world's art. New York, Lothrop, Lee & Shepard Co. [1970] 144 p. illus., maps. 29 cm. Describes, with the help of accompanying black and white reproductions, the portrayal of children in art from ancient times to the twentieth century. [N7640.D63] 69-14327 5.95
1. Children in art—Juvenile literature. I. Title.

SEDGWICK, Kate. 757'.5
Children in art / by Kate Sedgwick and Rebecca Frischkorn. New York : Holt, Rinehart and Winston, c1978. 56 p. : ill. ; 24 cm. A collections of stories, most of them based on true facts, about famous paintings and pieces of sculpture that depict children. [N7642.S4] 77-10833 ISBN 0-03-020896-3 lib. bdg. : 6.95
1. Children in art—Juvenile literature. 2. Art appreciation—Juvenile literature. I. Frischkorn, Rebecca, joint author. II. Title. BIP

Children in Ceylon—Pictorial works.

THWAITES, Jeanne. 779'.25'095493
Mother and child. South Brunswick [N.J.] A. S. Barnes [1967] 136 p. (chiefly illus.) 29 cm. [HQ792.C4T48] 67-12208
1. Children in Ceylon—Pictorial works. I. Title.

Children in China—Pictorial works.

BARNSTONE, Willis, 1927- 778.9'25'0951
New faces of China. Bloomington, Indiana University Press [1973] 1 v. (unpaged) illus. 32 cm. Poems. [DS727.B37 1973] 73-81160 ISBN 0-253-15660-2 10.00
1. Children in China—Pictorial works. 2. Photography of children. I. Title.

Children—Portraits.

BLAHOVE, Marcos, 1928- 751.4'5
Painting children in oil / by Marcos Blahove and Joe Singer. New York : Watson-Guptill, 1978. 152 p. : ill (some col.) ; 29 cm. Includes index. Bibliography: p. 149. [ND1329.3.C45B55 1978] 77-28845 ISBN 0-8230-3594-8 : 16.95
1. Children—Portraits. 2. Painting—Technique. I. Singer, Joe, 1923- joint author. II. Title. BIP

THE Family of children 779'.25
/ [editor and publisher, Jerry Mason ; art director, Albert Squillace ; project director, Ken Heyman ; quotations edited by Sylvia Cole]. New York : Grosset & Dunlap, 1977. 192 p. : chiefly ill. ; 29 cm. "A Ridge Press book." [TR681.C5F35] 77-72646 ISBN 0-448-14412-3 : 14.95
1. Children—Portraits. 2. Photography of children. I. Mason, Jerry.

LANGSTON, Shelley 779.25
The child, by Hubert Bermont. Photos. by Shelley Langston. New York, Trident Pr. [c.]1965. 1v. (chiefly illus.) 24cm. (Pocket Bk. special) [TR680.L33] 65-28092 3.95; 1.00 bds., pap.,
1. Children—Portraits. I. Bermont, Hubert Ingram. II. Title. BIP

NORTON, John, 1919- 757'.5
Painting and drawing children. New York, Watson-Guptill Publications [1974] 175 p. illus. 29 cm. Bibliography: p. 171-172. [N7643.N67 1974] 73-18055 ISBN 0-8230-3555-7 15.95
1. Children—Portraits. 2. Children in art. I. Title. BIP

REICH, Hanns 779.24
Children and their mothers. New York, Hill & Wang [1964] 15p. [64]p. ofillus. 23cm. (Terra magica bk.) 64-24833 3.50
1. Children—Portraits. 2. Mothers—Portraits. 3. Children Poetry. 4. Mothers—Poetry. I. Title. BIP

[ROSENBERG, Ethel (Clifford)] 1915- 779.25
Your face is a picture [by] Ethel and David Clifford [pseud.] Educ. consultant: Leo Fay. Indianapolis, E. C. Seale, c.1963. 63p. chiefly illus. 32cm. 63-20261 4.95
1. Hildren—Portraits. I. Rosenber, David, 1914- II. Title.

Children—Portraits—Exhibitions.

MARSHALL, Rosalind Kay. 757'.5'09411074094134
Childhood in seventeenth century Scotland : the Scottish National Portrait Gallery, 19 August-19 September 1976 / [by] Rosalind K. Marshall. Edinburgh : Trustees of the National Galleries of Scotland, 1976. 67 p. : ill., ports. ; 30 cm. An Edinburgh Festival Exhibition. Includes bibliographical references. [ND1329.3.C45M37] 77-361409 £1.25
1. Children—Portraits—Exhibitions. 2. Portrait painting, Scottish—Exhibitions. I. Edinburgh. Scottish National Portrait Gallery. II. Title.

SUBJECT INDEX CHINA—ANTIQUITIES.

Children—Yearbooks.

MCCALLS children's annual. 745
v.1- [New York, 1953- v. illus. 35cm. [TT635.M3] 53-69565
1. Children—Yearbooks. 2. Children's clothing. 3. Handicraft.

Children's art.

CATALDO, John W. 372.5'2
Words & calligraphy for children [by] John W. Cataldo. New York, Reinhold Book Corp. [1969] [60] p. illus. (part col.) 27 x 28 cm. Most of the illustrations by children from 5 through 11 years of age. [N352.C37] 68-22737
1. Children's art. 2. Children's writings. I. Title.

COLE, Natalie Robinson, 1901- 704.073
Children's arts from deep down inside. New York, John Day Co. [1966] 210 p. illus. 24 cm. (John Day books in contemporary education) [N352.C64] 66-15095
1. Children's art. I. Title.

GREENBERG, Pearl, 1927- 372.52
Children's experiences in art: drawing and painting. Photos. by Pearl and Murray Greenberg. New York, Reinhold Pub. Corp. [1966] 132 p. illus. (part col.) 27 cm. [N352.G72] 66-11936
1. Children's art. 2. Creation (Literary, artistic, etc.) I. Title.

NICKERSON, Betty. 741.9
Celebrate the sun; a heritage of festivals interpreted through the art of children from many lands. Philadelphia, Lippincott [1969] xv, 128 p. col. illus. 28 cm. Fifty-one illustrations by children recording the celebration of various festivals and holidays. [N352.N5 1969] 78-92874 6.95
1. Children's art. 2. Festivals—Juvenile literature. I. Title.

PELLOWSKI, Anne, comp. 808.8'99282
Have you seen a comet? Children's art and writing from around the world [compiled by] Anne Pellowski, Helen R. Sattley [and] Joyce C. Arkhurst. New York, John Day Co. [1971] 120 p. col. illus. 24 x 27 cm. Color illustrations, poems, stories, essays, anecdotes, and letters by children aged six to sixteen from seventy-five countries of the world. Includes both the original and its translation for those works not originally written in English. [N352.P415 1971] 78-135280
1. Children's art. 2. Children's writings. I. Sattley, Helen R., joint comp. II. Arkhurst, Joyce Cooper, joint comp. III. Title.

PRAGUE. Statni Zidovske museum. 741.9'437'1
I never saw another butterfly : children's drawings and poems from Terezin Concentration Camp, 1942-1944 / [edited by Hana Volavkova ; translated into English by Jeanne Nemcova]. 2d ed. New York : Schocken Books, 1978. p. cm. Translation of Detske kresby na zastavce k smrti, Terezin, 1942-1944. [N352.P713 1978] 78-3542 ISBN 0-8052-0598-5 pbk. : 4.95
1. Children's art. 2. Children's writings. 3. Terezin (Concentration camp) I. Volavkova, Hana. II. Title. III. Title: Children's drawings and poems from Terezin Concentration Camp, 1942-1944.
BIP

RIEGER, Shay. 731'.83'2
Gargoyles, monsters, and other beasts. New York, Lothrop, Lee & Shepard [1972] 62 p. illus. 27 cm. Photographs of and brief comments on sculptures of gargoyles, monsters, and other imaginary beasts from art of the past and by children and the author. [NB1940.R5] 72-1091 ISBN 0-688-40011-6 4.95
1. Children's art. 2. Animals in art. 3. Monsters in art. I. Title.

WYSE, Anne. 760'.0971
The one to fifty book [by] Anne and Alex Wyse. [Toronto] University of Toronto Press [1973] 1 v. (chiefly illus., part col.) 17 x 26 cm. [N352.W97] 73-85360 ISBN 0-8020-6222-9
1. Children's art. 2. Picture-books for children. I. Wyse, Alex, joint author. II. Title.
BIP

Children's art—Great Britain.

BERGSTROM, Theo. 741.9'42
Creature's progress / by Theo Bergstrom ; from drawings by Edmund Bergstrom ... [et al.]. [London] : Bergstrom and Boyle Books Limited, 1976. [52] p. of ill. ; 21 cm. A collage of his children's drawings. [N352.B47] 76-377652 ISBN 0-903767-06-6 : £1.00
1. Children's art—Great Britain. I. Bergstrom, Edmund, joint author. II. Title.

Children's art—Terezin, Czechoslovak Republic.

PRAGUE. Statni zidovske museum. 741.9437
I never saw another butterfly. Children's drawings and poems from Theresienstadt Concentration Camp, 1942-1944. New York, McGraw-Hill [1964] 80 p. illus. (part col.) 29 cm. Translation of Detske kresby na zastavce k smrti, Terezin 1942-1944. [N352.P713 1964] 64-15573
1. Children's art—Terezin, Czechoslovak Republic. 2. Children's writing, Russian. 3. Terezin (Concentration Camp) I. Title. II. Title: Children's drawings and poems from Theresienstadt Concentration Camp, 1942-1944.

Children's art—United States.

GRIGGS, Tamar. 759.1
There's a sound in the sea : a child's-eye view of the whale / collected by Tamar Griggs. San Francisco : Scrimshaw Press, 1975. 93 p. : ill. (some col.) ; 21 x 23 cm. Paintings and poems by school children expressing their feelings about the plight of the whale. [NX304.A1G74] 75-4784 ISBN 0-912020-47-4 : 10.95
1. Children's art—United States. 2. Children's art—Canada. 3. Children's writings, American. 4. Children's writings, Canadian. 5. Whales in art. I. Title. BIP

Children's books, Illustrated.

FEAVER, William. 741.64'2
When we were young : two centuries of children's book illustration / William Feaver. 1st ed. New York : Holt, Rinehart and Winston, c1977. 96 p. : ill. (some col.) ; 29 cm. "Annotated list of illustrations": p. 89-96. [NC965.F42 1977] 76-29901 ISBN 0-03-020306-6 : 9.95 ISBN 0-03-020301-5 pbk. : 5.95
1. Children's books, Illustrated. 2. Illustration of books. I. Title. BIP

Children's coverlets—United States—Exhibitions.

JOHNSON, Bruce, 1948-1976. 746.9'7
A child's comfort : baby and doll quilts in America folk art / Bruce Johnson, in collaboration with Susan S. Connor, Josephine Rogers, and Holly Sidford. 1st ed. New York : Harcourt Brace Jovanovich, c1977. xi, 116 p. : ill. ; 24 cm. Catalogue of an exhibition held Oct. 5, 1976, through Jan. 23, 1977, at the Museum of American Folk Art, New York. [NK9112.J63 1977] 76-27407 ISBN 0-15-117184-X : 12.95 ISBN 0-15-117185-8 pbk. : 6.95
1. Children's coverlets—United States—Exhibitions. 2. Doll coverlets—United States—Exhibitons. 3. Quilting. I. Museum of American Folk Art. II. Title. BIP

Children's dreams—Pictorial works.

TRESS, Arthur. 779'.9'154630924
The dream collector. Text by John Minahan. Richmond, Va., Westover Pub. Co. [1972] 1 v. (unpaged) illus. 29 cm. [BF1091.T73] 72-88362 ISBN 0-87858-032-8 9.95
1. Children's dreams—Pictorial works. I. Minahan, John. II. Title. BIP

Children's furniture.

BAKER, Bill. 684
Children's furniture you can build. [Greenwich, Conn., Fawcett Publications, c1956] 144p. illus. 24cm. (A Fawcett how-to book, 322) [TT197.5.C5B2] 57-2472
1. Children's furniture. I. Title.

DAL Fabbro, Mario, 1913- 684.1'04
How to make children's furniture and play equipment. 2d ed. New York, McGraw-Hill, 1974 [c1975] viii, 192 p. illus. 25 cm. [TT197.5.C5D3 1975] 74-9677 ISBN 0-07-015186-5 7.95
1. Children's furniture. 2. Playgrounds—Apparatus and equipment. 3. Toy making. I. Title.

DAL FABBRO, Mario, 1913- 684
How to make children's furniture and play equipment. New York, McGraw-Hill [1963] vii, 192 p. diagrs., tables 26 cm. [TT197.5.C5D3] 62-20184
1. Children's furniture. 2. Playgrounds—Apparatus and equipment. 3. Toys. I. Title. BIP

HOFMANN, Ruth B. 684.1
How to build special furniture and equipment for handicapped children, by Ruth B. Hofmann. Springfield, Ill., Thomas [1971] ix, 88 p. illus. 25 cm. [TT197.5.C5H6] 70-115385
1. Children's furniture. 2. Furniture making—Amateurs' manuals. 3. Handicapped children. I. Title. BIP

PALMER, Bruce. 684.1
Making children's furniture and play structures / by Bruce Palmer ; ill. by Judith Lane. New York : Workman Pub. Co., 1974. xiv, 144 p. : ill. ; 21 x 24 cm. [TT197.5.C5P34] 75-8813 ISBN 0-911104-24-0 : 8.95 ISBN 0-911104-25-9 pbk. : 3.95
1. Children's furniture. 2. Toy making—Amateurs' manuals. I. Title. BIP

Children's furniture—Catalogs.

FOA, Linda, 1942- 684
Kids' stuff / by Linda Foa and Geri Brin. 1st ed. New York : Pantheon Books, c1978. p. cm. [TT197.5.C5F63] 78-14343 ISBN 0-394-41558-2 : 17.95. ISBN 0-394-73658-3 pbk. : 8.95
1. Children's furniture—Catalogs. 2. Children's paraphernalia—Catalogs. I. Brin, Geri, 1947- joint author. II. Title. BIP

Children's literature—Illustrations—Juvenile literature.

THE Children's picture gallery : 30 favorite color illustrations to clip and frame / edited by Pasquale Cool. New York : Bounty Books, c1976. [64] p. : col. ill. ; 28 cm. Representative works of some early great children's book illustrators: Robinson, Potter, Rackham, Greenaway, Denslow, Brooke, Crane, and Caldecott. [NC965.C45] 76-2464 ISBN 0-517-52593-3 : 3.95 741.64'2
1. Children's literature—Illustrations—Juvenile literature. I. Cool, Pasquale, 1947-
BIP

Children's paraphernalia—Collectors and collecting.

MACKAY, James Alexander. 745.1
Childhood antiques / James Mackay. Toronto : Fitzhenry & Whiteside, c1976. 136 p. : ill. (some col.) ; 27 cm. Includes index. [NK1125.M3453 1976b] 77-367989 16.95
1. Children's paraphernalia—Collectors and collecting. I. Title. BIP

MACKAY, James Alexander. 745.1
Childhood antiques / James Mackay. New York : Taplinger Pub. Co., 1976. 136 p. : ill. (some col.) ; 27 cm. Includes index. [NK1125.M3453 1976] 76-11668 ISBN 0-8008-1442-8 : 14.95
1. Children's paraphernalia—Collectors and collecting. I. Title.

Children's paraphernalia—Collectors and collecting—U.S.

MCCLINTON, Katharine (Morrison) 745.1'0973
Antiques of American childhood. [1st ed.] New York, C. N. Potter; distributed by Crown [1970] 351 p. illus., facsims. 26 cm. Bibliography: p. 340-344. [NK805.M3 1970] 78-83755 12.50
1. Children's paraphernalia—Collectors and collecting—U.S. I. Title.

Children's rooms.

CHILDREN'S spaces : 747'.77
50 architects & designers create environments for the young / [edited by] Molly & Norman McGrath. New York : Morrow, c1978. p. cm. [NK2117.C4C47] 78-15324 ISBN 0-688-03329-6 : 25.00
1. Children's rooms. 2. Interior decoration. I. McGrath, Molly. II. McGrath, Norman.
BIP

GELSON, Hilary. 747'.8'8
Children about the house / Hilary Gelson ; [illustrated by Derek Higley et al.]. London : Design Council, 1976. 70 p. : ill. (some col.) ; 20 x 21 cm. (A Design Centre book) Includes index. [NK2117.C4G44] 77-366176 ISBN 0-85072-024-9 : £1.75
1. Children's rooms. 2. Children's paraphernalia. I. Title. BIP

STODDARD, Alexandra. 747'.77
A child's place : how to create a living environment for your child / Alexandra Stoddard ; illustrated by Mona Mark. 1st ed. Garden City, N.Y. : Doubleday, 1977. xii, 168 p. : ill. ; 27 cm. Bibliography: p. [167]-168. [NK2117.C4S8] 74-33665 ISBN 0-385-07939-7 : 9.95
1. Children's rooms. 2. Interior decoration. I. Title. BIP

Chillida, Eduardo, 1924-

HOUSTON, Tex. Museum of Fine Arts. 730.924
Eduardo Chillida; [exhibition at] the Museum of Fine Arts, Houston, Texas. (Houston, Tex., 1966] 59 p. illus., map, port. 28 cm. [NB813.C45H8] 66-30809
1. Chillida, Eduardo, 1924- I. Sweeney, James Johnson, 1900- II. Title. III. Title: Text by James Johnson Sweeney. Catalogue: p. 26-29.

China—Antiquities.

CHUNG YANG YEN CHIU YUAN. 913.51
LI SHIH YU YEN CHIU SO, Nan-king, Formosa.
Ch'eng-tzu-yai: the black pottery culture site at Lung-shan-chen in Li-ch'eng-hsien, Shantung Province [by] Li Chi, editor-in-chief [and others] Translated by Kenneth Starr. New Haven, Published for the Dept. of Anthropology, Yale University, by the Yale University Press, 1956. 232 p. illus., plates, maps, diagrs. 25 cm. (Yale University publications in anthropology, no. 52) "The original report, printed in two editions (one entirely in Chinese and the other with an appended English summary), was published in 1934 as the first number of the series Archaeologia Sinica, edited by Li Chi, Liang Ssu-yung, und Tung Tso-pin." Bibliography: p. 220-226. [GN2.Y3 no.52] [E77.Y3 no. 52] [NK4165.A25] 56-10099
1. China — Antiq. 2. Pottery, Chinese. I. Li, Chi, 1896- ed. II. Title. III. Series. IV. Series: Yale University. Dept. of Anthropology. Yale University publications in anthropology, no. 52

LAUFER, Berthold, 1874-1934. 732'.7
Chinese clay figures. Part I: Prolegomena on the history of defensive armor. [New York, Kraus Reprint Corp., 1967] 73-315 p. illus., 64 plates. 23 cm. (Field Museum of Natural History. Anthropological series, v. 13, no. 2) ([Field Museum of Natural History] Publication 177.) Title page includes original imprint: Chicago, 1914. "The Mrs. T. B. Blackstone Expedition."

No more published? [GN2.F4 vol. 13, no. 2] 68-3026
1. China—Antiquities. 2. Sculpture—China. 3. Arms and armor, Chinese. I. Title. II. Series. III. Series: Fieldiana: anthropology, v. 13, no 2.

China—Description and travel—Views.

TOPOLSKI, Feliks, 1907- 741.9'438
Holy China. Boston, Houghton Mifflin Co., 1968. 1 v. (chiefly 194 illus., 1 col.) 29 cm. [DS711.T63 1968b] 68-30732 12.95
1. China—Description and travel—Views. I. Title.

China—History—Pictorial works.

RATHBUN, Hope Willis, 1885- 759.13
Echoes of Chinese history, transcribed in the words and paintings of Hope Willis Rathbun. [1st ed.] Rutland, Vt., C. E. Tuttle Co. [1967] 116 p. 53 col. plates. 19 cm. [ND237.R173A44] 66-25437
1. China—History—Pictorial works. I. Title.

China in art.

CHEN, Chi, 1912- 741.9'51
China from the sketchbooks of Chen Chi. [New York, Chen Chi Studio, 1974] 1 v. (chiefly illus., part col.) 25 cm. [NC350.C47A43 1974] 73-92748
1. Chen, Chi, 1912- 2. China in art. I. Title.

MUSEUM of the American China Trade. 741.9'42
Warner Varnham: a visual diary of China and the Philippines, 1835 to 1843. Catalogue of an exhibition of drawings and watercolors, May through October 1973, with a checklist of other known works. Milton, Mass., 1973. viii, 23 p. illus. 28 cm. Cover title: Warner Varnham: exhibition of drawings and watercolors. Includes bibliographical references. [NC242.V33M87 1973] 74-157055
1. Varnham, Warner. 2. China in art. 3. Philippine Islands in art. I. Varnham, Warner. II. Title. III. Title: A visual diary of China and the Philippines, 1835 to 1843.

China—Intellectual life.

SCOTT, Adolphe Clarence, 1909- 700'.951
Literature and the arts in twentieth century China, by A. C. Scott. Gloucester, Mass., P. Smith, 1968 [c1963] xv, 212 p. illus. 21 cm. Bibliography: p. 189-196. [DS721.S37 1968] 68-3339
1. China—Intellectual life. I. Title. BIP

China painting.

CAMPANA, Domenic Mathews, 1871- 738.22
The teacher of china painting. [Chicago, 1949, '1950] 138 p. illus. 20 cm. (Campana's educational art library, 15) [NK4605.C3 1950] 50-13467
1. China painting. I. Title. BIP

CERAMIC decorating techniques. 738.1'5
[Los Angeles] Popular Ceramics Publications [1969] 30 p. illus. 16 x 23 cm. Cover title. [NK4605.C4] 70-17663 0.50
1. China painting. I. Popular Ceramics Publications.

GALLOWAY, Gladys. 738.1'5
China painting : fun & basics / Gladys Galloway. Caro, Mich. : R. Petzold, 1975. 140 p. : ill. (some col.) ; 22 cm. Includes index. [NK4605.G35] 75-10598
1. China painting. I. Title.

JoRGENSEN, Gunhild, 1919- 738.1'5
The techniques of China painting. [Translated from the Danish by Hugh Young] New York, Van Nostrand Reinhold [1974] 112 p. illus. (part col.) 21 x 22 cm. Translation of Porcelansmaling strog for strog. [NK4605.J613] 73-3941 ISBN 0-442-29989-3 6.95
1. China painting. I. Title.

LITTLE, Ruth. 738.15
Painting china for pleasure and profit. Lubbock, Tex., Brack Publications [1963] 290 p. illus. 21 cm. [NK4605.L5] 63-3124
1. China painting. I. Title. BIP

MCCARTHY, Jessie (Stubblefield). 738.22
The art of china painting. Dallas, Story Book Press [1952] 273 p. illus. 20 cm. [NK4605.M185] 52-14908
1. China painting. I. Title.

MCCARTHY, Jessie (Stubblefield). 738.22
Painting roses on china. Fort Worth, Tex [1957] 63p. illus. 29cm. [NK4605.M187] 58-18000
1. China painting. 2. Roses. I. Title.

MISEREZ-SCHIRA, Georges. 738.1'5
The art of painting on porcelain. Translated by Camilla Sykes. Radnor, Pa., Chilton Book Co. [1974] 132 p. illus. (part col.) 27 cm. Translation of Peinture sur porcelaine. [NK4605.M5413] 74-6404 ISBN 0-8019-6155-6 19.95
1. China painting. I. Title. BIP

MONACHESI, Nicola di Rienzi. 738.1'5
A manual for china painters : being a practical and comprehensive treatise on the art of painting china and glass with mineral colors / by Nicola di Rienzi Monachesi. Rev. and enl. ed. Detroit : Gale Research Co., 1975 [c1907] p. cm. Reprint of the ed. published by Lothrop, Lee & Shepard Co., Boston. [NK4605.M73 1975] 72-174084 ISBN 0-8103-4275-8 : 14.00
1. China painting. 2. Glass painting and staining. 3. Colors. I. Title.

PILLET, Nettie Ethel, 1877- 738.22
China painting. [Pasadena! Calif., 1954] 159p. illus. 21cm. [NK4605.P5] 54-36471
1. China painting. I. Title.

ROCHESTER, N. Y. Mercantile Institute of Applied Arts. 738.15
System of china painting instruction; year book. Rochester, N. Y. v. 26cm. Cover title, 19 : China painting and decorating. [NK4605.R75] 52-66791
1. China painting. I. Title.

SALYER, Pauline A. 738.15
The great artists of china decoration [by Pauline A. Salyer] [1st ed.] Oklahoma City, Salyer Pub. Co. [1964] 198 p. illus. (part col.) coats of arms, col. plates, ports. 29 cm. [NK4605.S2] 64-55015
1. China painting. I. Title. BIP

SHARP, Edith M. 738.1'5
China painting; the soft look technique, [by] Edith M. Sharp. [Melbourne] Lansdowne [1968] 96 p. illus. (part col.) 25 cm. [NK4605.S5] 68-17695 8.50
1. China painting. I. Title.

TAYLOR, Doris W. 738.15
Ceramic painting; step by step [by] Doris W. Taylor [and] Anne Button Hart. Wharf scene by Lee R. Brooks. Photos. by Robert C. Foster. Princeton, N.J., Van Nostrand [1966] x, 144 p. illus. (part col.) 25 cm. [NK4605.T28] 66-27525
1. China painting. 2. Pottery. I. Hart, Anne Button, joint author. II. Title.

TAYLOR, Doris W. 738.15
China painting, step by step [by] Doris W. Taylor [and] Anne Button Hart. Photos. by Darlene Bekhedal. Princeton, N.J., Van Nostrand [1962] x, 234 p. illus., col. plates. 25 cm. [NK4605.T3] 62-53305
1. China painting. I. Hart, Anne Button, joint author.

China painting—Exhibitions.

CHICAGO, Judy, 1939- 738
The dinner party : a symbol of our heritage. 1st ed. Garden City, N.Y. : Anchor Press, 1979. p. cm. Includes index. [NK4605.C45] 78-69653 ISBN 0-385-14566-7 : 24.95. ISBN 0-385-14567-5 pbk. : 9.95
1. China painting—Exhibitions. 2. Needlework—Exhibitions. 3. Women in art—Exhibitions. I. Title. BIP

China trade art—Exhibitions.

PEABODY Museum of Salem, Salem, Mass. 709'.51
A catalogue of Chinese export paintings, furniture, silver, and other objects, 1785 to 1865, by Carl L. Crossman. Salem, Mass., 1970. 48 p. illus. 22 cm. Exhibition from the collections of the museum and outside lenders. [N7343.5.P42 1970] 73-166201
1. China trade art—Exhibitions. 2. China trade art—Salem, Mass. I. Crossman, Carl L. II. Title.

China trade art—History.

CROSSMAN, Carl L. 709'.51
The China trade; export paintings, furniture, silver & other objects [by] Carl L. Crossman. With a foreword by Ernest S. Dodge. [1st ed.] Princeton [N.J.] Pyne Press [1972] xii, 275 p. illus. (part col.) 29 cm. Bibliography: p. 266-267. [N7343.5.C76] 72-79149 25.00
1. China trade art—History. 2. China trade art—United States. I. Title.

China trade porcelain.

PALMER, Arlene M. 738.2'0951'07401511
A Winterthur guide to Chinese export porcelain / Arlene M. Palmer. New York : Crown, 1976. p. cm. "A Winterthur book/Rutledge." Bibliography: p. [NK4565.5.P34 1976] 76-10848 ISBN 0-517-52178-4 pbk. : 3.95
1. Henry Francis du Pont Winterthur Museum. 2. China trade porcelain. I. Henry Francis du Pont Winterthur Museum. II. Title. BIP

China trade porcelain—Catalogs.

HOWARD, David Sanctuary. 738.2'0951
China for the West : Chinese porcelain & other decorative arts for export illustrated from the Mottahedeh Collection / David Howard and John Ayers ; foreword by Nelson A. Rockefeller. London ; New York : Sotheby Parke Bernet, 1978. 2 v. (698 p.) : ill. (some col.) ; 34 cm. Includes index. Bibliography: p. 673-678. [NK4565.5.H67] 78-319971 ISBN 0-85667-035-9 : 170.00 (2 vols.)
1. Mottahedeh, Rafi—Art collections—Catalogs. 2. Mottahedeh, Mildred—Art collections—Catalogs. 3. China trade porcelain—Catalogs. 4. China trade art—Catalogs. I. Ayers, John, joint author. II. Title. BIP

LE CORBEILLER, Clare. 382'.45'73820951
China trade porcelain: patterns of exchange; additions to the Helena Woolworth McCann Collection in the Metropolitan Museum of Art. Foreword by John Goldsmith Phillips. [New York] Metropolitan Museum of Art; [distributed by New York Graphic Society, 1974] 134 p. illus. (part col.) 28 cm. Includes bibliographical references. [NK4565.5.L43] 74-2097 ISBN 0-87099-089-6
1. McCann, Helena Woolworth—Art collections. 2. China trade porcelain—Catalogs. I. Title.

China trade porcelain—Collectors and collecting—United States.

GORDON, Elinor. 738.2'0951
Collecting Chinese export porcelain / Elinor Gordon ; foreword by J. A. Lloyd Hyde ; [col. photos. by Helga Photo Studio]. 1st ed. New York : Universe Books, 1977. 158 p., [8] col. leaves of plates : ill. ; 25 cm. "A Main Street Press book." Includes index.. Bibliography: p. 158. [NK4565.5.G67] 77-70474 ISBN 0-87663-295-9 : 14.95
1. China trade porcelain—Collectors and collecting—United States. 2. China trade porcelain—Collectors and collecting—Europe. I. Title. BIP

China trade porcelain—Exhibitions.

EFIRD, Callie Huger. 738.2'0951
Chinese export porcelain from the Reeves Collection at Washington and Lee University, Lexington, Virginia. [Exhibition and catalogue prepared by Callie Huger Efird and Katharine Gross Farnham. Lexington, Va., Washington and Lee University, 1973] 56 p. illus. 28 cm. "These Chinese export pieces from the Reeves Collection were first exhibited to the public at the High Museum of Art, Atlanta, Georgia, February 23rd to April 8th, 1973." Bibliography: p. 56. [NK4565.5.E33] 73-76576
1. Reeves, Euchlin D.—Art collections. 2. Reeves, Louise C. Herreshoff—Art collections. 3. China trade porcelain—Exhibitions. I. Farnham, Katharine Gross, joint author. II. Washington and Lee University, Lexington, Va. III. High Museum of Art. IV. Title. BIP

LE CORBEILLER, Clare. 738.2'0951
China trade porcelain; a study in double reflections. New York, China House Gallery [1973] 80 p. illus. 24 cm. Catalog of an exhibition held at the China House Gallery, Oct. 25, 1973-Jan. 27, 1974. Bibliography: p. 15. [NK4565.5.L42] 73-88150
1. China trade porcelain—Exhibitions. I. China House Gallery. II. Title.

China trade silverwork.

FORBES, Henry A. Crosby. 739.2'3'751
Chinese export silver, 1785 to 1885 / by H A Crosby Forbes John Devereux Kernan and Ruth S. Wilkins. Milton, Mass. : Museum of the American China Trade, 1975. xvi, 303 p. : ill. ; 29 cm. Includes indexes. Bibliography: p. 261-276. [NK7183.A1F67] 75-12401 55.00
1. China trade silverwork. 2. Hall-marks. I. Kernan, John Devereux, 1911- joint author. II. Wilkins, Ruth S., 1926- joint author. III. Museum of the American China Trade. IV. Title. BIP

Chinese Americans—New York (City)

GLICK, Carl, 1890- 917.47'1'06951
Shake hands with the dragon. Illustrated by Donald McKay. New York, Whittlesey House. Ann Arbor, Mich., Gryphon Books, 1971 [c1941] vii, 327 p. illus. 22 cm. [F128.9.C5G5 1971] 75-162513
1. Chinese Americans—New York (City) I. Title.

Chinese language—Writing.

DRISCOLL, Lucy. 741
Chinese calligraphy [by] Lucy Driscoll and Kenji Toda. 2d ed. New York, Paragon Book Reprint Corp., 1964. vii, 70 p. illus. 26 cm. Bibliographical references included in "Notes" (p. 65-68) [PL1171.D7 1964] 64-24329
1. Chinese language—Writing. 2. Paleography, Chinese. I. Toda, Kenji, joint author. II. Title. BIP

Chippendale, Thomas, 1718-1779.

HEWITT, Linda, 1940- 749.2'2
Chippendale and all the rest; some influences on eighteenth-century English furniture. Illus. by Robert G. Hewitt. South Brunswick, A. S. Barnes [1974] 161 p. illus. 26 cm. Bibliography: p. 141-144. [NK2529.H49] 72-6386 ISBN 0-498-01188-7
1. Chippendale, Thomas, 1718-1779. 2. Furniture, English. 3. Cabinet-workers—England. I. Title.

749.2'2
Chippendale and his contemporaries [by] John Kenworthy-Browne. New York, World Pub. [1973] p. (Connoisseur's library) Bibliography: p. [NK2529.K45] 72-10603 ISBN 0-529-05013-7
1. Chippendale, Thomas, 1718-1779. 2. Cabinet workers—England. 3. Decoration and ornament—Georgian style. I. Title. II. Series: Connoisseur's library (New York)

LOUGHLIN, David. 749'.3
The case of Major Fanshawe's chairs / David Loughlin. New York : Universe Books, 1978. 160 p. : ill. ; 22 cm. Includes bibliographical references and index. [NK2715.L63] 78-52196 ISBN 0-87663-317-3 : 10.95

1. Fanshawe, R. G. 2. Chippendale, Thomas, 1718-1779. 3. Chairs—Ireland—Collectors and collecting. 4. Decoration and ornament—Chippendale style. I. Title. II. Title: Fanshawe's chairs. BIP

Chippewa Indians.

HOUSTON, James A., 1921- 779'.9'9703
Ojibwa summer. Text by James Houston. Photos. by B. A. King. Barre, Mass., Barre Publishers, 1972. [96] p. illus. 28 cm. [E99.C6H67] 72-83228 ISBN 0-8271-7244-3 5.95
1. Chippewa Indians. I. King, B. A., illus. II. Title.

Chippewa Indians—Juvenile literature.

KOSTICH, Dragos D. 759.13 B
George Morrison / by Dragos D. Kostich. Minneapolis : Dillon Press, c1976. 66 p. : ill. ; 24 cm. (The Story of an American Indian) A biography of the Chippewa Indian whose many artistic achievements were crowned when in 1970 he began teaching at the University of Minnesota not only art, but American Indian studies. [E99.C6M864] 92 75-45210 ISBN 0-87518-110-4 : 4.95
1. Morrison, George, 1919- —Juvenile literature. 2. Chippewa Indians—Juvenile literature. I. Title. BIP

Chirico, Giorgio de, 1888—

CHIRICO, Giorgio de, 1888- 709'.2'4
G. de Chirico : [catalogue of an exhibition held at the Wildenstein Gallery] 7th to 28th April 1976. London : Wildenstein, [1976] 48 p. : chiefly ill. (some col.), port. ; 24 cm. English or French. Bibliography: p. 47-48. [N6923.C5W54] 76-372764 ISBN 0-902128-21-3 : £3.00
1. Chirico, Giorgio de, 1888- I. Wildenstein and Company, ltd., London.

CHIRICO, Giorgio de, 1888- 759.5
The memoirs of Giorgio de Chirico. Translated from the Italian and with an introd. by Margaret Crosland. Coral Gables, Fla., University of Miami Press [1971] 262 p. illus. 23 cm. Translation of Memorie della mia vita, di Giorgio de Chirico. Bibliography: p. 253-258. [ND623.C56A2713 1971b] 74-102694 ISBN 0-87024-125-7 12.50
1. Chirico, Giorgio de, 1888- 2. Painters—Italy—Correspondence, reminiscences, etc. I. Title. BIP

SOBY, James Thrall, 1906- 759.5
The early Chirico. New York, Arno Press [1969, c1941] xii, 119 p. 69 plates, port. 27 cm. (Arno series of contemporary art, no. 33) Bibliography: p. 113-116. [ND623.C56S6 1969] 79-91380
1. Chirico, Giorgio de, 1888- I. Title. BIP

SOBY, James Thrall, 1906- 927.5
Giorgio de Chirico. New York, Museum of Modern Art [1955] 267 p. illus. (part mounted col.) ports. 25 cm. A revision of The early Chirico, published in 1941. Bibliography: p. 254-258. [ND623.C56S6 1955] 55-5422
1. Chirico, Giorgio de, 1888- BIP

VALSECCHI, Marco. 759.5
Italian moderns; De Chirico, Carra, Morandi. New York, Abrams [1959] 75 p. 36 illus. (part col.) 17 cm. (The Pocket library of great art, A33) Bibliography: p. 75. [ND623.C56V3] 59-7242
1. Chirico, Giorgio de, 1888- 2. Carra, Cario, 1881- 3. Morandi, Giorgio, 1890- I. Title.

Chiropractic clinics—United States—Design and construction.

101 select chiropractic clinics and offices; plans layouts designs. 725'.23
[Fort Worth, Tex., Parker Chiropractic Research Foundation, 1972] 252 p. illus. 29 cm. "Compiled by the Professional Services Division of the Parker Chiropractic Research Foundation." [RZ242.O53] 72-89849
1. Chiropractic clinics—United States—Design and construction. I. Parker Chiropractic Research Foundation. Professional Services Division.

Chisholm Trail—Poetry.

CHISHOLM, Alexander, 1892- 811.54
The old Chisholm Trail. Illus. by Jim Pratt. [1st ed.] Salt Lake City, Hankdraft Art and Pub. Co. [1964] 584 p. illus., ports., maps. 24 cm. In verse. Bibliography: p. 569-584. [PS3553.H5O4] 64-2452
1. Chisholm Trail—Poetry. I. Title.

Choir-stalls—Gt. Brit.—Catalogs.

REMNANT, G. L. 729'.93
A catalogue of misericords in Great Britain, by G. L. Remnant; with an essay on their iconography by M. D. Anderson. Oxford, Clarendon P., 1969. xl, 221 p. 48 plates. 24 cm. Bibliography: p. 203-205. [NA5463.R4] 78-374990 63/-
1. Choir-stalls—Gt. Brit.—Catalogs. I. Title. BIP

Choir-stalls—Lincoln, Eng.

ANDERSON, Mary Desiree, 1902- 729'.93
The choir stalls of Lincoln Minster, by M. D. Anderson. 2nd ed. Lincoln, Friends of Lincoln Cathedral, 1967. 2-51 p. illus., plans. 24 cm. [NA5471.L7A6 1967] 76-547622 7/6
1. Lincoln Cathedral. 2. Choir-stalls—Lincoln, Eng. I. Title.

Choju giga.

THE Animal frolic, 741.9'52
by Toba Sojo. [Text by Velma Varner] New York, Putnam [1954] [48] p. illus. 20 x 24 cm. The illus. are reproduced from the Choju giga or Scrolls of animal caricatures, attributed to Toba Sojo (Kakuyu), which are in Kozan-ji, Kyoto. [ND1059.6.C46C46132] 54-5500
1. Choju giga. I. Toba Sojo, 1053-1140, illus. II. Varner, Velma.

CHOJU giga. 741.9'52
Scrolls of animal caricatures. Honolulu, East-West Center Press [1969] 2 v. (in case) 32 cm. Consists of reproductions of 4 scrolls, attributed to Toba Sojo, which are in Kozan-ji, Kyoto. Vol. 1 has an introd. adapted by Shigetaka Kaneko from the Japanese text by Hideo Okudaira, and scrolls B, C, and D in reduced size; v. 2 consists of scroll A, an actual-size reproduction in folding-book format. [ND1059.3.C513] 70-12471 ISBN 0-8248-0087-7
1. Choju giga. I. Toba Sojo, 1053-1140, illus. II. Okudaira, Hideo, 1905- III. Kaneko, Shigetaka, 1914- tr. IV. Title: Scrolls of animal caricatures.

Christ-Janer, Albert, 1910-1973.

GEORGIA Museum of Art. 760'.092'4
Albert Christ-Janer : [exhibition], February 22-March 28, 1976, Georgia Museum of Art, the University of Georgia, Athens, Georgia. Athens, Ga. : The Museum, c1976. 118 p. : ill. (some col.) ; 22 x 26 cm. Bibliography: p. 101-104. [N6537.C497G46 1976] 76-366543
1. Christ-Janer, Albert, 1910-1973. I. Christ-Janer, Albert, 1910-1973.

Christian antiquities.

LOWRIE. WALTER. 1868- 709.015
Art in the early church. Rev. ed. [Gloucester. Mass., P. Smith. 1965, c.1947] xi, 229p. illus. 21cm. (Harper torchbk., Cloister lib., TB124 rebound) First pub. in 1901 by Macmillan under title Monuments of the early church (in England under title Christian art and archaeology) Bibl. [N7832.L57] 4.75
1. Christian antiquities. 2. Christian art and symbolism. 3. Church architecture. I. Lowrie, Walter. 1868- Monuments of the early church. II. Title. BIP

Christian art

WALTERS, Art Gallery, Baltimore. 704.948'2
Liturgical objects in the Walters Art Gallery. Baltimore [1967] 1. v. (unpaged) illus. 24 cm. (A Walters Art Gallery picture book) [N7823.B3W3] 67-9432
1. Christian art and symboilsm — Exhibitions. I. Title. II. Series.

Christian art and symbolism.

BARBOUR, Russell B 704.948
Religious ideas for arts and crafts [by] Russell and Ruth Barbour. Philadelphia, Christian Education Press [1959] 95 p. illus. 28 cm. Includes bibliography. [N7829.5.B3] 59-9446
1. Christian art and symbolism. 2. Art—Study and teaching. Handicraft. I. Barbour, Ruth, joint author. II. Title.

BLES, Arthur de, 1876- 755'.6
How to distinguish the saints in art by their costumes, symbols, and other attributes / by Arthur de Bles. Detroit : Gale Research Co., 1975, c1929. 168 p. : ill. ; 28 cm. Reprint of the ed. published by Art Culture Publications, New York. Includes indexes. Bibliography: p. 163. [N8080.B5 1975] 68-18019 ISBN 0-8103-4125-5
1. Christian art and symbolism. 2. Saints—Art. I. Title.

CHICAGO. Art Institute. 755.2
Masterpieces of religious art; exhibition held in connection with the Second Assembly of the World Council of Churches, July 15 through August 31, 1954. [Chicago, 1954] 60p. (chiefly illus.) 26cm. [N7827.C5] 55-43925
1. Christian art and symbolism. 2. Paintings—Exhibitions. I. World Council of Churches. 2d Assembly, Evanston, Ill. II. Title.

DENNY, Don. 704.948'4
The Annunciation from the right : from early Christian times to the sixteenth century / Don Denny. New York : Garland Pub., 1977. p. cm. (Outstanding dissertations in the fine arts) Originally presented as the author's thesis, New York University, 1965. Bibliography: p. [N8070.D46 1977] 76-23611 ISBN 0-8240-2683-7 lib.bdg. : 32.50
1. Mary, Virgin—Art. 2. Mary, Virgin—Annunciation—Pictorial works. 3. Christian art and symbolism. 4. Christian art and symbolism—Renaissance, 1450-1600. I. Title. II. Series. BIP

DILLENBERGER, Jane. 704.948'2
Secular art with sacred themes. Nashville, Abingdon Press [1969] 143 p. illus. 23 x 26 cm. Bibliography: p. [131]-137. [N7880.D53] 76-87026 7.50
1. Christian art and symbolism. 2. Art, Modern—20th century. I. Title.

ESPINOSA, Jose Edmundo 730.979
Saints in the valleys Christian sacred images in the history, life, and folk art of Spanish New Mexico. Albuquerque, University of New Mexico Press, [c.]1960. xiii, 122p. Bibliography: p.101-107. Introd. by Fray Angelico Chavez illus., endpaper map 32cm. 60-5656 6.50
1. Christian art and symbolism. 2. Saints—Art. 3. Folk art—New Mexico. 4. Art, Spanish-American. 5. New Mexico—Hist. I. Title.

EVANS, Edward Payson, 1831-1917. 726.59
Animal symbolism in ecclesiastical architecture. London, W. Heinemann, 1896. Detroit, Gale Research Co., 1969. xii, 375 p. illus. 22 cm. Bibliography: p. [343]-349. [N7831.E8 1969] 68-18023
1. Christian art and symbolism. 2. Animal sculpture. 3. Church architecture—Details. I. Title. BIP

FERGUSON, George Wells, 1899- 704.9482
Signs & symbols in Christian art. Illus. from paintings of the Renaissance. [Popular ed.: complete and unabridged] New York, Oxford [1961] 123p. illus. (part col.) (Hesperides bk. HS1) 2.95 pap.,
1. Christian art and symbolism. I. Title.

FERGUSON, George Wells, 1899- 704.9482
Signs & symbols in Christian art. With illus. from paintings of the Renaissance. [Popular ed.: complete and unabridged] New York, Oxford University Press [1959] 123 p. illus., plates (part col.) 29 cm. [N7830.F37 1959] 59-4639
1. Christian art and symbolism. I. Title. BIP

HEATH, Sidney Herbert, 1872- 704.948'2
The romance of symbolism and its relation to church ornament and architecture / by Sidney Heath. Detroit : Gale Research Co., 1975. p. cm. Reprint of the 1909 ed. published by F. Griffiths, London. Includes index. [N7831.H4 1975] 70-174054 ISBN 0-8103-4302-9 : 14.00
1. Christian art and symbolism. 2. Church architecture. 3. Church decoration and ornament. I. Title. BIP

HIRN, Yrjo, 1870-1952. 704.9482
The sacred shrine; a study of the poetry and art of the Catholic Church. Boston, Beacon Press [1957] 574p. 22cm. [N7832.H5 1957] 57-1935
1. Christian art and symbolism. 2. Catholic Church.Liturgy and ritual. I. Title.

HULME, Edward. 704.948'2
Symbolism in Christian art / Edward Hulme. Revised and illustrated ed. Poole : Blandford Press, 1976. [6], 225 p. : ill. ; 23 cm. Previous ed., by F. E. Hulme, published under title: The history, principles, and practice of symbolism in Christian art. Includes index. [N8010.H84 1976] 77-378068 ISBN 0-7137-2501-X : 13.95
1. Christian art and symbolism. I. Hulme, Frederick Edward, 1841-1909. The history, principles, and practice of symbolism in Christian art. II. Title.
Distributed by Standing Orders Patterson, New York 12563 BIP

HULME, Frederick Edward, 1841-1909. 704.948'2
The history, principles, and practice of symbolism in Christian art. Detroit, Gale Research Co., 1969. 234 p. illus. 23 cm. Reprint of the 1891 ed. [N7830.H8 1969] 68-18027
1. Christian art and symbolism. I. Title. II. Title: Symbolism in Christian art. BIP

IRELAND, Marion P. 247.7
Textile art in the Church; vestments, paraments, and hangings in contemporary worship, art, and architecture [by] Marion P. Ireland. Nashville, Abingdon Press [1971] 283 p. illus., col. plates. 36 cm. Bibliography: p. 271-275. [NK8810.I7] 70-139750 ISBN 0-687-41363-X 27.50
1. Christian art and symbolism. 2. Textile fabrics. 3. Art, Modern—20th century. I. Title.

JAMESON, Anna Brownell Murphy, 1794-1860. 704.948'52
The history of our Lord as exemplified in works of art : with that of His types, St. John the Baptist, and other persons of the Old and New Testament / commenced by the late Mrs. Jameson, continued and completed by Lady Eastlake. New ed. Detroit : Gale Research Co., 1975. p. cm. Reprint of the 1890 ed. published by Longmans, Green, London. Includes indexes. [N7830.J3 1975] 72-167006 ISBN 0-8103-4304-5 : 29.00(2 vol. set)
1. Jesus Christ—Art. 2. Christian art and symbolism. I. Eastlake, Elizabeth Rigby, Lady, 1809-1893. II. Title.

JAMESON, Anna Brownell (Murphy) 1794-1860. 704.948'2
Sacred and legendary art, by Mrs. Jameson. [1st AMS ed.] New York, AMS Press [1970] 2 v. illus. 23 cm. Reprint of the 1896 ed. [N7830.J2 1970] 71-124594 ISBN 0-404-03551-5
1. Christian art and symbolism. 2. Christian saints in art. I. Title. BIP

JAMESON, Anna Brownell (Murphy) 1794-1860. 704.948'2
Sacred and legendary art. Edited, with additional notes, by Estelle M. Hurll and abundantly illustrated with designs from ancient and modern art. Boston, Houghton-Mifflin, 1896 [c1895] St. Clair Shores, Mich., Scholarly Press, 1972. 2 v. (xliv, 800 p.) illus. 22 cm. "The writings on

art of Anna Jameson." [N7830.J2 1972] 72-145108 ISBN 0-403-01045-4
1. Christian art and symbolism. 2. Christian saints in art. I. Hurll, Estelle May, 1863-1924, ed. II. Title.

LEHMANN, Arno. 704.948'2
Christian art in Africa and Asia. Translators: Erich Hopka, Jalo E. Nopola [and] Otto E. Sohn. Saint Louis, Concordia Pub. House [1969] 283 p. illus. (part col.) 30 cm. Translation of Afroasiatische christliche Kunst. Includes bibliographical references. [N7987.L413] 68-20840 12.50
1. Christian art and symbolism. 2. Art, African. 3. Art, Asian. I. Title.

MALE, Emile, 1862-1954. 704.948'2
The Gothic image; religious art in France in the thirteenth century. Translated by Dora Nussey. New York, Harper [1972] xxiv, 414 p. illus. 22 cm. (Icon editions, IN32) Translation of L'art religieux du XIIIe siecle en France. Includes bibliography. [N7949.M313 1958] pap., 3.95
1. Christian art and symbolism. 2. Art—France—History. 3. Art, Medieval. I. Title.
L.C. card for orig. ed.: 58-10152

MALE, Emile, 1862-1954. 709'.44
Religious art in France, the twelfth century : a study of the origins of medieval iconography / Emile Male. Princeton, N.J. : Princeton University Press, 1977 p. cm. (His Studies in religious iconography) (Bollingen series ; 90:1) Translation of L'art religieux du XIIe siecle en France. Includes bibliographical references and index. [N7949.A1M3413] 72-14029 ISBN 0-691-09912-X : 40.00 pbk. : 3.95
1. Christian art and symbolism. 2. Art, Romanesque—France. 3. Art, French. I. Title. II. Series.

MARTIN, F. David, 1920- 701
Art and the religious experience: the "language" of the sacred [by] F. David Martin. Lewisburg [Pa.] Bucknell University Press [1972] 288 p. illus. 22 cm. Bibliography: p. 258-274. [NX650.C5M3] 75-161508 ISBN 0-8387-7935-2 15.00
1. Christian art and symbolism. 2. The arts—Psychology. I. Title.

MOREY, Charles Rufus, 1877- 704.9483
Early Christian art; an outline of the evolution of style and iconography in sculpture and painting from antiquity to the eigth century. [2d ed.] Princeton, Princeton University Press, 1953. 296p. illus. 31cm. Bibliographical references included in 'Notes' (p. 201-232) [N7832.M67 1953] 53-10141
1. Christian art and symbolism. 2. Sculpture, Medieval. 3. Painting. Medieval. I. Title.

MOREY, Charles Rufus, 1877-1955. 246
Christian art. New York, Norton [1958, c1935] 120p. illus. 21cm. (The Norton library) [N7832.M66 1958] 58-11664
1. Christian art and symbolism. I. Title. BIP

NATHAN, Walter Ludwig, 1905-1961. 246
Art and the message of the church. Philadelphia, Westminster Press [1961] 208p. illus. 21cm. (Westminster studies in Christian communication) Includes bibliography. [N7831.N3] 61-7258
1. Christian art and symbolism. I. Title.

NEWTON, Eric, 1893-1965. 704.9482
2000 years of Christian art [by] Eric Newton and William Neil, New York, Harper & Row [1966] 318 p. illus., facsims., 17 col. plates, ports. 24 cm. [N7830.N4] 66-10230
1. Christian art and symbolism. I. Neil, William, 1909- joint author. II. Title.

NOLAN, James Lee, 1930- 979.4'98
Discovery of the lost art treasures of California's first mission / by James L. Nolan ; commissioned by Helen K. Copley ; edited by Richard F. Pourade. [La Jolla, Calif. : Copley Books, c1978] ix, 118 p. : ill. (some col.) ; 29 cm. Includes bibliographical references and index. [N7910.C2N64] 78-73173 ISBN 0-913938-20-3 : 20.00
1. San Diego mission. 2. Christian art and symbolism—Modern period, 1500- — California. I. Pourade, Richard F. II. Title. BIP

REGAMEY, Raymond, 1900- 200
Religious art in the twentieth century. [New York] Herder and Herder [1963] 256 p. 21 cm. Bibliographical footnotes. [N7831.R413] 63-18157
1. Christian art and symbolism. 2. Art, Modern — 20th cent. I. Title.

SCHAPIRO, Meyer, 1904- 704.948'4
Words and pictures. On the literal and the symbolic in the illustration of a text. The Hague, Mouton, 1973. 74 p. , 34 p. of photos. 23 cm. (Approaches to semiotics. Paperback series, 11) "The substance of this book was presented at a symposium, 'Language, Symbol, Reality', held at St. Mary's College, Notre Dame, Indiana, on November 7, 1969." Includes bibliographical references. [N8020.S32] 73-176481
1. Bible—Pictures, illustrations, etc. 2. Christian art and symbolism. 3. Artists—Psychology. I. Title. II. Series.
Distributed by Humanities Press, 8.25 (pbk.) BIP

SENCOURT, Robert, 1890- 704.948'2
The consecration of genius; an essay to elucidate the distinctive significance and quality of Christian art and literature by analysis and comparison of certain masterpieces. Port Washington, N.Y., Kennikat Press [1970] xxii, 329 p. illus., port. 23 cm. Reprint of the 1947 ed. Includes bibliographical references. [NX650.C5S4 1970] 76-105833
1. Christian art and symbolism. I. Title.

STRZYGOWSKI, Josef, 1862-1941. 709'.02
Origin of Christian church art; new facts and principles of research. Translated from the German by O. M. Dalton and H. J. Braunholtz. New York, Hacker Art Books, 1973. xvii, 267 p. illus. 26 cm. "Eight lectures delivered for the Olaus-Petri Foundation at Upsala, to which is added a chapter on Christian art in Britain." Translation of Ursprung der christlichen Kirchenkunst. Reprint of the 1923 ed. published by the Clarendon Press, Oxford, Eng. Bibliography: p. [253]-259. [NA4800.S72 1973] 72-95118 ISBN 0-87817-127-4 30.00
1. Christian art and symbolism. 2. Church architecture. I. Title.

VAN TREECK, Carl. 246
Symbols in the church [by] Carl Van Treeck and Aloysius Croft. [2d ed.] Milwaukee, Bruce Pub. Co. [c1960] 111 p. illus. 24 cm. [N7830.V3] 61-494
1. Christian art and symbolism. I. Croft, Aloysius, joint author. II. Title.

WATERS, Clara Erskine Clement, 1834-1916. 704.948'2
A handbook of Christian symbols and stories of the saints as illustrated in art. Edited by Katherine E. Conway. Boston, Ticknor, 1886. Detroit, Gale Research Co., 1971. xiv, 349 p. illus. 22 cm. [N8010.W38 1971] 70-159863
1. Christian art and symbolism. 2. Christian saints. I. Title. BIP

WEBBER, Frederick Roth, 1887-1963. 704.948'2
Church symbolism; an explanation of the more important symbols of the Old and New Testament, the primitive, the mediaeval, and the modern church. Introd. by Ralph Adams Cram. 2d ed., rev. Detroit, Gale Research Co., 1971. ix, 413 p. illus. 22 cm. "Facsimile reprint of the 1938 edition." Bibliography: p. 389-394. [BV150.W4 1938a] 79-107627
1. Christian art and symbolism. I. Title. BIP

WILSON, Winefride. 247
Modern Christian art. [1st ed.] New York, Hawthorn Books [1965] 175 p. illus. 22 cm. (The Twentieth century encyclopedia of Catholicism, v. 123. Section 12: Catholicism and the arts) Bibliography: p. [174]-175. [N7831.W5 1965] 65-13399
1. Christian art and symbolism. 2. Art and religion. 3. Art — Hist. — 19th cent. 4. Art — Hist. — 20th cent. I. Title. II. Series: The Twentieth century encyclopedia of Catholicism, v. 123

Christian art and symbolism—Exhibitions.

BUFFALO Fine Arts Academy. 704.948'2
Religious art from Byzantium to Chagall. [The Buffalo Fine Neighbor's Faith. A loan exhibition, December 13, 1964 -- January 10, 1965. Editors: Heather A. Moden and Jan von Adlmann. Buffalo, 1964] 1 v. (unpaged) illus. (part col.) 31 cm. [N7823.B9R4] 67-8035
1. Christian art and symbolism — Exhibitions. 2. Jewish art and symbolism — Exhibitions. I. Your Neighbor's Faith (Group) II. Title.

TARALON, Jean 704.9482
Treasures of the churches of France [by] Jean Taralon with Roseline Maitre Devallon. [Tr. from French by Mira Intrator] New York. Braziller [1966] 304p. illus. (pt. col.) 31cm. Bibl. [NK2190.T313] 66-23097
1. Christian art and symbolism—Exhibitions. 2. Church decoration and ornament—France—Exhibitions. I. Title. BIP

Christian art and symbolism—Handbooks, manuals, etc.

SILL, Gertrude Grace. 704.948'2
A handbook of symbols in Christian art / by Gertrude Grace Sill. New York : Macmillan, 1975. p. cm. Includes index. Bibliography: p. [N8010.S54 1975b] 75-26557 ISBN 0-02-610920-4 : 10.95
1. Christian art and symbolism—Handbooks, manuals, etc. I. Title. BIP

SILL, Gertrude Grace. 704.948'2
A handbook of symbols in Christian art / by Gertrude Grace Sill. New York : Collier Books, 1975. xii, 241 p. : ill. ; 21 cm. Includes index. Bibliography: p. 221. [N8010.S54 1975] 75-26560 ISBN 0-02-000850-3 : 4.95
1. Christian art and symbolism—Handbooks, manuals, etc. I. Title.

Christian art and symbolism—Hist.

APPLETON, LeRoy H 704.948
Symbolism in liturgical art, by LeRoy H. Appleton and Stephen Bridges. Introd. by Maurice Lavanoux. New York, Scribner [1959] 120p. illus. 22cm. [N7825.A7] 59-7203
1. Christian art and symbolism—Dictionaries. I. Bridges, Stephen, joint author. II. Title.

DILLENBERGER, Jane 704.9482
Style and content in Christian art; from the catacombs to the chapel designed by Matisse at Vence, France. Nashville, Abingdon [c.1965] 240p. illus. 23cm. Bibl. [N7830.D63] 65-22293 2.95 pap.,
1. Christian art and symbolism—Hist. I. Title.

MCCLINTON, Katherine (Morrison) 704.9482
Christian church art through the ages. New York, Macmillan [c.]1962. 160p. illus. Bibl. 62-7245 6.50
1. Christian art and symbolism—Hist. I. Title.

RICE, David Talbot, 1903- 704.9482
The beginnings of Christian art. Nashville, Abingdon Press [c1957] 223p. illus., plates (part col.) map (on lining papers) 23cm. Includes bibliographies. [N7832.R48 1957a] 58-1506
1. Christian art and symbolism—Hist. I. Title.

SYNDICUS, Edward, 1915- 709.02
Early Christian art. Translated from the German by J. R. Foster. [1st ed.] New York, Hawthorn Books [1962] 188 p. illus. 21 cm. The Twentieth century encyclopedia of Catholicism, v. 121. Section 12: Catholicism and the arts] [N7832.S953] 62-11412
1. Christian art and symbolism — Hist. 2. Art, Medieval — Hist. I. Title.

Christian art and symbolism—Roman influences.

SWIFT, Emerson Howland, 1889- 723'.1
Roman sources of Christian art, by Emerson H. Swift. Westport, Conn., Greenwood Press [1970, c1951] xx, 248 p. illus., plans, 48 plates. 27 cm. Bibliography: p. [227]-236. [N7831.S9 1970] 73-100181
1. Christian art and symbolism—Roman influences. I. Title. BIP

Christian biography.

MOLNAR, Enrico S., 1913- 741.9'437'1
Five Bohemian windows; historical vignettes in pen and ink, by Enrico S. Molnar. Los Angeles, 1965. [16] p. illus. 22 cm. Cover title. [BR1700.2.M63] 75-284599
1. Christian biography. 2. Bohemia—Biography. I. Title.

Christian IV, King of Denmark and Norway, 1577-1648.

*SKOVGAARD, Joakim A. 724.1
A king's architecture; Christian IV and his buildings, [by] Joakim A. Skougaard. London, Hugh Evelyn [1974, c1973] viii, 143 p. illus. 26 cm. Bibliography: p. 136-139. [NA1215] ISBN 0-8277-2830-1
1. Christian IV, King of Denmark and Norway, 1577-1648. 2. Architecture, Renaissance. I. Title.
Distributed by British Book Centre, Elmsford, N.Y. for 25.00 BIP

Christian martyrs in art.

LUIKEN, Jan, 1649-1712. 769'.92'4
The drama of the martyrs : from the death of Jesus Christ up to the recent times / drawn and engraved on copper by Jan Luyken ; with an introductory essay by Jan Gleysteen. Lancaster, Pa. : Mennonite Historical Associates, [1975] 141 p. : chiefly ill. ; 19 x 25 cm. Illustrations originally published in the 2d ed., 1685, of Het bloedig tooneel ... by T. J. van Bracht, and subsequently published separately under title: Theatre des martyrs .... [NE670.L8A43] 75-12518 pbk. : 5.95
1. Luiken, Jan, 1649-1712. 2. Christian martyrs in art. I. Bracht, Tieleman Janszoon van, 1625-1664. Het bloedig tooneel. II. Title.

Christian saints in art.

AHLBORN, Richard E. 731'.88'6
The sculpted saints of a borderland mission : los bultos de San Xavier del Bac : with notes on the statues of Tumacacori / by Richard Eigme Ahlborn ; photos. by Helga Teiwes-French. Tucson, Ariz. : Southwestern Mission Research Center, 1974. 124 p. : ill. ; 29 cm. Cover title: Saints of San Xavier. Bibliography: p. 121-124. [NB230.A6A34] 74-18171 ISBN 0-915076-03-9
1. San Xavier del Bac Mission. 2. Christian saints in art. 3. Sculpture, Baroque—Arizona. 4. Sculpture, Spanish American—Arizona. I. Title. II. Title: Saints of San Xavier.

DRAKE, Maurice, 1875-1923. 704.948'6
Saints and their emblems, by Maurice & Wilfred Drake. Illustrated by 12 plates from photos. and drawings by Wilfred Drake. With a foreword by Aymer Vallance. London, T. W. Laurie, 1916. Detroit, Gale Research Co., 1971. xiii, 235 p. illus. 30 cm. [N8080.D7 1971b] 68-18021
1. Christian saints in art. 2. Emblems. I. Drake, Wilfred James, 1879-1948, joint author. II. Title. BIP

DRAKE, Maurice, 1875-1923. 704.948'6
Saints and their emblems, by Maurice & Wilfred Drake. Illustrated by XII plates from photos. and drawings by Wilfred Drake. With a foreword by Aymer Vallance. New York, B. Franklin [1971] xiii, 235 p. illus. 32 cm. (Burt Franklin research & source works series, 705)

Reprint of the 1916 ed. [N8080.D7 1971] 78-122225 ISBN 0-8337-0902-X
1. Christian saints in art. 2. Emblems. I. Drake, Wilfred James, 1879-1948, joint author. II. Title.

JAMESON, Anna Brownell Murphy, 1794-1860. 704.948'6
Legends of the monastic orders as represented in the fine arts. Forming the second series of sacred and legendary art. London, New York, Longmans, Green, 1905. Detroit, Gale Research Co., 1974. p. cm. [N8080.J4 1974] 74-19210 ISBN 0-8103-4093-3
1. Christian saints in art. 2. Monasticism and religious orders. 3. Christian art and symbolism. I. Title. BIP

JAMESON, Anna Brownell Murphy, 1794-1860. 704.948'6
Legends of the monastic orders, as represented in the fine arts : forming the second series of sacred and legendary art / by Mrs. Jameson. New York : AMS Press, 1978. xv, 489 p. : port. ; 19 cm. Reprint of the corr. and enl. ed. published by Ticknor and Fields, Boston, 1866. [N8080.J4 1978] 75-41154 ISBN 0-404-14767-4 : 26.00
1. Christian saints in art. 2. Monasticism and religious orders. 3. Christian art and symbolism. I. Title.

VLIEGHE, Hans. 759.9493 s
Saints. [Translated from the Dutch, by P. S. Falla] London, New York, Phaidon [distributed in the USA by Praeger, New York, 1972-73] 2 v. illus. 27 cm. (Corpus Rubenianium Ludwig Burchard, pt. 8) Includes bibliographical references. [ND673.R9C63 pt. 8] [N6973.R9] 759.9493 72-185770 ISBN 0-7148-1505-5 (v. 1) 42.50 (U.S.) (v. 2)
1. Rubens, Peter Paul, Sir, 1577-1640. 2. Christian saints in art. I. Title. II. Series.

WATERS, Clara Erskine Clement, 1834-1916. 704.948'6
Saints in art. Boston, L. C. Page. Detroit, Gale Research Co., 1974 [c1899] 428 p. illus. 18 cm. Original ed. issued in series: Art lovers' series. [N8080.W32 1974] 77-89303 ISBN 0-8103-3030-X 14.00
1. Christian saints—Art. I. Title. II. Series: Art lovers' series.

Christianity and the arts.

ROOKMAAKER, Hendrik Roelof, 1922-1977. 701
Art needs no justification / H. R. Rookmaaker. Downers Grove, Ill. : Inter-Varsity Press, c1978. 61 p. ; 22 cm. Includes bibliographical references. [BR115.A8R66 1978] 78-13798 ISBN 0-87784-323-6 : 1.95
1. Christianity and the arts. 2. Artists—Psychology. I. Title. BIP

Christmas.

BEILENSON, Edna, 1909- 394.268
The Christmas stocking book. Drawn by Vee Guthrie. Mount Vernon, N. Y., Peter Pauper Press [1957] 60p. illus. 19cm. [TT155.B46] 57-43258
1. Christmas. 2. Handicraft. 3. Cookery. I. Title.

Christmas cards.

BUDAY, Gyorgy, 1907- 741.68
The history of the Christmas card, by George Buday. London, Rockliff [1954] Detroit, Tower Books, 1971. xxiii, 304 p. illus. 23 cm. Includes bibliographical references. [NC1866.C5B8 1971] 74-174012
1. Christmas cards. I. Title. BIP

MCGOWAN, Harold, 1909- 730'.92'4
The spirit of Christmas in words and sculpture : Christmas cards / by Harold McGowan ; introd. by Lee Marc Stein. 1st ed. Central Islip, N.Y. : Metaprobe Institute, [1974] 96 p. (p. 95-96 advertisements) : col. ill. ; 26 cm. [NC1868.M32A56] 74-81246 ISBN 0-682-48082-7 : 35.00
1. McGowan, Harold, 1909- 2. Christmas cards. I. Title.
Publisher's address: 900 S. Oyster Bay Rd. Hicksville, New York 11801.

PERRY, Margaret Curtiss. 745.59'41
Christmas card magic; the art of making decorations and ornaments with Christmas cards. Photos. and drawings by the author. [1st ed.] Garden City, N.Y., Doubleday, 1967. 127 p. illus., col. plates. 22 cm. [TT870.P47] 67-19802
1. Christmas cards. 2. Christmas decorations. 3. Paper work. I. Title.

Christmas in art.

THE Christmas book / 741.65
edited by David Larkin. 1st U.S. ed. New York : Scribner, 1975. [96] p. : chiefly col. ill. ; 31 cm. "An original Peacock Press/Bantam book." [NC968.5.C45C47 1975] 75-11193 ISBN 0-684-14417-4 : 10.00
1. Christmas in art. 2. Magazine illustration. 3. Illustration of books. I. Larkin, David. BIP

HOOPER, Van B., 1897- ed. 759.9
A treasure of Christmas religious art. Milwaukee, Ideals [1962]c.1961. unpaged. col. illus. 29cm. 1.50 bds.,
I. Title.

NAST, Thomas, 1840-1902. 741.9'73
Thomas Nast's Christmas drawings / by Thomas Nast ; with an introd. by Thomas Nast St. Hill. New York : Dover Publications, 1978. viii, 69 p. : chiefly ill. ; 29 cm. Reprint of the 1890 ed. published by Harper, New York, under title: Thomas Nast's Christmas drawings for the human race: with new introd. [NC139.N3A4 1978] 78-52251 ISBN 0-486-23660-9 pbk. : 3.50
1. Nast, Thomas, 1840-1902. 2. Christmas in art. I. Title. II. Title: Christmas drawings. BIP

WESTMAN, Barbara. 759.13
A Beacon Hill Christmas / by Barbara Westman. Boston : Houghton Mifflin, 1976. 41 p. : col. ill. ; 27 cm. [ND237.W54A42] 76-18147 ISBN 0-395-24726-8 : 8.95
1. Westman, Barbara. 2. Christmas in art. 3. Beacon Hill, Boston—Pictorial works. 4. Boston in art. I. Title. BIP

Christmas—Pictorial works.

CURRIER and Ives. 769'.92'4
Christmas in the country / Currier & Ives ; edited by Margery Darrell. 1st ed. Princeton [N.J.] : Pyne Press, [1974] [59] p. : ill. (some col.) ; 22 x 26 cm. [NE2312.C8D37] 74-80489 ISBN 0-87861-078-2 : 6.95
1. Currier and Ives. 2. Christmas—Pictorial works. I. Darrell, Margery, ed. II. Title.

FORD, Lauren, 1891- 759.13
Lauren Ford's Christmas book. Text and pictures by Lauren Ford. Scripture from the Gospel of St. Luke. New York, Dodd, Mead [1963] 1 v. (unpaged) illus. (part col.) 20 x 25 cm. Full name: Julia Lauren Ford. [ND237.F49A5] 63-18780
I. Title. II. Title: Christmas book.

NAST, Thomas, 1840-1902. 741.9'73
Christmas drawings for the human race. With introd. and epilogue by Thomas Nast St. Hill. [1st ed.] New York, Harper & Row [1971] 126 p. illus. 29 cm. Reprint of the 1890 ed. (p. [53]-[98]) with new introd. and afterword. [NC139.N3S2 1971] 70-160650 ISBN 0-06-013157-8 7.50
1. Christmas—Pictorial works. I. Title.

Christo, 1935-

CHRISTO, 1935- 730'.92'4
Christo. Text by David Bourdon. New York, H. N. Abrams [1972] 321 p. illus. 28 x 30 cm. Bibliography: p. 321. [NB893.C5B6] 70-165543 ISBN 0-8109-0051-3 35.00
I. Bourdon, David. BIP

CHRISTO, 1935- 730'.924
Christo [by] Lawrence Alloway. New York, Abrams [1970, c1969] xi, [12] p., 71 illus. (3 col.) 21 x 23 cm. (Modern artists) Bibliography: p. [5]-[8] [NB893.C5A7 1970] 72-82873 5.95
I. Alloway, Lawrence, 1900-

CHRISTO, 1935- 709'.2'4
Christo: Valley Curtain, Rifle, Colorado, 1970-72. Photos.: Harry Shunk. [1st ed.] New York, H. N. Abrams [1973] 1 v. (chiefly illus., part col.) 31 cm. [N7193.C5A43] 73-173891 ISBN 0-8109-0050-5 35.00
1. Christo, 1935- 2. Art—Rifle, Colo. I. Title. II. Title: Valley Curtain, Rifle, Colorado, 1970-72.

CHRISTO, 1935- 709'.2'4
Christo's running fence / photos. by Gianfranco Gorgoni ; pref. by Calvin Tomkins ; captions by David Bourdon. New York : Abrams, 1978. p. cm. [N7193.C5A44] 77-13109 ISBN 0-8109-0761-5 pbk. : 9.95
1. Christo, 1935- Running fence. I. Title.

PENNSYLVANIA. University. Institute of Contemporary Art. 709'.24
Christo; monuments and projects. [Exhibit] October 5 to November 11, 1968. Philadelphia [1968] [16] p. illus. 23 cm. Bibliography: p. [14]-[15] [NB623.C38P4] 70-97
1. Christo, 1935-

Christodoulos, Constantine.

SBORONOS, Ioannes N., 1863-1922. 737.4
Christodoulos the counterfeiter / J. Svoronos. Chicago : Ares Publishers, 1974. 38 p. [9] leaves of plates : ill. ; 28 cm. Consists of the original French text published in Athens in 1922 under title: C. Christodoulos et les faussaires d'Athenes and an English translation. [CJ245.S2613 1974] 74-77899
1. Christodoulos, Constantine. 2. Coins, Ancient. 3. Counterfeits and counterfeiting. I. Title.

Christy, Howard Chandler, 1873-1952—Exhibitions.

CHRISTY, Howard Chandler, 1873-1952. 760'.092'4
Howard Chandler Christy, artist/illustrator of style : September 25 through November 6, 1977, Allentown Art Museum. [Allentown, Pa.] : The Museum, c1977. [56] p. : ill. (some col.) ; 28 cm. Catalogue of the exhibition. [N6537.C4973A4 1977] 77-74176
1. Christy, Howard Chandler, 1873-1952—Exhibitions. I. Allentown, Pa. Art Museum. II. Title.

Chromolithography—France.

CATE, Phillip Dennis. 764'.2'0944
The color revolution : color lithography in France, 1890-1900 / by Phillip Dennis Cate and Sinclair Hitchings ; with a translation by Margaret Needham of Andre Mellerio's 1898 essay La lithographie originale en couleurs. Santa Barbara : P. Smith, 1978. p. cm. [NE2500.C37] 78-13809 pbk. : 9.95
1. Chromolithography—France. I. Hitchings, Sinclair H., joint author. II. Mellerio, Andre, 1862- La lithographie originale en couleurs. English. 1978. III. Title.

Chryssa, Varda, 1933—

CHRYSSA, Varda, 1933- 730'.924
Chryssa: selected works, 1955-1967, by Diane Waldman. New York, Pace Gallery [1968] 48 p. illus. 23 cm. Bibliography: p. 47-48. [NB237.C48W3] 68-22600
I. Waldman, Diane. II. Pace Gallery. III. Title.

CHRYSSA, Vordo, 1933- 709'.2'4
Chryssa / Pierre Restany ; translated by John Shepley. New York : H. N. Abrams, [1977] p. cm. (Contemporary artists series) Includes index. Bibliography: p. [NB237.C48R4713] 77-1916 ISBN 0-8109-0366-0 : 45.00
1. Chryssa, Varda, 1933- I. Restany, Pierre. II. Title. III. Series.

HUNTER, Sam, 1923- 730'.92'4
Chryssa. New York, H. N. Abrams [1974] [NB237.C48H86] 74-6199 7.50 (pbk.)
1. Chryssa, Varda, 1933- BIP

Chumley, John, 1928—

NORTON (R. W.) Art Gallery. 759.13
John Chumley's rural America; a retrospective exhibition, October 1-November 5, 1972. [Shreveport, La., 1972] 36 p. illus. (part col.) 28 cm. [ND1839.C56N67] 76-187913 ISBN 0-913060-00-3
1. Chumley, John, 1928- I. Title. BIP

Chun, Soo Ja, 1942—

CHUN, Soo Ja, 1942- 759.9519
Soo Ja Chun. [Edited by Judson Rosebush] Syracuse, N.Y., Everson Museum of Art [1973] [8] p. illus. 21 x 24 cm. Cover title. Catalog of an exhibition held June 23-Aug. 20, 1973. "Sponsored in part by the New York State Council on the Arts." [ND2073.6.Z8C48] 73-84245
1. Chun, Soo Ja, 1942- I. Rosebush, Judson, ed. II. Everson Museum of Art of Syracuse and Onondaga County. III. New York (State). State Council on the Arts.

Church architecture.

ARCHITECTURAL record. 726.5
Religious buildings for today; edited by John Knox Shear. [New York] F. W. Dodge Corp., c1957. 183p. illus. 20cm. (An Architectural record book) Articles previously published in issues of Architectural record. [NA4600.A7] 57-9272
1. Church architecture. 2. Churches. 3. Synagogues. I. Shear, John Knox, ed. II. Title.

BETTS, Darby Wood, 1912- ed. 726
Architecture and the church. With a foreword by G. Ashton Oldham. Greenwich, Conn., Seabury Press, 1952. 55p. illus. 24cm. 'An official publication of the Joint Commission on Architecture and the Allied Arts.' Includes bibliography. [NA4800.B42] 52-14237
1. Church architecture. I. Protestant Episcopal Church in the U. S. A. Joint Commission on Architecture and the Allied Arts. II. II. Title.

BIELER, Andre. 726.5
Architecture in worship: the Christian place of worship; a sketch of the relationships between the theology of worship and the architectural conception of Christian churches from the beginnings to our day. With an essay by Karl Barth: The architectural problem of Protestant places of worship. 45 original drawings by R. Schaffert. Translated by Odette and Donald Elliott. Philadelphia, Westminster Press [1965] x, 96 p. plans. 20 cm. Translation of Liturgie et architecture. Bibliographical footnotes. [NA4800.B533] 65-10153
1. Church architecture. 2. Architecture and religion. 3. Christian art and symbolism. I. Title.

BRIEFS for church 726.5
builders. no. 1- [New York, 1956- v. illus. 28cm. 'Published for the Dept. of Church Building, National Council of the Churches of Christ in the U. S. A. by the Office of Publication and Distribution.' [NA4800.B66] 56-12948
1. Church architecture. I. National Council of the Churches of Christ in the United States of America. Dept. of Church Building.

BRUGGINK, Donald J 726.5855
Christ and architecture; building Presbyterian Reformed churches [by] Donald J. Bruggink [and] Carl H. Droppers. Grand Rapids, Eerdmans [1965] ix, 708 p. illus., plans. 23 cm. Bibliography: p. [691]-693. [NA4800.B69] 63-11498
1. Church architecture. 2. Churches, Presbyterian. 3. Churches. Reformed. I. Droppers, Carl H., joint author. II. Title. BIP

CHRISTIAN herald (New York, 1878-). 726.5
Church builder. [New York, 1950] 64 p. illus., plans. 28 cm. Cover title. "Compiled ... by the editors of Christian herald from material previously appearing in that magazine." [NA4800.C45] 51-1627

1. Church architecture. 2. Church architecture—Designs and plans. I. Title.

CHRIST-JANER, Albert William, 1910- 726.5
Modern church architecture; a guide to the form and spirit of 20th century religious buildings, by Albert Christ-Janer, Mary Mix Foley. New York, Dodge Bk. Dept., McGraw, 1962. 333p. illus. 30cm. (Dodge bks.) 61-8035 9.75
1. Church architecture. 2. Church decoration and ornament. I. Foley, Mary Mix, joint author. II. Title.

CLARK, William Samuel, 1919- 726.5
Building the new church. Jenkintown, Pa., Religious Pub. Co., 1957. 68p. illus. 22cm. Includes bibliography. [NA4800.C55] 57-14821
1. Church architecture. I. Title.

CLARK, William Samuel, 1919- ed. 726
Planning church buildings, by Philip M. Larson, Jr. [and others] Jenkintown, Pa., Foundation Books, 1962. 63p. 22cm. [NA4800.C56] 62-15398
1. Church architecture. I. Larson, Philip M. II. Title.

COPE, Gilbert Frederick, ed. 726.583
Making the building serve the liturgy: studies in the reordering of churches. Pref. by the Bishop of Woolwich. London, A. R. Mowbray [dist. Westminister, M.D. Cantebury Pr., c.1962] 71p. plans. 26cm. Bibl. 63-868 3.75
1. Church architecture. 2. Liturgics. I. Title.

DAHINDEN, Justus. 726
New trends in church architecture [1st Amer. ed.] New York, Universe [1967,i.e. 1968] 144p. illus. plans. 24cm. Tr. of Bauen fur die Kirche in der Welt. [NA4825 D313] 67-14876 10.00
1. Church architecture. 2. Architecture, Modern—20th cent. I. Title.

FILTHAUT, Theodor. 726'.58'2
Church architecture and liturgical reform. With a foreword by Robert W. Hovda. Translated by Gregory Roettger. Baltimore, Helicon [1968] 109 p. illus., plans. 21 cm. (A Challenge book) Translation of Kirchenbau and liturglereform. [NA4800.F5513] 67-13791
1. Church architecture. 2. Christian art and symbolism. I. Title.

FREY, Edward Snively 726.5
This before architecture. Introd. by Harold E. Wagoner. Lenkintown. Pa. Foundation Bks. 122 Old York Rd. [c.]1963 127p. illus. 24cm. 63-14304 3.50
1. Church architecture. I. Title.

GIESELMANN, Reinhard 726.5
Kirchenbau [by] Reinhard Gieselmann, Werner Aebli. [dist. New York, Heinman, 1961, c.1959] 151p. illus., plans. Bibl. 60-44215 9.00
1. Church architecture. I. Aebli, Werner, joint author. II. Title.

HAMILTON, John Arnott. 723'.2
Byzantine architecture and decoration. Freeport, N.Y., Books for Libraries Press [1972] vi, 172 p. illus. 23 cm. Reprint of the 1933 ed. Bibliography: p. 155-165. [NA4829.B9H3 1972] 77-39658 ISBN 0-8369-9937-1
1. Church architecture. 2. Architecture, Byzantine. 3. Church decoration and ornament, Byzantine. I. Title. BIP

HAMMOND, Peter, 1921- 726.5
Liturgy and architecture. Foreword by F. W. Dillistone. New York, Columbia, 1961[c.1960] 191p. illus. Bibl. 61-17294 6.00
1. Church architecture. 2. Liturgies. I. Title. BIP

HARRELL, William Asa, 1903- 726.5
Planning better church buildings. Rev. ed. Nashville, Convention Press [1957] 132p. illus. 22cm. [NA4800.H3 1957] 57-6332
1. Church architecture. 2. Church architecture—Designs and plans. I. Title.

HENZE, Anton. 726.5
Contemporary church art, by Anton Henze and Thedoor Filthaut. Translated by Cecily Hastings; edited by Maurice Lavanoux. New York, Sheed & Ward [1956] 64, 128p. (p. 3-127 illus.) 29cm. [NA4800.H442] 56-9527
1. Church architecture. 2. Church decoration and ornament. I. Filthaut, Theodor. II. Title.
Contents omitted.

LUTHERAN Church-Missouri Synod. Commission on Church Architecture. 726.5841
Architecture and the church. Bernard W. Guenther, chairman. St. Louis, Concordia [c.1965] 85p. illus. 28cm. [NA4800.L83] 65-22698 3.00 pap.,
1. Church architecture. I. Guenther, Bernard W. II. Title.

MCCLINTON, Katharine (Morrison) 726.5
The changing church; its architecture, art, and decoration. New York, Morehouse-Gorham Co., 1957. 144p. illus. 28cm. Includes bibliography. [NA4800.M2] 57-7178
1. Church architecture. 2. Church decoration and ornament. 3. Churches—U.S. I. Title. BIP

MAGUIRE, Robert Alfred 726.5
Modern churches of the world [by] Robert Maguire, Keith Murray. [London, Studio Vista, Ltd., New York, Dutton, c.1965] 160p. illus., plans. 19cm. (Dutton Vista pictureback, 10) Bibl. [NA4815.M3] 65-3480 1.75 pap.,
1. Church architecture. 2. Churches. I. Murray, Keith, joint author. II. Title.

MILLS, Edward David. 726.5
The modern church. New York, Praeger [1956] 188, [1] p. illus., diagrs., plans. 25 cm. (Books that matter) Bibliography: p. 187-[189] [NA4800.M5 1956a] 55-12018
1. Church architecture. 2. Church architecture—Designs and plans. 3. Churches. I. Title.

NOTRE Dame, Ind. University. 726.082
Seminar on symbolism as applied to church art and architecture, a report. [Held at the Morris Inn, University of Notre Dame, July 12-14, 1957. [Notre Dame, Ind.] c1957, 1v. (various pagings) 29cm. [NA4800.N6 1957c] 58-22111
1. Church architecture. 2. Christian art and symbolism. I. Title.

PROTESTANT Episcopal Church in the U. S. A. Joint Commission on Architecture and the Allied Arts. 726.5
Church buildings and furnishings; a survey of requirements. Edited by Jonathan G. Sherman. Greenwich, Conn., Seabury Press, 1958. 130p. illus. 24cm. Includes bibliography. [NA4800.P75] 58-10391
1. Church architecture. 2. Theology—Dictionaries. I. Sherman, Jonathan Goodhue, ed. II. Title.

SCHWARZ, Rudolf, 1897- 726.5
The church incarnate; the sacred function of Christian architecture. Translated by Cynthia Harris. Chicago, H. Regnery Co. [1958] 231p. illus. 26cm. Translation of Vom Bal der Kirche. [NA4800.S3513] 58-10536
1. Church architecture. I. Title.

THIRY, Paul, 1904- 726
Churches & temples, by Paul Thiry, Richard M. Bennett, and Henry L. Kamphoefner. Illus. in historical pref. and Protestant church sections by Duncan R. Stuart. New York, Reinhold Pub. Corp. [1954, c1953] 1 v. (various pagings) illus., plans. 31cm. (Progressive architecture library) Includes bibliography (5 p.) [NA4600.T47] 52-6116
1. Church architecture. 2. Synagogues. I. Title.

Church architecture—Boston.

TUCCI, Douglass Shand. 917.44'61
Church building in Boston, 1720-1970 : with an introduction to the work of Ralph Adams Cram and the Boston Gothicists : issued by the trustees of the Dorchester Savings Bank in observation of the Bicentennial of the United States / Douglass Shand Tucci. 1st ed. Concord [Mass.] : Rumford Press, 1974. 134 p. : ill. (some col.) ; 21 x 21 cm. Includes bibliographical references and index. [NA5235.B7T82] 75-314879 7.50
1. Cram, Ralph Adams, 1863-1942. 2. Church architecture—Boston. 3. Gothic revival (Architecture)—Boston. I. Dorchester Savings Bank. II. Title. BIP

Church architecture—California.

NEWCOMB, Rexford, 1886-1968. 726'.9
The Franciscan mission architecture of Alta California. New York, Dover Publications [1973] xiii, 74 p. of plates. 29 cm. Reprint of the 1916 ed. [NA5230.C2N48 1973] 72-80877 ISBN 0-486-21740-X 3.00
1. Church architecture—California. 2. Spanish missions of California. I. Title. BIP

Church architecture—Cotswold Hills.

VEREY, David, 1913- 914.24'17'04857
Cotswold churches / David Verey. London : B. T. Batsford, 1976. 200 p., [16] leaves of plates : ill. ; 23 cm. Includes bibliographical references and index. [NA5495.C67V47] 76-361445 ISBN 0-7134-3054-0 : £5.50
1. Church architecture—Cotswold Hills. 2. Churches—England—Cotswold Hills—Guide-books. I. Title.

Church architecture—Designs and plans.

GIESELMANN, Reinhard. 726'.5'0904
New churches. New York, Architectural Book Pub. Co. [1972] 173 p. illus. 29 cm. English and German. [NA4825.G53 1972] 72-171014 ISBN 0-8038-0185-8 20.00
1. Church architecture—Designs and plans. 2. Architecture, Modern—20th century. I. Title.

SEVENTH-DAY Adventists. General Conference. 726.5867
Planning church and church school buildings. Washington, Review and Herald Pub. Association [1953] 151p. illus. 31cm. Bibliography: p. 151. [NA4821.S4A5] 53-39882
1. Church architecture—Designs and plans. I. Title.

UPJOHN, Richard, 1802-1878. 720
Upjohn's rural architecture; designs, working drawings, and specifications for a wooden church, and other rural structures. New York, Da Capo Press, 1974, [i.e.1975] [13] p., 25 plates. 31 x 43 cm. (Da Capo Press series in architecture and decorative art) Reprint of the ed. published by Putnam, New York. [NA4811.U7 1975] 74-16022 ISBN 0-306-70639-3 29.50 (lib. bdg.)
1. Church architecture—Designs and plans. 2. Building, Wooden. I. Title. BIP

Church architecture—Dorset, Eng.

MORSHEAD, Owen Frederick, Sir, 1893- 942.3'3
Dorset churches / by Sir Owen Morshead. Dorchester : Dorset Historic Churches Trust, 1975. 64 p. : ill., map, ports. ; 25 cm. [NA5469.D7M67] 76-350410 ISBN 0-9504432-0-4 : £0.60
1. Church architecture—Dorset, Eng. 2. Churches—England—Dorset—Guide-books. I. Title.

Church architecture—England.

BOWEN, David. 726'.5'0942
Looking at churches / David Bowen. Newton Abbot ; North Pomfret, Vt. : David and Charles, 1976. 127 p. : ill., plans ; 22 cm. (David & Charles leisure & travel series) Includes index. Bibliography: p. 124. [NA5461.B74] 76-8622 ISBN 0-7153-7011-1 : 4.95
1. Church architecture—England. 2. Church architecture—Details. I. Title.

†BOWYER, Jack. 726'.5'0942
The evolution of church building / Jack Bowyer. New York : Whitney Library of Design, 1977. viii, 139 p. : ill., plans ; 24cm. Includes index. [NA5461.B746 1977b] 77-89256 ISBN 0-8230-7163-4 : 14.95
1. Church architecture—England. I. Title.

CLARKE, Basil Fulford Lowther. 726'.5'0942
Church builders of the nineteenth century; a study of the Gothic revival in England, by Basil F. L. Clarke. With a pref. by Sir Charles Nicholson. New York, A. M. Kelley, 1969. xx, 296 p. illus., ports. 23 cm. Reprint of the 1938 ed. with new pref., corrections, and annotations by the author. Bibliographical footnotes. [NA5467.C55 1969] 69-10849
1. Church architecture—England. 2. Gothic revival (Architecture)—England. I. Title. BIP

CLARKE, Basil Fulford Lowther. 726'.5'0942
English churches [by] Basil Clarke and John Betjeman. New York, London House & Maxwell [1964] 208 p. illus. 26 cm. "Basil Clarke has been mainly responsible for the text, and John Betjeman for the choice of illustrations." [NA5461.C47 1964b] 64-25398
1. Church architecture—England. 2. Churches—England. I. Betjeman, John, 1906- II. Title. BIP

COX, John Charles, 1843-1919 726.50942
Parish churches [by] J. C. Cox, C. B. Ford. Rev. by Bryan Little [Dist. New York, Norton, 1962, c.1961] 187p. illus. (Batsford paperbacks, 5) First pub. in 1934 under title: The parish churches of England. 62-2137 1.50 pap.,
1. Church architecture—England. 2. Church furniture. 3. Churches—England. I. Ford, Charles Bradley, joint author. II. Title.

DURANT, Gladys May 726.50942
Landscape with churches. London, Museum Pr. [Chester Springs, Pa., Dufour 1966, c.1965] 224p. illus. 23cm. Bibl. [NA5463.D8] 66-4084 6.95
1. Church architecture—England. 2. Architecture, Medieval. 3. Church decoration and ornament. 4. Decoration and ornament. Medieval. I. Title.

JONES, Lawrence Elmore. 726.50942
The observer's book of old English churches, by Lawrence E. Jones. Describing the principal exterior & interior features, with 44 plates from photos, and text drawings by A.S.B. New. London, New York. F. Warne [1965] x. 214 p. illus. (part col.) plans. 15 cm. (The Observer's pocket series, 36) Bibliography: p. 207-208. [NA5461.J6] 65-15723
1. Church architecture—England. 2. Churches—England. I. Title. II. Series. BIP

MOORE, Charles Herbert, 1840-1930. 726'.5'0942
The mediaeval church architecture of England With twenty-three plates in half-tone and one hundred and forty-nine illustrations in the text. Freeport, N.Y., Books for Libraries Press [1972] xxiii, 237 p. illus. 23 cm. Reprint of the 1912 ed. [NA5463.M6 1972] 74-37900 ISBN 0-8369-6738-0
1. Church architecture—England. 2. Architecture, Medieval—England. I. Title. BIP

Church architecture—England—Essex—Conservation and restoration.

ESSEX, Eng. County Planning Dept. 726'.5'094267
Redundant churches in Essex / [prepared by Christine Couchman and John Hedges]. Chelmsford : [Essex County Planning Department], 1976. [2], 49 p. : ill., forms, map, plans ; 30 cm. Bibliography: p. 46-47. [NA5469.E8E87 1976] 77-363476 ISBN 0-901355-69-0 : £1.00
1. Church architecture—England—Essex—Conservation and restoration. 2. Churches—England—Essex. I. Couchman, Christine. II. Hedges, John. III. Title.

Church architecture—England—Hist.

FISHER, Ernest Arthur 726.50942
The greater Anglo-Saxon churches; an architectural historical study. London,

University of California Press, 1962. xxii, 126 p. illus., 163 plates (part col.) maps, plans. 29 cm. Bibliography: p. [70]-78. [NA5253.B3] 62-13073
1. Church architecture—Mexico—History. 2. Churches—Mexico. I. Rudinger, Hugo, illus. II. Title. BIP

Church architecture—New England—History.

MAZMANIAN, Arthur B. 726'.5'0974
The structure of praise; a design study architecture for religion in New England from the 17th century to the present [by] Arthur B. Mazmanian. Boston, Beacon Press [1970] 151 p. illus. 26 cm. [NA5215.M38 1970] 74-101323 19.95
1. Church architecture—New England—History. I. Title.

MAZMANIAN, Arthur B. 726'.5'0974
The structure of praise; a design study architecture for religion in New England from the 17th century to the present. Barre, Mass., Barre Publishers [1973, c.1970] 151 p. illus. 26 cm. [NA5215.M38] ISBN 0-8271-7260-5 5.95 (pbk.)
1. Church architect—New Negland—History. I. Title.
L.C. card no. for the hardbound ed.: 74-101323.

Church architecture—New Mexico.

KUBLER, George, 1912- 726'.5'09789
The religious architecture of New Mexico; in the colonial period and since the American occupation. [4th ed.] Albuquerque, Published for the School of American Research by University of New Mexico Press [1973, c1940] xxvii, 232 p. illus., col. fold. map (in pocket) 31 cm. Originally presented as the author's thesis, Yale, 1940. Bibliography: p. [149]-159. [NA5230.N6K8 1973] 72-86823 15.00
1. Church architecture—New Mexico. 2. Spanish missions of New Mexico. 3. Churches—New Mexico. I. Title.

KUBLER, George, 1912- 726.509789
Religious architecture of New Mexico. [Chicago, Rio Grande Press, 1962] xxi, 232 p. illus., maps, plans. 29 cm. (A Rio Grande classic) Reproduction of the 1940 ed., published by Taylor Museum, Colorado Springs, issued as thesis, Yale University, in the series, Contributions of the Taylor Museum of the Colorado Springs Fine Art Center. Full name: George Alexander Kubler. Bibliography: p. [149] -- 159. [NA5230.N6K8] 62-20277
1. Church architecture — New Mexico. 2. Spanish missions of New Mexico. 3. Churches — New Mexico. I. Title. BIP

KUBLER, George Alexander, 1912- 726.509789
Religious architecture of New Mexico. [Chicago, Rio Grande, 1963, c.1940] xxi, 232p. illus., maps, plans. 29cm. (Rio Grande classic) Reproduction of the 1940 ed., pub. by Taylor Museum, Colorado Springs, issued as thesis, Yale Univ., in the series, Contributions of the Taylor Museum of the Colorado Springs Fine Art Center. Bibl. 62-20277 12.00
1. Church architecture—New Mexico. 2. Spanish missions of New Mexico. 3. Churches—New Mexico. I. Title.

Church architecture—Norfolk, Eng. (County)

MANSFIELD, H. O., 1901- 942.6'1
Norfolk churches : their foundations, architecture, and furnishings / by H. O. Mansfield ; foreword by Lady Harrod. Lavenham [Eng.] : T. Dalton, 1976. 207 p. : ill. ; 24 cm. Includes index. Bibliography: p. 198-199. [NA5469.N5M36] 76-376403 ISBN 0-900963-57-3 : £6.80
1. Church architecture—Norfolk, Eng. (County) 2. Churches—England—Norfolk (County) I. Title. BIP

Church architecture—Oaxaca, Mexico (State)

MULLEN, Robert James. 726'.5'09727
Dominican architecture in sixteenth century Oaxaca, by Robert James Mullen. [Tempe] Center for Latin American Studies, Arizona State University, 1975. xix, 260 p. illus. 24 cm. Bibliography: p. 247-254. [NA5256.O25M84] 74-18032 ISBN 0-87918-016-1 12.95
1. Church architecture—Oaxaca, Mexico (State) 2. Dominicans in Oaxaca, Mexico (State) I. Title. BIP

Church architecture—Ravenna.

SIMSON, Otto Georg von, 1912- 726.582
Sacred fortress; Byzantine art and statecraft in Ravenna [Reissue] Chicago, Univ. of Chic. Pr. [1965, c.1948] xv, 149p. [49] plates. 29cm. Bibl. [NA5621.R3S5] 48-8992 price unreported
1. Church architecture—Ravenna. 2. Art, Byzantine. 3. Ravenna—Hist. I. Title. BIP

Church architecture—Rhine Valley.

GALL, Ernst, 1888-1958. 726.6
Cathedrals and abbey churches of the Rhine. Translated and adapted by Olive Cook. Photos. by H. Schmidt-Glassner. New York, Abrams [1963] 78 p. illus., 200 plates, maps, plans. 28 cm. [NA5579.G313] 63-9794
1. Church architecture—Rhine Valley. 2. Churches—Rhine Valley. I. Schmidt-Glassner, Helga. II. Title.

Church architecture—Russia—History.

FAENSEN, Hubert. 726'.5'0947
Early Russian architecture / Hubert Faensen, Vladimir Ivanov ; photos. by Klaus G. Beyer. New York : Putnam, c1975. 536 p. : ill. (some col.) ; 33 cm. Translation of Altrussische Baukunst. Includes index. Bibliography: p. 516-527. [NA5681.F3313 1975] 73-87578 ISBN 0-399-11293-6 : 42.50
1. Church architecture—Russia—History. 2. Churches—Russia. I. Ivanov, Vladimir Nikolaevich, joint author. II. Beyer, Klaus G., 1922- III. Title. BIP

Church architecture—Southern States.

HOLLIS, Daniel Walker, 1922- 726.5851
Look to the rock; one hundred ante-bellum Presbyterian Churches of the South. Photos. by Carl Julien. Text by Daniel W. Hollis. Richmond, Va., John Knox Press [c.]1961. xi, 142p. 32cm. 61-11612 10.00
1. Church architecture—Southern States. 2. Churches—Southern States. 3. Presbyterian Church in the U.S. I. Julien, Carl Thomas, 1897- illus. II. Title.

Church architecture—Spain.

STREET, George Edmund, 1824-1881. 726'.5'0945
Some account of Gothic architecture in Spain. Edited by Georgiana Goddard King. New York, B. Blom [1969] 2 v. illus., plans. 25 cm. Running title: Gothic architecture in Spain. Reprint of the 1914 ed. Bibliographical footnotes. [NA470.S8 1969] 68-56490
1. Church architecture—Spain. 2. Architecture, Gothic—Spain. I. Title. II. Title: Gothic architecture in Spain.

Church architecture—United States.

DORSEY, Stephen Palmer. 726.5
Early English churches in America 1607-1807. New York, Oxford University Press, 1952. xvi, 206 p. 118 illus. (incl. ports.) maps (on lining-papers) 29 cm. Bibliography: p. 195-199. [NA5207.D6] 52-9429
1. Church architecture—U. S. 2. Protestant Episcopal Church in the U. S. A. I. Title.

UPJOHN, Everard Miller, 1903- 720'.924 B
Richard Upjohn, architect and churchman, by Everard M. Upjohn. New York, Da Capo Press, 1968 [c1939] xvii, 243 p. illus., plans, port. 24 cm. (Da Capo Press series in architecture and decorative art, v. 15) Bibliography: p. [227]-228. [NA737.U6U6 1968] 68-26119
1. Upjohn, Richard, 1802-1878. 2. Church architecture—United States.

WATKIN, William Ward, 1886- 726.5
Planning and building the modern church. New York, F. W. Dodge Corp., 1951. 163 p. illus. 30 cm. [NA5212.W3] 51-13162
1. Church architecture — U.S. 2. Church architecture — Designs and plans. I. Title.

Church architecture—United States—Bibliography.

STARBUCK, James C. 016.3092 s
Modern American religious buildings / James C. Starbuck. Monticello, Ill. : Council of Planning Librarians, 1977. 2 v. ; 29 cm. (Exchange bibliography - Council of Planning Librarians ; 1357-1358) Cover title. Contents.Contents.—pt. 1. A bibliography of books and magazine articles of national or regional scope.—pt. 2. An indexed bibliography of books and magazine articles arranged State-by-State according to zip code abbreviations. [Z5942.C68 no. 1357-1358] [Z5944.U5] [NA5212] 016.726'0973 77-376466 1.50 (v. 1) : $5.50 (v. 2)
1. Church architecture—United States—Bibliography. 2. Synagogues—United States—Bibliography. 3. Architecture, Modern—20th century—United States—Bibliography. I. Title. II. Series: Council of Planning Librarians. Exchange bibliography ; 1357-1358.

Church, Barton, 1926—

RUTGERS University, New Brunswick, N.J. University Art Gallery. 760'.0924
Barton Church; paintings. [Exhibition] December 10, 1967, through February 11, 1968. [New Brunswick, N.J., 1967] 28 p. illus. 24 cm. (Its Bulletin, v. 1, no. 4) Text by Richard J. Wattenmaker, Director, University Art Gallery. [N722.A3 vol. 1, no. 4] 68-66543
1. Church, Barton, 1926- I. Wattenmaker, Richard J. II. Title. III. Series.

Church camps.

NATIONAL Council of the Churches of Christ in the United States of America. Committee on Camps and Conferences 726.9
Site selection and development; camps, conferences, retreats. Philadelphia. Pub. for the Cooperative Pubn. Assn. [by] United Church Pr. [c.1965] 174p. illus. (pt. col.) foms. plans. 28cm. Bibl. [NA8470N35] 65-13500 12.50. pap., plastic bdg.,
1. Church camps. 2. Architecture—Design and plans. I. Title. BIP

Church decoration and ornament.

EDWARDS, Joan, designer. 729'.9
Church kneelers. London, Batsford; Newton Centre, Mass., C. T. Branford Co., 1967. 71 p. illus. 22 cm. unpriced. [TT775.E3] 67-20992
1. Church decoration and ornament. I. Title. BIP

FRERE-COOK, Gervis. 704.948'2
Art and architecture of Christianity. Cleveland, Press of Case Western Reserve University, 1972. 296 p. illus. (part col.) 32 cm. [NK1650.F68 1972b] 72-86354 ISBN 0-8295-0242-4 29.95
1. Church decoration and ornament. 2. Christian art and symbolism. I. Title.

Church decoration and ornament—Terminology.

DIRSZTAY, Patricia. 726'.5'0942
Church furnishings : a NADFAS guide / Patricia Dirsztay ; illustrated by Caroline Cook, Frances Curwen and Paul Vincent. London : Routledge & K. Paul, 1978. vii, 246 p. : ill. ; 22 cm. Includes bibliographies and index. [NK1648.D57] 78-317143 ISBN 0-7100-8820-5 : 11.95 ISBN 0-7100-8897-3 pbk. : 5.95
1. Church decoration and ornament—Terminology. I. National Association of Decorative and Fine Arts Societies. II. Title.
Distributed by Routledge & Kegan Paul, Boston BIP

Church facilities.

LYNN, Edwin Charles. 726'.5
Tired dragons; adapting church architecture to changing needs. Boston, Beacon Press [1972] x, 276 p. illus. 24 cm. Includes bibliographical references. [NA4825.L9] 72-75540 ISBN 0-8070-1132-0 12.50
1. Church facilities. 2. Church architecture—Philosophy. 3. Architecture, Modern—20th century. I. Title.

Church facilities—Planning.

MORSE, John E., 1923- 726'.5
To build a church, by John E. Morse. Introd. by E. A. Sovik. [1st ed.] New York, Holt, Rinehart and Winston [1969] xviii, 171 p. 22 cm. Bibliography: p. [164]-169. [BV604.M67] 68-10073 5.95
1. Church facilities—Planning. 2. Church architecture. I. Title.

WIDBER, Mildred, C. 726'.4
Focus: Building for Christian education, by Mildred C. Widber and Scott Turner Ritenour. Philadelphia, Published for the Cooperative Publication Association [by] Pilgrim Press [1969] xii, 146 p. illus., plans. 29 cm. [BV604.W5] 70-76087 6.95
1. Church facilities—Planning. I. Ritenour, Scott Turner, joint author. II. Cooperative Publication Association. III. Title.

Church, Frederick Edwin, 1826-1900.

CANTOR, Jay E. 741.9'73'074014771
Drawn from nature/drawn from life. Studies and sketches by Frederick Church, Winslow Homer and Daniel Huntington, from the collection of the Cooper-Hewitt Museum of Decorative Arts and Design, Smithsonian Institution. An exhibition prepared by Jay E. Cantor for the Ithaca College Museum of Art, Ithaca, N.Y., Mar. 23-Apr. 18, 1971. [New York, American Federation of Arts, 1971? c1972] [20] p. illus. 21 cm. Exhibition no. 72-3, circulated by the American Federation of Arts, New York, 1972-1973. [NC107.C3] 72-186227
1. Church, Frederick Edwin, 1826-1900. 2. Homer, Winslow, 1836-1910. 3. Huntington, Daniel, 1816-1906. I. Church, Frederick Edwin, 1826-1900. II. Homer, Winslow, 1836-1910. III. Huntington, Daniel, 1816-1906. IV. Cooper-Hewitt Museum of Decorative Arts and Design. V. Ithaca College, Ithaca, N.Y. Museum of Art. VI. American Federation of Arts. VII. Title. BIP

HUNTINGTON, David C. 759.13
The landscapes of Frederic Edwin Church; vision of an American era, by David C. Huntington. New York, G. Braziller [1966] xii, 210 p. illus. (part col.) 21 x 23 cm. Bibliographical references included in "Notes" (p. [197]-204) [ND237.C52H8] 66-16675
1. Church, Frederick Edwin, 1826-1900. I. Title.

SMITHSONIAN Institution. National Collection of Fine Arts. 759.13
Frederic Edwin Church. An exhibition organized by the National Collection of Fine Arts, Smithsonian Institution. Washington, 1966. 85 p. illus. (part col.) 21 x 23 cm. (Smithsonian publication 4657) Catalog of the exhibition shown at the National Collection of Fine Arts, Smithsonian Institution, Feb. 12 to Mar. 13, 1966; Albany Institute of History and Art, Albany, N.Y., Mar. 30 to Apr. 30, 1966; M. Knoedler and Company, New York, June 1 to 30, 1966. [ND237.C52S6] 66-61709
1. Church, Frederick Edwin, 1826-1900. I. Albany Institute of History and Art. II. Knoedler (M.) and Company, inc.

SMITHSONIAN Institution. National Collection of Fine Arts. 759.13
Frederick Edwin Church. An exhibition organized by the National Collection of Fine Arts, Smithsonian Institution. Washington, 1966. 85 p. illus. (part col.) 21 x 23 cm. (Smithsonian publication 4657) Catalog of the exhibition shown at the National Collection of Fine Arts, Smithsonian Institution, Feb. 12 to Mar. 13, 1966; Albany Institute of History and Art, Albany, N.Y., Mar. 30 to Apr. 30,

1966: M. Knoedler Company, New York, June 1 to 30, 1966. [ND237.C52S6] 66-61709
1. Church, Frederick Edwin, 1826-1900. I. Albany Institute of History and Art. II. Knoedler (M.) and Company, inc. III. Title.

Church, Frederick Edwin, 1826-1900— Exhibitions.

CHURCH, Frederick Edwin,   759.13
1826-1900.
Close observation : selected oil sketches by Frederick E. Church : from the collections of the Cooper-Hewitt Museum / Theodore E. Stebbins, Jr. Washington : Published by the Smithsonian Institution Press for the Smithsonian Institution Traveling Exhibition Service, [1978] p. cm. Includes bibliographical references. [ND237.C52A4 1978] 78-16111 17.50 pbk. : 10.00
1. Church, Frederick Edwin, 1826-1900— Exhibitions. I. Stebbins, Theodore E. II. Cooper-Hewitt Museum of Decorative Arts and Design. III. Smithsonian Institution. Traveling Exhibition Service. IV. Title.   **BIP**

Church furniture.

ANSON, Peter Frederick   729.9
Fashions in church furnishings, 1840-1940. London, Faith Press [dist. New York, Macmillan, 1960] 383p. illus. 26cm. 60-3044 10.00
1. Church furniture. 2. Church decoration and ornament—Gt. Brit. I. Title.

ANSON, Peter Frederick,   729'.9
1889-
Fashions in church furnishings, 1840-1940, by Peter F. Anson. [New York] London House & Maxwell [1966] 383 p. illus. 27 cm. Bibliography: p.   368-374. [NA5050.A55 1966] 66-25523
1. Church furniture. 2. Church decoration and ornament—Great Britain. I. Title.

DELDERFIELD, Eric R.   247
A guide to church furniture, by Eric R. Delderfield. New York, Taplinger [1967, c1966] 157p. illus. 21cm. Bibl. [NA5050.D4 1967] 67-14049 5.00 bds.,
1. Church furniture. I. Title.

HOEFLER, Richard Carl.   247
Designed for worship; a study of the furniture, vessels, linens, paraments, and vestments of worship. Illus. by author. [Columbia, S.C., State Print. Co., c1963] viii, 77 p. illus., plans 28 cm. [NA5050.H6] 64-4499
1. Church furniture. 2. Church vestments. I. Title.

Church furniture—England.

COX, John Charles,   729'.9'0942
1843-1919.
English church furniture / by J. Charles Cox and Alfred Harvey. Wakefield : E. P. Publishing, 1973. xvi, 397 p., [32] leaves of plates : ill. ; 23 cm. Includes index. [NA5461.C738 1973] 74-189216 ISBN 0-85409-876-3 : £4.00
1. Church furniture—England. I. Harvey, Alfred, joint author. II. Title.

Church gardens.

WILDS, Nancy A   712.7
Church grounds and gardens, by Nancy A. Wilds. New York, Seabury Press, 1964. 98 p. illus., plans. 23 cm. [SB476.W63] 64-14887
1. Church gardens. I. Title.

Church maintenance and repair.

CATHEDRAL   690'.66'0942532
craftsman - past and present. [Lincoln, Lincoln Cathedral Fabric Fund, 1973] [16] p. illus., ports. 26 cm. Cover title. Guide to a display designed by Lincoln College of Art in the Cathedral. [NA5471.L7C35] 74-179637 ISBN 0-9502690-1-8 Free.
1. Lincoln Cathedral. 2. Church maintenance and repair. I. Lincoln College of Art.

Church of the Holy Cross, Aktamar Island.

DER NERSESSIAN,   726.5095662
Sirarpie, 1896-
Aght'amar, Church of the Holy Cross. Cambridge, Mass., Harvard University Press, 1965. 60 p. map, plan, plates (part col.) 32 cm. (Harvard Armenian texts and studies, 1) Bibliographical references included in "Notes" (p. [55]-60) [NA5975.A34D4] 64-21241
1. Church of the Holy Cross, Aktamar Island. 2. Art, Armenian. I. Title. II. Series.

Church of the Holy Trinity, Stratford-upon-Avon.

BLOOM, James Harvey,   283'.42'48
1860-
Shakespeare's church, otherwise the collegiate Church of the Holy Trinity of Stratford-upon-Avon; an architectural and ecclesiastical history of the fabric and its ornaments, by J. Harvey Bloom. Illustrated by L. C. Keighley-Peach. New York, Haskell House, 1971. xiv, 292 p. illus. 23 cm. Reprint of the 1902 ed. [DA690.S92B6 1971] 73-116790 ISBN 0-8383-1032-X
1. Church of the Holy Trinity, Stratford-upon-Avon. I. Title.

Church plate, American—Exhibitions.

VIRGINIA Museum of   739.2'3'82
Fine Arts, Richmond.
Church silver of Colonial Virginia. An exhibition organized by the Virginia Museum, February 2-March 8, 1970; [catalogue. George A. Cruger, ed. Richmond, 1970] 112 p. illus., map, port. 22 x 26 cm. [NK7215.V55] 77-102030
1. Church plate, American—Exhibitions. 2. Church plate—Virginia (Colony) I. Cruger, George A., ed. II. Title.

Church plate—Exhibitions.

EUCHARISTIC vessels of   739.2'282
the Middle Ages. [Cambridge, Mass.] : Busch-Reisinger Museum, 1975. xii, 130 p. : ill. ; 22 cm. Catalogue of an exhibition held at the Busch-Reisinger Museum. Bibliography: p. 111-116. [NK7215.E67] 75-3522
1. Church plate—Exhibitions. 2. Liturgical objects—Exhibitions. 3. Art objects, Medieval—Exhibitions. I. Harvard University. Busch-Reisinger Museum of Germanic Culture.

†EUCHARISTIC vessels of   739.2'282
the Middle Ages : Busch-Reisinger Museum. New York : Garland Pub., [1977] c1975. 130 p. : ill. ; 22 cm. Catalog of an exhibition held at the Busch-Reisinger Museum. Errata slip inserted. Bibliography: p. 111-116. [NK7215.E67 1977] 77-9913 ISBN 0-8240-1960-1 : 21.00
1. Church plate—Exhibitions. 2. Liturgical objects—Exhibitions. 3. Art objects, Medieval—Exhibitions. I. Harvard University. Busch-Reisinger Museum of Germanic Culture.

Church plate—Gt. Brit.

OMAN, Charles Chichele,   739.2182
1901-
English church plate, 597-1830 London, New York, Oxford University Press, 1957. xxx, 326p. 200 plates. 28cm. Bibliography: p.[291]-297. [NK721.O5] 58-445
1. Church plate—Gt. Brit. I. Title.

Church plate—Italy—Venice—Catalogs.

PAZZI, Piero.   739'.094531
Le oreficerie gotiche e rinascimentali del tesoro della Basilica di Santa Maria Gloriosa dei Frari / a cura di Pazzi Piero. Venezia : La tipografica, [1976- v. : ill. ; 24 cm. English, German and Italian. Contents.Contents.—Pt. 1. I secoli XIV, XV e XVI. [NK7215.P34] 77-454790
1. Church plate—Italy—Venice—Catalogs. 2. Goldwork, Gothic—Italy—Venice—Catalogs. 3. Goldwork, Renaissance—

Italy—Venice—Catalogs. 4. Basilica di Santa Maria Gloriosa dei Frari. I. Title.

Church—Virginia.

RAWLINGS, James Scott   726.509745
Virginia's colonial churches, an architectural guide; together with their surviving books, silver & furnishings. Richmond, Va., Garrett & Massie [c.]1963. xi, 286p. col. illus., map (on lining papers) diagrs. 25cm. Bibl. 63-14627 9.50, lim. ed.
1. Church—Virginia. 2. Church architecture—Virginia. 3. Architecture, Colonial. I. Title.   **BIP**

Church, William, 1779-1863.

HUSS, Richard E.   681'.62'0924 B
Dr. Church's "hoax" : an assessment of Dr. William Church's typographical inventions in which is enunciated Church's law / by Richard E. Huss. Lancaster, Pa. : Graphic Crafts, 1976. xiv, 78 p. : ill. ; 24 cm. Includes index. Bibliography: p. 77-78. [Z249.H88] 75-44946 12.00
1. Church, William, 1779-1863. 2. Printing machinery and supplies—History. I. Title.   **BIP**

Churches.

ANDERSON, Martin, 1882-   254.8
A guide to church building and fund raising. Minneapolis, Augsburg Pub. House. [1959] 69p. illus. 29cm. [BV604.A5] 59-5611
1. Churches. 2. Church architecture. 3. Fund raising. I. Title.

SCOTFORD, John Ryland,   726.5
1888-
When you build your church. 2d ed. Great Neck, N. Y., Channel Press [1958] 245p. illus. 21cm. [BV604.S35 1958] 58-8051
1. Churches. 2. Church architecture. I. Title.

SCOTFORD, John Ryland,   726'.5
1888-
When you build your church, by John R. Scotford. 3d ed. New York, Meredith Press [1969, c1968] ix, 230 p. illus. 21 cm. [BV604.S35 1969] 68-56863 4.95
1. Churches. 2. Church architecture. I. Title.

Churches, Catholic.

CAPUTO, Mario Vincent.   726'.58'2
The parish church, by Mario V. Caputo. Belmont, Mass. [1967] 100 p. illus., plans. 31 cm. [NA4820.C3] 67-6734
1. Churches, Catholic. 2. Church architecture—Designs and plans. I. Title.

SEASOLTZ, R Kevin.   246
The house of God; sacred art and church architecture. [New York] Herder and Herder [1963] 272 p. diagrs. 21 cm. Bibliography: p. [251]-267. [NA4820.S4] 63-18161
1. Churches, Catholic. 2. Church architecture. 3. Christian art and symbolism. I. Title.

Churches—Connecticut—Pictorial works.

COIT, Richard M.   779'.4'0924
Churches in Episcopal Connecticut : photographs / by Richard M. Coit ; edited by Kenneth Walter Cameron. Hartford : Transcendental Books, [1974] 186 leaves : chiefly ill. ; 29 cm. [BX5917.C8C64] 74-193173
1. Protestant Episcopal Church in the U.S.A.—Connecticut. 2. Churches—Connecticut—Pictorial works. I. Title.

Churches —England.

BETJEMAN, John, 1906- ed.   726.583
An American's guide to English parish churches, including the Isle of Man. New York, McDowell, Obolensky [1959, c1958] 480 p. illus. 22 cm. [NA5461.B4] 59-559
1. Churches—England. 2. Churches, Anglican. 3. England—Description and travel—Guide-books. I. Title. II. Title: English parish churches.

COOK, George Henry.   726.583
English collegiate churches of the Middle Ages. New York, Macmillan, 1960 [c1959] 228 p. illus. 23 cm. Includes bibliography. [NA5463.C64 1960] 60-9429
1. Churches—England. 2. Church architecture—England. 3. Architecture, Medieval. 4. Chapters, Cathedral, collegiate, etc.—England. I. Title.

COOK, George Henry   726.50942
The English mediaeval parish church [3d ed.] London, Phoenix House [dist. Mystic. Conn., Verry, 1965] 302p. illus., plans. 23cm. Bibl. [NA5463.C65] 65-2104 8.00
1. Churches—England. 2. Church architecture—England. 3. Architecture, Mediaeval. I. Title.

HUTTON, David Graham, 1904-   726.5
English parish churches. 226 photos. by Edwin Smith. Boston, Houghton Mifflin, 1953. 64p. plates, map (on lining paper) plans. 32cm. [NA5461.H88 1953] 53-10432
1. Churches —England. I. Smith, Edwin, photographer. II. Title.

KERSTING, A. F.   726.50942
A portrait of English churches; a selection of photographs by A. F. Kersting, text by Edmund Vale. [New York, Norton, 1961] 95p. illus. 31cm. 5.95
1. Churches — England. I. Vale, Edmund, 1888- II. Title.

SMITH, Edwin, 1912-   726'.5'0942
1971.
English parish churches / 214 photographs by Edwin Smith ; introductory texts by Graham Hutton ; notes on the plates by Olive Cook. London : Thames & Hudson, c1976. 252 p. : chiefly ill. ; 22 cm. Includes index. Bibliography: p. 246. [NA5461.S57 1976] 76-381115 ISBN 0-500-18145-4 : £4.50
1. Churches—England. 2. Church architecture—England. I. Hutton, Graham. II. Cook, Olive. III. Title.   **BIP**

Churches—England—Essex.

ESSEX, Eng. Record   914.26'7'008 s
Office.
Medieval Essex churches. Chelmsford, Essex County Council, 1972. [28] p. illus. 25 cm. (Essex Record Office publications, no. 60) [DA670.E7A17 no. 60] [NA5469.E8] 914.26'7'0485 73-150081 ISBN 0-900360-15-1 £0.15
1. Churches—England—Essex. 2. Architecture, Medieval—Essex, England. 3. Church architecture—Details. I. Title. II. Series: Essex, Eng. Record Office. Publications, no. 60.

Churches—England—Somerset.

WICKHAM, Archdale   726.5094238
Kenneth, 1897-1951
Churches of Somerset. New ed. Foreword by Robert Birley. New pref. by Bryan Little. Dawlish [Eng.] David & Charles [New York, Taplinger c.]1965. 178p. maps plates. 26cm. Bibl. [NA5469.S5W5] 65-29884 7.50
1. Churches—England—Somerset. 2. Church architecture—Somerset. Eng. I. Title.

Churches—Gt. Brit.

SMITH, Edwin   726.50942
British churches [Photos.] by Edwin Smith [text by] Olive Cook [London, Studio Vista; New York, Dutton, c.1964) 157p. illus. 19cm. (Dutton Vista pictureback, 6) 64-57003 1.75 pap.,
1. Churches—Gt. Brit. 2. Church architecture—Gt Brit. 3. Church decoration and ornament—Gt. Brit. I. Cook, Olive. II. Title.

Churches—Juvenile literature.

HILLER, Carl E.   726
Caves to cathedrals; architecture of the world's great religions, by Carl. E. Hiller. [1st ed.] Boston, Little, Brown [1974] 138 p. illus. 26 cm. Bibliography: p. 133-135. Briefly examines the sacred structures of various religions and the way their design and construction expresses the philosophy

of the religion each represents. [NA4600.H54] 74-16188 ISBN 0-316-36395-2
1. Churches—Juvenile literature. 2. Synagogues—Juvenile literature. 3. Temples—Juvenile literature. 4. Mosques—Juvenile literature. I. Title. **BIP**

Churches—Melbourne.

FREELAND, John 726.509945
Maxwell, 1920-
Melbourne churches, 1836-1851; an architectural record Parkville, Victoria] Melbourne Univ. Pr. [dist. New York, cambridge, 1964] 170p. illus., map. 26cm. Bibl. 64-1058 18.50 lim. ed., bxd.
1. Churches—Melbourne. 2. Church architecture—Melbourne. I. Title. **BIP**

Churches—Mexico—Sonora.

ECKHART, George Boland, 917.2'1
1897-
Temples in the wilderness : the Spanish churches of northern Sonora, their architecture, their past and present appearance, and how to reach them / George Boland Eckhart, James Seavey Griffith. Tucson, Ariz. : Arizona Historical Society, [1975] p. cm. (Historical monograph ; no. 3) Bibliography: p. [NA5256.S6E3] 75-29478
1. Churches—Mexico—Sonora. 2. Church architecture—Sonora, Mexico. 3. Sonora, Mexico—Description and travel. I. Griffith, James S., joint author. II. Title. III. Series.

Churches — New England.

DONNELLY, Marian 726.'5'0974
Card.
The New England meeting houses of the seventeenth century. [1st ed.] Middletown, Conn., Wesleyan University Press [1968] x, 165 p. illus. 24 cm. Bibliography: p. 145-156. [NA5215.D6] 68-27546 7.50
1. Churches—New England. 2. Church architecture — New England. I. Title. **BIP**

LATHROP, Elise L 277.4
Old New England churches. Illustrated by Welsh. Rutland, Vt C. E. Tuttle Co [c1963] 171 p. illus. 27 cm. Bibliography: p. 167-171. [NA5215.L3 1963] 63-22540
1. Churches — New England. 2. Church architecture — New England. I. Title.

SINNOTT, Edmund Ware, 726.50974
1888-
Meetinghouse & church in early New England. Jerauld A. Manter; photographic collaborator. [1st ed.] New York, McGraw-Hill [1963] 243 p. illus. 26 cm. Bibliographical references included in "Introduction" (p. 2) [NA5215.S5] 63-16197
1. Churches—New England. 2. Church architecture—New England. 3. New England—Social life and customs. I. Title.

Churches—Palestine.

CROWFOOT, John 726'.581'095694
Winter, 1873-
Early churches in Palestine, by J. W. Crowfoot. College Park, Md., McGrath Pub. Co., 1971. xiv, 166 p. illus. 24 cm. Reprint of the 1941 ed. issued in series: The Schweich lectures, 1937. Includes bibliographical references. [NA5977.C7 1971] 71-119257 ISBN 0-8434-0127-3
1. Churches—Palestine. I. Title. II. Series: The Schweich lectures, 1937.

Churches, Protestant.

WHITE, James F 726.584
Protestant worship and church architecture; theological and historical considerations [by] James F. White. New York, Oxford University Press, 1964. xi, 224 p. illus. 21 cm. Bibliography: p. 208-218. [NA4800.W48] 64-22367
1. Churches, Protestant. 2. Church architecture. 3. Public worship. I. Title.

Churches—U.S.

BRODERICK, Robert C., 1913- 726.5
Historic churches of the United States. Drawings by Virginia Broderick. New York, W. Funk [1958] 262 p. illus. 24 cm. [NA5205.B7] 58-7142
1. Churches—U.S. 2. U.S.—Church history. I. Title.

ROSE, Harold Wickliffe. 726.50973
The colonial houses of worship in America: built in the English colonies before the Republic, 1607-1789, and still standing. Ad majorem gloriam Dei. With photos. and maps by the author. New York, Hastings House [1964, c1963] xiv, 574 p. illus., maps. 28 cm. Bibliography: p. 543-550. [NA5207.R6] 63-19175
1. Churches—U.S. 2. Church architecture—U.S. 3. U.S.—Church history. I. Title.

Churches — Virginia.

RAWLINGS, James Scott. 726'.9
Virginia's colonial churches, an architectural guide together with their surviving books, silver & furnishings. Richmond, Garrett & Massie, 1963. xi, 286 p. col. illus., map (on lining papers) diagrs. 25 cm. Corrigenda slip mounted on p. [274] Bibliography: p. 271-273. [Architecture, Colonial.] [NA5230.V8R3] 63-14627
1. Churches — Virginia. 2. Church architecture — Virginia. I. Title.

Churches—Wight, Isle of.

GREEN, Margaret 726'.5'094228
Joan, 1922-
Churches of the Isle of Wight [by] Margaret Green. Winchester (Hants.) Winton Publications, 1969. 109 p. illus. 23 cm. Map on lining papers. Bibliography: p. 10. [NA5495.W6G7] 74-473128 24/-
1. Churches—Wight, Isle of. 2. Architecture, Medieval—Wight, Isle of. I. Title.

Churchill, Winston Leonard Spencer, Sir, 1874-1965—Portraits, caricatures, etc.

BRUCE, George, writer on 923.242
Churchill.
Churchill; a life in pictures] A memorial ed. [New York, Dell Pub. Co.,] 1965] 1 v. (unpaged) illus., ports. 29 cm. Cover title. [DA566.9.C5B78] 65-20265
1. Churchill, Sir Winston Leonard Spencer, 1874-1965 — Portraits, Caricatur I. Title.

CHURCHILL, Randolph 923.242
Spencer, 1911-1968, ed.
Churchill, his life in photographs, edited by Randolph S. Churchill and Helmut Gernsheim. New York, Rinehart [1955] unpaged. illus. 29 cm. [NA5215.S5] 63-16197
55-14646
1. Churchill, Winston Leonard Spencer, Sir, 1874-1965—Portraits, caricatures, etc. I. Gernsheim, Helmut, 1913- joint ed. II. Title.

FERRIER, Neil, ed. 923.242
Churchill, the man of the century; a pictorial biography. Garden City, N.Y., Doubleday, 1965. 60p. illus., facsims., ports. 28cm. [DA566.9.C5F43] 65-3144 2.95 bds.
1. Churchill, Winston Leonard Spencer, Sir 1874-1965—Portraits, carictures, etc. I. Title.

GILBERT, Martin, 942.082'092'4
1936- comp.
Churchill; a photographic portrait. [1st American ed.] Boston, Houghton Mifflin, 1974. 1 v. (unpaged) illus. 25 cm. [DA566.9.C5G444 1974] 74-4204 ISBN 0-395-19405-9 12.50
1. Churchill, Winston Leonard Spencer, Sir, 1874-1965—Portraits, caricatures, etc. I. Title.

MILLER, Harry Tatlock, 923.242
comp.
Churchill: the walk with destiny, compiled and designed by H. Tatlock Miller [and] Loudon Sainthill. New York, Macmillan [1959] 253p. (chiefly illus., plates (part

col.) ports. (part col.) coats of arms (part col.)) 33cm. [DA566.9.C5M55] 59-65213
1. Churchill, Sir Winston Leonard Spencer, 1874—Portraits, caricatures, etc. I. Sainthill, Loudon, joint comp. II. Title.

WINSTON S. Churchill: 820'.9'0091
youth, 1874-1900. Based upon Randolph S. Churchill's book "Winston S. Churchill." A Giniger portfolio published in association with University Microfilms [Ann Arbor, Mich., 1966] [16] p., 15 illus. (incl. facsims., ports.) 37 cm. "A Documents of history portfolio." In portfolio; title from portfolio. [DA566.9.C5A396] 68-6091
1. Churchill, Winston Leonard Spencer, Sir, 1874-1965—Portraits, caricatures, etc. I. Churchill, Randolph Spencer, 1911- Winston S. Churchill.

Ciba-Geigy Corporation—Art collections.

TEXAS. University at 759.13
Austin. Art Museum.
Visual r & d: a corporation collects; the Ciba-Geigy Collection of contemporary paintings, June 10-August 12, 1973 [catalogue. Austin] University Art Museum, University of Texas at Austin [1973] [24] p. col. illus. 26 cm. [ND212.T42 1973] 74-171008
1. Ciba-Geigy Corporation—Art collections. 2. Paintings, American—Exhibitions. 3. Painting, Modern—20th century—United States. I. Ciba-Geigy Corporation. II. Title.

Cimabue.

BATTISTI, Eugenio. 759.5
Cimabue. Translated from the Italian by Robert and Catherine Enggass. University Park, Pennsylvania State University Press [1967] xix, 136 p. illus., plates (part col.) 32 cm. Bibliography: p. 115-130. [ND623.C65B33] 66-25463
1. Cimabue. **BIP**

NICHOLSON, Alfred, 1898- 759.5
Cimabue; a critical study. Port Washington, N.Y., Kennikat Press [1972, c1932] xiii, 60 p. illus. 24 cm. Bibliography: p. [44] [ND623.C65N5 1972] 71-159097 ISBN 0-8046-1640-X
1. Cimabue.

Cincinnati. Tyler Davidson Fountain.

SMALLEY, Stephen B. 731.7'22
The Tyler Davidson Fountain, Cincinnati, Ohio, 1871. Compiled by Stephen B. Smalley. [Cincinnati, 1969] [25] p. (chiefly illus.) 22 cm. [NA9410.C5S6] 70-8899
1. Cincinnati. Tyler Davidson Fountain. I. Title.

Cincinnati. Union Terminal Station.

ART deco and the 709'.04
Cincinnati Union Terminal; an exhibition organized by the Art History Dept., University of Cincinnati, in cooperation with the Contemporary Arts Center, January 11 to February 10, 1973. Cincinnati, Ohio, Contemporary Arts Center [1973] 47, [1] p. illus. 31 cm. Bibliography: p. [48] [N6512.5.A7A87] 72-96930
1. Cincinnati. Union Terminal Station. 2. Art deco—Exhibitions. 3. Art deco—Cincinnati. I. Cincinnati. University. Dept. of Art History. II. Contemporary Arts Center, Cincinnati.

Cinematography.

CORNWELL-CLYNE, Adrian, 778.5
1892-
Three D cinematography and new screen techniques [London, New York] Hutchinson's Scientific and Technical Publications [1954] 266p. illus. 24cm. [TR850.C56] 54-4842
1. Cinematography. I. Title.

Circle.

MUNARI, Bruno 704.946
The discovery of the circle. [Eng. tr. from Italian by Marcello and Edna Maestro]

New York, Wittenborn [1966] 82, [1]p. illus. 16cm. Bibl. [GR950.C5M83] 65-28791 4.50 pap.,
1. Circle. I. Title.

Circus.

BRAITHWAITE, David. 725'.76
Fairground architecture; the world of amusement parks, carnivals, and fairs. New York, F. A. Praeger [1968] xi, 195 p. illus. (part col.), plans. 25 cm. (Excursions into architecture) Bibliography: p. 183-184. [GV1826.B7 1968b] 68-27429 12.50
1. Circus. I. Title.

BRAITHWAITE, David. 725'.76
Fairground architecture / by David Braithwaite. 2d ed., rev. London : H. Evelyn, 1976. 195 p : ill. ; 25 cm. (Excursions into architecture) Includes index. Bibliography: p. 183-184. [GV1826.B7 1976] 76-372892 ISBN 0-238-78997-7 : £8.50
1. Circus. I. Title. **BIP**

Circus in art.

THE Circus 704.94'9'7913074015961
in art : January 20-March 6, 1977, John and Mable Ringling Museum of Art, Sarasota, Florida, March 20-April 20, 1977, University Gallery, University of Florida. [Sarasota : The Museum, 1977] [32] p. : ill. ; 29 cm. [N6487.S28J633] 76-52264
1. Circus in art. 2. Art, Modern—20th century—Exhibitions. I. John and Mable Ringling Museum of Art, Sarasota, Fla. II. Florida. University, Gainesville. University Gallery.

HARKONEN, Helen B 704.9497913
Circuses and fairs in art, by Helen B. Harkonen. Designed by Robert Clark Nelson. Minneapolis, Lerner Publications Co. [1965] 64 p. illus. (part col.) 27 cm. [N8217.C3H3] 64-8205
1. Circus in art. 2. Fairs in art. I. Nelson, Robert Clark. II. Title. **BIP**

TOULOUSE-LAUTREC Monfa, 741.9'44
Henri Marie Raymond de, 1864-1901.
At the circus, a suite of color drawings. With an introd. by William C. Seitz. New York, H. N. Abrams [1967] [7] p., 22 col. plates (in portfolio) 45 cm. On cover: Facsimile reproductions from the original portfolio. Plate with title Female clown mounted on cover of portfolio. [NC1135.T6S4] 65-21827
1. Circus in art. I. Seitz, William Chapin. II. Title.

Circus—Posters.

AMERICAN circus posters in 769'.5
full color / edited by Charles Philip Fox. New York : Dover Publications, 1978. 43 p. : chiefly col. ill. ; 37 cm. [GV1826.A46 1978] 78-54311 ISBN 0-486-23693-5 : 6.95
1. Circus—Posters. I. Fox, Charles Philip, 1904-

Cirencester, Eng.—Antiquities—Addresses, essays, lectures.

STUDIES in the 942.4'17
archaeology and history of Cirencester : based on papers presented to a research seminar on the post-Roman development of Cirencester held at the Corinium Museum, November 1975 / edited by Alan McWhirr. Oxford [Eng.] : British Archaeological Reports, 1976. 200 p. : ill. ; 30 cm. (British archaeological reports ; 30) Includes bibliographical references. [DA690.C61S78] 77-352089 £3.90
1. Cirencester, Eng.—Antiquities—Addresses, essays, lectures. I. McWhirr, Alan. II. Title. III. Series.

Ciriaco de' Pizzicolli, of Ancona, 1391-1457?

LEHMANN, Phyllis Lourene 709'.38
(Williams) 1912-
Samothracian reflections; aspects of the revival of the antique, by Phyllis Williams Lehmann and Karl Lehmann. [Princeton, N.J.] Princeton University Press [1973]

xxiii, 278 p. illus. 27 cm. (Bollingen series, 92) [N6915.L38] 71-163867 ISBN 0-691-09909-X 20.00
1. Ciriaco de' Pizzicolli, of Ancona, 1391-1457? 2. Mantegna, Andrea, 1431-1506. Parnassus. 3. Victoria (Goddess)—Art. 4. Samothrace—Antiquities. 5. Renaissance—Italy. I. Lehmann, Karl, 1894-1960, joint author. II. Title. III. Series.

Cisneros, Jose, 1910—

CISNEROS, Jose, 1910- 741.9'73
Faces of the borderlands : twenty-one drawings / by Jose Cisneros, with text by the artist. [El Paso] : Texas Western Press, c1977. [58] p. : ill. ; 23 cm. (Southwestern studies ; monograph no. 52) Bibliography: p. [58] [NC139.C56A45] 77-359189 ISBN 0-87404-111-2 : 3.00
1. Cisneros, Jose, 1910- 2. Southwest, New, in art. I. Title. II. Series: Southwestern studies (El Paso, Tex.) ; monograph no. 52. BIP

Cities and towns — Byzantine Empire.

OSTROGORSKI, Georgije. 246
Byzantine cities in the early Middle Ages. (In Dumbarton Oaks papers. Cambridge, Mass. 30 cm. no. 13 (1959) p. [45]-66) Bibliographical footnotes. [N5970.D8] A 65
1. Cities and towns — Byzantine Empire. I. Title.

Cities and towns—Europe—Bibliography.

WATERHOUSE, Alan. 016.3092'08 s
Urban development in Mediaeval Europe: a bibliography. Monticello, Ill., Council of Planning Librarians, 1971. 20 l. 28 cm. (Council of Planning Librarians. Exchange bibliography 232) Cover title. [Z5942.C68 no. 232] [Z7164.U7] 016.30136'3'094 74-160788 2.00
1. Cities and towns—Europe—Bibliography. 2. Cities and towns, Medieval—Bibliography. I. Title. II. Series.

Cities and towns—Gt. Brit.—History.

BELL, Colin, 1938- 711'.4'0942
City fathers; town planning in Britain from Roman times to 1900 [by] Colin & Rose Bell. New York, Praeger [1969] 216 p. illus., maps, ports. 26 cm. Bibliography: p. 214. [HT169.G7B4] 78-98346 15.00
1. Cities and towns—Gt. Brit.—History. I. Bell, Rose, joint author. II. Title.

Cities and towns in art.

COOPER, Mario. 760
Drawing and painting the city. New York, Reinhold Pub. Corp. [1967] 128 p. illus. (part col.) 21 cm. [ND1341.C58] 66-22684
1. Cities and towns in art. 2. Painting—Technique. 3. Drawing—Instruction. I. Title.

DAVIS, Charles F., 1927- FIC
All around our town / by Charlie Davis ; ink drawings, Frank Kraft ; introd., Louis C. Jones. Oswego, N.Y. : Mathom Pub. Co., c1977. 128 p. : ill. ; 23 cm. [PZ4.D2595Al] [PS3554.A9328] 813'.5'4 77-80398 ISBN 0-930000-03-X : 12.00
I. Title. BIP

GATTO, Joseph A. 704.94'4
Cities / Joseph A. Gatto. Worcester, Mass. : Davis Publications, c1977. 112 p. : ill. ; 27 cm. (Insights to art series) [N8217.C35G37] 76-50509 ISBN 0-87192-087-5 : 8.95
1. Cities and towns in art. 2. Visual perception. I. Title. II. Series. BIP

GRAHAM, Robert John, 811'.5'4
1932-
Urban rhapsody; a picture and word portrayal of our times. Detroit, Harlo [1973] 95 p. illus. 23 cm. [PS3557.R22] 74-157937
I. Title.

LINKS, J. G. 704.94'4
Townscape painting and drawing [by] J. G. Links. New York, Harper & Row [1972] xviii, 261 p. illus. 26 cm. Includes bibliographical references. [N8217.C35L5] 74-157504 20.00
1. Cities and towns in art. I. Title.

Cities and towns in art—Juvenile literature.

CORNELIUS, Chase 709
The city in art. by Chase and Sue Cornelius. Designed by Wendell Carroll. Minneapolis, Lerner [1966] 71p. illus. (pt. col.) 27cm. (Fine art bks. for young people) [ND1146.O64-758] 65-29036 3.95 lib. ed.,
1. Cities and towns in art—Juvenile literature. 2. Paintings—Juvenile literature. I. Cornelius, Sue, joint author. II. Title. BIP

Cities and towns, Medieval.

SAALMAN, Howard. 711'.4'09
Medieval cities. New York, Braziller [1968] 127 p. illus., maps, plans. 25 cm. (Planning and cities) Bibliography: p. 116-118. [HT115.S2] 68-24702 5.95
1. Cities and towns, Medieval. I. Title. BIP

Cities and towns—Near East—History.

MIDDLE Eastern 711'.4'0956
cities; a symposium on ancient, Islamic, and contemporary Middle Eastern urbanism. Edited by Ira M. Lapidus. Berkeley, University of California Press, 1969. xi, 206 p. map. 24 cm. Organized by the Committee for Middle Eastern Studies of the University of California at Berkeley and held on Oct. 27-29, 1966. Bibliographical footnotes. [HT147.N4M53] 72-81939 6.00
1. Cities and towns—Near East—History. I. Lapidus, Ira Marvin, ed. II. California. University. Committee for Middle Eastern Studies. BIP

Cities and towns—Planning.

AMERICAN Institute of 711.43
Planners.
The planner in emerging urban society; a confrontation. Washington, D.C. [1965] xi, 104 p. illus., ports. 28 cm. [HT166.A68 1965] 66-2153
1. Cities and towns — Planning. I. Title.

ARGAN, Giulio Carlo. 711'.4
The Renaissance city [by] Giulio C. Argan. [Translated by Susan Edna Bassnett] New York, G. Braziller [1970, c1969] 128 p. illus., maps, plans. 25 cm. (Planning and cities) Bibliography: p. 122-[124] [NA9094.A713] 70-90409 5.95
1. Cities and towns—Planning. 2. Architecture, Renaissance. I. Title. BIP

ATLANTIC Research 711.409759381
Corporation, South Miami, Fla.
Metropolitan Miami. South Miami 1962] 98p. illus., maps (part col.) 36cm. (Its Metropolitan area and regional stuides, study no. 1) Bibliography: p. 98. [HT334.U5As] 62-15150
1. Mami metropolitan area. I. Title.

BLUMENFELD, Hans. 711'.4
The modern metropolis; its origins, growth, characteristics, and planning. Selected essays. Edited by Paul D. Spreiregen. Cambridge, Massachusetts Institute of Technology [1967] xv, 377 p. illus., maps. 26 cm. "List of other articles published by Hans Blumenfeld": p. 371-374. [HT166.B54] 67-13391
1. Cities and towns—Planning. I. Title. BIP

ESHER, Lionel Gordon 711'.4
Baliol Brett, 4th viscount, 1913-
Architecture in a crowded world; vision and reality in planning [by] Lionel Brett. New York, Schocken Books [1971, c1970] 181 p. 22 cm. First published in 1970 under title: Parameters and images. Bibliography: p. 171-173. [NA9050.E83 1971] 73-148713
1. Cities and towns—Planning. 2. Architects and community. I. Title. BIP

JEANNERET-GRIS, Charles 711'.4
Edouard 1887-1965.
The radiant city; elements of a doctrine of urbanism to be used as the basis of our machine-age civilization [by] Le Corbusier. New York, Orion Press [1967] 344 p. illus. (part col.), maps, plans. 24 x 31 cm. Translation of La ville radieuse. At head of title: This work is dedicated to Authority, Paris, May 1963. [NA9030.J4213] 67-12936
1. Cities and towns—Planning. I. Title.

LINDLEY, Kenneth Arthur, 711'.4
1928-
Landscape and buildings, by Kenneth Lindley. [1st ed.] Oxford, New York, Pergamon Press [1972] 58 p. illus. 19 x 26 cm. (Appreciation of architecture) (The Commonwealth and international library. Painting, sculpture, and fine arts division) [NA9035.L5 1972] 74-135097 ISBN 0-08-016406-4
1. Cities and towns—Planning. 2. Architecture. I. Title.

SITTE, Camillo, 1843-1903. 711'.4
City planning according to artistic principles. Translated from the German by George R. Collins and Christiane Crasemann Collins. New York, Random House [1965] xvii, 205 p. illus., plans, plates. 21 cm. (Columbia University studies in art history and archaeology, no. 2) Companion volume to Camillo Sitte and the birth of modern city planning, by G. R. and C. C. Collins. Translation of Der Stadte-Bau nach seinen kunstlevischen Grundsatzen. [NA9030.S613 1965] 64-17102 2.95
1. Cities and towns—Planning. I. Title. II. Series.

Cities and towns—Planning—1945-

AMERICAN Society of 711'.4'0904
Civil Engineers. Committee on Review of Urban Planning Guide.
Urban planning guide. Wm. H. Claire, editor. New York, 1969. v, 299 p. illus., maps. 23 cm. (ASCE manuals and reports on engineering practice, no. 49) Bibliographical footnotes. [HT166.A7] 69-19544 8.00
1. Cities and towns—Planning—1945- I. Claire, William H., ed. II. Title. III. Series: American Society of Civil Engineers. Manuals and reports on engineering practice, no. 49

BREESE, Gerald William, 711'.4
ed.
An approach to urban planning, edited by Gerald Breese and Dorothy E. Whiteman. New York, Greenwood Press [1969, c1953] ix, 147 p. 23 cm. "These chapters constitute revisions of a public lecture series sponsored during the autumn of 1951 by the Bureau of Urban Research, Princeton University." Bibliography: p. 111-147. [NA9040.B73 1969] 73-90474
1. Cities and towns—Planning—1945- I. Whiteman, Dorothy E., joint ed. II. Princeton University. Bureau of Urban Research. III. Title.

CITIES and space: 711.4
the future use of urban land; essays from the fourth RFF forum, by Lowdon Wingo, Jr. [and others] Edited by Lowdon Wingo, Jr. Baltimore, Published for Resources for the Future by the Johns Hopkins Press [1963] 261 p. illus. 24 cm. "Based on papers prepared by authorities who participated in the 1962 RFF Forum on the Future Use of Urban Space." Bibliographical footnotes. [HT166.C47] 63-18694
1. Cities and towns—Planning—1945- 2. Cities and towns—Planning—United States. I. Wingo, Lowdon, ed. II. Resources for the Future. III. RFF Forum on the Future Use of Urban Space, Washington, D.C., 1962. BIP

COOK, Theodore Stuart. 711'.4
City planning theory; the destiny of our cities. New York, Philosophical Library [1969] 92 p. illus. 23 cm. Bibliography: p. 89-92. [HT166.C626] 69-15530 5.00
1. Cities and towns—Planning—1945- I. Title. BIP

CROSBY, Theo. 711.01091732
Architecture: city sense. London, Studio Vista; New York, Reinhold Pub. Co. [1965] 95, [1] p. illus. 21 cm. (A Studio Vista/Reinhold art paperback) Bibliography: p. 95-[96] [NA9031.C7 1965] 65-14036
1. Cities and towns — Planning — 1945- I. Title.

CROSBY, Theo 711.01091732
Architecture: city sense. London, Studio Vista; New York, Reinhold [c.1965] 95[1] p. illus. (pt. col.) 21cm. (Studio Vista/Reinhold art paperback) Bibl. [NA9031.C7] 65-14036 4.95; 2.25 pap.,
1. Cities and towns—Planning—1945- I. Title.

DAHINDEN, Justus. 711'.4
Urban structures for the future. Translated by Gerald Onn. New York, Praeger Publishers [1972] 219 p. illus. 26 cm. Translation of Stadtstrukturen fur Morgen. Bibliography: p. 216-218. [NA9031.D2513] 74-136741 25.00
1. Cities and towns—Planning—1945- I. Title.

FERGUSON, Francis. 309.2'62
Architecture, cities and the systems approach / Francis Ferguson. New York : G. Braziller, [1975] 168 p. : ill. ; 27 cm. (Planning and cities) Includes index. Bibliography: p. 157-162. [NA9031.F47 1975] 74-80660 ISBN 0-8076-0763-0 : 15.00. ISBN 0-8076-0764-9 pbk. : 5.95
1. Cities and towns—Planning—1945- 2. System analysis. I. Title. BIP

GIBBERD, Frederick. 711'.4
Town design. 5th ed. New York, Praeger [1967] 372 p. illus., plans. 28 cm. [NA9031.G5 1967] 67-13491
1. Cities and towns—Planning—1945- I. Title.

GOODMAN, Percival. 711.4
Communitas; means of livelihood and ways of life [by] Percival and Paul Goodman. [2d ed., rev.] New York, Vintage Books [1960] 248 p. illus. 19 cm. [NA9030.G6 1960] 60-6381
1. Cities and towns—Planning—1945- I. Goodman, Paul, 1911- joint author. II. Title.

JEANNERET-GRIS, Charles 711.4
Edouard, 1887-1965.
Looking at city planning [by] Le Corbusier. Translated from the French by Eleanor Levieux. New York, Grossman Publishers, 1971. 176 p. illus. 27 cm. (An Orion Press book) Translation of Maniere de penser l'urbanisme. [NA9031.J3513 1971] 76-157865 ISBN 0-670-44044-2 12.95
1. Cities and towns—Planning—1945- I. Title.

LYNCH, Kevin. 711'.4
Site planning. 2d ed. Cambridge, M.I.T. Press [1971] 384 p. illus. 24 cm. Includes bibliographical references. [NA9031.L94 1971] 75-158161 ISBN 0-262-12050-X 10.00
1. Cities and towns—Planning—1945- I. Title. BIP

PAPAGEORGIOU, Alexandros 711'.4
Demetrios Nikolaou, 1933-
Continuity and change; preservation in city planning [by] Alexander Papageorgiou. With a pref. by Frederick Gutheim. [Translated by Gerald Onn] New York, Praeger [1971] 185 p. illus., plans. 27 cm. Translation of Stadtkerne im Konflikt. Bibliography: p. 11-13. [NA9053.C6P313 1971] 78-111073 29.00.
1. Cities and towns—Planning—1945- 2. Architecture—Conservation and restoration. I. Title.

SMITHSON, Alison Margaret. 711/.4
Urban structuring: studies of Alison & Peter Smithson. London, Studio Vista; New York, Reinhold [1967] 96p. front., illus., plans diagrs. 21cm. (Studio Vista/Reinhold art paperback) [NA9031.S6 1967] 67-27747 5.50; 2.45 pap.,
1. Cities and towns—Planning—1945- I. Smithson, Peter. joint author. II. Title.

SOLERI, Paolo, 1919- 711'.4
Arcology: the city in the image of man. Cambridge, Mass., MIT Press [1969] 122 p. illus., plans. 37 x 63 cm. [NA9053.P55S6] 73-87308
1. Cities and towns—Planning—1945- I. Title.

SOLERI, Paolo, 1919- 711'.4
The bridge between matter & spirit is matter becoming spirit; the arcology of Paolo Soleri. [1st ed.] Garden City, N.Y., Anchor Books, 1973. xiii, 253 p. 19 cm.

[NA9031.S63] 72-87501 ISBN 0-385-02361-8 2.95 (pbk.)
1. Cities and towns—Planning—1945- 2. Human ecology. I. Title. II. Title: Matter becoming spirit. III. Title: The arcology of Paolo Soleri. BIP

SOLERI, Paolo, 1919- 711'.4
The sketchbooks of Paolo Soleri. [Cambridge, Mass., MIT Press, 1971] 419 p. illus. 22 x 28 cm. [NA9085.S6A2] 70-148853 9.95
1. Cities and towns—Planning—1945-

SPREIREGEN, Paul D. 711.4
Urban design: the architecture of towns and cities, written and illustrated by Paul D. Spreiregen. New York, McGraw-Hill [1965] xi, 243 p. illus. 28 cm. Bibliography: p. 231-238. [NA9031.S65] 65-25520
1. Cities and towns—Planning—1945- I. Title.

WRIGHT, Frank Lloyd, 1869-1959. 711.4
The living city. New York, Horizon Press, 1958. 222 p. illus., port., plans. 27 cm. [NA9030.W72] 58-13550
1. Cities and towns—Planning—1945- I. Title. BIP

WRIGHT, Frank Lloyd, 1869-1959. 771.4
The living city. [New York] New American Library [1963, c1958] 255 p. illus., plans, port. 19 cm. (A Mentor book, MT470) [NA9031] 66-1553
1. Cities and towns — Planning — 1945- I. Title.

Cities and towns—Planning—1945- — Handbooks, manuals, etc.

DE CHIARA, Joseph, 1929- 711
Planning design criteria [by] Joseph De Chiara [and] Lee Koppelman in cooperation with the School of Architecture, Pratt Institute. New York, Van Nostrand Reinhold Co. [1969] 386 p. illus. (part col.), maps. 24 x 32 cm. Second ed. published in 1974 under title: Urban planning and design criteria. [NA9031.D4] 69-19592
1. Cities and towns—Planning—1945- — Handbooks, manuals, etc. I. Koppelman, Lee, joint author. II. Pratt Institute, Brooklyn. School of Architecture. III. Title.

DE CHIARA, Joseph, 1929- 711
Urban planning and design criteria [by] Joseph De Chiara [and] Lee Koppelman. 2d ed. New York, Van Nostrand Reinhold [1975] 646 p. illus. 23 x 31 cm. First published in 1969 under title: Planning design criteria. [NA9031.D4 1975] 74-16413 ISBN 0-442-22055-3 35.00
1. Cities and towns—Planning—1945- — Handbooks, manuals, etc. I. Koppelman, Lee, joint author. II. Title. BIP

Cities and towns—Planning—Addresses, essays, lectures.

GRIMM, Sergei N 711.4
Physical urban planning; system of general concepts and principal features. Syracuse, N. Y., School of Architecture, Syracuse University, 1961. 87p. 23cm. [NA9045.G75] 61-12433
1. Cities and towns—Planning—Addresses, essays, lectures. I. Title.

PLANNING and architecture 700
[by] Walter Bor [others] Ed. by Dennis Sharp. [1st ed.] New York, Wittenborn [1967] 169 p. illus., plans, ports. 31cm. Essays presented to Arthur Korn by the Architectural Assn. [NA9040.P55 1967] 67-27719 10.50
1. Cities and towns—Planning—Addresses, essays, lectures. 2. Architecture—Addresses. essays, lectures. I. Bor, Watter G. II. Sharp, Dennis. ed. III. Korn, Arthur, 1891- IV. Title: Architectural Association, London.

Cities and towns—Planning—Colorado—Collections.

COLORADO. State Planning Office. 711'.3'09788
[Urban planning grant publications. Denver, 1969- v. illus. 28 cm. (some vols.: 28 x 44 cm.) Issued with various titles (e.g., Capital improvements plan, Comprehensive development study, Comprehensive plan, Land control codes, Neighborhood analysis, etc.), each volume covering a community of Colorado. Prepared by various consultant firms for local planning agencies under contract with Colorado State Planning Office. [HT167.5.C6A54] 72-612275
1. Cities and towns—Planning—Colorado—Collections. I. Title.

Cities and towns—Planning—Congresses.

AIA-ACSA Teacher Seminar, Cranbrook Academy of Art, 1962. 711.4
The architect and the city; papers from the AIA-ACSA Teacher Seminar, Cranbrook Academy of Art, June 11-22, 1962. Ed.: Marcus Whiffen. Cambridge, Mass., M.I.T. Pr. [1966] xi, 173p. illus., plans. 21cm. Seventh annual seminar held under the jt. auspices of the Amer. Inst. of Archs. and the Assn. of Collegiate Schs. of Arch. [NA9010.A15 1962a] 66-23801 5.95
1. Cities and towns—Planning—Congresses. I. Whiffen, Marcus, ed. II. American Institute of Architects. III. Association of Collegiate Schools of Architecture. IV. Cranbrook Academy of Art Bloomfield Hills, Mich. V. Title.

Cities and towns—Planning—Exhibitions.

KOSTOF, Spiro K. 711'.4'0945632
The third Rome, 1870-1950: traffic and glory [by] Spiro Kostof. An exhibition organized by the University Art Museum, Berkeley, in collaboration with the Gabinetto fotografico nazionale, Rome. [Berkeley, University Art Museum, 1973] 88 p. illus. (part col.) 26 cm. Exhibition held at the University Art Museum, Berkeley, Mar. 28-May 13, 1973, the Art Galleries, University of California, Santa Barbara, Nov. 13-Dec. 23, 1973, and the Hayden Gallery, M.I.T., Cambridge, Feb. 15-Mar. 8, 1974. Includes bibliographical references. [NA9204.R7K67] 73-620012 5.25 (pbk.)
1. Cities and towns—Planning—Exhibitions. 2. Cities and towns—Planning—Rome (City) I. California. University. Art Museum. II. Gabinetto fotografico nazionale. III. California. University, Santa Barbara. Art Galleries. IV. Hayden Gallery. V. Title.

NEW York (City). Museum of Modern Art. 711.4'074'01471
The new city; architecture and urban renewal. [New York, 1967] 46 p. illus. (part col.), maps, plans. 31 cm. Catalog of an exhibition held Jan. 23 to Mar. 13, 1967, at the Museum of Modern Art. [NA9015.N48] 67-28526
1. Cities and towns—Planning—Exhibitions. 2. Cities and towns—Planning—New York (City) I. Title.

Cities and towns—Planning—Greece.

DOXIADES, Konstantinos Apostolou, 1913- 711'.4'0938
Architectural space in Ancient Greece [by] C. A. Doxiadis. Translated and edited by Jaqueline Tyrwhitt. Cambridge, Mass., MIT Press [1972] xxxvii, 184 p. illus. 29 cm. Translation of the author's thesis, prepared at the Berlin Charlottenburg Technische Hochschule and published in 1937 under title: Raumordnung im griechischen Stadtebau. Includes bibliographies. [NA9201.D613] 74-87300 ISBN 0-262-04021-2 12.50
1. Cities and towns—Planning—Greece. 2. Architecture, Greek. I. Title. BIP

WYCHERLEY, Richard Ernest. 711'.4'0938
How the Greeks built cities / by R. E. Wycherley. 2d ed. New York : Norton, [1976] c1962. p. cm. (The Norton library) Reprint of the ed. published by Macmillan, London. Includes index. Bibliography: p. [NA9201.W85 1976] 76-10762 ISBN 0-393-00814-2 pbk. : 3.95
1. Cities and towns—Planning—Greece. 2. Architecture—Greece. I. Title. BIP

Cities and towns—Planning—History.

RASMUSSEN, Steen Eiler, 1898- 301.31
Towns and buildings described in drawings and words. Cambridge, Harvard University Press, 1951. iv, 203 p. illus., maps. 25 cm. Revised from the Danish ed. of 1949. Cf. Pref. [NA9090.R] A 52
1. Cities and towns — Planning — Hist. 2. Architecture. I. Title.

Cities and towns—Planning—History.

GEDDES, Patrick, Sir, 1854-1932. 711'.4'09
Cities in evolution; an introduction to the town planning movement and to the study of civics. With a new introd. by Percy Johnson-Marshall. New York, H. Fertig, 1968. xxxv, 409 p. illus., maps, plans. 23 cm. Reprint of the 1915 ed. "Suggestions as to books": p. 403-406. [NA9030.G4 1968] 68-54893 11.00
1. Cities and towns—Planning—History. I. Title. BIP

MOHOLY-NAGY, Dorothea Maria Pauline Alice Sibylle (Pietzsch) 711'.4'09
Matrix of man; an illustrated history of urban environment [by] Sibyl Moholy-Nagy. New York, Praeger [1968] 317 p. illus., maps, plans. 27 cm. Bibliography: p. 304-308. [NA9090.M58] 68-11320 15.00
1. Cities and towns—Planning—History. I. Title.

RASMUSSEN, Steen Eiler, 1898- 711'.4'09
Towns and buildings described in drawings and words. Cambridge, Mass., M.I.T. Press [1969, c1951] viii, 203 p. illus., maps, plans, port. 24 cm. Translation of Byer og bygninger skildret i tegninger og ord. Revised from the Danish ed. of 1949. [NA9090.R313] 69-13127 2.95
1. Cities and towns—Planning—History. 2. Architecture. I. Title.

ROSENAU, Helen. 711'.4'094
The ideal city, its architectural evolution / Helen Rosenau. 1st U.S. ed. New York : Harper & Row, [1975] c1972. 176 p. : ill. ; 26 cm. (Icon editions) Published in 1959 under title: The ideal city in its architectural evolution. Includes index. Bibliography: p. 169-171. [NA9090.R6 1975] 74-188931 ISBN 0-06-438461-6 : 20.00.
1. Cities and towns—Planning—History. I. Title.

WARD-PERKINS, John Bryan 1912- 711'.4'0938
Cities of ancient Greece and Italy; planning in classical antiquity [by] J. B. Ward-Perkins. New York, G. Braziller [1974] 128 p. illus. 25 cm. (Planning and cities) Bibliography: p. 113-114. [HT166.W25 1974] 72-94955 ISBN 0-8076-0679-0 6.95
1. Cities and towns—Planning—History. 2. Cities and towns, Ancient. I. Title.
Pbk. 2.95; ISBN 0-8076-0678-2 BIP

Cities and towns—Planning—Indexes.

CHICOREL, Marietta. 016.3092'62
Chicorel index to urban planning and environmental design / edited by Marietta Chicorel. 1st ed. New York : Chicorel Library Pub. Corp., c1975. p. cm. (Her Chicorel index series ; v. 17-17a) Includes bibliographies. [Z5942.C5] [HT166] 75-30637 60.00 per vol.
1. Cities and towns—Planning—Indexes. 2. Environmental engineering—Indexes. I. Title. II. Title: Index to urban planning and environmental design. BIP

Cities and towns—Planning—Paris.

SAALMAN, Howard. 711'.4'0944361
Haussmann: Paris transformed. New York, G. Braziller [1971] 128 p. illus. 25 cm. (Planning and cities) Bibliography: p. 121-122. [HT169.F72P367 1971] 76-143399 ISBN 0-8076-0583-2 5.95
1. Haussmann, Georges Eugene, Baron, 1809-1891. 2. Cities and towns—Planning—Paris. I. Title.

Cities and towns—Planning—Paris—History.

COUPERIE, Pierre. 711'.4'094436
Paris through the ages; an illustrated historical atlas of urbanism and architecture. [Translated by Marilyn Low.] New York, G. Braziller [1971, c1968] 1 v. (unpaged) illus., col. maps. 22 x 25 cm. Translation of Paris au fil du temps. Includes a bibliography. [NA9198.P2C613] 77-104697 ISBN 0-8076-0556-5 12.50
1. Cities and towns—Planning—Paris—History. 2. Architecture—Paris—History. I. Title. BIP

Cities and towns—Planning—Rome (City)

FRIED, Robert C. 711'.4'0945632
Planning the eternal city; Roman politics and planning since World War II, by Robert C. Fried. New Haven, Yale University Press, 1973. xvii, 346 p. illus. 25 cm. Bibliography: p. 321-331. [HT169.I84R636] 72-91312 13.50
1. Cities and towns—Planning—Rome (City) 2. Rome (City)—Politics and government. 3. Rome (City)—Economic policy. I. Title.

WESTFALL, Carroll William. 711'.4'0945632
In this most perfect paradise; Alberti, Nicholas V, and the invention of conscious urban planning in Rome, 1447-55. University Park, Pennsylvania State University Press [1974] xvi, 228 p. illus. 28 cm. Bibliography: p. [185]-214. [NA9204.R7W47] 73-3352 ISBN 0-271-01175-0
1. Alberti, Leone Battista, 1404-1472. 2. Nicolaus V, Pope, d. 1455. 3. Cities and towns—Planning—Rome (City) I. Title. BIP

Cities and towns—Planning—Russia.

EGOROV, IUrii Alexseevich. 711'.40947'45
The architectural planning of St. Petersburg, by Iurii Alekseevich Egorov. Translated by Eric Dluhosch. Athens, Ohio University Press, 1969. xxix, 237 p. illus., map, plans. 25 cm. Translation of Ansambl' v gradostroitel'stve SSSR (romanized form) Bibliography: p. 213-222. [NA9211.E413] 67-24283 15.00
1. Cities and towns—Planning—Russia. I. Title.

Cities and towns—Planning—Salisbury, Mass.

METCALF & Eddy. 711'.4'097445
Master plan for Salisbury, Massachusetts. Prepared for Salisbury Planning Board and Massachusetts Dept. of Community Affairs. [Boston] 1969. ix, 310, [30] p. illus., maps (part fold.), fold. plans. 29 cm. On cover: Salisbury, 1980. [HT168.S19M48] 72-628555
1. Cities and towns—Planning—Salisbury, Mass. I. Salisbury, Mass. Planning Board. II. Massachusetts. Dept. of Community Affairs. III. Title. IV. Title: Salisbury, 1980.

Cities and towns—Planning—Study and teaching.

PERLOFF, Harvey S 711.071173
Education for planning: city, state & regional. [Essays] Baltimore. Published for Resources for the Future by Johns Hopkins Press [1957] 189p. illus.22cm. Includes bibliography. [NA9012.P4] 57-12448
1. Cities and towns—Planning—Study and teaching. 2. Regional planning--Study and teaching. I. Title.

Cities and towns—Planning—Toronto.

VASS, Benjamin. 711'.4'09713541
Toronto: a photo study of urban development. Toronto, New York, Ryerson Educational Division, McGraw-Hill Ryerson, c1971. 93 p. illus. 31 cm. [HT169.C32T488] 72-171077 ISBN 0-07-092887-8
1. Cities and towns—Planning—Toronto. 2. Cities and towns—Growth. I. Title.

1. Classicism in art. 2. Romanticism in art. 3. Art—Historiography. I. Title.

HAWLEY, Henry 709.033
Neo-classicism: style and motif. With an essay by Remy G. Saisselin. Cleveland Mus. of Art; dist. New York, Abrams [1965, c.1964] v, 167p. illus. 26cm. Bibl. [N6410.H34] 64-24988 6.00
1. Classicism in art. 2. Art—Exhibitions. I. Title.

HAWLEY, Henry. 709.033
Neo-classicism: style and motif. With an essay by Remy G. Saisselin. [Cleveland] Cleveland Museum of Art; distributed by H. N. Abrams, New York [1964] v, 167 p. illus. 26 cm. Errata slip inserted. Bibliography: p. 20. [N6410.H34] 64-24988
1. Classicism in art. 2. Art—Exhibitions. I. Title.

MOORE, Richard A. 709'.4
The dialectic norm of nineteenth and twentieth century art, by Richard A. Moore. Atlanta, Georgia State College, 1968. v, 110 p. illus. 23 cm. (School of Arts and Sciences research papers, Georgia State College, no. 20) Bibliography: p. 110. [AS36.G378A3 no. 20] 79-626813
1. Classicism in art. 2. Romanticism in art. 3. Art—Technique. I. Title. II. Series: Georgia. State College, Atlanta. School of Arts and Sciences. Research papers, no. 20

ROWLAND, Benjamin, Jr. 1904- 709.4
The classical tradition in Western art. Cambridge, Mass., Harvard [c.]1963. xx, 379p. plates. 25cm. Bibl . 63-17211 12.95
1. Classicism in art. 2. Art—Hist. I. Title.

Clay.

GRIMSHAW, Rex W. 666'.4'2
The chemistry and physics of clays and allied ceramic materials, by Rex W. Grimshaw. 4th ed. rev. New York, Wiley-Interscience [1971] 1024 p. illus. 24 cm. Previous editions, written by A. B. Searle and R. W. Grimshaw, have title: The chemistry and physics of clays and other ceramic materials. [TP810.5.G75 1971] 76-178139 ISBN 0-471-32780-8
1. Clay. 2. Ceramic materials. I. Searle, Alfred Broadhead, 1877-1967. The chemistry and physics of clays and other ceramic materials. II. Title.

PASCALE, Gus V 738
Industrial arts: resource book on ceramic materials. Prepared by Gus V. Pascale. New Brunswick, N.J., Vocational Division, Curriculum Laboratory [1961] vi, 346 p. illus. 28 cm. Cover title: Resource book on ceramic materials. Bibliography: p. 344-346. [TP807.P35] A61
1. Clay. 2. Ceramic materials 3. Pottery—Hist. I. New Jersey. Division of Vocational Education. Curriculum Laboratory, New Brunswick. II. Title. III. Title: Resource book on ceramic materials.

SEARLE, Alfred Broadhead, 1877- 666.42
The chemistry and physics of clays and other ceramic materials. by Alfred B. Searle and Rex W. Grimshaw. 3d ed. entirely rev. and enl. New York, Interscience Publishers [1959] 942p. illus. 24cm. Includes bibliography. [TP815.S15 1959] 59-2111
1. Clay. 2. Ceramic materials. I. Grimshaw, Rex W., joint author. II. Title.

WORRALL, W. E. 666'.4'2
Clays and ceramic raw materials / W. E. Worrall. New York : Wiley, [1975] vii, 203 p. : ill. 23 cm. "A Halsted Press book." Includes bibliographies and index. [TP811.W65] 75-12684 ISBN 0-470-96085-X : 21.50
1. Clay. 2. Ceramic materials. I. Title. BIP

WORRALL, W. E. 553'.61
Clays: their nature, origin, and general properties, by W. E. Worrall. [1st American ed.] New York, Transatlantic Arts [1968] xi, 128 p. illus. 23 cm. Includes bibliographies. [TP811.W66] 68-6224 8.75
1. Clay. I. Title.

Clay — Addresses, essays, lectures.

LAWRENCE, Willis Grant, 1916- ed. 620.19
Clay-water systems. W. G. Lawrence, editor. [Alfred, State University of New York College of Ceramics, 1965] 176 p. illus. 22 cm. Cover title. Papers from a symposium sponsored by the Ceramic Association of New York and the State University of New York College of Ceramics and held at Alfred University in 1962. Includes bibliographies. [TP811.L38] 66-3089
1. Clay — Addresses, essays, lectures. I. Ceramic Association of New York. II. New York. State College of Ceramics, Alfred. III. Alfred University. IV. Title.

Clay industries—Drying—Congresses.

SYMPOSIUM on Drying Claywares, Alfred University, 1967. 666'.4
Drying claywares. George A. Kirkendale, editor. Alfred, State University of New York College of Ceramics at Alfred University, 1967. iv, 90 p. illus. 23 cm. Symposium held at State University College of Ceramics at Alfred University on Feb. 6-8, 1967. [TP815.S95 1967] 67-65050
1. Clay industries—Drying—Congresses. I. Kirkendale, George Alderson, 1907- ed. II. New York. State College of Ceramics, Alfred. III. Alfred University. IV. Title.

Clay tobacco pipes—Wyoming.

WILSON, Rex L. 688'.4
Clay tobacco pipes from Fort Laramie National Historic Site and related locations, by Rex L. Wilson. [Washington] Division of Archeology and Anthropology, Office of Archeology and Historic Preservation, 1971. i l., 80 p. illus. 27 cm. Bibliography: p. 57-58. [NK4695.T55W5] 72-601087
1. Clay tobacco pipes—Wyoming. 2. Clay tobacco pipes—Montana. I. United States. Office of Archeology and Historic Preservation. Division of Archeology and Anthropology. II. Title.

Claypoole, Johnny.

GEPHART, Kay. 745.4'49'24 B
Painting hex signs "chust for nice"! Origin of hex artistry and how a modern artisan perpetuates folk art. With comments by Johnny Claypoole. Annandale, Va., Printed by C. Baptie Studios [1973] 15 p. illus. 22 cm. [NK1535.G46C55] 73-85526
1. Claypoole, Johnny. 2. Hex signs. I. Title.

Cleland, Thomas Maitland, 1880-1964.

ECKMAN, James Russell, 1908- 681'.62 B
Week ends with Tom Cleland [by] James Eckman. Rochester, Minn., Doomsday Press, 1971. 12 p. ports. 21 cm. 150 copies printed. First presented as the 2d lecture of the 13th series of lectures delivered at Gallery 303, New York City under the title: "Heritage of the graphic arts." [N6537.C5E3] 79-179674
1. Cleland, Thomas Maitland, 1880-1964. I. Title. II. Title: Heritage of the graphic arts.

Clergy—Caricatures and cartoons.

CARTWRIGHT, Charles. 253'.02'07
Choice chuckles. Grand Rapids, Kregel Publications [1968] [64] p. (chiefly illus.) 19 cm. (His Church chuckles cartoon series) [NC1429.C4A44] 68-31127 1.00
1. Clergy—Caricatures and cartoons. I. Title.

DILLARD, Samuel D. 817'.5'4
Bro. Blotz the builder, by Doug Dillard. Nashville, Tenn., Broadman Press [1967] 1 v. (chiefly illus.) 21 cm. Cartoons. [NC1429.D52D52] 67-22026
1. Clergy—Caricatures and cartoons. I. Title.

RON Carey's irreverent comedy. 741.5973
Created by Chet Dowling. Written by Chet Dowling [and others] Illustrated by Ron De Vito [1st ed.] New York, Hawthorn Books [1968] [63] p. (chiefly illus.) 21 cm. [NC1429.D324A56 1968] 68-30715 1.95
1. Clergy—Caricatures and cartoons. I. Carey, Ron. II. Dowling, Chet. III. De Vito, Ron, illus. IV. Title: Irreverent comedy.

SAVILE'S selection : 741.5'942
a collection of cartoons / compiled and introduced by Jimmy Savile. London : Mowbrays, [1976] 2-62 p. : of ill., port. ; 22 cm. Includes index. [NC1476.S28] 77-364773 ISBN 0-264-66270-9 : £0.95
1. Clergy—Caricatures and cartoons. 2. English wit and humor, Pictorial. I. Savile, Jimmy.

Cleve, Joos van, d. ca. 1540.

HAND, John, 1941- 759.9493
Joos van Cleve and the Saint Jerome in the Norton Gallery and School of Art. [West Palm Beach, Fla., Norton Gallery, c1972] [20] p. (incl. cover) illus. 29 cm. (Norton Gallery studies, 1) Includes bibliographical references. [ND673.C315H36] 73-157070
1. Cleve, Joos van, d. ca. 1540. Saint Jerome. I. Norton Gallery and School of Art, West Palm Beach, Fla. II. Title.

Cleveland. Institute of Art.

BENSON, Emanuel Mervin, 1904- 707'.11
A pilot research study of art facilities in six colleges and universities: Cleveland Institute of Art, Massachusetts Institute of Technology, New York University, Pratt Institute, Sarah Lawrence College, University of Michigan. Emanuel M. Benson, chief investigator. Brooklyn, 1966. 53 l. illus. (on covers) 28 cm. Bibliography: leaves 50-53. [N330.A1B4] 67-62655
1. Cleveland. Institute of Art. 2. Massachusetts Institute of Technology. 3. New York University. 4. Pratt Institute, Brooklyn. 5. Sarah Lawrence College, Bronxville, N. Y. 6. Michigan. University. 7. Art in universities and colleges. I. Title.

Cleveland Museum of Art.

WITTKE, Carl Frederick, 1892- 708.17132
The first fifty years: the Cleveland Museum of Art, 1916-1966 [by] Carl Wittke. [Cleveland] John Huntington Art and Polytechnic Trust, Cleveland Museum of Art: [distributed by the Press of Western Reserve University, 1966] xi, 161 p. illus., ports. 24 cm. Bibliographical references included in "Notes to the text" (p. 147-156) [N552.W5] 66-21227
1. Cleveland Museum of Art. I. Title.

Cliff-dwellings—Colorado—Mesa Verde.

NORDENSKIOLD, Gustaf Erik Adolf, 1868-1895. 970.4'88'27
The cliff dwellers of the Mesa Verde, southwestern Colorado: their pottery and implements. Translated by D. Lloyd Morgan. With a new introd. by Watson Smith. New York, Published by AMS Press for Peabody Museum of Archaeology and Ethnology, Harvard University, Cambridge, 1973. 1 v. (various pagings) illus. 27 cm. (Antiquities of the New World, v. 12) Reprint of the 1893 ed. Translation of Ruiner af klippboningar i Mesa Verde's canons. Includes bibliographical references. [E78.C6N6713 1973] 72-5006 ISBN 0-404-57312-6 84.50
1. Cliff-dwellings—Colorado—Mesa Verde. 2. Mesa Verde. I. Title. II. Series. BIP

Clive House Museum.

CLIVE House Museum. 738.2'7
Caughley and Coalport porcelain in the collection of Clive House, Shrewsbury : a catalogue / prepared by Michael Messenger. London : Remploy, 1976. [7], 383 p., plate : ill. ; 27 cm. Includes indexes. [NK4399.C3C56 1976] 77-358511 ISBN 0-7066-0639-6 : £15.00
1. Clive House Museum. 2. Caughley porcelain—Catalogs. 3. Coalport porcelain—Catalogs. 4. Porcelain—England—Shrewsbury—Catalogs. I. Messenger, Michael Frederick. II. Title: Caughley and Coalport porcelain ...

Cloar, Carroll.

†CLOAR, Carroll. 759.13
Hostile butterflies, and other paintings / by Carroll Cloar ; introd. by Guy Northrop. [Memphis] : Memphis State University Press, c1977. 187 p., [8] leaves of plates : chiefly ill. (some col.) ; 28 cm. [ND237.C573A47] 77-7549 35.00
1. Cloar, Carroll. I. Title.

Clock and watch makers—Vermont.

CARLISLE, Lilian Baker. 681'.11'09743
Vermont clock and watchmakers, silversmiths, and jewelers, 1778-1878. Burlington, Vt. [Distributed by The Stinehour Press, Lunenburg, Vt.] 1970. xi, 313 p. illus., facsims. 29 cm. [NK7110.C36] 72-114620 ISBN 0-87792-008-7 35.00
1. Clock and watch makers—Vermont. 2. Silversmiths—Vermont. 3. Jewelers—Vermont. I. Title.

Clock and watch making—Japan.

MODY, N. H. N. 681/.113/0952
Japanese clocks, by N. H. N. Mody. Rutland, Vt., Tuttle [1967] 46p., 136 plates (pt. fold.) 27cm. (romanized: Nihon tokei ishu) First ed., 1932, has title: A collection of Japanese clocks. Includes text in Japanese with added t. p.: [NK7495.J3M6 1967] 67-21931 17.50
1. Clock and watch making—Japan. I. Title. BIP

Clocks and watches, American.

ECKHARDT, George H. 681.113
Pennsylvania clocks and clockmakers; an epic of early American science, industry, and craftsmanship. New York, Devin-Adair Co., 1955. xviii, 229 p. illus., facsims. 26 cm. Among the facsims. are words and music for "Grandfather's clock," and "Sequel to Grandfather's clock," by Henry C. Work (p. 152-159) [NK7492.E4] 55-7743
1. Clock and watches, American. 2. Clock and watch makers—Pennsylvania. I. Title.

Clocks and watches.

BASSERMAN-JORDAN, Ernst von, 1876-1932. 681.11
The book of old clocks and watches. 4th ed., fully rev, by Hans von Bertele. New York, Crown Publishers [1964] xiii, 522 p. illus. (part col.) 25 cm. Translation of Uhren. Bibliography: p. 495-506. [NK7484.B313] 63-21111
1. Clocks and watches. I. Bertele, Hans von. II. Title.

*CLUTTON, Cecil. 681.113
Clocks and watches; the collection of the worshipful company of clockmakers, [by] Cecil Clutton and George Daniels. [London], New Jersey, Sotheby Parke Bernet Publications, [1975] xx, 123 p. ill. (part col.) 29 cm. Includes index. [NK7483] ISBN 0-85667-019-7 42.00.
1. Clocks and watches. 2. Clock and watch makers. I. Daniels, George. joint author. II. Title.

GENERAL Time Corporation. Westclox Division. 749.3
Clocks in home decoration, ed. with Good Housekeeping magazine by Westclox Div. of General Time. La Salle, Ill., Author [c.1965] 98p. illus. (pt. col.) port. 28cm. [NK7484.G4] 65-2318 1.25; pap., gratis to libs.
1. Clocks and watches. 2. Interior decoration. I. Title.

GENERAL Time Corporation. Westclox Division. 749.3
Clocks in home decoration, edited in collaboration with Good Housekeeping magazine by Westclox Division of General

Time. [La Salle, Ill., c1965] 98 p. illus., (part col.) port. 28 cm. [NK7484.G4] 65-2318
1. Clocks and watches. 2. Interior decoration. I. Title.

NICHOLLS, Andrew. 681'.113
Clocks in color / Andrew Nicholls ; photography, Bob Loosemore. 1st American ed. New York : Macmillan, 1976, c1975. 204 p. : ill. ; 20 cm. Includes index. Bibliography: p. 197. [NK7484.N53 1976] 75-17890 ISBN 0-02-589460-9 : 6.95
1. Clocks and watches. I. Title. BIP

NUTTING, Wallace, 1861- 681'.113
1941.
The clock book : being a description of foreign and American antique clocks, and a list of their makers / by Wallace Nutting. Facsim. ed. Greens Farms, Ct. : Modern Books and Crafts, [1975] 312 p. : ill. ; 26 cm. Photoreprint ed. of the 1924 ed. published by Old American Co., Framingham, Mass. Includes index. [NK7486.N8 1975] 75-316435 ISBN 0-913274-04-6 : 15.00
1. Clocks and watches. 2. Clocks and watch makers. I. Title. BIP

ULLYETT, Kenneth 681.113
In quest of clock, London. Rocklift [New York, Dover. 1965. c.1950] xv.264p. illus., ports. 23cm. [NK7495.G7U4] 51-684 5.00
1. Clocks and watches. 2. Clocks and watches—Collectors and collecting. 3. Clock and watch makers—Gt. Brit. I. Title.

WENHAM, Edward, 1884- 681.111
Old clocks for modern use, with a guide to their mechanism; illustrated by Edgar Holloway. [London] Studio Publications, in association with Crowell, New York [c1952] 174p. illus. 23cm. [NK7484] 52-8170
1. Clocks and watches. I. Title.

WILLSBERGER, Johann, 681'.113
1941-
Clocks & watches : six hundred years of the world's most beautiful timepieces / Johann Willsberger ; introd. by Arnold Toynbee ; translated by Renee Vera Cafiero. New York : Dial Press, 1975. ca 200 p. : chiefly col. ill. ; 29 cm. Translation of Zauberhafte Gehause der Zeit. [NK7485.W4413] 74-28148 ISBN 0-8037-4475-7 : 30.00
1. Clocks and watches. I. Title. BIP

Clocks and watches, American.

MAUST, Don, comp. 739.3'773
Early American clocks; a collection of essays on early American clocks and their makers, a practical reference. Uniontown, Pa., E. G. Warman Pub. Co., 1971-73. 2 v. illus., facsims., ports. 28 cm. Subtitle varies. Includes bibliographical references. [NK7492.M3] 73-291754 5.95 per vol.
1. Clocks and watches, American. 2. Clock and watch makers—United States. I. Title. BIP

SCHWARTZ, Marvin D. 681'.113'0973
Collectors' guide to antique American clocks, by Marvin D. Schwartz. [1st ed.] Garden City, N.Y., Doubleday [1975] xvi, 175 p. illus. 27 cm. Bibliography: p. [167]-168. [NK7492.S37] 73-83668 ISBN 0-385-02922-5 6.95
1. Clocks and watches, American. 2. Clock and watch makers—United States. 3. Clocks and watches—Collectors and collecting. I. Title. BIP

THOMSON, Richard. 739.3'7'73
Antique American clocks & watches. Line drawings by Gordon Converse, Jr. Princeton [N.J.] Van Nostrand [1968] 192 p. illus. 24 cm. [NK7492.T5] 68-29920 5.95
1. Clocks and watches, American. I. Title.

YALE University. 681'.113'0973
Art Gallery.
The American clock, 1725-1865; the Mabel Brady Garvan and other collections at Yale University. Essay and technical notes by Edwin A. Battison. Commentary by Patricia E. Kane. Foreword by Charles F. Montgomery. Introd. by Derek de Solla Price. Greenwich, Conn., New York Graphic Society [1973] 207 p. illus. 27 cm. Bibliography: p. 204-205. [NK7492.Y34 1973] 72-93856 ISBN 0-8212-0493-9 16.95
1. Yale University. Mabel Brady Garvan Collection. 2. Clocks and watches, American. I. Battison, Edwin A. II. Kane, Patricia E. III. Title. BIP

Clocks and watches, American—New Jersey.

DROST, William E. 739.3'7'749
Clocks and watches of New Jersey [by] William E. Drost. Elizabeth, N. J., Engineering Publishers [c1966] xi, 291 p. illus., facsims., ports. 27 cm. $15.00 [NK7492.D76] 66-26780
1. Clocks and watches, American—New Jersey. I. Title.

Clocks and watches—Catalogs.

ANSONIA Clock 681'.113'074019452
Company.
Ansonia clocks; catalogue. [New York, 1969] 140 p. illus. 28 cm. Cover title. [NK7497.A5A5] 77-21438 5.50
I. Title.

COLLECTORS guide to 681'.113'075
clocks; price guide. [Gas City, Ind., L-W Promotions, 1973] 61 p. illus. 28 cm. Cover title. [NK7485.C64] 73-166227 4.95
1. Clocks and watches—Catalogs. 2. Clocks and watches—Collectors and collecting.
Publisher's Address: 144 E. Main St., Gas City, Ind.

EHRHARDT, Roy. 681'.113'075
Clock : identification and price guide / author and compiler, Roy Ehrhardt ; text and research by Malvern "Red" Rabeneck. Kansas City, Mo. : Heart of America Press, 1977. 198 p. : ill. ; 29 cm. Includes index. [NK7485.E36] 77-364874 ISBN 0-913902-23-3 : 15.00
1. Clocks and watches—Catalogs. 2. Clocks and watches—Collectors and collecting. I. Rabeneck, Malvern, joint author. II. Title.

FRIED, Henry B., 1907- 739.3
Cavalcade of time; a visual history of watches [by] Henry B. Fried. [1st ed. Dallas 1968] 126 p. col. illus. 23 cm. "From the private collection of the Zale Corporation." [NK7483.F7] 68-23804
1. Zale Corporation—Art collections. 2. Clocks and watches—Catalogs. I. Title. II. Title: A visual history of watches.

HAGENS' 681'.113'0944074019493
Clock Museum, Evergreen, Colo.
Horological collections. Denver, Golden Bell Press [1964] 72 p. illus., facisms., map, ports. 29 cm. The collection of Orville R. and Josephine Hagans who finance and maintain the museum which is operated as a non-profit foundation. [NK7482.E9H3] 64-7241
1. Clocks and watches — Catalogs. I. Hagans, Orville Roberts, 1897- II. Hagans, Josephine, 1910- III. Title.

INGRAHAM (E.) & Co. 749'.3
Illustrated catalogue and price list of clocks, manufactured by E. Ingraham & Co. Bristol, Conn., 1880. [Bristol, Conn., Ken Roberts Pub. Co., 1972] 62 p. illus. 22 cm. Bibliography: p. 61. [TS549.I54] 73-186871 ISBN 0-9600264-5-2
1. Clocks and watches—Catalogs. I. Title.

Clocks and watches—Collectors and collecting.

BECKER, Walter M. 681'.113
The clock collector's handbook / Walt Becker. New Castle, N.H. : Becker, c1975. 88 p. : ill. ; 22 cm. [NK7484.B36] 75-332703
1. Clocks and watches—Collectors and collecting. I. Title.

BRUTON, Eric. 681'.113
Antique clocks and clock collecting / Eric Bruton. London ; New York : Hamlyn, 1974. 96 p. : ill. (some col.) ; 29 cm. Ill. on lining papers. Includes index. Bibliography: p. 94. [NK7484.B78] 75-318038 ISBN 0-600-31795-1 : £1.95
1. Clocks and watches—Collectors and collecting. I. Title.

CUMHAILL, P W 739.3'075
Investing in clocks and watches [by] P. W. Cumhaill. New York, C. N. Potter [1967] 159 p. illus. (part col.) 30 cm. Bibliography: p. 138-152. [NK7484.C8 1967b] 67-24608
1. Clocks and watches—Collectors and collecting. I. Title.

CURTIS, Tony. 681'.113'075
Clocks and watches / compiled and edited by Tony Curtis. Galashiels : Lyle Publications, 1976. 126 p. : chiefly ill. ; 16 cm. (Antiques and their values) Includes index. [NK7485.C87] 76-383842 ISBN 0-902921-44-4 : £1.50
1. Clocks and watches—Collectors and collecting. 2. Clocks and watches—Prices. I. Title.

CUTMORE, M. 681'.114'075
The watch collector's handbook / by M. Cutmore. Newton Abbot [Eng.] : David & Charles, c1976. 159 p. : ill. ; 23 cm. Includes index. Bibliography: p. 153-154. [NK7484.C86] 76-357709 ISBN 0-7153-7028-6 : £4.95
1. Clocks and watches—Collectors and collecting. I. Title.

CUTMORE, M. 681'.114
The watch collector's handbook / by M. Cutmore. Rutland, Vt. : C. E. Tuttle Co., c1976. 159 p. : ill. ; 23 cm. Includes index. Bibliography: p. 153-154. [NK7484.C86 1976b] 75-42563 ISBN 0-8048-1174-1 : 12.50
1. Clocks and watches—Collectors and collecting. I. Title. BIP

HARRIS, Henry 681'.113'075
Gordon.
Collecting and identifying old clocks / H. G. Harris. Buchanan, N.Y. : Emerson Books, 1977. 256 p. : ill. ; 21 cm. Includes index. Bibliography: p. 238-239. [NK7484.H25] 76-21577 ISBN 0-87523-187-X : 11.95
1. Clocks and watches—Collectors and collecting. I. Title. BIP

†HARRIS, Henry 681'.114'075
Gordon.
Collecting and identifying old watches / H. G. Harris. Buchanan, N.Y. : Emerson Books, 1977, i.e.1978 256 p. : ill. ; 21 cm. Includes index. Bibliography: p. 251-252. [NK7484.H26] 77-89902 ISBN 0-87523-190-X : 12.95
1. Clocks and watches—Collectors and collecting. I. Title. II. Title: Old watches. BIP

LLOYD, H Alan. 681.1109
Old clocks, [2d ed., rev. and reset] London, E. Benn [1958; label: Fair Lawn, N. J., Essential Books, 1959] 176p. illus. 23cm. (Practical handbooks for collectors) Includes bibliography. [NK7486.L55 1958] 59-16009
1. Clocks and watches—Collectors and collecting. 2. Clock and watch making—Hist. I. Title.

LLOYD, Herbert Alan. 681.1109
Old clocks. [2d ed., rev. and reset] London, E. Benn [1958; label: Fair Lawn, N.J., Essential Books, 1959] 176 p. illus. 23 cm. (Practical handbooks for collectors) Includes bibliography. [NK7486.L55 1958] 59-16009
1. Clocks and watches — Collectors and collecting. 2. Clock and watch making — Hist. I. Title.

PALMER, Brooks. 739.3'7'73
A treasury of American clocks. New York, Macmillan [1967] xi, 371 p. 559 illus. (incl. facsims.) 27 cm. [NK7492.P33] 67-28469
1. Clocks and watches—Collectors and collecting. 2. Clocks and watches, American. I. Title. BIP

ULLYETT, Kenneth. 681'.114'075
Watch collecting. Chicago, Regnery [1972, c1970] 144 p. illus. 22 cm. [NK7484.U44 1972] 72-80949 7.95
1. Clocks and watches—Collectors and collecting. I. Title.

WESCOT, Alex. 681'.113'0974
The standard antique clock value guide / by Alex Wescot. Paducah, Ky. : Collector Books, c1977. 215 p. : chiefly ill. ; 28 cm. [NK7485.W37] 77-374210 ISBN 0-89145-035-1 : 11.95
1. Clocks and watches—Collectors and collecting. 2. Clocks and watches—Catalogs. I. Title. BIP

Clocks and watches — England.

SYMONDS, Robert Wemyss, 926;8111
1889-
Thomas Tompion, his life & work. London, New York, Batsford [1951] xvi, 320 p. illus. (part col.) ports. 30 cm. [NK7417.T6S8] 52-35554
1. Tompion, Thomas, 1639-1713. 2. Clocks and watches — England. I. Title.

Clocks and watches, English.

CESCINSKY, Herbert, 681'.113'0942
1875-
English domestic clocks [by] Herbert Cescinsky & Malcolm R. Webster; Illustrated from drawings and photographs by the authors. Feltham, New York, Spring Books, 1969. 3-354 p. illus. 32 cm. [NK7495.G7C4 1969] 70-579806 ISBN 0-600-00897-5 £2.95
1. Clocks and watches, English. I. Webster, Malcolm R., joint author. II. Title.

Clocks and watches, French.

EDEY, Winthrop. 739.3'7'44
French clocks. New York, Walker [1967] 83 p. illus. (part col.) 22 cm. (Collector's blue books) [NK7495.F7E3 1967] 67-23091
1. Clocks and watches, French. I. Title.

Clocks and watches—Great Britain.

LOOMES, Brian. 681'.113'0941
Complete British clocks / Brian Loomes. Newton Abbot [Eng.] ; North Pomfret, Vt. : David & Charles, c1978. 256 p. : ill. ; 24 cm. Includes index. Bibliography: p. 251-252. [NK7495.G7L66] 78-66804 ISBN 0-7153-7567-9 : 19.95
1. Clocks and watches—Great Britain. I. Title. BIP

Clocks and watches, History.

LLOYD, H. Alan 749.3
The complete book of old clocks. New York, Putnam [1965, c.1964] 176p. illus. 23cm. Bibl. [NK7486.L54] 65-15537 5.95
1. Clocks and watches—Hist. I. Title.

Clocks and watches—History.

BRUTON, Eric. 739.3
The longcase clock. New York, F. A. Praeger [1968, c1964] 146 p. illus. 23 cm. [NK7486.B78 1968] 68-27091 4.95
1. Clocks and watches—History. I. Title. BIP

CLUTTON, Cecil. 681.114
Watches [by] Cecil Clutton and George Daniels. New York, Viking Press [1965] xvi, 159 p. illus. (part col.) 31 cm. (A Studio book) [NK7489.C55] 65-15108
1. Clocks and watches—History. I. Daniels, George, 1926- II. Title. BIP

CUSS, Theodore Patrick 739.3'7'03
Camerer.
Early watches [by] T. P. Camerer Cuss. Feltham, Hamlyn, 1971. 63 p. illus. 19 cm. (Country Life collectors' guides) [NK7489.C8] 75-597298 ISBN 0-600-43079-0 £0.65
1. Clocks and watches—History. I. Title.

DREPPERD, Carl William, 681.113
1898-1956.
American clocks & clockmakers. Enl. [i. e. 2d] ed. Boston, C. T. Branford Co., 1958 [c1947] 312, 52 p. illus., facsims. 23 cm. A list of American clockmakers: p. 196-293 and p. 3-52 (2d group) Bibliography: p. 312. [NK7492.D7 1958] 58-2993
1. Clocks and watches—History. 2. Clock and watch makers—U.S. 3. Clocks and watches—Collectors and collecting. I. Title. BIP

FLEET, Simon. 749.3
Clocks. New York, Putnam [1961] 128 p. illus. (part col.) (Pleasure and treasures) [NK7486.F5] 61-12199

1. Clocks and watches—History.

Clocks and watches—Malibu, Calif.—Catalogs.

GETTY (J. Paul) Museum. 681'.113'0944074019493
Clocks in the collection of the J. Paul Getty Museum / Gillian Wilson. Malibu, Calif. : The Museum, [1976] p. cm. Includes bibliographies. [NK7482.M34G473] 76-25150 ISBN 0-89236-004-6 : 3.95
1. Getty (J. Paul) Museum. 2. Clocks and watches—Malibu, Calif.—Catalogs. I. Wilson, Gilliam, 1941- II. Title.

Clocks and watches—Michigan—Dearborn—Catalogs.

EDISON Institute (Henry Ford Museum and Greenfield Village) Dearborn, Mich. 681'.113'074017433
The clock collection / [by William H. Distin]. Dearborn, Mich. : Greenfield Village & Henry Ford Museum, [1977?] 28, [1] p. : ill. ; 26 cm. Cover title. Bibliography: p. 28-[29] [NK7482.D42E344] 77-154049
1. Edison Institute (Henry Ford Museum and Greenfield Village) Dearborn, Mich. 2. Clocks and watches—Michigan—Dearborn—Catalogs. I. Distin, William H. II. Title.

Clocks and watches — Private collections.

NATIONAL Association of Watch and Clock Collectors. New York Chapter. 739.3
Pocket timepieces of New York Chapter members. [New York, 1968] [36] p. illus. 22 cm. Cover title. [NK7483.N3] 68-5002
1. Clocks and watches—Private collections. I. Title.

TERWILLIGER, Charles. 681.113
The Horolovar collection;[a comprehensive history and catalogue of 400-day clocks, 1880-1912. Bronxville, N.Y., Horolovar Co., 1962] 143 p. illus. 20 x 23 cm. [NK7483.T4] 62-16943
1. Clocks and watches — Private collections. 2. Clock and watch making — Germany. I. Title.

Clocks and watches—U.S.

PALMER, Brooks. 681.11
The book of American clocks. New York, Macmillan, 1950. viii, 318 p. 312 illus. 27 cm. "Based ... on the clock sections of Wallace Nutting's ... Furniture treasury."—Dust jacket. "List of clockmakers": p. [133]-316. Bibliography: p. 317-318. [NK7492.P3 1950] 50-11068
1. Clocks and watches—U.S. 2. Clocks and watches—Collectors and collecting. 3. Clock and watch makers—U.S. BIP

Cloisonne.

ALEXANDER, William Foster, 1914- 738.4
Cloisonne extraordinaire / by William F. Alexander and Donald Keith Gerber. Des Moines, Iowa : Wallace-Homestead Book Co., c1977. 180 p. : ill. (some col.) ; 26 cm. Includes index. Bibliography: p. 180. [NK5010.A44] 76-3154 ISBN 0-87069-159-7 : 11.95
1. Cloisonne. I. Gerber, Donald Keith, joint author. II. Title.

GARNER, Harry Mason, Sir 1891- 738.4
Chinese and Japanese cloisonne enamels. Rutland, Vt., Tuttle [c.1962] 120p. illus. (pt. col.) 26cm. Bibl. 62-6452 12.50
1. Cloisonne. I. Title. BIP

Cloisonne—China.

CHU, Arthur. 738.4
Oriental cloisonne : a guide to collecting and repairing / Arthur and Grace Chu. New York : Crown Publishers, [1975] p. cm. Includes index. Bibliography: p. [NK5015.C45 1975] 75-23441 ISBN 0-517-52352-3 : 9.95
1. Cloisonne—China. 2. Cloisonne—Japan. 3. Cloisonne—Collectors and collecting. I. Chu, Grace, joint author. II. Title.

Cloisonne—China—Catalogs.

OGITA, Tomoo. 738.4
Asian cloisonne enamels / by Tomoo Ogita & Richard Petterson. Los Angeles : Dorothy Adler Routh Publications, c1975. xvi, 83 p. : ill. (some col.) ; 29 cm. Published in 1974 under title: Asian cloisonne enamels from the Dorothy Adler Routh Collection. Bibliography: p. 81-82. [NK5015.O34 1975] 75-326567 27.50
1. Routh, Dorothy Adler—Art collections. 2. Cloisonne—China—Catalogs. 3. Cloisonne—Japan—Catalogs. I. Petterson, Richard B., joint author. II. Title.
Distributed by Paragon Books

Cloisonne, Chinese—Catalogs.

OGITA, Tomoo. 738.4
Asian cloisonne enamels from the Dorothy Adler Routh Collection, by Tomoo Ogita and Richard Petterson. [1st ed. Claremont, Calif., Printing by Claremont College Print Shop, 1974] 83 p. col. illus. 28 cm. Bibliography: p. 82. [NK5015.O34] 74-180332
1. Cloisonne, Chinese—Catalogs. 2. Cloisonne, Japanese—Catalogs. 3. Routh, Dorothy Adler—Art collections. I. Petterson, Richard B., joint author. II. Title.

Clothing and dress.

ANTOINE-DARIAUX, Genevieve. 646
Elegance; a complete guide for every women who wants to be well and properly dressed on all occasions. [1st ed.] Garden City, N.Y., Doubleday, 1964. xvi, 319 p. illus. 24 cm. Translation of Les voies de l'elegance. [TT507.A713] 64-11741
1. Clothing and dress. 2. Fashion. I. Title.

APPAREL engineering and needle trades handbook. New York, Kogos International Corp., c1960. 388p. illus. 32cm. [TT497.A7] 59-15511 687
1. Clothing and dress. 2. Clothing trade.

BAKER, Oleda, 1934- 391'.07'2
How to create the illusion of a more perfect figure / Oleda Baker and Francey Petty ; illustrated by Paul Hoover. Englewood Cliffs, N.J. : Prentice-Hall, c1978. 112 p. : ill. ; 25 cm. Includes index. [TT507.B34] 77-22825 ISBN 0-13-404475-4 : 8.95
1. Clothing and dress. I. Petty, Francey, joint author. II. Title. BIP

BISHOP, Edna Bryte. 646.4
The Bishop method of clothing construction [by] Edna Bryte Bishop [and] Marjorie Stotler Arch. Sketches by Dorothy L. Davids. Photos. by Stewart Love. Chicago, Lippincott [1959] 220 p. illus. 28 cm. [TT515.B55] 59-16129
1. Clothing and dress. I. Arch, Marjorie Stotler, joint author. II. Title.

CHAMBERS, Bernice Gertrude. 646
Color and design; fashion in men's and women's clothing and home furnishings. New York, Prentice-Hall, 1951. 603 p. illus. 24 cm. (Prentice-Hall retailing series) Published in 1942 under title: Color and design in apparel. [TT507.C48 1951] 51-7360
1. Clothing and dress. 2. Color. I. Title.

CHAMBERS, Helen G. 646
Clothing selection; fashions, figures, fabrics [by] Helen G. Chambers [and] Verna Moulton. 2d ed. Philadelphia, Lippincott [1969] viii, 471 p. illus. (part col.) 24 cm. [TT507.C52 1969] 69-17195
1. Clothing and dress. 2. Fashion. I. Moulton, Verna, joint author. II. Title.

CRAIG, Hazel Thompson, 1904- 646
Clothes with character, by Hazel Thompson Craig and Ola Day Rush. Rev. ed. Boston, Heath [1954] 277p. illus. 22cm. [TT507.C83 1954] 54-3953
1. Clothing and dress. I. Rush, Ola Day, 1890- joint author. II. Title.

ERTE. 746.9'2'0924
Erte fashions / Erte. London : Academy Editions ; New York : St. Martin's Press, 1972, 1976 printing. [112] p. : chiefly ill. (some col.) ; 30 cm. [TT507.E69 1976] 77-150056 8.95
1. Erte. 2. Clothing and dress. 3. Dress accessories. I. Title.

FASHION; 1000 hints. v. 1- [New York, Dell Pub. Co.] 1952- v. illus. annual. Cover title, v.1-1000 hints fashion [TT507.F34] 55-37727 646.05
1. Clothing and dress.

FOGARTY, Anne. 646.01
Wife-dressing. New York, J. Messner [1959] 191 p. illus. 22 cm. [TT507.F6] 59-8835
1. Clothing and dress. 2. Fashion. I. Title.

FOURT, Lyman Edwin, 1912- 687
Clothing; comfort and function [by] Lyman Fourt and Norman R. S. Hollies. New York, M. Dekker, 1970. ix, 254 p. illus. 24 cm. (Fiber science series) Bibliography: p. 203-237. [TT507.F66] 70-134699 ISBN 0-8247-1214-5
1. Clothing and dress. I. Hollies, Norman R. S., 1922- joint author. II. Title.

HARLOW, Eve. 646.4
The jeans scene. Illustrated by David Roe. New York, Drake Publishers [1973] 117 p. illus. (part col.) 28 cm. [TT552.H37] 73-5572 ISBN 0-87749-517-3 3.95 (pbk.)
1. Clothing and dress. 2. Fancy work. I. Title.

HAWEIS, Mary Eliza Joy, 1852-1898. 646'.34
The art of beauty and The art of dress / Eliza Haweis. New York : Garland Pub., 1978. xiv, 297, 127 p. : ill. ; 19 cm. (The Aesthetic movement & the arts and crafts movement) Reprint of the 1878 ed. of the first work published by Harper, New York and of the 1879 ed. of the second work published by Chatto & Windus, London. [TT507.H28] 76-17760 ISBN 0-8240-2465-6 : lib.bdg. : 35.00
1. Clothing and dress. 2. Beauty, Personal. I. Haweis, Mary Eliza Joy, 1852-1898. The art of dress. 1978. II. Title. III. Series.

HEAD, Edith. 646.01
How to dress for success, by Edith Head with Joe Hyams. Illustrated by Edith Head. New York, Random House [1967] xi, 211 p. illus. 21 cm. [TT507.H35] 66-12021
1. Clothing and dress. I. Hyams, Joseph. II. Title. BIP

HOLDERNESS, Esther R. 646.4
Peasant chic : a guide to making unique clothing using traditional folk designs / Esther R. Holderness ; photos. by Joan Hadden and David Monley ; drawings by Kay Sherry Hirsh. New York : Hawthorn Books, c1977. ix, 147 p., [4] leaves of plates : ill. (some col.) ; 28 cm. [TT560.H64] 76-7833 ISBN 0-8015-5811-5 : pbk. : 7.95
1. Clothing and dress. 2. Costume. I. Title. BIP

LAURY, Jean Ray. 746.9'2
Creating body coverings [by] Jean Ray Laury [and] Joyce Aiken. Photos. by Cam Smith. New York, Van Nostrand Reinhold [1974, c1973] 152 p. illus. 21 cm. [TT507.L34] 73-1631 ISBN 0-442-24698-6 9.95
1. Clothing and dress. 2. Fancy work. 3. Decoration and ornament. I. Aiken, Joyce, joint author. II. Title.
Pbk. 4.95; ISBN 0-442-246927

LEWIS, Dora S 646
Clothing construction and wardrobe planning [by] Dora S. Lewis, Mabel Goode Bowers [and] Marietta Kettunen. New York, Macmillan [1955] 534p. illus. 25cm. [TT518.L4] 55-1557
1. Clothing and dress. 2. Dressmaking. I. Title.

LEWIS, Dora S 646.4
Clothing construction and wardrobe planning [by] Dora S. Lewis, Mabel Goode Bowers [and] Marietta Kettunen. New York, Macmillan, 1960. 565p. illus. 24cm. Includes bibliography. [TT518.L4 1960] 60-560
1. Clothing and dress. 2. Dressmaking. I. Title.

MCCARDELL, Claire, 1905- 646
What shall I wear? The what, where, when, and how much of fashion. Illustrated by Annabrita. New York, Simon and Schuster, 1956. 161 p. illus. 24 cm. [TT507.M28] 56-11190
1. Clothing and dress. 2. Fashion. I. Title.

MESHKE, Edna Dorothy, 1906- 646.4
Textiles and clothing analysis and synthesis. Minneapolis, Burgess Pub. Co. [1961] 135p. illus. 28cm. [TT518.M45] 61-15214
1. Clothing and dress. 2. Dressmaking. I. Title.

OERKE, Bess Viola. 646.0712
Dress. [Rev. ed.] Peoria, Ill., C. A. Bennett Co. [c1960] 575p. illus. 24cm. Includes bibliography. [TT507.O4 1960] 61-495
1. Clothing and dress. I. Title.

PATRICK, Julia Mockett. 646
Distinctive dress. New York, Scribner [1969] x, 308 p. illus. 24 cm. Includes bibliographical references. [TT507.P34] 69-14350
1. Clothing and dress. I. Title.

Clothing and dress—Alteration.

TUIT, Ann. 646.4'04
How to fit clothes. New York, Drake Publishers [1972] 72 p. illus. 31 cm. [TT520.T88] 75-180140 ISBN 0-87749-170-4 6.95
1. Clothing and dress—Alteration. I. Title.

Clothing and dress—Catalogs.

FASHION portfolio for man and women. Philadelphia, Graphic Fashions. v. illus. (part col.) 37 cm. [TT555.F3] 67-33627 338.4'7'68712
1. Clothing and dress — Catalogs.

GOTTWALD, Laura, comp. 391'.42
Fredericks of Hollywood, 1947-1973; 26 years of mail order seduction. Edited by Laura & Janusz Gottwald. New York, Drake Publishers [1973, i.e. 1974] 255 p. illus. 31 cm. "A Strawberry Hill book." [TT555.G67] 73-17466 ISBN 0-87749-582-3 12.98; 7.95 (pbk.)
1. Frederick's of Hollywood. 2. Clothing and dress—Catalogs. I. Gottwald, Janusz, joint comp. II. Title.

LORD & Taylor. 687'.02'9
Clothing and furnishings; women's suits, walking costumes and dresses, wrappers, shawls, underwear, corsets, shoes, trimmed hats; bridal dresses and sets; men furnishings and boys' clothing; laces and embroideries. Lord & Taylor, 1881, illustrated catalog and historical introduction. [1st ed.] Princeton [N.J.] Pyne Press [1971] 174, [9] p. illus. 23 cm. (American historical catalog collection) Bibliography: p. [182] [TT555.L66] 74-162360 ISBN 0-87861-013-8 4.00
1. Clothing and dress—Catalogs. I. Title. II. Series.

TOBE Associates. 338.4'7'68712
Contemporaries; special report from Tobe, May 20, 1969. New York [1969] 84 p. illus., samples. 28 cm. Caption title. At head of title: Report from Tobe. [TT555.T6] 75-10134
1. Clothing and dress—Catalogs. I. Title. II. Title: Report from Tobe.

Clothing and dress—Dictionaries.

PICKEN, Mary (Brooks) 1886- 646.03
The fashion dictionary; fabric. sewing. and dress as expressed in the language of fashion. Claire Valentine. editorial associate. New York, Funk & Wagnalls [1957] 397p. illus. 24cm. 'Based on [the author's] The language of fashion.' [TT503.P49] 57-10114
1. Clothing and dress—Dictionaries. 2. Textile industry and fabrics—Dictionaries. I. Title.

PICKEN, Mary (Brooks) 1886- 391'.003
The fashion dictionary; fabric, sewing, and apparel as expressed in the language of fashion. Rev. and enl. New York, Funk & Wagnalls [1973] xii, 434 p. illus. 24 cm.

friend of Ruskin and William Morris and director of the Fitzwilliam Museum, Cambridge. [1st Amer. ed.] New York, Knopf, 1965[c.1964] xviii, 385p. illus., facsim., ports. 22cm. [N8375.C6B55] 65-11117 7.50
1. Cockerell, Sir Sydney Carlyle, 1867-1962. I. Title.

Codice Campos.

STARR, Frederick, 1858-1933. 759.01'1
The Mapa de Cuauhtlantzinco : or, Codice Campos / by Frederick Starr. New York : AMS Press, [1976] A commentary on the Codice Campos with reproductions of the paintings, chiefly by Tepostecatzin, together with the Spanish inscriptions (translated from the original Nahuatl text by Jose Vicente Campos) and with an English translation from the Spanish. Reprint of the 1898 ed. published by the University of Chicago, which was issued as Bulletin no. 3 of the University of Chicago, Dept. of Anthropology. [F1219.C75453 1976] 74-9026 ISBN 0-404-11904-2 : 12.50
1. Codice Campos. I. Tepostecatzin, Aztec chief, 16th cent. II. Campos, Jose Vicente, fl. 1836-1855. III. Title. IV. Series: Chicago. University. Dept. of Anthropology. Bulletin ; no. 3. BIP

Codman, Ogden.

CODMAN, Florence. 720'.924 B
The clever young Boston architect. [Augusta, Me., Designed and Printed by KJ Litho, 1970] 39 p. illus., plan, ports. 31 cm. [NA737.C6C6] 71-14960
1. Codman, Ogden. I. Title.

Cogswell, Arthur Edward, 1858-1934.

NASH, Andy. 720'.92'4
A. E. Cogswell, architect within a Victorian city / [by] Andy Nash. Portsmouth : School of Architecture, Portsmouth Polytechnic, 1975. [3], 115, viii, iii leaves : ill., map, plans ; 30 cm. Cover title. Bibliography: leaves i-iii. [NA997.C64N37] 76-359799 ISBN 0-905320-00-X : £3.50
1. Cogswell, Arthur Edward, 1858-1934. 2. Architecture, Victorian—Portsmouth, Eng. I. Title.

Cohonina culture

MCGREGOR, John Charles, 1903- 913.791
The Cohonina culture of northwestern Arizona. Urbana, University of Illinois Press, 1951. 158 p. illus. 23 cm. Bibliography: p. 152-153. [E78.A7M15] 51-5800
1. Cohonina culture 2. Arizona—Antiq. 3. Excavations (Archeology)—Arizona. I. Title.

Coin banks.

MEYER, John Daniel, 1874- 738.8
Old penny banks: Mechanical, by John D. Meyer. Stills, by Larry Freeman. Watkins Glen, N.Y., Century House [1960] 1 v. illus. 23 cm. Meyer's work is a reissue of his A handbook of old mechanical penny banks, first published in 1948. [NK4698.M4 1960] 60-13061
1. Coin banks. I. Freeman, Graydon La Verne, 1904- II. Title.

ROGERS, Carole G. 688.7'28
Penny banks : a history and a handbook / by Carole G. Rogers ; photos. by Terry Clough. 1st ed. New York : Dutton, c1977. 102, 16 p. : ill. ; 23 cm. "A Subsistence Press book." Includes index. Bibliography: p. 97-98. [NK4698.R56 1977] 77-79802 ISBN 0-525-47468-4 : 8.95
1. Coin banks. I. Title. BIP

WHITING, Hubert B. 739'.48
Old iron still banks, by Hubert B. Whiting. [1st ed.] [Manchester, Vt.] [Forward's Color Productions] [1968] 1 v. (unpaged) col. illus. 23 cm. Cover title. [NK4698.W52] 68-6582
1. Coin banks. I. Title.

Coin dealers—Direct.

MERCER, Robert W., ed. 737.4058
The Numismatic directory. 1881- Cincinnati. v. 23 cm. Editor: 1881- R. W. Mercer [CJ63N7] 51-35775
1. Coin dealers—Direct. I. Title.

Coin dealers—Gt. Brit.

DEALERS in coins; 737.4'025'42
the directory of dealers in coins & medals in the British Isles, edited by John M. Henshall. 1969-70 ed. Richmond, Numismatic Directories [1969] 120 p. maps. 21 cm. [CJ63.D44] 73-454288 9/6
1. Coin dealers—Gt. Brit. I. Henshall, John M.

Coin hoards—Agrinion, Greece.

THOMPSON, Margaret, 1911- 737.49'38
The Agrinion hoard. New York, American Numismatic Society, 1968. v, 130, lvi p. plates. 23 cm. (Numismatic notes and monographs, no. 159) Includes bibliographical references. [CJ393.A33T45] 68-21876
1. Coin hoards—Agrinion, Greece. 2. Coins, Greek. I. American Numismatic Society. II. Title. III. Series: Numismatic notes and monographs (New York) no. 159

Coin hoards—Scandinavia.

FAGERLIE, Joan M. 737.4
Late Roman and Byzantine solidi found in Sweden and Denmark, by Joan M. Fagerlie. New York, American Numismatic Society, 1967. xxv, 213 p. 33 plates. 23 cm. (Numismatic notes and monographs no. 157) A revision of the author's thesis, University of Washington. Bibliography: p. xiii-xviii. [CJ3094.F3 1967] 67-8456
1. Coin hoards—Scandinavia. 2. Solidus. I. Title. II. Series: Numismatic notes and monographs (New York) no. 157. BIP

Coinage—America—History.

COINAGE of the 737.4'097
Americas. Edited by Theodore V. Buttrey, Jr. New York, American Numismatic Society, 1973. 139 p. illus. 22 cm. [HG265.C63] 73-75064 8.50 (pbk.)
1. Coinage—America—History. I. Buttrey, Theodore V., ed. II. American Numismatic Society. BIP

Coinage—Australia—Juvenile literature.

THOMAS, Mary. 759'.559'94
Paper Collar Gully, [Illustrations by F. H. Thomas. Albany, W. A., The Author, 18 Parade St., 1968] 1 v. (unpaged) illus. 26 cm. Cover title. [PZ9.T5Pap] 71-453660 unpriced
1. Coinage—Australia—Juvenile literature. 2. Paper money—Australia—Juvenile literature. I. Title.

Coinage—Byzantine Empire.

METCALF, David Michael. 737.49'495
The origins of the Anastasian currency reform, by D. M. Metcalf. Chicago, Argonaut, 1969. vi, 105 p. illus. 26 cm. Bibliography: p. 103-105. [HG237.M43 1969] 78-4555
1. Anastasius I, Emperor of the East, 430 (ca.)-518. 2. Coinage—Byzantine Empire. 3. Coinage—Rome—History. I. Title.

Coinage—California—History.

ADAMS, Edgar Holmes, 1868- 737.4'9'794
Private gold coinage of California, 1849-55, its history and its issues / by Edgar H. Adams. [Harrisburg, Pa.] : Stackpole Books, [1974] c1912. xxviii, 110 p., [11] leaves of plates : ill. ; 27 cm. Reprint of the 1913 ed. published by the author, Brooklyn. [HG551.A3 1974] 74-189526 15.00
1. Coinage—California—History. 2. Gold coins. I. Title.

Coinage — China.

WANG, Yu-ch'uan. 737.4
Early Chinese coinage. New York, American Numismatic Society, 1951. viii, 254 p. plates, maps. 23 cm. (Numismatic notes and monographs, no. 122) [HG1223.W3] 52-1639
1. Coinage — China. I. Title. II. Series.

Coinage—Greece.

MILNE, Joseph Grafton, 1867-1951. 737.49'38
Greek and Roman coins and the study of history. Westport, Conn., Greenwood Press [1971] 128 p. 16 plates. 23 cm. Reprint of the 1939 ed. Includes bibliographical references. [CJ351.M5 1971] 75-109793 ISBN 0-8371-4283-0
1. Coinage—Greece. 2. Coinage—Rome. I. Title. BIP

Coinage—Rome—Hist.

MATTINGLY, Harold, 1884- 737.4937
Roman coins from the earliest times to the fall of the Western Empire. [2d ed. rev. and reset] Chicago, Quadrangle Books [1960] xiii, 303p. 64plates. 23cm. Bibliography: p. 259-272. [CJ833.M3 1960] 60-12823
1. Coinage—Rome—Hist. 2. Numismatics, Roman. I. Title.

Coinage—Salvador.

ALMANZAR, Alcedo. 737.4'9'7284
The coins and paper money of El Salvador, by Alcedo F. Almanzar & Brian R. Stickney. San Antonio, Tex., Almanzar's Coins of the World [1973] 88 p. illus. 22 cm. Bibliography: p. 87-88. [HG733.A7] 73-76731 ISBN 0-88242-007-0 pap. 3.00
1. Coinage—Salvador. 2. Paper money—Salvador. I. Stickney, Brian R., joint author. II. Title.

Coins.

AMERICAN Auction Association. 737.4'021'6
The American Auction Association, division of Bowers and Ruddy Galleries, inc., presents The Dr. Curtis R. Paxman collection, and other important properties, including the Rev. Henry J. Nagorka collection of coins of Poland, to be offered at mail bid and public auction sale, November 4, 5, 6, 1974 : sale to be held in ... Sheraton-Universal Hotel ... Los Angeles, California : sale conducted by the American Auction Association. Los Angeles : The Association, [1974] 176 p. : ill. ; 28 cm. Includes index. [CJ1517.A45 1974b] 74-193222
1. Coins. 2. Coins, American. 3. Coins, Polish. I. Title: The Dr. Curtis R. Paxman collection.

AMERICAN Auction Association. 737.4'021'6
The American Auction Association presents the Stanislaw Herstal collection and other important properties to be offered at mail bid and public auction sale in conjunction with the Numismatic Association of Southern California convention, February 7, 8, 9, 1974 : [catalogue / written by Q. David Bowers and staff]. Hollywood, Calif. : American Auction Association, [1974] 160 p. : ill. ; 28 cm. On spine: Stanislaw Herstal collection. Sale conducted by the American Auction Association at the Los Angeles Hilton Hotel. Includes index. [CJ1517.A45 1974] 74-193251
1. Coins. I. Bowers, Q. David. II. Numismatic Association of Southern California. III. Title: The American Auction Association presents the Stanislaw Herstal collection ... IV. Title: Stanislaw Herstal collection.

ANDREWS, Charles J 737.4
Fell's international coin book. [1st]-ed. New York, Fell 1953- v. illus. 20 cm. First-ed. by J. Del Monte. [CJ89.A5] 58-2154
1. Coins. I. Del Monte, Jacques, 1902- Fell's international coin book. II. Title. III. Title: International coin book.

ANDREWS, Charles J. 737.4
Fell's international coin book / by Charles J. Andrews. 6th rev. ed. New York : F. Fell Publishers, [1976] p. cm. [CJ89.A5 1976] 53-11213 ISBN 0-88391-052-7 : 3.95 ISBN 0-8119-0264-1 : 5.95
1. Coins. I. Title. II. Title: International coin book.

BROWN, Laurence A 737.4075
Coins and coin collecting made simple Drawings by Ann Pemberton. [1st ed.] Garden City, N.Y., Doubleday, 1963. 180 p. illus. 26 cm. (The Made simple books, MS52) [CJ89.B7] 63-13077
1. Coins. I. Title.

CRAIG, William D. 737.4
Coins of the world, 1750-1850, by William D. Craig. 1st ed. Racine, Wis., Whitman Pub. Co. [1966] 756 p. (754-756 blank for "Notes") illus., map. 20 cm. [CJ1751.C7] 66-5674
1. Coins. I. Title. BIP

DEL MONTE, Jacques, 1902- 737.4
Fell's international coin book. New York, F. Fell [1953] 192p. illus. 20cm. [CJ89.D4] 53-11213
1. Coins. I. Title. II. Title: International coin book. BIP

FREEMASONS. U.S. Scottish 737.4
Rite. Supreme Council for the Southern Jurisdiction. Library. Hanauer Collection. *Masonic chapter pennies.* By E. A. King. [Waltham, Mass., Quarterman Pub. [1972] 360 p. illus. 22 cm. [HS433.F7 1972] 73-189167 ISBN 0-88000-000-7
1. Freemasons—Medals. 2. Freemasons. Royal Arch Masons. 3. Freemasons—Symbolism. 4. Coins. I. King, Edward A., 1877- II. Title.

GALLETA, Gene. 737.4
Crowns of the world; a guide for silver coins from Afghanistan to Zanzibar. Edited by Eric W. Roberts. Lynbrook, N. Y., World-Wide Numismatic [1965] 87 p. illus. 22 cm. [CJ115.G3] 65-9563
1. Coins. 2. Crown (Coin) I. Title.

GALLETTA, Gene. 737.4
Crowns of the world; a guide for silver coins from Afghanistan to Zanzibar, by Gene Galleta [sic] Edited by Eric W. Roberts. Lynnbrook, N. Y., World-Wide Numismatic [1965] 87 p. illus. 22 cm. [CJ115.G3] 65-9563
1. Coins 2. Crown (Coin) I. Title.

HOBSON, Burton. 737.4
Coin identifier. New York, Sterling Pub. Co. [1966] 88 p. illus. 21 cm. [CJ89.H57] 66-25207
1. Coins. I. Title.

HOBSON, Burton. 737.4
Coins and coin collecting. New York, Dover Publications [1971, c1965] 124 p. illus. 24 cm. Originally published under title: Hidden values in coins. [CJ89.H62 1971] 70-168904 ISBN 0-486-22763-4 1.75
1. Coins. I. Title.

HOBSON, Burton. 737.4
Hidden values in coins; what you should know about coins & coin collecting. New York, Sterling Pub. Co. [1965] 124 p. illus. 23 cm. [CJ89.H62 1965] 65-24386
1. Coins. I. Title.

HOBSON, Burton 737.4075
International guide to coin collecting. New York, New Amer. Lib. [1966] 142p. illus. 18cm. (Signet bk. P3048) [CJ89.H623] 66-31229 .60 pap.,
1. Coins. I. Title.

HOBSON, Burton 737.4075
What you should know about coins & coin collecting. Greenwich, Conn., Fawcett [c.1965] 192p. illus. 18cm. (Gold medal bks., d1554 [CJ89.H63] 65-4948 .50 pap.,
1. Coins. I. Title.

KRAUSE, Chester L. 737.4'021'6
Standard catalog of world coins, by Chester L. Krause and Clifford Mishler. Contributing editors: Clement F. Bailey [and others] Photography by Fred Baerwald. [Iola, Wis., Krause Publications,

1972] 792 p. illus. 28 cm. [CJ1755.K7] 73-185649 10.00
1. Coins. I. Mishler, Clifford, joint author. II. Title. BIP

KRAUSE, Chester L. 737.4'021
Standard catalog of world coins, by Chester L. Krause and Clifford Mishler. Contributing editors: Carl Allenbaugh [and others] Photography: Fred Baerwald and David L. Heise. [2d ed. Iola, Wis., Krause Publications, 1973] 864 p. illus. 28 cm. "Incorporating a comprehensive listing of 20th century non-circulating legal tender coins by Charles R. Hosch." [CJ1755.K7 1973] 73-88957 12.50
1. Coins. I. Mishler, Clifford, joint author. II. Title.

KRAUSE, Chester L. 737.4'021'6
Standard catalog of world coins / by Chester L. Krause and Clifford Mishler. 3d ed., 2d print. / Colin R. Bruce II, coordinating editor ; Charles R. Hosch, NCLT cataloger ; contributing editors, Steve Album ... [et al.] ; photography, David L. Heise. Iola, Wis. : Krause Publications, c1975. 1376 p. : ill. ; 28 cm. "1976 edition." Includes indexes. [CJ1755.K7 1975] 75-15251 ISBN 0-87341-006-8 : 19.50
1. Coins. I. Mishler, Clifford, joint author. II. Title.

LINDHEIM, Leon. 737.4
Facts & fictions about coins. [1st ed.] Cleveland, World Pub. Co. [1967] viii, 280 p. illus. 22 cm. Based on the author's newspaper column, "Coin-wise", published in the Plain dealer since 1960. Bibliography: p. 273-276. [CJ36.L5] 66-25885
1. Coins. I. Title. II. Title: Coin-wise.

MCCLURE, Dudley L. 737.4
Tales of the golden beavers / by Dudley L. McClure. Iola, Wis. : Krause Publications, c1977. 64 p. (p. 63-64 blank for notes) : ill. ; 28 cm. Bibliography: p. 61-62. [CJ1848.O7M32] 78-71682 pbk. : 3.50
1. Beaver (Coin) I. Title. BIP

*NEUMANN, Josef 737.4
Beschreibung der bekanntesten Kupfermunzen; 7t. New York, Johnson Reprint, 1966. 7v. (various p.) 23cm. Facsim. reprint of the ed. first pub. in Prague between 1858-1872. 100.00; 15.00 set, ea.,
1. Coins. I. Title. BIP

PORTEOUS, John. 737.49
Coins. New York, Putnam [1964] 128 p. illus. (part col.), ports. 22 cm. (Pleasures and treasures) [CJ89.P6] 64-16767
1. Coins.

RAYMOND, Wayte, 1886- ed. 737.4
Coins of the world, twentieth century issues, 1901-1954; containing a complete list of all the coins issued by the countries of the whole world, their colonies or dependencies, with illustrations of most of the types and the average valuation among collectors and dealers. 5th ed. New York, W. Raymond, inc. [1955] 326p. illus. 24cm. [CJ1755.R3 1955] 55-2551
1. Coins. I. Title.

RAYMOND, Wayte, 1886- ed. 737.4
Coins of the world: nineteenth century issues; containing an extensive list of the silver and minor coins issued by the countries of the whole world, their colonies or dependencies, with illustrations of the principal or most interesting types and giving the average valuation among collectors and dealers. 2d ed. New York, W. Raymond, inc. [1953] 251 p. illus. 24 cm. [CJ1753.R3 1953] 53-13551
1. Coins. I. Title.

RAYMOND, Wayte, 1886- ed. 737.4
Coins of the world. Twentieth century issues, 1901-1950; containing a complete list of all the coins issued by the countries of the whole world, their colonies or dependencies, with illustrations of most of the types and the average valuation among collectors and dealers. 4th ed. New York, W. Raymond, inc. [c1951] 296 p. illus. 24 cm. [CJ1755.R3 1951] 52-621
1. Coins. I. Title.

REINFELD, Fred 737.4085
Catalogue of the world's most popular coins. Expanded ed. Rev. by Burton Hobson. Garden City, N.Y., Doubleday [c.1956-1965] 288p. illus. 26cm. 7.50
1. Coins. I. Title. BIP

REINFELD, Fred 737.4937
Catalogue of the world's most popular coins, by Fred Reinfeld, Rev. by Burton Hobson. Expanded ed. Garden City, N.Y., Doubleday [1967, c.1965] 288p. illus. 26cm. 7.50
1. Coins. I. Hobson, Burton, ed. II. Title.

REINFELD, Fred, 1910- 737.4085
A catalogue of the world's most popular coins. Rev. ed. New York, Sterling [1963] 265p. illus. 26cm. 63-24020 6.95
1. Coins. I. Title.

REINFELD, Fred, 1910- 737.4
Treasury of the world's coins. [Rev. ed.] New York Dover Publications [c1955] 224p. illus. 26cm. [CJ89.R4 1955] 58-2254
1. Coins. I. Title.

REINFELD, Fred, 1910-1964. 737.4
Catalogue of the world's most popular coins. Expanded ed. Rev. by Burton Hobson. New York, Sterling Pub. Co. [1965, c1964] 288 p. illus. 26 cm. [CJ63.R4 1965] 64-24677
1. Coins. I. Hobson, Burton. II. Title.

REINFELD, Fred, 1910-1964. 737.4'025'42
Catalogue of the world's most popular coins. Expanded ed. Rev. by Burton Hobson. New York, President Coin Corp. [1967] 288 p. illus. 26 cm. [CJ63.R4 1967] 67-4835
1. Coins. I. Hobson, Burton. II. Title.

REINFELD, Fred, 1910-1964. 737.4085
A catalogue of the world's most popular coins. Rev. ed. New York, Sterling Pub. Co.; distributed to the coin trade by President Coin Corp. [1960] 265 p. illus. 26 cm. [CJ63.R4 1960] 60-50897
1. Coins.

REINFELD, Fred, 1910-1964. 737.4'075
Catalogue of the world's most popular coins. Enl. and rev. ed., rev. by Burton Hobson. New York, President Coin Corp. [1969] 416 p. illus. 26 cm. [CJ63.R4 1969] 77-7641 8.95
1. Coins. I. Hobson, Burton, ed. II. Title.

REINFELD, Fred, 1910-1964. 737.4'02'9
Catalogue of the world's most popular coins, by Fred Reinfeld. Rev. by Burton Hobson. Rev. ed. Garden City, N.Y., Doubleday [1971] 416 p. illus. 26 cm. [CJ63.R4 1971] 74-24249 8.95
1. Coins. I. Hobson, Burton. II. Title.

REINFELD, Fred, 1910-1964. 737.4
Catalogue of the world's most popular coins, by Fred Reinfeld. Rev. by Burton Hobson. Enl. and rev. ed. Garden City, N.Y., Doubleday [1969] 416 p. illus. 27 cm. [CJ63.R4 1969b] 74-7233 8.95
1. Coins. I. Hobson, Burton. II. Title.

REINFELD, Fred, 1910-1964. 737.4
New treasury of the world's coins. Rev. by Burton Hobson. [Rev. and updated ed.] New York, Bantam Books [1967] 248 p. illus. 18 cm. Other editions, 1953-1967, published under title: Treasury of the world's coins. [CJ89.R4 1967a] 67-6131
1. Coins. I. Hobson, Burton. II. Title.

REINFELD, Fred, 1910-1964. 737.4
Treasury of the world's coins. New York, Sterling Pub. Co. [1953] 224 p. illus. 26 cm. [CJ89.R4] 53-13410
1. Coins. I. Title.

REINFELD, Fred, 1910-1964 737.4
Treasury of the world's coins. [Rev. ed.] New York, Sterling [1967] 221p. illus. 27cm. [CJ89.R4 1967] 67-6175 3.95; 3.99 lib. ed.,
1. Coins. I. Title.

SCHON, Gunter. 737.4'09'04
Simon and Schuster world coin catalogue, 1979-1980, twentieth century / by Gunter Schon. Rev. and expanded ed. New York : Simon and Schuster, c1978. p. cm. "Translated from the third edition of Weltmunzkatalog, XX. Jahrhundert." Edition published in 1973 under title: World coin catalogue, twentieth century. [CJ1755.S3413 1978] 78-13192 ISBN 0-671-24638-0 : 16.50. ISBN 0-671-24639-9 pbk. : 9.95
1. Coins. I. Title. II. Title: World coin catalogue, 1979-1980, twentieth century.

SCHON, Gunter. 737.4'09'04
World coin catalogue, twentieth century. Translated by George Muller. New York, Simon & Schuster [1973, c1972] 911 p. illus. 19 cm. Translation of Weltmunzkatalog, XX. Jahrhundert. [CJ1755.S3413 1973] 72-83922 ISBN 0-671-21378-4 10.00
1. Coins. I. Title.

THOMPSON, John, 1800-1891. 737.4'09
The coin chart manual, issued from the office of the Bank note and commercial reporter / arranged by J. Thompson. Chicago : Obol International, 1974. 48 p. : all ill. ; 26 cm. Reprint of the 1855? ed. published by the Bank note and commercial reporter, New York. [CJ1753.T47 1974] 75-310185
1. Coins. I. Title.

YEOMAN, R. S. 737.40838
A catalog of modern world coins. 4th. rev. ed. Racine, Wis., Whitman Pub. Co., c.1961 509p. illus. 4.00
1. Coins. I. Title. II. Title: Modern world coins.

*YEOMAN, R. S. 737.4
A catalog of modern world coins: 1850-1950. [By] R. S. Yeoman. Racine, Wisc. Western Pub. Co. [1974] 512 p. illus. 20 cm. [CJ1751] ISBN 0-307-09053-1 7.00
1. Coins. I. Title.

*YEOMAN, R.S. 737.4
A catalog of modern world coins, 1850-1964. Racine, Wis. : Western Pub. Co. The twelfth ed., 1978, is available for 5.95 (pbk.) ISBN 0-307-90538-1 ; L.C. card no.: 57-3057.

YEOMAN, Richard S 737.4
A catalog of modern world coins. 1st ed. Racine, Wis., Whitman Pub. Co., c1957. 509 p. illus. 20 cm. [CJ1753.Y4] 57-3057
1. Coins. I. Title. II. Title: Modern world coins. BIP

YEOMAN, Richard S 737.40838
A catalog of modern world coins. 3d rev. ed. Racine, Wis., Whitman Pub. Co., c1959. 509 p. illus. 20 cm. [CJ1753.Y4 1959] 60-22684
1. Coins. I. Title. II. Title: Modern world coins.

YEOMAN, Richard S. 737.40838
A catalog of modern world coins. 4th rev. ed. Racine, Wis., Whitman Pub. Co., c1961. 509 p. illus. 20 cm. [CJ1753.Y4 1961] 61-4597
1. Coins. I. Title: Modern world coins.

YEOMAN, Richard S 737.4
A catalog of modern world coins; includes coins of all countries of the world in all metals issued during approximately the past 100 years. 2d ed. Racine, Wis., Whitman Pub. Co., c1957. 509 p. illus. 20 cm. [CJ1753.Y4 1957] 58-217
1. Coins. I. Title. II. Title: Modern world coins.

YEOMAN, Richard S 737.4
Current coins of the world, by R. S. Yeoman. 2d ed. Racine, Wis. Western Pub. Co. [1968] 256 p. illus. 20 cm. [CJ1755.Y4] 68-5421
1. Coins. I. Title. BIP

YEOMAN, Richard S. 737.4
Current coins of the world, by R. S. Yeoman. 1st ed., profusely illus. Racine, Wis., Whitman Pub. [1966] 250p. illus. 20cm. [CJ1755.Y4] 66-31883 2.00 bds.,
1. Coins. I. Title.

YEOMAN, Richard S. 737.4
Current coins of the world, by R. S. Yeoman. 3d ed. Racine, Wis., Western Pub. Co., Whitman Hobby Division [1969] 256 p. illus. 20 cm. [CJ1755.Y4 1969] 75-10911
1. Coins. I. Title.

YEOMAN, Richard S. 737.4'075
Current coins of the world, by R. S. Yeoman. 5th ed. [Racine, Wis.] Whitman Coin Products, c1972. 256 p. illus. 20 cm. [CJ1755.Y4 1972] 73-154580 3.95
1. Coins. I. Title.

ZUCKER, Don. 737.4075
Complete guide to coin collecting; how to collect, evaluate, buy and sell. Plus big catalog section. [Los Angeles, Trend Books, 1961] 128 p. illus. 23 cm. (Trend book 203) [CJ89.Z8] 61-34269
1. Coins. I. Title.

Coins—Addresses, essays, lectures.

COIN world, 737.4973
Sidney, Ohio Coin world guide to coins [by the eds. of Coin world. Greenwich, Conn., Fawcett. c.1964] 112p. illus. 24cm. [CJ35.C6] 64-57916 .75 pap.,
1. Coins—Addresses, essays, lectures. I. Title: Guide to coins.

COIN world, Sidney, Ohio 737.4973
Coin world; guide to coins, by the eds. of Coin world. NewYork, Arco [1965, c.1964] 110p. illus., ports. 24cm. (Arco hobby lib.) [CJ35.C6] 65-18476 2.50
1. Coins—Addresses, essays, lectures. I. Title. II. Title: Guide to coins.

Coins, American.

AKERS, David W. 737.4'9'73
United States gold coins : an analysis of auction records / by David W. Akers ; photography by Thomas A. Mulvaney. Englewood, Ohio : Paramount Publications, c1975- v. : ill. ; 27 cm. Contents.Contents.—v. 1. Gold dollars, 1849-1889. [CJ1834.A38] 75-24518
1. Coins, American. 2. Gold coins. I. Title.

AMERICAN Auction Association. 737.4'021'6
The American Auction Association presents the Matt Rothert collection and other important consignments, including the Dr. W. E. Caldwell collection of U.S. half dimes, the George A. Merriweather collection of U.S. colonials, choice U.S. copper, silver, and gold coins, important coins of the world, to be offered at mail bid and public auction sale, November 16, 17, 1973 : sale conducted by the American Auction Association : [catalogue / written by Q. David Bowers ; photography by Robert Budinger]. Hollywood, Calif. : The Association, 1973. 128 p. : ill. ; 28 cm. Includes index. [CJ1826.A57 1973] 74-193245
1. Coins, American. 2. Paper money—United States—Catalogs. I. Bowers, Q. David. II. Title: The American Auction Association presents the Matt Rothert collection ... III. Title: The Matt Rothert collection.

AMERICAN Auction Association. 380.1'45'7374973
The American Auction Association presents the Newport collection and other important properties, to be offered at mail bid and public auction sale, in conjunction with the Long Beach International Coin and Stamp Exposition, Jan. 30, 31, Feb. 1, 1975 : sale to be held at the Long Beach Municipal Arena, Long Beach, California : sale conducted by the American Auction Association / Bowers and Ruddy Galleries, inc. Hollywood, Calif. : The Association, c1974. 180 p. : ill. ; 28 cm. Includes index. [CJ1826.A57 1974a] 75-316446
1. Coins, American. 2. Coins. I. Title: The Newport collection.

AMERICAN coin book and standard retail premium list of all United States coins. 737.4
Los Angeles [etc.] American Numismatic Co.[etc.] v. illus. 21cm. Title varies: The American catalog of all United States coins (varies slightly)--1934, The Federal catalog of all United States coins--American standard United States coin book Compiler R. A. Wilson. [CJ1826 A6] 54-2072
1. Coins, American. I. Wilson, Rinaldo Alexander, 1888- comp.

AMERICAN Numismatic Association. 737.406273
A. N. A. convention sale catalog. [New York?] v. 22-26cm. annual. Title varies slightly. [CJ15.A48] 48-33039
1. Coins, American. I. Title.

BIELER, James M. 737.4'9'73
Coin charts of United States coins / by James M. Bieler. 1st ed. Lanham, Md. : [Coin Charts], 1977. viii, 96 p. ; 23 cm. At head of title: The plum book of United States coins. [CJ1826.B5] 77-355844 5.00
1. Coins, American. 2. Coins—Prices. 3. Coins as an investment. I. Title.

BOWERS, Q. David. 737.4'9'73
Collecting rare coins for profit [by] Q. David Bowers. [1st ed.] New York, Harper & Row [1975] ix, 326 p. illus. 24 cm. Bibliography: p. 317-318. [CJ1830.B63 1975] 74-5788 ISBN 0-06-010426-0 10.00
1. Coins, American. 2. Numismatics—Collectors and collecting. 3. Coins as an investment. I. Title. BIP

BOWERS, Q. David. 332.6'7
High profits from rare coin investment / by Q. David Bowers. Los Angeles : Bowers and Ruddy Galleries, 1974. 208 p. : ill. ; 22 cm. Includes index. [CJ1832.B65] 74-76717 ISBN 0-914490-03-6
1. Coins, American. 2. Coins as an investment. I. Title.

BRESSETT, Kenneth E. 737.4'9'73
Buying and selling United States coins, by Ken Bressett. [5th ed.] Racine, Wis., Western Pub. Co. [1974] 128 p. illus. 18 cm. (An Official Whitman coin guide) [CJ1826.B67 1974] 74-172720 1.00 (pbk.).
1. Coins, American. I. Title. BIP

BRESSETT, Kenneth E. 737.4'9'73
Buying and selling United States coins : an illustrated valuation guide of all regular mint issues from 1792 to date / by Ken Bressett. 9th ed. Racine, Wis. : Western Pub. Co., c1978. 192 p. ; 18 cm. (Official Whitman coin guide) Includes index. [CJ1826.B67 1978] 78-107489 ISBN 0-307-09052-3 : 1.25
1. Coins, American. I. Title.

BROWN, Martin R 737.4973
A guide to the grading of United States coins, by Martin R. Brown and John W. Dunn. [1st ed.] Oklahoma City, 1958. 66p. illus. 19cm. [CJ1826.B7] 60-27728
1. Coins, American. I. Dunn, John Wallace, 1933- joint author. II. Title.

BROWN, Martin R 737.4973
A guide to the grading of United States coins, by Martin R. Brown and John W. Dunn. [Rev. ed.] Oklahoma City, 1961. 111p. illus. 19cm. [CJ1826.B7 1961] 61-43698
1. Coins, American. I. Dunn, John Wallace. 1963- joint author. II. Title.

BROWN, Martin R. 737.4973
A guide to the grading of United States coins, by Martin R. Brown and John W. Dunn. [4th ed.] Racine, Wis., Whitman Pub. Co., 1964. 206 p. illus. 20 cm. "No. 9096." [CJ1826.B7 1964] 64-3911
1. Coins, American. I. Dunn, John Wallace, 1933- joint author. II. Title.

BROWN, Martin R. 737.49'73
A guide to the grading of United States coins, by Martin R. Brown and John W. Dunn. Illus. by Arthur Mueller. 5th ed. Racine, Wis., Western Pub. Co. [1969] 206 p. illus. 20 cm. "No. 9096." "Official Brown and Dunn grading system." [CJ1826.B7 1969] 70-13439
1. Coins, American. I. Dunn, John Wallace, 1933- joint author. II. Title. III. Title: Grading of United States coins.

BROWN, Martin R 737.4973
Market value index for circulated United States coins, by Martin R. Brown and John W. Dunn. 1962 ed. Oklahoma City, 1961. vii, 103p. illus. 19cm. [CJ1826.B72] 61-19304
1. Coins, American. I. D 1963- joint author. II. Title.

BROWN, Martin R 332.4'042'0973
Market value index for circulated United States coins, by Martin R. Brown and John W. Dunn. 1963 ed. Oklahoma City, 1962. vii, 111p. illus. 19cm. [CJ1826.B72 1962] 62-4469
1. Coins, American. I. D 1963- joint author. II. Title.

COIN dealer newsletter. 737.4973
Coin investors manual. 1st-ed.; 1965- Gardena, Calif., Payne Pub. Co. v. illus. 23 cm. "Data compiled from the Coin dealer newsletter." [CJ1826.C6] 65-1952
1. Coins, American. I. Title.

COIN World, Sidney, Ohio 737.4075
Coin collecting for fun and profit, by the eds. of Coin world. New York, Arco [1964, c.1963] 104p. illus., ports. 25cm. (Arco hobby lib.) 64-18186 2.50 bds.,
1. Coins, American. I. Title.

CROSBY, Sylvester Sage, d.1914. 737.4'9'73
The early coins of America / Sylvester S. Crosby. Lawrence, Mass. : Quarterman Publications, [1974] xiv, 378, [22] p., [7] leaves of plates : ill. ; 29 cm. Reprint of the ed. published in Boston in 12 parts in 1873-75. A Centennial foreword and bibliographical appendix have been added. Includes bibliographical references and index. [CJ1841.C8 1974] 77-189168 ISBN 0-88000-035-X : 35.00
1. Coins, American. 2. Tokens—United States. I. Title. BIP

CROSBY, Sylvester Sage, d.1914. 737.49'73
The early coins of America and the laws governing their issue; comprising also descriptions of the Washington pieces, the Anglo-American tokens, many pieces of unknown origin of the seventeenth and eighteenth centuries and the first patterns of the United States mint. New York, B. Franklin [1970] 378 p. illus., facsims. 27 cm. (Burt Franklin research & source works series, 544) (American classics in history & social science, 145.) Reprint of the 1875 ed. Includes bibliographical references. [CJ1841.C8 1970] 70-118743
1. Coins, American. 2. Tokens—U.S. I. Title.

DAVIS, Norman M., 1936- 737.49'73
The complete book of United States coin collecting [by] Norman M. Davis. New York, Macmillan [1971] xii, 336 p. illus. 21 cm. Bibliography: p. [301]-304. [CJ1830.D36] 70-117963 7.95
1. Coins, American. I. Title. BIP

DAVIS, Norman M., 1936- 737.4'9'73
The complete book of United States coin collecting / Norman M. Davis. Rev. ed. New York : Macmillan, 1976. x, 341 p. : ill. ; 22 cm. Includes index. Bibliography: p. [308]-311. [CJ1830.D36 1976] 76-362977 9.95
1. Coins, American. I. Title.

DELLQUEST, Augustus Wilfrid, 1901- 737.4
United States coins, a guide to values. New York, M. Barrows [1951] 187 p. illus. 15 cm. (Collectors' little-book library) [CJ1826.D415] 51-10716
1. Coins, American. I. Title.

DEL MONTE, Jacques, 1902- 737.4
Fell's United States coin book. New, rev. ed. New York, F. Fell [1952] 127p. illus. 20cm. [CJ1826.D42 1952] 52-12471
1. Coins, American. I. Title. II. Title: United States coin book.

DEL MONTE, Jacques, 1902- 737.4
Fell's United States coin book. 4th rev. ed. New York, F. Fells [1958] 127 p. illus. 20 cm. [CJ1826.D42 1958] 58-2168
1. Coins, American. I. Title. II. Title: United States coin book.

DEL MONTE, Jacques, 1902- 737.4
Fell's United States coin book. New York, F. Fell [1950, c1949] 121 p. illus. 20 cm. "Suggested readings": p. 119-120. [CJ1826.D42] 49-50419
1. Coins, American. I. Title. II. Title: United States coin book.

DEL MONTE, Jacques, 1902- 737.4
Fell's United States coin book. 3d rev. ed. New York, F. Fell [1955] 127 p. illus. 20 cm. Bibliography: p. 119-120. [CJ1826.D42 1955] 55-1201
1. Coins, American. I. Title. II. Title: United States coin book.

DEUTCH, Howard E., 1932- 737.4'9'73
High profits without risk : how you can earn more than 50% on your investment with absolute safety / by Howard E. Deutch. 1st ed. Monroeville, Pa. : Jefren Pub. Co., c1976. 223 p. : ill. ; 24 cm. Includes index. [CJ1832.D48] 76-19925 ISBN 0-917244-01-X
1. Coins, American. 2. Coins as an investment. I. Title. BIP

DRYFHOUT, John, 1940- 332.4'042'0973
The 1907 United States gold coinage [by John H. Dryfhout.] Cornish, N.H., Eastern National Park & Monument Association, 1972] 12 p. illus. 28 cm. Caption title. Bibliography: p. 12. [CJ1834.D79] 74-152641
1. Saint-Gaudens, Augustus, 1848-1907. 2. Coins, American. 3. Gold coins. I. Title.

FERGUSON, Herbert P. 737.4973
Collectors' guide to standard U.S. coins. Illus. by J. Marcel Suid. 3d ed. rev. New York, Ballantine [c.1961-1965] 167p. illus. 18cm. (H2914) Bibl. [CJ1826.F4] .60 pap.,
1. Coins, American. I. Title.

FERGUSON, Herbert P. 737.4973
Collectors' guide to standard U.S. coins. 2d ed., rev. Illus. by J. Marcel Suid. New York, Bantam [1963] 167p. illus. 18cm. (Bantam reference lib., HR53) Bibl. 63-15227 .60 pap.,
1. Coins, American. I. Title.

FERGUSON, Herbert P 737.4973
Collectors' guide to standard U.S. coins, by Herbert P. Ferguson. Illus. by J. Marcel Suid. 3d ed. rev. Toronto, New York, Bantam Books [1965] viii, 167 p. illus. 18 cm. "H2914, 4, misc." [CJ1826.F4] 65-3272
1. Coins, American. I. Title.

FORMAN, Harry J. 381'.45'7374973
How you can make big profits investing in coins [by] Harry J. Forman. New York, Nummus Press [1972] 160 p. 24 cm. [CJ1826.F67] 77-174309 ISBN 0-87841-002-3 6.50
1. Coins, American. I. Title.

FRENCH, Charles 737.497
American guide to U.S. coins. 1967 ed. New York, Cornerstone [1967, c.1965] 176p. illus. 21cm. (CN132) [CJ1830.F7] 1.00 pap.,
1. Coins, American. I. Title. BIP

FRENCH, Charles F. 737.4973
American guide to U.S. coins. 1966 ed. New York, Cornerstone [c.1964, 1965] 176p. illus. 21cm. (CN106) [CJ1830.F7] 65-5856 1.00 pap.,
1. Coins, American. I. Title.

FRENCH, Charles F. 737.49'73
American guide to U.S. coins, by Charles French. 1967 ed. New York, Cornerstone Library, 1967. 176 p. illus. 21 cm. [CJ1830.F7 1967] 67-3445
1. Coins, American. I. Title.

FRIEDBERG, Robert, 1912- ed. 737.497
Appraising and selling your coins; a complete illustrated catalogue of U. S. coins and bills and their cash premium values from 1652 to the present and the complete coinage of Canada and Newfoundland from 1858 to date. 3d ed. New York, Coin & Currency Inst. [1963] 174p. illus. 20cm. (Green coin bk.) 63-6297 1.95
1. Coins, American. 2. Coins, Canadian. I. Title.

FRIEDBERG, Robert 1912- ed. 332.4'042'0973
Appraising and selling your coins. [1st]-ed.; 1960- New York, Coin and Currency Institute. v. illus. 20 cm. (The Green coin book) First edition has label mounted on t. p.: Distributed by Sterling Pub. Co., New York. Editors: 1960- R. Friedberg (with J. Friedberg, 1964-) [CJ1826.A72] 66-18756
1. Coins, American. 2. Coins, Canadian. I. Friedberg, Jack, ed. 1912- II. Title.

**A guide book of United States coins.* Racine, Wis. : Western Pub. Co. 737
The 1979 32nd Rev. ed. by R.S. Yeoman, is available for 3.95. ISBN 0-307-90519-5. L.C. card no: 76-9533.

A guide book of United States coins. Racine, Wis. : Western Pub. Co. 737.
The 30th Rev. ed.,1977,c1976, by R.S. Yeoman is available for 3.95. ISBN 0-307-09051-3. L.C. card no.:76-9533. BIP

GUIDE book of United States coins (A), 1964. 737.4
Catalog and price list, 1616 to date. Including a brief history of American coinage, early American coins and token, early mint issue, regular mint issues, private, state and territorial gold, silver and gold commemorative issues proofs, by R. S. Yeoman. 17th rev. ed. Racine, Wis., Whitman Pub., c.1963. 255p. illus. 20cm. At head of title: The red book of United States coins. annual. 47-22284 1.75
1. Coins, American. I. Yoeman, R. S., ed.

GUIDE book of United States coins, 1963 (A); 737.4
Catalog and price list, 1616 to date. Including a brief history of American coinage, early American coins and tokens, early Mint issues, regular Mint issues, private, state and territorial gold, silver and gold commemorative issues, proofs, by R. S. Yeoman. 16th rev. ed. Racine, Wisc. Whitman, c.1962. 255p. illus. 20cm. At head of title: The Red book of United States coins Annual. 47-22284 1.75
1. Coins, American. I. Yeoman, R.S., ed.

GUIDE book of United States coins (A); 737.4
fully illustrated catalog and price list, 1616 to date, by R. S. Yeoman; including a brief history of American coinage, early American coins and tokens, early mint issues regular mint issues, private, state and territorial gold, silver and territorial gold, silver and gold commemorative issues, proofs. [15th ed.] Racine, Wis., Whitman, c.1961 255p. illus. 47-22284 1.75
1. Coins, American. I. Yeoman, R. S.

GUIDE book of United States coins (A) 1966. 737.4
Catalog and price list, 1616 to date, including a brief hist. of American coinage, early American coins and tokens, early mint issues, regular mint issues, private, state, and territorial gold, silver and gold commemorative issues, proofs, by R. S. Yeoman. 19th rev. ed. Racine, Wis., Whitman [1965] 255p. illus. 20cm. At head of title: Red book of United States coins. annual. 47-22284 1.75 bds.,
1. Coins, American. I. Yeoman, R. S.

GUIDE book of United States coins (A) 1968. 737.4
Catalog and price list, 1616 to date including a brief hist of American coinage, early American coins and tokens, early mint issues, regular mint issues, private, state, and territorial gold, silver and gold commemorative issues, proofs by R. S. Yeoman. 21st rev. ed. Racine, Wis., Whitman Pub., 1967. 20cm. At head of title: Red book of United States coins. annual. [CJ1826.G785] 47-22284 2.00 bds.,
1. Coins, American. I. Yeoman, R. S. BIP

GUIDE Book of United States coins (A), 1965. 737.4
Catalog and price list, 1616 to date. Including a brief history of American coinage, early American coins and tokens, early mint issues, regular mint issues, private, state and territorial gold, silver and gold commemorative issues proofs, by R. S. Yeoman. 18th rev. ed. Racine, Wis., Whitman Pub., c.1964. 255p. illus. 20cm. At head of title: The red book of United States coins. Annual. 47-22284 1.75 bds.,
1. Coins, American. I. Yeoman, R. S.

GUIDE book of United States coins (A) 1967. 737.4
Catalog and price list, 1616 to date including a brief hist. of American coinage, early American coins and tokens, early mint issues, regular mint issues, private, state, and territorial gold, silver and gold commemorative issues, proofs by R. S. Yeoman. 20th rev. ed. Racine, Wis., Whitman Pub., c.1966. 255p. illus. 20cm. At head of title: Red book of United States coins. annual. [CJ1826.G785] 47-22284 1.75 bds.,
1. Coins, American. I. Yeoman, R.S.

GUITON, Harold H 737.49'73
Guiton's coin grading guide for grading United States coins, by Harold H. Guiton. Terre Haute Ind. [Moore-Langden, Print. and Pub. Co.] 1966. 105 p. illus. 23 cm. [CJ1832.G9] 67-2508
1. Coins, American. I. Title. II. Title: Coin

grading guide for grading United States coins.

GUTTAG, Julius. 737.4'9'8
The Julius Guttag collection of Latin American coins / arr. by Edgar H. Adams. Lawrence, Mass. : Quarterman Publications, [1974] 527 p. : ill. ; 24 cm. Published in 1929 under title: Catalogue of the collection of Julius Guttag. Includes index. [CJ1803.2.G87G87 1974] 74-80921 ISBN 0-88000-027-9 : 35.00
1. Guttag, Julius—Coin collections. 2. Coins, American. 3. Coins, Latin American. I. Title. **BIP**

HANDBOOK of United 737'.0973
States coins, with premium list.
The 26th edition, 1969 is now available from Western Pub. Co. (Whitman Hobby Div.) Racine, Wis., for $1.25. L. C. card order no.: 42-16475.

HANDBOOK of United 737.0973
States coins, with premium list. 23rd ed. 1966 Racine, Wis., Whitman Pub., c.1965. 126p. 20cm. Ed.: 1965 R. S. Yeoman. 42-16475 1.00 bds.,
1. Coins, American. I. Yeoman, R. S., ed.

HANDBOOK of United 737.0973
States coins, with premium list [21st ed.] 1964. Racine, Wis., Whitman Pub., c.1963. 126p. illus. 20cm. Ed.: 1964, R. S. Yeoman. 42-16475 1.00
1. Coins, American. I. Yeoman, R. S., ed.

HANDBOOK of United 737.0973
States coins, with premium list. 20th ed. 1963. Racine, Wis., Whitman, c.1962. 126p. illus. 20cm. Ed.: 1963: R. S. Yeoman. 42-16475 1.00 bds.,
1. Coins, American. I. Yeoman, R. S., ed.

HANDBOOK of United 737.0973
States coins, with premium list. 22nd ed. 1965. Racine, Wis., Whitman Pub., c.1964. 126p. illus. 21cm. Ed.: 1965 R. S. Yeoman. 42-16475 1.00 bds.,
1. Coins, American. I. Yeoman, R. S., ed.

HANDBOOK of United 737.0973
States coins, with premium list. 1967. Racine, Wis. Whitman Pub. 24th ed -1966. 136p. illus 20cm. Eds.: 1966- R. S. Yeoman. [CJ1826.H3] 42-16475 1.00
1. Coins. American. I. Yeoman. R. S., ed.

HANDBOOK of United 737.0973
States coins, with premium list, 1968. 25th ed. Racine, Wis., Whitman Pub., 1967. v. illus. 20cm. Ed 1967- R.S. Yeoman. [CJ1826.H3] 42-16475 1.00
1. Coins, American. I. Yeoman, R.S., ed. **BIP**

HANDBOOK of United 737.0973
States coins, with premium list; 19th ed. Racine, Wis., Whitman, c.1961. 126p. illus. 42-16475 1.00
1. Coins, American. I. Yeoman, R. S., ed. II. Hewitt, Lee F., ed. III. Green, Charles, Elmore, ed.

HERBERT, Alan. 737.4'9'37
The official price guide to mint errors and varieties / by Alan Herbert. 2d ed. Orlando, Fla. : House of Collectibles, c1978. 182 p. : ill. ; 21 cm. First published in 1974 under title: The official guide to mint errors. [CJ125.H47 1978] 78-67027 ISBN 0-87637-103-9 : 3.95
1. Coins—Errors. 2. Coins, American. I. Title.

*HOBSON, Burton. 737.49'73
Coin collecting as a hobby. Enl. and rev. ed. New York, Cornerstone Library [1973] 192 p. illus. 20 cm. (Cornerstone Library, 12118) [CT1830] 1.50 (pbk.)
1. Coins, American. 2. Numismatics. I. Title.
L.C. card no. for the 1967 edition: 67-27759.

HUDSON, Addie Belle. 737.4973
Modern U.S. coins. [San Diego, Calif., 1969] 91 l. illus., facsims. 28 cm. Cover title. Includes bibliographies. [CJ1830.H8] 75-1914
1. Coins, American. I. Title.

KNIGHT, Hugh McCown 737.4973
A simplified guide to collecting American coins. Introd. by Richard S. Yeoman. Illus. by the author. New rev., enl. ed. Garden City, N.Y., Doubleday [1963, c.1962] 187p. illus. 27cm. 62-17355 3.95
1. Coins, American. I. Title.

KNIGHT, Hugh McCown. 737.4973
A simplified guide to collecting American coins. Introd. by Richard S. Yeoman. Illustrated by the author. [1st ed.] Garden City, N.Y., Hanover House, 1959. 157 p. illus. 27 cm. [CJ1826.K53] 58-8094
1. Coins, American.

KOSOFF, A 332.4'042'0973
An illustrated history of United States coins. depicting the proposed designs as well as the accepted types. Encino, Calif., 1962. 76p. illus. 28cm. [CJ1830.K6] 62-36815
1. Coins, American. I. Title.

LIEBERS, Arthur, 737.4973075
1913-
United States coins; the collector's guide and handbook of values. New York, Putnam [c.1965] 212p. illus. 22cm. [CJ1826.L5] 65-10857 5.95
1. Coins, American. I. Title.

MASSEY, Joseph Earl. 737.49'73
America's money; the story of our coins and currency [by] J. Earl Massey. New York, Crowell [1968] x, 278 p. illus. 21 cm. [CJ1839.M3] 68-31772 5.95
1. Coins, American. I. Title.

MILLS, Brad. 737.4'9'73
The official guide to coin collecting. [New York, House of Collectibles, 1974] 192 p. illus. 19 cm. [CJ1832.M5] 73-93248 ISBN 0-87637-238-8 2.95
1. Coins, American. 2. Numismatics—Collectors and collecting. I. Title. II. Title: Coin collecting. **BIP**

NEFSKY, William F. 737.4'9'73
A short code to United States coins [by] William F. Nefsky. [Lincoln, Neb., c1970] v, 34 p. 22 cm. Cover title. [CJ1832.N4] 72-170032
1. Coins, American. 2. Numismatics—Collectors and collecting. I. Title.

THE New official guide 737.49'73
to United States coinage; fully illustrated with mint records and prices 1793 to date. Gene Hessler, coordinating editor. Designed by Donald Afsanick. 1971 ed. N.Y., Dafran House [1970] 192 p. illus. 18 cm. [CJ1830.N4] 70-19483 1.00
1. Coins, American. I. Hessler, Gene, ed.

NORTH American coins 737.49'73
... a price guide to current values: United States 1793 to date, Canada 1864 to date, Mexico 1905 to date. [Iola, Wis., Krause, 1967] 48 p. illus. 28 cm. Cover title. [CJ1826.N66] 67-31847
1. Coins, American. 2. Coins—Prices.

RAYMOND, Wayte, 1886- 737.4
The Standard catalogue of United States coins from 1616 to present day. [1st]- ed.; 1935- New York. v. illus. facsims. 24 cm. annual (irregular) Title varies: 1st-17th. The Standard catalogue of United States coins from 1652 to present day (varies slightly) "Compiled and published by Wayte Raymond, inc." A "1943 supplement" takes the place of a complete 1943 ed. [CJ1826.S85] 34-33842
1. Coins, American. 2. Paper money — U.S. 3. Tokens — U.S. I. Title.

REED, Fred Morton. 737.4'973
Coins: an investor's & collector's guide [by] Mort Reed. Chicago, Regnery [1973] x, 403 p. illus. 24 cm. [CJ1830.R417] 72-11187 10.00
1. Coins, American. 2. Numismatics—Collectors and collecting. 3. Coins as an investment. I. Title.

REED, Fred Morton. 737.4'9'73
The complete coin collector / Mort Reed. Chicago : H. Regnery Co., c1976. p. cm. [CJ1830.R418 1976] 76-6283 ISBN 0-8092-8045-0 : 14.95
1. Coins, American. 2. Numismatics—Collectors and collecting. I. Title. **BIP**

REED, Fred Morton. 737.49'73
Cowles complete encyclopedia of U.S. coins, by Mort Reed. Foreword by Gilroy Roberts. [1st ed.] New York, Cowles Book Co. [1969] xx, 300 p. illus. 24 cm. 1972 ed. published under title: Encyclopedia of U.S. coins. Bibliography: p. 293-294. [CJ1830.R42 1969] 70-90063 ISBN 0-402-01111-2 7.95
1. Coins, American. 2. Coins—United States. I. Title.

REED, Fred Morton. 737.4'9'73
Encyclopedia of U.S. coins [by] Mort Reed. Foreword by Gilroy Roberts. Completely rev., updated ed. Chicago, Regnery [1972] xx, 303 p. illus. 24 cm. 1969 ed. published under title: Cowles complete encyclopedia of U.S. coins. Bibliography: p. 296-297. [CJ1830.R42 1972] 70-186778
1. Coins, American. 2. Coinage—United States. I. Title.

REINFELD, Fred, 1910- 737.4973
1964.
A treasury of American coins. Garden City, N. Y., Hanover House [1961] 124 p. illus. 27 cm. [CJ1839.R4] 61-14719
1. Coins, American. I. Title.

RUDDY, James F. 737.49'73
Photograde; a photographic grading guide for United States coins, by James F. Ruddy. Hollywood, Calif., Ruddy Investments [1970] 207 p. illus. 23 cm. Title on spine: New photograde: coin trading guide. [CJ1826.R8] 78-132061
1. Coins, American. I. Title. II. Title: New photograde: coin trading guide.

RUDDY, James F. 737.4'9'73
Photograde; a photographic grading guide for United States coins, by James F. Ruddy. Hollywood, Calif., Bowers and Ruddy Galleries [1973, c1972] 111 p. illus. 22 cm. On spine: New photograde: coin grading guide. [CJ1826.R8 1973] 74-188572
1. Coins, American. I. Title. II. Title: New photograde: coin grading guide.

SPADONE, Frank G. 737.49'73
Major variety-oddity guide of United States coins, listing all U.S. coins from half cents through gold coins, by F. G. Spadone. Fully illustrated, with values. 4th ed. Iola, Wis., Krause Publications [1967] 128 p. illus. 22 cm. [CJ1832.S6 1967] 67-18968
1. Coins, American. 2. Numismatics—Collectors and collecting. I. Title.

SPADONE, Frank G. 737.4'9'73
Major variety-oddity guide of United States coins, listing all U.S. coins from half cents through gold coins, fully illustrated, with values / by F. G. Spadone. 7th ed. Florence, Ala. : Anco, c1977. 128 p. : ill. ; 22 cm. Includes index. [CJ1832.S6 1977] 77-91397 ISBN 0-87637-211-6 pbk. : 2.95
1. Coins, American. 2. Numismatics—Collectors and collecting. I. Title.

SPANBAUER, Larry. 737.4'9'73
Counterfeits of United States coins / by Larry Spanbauer. [Oshkosh, Wis.] : Spanbauer, [1975] 75 p. : ill. ; 22 cm. [CJ1832.S63] 75-4159
1. Coins, American. 2. Counterfeits and counterfeiting—United States. I. Title.

STACK, Norman. 737.4973
U.S. coins of value. [New York Dell pub. Co. 1965] 223 p. illus. 18 cm. "9230." [CJ1826.S78] 65-1320
1. Coins, American. I. Title.

STACK, Norman. 737.4973
U.S. coins of value. [New York, Dell Pub. Co., 1966] 223 p. illus. 18 cm. "Revised 1966 prices." [CJ1826.S78 1966] 66-881
1. Coins, American. I. Title.

STACK, Norman. 737.4973
U.S. coins of value. [New York] Dell [1967] 222p. illus. 18cm. (9248) Rev. 1968 prices. [CJ1826.S78] 66-881 .75 pap.,
1. Coins, American. I. Title. **BIP**

STACK, Norman. 737.4'9'73
U.S. coins of value. [New York] Dell [1976] 224 p. illus. 18 cm. "New 1976 prices" [CJ1826.S78] 1.50 (pbk.)
1. Coins, American. I. Title.
Earlier edition carried L.C. no.: 74-157833.

STACK, Norman. 737.4'9'73
U.S. coins of value. [New ed. New York, Dell Pub. Co., 1974] 224 p. illus. 18 cm. "1974 prices." [CJ1826.S78 1974] 74-157833 0.95 (pbk.)
1. Coins, American. I. Title.

STERNFELD, 332.4'042'0973
Bernard.
How to grow money. Brooklyn, How-To Publications [1961] 124 p. illus. 28 cm. [CJ1826.S87] 61-16309
1. Coins, American. I. Title.

SVENSSON, Robert 737.4075
The complete coin collector's guide [New York, Avon, 1965] 180p. illus. 18cm. (V2118) [CJ1830.S85] 65-2523 .75 pap.,
1. Coins, American. I. Title.

TAXAY, Don. 737.4'9'73
The comprehensive catalogue and encyclopedia of United States coins. Prepared and edited by Don Taxay. 1st ed. New York, Scott Pub. Co., 1971 [c1970] xiv, 397 p. illus. 25 cm. On spine: Scott's comprehensive catalogue and encyclopedia of U.S. coins. Includes bibliographies. [CJ1826.T38] 73-176464 15.00
1. Coins, American. 2. Tokens—United States. 3. Coins—Prices. I. Scott Publishing Co. II. Title. III. Title: Scott's comprehensive catalogue and encyclopedia of U.S. coins.

TAXAY, Don. 332.9
Counterfeit, mis-struck, and unofficial U.S. coins, a guide for the detection of cast and struck counterfeits, electrotypes, and altered coins. Introd. by John J. Ford, Jr. New York, Arco Pub. Co. [1963] 221 p. illus. 25 cm. [CJ1822.T3] 62-20291
1. Coins, American. 2. Counterfeits and counterfeiting—U.S. I. Title. **BIP**

VLACK, Robert A 737.4973
Early American coins; a comprehensive listing with valuations of early American coins and tokens used in the American Colonies and early America, prior to the establishment of the United States Mint issue of 1793, including the Washington issues up to 1796, by Robert A. Vlack. 2d ed. Johnson City, N.Y., Windsor Research Publications, 1965. 120 p. illus. 23 cm. Bibliography: p. 117-118. [CJ1842.V5] 65-27408
1. Coins, American. I. Title.

WILSON, Rinaldo Alexander, 737.4
1888-
American standard United States coin book, giving a price range on each coin to allow for the condition. Also a mint list, figures of the Government mints, which will show the number of coins made. Prices paid. 23d ed. Los Angeles, American Numismatic Co. [1953, c1954] 104p. illus., port. 18cm. Cover title: American coin book. Published in 1933 under title: The American catalog of all United States coins and currency. [CJ1826.W6 1954] 54-2072
1. Coins, American. I. Title. II. Title: American coin book.

WRIGHT, Glenn. 737.4'9'73
Standard guide to U.S. coin and paper money valuations / by Glenn Wright and Clifford Mishler. [Iola, Wi. : Krause Publications, c1975] 194 p. (p. 194 advertisement) : ill. ; 18 cm. Cover title. [CJ1826.W74] 75-37439 ISBN 0-87341-007-6 : 1.50
1. Coins, American. 2. Paper money—United States—Catalogs. I. Mishler, Clifford, joint author. II. Title. **BIP**

Coins, American—Collectors and collecting.

**CHECK list and record* 737'.09'73
book of United States and Canadian coins. Racine, Wis., Whitman Pub. (Hobby Div.) 1968. 112p. illus. 15cm. .49 pap.,
1. Coins, American—Collectors and collecting. 2. Coins, Canadian—Collectors and collecting.

Coins, American—Juvenile literature.

BROWIN, Frances 737.4973
(Williams) 1898-
Coins have tales to tell; the story of American coins. [1st ed.] Philadelphia, Lippincott [1966] 152 p. illus. 26 cm. [CJ1832.B7] 66-10901
1. Coins, American — Juvenile literature. I. Title.

CAMPBELL, Elizabeth Anderson 737.4973
Nails to nickels; the story of American coins old and new. Illustrated by Leonard Weisgard. Boston, Little, Brown [c.1960] 58p. illus. 27cm. 60-5863 3.00
1. Coins, American—Juvenile literature. I. Title.

Coins, American—Massachusetts.

NOE, Sydney Philip. 737.4'9'744
The silver coinage of Massachusetts. Lawrence, Mass., Quarterman Publications [1974, c1973] xiv, 246 p. illus. 24 cm. Includes bibliographical references. [CJ1848.M4N66 1974] 72-77024 ISBN 0-88000-005-8 20.00
1. Coins, American—Massachusetts. 2. Silver coins. I. Title. BIP

Coins, American—New Jersey.

MARIS, Edward. 737.4'9749
The coins of New Jersey. Lawrence, Mass., Quarterman Publications [1974] viii, 21 p. plates. 42 cm. Reprint of the 1881 ed. printed by W. K. Bellows, Philadelphia under title: A historic sketch of the coins of New Jersey, with a new foreword and price guide. [CJ1848.N5M3 1881a] 74-76492 ISBN 0-88000-038-4
1. Coins, American—New Jersey. I. Title. BIP

Coins, American—Prices.

**HANDBOOK of United* 737'.0973
States coins, with premium list. Racine, WI : Western Publishing Co.
The 34th 1977 ed and 35th 1978 ed. by R.S. Yeoman are available for 2.95 each. ISBN 0-307-09050-7. 0-307-90508-X. L.C. card no.: 42-16475.

WILHITE, Robert. 737.4'9'73
Standard guide to U.S. coin and paper money valuations / by Robert Whilite and Clifford Mishler. 4th ed. Iola, WI : Krause Publications, 1978, c1977 194 p. : ill. ; 18 cm. Cover title. Edition for 1975 by G. Wright. [CJ1826.W74 1977] 77-93060 ISBN 0-87341-015-7 : pbk. : 1.50
1. Coins, American—Prices. 2. Paper money—United States—Catalogs. I. Mishler, Clifford, joint author. II. Wright, Glenn. Standard guide to U.S. coin and paper money valuations. III. Title.

Coins, American—Prices—Catalogs.

WILHITE, Robert. 737.4'9'73
Standard guide to U.S. coin and paper money valuations / by Robert Wilhite and Clifford Mishler. 5th ed. [Iola, WI : Krause Publications, c1978] 194 p. (p. 194 advertisement) : ill. ; 18 cm. Cover title. [CJ1826.W74 1978] 78-60747 ISBN 0-87341-021-1 : 1.50
1. Coins, American—Prices—Catalogs. 2. Paper money—United States—Catalogs. I. Mishler, Clifford, joint author. II. Title. III. Title: U.S. coin and paper money valuations.

Coins, Ancient.

RAYMOND, Wayte, 1886- 737.4
Guide to ancient coins. [3d ed.] New York [1950] 28 p. illus. 23 cm. (The Coin collector series, no. 11) Cover title. [CJ221.R33 1950] 50-3608
1. Coins, Ancient. I. Title. II. Series.

REINFELD, Fred, 1910- 737.4075
Picture book of ancient coins, by Fred Reinfeld and Burton Hobson. London, Oak Tree Press; New York, Sterling Pub. Co. [1963] 64 p. illus. 26 cm. (Visual history series) [CJ241.R4] 63-11596
1. Coins, Ancient. I. Hobson, Burton, joint author. II. Title.

SBORONOS, Ioannes N., 1863-1922. 737.4
Christodoulos the counterfeiter / J. Svoronos. Chicago : Ares Publishers, 1974. 38 p. [9] leaves of plates : ill. ; 28 cm. Consists of the original French text published in Athens in 1922 under title: C. Christodoulos et les faussaires d'Athenes and an English translation. [CJ245.S2613 1974] 74-77899
1. Christodoulos, Constantine. 2. Coins, Ancient. 3. Counterfeits and counterfeiting. I. Title.

Coins, Ancient—Juvenile literature.

CURRIER, Richard L. 737.4'09
Coins of the ancient world / by Ya'akov Meshorer ; retold for young readers by Richard L. Currier. Minneapolis : Lerner Publications Co., 1975, c1974. 94 p. : ill. ; 21 cm. (The Lerner archaeology series) (Digging up the past) Includes index. Discusses the many different kinds of coins found in the Holy Land explaining how they were made and stamped with designs indicating their value and origin. [CJ255.C87 1975] 72-10795 ISBN 0-8225-0835-4 lib.bdg. : 6.95
1. Bible—Numismatics—Juvenile literature. 2. Coins, Ancient—Juvenile literature. I. Meshorer, Ya'akov, 1935- II. Title. BIP

Coins, Arab—Crete.

MILES, George Carpenter, 1904- 737.4'94998
The coinage of the Arab amirs of Crete, by George C. Miles. New York, American Numismatic Society, 1970. x, 86 p. illus. 24 cm. (Numismatic notes and monographs, no. 160) Includes bibliographical references. [CJ3428.C73M54] 71-135738
1. Coins, Arab—Crete. 2. Coins, Islamic. 3. Coins, Medieval. I. Title. II. Series: Numismatic notes and monographs (New York) no. 160. BIP

Coins—Arcadia.

WILLIAMS, Roderick T. 737.49388
The confederate coinage of the Arcadians in the fifth century B. C., New York, Amer. Numismatic Soc. [1966] xix. 141. xiv. p. map. plates. 23cm. (Numismatic notes and monographs, no. 155) [CJ403.W5] 66-4081 4.50 pap.,
1. Coins—Arcadia. I. American Numismatic Society. II. Title. III. Series.

Coins as an investment.

COIN investors manual. 737.4973
1st ed.; 1965. Gardena, Calif., Payne Pub. Co. 16408 So. B'way. [c.1965] 23cm. Contrib. eds.: Geo. W. Haylings, James G. Miladin, Allen Harriman. Data comp. from the Coin dealer newsletter. [CJ1826.C6] 65-1952 7.50 bds.,

HOUSEL, Paul H. 737.4
Discovered: the poor man's money plant, by Paul H. Housel. Lanoka Harbor, N.J., Paradise House, c1962. 13 l. illus. 29 cm. [CJ101.H68] 73-1612
1. Coins as an investment. I. Title.

Coins, Australian.

GARTNER, John, ed. 737.49'9
The Australian coin catalogue; the complete coinage of Australia, New Zealand, New Guinea, Fiji. 6th ed. Melbourne, Hawthorn Press [1970] 80 p. illus., tables. 22 cm. [CJ4404.G3 1970] 77-587623 ISBN 0-7256-0024-1 1.25
1. Coins, Australian. 2. Coins, New Zealand. 3. Coins, New Guinea. 4. Coins, Fijian. I. Title.

Coins, Austrian.

SZEGO, Alfred. 737.49'436
The coinage of medieval Austria, 1156-1521; a basic outline. Oakdale, N.Y. [1970] viii, 56 p. illus., map. 22 cm. [CJ2591.S9] 71-269544
1. Coins, Austrian. I. Title.

Coins—Bibliography—Catalogs.

AMERICAN Numismatic Society. Library. 016.7374
Auction catalogue of the Library of the American Numismatic Society. Boston : G. K. Hall, 1962. p. 5195-5920 ; 36 cm. [Z6870.A52 1962] [CJ47] 76-356267
1. American Numismatic Society. Library. 2. Coins—Bibliography—Catalogs. I. Title.

Coins, British.

BRESSETT, Kenneth E. 737.4'9'41
A guide book of English coins, nineteenth and twentieth centuries / by Kenneth E. Bressett. 8th ed. Racine, Wis. : Western Pub. Co., c1975. 144 p. : ill. ; 20 cm. Includes index. Bibliography: p. 144. [CJ2495.B7 1975] 76-358118 ISBN 0-307-09060-4
1. Coins, British. 2. Great Britain—History. I. Title.

EDMUNDSON, Joseph. 332.6'7
Coins for investment. London, New York, W. H. Allen, 1972. viii, 163, [8] p. illus. 22 cm. Bibliography: p. 154-157. [CJ2480.E35] 73-170090 ISBN 0-491-00377-3 £2.25
1. Coins, British. 2. Coins as an investment. 3. Numismatics—Collectors and collecting. I. Title.

SYLLOGE of coins of the 737.4942
British Isles. London, Pub. for the British Academy by Oxford Univ. Pr., 1966. xiv. 148p. (inc. 71 plates) 25cm. Contents.--4. pt. 2 Royal collection of coins and pt. 2. Anglo-Saxon coins. *aethelraed II Bibl. [CJ2482.S9] 64-54848 20.80
1. Coins, British. I. Copenhagen. National museet.
Available from publisher's New York office. BIP

SYLLOGE of coins of the 737.4942
British Isles [no. 4] pt. 1. [New York] Pub. for the British Acad. by Oxford [c.]1964. 116p. fold. map. plates. 25cm. Contents.[no. 4] Royal collection of coins and medals, National Museum, Copenhagen: pt. 1. Ancient British and Anglo-Saxon coins before Aethelred II, by Georg Galster. Bibl. 64-54848 16.10
1. Coins, British. I. Copenhagen, National museet.

TROWBRIDGE, Richard J. 737'.0942
History, coinage, paper notes and medals of Edward VIII of Great Britain, by Richard J. Trowbridge. [1st ed. Long Beach, Calif., 1970] 55 p. illus., facsims., ports. 22 cm. Includes bibliographical references. [CJ2476.T75] 77-25094
1. Edward VIII, King of Great Britain, 1894- 2. Coins, British. 3. Paper money—Gt. Brit. 4. Medals—Gt. Brit. I. Title.

Coins, Byzantine.

ADELSON, Howard L. 737.4
Light weight solidi and Byzantine trade during the sixth and seventh centuries. New York. American Numismatic Society. 1957. ix, 187p. illus., fold. map. 23cm. (Numismatic notes and monographs, no. 138) Bibliographical footnotes. [CJ1281.A3] 57-13895
1. Coins, Byzantine. 2. Byzantine Empire—Comm. I. Title. II. Series.

BATES, George Eugene. 737.49'495
Byzantine coins [by] George E. Bates. Cambridge, Harvard University Press, 1971. x, 159 p. illus., maps. 29 cm. (Archaeological Exploration of Sardis. Monograph 1) [CJ1281.B36] 76-95917 ISBN 0-674-08965-0 15.00
1. Coins, Byzantine. 2. Sardis—Antiquities. I. Title. II. Series.

BRECKENRIDGE, James Douglas. 737.49495
The numismatic iconography of Justinian II(685-695, 705-711 A.D.) New York, American Numismatic Society, 1959. x, 104p. 10plates. 23cm. (Numismatic notes and monographs, no. 144) Issued also in 1958 in microfilm form, as thesis, Princeton University, under title: The numismatic iconography of the Byzantine emperor Jastinian ii. Bibliographical footnotes. [CJ1281.B7 1959] 60-2318
1. Justinianus ii, Rhinotmetus, Emperor of the East, 669-711. 2. Coins, Byzantine. I. Title. II. Series.

DUMBARTON Oaks. 737.49'495
Catalogue of the Byzantine coins in the Dumbarton Oaks collection and in the Whittemore collection, edited by Alfred R. Bellinger and Philip Grierson. Washington, Dumbarton Oaks Center for Byzantine Studies, Trustees for Harvard University; [distributed by J. J. Augustin, Locust Valley, N.Y., 1966- v. plates. 30 cm. (Dumbarton Oaks catalogues) Contents.Contents.—v. 1. Anastasius I to Maurice, 491-602, by A. R. Bellinger.—v. 2. pt. 1. Phocas and Heraclius (602-641) pt. 2. Heraclius Constantine to Theodosius III (641-717). By P. Grierson.—v. 3. pt. 1. Lev III to Michael III (717-867). pt. 2. Basil I to Nicephorus III (867-1081). By P. Grierson. Bibliography: v. 1, p. xxii-xxvi. [CJ1217.D8] 67-9186
1. Coins, Byzantine. I. Bellinger, Alfred Raymond, 1893- ed. II. Grierson, Philip, ed. III. Title. IV. Title: Byzantine coins in the Dumbarton Oaks collection and in the Whittemore collection. BIP

RYNEARSON, Paul F. 737.49'495
Byzantine coin values; a guide. by Paul F. Rynearson. San Diego, Calif., Pegasus [c1967] 103p. illus., map. 23cm. Bibl. [CJ1237.R9] 68-2756 3.00 pap.,
1. Coins, Byzantine. 2. Coins—Prices. I. Title.

Coins, Canadian.

CHARLTON, James Edward, 1911- 737.4971
Standard grading guide to Canadian decimal coins, by James E. Charlton, Robert C. Willey. Racine, Wis., Whitman Pub. [c.1965] 157p. illus. 20cm. [CJ1866.C47] 65-5732 price unreported
1. Coins, Canadian. I. Willey, Robert C., joint author. II. Title.

HAXBY, James A. 737.4'9'71
Coins of Canada / by J. A. Haxby and R. C. Willey. 3rd ed. Racine, Wis. : Western Pub. Co., c1977. 192 p. : ill. ; 20 cm. (Whitman official coin guide) [CJ1864.H38 1977] 76-49265 ISBN 0-307-09058-2 pbk. : 2.75
1. Coins, Canadian. I. Willey, Robert C., joint author. II. Title. BIP

STANDARD catalogue of 737.4971
Canadian coins, tokens, and paper money fully illustrated 1670 to date 1967. 15th ed. Racine, Wis., Whitman Pub. Co. [1966. illus. 20cm. annual. Title varies. 15th ed. by J. E. Charlton [CJ1861.S8] 60-473 1.25
1. Coins, Canadian. 2. Paper money, Canadian. I. Charlton, James Edward, 1911-

STANDARD catalogue of 737.4917
Canadian coins, tokens, and paper money; 11th ed., 1963. Racine, Wis., Whitman [c.1962] 126p. illus. 20cm. annual Title varies. 1.00
1. Coins, Canadian. 2. Paper money—Canada.

STANDARD catalogue of 737.4971
Canadian coins, tokens, and paper money, fully illustrated 1670 to date; 14th ed., 1966. Racine, Wis., Whitman [c.1965] 126p. illus. 20cm. annual. Title varies. 14th ed. by J. E. Charlton. [CJ1861.S8] 60-473 1.00 bds.,
1. Coins, Canadian. 2. Paper money—Canada. I. Charlton, James Edward, 1911-

STANDARD catalogue of 737.4971
Canadian coins, tokens, and paper money, fully illustrated 1670 to date. 16th ed. 1968. Racine, Wis., Whitman Pub. [1968] v. illus. 20cm. annual. Title varies. 16th ed. ed. by J. E. Charlton. [CJ1861.S8] 60-473 1.50 bds.,
1. Coins, Canadian. 2. Paper money—Canada. I. Charlton, James Edward, 1911-

Coins, Central America.

ROBINSON, Charles M. 737.49728
The coins of Central America, 1733-1965; an illustrated guide to Central American coinage, with pricing aids, by Charles M. Robinson, iii [San Benito? Texas, 1965] 131 p. illus., maps. 28 cm. Bibliography: p. 127-130. [CJ1916.R6] 66-797
1. Coins, Central America. I. Title.

Coins, Chinese.

COOLE, Arthur Braddan, 1900- 737.4'0951
Ch i heavy sword coins of the Chou

Coins — Europe.

HARRIS, Robert P 737.4940216
A guide book of modern European coins, by Robert P. Harris. Racine, Wis., Whitman Pub. Co. [1965] 202 p. 20 cm. [CJ2454.H36] 65-6327
1. Coins — Europe. I. Title.

Coins, European.

DAVENPORT, John Stewart, 1907- 737.4'094
European crowns, 1600-1700 / by John S. Davenport. Galesburg, Ill. : Davenport, 1974. viii, 634 p. : chiefly ill. ; 24 cm. Bibliography: p. 631-633. [CJ2456.D28] 75-305525
1. Coins, European. 2. Crown (Coin) 3. Taler. I. Title.

DAVENPORT, John Stewart, 1907- 737.4'094
European crowns, 1700-1800, by John S. Davenport. 3d ed. Galesburg, Ill., 1971. 334 p. illus. 24 cm. Bibliography: p. 332-334. [CJ2456.D29 1971] 72-178511
1. Coins, European. 2. Crown (Coin) 3. Taler. I. Title.

HEWITT Brothers. 737.4'094
Price catalog of modern European gold coins. Chicago [1969] 32 p. illus. 20 cm. (Hewitt's numismatic information series) [CJ2458.H48] 75-286341 1.00
1. Coins, European. 2. Gold Coins. I. Title.

Coins, Foreign—U. S.

SCHILKE, Oscar G. 737.4973
America's foreign coins; an illustrated standard catalogue with valuations of foreign coins with legal tender status in the United States. 1793-1857, by Oscar G. Schilke, Raphael E. Solomon. New York, Coin Currency [hist. Sterling, 1966, c.1964] xvii, 211p. illus. 24cm. Bibl. [CJ1832.S3] 64-19722 7.50
1. Coins, Foreign—U. S. I. Solomon, Raphael E., joint author. II. Title. BIP

Coins, French.

KIRBY, Norman H. 737.4944
Crowns of France: Louis XVI-De Gaulle by Norm H. Kirby [Chicago, Ill., Printed by Hewitt Bros., 1968] vii, 64 p. illus. 24 cm. Bibliography: p. 64. [CJ2684.K56] 68-5401
1. Coins, French. I. Title.

MORRISON, Karl Frederick. 737.49'44
Carolingian coinage, by Karl F. Morrison. With the collaboration of Henry Grunthal. New York, American Numismatic Society, 1967. xii, 465 p. illus., maps, plates. 23 cm. (Numismatic notes and monographs, no. 158) [CJ2682.M6] 68-662
1. Coins, French. 2. Carlovingians. I. Title. II. Series: Numismatic notes and monographs (New York) no. 158

Coins, German.

ARNOLD, Paul, fl.1967- 737.4'9'73
Catalogue of German coins; gold, silver and minor coins since 1800, with their valuations, by P. Arnold, D. Steinhilber and H. Kuthmann. New York, Sterling Pub. Co. [1972] 320 p. illus. 26 cm. Translation of Grosser deutscher Munzkatalog von 1800 bis heute. [CJ2725.A7513 1972] 72-126855 ISBN 0-8069-6028-0
1. Coins, German. I. Kuthmann, Harald, joint author. II. Steinhilber, Dirk, joint author. III. Title.

Coins—Grading—Addresses, essays, lectures.

GRADING coins : 737.4
a collection of readings / edited by Richard Bagg and James J. Jelinski. Portsmouth, N.H. : Essex Publications, 1977. vii, 210 p. : ill. ; 23 cm. Includes bibliographical references and index. [CJ101.G7] 77-82246 ISBN 0-930332-01-6 pbk. : 9.95
1. Coins—Grading—Addresses, essays, lectures. 2. Coins—Prices—Addresses, essays, lectures. I. Bagg, Richard. II. Jelinski, James J.
Publisher's address : Portsmouth, NH 03801. BIP

Coins, Greek.

AMERICAN Numismatic Society. 737.4'9'38
The Burton Y. Berry Collection. New York, 1961-62. 2 v. plates. 40 cm. (Its Sylloge nummorum Graecorum) Contents.Contents.—pt. 1. Macedonia to Attica.—pt. 2. Megaris to Egypt. [CJ309.A4 vol. 1] 73-176717
1. Berry, Burton Yost—Coin collections. 2. Coins, Greek.

AMERICAN Numismatic Society 737.4938
Sylloge nummorum Graecorum [1] New York [32, Author, Broadway at 156 St.] 1961. unpaged, 27 plates. 40cm. Contents.[1] The Burton Y. Berry Collection. Pt. 1. Macedonia to Attica. 61-19327 15.00 pap.,
1. Coins, Greek. I. Title.

BOSTON. Museum of Fine Arts. 737.4
Catalogue of Greek coins, by Agnes Baldwin Brett. Boston, 1955. xvi, 340p. 116plates. 31cm. Includes bibliographies. [CJ335.B6] 55-10223
1. Coins, Greek. I. Brett, Agnes (Baldwin) 1876-1955. II. Title.

BOSTON. Museum of Fine Arts. 737.4
Catalogue of Greek coins, by Agnes Baldwin Brett. Boston, 1955. xvi, 340 p. 116 plates. 31 cm. 78 p. 30 plates. 30 cm. Greek coins, 1950 to 1963. Boston [1964] Includes bibliographies. [CJ335.B6] CJ335 55-10223
1. Coins, Greek. I. Brett, Agnes (Baldwin) 1876-1955. II. Title. III. Title: Greek coins, 1950 to 1963. BIP

BOSTON. Museum of Fine Arts. 737.4'9'38
Catalogue of Greek coins / by Agnes Baldwin Brett, honorary curator of classical coins, Museum of Fine Arts, Boston ; with a new introd. by Mary B. Comstock and Cornelius C. Vermeule, Jr. New York : Attic Books, 1974. xvii, 340 p., [58] leaves of plates : ill. ; 29 cm. Reprint of the 1955 ed. published by the museum. Includes bibliographies and indexes. [CJ315.U52B673 1974] 75-305887 ISBN 0-915018-04-7
1. Boston. Museum of Fine Arts. 2. Coins, Greek. I. Brett, Agnes Baldwin, 1876-1955. II. Title.

BOSTON, Museum of Fine Arts 737.4
Greek Coins, 1950 to 1963 [By Agnes Baldwin Brett] Author dist. New York, October House, c. 1964 78p. illus. 30cm. 64-21983 12.50
1. Coins, Greek. I. Brett, Agnes (Baldwin) 1876-1955. II. Title.

BRETT, Agnes (Baldwin) 1876-1955. 737.49'38
Facing heads on ancient Greek coins, by Agnes Baldwin. Closter, N.J., Reprinted by C. H. McSorley, 1968. 23 p. 4 plates. 29 cm. Imprint covered by label: Distributed by Argonaut, Chicago. [CJ351.B67] 68-4847
1. Coins, Greek. I. Title.

BRITISH Museum. Dept. of Coins and Medals. 737.4'09'014
Guide to the principal gold & silver coins of the ancients, from circa B.C. 700 to A.D. 1, by Barclay V. Head. Chicago, Argonaut, 1968. xviii, 128 p., 70 plates. port. 25 cm. (Argonaut library of antiquities) On spine: Guide to the coins of the ancients. "Reprint of the second edition of 1881, with the addition of a new preface and select bibliography." Bibliography: p. xv-xviii. [CJ215.B8 1968] 68-3656
1. Coins, Greek. 2. Coins, Roman. I. Head, Barclay Vincent, 1844-1914. II. Title. III. Title: Guide to the coins of the ancients.

CAMBRIDGE. University. Corpus Christi College. 737.4'938 s
The Lewis Collection in Corpus Christi College, Cambridge. London, Oxford University Press for the British Academy, 1972- v. illus. 39 cm. (Sylloge nummorum graecorum, v. 6) Includes index. Contents.Contents.—pt. 1. The Greek and Hellenistic coins (with Britain and Parthia) [CJ314.B7 vol. 6] [CJ315.G672] 737.4'938'0740259 74-174825 ISBN 0-19-725924-3 (v. 1) £8.00 (v. 1)
1. Cambridge. University. Corpus Christi College. 2. Lewis, Samuel Savage, 1836-1891—Coin collections. 3. Coins, Greek. I. Title. II. Series: British Academy, London (Founded 1901) Sylloge nummorum graecorum, v. 6

DAVIS, Norman, 1897- 737.49'38
Greek coins & cities. Illustrated from the collection at the Seattle Art Museum. [Seattle] Seattle Art Museum [1967] 221 p. illus., maps. 27 cm. Bibliography: p. 215. [CJ335.D38] 68-353
1. Davis, Norman, 1897- —Coin collections. 2. Coins, Greek. I. Seattle. Art Museum. II. Title.

DAVIS, Norman M., 1907- 737.49'38
Greek coins & cities. Illustrated from the collection at the Seattle Art Museum. [Seattle] Seattle Art Museum [1967] 221 p. illus., maps. 27 cm. Bibliography: p. 215. [CJ335.D38] 68-353
1. Coins, Greek. I. Seattle. Art Museum. II. Title.

FORRER, Leonard. 737.49'38
Portraits of royal ladies on Greek coins. Chicago, Argonaut, 1969. viii, 72 p. illus., port. 25 cm. "Original appeared first in the Numismatic chronicle of 1938." Bibliographical footnotes. [CJ385.F67] 79-4507
1. Coins, Greek. 2. Queens—Portraits. I. Title.

IMHOOF-BLUMER, Friedrich, 1838-1920 737.4938
Ancient coins illustrating last masterpieces of Greek art; a numismatic comentary on Pausanias, by F. W. Imhoof-Blumer, Percy Gardner. New enl. ed. with introd., commentary, notes by Al. N. Oikonomides [1st Amer. ed.] Chicago, Argonaut [c.] 1964. 1xxx, 176p. illus., map, plates. 22cm. (Argonaut lib. of antiquities) First pub. in Jour. of Hellenic studies, v.6 1885, v.7, 1886, v.8. 1887, under title: Numismatic commentary on Pausanias. Includes tr. of the Greek quotations from Palsanias and A new commentary on the statues represented on Athenian coins' by the ed. Bibl. 64-23435 10.00
1. Coins, Greek. 2. Pausanias, Descriptio Graeciae. 3. Sculpture, Greek. I. Gardner, Percy, 1846-1937, joint author. II. Oikonomides, Al. N., ed. III. Title.

IMHOOF-BLUMER, Friedrich, 1838-1920. 737.4938
Ancient coins illustrating lost masterpieces of Greek art; a numismatic commentary on Pausanias, by F. W. Imhoof-Blumer [and] Percy Gardner. New enl. ed. with introd., commentary and notes by Al. N. Oikonomides. [1st American ed,] Chicago, Argonaut, 1964. 1xxx, 176 p. illus., map, plates. 22 cm. (Argonaut library of antiquities) First published in Journal of Hellenic studies, v. 6, 1885, v. 7, 1886, and v. 8, 1887, under title: Numismatic commentary on Pausanias. Includes translations of the Greek quotations from Pausanias and "A new commentary on the statues represented on Athenian coins" by the editor. Bibliography: p. [175]-176. [CJ351.I5 1964] 64-23435
1. Coins, Greek. 2. Pausanias. Descriptio Graeciae. 3. Sculpture, Greek. I. Gardner, Percy 1846-1937, joint author. II. Oikonomides, Al. N., ed. III. Title.

JENKINS, Kenneth. 737.4'9'378
Coins of Greek Sicily / [by] Kenneth Jenkins. 2nd ed. London : British Museum Publications Ltd for the Trustees of the British Museum, 1976. 64 p. : ill., map ; 23 cm. Bibliography: p. 63-64. [CJ549.J4 1976] 77-354566 ISBN 0-7141-0838-3 : £2.50. ISBN 0-7141-0837-5 pbk.
1. Coins, Greek. 2. Numismatics—Sicily. I. British Museum. II. Title. BIP

KLAWANS, Zander H 737.4938
An outline of ancient Greek coins. Racine, Wis., Whitman Pub. Co., c1959. 208p. illus. 20cm. [CJ339.K53] 59-40274
1. Coins, Greek. I. Title.

KRAAY, Colin M. 737.49'38
Greek coins and history; some current problems [by] Colin M. Kraay. New York, Barnes & Noble [1969] x, 81 p. 8 plates. 23 cm. [CJ351.K7 1969b] 72-8925 6.50
1. Coins, Greek. 2. Greeks in Sicily. I. Title.

OLESON, John. 737.4'9'3807401444
Greek numismatic art : coins of the Arthur Stone Dewing collection / by John Oleson. [Cambridge] : Fogg Art Museum, Harvard University, 1975. [59] p. : ill. ; 18 x 21 cm. Errata slip inserted. Bibliography: p. [5] [CJ317.U62D486] 75-15059
1. Dewing, Arthur Stone, 1880-1971—Coin collections. 2. Coins, Greek. I. Title.

ROBINSON, David Moore, 1880- 737.4
A hoard of silver coins from Carystus. New York, American Numismatic Society, 1952. 62p. plates. 23cm. (Numismatic notes and monographs, no.124) Bibliographical footnotes. [CJ481.R6] 53-570
1. Coins, Greek. 2. Numismatics—Karistos, Greece. I. Title. II. Series.

STILLMAN, William James, 1828-1901. 737.4'9'38
The coinage of the Greeks / William J. Stillman. Chicago : Obol International, 1975. 16 p. : ill. ; 26 cm. Reprinted from Century illustrated magazine, v. 33, p. [788]-799, March 1887. [CJ335.S74] 75-325889 3.00
1. Coins, Greek. I. Title. BIP

TROXELL, Hyla A. 737.49'38'074
The Norman Davis Collection, by Hyla A. Troxell. New York, American Numismatic Society, 1969. 53 p. 28 plates. 28 cm. (Greek coins in North American collections) [CJ317.T76] 76-281687
1. Davis, Norman, 1907- —Coin collections. 2. Coins, Greek. I. Title. II. Series. BIP

Coins, Greek—Addresses, essays, lectures.

ESSAYS in Greek coinage, presented to Stanley Robinson; 737.49'38
edited by C. M. Kraay and G. K. Jenkins. Oxford, Clarendon P., 1968. ii-xii, 268 p. 34 plates, illus., port. 26 cm. Contents.Contents.—An interpretation of Ath. pol. ch. 10, by C. M. Kraay.—Electrum coins from Gordion, by A. R. Bellinger.—Observations on the Wappenmunzen, by R. J. Hopper.—Problems of the earliest owls of Athens, by E. J. P. Raven.—Early Tarentine chronology, by H. A. Cahn.—The fifth-century diskoboloi of Kos, by J. P. Barron.—Early Greek bronze coinage, by M. J. Price.—New evidence for the gold-silver ratio, by D. M. Lewis.—Lycian coin portraits, by W. Schwabacher.—The trihemidrachms of Corinth, by J. Warren.—Electrum coinage at Syracuse, by G. Kenneth Jenkins.—The mints of Lysimachus, by M. Thompson.—Monnaies hellenistiques de Byzance et de Calcedoine, by H. Seyrig.—A tyrant of Karystos, by W. P. Wallace.—New light on the Roman victoriate, by H. B. Mattingly.—Les arsinoeens de Crete, by G. le Rider.—The coinages of Ariarathes VIII and Ariarathes IX of Cedited by C. M. Kraay and G. K. Jenkins. Oxford, Clarendon P., 1968. ii-xii, 268 p. 34 plates, illus., port. 26 cm. Contents.Contents.—An interpretat
1. Coins, Greek—Addresses, essays, lectures. I. Robinson, Stanley. II. Kraay, Colin M., ed. III. Jenkins, G. Kenneth, ed. BIP

Coins, Greek—Asia, Western.

CUNNINGHAM, Alexander, Sir, 1814-1893. 737.49'39'6
Coins of Alexander's successors in the East (Bactria, Ariana & India). [1st American ed.] Chicago, Argonaut, 1969. 337 p. 14 illus., map. 24 cm. (The Argonaut library of antiquities) Reprint of the 1884 ed. Bibliographical footnotes. [CJ668.C8 1969] 77-6601
1. Coins, Greek—Asia, Western. I. Title.

Coins, Greek—Athens.

KLEINER, Fred S. 737.4'9'38
Greek and Roman coins in the Athenian Agora / [prepared by Fred S. Kleiner ; photos. by Eugene Vanderpool, Jr.]. Princeton, N.J. : American School of Classical Studies at Athens, 1975. [32] p. : ill. ; 22 cm. (Excavations of the Athenian Agora : picture book ; no. 15) [CJ459.A8K55] 76-359399 1.00
1. Coins, Greek—Athens. 2. Coins, Roman—Athens. 3. Athens. Agora. 4. Greece—Antiquities. 5. Rome—Antiquities. I. Title. II. Series. **BIP**

KRAAY, Colin Mackennal. 737.49'385
Coins of ancient Athens, by C. M. Kraay. Newcastle upon Tyne, Corbitt and Hunter, 1968. [2], 39 p. illus. 22 cm. (Minerva numismatic handbooks, no. 2) Bibliography: p. 22. [CJ459.A8K7] 75-363162 12/6
1. Coins, Greek—Athens. I. Title.

Coins, Greek—Cyprus.

NEWELL, Edward Theodore, 1886-1941. 737.4'9'3937
Some Cypriote "Alexanders" / by E. T. Newell. Chicago : Obol International, 1974. 29 p., [3] leaves of plates : ill. ; 22 cm. Pages also numbered 294-322. Reprinted from the Numismatic chronicle and journal of the Royal Numismatic Society, 4th series, v. 15, no. 59, 1915. Includes bibliographical references. [CJ684.N37 1974] 74-188861
1. Alexander the Great, 356-323 B.C. 2. Coins, Greek—Cyprus. I. Title. **BIP**

Coins, Greek—India.

NARAIN, A. K. 737.49'34
The coin types of the Indo-Greek kings, by A. K. Narain. Chicago, Argonaut, 1968. 37 p. geneal. table, map. 23 cm. "First published in J[ournal of the] N[umismatic] S[ociety of] I[ndia], vol. xvi, pt. ii, pp. 293-331. In 1955 published independently as NNM no. 1 of the Numismatic Society of India." Reprint ed. sponsored by the Ancient Coin Club of America. Bibliography: p. [2] [CJ667.N3] 68-4738
1. Coins, Greek—India. I. Ancient Coin Club of America. II. Title. **BIP**

WHITEHEAD, Richard Bertram. 737.4938
Indo-Greek numismatics. Chicago, Argonaut, 1970. 144 p. illus., 8 plates. 24 cm. "The four ... articles which form the present volume were all published originally in the Numismatic chronicle." Bibliographical footnotes. [CJ668.W5 1970] 76-9828
1. Coins, Greek—India. I. Title.

Coins, Greek—Philippi.

LAMPROS, Paulos, 1819-1887. 737.4'9'381
Gold coins of Philippi = [Peri hex chryson anekdoton nomismaton ton Philippon. (romanized form)] / Paul Lambros ; translated by Betty Gardiakos. Chicago : Obo International, 1975, c1970. 19 p. : ill. ; 22 cm. English translation followed by original text. First published in Greek in Nea pandora, v. 80, 1854. [CJ547.P48L3513 1975] 75-327921 2.00
1. Coins, Greek—Philippi. 2. Gold coins. 3. Philippi—Antiquities. I. Title. II. Title: Peri hex chryson anekdoton nomismaton ton Philippon. **BIP**

Coins, Haitian.

ARROYO, Carmen. 739.49'7294
Coins of Haiti, 1803-1970. Coordinating editor: Dale A. Seppa. Associate editor: Grecia Arroyo. San Antonio, Almanzar's Coins of the World [1970] 52 p. illus. 22 cm. Introd. also in Spanish. [CJ2136.A85] 74-96261
1. Coins, Haitian. I. Title.

Coins—History.

BECKER, Thomas W. 737'.08 s
The heritage of coins, by Thomas W. Becker. [Saddle Brook, N.J.] International Numismatic Collector Society [1970] 64 p. illus., 18 col. slides. 2 x 2 in. 29 cm. (International Numismatic Collector Society. Series, library 1, v. 1) [CJ35.I6 library 1, vol. 1] [CJ75] 737.4'09 71-31077
1. Coins—History. I. Title. II. Series.

KEARY, Charles Francis, 1848-1917. 737.4'09
The morphology of coins. Chicago, Argonaut, 1970. 89 p. illus., plates. 24 cm. "Reprinted from the Numismatic chronicle, vol. V, third series, pages 165-198, vol. VI, pages 41-95. London: 1886." Includes bibliographical references. [CJ75.K4] 79-11203 10.00
1. Coins—History. I. Title.

Coins, Hungarian.

*SEY, Katalin B. 737.4'075
Coins and medals [by] Katalin B. Sey and Istvan Gedai Budapest, Corvina Press, 1973 46 p. col. plates 27 cm. [CJ81]
1. Coins, Hungarian. 2. Medals. I. Gedai, Istvan, joint author II. Title.
Distributed by International Publications Service, N.Y. for 7.50. **BIP**

Coins, Indic.

BRITISH Museum. Dept. of Coins and Medals 737.4396
The coins of the Greek and Scythic kings of Bactria and India in the British Museum, by Percy Gardner. Ed. by Reginald Stuart Poole. Chicago, Argonaut [c.] 1966. lxxvi, 193p. illus., map. 25cm. [CJ3532.B8 1966] 66-25813 15.00
1. Coins, Indic. 2. Coins, Bactrian. 3. Coins, Greek. I. Gardner, Percy, 1846-1937, comp. II. Poole, Reginald Stuart, 1832-1895, ed. III. Title.

BRITISH Museum: Dept. of Coins and Medals. 737.4396
The coins of the Greek and Seythic kings of Bactria and India in the British Museum, by Percy Gardner. Edited by Reginald Stuart Poole. Chicago, Argonaut, 1966. ixxvi. 193 p. illus., map. 25 cm. [CJ3532.B8 1966] 66-25813
1. Coins, Indie 2. Coins, Bactrian. 3. Coins, Greek. I. Gardner, Percy, 1846-1937, comp. II. Poole, Reginald Stuart, 1832-1895, ed. III. Title.

LAHORE. Central Museum. 737.4'074'09549143
Catalogue of coins in the Rahjab Museum, Lahore, by R. B. Whitehead. Chicago, Argonaut, 1969- v. illus., plates. 24 cm. Reprint of the 1914 ed. Contents.Contents.—v. 1. Indo-Greek coins. [CJ3532.L32] 79-9956 20.00 (v. 1)
1. Coins, Indic. 2. Coins, Greek. 3. Coins, Islamic. 4. Coins, Iranian. I. Whitehead, Richard Bertram, comp. II. Title.

Coins, Iranian.

HILL, George Francis, Sir, 1867-1948. 737.4'9'55
Imperial Persian coinage / G. F. Hill. Chicago : Obol International, 1977. 17 p., 1 leaf of plates : ill. ; 26 cm. Reprinted from Journal of Hellenic studies, 1919. Includes bibliographical references. [CJ3756.H54 1977] 77-368269 ISBN 0-916710-32-7 : 2.00
1. Coins, Iranian. I. Title. **BIP**

Coins, Islamic.

MILES, George Carpenter, 1904- 722'.8
The Islamic coins / by George C. Miles. Princeton, N.J. : American School of Classical Studies at Athens, 1962. vi, [2], 61 p., [3] leaves of plates : ill. ; 31 cm. (The Athenian Agora ; v. 9) Includes index. Bibliography: p. [viii] [DF287.A23A5 vol. 9] [CJ3410] 737.4'0917'671 75-328018
1. Coins, Islamic. 2. Athens. Agora. I. Title. II. Series: American School of Classical Studies at Athens. The Athenian Agora ; v. 9.

Coins, Islamic—India.

HULL, Donald B. 737.4'9'54
Collectors' guide to Muhammadan coins of India, 1200 A.D. to 1860 A.D. [by] Donald B. Hull. [Alhambra, Calif., Printed by Cunningham Press, 1972] 789 p. illus. 29 cm. "250 copies." "Estimated values, June 1972" (11 p.) in pocket. Includes bibliographies. [CJ3536.H83] 72-188355
1. Coins, Islamic—India. 2. Coins, Indic. I. Title.

Coins, Israeli.

BERTRAM, Fred. 737.49'5694
Israel's 20-year catalog of coins and currency, including Palestine Mandate and state medals, by Fred Bertram and Robert Weber. New York, Louis Denberg Foundation [1968] 127 p. illus. 23 cm. [CJ3867.B42] 67-29649
1. Coins, Israeli. I. Weber, Robert, 1927- joint author. II. Title.

ISRAEL'S money and medals / [edited by Sylvia Haffner]. 2d ed. 737.4'9'5694
Valley Stream, N.Y. : A. H. Kagan, 1976, c1974. 1 v. : ill. ; 26 cm. Loose-leaf for updating. [CJ3867.I84 1976] 75-46129
1. Coins, Israeli. 2. Medals—Israel. 3. Paper money—Israel—Catalogs. I. Haffner, Sylvia.

Coins, Japanese.

JACOBS, Norman, 1924- 737.4
Japanese coinage [by] Norman Jacobs [and] Cornelius C. Vermeule III. New York, Numismatic Review, 1972. 151 p. illus. 26 cm. Price list in pocket in rear. [CJ3706.J3] 53-2547
1. Coins, Japanese. 2. Numismatics—Japan. I. Vermeule, Cornelius Clarkson, 1925- II. Title.

JACOBS, Norman, 1924- 737.4
Japanese coinage [by] Norman Jacobs [and] Cornelius C. Vermeule III. New York, Numismatic Review, 1953. 142p. illus. 26cm. [CJ3706.J3] 53-2547
1. Coins, Japanese. 2. Numismatics—Japan. I. Vermeule, Cornelius Clarkson. II. Title.

Coins, Jewish.

JEWISH coins of the Second Temple period. 737.49'5694
Tr. from Hebrew by I. H. Levine. Tel Aviv, Am Hassefer [1967] 184p. 32 plates. 28cm. Somewhat enl., rev. version of the orig. Hebrew. Tr. of (romanized) Matabe'ot ha-Yehudim bi-yeme Bavit sheni. Bibl. [CJ1375.M413] [PL480.Is-6099] HE67 15.00
1. Coins, Jewish. I. Meshorer, Ya'akov, 1935-

Coins,Korean

CRAIG, Alan David, 1930 737.4
Coins of Korea and an outline of early Chinese coinages Berkeley, Calif., c1955 96p. illus. 22cm. [CJ3736.C7] 56-16643
1. Coins,Korean 2. Coins,Chinese I. Title.

MANDEL, Edgar J. 737.4'9'519
Cast coinage of Korea [by] Edgar J. Mandel. Racine, Wis., Western Pub. Co., c1972. 160 p. illus. 22 cm. Bibliography: p. 154-155. [CJ3736.M36] 73-157530 7.50
1. Coins, Korean. 2. Coins, Chinese. I. Title.

Coins, Latin American.

ELIZONDO, Carlos A. 737.4'098
Eight reales and pesos of the New World [by Carlos A. Elizondo, Jr.] 1st ed. San Antonio, Tex., Roy's Coin Center [1968] 141 [2] p. illus. 23 cm. Bibliography: p. [143] [CJ1819.E4] 70-676
1. Coins, Latin American. I. Title.

HARRIS, Robert P. 737.498
A guide book of modern Latin American coins, by Robert P. Harris. Racine, Wis., Whitman [c.1966] 125p. illus. 20cm. Bibl. [CJ1819.H3] 67-967 1.50 bds.,
1. Coins, Latin-American. I. Title.

Coins, Lycian.

FELLOWS, Charles, Sir, 1799-1860. 737.4'9'3928
Coins of ancient Lycia before the reign of Alexander : with an essay on the relative dates of the Lycian monuments in the British Museum / by Sir Charles Fellows. Chicago : O[bol] I[nternational], 1976. 20 p., 19 leaves of plates : ill. ; 27 cm. Reprint of the ed. published in 1855 by J. Murray, London. [CJ614.F5 1976] 77-366956
1. Coins, Lycian. I. Title.

Coins, Medieval.

BRITISH Museum. Dept. of Coins and Medals. 737.407402
Western & provincial Byzantine coins of the Vandals, Ostrogoths, and Lombards, and of the empires of Thessalonica, Nicaea, and Trebizond, in the British Museum, by Warwick Wroth, assistant-keeper of the coins and medals. Introd. and 43 plates. [1st Amer. ed.] Chicago, Argonaut, 1966. xciv, 344p. illus. 25cm. Reprint of the work pub. in 1911 under title: Catalogue of the coins of the Vandals, Ostrogoths, and Lombards, and of the Empires of Thessalonica, Nicaea, and Trebizond in the British Mus. Suppls. the two vs. of the Catalogue of imperial Byzantine coins in the British Museum pub. in 1908. [CJ1215.B73 1966] 66-25814 25.00
1. Coins, Medieval. 2. Numismatics—Byzantine Empire. I. Worth, Warwick William, 1858-1911. II. Title.

Coins, Mexican.

BUTTREY, Theodore V. 737.49'72
A guide book of Mexican coins, 1822 to date, by Theodore V. Buttrey. Supplementary data and values compiled by Holland Wallace and Neil Shafer. Cover art and maps by Robert B. Kissner. [Racine, Wis., Western Pub. Co., 1969] 256 p. illus., maps. 20 cm. Bibliography: p. 255-256. [CJ1907.B82] 75-13625
1. Coins, Mexican. I. Wallace, Holland. II. Shafer, Neil. III. Title.

BUTTREY, Theodore V. 737.4'9'72
A guide book of Mexican coins, 1822 to date / by Theodore V. Buttrey, Jr., and Clyde Hubbard ; valuations compiled by Pat Johnson ; maps by Robert B. Kissner. 3d ed. Racine, Wis. : Western Pub. Co., c1977. 256 p. : ill. ; 20 cm. Bibliography: p. 252-253. [CJ1907.B82 1977] 76-49264 ISBN 0-307-09098-1 : 6.50
1. Coins, Mexican. I. Hubbard, Clyde, joint author. II. Johnson, Pat, 1944- III. Title.

BUTTREY, Theodore V. 737.4'9'72
A guide book of Mexican coins, 1822 to date, by Theodore V. Buttrey, Jr., and Clyde Hubbard. Supplementary data and values compiled by Holland Wallace and Neil Shafer. Cover art and maps by Robert B. Kissner. 2d ed. [Racine, Wis., Western Pub. Co., c1971] 256 p. illus. 20 cm. Bibliography: p. 255-256. [CJ1907.B82 1971] 72-177702
1. Coins, Mexican. I. Hubbard, Clyde, joint author. II. Wallace, Holland. III. Shafer, Neil. IV. Title.

BUTTREY, Theodore V. 737.4972
A guide book of Mexican decimal coins, 1863-1963; a comprehensive illustrated valuation catalog of Mexican decimal coins with official reports of coinage and historical notes about each issue. Hist. supp. data by Neil Shafer. Racine, Wis., Whitman [1963] 122p. illus. 20cm. Bibl. 63-4607 1.50
1. Coins, Mexican. I. Title.

GUTHRIE, Hugh S. 737.4'9'72
Mexican revolutionary coinage, 1913-1917 : based on the Bothamley collection / by Hugh S. Guthrie, in collaboration with Merrill Bothamley ; photography by Mark E. Goldberg. Beverly Hills : Superior Stamp & Coin Co., 1976. [12], 93 p., [6] leaves of plates : ports. ; 29 cm. Bibliography: p. [9] (1st group) [CJ1907.G87] 76-363314
1. Coins, Mexican. 2. Mexico—History—1910-1946. I. Bothamley, Merrill, joint author. II. Title.

HANKS, William Lawrence. 737.4'9'72
The comprehensive catalog and encyclopedia of Republic Mexican coins / by W. Larry Hanks ; photography by H. S. Ulan, Mark Goldberg ; edited by Judith M. Hanks, Gaye Dawn Christiansen, David D. Wilson ; ill. by Oscar L. Mireles. 1st ed., 1977. [s.l.] : Hanks, c1976. viii, 234 p. : ill. ; 23 cm. Bibliography: p. 234. [CJ1907.H37] 76-150243 10.00
1. Coins, Mexican. I. Title.

LONG, Richard A. 737.49'72
The availability of 20th century Mexican coins [by] Richard A. Long. [1st ed.] Corpus Christi, Tex., 1969] viii, 116 p. illus. 22 cm. Bibliography: p. 116. [CJ1907.L65] 75-15035 3.50
1. Coins, Mexican. I. Title.

SOTHEBY, Parke-Bernet Los Angeles. 737.4'9'72
Treasure of the Spanish Main; gold and silver coins and artifacts. Los Angeles [1973] 135 p. illus. 27 cm. Exhibition held June 13-16, 1973; public auction held June 17-19, 1973. [CJ1905.S67 1973] 74-152550 3.00
1. Coins, Mexican. 2. Coins, Latin American. 3. Gold coins. 4. Silver coins. 5. Treasure-trove—Caribbean area—Catalogs. I. Title.

SOUTH American Import Corporation, McAllen, Tex. v. 12
Coins of Mexico, by SAICO. McAllen, Tex., c1963. 75 p. illus. 28 cm. Priced catalog. [CJ1896.S6] 63-28854
1. Coins, Mexican. I. Title.

VOGT, George W. 737.4'9'72
Standard catalog of Mexican coins, paper money, and medals / by George W. Vogt ; edited by Colin R. Bruce II, William A. Pettit, coordinating editor, Carl Allenbaugh ... [et al.] contributing editors ; Bonnie Webb, photography. Iola, Wis. : Krause Publications, c1978. 256 p. : ill. ; 28 cm. [CJ1894.V63] 77-93671 ISBN 0-87341-016-5 pbk. : 12.50
1. Coins, Mexican. 2. Paper money—Mexico—Catalogs. 3. Medals—Mexico. I. Bruce, Colin R. II. Title. BIP

Coins, Mohammedan.

MILES, George Carpenter, 1904- 737.4
Rare Islamic coins. New York, American Numismatic Society, 1950. xi, 138 p. 10 plates. (Numismatic notes and monographs, no. 118) Bibliographical footnotes. [CJ3404.A6M5] 51-752
1. Coins, Mohammedan. I. Title. II. Series.

Coins, Omayyad.

LANE-POOLE, Stanley 1854-1931 737.4'09176'7
Coins of the Amawi Khalifehs. Chicago, Argonaut, 1968. viii, 38 p. illus. 22 cm. (Argonaut library of antiquities) At head of title: Catalogue of the collection of oriental coins belonging to Col. C. Seton Guthrie. Reprint of the 1874 ed. [CJ3421.L3 1968] 68-5555
1. Coins, Omayyad. I. Guthrie, Charles Seton, 1808-1874. II. Title.

Coins, Papal.

SADOW, Joseph. 737.4'9'45634
The coins & medals of the Vatican / by Joseph Sadow & Thomas Sarro, Jr. New York : S. J. Durst Numismatic Publications, c1977. 123, [1] p. : ill. ; 24 cm. Includes index. Bibliography: p. [124] [CJ2928.P3S23] 76-40814 ISBN 0-915262-06-1 : 12.95
1. Coins, Papal. 2. Medals, Papal. I. Sarro, Thomas, joint author. II. Title. BIP

Coins, Peruvian.

ALMANZAR, Alcedo. 737.4'9'85
The coins of Peru, 1822-1972, by Al Almanzar and Dale A. Seppa. San Antonio, Almanzar's Coins of the World [1972] 83 p. illus. 21 cm. Bibliography: p. 81. [CJ2397.A47] 78-96262 ISBN 0-88242-000-3
1. Coins, Peruvian. I. Seppa, Dale Allan, joint author. II. Title.

Coins, Philippine.

BASSO, Aldo P. 737'.09914
Coins, medals, and tokens of the Philippines [by] Aldo P. Basso. Menlo Park, Calif., Chenby Publishers, 1968. 136 p. illus. 24 cm. Bibliography: p. 136. [CJ3666.B33] 68-6276
1. Coins, Philippine. 2. Medals—Philippine Islands. 3. Tokens—Philippine Islands. I. Title.

SHAFER, Neil. 737.49914
United States territorial coinage for the Philippine Islands; an illustrated history and price list of coins, tokens, and medals, issued for the Philippine Islands as a United States Territory. Racine, Wis., Whitman Pub. Co. [1961] 63 p. illus. 20 cm. [CJ3677.S5] 61-66202
1. Coins, Philippine. I. Title.

Coins — Prices.

ACME'S authentic coin price v. 12
book of the United States and Canadian coins. [n.p., 1965] 126 p. illus. 22cm. Covert title. [CJ1804.A25] 67-8394
1. Coins — Prices. 2. Coins, American. 3. Coins, Canadian. I. Title: Authentic coin price book.

HAYLINGS, George W 737.4
The profit march of your coins from 1935 to 1968. Lim. ed. reprint. Gardena, Calif., 90249, 16408 S. Bway Payne Pub. Co., [1965, c.1960] 96p. 22cm. [CJ1826.H36] 2.50, pap., lim. ed.
1. Coins—Prices. I. Title.

HAYLINGS, George Wilfred 737.4
The profit-march of your coin investment. 1935-1971 [Rev. ed.] Gardena, Calif., Payne Pub. Co., 13725 Normandie Ave. [c.1964] xiv, 210p. 23cm. Bibl. 64-5307 4.95
1. Coins—Prices. I. Title.

INTERNATIONAL coin 737.4
catalogue and price list. New York, Coin and Currency Pub. Institute. v. illus. 23cm. Compiler:19 R. Friedberg. [CS49.I5] 56-32302
1. Coins—Prices. I. Friedberg, Robert, 1912- comp.

REINFELD, Fred, 1910- 737.4085
Cash for your coins. New York, Sterling Pub. Co. [1956] 128p. illus. 16cm. [CJ1826.R4] 56-7700
1. Coins —Prices. I. Title.

REINFELD, Fred, 1910- 737.4085
Cash for your coins. [Rev. ed.] New York, Sterling Pub. Co. [1957] 128p. illus. 16cm. [CJ1826.R4 1957] 58-267
1. Coins—Prices. I. Title.

REINFELD, Fred, 1910-1964 737.4029
Cash for your coins. [Rev. ed.] New York, Sterling [1966] 128p. illus. 16x12cm. [CJ1826.R4 1966] 66-5014 .50 pap.,
1. Coins—Prices. I. Title.

Coins, Roman.

BOYNE, William, d.1893. 737.49'37
A manual of Roman coins; from the earliest period to the extinction of the Empire; with rarity guide & 22 plates. With an introd. to the historical study of Roman republican and imperial coinage by Hugh Stuart Jones. Chicago, Ammon Press [1968] xviii, 86 p., 21 plates. illus., maps. 22 cm. On spine: Roman coins: manual & rarity-guide. Includes bibliographies. [CJ833.B88] 68-4123
1. Coins, Roman. I. Title. II. Title: Roman coins: manual & rarity-guide.

BREGLIA, Laura. 737.4
Roman imperial coins, their art & technique. Introd. by Ranuccio Bianchi Bandinelli. New York, F. A. Praeger [1968] 236 p. illus. 25 cm. Translation of L'arte romana nelle monete dell'eta imperiale. Bibliography: p. 232-233. [CJ969.B713 1968b] 68-8947 20.00
1. Coins, Roman. I. Title.

CRAWFORD, Michael H., 1939- 737.4'9'37
Roman Republican coinage / Michael H. Crawford. London ; New York : Cambridge University Press, c1974- v. : ill. ; 27 cm. Includes index. Bibliography: v. 1, p. 797-819. [CJ909.C7] 77-164450 ISBN 0-521-07492-4 (set)
1. Coins, Roman. I. Title. BIP

GLASGOW. University. Hunterian Museum. 737.49'37
Roman imperial coins in the Hunter Coin Cabinet, University of Glasgow / by Anne S. Robertson. London ; New York : Published for the University of Glasgow by the Oxford University Press, 1962- c1977. v. : ill., plates ; 26 cm. (Glasgow University publications) Contents.Contents: -v.3. Pertinax t0 Aemilian. [CJ815.G6] 78-24763 ISBN 0-19-713306-1 (v.3) : 72.50
1. Coins, Roman. I. Robertson, Anne S. II. Title. BIP

GRANT, Michael. 737.4
Roman imperial money. London, New York, Nelson [1954] x, 324p. illus., map (on lining papers) 21cm. Includes bibliographical references. [CJ969.G7] 54-4093
1. Coins, Roman. I. Title.

GRANT, Michael, 1914- 737.49'37
Roman history from coins; some uses of the imperial coinage to the historian. Cambridge, Cambridge U.P., 1968. 96 p. 32 plates, illus., map. 20 cm. Bibliography: p. 90-91. [CJ833.G7 1968] 68-54225 ISBN 0-521-09549-2 10/-
1. Coins, Roman. 2. Rome—History. I. Title. BIP

KENT, John Philip Cozens. 737.4'9'37
Roman coins / J. P. C. Kent ; photos. by Max and Albert Hirmer. Rev. ed. New York : H. N. Abrams, 1978. 368 p., [100] leaves of plates : ill. ; 32 cm. Revised translation of Die romische Munze. Includes index. Bibliography: p. 360-361. [CT833.K4613 1978] 77-77534 ISBN 0-8109-1584-7 : 60.00
1. Coins, Roman. I. Title. BIP

KIANG, Dawson. 737.4'9'37
Studies on the iconography of Julius Caesar. [New York?] 1968. viii, 105 l. 29 cm. Thesis—Columbia University. Bibliography: leaves 97-105. [N7589.C2K5] 75-330714
1. Caesar, C. Julius—Art. 2. Coins, Roman. I. Title.

KLAWANS, Zander H 737.4
Reading and dating Roman imperial coins. Racine, Wis., Whitman Pub. Co., c1953. 125p. illus. 20cm. [CJ965.K5] 53-2836
1. Coins, Roman. I. Title.

KLAWANS, Zander H 737.4937
Reading and dating Roman imperial coins. 2d ed. Racine, Wis., Whitman Pub. Co., c1959. 128p. illus. 20cm. [CJ965.K5 1959] 59-3123
1. Coins, Roman. I. Title.

KLAWANS, Zander H. 737.4937
Reading and dating Roman imperial coins. 3d ed. Racine, Wis., Whitman [1964] 128p. illus. 20cm. Bibl. 64-5306 2.00
1. Coins, Roman. I. Title. II. Title: Roman imperial coins.

OXFORD. University. Ashmolean Museum. 737.4'9'37
Catalogue of coins of the Roman Empire in the Ashmolean Museum. Oxford [Eng.] : Clarendon Press, 1975- v. : ill. ; 39 cm. Includes indexes. Contents.Contents.—pt. 1. Sutherland, C. H. V. and Kraay, C. M. Augustus (c. 31 B.C.-A.D. 14) Bibliography: pt. 1, p. xi. [CJ969.O93 1975] 76-352677 ISBN 0-19-813189-5 : 56.00
1. Oxford. University. Ashmolean Museum. 2. Coins, Roman. I. Title.
Dist. by Oxford U. Press N.Y. N.Y. BIP

RAYMOND, Wayte, 1886- 737.4
The J. Pierpont Morgan collection; catalogue of the Greek and Roman coins, Abukir medallions [and] Roman gold bar. With an introd. by Sydney P. Noe. New York, W. Raymond, inc. [1953] 59p. illus. 23cm. [CJ317.R35] 53-35940
1. Coins, Roman. 2. Coins, Greek. I. Morgan, John Pierpont, 1837-1913. II. Title.

SUTHERLAND, Carol Humphrey Vivian. 737.4'9'37
Roman coins / by C. H. V. Sutherland. New York : Putnam, 1974. 311 p. : ill. (some col.) ; 25 cm. (The World of numismatics) Includes index. Bibliography: p. 299-300. [CJ833.S9 1974] 73-81400 ISBN 0-399-11239-1 : 25.00
1. Coins, Roman. I. Title. II. Series.

SYDENHAM, Edward Allen, 1873-1948. 737.4'9'37
The coinage of the Roman Republic / by Edward Allen Sydenham ; rev. with indexes by G. C. Haines ; edited by L. Forrer and C. A. Hersh. New York : Arno Press, 1975. p. cm. (Roman history) Reprint of the 1952 ed. published by Spink, London. Bibliography: p. [CJ909.S9 1975] 75-7345 ISBN 0-405-07066-7 : 26.00
1. Coins, Roman. I. Haines, Geoffrey Colton, 1899- II. Title. III. Series. BIP

THOMPSON, Margaret, 1911- 722.6
Coins from the Roman through the Venetian period. Princeton, N. J., The American School of Classical Studies at Athens, 1954. viii, 122p. 4plates. 31cm. (The American School of Classical Studies at Athens. Athenian Agora, v. 2) [DF287] A55
1. Coins, Roman. I. Title. II. Series.

Coins, Roman—Athens.

THOMPSON, Margaret, 1911- 938'.5 s
Coins from the Roman through the Venetian period / by Margaret Thompson. Meriden, Conn. : Meriden Gravure Co., 1961. vii, 122 p., [2] leaves of plates : ill. ; 31 cm. (The Athenian Agora ; v. 2) (Reprint of the 1954 ed. published by the American School of Classical Studies at Athens, Princeton, N.J.) Includes indexes. Bibliography: p. [8] [DF287.A23A5 vol. 2] [CJ893.A8] 737.4'9'37 75-328019
1. Coins, Roman—Athens. 2. Coins, Byzantine—Athens. 3. Athens. Agora. I. Title. II. Series: American School of Classical Studies at Athens. The Athenian Agora ; v. 2.

Coins, Roman—England.

MILLER, David. 737.4'9'37
Coins of Roman Britain / [by] David Miller. London : Gibbons, 1976. 32 p. : ill., map ; 20 cm. (Stanley Gibbons guides) Bibliography: p. 31. [CJ1102.M54] 77-360392 ISBN 0-85259-845-9 : £0.75
1. Coins, Roman—England. I. Title.

Coins, Russian.

HARRIS, Robert P. 737.49'47
A guidebook of Russian coins, 1725 to 1970, by Robert P. Harris. 1st ed. Santa Cruz, Calif., Bonanza Press, 1971. 160 p. illus. 21 cm. Bibliography: p. 158-160. [CJ3006.H34] 79-23158
1. Coins, Russian. I. Title.

Coins, Scandinavian.

HOBSON, Burton. 737.49'48
Catalogue of Scandinavian coins; gold, silver, and minor coins since 1534, with their valuations. New York, Sterling Pub. Co. [1970] 128 p. illus. 26 cm. [CJ3086.H6 1970] 79-90813
1. Coins, Scandinavian. I. Title.

HOBSON, Burton. 737.4'9'48
Catalogue of Scandinavian coins; gold, silver, and minor coins since 1534, with their valuations. 2d [rev.] ed. New York, Sterling Pub. Co. [1972] 134 p. illus. 27 cm. [CJ3086.H6 1972] 72-178589
1. Coins, Scandinavian. I. Title.

Coins, Scottish.

ROBERTSON, John Drummond, 1857-1934. 737.4941
A handbook to the coinage of Scotland, giving a description of every variety issued by the Scottish Mint in gold, silver, billon,

SUBJECT INDEX COLLAGE.

and copper, from Alexander I to Anne Stuart, with an introductory chapter on the implements and processes employed. Chicago, Argonaut, 1968. xxvii, 146 p. illus. 22 cm. Reprint of the 1878 ed. "With rarity guide for all coins catalogued." Bibliographical footnotes. [CJ2530.R6 1968] 68-6032
1. Coins, Scottish. I. Title.

Coins, Swiss.

CLARKE, Robert L. 737.49'494
The coinage of Switzerland, 1850 to date; an up-to-date pricing guide, by Robert L. Clarke. [1st ed. San Diego, Calif., Malter-Westerfield Pub. Co. [1968] 64 p. illus. 24 cm. Imprint covered by label: Argonaut, Chicago, 1967. Includes bibliographical references. [CJ3265.C55] 68-5107
1. Coins, Swiss. I. Title.

Coins—U.S.

FRIEDBERG, Robert, 1912- 737.4973
Appraising and selling your coins; a complete, illustrated catalogue of U.S. coins and bills and their cash premium values, from 1652 to the present, and the complete coinage of Canada and Newfoundland from 1858 to date. Edited by Jack Friedberg. 5th ed. New York, Coin and Currency Institute [1966] 174 p. illus. 20 cm. (The Green coin book) [CJ1826.F7 1966] 66-18756
1. Coins—U.S. I. Friedberg, Jack, ed. II. Title.

HOBSON, Burton 737.4075
Manual for coin collectors and investors, by Burton Hobson, Fred Reinfield. New York, Sterling [1963] 160p. illus. 20cm. (Worthwhile how-to-paperbacks, 402) 63-19156 1.50 pap.,
1. Coins—U.S. I. Reinfeld, Fred, 1910- joint author. II. Title.

THE Official black book 737.49'73
of United States coins. Ralph DeVincenzo, co-ordinating editor. New York, HC Publishers [1968] 160 p. illus. 18 cm. [CJ1830.O3] 68-57353
1. Coins—United States. I. DeVincenzo, Ralph, ed.

THE Official black book 737.49'73
of United States coins; fully illustrated containing mint records and prices 1616 to date. Ralph DeVincenzo, co-ordinating and contributing editor. Hal L. Cohen, design & editorial. [Completely rev. 7th ed.] New York, HC Publishers, 1970] 192 p. illus. 18 cm. [CJ1830.O3 1970] 78-253529
1. Coins—United States. I. DeVincenzo, Ralph, ed.

Coins. U.S. Mint.

ALTZ, Charles G 737.4
]foreign coins struck at United States mints. by Charles G. Altz and E. H. Barton. Racine, Wis., Whitman Pub. Co. [1965] 63 p. illus. 20 cm. Bibliography: p. 63. [CJ63.A5] 65-9190
1. Coins. U.S. Mint. I. Barton, E. H., joint author II. Title.

Colchester, Eng.—History.

MORANT, Philip, 1700- 942.6'7
1770.
The history and antiquities of the most ancient town and borough of Colchester. [1st ed.] reprinted with a new introduction and ntoes by John S. Appleby. Wakefield, S.R. Publishers, 1970. xxiii, [246] p., 3 fold. plates. illus., geneal. tables, map, port. 36 cm. Reprint of the 1748 ed. [DA690.C7M67 1970] 71-871478 ISBN 0-85409-641-8 £5.25
1. Colchester, Eng.—History. I. Title. **BIP**

Cole, Thomas, 1801-1848.

COLE, Thomas, 1801-1848. 759.13
Thomas Cole. Introd. and catalogue by Howard S. Merritt. [Rochester, N.Y., Printed by Rochester Lithographics, 1969] 120 p. plates (part col.) 24 cm. Catalog of a loan exhibition organized by the Memorial Art Gallery of the University of Rochester and exhibited at the Memorial Art Gallery of the University of Rochester Feb. 14-Mar. 23, 1969; at the Munson-Williams-Proctor Institute Apr. 7-May 4, 1969; at the Albany Institute of History and Art May 9-June 20, 1969; and at the Whitney Museum of American Art June 30-Sept. 1, 1969. Bibliography: p. 115-117. [ND237.C6M4] 76-4612
I. Merritt, Howard S. II. Rochester, N.Y., University. Memorial Art Gallery.

NOBLE, Louis Legrand, 1813- 927.5
1882.
The life and works of Thomas Cole. Edited by Elliot S. Vesell. Cambridge, Belknap Press of Harvard Univeristy Press, 1964. xxxix, 333 p. illus. 25 cm. (The John Harvard library) Bibliographical references included in "Notes": p. 313-324. [ND237.C6N6] 64-22725
1. Cole, Thomas, 1801-1848. I. Title. II. Series.

STUDIES on Thomas 708.152'6 s
Cole, an American romanticist. Baltimore, Museum of Art, 1967. 129 p. illus. 27 cm. (The Baltimore Museum of Art. Annual 2) Contents.Contents.—Rosenthal, G. The story of two acquisitions.—Merritt, H. S. A wild scene, genesis of a painting.—Gerdts, W. H. Cole's painting: After the temptation.—Silberfeld, K. Treatment of Cole's painting A wild scene.—Thomas Cole: paintings by an American romanticist. Includes bibliographical references. [N515.A18 no. 2] [ND237.C6] 759.13 73-173337 4.00
1. Cole, Thomas, 1801-1848. I. Baltimore. Museum of Art. II. Series: Baltimore. Museum of Art. Annual 2.

Coleridge, Samuel Taylor, 1772-1834—Illustrations.

A Portfolio of twenty 741.9
drawings commemorating the bicentenary of the birth of Coleridge. Works of Carl Aldana [and others] and with forewords on Coleridge illustration by Walter Crawford and Richard Oden. Los Angeles, Printed by Anderson, Ritchie and Simon for the Foundation of the California State University, Long Beach, 1972. 1 portfolio (20 plates) 50 cm. Title and text on portfolio. "Edition of five hundred." Issued in a case. [PR4482.P6] 73-153846
1. Coleridge, Samuel Taylor, 1772-1834—Illustrations. 2. Coleridge, Samuel Taylor, 1772-1834—Anniversaries, etc., 1972. I. Crawford, Walter Byron. II. Oden, Richard.

Coletti, Luigi, 1886-

GIORGIONE, Giorgio 759.5
Barbarelli, 1477-1511
All the paintings of Giorgione. text by Luigi Coletti. tr. by Paul Colaicicchi. New York, Hawthorn [1962, c.1961] 80p. illus. (pt. col.) (Complete lib. of world art, v. 3) Bibl. 62-10517 3.95
1. Coletti, Luigi, 1886- I. Title. II. Series.

Colin, Paul, 1892- — Catalogs.

COLIN, Paul, 1892- 741.9'44
100 posters of Paul Colin / compiled by Jack Rennert. New York : Images Graphiques, 1977. 112 p. : chiefly ill. (some col.) ; 41 cm. (The Poster art library) [NC1850.C64A4 1977] 77-93005 ISBN 0-89545-004-6 : 19.95 ISBN 0-89545-005-4 pbk. : 8.95
1. Colin, Paul, 1892- — Catalogs. I. Rennert, Jack. II. Title.

Coll, Joseph Clement, 1881-1921.

COLL, Joseph Clement, 741.9'73
1881-1921.
The magic pen of Joseph Clement Coll / compiled by Walt Reed ; introd. by J. Thomson Willing. Westport, Conn. : North Light Publishers, 1978. p. cm. [NC139.C59A4 1978] 77-99225 ISBN 0-89134-009-2 pbk. : 8.95
1. Coll, Joseph Clement, 1881-1921. I. Reed, Walt. II. Title. **BIP**

Collage.

ADLER, Samuel, 1898- 759.13
Samuel Adler: recent collages. Athens, Georgia Museum of Art [1968] [62] p. (chiefly illus.) 28 cm. [N6537.A33G46] 73-157736
I. Georgia Museum of Art. II. Title.

ASHURST, Elizabeth. 745.59'4
Collage / Elizabeth Ashurst. London ; New York : Marshall Cavendish, 1976. 105 p. : ill. (chiefly col.) ; 30 cm. Ill. on lining papers. [TT910.A83] 77-368562 ISBN 0-85685-160-4 : £2.50
1. Collage. I. Title.

BEANEY JAN. 751.4'9
Adventures with collage. With 50 photos by Alan Wysman. New York, F. Warne [1970] 63 p. illus. 26 cm. (Adventures in learning) Bibliography: p. 63. An introduction to the collage, a picture or pattern built up wholly or partly from pieces of paper, cloth, and/or other materials stuck onto a background. [N6494.C6B4] 79-128406 3.50
1. Collage. I. Wysman, Alan, illus. II. Title. **BIP**

BRIGADIER, Anne. 751.4'93
Collage: a complete guide for artists. New York, Watson-Guptill Publications [1970] 192 p. illus. (part col.) 29 cm. [N6494.C6B7] 72-118982 ISBN 0-8230-0650-6 14.50
1. Collage. I. Title.

BROW, Francis 745.5
Collage. Tech. photos. by John Linsley. New York, Pitman [c.1963] 32p. illus. (pt. col.) 20x26cm. (Pitman art bks., 46) 1.00 pap.,
1. Collage. I. Title.

CAPON, Robin. 751.4'93
Paper collage / Robin Capon. Newton, Mass. : C. T. Branford Co., 1975. 96 p. : ill. ; 21 cm. Bibliography: p. 96. [N7433.7.C36] 75-313873 ISBN 0-8231-7035-7 : 9.50
1. Collage. I. Title. **BIP**

D'ARBELOFF, Natalie. 745.54
Creating in collage; illus. by Jack Yates. London, Studio Vista; New York, Watson-Guptill [1967] 104p. illus. (some col.) 19cm. [TT910.D3] 68-10159 2.50 bds.,
1. Collage. I. Title.

D'ARBELOFF, Natalie. 745.54
Creating in college; with illustrations by Jack Yates. London, Studio Vista; New York Watson-Guptill [1967] 104 p. illus. (some col) 19 cm. Bibliography: p. 101. [TT910.D3] 68-10159
1. Collage. I. Title.

FARNWORTH, Warren. 702'.8
Approaches to collage / Warren Farnworth. New York : Taplinger, 1976. 96 p., [2] leaves of plates : ill. (some col.) ; 26 cm. Bibliography: p. 95. [N7433.7.F37 1976b] 75-42539 ISBN 0-8008-0280-2 : 9.95
1. Collage. I. Title.

FARNWORTH, Warren. 702'.8
Approaches to collage / [by] Warren Farnworth. London : Batsford, 1976. 96 p., 4 p. of plates : ill. (incl. 4 col.) ; 26 cm. Bibliography: p. 95. [N7433.7.F37 1976] 76-373163 ISBN 0-7134-3105-9 : £3.95
1. Collage. I. Title. **BIP**

FRENCH, Brian. 745.59'4
Practice of collage / [by] Brian French, Anne Butler. London : Mills and Boon, 1975 [i.e. 1976] [86] p. : ill. (some col.) ; 26 cm. Label mounted on t.p.: Transatlantic Arts, Levittown, N.Y., sole distributor for the U.S.A. Bibliography: p. [86] [N7433.7.F74 1976] 76-377916 ISBN 0-263-05711-9 : 9.95
1. Collage. I. Butler, Anne, joint author. II. Title. **BIP**

FRENCH, Brian. 702'.8
Principles of collage / Brian French. Buchanan, N.Y. : Emerson Books, 1978. 118 p., [2] leaves of plates : ill. ; 21 cm. Bibliography: p. 117-118. [N7433.7.F743 1978] 78-67955 ISBN 0-87523-188-8 : 9.95
1. Collage. I. Title. **BIP**

GILLON, Edmund Vincent, 745.54
comp.
Picture sourcebook for collage and decoupage / edited by Edmund V. Gillon, Jr. ; with introductions by Jean-Claude Suares and Eleanor Hasbrouck Rawlings. New York : Dover Publications, 1974. xx p., 77 leaves : chiefly ill. (some col.) ; 31 cm. (Dover pictorial archive series) Bibliography: p. xx. [TT910.G55] 74-82206 ISBN 0-486-23095-3 pbk. : 3.95
1. Collage. 2. Decoupage. I. Title. **BIP**

HARTER'S picture 769'.90'4
archive for collage and illustration : over 300 19th-century cuts / edited by Jim Harter. New York : Dover Publications, 1978. [4], 90 leaves of plates : chiefly ill. ; 30 cm. (Dover pictorial archive series) [TT910.H36] 78-54868 ISBN 0-486-23659-5 pbk. : 4.50
1. Collage. 2. Pictures. I. Harter, Jim. II. Title: Picture archive for collage and illustration. **BIP**

HUTTON, Helen. 751.4'9
The technique of collage. London, Batsford; New York, Watson-Guptill, 1968. 144p. 8 plates., 123 illus. (9 col.). 26cm. [N6494.C6H8 1968] 68-20446 10.95
1. Collage. I. Title.

JANIS, Harriet (Grossman) 751.4'9
Collage: personalities, concepts [and] techniques [by] Harriet Janis and Rudi Blesh. [Rev. ed.] Philadelphia, Chilton Book Co. [1967] 342 p. 497 illus. 28 cm. Bibliographical footnotes. [N6490.J3 1967] 67-5494
1. Collage. I. Blesh, Rudi, 1899- joint author. II. Title.

JANIS, Harriet (Grossman) 751.4
Collage; personalities, concepts, techniques [by] Harriet Janis and Rudi Blesh. [1st ed.] Philadelphia, Chilton Co., Book Division [1962] 302 p. illus. 27 cm. (Arts and crafts series) [N6490.J3] 61-14961
1. Collage. 2. Art, Modern—20th century. I. Blesh, Rudi, 1899- joint author.

JANITCH, Valerie. 391'.07'20903
Fun with historical costume / by Valerie Janitch. London : Kaye and Ward, 1975. 63 p. : ill., ports. ; 26 cm. Stamped on t.p.: Distributed by Sportshelf, New Rochelle, N.Y. [TT910.J38] 76-364663 ISBN 0-7182-0092-6 : 10.50
1. Collage. 2. Costume—History. I. Title. **BIP**

LALIBERTE, Norman. 751.4'93
Collage, montage, assemblage: history and contemporary techniques [by] Norman Laliberte [and] Alex Mogelon. New York, Van Nostrand Reinhold Co. [1971] 80 p. illus. 21 cm. (An Art horizons book) [N6494.C6L3] 75-150506
1. Collage. 2. Assemblage (Art) I. Mogelon, Alex, joint author. II. Title.

LIEBMAN, Oscar, 1918- 702'.8
Collage fundamentals : two- and three-dimensional techniques for illustration and advertising / by Oscar Liebman. New York : Stravon Educational Press, c1979. 108 p. : ill. (some col.) ; 28 cm. Includes index. [N7433.7.L53] 79-262 ISBN 0-87396-079-3 : 10.95
1. Collage—Technique. I. Title. **BIP**

LYNCH, John, 1904- 751.4
How to make collages. New York, Viking Press [1961] 136 p. illus. (part col.) 24 cm. (A Studio book) [ND1265.L9] 61-9862
1. Collage. I. Title.

MCCONNELL, Gerald, 1931- 702'.8
Assemblage : three-dimensional picture making / Gerald McConnell ; designed and edited by Howard Munce. New York : Van Nostrand Reinhold Co., 1976. 95 p. : ill. ; 27 cm. [TT910.M3 1976] 76-4451 ISBN 0-442-25264-1 : 10.95 ISBN 0-442-25263-3 pbk. : 6.95 pbk. :
1. Collage. 2. Assemblage (Art) I. Title.

MARKS, Mickey Klar. 745.5
Collage. Collages by Edith Alberts. Photos. by David Rosenfeld. New York, Dial Press [1968] 48 p. illus. (part col.) 21 cm. Instructions for making simple and more complicated collages using paper cutouts and other materials. [N6494.C6M3] AC 68
1. Collage. I. Alberts, Edith, illus. II. Title.

MAYER, Mary Jane. 751.4'93
New ways in collage [by] Mary Jane Mayer and Mary Webb. New York, Van Nostrand Reinhold [1973] 95 p. illus. (part col.) 25 cm. [N7433.M33] 74-149267 ISBN 0-442-29234-1 12.95
1. Collage. I. Webb, Mary, joint author. II. Title. BIP

MEILACH, Dona Z. 751.4'93
Collage and assemblage; trends and techniques, by Dona Z. Meilach and Elvie Ten Hoor. New York, Crown Publishers [1973] vii, 246 p. illus. 27 cm. [N7433.M36 1973] 73-82320 ISBN 0-517-50577-0 8.95
1. Collage. 2. Assemblage (Art) I. Ten Hoor, Elvie, joint author. II. Title. BIP

MEILACH, Dona Z. 751.49
Collage and found art [by] Dona Meilach [and] Elvie Ten Hoor. New York, Reinhold Pub. Corp. [1964] 68 p. illus. (part col.) 21 cm. (An Art horizons book) [N6490.M43] 63-19227
1. Collage. 2. Found objects (Arts) I. Ten Hoor, Elvie, joint author. II. Title.

PORTCHMOUTH, John. 751.4'93
Working in collage. With illus. by the author. New York, Viking Press [1974, c1973] 128 p. illus. (part col.) 26 cm. (A Studio book) [N7433.P67 1974] 73-9277 ISBN 0-670-78289-0 8.95
1. Collage. I. Title.

VANDERBILT, Gloria, 1924- 745.59
Gloria Vanderbilt book of collage [by] Gloria Vanderbilt, with Alfred Allen Lewis. New York, Van Nostrand Reinhold [1970] 111 p. illus. (part col.) 29 cm. [N6494.C6V3 1970] 78-103625
1. Collage. I. Title. II. Title: Book of collage.

VARIAN, Elayne H. 709.04
Art in process; the visual development of a collage. Prepared by Elayne H. Varian with statements by the artists. Special photographic assistance, Bill Wilson. [Exhibition] Opening March 9, 1967. New York [1967] [32] p. ports. 22 x 29 cm. "Circulated under the auspices of the American Federation of Arts." [N6494.C6V34] 67-21455
1. Collage. 2. Art, Modern—20th century. I. Finch College, New York. Museum of Art. Contemporary Study Wing. II. Wilson, Bill, 1926- III. American Federation of Arts. IV. Title. V. Title: The visual development of a collage.

WESCHER, Herta. 759.06
Collage. Translated by Robert E. Wolf. New York, Abrams [1971, c1968] 417 p. illus. (part col.) 31 cm. [N6494.C6W413] 79-161620 ISBN 0-8109-0184-6
1. Collage.

Collage—History.

WOLFRAM, Eddie. 709'.04
History of collage : an anthology of collage, assemblage and event structures / by Eddie Wolfram. 1st American ed. New York : Macmillan, 1975. 192 p. : ill. (some col.) ; 26 cm. Includes index. Bibliography: p. 187. [N6494.C6W64 1975] 75-24650 16.95
1. Collage—History. 2. Assemblage (Art)—History. 3. Art, Modern—20th century—History. I. Title. BIP

Collage—Juvenile literature.

GERTH, Gayle. 702'.8
Photocollage made simple / Gayle and Teja Gerth. Garden City, N.Y. : Amphoto, c1978. 95 p., [4] leaves of plates : ill. (some col.) ; 29 cm. Step-by-step instructions for constructing collages from photographs. Tracing-paper patterns are included. [TT910.G47] 77-90001 ISBN 0-8174-2431-8 : 11.95 ISBN 0-8174-2112-2 pbk. : 6.95
1. Collage—Juvenile literature. 2. Photographs—Juvenile literature. I. Gerth, Teja, joint author. II. Title. BIP

MARKS, Mickey Klar. 372.5'2
Collage. Collages by Edith Alberts. Photos. by David Rosenfeld. New York, Dial Press [1968] 48 p. illus. (part col.) 21 cm. [N6494.C6M3] 68-15253 3.95
1. Collage—Juvenile literature. I. Alberts, Edith, illus. II. Title.

WEISS, Harvey. 731
Collage and construction. New York, Young Scott Books [1970] 62 p. illus. (part col.) 28 cm. (Beginning artists library) Instructions for making collages and constructions from a variety of easily available materials. [N6494.C6W37] 76-98115 3.95
1. Collage—Juvenile literature. 2. Sculpture—Juvenile literature. I. Title. BIP

Collages.

BEANEY, Jan. 704.94'36
Landscapes : in picture, collage, and design / by Jan Beaney. Woodbury, N.Y. : Barron's Educational Series, inc., 1978, c1976. p. cm. (Craft and design) Bibliography: p. [TT910.B3 1978] 77-28445 ISBN 0-8120-5167-X : 3.95
1. Collages. 2. Design, Decorative. 3. Landscape drawing. I. Title. II. Series.

JANITCH, Valerie. 746.3
Country collage / Valerie Janitch. 1st ed. Radnor, Pa. : Chilton Book Co., c1975. 96 p. : ill. (some col.) ; 27 cm. (Chilton's creative crafts series) [TT910.J36 1975] 74-7841 ISBN 0-8019-6394-X : 10.95. ISBN 0-8019-6395-8 pbk. : 6.95
1. Collages. I. Title. BIP

PRIOLO, Joan B. 751.4'93
Ideas for collage, by Joan B. Priolo. New York, Sterling Pub. Co. [1972] 48 p. illus. (part col.) 20 cm. (Little craft book series) Instructions for making a variety of collages with emphasis on the use of different kinds of paper. [TT910.P75 1972] 79-180456 ISBN 0-8069-5198-2
1. Collages. I. Title.

Collages, American—Exhibitions.

INDIANA. Ball State University, Muncie. Art Gallery. 759.13'074'017265
Collages by American artists. [Muncie, Ind., 1971] 1 v. (unpaged) illus. 18 cm. Catalog of the exhibition held in October 1971 at the gallery. [N6512.5.C55I5] 70-198446
1. Collages, American—Exhibitions. I. Title.

Collages—Exhibitions.

GALERIE Beyeler, Basel. 709'.04
Autres dimensions : collages, assemblages, reliefs ... [Horst Antes e.a. : exposition, Galerie Beyeler, Basel, juin-septembre 1976 : catalogue]. [Basel : La Galerie, 1976] [68] p. : col. ill. ; 31 cm. English, French, or German. [N6494.C6G34 1976] 77-356312 35.00F
1. Collages—Exhibitions. 2. Assemblages—Exhibitions. 3. Relief (Sculpture)—Exhibitions. 4. Art, Modern—20th century—Exhibitions. I. Title.

Collagraph printing.

STOLTENBERG, Donald. 760
Collagraph printmaking / Donald Stoltenberg ; photos. by Ralph Snow MacKenzie. Worcester, Mass. : Davis Publications, [1975] 95 p. : ill. (some col.) ; 27 cm. [NE2232.S86] 74-27699 ISBN 0-87192-067-0 : 9.95
1. Collagraph printing. I. MacKenzie, Ralph Snow. II. Title. BIP

WENNIGER, Mary Ann. 760
Collagraph printmaking / by Mary Ann Wenniger ; photos. by Mace Wenniger. New York : Watson-Guptill Publications, 1975. 184 p. : ill. (some col.) ; 29 cm. Includes index. Bibliography: p. 182. [NE2232.W46 1975] 74-28324 ISBN 0-8230-0665-4 : 14.50
1. Collagraph printing. I. Title. BIP

Collectors and collecting.

BROOKE, Milton. 769.5
Guide to color prints [by] Milton Brooke and Henry J. Dubester. Washington, Scarecrow Press, 1953. xii, 257p. 22cm. [NE1860.A2B7] 53-10394
1. Color prints—Catalogs. I. Dubester, Henry Joachim, 1917- II. Title.

GORDON, Hampden Charles, 1885- 708.051
The lure of antiques: looking and learning today. New York, Macmillan [c.]1961. 130p. illus. 61-4238 3.00 bds.,
1. Collections and collecting. 2. Art objects—Collectors and collecting. I. Title. BIP

Collective bargaining — Municipal employees — U.S.

LANG, William A v. 12
The development and techniques of collective bargaining in the municipal service. [Washington] International Association of Fire Fighters, AFL-CIO, CLC, 1966. 69 p. 24 cm. [NDLC] 67-100765
1. Collective bargaining — Municipal employees — U.S. 2. Collective labor agreements — Municipal employees — U.S. I. International Association of Fire Fighters. II. Title.

Collectors and collecting.

ANTIQUES 708.051
Collectors & collections: the Antiques anniversary book. Ed. by Alice Winchester, staff of Antiques magazine. New York [dist. Dutton] [c.]1961. 165p. illus. (pt. col.) 31cm. 61-16817 9.50; until Jan. 1, 8.95 bds.,
1. Collectors and collecting. 2. Art objects—Collectors and collecting. I. Winchester, Alice, ed. II. Title.

ANTIQUES year book (The); 705.8
encyclopedia & directory. 1960-61. Edited by Donald Cowie. London, Tantiry Press [dist. New York, International Pubns. Service, 1960] 852 p. illus., maps 20 cm 49-53305 bds., 3.25
1. Collectors and collecting. 2. Collectors and collecting—Direct. 3. Art—Yearbooks. I. Cowie, Donald, ed.

BRADFORD, Ernle Dusgate Selby 708.04
Dictionary of antiques. London, English Univ. Pr. [dist., Newton Centre, Mass., Branford, 1964, c.1963] 151p. illus. 18cm. (Teach yourself bks.) [NK 1125.B73] 63-25207 2.95 bds.,
1. Collectors and collecting. I. Title.

BRICKER, William Paul. 708.051
The complete book of collecting hobbies. New York, Sheridan House [1951] 316 p. 22 cm. [AM231.B7] 51-14832
1. Collectors and collecting.

HENRY, Stella (Vitty) 708.051
Better than riches: a story of family possessions. Hartland, Vt., Solitarian Press. 1956. 90p. 24cm. [NK1125.H4] 56-39730
1. Collectors and collecting. 2. Art objects—Collectors and collecting. 3. Vermont—soc. life & cust. I. Title.

LEEK, Sybil. 706.994
A shop in the High Street. Decorations by Douglas Hall. [1st American ed.] New York, D. McKay Co. [1964, c1962] 207 p. 21 cm. [NK1125.L42 1964] 64-15886
1. Collectors and collecting. 2. Art dealers. I. Title.

LEEMING, Joseph, 1897-1968. 708.051
Fun for young collectors; an introduction to thirty-two collection projects with information on sources for finds and on making cases for effective display. Illustrated by Jessie Robinson. [1st ed.] Philadelphia, Lippincott [1953] 88 p. illus. 26 cm. Includes bibliography. [NK1125.L43] 52-12904
1. Collectors and collecting. 2. Art objects—Collectors and collecting. I. Title.

MCCLINTON, Katharine (Morrison). 708.051
Antique collecting. [Greenwich, Conn., Fawcett Publications, 1952] 144 p. illus. 24 cm. (A Fawcett book, no. 153) "Abridged from Antique collecting for everyone." [NK1125.M324] 52-39321
1. Collectors and collecting. 2. Art objects—Collectors and collecting. I. Title. II. Title: Antique collecting for everyone.

MCCLINTON, Katharine (Morrison). 708.051
Antique collecting for everyone. Illustrated with over 200 photos. New York, McGraw-Hill [1951] xii, 252 p. illus. 26 cm. Includes bibliographies. [NK1125.M32] 51-4768
1. Collectors and collecting. 2. Art objects—Collectors and collecting. I. Title.

MCCLINTON, Katharine (Morrison) 745.1
The complete book of small antiques collecting New York, Coward [c.1965] 255p. illus. 22cm. [AM231.M23] 65-20402 5.95
1. Collectors and collecting. I. Title.

*MEBANE, John, 1909- 708.04
Collecting nostalgia; the first guide to the antiques of the 30s and 40s. New York, Popular Lib. [1973 c.1972] 367 p. illus. 18 cm. [NK1125] 66-27974 1.50 (pbk)
1. Collectors and collecting. I. Title. BIP

MEBANE, John, 1909- 708.04
Treasure at home. New York, A. S. Barnes [1964] 268 p. illus., facsims., ports. 26 cm. Based on a column published in the combined Sunday edition of the Atlanta journal and the Atlanta constitution under the byline Harold Heartman. Bibliography: p. 255-268. [NK1125.M36] 64-13891
1. Collectors and collecting. 2. Art objects—Collectors and collecting. I. Title.

MITCHELL, Edwin Valentine, 1890- 745
The romance of New England antiques. New York, Current Books, 1950. 265 p. illus. 22 cm. [NK1125.M5] 50-9718
1. Collectors and collecting. I. Title.

NOEL Hume, Ivor. 745.1
All the best rubbish. [1st ed.] New York, Harper & Row [1974] xiv, 320 p. illus. 24 cm. Bibliography: p. 309-310. [AM231.N63] 73-4093 ISBN 0-06-011997-7 10.00
1. Collectors and collecting. I. Title. BIP

ORMSBEE, Thomas Hamilton, 1890- 708.51
Collecting antiques in America. [3d ed. New York] Deerfield Books; distributed by Hearthside Press [c1962] 321 p. illus. 25 cm. [NK1125.O7] 62-19046
1. Collectors and collecting. 2. Art objects — collectors and collecting. 3. Art industries and trade — U.S. — Hist. I. Title.

ORMSBEE, Thomas Hamilton, 1890- 708.051
Know your heirlooms. New York, McBride [1956] 128p. illus. 27cm. [NK1125.O716] 56-12015
1. Collectors and collecting. 2. Art industries and trade—U. S. 3. Art objects—U. S. 4. Furniture, American. I. Title.

SCOTT, Amoret. 745.1
Collecting bygones [by] Amoret and Christopher Scott. Illustrated by Jannat Houston. With 12 photos. by Christopher Scott. [1st American ed.] New York, D. McKay Co. [1965, c1964] 142 p. illus. 21 cm. [AM231.S3 1965] 65-22008
1. Collectors and collecting. I. Scott, Christopher, joint author. II. Title.

SHEPARD, Louise. 708.051
The antique shop; illustrated by Sally Shepard Raglin. New York, Rosenthal & Smythe, 1952. 160 p. illus. 20 cm. [NK1125.S48] 52-4909
1. Collectors and collecting. 2. Art objects—Collectors and collecting. I. Title.

WINCHESTER, Alice 708.051
How to know American antiques; illus. by Pauline W. Inman. New York, New Amer. Lib. [1965, c.1951] 191p. illus. 18cm. (Signet Key bk. KP382) [NK1125.W53] .60 pap.,
1. Collectors and collecting. 2. Art objects—Collectors and collecting. I. Title.

WINCHESTER, Alice. 708.051
How to know American antiques; illustrated by Pauline W. Inman. [New York] New American Library [1951] 191 p. illus. 18 cm. (A Mentor book, 62) [NK1125.W53] 51-5073
1. Collectors and collecting. 2. Art objects—Collectors and collecting. I. Title.

YATES, Raymond Francis, 1895- comp. 708.051
The antique collector's manual: a price guide and data book. [1st ed.] New York, Harper [1952] viii, 303 p. illus. 22 cm. [NK1125.Y28] 51-11968
1. Collectors and collecting. 2. Art objects — Collectors and collecting. 3. Art — Prices. I. Title.

YATES, Raymond Francis, 1895- comp. 708.051
The antique collector's manual: a price guide and data book. Washington 4, D. C., Paul A. Ruddell, 461 Ben Franklin Station [1962, c.1952] viii, 303p. illus. 22cm. 5.00
1. Collectors and collecting. 2. Art objects—Collectors and collecting. 3. Art—Prices. I. Title.

Collectors and collecting—Anecdotes, facetiae, satire, etc.

TARKINGTON, Booth, 1869-1946. 745.1'075
The collector's whatnot; a compendium, manual, and syllabus of information and advice on all subjects appertaining to the collection of antiques, both ancient and not so ancient. Compiled by Cornelius Obenchain Van Loot, Milton Kilgallen, and Murgatroyd Elphinstone. With new introductory notes by Larry Freeman. Watkins Glen, N.Y., American Life Foundation & Study Institute, 1969 [c1923] 112 p. illus. 22 cm. An abridgement of the work first published in 1923, which was written under pseudonyms by Booth Tarkington, Kenneth Lewis Roberts, and Hugh MacNair Kahler. [PN6231.C58T32 1969] 77-96941
1. Collectors and collecting—Anecdotes, facetiae, satire, etc. I. Roberts, Kenneth Lewis, 1885-1957, joint author. II. Kahler, Hugh MacNair, 1883-1969, joint author. III. Title. BIP

Collectors and collecting—Direct.

THE Antique trader directory of antique dealers. 745.1'025'7471 [Kewanee, Ill., Babka Pub. Co.] v. 20 cm. annual. [NK1127.A5] 64-4643
1. Collectors and collecting — Direct. 2. Art industries and trade — U.S. — Direct. I. Title: Directory of antique dealers.

BUXTON, Wilbert John ed. 1924- 708.04
Buxton's guide: New England antique shops. 1963-64 ed. Greenwich, Conn., J. S. Herold, 1963] 168 p. illus., ports., maps (part fold.) 26 cm. Cover title. Edited by John Buxton. Bibliography: p. 162-163. [NK1127.B8] 63-24840
1. Collectors and collecting—Direct. 2. Art industries and trade—New England—Direct. I. Title. II. Title: New England antique shops.

BUXTON'S guide: New England antique shops 708.04 [2d ed. Greenwich, Conn., J. S. Herold, c.1964] 168p. illus., ports., maps (pt. fold.) 26cm. Cover title. Ed. by John Buxton. Bibl. 63-24840 2.95 pap.,
1. Collectors and collecting—Direct. 2. Art industries and trade—New England—Direct. I. Buxton, Wilbert John, 1924- ed. II. Title: New England antique shops.

CALLAHAN, Claire Wallis. 708.04
Hitting the antiques trail, by Ann Kilborn Cole [pseud. 1st ed.] New York, D. McKay Co. [1961] 211p. 22cm. [NK1127.C3] 61-10275
1. Collectors and collecting—Direct. 2. Art objects—Collectors and collecting. 3. Art industries and trade—Atlantic States. I. Title.

COLE, Ann Kilborn 708.04
Hitting the antiques trail. New York, McKay [c.1961] 211p. map 61-10275 4.50
1. Collectors and collecting—Direct. 2. Art objects—Collectors and collecting. 3. Art industries and trade—Atlantic States. I. Title.

KRAUSS, Ethel. 708.14058
Buxton's guide New England antique shops. [2d ed.] Greenwich, Conn., J. S. Herold, 1964. 224 p. illus., maps. 23 cm. Text on p. [3] of cover. Prepared by Ethel Krauss and John Buxton. Bibliography: p. 213. [NK1127.B8] 64-4700
1. Collectors and collecting—Direct. 2. Art industries and trade—New England—Direct. I. Buxton, Wilbert John, 1924- II. Title. III. Title: New England antique shops.

NATIONAL travel guide to antique shops. 745.1'025'7471 [Casper, Wyo., Antique Enterprises] v. 23 cm. [NK1127.N3] 65-4691
1. Collectors and collecting — Direct.

WEBSTER, Isabel Stevens. 708.051
Antique collectors' guide to New England; Antique shops, auction houses, museums & historic homes [by] Polly Websters. New York, Grossett & Dunlap [1961] 165 p. illus. 21 cm. [NK1127.W4] 61-3263
1. Collectors and collecting — Direct. 2. Art industries and trade — New England — Direct. 3. Art — New England — Galleries and museums. 4. New England — Historic houses, etc. I. Title.

Collectors and collecting—Yearbooks.

INTERNATIONAL antiques yearbook, encyclopaedia & directory, 1962-63. 705.8 Ed. by Donald Cowie. London, Tantivy Pr. [dist. New York, A. S. Barnes, 1962] 808p. illus., maps. 19cm. Title varies. 49-53305 4.95 bds.,
1. Collectors and collecting—Yearbooks. 2. Collectors and collecting—Direct. 3. Art—Yearbooks. 4. Booksellers and bookselling—Direct. I. Cowie, Donald, ed.

INTERNATIONAL antiques yearbook; 1966-1967. 705.8 Amer. ed. ed. by Antiques Magazine. with Philip Wilson. New York, Crown [c.1966] 1110p. illus. (pt. col.) 20cm. annual. Title varies. Pub. in England by Studio Vista. [NK1125.A315] 49-53305 5.95 bds.,
1. Collectors and collecting—Yearbooks. 2. Collectors and collecting—Direct. 3. Art—Yearbooks. 4. Booksellers and bookselling—Direct. I. Wilson, Philip, ed. II. Antiques magazine.

**INTERNATIONAL antiques yearbook 1976 /* 745.1 compiled by Marcelle d'Argy Smith and Elizabeth Dick. 26th edition London : Antiques Yearbooks, 1976 918p. : ill ; 18 cm. Includes index. [NK1125] ISBN 0-90030-512-6 : 25.00
1. Collectors and collecting-Yearbooks. 2. Collectors and collcting-Directories. 3. Art-Yearbooks. 4. Booksellers and bookselling-Directories.
Distributed by International Publications Service

INTERNATIONAL antiques yearbook, encyclopaedia and directory. 705.8 1963-64. Ed. by Donald Cowie. London, Tantivity Pr. [dist.] New York, A. S. Barnes [c.1963] 852p. illus., maps. 19cm. Title varies. annual. 49-53303 4.95 bds.,
1. Collectors and collecting—Yearbooks. 2. Collectors and collecting—Direct. 3. Art—Yearbooks. 4. Booksellers and bookselling—Direct. I. Cowie, Donald, ed.

College Park, Md.—Exhibitions.

HINDMAN, Sandra, 1944- 091'.074'015251
Pen to press : manuscripts and printed books in the first century of printing / by Sandra Hindman and James Douglas Farquhar. [College Park] : Art Dept., University of Maryland, 1977. p. cm. "An exhibition at the University of Maryland, Art Department Gallery, College Park, Maryland, September 15-October 23, 1977." Sponsored jointly by the Art Dept., University of Maryland and the Dept. of the History of Art, Johns Hopkins University. Includes index. Bibliography: p. [Z121.H6] 77-15026
1. College Park, Md.—Exhibitions. 2. Manuscripts—Exhibitions. 3. Bibliographical exhibitions. 4. Illumination of books and manuscripts—Exhibitions. I. Farquhar, James Douglas, 1941- joint author. II. Maryland. University. Dept. of Art. III. Johns Hopkins University. Dept. of the History of Art. IV. Maryland. University. Art Gallery. V. Title.

College teachers as artists.

CALIFORNIA Palace of the Legion of Honor, San Francisco. 741.973
Painters behind painters; an exhibition of central California artists teaching at the college level, California Palace of the Legion of Honor, Lincoln Park, San Francisco, 13 May-25 June, 1967. [San Francisco? 1967] 1 v. (unpaged) illus. (part col.) 19 x 26 cm. [N6512.C3] 67-68162
1. College teachers as artists. 2. Art, American—Exhibitions. I. Title.

Collins, Isaac, 1746-1817.

HIXSON, Richard F. 655.1'73
Isaac Collins, a Quaker printer in 18th century America [by] Richard F. Hixson. New Brunswick, N.J., Rutgers Univ., Pr. [1968] xi, 241p. illus., facisms., port. 23cm. A list of Collins imprints p. [187]-204. Bibl. ref. [Z232.C703H5] 67-31169 8.00
1. Collins, Isaac, 1746-1817. I. Title.

Collins, Jess.

COLLINS, Jess. 759.13
Translations, salvages, paste-ups by Jess : an exhibition organized by the Dallas Museum of Fine Arts, April 6 through May 15, 1977, with the participation of University Art Museum, Berkeley, June 7 through July 24, 1977, Des Moines Art Center, October 26 through December 4, 1977. [Dallas : Dallas Museum of Fine Arts], 1977. [32] p. : ill. (some col.) ; 26 cm. [ND237.C673D34] 77-365065 5.00
1. Collins, Jess. I. Dallas. Museum of Fine Arts. II. California. University. Art Museum. III. Des Moines Art Center. IV. Title.

Collins, Paul.

†COLLINS, Paul. 759.13
Gerald R. Ford : a man in perspective : as portrayed in the Gerald R. Ford mural by Paul Collins / photography by John R. Fulton Jr. and Candace Brown ; text by Tom LaBelle ; design by Candace Brown ; pref. by Fred Myers ; poetry by W. Randolph Brown. Grand Rapids : Eerdmans, c1976. 39 p. : ill. (some col.) ; 22 cm. [ND237.C674A46] 76-151475 ISBN 0-8028-1669-X : 2.95
1. Collins, Paul. Gerald R. Ford mural.

Collodi, Italy. Castello Garzoni.

ANDREINI Galli, Nori. 914.5'53
The Garzoni garden and castle at Collodi / texts by Nori Andreini Galli and Francesco Gurrieri ; English adaptation by Evelyn M. Piazza. Collodi : Societa Dilezza, 1976. 92, [7] p. : ill. ; 20 cm. Translation of Il giardino e il castello Garzoni a Collodi. Bibliography: p. [94]-[95] [NA7595.C64A5213] 77-556404
1. Collodi, Italy. Castello Garzoni. 2. Collodi, Italy. Castello Garzoni. Giardino. I. Gurrieri, Francesco, joint author. II. Title.

Collodion process.

SOBIESZEK, Robert A., 1943- comp. 772'.14
The collodion process and the ferrotype: Three accounts, 1854-1872. Edited by Robert A. Sobieszek. New York, Arno Press, 1973. 100, 27, 80 p. illus. 22 cm. (The Literature of Photography) Reprint of the Collodion process on glass, by F. S. Archer, first published 1854; of On the intervention of art in photography, by L. D. Blanquart-Evrard, first published 1864; and of Trask's practical ferrotyper, by A. K. P. Trask, first published 1872. [TR390.S6 1973] 72-9190 ISBN 0-405-04900-5 12.00
1. Collodion process. 2. Tintype. 3. Photography. I. Archer, Frederick Scott. The collodion process on glass. 1973. II. Blanquart-Evrard, Louis Desire, 1802-1872 On the intervention of art in photography. 1973. III. Trask, Albion K. P. Trask's practical ferrotyper. 1973. IV. Title. V. Series.

Colman, Samuel.

PARKINSON, Ronald. 759.2
Samuel Colman, fl. 1816-1840 : four apocalyptic themes / [by Parkinson] [London] : Tate Gallery Publications, [1976] [12] p. : ill. ; 21 cm. Cover title. Catalogue of an exhibition held at the Tate Gallery. [ND497.C644P37] 76-383871 ISBN 0-905005-40-6 : £0.25
1. Colman, Samuel. 2. Apocalyptic art. I. Colman, Samuel. II. Tate Gallery, London.

Colonial revival (Architecture)—United States.

RHOADS, William B. 720'.973
The Colonial revival / William B. Rhoads. New York : Garland Pub., 1977. 2 v. (xxxiv, 1134 p.) : ill. ; 21 cm. (Outstanding dissertations in the fine arts) Originally presented as the author's thesis, Princeton, 1974. Bibliography: p. 945-1015. [NA710.5.V5R48 1977] 76-23695 ISBN 0-8240-2722-1 : lib.bdg. : 100.00 (2 vols)
1. Colonial revival (Architecture)—United States. 2. Architecture, Victorian—United States. I. Title. II. Series. BIP

Colonial Williamsburg, inc.

UNITED Federation of Doll Clubs. Region 11. 745.59'22
Dolls, a sampler: souvenir booklet; meeting, Colonial Williamsburg, 1972. [Washington, Dollology Club of Washington, D.C., 1972] 43 p. illus. 28 cm. On cover: Williamsburg. [NK4893.U53] 73-151478
1. Colonial Williamsburg, inc. 2. Dolls. I. Title. II. Title: Williamsburg.

Colonial Williamsburg, inc. Dept. of Collections.

†COLONIAL Williamsburg Foundation. 738.2'7
Chelsea porcelain at Williamsburg / by John C. Austin. Williamsburg, Va. : Colonial Williamsburg Foundation ; Charlottesville : distributed by the University Press of Virginia, c1977. xii, 227 p. : ill. (some col.) ; 29 cm. (The Williamsburg decorative art series) Includes index. Bibliography: p. xi-xii. [NK4399.C5C64 1977] 76-49537 ISBN 0-87935-023-7 : 30.00
1. Colonial Williamsburg, inc. Dept. of Collections. 2. Chelsea porcelain—Catalogs. 3. Porcelain—Williamsburg, Va.—Catalogs. I. Austin, John Cecil, 1931- II. Title. III. Series. BIP

Color.

BIRREN, Faber, 1900- 752
Color, form, and space. New York, Reinhold Pub. Corp. [1961] 128 p. illus. (part col.) 27 cm. Bibliography: p. 124. [ND1280.B567] 61-14819
1. Color. 2. Polychromy. I. Title.

BIRREN, Faber, 1900- 752
Creative color. New York, Reinhold Pub. Corp. [1961] 128 p. illus. (part col.) 27 cm. Bibliography: p. 124. [ND1280.B57] 61-6947
1. Color. 2. Painting—Technique. I. Title. BIP

BIRREN, Faber, 1900- 752.09
History of color in painting, with new principles of color expression. New York, Reinhold [c.1965] 372p. illus., facsims., 32 col. plates, ports. 31cm. Includes a color chart of pigments and palettes. Bibl. [ND1280.B574] 64-22424 25.00
1. Color. 2. Painting—Hist. I. Title. II. Title: Color in Painting.

BIRREN, Faber, 1900- 752.4
New horizons in color. New York, Reinhold Pub. Corp. [1955] 200p. illus. 27cm. [ND1280.B58] 55-6281
1. Color. 2. Interior decoration. 3. Polychromy. I. Title.

BIRREN, Faber, 1900- 751.4
Principles of color; a review of past traditions and modern theories of color harmony. New York, Van Nostrand Reinhold Co. [1969] 96 p. illus. (part col.)

21 cm. Bibliography: p. 79-80. [ND1283.B47] 69-15895
1. Color. I. Title. BIP

CAMPBELL, Ann Raymond. 701.8 (j)
Let's find out about color, by Ann Campbell. Pictures by the author. New York, F. Watts [1966] 31 p. illus. (part col.) 22 cm. [N361.C3] 66-14563
1. Color. 2. Art—Study and teaching (Primary) I. Title. BIP

CHESKIN, Louis, 1907- 659.1325
Color for profit. New York, Liveright [1951] 164 p. illus. (part col.) 23 cm. [ND1280.C47] 51-9095
1. Color. 2. Commercial art. I. Title. BIP

CREWDSON, Frederick Mason, 1893- 752
Color in decoration and design. Wilmette, Ill., F. J. Drake [1953] 232 p. illus. 19 cm. [ND1280.C74] 53-12208
1. Color. I. Title.

DERGE, Wana Marie, 1887- 700.8
Color, form and composition, by Wana Derge. [1st ed.] [Berkeley, Calif.] [Wana Derge Art Association] [1966] 111 p. illus. (part col.) 28 cm. [ND1280.D43] 66-8523
1. Color. 2. Form (Art) 3. Floral decoration. I. Title.

DIVALENTIN, Maria Messuri, 1911- 752
Color in oil painting [by] Maria and Louis DiValentin. New York, Sterling Pub. Co. [1966] 79 p. illus. (part col.) ports. 29 cm. [ND1280.D5] 65-24382
1. Color. 2. Painting—Technique. I. DiValentin, Louis, joint author. II. Title.

ELLINGER, Richard Gordon 752
Color structure and design. Scranton, Pa., Intl. Textbk. [c.1963] xiii, 144p. illus. (pt. col.) 24cm. (Intl. textbks. in art educ.) Bibl. 63-13870 6.75
I. Title.

EMBERLEY, Ed. JUV
Green says go. [1st ed.] Boston, Little, Brown [1968] 32 p. col. illus. 27 cm. A brief explanation of colors and the results of mixing them, followed by the meanings and connotations of various colors, such as red for stop, green for envy, and pink for girl. [PZ7.E565Gr] 701.8 AC 68
1. Color. I. Title. BIP

FABRI, Ralph, 1894- 752
Color; a complete guide for artists. New York, Watson-Guptill Publications [1967] 175 p. illus. (part col.) 29 cm. [ND1280.F3] 67-13741
1. Color.

GIRARD, Robert, professeur de dessin. 752
Color and composition; a guide for artists. [Translated from the French by Juri Gabriel] New York, Van Nostrand Reinhold Co. [1974] p. cm. Translation of Couleur et composition. Bibliography: p. [ND1488.G5713] 73-16705 ISBN 0-442-30030-1 10.95
1. Color. 2. Composition (Art) I. Title.

GRAVES, Maitland E, 1902- 752
Color fundamentals; with 100 color schemes. 1st ed. New York, McGraw-Hill, 1952. 206 p. illus. 25 cm. [ND1280.G7] 51-12549
1. Color. I. Title.

GUPTILL, Arthur Leighton, 1891-1956 752
Color manual for artists. Ed.: Catherine Sullivan. New York, Reinhold [1963] 128p. illus. (pt. col.) 26cm. Bibl. 62-10321 10.00
1. Color. 2. Painting—Technique. I. Title.

ITTEN, Johannes, 1888-1967. 752
The Elements of color : study material / Johannes Itten. New York : Van Nostrand Reinhold Co., [1976] 1 portfolio (33 pieces) : chiefly col. ill. ; 21 cm. Cover title. Translation of Zur Farbenlehre Johannes Itten. For use in conjunction with the author's The art of color and the 1970 Study edition, the elements of color. [ND1493.I83213] 75-24991 ISBN 0-442-24036-8 : 6.95
1. Color. I. Title. BIP

ITTEN, Johannes, 1888-1967. 701.8
The elements of color; a treatise on the color system of Johannes Itten, based on his book The art of color. Edited, and with a foreword and evaluation, by Faber Birren. Translated by Ernst van Hagen. New York, Van Nostrand Reinhold Co. [1970] 96 p. illus. (part col.), port. 21 cm. (A Basic color library) "A simplification and condensation of ... The art of color, published in Germany in 1961 [under title: Kunst der Farbe]" [ND1493.I81813 1970] 77-124314
1. Color. I. Birren, Faber, 1900- ed. II. Title.

JACOBS, Michel, 1877- 752.1
The study of colour; with lessons and exercises, arranged for instruction of teachers, artists, students, and parents. 6th print. Rumson, N. J., Primatic Art Co. [1956] 161p. illus. 28cm. [ND1280.J33 1956] 56-3647
1. Color. I. Title.

JACOBS, Michel, 1887- 752
The art of colour. [3d ed.] Rumson, N.J., Primatic Art Co. [1956] 66p. illus. 28cm. [ND1280.J3 1956] 56-3648
1. Color. I. Title.

JUSTEMA, William, 1904- 746.4
Weaving & needlecraft color course [by] William & Doris Justema. New York, Van Nostrand Reinhold Co. [1971] 160 p. illus. (part col.) 27 cm. Bibliography: p. 156-158. [TT751.J87] 77-126875
1. Color. 2. Needlework. 3. Hand weaving. I. Justema, Doris, joint author. II. Title.

KOBLO, Martin. 701.8
World of color; an introduction to the theory and use of color in art. Translated by Ian F. Finlay. New York, McGraw-Hill [1963] 240 p. illus. 25 cm. [ND1280.K613] 62-17513
1. Color. 2. Painting—Technique. I. Title.

LIBBY, William Charles. 701'.8
Color and the structural sense. Englewood Cliffs, N.J., Prentice-Hall [1974] xi, 114 p. col. illus. 24 cm. [ND1488.L52] 73-20370 ISBN 0-13-151316-8 7.95
1. Color. I. Title. BIP

RENNER, Paul, 1878- 701.8
Color: order and harmony; a color theory for artists and craftsmen. Translated by Alexander Nesbitt. New York, Reinhold Pub. Corp. [1965, c1964] 80 p. illus. (part mounted, part col.) 28 cm. Translation of Ordnung und Harmonie der Farben. [ND1280.R453] 64-22423
1. Color. I. Title.

SARGENT, Walter, 1868- 752
The enjoyment and use of color [Gloucester, Mass., P. Smith, 1965, c.1923-1964] ix, 274p. illus. (pt. col.) 21cm. (Dover bk. rebound) [ND1283.S3] 4.00
1. Color. I. Title.

SARGENT, Walter, 1868- 752
The enjoyment and use of color. New York, Dover Publications [1964] ix, 274 p. illus (part col.) 21 cm. "Corrected and revised republication of the work first published ...in 1923." [ND1283.S3 1964] 63-20254
1. Color. I. Title. BIP

SPEARS, Charleszine (Wood) 646'.34
How to wear colors, with emphasis on dark skins. 5th ed. Minneapolis, Burgess Pub. Co. [1973, c1974] x, 83 p. illus. 23 cm. Includes bibliographies. [TT507.S7 1973] 73-89010 ISBN 0-8087-1927-0 3.00 (pbk.)
1. Color. 2. Clothing and dress. I. Title.

SPEARS, Charleszine (Wood) 646
How to wear colors, with emphasis on dark skins. 4th ed. Minneapolis, Burgesss Pub. Co. [1965] ii, 67 p. illus. 23 cm. "Color guide" (4 cards of mounted colored samples) in pocket. Includes bibliographies. [TT507.S7 1965] 65-22198
1. Color. 2. Clothing and dress. I. Title. BIP

TAYLOR, Frank A. 752
Colour technology for artists, craftsmen, and industrial designers. New York, Oxford [c.]1962. 140p. illus. (pt. col.) 62-1293 4.80 bds.,
1. Color. I. Title.

TAYLOR, Frank A 752
Colour technology for artists, craftsmen, and industrial designers. London, New York, Oxford University Press, 1962. 140 p. illus. 23 cm. Includes bibliography. [ND1280.T] 62-1293
1. Color. I. Title.

Color—Bibliography.

PARKS, Berkeley. 016.3092'08 s
Color theory : selected bibliography / Berkeley Parks. Monticello, Ill. : Council of Planning Librarians, 1975. 6 p. ; 28 cm. (Exchange bibliography - Council of Planning Librarians ; 886) Cover title. [Z5942.C68 no. 886] [Z7144.C7] [QC495] 016.5356 76-355243 pbk. : 1.50
1. Color—Bibliography. I. Title. II. Series: Council of Planning Librarians. Exchange bibliography ; 886.

Color cinematography.

SOCIETY of Motion Picture and Televsion Engineers. 778.5342
Elements of color in professional motion pictures, prepared by a special committee: Wilton R. Holm, chairman [and others] New York, [1957] 104 p. illus. (part col.) 28 cm. [TR853.S6] 57-4163
1. Color cinematography. I. Title. II. Title: Color in professional motion pictures.

Color-field painting—Exhibitions.

BOSTON. Museum of Fine Arts. 759.13'074'014461
Abstract painting in the 70's; a selection. [An exhibit Museum of Fine Arts, Boston, April 14 - May 21, 1972 [Boston, 1972] 1 v. (unpaged) col. illus. 29 cm. [ND212.5.C6B6] 72-79442 ISBN 0-87846-066-7
1. Color-field painting—Exhibitions. 2. Color-field painting—United States. I. Title. BIP

CARMEAN, E. A. 759.06
The great decade of American abstraction; modernist art 1960 to 1970; inaugural exhibition for the Brown Pavilion, the Museum of Fine Arts, Houston, January 15-March 10, 1974. With an introductory note by Philippe de Montebello, and text and catalogue by E. A. Carmean, Jr. [Houston, Museum of Fine Arts, 1974] 138 p. illus. (part col.) 24 x 28 cm. Errata slip inserted. Bibliography: p. 68-71. [ND212.5.C6C37] 73-94140 7.50 (pbk.)
1. Color-field painting—Exhibitions. 2. Color-field painting—United States. 3. Minimal sculpture—Exhibitions. 4. Minimal sculpture—United States. I. Houston, Tex. Museum of Fine Arts. II. Title.

PENNSYLVANIA. University. Institute of Contemporary Art. 752'.0973
Two generations of color painting. [Philadelphia] c1970. [24] p. illus. (part col.) 22 cm. Text by S. S. Prokopoff. Catalog of an exhibition held Oct. 1-Nov. 6, 1970 at the Institute of Contemporary Art, University of Pennsylvania. [ND212.5.C6P4] 70-29197
1. Color-field painting—Exhibitions. 2. Color-field painting—U.S. I. Prokopoff, Stephen S. II. Title. BIP

Color in advertising.

BIGGS, Ernest. 659.1325
Colour in advertising. London, New York, Studio Publications [1956] 160p. col. illus. 26cm. Bibliography: p. 157. [HF5839.B5] 56-58356
1. Clcolor in advertising. I. Title.

BIRREN, Faber, 1900- 659.1325
Selling color to people; a book on how to sell color in commercial products and advertising to the American public, based on practical methods of consumer research, styling, merchandising, promotion, and public relations. New York, University Books [1956] 219p. illus. 26cm. [HF5839.B55] 56-7835
1. Color in advertising. 2. Color—Psychology. I. Title.

CHESKIN, Louis, 1907- 659.1325
Color guide for marketing media. New York, Macmillan [1954] 209p. illus. 22cm. [HF5839.C47] 54-12932
1. Color in advertising. I. Title.

KETCHAM, Howard, 1902- 659.1325
Color planning for business and industry. [1st ed.] New York, Harper [1958] 274 p. illus. 25 cm. [HF5839.K4] 58-11387
1. Color in advertising. I. Title.

Color in architecture.

COLOR for architecture / 729
[edited by] Tom Porter and Byron Mikellides. New York : Van Nostrand Reinhold, 1976. 150 p. : ill. (some col.) ; 31 cm. Includes index. Bibliography: p. 145-146. [NA2795.C64 1976] 76-17745 ISBN 0-442-26619-7 : 20.00
1. Color in architecture. I. Porter, Tom. II. Mikellides, Byron. BIP

COLOUR for architecture / 729
[edited by] Tom Porter and Byron Mikellides. London : Studio Vista, 1976. 151 p. : ill. (some col.) ; 31 cm. American ed. published simultaneously under title: Color for architecture. Includes index. Bibliography: p. 145-146. [NA2795.C64 1976b] 77-365845 ISBN 0-289-70611-4 : £12.50
1. Color in architecture. I. Porter, Tom. II. Mikellides, Byron.

FAULKNER, Waldron. 721
Architecture and color. New York, Wiley-Interscience [1972] xv, 146 p. illus. 26 cm. Bibliography: p. 135. [NA2795.F38] 77-179419 ISBN 0-471-25630-7
1. Color in architecture. 2. Color in art. I. Title. BIP

GATZ, Konrad. 724.9
Colour and architecture [by] Konrad Gatz and Gerhard Achterberg. [1st English language ed.] New York, Architectural Book Pub. Co. [1967, c1966] 279 p. 477 illus. (part col.) 30 cm. Translation of Architektur farbig. [NA2795.G2813] 66-27872
1. Color in architecture. 2. Architecture, Modern—20th century. I. Achterberg, Gerhard, joint author. II. Title.

NATIONAL Research Council. Building Research Institute. Conferences. Washington, D.C., Fall, 1961. 667.6
Identification of colors for building. Report of a program held as part of the BRI 1961 Fall Conferences. [Washington] Building Research Institute, 1962. ii, 68 p. illus., diagrs. 23 cm. (Building Research Institute. Publication no. 1001) Includes bibliographies. [NA2795.N3] 62-64826
1. Color in architecture. 2. Colors. I. Title. II. Series.

VAN ZANTEN, David, 1943- 729'.4
The architectural polychromy of the 1830's / David Van Zanten. New York : Garland Publishing, 1977. 442 p., [70] leaves of plates : ill. ; 21 cm. (Outstanding dissertations in the fine arts) Reprint of the ed. originally presented as the author's thesis, Harvard University, 1970. Bibliography: p. 412-442. [NA2795.V36 1977] 76-23648 ISBN 0-8240-2733-7 : 45.00
1. Color in architecture. 2. Architecture—Greece. 3. Architecture, Modern—19th century. I. Title. II. Series. BIP

Color in art.

BIRREN, Faber, 1900- 752
Color perception in art / by Faber Birren. New York : Van Nostrand Reinhold Co., 1976. 63 p., 12 leaves of plates : ill. (some col.) ; 21 cm. Includes index. Bibliography: p. 59-60. [ND1495.P8B57] 75-32207 ISBN 0-442-20784-0 : 12.50 ISBN 0-442-20782-4 pbk. :
1. Color in art. 2. Color—Psychology. 3. Visual perception. I. Title. BIP

CARPENTER, James Morton, 1914- 752
Color in art; a tribute to Arthur Pope. With an introd. to color by Howard T. Fisher. Catalogue and text by James M. Carpenter. [Cambridge, Mass.] Fogg Art Museum, Harvard University [1974] 134 p. illus. (part col.) 27 cm. Exhibition held Apr. 24-June 16, 1974, at the Fogg Art Museum. Bibliography: p. 130. [ND1493.P66C37] 74-78661
1. Pope, Arthur, 1880- 2. Color in art. I.

SUBJECT INDEX

COLOR PHOTOGRAPHY.

Pope, Arthur, 1880- II. Harvard University. William Hayes Fogg Art Museum.

CHEVREUL, Michel Eugene, 1786-1889. 701.8
The principles of harmony and contrast of colors and their applications to the arts. With a special introd. and explanatory notes, by Faber Birren. New York, Reinhold Pub. Corp. [1967] 256 p. illus. (part col.), facsims., ports. 29 x 32 cm. "Based on the first English edition of 1854 as translated from the first French edition of 1839, De la loi du contraste simultane des couleurs. [ND1280.C57 1967] 66-24553
1. Color in art. I. Birren, Faber, 1900- ed. II. Title. **BIP**

COLOR Forum. 701'.8
Color Forum: University Art Museum, the University of Texas at Austin, February 27-April 16, 1972. [Austin, Printed by Printing Division, University of Texas at Austin, 1972] 55 p. col. illus. 24 cm. [ND195.C57] 72-181445
1. Color in art. 2. Paintings, Modern—20th century—Exhibitions. I. Texas. University at Austin. Art Museum.

CRUZ Diez, Carlos, 1923- 701'.8
Physichromies, couleur additive, induction chromatique, chromointerferences [by] Cruz-Diez. New York, Galerie Denise Rene, 1971. [20] p. (chiefly illus., part col.) 27 cm. Bibliography: p. [20] [N6739.C7A49] 79-198491
1. Color in art. 2. Light in art. I. Galerie Denise Rene. II. Title.

CURTIS, Roger William, 1910- 751.4'5
Color in outdoor painting / by Roger W. Curtis ; edited by Charles Movalli. New York : Watson-Guptill Publications, 1977. 152 p. : ill. (some col.) ; 30 cm. Includes index. Bibliography: p. 149. [ND1488.C87 1977] 76-49653 ISBN 0-8230-0740-5 : 16.95
1. Color in art. 2. Painting—Technique. I. Title. **BIP**

DELAUNAY, Robert, 1885-1941. 752
The new art of color : the writings of Robert and Sonia Delaunay / edited and with an introd. by Arthur A. Cohen. New York : Viking Press, [1978] p. cm. (The Documents of 20th-century art) Includes index. Bibliography: p. [ND1489.D44] 77-28840 ISBN 0-670-50636-2 : 12.95
1. Color in art. 2. Painting, Abstract. 3. Painting, Modern—20th century. I. Delaunay, Sonia, 1885- joint author. II. Cohen, Arthur Allen, 1928- III. Title. IV. Series. **BIP**

GREGORY, Albert. 752
Color/moire. Cambridge, Mass., 1969. 1 portfolio ([4] l., 23 col. plates) 75 cm. "X of 100 copies. Artists proof. [Signed] Albert Gregory." Five of the plates are printed on col. acetate sheets to be used as overlays on 5 plates to create moire patterns. "A reprint and enlargement of an earlier book, Color in line ... published in 1960." [ND1285.G72] 78-222761
1. Color in art. 2. Line (Art) I. Title.

GRUPPE, Emile A., 1896- 751.4'5
Gruppe on color / by Emile Gruppe ; edited by Charles Movalli. New York : Watson-Guptill Publications, 1979. p. cm. Includes index. Bibliography: p. [ND1489.G75 1979] 78-27121 ISBN 0-8230-2155-6 : 19.50
1. Color in art. 2. Landscape painting—Technique. 3. Marine painting—Technique. I. Movalli, Charles. II. Title. **BIP**

ROOD, Ogden Nicholas, 1831-1902. 752
Modern chromatics; students' text-book of color, with applications to art and industry. Including a facsim. of the 1st American ed. of 1879. Pref., introd., and commentary notes by Faber Birren. New York, Van Nostrand Reinhold Co. [1973, i.e.1974] 257 p. illus. (part col.) 23 x 29 cm. Original t.p. reads: Modern chromatics, with applications to art and industry, by Ogden N. Rood ... New York, D. Appleton and Company ... 1879. Original ed. issued as v. 26 of The International scientific series. Bibliography: p. 60-61. [ND1488.R66 1879a] 73-1627 ISBN 0-442-27028-3 14.95
1. Color in art. 2. Painting. I. Birren, Faber, 1900- II. Title. III. Series: The International scientific series (New York) v. 26.

SCHMID, H. Rainer. 117
Lux incorporata : zur ontologischen Begrundung einer Systematik des farbigen Aufbaus in der Malerei / H. Rainer Schmid. Hildesheim ; New York : G. Olms, 1975. 104 p. ; 21 cm. (Studien zur Kunstgeschichte ; Bd. 5) Originally presented as the author's thesis, Munich, 1971. Bibliography: p. 101-104. [ND1488.S35 1975] 76-452198 ISBN 3-487-05718-2
1. Color in art. 2. Light in art. 3. Painting—Technique. I. Title. II. Series.

Color in art—Exhibitions.

POLING, Clark V. 709'.04'074013
Bauhaus color : an exhibition organized by the High Museum of Art and supported by a grant from the National Endowment for the Arts / by Clark V. Poling. Atlanta : High Museum of Art, [1975] 71 p. : ill. (some col.) ; 24 cm. Exhibition to be held Jan. 31-Mar. 14, 1976 at the High Museum of Art, Atlanta, Apr. 8-May 30, 1976 at the Museum of Fine Arts, Houston, and Aug. 1-Sept. 21, 1976 at the Fine Arts Gallery of San Diego. Bibliography: p. 71. [N332.G33B475] 75-39143
1. Bauhaus. 2. Color in art—Exhibitions. 3. Art, Modern—20th century—Exhibition. I. High Museum of Art. II. Title.

Color in art—Juvenile literature.

CAMPBELL, Ann Raymond. 701'.8
Let's find out about color / by Ann Campbell ; pictures by Boche Kaplan and Roz Abisch. Rev. full color ed. New York : Watts, 1975. 40 p. : col. ill. ; 23 cm. Discusses the primary colors from which all other colors are made. [N361.C3 1975] 74-3502 ISBN 0-531-00015-X lib.bdg. : 4.90
1. Color in art—Juvenile literature. 2. Art—Study and teaching (Primary)—Juvenile literature. I. Kaplan, Boche. II. Abisch, Roz. III. Title.

GATTO, Joseph A. 701'.8
Color and value / Joseph A. Gatto. Worcester, Mass. : Davis Publications, [1974] 80 p. : ill. (some col.) ; 26 cm. (Elements of design) Includes index. Text and photographs explore the importance of color and of value (the lightness and darkness of color) in enchancing design. [ND1490.G37] 75-321024 ISBN 0-87192-065-4
1. Color in art—Juvenile literature. 2. Color—Psychology—Juvenile literature. I. Title. II. Series. **BIP**

Color in interior decoration.

BIRREN, Faber, 1900- 747
Color for interiors, historical and modern; an essential reference work covering the major period styles of history and including modern palettes for the authentic decoration of homes, institutional and commercial interiors. New York, Whitney Library of Design [1963] ix, 210 p. illus., mounted col. samples. 27 cm. 63-11888
1. Color in interior decoration. I. Title.

BLAKE, Jill. 747'.8'83
Colour and pattern in the home / Jill Blake. 1st ed. New York : Quick Fox, 1978. 83 p. : ill. (some col.) ; 20 x 21 cm. (A Design Centre book) Bibliography: p. 82. [NK2115.5.C6B57] 78-58485 ISBN 0-8256-3137-8 pbk. : 7.95
1. Color in interior decoration. 2. Textile fabrics in interior decoration. 3. Antiques in interior decoration. I. Title.

HALSE, Albert O., 1910- 747
The use of color in interiors [by] Albert O. Halse. New York, McGraw-Hill [1968] viii, 134 p. illus. 29 cm. Bibliography: p. 127-128. [NK2113.H23] 68-11607
1. Color in interior decoration. I. Title. **BIP**

HALSE, Albert O., 1910- 747
The use of color in interiors / Albert O. Halse. 2d ed. New York : McGraw-Hill, c1978. viii, 152 p., [16] leaves of plates : ill. ; 29 cm. Includes index. Bibliography: p. 147-149. [NK2115.5.C6H34 1978] 77-14472 ISBN 0-07-025624-1 : 24.95
1. Color in interior decoration. I. Title.

PLUMB, Barbara. 747
Young designs in color. New York, Viking Press [1972] 176 p. illus. 29 cm. (A Studio book) [NK2115.5.C6P55 1972] 72-79113 ISBN 0-670-79437-6 15.95
1. Color in interior decoration. I. Title.

VARNEY, Carleton. 747
Decorating with color. [Des Moines] Creative Home Library [1972] x, 173 p. illus. 27 cm. [NK2115.5.C6V3] 77-145625 ISBN 0-696-18600-4 8.95
1. Color in interior decoration. I. Title.

WALCH, Margaret. 701'.8
Color source book / Margaret Walch. New York : Scribner, [1979] p. cm. [ND1488.W34] 79-585 ISBN 0-684-16134-6 : 50.00
1. Color. 2. Color guides. I. Title. **BIP**

WILSON, Jose. 747
Color in decoration, by Jose Wilson and Arthur Leaman. New York, Van Nostrand Reinhold Co. [1973?] 159 p. illus. 32 cm. Bibliography: p. 159. [NK2115.5.C6W54 1973] 79-90332 ISBN 0-289-70220-8 24.95
1. Color in interior decoration. I. Leaman, Arthur, joint author. II. Title.

Color in the ceramic industries.

DUCRET, Siegfried. 738.2'094
The color treasury of 18th century porcelain / text by Siegfried Ducret; photos. by Michael Wogensinger; translated by Christine Friedlander. New York : Crowell, c1976. p. cm. [NK4373.D7813 1976] 76-10734 ISBN 0-690-01124-5 : 9.95
1. Color in the ceramic industries. 2. Porcelain. I. Wogensinger, Michael. II. Title.

SHAW, Kenneth. 666/.4/5
Ceramic colours and pottery decoration. London, Maclaren [1962] 196p. illus. 23cm. Bibl. [TP823.S48] 67-103850 8.00
1. Color in the ceramic industries. I. Title. American distributor: Transatlantic, Levittown, N.Y.

Color photography.

ANSCO. 778.6
Color photography made easy with Ansco color film and Ansco color printon. [Binghamton, N. Y., 1954] 96p. illus. 19cm. [TR510.A5] 54-2059
1. Color photography. I. Title.

ASHTON, George 778.6
Taking colour photographs. London, Fountain [dist. New York, Morgan & Morgan, 1964, c.1959] 122p. illus. 20cm. 55-56313 3.50
1. Color photography. I. Title.

BAGBY, Robert. 778.66
Anscochrome and Ektachrome home processing. Rev. Philadelphia, Chilton Co., Book Division, c1961. 125p. illus. 20cm. (Modern camera guide series, 246) First published in 1957 under title: Anscochrome and Ektachrome processing at home. [TR520.B3 1961] 61-14783
1. Color photography. 2. Photography—Films. I. Title.

BAILEY, Adrian, 1928- 778.6
The book of color photography / by Adrian Bailey and Adrian Holloway. New York : Knopf, 1979. p. cm. Cover title. Includes index. [TR510.B23] 78-20606 ISBN 0-394-41607-4 : 17.95
1. Color photography. I. Holloway, Adrian, joint author. II. Title. **BIP**

BENSER, Walther 778.6
Better colour with Walther Benser. Tr. [from German] by F. Bradley. London, Fountain Pr. [dist. New York, Morgan & Morgan, 1964, c.1959] 80p. col. illus. 21x22cm. 64-3125 6.5
1. Color photography. I. Title.

BENSER, Walther 778.6
Photographng colour with Walther Benser [Tr. from German by F. Bradley] London, Fountain Pr. [dist. New York, Morgan & Morgan, 1964, c.1961] 202p. illus., col. plates. 23cm. 64-3077 7.95
1. Color photography I. Title.

BOMBACK, Edward S. 770.24
Beginner's guide to colour photography, by Colin Day [pseud.] New York, McBride Books [1962] 127 p. illus. 19 cm. [TR510] 62-13551
1. Color photography. I. Title.

BOMBACK, Edward S. 778.6
Manual of color photography. London, Fountain Pr. [dist. New York, Morgan & Morgan. 1965, c.1964] 412p. illus. (pt. col.) 23cm. [TR510.B6115] 65-5432 9.95 bds.,
1. Color photography. I. Title.

BOMBACK, Edward S. 778.6
Manual of colour photography. [by] E. S. Bomback. [2d ed.] London, Fountain Press [1973, c.1972] 362 p. illus. 23 cm. [TR510.B6115] 75-188332 ISBN 0-852-42095-1
1. Color Photography. I. Title.
Available from International Publications Service, New York, for 13.50.

BOMBACK, Edward S. 778.6
Photography in colour. Illus by the author. [Rev. ed.] London, Fountain [dist. New York, Morgan & Morgan, 1964] 112p. col. plates. 23cm. (Fountain photobk.) First pub. in 1957 under title: Photography in colour with Kodak films. 64-6655 3.95
1. Color photography. I. Title.

BOMBACK, Edward S. 778.6
Your A-Z guide to colour photography. London, Fountain [dist. New York, Morgan & Morgan, 1964, c.1961] 126p. illus. (pt. col.) 17cm. (Fountain photobk.) 64-3078 3.50 bds.,
1. Color photography. I. Title.

BOND, Fred, 1893- 778.6
Making better color slides. All illus. by the author unless otherwise designated. [1st ed.] San Francisco, Camera Craft Pub. Co. [1951] 2v. illus. (part col.) 24 cm. [TR510.B62] 51-11600
1. Color photography. I. Title.

CATLING, Gordon. 778.6
Colour for the young cameraman. London, N. Kaye stamped: distributed by Sportshelf, New Rochelle, N. Y. [1961] 128p. illus. 19cm. [TR510.C32] 61-19817
1. Color photography. I. Title.

CAULFIELD, Patricia 778.66
Complete guide to Kodachrome I New York, Universal. [Dist. Amphoto, c.1962] 128p. illus. (pt. col.) 21cm. 62-12122 1.95 pap.,
1. Color photography. 2. Photography—Films. I. Title. II. Title: Kodachrome

CAULFIELD, Patricia. 778.66
Complete guide to Kodachrome II. New York, Universal Photo Books [1962] 128p. illus. 21cm. [TR510.C34] 62-12122
1. Color photography. 2. Photography—Films. I. Title.

CAULFIELD, Patricia. 778.6'6
Complete guide to Kodachrome II, Kodachrome-X. 2d ed. Philadelphia, Chilton Books [1967, c1964] 128 p. illus. (part col.) 21 cm. [TR510.C34 1967] 67-1678
1. Color photography. 2. Photography—Films. I. Title.

CAULFIELD, Patricia 778.66
Complete guide to Kodachrome ii, ,kodacrome-X. 2d ed. New York, Universal Photo Bks.; Philadelphia, ,chilton [1967,c.1964] 128p. illus. (pt. col.) 21cm. 2.95
1. Color ,photography. 2. Photography-Films. I. Title. II. Title: Kodachrome-X.

COOTE, Jack Howard Roy. 778.6
Making colour prints; practical photographic methods. 17th ed. London, New York, Focal Press [1953] 128p. illus. 19cm. [TR510.C6 1953] 53-13166
1. Color photography. 2. Photography—Printing processes. I. Title.

COSTA, Joseph. 778.6
Beginner's guide to color photography. New York, Greenberg [1955] 104p. illus. 20cm. (The Modern camera guide series) [TR510.C63] 54-11248

1. Color photography. I. Title.

*CRAIG, Walt. 778.6
Concepts in color photography: color temperature and filters. Columbus, Ohio, [Grid] [1973] iv, 51 p. 22 cm. [TR510] ISBN 0-88244-050-0 3.45 (pbk.)
1. Color photography. I. Title.

DANTZIC, Jerry. 778.6
How to take better color pictures. New York, American Photographic Book Pub. Co.; distributed to the book trade by Grosset & Dunlap [1964] 96 p. illus. 22 cm. (Better photo guides) "432." [TR510.D3] 63-22235
1. Color photography. I. Title.

DAY, Colin 770.24
Beginner's guide to colour photography. New York, McBride Bks. [c. 1962] 127p. col. illus. 19cm. 62-13551 2.95bds.,
1. Color photography. I. Title.

DE MARE, Eric Samuel, 1910- 778.6
Colour photography [by] Eric De Mare. Baltimore, Penguin [1968] 158p. illus. (pt. col.) 20cm. (Penguin handbks., PH136) Companion vol. to the author's Photography. [TR510.D45] 68-5261 2.25 pap.,
1. Color photography. I. Title. BIP

DE MARE, Eric Samuel, 778.6
1910-
Colour photography [by] Eric de Mare. [2d ed.] [Baltimore] Penguin Books [1973] 160 p. col. illus., tables. 20 cm. (Penguin handbooks, PH136) "Companion vol. to the author's Photography." [TR510.D45] 68-5261 ISBN 0-14-046136-1 2.65 (pbk.)
1. Color photography. I. Title.

DUNN, Carlton E. 778.6
Natural color processes. [5th ed.] Minneapolis, American Photographic Pub. Co., 1950. viii, 286 p. illus. 20 cm. [TR510.D83 1950] 50-10101
1. Color photography. I. Title. II. Title: Color processes.

DURNING, William P 778.6
Modern color photography Black-and-white photography by Rus Arnold. Rev. ed. New York, Crown Publishers [1954] 112p. illus. 18cm. (Little technical library, 41) [TR510.D86 1954] 54-6546
1. Color photography. I. Title.

EASTMAN Kodak Company. 778.6
Adventures in color-slide photography : a photo idea book from Kodak. [Rochester, N.Y. : Eastman Kodak Co., c1976] 336 p. : col. ill. ; 23 cm. Includes index. [TR510.E2 1976] 75-34515 ISBN 0-87985-162-7 : 10.95
1. Color photography. 2. Slides (Photography) I. Title. BIP

EASTMAN Kodak Company. 778.6
Kodak color handbook: materials, processes, techniques. [Rochester, N. Y.] c1950. 68, 56, 64, 60p. illus. (part col.) 23cm. (Kodak color data books) [TR510.E16] 50-14948
1. Color photography. I. Title.
Contents omitted.

EASTMAN Kodak Company. 778.6
Vacation Europe with your color camers. [Rochester, N. Y.] c1954. 64p. illus. 22cm. (Kodak publication no. C-29) [TR510.E2] 54-4105
1. Color photography. 2. Europe—Descr. & trav.—Views. I. Title.

EASTMAN Kodak Company. 778.6
Vacation USA with your color camera. [Rochester, 1953] 64p. illus. 22cm. 'A Kodak publication.' [TR660.E3] 53-2923
1. Color photography. 2. U. S.—Descr. & trav.—Views. I. Title.

ELISOFON, Eliot 778.6
Color photography. New York, Viking [c.1961] 153p. illus., plates (part col.) 32cm. (Studio bk.) 61-17410 10.00 bds.,
1. Color photography. I. Title.

EVANS, Ralph Merrill. 778.6
Eye, film, and camera in color photography / Ralph M. Evans. Huntington, N.Y. : R. E. Krieger Pub. Co., 1979 [c1959] p. cm. Reprint of the ed. published by Wiley, New York. Includes index. Bibliography: p. [TR510.E83 1979] 78-21990 ISBN 0-88275-798-9 lib.bdg. : 21.50
1. Color photography. I. Title. BIP

EVANS, Ralph Merrill. 778.6
Principles of color photography [by] Ralph M. Evans, W. T. Hanson, Jr. [and] W. Lyle Brewer. New York, Wiley [1953] 709 p. illus. 24 cm. Includes bibliography. [TR510.E85] 53-6722
1. Color photography. 2. Color-sense.

FEININGER, Andreas, 1906- 778.6
Successful color photography. 2d ed. Englewood Cliffs, N. J., Prentice-Hall [1955] 271p. illus. 24cm. [TR510.F44 1955] 55-11436
1. Color photography. I. Title.

FEININGER, Andreas, 1906- 778.6
Successful color photography. 4th ed. Englewood Cliffs, N. J., Prentice [1966] xv, 271p. illus. (pt. col.) 24cm. [TR510.F44 1966] 66-22365 7.95
1. Color photography. I. Title.

FOININGER, Andreas, 1906- 778.6
Basic color photography. New York, Amphoto [1972] 128 p. illus. (part col.) 22 cm. [TR510.F4] 72-159329 ISBN 0-8174-0542-9 6.95
1. Color photography. I. Title. BIP

FROST, Conrad 778.6
Taking and processing amateur colour negatives. London, Fountain [dist. New York Morgan & Morgan, 1964, c.1963] 95p. illus. 17cm. (Fountain photobk. ser.) 64-3082 2.95 bds.,
1. Color photography. 2. Photography—Developing and developers. 3. Photography—Negatives. I. Title.

HAAS, Ernst, 1921- 779'.3
The creation. New York, Viking Press [1971] 159 p. (chiefly col. illus.) 24 x 35 cm. (A Studio book) [TR510.H25] 75-155659 ISBN 0-670-24583-6 25.00
1. Color photography. 2. Photography, Artistic. 3. Creation. I. Title.

HAAS, Ernst, 1921- 779'.3
The creation / Ernst Haas. New York : Penguin Books, 1976, c1971. p. cm. [TR510.H25 1976] 76-18761 ISBN 0-14-004284-9 pbk. : 9.95
1. Color photography. 2. Photography, Artistic. 3. Creation. I. Title. BIP

HEDGECOE, John. 778.6
The art of color photography / by John Hedgecoe. New York : Simon and Schuster, [1978] p. cm. Includes index. [TR510.H37] 78-2093 ISBN 0-671-24274-1 : 29.95
1. Color photography. I. Title. BIP

HUNT, Robert William 778.6
Gainer.
The reproduction of colour, by R. W. G. Hunt. With a foreword by W. D. Wright. [2d ed. New York] Wiley [1967] 500 p. illus. (part col.) 23 cm. Includes bibliographies. [TR510.H84 1967b] 68-3125
1. Color photography. 2. Color television. 3. Color-printing. I. Title.

HUNT, Robert William 778.6
Gainer.
The reproduction of colour / R. W. G. Hunt ; with a foreword by W. D. Wright. 3d ed. New York : Wiley, 1975. xxi, 614 p., [6] leaves of plates : ill. (some col.) ; 22 cm. "A Halsted Press book." Includes bibliographies and index. [TR510.H84 1975] 76-6096 ISBN 0-470-15085-8 : 25.00
1. Color photography. 2. Color television. 3. Color-printing. I. Title.

ISERT, Gerhard. 778.6
The art of colour photography [by] G. Isert. New York, Van Nostrand Reinhold [1971] 411 p. illus. (part col.) 24 cm. Translation of Das Goldene Buch der Farbfotografie. [TR510.I7813 1971] 79-142180 ISBN 0-240-50725-8 17.95
1. Color photography. I. Title.

ISERT, Gerhard. 778.6
The art of colour photography [by] G. Isert [translated from the German by Leonard Gaunt]. London, New York, Focal Press, 1970. 412 p. illus. (some col.) 24 cm. Translation of Das Goldene Buch der Farbfotografie. [TR510.I7813 1970] 79-580313 ISBN 0-240-50725-8 £4.50
1. Color photography. I. Title.

JAFFE, Erwin. 778.6
Color separation photography for offset lithography, with an introduction to masking, by Erwin Jaffe [and others. 1st ed.] New York, Lithographic Technical Foundation [1959] 222p. illus. 22cm. [TR510.J3] 59-7087
1. Color photography. 2. Offset printing. I. Title.

JOHNSON, Kenneth S 778.66
How to make perfect color transparencies every time. [3d ed. Englewood, N. J., R. Maschke Pub. Co., c1960] 64p. illus. 19cm. [TR510] 61-14598
1. Color photography. 2. Transparencies. I. Title.

KRAMER, Arthur. 778.6
Color photography techniques. New York, Universal PhotoBooks [1958] 120p. illus. 21cm. (A Universal photo guide) [510.K73] 57-10341
1. Color photography. I. Title.

LANGLEY, Russell A. 778.6
How to use all kodachrome films [by] Russell A. Langley. [2d ed.] New York, Amphoto [1969] 72 p. illus. (part col.) 18 cm. (Viewfinder book) [TR520.L34 1969] 72-95774 1.25
1. Color photography. 2. Photography—Films. I. Title.

LILLEY, Geoffery I. 771.1
Make your own darkroom for colour printing. London, Fountain Pr. [dist. New York, Morgan & Morgan, 1964,c. 1962] 86p. illus. 17cm. (Fountain photobk. ser.) 64-4260 2.95bds.,
1. Color photoraphy—Printing processes. 2. Photography—Studios and dark rooms. I. Title.

LORELLE, Lucien, 1894- 778.6
The colour book of photography. 5th ed. New York, Focal Press [dist. Amer. Photographic Pub. Co. 1960] 211p. illus. (part col.), diagrs. 'Translated and adapted by Gerald R. Sharp . . . from the French' 60-52051 3.00 bds.,
1. Color photography. I. Title.

MANTE, Harald. 778.6
Color design in photography. [English translation by E. F. Linssen] New York, Van Nostrand Reinhold [1972] 108 p. illus. 26 x 28 cm. Translation of Farb-Design in der Fotografie. [TR510.M2813] 77-176303 15.95
1. Color photography. 2. Photography, Artistic. I. Title. BIP

MUTTER, Edwin, 1902- 778.6
Farbphotographie; Theorie und Praxis. Wien. New York, Springer- Verlag, 1967. xx, 463p. illus. (pt. col.) 25cm. (Die Wissenschaftliche und angewandte Photographie, 4 Bd.) Bibl. [TR145.W76 Bd.4] 67-11661 39.25
1. Color photography. I. Title. II. Series.

ROTHSTEIN, Arthur, 1915- 778.6
Color photography now. Philadelphia, Chilton Book Co. [1970] 159 p. illus. (part col.) 24 cm. [TR510] 70-13862
1. Color photography. I. Title.

ROTHSTEIN, Arthur, 1915- 778.6
Color photography now. New York, American Photographic Book Pub. Co. [1970] 159 p. illus. (part col.) 24 cm. [TR510.R63] 70-117627 7.95
1. Color photography. I. Title.

ROTHSTEIN, Arthur, 1915- 778.6
Creative color in photography. Philadelphia, Chilton Books, c1963. 96 p. 21 cm. [TR510.R64] 63-12445
1. Color photography. 2. Photography, Artistic. I. Title.

SKOGLUND, Gosta. 778.6
Colour in your camera; a book of colour photographs to show how to make colour photographs. New York, Ziff-Davis Pub. Co. [1960, c1959] 168 p. illus. 22 cm. [TR510.S57 1960] 60-4078
1. Color photography. I. Title.

SKOGLUND, Gosta. 778.6
Colour in your camera; a book of colour photographs to show how to make colour photographs. 5th rev. ed. Philadelphia, Chilton Book Co. [1969] 164 p. illus. (part col.) 22 cm. [TR510.S57 1969b] 69-16643 8.95
1. Color photography. I. Title.

SPENCER, Douglas Arthur, 778.6
1901-
Colour photography in practice [by] D. A. Spencer. Completely revised ed. by L. Andrew Mannheim and Viscount Hanworth. London, New York, Focal P., 1966. 410 p. illus., col. plates, tables, diagrs. 25 cm. (The Focal library) 5/5/- (B66-21772) Bibliography: p. 401-404. [TR510.S7 1966] 67-72610
1. Color photography. I. Mannheim, Ladislaus Andrew, 1925- ed. II. Hanworth, David Bertram Pollock, 2d viscount, 1916- ed. III. Title.

SPENCER, Douglas Arthur, 778.6
1901-
D. A. Spencer's Colour photography in practice. Rev. ed. by L. Andrew Mannheim and Viscount Hanworth. New York, Amphoto [1969, c1966] 410 p. illus. (part col.) 25 cm. (The Focal library) Bibliography: p. 401-404. [TR510.S7 1969] 76-133457 13.95
1. Color photography. I. Mannheim, Ladislaus Andrew, 1925- II. Hanworth, David Bertram Pollock, 2d Viscount, 1916- III. Title: Colour photography in practice.

THOMSON, C. Leslie 778.6
Successful colour photography. New York, Amphoto Press [1959] 144p. illus. (part col.) 19cm. (Focal photobk.) 59-65047 1.95 flex. plastic,
1. Color photography. I. Title.

THOMSON, C. Leslie. 778.6
Colour films; the technique of working with colour materials [by] C. Leslie Thomson. 4th rev. ed. Philadelphia, Chilton Book Co. [1969] 278 p. illus. (part col.) 22 cm. (A Focal manual of photo technique) Includes bibliographical references. [TR510.T47 1969] 69-11443 10.95
1. Color photography. I. Title.

THOMSON, C. Leslie. 778.6
Colour films: the technique of working with colour materials, [by] C. Leslie Thomson. 5th ed. London, New York, Focal Press, 1971. 278 p. illus. (some col.) 22 cm. (The manuals of photo-technique) Includes bibliographical references. [TR510.T47 1971] 72-189473 ISBN 0-240-44747-6 £3.00
1. Color photography. I. Title.

THOMSON, C. Leslie. 778.6
Successful colour photography. London, New York, Focal Press [1959] 144 p. illus. 19 cm. [TR510.T5] 59-65047
1. Color photography. I. Title.

TIME-LIFE Books. 778.6
Color / by the editors of Time-Life Books. New York : Time-Life Books, c1976. 240 p. : ill. (some col.) ; 27 cm. (Life library of photography) Includes index. [TR510.T55 1976] 76-372131 7.95
1. Color photography. I. Title.

TIME-LIFE Books. 778.6
Color / by the editors of Time-Life Books. Alexandria, Va. : Time-Life Books, c1978. 240 p. : ill. (some col.) ; 27 cm. (Life library of photography) Includes index. Bibliography: p. 235. [TR510.T55 1978] 78-103738 ISBN 0-8094-1019-2 : 11.95
1. Color photography. I. Title.

VICKERS, John, 1916- 778.6
Making and printing cplour negatives. London, Fountain Pr. [dist. New York, Morgan & Morgan, 1964, c.1959] 194p. illus. (pt. col.) 23cm. (Fountain photobk.) Bibl. 64-3085 6.95
1. Color photography. 2. Photography—Developing and developers. 3. Color photography—Printing processes. I. Title.

WALL, Edward John, 1860- 778.6'09
1928.
The history of three-color photography, by E. J. Wall. London, New York, Focal P., 1970. [14], 747 p. illus. 25 cm. (The Focal library) Reprint of 1st ed., Boston, American Photographic Publishing Co., 1925. Bibliography: p. 682-684. [TR520.W3 1970] 75-865962 ISBN 0-240-50702-9 £8.00

1. Color photography. I. Title. BIP

WELLS, George, F.R.P.S. 778.6
How to shoot outdoor colour [by] George Wells & Felix Smith. [2d ed.] New York, Amphoto [1969] 69 p. illus. (part col.) 18 cm. (Viewfinder book) [TR510.W4 1969] 76-95775 1.25
1. Color photography. I. Smith, Felix, joint author. II. Title.

YULE, John A. C. 778.6
Principles of color reproduction, applied to photomechanical reproduction, color photography, and the ink, paper, and other related industries [by] J. A. C. Yule. New York, Wiley [1967] xiii, 411 p. illus. (part col.) 24 cm. (Wiley series on photographic science and technology and the graphic arts) Bibliography: p. 385-394. [TR977.Y8] 66-26764
1. Color photography. 2. Color-printing. 3. Photomechanical processes. I. Title.

YULSMAN, Jerry. 778.6
Color photography simplified / by Jerry Yulsman. Garden City, N.Y. : Amphoto, c1977. 96 p., [4] leaves of plates : ill. ; 27 cm. (A Modern photoguide) Includes index. [TR510.Y84] 77-73134 ISBN 0-8174-2425-3 : 10.95. ISBN 0-8174-0176-8 pbk. : 5.95
1. Color photography. I. Title. BIP

Color photography—Congresses.

COLOR : 778.6
theory and imaging systems / editor Raymond A. Eynard. 1st ed. Washington : Society of Photographic Scientists and Engineers, 1973. xxi, 429 p. : ill. (some col.) ; 23 cm. Papers presented at a seminar sponsored by the Rocky Mountain Chapter of the Society of Photographic Scientists and Engineers, and held in Denver, Nov. 1972. Includes bibliographical references and index. [TR510.C54] 72-93870
1. Color photography—Congresses. 2. Color television—Congresses. I. Eynard, Raymond A. II. Society of Photographic Scientists and Engineers. Rocky Mountain Chapter.

Color photography—Developing and developers.

CURRENT, Ira B. 778.6'6
How to process color films at home [by] Ira B. Current. 2d ed. New York, Amphoto [1969? c1968] 124 p. illus. 21 cm. [TR530.C87 1969] 79-10797 2.95
1. Color photography—Developing and developers. I. Title.

CURRENT, Ira B. 778.6'6
How to process color films at home [by] Ira B. Current. 2d ed. Philadelphia, Chilton Book Co. [1968] 124 p. illus. 21 cm. [TR545.C8 1968] 68-16459 3.50
1. Color photography—Developing and developers. I. Title.

Color photography—Developing and developers—Handbooks, manuals, etc.

MORGAN and Morgan, inc. 778.6
Pocket color processing data book. Hastings-on-Hudson, N.Y., Author [c.1966] 96p. 1v. (loose-leaf) 18cm. [TR530.M6] 66-20079 3.95, loose-leaf ringbinder
1. Color photography—Developing and developers—Handbooks, manuals, etc. 2. Color photography—Printing processes—Handbooks, manuals, etc. I. Title. II. Title: Color processing data book.

Color photography—Handbooks, manuals, etc.

FEININGER, Andreas, 1906- 778.6
The color photo book. Englewood Cliffs, N.J., Prentice-Hall [1969] viii, 408 p. illus. (part col.) 22 cm. [TR510.F42] 69-12820 ISBN 1-315-21810- 12.95
1. Color photography—Handbooks, manuals, etc. I. Title. BIP

GAUNT, Leonard. 778.6'2'0202
Take color. New York, Amphoto [1970] 168 p. illus. (part col.) 19 cm. [TR510.G34] 74-103301 7.95
1. Color photography—Handbooks, manuals, etc. I. Title. BIP

KODAK color films. 778.6
4th ed. [Rochester, N. Y.] Eastman Kodak, c.1950-1961. 49p. illus. (pt. col.) (Kodak pubn. no. E-77) 1.00 pap.,
1. Color photography—Handbooks, manuals, etc.

THOMSON, C. Leslie. 778.6
How to choose and use colour films [by] C. Leslie Thomson. [2d ed.] New York, Amphoto [1969] 69 p. illus. (part col.) 18 cm. (Viewfinder book) [TR510.T474 1969] 71-92579 1.25
1. Color photography—Handbooks, manuals, etc. I. Title.

Color photography—History.

FRIEDMAN, Joseph Solomon, 1899- 778.6
History of color photography, by Joseph S. Friedman. 2nd ed.; with introduction and appendix by Lloyd E. Varden. London, New York, Focal P., 1968. xvi, 565 p. illus. 25 cm. ([Focal library classics]) Includes bibliographies. [TR510.F7 1968] 70-356663 7/7/-
1. Color photography—History. 2. Color photography. I. Title. BIP

SIPLEY, Louis Walton. 778.6
A half century of color. New York, Macmillan [1951] xv, 216 p. illus. (part col.) ports. 27 cm. [TR510.S5] 51-13148
1. Color photography—History. 2. Color-printing—History. I. Title.

Color photography—Printing processes.

BAGBY, Robert. 778.6
Make your own color prints. [1st ed.] New York, McGraw-Hill [1961] 168 p. illus. 21 cm. [TR545.B3] 60-12758
1. Color photography—Printing processes. I. Title.

COOTE, Jack Howard Roy. 778.6
Colour prints; the photographic techniques of the colour positive. [1st ed.] London, New York, Focal Press [1956] 327p. illus. 19cm. (The Manual of photo-technique) [TR545.C6] 56-59220
1. Color photography—Printing processes. I. Title. BIP

COOTE, Jack Howard Roy. 778.6
Colour prints; the photographic technique of the colour positive [by] Jack H. Coote. [3d rev. ed.] Philadelphia, Chilton Book Co. [1968] 252 p. illus. (part col.) 22 cm. (The Manuals of photo-technique) Includes bibliographies. [TR545.C6 1968] 68-5209 ISBN 0-240-44750-6 10.95
1. Color photography—Printing processes. I. Title.

COOTE, Jack Howard Roy. 778.6
Colour prints : the photographic technique of the colour positive / [by] Jack H. Coote. 5th ed., revised. London ; New York : Focal Press, 1974. 274 p. : ill. (some col.). ; 22 cm. (The Manual of photo-technique) Includes bibliographical references and index. [TR545.C6 1974] 75-325537 ISBN 0-240-44750-6 : £3.75
1. Color photography—Printing processes. I. Title.

ENGDAHL, David A. 778.66
Color printing: materials, processes, color control. Philadelphia, Chilton, c.1962. 126p. illus. 20cm. (Modern camera guide ser., 907) 62-12681 1.95 pap.,
1. Color photography—Printing processes. I. Title.

ENGDAHL, David A. 778.6
Color printing; materials, processes, color control [by] David A. Engdahl. Philadelphia, Chilton Books [1967] 128 p. illus. (part col.) 24 cm. [TR545.E5 1967] 67-925
1. Color photography — Printing processes. I. Title.

ENGDAHL, David A. 778.66
Color printing: materials, processes, color control. New York, Amphoto; Philadelphia, Chilton [1967] 128p. illus. (pt. col.) 24cm. Orig. pub. in 1962 in Modern camera guide 6.95 ser.
1. Color photography—Printing processes. I. Title.

ENGDAHL, David A. 778.6
Color printing : materials, processes, color control / David A. Engdahl. 4th ed. Garden City, N.Y. : American Photographic Book Pub. Co., c1977. 128 p., [4] leaves of plates : ill. (some col.) ; 24 cm. Includes index. [TR545.E5 1977] 77-362791 ISBN 0-8174-2420-2 : 9.95
1. Color photography—Printing processes. I. Title.

ENGDAHL, David A. 778.6
Color printing; materials, processes, color control [by] David A. Engdahl. Philadelphia, Chilton Books [1967] 128 p. illus. (part col.) 24 cm. [TR545.E5 1967] 67-925
1. Color photography—Printing processes. I. Title.

MITCHELL, Bob. 778.6
Color printing / by Bob Mitchell. Los Angeles : Petersen Pub. Co., c1975. 80 p. : ill. (some col.) ; 28 cm. (Petersen's how-to photographic library) [TR545.M57] 75-8142 ISBN 0-8227-0101-4 pbk. : 2.95
1. Color photography—Printing processes. I. Title. BIP

NADLER, Bob. 778.6
The color printing manual / Bob Nadler. Garden City, N.Y. : Amphoto, c1978. ca. 350 p. in various pagings : ill. (some col.) ; 29 cm. Includes index. [TR545.N3] 77-90000 ISBN 0-8174-2435-0 : 27.50
1. Color photography—Printing processes. I. Title. BIP

THOMSON, C Leslie. 770.24
Colour films; the technique of working with colour materials, [by] C. Leslie Thomson. 3d ed. London, New York, Focal Press [1963. c1956] 280 p. illus. (part col.) 22 cm. (The manuals of phot-technique) [TR510.T47] 65-6399
1. Clor photography. I. Title. II. Series.

Color photography—Processing.

CURRENT, Ira B. 778.66
How to process color film at home. New York, Amphoto [c.1961] 118p. illus. 61-8774 2.50 bds.,
I. Title.

EASTMAN Kodak Company. 778.6'6
Basic developing, printing, enlarging in color. [Rochester, N.Y.] : Kodak, [c1977] 91 p. : col. ill. ; 22 cm. (Kodak photo book ; AE-13) Cover title. [TR530.E3 1977] 78-103815 ISBN 0-87985-205-4 : 3.75
1. Color photography—Processing. I. Title. BIP

WATKINS, Derek. 778.6'6
The Focalguide to colour film processing / Derek Watkins. London : Focal Press ; New York : Focal/Hastings House, c1978. 200 p. : ill. (some col.) ; 19 cm. Includes index. [TR530.W37] 78-319682 ISBN 0-8038-2362-2 (Focal/Hastings) : 6.95
1. Color photography—Processing. I. Title. II. Title: Colour film processing.

Color photography—Processing—Handbooks, manuals, etc.

CARROLL, John S., 1911- 778.6
Amphoto color film & color processing data book [by] John S. Carroll. 1st ed. New York, Amphoto, 1972. 168 p. 18 cm. [TR530.C38] 71-187822 ISBN 0-8174-0550-X 5.95
1. Color photography—Processing—Handbooks, manuals, etc. 2. Photography—Films—Handbooks, manuals, etc. I. Title. II. Title: Color film & color processing data book.

CARROLL, John S., 1911- 778.6
Amphoto color film & color processing data book / John S. Carroll. 2d rev. ed. Garden City, N.Y. : Amphoto, 1975. 160 p. ; 17 cm. [TR530.C38 1975] 75-329763 ISBN 0-8174-1550-5 pbk. : 3.95
1. Color photography—Processing—Handbooks, manuals, etc. 2. Photography—Films—Handbooks, manuals, etc. I. Title. II. Title: Color film & color processing data book.

Color photography —Three-color process.

BOND, Fred, 1893- 778.6
Kodachrome and Ektachrome color photography from all angles, applicable to the common problems of all color photography enthusiasts; 35mm., Bantam, 120 size, movie and cut sheet color films. All illus. by the author except where otherwise designated. [4th ed.] San Francisco, Camera Craft Pub. Co. [1955] 252p. illus. 28cm. First ed. published in 1942 under title: Kodachrome and Kodacolor from all angles. [TR520.B6 1955] 55-10365
1. Color photography —Three-color process. 2. Color. I. Title.

HANWORTH, David Bertram Pollock, 2d viscount, 1916- 778.66
Amateur carbro colour prints. London, New York, Focal Press [1950] 160 p. (p. 159-160 advertisements) illus. 19 cm. [TR520.H35] 50-54828
1. Color photography—Three-color process. I. Title. II. Title: Carbro color prints.

Color photography—Yearbooks.

COLOR photography 770.24
annual. 1956- [New York, Ziff-Davis Publishing Co.] v. illus. (part col.) 28cm. [TR510.C53] 56-40970
1. Color photography—Yearbooks.

POPULAR photography (Chicago) 778.6058
Color annual. [New York] [Ziff-Davis Pub. Co.] 1956- v. illus. (part col.) 29 cm. Title varies: 1956, Color photography annual. [TR510.P6] 56-40970
1. Color photography—Yearbooks. I. Title.

Color-printing.

HARDIE, Martin, 1875-1952. 741.64'0942
English coloured books. With an introd. by James Laver. Totowa, N.J., Rowman and Littlefield [1973] xxiv, 339 p. plates (part col.) 26 cm. Reprint of the 1906 ed. [Z258.H37 1973] 72-11974 ISBN 0-87471-165-7 25.00
1. Color-printing. 2. Illustration of books—Great Britain. 3. Illustrated books. I. Title. BIP

MILWAUKEE journal. 655.32
Production of r. o. p. color in the Milwaukee journal. [Milwaukee, 1950] vii (i.e. viii), 177 p. illus. (part col.) 29 cm. Bibliography: p. 177. [Z258.M6] 50-4513
1. Color-printing. I. Title.

PRINCETON University Press. 686.2'3
The Princeton University Press color kit; a designers' and printers' aid for selecting two-color, solid, and screened ink combinations on assorted stocks. Princeton, N.J., 1973. 1. portfolio (108 col. plates) 55 x 46 cm. Title from portfolio. [Z258.P75 1973] 74-157759 50.00
1. Color-printing. I. Title.

SMITH, Charles William, 1893- 761
Experiments in relief print making. [Charlottesville] University of Virginia Press, 1954. 1v. (unpaged) illus. (part col.) 26cm. 300 copies printed. [Z258.S6] 54-21769
1. Color-printing. I. Title.

Color-printing—Congresses.

SEMINAR on Color in Print, 2d, New York, 1965. 686.2'3
Transcript, Second Seminar on Color in Print. Copy preparation for color. [New York] American Institute of Graphic Arts [1966?] 52 p. ports. 28 cm. Cover title. Held Dec. 4, 1965. [Z258.S45 1965] 74-191950
1. Color-printing—Congresses. I. American Institute of Graphic Arts.

Color-printing—Exhibitions.

UNITED States. Library of Congress. 686.2'3
Color and the graphic arts : selections

from an exhibition at the Library of Congress, October 1974 through March 1975. [Washington : The Library, 1975] 190-206 p. : ill. ; 27 cm. "Reprinted from the Quarterly journal of the Library of Congress, volume 31, number 4, October 1974." [Z258.U57 1975] 74-31445 ISBN 0-8444-0152-8
1. United States. Library of Congress. 2. Color-printing—Exhibitions. 3. Color prints—Exhibitions. I. Title.

Color prints.

FERN, Alan Maxwell, 1930- 769'.945
The "Pembroke" album of chiaroscuro woodcuts, by Alan M. Fern and Karen F. Jones. [Washington, Library of Congress, 1970] [16] p. illus. 27 cm. Reprinted from Jan. 1969 issue of Quarterly journal of the Library of Congress (list of prints from Jan. 1970 issue) Includes bibliographical references. [NE1300.2.F47] 74-604690
1. Color prints. I. Beall, Karen F., 1938- joint author. II. Title. III. Title: Chiaroscuro woodcuts.

KAMPMANN, Lothar. 760
Creating with printing material. New York, Van Nostrand Reinhold [1969] 72 p. illus. (part col.) 22 cm. (Art media series) Translation of Farbiges Drucken. Describes basic techniques and materials for relief and intaglio printing. [NE1850.K313 1969b] 74-83387
1. Color prints. I. Title.

PLATTE, Hans. 769'.922
Color prints international. Introd. by Hans Platte. New York, Universe Books [1969, c1960] 129 p. col. illus. 35 cm. Translation of Farbige Graphik unserer Zeit. [NE1858.P6313 1969] 79-88588 22.50
1. Color prints. I. Title. BIP

STROSE, Susanne. 769
Coloring papers. [Translated by Paul Kuttner] New York, Sterling Pub. Co. [1968] 48 p. illus. (part col.) 20 cm. (Little craft book series) Translation of Bunte Papiere. [NE1850.S713] 68-8762
1. Color prints. I. Title.

TAYLOR, William Ferguson. 769'.9428'42
Engravings. [by] William F. Taylor. Harrogate : Palliser Press for the Publishing Group of the British Printing Society, 1976. [17] p. : of ill. ; 21 cm. Limited ed. of 110 numbered copies. No. 17. "A second book of blocks in use at the Palliser Press." [Z232.P15T38] 77-362613 ISBN 0-9504112-1-3 : £1.00
1. Palliser Press. 2. Color-prints. I. Title.

WAKEMAN, Geoffrey. 769'.941
The production of nineteenth century colour illustration / [by] Geoffrey Wakeman. [Loughborough] : Plough Press, 1976. [5] p., [1], [17] leaves, [3] leaves of plates (2 fold.) : ill. (chiefly col.), facsim. ; 39 cm. Limited ed. of 100 copies. No. 56. Some plates tipped in. [NE1857.W34] 76-383741 ISBN 0-902813-07-2 : £35.00
1. Color prints. 2. Illustrated books—19th century. I. Title.

Color prints, American.

THE Business week (New York) 769.973
Woodcuts of fifteen American cities from the Business Week collection. [New York, McGraw-Hill, 1963] v, 63 p. col. plates. 38 cm. Includes biographical sketches of the artists. [NE1874.B8] 63-11123
1. Color prints, American. 2. U.S. — Descr. & trav. — Views. 3. Art and industry. I. Title.

MCGRATH, Daniel Francis, 1935- 764'.2'0973
American colorplate books, 1800--1900. American colorplate books eighteen hundred--nineteen hundred [Ann Arbor, 1966] iv, 231 l. Thesis—University of Michigan. Photocopy of typescript. Ann Arbor., Mich., University Microfilms, 1970. 23 cm. "List of colorplate books": leaves 182-231. [NE507.M3 1966a] 73-20413
1. Color prints, American. I. Title.

Color prints—Catalogs.

BALL, Abraham, 1908- 769'.92'4
The price guide to Baxter prints / [text] by A. Ball and M. Martin. Woodbridge : Antique Collectors' Club, 1974. [8], 275 p. : chiefly ill. (some col.), port., 28 cm. Includes index. [NE1860.B2B35] 75-310254 ISBN 0-902028-23-5 : £8.75
1. Baxter, George, 1804-1867. 2. Color prints—Catalogs. I. Martin, Michael, 1935- joint author. II. Baxter, George, 1804-1867. III. Title. IV. Title: Baxter prints.

BARTRAN, Margaret. 769.30216
A guide to color reproductions. New York, Scarecrow Press, 1966. 382 p. 22 cm. [NE1850.B3] 65-22751
1. Color prints—Catalogs. I. Title. II. Title: Color reproductions.

BARTRAN, Margaret. 338.4'7'76902573
A guide to color reproductions. 2d ed. Metuchen, N.J., Scarecrow Press, 1971. 625 p. 22 cm. [NE1850.B3 1971] 74-142231 ISBN 0-8108-0343-7
1. Color prints—Catalogs. I. Title. II. Title: Color reproductions.

KAPLAN (ARTHUR A.) COMPANY, inc., New York. 769'.92'4
Catalog of decorative pictures in full color. New York [1964] 127 p. (chiefly illus.) 21 x 30 cm. [NE1860.K35A3] 66-1076
1. Color prints — Catalogs. I. Title.

KASS, Benjamin. 769.5
The complete guide to free prints. with a section on lowcost framing by Elaine Rapp. New York, Citadel Press [1958] 112p. illus. 21cm. [NE1860.A2K3] 58-10598
1. Color prints—Catalogs. 2. Picture frames and framing. I. Title.

NEW York Graphic Society. 759.0838
Fine art reproductions, old & modern masters. [Anniversary ed.] [New York, 1951] 399 p. illus. (part col.) 29 cm. [NE1860.N4A32] 51-3547
1. Color prints — Catalogs. I. Title. BIP

NEW York Graphic Society. 750.216
Fine art reproductions of old and modern masters; a comprehensive illustrated catalog of art through the ages. Greenwich, Conn. [1965] 540 p. (chiefly col. illus.) 33 cm. [NE1860.N4A3 1965] 65-9117
1. Color prints—Catalogs. I. Title.

NEW York Graphic Society. 759.0838
Fine art reproductions, old & modern masters, 1925-1950, including 1954 and 1956 supplements. [Greenwich. Conn., c1956] [Greenwich, Conn., 1958] 671p. illus. (part col.) 29cm. 673-696 p. illus. 29cm. Bound with main work. [NE1860.N4A32 1956] 57-2989
1. Color prints—Catalogs. I. Title. II. Title: —1958 supplement.

NEW York Graphic Society. 759.0838
Fine art reproductions, old & modern masters, 1925-1950, including 1954 and 1956 supplements. [Greenwich, Conn., c1956] 671p. illus. (part col.) 29cm. [NE1860.N4A32 1956] 57-2989
1. Color prints—Catalogs. I. Title.

NEW York Graphic Society. 759.0838
Fine art reproductions, old modern masters. [Anniversary ed. New York, 1951] [New York, 1954] 399p. illus. (part col.) 29cm. viii, 381-547p. illus. (part col.) 29cm. [NE1860.N4A32 1951] 51-3547
1. Color prints—Catalogs. I. Title. II. Title: —Supplement.

NEW York Graphic Society. 769.0838
Reproductions of American paintings, selected from Fine art reproductions of old and modern masters. Greenwich, Conn. [1962] xv, 132 p. col. illus. 33 cm. Bibliography: p. xi. [NE1860.N4A32 1962a] 63-24384
1. Color prints—Catalogs. I. Title.

NEW York Graphic Society. 769.0838
Reproductions of American paintings, selected from Fine art reproductions of old and modern masters. Greenwich, Conn. [1962] xv, 132 p. col. illus. 33 cm. Bibliography: p. xi. [NE1860.N4A32 1962a] 63-24384
1. Color prints — Catalogs. I. Title.

OESTREICHER'S, New York. 769'.92'4
Oestreicher's. the world's largest collection of fine color art reproductions, [catalog. New York, 195-] 95p. illus. 28cm. [NE1860.O38A49] 56-58043
1. Color prints—Catalogs. I. Title. II. Title: The world's largest collection of fine color art reproductions.

OESTREICHER'S, New York. 769'.92'4
Oestreicher's. the world's largest collection of fine color art reproductions, [catalog. New York, 195-] 95p. illus. 28cm. [NE1860.O38A49] 56-58043
1. Color prints—Catalogs. I. Title. II. Title: The world's largest collection of fine color art reproductions.

OESTREICHER'S Prints, inc., New York. 769'.92'4
Oestreicher's Prints, inc., the world's largest collection of fine color art reproductions, [catalog. New York, 1964] 171 p. illus. (part col.) 28 cm. Cover title. [NE1860.O38A49 1964] 68-45146
1. Color prints—Catalogs. I. Title: The world's largest collection of fine color art reproductions.

OESTREICHER'S Prints, inc., New York. 769'.92'4
Oestreicher's Prints, inc., the world's largest collection of fine color art reproductions, [catalog. New York, 1964] 171 p. illus. (part col.) 28 cm. Cover title. [NE1860.O38A49] 68-45146
1. Color prints—Catalogs. I. Title. II. Title: The world's largest collection of fine color art reproductions.

OESTREICHER'S Prints, inc., New York. 769'.92'4
Oestreicher's, the world's largest collection of fine color art reproductions, catalog. New York, 195- 95 p. illus. 28 cm. [NE1860.O38A49] 56-58043
1. Color prints—Catalogs. I. Title. II. Title: The world's largest collection of fine color art reproductions.

UNITED Nations Educational, Scientific and Cultural Organization. 759.0838
Catalogue de reproductions en couleur de peintures. Catalogue of colour reproductions of paintings Catalogo de reproducciones en color de pinturas. 1860/1949- [6th ed., rev. & enlarged] New York, Columbia Univ. Pr. [c.]1961 485p. illus. 58-975 6.00 pap.,
1. Color prints—Catalogs. I. Title. II. Series: United Nations Educational Scientific and Cultural Organizations. UNESCO publication no. 409

UNITED Nations Educational, Scientific and Cultural Organization. 759.0838
Catalogue de reproductions en couleur de peintures. Catalogue of colour reproductions of paintings. Catalogo de reproducciones en color de pinturas. 1860/1963. Paris, Unesco [dist. New York, Columbia, c 1963] 519p. illus. 23cm. Catalogue for 1963 issued as the Organization's Pubn. no. CUA.63/IX.I.07/AFS. Title varies slightly. 58-975 6.00 pap.,
1. Color prints—Catalogs. I. Title. II. Series: United Nations Educational, Scientific and Cultural Organizations. UNESCO publication no. CUA.63/IX.I.07/AFS

UNITED Nations Educational, Scientific, and Cultural Organization 759.0838
Catalogue de reproductions en couleurs de peintures anterieures a 1860. Catalogue of colour reproductions of paintings prior to 1860. Catalogo de reproducciones en color de pinturas anteriores a 1860 Paris, UNESCO [dist. New York, UNESCO Pubns. Ctr., 1965, c.1964] 379p. illus. 23cm. [NE1860.A2U5] 58-21049 6.00 pap.,
1. Color prints—Catalogs. I. Title. II. Series: United Nations Educational, Scientific and Cultural Organization. UNESCO Publication no. 629

UNITED Nations Educational, Scientific and Cultural Organization. 759.0838
Catalogue de reproductions en couleurs de peintures anterieures a 1860. Catalogue of colour reproductions of paintings prior to 1860. Catalogo de reproducciones en color de pinturas anteriores a 1860. [dist. New York, Columbia University Press, 1960] 281p. illus. 23cm. In French, English and Italian The 1st ed. issued in French and English only. (UNESCO publication CUA. 59/IX.II.04/AFS) 58-21049 4.50 pap.,
1. Color prints—Catalogs. I. Title. II. Series: United Nations Educational Scientific and Cultural Organization. UNESCO publication no. 629

UNITED Nations Educational, Scientific and Cultural Organization. 759.0838
The Unesco catalogue of colour reproductions of paintings prior to 1860, New York, Author [dist.] Columbia Intl. Documents Serv. [1963, c.1962] 328p. illus. 23cm. Title varies. 58-975 6.00 pap.,
1. Color prints—Catalogs. I. Title.

Color prints, Chinese.

TSCHICHOLD, Jan, 1902- 769'.951
Chinese color prints from the Ten Bamboo Studio. With 24 reproductions in full-color facsim. of prints from the masterpiece of Chinese color printing from the Ming period. New York, McGraw-Hill [1972] 55 p. illus., 24 col. plates. 32 x 35 cm. "Some parts of the text ... have been adapted from the writer's previous books : Der fruhe chinesische Farbendruck, Basle, 1940; Der Holzschneider und Bilddrucker, Hu Cheng-yen, Basle, 1943; and Chinesisches Gedichtpapier vom Meister der Zehnbambushalle, Basle, 1947." Bibliography: p. 51-53, 55. [NE1300.8.C6T72] 76-37748 ISBN 0-07-065390-9
1. Color prints, Chinese. I. Hu, Cheng-yen, ca. 1582-ca. 1672. Shih chu chai chien p'u. II. Title.

Color prints, German—Catalogs.

STRAUSS, Walter L. 796'.92'2
Chiaroscuro: the clair-obscur woodcuts by the German and Netherlandish masters of XVIth and XVIIth centuries; a complete catalogue with commentary, by Walter L. Strauss. Greenwich, Conn., New York Graphic Society [1973] xx, 393 p. illus. 29 cm. "Exhibitions": p. 387. Bibliography: p. 388-390. [NE1300.8.G3S77] 73-76179 ISBN 0-8212-0501-3 25.00
1. Color prints, German—Catalogs. 2. Color prints, Dutch—Catalogs. 3. Color prints, Flemish—Catalogs. 4. Chiaroscuro. I. Title.

Color prints, Japanese.

CHICAGO. Art Institute. 745.5
The Clarence Buckingham collection of Japanese prints. Catalogue by Helen C. Gunsaulus. [Chicago, 1955- v. illus., col. plates. 40cm. 'This edition is limited to 500 numbered catalogues ... [Vol. 1] Number 20.' Contents.[1] The primitives. Bibliography: v. 1, p. 278. [NE1310.C43] A55
1. Buckingham, Clarence. 2. Color printeseJapanses. I. Gunsaulus, Helen Cowen, ed. II. Title. III. Title: The primitives.

CHICAGO. Art Institute. 761.2830838
Masterpieces of Japanese prints. March 10-April 17, 1955. [Chicago, 1955] 1v. (unpaged) illus. 26cm. Catalogue of an exhibition of prints from the Clarence Buckingham collection. [NE1315.C52] 55-2586
1. Color prints, Hapanese—Exhibitions. 2. Engravings, Japanese—Exhibitions. I. Buckingham, Clarence. II. Title.

Color prints, Italian.

ITALIAN chiaroscuro woodcuts (Bartsch volume XII) Edited by 769'.945

Color—Psychology.

ITTEN, Johannes, 1888-1967. 752
The art of color; the subjective experience and objective rationale of color. Translated by Ernst van Haagen. New York, Reinhold Pub. Corp. [1961] 155 p. mounted illus. (part col.) 29 x 32 cm. [ND1280.I813] 61-11190
1. Color—Psychology. 2. Painting—Technique. 3. Aesthetics. I. Title. BIP

MANY, Fillette. 752
Personality and color: in dress, in the home, and in the garden. New York, Vantage Press [c1953] 66p. illus. 23cm. [BF789.C7M3] 53-11635
1. Color—Psychology. 2. Clothing and dress. 3. Interior decoration. I. Title.

Color—Psychology—Bibliography.

BARTHOLOMEW, Robert. 016.3092 s
The use of color in physical environment planning / Robert Bartholomew. Monticello, Ill. : Council of Planning Librarians, 1976. 9 p. ; 29 cm. (Exchange bibliography ; 1050) Cover title. [Z5942.C68 no. 1050] [Z7204.C58] [BF789.C7] 016.729 76-373895 pbk. : 1.50
1. Color—Psychology—Bibliography. 2. Color in architecture—Bibliography. 3. Environmental psychology—Bibliography. I. Title. II. Series: Council of Planning Librarians. Exchange bibliography ; 1050.

PARKS, Berkeley. 016.1521'45
Psychological response to surface color / Berkeley Parks. Monticello, Ill. : Council of Planning Librarians, 1976 17 p. ; 29 cm. (Council of Planning Librarians exchange bibliography ; 902) Cover title. [Z5942.C68 no. 902] [Z7204.C58] [BF789.C7] 77-356765 pbk. : 1.50
1. Color—Psychology—Bibliography. I. Title. II. Series: Council of Planning Librarians. Exchange bibliography ; 902.

Color sensitometry (Photography)

SOCIETY of Motion Picture and Television Engineers. Color Committee. Color Sensitometry Subcommittee. 778.6
Principles of color sensitometry; a report. [Rev. ed.] New York, Society of Motion Picture and Television Engineers [1963] 102 p. illus. 23 cm. Includes bibliographies. [TR515.S6 1963] 63-19745
1. Color sensitometry (Photography) I. Title.

Color—Study and teaching.

ALBERS, Josef. 701.8
Interaction of color. New Haven, Yale University Press, 1971. xiv, 74 p. illus. (part col.) 22 cm. "Text of the original edition with selected plates." [ND1489.A4 1971] 74-147901 ISBN 0-300-01474-0
1. Color—Study and teaching. I. Title. BIP

ALBERS, Josef. 701'.8
Interaction of color : text of the original edition with revised plate section / Josef Albers. Rev. pocket ed. New Haven : Yale University Press, 1975. ix, 81 p., [4] leaves of plates : ill. (some col.) ; 21 cm. [ND1489.A4 1975] 74-15585 ISBN 0-300-01845-2 : 10.00. ISBN 0-300-01846-0 pbk. : 4.95
1. Color—Study and teaching. I. Title.

CARLSON, Charles, 1902- 752.4
Simplified color mixing. [New York, Melior Books, 1956?] 48p. illus. 31cm. (His Art instruction series) [ND1280.C3] 56-47556
1. Color—Study and teaching. 2. Painting—Technique. I. Title. II. Title: Color mixing.

SALEMME, Lucia A. 752
Color exercises for the painter, by Lucia A. Salemme. Foreword by Alexander Calder. New York, Watson-Guptill Publications [1970] 160 p. col. illus. 29 cm. [ND1280.S25] 77-98989 12.50
1. Color—Study and teaching. I. Title. BIP

SMITH, Charles N. 752
Student handbook of color, by Charles N. Smith. New York, Reinhold [1965] 95 p. illus. (part col.) 21 cm. Bibliography: p. 95. [ND1283.S6] 65-24059
1. Color—Study and teaching. I. Title.

Colorado — Antiq. — Addresses, essays, lectures.

OSBORNE, Douglas, comp. 917.882
Contributions of the Wetherill Mesa archeological project, assembled by Douglas Osborne; Bernard S. Katz, Project editor. Salt Lake City [Society for American Archaeology] 1965. xvii, 230 p. illus., maps. 26 cm. (Memoirs of the Society for American Archaeology, no. 19) "Issued as American antiquity, volume 31, number 2, part 2, October 1965." Includes bibliographies. [E51.S7] 66-6390
1. Colorado — Antiq. — Addresses, essays, lectures. 2. Pueblo Indians — Antiq. — Addresses, essays, lectures. 3. Excavations (Archaeology) — Colorado — Addresses, essays, lectures. 4. Mesa Verde National Park. I. American antiquity. II. Title. III. Title: Wetherill Mesa archeological pro- ject. IV. Series: Society for American Archaeology. Mem- oirs, no. 19

Colorado — Antiq. — Collected works.

COLORADO. University. Dept. of Anthropology. 917.8963044
Contributions to Mesa Verde archaeology. Boulder, University of Colorado Press, 1964- v. illus., maps. 26 cm. (University of Colorado studies. Series in anthropology, no. 9 Contents.Site 499, by R. H. Lister. Bibliography: v. 1, p. 91. [E78.C6C63] 65-64910
1. Colorado — Antiq. — Collected works. 2. Pueblo Indians — Antiq. — Collected works. 3. Mesa Verde National Park. I. Title. II. Title: (Series: Colorado. University. University of Colorado studies. Series in anthropology, no. 9. III. Series.

Colorado—Antiq.—Collections.

LISTER, Robert Hill, 1915- 917.88'03
Contributions to Mesa Verde archaeology. Boulder, University of Colorado Press, 1964- v. illus., maps. 26 cm. (University of Colorado studies. Series in anthropology, no. 9, 11-13) Results of an archaeological program accomplished by the Dept. of Anthropology, University of Colorado during the summers of 1953-1956. Includes bibliographies. [E78.C6L5] 65-64910
1. Colorado—Antiq.—Collections. 2. Pueblo Indians—Antiq.—Collections. 3. Excavations (Archaeology)—Colorado—Collections. 4. Mesa Verde National Park. I. Colorado. University. Dept. of Anthropology. II. Title. III. Series: Colorado. University. University of Colorado studies. Series in anthropology, no. 9, etc.

Colorado City, Tex.—Description—Views.

COLORADO City, 779'.9'9764729
Texas / photographers, Jim Eppler ... [et al.]. [Odessa, Tex.] : Backroads Graphics, 1976. 80 p. : chiefly ill. ; 21 x 26 cm. [F394.C695C64] 76-21154
1. Colorado City, Tex.—Description—Views. 2. Colorado City, Tex.—Social life and customs—Pictorial works. I. Eppler, Jim.

Colorado—Description and travel—1951- —Views.

CROUTER, George. 779'.9'91788043
The majestic fourteeners ... Colorado's highest / photographed by George Crouter ; edited by Carl Skiff. Silverton, Colo. : Sundance Books, 1977. 144 p. : col. ill. ; 29 cm. Title on spine: Colorado's highest. [F777.C76] 77-155102 ISBN 0-913582-22-0 : 14.95
1. Colorado—Description and travel—1951- —Views. 2. Rocky Mountains. I. Skiff, Carl. II. Title. III. Title: Colorado's highest.

MUENCH, David. 779'.9'91788
Colorado / photography, David Muench ; text, David Sumner. [Portland, Or.] : C. H. Belding, c1978. 192 p. : chiefly col. ill. ; 36 cm. [F777.M82] 78-51219 ISBN 0-912856-42-4 : 27.50
1. Colorado—Description and travel—1951- —Views. I. Sumner, David. II. Title. BIP

Colorado River in art.

†ABBEY, Rita Deanin. 759.13
Rivertrip / Rita Deanin Abbey ; foreword by Frank Waters. 1st ed. Flagstaff, Ariz. : Northland Press, 1976,c1977 69 p. : ill. (some col.) ; 24 x 31 cm. [ND1839.A18A55] 77-371305 ISBN 0-87358-152-0 : 14.95
1. Abbey, Rita Deanin. 2. Colorado River in art. 3. Colorado River—Poetry. 4. Poetry of places—Colorado River. I. Title. BIP

Colors.

ENABNIT, Merlin. 752
Nature's basic color concept / Merlin Enabnit. Des Moines : [Midwest Advertising Service?], 1975. 129 p. : ill. (some col.) ; 31 cm. [ND1492.E52] 75-326996
1. Colors. 2. Color in art. I. Title. II. Title: Basic color concept.

HAGEN, Catherine. 751.4'5
Color : a guide for every painter / Catherine Hagen. New York : H. Z. Walck, c1976. p. cm. Lessons and exercises in color principles designed to build memory patterns in students which will enable them to produce predictable color. [ND1510.H33] 75-43035 ISBN 0-8098-5002-8
1. Colors. I. Title. BIP

KORNERUP, Andreas. 752
Reinhold color atlas, by A. Kornerup and J. H. Wanscher. New York, Reinhold [1962, c1961] 224 p. illus col. plates. 18cm. [ND1285.K6 1962] 62-8756
1. Colors. 2. Color—Terminology. I. Wanscher, J. H., joint author. II. Title.

PROVENSEN, Alice. JUV
What is a color? By Alice and Martin Provensen. New York, Golden Press [1967] [32] p. col. illus. 33 cm. (A Big golden book) Tells and illustrates what things are yellow, purple, blue, red, green, brown, orange, white, or black. [PZ7.P9457Wh] 701.8 AC 67
1. Colors. I. Provensen, Martin, joint author. II. Title.

Colors—Juvenile literature.

LYTTLE, Richard B. 667
Paints, inks, and dyes, by Richard B. Lyttle. New York, Holiday House [1974] 178 p. illus. 24 cm. Bibliography: p. [168]-172. A history of paints, inks, and dyes—their origins in prehistoric times, and their uses then and now. [ND1510.L97] 73-16876 ISBN 0-8234-0240-1 6.50
1. Colors—Juvenile literature. I. Title. BIP

Colt firearms.

SUTHERLAND, Robert Q., 1918- 683'.4
The book of Colt firearms [by] R. Q. Sutherland [and] R. L. Wilson. Kansas City, Mo. [1971] xv, 604 p. illus. 32 cm. Bibliography: p. 588-589. [TS534.5.S92] 72-175675
1. Colt, Samuel, 1814-1862. 2. Colt firearms. I. Wilson, Robert Lawrence, 1939- joint author. II. Title.

Colt Industries, inc.

WILSON, Robert Lawrence, 1939- 683'.4'00275
The rampant colt; the story of a trademark [by] R. L. Wilson. Spencer, Ind., T. Haas [1969] v, 107 p. illus., ports. 27 cm. Bibliography: p. 107. [TS533.2.W56] 79-15509
1. Colt Industries, inc. 2. Trade-marks. I. Title.

Colt revolver.

BADY, Donald B. 683'.43
Colt automatic pistols / by Donald B. Bady. Rev. & enl. ed. Alhambra, Calif. : Borden Pub. Co., 1973. 354 p., [1] leaf of plates : ill. ; 24 cm. Includes index. Bibliography: p. 344-345. [TS537.B3 1973] 72-85928 12.50
1. Colt revolver. I. Title.

BROWN, David M 623.443
The 36 calibers of the Colt single action army, by David M. Brown. Edited by E. B. Mann. Albuquerque N.M. [c1965] 223 p. illus. 29 cm. [TS537.B78] 66-5774
1. Colt revolver. I. Title.

BROWN, David M. 683'.43
The 36 calibers of the Colt single action army, by David M. Brown. Edited by E. B. Mann. [Rev. ed.] Albuquerque, N.M. [1971] viii, ix, 206 p. illus. 29 cm. [TS537.B78 1971] 72-31384
1. Colt revolver. I. Title.

COCHRAN, Keith A. 683'.43
Peacemaker : evolution and variations / by Keith A. Cochran. Rapid City, S.D. : Colt Collector Press, c1975. 48 p. (p. 47-48 blank for "Notes") : ill. ; 22 cm. [TS537.C58] 75-325763
1. Colt revolver. I. Title.

GRAHAM, Ron. 683'.43
A study of the Colt single action Army revolver / by Ron Graham, John A. Kopec, C. Kenneth Moore. 1st ed. [s.l. : s.n.], 1976 (Dallas : Taylor Pub. Co.) xxviii, 522 p. : ill. ; 29 cm. Includes index. Bibliography: p. 326-327. [TS537.G7] 75-42934
1. Colt revolver. I. Kopec, John A., joint author. II. Moore, C. Kenneth, joint author. III. Title.

LARSON, E. Dixon. 683'.43
Colt tips, by E. Dixon Larson. [Union City, Tenn., Pioneer Press, 1972] 140 p. illus. 29 cm. [TS537.L37] 79-185227
1. Colt revolver. I. Title. BIP

RYWELL, Martin, 1905- ed. 623.4434
Colt guns. Harriman, Tenn., Pioneer Press [1957] 134p. illus. 23cm. [TS537.R97 1957] 57-13835
1. Colt revolver. I. Title.

SHUMAKER, P L 623.4434
Colt's variations of the old model pocket pistol, 1848-1872. Illustrated by C. H. Penco, Jr. [Beverly Hills, Calif.] Fadco Pub. Co. [1957] 150 p.illus. 24 cm. [NK6912.S45] 57-14424
1. Colt revolver. 2. Firearms — Collectors and collecting. I. Title. BIP

SMITH, Loren W 1912- 623.4434
Home gunsmithing the Colt single action frontier revolver; operation, repair [and] rework of the Colt peacemaker. Kenmore, N. Y., Gunroom Pub. Co., 1955. 117p. illus. 24cm. [TS537.S53] 55-4354
1. Colt revolver. I. Title.

SWAYZE, Nathan L. 623.4'43
'51 Colt Navies, by Nathan Swayze. [Yazoo City, Miss., Gun Hill Pub. Co., 1967] 243 p. illus., facsims., maps, ports. 29 cm. Bibliography: p. 236-237. [TS537.S85] 67-19544
1. Colt revolver. I. Title.

VIRGINES, George E. 623.4'43
Saga of the Colt six-shooter and the famous men who used it, by George E. Virgines. Illustrated by Ernest L. Reedstrom. New York, F. Fell [1969] 220 p. illus., ports. 24 cm. Bibliography: p. 215-220. [TS537.V56 1969] 69-10772 7.95
1. Colt revolver. I. Title.

WADSWORTH Atheneum, Hartford. 739.7
Samuel Colt presents: a loan exhibition of presentation percussion Colt firearms. Wadsworth Atheneum, Hartford, 3 November 1961 to 14 January 1962. Pref. by C. C.Cunningham; foreword by John S. duMont; catalogue by R. L. Wilson. [Hartford, 1961] xx, 293 p. illus. 28 cm. Bibliography: p. 292. [NK6912.W3] 62-1081
1. Colt revolver. 2. Firearms — Exhibitions. I. Title.

SUBJECT INDEX

COMIC BOOKS, STRIPS

WATSON, Albert. 683'.43
Those other Colts : or, Colt conversions : a study of factory alterations to holster revolvers from percussion cap to the self-contained metallic cartridge / by Albert Watson III. Rapid City, SD : Colt Collector Press, c1975. 32 p. : ill. ; 22 cm. Includes bibliographical references. [TS537.W37] 75-330248
1. Colt revolver. I. Title. II. Title: Colt conversions.

WILSON, Robert Lawrence, 1939- 739.7'4'43
The book of Colt engraving / by R. L. Wilson. Los Angeles : W. Beinfeld Publications, [1974] viii, 422 p., [1] leaf of plates : ill. (some col.) ; 32 cm. Includes indexes. Bibliography: p. 405-408. [TS537.W518] 74-21631 29.95
1. Colt revolver. 2. Engraving (Metal-work) I. Title.

WILSON, Robert Lawrence, 1939- 683'.43
Colt pistols, 1836-1976 / by R. L. Wilson, in association with R. E. Hable. Dallas : J. Arms, c1976. xv, 380 p. : ill. (some col.) ; 24 x 32 cm. [TS537.W523] 76-29140
1. Colt revolver. 2. Colt firearms. I. Hable, R. E., joint author. II. Title.

WINDERS, Gertrude (Hecker) 926.7
Sam Colt and his gun; the life of the inventory of the revolver. With sketches by the author. New York, J. Day Co. [1959] 159 p. illus. 21 cm. [TS535.C6W5] 59-6723
1. Colt revolver. I. Colt, Samuel, 1814-1862. II. Title.

Colt revolver—Dictionaries.

COCHRAN, Keith A. 683'.43
Colt peacemaker dictionary & encyclopedia / Keith Cochran. Rapid City, S.D. : Colt Collector Press, c1976. 256 p. : ill. ; 27 cm. [TS537.C57] 77-150364
1. Colt revolver—Dictionaries. I. Title.

Colt revolvers.

BADY, Donald B 623.4433
Colt automatic pistols. 1896-1955. [Beverly Hills. Calif., FADCO Pub. Co., c1956] 281p. illus. 24cm. [TS537.B3] 57-23530
1. Colt revolvers. I. Title. BIP

Colt, Samuel, 1814-1862.

ALBAUGH, William A 1908 623.4434
The original Confederate Colt; the story of the Leach & Rigdon and Rigdon-Ansley revolvers, by William A. Albaugh, III, and Richard D. Steuart. New York, Greenberg [1953] 62p. illus., map. 27cm. [TS537.A4] 53-5532
1. Colt, Samuel, 1814-1862. 2. Revolvers. 3. Confederate States of America. Army—Firearms. I. Steuart. Richard Dennis, 1882- joint author. II. Title.

BARNARD, Henry, 1811-1900, ed. 683'.43'0924 B
Armsmear : the home, the arm, and the armory of Samuel Colt : a memorial. [s.l. : s.n.], c1976. xviii, 399 p., [13] leaves of plates : ill. ; 27 cm. Reprint of the 1866 ed. privately printed by Alvord, New York. [TS533.3.C8C642 1976] 76-20422
1. Colt, Samuel, 1814-1862. 2. Manufacturers—Connecticut—Biography. I. Title.

MITCHELL, James L ed. 623.443
Colt; a collection of letters and photographs about the man, the arms, the company. Harrisburg, Pa., Stackpole Co. [1959] 265, [4]p. illus., ports. 29cm. Bibliography: p. [267-269] [TS535.C6M5] 59-14382
1. Colt, Samuel, 1814-1862. 2. Colt's Patent Fire Arms Manufacturing Company. I. Title.

SUTHERLAND, Robert Q., 1918- 683'.4
The book of Colt firearms [by] R. Q. Sutherland [and] R. L. Wilson. Kansas City, Mo. [1971] xv, 604 p. illus. 32 cm. Bibliography: p. 588-589. [TS534.5.S92] 72-175675
1. Colt, Samuel, 1814-1862. 2. Colt firearms. I. Wilson, Robert Lawrence, 1939- joint author. II. Title.

Colt's Patent Fire Arms Manufacturing Company.

MITCHELL, James L ed. 623.443
Colt; a collection of letters and photographs about the man, the arms, the company. Harrisburg, Pa., Stackpole Co. [1959] 265, [4]p. illus., ports. 29cm. Bibliography: p. [267-269] [TS535.C6M5] 59-14382
1. Colt, Samuel, 1814-1862. 2. Colt's Patent Fire Arms Manufacturing Company. I. Title.

Columba delegorguei.

BENSON, Constantine Walter. v. 12
The bronze-naped pigeon Columba delegorguei(Delegorgue) in Rhodesia, by C. W. Benson and M. P. Stuart Irwin. [Bulawayo?] National Museums of Southern Rhodesia, 1966. 3.[1] p. table. 23 cm. (Arnoldia [Rhodesia] v. 2, no. 23) Bibliography: p. [4] [NUC68-108626]
1. Columba delegorguei. 2. Pigeons-Rhodesia, Southern. I. Irwin, Michael P. Stuart, joint author. II. Title.

Columbia Art Association.

THE Columbia Art Association, 1915-1975, the Columbia Museum of Art, 1950-1975, Columbia, South Carolina : a history. [Columbia, S.C.] : Columbia Museums of Art & Science, 1975. iii, 59 p. : ill. ; 27 cm. [N11.C583C65] 75-7809 700'.6'275771
1. Columbia Art Association. 2. Columbia, S.C. Museum of Art.

Columbia River Valley—Antiq.

SMITH, Marian Wesley, 1907- *913.7973
Archaeology of the Columbia-Fraser region [by] Marian W. Smith. Cattle Point, a stratified site in the southern northwest coast region [by] Arden R. King. [Menasha, Wis.] Society for American Archaeology [1950] viii, 46, xii, 94 p. illus. 26 cm. (Memoirs of the Society for American Archaeology, no. 6-7) Cover title. "Supplement to American antiquity, volume xv, number 4, part 2, April 1950." Includes bibliographies. [E51.S7 no. 6-7] 52-2412
1. Columbia River Valley—Antiq. 2. San Juan Islands—Antiq. I. King, Arden. II. American antiquity. Supplement. III. Title. IV. Series: Society for American Archaeology. Memoirs, no. 6-7

Columbia University.

PETERS, John Edward. 686.2'21
The type punches at Columbia University; an inventory by John Peters & Peter M. VanWingen. [New York] School of Library Service, Columbia University, 1974. 40 p. illus. 23 cm. Bibliography: p. 13-16. [Z250.A2P47] 74-180508 1.50.
1. Columbia University. 2. Type and type-founding—History. I. VanWingen, Peter M., joint author. II. Title.

Columbia University. Libraries. Avery Architectural Library.

COLUMBIA University. Libraries. Avery Architectural Library. 016.72
Catalog of the Avery Memorial Architectural Library of Columbia University. 2d ed., enl. Boston : G. K. Hall, 1968. 19 v. ; 37 cm. Published in 1895 under title: Catalogue of the Avery Architectural Library. [Z5945.C653 1968] [NA2520] 76-358000
1. Columbia University. Libraries. Avery Architectural Library. 2. Architecture—Bibliography—Catalogs. 3. Art—Bibliography—Catalogs.

Columbia University. School of Architecture.

ROHDENBURG, Theodor Karl. 720.711747
A history of the School of Architecture, ColumbiaUniversity. New York, Columbia University Press, 1954. x, 114p. illus., facsims. 26cm. (The Bicentennial history of Columbia University) Bibliography: p. [105]-108. [NA2300.C65R6] 54-5196
1. Columbia University. School of Architecture. I. Title. II. Series.

Columbus, Ohio—Dwellings.

ELMER, Frank L. 711'.58
German Village; a case study in privately financed restoration [by Frank L. Elmer. Columbus? Ohio, 1970] iv l., 72 p. (incl. cover) illus., maps. 28 cm. [F499.C7E4] 72-24992
1. Columbus, Ohio—Dwellings. 2. Architecture—Conservation and restoration. I. Title.

Columns.

WEIBEZAHN, Ingrid. 720.9'4
Geschichte und Funktion des Monopteros' : Untersuchungen zu einem Gebaudetyp des Spatbarock und des Klassizismus / Ingrid Weibezahn. Hildesheim ; New York : Olms, 1975. 2 v. in 1 (146, 152 p.), [35] leaves of plates : ill. ; 21 cm. (Studien zur Kunstgeschichte ; Bd. 3) Originally presented as the author's thesis, Gottingen. Erratum slip inserted. Includes bibliographies and index. [NA590.W4 1975] 76-451221 ISBN 3-487-05764-6
1. Columns. 2. Architecture, Baroque. 3. Neoclassicism (Architecture) I. Title. II. Series.

Comacine Masters (Builders)

BAXTER, Lucy E. Barnes, 1837-1902. 726'.6'0945
The cathedral builders : the story of a great Masonic guild / by Leader Scott [i.e. L. E. B. Baxter]. Boston : Longwood Press, 1978. p. cm. Reprint of the 1899 ed. published by Scribner, New York. Includes index. Bibliography: p. [NA5613.B3 1978] 78-58191 ISBN 0-89341-354-2 : 50.00
1. Comacine Masters (Builders) 2. Freemasons. Italy. 3. Cathedrals—Italy. 4. Architecture, Medieval—Italy. I. Title.

Combs, Ann, 1935—

COMBS, Ann, 1935- 979.7'76 B
Helter shelter / Ann Combs. 1st ed. Philadelphia : Lippincott, 1979. p. cm. [CT275.C73A36] 78-26921 ISBN 0-397-01334-5 : 8.95
1. Combs, Ann, 1935- 2. Bainbridge Island, Wash.—Biography. I. Title. BIP

Comic art paraphernalia—Collectors and collecting.

LESSER, Robert. 790.13'2
A celebration of comic art and memorabilia / Robert Lesser ; photos. by Stefan Congrat-Butlar. New York : Hawthorn Books, [1975] 292 p., [8] leaves of plates : ill. (some col.) ; 29 cm. Includes index. [NK808.L47 1975] 74-22928 ISBN 0-8015-1456-8 : 24.50
1. Lesser, Robert—Art collections. 2. Comic art paraphernalia—Collectors and collecting. 3. Comic art paraphernalia—United States. I. Title.

Comic book covers—United States.

O'BRIEN, Richard, 1934- 741.5'973
The golden age of comic books, 1937-1945 / by Richard O'Brien. 1st ed. New York : Ballantine Books, 1977. 21, [2] p., 40 leaves of plates : ill. (some col.) ; 30 cm. Bibliography: p. [22] [PN6726.O2] 76-56755 ISBN 0-345-25535-6 pbk. : 6.95
1. Comic book covers—United States. I. Title. BIP

Comic books and children.

WERTHAM, Frederic, 1895- 741.5
Seduction of the innocent. New York, Rinehart [1954] 400p. illus. 22cm. [HQ784.C6W4] 54-5890
1. Comic books and children. 2. Comic books, stripps. etc.—Hist. & crit. I. Title.

Comic books, strips, etc.

BUSCH, Wilhelm, 1832-1908. 709.43
Max and Moritz; with many more mischief-makers more or less human or approximately animal. Edited and annotated by H. Arthur Klein. Translated by H. Arthur Klein and others. New York, Dover Publications [1962] 216p. illus. 22cm. English and German. [PT2603.U8M33 1962] 62-52768
I. Title. BIP

BUSCH, Wilhelm, 1832-1908. 709.43
Max and Moritz; with many more mischief-makers more or less human or approximately animal. Edited and annotated by H. Arthur Klein. Translated by H. Arthur Klein and others. New York, Dover Publications [1962] 216p. illus. 22cm. English and German. [PT2603.U8M33 1962] 62-52768
I. Title. BIP

*CHILDRESS, James. 741.5'973
Conchy : living in tomorrow's past. New York : Grosset & Dunlap, 1976. unpaged : ill. ; 18 cm. (Tempo books) [NC1428] ISBN 0-448-12353-3 pbk. : 0.95
1. Comic books, strips, etc. 2. American wit and humor, Pictorial. I. Title.

DE BECK, Billy, 1890-1942. 741.5'973
Barney Google : a complete compilation, 1919-1920 / Billy De Beck ; introd. by Bill Blackbeard. Westport, Conn. : Hyperion Press, [1977] p. cm. (The Hyperion library of classic American comic strips) [PN6728.B33D4 1977] 76-53038 ISBN 0-88355-631-6 : 15.95. ISBN 0-88355-630-8 pbk. : 6.95
I. Title. II. Series. BIP

HERRIMAN, George, 1880-1944. 741.5'973
Baron Bean : a complete compilation, 1916-1917 / George Herriman ; introd. by M. Thomas Inge. Westport, Conn. : Hyperion Press, c1977. ix, 101 p. : ill. ; 22 x 28 cm. (The Hyperion library of classic American comic strips) [PN6728.B35H4 1977] 76-53043 ISBN 0-88355-641-3 : 14.50. ISBN 0-88355-640-5 pbk. : 5.95
I. Title. II. Series. BIP

HERRIMAN, George, 1880-1944. 741.5'973
The family upstairs : introducing Krazy Kat : the complete strip, 1910-1912 / George Herriman ; introd. by Bill Blackbeard. Westport, Conn. : Hyperion Press, c1977. 212 p. : ill. ; 22 x 29 cm. (The Hyperion library of classic American comic strips) [PN6728.F3H4 1977] 76-53044 ISBN 0-88355-643-X : 17.95. ISBN 0-88355-642-1 pbk. : 8.95
I. Title. II. Series. BIP

75 years of the comics. 741'.59
Introd. by Maurice Horn Boston, Boston Book & Art [1971] 109 p. (p. 18-102 illus.) 34 cm. Published in conjunction with the exhibition held at the New York Cultural Center. Bibliography: p. 107-109. [NC1355.S4] 75-162320 ISBN 0-8435-1010-2 9.95
1. Comic books, strips, etc. I. Horn, Maurice. II. New York Cultural Center.

Comic books, strips, etc.—American.

ADAMSON, Joe. 791.43'0233'0924
Tex Avery, king of cartoons / by Joe Adamson. New York : Popular Library, c1975. 237 p. : ill. ; 28 cm. (The Big apple film series) (Big apple books) Filmography: p. [201]-[233] [NC1766.U52A922] 76-357684 pbk. : 3.95
I. Title.

CANIFF, Milton Arthur, 1907- 741.5'973
Terry and the pirates : the Normandie affair / Milton Caniff. New York : Nostalgia Press, c1977. [96] p. ; 22 x 28

cm. (The Golden age of the comics) Chiefly comics, first published in 1935 in syndication. Terry, Pat, and Connie find adventure, intrigue, and love in Singapore. [PN6728.T4C35] 77-75668 ISBN 0-87897-014-2 pbk. : 6.95
I. Title. BIP

CANIFF, Milton Arthur, 1907- 741.5'973
Terry and the pirates, China journey / Milton Caniff. New York : Nostalgia Press, c1977. [108] p. : chiefly ill. ; 21 x 28 cm. (The Golden age of the comics) [PN6728.T4C34] 77-75667 ISBN 0-87897-013-4 : 6.95
I. Title. II. Title: China journey.
Publisher's address: P.O. Box 293 Franklin Square N.Y. 11010

CRUMB, R. 741.5973
Head comix. Introd. by Paul Krassner. New York, Viking Press [1968] [64] p. (chiefly illus.) 28 cm. "A William Cole book." [NC1429.C83A45 1968] 68-28025 ISBN 0-670-01899-6 2.50
I. Title.

DILLE, Robert C., comp. 741.5'973
The collected works of Buck Rogers in the 25th century / Robert C. Dille, editor ; introd. by Ray Bradbury. New rev. ed. New York : A & W Publishers, c1977. xiv, 288 p. : ill. (some col.) ; 31 cm. (A & W visual library) Extracts from Buck Rogers in the 25th century, a serialized comic strip issued between 1929 and 1967. The extracts chosen were the work of Phil Nowlan, Dick Calkins, and Rick Yager. [PN6728.B8D5 1977] 76-39700 ISBN 0-89104-062-5 : 8.95
I. Nowlan, Phil. II. Calkins, Dick. III. Yager, Rick. IV. Buck Rogers in the 25th century. V. Title. VI. Series. BIP

GODWIN, Frank, 1889- 741.5'973
Connie, a complete compilation, 1929-1930 / Frank Godwin ; introd. by Maurice Horn. Westport, Conn. : Hyperion Press, c1977. xiii, 161 p. : ill. ; 18 x 27 cm. (The Hyperion library of classic American comic strips) [PN6728.C66G6] 76-53041 ISBN 0-88355-637-5 : 15.95. ISBN 0-88355-636-7 pbk. : 6.95
I. Title. II. Series.

GOODRICK, Susan, comp. 741.5'973
The Apex treasury of underground comics / edited by Susan Goodrick and Don Donahue ; featuring Willie Murphy ... [et al.]. New York : Links Books : distributed by Quick Fox, [1974] 192 p. : chiefly ill. ; 27 cm. [PN6726.G6] 73-21074 ISBN 0-8256-3042-8 : 4.95
1. Comic books, strips, etc.—American. I. Donahue, Don, joint comp. II. Murphy, Willy, 1936- III. Title. BIP

HOGARTH, Burne. 741.5'973
The golden age of Tarzan, 1939-42 / by Edgar Rice Burroughs ; [illustrated by Burne Hogarth ; edited by Maurice Horn]. Limited facsim. ed. New York : Chelsea House Publishers, 1977. p. cm. Photoreprints of the Sunday Tarzan color pages as drawn by B. Hogarth. [PN6728.T3H58 1977] 77-24461 ISBN 0-87754-055-1 : 150.00
I. Burroughs, Edgar Rice, 1875-1950. II. Title. BIP

HOGARTH, Burne. 741.5'973
Jungle tales of Tarzan / by Burne Hogarth ; original text by Edgar Rice Burroughs ; introd. by Walter James Miller. New York : Watson-Guptill Publications, 1975. p. cm. Includes bibliographical references. [PN6728.T3H59 1975] 75-23021 ISBN 0-8230-2576-4 pbk. : 8.95
I. Burroughs, Edgar Rice, 1875-1950. Jungle tales of Tarzan. II. Hodes, Robert M. III. Title.

LUPOFF, Richard A., 1935- 741.5'973
All in color for a dime [edited] by Dick Lupoff and Don Thompson. New Rochelle, N.Y., Arlington House [1970] 263 p. illus. (part col.) 24 cm. [PN6725.L8] 71-93454 ISBN 0-87000-062-4 11.95
1. Comic books, strips, etc.—American. I. Thompson, Don, joint author. II. Title. BIP

MCBRIDE, Clifford, 1901- 741.5'973
Napoleon : a complete compilation, 1932-1933 / Clifford McBride ; introd. by Jack Herbert. Westport, Conn. : Hyperion Press, c1977. x, 101 p. : ill. ; 22 x 28 cm. (The Hyperion library of classic American comic strips) [PN6728.N3M3] 76-53047 ISBN 0-88355-649-9 : 14.50. ISBN 0-88355-648-0 pbk. : 5.95.
I. Title. II. Series.

MCCAY, Winsor. 741.5'973
Dreams of the rarebit fiend. New York, Dover Publications [1973] xiii, 62 p. illus. 29 cm. Reprint of the 1905 ed. published by F. A. Stokes, New York. "Reproductions of a comic series [which appeared] ... in the New York Evening telegram [1905]" [PN6728.D7M3 1973] 73-75868 ISBN 0-486-21347-1 2.00
I. Title. BIP

MCCAY, Winsor. 741.5'973
Little Nemo in the palace of ice, and further adventures / Winsor McCay. New York : Dover Publications, [1976] 32 p. : col. ill. ; 37 cm. Caption title. Originally published in the New York herald Jan. 20-Sept. 22, 1907, as installments in the author's comic strip Little Nemo in Slumberland. [PN6728.L54M3 1976] 75-19834 ISBN 0-486-23234-4 pbk. : 3.50
I. McCay, Winsor. Little Nemo in Slumberland. II. Title. BIP

MCCAY, Winsor. 741.5'973
Winsor McCay's dream days : an original compilation, 1903-1914 / Winsor McCay ; introd. by Woody Gelman. Westport, Conn. : Hyperion Press, [1977] p. cm. (The Hyperion library of classic American comic strips) [PN6727.M25W5] 76-53048 ISBN 0-88355-651-0 : 17.95. ISBN 0-88355-650-2 pbk. : 8.95.
I. Title. II. Title: Dream days. III. Series.

MOORES, Dick. 741.5'973
Gasoline Alley / by Dick Moores ; with introd. by Nat Hentoff. New York : Avon Books, c1976. 137 p. : ill. ; 28 cm. (A Flare book) Chiefly cartoons. [PN6728.G3M6] 77-357245 ISBN 0-380-00761-4 : 3.95
I. Title. BIP

OPPER, Frederick Burr, 1857-1937. 741.5'973
Happy Hooligan : a complete compilation, 1904-1905 / Frederick Burr Opper ; introd. by Richard Marschall. Westport, Conn. : Hyperion Press, [1977] p. cm. (The Hyperion library of classic American comic strips) [PN6728.H36O66 1977] 76-53052 ISBN 0-88355-659-6 : 14.95. ISBN 0-88355-658-8 pbk. : 6.50
I. Title. II. Series. BIP

OUTCAULT, Richard Felton, 1863-1928. 741.5'973
Buster Brown : a complete compilation, 1906 / Richard F. Outcault ; introd. by Richard Marschall. Westport, Conn. : Hyperion Press, [1977] p. cm. (The Hyperion library of classic American comic strips) [PN6728.B87O9 1977] 76-53053 ISBN 0-88355-661-8 : 14.95. ISBN 0-88355-660-X : 6.50
I. Title. II. Series. BIP

RAYMOND, Alex, 1909- 741.5973
Flash Gordon [comic strips] New York, Nostalgia Press [1967] 1 v. (chiefly illus., port.) 29 x 37 cm. [NC1429.R34.A43] 67-28204
I. Title.

RAYMOND, Alex, 1909-1956. 741.5'973
Flash Gordon / Alex Raymond ; editor & publisher Woody Gelman ; designer Bill Chadbourne. New York : Nostalgia Press, c1974. 2 v. : chiefly ill. ; 32 cm. (Classics from the golden age of comics) Contents.Contents.—v. 1. The Planet Mongo.—v. 2. Into the water world of Mongo. [PN6728.F55R37 1974] 74-81370 12.95 ea.
I. Title.

SEGAR, Elzie Crisler, 1894-1938. 741.5'973
Thimble theater, introducing Popeye : a complete compilation of the first adventures of Popeye, 1928-1930 / Elzie C. Segar ; introd. by Bill Blackbeard. Westport, Conn. : Hyperion Press, c1977. xv, 173 p. : ill. ; 22 x 28 cm. (The Hyperion library of classic American comic strips) [PN6728.T5S39 1977] 76-53054 ISBN 0-88355-663-4 : 17.95. ISBN 0-88355-662-6 pbk. : 8.95
I. Title. II. Series.

SEGAR, Elzie Crisler, 1894-1938. 741.5'973
Thimble theater, starring: Popeye the sailor. [New York, Nostalgia Press, c1971] 1 v. (chiefly illus.) 23 x 29 cm. (The Golden age of the comics [no. 8]) On spine: 1936-1937. "Reprinted just as they originally appeared in the daily newspapers of 1936[-37]" Contents.Contents.—Popeye and the jeep.—Popeye's search for his poppa.—Popeye and the mystery melody. [PN6728.T5S4 1971] 79-168727
I. Title. II. Title: Popeye the sailor.

SMITH, Sidney, 1877-1935. 741.5'973
Sidney Smith's The Gumps / editor, Herb Galewitz ; Don Winslow, design. New York : Scribner, [1974] xiv, 162 p. : ill. ; 24 x 26 cm. Comic-strip published by The Chicago tribune from 1917-59. [PN6728.G8S6 1974] 74-6760 ISBN 0-684-13997-9 : 9.95
I. Title. II. Title: The Gumps.

STERANKO, James. 741.5
The Steranko history of comics. [Reading, Pa., Supergraphics, 1970- v. illus. 36 cm. (A Supergraphics publication) [NC1429.S62A56] 72-20236
I. Title. II. Title: History of comics. BIP

TUTHILL, Harry J. 741.5'973
The Bungle family : a complete compilation, 1928 / Harry J. Tuthill ; introd. by Bill Blackbeard. Westport, Conn. : Hyperion Press, c1977. 134 p. : ill. ; 18 x 26 cm. (The Hyperion library of classic American comic strips) [PN6728.B85T8] 76-53057 ISBN 0-88355-669-3 : 14.95. ISBN 0-88355-668-5 pbk. : 6.50
I. Title. II. Series.

Comic books, strips, etc.—American—Biography.

BAILS, Jerry G. 741'.092'2 B
The who's who of American comic books. Editors: Jerry Bails and Hames Ware. 1st ed. [Detroit, 1973- v. illus. 28 cm. [PN6725.B3] 73-174050
1. Comic books, strips, etc.—American—Biography. I. Ware, Hames, joint author. II. Title.

Comic books, strips, etc.—American—History and criticism.

ROBINSON, Jerry. 741.5'973
The comics : an illustrated history of comic strip art / by Jerry Robinson. New York : Putnam, [1974] 256 p., [16] leaves of plates : ill. (some col.) ; 31 cm. Includes indexes. [PN6725.R6 1974] 72-94257 ISBN 0-399-10937-4 : 15.00
1. Comic books, strips, etc.—American—History and criticism. I. Title.

SHERIDAN, Martin, 1914- 741.5'973
Classic comics & their creators; life stories of American cartoonists from the golden age. Arcadia, Ca[lif.] Post-Era Books [1973] 304 p. illus. 24 cm. Reprint of the 1942 ed. published by Cushman and Flint, Boston, under the title: Comics and their creators. [PN6725.S5 1973] 73-83508 ISBN 0-911160-59-0
1. Comic books, strips, etc.—American—History and criticism. 2. Cartoonists—United States—Biography. I. Title. BIP

SHERIDAN, Martin, 1914- 741.5'973
Comics and their creators; life stories of American cartoonists. New York, Luna Press [1971, c1944] 304 p. illus. 23 cm. [PN6725.S5 1971] 78-176227 4.00
1. Comic books, strips, etc.—American—History and criticism. 2. Cartoonists—United States—Biography. I. Title. BIP

WAUGH, Coulton, 1896-1973. 741.5'973
The comics. New York, Luna Press [1974, c1947] p. cm. Reprint of the ed. published by Macmillan, New York. [PN6725.W3 1974] 74-4071 ISBN 0-914466-02-X 8.00 (lib bdg.)
1. Comic books, strips, etc.—American—History and criticism. I. Title.
Pbk. 5.00

Comic books, strips, etc.—Collectors and collecting.

CARLSON, Raymond. 741.5
A guide to collecting and selling comic books : how to establish an interesting and rewarding hobby / by Raymond Carlson. New York : Pilot Books, c1976. 24 p. ; 22 cm. Offers simple step-by-step instructions for collecting, trading, and selling comic books. [PN6714.C3] 76-2461 ISBN 0-87576-056-2 pbk. : 2.00
1. Comic books, strips, etc.—Collectors and collecting. I. Title. BIP

Comic books, strips, etc.—Congresses.

NEW York Comic Art Convention, 1974. 741.5'973
Welcome to the 1974 New York Comic Art Convention. Brooklyn, N.Y. : P. Seuling, [1974] 98 p. : ill. (some col.) ; 22 cm. [PN6702.N4 1974] 75-302437 3.50
1. Comic books, strips, etc.—Congresses. I. Title.

Comic books, strips, etc.—Dictionaries.

THE World encyclopedia of comics / edited by Maurice Horn. New York : Chelsea House Publishers, 1976. p. cm. Includes index. Bibliography: p. [PN6710.W6 1976b] 76-7322 ISBN 0-87754-042-X : 22.50 741.5'03
1. Comic books, strips, etc.—Dictionaries. I. Horn, Maurice. BIP

Comic books, strips, etc.—Great Britain.

VICTORIAN comics / 741.5'941
[compiled by] Denis Gifford. London : Allen and Unwin, 1976. 128 p. : chiefly ill., facsims. ; 29 cm. Ill. on lining papers. [PN6736.V5] 77-354596 ISBN 0-04-741002-7 : 12.95
1. Comic books, strips, etc.—Great Britain. I. Gifford, Denis.
Distributed by Allen & Unwin, 198 Ash St. Reading, Mass. 01867 BIP

Comic books, strips, etc.—Hist.

PERRY, George. 809.3'6
The Penguin book of comics; a slight history devised by George Perry, Alan Aldridge. [Baltmore], Penguin, 1967. 256p. facsims. 29cm. [NC1340.P4] 68-31925 4.50 pap.,
1. Comic books, strips, etc.—Hist. I. Aldridge, Alan. II. Title.

Comic books, strips, etc.—History and criticism.

FUCHS, Wolfgang J., 1945- 741.5'973
Comics; anatomy of a mass medium [by] Reinhold Reitberger [and] Wolfgang Fuchs. [Translated from the German by Nadia Fowler. 1st American ed.] Boston, Little, Brown [1972] 264 p. illus. 30 cm. Bibliography: p. 257-258. [PN6710.F813 1972] 72-1826 12.50
1. Comic books, strips, etc.—History and criticism. I. Reitberger, Reinhold C., 1946- joint author. II. Title.
Paperback ed. 6.95.

A History of the comic strip, by Pierre Couperie [and others] Translated from the French by Eilleen B. Hennessy. New York, Crown Publishers [1968] 256 p. illus. 28 cm. Translation of Bande dessinee et figuration narrative. "Created in conjunction with the exhibition of comic-strip art at Musee des arts decoratifs, Palais du Louvre." [NC1355.B28513] 68-20471 741.5'09
1. Comic books, strips, etc.—History and criticism. I. Couperie, Pierre. BIP

MASTERS of comic book art / Will Eisner ... [et al. ; text] by P. R. Garriock. New York : Images Graphiques, 1978. 123, [5] p. : ill. (some col.) ; 31 cm. Bibliography: p. [126]-[128] [PN6710.M3 1978b] 78-55024 ISBN 0-89545-021-6 : 9.95 741'.092'2
1. Comic books, strips, etc.—History and criticism. I. Garriock, P. R.

SUBJECT INDEX COMMEMORATIVE POSTAGE STAMPS—CANADA.

Pub address: 37Riverside Drive. new york NY

PERRY, George C. 741.59'09
The Penguin book of comics; a slight history, devised by George Perry and Alan Aldridge. [Rev. ed. Harmondsworth, Eng., Baltimore, Md.] Penguin Books, [1971] 272 p. illus. (part col.) 29 cm. [PN6710.P4 1971] 79-31978 ISBN 0-14-002802-1 (pbk) 4.95 (pbk)
1. Comic books, strips, etc.—History and criticism. I. Aldridge, Alan. II. Title.

REITBERGER, Reinhold C., 1946- 741.5'03
Comics : die Welt der Bildgeschichten : 12. Ausstellung im Haus Deutscher Ring, Hamburg, 21. Januar bis 16. Marz 1975. Hamburg : Deutscher Ring Lebensversicherungs-Aktiengesellschaft, [1975] [22] leaves : ill. ; 30 cm. Cover title. Additional text by Reinhold Reitberger ([17] leaves) inserted. [PN6710.R38] 75-507925
1. Comic books, strips, etc.—History and criticism. I. Deutscher Ring Lebensversicherungs-Aktiengesellschaft. II. Title.

*STANLEY, John 741.59
The great comics game [by] John Stanley, Mal Whyte. Los Angeles. Price/Stern/Sloan [1966] 1 v. (unpaged) col. illus. 19cm. (10410) 1.00 pap.,
I. Title.
Available from Trident in New York.

Comic books, strips, etc.—Illustrations.

LEE, Stan. 741.5
How to draw comics the marvel way / by Stan Lee and John Buscema. New York : Simon and Schuster, c1977 p. cm. 741.5 [NC1764.L4] 77-20226 ISBN 0-671-22548-0 : 7.95
1. Comic books, strips, etc.—Illustrations. 2. Drawing—Technique. I. Buscema, John. II. Title. BIP

Comic books, strips, etc.—Illustrations—Juvenile literature.

TALLARICO, Anthony. 741.5
Let's draw comics / by Tony Tallarico. New York : Grosset & Dunlap, c1976. [64] p. : ill. ; 28 cm. (Elephant books) [NC1764.T34] 76-4260 ISBN 0-448-12514-5 : 1.50 ISBN 0-448-13388-1 lib.bdg. : 2.99
1. Comic books, strips, etc.—Illustrations—Juvenile literature. 2. Drawing—Instruction—Juvenile literature. I. Title.

Comic books, strips, etc.—Prices.

OVERSTREET, Robert M. 741.5973
The comic book price guide, books from 1933-present included; catalogue and price list, illustrated. Robert M. Overstreet, publishing editor [and] Jerry G. Bails, associate editor. 1st ed. Cleveland, Tenn. [1970] 228 p. illus. 22 cm. [Z1000.O9] 71-23716 5.00
1. Comic books, strips, etc.—Prices. 2. Comic books, strips, etc.—Bibliography. I. Bails, Jerry G., joint author. II. Title.

Comic books, strips, etc.—United States.

DANIELS, Les, 1943- 741.59'73
Comix: a history of comic books in America. [New York] Outerbridge & Dienstfrey; distributed by E. P. Dutton [1971] x, 198 p. illus. (part col.) 29 cm. "A Fusion book." Bibliography: p. 194. [NC1426.D3 1971] 75-169104 ISBN 0-87690-034-1
1. Comic books, strips, etc.—United States. I. Title.

DWIGGINS, Clare Victor, 1874-1958. 741.5'973
School days : a complete compilation, 1923-1924 / Clare V. Dwiggins ; introd. by Cal Dobbins. Westport, Conn. : Hyperion Press, [1977] p. cm. (The Hyperion library of classic American comic strips) [PN6728.S3D8 1977] 76-53039 ISBN 0-88355-633-2 : 14.95. ISBN 0-88355-632-4 pbk. : 6.95
I. Title. II. Series. BIP

GOLDBERG, Reuben Lucius, 1883-1970. 741.5'973
Bobo Baxter, the complete daily strip, 1927-1928 / by Rube Goldberg ; introd. by Bill Blackbeard. Westport, Conn. : Hyperion Press, c1977. xvii, 151 p. : ill. ; 22 x 28 cm. (The Hyperion library of classic American comic strips) [PN6728.B6G64 1977] 76-53042 ISBN 0-88355-639-1 : 16.95. ISBN 0-88355-638-3 pbk. : 7.95
I. Title. II. Series.

GOULD, Chester. 741.5973
The celebrated cases of Dick Tracy, 1931-1951. Edited by Herb Galewitz. Introd. by Ellery Queen. [1st ed.] New York, Chelsea House [1970] xxviii, 291 p. illus. (part col.) 32 cm. [NC1429.G58A43] 70-127010 15.00
I. Title.

HERSHFIELD, Harry, 1885-1974. 741.5'973
Abie the agent : a complete compilation, 1914-1915 / Harry Hershfield ; introd. by Peter C. Marzio. Westport, Conn. : Hyperion Press, c1977. xiii, 98 p. : ill. ; 22 x 28 cm. (The Hyperion library of classic American comic strips) [PN6728.A2H4 1977] 76-53045 ISBN 0-88355-645-6 : 14.50. ISBN 0-88355-644-8 pbk. : 5.95
I. Title. II. Series. BIP

HOGARTH, Burne. 741.59'73
Tarzan of the apes. [Drawings] by Burne Hogarth. Introd. by Maurice Horn. Original text of Edgar Rice Burroughs adapted by Robert M. Hodes. New York, Watson-Guptill Publications [1972] 32 p., [122] p. of col. illus. 29 cm. Bibliography: p. 29-31. [NC1429.H553A44] 72-2446 ISBN 0-8230-5060-2 9.95
I. Burroughs, Edgar Rice, 1875-1950. Tarzan of the apes. II. Title. III. Title: Tarzan of the apes.

LEE, Stan. 741.5'973
Marvel's greatest superhero battles / Stan Lee. New York : Simon and Schuster, c1978. 253 p. : ill. ; 26 cm. [PN6726.L4] 78-12877 ISBN 0-671-24544-9 : 12.95 ISBN 0-671-24391-8 pbk. : 6.95
1. Comic books, strips, etc.—United States. I. Marvel Comics Group. II. Title. BIP

LEE, Stan. 741.5'973
Origins of Marvel Comics. New York, Simon and Schuster [1974] 254 p. illus. 26 cm. [PN6725.L4] 74-11141 ISBN 0-671-21864-6
1. Marvel Comics Group. 2. Comic books, strips, etc.—United States. I. Title. BIP

LEE, Stan. 741.5'973
Son of Origins of Marvel Comics / Stan Lee. New York : Simon and Schuster, [1975] 249 p. : col. ill. ; 26 cm. [PN6725.L44] 75-20029 ISBN 0-671-22170-1 : 10.95 ISBN 0-671-22166-3 pbk. : 6.95
1. Marvel Comics Group. 2. Comic books, strips, etc.—United States. I. Title. BIP

LEE, Stan. 741.5'973
The superhero women / by Stan Lee. New York : Simon and Schuster, c1977. p. cm. [PN6725.L424] 77-9500 ISBN 0-671-22766-1 : 10.95 ISBN 0-671-22928-1 pbk. : 6.95
1. Marvel Comics Group. 2. Comic books, strips, etc.—United States. 3. Women—Caricatures and cartoons. I. Title. BIP

SHAZAM! : 741.5'973
From the forties to the seventies / introd. by E. Nelson Bridwell. New York : Harmony Books, c1977. 352 p. : ill. (some col.) ; 27 cm. Bibliography: p. 351-352. [PN6726.S49] 77-84980 ISBN 0-517-53127-5 : 10.00
1. Comic books, strips, etc.—United States.

SMITHSONIAN Institution. 741.5'973
The Smithsonian collection of newspaper comics / edited by Bill Blackbeard and Martin Williams ; foreword by John Canaday. Washington : Smithsonian Institution Press, [1977] 336 p. : chiefly ill. ; 36 cm. Includes index. Bibliography: p. 324. [PN6726.S6 1977] 77-608090 ISBN 0-87474-167-X pbk. : 12.50
1. Comic books, strips, etc.—United States. I. Blackbeard, Bill. II. Williams, Martin T. III. Title. BIP

Comic books, strips, etc.—United States—Dictionaries.

CRAWFORD, Hubert H. 741.5'0973
Crawford's Encyclopedia of comic books / by Hubert H. Crawford. Middle Village, N.Y. : Jonathan David Publishers, c1977. p. cm. Includes bibliographical references and indexes. [PN6725.C7] 77-24738 ISBN 0-8246-0221-8 : 20.00
1. Comic books, strips, etc.—United States—Dictionaries. I. Title. II. Title: Encyclopedia of comic books. BIP

FLEISHER, Michael. 741.5'973
The encyclopedia of comic book heroes / by Michael L. Fleisher, assisted by Janet E. Lincoln. New York : Collier Books, 1976- p. cm. Contents.Contents.—v. 2. The Wonder Woman encyclopedia. [PN6725.F5 1976b] 76-956 ISBN 0-02-538700-6 : 16.95
1. Comic books, strips, etc.—United States—Dictionaries. I. Title. BIP

FLEISHER, Michael L. 741.5'909
The Encyclopedia of comic book heroes / by Michael L. Fleisher, assisted by Janet E. Lincoln. New York : Macmillan, c1976- v. : ill. ; 29 cm. Contents.Contents.—v. 1. Batman. [PN6725.F5] 75-19237 ISBN 0-02-538700-6 : 16.95
1. Comic books, strips, etc.—United States—Dictionaries. I. Lincoln, Janet E., joint author. II. Title.

Comic books, strips, etc.—United States—Exhibitions.

BRONX Museum of the Arts. 741.5'973'0740147275
80 years of the comics : [catalogue of an exhibition May 7-June 29, 1975 Bronx, N.Y. : Bronx Museum of the Arts, [1975] 32 p. : ill. ; 26 cm. Text in English and Spanish. [PN6705.U5B7 1975] 75-320679
1. Comic books, strips, etc.—United States—Exhibitions. I. Title.

O'SULLIVAN, Judith. 741.5973'074'015251
The art of the comic strip. With an introductory note by Don Denny. [College Park] University of Maryland Dept. of Art [1971] 95 p. illus. 22 x 27 cm. Exhibition held at University of Maryland Art Gallery, Apr. 1-May 9, 1971. Includes bibliographies. [NC1427.C63O8] 77-634302
1. Comic books, strips, etc.—United States—Exhibitions. I. Maryland. University. Art Gallery. II. Title.

Comic books, strips, etc.—United States—History and criticism.

GOULART, Ron, 1933- 741.5
The adventurous decade / Ron Goulart. New Rochelle, N.Y. : Arlington House, [1975] 224 p. : ill. ; 25 cm. Includes index. [PN6725.G6] 75-6725 ISBN 0-87000-252-X : 8.95
1. Comic books, strips, etc.—United States—History and criticism. 2. American newspapers—Sections, columns, etc.—Comics. I. Title. BIP

HORN, Maurice. 741.5'973
Women in the comics / by Maurice Horn. New York : Chelsea House Publishers, 1977. p. cm. Includes index. [PN6725.H6] 77-24317 ISBN 0-87754-056-X : 15.00
1. Comic books, strips, etc.—United States—History and criticism. 2. Women in literature. 3. Women in art. I. Title. BIP

THOMPSON, Don. 741.5'973
The comic-book book. Edited by Don Thompson and Dick Lupoff. New Rochelle, N.Y., Arlington House [1974, c1973] 360 p. illus. 24 cm. [PN6725.T5 1974] 73-22448 ISBN 0-87000-193-0
1. Comic books, strips, etc.—United States—History and criticism. I. Lupoff, Richard A., 1935- joint author. II. Title. BIP

WALKER, Mort. 741.5'973
Backstage at the strips / by Mort Walker. 1st ed. New York : Mason/Charter, 1975. vii, 311 p. : ill. ; 29 cm. Includes index. [PN6725.W28] 75-34156 ISBN 0-88405-117-X
1. Comic books, strips, etc.—United States—History and criticism. 2. Cartoonists—United States. I. Title. BIP

Commemorative coins.

BECKER, Thomas W. 737.4
Pageant of world commemorative coins, their meaning and symbolism. Racine, Wis., Whitman, c.1962. 197p. illus. 24cm. 62-4147 3.75
1. Commemorative coins. I. Title.

BECKER, Thomas W 737.4
Pageant of world commemorative coins, their meaning and symbolism. Racine, Wis., Whitman Pub. Co., c1962. 197p. illus. 24cm. [CJ1539.B4] 62-4147
1. Commemorative coins. I. Title.

HIBLER, Harold E. 737.2085
So-called dollars; an illustrated standard catalog with valuations, by Harold E. Hibler, Charles V. Kappen. New York, Coin & Currency Inst. [c.1963] xi, 156p. illus. 29cm. 63-11546 12.50
1. Commemorative coins. 2. Medals—U. S. I. Kappen, Charles V., joint author. II. Title.

RUBY, Warren A 332.4'042'0973
Commemorative coins of the United States (gold and silver) Lake Mills, Iowa, Graphic Pub. Co. [1961] unpaged. illus. 23cm. [CJ1839.R8] 61-47618
1. Commemorative coins. I. Title.

SLABAUGH, Arlie R 737.4973
United States commemorative coins; the drama of America as told by our coins. Racine, Wis., Whitman Pub. Co. [1962] 144 p. illus. 20 cm. [CJ1839.S6] 62-5748
1. Commemorative coins. 2. Coins, American. I. Title.

Commemorative coins—U.S.

IACOVO, James S. 737.4'9'73
A comprehensive guide to United States commemorative coins / by James S. Iacovo. Dallas : Ivy Press, c1979. x, 130 p. : ill. ; 24 cm. Includes bibliographical references. [CJ1839.I18] 78-71956 ISBN 0-933372-00-0. : 12.95
1. Commemorative coins—United States—Catalogs. 2. Coins, American—Catalogs. I. Title. BIP

THE National Commemorative Society and its first fifty issues [by Joseph M. Segel and others. Philadelphia, National Historical Foundation, c1969] 166 p. illus., ports. 32 cm. [CJ1820.N35] 72-110053 737.4
1. National Commemorative Society. 2. Commemorative coins—U.S. I. Segel, Joseph M. II. National Historical Foundation.

TAXAY, Don. 737.49'73
An illustrated history of U.S. commemorative coinage. New York, Arco Pub. Co. [1967] viii, 256 p. illus., ports. 27 cm. [CJ1839.T3] 67-10696
1. Commemorative coins—United States. I. Title. BIP

Commemorative postage stamps.

TYRRELL, M. William. 769'.563
The Universal Postal Union, members & stamps, 1874-1974 / edited by M. William Tyrrell. Albany, Or. : Van Dahl Publications, [1974] 354 p. : ill. ; 25 cm. Includes index. [HE6271.T93] 74-19565 10.00
1. Union postale universelle. 2. Commemorative postage stamps. I. Title.

Commemorative postage stamps—Canada.

SEARY, Victor Perrin, 1903- 769'.563'0971
A postage stamp history of Canada [by] Victor Seary. Toronto, New York, McGraw-Hill Ryerson [1972] 168 p. illus. 23 cm. Bibliography: p. 157-158. [HE6185.C2S4] 74-39022 ISBN 0-07-077327-0
1. Commemorative postage stamps—Canada. I. Title.

Commemorative postage stamps—Gt. Brit.

HAVERBECK, H D S 383.22
The commemorative stamps of the British Commonwealth. New York, Van Nostrand [1955?] 239p. illus. 23cm. [HE6185.G6H36] 55-2764
1. Commemorative postage stamps—Gt. Brit. I. Title.

Commemorative postage stamps—U.S.

BYKOWSKI, Stanley J. 769.569'438
Poland's millenium in philately, 966-1966, comp., ed. by Stanley Bykowski. Layout by Paul Mastrangelo. Hyde Park, Mass. [1967] 1 v. (unpaged) illus., facsims., ports. 22cm. On cover: Millennium Polski chrzescijanskiej. [HE6185.U6B9] 67-7684 2.50 pap.,
1. Commemorative postage stamps—U. S. I. Title. II. Title: Millennuim Polski chrzescijanskiej.
Available from the author at 14 Cleveland St., Hyde Park, Mass. 02136.

BYKOWSKI, Stanley J. 769.56973075
Poland's millennium in philately, 966-1966, compiled and editored by Stanley Bykowski. Layout by Paul Mastrangelo. Hyde poark, Mass. [1967] 1 v. (unpaged) illus. facsims., ports. 22 cm. On cover: Millennium Poiski chrezescijanskiej. [HE6185.UgB9] 67-7684
1. Commemorative postage stamps—U.S. I. Title. II. Title: Millennium Polski chrzescijanskiej.

HOBSON, Burton. 383.223
U.S. commemorative coins and stamps, by Burton Hobson and Fred Reinfeld. New York, Sterling Pub. Co. [1964] 64 p. illus. 27 cm. (Visual history series) [HE6185.U6H55] 64-15119
1. Commemorative postage stamps—U.S. 2. Commemorative coins—U.S. I. Reinfeld, Fred, 1910-1964. II. Title.

MOOLMAN, Valerie. 383.223
The complete illustrated guide to U. S. commemorative stamps. New York, Cornerstone Library; [distributed by Affiliated Publishers] [1964] 157 p. facsims. 21 cm. "CN 90." [HE6185.U6M6] 64-7638
1. Commemorative postage stamps—U. S. I. Title.

REINFELD, Fred, 1910- 383.22
Commemorative stamps of the U. S. A.; an illustrated history of our country. New York, Crowell [c1956] 359p. illus. 23cm. [HE6185.U5R4 1956] 57-4182
1. Commemorative postage stamps—U. S. I. Title.

REINFELD, Fred, 1910-1964. 383.22
Commemorative stamps of the U. S. A.; an illustrated history of our country. New York, Crowell [1954] 344 p. illus. 23 cm. [HE6185.U5R4] 54-5616
1. Commemorative postage stamps—U.S. I. Title.

Commemorative postage stamps—U. S.—Albums.

BLUMENTHAL, Ben. 769'.563'0973
American commemorative stamp album, from 1893 to date. New York, Minkus Pubns. 220p. 18cm. (A340S) [TX6185.U5B5172] 68-2669 8.00
1. Commemorative postage stamps—U. S.—Albums. I. Title.
Publisher's address: 116 W. 32nd St., New York, N.Y. 10001.

BLUMENTHAL, Ben. 769'.563'0973
American commemorative stamp album, from 1893 to date. New York, Minkus Publications [1968]- 1 v. (loose-leaf) illus. 29 cm. [HE6185.U5B5172] 68-2669
1. Commemorative postage stamps—United States—Albums. I. Title.

Commemorative postage stamps—U. S.—Catalogs.

CRAMER, H W 383.22
Index to United States commemorative issues, 1893-1954. La Crosse, Kan., Clymer Philatelic Publications, c1955. 102p. illus. 16cm. [HE6185.U6C7] 55-26998
1. Commemorative postage stamps—U. S.—Catalogs. I. Title.

Commemorative postage stamps—United States—Juvenile literature.

TOWER, Samuel A. 769'.563'0973
Makers of America : stamps that honor them / by Samuel A. Tower. New York : Messner, c1978. 96 p. : ill. ; 22 cm. Includes index. [HE6185.U5T65] 77-26060 ISBN 0-671-32869-7 lib.bdg. : 7.29
1. Commemorative postage stamps—United States—Juvenile literature. 2. United States—Biography—Juvenile literature. 3. United States—History—Juvenile literature. I. Title. BIP

Commemorative pottery—Great Britain.

MAY, John, 1926- 738.3'0942
Commemorative pottery, 1780-1900; a guide for collectors [by] John and Jennifer May. New York, Scribner [1973, c1972] 180 p. illus. (part col.) 26 cm. [NK4085.M39 1973] 73-3007 ISBN 0-684-13403-9 12.50
1. Commemorative pottery—Great Britain. 2. Pottery—Collectors and collecting. I. May, Jennifer, joint author. II. Title.

Commemorative pottery—United States.

KLAMKIN, Marian. 738'.0973
American patriotic and political china. New York, Scribner [1973] viii, 215 p. illus. 27 cm. Bibliography: p. 210-211. [NK4005.K52] 72-6557 ISBN 0-684-13182-X 14.95
1. Commemorative pottery—United States. 2. Commemorative porcelain—United States. I. Title.

Commerce Trust Co., Kansas City, Mo.—Art collections.

MODERN 759.13'074'0178411
American painting from the Commerce Trust Company Collection. [Lawrence, Kan., 1966] 1 v. (unpaged) illus. 16 x 23 cm. (Miscellaneous publications of the Museum of Art, no. 64) "Catalogue ... prepared by art history students at the University of Kansas in a seminar on museum techniques, directed by Mr. Bret Waller [for the exhibition held at the museum Dec. 4, 1966-Jan. 1, 1967]" [ND212.M6] 68-63544
1. Commerce Trust Co., Kansas City, Mo.—Art collections. 2. Paintings, American—Exhibitions. 3. Painting, Modern—20th century—U.S. I. Kansas. University. Museum of Art. II. Series: Kansas. University. Museum of Art. Miscellaneous publications, no. 64

Commercial art.

ADVERTISING art: 741.67058
international, 1961/62. New York, Hastings [c.1961] 167p. illus. (pt. col.) 29cm. (Modern publicity, v.31) 26-17746 10.00

ADVERTISING art in 741.67'09'042
the Art Deco style / selected by Theodore Menten. New York : Dover Publications, 1975. [172] p. : all ill. (some col.) ; 29 cm. Includes bibliographical references and index. [NC998.45.A7A38] 74-27703 ISBN 0-486-23164-X pbk. : 5.00
1. Commercial art. 2. Art deco. I. Menten, Theodore.

ADVERTISING directions: 659.13
trends in visual advertising. [1]- New York, Art Directions Book Co. [1959- v. illus. 28cm. Editors: 1- E. Gottschall. A. Hawkins. [NC997.A682] 59-14827
1. Commercial art. I. Gottschall, Edward M., ed. II. Hawkins, Arthur, ed.

ANNUAL of advertising & 659.106
editorial art & design of the Art Directors Club of New York; 45th Art director: Mo Lebowitz, ed.: larry ottino [New York, Comet Pr. dist. Reinhold, 1966] v. illus. (pt. col.) 30cm. Pub. for the Art Directors Club. Title varies: 1921, Annual of advertising art in the United States.--1922, Annual of illustrations for advertisements in the United States.--1923-27, Annual of advertising art.--1938-46, Art directors annual of advertising art (varies) Other slight variations in title. [NC997.A1A69] 22-5058 16.50
1. Commercial art. 2. Commercial art—Societies, etc. I. Art Directors Club.

ANTEBI, Michael. 741.6'08
The art of creative advertising; a visual/verbal problem-solving approach. New York, Reinhold Book Corp. [1968] 1 v. (unpaged) illus. 31 cm. Includes bibliography. [NC997.A687] 68-16025
1. Commercial art. I. Title.

ART Directors Club of New York. 741.67
Art directing for visual communication and selling. New York, Hastings House [1957] 240 p. illus. 28 cm. (Visual communication books) [NC997.A693] 57-8644
1. Commercial art. I. Title.

ART Instruction, inc., Minneapolis. 741.67
Commercial art and design. Division 1- Minneapolis [1951- v. in illus. (part col., part inserted) 35cm. Cover title;each vol. has also speical t. p. The various divisions are frequently revised. This set includes all editions with this title in the Library. Originally published under title: Commercial designing. [NC997.A766] 53-16483
1. Commercial art. I. Title.

ART Instruction, inc., Minneapolis. 741.6
Master artists series. Minneapolis [1951- v. illus. (part col.) 35cm. Cover title. 'Home study art course ... supplementary reference texts. Contents.[1] The technique of Hy Rudin.--[2] The technique of John Clymer. [NC997.A767] 51-28913
1. Commercial art. I. Title.

ART Instruction, inc., Minneapolis. 741.67
[Textbooks]... arr. and edited by Walter J. Wilwerding [and] Lee S. Preston. Minneapolis [1956- v. illus. 34cm. Contents.1. Basic drawing.--2. Ink and wash drawing, by F. M. Wing and others.--3. Basic composition, color, perspective. [NC997.A768] 56-2744
1. Commercial art. I. Wilwerding, Walter Joseph, 1891- ed. II. Preston, Lee S., 1921- ed. III. Title.

BIEGELEISEN, Jacob Israel, 1910- 741.6069
Careers and opportunities in commercial art. New rev. ed. with added material. New York, Dutton, 1963 [c.1944-1963] 244p. illus. 21cm. Previous eds. pub. under title: Careers in commercial a rt. Bibl. 63-8608 4.95
1. Commercial art. 2. Art industries and trade. I. Title.

BIEGELEISEN, Jacob Israel, 1910- 740.69
Careers in commercial art. New and enl. ed. New York, Dutton [1952] 255 p. illus. 21 cm. [NC997.B46 1952] 52-10060
1. Commercial art. 2. Art industries and trade. I. Title.

CAMPANA, Domenic Mathews, 1871- 741.67
The teacher of advertising. Chicago, '1950. 127 p. illus. 20 cm. (Campana's popular art library) Cover title: The teacher of advertising and lettering. [NC997.C33] 51-584
1. Commercial art. 2. Lettering. I. Title.

CARBONI, Erberto, 1899- 741.67
Twenty five publicity campaigns. Greenwich, Conn., New York Graphic Society [c1961] 174p. illus. (part col.) 30cm. English, German, French, and Italian. [NC1155.C25A55] 62-6860
1. Commercial art. I. Title.

CHIN, Kay, 1920- 741.67
Commercial artists' guide. [New York, Commercial Artists Guide, 1956] 79p. 20cm. [NC997.C54] 56-2683
1. Commercial art. 2. Art as a profession. I. Title.

EBERMAN, Edwin. 655.3
How to make money in commercial art, illustration, and cartooning. Westport, Conn., Famous Artists Schools [1956] 74p. illus. 28cm. Published in 1952 under title: How to make money in commercial art and illustration. [NC997.E2 1956] 56-58203
1. Commercial art. I. Title.

EKSELL, Olle, 1918- 741.6
Corporate design programs. Tr. from the Swedish by Charles Harrison-Wallace. London, Studio Vista; New York, Reinhold [1967] 96p. illus. 20cm. (Studio Vista/Reinhold art paperback) [NC997.E3513] 67-25858 5.50; 2.45 pap.,
1. Commercial art. 2. Graphic arts—Technique. I. Title.

FELTEN, Charles J 1898- 741.67
Layout; the practical application of the principles of design to advertising and printing. 3d ed. New York, Appleton-Century-Crofts [1954] 170p. illus. 29cm. [NC997.F4 1954] 54-9525
1. Commercial art. I. Title.

FLETCHER, Alan. 741.6
Graphic design: visual comparisons, by Alan Fletcher, Colin Forbes [and] Bob Gill. New York, Reinhold [1964] 94 p. illus. 20 cm. (Reinhold paperbacks) [NC997.F55] 64-14628
1. Commercial art. I. Title.

GAMES, Abram 741.6
Over my shoulder. [New York] Macmillan [1960] 84p. illus. (part col.) 26cm. 60-50767 5.00 bds.,
1. Commercial art. I. Title.

GARLAND, Ken 659.13
Graphics handbook. London, Studio Vista; New York, Reinhold, [1966] 96p. front. (port.), illus., tables, diagrs. 20cm. Bibl. [NC997.G32 1966] 66-24540 5.50; 2.45 pap.,
1. Commercial art. I. Title.

GOLDEN, Cipe Pineles, ed. 741.6
The visual craft of William Golden. Eds.: Cipe Pineles Golden, Kurt Weihs, Robert Strunsky. New York, Braziller [c.]1962. 156p. illus. 22x28cm. 62-9694 12.50
1. Golden, William, 1911-1959. 2. Commercial art. 3. Columbia Broadcasting System, inc. CBS Television. I. Title.

HAWKINS, Arthur, ed. 741.67
The art director at work; how 15 medal-winning exhibits were conceived and executed. George Giusti, designer; Eugene Milbauer, art director. New York, Published for Art Directors Club of New York [by] Hastings House [1959] unpaged. illus. 26cm. (Visual communication books) [NC997.H28] 59-10848
1. Commercialart. 2. Art as a profession. I. Title.

HINWOOD, Tony, 1935- 745.4
Graphic design; time and money-saving tricks of the trade. New York, Drake [1973] 175 p. illus. 25 cm. [NC1000.H56] 74-18440 ISBN 0-87749-526-2 7.95
1. Commercial art. 2. Graphic arts—Technique. I. Title.

HOBBS, Eric. 741.67
Drawing for advertising. London, New York, Studio Publications [1956] 96p. illus. 26cm. (The How to do it series, 63) [NC997.H55] 56-58559
1. Commercial art. I. Title.

HORNUNG, Clarence Pearson. 741.67
Handbook of early advertising art, mainly from American sources. 3d ed. New York, Dover Publications [c1956] 2v. illus. 32cm. Contents.[1] Pictorial.--[2] Typographical and ornamental. Includes bibliographies. [NC997.H58 1956] 57-3530
1. Commercial art. I. Title. BIP

HORNUNG, Clarence Pearson. 741.67
Handbook of early advertising art, mainly from American sources. 3d ed. New York, Dover Publications [c1956] 2v. illus. 32cm. Contents.[1] Pictorial.--[2] Typographical and ornamental. Cnvludes bibliographies. [NC997.H58 1956] 57-3530
1. Commercial art. I. Title.

HORNUNG, Clarence Pearson. 741.67
Handbook of early American advertising art. 2d ed., completely rev. and greatly

expanded. New York, Dover Publications [1953] 2v. illus. 32cm. Contents.[1] Pictorial.--[2] Typographical and ornamental. Includes bibliographies. [NC997.H58 1953] 54-9264
1. Commercial art. I. Title.

KARO, Jerzy. 741.6
Graphic design : problems, methods, and solutions / Jerzy Karo. New York : Van Nostrand Reinhold, [1975] p. cm. Includes index. [NC1000.K37] 74-6791 ISBN 0-442-30069-7 : 9.95
1. Commercial art. 2. Graphic arts—Technique. I. Title.

KINGHAN, Charles R 741.67
Rendering techniques for commercial art and advertising. New York, Reinhold Pub. Corp. [1957] 159p. illus. 27cm. [NC997.K45] 57-9461
1. Commercial art. I. Title.

LUDEKENS, Fred, 1900- 741
How I make a picture. Westport, Conn., Institute of Commercial Art, c1951. 98 p. illus., ports. 35 cm. [NC997.L8] 52-1513
1. Commercial art. I. Westport, Conn. Institute of Commercial Art, Inc. II. Title.

MAURELLO, S. Ralph, 1911- 741.67
Commercial art techniques; a practical self-instruction course and reference handbook. Over 500 illus. of methods and procedures. New York, Tudor Pub. Co. [1952] 126 p. illus. 29 cm. [NC997.M35] 52-7830
1. Commercial art. I. Title. BIP

MINNEAPOLIS. Art Instruction. 741
Commercial design. [A series of texts with charts prepared for Art Instruction, inc., dealing with the various departments of illustrating and designing for advertising purposes.] Minneapolis [1950] no. in illus. 28 cm. Cover title. Folded "Chart[s]" laid in. First published in 1922 under title: Commercial designing. Contents.Contents. -- division 4. pt. 1. Advertising layout. [NC997.M532] 50-14647
1. Commercial art. I. Title.

MINNEAPOLIS. Art Instruction. 741.6
Master artists series. Minneapolis [1951- v. illus. (part col.) 35 cm. Cover title. "Home study art course ... supplementary reference texts." Contents.Contents. -- [1] The technique of Hy Rubin. [NC997.M522] 51-28913
1. Commercial art. I. Title.

MULLER-BROCKMANN, Josef, 1914- 741.6
Gestaltungsprobleme des Grafikers; gestalterische und erziekerische Probleme in der Werbegrafik—die Ausbildung des Grafikers. The graphic artist and his design problems; creative problems of the graphic designer; design and training in commercial art. Les probemes d'un artiste graphique; typographie, dessin, photo, labels, couleurs, etc. English version: D. Q. Stephensen. Version francaise: M. Menzel-flocon et J. P. Samson. New York, Hastings-House [1961] 186 p. illus. (part col.) typog. specimens. 24 x 27 cm. (Visual communication books) [NC997.M8] 61-66339
1. Commercial art. 2. Graphic arts—Technique. I. Title.

NELSON, Roy Paul 741.6
Fell's Guide to commercial art, by Roy Paul Nelson, Byron Ferris. With examples and illus. by the authors. Chris Arvetis [others] New York, Fell [c.1966] 118p. illus. 29cm. Bibl. [NC997.N37] 66-14801 5.95 bds.,
1. Commercial art. I. Ferris, Byron, joint author. II. Title. III. Title: Guide to commercial art. BIP

RODEWALD, Fred C. 741.6
Commercial art as a business. New York, Viking Press, 1954. 129 p. illus. 26 cm. [NC997.R58] 54-5756
1. Commercial art. I. Title.

RODEWALD, Fred C. 741.6
Commercial art as a business, by Fred C. Rodewald and Edward M. Gottschall. Rev. ed. New York, Viking Press, 1960. 180 p. illus. 24 cm. [NC997.R58 1960] 60-9776
1. Commercial art. I. Gottschall, Edward M., joint author. II. Title.

ROSS, Robert, 1927- 741.6
Illustration today. Scranton, International Textbook Co. [c1963] xii, 292 p. illus. (part col.) 27 cm. (International textbooks in art education) Bibliography: p. 290. [NC997.R63] 62-21507
1. Commercial art. 2. Illustration of books. I. Title.

SCANDINAVIAN advertising art; advertising art in Norway, 741.670948
Finland, Sweden, and Denmark. New York, Praeger [1967] 117 p. (chiefly illus., part col.) 31 cm. Cover title: Scan ad art. [NC997.S3] 67-11609
1. Commercial art. 2. Graphic arts, Swedish. I. Title. II. Title: Scan ad art.

SCHLEMMER, Richard M. 655.3
Handbook of advertising art production [by] Richard M. Schlemmer. With illus. by the author. Englewood Cliffs, N.J., Prentice-Hall [1966] xi, 285 p. illus. 22 cm. Bibliography: p. 266. [TR925.S3] 66-13644
1. Commercial art. 2. Photomechanical processes. I. Title. BIP

SCHORR, Harry Dreve. 741.67
The style and technique of Harry Dreve Schorr as applied to advertising layout. [1st ed.] New York, G. Efron [1956] unpaged. illus. 33cm. [NC997.S423] 56-7397
1. Commercial art. I. Title.

SOCIETY of Industrial Artists and Designers, London. 741.6
Designers in Britain; a review of graphic and industrial design 6. Ed. by David Caplan [New York, Universe, c.1964] v. illus. (pt. col.) 32cm. Formerly called Society of Industr ial Artists. cover title. Subtitle varies. annual. 48-4556 15.00 bds.,
1. Commercial art. 2. Design, Industrial. I. Caplan, David, ed. II. Title.

STONE, David K 655.3
Art in advertising. New York, Pitman Pub. Corp., 1961. unpaged. illus. 20 x 27 cm. (Pitman art series, 35) [NC997.S83] 61-16642
1. Commercial art. I. Title.

SUTNAR, Ladislav. 741.6
Visual design in action : principles, purposes. [New York, Hastings House, 1961] v. (unpaged) illus. (part. col.) 82 cm. [NC997.S85] 61-9378
1. Commercial art. 2. Design I. Title.

ZUCKER, Irving, comp. 741.67
A source book of French advertising art. With over 5000 illus. from the turn of the century. New York, Braziller [1964] 256 p. (chiefly illus.) 29 cm. [NC997.Z8] 64-14689
1. Commercial art. 2. Printing — Specimens. 3. France — Soc. life & cust. — Illustrations. I. Title.

Commercial art as a profession.

BALLINGER, Raymond A., 1907- 760'.023
Opportunities in graphic arts careers, by Raymond A. Ballinger. New York, Educational Books Division of Universal Pub. and Distributing Corp. [1968] 128 p. illus. 21 cm. (Vocational guidance manuals, Career series V169) Bibliography: p. 120-123. [NC1001.B3] 68-55526 1.65
1. Commercial art as a profession. I. Title. II. Title: Graphic arts careers.

FUJITA, S. Neil. 741.6
Aim for a job in graphic design/art, by S. Neil Fujita. [1st ed.] New York, Rosen Press [1968] 146 p. illus., ports. 22 cm. (Aim high vocation series) Defines graphic design and where and how it may be used. Also includes details on the necessary aptitudes for the work, suggestions for training, how to look for a job and biographies of some important people in the field. [NC1001.F8] AC 68
1. Commercial art as a profession. I. Title. BIP

Commercial art—Dictionaries.

THOMPSON, Philip. 741.6'01'48
A dictionary of graphic cliches / compiled by Philip Thompson & Peter Davenport. London : Pentagram Design, [1976- v. : ill., facsims. ; 21 cm. (Pentagram papers ; 1-) Contents.Contents.—[v. 1] [ABC] [NC998.4.T47] 77-361414 ISBN 0-905739-00-0 (v. 1) : £1.00 (v. 1)
1. Commercial art—Dictionaries. I. Davenport, Peter, joint author. II. Title. BIP

Commercial art—Europe.

GRAPHIC designers in Europe. 741.6'094 [Edited by Henri Hillebrand] New York, Universe Books [1971-73] 4 v. illus. (part col.) 27 cm. Text in English, French, and German. Contents.Contents.—1. Jan Lenica. Jean-Michel Folon. Josef Muller-Brockmann. Dick Elffers.—2. Giovanni Pintori. Edward Bawden. Hans Hillmann. Herbert Leupin.—3. Karl Gerstner. Crosby/ Fletcher/ Forbes. Andre Francois. Bob Gill.—v. 4. Franco Grignani. Heinz Edelmann. Jacques Richez. Celestino Piatti. [NC998.6.E87G72] 72-147894 ISBN 0-87663-143-X (v. 1) varies 7.95 per vol.
1. Commercial art—Europe. 2. Commercial artists—Europe. I. Hillebrand, Henri, ed.

Commercial art-Exhibitions.

CREATIVITY seventy six. 659.13
a photographic review of Creativity '76 displayed at the Conrad Hilton, Chicago, October 6,7,8, 1976, at the New York Hilton, New York, November 9,10,11, 1976 and at the Los Angeles Hilton, Los Angeles, April 19,20,21, 1977 New York : Art Direction Book Co., c1977. 1v. : ill. (part col) ; 28 cm. (Advertising directions ; v. 10) The Annualvol. of Creativity starts in 1972 as vol. 5 of Advertising Directions. [NC997.A682] 74-168254 ISBN 0-910158-25-8(v.10) : 21.50
1. Commercial art-Exhibitions. 2. Commercial art-United States.
Book carries L.C. card no.: 59-14827.

Commercial art—Germany, East.

GEBRAUCHSGRAPHIK in der DDR 655.3
/ hrsg. vom Verband Bildender Kunstler der DDR, Sektion Gebrauchsgraphik ; einfuhrender Text von Hellmut Rademacher. Dresden : Verlag der Kunst, 1975. 349 p. : 1400 ill. (some col.) ; 28 cm. [NC998.6.G42G42] 75-520630 98.00M
1. Commercial art—Germany, East. I. Verband Bildender Kunstler Deutschlands. Sektion Gebrauchsgrafik. II. Rademacher, Hellmut.

Commercial art—Handbooks, manuals, etc.

SNYDER, John. 741.6'028
Commercial artist's handbook. New York, Watson-Guptill Publications [1973] 264 p. illus. 26 cm. [NC1000.S68] 72-10220 ISBN 0-8230-0764-2 10.00
1. Commercial art—Handbooks, manuals, etc. 2. Artists' materials—Handbooks, manuals, etc. I. Title. BIP

Commercial art—Period.

PAGINA. 760.05845
2. June, 1963[International magazine of graphic design. Milano, Editorial Metro S.p.A. dist. New York, Wittenborn, 1963] 115p. illus. (pt. col., pt. fold) 32cm. English, Italian or French. annual. 63-1820 6.00 pap.,
1. Commercial art—Period. 2. Advertising—Period.

Commercial art—Printing.

SCHLEMMER, Richard M. 686.2
Handbook of advertising art production / Richard M. Schlemmer ; with ill. by the author. 2d ed. Englewood Cliffs, N.J. : Prentice-Hall, [1975] p. cm. Includes index. Bibliography: p. [Z257.S33 1975] 75-28157 ISBN 0-13-372524-3 : 11.95 ISBN 0-13-372516-2 pbk. : 7.95
1. Commercial art—Printing. 2. Photomechanical processes. I. Title.

Commercial art—Sweden.

SCANDINAVIAN 741.670948
advertising art; advertising art in Norway, Finland, Sweden, and Denmark. New York, Praeger [1967] 117 p. (chiefly illus., part col.) 31 cm. Cover title: Scan ad art. [NC997.S3] 67-11609
1. Commercial art—Sweden. 2. Graphic arts, Swedish. I. Title: Scan ad art.

Commercial art—Technique.

TUBAU Comamala, Juan, 1937- 741.6
How to attract attention with your art; a guide for graphic artists. [Translated by Jennifer Mellen.] New York, Sterling Pub. Co. [1970] 96 p. illus. (part col.) 22 cm. Translation of Diseno publicitario. [NC1000.T813] 79-126846 ISBN 0-8069-5154-0
1. Commercial art—Technique. I. Title.

Commercial art—United States.

GRAPHIC designers in the USA. 741.6'092'2 [Edited by Henri Hillebrand] New York, Universe Books [1971- v. illus. (part col.) 27 cm. Text in English, French, and German. Contents.Contents.—1. Louis Danziger. Herb Lubalin. Peter Max. Henry Wolf.—2. R. O. Blechman. Chermayeff & Geismar. Paul Davis. Rudolph de Harak.—3. Louis Dorfsman. Milton Glaser. George Tscherny. Tomi Ungerer. [NC998.5.A1G7] 76-147895 ISBN 0-87663-141-3 (v. 1) 7.95 per vol.
1. Commercial art—United States. 2. Commercial artists—United States. I. Hillebrand, Henri, ed.

PITZ, Henry Clarence, 1895-1976. 741.6'0973
200 years of American illustration / text by Henry C. Pitz;edited and designed by Bob Crozier;foreword by Norman Rockwell New York : Random House, c1977. p. cm. Includes index. Bibliography: p. [NC998.5.A1P57 1977] 77-5961 ISBN 0-394-41474-8 : 39.95
1. Commercial art—United States. I. Crozier, Bob. II. Title.

SHUKLE, Terrance, 1946- 741.67
Giraffe raps : a tale of advertising in America / Terrance Shukle. Ann Arbor, Mich. : Giraffe : distributed in the U.S. by Street Fiction Press, c1976. p. cm. [NC998.5.A1S45] 75-19944 ISBN 0-914908-94-4 : 5.95
1. Commercial art—United States. 2. Advertising—Psychological aspects. I. Title. BIP

Commercial art—United States—Catalogs.

AMERICAN Institute of Graphic Arts. 741.6'0973'074
AIGA catalog omnibus 1975-1976. [New York : American Institute of Graphic Arts, 1976] ca. 250 p. : ill. ; 26 cm. Title from spine. Includes indexes. Contents.Contents.—Cover '75/catch the eye.—LMS 1975.—Packaging: 76.—Communication graphics, 1975-76. [NC998.5.A1A45 1976] 77-363452
1. Commercial art—United States—Catalogs. I. Title.

Commercial art—United States—Exhibitions.

THE Design 741.6'0973'074
response : an exhibition / presented by the Federal Design Council. Washington : The Council, [1976?] [96] p. : chiefly ill. ; 28 cm. [NC998.5.A1D47] 76-380579
1. Commercial art—United States—Exhibitions. 2. Art and state—United States—Exhibitions. 3. Design—United States—Exhibitions. I. Federal Design Council.

Commercial art—Yearbooks.

ANNUAL of advertising 741.60952
art in Japan. 1966 [Tokyo, Bijutsu ShuppanSha] New York, Universe Bks. [1966.i.e.1967] v. illus. (pt. col.) 30cm. Began pubn. with 1957 issue. Added title in Japanese. English & Japanese. Vs. for

1957-1966 ed. by Art Directors Club of Tokyo [NC997.A1A62] 61-66515 17.50
1. Commercial art—Yearbooks. I. Tokyo Ato Direkutazu Kurabu.

GRAPHICS annual, 741.67058
International yearbook of advertising art ed. by Walter Herdeg [dist. New York, Praeger, 1960] Zurich, Amstutz & Herdeg 212p. illus. (part col.) 31cm. 56-24907 15.00
1. Commercial art— Yearbooks.

GRAPHIS annual, 741.67058
'64/65. International yearbook of advertising art. Ed. by Walter Herdeg. Zurich, Graphis Pr. [dist. New York, Hastings [c.]1964) 229p. 31cm. English, German, and French. 56-24907 16.00
1. Commercial art—Yearbooks.

GRAPHIS annual, 741.67058
'66/67. International annual of advertising graphics. Zurich. Graphis Pr. [New York, Hastins, c.1966] 266p. illus. (pt. col.) 31cm. Ed.: 1966-Walter Herdeg. English, German & French. 56-24907 17.50
1. Commercial art—Yearbooks. I. Herdeg, Walter, ed.

GRAPHIS annual, 741.67058
'65/66 International yearbook of advertising art. Ed. by Walter Herdeg. Zurich, Switzerland, Graphis Pr. [dist. New York, Hastings, c.1965] 245p. illus. (pt. col.) 31cm. English. German, and French. 56-24907 16.00
1. Commercial art—Yearbooks. I. Herdeg, Walter, ed.

GRAPHIS annual, 741.67058
International annual of advertising graphics; Internationales Jahrbuch der Werbegraphik; art publicitaire graphique international. Walter Herdeg, The Graphis Pr., Zurich [1967] v. illus. (pt. col.) 30cm. Ed. 1967/68. W. Herdeg Title varies. 1952/53: International advertising art; internationales Jahrbuch der Werbekunst; art publicitaire international. [NC997.A1G75] 56-24907 17.50
1. Commercial art— Yearbooks. American distributor: Hastings House, New York.

GRAPHIS annual, 62/63 741.67058
International yearbook of advertising art; internationales jahrbuch der werbekunst art publicitaire international ed. by walter herdeg. [dist. New York, Hastings, c.1962] Zurich. amstutz & herdeg 236p. illus. (pt. col.) 31cm. 56-24907 15.00
1. Commercial art—Yearbooks.

Commercial artists—United States.

NEW York. Art Students' 655.3 League.
The Art Students League of New York presents its eight instructor-artists in the fields of editorial illustration, fashion illustration, advertising layout and design, textile design, and lettering. Ray Prohaska [and others. New York, 1962?] 1 v. (unpaged) illus., ports. 23 cm. [NC997.N398] 68-128046
1. Commercial artists—United States. I. Prohaska, Ray. II. Title.

Commercial paraphernalia—Collectors and collecting.

GROSSHOLZ, Roselyn N. 680
The collectible classics from commerce / by Roselyn N. Grossholz. Erie, Pa. : Grossholz, c1975. 79 p. : ill. ; 28 cm. Bibliography: p. 79. [NK1125.G755] 76-353740
1. Commercial paraphernalia—Collectors and collecting. I. Title.

Commerical art as a profession.

RODEWALD, Fred C. 741.6'023
Commercial art as a business [by] Fred C. Rodewald and Edward M. Gottschall. 2d rev. ed. New York, Viking Press [1971] xvi, 173 p. forms. 24 cm. [NC1001.R6 1971] 79-125246 ISBN 0-670-23275-0 7.50
1. Commerical art as a profession. I. Gottschall, Edward M., joint author. II. Title.

Commerical art — Period.

SOCIETY of Modern Art. 655.3
M. A. C.; modern art collector. v. 1, no. 1-11; Sept. 1915-[1917? New York, Society of Modern Art] 1 v. in 2. illus. (part mounted, part col.) plates (part col.) 32 cm. monthly (irregular) No more published? Supplements with titles Poster art stamp supplement and Students supplement accompany some issues. [NC997.A1M22] 63-5166
1. Commerical art — Period. 2. Art — Period. I. Title. II. Title: Modern art collector.

Commerical art—Russia.

BOJKO, Szymon. 741.6'0947
New graphic design in revolutionary Russia [by] Szymon Bojko. [Translated from the Polish by Robert Strybel and Lech Zembrzuski]. New York, Praeger [1972] 156 p. illus. 21 x 22 cm. Bibliography: p. 154-155. [NC998.6.R9B6413] 72-78338 12.50
1. Commerical art—Russia. 2. Constructivism (Art)—Russia. I. Title. Pap. 5.95.

Communes (China)

CHIEN CHU HSUEH PAO. 711.40951
Plans and data on four Chinese communes. New York, U. S. Joint Publications Research Service, 1959. 79p. illus., maps. 27cm. (JPRS: 564-D) 'CSO: 2556-D.' Translated articles from Chien chu hsiien pao, no. 10 (1958) [AS36.U56 no. 564] 59-60974
1. Communes (China) I. Title. II. Series: U. S. Joint Publications Research Service, JPRS/DC-564

Communication—History.

MASSIN, 769'.5
Letter and image. Translated by Caroline Hillier and Vivienne Menkes. New York, Van Nostrand Reinhold Co. [1970] 286 p. illus. (part col.) 29 cm. Bibliography: p. 282-284. [NC997.M2913 1970] 72-114166
1. Communication—History. 2. Graphic arts—History. I. Title. BIP

Communication in architectural design.

KLIMENT, Stephen A. 658.4'5
Creative communications for a successful design practice / by Stephen A. Kliment. New York : Whitney Library of Design, 1977. 190 p. : ill ; 29 cm. Includes index. Bibliography: p. 181-183. [NA2750.K54 1977] 76-56257 ISBN 0-8230-7133-2 : 24.95
1. Communication in architectural design. 2. Communication in design. I. Title. BIP

Communication in design.

LEACH, Sid Delmar. 658'.91'729
Techniques of interior design rendering and presentation / Sid Delmar Leach. New York : Architectural Record Book, c1978. 213 p. : ill. (some col.) ; 23 x 28 cm. Includes index. [NK1510.L46] 77-13528 ISBN 0-07-036805-8 : 24.95
1. Communication in design. 2. Communication in architectural design. I. Title. BIP

Communication in design—Congresses.

FEDERAL Regional Design 729
Assembly/Western States, 1st, Colorado Women's College, 1975.
Federal Regional Design Assembly, Western States : Federal Regions VIII, IX, X, October 30-31, 1975, Denver, Colorado, Colorado Women's College, Houston Fine Arts Center / sponsored by the National Endowment for the Arts, with assistance from Department of the Interior, General Services Administration ; [editor, Mildred S. Friedman]. [Minneapolis : Walker Art Center, 1976?] 41 p. : ill. ; 28 cm. [NK1510.F37 1975] 77-355672
1. Communication in design—Congresses. 2. Federal government—United States. I.

Friedman, Mildred S. II. National Endowment for the Arts. III. United States. Dept. of the Interior. IV. United States. General Services Administration. V. Title.

Communism and art.

*BAXANDALL, Lee. comp. 335.438701
Marx & Engels on literature & art. St. Louis, Telos Press [1974, c1973] 175 p. 19 cm. Bibliography: p. 157-172. [HX521.S63] 73-93501 ISBN 0-914386-01-8 6.95
1. Marx, Karl, 1818-1883. 2. Engels, Friedrich, 1820-1895. 3. Communism and art. I. Morawski, Stefan. joint comp. II. Title.
Pbk. 2.95; ISBN 0-914386-02-6. BIP

LANG, Berel, comp. 701
Marxism and art; writings in aesthetics and criticism. Edited by Berel Lang and Forrest Williams. New York, McKay [1972] viii, 470 p. 23 cm. [HX521.L34] 77-185134
1. Communism and art. I. Williams, Forrest, joint comp. II. Title. BIP

SANCHEZ-VAZQUEZ, 700'.1
Art and society; essays in Marxist aesthetics, by Adolfo Sanchez Vasquez. Translated by Maro Riofrancos. New York, Monthly Review Press [1974, c1973] 287 p. 21 cm. Translation of Las ideas esteticas de Marx. Includes bibliographical references. [HX521.S313] 72-92025 ISBN 0-85345-269-5
1. Communism and art. 2. Communist aesthetics. I. Title. BIP

SANCHEZ VAZQUEZ, Adolfo 111.85
Art and society; essays in Marxist aesthetics. New York, Monthly Review Press, [1974, c1973] 287 p. 21 cm. Translation of Las ideas esteticas de Marx. Includes bibliographical references. [HX521.S313] ISBN 0-85345-269-5 3.95 (pbk.)
1. Communism and art. 2. Communist desthetics. I. Title.
L.C. card number for original ed.: 72-92025.

Communism and art—Addresses, essays, lectures.

SOLOMON, Maynard, 335.43'8'7011 comp.
Marxism and art; essays classic and contemporary, selected and with historical and critical commentary by Maynard Solomon. [1st ed.] New York, Knopf; [distributed by Random House] 1973. xvii, 649, xxvi p. ports. 25 cm. Includes bibliographies. [HX521.S63] 77-154902 ISBN 0-394-46195-9 15.00
1. Communism and art—Addresses, essays, lectures. I. Title.

SOLOMON, Maynard, 335.43'8'7011 comp.
Marxism and art: essays classic and contemporary, selected and with historical and critical commentary by Maynard Solomon. [1st ed.] New York, Vintage Books [1974, c1973] xvii, 649, xxvi p. illus. 21 cm. Bibliography: p. [611]-626. [HX521.S63 1974] 74-6340 ISBN 0-394-71228-5
1. Communism and art—Addresses, essays, lectures. I. Title.

Communism—China.

HUNTER, Edward, 1902- 777.55
The black book on Red China; the continuing revolt. New York, The Bookmailer [1958] 172p. 18cm. 'A Free Enterprise publication.' On cover: Review copy. 'Prepared ... for the Committee of One Million (against the Admission of Communist China to the United Nations) in cooperation with International Research on Communist Techniques, inc.' A59
1. Communism—China. 2. United Nations—China (People's Republic of China, 1949-) I. Title.

Communism—Russia—Caricatures and cartoons.

APON Record Corporation, 422.088
New York.
Komunisticky zverinee. Communist zoo. New York, c1961. unpaged (chiefly illus) 18x21cm. French and English. [NC1426.A6] 61-46014
1. Communism—Russia—Caricatures and cartoons. I. Title. II. Title: Communist zoo.

Communist aesthetics—Addresses, essays, lectures.

MARXIST-LENINIST 335.43'8'11185
aesthetics and life : a collection of articles [editors, I. Kulikova and A. Zis]. Moscow : Progress Publishers, 1976. 268 p. ; 21 cm. Translation of Marksistsko-leninskaia estetika i zhizn'. Includes bibliographical references. [BH41.M3513] 77-356779
1. Communist aesthetics—Addresses, essays, lectures. I. Kulikova, Irina Sergeevna. II. Zis', IA.

Community art projects.

ROSENBERG, Lilli Ann 709'.7471
Killen.
Children make murals and sculpture; experiences in community art projects. Photography by Ken Wittenberg. New York, Reinhold Book Corp. [1968] 132 p. illus. (part col.) 21 cm. [N352.R6] 68-16022
1. Community art projects. 2. Children as artists. I. Wittenberg, Ken, illus. II. Title.

Community art projects—United States.

MURPHY, Judith. 338.4'7'7
The place of the arts in new towns; a report [by Judy Murphy. New York] Educational Facilities Laboratories [1973] 72 p. illus. 28 cm. Includes bibliographical references. [NX504.M87] 73-90112 3.00 (pbk.)
1. Community art projects—United States. I. Educational Facilities Laboratories. II. Title. BIP

Community centers.

ALEXANDER, Christopher. 727'.9
A pattern language which generates multi-service centers [by] Christopher Alexander, Sara Ishikawa [and] Murray Silverstein. Berkeley, Calif., Center for Environmental Structure [1968] 283 p. illus. 28 cm. Includes bibliographical references. [HN42.A43] 78-548
1. Community centers. I. Ishikawa, Sara, joint author. II. Silverstein, Murray, joint author. III. Center for Environmental Structure. IV. Title.

STERNBERG, Eugene D. 725'.8
Community centers and student unions [by] Eugene and Barbara Sternberg. New York, Van Nostrand Reinhold Co. [1971] 319 p. illus., plans. 23 x 29 cm. Includes bibliographical references. [NA4510.C7S8 1971] 70-151719
1. Community centers. 2. Student unions. 3. Architecture—Designs and plans. I. Sternberg, Barbara, 1923- joint author. II. Title. BIP

Compasses (Mathematical instruments)

KOSTOVSKII, Aleksandr 513.1
Nikitich.
Geometrical constructions using compasses only. Translated from the Russian by Halina Moss, Translation editor: Ian N. Sneddon. Oxford, New York, Pergamon Press, 1961. 79p. illus. 22cm. (Popular lectures in mathematics series, v. 4) [QA464.K653 1961] 61-11527
1. Compasses (Mathematical instruments) 2. Circle. I. Title.

Composition (Art)

BETHERS, Ray, 1902- 751.4
Composition in pictures. 3d ed. New York, Pitman [1962] 244p. illus. 23cm. [ND1263.B4 1962] 62-5188

17cm. (Fountain photobk. ser.) 64-4261 2.95 bds.,
1. Composition (Photography) I. Title.

POORE, Henry Rankin, 1859-1940. 770'.11
Pictorial composition / Henry R. Poore. New York : Arno Press, 1979, [c1903] p. cm. (The Sources of modern photography) Reprint of the ed. published by Putnam, New York, under title: Pictorial composition and the critical judgment of pictures. [TR179.P66 1979] 76-24676 ISBN 0-405-09652-6 : 22.00
1. Composition (Photography) 2. Composition (Art) I. Title. II. Series.

WAGG, Alfred. 770.1
Composition in photography. New York, Greenberg, e1957. 128 p. illus. 20 cm. (The Modern camera guide series) [TR179.W3] 57-7368
1. Composition (Photography) I. Title.

Computer animation.

LEVITAN, Eli L. 778.5
Electronic imaging techniques : a handbook of conventional and computer-controlled animation, optical, and editing processes / Eli L. Levitan. New York : Van Nostrand Reinhold Co., 1977. 195 p. : ill. ; 24 cm. Includes index. [TR897.5.L48] 76-24376 ISBN 0-442-24771-0 : 16.50
1. Computer animation. 2. Video tape recorders and recording. 3. Video tapes—Editing. I. Title.

Computer art.

ARTIST and computer / 702.854
edited by Ruth Leavitt. New York : Harmony Books, c1976. ix, 121 p. : ill. (some col.) ; 28 cm. [N7433.8.A77] 76-440 ISBN 0-517-52787-1 : 10.95 ISBN 0-517-52735-9 pbk. : 4.95
1. Computer art. 2. Art, Modern—20th century. I. Leavitt, Ruth.

Computer art—Exhibitions.

COMPUTER 709'.73'074014766
genesis : a vision of the '70's : Joe and Emily Lowe Art Gallery, Sims Hall, Syracuse University, Syracuse, New York ... March 31 through May 3, 1977. Syracuse : The Gallery, c1977. [24] p. : ill. ; 27 cm. Catalog of an exhibition. Includes a bibliography. [N7433.8.C65] 77-151537
1. Computer art—Exhibitions. I. Joe and Emily Lowe Art Gallery.

Computer drawing.

FRANKE, Herbert W., 1927- 760'.028'5
Computer graphics; computer art [by] Herbert W. Franke. [London, New York] Phaidon [1971] 133 p. illus. 25 cm. Translation of Computergraphik-Computerkunst. Distributed in the U.S.A. by Praeger Publishers, 111 Fourth Ave., New York, N.Y. Bibliography: p. 126-131. [NC740.F713] 72-162314 ISBN 0-7148-1503-9 13.50 (U.S.)
1. Computer drawing. I. Title.

PRUEITT, Melvin L. 001.6'443
Computer graphics : 118 computer-generated designs / by Melvin L. Prueitt. New York : Dover Publications, 1975. viii, 69 p. : ill. (some col.) ; 28 cm. (Dover pictorial archive series) [NC740.P85] 74-18611 ISBN 0-486-23178-X pbk. : 3.00
1. Computer drawing. I. Title.

SUMNER, Lloyd. 744
Computer art and human response. [1st ed.] Charlottesville, Va., P. B. Victorius, 1968. 96 p. illus. (part col.) 16 x 24 cm. [NC740.S9] 70-2847 7.50
1. Computer drawing. I. Title.

Computer graphics.

CHENG, Tien-Ren Richard, 1934- 001.6'4'08 s
Coefficient generator and cursor for the stereomatrix 3-D display system, by Richard Tien-Ren Cheng. Urbana, Dept. of Computer Science, University of Illinois, 1971. viii, 90 p. illus. 28 cm. (UIUCDCS-R-71-484) Thesis—University of Illinois at Urbana-Champaign. "Supported in part by contract no. Atomic Energy Commission AT(11-1)1469." Bibliography: p. 81. [QA76.I4 no. 484] [T385] 621.3819'532 72-610342
1. Computer graphics. 2. Information display systems. I. Title. II. Series: Illinois. University at Urbana-Champaign. Dept. of Computer Science. Report no. 484.

FETTER, William A 744
Computer graphics in communication [by] William A. Fetter. New York, McGraw-Hill [1965] xii, 110 p. illus. 24 cm. (Engineering graphics monograph series) "Written for the Course content development study in engineering graphics." Bibliography: p. 105. [T357.F4] 65-21581
1. Computer graphics. I. Title.

KELLEY, Karl Cornell. 658.1
A computer graphics program for the generation of half-tone images with shadows. Detroit, Management Information Services, 1970. iv, 93 l. illus. 28 cm. Thesis (M.S.)—University of Illinois. Bibliography: leaves 92-93. [T385.K4] 79-127835
1. Computer graphics. I. Title.

SIDERS, R. A. 620.001
Computer graphics; a revolution in design. Authors: R. A. Siders [and others] New York, American Management Association [1966] 160 p. illus. 24 cm. Bibliography: p. 157-160. [T385.S5] 66-24180
1. Computer graphics.

SUGAYA, Hirotsugu. 001.6'4'08 s
Display of directed graphs for visual communication / by Hirotsugu Sugaya. Urbana : Dept. of Computer Science, University of Illinois at Urbana-Champaign, 1975. vi, 54 p. : ill. ; 28 cm. ([Report] - UIUCDCS-R-75 ; 735) Originally presented at the author's thesis (M.S.), University of Illinois. Bibliography: p. 53-54. [QA76.I4 no. 735] [T385] 001.55 75-623958
1. Computer graphics. I. Title. II. Series: Illinois. University at Urbana-Champaign. Dept. of Computer Science. Report ; 735.

Concentration camps—Pictorial works.

KANTOR, Alfred, 1923- 759.13
The book of Alfred Kantor. With a pref. by John Wykert. [1st ed.] New York, McGraw-Hill [1971] [42] p., 127 l. of col. illus. 25 cm. Some leaves have also illus. on verso. A facsimile of drawings made in 1945 of the author's experiences in the concentration camps of Terezin, Auschwitz and Schwarzheide during the period Dec. 1941-May 1945. [NC139.K3A43] 76-154228 ISBN 0-07-033275-4 17.95
1. Concentration camps—Pictorial works.

Conceptual art.

CELANT, Germano. 709'.046
Art povera. New York, Praeger Publishers [1969] 240 p. illus. 24 cm. Some captions in Italian or German. [N6494.C63C38 1969] 70-84095 8.95
1. Conceptual art. 2. Art, Modern—20th century. I. Title.

HIGGINS, Richard Carter. 720
Fantastic architecture [by] Wolf Vostell [and] Dick Higgins. [New York] Something Else Press [1971, c1969] 1 v. (unpaged) illus., facsims., maps, ports. 21 cm. Translation of Pop Architektur, by D. Higgins and W. Vostell. [N6494.C63H513] 74-117198 ISBN 0-87110-089-4 6.95
1. Conceptual art. 2. Architecture in art. I. Vostell, Wolf, 1932- joint author. II. Title.

LIPPARD, Lucy R. 709'.04
Six years: the dematerialization of the art object from 1966-1972 a cross-reference book of information on some esthetic boundaries ... edited and annotated by Lucy R. Lippard. New York, Praeger [1973] 272 p. illus. 23 cm. [N6494.C63L56] 78-189913 12.50
1. Conceptual art. 2. Art, Modern—20th century. I. Title.

MEYER, Ursula, 1915- comp. 709'.04
Conceptual art. [1st ed.] New York, Dutton, 1972. xx, 227 p. illus. 21 cm. Bibliography: p. 223-227. [N6494.C63M49 1972] 72-195118 ISBN 0-525-47271-1 3.45
1. Conceptual art. 2. Art, Modern—20th century. BIP

Conceptual art—Addresses, essays, lectures.

BATTCOCK, Gregory, 1937- comp. 709'.04
Idea art; a critical anthology. [1st ed.] New York, Dutton, 1973. xii, 203 p. illus. 19 cm. [NX600.C6B37 1973] 73-174858 ISBN 0-525-47344-0 3.50
1. Conceptual art—Addresses, essays, lectures. I. Title.
Contents omitted. BIP

Conceptual art—Exhibitions.

CONTEMPORARY Arts Museum. 709'.73'0740164
10 [Houston, Tex., 1972] 35 p. illus. (part col.) 22 cm. Cover title. "An exhibition organized by the Contemporary Arts Museum Houston, Texas, March 20-June 4, 1972." Contents.—John Alberty.—David Deutsch.—Robert Grosvenor.—Newton Harrison.—Paul Sharits.—Vera Simons.—Michael Snow.—Richard Van Buren.—Ellen Van Fleet.—William Wegman. [NX600.C6C6] 72-81108
1. Conceptual art—Exhibitions. I. Title.

DALY, Norman. 730'.92'4
The civilization of Llhuros; an exhibition of artifacts from the recent excavations of Vanibo, Houndee, Draikum, and other sites. Ithaca, N.Y. [Office of University Publications, Cornell University, 1972, c1971] 55 p. illus. 29 cm. Catalogue of a "pseudoanthropological" exhibition "organized by the Andrew Dickson White Museum of Art, Cornell University ... 1972." Llhuros was conceived and its artifacts executed by N. Daly. [NK839.D3C6] 72-188881
1. Cornell University. Andrew Dickson White Museum of Art. II. Title.

FORMULATION. 707.4'0144'5
[Andover, Mass., Addison Gallery of American Art, 1971] 1 v. (unpaged) illus. 21 cm. Cover title. Catalogue of an exhibition of ten European artists, held at the Addison Gallery of American Art, Jan. 8-Feb. 14, 1971. [N6494.C63F6] 76-198434
1. Conceptual art—Exhibitions. 2. Art, Modern—20th century—Europe. I. Philips Academy, Andover, Mass. Addison Gallery of American Art.

LICHT, Jennifer. 709'.04
Eight contemporary artists : [exhibition held at the Museum of Modern Art, New York, October 9, 1974-January 5, 1975] / Jennifer Licht. New York : Museum of Modern Art, c1974. 56 p., [1] fold. leaf of plates : ill. (some col.) ; 18 cm. Includes bibliographies. [NX600.C6L52] 74-84690 ISBN 0-87070-315-3
1. Conceptual art—Exhibitions. 2. Arts, Modern—20th century—Exhibitions. I. New York (City). Museum of Modern Art. II. Title.

THIS book is a movie; 700
an exhibition of language art & visual poetry, edited by Jerry G. Bowles & Tony Russell. [New York, Dell Pub. Co., 1971] 313 p. illus. 21 cm. (A Delta original) Cover title. [NX600.C6T5] 71-30786 3.25 ($3.75 Can)
1. Conceptual art—Exhibitions. I. Bowles, Jerry G., ed. II. Russell, Tony, 1935- ed. BIP

Conceptual art—United States.

ART work, no commercial value. 700'.973
Edited by Jerry G. Bowles. [New York, Grossman Publishers, 1972] 1 v. (unpaged) illus. 29 cm. [NX504.A85] 70-170612 ISBN 0-670-13721-9 10.00
1. Conceptual art—United States. I. Bowles, Jerry G., ed.

Conceptual art—United States—Addresses, essays, lectures.

INDIVIDUALS : 700'.973
post-movement art in America / edited by Alan Sondheim. New York : Dutton, c1977. xxx, 316 p. : ill. ; 21 cm. [NX504.I53 1977] 76-151894 ISBN 0-525-47428-5 : 7.95
1. Conceptual art—United States—Addresses, essays, lectures. 2. Arts, Modern—20th century—United States—Addresses, essays, lectures. 3. United States—Popular culture. I. Sondheim, Alan.

Concrete blocks.

GAGE, Michael Terence. 721'.044'4
Design in blockwork / Michael Gage, Tom Kirkbride. 2nd ed. London : Architectural Press, 1976. 121 p. : ill., diags., graphs, ports. ; 30 cm. Incorporates a revised version of Guide to concrete blockwork by M. Gage. Includes bibliographical references. [TH1491.G32 1976] 76-380537 ISBN 0-85139-161-3 : £4.95
1. Concrete blocks. 2. Concrete construction. I. Kirkbride, Tom W., joint author. II. Gage, Michael Terence. Guide to concrete blockwork. III. Title. BIP

Concrete construction.

COLLINS, Peter. 693.54
Concrete: the vision of a new architecture; a study of Auguste Perret and his precursors. New York, Horizon Press [1959] 307 p. illus., plans. 26 cm. Bibliographical references: p. 288-300. [NA4125.C6] 59-1958
1. Perret, Auguste, 1874-1954. 2. Concrete construction. 3. Architecture. I. Title.

Conde, Miguel.

CONDE, Miguel. 759.13
Miguel Conde, paintings and drawings : [catalogue of an exhibition held at] the Fruit Market Gallery, Edinburgh, Scotland, 10 July-7 August 1976. Edinburgh : Scottish Arts Council, 1976. [17] p. : chiefly ill. (some col.), port. ; 15 x 21 cm. At head of title: A Scottish Arts Council exhibiton. [N6537.C6F78] 77-363178 ISBN 0-902989-32-4 : £0.40
1. Conde, Miguel. I. Fruit Market Gallery. II. Scottish Arts Council.

Conder, Charles, 1868-1909.

HOFF, Ursula. 759.2
Charles Conder. [Melbourne, Lansdowne Press, 1972] 104 p. illus. (part col.) 31 cm. (Lansdowne Australian art library) Includes bibliographical references. [ND497.C65H59] 74-176947
1. Conder, Charles, 1868-1909. I. Title.

Conduct of life.

SEEGER, Dick. 760'.092'4
I've been thinking / thoughts by Dick Seeger ; graphics from Dick Seeger Designs ; assisted by Susan Ahearn. Scottsdale, Ariz. : Seeger, c1976. ca. 250 p. : ill. ; 23 cm. [BJ1581.2.S425] 76-45522
1. Conduct of life. I. Title.

Cone, Claribel.

POLLACK, Barbara. 706.992
The collectors: Dr. Claribel and Miss Etta Cone. With a portrait by Gertrude Stein. [1st ed.] Indianapolis, Bobbs-Merrill [1962] 320 p. illus., ports. 22 cm. "Two women, by Gertrude Stein": p. [273]-300. [N8384.C6P6] 61-9937
1. Cone, Claribel. 2. Cone, Etta. 3. Art—Collectors and collecting. I. Stein, Gertrude, 1874-1946. Two women. II. Title.

Coney, John, 1655-1722.

CLARKE, Hermann Frederick, 1882-1947. 739.2'3'724
John Coney, silversmith, 1655-1722. Introd. by Hollis French. New York, Da Capo Press, 1971 [c1932] xv, 59, [46] p. illus. 26 cm. (Da Capo Press series in

architecture and decorative art, v. 38) Includes bibliographical references. [NK7198.C6C6 1971] 71-87562 ISBN 0-306-71393-4
1. Coney, John, 1655-1722. **BIP**

Confectionery.

BARTON, Peggy Ann. 745.59'41
Step-by-step sugar artistry. Foreword by Richard V. Snyder. Photos. by John Barton and Leonard Shaffer. [1st ed.] Jericho, N.Y., Exposition Press [1974] 80 p. illus. 22 cm. (An Exposition-banner book) [TX799.B37] 74-75055 ISBN 0-682-47741-9 6.00
1. Confectionery. I. Title. **BIP**

Confectionery—Pictorial works.

ALCOSSER, Murray, 1937- 779'.9'664153
Sweets / by Murray Alcosser. New York : H. N. Abrams, [1978] p. cm. [TX791.A62] 78-9668 ISBN 0-8109-1629-0 : 17.50. ISBN 0-8109-2176-6 pbk. : 9.95
1. Confectionery—Pictorial works. I. Title. **BIP**

Conlon, William, 1941—

DALLAS. Museum of Fine Arts. 759.13
Four painters: Conlon, Cote, Hacklin, Rafoss. [Exhibition] Dallas Museum of Fine Arts, May 12-June 20, 1971. Dallas, [1971] [32] p. illus. (part col.) 22 x 25 cm. Bibliography: p. [31]-[32] [ND236.D3] 71-26592
1. Conlon, William, 1941- 2. Cote, Alan, 1937- 3. Hacklin, Allan, 1943- 4. Rafoss, Kaare, 1941- I. Title.

Connard, Philip, 1876-1958.

ORLEANS House Gallery. 759.2
Philip Connard: an exhibition of his work [held at] Orleans House Gallery, Twickenham, 26 May to 23 September 1973; with an introduction by Jane Connard. Richmond, [Amenities Committee of the London Borough of Richmond upon Thames], [1973]. 20 p. 23 x 11 cm. [ND497.C655O74 1973] 73-174475 ISBN 0-903704-14-5 £0.10
1. Connard, Philip, 1876-1958.

Connecticut—Capital and capitol.

CONNECTICUT Capitol Center. 711'.551
[Prepared on behalf of the Connecticut State Capitol Government Center Committee. Sketches by Nicholas Solovioff. Report presentation by the Barton-Gillet Company. Hartford, State Capitol Government Center Committee, 1967] 28 p. illus. (part col.), col. maps, plans. 28 cm. Issued in a case. [JK1651.C73C6 1967] 70-9356
1. Connecticut—Capital and capitol. I. Connecticut. State Capitol Government Center Committee. II. Barton-Gillet Company.

Conner, Bruce.

BRANDEIS University, Waltham, Mass. Poses Institute of Fine Arts. 741.9'73
Bruce Conner; sculpture, assemblages, drawings, films; a loan exhibition of the Poses Institute of Fine Arts. The Rose Art Museum, Bradeis University, September 20 -- October 24, 1965. [Waltham? Mass., 1965] 1 v. (unpaged) illus. 24 cm. [N6537.C65B7] 66-343
1. Conner, Bruce. I. Title.

PENNSYLVANIA. University. Institute of Contemporary Art. 709'.73
Bruce Conner: sculpture, assemblages, collages, drawings, films. [Philadelphia, 1967?] [24] p. illus. 22 cm. On label on t. p.: Supplied by Worldwide Books, New York. Exhibition held Nov. 29-Dec. 31, 1967, at the Institute of Contemporary Art, University of Pennsylvania. Bibliography: p. [22]-[23] [NB237.C615P4] 68-30098
I. Conner, Bruce. II. Title.

PENNSYLVANIA. University. Institute of Contemporary Art. 709'.73
Bruce Conner: sculpture, assemblages, collages, drawings, films. [Philadelphia, 1967?] [24] p. illus. 22 cm. On label on t.p.: Supplied by Worldwide Books, New York. Exhibition held Nov. 29-Dec. 31, 1967, at the Institute of Contemporary Art, University of Pennsylvania. Bibliography: p. [22]-[23] [NB237.C615P4] 68-30098
1. Conner, Bruce.

Connor, Russell.

KATSUSHIKA, Hokusai, 1760-1849. 759.952
Hokusai [by] Russell Connor. New York, Crown [1962] 19p. illus., col. plates. (Art of the East lib.) 62-1507 1.45 pap.,
1. Connor, Russell. I. Title. II. Series.

Constable, John, 1776-1837.

ALLHUSEN, Edward. 759.2
John Constable / by Edward Allhusen. London : Medici Society, 1976. 24 p. : ill. (chiefly col.), map, ports. (1 col.) ; 19 x 22 cm. (Medici art books) [ND497.C7A78] 76-380636 ISBN 0-85503-038-0 : £0.60
1. Constable, John, 1776-1837. I. Constable, John, 1776-1837.

CONSTABLE, John, 1776-1837. 759.2
Constable oil sketches [by] John Baskett. New York, Watson-Guptill Publications [1966] 82 p. 32 col. illus. 26 x 33 cm. Bibliography: p. 17-18. [ND497] 66-21806
I. Basket, John. II. Title.

CONSTABLE, John, 1776-1837. 759.2
Constable: paintings, drawings and watercolours; [text by] Basil Taylor. London, Phaidon, 1973. 240 p. chiefly illus. (some col.), facsim., ports. 29 cm. Distributed in the U.S.A. by Praeger, New York. Includes index. Bibliography: p. [236] [ND497.C7T38 1973] 72-79554 ISBN 0-7148-1594-2 25.00
1. Constable, John, 1776-1837. I. Taylor, Basil. II. Title.

CONSTABLE, John, 1776-1837. 759.2
John Constable. Text by Lawrence Gowing. New York, H. N. Abrams [1971] 24 p. illus. (part col.) 33 cm. (The Library of great painters. Portfolio ed.) Originally published under title: Constable, 1776-1837. [ND497.C7G6 1971] 78-130292 ISBN 0-8109-3000-5
I. Gowing, Lawrence. II. Title.

CONSTABLE, John, 1776-1837. 741.9'42
John Constable R. A., 1776-1837 : a catalogue of drawings and watercolours, with a selection of mezzotints by David Lucas after Constable for "English landscape scenery", in the Fitzwilliam Museum, Cambridge / [text by] Reg Gadney. [London] : Arts Council of Great Britain, 1976. 151 p. : ill. (some col.), facsims., ports. ; 24 cm. Includes index. Title on spine: Drawings & watercolours. [NC242.C5G33] 77-361638 ISBN 0-7287-0099-9
1. Constable, John, 1776-1837. I. Gadney, Reg, 1941- II. Cambridge. University. Fitzwilliam Museum. III. Arts Council of Great Britain. IV. Title: Drawings & watercolours.

FRASER, John Lloyd. 759.2 B
John Constable, 1776-1837 : the man and his mistress / John Lloyd Fraser. London : Hutchinson, 1976. 253 p., [9] leaves of plates : ill. ; 24 cm. Includes index. Bibliography: p. [239]-241. [ND497.C7F72] 76-362067 ISBN 0-09-125540-6 : £6.95
1. Constable, John, 1776-1837.

GADNEY, Reg, 1941- 759.2 B
Constable and his world / Reg Gadney. London : Thames and Hudson, c1976. 128 p. : ill. ; 24 cm. Includes index. Bibliography: p. 116. [ND497.C7G23] 76-357781 ISBN 0-500-13056-6 : £3.50
1. Constable, John, 1776-1837. I. Title.

GADNEY, Reg, 1971- 759.2 B
Constable and his world / Reg Gadney. 1st American ed. New York : Norton, 1976. 128 p. : ill. ; 24 cm. Includes index. Bibliography: p. 116. [ND497.C7G23 1976b] 76-365643 ISBN 0-393-04440-8 : 10.00
1. Constable, John, 1776-1837. I. Title.

GRETTON, Mary (Sturge) 759.2
Constable, by Mary Sturge Henderson. Freeport, N.Y., Books for Libraries Press [1971] xii, 239 p. illus. 23 cm. Reprint of the 1905 ed. Includes bibliographical references. [ND497.C7G7 1971] 70-165641 ISBN 0-8369-5950-7
1. Constable, John, 1776-1837.

PARRIS, Leslie. 759.2
Constable : paintings, watercolours & drawings / Leslie Parris, Ian Fleming-Williams, Conal Shields. London : Tate Gallery, 1976. 204 p., [9] leaves of plates : ill. (some col.) ; 30 cm. Catalog of an exhibition. Includes bibliographical references. [ND497.C7P37] 76-364252 ISBN 0-905005-05-8. ISBN 0-905005-00-7 pbk.
1. Constable, John, 1776-1837. I. Constable, John, 1776-1837. II. Fleming-Williams, Ian, joint author. III. Shields, Conal, joint author.

PAWSEY, James Thomas. 759.2 B
John Constable : paintings and countryside / written by James Pawsey. Ipswich : F. W. Pawsey and Sons, [1976] [1], 25 p. (2 fold.) : ill. (chiefly col.), map, ports. (1 col.) ; 25 cm. English text; English, French, and German foreword and captions. Bibliography: p. 2. [ND497.C7P39] 76-374582 £0.50
1. Constable, John, 1776-1837. 2. East Anglia in art. 3. East Anglia—Description and travel—Views. I. Constable, John, 1776-1837.

PEACOCK, Carlos 759.2
John Constable: the man and his work. Greenwich, Conn., N.Y. Graphic [c.1965] 148p. illus. (pt. col.) 30cm. [ND497.C7P4] 65-23505 12.00
1. Constable, John, 1776-1837. I. Title.

PEACOCK, Carlos. 759.2
John Constable: the man and his work. [Rev. ed.] Greenwich, Conn., New York Graphic Society [1971, c1965] 144 p. illus. (part col.) 30 cm. [ND497.C7P4 1971] 79-164882 ISBN 0-8212-0408-4 15.00
1. Constable, John, 1776-1837.

PEACOCK, Carlos. 759.2
John Constable: the man and his work. Greenwich, Conn., New York Graphic Society [1965] 148 p. illus. (part col.) 30 cm. [ND497.C7P4] 65-23505
1. Constable, John, 1776-1837.

POOL, Phoebe 759.2
John Constable. New York, Barnes & Noble [1964, c1963] 90p. illus. (pt. col.) port. 18cm. (Barnes & Noble art ser. No. 614) 64-1803 .75 pap.,
1. Constable, John 1776-1837. I. Title.

REYNOLDS, Graham. 759.2
Constable, the natural painter. New York, McGraw-Hill [1965] 238 p. plates (part mounted col.) 26 cm. Bibliography: p. 135-136. [ND497.C7R4] 65-25519
1. Constable, John, 1776-1837. I. Title.

REYNOLDS, Graham. 759.2
Constable, the natural painter. New York, Schocken Books [1969, c1965] 238 p. illus. 21 cm. Bibliography: p. 135-136. [ND497.C7R4 1969] 70-88217 2.95
1. Constable, John, 1776-1837. I. Title.

WALKER, John, Dec.24,1906- 759.2
John Constable / text by John Walker. New York : Abrams, 1979. p. cm. (The Library of great painters) Includes index. Bibliography: p. [ND497.C7W34] 78-2842 ISBN 0-8109-0752-6 : 28.50
1. Constable, John, 1776-1837. I. Constable, John, 1776-1837.

Constructivism.

RICKEY, George. 701.8
Constructivism; origins and evolution. New York, G. Braziller [1967] xi, 305 p. illus. 25 cm. Bibliography: p. 247-300. [N6490.R54] 67-24210
1. Constructivism. I. Title.

Constructivism (Architecture)—Russia.

KOPP, Anatole. 711.4'0947
Town and revolution; Soviet architecture and city planning, 1917-1935. Translated by Thomas E. Burton. New York, G. Braziller [1970] xii, 274 p. illus. 22 x 26 cm. Translation of Ville et revolution. Bibliography: p. 261-267. [NA1188.K613 1970] 70-103169 ISBN 0-8076-0554-9 15.00
1. Constructivism (Architecture)—Russia. 2. Architecture, Modern—20th century—Russia. 3. Cities and towns—Planning—Russia. I. Title. **BIP**

Constructivism (Art)

CIRCLE; international survey of constructive art. 709.04
Editors: J. L. Martin, Ben Nicholson [and] N. Gabo. New York, Praeger Publishers [1971] viii, 291 p. illus., plans. 27 cm. Bibliography: p. 282-284. [N6494.C64C5 1971] 78-118819 18.50
1. Constructivism (Art) I. Martin, John Leslie, Sir, 1908- ed. II. Nicholson, Ben, 1894- ed. III. Gabo, Naum, 1890- ed.

Constructivism (Art)—Addresses, essays, lectures.

BANN, Steven, comp. 709'.04
The tradition of constructivism. Edited and with an introd. by Steven Bann. New York, Viking Press [1974] xlix, 334 p. illus. 22 cm. (The Documents of 20th-century art) Bibliography: p. 303-334. [N6494.C64B36 1974] 72-75748 ISBN 0-670-72301-0 16.50
1. Constructivism (Art)—Addresses, essays, lectures. 2. Art, Modern—20th century—Addresses, essays, lectures. I. Title. II. Series.
Pbk; 4.95, ISBN 0-670-01956-9. **BIP**

Constructivism (Art)—Exhibitions.

ROWELL, Margit. 709'.04
The planar dimension : Europe, 1912-1932 / by Margit Rowell. New York : Solomon R. Guggenheim Foundation, 1979. 159 p. : ill. (some col.) ; 28 cm. Cover title: Planes. "Exhibition 79/1." Catalogue of an exhibition held at the Solomon R. Guggenheim Museum, New York. Includes bibliographical references. [N6494.C64R68] 78-74711 ISBN 0-89207-017-X pbk. : 12.95
1. Constructivism (Art)—Exhibitions. 2. Art, Modern—20th century—Exhibitions. I. Solomon R. Guggenheim Museum, New York. II. Title. III. Title: Planes. **BIP**

RUSSIAN art of the revolution. 709'.47'074014771
Works by Yurii Annenkov [and others. Exhibition] Andrew Dickson White Museum of Art, Feb. 24 through Mar. 25, 1971, Brooklyn Museum of Art, June 14 through July 25, 1971. Assisted by a grant from the New York State Council on the Arts. [Edited by Nita Jager. Ithaca, N.Y., Office of University Publications, Cornell University, c1970] [42] p., 56 plates. illus., ports. 25 cm. Introductory essay, chronology, and artists' biographies, by Sarah Bodine. Includes bibliographical references. [N6988.5.C64R8] 72-152344
1. Constructivism (Art)—Exhibitions. 2. Art, Modern—20th century—Russia. I. Jager, Nita, ed. II. Bodine, Sarah. III. Cornell University. Andrew Dickson White Museum of Art. IV. Brooklyn Institute of Arts and Sciences. Museum.

Constructivism (Art)—History.

ROTZLER, Willy. 709'.04
Constructive concepts : a history of constructive art from cubism to the present / Willy Rotzler. New York : Rizzoli, 1977. 299 p. : ill. (some col.) ; 29 cm. Translation of Konstruktive Konzepte. "The works of art illustrated are in the collection of the McCrory Corporation." "Catalog, collection of the McCrory Corporation, New York": p. 255-294. Includes bibliographical references and index. [N6494.C64R6713] 77-89937 38.50
1. Constructivism (Art)—History. 2. Art, Modern—20th century—History. I. McCrory Corporation. II. Title.

Constructivism (Art)—Russia—Catalogs.

CONSTRUCTIVISM & futurism 016.7
: Russian & other : [catalogue]. New York : Ex Libris, c1977. [160] p. : 776 ill. ; 31 cm. (Ex libris ; 6) Includes index. Bibliography: p. [160] [NX556.A1C66] 77-71400
1. Constructivism (Art)—Russia—Catalogs. 2. Arts, Modern—20th century—Russia—Catalogs. 3. Futurism (Art)—Italy—Catalogs. 4. Arts, Modern—20th century—Italy—Catalogs.

Contaflex camera.

COOPER, Joseph David, 1917- 771.31
Contaflex pocket companion. [New York] Universal Photo Bks. [dist. Amphoto, 1962, 1962, c. 1961] 94p. illus. 15cm (U-262) 62-14417 1.95, wire bdg.
1. Contaflex camera. 2. Photography—Handbooks. manuals, etc. I. Title.

FREYTAG, Heinrich. 770.2
The Contaflex way; the Contaflex photographer's companion. [English ed. translated and adapted by Hans Wolff] London, New York, Focal Press [1957] 312p. illus. 22cm. [TR263.C58F73] 57-3153
1. Contaflex camera. 2. Photography—Handbooks, manuals, etc. I. Title.

Contarex camera.

EMANUEL, Walter Daniel, 1908- 771.31
Contarex guide; how to use the Contarex and Contarex special single lens reflex cameras. New York, Focal Press; dist. Amphoto, New York [c. 1960] 95p. illus. 17cm. (The Camera guide)p 1.95plastic, 60-52171
1. Contarex camera. 2. Photography—Handbooks, manuals, etc. I. Title.

FREYTAG, Heinrich Walter 771.31
The Contarex way; the Contarex photograper's companion.[Tr. from German] New York, Focal Pr.[1961 dist. Amphoto, New York] 360p. illus. Bibl. 61-66235 8.95bds.,
1. Contarex camera. 2. Photography—Handbooks, manuals, etc. I. Title.

Contax camera.

EMANUEL, Walter Daniel, 1908- 770.2
Contax guide; working with Contax cameras. 6th rev. American ed. Hollywood-by-the Sea, Fla., Transatlantic Arts, 1953. 112 p. illus. 17 cm. (The Camera guide) A Focal Press book. [TR263.C6E5 1953] 53-12477
1. Contax camera. I. Title.

TYDINGS, Kenneth S 770.2
The Contax 35mm guide. New York, Greenberg, c1953. 127p. illus. 20cm. (The Modern camera guide series) [TR263.C6T9] 53-3534
1. Contax camera. I. Title.

Conversation piece (Portrait painting)

ENGLISH conversation 757'.9'0942
pictures of the eighteenth and early nineteenth centuries / with an introd. and notes by G. C. Williamson. New York : Hacker Art Books, 1975. viii, 31 p., [44] leaves of plates : ill. ; 29 cm. Reprint of the 1931 ed. published by B. T. Batsford, London, which contained some col. plates. Includes bibliographical references and index. [ND1304.E53 1975] 74-78420 ISBN 0-87817-157-6 lib.bdg. : 40.00
1. Conversion piece (Portrait painting)—Great Britain. I. Williamson, George Charles, 1858-1942.

PRAZ, Mario, 1896- 757.9
Conversation pieces; a survey of the informal group portrait in Europe and America. University Park, Pennsylvania State University Press [1971] 287 p. illus. (part col.) 29 cm. Translation of Scene di conversazione. Includes bibliographical references. [ND1304.P713] 76-127380 ISBN 0-271-00132-1 19.50
1. Conversation piece (Portrait painting) I. Title. BIP

Cooke, Jean, 1927—

WOODLANDS Art Gallery. 759.2'074'02162
Jean Cooke and Diana Cumming paintings and drawings : [catalogue of an exhibition held] 5 to 27 June 1976 [at] Woodlands Art Gallery. London : London Borough of Greenwich, [1976] [11] p. : ill. ; 21 cm. [N6797.C65W66] 77-367508 ISBN 0-9504033-9-3
1. Cooke, Jean, 1927- 2. Cumming, Diana. I. Cooke, Jean, 1927- II. Cumming, Diana. III. Title.

Cookery—Juvenile literature.

COBB, Vicki. 745.5
Arts and crafts you can eat. Illustrated by Peter Lippman. [1st ed.] Philadelphia, Lippincott [1974] 127 p. illus. 21 cm. Instructions for creating such artistic cuisine as mosaic salad, cheese intaglio, carved chocolate, pasta mobile, and peach pit ring. [TX652.5.C62] 73-13864 ISBN 0-397-31491-4 1.95 (pbk.)
1. Cookery—Juvenile literature. 2. Handicraft—Juvenile literature. I. Lippman, Peter J., illus. II. Title. BIP

HETZER, Linda. 745.5
Hobby crafts / crafts by Linda Hetzer ; photos. by Steven Mays, ill. by Sally Shimizu and Lynn Matus. Milwaukee : Raintree, c1978. p. cm. Includes instructions for projects involving cooking, tye-dyeing, and batiking and directions for constructing airplanes and kites. [TX652.5.H47] 77-28949 ISBN 0-8172-1180-2 lib.bdg. : 7.93
1. Cookery—Juvenile literature. 2. Tie-dyeing—Juvenile literature. 3. Batik—Juvenile literature. 4. Airplanes—Models—Juvenile literature. 5. Kites—Juvenile literature. I. Mays, Steven. II. Shimizu, Sally. III. Matus, Lynn. IV. Title. BIP

Cookery, Thai.

LAPCHAROEN, Supajee. 745.92'4'09593
Floral vegetable arrangements and recipes from Thailand / Supajee Lapcharoen. Silver Spring, Md. : Thai-American Pub. Co., [c1976] 51 p. : ill. (some col.) ; 23 cm. Cover title. [TX724.5.T5L36] 76-45491 6.00
1. Cookery, Thai. 2. Vegetable carving. 3. Artificial flowers. I. Title.

Cooky molds.

GREASER, Arlene. 745.5
Cookie cutters and molds; a study of cookie cutters, Turk's head molds, butter molds, and ice cream molds, by Arlene and Paul H. Greaser. Allentown, Pa., c1969. 171 p. illus. (part col.) 24 cm. Bibliography: p. 168-171. [NK8490.G7] 70-98944
1. Cooky molds. I. Greaser, Paul H., joint author. II. Title.

Cooky molds—Exhibitions.

HARDING, Anneliese. 745
The edible mass medium : traditional European cookie molds of the seventeenth, eighteenth, and nineteenth centuries : [catalogue] / by Anneliese Harding. Cambridge, Mass. : Busch-Reisinger Museum, Harvard University, 1975. p. cm. "Prepared to accompany the exhibition Traditional European cookie molds, November 6, 1975 through January 17, 1976 [Busch-Reisinger Museum, Harvard University]" Bibliography: p. [NK8490.H37] 75-34350 2.50
1. Cooky molds—Exhibitions. 2. Folk art—Europe, Northern—Exhibitions. I. Harvard University. Busch-Reisinger Museum of Germanic Culture. II. Title.

Coomaraswamy, Ananda Kentish, 1877-1947.

IYER, K. Bharatha, ed. 704
Art and thought, issued in honor of Dr. Ananda K Coomaraswamy on the occasion of his 70th birthday [Reissue] London, Luzac [dist. Mystic, Conn., Verry, 1965] xvi, 259p. illus. 26cm. Bibl. [N7443.C57] 49-4227 12.50
1. Coomaraswamy, Ananda Kentish, 1877-1947. 2. Art—Addresses, essays, lectures. 3. Philosophy—Addresses, essays, lectures. I. Title.

Coomaraswamy, Ananda Kentish, 1877-1947—Addresses, essays, lectures.

NARAVANE, Vishwanath S. 700'.92'4
Ananda K. Coomaraswamy / Vishwanath S. Naravane. Boston : Twayne Publishers, 1978, c1977. p. cm. (Twayne's world leaders series ; TWLS 75) Includes index. Bibliography: p. [DS435.7.C66N37] 78-5580 ISBN 0-8057-7722-9 lib. bdg. : 10.95
1. Coomaraswamy, Ananda Kentish, 1877-1947—Addresses, essays, lectures. BIP

Cooper, Ron, 1943—

COOPER, Ron, 1943- 709'.2'4
Ron Cooper; an exhibition organized by the La Jolla Museum of Contemporary Art, La Jolla, California, May 13-July 1, 1973. [La Jolla? Calif., 1973] 24 p. illus. (part col.) 23 x 30 cm. Catalog. [N6537.C657L34] 73-82571
1. Cooper, Ron, 1943- I. La Jolla Museum of Contemporary Art.

Cooper, Thomas Sidney, 1803-1902.

SARTIN, Stephen. 759.2 B
Thomas Sidney Cooper, C.V.O., R.A., 1803-1902 / [compiled] by Stephen Sartin. Leigh-on-Sea : F. Lewis, 1976. 79 p., [40] p. of plates : ill. (incl. 1 tipped in) ; 30 cm. Limited ed. of 500 copies. Bibliography: p. 79. [ND497.C73S27] 77-354191 ISBN 0-85317-037-1 : £15.50
1. Cooper, Thomas Sidney, 1803-1902. 2. Painters—Great Britain—Biography.

Cooper Union for the Advancement of Science and Art, New York. School of Art and Architecture.

COOPER Union for the Advancement of Science and Art, New York. School of Art and Architecture. 720'.71'17471
Education of an architect: a point of view. An exhibition by the Cooper Union School of Art & Architecture at the Museum of Modern Art, New York City, November 1971. [New York, 1971] 323 p. illus. (part col.) 31 cm. [NA2440.N47M873 1971] 74-184158
1. Cooper Union for the Advancement of Science and Art, New York. School of Art and Architecture. 2. Architecture—Exhibitions. 3. Architecture—Study and teaching—New York (City) I. New York (City). Museum of Modern Art. II. Title.

Cooper Union for the Advancement of Science and Art, New York (The building)

WAITE, John G., comp. 725'.21'097471
Iron architecture in New York City; two studies in industrial archeology: The Edgar Laing stores (1849), by John G. Waite [and] The Cooper Union (1853-59), compiled by William Rowe, III. Edited by John G. Waite. [Albany] New York State Historic Trust, 1972. 83, [17] p. illus. 29 cm. Includes bibliographical references. [NA6220.W34] 73-621396
1. Cooper Union for the Advancement of Science and Art, New York (The building) 2. New York (City). Edgar Laing Stores (The building) 3. Building, Iron and steel. 4. Architecture—Details. I. Waite, John G. The Edgar Laing stores (1849). 1972. II. Rowe, William, 1941- The Cooper Union (1853-59) 1972. III. Title.

Coorte, Adriaen, fl. 1683-1707.

BOL, Laurens Johannes, 1898- 759.9492
Adriaen Coorte : a unique late seventeenth century Dutch still-life painter / Laurens J. Bol ; [translated from the Dutch manuscript by Mrs. A. M. de Bruin]. Assen : Van Gorcum, 1977. vii, 122 p. : ill. (some col.) ; 26 cm. Includes bibliographical references and index. [ND653.C58B6413] 78-306569 ISBN 9-02-321516-8 : 21.75
1. Coorte, Adriaen, fl. 1683-1707.
Distributed by Humanities Press, Atlantic Highlands,NJ 07716 BIP

Copan, Honduras.

LONGYEAR, John Munro, 1914- 972
Copan ceramics: a study of southeastern Maya pottery. Washington, 1952. xiii, 114p. plates, maps (1 fold.) 30cm. (Carnegie Institution of Washington. Publication 597) Bibliography: p. 113-114. [F1435.1.C7L65] [F1435.1.C7L65] 970.657155 A53 A53
1. Copan, Honduras. 2. Pottery, Maya. I. Title. II. Series. BIP

Copenhagen. Kongelige Porcelonsfabrik.

OWEN, Pat. 738.27
The story of royal Copenhagen Christmas plates. [1st ed.] Dayton, Ohio, Viking Import House [1961- 1 v. (loose-leaf) illus. 24 cm. [NK4399.C6O94] 61-14905
1. Copenhagen. Kongelige Porcelonsfabrik. 2. Copenhagen porcelain.

Copenhagen porcelain.

OWEN, Pat 738.28
The story of Bing & Grondahl Christmas plates. Dayton, Ohio, Viking Import House, 1975 Burnham Lane [c.1962] 154p. illus. 24cm. 62-20284 7.50; loose-leaf bdg.
1. Copenhagen porcelain. 2. Bing & Grondahls porcelxnsfabrik, Aktieseskabet, Copenhagen. I. Title. BIP

OWEN, Pat 738.27
The story of royal Copenhagen Christmas plates. Dayton, Ohio, Viking Import House [1962]c.1961. 130p. (loose-leaf) illus. 23cm. 7.00
1. Copenhagen porcelain. 2. Copenhagen. Kongelige Porcelaensfabrik. I. Title. BIP

OWEN, Pat. 738.27
The story of royal Copenhagen Christmas plates. [1st ed.] Dayton, Ohio, Viking Import House [1961- 1 v. (loose-leaf) illus. 24 cm. [NK4399.C6O94] 61-14905
1. Copenhagen. Kongelige Porcelonsfabrik. 2. Copenhagen porcelain.

Copley, John Singleton, 1737-1815.

AMORY, Martha Babcock (Greene) 1812-1880. 759.13
The domestic and artistic life of John Singleton Copley. New York, Kennedy Galleries, 1969 [c1882] xii, 478 p. port. 24 cm. (Library of American art) "With notices of his works, and reminiscences of his son, Lord Lyndhurst, Lord High Chancellor of Great Britain." Includes bibliographical references. [ND237.C7A5 1969] 71-77698
1. Copley, John Singleton, 1737-1815. 2. Lyndhurst, John Singleton Copley, Baron, 1772-1863. I. Title.

AMORY, Martha Babcock (Greene) 1812-1880. 759.13 B
The domestic and artistic life of John Singleton Copley, R.A. With notices of his works, and reminiscences of his son, Lord Lyndhurst, High Chancellor of Great Britain. Freeport, N.Y., Books for Libraries Press [1970] xii, 478 p. port. 23 cm. Reprint of the 1882 ed. [ND237.C7A5 1970] 70-119925
1. Copley, John Singleton, 1737-1815. 2. Lyndhurst, John Singleton Copley, Baron, 1772-1863. I. Title. BIP

PROWN, Jules David 759.13
John Singleton Copley; 2v. Cambridge, Mass., Pub. for the Natl. Gallery of Art, Washington [by] Harvard [c.]1966. 2v.

(xxiv, 491p.) illus., geneal. tables, ports. 29cm. (Ailsa Mellon Bruce studies in Amer. art, 1) Contents.v.1. In America, 1738-1774.--v.2. In England, 1774-1815 Bibl. [ND237.C7P7] 66-13183 25.00 set, bxd.
1. Copley, John Singleton, 1737-1815. I. U.S. National Gallery of Art. II. Title. III. Series. BIP

RIPLEY, Elizabeth. 759.13 B
Copley; a biography. [1st ed.] Philadelphia, Lippincott [1967] 72 p. illus., ports. 26 cm. Bibliography: p. 70. A biography of the New England portrait painter who gained fame in both the colonies and England. Illustrated with reproductions of his works, and includes information on the subjects of his paintings. [ND497.C738R5] 92 AC 68
1. Copley, John Singleton, 1737-1815. I. Title.

U.S. National Gallery of Art 759.13
John Singleton Copley, 1738-1815 [catalogue of exhibition held at] National Gallery of Art, Smithsonian Institution, Washington; Metropolitan Museum of Art, New York; Museum of Fine Arts, Boston. New York, [October House, c.1965] 142p. illus. (pt. col.) port. 26cm. Bibl. [ND237.C7U5] 65-24371 12.00; 3.75 bds., pap.,
1. Copley, John Singleton, 1737-1815. I. New York. Metropolitan Museum of Art. II. Boston. Museum of Fine Arts. III. Title.

Copley, John Singleton, 1737-1815—Juvenile literature.

FLEXNER, James Thomas, 1908- 759.13 B
The double adventure of John Singleton Copley, first major painter of the new world. [1st ed.] Boston, Little, Brown [1969] 169 p. illus., ports. 22 cm. "This book is a reworking of material previously published in the author's books America's old masters and John Singleton Copley." Bibliography: p. [157]-158. A biography of the eighteenth-century painter who was America's first major artist. [ND237.C7F58] 92 69-10659 4.95
1. Copley, John Singleton, 1737-1815—Juvenile literature. I. Title.

Copley, John Singleton, 1738-1815.

PLATE, Robert. 759.13
John Singleton Copley; America's first great artist. [New York] McKay [1969] vi, 154 p. 16 plates. 22 cm. Bibliography: p. 146-149. A biography of America's first great artist who captured on canvas the great patriots of the Revolutionary War and whose precise techniques made him world famous. [ND237.C7P55] 92 69-12952 3.95
1. Copley, John Singleton, 1738-1815. I. Title.

Copperwork.

ELLIOT, Zena Marjorie. 739'.511
Working with copper / [Zena Elliot]. New York : Drake, 1976. 128 p. : ill. (some col.) ; 25 cm. Includes index. [TT250.E45] 76-1344 ISBN 0-8473-1078-7 : 7.95
1. Copperwork. I. Title. BIP

KRAMER, Karl Robert. 739.51
Coppercraft and silver made at home, by Karl Robert Kramer and Nora Kramer. Drawings by Joan Stoliar. Photos. by Keith B. Norris. New York, Greenberg [1957] 175p. illus. 27cm. (Arts and crafts series) [NK8100.K7] 57-11906
1. Copperwork. 2. Silversmithing. I. Kramer, Nora, joint author. II. Title. BIP

KRAMER, Karl Robert. 739'.511
Coppercraft and silver made at home, by Karl Robert Kramer and Nora Kramer. Drawings by John Stoliar, photos. by Keith B. Norris. New York, Dover Publications [1972] 175 p. illus. 26 cm. Reprint of the 1957 ed., issued in series: Arts and crafts series. [TT250.K73 1972] 70-178088 ISBN 0-486-22790-1 3.00
1. Copperwork. 2. Silverwork. I. Kramer, Nora, joint author. II. Title.

Copy art—United States—Addresses, essays, lectures.

COPY art : 760
the first complete guide to the copy machine / by Patrick Firpo ... [et al.]. New York : R. Marek Publishers, c1978. p. cm. Bibliography: p. [NE3000.C66] 78-15827 ISBN 0-399-90016-0 pbk. : 8.95
1. Copy art—United States—Addresses, essays, lectures. I. Firpo, Patrick. BIP

Copyists.

TRITHEMIUS, Johannes, 1462-1516. 745.6'1
In praise of scribes. De laude scriptorum. Edited with introd. by Klaus Arnold. Translated by Roland Behrendt. Lawrence, Kan., Coronado Press, 1974. viii, 111 p. illus. 22 cm. Includes bibliographical references. [Z105.T7413 1974] 74-77102 ISBN 0-87291-066-0 6.50
1. Copyists. I. Title. II. Title: De laude scriptorum.

Corcoran Gallery of Art, Washington, D.C.

CORCORAN Gallery of Art, Washington, D.C. Education Dept. 658'.91'708
Summer intern handbook / the Corcoran Gallery of Art, Education Department. Washington : The Gallery, 1977. [77] leaves : forms ; 29 cm. [N850.A87] 77-86471
1. Corcoran Gallery of Art, Washington, D.C. I. Title.

Cordoba. Catedral.

FOTOGRAFIA Industrial, S.A. 914.6'84
La Mezquita de Cordoba / [texto, fotografias, compaginacion, reproduccion, impresion y encuadernacion realizados por los equipos tecnicos de F.I.S.A.]. 1. ed. Barcelona : Escudo de Oro, 1976. 31 p. : ill. ; 24 cm. (Serie Monografias Escudo de Oro) Cover title. Text in English, French, German, and Spanish. [NA5811.C62F67 1976] 77-465054
1. Cordoba. Catedral. I. Title.

Corinth, Greece—Antiquities.

BRONEER, Oscar Theodore, 1894- 938'.7 s
The South Stoa and its Roman successors / by Oscar Broneer. Princeton, N.J. : American School of Classical Studies at Athens, 1954. xviii, 167 p., [42] leaves of plates (6 fold.) : ill. ; 31 cm. (Corinth ; v. 1, pt. 4) Includes bibliographical references and index. [DF261.C65A6 vol. 1, pt. 4] [NA285.C6] 938'.7 75-25700
1. Corinth, Greece. South Stoa. 2. Corinth, Greece—Antiquities. I. Title. II. Series: American School of Classical Studies at Athens. Corinth ; v. 1, pt. 4. BIP

Corinth, Greece. Odeum.

STURGEON, Mary Carol, 1943- 938'.7 s
Sculpture : the reliefs from the theater / by Mary C. Sturgeon. Princeton, N.J. : American School of Classical Studies at Athens, 1977. p. cm. (Corinth ; v. 9, pt. 2) A revision of the author's thesis, Bryn Mawr College, 1971. Bibliography: p. [DF261.C65A6 vol. 9, pt. 2] [NB91.C615] 733'.3'09387 77-383 ISBN 0-87661-092-0
1. Corinth, Greece. Odeum. 2. Friezes—Greece—Corinth. 3. Relief (Sculpture)—Greece—Corinth. I. Title. II. Series: American School of Classical Studies at Athens. Corinth ; v. 9, pt. 2.

Corinth, Greece. South Stoa.

BRONEER, Oscar Theodore, 1894- 938'.7 s
The South Stoa and its Roman successors / by Oscar Broneer. Princeton, N.J. : American School of Classical Studies at Athens, 1954. xviii, 167 p., [42] leaves of plates (6 fold.) : ill. ; 31 cm. (Corinth ; v. 1, pt. 4) Includes bibliographical references and index. [DF261.C65A6 vol. 1, pt. 4] [NA285.C6] 938'.7 75-25700
1. Corinth, Greece. South Stoa. 2. Corinth, Greece—Antiquities. I. Title. II. Series: American School of Classical Studies at Athens. Corinth ; v. 1, pt. 4. BIP

Corinth, Louis,1858-1925.

CORINTH, Louis, 1858-1925. 769'.92'4
Graphik von Lovis Corinth, 1858-1925 : [Austellung] Altonaer Museum in Hamburg, Norddeutsches Landesmuseum, 20. November 1974 bis 21. Januar 1975. [Katalogbearbeitung, Christine Knupp]. Hamburg : Altonaer Museum in Hamburg, 1975. [36] p. : ill. ; 24 cm. Bibliography: p. [35] [NE654.C64K58] 75-505028
1. Corinth, Louis, 1858-1925. I. Knupp, Christine. II. Altonaer Museum in Hamburg.

NEW York. Gallery of Modern Art Including the Huntington Hartford Collection. 759.3
Lovis Corinth; a retrospective exhibition in the Gallery of Modern Art, 22 September through 1 November 1964. New York, Foundation for Modern Art [1964] 53 p. illus. 24 cm. Bibliography: p. 38. [ND588.C5N4] 64-8059
1. Corinth, Louis,1858-1925. I. Title.

Cork craft.

PLOQUIN, Genevieve. 745.59'2
Cork toys you can make / by Genevieve Ploquin ; photos. by Jean-Pierre Tesson ; [translated by Maxine Hobson]. New York : Sterling Pub. Co., c1976. 32 p. : ill. (some col.) ; 22 cm. (Easy craft series) Translation of Bouchons dociles. Includes index. [TT190.5.P5613] 76-19817 ISBN 0-8069-5402-7 : ISBN 0-8069-5400-0 : 3.95 lib bdg : 3.99
1. Cork craft. 2. Toy making. I. Title. II. Series. BIP

Cork craft—Juvenile literature.

NEWSOME, Arden J. 745.51
Cork & wood crafts, by Arden J. Newsome. Illustrated by Nancy Coner. New York, Lion Press [1970] 63 p. illus. 27 cm. Instructions for making toys, gifts, party props, holiday decorations, and other objects from corks and pieces of wood found around the house. [TT190.5.N48 1970] 72-112370 ISBN 0-87460-228-9
1. Cork craft—Juvenile literature. 2. Woodwork—Juvenile literature. I. Coner, Nancy, illus. II. Title. BIP

Corne, Michele Felice, 1752-1845.

CORNE, Michele Felice, 1752-1845. 759.5
Michele Felice Corne, 1752-1845; versatile Neapolitan painter of Salem, Boston, & Newport. Foreword & notes by Philip Chadwick Foster Smith. Introd. by Nina Fletcher Little. [Salem, Mass.] Peabody Museum of Salem, 1972. xiv, 44 p. illus. (part col.) 28 cm. Catalog of a summer exhibition held in 1972 by the Peabody Museum of Salem. [ND623.C6977P42] 72-83502 ISBN 0-87577-042-8
1. Corne, Michele Felice, 1752-1845. I. Peabody Museum of Salem, Salem, Mass. BIP

Cornell, Joseph.

ASHTON, Dore. 709'.2'4
A Joseph Cornell album. With special contributions by John Ashbery [and others] and assorted ephemera, readings, decorations, and reproductions of works by Joseph Cornell. New York, Viking Press [1974] xiv, 240 p. illus. 23 x 25 cm. Includes bibliographical references. [N6537.C66A93 1974] 74-10815 ISBN 0-670-40884-0
1. Cornell, Joseph. I. Title.

CORNELL, Joseph. 709.73
An exhibition of works by Joseph Cornell. [Pasadena, Calif., Pasadena Art Museum, 1967?] 76 p. illus. (part col.) 18 cm. On label on t.p.: Supplied by Worldwide Books, New York. Catalog of an exhibition held Dec. 27, 1966 to Feb. 11, 1967, at the Pasadena Art Museum. [ND237.C74A43] 67-31771
1. Pasadena, Calif. Art Museum. II. Title.

CORNELL, Joseph. 709'.73
Joseph Cornell. New York, Solomon R. Guggenheim Museum, [1967] 55 p. illus. (part col.) 26 cm. Catalogue of an exhibition selected and presented by Diane Waldman at the Solomon R. Guggenheim Museum, May-June 1967. [ND237.C74S66] 67-25057
I. Waldman, Diane. II. Solomon R. Guggenheim Museum, New York.

CORNELL, Joseph. 709'.2'4
Joseph Cornell portfolio. [New York : Leo Castelli Gallery, c1976] 1 portfolio ([10] pieces, 43 leaves of plates : 44 ill.) ; 26 cm. Title from portfolio. "Portfolio-catalogue designed and edited by Sandra Leonard Starr." Catalogue of the exhibition held Feb. 28-Mar. 20, 1976 at the Leo Castelli Gallery, New York. Contents.Contents.—Barthelme, D. Cornell, prose-poem.—Copley, B. Joseph Cornell.—Curtis, T. A letter.—Hussey, H. L'esprit Cornell.—Kent, A. Joseph Cornell.—Levy, J. Joseph Cornell.—Mekas, J. Notes on films of Joseph Cornell.—Motherwell, R. Preface to a Joseph Cornell exhibition.—Namuth, H. A photograph of Cornell taken in the garden at Utopia Parkway, 1969.—Starr, S. L. Bibliography and catalogue of the exhibition. [NX512.Z9C67] 76-5561
1. Cornell, Joseph. I. Starr, Sandra Leonard. II. Leo Castelli Gallery. III. Title.

WALDMAN, Diane. 709'.2'4
Joseph Cornell / by Diane Waldman. New York : G. Braziller, 1976. p. cm. Bibliography: p. [N6537.C66W34] 76-16446 ISBN 0-8076-0833-5 : 17.50. ISBN 0-8076-0834-3 pbk. : 8.95
1. Cornell, Joseph. I. Cornell, Joseph. BIP

Cornhusk craft.

CRAWFORD, Marguerite Cain. 745.5
Cornshuck crafts; an illustrated handbook for teachers and hobbyists, by Marguerite Cain Crawford and Marietta Cain Fuller. [1st ed.] New York, Exposition Press [1967] 80 p. illus. 21 cm. [TT878.C7] 67-24260
1. Cornhusk craft. I. Fuller, Marietta Cain, joint author. BIP

Cornhusk craft—Juvenile literature.

FACKLAM, Margery. 745.5
Corn-husk crafts, by Margery Facklam & Patricia Phibbs. New York, Sterling Pub. Co. [1973] 48 p. illus. (part col.) 20 cm. (Little craft book series) Directions for dyeing, softening, and preserving corn husks and for making both useful and decorative items from this natural material. [TT878.F3 1973] 73-83446 ISBN 0-8069-5276-8 2.95
1. Cornhusk craft—Juvenile literature. I. Phibbs, Patricia, joint author. II. Title.
Library binding; 2.69, ISBN 0-8069-5275-X.

Cornwell, Dean, 1892-1960.

CORNWELL, Dean, 1892-1960. 759.13 B
Dean Cornwell : dean of illustrators / Patricia Janis Broder ; pref. By Norman Rockwell. New York : Balance House : distrubuted by Watson-Guptill Publications, 1978. 239 p. : chiefly ill. (some col.) ; 28 x 30 cm. Includes index. Bibliography: p. 235-236. [NC975.5.C65A4 1978] 78-4621 ISBN 0-8230-1269-7 : 35.00
1. Cornwell, Dean, 1892-1960. I. Broder, Patricia Janis. BIP

Corot, Jean Baptiste Camille, 1796-1875.

HOURS, Madeleine, 1913- 759.4
Jean-Baptiste-Camille Corot. New York, H. N. Abrams [1972] 167 p. illus. (part col.) 34 cm. (The Library of great painters) Bibliography: p. 167. [ND553.C8H77] 79-99240 ISBN 0-8109-0058-0 18.50
I. Corot, Jean Baptiste Camille, 1796-1875.

LEYMARIE, Jean. 759.4
Corot; biographical and critical study. Translated from the French by Stuart Gilbert. [Geneva] Skira; [distributed in the U.S. by World Pub. Co., Cleveland, 1966] 137 p. col. plates 19 cm. (The Taste of our time, v. 44) Bibliography: p. 121-[124] [ND553.C8L43] 66-15282
1. Corot, Jean Baptiste Camille, 1796-1875.

TAILLANDIER, Yvon. 759.4
Corot. [Translated from the French by Anne Ross] New York, Crown Publishers [1967] 93, [2] p. illus. (part col.) 29 cm. Bibliography: p. 93-[94] [ND553.C8T33] 67-31825
1. Corot, Jean Baptiste Camille, 1796-1875. BIP

Correctional institutions—Design and construction—Competitions.

HUTCHINGS, Bruce L. 725'.6
National student competition on correctional architecture : co-sponsored by the American Institute of Architects ... National Clearinghouse for Criminal Justice Planning and Architecture ... / Bruce L. Hutchings ; assisted by James M. Smith, Larry M. Buckley, Diane Vanko. Urbana : National Clearinghouse for Criminal Justice Planning and Architecture, Dept. of Architecture, University of Illinois, c1973. 84 p. : ill. ; 28 cm. Bibliography: p. 83-84. [HV8805.H87] 74-623291
1. Correctional institutions—Design and construction—Competitions. I. American Institute of Architects. II. National Clearinghouse for Criminal Justice Planning and Architecture. III. Title.

Correggio, Antonio Allegri, known as, 1489?-1534.

GHIDIGLIA Quintavalle, 759.5
Augusta.
Correggio; the frescoes in San Giovanni Evangelista in Parma. Pref. by Roberto Longhi. [Translated by Olga Ragusa] New York, H. N. Abrams [1964?] 61 p. illus. (1 mounted col.) facsim., 42 col. plates. 33 cm. Translation of Gil affreschi del Correggio in San Giovanni Evangelista a Parma. Bibliographical references included in "Notes" (p. 59-60) Bibliography: p. 61. [ND623.C7G513] 64-10758
1. Correggio, Antonio Allegri, known as, 1494-1534. 2. Parma. San Giovanni Evangelista (Church) I. Longhi, Roberto, 1390- . II. Title.

GOULD, Cecil Hilton Monk, 759.5
1918-
The paintings of Correggio / Cecil Gould. Ithaca, N.Y. : Cornell University Press, 1976. 307 p., [102] leaves of plates : ill. (some col.) ; 29 cm. Includes index. Bibliography: p. 290-295. [ND623.C7G58] 75-16813 ISBN 0-8014-0973-X : 85.00
1. Correggio, Antonio Allegri, known as, 1489?-1534. I. Title. BIP

POPHAM, Arthur Ewart, 741.91
1889-
Correggio's drawings. London, Published for the British Academy by Oxford University Press, 1957. xix, 218p. illus., 110 plates. 30cm. Catalogue: p. [147]-210. Bibliography: p. xiv. [ND623.C7P6] 58-1175
1. Correggio, Antonio Allegri, known as, 1494-1534. I. Title.

Corsages.

ALDRIDGE, Dora Maud 635.9664
(Thompson)
Make your own corsage;you don't need orchids. Edited by Elizabeth Thompson and Catherine Laughlin; photography by Jimmie Jones Studios. Philadelphia, Dorrance [1955] 118p. illus. 24cm. [SB449.5.C6A4] 55-10984
1. Corsages. I. Title.

BIDDLE, Dorothy, 1887- 635.9664
Making corsages at home [by] Dorothy Biddle and Dorothea Blom. Drawings by Georgina Falk. New York, M. Barrows [1952] 64 p. illus. 21 cm. [SB449.5.C6B5] 52-8924
1. Corsages. I. Title.

DRUMMOND, Mary Hazel. 635.9664
Styling corsages with garden flowers. Drawings by Lani. New York, Macmillan, 1953. 247 p. illus. 21 cm. [SB449.5.C6D78] 53-1258
1. Corsages. I. Title.

LOCHRY, Marie Antonette, 635.9664
1891-
Corsages of pods and cones; a handbook for the hobbyist. [Seattle?] Chieftain Press, 1955. 89 p. illus. 24 cm. [SB449.5.C6L6] 56-22938
1. Corsages. I. Title.

REUSCH, Glad, 1891- 635.9664
Corsage craft, by Glad Reusch and Mary Noble. Sketches by Glad Reusch. Princeton, N.J., Van Nostrand [1960] 189 p. illus. 24 cm. [SB449.5.C6R49 1960] 60-10290
1. Corsages. I. Noble, Mary, joint author. II. Title.

Cosmas, Saint—Art.

SKROBUCHA, Heinz 704.9486
The patrons of doctors. [Tr. from German by Hans Hermann Rosenwald] Recklinghausen, A. Bongers; dist. by Taplinger [New York, 1965] 66 p. illus. (pt. col.) 18cm. (Pictorial lib. of Eastern Church art, v. 7) Tr. of Lpsmas und Damian. [N8080.S5513] 67-16579 2.50 bds.,
1. Damianus, Saint—Art. 2. Cosmas, Saint—Art. I. Title.

Cosmetics—History.

ANGELOGLOU, Maggie. 391'.63'09
A history of make-up. [1st American ed. New York] Macmillan [1970] 143 p. illus. (part col.), ports. 26 cm. Bibliography: p. 141-142. [GT2340.A5 1970] 74-114232 8.95
1. Cosmetics—History. I. Title.

CORSON, Richard. 391'.63'09
Fashions in makeup; from ancient to modern times. New York, Universe Books [1972] xxiv, 614 p. illus. 26 cm. Bibliography: p. 594-600. [GT2340.C67] 71-186143 ISBN 0-87663-152-9 30.00
1. Cosmetics—History. I. Title.

Cosmology in art.

PIPER, Raymond Frank. 709'.04
Cosmic art / Raymond F. Piper and Lila K. Piper ; edited and with foreword by Ingo Swann. New York : Hawthorn Books, c1975. xxii, 152 p., [8] leaves of plates : ill. (some col.) ; 29 cm. Includes index. Bibliography: p. 143-147. [N6490.P535 1975] 73-19379 ISBN 0-8015-1774-5 : 16.50
1. Cosmology in art. 2. Art, Modern—20th century. I. Piper, Lila K., 1896- joint author. II. Title.

Costume.

ARADOON, Zarifa. 646.4'7
The belly dance costume book : all of the lore, lure, and merriment of making a costume / Zarifa Aradoon. Stanford, Calif. : Dream Place Publications, c1978. 202 : ill. ; 28 cm. Bibliography: p. 190. [TT633.A73] 77-88919 ISBN 0-930486-00-5 : 10.95
1. Costume. 2. Belly dance. I. Title. BIP

BROOKE, Iris. 746.9'09
Medieval theatre costume: a practical guide to the construction of garments. New York, Theatre Arts Books [1967] 111 p. illus. 26 cm. [PN2067.B75 1967b] 67-25699
1. Costume. I. Title. BIP

IVES, Suzy. 646.4'7
Creating children's costumes from paper and card. New York, Taplinger Pub. Co. [1973] 95 p. illus. 23 cm. Instructions for using inexpensive or waste materials to make head and body coverings for owl, bird, dragon, elephant, hippopotamus, and other costumes. [TT633.I9 1973] 72-12431 ISBN 0-8008-1985-3 6.50
1. Costume. 2. Paper work. I. Title. BIP

LOBLEY, Priscilla. 646.4'06
Making children's costumes. New York, Taplinger Pub. Co. [1972] 95 p. illus. 26 cm. [GT1750.L6] 77-185256 ISBN 0-8008-5077-7 7.95
1. Costume. 2. Dressmaking. I. Title.

PARISH, Peggy. 646.4'7
Costumes to make. Illustrated by Lynn Sweat. [New York] Macmillan [1970] 111 p. illus. 25 cm. Detailed instructions for making costumes representative of historical periods, foreign countries, holidays, and storybook characters. [TT560.P36] 75-102969 3.95
1. Costume. I. Sweat, Lynn, illus. II. Title. BIP

POINTILLART, Marie- 745.59'41
Blanche.
Costumes from crepe paper. [Translated by Manly Banister] New York, Sterling Pub. Co. [1974] 48 p. illus. (part col.) 20 cm. (Little craft book series) Translation of Savoir faire des costumes en papier crepon. Gives instructions for using crepe paper to make ten costumes, including buttercup, clown, Egyptian girl, and Indian costumes. [TT633.P6413 1974] 73-93599 ISBN 0-8069-5302-0 3.50
1. Costume. 2. Paper work. I. Title.
Library binding, 3.29; ISBN 0-8069-5303-9 BIP

Costume—Australia—History.

MARTYN, Norma. 746.9'2'0994
The look : Australian women in their fashion / by Norma Martyn. Stanmore, N.S.W. : Cassell Australia, 1976. ix, 227 p. : ill. ; 30 cm. [GT1590.M37] 76-370656 ISBN 0-7269-5445-4
1. Costume—Australia—History. I. Title.

Costume—China.

CAMMANN, Schuyler. 391.0951
China's dragon robes. New York, Ronald Press Co. [1952] vii, 230 p. illus. 24 cm. Bibliographical footnotes. "Bibliography of the principal oriental sources":p. 187-188. [GT1755.C5C3] 52-94620
1. Costume—China. 2. China—Court and courtiers. I. Title.

Costume, Chinese—Exhibitions.

NEW York (City). 746.9'2
Metropolitan Museum of Art.
Costumes from the Forbidden City, by Alan Priest, curator of Far Eastern Art. New York, Metropolitan Museum of Art, 1945. [New York] Arno Press, 1974. 16 p., 56 p. of illus. 29 cm. Catalog of an exhibition held Mar.-May 1945. [NK4783.P44N48 1974] 74-168427 ISBN 0-405-02265-4
1. Costume, Chinese—Exhibitions. 2. Costume, Chinese—Peking. 3. Embroidery—China—Exhibitions. 4. Textile fabrics—China—Exhibitions. I. Priest, Alan, 1898-1969. II. Title. BIP

Costume design.

BROCKMAN, Helen L 687.101
The theory of fashion design [by] Helen L. Brockman. New York, Wiley [1965] xii, 332 p. illus., ports. 27 cm. Bibliography: p. 325. [TT507.B68] 65-25852
1. Costume design. I. Title. BIP

CAIN, Gertrude, 1899- 687.12
The American way of designing. New York, Fairchild Publications [1950] 115 p. illus. 22 cm. Includes bibliographies. [TT507.C3] 51-9144
1. Costume design. I. Title.

CHIERICHETTI, David. 791.43'02'6
Hollywood costume design / David Chierichetti. New York : Harmony Books, c1976. 192 p. : ill. ; 29 cm. Includes index. Filmography: p. 169-188. [TT507.C54 1976] 76-6729 ISBN 0-517-52637-9 : 15.00
*1. Costume design. 2. Costume. I. Title.*BIP

DOTEN, Hazel Ruth, 1892- 741.67
Fashion drawing, how to do it, by Hazel R. Doten and Constance Boulard. Rev. ed. New York, Harper [1953] 224 p. illus. 29 cm. [TT509.D67 1953] 53-8025
1. Costume design. 2. Drawing—Instruction. 3. Anatomy, Artistic. 4. Clothing and dress. 5. Costume. I. Boulard, Constance Augusta, 1899- joint author. II. Title.

EVANS, Mary, 1890- 646.4'7
How to make historic American costumes / by Mary Evans ; illustrated by Elizabeth Brooks. Detroit : Gale Research Co., 1976, c1942. xii, 178 p. : ill. ; 24 cm. Reprint of the ed. published by A. S. Barnes, New York. Includes index. Bibliography: p. 171-173. [TT507.E83 1976] 78-159952 ISBN 0-8103-4141-7 : 11.00
1. Costume design. 2. Costume—United States. I. Title. BIP

FERNALD, Mary. 746.9
Costume design & making: a practical handbook, by Mary Fernald in collaboration with Eileen Shenton. [2d ed.] New York, Theatre Arts Books [1967] 159 p. illus. 23 cm. Bibliography: p. 159. [PN2067.F4 1967] 67-14505
1. Costume design. 2. Costume—History. 3. Garment cutting. I. Shenton, Eileen. II. Title. BIP

HILLHOUSE, Marion Strong, 646.3
1900-
Dress selection and design. New York, Macmillan [1963] 216 p. illus. 29 cm. (The Macmillan college home economics series) [TT507.H53] 63-7779
1. Costume design. 2. Clothing and dress. I. Title.

IRELAND, Patrick John. 746.9'2
Every woman's book of fashion design, by P. J. Ireland. New York, Drake Publishers [1972] 128 p. illus. 21 cm. [TT507.I67] 76-188255 ISBN 0-87749-233-6 5.95
1. Costume design. I. Title.

JAFFE, Hilde. 746.9'2
Draping for fashion design / Hilde Jaffe, Nurie Relis. Reston, Va. : Reston Pub. Co., [1975] c1973. x, 166 p. : ill. ; 25 cm. Includes index. [TT507.J34 1975] 75-9791 ISBN 0-87909-210-6 : 10.95
1. Costume design. 2. Dressmaking—Pattern design. I. Relis, Nurie, 1929- joint author. II. Title. BIP

LEESE, 791.43'026'0922 B
Elizabeth, 1937-
Costume design in the movies / [by] Elizabeth Leese. Bembridge : BCW Publishing Ltd, 1976. 166, [2] p. : ill. (some col.), ports. ; 31 cm. Ill., port. on lining papers. Includes index. [TT507.L42] 77-361474 ISBN 0-904159-32-9 : £8.50
1. Costume design. 2. Costume designers. 3. Costume. I. Title. BIP

LEWIS, Diehl. 646.4
Patternless fashions [by] Diehl Lewis & May Loh. [Newly rev. ed.] Washington, Acropolis Books [1973] xi, 243 p. illus. 26 cm. At head of title: Make it yourself from a picture. Earlier (1968) ed., by May Loh and Diehl Lewis, published under title: Patternless fashion design. [TT520.L66 1973] 73-168299 5.95
1. Costume design. 2. Dressmaking. I. Loh, May, joint author. II. Title.

LIPSON, Louis. *687.12 646
Textbook of practical costume designing ... [3d, rev. ed. Los Angeles, 1951, c1950] 220 p. illus. 37 cm. First published in 1940 under title: Textbook of Lipson's complete practical artistic costume design. [TT507.L56 1951] 52-24489
1. Costume design. 2. Textile industry and fabrics. I. Title.

LOH, May. 646.4
Patternless fashion design, by May Loh & Diehl Lewis. Illus. by Lin Cheng-chun. [Manassas, Va., D. Lewis] 1968. x, 232 p. illus. 27 cm. Newly rev. ed. (1973) by Diehl Lewis and May Loh published under title: Patternless fashions. [TT520.L83] 79-2490
1. Costume design. 2. Dressmaking. I. Lewis, Diehl, joint author. II. Title.

MCJIMSEY, Harriet Tilden. 646'.3
Art and fashion in clothing selection [by] Harriet T. McJimsey. 2d ed. Ames, Iowa

State University Press, 1973. ix, 284 p. illus. 23 cm. Published in 1956 under title: Costume selection. Bibliography: p. 276-277. [TT507.M34 1973] 72-1958 ISBN 0-8138-0150-8 12.50
1. Costume design. 2. Fashion. I. Title. **BIP**

MCJIMSEY, Harriet Tilden. 646.01
Art in clothing selection. New York, Harper & Row [1963] 300 p. illus. 24 cm. (Harper's home economics series) "In its original version, this book was published ... under the title Costume selection." [TT507.M34 1963] 63-7104
1. Costume design. 2. Fashion. I. Title.

MCJIMSEY, Harriet Tilden. 646.01
Costume selection. [Rev. ed.] Minneapolis, Burgess Pub. Co. [1956, c1955] 143p. illus. 28cm. [TT507.M34 1956] 57-1139
1. Costume design. I. Title.

MOTLEY, pseud. 792.026
Designing and making stage costumes. [American ed. adapted by Susan E. Meyer] New York, Watson-Guptill Publications [1965, c1964] 143 p. illus. (part col.) 27 cm. Bibliography: p. 140-141. [TT507.M73 1965] 65-25308
1. Costume design. I. Title.

NAYLOR, Brenda. 687/.101
The technique of dress design. London, Batsford; Newton Centre, Mass., Branford, 1967. [1], 154p. illus. (some col) 26cm. [TT507.N3 1967] 67-23469 11.95
1. Costume design. I. Title.

PHILIPSON, Norman W. 745.4'02'46464
Creative design for fashion and embroidery / [by] Norman W. Philipson. London : Studio Vista, 1976. 96 p. : ill. (some col.) ; 26 cm. Includes index. Bibliography: p. 94. [TT507.P45] 77-354087 ISBN 0-289-70588-6 : £3.95
1. Costume design. 2. Embroidery. 3. Design. I. Title.

PICKEN, Mary (Brooks) 1886- 687.1
Dressmakers of France; the who, how, and why of the French couture, by Mary Brooks Picken and Dora Loues Miller. Layout and book design by Claire Valentine; drawings by Patricia Rowe Waters. New York, Harper [1956] New York, Harper [1959] 178p. illus. 24cm. 8p. 23cm. TT505.A1P5 Suppl. [TT505.A1P5] 56-6040
1. Costume design. 2. Fashion. I. Miller, Dora Loues, joint author. II. Title. III. Title: —Eight new designers a supplement.

SHARAFF, Irene. 746.9'2'0924 B
Broadway & Hollywood : costumes designed by Irene Sharaff / Irene Sharaff. New York : Van Nostrand Reinhold Co., 1976. 136 p. : ill. (some col.) ; 24 cm. Includes index. [TT505.S5A33] 75-43903 ISBN 0-442-27527-7 : 12.50
1. Sharaff, Irene. 2. Costume design. I. Title.

SHELDEN, Martha Gene. 646.4'3'04
Design through draping. Illustrated by Ray W. Hellberg. Minneapolis, Burgess Pub. Co. [1967] iii, 153 p. illus. 26 cm. Includes bibliographies. [TT507.S53] 67-26277
1. Costume design. 2. Dressmaking. I. Title. **BIP**

SHELDEN, Martha Gene. 646.4'3'04
Design through draping. Illustrated by Laura Lathrop Haynie. 2d ed. Minneapolis, Burgess Pub. Co. [1974] vi, 138 p. illus. 28 cm. Bibliography: p. 130-131. [TT507.S53 1974] 74-78568 ISBN 0-8087-1906-8 4.95 (pbk.)
1. Costume design. 2. Dressmaking—Pattern design. I. Title.

TATE, Sharon Lee. 746.9'2
Inside fashion design / Sharon Lee Tate ; illustrated by Mona Shafer Edwards ; photos. by Larry Kastendiek. San Francisco : Canfield Press, c1977. 308 p. : ill. ; 29 cm. Includes index. [TT507.T38] 76-44872 ISBN 0-06-453504-5 : 13.95
1. Costume design. I. Title. **BIP**

TIME-LIFE Books. 746.9'2
Creative design / by the editors of Time-Life Books. New York : Time-Life Books, [1975] 184 p. : col. ill. ; 29 cm. (The Art of sewing) [TT507.T53 1975] 74-29449 8.95
1. Costume design. 2. Needlework. I. Title. **BIP**

TOMPKINS, Julia. 646.4'7
Easy-to-make costumes for stage and school / Julia Tompkins ; with drawings by Joyce Asser ; diagrs. by the author. Boston : Plays, inc., 1976, c1975. viii, 152 p. : ill. ; 23 cm. First published under title: More stage costumes and how to make them. Includes index. [TT507.T63 1976] 75-28277 ISBN 0-8238-0205-1 : 7.95
1. Costume design. I. Title.

TRIPPON, George W. 746.9'2
Becoming a dress designer; what every designer should know, by George W. Trippon. [Los Angeles, Trippon Fashion Center, 1970] 157 p. illus., port. 29 cm. [TT507.T84] 70-146213
1. Costume design. I. Title.

WESTERMAN, Maxine. 746.9'2
Elementary fashion design and trade sketching : [a workbook for the beginner] / written and illustrated by Maxine Westerman. New York : Fairchild Publications, [1973] 111 p., [6] leaves of plates : ill. ; 31 cm. [TT507.W43] 75-306464 ISBN 0-87005-103-2 : 6.95
1. Costume design. 2. Fashion drawing. I. Title. **BIP**

Costume design—History.

LYNAM, Ruth. 746.9'2
Couture; an illustrated history of the great Paris designers and their creations. Edited by Ruth Lynam, with an introd. by Nancy White. [1st ed. in the U.S.A.] Garden City, N.Y., Doubleday, 1972. 256 p. illus. 31 cm. [TT507.L96] 72-80012 25.00
1. Costume design—History. 2. Fashion—History. 3. Costume designers—Paris—Biography. 4. Paris—Biography. I. Title.

Costume design—Vocational guidance.

FASHION Group. 746.9
Your future in fashion design. Contributors: Stephanie Cartwright [others] Rebecca Warfield, coordinator. Portraits by Dora. [1st ed.] New York, Rosen [1966] 143p. ports. 22cm. (Careers in depth) [TT507.F35] 66-10996 3.78 lib. ed.,
1. Costume design—Vocational guidance. I. Title.

FASHION Group. 746.9
Your future in fashion design. Contributors: Stephanie Cartwright [and others] Rebecca Warfield, Coordinator. Portraits by Dora. [1st ed.] New York, R. Rosen Press [1966] 143 p. ports. 22 cm. (Careers in depth) [TT507.F35] 66-10996
1. Costume design — Vocational guidance. I. Title.

FASHION Group. 746.9'2
Your future in fashion design [by] members of Fashion Group, inc. Contributors: Stephanie Cartwright [and others] Rebecca Warfield, coordinator. Portraits by Dora. [Rev. ed.] New York, Arco [1971] 143 p. illus., ports. 21 cm. (Arco-Rosen career guidance series) Fifteen prominent designers in the fashion industry discuss the rewards and requirements of careers in their design specialities, such as separates, custom order clothes, sportswear, accessories, and shoes. [TT507.F35 1971] 72-114123 ISBN 0-668-02243-4 1.95
1. Costume design—Vocational guidance. I. Dora, illus. II. Title.

KOLODNY, Rosalie. 687'.12'023
Fashion design for moderns. New York, Fairchild Pubns. [1968] 128p. illus., ports. 26cm. Bibl. [TT507.K725] 67-16799 5.95; 4.25 pap.,; text, 3.40
1. Costume design—Vocational guidance. I. Title. **BIP**

Costume designers—Biography.

AMERICAN fashion 746.9'2'0922 B
: the life and lines of Adrian, Mainbocher, McCardell, Norell, and Trigere / edited by Sarah Tomerlin Lee for the Fashion Institute of Technology. New York : Quadrangle/New York Times Book Co., [1975] p. cm. Bibliography: p. [TT505.A1A44] 75-8295 ISBN 0-8129-0524-5 : 25.00
1. Costume designers—Biography. I. Lee, Sarah. II. New York. Fashion Institute of Technology.

EPSTEIN, Beryl (Williams) 746.9'2
1910-
Fashion is our business. Freeport, N.Y., Books for Libraries Press [1970, c1945] 204 p. illus., ports. 23 cm. (Essay index reprint series) Contents.Contents.—You are interested in clothes.—Clare Potter.—Emily Wilkens.—Hattie Carnegie.—Claire McCardell.—Norman Norell.—Jo Copeland.—Philip Mangone.—Edith Head.—Louella Ballerino.—Mariska Karasz.—Mabs and Voris. [TT505.A1E6 1970] 72-117787 ISBN 0-8369-1920-3
1. Costume designers—Biography. 2. Fashion. I. Title. **BIP**

WATKINS, Josephine Jay. 746.9'2'0922 B
Who's who in fashion. [New York] Office of Community Resources, Fashion Institute of Technology [1972] 150 l. 28 cm. [TT505.A1W37] 72-190664
1. Costume designers—Biography. I. Title.

Costume designers—United States.

HEAD, Edith. 646.01
The dress doctor, by Edith Head and Jane Kesner Ardmore. Sketches by Edith Head. [1st ed.] Boston, Little, Brown [1959] 249 p. illus. 21 cm. Autobiographical. [TT505.H4A3 1959] 59-5935
I. Ardmore, Jane Kesner Morris. II. Title.

WALZ, Barbra. 779'.9'746920922
The fashion makers / Barbra Walz, photos. ; Bernadine Morris, text. 1st ed. New York : Random House, c1978. 223 p. : ill. ; 29 cm. [TT507.W218] 77-6028 ISBN 0-394-41166-8 : 15.00
1. Costume designers—United States. I. Morris, Bernadine. II. Title.

Costume—Exhibition.

HARRIS, Karyn Jean. 069'.53
Costume display techniques / Karyn Jean Harris. Nashville : American Association for State and Local History, c1977. v, 90 p. : ill. ; 14 x 22 cm. Bibliography: p. 87-90. [NK4704.H37] 77-5404 ISBN 0-910050-27-9 pbk. : 5.75
1. Costume—Exhibition. 2. Museum techniques. I. American Association for State and Local History. II. Title. **BIP**

Costume—History.

BOEHN, Max von, 1860- 391'.44'09
1932.
Ornaments; lace, fans, gloves, walking-sticks, parasols, jewelry, and trinkets. [New York] B. Blom [1970] xix, 273 p. 257 illus. 24 cm. "Modes & manners: supplementary volume." Reprint of the 1929 ed. published under title: Modes & manners: ornaments. Translation of Das Beiwerk der Mode. [GT2050.B613 1970] 70-148467
1. Costume—History. 2. Fashion—History. 3. Laces and lace making—History. 4. Jewelry—History. I. Title.

BOUCHER, Francois Leon 746.9'09
Louis, 1885-
20,000 years of fashion; the history of costume and personal adornment [by] Francois Boucher. New York, H. N. Abrams [1967] 441 p. illus. (part col.) fold. maps. 29 cm. Translation of Histoire du costume en Occident. Includes bibliographies. [GT510.B6713 1967a] 66-12103
1. Costume—History. I. Title.

BROOKE, Iris. 746.9'09
Medieval theater costume: a practical guide to the construction of garments. New York, Theater Arts Books [1967] 111 p. illus. 26 cm. [GT575.B76 1967b] 67-25699
1. Costume—Hist.—Medieval. I. Title.

HILER, Hilaire, 1898-1966. 391
From nudity to raiment; an introduction to the study of costume. New York, Gordon Press [1974] p. cm. Reprint of the 1930 ed. published by Educational Press, New York. Bibliography: p. [GN799.C5H54 1974] 74-10733 ISBN 0-87968-156-X 50.75 (lib. bdg.)
1. Costume—History. 2. Man, Prehistoric. I. Title. **BIP**

LOWNDES, Rosemary. 745.59'22
A world of costumes in cutout / written and designed by Rosemary Lowndes and Claude Kailer. New York : Holt, Rinehart and Winston, c1977. [98] p. : ill. ; 30 cm. [TT504.L68] 77-73858 ISBN 0-03-020936-6 pbk. : 7.95
1. Costume—History. 2. Paper work. I. Kailer, Claude, joint author. II. Title. **BIP**

Costume—History—Catalogs.

WADSWORTH Atheneum, 391'.2'09
Hartford.
Dress from three centuries : Wadsworth Atheneum / compiled and with an introd. by J. Herbert Callister. Hartford, [Conn.] : Wadsworth Atheneum, c1976. 86 p. : ill. (some col.) ; 29 cm. [GT505.W32 1976] 76-14506
1. Wadsworth Atheneum, Hartford. 2. Costume—History—Catalogs. I. Callister, J. Herbert. II. Title.

Costume in art.

HOLLANDER, Anne. 704.94'2
Seeing through clothes / Anne Hollander. New York : Viking Press, [1978] p. cm. Includes index. Bibliography: p. [N8217.C63] 78-15598 ISBN 0-670-63174-4 : 20.00
1. Costume in art. 2. Human figure in art. 3. Art—Psychology. I. Title. **BIP**

Costume jewelry—Collectors and collecting—Catalogs.

HENZEL, S. Sylvia. 745.59'42'075
Old costume jewelry, a collector's dream : with prices / by S. Sylvia Henzel. Des Moines, Iowa : Wallace-Homestead Book Co., c1978. 50 p., [1] leaf of plates : col. ill. ; 23 cm. [NK4890.C67H46] 78-112677 ISBN 0-87069-228-3 : 7.95
1. Costume jewelry—Collectors and collecting—Catalogs. I. Title.

HENZEL, S. Sylvia. 745.59'42'075
Old costume jewelry, a collector's dream : with prices / by S. Sylvia Henzel. Des Moines, Iowa : Wallace-Homestead Book Co., c1978. 50 p., [1] leaf of plates : col. ill. ; 23 cm. [NK4890.C67H46] 78-112677 ISBN 0-87069-228-3 : 7.95
1. Costume jewelry—Collectors and collecting—Catalogs. I. Title.

Costume—Juvenile literature.

BOYES, Janet. 646.4'7
Making paper costumes. [1st American ed.] Boston, Plays, inc. [1974] 88 p. illus. 21 cm. Instructions for making, decorating, and fireproofing paper costumes for both younger and older children. [TT633.B69 1974] 73-5841 ISBN 0-8238-0147-0 6.95
1. Costume—Juvenile literature. 2. Paper work—Juvenile literature. I. Title. **BIP**

CHERNOFF, Goldie Taub. 745.54
Easy costumes you don't have to sew / by Goldie Taub Chernoff ; costumes designed and illustrated by Margaret A. Hartelius. New York : Four Winds Press, 1977c1975 41 p. : ill. (some col.) ; 21 x 24 cm. Instructions for easily constructed costumes which do not require sewing. [TT633.C48] 76-46428 ISBN 0-590-07491-1 : 6.95
1. Costume—Juvenile literature. 2. Paper work—Juvenile literature. I. Hartelius, Margaret A. II. Title. **BIP**

EISNER, Vivienne. 646.4'7
Quick and easy holiday costumes / written by Vivienne Eisner ; illustrated by Carolyn Bentley. New York : Lothrop, Lee & Shepard Co., c1977. p. cm. Describes how to make almost instantly more than five dozen costumes for twenty-three holidays with inexpensive and easily available tools and materials. [TT633.E38] 77-21987 ISBN 0-688-41809-0 : 6.95 ISBN 0-688-51809-5 lib.bdg. : 6.43
1. Costume—Juvenile literature. I. Bentley, Carolyn. II. Title. **BIP**

Costume—Norway (continued)

GILBREATH, Alice 646.4'7
Thompson.
Making costumes for parties, plays, and holidays, [by] Alice Gilbreath. Pictures by Timothy Evans. New York, Morrow, 1974. 93 p. illus. 24 cm. Instructions for making a variety of costumes from easily available materials. [TT633.G53] 73-13996 ISBN 0-688-20103-2 3.95
1. Costume—Juvenile literature. I. Evans, Timothy, illus. II. Title.
Library binding 3.78; ISBN 0-688-30103-7.
BIP

GLOVACH, Linda. 646.4'7
The little witch's black magic book of disguises. Englewood Cliffs, N.J., Prentice-Hall [1973] 48 p. col. illus. 24 cm. Directions for making such disguises as Peter Pan, Alice in Wonderland, a ski accident, and various holiday costumes requiring inexpensive materials and no sewing. [TT633.G56] 72-13704 ISBN 0-13-537910-5 4.95
1. Costume—Juvenile literature. 2. Dressmaking—Juvenile literature. I. Title. II. Title: Disguises.
BIP

SCHNURNBERGER, Lynn 646.4'7
Edelman.
Kings, queens, knights, and jesters : making Medieval costumes / by Lynn Edelman Schnurnberger in association with the Metropolitan Museum of Art ; drawings by Alan Robert Showe ; photos. by Barbara Brooks and Pamela Hart. 1st ed. New York : Harper & Row, c1978. p. cm. Instructions for making medieval costumes such as king, monk, knight, peasant, and minstrel, with facts about the medieval period. [TT633.S3] 77-25682 ISBN 0-06-025241-3 : 6.95. ISBN 0-06-025242-1 lib. bdg. : 6.79
1. Costume—Juvenile literature. 2. Costume—History—Medieval, 500-1500—Juvenile literature. I. Showe, Alan Robert. II. Brooks, Barbara. III. Hart, Pamela. IV. New York (City). Metropolitan Museum of Art. V. Title. VI. Title: Medieval costumes.
BIP

SNOOK, Barbara. 391'.07'3
Costumes for children. Newton, Mass., C. T. Branford Co. [1970, c1969] 96 p. illus. 23 cm. More than one-hundred costume designs that can be executed by children. [GT1750.S56 1970] 78-97870
1. Costume—Juvenile literature. I. Title.
BIP

Costume—Norway.

TRAETTEBERG, Gunvor 746.909481
Ingstad, 1897-
Folk-costumes of Norway. Oslo, Dreyer, 1966. 40p. illus. 28cm. [GT1150.T7] 67-70401 4.50 pap.
1. Costume—Norway. I. Title.
American distributor: Vanous, New York.

Costume—Palestine—Catalogs.

STILLMAN, 391'.0095694'074018956
Yedida Kalfon, 1946-
Palestinian costume and jewelry / Yedida Kalfon Stillman. 1st ed. Albuquerque : University of New Mexico Press, 1978. p. cm. "Published for the Museum of New Mexico and the International Folk Art Foundation." Includes index. Bibliography: p. [NK7373.7.A1S75] 78-55711 ISBN 0-8263-0490-7 pbk. : 12.50
1. Santa Fe, N.M. Museum of New Mexico—Catalogs. 2. Costume—Palestine—Catalogs. 3. Jewelry—Palestine—Catalogs. I. Santa Fe, N.M. Museum of New Mexico. II. International Folk Art Foundation. III. Title.
BIP

Costume—Societies, etc.—Directories.

HUENEFELD, Irene 391'.0025
Pennington.
International directory of historical clothing. Metuchen, N.J., Scarecrow Press, 1967. 175 p. 22 cm. [NK4700.H8] 67-10186
1. Costume—Societies, etc.—Directories. I. Title.

Cottages.

WOODFORDE, John. 747'.8'864
Furnishing a country cottage; introduction by Audrey Powell. Newton Abbot, David and Charles, [1973, c1972] 135 p. illus., plans. 23 cm. [NK2195.R87W66] 73-160985 ISBN 0-7153-5748-4
1. Cottages. 2. Interior decoration. I. Title.
Distributed by David & Charles, N. Pomfret, Vt., 7.50.

Couffer, Jack.

BEARDWOOD, Valerie. 778.930924
The still hunt; the story of naturalist-wildlife photographer, Jack Couffer. With photos. by Jack Couffer. New York, McKay, 1965. x. 148 p. illus. ports. 21 cm. Bibliography: p. 144. [QH31.C84B4] 65-18876
1. Couffer, Jack. I. Title.

Coughtry, John Graham, 1931—

COUGHTRY, John Graham, 759.11
1931-
Graham Coughtry retrospective / [written by] Barrie Hale. Oshawa, [Ont.] : Robert McLaughlin Gallery, [1976?] 36 p. : ill. (some col.) ; 21 x 25 cm. Exhibition shown at the Robert McLaughlin Gallery, Oshawa, Ont., Mar. 3-28, 1976, and other museums. Includes bibliographical references. [ND249.C67H33] 77-369228
1. Coughtry, John Graham, 1931- I. Hale, Barrie. II. Robert McLaughlin Gallery. III. Title.

Counihan, Noel, 1913—

DIMMACK, Max. 709'.2'4
Noel Counihan / [by] Max Dimmack. [Carlton South, Vic.] : Melbourne University Press, 1974. 128 p. : ill. ; 23 x 31 cm. Includes index. Bibliography: p. 125-126. [N7405.C68D55] 75-305894 ISBN 0-522-84060-4 : 47.00
1. Counihan, Noel, 1913- I. Counihan, Noel, 1913-
Distributed by International Scholarly Book Services.
BIP

Counted thread embroidery.

COATS Sewing Group. 746.4'4
50 counted thread embroidery stitches / New York : Scribner, 1978,c1977 116 p. : ill. ; 15 cm. (The Scribner library) Includes index. [TT778.C65C6 1977] 78-50729 ISBN 0-684-15643-1 pbk. : 2.25
1. Counted thread embroidery. I. Title. II. Title:

KINMOND, Jean. 746.4'4
Counted thread embroidery / Jean Kinmond. New York : Scribner, c1976. 127 p. : ill. (some col.) ; 28 cm. [TT778.C65K56 1976] 75-38406 ISBN 0-684-14238-4 : 10.00
1. Counted thread embroidery. I. Title.

Counter-Reformation in art.

GLEN, Thomas L. 759.9493
Rubens and the Counter Reformation : studies in his religious paintings between 1609 and 1620 / Thomas L. Glen. New York : Garland Pub., 1977. p. cm. (Outstanding dissertations in the fine arts) Originally presented as the author's thesis, Princeton University, 1975. Bibliography: p. [ND673.R9G535 1977] 76-23621 ISBN 0-8240-2692-6 lib.bdg. : 40.00
1. Rubens, Peter Paul, Sir, 1577-1640. 2. Counter-Reformation in art. I. Title. II. Series.
BIP

Counterfeits and counterfeiting.

BLOOM, Murray Teigh, 1916- 332.9
Money of their own; the great counterfeiters. New York, Scribner [1957] 302 p. 22 cm. [HG335.B6] 57-6065
1. Counterfeits and counterfeiting. I. Title.

Counterfeits and counterfeiting—Connecticut.

SCOTT, Kenneth. 332.9
Counterfeiting in colonial Connecticut. New York, American Numismatic Society, 1957. 243p. map, 46 facsims. 23cm. (Numismatic notes and monographs, no. 140) Bibliographical footnotes. [HG336.U52C66] 58-1001
1. Counterfeits and counterfeiting—Connecticut. I. Title. II. Series.

Counterfeits and counterfeiting—New York (State)—Hist.

SCOTT, Kenneth. 332.9
Counterfeiting in colonial New York. New York, American Numismatic Society, 1953. 222p. plates. 23cm. (Numismatic notes and monographs, no. 127) Bibliographical footnotes. [HG336.U5N4] 53-10831
1. Counterfeits and counterfeiting—New York (State)—Hist. I. Title. II. Series. **BIP**

Counterfeits and counterfeiting—U.S.

GLASER, Lynn. 332.9
Counterfeiting in America; the history of an American way to wealth. [1st ed. New York] C.N. Potter; distributed by Crown Publishers [1967, 1968] 274 p. illus. 22cm. Bibliographical references included in "Notes" (p. 263-271) [HG336.U5G55] 67-16523
1. Counterfeits and counterfeiting—U.S. I. Title.

LANDRESS, M. M. 364.1'33'0924 B
I made it myself, by M. M. Landress, with Bruce Dobler. New York, Grosset & Dunlap [1973] x, 276 p. 22 cm. [HG336.U5L35] 72-90844 ISBN 0-448-02206-0 6.95
1. Landress, M. M. 2. Counterfeits and counterfeiting—United States. I. Dobler, Bruce. II. Title.

SCOTT, Kenneth. 332.9
Counterfeiting in colonial America. With a foreword by U. E. Baughman. New York, Oxford University Press, 1957. 283 p. illus. 21 cm. Includes bibliography. [HG336.U5S35] 57-6478
1. Counterfeits and counterfeiting—U.S. I. Title.

Country furniture—Ontario.

PAIN, Howard. 749.2'113
The heritage of country furniture, 1780-1900 / Howard Pain. New York : Van Nostrand Reinhold Co., [1978] p. cm. Includes index. Bibliography: p. [NK2442.O6P34] 78-15501 ISBN 0-442-29828-5 : 49.95
1. Country furniture—Ontario. I. Title. **BIP**

Country furniture—United States—Handbooks, manuals, etc.

VOSS, Thomas M., 1945- 749.2
Antique American country furniture : a field guide / by Thomas M. Voss ; illustrated by Donald Bender. 1st ed. Philadelphia : Lippincott, c1978. p. cm. Inludes indexes. Bibliography: p. [NK2405.V67] 77-15649 ISBN 0-397-01219-5 : 9.95 ISBN 0-397-01267-5 pbk. : 6.95
1. Country furniture—United States—Handbooks, manuals, etc. I. Title. **BIP**

Country homes.

DOWNING, Andrew Jackson, 728.6
1815-1852.
The architecture of country houses, by A. J. Downing. New introd. by George B. Tatum. New York, Da Capo Press, 1968. xx, x, 484 p. illus., plans. 24 cm. (Da Capo Press series in architecture and decorative art, v. 11) A Da Capo Press reprint edition. Reprint of the 1850 ed. [NA7561.D75 1968] 68-16230
1. Country homes. I. Title.
BIP

DOWNING, Andrew Jackson, 728.6
1815-1852.
The architecture of country houses; including designs for cottages, and farmhouses, and villas, with remarks on interiors, furniture, and the best modes of warming and ventilating. [1st ed.] New York, Dover Publications [1969] xxiv, 484 p. illus., plans. 22 cm. Reprint of the 1850 ed., with a new introd. by J. Stewart Johnson. [NA7561.D75 1969] 69-17702 ISBN 0-486-22003-6
1. Country homes. I. Title.

Country homes—Gt. Brit.

GIROUARD, Mark, 728.8'3'0942
1931-
The Victorian country house. Oxford, Clarendon Press, 1971. xxii, 220 p., 162 plates (1 fold.) illus., facsims. (on lining papers)., maps, plans, ports. 32 cm. [NA7562.G5] 75-884893 ISBN 0-19-817183-8 £12.00
1. Country homes—Gt. Brit. 2. Architecture, Victorian—Gt. Brit. I. Title.

Country homes—Spain.

RIBALTA, Marta. 728.3
Vivir en el campo = Living in the country = Vivre a la campagne / Director ... Marta Ribalta. 1. ed. Barcelona : Blume, 1977. 181 p. : ill. (some col.) ; 26 cm. (Habitat ; 5) English, French, and Spanish. "Distributed by Universe Books, New York." [NA7566.S7R5] 79-301534 ISBN 8-470-31046-1 pbk. : 5.95
1. Country homes—Spain. 2. Decoration and ornament, Rustic—Spain. I. Title. II. Title: Living in the country. III. Title: Vivre a la campagne. IV. Series: Habitat (Barcelona) ; 5.

Country homes—United States.

ARTISTIC country-seats : 728
types of recent American villa and cottage architecture, with instances of country club-houses / edited by George William Sheldon. New York : Da Capo Press, 1978. p. cm. (Da Capo Press series in architecture and decorative art) Reprint of v. 1-2 of the 1886 ed. published by D. Appleton, New York. [NA7610.A8 1979] 78-17476 ISBN 0-306-70829-9 : 110.00
1. Country homes—United States. 2. Country homes—Designs and plans. I. Sheldon, George William, 1843-1914.

Country houses—England.

WILSON, Michael I. 942
The English country house and its furnishings / Michael I. Wilson. New York : Architectural Book Pub. Co., 1978. p. cm. Includes bibliographical references and index. [NA7620.W543] 77-12100 ISBN 0-8038-0074-6 : 12.95
1. Country houses—England. 2. Historic buildings—England. 3. Furniture—England. I. Title.

Courbet, Gustave,

MACK, Gerstle, 1894- 927.5
Gustave Courbet. [1st ed.] New York, Knopf, 1951. xv, 406, xix p. illus, ports., fold. map. 25 cm. Bibliography: p. 397-406. [ND553.C9M3] 51-11099
1. Courbet, Gustave, I. Title. **BIP**

Courbet, Gustave, 1819-1877.

BOAS, George, 1891- ed. 700.1
Courbet and the naturalistic movement; essays read at the Baltimore Museum of Art, May 16, 17, 18, 1938. New York, Russell & Russell [1967, c1938] x, 249 p. illus., ports. 23 cm. Bibliographical footnotes. [ND553.C9B6] 66-27041
1. Courbet, Gustave, 1819-1877. 2. Naturalism in art. 3. Naturalism in literature. I. Title.
Contents Omitted **BIP**

BOUDAILLE, Georges. 759.4
Gustave Courbet, painter in protest. [Translated from the French by Michael Bullock] Greenwich, Conn., New York Graphic Society [1970, c1969] ix, 151 p. illus. (part col.), facsims., ports. 29 cm. Bibliography: p. 146-147. [ND553.C9B6813] 73-86264
1. Courbet, Gustave, 1819-1877.

SUBJECT INDEX

COVERLETS.

BOWNESS, Alan. 759.4
Courbet's L'Atelier du peintre. [Newcastle upon Tyne] University of Newcastle upon Tyne, 1972. 30 p. illus., port. 25 cm. (Charlton lectures on art, 50) Bibliography: p. 30. [ND553.C9B69] 73-160115 ISBN 0-900565-73-X £1.00
1. Courbet, Gustave, 1819-1877. Painter's studio. I. Title. II. Series: Charlton lecture, 50, 1967.

FERNIER, Robert. 759.4
Gustave Courbet. With an introd. by Rene Huyghe. [Translated from the French by Marcus Bullock] New York, Praeger [1969] 139 p. illus. (part col.), facsims., ports. 28 cm. Bibliography: p. 135. [ND553.C9F4153] 70-84856 15.00
1. Courbet, Gustave, 1819-1877. I. Title.

FOUCART, Bruno. 759.4
G. Courbet / by Bruno Foucart ; [translated from the French by Alice Sachs]. New York : Crown Publishers, c1977. 96 p. : ill. (some col.) ; 29 cm. Bibliography: p. 94-95. [ND553.C9F6813] 77-17224 ISBN 0-517-53285-9 : 4.95
1. Courbet, Gustave, 1819-1877. I. Courbet, Gustave, 1819-1877.

MACK, Gerstle, 1894- 759.4 B
Gustave Courbet. Westport, Conn., Greenwood Press [1970, c1951] xv, 406, xix p. illus., map, ports. 23 cm. Bibliography: p. 397-406. [ND553.C9M3 1970] 73-110833 ISBN 0-8371-2588-X
1. Courbet, Gustave, 1819-1877.

NICOLSON, Benedict. 759.4
Courbet: The studio of the painter. New York, Viking Press [1973] 98 p. illus. (1 fold. col.) 24 cm. (Art in context) Bibliography: p. [83]-84. [ND553.C9N53 1973b] 72-78199 ISBN 0-670-24425-2 7.95
1. Courbet, Gustave, 1819-1877. Painter's studio. I. Title.

NOCHLIN, Linda. 759.4
Gustave Courbet : a study of style and society / Linda Nochlin. New York : Garland Pub., 1976. xvii, 240 p., [33] leaves of plates : ill. ; 21 cm. (Outstanding dissertations in the fine arts) Originally presented as the author's thesis, New York University, 1963, under the title: The development and nature of realism in the work of Gustave Courbet. Bibliography: p. 233-240. [ND553.C9N62 1976] 75-23803 ISBN 0-8240-1998-9 lib.bdg. : 27.50
1. Courbet, Gustave, 1819-1877. 2. Realism in art—France. I. Title. II. Series.

PHILADELPHIA Museum of Art. 759.4
Gustave Courbet, 1819-1877. [Exhibition] 1959-1960, Philadelphia Museum of Art, Museum of Fine Arts, Boston. [Philadelphia, c1959] 1v. (unpaged) illus. (part col.) 26cm. Erratum slip inserted. Includes bibliography. [ND553.C9P45] 60-2929
1. Courbet, Gustave, 1819-1877. I. Boston. Museum of Fine Arts. II. Title.

ZAHAR, Marcel. 759.4
Gustave Courbet. [Translated by D. I. Wilton. 1st American ed.] New York Harper [1950] 17, [2] p. 39 plates (part col.) 28 cm. (Masters of painting) Harper's art library. Bibliography: p. [18] [ND553.C9Z3] [927.5] 50-10788
1. Courbet, Gustave, 1819-1877. I. Title. II. Series: Masters of painting (New York)

Courbet, Gustave, 1819-1877—Addresses, essays, lectures.

COURBET in perspective / 759.4
[compiled by] Petra ten-Doesschate Chu. New York : Prentice-Hall, [1976] p. cm. (The Artists in perspective series) (A Spectrum book) Bibliography: p. [ND553.C9C58] 76-44418 ISBN 0-13-184432-6 : 10.95 pbk. : 3.95
1. Courbet, Gustave, 1819-1877—Addresses, essays, lectures. I. Doesschate Chu, Petra ten.

Court-houses—Iowa.

†STANEK, Edward. 977.7
Iowa's magnificent county courthouses / by Edward & Jacqueline Stanek. Des Moines : Wallace-Homestead Book Co., c1976. 213 p. : ill. ; 23 cm. Includes bibliographical references. [NA4472.I8S7] 76-6608 ISBN 0-87069-189-9 : 7.95
1. Court-houses—Iowa. 2. Iowa—Public buildings. I. Stanek, Jacqueline, joint author.

Court-houses—Michigan.

COLE, Maurice F. 977.4
Michigan's courthouses, old and new / by Maurice F. Cole. [Royal Oak? Mich. : Cole?, 1974?] 167 p., [1] leaf of plates : ill. ; 29 cm. Includes bibliographical references. [NA4472.M5C65] 74-27625
1. Court-houses—Michigan. I. Title.

Court-houses—United States.

ALFINI, James J., comp. 725'.15
Courthouses and courtrooms; selected readings. Compiled by James J. Alfini. Edited by Glenn R. Winters. Chicago, American Judicature Society, 1972. 81 p. illus. 26 cm. (American Judicature Society selected readings, 5) Bibliography: p. 81. [NA4471.A73] 72-91935
1. Court-houses—United States. 2. Court-houses—United States—Designs and plans. I. Winters, Glenn R., ed. II. Title. III. Series: American Judicature Society. Selected readings, 5.

MICHIGAN. University. Law School. 725'.15
The American courthouse, a planning and design guide for its future development. Conceived and sponsored by the ABA-AIA Joint Committee on Judicial Facilities [of] American Bar Association, Section of Judicial Administration, [and] American Institute of Architects. Prepared by the University of Michigan, Ann Arbor: Law School, the Institute of Continuing Legal Education [and] College of Architecture and Design, Architectural Research Laboratory. [Ann Arbor, University of Michigan, Architectural Research Laboratory, 1971] 2 v. illus., plans. 28 cm. "The University of Michigan. O.R.A. project 30387, 'judicial facilities study'." [NA4471.M5] 72-181687
1. Court-houses—United States. 2. Court-houses—Designs and plans. I. Institute of Continuing Legal Education, Ann Arbor, Mich. II. Michigan. University. Architectural Research Laboratory. III. ABA-AIA Joint Committee on Judicial Facilities. IV. Title.

MICHIGAN. University. Law School. 725'.15
The American courthouse; planning and design for the judicial process. The American Bar Association and the American Institute of Architects Joint Committee on the Design of Courtrooms and Court Facilities. A. Benjamin Handler, Project director. Ann Arbor, Mich., Institute of Continuing Legal Education [1973] xiii, 320 p. illus. 29 cm. One folded chart inserted. "The projet was conducted under the general supervision of the Joint Committee and the research was done at The University of Michigan in Ann Arbor by a project staff representing both the Law School and the College of Architecture and Design." A revision of the work first issued in 1971 under title: The American courthouse, a planning and design guide for its future development. Includes bibliographical references. [NA4471.M5 1973] 72-89627 40.00
1. Court-houses—United States. 2. Court-houses—Designs and plans. I. Handler, A. Benjamin, 1911- II. Michigan. University. College of Architecture and Design. III. American Bar Association and the American Institute of Architects Joint Committee on the Design of Courtrooms and Court Facilities. IV. Institute of Continuing Legal Education, Ann Arbor, Mich. V. Title.

Court-houses—United States—Conservation and restoration.

A Courthouse conservation handbook. 725'.15
Washington : Preservation Press, 1976. 75 p. : ill. ; 27 cm. A project of the National Trust for Historic Preservation in cooperation with the National Clearinghouse for Criminal Justice Planning and Architecture; prepared for use at the National Conference on Historic Courthouses held March 31-April 2, 1976, St. Louis, Mo. Bibliography: p. 71-72. [NA4471.C68] 76-1039 ISBN 0-89133-036-4 : 30.00
1. Court-houses—United States—Conservation and restoration. I. National Trust for Historic Preservation in the United States. II. National Clearinghouse for Criminal Justice Planning and Architecture. III. National Conference on Historic Courthouses, St. Louis, 1976. BIP

Courtauld family.

HAYWARD, John Forrest, 1916- 739.2'3'722
The Courtauld silver : an introduction to the work of the Courtauld Family of Goldsmiths / J. F. Hayward. London ; New York : Sotheby Parke Bernet, [1975] 62 p. : ill. ; 26 cm. [NK7198.C63H38] 75-316374 ISBN 0-85667-018-9 : 15.00
1. Courtauld family. 2. Plate, English. I. Title. BIP

Courtyards—United States—Bibliography.

STARBUCK, James C. 016.3092 s
Atriums : a bibliography on an architectural vogue / James C. Starbuck. Monticello, Ill. : Council of Planning Librarians, 1976. 10 p. ; 28 cm. (Exchange bibliography ; 1104) Cover title. [Z5942.C68 no. 1104] [NA8375] 721 77-350696 pbk. : 1.50
1. Courtyards—United States—Bibliography. I. Title. II. Series: Council of Planning Librarians. Exchange bibliography ; 1104.

Couture, Thomas, 1815-1879.

COUTURE, Thomas, 1815-1879. 741.9'44
Thomas Couture; [drawings and some oil sketches] Essay by Albert Boime. Catalog by Robert Kashey and Martin L. H. Reymert. [New York, Shepherd Gallery, 1971] [62] p. illus., port. 22 cm. Catalog of the exhibition held May-June 1971 at the Shepherd Gallery, New York. [NC248.C69B6] 79-198187
I. Boime, Albert. II. Kashey, Robert. III. Reymert, Martin L. H. IV. Shepherd Gallery.

VAN NIMMEN, Jane, 1937- 760'.0924
Thomas Couture: paintings and drawings in American collections. With an introductory note by George Levitine, and essays by Alain de Leiris and Jane Van Nimmen. Catalogue by Jane Van Nimmen. [College Park] University of Maryland, Dept. of Art [1970] 62, [34] p. illus. 22 x 26 cm. Exhibition held at University of Maryland Art Gallery, Feb. 5-Mar. 15, 1970. [ND553.C9565V3] 73-116139
1. Couture, Thomas, 1815-1879. I. De Leiris, Alain. II. Maryland. University. Art Gallery. III. Title.

Covent Garden, London.

BORER, Mary Irene Cathcart. 942.1'3
Covent Garden: photographs by A. F. Kersting, text by Mary Cathcart Rover. London, New York [etc.] Abelard-Schuman, 1967. 144 p. illus., maps, plans. 22 1/2 cm. 30/- (B 67-6678) Bibliography: p. 140. [DA685.C7B6] 67-19420
1. Covent Garden, London. I. Kersting, A. F. II. Title.

Coventry Cathedral.

SPENCE, Basil, Sir 1907- 726.65094248
Phoenix at Coventry; the building of a cathedral. New York, Harper & Row [1962] 141 p. illus. 24 cm. [NA5471.C95456] 62-20256
1. Coventry Cathedral. I. Title.

SPENCE, Basil Urwin, Sir 1907- 726.65094248
Phoenix at Coventry; the building of a cathedral. New York, Harper [c.1962] 141p. illus. (pt. col.) 24cm. 62-20256 6.95
1. Coventry Cathedral. I. Title.

Coventry, Eng.

STEANE, Leonard. 914.24'8
Coventry cameos. Coventry, L. Steane [1972] [1], 14 p., leaf 1 illus. 22 cm. [DA690.C75S8] 72-185949 ISBN 0-9502238-0-8 £0.20
1. Coventry, Eng. I. Title.

Coventry, Eng.—Description—Views.

NEWBOLD, E. B. 914.24'98
Coventry old and new / [compiled by] E. B. Newbold. Wakefield : EP Publishing, 1974 [i.e.1975] [5], 99 p. : of ill., leaf 1 ill., plans ; 18 x 24 cm. [DA690.C75N47] 75-309917 ISBN 0-7158-1061-8 pbk. : 8.50
1. Coventry, Eng.—Description—Views. I. Title.
Distributed by British Book Center, New York BIP

Covered bridges.

PETERSEN, Hegen 725.98
Kissing bridges. Foreword by Richard Sanders Allen. Brattleboro, Vt., S. Greene [c.] 1965. 48p. illus., map. 22cm Bibl. [TG23.P46] 65-14694 3.50; 1.50 pap.,
1. Covered bridges. 2. Bridges—U.S. I. Title.

Coverlets.

BRIGHTBILL, Dorothy. 746.46
Quilting as a hobby. New York, Sterling Pub. Co. [1964, c1963] 96 p. illus. 22 cm. [TT835.B7 1964] 63-19159
1. Coverlets. I. Title.

CARLISLE, Lilian Baker. 745.46
Pieced work and applique quilts at Shelburne Museum. Shelburne, Vt., Shelburne Museum [1957] 95p. illus. 23cm. (Museum pamphlet series, no. 2) [F59.S49S47 no. 2] 57-14118
1. Coverlets. I. Title. BIP

CARLISLE, Lilliam Baker. 745.46
Pieced work and applique quilts at Shelburne Museum. Shelburne, Vt., Shelburne Museum [1957] 95p. illus. 23cm. (Museum pamphlet series, no. 2) [F59.S49S47 no.2] 57-14118
1. Coverlets. I. Title.

COLBY, Averil. 746.46
Patchwork quilts. [New York] Scribner [1966] 94 p. illus. (part col.) 23 cm. [NK9104.C65 1966] 66-10941
1. Coverlets. 2. Patchwork. I. Title. BIP

COLONIAL Coverlet Guild of America. 745.5262
Heirlooms from old looms; a catalogue of coverlets owned by the Colonial Coverlet Guild of America and its members. Rev. Edited by Mrs. Luther M. Swygert. Chicago, 1955. viii, 406p. (chiefly illus.) 25cm. [NK9112.C6 1955] 55-35811
1. Coverlets. I. Swygert, Mildred (Kercher) ed. II. Title.

FINLEY, Ruth (Ebright) 1884-1955. 746.4'6
Old patchwork quilts and the women who made them. Newton Centre, Mass., C. T. Branford Co. [1970, c1929] 202 p. illus. 21 cm. [NK9112.F5 1970] 78-20748
1. Coverlets. 2. Needlework—Patterns. I. Title.

HALL, Carrie A., 1866- 746.4'6
The romance of the patchwork quilt in America [by Carrie A. Hall and Rose G. Kretsinger] Photos by Mary Ellen Everhard. New York, Bonanza Books [1969? c1935] 299 p. illus. 24 cm. Contents.Contents.—History and quilt patches, by C. A. Hall.—Quilts: antiques and modern, by C. A. Hall.—Quilting and quilting designs, by R. G. Kretsinger.—Bibliography (p. [292]) [NK9112.H3 1969] 76-17469
1. Coverlets. 2. Needlework—U.S. I. Kretsinger, Rose (Good) II. Title.

HELSEL, Marjorie Borradaile. 746.9
The interior designer's bedspread and canopy sketchfile / edited by Marjorie Borradaile Helsel. New York : Whitney Library of Design, 1975. ca. 200 p. : chiefly ill. ; 29 cm. Includes index.

[TT403.H44] 74-26755 ISBN 0-8230-7290-8 : 13.50
1. Coverlets. I. Title. II. Title: Bedspread and canopy sketchfile. BIP

HINSON, Dolores A. 746.46
Quilting manual [by] Dolores A. Hinson. Drawings by the author. New York, Hearthside [1966] 192p. illus. 25cm. [TT835.H5] 66-15788 4.95 bds.,
1. Coverlets. I. Title. BIP

ICKIS, Marguerite, 1897- 746.46
The standard book of quilt making and collecting. New York, Dover Publications [1961, c1949] 276p. illus. 25cm. [TT835] CD62
1. Coverlets I. Title. II. Title: Quilt making. BIP

ICKIS, Marguerite [Gourlay] 746.46
The standard book of quilt making and collecting. New York, Dover Pubns. [1960, c.1949] xi, 276p. illus. (col. front.) 25cm. (T582) 2.00 pap.,
1. Coverlets. I. Title. II. Title: Quilt making.

LAURY, Jean Ray 746.4'6
Quilts and coverlets; a contemporary approach. Photos by Gayle Smalley. New York, Van Nostrand Reinhold Co. [1975 c1970] 128 p. illus. (part col.) 26 cm. [TT835.L37] 70-126873 ISBN 0-442-24703-6 4.95 (pbk.)
1. Coverlets. 2. Quilting. I. Title.
Hardcover, 9.95; 0-442-24694-3. BIP

MCKIM, Ruby Short. 746.46
One hundred and one patchwork patterns; quilt name stories, cutting designs, material suggestions, yardage estimates, definite instructions for every step of quilt making. [Rev. ed.] New York, Dover Publications [1962] 124 p. illus. 28 cm. [TT835.M3 1962] 63-1453
1. Coverlets. 2. Needlework—Patterns. I. Title. II. Title: Patchwork patterns.

MCKIM, Ruby Short 746.46
One hundred and one patchwork patterns; quilt name stories, cutting designs, material suggestions. yardage estimates, definite instructions for every step of quilting [Rev. ed. Gloucester, Mass., P. Smith, 1964, c.1962] 124p. illus. 28cm. (Dover bk. T773 rebound) [TT835.M3] 4.25
1. Coverlets 2. Needlework—Patterns. I. Title. II. Title: Patchwork quilts. BIP

MARSTON, Doris Elizabeth. 747.77
Patchwork today, a practical introduction. Newton, Mass., C. T. Branford Co. [1968] 92 p. illus. 21 cm. [NK9104.M306]
1. Coverlets. I. Title. BIP

OBENCHAIN, Eliza Caroline (Calvert) 1856- 746.1
A book of hand-woven coverlets. by Eliza Calvert Hall. Rutland, Vt., Tuttle [1966] 411p. illus. (pt col) 22cm. First pub. in 1912. [NK8903.O3 1966] 66-23536 8.75
1. Coverlets. I. Title.

WEBSTER, Marie (Daugherty) 1859- 746.4'6
Quilts: their story and how to make them. Garden City, N.Y., Doubleday, Page, 1915. Detroit, Gale Research Co., 1972. xviii, 178 p. illus. 19 cm. Includes bibliographical references. [NK9104.W4 1972] 75-174137
1. Coverlets. 2. Quilting. I. Title.

Coverlets, American.

MONTGOMERY, Pauline. 746.9'7 B
Indiana coverlet weavers and their coverlets / Pauline Montgomery. Indianapolis : Hoosier Heritage Press, 1974. vii, 138 p. : ill. (some col.) ; 29 cm. Includes bibliographical references and index. [TT835.M66] 75-314888 14.95
1. Coverlets, American. 2. Hand weaving. 3. Weavers—Indiana. I. Title.

ORLOFSKY, Patsy. 746.9'7
Quilts in America [by] Patsy and Myron Orlofsky. New York, McGraw-Hill [1974] xiv, 368 p. illus. 26 cm. Bibliography: p. 351-357. [NK9112.O74] 74-6160 ISBN 0-07-047725-6 17.95
1. Coverlets, American. I. Orlofsky, Myron, joint author. II. Title. BIP

SAFFORD, Carleton L. 746.9'7
America's quilts and coverlets, by Carleton L. Safford and Robert Bishop. [1st ed.] New York, Dutton, 1972. 313 p. illus. 29 cm. Bibliography: p. 310. [NK9112.S23 1972] 72-82707 ISBN 0-525-05395-6 25.00
1. Coverlets, American. I. Bishop, Robert Charles, joint author. II. Title.

Coverlets, American—Catalogs.

CHICAGO. Art Institute. 746.9'7
American quilts from The Art Institute of Chicago [by] Mildred Davison. [Chicago?] 1966. 1 v. (chiefly illus.) 22 cm. Includes bibliography. [NK9112.C47] 68-514
1. Coverlets, American—Catalogs. I. Davison, Mildred. II. Title.

CHICAGO. Art Institute. 746.9'7
Coverlets; a handbook on the collection of woven coverlets in the Art Institute of Chicago, by Mildred Davison and Christa C. Mayer-Thurman. [Chicago] 1973. 228 p. illus. (part col.) 26 cm. Bibliography: p. 227-228. [NK9112.C48] 73-82570 7.50 (pbk.)
1. Chicago. Art Institute. 2. Coverlets, American—Catalogs. 3. Coverlets—Chicago—Catalogs. I. Davison, Mildred. II. Mayer-Thurman, Christa C. III. Title.

KANSAS. University. Museum of Art. 746.9'7
150 years of American guilts. [Lawrence] 1973. [56] p. illus. 26 cm. (Its Miscellaneous publications, no. 90) Bibliography: p. [52]-[54] [NK9102.L42K364 1973] 73-622705
1. Kansas. University. Museum of Art. 2. Coverlets, American—Catalogs. 3. Coverlets—Lawrence, Kan.—Catalogs. I. Title. II. Series.

Coverlets, American—Exhibitions.

HOLSTEIN, Jonathan. 746.9'7
American pieced quilts. New York, Viking Press [1973, c1972] 94 p. illus. (part col.) 17 cm. (A Studio book) Catalogue of an exhibition first held at the Musee des arts decoratifs, Lausanne; later shown at the Renwick Gallery, Washington, D.C., Oct. 14, 1972-Jan. 8, 1973; and to be circulated by the Smithsonian Institution Traveling Exhibition Service, 1972-74. Bibliography: p. 15-16. [NK9112.H62 1973] 72-11905 ISBN 0-670-12004-9 5.95
1. Coverlets, American—Exhibitions. I. Musee des arts decoratifs, Lausanne. II. Renwick Gallery. III. Smithsonian Institution. Traveling Exhibition Service. IV. Title. BIP

NEBRASKA. University. Sheldon Memorial Art Gallery. 746.9'7
Quilts from Nebraska collections : [catalogue of an exhibition presented in collaboration with the Lincoln Quilters Guild, Sheldon Memorial Art Gallery, University of Nebraska, Lincoln, September 17-October 13, 1974]. [Lincoln] : The Gallery, [1974] [75] p. : chiefly ill. (some col.) ; 22 x 23 cm. Cover title. [NK9112.N3 1974] 75-621730
1. Coverlets, American—Exhibitions. I. Lincoln Quilters Guild. II. Title.

NEW York (City). Metropolitan Museum of Art. American Wing. 746.9'7
12 great quilts from the American Wing; catalogue, by Marilyn Johnson Bondes, Associate Curator. The American Wing [New York, Metropolitan Museum of Art, 1974] [36] p. illus. (part col.) 21 cm. Catalog of an exhibition. Bibliography: p. [36] [NK9112.N37 1974] 74-180367
1. Coverlets, American—Exhibitions. I. Bordes, Marilynn Johnson. II. Title.

WADSWORTH Atheneum, Hartford. 746.9'7
Bed ruggs/1722-1833. [Hartford, Conn., 1972] 80 p. illus. 29 cm. Catalog of loan exhibition held 9 Nov.-31 Dec., 1972. [NK9112.W32] 72-88680
1. Coverlets, American—Exhibitions. 2. Coverlets—New England. I. Title. BIP

Coverlets, American—History.

HOLSTEIN, Jonathan. 746.9'7
The pieced quilt; an American design tradition. Greenwich, Conn., New York Graphic Society [1973] 187, [5] p. illus. (part col.) 29 cm. Bibliography: p. [188]-[189] [NK9112.H63] 73-79991 17.50
1. Coverlets, American—History. I. Title.

HOLSTEIN, Jonathan. 746.97
The pieced quilt : an American design tradition. Boston : New York Graphic Society [1976c1973] 192p. : ill. ; 28 cm. Includes index. Bibliography: p. 188-189. [NK9112.H63] ISBN 0-8212-0686-9 pbk. : 8.95
1. Coverlets, American-History. I. Title.
L. C. card no. for original edition: 73-79991. BIP

Coverlets, Amish.

HADERS, Phyllis. 746.9'7
Sunshine and shadow : the Amish and their quilts / by Phyllis Haders. New York : Universe Books, c1976. 71 p. : ill. (some col.) ; 22 cm. [NK9112.H26] 76-5094 ISBN 0-87663-236-3 : 5.95
1. Coverlets, Amish. 2. Amish. I. Title. BIP

Coverlets—Denver—Catalogs.

DENVER. Art Museum. 746.9'7
Quilts and coverlets / The Denver Art Museum ; Imelda G. DeGraw. [Denver] : The Museum, [1974] [160] p. : ill. (some col.) ; 20 cm. Bibliography: p. [158]-[159] [NK9102.D46D466 1974] 74-7687 ISBN 0-914738-02-X
1. Denver. Art Museum. 2. Coverlets—Denver—Catalogs. I. DeGraw, Imelda G. II. Title.

Coverlets, Hawaiian—Exhibitions.

JONES, Stella M. 746.9'7
Hawaiian quilts [by] Stella M. Jones. [Rev. 2d ed.] Honolulu, Daughters of Hawaii, 1973. 78 p. illus. 26 cm. "Including a catalog of the exhibition, 'The quilt—a Hawaiian heritage,' held at the Honolulu Academy of Arts, October 13-November 18, 1973": p. [19]-78. [NK9112.J66 1973] 73-88714
1. Coverlets, Hawaiian—Exhibitions. 2. Needlework, Hawaiian—Exhibitions. I. Honolulu Academy of Arts. The quilt—a Hawaiian heritage. 1973. II. Title. III. Title: The quilt—a Hawaiian heritage.

Coverlets—Pennsylvania—West Chester—Catalogs.

CHESTER County Historical Society, West Chester, Pa. 746.9'7
Coverlets in the collection of the Chester County Historical Society : from an exhibition, June 6th to October 2nd, 1976, 225 North High Street, West Chester, Pennsylvania / [editor, Ruth K. Hagy ; consultants, Jane A. Bolster ... et al. ; photography, Dan Coxe]. [West Chester, Pa.] : The Society, c1976. 28 p. : chiefly ill. ; 26 cm. [NK9112.C45 1976] 76-371684
1. Chester County Historical Society, West Chester, Pa. 2. Coverlets—Pennsylvania—West Chester—Catalogs. I. Hagy, Ruth K. II. Title.

Coverlets—United States.

BISHOP, Robert Charles. 746.9'7
New discoveries in American quilts / Robert Bishop, Patricia Coblentz. 1st ed. New York : Dutton, 1975. 127 p. : ill. (some col.) ; 29 cm. Bibliography: p. 127. [NK9112.B57 1975] 75-24533 ISBN 0-525-16552-5 : 17.95. ISBN 0-525-47410-2 pbk. : 9.95
1. Coverlets—United States. I. Coblentz, Patricia, joint author. II. Title. BIP

MAINARDI, Patricia. 746.9'7
Quilts, the great American art / Patricia Mainardi. San Pedro, [Calif.] : Miles & Weir, 1978. xix, 57 p. : 10 ill. ; 12 x 15 cm. (A Peace and plenty quilt book) Bibliography: p. 56-57. [NK9112.M34] 77-95430 ISBN 0-917300-06-8 : 7.95 ISBN 0-917300-01-7 pbk. : 2.95
1. Coverlets—United States. I. Title. II. Series.

PETO, Florence. 746.4'6
Historic quilts / by Florence Peto. Detroit : Gale Research Co., 1975. p. cm. Reprint of the 1939 ed. published by the American Historical Co., New York. [NK9112.P47 1975] 72-180954 ISBN 0-8103-4199-9 : 14.00
1. Coverlets—United States. 2. Needlework—Patterns. I. Title.

Coverlets—United States—Exhibitions.

AMERICAN Museum in Britain. 746.9'7
The American quilt tradition : an exhibition to mark the Bi-centenary of American Independence / arranged by the American Museum in Britain and the Commonwealth Institute, [held at the] Commonwealth Art Gallery ... 23 July unitl 2 September 1976 ; [text by Shiela Betterton]. [Bath] : American Museum, 1976. 57 p. : ill. (some col.) ; 21 cm. Bibliography: p. [57] [NK9112.A53 1976] 77-361412 ISBN 0-9504971-0-X
1. Coverlets—United States—Exhibitions. I. Betterton, Shiela. II. London. Commonwealth Institute. III. Title.

BALTIMORE. Museum of Art. 746.9'7
The great American cover-up: counterpanes of the eighteenth and nineteenth centuries. [Baltimore, Md., 1971] 48 p. illus. 26 cm. Catalog of counterpanes, chiefly from the museum's collections. Introd. signed by Dena S. Katzenberg. Bibliography: p. 48. [NK9112.B35] 76-31369
1. Coverlets—United States—Exhibitions. I. Katzenberg, Dena S. II. Title.

ELVEHJEM Art Center. 746.9'7
American coverlets of the nineteenth century, from the Helen Louise Allen textile collection : [exhibition and catalogue / organized by the Elvehjem Art Center and the School of Family Resources and Consumer Sciences]. Madison, Wis. : The Center, 1974. ix, 95 p. : ill. ; 26 cm. "The exhibition was shown at the Elvehjem Art Center, November 3, 1974-January 5, 1975." Bibliography: p. 95. [NK9112.E48 1974] 75-622430
1. Coverlets—United States—Exhibitions. 2. Allen, Helen Louise—Art collections. I. Wisconsin. University—Madison. School of Family Resources and Consumer Sciences. II. Title.

HOLSTEIN, Jonathan. 746.9'7
Abstract design in American quilts. New York, Whitney Museum of American Art [1971] 15, [1] p. illus. 21 cm. Catalog of an exhibition held at the Whitney Museum of American Art, July 1-September 12, 1971. Bibliography: p. [16] [NK9112.H6] 71-168575
1. Coverlets—United States—Exhibitions. 2. Design, Decorative—United States. I. Whitney Museum of American Art, New York. II. Title.

Coverlets—United States—History—20th century—Catalogs.

CHASE, Pattie. 746.9'7
The contemporary quilt : new American quilts and fabric art / by Pattie Chase, with Mimi Dolbier ; foreword by Radka Donnell. 1st ed. New York : Dutton, 1978. 80 p., [1] leaf of plates : 141 col. ill. ; 28 cm. Includes index. [NK9112.C44 1978] 78-59313 ISBN 0-525-17441-9 : 17.50 ISBN 0-525-47523-0 pbk. : 9.95
1. Coverlets—United States—History—20th century—Catalogs. 2. Needlework—United States—History—20th century—Catalogs. I. Dolbier, Mimi, joint author. II. Title. BIP

Covers (Philately)

AMERICAN Air Mail Society. 383.22
The American air mail catalogue of air letter sheets, including military and prisoner of war air letter cards; edited by American Air Mail Society, Catalogue 'Committee. 1953 ed. [Albion, Pa., 1953] 147p. illus. 22cm. 'An official publication of the American Air Mail Society.'sAir mail stamps--Catalogs. [HE6230.A56] 53-35981
1. Covers (Philately) 2. Covers (Philately). I. Title.

BARTELS, John Murray, 1871-1944. 383.22
Thorp-Bartels Catalogue of the stamped envelopes and wrappers of the United States; compiled, completely rev. and edited by Prescott Holden Thorp. Editorial board: L. H. Barkhausen [and others] Alice Ruth Thorp, assistant to the editor. William Carroll, photography. 6th (Century) ed. Netcong, N.J., H. Thorp [1954] 597p. illus. 24cm. [HE6185.U6B32 1954] 54-37552
1. Covers (Philately) 2. Postage-stamps—U. S.—Catalogs. I. Thorp, Prescott Holden, ed. II. Title.

BOND, Nelson Slade, 1908- 383.22
The postal stationery of Canada, a reference catalogue. [1st ed.] Shrub Oak, N. Y., H. Herst, Jr. [1953] 132p. illus. 23cm. [HE6185.C2B66] 54-15653
1. Covers (Philately) 2. Postal cards—Catalogs. 3. Postage stamps—Canada—Catalogs. I. Title.

CONNETT, Eugene Virginius, 1891- 383.22
Adventures in cover collecting. New York, Van Nostrand [1955] 72p. illus. 23cm. [HE6230.C6] 55-14325
1. Covers (Philately) I. Title.

HART, Creighton C. 769'.569'73
Directory of 10 cent 1847 covers. Compiled by Creighton L. Hart and Susan M. McDonald. 2d. ed Kansas City, Mo., Reserve Plan, 1970. xv, 156 l. 24 cm. [HE6184.C65H35 1970] 78-274052
1. Covers (Philately) 2. Postage-stamps—U.S. I. McDonald, Susan M., joint author. II. Title.

HART, Creighton C. 769'.569'73
Directory of 10 [cent] 1847 covers. Compiled by Creighton C. Hart and Susan M. McDonald. Kansas City, Mo., Reserve Plan, 1969. 12, [124] l. 24 cm. [HE6184.C65H35] 74-6804
1. Covers (Philately) 2. Postage-stamps—U.S. I. Title.

HARVEY, Jack V. 769'.569'73
First day covers of the regular postage issue of 1922-1935, by Jack V. Harvey. Cranford, N.J., American First Day Cover Society [1967] vi, 64 p. facsims. 23 cm. (AFDS handbook, no. 2) Bibliography: p. 64. [HE6185.U52H3] 68-955
1. Covers (Philately) 2. Postage-stamps—United States. I. Title. II. Series.

MILGRAM, James W. 769.56973075
The western mails, by James W. Milgram. [Cincinnati] Society of Philatelic Americans [196-] 62 p. illus., facsims. 23 cm. [HE6185.U5M5] 67-6219
1. Covers (Philately) 2. Postal service — U.S. — Hist. 3. U.S. — Hist. I. Title.

Covers (Philately)—Catalogs.

†MELLONE, Michael. 769'.56
Discovering the fun in first day covers : complete up-to-date catalogue / compiled and edited by Michael Mellone and Barry Newton. 1st ed. Stewartsville, NJ : F.D.C. Pub. Co., c1977. xxv, 98 p. : ill. ; 19 cm. [HE6184.C65M443] 78-103028 pbk. : 2.95
1. Covers (Philately)—Catalogs. I. Newton, Barry, joint author. II. Title.
Publisher's address : Box 206, Stewartsville, NJ 08886 BIP

Covers (Philately)—United States—Catalogs.

†MELLONE, Michael. 769'.56
The cachet identifier of U.S. cacheted first day covers / by Michael Mellone & Barry Newton. 2d ed. Stewartsville, N.J. : F.D.C. Pub. Co., 1977. 60 p. : ill. ; 23 cm. Includes indexes. [HE6184.C65M44 1977] 78-102950 pbk. : 6.95
1. Covers (Philately)—United States—Catalogs. I. Newton, Barry, joint author. II. Title.
Publisher's address : Box 206, Stewartsville, NJ 08886 BIP

PLANTY, Earl Gerald. 769'.56
U.S. first day cover catalog of classic cachets, 1923-1933, with cachet descriptions, identification by number, and prices, by Earl Planty. Coral Springs, Fla., 1974. 155 l. 28 cm. [HE6184.C65P55] 74-84517 3.50
1. Covers (Philately)—United States—Catalogs. I. Title.

Covers (Philately)—United States—History.

GRANT, Robert W. 769'.5
The handbook of Civil War patriotic envelopes and postal history / Robert W. Grant ; Gordon P. McKinnon, editor. Hanover, Mass. : Grant, c1977- v. : ill. ; 31 cm. Loose-leaf for updating. Bibliography, v. 1, p.: B1-B4. [HE6184.C65G73] 77-72273 ISBN 0-9601218-1-1 loose-leaf : 42.50
1. Covers (Philately)—United States—History. 2. Postal service—United States—History. I. Title.
Publisher's address : P.O. Box 2060, Hanover, MA 02339 BIP

Cowboys in art.

AINSWORTH, Edward Maddin, 1902-1968. 704.94'9'63608
The cowboy in art, by Ed Ainsworth. New York, World Pub. Co. [1968] xiii, 242 p. illus., ports. (both part col.) 29 cm. [N8217.C75A35] 68-23975 15.00
1. Cowboys in art. I. Title.

PHIPPEN, George. 709'.24
The life of a cowboy, told through the drawings, paintings, and bronzes of George Phippen, as selected by Louise Phippen. Tucson, University of Arizona Press [1969] 104 p. illus. (part col.), port. 24 x 32 cm. [N6537.P45A49] 70-101102 ISBN 8-16-502056- 15.00
1. Cowboys in art. I. Phippen, Louise, comp. II. Title. BIP

Cowherd, Barney, 1922-1972.

COWHERD, Barney, 1922-1972. 779'.092'4
Barney Cowherd, photographer. By Bill Strode. [Louisville, Ky.] The Courier-Journal [1973] 152 p. illus. 23 x 27 cm. Bibliography: p. 151. [TR654.C68] 73-89551 4.95
1. Cowherd, Barney, 1922-1972. 2. Photography, Artistic. I. Strode, Bill.
Publisher's address: 525 W Broadway, Louisville, Kentucky 40202.

Cox, Palmer, 1840-1924.

CUMMINS, Roger W. 741'.092'4 B
Humorous but wholesome; a history of Palmer Cox and the Brownies [by] Roger W. Cummins. Watkins Glen, N.Y., Century House [1973] 254 p. illus. 26 cm. Bibliography: p. 235-250. [PS3505.O9633Z6] 72-97477
1. Cox, Palmer, 1840-1924. I. Title. BIP

Coye, Lee Brown.

PICKER Gallery. 709'.24
Lee Brown Coye; retrospective exhibition. [Hamilton, N.Y., 1968] [8] p. illus., port. 24 cm. Catalogue of an exhibition held at the Picker Gallery, Charles A. Dana Art Center, Colgate University, Hamilton, N.Y., Apr. 7-28, 1968. [N6537.C67P5] 68-5221
1. Coye, Lee Brown.

Cozens, Alexander, 1717 (ca.)-1786.

OPPE, Adolf Paul, 1878- v. 12
Alexander & John Robert Cozens. With a reprint of Alexander Cozens' A new method of assisting the invention in drawing original compositions of landscape. Cambridge, Harvard University Press, 1954. xii, 196p. illus., 49 plates. 23cm. Bibliographical footnotes. [NC497.C85O] A54
1. Cozens, Alexander, 1717 (ca.)-1786. 2. Cozens, John Robert, 1752-1797. I. Cozens, Alexander, 1717 (ca.)-1786. A new method of assisting the invention in drawing original compositions of landscape. II. Title.

Crackle.

NUSSBAUMER, Hanny. 745.7'2
Lacquer & crackle. [Translated by Manly Banister. Adapted by Louisa Hellegers] New York, Sterling Pub. Co. [1972] 48 p. illus. 20 cm. (Little craft book series) Translation of Craquelee und Lackarbeiten. Instructions for decorating a variety of things in the home including wastebaskets, boxes, and ceramic wares with crackle, a technique for creating fine cracks in a lacquer finish. [TT378.N8713] 72-80664 ISBN 0-8069-5200-8
1. Crackle. 2. Lacquer and lacquering. I. Title. BIP

Craig, Edward Gordon, 1872-1966.

BABLET, Denis. 792.0250924
Edward Gordon Craig. Translated by Daphne Woodward. [New York] Theatre Arts Books [1966] ix, 207 p. illus., ports. 23 cm. Includes bibliographical references. [PN2091.S8B223 1966a] 66-23134
1. Craig, Edward Gordon, 1872-1966. 2. Theaters—Stage-setting and scenery. BIP

NASH, George. 792'.0924
Edward Gordon Craig, 1872-1966. London, H. M. S. O., 1967. [2], 30 p. front., 36 plates (incl. ports., facsims.) 25cm. (Large picture bk. no. 35) At head of title: Victoria & Albert Mus. [N1150.A752 no. 35] 68-30057 2.50 pap.,
1. Craig, Edward Gordon, 1872-1966. I. Title. II. Series: Victoria and Albert Museum, South Kensington. Large picture books, no. 35
Available from British Info., New York.

ROOD, Arnold. 792'.0924
Edward Gordon Craig, artist of the theatre, 1872-1966; a memorial exhibition in the Amsterdam Gallery. Catalogue by Arnold Rood with an introd. by Donald Oenslager. New York, New York Public Library [1967] 57 p. illus. 26 cm. "Preprinted from the Bulletin of the New York Public Library, September, October 1967." [PN2091.S8R58] 67-28540
1. Craig, Edward Gordon, 1872-1966. I. Shelby Cullom Davis Museum. Amsterdam Gallery. BIP

Cram, Ralph Adams, 1863-1942.

TUCCI, Douglass Shand. 917.44'61
Church building in Boston, 1720-1970 : with an introduction to the work of Ralph Adams Cram and the Boston Gothicists : issued by the trustees of the Dorchester Savings Bank in observation of the Bicentennial of the United States / Douglass Shand Tucci. 1st ed. Concord [Mass.] : Rumford Press, 1974. 134 p. : ill. (some col.) ; 21 x 21 cm. Includes bibliographical references and index. [NA5235.B7T82] 75-314879 7.50
1. Cram, Ralph Adams, 1863-1942. 2. Church architecture—Boston. 3. Gothic revival (Architecture)—Boston. I. Dorchester Savings Bank. II. Title. BIP

TUCCI, Douglass Shand. 720'.92'4
Ralph Adams Cram, American medievalist / by Douglass Shand Tucci. [Boston] : Boston Public Library, 1975. 49 p., [2] fold. leaves of plates : ill. ; 27 cm. Catalogue of an exhibition held at the Boston Public Library. Bibliography: p. 45-49. [NA737.C7T82] 76-358972
1. Cram, Ralph Adams, 1863-1942. 2. Romanesque revival (Architecture)—United States. 3. Gothic revival (Architecture)—United States. I. Boston. Public Library. II. Title. BIP

Cranach, Lucas, 1472-1553.

CRANACH, Lucas, 1472-1553. 759.3
Cranach, by E. Ruhmer. [Translated from the German by Joan Spencer. London] Phaidon Publishers distributed by New York Graphic Society Greenwich Conn. [c1963] 87 p. illus. (part col.) port. 31 cm. Includes bibliographical references. [ND588.C8R8] 63-25190
I. I. Ruhmer, Eberhard. II. Title.

CRANACH, Lucas [original name: Lucas Sunder or Lucas Muller] 1472-1553. 759.3
Cranach, by E. Ruhmer [Tr. from German by Joan Spencer. London] Phiadon Pubs., dist. N.Y. Graphic Soc., Greenwich, Conn. [c.1963] 87p. illus. (pt. col.) port. 31cm. Bibl. 63-25190 5.95
I. Ruhmer, Eberhard. II. Title.

DESCARGUES, Pierre 759.03
Cranach. [Tr. from French by Helen Ramsbotham] new York, Abrams [1962] 87p. col. illus. (Student's ser. of great artists) 61-11936 1.95
1. Cranach, Lucas, 1472-1553. I. Title.

FRIEDLANDER, Max J., 1867-1958. 759.3
The paintings of Lucas Cranach / Max J. Friedlander & Jakob Rosenberg ; [catalogue translated by Heinz Norden ; introd. translated by Ronald Taylor.] Rev. ed. Ithaca, N.Y. : Cornell University Press, c1978. p. cm. Translation of Die Gemalde von Lucas Cranach. Includes indexes. Bibliography: p. [ND588.C8A413 1978] 77-18410 85.00
1. Cranach, Lucas, 1472-1553—Catalogs. I. Rosenberg, Jakob, 1893- joint author. II. Cranach, Lucas, 1472-1553. III. Title. BIP

Cranbrook Academy of Art, Bloomfield Hills, Mich.

CRANBROOK Academy of Art, Bloomfield Hills, Mich. Museum. 745.4'49'22
The creative spirit of Cranbrook; the early years: Eliel Saarinen, Loja Saarinen, Maija Grotell [and] Zoltan Sepeshy. Bloomfield Hills, Mich. [1972] 20 p. illus. 26 cm. Catalog of an exhibition held at the Museum Oct. 30, 1972-Oct. 14, 1973. Bibliography: p. 19. [NK410.B55C72 1972] 73-88751
1. Cranbrook Academy of Art, Bloomfield Hills, Mich. 2. Design—Exhibitions. I. Title.

CRANBROOK ACADEMY OF ART, Bloomfield Hills, Mich. 707.11774
News letter. Bloomfield Hills. no. 23cm. annual. [N330.B55C725] 54-16212
I. Title.

Cranch, Christopher Pearse,

CRANCH, Christopher Pearse, 1813-1892. 759.13 B
The life and letters of Christopher Pearse Cranch, by his daughter Leonora Cranch Scott. New York, AMS Press [1969] xii, 395 p. illus., ports. 23 cm. Reprint of the 1917 ed. [PS1449.C8Z5] 72-90096
I. Scott, Leonora (Cranch) 1848- II. Title. BIP

MILLER, Frederick De Wolfe. 928.1
Christopher Pearse Cranch and his caricatures of New England transcendentalism. Cambridge, Harvard University Press, 1951. xi, 81 p. illus. 22 cm. Bibliography [and] notes": p. [67]-77. [PS1449.C8Z8] 51-10752
1. Cranch, Christopher Pearse, 1813-1892. 2. Transcendentalism (New England) I. Title.

Crane, Walter, 1845-1915.

CRANE, Walter, 1845-1915. 760'.0924
An artist's reminiscences. With 12 illus. by the author, and others from photos. London, Methuen, 1907. Detroit, Singing Tree Press, 1968. xvi, 520 p. illus., ports. 22 cm. [ND497.C86A5 1968] 68-21763
I. Title. BIP

SPENCER, Isobel. 760'.092'4 B
Walter Crane / Isobel Spencer. 1st American ed. New York : Macmillan, 1975. 208 p. : ill. ; 28 cm. Includes index. Bibliography: p. 200-205. [ND497.C86S63 1975] 75-18567 25.00
1. Crane, Walter, 1845-1915. BIP

Crawford, John M.—Art collections.

WILSON, Marc F. 745.6'1'9951
Friends of Wen Cheng-ming : a view from the Crawford Collection : [catalogue of the exhibition] : October 24, 1974 through January 26, 1975 / by Marc F. Wilson and Kwan S. Wong. New York : China House Gallery, China Institute in America, [1974]

128 p. : ill. (some col.) ; 24 cm. "After January 26, 1975, this collection will be exhibited at ... the William Rockhill Nelson Gallery of Art and Atkins Museum of Fine Arts, Kansas City, Missouri [and] Seattle Art Museum, Seattle, Washington." Bibliography: p. 127-128. [ND1042.W54] 74-84780
1. Crawford, John M.—Art collections. 2. Paintings, Chinese—Exhibitions. 3. Calligraphy, Chinese—Exhibitions. I. Wong, Kwan S., joint author. II. China House Gallery. III. Title.

Crawford, Ralston, 1906—

CRAWFORD, Ralston, 1906- 741.9'73
Graphics '73: Ralston Crawford [by] Richard B. Freeman. Lexington, 1973. 96 p. (p. 17-96 illus. (part col.)) 29 cm. Catalog of the exhibition held Feb. 11-Mar. 4, 1973 and organized by the University of Kentucky Art Gallery. [NC139.C72F73] 73-161354
1. Crawford, Ralston, 1906- I. Freeman, Richard B., 1908- II. Kentucky. University. Art Gallery. III. Title.

CRAWFORD, Ralston, 1906- 769.973
Lithographs. [By] Richard B. Freeman. [Lexington] Univ. of Kentucky Pr. [c.1962] 72, [1]p. illus. (pt. col.) 29x39cm. Bibl. 62-13460 10.00 bds.,
I. Freeman, Richard B., 1908- II. Title.

Crawford, Thomas, 1813-1857.

GALE, Robert L 927.3
Thomas Crawford, American sculptor. [Pittsburgh] University of Pittsburg Press [1964] viii, 241 p. 24 cm. "Bibliography and notes": p. 199-229. [NB237.C8G3] 64-12496
1. Crawford, Thomas, 1813-1857. I. Title.

Crawhall, Joseph, 1821-1896.

CRAWHALL, Joseph, 1821- 769'.92'4 1896.
Quaint cuts in the chap book style. Selected and arr. by Theodore Menten. New York, Dover Publications [1974] 88 p. (chiefly illus.) 29 cm. (Dover pictorial archive series) [NE1147.6.C7A55 1974] 73-94349 ISBN 0-486-23020-1 2.50 (pbk.)
1. Crawhall, Joseph, 1821-1896. I. Title. BIP

FELVER, Charles 769'.92'4 B Stanley, 1916-
Joseph Crawhall: the Newcastle wood engraver (1821-1896), by Charles S. Felver. Newcastle upon Tyne, Graham, [1973]. viii, 144 p. illus., facsims. 22 cm. Bibliography: p. 137-141. [NE1147.6.C7F44] 73-161709 ISBN 0-902833-07-3 £3.00
1. Crawhall, Joseph, 1821-1896.

Crayon drawing.

BENNETT, Maggi. 741.2'3
Creative crayon techniques [by] Maggi Bennett, Sarajean Capua [and] Jeanette McArthur. [1st ed.] Hollywood, Fla., Dukane Press [1971, c1970] 32 p. col. illus. 32 cm. Text and color photographs illustrate the versatility of crayon. [NC855.B45] 72-127619 ISBN 0-87800-028-3
1. Crayon drawing. I. Capua, Sarajean, joint author. II. McArthur, Jeanette, 1919- joint author. III. Title.

BOYLSTON, Elise Reid. 372.52
Creative expression with crayons. [Worcester, Mass.] [Davis Press] [1954] 98 p. illus. 25 cm. [NC855.B6 1954] 55-18220
1. Crayon drawing. 2. Drawing—Instruction. I. Title.

BOYLSTON, Elise Reid. 372.52
Creative expressions with crayons. [Worcester, Mass, Davis Press, 1953] 98p. illus. 26cm. [NC855.B6] 53-11790
1. Crayon drawing. 2. Drawing—Instruction. I. Title.

HORN, George F. 741.2'3
The crayon; a versatile medium for creative expression [by] George F. Horn. [Worcester, Mass., Davis Publications, 1969] 64 p. illus. (part col.) 24 x 25 cm. Bibliography: p. 62-63. [NC855.H6] 76-78029 6.95
1. Crayon drawing. I. Title. BIP

KAMPMANN, Lothar. 741.2'3
Creating with crayons. New York, Reinhold Book Corp. [1968] 76 p. illus. (part col.) 21 cm. (Art media series) Translation of Wachsmalstifte. [NC855.K313] 68-26804
1. Crayon drawing. I. Title.

LALIBERTE, Norman. 741.2'3
Painting with crayons: history and modern techniques [by] Norman Laliberte [and] Alex Mogelon. New York, Reinhold [1967] 119 p. (chiefly illus. (part col.)) 21 cm. (An Art horizons book) [NC855.L3] 67-14976
1. Crayon drawing. I. Mogelon, Alex. II. Title.

PLUCKROSE, Henry Arthur. 741.2'3
Introducing crayon techniques [by] Henry Pluckrose. London, Batsford; New York, Watson-Guptill, 1967. 100p. illus. (incl. 1 col.). 22x21cm. Bibl. [NC855.P5] 68-10021 6.95 bds.,
1. Crayon drawing. I. Title.

RAINEY, Sarita R. 741.2'3
Crayon resist techniques [by] Sarita Rainey [and] Burton Wasserman. Worcester, Mass., Davis Publications [1972] 35 p. illus. 20 x 27 cm. (Basic concept series, no. 4) [NC855.R34] 72-79635 ISBN 0-87192-049-2 1.95
1. Crayon drawing. 2. Artists' materials. I. Wasserman, Burton, joint author. II. Title. BIP

ROMBERG, Jenean. 741.2'3
Let's discover crayon. New York, Center for Applied Research in Education [1973] 64 p. illus. 28 cm. (Her Arts and crafts discovery units) [NC855.R65] 73-14840 ISBN 0-87628-523-X 3.95
1. Crayon drawing. 2. Art—Study and teaching (Elementary) I. Title. BIP

Crayon drawing—Juvenile literature.

ALKEMA, Chester Jay. 741.2'3
The complete crayon book, in color. New York, Sterling Pub. Co. [1969] 156 p. illus. (part col.) 21 x 25 cm. Describes many different techniques for using crayon in art work. [NC870.A47] 69-19486
1. Crayon drawing—Juvenile literature. I. Title.

SCOTT, Guy. 741.2'3
Let's crayon. New York, Van Nostrand Reinhold [1972] c1971. 32 p. illus. (part col.) 22 cm. (Starting points) Describes various techniques for creating designs and pictures with crayons. [NC870.S36 1972] 79-188509 ISBN 0-442-27522-6 1.45
1. Crayon drawing—Juvenile literature. I. Title.

Crazy Horse, Oglala Indian, 1842 (ca.)-1877—Juvenile literature.

KOTZWINKLE, William. 736'.5
Return of Crazy Horse. Pictures by Joe Servello. [1st ed.] New York, Farrar, Straus and Giroux [1971] [39] p. col. illus. 30 cm. Describes the efforts of Korczak Ziolkowski to carve a monument to Crazy Horse, Sioux Chief, out of Thunderhead Mountain in the Black Hills of South Dakota. [E99.O3K6] 78-149217 ISBN 0-374-36246-7 4.95
1. Crazy Horse, Oglala Indian, 1842 (ca.)-1877—Juvenile literature. 2. Ziolkowski, Korczak, 1908-—Juvenile literature. 3. Thunderhead Mountain, S.D.—Juvenile literature. I. Servello, Joe, illus. II. Title.

Creamware.

TOWNER, Donald C. 738.3'7
Creamware / by Donald Towner. London ; Boston : Faber and Faber, 1978. 240 p., [4] p. of plates : ill. (some col.) ; 26 cm. (The Faber monographs on pottery and porcelain) Includes index. Bibliography: p. [233]-234. [NK4278.T68] 78-320727 ISBN 0-571-04964-8 : 37.50
1. Creamware. 2. Pottery, English. I. Title. Distributed by Faber & faber, Salem, NH BIP

Creation—Art.

WORLD Council of Christian 755.48 Education and Sunday School Association
In the beginning; paintings of the creation by boys and girls around the world. New York, Nelson [c.1965] [32]p. (chiefly col. illus.) 23x28cm. [N8180.W67] 65-12531 3.50 bds.,
1. Creation—Art. 2. Bible. O. T. Genesis—Pictures, illustrations, etc. 3. Children as artists. I. Title.

Creation in art.

YEARBURY, Pauline 759.9931 Kahurangi.
The children of Rangi and Papa : the Maori story of creation / Pauline Kahurangi Yearbury. Christchurch : Whitcoulls, 1976. 36 p. : col. ill. ; 36 cm. [ND1108.Y4A43] 77-363030 ISBN 0-7233-0449-1 : 25.00
1. Yearbury, Pauline Kahurangi. 2. Creation in art. 3. Mythology, Maori—Poetry. I. Title. BIP

Creation (Literacy, artistic, etc.)—Psychological aspects.

GETZELS, Jacob W. 707'.1'173
Creative thinking in art students: an exploratory study [by] Jacob W. Getzels and Mihaly Csikszentmihalyi. Chicago, University of Chicago, 1964. vii, 202 p. illus. 28 cm. Cooperative research project no. E-008, Office of Education, U.S. Dept. of Health, Education, and Welfare. Includes bibliographical references. [N345.G4] 65-60624
1. Creation (Literary, artists, etc.) 2. Art — Study and teaching. 3. Artists — Psychology. I. Csikszentmihalyi, Mihaly, joint author. II. Chicago. University. III. Title.

PICASSO, Pablo, 1881- 709'.2'4 1973.
Child and caveman : elements of Picasso's creativity / [compiled by] Josep Palau i Fabre. New York : Rizzoli, [1978, c1977] 20, 69 p. : chiefly ill. (some col.) ; 21 cm. Bibliography: p. 20 (1st group) [N6853.P5A4 1978] 77-95343 ISBN 0-8478-0165-9 : 9.95
1. Picasso, Pablo, 1881-1973. 2. Creation (Literary, arrtistic, etc.)—Psychological aspects. I. Palau y Fabre, Jose. II. Title. BIP

Creation (Literary, artistic, etc.)

ALLAND, Alexander, 1931- 700'.1
The artistic animal : an inquiry into the biological roots of art / Alexander Alland, Jr. 1st ed. Garden City, N.Y. : Anchor Books, 1977. xii, 153 p., [8] leaves of plates : ill. ; 21 cm. Includes index. Bibliography: p. 143-145. [NX165.A455] 76-53408 ISBN 0-385-09771-9 pbk. : 3.95
1. Creation (Literary, artistic, etc.) 2. Arts—Psychology. I. Title. BIP

BERDIAEV, Nikolai 155.333 Aleksandrovich, 1874-1948.
The meaning of the creative act. Translated by Donald A. Lowrie. New York, Harper [1955?] 344p. 21cm. [BF408.B413] 55-14509
1. Creation (Literary, artistic, etc.) I. Title.

BOSTON. Institute of 155.333 Contemporary Art.
Conference on motivating the creative process, May 7-10, 1957, Arden House, Harriman, New York; the second in a series of three conferences organized by the Institute of Contemporary Art, with the assistance of William J. J. Gordon and Jerome S. Bruner. Cover design by Carl F. Zahn. [Boston, 1957] 137p. 28cm. [BF408.B58] 57-49208
1. Creation (Literary, artistic, etc.) I. Title. II. Title: Motivating the creative process.

CENTENO, Augusto, 1901- ed. 701
The intent of the artist, by Sherwood Anderson [and others] New York, Russell & Russell [1970, c1941] 162 p. illus. 22 cm. Contents.Contents.—Man and his imagination, by S. Anderson.—Some thoughts on playwrighting, by T. Wilder.—The composer and his message, by R. Sessions.—These documents called buildings, by W. Lescaze. [BF408.C4 1970] 71-81455
1. Creation (Literary, artistic, etc.) 2. Imagination. I. Anderson, Sherwood, 1876-1941. II. Title.

CHICAGO. University. 155 Committee on Social Thought.
The works of the mind, by Mortimer J. Adler [others] Ed. for the Comm. on Soc. Thought by Ro]ert B. Heywood. Pref. & new foreword by John U. Nef. Chicago, Univ. of Chicago Pr. [1966, c.1947] xix, 246p. music. 21cm. (Phonix ed., P239) Paps. -- offered as a set of lects. at the Univ. of Chicago during 1946. [BF408.C5] 47-11992 2.45 pap.,
1. Creation (Literary, artistic, etc.) I. Adler, Mortimer Jerome, 1902- II. Heywood, Robert B., 1918- ed. III. Title. Contents omitted. The clothbound edition is still available.

THE Creative expression 153.3'5 / edited by Stanley Rosner and Lawrence Edwin Abt. Croton-on-Hudson, N.Y. : North River Press, c1976. v, 383 p. : ports. ; 23 cm. Bibliography: p. 383. [BF408.C746] 75-37977 ISBN 0-88427-015-7 : 17.50
1. Creation (Literary, artistic, etc.) I. Rosner, Stanley, 1928- II. Abt, Lawrence Edwin, 1915-
Contents omitted BIP

EZELL, Mancil. 153.3'5
Being creative [by] Mancil and Suzanne Ezell. Illustrated by Mancil Ezell. Nashville, Broadman Press [1974] 88 p. illus. 13 x 20 cm. [BF408.E93] 73-91608 ISBN 0-8054-6913-3 1.95 (pbk.)
1. Creation (Literary, artistic, etc.) I. Ezell, Suzanne, joint author. II. Title. BIP

GILSON, Etienne Henry, 1884- 155
Choir of muses; translated by Maisie Ward. New York, Sheed and Ward, 1953. 196p. 21cm. Translation of L'ecole des muses. [BF408.G513] 53-9809
1. Creation (Literary, artistic, etc.) I. Title.

HALPRIN, Lawrence. 701.15
The RSVP cycles; creative processes in the human environment. New York, G. Braziller [1970, c1969] 207 p. illus. 23 cm. Bibliography: p. 206-207. [NX175.H3 1970] 73-107750 15.00
1. Creation (Literary, artistic, etc.) 2. Human ecology. I. Title. BIP

HEPPER, Alfred H B 159.954433
How to get original ideas; a course of thirty-six lessons in developing originality, by Edward Wortley [pseud.] New York, Park Row Pub. House [1941] xvii, 234p. 24cm. Includes bibliographies. [BF408.H4] 155.333 41-8052
1. Creation (Literary, artistic, etc.) 2. Inventions. 3. Thought and thinking. I. Title.

JEANNERET-GRIS, Charles 709.44 Edouard, 1887-
Creation is a patient search [by] Le Corbusier [pseud.] Translated by James Palmes. Introd. by Maurice Jardot. New York, Praeger [1960] 308, [4]p. illus., maps, plans. 29cm. (Books that matter) Bibliography: p. [310]-[311] [NA1053.J4A5] 60-53113
1. Creation (Literary, artistic, etc.) 2. Art, Modern—20th cent. I. Title.

KEPES, Gyorgy, 1906- ed. 701
The man-made object. New York, G. Braziller [1966] 230 p. illus. 29 cm. (Vision+value series) Includes bibliographies. [N7428.K4] 66-13046
1. Creation (Literary, artistic, etc.) 2. Art—Philosophy. 3. Art—Technique. I. Title.

KOESTLER, Arthur, 1905- 155.3
The act of creation. New York, Macmillan [1964] 751 p. illus. 24 cm. Bibliography: p. 700-728. [BF408.K6] 64-25194
1. Creation (Literary, artistic, etc.) I. Title. BIP

LEHMAN, Harvey Christian. 155
Age and and achievement. [Princeton] Published for the American Philosophical Society by Princeton University Press, 1953. xi, 358p. diagrs. 25cm. (Memoirs of the American Philosophical Society, v. 33)

Bibliography: p.333-341. [BF408.L56] 52-13159
1. Creation (Literary, artistic, etc.) I. Title. II. Series: American Philosophical Society. Philadelphia. Memoirs, v. 33

LIFE class 001.2
[conducted by] Charles Schorre. Houston, Tex. [Rice University; distributed by Wittenborn, New York] 1968. 1 v. (unpaged) 19 cm. (Architecture at Rice 24) [NA1.A785 no. 24] [BF408] 720.05 68-57035 4.00
1. Creation (Literary, artistic, etc.) 2. Visual perception. I. Schorre, Charles. II. Series: Architecture at Rice University 24

MCKELLAR, Peter. 155.333
Imagination and thinking; a psychological analysis. New York, Basic Books [1957] 219p. illus. 22cm. [BF408.M2 1957a] 57-3802
1. Creation (Literary, artistic, etc.) 2. Imagination I. Title.

MARITAIN, Jacques, 1882- 155.333
Creative intuition in art and poetry. New York, Meridian Books, 1955[c1953] 339p. illus. 18cm. (The A. W. Mellon lectures in the fine arts. 1) Meridian books, M8. [BF408.M25 1955] 55-5167
1. Creation (Literary, artistic, etc.) I. Title. BIP

MARITAIN, Jacques, 1882- 155.333
Creative intuition in art and poetry. [New York] Pantheon Books [1953] xxxii, 423 p. 69 plates (1 col.), diagrs. 26 cm. (Bollingen series, 35. The A. W. Mellon lectures in the fine arts, 1) Includes bibliographical references. [BF408.M25 1953] 53-5537
1. Creation (Literary, artistic, etc.) I. Title. II. Series: Bollingen series, 35. III. Series: The A. W. Mellon lectures in the fine arts, 1.

MARSHALL, George O ed. 001.9
Creativity and the arts. Athens, University of Georgia, Center for Continuing Education [1961] 104p. illus. 22cm. (Basic issues of man, no. 4) Includes bibliography. [BF408.M26] 62-326
1. Creation (Literary, artistic, etc.) I. Title.

MAUE, Kenneth. 701'.15
Water in the lake : real events for the imagination / by Kenneth Maue. 1st ed. New York : Harper & Row, c1979. p. cm. Bibliography: p. [BF408.M327] 78-4737 ISBN 0-06-012952-2 : 9.50. ISBN 0-06-090670-7 pbk. : 4.95
1. Creation (Literary, artistic, etc.) 2. Imagination. I. Title. BIP

MAY, Rollo. 153.3'5
The courage to create / Rollo May. 1st ed. New York : Norton, [1975] 143 p. ; 21 cm. Includes bibliographical references. [BF408.M33 1975] 75-23055 ISBN 0-393-01119-4 : 7.95
1. Creation (Literary, artistic, etc.) I. Title. BIP

OSBORN, Alexander Faickney, 1888- 155.333
Applied imagination; principles and procedures of creative thinking. Rev. ed. New York, Scribner [1957] 379 p. 21 cm. Includes bibliographies. [BF408.O775 1957] 57-7589
1. Creation (Literary, artistic, etc.) I. Title. BIP

OSBORN, Alexander Faickney, 1888- 155.3
Applied imagination; principles and procedures of creative problem-solving. 3d rev. ed. New York, Scribner [1963] 417 p. 21 cm. [BF408.O775 1963] 63-15514
1. Creation (Literary, artistic, etc.) I. Title.

RIBOT, Theodule Armand, 1839-1916. 153.3'5
Essay on the creative imagination. New York, Arno Press, 1973 [c1906] xix, 370 p. 23 cm. (Classics in psychology) Translation of Essai sur l'imagination creatrice. Reprint of the ed. published by Open Court Pub. Co., Chicago. Includes bibliographical references. [BF408.R3513 1973] 73-2987 ISBN 0-405-05159-X 18.00
1. Creation (Literary, artistic, etc.) 2. Imagination. I. Title. II. Series. BIP

ROMEY, William D. 158
Consciousness and creativity : transcending science, humanities, and the arts / Bill Romey ; drawings by Lucretia Romey. Canton, N.Y. : Ash Lad Press, [1975] 278 p. : ill. ; 23 cm. Includes bibliographical references. [BF408.R63] 75-5095 ISBN 0-915492-00-8
1. Creation (Literary, artistic, etc.) 2. Consciousness. I. Title. BIP

SACHS, Hanns, 1881-1947. 001.9
The creative unconscious; studies in the psychoanalysis of art. 2d enl. ed. edited by A. A. Roback. Cambridge, Mass., Sci-Art Publishers, 1951. 358 p. 20 cm. [[BF408.S...]] A 52
1. Creation (Literary, artistic, etc.) 2. Aesthetics. 3. Psychoanalysis. I. Title.

SORELL, Walter, 1905- 701
The duality of vision: genius and versatility in the arts. Indianapolis, Bobbs-Merrill [1970] 360 p. illus. (part col.) 26 cm. Bibliography: p. 342-344. [NX175.S65 1970] 74-98290 15.00
1. Creation (Literary, artistic, etc.) 2. Genius. I. Title.

SUMMERFIELD, Jack D ed. 155.3
The creative mind and method: exploring the nature of creativeness in American arts, sciences, and professions. With commentary by Lyman Bryson. Edited by Jack D. Summerfield and Lorlyn Thatcher. Austin, University of Texas Press [1960] 118 p. illus. 26 cm. "Supplement to the Texas quarterly, volume three, number two." Includes bibliography. [BF408.S85] 60-14308
1. Creation (Literary,artistic, etc.) I. Thatcher, Lorlyn, joint ed. II. The Texas quarterly, Supplement. III. Title.

TAYLOR, Jack Wilson, 1915- 155.3
How to create new ideas. Englewood Cliffs, N.J., Prentice-Hall [1961] 242 p. illus. 24 cm. Includes bibliography. [BF408.T3] 61-12003
1. Creation (Literary, artistic, etc.) I. Title.

TOMAS, Vincent, ed. 155.3082
Creativity in the arts. Englewood Cliffs, N.J., Prentice-Hall [1964] ix, 110 p. illus. 22 cm. (Contemporary perspectives in philosophy series) Bibliography: p. 110. [BF408.T6] 64-11552
1. Creation (Literary, artistic, etc.) I. Title.

VISUAL Communications Conference. 3d, New York, 1958. 155.3082
Creativity, an examination of the creative process; a report on the third communications conference of the Art Directors Club of New York. Paul Smith, editor. New York, Hastings House [1959] 210 p. illus. 26 cm. (Communication arts books) [BF408.V5 1958] 58-14479
1. Creation (Literary, artistic, etc.) I. Smith, Paul, 1907- ed. II. Title.

VISUAL Communications Conference, 3d, New York, 1958. 153.3'5
Creativity, an examination of the creative process; a report on the third communications conference of the Art Directors Club of New York. Paul Smith, editor. Freeport, N.Y., Books for Libraries Press [1972, c1959] 210 p. illus. 27 cm. (Essay index reprint series) [BF408.V5 1958a] 77-167306 ISBN 0-8369-2578-5
1. Creation (Literary, artistic, etc.) I. Smith, Paul, 1907- ed. II. Art Directors Club of New York. III. Title.

WHITING, Charles S 155
Creative thinking. New York, Reinhold [1958] 168 p. illus. 23 cm. (Reinhold management science series) [BF408.W46] 58-13586
1. Creation (Literary, artistic, etc.) I. Title.

Creation (Literary, artistic, etc.)—Addresses, essays, lectures.

NEUMANN, Erich. 150'.19'5
Art and the creative unconscious : four essays / Erich Neumann ; translated from the German by Ralph Manheim. Princeton, N.J. : Princeton University Press, 1971, c1959. 232 p., 7 leaves of plates : ill. ; 21 cm. (Bollingen series, 61) "A translation of Kunst und schopferisches Unbewusstes, which was published in 1954...as the third of a series of volumes of collected essays...under the common title of 'Umkreisung der Mitte.' To the three original essays a fourth has been added." Includes index. Contents.Contents.—Leonardo di Vinci and the mother archetype.—Art and time.—A note on Marc Chagall.—Creative man and transformation. Bibliography: p. 209-215. [BF408.N3813 1971] 75-312938 ISBN 0-691-01773-5
1. Creation (Literary, artistic, etc.)—Addresses, essays, lectures. 2. Subconsciousness—Addresses, essays, lectures. I. Title. II. Series.

NEUMANN, Erich. 150'.19'5
Art and the creative unconscious : four essays / Erich Neumann ; translated from the German by Ralph Manheim. New York : Harper & Row, 1966, c1959. 226 p., [7] leaves of plates : ill. ; 20 cm. (Harper torchbooks, TB 2022K : The Bollingen library ; 61) "A translation of Kunst und schopferisches Unbewusstes, which was published in 1954 ... as the third of a series of volumes of collected essays ... under the common title 'Umkreisung der Mitte.' To the three original essays a fourth has been added." Includes index. Contents.Contents.—Leonardo di Vinci and the mother archetype.—Art and time.—A note on Marc Chagall.—Creative man and transformation. Bibliography: p. 206-212. [BF408.N3813 1966] 75-312939
1. Creation (Literary, artistic, etc.)—Addresses, essays, lectures. 2. Subconsciousness—Addresses, essays, lectures. I. Title. BIP

Creative ability.

BARRON, Frank X., 1922- 153.3'5
Creative person and creative process [by] Frank Barron. New York, Holt, Rinehart and Winston [1969] x, 212 p. 22 cm. Bibliography: p. 195-208. [BF408.B355] 76-75918
1. Creative ability. I. Title.

BARRON, Frank X., 1922- 153.9'2
An eye more fantastical [by] Frank Barron. Washington, National Art Education Association, 1967. 13 p. 23 cm. (Research monograph 3) [BF408.B349] 74-256057
1. Creative ability. 2. Perception. I. Title. II. Series: National Art Education Association. Research monograph no. 3

KOESTLER, Arthur, 1905- 153.3
The act of creation. [New York] Macmillan [1969] 491 p. 21 cm. (The Danube edition) [BF408.K6 1969b] 73-85780 7.95
1. Creative ability. I. Title.

Creative activities and seat work.

ELLIOTT, Ann. 745.5
Eyes to see God : [a book of arts and crafts activities] / Ann Elliott. Wilton, Conn. : Morehouse-Barlow Co., c1977. 95 p. : ill. ; 28 cm. Includes index. [BV1536.E43] 77-70796 ISBN 0-8192-1225-3 : 5.95
1. Creative activities and seat work. 2. Christian education of children. I. Title. BIP

HAUPT, Dorothy 745.5
Creative activities for young children [by] D. Keith Osborn, Dorothy Haupt [Rev. ed.] Detroit, Merrill-Palmer Inst. of Human Development and Family Life, 71 E. Ferry Ave., 1964. 105p. illus. 23cm. Author's names in reverse order in 1956 ed. pub. under title: Creative activities. Bibl. [LB1537.H35] 64-8104 1.50 pap.,
1. Creative activities and seat work. I. Osborn, D. Keith, joint author. II. Title.

HORTH, Lillie B 793.7
101 things for children to do, by L. B. & A. C. Horth. Rev. by M. Metcalfe. [7th ed.] New York, Lippincott, 1957. 220p. illus. 20cm. First published in 1936 under title: 101 things for little folks to do. [GV1218.P3H6 1957] 57-59044
1. Creative activities and seat work. 2. Paper work. I. Horth, Arthur Cawdron, 1874- joint author. II. Title.

LARSON, Katherine A. 702'.8
Let's make something with shapes & colors / Katherine A. Larson & Frederick A. Rodgers ; [ill., Jody Grovier]. Champaign, Ill. : CEPCO, 1978. 96 p. : ill. ; 21 x 26 cm. (Let's do it) Bibliography: p. 95. Suggested art projects simulate how an artist thinks and works. Includes brief discussions of color, shapes, drawing and painting techniques, and art supplies. [LB1537.L29] 78-55561 ISBN 0-89469-102-3 lib. bdg. : 11.95 ISBN 0-89469-101-5 pbk. : 8.50
1. Creative activities and seat work. I. Rodgers, Frederick A., joint author. II. Grovier, Jody. III. Title. BIP

PLUCKROSE, Henry Arthur. 372.5
Creative arts and crafts; a handbook for teachers in primary schools [by] H. Pluckrose. With photos. by G. W. Hales. New York, Roy Publishers [1967, c1966] xv, 232 p. illus. 23 cm. [N361.P55 1967] 67-20234
1. Creative activities and seat work. 2. Art—Study and teaching (Primary) I. Title.

RAZZI, James. 745.59
Easy does it! Things to make and do. Edited by Anne Walentas. New York, Parents' Magazine Press [1969] 61 p. col. illus. 19 x 27 cm. Instruction for simple handicrafts, magic tricks, puzzles, and games. [GV1201.R35] 75-77794 3.50
1. Creative activities and seat work. I. Title. II. Title: Things to make and do.

Creative Artists Public Service Program.

CREATIVE Artists Public Service Program. 658'.91'70079
Caps in capsule : a fellowship program for individual artists. [New York : Creative Artists Public Service Program, c1975] 67 p. : ill. ; 26 cm. Cover title. [NX742.N7C73 1975] 75-24028
1. Creative Artists Public Service Program. 2. Arts—Scholarships, fellowships, etc.—New York (State) I. Title.

Creative thinking—Abstracts.

†GRANT, Donald P. 620'.004'2
A partially annotated bibliography on the morphological approach to plan generation / Donald P. Grant. Monticello, Ill. : Council of Planning Librarians, 1976. 26 p. ; 29 cm. (Exchange bibliography ; 1125) Cover title. Includes indexes. [Z5942.C68 no. 1125] [BF408] 77-362766 pbk. : 2.50
1. Creative thinking—Abstracts. 2. Engineering design—Abstracts. 3. Architectural design—Abstracts. I. Title: A partially annotated bibliography on the morphological approach ... II. Series: Council of Planning Librarians. Exchange bibliography ; 1125.

Creative thinking (Education)

SMITH, James A. 372.5
Creative teaching of the creative arts in the elementary school [by] James A. Smith. Foreword by E. Paul Torrance. Boston, Allyn [1967] xvi, 186p. illus. 22cm. (Allyn ser. in creative teaching, 4) Includes music. Bibl. [N362.S6] 67-15070 3.95 pap.,
1. Creative thinking (Education) 2. Art—Study and teaching (Elementary) 3. Performing arts—Study and teaching. I. Title.

Cree Indians—Pictorial works.

SAPP, Allen, 1929- 759.11
A Cree life : the art of Allen Sapp / introd. by John Anson Warner & Thecla Bradshaw. Vancouver : J. J. Douglas, c1977. 126 p. : ill. (some col.), port. ; 31 cm. Bibliography: p. 121-122. [ND249.S27A4 1977] 78-304465 ISBN 0-88894-149-8 : 24.95
1. Sapp, Allen, 1929- 2. Cree Indians—Pictorial works. I. Title.
Distributed by ISBS

Crests.

HONDA, Isao, 1888- 745.44052
Monsho; family crests for symbolic design. [Translated by Masatsugu Tsuzawa and Donald C. Mann] Rutland, Vt., Japan Publications Trading Co. [1963] 90 p. (chiefly illus.) 27 cm. [CR57.J3H613] 63-22580
1. Crests. 2. Heraldry — Japan. I. Title. II. Title: Family crests for symbolic design.

Cret, Paul Philippe, 1876-1945.

WHITE, Theophilus 720'.92'4
Ballou, 1903-
Paul Philippe Cret, architect and teacher. Edited, with introductory text by Theo B. White. Foreword by John F. Harbeson. Philadelphia, Art Alliance Press [1973] 94 p. illus. 29 cm. "Appendix B: Selected papers and articles by Paul Philippe Cret": p. [47]-91. Bibliography: p. 91. [NA737.C74W45] 72-7856 ISBN 0-87982-008-X 10.00
1. Cret, Paul Philippe, 1876-1945. I. Cret, Paul Philippe, 1876-1945.

Crewelwork.

ALFERS, Betty. 746.4'4
Creative crewel. New York, Grosset & Dunlap [1970] 95 p. illus. 22 cm. [TT778.C7A4] 76-86672 3.95
1. Crewelwork. I. Title.

EDWARDS, Joan, designer. 746.4'4
Crewel embroidery in England / Joan Edwards. New York : Morrow, c1975. 248 p. : ill. (some col.) ; 29 cm. Includes index. Bibliography: p. 235-238. [TT778.C7E38 1975] 74-29088 ISBN 0-688-02919-1 : 17.50
1. Crewelwork. 2. Embroidery, English. I. Title.

FRANCINI, Audrey A. 746.4'4
Crewel embroidery / Audrey A. Francini. New York : Van Nostrand Reinhold Co., 1979. p. cm. Includes index. Bibliography: p. [TT778.C7F72] 78-27160 ISBN 0-442-21651-3 : 15.00
1. Crewelwork. I. Title. BIP

HEDLUND, Catherine A. 746.4'4
A primer of New England crewel embroidery, by Catherine A. Hedlund. [5th ed.] Sturbridge, Mass., Old Sturbridge Village [1973] 76 p. illus. 22 cm. (Old Sturbridge Village booklet series) [TT778.C7H4 1973] 73-176025
1. Crewelwork. 2. Embroidery—New England—History. I. Title. II. Series.

HEDLUND, Catherine A. 746.4'4
A primer of New England crewel embroidery, by Catherine A. Hedlund. [2d ed.] Sturbridge, Mass., Old Sturbridge Village [1967] 64 p. illus. 22 cm. (Old Sturbridge Village booklet series no. 17) [TT771.H25 1967] 68-257
1. Crewelwork. 2. Embroidery—New England—History. I. Title. II. Title: Crewel embroidery. III. Series.

HOWE, Margery Burnham. 746.4'4
Deerfield embroidery / Margery Burnham Howe. New York : Scribner, [1975] p. cm. Includes index. Bibliography: p. [TT778.C7H68] 75-14020 ISBN 0-684-14377-1 : 12.50
1. Crewelwork. 2. Embroidery, American. 3. Deerfield, Mass.—History. I. Title. BIP

*JONES, Mary Eirwen. 746.4'4
English crewell designs. New York, Morrow [1974] 160 p. illus (part col.) 26 cm. Bibliography: p. 160. [TT778] 74-7633 ISBN 0-688-00288-9 9.95
1. Crewelwork. I. Title.

LANDON, Mary Taylor. 746.4'4
American crewelwork [by] Mary Taylor Landon and Susan Burrows Swan. Illustrated by Susan Burrows Swan. [New York] Macmillan [1970] 192 p. illus. (part col.) 26 cm. [TT778.C7L3] 79-104869
1. Crewelwork. 2. Embroidery, American. I. Swan, Susan Burrows, joint author. II. Title. BIP

MCBRIDE, Regina 746.4'4
Creative crewel embroidery; a complete illustrated guide to mastering the stitches and exploring design. [1st ed.] Garden City, N.Y., Doubleday, 1974. xiii, 385 p. illus. 27 cm. [TT778.C7M32] 73-11716 ISBN 0-385-02400-2 12.95
1. Crewelwork. I. Title.

MCCLENNEN, Barbara C. 746.4'4
Crewel embroidery made easy [by] Barbara C. McClennen. [1st ed.] Garden City, N.Y., Doubleday, 1972. xii, 179 p. illus. 22 cm. [TT778.C7M33] 71-159543 5.95
1. Crewelwork. I. Title.

PERRONE, Lisbeth. 746.4'4
The new world of crewel / Lisbeth Perrone. New York : Random House, [1975] p. cm. Includes index. [TT778.C7P47] 75-10290 ISBN 0-394-48979-9 : 9.95
1. Crewelwork. I. Title. BIP

SPRINGER, Jo. 746.4'4
Pleasures of crewel; a book of elementary to elegant stitches and new embroidery designs. New York, Universal Pub.; distributed by Scribner [1972] 166 p. illus. 27 cm. (The Betty Crocker home library) [TT778.C7S67] 70-177368 ISBN 0-684-12867-5 8.95
1. Crewelwork. I. Title.

STEARNS, Martha (Genung) 746.44
Homespun and blue; a study of American crewel embroidery. New York, Scribner [1963] xiii, 96 p. illus. (part col.) 23 cm. [NK9212.S8 1963] 63-19875
1. Crewelwork. 2. Embroidery, American—History. I. Title.

WILSON, Erica. 746.4'4
The craft of crewel embroidery. Illustrated with drawings by Vladimir Kagan, and with photos. New York, Scribner [1971] 96 p. illus. 28 cm. (The Scribner library, SL211 Emblem editions) Abridged from [the author's] Crewel embroidery published in 1962. [TT778.C7W54] 76-165167 ISBN 0-684-12501-3 2.95
1. Crewelwork. I. Title. BIP

WILSON, Erica. 746.44
Crewel embroidery. Illustrated with drawings by Vladimir Kagan, and with photos. New York, Scribner [1962] 153 p. illus. 27 cm. [TT771.W73] 62-9637
1. Crewelwork. I. Title.

Crewelwork—Juvenile literature.

YOUNG, Eleanor R. 746.4'4
Crewel embroidery / by Eleanor R. Young. New York : Watts, 1976. 63 p. : ill. ; 24 cm. (A Concise guide) Includes index. A guide to crewel embroidery covering materials, design, stitches, and suggested projects. [TT778.C7Y68] 76-16534 ISBN 0-531-00341-8 lib.bdg. : 4.33
1. Crewelwork—Juvenile literature. I. Title. BIP

Crewelwork—Patterns.

SNOOK, Barbara. 746.4'4
Embroidery designs from pre-columbian art / by Barbara L. Snook. New York : Scribner, c1975. x, 134 p., [8] leaves of plates : ill. (some col.) ; 28 cm. Includes index. Bibliography: p. 132. [TT778.C7S65] 73-2552 ISBN 0-684-13988-X : 12.95
1. Crewelwork—Patterns. 2. Canvas embroidery—Patterns. 3. Indians—Art. I. Title.

Crib in Christian art and tradition.

BOSTON. Museum of Fine 731.8'856
Arts.
An 18th century creche. Introd. by Hams Swarzenski. Boston [1967] 54 p. 19 plates (part col.) 23 cm. Bibliography: p. 15. [N8180.B64] 66-25450
1. Crib in Christian art and tradition. 2. Sculpture—Boston. I. Swarzenski, Hanns, 1903- II. Title.

DE ROBECK, Nests. 704.9485
The Christmas crib. Milwaukee, Bruce Pub. Co. [1956] 119p. illus. 23cm. [N8180.D4 1956] 56-11151
1. Crib in Chiristian art and tradition. I. Title.

MAURON, Marie 738.38
Santons of Provence. [Translated from the French by Melvin Askew and Elena Fels Noth] New York, Oxford University Press. [c.]1959. 30p. col. illus. (col.) 12x16 cm. 59-65493 apply pap.,
1. Crib in Christian art and tradition. 2. Pottery—Provence. I. Title.

THE 704.948'55'07401471
Nativity; the Christmas creche at the Metropolitan Museum of Art; the Loretta Hines Howard Collection, photographed by Lee Boltin. Commentary by Olga Raggio. [1st ed.] Garden City, N.Y., Doubleday [1969] [62] p. col. illus. 29 cm. [N8065.B6] 75-81519 7.95
1. Howard, Loretta Hines—Art collections. 2. Crib in Christian art and tradition. I. Raggio, Olga, 1926- II. New York (City). Metropolitan Museum of Art.

Criticism.

BOAS, George, 1891- 700'.1
A primer for critics. New York, Phaeton Press, 1968. viii, 153 p. front. 23 cm. Reprint of the 1937 ed. [BH39.B6 1968b] 68-59377
1. Criticism. 2. Aesthetics. I. Title. BIP

GREENE, William Chace, 701.1
1901-
The choices of criticism. Cambridge, Mass., M.I.T. [c.1965] vi, 207p. illus. 21cm. [PN81.G73] 65-26664 7.50
1. Criticism. I. Title.

TSUGAWA, Albert Genyo, 701.17
1927-
The idea of criticism, by Albert Tsugawa. University Park, Pennsylvania State University [1967] 157 p. 23 cm. (The Pennsylvania State University studies, no. 20) Errata slip inserted. Includes bibliographical references in "Notes" (p. 145-151) [BH39.T75] 67-63894
1. Criticism. 2. Aesthetics. I. Title. II. Series: Pennsylvania. State University. The Pennsylvania State University studies, no. 20

Criticism—Addresses, essays, lectures.

READ, Herbert Edward, Sir, 701
1893-1968.
The tenth muse; essays in criticism. Freeport, N.Y., Books for Libraries Press [1969, c1957] ix, 330 p. 8 illus. 23 cm. (Essay index reprint series) Includes bibliographical references. [PN85.R4 1969] 73-99646
1. Criticism—Addresses, essays, lectures. 2. The arts—Addresses, essays, lectures. I. Title. BIP

Critics—England—Biography.

ROSSETTI, William 700'.92'4 B
Michael, 1829-1919.
The diary of W. M. Rossetti 1870-1873 / edited with an introd. and notes by Odette Bornand. Oxford [Eng.] : Clarendon Press, 1978 xxiii, 302 p., [1] leaf of plates : port. ; 22 cm. Includes bibliographical references and index. [PR5249.R2A799 1977] 78-312738 ISBN 0-19-812458-9 : 26.50
1. Rossetti, William Michael, 1829-1919. 2. Rossetti Family. 3. Critics—England—Biography. 4. Art critics—England—Biography. 5. Poets, English—19th century—Biography. I. Bornand, Odette. II. Title.
Distributed by Oxford University Press, NY BIP

Crocheting.

AYTES, Barbara. 746.4'3
Adventures in crocheting; more than 100 easy-to-make patterns, with photographs, drawings and detailed instructions. [1st ed.] Garden City, N.Y., Doubleday, 1972. x, 244 p. illus. 24 cm. [TT820.A88] 77-186001 7.95
1. Crocheting. I. Title. BIP

BETTER homes and gardens 746.4'3
crocheting & knitting. 1st ed. Des Moines, Iowa : Meredith Corp., c1977. 96 p. : ill. ; 27 cm. (Better homes and gardens books) [TT820.B62] 76-47271 ISBN 0-696-00155-1 : 2.95
1. Crocheting. 2. Knitting. I. Title: Crocheting & knitting. BIP

BROCK, Delia. 746.4'3
The adventurous crocheter [by] Delia Brock & Lorraine Bodger. Illus. by Lorraine Bodger. [New York], Simon and Schuster [1974, c1972] 286 p. illus., 20 cm. [TT820.B74] 75-189749 ISBN 0-671-21755-0 3.95 (pbk.)
1. Crocheting. I. Bodger, Lorraine, joint author. II. Title. BIP

CHATTERTON, Pauline. 746.4'3
Crochet: fashions & furnishings. Chicago, H. Regnery Co. [1973] 152 p. illus. 27 cm. [TT820.C484] 72-80945 6.95
1. Crocheting. I. Title.

COATS Sewing Group. 746.4'34
Crochet stitches & edgings / Coats Sewing Group. New York : Scribner, 1978,c1976. 110 p. : ill. ; 25 cm. (The Scribner library) [TT820.C69 1976] 78-50728 ISBN 0-684-15642-3 pbk. : 2.25
1. Crocheting. I. Title. II. Title: Edgings. BIP

COPELAND, Judith. 746.9'2
Modular crochet : a revolutionary new method for creating custom-design pullovers / by Judith Copeland. New York : M. Evans, c1978. 192 p. : ill. ; 29 cm. [TT825.C66] 78-3704 ISBN 0-87131-256-5 : 12.50
1. Crocheting. 2. Sweaters. I. Title. BIP

CROCHETING tablecloths 746.9'6
and placemats / edited by Florence Weinstein. New York : Dover Publications, [1975?] 140 p. : ill. ; 28 cm. Cover title. "Unabridged republication of five crochet booklets published between 1937 and 1944." [TT825.C76] 75-321276 ISBN 0-486-20659-9 pbk. : 3.50
1. Crocheting. 2. Table-cloths. 3. Doilies. I. Weinstein, Florence. BIP

DESIGN crochet / 746.4'34
Lillian Bailey ... [et al.] ; edited by Mark Dittrick ; photos. by Jeffrey Fox. New York : Hawthorn Books, c1978. ix, 221 p., [8] leaves of plates : ill. ; 29 cm. [TT820.D398 1978] 78-53417 ISBN 0-8015-2019-3 : 14.95
1. Crocheting. I. Bailey, Lillian L. II. Dittrick, Mark. BIP

DITTRICK, Mark. 746.4'34
Hard crochet / Mark Dittrick ; [photos. by Lloyd Freidus]. New York : Hawthorn Books, c1978. 154 p., [4] leaves of plates: ill. (some col.) ; 29 cm. Includes index. [TT820.D57] 76-56512 ISBN 0-8015-3279-5 : 12.95
1. Crocheting. I. Title. BIP

EDSON, Nicki Hitz, 1941- 746.4'3
Creative crochet, by Nicki Hitz Edson and Arlene Stimmel. New York, Watson-Guptill Publications [1973] 143 p. illus. (part col.) 19 x 27 cm. Bibliography: p. 141. [TT820.E46 1973] 73-6784 ISBN 0-8230-1040-6 10.75
1. Crocheting. I. Stimmel, Arlene, 1945- joint author. II. Title.

FELDMAN, Annette. 746.4'34
Crochet and creative design / Annette Feldman. New York : Galahad Books, [1976] c1973. ix, 177 p. : ill. ; 27 cm. Originally published by Harper & Row, New York. Includes index. [TT820.F43 1976] 75-34986 ISBN 0-88365-334-6 : 8.95
1. Crocheting. I. Title.

FELDMAN, Del Pitt. 746.4'3
Crochet: discovery and design. Drawings by Marian Weissberg. Original photography by Malcolm Varon. [1st ed.] Garden City, N.Y., Doubleday, 1972. 96 p. illus. 26 cm. Bibliography: p. 90. [TT820.F45] 72-76227 ISBN 0-385-05133-6 3.95
1. Crocheting. I. Title.

FELDMAN, Del Pitt. 746.4'34
The crocheter's art; new dimensions in free-form crochet. [1st ed.] Garden City, N.Y., Doubleday, 1974. 146 p. illus. (part col.) 27 cm. [TT820.F453] 73-17725 ISBN 0-385-05134-4 14.95
1. Crocheting. 2. Soft sculpture. I. Title.

GRONSAND, Sally Ann. 745.59'22
Storybook crochet : over 25 easy-to-crochet miniature dolls, including their costumes and accessories / Sally Ann Gronsand. New York : Butterick Pub., c1977. 172 p. : ill. ; 27 cm. [TT825.G7] 76-57295 ISBN 0-88421-030-8 : 9.95
1. Crocheting. 2. Dollmaking. I. Title.

HALLIDAY, Anne. 746.9
Decorating with crochet / by Anne Halliday ; illustrated with photos. and diagrs. Boston : Houghton Mifflin, 1975. p. cm. [TT820.H23] 75-15893 ISBN 0-395-20992-7 : 14.95

1. Crocheting. 2. House furnishings. I. Title. BIP

*HORNE, Caroline 746
Crochet- pretty and practical. London, Mills & Boon, 1973 [120 p.] illus. 22 cm. [TT820] ISBN 0-263-05151-X
1. Crocheting. I. Title.
Distributed by Transatlantic Arts, Inc., Levittown, N.Y. for 7.50 BIP

HORNE, Caroline. 746.4'3
Fashion crochet. New York, Hearthside Press [1970] 128 p. illus. 22 cm. [TT820.H78 1970] 77-130537 5.95
1. Crocheting. I. Title. BIP

HURLBURT, Regina. 746.4'34
Left-handed crochet / Regina Hurlburt ; drawings by Prue Campbell-Smith. New York : Van Nostrand Reinhold Co., [1978] p. cm. [TT820.H86] 78-17162 ISBN 0-442-23590-9 pbk. : 6.00
1. Crocheting. I. Title.

KLIP, Rite van der. 746.4'34
Crochet / Rite van der Klip. New York : Two Continents Pub. Group, c1977. p. cm. Translation of Haken. [TT820.K69213 1977] 76-52781 ISBN 0-8467-0240-1 : 6.95
1. Crocheting. 2. Soft sculpture. I. Title.

LIGHTBODY, Donna M. 746.4'34
Hooks and loops : beginning crochet / Donna M. Lightbody. New York : Lothrop, Lee & Shepard Co., [1975] p. cm. Bibliography: p. [TT820.L63] 75-15996 ISBN 0-688-41707-8 : 5.95 ISBN 0-688-51707-2 lib.bdg. : 5.11
1. Crocheting. I. Title.

LIND, Vibeke. 746.4'3
Practical modern crochet. New York, Van Nostrand Reinhold Co. [1973] 104 p. illus. 28 cm. [TT820.L66 1973] 72-9376 ISBN 0-442-29970-2 4.95
1. Crocheting. I. Title.

MATHIESON, Elizabeth Laird, 1898- 746.4'34
The complete book of crochet / Elizabeth E. Mathieson. Rev. ed. New York : Crowell, c1977. viii, 264 p. : ill. ; 27 cm. Includes index. [TT820.M36 1977] 76-28737 ISBN 0-690-01156-3 : 11.95
1. Crocheting. I. Title. BIP

NORTON, Maggi Jo. 746.4'34
Crochet designs from simple motifs / Maggi Jo Norton. London : B. T. Batsford, 1978. 112 p., [12] leaves of plates : ill. ; 26 cm. Includes index. [TT820.N674] 78-320426 ISBN 0-7134-1238-0 : 8.50
1. Crocheting. I. Title.
Distributed by Hippocrene Books, New York, NY

NORTON, Maggi Jo. 746.4'34
Crochet designs from simple motifs / Maggi Jo Norton. New York : Larousse, 1978. 112 p., [2] leaves of plates : ill. ; 26 cm. On spine: The complete book of crochet design. Includes index. [TT820.N674 1978b] 78-54047 ISBN 0-88332-091-6 : 10.95
1. Crocheting. I. Title. II. Title: The complete book of crochet design. BIP

RAMSAY, Margaret. 746.4'34
Crocheting for the home / Margaret Ramsay and Sondra Miller ; [photography, Arie deZanger ; ill., Carol Hines]. 1st ed. Des Moines : Creative Home Library, c1977. 208 p. : ill. (some col.) ; 27 cm. Includes index. [TT820.R33] 75-40625 ISBN 0-696-18300-5 : 12.95
1. Crocheting. I. Miller, Sondra, joint author. II. Title.

SOMMER, Elyse. 746.4'34
A new look at crochet : using basic stitches to create modern designs / by Elyse Sommer and Miles Sommer. New York : Crown Publishers, [1975] ix, 276 p. : ill. ; 27 cm. Includes index. Bibliography: p. 269-272. [TT820.S62 1975] 74-30265 ISBN 0-517-51607-1 : 10.95 ISBN 0-517-51608-X pbk. : 4.95
1. Crocheting. I. Title. BIP

TAYLOR, Gertrude. 746.4'3
Americas's crochet book. Illustrated by Cathy Goodale. Photos. by Saul Pliuskonis. New York, Scribner [1972] 309 p. illus. 24 cm. [TT820.T32] 72-1209 ISBN 0-684-12976-0 9.95
1. Crocheting. I. Title.

VENTRE, Mary Tibbals. 746.4'3
Crochet; a basic manual for creative construction. Photos. by Paul Brandford and others. [1st ed.] Boston, Little, Brown [1974] 136 p. illus. 22 cm. (The Crafts series) Bibliography: p. [133]-136. [TT820.V45] 73-20397 ISBN 0-316-89960-7 7.95
1. Crocheting. I. Title.
Pbk. 3.95, ISBN 0-316-89961-5.

VOGUE guide to crochet. 746.4'34
/ [editor, Judy Brittain]. New York : Galahad Books, [1977] c1971. 80 p. : ill. ; 28 cm. [TT820.V62 1977] 76-46746 ISBN 0-88365-385-0 : 6.95
1. Crocheting. I. Brittain, Judy. II. Vogue.
Distributed by A & W Promotional Book Corp., 95 Madison Ave., New York, NY 10016

WILDMAN, Emily. 746.4'3
Step-by-step crochet; a complete introduction to the craft of crocheting. Conceived and edited by William and Shirley Sayles. New York, Golden Press [1972] 80 p. illus. 29 cm. (The Golden Press step-by-step craft series) [TT820.W597] 72-75850 2.95
1. Crocheting. I. Title.

THE Woman's day book of granny squares and other carry-along crochet. 746.4'34
New York : Simon and Schuster, [1975] 157 p. : ill. ; 25 cm. [TT825.W63] 74-32183 ISBN 0-671-21961-8 : 7.95
1. Crocheting. BIP

ZUKERMAN, Dianne. 746.4'34
Get hooked : creative crocheting / by Dianne Zukerman. 1st ed. Blue Ridge Summit, Pa. : Tab Books, c1977. 192 p., [2] leaves of plates : ill. ; 22 cm. Includes index. [TT820.Z84] 76-8615 pbk. 9.95
1. Crocheting. I. Title.

Crocheting—Australia—Patterns.

AUSTRALIAN book of crochet. 746.4'3
Sydney, New York, Hamlyn, 1972. 191 p. illus. 30 cm. [TT820.A85] 73-153967 ISBN 0-600-07066-2 3.95
1. Crocheting—Australia—Patterns.

Crocheting—Hungary—Patterns.

RAY, Juliana. 746.4'3
Crochet designs from Hungary [by] Juliana Ray and Madeleine Bokoli. Edited by Jean Kinmond. New York, Dover Publications [1973] 71 p. illus. 24 cm. Reprint of the 1959 ed. published by B. T. Batsford, London. [TT820.R38 1973] 73-79488 ISBN 0-486-20391-3 2.50 (pbk.)
1. Crocheting—Hungary—Patterns. I. Bokoli, Madeleine, joint author. II. Title. BIP

Crocheting— Juvenile literature.

CHAPMAN, Jane A 646.26
Child's book of crochet. New York, Greenberg [1954] 96p. illus. 23cm. [TT820.C48] 54-7112
1. Crocheting— Juvenile literature. I. Title.

RUBENSTONE, Jessie. 746.4'3
Crochet for beginners. Photos. by Edward Stevenson. [1st ed.] Philadelphia, Lippincott [1974] 64 p. illus. 23 cm. Describes the materials and basic stitches for the beginning crocheter and gives directions for making such crocheted items as a headband, belt, pot holder, rug, poncho, and others. [TT820.R778] 74-4462 ISBN 0-397-31547-3 5.95
1. Crocheting—Juvenile literature. I. Stevenson, Edward, illus. II. Title.
Pbk 2.25, ISBN 0-397-31548-1 BIP

Crocheting—Patterns.

ASHLEY, Roberta. 746.4'3
Crocheting, the new look. New York, Grosset & Dunlap [1970] 96 p. illus. 22 cm. "Published in association with Parade magazine." [TT825.A8] 74-125399 3.95
1. Crocheting—Patterns. I. Title.

BLACKWELL, Liz. 746.4'3
The craft of crocheted afghans. New York, Scribner [1973] 96 p. illus. 28 cm. (Emblem editions. SL472) Originally published as part of the author's A treasury of crochet patterns, 1971. [TT825.B53] 73-5169 ISBN 0-684-13574-4 3.95
1. Crocheting—Patterns. I. Title.

BLACKWELL, Liz. 746.4'3
A treasury of crochet patterns. New York, Scribner [1971] viii, 213 p. illus. 27 cm. [TT825.B54] 71-143947 ISBN 0-684-12331-2 12.50
1. Crocheting—Patterns. I. Title. BIP

HORNE, Caroline. 746.4'3
Fashion crochet for your doll. New York, Drake Publishers [1971] 112 p. illus., col. plates. 22 cm. Crocheting patterns for a wide variety of doll clothes. Includes instructions for the new metric sizes also. [TT825.H67 1971] 77-175968 ISBN 0-87749-076-7
1. Crocheting—Patterns. 2. Doll clothes. I. Title.

MCCALL'S super-book of afghans 746.9'7
/ by the editors of McCall's needlework & crafts. New York : McCall Pattern Co., c1978- v. : ill. (some col.) ; 28 cm. Cover title. Includes index. [TT825.M23] 78-108938 pbk. : 2.95
1. Crocheting—Patterns. 2. Embroidery—Patterns. 3. Knitting—Patterns. I. McCall's needlework & crafts.

RATHBONE, Iris. 746.4'3
More crochet. New York, Drake Publishers [1973] 80 p. illus. 29 cm. [TT825.R33] 72-10522 ISBN 0-87749-431-2 5.95
1. Crocheting—Patterns. I. Title.

SCHARF, Bella. 746.4'34
Illustrated patchwork crochet : contemporary granny squares for clothing and home decorating / Bella Scharf ; [ill. by Bella Scharf, photography by Bob Connolly]. New York : Butterick Pub., c1976. 184 p. : ill. (some col.) ; 26 cm. Includes index. [TT825.S38] 75-43282 ISBN 0-88421-052-9 : 9.95
1. Crocheting—Patterns. 2. Patchwork—Patterns. I. Butterick Publishing. II. Title. BIP

Crocheting — Yearbooks.

WOMAN'S day. 646.27
Crochet annual. [New York] v. illus. 24 cm. [TT820.W635] 51-37272
1. Crocheting — Yearbooks. I. Title.

Crocker Art Gallery, Sacramento, Calif.

CROCKER Art Gallery, Sacramento, Calif. 708'.194'54
E.B. Crocker Art Gallery report, 1973-75. Sacramento, Calif. : Art Museum of the City of Sacramento, c1976. 50 p. : ill. ; 28 cm. [N726.A17 1976] 77-359570
1. Crocker Art Gallery, Sacramento, Calif.

Crome, John, 1768-1821.

CLIFFORD, Derek Plint. 760'.0924
John Crome, by Derek Clifford and Timothy Clifford. Greenwich, Conn., New York Graphic Society [1968] 301 p. illus. (part col.) 26 cm. Bibliography: p. 285-289. [ND497.C9C5 1968b] 68-25739 18.50
1. Crome, John, 1768-1821. I. Clifford, Timothy, joint author. BIP

GOLDBERG, Norman L. 759.2
John Crome the elder / Norman L. Goldberg. New York : New York University Press, 1978. 2 v. : ill. (some col.) ; 30 cm. Contents.Contents.—1. Text and a critical catalogue.—2. Illustrations. Bibliography: v. 1, p. 165-166. [ND497.C9G64] 75-27046 ISBN 0-8147-2957-6 (v. 1) ISBN 0-8147-2968-1(v. 2) : 60.00 set
1. Crome, John, 1768-1821. I. Title. BIP

Cropsey, Jasper Francis, 1823-1900.

TALBOT, William S. 759.13 B
Jasper F. Cropsey, 1823-1900 / William S. Talbot. New York : Garland Pub., 1977. xviii, 578 p., [56] leaves of plates : ill. ; 21 cm. (Outstanding dissertations in the fine arts) Originally presented as the author's thesis, New York University, 1972. Bibliography: p. 570-578. [ND237.C819T342 1977] 76-23652 ISBN 0-8240-2731-0 lib.bdg. : 60.00
1. Cropsey, Jasper Francis, 1823-1900. 2. Landscape painters—United States—Biography. I. Title. II. Series.

Crosby, Percy Leo, 1891-1964.

ROBINSON, Jerry. 741.5'973 B
Skippy and Percy Crosby / Jerry Robinson ; with the art of Percy Crosby. 1st ed. New York : Holt, Rinehart and Winston, c1978. x, 155 p. : ill. (some col.) ; 29 cm. [NC1429.C76R62] 78-53777 ISBN 0-03-018491-6 : 16.95
1. Crosby, Percy Leo, 1891-1964. 2. Cartoonists—United States—Biography. I. Crosby, Percy Leo, 1891-1964. II. Title.

Cross-stitch.

NEWMAN, Thelma R. 746.4'4
The complete cross-stitch : 52 stitches in embroidery and gros point in new and traditional designs and methods / Thelma R. Newman. New York : Crown Publishers, c1978. p. cm. Includes index. Bibliography: p. [TT778.C76N48 1978] 77-25237 ISBN 0-517-52839-8 : 12.95 ISBN 0-517-52840-1 pbk. : 6.95
1. Cross-stitch. 2. Cross-stitch—Patterns. I. Title. BIP

Cross-stitch—Central Europe—Patterns.

KOCSIS, Maria Szirmai Foris. 746.4'4
Charted folk designs for cross-stitch embroidery : 278 charts of ancient folk embroideries from the countries along the Danube / collected by Maria Foris ; edited by Andreas Foris ; translated and introduced by Heinz Edgar Kiewe. New York : Dover Publications, 1975. 77 p. : chiefly ill. (some col.) ; 28 cm. (Dover needlework series) Translation of Kreuzstich-Vorlagen. "An unabridged and unaltered republication of the work originally published by Sebaldus-Verlag, Nuremberg in 1950 under the title Susann folk cross-stitch charts." [TT778.C76K613 1975] 75-9175 ISBN 0-486-23191-7 pbk. : 2.00
1. Cross-stitch—Central Europe—Patterns. I. Title. BIP

Cross-stitch—Denmark—Patterns.

SELSKABET til haandarbejdets fremme. 746.4'4
Cross-stitch patterns in color [by] Danish Handcraft Guild. Designs by Gerda Bengtsson. New York, Van Nostrand Reinhold [1974] 79 p. illus. (part col.) 21 cm. Translation of Vilde roser og andre motiver fra haandarbejdets fremme. [TT778.C76S4413] 74-7824 ISBN 0-442-21984-9 6.50 (lib. bdg.)
1. Cross-stitch—Denmark—Patterns. I. Title.
Pbk. 3.50; ISBN 0-442-21985-7.

Cross-stitch-Patterns.

*BENGTSSON, Gerda. 746.4'4
Flower designs in cross-stitch [by] Gerda Bengtsson [and] Else Thordur-Hansen.. [Translated from Swedish by P. Palmer] New York, Van Nostrand Reinhold [1973, c1972] 79 p. illus. 21 cm. [TT778.] 73-3937 ISBN 0-442-29988-5. 3.50 (pbk.)
1. Cross-stitch—Patterns. 2. Embroidery—Patterns. I. Thordur-Hansen, Else. joint author. II. Title. BIP

BENGTSSON, Gerda. 746.4'4
Gerda Bengtsson's Book of Danish stitchery. [Translated by Paula Hostrup-Jessen] New York, Van Nostrand Reinhold [1972] 135 p. 29 cm. [TT778.C76B4613] 73-155897 10.95
1. Cross-stitch—Patterns. 2. Embroidery—Patterns. 3. Embroidery, Danish. I. Title. II. Title: Danish stitchery.

BENGTSSON, Gerda. 746.4'4
Herbs and medicinal plants in cross-stitch from the Danish Handcraft Guild / Gerda

Bengtsson. New York : Van Nostrand Reinhold, [1978] p. cm. [TT778.C76B46133] 78-8618 ISBN 0-442-20677-1 pbk. : 6.95
1. Cross-stitch—Patterns. 2. Design, Decorative—Plant forms. 3. Herbs. 4. Materia medica, Vegetable. I. Danish Handcraft Guild. II. Title.

BENGTSSON, Gerda. 746.4'4
U.S. State flowers in counted cross-stitch / Gerda Bengtsson and the Danish Handcraft Guild, with Ginnie Thompson. New York : Van Nostrand Reinhold Co., [1976] p. cm. Includes index. [TT778.C76B47] 76-16681 ISBN 0-442-20683-6 pbk. : 8.95
1. Cross-stitch—Patterns. 2. State flowers. I. Thompson, Ginnie, joint author. II. Danish Handcraft Guild. III. Title. BIP

GIERL, Irmgard. 746.4'4
Cross stitch patterns / Irmgard Gierl. New York : Scribner, [1977] c1973. 88 p. : chiefly ill. ; 23 cm. (The Scribner library : Emblem editions) Contains the illustrations from the author's Stickereien in Bauernstuben. [TT778.C76G513] 77-75315 ISBN 0-684-15231-2 : 7.95. ISBN 0-684-15232-0 pbk. : 3.95
1. Cross-stitch—Patterns. I. Title. BIP

*ROTH, Ann. 746.'4
America in cross-stitch / designs by Ann Roth. Englewood Cliffs, N.J. : Prentice-Hall, c1976. 111p. : ill. ; 23 x 27 cm. [TT773] 76-27326 ISBN 0-13-024125-3 : 12.95
1. Cross-stitch-Patterns. 2. Embroidery. I. Title.
Needle work.

†SELSKABET til haandarbejdets fremme. 746.4'4
Cross-stitch designs for Christmas / by Danish Handcraft Guild. New York : Scribner, 1977. p. cm. First published in Danish and English under title: Sy julekorssting. Cross-stitch designs for Christmas. [TT778.C76S4413 1978] 78-19181 ISBN 0-684-15231-2 : 7.95 ISBN 0-684-15232-0 pbk. : 3.95
1. Cross-stitch—Patterns. 2. Christmas decorations. I. Title.

THOMPSON, Ginnie. 746.4'4
Favorite illustrations from children's classics in counted cross-stitch / Ginnie Thompson. New York : Dover Publications, 1976. vi, 42 p. : ill. ; 28 cm. (Dover needlework series) [TT778.C76T43 1976] 76-18404 ISBN 0-486-23394-4 pbk. : 1.50
1. Cross-stitch—Patterns. I. Title. BIP

THORNE-THOMSEN, Kathleen. 746.4'4
Alice in stitches / by Kathleen Thorne-Thomsen. 1st ed. New York : Holt, Rinehart and Winston, c1979. p. cm. Includes the author's version of Lewis Carroll's Alice in Wonderland. [TT778.C76T44] 79-4045 ISBN 0-03-020796-7. : 12.95 ISBN 0-03-052761-9 pbk. : 7.95
1. Cross-stitch—Patterns. 2. Canvas embroidery—Patterns. I. Dodgson, Charles Lutwidge, 1832-1898. Alice in Wonderland. II. Title.

Cross-stitch—Romania—Transylvania—Patterns.

SIGERUS, Emil. 746.4'4
Charted peasant designs from Saxon Transylvania / edited and introduced by Heinz Edgar Kiewe. New York : Dover Publications, 1977, c1964. 14, xl p., [1] leaf of plates : ill. ; 28 cm. (Dover needlework series) Reprint of the ed. published by H. Meschendorfer, Munich, under title: Folk cross-stitch design collected by Emil Sigerus. Originally published in 1961 by Meschendorfer under title: Siebenburgisch-sachsische Leinenstickereien. Bibliography: p. 14. [TT778.C76S53 1977] 76-24564 ISBN 0-486-23425-8 pbk. : 2.75
1. Cross-stitch—Romania—Transylvania—Patterns. 2. Design, Decorative—Romania—Transylvania. I. Kiewe, Heinz Edgar. II. Sigerus, Emil. Siebenburgisch-sachsische Leinenstickereien. III. Title. BIP

Cross-stitch—Switzerland—Patterns.

PAROLINI-RUFFINI, Elvira. 746.4'4
Charted Swiss folk designs / collected by Elvira Parolini-Ruffini ; rendered by Hanna Reinolter. New York : Dover Publications, 1978. 30 p. : all ill. ; 28 cm. (Dover needlework series) Reprint of "all of the charted designs from Engadiner Kreuzstichmuster, first published in 1976." [TT778.C76P3713] 77-87356 ISBN 0-486-23574-2 pbk. : 1.50
1. Cross-stitch—Switzerland—Patterns. 2. Design, Decorative—Switzerland. 3. Folk art—Switzerland. I. Title. BIP

Cross-stitch—United States—Patterns.

ROTH, An. 746.4'4
America in cross-stitch / designs by Ann Roth. Englewood Cliffs, N.J. : Prentice-Hall, c1976. p. cm. "Twenty American landscapes and landmarks with descriptions and detailed instructions for cross-stitching." [TT778.C76R67] 76-26575 ISBN 0-13-024125-3 : 12.95
1. Cross-stitch—United States—Patterns. I. Title. BIP

THORNE-THOMSEN, Kathleen. 746.4'4
American cross-stitch [by] Kathleen Thorne-Thomsen [and] Hildy Paige Burns. [New York, Van Nostrand Reinhold, 1974] 104 p. (chiefly illus.) 21 x 26 cm. [TT778.C76T45] 73-10746 ISBN 0-442-28514-0 8.95
1. Cross-stitch—United States—Patterns. I. Burns, Hildy Paige, joint author. II. Title. BIP

Croton-on-Hudson. N. Y. Van Cortlandt Manor.

BUTLER, Joseph T. 745.1
The family collections at Van Cortlandt Manor [by] Joseph T. Butler. Tarrytown. N. Y., Sleepy Hollow Restorations [1967] 127p. illus., coat of arms, facsims., geneal. table, ports. 28cm. Includes catalogue. Bibl. [NK460 C7B8] 67-28473 6.50; 5.00 pap.,
1. Croton-on-Hudson. N. Y. Van Cortlandt Manor. 2. Van Cortlandt family—Art collections. I. Title. BIP

Crowds in art.

JOHNSON, Lester, 1919- 759.13
The kaleidoscopic crowd : [Lester Johnson paintings, 1970-1974 / introd. by Burt Chernow ; with a statement by Harold Rosenberg]. [New York] : D. Anderson, [1975]. 67, [4] p. : ill. (some col.) ; 22 x 22 cm. Bibliography: p. [71] [ND237.J724C47] 74-34550
1. Johnson, Lester, 1919- 2. Crowds in art. I. Chernow, Burt. II. Title.

Crown (Coin)

TROWBRIDGE, Richard J. 737.49'42
Crowns of the British Empire, by Richard J. Trowbridge. 2d ed. Iola, Ill., Krause Publications, 1971] 170 p. illus., port. 24 cm. Bibliography: p. 167-170. [CJ2485.T7 1971] 78-160115
1. Crown (Coin) I. Title.

TROWBRIDGE, Richard J. 737.49'42
Crowns of the British Empire, by Richard J. Trowbridge. [1st ed. Long Beach, Calif., 1970] vi, 164 p. illus. 23 cm. "Complete from 1551 to date." Bibliography: p. 160-164. [CJ2485.T7] 76-11989
1. Crown (Coin) I. Title. BIP

Crown jewels—Iran.

MEEN, V. B. 739.27'0955
Crown jewels of Iran [by] V. B. Meen and A. D. Tushingham; photographed by Leighton Warren. [Toronto] University of Toronto Press, 1968. 159 p. illus. (part col.) 36 cm. Bibliographical references included in "Notes" (p. 147-150) [NK7415.I7M4] 68-134808 ISBN 0-8020-1519-0 20.00 Can.
1. Crown jewels—Iran. I. Tushingham, A. Douglas, 1914- joint author. II. Title. BIP

Crown jewels—Russia.

POST, Marjorie Merriweather. 739.27
The art of Karl Faberge and his comtemporaries; Russian imperial portraits and mementoes (Alexander III—Nicholas II) Russian imperial decorations and watches, by Marvin C. Ross. With a foreword by Marjorie Merriweather Post. [1st ed.] Norman, University of Oklahoma Press [1965] xviii, 238 p. illus., col. plates, ports. (part col.) 24 cm. (Her The Collections of Marjorie Merriweather Post) Bibliography: p. 229-233. [NK7417.F3P6] 65-14804
1. Faberge, Karl Gustavovich, 1846-1920. 2. Crown jewels—Russia. I. Ross, Marvin Chauncey, 1904- II. Title.

Crown jewels—Russia—Catalogs.

LESLEY, Parker. 739.2'092'4
Faberge : a catalog of the Lillian Thomas Pratt Collection of Russian imperial jewels / by Parker Lesley. Richmond : Virginia Museum, c1976. 160 p. : col. ill. ; 29 cm. Published in 1960 under title: Handbook of the Lillian Thomas Pratt Collection. [NK7417.F3L47 1976] 76-16557 ISBN 0-917046-00-5 : 17.50
1. Faberzhe, Karl Gustavovich, 1846-1920. 2. Pratt, Lillian Thomas—Art collections. 3. Crown jewels—Russia—Catalogs. I. Virginia Museum of Fine Arts, Richmond. BIP

Crowns.

KELLEHER, Patrick J. 739.27
The holy crown of Hungary. [Rome] American Academy in Rome, 1951. ix, 124 p. illus. 25 cm. (Papers and monographs of the American Academy in Rome, v. 13) Bibliography: p. [112]-118. [NK7415.H8K4] 52-2685
1. Crowns. 2. Crown jewels—Hungary. 3. Hungary—Hist. I. Title. II. Series: American Academy in Rome. Papers and monographs, v. 13

Crozier, Robin.

PORTRAIT of Robin 828'.9'1407
Crozier / [edited by Robin Crozier]. Sunderland : Ceolfrith Press, 1975. [70] p. : chiefly ill. ; 19 cm. Cover title. [NC773.P67] 75-316327 £0.75
1. Crozier, Robin. 2. Portrait drawing. I. Crozier, Robin.

Cruets—Catalogs.

MURRAY, Dean L. 748.8
More cruets only. [Illustrated by Dean L. Murray. Phoenix, Ariz., Killgore Graphics, 1973] 78 p. col. illus. 23 cm. [NK5440.C75M87] 73-168224 7.95
1. Murray, Dean L.—Art—Collections. 2. Cruets—Catalogs. I. Title.
Publisher's Address: 1401 E. Washington Ave., Phoenix, Ariz. 85004. BIP

Cruikshank, George, 1792-1878.

COHN, Albert Mayer. 016.7419'42
George Cruikshank; a catalogue raisonne, by Albert M. Cohn. [New York] Collectors Editions [1969] xvi, 375 p. illus., port. 29 cm. Reprint of the 1924 ed. Bibliography: p. 357-359. [NC1479.C9C72 1969] 71-102791
1. Cruikshank, George, 1792-1878.

EVANS, Hilary, 1929- 760'.092'4 B
The life & art of George Cruikshank, 1792-1878 : the man who drew The Drunkard's daughter / Hilary and Mary Evans. New York : S. G. Phillips, 1978. p. cm. [NC1479.C9E82] 77-19166 ISBN 0-87599-227-7 : 35.00
1. Cruikshank, George, 1792-1878. 2. Cartoonists—England—Biography. I. Evans, Mary, 1890- joint autor. II. Title. BIP

THE Inimitable George 760'.0924
Cruikshank: an exhibition of illustrated books, prints, drawings and manuscripts from the collection of David Borowitz, J. B. Speed Art Museum, October 12-November 15, 1968. With an essay by Richard A. Vogler. Catalogue and exhibition organized and arranged by Nathalie T. Andrews and Margaret M. Bridwell. Louisville, Ky., University of Louisville Libraries, 1968. 55 p. illus. (part col.) 23 cm. Bibliography: p. [39]-53. [NC242.C715] 71-1483
1. Cruikshank, George, 1792-1878. 2. Borowitz, David, 1906- —Art collections. I. Andrews, Nathalie T. II. Bridwell, Margaret Morris, 1905- III. Speed Art Museum, Louisville, Ky. IV. Louisville, Ky. University. Library.

WARDROPER, John. 741'.092'4
The caricatures of George Cruikshank / John Wardroper. 1st U.S. ed. Boston : D. R. Godine, 1978. 144 p. : ill. (some col.) ; 24 x 26 cm. Includes index. Bibliography: p. 142. [NC1479.C9A4 1978] 77-94112 ISBN 0-87923-231-5 : 30.00
1. Cruikshank, George, 1792-1878. 2. English wit and humor, Pictorial. I. Title. BIP

WARDROPER, John. 741.5'942
The caricatures of George Cruikshank / [text by] John Wardroper. London : Gordon Fraser Gallery, 1977, i.e.1978 144 p. : chiefly ill. (some col.), facsim., port. ; 24 x 25 cm. Includes index. Bibliography: p. 142. [NC1479.C9A4 1977] 78-307169 ISBN 0-900406-85-2 : 30.00
1. Cruikshank, George, 1792-1878. 2. English wit and humor, Pictorial. I. Cruikshank, George, 1792-1878. II. Title.
Available from Godine

Cruikshank, Isaac, 1756?-1811?

KRUMBHAAR, Edward Bell, 1882- 741.5942
Isaac Cruikshank; a catalogue raisonne, with a sketch of his life and work, by E. B. Krumbhaar. Philadelphia, University of Pennsylvania Press [1966] 177 p. plates. 20 cm. Bibliography: p. 174-175. [NC1479.C95K7] 61-6617
1. Cruikshank, Isaac, 1756?-1811? I. Title.

WARK, Robert R. 741.942
Isaac Cruikshank's drawings for drolls, with an introd. and notes by Robert R. Wark. San Marino, Calif., Huntington Library, 1968. 20, [75] p. illus. 16 x 24 cm. Catalog of a bound volume of drawings in the collection of the Henry E. Huntington Library. [NC1479.C95W3] 68-31202
1. Cruikshank, Isaac, 1756?-1811? I. Henry E. Huntington Library and Art Gallery, San Marino, Calif. II. Title. III. Title: Drawings for drolls.

Cruise, Boyd.

CRUISE, Boyd. 759.13
Boyd Cruise. 1st ed. New Orleans : Kemper and Leila Williams Foundation, c1976. 72 p. : ill. (some col.) ; 29 cm. Published in conjunction with the artist's exhibition held at the Historic New Orleans Collection, December 1976-February 1977. "Biography of the artist [by] Mary Louise Christovich": p. 2-13. [ND237.C843C48] 76-24712 ISBN 0-917860-01-2
1. Cruise, Boyd. 2. Painters—Louisiana—New Orleans—Biography. I. Christovich, Mary Louise. II. Historic New Orleans Collection.

Crutchfield, William, 1932—

CRUTCHFIELD, William, 1932- 741.9'73
Owl feathers / by William Crutchfield. Rev. ed. Pasadena [Calif.] : W. Ritchie Press, c1975. [94] p. : chiefly ill. ; 18 cm. [NC139.C78A56 1975] 75-18100 ISBN 0-378-02884-7
1. Crutchfield, William, 1932- I. Title.

Crutis, Edward S., 1868-1952.

CURTIS, Edward S., 1868-1952. 779'.9'97000497
Edward Sheriff Curtis : visions of a vanishing race / by Florence Curtis Graybill and Victor Boesen ; photos. prepared by Jean-Anthony du Lac. New York : Crowell, [1976] p. cm. [E77.5.C78 1976] 76-16579 ISBN 0-690-01162-8 : 35.00

1. Crutis, Edward S., 1868-1952. 2. Indians of North America—Pictorial works. I. Graybill, Florence Curtis. II. Boesen, Victor. BIP

Crypts—Lorraine.

SANDERSON, Warren. 726'.8'094438
Monastic reform in Lorraine and the architecture of the outer crypt, 950-1100. Philadelphia, American Philosophical Society, 1971. 36 p. illus. 30 cm. (Transactions of the American Philosophical Society, new ser., v. 61, pt. 6) Bibliography: p. 36. [NA5570.S25] 79-153383
1. Crypts—Lorraine. 2. Architecture, Medieval—Lorraine. 3. Abbeys—Lorraine. I. Title. II. Series: American Philosophical Society, Philadelphia. Transactions, new ser., v. 61, pt. 6.

Cubism.

APOLLINAIRE, Guillaume, 1880-1918 759.915
The cubist painters; aesthetic meditations, 1913. Tr. from French by Lionel Abel. [2d rev. ed.] New York, Wittenborn, 1962[c.1949] vi, 65p. illus. 26cm. (Documents of modern art, 1) Bibl. 2.50 pap.,
1. Cubism. I. Title. II. Series. BIP

FRY, Edward F. 759.06
Cubism [by] Edward F. Fry. New York, McGraw-Hill [1966] 200 p. illus., facsims., plates (part col.), ports. 21 cm. (McGraw-Hill paperbacks) Bibliography: p. 176-187. [ND1265.F7] 66-24888
1. Cubism. I. Title.

FRY, Edward F. 759.06
Cubism / Edward F. Fry. New York : Oxford University Press, 1978, c1966. p. cm. (The World of art) Reprint of the ed. published by Thames & Hudson, London. Includes index. Bibliography: p. [N6494.C8877 1978] 78-7541 ISBN 0-19-520069-1 pbk. : 6.95
1. Cubism. 2. Art, Modern—20th century. I. Title. II. Series.

GOLDING, John. 759.06
Cubism: a history and an analysis, 1907-1914. [Rev. American ed.] Boston, Boston Book & Art Shop [1968] 208 p. 100 plates (4 col.) 26 cm. Bibliography: p. 188-200. [ND196.C8G6 1968b] 76-12087
1. Cubism.

GRAY, Christopher. 759.06
Cubist aesthetic theories. Baltimore, Johns Hopkins Press [1953] 190p. illus. 21cm. [ND1265.G695] 759.915 53-6493
1. Cubism. I. Title.

HABASQUE, Guy. 759.06
Cubism: biographical and critical study. Translated by Stuart Gilbert. [New York] Skira [1959] 169 p. mounted col. illus. 19 cm. (The Taste of our time, v. 27) Bibliography: p. 154-157. [ND1265.H313] 59-7254
1. Cubism.

HILTON, Timothy, 1941- 759.4
Picasso / Timothy Hilton. New York : Praeger, 1975. p. cm. (World of art) Includes index. Bibliography: p. [ND553.P5H54] 75-48 ISBN 0-275-49780-1 : 12.50. ISBN 0-275-71750-X pbk. : 6.95
1. Picasso, Pablo, 1881-1973. 2. Cubism.

JUDKINS, Winthrop. 759.06
Fluctuant representation in synthetic cubism : Picasso, Braque, Gris, 1910-1920 / Winthrop Judkins. New York : Garland, 1976. viii, 526 p. : ill. ; 22 cm. (Outstanding dissertations in the fine arts) Originally presented as the author's thesis, Harvard, 1954, under title: The nature and techniques of fluctuant representation in synthetic cubism: Picasso, Braque, Gris. Bibliography: p. 329-330. [ND196.C8J82 1976] 75-23796 ISBN 0-8240-1991-1 lib.bdg. : 35.00
1. Picasso, Pablo, 1881-1973. 2. Braque, Georges, 1882-1963. 3. Gris, Juan, 1887-1927. 4. Cubism. 5. Painting, Modern—20th century. I. Title. II. Series. BIP

KOZLOFF, Max 759.06
Cubism futurism. New York, Harper & Row, [1974, c1973] xvii, 234 p. illus. 22 cm. Bibliography: p. 221-222 [N6494.C8K69] ISBN 0-06-430059-5 4.95 (pbk.)
1. Cubism. 2. Futurism (Art) I. Title.
L.C. card no. for original ed: 72-84221

KOZLOFF, Max. 759.06
Cubism/futurism. New York, Charterhouse [1973] xix, 234 p. illus. 23 cm. Bibliography: p. 221-222. [N6494.C8K69] 72-84221 9.95
1. Cubism. 2. Futurism (Art) I. Title. BIP

NEW Mexico. University. Art Museum 759.06
Cubism; its impact in the USA, 1910-1930. [Albuquerque, 1967] 64p. illus. (pt. col.) 23cm. An exhibition co-sponsored by the Univ. of N.M. Art Mus. and the Junior League of Albuquerque, and shown at the following institutions: Univ. of N.M. Art Mus., Albuquerque; Marion Koogler McNay Art Inst., San Antonio; San Francisco Mus. of Art. San Francisco; Los Angeles Municipal Art Gallery, Los Angeles. Bibl. [ND212.N369] 66-65561 2.00 pap.,
1. Cubism. 2. Paintings, American — Exhibitions. I. Junior League of Albuquerque. II. Title.

NEW York. Museum of Modern Art. 709.04
Cubism and abstract art, by Alfred H. Barr, Jr. Reprint ed. New York, Published for the Museum of Modern Art by Arno Press, 1966 [c1936] 249 p. illus. 27 cm. Includes catalog of an exhibition. Bibliography: p. 234-249. [ND6494.C8] 66-26123
1. Cubism. 2. Art, Abstract. I. Barr, Alfred Hamilton, 1902- II. Title. BIP

ROSENBLUM, Robert. 759.06
Cubism and twentieth-century art. New York, Abrams [1961, c1960] 327 p. mounted col. illus., plates 31 cm. Bibliography: p. 312-316. [ND1265.R63] 61-7155
1. Cubism. 2. Art, Modern—20th century. 3. Paintings.

ROSENBLUM, Robert. 759.06
Cubism and twentieth-century art / Robert Rosenblum. Englewood Cliffs, N.J. : Prentice-Hall, 1976. 346 p. : ill. (some col.) ; 25 cm. Includes index. Bibliography: p. 333-336. [N6494.C8R67 1976] 76-150796 ISBN 0-13-195065-7 pbk. : 9.95
1. Cubism. 2. Art, Modern—20th century. I. Title. BIP

SCHMELLER, Alfred. 759.06
Cubism. [Translated by Hilde Spiel] New York, Crown [195-] 62p. illus. 19cm. (Movements in modern art) [ND1265.S333] 59-47666
1. Cubism. 2. Paintings, French. I. Title.

SCHWARTZ, Paul Waldo. 759.06
Cubism. New York, Praeger [1971] 216 p. illus. (part col.) 22 cm. (Praeger world of art series) Bibliography: p. 203-205. [NX600.C8S37] 70-100034 8.50
1. Cubism.

Cubism—Exhibitions.

COOPER, Douglas, 1911- 759.06
The Cubist epoch. [London] Phaidon in association with the Los Angeles County Museum of Art & the Metropolitan Museum of Art [distributed by Praeger, New York, 1971] 320 p. illus. (part col.) 25 cm. Catalog of an exhibition. Bibliography: p. 270-272. [N6494.C8C6 1971b] 73-585644 ISBN 0-7148-1448-2
1. Cubism—Exhibitions. 2. Art, Modern—20th century. I. Los Angeles Co., Calif. Museum of Art, Los Angeles. II. New York. Metropolitan Museum of Art. III. Title.

LOOK back; 709'.22
an exhibition of cubist paintings and sculptures from the Menil family collection. [Houston, Printed by Gulf Pub. Co., 1968] 105 p. (chiefly illus.) 23 cm. Catalogue of an exhibition of the John de Menil family collection held at the University of St. Thomas, Houston, Mar. 13-Sept. 13, 1968, and later at 8 other museums in the United States and Canada. Includes bibliographies. [N6494.C8L6] 68-8356 2.75
1. De Menil, John—Art collections. 2. Cubism—Exhibitions. I. De Menil, John. II. Houston, Tex. University of St. Thomas.

WEST, Richard V. 759.06
Painters of the Section d'or; the alternatives to cubism. Buffalo, Albright-Knox Art Gallery, 1967. 59 p. illus. 26 cm. Catalog, by Richard V. West, of an exhibition held Sept. 27-Oct. 22, Albright-Knox Art Gallery, Buffalo. Includes bibliographies. [ND1265.W53] 67-9328
1. Cubism—Exhibitions. I. Albright-Knox Art Gallery. II. Title.

Cubism—Paris—History.

WARNOD, Jeanine. 759.4
Washboat days. Translated from the French by Carol Green. New York, Grossman, 1972. xi, 241 p. illus. 21 cm. (An Orion Press book) [NX549.P2W3613 1972] 70-157868 ISBN 0-670-75005-0 16.95
1. Le Bateau-Lavoir, Paris. 2. Cubism—Paris—History. I. Title.

Cubitt, Thomas, 1788-1855.

HOBHOUSE, Hermione. 711'.4'0924 B
Thomas Cubitt; master builder. New York, Universe Books [1971] xx, 568 p. illus. 25 cm. Bibliography: p. 551-552. [NA997.C8H6] 79-122323 ISBN 0-87663-706-3 32.50
1. Cubitt, Thomas, 1788-1855. I. Title.

Cuesta, Juan de la, fl. 1605.

SCHNEER, Richard James. 070.5'0946'41
Juan de la Cuesta, first printer of Don Quixote de la Mancha; a bibliographic record of his works, 1604-1625. University, University of Alabama Press [1973] xii, 89 p. 22 cm. [Z232.C963S35] 72-11809 ISBN 0-8173-9513-X 6.00
1. Cuesta, Juan de la, fl. 1605.

Cultural property, Protection of.

STOLOW, Nathan 658.78840185
Controlled environment for works of art in transit. London, [pub. for the] Intl. Centre for the Study of the Conservation of Cultural Property [by] Butterworths. 1966. v, 46p. illus, tables, diagrs. 25cm. Bibl. [N8750.S78] 66-78084 4.00 pap.,
1. Cultural property, Protection of. 2. Transportation—Research. I. International Centre for the Study of the Conservation of Cultural Property. II. Title.
Available from the publisher's Washington, D.C., office.

Culture—Addresses, essays, lectures.

THE Production of culture 301.2'1
/ edited by Richard A. Peterson. Beverly Hills, Calif. : Sage Publications, 1976. 144 p. ; 22 cm. (Sage contemporary social science issues ; 33) Originally appeared as a special issue of American behavioral scientist, v. 19, no. 6, July/August 1976. Includes bibliographies. [NX180.S6P76] 76-41102 ISBN 0-8039-0734-6 pbk. : 3.95
1. Culture—Addresses, essays, lectures. 2. Arts and society—Addresses, essays, lectures. I. Peterson, Richard A.

Cumbria, Eng., in art.

CARLISLE, Eng. Museum and Art Gallery. 942.7'8
The landscape of Cumbira : [catalogue of an exhibition held at] Carlisle Art Gallery [7th November-7th December 1974] / [exhibition organised and catalogue produced by D. R. Perriam] [Carlisle] : Carlisle Art Gallery, [1974] [1], 40 p. : ill. ; 21 cm. Cover title. [N8214.5.G7C37 1974] 75-312800 ISBN 0-9502457-4-7 : £0.10
1. Cumbira, Eng., in art. 2. Art, British—Exhibitions. I. Perriam, D. R. II. Title.

Cumming, Charles Atherton, 1858-1932.

FERGUSON, Bess. 759.13
Charles Atherton Cumming. Iowa's pioneer artist-educator [by] Bess Ferguson with Velma Wallace Rayness and Edna Patzig Gouwens. [Des Moines] Iowa Art Guild, 1972. ix, 54 p. illus. 27 cm. [ND237.C848F47] 72-87322
1. Cumming, Charles Atherton, 1858-1932. I. Rayness, Velma Wallace, 1896- II. Gouwens, Edna Patzig.

Cummings, Nathan—Art collections.

CHICAGO. Art Institute. 709'.03'4
Major works from the Collection of Nathan Cummings; [catalogue of the exhibition] the Art Institute of Chicago, October 20-December 9, 1973. [Chicago, 1973] 95 p. (chiefly illus. (part col.)) 26 cm. [N6867.C47 1973] 73-87962
1. Cummings, Nathan—Art collections. 2. Art, Modern—19th century—Exhibitions. 3. Art, Modern—20th century—Exhibitions. I. Title.

U.S. National Gallery of Art. 759.06'074'0153
Selections from the Nathan Cummings Collection. [Exhibition] National Gallery of Art, Washington, June 28-September 11, 1970; the Metropolitan Museum of Art, New York, July 1-September 7, 1971. [Catalogue notes by Carol Cutler. Photography by Malcolm Varon. Washington, 1970] 96 p. illus. (part col.) 27 cm. [N6867.U5] 71-606524
1. Cummings, Nathan—Art collections. 2. Art, Modern—19th century—Exhibitions. 3. Art, Modern—20th century—Exhibitions. I. New York (City). Metropolitan Museum of Art. II. Title.

Cunningham, Imogen, 1883—

CUNNINGHAM, Imogen, 1883- 779'.092'4
Imogen! Imogen Cunningham photographs, 1910-1973. Introd. by Margery Mann. Seattle, Published for the Henry Art Gallery by the University of Washington Press [1974] 110 p. illus. 29 cm. (Index of art in the Pacific Northwest no. 7) "Published in connection with an exhibition shown at the Henry Art Gallery, University of Washington, March 23-April 21, 1974." Bibliography: p. 109-110. [TR647.C8H45] 74-2490 ISBN 0-295-95332-2 15.00
1. Cunningham, Imogen, 1883- 2. Photography, Artistic—Exhibitions. I. Henry Art Gallery. II. Title. III. Series.

Cup plates.

ROSE, James Harry, 1899- 748.8
Cup plate discoveries since 1948; the cup plate notes of James H. Rose. Compiled by John E. Bilane. [New York? c1971] 41 p. illus. 28 cm. Cover title. Additions to the data in American glass cup plates, by R. W. Lee and J. H. Rose, first published in 1948. [NK5440.C8R6] 72-176591
1. Cup plates. 2. Glassware, American. I. Bilane, John E. II. Lee, Ruth Webb, 1894- American glass cup plates. III. Title.

Cupid—Art.

KUNSTMANN, Josef 704.9425
The transformation of Eros. Tr. [from German] by M. von Herzfeld, R. Gaze [Chester Springs, Pa.] Dufour, 1965 [c.1964] 73, 80p. illus. (pt. col.) 19cm. (Realms of art, 2) [N7760.K8413] 65-18354 5.95
1. sCupid—Art. 2. Sculpture, German. I. Title. BIP

Currey, Thomas Lane, 1922—

CURREY, Thomas Lane, 1922- 759.13
The Smoky Hill Trail / paintings, Thomas Lane Currey ; narrative, Betty Radcliffe Jackson. Colby, Kan. : H. F. Davis Memorial Library, Colby Community College, c1976. [40] p. : ill. (some col.) ; 29 x 37 cm. (Western plains heritage publications ; no. 3) [ND1839.C87J33] 77-360307

1. Currey, Thomas Lane, 1922- 2. Smoky Hill Trail in art. 3. Smoky Hill Trail, Kan. and Colo. I. Jackson, Betty Radcliffe. II. Title. III. Series.

Curriculum planning—United States.

THE Arts, human development, and education / edited by Elliot W. Eisner. Berkeley, Calif. : McCutchan Pub. Corp., c1976. xvi, 226 p. : ill. ; 24 cm. Includes bibliographical references. [LB1570.A78] 75-46106 ISBN 0-8211-0414-4 : 11.50 707'.1
1. Curriculum planning—United States. 2. Child development. 3. The arts. I. Eisner, Elliot W.

Currier & Ives.

CONNINGHAM, Frederic Arthur, 1890- 763
Currier & Ives. Cleveland, World Pub. Co. [1950] 63 p. illus., col. plates, port. 20 cm. (The American arts library, 1583) Bibliography: p. 63. [NE2415.C7C616] 50-58061
1. Currier & Ives. 2. Lithograph, American. 3. Lithographers, American.

CONNINGHAM, Frederic Arthur, 1890- 769'.02'9
Currier & Ives prints; an illustrated check list, by Frederic A. Conningham. Updated by Colin Simkin. [Rev. ed.] New York, Crown Publishers [1970] xx, 300 p. illus. 24 cm. [NE2415.C7C62 1970] 77-105958 12.50
1. Currier and Ives. 2. Lithographs—Catalogs. I. Simkin, Colin. II. Title.

CURRIER and Ives. 769'.92'4
Christmas in the country / Currier & Ives ; edited by Margery Darrell. 1st ed. Princeton [N.J.] : Pyne Press, [1974] [59] p. : ill. (some col.) ; 22 x 26 cm. [NE2312.C8D37] 74-80489 ISBN 0-87861-078-2 : 6.95
1. Currier and Ives. 2. Christmas—Pictorial works. I. Darrell, Margery, ed. II. Title.

KING, Roy. 769'.922
The world of Currier & Ives, by Roy King & Burke Davis. New York, Random House [1968] 140 p. 60 col. illus. 37 x 49 cm. The 60 prints reproduced were selected from the Roy King Collection as representative of the work of Currier & Ives. "A selected list of two hundred [and fifty] Currier & Ives prints with their values": p. 136-140. [NE2415.C7K5] 68-28542 30.00
1. Currier and Ives. 2. Lithographs, American—Catalogs. 3. Lithographs—Private collections. I. Currier and Ives. II. Davis, Burke joint author. III. Title.

NEWMAN, Ewell L. 769'.92'4
A guide to collecting Currier & Ives / by Ewell L. Newman in collaboration with Ladd MacMillan. New York : Pyramid Books, 1975. 158, [2] p. : ill. (some col.) ; 14 x 21 cm. "A Pyramid prestige edition." Includes index. Bibliography: p. [159] [NE2312.C8N48] 76-351422 pbk. : 4.95
1. Currier and Ives. 2. Lithographs—Collectors and collecting. 3. United States in art. I. Macmillan, Ladd. II. Title. BIP

PETERS, Harry Twyford, 1881-1948. 769'.92'4
Currier & Ives, printmakers to the American people / Harry T. Peters. New York : Arno Press, 1976, c1929-1931. p. cm. (America in two centuries, an inventory) Reprint of the ed. published by Doubleday, Doran, Garden City, N.Y. [NE2312.C8P47 1976] 75-22834 ISBN 0-405-07741-6 : 300.00
1. Currier and Ives. 2. Lithographs, American. I. Title. II. Series.

SCHURRE, Jacques. 769'.92'4
Currier & Ives : a checklist of unrecorded prints produced by Currier & Ives, N. Currier, and C. Currier / compiled by Jacques Schurre. Rev. ed. [New York : s.n.], c1976. ii, 28 p. ; 22 cm. Cover title. [NE2312.C8S34 1976] 76-383236
1. Currier and Ives. 2. Lithographs—United States—Catalogs. I. Title.

SCHURRE, Jacques. 769'.02'9
Currier & Ives prints; a checklist of unrecorded prints produced by Currier & Ives, N. Currier, and C. Currier. [New York, 1970] [23] p. 22 cm. "The checklist ... is a complete compilation of prints not listed in the recently published revised edition of Conningham's." [NE2312.C8S39] 72-25031
1. Currier and Ives. 2. Lithographs—Catalogs. I. Conningham, Frederic Arthur, 1890- Currier & Ives prints. II. Title. BIP

WARMAN, Edwin G., 1915- 769'.973
Fourth print price guide : a check-list and price guide to N. Currier, Currier & Ives, and Currier & Ives reproductions, including Audubon, Icart, Nutting, Parrish, Prang, and other printmakers / Edwin G. Warman. Rev. and enl. ed. Uniontown, Pa. : E. G. Warman Pub., c1976. 145 p. ; 22 cm. Edition of 1955 published under title: Print price guide; 1959 ed. under title: New print price guide; 1969 ed. under title: Third print price guide. [NE2303.7.W3 1976] 76-356023 7.95
1. Currier and Ives. 2. Lithographs, American—Catalogs. 3. Printmakers—United States. 4. Prints, American—Catalogs. I. Title. BIP

WARMAN, Edwin G., 1915- 763.085
Print price guide; a check-list and price guide to N. Currier, Currier & Ives, Kellogs, and other printmakers. Uniontown, Pa., Warman Pub. Co. [1955] 136p. 20cm. [NE2415.C7W36] 56-521
1. Currier and Ives. 2. Lithographs—Prices. 3. Lithographers, American. I. Title.

Currier and Ives—Catalogs.

CURRIER and Ives. 769'.92'4
50 Currier & Ives favorites, from the Museum of the City of New York / introd. and commentary by A. K. Baragwanath. New York : Crown Publishers, [1978] 104 p. : col. ill. ; 38 cm. "An Artabras book." [NE2312.C8A4 1978] 78-2205 ISBN 0-89660-007-6 pbk. : 7.98
1. Currier and Ives—Catalogs. 2. New York (City). Museum of the City of New York. 3. United States in art—Catalogs. 4. Lithography—19th century—United States—Catalogs. I. Baragwanath, A. K. II. New York (City). Museum of the City of New York. III. Title.

Currier (N.) (firm)

PRATT, John Lowell, comp. 769'.924
Currier & Ives chronicles of America; color plates reproduced from the original hand colored stone prints by N. Currier and Currier & Ives. Edited by John Lowell Pratt. Introd. by A. K. Baragwanath. Maplewood, N.J., Hammond [1968] 256 p. illus. (part col.), col. map. 32 cm. [NE2312.C8P72 1968] 68-13933 14.95
1. Currier (N.) (Firm) 2. United States in art. I. Currier (N.) (Firm) II. Currier and Ives. III. Title. IV. Title: Chronicles of America.

PRATT, John Lowell, comp. 769'.973
Currier & Ives chronicles of America : color plates reproduced from the original hand colored stone prints by N. Currier and Currier & Ives / edited by John Lowell Pratt ; introd. by A. K. Baragwanath. [New York] : Promontory Press, [1974?] c1968. 256 p. : chiefly col. ill. ; 32 cm. Includes index. [NE2312.C8P72 1974] 74-77002 ISBN 0-88394-031-0 : 17.50
1. Currier (N.) (Firm) 2. United States in art. I. Currier (N.) (Firm) II. Currier and Ives. III. Title. IV. Title: Chronicles of America.

WARMAN, Edwin G., 1915- 769'.029
Third print price guide; a check-list and price guide to N. Currier, Currier & Ives, Kellogg and other printmakers. [Rev. ed.] Uniontown, Pa., E. G. Warman [1969] 139 p. 22 cm. First published in 1955 under title: Print price guide; in 1959, under title: New print price guide. [NE2303.7.W3 1969] 70-17679 4.75
1. Currier (N.) (firm) 2. Lithographs—Prices. 3. Lithographers—United States. I. Title.

Currier, Nathaniel, 1813-1888.

KENNEDY Galleries, inc., New York. 708'.147'1 s
Mr. Currier & Mr. Ives: an American phenomenon. New York [1970] 78-124 p. illus. 23 cm. (The Kennedy quarterly, v. 10, no. 2) [N8640.K4 vol. 10, no. 2] [NE2312] 769.92'4 72-170863 2.00
1. Currier, Nathaniel, 1813-1888. 2. Ives, James Merritt, d. 1895. 3. Currier and Ives. I. Title. II. Series.

Curtain walls.

CURTAIN wall construction. Ed.-inchief: Konrad Gatz, with Hans-Jurgen Meier-Menzel, Fritz Hierl. [Text contributions by G. Schellbach, others. Tr. by David Stern, Felix G. Winkler] New York, Praeger [1967, [c.1965] 174p. illus. (pt. col.), plans. 31cm. [TH2238.G3813 1967b] 67-29398 15.00 729'.1
1. Curtain walls. I. Gatz, Konrad. ed. BIP

Curtis, Edward S., 1868-1952—Juvenile literature.

BOESEN, Victor. 779'.9'970004970924 B
Edward S. Curtis, photographer of the North American Indian / Victor Boesen and Florence Curtis Graybill. New York : Dodd, Mead & Co., [1977] p. cm. Includes index. A biography of Edward Curtis who spent many years photographing, writing about, and recording the songs of the North American Indians. [TR140.C82B63] 92 76-53435 ISBN 0-396-07430-8 : 6.95
1. Curtis, Edward S., 1868-1952—Juvenile literature. 2. Photographers—United States—Biography—Juvenile literature. 3. Indians of North America—Juvenile literature. I. Graybill, Florence Curtis, joint author.

Curtis, Philip C.

PALM Springs, Calif. Desert Museum. 759.13
Philip C. Curtis; an exhibition organized by the Palm Springs Desert Museum, with the participation of the UCLA Art Galleries. Comments by Frederick W. Sleight and Henry J. Seldis. [Flagstaff, Ariz., Printed by Northland Press, 1971] 56 p. illus. (part col.) 26 cm. Catalogue of an exhibition to be held at Palm Springs Desert Museum, Nov.-Dec., 1971; UCLA Art Galleries, Jan.-Feb., 1972, and Utah Museum of Fine Arts, Aug. 1-Sept. 15, 1972. [ND237.C884P3] 77-183531 ISBN 0-87358-091-5
1. Curtis, Philip C. I. California. University. University at Los Angeles. Art Galleries. II. Utah Museum of Fine Arts.

Cust, Charles Leopold, Sir, 3d, bart., 1864- —Art collections.

CUST, Charles Leopold, Sir, 3d, bart., 1864- 769'.4'99047
Naval battles from the collection of prints formed and owned by Commander Sir Charles Leopold Cust, bart. The chronological arrangement of the prints with descriptive and historical notes by Harry Parker, and an introd. by Charles Napier Robinson. New York, B. Franklin [1974] Reprint of the 1911 ed. published by T. H. Parker, London. [NE957.C8 1974] 74-9854 ISBN 0-8337-4668-5 19.50 (lib. bdg.)
1. Cust, Charles Leopold, Sir, 3d, bart., 1864- —Art collections. 2. Naval battles in art. 3. Naval prints—Catalogs. I. Parker, Harry, 1884- II. Title.

Custard glass.

BRAHMER, Bonnie J. 748.2'913
Custard glass [by] Bonnie J. Brahmer. [1st ed.] Springfield? Mo., 1966] 63 p. illus. 22 cm. Pages 59-63 blank for "Notes." [NK5112.B65] 67-2461
1. Custard glass. 2. Glassware—Collectors and collecting. I. Title.

GADDIS, James H. 748.2'913
Keys to custard glass identification. By James H. Gaddis. [1st ed. Pontiac, Ill., Early America Co., 1966-69] 6 v. (chiefly illus.) 28 cm. Cover title. [NK5112.A1G3] 73-23632 2.95 per vol.
1. Custard glass. I. Title.

Cut glass.

ELVILLE, E. M. 748.6
English and Irish cut glass, 1750-1950. London, Country Life [dist. New York, Taplinger, 1963, c.1953] 95p. illus. 26cm. 6.95
1. Cut glass. 2. Glassware—Gt. Brit. I. Title.

Cut glass, American.

BOGGESS, Bill. 748.2'913
American brilliant cut glass / by Bill and Louise Boggess. New York : Crown Publishers, c1977. vii, 183 p. : ill. ; 29 cm. Includes index. [NK5203.B63 1977] 76-14479 ISBN 0-517-52525-9 : 12.95
1. Cut glass, American. I. Boggess, Louise, joint author. II. Title. BIP

PEARSON, J. Michael. 748.6
American cut glass for the discriminating collector [by] J. Michael Pearson and Dorothy T. Pearson. [1st ed.] New York, Vantage Press [1965] 204 p. illus. (part col.) 27 cm. [NK5112.P4] 65-26205
1. Cut glass, American. 2. Glassware, American. 3. Glassware—Collectors and collecting. I. Pearson, Dorothy T., joint author. II. Title. BIP

PEARSON, J. Michael. 748.2'913
Encyclopedia of American cut and engraved glass, 1880-1917 / by J. Michael Pearson. 1st ed. Miami Beach, Fla. : Pearson, c1975- v. : ill. ; 29 cm. Includes indexes. Contents.Contents.—v. 1. Geometric conceptions. [NK5203.P42] 74-18615 ISBN 0-916528-01-4 : 25.00 (v. 1)
1. Cut glass, American. 2. Engraved glass, American. I. Title. BIP

STEUBEN Glass, inc. 748.2'9147'83
Five masterworks. [1st ed. New York, 1972] 27 p. col. plates. 32 cm. "The artists": p. 27. [NK5112.S762 1972] 74-152329
1. Steuben Glass, inc. 2. Cut glass, American. 3. Engraved glass—United States.

Cut glass, American—Catalogs.

EHRHARDT, Alpha. 748.2'913
Cut glass price guide to 1500 pieces. [Kansas City, Mo., Heart of America Press, 1973- v. illus. 29 cm. Cover title. Bibliography: v. 1., p. 4. [NK5112.E35] 74-155413 6.95 (v. 1)
1. Cut glass, American—Catalogs. I. Title.

WILLEY, Harold E. 748.2'9171'54
Heisey's cut handmade glassware / by Harold E. Willey. [Newark? Ohio] : Willey, c1974. 147 p. : ill. ; 23 cm. Cover title. Includes index. [NK5198.H4W54] 75-308357
1. Heisey (A. H.) & Co. 2. Willey, Harold E.—Art collections. 3. Cut glass, American—Catalogs. I. Title.

Cut glass, American—New York (State)—Corning—Exhibitions.

SPILLMAN, Jane Shadel. 748.2'9147'83
The cut and engraved glass of Corning, 1868-1940 / Jane Shadel Spillman, Estelle Sinclaire Farrar. Corning, N.Y. : Corning Museum of Glass, 1977. 101 p. : ill. ; 28 cm. Exhibition held at the Corning Museum of Glass, Corning, N.Y. Bibliography: p. 101. [NK5203.S65] 77-73626
1. Cut glass, American—New York (State)—Corning—Exhibitions. 2. Engraved glass, American—New York (State)—Corning—Exhibitions. I. Farrar, Estelle Sinclaire, joint author. II. Corning, N.Y. Museum of Glass. III. Title. BIP

Bibliography: p. 169-170. [TR365.N4] 61-10389
1. Daguerreotype. 2. Photography—History—United States. 3. Photographers. BIP

POBBORAVSKY, Irving, 1933- 772'.12
Study of iodized daguerreotype plates. Rochester, N.Y., Information Service, Graphic Arts Research Center, Rochester Institute of Technology [1971] 60 p. illus. 28 cm. ([Rochester Institute of Technology, Rochester, N.Y. Graphic Arts Research Center] Report no. 142) "In partial fulfillment of a masters degree in photographic science, School of Photographic Arts and Science, Rochester Institute of Technology." Bibliography: p. 58-60. [TR365.P63] 76-30893
1. Daguerreotype. 2. Silver iodide. I. Title. II. Series.

RINHART, Floyd. 772'.12'0973
American Daguerreian [sic] art [by] Floyd and Marion Rinhart. New York, C. N. Potter; distributed by Crown Publishers [1967] ix, 135 p. illus. (part col.) 29 cm. Bibliography: p. 133-134. [TR365.R47] 67-16521
1. Daguerreotype. 2. Photography—History—United States. I. Rinhart, Marion, joint author. II. Title.

RUDISILL, Richard. 770'.973
Mirror image; the influence of the daguerreotype on American society. [1st ed.] Albuquerque, University of New Mexico Press [1971] ix, 342 p. illus., 202 plates (incl. ports.) 29 cm. Originally presented as the author's thesis, University of Minnesota, 1967. Bibliography: p. 239-255. [TR365.R83] 79-137880 30.00
1. Daguerreotype. 2. Photography—History—U.S. I. Title. BIP

SOBIESZEK, Robert A., 1943-comp. 772'12
The daguerreotype process: Three Treatises, 1840-1849: edited by Robert A. Sobieszek. New York, Arno Press, 1973. 12, 16, 81 p. illus. 23 cm. (Literature of Photography) Reprint of researches on the theory of the principal phaenomena of photography in the Daguerreotype process, by A. Claudet, from the London, Edinburgh, and Dublin Philosophical Magazine and Journal of Science for Nov. 1849; of description of the daguerreotype process, or a summary of M. Gouraud's public lectures, according to the principles of M. Daguerre; with a description of a provisory method for taking human portraits, first published in 1840; and of a system of photography, containing an explicit detail of the whole process of daguerreotype, by S. D. Humphrey and M. Finley, first published in 1849. [TR365.S6 1973] 72-9192 ISBN 0-405-04902-1. 10.00.
1. Daguerreotype. I. Claudet, Antoine Fran cois Jean, 1797-1867. Description of the daguerreotype process. 1973 II. Fauvel-Gouraud, Francois. Description of the daguerreotype process. 1973. III. Humphrey, Samuel D. A system of photography. 1973. IV. Title. V. Series.

Daguerreotype—Exhibitions.

HEYMAN, Therese Thau. 779'.9'91794
Mirror of California; daguerreotypes. The Oakland Museum Oakes Gallery, November 6, 1973 through January 27, 1974. [Oakland, Calif., Oakland Museum, Art Dept., c1973] 32 p. illus. 22 x 26 cm. Bibliography: p. 26-27. [TR365.H49] 73-91764
1. Daguerreotype—Exhibitions. 2. California—History—1850-1950—Exhibitions. I. Oakland Museum. II. Title.

SOBIESZEK, Robert A., 1943- 779'.2'0924
The spirit of fact : the daguerreotypes of Southworth & Hawes, 1843-1862 / Robert A. Sobieszek and Odette M. Appel ; with research assistance by Charles R. Moore. Boston : D. R. Godine, c1976. xxv, 163 p. : ill. ; 28 x 32 cm. Catalogue of an exhibition held at the International Museum of Photography at the George Eastman House, Rochester, Feb.-June 1976; at the National Portrait Gallery, Washington, July-Dec. 1976; and at the Museum of Fine Arts, Boston, Jan.-Feb. 1977. Bibliography: p. 161-163. [TR365.S6] 75-43054 ISBN 0-87923-179-3 : 27.50
1. Southworth, Albert Sands, 1811-1894. 2. Hawes, Josiah Johnson, 1808-1901. 3. Daguerreotype—Exhibitions. I. Appel, Odette M., joint author. II. Moore, Charles R. III. International Museum of Photography at George Eastman House. IV. National Portrait Gallery, Washington, D.C. V. Boston. Museum of Fine Arts. VI. Title. BIP

Daguerreotype—History.

THE Daguerreotype in 772'.12
Germany : three accounts / ed. by Robert Sobieszek. New York : Arno Press, 1979. p. cm. (The Sources of modern photography) Text in German. The first contribution is reprinted from the 1843 ed., published by Berendsohn, Hamburg; the second contribution from the 1922 ed. published by Bredow, Berlin; the third contribution from the 1915 ed. published by Meissen, Hamburg and issued as Beiheft zum Jahrbuch dew hamburgischen wissenschaftlichen Anstalten, 1. Contents.Contents.—Cephir. Der Dagerreotypen-Krieg in Hamburg.—Dost, W. Die Daugerreotypie in Berlin 1839-1860.—Weimar, W. Die Daguerreotypie in Hamburg 1839-1860. [TR73.D33] 76-23344 ISBN 0-405-09598-8 : 30.00
1. Photography—Germany—History—Collected works. 2. Daguerreotype—Collected works. I. Sobieszek, Robert A., 1943- II. Cephir. Der Dagerreotypen-Krieg in Hamburg. 1979. III. Dost, Wilhelm. Die Daguerreotpie in Berlin 1839-1860. 1979. IV. Weimar, Wilhelm, 1859-1914. Die Daguerreotypie in Hamburg, 1839-1860. 1979. V. Title. VI. Series.

NEWHALL, Beaumont, 1908- 772'.12
The daguerreotype in America / by Beaumont Newhall. 3d rev. ed. New York : Dover Publications, 1976. 175 p., [48] leaves of plates : ill. ; 29 cm. Includes index. Bibliography: p. 169-170. [TR365.N4 1976] 76-691 ISBN 0-486-23322-7 pbk. : 6.00
1. Daguerreotype—History. 2. Photography—United States—History. I. Title.

Daingerfield, Elliott, 1859-1932.

HOBBS, Robert. 759.13
Elliott Daingerfield retrospective exhibition. [Charlotte, N.C., Mint Museum of Art, 1971] 64 p. illus. 27 cm. Catalog of the exhibition held at the Mint Museum of Art, Charlotte, N.C., April 14-May 16, 1971, and at the North Carolina Museum of Art, Raleigh, N.C., May 23-June 20, 1971. Bibliography: p. 61. [N6537.D3H6] 76-161125
1. Daingerfield, Elliott, 1859-1932. I. Mint Museum of Art. II. North Carolina. Museum of Art, Raleigh.

Dakin, James H.

SCULLY, Arthur. 720'.92'4
James Dakin, architect, his career in New York and the South. Baton Rouge, Louisiana State University Press [1973] xiv, 209 p. illus. 26 cm. Bibliography: p. [205]-206. [NA737.D27S38] 72-89897 ISBN 0-8071-0213-X 15.00
1. Dakin, James H. 2. Architecture—New York (State) 3. Architecture—Southern States. I. Title.

Dakota Indians—Art—Exhibitions.

UNITED States. Indian Arts and Crafts Board. 759.13'074'018393
Contemporary Sioux painting; an exhibition organized by the Indian Arts and Crafts Board of the United States Department of the Interior. [Rapid City, S.D., Tipi Shop, 1970] 80 p. illus. 25 cm. Bibliography: p. 80. [E99.D1U75] 70-119593
1. Dakota Indians—Art—Exhibitions. I. Title.

Daland, John Tucker, 1795-1858.

TOLLES, Bryant Franklin, 1939- 974.4'5
The John Tucker Daland House / by Bryant F. Tolles, Jr. ; foreword by Anne Farnam. Salem, Mass. : Essex Institute, 1978. 27 p., [4] leaves of plates : ill. ; 23 cm. (Historic house booklet series ; no. 7) Includes bibliographical referendes. [NA7238.S3T64] 76-27382 ISBN 0-88389-065-8 : 2.00
1. Daland, John Tucker, 1795-1858. 2. Salem, Mass. John Tucker Daland House. I. Title. II. Series.
Publisher's address : 132 Essex St., Salem, MA 01970 BIP

Dali, Salvador, 1904—

BOSQUET, Alain, 1919- 759.6
Conversations with Dali. Translated from the French by Joachim Neugroschel. [1st ed.] New York, Dutton, 1969. 123 p. 21 cm. Translation of Entretiens avec Salvador Dali. [ND813.D3B613] 78-87186 3.95
I. Dali, Salvador, 1904- II. Title.

COWLES, Fleur. 759.6
The case of Salvador Dali. [1st American ed.] Boston, Little, Brown [1960, c1959] 334 p. illus. 22 cm. [ND813.D3C6 1960] 60-5366
1. Dali, Salvador, 1904- I. Title.

DALI, Salvador, 1904- 760'.092'4
Dali : the wines of gala / by Salvador Dali. New York : Abrams, [1977] p. cm. [N7113.D3A44] 77-8625 ISBN 0-8109-0802-6 : 50.00
1. Dali, Salvador, 1904- 2. Wine in art.

DALI, Salvador, 1904- 760'.0924
Dali. Edited and arranged by Max Gerard. Translated by Eleanor R. Morse. New York, H. N. Abrams [1968] 1 v. (chiefly illus. (part col.)) 31 cm. Cover title: Dali de Draeger. [ND813.D3G413] 68-28386
I. Gerard, Max, ed. BIP

DALI, Salvador, 1904- 759.6
Dali / with an introd. by J. G. Ballard ; edited by David Larkin. New York : Ballantine Books, 1974. [14] p., [40] leaves of plates : chiefly col. ill. ; 30 cm. [ND813.D3L34] 75-315871 ISBN 0-345-23782-X : 4.95
1. Dali, Salvador, 1904- I. Larkin, David.

DALI, Salvador, 1904- 759.6
Dali ... Dali ... Dali ... / text by Max Gerard ; introd. by Pierre Roumeguere. Abridged ed. New York : H. N. Abrams, [1974] [144] p. : ill. (some col.) ; 31 cm. [ND813.D3G3913] 74-4169 ISBN 0-8109-0223-0 : 15.00
1. Dali, Salvador, 1904- I. Gerard, Max. II. Title.

DALI, Salvador, 1904- 741.9'46
Dali: paintings and drawings, 1965-70 [by] Thomas B. Hess. [Exhibition, March 10-April 4, 1970. New York] M. Knoedler [1970] 11, [11] p. illus. (part col.) 22 cm. [ND813.D3A33] 77-120086
I. Hess, Thomas B. II. Title.

DALI, Salvador, 1904- 759.6
Diary of a genius. Foreword, notes by Michel Deon. Tr. from French by Richard Howard. [1st ed. in the U.S.A.] New York, Doubleday [c.1964, 1965] ix, 230p. illus., ports. 22cm. [ND813.D3A353] 65-25448 5.95
I. Title.

DALI, Salvador, 1904- 759.6
Salvador Dali. Text by Robert Descharnes. Translated by Eleanor Morse. New York, Abrams [1975] p. cm. (The Library of great painters) Bibliography: p. [ND813.D3D4413] 74-4257 ISBN 0-8109-0222-2 : 22.50
1. Dali, Salvador, 1904- I. Descharnes, Robert.

DALI, Salvador, 1904- 709'.2'4
Salvador Dali (Spanish—1904-): a guide to his works in public museums. Cleveland, Privately published by the Dali Museum for the Reynolds Morse Foundation [1974, c1973] xiii, 92 p. (chiefly illus.) 26 x 31 cm. Cover title: A guide to works by Salvador Dali in public museum collections. Text by A. Reynolds Morse. Edition of 1956 published under title: Guide to works by Salvador Dali in public museum collections. Includes bibliographical references. [N7113.D3M67] 73-92363
1. Dali, Salvador, 1904- I. Morse, Albert Reynolds, 1914- II. Salvador Dali Museum. III. Reynolds Morse Foundation. IV. Title. V. Title: A guide to works by Salvador Dali in public museum collections.

DALI, Salvador, 1904- 759.6 B
The unspeakable confessions of Salvador Dali / as told to Andre Parinaud ; translated from the French by Harold J. Salemsom. New York : Morrow, 1976. 300 p., [9] leaves of plates : ill. ; 24 cm. Translation of Comment on devient Dali. [ND813.D3P3713] 75-25924 ISBN 0-688-02995-7 : 10.00
1. Dali, Salvador, 1904- 2. Painters—Spain—Correspondence, reminiscences, etc. I. Parinaud, Andre, 1924- II. Title.

DESCHARNES, Robert. 927.5
The world of Salvador Dali [Translation by Albert Field. 1st ed.] New York, Harper & Row [1962] 228 p. illus. (part mounted; part col.), ports. 31 cm. Captions of the illustrations by Dali; translated by Haakon Chevalier. Translation of Dali de Gala. [ND813.D3D43] 62-15741
1. Dali, Salvador, 1904- I. Title.

HALSMAN, Philippe. 759.6
Dali's mustache, a photographic interview by Salvador Dali and Philippe Halsman. New York, Simon and Schuster [1954] 126p. illus. 18cm. [ND813.D3H3] 927.5 54-13184
1. Dali, Salvador, 1904- I. Dali, Salvador, 1904- II. Title.

LAKE, Carlton. 759.6
In quest of Dali. New York, Putnam [1969] 316 p. 22 cm. [ND813.D3L3] 70-77633 6.95
1. Dali, Salvador, 1904- I. Title.

MADDOX, Conroy. 759.6 B
Dali / Conroy Maddox. New York : Harmony Books, [1979] p. cm. [N7113.D3M32] 78-9924 ISBN 0-517-53675-7 : 9.95
1. Dali, Salvador, 1904- 2. Artists—Spain—Biography. I. Title. BIP

MORSE, Albert Reynolds, 1914- 759.6
Dali: a study of his life and work. Text by A. Reynolds Morse and a special appreciation by Michel Tapie. Descriptive captions for the color plates written especially for this volume by Salvador Dali. [1st American ed.] Greenwich, Conn., New York Graphic Society [1958] 96p. illus. (17 mounted col.) ports. 35 x 37cm. [ND813.D3M58] 927.5 58-6725
1. Dalf, Salvador, I. Title.

MORSE, Albert Reynolds, 1914- 759.6
The Dali adventure, 1943-1973; a photo album, by A. Reynolds Morse and Eleanor R. Morse. Cleveland, Salvador Dali Museum [1973] 1 v. (unpaged) illus. 26 x 31 cm. Pt. 2, Romantic Ampurdan, originally published in 1972 in Dali ... a collection, by A. R. Morse. [ND813.D3M583] 73-78993
1. Dali, Salvador, 1904- I. Morse, Eleanor R., joint author. II. Salvador Dali Museum. III. Title.

MORSE, Albert Reynolds, 1914- 759.6
A new introduction to Salvador Dali. Cleveland, Reynolds-Morse Foundation, c1960. 88p. illus. (part col.) ports. 21cm. [ND813.D3M59] 60-43285
1. Dalf, Salvader, 1904- I. Title.

MORSE, Albert Reynolds, 1914- 759.6
Salvador Dali, Pablo Picasso—Pablo Picasso, Salvador Dali; a preliminary study in their similarities and contrasts, by A. Reynolds Morse. Cleveland, Salvador Dali Museum [1973] 112 p. illus. 26 x 31 cm. English, French, or Spanish. [ND813.D3M64] 73-78992 9.95
1. Dali, Salvador, 1904- 2. Picasso, Pablo, 1881-1973. I. Dali, Salvador, 1904- II. Picasso, Pablo, 1881-1973. III. Salvador Dali Museum.

Publisher's Address: 24050 Commerce Park, Cleveland, Ohio 44122.

NEW York. Gallery of Modern   759.6
Art Including the Huntington Hartford Collection
Salvador Dali, 1910-1965; an exhibition in the Gallery of Modern Art Including the Huntington Hartford Collection, 18 Dec. 1965-28 Feb. 1966, with the Reynolds Morse collection [Greenwich, Conn., N.Y. Graphic, 1966, c.1965] 160p. illus. (pt. col.) 28cm. Catalogue of the exhibition: p.149-160 [ND813.D3N4] 65-29182 12.50
1. Dali, Salvador, 1904- I. Morse, Albert Reynolds, 1914- II. Title.

OWEN Cheatham Foundation,   709'.24
New York.
Dali, a study of his art-in-jewels: the collection of the Owen Cheatham Foundation. Foreword by A. Hyatt Mayor. Comments and captions by the artist. Edited by Lida Livingston. Greenwich, Conn., New York Graphic Society [1959] 67p. mounted col. illus: 29cm. [NK7398.D25O9] 62-1828
1. Dalí, Salvador, 1904- 2. Jewelry. I. Title.

OWEN Cheatham Foundation,   739.27
New York.
Dali, a study of his art-in-jewels: the collection of the Owen Cheatham Foundation. Foreword by A. Hyatt Mayor. Comments and captions by the artist. Edited by Lida Livingston. Greenwich, Conn., New York Graphic Society [1970] 85 p. 36 col. illus. ; part. 29 cm. [NK7398.D25O9 1970] 79-21145
1. Dali, Salvador, 1904- 2. Jewelry—Catalogs. I. Title.

SALVADOR Dali.   759.6
[Cleveland 1954] 64 p. illus., port., map. 14 cm. 'The paintings reproduced in this catalog are from the collection of Mr. and Mrs. A. Reynolds Morse Clevdrland, Ohio.' [ND813.D3M6] [ND813.DM6] 927.5 55-18275 55-18275
1. Dali Salvador, 1904- II. Morse, Albert Reynolds, 1914-

SALVADOR Dali Museum.   759.6
Salvador Dali: catalog of a collection; ninety-three oils, 1917-1970. [1st deluxe limited ed.] Cleveland (Beachwood), Ohio [1972] 226, xxxvi p. illus. (part col.) 27 x 32 cm. On cover: Salvador Dali: a collection. "Written ... by A. Reynolds Morse." Five hundred copies printed. No. 44. "The paintings in this catalog are in the Collection of Mr. and Mrs. A. Reynolds Morse." [ND813.D3S34] 73-152939
1. Dali, Salvador, 1904- 2. Morse, Albert Reynolds, 1914- —Art collections. I. Morse, Albert Reynolds, 1914- II. Title.

SOBY, James Thrall, 1906-   759.6
Salvador Dali. [New York] Museum of Modern Art. Reprint ed. [New York] Published for the Museum of Modern Art by Arno Press [1969, c1946] 108 p. illus. 27 cm. Bibliography: p. 97-108. [ND813.D3S6 1969] 68-8368
1. Dali, Salvador, 1904- I. New York. Museum of Modern Art.   **BIP**

WALTON, Paul H.   759.6
Dali/Miro. Text and notes by Paul H. Walton. New York, Tudor Pub. Co. [1967] 36 p., 92 col. plates. 18 cm. Bibliography: p. 14. [ND812.W3] 67-19837 2.95
1. Dali, Salvador, 1904- 2. Miro, Joan, 1893-

Dali, Salvador, 1904—Juvenile literature.

CEVASCO, George A.   759.6
Salvador Dali: master of surrealism and modern art, by G. A. Cevasco. Charlotteville, N.Y., SamHar Press, 1971. 31 p. 22 cm. (Outstanding personalities, no. 5) Bibliography: p. 31. A brief biography of the Spanish artist whose art reflects his interest in surrealism. [ND813.D3C4] 92 79-185661
1. Dali, Salvador, 1904—Juvenile literature. I. Title.

Dallas—Buildings.

AMERICAN Institute   720'.9764'2812
of Architects. Dallas Chapter.
Dallasights : an anthology of architecture and open spaces / [editor, Alan R. Sumner]. 1st ed. [Dallas] : American Institute of Architects, Dallas Chapter, 1978. 191 p. : ill. ; 26 cm. Includes indexes. [NA735.D2A4 1978] 78-54082 ISBN 0-913962-05-8 : 12.95
1. Dallas—Buildings. 2. Dallas—Plazas. I. Sumner, Alan R. II. Title.
Publisher's address: 2800 Routh, Suite 141, Dallas, TX75201

Dallas. Museum of Fine Arts.

GOGH, Vincent van, 1853-   709/.492
1890
Vincent van Gogh; drawings, watercolors. [Zaandam? 1967?] 1v. (unpaged) illus. (pt. col.) 25cm. Exhibition held at the Dallas Mus. of Fine Arts, Oct. 6-Nov. 4, 1967 and others. [NC263.G56A58] 68-72974 2.50 pap.
1. Dallas. Museum of Fine Arts. I. Title.
Order from the Museum Shop, Dallas Mus. of Fine Arts, Fair Park, Dallas, Tex. 75226.

Dallin, Cyrus Edwin, 1861-1944.

FRANCIS, Rell G.,   730'.92'4 B
1928-
Cyrus E. Dallin : let justice be done / Rell G. Francis. Springville, Utah : Francis, c1976. xv, 262 p. : ill. ; 29 cm. "Published for Springville Museum of Art ... in cooperation with Utah American Revolution Bicentennial Commission." Includes index. Bibliography: p. 255-258. [NB237.D25F72] 76-12352 15.95
1. Dallin, Cyrus Edwin, 1861-1944. I. Springville Museum of Art.

Dalou, Jules, 1838-1902.

HUNISAK, John M., 1944-   730'.92'4
The sculptor Jules Dalou : studies in his style and imagery / John M. Hunisak. New York : Garland Pub., 1977. p. cm. (Outstanding dissertations in the fine arts) Reprint of the author's thesis, New York University, 1975. Bibliography: p. [NB553.D25H86 1977] 76-23629 ISBN 0-8240-2699-3 : 42.50
1. Dalou, Jules, 1838-1902. I. Title. II. Series.   **BIP**

Dalton, Harry L.

NORTH Carolina. Museum   708.15'6
of Art, Raleigh.
Selections from the collection of Mr. and Mrs. Harry L. Dalton, September 19-October 10, 1965, North Carolina Museum of Art, Raleigh. [Raleigh, 1966?] 1 v. (unpaged) illus. (part col.) 26 cm. Catalog of the exhibition. [N5020.R34] 66-64856
1. Dalton, Harry L. 2. Art—Exhibitions. I. Title.   **BIP**

Dalton, Harry L.—Art collections.

DUKE University,   750'.74'05656
Durham, N.C.
Older European paintings from the Collection of Harry L. Dalton. A loan exhibition, Duke University, Durham, N.C., February 28-April 4, 1965. [Durham, 1965?] 1 v. (unpaged) illus. 23 cm. [ND454.D8] 67-63858
1. Dalton, Harry L.—Art collections. 2. Paintings, European—Exhibitions. I. Title.

DUKE   709'.73'0740156563
University, Durham, N.C. Art Museum.
America the beautiful : a Bicentennial exhibition of American art from the Dalton Collection, the Duke University Museum of Art, July 1976. Durham, N.C. : The Museum, c1976. 63 p. : chiefly ill. (some col.) ; 22 cm. [N6505.D85 1976] 76-335221
1. Dalton, Harry L.—Art collections. 2. Dalton, Mary—Art collections. 3. Art, American—Exhibitions. I. Title.

Dalton, Mary—Art collections.

DUKE University, Durham,   759.6
N.C. Art Museum.
The Italian paintings from the Mary and Harry L. Dalton Collection : the Duke University Museum of Art, September 29-November 12, 1974 : [catalog] [Durham, N.C.] : The Museum, [1974] [71] p. : ill. (some col.) ; 22 cm. [ND614.D84 1974] 74-195180
1. Dalton, Mary—Art collections. 2. Dalton, Harry L.—Art collections. 3. Paintings, Italian—Exhibitions. 4. Painting, Modern—Italy. I. Title.

Damianus, Saint—Art.

SKROBUCHA, Heinz   704.9486
The patrons of doctors. [Tr. from German by Hans Hermann Rosenwald] Recklinghausen, A. Bongers; dist. by Taplinger [New York, 1965] 66 p. illus. (pt. col.) 18cm. (Pictorial lib. of Eastern Church art, v. 7) Tr. of Lpsmas und Damian. [N8080.S5513] 67-16579 2.50 bds.,
1. Damianus, Saint—Art. 2. Cosmas, Saint—Art. I. Title.

Danby, Francis, 1793-1861.

ADAMS, Eric.   759.9429
Francis Danby: varieties of poetic landscape. New Haven, Published for the Paul Mellon Centre for Studies in British Art by Yale University Press, 1973. xviii, 207, [96] p. 166 illus. (part col.) 32 cm. (Studies in British art) Bibliography: p. 164-168. [ND497.D32A65] 72-75185 ISBN 0-300-01538-0 27.50
1. Danby, Francis, 1793-1861. 2. Landscape in art. I. Title. II. Series.

Danby, Ken, 1940—

DUVAL, Paul.   760'.092'4 B
Ken Danby / by Paul Duval. Toronto : Clarke, Irwin, c1976. 192 p. : ill. (some col.) ; 28 cm. Includes index. [N6549.D36D83] 77-354056 ISBN 0-7720-1093-5
1. Danby, Ken, 1940- I. Danby, Ken, 1940-

Dance of death.

CHARLOT, Jean, 1898-   741.5
Dance of death; 50 drawings and captions New York, Sheed & Ward [1951] unpaged. illus. 16 x 24 cm. [N7720.C5A43] 51-12426
1. Dance of death. I. Title.

KUBIN, Alfred, 1877-   741.9'436
1959.
Kubin's Dance of death, and other drawings. 83 works, by Alfred Kubin. With a new introd. by Gregor Sebba. New York, Dover Publications [1973] xii p., 83 plates. 29 cm. Includes Die Blatter mit dem Tod originally published in 1918, and Funfzig Zeichnungen originally published in 1923, with captions in German and English. [NC245.K8A52] 72-81285 ISBN 0-486-22884-3 2.50 (pbk.)
1. Kubin, Alfred, 1877-1959. 2. Dance of death. I. Kubin, Alfred, 1877-1959. Die Blatter mit dem Tod. 1973. II. Kubin, Alfred, 1877-1959. Funfzig Zeichnungen. 1973. III. Title. IV. Title: Dance of death.   **BIP**

ROWLANDSON, Thomas, 1756-   741.942
1827.
Drawings for The English dance of death [by William Combe] With an introd. and notes by Robert R. Wark. San Marino, Calif., Huntington Library, 1966. xiii, 178 p. illus. (part col.) 16 x 25 cm. (Huntington Library publications) [NC242.R66W3] 66-21941
1. Dance of death. I. Combe, William, 1742-1823. The English dance of death. II. Wark, Robert R., ed. III. Title. IV. Series: Henry E. Huntington Library and Art Gallery, San Marino, Calif. Huntington Library publications.

WARTHIN, Aldred Scott,   016.76
1866-1931.
The physician of the dance of death / Aldred Scott Warthin. New York : Arno

Press, 1977. xvi, 142 p. : ill. ; 26 cm. (The Literature of death and dying) Reprint of the 1931 ed. published by P. B. Hoeber, New York. [N7720.A1W37 1977] 76-19592 ISBN 0-405-09587-2 : 12.00
1. Dance of death. 2. Death in art. 3. Dance of death—Bibliography. I. Title. II. Series.   **BIP**

Dance posters.

100 years of dance posters   769'.5
/ by Walter Terry and Jack Rennert New York : Universe Books, 1975. 112 p. : ill.(some col.) ; 41 cm. (The Poster art library) [GV1781.O53] 75-21874 ISBN 0-87663-270-3 : 14.95
1. Dance posters. 2. Dancing—History. I. Terry, Walter. II. Rennert, Jack.

Dancers.

ZAIDENBERG, Arthur, 1903-   741.4
How to draw ballet and other dancers. London, New York [etc.] Abelard-Schuman [1968] 64 p. illus. 27 cm. [NC785.Z32] 68-8560 3.50
1. Dancers. 2. Action in art. I. Title.   **BIP**

Dancers—Portraits.

WALDMAN, Max.   778.9'9'79280922
Waldman on dance / by Max Waldman ; with an introd. by Clive Barnes. New York : Morrow, 1977. ca. 150 p. : chiefly ill. ; 29 cm. [GV1785.A1W26] 77-6627 ISBN 0-688-03227-3 : 14.95
1. Dancers—Portraits. I. Title.   **BIP**

Dancing—Greece.

WRIGHT, Frederick Adam, 1869-   700
1946.
The arts in Greece; three essays. Port Washington, N.Y., Kennikat Press [1969] viii, 111 p. 22 cm. (Kennikat classics series) Reprint of the 1923 ed. Contents.Contents.—The dance.—Music.—Painting. [DF78.W7 1969] 75-101054
1. Dancing—Greece. 2. Music, Greek and Roman. 3. Painting, Greek. I. Title.   **BIP**

Dancing in art.

THE Dance in art.   741.9'24
Introd. by Stephen Longstreet. [1st ed.] Alhambra, Calif., Borden Pub. Co. [1968] [42] p. (chiefly illus.) 31 cm. (Master draughtsman series) [N8217.D3D3] 68-28183
1. Dancing in art. I. Borden Publishing Company.   **BIP**

KOVALEVSKY, Olga.   741.9'47
Studies in movement of Doris Niles and Serge Leslie, drawn by Olga Kovalevsky. Los Angeles [United Printing and Lithograph Co.] 1951. 1 portfolio (iv p. 18 plates (part col.)) 29 cm. "The American edition of this folio is limited to two hundred and fifty numbered copies of which this is number 123." [NC269.K673N54] 75-318291
1. Kovalevsky, Olga. 2. Niles, Doris. 3. Leslie, Serge. 4. Dancing in art. 5. Movement, Aesthetics of. I. Title.

Dancing in art—Exhibitions.

NEW York (City).   793.3'074'01471
Public Library. Library & Museum of the Performing Arts.
A decade of acquisitions; the dance collection, 1964-1973, Vincent Astor Gallery & Dance Collection Reading Room, Performing Arts Research Center, New York Public Library at Lincoln Center, April 9-June 2, 1973. [New York, 1973] 28 p. 23 cm. Cover title. Catalog of an exhibition. [N8217.D3Nr8 1973] 75-304010
1. Dancing in art—Exhibitions. 2. Art, Modern—Exhibitions. I. Title.

Daniels, David—Art collections.

BENNETT, Mary   741'.074'0176579
Lee.
Selections from the drawing collection of

David Daniels; loan exhibition. [Catalogue compiled by Mary Lee Bennett and Agnes Mongan. Cambridge? Mass., 1968] 10 p., 86 l. illus. 22 cm. Spine and half title: Drawings from the David Daniels Collection. Held at the Minneapolis Institute of Arts, Minneapolis, Minn.; Art Institute of Chicago, Chicago, Ill.; Nelson Gallery-Atkins Museum, Kansas City, Mo.; and Fogg Art Museum, Harvard University, Cambridge, Mass. Includes bibliographical references. [NC33.B4] 68-3317
1. Daniels, David—Art collections. 2. Drawings—Exhibitions. I. Mongan, Agnes, joint author. II. Minneapolis. Institute of Arts. III. Title. IV. Title: Drawings from the David Daniels Collection.

Dansk Ostindisk Compagni.

GRAY, John C. F. 737.49'5482
Tranquebar: a guide to the coins of Danish India, circa 1620 to 1845. [By] John C. F. Gray. Lawrence, Mass., Quarterman Publications, [1975, c1974] 83 p. illus. 24 cm. Bibliography: p. [34]-35. [CJ3119.T7.G73] 74-84564 ISBN 0-88000-054-6 12.50
1. Dansk Ostindisk Compagni. 2. Dansk Asiatisk Compagni. 3. Coins, Danish—Tranquebar. 4. Numismatics—Tranquebar. I. Title. BIP

Dantan, Jean Pierre, 1800-1869.

SELIGMAN, Janet. 738.84
Figures of fun; the caricature-statuettes of Jean-Pierre Dantan. London, New York, Oxford University Press, 1957. 158p. illus. 23cm. [NB553.D27S4] 57-3529
1. Dantan, Jean Pierre, 1800-1869. I. Title.

Dante Alighieri, 1265-1321.

DORE, Gustave, 1832-1883. 769'.92'4
The Dore illustrations for Dante's Divine comedy : 136 plates / by Gustave Dore. New York : Dover Publications, 1976. vii, 136 p. : chiefly ill. ; 31 cm. [PQ4329.D625 1976] 75-17176 ISBN 0-486-23231-X pbk. : 4.50
1. Dante Alighieri, 1265-1321. Divina Commedia—Illustrations. I. Dante Alighieri, 1265-1321. Divina Commedia. II. Title.

Dante Alighieri, 1265-1321—Illustrations.

BLAKE, William, 1757-1827. 741.9'42
Blake's illustrations for Dante; selections from the originals in the National Gallery of Victoria, Melbourne, Australia and the Fogg Art Museum, Cambridge, Massachusetts. [Cambridge] 1953. [49] p. illus. 14 x 20 cm. (Fogg picture book no. 2) [N527.A55 no. 2] 78-235410
1. Dante Alighieri, 1265-1321—Illustrations. I. Dante Alighieri, 1265-1321. II. Victoria, Australia. National Gallery, Melbourne. III. Harvard University. William Hayes Fogg Art Museum. IV. Title. V. Series.

BLAKE, William, 1757-1827. 741.9'42
Illustrations to the Divine comedy of Dante. [2d ed.] New York, Da Capo Press, 1968. 1 portfolio ([6] p., 109 plates) 44 cm. A slightly enlarged version; the drawings of the ed. priv. print. by E. Walker Limited for the subscribers of the National Art-Collections Fund, London, 1922, have been reproduced in facsimile. [NC1115.B63 1968] 68-30552
1. Dante Alighieri, 1265-1321—Illustrations. I. Title.

BRIEGER, Peter H., 1898- 745.6'7
Illuminated manuscripts of the Divine comedy, by Peter Brieger, Millard Meiss [and] Charles S. Singleton. [Princeton, N.J.] Princeton University Press [1969] 2 v. facsims. (part col.), plates (part col.) 32 cm. (Bollingen series, 81) Contents.Contents.—v. 1. Text.—v. 2. Plates. Bibliography: v. 1, p. [341]-350. [PQ4366.B7] 68-20867 45.00
1. Dante Alighieri, 1265-1321—Illustrations. 2. Illumination of books and manuscripts—Specimens, reproductions, etc. I. Meiss, Millard. II. Singleton, Charles Southward, 1909- III. Title. IV. Series. BIP

FLAXMAN, John, 1755-1826. 851'.1
Flaxman designs for Dante: Inferno, Purgatorio, Paradiso. Edited by Bill Tate. [1st ed. Truchas, N.M.] Tate Gallery [1968] 83 p. 34 illus., facsim. 29 cm. With selections translated into English verse by I. C. Wright, and illus. reproduced from an 1877 ed. of Dante. [NC1115.F6T32] 70-3257
1. Dante Alighieri, 1265-1321—Illustrations. I. Dante Alighieri, 1265-1321. Divina Commedia. II. Wright, Ichabod Charles, 1795-1871, tr. III. Tate, Bill, ed. IV. Title.

Darley, Felix Octavius Carr, 1822-1888.

BOLTON, Theodore, 1889- 016.74164
The book illustrations of Felix Octavius Carr Darley, Worcester, Mass., The Society, 1952. 138-182 p. port. 25 cm. At head of title: American Antiquarian Society. "Reprinted from the Proceedings of the American Antiquarian Society for April 1951." [NC139.D37B6] 52-64322
1. Darley, Felix Octavius Carr, 1822-1888. I. Title.

KING, Ethel M. 927.4
Darley, the most popular illustrator of his time, by Ethel King. Brooklyn, N.Y., T. Gaus' Sons [c1964] 156 p. plates, port. 23 cm. Bibliography: p. 151-152. [NC139.D37K5] 64-8864
1. Darley, Felix Octavius Carr, 1822-1888. I. Title.

Darling, Jay Norwood, 1876-1962.

LENDT, David L. 741'.092'4 B
Ding : the life of Jay Norwood Darling / David L. Lendt. 1st ed. Ames : Iowa State University Press, 1978. p. cm. Includes index. Bibliography: p. [NC1429.D237L46] 78-10321 ISBN 0-8138-0010-2 : 7.95
1. Darling, Jay Norwood, 1876-1962. 2. Cartoonists—United States—Biography. I. Title. BIP

Dartington Hall, Totnes, Eng.

EMERY, Anthony. 728.8'3'094235
Dartington Hall. Oxford, Clarendon P., 1970. [12], 292 p., 2 fold. plates. illus., facsms., geneal. tables, maps, plans, ports. 32 cm. [NA7333.T66E4] 74-17542 6/10/-
1. Dartington Hall, Totnes, Eng. BIP

Dartmouth College—Description—Views.

PLOWMAN, George Taylor, 1869-1932. 741.973
Dartmouth drawings. With an introd. by E. Grosvenor Plowman. Hanover, N.H., Dartmouth College Library [1970] 1 v. (chiefly illus.) 32 cm. Cover title. [NC139.P55A44] 75-15725
1. Dartmouth College—Description—Views. I. Title.

Dasburg, Andrew.

AMERICAN Federation of Arts. 759.13
Andrew Dasburg, by Jerry Bywaters. New York, Author, 1083 Fifth Ave. c.1959. 28p. (Bibl.: p.21-23) illus. (part col.) port. 18cm. 60-2726 2.00; .50 pap.,
1. Dasburg, Andrew. I. Bywaters, Jerry. II. Title.

Daubigny, Charles Francois, 1817-1878.

PAINE Art Center and Arboretum. 707
The first American retrospective exhibition of paintings, drawings and prints by Charles Francois Daubigny at the Paine Art Center & Arboretum, Oshkosh, Wisconsin, May 1 through 31, 1964. [Oshkosh, Wis., 1964] 1 v. (unpaged) illus. 14 x 22 cm. Caption title. Cover title: Charles Francois Daubigny at the Paine Art Center. Catalog of the exhibition. [N6853.D29P3] 72-209802
1. Daubigny, Charles Francois, 1817-1878. I. Title.

Daumier, Honore Victorin, 1808-1879.

DAUMIER, Honore Victorin, 1808-1879. 769'.92'4
Daumier, 120 great lithographs / edited by Charles F. Ramus. New York : Dover Publications, 1978. xx, 138 p. : ill. ; 31 cm. (Dover art collections) Bibliography: p. [137]-138. [NC1499.D3A4 1978] 77-83928 ISBN 0-486-23512-2 : 5.00
1. Daumier, Honore Victorin, 1808-1879. 2. French wit and humor, Pictorial. I. Ramus, Charles F. II. Title.

DAUMIER, Honore Victorin, 1808-1879. 709.24
Honore Daumier. Text by Robert Rey. [Tr. by Norbert Guterman] New York, Abrams [1966] 160p. illus. facsims., col. plates (pt. fold.) ports. 33cm. (Lib. of great painters) Bibl. [ND533.D24R48] 65-19225 15.00
I. Title.

DAUMIER, Honore Victorin, 1808-1879. 769'.924
Selected works. Edited by Bruce and Seena Harris. With an appreciation by Frank and Dorothy Getlein. New York, Bounty Books [1969] xiii, 209 p. (chiefly illus.) 32 cm. Texts to the satirical lithographs in French and English. [NC1499.D3A27] 72-75093
I. Harris, Bruce S., comp. II. Harris, Seena, comp.

LARKIN, Oliver W. 709.24
Daumier, man of his time. New York. McGraw [c.1966] x, 245p. illus., facsim., col. plates, ports. 24cm. Bibl. [ND553.D24L37] 65-28729 9.95
1. Daumier, Honore Victorin, 1808-1879. I. Title.

LOS Angeles Co., Calif. Museum, Los Angeles. 769.944
Honore Daumier; exhibition of prints, drawings, water-colors, paintings, and sculpture. [Los Angeles] 1958. 71 p. illus. 26 cm. [NE2415.D2L6] 59-618
1. Daumier, Honore Victorin, 1808-1879. I. Title.

VINCENT, Howard Paton, 1904- 760'.0924
Daumier and his world [by] Howard P. Vincent. Evanston [Ill.] Northwestern University Press, 1968. xvii, 267 p. illus., facsims., ports. 28 cm. Bibliographical references included in "Notes" (p. 239-261) [ND553.D24V5] 66-12961
1. Daumier, Honore Victorin, 1808-1879. I. Title. BIP

WASSERMAN, Jeanne L. 730'.924
Daumier sculpture; a critical and comparative study, by Jeanne L. Wasserman, assisted by Joan M. Lukach and Arthur Beale. [Exhibition] Fogg Art Museum, Harvard University, May 1-June 23, 1969. Greenwich, Conn., Distributed by New York Graphic Society [1969] xiii, 265 p. illus., facsims., ports. 28 cm. Bibliography: p. 259-263. [NB553.D29W3] 79-84763 32.50
1. Daumier, Honore Victorin, 1808-1879. I. Harvard University. William Hayes Fogg Art Museum. II. Title.

Davenport, Homer Calvin, 1867-1912.

HUOT, Leland. 741.5'973 B
Homer Davenport of Silverton; life of a great cartoonist, by Leland Huot and Alfred Powers. Bingen, Wash., West Shore Press [1973] 260, [189] p. illus. 26 cm. [NC1429.D3H86] 73-156268
1. Davenport, Homer Calvin, 1867-1912. I. Powers, Alfred, joint author.

David and Bathsheba tapestries (Paris)—Exhibitions.

NEW York (City). Metropolitan Museum of Art. 746.3
David & Bathsheba; ten early sixteenth-century tapestries from the Cluny Museum in Paris. New York [1974] [28] p. illus. 22 x 29 cm. Exhibition held May 14-Sept. 2, 1974. [NK3055.S76N48 1974] 74-177241
1. David and Bathsheba tapestries (Paris)—Exhibitions. 2. Tapestry—Brussels. I. Paris. Musee des Thermes et de l'Hotel de Cluny. II. Title.

David E. Bright Collection.

MONTE, James. 708.194'93
The David E. Bright Collection, Los Angeles County Museum of Art. [Catalog information: James Monte, Helene Winer, Ellen Landis; commentaries: James Monte. Los Angeles, 1967] 57 p. illus. (part col.) 26 cm. [N582.L7M6] 67-30743
1. David E. Bright Collection. 2. Paintings—Los Angeles—Catalogs. I. Los Angeles Co., Calif. Museum of Art, Los Angeles. II. Title.

David, Jacques Louis, 1748-1825.

BROOKNER, Anita. 759.4
Jacques-Louis David, a personal interpretation : lecture on aspects of art, Henriette Hertz Trust of the British Academy, 1974 / by Anita Brookner. London : Oxford University Press for the British Academy, 1974. 23 p., xiii p. of plates : ill. ; 25 cm. (Lecture on aspects of art, Henriette Hertz Trust of the British Academy ; 1974) Includes bibliographical references. [ND553.D25B7] 75-333067 ISBN 0-19-725719-4 : £1.00
1. David, Jacques Louis, 1784-1825. I. Title. II. Series: British Academy, London (Founded 1901). Annual lecture on aspects of art, Henriette Hertz Trust ; 1974.

DOWD, David Lloyd. 944.04'0924
Pageant-master of the Republic; Jacques-Louis David and the French Revolution. Freeport, N.Y., Books for Libraries Press [1969, c1948] xiv, 205 p. illus., ports. 24 cm. (Select bibliographies reprint series) Includes bibliographical references. [ND553.D25D6 1969] 72-75507
1. David, Jacques Louis, 1748-1825. 2. France—History—Revolution, 1789-1799—Pictorial works. I. Title. BIP

HOWARD, Seymour, 1928- 741.9'44
A classical frieze by Jacques Louis David : Sacrifice of the hero : the Roman years / Seymour Howard. Sacramento, Calif. : E. B. Crocker Art Gallery, c1975. 132 p. : ill. ; 28 cm. (Monograph series - E. B. Crocker Art Gallery) Includes bibliographical references and index. [NC248.D35H68] 75-16779
1. David, Jacques Louis, 1748-1825. Burial of Patroclus. 2. Neoclassicism (Art)—France. I. David, Jacques Louis, 1748-1825. II. Title. III. Title: Sacrifice of the hero. IV. Series: Crocker Art Gallery, Sacramento, Calif. Monograph series — E. B. Crocker Art Gallery.

Davies, Arthur B.

**ARTHUR B. Davies; essays on his art* [Edited by Martin S. and Diane L. Ackerman]. New York, Arco, 1974. 1v. (unpaged) illus 31 cm. (Arco collectors' series) Essays by Dwight Williams [and others] [N5210] 74-76369 ISBN 0-668-03489-0 8.95 (pbk.). 741.9
1. Davies, Arthur B. 2. Art—Private collections. 3. Art criticism. I. Ackerman, Martin S. ed. II. Ackerman, Diane L. joint ed. III. Williams, Dwight

CZESTOCHOWSKI, Joseph S. 759.13
Arthur B. Davies / Joseph S. Czestochowski ; with a foreword by Mahonri Sharp Young. Chicago : University of Chicago Press, c1979. p. cm. (Chicago visual library) Includes index. Bibliography: p. [N6537.D34A4 1979] 79-11546 ISBN 0-226-68946-8 : 65.00
1. Davies, Arthur Bowen, 1862-1928—Catalogs.

Davies, Ken, 1926—

DAVIES, Ken, 1926- 759.13
Ken Davies, artist at work / by Ken Davies. New York : Watson-Guptill Publications, 1978. p. cm. Includes index. [ND237.D32A4 1978] 78-17520 ISBN 0-8230-2578-0 : 18.50.

[1968, c1967] [27] l. (chiefly illus.) 26 cm. [NC1075.D372A45] 67-30379

DE KOONING, Willem, 1904- 759.13
De Kooning; recent paintings [by] Thomas B. Hess. New York, Walker [1968, c1967] 63 p. illus. (part col.), port. 22 cm. Catalog, by T. B. Hess, of an exhibition held at M. Knoedler and Company from November 14 through December 2, 1967. [ND237.D334H38] 67-30380
I. Hess, Thomas B. II. Knoedler (M.) and Company, inc.

DE KOONING, Willem, 1904- 759.13
Willem de Kooning, by Thomas B. Hess. New York, Museum of Modern Art; distributed by New York Graphic Society. Greenwich, Conn. [1969, c1968] 170 p. illus. (part col.), port. 26 cm. Catalog of an exhibition held at the Museum of Modern Art, New York, Mar. 6-Apr. 27, 1969, and at 4 other museums. "Bibliography by Bernard Karpel:" p. 151-159. [ND237.D334H42] 68-54925 8.95
I. Hess, Thomas B. II. New York (City) Museum of Modern Art.

DE KOONING, Willem, 1904- 759.13
Willem de Kooning. Texts by Dore Ashton and Willem de Kooning. Exhibition Smith College Museum of Art. April 8-May 2. The Hayden Gallery, Massachusetts Institute of Technology, May 10-June 16. [Northampton, Mass.] Smith College Museum of Art, 1965. [48] p. illus., port. 25 cm. (Louise Lindner Eastman memorial lectures, 3) Bibliography: p. [39]-[44] [ND237.D334A9] 78-253754
I. Ashton, Dore. II. Smith College. Museum of Art. III. Hayden Gallery. IV. Title. V. Series.

DE KOONING, Willem, 741.9'73
1904-
Willem de Kooning drawings. [Text by] Thomas B. Hess. Greenwich, Conn., New York Graphic Society [1972] 296 p. illus. (part col.) 32 cm. (A Paul Bianchini book) Bibliography: p. 277-288. [NC139.D45H47 1972b] 70-181345 ISBN 0-8212-0418-1 27.50
1. De Kooning, Willem, 1904- I. Hess, Thomas B.

HESS, Thomas B. 759.13
tWillem de Kooning New York, G. Braziller, 1959. 128 p. illus. (part col.) ports. 26 cm. (The Great American artists series) Bibliography: p. 119-124. [ND237.D334H4] 59-12224
1. De Kooning, Willem, 1904-

JANIS, Harriet (Grossman) 759.13
De Kooning, by Harriet Janis and Rudi Blesh. New York, Grove Press [1960] 71p. illus. 21cm. (Evergreen gallery book 8--E-191) [ND237.D334J3] 59-14402
1. De Kooning, William, 1904- I. Blesh, Rudi, 1899- joint author. II. Title.

De Menil, John—Art collections.

LOOK back; 709'.22
an exhibition of cubist paintings and sculptures from the Menil family collection. [Houston, Printed by Gulf Pub. Co., 1968] 105 p. (chiefly illus.) 23 cm. Catalogue of an exhibition of the John de Menil family collection held at the University of St. Thomas, Houston, Mar. 13-Sept. 13, 1968, and later at 8 other museums in the United States and Canada. Includes bibliographies. [N6494.C8L6] 68-8356 2.75
1. De Menil, John—Art collections. 2. Cubism—Exhibitions. I. De Menil, John. II. Houston, Tex. University of St. Thomas.

De Morgan, William Frend, 1839-1917.

GAUNT, William, 1900- 738'.0924
William De Morgan: Pre-Raphaelite ceramics, by William Gaunt and M. D. E. Clayton-Stamm. Greenwich, Conn., New York Graphic Society [1971] 176 p. illus. (part col.) 29 cm. Bibliography: p. 173-174. [NK4210.D4G3] 75-161611 ISBN 0-8212-0390-8 20.00
1. De Morgan, William Frend, 1839-1917. I. Clayton-Stamm, Maxwell David Eugene, joint author. II. Title.

De Staebler, Stephen, 1933—

DE STAEBLER, Stephen, 730'.92'4
1933-
Stephen De Staebler, sculpture : the Oakland Museum, Art Special Gallery, September 10-November 10, 1974. Oakland, CA. : Oakland Museum, [1974] [32] p. : ill. (some col.) ; 22 x 28 cm. [NB237.D49O24] 74-19891
1. De Staebler, Stephen, 1933- I. Oakland Museum. II. Title.

De Stijl.

BARR, Alfred Hamilton, 1902- v. 12

De Stijl, 1917-1928 With a pref. by Phillip C. Johnson. New York, Museum of Modern Art; distributed by Doubleday, Garden City, N.Y., 1961. 15 p. illus. 26 cm. "The first edition ... was published as an introduction to the exhibition, de Stijl, organized by the Stedelijk Museum, Amsterdam ... and shown at the Museum of Modern Art, December 1952-February 1953. The text is adapted from Cubism and abstract art, the Museum of Modern Art, 1936." [[N6948]] 63-6775 CD
1. De Stijl. I. Title.

De Unger, Edmund—Art collections.

FEHERVARI, Geza.
Islamic metalwork of the eighth to the fifteenth century in the Keir Collection / Geza Fehervari ; with a foreword by Ralph Pinder-Wilson. London : Faber and Faber, 1976, i.e. 1977 143 p., [36] leaves of plates : ill. (some col.) ; 29 cm. (The Keir Collection) Bibliography: p. [19]-20. [NK6408.9.F44 1976] 76-376866 ISBN 0-571-09740-5 : 62.50
1. De Unger, Edmund—Art collections. 2. Art metal-work, Islamic—Catalogs. I. Title. II. Series.
Distributed by Faber and Faber, Salem, NH

GRUBE, 738.3'0917'67107402176
Ernst J.
Islamic pottery of the eighth to the fifteenth century in the Keir Collection / Ernst J. Grube. London : Faber and Faber, 1976, i.e. 1977 378 p., [14] col. leaves of plates : ill. (some col.) ; 29 cm. (The Keir Collection) Includes index. General bibliography: p. 308-332. [NK3880.G78] 76-383703 ISBN 0-571-09953-X : 75.00
1. De Unger, Edmund—Art collections. 2. Pottery, Islamic—Catalogs. I. Title. II. Series.
Distributed by Faber and Faber, Salem, New Hampshire

De Unger, Edmund—Art collections—Catalogs.

SPUHLER, 746.7'5'07402176
Friedrich.
Islamic carpets and textiles in the Keir Collection / Friedrich Spuhler ; with an introd. by George Wingfield Digby ; translated by George and Cornelia Wingfield Digby. London : Faber and Faber, 1978. 251 p. : ill. (some col.) ; 29 cm. (The Keir collection) Includes bibliographical references and index. [NK2809.I8S6813] 78-310307 ISBN 0-571-09783-9 : 84.95
1. De Unger, Edmund—Art collections—Catalogs. 2. Rugs, Islamic—Catalogs. 3. Textile fabrics, Islamic—Catalogs. I. Title. II. Series.
Distributed by Faber & Faber, Salem, NH

De Wint, Peter, 1784-1849.

USHER Gallery. 759.2
Peter De Wint, 1784-1849, the Usher Gallery, Lincoln. Lincoln, Usher Gallery, [1973] (2), 25 p. col. illus., col. port. 19 cm. Cover title. Bibliography: p. 20-[21] [ND497.D45U83 1973] 74-165619
1. De Wint, Peter, 1784-1849.

De Wolfe, Elsie, 1865-1950.

BEMELMANS, Ludwig, 1898- 927.47
1962.
To the one I love the best. New York, Viking Press, 1955. 255 p. illus. 22 cm. [CT275.D382B4] 54-9596
1. De Wolfe, Elsie, 1865-1950. I. Title.

DE WOLFE, Elsie, 1865- 910'.03 B
1950.
After all. New York, Arno Press, 1974 [c1935] x, 278 p. illus. 23 cm. (Women in America: from colonial times to the 20th century) Autobiography. Reprint of the 1st ed. published by Harper, New York. [CT275.D382A3 1974] 74-3938 ISBN 0-405-06085-8
1. De Wolfe, Elsie, 1865-1950. I. Title. II. Series. BIP

De Young, Harry Anthony, 1893-1956.

DEYOUNG, Harry Anthony, 741.9'73
1893-1956.
Texas out back / sketches by Harry Anthony DeYoung ; text by Leon Hale. 1st ed. Austin, Tex. : Madrona Press, c1973. 65 p. : ill. ; 24 cm. [NC139.D48H34] 75-314512
1. De Young, Harry Anthony, 1893-1956. 2. Privies in art. 3. Texas in art. I. Hale, Leon. II. Title. BIP

Dead Sea scrolls—Juvenile literature.

CURRIER, Richard L. 417'.7
Ancient scrolls, by Michael Avi-Yonah. Retold for young readers by Richard L. Currier. Minneapolis, The Lerner Publications Co. [1974, c1973] 95 p. illus. (part col.) 21 cm. (Digging up the past) (The Lerner archaeology series) A history of manuscripts, including discussions of early writing materials, preparation of scrolls and manuscripts, examples of surviving ancient literature, and the story of the Dead Sea Scrolls. [Z107.C87 1974] 72-10792 ISBN 0-8225-0827-3 (lib. bdg.)
1. Dead Sea scrolls—Juvenile literature. 2. Manuscripts—History—Juvenile literature. 3. Paleography—Juvenile literature. I. Avi-Yonah, Michael, 1904- II. Title. BIP

DeArmond, Dale.

DEARMOND, Dale. 769'.92'4
Juneau; a book of woodcuts. [Anchorage, Alaska Northwest Pub. Co., 1973] [53] p. illus. (part col.) 21 x 26 cm. Brief text and woodcuts trace the history of Juneau, Alaska, from its founding as a mining town to its present status as capital of the forty-ninth state. [NE1112.D42A48] 73-82791 ISBN 0-88240-021-5 10.20 (pbk.)
1. DeArmond, Dale. 2. Juneau, Alaska, in art. I. Title.

DEARMOND, Dale. 769'.92'4
Raven : a collection of woodcuts / by Dale Burlison DeArmond. Anchorage : Alaska Northwest Pub. Co., [1975] [128] p. : col. ill. ; 32 cm. Stories adapted from John Swanton's Tlingit myths and texts published in 1909 by the Bureau of American Ethnology in Bulletin 39. [NE1112.D42A56] 75-23002 ISBN 0-88240-040-1 : 100.00
1. DeArmond, Dale. 2. Ravens in art. I. Swanton, John Reed, 1873-1958. Tlingit myths and texts. II. Title. BIP

Death in art.

CUMONT, Franz Valery 733'.5
Marie, 1868-1947.
Recherches sur le symbolisme funeraire des Romains / Franz Cumont. New York : Arno Press, 1975. iv, 543 p., [46] leaves of plates : ill. ; 26 cm. (Ancient religion and mythology) Reprint of the 1942 ed. published by Librairie orientaliste Paul Geuthner, Paris, which was t. 35 of Bibliotheque archeologique et historique. Includes bibliographical references and indexes. [N8217.D5C8 1975] 75-10632 ISBN 0-405-07007-1
1. Death in art. 2. Symbolism in art. 3. Sepulchral monuments—Rome. 4. Sculpture, Roman. 5. Art and mythology. 6. Bas-relief. I. Title. II. Series: Bibliotheque archeologique et historique ; t. 35. BIP

WEBER, Frederick Parkes, 700
1863-
Aspects of death and correlated aspects of life in art, epigram, and poetry; contributions towards an anthology and an iconography of the subject, illustrated especially by medals, engraved gems, jewels, ivories, antique pottery, &c. 4th ed., rev. and much enl. College Park, Md., McGrath Pub. Co., 1971. xliv, 851 p. illus. 23 cm. Reprint of the 1922 ed. Includes bibliographical references. [NX650.D4W4 1971] 70-119251 ISBN 0-8434-0073-0
1. Death in art. 2. Death in literature. I. Title.

Death Valley, Calif.—Antiq.

HUNT, Alice. 970.4
Archeology of the Death Valley salt pan California. [Salt Lake City, University of Utah Press] 1960. xvi, 313p. illus., maps. 28cm. (University of Utah. Dept. of Anthropology. Anthropological papers, no. 47) Bibliography: p.293-305. [E51.U8 no.47] 60-64334
1. Death Valley, Calif.—Antiq. 2. Indians of North America—California—Death Valley. 3. Indians of North America—Antiq. I. Title. II. Series: Utah. University. Dept. of Anthropology. Anthropological papers BIP

Decalcomania.

KULP, George Ellwood. 738.2
Teaching the designing of decal and handpainted china; lustre colors, and effects, gold work, lost arts. [1st ed. Miami, Fla., Printed by Atlantic Printers & Lithographers, 1970] 128 p. illus. (part col.) 30 cm. Alternate pages of text blank for notes. [NK4607.K8] 78-142196
1. Decalcomania. 2. China painting. I. Title.

STEVENS, Harold. 745.74
Relief and design transfer : creating a three-dimensional illusion on a flat surface. New York : Hawthorn Books [1976c1974] 80p. : ill. ; 25 cm. [NK9510S75] 75-28702 ISBN 0-8015-6277-5 pbk. : 3.95
1. Decalcomania. 2. Transfer-printing. I. Title.

STEVENS, Harold. 760
Transfer: designs, textures, and images. Worcester, Mass., Davis Publications [1974] 80 p. illus. 27 cm. [NK9510.S75] 73-93380 ISBN 0-87192-058-1 7.95
1. Decalcomania. 2. Transfer-printing. I. Title.

Decamps, Alexandre Gabriel, 1803-1860.

MOSBY, Dewey F., 1942- 759.4 B
Alexandre-Gabriel Decamps, 1803-1860 / Dewey F Mosby New York : Garland Pub., 1977. 2 v. (xli, 699 p., 232 leaves of plates) : ill. ; 21 cm. (Outstanding dissertations in the fine arts) Thesis—Harvard, 1973. Bibliography: v. 2, p. [665]-699. [ND553.D29M83 1977] 76-23651 ISBN 0-8240-2714-0 : 95.00
1. Decamps, Alexandre Gabriel, 1803-1860. 2. Painters—France—Biography. I. Title. II. Series. BIP

Decatur House, Washington, D.C.

NATIONAL Trust for Historic 975.3
Preservation in the United States.
Decatur House. Senior editor: Helen Duprey Bullock. Editor: Terry B. Morton. Washington [1967 or 8] 104 p. illus., facsims., ports. 23 cm. First published in Historic preservation, v. 19, no. 3-4, July-Dec., 1967. [F204.D4N3] 68-2718
1. Decatur, Stephen, 1779-1820. 2. Decatur House, Washington, D.C. I. Bullock, Helen Claire (Duprey) 1905- ed. II. Morton, Terry B., ed. BIP

Decatur, Stephen, 1779-1820.

NATIONAL Trust for Historic 975.3
Preservation in the United States.
Decatur House. Senior editor: Helen Duprey Bullock. Editor: Terry B. Morton. Washington [1967 or 8] 104 p. illus., facsims., ports. 23 cm. First published in Historic preservation, v. 19, no. 3-4, July-Dec., 1967. [F204.D4N3] 68-2718
1. Decatur, Stephen, 1779-1820. 2. Decatur House, Washington, D.C. I.

SUBJECT INDEX

DECORATION AND ORNAMENT

Bullock, Helen Claire (Duprey) 1905- ed. II. Morton, Terry B., ed. BIP

Decision-making in architecture.

AMERICAN Institute of Architects. 338.4'7'7280973
The architect and the shelter industry / [Beverly Willis] ; the American Institute of Architects. [Washington] : The Institute, c1975. iv, 24 p. : ill. ; 28 cm. [NA2540.A43 1975] 75-325678
1. Decision-making in architecture. 2. Architects and community. 3. Housing—United States. I. Willis, Beverly. II. Title.

Decoration and ornament.

ALEXANDER, Mary Jean 745.4
Handbook of decorative design and ornament. New York, Tudor [c.1965] 128p. illus. 28cm. [NK1530.A27] 65-20752 4.95; 1.95 pap.,
1. Decoration and ornament. 2. Design, Decorative. I. Title. BIP

†DAY, Lewis Foreman, 1845-1910. 745.4
The application of ornament / Lewis F. Day. New York : Garland Pub., 1977. xi, 73 p., 42 leaves of plates : ill. ; 19 cm. (The Aesthetic movement & the arts and crafts movement) Reprint of the 1888 ed. published by B. T. Batsford, London, which was issued as no. 3 of Text-books of ornamental design. [NK1510.D34 1977] 78-1333 ISBN 0-8240-2471-0 : lib.bdg. : 35.00
1. Decoration and ornament. 2. Design, Decorative. I. Title. II. Series. III. Series: Text-books of ornamental design ; 3. BIP

DAY, Lewis Foreman, 1845-1910. 745
Every-day art / Lewis F. Day. New York : Garland Pub., 1977. xii, 283 p., [1] leaf of plates : ill. ; 19 cm. (The Aesthetic movement & the arts and crafts movement) Reprint of the 1882 ed. published by B. T. Batsford, London. [NK1510.D36 1977] 76-17763 ISBN 0-8240-2468-0 lib.bdg. : 35.00
1. Decoration and ornament. 2. Interior decoration. I. Title. II. Series. BIP

DAY, Lewis Foreman, 1845-1910. 745'.4'49'24
Instances of accessory art / Lewis F. Day. New York : Garland Pub., 1978. p. cm. (The Aesthetic movement & the arts and crafts movement) Reprint of the 1880 ed. published by B. T. Batsford, London. [NK1535.D3A4 1978] 76-17762 ISBN 0-8240-2467-2 lib.bdg. : 35.00
1. Day, Lewis Foreman, 1845-1910. 2. Decoration and ornament. 3. Arts and crafts movement. I. Title. II. Series. BIP

DAY, Lewis Foreman, 1845-1910. 745
Ornament & its application; a book for students treating in a practical way of the relation of design to material, tools, and methods of work. Detroit, Gale Research Co., 1970. xxxii, 319 p. illus. 23 cm. Reprint of the 1904 ed. [NK1510.D37 1970] 71-136735
1. Decoration and ornament. I. Title. BIP

DAY, Lewis Foreman, 1845-1910. 745.4
The planning of ornament / Lewis F. Day. New York : Garland Pub., 1977. xi, 49 p., [38] leaves of plates : ill. ; 19 cm. (The Aesthetic movement & the arts and crafts movement) Reprint of the 1887 ed. published by B. T. Batsford, London, which was issued as no. 2 of Text books of ornamental design. [NK1510.D385 1977] 76-17766 ISBN 0-8240-2470-2 lib.bdg. : 35.00
1. Decoration and ornament. 2. Design, Decorative. I. Title. II. Series. III. Series: Text-books of ornamental design ; no. 2. BIP

FRASER, B. Kay. 745.7'2
Tole painting, by B. Kay Fraser. Photos. by the author. New York, Sterling Pub. Co. [1971] 48 p. illus. (part col.) 20 cm. (Little craft book series) Instructions for tole painting in which one "basic stroke" is used to create all the designs. [TT325.F68 1971] 78-167672
1. Decoration and ornament. 2. Painting. I. Title.

HALLEN, Julienne, 1923- 745
300 projects for hand decorating [New York] Homecrafts [1950] 188 p. illus. 25 cm. [NK1510.H28] 50-8089
1. Decoration and ornament. 2. Design, Decorative. I. Title.

JONES, Owen, 1809-1874. 745.4
The grammar of ornament. Illustrated by examples from various styles of ornament. New York, Van Nostrand Reinhold Co. [1973 c1972] 157 p. illus., 112 col. plates. 34 cm. First published in 1856. With contributions by J. B. Waring, J. O. Westwood, and M. D. Wyatt. Includes bibliographies. [NK1510.J7 1972] 72-1444 ISBN 0-442-24175-5 35.00
1. Decoration and ornament. 2. Design, Decorative. I. Title.

MEYER, Franz Sales, 1849- 745
Handbook of ornament; a grammar of art, industrial and architectural designing in all its branches for practical as well as theoretical use. New York, Dover Publications [1957] xiv, 548 p. illus. 21 cm. "An unabridged and unaltered republication of the English translation of the last revised edition of Handbook of ornament." [NK1510.M6 1957] 57-14417
1. Decoration and ornament. 2. Design, Decorative. 3. Art objects. BIP

PRIOLO, Joan B. 745.43
Designs, and how to use them. New York, Sterling Pub. Co. [1956] 134 p. illus. (part col.) 30 cm. [NK1130.P75] 56-7696
1. Decoration and ornament. 2. Design, Decorative. I. Title.

RACINET, Albert Charles Auguste, 1825-1893. 745.4
Handbook of ornaments in color : one hundred color plates highlighted with gold and silver ... : a practical and historical collection / written under the direction of A. Racinet ; English translation by J. A. Underwood. New York : Van Nostrand Reinhold, 1978- p. cm. Translation of L'ornement polychrome. [NK1530.R313 1978] 77-25047 ISBN 0-442-26794 (v.1) : 27.50
1. Decoration and ornament. 2. Design, Decorative. I. Title. BIP

SHAW, Henry, 1800-1873. 745.4
The encyclopedia of ornament / Henry Shaw. New York : St. Martin's Press, 1974. vi p., [33] leaves of plates : chiefly ill. (some col.) ; 30 cm. Reprint of the 1842 ed. published by W. Pickering, London. [NK1530.S5 1974] 73-92616 5.95
1. Decoration and ornament. 2. Design, Decorative. I. Title. BIP

SPELTZ, Alexander 745.44
The styles of ornament [Tr. from 2d. German ed. by David O'Conor] [Gloucester, Mass., P. Smith, 1964] vii, 647p. illus. 22cm. (Dover bk. rebound) Bibl. 4.50
1. Decoration and ornament. I. Title.

SPELTZ, Alexander. 745.44
The styles of ornament. New York, Dover Publications [1959] vii, 647 p. illus. 22 cm. "Republication of David O'Connor's translation from the second German edition." Bibliography: p. [627]-629. [NK1530.S72 1959] 59-65147
1. Decoration and ornament. I. Title. BIP

WAUGH, Dorothy. 745.5
Festive decoration the year round. Illustrated with 464 pen diagrs. and photos. of 17 original decorations by the author. New York, Macmillan, 1962. 160 p. illus. 24 cm. [TT157.W358] 61-14714
1. Decoration and ornament. 2. Festivals. I. Title.

YOUNG, Marjorie W 1962- 747.93
Decorating for joyful occasions. Scranton, Laurel Publishers; distributed by Grosset & Dunlap New York [1952] 120 p. illus. 23 cm. (Books for better living) [TT157.Y6] 52-10748
1. Decoration and ornament. 2. Entertaining. 3. Table. I. Title.

Decoration and ornament, American.

SABINE, Ellen S. 745.44973
Early American decorative patterns and how to paint them. Drawings by the author. Color photos. by Hilda Borcherding. Princeton, N. J., Van Nostrand [1962] 199 p. illus. 28 cm. [NK1403.S3] 62-4487
1. Decoration and ornament, American. 2. Design, Decorative. 3. Painting—Technique. I. Title.

SLAYTON, Mariette Paine. 745.7'2'0973
Early American decorating techniques; step-by-step directions for mastering traditional crafts. New York, Macmillan [1972] xi, 244 p. illus. 29 cm. Bibliography: p. 240-241. [TT385.S55] 75-180297 12.95
1. Decoration and ornament, American. 2. Painting—Technique. 3. Stencil work. I. Title. BIP

Decoration and ornament, American—Hist.

DECORATOR, (The) 747.213
The Decorator digest; chapters in the history of early American decoration and its European background. selected from The Decorator. Ed. by Natalie Allen Ramsey. Rutland, Vt., Tuttle [c.1965] x, 372p. illus., facsims., ports. 24cm. Pubn. of the Hist. Soc. of Early Amer. Decoration [NK1403.D4] 65-6760 8.95
1. Decoration and ornament, American—Hist. 2. Art industries and trade, American—Hist. I. Ramsey, Natalie Allen, ed. II. Historical Society of Early American Decoration.

Decoration and ornament—Amur Valley.

LAUFER, Berthold, 1874-1934. 745.5'0957'7
The decorative art of the Amur tribes / by Berthold Laufer. New York : AMS Press, 1975. 86 p., 33 [i.e. 28] leaves of plates : ill. ; 24 cm. Reprint of the 1902 ed. published in New York, which was issued as v. 7 of Memoirs of the American Museum of Natural History, Anthropology, v. 6, pt. 1, and as v. 4, pt. 2 of Publications of the Jesup North Pacific Expedition. [NK1483.A3A454 1975] 73-3524 ISBN 0-404-58104-8 : 72.50
1. Decoration and ornament—Amur Valley. I. Title. II. Series: American Museum of Natural History, New York. Memoirs ; v. 7. III. Series: The Jesup North Pacific Expedition. Publications ; v. 4, pt. 2. BIP

Decoration and ornament, Architectural.

BITTERMANN, Eleanor. 729
Art in modern architecture. New York, Reinhold [1952] 178 p. illus. 27 cm. [NA3503.A1B5] 52-10119
1. Decoration and ornament, Architectural. 2. Architecture—Details. 3. Architecture—U.S. I. Title.

BROOKLYN Institute of Arts and Sciences. Museum. 730.74014723
The Frieda Schiff Warburg Memorial Sculpture Garden. [Brooklyn] Brooklyn Museum [1966] 31 p. illus. 23 cm. The essay Fragmentary landmarks is signed: Frederick Fried. Bibliography: p. [21] [NA3503.A1B7] 66-22570
1. Decoration and ornament, Architectural. 2. Decoration and ornament, American. I. Fried, Frederick. II. Title.

CHAMBERS, William, Sir, 1726-1796 729
A treatise on the decorative part of civil architecture. Introd. by John Harris. New York, B. Blom, 1968. v, 137, [20] p. illus., facsim., plans. 34 cm. First ed., 1759, has title: A treatise on civil architecture. Reprint of the "third edition, considerably augmented" published in London in 1791. [NA3321.C5 1968] 68-17154
1. Decoration and ornament, Architectural. 2. Architecture—Details. 3. Architecture, Greek. I. Title. II. Title: Civil architecture.

DIETTERLIN, Wendel, 1550?-1599? 720'.924
The fantastic engravings of Wendel Dietterlin; the 203 plates and text of his Architectura. With an introd. by Adolf K. Placzek. New York, Dover Publications [1968] 209 p. (chiefly illus.) 32 cm. (Dover pictorial archives series) "T1944." "Unabridged republication of the German-language 1598 Nuremberg edition of Architectura." New introd. in English. [NA3310.D5 1968] 68-14970 4.00
1. Decoration and ornament, Architectural. 2. Architecture—Details. I. Title. II. Series. BIP

HOLMES, John M. 729
The art of interior design and decoration. London, New York, Longmans, Green [1951] 195 p. illus. 23 cm. Bibliography: p. 192. [NA3320.H6] 51-128806
1. Decoration and ornament, Architectural. I. Title.

KARP, Ben 729.3
Wood motifs in American domestic architecture; phantasy in wood. South Brunswick [N.J.] A. S. Barnes [1966] 255p. (chiefly illus.) 23x29cm. [NA4110.K3] 66-13771 12.50
1. Decoration and ornament. Architectural. 2. Wood-carving, American. I. Title.

LANGLEY, Batty, 1696-1751. 729
The city and country builder's and workman's treasury of designs. New York, B. Blom, 1967. 22 p. illus. 26 cm. Reprint of the 1756 ed. Title page includes original imprint: London, Printed by S. Harding, 1750. [NA3310.L3 1967] 67-18424
1. Decoration and ornament, Architectural. 2. Architecture—Details. 3. Architecture—Orders. I. Title. BIP

REDSTONE, Louis G. 720
Art in architecture, by Louis G. Redstone. Introd. by Jacques Lipchitz. Foreword by Robert L. Durham. New York, McGraw-Hill [1968] ix, 256 p. illus. (part col.) 28 cm. [NA3485.R4] 68-13098
1. Decoration and ornament, Architectural. 2. Art, Modern—20th century. I. Title. BIP

SULLIVAN, Louis Henry, 1856-1924 729
A system of architectural ornament according with a philosophy of man's powers, by Louis H. Sullivan. Together with drawings for the Farmers' and Merchants' Union Bank of Columbus, Wisconsin. & a note by Ada Louise Huxtable. New York, Eakins Pr. [1967] [75]p. plans, 20 plates. 26cm. The plates are reproduced in a reduced sixe from the orig. ed. of 1924 [NA3321.S8 1967] 67-17016 7.50
1. Decoration and ornament, Architectural. I. Title. BIP

SULLIVAN, Louis Henry, 1856-1924. 729
A system of architectural ornament according with a philosophy of man's powers, by Louis H. Sullivan. Together with drawings for the Farmers' and Merchants' Union Bank of Columbus, Wisconsin, & a note by Ada Louise Huxtable. New York, Eakins Press [1967] [75,] p. plans, 20 plates 26 cm. "The plates...are reproduced in a reduced size from the original edition of 1924" [NA3321.S8 1967] 67-17016
1. Decoration and ornament. Architectural. I. Title.

Decoration and ornament, Architectural—Catalogs.

ELMSLIE, George Grant, 1871-1952. 729'.022'3
Drawings for architectural ornament, 1902-1936. Catalogue designed by David Gebhard. Santa Barbara, Printed by Haagen Printing & Offset [1968] 3 p., 12 plates (in portfolio) 38 cm. 250 copies printed. "Catalogue published in conjunction with an exhibition of original drawings by George Grant Elmslie held at the Art Gallery, University of California, Santa Barbara, January 4 through January 31, 1968." [NA737.E37G4] 68-63140
1. Decoration and ornament, Architectural—Catalogs. 2. Architecture—Sketch-books. I. Gebhard, David. II. California. University, Santa Barbara. Art Galleries. III. Title.

Decoration and ornament, Architectural—Great Britain.

BARNARD, Julian. 729'.3
The decorative tradition. Princeton [N.J.] Pyne Press; [distributed by Scribner, New York, 1974, c1973] 144 p. illus. 26 cm. Bibliography: p. 142. [NA3543.B37 1974] 73-91328 ISBN 0-87861-064-2 12.95
1. Decoration and ornament, Architectural—Great Britain. 2. Decoration and ornament—Victorian style. I. Title.

Decoration and ornament, Architectural—India.

NATH, R. 729'.0954
History of decorative art in Mughal architecture / R. Nath. 1st ed. Delhi : Motilal Banarsidass, 1976. xxiii, 188 p., [35] leaves of plates : ill. ; 22 cm. A revision of a part of the author's thesis, Agra University, 1969. Includes index. Bibliography: p. [169]-183. [NA3576.A1N372 1976] 76-905414 Rs50.00
1. Decoration and ornament, Architectural—India. 2. Decoration and ornament, Islamic—India. 3. Architecture, Mogul. I. Title. BIP

Decoration and ornament, Architectural—Middle West—Indexes.

GILFILLEN, Statler. 721'.0443'0977
The American terra cotta index / edited by Statler Gilfillen. [Palos Park, Ill. : Prairie School Press, 1972?] xi, 487 p. ; 28 cm. [NA3507.G54] 75-322634
1. Decoration and ornament, Architectural—Middle West—Indexes. 2. Terra-cottas—Middle West—Indexes. I. Title.

Decoration and ornament, Architectural—Near East.

SEHERR-THOSS, Sonia P. 709'.5
Design and color in Islamic architecture; Afghanistan, Iran, Turkey [by] Sonia P. Seherr-Thoss. Hans C. Seherr-Thoss, photography. Donald N. Wilber, introd. Washington, Smithsonian Institution Press, 1968. 312 p. illus. (part col.), map. 30 cm. (Smithsonian publication 4741) Bibliography: p. 309-312. [NA3573.S4] 68-28138 27.50
1. Decoration and ornament, Architectural—Near East. 2. Decoration and ornament, Islamic—Near East. I. Seherr-Thoss, Hans Christoph, 1912- illus. II. Title.

Decoration and ornament, Architectural—New York (City)

JACOBY, Stephen M. 729'.5'097471
Architectural sculpture in New York City / Stephen M. Jacoby ; with an introd. by Clay Lancaster. New York : Dover Publications, 1975. ca. 150 p. : chiefly ill. ; 24 cm. [NA3511.N48J32 1975] 74-15247 ISBN 0-486-23120-8 pbk. : 3.00
1. Decoration and ornament, Architectural—New York (City) 2. Sculpture—New York (City) I. Title. BIP

ROBINSON, Cervin. 720'.9747'1
Skyscraper style : art deco, New York / Cervin Robinson, Rosemarie Haag Bletter. New York : Oxford University Press, 1975. 88 p., [65] leaves of plates : ill. (some col.) ; 29 cm. Includes bibliographical references. [NA3511.N48R6] 74-22885 ISBN 0-19-501873-7 : 20.00
1. Decoration and ornament, Architectural—New York (City) 2. Art deco—New York (City) 3. Skyscrapers. I. Bletter, Rosemarie Haag, joint author. II. Title. BIP

VLACK, Don. 720'.9747'1
Art deco architecture in New York, 1920-1940 / Don Vlack photos by Ralph Appelbaum 1st ed. New York : Harper & Row, c1974. 179 p. : 184 ill. ; 27 cm. (Icon editions) Includes index. Bibliography: p. 175-177. [NA3511.N48V55 1974] 74-6577 ISBN 0-06-438850-6 : 15.00
1. Decoration and ornament, Architectural—New York (City) 2. Art deco—New York (City) I. Appelbaum, Ralph, ill. II. Title. BIP

Decoration and ornament, Architectural—Provence.

BORG, Alan. 729'.5
Architectural sculpture in Romanesque. Provence. Oxford, Clarendon Press, 1972. x, 144 p. illus. 30 cm. (Oxford studies in the history of art and architecture) Bibliography: p. [133]-142. [NA3549.A3P762] 73-152045 ISBN 0-19-817192-7
1. Decoration and ornament, Architectural—Provence. 2. Sculpture, Romanesque—Provence. I. Title. II. Series. Distributed by Oxford University Press N.Y. 32.00.

Decoration and ornament, Architectural—Quebec (Province)—Montreal.

HATTON, Warwick Trevor, 1943- 728'.09714'281
A feast of gingerbread from our Victorian past = Patisserie maison de notre charmant passe / by Warwick and Beth Hatton ; traduction de Rene Chicoine. Montreal : Tundra Books of Montreal, c1976. 96 p. : ill. ; 31 cm. English and French. Includes index. Bibliography: p. 96. [NA3513.M66H37] 75-2792 ISBN 0-88776-057-0 : 9.95
1. Decoration and ornament, Architectural—Quebec (Province)—Montreal. 2. Wood-carving—Quebec (Province)—Montreal. 3. Architecture, Victorian—Quebec (Province)—Montreal. I. Hatton, Beth, 1943- joint author. II. Title. III. Title: Patisserie maison de notre charmant passe.

Decoration and ornament, Architectural—Sydney.

ROBERTSON, Edward Graeme. 739'.47944
Sydney lace; ornamental cast iron in architecture in Sydney [by] E. Graeme Robertson. Melbourne, Georgian House [1962] xvi, 198 p. illus. 29 cm. [NA3590.S95R62] 73-171324
1. Decoration and ornament, Architectural—Sydney. 2. Ironwork—Sydney. I. Title.

Decoration and ornament—Art deco.

HULL, John, 1942- 709'.04
Art Deco : design motifs of the 20's & 30's / by John Hull. San Francisco : Troubador Press, c1975. p. cm. (Design resource series) [NK789.5.A7H84] 75-37604 ISBN 0-912300-62-0 : 2.95
1. Decoration and ornament—Art deco. 2. Art industries and trade. I. Title.

Decoration and ornament—Art nouveau.

THE Art nouveau style in jewelry, metalwork, glass, ceramics, textiles, architecture, and furniture / edited by Roberta Waddell. New York : Dover Publications, 1977. xi, 288 p. : chiefly ill. ; 29 cm. Selections from the Paris journal Art et decoration, 1897-1911. Includes index. [NK1380.A76 1977] 77-80034 ISBN 0-486-23515-7 : 6.95 745.4'44
1. Decoration and ornament—Art nouveau. 2. Decoration and ornament, Architectural. I. Waddell, Roberta. II. Art et decoration.

TILBROOK, Adrian J. 739.2'3'724
The designs of Archibald Knox for Liberty & Co. / by A. J. Tilbrook ; jointly edited with Gordon House. 1st ed. London : Ornament Press, 1976. 283 p. : ill., port. ; 22 cm. Includes index. Bibliography: p. 279-280. [NK1535.K58T54] 77-368961 ISBN 0-905464-00-1 : £10.60
1. Knox, Archibald, 1864-1933. 2. Liberty & Co. 3. Decoration and ornament—Art nouveau. 4. Design—England. I. Knox, Archibald, 1864-1933. II. Title.

VERNEUIL, Maurice Pillard, 1869- 745.4
Art nouveau designs in color / Alphonse Mucha, Maurice Verneuil & Georges Auriol. New York : Dover Publications, [1974] [62] p. : 60 col. ill. ; 21 x 24 cm. First published in 1900 (?) as Combinaisons ornementales by M. P. Verneuil, G. Auriol, and A. Mucha. [NK1380.V4713] 74-79935 ISBN 0-486-22885-1 pbk. : 4.00
1. Decoration and ornament—Art nouveau. 2. Design, Decorative. I. Auriol, George, 1863-1938. II. Mucha, Alphonse Marie, 1860-1939. III. Title. BIP

Decoration and ornament, Celtic.

BAIN, George. 745.4'49'41
The methods of construction of Celtic art. New York, Dover Publications [1973] 159 p. illus. 31 cm. Half title: Celtic art. Reprint of the 1951 ed. published by W. MacLellan, Glasgow. [NK1264.B3 1973] 73-75875 ISBN 0-486-22923-8 2.50
1. Decoration and ornament, Celtic. I. Title. II. Title: Celtic art. BIP

Decoration and ornament, Chinese.

KUO, Nancy, 1921- 745.54
Chinese paper-cut pictures, old and modern. Photos. by Guy Davis. [1st American ed.] New York, Taplinger Pub. Co. [1965] 20 p. 75 plates (part col.), map. 23 cm. Bibliography: p. 19. [NK1483.K85 1965] 65-14389
1. Decoration and ornament, Chinese. 2. Design, Decorative. 3. Paper work. I. Davis, Guy, illus. II. Title.

KUO, Nancy, 1921- 745.54
Chinese paper-cut pictures, old and modern, Photos. by Guy Davis. [1st Amer. ed.] New York, Taplinger [c.1965] 20p. 75 plates (pt. col.), map. 23cm. Bibl. [NK1483.K85] 65-14389 6.75 bds.,
1. Decoration and ornament, Chinese. 2. Design, Decorative. 3. Paper work. I. Davis, Guy, illus. II. Title.

PETELN, Theodor A., 1933- 745.4495
Oriental motifs for creative people, by Theodor A. Peteln. [1st ed.] Rutland, Vt., C. E. Tuttle Co. [1965] 70 p. illus. (part col.) 20 cm. [NK1482.P4] 65-16744
1. Decoration and ornament, Chinese. 2. Decoration and ornament, Japanese. 3. Design, Decorative—China. 4. Design, Decorative—Japan. 5. Prints—Technique. I. Title.

Decoration and ornament—Dictionaries.

DIZIK, A. Allen. 747'.03
Encyclopedia of interior design and decoration / A. Allen Dizik. [1st ed.] [Burbank, Calif. : Stratford House Pub. Co., c1976] 192 p. : ill. ; 27 cm. Bibliography: p. 165-168. [NK1165.D59] 76-370398
1. Decoration and ornament—Dictionaries. 2. Interior decoration—Dictionaries. I. Title.

PEGLER, Martin. 747.03
The dictionary of interior design. New York, Crown Publishers [1966] 500 p. illus. 26 cm. [NK1165.P4] 66-15127
1. Decoration and ornament—Dictionaries. I. Title.

STAFFORD, Maureen. 745.4'03
An illustrated dictionary of ornament / by Maureen Stafford and Dora Ware ; with an introd. by John Gloag. New York : St. Martin's Press, [1975, c1974] 246 p. : ill. ; 25 cm. Includes index. Bibliography: p. 243-244. [NK1165.S72 1975] 74-21095 15.00
1. Decoration and ornament—Dictionaries. I. Ware, Dora, joint author. II. Title. BIP

WEISS, Lillian. 747'.03
The concise dictionary of interior decorating. Garden City, N.Y., Doubleday [1973] 188 p. illus. 25 cm. Bibliography: p. 187-188. [NK1165.W44] 72-89358 ISBN 0-385-05163-8 7.95
1. Decoration and ornament—Dictionaries. 2. Interior decoration—Dictionaries. I. Title.

Decoration and ornament, Egyptian.

FORTOVA-SAMALOVA, Pavla 745.0932
Egyptian ornament. Text by M. Vilimkova [Tr. by Till Gottheiner] London, A. Wingate [New York, dist. Crown, 1964, c.1963] 162p. 343 col. illus. 30cm. Bibl. 64-2811 12.50
1. Decoration and ornament, Egyptian. I. Vilimkova, Milada. II. Title.

Decoration and ornament—Empire style.

APRA, Nietta. 745.4'44
Empire style. New York, World Pub. [1973] p. (Connoisseur's library) Bibliography: p. [NK1372.A67] 72-10533 ISBN 0-529-05018-8
1. Decoration and ornament—Empire style. I. Title. II. Series: Connoisseur's library (New York)

BEUNAT, Joseph. 745.4
Empire style designs and ornaments : a reprint of Recueil des dessins d'ornements d'architecture, c. 1813 / Joseph Beunat ; with a new introd. by David Irwin. New York : Dover Publications, 1974. x, [97] p. : chiefly ill. ; 32 cm. (Dover pictorial archive series) [NK1372.B4813] 73-91877 ISBN 0-486-22984-X pbk. 3.50
1. Decoration and ornament—Empire style. 2. Design, Decorative. I. Title. BIP

GRANDJEAN, Serge 749.24
Empire furniture, 1800 to 1825. [1st Amer. ed.] New York, Taplinger [c.1966] 120p., 100 plates (4 col.) 26cm. (Faber monographs on furniture) Bibl. [NK2548.G7] 66-11303 17.50
1. Decoration and ornament—Empire style I. Title. BIP

Decoration and ornament, English.

BEARD, Geoffrey W. 729'.3
Georgian craftsmen and their work [by] Geoffrey Beard. [1st American ed.] South Brunswick [N.J.] A. S. Barnes [1967, c1966] 206 p. illus., geneal. tables, ports. 29 cm. Bibliography: p. 190-198. [NA3544.A1B4 1967] 67-20199
1. Decoration and ornament, English. 2. Decoration and ornament, Architectural. I. Title.

EARLY English decorative detail from contemporapy source books and some early drawings. Introd. by John Gloag. London, A. Tiranti. On label mounted on t.p.:[dist. Transatlantic, New York.] 1965. On label mounted on t.p.: dist. Transatlantic, New York. 19p. facsims., plates. 29cm. (Master hands ser.) [NK1334.E18] 67-31914 13.50 745.44942
1. Decoration and ornament, English. 2. Decoration and ornament, Architectural. I. Gloag, John.

FOWLER, John, 1906- 942.07
English decoration in the 18th century / John Fowler and John Cornforth Princeton, [N.J.] : Pyne Press, [1974] 288 p., [16] leaves of plates : ill. (some col.) ; 31 cm. Includes indexes. Bibliography: p. 267-269. [NK1443.F68] 74-81180 ISBN 0-87861-075-8 : 30.00
1. Decoration and ornament, English. 2. Decoration and ornament—Neoclassicism. I. Cornforth, John, 1937- joint author. II. Title. BIP

Decoration and ornament—Europe.

EVANS, Joan, 1893- 745.4'49'4
Pattern : a study of ornament in Western Europe from 1180 to 1900 / by Joan Evans. New York : Hacker Art Books, 1975. 2 v. : ill. ; 27 cm. Reprint of the 1931 ed. published by Clarendon Press, Oxford. Includes bibliographical references and index. [NK1442.E8 1975] 73-90614 ISBN 0-87817-151-7 : 75.00
1. Decoration and ornament—Europe. I. Title.

EVANS, Joan, 1893- 745.4'49'4
Pattern : a study of ornament in Western Europe from 1180 to 1900 / by Joan Evans. New York : Da Capo Press, 1976. 2 v. : ill. ; 28 cm. (A Da Capo paperback) Reprint of the 1931 ed. published at the Clarendon Press, Oxford. Contents.—v. 1.

The Middle Ages.—v. 2. The Renaissance to 1900. Includes bibliographical references and index. [NK1442.E8 1976] 76-10682 ISBN 0-306-80040-3]v.1[pbk. : 9.95 ISBN 0-306-80041-1 (v. 2)
1. Decoration and ornament—Europe. I. Title.

Decoration and ornament, French.

HENRY E. Huntington 754'.00944 Library and Art Gallery, San Marino, Calif.
French decorative art in the Huntington collection [by] Robert R. Wark. [2d ed.] San Marino, Calif., 1968. xxiv, 128 p. illus. 27 cm. (Its Huntington Library publications) [NK1449.H4 1968] 68-31203
1. Decoration and ornament, French. 2. Art industries and trade—France. 3. Art, Decorative. I. Wark, Robert R. II. Title. III. Series. BIP

HENRY E. Huntington 745.0944 Library and Art Gallery, San Marino, Calif.
French decorative art in the Huntington collection [by] Robert R. Wark. San Marino, 1961. xxiv, 123p. illus. 26cm. (Huntington Library publications) [NK1449.H4] 60-15414
1. Decoration and ornament, French. 2. Art Industries and trade—France. 3. Art, Decorative. I. Wark, Robert R. II. Title. III. Series: Henry E. Huntington Library and Art Gallery, San Marino, Calif. Huntington Library publications

Decoration and ornament—History.

EVANS, Joan, 1893- 745.44
Style in ornament. London, New York, Oxford University Press, 1950. 63 p. illus. 20 cm. [NK600.E9] 51-10705
1. Decoration and ornament—Hist. I. Title.

Decoration and ornament—History.

AUDSLEY, William James, 745.4'4 b.1833.
Designs and patterns from historic ornament [by] W. & G. Audsley. New York, Dover Publications [1968] 14, [74] p. illus. 31 cm. (Dover pictorial archive series) "An unabridged republication of the work originally published ... in 1882 under the title Outlines of ornament in the leading styles." [NK1530.A8 1968] 68-19174
1. Decoration and ornament—History. 2. Design, Decorative. I. Audsley, George Ashdown, 1838-1925, joint author. II. Title. III. Series. BIP

EASTLAKE, William. FIC
The bamboo bed. New York, Simon and Schuster [1969] 350 p. 22 cm. [PZ4.E1327Bam] [PS3555.A7] 813'.5'4 70-79630 6.50
I. Title.

HAMLIN, Alfred Dwight 745.4 Foster, 1855-1926.
A history of ornament / by A. D. Hamlin. New York : Cooper Square Publishers, 1973, c1916-1923. 2 v. : ill. (some col.) ; 24 cm. Contents.Contents.—[1] Ancient and medieval.—[2] Renaissance and modern. Includes bibliographies. [NK1175.H3 1973] 72-92374 ISBN 0-8154-0450-6
1. Decoration and ornament—History. I. Title.

HAMLIN, Alfred Dwight 745.4'4 Foster, 1855-1926.
A history of ornament / by A. D. F. Hamlin. Boston : Longwood Press, 1978. p. cm. Reprint of the 1916-1923 ed. published by the Century Co., New York. Contents.Contents.—[v. 1] Ancient and medieval. Includes bibliographies and index. [NK1175.H3 1978] 78-16002 ISBN 0-89341-360-7 : 40.00
1. Decoration and ornament—History. I. Title. BIP

HULME, Frederick Edward, 745.4 1841-1909.
The birth and development of ornament. London, S. Sonnenschein; New York, Macmillan, 1893. Detroit, Gale Research Co., 1974. xii, 340 p. illus. 22 cm. [NK1175.H8 1974] 79-78173 ISBN 0-8103-4026-7 17.50
1. Decoration and ornament—History. I. Title. BIP

WARD, James, 1851-1924. 745.4
Historic ornament : treatise on decorative art and architectural ornament / by James Ward. Portland, Me. : Longwood Press, 1977. 856 p. in various pagings : ill. ; 22 cm. Reprint of the 1897 ed. published by Scribner, New York. [NK1175.W3 1977] 77-1703 ISBN 0-89341-107-8 lib.bdg. : 60.00
1. Decoration and ornament—History. 2. Architecture—History. 3. Art, Decorative—History. I. Title. BIP

WARD, James, 1851-1924. 745.4
Historic ornament; treatise on decorative art and architectural ornament. Boston, Milford House [1973] p. Reprint of the 1897 ed. published by Scribner, New York. Contents.Contents.—1. Treats of prehistoric art; ancient art and architecture: Eastern, early Christian, Byzantine, Saracenic, Romanesque. Gothic, and Renaissance architecture and ornament.—2. Pottery, enamels, ivories, metal-work, furniture, textile fabrics, mosaics, glass, and book decoration. [NK1175.W3 1973] 73-10011 60.00 (lib. bdg.)
1. Decoration and ornament—History. 2. Architecture—History. 3. Art, Decorative—History. I. Title.

Decoration and ornament, Islamic.

BOURGOIN, Jules, 745.4'49'17671 1838-
Arabic geometrical pattern and design. New York, Dover Publications [1973] 189 p. (chiefly illus.) 28 cm. (Dover pictorial archive series) Consists of all the illus. from Les elements de l'art arabe. [NK1270.B613 1973] 72-90630 ISBN 0-486-22924-6 3.50
1. Decoration and ornament, Islamic. I. Title. BIP

Decoration and ornament—Louis XIV style.

SAVAGE, George, 1909- 745'.00944
French decorative art, 1638-1793. New York, Praeger [1969] xi, 188 p. illus. (part col.) 28 cm. Bibliography: p. 179-[180] [NK1340.S2 1969b] 79-81560 15.00
1. Decoration and ornament—Louis XIV style. 2. Decoration and ornament—Louis XV style. 3. Decoration and ornament—Louis XVI style. I. Title.

Decoration and ornament—Louis XVI Style.

VERIET, Pierre. 747.24
The eighteenth century in France; society, decoration, furniture. [Translated from the original French language ed. by George Savage] Rutland, Vt., Charles E. Tuttle Co. [1967] viii, 291 p. illus. (part col.) 32 cm. Translation of La Maison du XVII siecle en France. [NK1930.V413] 67-4313
1. Decoration and ornament — Louis XVI Style. 2. Furniture, French — Hist. 3. France — Soc. life & cust. — Illustrations. I. Title.

VERLET, Pierre. 747.24
The eighteenth century in France; society, decoration, furniture. [Translated from the original French language ed. by George Savage] Rutland, Vt., Charles E. Tuttle Co. [1967] viii, 291 p. illus. (part col.) 32 cm. Translation of La Maison du XVIIe siecle en France. [NK1930.V413] 67-4313
1. Decoration and ornament—Louis XVI Style. 2. Furniture, French—History. 3. France—Social life and conditions—Pictorial works. I. Title.

Decoration and ornament, Melanesian.

REICHARD, Gladys Amanda, 736 1893-1955.
Melanesian design; a study of style in wood and tortoiseshell carving. New York, Hacker Art Books, 1969. 2 v. in 1. illus., fold. map, 151 plates. 29 cm. Reprint of the 1933 ed. Bibliography: p. [155]-157. [NK1496.M4R4 1969] 68-9012 35.00
1. Decoration and ornament, Melanesian. 2. Wood-carving, Melanesian. I. Title. BIP

REICHARD, Gladys 736'.4'0993 Amanda, 1893-1955.
Melanesian design; a study of style in wood and tortoiseshell carving. New York, AMS Press [1969] x, 172, 14, [169] p. illus., 151 plates. 29 cm. Reprint of the 1933 ed., which was issued as no. 18 of Columbia University contributions to anthropology. Bibliography: p. [155]-157. [NK1496.M4R4 1969b] 70-82256
1. Decoration and ornament, Melanesian. 2. Wood-carving, Melanesian. I. Title. II. Series: Columbia University, Columbia University contributions to anthropology, no. 18.

Decoration and ornament—New Guinea.

LEWIS, Albert Buell, 745.4'41 1867-
Decorative art of New Guinea; consisting of the two complete publications: Decorative art of New Guinea, incised designs and Carved and painted designs from New Guinea. New York, Dover Publications [1973] 113 p. illus. 31 cm. [NK1496.N4L39] 72-95080 ISBN 0-486-22783-9 3.00 (pbk.)
1. Decoration and ornament—New Guinea. 2. Decoration and ornament, Primitive—New Guinea. 3. Design, Decorative—New Guinea. I. Lewis, Albert Buell, 1867- Carved and painted designs from New Guinea. 1973. II. Title. III. Title: Decorative art of New Guinea, incised designs. IV. Title: Carved and painted designs from New Guinea.

Decoration and ornament, Primitive.

BOSSERT, Helmuth Theodor, 745 1889-
Folk art of primitive peoples: six hundred decorative motifs in color, forming a survey of the applied art of Africa, Asia, Australia, and Oceania, North, Central, and South America. New York, Praeger [1955] 15 p. 40 col. plates. 35 cm. (Books that matter) Translation of Ornamente der Volker. [NK1177.B612] 55-11523
1. Decoration and ornament, Primitive. 2. Art, Primitive. I. Title.

Decoration and ornament—Regency style.

HOPE, Thomas, 1770?-1831. 747.22
Household furniture and interior decoration; classic style book of the Regency period. With a new introd. by David Watkin. New York, Dover Publications [1971] xiii, 140 p. illus., plan, port. 31 cm. "An unabridged republication, with minor corrections, of the work originally published in London in 1807." [NK2135.H7M8 1971] 75-132319 ISBN 0-486-21710-8 3.50
1. Decoration and ornament—Regency style. I. Title. BIP

Decoration and ornament, Rustic.

LIMAN, Ellen. 747'.8'86
Decorating your country place. New York, Coward, McCann & Geoghegan [1973] 255 p. illus. 24 cm. Bibliography: p. 249-250. [NK1986.R8L55 1973] 72-94126 ISBN 0-698-10518-4 8.95
1. Decoration and ornament, Rustic. 2. Interior decoration. I. Title.

Decoration and ornament—U.S.

HALL, Peg, 1897- 745.44
Early American decorating patterns. Drawings and color renderings by the author. New York, M. Barrows [1951] 150 p. illus. 28 cm. [NK1115.H6] 51-14161
1. Decoration and ornament—U.S. 2. Stencil work. 3. Design, Decorative. I. Title.

SABINE, Ellen S. 745.43
American antique decoration. With drawings by the author, photos. by Hilda Borcherding. Princeton, N. J., Van Nostrand [1956] x, 132 p. illus. (part col.) 28 cm. [NK1130.S18] 56-12094
1. Decoration and ornament—U.S. 2. Design, Decorative. I. Title.

Decoration and ornament, Victorian—Exhibitions.

DRESSER, Christopher. 745.4'44
Development of ornamental art in the International Exhibition / Christopher Dresser. New York : Garland Pub., 1978. 192 p. ; 19 cm. (The Aesthetic movement & the arts and crafts movement) Reprint of the 1862 ed. published by Day and Son, London. [NK1378.D73 1978] 76-17750 ISBN 0-8240-2452-4 : 35.00
1. London. International Exhibition, 1862. 2. Decoration and ornament, Victorian—Exhibitions. I. Title. II. Series. BIP

Decoration and ornament—Victorian style.

FREEMAN, John Crosby, 749.204 comp.
Late Victorian decor from Eastlake's Gothic to Cook's House beautiful, edited by Hugh Guthrie. [Watkins Glen, N.Y.] American Life Foundation; [distributed by Century House] 1968. 208 p. illus. 24 cm. (Library of Victorian culture) [NK1960.F7] 68-55036
1. Decoration and ornament—Victorian style. I. Eastlake, Charles Locke, 1833-1906. Hints on household taste. 1968. II. Cook, Clarence Chatham, 1828-1900. The house beautiful. 1968. III. Title.

GLOAG, John, 1896- 745.4'44
Victorian comfort; a social history of design from 1830-1900. [2d ed.] New York, St. Martin's Press [1974, c1973] xvi, 252 p. illus. 26 cm. Companion volume to the author's Georgian grace and his Victorian taste. Includes bibliographical references. [NK1443.G55 1974] 73-85380 10.95
1. Decoration and ornament—Victorian style. 2. Design, Decorative—Great Britain. 3. Architecture, Victorian—Great Britain. 4. Design, Industrial—Great Britain. I. Title.

Decoration and ornament—Victorian style—Exhibitions.

MARGARET Woodbury 745.1'09'034 Strong Museum.
A scene of adornment : decoration in the Victorian home from the collections of the Margaret Woodbury Strong Museum : exhibited at Memorial Art Gallery of the University of Rochester, March 7-April 13, 1975. [Rochester : s.n.], c1975. 109, [2] p. : ill. (some col.) ; 27 cm. Bibliography: p. [110]-[111]. [NK1378.M37 1975] 76-351727
1. Decoration and ornament—Victorian style—Exhibitions. 2. Art industries and trade, Victorian—Exhibitions. I. Rochester, N.Y. University. Memorial Art Gallery. II. Title.

Decorations of honor.

MERICKA, Vaclav. 737'.2
The book of orders and decorations / test by Vaclav Mericka ; [translated from the Czech by Ruth Shepherd and Eliska Rihova] ; photographs by Jindrich Marco ; [edited by Alec A. Purves]. London ; New York : Hamlyn, 1976, i.e.1977 248 p. : ill. (some col.), ports. ; 29 cm. "A further development of" the author's Orders and decorations. Ports. on lining papers. Bibliography: p. 239-241. [CR4509.M39] 78-315897 ISBN 0-600-36731-2 : 15.00
1. Decorations of honor. I. Title.

ROSIGNOLI, Guido. 737'.2
Ribbons of orders, decorations, and medals / by Guido Rosignoli. New York : Arco Pub. Co., 1977, c1976 p. cm. (Arco color series) Includes index. Bibliography: p. [CR4661.R67] 76-28307 ISBN 0-668-04104-8 pbk. : 6.95
1. Decorations of honor. 2. Orders of knighthood and chivalry—Insignia. 3. Medals. I. Title. BIP

Decorations of honor—Great Britain.

ABBOTT, Peter Edward. 355.1'34
British gallantry awards [by] P. E. Abbott [and] J. M. A. Tamplin. Garden City, N.Y., Doubleday [1972] 359 p. illus. 25 cm. Bibliography: p. 15-17. [CR4801.A63 1972] 70-180905 14.95
1. Decorations of honor—Great Britain. 2. Medals—Great Britain. I. Tamplin, J. M. A., joint author. II. Title.

JOSLIN, Edward C. 355.1'34'0941
The observer's book of British awards and medals / Edward C. Joslin. London ; New York : F. Warne, [1975] c1974 191 p., 8 p. of plates : ill. (some col.) ; 15 cm. (The Observer's pocket series ; 55) Includes bibliographical references and index. [CR4801.J58] 74-80608 ISBN 0-7232-1538-3 : 2.50
1. Decorations of honor—Great Britain. I. Title. II. Series.

JOSLIN, Edward C. 737'.2
The standard catalogue of British orders, decorations, and medals / [by] E. C. Joslin. 3rd ed. London : Spink, 1976. xvi, 39, [8] p., [8], 61 p. of plates, leaf of plate : ill. (chiefly col.) ; 26 cm. Includes index. [CR4801.J6 1976] 77-350729 ISBN 0-900696-69-9 : £5.50
1. Decorations of honor—Great Britain. I. Title. II. Title: British orders, decorations, and medals. BIP

Decorations of honor—Russia.

WERLICH, Robert. 737.2
Russian orders, decorations, and medals; including those of Imperial Russia, the Provisional Government, and the Soviet Union. [Washington, Quaker Press, 1968] 139 p. illus. (part col.) 29 cm. Bibliography: p. 137. [CR5657.W47] 68-6700 20.00
1. Decorations of honor—Russia. I. Title. BIP

Decoupage.

AUDUBON, John James, 1785-1851. 745.54
Audubon's birds in color for decoupage / selected and with instructions by Eleanor Hasbrouck Rawlings. New York : Dover Publications, 1977. viii p., 24 leaves of plates : col. ill. ; 28 cm. Includes index. Bibliography: p. vii. [TT870.A92 1977] 77-70050 ISBN 0-486-23492-4 pbk. : 2.50
1. Decoupage. 2. Design, Decorative—Animal forms. I. Rawlings, Eleanor Hasbrouck. II. Title. III. Title: Birds in color for decoupage. BIP

DOVER Publications, inc., New York. 745.54
Decoupage : the big picture sourcebook / edited and introduced by Eleanor Hasbrouck Rawlings. New York : Dover Publications, 1975. viii p., 92 leaves of plates : chiefly ill. ; 32 cm. (Dover pictorial archive series) Bibliography: p. vii-viii. [TT870.D65 1975] 75-11080 ISBN 0-486-23182-8 pbk. : 5.00
1. Decoupage. I. Rawlings, Eleanor Hasbrouck. II. Title.

FOY, Elizabeth Gilmour. 745.54
Decoupage; the ancient art of surface finishing and antiquing. Illustrated by John G. Schurer, Jr. Charlott[e]ville, N.Y., Story House Corp, 1971. 32 p. illus. 22 cm. (Hand crafts and hobbies) Describes the tools, materials, and techniques for using decoupage to decorate a variety of objects. [TT870.F68] 73-185673
1. Decoupage. I. Schurer, John G., illus. II. Title.

HARLOW, Eve. 745.54
Decoupage. New York, Drake Publishers [1973] p. [TT870.H33] 73-5574 ISBN 0-87749-502-5 7.95
1. Decoupage. I. Title.

HARROWER, Dorothy. 745
Decoupage, a limitless world in decoration. New York : Bonanza Books, c1958. 191 p. ; ill. (part col.) ; 29 cm. [NK1520.H3] 58-12133
1. Decoupage. 2. Design, Decorative. I. Title.

*HYMAN, Rebecca. 745.45
The beginner's book of decoupage. [New York, Bantam Books, 1974] vii, 87 p. 14 cm. (A Bantam minibook) [TT870] 0.60 (pbk.)
1. Decoupage. I. Title.

KAMPMANN, Lothar. 745.54
Creating with colored paper. New York, Reinhold Book Corp. [1968] 77 p. illus. (part col.) 21 cm. (Art media series) Translation of Bunte Papiere. [NK1520.K343] 68-26802
1. Decoupage. 2. Color—Study and teaching. I. Title. BIP

LINSLEY, Leslie. 745.54
Decoupage designs : 75 projects you can do with color prints / by Leslie Linsley ; line drawings by Jon Aron. 1st ed. Garden City, N.Y. : Doubleday, 1975. 96 p. : ill. ; 28 cm. [TT870.L54] 74-32572 ISBN 0-385-02720-6 pbk. : 4.95
1. Decoupage. I. Title.

LINSLEY, Leslie. 745.54
Decoupage on glass, wood, metal, rocks, shells, wax, soap, plastic, canvas, ceramic / Leslie Linsley ; photos. by Jon Aron. Radnor, Pa. : Chilton Book Co., c1977. xi, 147 p., [4] leaves of plates : ill. (some col.) ; 27 cm. [TT870.L5416] 77-3527 ISBN 0-8019-6497-0 : 12.50. ISBN 0-8019-6498-9 pbk. : 6.95
1. Decoupage. I. Title.

LINSLEY, Leslie. 745.54
The decoupage workshop / by Leslie Linsley ; photography by Jon Aron. 1st ed. Garden City, N.Y. : Doubleday, 1976. 191 p., [4] leaves of plates : ill. (some col.) ; 27 cm. A detailed explanation of the decoupage process with suggestions for projects and designs. [TT870.L542] 76-2790 ISBN 0-385-07702-5 : 12.95
1. Decoupage. I. Aron, Jon. II. Title. BIP

LINSLEY, Leslie. 745.54
You can decoupage the plain and uglies around your house / by Leslie Linsley ; ill. by Jon Aron. Norwalk, Conn. : C. R. Gibson Co., [1975] 48 p. : ill. ; 22 cm. [TT870.L545] 74-77821 ISBN 0-8378-3004-4 : 2.00
1. Decoupage. I. Title. II. Title: Decoupage the plain and uglies around your house.

MANNING, Hiram. 745.54
Manning on decoupage. New York, Hearthside Press [1969] 254 p. illus. (part col.) 25 cm. [NK1520.M3] 76-76154 10.00
1. Decoupage. I. Title: On decoupage.

MILLARD, Adele. 745.54
Three-dimensional decoupage : how to transform any print into an "in-depth" picture / by Adele Millard ; photos. by Marc Feldman. New York : Sterling Pub. Co., [1975] 96 p. : ill. (some col.) ; 26 cm. Includes index. [TT870.M44] 74-31704 ISBN 0-8069-5322-5 : 8.95 ISBN 0-8069-5323-3 lib.bdg. : 7.89
1. Decoupage. I. Title. BIP

MITCHELL, Marie, 1907- 745.54
The art of decoupage. Rev. Detroit, Marie Mitchell's Decoupage Center, 1968, c1966. 20 p. illus. 23 cm. [TT870.M47 1968] 72-191586
1. Decoupage. I. Title.

NEWMAN, Thelma R. 745.54
Contemporary decoupage; new plastic materials, new and traditional processes [by] Thelma R. Newman. New York, Crown Publishers [1972] x, 214 p. illus. (part col.) 27 cm. Bibliography: p. 201. [TT870.N48 1972] 72-84321 ISBN 0-517-50090-6 7.95
1. Decoupage. I. Title.

NIMOCKS, Patricia E. 745.54
The craft of decoupage [by] Patricia Nimocks. New York, Scribner [1972] 128 p. illus. (part col.) 28 cm. [NK1520.N49] 75-179551 ISBN 0-684-12741-5 3.95
1. Decoupage. I. Title. BIP

NIMOCKS, Patricia E. 745.54
Decoupage [by] Patricia Nimocks. New York, Scribner [1968] 176 p. illus. (part col.) 27 cm. Bibliography: p. 171-172. [NK1520.N5 1968] 68-11372
1. Decoupage.

PRIOLO, Joan B. 745.54
Decoupage, simple and sophisticated, by Joan B. Priolo. New York, Sterling Pub. Co. [1974] 48 p. illus. (part col.) 20 cm. (Little craft book series) Introduces the materials and techniques of decoupage and gives suggestions for simple and advanced projects. [TT870.P8 1974] 73-93597 ISBN 0-8069-5300-4 3.50
1. Decoupage. I. Title.
Library binding 3.69, ISBN 0-8069-5301-2.

SOMMER, Elyse. 745.54
Decoupage old and new. New York, Watson-Guptill [1971] 175 p. illus. (part col.) 27 cm. Bibliography: p. 170. [TT870.S65] 74-157650 ISBN 0-8230-1316-2 9.95
1. Decoupage. I. Title.

SOMMER, Elyse. 745.54
Decoupage old and new. New York, Lancer [1973? c.1971] 288 p. illus., col. plates. 19 cm. (Larchmont Books, 76324) Bibliography: p. 275-277. [TT870.S65] pap., 3.95
1. Decoupage. I. Title.

Decoupage—Juvenile literature.

GILBREATH, Alice Thompson. 745.54
Simple decoupage : having fun with cutouts / by Alice Gilbreath ; illustrated by Marika. 1st ed. New York : Morrow, 1978. 62 p. : ill. ; 25 cm. Thirteen decoupage projects suitable for beginners and using accessible materials. Includes lampshade, necklace, holiday ornaments, flowerpot, and key ring. [TT870.G46] 77-22088 ISBN 0-688-22134-3 : 5.50 ISBN 0-688-32134-8 lib.bdg. : 5.09
1. Decoupage—Juvenile literature. I. Marika. II. Title. BIP

LINSLEY, Leslie. 745.54
Decoupage for young crafters / by Leslie Linsley ; photos. by Jon Aron. 1st ed. New York : Dutton, c1977. vii, 56 p. : ill. ; 21 x 23 cm. Instructions for decorating a shell necklace, planter, pins and barrettes, boxes, and other things with cutout paper designs. [TT870.L5414 1977] 76-53572 ISBN 0-525-28614-4 : 6.95
1. Decoupage—Juvenile literature. I. Aron, Jon. II. Title. BIP

LORRIMAR, Betty. 745.54
Ideas for decoupage and decoration / Betty Lorrimar and Margaret Hickson. New York : Van Nostrand Reinhold Co., [1975] 81 p. : ill. ; 21 x 22 cm. Includes index. Bibliography: p. 78. Describes the tools and techniques of decoupage with instructions for projects. [TT870.L73] 74-6793 ISBN 0-442-30070-0 : 8.95
1. Decoupage—Juvenile literature. 2. Design, Decorative—Juvenile literature. 3. Decoration and ornament—Juvenile literature. I. Hickson, Margaret, joint author. II. Title. BIP

SOMMER, Elyse. 745.54
Designing with cutouts: the art of decoupage. Illustrated by Giulio Maestro. New York, Lothrop, Lee & Shepard Co. [1973] 96 p. illus. 24 cm. Bibliography: p. 94. Describes the necessary materials and techniques for creating designs with paper cutouts on a variety of surfaces and objects. [TT870.S66] 72-9363 ISBN 0-688-40043-4 4.25
1. Decoupage—Juvenile literature. I. Maestro, Giulio, illus. II. Title.
Lib. Ed. 3.94; ISBN 0-688-45043-1. BIP

TEMKO, Florence. 745.54
Decoupage crafts / by Florence Temko ; illustrated by Linda Winchester. 1st ed. Garden City, N.Y. : Doubleday, [1976] 64 p. : ill. (some col.) ; 22 cm. Bibliography: p. 63. Introduces the beginner to the art of decoupage and gives instructions for a variety of projects. [TT870.T444] 74-33666 ISBN 0-385-01503-8 : 5.95
1. Decoupage—Juvenile literature. I. Winchester, Linda. II. Title. BIP

WAGNER, Lee. 745.54
How to have fun with decoupage. Illustrated by Nancy Inderieden. [Mankato, Minn., Creative Education; distributed by Childrens Press, Chicago, 1974] p. cm. (Creative education craft series) Briefly traces the origins of decoupage and gives instructions for three projects that introduce the basic techniques of this type of paper craft. [TT870.W25] 74-9829 ISBN 0-87191-366-6 4.45 (lib. bdg.).
1. Decoupage—Juvenile literature. I. Inderieden, Nancy, illus. II. Title. BIP

Decoys—Exhibitions.

THE Bird decoy : 745.59'3
an American art form : a catalog of carvings exhibited at the Sheldon Memorial Art Gallery, Lincoln, Nebraska / edited by Paul A. Johnsgard. Lincoln : University of Nebraska Press, c1976. x, 190 p., [2] leaves of plates : ill. ; 27 cm. Includes indexes. Bibliography: p. [185] [NK9712.B57] 76-2072 ISBN 0-8032-0887-1 : 17.95
1. Decoys—Exhibitions. 2. Wood-carving—United States—Exhibitions. I. Johnsgard, Paul A. II. Sheldon Memorial Art Gallery. BIP

Decoys (Hunting)

CONNETT, Eugene Virginus, 1891- 799.24841
Duck decoys: how to make them, how to paint them, how to rig them; illustrated by Edgar Burke and the author. [1st ed.] New York, Van Nostrand [1953] 116p. illus. 24cm. [SK335.C65] 53-8764
1. Decoys (Hunting) 2. Duck shooting. I. Title.

FRANK, Charles W., 1922- 745.59'3
Louisiana decoys / by Charles W. Frank, Jr. New Orleans : Frank, c1975. 124 p., [1] leaf of plates : ill. (some col.) ; 22 x 28 cm. Cover title: Louisiana duck decoys. Includes index. [NK9712.F72] 75-35437
1. Decoys (Hunting) 2. Wood-carving—Louisiana. 3. Wood-carvers—Louisiana. I. Title. II. Title: Louisiana duck decoys.

FRANK, Charles W., 1922- 745.59'3
Louisiana duck decoys / by Charles W. Frank, Jr. Gretna, La. : Pelican Pub. Co., 1978, c1975. p. cm. Published in 1975 under title: Louisiana decoys. Includes index. A survey of the duck decoy carvers of Louisiana with examples of their work in full color. [VK9712.F722] 78-7575 ISBN 0-88289-191-X : 19.95
1. Decoys (Hunting) 2. Wood-carving—Louisiana. 3. Wood-carvers—Louisiana. I. Title. BIP

MACKEY, William J., Jr. 745.59
American bird decoys. With a chapter on American decoys as folk art by Quintina Colio. New York, Dutton [c.]1965. 256p. illus. (pt. col.) 28cm. [SK335.M3] 65-19954 10.00
1. Decoys (Hunting) I. Title.

MURPHY, Stanley. 745.59'3
Martha's Vineyard decoys / Stanley Murphy ; photos. by George Moffett. Boston : D. R. Godine, c1978. viii, 165 p. : ill. (some col.) ; 25 x 26 cm. [SK335.M88] 78-58592 ISBN 0-87923-260-9 : 25.00
1. Decoys (Hunting)—Massachusetts—Martha's Vineyard. 2. Wood-carvers—Massachusetts—Martha's Vineyard—Biography. 3. Martha's Vineyard, Mass.—Biography. I. Moffett, George. II. Title. BIP

PARMALEE, Paul Woodburn. 736'.4
Decoys and decoy carvers of Illinois [by] Paul W. Parmalee and Forrest D. Loomis. DeKalb, Northern Illinois University Press [1969] xi, 506 p. illus. (part col.), facsims., map, ports. 24 cm. Bibliography: p. 491-492. [SK335.P36] 69-19824
1. Decoys (Hunting) 2. Waterfowl shooting—Illinois—History. I. Loomis, Forrest D., joint author. II. Title.

STARR, George Ross. 745.59'3
Decoys of the Atlantic flyway / George Ross Starr, Jr. ; photos. by George Dow. New York : Winchester Press, [1974] ix, 308 p., [6] leaves of plates : ill. (some col.) ; 29 cm. Bibliography: p. 304. [SK335.S7] 74-78699 ISBN 0-87691-141-6 : 17.95
1. Decoys (Hunting) I. Title. BIP

STARR, George Ross. 688.7
How to make working decoys / George Ross Starr, Jr. ; photography by Andrea Pape. New York : Winchester Press, c1978. p. cm. Includes index. [SK335.S73] 78-15737 ISBN 0-87691-260-9 : 12.50
1. Decoys (Hunting) I. Title.

SUBJECT INDEX DEGAS, HILAIRE GERMAIN

WEILER, Milton C. 759.13
Classic shorebird decoys: a portfolio of paintings, by Milton C. Weiler. Text by William J. Mackey, Jr. Foreword by Ed Zern. New York, Winchester Press, 1971. [61] p. 24 illus., 24 col. plates. 39 cm. In portfolio. [ND237.W39M3] 74-163778 ISBN 0-87691-048-7
1. Decoys (Hunting) I. Mackey, William J. II. Title.

WEILER, Milton C. 736'.4
The classics decoy series; a portfolio of paintings by Milton C. Weiler. Text by Ed Zern. Foreword by William J. Mackey, Jr. New York, Winchester Press, 1969. [58] p. 24 col. plates. 34 cm. [ND237.W39Z4] 71-99746
1. Decoys (Hunting) I. Zern, Edward Geary, 1910- II. Title.

Decoys (Hunting) — Collectors and collecting.

SORENSON, Harold D., 731.4'62'075 ed.
Decoy collector's guide. [Burlington, Iowa] v. illus. 22 cm. annual. Editor: H. D. Sorenson. [NK9705.D4] 67-1078
1. Decoys (Hunting) — Collectors and collecting. I. Title.

Decoys (Hunting)—Collectors and collecting—Susquehana Valley.

BUCKWALTER, Harold R. 745.59'3
Susquehanna River decoys / Harold R. Buckwalter ; edited by Nancy B. Brown ; photography by Richard Le Grande ; drawings by Terry Buckwalter. [Dallastown, Pa.] : H. R. Buckwalter, c1978. ix, 162 p. : ill. ; 27 cm. Includes index. Bibliography: p. 159. [SK335.B8] 78-66823 12.95
1. Decoys (Hunting)—Collectors and collecting—Susquehana Valley. 2. Wood-carvers—Pennsylvania. I. Title.

Decoys (Hunting)—Design and construction.

MURPHY, Charles F. 745.59'3
Working plans for working decoys / Charles F. Murphy. New York : Winchester Press, c1979. p. cm. Bibliography: p. [SK335.M87] 79-803 ISBN 0-87691-286-2 : 12.50
1. Decoys (Hunting)—Design and construction. I. Title. **BIP**

Decoys (Hunting)—Pictorial works.

SMITH, Elmer Lewis. 745.59'3
American wildfowl decoys from folk art to factory : a sampler of the collectibles. Lebanon, Pa. : Applied Arts, [1974] 32 p. : chiefly ill. ; 28 cm. [SK335.S55] 74-192528
1. Decoys (Hunting)—Pictorial works. I. Title.

Dedham Pottery—Exhibitions.

HAWES, Lloyd E., 1912- 738.3'7
The Dedham Pottery and the earlier Robertson's Chelsea potteries, by Lloyd E. Hawes. With contributions from Marion K. Conant, Paul F. Evans and Nina Fletcher Little. Dedham, Mass., Dedham Historical Society, 1968. 52 p. illus., facsims., geneal. table, ports. 27 cm. Catalog of an exhibition held at the Dedham Historical Society, Aug. 15-Oct. 31, 1968. Bibliography: p. 52. [NK4340.D4H3] 78-5150
1. Dedham Pottery—Exhibitions. I. Dedham Historical Society. II. Title.

Deerfield, Mass.—Descr.—Views.

CHAMBERLAIN, Samuel, 1895- 917.442
Frontier of freedom; the soul and substance of America portrayed in one extraordinary village, Old Deerfield, Massetts, by Samuel Chamberlain and Henry N. Flynt. Illustrated by Samuel Chamberlain. New York, Hastings House [1952] 154 p. illus. 24 cm. [F74.D4C47] 52-9645
1. Deerfield, Mass.—Descr.—Views.SDeerfield, Mass.—Historic houses, etc. I. Title.

CHAMBERLAIN, Samuel, 1895- 917.442
Historic Deerfield: houses and interiors, by Samuel Chamberlain, Henry N. Flynt. Illus. by Samuel Chamberlain. New York, Hastings [1965] 182p. illus., map (on lining papers) 26cm. Rev., enl. ed. of the authors' 'Frontier of freedom.' [F74.D4C47] 65-17610 8.50
1. Deerfield, Mass.—Descr.—Views. 2. Deerfield, Mass.—Historic houses, etc. I. Flynt, Henry N., joint author. II. Title.

Deerfield, Mass.—Historic houses, etc.

CHAMBERLAIN, Samuel, 1895- 917.44'22
Historic Deerfield: houses and interiors, by Samuel Chamberlain and Henry N. Flynt. Illustrated by Samuel Chamberlain. New York, Hastings House [1972] 188 p. chiefly illus. 25 cm. "Revised and enlarged edition of [the authors'] 'Frontier of freedom.'" [F74.D4C47 1972] 72-4447 ISBN 0-8038-3027-0
1. Deerfield, Mass.—Historic houses, etc. I. Flynt, Henry N., joint author. II. Title.

DeForest, Lockwood, 1850-1932.

LEWIS, Anne Suydam. 709'.2'4 B
Lockwood de Forest, painter, importer, decorator / foreword by Eva Ingersoll Gatling ; essay by Anne Suydam Lewis. Huntington, N.Y. : Heckscher Museum, 1976. 52 p. : ill. ; 28 cm. & catalog in pocket. Errata sheet inserted. Bibliography: p. 42-43. [N6537.D36L48] 76-53309
1. DeForest, Lockwood, 1850-1932. 2. Artists—United States—Biography. I. DeForest, Lockwood, 1850-1932. II. Heckscher Museum. III. Title.

Degas, Hilaire Germain Edgar, 1834-1917.

BOGGS, Jean Sutherland. 759.4
Portraits by Degas. Berkeley, University of California. Press, 1962. xv, 142p. plates (part col.) 29cm. (California studies in the history of art, 2) Bibliographical references included in 'Notes' (p. [83]-97) Bibliography: p. [99]-102. [ND553.D3B6] 62-11142
1. Degas, Hilaire Germain Edgar, 1834-1917. I. Title. II. Series. **BIP**

BOURET, Jean 759.4
Degas. [Tr. from French by Daphne Woodward] New York, Tudor [1966, c.1965] 272p. illus. (pt. col.) ports. (pt. col.) 22cm. [ND553.D3B683] 66-4672 5.95
1. Degas, Hilaire Germain Edgar, 1834-1917. I. Title.

BULLARD, Edgar John, 1942- 759.4
Degas [by] E. John Bullard. New York, McGraw-Hill [1971] 48 p. illus., port., slide set (20 col. slides 2 x 2 in.) 29 cm. (Color slide program of the great masters) On spine: Edgar Degas. Bibliography: p. 48. [ND553.D3B8] 75-127921 ISBN 0-07-008860-8
1. Degas, Hilaire Germaine Edgar, 1834-1917. I. Title. II. Series.

CABANNE, Pierre 759.4
Degas: dancers. [Tr. from French by Diana Imber] New York 20 French & European Pubns., 610 Fifth Ave. [1963] 62p. mounted col. illus. 21cm. (Rhythm & colour, 4) Bibl. 63-3611 3.95
1. Degas, Hilaire Germain Edgar, 1834-1917. I. Title.

CABANNE, Pierre. 759.4
Edgar Degas. [Translated by Michel Lee Landa] Paris, P. Tisne New York, Universe Books [1958] 138p. illus., 160 plates (incl. ports.; part col.) 29cm. Bibliography: p. 127-131. [ND553.D3C313] [ND553.D3C313] 927.5 58-8338 58-8338
1. Degas, Hilaire Germain Edgar, 1834-1917. I. Title.

CHARENSOL, Georges, 1899- 759.4
Degas. [Translated from the French by James Oliver] New York, H. N. Abrams [1959] 87p. col. illus. 19cm. [ND553.D3C453] 59-11866
1. Degas, Hilaire Germain Edgar, 1834-1917. I. Title.

CITIZENS' Committee for Children of New York City. 759.4
Degas; loan exhibition, for the benefit of the Citizens' Committee for Children of New York inc, April 7-May 7, 1960. New York, Wildenstein [1960] [98]p. plates. 24cm. [ND553.D3C5] 61-35750
1. Degas, Hilaire Germain Edgar, 1834-1917. I. Title.

THE Degas bronzes. 730'.92'4
[Fair Park, Dallas Museum of Fine Arts, 1974] [30] p. illus. 28 cm. Cover title. "An exhibition presented by the Dallas Museum of Fine Arts, February 6-March 24, 1974, sponsored by the Atlantic Richfield Foundation." Includes an essay by Charles W. Millard. [NB553.D4D43] 74-653
1. Degas, Hilaire Germain Edgar, 1834-1917. I. Degas, Hilaire Germain Edgar, 1834-1917. II. Millard, Charles W. III. Dallas. Museum of Fine Arts.

DEGAS, Hilaire Germain Edgar, 1834-1917 759.4
Degas [by] Raymond Cogniat. [Tr. from French by John Garrett] New York, Crown [196-] 45p. illus. (pt. col.) 19cm. (Basic art lib.) [ND553.D3C613] 68-20463 1.00 bds.,
I. Cogniat, Raymond, 1896- II. Title.

DEGAS, Hilaire Germain Edgar, 1834-1917. 759.4
Degas [by] Raymond Cogniat. [Translated from the French by John Garrett] New York, Crown Publishers [196-] 45 p. illus. (part col.) 19 cm. (Basic art library) [ND553.D3C613] 68-20463
I. Cogniat, Raymond, 1896-

DEGAS, Hilaire Germain Edgar, 1834-1917. 769'.92'4
Degas : the complete etchings, lithographs and monotypes / Jean Adhemar and Francoise Cachin ; foreword by John Rewald ; [translated by Jane Brenton]. New York : Viking Press, c1974. 288 p. : ill. (some col.) ; 34 cm. (A Studio book) Translation of Edgar Degas; gravures et monotypes. Bibliography: p. 287. [NE650.D45A6613] 74-7504 ISBN 0-670-26615-9 : 32.50
1. Degas, Hilaire Germain Edgar, 1834-1917. I. Adhemar, Jean. II. Cachin, Francoise.

DEGAS, Hilaire Germain Edgar, 1834-1917. 741.9'44
Degas' drawings. New York, Dover, [1973] ix, 92 p. (chiefly illus., part col.) 31 cm. "This Dover edition ... reproduces all the illustrations in the portfolio Les Dessins de Degas Reproduits en fac-simile, edited by Henri Riviere and published by Demotte, Paris, in the series Les Dessins des grands artistes francais ... 1922 and 1923." [NC248.D38A44 1973] 73-80952 ISBN 0-486-21233-5 3.50 (pbk.)
1. Degas, Hilaire Germain Edgar, 1834-1917. I. Title. **BIP**

DEGAS, Hilaire Germain Edgar, 1834-1917. 741.9'44
Drawings [by] Degas; [selected and with an introduction] by Ronald Pickvance and Jaromir Pecirka. New ed; rewritten by Ronald Pickvance. Feltham, New York, Hamlyn, 1969. 31 p., 64 plates. 64 illus. (some col.). 31 cm. Bibliography: p. 29. [NC1135.D4P5 1969] 75-464182 50/-
I. Pickvance, Ronald. II. Pecirka, Jaromir.

DEGAS, Hilaire Germain Edgar, 1834-1917. 741.9'0924
Drawings by Degas; essay and catalogue by Jean Sutherland Boggs. [St. Louis] City Art Museum of Saint Louis [1966] 237 p. illus. (part col.) 25 cm. Exhibited at City Art Museum of Art, Mar. 10-Apr. 30, 1967, and the Minneapolis Society of Fine Arts, May 18-June 25, 1967. Bibliography: p. 234-235. 67-14008
I. Boggs, Jean Sutherland. II. St. Louis. City Art Museum. III. Philadephia Museum of Art. IV. Minneapolis Society of Fine Arts. V. Title.

DEGAS, Hilaire Germain Edgar, 1834-1917. 741.9'44
Drawings by Degas; essay and catalogue by Jean Sutherland Boggs. [St. Louis] City Art Mus. of St. Louis [c.1966] 237p. illus. (pt. col.) 25cm. Exhibited at City Art Mus. of Saint Louis, Jan. 20.-Feb. 26, 1967, Philadelphia Mus. of Art. Mar. 10-Apr. 30, 1967, and the Minneapolis Soc. of Fine Arts, May 18-June 25, 1967. Bibl. [NC1135.D4B6] 67-14008 12.50
I. Boggs, Jean Sutherland. II. St. Louis. City Art Museum. III. Philadelphia Museum of Art. IV. Minneapolis Society of Fine Arts. V. Title.
Distributed by Abrams, New York. **BIP**

DEGAS, Hilaire Germain Edgar, 1834-1917. 759.4
Edgar-Hilaire-Germain Degas. Text by Daniel Catton Rich. New York, H. N. Abrams [197-?] 126 p. illus. (part col.) 33 cm. (The Library of great painters) [ND553.D3R45 1972z] 66-27983
I. Rich, Daniel Catton, 1904-

DEGAS, Hilaire Germain Edgar, 1834-1917. 759.4
Edgar Hilaire Germain Degas. Text by Daniel Catton Rich. [1st ed.] New York, H. N. Abrams [1951] 126 p. illus., col. plates. 34 cm. (The Library of great painters) [ND553.D3R45] 52-6130
I. Rich, Daniel Catton, 1904-

DEGAS, Hilaire Germain Edgar, 1834-1917. 759.4
Edgar-Hilaire-Germain Degas. Text by Daniel Catton Rich. New York, H. N. Abrams [1969] 24 p. illus. (part col.) 33 cm. (The Library of great painters. Portfolio ed.) [ND553.D3R45 1969] 69-14742
I. Rich, Daniel Catton, 1904-

DEGAS, Hilaire Germain Edgar, 1834-1917. 927.5
My friend Degas [by] Daniel Halevy. Translated and edited with notes by Mina Curtiss. [1st American ed.] Middletown, Conn., Wesleyan University Press [1964] 127 p. illus., ports. 22 cm. Translation of Degas parle. [ND553.D3H273] 64-22375
I. Halevy, Daniel, 1872- II. Title.

DEGAS, Hilaire Germain Edgar, 1834-1917. 016.7594
The notebooks of Edgar Degas : a catalogue of the thirty-eight notebooks in the Bibliotheque Nationale and other collections / Theodore Reff. Oxford : Clarendon Press, 1976. 2 v. : ill. (some col.) ; 34 cm. Includes indexes. Bibliography: v. 1, p. [153]-154. [NC248.D38R43] 77-361665 ISBN 0-19-817333-4 : 97.50 (2 vols.)
1. Degas, Hilaire Germain Edgar, 1834-1917. I. Reff, Theodore. II. Paris. Bibliotheque Nationale. III. Title.
Distributed by Oxford University Press New York, N. Y. **BIP**

EDGAR-HILAIRE-GERMAIN Degas 759.4
(1834-1917) Text by Daniel Catton Rich. New York, H. N. Abrams in association with Pocket Books [1953] [74]p. 39 illus. (part col.) 18cm. (The Pocket library of great art, A1) An Abrams art book. Bibliography: p.[74] [ND553.D3R45 1953] [ND553.D3R45 1953] 927.5 54-16486 54-16486
1. Degas, Hilaire Germain Edgar, 1834-1917. II. Rich, Daniel Catton, 1904-

HUTTINGER, Eduard. 759.4
Degas. [Translated by Ellen Healy] New York, Crown Publishers. 1960 92 [3] p. illus. (part mounted, part col.) 29 cm. Bibliography: p. [89]-[93] [ND553.D3H83] [ND553.D3H83] 759.4 60-51440 60-51440
1. Degas, Hilaire Germain Edgar, 1834-1917. I. Title. **BIP**

ITTMANN, William M. 769'.924
Lithographs by Edgar Degas. An exhibition held at Steinberg Hall, Washington University, St. Louis, Jan. 7-28 [and] the Museum of Art, the University of Kansas, Lawrence, Feb. 8-Mar. 4, 1967. [Lawrence, 1967?] 31 p. illus. 23 cm. (University of Kansas. Miscellaneous publications of the Museum of Art, no. 65) Catalogue of the exhibition: p. [13]-31. Bibliography: p. 12. [NE2349.5.D418] 67-64706
1. Degas, Hilaire Germain Edgar, 1834-1917. I. Washington University, St. Louis. II. Kansas. University. Museum of Art. III. Title. IV. Series: Kansas. University. Museum of Art. Miscellaneous publications, no. 65

JANIS, Eugenia Parry. 769'.924
Degas monotypes; essay, catalogue & checklist. [Cambridge] Fogg Art Museum, Harvard University; distributed by New York Graphic Society, Greenwich, Conn. [1968] [299] p. illus. 29 cm. On spine: Degas; a critical study of the monotypes. Exhibition held at the Fogg Art Museum, Harvard University, April 25-June 14, 1968. Includes bibliographical references. [NE650.D45J3] 68-27094 17.50
1. Degas, Hilaire Germain Edgar, 1834-1917. I. Harvard University. William Hayes Fogg Art Museum. II. Title. III. Title: Degas; a critical study of the monotypes.

LOS Angeles Co., Calif. 759.4
Museum, Los Angeles.
An exhibition of works by Edgar Hilaire Germain Degas, 1834-1917. [Los Angeles] 1958. 99 p. illus. (part col.) 28 cm. [ND553.D3L75] 59-1378
1. Degas, Hilaire Germain Edgar. 1834-1917. I. Title.

MILLARD, Charles W. 730'.92'4
The sculpture of Edgar Degas / Charles W. Millard. Princeton, N.J. : Princeton University Press, c1976. p. cm. Includes index. Bibliography: p. [NB553.D4M44] 73-2485 ISBN 0-691-03898-8 : 20.00
1. Degas, Hilaire Germain Edgar, 1834-1917. 2. Sculpture, French. 3. Sculpture, Modern—19th century. I. Degas, Hilaire Germain Edgar, 1834-1917. II. Title. BIP

NEW York (City). 709'.2'4
Metropolitan Museum of Art.
Degas in the Metropolitan, February 26, 1977-September 4, 1977 : a complete checklist of the works by Degas in the Metropolitan Museum of Art / compiled by Charles S. Moffett. [New York] : The Museum, c1977. [26] p. : ill. ; 27 cm. [N6853.D33N48] 77-358210
1. Degas, Hilaire Germain Edgar, 1834-1917. I. Degas, Hilaire Germain Edgar, 1834-1917. II. Moffett, Charles S. III. Title.

REFF, Theodore. 759.4
Degas : the artist's mind / Theodore Reff. [New York] : Metropolitan Museum of Art, c1976. 352 p. : ill. (some col.) ; 26 cm. Includes index. Includes bibliographical references. [ND553.D3R38 1976] 75-45190 ISBN 0-87099-146-9 : 25.00
1. Degas, Hilaire Germaine Edgar, 1834-1917.

REFF, Theodore. 759.4
Degas, the artist's mind / [by] Theodore Reff. London : Thames and Hudson, 1976. 352 p. : ill. (some col.), facsims., ports. ; 26 cm. Includes bibliographical references and index. [ND553.D3R38 1976b] 77-358370 ISBN 0-500-09120-X : £15.00
1. Degas, Hilaire Germaine Edgar, 1834-1917.

ROUART, Denis. 759.4
The unknown Degas and Renoir in the National Museum of Belgrade. New York, McGraw-Hill, 1964. xxix, 111 p. illus. (part mounted col.) 32 cm. [ND553.D3R63] 64-22728
1. Degas, Hilaire Germain Edgar, 1834-1917. 2. Renoir, Auguste, 1841-1919. I. Belgrad. Narodni muzej. II. Title.

SHAPIRO, Barbara S. 709'.2'4
Edgar Degas; the reluctant impressionist, by Barbara S. Shapiro. [Exhibition: June 20-September 1, 1974] Boston, Museum of Fine Arts [1974] [24] p. illus. (part col.) 27 cm. Catalog. [N6853.D33S48] 74-82699 ISBN 0-87846-084-5
1. Degas, Hilaire Germain Edgar, 1834-1917. I. Degas, Hilaire Germain Edgar, 1834-1917. II. Boston. Museum of Fine Arts.

STERLING and Francine Clark 759.4
Art Institute, Williamstown, Mass.
An exhibition of the works of Edgar Degas (1834-1917) at the Sterling and Francine Clark Art Institute, with selected loans from other collections, January 8 - February 22, 1970. Williamstown, Mass. [1970] 20 p. illus. 26 cm. [ND553.D3S76] 72-264224
1. Degas, Hilaire Germain Edgar, 1834-1917. I. Title.

TERRASSE, Antoine. 759.4
Degas. [1st U.S. ed.] Garden City, N.Y., Doubleday [1974, c1973] 95 p. illus. (part col.) 34 cm. (The Great impressionists) Includes bibliographical references. [ND553.D3T4713 1974] 73-11047 ISBN 0-385-09543-0 9.95
1. Degas, Hilaire Germain Edgar, 1834-1917.

WERNER, Alfred, 1911- 741'.0924
Degas pastels. New York, Watson-Guptill Publications [1968] 87 p. 32 col. plates. 29 cm. Bibliography: p. 84. [NC1135.D4W4] 68-31215
1. Degas, Hilaire Germain Edgar, 1834-1917. I. Title. BIP

DeGrazia, Ted Ettore, 1909-

DEGRAZIA, Ted Ettore, 759.13
1909-
De Grazia. Tucson, University of Arizona Museum of Art [1973] 126, [16] p. illus. (part col.) 32 cm. "Jeffrey Mitchell ... designed and assembled the catalogue." Bibliography: p. [127]-[137] [ND237.D3337M57] 73-88413
1. DeGrazia, Ted Ettore, 1909- I. Mitchell, Jeffrey. II. Arizona. University. Museum of Art.

DEGRAZIA, Ted Ettore, 739.2'092'4
1909-
De Grazia Moods in gold, silver, precious gems, and cookies. Artist proof ed. Tucson, Ariz. : De Grazia Gallery in the Sun, [1974] 47 p. : ill. (some col.) ; 32 cm. [NK7198.D43A44] 74-190646
1. DeGrazia, Ted Ettore, 1909- 2. Silversmithing, American. I. Title: Moods in gold, silver, precious gems, and cookies.

DEGRAZIA, Ted Ettore, 759.13
1909-
De Grazia paints Cabeza de Vaca; the first non-Indian in Texas, New Mexico, and Arizona, 1527-1536. Artist's proof ed. Tucson, Ariz., De Grazia Gallery in the Sun, 1973. 68 p. illus. (part col.) 32 cm. [ND237.D3337A43] 73-168814 13.50
1. DeGrazia, Ted Ettore, 1909- 2. Nunez Cabeza de Vaca, Alvar, 16th century. 3. Indians of North America—Southwest, Old. 4. Indians of North America—Art. I. Title. BIP

LOS Angeles. Southwest 701
Museum.
Padre Kino, memorable events in the life and times of the immortal priest-colonizer of the Southwest depicted in drawings by DeGrazia. With commentaries on the artist and his work by noted authorities on southwestern history and art. Los Angeles, 1962. 54 p. illus., map. 27 cm. [NC139.D4L6] 62-53443
1. Kino, Eusebio Francisco, 1644-1711. 2. DeGrazia, Ted Ettore, 1909- I. Title.

REED, William, 1929- 709'.24
De Grazia, the irreverent angel. San Diego, Calif., Frontier Heritage Press, 1971. ix, 191 p. illus. (part col.) 24 x 32 cm. Bibliography: p. [186]-191. [N6537.D4R4] 72-157994 14.95
1. DeGrazia, Ted Ettore, 1909- I. Title.

ROSENFELD, Dorcas. 759.13
DeGrazia as I know him. [Phoenix, Ariz., O'Sullivan Woodside, 1974] p. cm. [ND237.D3337R67] 74-17066 ISBN 0-89019-042-9 7.95
1. DeGrazia, Ted Ettore, 1909- I. Title.

DeGrazia, Ted Ettore, 1909- — Portraits, etc.

KEW, George. 779'.23'0924
De Grazia in chiaroscuro; photographic studies. Tucson, Ariz., Photocenter, c1963. [28] p. illus. 36 cm. [N6537.D4K48 Fol] 75-508500
1. DeGrazia, Ted Ettore, 1909- —Portraits, etc. 2. Kew, George. I. Title.

DeHavenon, Gaston T.—Art collections.

MUSEUM of African Art. 732'.2
The deHavenon collection. Washington [1971] 1 v. (unpaged) illus. (part col.) 26 cm. Catalogue of a loan exhibition held at the opening of the museum's enlarged galleries, 1971. [NB1080.M83] 70-198245
1. DeHavenon, Gaston T.—Art collections. 2. Sculpture, African—Exhibitions. 3. Wood-carving, African—Exhibitions. I. Title.

Dehner, Dorothy.

JEWISH Theological 730'.92'4
Seminary of America Jewish Museum.
Dorothy Dehner; ten years of sculpture. [New York, 1965] 1 v. (unpaged) illus. 24 cm. Catalogue of the exhibition held March 11-April 11, 1965. [NB237.D46J4] 65-19747
1. Dehner, Dorothy. I. Title.

Delacroix, Eugene, 1798-1863.

DELACROIX, Eugene, 1798- 759.4
1863
Delacroix [by] Gaston Diehl. [Tr. from French by Anne Ross] New York, Crown [196-] 46p. illus. (pt. col.) 19cm. (Basic art lib.) [ND553.D33D513] 68-20464 1.00 bds.,
I. Diehl, Gaston. II. Title.

DELACROIX, Eugene, 1798- 759.4
1863.
Eugene Delacroix. Text by Maurice Serullaz. New York, H. N. Abrams [1971] 168 p. 90 illus. (part col.), 48 col. plates. 33 cm. (The Library of great painters) Bibliography: p. 168. [ND553.D33S36] 73-99244 ISBN 0-8109-0069-6
I. Serullaz, Maurice.

DELACROIX, Eugene, 1798- 759.4 B
1863.
The journal of Eugene Delacroix. Translated from the French by Walter Pach. Illustrated with reproductions of drawings by the artist. New York, Viking Press [1972] 762 p. illus. 20 cm. (A Viking compass book, C335) Bibliography: p. 737-740. [ND553.D33A32 1972] 70-182804 ISBN 0-670-00335-2 4.95

DELACROIX, Eugene, 1798- 927.5
1863.
The Journal of Eugene Delacroix; a selection edited with an introd. by Hubert Wellington, translated from the French by Lucy Norton. New York, Phaidon Publishers; distributed by Oxford University Press [1951] xxxiv, [1]. 504 p. plates, ports., facsim. 20 cm. (Phaidon pocket series] Bibliography: p. [xxxv] [ND553.D33A318 1951] 52-11273
I. Title.

DELACROIX, Eugene, 741.9'44
1798-1863.
More drawings of Delacroix. Introd. by Stephen Longstreet. [1st ed.] Alhambra, Calif., Borden Pub. Co. [1973] [48] p. (chiefly illus.) 31 cm. (Master draughtsman series) [NC248.D4L66] 72-84101 4.95; 2.25 (pbk.)
1. Delacroix, Eugene, 1798-1863. I. Longstreet, Stephen, 1907- II. Title. BIP

DESLANDRES, Yvonne 759.4
Delacroix, a pictorial biography. [Tr. from French by Jonathan Griffin] New York, Viking c.1963] 144p. illus. 24cm. (Studio bk.) 63-9301 6.50
1. Delacroix, Eugene, 1798-1863. I. Title.

HUYGHE, Rene 759.4
Delacroix. 56 colour plates, 405 black and white illus. [Tr. from French by Jonathan Griffin. New York, Abrams, 1963] 564p. illus., plates (pt. col.) ports., facsims. 31cm. Bibl. 63-19565 35.00
1. Delacroix, Eugene, 1798-1863. I. Title.

JOHNSON, Lee 759.4
Delacroix. New York, Norton [1963] 123p. plates (pt. col.) 21cm. (Masters & movements) Bibl. 62-17878 3.95.
1. Delacroix, Eugene, 1798-1863. I. Title.

LASSAIGNE, Jacques, 1910- 759.4
Eugene Delacroix. [1st American ed. Translated from the French by D. I. Wilton] New York, Harper [1950] 16, [4] p. 40 plates (part col.) 27 cm. (Masters of painting) Harper's art library. Bibliography: p. [18] [ND553.D33L34] 50-5883
1. Delacroix, Eugene, 1798-1863. I. Series: Masters of painting (New York)

MRAS, George P. 701
Eugene Delacroix's theory of art, by George P. Mras. Princeton, N.J., Princeton University Press, 1966. xiv, 160 p. illus. 25 cm. (Princeton monographs in art and archaeology, 37) "Published for the Department of Art and Archaeology, Princeton University." Bibliography: p. 139-151. [ND553.D33M83] 66-17704
1. Delacroix, Eugene, 1798-1863. I. Princeton University. Dept. of Art and Archaeology. II. Title. III. Series.

POOL, Phoebe. 759.4
Delacroix. London, New York, Hamlyn, 1969. 40 p., 49 plates. 53 illus. (49 col.), port. 28 cm. (The Colour library of art) [ND553.D33P6] 75-482101 17/6
1. Delacroix, Eugene, 1798-1863.

PRIDEAUX, Tom. 759.4
The world of Delacroix, 1798-1863, by Tom Prideaux and the editors of Time-Life Books New York, Time, inc. [1966] 196 p. illus. (part col.) 31 cm. (Time-Life library of art) Bibliography: p. 192-193. [ND553.D33P7] 66-21130
1. Delacroix, Eugene, 1798-1863. I. Time-Life Books. II. Title. BIP

ROGER-MARX, Claude, 1888- 759.4
Delacroix [by] Claude Roger-Marx [and] Sabine Cotte. [Translated by Lynn Michelman] New York, G. Braziller [1971, c1970] 99 p. illus. (part col.) 25 cm. (The Great draughtsmen) Translation of L'univers de Delacroix. [ND553.D33R633] 70-132366 7.95
1. Delacroix, Eugene, 1798-1863. I. Cotte, Sabine, joint author. BIP

SPECTOR, Jack J. 759.4
Delacroix : The Death of Sardanapalus / Jack J. Spector. New York : Viking Press, 1974. 135 p. : ill. ; 23 cm. (Art in context) Includes bibliographical references and index. [ND553.D33S62] 73-10559 ISBN 0-670-26636-1 : 9.95
1. Delacroix, Eugene, 1798-1863. Death of Sardanapalus. I. Title.

SPECTOR, Jack J. 759'.4
The murals of Eugene Delacroix at Saint-Sulpice [by] Jack J. Spector. New York, College Art Association of America, 1967. 171 p. illus. (part col.) 28 cm. (Monographs on archaeology and the fine arts, 16) Revision of the author's thesis, Columbia University. Includes bibliographical references. [ND553.D33S63 1967] 67-30384
1. Delacroix, Eugene, 1798-1863. 2. Paris. Saint-Sulpice (Church) I. Title. II. Series. BIP

TRAPP, Frank Anderson. 759.4
The attainment of Delacroix. Baltimore, Johns Hopkins Press [1970] xix, 371 p. illus., col. plates, ports. 29 cm. Includes bibliographical references. [ND553.D33T77] 70-79728 35.00
1. Delacroix, Eugene, 1798-1863. I. Title. BIP

DeLap, Tony, 1927—

CALIFORNIA. University, 730'.924
Irvine. Art Gallery.
Tony DeLap: the last five years, 1963-1968. [Exhibition] Art Gallery, University of California, Irvine. January 28 to March 9,1969. [Irvine, Calif., 1969] 49 p. illus. (part col.) 24 cm. "Tony DeLap, by Alan Solomon": p. 7-14. Bibliography: p. 48-49. [NB237.D43C3] 73-625170
1. DeLap, Tony, 1927- I. Solomon, Alan R.

Delaroche, Hippolyte, called Paul, 1797-1856.

ZIFF, Norman D. 759.4 B
Paul Delaroche : a study in nineteenth-century French history painting / Norman D. Ziff. New York : Garland Pub., 1977. xv, 410 p. : ill. ; 21 cm. (Outstanding dissertations in the fine arts) Originally presented as the author's thesis, New York University, 1974. Bibliography: p. 308-328. [ND553.D3553 1977] 76-23663 ISBN 0-8240-2741-8 lib.bdg. 40.00
1. Delaroche, Hippolyte, called Paul, 1797-1856. 2. Painters—France—Biography. 3. History in art. I. Delaroche, Hippolyte, called Paul, 1797-1856. II. Title. III. Series.

Denon, Dominique Vivant, Baron, 1747-1825.

NOWINSKI, Judith. 709'.24
Baron Dominique Vivant Denon (1747-1825); hedonist and scholar in a period of transition. Rutherford, Fairleigh Dickinson University Press [1970] 280 p. plates (incl. ports) 23 cm. Bibliography: p. 263-272. [PQ1977.D33N6] 78-86651 ISBN 0-8386-7470-4 8.50
1. Denon, Dominique Vivant, Baron, 1747-1825. BIP

Denslow, William Wallace, 1856-1915.

GREENE, Douglas G. 741'.092'4 B
W. W. Denslow / by Douglas G. Greene and Michael Patrick Hearn ; with an introd. by Patricia Denslow Eykyn. [Mount Pleasant] : Clarke Historical Library, Central Michigan University, c1976. vii, 225 p. : ill. ; 24 cm. (Juvenile series ; no. 2) "A bibliography of the work of W. W. Denslow": p. 168-211. [NC975.5.D46G73] 77-353964
1. Denslow, William Wallace, 1856-1915. 2. Illustrators—United States—Biography. I. Hearn, Michael Patrick, joint author. II. Series: Juvenile series (Mount Pleasant, Mich.) ; no. 2.

Dent, Charles C.—Art collections.

ALLENTOWN, Pa. Art Museum. 739'.512
Bronzes from the Charles C. Dent Collection. Introd. by Richard C. Hirsch, director. Selected from the collection shown originally at the Allentown Art Museum, Allentown, Pa. Organized and circulated by the American Federation of Arts. [New York, Printed by S. C. Scott Print. Co., c1967] 30 p. illus. 23 x 21 cm. [NK7903.C5A4] 67-31676
1. Dent, Charles C.—Art collections. I. Hirsch, Richard C. II. American Federation of Arts. III. Title.

Dentistry in art.

PINDBORG, Jens Jorgen, ed. 704.9496176
The dentist in art, by J. J. Pindborg and L. Marvitz. [Translated from the Danish by Gillian Hartz] Chicago, Quadrangle Books [1960] 144p. Bibliography: p.138-140. illus. (part mounted col.) 25cm. 59-15686 12.50
1. Dentistry in art. I. Marvitz, Leif, joint ed. II. Title.

Denver. Art Museum.

CONN, Richard. 746.9'2
Robes of white shell and sunrise : personal decorative arts of the native American : [catalog of an exhibition] Denver Art Museum, November 9, 1974-January 19, 1975 / by Richard Conn. Denver : Denver Art Museum, [1974] 150 p. : ill. (some col.) ; 22 x 28 cm. Bibliography: p. 150. [E98.C8C66] 74-16739 ISBN 0-914738-04-6
1. Denver. Art Museum. 2. Indians of North America—Costume and adornment—Exhibitions. I. Denver. Art Museum. II. Title. BIP

DENVER. Art Museum. 704'.7 B
The Denver Art Museum, major patrons and donors : [catalog / written and edited by Cile M. Bach and Marlene Chambers]. [Denver] : The Museum, c1973. 60 p. : ill. ; 21 cm. [N5215.D46 1973] 75-311544
1. Denver. Art Museum. 2. Art patrons—United States. 3. Art—Denver—Catalogs. I. Bach, Cile M. II. Chambers, Marlene.

DENVER. Art Museum. 709'.01'1
Native American art in the Denver Art Museum / by Richard Conn. [Denver] : Denver Art Museum ; Seattle : distributed by the University of Washington Press, c1979. 350, [1] p. ill. (some col.) ; 30 cm. Bibliography: p. [351] [E98.A7D37 1979] 78-62396 ISBN 0-295-95637-2 : 40.00 ISBN 0-295-95638-0 pbk. : 19.95
1. Denver. Art Museum. 2. Indians of North America—Art. 3. Indians of North America—Industries. I. Conn, Richard. II. Title. BIP

DENVER. Art Museum. 746.9'7
Quilts and coverlets / The Denver Art Museum ; Imelda G. DeGraw. [Denver] : The Museum, [1974] [160] p. : ill. (some col.) ; 20 cm. Bibliography: p. [158]-[159] [NK9102.D46D466 1974] 74-7687 ISBN 0-914738-02-X
1. Denver. Art Museum. 2. Coverlets—Denver—Catalogs. I. DeGraw, Imelda G. II. Title.

Denvir, Bernard.

CHARDIN, Jean Baptiste Simeon, 1699-1779. [927.5]
Chardin, by Bernard Denvir. [1st American ed.] New York, Harper [1950] 16, [1] p. 39 plates (part col.) 28 cm. (Masters of painting) Harper's art library. Bibliography: p. [17] [ND553.C4D43] 759.4 50-7873
1. Denvir, Bernard. I. Title. II. Series: Masters of painting (New York)

Denys Lasdun and Partners.

DENYS Lasdun and Partners. 720'.6'5421
A language and a theme : the architecture of Denys Lasdun & Partners. London : RIBA Publications, 1976. 119 p. : chiefly ill., plans ; 20 x 21 cm. Bibliography: p. 117-118. [NA997.D46A47 1976] 76-378550 ISBN 0-900630-49-3 : £3.50
1. Denys Lasdun and Partners. 2. Architecture, Modern—20th century—Great Britain. I. Title.

Depression glass.

ANDERTON, Johana Gast. 748.2'913
The glass rainbow; depression glass: its origins and patterns, with a price guide for collectors. [North Kansas City, Mo., Trojan Press, 1969] 111 p. illus., facsims., port. 22 cm. (The Collectibles series, no. 1) [NK5103.A55] 77-19939 7.50
1. Depression glass. I. Title.

KLAMKIN, Marian. 748.2'075
The collectors [sic] guide to depression glass. Photos. by Charles Klamkin. New York, Hawthorn Books [1973] 225 p. illus. 29 cm. Bibliography: p. 214. [NK5112.K55 1973] 73-345 13.95
1. Depression glass. 2. Glassware—Collectors and collecting. I. Title. II. Title: Depression glass.

STOUT, Sandra McPhee. 748.2'904
Depression glass in color. [Des Moines, Iowa, Wallace-Homestead Book Co., 1970-71] 2 v. col. plates. 23 cm. Cover title. [NK5112.S77] 70-22716
1. Depression glass. 2. Glass, Colored. 3. Glassware—United States. I. Title. BIP

Depression glass—Catalogs.

CONWAY, Darlyne. 338.4'3748'2
Depression era glass handbook & pricing guide. Photos by Joe A. Gibson. San Angelo, Tex., Educator Books, c1971. 168 p. illus. 22 cm. Bibliography: p. 167. [NK5104.C6] 75-184288 ISBN 0-912092-41-6 8.95
1. Depression glass—Catalogs. I. Title. BIP

FLORENCE, Gene, 1944- 748.2'913
The collectors encyclopedia of depression glass. Photos. by Donahue Studios, Evansville, Ind. 2d ed. Paducah, Ky., Collectors Books [1974] 174 p. illus. 28 cm. [NK5112.F57] 74-170411 9.95
1. Depression glass—Catalogs. I. Title. II. Title: Depression glass.

FLORENCE, Gene, 1944- 748.2'913
The collectors encyclopedia of depression glass / by Gene Florence. 3d ed. Paducah, Ky. : Collectors Books, c1977. 208 p. : ill. ; 29 cm. [NK5439.D44F56 1977] 77-354859 ISBN 0-89145-026-2 : 14.95
1. Depression glass—Catalogs. I. Title. II. Title: Depression glass. BIP

KLAMKIN, Marian. 748.2'913
The Depression glass collector's price guide / by Marian Klamkin ; photos. by Charles Klamkin. New York : Hawthorn Books, c1974. xii, 102 p. : ill. ; 21 cm. Supplement to her The collector's guide to depression glass. [NK5112.K56 1974] 74-6663 ISBN 0-8015-2018-5 : 3.50
1. Depression glass—Catalogs. 2. Depression glass—Collectors and collecting. I. Title. BIP

WEATHERMAN, Hazel Marie, 1920- 748.2
Colored glassware of the Depression Era. [2d ed. Springfield, Mo., Printed by Midwest Litho, 1970-74. 2 v. illus. (part col.) 22 cm. First ed. published in 1969 under title: A guidebook to colored glassware of the 1920's and 1930's. Vol. 2 without ed. note; published by Weatherman Glassbooks, Springfield, Mo. [NK5105.W4 1970] 70-19184 10.00 (v. 1)
1. Depression glass—Catalogs. 2. Glassware—Collectors and collecting. I. Title. BIP

WEATHERMAN, Hazel Marie, 1920- 748.5
A guidebook to colored glassware of the 1920's and 1930's. Springfield, Mo., Printed by Fay Printing Center [1969] 83 p. illus., port. 21 cm. [NK5105.W4] 74-8048
1. Depression glass—Catalogs. 2. Glassware—Collectors and collecting. I. Title. II. Title: Colored glassware of the 1920's and 1930's.

Derain, Andre, 1880-1954.

DERAIN, Andre, 1880-1954. 759.4
Andre Derain / [compiled and introduced by N. Kalitina ; notes by E. Georgiyevskaya and A. Barskaya ; translated by Yu. Nemetsky]. Leningrad : Aurora Art, c1976. 147 p. : chiefly col. ill. ; 34 cm. Includes bibliographical references. [ND553.D37K34] 77-359847
1. Derain, Andre, 1880-1954. I. Kalitina, Nina Nikolaevna.

DIEHL, Gaston. 759.4
Derain. [Translated from the French by A. P. H. Hamilton] New York, Crown Publishers [1964] 92, [2] p. illus. (part col, part mounted col.) 29 cm. Bibliography: p. 92-[93] [ND553.D37D54] 64-3284
1. Derain, Andre, 1880-1954. BIP

Derby, Eng.—Description—Views.

DERBY Borough Libraries. 914.25'1
Old Derby: an illustrated introduction to some buildings and places of historic interest. Derby (Wardwick, Derby, DE1 1HS), Derby Borough Libraries, 1971. [2], 27 p. of illus., maps, 2 fold. plates. 22 cm. [DA690.D4D45] 73-154827 ISBN 0-903188-00-7 £0.20
1. Derby, Eng.—Description—Views. 2. Derby, Eng.—Historic houses, etc. I. Title.

RODGERS, Frank. 779'.9'9425170924
Derby, old and new / [compiled and photographed by] Frank Rodgers. Wakefield : EP Publishing, 1975. [5], 98 p. : chiefly ill. ; 18 x 24 cm. [DA690.D4R6] 75-325268 ISBN 0-7158-1082-0 :
1. Derby, Eng.—Description—Views. I. Title.
Distributed by British Book Center for 8.50 (pbk.)

Derby porcelain.

GILHESPY, F. Brayshaw 738.27
Derby porcelain. London, MacGibbon & Kee, dist. New York, Archer 1963 c.1961 144p. plates (pt. col.) 29cm. Bibl. 62-640 35.00
1. Derby porcelain. I. Title.

HASLEM, John, 1808-1884. 666'.3'942517
The old Derby China Factory; the workmen and their productions; containing biographical sketches of the chief artist workmen, the various marks used, facsimiles copied from the old Derby pattern books, the original price list of more than 400 figures and groups etc., etc. [1st ed. reprinted] with a new foreword by A. L. Thorpe. Wakefield, E. P. Publishing, 1973. xv, iii-xvi, 255 p., [2], xi leaves of plates. illus. 27 cm. Reprint of the 1876 ed. published by T. Bell, London. Includes index. Bibliography: p. xiv-xv. [NK4399.D4H37 1973] 74-178555 ISBN 0-85409-904-2 £3.50
1. Derby porcelain. I. Title. BIP

TWITCHETT, John. 738.2'7
Royal Crown Derby / John Twitchett and Betty Bailey. London : Barrie & Jenkins, 1976. 224 p., [10] leaves of plates : ill. ; 30 cm. Includes index. Bibliography: p. 218. [NK4399.D4T85 1976b] 76-372302 ISBN 0-214-20044-2 : £15.00
1. Derby porcelain. I. Bailey, Betty, joint author. II. Title. BIP

Design.

ALEXANDER, Christopher. 745.4
Notes on the synthesis of form. Cambridge, Harvard University Press, 1964. 216 p. diagrs. 22 cm. Bibliographical references included in "Notes" (p. 193-216) [NK1505.A4] 64-13417
1. Design. I. Title. BIP

ALEXANDER, Harold H. 745.4
Design : criteria for decisions / Harold H. Alexander. New York : Macmillan, c1976. ix, 556 p., [4] leaves of plates : ill. ; 24 cm. Includes index. Includes bibliographical references and index. [NK1510.A57] 75-9697 ISBN 0-02-301660-4 : 14.95
1. Design. I. Title. BIP

ANDERSON, Donald M. 745.4
Elements of design. New York, Holt, Rinehart and Winston [1961] 218 p. illus. 22 x 27 cm. [NK1510.A63] 61-8584
1. Design. 2. Art.

BALLINGER, Louise Bowen 745.4
Design: sources and resources [by] Louise Bowen Ballinger, Thomas F. Vroman. New York, Reinhold [c.1965] 96p. illus. (pt. col.) 21cm. Bibl. [NK1520.B3] 64-22419 5.75
1. Design. I. Vroman, Thomas F., joint author. II. Title.

BALLINGER, Louise Bowen. 745.4
Design: sources and resources [by] Louise Bowen Ballinger [and] Thomas F. Vroman. New York, Reinhold Pub. Corp. [1965] 96 p. illus. (part col.) 21 cm. Bibliography: p. 95. [NK1520.B3] 64-22419
1. Design. I. Vroman, Thomas F., joint author. II. Title.

BATES, Kenneth Francis, 1904- 745.4
Basic design; principles and practice. Foreword by William M. Milliken. [1st ed.] Cleveland, World Pub. Co., [1960] 174 p. illus. 25 cm. Includes bibliography. [NK1510.B46] 60-11456
1. Design.

BAYNES, Ken. 745.4
About design / [by] Ken Baynes. London : Design Council Publications : Distributed by Heinemann Educational, 1976. 159 p. : ill., facsims., plans ; 21 x 22 cm. Ill. on lining papers. Bibliography: p. 155-156. [NK1510.B47] 77-358236 ISBN 0-435-58063-9 : £6.90. ISBN 0-435-58064-7 pbk.
1. Design. I. Title.

BEITLER, Ethel Jane. 754.4
Design for you [by] Ethel Jane Beitler [and] Bill Lockhart. 1st ed. New York, Wiley [1961] 206p. illus. 24cm. [NK1510.B48] 61-14810
1. Design. I. Lockhart, Bill Clarence, 1926- joint author. II. Title.

BEITLER, Ethel Jane. 745.4
Design for you [by] Ethel Jane Beitler [and] Bill Lockhart. 2d ed. New York, Wiley [1969] xxii, 247 p. illus. 24 cm. Bibliography: p. 229-231. [NK1510.B48 1969] 73-76050
1. Design. I. Lockhart, Billy Clarence, 1926- joint author. II. Title. BIP

BEVLIN, Marjorie Elliott. 745.4
Design through discovery. New York, Holt, Rinehart and Winston [1963] 388 p. illus. 25 cm. [NK1510.B53] 63-15112
1. Design. I. Title. BIP

BEVLIN, Marjorie Elliott. 745.4
Design through discovery. 2d ed. New York, Holt, Rinehart and Winston [1970] ix, 382 p. illus. (part col.) 26 cm. Bibliography: p. 367-371. [NK1510.B53 1970] 72-85753
1. Design. I. Title.

to create space figures. New York, Harper [1959] 169 p. illus. 19 cm. [NK1570.W6] 59-9933
1. Design. 2. Geometrical drawing. I. Title. BIP

WOLCHONOK, Louis. 745.4
The art of three-dimensional design; how to create space figures. New York, Dover Publications [1969, c1959] xii, 169 p. illus. 28 cm. [NC740.W6 1969b] 75-86322 2.75
1. Design. 2. Geometrical drawing. I. Title.

Design—Addresses, essays, lectures.

BANHAM, Reyner, comp. 745.4
The Aspen papers; twenty years of design theory from the International Design Conference in Aspen. Edited and with commentary by Reyner Banham. New York, Praeger [1974] 224 p. illus. 25 cm. [NK1510.B26] 73-14559
1. Design—Addresses, essays, lectures. 2. Design, Industrial—Addresses, essays, lectures. I. International Design Conference. II. Title.

DESIGN and planning. 745.408
Edited by Martin Krampen. New York, Hastings House [1965] 171 p. illus. 28 cm. Based on rewritten contributions to the National Design Seminar, held at the University of Waterloo, Ontario, from May 4 to 6, 1964. Includes bibliographies. [NK1525.D4] 65-22998
1. Design—Addresses, essays, lectures. 2. Design, Industrial—Addresses, essays, lectures. I. Krampen, Martin, ed. II. National Design Seminar, University of Waterloo, 1964.

NATIONAL Design Seminar, University of Waterloo, 1966 745.408
Design and planning, 2, ed. by Martin Krampen, Peter Seitz. New York, Hastings [1967] v. illus. 28cm. Rewritten papers, orig. prepd. for and presented at the seminar, org. by the Design Studies Group at the Univ. of Waterloo, Ontario, in conjunction with the Doon School of Fine Arts. Bibl. [NK1525.N3 1964] 65-22998 10.00 pap.,
1. Design—Addresses, essays, lectures. 2. Design, Industrial—Addresses, essays, lectures. I. Krampen, Martin. ed. II. Waterloo, Ont. University. Dept. of Environmental Design. III. Doon, Ont. School of Fine Arts. IV. Title.

Design— Congresses.

THE Design necessity; 745.4'49'73
a casebook of federally initiated projects in visual communications, interiors and industrial design, architecture, landscaped environment [by] Ivan Chermayeff [and others] Cambridge, Mass., MIT Press [1973] 80 p. illus. 24 x 31 cm. "Prepared for the first Federal Design Assembly." [NK1164.D47] 73-2022 ISBN 0-262-03047-0 6.00 (pbk.)
1. Design—Congresses. 2. Architectural design—Congresses. I. Chermayeff, Ivan. II. Federal Design Assembly, 1st, Washington, D.C., 1973.
ISBN 0-262-53-026-0 (pbk); 6.00

FEDERAL Design Assembly, 2d, Washington, D.C., 1974 745'.05 s
The design reality / Second Federal Design Assembly ; editor, Mildred S. Friedman. Minneapolis : Walker Art Center, [1975] 76 p. : ill. (some col.) ; 29 cm. (Design quarterly ; 94/95) "Sponsored by the Federal Council on the Arts and the Humanities, administered by the National Endowment for the Arts." [NK1.E9 no. 94/95] [NK1164] 745.4'49'73 75-308777 pbk. : 1.60
1. Design—Congresses. 2. Architectural design—Congresses. I. Friedman, Mildred S. II. Federal Council on the Arts and the Humanities. III. National Endowment for the Arts. IV. Title. V. Series.

INTERNATIONAL Design Conference. 745.4
Man/problem solver. Conference papers, 11th International Design Conference in Aspen, June 18-24, 1961. Chicago 1, Author [6 E. Lake St., c.1961] various p. 29cm. 56-35731 5.00, pap., unbound
1. Design—Congresses. I. Title.

INTERNATIONAL Design Conference. v. 12
Program. Conference papers. 1955- Aspen [Colo.] v. 29cm. [NC5.I53] 56-357317
1. Design— Congresses. I. Title.

Design, Decorative.

THE American home. 745
Patterns; 1064 designs, over 109 never before published in book form, something for every skill and craft. [Forest Hills, N. Y., 1959] 202p. illus. 32cm. [NK1115.A7] 55-891
1. Design, Decorative. 2. Decoration and ornament. 3. Interior decoration. I. Title.

ANTIQUE Designs, inc. 745.4
Decorative material; borders, braces, flowers, headbands, tailpieces, initials, etc. All pieces designed prior to 1928 by world famous decorative artists. Compiled by Ted Rombach. Cleveland, [1968] iv, 118 p. (chiefly illus.) 32 cm. The decorative material is from the collection of the Antique Designs, inc. [NK1530.A5] 79-1627
1. Design, Decorative. I. Rombach, Ted, comp. II. Title.

BERGLING, John Mauritz, 1866-1933 745.4
Ornamental designs and illustrations; studies of the human figure, plant and animal life. An encyclopedia of subjects for the use of engravers, designers and all lovers of art. 4th ed. Coral Gables 34, Fla., V. C. Bergling, Box 34-523 [1963, c.1913-1964] 106p. illus. 28cm. 63-22578 10.00
1. Design, Decorative. I. Title. BIP

BRADLEY, Amos Day, 1905- 745.4
The geometry of repeating design and geometry of design for high schools, by A. Day Bradley. New York, Bureau of Publications, Teachers College, Columbia University, 1933. [New York, AMS Press, 1973, c1972] vi, 131 p. illus. 22 cm. Reprint of the 1933 ed., issued in series: Teachers College, Columbia University. Contributions to education, no. 549. Originally presented as the author's thesis, Columbia. Bibliography: p. 129-131. [NK1570.B68 1972] 72-176586 ISBN 0-404-55549-7 10.00
1. Design, Decorative. 2. Geometrical drawing. I. Title. II. Series: Columbia University. Teachers College. Contributions to education, no. 549. BIP

BRAGDON, Claude Fayette, 1866-1946. 745.4
Projective ornament. Brighton, Seattle, Unicorn Bookshop, 1972. [10], 79 p. illus. 22 cm. Reprint of the 1915 ed. [NK1570.B7 1972] 73-155671 ISBN 0-85659-000-2 £0.95 ($3.00 U.S.)
1. Design, Decorative. 2. Fourth dimension. I. Title.

BROD, Fritzi (Shermer) 1900- 745.4
Decorative design. New York, Pitman Pub. Corp. [1958] unpaged (chiefly illus.) 20 x 26cm. (Pitman drawing series) [NK1510.B78 1958] 58-13046
1. Design, Decorative. I. Title.

CARTOUCHES and decorative small frames 749'.7
/ edited by Edmund V. Gillon, Jr. New York : Dover Publications, 1975. 120, [2] p. : chiefly ill. ; 29 cm. (Dover pictorial archive series) Bibliography: p. [121]-[122] [NK1530.C37 1975] 74-15173 ISBN 0-486-23122-4 pbk. : 3.00
1. Design, Decorative. I. Gillon, Edmund Vincent.

CHAPMAN, Suzanne E 745.43
Early American design motifs. New York, Dover Publications [1952] 191p. illus. 28cm. [NK1115.C47] 52-13843
1. Design, Decorative. 2. Decoration and ornament—U. S. I. Title. BIP

CHRISTENSEN, Erwin Ottomar, 1890- 745.44
Early American designs: toleware. New York, Pitman Pub. Corp. [1952] unpaged illus. 28 cm. [NK1403.C49] 52-14604
1. Design, Decorative. 2. Decoration and ornament—U.S. 3. Tinware. I. Title.

CHRISTIE, Archibald H. 745.4
Pattern design; an introduction to the study of formal ornament, by Archibald H. Christie. New York, Dover Publications [1969] xii, 313 p. illus. 22 cm. Reprint of the 1929 ed. first published under title: Traditional methods of pattern designing. Bibliographical footnotes. [NK1510.C5 1969] 72-79234 3.00
1. Design, Decorative. I. Title.

D'ARBELOFF, Natalie. 745.4
Designing with natural forms. Photography by Ted Sebley. New York, Watson-Guptill Publications [1973] 96 p. illus. 22 cm. Includes bibliographical references. [NK1553.D23] 72-6451 ISBN 0-8230-1318-9 7.95
1. Design, Decorative. 2. Nature (Aesthetics) I. Title.

DAY, Lewis Foreman, 1845-1910. 745.4
The anatomy of pattern / Lewis F. Day. New York : Garland Pub., 1977. xi, 53 p., [35] leaves of plates : ill. ; 19 cm. (The Aesthetic movement & the arts and crafts movement) Reprint of the 1887 ed. published by B. T. Batsford, London, in series: Text-books of ornamental design. [NK1510.D3 1977] 76-17764 ISBN 0-8240-2469-9 lib.bdg. : 35.00
1. Design, Decorative. I. Title. II. Series. III. Series: Text-books of ornamental design. BIP

DRESSER, Christopher. 745.4
The art of decorative design / Christopher Dresser. New York : Garland Pub., 1977. xi, 241 p., [28] leaves of plates : ill. ; 23 cm. (The Aesthetic movement & the arts and crafts movement) Reprint of the 1862 ed. published by Day and Son, London. [NK1510.D75 1977] 76-17751 ISBN 0-8240-2453-2 : 35.00
1. Design, Decorative. 2. Design, Decorative—Plant forms. 3. Botany. I. Title. II. Series. BIP

DRESSER, Christopher. 745.4
Modern ornamentation / Christopher Dresser. New York : Garland Pub., 1978. p. cm. (The Aesthetic movement & the arts and crafts movement) [NK1530.D73] 76-17771 ISBN 0-8240-2475-3 : lib.bdg. : 35.00z
1. Design, Decorative. 2. Arts and crafts movement. I. Title. II. Series. BIP

FLAM, David S., 1920- 745.43
1001 designs for hand decorating. New York, Homecrafts, 1950. 96 p. (chiefly illus.) 26 cm. [NK1530.F55] 50-6222
1. Design, Decorative. I. Title.

GILLON, Edmund Vincent. 741.6
Decorative frames and borders: 396 examples from the Renaissance to the present day. Selected by Edmund V. Gillon, Jr. New York, Dover Publications [1973] 173 p. illus. 29 cm. (Dover pictorial archives series) [NK1530.G54 1973] 72-96186 ISBN 0-486-22928-9 3.50 (pbk)
1. Design, Decorative. I. Title.

HANDBOOK of designs and motifs; 745.44
nearly 7,000 designs, motifs, patterns, forms and symbols based on Japanese family crests ... Introd. by P. K. Thomajan. New York, Tudor [1950] 1 v. (unpaged) of illus. 21 x 28 cm. [NK1530.H28] 50-8098
1. Design, Decorative. I. Thomajan, Puzant Kevork, 1902-

HOLIDAY, Ensor. 745.4
Altair design. [New York] Pantheon Books [1973] c1970. 1 v. chiefly illus. (part col.) 21 x 26 cm. [NK1510.H56] 72-13052 ISBN 0-394-82548-9 1.95
1. Design, Decorative. I. Title. BIP

HOLIDAY, Ensor. 745.4
Altair design 4 / developed by Ensor Holiday. [New York] : Pantheon, c1978. ca. 150 p. : chiefly ill. (some col.) ; 21 x 26 cm. [NK1570.H57] 77-17417 ISBN 0-394-83794-0 pbk. : 2.95
1. Design, Decorative. 2. Geometry. I. Title.

HORNUNG, Clarence Pearson. 745.4
Allover patterns for designers and craftsmen / Clarence P. Hornung. New York : Dover Publications, 1975. [118] p. : chiefly ill. (some col.) ; 31 cm. (Dover pictorial archive series) [NK1530.H66 1975] 75-13125 ISBN 0-486-23179-8 pbk. : 4.50
1. Design, Decorative. I. Title. BIP

HORNUNG, Clarence Pearson. 745.4
Background patterns, textures and tints : 92 full-page plates for artists and designers / Clarence P. Hornung. New York : Dover Publications, 1976. [95] p. : chiefly ill. ; 28 cm. (Dover pictorial archive series) [NK1530.H67 1976] 75-44715 ISBN 0-486-23260-3 pbk. : 3.00
1. Design, Decorative. 2. Texture (Art) 3. Tinting. I. Title. BIP

HUMBERT, Claude, comp. 745.4
Ornamental design; a source book with 1000 illustrations chosen and introduced by Calude Humbert. New York, Viking Press [1970] 236 p. (chiefly illus., part col.) 28 cm. (A Studio book) English, French, and German. [NK1530.H85 1970] 78-101785 ISBN 0-670-52877-3 16.95
1. Design, Decorative.

LANG, John, 1886- 745.44
Geometric designs for artists and craftsmen; a new, simplified method for decorative pattern- making in wood, metal, leather, fabric and title. Illustrated by the author. [1st ed.] New York, Exposition Press [1959] 85p. illus. 24cm. (An Exposition-university book) [NK1570.L3] 59-16268
1. Design, Decorative. I. Title.

THE Language of pattern; 745.4
an enquiry inspired by Islamic decorations [by] Keith Albarn [and others. 1st U.S. ed.] New York, Harper & Row [1974] 112 p. illus. 29 cm. (Icon editions) Bibliography: p. 112. [NK1505.L33 1974b] 73-20057 ISBN 0-06-430050-1 5.95 (pbk.)
1. Design, Decorative. 2. Arabesques. I. Albarn, Keith.

LEIGHTON, John, 1822-1912. 745.4
Suggestions in design : three thousand years of ornaments, styles, motifs / more than 1000 original drawings by John Leighton ; with a new introduction by Edward Lucie-Smith. New York : Paddington Press ; distributed by Grosset & Dunlap, c1977. 9, 101, [17] p. : chiefly ill. ; 28 cm. Reprint of the plates from the 1880 ed. published by Blackie, London. [NK1510.L493 1977] 76-53617 ISBN 0-448-22615-4 pbk. : 4.95
1. Design, Decorative. 2. Decoration and ornament. I. Title. BIP

LIPMAN, Jean (Herzberg), 1909- 745.3
American folk decoration, by Jean Lipman, with practical instruction by Eve Meulendyke. New York, Oxford University Press, 1951. xii, 163 p. illus. (part col.) 29 cm. Bibliography: p. 157-159. [NK806.L5] 51-11035
1. Design, Decorative. 2. Decoration and ornament—U. S. 3. Folk art—U. S. I. Meulendyke, Eve. II. Title. BIP

LORCH, Adolf. 745.4
Modern geometric design. New York, Sterling Pub. Co. [1971] 79 p. (chiefly col. illus.) 29 cm. [NK1570.L613 1971] 72-151714 ISBN 0-8069-5164-8
1. Design, Decorative. 2. Geometrical drawing. I. Title.

MIROW, Gregory. 745.4
A treasury of design of artists and craftsmen. New York, Dover Publications [1969] 1 v. (chiefly illus., part col.) 28 cm. (Dover pictorial archive series) Includes bibliographies. [NK1530.M53] 69-18877 2.50
1. Design, Decorative. I. Title. BIP

MORRIS, William, 1834-1896. 745.4'49'24
William Morris: wallpapers and chintzes. [Edited by] Fiona Clark. With a biographical note by Andrew Melvin. New York, St. Martin's Press [1973] 95 p. 91 illus. (part col.). 30 cm. Includes bibliographical references. [NK1535.M67C55 1973] 73-89359 6.95
1. Morris, William, 1834-1896. 2. Design, Decorative. I. Clark, Fiona. II. Title.

NELSON, George, 1908- 745.4
Problems of design. [2d ed. New York, Whitney Library of Design, 1965] ix, 204 p. illus., plans. 22 cm. [NK1505.N4 1965] 65-29814
1. Design, Decorative. 2. Design,

SUBJECT INDEX

DESIGN, DECORATIVE—NEW YORK

Industrial. 3. Architecture — Designs and plans. I. Title.

NELSON, George, 1908- 745.43
Problems of design. [2d ed. New York, Whitney Pubns., 18 E. 50th St., c.1957, 1965] ix, 204p. illus., plans. 21cm. [NK1505.N4] 57-14401 3.95 pap.,
1. Design, Decorative 2. Design, Industrial. 3. Architecture—Designs and plans. I. Title. BIP

NELSON, George, 1908- 745.43
Problems Whitney Publications, 1957] ix, 205p. illus., plans. 23cm. [NK1505.N4] 57-14401
1. Design, Decorative. 2. Design, Industrial. 3. Architecture—Designs and plans. I. Title.

O'BRIEN, James Francis, 1917- 745.4
Design by accident, by James F. O'Brien. New York, Dover Publications [1968] 215 p. illus. (part col.) 29 cm. [NK1520.O26 1968] 68-10779 3.00
1. Design, Decorative. 2. Art—Technique. 3. Artists' materials. I. Title. BIP

PERGOLESI, Michel Angelo. 745.4
Classical ornament of the eighteenth century, designed and engraved by Michelangelo Pergolesi Magnolia, Mass., Peter Smith [1973 c1970] vii, 99 p. (chiefly illus.) 35 cm. (Dover book rebound) "Unabridged repub. of an untitled & undated vol. of ornamental sheets ... pub. in London ... between 1777 & 1792," with a new introd. by Edward A. Maser Bibl. [NK1535.P4A43] 75-82792 ISBN 0-8446-4595-8 7.50
I. Title. BIP

PROCTOR, Richard M. 745.4
The principles of pattern for craftsmen and designers [by] Richard M. Proctor. New York, Van Nostrand Reinhold [1969] 135 p. (chiefly illus.) 22 cm. Bibliography: p. 134-135. [NK1505.P7 1969] 79-90308
1. Design, Decorative. I. Title. BIP

REICHEK, Jesse 745.44
Etcetera [New Directions. dist. Philadelphia, Lippincott, c.1965] 1v. (chiefly illus.) 20cm. (ND196) [NC1075.R45] 65-15671 1.60 pap.,
I. Title.

SMEETS, Rene. 745.4
Signs, symbols & ornaments / Rene Smeets ; [translated by Audrey Hutchison]. New York : Van Nostrand Reinhold, [1975] 176 p. : ill. ; 24 cm. Translation of Ornament, symbool & teken. Includes index. [NK1520.S613] 75-2823 ISBN 0-442-27849-7 : 9.95
1. Design, Decorative. 2. Decoration and ornament. 3. Symbolism in art. I. Title. BIP

SNEAD, Jane Wanger, 1906- 745.44
Pennsylvania Dutch designs. Chicago, J. Snead, c1950. [50] p. (incl. cover; chiefly illus.) 29 cm. Title from p. [2] [NK1533.S58] 50-14843
1. Design, Decorative. 2. Art, Pennsylvania German. I. Title.

SPEARS, Ruth (Wyeth) 1895-- 747
Painting patterns for home decorators. New York, M. Barrows, 1954 [c1947, 49] 2v. inl. illus. 29cm. Vol. 2 has title: More painting patterns for home decorators. [NK1535] 54-10311
1. Design, Decorative. 2. Interior decoration. 3. Stencil work. I. Title. II. Title: More painting patterns for home decorators.

SUTPHEN, Richard 745.4
Design devices; a copyright free handbook, comp. by Dick Sutphen. [Minneapolis, Dick Sutphen Studio, 1967] 80 1. (chiefly illus.) 30cm. [NK1530.S9] 67-27674 12.00 loose-leaf ring binder
1. Design, Decorative. I. Title.
Publisher's address: Box 8408, Minneapolis, Minn., 55426.

WADSWORTH, Beula. 745.44
Design motifs of the Pueblo Indians; with applications in modern decorative arts. [San Antonia] Maylor Co. [1957] 96 p. illus. 28 cm. [NK1533.W3] 57-4772
1. Design, Decorative. 2. Pueblo Indians—Art. I. Title.

WING, Frances S. 745.7
The complete book of decoupage, by Frances S. Wing. New York, Coward McCann [1965] 205 p. illus. 22 cm. Bibliography: p. 199-201. [NK1520.W55] 65-25502
1. Design, Decorative. 2. Paper work. I. Title. BIP

WING, Frances S. 745.7
The complete book of decoupage, by Frances S. Wing. Rev. ed. New York, Coward-McCann [1970] 205 p. illus. 22 cm. Bibliography: p. 199-201. [NK1520.W55 1970] 71-113166 5.95
1. Design, Decorative. 2. Paper work. I. Title.

WING, Francis S. 745.7
The complete book of decoupage [by] Francis S. Wing Rev. ed. [New York] Berkley Pub. Co. [1976 c1970] 205 p. illus. 20 cm. [NK1520.W55] ISBN 0-425-03012-1 2.95 (pbk.)
1. Design, Decorative. 2. Paper work. I. Title.
L.C. card no. for original edition: 71-113166.

Design, Decorative—Africa.

JEFFERSON, Louise E. 745'.096
The decorative arts of Africa [by] Louise E. Jefferson. New York, Viking Press [1973] 191 p. illus. (part col.) 29 cm. (A Studio book) Bibliography: p. 188-189. [NK1487.A1J43 1973] 72-12055 ISBN 0-670-26285-4 14.95
1. Design, Decorative—Africa. 2. Decoration and ornament—Africa. I. Title.

WILLIAMS, Geoffrey. 745.4'41
African designs from traditional sources. New York, Dover Publications [1971] xxii, 200 p. of illus. 24 cm. (Dover pictorial and archive series) Bibliography: p. xxi-xxii. [NK1487.W5] 76-162027 ISBN 0-486-22752-9 3.00
1. Design, Decorative—Africa. I. Title. BIP

Design, Decorative—Africa, Sub-Saharan.

TROWELL, Kathleen Margaret. 745.44967
African design. New York, Praeger [1960] 78 p. 77 plates. 29 cm. (Books that matter) [NK1487.T7] 60-11832
1. Design, Decorative—Africa, Sub-Saharan. 2. Decoration and ornament, Primitive. 3. Black art. I. Title.

TROWELL, Kathleen Margaret. 745.44967
African design [by] Margaret Trowell. [2d ed.] New York, F. A. Praeger [1966, c1960] 78 p. map, 78 plates (2 col.) 29 cm. Bibliographical footnotes. [NK1487.T7 1966] 65-20075
1. Design, Decorative—Africa, Sub-Saharan. 2. Negro art—Africa, Sub-Saharan. I. Title.

TROWELL, Kathleen Margaret. 745.4'41
African design [by] Margaret Trowell. [3d ed.] New York, Praeger [1971, c1960] 78, [76] p. map, 78 plates (2 col.) 29 cm. Includes bibliographical references. [NK1487.A3S97 1971] 76-112635 12.50
1. Design, Decorative—Africa, Sub-Saharan. 2. Negro art—Africa, Sub-Saharan. I. Title.

Design, Decorative—Animal forms.

ROSTOVTSEV, Mikhail Ivanovich, 1870-1952. 731'.83'2
The animal style in South Russia and China [by] M. Rostovtzeff. New York, Hacker Art Books, 1973. xvi, 112 p., 33 plates. illus. 29 cm. Includes bibliographical references. [NK1456.A3R877 1973] 75-143361 ISBN 0-87817-080-4 25.00
1. Design, Decorative—Animal forms. 2. Decoration and ornament—Russia, Southern. 3. Russia, Southern—Antiquities. 4. Decoration and ornament, Chinese. 5. China—Antiquities. I. Title. BIP

Design, Decorative—Central Europe.

SIBBETT, Ed. 745.4'49'4
Peasant designs for artists and craftsmen / by Ed Sibbett, Jr. New York : Dover Publications, 1977. 100 p. : all ill. ; 29 cm. (Dover pictorial archives series) [NK142.S53 1977] 76-58079 ISBN 0-486-23478-9 pbk. : 3.00
1. Design, Decorative—Central Europe. 2. Design, Decorative—Europe, Eastern. 3. Folk art—Central Europe. 4. Folk art—Europe, Eastern. I. Title. BIP

Design, Decorative—China.

HAWLEY, Willis Meeker, 1896- ed. 736'.98
Chinese folk designs; a collection of 300 cut-paper designs used for embroidery together with 160 Chinese art symbols and their meanings. [By] W. M. Hawley. New York, Dover Publications [1971, c1949] [319] p. (chiefly illus.) 299 plates. 24 cm. (Dover pictorial archive series) "Supplement: ... Chinese art symbols ... drawn from the Chinese originals for Oriental culture chart 12, by Francess Hawley Seyssel." [NK1483.A1H3 1971] 77-179790 ISBN 0-486-22633-6 3.50
1. Design, Decorative—China. 2. Embroidery, Chinese. 3. Signs and symbols—China. I. Seyssel, Francess Hawley. II. Title. BIP

Design, Decorative—England.

GLOAG, John, 1896- 745.44942
The English tradition in design. New York, Macmillan, 1960. 89p. illus., 40 plates. 24cm. 60-50462 5.00
1. Design Decorative—England. 2. Design, Industrial. 3. Art industries and trade—England. I. Title.

GLOAG, John, 1896- 745.4
The English tradition in design. [Enl., rev. ed.] London. A. ; C. Black [New York, Hillary House. 1966.c.1959] x. 89p. illus., 43 plates. 24cm. [NK928] 56-1097 ISBN /CD 5.00
1. Design, Decorative—England. 2. Design, Industrial—England. 3. Art industries and trade, England. I. Title.

Design, Decorative—Greece, Modern.

ETHNIKOS Organismos Hellenikes Cheirotechnias. 745.4'49'38
Greek ornament. Translation and introd. by Patrick Connell. [1st English language ed.] New York, Dover Publications [1968] 127 p. (chiefly illus.) 26 cm. Translation of Hellenika diakosmetika themata. Bibliography: p. 10. [NK1451.A1E813 1968b] 68-57488
1. Design, Decorative—Greece, Modern. I. Title.

Design, Decorative—History—Pictorial works.

GRIESBACH, C. B. 745.4'4
Historic ornament : a pictorial archive : 900 fine examples from ancient Egypt to 1800, suitable for reproduction / C. B. Griesbach. New York : Dover Publications, 1975. 280 p. : all ill. ; 29 cm. (The Dover pictorial archive series) "Contains 280 plates from the portfolio Muster-Ornamente aus allen Stilen in historischer Anordnung, originally published by C. B. Griesbach in Gera, Germany, n.d. (late nineteenth century). [NK1530.G7413 1975] 76-352598 ISBN 0-486-23215-8 pbk. : 5.00
1. Design, Decorative—History—Pictorial works. I. Title. BIP

Design, Decorative—Japan.

BLAKEMORE, Frances. 745.4
Japanese design through textile patterns / Frances Blakemore. 1st ed. New York : Weatherhill, 1978. 272 p. : ill. ; 21 cm. Includes index. [NK1484.A1B55 1978] 78-2430 10.95
1. Design, Decorative—Japan. 2. Textile design. 3. Stencil work. I. Title.

KAIYAMA, Kyusaburo. 745.4
The book of Japanese design; Banshoku shin hinagata, bijutsu oyo. Translation and commentary by Sylvia Price Mueller. New York, Crown Publishers [1969] 186 p. illus. 16 x 24 cm. [NK1484.K3 1969] 70-75060 4.95
1. Design, Decorative—Japan. I. Mueller, Sylvia Price, ed. II. Title. III. Title: Banshoku shin hinagata, bijutsu oyo.

KOJIRO, Yuichiro, 1922- 745.44952
Forms in Japan. Tr. [from Japanese] by Kenneth Yasuda. Photos by Yukio Futagawa. Honolulu, East-West Ctr Pr. [1965, c.1963] 184 p. illus. 29 cm. [NK1484.K613] 64-7591 15.00
1. Design, Decorative—Japan. 2. Design, Industrial—Japan. I. Futagawa. Yukio, 1932- illus. II. Title.

KOJIRO, Yulchiro, 1922- 745.44952
Forms in Japan, Translated by Kenneth Yasuda. Photos, by Yukio Futagawa. Honolulu, East-West Center Press [1965, c1963] 184 p. illus. 29 cm. Erratum slip inserted. [NK1484.K613] 64-7591
1. Design, Decorative—Japan. 2. Design, Industrial—Japan. I. Futagawa, Yukio, 1932- illus. II. Title.

MIZOGUCHI, Saburo, 1896- 745.4'4952
Design motifs. Translated and adapted by Louise Allison Cort. [1st ed.] New York, Weatherhill [1973] 143 p. illus. (part col.) 24 cm. (Arts of Japan, 1) Translation of Monyo. [NK1484.A1M5813] 72-89447 ISBN 0-8348-2700-X 7.95
1. Design, Decorative—Japan. I. Title.

OUCHI, Hajime. 741.9'52
Japanese optical and geometrical art / Hajime Ouchi. New York : Dover Publications, 1977. 170 p. : all ill. ; 28 cm. (Dover pictorial archive series) Selections from the author's Leading part 1. [NK1484.A1O82 1977] 77-82360 ISBN 0-486-23553-X : 4.50
1. Design, Decorative—Japan. 2. Optical art—Japan. 3. Geometrical drawing. I. Title. BIP

TRADITIONS in 745.4'49'52
Japanese design, by Hirokazu Arakawa [and others] Photos. by Bin Takahashi. Translated by Alan Turney. [1st ed.] Tokyo, palo Alto, Calif., Kodansha International [1967- v. illus., col. plates. 25 x 26 cm. Captions in Japanese and English. Contents.Contents.—v. 1. Kacho: bird and flower motifs. [NK1484.T73] 67-16774
1. Design, Decorative—Japan. 2. Birds in art. 3. Flowers in art. I. Arakawa, Hirokazu.

Design, Decorative—Japan—Pictorial works.

JAPANESE border 745.4'49'52
designs / selected and edited by Theodore Menten. New York : Dover Publications, 1975. 93 p. : all ill. ; 24 cm. (Dover pictorial archive series) "A selection of illustrations from the Japanese book Kodai moshiki zuko." [NK1484.A1J36] 75-13124 ISBN 0-486-23180-1 pbk. : 2.00
1. Design, Decorative—Japan—Pictorial works. 2. Decoration and ornament—Japan—Pictorial works. I. Menten, Thomas

Design, Decorative—Mexico.

SHIPWAY, Verna (Cook) 1890- 729
Decorative design in Mexican homes, by Verna Cook Shipway, Warren Shipway. New York, Architectural Bk. [c.1966] xix, 249p. illus., plans. 28cm. [NK1414.S5] 66-18356 12.95
1. Design, Decorative—Mexico. 2. Decoration and ornament, Mexican. 3. Interior decoration. I. Shipway, Warren, joint author. II. Title. BIP

Design, Decorative—New York (City)—Direct.

KALINS, Dorothy G 745.4'025'7471
Researching design in New York: interiors, furniture, decorative arts, written and illustrated by Dorothy G. Kalins. New York, Fairchild Publications [1967] xv, 127 p. illus., plans. 23 cm. [NK460.N4K3] 67-22389

1. Design, Decorative—New York (City)—Direct. I. Title.

KALINS, Dorothy G. 745.4'025'7471
Researching design in New York: interiors, furniture, decorative arts, written and illustrated by Dorothy G. Kalins. New York, Fairchild Publications [1967] xv, 127 p. illus., plans. 23 cm. [NK460.N4K3] 67-22389
1. Design, Decorative—New York (City)—Direct. I. Title.

Design, Decorative — Plant forms.

BLOSSFELDT, Karl, 1865- 745
Art forms in nature; enlarged photographs of plant forms. With an introd. by Karl Nierendorf. New York, Universe Books [1967] 112 p. (chiefly illus.) 30 cm. [NK1560.B52] 67-14873
1. Design, Decorative — Plant forms. I. Title.

DAY, Lewis Foreman, 1845-1910. 745.4
Nature and ornament; nature, the raw material of design. With an additional chapter by Mary Hogarth. 2d ed., rev. Detroit, Gale Research Co., 1970. xv, 126 p. illus. 23 cm. "A facsimile reprint of the 1930 edition." [NK1553.D32 1930a] 74-137355
1. Design, Decorative—Plant forms. 2. Nature (Aesthetics) I. Hogarth, Mary. II. Title.

DAY, Lewis Foreman, 1845-1910. 745.4
Nature in ornament. 3d ed. London, B. T. Batsford, 1898. Detroit, Gale Research Co., 1971. xxiii, 260 p. illus. 19 cm. (Text books of ornamental design) [NK1553.D25 1971] 70-159852
1. Design, Decorative—Plant forms. 2. Nature (Aesthetics) I. Title. II. Series. BIP

DAY, Lewis Foreman, 1845-1910. 745.4
Nature in Ornament / Lewis F. Day. New York : Garland Pub., 1977. xxiii, 247 p., 123 leaves of plates : ill. ; 19 cm. (The Aesthetic movement & the arts and crafts movement ; 23) Reprint of the 1892 ed. published by B. T. Batsford, London, and Scribner, New York, in series: Text books of ornamental design. [NK1553.D25 1977] 76-17768 ISBN 0-8240-2472-9 lib.bdg. : 35.00
1. Design, Decorative—Plant forms. 2. Nature (Aesthetics) I. Title. II. Series. III. Series: Text-books of ornamental design.

HATTON, Richard George, 1864-1926. 745.44
Handbook of plant and floral ornament; selected from the herbals of the sixteenth century, and exhibiting the finest examples of plant-drawing found in those rare works, whether executed in wood-cuts or in copperplate engravings, arranged for the use of the decorator with supplementary illustrations and some remarks on the use of plant-form in design. New York, Dover Publications [1960] ix, 539p. illus. 24cm. 'Formerly titled: The craftsman's plant-book; or, Figures of plants.' 'List of the chief ancient herbals': p.49-50. [NK1560.H3 1960] 60-50719
1. Design, Decorative—Plant forms. 2. Botany—Pre-Linnean works. I. Title.

KLIMSCH, Karl, 1812-1890. 745.4'49'24
Florid Victorian ornament / Karl Klimsch. New York : Dover Publications, 1977. [52] leaves of plates : all ill. ; 29 cm. (Dover pictorial archive series) Reprint of the 1877? ed. published by Asher, London, under title: Ornaments invented & designed by Charles Klimsch. [NK1535.K55A52 1977] 76-58573 ISBN 0-486-23490-8 pbk. : 3.50
1. Klimsch, Karl, 1812-1890. 2. Design, Decorative—Plant forms. 3. Decoration and ornament—Victorian style. I. Title. BIP

LILLEY, A. E. V. 745.4
A book of studies in plant form with some suggestions for their application to design, by A. E. V. Lilley and W. Midgley. Detroit, Tower Books, 1971. xvi, 131 p. illus. 23 cm. Reprint of the 1895 ed. [NK1560.L7 1971] 70-89276
1. Design, Decorative—Plant forms. I. Midgley, W., joint author. II. Title.

MILES, Sally. 745.92'8
Natural collage : the making of pictures with seeds, leaves, and grasses / Sally Miles ; with line drawings by Anthony Loynes. New York : Scribner, c1973. 127 p. : ill. (some col.) ; 26 cm. Includes index. [NK1535.M47A52] 74-5964 ISBN 0-684-13895-6 : 9.95
1. Miles, Sally. 2. Design, Decorative—Plant forms. 3. Design, Decorative—Animal forms. 4. Collage. I. Title. BIP

PLANT and floral 769'.4'34
woodcuts for designers and craftsmen : 419 illustrations from the Renaissance herbal of Carolus Clusius / selected and arr. by Theodore Menten. New York : Dover Publications, 1974. 184 p. : chiefly ill. ; 29 cm. (Dover pictorial archive series) [QK41.L423P55 1974] 74-77285 ISBN 0-486-20722-6 pbk. : 4.00
1. L'Ecluse, Charles de, 1526-1609. Rariorum plantarium historia. 2. Design, Decorative—Plant forms. 3. Botany—Pictorial works. 4. Botany—Pre-Linnean works. I. Menten, Theodore. II. L'Ecluse, Charles de, 1526-1609. Rariorum plantarium historia. BIP

ROMNES, Harriet. 745.7'2
Rosemaling; an inspired Norwegian folk art. [Rev. 10th ed. Madison, Wis., 1970] 36 p. illus. (part col.), ports. 28 cm. [NK991.R6 1970] 78-19426
1. Design, Decorative—Plant forms. 2. Folk art—Norway. I. Title.

ROWE, William, 1941- 745.4
Flora and fauna design fantasies / by William Rowe. New York : Dover Publications, 1976. 72 p. : all. ill. ; 29 cm. (Dover pictorial archive series) [NK1560.R64] 75-43149 ISBN 0-486-23289-1 pbk. : 3.00
1. Design, Decorative—Plant forms. 2. Design, Decorative—Animal forms. I. Title. BIP

SEGUY, E. A. 745.4'49'24
Exotic floral patterns in color / by E.-A. Seguy. New York : Dover Publications, 1974. [5] p., 40 leaves of plates : col. ill. ; 31 cm. Unabridged republication of two of the author's portfolios originally published by C. Massin, Paris: Bouquets et frondaisons, published in 1926 and Suggestions pour etoffes et tapis, published in 1923. [NK9502.2.S43A45] 74-77178 ISBN 0-486-23041-4
1. Seguy, E. A. 2. Design, Decorative—Plant forms. I. Title. BIP

WADSWORTH, John W. 745.4
Designs from plant forms / John W. Wadsworth. New York : Universe Books, 1977. 124 p. : chiefly ill. ; 22 x 28 cm. Reprint of the 1910 ed. published by Chapman and Hall, London under title: Designing from plant forms. [NK1560.W3 1977] 76-21223 ISBN 0-87663-943-0 pbk. : 3.95
1. Design, Decorative—Plant forms. I. Title. BIP

WHITE, Gwen. 745.4
A world of pattern. Boston, C. T. Branford Co. [1958] 76 p. illus. (part col.) 21 x 27 cm. (A Life-up book) [NK1553.W46] 57-13044
1. Design, Decorative—Plant forms. 2. Design, Decorative—Animal forms. I. Title.

Design, Decorative—Russia.

GILLON, Edmund Vincent, comp. 745.4'4947
Russian geometric design and ornament; 374 illustrations for artists and designers. Selected by Edmund V. Gillon Jr. Magnolia, Mass., Peter Smith [1973 c1969] 66 p. of illus 28 cm. (Dover bk rebound) "The illustrations in this volume have been selected from Ornament by Y. Chernikhov, published (in Russian) by the author in Leningrad in 1930." [NK1456.A1G5 1969] 76-97126 ISBN 0-8446-4547-8 4.50
1. Design, Decorative—Russia. I. Chernikhov, Iakov Georgievich. Ornament. II. Title.

Design, Decorative—Themes, motives—History.

JUSTEMA, William, 1904- 745.4
Pattern : a historical panorama / William Justema. 1st ed. Boston : Little, Brown, c1976. p. cm. Includes index. Bibliography: p. [NK1520.J87] 76-8451 ISBN 0-8212-0665-6 : 15.00
1. Design, Decorative—Themes, motives—History. I. Title.

Design, Decorative—Tunisia.

REVAULT, Jacques. 746.7'961'1
Designs & patterns from North African carpets & textiles. New York, Dover Publications [1973] xii p., 121 p. of illus. 29 cm. (Dover pictorial archive series) "New selection ... of plates from the four portfolios of Tapis tunisiens, by L. Poinssot and J. Revault." [NK1487.85.A1R48 1973] 72-93604 ISBN 0-486-22850-9 3.50 (pbk.)
1. Design, Decorative—Tunisia. 2. Rugs, Tunisian. 3. Textile industry and fabrics, Tunisian. I. Poinssot, Louis. Tapis tunisiens. II. Title. BIP

Design, Decorative—United States.

CHAPMAN, Suzanne E. 745.4'49'73
Early American design motifs / Suzanne E. Chapman. 2d rev. & enl. ed. New York : Dover Publications, 1974. xviii, [i], 138 p., [4] leaves of plates : chiefly ill. ; 29 cm. (Dover pictorial archive series) Includes index. Bibliography: p. [xix] [NK1403.5.C45 1974] 73-86040 ISBN 0-486-23084-8 : 6.95 ISBN 0-486-22985-8 pbk. : 3.50
1. Design, Decorative—United States. I. Title.

LIPMAN, Jean (Herzberg), 1909- 745.4
American folk decoration. By Jean Lipman, with practical instruction by Eve Meulendyke. Magnolia, Mass., Peter Smith [1973, c1951] xii, 163 p. illus. 29 cm. (Dover bk rebound) [NK806.L5 1972] 77-182096 ISBN 0-8446-4573-7 5.00
1. Design, Decorative—United States. 2. Decoration and ornament—United States. 3. Folk art—United States I. Meulendyke, Eve. II. Title.

Design—Exhibitions.

CRANBROOK Academy of Art, Bloomfield Hills, Mich. Museum. 745.4'49'22
The creative spirit of Cranbrook; the early years: Eliel Saarinen, Loja Saarinen, Maija Grotell [and] Zoltan Sepeshy. Bloomfield Hills, Mich. [1972] 20 p. illus. 26 cm. Catalog of an exhibition held at the Museum Oct. 30, 1972-Oct. 14, 1973. Bibliography: p. 19. [NK410.B55C72 1972] 73-88751
1. Cranbrook Academy of Art, Bloomfield Hills, Mich. 2. Design—Exhibitions. I. Title.

Design—Finland.

HARD af Segerstad, Ulf. 745.2'09471
Modern Finnish design. New York, Praeger [1969] 62 p. illus., 64 plates (part col.) 20 cm. Translation of Finskt konsthantverk. [NK976.F5H313] 69-17304 4.50
1. Design—Finland. 2. Art industries and trade—Finland. I. Title.

Design—Great Britain—History—20th century.

LIVING by design / 745.4'49'41
the partners of Pentagram, Theo Crosby ... [et al.] ; editor, Peter Gorb. London : L. Humphries ; New York : Whitney Library of Design, 1978. 300 p. : ill. (some col.) ; 20 x 21 cm. [NK1535.P39L38] 77-95220 ISBN 0-8230-7355-6 (Whitney) : 15.00
1. Pentagram Design Partnership. 2. Design—Great Britain—History—20th century. I. Pentagram Design Partnership. II. Crosby, Theo. III. Gorb, Peter.

Design, Industrial.

ALGER, John R M 745.2
Creative synthesis in design [by] John R. M. Alger [and] Carl V. Hays. Englewood Cliffs, N.J. Prentice-Hall [1964] 92 p. illus. 24 cm. (Prentice-Hall series in engineering design) Bibliography: p. 87-89. [TA153.A38] 64-12216
1. Design, Industrial. I. Hays, Carl V, joint author. II. Title.

ANDERSON, Arthur D 745.2
A designer's notebook [by] Arthur D. Anderson. [1st ed.] Bloomington, Ill., McKnight & McKnight Pub. Co. [1966] xi, 228 p. illus. (part col.) 21 x 24 cm. [TT149,A5] 65-29122
1. Design, industrial. 2. Manual training. I. Title.

ASHFORD, Frederick Charles. 745.2
Designing for industry; some aspects of the product designer's work. New York, Philosophical Library [1955] 222p. illus. 23cm. [TS149] 55-12760
1. Design, Industrial. I. Title.

DOBLIN, Jay, 1920- 745.2
One hundred great product designs. New York, Van Nostrand Reinhold Co. [1970] 128 p. illus. 24 cm. [TS171.D63] 69-16381
1. Design, Industrial. I. Title.

DREYFUSS, Henry, 1904- 745.43
Designing for people. New York, Simon and Schuster, 1955. 240 p. illus. 25 cm. [NK1105.D7] 55-5950
1. Design, Industrial. 2. Human engineering. I. Title.

DREYFUSS, Henry, 1904- 745.2
A record of industrial designs, 1929 through 1947. New York [19--] unpaged. illus. 25cm. [TS149.D69] 56-47214
1. Design, Industrial. I. Title.

GEDDES, Norman Bel, 1893-1958. 745.4
Horizons. Freeport, N.Y., Books for Libraries Press [1972] xix, 293 p. illus. 29 cm. Reprint of the 1932 ed. [TS171.G43 1972] 72-92 ISBN 0-8369-9954-1
1. Design, Industrial. 2. Architecture—Designs and plans. I. Title.

GEDDES, Norman Bel, 1893-1958. 745.4
Horizons / Norman Bel Geddes. New York : Dover Publications, 1977. xix, 292 p. : ill. ; 26 cm. [TS171.G43 1977] 77-77637 ISBN 0-486-23514-9 : 6.95
1. Design, Industrial. 2. Architecture—Designs and plans. I. Title. BIP

HANKS, Kurt, 1947- 745.2
Design yourself! / Kurt Hanks, Larry Belliston, Dave Edwards. Experimental ed. Los Altos, Calif. : W. Kaufmann, 1977. 142 p. : ill. ; 28 cm. Includes index. Bibliography: p. 140. [TS171.H34] 76-56620 ISBN 0-913232-38-6 pbk. : 5.95
1. Design, Industrial. 2. Design. 3. Problem solving. I. Belliston, Larry, 1949- joint author. II. Edwards, Dave, 1949- joint author. III. Title. BIP

LEVENS, Alexander Sander, 1900- 744.422
Graphics, with an introduction to conceptual design. New York, Wiley [1962] 743 p. illus. 25 cm. [TA175.L4] 62-15183
1. Design, Industrial. 2. Engineering drawings. I. Title.

LEVENS, Alexander Sander, 1900- 744.4'22
Graphics, analysis and conceptual design [by] A. S. Levens. 2d ed. New York, Wiley [1968] xi, 771 p. illus. 25 cm. First ed. published in 1962 under title: Graphics, with an introduction to conceptual design. [T353.L628 1968] 67-29941
1. Design, Industrial. 2. Engineering graphics. I. Title. BIP

LINDBECK, John Robert. 745.4
Designing; today's manufactured products [by] John R. Lindbeck. [2d ed.] Bloomington, Ill., McKnight & McKnight Pub. Co. [1972] xiii, 400 p. illus. 24 cm. First ed. published in 1963 under title: Design textbook. Bibliography: p. 374-388. [TS171.L56 1972] 72-79110 ISBN 0-87345-440-5 9.32
1. Design, Industrial. I. Title. BIP

Design, Industrial—Vocational guidance.

ANGEL, Juvenal Londono 745.2069
Careers and opportunities in industrial design. New York, World Trade Academy Press, c.1960. 22p. illus. 27cm. (Modern vocational trends career monographs, 66) 60-3401 1.25 pap.,
1. Design, Industrial—Vocational guidance. I. Title.

PULOS, Arthur J. 745.2'023
Opportunities in industrial design careers, by Arthur J. Pulos. New York, Vocational Guidance Manuals [1970] 160 p. illus. 20 cm. (VGM career series, V175) Bibliography: p. 158. [TS171.4.P85] 70-111533
1. Design, Industrial—Vocational guidance. I. Title.

Design, Industrial—Yearbooks.

IDEA; international 745.058
design annual. 1953- New York, Wittenborn, Schultz. v. illus. 30cm. Vols. for 1953- have subtitle and text also in French and German. Editor: 1953- G. Hatje. [NK9.I33] 53-3014
1. Design, Industrial—Yearbooks. 2. Art and industry. I. Hatje, Gerd, ed.

Design—Juvenile literature.

HELFMAN, Harry Carmozin, 760'.028
1910-
Making designs by chance, by Harry Helfman. Photos. by the author. New York, Morrow, 1974. 47 p. illus. 23 cm. Describes various techniques for creating "accidental art" with common household objects. [NK1520.H44 1974] 73-16310 ISBN 0-688-20107-5 3.75
1. Design—Juvenile literature. I. Title. BIP

LOVOOS, Janice. 741
Design is a dandelion. San Carlos, Calif., Golden Gate Junior Books [1966] 62 p. illus. (part col.) 29 cm. [PZ10.L788De] 66-10802
1. Design—Juvenile literature. I. Title.

STEINEN, Robert, 1916- 745.4
Introduction to design / Robert Steinen. Englewood Cliffs, N.J. : Prentice-Hall, c1977. 117 p. : ill. ; 24 cm. (Modular exploration of technology series) Includes index. Presents basic facts about the history, elements, raw materials, process, and importance of design and considers the problem of combining function and aesthetics. [NK1510.S73] 76-18146 ISBN 0-13-481176-3 : 5.96 ISBN 0-13-481168-2 pbk. : 3.12
1. Design—Juvenile literature. I. Title.

Design services—Marketing.

BACHNER, John 658.8'09'74544'973
Philip.
Marketing and promotion for design professionals / John Philip Bachner, Naresh Kumar Khosla. New York : Van Nostrand Reinhold Co., c1977. xiv, 354 p. : ill. ; 24 cm. Includes index. [NK1504.B3 1977] 76-57975 ISBN 0-442-20478-7 : 17.95
1. Design services—Marketing. I. Khosla, Naresh Kumar, joint author. II. Title.

Design—Study and teaching.

EGGLESTON, John. 745.4'07'1041
Developments in design education / [by] John Eggleston. London : Open Books, 1976. x, 138 p. : ill., plans ; 21 cm. (The Changing classroom) Includes index. Bibliography: p. 133-136. [NK1170.E35] 77-361408 ISBN 0-7291-0097-9 : £3.90. ISBN 0-7291-0092-8 pbk.
1. Design—Study and teaching. I. Title. BIP

MAIER, Manfred. 745.4'07
Basic principles of design / Manfred Maier. New York : Van Nostrand Reinhold, 1977. 4 v. : ill. ; 30 cm. At head of title: The foundation program at the School of Design, Basel, Switzerland. Translation of Elementare Entwurfs- und Gestaltungsprozesse. Contents.Contents.—v. 1. Object drawing, object and museum drawing, nature drawing.—v. 2. Memory drawing, technical drawing and perspective, lettering.—v. 3. Material studies, textile design, color 2.—v. 4. Color 1, graphic exercises, dimensional design. [NK1170.M3413] 77-3493 ISBN 0-442-24977-2 (v. 1) : 10.00 per vol.
1. Design—Study and teaching. I. Basel. Kunstgewerbeschule. II. Title. BIP

ROWLAND, Kurt F. 745.2
Pattern and shape, by Kurt Rowland. New York, Van Nostrand Reinhold Co. [1964] 126 p. illus. 27 cm. (His Looking and seeing 1) Gives examples of patterns in the world around us and explains how they relate to "environment, social forces, and character." [NK1510.R6] 70-97064
1. Design—Study and teaching. 2. Design—Juvenile literature. I. Title.

Design—United States.

SHERWOOD, Ruth F. 643'.0973
Homes: today and tomorrow, by Ruth F. Sherwood, with George H. Sherwood. Peoria, Ill., C. A. Bennett Co. [1972] 496 p. illus. 25 cm. Includes bibliographies. [NK1403.A1S49] 72-80327 ISBN 0-87002-131-1
1. Design—United States. 2. Interior decoration—United States. 3. House buying. I. Title. BIP

Desks.

POPULAR homecraft. 684
24 desks: colonial, early American, modern Edited by Perry S. Graffam [Chicago, General Pub. Co., 1950] 80 p. illus., diagrs. 23 cm. (The Home workshop library) Hobby books. Cover title. Reprints of articles from Popular homecraft magazine. [TT197.5.D4P6] 50-14574
1. Desks. I. Graffam, Perry S., 1800- ed. II. Title.

Dessau Bauhaus.

BAYER, Herbert, 1900- ed. 709
Bauhaus, 1919-1928, ed. by Herbert Bayer, Walter Gropius [and] Isc Gropius. Boston, C. T. Branford Co., 1952. 223 p. illus., ports. 27 cm. Cover title: Bauhaus. Weimar. 1919-25; Dessau, 1925-28. [N332.D4B] A 52
1. Dessau Bauhaus. I. Title.

SCHLEMMER, Oskar, 1888- 792.025
1943.
The Theater of the Bauhaus [by] Oskar Schlemmer, Laszlo Moholy-Nagy [and] Farkas Molnar. Edited and with an introd. by Walter Gropius. Translated by Arthur S. Wensinger. [1st ed.] Middletown, Conn., Wesleyan University Press [1961] 109 p. illus. 26 cm. Translation of Die Buhne im Bauhaus. [N332.D4B83] 61-14239
1. Dessau. Bauhaus. 2. Theaters — Stage-setting and scenery. I. Title. BIP

Detmold, Edward Julius, 1883-1957.

DETMOLD, Edward Julius, 759.2
1883-1957.
The fantastic creatures of Edward Julius Detmold / edited by David Larkin ; introd. by Keith Nicholson. 1st U.S. ed. New York : Scribner, 1976. [96] p. : col. ill. ; 31 cm. [NC978.5.D47L37 1976c] 76-378147 ISBN 0-684-14587-1 : 12.00
1. Detmold, Edward Julius, 1883-1957. 2. Animals in art. I. Title. BIP

DETMOLD, Edward Julius, 759.2
1883-1957.
The fantastic creatures of Edward Julius Detmold / edited by David Larkin ; introd. by Keith Nicholson. Toronto ; New York : Peacock Press/Bantam Book, c1976. [14] p., [40] leaves of plates : col. ill. ; 30 cm. [NC978.5.D47L37 1976] 76-372121 6.95
1. Detmold, Edward Julius, 1883-1957. 2. Animals in art. I. Larkin, David. II. Title.

Detroit. Institute of Arts.

DETROIT. Institute of 708.174'34
Arts.
The Detroit Institute of Arts illustrated handbook. Frederick J. Cummings and Charles H. Elam, editors. Detroit, Published for the Detroit Institute of Arts by Wayne State University Press, 1971. 215 p. illus. 20 cm. [N560.A532] 76-168631 ISBN 0-8143-1457-0(hbd)
I. Cummings, Frederick J., ed. II. Elam, Charles H., ed. III. Title. BIP

DETROIT. 739.2'3'7714074017434
Institute of Arts.
Quebec and related silver at the Detroit Institute of Arts : [catalogue] / by Ross Allan C. Fox. Detroit : Published for Founders Society, Detroit Institute of Arts by Wayne State University Press, 1977. p. cm. Includes bibliographical references and index. [NK7113.A3Q33] 77-4850 ISBN 0-8143-1575-5 : 17.50
1. Detroit. Institute of Arts. 2. Silverwork—Quebec (Province)—Catalogs. 3. Church plate—Quebec (Province)—Catalogs. 4. Silversmiths—Quebec (Province)—Biography. I. Fox, Ross Allan C., 1945- II. Founders Society. III. Title. BIP

Detroit metropolitan area.

DOXIADES, 711.40977434
Konstantinos Apostalou, 1913-
Emergence and growth of an urban region: the developing urban Detroit area, by Constantinos A. Doziadis. [Detroit] Detroit Edison Co., 1966- v. illus. (part col.) maps (part col.) 29 cm. "Sources for figures": v. 1, p. 329-334. Contents.-- v. 1. Analysis. [HC108.D6D4] 66-29622
1. Detroit metropolitan area. 2. Great Lakes region — Econ. condit. I. I. Doxiades. Konstantinos Apostalou, 1913- II. Title. BIP

Detroit Publishing Company.

LOWE, James L. 769'.5
Detroit Publishing Company collectors' guide / James L. Lowe and Ben Papell. 1st ed. Newton Square, Pa. : Deltiologists of America, c1975. 288 p. : ill. ; 28 cm. Includes index. [NC1872.L59] 75-4127 ISBN 0-913782-07-6
1. Detroit Publishing Company. 2. Postal cards—Collectors and collecting. I. Papell, Ben, joint author. II. Title.

Detroit Society of Women Painters and Sculptors.

MOORE, Julia Gatlin, 706.2774
1875-
History of the Detroit Society of Women Painters and Sculptors, 1903-1953. [Detroit? 1953] 96p. illus. 24cm. [N11.D558M6] 53-25797
1. Detroit Society of Women Painters and Sculptors. I. Title.

Deutscher Werkbund.

CAMPBELL, Joan, 1929- 745'.06'243
The German Werkbund : the politics of reform in the applied arts / by Joan Campbell. Princeton, N.J. : Princeton University Press, 1977. p. cm. Includes index. Bibliography: p. [NK951.C35] 77-71974 ISBN 0-691-05250-6 : 20.00
1. Deutscher Werkbund. 2. Art industries and trade—Germany. I. Title. BIP

Devil—Art.

LEHNER, Ernst, 1895- 769'.4'87
Devils, demons, death, and damnation [by] Ernst and Johanna Lehner. New York, Dover Publications [1971] xvi, 174 p. (chiefly illus.) 28 cm. (Dover pictorial archive series) [N8140.L35] 72-137002 ISBN 0-486-22751-0 3.50
1. Devil—Art. 2. Death in art. 3. Hell in art. I. Lehner, Johanna, joint author. II. Title. BIP

Devonshire, Andrew Robert Buxton Cavendish, 11th duke of, 1920- —Art collections.

BYAM Shaw, James, 1903- 741.9'4
Old master drawings from Chatsworth; a loan exhibition from the Devonshire Collection. Introd. and catalogue by James Byam Shaw. Foreword by Thomas S. Wragg. [Meriden, Conn., Produced by the Meriden Gravure Co. and the Stinehour Press, Lunenburg, Vt., 1969] 50 p., [111] p. of illus. 26 cm. Circulated by the International Exhibitions Foundation, 1969-70. Participating museums: National Gallery of Art, Washington, D.C., and others. Includes bibliographies. [NC225.B9] 74-97171
1. Devonshire, Andrew Robert Buxton Cavendish, 11th duke of, 1920- —Art collections. 2. Drawings, European—Exhibitions. I. International Exhibitions Foundation. II. U.S. National Gallery of Art. III. Title.

Dewing, Arthur Stone, 1880-1971—Coin collections.

OLESON, John. 737.4'9'3807401444
Greek numismatic art : coins of the Arthur Stone Dewing collection / by John Oleson. [Cambridge] : Fogg Art Museum, Harvard University, 1975. [59] p. : ill. ; 18 x 21 cm. Errata slip inserted. Bibliography: p. [5] [CJ317.U62D486] 75-15059
1. Dewing, Arthur Stone, 1880-1971—Coin collections. 2. Coins, Greek. I. Title.

Dexter, Henry, 1806-1876.

ALBEE, John, 1833-1915. 730'.92'4
Henry Dexter, sculptor; a memorial, by John Albee. [Cambridge, Mass,] Priv. print., 1898. 117 p. front. (port.) 22 1/2 cm. "Catalogue of the works of Henry Dexter": p.[111]-117. [NB237.D5A3] 0-6994
1. Dexter, Henry, 1806-1876. I. Title.

Di Suvero, Mark, 1933—

DI SUVERO, Mark, 1933- 730'.92'4
Mark di Suvero : [exhibition], November 13, 1975-February 8, 1976, Whitney Museum of American Art, New York / James K. Monte. New York : The Museum, c1975. 92 p. : chiefly ill. (some col.) ; 24 x 26 cm. Bibliography: p. 90-92. [NB237.D57M66] 75-31046
1. Di Suvero, Mark, 1933- I. Monte, James K. II. Whitney Museum of American Art, New York.

Diamonds.

COPELAND, Lawrence L. 736.2
Diamonds, famous, notable and unique, by Lawrence L. Copeland. Artwork. design, photo by Jeanne G. M. Martin. [1st ed. Los Angeles] Gemological Inst. of Amer. [1966] ix, 188p. illus., col. plates, ports. 22cm. [TS753.C6] 66-6158 7.50
1. Diamonds. I. Gemological Institute of America. II. Title.
11940 San Vicente Blvd., Los Angeles, Calif. 90049

DICKINSON, Joan (Younger) 736.2
1916-
The book of diamonds: their history and romance from ancient India to modern times. Introd. by Harry Winston. New York, Crown [c.1965] ix, 226. [13]p. illus., facsim., map, ports. 24cm. [TS753.D5] 65-15844 5.95
1. Diamonds. I. Title.

DICKINSON, Joan (Younger) 736.2
1916-
The book of diamonds: their history and romance from ancient India to modern times. Introd. by Harry Winston. New York, Crown Publishers [1965] ix, 226, [13] p. illus., facsim., map, ports. 24 cm. Bibliography: p. [227]-[230] [TS753.D5] 65-15844
1. Diamonds. I. Title.

STREETER, Edwin William. 736'.23
The great diamonds of the world. Their history and romance. Collected from official, private, and other sources during many years of correspondence and inquiry, by Edwin W. Streeter. Edited and annotated by Joseph Hatton and A. H. Keane. Ann Arbor, Mich., Gryphon Books, 1971. 321 p. 22 cm. Reprint of the 1882 ed. [TS753.S91 1971] 76-78238
1. Diamonds. I. Title.

Diamonds—Dictionaries.

GEMOLOGICAL Institute of America. 736'.23'03
The diamond dictionary. 2d ed. / by Robert A. P. Gaal. Santa Monica, Calif. : Gemological Institute of America, 1977. vii, 342 p. : ill. ; 22 cm. Bibliography: p. 338-339. [TS753.G4 1977] 77-369451 ISBN 0-87311-008-0 : 16.95
1. Diamonds—Dictionaries. I. Gaal, Robert A. P. II. Title. BIP

Diazo compounds.

DINABURG, Maks Solomonovich. 773'.7
Photosensitive diazo compounds and their uses [by] M. S. Dinaburg; tr. from Russian by F. Lachman, ed. by D. J. Fry, E. A. Sutherns, others. London, New York, Focal 1967. 240p. tables, diagrs. 25cm. (Focal lib.) Tr. (romanized): Svetochuvstvitel'nye diazosoedineniia i ikh primenenie Bibl. [TP248.N8D513] 68-78636 35.00
1. Diazo compounds. 2. Photochemistry. 3. Copying processes. I. Title.

Dickens, Charles, 1812-1870—Illustrations.

BROWNE, Hablot Knight, 1815-1882. 767.2
Phiz illustrations from the novels of Charles Dickens, by Albert Johannsen. [Chicago] University of Chicago Press [1956] xi, 442 p. illus., ports. 23 x 28 cm. "Corrigenda" slip inserted. Bibliography: p. ix. [NE2195.B77J6] 56-10998
1. Dickens, Charles, 1812-1870—Illustrations. I. Johannsen, Albert, 1871-1962. II. Title.

Dickens, Charles—Illustrations.

BROWNE, Habiot Knight, 1815-1882. 767.2
Phiz illustrations from the novels of Charles Dickens, by Albert Johannsen. [Chicago] University of Chicago Press [1956] xi, 442p. illus., ports. 22x28cm. 'Corrigenda' slip inserted. Bibliography: p. ix. [NE2195.B77J6] 56-10998
1. Dickens, Charles—Illustrations. I. Johannsen, Albert, 1871- II. Title.

Dickinson, Edwin Walter, 1891-

THE Dickinson family heritage: paintings and drawings, by Edwin Dickinson; [exhibition] presented by the Institute of Contemporary Art and the Weeden Gallery, October 11-November 7, 1970, Weeden Gallery ... Boston. [Boston, Printed by Unique Press, 1970] 24 p. illus., ports. 26 cm. Bibliography: p. 21-22. [ND237.D46D5] 72-141054 759.13
I. Dickinson, Edwin Walter, 1891- II. Boston. Institute of Contemporary Art. III. Weeden Gallery.

WHITNEY, Museum of American Art, New York 759.13
Edwin Dickinson, by Lloyd Goodrich. New York, Author [c.1965] 55p. illus. (pt. col.) ports. (pt. col.) 25cm. Catalog of an exhibition held at the Whitney Mus., Oct. 20-Nov. 28, 1965. Bibl. [ND237.D46W5] 65-29633 2.00 pap.,
1. Dickinson, Edwin Walter, 1891- I. Goodrich. Lloyd, 1897- II. Title.

WHITNEY Museum of American Art, New York. 759.13
Edwin Dickinson, by Lloyd Goodrich. New York, Published for the Whitney Museum of American Art, by Praeger [1966, c1965] 55 p. illus. (part col.) 25 cm. Catalog of an exhibition held at the Whitney Museum of American Art. Bibliography: p. 53-54. [ND237.D46W5] 65-28405
1. Dickinson, Edwin Walter, 1891- I. Goodrich, Lloyd, 1897- II. Title.

Die Brucke (Dresden)

CORNELL University. Andrew Dickson White Museum of Art. 759.3'074'0147
Brucke. [Exhibition] Andrew Dickson White Museum of Art, Cornell University, Feb. 11 to Mar. 22, 1970 [and] Memorial Art Gallery, University of Rochester, Apr. 2 to May 10, 1970. [Ithaca, Cornell University, Office of University Publications, 1970] 29, [65] p. illus. (part col.) 26 cm. Label mounted on t.p.: Supplied by Worldwide Books, Boston. [N6868.5.E9C6] 77-112768
1. Die Brucke (Dresden) 2. Art, German—Exhibitions. I. Rochester, N.Y. University. Memorial Art Gallery.

Diebenkorn, Richard, 1922-

DIEBENKORN, Richard, 1922- 759.13
Richard Diebenkorn : paintings and drawings, 1943-1976 / with essays by Robert T. Buck, Jr. ... [et al.]. Buffalo : Albright-Knox Art Gallery, c1976. 122 p. : ill. (some col.) ; 28 cm. Exhibition held at the Albright-Knox Art Gallery, Buffalo, N.Y., Nov. 12, 1976-Jan. 9, 1977, and at other museums. [ND237.D465B8] 76-47104 ISBN 0-914782-07-X : 9.50
1. Diebenkorn, Richard, 1922- I. Buck, Robert T. II. Albright-Knox Art Gallery.

WASHINGTON, D. C. Gallery of Modern Art. 759.13
Richard Diebenkorn; [a retrospective exhibition organized by the Washington Gallery of Modern Art. Washington, 1965] 37 p. illus. (part col.) 27 cm. "Washington Gallery of Modern Art, Washington, D. C., Nov. 6 to Dec. 31. 1964. The Jewish Museum, New York, Jan 13 to Feb. 21, 1965. Pavillion Gallery, Newport Beach, California, Mar. 14 to Apr. 15, 1965." Bibliography: p. 56-57. [ND237.D465W3] 66-2735
1. Diebenkorn, Richard, 1922- I. Jewish Theological Seminary of America. Jewish Museum. II. Balboa, Calif. Pavillion Gallery. III. Title.

Diehl, Gaston.

MATISSE, Henri, 1869-1954 759.4
Matisse, by Gaston Diehl. New York, Crown [1963] 36p. chiefly illus. (pt. col.) 18cm. (Little bks. on great artists)gbBiographical sketch in French, English, and German. 63-24494 .69 bds.,
1. Diehl, Gaston. I. Title.

Differential equations.

CHORLTON, Frank 517.38
Art in Life. Supplement--1965. New York, Scarecrow [c.]1965. 379p. 23cm. First suppl. covers the years 1957-63. [N7525.C55] 65-13552 8.50
1. Differential equations. 2. Difference equations. I. Title.

Dine, james 1935—

DINE, James. 709'.24
Jim Dine, by John Gordon. New York, Published for the Whitney Museum of American Art by Praeger [1970] 1 v. (unpaged) illus. (part col.), ports. 27 cm. "Published on the occasion of the ... retrospective exhibition of the work of Jim Dine, held at the Whitney Museum of American Art from February 27 through April 19, 1970." Includes bibliography, by L. W. Seaberg. [N6537.D5G6] 72-116144 6.95
I. Gordon, John, 1912- II. Whitney Museum of American Art, New York. III. Title.

DINE, James. 769'.92'4
Jim Dine prints, 1970-1977. 1st ed. New York : Published in association with the Williams College artist-in-residence program by Harper & Row, c1977. 134 p. : ill. (some col.) ; 31 cm. (Icon editions) Catalogue of an exhibition held Oct. 3-Nov. 5, 1976, at Williams College Museum of Art and at other places. Bibliography: p. 131-134. [NE539.D5A4 1977] 77-3758 ISBN 0-06-430083-8 : 11.00
1. Dine, James—Exhibitions. I. Williams College. Museum of Art. II. Title. BIP

DINE, Jim, 1935- 709'.2'4
Jim Dine, the Summers Collection; an exhibition organized by the La Jolla Museum of Contemporary Art, La Jolla, California, May 18-July 7, 1974. La Jolla, Calif., La Jolla Museum of Contemporary Art, 1974] [28] p. illus. 28 cm. Bibliography: p. [26] [N6537.D5L34] 74-81586
1. Dine, Jim, 1935- 2. Summers, Gene R.—Art collections. I. La Jolla Museum of Contemporary Art.

Diners and dining in art.

DINING & drinking / under the general editorship of Harold H. Hart ; compiled by Pam Pollack. New York : Hart Pub. Co., c1977. 96 p. : all ill. ; 32 cm. (Hart picture archives) Bibliography: p. 95-96. [N8217.D67D56] 77-151873 ISBN 0-8055-1211-X : 10.95 ISBN 0-8055-0304-8 pbk. : 4.95 769'.4'939412
1. Diners and dining in art. 2. Drinking in art. 3. Pictures. I. Pollack, Pam. BIP

Diners (Restaurants) in art.

BAEDER, John. 759.13
Diners / by John Baeder. New York : H. N. Abrams, [1978] p. cm. [ND237.B215A44] 77-13203 ISBN 0-8109-2078-6 pbk. : 7.95
1. Baeder, John. 2. Diners (Restaurants) in art. I. Title. BIP

Dining room furniture.

POPULAR homecraft. 684
Dining room furniture; 5 suites, 15 odd pieces. Edited by Perry S. Graffam. [Chicago, General Pub. Co., 1950] 96 p. illus., diagrs. 23 cm. (The Home workshop library) Hobby books. Cover title. Reprints of articles from Popular homecraft magazine. [TT197.5.D5P6] 50-14573
1. Dining room furniture. I. Graffam, Perry S. 1890- ed. II. Title.

Dining rooms.

LOFTIE, M. J. 747'.7
The dining-room / by M. J. Loftie. The drawing-room / by Lucy Orrinsmith. The bedroom and boudoir / by Lady Barker. New York : Garland Pub., 1978. 423 p. in various pagings : ill. ; 19 cm. (Reprint of 3 works: the 1st published in 1878; the 2d in 1877, and the 3d in 1878, by MacMillan, London, in the Art at home series.) (The Aesthetic movement & the arts and crafts movement) [NK2117.D5L64] 76-18321 ISBN 0-8240-2461-3 : 35.00
1. Dining rooms. 2. Living rooms. 3. Bedrooms. 4. Interior decoration—Great Britain. I. Orrinsmith, Lucy. The drawing room. 1978. II. Broome, Mary Anne Stewart Barker, Lady, 1831-1911. The bedroom and the boudoir. 1978. III. Title. IV. Series. V. Series: Art at home series.

MEYER, Genevieve. 747'.76
Dining rooms. Garden City, N.Y., Doubleday [1970] 70 p. illus. (part col.) 24 cm. (The Doubleday home decorating program) [NK2117.M38] 70-22642
1. Dining rooms. 2. Interior decoration.

Dinnerstein, Harvey.

DINNERSTEIN, Harvey. 759.13
Harvey Dinnerstein : artist at work / by Harvey Dinnerstein. New York : Watson-Guptill, 1978. p. cm. Includes index. Bibliography: p. [N6537.D52A4 1978] 78-17847 ISBN 0-8230-2210-2 : 18.50
1. Dinnerstein, Harvey. 2. Art—Technique. I. Title: Artist at work. BIP

Dinosauria in art.

AMES, Lee J. 743'.6
Draw 50 dinosaurs and other prehistoric animals / Lee J. Ames ; with a foreword by George Zappler. 1st. ed. Garden City, N.Y. : Doubleday, c1977. [63] p. : ill. ; 32 cm. Step-by-step instructions for drawing fifty different dinosaurs and other prehistoric animals. [NC780.A482] 76-7285 ISBN 0-385-11134-7 : 5.95.
1. Dinosauria in art. 2. Extinct animals in art. 3. Animal painting and illustration. I. Title.

Diplomats—United States—Correspondence, reminiscences, etc.

BERRY, Burton Yost. 704'.7 B
Out of the past : the Istanbul Grand Bazaar / by Burton Y. Berry ; illustrated by Azzedine El-Aaji. New York : Arco Pub. Co., c1976. p. cm. [N5220.B46A52] 74-29791 ISBN 0-668-03778-4 : 12.50
1. Berry, Burton Yost—Art collections. 2. Istanbul. Kapalicarsi. 3. Diplomats—United States—Correspondence, reminiscences, etc. I. Title. BIP

Disney, Walt, 1901-1966.

FINCH, Christopher. 791'.092'4
The art of Walt Disney: from Mickey Mouse to the Magic Kingdoms. New concise ed. New York, H. N. Abrams [1975] 160 p. illus. (part col.) 29 cm. [NC1766.U52D533 1975] 74-8435 ISBN 0-8109-9007-5 45.00
1. Disney, Walt, 1901-1966. 2. Disney (Walt) Productions. I. Title.

FINCH, Christopher. 791'.092'4
The art of Walt Disney; from Mickey Mouse to the Magic Kingdoms. With a special essay by Peter Blake. New York, H. N. Abrams [1973] 458 p. illus. (part col.) 35 cm. Bibliography: p. [453]-454. [NC1766.U52D53] 73-4639 ISBN 0-8109-0122-6 45.00
1. Disney, Walt, 1901-1966. 2. Disney (Walt) Productions. I. Title. BIP

Disney (Walt) Productions.

DISNEY (Walt) Productions. 769'.5
The Disney poster book / introd. by Maurice Sendak. New York : Harmony Books, c1977. 47 p. : chiefly col. ill. ; 39 cm. [NC1850.D5744 1977] 76-56735 ISBN 0-517-52936-X pbk. : 5.95
1. Disney (Walt) Productions. 2. Posters, American. I. Title. BIP

Disney (Walt) Productions—Collectibles.

MUNSEY, Cecil. 745'.075
Disneyana : Walt Disney collectibles / Cecil Munsey. New York : Hawthorn Books, [1974] xiv, 385 p., [8] leaves of plates : ill. (some col.) ; 29 cm. Includes index. [NK808.M86 1974] 73-19381 ISBN 0-8015-2138-6 : 19.95
1. Disney (Walt) Productions—Collectibles. I. Title.

Disney (Walt) Productions—History.

MICKEY Mouse : 741.5'973
fifty happy years / edited by David Bain and Bruce Harris. New York : Harmony Books : distributed by Crown Publishers, c1977. p. cm. Filmography: p. [NC1766.U52D55 1977] 77-11076 ISBN 0-517-52962-9 : 10.00
1. Disney (Walt) Productions—History. 2. Mickey Mouse (Cartoon character) I. Bain, David, 1949- II. Harris, Bruce S. BIP

Disneyland.

EVANS, Alfred Morgan, 1910- 712.6
Walt Disney Disneyland world of flowers, by Morgan Evans. Color photos. by William C. Aplin [others] Burbank, Calif., Walt Disney Productions, 1965. 72p. col. illus., port. 29cm. [SB479.D5E8] 65-9518 price unreported
1. Disneyland. 2. Landscape gardening—California, Southern. I. Aplin William C., illus. II. Title. III. Title: Disneyland world of flowers.

Display of collectibles—Handbooks, manuals, etc.

WILLIAM, V. A. 069'.53
Keepsake crafts : a craft book showing how to display keepsakes, collectibles, and antiques : 140 ideas with history and illustrations of each item / by V. A. William. Des Moines : Wallace-Homestead Book Co., c1977. 202 p. : ill. ; 28 cm. [NK805.W48] 77-152227 ISBN 0-87069-195-3 : 9.95

1. Display of collectibles—Handbooks, manuals, etc. 2. Americana. I. Title.

Display of merchandise.

KASPAR, Karl. 747'.8'521
Shops and showrooms: an international survey. [Translated from the German by Lieselotte Mickel] New York, F. A. Praeger [1967] 167 p. illus., plans. 29 cm. English and German. Translation of Ladenbauten - international. [HF5845.K3] 67-20402
1. Display of merchandise. I. Title.

Display of merchandise—Pictorial works.

THE Golden age of shop 747'.8'521
design : European shop interiors, 1880-1939 / edited by Alexandra Artley. New York : Whitney Library of Design, 1976, c1975. 128 p. : chiefly ill. ; 31 cm. Bibliography: p. 128. [HF5845.G54 1976] 75-19437 ISBN 0-8230-7215-0 : 22.50
1. Display of merchandise—Pictorial works. 2. Department stores—Europe—History—Pictorial works. I. Artley, Alexandra. BIP

Dissident art—Russia.

GOLOMSHTOK, I. N. 709'.47
Soviet art in exile / by Igor Golomshtok and Alexander Glezer ; introd. by Sir Roland Penrose ; edited by Michael Scammell. 1st American ed. New York : Random House, c1977. p. cm. Bibliography: p. [N6988.G58 1977] 77-3344 ISBN 0-394-41644-9 : 17.50
1. Dissident art—Russia. 2. Art, Modern—20th century—Russia. 3. Dissenters, Artistic—Russia—Biography. I. Glezer, Aleksandr, joint author. II. Title. BIP

KOMAR, Vitali. 759.7
Komar/Melamid, two Soviet dissident artists / edited by Melvyn B. Nathanson ; with an introd. by Jack Burnham. Carbondale : Southern Illinois University Press, c1979. xxxix, 59 p. : ill. ; 29 cm. Bibliography: p. xiii. [ND699.K557A4 1979] 78-14254 ISBN 0-8093-0887-8 : 15.00
1. Komar, Vitali. 2. Melamid, Aleksandr. 3. Dissident art—Russia. I. Melamid, Aleksandr, joint author. II. Nathanson, Melvyn B., 1944- III. Title.

Dixon, Maynard, 1875-1946.

BURNSIDE, Wesley M. 759.13
Maynard Dixon, artist of the West [by] Wesley M. Burnside. Provo, Utah, Brigham Young University Press [1973] xvi, 237 p. illus. (part col.) 28 x 34 cm. Developed from the author's thesis, Ohio State University, 1970. "250 limited special edition." Bibliography: p. 225-227. [ND237.D5B87] 73-18262 ISBN 0-8425-0912-7 28.95
1. Dixon, Maynard, 1875-1946. 2. The West in art. I. Dixon, Maynard, 1875-1946. II. Title.

Do-it-yourself work—Dictionaries.

COMPLETE handyman do-it- 643'.7
yourself encyclopedia : a compilation of special interest projects and manuals for the repair and care of homes, autos, appliances, hobby equipment / by the editors of Science & mechanics. New York : H. S. Stuttman Co., c1978- v. : ill. ; 27 cm. [TT9.C65 1978] 78-101407 ISBN 0-87475-700-2 : 112.00 (21 vols.)
1. Do-it-yourself work—Dictionaries. I. Science and mechanics. II. Title: Do-it-yourself.

Dodgson, Campbell, 1867-1948.

DURER, Albrecht, 1471-1528 760'.0924
Albrecht Durer; engravings and etchings, by Campbell Dodgson. New York, Da Capo, 1967. xii, 145p. illus. 27cm. (Da Capo Pr. ser. in graphic art, v. 1) Da Capo Pr. reprint edn. Reprint of 1st ed., London, 1926. [NE654.D9A54 1967] 67-27451 12.50
1. Dodgson, Campbell, 1867-1948. I. Title.

Dodgson, Charles Lutwidge, 1832-1898.

GERNSHEIM, Helmut, 1913- 928.2
Lewis Carroll, photographer. With 64 plates in photogravure. [2d ed.] New York, Chanticleer Press, 1950. xi, 126p. illus., ports. 23cm. Bibliography: p. 103-104. [PR4612.G4 1950] 52-67456
1. Dodgson, Charles Lutwidge, 1832-1898. I. Title.

GERNSHEIM, Helmut, 1913- 770'.924
Lewis Carroll, photographer. Rev. ed. New York, Dover Publications [1969] ix, 127 p., [62] p. of ports. illus. 24 cm. Includes bibliographical references. [PR4612.G4 1969] 68-8045 2.50
1. Dodgson, Charles Lutwidge, 1832-1898.

Dodgson, Charles Lutwidge, 1832-1898 —Criticism and interpretation—Addresses, essays, lectures.

LEWIS Carroll observed 828'.8'09
: a collection of unpublished photographs, drawings, poetry, and new essays / edited by Edward Guiliano for the Lewis Carroll Society of North America. New York : C. N. Potter : distributed by Crown Publishers, c1976. viii, 216 p. : ill. ; 29 cm. Includes index. Bibliography: p. 208-209. [PR4612.L454 1976] 76-14836 ISBN 0-517-52497-X : 12.95
1. Dodgson, Charles Lutwidge, 1832-1898 —Criticism and interpretation—Addresses, essays, lectures. I. Guiliano, Edward. II. Lewis Carroll Society of North America.

Doesburg, Theo van, 1883-1931.

BALJEU, Joost. 709'.2'4 B
Theo van Doesburg. [1st American ed.] New York, Macmillan [1974] 232 p. illus. (part col.) 26 cm. Bibliography: p. 205-219. [N6953.D57B34 1974] 74-7400 ISBN 0-02-506440-1 15.95
1. Doesburg, Theo van, 1883-1931. I. Doesburg, Theo van, 1883-1931. Selected works. 1974.

Dogs—Car1catures and cartoons.

MCKIE, Roy. 741.5
The dog; a cartoon inquiry concerning man's relationship to his best friend. New York, Simon and Schuster [1954] unpaged (chiefly illus.) 25cm. [NC1429.M245A44] 54-3861
1. Dogs—Car1catures and cartoons. I. Title. BIP

Dogs—Caricatures and cartoons.

ANDERSON, Brad. 741.5'973
The Marmaduke treasury / by Brad Anderson ; foreword by Charles M. Schulz. Kansas City : Sheed, Andrews, and McMeel, c1978. 224 p. : chiefly ill. (some col.) ; 29 cm. (Sheed, Andrews, and McMeel treasury series) [NC1429.A58A4 1978] 78-54706 ISBN 0-8362-1108-1 : 12.95. ISBN 0-8362-1107-3 pbk. : 7.95
1. Dogs—Caricatures and cartoons. 2. American wit and humor, Pictorial. I. Title. BIP

STEADMAN, Ralph. 741.5'942
Dogs bodies / Ralph Steadman. New York : Paddington Press : distributed by Grosset & Dunlap, c1977. [32] p. : chiefly ill. ; 23 cm. [NC1479.S79A44] 76-62523 ISBN 0-448-22975-7 : 1.25
1. Dogs—Caricatures and cartoons. 2. English wit and humor, Pictorial. I. Title. BIP

Dogs in art.

COOK, Gladys Emerson, 1899- 743.6974442
Drawing dogs. New York, Pitman Pub. Corp. [1958] 1 v. unpaged. illus. 20 x 26 cm. (Pitman drawing series) [NC780.C62] 58-9183
1. Dogs in art. I. Title. BIP

THORNE, Diana, 1895- 743.6974442
How to draw the dog, a technical treatise; illustrated by the author. [1st ed.] New York, Watson-Guptill Publications, 1950. vii, 82 p. illus. 27 cm. (Step-by-step series) [NC780.T52] 50-7890
1. Dogs in art. I. Title.

Dogs in art—Juvenile literature.

FRAME, Paul, 1913- 743'.69'74442
Drawing dogs and puppies / by Paul Frame. New York : F. Watts, 1978. 72 p. : ill. ; 26 cm. (A How-to-draw book) A step-by-step guide to drawing dogs and puppies including a list of basic materials and warm-up exercises to improve drawing technique. [NC780.F68] 78-5289 ISBN 0-531-01452-5 lib. bdg. : 5.90
1. Dogs in art—Juvenile literature. 2. Drawing—Technique—Juvenile literature. I. Title.

Dogs—Pictorial works.

ERWITT, Elliott. 779'.32
Son of bitch / by Elliott Erwitt ; unleashed by P. G. Wodehouse. New York : Grossman Publishers, 1974. 127 p. : chiefly ill. ; 26 cm. [SF430.E78 1974] 73-16568 ISBN 0-670-65722-0 : 15.00. ISBN 0-670-00582-7 pbk. : 5.95
1. Dogs—Pictorial works. I. Title.

Dogs—Pictures, illustrations, etc.

SENSENEY, Dan. 779.32
Dogs. Photos by Walter Chandoha. New York, Random House [1957] 144p. illus. 24cm. [SF430] 57-7814
1. Dogs—Pictures, illustrations, etc. I. Chandoha, Walter, illus. II. Title.

SENSENEY, Dan. 779.32
Dogs: facts, lore, legends, all popular breeds. Over 100 photos. by Walter Chandoha. [New York, Maco Magazine Corp., c1957] 144p. illus. 24cm. (Maco 58) [SF430.S4] 58-37975
1. Dogs—Pictures, illustrations, etc. I. Chandoha, Walter, illus. II. Title.

Doilies.

CROCHETING doilies / 746.9'6
edited by Rita Weiss. New York : Dover Publications, 1976. 47 p. : ill. ; 29 cm. (Dover needlework series) [TT825.C754 1976] 76-24565 ISBN 0-486-23424-X pbk. : 1.50
*1. Doilies. 2. Crocheting. I. Weiss, Rita.*BIP

Dolce, Lodovico, 1508-1568.

ROSKILL, Mark W., 1933- 759
Dolce's Aretino and Venetian art theory of the Cinquecento, by Mark W. Roskill. [New York] Published for the College Art Association of America by New York University Press, 1968. 354 p. front. 22 cm. (Monographs on archaeology and fine arts, 15) Revision of the author's thesis, Princeton, 1961. Includes text and translation of Dolce's L'Aretino. Bibliographical footnotes. [ND1130.D573R6] 68-19901
1. Dolce, Lodovico, 1508-1568. L'Aretino. 2. Painting—Early works to 1800. I. Title. II. Series.

Dolet, Etienne, 1508-1546.

CHRISTIE, Richard Copley, 1830-1901. 686.2'092'4 B
Etienne Dolet, the martyr of the Renaissance, 1508-1546; a biography. New ed., rev. and corr. Freeport, N.Y., Books for Libraries Press [1972] p. Reprint of the 1899 ed. Bibliography: p. [Z232.D66C5 1972] 72-8440 ISBN 0-8369-6999-5
1. Dolet, Etienne, 1508-1546.

Doll clothes.

ANDERTON, Johana Gast. 745.59'22
Sewing for twentieth century dolls. North Kansas City [Mo.] Trojan Press [1972] 264 p. illus. 29 cm. [TT175.7.A5] 72-77829 17.50
1. Doll clothes. I. Title. BIP

BAILEY, Albina. 745.59'22
Dressing dolls in nineteenth century fashions / Albina Bailey. North Kansas City, Mo. : Athena Pub. Co., 1975. 200 p., [1] leaf of plates : ill. ; 29 cm. Bibliography: p. 193. [TT175.7.B34] 74-29003
1. Doll clothes. 2. Costume—History—19th century. I. Title. BIP

BARLOW, Iola. 745.5922
Dolls in national costume. Newton, Mass., C. T. Branford [1966] 87 p. illus. 22 cm. [TT715.B37 1966a] 66-18103
1. Doll clothes. I. Title. BIP

CARTER, Eleanor-Jean. 745.59'22
Doll modes; doll fashions with patterns. [Hyattsville, Md., Carter Craft Doll House, 1972- v. illus. 28 cm. Contents.Contents.—[1] 10"-12" dolls, 1900-1930. [TT175.7.C37] 72-76726
1. Doll clothes. I. Title.

CRAVEN, Winifred M. 745.5922
Costume dolls and how to make them, by Winifred M. Craven. London, I. Pitman [1962] 109p. illus. 26cm. [TT715.C7 1962] 66-31345 6.75 bds.,
1. Doll clothes. 2. Dolls. I. Title.

JOHNSON, Audrey. 745.59'22
Dressing dolls. Newton, Mass., C. T. Branford Co. [1969] 191 p. illus. 28 cm. [TT715.J6 1970] 69-19643
1. Doll clothes. 2. Dollmaking. I. Title. BIP

ROTH, Charlene Davis, 1945- 745.59'22
Dressing dolls : clothing patterns for rag, baby, toddler, older action and fashion dolls, and many, many others / Charlene Davis Roth ; photography, by James A. Davis. New York : Crown Publishers, c1976. vii, 112 p., [2] leaves of plates : ill. ; 28 cm. Includes index. [TT175.7.R67] 76-801 ISBN 0-517-52393-0 pbk. : 4.95
1. Doll clothes. I. Title. BIP

Doll clothes—Collectors and collecting.

COLEMAN, Dorothy S. 745.59'22
The collector's book of dolls' clothes : costumes in miniature, 1700-1929 / by Dorothy S., Elizabeth A., and Evelyn J. Coleman. New York : Crown Publishers, [1975] 794 p., [8] leaves of plates : ill. ; 29 cm. Includes index. Bibliography: p. 623-624. [NK4893.C59 1975] 75-9564 ISBN 0-517-52031-1 : 25.00
1. Doll clothes—Collectors and collecting. I. Coleman, Elizabeth A., joint author. II. Coleman, Evelyn J., joint author. III. Title. BIP

Doll clothes—Juvenile literature.

HOLLIS, Nesta. 745.59'22
Top outfits for teenage dolls; a doll-dressing book designed for the popular "teenage" dolls ... By Nesta Hollis with Valerie Janitch. Illus. by Nesta Hollis. Diagrs. by Roger Handcock. Photos. by Alphaplus Ltd. New York, Taplinger Pub. Co. [1973, c1972] 110 p. illus. (part col.) 29 cm. Instructions and patterns for making thirty-six outfits for teenage dolls, including pants suit, bathing suit, rain coat, riding outfit, and bridal gown. [TT175.7.H64 1973] 72-7215 ISBN 0-8008-7768-3 9.95
1. Doll clothes—Juvenile literature. 2. Sewing—Juvenile literature. I. Janitch, Valerie. II. Title. BIP

Doll furniture.

FALK, Kathryn. 745.59'23
Miniature needlepoint and sewing projects for dollhouses / by Kathryn Falk and the staff of Mini Mundus ; photos. by Sydnie Michel. New York : Hawthorn Books, c1977. 184 p. : ill. ; 29 cm. Includes index. Bibliography: p. 167-168. [TT175.5.F34 1977] 76-53393 ISBN 0-8015-5072-6 : 12.95
1. Doll furniture. 2. Canvas embroidery. 3. Sewing. I. Michel, Sydnie. II. Mini Mundus Shop. III. Title. BIP

GLICK, Ruth, 1942- 745.59'23
Dollhouse furniture you can make / by Ruth Glick and Nancy Baggett ; photos. by Charlie C. Baggett, Jr. ; ill. by Christine

P. Tischer. South Brunswick, N.J. : A. S. Barnes, c1977. p. cm. Presents step-by-step directions for building a doll house and using household items to make furniture, accessories, and appliances. [TT175.5.G54] 76-50189 ISBN 0-498-01994-2 : 12.00
1. Doll furniture. I. Baggett, Nancy, 1943- joint author. II. Baggett, Charlie C. III. Tischer, Christine P. IV. Title. BIP

JOHNSON, Audrey. 745.59'23
Furnishing dolls' houses. Newton Centre, Mass., C. T. Branford Co. [1972] 284 p. illus. 26 cm. [TT175.5.J64 1972b] 72-75079
1. Doll furniture. 2. Doll-houses. I. Title. BIP

MCELROY, Joan 745.59'23
Joan McElroy's dolls' house furniture book / by Joan McElroy. 1st ed. New York : Knopf : distributed by Random House, 1976. p. cm. Includes index. Bibliography: p. [TT175.5.M28 1976] 76-13703 ISBN 0-394-40057-7 : 15.00
1. Doll furniture. I. Title. II. Title: Dolls' house furniture book. BIP

MERCER, Eileen. 688.723
Let's make doll furniture. Photos. and drawings by H. Lee McQuilliams. [1st ed.] New York, Harper [1962] 114 p. illus. 22 cm. [TT200.M4] 62-9898
1. Doll furniture. I. Title. BIP

MERCER, Eileen. 745.59'23
Let's make doll furniture / by Eileen Mercer ; photos. and drawings by H. Lee McQuilliams. New York : Schocken Books, 1975, c1962. p. cm. Reprint of the ed. published by Harper, New York. [TT175.5.M47 1975] 75-13753 ISBN 0-8052-3601-5 : 5.95
1. Doll furniture. I. Title.

MIDKIFF, Pat. 745.59'23
Colonial furniture for doll houses & miniature rooms / Pat Midkiff. New York : Drake Publishers, 1977, c1976. 123 p. : ill. ; 28 cm. [TT175.5.M5 1977] 76-27807 ISBN 0-8473-1405-7 : 5.95
1. Doll furniture. 2. Furniture, Colonial. I. Title. BIP

ROCHE, Patricia K. 745.59'23
Dollhouse magic : how to make and find simple dollhouse furniture / by P. K. Roche ; drawings by Richard Cuffari ; photos. by John Knott. New York : Dial Press, c1977. p. cm. [TT175.5.R6] 76-42932 ISBN 0-8037-2122-6 : 6.95. ISBN 0-8037-2123-4 lib. bdg. : 6.46
1. Doll furniture. I. Cuffari, Richard, 1925- II. Knott, John. III. Title. BIP

Doll furniture—Juvenile literature.

KAHANE, Melanie. 745.59'23
There's a decorator in your doll house / written and illustrated by Melanie Kahane. New York : Galahad Books, c1968. 183 p. : ill. (some col.) ; 30 cm. Includes index. [TT175.5.K33] 74-77015 ISBN 0-88365-280-3 : 12.95
1. Doll furniture—Juvenile literature. 2. Doll-houses—Juvenile literature. I. Title.

KAHANE, Melanie. 745.59'23
There's a decorator in your doll house. Written and illustrated by Melanie Kahane. [1st ed.] New York, Atheneum, 1968. 183 p. illus. (part col.) 30 cm. Instructions for making miniature furniture for all rooms in a dollhouse and such accessories as lamps, rugs, and curtains. [TT200.K33] 68-18448 9.95
1. Doll furniture—Juvenile literature. 2. Doll-houses—Juvenile literature. I. Title.

Doll-houses.

BLAUER, John M. v. 12
Maynard Manor; the miniature world of a modern Gulliver, by John M. Blauer. San Francisco, c1965. 24 p. (chiefly illus.) 15 x 23 cm. [NI4892.S3] 67-1977
1. Doll-houses. 2. Furniture — Models I. Title.

BRANN, Donald R. 745-59'23
How to build dollhouses and furniture / by Donald R. Brann. Briarcliff Manor, N.Y. : Directions Simplified, 1976. 194 p. : ill. ; 23 cm. (Easi-bild home improvement library ; no. 753) "A Business of your own book." [TT175.3.B7] 75-32052 ISBN 0-87733-753-5 pbk. : 2.50
1. Doll-houses. 2. Doll furniture. I. Title. BIP

CALLICOTT, 745.59'23'0740168
Catherine Dorris.
In praise of dollhouses : the story of a personal collection / Catherine Dorris Callicott & Lawson Holderness ; photos. by Robert Brandau. 1st ed. New York : W. Morrow, c1978. 144 p. : ill. ; 29 cm. [TT175.3.C34] 78-17316 ISBN 0-688-03328-8 : 15.95
1. Doll-houses. I. Holderness, Lawson, joint author. II. Title.

COLE, Christopher. 745.59'23
Make your own doll's house : a practical guide showing how to make in miniature the building of your choice / Christopher Cole. New York : Van Nostrand Reinhold, 1976. p. cm. [TT175.3.C64] 76-14481 ISBN 0-442-21618-1 : 8.95
1. Doll-houses. I. Title. BIP

CREEKMORE, Betsey 745.59'23
Beeler.
Your world in miniature : a guide to making small-scale rooms and scenes / Betsey B. Creekmore and Betsey Creekmore. 1st ed. Garden City, N.Y. : Doubleday, 1975. p. cm. Includes index. Bibliography: p. [TT175.3.C73] 73-83622 ISBN 0-385-06521-3 : 7.95
1. Doll-houses. 2. Doll furniture. I. Creekmore, Betsey, joint author. II. Title.

DUDA, Margaret B. 745.59'23
Dollhouse accessories; how to design and make them, by Margaret B. Duda. Photography by Jon Sheckler. South Brunswick, A. S. Barnes [1975] 129 p. illus. 26 cm. Bibliography: p. 129. [TT175.3.D82 1975] 74-9281 ISBN 0-498-01557-2 9.95
1. Doll-houses. 2. Doll furniture. I. Title.

FISHER, Elizabeth Andrews. 634.98
Miniature stuff, [Written in part and compiled by Elizabeth Andrews Fisher. Middletown, Conn, 1964] 128 p. illus., plans. 23 cm. [TT200.F5] 64-55938
1. Doll-houses. 2. Furniture — Models. I. Title.

FLICK, Pauline. 745.59'23
The dollhouse idea book : furniture and decoration / Pauline Flick and Valerie Jackson ; illustrated by Ian Douglass. New York : Hawthorn Books, c1976. vi, 120 p. : ill. ; 24 cm. Originally published in 1974 under title: Doll's houses. Includes index. [TT175.3.F58 1976] 75-20912 ISBN 0-8015-2152-1 : 3.50
1. Doll-houses. 2. Doll furniture. I. Jackson, Valerie, joint author. II. Title. BIP

GOODFELLOW, 745.59'23'09420740215
Caroline.
Dolls' house / [text by] Caroline Goodfellow. London : H.M.S.O., 1976. [12] p. : chiefly col. ill. ; 16 cm. (Victoria and Albert Museum small colour book ; 10) At head of title: Victoria & Albert Museum and Bethnal Green Museum. Obtainable from Pendragon House, Palo Alto, Calif. [NK4893.G68] 77-353424 ISBN 0-11-290232-4 : £0.35
1. Doll-houses. I. Victoria and Albert Museum, South Kensington. II. Bethnal Green Museum. III. Title. IV. Series: Victoria and Albert Museum, South Kensington. Small colour book ; 10.

HINES, Millie. 745.59'23
The most wonderful dollhouse book : easy-to-make, inexpensive houses with furnishings and loveable doll families / Millie Hines. New York : Butterick Pub., c1979. 200 p. : ill. ; 26 cm. Includes index. [TT175.3.H56] 78-11766 ISBN 0-88421-076-6 : 12.95
1. Doll-houses. 2. Dollmaking. I. Title.

HINES, Millie. 745.59'23
The most wonderful dollhouse book : easy-to-make, inexpensive houses with furnishings and loveable doll families / Millie Hines. New York : Butterick Pub., c1979. 200 p. : ill. ; 26 cm. Includes index. [TT175.3.H56] 78-11766 ISBN 0-88421-076-6 : 12.95
1. Doll-houses. 2. Dollmaking. I. Title. BIP

HODGES, Lewis H. 745.59'23
How to build your own fine doll houses and furnishings / Lewis H. Hodges. Blue Ridge Summit, Pa. : Tab Books, 1979. p. cm. Includes index. [TT175.3.H62] 78-11254 ISBN 0-8306-9853-1 : 14.95. ISBN 0-8306-1102-9 pbk. : 9.95
1. Doll-houses. 2. Doll furniture. I. Title. BIP

JACOBS, Flora Gill. 649.55
A history of doll houses; four centuries of the domestic world in miniature. New York, Scribner, 1953. viii, 322 p. illus. 26 cm. Bibliography: p. [315]-316. [NK4894.A2J3] 53-6996
1. Doll-houses. BIP

JACOBS, Flora Gill. 745.5923
A history of dolls' houses. New York : Charles Scribner's Sons [1976c1965] x, 342p. : ill. ; 27 cm. Includes index. Bibliography: p. 335-336. [NK4894.A2J3] ISBN 0-684-14538-3 pbk. : 8.95
1. Doll-houses. I. Title.
L. C. card no. for original edition: 65-24648

JELLISON, Phyllis Gift. 745.59'23
The colonial dollhouse : how to make your own early American dollhouse with colonial furniture and accessories for under $50 / Phyllis Gift Jellison. New York : Van Nostrand Reinhold, 1977. 128 p. : ill. ; 28 cm. Includes index. [TT175.3.J44] 76-42594 ISBN 0-442-24129-1 : 7.95
1. Doll-houses. 2. United States—Social life and customs—Colonial period, ca. 1600-1775. I. Title. BIP

JELLISON, Phyllis Gift. 745.59'23
The "remember when" dollhouse / Phyllis Gift Jellison. New York : Van Nostrand Reinhold, 1978. 144 p. : ill. ; 28 cm. Includes index. [TT175.3.J45] 78-8127 ISBN 0-442-24128-3 pbk. : 7.95
1. Doll-houses. 2. Doll furniture. I. Title. BIP

JOHNSON, Audrey. 649.55
How to make dolls' houses. London, G. Bell [1957; label: Boston, C.T. Branford Co.] 112p. illus. 21cm. [TS2301.T7J55] 57-4416
1. Doll-houses. I. Title. BIP

JOYNER, Nina Glenn. 745.59'23
Dollhouse construction and restoration / Nina Glenn Joyner. Radnor, Pa. : Chilton Book Co., c1977. viii, 123 p. : ill. ; 27 cm. (Chilton's creative crafts series) Includes index. [TT175.3.J68 1977] 77-6117 ISBN 0-8019-6462-8 : 10.95 ISBN 0-8019-6463-6 pbk. : 5.95
1. Doll-houses. I. Title. BIP

LATHAM, Jean. 745.59'23
Dolls' houses; a personal choice. New York, Scribner [1969] 200 p. illus. (part col.) 29 cm. Bibliography: p. [195]-196. [NK4893.L3] 79-82079 12.50
1. Doll-houses. I. Title.

MACLAREN, Catherine B. 745.59'23
This side of yesterday in miniature / Catherine B. MacLaren. La Jolla, CA : Nutshell News, 1975. 160 p. : ill. ; 28 cm. [NK4893.M32] 75-324879 9.50
1. Doll-houses. 2. Doll furniture. 3. Miniature objects. I. Title.

MILSTEIN, Jeff. 745.59'23
Building cardboard dollhouses / written, photographed, and illustrated by Jeff Milstein. 1st ed. New York : Harper & Row, 1978. 78 p. : ill. ; 23 cm. (Harper Colophon books) Instructions for making dollhouses out of cardboard. Includes several styles: colonial, Georgian, Greek Revival, Victorian, and Italianate. [TT175.3.M54] 78-19235 ISBN 0-06-090612-X : 3.95
1. Doll-houses—Juvenile literature. 2. Paperboard—Juvenile literature. I. Title. BIP

NEWMAN, Thelma R. 646.4'3'04
The complete book of making miniatures : for room settings and dollhouses / by Thelma R. Newman and Virginia Merrill. New York : Crown Publishers, [1975] 308 p. [4] leaves of plates : ill. (some col.) ; 27 cm. Includes index. Bibliography: p. 285-288. [TT175.3.N48 1975] 75-16456 ISBN 0-517-52460-0 pbk. : 5.95 ISBN 0-517-52318-3 : 10.95
1. Doll-houses. 2. Miniature rooms. I. Merrill, Virginia, joint author. II. Title. BIP

O'BRIEN, Marian Maeve. 745.59'23
The collector's guide to dollhouses and dollhouse miniatures. With photos. by Elinor Coyle. New York, Hawthorn Books [1974] xxv, 213 p. illus. 29 cm. [NK4893.O27 1974] 73-11742 13.95
1. Doll-houses. 2. Doll furniture. 3. Miniature objects. I. Coyle, Elinor Martineau, illus. II. Title. BIP

O'BRIEN, Marian Maeve. 745.59'23
Make your own dollhouses and dollhouse miniatures / Marian Maeve O'Brien ; drawings by Eileen Kramer. New York : Hawthorn Books, c1975. xi, 274 p., [4] leaves of plates : ill. (some col.) ; 29 cm. Includes index. [TT175.3.O27 1975] 74-20297 ISBN 0-8015-4801-2 : 15.00
1. Doll-houses. 2. Doll furniture. I. Title. BIP

ROSNER, Bernard. 745.59'23
Inside the world of miniatures & dollhouses : a comprehensive guide to collecting and creating / Bernard Rosner and Jay Beckerman. New York : McKay, c1976. p. cm. Includes index. Bibliography: p. [NK4893.R67] 76-16458 ISBN 0-679-50617-9 : 14.95 ISBN 0-679-50620-9 pbk. :
1. Doll-houses. 2. Doll furniture. 3. Miniature objects. I. Beckerman, Jay, joint author. II. Title. BIP

WILLIAMS, Guy R. 688.723
Making a miniature house. Diagrs. by the author. [New York] Oxford 1965 [c.]1964. 96p. illus(pt. col.) 26cm. [TT200.W54] 65-791 3.40 bds.,
1. Doll-houses. 2. Furniture—Models. I. Title. BIP

WORRELL, Estelle 745.5923
(Ansley) 1929-
The dollhouse book. Basic house plans and photography by Norman Worrell. [pseud.] Princeton, N.J., Van Nostrand [1964] ix, 125p. illus. (pt. col.) 29cm. Patterns for dolls' furniture, dollhouse plans, needlework and accessories: p.53-118. Bibl. 64-57228 6.50
1. Doll-houses. 2. Furniture—Models. I. Title. BIP

Doll-houses—England.

HOSMER, Herbert 745.59'23'0942
Henry, 1913-
Four dolls' houses—plus two (a study in relationship) by Herbert H. Hosmer. South Lancaster, Mass., Toy Cupboard Museums, c1973. [40] p. illus. 19 cm. [NK4894.G7H67] 74-162946
1. Doll-houses—England. I. Title.

Doll-houses—England—History.

GREENE, Vivien. 745.59'23'0942
Family dolls' houses. [U.S. ed.] Newton, Mass., C. T. Branford Co. [1973] 176 p. illus. 25 cm. Includes bibliographical references. [NK4894.E5G73] 73-6565 21.50
1. Doll-houses—England—History. I. Title. BIP

Doll-houses—Hist.

JACOBS, Flora Gill 745.5923
A history of dolls' houses. [Rev., enl., ed.] New York, Scribners [c.1953, 1965] x, 342p. illus. 26cm. First pub. in 1953 under title: A history of doll houses. Bibl. [NK4894.A2J3] 65-24648 12.50
1. Doll-houses—Hist. I. Title.

Doll-houses—Juvenile literature.

GARDNER, Richard M. 745.59'23
Make your own dollhouses / written and illustrated by Richard Cummings [i.e. R. M. Gardner]. New York : McKay, c1978. 149 p. : ill. ; 24 cm. Includes index. Bibliography: p. 142-143. Instructions for building dollhouses in various styles including a basic house, Cape Cod, Colonial, Victorian, and an eight-unit apartment building. [TT175.3.G37] 77-20088 ISBN 0-679-20439-3 : 8.95
1. Doll-houses—Juvenile literature. I. Title.

HELBERG, Kristin. 745.59'23
The elegant dollhouse book / by Kristin

Helberg ; cartoons and calligraphy by Daniel Lewis ; photography by Jim Goodwin. [Berkeley, Calif.] : Wingbow Press : distributed by Bookpeople to the World, c1976. 89 p. : ill. ; 28 cm. "A Rainy Day book." Bibliography: p. 88-89. Instructions for constructing a dollhouse and its furniture from cardboard boxes and objects around the house. [TT175.3.H44] 76-45559 ISBN 0-914728-18-0 : 4.50
1. Doll-houses—Juvenile literature. 2. Doll furniture—Juvenile literature.

JACOBS, Flora Gill 745.5923
A world of doll houses. Chicago, Rand McNally [c.1965] 144p. illus. 22cm. [NK4894.A2J32] 65-14279 3.50
1. Doll-houses—Juvenile literature. I. Title.

KELLY, Karin. 745.59'23
Doll houses. Pictures by George Overlie. Minneapolis, Lerner Publications Co. [1973, c1974] 32 p. illus. 20 cm. (An Early craft book) Instructions for making a doll house from a cardboard box and furnishing it with objects made from spools, fabric, clay, cardboard, and other materials. Also includes dollmaking and other projects. [TT175.3.K44] 72-13338 ISBN 0-8225-0854-0 3.95 (lib. bdg.)
1. Doll-houses—Juvenile literature. 2. Doll furniture—Juvenile literature. 3. Dollmaking—Juvenile literature. I. Overlie, George, illus. II. Title. BIP

PFLUG, Betsy. 745.59'23
Boxed-in doll houses. [1st ed.] Philadelphia, Lippincott [1971] 48 p. col. illus. 26 cm. Instructions for making doll houses and furniture from boxes and various household items. [TT175.3.P45] 71-137219 3.95
1. Doll-houses—Juvenile literature. 2. Furniture—Models—Juvenile literature. I. Title. BIP

TANGERMAN, Elmer John, 1907- 745.59'23
Build your own inexpensive dollhouse with one sheet of 4' x 8' plywood and home tools / by E. J. Tangerman. New York : Dover Publications, 1977. 44 p. : ill. ; 28 cm. Offers instructions for constructing a basic dollhouse, with design options, for the reader with no carpentry skills. [TT175.3.T36 1977] 76-50272 ISBN 0-486-23493-2 : 1.50
1. Doll-houses—Juvenile literature. I. Title.

Doll-houses—United States.

JACOBS, Flora Gill. 745.59'23'0973
Dolls' houses in America; historic preservation in miniature. New York, Scribner [1974] xii, 395 p. illus. 29 cm. Includes bibliographical references. [NK4894.U6J32] 73-1100 ISBN 0-684-13583-3
1. Doll-houses—United States. I. Title. BIP

MOORE, Colleen, 1902- 745.59'23
Colleen Moore's doll house. Photographed by Will Rousseau. Garden City, N.Y., Doubleday, [1971?] 96 p. col. illus. 29 cm. [NK4892.5.M6A43] 79-125881 9.95
1. Doll-houses—United States. I. Title. BIP

Dollar.

BOLENDER, Milferd Henry, 1894- 737.4
The United States early silver dollars from 1794 to 1803. Freeport. Ill., 1950. 75 p. 9 plates. 32 cm. One illus., on plate 3, covered by mounted illus. [CJ1835.B65] 50-31638
1. Dollar. I. Title.

NEWMAN, Eric P. 737.4973
The fantastic 1804 dollar, by eric. P. Newman and Kenneth E. Bressett. Associates in research: Walter H. Breen and Lynn Glaser. Racine, Wis., Whitman Pub. Co. [1962] 144 p. illus. 24 cm. [CJ1835.N53] 62-19453
1. Dollar. I. Bressett, Kenneth E., joint author. II. Title.

RAYMOND, Wayte, 1886-1956 737.497
The silver dollars of North and South America; an illustrated catalog of all major types of dollarsize coins of the Western Hemisphere, with valuations. 2d ed. rev., ed. by imre Molnar [others] Racine, Wis., Whitman [1964] 125p. 24cm. Bibl. 64-5518 1.00
1. Dollar. I. Title.

TOM'S Stamp and Coin Service, Norwalk, Conn. 737.4
One dollar issues, new (small) series, 1928 to date. Norwalk, c1961. unpaged. illus. 30 cm. (Tom's original currency albums) [CJ1832.T6] 62-2664
1. Dollar. I. Title.

VAN ALLEN, Leroy C 737.4973
Morgan and peace dollar varieties; a comprehensive guide and reference book on U.S. silver dollars, by Leroy C. Van Allen. Baltimore, c1965. 183 p. illus. 23 cm. [CJ1835.V35] 66-3139
1. Dollar. I. Title.

Dollar, American (Coin)

VAN ALLEN LEROY C. 737.4'9'73
The comprehensive catalog and encyclopedia of U. S. Morgan and peace silver dollars / by Leroy C. Van Allen, A.George Mallis. Rev. ed. New York : Arco Pub. Co., [1976] p. cm. First ed. published in 1971 under title: Guide to Morgan and peace dollars. Bibliography: p. [CT1835.V346 1976] 76-18299 ISBN 0-668-04021-1 : 19.50
1. Dollar, American (Coin) 2. Silver coins. I. Mallis, A. George, joint author. II. Title. BIP

Dollar (Coin)

BACHTELL, Lee M. 737.4'09
World dollars, 1477-1877 : pictorial guide / by Lee M. Bachtell Ludowici, Ga. : Bachtell, [1974] iii, 606 p. : ill. ; 29 cm. Includes indexes. [CJ1546.B3] 75-303154
1. Dollar (Coin) 2. Taler. 3. Silver coins. I. Title.

HOSKINS, Charles R. 737.08 s
The story of the dollar, by Charles R. Hoskins. [Saddle Brook? N.J., International Numismatic Collector Society, 1970] 65 p. illus. (part col.), 18 col. slides. 2 x 2 in. 29 cm. (International Numismatic Collector Society. [Series] Library 1, v. 2) [CJ35.I6 library 1, vol. 2] [CJ1835] 737.4 73-31100
1. Dollar (Coin) 2. Silver coins. 3. Taler. I. Title. II. Series.

Dollars, American (Coin)

OSBON, James B. 737.4'9'73
Jim Osbon's Silver dollar encyclopedia / by James B. Osbon. Richmond, Va. : Headquarters Pub. Co., c1976. 271 p. : ill., graphs ; 28 cm. Includes index. Bibliography: p. 269. [CJ1835.O7] 76-363555 15.00
1. Dollars, American (Coin) 2. Silver coins. I. Title. II. Title: Silver dollar encyclopedia.

Dollmakers—U.S.

KRECHNIAK, Helen Bullard, 1902- 745.5922
The American doll artist [by] Helen Bullard. [Newton Centre] Mass., Branford [c.1965] ix, 217p. illus., ports. 24cm. Bibl. [TS2301.T7K7] 65-22379 12.00
1. Dollmakers—U.S. I. Title. BIP

Dollmaking.

BENBOW, Mary. 745.59'22
Dolls traditional and topical and how to make them, by Mary Benbow, Edith Dunlop and Joyce Luckin. Illustrated by Mary Benbow. Photos. by F. H. Newbold and T. J. Moore. [1st American ed.] Boston, Plays, inc. [1970] 93 p. illus. (part col.) 27 cm. [TT157.B37 1970] 75-133316 ISBN 8-238-00903- 6.95
1. Dollmaking. I. Dunlop, Edith, joint author. II. Luckin, Joyce, joint author. III. Title.

CASSIN-SCOTT, Jack. 745.59'22
Making historical costume dolls / Jack Cassin-Scott. Newton Centre, Mass. : C. T. Branford Co., 1975. 96 p. : ill. ; 21 cm. [TT175.C37] 74-26667 ISBN 0-8231-3031-2 : 8.25
1. Dollmaking. 2. Doll clothes. I. Title. BIP

COYNE, John. 745.59'22
How to make upside-down dolls / by John Coyne and Jerry Miller. Indianapolis : Bobbs-Merrill, [1977] p. cm. [TT175.C69] 77-76889 ISBN 0-672-52157-1 : 12.95
1. Dollmaking. I. Miller, Jerry, 1946- joint author. II. Title. BIP

GOTTILLY, Doris Rockwell. 745.59'22
Creative dollmaking : from papier mache, cloth, clothespins & appleheads to yarn, corn cob, bottle & seashell dolls / by Doris Rockwell Gottilly ; with doll and costume designs by the author. Watkins Glen, N.Y. : Century House Pub. Co., c1976. 142 p. : ill. ; 23 cm. [TT175.G67] 76-23722 ISBN 0-87282-103-X : 8.95
1. Dollmaking. I. Title. BIP

GRAY, Ilse. 745.59'22
Designing and making dolls. Drawings by David Gray. Photos. by Michael Wickham. New York, Watson-Guptill [1972] 96 p. illus. (part col.) 25 cm. Bibliography: p. 95. [TT175.G7] 72-1449 ISBN 0-8230-2991-3 (Watson-Guptill) 8.95
1. Dollmaking. I. Title. BIP

GREENHOWE, Jean. 745.59'22
Dolls in national and folk costume / Jean Greenhowe. Newton Center, Mass. : C. T. Branford Co., 1978. 112 p., [2] leaves of plates : ill. ; 26 cm. Bibliography: p. 112. [TT175.G72] 78-105141 ISBN 0-8231-3033-9 : 10.95
1. Dollmaking. 2. Doll clothes. 3. Costume. I. Title. BIP

HARTMAN, Grietje. 745.59'22
Popmooi : European dolls to make yourself / Greitje Hartman and Ellen Lens ; translated by Ria Leigh-Loo-huizen. San Francisco : Chronicle Books, [1979] p. cm. [TT175.H3413] 78-31240 ISBN 0-87701-131-1 pbk. : 5.95
1. Dollmaking. I. Lens, Ellen, joint author. II. Title. BIP

HOLMES, Anita. 745.59'22
Making dolls for pleasure & profit / Anita Holmes. New York : Arco Pub. Co., [1978] c1976. p. cm. [TT175.H65 1978] 77-25288 ISBN 0-668-04534-5 : 7.95
1. Dollmaking. I. Title. BIP

IVES, Suzy. 745.59'22
Making and dressing a rag doll. New York, Drake Publishers [1972] 96 p. illus. 23 cm. [TT175.I84] 72-1258 ISBN 0-87749-248-4 5.95
1. Dollmaking. 2. Doll clothes. I. Title.

JANITCH, Valerie. 745.59'22
Doll houses and doll house families / by Valerie Janitch. Woodbury, N.Y. : Barron's, 1978. p. cm. London ed. published under title: Dolls' houses and dolls' house families. [TT175.J34 1978] 77-28371 ISBN 0-8120-5166-1 pbk. : 3.95
1. Dollmaking. 2. Doll clothes. 3. Doll-houses. I. Title.

JANITCH, Valerie. 745.59'22
Dolls in miniature / Valerie Janitch. 1st ed. Radnor, Pa. : Chilton Book Co., c1976. p. cm. (Chilton's creative crafts series) [TT175.J35 1976] 75-30782 ISBN 0-8019-6412-1 : 10.95 ISBN 0-8019-6413-X pbk. :
1. Dollmaking. I. Title. BIP

JONES, Genevieve Priscilla. 745.59'22
Easy-to-make dolls with nineteenth-century-costumes / by G. P. Jones. New York : Dover Publications, 1977. 89 p. : ill. ; 28 cm. (Dover needlework series) [TT175.J66 1977] 76-24566 ISBN 0-486-23426-6 pbk. : 2.75
1. Dollmaking. 2. Doll clothes. I. Title. BIP

JONES, Genevieve Priscilla. 745.59'22
An easy-to-make Godey doll, with instructions and ready-to-use patterns for a complete wardrobe / G. P. Jones. New York : Dover Publications, 1978. 27 p., 24 leaves of plates : ill. ; 28 cm. (Dover needlework series) [TT175.J653 1978] 78-56762 ISBN 0-486-23710-9 : 2.00
1. Dollmaking. 2. Doll clothes. I. Title.

JONES, Iris Sanderson, 1932- 745.59'22
Early North American dollmaking : a narrative history and craft instructions / Iris Sanderson Jones ; drawings by Catherine Claytor-Becker ; photos. by Micky Jones. San Francisco : 101 Productions ; New York : distributed by Scribner, c1976. 144 p. : ill. ; 21 cm. Includes index. [TT175.J66] 76-44413 ISBN 0-89286-107-X : 8.95. ISBN 0-89286-108-8 pbk. : 4.95
1. Dollmaking. 2. Dolls—North America—History. I. Title. BIP

LAURY, Jean Ray. 745.59'22
Doll making: a creative approach. Photos by Gayle Smalley. New York, Van Nostrand Reinhold [1975 c1970] 135 p. illus (17 col.) 26 cm. [TT157.L27] 79-126984 ISBN 0-442-24702-8 4.95 (pbk.)
1. Dollmaking. I. Title.
Hardcover, 9.95; 0-442-24693-5. BIP

MCLAUGHLIN, Eve. 745.59'22
Costume doll making / Eve McLaughlin. New York : Larousse, 1975. 120 p., [4] leaves of plates : ill. (some col.) ; 26 cm. (The Larousse craft series) Includes index. Bibliography: p. 117. [TT175.M32] 75-2712 ISBN 0-88332-071-1 : 7.95. ISBN 0-88332-072-X pbk. : 4.95
1. Dollmaking. 2. Doll clothes. I. Title. BIP

*MORTON, Brenda 745.59'22
Cuddly dolls and how to dress them Brenda Morton ; with drawings by Juliet Renny. New York : Taplinger, c1976. 159 p. : ill. ; 22 cm. [TT175] 75-37044 ISBN 0-8008-2090-8 lib.bdg. : 8.50
1. Dollmaking. 2. Doll clothes. I. Title. BIP

ROBERTS, Catherine Christopher, 1905- 745.59'22
The complete book of doll making and collecting, by Catherine Christopher. 2d rev. ed. New York, Dover Publications [1971] 290 p. illus. 23 cm. [TT175.R62 1971] 76-102176 ISBN 0-486-22066-4 3.00
1. Dollmaking. 2. Dolls—Collectors and collecting. I. Title.

ROGOWSKI, Gini, 1931- 745.59'22
Making American folk art dolls / Gini Rogowski and Gene DeWeese ; [photos. by Robert Way ; drawings by Paul Sintak]. 1st ed. Radnor, Pa. : Chilton Book Co., c1975. p. cm. (Chilton's creative crafts series) Includes index. [TT175.R64 1975] 75-24965 ISBN 0-8019-6122-X : 12.50 ISBN 0-8019-6123-8 pbk. : 6.95
1. Dollmaking. 2. Folk art—United States. I. DeWeese, Gene, joint author. II. Title. BIP

SEELEY, Mildred. 745.59'22
The doll house doll : directions for making the dolls, body patterns, costume patterns, study photos of old dolls, everything you need to know about doll house dolls / by Mildred Seeley ; photos. by Jay Seeley and Vernon Seeley ; illustrated by Dubie Seeley. [Oneonta, N.Y. : Seeley's Ceramic Service, c1976] 86 p. : ill. ; 28 cm. Text on p. [3] of cover. [TT175.S43] 76-373874
1. Dollmaking. I. Title.

SEYFFERTH, Claire J. 745.59'22
Fruit head dolls : a new method for making fruit head dolls / Clarie J. Seyfferth. 1st ed. New York : Vantage Press, c1976. 19 p. : ill. ; 21 cm. [TT175.S49] 76-375223 ISBN 0-533-02160-X : 4.95
1. Dollmaking. I. Title.

SNOOK, Barbara. 745.59/2
Making clowns, witches and dragons. London, Batsford; Newton Centre (Mass.), Branford, 1967. 96p. illus. 22cm. [TT157.S58 1967] 67-20993 3.50 bds.,
1. Dollmaking. 2. Handicraft. I. Title.

TYLER, Mabs. 745.59'22
The big book of dolls / Mabs Tyler ; photos. by Gina Harris, line drawings by Janine Kirwan. New York : Dial Press, 1976. 191 p. : ill. (some col.) ; 27 cm. [TT175.T9 1976] 75-23222 ISBN 0-8037-0580-8 : 12.95
1. Dollmaking. I. Title. BIP

WITZIG, Hans. 745.59'22
Making dolls, by H. Witzig and G. E. Kuhn. [Translated by Ingrid Froehlich] New York, Sterling Pub. Co. [1969] 96 p. illus. 22 cm. Translation of Puppen. [TS2301.T7W533 1969] 69-19492
1. Dollmaking. I. Kuhn, Gertrud Elisabeth, 1920- joint author. II. Title.

WORRELL, Estelle Ansley, 1929- 745.59'22
Dolls, puppedolls, and teddy bears / by Estelle Ansley Worrell. New York : Van Nostrand Reinhold Co., [1977] p. cm. Includes index. [TT175.W67] 77-7246 ISBN 0-442-29541-3 : 11.95
1. Dollmaking. 2. Puppet making. 3. Teddy bears. I. Title. BIP

YOUNG, Helen. 745.59'22
Dollmaking for everyone / Helen Young. South Brunswick, [N.J.] : A. S. Barnes, c1977. 198 p. : ill. ; 25 cm. Includes index. [TT175.Y68 1977] 75-38447 ISBN 0-498-01867-9 : 9.95
1. Dollmaking. I. Title. BIP

Dollmaking—Amateurs' manuals.

WENDORFF, Ruth. 745.59'22
How to make cornhusk dolls. New York, Arco [1973] 76 p. illus. 24 cm. Instructions for using cornhusks to make a variety of dolls, animals, flowers, and other accessories. Gives suggestions for using these objects for decorating or for money-making projects. [TT175.W46] 72-90906 ISBN 0-668-02883-1 4.95
1. Dollmaking—Amateurs' manuals. 2. Cornhusk craft. I. Title. BIP

Dollmaking—Juvenile literature.

DOLLS and toy animals 745.59'22
[by] Vibeke Lind [and] Lis Albrectsen. [Translation from the Danish by Christine Hauch. New York, Van Nostrand Reinhold Co., 1973] 94 p. illus. 21 cm. (A Rheinhold craft paperback) Translation of Blodedukker by Vibeke Lind, and Sovedyr by Lis Albrectsen. Directions for making dolls and toy animals from felt, handkerchiefs, rice, socks, and other materials. [TT175.D64] 72-9377 ISBN 0-442-29968-0 2.95
1. Dollmaking—Juvenile literature. 2. Soft toy making—Juvenile literature. I. Lind, Vibeke. Blodedukker. English. 1973. II. Albrectsen, Lis. Sovedyr. English. 1973.

HANAUER, Elsie V. 745.59'22
How to make egg carton figures, by Elsie Hanauer. South Brunswick, A. S. Barnes [1972] 71 p. illus. 22 cm. Instructions for creating a variety of egg carton dolls using a pencil, scissors, knife, and awl as the only essential tools. [PZ10.H1477Ho] 70-37812 ISBN 0-498-01016-3 4.95
1. Dollmaking—Juvenile literature. I. Title.

HEADY, Eleanor B. 745.59'22
Make your own dolls, by Eleanor B. Heady. Illustrated by Harold F. Heady. New York, Lothrop, Lee & Shepard Co. [1974] 94 p. illus. 24 cm. Instructions for making a variety of dolls from such materials as clothespins, pipe cleaners, soap, bottles, and nylon stockings. [TT175.H37] 73-17712 ISBN 0-688-41570-9 4.75
1. Dollmaking—Juvenile literature. I. Heady, Harold F., illus. II. Title.
Library binding; 4.32, ISBN 0-688-51570-3.

HOFFSOMMER, Alan. 745.59'22
Rope dolls : how to make them for pleasure and profit / Alan Hoffsommer. New York : Drake Publishers, 1977. 127 p. : ill. ; 26 cm. Text and photographs introduce basic techniques for making various rope dolls. [TT175.H64] 77-72390 ISBN 0-8473-1550-9 pbk. : 5.95
1. Dollmaking—Juvenile literature. 2. Rope—Juvenile literature. I. Title. BIP

Dolls.

ACKLEY, Edith (Flack), 1887- 649.55
Dolls to make for fun and profit. Drawings by Telka Ackley. [Rev. ed.] Philadelphia, Lippincott [1951] 126 p. illus. 26 cm. [TS2301.T7A42 1951] 51-13176
1. Dolls. I. Title. BIP

BACHMANN, Manfred. 745.59'22
Dolls the wide world over, by Manfred Bachmann and Claus Hansmann. Translated by Ruth Michaelis-Jena, with the collaboration of Patrick Murray. New York, Crown Publishers [1973] 203, [1] p. illus. (part col.) 28 cm. Translation of Das grosse Puppenbuch. Bibliography: p. [200]-[204] [NK4893.B313 1973b] 72-94617 14.95
1. Dolls. I. Hansmann, Claus, 1918- illus. II. Title.

BASS, Flora (Gardner) 1916- 396
Philippine women and dolls. [Laguna Beach, Calif., Mermaid Books, 1955] 111p. illus. 23cm. [NK4894.P5B3] 55-14730
1. Dolls. 2. Women in the Philippine Islands. I. Title.

BENBOW, Mary. 745.59'22'028
Dolls and doll-making, by Mary Benbow, Edith Dunlop, and Joyce Luckin. Illustrated by Mary Benbow. Photos. by Rodney Morse. [1st American ed.] Boston, Plays, inc. [1968] 95 p. illus. (part col.) 27 cm. [GV1219.B4 1968] 68-20354 6.95
1. Dolls. I. Dunlop, Edith, joint author. II. Luckin, Joyce, joint author. III. Title.

BOEHN, Max von, 1860-1932. 394'.3
Dolls. Translated by Josephine Nicoll. New York, Dover Publications [1972] 269 p. illus. 22 cm. Translation of v. 1 of Puppen und Puppenspiele. Bibliography: p. 253-260. [GV1219.B62 1972] 73-189341 3.00 (pbk)
1. Dolls. 2. Idols and images.

BOEHN, Max von, 1860-1932. 649.55
Dolls and puppets. Translated by Josephine Nicoll, with a note on puppets by George Bernard Shaw. Rev. ed. Boston, C. T. Branford Co. [1956] 521p. illus. (part col.) plan. 22cm. Bibliography: p. 481-506. [GV1219.B62 1956] 57-3084
1. Dolls. 2. Puppets and puppet-plays. 3. Idols and images. I. Title.

BOEHN, Max von, 1860-1932. 394.3
Dolls and puppets. Translated by Josephine Nicoll, with a note on puppets by George Bernard Shaw. New York, Cooper Square Publishers, 1966. 521 p. illus., 30 col. plates. 24 cm. Translation of Puppen und Puppenspiele. Bibliography: p. 481-506. [GV1219.B62 1966] 65-25496
1. Dolls. 2. Puppets and puppet-plays. 3. Idols and images. I. Title.

BRINLEY, Rosemary. 688.7
Dolls and stuffed toy making; edited by Marjorie O'Shaughnessy. [New York] Dover Publications [1953] 1952] 93p. illus. 20cm. (Dover- Foyle handbooks) [TS2301.T7B7] 53-9942
1. Dolls. 2. Toys. I. Title.

BUTLER, Winifred. 646.2
Dolls' dressmaking. Diagrs. by Ionicus. Photos. by Fact Photography. Princeton, N.J., Van Nostrand [1964, c1962] 142 p. illus., col. plates. 26 cm. [TT715.B88 1964] 64-25982
1. Dolls. 2. Sewing. I. Title.

CHRISTOPHER, Rosemary Brinley, 1918- 688.7
Dolls and stuffed toy making; edited by Marjorie O'Shaughnessy. [New York] Dover Publications [1953, c1952] 93p. illus. 20cm. (Dover-Foyle handbooks) [TS2301.T7C4] 53-9942
1. Dolls. 2. Toys. I. Title.

COCKETT, Mary. 745.59'22
Dolls and puppets / [by] Mary Cockett. Newton Abbot ; North Pomfret, Vt. : David & Charles, 1974. 80 p. : ill. ; 22 cm. Includes index. [NK4893.C57] 74-190267 ISBN 0-7153-6311-5 : 4.95
1. Dolls. 2. Puppets. I. Title. BIP

DARRAH, Marjorie Merritt. 745.59'22
Dolls in color. [Des Moines, Iowa, Wallace-Homestead Book Co., c1971] [49] p. illus. 23 cm. [NK4893.D3] 72-175881
1. Dolls. I. Title. BIP

DESMONDE, Kay. 745.59'22
Dolls and dolls houses. [1st American ed.] New York, World Pub. Co. [1972] 80 p. illus. 22 cm. Bibliography: p. 80. [NK4893.D4 1972] 77-173021 5.95
1. Dolls. 2. Doll-houses. I. Title.

DOW, Emily R., 1904- 646.2
How to make doll clothes; a book for daughters, mothers, & grandmothers, written and illustrated by Emily R. Dow. New York, Coward-McCann [1953] 96 p. illus. 22 cm. [TT715.D6] 53-9566
1. Dolls. 2. Sewing. I. Title. BIP

EATON, Faith. 745.59'22
Dolls in color / Faith Eaton ; photography, Bob Loosemore. 1st American ed. New York : Macmillan, 1976, c1975. 187 p. : col. ill. ; 20 cm. Includes index. Bibliography: p. 184. [NK4893.E33 1976] 75-17668 ISBN 0-02-534710-1 : 6.95
1. Dolls. I. Title.

FISHER, Elizabeth Andrews. 745.5922
Doll stuff again. [Written in part and compiled by Elizabeth Andrews Fisher. Middletown, Conn., 1965] 319 p. illus. 23 cm. Much of the material originally appeared in the Toy trader. Doll patterns (8 sheets) in pocket. [TS2301.T7F52] 66-2007
1. Dolls. I. Title.

FISHER, Elizabeth Andrews. 745.5922
Doll stuff again. [Written in part and compiled by Elizabeth Andrews Fisher. Middletown, Conn., 1961] 319 p. illus. 23 cm. Much of the material originally appeared in the Toy trader. Doll patterns (8 sheets) in pocket. [TS2301.T7F52] 66-43673
1. Dolls. I. Title.

FOX, Carl, 1913- 745.59'22
The doll. Photos. by H. Landshoff. New York, H. N. Abrams [1972] 343 p. illus. (part col.) 28 x 30 cm. Bibliography: p. 341-343. [NK4893.F69] 77-160218 ISBN 0-8109-0078-5 35.00
1. Dolls. I. Landshoff, H., illus. II. Title.

FREEMAN, Ruth Sunderlin. 688.7'22
Cavalcade of dolls : basic source book for collectors / by Ruth S. Freeman. Watkins Glen, N.Y. : Century House Pub. Co., c1978. 362 p., [4] leaves of plates : ill. ; 29 cm. Includes index. Bibliography: p. 345-359. [TS2301.T7F76] 75-30167 ISBN 0-87282-001-7 : 35.00
1. Dolls. I. Title. BIP

HALLEN, Julienne, 1923- 649.55
How to make foreign dolls and their costumes. New York, Homecrafts, 1950. 93 p. illus. 25 cm. [TS2301.T7H28] 50-11131
1. Dolls. 2. Costume. I. Title.

HART, Luella Tilton, 1897- 704.94964955
The Japanese doll. [Middletown, Conn., Printed by E. A. Fisher, 1952] 92 p. illus. 16 cm. [NK4894.J3H3] 52-42559
1. Dolls. I. Title.

HOLT, Florrie Bell. 745.59'23
Antique Turpin dolls. Cincinnati [Talaria] 1961. 94p. illus. 24cm. (A Talaria book) [NK4892.C55 1961] 61-40070
1. Dolls. 2. Turpin family. I. Title.

JOHL, Janet (Pagter) 745.59'22
The fascinating story of dolls. Watkins Glen, N.Y., Century House [1970, c1941] 270 p. illus. 24 cm. [NK4893.J58 1970] 77-96933
1. Dolls. I. Title.

NOBLE, John, 1923- 745.59'22
A treasury of beautiful dolls. With color plates by Peter Reinstorff. Foreword by Dorothy, Elizabeth, and Evelyn Coleman. New York, Hawthorn Books [1971] xxiii, 210 p. illus. (part col.) 29 cm. [NK4894.A2N6 1971] 71-158022 17.50
1. Dolls. I. Reinstorff, Peter, illus. II. Title.

PIERCY, Caroline Behlen, 1886- 649.55
Victoria enters a doll museum; a Staffordshire doll tells her story. [1st ed.] New York, Pageant Press [1953] 64p. illus. 22cm. [GV1219.P5] 53-8061
1. Dolls. I. Title.

ROBERTS, Catherine Christopher, 1905- 649.55
The real book about making dolls and doll clothes; illustrated by the author. Garden City, N.Y., Garden City Books, by arrangement with F. Watts [New York, 1951] 191 p. illus. 21 cm. (Real books) [TS2301.T7R73] 51-12263
1. Dolls. I. Title.

ST. George, Eleanor. 649.55
Dolls of three centuries. New York, Scribner, 1951. 205 p. illus. 26 cm. [NK495.S3] 51-13769
1. Dolls. I. Title.

ST. George, Eleanor. 649.55
Old dolls. New York, Barrows [1950] 176 p. 77 illus. 15 cm. (Collectors' little-book library) [NK4893.S33] 50-8733
1. Dolls. I. Title.

TOKYO Ningyo Gakuin. 745.5922
The world of Japanese dolls, by the Tokyo Doll School. [Translated by C. A. Pomeroy] Tokyo, Rutland, Vt., C. E. Tuttle Co. [1962] 115 p. illus. (part mounted, part col.) 31 cm. "Paper patterns" (fold. leaf) in pocket. [NK4894.J3.T613] 62-15061
1. Dolls. I. Title.

UNITED Federation of Doll Clubs. Region 11. 745.59'22
Dolls, a sampler: souvenir booklet; meeting, Colonial Williamsburg, 1972. [Washington, Dollology Club of Washington, D.C., 1972] 43 p. illus. 28 cm. On cover: Williamsburg. [NK4893.U53] 73-151478
1. Colonial Williamsburg, inc. 2. Dolls. I. Title. II. Title: Williamsburg.

WENHAM HISTORICAL ASSOCIATION, Wenham, Mass. Dolls Museum. 704.94964955
Notes on the collection of dolls and figurines at the Wenham Museum, Claflin-Richards House, Wenham, Mass. Compiled by Adeline P. Cole. Edited and published by the Wenham Historical Association. [Wenham] 1951. 171, [2] p. illus. 24 cm. Bibliography: p. [173] [NK495.W4] 51-7663
1. Dolls. I. Cole, Adeline P. II. Title.

WHITE, Gwen. 745.5922
Dolls of the world. [U.S. ed.] Newton Centre, Mass., C. T. Branford Co. [1963, c1962] 256 p. illus. (part col.) 26 cm. Bibliography: p. 248-249. [GV1219.W48 1963] 62-20818
1. Dolls.

YAMANASHI, Taeko 745.5922
Japanese paper dolls. Tokyo, T. Shuppan Co.; Rutland, Vt., Japan Pubns. [c.1964] 25p. illus. (pt. col.) mounted col. samples. 31cm. 64-4195 3.75 bds.,
1. Dolls. 2. Paper work. I. Title.

YAMANASHI, Taeko 745.5922
Paper dolls of old Japan. [Tr. by C. A. Pomeroy] Rutland, Vt., Tuttle [1962, c.1961] 49p. col. illus. 31cm. 62-15062 3.95 bds.,
1. Dolls. 2. Paper work. I. Title.

Dolls—Addresses, essays, lectures.

ANDERTON, Johana Gast. 745.59'22
Johana's dolls : a reprint of her doll columns and articles / Johana Gast Anderton. North Kansas City, Mo. : Athena Pub. Co., c1975. 97 p. (incl. cover) : ill. ; 28 cm. Includes index. [NK4893.A45] 75-14528 ISBN 0-89161-004-9 pbk. : 6.95
1. Dolls—Addresses, essays, lectures. I. Title. BIP

Dolls, American.

WATSON, Eleanor Schwingle. 688.7'22
Wee friends : a collection of 8" Madame Alexander dolls / by Eleanor Schwingle Watson. [Little Rock, Ark.] : Watson, [1974] v, 81 p. : ill. ; 27 cm. Includes index. [NK4894.2.A44W37] 75-300677
1. Alexander Doll Company. 2. Dolls, American. I. Title. II. Title: Madame Alexander dolls.

Dolls—Catalogs.

HOPKINSON, Isabella. 745.59'22
Dolls and miniatures with their prices at auction, by Isabella and William Hopkinson. [1st ed. Concord, N.H., Printed by Rumford Press, c1970] 51 p. col. illus. 22 cm. Cover title. [NK4893.H6] 75-281668
1. Dolls—Catalogs. 2. Miniature objects—Catalogs. I. Hopkinson, William, joint author. II. Title.

KAMMER und Reinhardt. 688.7'22
"My darling" dolls. Edited by Dorothy S. Coleman. [1st ed.] Princeton, Pyne Press; distributed by Scribner, New York [1972] 67 p. illus. 28 cm. Text in English, French, German, and Spanish. Reprint of the firm's catalog published in 1927 without title. [TS2301.T7K34] 72-79148 ISBN 0-87861-030-8 5.95 (pbk)
1. Dolls—Catalogs. I. Coleman, Dorothy S., ed. II. Title.

MERRILL, Madeline O. 745.59'22
Handbook of collectible dolls [by] Merrill & Perkins. [Photography by Richard Merrill. Melrose, Mass.? 1969- 2 v. (loose-leaf) illus. 20 cm. [NK4893.M4] 70-86337 23.00 (v. 1-2)
1. Dolls—Catalogs. 2. Dolls—Collectors and collecting. I. Perkins, Nellie W., joint author. II. Title. III. Title: Collectible dolls.

SELFRIDGE, Jim. 745.59'22
Dolls: images of love, by Jim and Madalaine Selfridge. [Irvine, Calif., c1973- v. illus. 28 cm. [NK4893.S42] 74-161006
1. Dolls—Catalogs. I. Selfridge, Madalaine, joint author. II. Title.

SMITH, Patricia R. 688.7'22
Teen dolls : identification and value guide / by Patricia R. Smith. Paducah, Ky. : Collector Books, c1977. 139 p. : ill. ; 22 cm. [TS2301.T7S59] 77-153171 ISBN 0-89145-051-3 : 7.95
1. Dolls—Catalogs. 2. Dolls—Collectors and collecting. I. Title.

Dolls—Collectors and collecting.

ANDERTON, Johana Gast. 688.7'22
More twentieth century dolls from bisque to vinyl / Johana Gast Anderton. North Kansas City, Mo. : Athena, 1974. p. 470-1191 : ill. ; 29 cm. Continues the paging of the author's earlier work, Twentieth century dolls. Includes index. [NK4893.A46] 74-84193 27.50
1. Dolls—Collectors and collecting. I. Title. BIP

ANDERTON, Johana Gast. 688.7'22
Twentieth century dolls; from bisque to vinyl. North Kansas City, Trojan Press [1971] 464 p. illus., facsims. 29 cm. [NK4893.A47] 75-165294 23.50
1. Dolls—Collectors and collecting. I. Title. BIP

ANGIONE, Genevieve. 738.8
All-bisque & half-bisque dolls. Photography: color plates by Louis Ouzer; black and white by Charles F. Angione. [Camden, N.J.,] T. Nelson [1969] 357 p. illus. (part col.) 23 cm. Bibliography: p. 357. [NK4893.A5] 76-77265 15.00
1. Dolls—Collectors and collecting. I. Title. BIP

ANGIONE, Genevieve. 688.7'22
All dolls are collectible / by Genevieve Angione and Judith Whorton. New York : Crown Publishers, c1977. 207 p. : ill. ; 29 cm. Includes index. [NK4893.A53] 77-79709 ISBN 0-517-53182-8 : 12.95
1. Dolls—Collectors and collecting. I. Whorton, Judith, joint author. II. Title. BIP

BROWN, Gearn. 745.59'22
Dolls of the United Nations. [1st ed.] New York, Vantage Press [1965] 210 p. illus. 21 cm. [NK4893.B7] 65-26705
1. Dolls — Collectors and collecting. I. Title.

COLEMAN, Dorothy S. 745.59'22'03
The collector's encyclopedia of dolls, by Dorothy S., Elizabeth A. and Evelyn J. Coleman. New York, Crown Publishers [1968] 697 p. illus., col. plates. 29 cm. Bibliography: p. 672-675. [NK4893.C6] 68-9101 25.00
1. Dolls—Collectors and collecting. 2. Dolls—Dictionaries. I. Coleman, Elizabeth A., joint author. II. Coleman, Evelyn J., joint author. III. Title. BIP

DICICCO, Laurel M. 745.5*22
Doll collectors' treasures [by] Laurel M. Dicicco. New York, Carlton Press [1970] 96 p. illus. 15 x 21 cm. (A Hearthstone book) [NK4893.D5] 73-24830 3.50
1. Dolls—Collectors and collecting. I. Title.

ELLENBURG, M. Kelly. 745.59'22
Effanbee: the dolls with the golden hearts [by] M. Kelly Ellenburg. North Kansas City [Mo.] Trojan Press [1973] 200 p. illus. 29 cm. Bibliography: p. 191. [TS2301.T7E44] 73-85390 14.95
1. Dolls—Collectors and collecting. 2. Dolls—Catalogs. I. Title. BIP

FAWCETT, Clara Evelyn 745.5922075 (Hallard)
Dolls; a new guide for collectors. Boston, C. T. Branford Co. [1964] 282 p. illus. 24 cm. "Bibliography—dolls" p. 268-272. "Bibliography—puppets and marionettes":p. 273. "Music composed for dolls": p. 274. [NK4893.F3 1964] 64-16263
1. Dolls—Collectors and collecting. I. Title.

FRASER, Antonia 745.592209 (Pakenham) Lady
Dolls. New York, Putnam [1963] 128 p. illus. (part col.) 22 cm. [NK4894.A2F7] 63-15526
I. Title.

GERKEN, Jo Elizabeth. 745.59'22
Wonderful dolls of wax [by] Jo Elizabeth Gerken. Lincoln, Neb., Doll Research Associates [1964] 135 p. illus. 28 cm. Bibliography: p. 127-129. [NK4893.G4] 64-25530
1. Dolls—Collectors and collecting. I. Title.

JOHL, Janet Pagter. 649.55
Your dolls and mine; a collectors' handbook. New York, H. L. Lindquist Publications, 1952. xvii, 384 p. illus. 27 cm. [NK4893.J6] 52-12550
1. Dolls—Collectors and collecting. I. Title.

NOBLE, John, 1923- 745.59'22'075
Dolls. New York, Walker [1967] 84 p. illus. (part col.) 22 cm. (Collectors' blue books) [NK4893.N6 1967] 67-23093
1. Dolls—Collectors and collecting. I. Title.

SELFRIDGE, Madalaine. 745.59'22
Wendy and friends; a practical guide to a fascinating hobby. [Escondido, Calif., Swadell Lithographers, Inc., c1969] iv, 92 p. illus. 28 cm. [NK4893.S44] 77-26276
1. Dolls—Collectors and collecting. I. Title.

SHOEMAKER, Rhoda. 745.59'22
Compo dolls: cute and collectible. [Menlo Park, Calif., 1971-73] 2 v. illus. 28 cm. Bibliography: v. 2, p. 114. [NK4893.S5] 74-30646
1. Dolls—Collectors and collecting. I. Title.

SMITH, Patricia R. 745.59'22
Antique collector's dolls : second series / by Patricia R. Smith ; edited by Karen Penner ; price guide editor, Kim McKim. Paducah, Ky. : Collector Books, c1976. viii, 248 p. : ill. ; 29 cm. Includes index. [NK4893.S632] 77-353963 ISBN 0-89145-021-1 : 17.95
1. Dolls—Collectors and collecting. I. Title. BIP

SMITH, Patricia R. 745.59'22'075
Armand Marseille dolls, 1865-1928 / by Patricia R. Smith ; edited by Dorothy Westbrook ; photo's by Dwight F. Smith. Paducah, Ky. : Collector Books, [1975] 144 p. : col. ill. ; 22 cm. Bibliography: p. 144. [TS2301.T7S58] 75-316885 7.95
1. Armand Marseille (Firm) 2. Dolls—Collectors and collecting. 3. Dolls—Catalogs. I. Title. BIP

SMITH, Patricia R. 745.59'22
Modern collector's dolls, by Patricia R. Smith. Photography by Dwight F. Smith. Edited by Dorothy Westbrook. 1st ed. Paducah, Ky., Collector Books, c1973. iv, 309 p. illus. 29 cm. Bibliography: p. 304. [NK4893.S64] 74-160943 17.95
1. Dolls—Collectors and collecting. I. Title. BIP

THE Standard antique 688.7'22
doll identification & value guide, 1700-1935. Paducah, Ky. : Collector Books, c1976. 103 p. : ill. ; 23 cm. Includes indexes. [NK4893.S86] 76-374774 ISBN 0-89145-014-9 : 7.95
1. Dolls—Collectors and collecting. 2. Dolls—Catalogs. 3. Dolls—Trade-marks. I. Title: Antique doll. BIP

THE Standard modern doll 688.7'22
identification & value guide, 1935-1976. Paducah, Ky. : Collector Books, c1976. 128 p. : ill. ; 23 cm. Includes index. [NK4893.S865] 76-374773 ISBN 0-89145-013-0 : 7.95
1. Dolls—Collectors and collecting. 2. Dolls—Catalogs. 3. Dolls—Trade-marks. I. Title: Modern doll. BIP

STEWART, Ethel. 688.7'22'075
A collector's guide to the Patsy dolls / Ethel Stewart and Katherine Dennis ; photography by Darryl Dennis. Seattle : Stewart, [1974] 44 p., 2 leaves of plates : ill. ; 28 cm. Bibliography: p. 44. [TS2301.T7S74] 75-305463 6.95
1. EFFanBEE Doll Corp. 2. Dolls—Collectors and collecting. 3. Dolls—Catalogs. I. Dennis, Katherine, joint author. II. Dennis, Darryl. III. Title.

TAVARES, Olinda. 745.59'22
The armchair museum of dolls. [1st ed.] New York, Vantage Press [1973] 138 p. illus. 24 cm. [NK4893.T38] 74-156279 ISBN 0-533-00621-X 13.95
1. Dolls—Collectors and collecting. I. Title.

YOUNG, Helen. 688.7'22
The complete book of doll collecting. New York, Putnam [1967] 312 p. illus. 22 cm. Bibliography: p. 285-287. [GV1219.Y58] 67-21216
1. Dolls—Collectors and collecting. I. Title. BIP

YOUNG, Helen. 745.5922
Here is your hobby: doll collecting. New York, Putnam [1964] 128 p. illus. 24 cm. (Here is your hobby series) Bibliography: p. 126. [GV1219.Y6] 64-14217
1. Dolls—Collectors and collecting. I. Title.

Dolls—Collectors and collecting—Congresses.

UNITED Federation of 745.59'22 Doll Clubs.
Silver anniversary convention / United Federation of Doll Clubs, inc. Lincoln, Neb. : The Federation, [1974] 206 p., (p. 127-204 advertisements), [1] leaf of plates : ill. ; 29 cm. Pages 205-206, blank for "Notes." Transactions of the convention held in Miami Beach, Aug. 5-11, 1974. [NK4893.U54 1974] 74-79033
1. United Federation of Doll Clubs—Congresses. 2. Dolls—Collectors and collecting—Congresses.

Dolls — Collectors and collecting — Period.

DOLL Collectors of 745.59'22 America.
Doll collectors manual. [Boston] Doll Collectors of America. v. illus. 26 cm. [NK4893.D6] 65-29362
1. Dolls — Collectors and collecting — Period. I. Title. BIP

Dolls—Collectors and collecting—United States.

CHISMAN, Evelyn Meade. 688.7'22
Small dolls & other collectibles / Evelyn Meade Chisman. New York : Drake Publishers, 1978. 144 p. : ill. ; 26 cm. Bibliography: p. 143-144. [NK4893.C48] 77-15903 pbk. : 6.95
1. Dolls—Collectors and collecting—United States. 2. Figurines—Collectors and collecting—United States. I. Title. BIP

Dolls, English.

HART, Luella 745.59'22'075 Tilton, 1897-
Directory of British dolls. [n. p., 1964] 52 p. illus., diagrs. 26 cm. Part 1 of the author's Doll directories, pt. 2 of which is the Directory of German dolls trademarks, 1875-1960. [TS2301.T7H34] 64-9115
1. Dolls, English. 2. Dolls — Patents — Direct. 3. Dolls — Trademarks — Direct. I. Title. II. Title: British dolls.

Dolls, French.

HART, Luella Tilton, 688.722 1897-
Complete French doll directory, 1801-1964, covers early doll makers, sellers, trademarks, patents, by Luella Hart. [n. p., 1965] 125 p. illus. 26 cm. Part 3 of the author's Doll directories, of which pt. 1 is the Directory of British dolls and pt. 2 is the Directory of German dolls trademarks. [TS2301.T7H33] 65-2186
1. Dolls, French. 2. Dolls — Patents — Direct. 3. Dolls — Trademarks — Direct. I. Title. II. Title: French doll directory, 1801-1964. III. Title: Doll directories.

Dolls, German — Trademarks.

HART, Luella Tilton, 688.722 1897-
Directory of German dolls trademarks 1875-1960, by Luella Hart [n. p., 1964] 75 p. illus. 26 cm. Part 2 of the author's Doll directories, the 1st of which is the Directory of British dolls. [TS2301.T7H35] 64-54552
1. Dolls, German — Trademarks. 2. Trademarks — Germany. I. Title. II. Title: German dolls trademarks, 1875-1960.

Dolls—Germany—Catalogs.

SMITH, Patricia R. 688.7'22
Kestner and Simon & Halbig dolls, 1804-1930 / by Patricia R. Smith ; edited by Tyral Jane Weiss ; photos. by Dwight F. Smith. Paducah, Ky. : Collector Books, c1976. 96 p. : col. ill. ; 22 cm. Bibliography: p. 96. [NK4894.2.K47S64] 76-150225 ISBN 0-89145-022-X : 7.95
1. Kestner (Firm) 2. Simon und Halbig. 3. Dolls—Germany—Catalogs. 4. Dolls—Collectors and collecting—United States. I. Title. BIP

Dolls—History.

BATEMAN, Thelma. 745.5922
Delightful dolls, antique and otherwise. Photos. by the author. Washington, Hobby House Press, 1966. xvi, 237 p. illus., facsims. 26 cm. Bibliography: p. 233-234. [NK4894.A2B27] 66-20359
1. Dolls—History. I. Title.

COLEMAN, Evelyn J. 745.592209
The age of dolls, by Evelyn, Elizabeth, and Dorothy Coleman. Washington, D.C. [D.S. Coleman, 4315 Van Ness N.W.] 1965. iv, 138p. illus. 29cm. [NK4894.A2C57] 65-23112 price unreported
1. Dolls—Hist. I. Coleman, Elizabeth A., joint author. II. Coleman, Dorothy S., joint author. III. Title. BIP

COLEMAN, Elizabeth 745.59'22'09 A.
Dolls; makers and marks, including addenda, by Elizabeth A. Coleman, in collaboration with Dorothy and Evelyn Coleman. [2d, rev. ed.] Washington, 1966- v. illus., facsims. 23 cm. [NK4894.A2C62] 66-25627
1. Dolls—History. 2. Dolls—Trade-marks. I. Title. BIP

FRASER, Antonia 745.592209 (Packenham)
Dolls. New York, Putnam [1963] 128 p. illus. (part col.) 22 cm. (Pleasures and treasures) [NK4894.A2F7] 63-15526
1. Dolls — Hist. I. Title.

FREEMAN, Ruth (Sunderlin). 688.7
American dolls. Watkins Glen, N. Y., Century House, '1952. 71 p. illus. 23 cm. [GV1219.F7] 649.55 52-14498
1. Dolls—Hist. I. Title.

GERKEN, Jo Elizabeth. 745.59'22
Wonderful dolls of papier mache. [Lincoln, Neb.] Doll Research Associates [1970] xv, 227 p. illus. (part col.), map. 29 cm. Bibliography: p. 223-224. [NK4894.A2G4] 77-120295
1. Dolls—History. I. Title.

GOLDING, Amy Thomas. 649.55
Miniature travelers. Francestown, N. H., M. Jones Co. [c1956] 160p. illus. 23cm. [GV1219.G64] 57-28906

1. Dolls—Hist. I. Title.

HILLIER, Mary. 745.59'22'09
Dolls and doll-makers. New York, Putnam [1968] 256 p. illus. (part col.) 26 cm. Bibliography: p. 254. [NK4894.A2H45] 68-20629 15.00
1. Dolls—History. I. Title.

JACOBS, Flora Gill. 745.59'2
A book of dolls & doll houses, by Flora Gill Jacobs and Estrid Faurholt. Rutland, Vt., C. E. Tuttle Co. [1967] 224 p. illus. (part col.) 32 cm. Contents.Contents.—Pt. 1. The dolls, by Estrid Faurholt.—Pt. 2. Doll houses and shops, by Flora Gill Jacobs. [NK4894.A2J28] 65-20615
1. Dolls—History. 2. Doll-houses—History. I. Faurholt, Estrid. II. Title.

JOHL, Janet (Pagter). 649.55
Still more about dolls. [1st ed.] New York, H. L. Lindquist Publications [1950] 300 p. illus. 26 cm. [GV1219.J595] 50-10445
1. Dolls—Hist. I. Title.

KING, Constance Eileen. 745.59'22
The collector's history of dolls / Constance Eileen King. New York : St. Martin's Press, [1977] p. cm. Includes index. Bibliography: p. [NK4894.A2K56] 77-6095 ISBN 0-312-15025-3 : 30.00
1. Dolls—History. 2. Dolls—Collectors and collecting. I. Title. BIP

WHITE, Gwen. 688.722
European and American dolls and their marks and patents. [1st American ed.] New York, Putnam [1966] 274 p. illus. 31 cm. Bibliography: p. 268. [NK4894.A2W46 1966a] 66-24567
1. Dolls—History. 2. Dolls—Trade-marks. I. Title.

Dolls—Japan—Catalogs.

CHANDLER, Ceil. 382'.45'688720952
Toys and dolls made in occupied Japan. Houston, Tex., Chandler's Discriminating Junk [1973] 9 p. illus. 22 cm. [NK4894.J3C46] 74-153437 15.00
1. Dolls—Japan—Catalogs. 2. Toys—Japan—Catalogs. I. Title.

Dolls, Japanese.

CHANDLER, Billie T. 745.59
Crafts and trades of Japan, with doll-and-flower arrangements. Photos. by Shigemasa Nagai. Rutland, Vt., Tuttle [1965, c.1964] 56p. col. illus. 18cm. [NK4894.J3C45] 64-24952 5.00
1. Dolls, Japanese. 2. Flower arrangement, Japanese. 3. Art industries and trade—Japan. I. Title.

Dolls—Juvenile literature.

GLUBOK, Shirley. 745.59'22
Dolls, dolls, dolls / Shirley Glubok ; special photography by Alfred Tamarin ; designed by Gerard Nook. Chicago : Follett Pub. Co., [1975] 64 p., [4] leaves of plates : ill. ; 27 cm. Text and illustrations trace the history of dolls from ancient Egyptian paddle dolls to stylish fashion dolls and clever mechanical dolls. Also includes a section on dollhouses. [NK4893.G55] 73-93559 ISBN 0-695-80483-9 : 5.95 ISBN 0-695-40483-0 lib.bdg. : 5.97
1. Dolls—Juvenile literature. I. Tamarin, Alfred H. II. Title. BIP

WORRELL, Estelle Ansley, 1929- 745.5922
The doll book [by] Estelle Ansley Worrell with Norman Worrell. Princeton, N.J., Van Nostrand [1966] xii, 135 p. illus. (part col.) 29 cm. [GV1219.W6] 66-27528
1. Dolls—Juvenile literature. I. Worrell, Norman. II. Title. BIP

WORRELL, Estelle(Ansley) 1929- 745.59'22
The dollbook / Estelle Ansley Worrell ; with Norman Worrell. New York : Van Nostrand Reinhold [1976]c1966. xii, 135p. : ill. (part col.) ; 28 cm. Includes index. [GV1219.W6] ISBN 0-442-29555-3 pbk. : 5.95
1. Dolls-Juvenile literature. I. Title.
L. C. card no. for original ed. 66-27528.

Dolls—Massachusetts—Salem.

MERRILL, Madeline O. 688.7'2'07401445
Dolls & toys at the Essex Institute / by Madeline & Richard Merrill ; photographs by Richard Merrill. Salem, Mass. : Essex Institute, c1976. 60 p. : ill. ; 21 cm. (Esses Institute museum booklet series ; 1) Bibliography: p. 60. [NK4892.U6S345] 76-40405 ISBN 0-88389-066-6 : 4.95
1. Essex Institute, Salem, Mass. 2. Dolls—Massachusetts—Salem. 3. Toys—Massachusetts—Salem. I. Merrill, Richard, 1908- joint author. II. Essex Institute, Salem, Mass. III. Title. IV. Series: Essex Institute, Salem, Mass. Essex Institute museum booklet series ; 1. BIP

Dolls—Prices.

MILLER, Robert William, 1922- 745.59'22
Wallace-Homestead price guide to dolls : pictures and identification of more than 850 dolls from all over the world / Robert W. Miller. Des Moines : Wallace-Homestead Book Co., [1975] 212 p. : chiefly ill. (some col.) ; 29 cm. Cover title. [NK4893.M5] 74-84522 ISBN 0-87069-117-1 : 7.95
1. Dolls—Prices. 2. Dolls—Collectors and collecting. I. Title. II. Title: Price guide to dolls. BIP

Dolls—Private collections.

JOHNSTON, LaVaughn C. 745.59'22
Open mouth dolls, by LaVaughn C. Johnston. [Downey, Calif., Printed by E. Quinn, 1974] 152 p. (chiefly illus.) 28 cm. [NK4892.5.J64A52] 74-174953
1. Dolls—Private collections. I. Title.

Dolls—Repairing.

GAYLIN, Evelyn. 745.59'22
Doll repair: from the Gay World of Dolls. [1st ed.] Portland, Or., Gay World of Dolls, 1967. 119 p. illus. 24 cm. [TS2301.T7G3] 67-8873
1. Dolls—Repairing. I. Title. BIP

GAYLIN, Evelyn. 745.59'22
Doll repair: from the Gay World of Dolls. [2d ed.] Oregon City, Or., Gay World of Dolls, 1971. 158 p. illus., facsims. 23 cm. [TS2301.T7G3 1971] 70-26076
1. Dolls—Repairing. I. Title.

JOHNSON, Audrey. 745.5922
How to repair and dress old dolls, written and illustrated by Audrey Johnson. [U.S. ed.] Newton, Mass., C. T. Branford Co. [1967] 128 p. illus. 21 cm. [TS2301.T7J57] 67-12386
1. Dolls—Repairing. 2. Doll clothes. I. Title. BIP

Dolls—Trade-marks.

SHEA, Ralph A. 688.7'22
Doll mark clues; by Ralph A. Shea. [1st ed.] Ridgefield, N.J., 1972- v. illus. 23 cm. Contents.Contents.—v. 1. Antique dolls dictionary, 1967-72 asking prices.—v. 2. Numbers in antique doll marks, 1968-1973 asking prices.—v. 3. Numbers in antique doll marks (part B) 1973-1974 asking price.—v. 4. Numbers in antique doll marks, part C: 1974-1975 asking prices. Includes bibliographies. [NK4893.S48] 72-197072 16.50 (v. 3)
1. Dolls—Trade-marks. 2. Dolls—Collectors and collecting. I. Title.

WHITE, Gwen. 745.59'2'0275
Toys and dolls : marks and labels / Gwen White. Newton, Mass. : C. T. Branford Co., 1975. 240 p. : ill. ; 26 cm. Includes indexes. [T257.V4D684] 75-332961 ISBN 0-8231-3032-0 : 24.50
1. Dolls—Trade-marks. 2. Trade-marks—Great Britain. I. Title. BIP

Dolls—United States.

BUSER, M. Elaine. 688.7'2'075
M. Elaine and Dan Buser's guide to Schoenhut's dolls, toys, and circus, 1872-1976. Paducah, Ky. : Collector Books, c1976. 104 p. : ill. (some col.) ; 29 cm. [NK4894.2.S3B98] 76-374765 12.95
1. Schoenhut (A.) Company. 2. Dolls—United States. 3. Toys—United States. I. Buser, Daniel S., joint author. II. Title: M. Elaine and Dan Buser's guide to Schoenhut's dolls, toys, and circus ... III. Title: Guide to Schoenhut's dolls, toys, and circus, 1872-1976.

SORENSEN, Lewis, 1910- 745.59'22
Lewis Sorensen's Doll scrapbook / by Lewis Sorensen ; compiled and edited by Don Thorup. A collector's ed. Alhambra, Calif. : Thor Publications, 1976- v. : ill. (some col.) ; 29 cm. [NK4894.2.S65A43] 76-7692
1. Sorensen, Lewis, 1910- 2. Dolls—United States. 3. Dolls—Collectors and collecting—United States. I. Title. II. Title: Doll scrapbook.

Dolls—United States—Catalogs.

MANOS, Susan. 688.7'2'075
Schoenhut dolls & toys : a loving legacy / by Susan Manos. 1st ed. Paducah, Ky. : Collector Books, c1976. 96 p. : ill. (some col.) ; 23 cm. Includes index. Bibliography: p. 94. [NK4894.2.S3M35] 76-374764 ISBN 0-89145-012-2 : 8.95
1. Schoenhut (A.) Company. 2. Dolls—United States—Catalogs. 3. Toys—United States—Catalogs. I. Title. BIP

Dolls—United States—Collectors and collecting.

SMITH, Patricia R. 791.43'028'0924
Shirley Temple dolls and collectibles / by Patricia R. Smith ; all photos. by Dwight F. Smith, unless noted ; editor, Karen Penner. Paducah, Ky. : Collector Books ; New York : distributed by Crown Publishers, c1977. vi, 144 p. : ill. ; 29 cm. [NK808.S6] 77-153173 ISBN 0-89145-053-X : 17.95
1. Temple, Shirley, 1928- —Collectibles. 2. Dolls—United States—Collectors and collecting. I. Penner, Karen. II. Title. BIP

Dolls—United States—Collectors and collecting—Catalogs.

SMITH, Patricia R. 688.7'22
Madame Alexander collector's dolls / by Patricia R. Smith ; editors, Beatrice Alexander, Karen Penner. Paducah, Ky. : Collector Books, [c1978] 315 p. : ill. ; 29 cm. & price guide. Includes index. [NK4894.2.A44A4 1978] 78-103728 19.95
1. Alexander Doll Company—Catalogs. 2. Dolls—United States—Collectors and collecting—Catalogs. I. Alexander, Beatrice. II. Penner, Karen. III. Title.

Dombrowski, Ernst, Ritter von, 1896—

DOMBROWSKI, Ernst, Ritter von, 1896- 741.9'43
Children : sketches, stories, and thoughts about children / Ernst von Dombrowski ; translated from the German by Norma and Garold Davis. Provo, Utah : Brigham Young University Press, c1976. 91 p. : chiefly ill. ; 29 cm. Translation of Kinder. [NC251.D65A4813] 75-43798 14.95
1. Dombrowski, Ernst, Ritter von, 1896- 2. Children in art. I. Title. BIP

Domes.

HJERSMAN, Peter. 729'.34
Dome notes / Peter Hjersman. [Berkeley, Calif.] : Erewon Press, c1975. 201 p. : ill. ; 27 cm. Includes index. Bibliography: p. 195-197. [NA2890.H54] 75-32589 ISBN 0-916342-01-8
1. Domes. I. Title. BIP

Domestic animals—U.S.—Pictorial works.

HARDING, Frank, 1911- 704.94'32
A livestock heritage; animals and people in art. [Geneva, Ill., 1971] [64] p. col. illus., col. facsims. 28 cm. [N6505.H29] 70-26826
1. Domestic animals—U.S.—Pictorial works. 2. The West in art. I. Title.

Domjan, Joseph, 1907—

DOMJAN, Joseph, 1907- 769'.92'4
The artist and the legend : a visit to China is remembered and the legends unfold : text and woodcuts / by Joseph Domjan. Tuxedo Park, N.Y. : Opus, c1974. [70] p. : ill. (some col.) ; 29 cm. [NE1300.6.D65A42] 74-81927
1. Domjan, Joseph, 1907- 2. Legends, Chinese, in art. I. Title. BIP

DOMJAN, Joseph, 1907- 769'.92'4
Bellringer / woodcuts by Domjan ; poems by Ruth Laurene. Tuxedo Park, N.Y. : Opus, c1974. 80 p. : col. ill. ; 33 cm. Bibliography: p. 72-73. [NE1112.D65L38] 74-75851
1. Domjan, Joseph, 1907- I. Laurene, Ruth. II. Title. BIP

DOMJAN, Joseph, 1907- 769'.92'4
Domjan, in the forest of the golden dragon [by] Pierre Mornand. [Translated by Mira Intrator. Tuxedo Park, N.Y.] Opus [1973] 128 p. illus. (part col.) 29 cm. English and French. Bibliography: p. 125-127. [NE1112.D65M67 1973] 73-76776
1. Domjan, Joseph, 1907- I. Mornand, Pierre, 1884-

CINCINNATI Museum Association. 927.6
Jozsef Domjan color woodcuts, October 21-November 25, 1958, Cincinnati Art Museum. [Cincinnati, 1958] unpaged. illus. 21cm. [NE1217.D63C5] 59-27868
1. Domjan, Jozsef, 1907- I. Title.

Domsaitis, Pranas, 1880-1965.

DOMSAITIS, Pranas, 1880-1965. 741.973
Pranas Domsaitis / [text] by Elsa Verloren van Themaat. Cape Town : Struik (C.), 1976. 64 p. : chiefly ill. (some col., 1 fold.) ; 25 x 28 cm. (South African art library ; 6) Includes index. Bibliography: p. 63. [ND588.D65V37] 77-558243 ISBN 0-86977-070-5 : R9.75
1. Domsaitis, Pranas, 1880-1965. 2. Painters—Germany—Biography. I. Verloren van Themaat, Elsa. II. Title. III. Series.

Donatello, i.e. Donato di Nicolo di Betto Bardi, 1386 (ca.)-1466.

CASTELFRANCO, Giorgio, 1896- 730.924
Donatello. [Translated from the Italian by R. H. Boothroyd] New York, Reynal [1965] 118 [119] p. illus., 40 col. plates. 32 cm. Bibliography: p. 115-118 (1st group) [NB623.D7C313] 66-3039
1. Donatello, i.e. Donato di Nicolo di Betto Bardi, 1386 (ca.)-1466. I. Title.

CRUTTWELL, Maud. 730'.92'4
Donatello. Freeport, N.Y., Books For Libraries Press [1971] xii, 161, [80] p. illus. 27 cm. Reprint of the 1911 ed., issued in series: Classics of art. Bibliography: p. 150-151. [NB623.D7C7 1971] 71-37334 ISBN 0-8369-6681-3
1. Donatello, i.e. Donato di Niccolo di Betto Bardi, 1386 (ca.)-1466. I. Series: Classics of art. BIP

DONATELLO, i.e. Donato di Niccolo di Betto Bardi, 1386(ca.)-1466 730.924
All the sculpture of Donatello. [Text] by Luigi Grassi. Translated by Paul Colacicchi. New York, Hawthorn Books [c1964] 2 v. (147 p., 224 plates (4 col.] illus. 18 cm. (The Complete library of world art, v. 23-24) "Bibliographical note": v. 2, p. 143-147. [NB623.D7G73] 64-24261
I. Grassi, Luigi, 1913- II. Title. III. Series.

FINN, David. 730'.92'4
Donatello, prophet of modern vision. Photos by David Finn. Text by Frederick Hartt. New York, Abrams [1973] 482 p.

illus (part. col.) 42 cm. Bibliography: p. 479 [NB623.D7H3] 72-10605 ISBN 0-8109-0121-8. 85.00
1. Donatello, i.e. Donato di Niccolo di Betto Bardi, 1386 (ca.)-1466. I. Hartt, Frederick. II. Title.

JANSON, Horst Woldemar, 1913- 730.945
The sculpture of Donatello. Incorporating the notes and photos. of Jeno Lanyi. Princeton, N. J., Princeton University Press, 1963. xix, 260 p. illus., 128 plates. 29 cm. "The complete text of the first edition [1957] but a less lavish pictorial apparatus." Bibliography: p. xviii-xix. "Selected Donatello bibliography, 1957-1962": p. [250]-[251] [NB623.D7J3] 62-7041
1. Donatello, i.e. Donato di Betto Bardi, 1386 (ca.)-1466. I. Lanyi, Jeno.

THE sculpture of 735.45
Donatello, by H. W. Janson, incorporating the notes and photos. of the late Jeno Lanyi. Princeton, Princeton University Press, 1957. 2 v. illus., plates. 31cm. Contents.v. 1. Plates.--v. 2. Critical catalogue. Includes bibliographical references. [NB623.D7J3] 927.3 57-5473
I. Janson, Horst Woldemar, 1913- II. Donatello, i. e. Donato di Niccolo di Betto Bardi, 1386 (ca.)-1466. III. Lanyi, Jeno.

Dongen, Kees van, 1877-1968.

DIEHL, Gaston. 759.9492
Van Dongen. [Translated from the French by Stephanie Winston] New York, Crown Publisher [1969] 94, [2] p. illus. (part col.), ports. (part col.) 29 cm. ([The Q.L.P. art series]) Bibliography: p. 94-[95] [ND653.D64D513] 77-13525 3.50
1. Dongen, Kees van, 1877-1968. BIP

DONGEN, Kees van, 1877-1968. 760'.0924
Cornelis Theodorus Marie van Dongen, 1877-1968. Hommages de William E. Steadman et Denys Sutton. [Tucson, Ariz.] University of Arizona Museum of Art, 1971. 198 p. illus. (part col.), ports. 29 cm. Catalogue of a retrospective exhibition of Dongen's paintings, watercolors, drawings and lithographs held at the University of Arizona Museum of Art and the William Rockhill Nelson Gallery of Art. Bibliography: p. 196-198. [N6953.D65S7] 75-634228
I. Steadman, William E. II. Sutton, Denys. III. Arizona. University. Museum of Art. IV. William Rockhill Nelson Gallery of Art and Mary Atkins Museum of Fine Arts, Kansas City, Mo.

DONGEN, Marc van, 1875- 759.9492
A comprehensive exhibition of paintings, 1900 to 1925, by Van Dongen, November 16 to December 18, 1965 Leonard Hutton Galleries, New York [New York, 1965] [24] p. illus. (part col.), port. (on cover) 27 cm. "Catalogue": p. [12] Previous exhibitions of the artist's work: p. [21] [ND653.D643L4] 68-7153
I. Leonard Hutton Galleries. II. Title.

LYONS. Musee des beaux-arts. 372.5
Van Dongen. [Exposition] Musee de Lyon, 1964. [Lyon, 1964] 1 v. (unpaged) illus., ports. 25 cm. At head of title: Festival de Lyon. Introductory text by R. Deroudille. [ND653.D64L9] 66-47118
1. Dongen, Klees van, 1887- I. Deroudille, Rene. II. Title.

Donkeys—Pictorial works.

REICH, Hanns, comp. 779'.32
Donkeys. Translated and adapted from a text by Eugen Skasa-Weiss. New York, Hill and Wang [1973] [7] p., 60 p. of illus. 24 cm. (Terra magica) Translation of Esel. [SF361.R4413 1973] 73-81579 ISBN 0-8090-2048-3 5.95
1. Donkeys—Pictorial works. I. Skasa-Weiss, Eugen, 1905- II. Title. BIP

Doodles.

URIS, Norman Burton, comp. 741.9
The doodle book. [New York] Collier Books [1970] 176 p. illus., facsims. 18 cm. [NC915.D6U7] 75-119128
1. Doodles. I. Title. BIP

Doors.

*CLERY, Val. 729'.38
Doors / Val Clery ; photos. by Gordon Beck [et al.] New York : Penguin Books, 1979, c1978. 157p. : col. ill. ; 22 cm. "A Jonathan James book." [NA3010] ISBN 0-14-005105-8 pbk. : 9.95
1. Doors. I. Title. BIP

CLERY, Val. 729'.38
Doors / text by Val Clery ; photos. by Gordon Beck ... [et al.]. New York : Viking Press, 1979, c1978. ca. 150 p. : col. ill. ; 23 cm. (A studio book) "A Jonathan-James book." [NA3010.C56 1979] 78-63154 ISBN 0-670-28039-9 : 14.95
1. Doors. 2. Doorways. I. Beck, Gordon. II. Title.

NATIONAL Research Council. Building Research Institute. 729.38
Public entrance doors; proceedings of a conference presented as part of the 1961 spring conferences of the Building Research Inst., Div. of Engin. and Industrial Research. Washington, D. C., Natl. Acad. of Scis.--Natl. Research Council, 1961. vii, 93p. 28cm. (Natl. Research Council. Pubn. 948) Bibl. 62-60013 6.00 pap.,
1. Doors. 2. Doorways. I. Title. II. Series. BIP

Doors—Exhibitions.

AMERICAN Craftsmen's Council. Museum of Contemporary Crafts. 721'.8
The door. [New York, 1968] [36] p. illus. 29 x 12 cm. Catalogue of an exhibition organized by the Museum of Contemporary Crafts and U.S. Plywood. [NB1285.A46] 72-194797
1. Doors—Exhibitions. I. U.S. Plywood Corp. II. Title.

Doors in art—Exhibitions.

ARKWRIGHT Arts Trust. 704.94'4'07402142
Doors : [catalogue of an exhibition held] 14 December 1976-30 January 1977 [at] Camden Arts Centre ... [organised by the Arkwright Arts Trust]. London : The Trust, [1976] 36 p. : ill. ; 30 cm. [N6488G7L627] 77-369112 ISBN 0-9505532-0-4 : £1.00
1. Doors in art—Exhibitions. 2. Art, Modern—20th century—Exhibitions. I. Camden Arts Centre. II. Title.

Doorstops—Collectors and collecting.

HAMBURGER, Marilyn G., 1941- 745.1
Collecting figural doorstops / Marilyn G. Hamburger and Beverly S. Lloyd. South Brunswick [N.J.] : A. S. Barnes, c1978. p. cm. Includes index. Bibliography: p. [NK4894.6.H35] 76-50219 ISBN 0-498-02082-7 : 12.95
1. Doorstops—Collectors and collecting. I. Lloyd, Beverly S., 1934- joint author. II. Title. BIP

Doorways.

LEISINGER, Hermann. 739.512
Romanesque bronzes; church portals in mediaeval Europe. New York, F. A. Praeger [1957] [16] p., 160 plates. 33 cm. [NB1282.L413] 57-11298
1. Doorways. 2. Bronzes, Romanesque. 3. Sculpture, Romanesque. I. Title.

Dore, Gustave, 1832-1883.

DE MARE, Eric Samuel, 1910- 914.21'03'81
The London Dore saw: a Victorian evocation [by] Eric de Mare. New York, St. Martin's Press [1973] 228 p. illus. 31 cm. Bibliography: p. 221-225. [NC248.D6D45 1973b] 72-93928 15.00
1. Dore, Gustave, 1832-1883. 2. London in art. I. Title.

**A Dore gallery.* 709.2
New York, Arco, [1974]. 304 p. illus. 31 cm. [N72.R4] 73-91686 ISBN 0-668-03444-0. 15.00
1. Dore, Gustave, 1832-1883. 2. Art—Galleries and museums.

DORE, Gustave, 1832-1883. 769'.92'4
The Dore Bible illustrations. With a new introd. by Millicent Rose. New York, Dover Publications [1974] xiii p., 241 p. of illus. 31 cm. [N8027.D82 1974] 73-87048 ISBN 0-486-23079-1. 5.00
1. Dore, Gustave, 1832-1883. 2. Bible—Pictures, illustrations, etc. I. Title. BIP

DORE, Gustave, 1832-1883. 769'.92'4
A Dore gallery / [text by Edmund Ollier]. London ; New York [etc.] : Spring Books, 1974. 304 p. : chiefly ill. ; 31 cm. Adapted from a 2 v. ed. published in London in 1870. [NE650.D646O44 1974] 75-308617 ISBN 0-600-32897-X : £3.95
1. Dore, Gustave, 1832-1883. I. Ollier, Edmund, 1827-1886. II. Title. BIP

DORE, Gustave, 1832-1883. 769'.924
A Dore treasury; a collection of the best engravings of Gustave Dore, edited and with an introd. by James Stevens. [New York] Bounty Books [1970] ix, 246 p. (chiefly illus.) 31 cm. [NC1135.D7S67 1970] 72-93414 10.00
I. Title.

DORE, Gustave, 1832-1883. 769'.92'4
Dore's illustrations for Rabelais : a selection of 252 illustrations / by Gustave Dore : [selection, introd. captions by Stanley Applebaum]. New York : Dover Publications, c1978. 153 p. : chiefly ill. ; 31 cm. Selections from Ouvres de Rabelais published by Garnier Freres, 188-? [NC248.D6A4 1978] 78-51529 ISBN 0-486-23656-0 : 5.00
1. Dore, Gustave, 1832-1883. 2. Rabelais, Francois, 1490 (ca.)-1557?—Illustrations. I. Applebaum, Stanley. II. Rabelais, Francois, 1490 (ca.)-1553? Works. 188-. III. Title. BIP

GOSLING, Nigel. 759.4
Gustave Dore. New York, Praeger [1974, c1973] 112 p. illus. 29 cm. Includes bibliographical references. [ND553.D7G67 1974] 73-13525 12.50
1. Dore, Gustave, 1832-1883.

JERROLD, Blanchard, 1826-1884. 759.4 B
Life of Gustave Dore. With one hundred and thirty-eight illus. from original drawings by Dore. London, W. H. Allen, 1891. Detroit, Singing Tree Press, 1969. vi, 415 p. illus., port. 22 cm. [NC248.D6J4 1969] 69-17492
1. Dore, Gustave, 1832-1883. I. Title. BIP

LEHMANN-HAUPT, Hellmut, 1903 741.9'44 B
The terrible Gustave Dore / by Hellmut Lehmann-Haupt. Westport, Conn. : Greenwood Press, 1976. p. cm. Reprint of the 1943 ed. published by Marchbanks Press, New York. "Originated as a lecture given before the Grolier Club in New York City on December 14, 1939." Bibliography: p. [NC248.D6L43 1976] 76-27880 ISBN 0-8371-9098-3 lib.bdg. : 11.50
1. Dore, Gustave, 1832-1883. I. Title. BIP

Dorflinger, Hans, 1941—

DORFLINGER, Hans, 1941- 759.3
Hans Dorflinger : recent paintings, drawings and gouaches : [catalogue of an] exhibition open 13 February-12 March 1976 [at] Fischer Fine Art Limited, London. London : Fischer Fine Art Limited, [1976] Folder (4 p.) : chiefly ill. (incl. 1 col.) ; 26 cm. Cover title. Text in English or German. [ND588.D63F57] 76-368175 ISBN 0-904867-04-8 : £0.15
1. Dorflinger, Hans, 1941- I. Fischer Fine Art Limited.

Dorfman, Elsa.

DORFMAN, Elsa. 770'.92'4 B
Elsa's housebook : a woman's photojournal / by Elsa Dorfman. Boston : D. R. Godine, [1974] 78 p. : ill. ; 23 cm. [TR140.D67A33] 74-81513 ISBN 0-87923-099-1 : 5.95
1. Dorfman, Elsa. I. Title. BIP

Dormitories—Designs and plans.

UNIVERSITY Facilities Research Center. 727.38
High rise or low rise? A study of decision factors in residence halls planning. [Madison, Wis.] University Facilities Research Center, with the Educational Facilities Laboratories, inc. [1963] 50 p. illus., plans, ports. 22 x 28 cm. (Its Monograph series) Cover title. [NA6602.D6U5] 64-5180
1. Dormities — Design and plans. I. Title.

Dorner, Alexander, 1893-1957.

CAUMAN, Samuel. 708
The living museum, experiences of an art historian and museum director: Alexander Dorner. With an introd. by Walter Gropius. [New York] New York University Press, 1958. ix, 216p. illus. (part fold.) facsims., plans. 26cm. Bibliography: p. 211. [N8375.D6C3] 57-13239
1. Dorner, Alexander, 1893-1957. 2. Art—Galleries and museums. I. Title. BIP

Dorothea, Saint, d. 311—Art.

SCHRODER, Anneliese 704.948'6
Dorothy [by] Anneliese Schroder. Text of story and legend by Leonhard Kuppers. [Tr. from German by Hans Hermann Rosenwald] Recklinghausen [Ger.]A. Bongers; dist by Taplinger [New York, 1967,c.1966] 71p. col. illus. 18cm. (Saints in legend and art, v. 7) [N8080.S3713] 67-16588 2.50 bds.,
1. Dorothea, Saint, d. 311—Art. I. Kuppers, Leonhard, 1903- II. Title.

Dossi, Battista, d. 1548.

GIBBONS, Felton Lewis, 1929- 759.5
Dosso and Battista Dossi; court painters at Ferrara, by Felton Gibbons. Princeton, N.J., Princeton University Press, 1968. xxi, 320 p. 238 illus. (1 col.) 31 cm. (Princeton monograph in art and archaeology, 39) "Catalogue raisonne": p. [163]-272. "Bibliographical appendix to chapter VI": p. 292-295. Bibliography: p. 296-306. [ND622.G5] 68-11441 30.00
1. Dossi, Battista, d. 1548. 2. Dossi, Dosso, d. 1542. I. Series: Princeton monographs in art and archaeology, 39 BIP

Doughty, Thomas, 1793-1856.

DOUGHTY, Thomas, 1793-1856. 759.13
Thomas Doughty, 1793-1856; an American pioneer in landscape painting. Selection and catalogue by Frank H. Goodyear, Jr. Philadelphia, Pennsylvania Academy of the Fine Arts [1973] 33 p. 52 plates. 22 x 27 cm. Catalog of the exhibition held at the Pennsylvania Academy of the Fine Arts, Oct. 19-Dec. 2, 1973, the Corcoran Gallery of Art, Dec. 14, 1973-Jan. 27, 1974, and the Albany Institute of History and Art, Feb. 14-Apr. 7, 1974. Includes bibliographical references. [ND237.D66G66] 73-89435
1. Doughty, Thomas, 1793-1856. 2. Landscape in art. I. Goodyear, Frank Henry, 1944- II. Pennsylvania Academy of the Fine Arts, Philadelphia. III. Corcoran Gallery of Art, Washington, D.C. IV. Albany Institute of History and Art. V. Title.

Douglass, Frederick, 1817?-1895.

TOOGOOD, Anna Coxe. 973.8'0924
Frederick Douglass Home, Cedar Hill. [Washington] Division of History, Office of Archeology and Historic Preservation, 1968. iv, 58 l., [36] p. illus. 27 cm. "Historic grounds report, historical data

section." Bibliography: leaves 54-56. [F204.C4T6] 77-612463
1. Douglass, Frederick, 1817?-1895. 2. Washington, D.C. Cedar Hill. I. Title.

Dove, Arthur Garfield, 1880-1946.

DOVE, Arthur Garfield, 1880-1946. 759.13
Arthur Dove : [exhibition], San Francisco Museum of Art / Barbara Haskell. Boston : New York Graphic Society, c1974. ca. 150 p. : ill. (some col.) ; 23 x 26 cm. Held Nov. 21, 1974-Jan. 5, 1975 at the San Francisco Museum of Art, Jan. 27-Mar. 2, 1975 at the Albright-Knox Art Gallery, Buffalo, N.Y., Apr. 3-May 25, 1975 at the St. Louis Art Museum, July 12-Aug. 31, 1975 at the Art Institute of Chicago, Sept. 22-Nov. 2, 1975 at the Des Moines Art Center, Des Moines, Iowa, and Nov. 24, 1975-Jan. 18, 1976 at the Whitney Museum of American Art, New York. Includes bibliography. [ND237.D67H37] 74-24700 ISBN 0-8212-0651-6
1. Dove, Arthur Garfield, 1880-1946. I. Haskell, Barbara. II. San Francisco. Museum of Art.

WIGHT, Frederick Stallknecht, 1902- [759.13] 927.5
Arthur G. Dove. Berkeley, University of California Press, 1958. 96 p. illus. 28 cm. Bibliography: p 91-94. [ND237.D67W7] 58-10625
1. Dove, Arthur Garfield, 1880-1946. I. Title.

Dover Castle.

COLVIN, Howard Montagu. 338.4'3
Building accounts of King Henry III; edited by H. M. Colvin. Oxford, Clarendon Press, 1971. iii-xvi, 472 p., 16 plates; illus., map, plans. 23 cm. English and Latin. Includes bibliographical references. [NA963.C77] 77-863490 ISBN 0-19-920013-0 £7.00
1. Henry III, King of England, 1207-1272. 2. Dover Castle. 3. Westminster Abbey. 4. Winchester, Eng. Castle. I. Title.

Dover, Del.—Public buildings.

DELAWARE. State Planning Office. 725'.1'09751
Dover capital complex plan. Dover, 1966. 1 v. (various pagings) illus., plans (part col.) 28 cm. Includes bibliography. [JK1651.D45A53] 68-64423
1. Dover, Del.—Public buildings. I. Title.

Dowell-Simpson sampler.

THE Dowell-Simpson sampler / edited by Mildred J. Davis ; [charts drawn by Sydelle C. Byer, Marion E. Scoular]. Richmond : Textile Resource and Research Center, Valentine Museum, c1975. 53 p. : ill. (1 fold. col.) ; 28 cm. The sampler was exhibited at the museum Apr. 15-Aug. 15, 1975. Bibliography: p. 48. [NK9143.D68] 76-351565 746.3'9426'12
1. Dowell-Simpson sampler. 2. Needlework—England. I. Davis, Mildred J. II. Valentine Museum, Richmond, Va. Textile Resource and Research Center.

Doxiades, Konstantinos Apostoiou, 1913-

GIGANTES, Gerassimos, 1923- . 711
Constantinos Doxiadis; master builder for free men, by Philip Deane. Dobbs Ferry, N.Y., Oceana Publications, 1965. 147 p. illus., maps, plans, port. 24 cm. [NA9085.D6G5] 64-21186
1. Doxiades, Konstantinos Apostoiou, 1913- I. Title.

Doyle, Charles Altamont.

DOYLE, Charles Altamont. 741'.092'4 B
The Doyle diary : the last great Conan Doyle mystery : with a Holmesian investigation into the strange and curious case of Charles Altamont Doyle / by Michael Baker. New York : Paddington Press, c1978. xxix, 91 p. : ill. ; 18 x 25 cm. Facsim. of the author's diary-sketchbook, with an additional introd., and a page transcription of the words of Charles Doyle as they appear in the diary. [N6797.D68A2 1978] 78-6356 ISBN 0-448-22068-7 : 12.95
1. Doyle, Charles Altamont. 2. Artists—England—Biography. I. Baker, Michael, 1948- II. Title. BIP

Dozier, Otis, 1904—

A Salute to the Doziers of Dallas : [catalogue of an exhibition] Dallas Museum of Fine Arts, September 20-Oct. 27, 1974, Marion Koogler McNay Art Institute, San Antonio, January 5-February 2, 1975 / sponsored by the Texas Commission on the Arts and Humanities, and the National Endowment for the Arts. [Dallas : Museum of Fine Arts, 1974] [56] p. : chiefly ill. ; 22 x 26 cm. [NC139.D69S24] 75-302445 741.9'73
1. Dozier, Otis, 1904- 2. Dozier, Velma Davis, 1901- I. Dozier, Otis, 1904- II. Dozier, Velma Davis, 1901- III. Dallas. Museum of Fine Arts. IV. Marion Koogler McNay Art Institute, San Antonio. V. Texas Commission on the Arts and Humanities. VI. National Endowment for the Arts. VII. Title.

Drachler, Jacob—Catalogs.

DRACHLER, Jacob. 730'.92'4
The boxworks of Jacob Drachler / with texts by the artist and Amy Goldin. Brooklyn : Gridgraffiti, 1977. [44] p. : chiefly ill. ; 18 x 23 cm. "Book two." [NB237.D7A4 1977] 78-302393 4.00
1. Drachler, Jacob—Catalogs. I. Goldin, Amy, joint author. II. Title.

Dragons—Pictures and illustrations.

SEIDELMAN, James E. 741.9
The 14th dragon. Text by James E. Seidelman and Grace Mintonye. Drawings by robert L. Anderson and others. New York, H. Quist; distributed by Crown Publishers, 1968] [31] p. illus. (part col.) 23 x 29 cm. Thirteen dragons are captured in verse and by paint brush. Each dragon is the creation of a different illustrator with the imagination and talent of the reader. [PZ8.3.S46Fo] AC 68
1. Dragons—Pictures and illustrations. I. Mintonye, Grace, joint author. II. Anderson, Robert Lindberg, illus. III. Title.

Drake, Gordon, 1917-1952.

BAYLIS, Douglas. 728.6
California houses of Gordon Drake [by] Douglas Baylis and Joan Parry. New York, Reinhold Pub. Corp. [1956] 91 p. illus. 23 cm. [NA737.D7B3] 56-11751
1. Drake, Gordon, 1917-1952. 2. Architecture, Domestic—California. I. Parry, Joan, joint author. II. Title.

Drama—History and criticism.

DUPIN, Jacques. 759.6
Miro. [Translated from the French by Norbert Guterman] Gerhard Nellhaus] and The marriage of Mr. Mississippi; a play [translated from the German by Michael Bullock] New York, Grove Press [1966? c1964] 596 p. illus. (part mounted, part col.) ports. 31 cm. (An Evergreen book, E-401) Bibliography: p. 577-591. [ND813.M5D83] 62-1913214
1. Miro, Joan, 1893- 2. Drama—History and criticism. I. Title: The marriage of Mr. Mississippi.

Drapery.

BAER, Barbara. 645.3
How to make curtains and draperies. New York, McBride [1950] 103 p. illus. 18 cm. Cover title: Making curtains & draperies. [TT390.B3 1950] 50-9616
1. Drapery. 2. Interior decoration. I. Title.

BRANN, Donald R. 747'.5
How to make cornice boards, draperies, valances, install traverse track, by Donald R. Brann. Rev. ed. Briarcliff Manor, N.Y., Directions Simplified, 1971. 66 p. illus. 23 cm. (Easi-bild simplified directions, 627) [TT390.B7 1971] 78-24073 1.50
1. Drapery. I. Title.

BROSTROM, Ethel. 645.4
How to make draperies & slipcovers, including bedspreads, curtains, lampshades, and their use in home decoration, by Ethel Brostrom & Harry Marinsky. New York, Crown Publishers [1951] ix, 182 p. illus. 24 cm. [TT390.B75] 51-10663
1. Drapery. 2. Slip covers. I. Marinsky, Harry. II. Title.

BUTLER, Margaret G. 746.9'4
Fashions for the home [by] Margaret G. Butler and Beryl S. Greves. New York, Drake Publishers [1972] 240 p. illus. 26 cm. [TT387.B88 1972.] 72-185254 ISBN 0-87749-211-5 8.95
1. Drapery. 2. Cushions. 3. Lampshades. 4. Coverlets. I. Greves, Beryl S., joint author. II. Title.

GRABER, Marie. 747'.5
The first official window decorating guide. [New York, Benjamin Co., 1967] 113 p. illus. 23 cm. (Benco edition) "An Essandess special edition." "Previously published ... as Marie Graber's window decorating book." "Special section on sewing by Singer": p. 92-111. [TT390.G7 1967] 67-29003
1. Drapery. I. Title. II. Title: Window decorating guide. BIP

HELSEL, Marjorie Borradaile. 747'.5
The interior designer's drapery sketchfile. [New York] Whitney Library of Design [1969] 1 v. (chiefly illus.) 29 cm. [NK3197.H44] 68-58182
1. Drapery. 2. Interior decoration. I. Title. BIP

KIRSCH Company. 645.3
Kirsch guide to window beauty. [Sturgis, Mich., 1961] 95p. illus. 31cm. [TT390.K52] 61-66057
1. Drapery. I. Title. II. Title: Window beauty.

OMEN, Mary. 645.3
Curtains, draperies, and slipcovers. [New York] Emily Post Institute [1964, c1963] viii, 113 p. illus. (part col.) 24 cm. (Emily Post's guidebooks for homemakers) [TT390.O4] 63-10472
1. Drapery. 2. Slip covers. I. Title.

RODERICK, Phyllis Hingston. 747'.8'8
McCall's do-it-yourself traditional decorating. [1st ed.] New York, Random House [1974] 127 p. illus. 29 cm. [TT387.R63] 74-6096 ISBN 0-394-49065-7 5.95
1. Drapery. 2. Coverlets. 3. Interior decoration—Amateurs' manuals. I. Title. II. Title: Do-it-yourself traditional decorating. BIP

SINGER Sewing Machine Company. Educational Dept. 645.3
Singer home decorations sewing book. Eula Hicks, editor. New York, Grosset & Dunlap [1961] 128 p. illus. 29 cm. [TT390.S5] 61-19890
1. Drapery. I. Hicks, Eula ed. II. Title. III. Title: Home decorations sewing book.

Drapery—History.

DUBOIS, Marius Joseph. 747.509
Curtains & draperies; a survey of the classic periods [by] M. J. Dubois. [Translated from the French by Violet M. Macdonald] New York, Viking Press [1967] 252 p. illus. (part col.) ports. 29 cm. (A Studio book) Translation of Rideaux et draperies classiques. [NK3200.D813] 67-10660
1. Drapery—History. I. Title.

Drapery in art.

BRIDGMAN, George Brant, 1864-1943 743.4
The female form, draped and undraped. Photos. by Ben Pinchot. [Rev. ed.] New York, Sterling [c.1963] 128p. illus. 20cm. (Worthwhile how-to paperbacks; 506) Combines the author's The seven laws of folds, pub. in 1942 and drawings, photos, taken from Ben Pinchot's Female form, pub. in 1935. 63-12586 1.00 pap.,
1. Drapery in art. 2. Anatomy, Artistic. 3. Figure drawing. I. Title.

Drawing.

BEITTEL, Kenneth R. 741.2
Mind and context in the art of drawing; an empirical and speculative account of the drawing process and the drawing series and of the contexts in which they occur [by] Kenneth R. Beittel. New York, Holt, Rinehart and Winston [1972] xiii, 274 p. illus. 25 cm. Includes bibliographies. [NC715.B44] 71-184950 ISBN 0-03-086045-8
1. Drawing. 2. Drawing, Psychology of. I. Title.

BERTRAM, Anthony, 1897- 741.9
One thousand years of drawing. London, Studio Vista; New York, Dutton [1966] 159 p. front., illus. 18 1/2 cm. (Dutton Vista paperback) (B 66-8513) [NC730.B4] 66-72501
1. Drawing. 2. Composition (Art) 3. Figure drawing. I. Title.

BLAKE, Vernon, 1875-1930. 741
The art and craft of drawing; a study both of the practice of drawing and of its aesthetic theory as understood among different peoples and at different epochs; especial reference being made to the construction of the human form from the practical draughtsman's point of view, by Vernon Blake. New York, Hacker Art Books, 1971. xvi, 414 p. illus. 27 cm. Reprint of the 1927 ed. [NC710.B55 1971] 75-116351 ISBN 0-87817-039-1
1. Drawing. I. Title. BIP

COSTUME drawing, by Hazel R. Do ten and Constance Boulard. 2d ed. New York, Pitman Pub. Corp. [c1956] unpaged. illus. 20x26cm. (Pitman drawing series) [TT509.D65 1956] [TT509.D65 1956] 743 56-12729 56-12729 741.67
1. Drawing. 2. Custume. 3. Clothing and dress. I. Doten, Hazel Ruth, 1892- II. Boulard, Constance Augusta, 1899- joint author. BIP

DRAWING Society. 741
Approaches to drawings [by] a collector: Philip Hofer; a curator: Jacob Bean [and] an artist: Gabor Peterdi. New York, 1963. 69 p. illus., ports. 23 cm. "Three lectures presented by the Drawing Society at the Metropolitan Museum of Art, New York, 1961-62." [NC720.D7] 63-22781
1. Drawing. 2. Drawings. I. Hofer, Philip, 1898- II. New York. Metropolitan Museum of Art. III. Title.

FAWCETT, Robert. 741.4
On the art of drawing; an informal textbook with illus. by the author. [1st ed.] [New York] Watson-Guptill Publications [1958] 136 p. illus., port. 32 cm. [NC710.F3] 58-8130
1. Drawing. I. Title.

HUTTER, Heribert. 741
Drawing; history and technique. New York, McGraw-Hill [1968] 152 p. illus. (part col.) 28 cm. Translation of Die Handzeichnung; Entwicklung, Technik, Eigenart. Bibliography: p. 148-149. [NC710.H813 1968b] 68-16484
1. Drawing. I. Title.

*JENSEN, C. H. 744.422
Drafting fundamentals [by] C. H. Jensen, F. H. S. Mason. New York, McGraw [c.1963] 201p. diagrs. 25cm. 4.00
I. Title.

JOPLING, Louise. 740
Hints and tips. New York, Pitman Pub. Corp. [1955?] 64p. illus. 19cm. (The Artist's handbooks, no. 2) [NC650] 55-4224
1. Drawing. 2. Painting. I. Title.

RUSKIN, John, 1819-1900. 741.2
The elements of drawing. With a new introd. by Lawrence Campbell. New York, Dover Publications [1971] xii, 228 p. illus. 22 cm. Reprinted from v. 15 (1904) of the library ed. of The works of John Ruskin. Includes bibliographical references. [NC710.R8 1971] 79-132553 ISBN 0-486-22730-8 2.50
1. Drawing. I. Title. BIP

RUSKIN, John, 1819-1900. 741'.01
The elements of drawing in three letters to beginners. New York, Maynard, Merrill. St. Clair Shores, Mich., Scholarly Press, 1972. p. Reprint of the 1893 ed. [NC710.R8 1972] 74-115264 ISBN 0-403-00307-5
1. Drawing. I. Title.

SCHULER, Josef Egon, ed. 741.9
Great drawings of the masters. Text by Rolf Hansler. [Translated from the German by Gillian Brydone. 1st American ed.] New York, Putnam [1963] 234 p. illus. (part mounted, part col.) 33 cm. Translation of Meisterzeichnungen von der Welt bewundert. [NC1005.S413] 63-12754
1. Drawing. I. Hansler, Rolf. II. Title.

WIRTH, Kurt, 1917- 741.6
Zeichnung: wann. wie. Drawing: when. how. New York, Hastings [c.1965] 120p. illus. 23x25cm. Text and captions in German, English, and French. [NC703.W5] 65-29832 10.95 bds.,
1. Drawing. 2. Composition (Art) I. Title. II. Title: Drawing: when. how.

ZIPPRICH, Anthony E 744.4
Freehand drafting, for technical sketching. With an introd. by Carl L. Svensen. 3d ed. New York, Van Nostrand [1954] 176p. illus. 24cm. [T359.Z5 1954] 54-9391
1. Drawing. 2. Geometrical drawing. I. Title.

Drawing—18th century—Exhibitions.

STEADMAN, David W. 741.9'4'074019493
18th century drawings from California collections : [exhibition], Montgomery Art Gallery, Pomona College, Claremont, January 16-February 29, 1976, the E. B. Crocker Art Gallery, Sacramento, March 14-April 11, 1976 / introd by David W. Steadman; catalogue by David W. Steadman and Carol M. Osborne. Claremont, Calif. : Galleries of the Claremont Colleges, Pomona College, [1976] 112 p. : ill. ; 26 cm. Includes index. [NC87.S73] 75-34964 ISBN 0-915478-09-9
1. Drawing—18th century—Exhibitions. 2. Drawing—Collectors and collecting—California. I. Osborne, Carol M., joint author. II. Pomona College, Claremont, Calif. Gallery. III. Crocker Art Gallery, Sacramento, Calif. IV. Title.

Drawing—20th century—Catalogs.

A Treasury of modern drawing : the Joan and Lester Avnet Collection in the Museum of Modern Art / William S. Lieberman. New York : Museum of Modern Art, c1978. 119 p. : ill. ; 19 x 21 cm. "Catalog of the collection," by M. A. Richards: p. 108-119. Includes bibliographical references. [NC95.T68] 78-50658 ISBN 0-87070-609-8 pbk. : 6.75 741.9'24
1. New York (City). Museum of Modern Art—Catalogs. 2. Drawing—20th century—Catalogs. 3. Drawing—New York (City)—Catalogs. 4. Avnet, Lester—Art collections—Catalogs. 5. Avnet, Joan—Art collections—Catalogs. I. Lieberman, William Slattery, 1924- II. New York (City). Museum of Modern Art. BIP

Drawing—20th century—Exhibitions.

WESTERN Australian Art Gallery. 741.9'24
Contemporary drawing / edited by Lou Klepac. Nedlands, W.A. : University of Western Australia Press with the Art Gallery of Western Australia, 1977. 108 p. : ill. ; 22 x 28 cm. Aus "1977 Perth international survey of drawing." Catalog of an exhibition. Bibliography: p. 106. [NC95.W47 1977] 78-301575 ISBN 0-85564-128-2 pbk. : 15.95
1. Drawing—20th century—Exhibitions. I. Klepac, Lou. II. Title.
Distributed by ISBS BIP

Drawing, American—Exhibitions.

DRAWING : 741.9'24
transparence = Disegno : trasparenza : Cannaviello studio d'arte, Roma / [text by] Achille Bonito Oliva. Pollenza [Italy] : La nuova foglio, c1976. [136] p. : chiefly ill. ; 28 cm. (Cataloghi altro) English and Italian. Catalog of an exhibition held at Cannaviello studio d'arte, Rome. [NC108.D73] 77-465036 L8000
1. Drawing, American—Exhibitions. 2. Drawing—20th century—United States—Exhibitions. 3. Drawing, Italian—Exhibitions. 4. Drawing—20th century—Italy—Exhibitions. I. Bonito Oliva, Achille. II. Cannaviello studio d'arte.

GOICHBERG, Rena. 811'.5'4
Spiked flower : poems and drawings / by Rena Goichberg. San Francisco, Calif. : Cassandra Publications, 1975. 37 p. : ill. ; 18 cm. [PS3557.O325S6] 75-7158 2.00
I. Title. BIP

GOODMAN, Sanford. 741.973
Incubator for savages; voiced drawings. [Topanga, Calif.] Crazy Horse Books, 1970. 1 v. (unpaged (chiefly illus., ports.)) 29 cm. [NC139.G62A47] 70-118876 12.50
I. Title.

HATCH, John Davis. 741.9'73'0740941835
100 American drawings : loan exhibition from the collection of John Davis Hatch ... [autumn exhibition] National Gallery of Ireland, Dublin, 7th September-8th October 1976. / [catalogue entries by Gary Burger Dublin : National Gallery of Ireland, [1976] [74] p., [50] leaves of plates : ill. ; 25 cm. (Heim exhibition catalogues ; no. 26) On spine: American drawings. Includes index. Bibliography: p. [72] [NC105.H26 1976] 77-363055
1. Hatch, John Davis—Art collections. 2. Drawing, American—Exhibitions. I. Burger, Gary. II. Dublin. National Gallery of Ireland. III. Heim Gallery. IV. Title. V. Title: American drawings. VI. Series: Heim exhibition catalogues (Dublin) ; no. 26.

HATCH, John Davis. 708'.21'32 s
100 American drawings : loan exhibition from the collection of John Davis Hatch ... [autumn exhibition] National Gallery of Ireland, Dublin, 7th September-8th October, 1976 / [catalogue entries by Gary Burger] London : Heim Gallery (London), [1976] [74] p., [50] leaves of plates : ill. ; 25 cm. (Heim exhibition catalogues ; no. 26) On spine: American drawings. Includes index. Bibliography: p. [72] [N8640.H4 no. 26] [NC105] 741.9'73'07402132 77-363084
1. Hatch, John Davis—Art collections. 2. Drawing, American—Exhibitions. I. Burger, Gary. II. Dublin. National Gallery of Ireland. III. Heim Gallery. IV. Title. V. Title: American drawings. VI. Series.

LATE nineteenth century American drawings and watercolors : the University Gallery, University of Massachusetts, Amherst, Massachusetts, May 14-June 5, 1977 / edited by Martha J. Hoppin. Amherst : The Gallery, c1977. 59 p., [2] leaves of plates : ill. ; 28 cm. An exhibition and catalog prepared by the students of the Art Department, University of Massachusetts at Amherst in conjunction with an art history seminar. Includes bibliographies. [NC107.L37] 77-77591 741.9'73'074014423
1. Drawing, American—Exhibitions. 2. Drawing—19th century—United States—Exhibitions. 3. Water-color paintings, American—Exhibitions. 4. Water-color painting—19th century—United States—Exhibitions. I. Hoppin, Martha J. II. University of Massachusetts at Amherst. University Gallery. III. University of Massachusetts at Amherst. Dept. of Art.

LEBRUN, Federico, 1900- 741.973
Rico Lebrun drawings. Foreword by James Thrall Soby. Berkeley, Univ. of California Press [c.]1961. vii, 100p. illus. 29cm. 60-16562 7.50
I. Title. BIP

LEBRUN, Federico, 1900- 711.973
Rico Lebrun drawings. Foreword by James Thrall Soby. Berkeley, University of California Press, 1961. vii, 100p. illus. 29cm. [NC1075.L35S6] 60-16562
I. Title.

NEWPORT Harbor Art Museum. 741.9'73'074019496
Three directions : Agnes Denes, Channa Horwitz, Joyce Cutler Shaw, October 23-November 28, 1976 : an exhibition / organized by Newport Harbor Art Museum. Newport Beach, Calif. : The Museum, c1976. [20] p., [6] leaves of plates : ill. ; 22 x 28 cm. Includes bibliographies. [NC108.N45 1976] 76-382775
1. Denes, Agnes. 2. Horwitz, Channa. 3. Shaw, Joyce Cutler. 4. Drawing, American—Exhibitions. 5. Women artists—United States. 6. Art—Philosophy—Exhibitions. 7. Visual perception—Exhibitions. I. Denes, Agnes. II. Horwitz, Channa. III. Shaw, Joyce Cutler. IV. Title.

PRINCETON University. Art Museum. 741.9'73'074014967
American drawings in the Art Museum, Princeton University : 130 selected examples : [exhibition] / Barbara T. Ross. Princeton, N.J. : [Art Museum, Princeton University] : distributed by Princeton University Press, c1976. ix, 130 p. : ill. ; 24 cm. Catalog of the exhibition held at the Art Museum, Princeton University, Oct. 3-Nov. 28, 1976. [NC105.P74 1976] 76-27117 ISBN 0-691-03921-6 : 16.00
1. Drawing, American—Exhibitions. I. Ross, Barbara T. II. Title.

SANTA Barbara, Calif. Museum of Art. 741.9'794'91074019491
Santa Barbara drawings, 1976 : [exhibition] , Santa Barbara Museum of Art, June 9-July 11, 1976. [Santa Barbara] : The Museum, [1976] [20] p. : chiefly ill. ; 22 x 27 cm. [NC138.S26S26 1976] 77-365774
1. Drawing, American—Exhibitions. 2. Drawing—20th century—California—Santa Barbara—Exhibitions. I. Title.

Drawing, American—History.

STEBBINS, Theodore E. 759.13
American master drawings and watercolors : a history of works on paper from colonial times to the present / by Theodore E. Stebbins, Jr. 1st ed. New York : Harper & Row, c1976. p. cm. Includes index. Bibliography: p. [ND1805.S73 1976] 75-37156 ISBN 0-06-014068-2 : 30.00. ISBN 0-06-014069-0 pbk. : 10.95
1. Drawing, American—History. 2. Water-color painting, American—History. I. Title. BIP

Drawing—Attribution.

NETTO-BOL, M. M. L. 707'.2
The so-called Maarten de Vos Sketchbook of drawings after the antique / M. M. L. Netto-Bol ; [translated from the Dutch by Gary Schwartz]. The Hague : Ministry of Cultural Affairs, Recreation and Social Welfare : Govt. Pub. Off., 1976. 116 p. : ill. ; 29 cm. (Kunsthistorische studien van het Nederlands Instituut te Rome ; deel 4) Includes bibliographical references and indexes. [N380.N38 d. 4] [NC266.V6] 741.9'493 77-469754 ISBN 9-01-200728-3 : fl 25.00
1. Vos, Maerten de, 1532-1603. 2. Drawing—Attribution. 3. Rome (City) in art. 4. Rome (City)—Antiquities—Pictorial works. I. Title. II. Series: Nederlands Historisch Instituut te Rome. Kunsthistorische studien ; deel 4.

Drawing books.

COLE, William [Harrison] ed. 741
The poetry-drawing book. Edited by William Cole and Julia Colmore. New York, Simon and Schuster [c.] 1960. unp)ged. illus. (part col.) 22x29cm. 60-10984 1.95, pap., spiral binding
1. Drawing books. 2. Children's poetry. I. Colmore, Julia, joint ed. II. Title.

CUBACUB, Arturo. 811'.5'4
In piecing a sun : a fantasy in verses and illustrations / by Arturo Cubacub. 1st ed. Chicago : Sahner Pub. Co., 1976. [45] p. : ill. (some col.) ; 21 cm. [PS3553.U23I5] 76-18012
I. Title.

MEMLING, Carl 741
My read and draw 'Magic slate' book. Illus. by Richard Scarry. New York, Golden [1962, c.1961] 48p. col. illus. 29cm. 61-18793 1.99 bds.,
1. Drawing books. I. Title.

Drawing books—Juvenile literature.

SACKSON, Sid. 793.9
Beyond tic tac toe : challenging and exciting new games to be played with colored pens or pencils / by Sid Sackson. New York : Pantheon Books, [1975] [142] p. : chiefly ill. (some col.) ; 21 cm. Seven games, each of which ultimately forms a drawing in the style of Mondrian, Miro, and other masters of abstract art. [NC670.S22] 75-2546 ISBN 0-394-83136-5. ISBN 0-394-93136-X lib. bdg.
1. Drawing books—Juvenile literature. 2. Games—Juvenile literature. I. Title. BIP

Drawing—Budapest.

VAYER, Lajos. 741.9
Master drawings from the collection of the Budapest Museum of Fine Arts, 14th-18th centuries. Introd. and notes by Lajos Vayer. New York, H. N. Abrams [1957, c1956] 31 p. 109 plates (part col.) 40 cm. [NC27.B9V3 1957] 58-42590
1. Drawing—Budapest. I. Budapest. Szepmuveszeti Muzeum. II. Title.

Drawing—Budapest—Catalogs.

PATAKY, Denes. 741.94391
Master drawings from the collection of the Budapest Museum, of Fine Arts, 19th and 20th centuries. New York, H. N. Abrams [1959] 27 p. 94 plates (part col.) 40 cm. Translation of A rajzmuveszet mesterel, xix, es xx. szazad. Includes bibliographies. [NC27.B9P283] 59-8844
1. Drawing—Budapest—Catalogs. 2. Drawing, French. I. Budapest. Szepmuveszeti Muzeum. II. Title.

Drawing, Chinese.

LAI, T'ien-ch'ang. 745.6'199'51
Treasures of a Chinese studio : ink, brush, inkstone, paper / T. C. Lai. Kowloon, Hong Kong : Swindon Book Co., c1976. 152 p. : ill. (some col.) ; 23 cm. Bibliography: p. 152. [NC348.L34] 77-363901
1. Drawing, Chinese. 2. Calligraphy, Chinese. 3. Artists' materials. I. Title.

Drawing—Conservation and restoration.

LEPELTIER, Robert. 760'.028
The restorer's handbook of drawings and prints / Robert Lepeltier ; [English translation, Anne G. Ward]. New York : Van Nostrand Reinhold Co., c1977. 130 p. : ill. ; 22 cm. Translation of Restauration des dessins et estampes. Includes index. Bibliography: p. 123-125. [NC930.L4613] 77-5591 ISBN 0-442-24765-6 : 22.50
1. Drawing—Conservation and restoration. 2. Prints—Conservation and restoration. I. Title.

Drawing, Dutch.

GELDER, Jan Gerrit van, 1903- 741.9492
Dutch drawings and prints, with 224 plates in black and white. New York, H. N. Abrams [1959] 54 p. illus. 35 cm. Bibliography: p. 54. [NC1030.G4] 58-13481
1. Drawing, Dutch. 2. Engraving, Dutch. I. Title.

Drawing, Dutch—Exhibitions.

REMBRANDT and his century : Dutch drawings of the seventeenth century : from the collection of Frits Lugt, Institut neerlandais, Paris, New York-Paris, 1977-1978. [New York : Pierpont Morgan Library, 1978] xxi, 251 p., [68] leaves of plates : ill. ; 26 cm. "Exhibitions: New York, the Pierpont Morgan Library ... 8th December 1977-19th February 1978 ...; Paris, Institut neerlandais ... 16th March-30th April 1978." Includes indexes. Bibliography: p. 223-244. [NC261.R46] 78-107157 pbk. : 15.95 741.9'492'07401471
1. Lugt, Frits, 1884-1970—Art collections—Exhibitions. 2. Drawing, Dutch—Exhibitions. 3. Drawing—17th

century—Netherlands—Exhibitions. I. Pierpont Morgan Library, New York. II. Institut neerlandais, Paris.

ROBINSON, Franklin Westcott. 741.9'492'074013
Seventeenth century Dutch drawings from American collections : a loan exhibition / Franklin W. Robinson ; organized and circulated by the International Exhibitions Foundation. [Washington] : The Foundation, 1977. xvii, 189 p. : ill. ; 27 cm. Participating museums: National Gallery of Art, Denver Art Museum, and Kimbell Art Museum. Includes bibliographical references and index. [NC261.R63] 76-48613
1. Drawing, Dutch—Exhibitions. 2. Drawing—17th century—Netherlands—Exhibitions. 3. Drawing, Dutch—United States—Exhibitions. I. International Exhibitions Foundation. II. United States. National Gallery of Art. III. Denver. Art Museum. IV. Kimbell Art Museum. V. Title. BIP

Drawing, European—Exhibitions.

EUROPEAN drawings from the Fitzwilliam : lent by the syndics of the Fitzwilliam Museum, University of Cambridge : organized and circulated by the International Exhibitions Foundation, 1976-1977 / introduction by Michael Jaffe. [Washington : International Exhibitions Foundation], c1976. xiv, 84 p., [61] leaves of plates : ill. ; 26 cm. "Participating museums: The Pierpont Morgan Library, New York, New York, Kimbell Art Museum, Fort Worth, Texas, The Baltimore Museum of Art, Baltimore, Maryland, The Minneapolis Institute of Arts, Minneapolis, Minnesota, Philadelphia Museum of Art, Philadelphia, Pennsylvania." Draft entries for the catalog prepared by M. Cormack and D. Robinson and edited by A. M. Jaffe. Includes index. [NC225.E97] 76-25622 741.9'4'074013
1. Cambridge. University. Fitzwilliam Museum. 2. Drawing, European—Exhibitions. I. Jaffe, Andrew Michael. II. Cormack, Malcolm. III. Robinson, Duncan. IV. International Exhibitions Foundation. V. Pierpont Morgan Library, New York. BIP

TAYLOR, Mary C. 741.9'4'074011
European drawings from Canadian collections, 1500-1900 = Dessins Europeens des collections Canadiennes, 1500-1900 / Mary Cazort Taylor. Ottawa : National Gallery of Canada, 1976. 150 p. : ill. ; 26 cm. English and French. Exhibition catalog. Includes bibliographical references. [NC225.T38] 77-552500 ISBN 0-88884-334-8
1. Drawing, European—Exhibitions. 2. Drawing, European—Canada—Exhibitions. I. Title. II. Title: Dessins Europeens des collections Canadiennes, 1500-1900.

Drawing—Exhibitions.

BASKETT and Day (Firm) 741.9'4'07402132
Exhibition [catalogue] of fifty Old Master drawings : Tuesday, 16th March-30th March, 1976. London : Baskett and Day, 1976. [50] p. : ill. (some col.) ; 25 cm. [NC17.G7L616 1976] 77-354575
1. Drawing—Exhibitions. I. Title.

FIRST Museum of Blind Arts and Sciences. 741.9'24
Drawings and paintings by the blind in perspective : catalogue of the Wally Collection : First Museum of Blind Arts and Sciences, Caguas, Puerto Rico, 1976 / [compiled, designed, edited by G. B. Wally]. Caguas, P.R. : World Research Center for the Blind, 1976. 151 p., [3] leaves of plates : ill. (some col.) ; 28 cm. "First edition, illustrated by the blind." [NC17.P9C333] 76-28871
1. Wally, George B.—Art collections. 2. Drawing—Exhibitions. 3. Painting—Exhibitions. 4. Perspective. 5. Artists, Blind. I. Wally, George B. II. Title.

†HARVARD University. William Hayes Fogg Art Museum. 741.9'074'01444
Memorial exhibition : works of art from the Collection of Paul J. Sachs (1878-1965) : given and bequeathed to the Fogg Art Museum, Harvard University, Cambridge, Massachusetts. New York : Garland Pub., [1977] c1965. 214 p. : ill. ; 23 cm. "Compiled by Agnes Mongan with the assistance of Mary Lee Bennett." Catalog of the exhibitions held at the Fogg Art Museum, Cambridge, Mass., Nov. 15, 1965-Jan. 15, 1966 and at the New York Museum of Modern Art, Dec. 19, 1966-Feb. 25, 1967. Reprint of the ed. published by William Hayes Fogg Art Museum, Harvard University, Cambridge. [NC25.C35H45 1977] 77-22978 ISBN 0-8240-1961-X : 35.00
1. Sachs, Paul Joseph, 1878-1965—Art collections. 2. Drawing—Exhibitions. I. Mongan, Agnes. II. Bennett, Mary Lee. III. New York (City). Museum of Modern Art. IV. Title.

NEW Testament narratives in master drawings : selected from the collections of the E. B. Crocker Art Gallery : an exhibition and catalogue / cosponsored by the Department of Art, University of California at Davis and the E. B. Crocker Art Gallery of Sacramento ; edited by Seymour Howard. Sacramento : The Gallery, 1976. 47 p. : ill. ; 28 cm. "Largely the work of graduate students in the history of art at the University of California, Davis—the product of a seminar dealing with problems of iconology and connoisseurship in master drawings." [NC15.S3C766] 76-47754 741.9'4'074019454
1. Bible. N.T.—Pictures, illustrations, etc.—Exhibitions. 2. Drawing—Exhibitions. I. Howard, Seymour, 1928- II. Crocker Art Gallery, Sacramento, Calif. III. California. University, Davis. Dept. of Art.

UNITED States. National Gallery of Art. 741.9'074'0153
Master drawings from the collection of the National Gallery of Art and promised gifts. Washington : The Gallery, 1978. 128 p. : chiefly ill. (some col.) ; 27 cm. Catalog of an exhibition held at the National Gallery of Art June 1-Oct. 1, 1978. Includes index. [NC15.W37U548] 78-3699 9.95
1. Drawing—Exhibitions. 2. Water-color painting—Exhibitions. I. Title.

Drawing, Florentine—History.

BERENSON, Bernhard, 1865-1959. 741.9'455'1
The drawings of the Florentine painters. Chicago, University of Chicago Press [1970] 3 v. illus. 29 cm. "Collector's edition." Text is that of first ed., 1938, with essential changes and additions and new appendices. Contents.Contents.—v. 1. Texts.—v. 2. Catalogue.—v. 3. Illustrations. Includes bibliographical references. [NC256.F5B4 1970] 73-114808 ISBN 0-226-04357-6
1. Drawing, Florentine—History. 2. Drawings, Florentine. 3. Painters—Italy—Florence. I. Title. BIP

BERENSON, Bernhard, 1865-1959. 741.9'45
The drawings of the Florentine painters, by Bernard Berenson. Amplified ed. New York, Greenwood Press [1969] 3 v. illus. 32 cm. (University of Chicago publications in art) "Originally published in 1938." Contents.Contents.—v. 1. Text.—v. 2. Catalogue.—v. 3. Illustrations. Bibliography: v. 2, p. v.-xii. [NC1045.B5 1969] 69-13822
1. Drawing, Florentine—History. 2. Drawings, Florentine. 3. Painters, Italian—Florence. I. Title. II. Series: Chicago. University. Publications in art

Drawing, French—Catalogs.

CHICAGO. Art Institute. 741.9'44'074017311
French drawings and sketchbooks of the eighteenth century / Harold Joachim ; compiled by Sandra Haller Olsen ; Art Institute of Chicago. Chicago : University of Chicago Press, 1977. vii, 112 p. ; 23 cm. & microfiche (4 sheets : ill. (some col.) ; 11 x 15 cm.) in pocket (A University of Chicago Press text/fiche) Bibliography: p. 109-112. [NC246.C45 1977b] 77-20132 ISBN 0-226-68795-3 : 45.00
1. Chicago. Art Institute. 2. Drawing, French—Catalogs. 3. Drawing—18th century—France—Catalogs. I. Joachim, Harold. II. Olsen, Sandra Haller. III. Title. BIP

CHICAGO. Art Institute. 741.9'44'074017311
French drawings and sketchbooks of the nineteenth century / The Art Institute of Chicago ; Harold Joachim ; compiled by Sandra Haller Olsen. Chicago : University of Chicago Press, 1978- p. cm. (Chicago visual library) Bibliography: v. 1, p. [NC246.C45 1978] 78-23641 ISBN 0-226-68796-1(v.1) : write for information
1. Drawing, French—Catalogs. 2. Drawing—19th century—France—Catalogs. I. Joachim, Harold. II. Olsen, Sandra Haller. III. Title. BIP

CHICAGO. Art Institute. 741.9'44'074017311
French drawings of the sixteenth and seventeenth centuries / Harold Joachim ; compiled by Sandra Haller Olsen. Chicago : University of Chicago Press, 1977. vii, 32 p. ; 23 cm. & microfiche (1 sheet : col. ill. ; 11 x 15 cm.) in pocket. (A University of Chicago Press text/fiche) Bibliography: p. 31-32. [NC246.C45 1977a] 77-9417 ISBN 0-226-68794-5 : 45.00
1. Chicago. Art Institute. 2. Drawing, French—Catalogs. 3. Drawing—16th century—France—Catalogs. 4. Drawing—17th century—France—Catalogs. 5. Drawing—Illinois—Chicago—Catalogs. I. Joachim, Harold. II. Olsen, Sandra Haller. III. Title. BIP

Drawing, French—Exhibitions.

NINETEENTH century French drawings : [exhibition] 20th May-18th June 1976, Stefanie Maison and Hazlitt, Gooden & Fox. [s.l. : s.n., 1976] ([s.l. : Lund Humphries]) 16 p., [18] leaves of plates : ill. ; 25 cm. [NC246.N56] 77-366590 741.9'44'07402132
1. Drawing, French—Exhibitions. 2. Drawing—19th century—France—Exhibitions. 3. Water-color painting, French—Exhibitions. 4. Water-color painting—19th century—France—Exhibitions. I. Stefanie Maison (Art gallery). II. Hazlitt, Gooden & Fox.

RUBIN, James Henry. 741.9'44'074014967
Eighteenth-century French life-drawing : selections from the Collection of Mathias Polakovits / James Henry Rubin, in collaboration with David Levine ; foreword by Pierre Rosenberg. Princeton, N.J. : Art Museum, Princeton University : distributed by Princeton University Press, c1977. 103 p. : ill. ; 29 cm. Catalog of the exhibition held at the Princeton University Art Museum, April 2-May 8, 1977. Foreword also in French. Includes bibliographical references. [NC246.R82] 76-56719 ISBN 0-691-03926-7 : 24.50
1. Polakovits, Mathias—Art collections. 2. Drawing, French—Exhibitions. 3. Drawing—18th century—France—Exhibitions. 4. Nude in art. 5. Men in art. I. Levine, David, 1951- joint author. II. Princeton University. Art Museum. III. Title.

Drawing—History.

DE TOLNAY, Charles, 1899- 741'.092'2
History and technique of old master drawings; a handbook. New York, Hacker Art Books, [1973, c1972] vii, 155 p. illus. 32 cm. Reprint of the 1943 ed. published by H. Bittner, New York. Includes bibliographical references. [NC53.D4 1972] 70-158334 ISBN 0-87817-107-X 40.00
1. Drawing—History. 2. Drawing—Instruction. 3. Drawings—Catalogs. I. Title. II. Title: Old master drawings. BIP

HILL, Edward. 741
The language of drawing. Englewood Cliffs, N.J. Prentice-Hall [1966] iv, 152 p. illus. 21 cm. Bibliography: p. 146-152. [NC390.H5] 66-28111
1. Drawing—History. 2. Drawing—Instruction. I. Title. BIP

KENIN, Richard. 741.9'074'02142
The art of drawing: from the dawn of history to the era of the Impressionists. [New York] Paddington Press [1974] 244 p. illus. 29 cm. [NC50.K46] 73-15023 ISBN 0-8467-0019-0 12.95
1. Drawing—History. 2. Drawings. I. Title.

MENDELOWITZ, Daniel Marcus. 740.9
Drawing. Supplement, [by] Daniel M. Mendelowitz. New york, Holt, Rinehart and Winston [1966] vi, 153 p. illus. 28 cm. [NC50.M4 suppl.]
1. Drawing—History. 2. Drawing. I. Title.

MENDELOWITZ, Daniel Marcus. 741.2
A guide to drawing / Daniel M. Mendelowitz. 2d ed. New York : Holt, Rinehart & Winston, [1975] p. cm. First ed. published in 1966 under title: Drawing. [NC50.M4 1975] 75-25923 ISBN 0-03-086565-4 pbk. : 8.95
1. Drawing—History. 2. Drawings. I. Title. BIP

SELZ, Jean. 741'.09'034
XIXth century drawings and water-colors. [Translated from the French by Rosalie Siegel New York, Crown Publishers [1968] 238 p. illus., ports. (both part col.) 33 cm. [NC90.S413] 68-9086 12.50
1. Drawing—History. 2. Water-color painting—History. 3. Drawings. 4. Water-colors. I. Title.

Drawing, Hungarian—Hist.

PATAKY, Denes 709.4391
Hungarian drawings and water-colours. Budapest, Corvina [dist. New York, Heinman, 1963] 66p. 191 plates (pt. col.) 25x27 cm. Bibl . 62-6226 17.50
1. Drawing, Hungarian—Hist. 2. Water-color painting—Hungary—Hist. I. Title.

Drawing, Indic—Exhibitions.

LOS Angeles Co., Calif. Museum of Art, Los Angeles. 741.9'54'074019494
The sensuous line : Indian drawings from the Paul F. Walter Collection / by Pratapaditya Pal and Catherine Glynn. Los Angeles : Los Angeles County Museum of Art, c1976. 72 p. : ill. ; 26 cm. Catalog of an exhibition. Bibliography: p. 72. [NC327.L67 1976] 76-18934 ISBN 0-87587-071-6 pbk. : 4.00
1. Walter, Paul F.—Art collections. 2. Drawing, Indic—Exhibitions. I. Pal, Pratapaditya. II. Glynn, Catherine, 1946- III. Title.

Drawing-Instruction.

AIRY, Anna, 1882- 741.07
Making a start in art. London, New York, Studio Publications [1951] 95 p. illus. 25 cm. (The how to do it series, no. 42) [NC730.A4] 52-7389
1. Drawing—Instruction. 2. Painting—Technique. I. Title.

ANDERSON, Douglas, 1919- 741
How to draw with the light touch, by Doug Anderson. Text by Mary Anne Guitar. New York, Sterling Pub. Co. [1954] 80 p. illus. 30 cm. [NC730.A6] 54-13068
1. Drawing—Instruction. I. Guitar, Mary Anne. II. Title.

ANDERSON, Douglas, 1919- 741
Let's draw a story: fifth easy drawing book. New York, Sterling Pub. Co. [1958] 127p. illus. 26cm. [NC620.A735] 58-12539
1. Drawing—Instruction. I. Title.

ANDERSON, Douglas, 1919- 741.4
New things to draw & how to draw them. New York, Dodd, Mead, 1959. 56p. (chiefly illus.) 18x25cm. [NC650.A43] 58-13101
1. Drawing—Instruction. I. Title.

ANDERSON, Douglas, 1919- 741.5
Third easy drawing book: humorous drawing made easy. New York, Sterling Pub. Co. [1956] 126p. (chiefly illus.) 26cm. [NC620.A733] 56-11138
1. Drawing—Instruction. I. Title. II. Title: Easy drawing book. III. Title: Humorous drawing made easy.

ART Instruction, inc., Minneapolis. 741
Illustrating and cartooning. no. 1- Minneapolis 1951- v. in illus. (part col., part inserted) 35cm. Cover title. The

various numbers are frequently revised. This set includes all editions in the Library published since 1951 with this title. [NC950.A77] 53-15221
1. Drawing—Instruction. 2. Illustration of books. 3. Caricature. I. Title.

ART Instruction, inc., Minneapolis. 741.6
A series of texts dealing with the various phases of art for commercial purposes, prepared especially for Art Instruction, inc. Arr. and edited by Walter J. Wilwerding [and] Lee S. Preston. Layont and typography by Frank Kofron. Minneapolis [1956- v. illus. 31cm. ommercial art. Vols. published 1957- have title: ... A series of texts dealing with the various phases of art. The various texts are frequently revised: this set covers all editions in the Library. Contents.1. Basic drawing.--2. Ink and wash drawing. by F. M. Wing and others--3. Basic composition. color, perspective.--4. Advertising layout, by C. A. Chatterton and D. R. Bohmbach. Jr.--4 [i. e. 5] Beginning cartooning arr. by C. Waugh.--[6] Outline drawing.--9. Fashion illustration. by J. H. de Leon.--[10] Cartoon techniques, by C. Waugh and others.--[11] Still life painting in oil. by F. Taubes.--12 Newspaper illustrating by J. Welter and others.--[13] Perspective.--[14] ink drawing. by F. M. Wing and others.--[15OA series of texts dealing with the various phases of art for commercial purposes, prepared especially for Art Instruction, inc. Arr. and edited by Walter J. Wilwerding [and] Lee S. Preston. Layont and typography by Frank Kofron. Minneapolis [1956- v. illus. 31cm. ommercial art. Vols. published 1957- have title: ... A series of texts dealing with the various phases of art. The various texts are frequently revised: this set covers all editions in the Library. Contents.1. Basic drawing.--2. Ink and wash drawing. by F. M. Wing and others--3. Basic composition. color, perspective.--4. Advertising layout, by C. A. Chatterton and D. R. Bohmbach. Jr.--4 [i. e. 5] Beginning cartooning arr. by C. Waugh.--[6] Outline drawing.--9. Fashion illustration. by J. H. de Leon.--[10] Cartoon techniques, by C. Waugh and others.--[11] Still life painting in oil. by F. Taubes.--12 Newspaper illustrating by J. Welter and others.--[13] Perspective.--[14] ink drawing. by F. M. Wing and others.--[15]OA series of texts dealing with the various phases of art for commercial purposes, p
1. Drawing—Instruction. I. Wilwerding. Walter Joseph, 1891- ed. II. Preston. Lee S., 1921- ed. III. Title.

BRANDT, Rexford Elson, 1914- 741'.07
The artists' sketchbook and its uses [by] Rex Brandt. New York, Reinhold Pub. Corp. [1966] 96 p. illus. (part col.) port. 27 cm. [NC735.B65] 66-24557
1. Drawing—Instruction. I. Title.

*BRIDGMAN, George Brant, 1864-1943 743.49
Heads features and faces. New York, Barnes & Noble [1966, c.1932-1962] 125p. illuu. 21cm. (Everyday handbks. no. 300) 1.00 pap.,
I. Title. BIP

BROMMER, Gerald F. 741.2
Drawing: ideas, materials, and techniques [by] Gerald F. Brommer. Worcester, Mass., Davis [1972] 144 p. illus. 26 cm. Bibliography: p. 140-141. [NC730.B65] 77-169729 ISBN 0-87192-041-7 9.95
1. Drawing—Instruction. 2. Artists' materials. I. Title.

BROOKS, Walter, 1921- ed. 741.4
The art of drawing; still life, flowers, trees, landscape perspective, the human figure, heads-hands-feet, animals, birds [Designed, by Walter Brooks. New York, Odyssey, c.1965] 1v. (unpaged) illus. (pt. col.) 32cm. (Grumbacher lib. bk.) [NC730.B66] 65-15429 1.00 pap.,
1. Drawing—Instruction. I. Title.

BROOKS, Walter, 1921- 741.2
Creative ways with drawing. Designed and edited by Walter Brooks. New York, Golden Press [1974] 32 p. illus. 29 cm. (The Golden Press art instruction series) [NC730.B67] 73-88429 1.25 (pbk.)
1. Drawing—Instruction. I. Title. II. Title: Drawing. BIP

BUCHANAN, Norman 741
Learn to draw. New York, Warne [1965, c.1964] 65p. illus. 29cm. [NC730.B78] 65-10017 2.95
1. Drawing—Instruction. I. Title.

CAPON, Robin. 741.2
Introducing drawing techniques. New York, Taplinger Pub. Co. [1974] 96 p. illus. 21 cm. Bibliography: p. 93-94. [NC730.C27 1974] 73-14367 ISBN 0-8008-4174-3 7.50
1. Drawing—Instruction. I. Title. BIP

CHAET, Bernard. 741.4
The art of drawing. New York, Holt, Rinehart and Winston [1970] viii, 288 p. illus. (part col.) 26 cm. [NC730.C45] 78-120910 ISBN 0-03-077125-0
1. Drawing—Instruction. I. Title.

CHEEK, Carl. 743.4
Drawing hands. New York, Pitman Pub. Corp. [1959] unpaged. illus. 20x26cm. (Pitman art series, 15) [NC774.C47] 59-6583
1. Drawing—Instruction. 2. Hand. I. Title. BIP

CHEEK, Carl. 741
Quick sketching. New York, Pitman Pub. Co. [c1961] unpaged. illus. 20x27cm. (Pitman art series, 34) [NC650.C53] 61-9082
1. Drawing—Instruction. I. Title. BIP

CLIFTON, Jack. 741.4
Manual of drawing & painting. New York, Watson-Guptill Publications [1957] 63p. illus. 27cm. [NC650.C63] 57-12738
1. Drawing—Instruction. 2. Painting—Techniques. I. Title.

COLLES, Dorothy. 757.5
Portraying children. London, New York, Studio Publications [1956] 96p. illus. 26cm. (How to do it, no. 66) [NC773.C6] 57-387
1. Drawing—Instruction. 2. Portrait painting. 3. Portraits. I. Title.

COLLIER, Graham. 741
Form, space, and vision; discovering design through drawing. Foreword by Herbert Read. 2d ed. Englewood Cliffs, N. J., Prentice-Hall [1967] xix, 263 p. illus. (1 col.) 29 cm. Bibliographical footnotes. [NC730.C6 1967] 67-12189
1. Drawing—Instruction. 2. Creation (Literary, artistic, etc.) I. Title. BIP

D'AMELIO, Joseph. 742
Perspective drawing handbook. New York, Tudor Pub. Co. [1964] 96 p. illus. 29 cm. [NC750.D3] 64-24726
1. Drawing—Instruction. 2. Perspective. I. Title. BIP

DANIELS, Alfred. 741.2
Drawing for fun / Alfred Daniels. 1st ed. Garden City, N.Y. : Doubleday, 1975. x, 198 p. : ill. ; 27 cm. [NC730.D27] 74-25100 ISBN 0-385-01543-7 : 7.95
1. Drawing—Instruction. I. Title.

DAWE, Cedric. 741.23
Conte. [London, New York] Studio Publications [1956 96p. illus. 26cm. (The How to do it series, no. 64) [NC730.D3] 56-58998
1. Drawing—Instruction. I. Title.

DE REYNA, Rudy, 1914- 741.2
How to draw what you see. New York, Watson-Guptill Publications [1972] 174 p. illus. 27 cm. [NC730.D4 1972] 72-152754 ISBN 0-8230-1460-6 9.95
1. Drawing—Instruction. I. Title. BIP

DILLER, Mary Black, 1899- 741.4
Drawing for young artists. New York, Pitman Pub. Corp., c1955. unpaged., illus. 20x23cm. [NC655.D5] 55-12073
1. Drawing—Instruction. I. Title. BIP

DILLER, Mary Black, 1899- 743.897913
Drawing the circus for young artists. New York, Pitman, c.1960. unpaged. col. illus. 20x26cm. (Pitman art series, 32) 60-13319 1.00 pap.,
1. Drawing—Instruction. I. Title.

DILLER, Mary Black, 1899- 741.4
The holiday drawing book. New York, Pitman Pub. Corp. [1953] 128 p. (chiefly illus.) 29 cm. [NC670.D5] 53-12406
1. Drawing—Instruction. I. Title.

DOHANOS, Stevan, 1907- 741.6
How I make a picture. Westport, Conn., Institute of Commercial Art, '1950. 86 p. illus., ports. 35 cm. [NC730.D57] 51-825
1. Drawing—Instruction. 2. Commercial art. I. Westport, Conn. Institute of Commercial Art. II. Title.

*DRAPER, G.F. 741.24
Basic drawing for beginners of any age. Text and illustrations by G.F. Draper. New York, Vantage [c.1966] 48p. 21cm. 2.50 bds.,
I. Title.

ELLENDER, Raphael. 741.4
Basic drawing; new ways to see and draw. [1st ed.] Garden City, N.Y., Doubleday, 1964. 128 p. illus., ports., diagrs. 27 cm. ([A Doubleday artcraft book]) [NC730.E4] 64-11387
1. Drawing — Instruction. I. Title.

ELLIS, Howard W. 741.7
How to draw and speak; for the artist who wants to speak and the speaker who wants to draw. Illus. by the author. Anderson, Ind., Warner Press [dist. Gospel Trumpet Press, c.1961] 64p. illus. 28cm. 61-8163 pap., 2.00, plastic binding
1. Drawing—Instruction. 2. Public speaking. 3. Chalk-talks. I. Title.

FAUSTLE, Alfred. 604'.2
Drafting techniques for the artist. [Translated by Manly Banister] New York, Sterling Pub. Co. [1972] 96 p. illus. 29 cm. Translation of Technisches Zeichnen; Leitfaden fur den Unterricht. [NC735.F3813] 72-83256 ISBN 0-8069-5208-3
1. Drawing—Instruction. 2. Geometrical drawing. I. Title.

FLETCHER, Geoffrey S. 741.4
Elements of sketching [by] Geoffrey Fletcher. [1st American ed.] South Brunswick [N.J.] A. S. Barnes [1968, c1966] 126 p. illus. 26 cm. [NC730.F55 1968] 68-16352
1. Drawing—Instruction. I. Title.

FLETCHER, Geoffrey S. 760'.028
Sketching in colour [by Geoffrey Fletcher] [1st American ed.] South Brunswick [N.J.] A. S. Barnes [1969, c1968] 86 p. illus. (part col.) 26 cm. [NC730.F56 1969] 69-14884 8.50
1. Drawing—Instruction. 2. Color—Study and teaching. I. Title.

FRANK, Arthur J. 741
Drawing for everyone; the natural way to draw expressively. New York, A. S. Barnes [c.1962] 220p. illus. 26cm. 62-14974 7.95
1. Drawing—Instruction. 2. Figure draming. I. Title.

FREEDMAN, Edward H. 743
How to draw. New York, Bantam [1965] 128p. illus. 18cm. [NC650.F74] 65-20344 .75 pap.,
1. Drawing—Instruction. I. Title.

FRYKLUND, Verne Charles 744.4
General drafting [by] Verne C. Fryklund [and] Frank Roy Kepler. [3d ed.] Bloomington, Ill., McKnight & McKnight Pub. Co. [dist. New York, Taplinger, c.1938-1960] 204p. (bibl.) illus. (diagrs.) 27cm. 60-833 3.40; 2.00 pap.,
1. Drawing—Instruction. 2. Mechanical drawing. I. Kepler, Frank Roy, joint author. II. Title.

GETTINGS, Fred. 741.4
Techniques of drawing. New York, Viking Press [1969] 112 p. illus., facsims. 26 cm. (A Studio book) [NC730.G4] 75-91749
1. Drawing—Instruction. I. Title.

GILLEN, Michael, 1911- 701.8
Drawing, painting & sculpture from models, by Michael Gillen, Herbert Kallem [and] Henry Kallem. New York, Stravon, 1951. 95 p. illus. 29 cm. [NC730.G5] 51-2072
1. Drawing—Instruction. 2. Painting—Technique. 3. Sculpture—Technique. I. Title.

GILMORE, Barbara Cram 740.7
Instant talent; personalized doodles. by Cram. [1st ed.] Rutland. Vt., Tuttle [1966. c.1967] 64p. illus. 18 x 19cm. [NC593.G5] 67-11432 1.25 pap.,
1. Drawing—Instruction. I. Title.

GIRARD, Robert, professeur de dessin. 741'.07
Learn art in one year. [Translated by E. W. Egan, and adapted by Barbara Klinger] New York, Sterling Pub. Co. [1968] 96 p. illus. 29 cm. Translation of Art et technique du dessin. [NC730.G5413 1968] 68-18789
1. Drawing—Instruction. I. Title.

GNAGY, Jon. 741
New television art instruction book. [Garden City, N.Y.] [Doubleday] [1950] 64 p. illus., port. 31 cm. Cover title. [NC730.G6] 50-10110
1. Drawing—Instruction. I. Title.

GOLDSTEIN, Nathan. 741'.018
The art of responsive drawing. Englewood Cliffs, N.J., Prentice-Hall [1973] xi, 276 p. illus. 29 cm. Bibliography: p. 271-[272] [NC740.G6] 72-12289 ISBN 0-13-048637-X 12.00
1. Drawing—Instruction. 2. Composition (Art) I. Title. BIP

GOLLWITZER, Gerhard, 1906- 741.4
Abstract art, how to draw and understand it, [Translated and adapted by Dale Cunningham] New York, Sterling Pub. Co. [1962] 107 p. illus. 21 cm. Translation of Schule des Sehena. [NC730.G6283] 62-18625
1. Drawing — Instruction. 2. Art. Abstract. I. Title.

GOLLWITZER, Gerhard, 1906- 741.4
Abstract art, how to draw and understand it. [Translated and adapted by Dale Cunningham] New York, Sterling Pub. Co. [1962] 107 p. illus. 21 cm. Translation of Schule des Sehens. [NC730.G6283] 62-18625
1. Drawing—Instruction. 2. Art, Abstract.

GOLLWITZER, Gerhard, 1906- 741.4
Drawing from nature. [Translated by Eric Greweldinger] New York, Sterling Pub. Co. [1970] 96 p. illus. 22 cm. Translation of Gegenstandliches Zeichnen. [NC735.G613] 76-90807
1. Drawing—Instruction. I. Title.

GOLLWITZER, Gerhard, 1906- 741.4
Express yourself in drawing. New York, Sterling Pub. Co. [1960] 156 p. illus. 21 cm. [NC730.G633] 60-14329
1. Drawing—Instruction. I. Title. BIP

GOLLWITZER, Gerhard, 1906- 741.4
The joy of drawing. New York, Sterling Pub. Co. [1962, c1961] 123 p. illus. 21 cm. [NC730.G623 1962] 61-15855
1. Drawing—Instruction. I. Title.

GORDON, David. 741
How to draw in the third dimension. simplified instructions New York, William-Frederick Press, 1955. unpaged. illus. 23cm. [NC650.G63] 55-8558
1. Drawing—Instruction. I. Title.

†GRAY, Bill. 760'.028
Studio tips for artists & graphic designers / Bill Gray. New York : Van Nostrand Reinhold, c1976. 128 p. : ill. ; 23 cm. Includes index. [NC735.G7] 75-11317 ISBN 0-442-22819-8 : 4.95
*1. Drawing—Instruction. 2. Graphic arts—Technique. 3. Artists' materials. I. Title.*BIP

HENKES, Robert. 741
Orientation to drawing and painting. Scranton, International Textbook Co. [1965] xvi, 187 p. illus. (part col.) 26 cm. [NC590.H4] 64-14431
1. Drawing — Instruction. 2. Painting — Study and teaching. I. Title.

HERTER, Christine, 1890- 744
Dynamic symmetry; a primer. [1st ed.] New York, Norton [1966] xiii, 236p. illus. 27cm. [NC660.H4] 64-10568 10.00
1. Drawing—Instruction. 2. Proportion (Art) I. Title. BIP

*HILL, Adrian 741
You can draw. New York, Hart [1966, c.1963] 192p. illus. 18cm. Orig. pub. in London by Pan Bks. in 1963. .75 pap.,
1. Drawing—Instruction. I. Title. BIP

HILL, Adrian Keith Graham, 1895- 741.2
Further steps in drawing and sketching, written and illustrated by Adrian Hill. London, Blandford Press [1972] 96 p. illus.

SUBJECT INDEX DRAWING-INSTRUCTION.

23 cm. Label mounted on t.p.: Transatlantic Arts, Inc., New York: sole distributor for the U.S.A. [NC730.H5] 73-174055 ISBN 0-7137-0560-4 3.95
1. Drawing—Instruction. I. Title. BIP

HILL, Adrian Keith Graham, 1895- 743
You can draw [by] Adrian Hill. New York, Hart Pub. Co. [1966] 192 p. illus. 18 cm. First published in 1963 under title: How to draw. [NC730.H52 1966] 67-7497
1. Drawing—Instruction. I. Title.

HOAGLAND, Clayton. 743'.8'3
The pleasures of sketching outdoors. 2d ed. New York, Dover Publications [1969] xi, 164 p. illus. 28 cm. Bibliography: p. 164. [NC650.H6 1969] 70-95244 2.50
1. Drawing—Instruction. 2. Landscape in art. I. Title. BIP

HOGARTH, Burne. 743.49
Drawing the human head. [1st ed.] New York, Watson-Guptill Publications [1965] 156 p. illus., ports. 29 cm. [NC770.H6] 64-14763
1. Drawing—Instruction. 2. Head. 3. Head in art. I. Title. BIP

JAMESON, Kenneth. 741.4
You can draw. London, Studio Vista; New York, Watson-Guptill [1967] 104p. front., illus. (some col.) 19cm. [NC730.J27] 68-10157 2.50 bds.,
1. Drawing—Instruction. I. Title.

JAXTHEIMER, Bodo W. 741.4
Reinhold drawing and painting book. New York, Reinhold Pub. Corp. [1962, c1961] 408 p. illus. (part col.) 23 cm. Translation of Knaurs Mal- und Zeichenbuch. [NC730.J313] 62-20452
1. Drawing—Instruction. 2. Painting—Technique. I. Title.

JELLICO, John. 701
Heads, hands, and feet. Serial 6484. [Ed. 1] Scranton, Pa., International Correspondence Schools [c1962] 75 p. illus. 28 cm. [NC770.J4] 63-1627
1. Drawing—Instructions. 2. Anatomy, Artistic. I. International Correspondence Schools, Scranton, Pa. II. Title.

JONES, William T. 720'.28
Freehand and ornamental drawing, by William T. Jones. [Ed. 1] Scranton, ICS [1972] 121 p. illus. 27 cm. "4511." Part of illustrative matter on fold. sheet inserted. [NC660.J6] 72-186586
1. Drawing—Instruction. 2. Design, Decorative. 3. Decoration and ornament, Architectural. I. International Correspondence Schools, Scranton, Pa. II. Title.

KAUPELIS, Robert. 741.4
Learning to draw; a creative approach to expressive drawing. New York, Watson-Guptill Publications [1966] 138, [6] p. illus. 27 cm. Bibliography: p. [142] [NC730.K36] 66-13002
1. Drawing—Instruction. I. Title. BIP

KESSLER, Leonard P 1920- 741
Art is everywhere. New York, Dodd, Mead, 1958. 87p. illus. 25cm. [NC655.K396] 58-10766
1. Drawing— Instruction. 2. Painting—Technique. I. Title.

KRUSE, Alexander Z., 1890- 741
How to draw and paint. Illustrated by the author. New York, Barnes & Noble [1953] 136 p. illus. 21 cm. (Everyday handbook series. 244) [NC650.K7] 53-8942
1. Drawing—Instruction. 2. Painting—Technique. I. Title. BIP

LAIDMAN, Hugh. 741.2
The complete book of drawing and painting. New York, Viking Press [1974] 192 p. illus. (part col.) 38 cm. (A Studio book) [NC730.L33 1974] 73-6071 ISBN 0-670-23398-6 15.95
1. Drawing—Instruction. 2. Painting—Technique. I. Title. BIP

LANING, Edward, 1906- 741.2
The act of drawing. [1st ed.] New York, McGraw-Hill [1971] 159 p. illus. (part col.) 27 cm. [NC730.L37] 70-148991 ISBN 0-07-036349-8 10.95
1. Drawing—Instruction. I. Title. BIP

LEARN to draw from master artists, by the eds. of Fawcett books. Text by Ray Gill. Technical advisor: Frank Reilly. New York, Arco Pub. Co. [1961, c.1960] 144p. illus. (Do-it-yourself series) 60-15533 2.50 741.4
1. Drawing—Instruction. I. Gill, Ray. II. Fawcett Publications, Inc.

LEARN to draw from master artists, by the editors of Fawcett books. Text by Ray Gill. Technical advisor: Frank Reilly. Greenwich, Conn., Fawcett Publications, 1960. 144p. illus. 24cm. (A Fawcett how-to book, 452) [NC650.L37] 60-50170 741.4
1. Drawing—Instruction. I. Gill, Ray. II. Fawcett Publications, inc.

LOOMIS, Andrew, 1892- 741.4
Successful drawing. New York, Viking Press, 1951. 160 p. illus. 32 cm. [NC730.L6] 51-11036
1. Drawing—Instruction. I. Title.

LOOMIS, Andrew, 1892- 741.4
Three-dimensional drawing. Rev. ed. New York, Viking Press, 1958. 160 p. illus. 31 cm. First published in 1951 under title: Successful drawing. [NC730.L6 1958] 58-6047
1. Drawing—Instruction. I. Title.

MACDONALD, Norman, 1941- 741.2
Artist on the spot. [Westport, Conn.] Fletcher Art Services; distributed by Van Nostrand Reinhold, New York [1972] 143 p. illus. (part col.) 27 x 29 cm. [NC730.M23] 72-81503 ISBN 0-442-25047-9 12.95
1. Drawing—Instruction. I. Title.

MACKAY, Richard. 741.4
Step-by-step drawing. New York, Hart Pub. Co. [c1958] 128p. illus. 28cm. [NC655.M2] 59-617
1. Drawing—Instruction. I. Title.

MARSHALL, Francis. 743.2
Sketching the ballet. [London, New York, Studio, 1950] 63 p. illus. 18 cm. (The How to draw series) [NC715.M3] 51-9168
1. Drawing—Instruction. I. Title. II. Series.

MEGLIN, Nick. 741.4
On-the-spot drawing, by Nick Meglin. New York, Watson-Guptill Publications [1969] 159 p. illus. 27 cm. Report of interviews with 12 illustrators, with selections from their drawings. [NC730.M38] 69-17668 10.95
1. Drawing—Instruction. I. Title. BIP

MINNEAPOLIS. Art Instruction. 741.07
Modern illustrating. Division 1- Compiled and edited by Chas. L. Bartholomew Minneapolis, c1950- no. illus. (part fold., inserted) 28 cm. First published under title: Illustrating and cartooning. [NC640.M5 1950] 50-14260
1. Drawing — Instruction. 2. Caricature. I. Bartholomew, Charles Lewis, 1869- ed. II. Almars, Joseph, 1884- joint ed. III. Title.

MOORE, Henry Spencer, 1898- 741.91
Heads, figures and ideas. With a comment by Geoffrey Grigson. Greenwich, Conn., New York Graphic Society, 1958. [66] p. (chiefly illus. [part col.]) 48 cm. [NC1115.M57G7] 58-4168
I. Title.

MORANZ, John, 1902- 741.07
Mastery of drawing. New York, R. R. Smith, 1950. 400 p. (chiefly illus., part col.) 31 cm. [NC710.M75] 50-9719
1. Drawing — Instruction. I. Title.

MORANZ, John, 1902- 740
The professional guide to drawing and illustration. Mastery of drawing. New York, Grosset [c1950] 400p. (chiefly illus., part col.) 31cm. Originally published (New York, Smith, 1950) under title: Mastery of drawing. [NC710.M] A53
1. Drawing—Instruction. I. Title. II. Title: Mastery of drawing.

MUGNAINI, Joseph A. 741.4
Drawing: a search for form [by] Joseph Mugnaini and Janice Lovoos. New York, Reinhold Pub. Corp. [1966, c1965] 159 p. illus. (part col.) 29 cm. [NC745.M8] 65-19673
1. Drawing—Instruction. 2. Form (Aesthetics) 3. Proportion (Art) I. Lovoos, Janice, joint author. II. Title.

MUGNAINI, Joseph A. 741.2
The hidden elements of drawing [by] Joseph Mugnaini. New York, Van Nostrand Reinhold Co. [1974] 211 p. illus. 29 cm. [NC735.M82] 73-3944 ISBN 0-442-25720-1
1. Drawing—Instruction. 2. Form (Aesthetics) I. Title. BIP

NELMS, Henning, 1900- 741.4
Thinking with a pencil. New York, Barnes & Noble [1964] xiii, 347 p. illus., maps, diagrs. 22 cm. (Everyday handbooks, no. 206) Bibliography: p. 331-335. [NC730.N4 1964] 64-14257
1. Drawing—Instruction. I. Title. BIP

NICOLAIDES, Kimon, 1891-1938. 741.2
The natural way to draw : a working plan for art study / by Kimon Nicolaides. Boston : Houghton Mifflin Co., 1975, c1941. xiv, 221 p. : ill. ; 24 cm. [NC650.N5 1975] 75-313761 ISBN 0-395-08048-7 : 7.95 ISBN 0-395-20548-4 pbk. : 4.95
1. Drawing—Instruction. I. Title. BIP

PALAZZO, Tony, 1905- 741.4
The magic crayon; drawings from simple shapes and forms. New York, Lion Press [1968] c1967. [42] p. col. illus. 22 cm. Shows how simple shapes such as curves and circles can be the basis for drawing many things. [PZ10.7.P3Mag] 67-18481 3.25
I. Title. BIP

PELIKAN, Alfred George, 1893- 701
Designs for faces & figures. Milwaukee, Bruce Pub. Co. [1962] 64p. illus. 26cm. [NC765.P36] 61-18287
1. Drawing—Instruction. 2. Figure drawing. I. Title.

PERARD, Victor Semon, 1870- 743.69725
Drawing horses. Rev. by Gladys Emerson Cook. New York, Pitman Pub. Corp. [1956] unpaged. illus. 20x27cm. (Pitman drawing series) [NC780.P38 1956] 55-12076
1. Drawing—Instruction. 2. Animal painting and illustration. 3. Horses—Pictures, illustrations, etc. 4. Action in art. I. Cook, Gladys Emerson, 1899- ed. II. Title. BIP

PERARD, Victor Semon, 1870- 741
Drawing sea & sky. New York, Pitman Pub. Corp. [c1957] unpaged. illus. 20x26cm. (Pitman drawing series) [NC825.S5P4 1957] 57-10744
1. Drawing—Instruction. 2. Sea in art. I. Title. BIP

PERARD, Victor Semon, 1870-1957. 741.4
How to draw. Contributing artists: Victor Perard [and others] New York, Pitman Pub. Corp. [1957] unpaged. illus. 24x32cm. [NC730.P46 1957] 57-7598
1. Drawing —Instruction. I. Title.

PERARD, Victor Semon, 1870-1957. 741.4
How to sketch. Contributing artists: Victor Perard and others New York, Pitman Pub. Corp. 1960 1 v. (unpaged chiefly illus.) 20 x 27 cm. (Pitman art series, 31) [NC650.P49] 60-13318
1. Drawing—Instruction. I. Title.

PERARD, Victor Semon, 1870-1957. 741.4
The new how to draw. Contributing artists: Victor Perard [and others] New York, Pitman Pub. Corp. [1963] 1 v. (unpaged) illus. 24 x 32 cm. [NC730.P47] 63-22149
1. Drawing—Instruction. I. Title.

PITZ, Henry Clarence, 1895- 741
Drawing outdoors [by] Henry C. Pitz. New York, Watson-Guptill Publications [1965] 144 p. illus. 27 cm. [NC650.P55] 65-15949
1. Drawing—Instruction. I. Title. BIP

POGANY, Willy, 1882-1955. 741.2
The art of drawing. [Rev. and enl. ed., including sketches and studies] South Brunswick [N.J.] A. S. Barnes [1969, c1946] [128] p. illus. 29 cm. This ed. first published in 1946 under title: Willy Pogany's drawing lessons. [NC650.P6 1969] 68-14415 7.50
1. Drawing—Instruction. I. Title.

POGANY, Willy, 1882-1955. 741.2
The art of drawing. [Rev. and enl. ed., including sketches and studies] Totowa, N.J., Littlefield, Adams, 1972 [c1946] 126 p. illus. 28 cm. (Littlefield quality paperbacks, no. 257) First published in 1946 under title: Willy Pogany's drawing lessons. [NC650.P6 1972] 72-86204 2.95
1. Drawing—Instruction. I. Title.

PRISCILLA, Louis, 1906- 740
Basic drawing. New York, Grayson Pub. Corp. [1954] 128p. illus. 29cm. [NC730.P75] 54-4127
1. Drawing—Instruction. I. Title.

RAWSON, Philip S. 741.4
Drawing [by] Philip Rawson. London, New York, Oxford U.P., 1969. xiv, 322 p. illus., ports. 21 cm. (The Appreciation of the arts, 3) [NC735.R35] 70-109895 50/- ($9.75)
1. Drawing—Instruction. I. Title.

RICHMOND, Leonard. 741
Sketching out of doors. New York, Pitman Pub. Corp. [1954] unpaged (chiefly illus.) 20x26cm. (Pitman drawing series) [NC730.R5] 54-3989
1. Drawing—Instruction. I. Title.

RICHMOND, Leonard. 741.24
Sketching out of doors. New York, Pitman Pub. Corp. 1958? c1954 1 v. (unpaged) illus. 20 x 26 cm. (Pitman art books) [NC730.R5 1958] 58-9730
1. Drawing—Instruction. I. Title. BIP

ROBERTS, Cliff. 741.4
Start with a dot. New York, F. Watts [1968, c1960] [39] p. illus. (part col.) 22 cm. 1960 edition published under title: The dot. A simple dot can be the start of a circle or a straight line and a combination of these can produce many interesting shapes. [PZ8.3.R53St] AC 68
1. Drawing—Instruction. I. Title.

ROTH, Harry. 740
At pencil's point, an enjoyable and sure way to become a good draughtsman. [Rev. and enl. ed.] New York, Stephen Daye Press [1950] 223 p. illus. 26 cm. [NC650.R6 1950] 51-9106
1. Drawing—Instruction. I. Title.

ROTTGER, Ernst. 741.4
Creative drawing, point and line [by] Ernst Rottger and Dieter Klante. New York, Reinhold Pub. Corp. [1964, c1963] 143 p. illus. 21 cm. ([Creative play series]) Translation of Punkt und Linie. [NC650.R58] 64-13649
1. Drawing—Instruction. I. Klante, Dieter, joint author. II. Title.

SARGEANT, Charles. 743.8962913338
How to draw rockets & spaceships. London, New York, Studio Publications [1958] 61p. illus. 18cm. [NC825.R6S3] 59-3351
1. Drawing—Instruction. 2. Rockets Aeronautics) 3. Spaceships. I. Title.

SIMON, Howard, 1902- 741.4
Primer of drawing, (Rev. ed.] New York, Sterling Pub. Co. [1958] 135 . illus. 29 cm. (A Bridgman art book) Published in 1953 under title: Primer of drawing for adults. [NC730.S45 1958] 58-7605
1. Drawing — Instruction. I. Title.

SIMON, Howard, 1903- 741.4
Primer of drawing. [Rev. ed.] New York, Sterling Pub. Co. [1958] 135 p. illus. 29 cm. (A Bridgman art book) Published in 1953 under title: Primer of drawing for adults. [NC730.S45 1958] 58-7605
1. Drawing — Instructions. I. Title.

SIMON, Howard, 1903- 741.4
Primer of drawing for adults. New York, Sterling Pub. Co., 1953. 137 p. illus. 30 cm. (A Bridgman art book) [NC730.S45] 53-1609
1. Drawing — Instruction. I. Title.

SIMON, Howard, 1903- 741.4
Techniques of drawing. London, Oak Tree Press; New York, Sterling Pub. Co. [1963] 135 p. illus. 28 cm. (A Bridgman giant) "First published as Primer of drawing for

adults ... 1953." [NC730.S45 1963] 63-6100
1. Drawing — Instruction. I. Title. BIP

SIMON, Howard, 1903- 741.2
Techniques of drawing. New York, Dover Publications [1972, c1963] 135 p. illus. 28 cm. First ed. published in 1953 under title: Primer of drawing for adults. [NC730.S45 1972] 72-87523 ISBN 0-486-21578-4 2.50
1. Drawing—Instruction. I. Title.

SIMPSON, Ian. 741
Drawing: seeing and observation. New York, Van Nostrand Reinhold [1973] 168 p. illus. 29 cm. Bibliography: p. 165. [NC735.S48] 77-39808 ISBN 0-442-27650-8 10.95
1. Drawing—Instruction. 2. Visual perception. 3. Perspective. I. Title.

SLOBODKIN, Louis, 1903- 741
The first book of drawing. New York, F. Watts, c1958. 68 p. illus. 23 cm. [First books, 88] [NC650.S5] 58-11352
1. Drawing—Instruction. I. Title. BIP

SMITH, Ronald, A. T. D. (Lond.) 741
Teach yourself to draw. New York, Roy Publishers [1954] 189p. illus. 19cm. (The Teach yourself books) [NC650] 54-5433
1. Drawing—Instruction. I. Title.

SMITH, Ronald, A.T.D. (LOND.) 741
Teach yourself to draw. London, English Universities Press [1951] 189 p. illus. 18 cm. (The Teach yourself series) [NC650.S63] 52-30676
1. Drawing—Instruction. I. Title.

SPEED, Harold, 1873- 741.2
The practice & science of drawing. 3d ed. New York, Dover Publications [1972] 296 p. illus. 22 cm. Reprint of the 1917 ed. [NC730.S674 1973] 72-83742 ISBN 0-486-22870-3 3.50
1. Drawing—Instruction. I. Title. BIP

*SPENCER, Avalee Boner 743.5
Paper, pencil, color. Scranton, Pa., Intl. Textbk. [1967] ix, 204p. illus.(pt. col.) 26cm. 4.95 pap., plastic bdg.
1. Drawing—Instruction. I. Title.

STEARN, Frank Charles, 1900- 741.07
Drawing for fun [by] Frank Stearn [and others] New York, Sentinel Books [1950] 95 p. illus. 20 cm. Bibliography: p. 94-95. [NC650.S8] 50-14548
1. Drawing — Instruction. I. Title.

TAUBES, Frederic, 1900- 741.4
The quickest way to draw well. New York, Studio Publications [1958] 94 p. illus. 25 cm. [NC650.T3] 58-10448
1. Drawing—Instruction. I. Title. BIP

TAYLOR, Benjamin DeBrie, 1923- 741.2
Design lessons from nature. New York, Watson-Guptill Publications [1974] 159 p. illus. 29 cm. Bibliography: p. 156-157. [NC735.T38] 73-22401 ISBN 0-8230-1323-5 12.50
1. Drawing—Instruction. 2. Nature (Aesthetics) I. Title.

TOMASCH, Elmer John. 741.4
A foundation for expressive drawing [by] E. J. Tomasch. Minneapolis, Burgess Pub. Co. [1969] 194 p. illus. 28 cm. [NC730.T6] 76-77328
1. Drawing—Instruction. I. Title. BIP

VAUGHAN-JACKSON, Genevieve. 741
Drawing for boys. New York, Pitman, c1956. unpaged. illus. 20 x 26 cm. (Pitman drawing series) [NC655.V3] 56-12127
1. Drawing—Instruction. I. Title.

VAUGHAN-JACKSON, Genevieve. 741
Drawing for boys. New York, Pitman [1959] c1956. unpage (chiefly illus.) 20 x 27 cm. (Pitman art series, 13) [NC655.V3] 59-7362
1. Drawing — Instruction. I. Title. BIP

VAUGHAN-JACKSON, Genevieve. 741.4
Drawing for girls. New York, Pitman [1960] Unpaged. illus. 20 x 26 cm. (Pitman art series, 30) [NC655.V32] 60-5518
1. Drawing — Instruction. I. Title. BIP

WALTER, Start. 741.4
Drawing for pleasure. [1st American ed. New York, Watson-Guptill Publications, 1967, c1962] 55 p. illus. 18 x 20 cm. (Watson-Guptill drawing books) [NC735.W25 1967] 65-19008
1. Drawing—Instruction. I. Title.

WATROUS, James. 741
The craft of old-master drawings. Madison, University of Wisconsin Press, 1957. 170 p. illus. 27 cm. [NC735.W36] 56-9307
1. Drawing — Instruction. 2. Drawing — Hist. 3. Drawings. I. Title. BIP

WATSON, Ernest William, 1884- 741.24
Ernest W. Watson's Sketch diary, with instructive text on brush and pencil techniques. New York, Reinhold [1965] 64p. illus. (pt. col.) 27cm. [NC1075.W36A45] 65-12979 4.50
I. Title. II. Title: Sketch diary.

WATSON, Ernest William, 1884-1969. 741
The Watson drawing book, by Ernest W. Watson and Aldren A. Watson. New York, Reinhold Pub. Corp. [1962] 160 p. illus. 27 cm. [NC730.W39] 62-19491
1. Drawing—Instruction. I. Watson, Aldren Auld, 1917- joint author. II. Title.

*WEISS, Harvey 741
Pencil, pen and brush. New York, Scholastic [1965, c.1961] 64p. illus. (pt. col.) 23cm. .50 pap.,
1. Drawing—Instruction. I. Title. BIP

WHITE, Peter, pseud. 372.52
The easy drawing book. New York, Sterling Pub. Cp., c1953. 127p. (chiefly illus.) 26cm. [NC620.W62] 53-8473
1. Drawing—Instruction. I. Title.

WHITE, Peter, pseud. 372.52
The easy drawing book. [Combined ed.] New York, Sterling [c. 1953, 1966] 124p. (chiefly illus.) 21cm. [NC620.W62] 66-3907 1.95 bds.,
1. Drawing-Instruction. I. Title.

WHITE, Peter, pseud. 372.52
The second easy drawing book. New York, Sterling Pub. Co., c1955. 126p. (chiefly illus.) 26cm. [NC620.W63] 55-7427
1. Drawing—Instruction. I. Title. II. Title: Easy drawing book.

WILLIAMS, Guy R. 741
Tackle drawing and painting this way. London, S. Paul [New Rochelle, N.Y., SportShelf, 1966, c.1965] 128p. illus. 20cm. [NC650.W53] 66-1502 3.75 bds.,
1. Drawing—Instruction. 2. Paintings—Technique. I. Title.

WILLIAMS, Guy R. 751.4
Taking up drawing and painting [by] Guy R. Williams. New York, Taplinger Pub. Co. [1973, c1971] 128 p. illus. 22 cm. (Taplinger's teach-yourself-crafts series) [NC650.W54 1973] 72-2200 ISBN 0-8008-7542-7 5.95
1. Drawing—Instruction. 2. Painting—Technique. I. Title.

WINSEY, Alexander Reid, 1905- 741.07
Drawing simplified. New York, Prentice-Hall, 1950. xxvii, 161 p. illus. 31 cm. "The major portion . . . is also published under the title of Freehand drawing manual." Bibliography: p. [153]-159. [NC730.W5] 50-10423
1. Drawing—Instruction. I. Title.

WINSEY, Alexander Reid, 1905- 741.07
Freehand drawing manual. New York, Prentice-Hall, 1950. xxvii, 161 p. illus. 32 cm. The major portion is also published under title: Drawing simplified. Bibliography: p. [158]-159. [NC730.W52] 50-12983
1. Drawing—Instruction. I. Title.

WOLCHONOK, Louis. 745.4
Design for artists and craftmen [Magnolia, Mass., Peter Smith, 1968, c. 1953] xiv, 207p. illus. 28cm. (Dover bk. rebound) [NC735W6] 5.00
1. Drawing—Instruction. 2. Design. I. Title.

WOLCHONOK, Louis. 745.4
Design for artists and craftsmen. New York, Dover Publications [1953] xiv, 207 p. illus. 28 cm. [NC735.W6] 54-9269
1. Drawing—Instruction. 2. Design. I. Title. BIP

WOOD, Charles. 743
Drawing at the circus. London, New York, Studio Publications [1953] 63p. illus. 18cm. (The How to draw series) [NC730.W57] 54-9356
1. Drawing—Instruction. I. Title.

WOOTTON, Frank A A 743.89629133
Drawing aircraft. [New York] Studio Publications [1959] 62 p. illus. 18 cm. (A Studio publication, 44) [NC825.A4W6] 59-16490
1. Drawing — Instruction. 2. Aeroplanes I. Title.

ZAIDENBERG, Arthur, 1903- 741.4
The draw anything book. New York, Harper [1950] 1 v. (chiefly illus.) 28 cm. [NC730.Z35] 50-10291
1. Drawing—Instruction. I. Title.

ZAIDENBERG, Arthur, 1903- 743'.8'97913
How to draw a circus. London, New York, Abelard-Schuman [1969] 63 p. illus. 26 cm. Stresses anatomy, movement, and balance for the beginning artist using circus animals and performers as models. [NC620.Z3] 69-17551 3.50
1. Drawing—Instruction. 2. Circus in art. I. Title.

ZAIDENBERG, Arthur, 1903- 741.2
How to draw and compose pictures. London, New York, Abelard-Schuman [1971] 64 p. illus. 26 cm. [NC740.Z3] 78-141862 ISBN 0-200-71772-3
1. Drawing—Instruction. 2. Composition (Art) I. Title. BIP

ZAIDENBERG, Arthur, 1903- 743.94
How to draw historic and modern bridges. London, New York, Abelard Schuman [1962] 64 p. illus. 26 cm. [NC825.B7Z3] 62-17043
1. Drawing—Instruction. 2. Bridges in art. I. Title.

ZAIDENBERG, Arthur, 1903- 743.4
How to draw people! A beginner's book for boys and girls. New York, Vanguard Press [1952] 60 p. illus. 28 cm. [NC765.Z288] 52-11123
1. Drawing—Instruction. 2. Human figure in art. I. Title. BIP

ZAIDENBERG, Arthur, 1903- 743.5
How to draw period costumes. New York, Abelard [c.1966] 64p. (chiefly illus.) 27cm. [NC825.C6Z3] 66-11894 3.00; 2.93 lib. ed.,
1. Drawing—Instruction. 2. Costume. I. Title.

ZAIDENBERG, Arthur, 1903- 743.4
How to draw portraits, a book for beginners. New York, Vanguard Press [1962] unpaged. 28 cm. [NC773.Z3] 62-11216
1. Drawing—Instructions. 2. Portraits. I. Title. BIP

ZAIDENBERG, Arthur, 1903- 743.89629
How to draw ships and trains, cars and airplanes. London, New York, Abelard-Schuman [1961] 62 p. illus. 26 cm. [NC650.Z28] 61-7145
1. Drawing — Instruction. I. Title.

ZAIDENBERG, Arthur, 1903- 741
New and easy ways to draw and paint. [Los Angeles, Trend Books, 1956] 128 p. illus. 24 cm. (Trend books, 141) [NC730.Z37] 56-12639
1. Drawing — Instructions. 2. Painting — Technique. I. Title.

ZAIDENBERG, Arthur, 1903- 741
Seeing with pencil and brush. [1st ed.] New York, Harper [1962] 171 p. illus. 28 cm. [NC730.Z39] 62-8619
1. Drawing — Instruction. 2. Painting — Technique. 3. Art — Hist. I. Title.

Drawing—Instruction—Juvenile literature.

ARESTEIN, Jean. 743
Cartooning and outline drawing. London, Oak Tree Press; New York, Sterling, Pub. Co. [1964, c1963] c1963] 128 p. (chiefly illus.) 20 cm. (Worthwhile hoe-to paperbacks, 507) Pages 114-128 blank for "Your own sketchbook." First published in 1958 under title: Fourth easy drawing book: How to draw people and animals. [NC620.A77] 63-20097
1. Drawing — Instruction — Juvenile leterature. I. Title.

Drawing—Instruction—Juvenile literature.

CAMPBELL, Ann Raymond. 741'.07 (j)
Start to draw. Written and drawn by Ann Campbell. New York, F. Watts [1968] 48 p. illus. (part col.) 22 cm. [NC625.C3] 68-25727 2.95
1. Drawing—Instruction—Juvenile literature. I. Title. BIP

DICKIE, Jimmie 741
Your child can draw, a book of fun. Foreword by Merel Armitage. Manzanita Pr. [dist. Fresno(Calif., Acad. Lib. Guild, 1962, c.1961] unpaged. illus. 28cm. 61-17476 2.50 bds.,
1. Drawing—Instruction—Juvenile literature. I. Title.

EMBERLEY, Ed. 741.2
Drawing book: make a world. [1st ed.] Boston, Little, Brown [1972] [32] p. col. illus. 20 x 26 cm. [NC655.E46] 70-154962 3.95
1. Drawing—Instruction—Juvenile literature. I. Title. II. Title: Make a world.

KATCHMER, Betsy 741.4
Little Rembrandt; a book of simple art instruction for boys and girls. New York, Exposition [c.1963] unpaged. illus. 21x27cm. 2.79
1. Drawing (Instruction)—Juvenile literature. I. Title.

KRINSKY, Norman. 372.5'2
How to draw a hippopotamus. New York, Van Nostrand Reinhold [1971] [32] p. illus. (part col.) 22 x 28 cm. Brief stories accompany illustrations that demonstrate how to draw a freighter, a hippopotamus, an astronaut, faces, a castle, and other objects beginning with the technique of "blocking in." [NC630.K74] 70-126876
1. Drawing—Instruction—Juvenile literature. I. Title.

LANCASTER, John, 1930- 741.2
Let's draw [by] John Lancaster. New York, Van Nostrand Reinhold [1972] 32 p. illus. (part. col.) 21 cm. (Starting points) Gives the beginning artist suggestions for gathering his equipment and experimenting with a variety of techniques and mediums. [NC655.L28] 73-188482 Pap. 1.45
1. Drawing—Instruction—Juvenile literature. I. Title.

LUTZ, Edwin George, 1868- 741.2'4
Drawing made easy; a step by step guide to drawing for young artists, by E. G. Lutz. New York, Scribner [1973, c1921] 95 p. illus. 20 cm. (The Scribner library. Emblem editions) Step-by-step instructions for sketching animals, faces and figures in action, flowers, landscapes, and other subjects. [NC655.L8 1973] 72-12164 ISBN 0-684-13324-5 2.95
1. Drawing—Instruction—Juvenile literature. I. Title.

WARSHAW, Jerry. 741.2
Jerry Warshaw's The I-can't-draw book. Photography by Dick Masek. Chicago, A. Whitman [1971] 31 p. col. illus. 24 cm. Simple instructions that can turn anyone into an artist of sorts. [NC655.W36 1971] 73-165824 ISBN 0-8075-3502-8
1. Drawing—Instruction—Juvenile literature. I. Masek, Dick, illus. II. Title. III. Title: The I-can't-draw book.

WEISS, Harvey. 741
Pencil, pen, and brush drawing for beginners. New York, Young Scott Books [1961] 63 p. illus. 28 cm. [NC655.W4] 61-2895
1. Drawing—Instruction—Juvenile literature. I. Title.

ZAIDENBERG, Arthur, 1903- 743.4
How to draw costumes and clothes. London, New York Abelard-Schuman

SUBJECT INDEX DRAWINGS.

[1964] 64 p. illus. 26 cm. [NC655.Z29] 64-22866
1. Drawing — Instruction — Juvenile literature. 2. Costume — Juvenile literature. I. Title.

ZAIDENBERG, Arthur, 1903- 743.8
How to draw landscapes, seascapes, and cityscapes. London, New York, Abelard-Schuman [1963] 64 p. illus. 27 cm. [NC655.Z3] 63-10467
1. Drawing — Instruction — Juvenile literature. 2. Landscape drawing — Juvenile literature. I. Title. BIP

ZAIDENBERG, Arthur, 1903- 743.5
How to draw military and civilian uniforms. London, New York, Abelard Schuman 1965 64 p. illus. 26 cm. [NC825.U5Z3] 65-12668
1. Drawing—Instruction—Juvenile literature. 2. Uniforms—Juvenile literature. I. Title.

Drawing, Italian—Catalogs.

ITALIAN 741.9'45'07402574
drawings in Oxford : from the collections of the Ashmolean Museum and Christ Church / text and commentary by Terisio Pignatti ; [translated from the Italian by Barbara Luigia la Penta]. Oxford : Phaidon, 1977. 256 p. : ill. (chiefly col.), ports. (some col.) ; 32 cm. Translation of I grandi disegni Italiani nelle collezione di Oxford. Includes index. Bibliography: p. 83-86. [NC255.G6613] 78-305501 ISBN 0-7148-1764-3 : 49.95
1. Oxford University. Ashmolean Museum. 2. Oxford University. Christ Church. Picture Gallery. 3. Drawing, Italian—Catalogs. 4. Drawing—England—Oxford—Catalogs. I. Pignatti, Terisio, 1920- II. Oxford. University. Ashmolean Museum. III. Oxford. University. Christ Church. Picture Gallery.

Drawing, Latin American—Exhibitions.

RECENT Latin American 741.9'8'074
drawings, 1969-1976 : lines of vision / essays by Barbara Duncan and Damian Bayon ; catalogue entries by Ana M. Casciero. Washington : International Exhibitions Foundation, c1977. 79 p. : ill. ; 28 cm. Exhibition organized and circulated by International Exhibitions Foundation, 1977-1978. [NC102.R42] 77-71639 ISBN 0-88397-000-7
1. Drawing, Latin American—Exhibitions. 2. Drawing—20th century—Latin America—Exhibitions. I. Duncan, Barbara, 1921- II. Bayon, Damian Carlos. III. Casciero, Ana M. IV. International Exhibitions Foundation. BIP

Drawing, Renaissance—Exhibitions.

EDINBURGH. 741.9'4'074094134
National Gallery of Scotland.
Old master drawings from the David Laing Bequest : [catalogue of an exhibition held] 14 June-24 July 1976 [at the National Gallery of Scotland]. Edinburgh : The Gallery, [1976] 43 p., leaf of plate, [20] p. of plates : ill., port. ; 24 cm. Errata slip inserted. [NC80.E33 1976] 77-358845 ISBN 0-903148-05-6 : £1.00
1. Laing, David, 1793-1878—Art collections. 2. Drawing, Renaissance—Exhibitions. 3. Drawing, Baroque—Exhibitions. 4. Drawing, Rococo—Exhibitions. I. Title.

Drawing-room practice.

AMERICAN Institute of Steel 744.4
Construction.
The A. I. S. C. textbook of structural shop drafting. 1st ed. New York, 1950- v. illus. 29 cm. Cover title: Structural shop drafting. [T352.A48] 50-12903
1. Drawing-room practice. 2. Structures, Theory of. I. Title. II. Title: Structural shop drafting.

KATZ, Hyman H 744.4
Handbook of layout and dimensioning for production. New York, Macmillan [1957] 479p. illus. 25cm. [T352.K3] 56-7313
1. Drawing-room practice. I. Title. II. Title: Layout and dimensioning for production.

Drawing—Self-instruction.

HILL, Adrian Keith Graham, 741.4
1895-
What shall we draw? The beginner's book of drawings, written and illustrated by Adrian Hill. New York, Emerson Books [1959] 64 p. illus. 23 cm. [NC710.H5] 59-9102
1. Drawing—Self-instruction. I. Title. BIP

Drawing—Technique.

BRO, Lu. 741.2
Drawing, a studio guide / by Lu Bro. 1st ed. New York : Norton, c1978. p. cm. Includes index. Bibliography: p. [NC735.B69 1978] 78-12136 14.95 pbk. : 7.95
1. Drawing—Technique. I. Title.

BROMMER, Gerald F. 741.2
Drawing : ideas, materials, and techniques / Gerald F. Brommer. Rev. ed. Worcester, Mass. : Davis Publications, c1978. 152 p. : ill. (some col.) ; 27 cm. Includes index. Bibliography: p. 140-143. [NC730.B65 1978] 78-59861 ISBN 0-87192-097-2 : 13.95
1. Drawing—Technique. 2. Artists' materials. I. Title.

CHAET, Bernard. 741.2
The art of drawing / Bernart Chaet. 2d ed. New York : Holt, Rinehart and Winston, c1978. x, 324 p. : ill., (some col.) ; 28 cm. Includes index. [NC730.C45 1978] 77-24195 ISBN 0-03-089960-5 : 18.95
1. Drawing—Technique. I. Title.

GOLDSTEIN, Nathan. 741
The art of responsive drawing / Nathan Goldstein. 2d ed. Englewood Cliffs, N.J. : Prentice-Hall, c1977. xii, 355 p. : ill. ; 29 cm. Includes index. Bibliography: p. 348. [NC740.G6 1977] 76-25001 ISBN 0-13-048629-9 : 14.95
1. Drawing—Technique. 2. Composition (Art)

GRAY, Bill. 702'.8
More studio tips for artists and graphic designers / Bill Gray. New York : Van Nostrand Reinhold Co., 1978. 128 p. : ill. ; 24 cm. Includes index. [NC735.G68] 77-10676 ISBN 0-442-22811-2 pbk. : 4.95
*1. Drawing—Technique. 2. Graphic arts—Technique. 3. Artists' materials. I. Title.*BIP

HAYES, Colin. 741.2
Complete guide to drawing and painting / by Colin Hayes. New York : Mayflower Books, 1979. p. cm. [NC730.H39] 78-25627 ISBN 0-8317-1615-0 : 19.95
1. Drawing—Technique. 2. Painting—Technique. I. Title.

LAIDMAN, Hugh. 741.2
The complete book of drawing and painting / Hugh Laidman. Harmondsworth, Eng. ; New York : Penguin Books, 1978, c1974. 192 p. : ill. (some col.) ; 37 cm. (A Penguin handbook) Reprint of the 1974 ed. published by Viking Press, New York, in series: A Studio book. [NC730.L33 1978] 78-6496 ISBN 0-14-046349-6 pbk. : 7.95
1. Drawing—Technique. 2. Painting—Technique. I. Title.

LENT, William T. 741.2
Speed sketching / William T. Lent. 1st ed. Garden City, N.Y. : Doubleday, 1978. 96 p. : ill. ; 21 x 27 cm. [NC730.L46] 77-82957 ISBN 0-385-13089-9 : 8.95
1. Drawing—Technique. I. Title. BIP

PORTER, Albert W. 741.2
The art of sketching Albert W. Porter. Worcester, Mass. : Davis Publications, c1977. 136 p. : chiefly ill. (some col.) ; 27 cm. [NC730.P66] 77-78826 ISBN 0-87192-092-1 : 10.95
1. Drawing—Technique. I. Title. BIP

RAUCH, Hans-Georg, 1939- 741.2
The lines are coming : a book about drawing / by Hans-Georg Rauch. New York : Scribner, [1978] p. cm. Briefly explains how to use various line combinations to form pictures. [NC730.R38] 78-12861 ISBN 0-684-15989-9 : 7.95
1. Drawing—Technique. I. Title. BIP

SIMMONS, Seymour. 741.2
Drawing : the creative process / by Seymour Simmons III and Marc S. A. Winer. Englewood Cliffs, N.J. : Prentice-Hall, c1977. p. cm. (A Spectrum book) Includes index. Bibliography: p. [NC730.S44 1977] 77-4982 ISBN 0-13-219378-7 : 17.95. ISBN 0-13-219360-4 : pbk. 8.95
1. Drawing—Technique. 2. Drawing—Themes, motives. 3. Artists' materials. I. Winer, Marc S. A., joint author. II. Title.

*TALBOT, Bernerd J. 744.4
Visual aid for bright ideas [a drawing technique for:the handyman, inventor. hobbysts, planner, de signer, and ali men of ideas [East Islip, N.Y., Author, c.1964] 63p. illus. 28cm. 4.98, pap., plastic bdg.
I. Title.

TAUBES, Frederic, 1900- 741.2
The quickest way to draw well / by Frederic Taubes. New York : Penguin Books, 1977. 94 p. : ill. ; 23 cm. (A Penguin handbook) [NC730.T38 1977] 77-1440 ISBN 0-14-046275-9 pbk. : 2.95
1. Drawing—Technique. I. Title.

Drawing—Technique—Juvenile literature.

SWEENEY, Morgan J. 741.2
The magic pear : twelve outline drawing lessons with directions for the amusement of little folks / Morgan J. Sweeney. New York : Hart Pub. Co., c1977. 31 p. : ill. ; 18 x 23 cm. Includes twelve lessons for drawing such subjects as a rabbit, cat, dog, and chicken, beginning with the basic shape of the pear. [NC670.S9 1977] 77-155308 ISBN 0-8055-0352-8 pbk. : 2.95
1. Drawing—Technique—Juvenile literature. 2. Amusements—Juvenile literature. I. Title. BIP

Drawing—Themes, motives.

BUCKINGHAM, Naida. 818.54
Straw in my camel's hair, by Naida Buckingham and Ingrid Etter. Line sketches by Anne Cleveland. [1st ed.] New York, Dutton, 1961. 214p. illus. 21cm. [CT788.B8763A3] 61-10837
I. Etter, Ingrid, joint author. II. Title.

FRANCK, Frederick, 1909- 741.973
My eye is in love; revelations on the act of seeing by drawing. New York, Macmillan [1963] 146 p. illus. 31 cm. [NC1145.F5A46] 63-15679
I. Title.

MARKS, Claude. 741.9
From the sketchbooks of the great artists. New York, Crowell [1972] 480 p. illus. 29 cm. Bibliography: p. 459-466. [NC53.M37 1972] 74-170998 ISBN 0-690-31999-1 25.00
1. Drawing—Themes, motives. 2. Drawings. 3. Art—Psychology. I. Title.

Drawings.

BRICE, William J. 741.9'0924
William Brice: Selection of drawings, 1955-1966. Forewords by Gerald Nordland, Thomas W. Leavitt and an appreciation by Frederic S. Wight. [Los Angeles] Ritchie. 1967. [55]p. 40 illus. 29cm. [NC1075.B72W5] 67-17110 7.95
I. Wight, Frederick Stallknecht, 1902- II. Title.
Distributed by Lane, Menlo Park, Calif.

COGNIAT, Raymond, 1896- 708.00904
XXth century drawings and watercolors. Trans. from the French by Anne Ross New York, Crown Publishers [1966] 222 p. illus. (part col.) 33 cm. [NC1060.C6] 66-26181
1. Drawings. 2. Water colors. I. Title.

DEVEAUX, Alexis, 1948- 818'.5'407
Spirits in the street. Drawings by the author. [1st ed.] Garden City, N.Y., Anchor Press [1973. 192 p. illus. 22 cm. [PS3554.E927S6] 72-96233 ISBN 0-385-03293-5 6.95
I. Title.

DEVEAUX, Alexis, 1948- 818.5407
Spirits in the street. Drawings by the author. Garden City, N.Y., Anchor Press, 1974 [c1973] 192 p. illus. 21 cm. (A Doubleday Anchor book) [PS3554.E927S6] ISBN 0-385-09017-X
I. Title.
L.C. card no. for original ed: 72-96233

GOODSELL, Jane. 817.54
I've only got two hands and I'm busy wringing them. Illustrated by Rob't Day. [1st ed.] Garden City, N.Y., Doubleday, 1966. 161 p. illus. 22 cm. [PS3557.O612] 66-12217
I. Title.

GRANT, Gordon 741.973
Sketchbook. Pref. by Wade Hampton de Fontaine. Introd. by Norman Kent. New York, Watson-Guptill Publications [c.1960] (unpaged, chiefly illus.) 27cm. 60-13375 4.50
I. Title.

HOLME, Bryan, 1913- 741
Drawings to live with. New York, Viking Press [1966] 155 p. illus. 27 cm. [NC735.H59] 66-15650
1. Drawings. 2. Drawing—Instruction. I. Title.

JOHNSON, Una E. 741.924
20th century drawings. New York, Shorewood Publishers [1964] 2 v. illus. (part col.) 25 cm. (Drawings of the masters) Contents.Contents.—pt. 1. 1900-1940.—pt. 2. 1940 to the present. Bibliography: pt. 1, p. 140-142; pt. 2, p. 140-141. [NC95.J6] 64-15862
1. Drawings. I. Title. II. Series.

JOHNSON, Una E. 741.9'4
20th century drawings : part I, 1900-1940 / text by Una E. Johnson. Boston : Little, Brown, [1976] c1964. p. cm. Reprint of vol. 1 of the 2 vol. ed. published by Shorewood Publishers, New York, in series: Drawings of the masters. Bibliography: p. [NC95.J6 1976] 75-25734 ISBN 0-316-46759-6 pbk. : 4.95
1. Drawings. I. Title. II. Series: Drawings of the masters.

KELLOGG, Rhoda, 1898- 372.52
What children scribble and why. Author's ed. [San Francisco?] 1955. 137p. illus. 28cm. [LB1139.D7K4] 55-28745
1. Drawings. 2. Child study. I. Title.

KRASNOW, Peter. 741.973
Drawings. Los Angeles, 1967. 78 p. (chiefly illus.) 31 cm. [NC139.K7A43] 67-6200

LEVY, Mervyn, ed. 743.4
The artist & the nude; an anthology of drawings. New York, Potter, dist. Crown, [c.1965] 155p. (chiefly illus.))) 32cm. [NC1060.L4] 65-24172 15.00 sNude in art.
1. Drawings. I. Title.

LEVY, Mervyn. 741.9
Drawing & sculpture. New York, Walker [1970] 165 p. illus., col. plates. 29 cm. Includes bibliographical references. [NC53.L48 1970b] 71-129566 20.00
1. Drawings. I. Title.

MOSKOWITZ, Ira, ed. 741.9
Great drawings of all time. New York, Shorewood Publishers [1962] 4 v. 1107 illus. (part col.) 35 cm. Contents.Contents.—v. 1. Italian, thirteenth through nineteenth century.—v. 2. German, Flemish and Dutch, thirteenth through nineteenth century—v. 3. French, thirteenth century to 1919.—v. 4. Oriental, Spanish, English, American and contemporary. Bibliography ([8] p. at end) [NC1005.M65] 62-19989
1. Drawings. BIP

ROMBOLA, John 741.973
Rombola, by Rombola; drawings by John Rombola. New York, A. S. Barnes [c.1965] 160p. (chiefly illus. (pt. col.)) 29cm. [NC1075.R79A55] 64-21358 10.00
I. Title.

ROMBOLA, John. 741.5973
Rombola's people. [Cranbury] N.J., A. S. Barnes [1970] 192 p. (chiefly illus., ports.) 29 cm. [NC1429.R753A53] 69-14878 10.00
I. Title.

ROSENBERG, Jakob, 1893- 741.94
Great draughtsmen from Pisanello to Picasso. Cambridge, Harvard University Press, 1959. xxvi, 142p. 256plates. 26cm. 'Presented as a series of eight lectures under the auspices of the Lowell Institute in Boston in January, 1956.' [NC80.R6] 59-7661
1. Drawings. 2. Drawing—Hist. 3. Artists. I. Title.
Contents omitted. BIP

ROWLAND, Benjamin, 1904- 741.9
Cave to Renaissance. New York, Shorewood [1965] 141p. illus. (pt. col.) 25cm. (Drawings of the masters) Bibl. [NC1010.R6] 65-16879 5.95
1. Drawings. I. Title. II. Series. BIP

ROWLAND, Benjamin, 1904- 741.9
1972.
Cave to Renaissance / text by Benjamin Rowland, Jr. Boston : Little, Brown, [1976] c1965. 141 p. : ill. (some col.) ; 24 cm. (Drawings of the masters) Bibliography: p. 141. [NC52.R68 1976] 75-25617 ISBN 0-316-75462-5 pbk. : 4.95
1. Drawings. I. Title. II. Series: Drawings of the masters (Boston).

SACHS, Paul Joseph, 1878- 741.9
The pocket book of great drawings. New York, Pocket Books [1951] xiv, 112 p. illus. 17 cm. [Pocket book, 765) Bibliography: p. 109-112. [NC1020.S3] 51-3286
1. Drawings. I. Title.

SACHS, Paul Joseph, 1878- 741.94
The pocket book of great drawings. [New York] Washington Square Press [dist. Pocket Books, 1961, c.1951] 112p. illus. (part col.) (W730) Bibl. .60 pap.,
1. Drawings. I. Title.

SPERRY, Vicci. 741.9'73
Drawings. Andre Sauret, editeur. Boston, Boston Book and Art Shop [1969] 1 v. (chiefly illus.) 29 cm. [NC1075.S715S2] 68-58697 201 A0013040SZABO, Marc.

SZABO, Marc. 702'.8
Drawing file for architects, illustrators, and designers / Marc Szabo. New York : Van Nostrand Reinhold, 1976. ca. 300 p. : ill. ; 31 cm. [NC52.S9] 75-29209 ISBN 0-442-27878-0
1. Drawings. I. Title. BIP

TONEY, Anthony, comp. 741.9
150 masterpieces of drawing. New York, Dover Publications [1963] xvi p., 150 plates. 29 cm. [NC1005.T6 1963] 63-5656
1. Drawings. I. Title. II. Title: Masterpieces of drawing.

WALTERS, Ernest, 1927- 741.9'73
Wiener Schwarzweiss; a portfolio of drawings. [Baltimore, Daedal Press, 1968] [2] p., 17 plates. 33 x 41 cm. [NC139.W35A58] 68-7149
I. Title.

ZWART, Piet, 1885- 741.9492
Piet Zwart. Ed.: Fridolin Muller. Introd. Peter F. Althaus. New York, Hastings [1966] 112p. illus. (pt. col.) port. 25cm. (Visual communication bks.) Documents in the visual arts, v.1. Parallel texts in English. German, & French. [NC1850.Z9M8] 66-31985 10.00 bds.,
I. Title.

Drawings, American.

ANGLUND, Joan Walsh 741.642
The Joan Walsh Anglund sampler; twelve drawings in color New York, Harcourt [1963] unpaged col. illus. 38cm. 4.25 bxd.
I. Title. BIP

BALDER, Alton Parker. 741.9752
Six Maryland artists, a study in drawings. Text by Alton Parker Balder; introd. by George Boas. [1st ed.] Baltimore, Balboa Publications, 1955. xix, 155 p. illus. 31 cm. [NC1070.B3] 55-13996
1. Drawings, American. 2. Artists, American—Maryland. I. Title.
Contents omitted.

BENTOV, Mirtala. 730'.92'4
Thought-forms : sculptures, poems / by Mirtala Bentov ; translated by Sylvia Juran. Boston : Branden Press, c1975. vii, 118 p. : col. ill. ; 20 x 23 cm. Includes translation of Stikhi. [PG3549.B45A24] 75-29847 ISBN 0-8283-1652-X : 15.00
I. Bentov, Mirtala. Stikhi. English. 1975. II. Title.

A book of sketches 759.13
by Anna Richards Brewster, published in her memory by William Tenney Brewster. [New York? 1954] 151p. plates (part col.) port. 32cm. 500 copies printed. [ND237.B862B7] [ND237.B862B7] 927.5 54-36473 54-36473
I. Brewster, Anna (Richards) 1870-1952.

BREWSTER, Anna(Richards) 759.13
1870-1952.
A book of sketches by Anna Richards Brewster, published in her memory by William Tenney Brewster. [Scarsdale N. Y., 1954- v. plates (part col.) parts., map. 32cm. Vols. 2- have general title on spine and a special t. p. only. Vol. 1, 500 copies: v. 2- 250 copies. Contents.[v. 1] A book of sketches.--v. 2. Sketches from the south county of Rhode Island.--v. 3. Sketches from the British Isles.-- v. 4. Italian and Sicillan sketches. [ND237.B862B7] 54-36473
I. Title. II. Title: Sketches from the south county of Rhode Island. III. Title: Sketches from the British Isles. IV. Title: Italian and Sicllian sketches.

CLARK, Tom, 1941- 811'.5'4
When things get tough on easy street : selected poems, 1963-1978 / Tom Clark. Santa Barbara, CA : Black Sparrow Press, 1978. p. cm. Edition limited to 200 hardcover copies numbered and signed by the author and 26 handbound copies, illustrated by author. [PS3553.L29W5] 78-13630 ISBN 0-87685-349-1 : 15.00. ISBN 0-87685-348-3 pbk. : 5.00
I. Title. BIP

CONGER, Lesley. 818.54
Adventures of an ordinary mind. Drawings by Doug Anderson. [1st ed.] New York, Norton [1963] 236 p. illus. 22 cm. [CT275.C7625A29] 63-9878
I. Title.

CUMMINGS, Paul. 741.9'73
American drawings : the 20th century / Paul Cummings. New York : Viking Press, 1976. 207 p. : ill. ; 29 cm. (A Studio book) Includes index. Bibliography: p. 205. [NC108.C85 1976] 76-21729 ISBN 0-670-11784-6 : 16.95
1. Drawings, American. 2. Artists—United States.

DEAN, Abner, 1910- 741.5973
Abner Dean's naked people; a selection of drawings ... New York, Stein and Day [c1963] 207 p. (chiefly illus.) 23 x 28 cm. [NC1429.D327] 63-18384
I. Title.

DEHN, Adolf Arthur, 741.9'73
1895-1968.
Adolf Dehn drawings. Selected by Virginia Dehn. Introd. by Carl Zigrosser. Columbia, University of Missouri Press, 1971. 208 p. illus. 23 x 29 cm. [NC139.D44D4] 71-134016 ISBN 0-8262-0100-8
I. Dehn, Virginia, comp. II. Title. BIP

DUFF, James, 1950- 811'.5'4
Gallery: color sketches and prose. Iowa City, Firemark Press, 1973. [20] p. 20 cm. "Limited to 48 copies." [PS3554.U318G3] 74-157945
I. Title.

DUNCAN, Robert Edward, 741.9'73
1919-
A selection of sixty five drawings from one drawing book, 1952-1956 [by] Robert Duncan. Los Angeles, Black Sparrow Press, 1970. 1 portfolio ([6] p., 65 illus.) 23 cm. On spine: 65 drawings. "This edition is limited to 300 numbered copies, and 26 lettered presentation copies each with an original drawing by Robert Duncan." This copy: for copyright. [NC139.D83A56] 72-181088
I. Title.

EICKE, Edna. 759.13
What's your name? [New York] Windmill Books; distributed by Harper & Row [1968] 1 v. (chiefly col. illus.) 31 cm. "All of the drawings in this book ... appeared originally as covers on issues of the New Yorker." [NC1075.E43A58] 68-16823 7.95
I. Title.

FAUST, Jan, 1944- 741.5973
The underground sketchbook of Jan Faust. New York, Dover [1971] 101 p. (chiefly illus.) 24 cm. (Dover pictorial archive series) [NC1429.F295A58] 78-151422 ISBN 0-486-22740-5 1.50
I. Title.

FILMUS, Anatol, 1908- 759.13
Tully Filmus. Introd. by Alfred Werner. Cleveland, World Pub. Co. [1963] 47 p. illus. (part col.) 81 plates (incl. ports., part col.) 32 cm. [ND237.F42F5] 63-18587
I. Werner, Alfred, 1911-

FILMUS, Anatol, 1908- 741.9'73
Tully Filmus; selected drawings. With an essay by Isaac Bashevis Singer. Introd. by George Albert Perret. [1st ed.] Philadelphia, Jewish Publication Society of America, 1971. xx, 76 p. of illus. 34 cm. [NC139.F45S5] 70-151314 12.50
I. Singer, Isaac Bashevis, 1904-

FRANCK, Frederick, 1909- 812'.5'4
Everyone : the timeless myth of "Everyman" reborn / handwritten and with drawings by Frederick Franck. 1st ed. Garden City, N.Y. : Doubleday, 1978. 187 p. : ill. ; 28 cm. [PS3556.R332E9] 77-25590 ISBN 0-385-14357-5 : 12.50 ISBN 0-385-13329-4 pbk. : 6.95
I. Elckerlijc. II. Title. III. Title: Every One. BIP

FROST, Celestine. 811'.5'4
An inhuman rival : poems & drawings / Celestine Frost. New York : New Rivers Press, 1977. 95 p. : ill. ; 23 cm. [PS3556.R597I5] 76-49678 ISBN 0-912284-83-8 : 3.00
I. Title.
Distributed by Serendipity Books BIP

GIBSON, Charles Dana, 741.5973
1867-1944.
The Gibson Girl; drawings. Edited by Steven Warshaw. [Berkeley, Calif.] Diablo Press [1968] 1 v. (chiefly illus.) 22 x 28 cm. [NC1429.G42W3] 76-116
I. Title.

GIBSON, Charles Dana, 741.973
1867-1944.
The Gibson girl and her America; the best drawings. Selected by Edmund Vincent Gillon, Jr., with an introductory essay by Henry C. Pitz. New York, Dover Publications [1969] xi, 144 p. (chiefly illus.) 21 x 29 cm. [NC1429.G42G5] 68-28065 ISBN 4-86219-860- 2.50 (pbk.)
I. Gillon, Edmund Vincent. II. Title. BIP

GILLON, Adam, 1921- 811'.5'4
Summer morn ... winter weather : poems twixt haiku and senryu / by Adam Gillon ; art work by Alice D. Phalen. New York : Astra Books, c1976. 155 p. : ill. ; 21 cm. [PS3557.I4S83] 75-38484 ISBN 0-913994-23-5 pbk. : 4.00
I. Title. BIP

HAYES, Bartlett H 1904- 741.973
American drawings. Text by Bartlett H. Hayes, Jr. New York, Shorewood Publishers [1965] 141 p. illus. (part col.) ports. (part col.) 25 cm. (Drawings of the masters) Bibliography: p. 139-141. [NC1070.H3] 64-66431
1. Drawings, American. I. Title. II. Series.

HAYES, Bartlett H., 741.9'73
1904-
American drawings / text by Bartlett H. Hayes, Jr. Boston : Little, Brown, [1975] c1965. 141 p. : ill. (some col.) ; 24 cm. (Drawing of the masters) Bibliography: p. 139-141. [NC105.H28 1975] 75-11518 ISBN 0-316-35170-9 pbk. : 3.95
1. Drawings, American. I. Title. II. Series: Drawings of the masters (Boston)

HURWITZ, Harry. 741.973
The notebook. Drawings and text by Harry Hurwitz. [New Paltz, N.Y., 1966] [39] p. illus. 21 cm. [NC139.H85A46] 76-17627
I. Title.

LAZZARI, Pietro, 1898- 741.9'73
Adam and Eve; 12 drawings. [Washington, Print. by Yazge] 1970. [1] p., 12 illus. 54 cm. In portfolio. [NC139.L38A42] 79-144118
I. Title.

LEVINE, David, 1926- 916
A summer sketchbook; drawings selected from 3 sketchbooks in the collection of David Daniels, Foreword by Peter A. Wick. New York, Mitchell Press [1963] [84] p. illus. (part col.) 16 x 23 cm. [Nc1075.L38W5] 64-4
I. Daniels, David. II. Wick, Peter A., ed. III. Title.

MCCALL, Taylor. 741.942
Behind us. Stockbridge (Hants.), Bocaccio Books, 1970. 104 p. (chiefly illus. (some col.)). 31 cm. Limited ed. of 300 signed and numbered copies, no. 54. In slip case. [NC139.M2A43] 70-514601 21/-/-
I. Title.

MALONEY, Francis J. 741.02*07
Bottle Cap: his family and his friends, by Francis J. Maloney. Illustrated by the author. New York, William-Frederick Press, 1971. [64] p. illus. 22 cm. [NC1429.M355A43] 70-130834 3.00
I. Title.

MILLER, Henry, 1891- 759.13
Henry Miller: watercolors, drawings, and his essay, The angel is my watermark! New York, Abrams [1962] 39p. illus. (pt. col.) 33cm. 62-11621 17.50
I. Title. II. Title: The angel is my watermark!

MOEN, Esten, 1904- 741.91
When I was little; [pen-and-ink sketches] Fosston, Minn., Thirteen Towns, 1955. unpaged. illus. 21cm. [NC1075.M75A55] 55-11679
I. Title.

OKAMURA, Arthur. 741.9'52
102030405060708090O. Drawings by Arthur Okamura; poem, by Robert Creeley. Berkeley, Shambala, 1971. [94] p. illus. 28 cm. [NC139.O43C7] 72-175682 ISBN 0-87773-013-X
I. Creeley, Robert, 1926- II. Title.

ONLY a little 779'.3'0924
planet. Edited, with a foreword, by David R. Brower. Lines by Lawrence Collins. Photos. by Martin Schweitzer. San Francisco, Friends of the Earth [1972] 127 p. col. illus. 29 cm. (Celebrating the earth, [1]) [PS3553.O4749O5] 72-187904 12.50
I. Brower, David Ross, 1912- ed. II. Collins, Lawrence. III. Schweitzer, Martin, illus. IV. Title. V. Series.

POLLACK, Reginald. 741.9'73
O is for overkill; a survival alphabet. Drawings by Reginald Pollack. Words by Merrill Pollack. New York, Viking Press [1968] [60] p. (chiefly illus.) 19 x 22 cm. (A Gemini Press book) [NC1075.P645P6 1968] 68-30692 ISBN 0-670-51898-0 5.00
I. Pollack, Merrill. II. Title.

PUTNAM, Wallace, 1899- 759.13
Miracle enough; a book of drawing and writing. Boston, Beacon Press [1969] 1 v. (chiefly illus.) 27 x 34 cm. [NC1075.P94A56] 74-86346 25.00
I. Title.

THOMASON, John William, 741.973
1893-1944.
A Thomason sketchbook: drawings. Edited with a foreword by Arnold Rosenfeld. Introd. by John Graves. Austin, University of Texas Press [1969] 128 p. illus., port. 32 cm. [NC1075.T48R6] 69-13711 ISBN 2-927841-47- 10.00
I. Rosenfeld, Arnold, ed. II. Title.

TIRSCH, Ignacio, 741.9'437
b.1733.
The drawings of Ignacio Tirsch, a Jesuit missionary in Baja California. Narrative by Doyce B. Nunis, Jr. Translation by Elsbeth Schulz-Bischof. Los Angeles, Dawson's Book Shop, 1972. 125 p. (chiefly plates, part col.) 23 cm. (Baja California travels series, 27) Captions in English and German. Includes bibliographical references. [NC245.T55N813] 76-169943
I. Nunis, Doyce Blackman. II. Title. III. Series. BIP

UNGERER, Tomi, 1931- 741.5973
The underground sketchbook of Tomi Ungerer. With a pref. by Jonathan Miller. New York, Viking [1964] 1 v. (chiefly illus., part col.) 19 x 23 cm. [NC1429.U5A55] 64-15060
I. Title.

SUBJECT INDEX DRAWINGS, DUTCH.

Drawings, American—Exhibitions.

ASHTON, Dore. 741.9'73'074019225
Drawings by New York artists. Selected by Dore Ashton. [Salt Lake City, Utah Museum of Fine Arts, 1972] [24] p. illus. 23 cm. Catalogue of an exhibition held at the Utah Museum of Fine Arts and others. [NC138.N4A9] 75-190626
1. Drawings, American—Exhibitions. 2. Artists, American—New York (City) I. Utah Museum of Fine Arts. II. Title.

BROOKLYN Institute of Arts and Sciences. Museum. 741.9'73
Drawings of the Hudson River School, 1825-1875, by Jo Miller. [Brooklyn, N.Y.] Brooklyn Museum [1969] 127 p. illus. 23 cm. The Brooklyn Museum: a special exhibition, Nov. 25, 1969-Feb. 22, 1970. Bibliography: p. 126-127. [NC107.B75] 70-104837
1. Drawings, American—Exhibitions. 2. Landscape in art. I. Miller, Jo. II. Title.

CALIFORNIA. University, Santa Barbara. Art Galleries. 741.9'794
Drawings 1970: California, Arizona, Nevada, Utah. [Santa Barbara, 1970] 28 p. illus. 22 cm. Catalog of the exhibition held Mar. 31-Apr. 26, 1970. [NC123.C3] 75-630001
1. Drawings, American—Exhibitions. 2. Drawings—The West. I. Title.

CHICAGO Society of Artists. 741.9'73'074014771
Black and white; annual exhibition. [Catalogue] [Chicago] v. illus. 28cm. [NC107.C47] 56-49848
1. Drawings, American—Exhibitions. I. Title.

DRAWING Society 741.973
The Drawing Society national exhibition, 1965. [New York] Amer. Federation of Arts; [dist. October House, [1966] 104p. (100 illus.) 23cm. Catalog of an exhibition circulated among 11 mus. and art galleries, 1965-1966. [NC108.D7] 65-28186 7.50; 2.50 pap.,
1. Drawings, American—Exhibitions. I. American Federation of Art. II. Title.

THE Drawing Society national exhibition 1970; 741.9'73 [catalogue. New York, Drawing Society, c1970] 96 p. illus. 23 x 22 cm. Cover title: Drawing. "Circulated by the American Federation of Arts." "AFA circulating exhibition: 70-20, 1970-72." [NC108.D72] 73-134910
1. Drawings, American—Exhibitions. I. Drawing Society. II. American Federation of Arts. III. Title: Drawing.

HAYES, Bartlett H 1904- 741.973
The American line; 100 years of drawing.iAndover, Mass., Addison Gallery of American Art, Phillips Academy [1959] unpaged. illus. 13x21cm. 'Published to accompany an exhibition surveying 100 years of American drawing circultated by the American Federation of Arts in the United States.' [NC105.H3] 59-16240
1. Drawings, American—Exhibitions. I. Title.

HENRY Art Gallery. 741.9'73
Drawings by Americans; recent work by thirteen contemporary artists. [Exhibition] Henry Gallery, University of Washington, Seattle, February 12 through March 19, 1967, presented by the Henry Gallery and the Junior League of Seattle. [Seattle? 1967?] 45 p. (chiefly illus.) 22 cm. [NC108.H45] 70-631096
1. Drawings, American—Exhibitions. I. Junior League of Seattle. II. Title.

KANSAS. University. Museum of Art. 741.9'73'074018165
American drawings and watercolors from the collection of the University of Kansas Museum of Art; [exhibition] University of Kansas Museum of Art, June 10-July 8, 1973. [Lawrence, 1973] 1 v. (unpaged) illus. 23 cm. (Its Miscellaneous publications, no. 92) [NC105.K26 1973] 73-623368
1. Drawings, American—Exhibitions. 2. Water-colors, American—Exhibitions. I. Title. II. Series.

KRAUSS, Rosalind E. 709'.73
Line as language: six artists draw [by] Rosalind Krauss. [Princeton, N.J.] The Art Museum, Princeton University, [1974] 36 p. illus. 21 cm. "Prepared in conjunction with an exhibition of works by Mel Bochner, Sol LeWitt, Robert Morris, Dorothea Rockburne, Richard Serra, and Richard Tuttle, held February 23 to March 31, 1974, at The Art Museum, Princeton University." Includes bibliographies. [NC108.K72] 74-165136 2.00
1. Drawings, American—Exhibitions. 2. Line (Art) I. Princeton University. Art Museum. II. Title.

LOS Angeles Co., Calif. Museum, Los Angeles. 741.91
Catalogue of the first biennial exhibition of drawings by American artists ... February 18 to April 22, 1945. [James Normile, editor. Los Angeles? 1945] 67 p. illus. 26 cm. [NC105.L6] 47-8209
1. Drawings, American — Exhibitions. I. Normile, James, ed. II. Title.

LOS Angeles Co., Calif. Otis Art Institute, Los Angeles. 760'.0973'074019225
Biennial invitational drawing exhibition. 1st-1964- Los Angeles. v. illus. 22 cm. [NC108.L6] 67-6706
1. Drawings, American — Exhibitions. I. Title.

MICHIGAN. University. Museum of Art. 741.973
One hundred contemporary American drawings. [Exhibition] February 24 through March 28, 1965. Ann Arbor [1965] 1 v. (unpaged) 100 illus. 23 x 26 cm. Correction slip inserted. [NC108.M5] 66-64352
1. Drawings, American — Exhibitions. I. Title.

MINNESOTA Museum of Art. 741.9'73'0740176581
Drawings in Saint Paul from the permanent collection of the Minnesota Museum of Art, Saint Paul, Minnesota, U.S.A. [Saint Paul, 1971] 1 v. (unpaged) illus. 24 cm. (Its Catalog 113) Catalog of the exhibition held Dec. 2, 1971-Jan. 23, 1972 at the museum. [NC108.M53] 71-185958
1. Drawings, American—Exhibitions. I. Title. II. Series.

MUNSON-WILLIAMS-PROCTOR Institute, Utica, N.Y. 741.9'73
American drawings and watercolors from the Munson-Williams-Proctor Institute. Sacramento, Calif. : E. B. Crocker Art Gallery, 1974. [28] p. : ill. ; 28 cm. Catalog of an exhibition held at the Crocker Art Gallery, Oct. 25-Nov. 24, 1974. Includes bibliographical references. [NC108.M86 1974] 74-24018
1. Drawings, American—Exhibitions. 2. Water-colors, American—Exhibitions. I. Crocker Art Gallery, Sacramento, Calif. II. Title.

NAYLOR, Maria. 760'.0973
American drawings, pastels and watercolors. New York, Kennedy Galleries [1967- v. illus. 26 cm. Catalogue of an exhibition held at Kennedy Galleries, inc., New York: Mar. 14-Apr.28, 1967. Apr. 16-May 6, 1968. Contents.Contents.—pt. 1. Works of the eighteenth and early nineteenth centuries. pt. 2. The nineteenth century, 1825-1890. [NC105.N34] 70-17112 1.00 per vol.
1. Drawings, American—Exhibitions. 2. Water-colors, American—Exhibitions. I. Kennedy Galleries, inc., New York. II. Title.

NEW York (City). New School for Social Research. New School Art Center. 741.9'73'07401471
American drawings of the sixties: a selection. [Exhibition] November 11, 1969-January 10, 1970. [New York, 1969] 49 p. (incl. cover) illus. 21 x 26 cm. (The Artistic thinking of our time) [NC108.N37] 72-176365
1. Drawings, American—Exhibitions. I. Title. II. Series.

NEW York. National Academy of Design. 741.9739
Exhibition of contemporary American drawings. New York. v. illus. 20 cm. annual. First exhibition held 1945. [NC108.N4] 51-34808
1. Drawings, American — Exhibitions. I. Title.

REICH, Sheldon. 760'.0973'074019225
Graphic styles of the American Eight : [exhibition and catalogue], Utah Museum of Fine Arts, University of Utah, Salt Lake City, Utah, 29 February-11 April, 1976 / by Sheldon Reich. Salt Lake City : Utah Museum of Fine Arts, c1976. 118 p. : ill. ; 22 x 27 cm. Bibliography: p. 102-116. [NC108.R44] 76-5654
1. Ashcan School. 2. Drawings, American—Exhibitions. 3. Water-colors, American—Exhibitions. 4. Prints, American—Exhibitions. I. Utah Museum of Fine Arts. II. Title.

ROTHSCHILD, Amalie, 1916- 741.9'73
Drawings. Introd. by Lincoln F. Johnson, Jr. Baltimore, 1968. 77 p. illus. (part col.) port. 30 cm. "Sponsored by Goucher College." [NC1075.R8] 68-23463
I. Johnson, Lincoln F. II. Goucher College, Baltimore.

SOLOMON, Elke. 741.9'73
American drawings, 1963-1973, by Elke M. Solomon [New York, Whitney Museum of American Art, 1973] 63 p. illus. 24 cm. An exhibition held at the Whitney Museum of American Art, May 25-July 22, 1973. [NC108.S59] 73-80909 3.00 (pbk.)
1. Drawings, American—Exhibitions. I. Whitney Museum of American Art, New York. II. Title.

SOLOMON R. Guggenheim Museum, New York. 741.973
American drawings [New York] Author [1964] 1v. (unpaged) illus. 26cm. Catalog of Exhibition 64/6, September-October, 1964. Bibl. 64-7660 3.00 pap.,
1. Drawings, American—Exhibitions. I. Title.

UTAH Museum of Fine Arts. 741.9'73'074019225
Twentieth century American drawings, from the Collection of Edward Jacobson; with an introd. by Vincent Price. [Salt Lake City, 1972] 1 v. (unpaged) illus. 23 cm. Catalog of an exhibition held Aug. 15-Sept. 5, 1971, and circulated by the University of Utah Museum of Fine Arts. [NC108.U83] 79-190627
1. Jacobson, Edward, 1922- —Art collections. 2. Drawings, American—Exhibitions. I. Title.

Drawings, American (Series)

HAYES, Bartlett , 1904- 741.973
American drawings. Text by Bartlett H. Hayes, Jr. New York, Shorewood [c.1965] 141p. illus. (pt. col.) ports. (pt. col.) 25cm. (Drawings of the masters) Bibl. [NC1070.H3] 64-66431 5.95
1. Drawings, American (Series) I. Title.

Drawings—Baltimore—Catalogs.

BALTIMORE. Museum of Art. 741.9'24'07401526
The Thomas Edward Benesch Memorial Collection; [catalogue. Baltimore, 1970] 1 v. (unpaged) illus. 26 cm. [NC31.B45B3] 76-26407
1. Benesch, Thomas Edward—Art collections. 2. Drawings—Baltimore—Catalogs. I. Title.

Drawings, British—Catalogs.

HARRIS, John, 1931- 741.9'42'074013
A catalogue of British drawings for architecture, decoration, sculpture and landscape gardening, 1550-1900, in American collections. Introd. by Henry-Russell Hitchcock. Upper Saddle River, N.J., Gregg Press [1971] xv, 355 p. illus. 35 cm. [NC228.H3] 75-93124 ISBN 0-8398-0766-X
1. Drawings, British—Catalogs. 2. Drawings, British—U.S. I. Title. BIP

Drawings, British—Exhibitions.

HENRY E. Huntington Library and Art Gallery, San Marino, Calif. 741.942
Early British drawings in the Huntington Collection, 1600-1750, by Robert R. Wark. San Marino, Calif., 1969. 231 p. illus. 27 cm. (Its Huntington Library Publications) [NC228.H45] 68-56148 12.50
1. Drawings, British—Exhibitions. I. Wark, Robert R. II. Title. III. Series. BIP

Drawings—Catalogs.

ISABELLA Stewart Gardner Museum, Boston. 740'.74'014461
Drawings. Edited by Rollin van N. Hadley. Boston, Published by the Trustees, 1968. viii, 67 p. illus. (part col.) 22 cm. [NC25.I8] 68-9482
1. Drawings—Catalogs. I. Hadley, Rollin van N., ed.

OLD master drawings from the Collection of Mr. & Mrs. Lester Francis Avnet. 741.9'23 [New York? c1968] [179] p. illus. (part col.) 23 cm. "Circulated by the American Federation of Arts, New York." [NC30.O4] 72-76721
1. Avnet, Lester—Art collections. 2. Avnet, Joan—Art collections. 3. Drawings—Catalogs. I. American Federation of Arts.

SCHAB, William H., firm, New York. 741.9'074'01471
A collection of fifty master drawings from the fifteenth to twentieth centuries; a critical catalogue augmented with related documents and bibliography from European archives. New York [1971?] 88 p. illus. (part col.) 23 x 29 cm. "Price list" ([1] p.) inserted. [NC38.S3] 73-29845
1. Drawings—Catalogs. 2. Drawings—Prices. I. Title. II. Title: Fifty master drawings.

WARK, Robert R. 760'.0942
Drawings from the Turner Shakespeare, by Robert R. Wark. With a bibliographical note by Shelley M. Bennett. San Marino, Calif., Henry E. Huntington Library and Art Gallery, 1973. 89 p. illus. 14 x 22 cm. Consists of a guide to some of the drawings (illustrations to Shakespeare) originally collected by T. Turner of Gloucester from approximately 1835-60. The 44 v. set of original drawings is now in the Henry E. Huntington Library. Includes bibliographical references. [PR2883.W3] 73-85885
1. Shakespeare, William, 1564-1616—Illustrations. 2. Turner, Thomas, of Gloucester, Eng.—Art collections. 3. Drawings—Catalogs. I. Title. BIP

Drawings—Conservation and restoration.

DOLLOFF, Francis W. 769'.1
How to care for works of art on paper, by Francis W. Dolloff and Roy L. Perkinson. Boston, Museum of Fine Arts [1971] 46 p. illus. 22 cm. "The publication of this guide was prompted by two exhibitions held at the Museum of Fine Arts, Boston in the spring of 1971." Bibliography: p. 45-46. [N8560.D64] 77-157703 ISBN 0-87846-055-1
1. Drawings—Conservation and restoration. 2. Prints—Conservation and restoration. 3. Picture frames and framing. I. Perkinson, Roy L., joint author. II. Boston. Museum of Fine Arts. III. Title. BIP

Drawings, Dutch.

REMBRANDT Harmenszoon van Rijn, 1606-1669. 741.9492
Drawings of Rembrandt, with a selection of drawings by his pupils and followers. With an introd., commentary, and supplementary material by Seymour Slive. New York, Dover Publications [1965] 2 v. 550 plates 31 cm. Based on the facsim. series, Original drawings by Rembrandt Harmensz van Rijn, published 1888-92. Includes bibliographies. [NC1055.R4S5] 65-12555
1. Drawings, Dutch. I. Slive, Seymour, 1920- II. Rembrandt Harmenszoon van Rijn, 1606-1669. Original drawings by Rembrandt Harmensz van Rijn.

REMBRANDT HERMANSZOON VAN RIJN, 1606-1669 741.9492
Drawings of Rembrandt, with a selection

of drawings by his pupils and followers; 2v. Introd., commentary, supplementary material by Seymour Slive. New York, Dover [c.1965] 2v. 550 plates. 31cm. (T1485/6) Based on the facsim. series, Orig. drawings by Rembrandt Harmensz van Rijn, pub. 1888-92. Bibl. [NC1055.R4S5] 65-12555 12.50; 3.00 set pap., ea.,
1. Drawings, Dutch. I. Slive, Seymour, 1920- II. Rembrandt Hermanszoon van Rijn, 1607-1669. Original drawings by Rembrandt Harmensz van Rijn. III. Title.

Drawings, Dutch—Exhibitions.

AMSTERDAM. Rijks-Museum. 741.9492 Prentenkabinet.
Dutch drawings, masterpieces of five centuries; exhibition organized by the Printroom of the Rijksmuseum, Amsterdam and circulated by the Smithsonian Institution [to] National Gallery of Art, Washington, D.C. [and others] 1958-1959. [Washington? 1958] 57p. illus., ports. 26cm. Bibliography: p.55. [NC261.A5] 58-62484
1. Drawings, Dutch—Exhibitions. I. Smithsonian Institution. II. U.S. National Gallery of Art. III. Title.

ROBINSON, Franklin 741.9492 Westcott.
Selections from the collection of Dutch drawings of Maida & George Abrams; a loan exhibition [by Franklin W. Robinson] Wellesley, Mass., Wellesley College Museum, 1969. xi, [132] p. illus. 22 cm. Cover title: Dutch drawings from the Abrams collection. Catalog of an exhibition held at Hopkins Center art galleries, Dartmouth College, Hanover, N.H., March 27-April 28, 1969; and at other museums. [NC261.R6] 78-77279
1. Abrams, Maida—Art collections. 2. Abrams, George—Art collections. 3. Drawings, Dutch—Exhibitions. I. Dartmouth College. Hopkins Center. II. Wellesley College. Jewett Arts Center. III. Title. IV. Title: Dutch drawings from the Abrams collection.

SCHATBORN, 741.9'492'074013 Peter.
Dutch genre drawings of the seventeenth century; a loan exhibition from Dutch museums, foundations, and private collections. Introd. by K. G. Boon. Circulated by the International Exhibitions Foundation, 1972-1973. [Meriden, Conn., Meriden Gravure Co., 1972] 65, [2] p., 85 p. of plates. 23 cm. Exhibition was organized by the Rijksprentenkabinet, Amsterdam, and held in the Pierpont Morgan Library, New York, the Museum of Fine Arts, Boston, and the Art Institute of Chicago. Bibliography: p. [67] (1st group) [NC261.S33] 72-86013
1. Drawings, Dutch—Exhibitions. 2. Genre (Art) I. International Exhibitions Foundation. II. Amsterdam. Rijks-Museum. Prentenkabinet. III. Pierpont Morgan Library, New York. IV. Boston. Museum of Fine Arts. V. Chicago. Art Institute. VI. Title.

STERLING and Francine 741.9'492 Clark Art Institute, Williamstown, Mass.
Things of this world; a selection of Dutch drawings from the Collection of Maida and George Abrams. Williamstown [1973] 67 p. illus. 21 cm. Catalog of an exhibition held at the Institute, Oct. 31, 1972-Feb. 25, 1973. "This is the second catalogue of drawings selected from the collection of Maida and George Abrams; all entries have been written by the students under the supervision of professor Franklin W. Robinson." Includes bibliographical references. [NC261.S74] 73-160648
1. Abrams, Maida—Art collections. 2. Abrams, George—Art collections. 3. Drawings, Dutch—Exhibitions. I. Robinson, Franklin Westcott. II. Title.

Drawings, English.

CARLISLE, Anne. 741.942
English drawings, XIX century. [Edited by Andre Gloeckner] London, New York, Heinemann, in association with Hyperion Press [1951] 100 p. illus. 21 cm. (Hyperion drawing series) [NC1110.C28] 51-9664
1. Drawings, English. I. Title.

LISTER, Raymond. 741.942
The emblems of Theodosius; or, The unity of Endymion and Prometheus. Cambridge, Golden Head P., 1969. [13] leaves of illus. 25 cm. Limited ed. of 50 numbered copies, no. 27. Also available 9 copies lettered A to I, bound in cloth, each containing one of the original drawings. [NC1115.L48A44] 76-438740 unpriced
I. Title.

OXFORD. 741.9'42'07402574 University. Ashmolean Museum. Dept. of Western Art.
Seventeenth and eighteenth century English drawings in the Ashmolean Museum [Department of Western Art]. Oxford ([University of Oxford, Oxford OX1 2PH]) : Ashmolean Museum, 1974. [4], 31 p. : (chiefly ill.). ; 19 cm. Cover title. [NC228.O93 1974] 75-320478 ISBN 0-900090-15-4 : £0.30
1. Oxford. University. Ashmolean Museum. Dept. of Western Art. 2. Drawings, English. I. Title.

WORMALD, Francis. 741.942
English drawings of the tenth and eleventh centuries. New York, Praeger [1953] 83p. plates. 26cm. (Books that matter) [NC1015.W6 1953] 52-13578
1. Drawings, English. I. Title.

Drawings, English—Exhibitions.

BASKETT, John. 741.9'42'07401471
English drawings and watercolors, 1550-1850, in the Collection of Mr. and Mrs. Paul Mellon [by John Baskett and Dudley Snelgrove] New York, Pierpont Morgan Library, 1972. xxi, 107 p. 150 plates (part col.) 29 cm. "Exhibition of the Mellon Collection, 13 April to 28 July 1972, the Pierpont Morgan Library." Bibliography: p. xvii-xx. [NC228.B3] 77-190656 ISBN 0-87598-035-X
1. Mellon, Paul—Art collections 2. Mellon, Rachel Lambert (Lloyd)—Art collections. 3. Drawings, English—Exhibitions. 4. Water-colors, English—Exhibitions. I. Snelgrove, Dudley, joint author. II. Pierpont Morgan Library, New York. III. Title.

YALE 741.9'42'07401468 University. Art Gallery.
English drawings and watercolors, from the collection of Mr. and Mrs. Paul Mellon, April 15 - June 20, 1965. [New Haven, c1965] [46] p. (chiefly illus.) 22 cm. [NC228.Y34] 73-168190
1. Mellon, Paul—Art collections. 2. Mellon, Rachel Lambert (Lloyd)—Art collections. 3. Drawings, English—Exhibitions. 4. Watercolors, English—Exhibitions. I. Title.

Drawings, European.

NEW York. Metropolitan 741.94 Museum of Art
100 European drawings in the Metropolitan Museum of Art / Introd. by Jacob Bean, curator of drawings Greenwich, Conn., Graphic N. Y. 1964 222p. illus. 30cm. Bibl. 64-22151 12.50
1. Drawings, European. I. Bean, Jacob. II. Title.

VAN SCHAACK, Eric. 741.94
Master drawings in private collections. New York, Lambert-Spector; distributed by Clarke & Way [1962] 90 p. 75 illus. 28 cm. Bibliography: p. 68. [NC1100.V3] 62-17541
1. Drawings, European. 2. Drawings — Private collections. I. Title.

WUNDER, Richard P 741.923
Extravagant drawings of the eighteenth century, from the collection of the Cooper Union museum. New York, Lambert-Spector: distributed by Clarks & Way [1962] 107 p. 79 illus. 28 cm. [NC1100.W8] 62-17477
1. Drawings, European. 2. Drawings — New York (City) — Catalogs. I. Cooper Union for the Advancement of Science and Art, New York. Museum for the Arts of Decoration. II. Title.

Drawings, European — Catalogs.

CHICAGO. Art 741.9'4'074017311 Institute.
The Helen Regenstein Collection of European drawings : catalogue / by Harold Joachim. [Chicago] : Art Institute of Chicago, 1974. 167 p. : ill. (some col.) ; 26 cm. [NC225.C53 1974] 74-79440
1. Regenstein, Helen—Art collections. 2. Chicago. Art Institute. 3. Drawings, European—Catalogs. 4. Drawings—Chicago—Catalogs. I. Joachim, Harold. II. Title.

SANTA Barbara, 741.9'4'074019491 Calif. Museum of Art.
European drawings in the collection of the Santa Barbara Museum of Art / Alfred Moir, editor. [Santa Barbara, Calif.] : The Museum, c1976. 298 p. : ill. ; 28 cm. Includes bibliographical references and index. [NC225.S2 1976] 76-4685
1. Santa Barbara, Calif. Museum of Art. 2. Drawings, European—Catalogs. 3. Drawings—Santa Barbara, Calif.—Catalogs. I. Moir, Alfred. II. Title.

SMITH College. 741.9'4'074013 Museum of Art.
Check list: European drawings. Northampton, Mass., 1958. unpaged. 28 cm. [NC225.S56] 62-5187
1. Drawings, European — Catalogs. 2. Drawings — Northampton, Mass. — Catalogs. I. Title.

WORCESTER, Mass. 741.9'4'074013 Art Museum.
A catalogue of the drawings by European masters in the Worcester Art Museum, by Horst Vey. Worcester, The Trustees, 1958. 71 p. 28 cm. [NC225.W65] 62-1992
1. Drawings. European — Catalogs. 2. Drawings — Worcester, Mass. — Catalogs. I. Vey, Horst. II. Title.

WORCESTER, Mass. 741.9'4'074013 Art Museum.
A catalogue of the drawings by European masters in the Worcester Art Museum, by Horst Vey. Worcester, The Trustees, 1958. 71 p. 28 cm. [NC225.W65] 62-1992
1. Drawings, European — Catalogs. 2. Drawings — Worcester, Mass. — Catalogs. I. Vey, Horst. II. Title.

YALE University. 741.9'4'07401468 Art Gallery.
European drawings and watercolors in the Yale University Art Gallery, 1500-1900, by E. Haverkamp-Begemann and Anne-Marie S. Logan. New Haven, Published for the Yale University Art Gallery by Yale University Press, 1970. 2 v. 69 illus., 321 plates. 26 cm. Contents.Contents.—v. 1. Catalogue raisonne.—v. 2. Plates. Includes bibliographical references. [NC225.Y34] 72-115372 ISBN 0-300-01291-8 25.00
1. Drawings, European—Catalogs. 2. Water-colors, European—Catalogs. I. Haverkamp Begemann, Egbert. II. Logan, Anne-Marie S. III. Title.

Drawings, European—Exhibitions.

AMERICAN Federation of 741.94 Arts
17th & 18th century European drawings. [Catalog of an exhibition] sponsored by the Samuel H. Kress Found. Selected byRichard P. Wunder, Org., circulated by the Amer. Fed. of Arts, Aug. 1966--July 1967. [New York, Dist. October House, 1966] 16p., 50 illus. on [47]p. 24cm. [NC225.A39] 66-25158 2.50 pap.,
1. Drawings, European—Exhibitions. I. Wunder, Richard P. II. Samuel H. Kress Foundation. III. Title.

BYAM Shaw, James, 1903- 741.9'4
Old master drawings from Chatsworth; a loan exhibition from the Devonshire Collection. Introd. and catalogue by James Byam Shaw. Foreword by Thomas S. Wragg. [Meriden, Conn., Produced by the Meriden Gravure Co. and the Stinehour Press, Lunenburg, Vt., 1969] 50 p., [111] p. of illus. 26 cm. Circulated by the International Exhibitions Foundation, 1969-70. Participating museums: National Gallery of Art, Washington, D.C., and others. Includes bibliographies. [NC225.B9] 74-97171
1. Devonshire, Andrew Robert Buxton Cavendish, 11th duke of, 1920- —Art collections. 2. Drawings, European—Exhibitions. I. International Exhibitions Foundation. II. U.S. National Gallery of Art. III. Title.

Drawings, European—United States.

TIETZE, Hans, 1880- 741.9'4'0973 1954.
European master drawings in the United States. New York, Hacker Art Books, 1973. xi, 326 p. illus. 32 cm. Reprint of the 1947 ed. published by J. J. Augustin, New York. Bibliography: p. [1] [NC225.T53 1973] 72-80903 ISBN 0-87817-114-2 40.00
1. Drawings, European—United States. 2. Drawings—United States—Catalogs. I. Title.

Drawings — Exhibition.

COLUMBIA University. Dept. 741.94 of Art History and Archaeology.
Great master drawings of seven centuries; a benefit exhibition of Columbia University for the scholarship fund of the Department of Fine Arts and Archaeology, held at M. Knoedler and Company, 14 East 57th Street, New York City, 13 October to 7 November, 1959. [Catalogue] New York, Distributed by Wittenborn [1959] xv, 94 p. plates. 25 cm. [NC15.N53] 59-15561
1. Drawings — Exhibition. I. Knoedler (M.) and Company, inc. II. Title.

Drawings—Exhibitions.

ALBRIGHT-KNOX 741.9'24'074014797 Art Gallery.
Drawings and watercolors from the Albright-Knox Art Gallery. [Exhibition] December 18, 1967 to January 31, 1968. Buffalo [1967] [18] p. illus. 18 x 21 cm. [NC25.B8A45] 72-176969
1. Drawings—Exhibitions. 2. Water-colors—Exhibitions. I. Title.

ARTS Club of 741.9'074'017311 Chicago.
A second talent; an exhibition of drawings and paintings by writers. [Chicago, 1971] 1 v. (unpaged) illus. 26 cm. Cover title. Catalog of the exhibition held Nov. 15-Dec. 31, 1971. [NC90.A77] 73-172313
1. Drawings—Exhibitions. 2. Paintings, Modern. 3. Authors as artists. I. Title.

BENNETT, Mary 741'.074'0176579 Lee.
Selections from the drawing collection of David Daniels; loan exhibition. [Catalogue compiled by Mary Lee Bennett and Agnes Mongan. Cambridge? Mass., 1968] 10 p., 86 l. illus. 22 cm. Spine and half title: Drawings from the David Daniels Collection. Held at the Minneapolis Institute of Arts, Minneapolis, Minn.; Art Institute of Chicago, Chicago, Ill.; Nelson Gallery-Atkins Museum, Kansas City, Mo.; and Fogg Art Museum, Harvard University, Cambridge, Mass. Includes bibliographical references. [NC33.B4] 68-3317
1. Daniels, David—Art collections. 2. Drawings—Exhibitions. I. Mongan, Agnes, joint author. II. Minneapolis. Institute of Arts. III. Title. IV. Title: Drawings from the David Daniels Collection.

BYAM Shaw, James, 741.9'4'0740153 1903-
Old master drawings from Christ Church, Oxford; a loan exhibition. Introd. and catalogue by James Byam Shaw. [Washington, International Exhibitions Foundations, 1972] 70 p., [114] p. of illus. 26 cm. Circulated by the International Exhibitions Foundation, 1972-73. Participating museums: National Gallery of Art, Washington, D.C., and others. [NC15.W37N372] 72-83826
1. Oxford. University. Christ Church. 2. Drawings—Exhibitions. I. International Exhibitions Foundation. II. United States. National Gallery of Art. III. Title. **BIP**

CALIFORNIA. University. 741'.0922 Art Museum.
Master drawings from California collections. Edited by Juergen Schulz. Berkeley; distributed by New York Graphic Society, Greenwich, Conn. [1968] 164 p. illus. 28 cm. Catalog of an

exhibition held at the University Art Museum, April 30-June 2, 1968, in honor of the University of California centennial, 1868-1968. Includes bibliographical references. [NC15.B4C34] 68-64558
1. Drawings—Exhibitions. 2. Drawings—California. I. Schulz, Juergen, ed. II. Title.

DRAWINGS from 741.9'4'074017366
four collections, May 6 through June 17, 1973 : catalogue / by graduate students in art history, Department of Art and Design ; introd. by Jerrold Ziff ; edited by Mary Beth Lewis. [Champaign] : Krannert Art Museum, College of Fine and Applied Arts, University of Illinois at Urbana-Champaign, [1973] 73 p., 7 leaves of plates : 7 ill. ; 23 cm. Includes index. [NC15.U72K72] 76-620668
1. Drawings—Exhibitions. 2. Drawings—Private collections—United States. I. Lewis, Mary Beth. II. Illinois. University at Urbana-Champaign. Dept. of Art and Design. III. Krannert Art Museum.

THE Elsa Durand Mower 741.9'4
Collection of French and Italian drawings. [Exhibition] the Art Museum, Princeton University, Feb. 13 through Mar. 17, 1968. [Princeton, 1968] [62] p. illus. 26 cm. [NC15.P7P74] 75-9458
1. Mower, Margaret—Art collections. 2. Drawings—Exhibitions. I. Princeton University. Art Museum.

HARVARD University. 741.97444
William Hayes Fogg Art Museum
Memorial exhibition; works of art from the collection of Paul J. Sachs, 1878-1965. Given and bequeathed to the Fogg Art Museum, Harvard University. [Comp. by Agnes Mongan with Mary Lee Bennet] Cambridge [1965] 214p. illus., port. 22cm. Catalogue of exhibitions held at the Fogg Art Mus., Cambridge, Nov. 15, 1965-Jan. 15, 1966, and at the Mus of Mod. Art. New York, Dec. 19, 1966-Feb. 26, 1967 [NC25.H34] 66-5586 9.50
1. Drawings—Exhibitions. I. Mongan, Agnes, ed. II. Bennett, Mary Lee, ed. III. Sachs, Paul Joseph, 1878-1965. IV. Title. Available from New York Graphic, Greenwich, Conn.

LICHTNER, Schomer. 916
Drawings, 1st ed. Milwaukee, Galley Press, c1964 71 p. illus. 19 x 21 cm. [NC1075.L63A44] 65-5092
I. Title.

LIEBERMAN, William 741.9'4
Slattery, 1924-
Drawings from the Kroller-Muller National Museum, Otterlo, Edited by William S. Lieberman. New York, Museum of Modern Art [1973] 89 p. illus. 19 x 21 cm. Catalog of an exhibition sponsored by the Netherlands Ministry of Cultural Affairs, Recreation, and Social Welfare; first held at Museum of Modern Art, New York, May 24-Aug. 19, 1973. [NC17.N4O874] 72-95074 ISBN 0-87070-297-1
1. Otterlo, Netherlands. Rijksmuseum Kroller Muller. 2. Drawings—Exhibitions. I. Netherlands (Kingdom, 1815-). Ministerie van Cultuur, Recreatie en Maatschappelijk Werk. II. New York (City). Museum of Modern Art. III. Title.

LINCKE, Hartmut, 1942- 741.9'43
Hartmut Lincke, drawings. [San Francisco? 1968?] 1 v. (unpaged) illus., port. 27 cm. Label mounted on t.p.: San Francisco Museum of Art, San Francisco, California, July-August 1968. [NC251.L54A46] 70-20183
I. San Francisco. Museum of Art.

MINNEAPOLIS. 760'.074'0176579
Institute of Arts.
A loan exhibition of drawings and watercolors from Minnesota private collections. [Minneapolis, 1971] 116 p. illus. 23 cm. Cover title: Drawings & watercolors from Minnesota private collections. Catalog of the exhibition held May 13-June 13, 1971. [NC30.M5] 71-26411
1. Drawings—Exhibitions. 2. Watercolors—Exhibitions. 3. Art—Private collections—Minnesota. I. Title. II. Title: Drawings & watercolors from Minnesota private collections.

MINNESOTA. 741.9'4'074019454
University. University Gallery.
20th century master drawings / catalogue by Sidney Simon and Emily Rauh. Minneapolis, 1963] [57] p. 42 plates. 28 cm. Exhibition held at the Solomon R. Gugenheim Museum, New York, Nov. 6, 1963-Jan. 1963-Jan. 5, 1964: University Gallery, University of Minnesota, Minneapolis, Feb. 3, Mar. 15, 1964; the Fogg Art Museum, Harvard University, Cambridge, Apr. 6-May 24, 1964. "Third in a series of yearly exhibitions initiated by the University of Minnesota in 1961." [NC15.M55] 64-1129
1. Drawings — Exhibitions. I. Simon, Sidney. II. Rauh, Emily. III. Title.

MINNESOTA. University. 741.924
University Gallery
The nineteenth century: one hundred twenty-five master drawings; a loan exhibition organized for the Solomon R. Guggenheim Museum, New York, by the University Gallery, University of Minnesota, Minneapolis. [Minneapolis, 1962] [95]p. illus., plates. 28cm. The exhibition to be held at the University Gallery, Mar. 26 to Apr. 23: at the Solomon R. Guggenhelm Museum, May 15 to July 1, 1962. [NC15.M54] 62-63690
1. Drawings—Exhibitions. I. Solomon R. Guggenhelm Museum, New York. II. Title.

MINNESOTA University. 741.924
Universtiy Gallery
The nineteenth century: one hundred twenty-five master drawings a loan exhibition organized for the Solomon R. Guggenheim Museum, New York, by the Univ. Gallery, Univ. of Minn., Minneapolis. [Minneapolis, Author, 1962] [95]p. illus., plates. 28cm. The exhibiti6n to be held at the University Galley, Mar. 26 th Apr. 23 at the Solomon R. Guggenheim Museum, May 15 to 1962. 62-63690 2.00
1. Drawings—Exhibitions. I. Solomon R. Guggenheim Museum, New York. II. Title.

MONGAN, Agnes, ed. 741.9'4
One hundred master drawings. Westport, Conn., Greenwood Press [1971, c1949] xv, 208 p. illus. 27 cm. Presented in honor of Paul J. Sachs. "Seventy master drawings," a loan exhibition at the Fogg Museum of Art, Nov. 1948-Jan. 1949, held on the occasion of the 70th birthday of Paul J. Sachs, and 30 additional drawings from the museum's collections. Bibliography: p. 203-204. [NC15.C3M6 1971] 75-95129 ISBN 0-8371-3989-9
1. Drawings—Exhibitions. I. Sachs, Paul Joseph, 1878-1965. II. Harvard University. William Hayes Fogg Art Museum. III. Title. BIP

NORTH Carolina. 760'.074'015655
Museum of Art, Raleigh.
A catalogue of drawings and watercolors. Raleigh, 1969. 79 p. illus. 26 cm. [NC95.N6] 75-286297
1. Drawings—Exhibitions. 2. Watercolors—Exhibitions. I. Title.

PARKE-BERNET 380.1'45'7 s
Galleries, inc., New York.
Highly important old master drawings including examples of Francois Boucher [and others]. Collected by Irma N. Straus and Jesse Isidor Straus ... Public auction, Wednesday evening, October 21 at 8 p.m. New York, 1970. 94 p. illus. 28 cm. On cover: The Irma N. Straus Collection of old master drawings. "Sale number 3096." [Z999.P23 no. 3096] [NC80] 741.9'4'0740471 74-189761 7.00
1. Straus, Irma N.—Art collections. 2. Straus, Jesse Isidor, 1872-1936—Art collections. 3. Drawings—Exhibitions. I. Title. II. Title: Old master drawings.

PHILADELPHIA MUSEUM OF ART. 741.9
Masterpieces of drawing: diamond jubilee exhibition, November 4, 1950 -- February 11, 1951. [Philadelphia, 1950] unpaged. illus. 23 cm. [NC15.P13] 52-819
1. Drawings — Exhibitions. I. Title.

SANTA Barbara, 740'.74'019491
Calif. Museum of Art.
Drawings; the Collection of the Santa Barbara Museum of Art; [an exhibition. Santa Barbara, Printed by the Triple R Press, 1970] 88 p. illus. 29 cm. [NC15.S36S32] 77-124582
1. Drawings—Exhibitions. I. Title.

STAMPFLE, Felice. 741.9'4
Drawings from the Collection of Lore and Rudolf Heinemann. Catalogue by Felice Stampfle and Cara D. Denison. With an introd. by James Byam Shaw. New York, Pierpont Morgan Library, 1973. 189 p. 120 plates. 28 cm. Catalog of an exhibition. Includes bibliographical references. [NC15.N56P537] 73-79034 ISBN 0-87598-040-6 7.50
1. Heinemann, Lore—Art collections. 2. Heinemann, Rudolf—Art collections. 3. Drawings—Exhibitions. I. Denison, Cara D., joint author. II. Pierpont Morgan Library, New York. III. Title. BIP

STAMPFLE, 741.9'4'07401471
Felice.
Drawings from the collection of Mr. & Mrs. Eugene V. Thaw : catalogue / by Felice Stampfle & Cara D. Denison ; with an introd. by Eugene V. Thaw. New York : The Pierpont Morgan Library, 1975. 105 p., [62] leaves of plates : ill. (some col.) ; 28 cm. Catalog of the exhibition held Dec. 10, 1975-Feb. 15, 1976 at the Pierpont Morgan Library, New York; Mar. 16-May 2, 1976 at the Cleveland Museum of Art; May 28-July 5, 1976 at the Art Institute of Chicago; and Aug. 6-Sept. 17, 1976 at the National Gallery of Canada, Ottawa. Includes bibliographies and index. [NC15.N56P538] 75-38424 ISBN 0-87598-052-X : 16.50
1. Thaw, Eugene V.—Art collections. 2. Drawings—Exhibitions. I. Denison, Cara D., joint author. II. Thaw, Eugene V. III. Pierpont Morgan Library, New York. IV. Title.

STOCKHOLM. 741.9'074'01471
Nationalmuseum.
Drawings from Stockholm: a loan exhibition from the Nationalmuseum. Compiled by Per Bjurstrom. [New York? 1969] 55 p., 139 plates. 27 cm. Catalog of an exhibition shown at the Pierpont Morgan Library, New York, the Museum of Fine Arts, Boston, and the Art Institute of Chicago, in 1969. Includes bibliographical references. [NC15.N557S75] 69-20400 ISBN 0-87598-001-5
1. Drawings—Exhibitions. I. Bjurstrom, Per. II. Pierpont Morgan Library, New York. III. Boston. Museum of Fine Arts. IV. Chicago. Art Institute. V. Title. BIP

VASSAR College. 707.4
Centennial loan exhibition; drawings & watercolors from alumnae and their families, Vassar College, Poughkeepsie, New York [May 19-June 11, 1961. Poughkeepsie, c1961] xxiv, 151 p. plates. 23 cm. Exhibition held at Wildenstein & Co., New York, June 14-Sept. 9, 1961. [NC15.P6] 61-12321
1. Drawings — Exhibitions. 2. Watercolors — Exhibitions. 3. Art — Private collections. I. Wildenstein and Company, inc., New York. II. Title.

VICTORIA, 741'.074'09945
Australia. National Gallery, Melbourne.
The art of drawing. [Melbourne, Aldine Press, 196-] [24] p. illus. 28 cm. Exhibition catalog includes 100 drawings from the Print Room of the National Gallery of Victoria and some other collections. [NC17.A78V527 1960z] 74-185418
1. Drawings—Exhibitions. I. Title.

WUNDER, Richard P. 720'.28
Architectural, ornament, landscape, and figure drawings / collected by Richard Wunder. Middlebury, Vt. : Middlebury College, 1975. 200 p. : ill. ; 28 cm. Catalogue of an exhibition. Includes bibliographical references and index. [NC15.M5M528] 74-28546 7.50
1. Wunder, Richard P.—Art collections. 2. Drawings—Exhibitions. 3. Artists' preparatory studies—Exhibitions. I. Middlebury College, Middlebury, Vt. II. Title.

Drawings—Exhibitions—Art collections.

FORSTER-HAHN, 741.9'074'094945
Franziska.
Old master drawings from the Collection of Kurt Meissner, Zurich. Catalogue by Francoise Forster-Hahn. [Stanford, Calif.] Dept. of Art, Stanford University [1969] 117 p. 88 illus. 24 cm. (Stanford art book 10) Catalogue of an exhibition held at Stanford Art Gallery, Nov. 2-Dec. 14, 1969; Detroit Institute of Arts, Jan. 27-Mar. 8, 1970; and Finch College Museum of Art, Apr. 1-June 15, 1970. Label mounted on t.p.: Supplied by Worldwide Books, inc., Boston. Includes bibliographical references. [NC33.S92M44] 70-21381 4.50
1. Meissner, Kurt, 1909- 2. Drawings—Exhibitions—Art collections. I. Stanford University. Thomas Welton Stanford Art Gallery. II. Detroit. Institute of Arts. III. Finch College, New York. Museum of Art. IV. Title. V. Series.

Drawings, Flemish.

DELEN, Adrien Jean 741.9493
Joseph, 1883-
Flemish master drawings of the seventeenth century. With 57 illus. [Translated by Robert Allen] New York, Harper [1950] 90 p. illus. 25 cm. (Master drawings) Harper's art library. [NC1030.D37] 50-9517
1. Drawings, Flemish. I. Title.

EISLER, Colin T. 741.9493
Flemish & Dutch drawings from the 15th to the 18th century. Text by Colin T. Eisler. New York, Shorewood [1964, c.1963] 140p. illus. (pt. col.) ports. (pt. col.) 25cm. (Drawings of the masters) Bibl. 63-19860 4.95
1. Drawings, Flemish. 2. Drawings, Dutch. I. Title. II. Series.

EISLER, Colin T. 741.9'492
Flemish & Dutch drawings : from the 15th to the 18th century / text by Colin T. Eisler. Boston : Little, Brown, [1976] c1963. 140 p. : ill. (some col.) ; 24 cm. (Drawings of the masters) Bibliography: p. 139-140. [NC258.E35 1976] 75-25674 ISBN 0-316-22521-5 pbk. : 4.95
1. Drawings, Flemish. 2. Drawings, Dutch. I. Title. II. Series: Drawings of the masters (Boston).

Drawings, French.

ADHEMAR, Jean. 741.944
French drawing of the XVI century; 99 reproductions Edited by Ed. Merniod-Lausanne. New York, Vanguard Press [1955] xxvii, 139p. plates. 29cm. (A Thames and Hudson book) 'Biographical notes': p. 99-118. [NC1035.A3] 55-7884
1. Drawings, French. I. Title.

BERGER, Klaus, 1901- ed. 741.944
French master drawings of the nineteenth century. [Translated by Robert Allen] With 57 illus. New York, Harper [1950] 90 p. illus. 25 cm. (Harper's art library) [NC1130.B413] 50-6872
1. Drawings, French. I. Title.

COCTEAU, Jean, 1889- 741.9'44
1963.
Drawings: 129 drawings from "Dessins." [Magnolia, Mass.] [Peter Smith] [1973, c1972] xii, 129 p. (chiefly illus.) 29 cm. (Dover paperback rebound) "Unabridged repubn. of the 3rd ed. (1924) of the book 'Dessins'." [NC1499.C6A313 1972] 78-182100 ISBN 0-486-20781-1 6.00
I. Title.

DIEHL, Gaston. 741.944
Drawing in France, XIX century; the romantics and realists. [Edited by Andre Gloeckner. Translated from French by L. Norton] London, New York, Heinemann, in association with Hyperion Press [1951] 100 p. (p. 21-100 illus.) maps (on lining papers) 21 cm. (Hyperion drawing series) Bibliography: p. 13-14. [NC1130.D5 1951] 52-44139
1. Drawings, French. I. Title.

DIEHL, Gaston. 741.944
Drawing in France, XIX century; the romantics and realists. [Edited by Andre Gloeckner. Translated from French by L. Norton] New York, Hyperion Press; distributed by Macmillan [1950] 100 p. (p. 21-100 illus.) maps (on lining papers) 21 cm. (Hyperion drawing series) Bibliography: p. 13-14. [NC1130.D5] 51-9669
1. Drawings, French. I. Title.

DU MAURIER, George 741'.0924
Louis Palmella Busson, 1834-1896.
The young George du Maurier; a selection of his letters, 1860-67. Edited by Daphne du Maurier, with a biographical appendix by Derek Pepys Whiteley and illus. from contemporary drawings by du Maurier. Westport, Conn., Greenwood Press [1969] xxi, 307 p. illus., ports. 23 cm. Reprint of the 1951 ed. [NC242.D8A32 1969] 73-97329
I. Du Maurier, Daphne, 1907- ed. II. Title.
BIP

FRENCH drawing of the 741.944
19th century 136 reproductions. Introd by Rene Huyghe. Biographical notes by Philippe Jaccottet. Edited by Ed. Merniod-Lausanne. New York, Vanguard Press [1956] xxxix, 174p. plates. 29cm. [NC1130.F75] 56-12042
1. Drawings, French. 2. Artists, French. I. Huyghe, Rene. II. Jaccottet, Philippe.

FRENCH drawing of the 741.944
20th century; 149 reproductions. Introd. by Jean Casson. Biographical notes by Philippe Jaccottet Edited by Ed. Merniod-Lausanne. New York, Vanguard Press [1955] xv, 184p. (chiefly illus.) 29cm. (A Thames and Hudson book) [NC1130.D482] 55-12957
1. Drawings, French. 2. Artists, French. I. Cassou, Jean, 1897- II. Jaccottet, Phillippe.

HUGO, Victor Marie 741.944
comte, 1805-1885
Victor hugo, dessinateur in french pref. de Gaetan Picon. Notes, tegendes de Roger Cornaille, Georges Herscher. [dist. New York, Wittenborn, 1964, c.1963] Paris editions du Minotaure 234p. (chieffy illus., pt. col., ports.) 25cm. (Le Cabinet fantastique, v.3) Bibl. 64-570 12.50
I. Title.

LALIRE, Adolphe, 1850- 741.044
The drawings of La Lyre. Introd. by Stephen Longstreet. [1st ed.] Alhambra, Calif., Borden Pub. Col [1966] 1 v. (unpaged) col. illus. 31 cm. (Master draughtsman series) [NC1135.L3L6] 66-7153
I. Longstreet, Stephen, 1907- II. Title. BIP

LEYMARIE, Jean. 741.9'44
Impressionist drawings from Manet to Renoir. Translated by Robert Allen. [Geneva] Skira [1969] 103 p. illus. 18 cm. (The Taste of our time) Distributed in the U.S.A. by the World Publishing Co., Cleveland, Ohio. [NC246.L48] 77-80454 7.95 (U.S.)
1. Drawings, French. 2. Impressionism (Art)—France. I. Title.

MOSKOWITZ, Ira, ed. 741.944
French impressionists; a selection of drawings of the French 19th century, selected and edited by Ira Moskowitz, with a text by Maurice Serullaz. New York, Shorewood Publishers [c1962] 140 p. (p. 33-[128] plates (part col.)] illus. 25 cm. (Drawings of the masters) Bibliography: p. 139-140. [NC1130.M6] 62-21091
1. Drawings, French. 2. Serullaz, Maurice. I. Title. II. Series.

MOSKOWITZ, Ira, ed. 741.9'44
French impressionists : a selection of drawings of the French 19th century / selected and edited by Ira Moskowitz ; with a text by Maurice Serullaz. Boston : Little, Brown, [1975] c1962. 140 p. : ill. (some col.) ; 24 cm. Reprint of the ed. published by Shorewood Publishers, New York, in the series: Drawings of the masters. Bibliography: p. 139-140. [NC246.M67 1975] 75-11514 ISBN 0-316-58560-2 pbk : 3.95
1. Drawings, French. 2. Impressionism (Art)—France. I. Serullaz, Maurice. II. Title.

VALLERY-RADOT, Jean, 741.944
1890-
French drawings from the 15th century through Gericault. Text by Jean Vallery-Radot New York, Shorewood Publishers [c1964] 141 p. illus. (part col.) ports. (part col.) 25 cm. (Drawings of the masters) Bibliography: p. 141. [NC1035.V33] 64-22717
1. Drawings, French. I. Title. II. Series.

VALLERY-RADOT, Jean, 741.9'44
1890-
French drawings from the 15th century through Gericault / text by Jean Vallery-Radot. Boston : Little, Brown, [1976] c1964. 141 p. : ill. (some col.) ; 24 cm. (Drawings of the masters) Translation of Les plus beaux dessins francais du XVe siecle a Gericault. Reprint of the ed. published by Shorewood Publishers, New York. Bibliography: p. 141. [NC246.V3413 1976] 76-2077 ISBN 0-316-89540-7 pbk. : 5.95
1. Drawings, French. I. Title. II. Series: Drawings of the masters (Boston)

VANTOURA, Andre, ed. 741.944
French drawings from Prud'hon to Daumier. Introd. by Maurice Serullaz. [Compiled and edited by Andre Vantoura with the assistance of O. H. Gasnier. Translated from the French by Florence Hammond Phillips] Greenwich, Conn., New York Graphic Society [1966] 1 v. (chiefly illus. (part col.)) 33 cm. [NC1130.V314] 66-19493
1. Drawings, French. I. Serullaz, Maurice. II. Title.

Drawings, French—Catalogs.

BJURSTROM, Per. 741.9'44'074085
French drawings : sixteenth and seventeenth centuries / Per Bjurstrom ; [utg. av] National-museum ; [English translation by Patrick Hort]. Stockholm : LiberForlag, 1976. xxxiv, 297 p. ; ill. ; 29 cm. (Drawings in Swedish public collections ; 2) Includes bibliographies and index. [NC246.B8413] 76-369323 ISBN 9-13-802345-8 : kr345.00
1. Drawings, French—Catalogs. 2. Drawings, French—Sweden—Catalogs. I. Title. II. Series.

SERULLAZ, Maurice. 741.944
Great drawings of the Louvre Museum, the French drawings [by] Maurice Serullaz with the collaboration of Lise Duclaux and Genevieve Monnier. [Translated from the French by Victoria Benedict] New York, G. Braziller [1968] 222 p. illus. (part col.) 30 cm. Translation of Dessins du Louvre, ecole francaise. Bibliography: p. 14. [NC1130.S413] 68-23040
1. Drawings, French—Catalogs. 2. Drawings—Paris—Catalogs. I. Paris. Musee national du Louvre. Cabinet des dessins. II. Title.

Drawings, French—Exhibitions.

ASSOCIATION francaise 741.944
d'action artistique.
French drawings; masterpieces from five centuries. A loan exhibition organized by l'Association francaise d'action artistique and circulated by the Smithsonian Institution, 1952-1953 [to the] national Gallery of Art Washington, D. C.the Cleveland Museum of Art, Cleveland, Ohio. •city Art Museum, St. Louis, Missouri, Fogg Art Museum, Harvard University [and] the Metropolitan Museum of Art, New York. [New York? 1952] 62p. 49 plates. 26cm. [NC246.A88] 53-60757
1. Drawings, French—Exhibitions. I. Smithsonian Institution. II. Title.

BATEAU-LAVOIR Le. Paris 741.944
Dessins de poetes, le Bataeu Lavoir. [Paris, 1966. Preface par Francois Chapon]. Paris, le Bateau Lavoir, 1966. unpaged. illus. 20cm. [NC246.B3] 67-81157 3.00 pap.,
1. Drawings, French—Exhibitions. 2. Art and literature. I. Title.
American distributor: Wittenborn, New York.

DAYTON Art 741'.0944'074017173
Institute, Dayton, Ohio.
French artists in Italy, 1600-1900. [Dayton, Ohio, 1971?] 31 p. illus. 23 cm. Catalog of an exhibition held at the Dayton Art Institute, Oct. 15-Nov. 28, 1971. [NC246.D3] 72-198131
1. Drawings, French—Exhibitions. 2. Artists, French—Italy. 3. Italy—Description and travel—Views. I. Title.

MICHIGAN. 741.9'44'07402132
University. Museum of Art.
A generation of draughtsmen; [exhibition] April 25-May 29, 1962. Ann Arbor [1962] unpaged. illus. 28cm. [NC246.M53] 62-63409
1. Drawings, French— Exhibitions. I. Title.

NEW York 741.9'44'07401471
(City). Museum of Modern Art.
Seurat to Matisse: drawing in France; selections from the collection of the Museum of Modern Art. Edited by William S. Lieberman. New York, [1974] 103 p. illus. 19 x 21 cm. Catalog of an exhibition held at the Museum of Modern Art, New York. [NC246.N48 1974] 73-91049 ISBN 0-87070-589-X
1. Drawings, French—Exhibitions. I. Lieberman, William Slattery, 1924- ed. II. Title.

PRINCETON 741.9'44'074014967
University. Art Museum.
19th and 20th century French drawings from the Art Museum, Princeton University: a introduction,. [Princeton, N.J.] Distributed by Princeton University Press [1972] 96 p. illus. 25 cm. Catalog of the exhibition held Mar. 4-Apr. 9, 1972. Prepared by the graduate students of the Dept. of Art and Archaeology, Princeton University. [NC246.P7] 77-187565 ISBN 0-691-03881-3 10.00
1. Drawings, French—Exhibitions. I. Princeton University. Dept. of Art and Archaeology. II. Title.

SLATKIN (CHARLES E.) 741.944
GALLERIES, New York.
French master drawings, Renaissance to modern. A loan exhibition, February 10 through March 7, 1959. New York [1959] unpaged. illus. 28 cm. [NC246.S55] 59-1666
1. Drawings, French — Exhibitions. I. Title.

Drawings, French—U.S.

BOUCHER, Francois, 741.9'44
1703-1770.
Francois Boucher in North American collections: 100 drawings. [Text by] Regina Shoolman Slatkin. [Washington, National Gallery of Art, 1973] xxv, 130 p. illus. 22 x 29 cm. Catalog of an exhibition to be held at National Gallery of Art, Dec. 23, 1973-Mar. 17, 1974, and the Art Institute of Chicago, Apr. 4-May 12, 1974. Bibliography: p. xxiii-xxiv. [NC248.B587S55] 73-89398 11.95
1. Boucher, Francois, 1703-1770. 2. Drawings, French—United States. 3. Drawings, French—Canada. I. Slatkin, Regina Shoolman, 1909- II. United States. National Gallery of Art. III. Chicago. Art Institute. IV. Title.
Pbk. 4.95

SHOOLMAN, Regina Lenore, 741.944
1909-
Six centuries of French master drawings in America [by]Regina Shoolman and Charles E. Latkin. New York, Oxford University Press, 1950. xxvii, 256 p. illus. 29 cm. Includes bibliographies. [NC1130.S5] 50-6159
1. Drawings, French—U.S. I. Slatkin, Charles Ell, 1907- joint author. II. Title.

Drawings, German.

EISLER, Colin T. 741.943
German drawings from the 16th century to the expressionists. New York, Shorewood [1964, c.1963] 139p. illus. (pt. col.) ports. (pt. col.) 25cm. (Drawings of the masters) Bibl. 64-20403 pprice unreported
1. Drawings, German. I. Title. II. Series.

EISLER, Colin T. 741.9'43
German drawings, from the 16th century to the expressionists / text by Colin T. Eister Boston : Little, Brown, [1975] c1963. 139 p. : ill. (some col.) ; 24 cm. (Drawings of the masters) Bibliography: p. 138-139. [NC249.E35 1975] 75-11516 ISBN 0-316-22520-7 pbk : 4.95
1. Drawings, German. I. Title. II. Series: Drawings of the masters (Boston

KLEY, Heinrich, 1863- 741.943
Drawings. New York, Dover Publications [1961] viii. 128p. illus. 28cm. Captions in English and German. 'Unabridged republication of Skizzenbuch--Hundert Federzeichnungen ... and Skizzenbuch II--Hundert Federzeichnungen. [NC1509.K46 1961] 61-4034
I. Title.

KLEY, Heinrich, 1863- 741.943
More drawings. New York, Dover Publications [1962] [4]p., 104p. of illus. 28cm. Captions in English and German. 'A selection ... from ... Leut' und Viecher. published ... in 1912 [and] Sammel-Album, published ... in 1923. [NC1509.K49 1962] 62-5906
I. Title.

Drawings, German—Catalogs.

BACOU, Roseline. 741.94
Great drawings of the Louvre Museum, the German, Flemish and Dutch drawings [by] Roseline Bacou with the collaboration of Arlette Calvet. [Translated from the French by Marguerite Hugo] New York, G. Braziller [1968] 222 p. illus. (part col.) 30 cm. Bibliography: p. 14. [NC27.F7P3523] 70-9769
1. Drawings, German –Catalogs. 2. Drawings, Flemish—Catalogs. 3. Drawings, Dutch—Catalogs. 4. Drawings—Paris—Catalogs. I. Paris. Musee national du Louvre. Cabinet des dessins. II. Title.

SCHILLING, 741.9'4'0740229
Edmund, 1888-
The German drawings in the collection of Her Majesty the Queen at Windsor Castle, by Edmund Schilling; and, Supplements to the catalogues of Italian and French drawings, with a history of the Royal Collection of Drawings, by Anthony Blunt. London, New York, Phaidon [1971] viii, 239 p. illus., facsims. 31 cm. (The Drawings at Windsor Castle) "Distributors in the United States: Praeger Publishers Inc." Includes bibliographical references. [NC249.S3] 73-111053 ISBN 0-7148-1446-6 £8.50
1. Windsor, House of—Art collections. 2. Drawings, German—Catalogs. 3. Windsor Castle. I. Blunt, Anthony, Sir, 1907- II. Title.

Drawings, German—Exhibitions.

GERMAN baroque 708'.21'32 s
drawings : loan exhibition from collections of various museums in the Federal Republic of Germany organized by the Kunstmuseum in Dusseldorf. London : Heim Gallery, [1976] [80] p., [42] leaves of plates : ill. ; 25 cm. (Heim exhibition catalogues ; no. 23) Held at the Heim Gallery, London from October 15-November 19, 1975, and at three other galleries from November 25, 1975-April 18, 1976. Includes index. Bibliography: p. [77]-[78] [N8640.H4 no. 23] [NC249] 741.9'43'07402132 76-377148
1. Drawings, German—Exhibitions. 2. Drawing, Baroque—Germany—Exhibitions. I. Dusseldorf. Kunstmuseum. II. Heim Gallery. III. Title. IV. Series.

HARVARD 741.9'43'07401444
University. Busch-Reisinger Museum of Germanic Culture.
German master drawings of the nineteenth century. [Cambridge, 1972] 1 v. (unpaged) 93 illus. 24 cm. Catalogue of an exhibition held at the Busch-Reisinger Museum, Harvard University, Cambridge, Oct. 5-Nov. 18, 1972, and other museums. [NC249.H36] 72-88047
1. Drawings, German—Exhibitions. I. Title.

SMITHSONIAN Institution. 741.943
German drawings; masterpieces from five centuries, A loan exhibition sponsored by the Federal Republic of Germany and circulated by the Smithsonian Institutional ;National Gallery of Art, Washington D.C.;the Cleveland Musuemof Art,Cleveland Ohio;Museum of Fine Arts, Boston, Massacusett;M. H deYoung Memorial Museum, San Francisco, California,1955-56 [Washington, 1955] 59p. plates. 26cm. Bibliography: p. 59. [NC249.S5] 56-60425
1. Drawings. German—Exhibitions. I. Title.

Drawings, Hungarian—Exhibitions.

SZABO, Katalin. 741.9'439'0740261
20th century Hungarian graphic art: catalogue of a loan exhibition, July 24 to August 29, 1971. Norwich (Castle Museum, Norwich, Norfolk, NOR 65B), City of Norwich Museums, 1971. [27] p. 23 cm. Exhibition prepared by the Hungarian Institute for Cultural Relations in collaboration with the Hungarian National Gallery. Catalogue by K. Szabo. [NC312.H8S95] 72-176211 ISBN 0-903101-01-7
1. Drawings, Hungarian—Exhibitions. 2. Water-colors, Hungarian—Exhibitions. I. Norwich Castle Museum, Norwich, Eng. II. Kulturalis Kapcsolatok Intezete. III. Budapest. Magyar Nemzeti Galeria. IV. Title.

Drawings, Indic.

EASTMAN, Alvan Clark. 741.954
The Nala-Damayanti drawings A study of a portfolio of drawings made for Raja Samsar Cand of Kangra (1774-1823), illustrating an early Indian romance; twenty-nine drawings now in the Museum of Fine Arts, Boston, with the addition of nineteen drawings from other American museums and from a private collection. Boston, Museum of Fine Arts, 1959. xix, 119 p. 47 plates. 23 x 28 cm. Bibliography: p. 113-115. [NC1250.E25] 59-14357
1. Mahabharata. Nalopakhyana. 2. Drawings, Indic. 3. Drawing—Kangra (District) Punjab. I. Boston, Museum of Fine Arts. II. Title.

TAGORE, Ranindranath, Sir 1861-1941 759.62-4486
Drawings and paintings of Rabindranath Tagore; centenary 1861-1961. [Dist. New York, Heinman, 1962. 15]p. col. illus. 38cm. 15.00
I. Title.

Drawings, Indic—Catalogs.

GREAT Britain. Office of Commonwealth Relations. India Office Library. 743.932
Natural history drawings in the India Office Library; [catalogue] by Mildred Archer. London, Pub. for the Commonwealth Relations Office by H. M. Stationery Off., [dist. New York, British Info., c.]1962. ix, 116p. 25 plates (pt. col.) 25cm. Bibl. 62-51947 5.50
1. Drawings, Indic—Catalogs. 2. Drawings—Catalogs. 3. Natural history—Pictorial works. 4. Natural history—Asia. I. Archer, Mildred. II. Title. BIP

Drawings, Indic—Exhibitions.

WELCH, Stuart Cary. 759.954'074'01471
Indian drawings and painted sketches, 16th through 19th centuries : [catalogue] / by Stuart Cary Welch. [New York] : Asia Society, 1975, c1976. 142 p. : ill. (some col.) ; 26 cm. "An Asia House Gallery publication." "Catalogue of an exhibition shown in the Asia House Gallery in the winter of 1976 as an activity of the Asia Society." Bibliography: p. 140-142. [NC327.W44] 75-29780 ISBN 0-87848-046-3 : 17.50
1. Drawings, Indic—Exhibitions. I. Asia House Gallery, New York. II. Asia Society. III. Title.

Drawings—Instruction.

KESSLER, Leonard P. 1920- 741.0713
What's in a line? New York, W. R. Scott, c1951. unpaged. illus. 26 cm. (Young Scott books) [DN655.K4] 51-11802
1. Drawings—Instruction. I. Title.

Drawings, Iranian.

ROBINSON, Basil William 741.955
Persian drawings from the 14th through the 19th century. Text by B. W. Robinson. New York. Shorewood [c.1965] 141p. illus. (pt. col.) ports. (pt. col.) 25cm. (Drawings of the masters) Bibl. [NC1050.I7R6] 65-16878 5.95
1. Drawings, Iranian. 2. Miniature painting, Iranian. I. Title. II. Series.

ROBINSON, Basil William. 760'.0955
Persian drawings from the 14th through the 19th century / text by B. W. Robinson. Boston : Little, Brown, [1976] c1965. 142 p. : ill. (some col.) ; 24 cm. (Drawings of the masters) Bibliography: p. 142. [NC321.R62 1976] 75-25673 ISBN 0-316-75142-1 pbk. : 4.95
1. Drawings, Iranian. 2. Miniature paintings, Iranian. I. Title. II. Series: Brawings of the masters (Boston). III. Series: Drawings of the masters.

ROBINSON, Basil Williams. 751.955
Persian drawings from the 14th through the 19th century. Text by B. W. Robinson. New York, Shorewood Publishers [1965] 141 p. illus. (part col.) ports. (part col.) 25 cm. (Drawings of the masters) Bibliography: p. 141. [NC1050.I7R6] 65-16878
1. Drawings, Iranian. 2. Miniature painting, Iranian. I. Title. II. Series.

Drawings, Italian.

AMES, Winslow. 741.945
Italian drawings from the 15th to the 19th century. Text by Winslow Ames. New York. Shorewood Publishers [c1963] 141 p. illus. (part col.) 25 cm. (Drawings of the masters) [NC1150.A5] 63-19843
1. Drawings, Italian I. Title. II. Series.

AMES, Winslow. 741.9'45
Italian drawings from the 15th to the 19th century / text by Winslow Ames. Boston : Little, Brown, [1976] c1963. 141 p. : ill. (some col.) ; 24 cm. (Drawings of the masters) Reprint of the ed. published by Shorewood Publishers, New York. Bibliography: p. 140-141. [NC255.A43 1976] 76-2076 ISBN 0-316-03688-9 pbk. : 5.95
1. Drawings, Italian. I. Title. II. Series: Drawings of the masters (Boston)

CHIRICO, Giorgio de, 1888- 741.9495
194 drawings. Selected by Ezio Gribaudo: Introductory essay by Luigi Carluccio. New York, H. N. Abrams [1969?] [6] p., 194 plates. 25 cm. Translation of 194 [i.e. Centonovantaquattro] disegni. [NC257.C56C313] 69-15435
I. Carluccio, Luigi. II. Title.

FENYO. IVAN 741.9450740391
North Italian drawings from the collection of the Budapest Museum of Fine Arts. New York, October House [1966, c.1965] 178p. 144p. of illus., xxxi p. illus. 24cm. Bibl. [NC1150.F413] 66-14731 15.00
1. Drawings. Italian. I. Budapest. Szepmuveszti Mureum. II. Title. BIP

LEONARDO da Vinci, 1452-1519. 741.9'45
Drawings. Introd. by Elmer Belt. [1st ed.] Los Angeles, Borden Pub. Co., [1962] unpaged. illus. 31 cm. (Master draughtsman series) [NC1055.L5A52] 62-19992
I. Belt, Elmer, 1893- II. Title.

MILLAR, Oliver, 1923- ed. 708.2
Italian drawings and paintings in the Queen's collection. New York, Viking [c.1965] xviii, 86 col. plates. 31cm. (Studio bk.) [NC1045.M5] 65-15680 35.00
1. Drawings, Italian. 2. Paintings, Italian. 3. Buckingham Palace. 4. Windsor Castle. I. Title.

VERMEULE, Cornelius Clarkson, 1925- 741.945
The Dal Pozzo-Albani drawings of classical antiquities in the British Museum. Philadelphia, American Philosophical Society, 1960. 78 p. illus. 30 cm. (Transactions of the American Philosophical Society, new ser., v. 50, pt. 5) Bibliography: p. 8. [Q11.P6] 60-11139
1. Pozzo, Cassiano del, d. 1657. Museum chartaceum. 2. Albani, Alexxandro, cardinal, 1692-1779. 3. Drawings, Italian. 4. Classical antiquities. 5. Sculpture, Ancient. 6. British Museum. Dept. of Greek and Roman Antiquities. I. Title. II. Title: Pozzo-Albani drawings of classical antiquities in the British Museum. III. Series: American Philosophical Society, Philadelphia. Transactions, new ser., v. 50 pt. 5

Drawings, Italian — Catalogs.

BACOU, Roseline. 741.945
Great drawings of the Louvre Museum, the Italian drawings [by] Roseline Bacou with the collaboration of Francoise Viatte. [Translated from the French by Victoria Benedict] New York, G. Braziller [1968] 222 p. illus. (part col.) 30 cm. Translation of Dessins du Louvre, ecole italienne. Bibliography: p. 209. [NC1150.B2613] 75-9675
1. Drawings, Italian—Catalogs. 2. Drawings—Paris—Catalogs. I. Paris. Musee national du Louvre. Cabinet des dessins. II. Title.

EDINBURGH. National Gallery of Scotland. 741.9'45
Catalogue of Italian drawings [by] Keith Andrews. London, Published for the Trustees of the National Galleries of Scotland by Cambridge U.P., 1968. 2 v. 200 plates. 29 cm. Contents.Contents.—v. 1. Text.—v. 2. Plates. [NC1150.E3] 68-22661 ISBN 0-521-07121-6 10/-/-
1. Drawings, Italian—Catalogs. I. Andrews, Keith. II. Title.

GIBBONS, Felton Lewis, 1929- 741.9'45'074014967
Catalogue of Italian drawings in the Art Museum, Princeton University / by Felton Gibbons. Princeton, N.J. : Princeton University Press, c1977. 2 v. : ill. ; 29 cm. "Published for the Department of Art and Archaeology, Princeton University." Includes index. Contents.Contents.—1. Text.—2. Plates. [NC255.G45] 76-3252 ISBN 0-691-03888-0 : 50.00
1. Princeton University. Art Museum. 2. Drawings, Italian—Catalogs. 3. Drawings—Princeton, N.J.—Catalogs. I. Princeton University. Art Museum. II. Princeton University. Dept. of Art and Archaeology. III. Title. BIP

ITALIAN master drawings, 1350-1800 from the Janos Scholz collection / selected and described by Janos Scholz. New York : Dover Publications, 1976. xxiv p., [75] leaves of plates : ill. ; 31 cm. [NC255.I82 1976] 75-19835 ISBN 0-486-23257-3 pbk. : 5.00 741.9'45'075
1. Scholz, Janos—Art collections. 2. Drawings, Italian—Catalogs. I. Scholz, Janos.

PRINCETON University. Art Museum. 741.945
Italian drawings in the Art Museum, Princeton University; 106 selected examples [Catalogue by Jacob Bean. New York, October House, 1966] 64 p. illus. 26 cm. Bibliography: p. 13. [NC1150.P7] 66-24379
1. Drawings, Italian—Catalogs. I. Bean, Jacob. II. Title. BIP

VERMEULE, Cornelius Clarkson, 1925- 740.0740229
The Dal Pozzo-Albani drawings of classical antiquities in the Royal Library at Windsor Castle [by] Cornelius C. Vermeule, III. Philadelphia, American Philosophical Society, 1966. 170 p. illus. 30 cm. (Transactions of the American Philosophical Society. New ser., v. 56, pt. 2, 1966) Bibliography: p. 7. [Q11.P6 n.s., vol. 56, pt. 2] 66-18701
1. Pozzo, Cassiano del, d. 1657. Museum chartaceum. 2. Albani, Alessandro, Cardinal, 1692-1779. 3. Drawings, Italian — Catalogs. 4. Classical antiquities — Catalogs. I. Windsor Castle. Royal Library. II. Title. III. Series: American Philosophical Society, Philadelphia. Transactions, new ser., v. 56, pt. 2 BIP

Drawings, Italian— collections,

STAMPFLE, Felice 741.9'45
The seventeenth century in Italy; [catalogue by] Felice Stampfle, Jacob Bean. [New York] Metropolitan Museum of Art [and] Pierpont Morgan Library; dist. by N.Y. Graphic Greenwich, Conn., [1967] 233p. illus. 27cm. (Drawings from New York Exhibitions. Exhibited at the Pierpont Morgan Lib., Museum of Art. Bibl. [NC255.S8] 67-13364 8.50
1. Drawings, Italian— collections, I. Bean, Jacob, joint author. II. New York. Metropolitan February 23-April 22, 1967. III. Pierpont Morgan Library, New York. IV. Title. V. Series.

Drawings, Italian—Exhibitions.

BACOU, Roseline. 741.9'45
Italian Renaissance drawings from the Musee du Louvre, Paris: Roman, Tuscan, and Emilian Schools, 1500-1575. [Catalog of an exhibition] the Metropolitan Museum of Art, October 11, 1974-January 5, 1975. [New York, Metropolitan Museum of Art, 1974] 1 v. (unpaged) illus. 25 cm. "Catalogue entries by Roseline Bacou and Francoise Viatte." Includes bibliographies. [NC255.B32] 74-12141 ISBN 0-87099-094-2 3.50 (pbk.).
1. Drawings, Italian—Exhibitions. 2. Drawings, Renaissance—Exhibitions. I. Viatte, Francoise, joint author. II. Paris. Musee national du Louvre. III. New York (City). Metropolitan Museum of Art. IV. Title.

BEAN, Jacob. 741.9'45
The eighteenth century in Italy; [catalogue by] Jacob Bean [and] Felice Stampfle. [New York] Metropolitan Museum of Art [and] Pierpont Morgan Library; distributed by New York Graphic Society, Greenwich, Conn. [1971] 443 p. illus., 300 plates. 27 cm. (Drawings from New York collections, 3) "Exhibited at the Metropolitan Museum of Art, January 30-March 21, 1971." Bibliography: p. 16-17. [NC255.B33] 77-134891 ISBN 0-87099-021-7 25.00
1. Drawings, Italian—Exhibitions. 2. Drawings, Italian—New York (City) I. Stampfle, Felice, joint author. II. New York (City). Metropolitan Museum of Art. III. Pierpont Morgan Library, New York. IV. Title. V. Series.

BROWN University. Dept. of Art. 741.9'45
Drawings and prints of the First Maniera, 1515-1535. [Providence, 1973] 115 p. illus. 21 x 26 cm. "An exhibition by the Department of Art, Brown University at the Museum of Art, Rhode Island School of Design ... February 22 through March 25, 1973." Errata slip inserted. Bibliography: p. 114-115. [NC255.B75 1973] 73-169812
1. Drawings, Italian—Exhibitions. 2. Prints, Italian—Exhibitions. 3. Mannerism (Art)—Italy. I. Rhode Island School of Design, Providence. Museum of Art. II. Title.

DARTMOUTH College. Hopkins Center. Art Galleries. 741.9'45
Italian drawings; selections from the Collection of Esther and Malcolm W. Bick; [exhibition. Edited by Franklin W. Robinson and John T. Paoletti] Hanover, N.H., 1971. 1 v. (unpaged) illus. 25 cm. Includes bibliographies. [NC255.D28 1971] 74-157102
1. Bick, Esther S.—Art collections. 2. Bick, Malcolm W.—Art collections. 3. Drawings, Italian—Exhibitions. I. Robinson, Franklin Westcott, ed. II. Paoletti, John T., ed. III. Title.

DRAWINGS by seventeenth century Italian masters from the Collection of Janos Scholz. A faculty-graduate student project, University of California, Santa Barbara. Edited by Alfred Moir. [Santa Barbara, Art Galleries, University of California, 1974] 150 p. illus. 27 cm. Catalog of an exhibition carried out as a project of the Dept. of Art, to be shown at the Art Galleries, University of California, Santa Barbara, and other museums, Feb. 26-Dec. 9, 1974. Bibliography: p. 148-150. [NC255.D72] 73-620185 741.9'45
1. Scholz, Janos—Art collections. 2. Drawings, Italian—Exhibitions. 3. Drawing, Baroque—Italy. I. Moir, Alfred, ed. II. California. University, Santa Barbara. Dept. of Art. III. California. University, Santa Barbara. Art Galleries.

FLORENCE. Galleria degli Uffizi. Gabinetto dei disegni e delle stampe. 741.945
Italian drawings: masterpieces of five centuries. [Catalogue of the] exhibition organized by the Gabinetto disegni, Galleria degli Uffizi, Florence, and

circulated by the Smithsonian Institution: National Gallery of Art, Washington, D. C.: the Art Institute of Chicago; Museum of Fine Arts. Boston; Metropolitan Museum of Art, New York. 1960-1961. 78p. illus. 26cm. (Tr. by John Freccero. Washington, D.C., Smithsonian Institution, 1960] 60-64671 apply pap.,
1. Drawings, Italian—Exhibitions. I. Smithsonian Institution. II. Title.

HOLLAND, Ralph. 741.9'45'07402876
Italian and other drawings, 1500-1800 / [by Ralph Holland]. [Newcastle upon Tyne] : Hatton Gallery, University of Newcastle upon Tyne, 1974. [66] p., [10] leaves of plates : ill. ; 24 cm. Exhibition catalog. [NC255.H64] 75-324383
1. Drawings, Italian—Exhibitions. 2. Drawings—Exhibitions. I. Hatton Gallery. II. Title.

JOHN and Mable 741.9'45'074015961
Ringling Museum of Art, Sarasota, Fla.
The Bick Collection of Italian religious drawings. [Exhibition] John & Mable Ringling Museum of Art. [Sarasota] 1970. 1 v. (unpaged) illus. 23 cm. [NC255.J6] 72-635854
1. Bick, Malcolm W.—Art collections. 2. Drawings, Italian—Exhibitions. I. Title.

KNOX, George. 741.9'45
Tiepolo: a bicentenary exhibition, 1770-1970; drawings, mainly from American collections, by Giambattista Tiepolo and the members of his circle. [Cambridge, Mass., Fogg Art Museum, Harvard University, 1970] xxvi, 232 p. illus., plates. 28 cm. Catalog of the exhibition held at the Fogg Art Museum, Harvard University, March 14-May 3, 1970. Bibliography: p. xxv-xxvi. [NC257.T5K55] 78-116743
1. Tiepolo, Giovanni Battista, 1696-1770. 2. Drawings, Italian—Exhibitions. I. Tiepolo, Giovanni Battista, 1696-1770. II. Harvard University. William Hayes Fogg Art Museum. III. Title.

LONDON. Queen's Gallery, 741.9'45
Buckingham Palace.
Drawings by Michelangelo, Raphael & Leonardo, and their contemporaries. London, 1973. 75 p. illus. 22 cm. Stamped on t.p.: Supplied by World Wide Books, Boston. Exhibition of drawings from the collection in the Royal Library at Windsor Castle. Bibliography: p. 8. [NC255.L66 1973] 73-198364
1. Drawings, Italian—Exhibitions. 2. Drawings, Renaissance—Italy. I. Buonarroti, Michel Angelo, 1475-1564. II. Raphael, 1483-1520. III. Leonardo da Vinci, 1452-1510. IV. Title. BIP

NEILSON, Nancy 741.9'45'074017866
Ward.
Italian drawings selected from mid-western collections. Introd. & catalogue by Nancy Ward Neilson. [St. Louis] St. Louis Art Museum [1972] 1 v. (unpaged) illus. 25 cm. Catalogue of an exhibition held at the St. Louis Art Museum, Feb. 25-April 16, 1972. Includes bibliography. [NC255.N4] 77-189996
1. Drawings, Italian—Exhibitions. 2. Drawings, Italian—Middle West. I. St. Louis. City Art Museum. II. Title.

NEW York (City). 741.9'45
Metropolitan Museum of Art.
Architectural and ornament drawings : Juvarra, Vanvitelli, the Bibiena family, & other Italian draughtsmen / catalogue by Mary L. Myers. [New York] : Metropolitan Museum of Art, 1975. 56 p., [44] leaves of plates : ill. ; 28 cm. [NC255.N45 1975] 74-32459 ISBN 0-87099-126-4 pbk. : 8.95
1. Drawings, Italian—Exhibitions. 2. Decoration and ornament, Architectura—Italy. 3. Decoration and ornament, Italian. 4. Artists' preparatory studies—Italy. I. Myers, Mary L., 1940- II. Title. BIP

NEW York 741.945'074'01471
(City). New School for Social Research. New School Art Center.
One hundred Italian drawings from the 14th to the 18th centuries from the Janos Scholz collection. New York [1971] 36 p. illus. 17 x 26 cm. (American private collections) Catalogue of an exhibition, Mar.-Apr. 1971. [NC255.N46] 72-192516
1. Scholz, Janos—Art collections. 2. Drawings, Italian—Exhibitions. I. Title.

NEW York. Metropolitan 741.945
Museum of Art.
The Italian Renaissance. [Catalogue by] Jacob Bean [curator of drawings, Metropolitan Museum of Art, and] Felice Stampfle [curator of drawings and prints, Pierpont Morgan Library. [New York] Metropolitan Museum of Art, Pierpont Morgan Library; distributed by New York Graphic Society, Greenwich, Conn. [1965] 246 p. illus. 27 cm. (Drawings from New York collections, 1) "Exhibited at the Metropolitan Museum of Art, November 8, 1965 -- January 9, 1966." Bibliography: p. 14-15. [NC255.N45] 65-24811
1. Drawings, Italian — Exhibitions. 2. Drawings — New York (City) I. Bean, Jacob. II. Stampfle, Felice. III. Pierpont Morgan Library, New York. IV. Title. V. Series.

NEWCOME, Mary. 741.9'45'182
Genoese baroque drawings. [Binghamton, University Art Gallery, State University of New York at Binghamton, 1972] xxiv, 61 p., [127] p. of illus. 28 cm. "A loan exhibition [at the] University Art Gallery, State University of New York at Binghamton, October 1 to 31, 1972 [and] Worcester Art Museum, November 8 to December 10, 1972." [NC256.G4N48] 73-170913
1. Drawings, Italian—Exhibitions. 2. Drawing, Baroque—Genoa. I. New York (State). State University at Binghamton. University Art Gallery. II. Worcester, Mass. Art Museum. III. Title.

OBERHUBER, Konrad. 741.9'45
Sixteenth century Italian drawings from the Collection of Janos Scholz [by] Konrad Oberhuber [and] Dean Walker. Washington, National Gallery of Art [1973] xv, 143 p. 28 cm. Catalog of an exhibition held at the National Gallery of Art, Washington, D.C., 23 Sept. to 25 Nov. 1973, and at the Pierpont Morgan Library, New York, 12 Dec. 1973 to 3 Feb. 1974. Includes bibliographical references. [NC255.O23] 73-86478 8.50
1. Scholz, Janos—Art collections. 2. Drawings, Italian—Exhibitions. 3. Drawing, Renaissance—Italy. 4. Drawing, Baroque—Italy. I. Walker, Dean, 1948- joint author. II. United States. National Gallery of Art. III. Pierpont Morgan Library, New York. IV. Title. BIP

OXFORD. 741.9'45'07402572
University. Ashmolean Museum.
Italian drawings from the Ashmolean Museum, Oxford. A loan exhibition in aid of the Friends of the Ashmolean Museum. New York, Wildenstein [1970] 1 v. (unpaged) plates, ports. 25 cm. Organization of exhibition and catalog introd. by Denys Sutton. Catalog of the exhibition held Oct. 15-Nov. 28, 1970, at Wildenstein and Company, inc. in New York. [NC255.O95 1970b] 77-199844
1. Drawings, Italian—Exhibitions. I. Sutton, Denys. II. Ashmolean Museum. Friends. III. Wildenstein and Company, inc., New York. IV. Title.

SCHOLZ, 741.59'45'07401471
Janos.
One hundred Italian drawings from the 14th to the eighteenth centuries from the Janos Scholz collection. [New York, New School Art Center, 1971] 36 p. illus. 17 x 26 cm. (American private collections) Catalog of the exhibition held March-April, 1971 at the New School Art Center in New York. [NC255.S32] 70-198443
1. Drawings, Italian—Exhibitions. 2. Drawings—Private collections. I. New York (City). New School for Social Research. New School Art Center. II. Title.

Drawings, Italian—Florence.

CHASTEL, Andre, 1912- 741.91
Florentine drawings, XIV-XVII centuries. Translated from French by Rosamund Frost. [Edited by Andre Gloeckner] London, New York, Heinemann, in association with Hyperion Press [1950] 104 p. illus. 21 cm. (Hyperion drawing series) [NC1045.C45] 52-1413
1. Drawings, Italian—Florence. I. Title.

Drawings, Italian—Great Britain.

BUONARROTI, Michel 741.9'45
Angelo, 1475-1564.
Drawings by Michelangelo in the collection of Her Majesty the Queen at Windsor Castle, the Ashmolean Museum, the British Museum, and other English collections : an exhibition held in the Department of Prints and Drawings in the British Museum. New York : Universe Books, 1975. 160 p. : ill. ; 26 cm. Includes bibliographical references. [NC257.B8B75] 75-561 ISBN 0-87663-221-5 : 12.50
1. Buonarroti, Michel Angelo, 1475-1564. 2. Drawings, Italian—Great Britain. I. British Museum. Dept. of Prints and Drawings. II. Title: Drawings by Michelangelo ...

Drawings, Japanese.

HILLIER, Jack Ronald 741.952
Japanese drawings from the 17th through the 19th century New York, Shorewood [c.1965] 139p. illus., plates (pt. col.) 25cm. (Drawings of the masters) Bibl. [NC1240.H5] 65-16877 5.95
1. Drawings, Japanese. I. Title. II. Series. BIP

HILLIER, Jack Ronald. 741.952
Japanese drawings from the 17th through the 19th century. Text by J. R. Hillier. New York, Shorewood Publishers [1965] 139 p. illus., plates (part col.) 25 cm. (Drawings of the masters) Bibliography: p. 139. [NC1240.H5] 65-16877
1. Drawings, Japanese. I. Title. II. Series.

HILLIER, Jack Ronald. 741.9'52
Japanese drawings, from the 17th through the 19th century / text by J. R. Hillier Boston : Little, Brown, [1975] c1965. 139 p. : ill. (some col.) ; 24 cm. (Drawings of the masters) Bibliography: 139. [NC351.H55 1975] 75-11513 ISBN 0-316-36394-4 pbk : 4.95
1. Drawings, Japanese. I. Title. II. Series: Drawings of the masters (Boston)

Drawings, Japanese—Exhibitions.

JAPANISCHE 741.952
Handzeichnungen von Itcho, Hokusai, Kuniyoshi, Kyosai, Chinnen, Eisen, Hiroshige, Kunisada, Hokkei, Hokuba, Isai : Horst Janssen, Kopien nach Kyosai und Hokusai / mit e. Vorw. von Basil W. Robinson ; hrsg. von Gerhard Schack ; [die Publication erscheint anlassl. d. Ausstellung "Meisterwerke japanischer Handzeichnung" in d. Kunsthalle Bielefeld] . Hamburg : Christians, 1975. 100 p. : ill. ; 33 cm. Bibliography: p. 98-100. [NC351.J36] 76-450640 ISBN 3-7672-0383-9
1. Drawings, Japanese—Exhibitions. I. Janssen, Horst, 1929- II. Schack, Gerhard, 1929- III. Richard Kaselowsky Haus, Kunsthalle der Stadt Bielefeld.

Drawings—London—Catalogs.

BRITISH Museum. Dept. of 741.945
Prints and Drawings
Italian drawings in the Department of Prints and Drawings in the British Museum. [By] A. E. Popham. London, Pub. by the Trustees of the British Mus., 1950-1967. v. plates 26cm. Contents.v. 2. pts. 1 & 2. Artists working in Parma in the sixteenth century: Catalogue. Plates. Bibl. [NC27.B87] 51-5446 16.80 2 v. set.,
1. Drawings—London—Catalogs. 2. Drawings, Italian. I. Popham, Arthur Ewart, 1889- II. Title.
Distributed by British Information Service, New York.

Drawings, Medieval.

EVANS, M. W. 741.9'4
Medieval drawings [by] M. W. Evans. Feltham, New York, Hamlyn, 1969. 43 p., 132 plates. illus., facsims. 32 cm. Includes bibliographical references. [NC70.E9] 78-550053 ISBN 0-600-02554-3 50/-
1. Drawings, Medieval. I. Title.

Drawings, Neopolitan—Exhibitions.

FINCH 741'.0945'7307401471
College, New York. Museum of Art.
In the shadow of Vesuvius; Neapolitan drawings from the Collection of Janos Scholz. New York [1969] 40 p. 57 illus. 23 cm. Foreword signed: Robert L. Manning. "[Catalogue of] a loan exhibition, Feb. 12-April 12, 1969." [NC256.N3F5] 70-17565
1. Scholz, Janos—Art collections. 2. Drawings, Neapolitan—Exhibitions. I. Manning, Robert L. II. Title.

FINCH 741.9'45'7307401471
College, New York. Museum of Art.
The Two Sicilies; drawings from the Cooper-Hewitt Museum. New York [1970] 40 p. illus. 23 cm. Catalogue of a loan exhibition, Feb. 4-Mar. 20, 1970, prepared by Elaine Evans Dee. [NC256.N3F53] 75-25360
1. Drawings, Neopolitan—Exhibitions. I. Dee, Elaine Evans. II. Cooper-Hewitt Museum of Decorative Arts and Design. III. Title.

Drawings — New London, Conn. — Catalogs.

LYMAN Allyn Museum, New 759.0838
London, Conn.
Complete list of American and European drawings, paintings, and watercolors in the collection of the Lyman Allyn Museum. New London, 1960. 63p. illus. 22cm. [N594.A55] 60-52025
1. Drawings—New London, Conn.—Catalogs. 2. Paintings—New London, Conn.—Catalogs. I. Title.

LYMAN Allyn Museum, New 708.1465
London, Conn.
Complete list of American and European drawings, paintings, and watercolors in the collection of the Lyman Allyn Museum. [New London, 1966] 71 p. 23 cm. [N594.A55 1966] 66-31424
1. Drawings — New London, Conn. — Catalogs. 2. Paintings — New London, Conn. — Catalogs. I. Title.

Drawings—New York (City)—Catalogs.

NEW York. Museum of 741.97471
Modern Art.
Drawings: recent acquisitions. [Introd. by William S. Lieberman. New York, 1967] 48 p. illus. 26 cm. [NC25.N43] 67-20270
1. Drawings—New York (City)—Catalogs. I. Lieberman, William Slattery, 1924- ed. II. Title.

PIERPONT Morgan Library, 741.9'4
New York.
Drawings. New York [1974] xxx, 103 p. 50 plates. 30 cm. (Its Major acquisitions, 1924-1974) [NC25.N4P536 1974] 73-92928 ISBN 0-87598-044-9 8.00 (pbk.)
1. Pierpont Morgan Library, New York. 2. Drawings—New York (City)—Catalogs. I. Title.

SLATKIN (Charles E.) 708'.147'1
Galleries, New York.
Selected drawings. New York [1968?] [5] p., 59 p. of illus. 28 cm. [NC25.N4S57 1968] 74-184378
1. Drawings—New York (City)—Catalogs.

Drawings—Oakland, Calif.—Catalogs.

MILLS College, 741.9'074'019466
Calif. Art Gallery.
Selections from the drawing and watercolor collection. Oakland, Calif., 1972. 111 p. illus. 29 cm. [NC25.O2M5] 72-180876
1. Drawings—Oakland, Calif.—Catalogs. 2. Water-colors—Oakland, Calif.—Catalogs. I. Title.

Drawings—Oberlin, Ohio—Catalogs.

OBERLIN College. 741.9'771'23
Dudley Peter Allen Memorial Art Museum.
Catalogue of drawings and watercolors in the Allen Memorial Art Museum, Oberlin

College / by Wolfgang Stechow. Oberlin, Ohio : Oberlin College, 1976. p. cm. Includes index. [NC25.O25O256] 76-23495 ISBN 0-521-20955-2 : 15.95
1. Oberlin College. Dudley Peter Allen Memorial Art Museum. 2. Drawings—Oberlin, Ohio—Catalogs. 3. Water-colors—Oberlin, Ohio—Catalogs. I. Stechow, Wolfgang, 1896-1974. II. Title.

Drawings—Oxford—Catalogs.

BYAM Shaw, James, 1903- 741.9'4'07402574
Drawings by old masters at Christ Church, Oxford / by James Byam Shaw. Oxford : Clarendon Press, 1976. 2 v. : ill. ; 31 cm. Contents.Contents.—v. 1. Catalogue. —v. 2. Plates. Includes bibliographical references and indexes. [NC27.G7O932] 76-375903 ISBN 0-19-817323-7 : 115.00
1. Oxford. University. Christ Church. 2. Drawings—Oxford—Catalogs. I. Title.
Dist. by Oxford University Press New York N.Y. BIP

Drawings—Private collections.

PICASSO, Pablo, 1881- 741.96
Picasso's private drawings; the artist's personal collection of his finest drawings, including 117 reproductions. With an introd. by Maurice Serullaz. New York, Simon and Schuster [1969] 141 p. (chiefly illus.) 25 cm. [NC33.P5] 74-87142 8.50
1. Drawings—Private collections. I. Serullaz, Maurice. II. Title. BIP

Drawings—Sacramento, Calif.—Catalogs.

CROCKER Art Gallery, Sacramento, Calif. 741.9'4
Classical narratives in master drawings. Selected from the collections of the E. B. Crocker Art Gallery. Edited by Seymour Howard. Davis [University of California] 1972. 64 p. illus. 29 cm. Catalog by art students at the University of California at Davis. Sponsored by the California Arts Commission, and others. Includes bibliographical references. [NC25.S2C66 1972] 73-622466
1. Drawings—Sacramento, Calif.—Catalogs. 2. Mythology, Classical, in art. I. Howard, Seymour, 1928- ed. II. California. University, Davis. III. California. Arts Commission. IV. Title.

CROCKER Art Gallery, Sacramento, Calif. 741.9'4'074019454
Master drawings from Sacramento. Sacramento [1971] viii, 169 p. illus. 28 cm. "European master drawings from the collection of Edwin Bryant Crocker (1818-1875) presented by his widow Margaret E. Crocker to the City of Sacramento in 1885, now part of the collections of the E. B. Crocker Art Gallery." [NC25.S2C7] 76-198111
1. Drawings—Sacramento, Calif.—Catalogs. I. Title.

Drawings, Shaker.

ANDREWS, Edward Deming, 1894-1964. 741.9'73
Visions of the heavenly sphere; a study in Shaker religious art [by] Edward Deming Andrews and Faith Andrews. Charlottesville, Published for the Henry Francis du Pont Winterthur Museum [by] the University Press of Virginia [1969] xiv, 138 p. illus. (part col.), port. 27 cm. Bibliography: p. [125]-132. [NC107.A68] 79-83652 15.00
1. Drawings, Shaker. 2. Shakers. I. Andrews, Faith, joint author. II. Henry Francis du Pont Winterthur Museum. III. Title. BIP

Drawings, Shaker—Exhibitions.

HANCOCK Shaker Village. 741.9'73
The gift of inspiration, religious art of the Shakers. Hancock, Mass. [1970] 12 p. illus. 24 cm. Catalog of an exhibition held June 27 to October 15, 1970. Introduction, by Eugene M. Dodd: [3] p. inserted. [NC105.H25] 73-30016
1. Drawings, Shaker—Exhibitions. I. Title.

Drawings, Spanish.

SANCHEZ Canton, Francisco Javier, 1891-1971 741.9'46
Spanish drawings from the 10th to the 19th century / text by F J Sanchez Canton Boston : Little, Brown, [1976] c1964. p. cm. Reprint of the ed. published by Shorewood Publishers, New York, issued in series: Drawings of the masters. Bibliography: p. [NC285.S28 1976] 76-1887 ISBN 0-316-12786-8 pbk. : 5.95
1. Drawings, Spanish. I. Title. II. Series: Drawings of the masters.

SANCHEZ CANTON, Francisco Javier, 1891- 741.946
Spanish drawings from the 10th to the 19th century. Text by F. J. Sanchez Canton. New York, Shorewood Publishers [1964] 141 p. illus. (part col.) ports. (part col.) 25 cm. (Drawings of the masters) Bibliography: p. 141. [NC1050.S752] 64-7857
1. Drawings, Spanish. I. Title. II. Series.

Drawings, Spanish—Exhibitions.

BROWN, Jonathan. 741.9'46
Murillo & his drawings / Jonathan Brown. Princeton, N.J. : Art Museum, Princeton University : distributed by Princeton University Press, c1976. 200 p. : ill. ; 23 x 27 cm. "Published in conjunction with an exhibition ... held at The Art Museum, December 12, 1976-January 30, 1977." Includes index. Bibliography: p. 193-196. [NC287.M87B76] 76-9395 ISBN 0-691-03916-X : 25.00

SMITH, Gridley McKim. 741.9'46'0973
Spanish baroque drawings in North American collections : [exhibition] October 19-November 24, 1974 / introd. and catalogue by Gridley McKim Smith. [Lawrence?] : University of Kansas Museum of Art, c1974. 68, [11] p., [23] leaves of plates : ill. ; 26 cm. (Miscellaneous publication of the Museum of Art ; no. 97) Bibliography: p. [1]-[9] (2d group) [NC285.S5] 74-17875
1. Drawings, Spanish—Exhibitions. 2. Drawing, Baroque—Spain—Exhibitions. 3. Drawings, Spanish—North America. I. Kansas. University. Museum of Art. II. Title. III. Series: Kansas. University. Museum of Art. Miscellaneous publications ; no. 97.

Drawings, Swiss—Exhibitions.

HUGELSHOFER, Walter, 1899- 741.9494
Swiss drawings; masterpieces of five centuries. Introd. and notes by Walter Hugelshofer. Organized by the Pro Helvetia Foundation. Washington, Smithsonian Institution Press, 1967. 176 p. illus. 26 cm. (Smithsonian publication, 4716) "Catalog of the Swiss drawings exhibition circulated by the Smithsonian Institution Traveling Exhibition Service to ... National Gallery of Art, Washington, D.C. ... [and others]" Bibliography: p. 173-175. [NC291.H8] 67-28923
1. Drawings, Swiss—Exhibitions. I. Pro Helvetia, Zurich. II. Smithsonian Institution. Traveling Exhibition Service. III. U. S. National Gallery of Art. IV. Title.

HUGELSHOFER, Walter, 1899- 741.9494
Swiss drawings; masterpieces of five centuries. Introd. and notes by Walter Hugelshofer. Organized by the Pro Helvetia Foundation. Washington, Smithsonian Institution Press, 1967. 176 p. illus. 26 cm. (Smithsonian publication, 4716) "Catalog of the Swiss drawings exhibition circulated by the Smithsonian Institution Traveling Exhibition Service to ... National Gallery of Art, Washington, D.C. ... [and others]" Bibliography: p. 173-175. [NC291.H8] 67-28923
1. Drawings, Swiss—Exhibitions. I. Pro Helvetia, Zurich. II. Smithsonian Institution. Traveling Exhibition Service. III. United States. National Gallery of Art. IV. Title.

Drawings, Tuscan—Exhibitions.

LOS Angeles Co., Calif. Museum of Art, Los Angeles. 741.9'45
Tuscan and Venetian drawings of the guattrocento from the collection of Janos Scholz. [Los Angeles, 1967] [20] p. illus. 31 cm. Catalog of the Janos Scholz Exhibition, presented for the Committee to Rescue Italian Art by Los Angeles County Museum of Art, July-Aug., 1967, and Seattle Art Museum, Aug.-Sept., 1967. Bibliography: p. [19] [NC256.T8L6] 67-27807
1. Drawings, Tuscan—Exhibitions. 2. Drawings, Venetian—Exhibitions. 3. Drawings—Private collections. I. Scholz, Janos. II. Committee to Rescue Italian Art. III. Seattle. Art Museum. IV. Title.

Drawings, Venetian—Catalogs.

TIETZE, Hans, 1880-1954. 741.9'45
The drawings of the Venetian painters in the 15th and 16th centuries, by Hans Tietze and Erica Tietze-Conrat. [New York] Collectors Editions [1970] 2 v. illus. 29 cm. Reprint of the 1944 ed. Contents.Contents.—[1] Text.—[2] Plates. Includes bibliographical references. [NC256.V4T5 1970] 71-101392
1. Drawings, Venetian—Catalogs. 2. Drawings, Renaissance—Venice. I. Tietze-Conrat, Erika, 1883-1958, joint author. II. Title. BIP

Drawings, Venetian- -Exhibitions.

HENRY Art Gallery. 741.9'45'31
Eighteenth century Venice: drawings from American academic collections, paintings from the Seattle Art Museum: a loan exhibition ogranized by the Henry Gallery, September 22-October 20 Seattle : University of Washington, 1974. 31 p. : ill. ; 31 cm. Includes bibliographies. [NC256.V4H46 1974] 74-19570
1. Drawings, Venetian—Exhibitions. 2. Drawing, Rococo—Venice—Exhibitions. 3. Paintings, Venetian—Exhibitions. 4. Painting, Rococo—Venice—Exhibitions. I. Seattle. Art Museum. II. Title.

MILLS College, Calif. Art Gallery. 741.9'45
Venetian drawings(1400-1630; [exhibition] Mills College Art Gallery, Oakland [and] H. M. [i. H.] DeYoung Museum, San Francisco. [Berkeley? Calif.] 1959. unpaged. illus. 23cm. Drawings from the collection of Janos Schoz.58 [NC256.V4M5] 59-2835
1. Drawings, Venetian— Exhibitions. 2. Drawings—Private collections. I. Schoiz, Janos. II. De Young Memorial Museum, San Francisco. III. Title.

MILLS College, Calif. Art Gallery. 741.945
Venetian drawings, 1600-1800; [exhibition] Mills College Art Gallery, Oakland [and] California Palace of the Legion of Honor, San Francisco. [Berkeley? Calif.] 1960. unpaged. illus. 25cm. 'Drawings from the collection of Janos Scholz.' [NC256.V4M52] 61-24250
1. Drawings, Venetian- -Exhibitions. 2. Drawings—Private collections. I. Scholz, Janos. II. California Palace of the Legion of Honor, San Francisco. III. Title.

PIGNATTI, Terisio, 1920- 741.9'45'31
Venetian drawings from American collections : a loan exhibition, organized and circulated by the International Exhibitions Foundation, 1974-1975 : introduction and catalogue / by Terisio Pignatti. [Washington] : International Exhibitions Foundation, [1974] xiii, 57 p., [70] leaves of plates : ill. ; 28 cm. Participating museums: National Gallery of Art, Kimbell Art Museum, and the St. Louis Art Museum. Bibliography: p. 3-4. [NC256.V4P52] 74-82717
1. Drawings, Venetian—Exhibitions. 2. Drawings, Venetian—United States. I. International Exhibitions Foundation. II. United States. National Gallery of Art. III. Kimbell Art Museum. IV. St. Louis Art Museum. V. Title. BIP

SMITHSONIAN Institution. Traveling Exhibition Service. 741.9'45
Eighteenth-century Venetian drawings from the Correr Museum, circulated by the Smithsonian Institution, 1963-1964: National Gallery of Art, Washington, D.C., the Museum of Fine Arts, Houston, Texas, Los Angeles County Museum of Art, Los Angeles, California, California Palace of the Legion of Honor, San Francisco, California. [Washington? 1963] 58 p. illus. 26 cm. (Smithsonian publication no. 4521) Bibliography: p. 23-26. [NC256.V4S6] 63-65416
1. Drawings, Venetian — Exhibitions. I. Venice, Museo civico Correr. II. Title.

Drawings—Williamstown, Mass.

HAVERKAMP, Begemann, Egbert 749.9
Drawings from the Clark Art Institute; a catalogue raisonne of the Robert Sterling Clark Collection of European and American Drawings, sixteenth through nineteenth centuries, at the Sterling and Francine Clark Art Institute, Williamstown; 2v. By Egbert Haverkamp-Begemann, Standish D. Lawder, Charles W. Talbot, Jr. New Haven, Conn., Yale [c.]1964. 2v. (various p.) illus. 31cm. Contents.v.1. The catalogue raisonne.--v.2. The plates. Bibl. [NC25.W5H3] 64-20922 37.50 set,
1. Drawings—Williamstown. Mass. I. Lawder, Standish D. II. Talbot, Charles W. III. Sterling and Francine Clark Art Institute. Williamstown, Mass. IV. Title.

STERLING and Francine Clark Art Institute, Williamstown, Mass. 741.9
Fifteen master drawings from the collection of the Sterling and Francine Clark Art Institute at Williamstown. Introd. by Egbert Haverkamp-Begemann. New Haven, Conn., Yale [c.]1965. 12p. 15 plates (pt. col.) 33cm. Issued in a case [NC25.S8] 65-15049 5.00, bxd.
1. Drawings—Williamstown, Mass. I. Title.

Drawn-work.

DRYSDALE, Rosemary. 746.4'4
Pulled work on canvas and linen / by Rosemary Drysdale. New York : Scribner, [1978] p. cm. Includes index. Bibliography: p. [TT785.D79] 78-17110 ISBN 0-684-14330-5 : 12.95
1. Drawn-work. I. Title. BIP

FANGEL, Esther. 746.4'4
Danish pulled thread embroidery=Sammentrakssyning : with English and Danish text / Esther Fangel, Ida Winckler & Agnete Wuldem Madsen. New York : Dover Publications, 1977. 100 p. : ill. ; 24 cm. (Dover needlework series) Part 1 first published in 1953 under title: Sammentrakssyning; pt. 2 first published in 1954 under title: Sammentrakssyning: nye monstre. First published in Danish and English in 1958 under title: Sammentrakssyning=Pulled thread work. [TT785.F3613 1977] 76-49327 ISBN 0-486-23474-6 pbk. : 3.00
1. Drawn-work. I. Winckler, Ida, joint author. II. Madsen, Agnete Wuldem, joint author. III. Title. IV. Title: Sammentrakssyning.

MCNEILL, Moyra. 746.4'4
Pulled thread embroidery. New York, Taplinger Pub. Co. [1972, c1971] 207 p. illus. 22 cm. First ed. published in 1971 under title: Pulled thread. Bibliography: p. 207. [TT785.M27 1972] 70-185624 ISBN 0-8008-6562-6 8.50
1. Drawn-work. I. Title.

MCNEILL, Moyra 746.44
Pulled thread embroidery. New York : Taplinger [1976c1971] 207p. : ill. ; 21 cm. Bibliography: p. 207. [TT785.M27] ISBN 0-8008-6562-6 : 9.95 ISBN 0-8008-6563-4 pbk. : 4.50
1. Drawn-work. I. Title.
L. C. card no. for original edition: 70-185624. BIP

Drawn-work—Patterns.

MELEN, Lisa, 1917- 746.4'4
Drawn threadwork [by] Lisa Melen. Edited by Lynette de Denne. [Translated from Swedish by Joan Bulman] New York, Van Nostrand Reinhold [1972] 96 p. illus. 23 cm. Translation of Naversom.

[TT785.M413] 70-156128 ISBN 0-442-05308-8
1. Drawn-work—Patterns. I. Title.

Drayton, John Grimke, 1815-1891.

LASHLEY, Dolores C. 712'.6'09757915
Legacy of beauty, by Dolores C. Lashley. Columbia, S.C., State Print. Co., 1969. 139 p. illus. (part col.), map (on lining papers) 23 cm. Bibliography: p. 133-139. [SB466.U7M34] 77-23633
1. Drayton, John Grimke, 1815-1891. 2. Magnolia Gardens, S.C. I. Title. BIP

Dresden, Gemalde- Galerie.

MENZ, Henner. 708.3
The Dresden Gallery. [Translated from the German by Daphne Woodward] New York, Abrams [1962] 320p. illus. (part col.) 22cm. [N2280.M413] 62-18732
1. Dresden, Gemalde- Galerie. 2. Paintings—Dresden. I. Title.

RUDLOFF-HILLE, Gertrud. 759.074
Dresden Gemaldegalerie. [Translated from the German by Kenneth Martin Leake] New York, T. Yoseloff [1961, 1960] 159 p. (ciefly illus. (part col.)) 28 cm. (Heritage of art series) From the collections of the Gemaldegalerie Alte Meister located in the Semper-Galerie. [N2280.R833] 61-19743
1. Dresden. Gemalde-Galerie. I. Dresden. Gemaldegalerie Alte Meister. II. Dresden. Semper-Galerie. III. Title.

Dresden. Historisches Museum.

DRESDEN. Historisches Museum. 739.7'074'0321
Fine arms and armor : treasures in the Dresden collection / by Johannes Schobel ; translated by M. O. A. Stanton ; photos. by Jurgen Karpinski ; pref. by Claude Blair. New York : Putnam, 1975. 255 p. : ill. (some col.) ; 31 cm. Translation of Prunkwaffen. Includes index. [NK6602.5.G35D73 1975] 73-94104 ISBN 0-399-11363-0 : 20.00
1. Dresden. Historisches Museum. 2. Arms and armor—Germany, West—Catalogs. I. Schobel, Johannes. II. Karpinski, Jurgen. III. Title.

Dresden. Staatliche Kunstsammlungen—Exhibitions.

THE Splendor of 707'.4'013
Dresden, five centuries of art collecting : an exhibition from the State Art Collections of Dresden, German Democratic Republic : the National Gallery of Art, Washington, June 1-September 4, 1978, the Metropolitan Museum of Art, New York, Oct. 21, 1978-January 13, 1979, the Fine Arts Museums of San Francisco, February 18-May 26, 1979. [New York] : Metropolitan Museum of Art, c1978. 279 p. : ill. (some col) ; 26 cm. Includes bibliographies. [N5020.W52N378] 78-6542 ISBN 0-87099-177-9 : 20.00
1. Dresden. Staatliche Kunstsammlungen—Exhibitions. 2. Art—Exhibitions. I. United States. National Gallery of Art. II. New York (City). Metropolitan Museum of Art. III. Fine Arts Museums of San Francisco.

Dress accessories.

HUMMEL, Edith M. 646.48
You can make your own bags and accessories. New York, Fairchild Publications [1952] 88 p. illus. 28 cm. [TT290.H7] 52-4170
1. Dress accessories. 2. Leather work. I. Title.

PELTZ, Leslie Ruth. 646'.02'4658
Fashion accessories. Indianapolis, H. W. Sams [1974] x, 166 p. illus. 28 cm. (Fashion merchandising series) Bibliography: p. 155-157. [TT560.P39] 74-10891 ISBN 0-672-26109-X
1. Dress accessories. I. Title. II. Series. BIP

SCOTT, Janie W. 646.48
Easy-to-make fashion accessories. Drawings by Barbara Carr. New York, Woman's Press and W. Morrow, 1953. 123 p. illus. 21 cm. [TT560.S4] 53-9167
1. Dress accessories. I. Title.

Dressmaking.

ALEXANIAN, Nvart Hampikian, 1899- 646.4'04
Couture by Nvart. [Southfield? Mich., 1971] 165 p. illus., 89 plates (part col.) 28 cm. Includes bibliographical references. [TT518.A47] 73-156748
1. Dressmaking. 2. Tailoring (Women's) I. Title.

BANE, Allyne 646.4
Creative clothing construction. 2d ed. New York, McGraw [c.1956, 1966] xiv, 329p. illus. 24cm. First pub. in 1956 under title: Creative sewing. [TT515.B33] 65-23818 7.50
1. Dressmaking. I. Title.

BANE, Allyne. 646.4
Creative clothing construction. 3d ed. New York, McGraw-Hill [1973] xiv, 529 p. illus. 24 cm. First published in 1956 under title: Creative sewing. [TT515.B33 1972] 70-38730 ISBN 0-07-003615-2 9.65
1. Dressmaking. I. Title.

BANE, Allyne. 646.4
Creative sewing; professional touches for the home dressmaker. New York, McGraw-Hill, 1956. 274 p. illus. 24 cm. [TT515.B33] 55-9535
1. Dressmaking. I. Title.

BISHOP, Edna Bryte 646.4
The Bishop method of clothing construction [by] Edna Brvte Bishop. Marjorie Stotler Arch. Sketches by Dorothy L. Davids. Photos. by Stewart Love. Rev. ed. Philadelphia. Lippincott [1966] 284p. illus. 28cm. [TT515.B55 1966] 66-5299 3.50: 2.10 pap., sch.ed.,
1. Dressmaking. 2. Tailoring (Women's): I. Arch. Marjorie Stotler. joint author. II. Title.

BRADLEY, Duane. 646.4'04
Practical and pretty fashions from simple shapes sewing / by Duane Bradley ; ill. by Eleanor Shull. Norwalk, Conn. : C. R. Gibson Co., [1975] 48 p. : ill. ; 22 cm. [TT515.B78] 74-76216 ISBN 0-8378-3003-6 : 2.00
1. Dressmaking. 2. Sewing. I. Title. II. Title: Simple shapes sewing.

CLARK, Winifred, 1906- 687
Dressmaking techniques for trade students [by] Winifred Clark. New York, Drake Publishers [1970] 120 p. illus. 22 cm. Bibliography: p. 7. An introduction to the tools, terminology, and techniques of dressmaking intended especially for those interested in a career in the clothing industry. [TT518.C55] 71-25481 ISBN 0-87749-036-8
1. Dressmaking. 2. Clothing trade. I. Title.

DOERR, Catherine M. 646.4'3
Smart sewing; the making of clothing [by] Catherine M. Doerr. New York, Macmillan [1967] xi, 228 p. illus. 28 cm. [TT515.D6] 66-23474
1. Dressmaking. 2. Sewing. I. Title.

DUNN, Lucille. 646.4'04
Steps in clothing skills [by] Lucille Dunn, Annetta Bailey [and] Wanda Vansickle. Peoria, Ill., C. A. Bennett Co. [1970] 528 p. illus. (part col.) 25 cm. [TT518.D85] 74-103387 ISBN 0-87002-000-5
1. Dressmaking. 2. Clothing and dress. 3. Beauty, Personal. I. Bailey, Annetta, joint author. II. Draper, Mary Wanda, joint author. III. Title. BIP

ERWIN, Mabel Deane. 646
Clothing for moderns. Rev. ed. New York, Macmillan [1957] 632p. illus. 22cm. Includes bibliography. [TT515.E7 1957] 57-5103
1. Dressmaking. 2. Clothing and dress. I. Title. BIP

ERWIN, Mabel Deane. 646
Clothing for moderns [by] Mabel D. Erwin [and] Lila A. Kinchen. 3d ed. New York, Macmillan [1964] v, 600 p. illus. 24 cm. Includes bibliographies. [TT515.E7] 64-10327
1. Dressmaking. 2. Clothing and dress. I. Kinchen, Lila A., joint author. II. Title.

ERWIN, Mabel Deane. 646
Clothing for moderns [by] Mabel D. Erwin [and] Lila A. Kinchen. 4th ed. [New York] Macmillan [1969] xii, 585 p. illus. 23 cm. Includes bibliographical references. [TT518.E7 1969] 69-10183
1. Dressmaking. 2. Clothing and dress. I. Kinchen, Lila A., joint author. II. Title.

ERWIN, Mabel Deane. 646.4'3'04
Clothing for moderns [by] Mabel D. Erwin [and] Lila A. Kinchen. 5th ed. New York, Macmillan [1974] x, 516 p. illus. 23 cm. Includes bibliographical references. [TT518.E7 1974] 72-12458 ISBN 0-02-334210-2 9.95
1. Dressmaking. 2. Clothing and dress. I. Kinchen, Lila A., joint author. II. Title.

ERWIN, Mabel Deane. 646.4'3'04
Clothing for moderns / Mabel D. Erwin, Lila A. Kinchen, Kathleen A. Peters. 6th ed. New York : Macmillan, c1979. p. cm. Includes bibliographical references and index. [TT518.E7 1979] 78-11350 ISBN 0-02-334220-X : 13.95
1. Dressmaking. 2. Clothing and dress. I. Kinchen, Lila A., joint author. II. Peters, Kathleen A., joint author. III. Title.

FIAROTTA, Phyllis. 646.4
Sewing without a pattern. New York, Sterling Pub. Co. [1971] 48 p. illus. 20 cm. (Little craft book series) [TT515.F48 1971] 71-151711 ISBN 0-8069-5162-1
1. Dressmaking. 2. Sewing. I. Title.

FIELDING, Jessie Lambert. 646.4
Elements of clothing construction, laboratory manual. Minneapolis, Burgess Pub. Co., '1952. 52 l. 28 cm. Includes bibliography. [TT508.F5] 52-9216
1. Dressmaking. I. Title. II. Title: Clothing construction.

GEHRET, Ellen J. 646.4'009748
Rural Pennsylvania clothing : being a study of the wearing apparel of the German and English inhabitants both men and women, who resided in southeastern Pennsylvania in the late eighteenth and early nineteenth century : also including sewing instructions and patterns which are profusely illustrated! / By Ellen J. Gehret ; Janet Gray Crosson, technical editor. York, Pa. : Liberty Cap Books, 1976. 309 p. : ill. ; 29 cm. Includes index. Bibliography: p. 292-302. [TT560.G36] 73-18534 ISBN 0-87387-064-6 : 25.00
1. Dressmaking. 2. Tailoring. 3. Costume—Pennsylvania—History. I. Title.
Publisher's address:R.D.7 York,Pennsylvania 17402. BIP

IOWA Home Economics Association. 646.404
Unit method of clothing construction. Illustrated by Harriet Allen. 4th ed. Ames, Iowa State University Press [1965] xi, 132 p. illus. 29 cm. Earlier editions published under title: Unit method of sewing. [TT508.I6 1965] 65-19383
1. Dressmaking. I. Title. BIP

IOWA Home Economics Association. 646.4'04
Unit method of clothing construction. Illustrated by Harriet Allen. 5th ed. Ames, Iowa State University Press [1972] vii, 130 p. illus. 29 cm. Published 1950-59 under title: Unit method of sewing. [TT518.I66 1972] 72-59 ISBN 0-8138-1710-2 4.25
1. Dressmaking. I. Title.

IOWA Home Economics Association. 646.4'04
Unit method of clothing construction / by the Iowa Home Economics Association ; [volume editors: Phyllis Brackelsberg, Bertha Shaw]. 6th ed. Ames, Iowa : Iowa State University Press, 1976. p. cm. Published 1950-1959 under title: Unit method of sewing. Includes index. [TT518.I66 1976] 76-26619 ISBN 0-8138-1710-2 : 5.95
1. Dressmaking. I. Brackelsberg, Phyllis, 1940- II. Shaw, Bertha, 1943- III. Title.

JOHNSON, Mary (Ritz) 1904- 646.4
Mary Johnson's guide to altering and restyling ready-made clothes. Illus. by Mary Johson rendered by Jeanette Foletar. [1st ed.] New York, Dutton, 1964. 251 p. illus. 25 cm. [TT550.J6] 64-11068
1. Dressmaking. I. Title. II. Title: Guide to altering and restyling ready-made clothes.

JOHNSON, Mary Ritz, 1904- 646.4'3'04
Sewing the easy way / Mary Johnson ; new ill. by Mary Johnson, rendered by Jeanette Foletar. New York : Barnes & Noble Books, 1974, c1966. 255 p. : diagrs. ; 21 cm. (A Barnes & Noble craft book ; EH 420) Reprint of the new, completely rev. and enl. ed. published by Dutton, New York. Includes index. [TT518.J6 1974] 75-308842 ISBN 0-06-463420-5 : 2.50
1. Dressmaking. 2. Sewing. I. Title. BIP

JONES, Helen S. 646.4
Hi-fashion sewing and tailoring [by] Helen S. Jones. Illus. by Nancy T. Bunce. [Salt Lake City, Utah, Lithographed by Publishers Press, 1970] 202 p. illus. 28 cm. [TT515.J58] 78-17125 5.95
1. Dressmaking. 2. Tailoring. I. Title.

KELLY, Sandra. 646.4'3'04
How to add designer touches to your wardrobe. New York, Sterling Pub. Co. [1972] 48 p. illus. 20 cm. (Little craft book series) Instructions for combining and changing clothes patterns and making fashionable accessories. [TT515.K4] 76-180458 2.95
1. Dressmaking. I. Title.
Library binding 2.69.

*KIDWELL, Claudia B. 687.105
Suiting everyone; the democratization of clothing in America, [by] Claudia B. Kidwell [and] Margaret C. Christman. Washington, Published for the National Museum of History and Technology by the Smithsonian Institution Press, 1974. 208 p. illus. 23 cm. [TT507] 11.05. (pbk.).
1. Dress making. 2. Costume design. I. Christman, Margaret C. joint author. II. Title.

KLEEBERG, Irene Cumming. 646.4'3'04
Fashion tops. New York, Drake [1973] 192 p. illus. (part col.) 27 cm. [TT515.K48] 72-10518 ISBN 0-87749-424-X 7.95
1. Dressmaking. I. Title.

LANE, Jean D. 646.4'3'04
Needlecraft construction techniques, by Jean D. Lane. Melbourne, Hall's Book Store [1967]- v. illus. 29 cm. [TT518.L35] 70-438086 unpriced (v. 2)
1. Dressmaking. 2. Needlework. I. Title.

LEWIS, Virginia Stolpe. 646.4
Comparative clothing construction techniques / Virginia Stolpe Lewis. Minneapolis : Burgess Pub. Co., c1976. xiv, 393 p., [12] leaves of plates : ill. ; 27 cm. Includes index. [TT518.L46] 75-43123 ISBN 0-8087-1230-6 : 15.95
1. Dressmaking. 2. Tailoring (Women's) 3. Tailoring. I. Title. BIP

LILLOW, Ira. 646.4304
Making a dress. New York, Hearthside Press [1965] 96 p. illus. 22 cm. [TT515] 65-28971
1. Dressmaking. I. Title. BIP

MACTAGGART, Ann. 646.4'04
Complete book of dressmaking / Ann Mactaggart. New York : Van Nostrand Reinhold Co., 1975. 168 p. : ill. ; 26 cm. Includes index. [TT515.M243] 75-3784 4.95
1. Dressmaking. I. Title. BIP

MANSFIELD, Evelyn A 1908- 646.4
Clothing construction. Boston, Houghton Mifflin [1953] 454p. illus. 25cm. [TT515.M26] [TT515.M26] 646.34 53-10408 53-10408
1. Dressmaking. I. Title. BIP

MANSFIELD, Evelyn A., 1908- 646.4'3'04
Clothing construction [by] Evelyn A. Mansfield [and] Ethel L. Lucas. 2d ed. Boston, Houghton Mifflin [1974] viii, 403 p. illus. 25 cm. [TT518.M36 1974] 73-8446 ISBN 0-395-16728-0 11.50
1. Dressmaking. I. Lucas, Ethel L., joint author. II. Title.

MAUCK, Frances Felice. 646.4
Modern sewing techniques. Edited by Dorothy L. Stepat. Illustrated by Beverly Silverman. New York, Macmillan [1963] 307 p. illus. 25 cm. [TT515.M29] 62-8913
1. Dressmaking. 2. Sewing. I. Title. BIP

NEW York (State) 687.1
University. Bureau of Vocational Curriculum Development and Industrial Teacher Training.
Operation series for course of instruction in garment making. Rochester, Paul Revere Trade School [1951- v. illus. 27 cm. [TT518.N45] 52-62294
1. Dressmaking. I. Title.

ROBINSON, Renee. 646.4
Streamlined dressmaking, by Renee & Julian Robinson. With an introd. by Ailsa Garland. New York, Crown Publishers [1967, c1966] 128 p. illus. 22 cm. [TT515.R784 1967] 67-17083
1. Dressmaking. I. Robinson, Julian, joint author. II. Title.

ROXANE. 646.4'04
The secret of couture sewing. [1st ed.] New York, McGraw-Hill [1972] x, 129 p. illus. 29 cm. [TT515.R832] 70-39045 ISBN 0-07-054163-9 7.95
1. Dressmaking. I. Title.

TIME-LIFE Books. 646.4'04
Boutique attire / by the editors of Time-Life Books. New York : Time-Life Books, c1975. 184 p. : ill. (some col.) ; 29 cm. (The Art of sewing) Includes index. [TT515.T55 1975a] 75-7826 6.95
1. Dressmaking. 2. Textile crafts. I. Title.
BIP

TIME-LIFE Books. 646.4'04
Delicate wear / by the editors of Time-Life Books. New York : Time-Life Books, [1975] 192 p. : col. ill. ; 29 cm. (The Art of Sewing) Includes index. [TT515.T55 1975] 74-21557 6.95
1. Dressmaking. 2. Sewing. 3. Needlework. I. Title. BIP

TIME-LIFE Books. 646.4'3'4
Exotic styling / by the editors of Time-Life Books. New York : Time-Life Books, [1974] 192 p. : col. ill. ; 29 cm. (The Art of sewing) Includes index. [TT560.T55 1974] 74-83437 8.95
1. Dressmaking. 2. Sewing. I. Title. BIP

TORBET, Laura. 646.4
Clothing liberation; out of the closets and into the streets. Illustrated by the author. New York, Praeger [1973] vi, 73 p. illus. 29 cm. [TT550.T67] 72-12294 5.95
1. Dressmaking. 2. Dress accessories. I. Title.

•VERCOLLONE, Flora M. 646'.4
The Flora form. Photographs by roland T. Sharrillo. [Winchester, Mass., Fauna Pr., 1973] 56 p. illus. 28 cm. [TT515] 3.95 (pbk.)
1. Dressmaking. 2. Patterns—Alteration. 3. Sewing. I. Title.
Publisher's address: 17A Ginn Rd., Winchester, Mass.

WARCH, Constance 646.4'3'04
Joyce.
Illustrated guide to sewing / by Constance Joyce Warch. Fullerton, Calif. : Plycon Press, c1975. 512 p. in various pagings : ill. ; 30 cm. Includes bibliography and index. [TT518.W28] 75-20973 pbk. : 13.95
1. Dressmaking. 2. Tailoring (Women's) 3. Tailoring. I. Title.

WARDEN, Jessie Aubrey, 646.4'04
1918-
Principles for creating clothing [by] Jessie A. Warden, Martha A. Golding [and] Judy Varyan Stam. New York, Wiley [1969] xiii, 273 p. illus. 22 cm. [TT518.W3] 69-13668
1. Dressmaking. I. Golding, Martha A., joint author. II. Stam, Judy Varyan, joint author. III. Title.

WELLS, Helen Taylor. 646.4'3
Helen Taylor Wells' Clothing construction book / illustrated by Judith Hoffman Corwin. New York : McKay, c1978. p. cm. Includes index. [TT518.W44] 78-16831 ISBN 0-679-20357-5 : 12.50
1. Dressmaking. 2. Tailoring. 3. Tailoring (Women's) I. Title. II. Title: Clothing construction book.

WILSON, Violet I 646
Sew a fine seam. Illus. by Margaret Messer. 2d ed. New York, McGraw-Hill [1964] xiv, 351 p. illus. (part col.) 24 cm.. Bibliography: p. 338-339. [TT518.W5 1964] 64-15872
1. Dressmaking. 2. Sewing. I. Title.

Dressmaking—Dictionaries.

LADBURY, Ann. 646.4'003
Ann Ladbury's book of dressmaking. [1st American ed.] South Brunswick, A. S. Barnes [1971] 127 p. illus. 25 cm. [TT503.L33 1971] 70-151124 ISBN 0-498-07920-1 6.95
1. Dressmaking—Dictionaries. I. Title. II. Title: Book of dressmaking.

Dressmaking—History.

ARNOLD, Janet 391.2
Patterns of fashion; Englishwomen's dresses & their construction, written, illus. by Janet Arnold. London, Wace. Washington, D. C., Hobby House Pr., 1966 v. illus. 27 x 37cm. Bibl. [v.2] c. 1860-1940. [TT504.A7] 65-80824 8.95 pap.,
1. Dressmaking—Hist. 2. Costume—Gt. Brit. I. Title.
Ditributor's address: 461 Ben Franklin Sta., Washington, D.C. 20044. BIP

ARNOLD, Janet. 646.4'3'040942
Patterns of fashion; Englishwomen's dresses & their construction. Written and illustrated by Janet Arnold. New York, Drama Book Specialists, 1972. 2 v. illus. 27 x 37 cm. Contents.Contents.—1. c. 1660-1860.—2. c. 1860-1940. Includes bibliographies. [TT504.A7 1972] 76-189820 20.00 (pbk)
1. Dressmaking—History. 2. Costume—Great Britain. I. Title.
Two Volumes 10.00 each, ISBN 0-910482-50-0

WAUGH, Norah. 391'.2'09
The cut of women's clothes, 1600-1930. With line diagrs. by Margaret Woodward. New York, Theatre Arts Books [1968] 336 p. illus., ports. (1 col.) 29 cm. Bibliography: p. 320-322. [TT504.W385 1968] 68-13408 21.00
1. Dressmaking—History. 2. Tailoring (Women's)—History. I. Woodward, Margaret. II. Title. BIP

Dressmaking—Pattern books.

KIMATA, Kikuyo. 646.4
Simplified drafting book for dressmaking. 1953 rev. ed. [Honolulu? 1953] 130, 20p. (chiefly illus.) 31cm. [TT520.K48 1953] 53-32796
1. Dressmaking—Pattern books. I. Title.

PERFECT fit; 646.4
the new method of grain-scored pattern alteration, by Bonnie Early [and others] New York, Greenberg [1953] 65p. illus. 27cm. [TT520.E3] [TT520.E3] 646.34 52-13112 52-13112
1. Dressmaking—Pattern books. I. Early, Bonnie.

PICKEN, Mary (Brooks) 1886- 646.4
Album of prize patterns. Greenwich, Conn., Fawcett Publications, c1955. 143p. illus. 24cm. (A Fawcett how-to book, 295) [TT520.P65] 56-1953
1. Dressmaking—Pattern books. I. Title.

Dressmaking—Pattern design.

ALDRICH, Winifred. 646.4'3'04
Metric pattern cutting / Winifred Aldrich. London : Mills and Boon, 1977 143 p. : ill. ; 26 cm. Label mounted on t.p.: Transatlantic Arts, Inc., Levittown, New York, sole distributor for the U.S.A. [TT520.A43] 77-372077 ISBN 0-263-06119-1 : 10.00
1. Dressmaking—Pattern design. I. Title.
BIP

BANE, Allyne. 646.4'04
Flat pattern design. New York, McGraw-Hill [1971, c1972] ix, 262 p. illus. 28 cm. [TT520.B23] 79-149709 ISBN 0-07-003603-9
1. Dressmaking—Pattern design. I. Title.
BIP

COLICCHIO, Antoinette J 646.4
Patternmaking and design. Prepared by Antoinette J. Colicchio. New Brunswick, N. J., Vocational-Technical Curriculum Laboratory, Rutgers, the State University, 1967. iv, 273 [1], 30, p. illus. 28 cm. Bibliography: p. [274] [TT520.C69] 67-65060
1. Dressmaking—Pattern design. I. Vocational-Technical Curriculum Laboratory. II. Title.

DE SANTIS, Lorna. 646.4
Basic pattern drafting for fashion design. Northbrook, Ill., Whitehall Co. [1970] viii, 90 p. illus. 24 cm. [TT520.D44] 70-101512
1. Dressmaking—Pattern design. I. Title.

ERWIN, Mabel Deane. 646.43
Practical dress design; principles of fitting and pattern making. Rev. ed. New York, Macmillan [1954] 178p. illus. 29cm. [TT520.E7 1954] 54-2864
1. Dressmaking—Pattern design. I. Title.

HANDFORD, Jack. 687'.12
Professional patternmaking for designers of women's wear. [1st ed.] Los Angeles, Handford Enterprises [1974] xi, 404 p. illus. 28 cm. [TT520.H225] 74-78635 ISBN 0-914658-01-8 12.50
1. Dressmaking—Pattern design. I. Title.
Publisher's address: 447 South St. Andrews Pl. Los Angeles, Ca. 90020. BIP

HEARN, Esther K. 646.4
Fitting your figure; the home dressmaker's guide to perfect measurement, by Esther K. Hearn. [1st ed.] Old Greenwich, Conn., Gross, Hinshaw & Lindberg [1967] ix, 113 p. illus. 29 cm. [TT520.H44] 67-25833
1. Dressmaking—Pattern design. I. Title.

HOLLEN, Norma R. 646.43
Flat pattern methods. 2d ed. Minneapolis, Burgess [c.1961, 1965] v, 167p. illus. (10 in pocket) 28cm. First ed. pub. in 1961 under title: Flat pattern methods with selected sewing suggestions [TT520.H64] 65-25041 4.00 pap., wire bdg.
1. Dressmaking—Pattern design. 2. Sewing. I. Title.

HOLLEN, Norma R 646.43
Flat pattern methods with selected sewing suggestions. Drawings by Harriet Allen. Photography by Lou Facto. [Minneapolis, Burgess Pub. Co., 1961] 151p. illus. 28cm. [TT520.H64] 61-806
1. Dressmaking—Pattern design. 2. Sewing. I. Title.

HOLLEN, Norma R. 646.4'3'04
Pattern making by the flat-pattern method / by Norma R. Hollen. 4th ed. Minneapolis, Minn. : Burgess Pub. Co., c1975. ix, 219 p. : ill. ; 29 cm. First ed. published in 1961 under title: Flat pattern methods with selected sewing suggestions. Second ed. published in 1965 under title: Flat pattern methods. [TT520.H64 1975] 75-13663 ISBN 0-8087-0856-2 : 5.95
1. Dressmaking—Pattern design. I. Title.

HOLLEN, Norma R. 646.4'3'04
Pattern making by the flat-pattern method, by Norma R. Hollen. 3d ed. Minneapolis, Burgess Pub. Co. [1972] ix, 206 p. illus. 29 cm. Part of illustrative matter in pocket. First published in 1961 under title: Flat pattern methods with selected sewing suggestions. Second ed. published in 1965 under title: Flat pattern methods. [TT520.H64 1972] 76-182077 ISBN 0-8087-0824-4
1. Dressmaking—Pattern design. I. Title.
BIP

KLIPFEL, Eve M 646.43
The art and science of pattern making. Buffalo, University Bookstore, 1956. 100p. illus. 28cm. [TT520.K7] 57-216
1. Dressmaking—Pattern design. I. Title.

KOPP, Ernestine. 687.1
Designing apparel through the flat pattern, by Ernestine Kopp, Vittorina Rolfo [and] Beatrice Zelin. Art production by Lee Gross. New York, Fairchild Publications [1960] 325p. illus. 28cm. (FIT-Fairchild series) [TT520.K76] 60-15680
1. Dressmaking—Pattern design. I. Title.
BIP

KOPP, Ernestine. 646.4
Designing apparel through the flat pattern, by Ernestine Kopp, Vittorina Rolfo [and] Beatric Zelin. Art production by Lee Gross. [2d ed.] New York, Book Division, Fairchild Publications [1962] 356p. illus. 29cm. (FIT: Fairchild series) [TT520.K76 1962] 62-52431
1. Dressmaking—Pattern design. I. Title.

KOPP. ERNESTINE 687.102
Designing apparel through the flat pattern. by Ernestine Kopp. Vittorino Rolfo. Beatrice Zelin. Art prod. by Lee Gross. [3d ed.] New York Bk. Div., Fairchild Pubns. [1966] viii. 355p. illus. 29cm. (Textbk of the FIT-Fairchild ser.) [TT520.K76 1966] 66-21441 10.00. bdg., plastic bdg.
1. Dressmaking—Pattern design. I. Rolfo. Vittorino. joint author. II. Zelin, Beatrice, Joint author. III. Title.

KOPP, Ernestine. 687'.101
How to draft basic patterns, by Ernestine Kopp, Vittorina Rolfo [and] Beatrice Zelin. Art production by Lee Gross. New York, Book Division, Fairchild Publications [1968] 83 p. illus. 28 cm. (Textbook of the FIT—Fairchild series) Includes "Designers neckline curve" (in pocket) [TT520.K765] 68-27530
1. Dressmaking—Pattern design. I. Rolfo, Vittorina, joint author. II. Zelin, Beatrice, joint author. III. Title.
BIP

KOPP, Ernestine. 687'.12
New fashion areas for designing apparel through the flat pattern, by Ernestine Kopp, Vittorina Rolfo [and] Beatrice Zelin. Art production by Lee Gross. [New York, Fairchild Publications, 1972] xvii, 247 p. illus. 29 cm. (Textbook of the FIT-Fairchild series) Sequel to Designing apparel through the flat pattern. [TT520.K767] 72-82160 ISBN 0-87005-111-3
1. Dressmaking—Pattern design. I. Rolfo, Vittorina, joint author. II. Zelin, Beatrice, joint author. III. Title. BIP

LITTMAN, Connie. 646.4'3'04
Basic pattern making : an individualized approach / Connie Littman. Albany : Delmar Publishers, c1977. 210 p. : ill. ; 26 cm. & instructor's guide. Includes index. [TT520.L768] 76-14097 ISBN 0-8273-0581-8 : 6.00
1. Dressmaking—Pattern design. 2. Tailoring—Pattern design. I. Title. BIP

LITTMAN, Connie. 646.4
Pattern making design / Connie Littman. Albany, N.Y. : Delmar Publishers, c1977- v. : ill. ; 27 cm. Contents.Contents.—[1] Skirts & pants.—[2] Sleeveless dresses.—[3] Sleeved & tailored garments. [TT520.L77] 76-14096 ISBN 0-8273-0583-4 (vol. 1) pbk. : 4.00
1. Dressmaking—Pattern design. 2. Tailoring—Pattern design. I. Title. BIP

MARGOLIS, Adele P 646.4
Pattern wise; how to make and use a basic pattern. [1st ed.] Garden City, N. Y., Doubleday [1961] 147p. illus. 19cm. (A Dolphin handbook original, C203) [TT520.M32] 61-7659
1. Dressmaking—Pattern design. I. Title.

MINOTT, Jan. 646.4'04
Coordinated pattern fit; a manual of instruction for making personal basic patterns, introducing a new method of commercial pattern adjustment. Illustrated by Kathy Pelta. Special effects by Elizabeth Kosa. Minneapolis, Burgess Pub. Co. [1970, c1969] vii, 171 p. illus. 28 cm. Bibliography: p. 168. [TT520.M653] 78-82112 ISBN 0-8087-1340-X 4.25
1. Dressmaking—Pattern design. I. Title.
BIP

MINOTT, Jan. 646.4'3
Fitting commercial patterns : the Minott method / Jan Minott. Minneapolis : Burgess Pub. Co., c1978. xi, 260 p. : ill. ; 28 cm. Includes index. [TT520.M654] 77-87335 pbk. : 10.95
1. Dressmaking—Pattern design. 2. Tailoring—Pattern design. I. Title. BIP

MOORE, Dorothy. 646.4'04
Pattern drafting and dressmaking. New York, Golden Press [1971] 191 p. illus. (part col.) 29 cm. Paper triangle and curve stick inserted. "Originally published as The oriental method of pattern drafting and dressmaking." [TT520.M76 1971] 72-163110 9.95

1. Dressmaking—Pattern design. I. Title. BIP

MORI, Maria. 646.4'3'04
Basic pattern cutting. New York, Taplinger Pub. Co. [1970] 160 p. illus. 26 cm. [TT520.M78 1970] 76-127025 ISBN 0-8008-0670-0 6.95
1. Dressmaking—Pattern design. I. Title. BIP

NORDQUIST, Barbara. 646.4'04
The complete guide to pattern-making, by Barbara K. Nordquist. New York, Drake Publishers [1974, c1973] 279 p. illus. 26 cm. [TT520.N66] 73-18041 ISBN 0-87749-595-5 14.95
1. Dressmaking—Pattern design. 2. Children's clothing—Pattern design. I. Title.

NORDQUIST, Barbara. 646.4'04
Creative West African fashion. Clothing: Barbara Nordquist. Fabrics: Jean Mettam. Interpretations: Peggy Hoyle. [Washington, 1972] 90 l. illus. 28 cm. [TT520.N67] 72-79902
1. Dressmaking—Pattern design. 2. Costume—Africa, West. I. Mettam, Jean, joint author. II. Hoyle, Peggy, joint author. III. Title. BIP

OBLANDER, Ruth. 646.4'3
The Sew/Fit manual : a guide to making patterns fit by pivoting and sliding / authors, Ruth Oblander, Doris Ekern, Nancy Luedtke Zieman ; artist, Janet Asbury ; photographer, J. J. Snook. La Grange, IL : Sew/Fit Co., c1978. 479 p. in various pagings : ill. ; 28 cm. [TT520.O24] 77-84538 26.00 pbk. : 21.50
1. Dressmaking—Pattern design. I. Ekern, Doris, joint author. II. Zieman, Nancy Luedtke, joint author. III. Title.
Publisher's address: 905 Hillgrove, Suite 6, La Grange, IL 60525 BIP

†OLD, Leila Sturgis. 646.4'3
Personalized apparel design : drafting and designing for the individual female figure / Leila Sturgis Old, Agnes Vimlati Csizinsky ; graphics by Kathleen Erin Old. Moscow : University Press of Idaho, c1977. xi, 392 p. : ill. ; 28 cm. Includes bibliographical references and index. [TT520.O45] 76-56466 ISBN 0-89301-040-5 pbk. : 11.50
1. Dressmaking—Pattern design. I. Csizinsky, Agnes Vimlati, joint author. II. Title. BIP

PRICE, Jeanne. 687'.102
Grading techniques for modern design, by Jeanne Price and Bernard Zamkoff. New York, Fairchild Publications [1974] ix, 132 p. illus. 31 cm. Errata slip inserted. [TT520.P93] 74-165121 ISBN 0-87005-102-4 12.50
1. Dressmaking—Pattern design. I. Zamkoff, Bernard, joint author. II. Title. BIP

ROHR, Mayer. 687'.12
Grading women's and misses' garment design, including junior, petite, and teens; supplement to Pattern drafting and grading, by M. Rohr. Waterford, Conn., Rohr Pub. Co., [1970] 32 p. illus. 28 cm. [TT520.R64] 70-91986
1. Dressmaking—Pattern design. I. Rohr, Mayer. Pattern drafting & grading. II. Title.

SONNELAND, Yvonne E 646.4
Let's alter your pattern; workbook for teaching the theory of pattern alteration. Minneapolis, Burgess Pub. Co. [1959] 104 p. illus 28 cm. [TT520.S73] 59-9207
1. Dressmaking — Pattern design. I. Title.

STEINHART, Joseph, 1904- 687.12
Pattern drafting and pattern grading; based on TS-5200A, the recommended commercial standard on body measurements for sizing of women's patterns and apparel. N[ew] Y[ork, 1955] 212p. illus. 29cm. [TT520.S8] 55-29771
1. Dressmaking—Pattern design. I. Title.

TANOUS, Helen Nicol, 1917- 646.4
Designing dress patterns. Peoria, Ill., C. A. Bennettt Co. [c1964] 208 p. illus. 28 cm. First published in 1951 under title: Designing your own dress patterns. [TT520.T16] 64-18146
1. Dressmaking—Pattern design. I. Title. BIP

TANOUS, Helen Nicol, 646.4'04
1917-
Designing dress patterns. 3d ed. Peoria, Ill., C. A. Bennett Co. [1971] 208 p. illus. 28 cm. First published in 1951 under title: Designing your own dress patterns. [TT520.T16 1971] 78-29297 ISBN 0-87002-112-5
1. Dressmaking—Pattern design. I. Title.

Dressmaking—Patterns.

FUKUMOTO, Sue S, 1904- 646.4
Scientific pattern drafting, as taught at Style Center School of Costume Design, Dressmaking and Millinery. [Honolulu? 1951] 201 p. illus. 29 cm. --Supplement. no. 1- [Honolulu? '1951- v. illus. 28 cm. [TT520.F9] 51-37500
1. Dressmaking—Patterns. I. Title.

KIRSCHNER, Jack. 646.4
Advanced pattern grading: wholesale, stack, mass, Chinatown. [New York] Fairchild Publications [1951] 210 p. illus. 29 cm. [TT520.K587] 51-8570
1. Dressmaking—Patterns. I. Title.

MAYER, Herbert, 1913- 646.4
Applied pattern designing, illustrated; based on the patternmaking methods of Abram Mayer. Developed and written by Herbert Mayer; technical assistance in compiling the text by Allyne Bane. Illustrated by Eleanor Harrington and Eve Stockhold. [New York] Mayer Pub. Co., c1950. vii, 192 p. (chiefly illus.) 29 cm. [TT520.M4] 51-2451
1. Dressmaking—Patterns. I. Title.

RUSSELL, Elizabeth. 646.4'7
Adaptable stage costume for women : a hundred-in-one costumes designed by Elizabeth Russell. New York : Theatre Arts Books, 1974 [i.e. 1975] viii, 95 p., [1] fold leaf of plates : ill. ; 26 cm. [TT560.R87 1975] 73-75920 ISBN 0-87830-007-4 : 10.75
1. Dressmaking—Patterns. 2. Costume. I. Title. BIP

Dressmaking—Programmed instruction.

REICH, Naomi A., 1926- 646.4'07'7
Essentials of clothing construction : the self-instructional programmed approach / Naomi A. Reich, Mark L. Berman, Joan Hresko-Evans. 2d ed. Englewood Cliffs, N.J. : Prentice-Hall, c1978. x, 163 p. : ill. ; 24 cm. [TT518.R42 1978] 78-1075 ISBN 0-13-284398-6 pbk. : 6.95
1. Dressmaking—Programmed instruction. 2. Tailoring—Programmed instruction. I. Berman, Mark L., joint author. II. Hresko-Evans, Joan, 1944- joint author. III. Title. BIP

Dressmaking—Study and teaching.

IOWA Home Economics Association. 646.4
Unit method of sewing. Illus. by Harriet Allen. Ames, Iowa State College Press [1950] 102 p. illus. 28 cm. [TT508.I 6] 50-3051
1. Dressmaking—Study and teaching. I. Title.

IOWA Home Economics Association. 646.4
Unit method of sewing. Illustrated by Harriet Allen. 2d ed. Ames, Iowa State College Press [1955] 112p. illus. 29cm. [TT508.I6 1955] 54-7655
1. Dressmaking— study and teaching. I. Title.

IOWA Home Economics Association. 646.4
Unit method of sewing. Illustrated by Harriet Allen. 3d ed. Ames, Iowa State University Press [1959] 143p. illus. 29cm. [TT508.I6 1959] 59-11783
1. Dressmaking —Study and teaching. I. Title.

Dressmaking—Study and teaching—Audio-visual aids.

VOGUE-BUTTERICK Pattern Service. Education Dept. 646.4'04'078
See and sew. [New York, 1969- Cases illus. (part col.) 33 x 28 cm. Contents.Contents.—v. 1. Inner construction. Couture closures. [TT508.V64] 75-12147
1. Dressmaking—Study and teaching—Audio-visual aids. I. Title.

Drexel, Francis Martin, 1792-1863.

FRANCIS Martin Drexel, 1792-1863 : an artist turned banker : [exhibition] the Drexel Museum Collection, Drexel University, Philadelphia, Pennsylvania, January 1976-December 1976. [Philadelphia : Drexel University, c1975] 40 p. : ill. (some col.) ; 26 cm. Bibliography: p. 39-40. [ND1329.D72F72] 76-358970 759.13
1. Drexel, Francis Martin, 1792-1863. I. Drexel Museum Collection.

Dried flower arrangement.

CLARK, Janet, 1936- 745.92
Botanical art / by Janet Clark, Mary Alice Collins and Gary Collins. Minneapolis, Minn. : Burgess Pub. Co., c1975. 61 p. : ill. ; 23 cm. On cover: The naturalist. [SB449.3.D7C57] 75-8462 ISBN 0-8087-0354-4 pbk. : 2.95
1. Dried flower arrangement. 2. Pressed flower pictures. 3. Plants—Drying. 4. Nature craft. I. Collins, Mary Alice, joint author. II. Collins, Gary, joint author. III. Title. IV. Title: The naturalist.

FLOYD, Harriet. 745.92
Plant it now, dry it later. [1st ed.] New York, McGraw-Hill [1973] viii, 231 p. illus. (part col.) 25 cm. Bibliography: p. [221]-222. [SB449.3.D7F5] 73-4260 ISBN 0-07-021387-9 12.95
1. Dried flower arrangement. 2. Flowers—Drying. 3. Flower gardening. 4. Flowers. I. Title.

KLAMKIN, Marian. 745.92'2
Flower arrangements that last; how to buy, dry, and arrange permanent flowers. New York, Macmillan Co. [1967, c1968] x, 182 p. illus. 21 cm. Bibliography: p. [175] [SB449.3.D7K55 1968] 68-10815
1. Dried flower arrangement. 2. Flowers—Drying. I. Title.

METZLER, Rejean. 745.92
Forever flowers. New York, Scribner [1972] 157 p. illus. (part col.) 27 cm. [SB449.3.D7M47] 72-37215 ISBN 0-684-12755-5 10.95
1. Dried flower arrangement. 2. Handicraft. I. Title.

MILLARD, Nancy. 745.92
Dried flower arrangements from garden, bush and seashore. Photography by Gilbert Millard. [6th ed.] Sydney, Murray [1973] 128 p. illus. (part col.) 25 cm. Stamped on t.p.: Distributed by Sportshelf, New Rochelle, N.Y. [SB449.3.D7M54 1973] 74-155436 ISBN 0-85566-138-0 11.25
1. Dried flower arrangement. 2. Flowers—Drying. I. Title.

MOFFITT, Roberta. 745.92
The step-by-step book of dried bouquets / by Roberta Moffitt. [Columbus, Ohio : Moffitt], c1975. 96 p. : ill. (some col.) ; 23 cm. [SB449.3.D7M63] 75-20781 7.95
1. Dried flower arrangement. I. Title.

ROHRER, Edwin. 745.92'2
Dried flower arrangement. New York, Van Nostrand Reinhold Co. [1973] 88 p. illus. 21 x 29 cm. Translation of Mit getrockneten Blumen gestalten. [SB449.3.D7R6613] 72-5962 ISBN 0-442-29965-6 5.95
1. Dried flower arrangement.

STEVENSON, Violet W. 745.92
Dried flowers for decoration, by Violet Stevenson. New York, Drake Publishers [1972] p. [SB449.3.D7S83 1972] 72-1288 ISBN 0-87749-241-7
1. Dried flower arrangement. I. Title.

THOMPSON, Dorothea Schnibben. 745.92
The new creative decorations with dried flowers. Drawings by Marion Seiler. Photos. by William Brinkhaus except where noted. Great Neck, [N.Y.] Hearthside Press [1972] 156 p. illus. (part col.) 24 cm. First published in 1965 under title: Creative decorations with dried flowers. [SB449.3.D7T47 1972] 73-185807 7.95
1. Dried flower arrangement. 2. Handicraft. 3. Flowers—Collection and preservation. I. Title.

VANCE, Georgia S. 745.92'24
The decorative art of dried flower arrangement [by] Georgia S. Vance. [1st ed.] Garden City, N.Y., Doubleday, 1972. xiv, 194 p. illus. 27 cm. [SB449.3.D7V33] 79-162025 9.95
1. Dried flower arrangement. 2. Flowers—Drying. 3. Flower arrangement—History. I. Title. BIP

WESTLAND, Pamela. 745.92
The art of dried and pressed flowers / Pamela Westland and Paula Critchley. New York : Crown, [1974] 128 p. : ill. (some col.) ; 27 cm. Includes index. [SB449.3.D7W47 1974] 74-80290 ISBN 0-517-51659-4 : 9.95
1. Dried flower arrangement. 2. Pressed flower pictures. 3. Flowers—Drying. I. Critchley, Paula, joint author. II. Title.

Driftwood arrangement.

ISHIMOTO, Tatsuo. 745.92'6
A treasury of driftwood, and dried arrangements. New York, Crown Publishers [1962] 124p. illus. 24cm. [SB449.3.D8 I 8] 62-20041
1. Driftwood arrangement. I. Title.

SCHAFFER, Florence M. 745.92'5
ABC of driftwood and dried-flower designs, by Florence M. Schaffer. Photography by Mel Manley. Great Neck, N.Y. [Hearthside Press, 1971] 160 p. illus. 24 cm. First published in 1957 under title: ABC of driftwood for flower arrangers. [SB449.3.D8S29 1971] 74-151456 5.95
1. Driftwood arrangement. I. Title.

SCHAFFER, Florence M 635.9663
Driftwood in the home. Photography by Mel Manley. New York, Hearthside Press [1960] 128p. illus. 25cm. [SB449.3.D8S3] 60-12958
1. Driftwood arrangement. I. Title.

SCHAFFER, Florence M. 745.92'5
Driftwood miniatures, including plants, rocks and shells [by] Florence M. Schaffer. New York, Hearthside Press [1967] 128 p. illus. 25 cm. [SB449.3.D8S32] 67-17837
1. Driftwood arrangement. 2. Decoration and ornament. I. Title.

THOMPSON, Mary E 635.9664
The driftwood book. With photos. by Leonid Skvirsky. Princeton, N.J., Van Nostrand [1960] 200 p. illus. 21 cm. [SB449.3.D8T45] 60-9037
1. Driftwood arrangement. I. Title.

THOMPSON, Mary E 745.925
The driftwood book, by Mary E. Thompson. With photos. by Leonid Skvirsky. 2d ed. Princeton, N.J., Van Nostrand [1966] xiii, 248 p. illus. 21 cm. [SB449.3.D8T45] 66-2065
1. Driftwood arrangement. I. Title.

Driftwood sculpture.

THORNBER, Jean, 1919- 745.51
Driftwood sculpture / Jean Thornber. Millbrae, Calif. : Celestial Arts, 1975. 117 p. : ill. ; 22 cm. [NB1250.T46] 74-24981 ISBN 0-89087-019-5 : 4.95
1. Driftwood sculpture. I. Title.

Drinking vessels.

ASH, Douglas 739.23742
How to identify English silver drinking vessels, 600-1830. London, G. Bell. [New Rochelle, N.Y., SportShelf, 1965, c.1964] 159p. illus., plates. 23cm. (How to identify ser.) Bibl. [NK7143.A67] 64-9023 8.00
1. Drinking vessels. 2. Silversmithing—Gt. Brit—Hist. I. Title.

Drinking vessels, English—Catalogs.

TURNBULL, George A. 748'.8
The price guide to English 18th century drinking glasses [by] George A. Turnbull [and] Anthony G. Herron; photographs by Arthur Chadwick. Woodbridge (Suffolk),

SUBJECT INDEX DUCHAMP, MARCEL, 1887-1968.

Antique Collectors' Club, 1970. [5], 359 p. illus. 22 cm. Bibliography: p. 358-359. [NK5143.A1T8] 70-597286 ISBN 0-902028-04-9 £3.50
1. Drinking vessels, English—Catalogs. 2. Drinking vessels—Prices. 3. Glassware, English—Catalogs. I. Herron, Anthony G., joint author. II. Title.

Druids and druidism.

KENDRICK, Sir Thomas Downing. v. 12
The Druids, a study in Keltic prehistory. [2d ed.] New York, Barnes & Noble [1966, 1928] 227 p. illus., port., maps, plans. [NUC68-50146]
1. Druids and druidism. 2. Celts—Religion. I. Title.

Du Fresnoy, Charles Alphonse, 1611-1665.

REYNOLDS, Joshua, Sir, 1723-1792. 759.2
The works. Edited by Edmond Malone. (1797) Hildesheim, New York, G. Olms, 1971. 2 v. port. 25 cm. (Anglistica & Americana 129) Facsimile of the ed. published in London in 1797. [N7445.2.R48 1797a] 76-866761
1. Du Fresnoy, Charles Alphonse, 1611-1665. De arte graphica. 2. Art—Collected works. 3. Flanders—Description and travel. 4. Netherlands—Description and travel. 5. Painters. I. Malone, Edmond, 1741-1812. II. Title. III. Series.

Du Maurier, George Louis Palmella Busson, 1834-1896.

ORMOND, Leonee. 741'.0924 B
George Du Maurier. [Pittsburgh, Pa.] University of Pittsburgh Press [1969] xv, 516 p. illus., ports. (part col.) 26 cm. Bibliography: p. [499]-501. [NC242.D8O7 1969b] 79-80031 14.95
1. Du Maurier, George Louis Palmella Busson, 1834-1896.

Du Pont de Nemours, Eleuthere Irenee, 1771-1834.

WILKINSON, Norman B. 712'.6'0922 B
E. I. du Pont, botaniste; the beginning of a tradition [by] Norman B. Wilkinson. Charlottesville, Published for the Eleutherian Mills-Hagley Foundation, University Press of Virginia [1972] xi, 139 p. illus. 27 cm. [SB63.D87W55] 76-171485 ISBN 0-8139-0399-8
1. Du Pont de Nemours, Eleuthere Irenee, 1771-1834. 2. Du Pont family (Pierre Samuel Du Pont de Nemours, 1739-1817) 3. Gardens—United States. I. Eleutherian Mills-Hagley Foundation, Greenville, Del. BIP

Du Tilleux, Jean, 1903—

DU TILLEUX, Jean, 1903- 738.2'092'4
Roses in porcelain. [Shreveport, La., R. W. Norton Art Foundation, 1973] 16 p. col. illus. 28 cm. Catalog of an exhibition held June 3 to July 15, 1973 at the R. W. Norton Art Gallery, Shreveport, La. [NK4210.D8N67] 73-81397 ISBN 0-913060-02-X
1. Du Tilleux, Jean, 1903- 2. Roses in art. 3. Porcelain, American. I. Norton (R. W.) Art Gallery. II. Title.

Dublin. University. College Historical Society.

DUBLIN. National Gallery of Ireland. 708.9418'3
Art & oratory; bicentenary of the College Historical Society, 1770-1970. [Exhibition] 2nd-31st March 1970. Dublin [1970] [54] p. illus., ports. 28 cm. [PN4177.C63D8 1970] 70-269581
1. Dublin. University. College Historical Society. I. Title.

Dublin. University. Library.

CROOKSHANK, Anne. 027.7418'35
The long room / Anne Crookshank. [Dublin : Gifford & Craven, c1976] 16 p. : ill. ; 25 cm. (Gatherum ; 6) Caption title. Includes bibliographical references. [Z679.C84] 77-351766 £0.45
1. Dublin. University. Library. 2. Library architecture—Ireland—Dublin. 3. Architecture, Modern—17th-18th centuries—Ireland—Dublin. I. Title.

Dubuffet, Jean, 1901—

CORDIER, Daniel. 741.944
The drawings of Jean Dubuffet. Translated from the French by Cecily Mackworth. New York, G. Braziller [1960] 1 v. (unpaged) 100 illus. 27 x 33 cm. [NC1135.D82C63] 60-14515
I. Dubuffet, Jean, 1901- II. Title.

DALLAS, Museum of Fine Arts 759.44
Jean Dubuffet: retrospective. [Dallas, 1966] 54p. illus. (pt. col.) 26cm. Catalog of an exhibition held Mar. 16-Apr. 17, 1966. [ND553.D772D3] 66-7842 2.00 pap.,
1. Dubuffet, Jean, I. Title.

DUBUFFET, Jean, 1901- 741.9'44
Drawings. Introd. by Virginia Allen. New York, Museum of Modern Art; distributed by New York Graphic Society, Greenwich, Conn. [1968] vii, 34 p. 39 illus. 25 cm. Bibliographical footnotes. [NC1135.D818N4] 68-54919
I. New York (City). Museum of Modern Art. II. Title.

DUBUFFET, Jean, 1901- 709'.24
Dubuffet; new sculpture and drawings. [Exhibition, April 13-May 18, 1968] New York, Pace Gallery [1968] 47 p. (chiefly illus., part col.) 26 cm. [NB553.D75P3] 68-28262
I. Pace Gallery.

DUBUFFET, Jean, 1901- 730'.92'4
Dubuffet: studies for a spectacle. New York [Pace Editions, 1973] [32] p. (chiefly illus.) 26 cm. Catalog of the exhibition held May 5-June 27, 1973, in the Pace Gallery, New York. [NB553.D75P32] 73-81326
1. Dubuffet, Jean, 1901- I. Pace Gallery. II. Title.

DUBUFFET, Jean, 1901- 730'.924
Edifices. [Translated by Teri Wehn] New York, Published by the author for the Museum of Modern Art [1968] 46 p. illus., plans (both part col.) 24 cm. [NB553.D75A453] 68-58413
I. New York (City). Museum of Modern Art. II. Title.

DUBUFFET, Jean, 1901- 730'.92'4
Edifices and monuments by Jean Dubuffet. Catalogue by A. James Speyer. An exhibition organized by the Art Institute of Chicago in collaboration with the Graham Foundation for Advanced Studies in the Fine Arts. [Chicago] Art Institute of Chicago [1970?] 39 p. illus. (part col.) 26 cm. Exhibition held Dec. 19, 1970-Jan. 31, 1971 at the Art Institute of Chicago. [NB553.D75S67] 73-172325
I. Speyer, A. James. II. Chicago. Art Institute. III. Graham Foundation for Advanced Studies in the Fine Arts. IV. Title.

DUBUFFET, Jean, 1901- 709'.2'4
Jean Dubuffet: a retrospective. [New York, Solomon R. Guggenheim Foundation, 1973] 304 p. 296 illus. (part col.) 28 cm. Errata slip inserted. "Exhibition 73/3." Catalogue of a loan exhibition organized by the Solomon R. Guggenheim Museum and the Centre national d'art contemporain; presented at the Solomon R. Guggenheim Museum, New York and the Grand Palais, Paris. Includes bibliographical references. [N6853.D78S64] 73-77081
1. Dubuffet, Jean, 1901- I. Solomon R. Guggenheim Museum, New York. II. Centre national d'art contemporain. III. Paris. Grand Palais.

DUBUFFET, Jean, 1901- 730'.92'4
Monuments, simulacres, praticables. An exhibition organized by Walker Art Center, cosponsored by Air France and l'Association francaise d'action artistique, 4 February-18 March, 1973. [Minneapolis, Walker Art Center, 1973] [20] p. (chiefly illus. (part col.)) 23 cm. Catalog of the exhibition. [N6853.D78W34] 72-97249
1. Dubuffet, Jean, 1901- I. Walker Art Center, Minneapolis. II. Air France. III. Association francaise d'action artistique. IV. Title.

DUBUFFET, Jean, 1901- 709'.24
Simulacres. [Exhibition, Nov. 8-Dec. 10, 1969, at] the Pace Gallery, New York. [New York, Pace Editions, 1969] 45 p. (chiefly illus.) 28 cm. Facsim. of author's signature at head of title. One illus. accompanied by 4 superposed transparent overlays. Illustrated cover. A letter in French from the author to A. Glimcher (p. 5-[7]) An essay in English by A. Glimcher entitled: Peintures monumentees (p. 39-42) [ND553.D772A57] 78-106008
I. Glimcher, Arnold B. II. Pace Gallery. III. Title.

RAGON, Michel. 759.4
Dubuffet. Photos. by Luc Joubert. Translated by Haakon Chevalier. New York, Grove Press [1959] 62 p. mounted col. illus. 21 cm. [ND553.D772R3] 59-10873
1. Dubuffet, Jean, 1901-

SELZ, Peter Howard, 1919- 759.4
The work of Jean Dubuffet, with texts by the artist. N[ew] Y[ork] Museum of Modern Art; distributed by Doubleday, Garden City, N.Y. [1962] 187 p. illus. 24 cm. Includes bibliography. [ND553.D772S4] 62-11971
1. Dubuffet, Jean, 1901-

SOLOMON R. Guggenheim Museum, New York. 759.4
Jean Dubuffet, 1962-66. [Exhibition] Solomon R. Geggenheim Museum, New York. [New York, 1966] 75 p. illus. (part col.) 26 cm. "[Cataloge of] Exhibition 66 Contents.Twenty third period of my works, by J. Dubuffet.--Introduction, by L. Alloway.--Bibliography, by D. Waldman (p. [72]-75) [ND553.D772S6] 66-28456
I. Dubuffet, Jean, 1901- II. Alloway, Lawrence, 1900- III. Title.

Ducat.

IVES, Herbert Eugene, 1882-1953. 737.4
The Venetian gold ducat and its imitations. Edited and annotated by Philip Grierson. New York, American Numismatic Society, 1954. viii, 37p. plates, 23cm. (Numimismatic notes and monographs, 128 Bibliographical footnotes. [CJ2928.V5I9] 55-966
1. Ducat. I. Title. II. Series.

Duchamp, Marcel 1887-1968.

D'HARNONCOURT, Anne. 709'.2'4
Marcel Duchamp; a retrospective exhibition organized by the Philadelphia Museum of Art and The Museum of Modern Art, New York, made possible in part by a grant from the Natural Endowment for the Arts. Exhibition prepared by Anne d'Harnoncourt and Kynaston McShine. [Philadelphia, Philadelphia Museum of Art, 1973] 40 p. illus. 26 cm. Catalog of the exhibition held at the Philadelphia Museum of Art, Sept. 22-Nov. 11, 1973, The Museum of Modern Art, New York, Dec. 3, 1973-Feb. 10, 1974, and the Art Institute of Chicago, Mar. 9-Apr. 21, 1974. [N6853.D8D53] 74-159894
1. Duchamp, Marcel, 1889-1968. I. McShine, Kynaston, joint author. II. Philadelphia Museum of Art. III. New York (City). Museum of Modern Art. IV. Chicago. Art Institute.

HOPPS, Walter 709.44
Marcel Duchamp; ready-mades, etc., 1913-1964 [by] Walter Hopps, Ulf Linde, Arturo Schwarz. Milano, Galleria Schwarz [c.1964] Imprint covered by label: Hacker Art Bks., New York. 93p. illus. (pt. col.) ports. 35cm. Italian, French, & English. [N6853.D8H6 964] 67-3628 15.00
1. Duchamp, Marcel, 1887- I. Linde, Ulf, joint author. II. Schwarz, Arturo, 1924- joint author. III. Title.

LEBEL, Robert 759.4
Marcel Duchamp. With chapters by Marcel Duchamp, Andre Breton, H. P. Roche. Tr. by George Heard Hamilton. [New York, Paragraphic. 1967] 201p. illus., ports. 28cm. Tr. of Sur Marcel Duchamp. Bibl. [ND553.D774L43 1967] 67-21258 3.50 pap.,
1. Duchamp, Marcel, 1887- I. Title.
Distributed by Grossman.

LEBEL, Robert. 759.4
Marcel Duchamp. With chapters by Marcel Duchamp, Andre Breton & H. P. Roche. Translation by George Heard Hamilton. New York, Grove Press [1959] 191p. illus., col. plates, ports., facsims. 32cm. Translation of Sur Marcel Duchamp. Bibliography: p.177-188. [ND553.D774L43] 59-13893
1. Duchamp, Marcel, 1887- I. Title.

PASADENA, Calif. Art Museum. 709.44
Marcel Duchamp, Pasadena Art Museum: a retrospective exhibition,October 8 through November 3, 1963 [Pasadena] Author [1964] 1v. (unpaged) illus. (pt. mounted, pt. col.) facsim., port. 28cm. 64-6293 2.50 pap.,
1. Duchamp, Marcel, 1887- I. Title.

TOMKINS, Calvin, 1925- 709.04
The bride & the bachelors; the heretical courtship in modern art. New York, Viking [c.1962-1965] 246p. illus., ports. 22cm. [ND553.D774T6] 65-14512 6.50 bds.,
1. Duchamp, Marcel, 1887- 2. Cage, John 3. Rauschenberg, Robert, 1925- 4. Tinguely, Jean, 1925- I. Title. BIP

TOMKINS, Calvin, 1925- 709.04
The world of Marcel Duchamp, 1887- by Calvin Tomkins and the editors of Time-Life Books New York, Time, inc. [1966] 192 p. illus. (part col.) ports. (part col.) 31 cm. (Time-Life library of art) Bibliography: p. 185. [N6853.D8T6] 66-28544
1. Duchamp, Marcel, 1887- I. Time-Life Books. II. Title. BIP

Duchamp, Marcel, 1887-1968.

ALEXANDRIAN, Sarane. 759.4 B
Marcel Duchamp / by Alexandrian ; [translated from the French by]. New York : Crown Publishers, c1977. p. cm. Bibliography: p. [ND553.D774A7613] 76-56831 ISBN 0-517-53008-2 : 4.95
1. Duchamp, Marcel, 1887-1968.

CABANNE, Pierre. 709'.2'2 B
The brothers Duchamp : Jacques Villon, Raymond Duchamp-Villon, Marcel Duchamp / text by Pierre Cabanne ; [translated from the French by Helga and Dinah Harrison]. 1st U.S. ed. Boston : New York Graphic Society, c1976. 269 p. : ill. (some col.) ; 29 cm. Translation of Les 3 Duchamp. Bibliography: p. 266. [N6853.D8C2213] 75-37285 ISBN 0-8212-0666-4 : 49.50
1. Duchamp, Marcel, 1887-1968. 2. Duchamp-Villon, Raymond, 1876-1918. 3. Villon, Jacques, 1875-1963. I. Title. BIP

CABANNE, Pierre. 759.4
Dialogues with Marcel Duchamp. Translated from the French by Ron Padgett. New York, Viking Press [1971] 136 p. illus., ports. 22 cm. (The Documents of 20th century art) Translation of Entretiens avec Marcel Duchamp. Bibliography: p. 121-132. [ND553.D774C313 1971] 77-83255 ISBN 0-670-24017-6 7.50
1. Duchamp, Marcel, 1887-1968. I. Duchamp, Marcel, 1887-1968. II. Title. III. Series. BIP

D'HARNONCOURT, Anne. 730'.924
Etant donnes: 10 la chute d'eau, 20 le gaz d'eclairage; reflections on a new work by Marcel Duchamp [by Anne d'Harnoncourt and Walter Hopps] Philadelphia, Philadelphia Museum of Art [1969] 57 p. 35 illus. (incl. facsim.) 24 cm. At head of title: Bulletin, Philadelphia Museum of Art. Originally issued as v. 14, no. 299-300 of the Bulletin. [N6853.D8D5] 75-27093
1. Duchamp, Marcel, 1887-1968. Given: 1. the waterfall, 2. the illuminating gas. I. Hopps, Walter, joint author. II. Philadelphia Museum of Art. III. Title.

DUCHAMP, Marcel, 1887-1968. 759.4
Marcel Duchamp. Text by Arturo Schwarz. New York, H. N. Abrams [1975, c1970] [51] p., [159] p. of illus. (part col.) 32 cm. Bibliography: 40th-42d prelim. page. [ND553.D774S31813] 73-16230 ISBN 0-8109-0087-4 37.50
1. Duchamp, Marcel, 1887-1968. I. Schwarz, Arturo, 1924-

DUCHAMP, Marcel, 1887- 769'.924
1968.
Notes and projects for the Large Glass [by] Marcel Duchamp. Selected, ordered and with an introd. by Arturo Schwarz. New York, H. N. Abrams [1969] 217 p. illus. (part col.) 44 cm. English and French. [ND553.D774S32] 69-11986
I. Schwarz, Arturo, 1924- II. Title.

DUCHAMP, Marcel, 1887-1968. 759.4
Salt seller; the writings of Marcel Duchamp. Marchand du sel. Edited by Michel Sanouillet and Elmer Peterson. New York, Oxford University Press, 1973. xii, 196 p. illus. 24 cm. Bibliography: p. 196. [N6853.D8A57] 73-87343 ISBN 0-19-519749-6 10.95
1. Duchamp, Marcel, 1887-1968. 2. Art—Philosophy. I. Title.

GOLDING, John. 709'.2'4
Marcel Duchamp: The Bride stripped bare by her bachelors, even. [New York, Viking Press, 1973, c1972] 116 p. illus. 23 cm. (Art in context) Bibliography: p. [107]-108. [N6853.D8G64] 77-180828 ISBN 0-670-28607-9 7.50
1. Duchamp, Marcel, 1887-1968. Bride stripped bare by her bachelors, even. I. Title.

MASHECK, Joseph, comp. 709'.2'4
Marcel Duchamp in perspective. Englewood Cliffs, N.J., Prentice-Hall [1974, c1975] xi, 184 p. illus. 23 cm. (Artists in perspective series) (A Spectrum book) Bibliography: p. 179-184. [N6853.D8M37] 74-13935 ISBN 0-13-556316-X
1. Duchamp, Marcel, 1887-1968. I. Title.

PAZ, Octavio, 1914- 759.4
Marcel Duchamp, appearance stripped bare / Octavio Paz ; translated by Rachel Phillips and Donald Gardner. New York : Viking Press, 1978. vii, 211 p. : ill. ; 22 cm. "A Richard Seaver book." Rev. and greatly enl. versions of two essays originally published separately. Contents.Contents.—The castle of purity.—water writes always in * plural. [ND553.D774P352 1978] 78-17560 ISBN 0-670-45502-4 : 8.95
1. Duchamp, Marcel, 1887-1968. I. Title.

SCHWARZ, Arturo, 1924- 709'.24
The complete works of Marcel Duchamp. New York, H. N. Abrams [1969] xxi, 630 p. illus., plates (part col.) 32 cm. Bibliography: p. 607-617. [ND553.D774S3] 69-11987
1. Duchamp, Marcel, 1887-1968. I. Title.

STEEFEL, Lawrence D. 759.4
The position of Duchamp's Glass in the development of his art / Lawrence D. Steefel, Jr. New York : Garland Pub., 1977. 423 p., [25] leaves of plates : ill. ; 21 cm. (Outstanding dissertations in the fine arts) Originally presented as the author's thesis, Princeton, 1960, under title: The position of La mariee mise a nu par ses celibataires, meme, (1915-1923) in the stylistic and iconographic development of the art of Marcel Duchamp. Includes bibliographical references. [N6853.D8S85 1977] 76-23647 ISBN 0-8240-2730-2 lib.bdg. : 45.00
1. Duchamp, Marcel, 1887-1968. 2. Duchamp, Marcel, 1887-1968. Bride stripped bare by her bachelors, even. I. Title. II. Series. BIP

†TOMKINS, Calvin, 1925- 709'.04
The world of Marcel Duchamp, 1887-1968 / by Calvin Tomkins and the editors of Time-Life Books. Rev. Alexandria, Va. : Time-Life Books ; Morristown, N.J. : school and library distribution by Silver Burdett Co., c1977. 192 p. : ill. (some col.) ; 31 cm. (Time-Life library of art) Includes index. Bibliography: p. 185. [N6853.D8T6 1977] 77-153784 ISBN 0-8094-0236-X : 10.95
1. Duchamp, Marcel, 1887-1968. 2. Surrealism. I. Time-Life Books. II. Title.

Duchamp-Villon, Raymond, 1876-1918.

AGEE, William C. 730'.924
Raymond Duchamp-Villon, 1876-1918; notes by William C. Agee. Introd. by George Heard Hamilton. New York, Walker [1968, c1967] 141 p. illus., ports. 23 cm. Catalog of an exhibition held at M. Knoedler and Company, Oct. 10-Nov. 4, 1967. "Writing by Duchamp-Villon": p. 109-125. Bibliography: p. 128-135. [NB553.D77A68 1968] 67-30378 7.50
1. Duchamp-Villon, Raymond, 1876-1918. I. Knoedler (M.) and Company, inc. BIP

Dufy, Raoul, 1877-1953.

COGNIAT, Raymond, 1896- 759.4
Raoul Dufy [Tr. from French by Thomas L. Callow] New York Crown, 1962. 92p. illus. (pt. col.) 29cm. 62-11813 3.50
1. Dufy, Raoul, 1877-1953. I. Title.

DUFY, Raoul, 1877-1953. 759.4
Raoul Dufy. Text by Sam Hunter. New York, H. N. Abrams [1972?] 24 p. illus. (part col.) 33 cm. (The Library of great painters. Portfolio ed.) On cover: Dufy. [ND553.D78H83 1972] 69-14743
I. Hunter, Sam, 1923-

DUFY, Raoul, 1877-1953. 759.4
Raoul Dufy. Text by Alfred Werner. [1st ed.] New York, H. N. Abrams [1970] 168 p. illus. (part col.) 34 cm. (The Library of great painters) Bibliography: p. 167-168. [ND553.D78W42 1970b] 73-120740 ISBN 0-8109-0083-1
I. Werner, Alfred, 1911-

DUFY, Raoul, 1877-1953. 759.4
Raoul Dufy [texte par] Raymond Cogniat New York [1950] [63] p. 60 illus. 17 cm. (Collection des maltres) Text in French, English and German. Bibliography: p. [63] [ND553.D78C56] 52-28621
I. Cogniat, Raymond, 1896- II. Title. III. Series: Collection "Les Maltres"

DUFY, Raoul, 1877-1953. 927.5
Raoul Dufy (1877-1953) Text by Alfred Werner New York, H. N. Abrams in association with Pocket Books [1953] [74] p. 34 illus. part col.) 18 cm. (The Pocket library of great art, A5) An Abrams art book. Bibliography: p. [74] [ND553.D78W4] 759.4 53-4518
I. Werner, Alfred, 1911-

Dulac, Edmund, 1882-1953.

*DULAC, Edmund. 741.642
Dulac edited by David Larkin, introduction by Brian Sanders New York, Peacock Press/Bantam Book [1975] [90 p. (chiefly ill plates), 30 cm. [NC965] 5.95 (pbk.)
1. Dulac, Edmund I. Larkin, David comp. II. Title. BIP

DULAC, Edmund, 1882- 741.9'42
1953.
Dulac / edited by David Larkin ; introd. by Brian Sanders. 1st U.S. ed. New York : Scribner, 1975. [56] p. : chiefly col. ill. ; 31 cm. "An original Peacock Press/Bantam Book." [ND1942.D84L37] 75-11189 ISBN 0-684-14414-X : 10.00
1. Dulac, Edmund, 1882-1953. I. Larkin, David.

WHITE, Colin. 741'.092'4 B
Edmund Dulac / Colin White. New York : Scribner, c1976. 205 p. : ill. (some col.) ; 29 cm. Includes bibliographical references and index. [NC980.5.D84W47] 76-9562 ISBN 0-684-14791-2 : 25.00
1. Dulac, Edmund, 1882-1953. 2. Illustrators—France—Biography. BIP

WHITE, Colin. 741'.092'4 B
Edmund Dulac / [by] Colin White. London : Studio Vista, 1976. 208 p. : ill. (some col.), facsims., map, music, plan, ports. ; 29 cm. Includes bibliographical references and index. [NC980.5.D84W47 1976b] 77-364635 ISBN 0-289-70751-X : £10.50
1. Dulac, Edmund, 1882-1953. 2. Illustrators—France—Biography.

Dumbarton Oaks.

DUMBARTON Oaks. 738.3'7
Classic Maya pottery at Dumbarton Oaks / Michael D. Coe. [Washington : Dumbarton Oaks, Trustees for Harvard University, 1975] 1 portfolio (30 p., [16] leaves of plates : ill. (some col.)) ; 45 cm. Bibliography: p. 29-30. [F1435.3.P8D84 1975] 75-1727
1. Dumbarton Oaks. 2. Mayas—Pottery. 3. Indians of Mexico—Pottery. 4. Indians of Central America—Pottery. I. Coe, Michael D. II. Title. BIP

WHITEHILL, Walter Muir, 975.3
1905-
Dumbarton Oaks; the history of a Georgetown house and garden, 1800-1966. Cambridge, Belknap Press of Harvard University Press, 1967. x, 147 p. illus., maps, ports. 25 cm. [F204.D8W47] 67-20887
1. Dumbarton Oaks. BIP

Dummer, Jeremiah, 1645-1718.

CLARKE, Hermann 739.2'3'0924
Frederick, 1882-1947.
Jeremiah Dummer, colonial craftsman & merchant, 1645-1718 [by] Hermann Frederick Clarke and Henry Wilder Foote. Foreward by E. Alfred Jones. New York, Da Capo Press, 1970 [c1935] xviii, 204 p. illus., facsims., ports. 26 cm. (Da Capo Press series in architecture and decorative art, v. 33) A Da Capo Press reprint edition. Reprint of the 1935 ed. [NK7198.D8C5 1970] 75-87563
1. Dummer, Jeremiah, 1645-1718. I. Foote, Henry Wilder, 1875- joint author. II. Title.

Dummy board figures.

SCOTT, Amoret. 749'.3
Dummy board figures, by Amoret and Christopher Scott. Cambridge, Golden Head P., 1966. 21 p. 15 plates. 21 1/2 cm. [NK9955.D8S3] 67-74671
1. Dummy board figures. I. Scott, Christopher, joint author.

Duncan & Miller Glass Company.

KRAUSE, Gail. 748.2'9148'82
The encyclopedia of Duncan glass / Gail Krause. 1st ed. Hicksville, N.Y. : Exposition Press, c1976. viii, 223 p. : ill. (some col.) ; 24 cm. [NK5198.D86K7] 76-366971 ISBN 0-682-48527-6 : 17.50
1. Duncan & Miller Glass Company. 2. Glassware—Pennsylvania—Washington. 3. Glassware—Collectors and collecting. I. Title. BIP

Duncan, Douglas Moerdyke, 1902-1968—Art patronage

JARVIS, Alan, 1915-1972. 704'.361
Douglas Duncan, a memorial portrait. Edited by Alan Jarvis. [Toronto, Buffalo] University of Toronto Press [1974] viii, 74 p. illus. (part col.) 18 x 23 cm. [N5230.C3D864] 72-97526 ISBN 0-8020-1977-3 7.50
1. Duncan, Douglas Moerdyke, 1902-1968—Art patronage. I. Title.

PICTURES from the 760'.0971
Douglas M. Duncan Collection / selected and introduced by Frances Duncan Barwick. Toronto ; Buffalo : University of Toronto Press, [1975] 146 p. : ill. (some col.) ; 23 x 26 cm. [N6545.P52] 74-75587 ISBN 0-8020-3322-9 : 15.00
1. Duncan, Douglas Moerdyke, 1902-1968—Art collections. 2. Art, Canadian—Catalogs. 3. Art, Modern—20th century—Canada. I. Barwick, Frances Duncan, 1909-

Duncan, John, 1920- —Art collections.

CENTER for Inter- 759.98'074'01471
American Relations. Art Gallery.
Latin American paintings and drawings from the Collection of John and Barbara Duncan. New York [1970] 32 p. illus. (part col.) 22 cm. Exhibition held July 9-Aug. 30, 1970. [N6502.C38] 70-25033
1. Duncan, John, 1920- —Art collections. 2. Duncan, Barbara, 1921- —Art collections. 3. Art, Latin American—Exhibitions. I. Title. BIP

Dunlap family.

THE Dunlaps & their 749.2'142
furniture. Manchester, N.H., Currier Gallery of Art [1970] 310 p. illus. 26 cm. Catalogue, by Charles S. Parsons, of an exhibition held at the Currier Gallery of Art, Aug.-13 Sept. 1970. "Transcription of Major John Dunlap's account book": p. [171]-310. Bibliography: p. 67-69. [NK2439.D86P37] 70-129914
1. Dunlap family. 2. Furniture, American—Exhibitions. I. Parsons, Charles Sumner, 1904- II. Dunlap, John, 1746-1792. III. Currier Gallery of Art, Manchester, N.H. BIP

Dunn, Harvey, 1884-1952.

KAROLEVITZ, Robert F. 759.13
The prairie is my garden; the story of Harvey Dunn, artist, by Robert F. Karolevitz. [Aberdeen, S.D., North Plains Press, 1969] 95 p. illus. (part col.), ports. 31 cm. Bibliography: p. 91. [ND237.D79K3] 77-83472 2.00
1. Dunn, Harvey, 1884-1952. I. Title. BIP

KAROLEVITZ, Robert F. 759.13 B
Where your heart is; the story of Harvey Dunn, artist, by Robert F. Karolevitz. [Aberdeen, S.D., North Plains Press, 1970] 208 p. illus. (part col.), ports. 32 cm. Expanded version of The prairie is my garden. [ND237.D79K3 1970] 78-125992 15.00
1. Dunn, Harvey, 1884-1952. I. Title. BIP

Dunning, Gerald Clough.

MEDIEVAL pottery from 738.3'094
excavations : studies presented to Gerald Clough Dunning : with a bibliography of his works / edited by Vera I. Evison, H. Hodges, and J. G. Hurst. New York : St. Martin's Press, 1974. 262 p., [9] leaves of plates : ill. ; 24 cm. Includes bibliographies and index. [TP793.M4 1974] 74-82134 14.95
1. Dunning, Gerald Clough. 2. Pottery—Europe—History—Addresses, essays, lectures. I. Dunning, Gerald Clough. II. Evison, Vera I. III. Hodges, Henry, 1920- IV. Hurst, John G., 1927-
Contents omitted. BIP

Dunstaffnage Castle.

SIMPSON, William Douglas, 941.38
1896-
Dunstaffnage Castle and the Stone of Destiny. Edinburgh, Oliver and Boyd [1958] 136 p. illus. 23 cm. [NA7746.D84S5] 58-41167
1. Dunstaffnage Castle. 2. Stone of Scone. I. Title.

Dunster Castle.

MUSGRAVE, Ernest 914.23'8
Illingworth.
Dunster Castle: an illustrated survey of the historic Somerset home of the Luttrell family: [text written by E. I. Musgrave. New ed.; revised by Walter Luttrell]. Derby, English Life Publications, 1968. [34] p. illus. (some col.), col. maps. 15 x 22 cm. [DA690.D85M8 1968] 72-425664 2/6
1. Dunster Castle.

Dura, Syria. Synagogue—Addresses, essays, lectures.

THE Dura-Europes 755'.9'6
synagogue; a re-evaluation (1932-1972). Edited by Joseph Gutmann. [Chambersburg, Pa.] American Academy of Religion, 1973. 190 p. illus. 21 cm. (Religion and the arts 1) Bibliography: p. [157]-159. [ND2819.S93D872] 73-85879 ISBN 0-88414-024-5
1. Dura, Syria. Synagogue—Addresses, essays, lectures. 2. Mural painting and

(A Studio book) Translation of Durer; eine Bildbiographie. [ND588.D9S843] 64-12234
1. Durer, Albrecht, 1471-1528. I. Title.

STRAND, Kenneth Albert, 769'.924 1927- comp.
Woodcuts to the Apocalypse in Durer's time; Albrecht Durer's woodcuts plus five other sets from the 15th and 16th centuries. Compilation and introductions by Kenneth A. Strand. [Ann Arbor, Mich.] Ann Arbor Publishers, 1968. 86 p. (chiefly illus.) 29 cm. [NE1205.D9S7] 73-3625 10.00
1. Durer, Albrecht, 1471-1528. Apocalypse. 2. Bible. N.T. Revelation—Pictures, illustrations, etc. I. Title.

STRAUSS, Walter L. 741.9'43
The complete drawings of Albrecht Durer / Walter L. Strauss. New York : Abaris Books, 1974. 6 v. (x, 3352 p.) : ill. ; 32 cm. Title on spine of v. 6: Architectural studies & index. Includes indexes. Contents.Contents.—v. 1. 1471-1499.—v. 2. 1500-1509.—v. 3. 1510-1519.—v. 4. 1520-1528.—v. 5. Human proportions.—v. 6. Appendices & index. Bibliography: p. 3295-3318. [NC251.D8S74] 73-80442 ISBN 0-913870-00-5 : 360.00
1. Durer, Albrecht, 1471-1528. I. Durer, Albrecht, 1471-1528. II. Title. **BIP**

STRIEDER, Peter. 760'.092'4
The hidden Durer / Peter Strieder ; [translated from the German by Vivienne Menkes]. Chicago : Rand McNally Co., 1978. 191 p. : ill (some col.) ; 34 cm. Translation of Albrecht Durer. Includes index. Bibliography: p. 189. [N6888.D8S7313] 78-50816 ISBN 0-528-81041-3 : 19.95
1. Durer, Albrecht, 1471-1528. I. Title. BIP

WAETZOLDT, Wilhelm, [759.3]927.5 1880-
Durer and his times. Translated from the German by R. H. Boothroyd] New York, Phaidon Publishers; distributed by Oxford University Press [1950] viii, 398 p. illus. plates (part col.) 27 cm. Full name: Adolf Wilheim Waetzoldt. [ND588.D9W132] 50-12885
1. Durer, Albrecht, 1471-1528. II. Title.

WOLFFLIN, Heinrich, 760'.0924 1864-1945.
The art of Albrecht Durer. Translated by Alastair & Heide Grieve. [New York] Phaidon [distributed in the U.S. by Praeger, 1971] 311 p. illus. 8 col. plates. 26 cm. Translation of Die Kunst Albrecht Durers. Bibliography: p. 303. [N6888.D8W613] 70-139837 ISBN 0-7148-1467-9 18.50
1. Durer, Albrecht, 1471-1528. I. Title.

Durer, Albrecht, 1471-1528—Adaptations.

DURER through 769'.94'07401441 other eyes : his graphic work mirrored in copies and forgeries of three centuries : an exhibition prepared by students in the Williams College-Clark Art Institute graduate program in art history, March 14 to June 15, 1975. Williamstown, Mass. : Sterling and Francine Clark Art Institute, c1975. 99 p. : ill. ; 27 cm. Errata sheet inserted. Includes index. Bibliography: p. 68-73. [NE42.W54S834] 76-354407
1. Durer, Albrecht, 1471-1528—Adaptations. 2. Durer, Albrecht, 1471-1528—Forgeries. 3. Prints—Exhibitions. I. Williams College. II. Sterling and Francine Clark Art Institute, Williamstown, Mass.

Durer, Albrecht, 1471-1528—Catalogs.

STRAUSS, Walter L. 741.9'43
The complete drawings of Albrecht Durer : supplement / Walter L. Strauss. New York : Abaris Books, c1977- v. : ill. ; 30 cm. Bibliography: v. 1, p. 15. [NC251.D8A4 1977] 78-322176 ISBN 0-913870-43-9 (v. 1)
1. Durer, Albrecht, 1471-1528—Catalogs. I. Durer, Albrecht, 1471-1528. II. Title. Available in set only ISBN no. 0-913870-00-5 price 360.00

Durer, Albrecht, 1471-1528—Juvenile literature.

RABOFF, Ernest Lloyd. 759.3
Albrecht Durer, by Ernest Raboff. Garden City, N.Y., Doubleday [1970] [31] p. illus. (part col.), ports. (part col.) 29 cm. (Art for children) (A Gemini Smith book.) Briefly discusses the influences upon Durer, the fifteenth-century German artist, and the outstanding features of some of his paintings. [ND588.D9R17] 78-121784 3.95
1. Durer, Albrecht, 1471-1528—Juvenile literature. I. Title.

Durham Castle.

COLGRAVE, Bertram. 942.81
Durham Castle: an illustrated survey of theancient castle of the bishops of Durham, now occupied by University College, Durham. Derby, Designed and produced by English Life Publications [1953] unpaged. illus. 14x22cm. [DA690.D96C6] 54-43929
1. Durham Castle. I. Title.

Durham Cathedral in art.

SUNDERLAND Art Gallery. 769'.4'4
Durham Cathedral: topographical prints from 16th to 20th centuries [catalogue of an exhibition held 15th February to 23rd March 1969] Sunderland (Durham), Sunderland Art Gallery, 1969. [2], 44 p., 8 plates. 89 illus. 23 cm. Cover title. Bibliography: p. 42-44. [NE628.S9] 76-492527 5/6
1. Durham Cathedral in art. 2. Prints, English—Exhibitions. I. Title.

Durham, Eng.

JOHNSON, Margot. 914.28'1
Durham City: a pictorial history. Washington (Co. Durham), Northern Notes, 1970. [2], 32, [2] p. (2 fold.). illus., facsims., maps. 22 cm. Maps on lining papers. Cover title. [DA690.D96J63] 72-175637 ISBN 0-901744-05-0 £0.37 1/2
1. Durham, Eng. I. Title.

Durham, Eng. (County)—Historic houses, etc.

WHITTAKER, Neville. 720'.9428'1
Historic architecture of County Durham, by Neville Whittaker and Ursula Clark; sponsored by the Civic Trust for the North East and Durham County Council. Newcastle upon Tyne, Oriel Press, 1971. 96 p. (chiefly illus., map, plan). 25 cm. Map on lining papers. [NA969.D9W5] 77-160364 ISBN 0-85362-129-2 £1.25
1. Durham, Eng. (County)—Historic houses, etc. 2. Architecture—Durham, Eng. (County) I. Clark, Ursula, joint author. II. Civic Trust for the North East. III. Durham, Eng. (County). County Council. IV. Title.

Durieux, Caroline, 1896-

DURIEUX, Caroline, 769'.92'4 1896-
Caroline Durieux's lithographs of the thirties and forties / text by Richard Cox. Baton Rouge : Louisiana State University Press, c1977. p. cm. [NE2312.D87C68] 77-16525 ISBN 0-8071-0372-1 : 14.95
1. Durieux, Caroline, 1896- I. Cox, Richard, 1942- II. Title. III. Title: Lithographs of the thirties and forties.

Dutton, Ninette.

DUTTON, Ninette. 738.4'092'4 B
Portrait of a year / Ninette Dutton. Melbourne : Nelson, 1976. viii, 176 p. ; 24 cm. [N7405.D87A56] 77-373787 ISBN 0-17-005089-0
1. Dutton, Ninette. 2. Artists—Australia—Biography. I. Title.

Duveen Brothers.

DUVEEN, James Henry, 1873- 706.9
The rise of the House of Duveen. [1st American ed.] New York, Knopf, 1957.

293 p. illus. 22 cm. [N8660.D8D8] 55-9282
1. Duveen Brothers. I. Title.

Duveen, Joseph Duveen, Baron, 1869-1939.

BEHRMAN, Samuel 706'.5 B Nathaniel, 1893-
Duveen [by] S. N. Behrman. Boston, Little, Brown [1972] 232 p. illus. (part. col.) 26 cm. [N8660.D8B4 1972] 78-183995 12.50
1. Duveen, Joseph Duveen, Baron, 1869-1939. 2. Art—Collectors and collecting.

BEHRMAN, Samuel Nathaniel, 927 1893-
Duveen. Illus. by Saul Steinberg. New York, Random House [1952] 302 p. illus. 22 cm. [N8386.D82B4] 52-5137
1. Duveen, Joseph Duveen, baron, 1869-1939. 2. Duveen brothers. 3. Art—Collectors and collecting. 4. Art dealers. 5. Collectors and collecting.

BEHRMAN, Samuel Nathaniel, 927 1893-
Duveen. Illus. by Saul Steinberg. [Gloucester, Mass., P. Smith, 1965, c1951, 1952] 176p. illus. 19cm. (Vintage bk. rebound) [N8386.D82B4] 3.25
1. Duveen, Joseph Duveen, baron, 1869-1939. 2. Art—Collectors and collecting. 3. Art dealers. 4. Duveen brothers. 5. Collectors and collecting. I. Title.

Duveneck, Frank, 1848-1919.

DUVENECK, Josephine 759.13 Whitney, 1891-
Frank Duveneck: painter-teacher, by Josephine W. Duveneck. San Francisco, John Howell-Books, 1970. 169 p. illus., facsims., col. plates, ports. 27 cm. Bibliography: p. 167-169. [ND237.D85D86] 79-20180
1. Duveneck, Frank, 1848-1919. I. Title.

Dwellings.

DANIELS, George Emery, 1914- 728
How to build or remodel your house; including How to buy your house or have it built [edited by Julian Roth] New York, Greystone Press [1953] 434 p. illus. 24 cm. At head of title: Mr. Fix-It. How to buy your house or have it built was first published in 1947 under title: A home of your own. [TX301.D3] 53-9261
1. Dwellings. 2. Building. 3. Architecture, Domestic. I. Roth, Julian, ed. How to buy your house or have it built. II. Title. III. Title: How to buy your house or have it built. IV. Title: Mr. Fix-It.

RODGERS, Dorothy F., 728.6'4 1909-
The house in my head [by] Dorothy Rodgers. [1st ed.] New York, Atheneum, 1967. x, 254 p. illus. (part col.), plans (on lining papers) 27 cm. Illus. from House beautiful, mostly by Ezra Stoller. [TH4811.R6] 67-25491
1. Dwellings. 2. Architecture, Domestic. 3. Cookery. I. Title. **BIP**

SHELTER. 728
[Bolinas, Calif.: Shelter Publications; distributed in the U.S. by Random House, New York, c1973] 176 p. illus. 37 cm. Cover title. Bibliography: p. 172-173. [NA7110.S53 1973] 73-5415 ISBN 0-394-48829-6 6.00
1. Dwellings. **BIP**

SHELTER II / 728
[edited by] Lloyd Kahn. Bolinas, Calif. : Shelter Publications : New York : distributed by Random House, [1978] p. cm. [TH4812.S53] 78-57133 ISBN 0-394-73611-7 pbk. : 9.50
1. Dwellings. 2. House construction. I. Kahn, Lloyd.

Dwellings—Case-studies.

UNITED Nations. Dept. of 300'.8 s Economic and Social Affairs.
Basic housing case studies / Department of Economic and Social Affairs. New York : United Nations, 1976. 110 p. : ill. ; 28 cm. ([Document] - United Nations ;

ST/ESA/19) (Design of low-cost housing and community facilities ; v. 2) "United Nations publication. Sales no. E.75.IV.2." [JX1977.A2 ST/ESA/19] [NA7125] 728'.1 77-374058 8.50
1. Dwellings—Case-studies. 2. Dwellings—Designs and plans. I. Title. II. Series. III. Series: United Nations. Document ; ST/ESA/19.

Dwellings—England—London metropolitan area—Designs and plans.

GREATER London 728'.09421 Council.
GLC preferred dwelling plans. London : Architectural Press, [1976?] 83 p. : plans ; 21 x 30 cm. [NA7331.L6G73 1976] 77-363470 ISBN 0-85139-252-0 : £3.75
1. Dwellings—England—London metropolitan area—Designs and plans. I. Title. **BIP**

Dwellings—Europe—Remodeling.

DEBAIGTS, Jacques. 728
New interiors for old houses. New York, Van Nostrand Reinhold [1973] 158 p. illus. (part col.) 27 cm. English ed. has title: Old houses, new interiors. English, French, and German. [TH4816.D36] 72-6921 ISBN 0-442-22056-1 19.95
1. Dwellings—Europe—Remodeling. 2. Architecture, Domestic—Europe—Designs and plans. I. Title. **BIP**

Dwellings—Ghana.

PRUSSIN, Labelle. 720'.9667
Architecture in Northern Ghana; a study of forms and functions. Berkeley, University of California Press, 1969. xi, 120 p. illus., maps. 16 x 24 cm. Bibliography: p. 119-120. [GN414.A1P7] 75-84789 8.95
1. Dwellings—Ghana. I. Title. **BIP**

Dwellings—Gt. Brit.

BARFOOT, Audrey 728.30942
Homes in Britain, from the earliest times to 1900. London, B. T. Batsford [dist. Chester Springs, Pa., Dufour, 1964, c1963] 96p. illus. 23cm. Bibl. 64-9195 2.95 bds.,
1. Dwellings—Gt. Brit. 2. Architecture, Domestic— Gt. Brit. 3. Interior Decoration—Gt. Brit. 4. Gt. Brit.—Soc. life & cust. I. Title.

Dwellings—Greece.

RIDER, Bertha Carr 728.0938
Ancient Greek houses: their history and development from the Neolithic period to the Hellenistic age [1st Amer. ed.] Chicago, Argonaut [c.]1964. xvi.272p. illus., plans. 22cm. (Argonaut lib. of antiquities) First pub. in London in 1916 under title: The Greek house. Bibl. 64-23438 8.50
1. Dwellings—Greece. 2. Architecture, Greek—Hist. 3. Classical antiquities. I. Title.

RIDER, Bertha Carr 722.8
The Greek house: its history and development from the Neolithic period to the Hellenistic age [Reissue, New York] Cambridge [1965] xii, 272p. illus. (incl. plans) 22cm. Bibl. [DF99.R5] 16-24977 4.00
1. Dwellings—Greece. 2. Architecture, Greek—Hist. 3. Classical antiquities. I. Title. **BIP**

Dwellings—Illinois—Vermilion Co.

JAKLE, John A. 728.3
The testing of a house typing system in two Middle Western counties : a comparative analysis of rural houses / by John A. Jakle ; Susan R. Gross, editor. [Urbana] : Geography Graduate Student Association, University of Illinois at Urbana-Champaign, 1976. 36 leaves : ill. ; 28 cm. (Occasional publications of the Department of Geography ; paper no. 11) Cover title. Includes bibliographical references. [NA7235.I4J34] 77-621769
1. Dwellings—Illinois—Vermilion Co. 2.

Caption title. Bibliography: p. 33. [GN2.F4 vol. 66, no. 2] [TT853] 667'.3'09664 76-11369
1. Kamara, Kadiato. 2. Dyes and dyeing—Sierra Leone. I. Title. II. Series: Field Museum of Natural History, Chicago. Publication ; 1230. III. Series: Fieldiana : Anthropology ; v. 66, no. 2.

Dyes and dyeing—Textile fibers.

THE Dyer's art : 746.6
ikat, plangi, batik / by Jack Lenor Larsen ... [et al.]. New York : Van Nostrand Reinhold Co., [1976] p. cm. Includes index. Bibliography: p. [TT853.D9] 76-14234 ISBN 0-442-24685-4 : 35.00
1. Dyes and dyeing—Textile fibers. I. Larsen, Jack Lenor. BIP

HAYWOOD, Hilary. 746.6
Enjoying dyes : how to pattern your own fabrics / Hilary Haywood. New York : Drake Publishers, 1975, c1974. 148 p. : ill. ; 25 cm. Includes index. Bibliography: p. 145. [TT853.H38 1975] 74-13516 ISBN 0-87749-726-5 : 8.95
1. Dyes and dyeing—Textile fibers. I. Title.

PROUD, Nora. 746.6
Textile dyeing and printing simplified / Nora Proud. New York : Arco Pub. Co., 1974. 96 p. : ill. (some col.) ; 22 cm. [TT853.P76] 76-350104 ISBN 0-668-03389-4 : 5.95
1. Dyes and dyeing—Textile fibers. 2. Textile printing. I. Title.

ROBINSON, Stuart. 746.6
Fabric dyeing and printing / [by Stuart and Patricia Robinson]. Leicester : Dryad Press, 1976. 3 v. : ill. (chiefly col.) ; 15 x 21 cm. (Dryad leaflet ; 500-502) Cover title. Contents.Contents.—1. Tiedye and batik.—2. Pad and block.—3. Screen printing. Includes bibliographies. [TT853.R6] 76-382227 ISBN 0-85219-096-4 (v. 1) : £0.45 per vol.
1. Dyes and dyeing—Textile fibers. 2. Textile printing. I. Robinson, Patricia, fl. 1966- joint author. II. Title.

Dyott, Thomas W.

MCKEARIN, Helen. 666'.19
Bottles, flasks, and Dr. Dyott. New York, Crown Publishers [1970] 160 p. illus., facsims., map., port. 26 cm. Bibliography: p. 155. [NK5198.D95M3 1970] 74-127499 5.95
1. Dyott, Thomas W. I. Title.

Dzubas, Friedel, 1915—

CARMEAN, E. A. 759.13
Friedel Dzubas, a retrospective exhibition, the Museum of Fine Arts, Houston, October 16-November 24, 1974 : with an introductory note / by William C. Agee ; text and catalogue by E. A. Carmean, Jr. Houston : The Museum, 1974. 31 p. : ill. (some col.) ; 22 x 28 cm. Includes bibliographical references. [ND237.D95C37] 74-21755
1. Dzubas, Friedel, 1915- I. Dzubas, Friedel, 1915- II. Houston, Tex. Museum of Fine Arts.

MOFFETT, Kenworth. 759.13
Friedel Dzubas : [catalogue of an exhibition] Museum of Fine Arts, Boston, March 13-May 18, 1975 / [Kenworth Moffett]. Boston : The Museum, 1975. [16] p. : ill. (some col.) ; 22 x 26 cm. Bibliography: p. [13]-[14] [ND237.D95M63] 75-4432 ISBN 0-87846-091-8
1. Dzubas, Friedel, 1915- I. Dzubas, Friedel, 1915- II. Boston. Museum of Fine Arts. BIP

Eagle in art.

ISAACSON, Philip M., 1924- 704.94'32
The American eagle / Philip M. Isaacson. 1st ed. Boston : New York Graphic Society, c1975. xiii, 210 p. : ill. (some col.) ; 29 cm. Includes index. Bibliography: p. 205-207. [NK1403.A1I82] 75-362 ISBN 0-8212-0612-5
1. Eagle in art. 2. Decoration and ornament, American. 3. United States—Seal. 4. Eagle (in religion, folk-lore, etc.) I. Title. BIP

Eakins, Thomas, 1844-1916.

EAKINS, Thomas, 1844-1916. 779'.2'0924
A family album : photographs by Thomas Eakins. New York : Coe Kerr Gallery, c1976. [27] p. : ill. ; 22 x 26 cm. Issued in conjunction with the exhibition held January, 1976 at the Philadelphia Art Alliance, Philadelphia, March, 1976 at the Chrysler Museum at Norfolk, Norfolk, Va., April, 1976 at the Hunter Museum of Art, Chattanooga, Tenn., and October, 1976 at the Amon Carter Museum, Fort Worth, Tex. [TR647.E2A43] 76-357337
1. Eakins, Thomas, 1844-1916. 2. Photography, Artistic—Exhibitions. I. Philadelphia Art Alliance. II. Title.

EAKINS, Thomas, 1844-1916. 730'.924
The sculpture of Thomas Eakins. [Catalog by] Moussa M. Domit. [Washington, Corcoran Gallery of Art, 1969] viii, 66 p. illus., port. 21 cm. An exhibition at the Corcoran Gallery of Art, May 3-June 10, 1969. Includes bibliographical references. [NB237.E17D6] 70-87934
I. Domit, Moussa M. II. Corcoran Gallery of Art, Washington, D.C. III. Title.

EAKINS, Thomas, 1844-1916. 759.13
Thomas Eakins, by Lloyd Goodrich. New York, Published for the Whitney Museum of American Art by Praeger [1970] 72 p. illus. (part col.), ports. 28 cm. "Published on the occasion of the Thomas Eakins Retrospective Exhibition organized by the Whitney Museum of American Art in the fall of 1970." [ND237.E15G59 1970] 78-134362 7.95
I. Goodrich, Lloyd, 1897- II. Whitney Museum of American Art, New York.

GOODRICH, Lloyd, 1897- 759.13
Thomas Eakins: his life and work. New York, Whitney Museum of Art, 1933. [New York, AMS Press, 1970] 225 p. 72 plates, port. 27 cm. Bibliography: p. [217]-220. [ND237.E15G6 1970] 71-138259 ISBN 0-404-02863-2
1. Eakins, Thomas, 1844-1916. BIP

HENDRICKS, Gordon. 759.13 B
The life and work of Thomas Eakins / Gordon Hendricks. New York : Grossman Publishers, 1974. xxx, 367 p., [25] leaves of plates : 306 ill. (some col.) ; 31 cm. Includes index. Bibliography: p. 305-314. [ND237.E15H46 1974] 73-4174 ISBN 0-670-42795-0 : 45.00
1. Eakins, Thomas, 1844-1916. I. Eakins, Thomas, 1844-1916. II. Title.

HIRSHHORN Museum and Sculpture Garden. 759.13
The Thomas Eakins collection of the Hirshhorn Museum and Sculpture Garden / introd. and text by Phyllis D. Rosenzweig. Washington : Published for the Hirshhorn Museum and Sculpture Garden, Smithsonian Institution, by the Smithsonian Institution Press ; for sale by the Supt. of Docs., U.S. Govt. Print. Off., 1977. 240 p. : ill. ; 30 cm. "Exhibition dates: May 24-September 5, 1977." Includes bibliographical references and index. [ND237.E15H57 1977] 77-608029 25.00
1. Eakins, Thomas, 1844-1916. I. Eakins, Thomas, 1844-1916. II. Rosenzweig, Phyllis D. III. Title. BIP

HOOPES, Donelson F. 759.13
Eakins watercolors, by Donelson F. Hoopes. New York, Watson-Guptill [1971] 87 p. illus. (part col.) 29 cm. Bibliography: p. 9-11. [ND1839.E2H6] 78-152785 ISBN 0-8230-1590-4 17.50
1. Eakins, Thomas, 1844-1916. I. Title.

PORTER, Fairfield. 759.13
Thomas Eakins. New York, G. Braziller, 1959. 127 p. illus. (part col.), port. 26 cm. (The Great American artist series) Bibliography: p. 121-122. [ND237.E15P6] 59-12225
1. Eakins, Thomas, 1844-1916.

SCHENDLER, Sylvan. 759.13
Eakins. [1st ed.] Boston, Little, Brown [1967] xix, 300 p. illus., ports. 25 cm. [ND237.E15S3] 67-18109
1. Eakins, Thomas, 1844-1916.

THE Trenton 069'.09749'66 s
Battle Monument Eakins bronzes. Edited by Zoltan Buki [and] Suzanne Corlette. Trenton, New Jersey State Museum, 1973. 85 p. illus. 22 cm. (New Jersey State Museum. Bulletin 14) Contents.—The Battle of Trenton.—The Trenton Battle Monument.—The Eakins bronzes.—Thomas Eakins, a chronology. Includes bibliographical references. [QH1.N5897 no. 14] [NB237.E17] 730'.92'4 75-188488
1. Eakins, Thomas, 1844-1916. 2. Trenton. Battle Monument. 3. Trenton, Battle of, 1776. I. Buki, Zoltan, ed. II. Corlette, Suzanne, ed. III. Series: New Jersey. State Museum, Trenton. Bulletin 14.

U.S. National Gallery of Art. 759.13
Thomas Eakins, a retrospective exhibition. National Gallery of Art, Smithsonian Institution; the Art Institute of Chicago; Philadelphia Museum of Art. [Washington, 1961] [Washington 1958] 131 p. illus. 26 cm. 131 p. illus. 26 cm. "Exhibition dates: National Gallery of Art, October 8 through November 12, 1961; the Art Institute of Chicago, December 1, 1961, through January 7, 1962; Philadelphia Museum of Art, February 1 through March 18, 1962." [ND237.E15U5] [ND237.H7U6] 759.13 62-60557 59-60282
1. Homer, Winslow, 1836-1910. 2. Eakins, Thomas, 1844-1916 I. U.S. National Gallery of Art. II. New York. Metropolitan Museum of Art. III. Title. IV. Title: Winslow Homer:

Eames, Charles.

EAMES, Charles. 749.2'13
Furniture from the design collection, the Museum of Modern Art, New York, by Arthur Drexler. [New York, Museum of Modern Art, 1973] 56 p. illus. 26 cm. [NK2439.E2D73] 73-76672 ISBN 0-87070-314-5 5.95
1. Eames, Charles. 2. Furniture, American. I. Drexler, Arthur. II. New York (City). Museum of Modern Art. III. Title.

Eardley, Joan.

BUCHANAN, William. 759.9411 B
Joan Eardley / by William Buchanan. Edinburgh : Edinburgh University Press, c1976. 91 p. : ill. (some col.) ; 16 x 22 cm. (Modern Scottish painters ; no. 5) Bibliography: p. 88. [ND497.E25B8] 77-360043 ISBN 0-85224-301-4 : 5.00
1. Eardley, Joan. 2. Painters—Scotland—Biography. I. Eardley, Joan.
Distributed by Edinburgh Univ. Press, c/o Biblio Distribution Center, 81 Adams Dr., Totowa, NJ07512

Earl, Ralph, 1754-1801.

GOODRICH, Laurence B. 759'.13
Ralph Earl, recorded for an era, by Laurence B. Goodrich. Albany, State University of New York [1967] vii, 96 p. illus., ports. (part col.) 27 cm. Bibliographical reference included in "Notes" (p. 95-96) [ND237.E18G6] 66-64728
1. Earl, Ralph, 1754-1801. I. Title. BIP

GOODRICH, Laurence B. 759'.13
Ralph Earl, recorder for an era, by Laurence B. Goodrich. [Albany] State Univ. of N. Y. [1967] vii, 96p. illus., ports. (pt col.) 27cm. Bibl. [ND237.E18G6] 66-64728 7.50
1. Earl, Ralph, 1751-1801. II. Title.

Earth sheltered houses.

MINNESOTA. University. Underground Space Center. 728
Earth sheltered housing design : guidelines, examples, and references / prepared by the Underground Space Center, University of Minnesota ; prepared for the Minnesota Energy Agency. New York : Van Nostrand Reinhold, [1978] p. cm. Bibliography: p. [TH4819.E27M56 1978] 78-25555 pbk. : 10.00 ISBN 0-442-26157-8 : 17.95
1. Earth sheltered houses. I. Minnesota. Energy Agency. II. Title. BIP

East Anglia in art.

PAWSEY, James Thomas. 759.2 B
John Constable : paintings and countryside / written by James Pawsey. Ipswich : F. W. Pawsey and Sons, [1976] [1], 25 p. (2 fold.) : ill. (chiefly col.), map, ports. (1 col.) ; 25 cm. English text; English, French, and German foreword and captions. Bibliography: p. 2. [ND497.C7P39] 76-374582 £0.50
1. Constable, John, 1776-1837. 2. East Anglia in art. 3. East Anglia—Description and travel—Views. I. Constable, John, 1776-1837.

East (Far East) in art.

OREGON. University. Museum of Art. 769'.92'4
Elizabeth Keith (1887-1956) : the Orient through Western eyes : an exhibition of works from the Murray Warner Collection in the Museum of Art, University of Oregon, Eugene, Oregon, September 22-November 3, 1974. [Eugene] : The Museum, 1974. [24] p. : ill. ; 22 cm. Bibliography: p. [24] [NE1300.8.G72K446 1974] 74-195089
1. Keith, Elizabeth. 2. Warner, Murray—Art collections. 3. East (Far East) in art. I. Title: The Orient through Western eyes.

Easter decorations.

DUNCAN Ceramic Products. 738.1'5
Decorating for Easter. Fresno, Calif., c1973. 39 p. illus. 28 cm. (Duncan library of ceramic decorating) [TT900.E2D86 1973] 74-162860 1.95
1. Easter decorations. 2. Pottery craft. I. Title.

Easter decorations—Juvenile literature.

WAGNER, Lee. 745.59'41
How to have fun making Easter decorations. Illustrated by Nancy Inderieden. [Mankato, Minn., Creative Education; distributed by Children's Press, Chicago, 1974] 28 p. illus. (part col.) 25 cm. (Creative education craft series) Directions for decorating eggs and making baskets for Easter. [TT900.E2W34] 74-10595 ISBN 0-87191-361-5
1. Easter decorations—Juvenile literature. I. Inderieden, Nancy, illus. II. Title. BIP

Easter eggs.

LUCIOW, Johanna. 745.59'4
Eggs beautiful : how to make Ukrainian Easter eggs / by Johanna Luciow, Ann Kmit, and Loretta Luciow. Minneapolis : Ukrainian Gift Shop, [1975] 96 p. : ill. (some col.) ; 27 cm. Includes index. Bibliography: p. 95. [TT896.7.L8] 75-638 6.95
1. Easter eggs. 2. Egg decoration. 3. Folk art—Ukraine. I. Kmit, Ann, joint author. II. Luciow, Loretta, joint author. III. Title.
Publisher's address: 2422 Central Ave., Minneapolis, Minn. 55418.

Easter eggs—Juvenile literature.

COLE, Marion. 745.59'41
Things to make and do for Easter / by Marion Cole and Olivia H. H. Cole ; pictures by Olivia H. H. Cole. New York : Watts, 1979. p. cm. (A things to make and do book) Includes recipes, puzzles, riddles, games, and instructions for making Easter eggs and an Easter basket. [TT896.7.C65] 78-12457 ISBN 0-685-65723-X lib. bdg. : 6.90
1. Easter eggs—Juvenile literature. 2. Games—Juvenile literature. 3. Riddles—Juvenile literature. 4. Easter—Juvenile literature. I. Cole, Olivia H. H., joint author. II. Title. BIP

Easter Island.

PICKER, Fred. 779'.9'919618
Rapa Nui. Photos. and text by Fred Picker. Historical summary by Thor Heyerdahl. New York, Paddington Press [1974] 131 p. illus. 29 cm. [F3169.P58] 73-15025 ISBN 0-8467-0021-2 14.95

1. Easter Island. I. Heyerdahl, Thor. II. Title.

Eastern Shore, Md.—Description and travel—Views.

SZABO, Steve. 779'.9'97521
The Eastern Shore / Steve Szabo. Danbury, N.H. : Addison House, c1976. [25] p., [28] leaves of plates : ill. ; 27 x 34 cm. [F187.E2S92] 76-42071 ISBN 0-89169-009-3. ISBN 0-89169-008-5 pbk.
1. Eastern Shore, Md.—Description and travel—Views. 2. Photography, Artistic. I. Title. BIP

Eastgate, Nigel.

EASTGATE, Nigel. 769'.563'09931
Stamp out kiwis / Nigel Eastgate. Dunedin [N.Z.] : J. McIndoe, 1976. [24] p. : ill. ; 22 cm. [CT2888.E2A37] 77-354610 ISBN 0-908565-15-1
1. Eastgate, Nigel. 2. New Zealand—Biography. 3. Postage-stamps—New Zealand—Miscellanea. I. Title.

Eastlake, Charles Lock, Sir, 1793-1865.

ROBERTSON, David 709'.2'4 B
Allan.
Sir Charles Eastlake and the Victorian art world / by David Robertson. Princeton, N.J. : Princeton University Press, c1976. p. cm. Includes bibliographical references and index. [N6797.E15R62] 75-43797 ISBN 0-691-03902-X : 40.00
1. Eastlake, Charles Lock, Sir, 1793-1865. 2. Art, Victorian—England. I. Title. BIP

Eastlake, Charles Locke, 1833-1906—Influence.

MADIGAN, Mary Jean 749.2'13
Smith.
Eastlake-influenced American furniture, 1870-1890; [catalogue of an exhibition] November 18, 1973-January 6, 1974, the Hudson River Museum. [Yonkers, N.Y., Hudson River Museum, 1973] [66] p. illus. 29 cm. Bibliography: p. [64]-[65] [NK2407.M32] 73-90034 ISBN 0-87100-043-1
1. Eastlake, Charles Locke, 1833-1906—Influence. 2. Furniture, American—Exhibitions. 3. Decoration and ornament—Victorian style. I. Hudson River Museum. II. Title. BIP

Eastman, George, 1854-1932.

ACKERMAN, Carl 338.7'61'77 B
William, 1890-
George Eastman, by Carl W. Ackerman. With an introd. by Edwin R. A. Seligman. Clifton [N.J.] A. M. Kelley, 1973 [c1930] xviii, 522 p. illus. 22 cm. (Library of early American business and industry, 54) [TR140.E3A3 1973] 70-128074 ISBN 0-678-03556-3
1. Eastman, George, 1854-1932. I. Title. BIP

Eastman, Seth, 1808-1875.

MCDERMOTT, John Francis, 759.13
1902-
Seth Eastman, pictorial historian of the Indian. [1st ed.] Norman, University of Oklahoma Press [1961] x, 270 p. plates (part col.) ports. 27 cm. "Checklist of works [by S. Eastman]": p. 228-255. Bibliography: p. 256-261. [ND237.E35M33] 61-15145
1. Eastman, Seth, 1808-1875. 2. Indians of North America—Pictures, illustrations, etc.

MCDERMOTT, John Francis, 759.13
1947-
Seth Eastman's Mississippi; a lost portfolio recovered. Urbana, University of Illinois Press [1973] xvii, 149 p. illus. 16 x 23 cm. Bibliography: p. 145-147. [ND1839.E23M32] 73-2457 ISBN 0-252-00192-3 10.00
1. Eastman, Seth, 1808-1875. 2. Mississippi River in art. I. Title. BIP

Eaton, Norman, 1902-1966.

HARROP-ALLIN, Clinton, 720'.92'4
1936-
Norman Eaton, architect : a study of the work of the South African architect Norman Eaton 1902-1966 / Clinton Harrop-Allin ; foreword by Alexis Preller. Cape Town : C. Struik, 1975. 128 p. : ill. ; 28 cm. Includes index. Bibliography: p. 125-126. [NA1596.E17H37] 76-350679 ISBN 0-86977-053-5 : 23.00
1. Eaton, Norman, 1902-1966. I. Title. Distributed by Verry

Ecclesiastical embroidery.

DEAN, Beryl. 746.4'4
Ideas for church embroidery. [Newton Centre, Mass.] C. T. Brandford Co. [1968] 192 p. illus. 26 cm. Bibliography: p. 186. [NK9310.D37 1968b] 69-10880 13.25
1. Ecclesiastical embroidery. 2. Church vestments. I. Title. BIP

Ecclesiastical embroidery—England—Great Bealings.

BROWN, Cynthia. 746.9'5
Hassocks for your church : how we made them at Great Bealings / [by] Cynthia Brown. [Great Bealings] : [St. Mary's Church], [1976] 36 p. : ill. ; 12 x 19 cm. [NK9310.B77] 77-364716 ISBN 0-9505054-0-4 : £0.95
1. St. Mary's Church, Great Bealings, Eng. 2. Ecclesiastical embroidery—England—Great Bealings. 3. Canvas embroidery. 4. Kneelers (Church furniture)—England—Bealings. I. Title.

Ecclesiastical embroidery—New Castle Co., Del.

CHRIST Church Christiana 746.4'4
Hundred, New Castle Co., Del.
Needlepoint cushions. Greenville, Del. [Needlepoint Committee, Christ Church, 1971- v. col. illus. 22 x 28 cm. [NK9310.C5] 71-182570
1. Ecclesiastical embroidery—New Castle Co., Del. 2. Canvas embroidery. 3. Kneelers (Church furniture) I. Title.

Ecclesiastical embroidery—Washington, D.C.

MONTGOMERY, Nancy S. 746.4'4
Stitches for God : the story of Washington Cathedral needlepoint / Nancy S. Montgomery. Washington : Cathedral Church of Saint Peter and Saint Paul, [1974] 32 p. : ill. (some col.) ; 23 cm. [NK9310.M66] 74-84715
1. Washington, D.C. Cathedral of St. Peter and St. Paul. 2. Ecclesiastical embroidery—Washington, D.C. 3. Canvas embroidery. I. Title.

Eccleston, Daniel, 1745-1816.

TYSON, Edith. 914.27'2 B
Daniel Eccleston. Lancaster, Lancaster City Museum and Art Gallery, [1971] [1], 13 p. 30 cm. "A Lancaster Museum monograph." [CT788.E25T97] 73-160360 ISBN 0-9500360-2-1 £0.04
1. Eccleston, Daniel, 1745-1816.

Eclecticism in architecture.

WATKIN, David, 1941- 724
Morality and architecture : the development of a theme in architectural history and theory from the Gothic revival to the modern movement / by David Watkin. Oxford [Eng.] : Clarendon Press, 1978. viii, 126 p. ; 23 cm. Includes bibliographical references and index. [NA645.5.E25W37] 77-6815 ISBN 0-19-817350-4 : 7.50
1. Eclecticism in architecture. 2. Architecture, Modern—19th century. 3. Architecture, Modern—20th century. I. Title. BIP

Eclecticism in architecture—France.

†THE Architecture of the 724
Ecole des beaux-arts / edited by Arthur Drexler ; essays by Richard Chafee ... [et al.]. New York : Museum of Modern Art ; Cambridge, Mass. : distributed by MIT Press, 1976,c1977 525 p. : ill. (some col.) ; 29 cm. Based on an exhibition shown at the Museum of Modern Art, New York, Oct. 29, 1975-Jan. 4, 1976. Includes bibliographical references and index. [NA1047.5.E34A69] 75-7649 ISBN 0-87070-244-0 : 45.00
1. Eclecticism in architecture—France. 2. Architecture, Modern—19th century—France. 3. Eclecticism in architecture—United States. 4. Architecture, Modern—19th century—United States. 5. Architecture, Modern—20th century—United States. I. Drexler, Arthur. II. Chafee, Richard. III. Paris. Ecole nationale superieure des beaux-arts. IV. New York (City). Museum of Modern Art.

Eclecticism in architecture—United States.

KIDNEY, Walter C. 720'.973
The architecture of choice: Eclecticism in America, 1880-1930 [by] Walter C. Kidney. New York, G. Braziller [1974] viii, 178 p. illus. 27 cm. Includes bibliographical references. [NA710.5.E25K52 1974] 73-88044 ISBN 0-8076-0730-4 12.50
1. Eclecticism in architecture—United States. 2. Architecture, Modern—19th century—United States. I. Title.

PLATT, Frederick, 1946- 720'.973
America's gilded age / Frederick Platt. South Brunswick : A. S. Barnes, [1975] p. cm. Includes index. Bibliography: p. [NA710.5.E25P42] 73-114 ISBN 0-498-01322-7 : 25.00
1. Eclecticism in architecture—United States. 2. Architecture, Modern—19th century—United States. 3. Architecture, Modern—20th century—United States. I. Title. BIP

Ecstasy.

PETERSSON, Robert Torsten. 701.15
The art of ecstasy; Teresa, Bernini, and Crashaw [by] Robert T. Petersson. [1st American ed.] New York, Atheneum, 1970. xv, 183 p. illus., col. plate. 25 cm. Includes bibliographical references. [NX652.T4P4 1970b] 79-108825 8.95
1. Teresa, Saint, 1515-1582. 2. Bernini, Giovanni Lorenzo, 1598-1680. 3. Crashaw, Richard, 1613?-1649. 4. Ecstasy. I. Title. BIP

Eddy, Oliver Tarbell, 1799-1868.

NEWARK Museum Association, 759.13
Newark, N.J.
Oliver Tarbell Eddy, 1799-1868; a catalogue of his works compiled by Edith Bishop in connection with an exhibition shown at the Newark Museum, March 28-May 7, 1950 [and] the Baltimore Museum of Art, May 28-June 25, 1950. [Newark, 1950] 68 p. illus., ports. 26 cm. "References": p. 38-39. [ND237.E39N4] 51-1733
1. Eddy, Oliver Tarbell, 1799-1868. 2. Paintings, American — Exhibitions. I. Bishop, Edith II. Baltimore. Museum of Art. III. Title.

Edinburgh—Description.

SASEK, Miroslav. 914.1
This is Edinburgh. New York, Macmillan [1961] 59 p. illus. 32 cm. A pictorial presentation of the capital of Scotland, with drawings of its famous sights, monuments, and buildings. [ND1946.S2A52] AC 68
1. Edinburgh—Description. I. Title. BIP

Edinburgh. Royal Scottish Academy of Painting, Sculpture, and Architecture.

EDINBURGH. Royal 708'.9413'4
Scottish Academy of Painting, Sculpture, and Architecture.
Report of the council. Edinburgh. v. 22cm. annual. [N12.R8A3] 55-40271
I. Title.

EDINBURGH. Royal 914.22'5
Scottish Museum.
The Royal Scottish Museum: art & ethnography, natural history, technology, geology. 1854-1954. Edinburgh, Oliver & Boyd [1955?] 54p. illus. 25cm. [AM101.E26] 55-37578
I. Title.

GORDON, Esme. 708'.9413'4
The Royal Scottish Academy of Painting, Sculpture and Architecture : 1826-1976 / Esme Gordon ; foreword by His Royal Highness, The Prince Philip, Duke of Edinburgh. Edinburgh : Skilton, 1976. xxiv, 272 p., [14] leaves of plates : ill. (1 col.), plans, ports. ; 26 cm. Ill. on lining papers. Includes index. Bibliography: p. 264-266. [N12.E353G67] 76-378719
1. Edinburgh. Royal Scottish Academy of Painting, Sculpture, and Architecture. I. Edinburgh. Royal Scottish Academy of Painting, Sculpture, and Architecture.

Edison Institute (Henry Ford Museum and Greenfield Village) Dearborn, Mich.

EDISON 681'.113'074017433
Institute (Henry Ford Museum and Greenfield Village) Dearborn, Mich.
The clock collection / [by William H. Distin]. Dearborn, Mich. : Greenfield Village & Henry Ford Museum, [1977?] 28, [1] p. : ill. ; 26 cm. Cover title. Bibliography: p. 28-[29] [NK7482.D42E344] 77-154049
1. Edison Institute (Henry Ford Museum and Greenfield Village) Dearborn, Mich. 2. Clocks and watches—Michigan—Dearborn—Catalogs. I. Distin, William H. II. Title.

EDISON 745'.0973'07417433
Institute (Henry Ford Museum and Greenfield Village) Dearborn, Mich.
Folk art and the street of shops / Henry Ford Museum. Dearborn : Edison Institute, c1971. 47 p. : ill. ; 26 cm. Cover title. [E161.E3 1971] 75-301777
1. Edison Institute (Henry Ford Museum and Greenfield Village) Dearborn, Mich. I. Title.

Editorial cartoons—History.

HOFF, Sydney, 1912- 741.5'909
Editorial and political cartooning : from earliest times to the present, with over 700 examples from the works of the world's greatest cartoonists / Syd Hoff. New York : Stravon Educational Press, c1976. 416 p. : ill. ; 28 cm. Includes index. [NC1325.H63] 75-45314 ISBN 0-87396-078-5 : 12.95
1. Editorial cartoons—History. 2. World politics—Caricatures and cartoons—History. I. Title. BIP

Edmonds, Francis William, 1806-1863.

MANN, Maybelle. 759.13 B
Francis William Edmonds, Mammon and art / Maybelle Mann. New York : Garland Pub., 1977. vii, 170 p., [8] leaves of plates : ill. ; 21 cm. (Outstanding dissertations in the fine arts) Originally presented as the author's thesis, New York University, 1972. Bibliography: p. 165-170. [ND237.E394M36 1977] 76-23638 ISBN 0-8240-2708-6 lib.bdg. : 30.00
1. Edmonds, Francis William, 1806-1863. 2. Painters—United States—Biography. I. Title. II. Series.

Edmondson, William, 1883?-1951.

EDMONDSON, William, 730'.92'4
1883?-1951.
Visions in stone: the sculpture of William Edmondson [by] Edmund L. Fuller. With photos. by Edward Weston. [Pittsburgh] University of Pittsburgh Press [1973] xi, 123 p. illus. 27 cm. [NB237.E35F84] 72-91108 ISBN 0-8229-3259-8 14.95
1. Edmondson, William, 1883?-1951. I. Fuller, Edmund L., 1941- II. Title.

Edouart, Augustin Amant Constance Fidele, 1789-1861.

EDOUART, Augustin Amant Constance Fidele, 1789-1861. 741.9'4
Auguste Edouart's Silhouettes of eminent Americans, 1839-1844 / Andrew Oliver. Charlottesville : Published for the National Portrait Gallery, Smithsonian Institution, by the University Press of Virginia, 1976. p. cm. "Catalogue of 3,800 named and dated American silhouette portraits by August Edouart" by E. Jackson: p. Includes index. [NC910.5.E3O44] 76-21073 ISBN 0-8139-0632-6 : 22.50
1. Edouart, Augustin Amant Constance Fidele, 1789-1861. 2. Silhouettes—United States. 3. United States—Biography—Portraits. I. Oliver, Andrew, 1906- II. Jackson, Emily, 1861- Catalogue of 3,800 named and dated American silhouette portraits by August Edouart, 1789-1861. 1976. III. Title. IV. Title: Silhouettes of eminent Americans, 1839-1844.
Distributed by University Press of Virginia.
BIP

JACKSON, Emily, 1861- 741.9'4
Ancestors in silhouette, cut by August Edouart. Illustrative notes and biographical sketches by Mrs. F. Nevill Jackson. Boston, Milford House [1973] p. Reprint of the 1921 ed. published by J. Lane, London, and J. Lane Co., New York. [NC910.5.E3J32 1973] 73-5522 ISBN 0-87821-141-1 45.00 (lib. bdg.)
1. Edouart, Augustin Amant Constance Fidele, 1789-1861. 2. Silhouettes. I. Title.
BIP

Education—Caricatures and cartoons.

DAUMIER, Honore Victorin, 1808-1879. 741.5944
Teachers and students. Pref., catalogue, and notes by Raymond Picard. [Translated from the French by Arnold Rosin] Boston, Boston Book and Art [1970] 94 p. illus. 33 cm. At head of title: Daumier and the University. Translation of Professeurs et moutards. Bibliography: p. 86-[87] [NC1499.D3P5313] 74-124158 15.00
1. Education—Caricatures and cartoons. I. Picard, Raymond, 1917- ed. II. Title. III. Title: Daumier and the University.

WADSWORTH, Pat 741.5973
Sex and violence at Happy Hill [Cranbury. N.J.] A. S. Barnes [c.1966] 71p. illus. 22cm. Cartoons. [NC1429 W15A54] 66-13769 2.95
1. Education—Caricatures and cartoons. I. Title.

Education in art.

EDUCATION. 704.94'937
[1st ed.] Greenwich, Conn., New York Graphic Society [1967] 64 p. illus., 20 plates (part col.) 32 cm. (Man through his art v. 4) "Published ... with the sponsorship of the World Confederation of Organizations of the Teaching Profession (WCOTP) and with the financial help of UNESCO." [N8217.E3E3] 66-15191
1. Education in art. I. World Confederation of Organizations of the Teaching Profession. II. Title. III. Series.

Educational innovations.

RENSSELAER Polytechnic Institute, Troy, N.Y. Center for Architectural Research. 727
Educational facilities with new media [by] Alan C. Green, editor [and others. Washington] Dept. of Audiovisual Instruction, National Education Association [1966] A55, B99, C55 p. illus. 28 cm. Final report of an architectural research study under Contract OE-316-031 with the U.S. Office of Education. Bibliography: p. C48. [LB1027.R43] 66-25154
1. Educational innovations. 2. School facilities. I. Green, Alan C., ed. II. Title.

Educational planning—Great Britain.

FALUDI, Andreas. 711'.07'11
Essays on planning theory and education / by Andreas Faludi. Oxford [Eng.] ; New York : Pergamon Press, 1978. viii, 186 p. : ill. ; 22 cm. (Pergamon international library of science, technology, engineering, and social studies) Includes bibliographies. [LA632.F33 1978] 77-30343 ISBN 0-08-021224-7 20.00
1. Educational planning—Great Britain. 2. Educational sociology—Great Britain. I. Title.
BIP

Edward VIII, King of Great Britain, 1894-

TROWBRIDGE, Richard J. 737'.0942
History, coinage, paper notes and medals of Edward VIII of Great Britain, by Richard J. Trowbridge. [1st ed. Long Beach, Calif., 1970] 55 p. illus., facsims., ports. 22 cm. Includes bibliographical references. [CJ2476.T75] 77-25094
1. Edward VIII, King of Great Britain, 1894- 2. Coins, British. 3. Paper money—Gt. Brit. 4. Medals—Gt. Brit. I. Title.

EFFanBEE Doll Corp.

STEWART, Ethel. 688.7'22'075
A collector's guide to the Patsy dolls / Ethel Stewart and Katherine Dennis ; photography by Darryl Dennis. Seattle : Stewart, [1974] 44 p., 2 leaves of plates : ill. ; 28 cm. Bibliography: p. 44. [TS2301.T7S74] 75-305463 6.95
1. EFFanBEE Doll Corp. 2. Dolls—Collectors and collecting. 3. Dolls—Catalogs. I. Dennis, Katherine, joint author. II. Dennis, Darryl. III. Title.

Effigies—Ireland.

HUNT, John, 1900- 730'.9415
Irish medieval figure sculpture, 1200-1600 : a study of Irish tombs with notes on costume and armour / John Hunt, with assistance and contributions from Peter Harbison ; with photos. by David H. Davison. Dublin : Irish University Press, [1974] 2 v. : 357 ill., fold. col. map ; 31 cm. Contents.Contents.—v. 1. Text and catalogue.—v. 2. Plates. Includes bibliographical references and indexes. [NB1820.H86 1974] 74-195906 ISBN 0-85667-012-X : 70.00
1. Effigies—Ireland. 2. Sculpture, Medieval—Ireland. 3. Sculpture—Ireland. 4. Costume—Ireland. 5. Arms and armor, Irish. I. Harbison, Peter. II. Title.
BIP

Egg decoration.

COSKEY, Evelyn, 1932- 745.59'41
Easter eggs for everyone [by] Evelyn Coskey. Drawings by Giorgetta Bell. Photographs unless otherwise indicated are by Sid Dorris. Nashville, Abingdon [1973] 191 p. diagrs. 25 cm. Bibliography: p. 187-188. Summary: Discusses the lore and legends of eggs, including Easter eggs, gives instructions for simple and elaborate ways to decorate eggs, and suggests uses for the final product. [TT896.7.C67] 72-6680 ISBN 0-687-11492-6 6.95
1. Egg decoration. I. Bell, Giorgetta A., illus. II. Dorris, Sid, illus. III. Title.
BIP

DISNEY, Rosemary. 745.59'4
The splendid art of decorating eggs. Great Neck, N.Y., Hearthside Press [1972] 192 p. illus. 25 cm. [TT896.7.D58] 77-185808 10.00
1. Egg decoration. I. Title. II. Title: Decorating eggs.
BIP

LANG, Nancy M. 745.59'41
Getting started in egg decoration [by] Nancy M. Lang. New York, Bruce Pub. Co. [1971] x, 86 p. illus. (part col.) 28 cm. (Getting started series) [TT896.7.L35] 78-160383 2.95
1. Egg decoration. I. Title.

NASSIET, Claude. 745.59'4
Egg art. Illus. by Marc Berthier. Photos: Promophot. New York, Drake Publishers [1973] 62 p. illus. (part col.) 23 cm. Translation of La feerie des oeufs. Suggestions for making a variety of decorative objects from egg shells, plaster eggs, or egg cartons. [TT896.7.N3613] 73-3721 ISBN 0-87749-476-2 3.95
1. Egg decoration. 2. Eggshell craft. I. Berthier, Marc, illus. II. Title.
BIP

NEWSOME, Arden J. 745.59'4
Egg decorating, plain & fancy, by Arden J. Newsome. New York, Crown Publishers [1973] 96 p. illus. (part col.) 29 cm. [TT896.7.N49 1973] 73-82940 ISBN 0-517-50595-9 5.95
1. Egg decoration. I. Title.

RIOTTE, Louise. 745.59'4
Egg decorating. New York, Drake [1973] 177 p. illus. (part. col.) 28 cm. [TT896.7.R56] 72-10494 ISBN 0-87749-417-7 8.95
1. Egg decoration. I. Title.

SZILVASY, Linda Markuly, 1940- 745.59'4
The jeweled egg : a handbook for beginning and advanced craftsmen / Linda Markuly Szilvasy. New York : Association Press, c1976. p. cm. Includes index. [TT896.7.S94] 76-14985 ISBN 0-8096-1916-4 : 9.95
1. Egg decoration. I. Title.
BIP

Egg decoration—Juvenile literature.

EDWARDS, H. Wayne. 745.59'4
Kalendar kreatures, by H. Wayne Edwards. San Antonio, Naylor Co. [1973] xi, 112 p. illus. 22 cm. Instructions for making eggshell figures for holidays and other occasions throughout the year. [TT896.7.E38] 73-747 ISBN 0-8111-0478-8 4.95
1. Egg decoration—Juvenile literature. I. Title.

NEWSOME, Arden J. 745.59'4
Egg craft, written and illustrated by Arden J. Newsome. New York, Lothrop, Lee and Shepard Co., [1973] 128 p. illus. 25 cm. Bibliography: p. [124] Demonstrates in text and illustrations the various techniques of decorating blown or cooked eggs. Includes a list of suppliers of materials used. [TT896.7.N48] 72-11993 ISBN 0-688-41512-1 4.50
1. Egg decoration—Juvenile literature. I. Title.
Library edition 4.14; ISBN 0-688-45512-3.
BIP

Eggenhofer, Nicholas, 1897—

EGGENHOFER, Nicholas, 1897- 741'.092'4
Eggenhofer : the pulp years / John M. Carroll ; introd. by Jeff Dykes. 1st ed. Fort Collins, Colo : Old Army Press, c1975. 145 p. : ill. (some col.) ; 29 cm. [NC975.5.E33C37] 75-333132 15.00
1. Eggenhofer, Nicholas, 1897- 2. The West in art. I. Carroll, John M.

Eggshell craft—Juvenile literature.

PFLUG, Betsy. 745.5
Egg-speriment; easy crafts with eggs and egg cartons. [1st ed.] Philadelphia, Lippincott [1973] 39 p. illus. 25 cm. Easy projects for creating such items as dolls, insects, houses, masks, and animals using simple materials, eggs, and egg cartons. [TT896.7.P47] 72-12522 ISBN 0-397-31460-4 4.95
1. Eggshell craft—Juvenile literature. 2. Egg carton craft—Juvenile literature. I. Title.

Egypt—Antiquities.

COTTRELL, Leonard. 709.32
The lost Pharaohs; the romance of Egyptian archaeology. New York, Philosoihocal Library [1951] 256p. plates, ports. 23cm. Bibliography: p. 248-249. [DT60.C] A 53
1. Egypt—Antiq. I. Title.
BIP

HAYES, William Christopher, 1903- 932
The scepter of Egypt; a background for the study of the Egyptian antiquities in the Metropolitan Museum of Art. New York, Harper in co-operation with the Metropolitan Museum of Art, 1953-1959. 2 v. illus., map. 26 cm. Contents.Contents.—pt. 1. From the earliest times to the end of the Middle Kingdom.—pt. 2. The Hyksos period and the new Kingdom (1675-1080 B.C.) Bibliography: pt. 1, p. [353]-374. [DT59.H43] 52-7286
1. Egypt—Antiquities. I. Title.
BIP

*KAMIL, Jill. 916.23
Luxor: a guide to ancient Thebes. Photographs by Alistair Duncan and George Allen, plans by Hassan Ibrahim. [New York, Longman, 1973] 175 p. maps, plates, illus., 19 cm. [DT73.T3] 0-582 3.00 (pbk.)
1. Egypt—Antiquities. 2. Luxor—Description and travel. I. Title.

LECLANT, Jean. 709.32
In the steps of the pharaohs. Photos. by Albert Raccah. New York, Hastings House [1958] 127p. plates (part col.) maps. 31cm. [DT61.L] A59
1. Egypt—Antiq. I. Itaccah, Albert. II. Title.

OTTO, Eberhard, 1913- 709.32
Aus der Sammlung des Agyptologischen Institutes der Universitat Heidelberg. Berlin, New York, Springer-Verlag, 1964. 99 p. plates (1 col.) 28 cm. (Werke der Kunst in Heidelberg, 1) "Beschrelbungen und Literaturhinweise": p. [87]-99. [DT59.O88] 64-7817
1. Egypt — Antiq. I. Heidelberg. Universitat. Agyptologisches Institut. II. Title. III. Series.

SILVERMAN, David P. 709'.32
Treasures of Tutankhamen / David P. Silverman. New York : Abbeville Press, [1978] p. cm. [DT87.5.S45] 78-12357 ISBN 0-89659-022-4 : 17.95
1. Tutankhamen, King of Egypt—Tomb. 2. Egypt—Antiquities. 3. Art objects, Egyptian. I. Title.

Egypt—Antiquities—Catalogs.

STEWART, H. M., B.A. 732'.8'07402142
Egyptian stelae, reliefs and paintings from the Petrie collection / H. M. Stewart. Warminster, Eng. : Aris & Phillips, c1976- v. : ill. ; 31 cm. Contents.Contents.—pt. 1. The New Kingdom. Includes bibliographical references and indexes. [DT59.L65S84] 76-372332 ISBN 0-85668-026-5(v.1) 27.50
1. Petrie Museum. 2. Egypt—Antiquities—Catalogs. 3. Stele (Archaeology)—Catalogs. 4. Bas-relief—Catalogs. 5. Sculpture, Egyptian—Catalogs. I. Petrie Museum. II. Title.
Distributed by International Scholarly Book Services.

VICTORIA and Albert Museum, South Kensington. 932'.0074'02134
Egyptian objects in the Victoria and Albert Museum / Barbara Adams. Warminster, Eng. : Aris & Phillips, 1977. 61 p. ; 30 cm. (Egyptology today ; no. 3) Includes bibliographical references. [DT59.S68V52 1977] 78-320285 ISBN 0-85668-103-2 : 19.50
1. Victoria and Albert Museum, South Kensington—Catalogs. 2. Egypt—Antiquities—Catalogs. I. Adams, Barbara G. II. Title. III. Series.
Distributed by International Scholarly Book Services Inc., P. O. Box 555 Forest Grove, OR
BIP

Egypt—Antiquities—Juvenile literature.

VAN DUYN, Janet H. (Dunning) 913.32'03'1
Builders on the desert; stone craftsmen of ancient Egypt, by Janet Van Duyn. Illustrated with photos. Drawings by William V. Judson. New York, J. Messner [1974] 96 p. illus. 22 cm. A brief description of ancient Egyptian civilization as revealed by the discoveries of archaeologists and scholars. [DT64.V36] 73-19234 ISBN 0-671-32649-X 6.25
1. Egypt—Antiquities—Juvenile literature. I. Judson, William V., illus. II. Title.
Library binding 5.79, ISBN 0-671-32650-3.
BIP

1. Electric power-plants—Connecticut—Design and construction.

Electronic data processing—Architectural design.

LAWRENCE, Howard Ray. 729'.028'54
Basic design process and visual communication products / Howard Ray Lawrence. University Park, Pa. : Lawrence, [1974] vi, 189 leaves. : ill. ; 24 x 28 cm. [NA2728.L38] 74-82911
1. Electronic data processing—Architectural design. I. Title.

LEE, Kaiman, comp. 729'.028'54
Computer aided architectural design; 16 ARK-2 articles. Boston, Center for Environmental Research, c1973. 1 v. (various pagings) 29 cm. Consists of articles, chiefly by C. D. Stewart and K. Lee, compiled from journals and conference proceedings. Includes bibliographical references. [NA2728.L43] 74-160961
1. Electronic data processing—Architectural design. I. Stewart, Clifford D. II. Title. BIP

LEE, Kaiman. 729'.028'54
A step towards an integrated computer aided design system for the architect/planner / by Kaiman Lee. Boston : Environmental Design & Research Center, [1974] 225 leaves : diagrs. ; 29 cm. Cover title: Integrated CAD system. Bibliography: leaves 78-79. [NA2728.L44] 74-182899 25.00
1. Electronic data processing—Architectural design. I. Title. II. Title: Integrated CAD system. BIP

REFLECTIONS on 729'.028'54
computer aids to design and architecture / edited by Nicholas Negroponte. New York : Petrocelli/Charter, 1975. p. cm. Includes index. Bibliography: p. [NA2728.R43 1975] 75-16358 ISBN 0-88405-305-9
1. Electronic data processing—Architectural design. I. Negroponte, Nicholas.

Electronic data processing—Architectural practice.

GUTTRIDGE, Bryan. 729'.028'54
Computers in architectural practice [by] Bryan Guttridge [and] Jonathan R. Wainwright. New York, J. Wiley [1973] p. "A Halsted Press book." Bibliography: p. [NA1996.G87] 72-11917 ISBN 0-470-33785-0
1. Electronic data processing—Architectural practice. I. Wainwright, Jonathan R., joint author. II. Title. BIP

Electronic data processing—Architecture.

AUGER, Boyd. 729'.028'54
The architect and the computer. New York, Praeger [1972] 135 p. illus. 24 cm. Includes bibliographical references. [NA1995.A77] 79-165855 13.50
1. Electronic data-processing—Architecture. I. Title.

HAVILAND, David S. 720'.78
The computer and the architectural profession, by David S. Haviland. [Troy, N.Y., Center for Architectural Research, School of Architecture, Rensselaer Polytechnic Institute, 1966] 51, [5] p. illus. 22 x 28 cm. "The first in an anticipated series of reports to be issued by the Center for Architectural Research." Bibliography: p. [53]-[56] [NA2005.H3] 66-25155
1. Electronic data processing—Architecture. I. Rensselaer Polytechnic Institute, Troy, N.Y. Center for Architectural Research. II. Title.

LEE, Kaiman. 720'.28
Computer-generated perspective drawings / by Kaiman Lee. Boston : Environmental Design & Research Center, [1974] 5, [32] leaves : chiefly ill. ; 29 cm. Cover title: Computer perspectives. [NA2728.L435] 75-305512 5.00
1. Perry, Dean and Stewart. 2. Electronic data processing—Architecture. 3. Computer drawing. I. Title. II. Title: Computer perspectives. BIP

NEGROPONTE, Nicholas. 720'.18
The architecture machine: toward a more human environment. Cambridge, M.I.T. Pr. [1972, c.1970] 153 p. illus. 19 cm. Bibl.: p. 123-153. [NA2750.N37] 75-95283 ISBN 0-262-64010-4 pap., 2.95
1. Electronic data processing—Architecture. 2. Electronic data processing—City planning. I. Title. BIP

NEGROPONTE, Nicholas. 729'.028'54
Soft architecture machines. Cambridge, Mass., The MIT Press [1973] p. Bibliography: p. [NA2540.N375] 73-8720 ISBN 0-262-14018-7 7.95
1. Electronic data processing—Architecture. I. Title. BIP

Electronic data processing—Architecture—Bibliography.

BUNSELMEIER, Erich. 016.3092'08 s
Computerized location-allocation. [Monticello, Ill.] Council of Planning Librarians, 1973. 51 p. 29 cm. (Council of Planning Librarians. Exchange bibliography no. 414) Cover title. [Z5942.C68 no. 414] [Z5943.E4] 016.72'028'54 74-185442 5.00
1. Electronic data processing—Architecture—Bibliography. I. Title. II. Series.

Electronic data processing—Arts.

MCCAULEY, Carole 700'.28'54
Spearin.
Computers and creativity. New York, Praeger [1974] 160 p. illus. 22 cm. Bibliography: p. 149-156. A brief history of computers and the people involved in their development and a discussion of the computer's past and potential use in creating music, literature, and other artistic works. [NX458.M32] 73-21346 ISBN 0-275-25850-5 7.50
1. Electronic data processing—Arts. I. Title.

Electronic data processing—Museums.

COMPUTERS and their 069'.01'8
potential applications in museums; a conference sponsored by the Metropolitan Museum of Art, April 15, 16, 17, 1968. New York, Published for the museum by Arno Press, 1968. xx, 402 p. illus. 27 cm. Includes bibliographical references. [AM133.C6] 68-58185
1. Electronic data processing—Museums. I. New York (City) Metropolitan Museum of Art. BIP

Electrophotography.

SCHAFFERT, Roland Michael, 778.3
1905-
Electrophotography [by] R. M. Schaffert. London, New York, Focal Press [1965] 463 p. illus. 25 cm. (The Focal library) Includes bibliographical references. [TR1035.S3] 65-18644
1. Electrophotography. 2. Xerography. I. Title. BIP

SCHAFFERT, Roland 686.4'4
Michael, 1905-
Electrophotography / R. M. Schaffert. Enl. and rev. ed. New York : Wiley, [1975] p. cm. "A Halsted Press book." Includes bibliographical references and indexes. [TR1035.S3 1975] 75-20099 ISBN 0-470-75696-9 : 77.50
1. Electrophotography. 2. Xerography.

Electrophotography—Congresses.

ABSTRACTS of papers for 686.4'4
second International Conference on Electrophotography : Marriott Twin Bridges Hotel, Washington, D.C., October 24-27, 1973 / Society of Photographic Scientists and Engineers. Washington : The Society, c1973. 61 p. ; 23 cm. Includes index. [TR1035.A27] 75-328169
1. Electrophotography—Congresses. I. International Conference on Electrophotography, 2d, Washington, D.C., 1973. II. Society of Photographic Scientists and Engineers.

COATING and Graphic Arts 686.4'4
Conference, St. Charles, Ill., Fall1974.
1974 Fall Coating and Graphic Arts Conference ; Atlanta : Technical Association of the Pulp and Paper Industry, c1974. 177 p. : ill. ; 28 cm. Sponsored by the Coating and Graphic Arts Division of TAPPI. Includes bibliographical references. [TR1035.C6 1974] 75-316980
1. Electrophotography—Congresses. I. Technical Association of the Pulp and Paper Industry. Coating and Graphic Arts Division.

INTERNATIONAL Conference 686.4'4
on Electrophotography, 2d, Washington, D.C., 1973.
Electrophotography : second international conference : [papers] / edited by Deane R. White ; sponsored by the Society of Photographic Scientists and Engineers. [Washington] : The Society, c1974. vi, 231 p. : ill. ; 30 cm. Includes bibliographical references and indexes. [TR1035.157 1973] 75-306784
1. Electrophotography—Congresses. I. White, Deane Rowland, 1902- II. Society of Photographic Scientists and Engineers. III. Title.

INTERNATIONAL Conference 686.4'4
on Electrophotography, 3d, Washington, D.C., 1977.
Advance printing of paper summaries / Third International Conference on Electrophotography. Washington : Society of Photographic Scientists and Engineers, c1977. 112 p. (p. 110-112 blank for "Notes") : ill. ; 23 cm. Includes bibliographical references and index. [TR1035.157 1977] 77-88455 ISBN 0-89208-093-0 pbk. : 12.00
1. Electrophotography—Congresses. I. Society of Photographic Scientists and Engineers.

TAPPI Reprography 686.4'4
Conference, San Francisco, 1976.
1976 Tappi Reprography Conference, October 11-13, San Francisco, Ca. : [papers. Atlanta : Technical Association of the Pulp and Paper Industry, c1976. iv, 84 p. ; 28 cm. Includes bibliographical references. [TR1035.T36 1976] 76-382182
1. Electrophotography—Congresses. I. Technical Association of the Pulp and Paper Industry. II. Title.

TECHNICAL Association of 686.4'4
the Pulp and Paper Industry. Coating and Graphic Arts Division.
1975 fall Coating and Graphic Arts Division Week : October 27-31, Philadelphia Marriott, Atlanta : Technical Association of the Pulp and Paper Industry, c1975. iv, 204 p. : ill. ; 28 cm. On cover: 1975 TAPPI fall Coating and Graphic Arts Division week: preprint. Includes bibliographical references. [TR1035.T4 1975] 75-333109
1. Electrophotography—Congresses. 2. Paper coatings—Congresses. 3. Photography—Printing papers. I. Title.

Electrophotography—Directories.

try.
TECHNICAL Association of the Pulp and Paper Industry.
The source book for electrophotography. Atlanta, 1972. 1 v. (unpaged) 28 cm. (Its CA report no. 42) [TR1025.T4] 72-190595 5.00
1. Electrophotography—Directories. I. Title. II. Series.

Elema (Papuan people)—Religion.

BEIER, Ulli. 301.29'953
Hohao; the uneasy survival of an art form in the Papuan Gulf [by] Ulli Beier & Albert Maori Kiki. [Melbourne, Thomas] Nelson [(Australia) 1970] 63 p. illus. 29 cm. [GN470.B3] 79-871950 ISBN 0-17-001912-8 4.95
1. Elema (Papuan people)—Religion. 2. Art, Elema. I. Kiki, Albert Maori, 1931- joint author. II. Title.

Elgar, Frank.

MATISSE, Henn 1869-1954 759.4
Matisse. Text by Frank Elgar. Greenwich, Conn., New York GraphicSociety [1961, c.1960] 14p. illus., 20col. plates. 41cm. 61-4063 65.00 bds.,
1. Elgar, Frank. I. Title.

Elgin marbles.

ROTHENBERG, Jacob. 733'.3'09385
"Descensus ad terram" : the acquisition and reception of the Elgin marbles / Jacob Rothenberg. New York : Garland Pub., 1977, i.e.1978 p. cm. (Outstanding dissertations in the fine arts) Originally presented as the author's thesis, Columbia, 1967. Bibliography: p. [NB92.R67 1977] 76-23716 ISBN 0-8240-2726-4 lib.bdg. : 50.00
1. Elgin marbles. I. Title. II. Title: The acquisition and reception of the Elgin marbles. III. Series.

VRETTOS, Theodore. 733'.3
A shadow of magnitude : the acquisition of the Elgin marbles / by Theodore Vrettos. New York : Putnam, [1974] 250 p., [4] leaves of plates : ill. ; 22 cm. Includes index. Bibliography: p. 225-229. [NB92.V73 1974] 74-194382 ISBN 0-399-11402-5 : 8.95
1. Elgin marbles. I. Title.

Elgin, Thomas Bruce, 7th Earl of, 1766-1841.

ST. Clair, William 733'.3'0924
Linn.
Lord Elgin and the marbles [by] William St. Clair. London, New York [etc.] Oxford U.P. 1967. x, 309 p. front., 10 plates (incl. ports., facsims.), map. 22 1/2 cm. 42/- (B 67-13030) Bibliography: p. [277]-279. [NB92.S7] 67-92112
1. Elgin, Thomas Bruce, 7th Earl of, 1766-1841. 2. Elgin marbles. I. Title.

Eliot, Charles, 1859-1897.

[ELIOT, Charles 712'.0924 B
William] 1834-1926.
Charles Eliot, landscape architect; a lover of nature and of his kind, who trained himself for a new profession, practised it happily and through it wrought much good. Freeport, N.Y., Books for Libraries Press [1971] xxiv, 770 p. illus., maps (part fold.), plans (part fold.), ports. 23 cm. Reprint of the 1902 ed. [SB470.E6E6 1971] 72-160971 ISBN 0-8369-5839-X
1. Eliot, Charles, 1859-1897. 2. Landscape architecture. I. Title. BIP

Eliot, George, pseud., i.e. Marian Evans afterwards Cross, 1819-1880.

BENNETT, Joan [Frankau] v. 12
George Eliot, her mind and her art. Cambridge [Eng.] University Press, 1962. 202 p. 21 cm. [NUC63-5999]
1. Eliot, George, pseud., i.e. Marian Evans afterwards Cross, 1819-1880. I. Title. BIP

Elisofon, Eliot.

MUSEUM of 732'.2'09660740153
African Art.
Tribute to Africa: the photography and the collection of Eliot Elisofon; a memorial exhibition at the Museum of African Art, June through December, 1974. Washington [1974] 48 p. illus. 28 cm. Catalog. Bibliography: p. 48. [TR140.E4M87 1974] 74-81895
1. Elisofon, Eliot. 2. Sculpture, African—Exhibitions. 3. Photography, Artistic—Exhibitions. I. Elisofon, Eliot. II. Title. BIP

Elizabeth II, Queen of Great Britain, 1926-

YOUNG, Sheila. 739.27'074'021
The Queen's jewellery; the jewels of H.M. Queen Elizabeth II. New York, Taplinger Pub. Co. [1969] 119 p. illus. (part col.), ports. (part col.) 26 cm. [NK7303.Y6 1969] 71-86660 8.95
1. Elizabeth II, Queen of Great Britain, 1926- 2. Jewelry—Private collections. I. Title.

Elizabeth, Queen of England, 1533-1603.

STRONG, Roy C. 757'.0942
The cult of Elizabeth : Elizabethan portraiture and pageantry / Roy Strong. London : Thames and Hudson, 1977. 227 p. : ill. (some col.) ; 26 cm. Includes bibliographical references and index. [DA356.S83] 77-378494 ISBN 0-500-23263-6 : 24.95
1. Elizabeth, Queen of England, 1533-1603. 2. Great Britain—History—Elizabeth, 1558-1603. I. Title.
Distributed by W.W. Norton. BIP

Elizabeth, Queen of England, 1533-1603 — Portraits, caricatures, etc.

STRONG, Roy C 923.142
Portraits of Queen Elizabeth I Oxford, Clarendon Press, 1963. xiv, 173 p. illus. (part col.) ports (part col.) 25 cm. Includes bibliographical references. [N7639.E4S8] 63-2810
1. Elizabeth, Queen of England, 1533-1603 — Portraits, caricatures, etc. I. Title.

Ellsworth, Clarence, 1885-1961.

WEARIN, Otha Donner, 1903- 759.13
Clarence Arthur Ellsworth, artist of the Old West 1885-1964. Shenandoah, Iowa World Pub. Co., 1967. 171 p. illus. (part col.), facsims., ports. 30 cm. Bibliography: p. 154-163. [ND237.E56W4] 67-31472
1. Ellsworth, Clarence, 1885-1961. I. Title.

Ellsworth, James Sanford, 1802-1873 or 4.

MITCHELL, Lucy B 1901- 759.13
The paintings of James Sanford Ellsworth, itinerant folk artist, 1802-1873.: catalog of an exhibition, by Lucy B. Mitchell. Williamsburg, Va., [The Colonial Williamsburg Foundation 1974 vii, 103 p. illus. 21 cm. Catalog of an exhibition presented by the Abby Aldrich Rockefeller Folk Art Collection, Williamsburg, Virginia, October 13-December 1, 1974. Bibliography: p. 101-103. [ND1337.U6E495] 74-14365 ISBN 0-87935-025-3 7.00 (pbk.)
1. Ellsworth, James Sanford, 1802-1873 or 4. 2. Primitivism in art—United States. I. Ellsworth, James Sanford, 1802-1873 or 4. II. Abby Aldrich Rockefeller Folk Art Collection, Williamsburg, Va. III. Title.

Ellwood, Craig.

MCCOY, Esther. 720'.924
Craig, Ellwood; architecture. Foreword by Peter Blake. New York, Walker [1968] 155 p. illus. (part col.), plans. 24 x 25 cm. [NA737.E36M3 1968b] 68-14007 15.00
1. Ellwood, Craig.

Elsevier, family of printers.

DAVIES, David William, 1908- 686'.2'0922 B
The world of the Elseviers, 1580-1712 [by David W. Davies] Westport, Conn., Greenwood Press [1971] vii, 159 p. 23 cm. Reprint of the 1954 ed. Includes bibliographical references. [Z232.E5D3 1971] 70-98751 ISBN 0-8371-3084-0
1. Elsevier, family of printers. I. Title. BIP

GOLDSMID, Edmund Marsden. 686.2'092'2
A complete catalogue of all the publications of the Elzevier presses at Leyden, Amsterdam, The Hague and Utrecht, with introd., notes, and an appendix containing a list of all works, whether forgeries or anonymous publications, generally attributed to these presses, by Edmund Goldsmid. Boston, Milford House [1973] p. Reprint of the 1885-88 ed. published privately in Edinburgh in series: Bibliotheca curiosa. A rev. and abridged translation of Les Elzeviers, by A. Willems. [Z232.E5G58 1973] 73-15704 ISBN 0-87821-199-3
1. Elsevier, family of printers. I. Willems, Alphonse Charles Joseph, 1839-1912. Les Elzevier. II. Title. III. Series: Bibliotheca curiosa. BIP

Elsheimer, Adam, 1578-1610.

ANDREWS, Keith. 760'.092'4
Adam Elsheimer : paintings, drawings, prints / Keith Andrews. New York : Rizzoli, 1977. 178 p. : ill. (some col.) ; 29 cm. Includes indexes. Bibliography: p. 171. [N6888.E63A5] 77-73365 ISBN 0-8478-0089-X : 60.00
1. Elsheimer, Adam, 1578-1610. 2. Artists—Italy—Rome (City)—Biography. 3. Artists—Germany—Biography. I. Elsheimer, Adam, 1578-1610.

Elvehjem Art Center.

ELVEHJEM Art Center. 704.948'2
Icons from the Elvehjem Art Center, by George Galavaris. [Madison, Wis., 1973] xxii, 127 p. illus. 27 cm. Bibliography: p. xv-xxii. [N8186.U6E454 1973] 74-167272
1. Elvehjem Art Center. 2. Icons—Madison, Wis.—Catalogs. I. Galavaris, George. II. Title.

Emblems.

BOUDARD, Giovanni Battista, d.1778. 704.94'6
Iconologie : Vienna, 1766 / J. B. Boudard. New York : Garland Pub., 1976. p. cm. (The Renaissance and the gods ; 43) Reprint of the 1766 ed. published by J. T. de Trattnern, Vienna. [N7740.B75 1976] 75-27888 ISBN 0-8240-2092-8 lib.bdg. : 40.00
1. Emblems. 2. Art—Early works to 1800. I. Title. II. Series. BIP

COLE, Herbert. 745.6'6
Heraldry and floral forms as used in decoration. With drawings by the author. London, J. M. Dent; New York, Dutton, 1922. Detroit, Tower Books, 1971. 248 p. illus. 24 cm. [NK1585.C6 1971] 74-164180
1. Emblems. 2. Heraldry. 3. Design, Decorative—Plant forms. I. Title. BIP

RIPA, Cesare, fl.1600. 704.94'6
Baroque and Rococo pictorial imagery. The 1758-60 Hertel edition of Ripa's 'Iconologia.' Introd., translations, and 200 commentaries by Edward A. Maser. New York, Dover Publications [1971] xxi, 200 (i.e. 400) p. 200 illus. 24 cm. (The Dover pictorial archives series) Includes bibliographical references. [N7740.R515 1971] 78-100544 ISBN 0-486-22748-0 6.00
1. Emblems. 2. Allegories. I. Maser, Edward Andrew, 1923- II. Title. BIP

RIPA, Cesare, fl.1600. 704.94'6
Iconologia / Cesare Ripa. New York : Garland Pub., 1976. p. cm. (The Renaissance and the gods ; v. 21) Reprint of the 1611 ed. published by P. P. Tozzi, Padua. Includes indexes. [N7740.R5 1976] 75-27865 ISBN 0-8240-2070-7 : 40.00
1. Emblems. I. Title. II. Series. BIP

Embroidery.

ANCHOR book of counted thread embroidery. 746.44
introd. by Dorothy A. Allsopp. London, B. T. Batsford [1960] [Label: Boston] [C. T. Branford Co.] 229 p. illus. (part col.) 28 cm. [TT771.A5] 60-1900
1. Embroidery. I. Title: Counted thread embroidery.

APPELL, Madeleine. 746.4'4
One-stitch stitchery / by Madeleine Appell ; drawings by Millicent Trikaminas. New York : Sterling Pub. Co., c1978. 47 p. : ill. ; 20 cm. (Little craft book series) Includes index. Directions for using 10 embroidery stitches and their standard variations to create a variety of stitchery paintings. [TT770.A66] 78-51063 ISBN 0-8069-5384-5 : 3.75 ISBN 0-8069-5385-3 lib.bdg. : 3.99
1. Embroidery. I. Trikaminas, Millicent. II. Title. BIP

BEANEY, Jan. 746.4
The young embroiderer; a how-it-is-done book of embroidery. New York, F. Warne [1967, c1966] 57 p. illus. 29 cm. Bibliography: p. 57. Considers threads, background fabrics, color schemes, and sewing equipment; explains stitches and presents stitchery exercises in the form of short projects; discusses allied embroidery decoration such as applique and padding; and introduces unique sources of patterns including rubbings, cut paper, and mathematical designs. Includes photographs of sample work. [TT770.B4] AC 68
1. Embroidery. I. Title.

BEESE, Pat. 746.9
Embroidery for the church / Pat Beese. Newton Centre, Mass. : C. T. Branford Co., [1975] 104 p. : ill. ; 26 cm. (A Studio handbook) Includes index. Bibliography: p. 103. [TT770.B43 1975] 74-32017 ISBN 0-8231-4034-2 : 15.95
1. Embroidery. 2. Church decoration and ornament. I. Title. BIP

BENNETT, Maggi. 746.4'6
Stitchery, by Maggi Bennett, Sarajean Capua [and] Jeanette McArthur. [1st ed.] Hollywood, Fla., Dukane Press [1971, c1970] 32 p. col. illus. 32 cm. Brief text and photographs introduce decorative stitchery demonstrating various stitches to be used for pictures, wall hangings, and clothing. [TT771.B364] 79-127618 ISBN 0-87800-010-0
1. Embroidery. I. Capua, Sarajean, joint author. II. McArthur, Jeanette, 1919- joint author. III. Title.

BETTER homes and gardens embroidery. 746.4'4
1st ed. Des Moines : Meredith Corp., c1978. 96 p. : ill. ; 27 cm. (Better homes and gardens books) [TT770.B47] 77-85857 ISBN 0-696-00425-9 : 3.95
1. Embroidery. I. Better homes and gardens. II. Title: Embroidery. BIP

BOYLES, Margaret. 746.4'4
The Margaret Boyles' Book of needle art. 1st ed. New York : Harcourt Brace Jovanovich, c1978. 160 p. : ill. ; 29 cm. Includes index. [TT770.B69 1978] 77-73064 ISBN 0-15-157100-7 : 17.95
1. Embroidery. I. Title. II. Title: Book of needle art. BIP

BRUDNER, Nettie Yanoff. 746.4'4
Painting with a needle; an introduction to the art and craft of creative stitchery. [1st ed.] Garden City, N.Y., Doubleday, 1972. 192 p. illus. 24 cm. Bibliography: p. 188-189. [TT770.B89] 79-180117 8.95
1. Embroidery. I. Title.

BUCHER, Jo. 746.4'4'03
The complete guide to embroidery stitches and crewel. [New York, Creative Home Library, 1971] 353 p. illus. (part col.) 27 cm. Bibliography: p. 347. [TT770.B9] 76-145622 ISBN 0-696-16500-7 8.95
1. Embroidery. I. Title.

BUTLER, Anne. 746.4'4
Embroidery stitches; an illustrated guide. New York, Praeger [1968] 128 p. illus. 21 cm. [TT771.B84] 68-23042
1. Embroidery. I. Title.

BUTLER, Anne. 746.4
Embroidery stitches; an illustrated guide. New York, Praeger [1968] 128 p. illus. 21 cm. Photographs and diagrams illustrate simple stitches used in hand embroidery. [TT771.B84] AC 68
1. Embroidery. I. Title.

CELESTIN, Gina. 746.4'4
Embroider your clothes and linens / by Gina Celestin. Indianapolis : Bobbs-Merrill, [1978] p. cm. [TT770.C44] 77-15445 ISBN 0-672-52073-7 : 12.95
1. Embroidery. I. Title.

CHAPMAN, Jane A 746.44
Girl's book of embroidery. With illus. and diagrs. by Walter Chapman. New York, Greenberg [1953] 96p. illus. 23cm. [TT770.C47] 52-13109
1. Embroidery. I. Title.

DAVIS, Mildred J. 746.44
The art of crewel embroidery. New York, Crown [c.1962] 224p. illus. (pt. col.) 29cm. 62-11810 10.00
1. Embroidery. I. Title. BIP

DAWSON, Barbara. 746.4'4
Metal thread embroidery. New York, Taplinger Pub. Co. [1969, c1968] 175 p. illus. (part col.) 26 cm. Bibliography: p. 167. [TT777.D3 1969] 69-11172 12.95
1. Embroidery. I. Title. BIP

DAWSON, Barbara. 746.4'4
Metal thread embroidery / Barbara Dawson. New ed. New York : Watson-Guptill Publications, 1976. p. cm. Includes index. Bibliography: p. [TT777.D3 1976] 75-44164 ISBN 0-8230-3044-X : 14.95
1. Embroidery. I. Title.

*DEDENNE, Lynnette. 746.4'4
Decorating with stitches / Lynette deDenne [and] Margaret F. Johnson. Newton, Mass : Charles T. Brandford Co., 1976. 144p. : ill. (part col.) ; 25 cm. Includes index. Bibliography: p. [141]-142. [TT770] ISBN 0-8231-5047-X pbk. : 13.50
1. Embroidery. I. Johnson, Margaret F. joint author. II. Title. BIP

DOUGLASS, Winsome 746.44
Discovering embroidery. [Dist. New York, Taplinger, 1962] 2.95 56-16297
1. Embroidery. I. Title. BIP

DOUGLASS, Winsome. 746.44
Discovering embroidery. New York, Studio Publications [1956, c1955] 167p. illus. 23cm. [TT770.D6 1956] 56-7998
1. Embroidery. I. Title.

DOUGLASS, Winsome. 746.44
Discovering embroidery. London, Mills & Boon [1971, c.1955] viii, 167 p. illus. 23 cm. [TT770.D6] ISBN 0-263-69981-1
1. Embroidery. I. Title.
Distributed by Transatlantic Arts, Levittown, N.Y., for 4.95. L.C. card no. 56-16297 rev.

DREESMANN, Cecile. 746.4'4
Embroidery. [1st American ed. New York] Macmillan [1969] 173 p. illus. 20 cm. Translation of Borduurkunst. Bibliography: p. 173. [TT770.D6823 1969] 75-82559
1. Embroidery.

DROOKER, Penelope B. 746.1'4
Embroidering with the loom : creative combinations of weaving and stitchery / Penelope B. Drooker ; drawings by Susan Damon Fritz-Herzberg ; photos. by Jan Lougee Bryant, Robert M. Wilson, and Douglas Barr. New York : Van Nostrand Reinhold Co., [1978] p. cm. Includes index. Bibliography: p. [TT770.D74] 78-17108 ISBN 0-442-22175-4 : 14.00
1. Embroidery. 2. Hand-weaving. I. Title. BIP

EMBROIDERY / 796.4'4
[editor, Mary Harding]. New York : Van Nostrand Reinhold Co., [1978] 127 p. : ill. ; 29 cm. Includes index. [TT770.E496] 77-92127 ISBN 0-442-23070-2 : 8.95
1. Embroidery. I. Harding, Mary. BIP

EMBROIDERY in easy steps / 746.4'4
edited by Christine Risley ; [photographs by Peter Kibbles]. London : Studio Vista, 1976. 64 p. : ill. (chiefly col.) ; 29 cm. Bibliography: p. 64. [TT770.E497] 77-362489 ISBN 0-289-70722-6 : £1.95
1. Embroidery. I. Risley, Christine. II. Kibbles, Peter.

EMBROIDERY step-by-step. 746.4'4
New York : Collier Books, 1976. p. cm. "A Studio Vista book." [TT770.E5 1976b] 76-8262 ISBN 0-02-011820-1 / 4.95
1. Embroidery.

EMBROIDERY step-by-step. 746.4'4
1st American ed. New York : Macmillan, 1976. p. cm. "A Studio Vista book." [TT770.E5 1976] 76-8267 ISBN 0-02-578250-9 : 6.95 pbk. : 4.95
1. Embroidery.

ENDACOTT, Violet M. 746.44
Design in embroidery. New York, Macmillan, 1964 [c.1963] vi, 133p. illus. (pt. col.) 26cm. 64-18410 7.50
1. Embroidery. I. Title.

ENTHOVEN, Jacqueline. 746.44
The stitches of creative embroidery. New York, Reinhold Pub. Corp. [1964] 212 p. illus. (part col.) 28 cm. [TT770.E58] 64-13643
1. Embroidery. I. Title. BIP

FRASER, B. Kay. 746.4'4
Modern stitchery : stitches, patterns, free-form designing / by B. Kay Fraser. New York : Crown Publishers, c1976. 108 p., [4] leaves of plates : ill. ; 29 x 18 cm.

Includes index. [TT770.F66 1976] 75-28078 ISBN 0-517-51864-3 : 6.95 ISBN 0-517-51865-1 pbk. : 4.95
1. Embroidery. I. Title. BIP

FREW, Hannah. 746.4'4
Three-dimensional embroidery / Hannah Frew. New York : Van Nostrand Reinhold Co., [1975] 104 p., [4] leaves of plates : ill. ; 27 cm. Includes index. Bibliography: p. 102. [TT770.F7] 74-9188 ISBN 0-442-30075-1 : 9.95 ISBN 0-442-30085-9 pbk. : 5.95
1. Embroidery. I. Title. BIP

GEDDES, Elisabeth 746.44
Design for flower embroidery. [Dist. New York, Taplinger, 1962, c.1961] 103p. illus. (pt. col.) 26cm. Bibl. 62-6608 5.95
1. Embroidery. 2. Flowers. I. Title.

GOSTELOW, Mary. 746.4'4
The complete international book of embroidery / Mary Gostelow ; [editor, Susannah Read]. New York : Simon and Schuster, c1977. 288 p. : col. ill. ; 30 cm. Includes index. Bibliography: p. 277-279. [TT770.G67] 77-91619 ISBN 0-671-22886-2 : 19.95
1. Embroidery. I. Read, Susannah. II. Title. BIP

GOSTELOW, Mary. 746.4'4
Mary Gostelow's embroidery book / ill. by the author ; col. photos. by Martin F. Gostelow. 1st American ed. New York : Dutton, 1979, c1978. 247 p. : ill. (some col.) ; 27 cm. "A Sunrise book." Includes index. Bibliography: p. 241-244. [TT770.G68 1979] 78-70937 ISBN 0-87690-344-8 : 15.95
1. Embroidery. I. Title. II. Title: Embroidery book. BIP

GUILD, Vera P. 746.4'4
Creative use of stitches. Worcester, Mass., Davis Publications [1964] 51 p. illus. 26 cm. [TT770.G94] 64-12773
1. Embroidery. I. Title.

GUILD, Vera P. 746.4'4
Creative use of stitches, by Vera P. Guild. [Rev. and enl.] Worcester, Mass., Davis Publications [1969, c1964] 63 p. illus. (part col.) 26 cm. [TT770.G94 1969] 77-88460 ISBN 0-87192-009-3 5.59
1. Embroidery. I. Title.

HANA, Nora. 746.4'4
Embroidery / Nora Hana. New York : Two Continents Pub. Group, c1977. p. cm. (Creative needlecraft) Includes index. Bibliography: p. [TT770.H1813 1977] 76-52841 ISBN 0-8467-0239-8 : 6.95
1. Embroidery. I. Title.

HARASZTY, Eszter. 746.4'4
Needlepainting, a garden of stitches [by] Eszter Haraszty and Bruce David Colen. New York, Liveright [1974] xiv, 114 p. illus. 28 cm. [TT770.H26] 74-13423 ISBN 0-87140-593-8 14.95
1. Embroidery. I. Colen, Bruce David, joint author. II. Title. BIP

HARDING, Valerie. 746.4'4
Textures in embroidery / Valerie Harding. New York : Watson-Guptill Publications, 1977. 84 p. : ill. ; 26 cm. Includes index. [TT770.H27] 76-55420 ISBN 0-8230-5341-5 : 10.95
1. Embroidery. I. Title.

HAUPT-BATTAGLIA, Heidi. 746.44
Let's embroider. [Rev. English ed.] London, Batsford [1960; label: Newton, Mass., C. T. Branford Co.] 200 p. illus. 26 cm. Translation of Wir sticken weiter. [NK9204.H313 1960] 60-2800
1. Embroidery. I. Title.

HOWARD, Constance. 746.4'4
Embroidery and color / Constance Howard. New York : Van Nostrand Reinhold, [1976] p. cm. Includes index. Bibliography: p. [TT770.H68 1976] 76-10763 ISBN 0-442-23556-9 : 16.95
1. Embroidery. 2. Color in the textile industries. I. Title.

HOWARD, Constance 746.4'4
Inspiration for embroidery. Newton Centre, Mass., Branford [1967, c.1966] 240p. illus. (pt. col.) 26cm. Bibl. [NK9204] 67-15952 12.50
1. Embroidery. 2. Design. I. Title. BIP

HULL, May. 746.4'4
Embroidery for Africa. London, Nairobi [etc.] Oxford U.P., 1967. [9] 86 p. illus., diagrs. 25 cm. 12/6 (B 67-13034) [TT770.H8] 67-102383
1. Embroidery. I. Title.

ILLES, Robert E. 746.4'4
Men in stitches / Robert E. Illes. New York : Van Nostrand Reinhold Co., [1975] 136 p. : ill. ; 25 cm. Includes index. [TT840.I42] 74-22512 ISBN 0-442-23630-1 : 13.95
1. Punched work. 2. Embroidery. 3. Needlework. I. Title. BIP

JOHN, Edith. 746.4'4
Creative stitches. Newton Centre, Mass., C. T. Branford Co. [1967] 112 p. illus. 26 cm. [TT770] 67-19870
1. Embroidery. I. Title. BIP

JOHN, Edith. 746.4'4
Creative stitches. New York, Dover Publications [1973, c1967] 112 p. illus. 26 cm. [TT720.J57 1973] 73-84802 ISBN 0-486-22972-6 2.00 (pbk.)
1. Embroidery. I. Title.

JOHN, Edith. 746.4'4
Experimental embroidery / Edith John. Newton Centre, Mass. : C. T. Branford Co., 1976. 120 p. : ill. ; 26 cm. Includes index. Bibliography: p. 114. [TT770.J578 1976] 75-9521 ISBN 0-8231-4255-8
1. Embroidery. I. Title. BIP

JOHN, Edith. 746.4'4
Filling stitches. Newton Centre, Mass., C. T. Branford [1967] 96 p. illus., 8 plates. 26 cm. [TT770.J58] 67-22707
1. Embroidery. I. Title. BIP

KARASZ, Mariska. 746.44
Adventures in stitches; a new art of embroidery, and more adventures—fewer stitches. Rev. and expanded ed. [New York] Funk & Wagnalls [1959] 127 p. illus. (part col.) diagrs. 23 x 28 cm. [TT770.K2 1959] 59-10899
1. Embroidery. I. Title. BIP

KASSELL, Hilda. 746.4'4
Stitches in time; the art and history of embroidery. [1st ed.] New York, Duell, Sloan and Pearce [1967, c1966] 108 p. illus. 21 cm. Bibliography: p. 107-108. [TT770.K22] 67-2273
1. Embroidery. 2. Embroidery—United States—History. I. Title.

KASSELL, Hilda. 746.4
Stitches in time: the art and history of embroidery. [1st ed.] New York, Duell, Sloan and Pearce [1967, c1966] 108 p. illus. 21 cm. Bibliography: p. 107-108. Describes the varieties of needlepoint and embroidery practiced by young ladies since colonial times; surveys the contemporary needle work designs of this century; and includes instructions for many embroidery stitches. [TT770.K22] AC 66
1. Embroidery. 2. Embroidery—United States—History. I. Title.

KATZENBERG, Gloria. 746.4'4
Art and stitchery: new directions. New York, Scribner [1974] xiii, 109 p. illus. 28 cm. Bibliography: p. 107. [TT770.K23] 73-19284 ISBN 0-684-13765-8 12.50
1. Embroidery. I. Title.

KENYON, Anne. 746.4'4
Embroidery and design on patterned fabric / Anne Kenyon. 1st American ed. South Brunswick : A. S. Barnes, 1975. 128 p. : ill. ; 25 cm. Includes index. Bibliography: p. 127. [TT770.K33 1975] 74-17802 ISBN 0-498-01679-X : 9.95
1. Embroidery. 2. Applique. 3. Collages. I. Title. BIP

KING, Bucky. 746.44
Creative canvas embroidery. New York, Hearthside Press [c1963] 125 p. illus., plates (part col.) 23 cm. [TT770.K5] 63-9931
1. Embroidery. I. Title.

KOHLER, Elsie Kay 746.44
Flower embroidery. [Label: Newton, Mass., C. T. Branford Co. 1961, c.1960] 119p. illus. (Embroidery handbooks [no. 3]) 61-4265 5.00
1. Embroidery. 2. Flowers. I. Title.

KREVITSKY, Nik 746.44
Stitchery: art and craft. New York, Reinhold [c.1966] 132p. chiefly illus. (pt. col.) ports. 2icm. (Art horizons bk. Bibl. [NK9200.K7] 65-19678 5.50
1. Embroidery. I. Title. II. Series.

*KREVITSKY, Nik. 746.44
Stitchery: art and craft. New York, Van Nostrand Reinhold [1973?] 132 p. illus., (some col.) 21 cm. (An Art horizons book) Bibliography: p. 132. [NK9200.K7] 65-19678 ISBN 0-442-24535-1 3.95 (pbk.)
1. Embroidery. I. Title. II. Series.

LILEY, Alison. 746.44
The craft of embroidery: a practical study. Newton Centre, Mass. [1961] 224p. illus. 22cm. Includes bibliography. [TT770.L5 1961] 61-14619
1. Embroidery. I. Title. BIP

LILEY. ALISON 746.44
Embroidery: a fresh approach. London. Mills & Boon [New York. Taplinger. 1965. c.1964] 236p. illus. (pt. col.) 23cm. [TT770.L52] 65-3056 6.50
1. Embroidery. I. Title.

LOPO, Ana G. 746.3
The sampler book / by Ana G. Lopo and Bruce W. Murphy. New York : Crown Publishers, c1978. p. cm. Includes index. Bibliography: p. [TT775.L66] 78-9465 ISBN 0-517-53038-4 : 10.95. ISBN 0-517-53461-4 pbk. : 9.95 pbk. : 5.95
1. Embroidery. 2. Samplers. I. Murphy, Bruce W., joint author. II. Title. BIP

MARKRICH, Lilo. 746.4'4
The principles of the stitch / Lilo Markrich. Chicago : H. Regnery Co., c1976. p. cm. Includes index. Bibliography: p. [TT770.M37 1976] 76-6271 ISBN 0-8092-8447-2 : 17.95. ISBN 0-8092-7964-9 pbk. : 7.95
1. Embroidery. I. Title. BIP

*MASON, Enid (Mann) 746.4'4
Embroidery design for students of all ages. London, Mills & Boon [1973, c.1970] 128 p. illus. (pt. col.) 26 cm. Bibliography: p. 128. [TT770]
1. Embroidery. 2. Needlework, Artistic. I. Title.
Available from Transatlantic Arts, Levittown, N.Y., for 6.95. BIP

MASON, Enid (Mann) 746.44
Ideas for machine embroidery. Drawings by the author. [Dist. New York, Taplinger, 1962, c.1961] 85p. illus. 26cm. 62-6719 5.95
1. Embroidery. I. Title. II. Title: Machine embroidery.

MAY, Marian. 746.44
Decorative stitchery. [1st ed.] Menlo Park, Calif., Lane Books [1965] 80 p. illus. 28 cm. (Sunset books) [TT770.M395] 65-16753
1. Embroidery. 2. Applique. I. Title.

MILLER, Irene Preston. 746.44
The stitchery book; embroidery for beginners, by Irene Preston Miller and Winifred Lubell. Drawings by Winifred Lubell. [1st ed.] Garden City, N.Y., Doubleday [1965] 96 p. illus. (part col.) 27 cm. [TT770.M54] 65-16370
1. Embroidery. I. Lubell, Winifred, joint author. II. Title. BIP

MILLER. IRENE PRESTON 746.44
The stitchery book; embroidery for beginners, by Irene Preston Miller, Winifred Lubell. Drawings by Winifred Lubell. Garden City. N.Y., Doubleday [c.1965] 96p. illus. (pt. col.) 27cm. [TT770.M54] 65-16370 4.95
1. Embroidery. I. Lubell. Winifred, joint author. II. Title.

MYERS, Carole Robbins. 746.4'4
A primer of left-handed embroidery. New York, Scribner [1974] 158 p. illus. 24 cm. [TT770.M9] 73-1105 7.95
1. Embroidery. I. Title. BIP

NICHOLS, Marion. 746.4'4
Encyclopedia of embroidery stitches, including crewel / Marion Nichols. New York : Dover Publications, 1974. xii, 218 p. : ill. ; 29 cm. Includes index. [TT770.N48] 72-97816 ISBN 0-486-22929-7 pbk. : 4.95
1. Embroidery. I. Title. BIP

NICHOLSON, Joan. 746.44
Creative embroidery. New York, Sterling Pub. Co. [1960] 136 p. illus. 23 cm. (Sterling craft books) [TT770.N5] 60-10377
1. Embroidery. I. Title.

NORBURY, James, 1904- 746.44
Counted-thread embroidery on linens and canvas. New York, Studio Publications [1956] 96 p. illus. 29 cm. [TT770.N84] 57-379
1. Embroidery. I. Title.

PALUDAN, Lis. 746.4'4
Easy embroidery / Lis Paludan ; translated by Christine Crowley. New York : Taplinger Pub. Co., 1975, c1970. 125 p. : ill. (some col.) ; 25 cm. Translation of Eva's broderibog. Includes index. Describes basic embroidery techniques and suggests various projects including those using potato prints, woven cord, and painted fabric. [TT770.P2213 1975] 75-10065 ISBN 0-8008-2358-3 : 9.95
1. Embroidery. 2. Applique. I. Title. BIP

PARKER, Betty. 746.4'4
Embroidery magic for patterned fabrics / by Betty Parker and Edith Martin. New York : Scribner, 1976. p. cm. Includes index. Bibliography: p. [TT770.P24] 76-14976 ISBN 0-684-14722-X : 14.95
1. Embroidery. 2. Textile fabrics. I. Martin, Edith, joint author. II. Title. BIP

PETERSEN, Grete 746.4'4
Handbook of stitches: 200 embroidery stitches, old and new, with descriptions, diagrams, and samplers by Grete Petersen and Elsie Svennas. Foreward by Jacqueline Enthoven. New York, Van Nostrand Reinhold [1975 c1970] 64 p. (chiefly illus.) 16 x 24 cm. Translation of Sting og sOmme. "To the pages of Sting og sOmme . . . [are] are added a few from Markbok." [TT770.P4813] 71-86644 ISBN 0-442-26533-6 3.95 (pbk.)
1. Embroidery. I. Svennas, Elsie, joint author. II. Title. BIP

*PETERSON, Grete. 746.4'4
Borders for embroidery. Translated by Anne Wilkins. New York, Van Nostrand Reinhold [1973 c.1971] 63 p. illus. 17 cm. [TT770] 72-9774 ISBN 0-442-26530-1. 3.95
1. Embroidery. I. Title. BIP

ROBINSON, Renee. 746.4'4
Streamlined decorative sewing [by] Renee Robinson [and] Julian Robinson. New York, St. Martin's Press [1971, c1970] 128 p. illus. 20 cm. [TT770.R64] 75-153508 2.95
1. Embroidery. 2. Sewing. I. Robinson, Julian, joint author. II. Title.

SAUNDERS, Everett E. 746.4
Stitchery [by Everett E. Saunders] Photos by Egons Tomsons. Racine, Wis., Whitman Pub. Co., c1967- v. col. illus. 30 cm. (A Whitman creative art book) Gives instructions for making various kinds of stitches and suggests their possible uses in a variety of creative stitchery projects. [TT771.S26] AC 68
1. Embroidery. I. Title.

SAYLES, Shirley. 746.4'4
Step-by-step stitchery : a complete introduction to the craft of stitchery / by Shirley Sayles ; conceived and edited by William Sayles ; stitchery projects designed and executed by Maida Silverman. New York : Golden Press, c1976. 80 p. : ill. (some col.) ; 29 cm. (The Golden Press step-by-step craft series) Bibliography: p. 79. [TT770.S29] 75-21846 ISBN 0-307-42018-3 pbk. : 2.95
1. Embroidery. I. Title. II. Title: Stitchery.

SEARNS, Martha (Genung) 746.44
Needle in hand. New York, Washburn [1950] 168 p. illus. 21 cm. Bibliography: p. 163-164. [TT770.S75] 50-10558
1. Embriodery. I. Title.

SMITH, Glenora. 746.4'4
Needlery : the connoisseur's album of adventures in needlepoint and embroidery / by Glenora Smith ; [editor, Carol Castellano ; illustrator, Janet Lombardo ; photographer, Edward Scibetta]. New York : Butterick Pub., c1978. 208 p. : ill. ; 22 x 27 cm. Bibliography: p. 208. [TT770.S653] 77-92604 ISBN 0-88421-045-6 : 12.95

1. Embroidery. 2. Needlework. I. Castellano, Carol. II. Lombardo, Janet. III. Title.

SNOOK, Barbara.   746.4'4
The creative art of embroidery. London, New York, Hamlyn, 1972. 176 p. illus. (some col.) 26 cm. Bibliography: p. 172. [TT770.S66] 73-157598 ISBN 0-600-31752-8 £1.50
1. Embroidery. I. Title.

SNOOK, Barbara.   746.4'4
Florentine embroidery. New York, Scribner [1967] 160 p. illus. (part col.) 27 cm. Bibliography: p. 158. [TT770.S67] 67-18133
1. Embroidery. I. Title.

SNOOK, Barbara   746.44
Learning to embroider. New York, Hearthside Press [c.1960] 112p. illus. Bibl. 61-2953 3.75 bds.,
1. Embroidery. I. Title.

SNOOK, Barbara.   746.44
Needlework stitches. New York, Crown Publishers [1963] 127 p. illus. 23 cm. Bibliography: p. 8. [TT771.S67] 63-21112
1. Embroidery. 2. Fancy work. I. Title.

SPEARS, Ruth (Wyeth) 1895-   746.44
The work basket embroidery book' illustrations of popular stitches. New York, M. Barrows [c1954] 127p. illus. 13cm. [TT760.S62 1954] 54-10309
1. Embroidery. 2. Needlework. I. Title.

THOMAS, Mary (Hedger), 1889-   746.44
Teach yourself embroidery. [U.S. ed.] Newton, Mass., C. T. Branford Co. [1962] 164 p. illus. 18 cm. (The Teach yourself books) [TT770.T53 1962] 62-12133
1. Embroidery. I. Title.

TURKIS, Ellen.   746.4'4
Fun with embroidery. New York, Watson-Guptill Publications [1973] p. [TT770.T9] 72-9782 ISBN 0-8230-1970-5
1. Embroidery. I. Title.

WELDONS, ltd., London.   746.44
Crewel embroidery, old and new, by Weldon's editors. New York, Hearthside Press [c1963] 96 p. illus. 23 cm. [TT770.W4] 63-21789
1. Embroidery. I. Title.

WHITE, Alice Violet.   746.44
Blackwork embroidery of today. London,Mills & Boon [1958; stamped: distributed by Sportshelf, New Rochelle, N. Y.] 90 p. illus. 22 cm. [TT771.W6] 58-4532
1. Embroidery. I. Title.

WHYATT, Betty.   746.4'4
Design for embroidery : an experimental approach / [by] Betty Whyatt & Jean Oxland. London : Mills and Boon, 1975 [i.e. 1976] 144 p., [16] p. of plates : ill. (some col.) ; 26 cm. Bibliography: p. [144] [TT770.W49 1976] 76-366425 ISBN 0-263-05893-X : 12.50
1. Embroidery. 2. Design. I. Oxland, Joan, joint author. II. Title.
Distributed by Transatlantic Arts.

WILLIAMS, Elsa S   746.4'4
Heritage embroidery [by]Elsa S. Williams. New York, Reinhold Pub. Corp. [1967] 112 p. illus. (part col.) 26 cm. [TT770.W495] 67-24700
1. Embroidery. I. Title.

WILLIAMS, Elsa S.   746.4'4
Heritage embroidery [by] Elsa S. Williams. New York, Reinhold Pub. Corp. [1967] 112 p. illus. (part col.) 26 cm. [TT770.W495] 67-24700
1. Embroidery. I. Title.

WILSON, Anna.   746.4'4
Enjoying embroidery / Anna Wilson; foreword by Constance Howard. New York : C. T. Branford Co., [1975] 96 p., [4] leaves of plates : 21 cm. Includes bibliographical references. [TT770.W53] 74-32170 ISBN 0-8231-4032-6 : 9.50
1. Embroidery. I. Title.   BIP

WILSON, Erica.   746.4'4
The craft of silk and gold thread embroidery and stump work / Erica Wilson. New York : Scribner, c1973. 96 p.

: ill. ; 27 cm. [TT770.W538] 77-23349 ISBN 0-684-15067-0 pbk. : 4.95
1. Embroidery. 2. Gold thread. 3. Silk thread. 4. Stump work. I. Title.   BIP

WILSON, Erica.   746.4'4
Erica Wilson's embroidery book. New York, Scribner [1973] x, 374 p. illus. 28 cm. Bibliography: p. 369. [TT770.W54] 78-123841 ISBN 0-684-10655-8 14.95
1. Embroidery. I. Title.   BIP

WILSON, Erica   746.44
Fun with crewel embroidery. New York, Scribners [c.1965] 41p. illus. (pt. col.) 27cm. [TT770.W55] 65-26942 3.50; 3.31 lib. ed.,
1. Embroidery. I. Title.   BIP

WILSON, Erica.   746.4'4
Needleplay / Erica Wilson. New York : Scribner, [1975] 189 p. : ill. (some col.) ; 24 cm. Includes index. [TT770.W57] 75-6036 ISBN 0-684-10655-8 : 9.95
1. Embroidery. I. Title.

Embroidery, American.

BAKER. MURIEL L.   746.44
A handbook of American crewel embroidery Rutland. Vt., Tuttle [1966] 67p. illus. (1 col.) 24cm. [NK9212.B3] 66-16722 3.75
1. Embroidery, American. I. Title.

DAVIS, Mildred J.   746.4'4'0973
Early American embroidery designs, by Mildred J. Davis. New York, Crown Publishers [1969] 159 p. illus. (part col.) 29 cm. Bibliography: p. 154-156. [NK9203.D3 1969] 68-9099 10.00
1. Embroidery, American. I. Title.

Embroidery—Bulgaria.

TCHOUKANOVA, Rossitza   746.44
Broderie nationale Bulgare [Bulgarian national embroidery] regions de l'ouest; introd. [by] Christo Vakarelski. [New York, Arthur Vanous, 406 E. 70th St., 1960] 135 col. plates 58-31532 14.80 bds.,
1. Embroidery—Bulgaria. I. Title.

Embroidery, Byzantine.

JOHNSTONE, Pauline.   746.4'4
The Byzantine tradition in church embroidery. [1st American ed.] Chicago, Argonaut, 1967. x, 144 p., 121 plates (part col.) illus. 26 cm. Bibliography: p. 132-135. [NK9310.J6] 67-17572
1. Embroidery, Byzantine. 2. Church Vestments. I. Title.

Embroidery—Central Europe—Patterns.

SIBBETT, Ed.   746.4'4
Peasant iron-on transfer patterns / Ed Sibbett, Jr. New York : Dover Publications, 1976. [24] leaves : chiefly ill. ; 28 cm. (Dover needlework series) Cover title. [TT771.S53 1976] 76-39752 ISBN 0-486-23456-8 pbk. : 1.50
1. Embroidery—Central Europe—Patterns. 2. Folk art—Central Europe.   BIP

Embroidery—China.

BAKER, Muriel L.   746.4'4
The blue and white : the cotton embroideries of rural China / by Muriel Baker and Margaret Lunt. New York : Scribner, c1977. ix, 102 p., [2] leaves of plates : col. ill. ; 28 cm. Bibliography: p. 102. [NK9283.A1B34] 76-57933 ISBN 0-684-14887-0 : 12.50
1. Embroidery—China. 2. Folk art—China. I. Lunt, Margaret, joint author. II. Title.   BIP

Embroidery—Collected works.

ANCHOR *embroidery book.*   746.44
no. 1- [London, New York, B.T.Batsford, 1952-- v. illus. 27cm. [TT770.A11] 54-31401
1. Embroidery—Collected works.

Embroidery, Croatian.

ZAGREB. Etnografski   746.4'4
muzej.
Yugoslavian Croatian folk embroidery : designs and techniques / [foreword by] Jelka Radaus Ribaric. New York : Van Nostrand Reinhold, 1976. p. cm. Illustrations and descriptions of samples from the Ethnographic Museum in Zagreb. Translation of Vezak vezla. [TT769.Y82C769 1976] 75-17280 ISBN 0-442-26905-6
1. Embroidery, Croatian. I. Radaus Ribaric, Jelka. II. Title.

Embroidery—England—Exhibitions.

WOODLANDS Art 746.3'942'07402162
Gallery.
Mary Rhodes, her embroiderers and tapestry-weavers : [catalogue of an exhibition held] 6 May to 1 June 1976 [at the] Woodlands Art Gallery. London : London Borough of Greenwich, [1976] [12] p. : ill. ; 21 cm. [NK9244.W66 1976] 77-368379 ISBN 0-9504033-8-5
1. Rhodes, Mary. 2. Embroidery—England—Exhibitions. 3. Tapestry—England—Exhibitions. I. Rhodes, Mary. II. Title.

Embroidery—England—Winchester.

CARBONELL,   746.4'4'09422735
Dorothy.
Winchester Cathedral embroideries / written and compiled by Dorothy Carbonell. Winchester : Friends of Winchester Cathedral, 1975. 32 p. : ill., facsims. ; 22 cm. Bibliography: p. 32. [NK9244.W55C37] 75-326840 ISBN 0-903346-06-0 : £0.30
1. Winchester Cathedral. 2. Embroidery—England—Winchester. I. Title.

Embroidery, English.

CAVE, Oenone   746.44
English folk embroidery. New York, Taplinger [1966, c.1965] 101, [3]p. illus. 26cm. Bibl. [NK9243.C3 1966] 66-11929 5.50 bds.,
1. Embroidery, English. 2. Smocking. I. Title.

GEDDES, Elisabeth   746.44
Blackwork embroidery [by] Elisabeth Geddes, Moyra McNeill [U.S.A. ed.] Newton Center. Mass.] Branford [1966, c.1965] 113p. illus., ports. 26cm. Bibl. [NK9423.G4] 66-10858 6.50
1. Embroidery, English. 2. Embroidery—Patterns. I. McNeill. Moyra. joint author. II. Title.

MORRIS, Barbara J.   746.440942
Victorian embroidery. Foreword by Hugh Wakefield. New York, Nelson [1963, c.1962] 238p. illus. 25cm. (Victorian collector ser.) Bibl. 62-17802 8.50
1. Embroidery, English. I. Title.

Embroidery, English—History.

SNOOK, Barbara.   746.4'4
English embroidery / Barbara Snook. London : Mills & Boon, 1974 [i.e.1975] 136 p. : ill. ; 23 cm. First ed. published in 1960 under title: English historical embroidery. L.C. copy imperfect: p. 33-48 bound upside down. Label mounted on t.p.: Transatlantic Arts, Levittown, N.Y., sole distributor for the U.S.A. Includes index. Bibliography: p. [131]-132. [NK9243.S6 1974] 75-312648 ISBN 0-263-05579-5 : 8.95
1. Embroidery, English—History. I. Title. Distributed by Transatlantic Arts, Levittown, N.Y., 8.95   BIP

Embroidery—Europe.

KINMOND, Jean.   746.44
Anchor book of European embroidery. Boston, C. T. Branford Co. [1964] 160 p. illus. (part col.) 28 cm. [TT770.K53] 64-55648
1. Embroidery—Europe. I. Title.

Embroidery—Greece, Modern.

PETRAKIS, Joan.   746.4'4
The needle arts of Greece : design and techniques / Joan Petrakis; graphs and maps by Martha Pangakis ; line drawings by Margery Nichols. New York : Scribner, c1977. xii, 175 p. : ill. ; 28 cm. Includes indexes. Bibliography: p. 169-171. [NK9151.A1P48] 76-49654 ISBN 0-684-14863-3 : 14.95
1. Embroidery—Greece, Modern. 2. Embroidery—Patterns. I. Title.

Embroidery—History.

GOSTELOW, Mary.   746.4'4
A world of embroidery / Mary Gostelow ; line drawings by the author and Janet Watson. New York : Scribner, [1975] 512 p., [14] leaves of plates : ill. (some col.) ; 26 cm. Includes index. Bibliography: p. 451-463. [NK9206.G67] 74-25172 ISBN 0-684-14230-9 : 20.00
1. Embroidery—History. I. Title.

SCHUETTE, Marie, 1878-   746.4409
A pictorial history of embroidery [by] Marie Schuette, Sigrid Muller-Christensen [Tr. from German by Donald King] New York, Praeger [1964, c.1963] xxiv, 336p. 484p. illus., 29 col. plates. 30cm. 64-13379 27.50
1. Embroidery—Hist. I. Muller, Sigrid Flammand (Christensen) 1904- II. Title.

Embroidery, Hungarian.

FEL, Edit.   746.44
Hungarian peasant embroidery [Tr. from Hungarian by Annie Barat and Lily Halapy. Dist. Newton, Mass., Branford, 1962, c.1961] 138p. illus. (pt. col.) 25cm. 62-668 10.50
1. Embroidery, Hungarian. I. Title.

Embroidery—India—Himachal Pradesh.

ARYAN, Subhashini   746.4'4
Himachal embroidery / Subhashini Aryan. New Delhi : Rekha Prakashan, [1976] 82 p., [24] leaves of plates : ill. ; 26 cm. [NK9276.A3H542] 77-900628 Rs80.00
1. Embroidery—India—Himachal Pradesh. I. Title.

Embroidery, Jewish.

FREEHOF, Lillian B.   746.4'4
(Simon) 1906-
Embroideries and fabrics for synagogue and home; 5000 years of ornamental needlework [by] Lillian S. Freehof and Bucky King. New York, Hearthside Press [1966] 224 p. illus. 24 cm. Bibliography: p. 217-219. [NK9273.F7] 66-15787
1. Embroidery, Jewish. 2. Decoration and ornament, Jewish. 3. Textile design. I. King, Bucky, joint author. II. Title.

Embroidery—Juvenile literature.

BEANEY, Jan.   746.4'4
The young embroiderer; a how-it-is-done book of embroidery. New York, F. Warne [1967, c1966] 57 p. illus. 29 cm. Bibliography: p. 57. [TT770.B4] 67-24708
1. Embroidery—Juvenile literature. I. Title.

HOLZ, Loretta.   746.4'4
Teach yourself stitchery. Illustrated with photos. and drawings by the author. New York, Lothrop, Lee & Shepard Co. [1974] 160 p. illus. 24 cm. Bibliography: p. 154-158. Instructions for making basic embroidery stitches and combining them creatively in various designs and projects. [TT770.H63] 73-17713 ISBN 0-688-41571-7 4.75
1. Embroidery—Juvenile literature. I. Title. Library binding; 4.32, ISBN 0-688-51571-1.   BIP

SAUNDERS, Everett E.   746 (j)
Stitchery [by Everett E. Saunders] Photos by Egons Tomsons. Racine, Wis., Whitman Pub. Co., c1967- v. col. illus. 30 cm. (A

Whitman creative art book) [TT771.S26] 68-3558
1. Embroidery—Juvenile literature. I. Title.

STANERSON, Lavon. 746.4'4
Creative stitchery / by Lavon Stanerson ; pictures by George Overlie. Minneapolis : Lerner Publications Co., c1976. p. cm. (An Early craft book) Introduces basic embroidery stitches and necessary materials. Includes design and project suggestions. [TT770.S7 1976] 76-13060 ISBN 0-8225-0885-0 lib.bdg. : 3.95
1. Embroidery—Juvenile literature. I. Overlie, George. II. Title. BIP

**STITCHERY.* 746
Racine, Wis., Whitman Pub., 1967. 1v. (unpaged) col. illus. 30cm. (Creative art bk., 1) 1.00 bds.,
1. Embroidery—Juvenile literature.

Embroidery, Machine.

BARTLEY, Regina. 746.4'4
The joy of machine embroidery / Regina Bartley. Chicago : H. Regnery, [1976] p. cm. Includes index. [TT772.B37] 76-6259 ISBN 0-8092-8346-8 : 12.95 ISBN 0-8092-7966-5 pbk. : 4.95
1. Embroidery, Machine. I. Title. BIP

FOSS, Mildred B. 746.4'4
Creative embroidery with your sewing machine / Mildred B. Foss. Englewood Cliffs, N.J. : Prentice-Hall, c1976. x, 118 p. : ill. ; 24 cm. (The Creative handcrafts series) (A Spectrum book ; S-CR-7) Includes index. [TT772.F67] 76-7588 ISBN 0-13-189365-3 : 10.95 ISBN 0-13-189357-2 pbk. :
1. Embroidery, Machine. I. Title. BIP

HOLT, Verna W. 746.4'4
Machine embroidery & yarn stitchery, by Verna W. Holt. [Las Vegas, Printed by A M I Print. Co., c1973] iv, 117 p. illus. 29 cm. On cover: Yarn stitchery on the sewing machine. [TT772.H64] 74-167226
1. Embroidery, Machine. I. Title. II. Title: Yarn stitchery on the sewing machine.

LILLOW, Ira. 746.4'4
Introducing machine embroidery. London, Batsford; New York, Watson-Guptill Publications, 1967. 3-72 p. illus., 2 col. plates. 21 1/2 cm. 25/- (B 67-13035) [TT772.L5] 68-10066
1. Embroidery, Machine I. Title.

MASON, Enid (Mann) 746.4'4
Ideas for machine embroidery, by Enid Mason, with drawings by the author. [2d (rev. and extended) ed.] London, Mills & Boon; distributor: Transatlantic Arts, New York [1973, c1961] 99 p. illus. 26 cm. [TT772.M37 1967] 73-161648 4.95
1. Embroidery, Machine. I. Title.

RISLEY, Christine. 746.44
Machine embroidery. With an historical survey by Patricia Wardle. Newton Centre, Mass., C. T. Branford Co. [1961] 128 p. illus. 26 cm. (Vista books) [TT771.R5 1961] 61-15587
1. Embroidery (Machine) I. Title.

SWIFT, Gay. 746.4'4
Machine stitchery / Gay Swift. Newton Centre, Mass. : C. T. Branford, [1975] c1974. 96 p., [4] leaves of plates : ill. ; 21 cm. [TT772.S95 1975] 74-23867 ISBN 0-8231-5046-1(Brandford) : 9.75
1. Embroidery, Machine. I. Title. BIP

Embroidery, Machine—Patterns.

LILLOW, Ira. 746.4'4
Designs for machine embroidery / Ira Lillow. Newton Centre, Mass. : C. T. Branford Co., 1975. 94 p. : chiefly ill. ; 21 cm. Bibliography: p. 94. [TT772.L48] 74-32174 ISBN 0-8231-4033-4 : 10.50
1. Embroidery, Machine—Patterns. I. Title. BIP

Embroidery, Medieval.

FREEMAN, Margaret Beam, 1899- 746.4'4
The St. Martin embroideries; a fifteenth-century series illustrating the life and legend of St. Martin of Tours [by] Margaret B. Freeman. [New York] Metropolitan Museum of Art; distributed by New York Graphic Society, Greenwich, Conn. [1968] 131, [1] p. illus. (part col.) 29 cm. Bibliography: p. 130-[132] [NK9208.F7] 68-21564 6.95
1. Martin, Saint, Bp. of Tours, 4th century—Art. 2. Embroidery, Medieval. I. Title. BIP

Embroidery—Patterns.

BATH, Virginia Churchill. 746.4'4
Embroidery masterworks; classic patterns and techniques for contemporary application. Photos. by Howard Kraywinkel, John Mahtesian [and] Richard Brittain. Chicago, H. Regnery Co. [1972] x, 225 p. illus. 29 cm. Bibliography: p. 222-223. [TT771.B32] 72-183818 15.00
1. Embroidery—Patterns. I. Title.

BRIGGS (Wm.) and Co. 746.4'4
Designs and patterns for embroiderers and craftsmen : 512 motifs from the Wm. Briggs and Company Ltd. "Album of transfer patterns" / edited by Marion Nichols. New York : Dover Publications, 1974. 145 p. : chiefly ill. ; 31 cm. Includes index. [TT771.B75 1974] 73-93081 ISBN 0-486-23030-9 pbk. : 3.50
1. Embroidery—Patterns. I. Nichols, Marion. II. Title. BIP

CAMPBELL, Etta. 746.44
Linen embroidery. London, Batsford [1957] [New York] [G. T. Branford Co.] 72 p. illus. 26 cm. [TT771.C26] 61-2334
1. Embroidery—Patterns. 2. Linen. 3. Samplers.

CHAPMAN, Suzanne E. 746.4'4
Historic floral and animal designs for embroiderers and craftsmen / Suzanne E. Chapman. New York : Dover Publications, 1977. vii, 71 p. : chiefly ill. ; 29 cm. (Dover pictorial archives series) [TT773.C5] 77-75740 ISBN 0-486-23526-2 : 3.00
1. Embroidery—Patterns. 2. Design, Decorative—Plant forms. 3. Design, Decorative—Animal forms. I. Title. BIP

EMBROIDERY designs, 1780-1820; 746.4'4
from the manuscript collection, the Textile Resource and Research Center, the Valentine Museum, Richmond, Virginia. Edited by Mildred J. Davis. New York, Crown Publishers [1971] xiii, 94 p. (chiefly illus. (part col.)) 29 cm. [TT771.E45 1971] 72-151024 7.50
1. Embroidery—Patterns. I. Davis, Mildred J., ed. II. Valentine Museum, Richmond, Va. Textile Resource and Research Center.

GIBBON. MABEL ANNIE 746.44
Canvas work: a practical guide. London, G. Bell [Newton Center, Mass., Branford, 1966, c.1965] 93, [2]p. illus. 21cm. [TT771.G5] 66-1663 3.75 bds.,
1. Embroidery—Patterns. I. Title.

HANSEN, Edith. 746.4'4
Counted thread embroidery [by] Edith Hansen & Ingrid Hansen. New York, Van Nostrand Reinhold Co. [1974, c1968] 76 p. illus. 21 x 22 cm. Danish original published under title: Tallesyning. Instructions with photographs for making original and traditional patterns with counted thread embroidery. [TT771.H2313 1974] 73-15284 ISBN 0-442-30024-7 4.95
1. Embroidery—Patterns. I. Hansen, Ingrid, joint author. II. Title.

HAUPT-BATTAGLIA, Heidi. 746.4'4
Practical embroidery. [1st American ed.] Newton Centre, Mass., C. T. Branford Co. [1968- c1963- v. illus. (part col.) 25 cm. Translation of Zeitloses Sticken. Contents.Contents.—v. 1. Mats, cloths, and runners. [TT771.H2332] 67-10690
1. Embroidery—Patterns. I. Title. BIP

JESSEN, Ellen. 746.4'4
Ancient Peruvian textile design in modern stitchery. New York, Van Nostrand Reinhold [1972] 64 p. illus. 22 x 26 cm. Bibliography: p. 64. [TT771.J45] 70-170674 7.95
1. Embroidery—Patterns. 2. Design, Decorative—Peru. I. Title.

LEY, Sandra. 746.4'4
Russian and other Slavic embroidery designs / Sandra Ley. New York : Scribner, c1976. 95 p., [2] leaves of plates : ill. ; 24 cm. Includes bibliographical references. [TT771.L49] 76-12479 ISBN 0-684-14734-3 : 12.50
1. Embroidery—Patterns. 2. Design, Decorative—Russia. 3. Design, Decorative—Europe, Eastern. I. Title.

ROSEN, Ike. 746.4'4
Modern embroidery. New York, Scribner [1972] 159 p. illus. 23 x 25 cm. [TT771.R56] 73-172973 ISBN 0-684-12620-6 10.00
1. Embroidery—Patterns. I. Title.

ROSSE, Allianora. 746.4'4
Flower embroidery. Photography by Rosanna H. Rosse. New York, Scribner [1975] 84 p. illus. 29 cm. Bibliography: p. 82-83. [TT773.R66] 74-13063 ISBN 0-684-14013-6
1. Embroidery—Patterns. 2. Design, Decorative—Plant forms. I. Title.

SCRASE, Pat 746.4'4
Let's start designing. London, Studio Vista; New York, Reinhold, [1966,i.e.1967] 60p. col. front., illus. (some col.). 26cm. [TT753.S47] 66-25544 6.50 bds.,
1. Embroidery—Patterns. 2. Textile design. I. Title.

SNOOK, Barbara. 746.4'4
Embroidery designs from the sea / Barbara Snook. New York : Taplinger Pub. Co., 1977, c1976. 96 p., [2] leaves of plates : ill. ; 26 cm. Includes index. Bibliography: p. 95. [TT771.S66 1977] 76-53872 ISBN 0-8008-2403-2 : 8.95
1. Embroidery—Patterns. 2. Design, Decorative—Animal forms. 3. Design, Decorative—Plant forms. 4. Sea in art. I. Title. BIP

THORNE-THOMSEN, Kathleen. 746.4'4
ThorneThomsen Kathleen
Mother Goose in stitches / Kathleen Thorne-Thomsen. 1st ed. New York : Holt, Rinehart and Winston, c1976. p. cm. [TT771.T43] 75-21486 ISBN 0-03-015201-1 : 9.95
1. Embroidery—Patterns. I. Title. BIP

Embroidery, Portuguese.

MOURA, Maria Clementina Carneiro de, 1898- 746.44
Traditional embroidery of Portugal, complete with designs. London, New York, B. T. Batsford [1952] 58p. illus. 27cm. (Anchor embroidery book, no. 1) In case. gMap on p. [2] of cover.3 fold, design sheets laid in. [TT770.A11 no.1] 54-31394
1. Embroidery, Portuguese. I. Title. II. Series.

Embroidery—Russia.

GOSTELOW, Mary. 746.4'4'0947
Embroidery of all Russia / Mary Gostelow ; line ill. and designs drawn and executed by the author, maps by John E. Damsell. New York : Scribner, c1977. 158 p., [8] leaves of plates : ill. (some col.) ; 26 cm. Includes index. Bibliography: p. 151-154. [TT769.R9G67] 77-73769 ISBN 0-684-15184-7 : 9.95
1. Embroidery—Russia. 2. Design, Decorative—Russia. I. Title. BIP

Embroidery—Scandinavia.

NIELSEN, Edith. 746.4'4
Scandinavian embroidery, past and present / by Edith Nielsen ; photography by Ben Marra and Peggy Nielsen ; diagrs. by Peggy Nielsen and Marlene Randall Richey. New York : Scribner, [1977] p. cm. Includes index. Bibliography: p. [TT769.S34N5] 77-7185 ISBN 0-684-15069-7 : 14.95
1. Embroidery—Scandinavia. 2. Design, Decorative—Scandinavia. I. Title.

Embroidery, Spanish.

A Devotional miscellany; 746.4'4
a printed replica of an embroidered book in the Elizabeth Day McCormick Collection, Museum of Fine Arts, Boston. Text by Margaret H. Swain. Boston [1966?] 1 v. (unpaged) col. illus. 15 cm. [NK9262.D4] 66-16609
1. Embroidery, Spanish. 2. Book ornamentation. I. Swain, Margaret H. II. Boston. Museum of Fine Arts.

Embroidery—Study and teaching.

BUTLER, Anne. 746.4'4
Embroidery for school children. [U.S. ed.] Newton, Mass., C. T. Branford Co. [1969] 95 p. illus. (part col.) 22 cm. Bibliography: p. 95. Describes the use of fabrics, threads, stitches, embroidery pictures, the use of material, and three-dimensional embroidery in the art of embroidery. [TT770.B948 1969] 79-90359
1. Embroidery—Study and teaching. I. Title.

KORNERUP, Ann-Mari. 746.4'4
Embroidery for children. Translated from Danish by Gerda M. Andersen. New York, Van Nostrand Reinhold Co. [1969] 70 p. illus. (part col.) 21 cm. Translation of Broderiformning. Gives suggestions for various embroidery projects and illustrates basic stitches. [TT770.K613] 75-86645
1. Embroidery—Study and teaching. I. Title.

Embroidery, Turkish.

CHICAGO. Art Institute. 746.4409561
Turkish and Greek island embroideries from the Burton Yost Berry Collection in the Art Institute of Chicago [compiled by] Margaret Gentles. [1st ed. Chicago] Art Institute of Chicago [1964] 53 p. 53 illus. (part col.) col. map (on lining papers) 29 cm. Bibliography: p. 53. [NK9265.C48] 64-11413
1. Embroidery, Turkish. 2. Embroidery, Greek. I. Berry, Burton Yost. II. Gentles, Margaret, comp. III. Title.

RAMAZANOGLU, Gulseren. 746.4'4
Turkish embroidery / Gulseren Ramazanoglu. New York : Van Nostrand Reinhold Co., 1976. 104 p. : ill. ; 25 cm. Includes index. [TT769.T9R35] 74-33892 ISBN 0-442-26799-1 : 10.95
1. Embroidery, Turkish. I. Title. BIP

Embroidery—Ukraine.

KMIT, Ann. 746.4'4
Ukrainian embroidery / Ann Kmit, Johanna Luciow, Loretta Luciow. New York : Van Nostrand Reinhold Co., [1978] p. cm. Includes index. Bibliography: p. [TT769.U35K54] 78-5659 ISBN 0-442-24465-7 : 13.95
1. Embroidery—Ukraine. 2. Design, Decorative—Ukraine. I. Luciow, Johanna, joint author. II. Luciow, Loretta, joint author. III. Title. BIP

Embroidery—U.S.

BAKER, Muriel L. 746.44
A handbook of American crewel embroidery, by Muriel L. Baker. [1st ed.] Rutland, Vt., C. E. Tuttle Co. [1966] 67 p. illus. (1 col.) 24 cm. Bibliography: p. 67. [NK9212.B3] 66-16722
1. Embroidery—U.S. I. Title. BIP

Embry, Norris, 1921—

EMBRY, Norris, 1921- 759.13
Norris Embry. Baltimore : Baltimore Museum of Art, c1975. 48 p. : ill. (some col.) ; 26 cm. "Dates of the exhibition: the Baltimore Museum of Art, December 16, 1975-January 18, 1976; Gruenbaum Gallery, New York, February 4-March 6, 1976; Louise E. Thorn Memorial Art Gallery, Keene, New Hampshire, October 1976." [N6537.E55B34] 76-352569
1. Embry, Norris, 1921- I. Baltimore. Museum of Art. BIP

Emerson, Peter Henry, 1856-1936.

NEWHALL, Nancy Wynne. 770'.92'4 B
P. H. Emerson : the fight for photography as a fine art / by Nancy Newhall. New York : Aperture, inc., c1975. 266 p. : ill. ; 24 x 27 cm. Also published as Aperture, v. 19, no. 3-4. Published to accompany an exhibition of British photographers prior to 1915 to be presented by the Alfred

Stieglitz Center in 1978. Bibliography: p. 262-265. [TR140.E43N48] 74-76911 ISBN 0-912334-58-4 : 22.50. ISBN 0-912334-59-2 pbk. : 12.95
1. Emerson, Peter Henry, 1856-1936. 2. Photography, Artistic. BIP

TURNER, Peter. 770'.92'4 B
P. H. Emerson : photographer of Norfolk / Peter Turner and Richard Wood. Boston : D. R. Godine, [1975] c1974. 108 p. : ill. ; 30 cm. (Godine photographic monographs ; 2) Includes bibliographical references. [TR140.E43T87 1975] 74-81518 ISBN 0-87923-106-8 : 19.95
1. Emerson, Peter Henry, 1856-1936. 2. Photography, Artistic. 3. Norfolk, Eng. (County)—Description and travel—Views. I. Wood, Richard, joint author.

Emerson. Ralph Waldo. 1803-1882.

HOPKINS, Vivian Constance, 1909- 701.170924
Spires of form; a study of Emerson's aesthetic theory New York, Russell & Russell, 1965 [c.1951] x, 276p. 23cm. Bibl. [PS1642.A3H6] 65-17901 7.50
1. Emerson, Ralph Waldo, 1803-1882. 2. Aesthetics. I. Title.

METZGER, Charles Reid, 1921- 101
Emerson and Greenough, transcendental pioneers of an American esthetic. Berkeley, University of California Press, 1954. 153p. 22cm. Includes bibliographies. [PS1633.G67M4] [PS1633.G67M4] 701.17 54-10438 54-10438
1. Emerson. Ralph Waldo. 1803-1882. 2. Greenough, Horatio, 1805-1852. 3. Aesthetics. I. Title.

METZGER, Charles Reid, 1921- 701.17
Emerson and Greenough; transcendental pioneers of an American esthetic [by] Charles R. Metzger. Westport, Conn., Greenwood Press [1970, c1954] 153 p. 23 cm. Bibliography: p. 149-150. [PS1633.G67M4 1970] 74-139140 ISBN 0-8371-5756-0
1. Emerson, Ralph Waldo, 1803-1882. 2. Greenough, Horatio, 1805-1852. 3. Aesthetics, American. I. Title.

Emerson, William Ralph, 1833-1917.

ZAITZEVSKY, Cynthia. 720'.924
The architecture of William Ralph Emerson, 1833-1917; catalogue. Photography by Myron Miller. [Cambridge? Mass. 1969] 100 p. illus., plans. 26 cm. Catalog of an exhibition presented by the Fogg Art Museum in collaboration with the Carpenter Center for the Visual Arts, Harvard University, May 30-June 20, 1969. Includes bibliographical references. [NA737.E4Z3] 79-89648
1. Emerson, William Ralph, 1833-1917. I. Harvard University. William Hayes Fogg Art Museum. II. Harvard University. Carpenter Center for the Visual Arts. III. Title.

Emmons, Chansonetta Stanley, 1858-1937.

PELADEAU, Marius B. 770'.92'4 B
Chansonetta : the life and photographs of Chansonetta Stanley Emmons, 1858-1937 / by Marius B. Peladeau ; introd. by Berenice Abbott. 1st ed. Waldoboro : Maine Antique Digest ; Dobbs Ferry, N.Y. : distributed by Morgan & Morgan, 1977. 96 p. : ill. ; 23 x 27 cm. Includes bibliographical references. [TR653.P44] 77-78057 ISBN 0-917312-01-5 pbk. : 8.95
1. Emmons, Chansonetta Stanley, 1858-1937. 2. Photography, Artistic. 3. Photographers—Maine—Biography. I. Emmons, Chansonetta Stanley, 1858-1937. II. Title. BIP

En Medio Shelter, N.M.

IRWIN-WILLIAMS, Cynthia. 917.89'57
Excavations at En Medio, Shelter, New Mexico; interim report of the Anasazi origins project of Eastern New Mexico University [by] C. Irwin-Williams and S. Tompkins. [Portales] Eastern New Mexico University, Paleo-Indian Institute, 1968. iv, 44 p. illus. 26 cm. (Contributions in anthropology, v. 1, no. 2) Bibliography: p. 21-22. [E78.N65I78] 74-622309
1. En Medio Shelter, N.M. 2. Pueblo Indians—Antiquities. 3. New Mexico—Antiquities. I. Tompkins, S., joint author. II. Title. III. Series.

Enamel and enameling.

BALL, Fred, 1945- 738.4
Experimental techniques in enameling. New York, Van Nostrand Reinhold [1972] 144 p. illus. (part col.) 24 cm. Bibliography: p. 140-141. [TT382.6.B35] 72-184823 ISBN 0-442-20542-2 9.95
1. Enamel and enameling. I. Title.

BATES, Kenneth Francis, 1904- 739.15
Enameling; principles and practice. [1st ed.] Cleveland, World Pub. Co. [1951] 208 p. illus. (part col.) 25 cm. Bibliography: p. 202-203. [NK5000.B3] 51-10773
1. Enamel and enameling. I. Title.

BATES, Kenneth Francis, 1904- 739'.15
The enamelist [by] Kenneth F. Bates. Cleveland, World Pub. Co. [1967] xvi, 246 p. illus. (part col.) 24 cm. Bibliography: p. 238-240. [TS700.B3] 67-13833
1. Enamel and enameling. I. Title.

CERAMIC industry. 666.2
101 ideas for the porcelain enameler, gathered by the engineering staff of Ceramic industry; theseitems appeared in issues over the past three years Chicago, c1953. 92p. illus. 23cm. [TP812.C4] 54-1452
1. Enamel and enameling. I. Title.

CLARKE, Geoffrey, 1924- 738.4
The technique of enameling [by] Geoffrey Clarke, Francis & Ida Feher. London, Batsford: New York, Reinhold, 1967. 104 p. col. front., 168 illus., 2 col. plates, tables, diagrs. 25 1/2 cm. 52/6 Bibliography: p. 101. [TP812.C55] 67-16841
1. Enamel and enameling. I. Feher, Francis, joint author. II. Feher, Ida, joint author. III. Title.

CLARKE, Geoffrey, 1924- 738.4
The technique of enamelling / Geoffrey Clarke, Francis & Ida Feher. Rev. ed. New York : Van Nostrand Reinhold Co., 1977. 112 p., [2] leaves of plates : ill. ; 26 cm. Includes index. Bibliography: p. 103. [TP812.C55 1977] 77-6625 ISBN 0-442-24255-7 : 9.95
1. Enamel and enameling. I. Feher, Francis, joint author. II. Feher, Ida, joint author. III. Title. BIP

DUTTON, Ninette. 738.4
The beautiful art of enamelling; a textbook for beginners. New York, Arc Books [1968, c1966] x, 81 p. illus. (part col.) 18 cm. [TP812.D8] 67-23062
1. Enamel and enameling. I. Title.

FRANKLIN, Geoffrey. 738.4
Simple enamelling. New York, Watson-Guptill Publications [1971] 103 p. illus. 24 cm. Bibliography: p. 102. [TT382.6.F7 1971] 77-133981 ISBN 0-8230-4833-0 7.95
1. Enamel and enameling. I. Title.

FROMENTEAU, Alb. 738.4
Painting with cold enamel. Illus. by Marc Berthier. New York, Drake [1973, c1971] 96 p. illus. (part col.) 19 cm. Translation of L'emaillage a froid. [TT382.6.F7613] 73-3716 ISBN 0-87749-466-5 2.95
1. Enamel and enameling. I. Title.

*HARPER, William. 738.4
Step-by-step enameling; a complete introduction to the craft of enameling, by William Harper. Conceived and edited by William and Shirley Sayles. New York, Golden Press [1973] 80 p. illus. (some col.) 28 cm. (Step-by-step craft series) Bibliography: p. 79 [TT382.6] 72-94424 2.95 (pbk.)
1. Enamel and enameling. I. Sayles, William. II. Sayles, Shirley. III. Title.

HUGHES, Therle. 739.15
English painted enamels [by] Therle & Bernard Hughes. Illustrated from the collections of Her Majesty Queen Mary and Mrs. Ionides. London, Country Life; New York, Scribner [1951] 156 p. plates (part col.) ports. (part col.) 26 cm. [NK5000.H8] 52-7336
1. Enamel and enameling. 2. Art objects, English. I. Hughes, G. Bernard, 1896- joint author. II. Title.

LAROM, Mary. 745.56
Enameling for fun and profit. Photos. by Ted Hewett. New York, D. McKay Co. [1954] 96 p. illus. 22 cm. [TS700.L33] 54-12750
1. Enamel and enameling. I. Title.

NEVILLE, Kenneth. 739.15
The craft of enamelling. Illus. by the author. New York, Taplinger Pub. Co. [1966] 149 p. illus. (part col.) 22 cm. Bibliography: p. 149. [TS700.N48 1966] 66-21871
1. Enamel and enameling. I. Title.

NEVILLE, Kenneth. 738'.4
The craft of enamelling; with illus. by the author. [1972, ie.1973] 156 p. illus. (1 col.) 22 cm. Label mounted on t.p.: Transatlantic Arts, Inc., Levittown, New York, Sole distributors for the U.S.A. Bibliography: p. 150. [TT382.6.N48 1972] 73-178946 ISBN 0-263-51654-7 6.95
1. Enamel and enameling. I. Title.

PELLE, Josette. 738.4
Enameling, by J. Pelle and A. Sainsard. New York, Drake Publishers [1973] p. Translation of Joies de l'email. Bibliography: p. [TT382.6.P4313] 73-3198 ISBN 0-87749-475-4
1. Enamel and enameling. I. Sainsard, Andree, joint author. II. Title.

REMENIH, Maurice. 738.4
Introduction to enameling, by Maurine Reminih [i.e. Remenih] Illus. by Ann Bruce Chamberlain. Los Angeles, Nash Pub. [1972] 133 p. illus. 21 cm. Bibliography: p. [123]-124. [TT382.6.R46] 72-81853 ISBN 0-8402-8052-1 2.45
1. Enamel and enameling. I. Title.

ROTHENBERG, Polly. 739'.15
Metal enameling. New York, Crown Publishers [1969] xi, 211 p. illus. (part col.), ports. 27 cm. Bibliography: p. 201. [TS700.R6] 70-75079 6.95
1. Enamel and enameling. 2. Art metal-work. I. Title. BIP

SCHILT, Stephen J. 738.4
Enamel without heat, by Stephen J. Schilt and Donna J. Weir. New York, Sterling Pub. Co. [1971] 47 p. illus. 20 cm. (Little craft book series) Pictures and text illustrate the variety of items that can be enameled with Polymer, a substance which does not require firing. [TT382.6.S34] 75-167658 ISBN 0-8069-5180-X
1. Enamel and enameling. I. Weir, Donna J., joint author. II. Title.

SEELER, Margaret. 739'.15
The art of enameling; how to shape precious metal and decorate it with cloisonne, champleve, plique-a-jour, mercury gilding and other fine techniques. New York, Van Nostrand Reinhold Co. [1969] 128 p. illus. (part col.) 29 cm. [NK5000.S37] 69-15891
1. Enamel and enameling. I. Title.

SEELER, Margaret. 739'.15
The art of enameling : how to shape precious metal and decorate it with cloisonne, champleve, plique-a-jour, mercury gilding and other fine techniques / Margaret Seeler. New York : Galahad Books, [1975] c1969. 128 p. : ill. ; 29 cm. Includes bibliographical references and index. [NK5000.S37 1975] 74-75598 ISBN 0-88365-239-0 : 14.95
1. Enamel and enameling. I. Title.

TAUBES, Lili. 738.4
Basic enameling. New York, Pitman [1970] 32 p. illus., port. 20 x 27 cm. (Pitman art books, 68) [NK5000.T35] 74-95903 1.00
1. Enamel and enameling. I. Title. BIP

TAYLOR, Louie S. 738.4
Copper enameling / Louie S. Taylor. South Brunswick : A. S. Barnes, [1976] p. cm. Includes index. [NK5000.T38] 75-38448 ISBN 0-498-01865-2 : 9.95
1. Enamel and enameling. I. Title. BIP

THOMPSON, Thomas Eugene, 1885- 666.2
Enameling on copper and other metals. Highland Park, Ill., T. C. Thompson Co. [1950] 39 p. (incl cover) illus. 23 cm. Bibliography: p. 37-38. [TS700.T52] 50-20529
1. Enamel and enameling. 2. Copperwork.

WINTER, Edward. 739.15
Enamel art on metals. New York, Watson-Guptill Publications [1958] 159 p. illus. 27 cm. [NK6510.W5] 58-8128
1. Enamel and enameling. 2. Art metal-work. I. Title.

WINTER, Edward. 738.4
Enameling for beginners. New York, Watson-Guptill Publications [1962] 116 p. illus. 27 cm. Includes bibliography. [TS700.W5] 61-15926
1. Enamel and enameling. I. Title.

ZECHLIN. KATHARINA 739.15
Creative enamelling and jewelry-making. [Tr. from German by Paul Kuttner. Rev., adapted by Jennifer Mellen] New York, Sterling [1966, c.1965] 104p. illus. 22cm. [TS700.Z413] 65-20877 3.95; 3.69 lib. ed.,
1. Enamel and enameling. 2. Jewelry. I. Title. BIP

Enamel and enameling, Byzantine—Catalogs.

WESSEL, Klaus. 738.4'09'02
Byzantine enamels, from the 5th to the 13th century. [Translated from the German by Irene R. Gibbons] Greenwich, Conn., New York Graphic Society [1968, c1967] 211 p. illus., plates (part col.) 28 cm. Translation of Die byzantinische Emailkunst. Includes bibliographical references. [NK5013.W413] 68-25736 22.50
1. Enamel and enameling, Byzantine—Catalogs. I. Title.

Enamel and enameling, Chinese.

COSGROVE, Maynard Giles. 738.4
The enamels of China and Japan; champleve and cloisonne, by Maynard G. Cosgrove. New York, Dodd, Mead [1974] vii, 115 p. col. plates. 24 cm. Bibliography: p. 109-112. [NK5004.C6C67] 72-7199 ISBN 0-396-06733-6 10.00
1. Enamel and enameling, Chinese. 2. Enamel and enameling, Japanese. I. Title. BIP

Enamel and enameling—England.

BENJAMIN, Susan, 1921- 738.4'0942
English enamel boxes : from the eighteenth to the twentieth century / Susan Benjamin. New York : Viking Press, [1978] p. cm. (A Studio book) Includes index. Bibliography: p. [NK5004.G7B46] 78-8344 ISBN 0-670-29679-1 : 15.95
1. Enamel and enameling—England. 2. Enamel boxes—England—Collectors and collecting. I. Title. BIP

Enamel and enameling, European.

BELLI Barsali, Isa. 738.4'094
European enamels; translated by Raymond Rudorff from the Italian. London, New York, Hamlyn, 1969. 3-158 p. col. illus. 20 cm. (Cameo) Translation of Lo smalto in Europa. [NK5004.E9B473] 71-454617 15/-
1. Enamel and enameling, European. I. Title.

Enamel and enameling—Exhibitions.

ROWE, Donald F. 738.4'094
Enamels: the XII to the XVI century; a special exhibition at the Martin D'Arcy Gallery of Art. Text by Donald F. Rowe. [Chicago, Loyola University of Chicago, 1970] 41 p. illus. (part col.) 26 cm. Catalog of the exhibition held Feb. 2-Mar. 2, 1970. Includes bibliographical references. [NK4999.C48M37] 76-111374
1. Enamel and enameling—Exhibitions. I. Martin D'Arcy Gallery of Art. II. Title.

Enamel and enameling, Georgian.

AMIRANASHVILI, Shalva IAsonovich, 1899- 738.474795
Medieval Georgian enamels of Russia. Text by Shalva Amiranashvili. [Translated by Francois Hirsch and John Ross] New York, H. N. Abrams [1964] 126 p. mounted col. illus. 33 cm. "Enamels in the Georgian National Museum of Fine Arts in Tiflis." -- Dust jacket. Bibliography: p. 125-126. [NK5000.A513] 64-11576
1. Enamel and enameling, Georgian. I. Tiflis. Muzel iskusstv Gruzinskol SSR. II. Title.

Enamel and enameling, German.

CORNING, N. Y. Museum of Glass 748.593
German enameled glass; the Edwin J. Beinecke collection and related pieces [by] Axel von Saldern. Corning, N.Y., Museum of Glass, Corning Glass Ctr. [1966, c.] 1965. 474p. illus. (pt. col.) col. map. 31cm. (Corning Mus. of Glass monographs, v. 2) Title. (Series: Corning N., Y. Museum of Glass. Monographs, v.2) Bibl. [NK5102.C64] 65-29139 38.00
1. Enamel and enameling, German. 2. Glassware—Corning, N. Y.—Catalogs. 3. Glassware, German—Catalogs. I. Saldern, Axel von. 1923- II. v8Beinecke. Edwin John, 1886- III. Title. IV. Series.

Enamel and enameling—Juvenile literature.

ELBERT, Virginie. 738.4
Easy enameling on metal / Virginie Fowler Elbert ; photos. and ill. by the author. New York : Lothrop, Lee & Shepard, [1975] 96 p. : ill. ; 24 cm. Includes index. Directions for decorating a variety of metal objects with quick-drying, liquid enamels that do not require the use of a kiln. [TT382.6.E38] 75-16457 ISBN 0-688-41710-8 : 4.95 ISBN 0-688-51710-2 lib.bdg. : 4.59
1. Enamel and enameling—Juvenile literature. I. Title. BIP

Enamel and enamelling.

*KUHNEMANN, Ursula. 738.4
Cold enamelling. New York, Taplinger [1973 c.1972] 64 p. illus. 22 cm. [TT382.6] 72-2181 ISBN 0-8008-1684-6 4.95
1. Enamel and enamelling. I. Title.
Pbk. 2.95, ISBN 0-8008-1685-4. BIP

Enameled ware—Catalogs.

†BOOHER, Fred. 666'.2
Graniteware : identification & value guide / by Fred and Rose Booher. Paducah, Ky. : Collector Books, c1977. 62 p. : ill. ; 22 cm. Includes index. [TS705.B66] 78-107688 ISBN 0-89145-067-X : 7.95
1. Enameled ware—Catalogs. 2. Enameled ware—Collectors and collecting. I. Booher, Rose, joint author. II. Title.

Enameled ware—History.

CAIGER-SMITH, A. 738.3
Tin-glaze pottery in Europe and the Islamic world; the tradition of 1000 years in maiolica, faience & delftware [by] Alan Caiger-Smith. London, Faber [1973, i.e.1974] 236 p. illus. 25 cm. Bibliography: p. [226]-228. [NK4290.C33] 73-181068 ISBN 0-571-09349-3
1. Enameled ware—History. I. Title.
Distributed by Humanities; 41.00

Endowments—United States.

MILLSAPS, Daniel W. 338.4'7'700973
Private foundations and business corporations active in arts, humanities, education, [by] Daniel Millsaps. [Washington] Washington International Arts Letter, [1974] iv, 264 p. 28 cm. (The Arts patronage) Vol. 1 has title: Private foundations active in the arts. [NX711.U5M54] 77-140925 ISBN 0-912072-05-9 45.00 (pbk., v 2.)
1. Endowments—United States. 2. Art patronage—United States. I. Washington international arts letter. II. Title. III. Series: The Arts patronage Series

Endowments—United States—Directories.

MILLSAPS, Daniel. 338.4'7'7002573
National directory of art support by private foundations : volume 3 / by Daniel Millsaps & editors of the Washington international arts letter. Washington : Washington international arts letter, c1977. iv, 264 p. ; 28 cm. (The Arts patronage series ; no. 6) Vol. 2 has title: Private foundations & business corporations active in arts/humanities/education. Includes index. [NX711.U5M53] 77-79730 ISBN 0-912072-07-5 pbk. : 45.00
1. Endowments—United States—Directories. 2. Art patronage—United States—Directories. I. Washington international arts letter. II. Title. III. Series.

Engebrechtsz, Cornelis, d. 1527.

GIBSON, Walter S. 759.9492
The paintings of Cornelis Engebrechtsz / Walter S. Gibson. New York : Garland Pub., 1977. xvi, 284 p., [36] leaves of plates : ill. ; 21 cm. (Outstanding dissertations in the fine arts) Originally presented as the author's thesis, Harvard, 1969. Bibliography: p. 273-284. [ND653.E58G52 1977] 76-23620 ISBN 0-8240-2691-8 lib.bdg. : 40.00
1. Engebrechtsz, Cornelis, d. 1527. I. Title. II. Series. BIP

Engineering design.

INTRODUCTION to creative design. D. Henry Edel, Jr., editor. 745.2
Contributors: Robert J. Christenson [and others] Englewood Cliffs, N.J., Prentice-Hall [1967] xiii, 237 p. illus. 24 cm. Includes bibliographies. [TA174.I5] 67-18914
1. Engineering design. 2. Design, Industrial. I. Edel, D. Henry, ed. II. Christenson, Robert J.

Engineering—Rome.

BLAKE, Marion Elizabeth, 1892- 722.7
Roman construction in Italy from Tiberius through the Flavians. Washington, D.C., Carnegie Institution of Washington, 1959; New York, Kraus Reprint, 1968. xvii, 195p. illus., plans. 29cm. (Carnegie Institution of Wash. Pubns. 616) Select. bibl. & abbreviations: p. xi-xvii [DG67.B56] 59-11715 19.50
1. Engineering—Rome. 2. Rome—Antiq. I. Title. II. Series. BIP

BLAKE, Marion Elizabeth, 1892- 722.7
Roman construction in Italy from Tiberius through theFlavians. Washington, Carnegie Institution of Washington, 1959. xvii, 195p. illus, plans. 29cm. (Carnegie Institution of Washington, Publication 616) 'Selected bibliography and abbreviations': p. xi-xvii. [DG67.B56] 59-11715
1. Engineering—Rome. 2. Rome—Antiq. I. Title. II. Series.

Engineering schools—Buildings.

MILLS, Edward David. 727'.4'6
The design of polytechnic institute buildings by Edward D. Mills and Harry Kaylor. Paris, Unesco, 1972. 96 p. illus. 27 cm. "SC.70/D.78/A" Bibliography: p. 95-96. [NA6602.E6M54] 73-180164 6.50 (U.S.)
1. Engineering schools—Buildings. I. Kaylor, Harry, joint author. II. Title.
Distributed by UNIPUB. BIP

Engineers — Legal status, laws, etc. — U.S.

TOMSON, Bernard, 1909- 720.69
Architectural & engineering law. New York, Reinhold [1951] xiii, 424 p. 24 cm. 51-14987
1. Engineers — Legal status, laws, etc. — U.S. I. Architects — Legal status, laws, etc. — U.S. II. Title.

England. Architecture.

PEVSNER, Nikolaus 720.942575
Buckinghamshire. [Baltimore. Md.] Penguin Bks., [c.1960] 340p. illus., map (Penguin--the Buildings of England BE 19) 2.50 pap.,
1. England. Architecture. 2. Buckinghamshire. County. England. Architecture. I. Title.

England—Civilization—20th century.

BENTLEY, Nicolas, 1907- 914.2'03'82
Edwardian album : a photographic excursion into a lost age of innocence / Nicolas Bentley ; photographic research by Andra Nelki. New York : Viking Press, [1974] 223 p. : ill. ; 26 cm. (A Studio book) Includes index. Bibliography: p. 217. [DA566.4.B47] 74-3518 ISBN 0-670-28975-2 : 10.00
1. England—Civilization—20th century. I. Title.

England—Description and travel—Views.

JAY, Bill. 779'.4'0924
Victorian cameraman; Francis Frith's views of rural England, 1850-1898. Newton Abbot, David & Charles [1973, i.e.1974] 112 p. illus. 25 cm. [DA667.J39] 73-164057 ISBN 0-7153-5895-2
1. Frith, Francis. 2. England—Description and travel—Views. I. Title.
Distributed by David and Charles, Vermont, 10.50.

England—Historic houses etc.

DUTTON, Ralph, 1898- 728.80942
The English country house. [Rev. ed. Dist. New York, Norton, c.1962] 200p. illus. (Batsford paperbacks, 16) 62-2136 1.50 pap.,
1. England—Historic houses, etc. 2. Architecture, Domestic—England. I. Title.

GREAT Britain Ministry of Housing and Local Government. 711'.4'0942
Historic towns: preservation and change. London, H. M. S. O., 1967. [8], 49p. illus. 31cm. [DA655.A55] 67-112856 4.95
1. England—Historic houses etc. 2. Architecture—Conservation and restoration 3. Cities and towns—England. I. Title.
American distributor: British Info., New York.

England in art.

WHITE, Christopher. 760'.0942'07401468
English landscape, 1630-1850 : drawings, prints & books from the Paul Mellon Collection : an exhibition, April 19-July 17, 1977 / by Christopher White. New Haven : Yale Center for British Art, c1977. xxv, 126 p., [91] leaves of plates : ill. (some col.) ; 29 cm. Catalogue of an exhibition held at Yale Center for British Art, New Haven. Includes bibliographical references. [N8214.5.G7W48] 77-71656
1. Mellon, Paul—Art collections. 2. England in art. 3. Art, English—Exhibitions. 4. Art, Modern—17th-18th centuries—England—Exhibitions. 5. Art, Modern—19th century—England—Exhibitions. I. Yale Center for British Art. II. Title.

England—Intellectual life.

HALLIDAY, Frank Ernest, 1903- 709'.42
An illustrated cultural history of England [by] F. E. Halliday. New York, Viking Press [1967] 320 p. illus. (part col.), facsims. (incl. music) 24 cm. [DA110.H315 1967a] 67-5109
1. England—Intellectual life. 2. Art, English—History. I. Title. II. Title: Cultural history of England.

England—Social life and customs.

ALDERSON, Frederick. 769'.5
The comic postcard in English life. [1st ed.] Rutland, Vt., C. E. Tuttle Co. [1970] 112 p. illus. (part col.) 26 cm. [DA566.4.A65 1970b] 75-113901
1. England—Social life and customs. 2. Postal cards—History. I. Title.

DITCHFIELD, Peter Hampson, 1854-1930. 942
Old village life ; or, Glimpses of village life through all ages / P. H. Ditchfield ; with forty illustrations and plans. Wakefield : EP Publishing, 1974. xv, 255 p., [8] leaves of plates : ill. ; 20 cm. Reprint of 2d ed. published in 1921 by Methuen, London. Includes index. [DA110.D66 1974] 75-305755 ISBN 0-85409-994-8 : £4.00
1. England—Social life and customs. 2. Villages—England. 3. England—Antiquities. I. Title. II. Title: Glimpses of village life through all ages.

ROWLANDSON, Thomas, 1756-1827. 914.2
Drawings for a tour in a post chaise. With an introd. and notes by Robert R. Wark. San Marino, Calif., Huntington Library, 1963. xiii, 150 p. illus. (part col.) maps. 16 x 25 cm. (Huntington Library publications) "A note on bibliography": p. [25]-28. [NC1115.R65W3] 62-18104
1. England—Social life and customs. I. Wark, Robert R. II. Series: Henry E. Huntington Library and Art gallery, San Marino, Calif Huntington Library publications.

WOODFORDE, John. 914.2
The truth about cottages. Fifty types of cottage specially drawn by Bertha Stamp. New York, A. M. Kelley [1970, c1969] 138 p. illus. 23 cm. Includes bibliographical references. [DA110.W67 1970] 76-115042
1. England—Social life and customs. 2. Cottages. I. Title. BIP

England—Social life and customs—1945- —Pictorial works.

RAY-JONES, Tony, 1941-1972. 779'.9'9420850924
A day off : 120 photographs / Tony Ray-Jones ; with an introd. by Ainslie Ellis. 1st U.S. ed. Boston : New York Graphic Society, [1977] c1974. p. cm. [DA566.4.R37 1977] 77-77327 ISBN 0-8212-0708-3 pbk.: 7.95
1. England—Social life and customs—1945- —Pictorial works. I. Title. BIP

England—Social life and customs—20th century—Juvenile literature.

BRADLEY, Helen, 1900- 914.2'03'82
And Miss Carter wore pink; scenes from an Edwardian childhood [Written and illustrated by] Helen Bradley. New York, Holt, Rinehart and Winston [1972, c1971] 31 p. col. illus. 27 x 30 cm. A grandmother recalls through paintings and text her turn-of-the century childhood in northern England. [DA566.4.B68 1972] 72-181489 ISBN 0-03-091336-5 6.95
1. England—Social life and customs—20th century—Juvenile literature. I. Title.

England—Social life and customs—20th century—Pictorial works.

THE Countryman's Britain in pictures / [compiled by] Crispin Gill. Newton Abbot ; North Pomfret, Vt. : David and Charles, 1977. 96 p. : chiefly ill., ports. ; 25 cm. Includes index. [DA566.4.C66] 77-89381 ISBN 0-7153-7450-8 : 11.95 942'.00973'4
1. England—Social life and customs—20th century—Pictorial works. 2. Country life—England—Pictorial works. I. Gill, Crispin. BIP

WINTER, Gordon. 942.082'3
The golden years 1903-1913 : a pictorial survey of the most interesting decade in English history, recorded in contemporary photographs and drawings / Gordon Winter. Newton Abbot [Eng.] : David & Charles, [1975] 112 p. : chiefly ill. ; 24 cm.

SUBJECT INDEX ENGRAVING—HISTORY.

[DA566.4.W57] 75-311150 ISBN 0-7153-6896-6 : 9.95
1. England—Social life and customs—20th century—Pictorial works. I. Title.
Distributed by David & Charles, Vermont.

English literature—19th century—History and criticism.

JACKSON, Holbrook, 1874-1948. 700'.942
The eighteen nineties; a review of art and ideas at the close of the nineteenth century. New York, Knopf. St. Clair Shores, Mich., Scholarly Press, 1972. 304 p. illus. 22 cm. Reprint of the 1922 ed. [PR461.J2 1972] 78-145104 ISBN 0-403-01041-1
1. English literature—19th century—History and criticism. 2. Great Britain—Intellectual life—19th century. 3. Art—Great Britain. I. Title.

English literature—Selections: Extracts, etc.

LOBAN, Walter, ed. v. 12
Adventures in appreciation. [Edited by] Walter Loban [and] Rosalind A. Olmsted. Laureate [paperback] ed. New York, Harcourt, Brace & World [c1963] 5 v. 21 cm. (Adventures in literature series) A school textbook. [NUC64-5252]
1. English literature—Selections: Extracts, etc. 2. American literature—Sections: Extractions, etc. I. Olmsted, Rosalind A., ed. II. Title.
Contents Omitted

English wit and humor, Pictorial.

DOYLE, Richard, 1824-1883. 741.5'942
The foreign tour of Messrs. Brown, Jones, and Robinson; being the history of what they saw, and did, in Belgium, Germany, Switzerland & Italy. [With a new introd. by A. E. Santaniello] London, Bradbury & Evans, 1855. [New York, B. Blom, 1972] xiii, 110 p. illus. 26 cm. [NC1479.D64A5 1972] 74-177503 15.75
1. English wit and humor, Pictorial. I. Title. BIP

GILLRAY, James, 1757-1815. 741.5'942
The satirical etchings of James Gillray / edited by Draper Hill. New York : Dover Publications, c1976. xxxii, 142 p., [4] leaves of plates : ill. (some col.) ; 31 cm. Includes bibliographical references. [NC1479.G5H52 1976] 75-41946 ISBN 0-486-23340-5 pbk. : 5.00
1. English wit and humor, Pictorial. I. Hill, Draper. II. Title. BIP

GREGO, Joseph, 1843-1908. 741.9'42
Rowlandson the caricaturist. [New York] Collectors Editions [1970] 2 v. illus. 29 cm. Reprint of the 1880 ed. published by Chatto and Windus, London. Lists of drawings by Rowlandson: v. 2, p. 412-431. Includes bibliographical references. [NC1479.R8G8 1970] 78-102790 ISBN 0-87681-038-5
1. Rowlandson, Thomas, 1756-1827. 2. English wit and humor, Pictorial. I. Rowlandson, Thomas, 1756-1827. II. Title.

MOLNAR, George, 1910- 741.5
Statues. [1st American ed. New York] Dutton, 1955 [c1954] 88p. (chiefly illus.) 26cm. [NC1479.M57A5 1955] 55-5467
1. English wit and humor, Pictorial. I. Title.

PUNCH (London) 741.5
The best cartoons from Punch, collected for Americans from England's famous humorous weekly; edited by Marvin Rosenberg and William Cole. [New York] Simon and Schuster, 1952. unpaged. illus. 28 cm. [NC1478.P8] 52-12710
1. English wit and humor, Pictorial. I. Title.

THELWELL, Norman, 1923- 741.5
Angels on horseback and elsewhere. [1st American ed.] [New York] Dutton [1958] 96 p. illus. 26 cm. [NC1479.T54A42 1958] 58-10111
1. English wit and humor, Pictorial. I. Title.

WARDROPER, John. 741'.092'4
The caricatures of George Cruikshank / John Wardroper. 1st U.S. ed. Boston : D. R. Godine, 1978. 144 p. : ill. (some col.) ; 24 x 26 cm. Includes index. Bibliography: p. 142. [NC1479.C9A4 1978] 77-94112 ISBN 0-87923-231-5 : 30.00
1. Cruikshank, George, 1792-1878. 2. English wit and humor, Pictorial. I. Title. BIP

WARDROPER, John. 741.5'942
The caricatures of George Cruikshank / [text by] John Wardroper. London : Gordon Fraser Gallery, 1977, i.e.1978 144 p. : chiefly ill. (some col.), facsim., port. ; 24 x 25 cm. Includes index. Bibliography: p. 142. [NC1479.C9A4 1977] 78-307169 ISBN 0-900406-85-2 : 30.00
1. Cruikshank, George, 1792-1878. 2. English wit and humor, Pictorial. I. Cruikshank, George, 1792-1878. II. Title.
Available from Godine

English wit and humor, Pictorial—History.

WYNN JONES, Michael. 741.5'942
The cartoon history of Britain. With foreword by Michael Cummings. [1st American ed.] New York, Macmillan [1973, c1971] 287 p. illus. 32 cm. Bibliography: p. [5] [NC1470.W9 1973] 72-84879 17.50
1. English wit and humor, Pictorial—History. I. Title.

Engraved glass.

MATTHEWS, Robert T. 748.2
Engraved glass and other decorated glass / by Robert T. Matthews. West Friendship, Md. : Matthews, c1978. 157 p. : ill. ; 28 cm. Includes index. Bibliography: p. 153. [NK5201.M37] 76-48555 ISBN 0-9601150-1-3 : 10.75
1. Engraved glass. 2. Glass, Ornamental. 3. Decoration and ornament. I. Title.

Engraved glass—Great Britain.

WHISTLER, Laurence, 1912- 748.6
Pictures on glass; engraved by Laurence Whistler. Ipswich, Cupid Press, 1972. 32, 80 p., leaf (chiefly illus.) 28 cm. [NK5198.W4A53] 73-159846 ISBN 0-903575-00-0 £7.50
1. Whistler, Laurence, 1912- 2. Engraved glass—Great Britain. I. Title. BIP

Engraved glass—United States.

MANNING, Reg, 1905- 748.2'913
Reg Manning's desert in crystal; photographs of the artist's copper wheel engravings on crystal glass and the brief story of how he became involved in the rare and ancient art. [1st ed.] Phoenix, Ariz., Reganson [1973] 63 p. illus. 23 cm. [NK5198.M36A54 1973] 73-91157 3.00 (pbk.)
1. Manning, Reg, 1905- 2. Engraved glass—United States. I. Title. II. Title: Desert in crystal.
Publisher's address: 5724 E. Cambridge Ave., Scottsdale, Az. 85251.

Engravers.

FAR Gallery Print Collectors' Club, New York. 760'.0922
The Far Gallery booklets on prints and printmakers. [New York, Far Gallery, 1962] 7 v. illus. 18 cm. In slide case. Reprinted from the original editions of the Print-collector's quarterly, 1911-1922. Contents.[1] The dry-points of Mary Cassatt, by F. Weitenkampf. -- [2] The awakening of the young print-collector to a sense of beauty, by F. Bullard. -- [3] Notes on Toulouse-Lautrec and his lithographs, by A. Symons. -- [4] Le Pere Corot. by R. J. Wickenden. -- [5] Francisco Goya y Lucientes, by C. H. Caffin. -- [6] Daumier's lithographs, by H. L. Seaver and W. M. Thackeray. -- [7] Giovanni Battista Piranesi, by B. B. Moore. [NE800.F3] 63-6424
1. Engravers. 2. Engraving. I. Title.

Engravers, American.

STAUFFER, David McNeely, 1845-1913. 769'.924
American engravers upon copper and steel. New York, B. Franklin [1964] 3 v. illus., ports. 27 cm. (Burt Franklin bibliography and reference series, 54) Vols. 1-2 originally published in 1907. Vol. 3, by Mantle Fielding, was published in 1917 as a supplement to Stauffer's work. Contents.Contents.—Pt. 1. Biographical sketches, illustrated. Index to engravings described, with check-list numbers and names of engravers and artists.—Pt. 2. Check-list of the works of the earlier engravers.—Pt. 3. Biographical sketches and check lists of engravings. [NE505.S8 1964] 78-6927
1. Engravers, American. I. Fielding, Mantle, 1865-1941. American engravers upon copper and steel. II. Title. BIP

Engravers—Correspondence. reminiscences, etc.

EVANS, Edmund, 1826-1905 769.942
The reminiscences of Edmund Evans; ed., introd. by Ruari McLean. Oxford, Clarendon Pr., 1967. xx, 92p. 2 fronts. (incl. 1 col.). illus. (incl. ports.). facsims. (incl. 3 col.), diagr. 22cm. Bibl. [NE539.E9A2 1967] 68-72949 10.40
1. Engravers—Correspondence. reminiscences, etc. I. McLean, Ruari, II. Title.
Available from Oxford Univ. Pr., New York.

Engraving.

ADHEMAR, Jean. 769'.904
Twentieth-century graphics. Translated from the French by Eveline Hart. New York, Praeger [1971] 256 p. illus. (part col.) 22 cm. Translation of La gravure original au XXe siecle. Bibliography: p. 243-244. [NE490.A313 1971] 72-150453
1. Engraving. 2. Engravers. I. Title.

BOWMAN, John J. 761.8
The jewelry engravers manual. New York, Van Nostrand [1954] 143 p. illus. 24 cm. [NE2710.B65] 54-11403
1. Engraving. 2. Lettering. 3. Monograms. I. Title.

CALIFORNIA Historical Society. v. 12
California pictorial lettersheets,1849-1859: museum reproductions of unique pictorial writing paper used in gold rush California. Selected from rare originals in the archives of the California Historical Society, San Francisco. [San Francisco, Reynard Press, c1961] portfolio (12 lettersheets, 12 envelopes) 31 cm. (Its Portfolio no. 2) Title from portfolio. [NELC3] 67-3946
1. Engraving. 2. California — Gold discoveries. 3. Stationery. I. Title. II. Series.

HAAS, Irvin. 769.084
A treasury of great prints. New York, T. Yoseloff [1956] 135 p. 60 illus. 29 cm. [NE900.H3] 55-11783
1. Engraving. 2. Engravers. I. Title.

STEFFENS, Robert N 1907- 760
Engraved stationery handbook. New York, Cronite Co., 1950. 430 p. illus. 27 cm. [NE2715.S7] 50-14844
1. Engraving. 2. Stationery. I. Title.

VICTORIA and Albert Museum, South Kensington. Dept. of Prints and Drawings. 769.942
The engraved work of Eric Gill. London, H.M.S.O. [dist. New York, British Info., 1964,c.1963] 94p. illus. 25cm. 2.50 pap.,
1. Engraving. I. Gill, Eric, 1882-1940. II. Title.

WECHSLER, Herman Joel, 1904- 760
An introduction to prints & print-making. [New York] FAR Gallery [dist. Cambridge, Mass., Fogg Art Mus., Harvard, 1963,c.1960] 126p. (chiefly illus.) 20cm. Bibl. 60-12704 2.50 pap.,
1. Engraving. 2. Engravings, French. I. Title. II. Title: Prints & print-making.

Engraving—Addresses, essays, lectures.

RUSKIN, John, 1819-1900. 765
Ariadne florentina; six lectures on wood and metal engraving ... given before the University of Oxford in Michaelmas term, 1872. With an introd. by Charles Eliot Norton. Brantwood ed. New York, Merrill, 1892. St. Clair Shores, Mich., Scholarly Press, 1972 [c1891] p. (The works of John Ruskin) Contents.Contents.—Definition of the art of engraving.—The relation of engraving to other arts in Florence.—The technics of wood engraving.—The technics of metal engraving.—Design in the German schools of engraving (Holbein and Durer)—Design in the Florentine schools of engraving (Sandro Botticelli)—Appendix: Notes on the present state of engraving in England. [NE865.R8 1972] 72-8272 ISBN 0-403-02057-3
1. Engraving—Addresses, essays, lectures. I. Title.

Engraving, American.

FREEMAN, Graydon La Verne, 1904-1963, comp. 769.4
Historical prints of American cities. Comments by Larry Freeman. Watkins Glen, N. Y., Century House [1952] 100 p. illus. 27 cm. [NE940.F7] 52-9808
1. Engraving, American. 2. U.S.—Description and travel—Views. I. Title.

Engraving, American—Exhibitions.

ART Association of Indianapolis, Indiana. John Herron Art Institute. 769.9772
Biennial exhibition 50 Indiana prints. 1st-1952- [Indianapolis] v. illus. 23cm. Sponsored by the art association of Indianapolis, Indiana, and the Indiana Society of Printmakers. [NE535.I5A7] 53-34130
1. Engraving, American—Exhibitions. 2. Lithographs, American—Exhibitions. I. Title.

Engraving—Early works to 1800.

FAITHORNE, William, 1616-1691. 760
The art of graveing and etching. New introd. by Jacob Kainen. New York, Da Capo Press, 1970. 1 v. (unpaged) illus., facsim. 19 cm. (Da Capo Press series in graphic art, v. 9) Reprint of the 1662 ed. [NE1760.F3 1970] 68-54841 ISBN 0-306-71049-8
1. Callot, Jacques, 1592?-1635. 2. Bosse, Abraham, 1602-1676. 3. Engraving—Early works to 1800. 4. Engraving—Technique. 5. Etching—Technique. I. Title. BIP

Engraving, French.

BLUM, Andre, 1881- 769'.944
The origin and early history of engraving in France / Andre Blum ; [translated from the French by J. Byam Shaw]. New York : Hacker Art Books, 1978. viii, 92 p., [78] leaves of plates : ill. ; 33 cm. Translation of Les origines de la gravure en France. Reprint of the 1930 rev. & enl. ed. published by E. Weyhe, New York. Bibliography: p. [81]-84. [NE647.B513 1978] 77-73881 ISBN 0-87817-216-5 lib.bdg. : 40.00
1. Engraving, French. 2. Engraving—15th century—France. I. Title.

Engraving—Germany.

BUCHHEIM, Lothar Gunther. 769.943
The graphic art of German expressionism. [1st American ed.] [New York] Universe Books [1960] 294 p. (chiefly illus.) (part col.)) 30 cm. Bibliography: p. 285-292. [NE651.B853] 60-8171
1. Engraving—Germany. 2. Engraving, German. 3. Expressionism (Art) I. Title.

Engraving—History.

HIND, Arthur Mayger, 1880-1957 765.09
A history of engraving & etching from the

15th century to the year 1914; being the third and fully rev. ed. of A short history of engraving and etching. [Gloucester, Mass., P. Smith, 1963] xviii,487p. illus. 22cm. (Dover bk. T954 rebound) Bibl. 4.75
1. Engraving—Hist. 2. Engravers. 3. Etching—Hist.   I.   Title.

ROGER-MARX, Claude, 1888-   760.9
Graphic art [of] the 19th century. [Tr. from French by E. M. Gwyer] New York, McGraw [1962] 254p. illus. (pt. col.) 22cm. 62-20257 6.95
1. Engraving—Hist. 2. Engravings. I. Title.

Engraving—History.

GETLEIN, Frank.   769
The bite of the print; satire and irony in woodcuts, engravings, etchings, lithographs and serigraphs [by] Frank and Dorothy Getlein. New York, C. N. Potter [1963] xxvi, 272 p. illus. Bibliography: p. [269]-272. [NE430.G4] 62-19294
1. Engraving—History. 2. Wit and humor, Pictorial—History. 3. Caricature—History. I. Getlein, Dorothy, joint author. II. Title.

HIND, Arthur Mayger, 1880-   765.09
1957.
A history of engraving & etching from the 15th century to the year 1914; being the 3rd and fully rev. ed. of A short history of engraving and etching. New York, Dover Publications [1963] xviii, 487 p. illus. 22 cm. "Unabridged and unaltered republication of the third, fully revised edition, as published ... in 1923." Bibliography: p. 393-419. [NE400.H66 1963] 63-5658
1. Engraving—History. 2. Etching—History.

SALAMON, Ferdinando.   769'.9
The history of prints and printmaking from Durer to Picasso; a guide to collecting. New York, American Heritage Press [1972] viii, 303 p. illus. (part col.) 31 cm. Translation of La collezione di stampe. Bibliography: p. 287-288. [NE400.S213 1972] 72-80702 ISBN 0-07-054460-3 22.50
1. Engraving—History. 2. Engravings. I. Title.

Engraving — Illst.

ADHEMAR, Jean.   v. 12
Graphic art of the 18th century. [Translated from the French by M. I. Martin, New York, McGraw-Hill [1964] 254 p. illus. (part col.) 22 cm. Bibliography: p. 237-240. [NE480.A314] 760 64-14334
1. Engraving — Illst. I. Title.

Engraving—Lombardy—History.

KRISTELLER, Paul, 1863-   v. 12
1931.
Die lombardische Graphik der Renaissance / Paul Kristeller. Nachdr. d. Ausg. Berlin 1913. Hildesheim ; New York : Olms, 1975. 171 p. 6 leaves of plates : ill. ; 22 cm. Reprint of the ed. published by B. Cassirer. "Verzeichnis von Bucher mit holzschnitten lombardischer und piemontesischer Druckstatten": p. [63]-170. [NE660.L6K7 1975] 76-458559 ISBN 3-487-05900-2 : DM78.00
1. Engraving—Lombardy—History. 2. Engravings, Renaissance—Lombardy—Catalogs. 3. Engravings, Italian—Lombardy—Catalogs. 4. Illustrated books—15th-16th centuries—Catalogs. I. Title.

Engraving (Metal-work)

MEEK, James B., 1901-   739.7'4'42
The art of engraving; a book of instructions, by James B. Meek. Book design, drawings and photos. by the author. Montezuma, Iowa, F. Brownell [1973] x, 196 p. illus. 29 cm. Bibliography: p. 188. [NE2700.M43] 73-84371 19.95
1. Engraving (Metal-work) I. Title.

Engraving, Mexican.

HAAB, Armin.   769.972
Mexican graphic art. [English version: C. C. Palmer] New York, G. Wittenborn

[1957] 126 p. (chiefly illus. (part col.) ports.) 24 cm. Includes brief biographies of the artists. [NE544.H3] 57-59264
1. Engraving, Mexican. 2. Engravers, Mexican. I. Title.

Engraving—Technique.

GORBATY, Norman   761
Print making with a spoon. New York, Reinhold Pub. Corp. [c.1960] 68p. illus. 27cm. 60-9671 3.95 bds.,
1. engraving—Technique. I. Title.

HAYTER, Stanley William,   760
1901-
About prints. New York, Oxford [c.1962] 176p. illus. (pt. col.) 25cm. Bibl. 62-4485 12.50
1. Engraving—Technique. 2. Engraving—Hist. I. Title.   BIP

HAYTER, Stanley William,   760
1901-
New ways of gravure; with a preface by Herbert Read. [Revised ed.] London, New York [etc.] Oxford U.P., 1966. xxiv, 208 p. front., illus. (incl. ports.) diagrs. 25 cm. 70/- Bibliography: p. [289]-294. [NE850.H4 1966] 66-70574
1. Engraving — Technique. I. Title.

LEWIS, Adele.   760
The print: an original art form for all, by Adele Lewis, Bertram Goodman [and] Harold Toledo. New York, 1959 [c1960] 32 p. illus. 29 cm. [NE860.L4] 60-626
1. Engraving—Technique. I. Title: An original art form for all.

MILLS, John, 1917-   761
Tackle printmaking this way. London, S. Paul [1962, c1961 stamped: distributed by Sportshelf, New Rochelle, N. Y.] 123p. illus. 20cm. [NE850.M5 1962] 62-6858
1. Engraving— Technique. I. Title.

WEISS, Harvey.   760
Paper, ink, and roller; print-making for beginners. New York, Young Scott Books [1958] 64 p. illus. 29 cm. Includes bibliography. [NE860.W42] 58-14993
1. Engraving—Technique. I. Title.   BIP

Engraving—Technique—Juvenile literature.

OTA, Koshi   760
Printing for fun, by Koshi Ota [and others] New York, Ivan Obolensky [1960] 53p. col. illus. 27cm. (An Astor book) 60-50872 3.95
1. Engraving—Technique—Juvenile literature. I. Title.

Engraving—Themes, motives.

ATTENTION getting old   769
engravings : a copyright free handbook / compiled by Dick Sutphen. New York : Art Direction Book Co., c1976. 192 p. : all ill. ; 29 cm. [NE951.A88] 76-40494 ISBN 0-910158-22-3 : 19.50
1. Engraving—Themes, motives. I. Sutphen, Richard.

Engraving—Washington, D.C.—Catalog.

U.S. Library of   016.779
Congress. Reference Dept.
Guide to the special collections of prints & photographs in the Library of Congress, compiled by Paul Vanderbilt. Washington, 1955. v, 200 p. 26 cm. [NE53.W3A52] 54-60020
1. Engraving—Washington, D.C.—Catalog. 2. Photographs—Catalogs. I. Vanderbilt, Paul. II. Title.

Engravings.

SCHOOFS, Rudolf, 1932-   769.943
Gravuren. Museum am Ostwall, Dortmund; Palm Springs, Desert Museum, California. Von der Heydt Museum der Stadt Wuppertal. [Wuppertal-Barmen, Druckerei A. Jung & Sohne [dist. New York, Wittenborn, 1963, c.1962] 24 1. (chiefly illus.) 36cm. Texts by Will Grohmann, Harald Seiler in German and English. 63-5620 4.50 pap.,

I. Grohmann, Will, 1887- II. Dortmund. Museum am Ostwall. III. Palm Springs, Calif. Desert Museum. IV. Title.

SUTPHEN, Richard.   765'.022'2
Antiques, filigree & rococo; copyright free engraving masterpieces. Compiled, edited and published by the Dick Sutphen Studio. Minneapolis [1966] 80 l. (chiefly illus.) 30 cm. [NE900.S8] 67-1758
1. Engravings. 2. Filigree. 3. Decoration and ornament, Rococo. I. Title.

SUTPHEN, Richard.   769
The encyclopedia of small spot engravings; a copyright-free handbook of material for reference or reuse in advertising or publications, without permission or payment. Compiled by Dick Sutphen. Phoenix, Valley of the Sun Pub. Co. [1969] 208 p. (chiefly illus.) 29 cm. [NE900.S82] 72-197858
1. Engravings. I. Title.   BIP

SUTPHEN, Richard.   769
Old engravings & illustrations, compiled, edited and published by the Dick Sutphen studio. Minneapolis, [1965] 2 v. of illus. 29 cm [NE940.S9] 65-29610
1. Prints. I. Title.

SUTPHEN, Richard, comp.   769
The wildest old engravings and illustrations; a copyright free handbook, comp. by Dick Sutphen. [Minneapolis, D Sutphen Studio, 1966] 191p. (chiefly illus.)29cm. [NE375.S9] 66-28210 10.00
1. Engravings. I. Title.
Box 8408, Minneapolis, Minn., 55426

VAN HOESEN, Beth, 1926   769'.92'4
A collection of wonderful things; intaglio prints. [San Francisco] Scrimshaw, 1972. 151 l. (chiefly illus., part col.) 27 cm. [NE539.V36A43] 72-88031 ISBN 0-912020-29-6 15.00
1. Title.   BIP

ZIGROSSER, Carl, 1891-   769
The book of fine prints; an anthology of printed pictures and introduction to the study of graphic art in the West and the East. [Rev. ed.] New York, Crown Publishers [c1956] 499p. (p. [241]-[476] illus.) 25cm. First published in 1937 under title: Six centuries of fine prints. Bibliography: p. 233-238. [NE430.Z5 1956] 56-1208
1. Engravings. I. Title.

ZIGROSSER, Carl, 1891- ed.   760
Prints; thirteen illustrated essays on the art of the print, selected for the Print Council of America. [1st ed.] New York, Holt, Rinehart and Winston [1962] x, 269 p. illus. (part col.) 29 cm. Includes bibliographical references. [NE900.Z5] 62-17344
1. Engravings. 2. Engravers. I. Print Council of America. II. Title.

Engravings, American.

BESNIA, Howard John.   759.13
The beetlepeople of Scarabank, fantasy on evolution. With 11 woodengravings by the author. Sterling Junction, Mass., Scarab Press, 1964. [32] p. (on double leaves) illus. 29 cm. "An additional suite of woodengravings printed on Moriki" in pocket. "One hundred copies were printed ... This is copy number iv. [Signed] Howard John Besnia." [NE1215.B44A42] 65-2352
I. Title.

FREEMAN, Graydon La Verne,   769.4
1904- comp.
Historical prints of American cities. Comments by Larry Freeman. Watkins Glen, N. Y., Century House [1952] 100 p. illus. 27 cm. [NE940.F7] 52-9808
1. Engravings, American. 2. U. S.—Descr. & trav.-Views. I. Title.

LEWIS, Benjamin Morgan,   769.973
1920-
A guide to engravings in American magazines, 1741-1810. New York, New York Public Library, 1959. iv, 60p. illus. 26cm. Bibliography: p. iv. [NE506.L4] 59-10239
1. Engravings, American. 2. American periodicals. I. Title. II. Title: Engravings in American magazines, 1741-1810.

MARTIN, Walt, 1924-   769.9758231
Martin, Perli, Reeves, Slattery, Wolf, Wolfe. [Designed, edited, and produced by Bill Slattery. Atlanta, Distributed by Atlanta Art Institute, c1958] 81p. (chiefly col. illus.) 33cm. 225 copies, no. 40. [NE538.A7M3] 59-38186
1. Engravings, American. 2. Engravers, American—Atlanta. I. Slattery, Bill, 1929- ed. II. Title.

MASSACHUSETTS 760'.0974'074014461
Historical Society, Boston.
Prints, maps and drawings, 1677-1822. 3d ed. Boston : Massachusetts Historical Society, 1976. [32] p. : chiefly ill. ; 22 x 28 cm. (A Massachusetts Historical Society picture book) [NE506.M3 1976] 76-363293
1. Engravings, American. 2. Drawings, American. I. Title. II. Series.   BIP

PETERDI, Gabor.   769'.924
Graphics, 1934-1969. Introd. by Una E. Johnson. New York, Touchstone Publishers [1970] 1 v. (chiefly illus., part col.) 33 cm. [NE539.P43P4] 75-102130
1. Title.

STEINHARDT, Jacob, 1887-   769.943
The graphic art of Jakob Steinhardt. With a critical appreciation by Haim Gamzu. New York, T. Yoseloff [1963] 24 p. 120 illus. 29 cm. [NE654.S69G3] 61-13932
1. Gamzu, Haim.

Engravings, American— Exhibitions.

BROOKLYN Institute of   769.974723
Arts and Sciences. Museum.
National print annual exhibition. [Catalog] [Brooklyn, New York, Brooklyn Museum] 1960 unpaged illus. First exhibition held in 1947. Cover title: Twelfth national print exhibition 1960. 23x11cm. 55-34393 .25 pap.,
1. Engravings, American — Exhibitions. I. Title.

BROOKLYN Institute of   769'.973
Arts and Sciences. Museum.
National print annual exhibition. [Catalog] [Brooklyn] v. illus. 24x10cm. First exhibition held in 1947. [NE508.B7] 55-34393
1. Engravings, American—Exhibitions. I. Title.

Engravings, American—Period.

AMERICAN prints today.   769.973
1959-- [New York 22, Print Council of America] 527 Madison Ave. [1959] unpaged illus. 31cm. 59-16916 1.25 pap.,
1. Engravings, American—Period. I. Print Council of America.

AMERICAN prints today   769.973
1959- [New York, Print Council of America] v. illus. 31cm. [NE10.A5] 59-16916
1. Engravings, American—Period. I. Print Council of America.

Engravings, British—Catalogs.

PETTER, Helen Mary.   769'.942
The Oxford almanacks / Helen Mary Petter. Oxford : Clarendon Press, 1974. xi, 128 p., 4 leaves of plates : ill. ; 23 x 29 cm. Includes bibliographical references and index. [NE628.P47] 74-185495 ISBN 0-19-817329-6 : 32.00
1. Oxford almanac—Illustrations. 2. Engravings, British—Catalogs. I. Title.
Distributed by Oxford University Press, N.Y.   BIP

Engravings—Collectors and collecting.

HAYDEN, Arthur, 1868-1946   769
Old prints by Arthur Hayden, Cyril G. E. Bunt. London, Benn [dist. New York, Dover, 1965] xvi, 199p. illus. 21cm. (Practical handbks. for collectors) [NE885.H43] 56-28865 3.00
1. Engravings—Collectors and collecting. 2. Engraving—Hist. I. Bunt, Cyril George Edwards, 1882- II. Title.

Entertainers—Portraits.

ABBE, James 779'.9'791430280922
Edward, 1883-1973.
Stars of the twenties / observed by James Abbe ; text by Mary Dawn Earley ; introd. by Lillian Gish. New York : Viking Press, 1975. 32 p., [48] leaves of plates : ports. ; 29 cm. (A Studio book) [PN1583.A2A2 1975] 74-29487 ISBN 0-670-66836-2 : 10.00
1. Entertainers—Portraits. I. Earley, Mary Dawn. II. Title. BIP

Entertainers—Portraits—Exhibitions.

HIXON, Orval, 1884- 779'.2'0924
Main Street Studio; an exhibition of photographs of famous vaudeville entertainers. [Exhibition organized and catalogue written and designed by James Enyeart. Exhibition held at] the University of Kansas Museum of Art, May 2-June 27, 1971. [Lawrence, University of Kansas Museum of Art; supplied by Worldwide Books, Boston, 1971] [76] p. illus. 26 cm. (Miscellaneous publications of the Museum of Art, no. 81) Bibliography: p. [74] [PN1583.H5A3] 79-198440
1. Entertainers—Portraits—Exhibitions. 2. Vaudeville—Exhibitions. I. Enyeart, James. II. Kansas. University. Museum of Art. III. Title. IV. Series: Kansas. University. Museum of Art. Miscellaneous publications, no. 81.

Entomology.

KLOTS, Alexander Barrett, 595.7
1903-
Living insects of the world, by Alexander B. Klots and Elsie B. Klots. With photos. by Andreas Feininger, and others. Line drawings by Su Zan Noguchi Swain. A Chanticleer Press ed. Garden City, N.Y., Doubleday [1959] 304 p. illus. 19 cm. (World of nature series) Includes bibliography. [QL463.K65] 59-9100
1. Entomology. 2. Insects—Pictorial works. I. Klots, Elsie Broughton, joint author. II. Title. BIP

Environment (Art)—Exhibitions.

COE, Ralph T. 700
The Magic Theater; art technology spectacular [by] Ralph T. Coe. Kansas City [Mo.] Circle Press [1970] 261 p. illus. 25 cm. Held at the Nelson Gallery of Art, Kansas City, Mo. [N6512.C5812] 78-115920
1. Environment (Art)—Exhibitions. 2. Environment (Art)—U.S. I. William Rockhill Nelson Gallery of Art and Mary Atkins Museum of Fine Art, Kansas City, Mo. II. Title.

RUTGERS 709'.04'074014942
University, New Brunswick, N.J. Art Gallery.
A response to the environment : [exhibition], Rutgers University Art Gallery, Voorhees Hall, New Brunswick, New Jersey, in association with Cook College, March 16-April 26, 1975. New Brunswick, N.J. : The Gallery, [1975] [8] p., [16] leaves of plates : ill. ; 22 x 28 cm. [N6494.E6R88 1975] 75-620001
1. Environment (Art)—Exhibitions. 2. Art, Modern—20th century—Exhibitions. I. Cook College. II. Title.

VENICE. Biennale d'arte. 709'.04
Environment, participation, cultural structures : general catalogue / La Biennale di Venezia, 1976. Venezia : Alfieri edizioni d'arte, c1976. 2 v. (386 p.) : ill. ; 25 cm. On cover: La Biennale di Venezia, Section of Visual Arts and Architecture. [N6494.E6V46 1976] 77-465647
1. Environment (Art)—Exhibitions. 2. Art, Modern—20th century—Exhibitions. 3. Architecture, Modern—20th century—Exhibitions. 4. Architecture—Environmental aspects—Exhibitions. I. Title.

WALKER Art Center, 709.73
Minneapolis.
Figures/environments: Alex Katz, Red Grooms, Jann Haworth, Duane Hanson, Paul Thek, Lynton Wells, George Segal, Robert Whitman; an exhibition organized by Walker Art Center. [Minneapolis, 1970] 43 p. illus. 28 cm. Held at the Walker Art Center, May 15-June 13, 1970; Cincinnati Art Museum, Oct. 2-Nov. 1, 1970; and Dallas Museum of Fine Arts, Dec. 13, 1970-Jan. 17, 1971. [N6512.W312] 72-123218
1. Environment (Art)—Exhibitions. 2. Art, Modern—20th century—United States. I. Cincinnati. Art Museum. II. Dallas. Museum of Fine Arts. III. Title.

Environmental engineering (Buildings)

FLYNN, John Edward, 1930- 729'.2
Architectural interior systems; lighting, air conditioning, acoustics [by] John E. Flynn [and] Arthur W. Segil. New York, Van Nostrand Reinhold [1970] xiii, 306 p. illus. 24 cm. (Van Nostrand Reinhold environmental engineering series) Bibliography: p. 294-295. [TH7011.F58 1970] 78-122678
1. Environmental engineering (Buildings) I. Segil, Arthur W., joint author. II. Title. BIP

Environments (Art)—Exhibitions.

PENNSYLVANIA. 709'.748'11
University. Institute of Contemporary Art.
Made in Philadelphia: Don Roger Gill, Ree Morton, Italo Scanga, Phillips Simkin [and] Dennis Will; [exhibition] March 24 to April 27, 1973. Philadelphia [1973] [28] p. illus. 22 x 28 cm. [N6535.P5P38 1973] 74-167239
1. Environments (Art)—Exhibitions. 2. Environments (Art)—Philadelphia. I. Title.

Epiphanius, Monastery of.

WINLOCK, Herbert Eustis, 913.32
1884-1950.
The monastery of Epiphanius at Thebes. New York, 1926. [New York] Arno Press, 1973. 2 v. illus. 32 cm. Reprint of the ed. which was issued as v. 3-4 of the Publications of the Metropolitan Museum of Art Egyptian Expedition. At head of title: The Metropolitan Museum of Art Egyptian Expedition. Contents.Contents.—pt. 1. Winlock, H. E. The archaeological material. Crum, W. E. The literary material.—pt. 2. Crum, W. E. Coptic ostraca and papyri; edited with translations and commentaries. Evelyn-White, H. G. Greek ostraca and papyri; edited with translations and commentaries. [DT73.T3W48 1973] 72-168413 ISBN 0-405-02249-2 40.00
1. Epiphanius, Monastery of. 2. Manuscripts, Coptic (Papyri) 3. Manuscripts, Greek (Papri) 4. Ostraka. I. Crum, Walter Ewing, 1865-1944. II. Evelyn-White, Hugh Gerard, d. 1924, ed. III. Title. IV. Series: New York (City). Metropolitan Museum of Art. Egyptian Expedition. Publications, v. 3-4. BIP

Epstein, Jacob, Sir, 1880-1959.

BUCKLE, Richard. 730.942
Jacob Epstein, sculptor. [1st ed.] Cleveland, World Pub. Co. [c1963] 448 p. illus., ports. 30 cm. [NB497.E6B8] 63-11957
1. Epstein, Sir Jacob, 1880-1959. I. Title.

EPSTEIN, Jacob, Sir, 730'.92'4 B
1880-1959.
Epstein, an autobiography / Jacob Epstein. [Rev. & extended ed.]. New York : Arno Press, 1975. x, 294 p., [47] leaves of plates : ill. ; 24 cm. (The Modern Jewish experience) Published in 1940 under title: Let there be sculpture. Reprint of the 1955 ed. published by Dutton, New York. Includes index. [NB497.E6A2 1975] 74-27978 ISBN 0-405-06707-0 : 26.00
1. Epstein, Jacob, Sir, 1880-1959. 2. Sculptors—Great Britain—Correspondence, reminiscences, etc. I. Title. II. Series.

EPSTEIN, Jacob, Sir, 741.942
1880-1959.
Epstein drawings. With notes by Lady Epstein, and an introd. by Richard Buckle. [1st American ed.] Cleveland, World Pub. Co. [1962] 150 p. 65 plates. 29 cm. [NC1115.E6E6 1962] 62-6636
I. Epstein, Kathleen, Lady. II. Title.

Eragny Press.

PITTSBURGH Bibliophiles. 686
The Eragny Press, 1894-1914; an exhibition catalogue. [Pittsburgh] 1967. [7] p. 23 cm. [Z232.P65P58] 73-284392
1. Eragny Press.

Erasmus, Desiderius, d. 1536.

BROCKWELL, Maurice 759.9492
Walter, 1869-1958.
Erasmus, humanist and painter : a study of a triptych in a private collection / by Maurice W. Brockwell. Folcroft, Pa. : Folcroft Library Editions, 1979. p. cm. Reprint of the 1918 ed. privately printed in New York. Includes bibliographical references and index. [ND653.E7A63 1979] 79-14635 ISBN 0-8414-9830-X lib. bdg. : 17.50
1. Erasmus, Desiderius, d. 1536. Christ on the Cross. I. Title.

EICHENBERG, Fritz, 769'.92'4
1901-
In praise of folly (Encomium moriae) [by] Desiderius Erasmus. Ten original prints from woodblocks by Fritz Eichenberg with excerpts of the Latin texts, selected and freely translated into English by the artist. New York, Aquarius Press, 1972. 1 portfolio ([47] p., 10 plates) 54 cm. One hundred sixty-one copies printed. "F. E. artist's copy." [NE1112.E32E72] 73-163962
1. Erasmus, Desiderius, d. 1536. Moriae encomium—Illustrations. I. Erasmus, Desiderius, d. 1536. Moriae encomium. English and Latin. Selections. 1972. II. Title.

Erickson, Carl Ebert, 1899-1966.

KNOWER, Ramona C., 748.2'913
1905-
Erickson freehand glass, Bremen, Ohio, 1943-1961, in color, by Ramona C. and Franklin H. Knower. [Columbus, Ohio, 1971] 33 p. illus. (part col.) 23 cm. Cover title. [NK5198.E7K5] 75-29745
1. Erickson, Carl Ebert, 1899-1966. I. Knower, Franklin Hayward, 1901- joint author. II. Title.

Ericson, Augustus William, 1848-1927.

ERICSON, Augustus 779'.9'9794
William, 1848-1927.
Fine California views : the photographs of A. W. Ericson / by Peter E. Palmquist. Eureka : Interface California Corp., c1975. 111 p. : ill. ; 27 cm. [TR140.E73A33 1975] 75-7846 ISBN 0-915580-02-0 : 20.95
1. Ericson, Augustus William, 1848-1927. 2. California—Description and travel—Views. I. Palmquist, Peter E. II. Title.
Publisher's address: 1806 E. St., Suite B., Eureka, Ca. 95501. BIP

Erivan. Matenadaran.

DURNOVE, Libiia 759.9566
Aleksandrovna.
Armenian miniatures. Text and notes by Lydia A. Dournovo. Pref. by Sirarpie Der Nersessian. [Text translated from the French by Irene J. Underwood] New York, H. N. Abrams [1961] 181 p. mounted illus. (part col.) col. map (on lining paper) 31 cm. [ND3239.A7D83] 61-15292
1. Erivan. Matenadaran. 2. Illumination of books and manuscripts—Armenia. I. Title.

Ernst, Max, 1891—

DIEHL, Gaston. 759.4
Max Ernst. [Translated from the French by Eileen B. Hennessy] New York, Crown [1973] 95 p. illus. (part col.) 29 cm. Bibliography: p. 91-93. [ND588.E75D5313] 72-84222 ISBN 0-517-50004-3 3.95
1. Ernst, Max, 1891-

ERNST, Max, 1891- 709'.2'4
Inside the sight. Houston, Tex., Institute for the Arts, Rice University, c1973. 159 p. illus. (part col.) 23 cm. Contributions by W. Hofmann and others. "An exhibition of paintings, drawings, and sculpture by Max Ernst from the Menil Family Collection. Circulated by the Institute for the Arts, Rice University, Houston and presented by ... Hamburg, Kunsthalle [and other museums]" Translation of Das innere Gesicht. Bibliography: p. [156]-157. [N6888.E7H613] 77-125283
1. Ernst, Max, 1891- 2. Menil family—Art collections. I. Hofmann, Werner, 1928- II. William Marsh Rice University, Houston, Tex. Institute for the Arts. III. Hamburg. Kunsthalle. IV. Title.

ERNST, Max, 1891- 709.24
Max Ernst. [New York, Byron Gallery, 1970] 1 v. (chiefly illus., part col.) 22 cm. Catalog of the exhibition held at the Byron Gallery, Oct. 28-Dec. 2, 1970. [N6888.E7A48] 72-199997
I. Byron Gallery.

ERNST, Max, 1891- 709.24
Max Ernst. [New York, Byron Gallery, 1970] 1 v. (chiefly illus., part col.) 22 cm. Catalog of the exhibition held at the Byron Gallery, Oct. 28-Dec. 2, 1970. [N6888.E7A48] 72-199997
I. Byron Gallery.

ERNST, Max, 1891- 769'.924
Max Ernst [by] Werner Spies. [Translated from the German by Joseph M. Bernstein] New York, H. N. Abrams [1969, c1968] xxvi, 59 p. illus. (part col.) 21 x 23 cm. (Modern artists) Bibliography: p. 59. [NC1145.E7S613 1969] 69-12795
I. Spies, Werner, fl. 1965-

ERNST, Max, 1891- 769'.924
Max Ernst [by] Werner Spies. [Translated from the German by Joseph M. Bernstein] New York, H. N. Abrams [1969, c1968] xxvi, 59 p. illus. (part col.) 21 x 23 cm. (Modern artists) Bibliography: p. 59. [NC1145.E7S613 1969] 69-12795
I. Spies, Werner, fl. 1965-

ERNST, Max, 1891- 709'.2'4
Max Ernst : a retrospective. New York : Solomon R. Guggenheim Museum, 1975. 271 p. : chiefly ill. (some col.) ; 28 cm. Sheet inserted: Additions to the exhibition. Bibliography: p. 257-269. [N6888.E7S62] 74-29415 pbk. : 14.75
1. Ernst, Max, 1891- I. Solomon R. Guggenheim Museum, New York.

ERNST, Max, 1891- 759.4
Max Ernst [by] Giuseppe Gatt. [Translated from the Italian] London, New York, Hamlyn, 1970. 96 p. illus. (some col.), port. 32 cm. (Twentieth-century masters) "Distributed in the United States of America by Crown Publishers." Bibliography: p. 96 [N6888.E7G3513] 76-30282 ISBN 0-600-35926-3 £2.25
I. Gatt, Giuseppe.

ERNST, Max, 1891- 759.4
Max Ernst [by] Giuseppe Gatt. [Translated from the Italian] London, New York, Hamlyn, 1970. 96 p. illus. (some col.), port. 32 cm. (Twentieth-century masters) "Distributed in the United States of America by Crown Publishers." Bibliography: p. 96 [N6888.E7G3513] 76-30282 ISBN 0-600-35926-3 £2.25
I. Gatt, Giuseppe.

ERNST, Max, 1891- 709'.2'4
Max Ernst. Conceived by Jean Saucet. Text by Sarane Alexandrian. Translated from the French by Eleanor Levieux. Chicago, J. P. O'Hara [1972] 72 p. illus. (part col.) 31 cm. "A Howard Greenfeld book." Bibliography: p. 72. [N6888.E7A7913] 79-189277 15.00
1. Ernst, Max, 1891- I. Alexandrian, Sarane.

ERNST, Max, 1891- 709'.2'4
Maximiliana : the illegal practice of astronomy : hommage a Dorothea Tanning / Max Ernst ; Peter Schamoni [editor]. Boston : New York Graphic Society, [1975] c1974. 89 p. : chiefly ill. (some col.) ; 25 cm. Issued also under title: Max Ernst, Maximiliana: die widerrechtliche Ausubung der Astronomie. Text in English, French, and German. [N6888.E7S248] 74-24832 ISBN 0-8212-0655-9 : 17.50

1. Ernst, Max, 1891- 2. Astronomy in art. I. Schamoni, Peter. II. Title.

ERNST, Max, 1891- 709'.2'4
Une semaine de bonte : a surrealistic novel in collage / Max Ernst ; [translated by Stanley Appelbaum]. New York : Dover Publications, 1976. ix, 208 p. : all ill. ; 28 cm. Originally published in 1934 in 5 volumes by J. Bucher, Paris. [N6888.E7A5613 1976] 75-17362 ISBN 0-486-23252-2 pbk. : 4.50
1. Ernst, Max, 1891- Semaine de bonte. I. Title. BIP

JEWISH Theological Seminary of America. Jewish Museum. 759.3
Max Ernst: sculpture and recent painting, ed. by Sam Hunter. Introd. essays by Lucy R. Lippard, Andre Pieyre de Mandiargues, John Russell, with a statement by the artist. [New York, 1966] 65, [3] p. illus. (pt. col.) ports. 25cm. Catalog of an exhibition held at the Jewish Mus., New York, March 3-April 17, 1966. Bibl. [ND588.E75J4] 66-18741 8.50
1. Ernst, Max, 1891- I. Hunter, Sam, 1923- ed. II. Title.
Available from October House in New York.

NEW York (City). Museum of Modern Art. 759.4
Max Ernst. Edited by William S. Lieberman. Reprint ed. [New York] Published for the Museum of Modern Art by Arno Press, 1972 [c1961] 62, [1] p. illus. 23 cm. Catalog of an exhibition held at the Museum of Modern Art, New York: March 1-May 7, 1961 and the Art Institute of Chicago: June 16-July 23, 1961. Bibliography: p. 61-[63] [N6888.E7N4 1972] 72-169307 ISBN 0-405-01566-6 12.00
1. Ernst, Max, 1891- I. Chicago. Art Institute. II. Lieberman, William Slattery, 1924- ed.

NEW York. Museum of Modern Art. 759.3
Max Ernst. [Exhibition dates: Museum of Modern Art, Mar. 1-May 7, 1961. Art Institute of Chicago, June 16-July 23, 1961] Ed. by William S. Lieberman. Garden City, N. Y., Dist. by Doubleday [c.1961] 63p. illus. (col. front.) Bibl. 61-11269 2.50 pap.,
1. Ernst, Max, 1891- I. Chicago, Art Institute. II. Lieberman, William Slattery, 1924- ed. III. Title.

PENROSE, Roland, Sir. 759.4
Max Ernst's Celebes. [Newcastle upon Tyne] University of Newcastle upon Tyne, 1972. 24 p. illus. 24 cm. (Charlton lecture, 52nd) "Delivered on 19th November 1969." [ND588.E75P46] 73-167510 £1.00
1. Ernst, Max, 1891- Celebes. I. Title. II. Series.

RUSSELL, John, 1919- 709'.44
Max Ernst: life and work. New York, H. N. Abrams [1967] 359 p. illus. (part col.), facsims., ports. 31 cm. Bibliography: p. 336-341. [N6888.E7R83 1967b] 67-22852
1. Ernst, Max, 1891-

SCHNEEDE, Uwe M. 759.4
Max Ernst [by] Uwe M. Schneede. Translated by R. W. Last. New York, Praeger [1973, c1972] 216 p. illus. (part col.) 22 cm. Bibliography: p. 204-205. [ND588.E75S3613 1973] 72-88535 10.00
1. Ernst, Max, 1891- BIP

SPIES, Werner, fl.1965- 759.4
The return of la belle jardiniere; Max Ernst 1950-1970. [Translated from the German by Walter Allen] New York, Abrams [1972, c1971] 147 p. illus., col. plates. 30 cm. Translation of Die Ruckkehr der schonen Gartnerin; Max Ernst 1950-1970. Bibliography: p. 143-147. [ND588.E75S613] 72-544 ISBN 0-8109-0105-6 20.00
1. Ernst, Max, 1891- I. Title. II. Title: Max Ernst 1950-1970.

Erotic art.

BAYROS, Franz, Marquis de, 1866-1924. 709.46
The amorous drawings of the Marquis von Bayros. Edited by Ludwig von Brunn] New York, Cythera Press [1968] 238 p. (chiefly illus.) 33 cm. [NC1145.B32B7] 68-20201
I. Title.

BERTRAND, Raymond. 741.9'44
The drawings of Raymond Bertrand / with an introd. by Emmanuelle Arsan. [New York] : Grove Press : distributed by Random House, [1974] [126] p. : chiefly ill. (some col.) ; 32 cm. Translation of Dessins erotiques de Bertrand. [NC248.B43A7713] 73-21034 ISBN 0-8021-0040-6 : 20.00
1. Bertrand, Raymond. 2. Erotic art. I. Arsan, Emmanuelle. II. Title.

BOYCE, John. 741.9'73
Aphrodisiac : erotic drawings / by John Boyce for selected passages from the works of Anais Nin. New York : Crown Publishers, c1976. p. cm. [NC139.B68A74 1976] 76-15163 ISBN 0-517-52678-6 : 7.95 ISBN 0-517-52679-4 pbk. :
1. Boyce, John. 2. Erotic art. I. Nin, Anais, 1903- II. Title. BIP

BRIDGEMAN, Harriet. 704.94'28
Erotic antiques, Galashiels (Glenmoyne, Galashiels, Selkirkshire, Scotland): Lyle Publications, 1974. 128 p. of ill.; 30 cm. [N8217.E6B67] 74-195831 ISBN 0-8277-2707-0 15.00
1. Erotic art. I. Title. II. Title: or, Love is an antique thing, III. Title: Love is an antique thing.
Distributed by British Book Centre. BIP

GERHARD, Poul. 704.94'9'30141
Pornography in fine art from ancient times up to the present. [Los Angeles] Elysium, 1969. xxv, 187 p. illus. 32 cm. [N8217.E6G4] 70-79622 18.95
1. Erotic art. I. Title.

LUCIE-SMITH, Edward. 704.94'2
Eroticism in Western art. New York, Praeger Publishers [1972] 287 p. illus. 22 cm. Bibliography: p. 276. [N8217.E6L8 1972b] 72-180729
1. Erotic art. I. Title. BIP

SMITH, Bradley, 1910- 704.94'28
Erotic art of the masters : the 18th, 19th & 20th centuries / by Bradley Smith. Secaucus, N.J. : L. Stuart, [1974]. xvi, 207 p. : chiefly ill. (some col.) ; 32 cm. (A Gemini-Smith, inc. book) Includes index. Bibliography: p. 198-199. [N8217.E6S58] 74-76371 ISBN 0-8184-0174-5 : 24.95
1. Erotic art. 2. Art, Modern. I. Title. BIP

UNGERER, Tomi, 1931- 741.9'73
Fornicon. [New York? 1969] 1 portfolio ([4] p., 62 plates (part col.)) 38 cm. "A limited edition of five hundred copies signed by the author." L.C. copy not signed. [NC1429.U5A46 1969b] 72-187585
I. Title.

ZICHY, Mihaly, grof, 1827-1906. 741.9'439'1
The erotic drawings of Mihaly Zichy; forty drawings. New York, Grove Press [1969] [4] p., 40 plates. 23 x 28 cm. [NC1145.Z5A44] 76-81073 25.00
I. Title.

Erotic art—Addresses, essays, lectures.

STUDIES in erotic art 704.94'9'30141
[by] Theodore Bowie [and others] Edited by Theodore Bowie and Cornelia V. Christenson. New York, Basic Books [1970] x, 395 p. illus. 28 cm. (Studies in sex and society, 3) Includes bibliographical references. Contents.Contents.—The scope and temperament of erotic art in the Greco-Roman world, by O. J. Brendel.—Sexual motifs in prehistoric Peruvian ceramics, by P. H. Gebhard.—Erotic aspects of Japanese art, by T. Bowie.—The metaphors of love and birth in Michelangelo's Pietas, by L. Steinberg.—Picasso and the anatomy of eroticism, by R. Rosenblum. [N8217.E6S8] 72-94288 ISBN 0-465-08266-1 15.00
1. Erotic art—Addresses, essays, lectures. I. Bowie, Theodore Robert, ed. II. Christenson, Cornelia V., ed. III. Title. IV. Series.

Erotic art—East (Far East)

RAWSON, Philip S. 704.94'9'30141
Erotic art of the East; the sexual theme in oriental painting and sculpture, by Philip Rawson. Introd. by Alex Comfort. New York, Putnam [1968] xiii, 880 p. illus., 32 col. plates. 29 cm. Bibliography: p. 376-378. [N7260.R35] 68-25429 20.00
1. Erotic art—East (Far East) 2. Art, Oriental. I. Title. BIP

Erotic art—Exhibitions.

EROTIC Art Gallery. 704.94'28
The Erotic Art Gallery; [exhibit of works by] Louise Bourgeois [and others] New York, February 8-March 30, 1974. [New York, 1974] 39 p. (chiefly illus.) 22 x 23 cm. [N8217.E6E67 1974] 74-176341
1. Erotic art—Exhibitions. I. Bourgeois, Louise, 1911-

Erotic art—Japan.

EVANS, Tom, 1949- 769'.4'28
Shunga : the art of love in Japan / Tom and Mary Anne Evans. New York : Paddington Press, [1975] p. cm. Bibliography: p. [N7353.E82] 75-11171 ISBN 0-8467-0063-8 : 35.00
1. Erotic art—Japan. 2. Ukiyoe. 3. Art, Japanese—Edo period, 1600-1868. 4. Japan—Social life and customs—1600-1868. I. Evans, Mary Anne, joint author. II. Title. BIP

Erotic art—Russia.

FLEGON, Alec. 704.94'28'0947
Eroticism in Russian art / A. Flegon. London : Flegon Press, 1976. 468, xxxvi p. : chiefly ill. (some col.) ; 22 x 23 cm. Includes index. [N6981.F57] 77-368323 £28.00
1. Erotic art—Russia. 2. Art, Russian. I. Title.

Erotica.

BACON, Jack. 704.94'9'30141
Eros in art. [Los Angeles, Elysium, 1969] 49 p. illus. (part col.) 29 cm. [HQ460.B3] 74-79623
1. Erotica. 2. Erotic art. I. Title. BIP

CHINESE erotic art, 709'.51
by Michel Beurdeley in collaboration with Kristofer Schipper, Chang Fu-Jui [and] Jacques Pimpaneau. [Translated from the French by Diana Imber] Rutland, Vt., C. E. Tuttle Co. [1969] xiii, 209 p. illus., col. plates. 37 cm. Bibliography: p. 207-208. [NX650.E7J483 1969] 74-83072 ISBN 0-8048-0695-0 32.50
1. Erotica. 2. The arts, Chinese. I. Beurdeley, Michel.

CREPAX, Guido. 741.5'944
Story of O / by Pauline Reage ; illustrated version by Guido Crepax. New York : Grove Press : distributed by Whirlwind Book Co., 1978. ca. 150 p. : chiefly ill. ; 29 cm. [PN6747.C7S8] 77-93975 ISBN 0-8021-0159-3 : 25.00. ISBN 0-8021-4111-0 pbk.
I. Reage, Pauline. Histoire d'O. English. II. Title.

EROTIC art of China : 769'.4'28
a unique collection of Chinese prints and poems devoted to the art of love / introd. by Abraham N. Franzblau ; postscript by Etiemble. New York : Crown Publishers, c1977. 160 p. : col. ill.; 29 cm. Bibliography: p. 160. [NX650.E7E76] 76-39804 ISBN 0-517-20674-9 : 12.95
1. Erotica. 2. Arts, Chinese. I. Franzblau, Abraham Norman, 1901-

EROTIC art of China : 769'.4'28
a unique collection of Chinese prints and poems devoted to the art of love / introd. by Abraham N. Franzblau ; postscript by Etiemble. New York : Crown Publishers, c1977. 160 p. : col. ill.; 29 cm. Bibliography: p. 160. [NX650.E7E76] 76-39804 ISBN 0-517-20674-9 : 12.95
1. Erotica. 2. Arts, Chinese. I. Franzblau, Abraham Norman, 1901-

L'AMOUR bleu / 700
Cecile Beurdeley ; translated from the French by Michael Taylor. New York : Rizzoli, 1978. 304 p. : ill. (some col.) ; 36 cm. Bibliography: p. 299. [NX650.H6A46] 77-77509 ISBN 0-8478-0129-2 : 65.00
1. Homosexuality in art. 2. Erotica. I. Beurdeley, Cecile.

PECKHAM, Morse. 176
Art and pornography; an experiment in explanation. New York, Basic Books [1969] viii, 306 p. 22 cm. (Studies in sex and society) [HQ460.P42] 78-94292 6.95
1. Erotica. I. Title. II. Series.

PECKHAM, Morse. 176.'7
Art and pornography; an experiment in explanation. New York, Harper & Row [1971, c1969] viii, 306 p. illus. 22 cm. (Sex and society series) (Icon editions, IN-12) [NX650.E7P42 1971] 72-195323 ISBN 0-06-430012-9 3.95
1. Erotica. I. Title. II. Series: Studies in sex and society.

WEBB, Peter. 700
The erotic arts / Peter Webb. 1st U.S. ed. Boston : New York Graphic Society, c1975. p. cm. [NX650.E7W4 1975b] 75-27441 ISBN 0-8212-0696-6 : 17.50
1. Erotica. 2. Arts. I. Title. BIP

WILSON, Colin, 1931- 301.41'8
L'Amour; the ways of love. Text by Colin Wilson. Photos. by Piero Rimaldi. New York, Crown Publishers [1972, c1970] 1 v. (unpaged) illus. 21 x 26 cm. [HQ460.W54] 71-133804
1. Erotica. 2. Sex. I. Title.

Erotica—Addresses, essays, lectures.

NOBILE, Philip, comp. 301.41'5
The new eroticism: theories, vogues and canons. [1st ed.] New York, Random House [1970] xii, 238 p. 22 cm. Contents.—Introduction, by P. Nobile.—The self and the other: Narcissus, by N. O. Brown.—Sexuality into eros, by H. Marcuse.—Revolution is Puritan, by E. J. Hobsbawm.—Everyman as pervert, by E. Becker.—Sexual perversion, by T. Nagel.—Voyeurism in New York, by D. Kalins.—The new homosexuality, by T. Burke.—Naked therapy, by P. Bindrim.—Body painting: the youngest profession, by J. Mancini.—Night words: human privacy and high pornography, by G. Steiner.—Dirty books can stay, by K. Tynan.—How to make the world safe for pornography, by P. Michaelson.—Inside Screw, by P. Nobile.—The sex sell, by J. Bugler.—Paydirt: notes on the sex explosion, by R. Craft.—Staged sexuality, by R. Wetzsteon.—Sex rock symbolism, by C. Hodenfeld.—Pop sex, by C. Karpel.—The desexualized society, by C. Winick.—Was it good for you, too? By D. Greenburg.—Liberating woman's orgasm, by S. Lydon.—ThOThe new eroticism: theories, vogues and canons. [1st ed.] New York, Random House [1970] xii, 238
1. Erotica—Addresses, essays, lectures. I. Title.

Erte

ERTE. 745.4'4924
Erte. [Exhibition, December 8 to January 13, 1971. New York, Sonnabend Gallery, c1970] [1] p., 24 p. of illus. 26 cm. Cover title. [NK1535.E7A43] 72-198015
I. Title.

ERTE. 746.9'2'0924
Erte fashions / Erte. London : Academy Editions ; New York : St. Martin's Press, 1972, 1976 printing. [112] p. : chiefly ill. (some col.) ; 30 cm. [TT507.E69 1976] 77-150056 8.95
1. Erte. 2. Clothing and dress. 3. Dress accessories. I. Title.

ERTE. 769'.92'4
Erte graphics : five complete suites reproduced in full color = Erte : cinq suites de lithographies / pref. by Salome Estorick. New York : Dover Publications, c1978. 46 p. : chiefly col. ill. ; 31 cm. Text in English and French. Contents.Contents.—The seasons. The alphabet. The numerals. The aces. The precious stones. [NE2356.5.E77A4 1978] 77-91513 ISBN 0-486-23580-7 : 5.00
I. Erte. II. Title.

ERTE. 745.4'49'24 B
Things I remember : an autobiography / Erte. New York : Quadrangle, [1975] p.

cm. Includes index. [TT505.E78A34] 75-8286 ISBN 0-8129-0575-X : 12.50
1. Erte. I. Title. BIP

SPENCER, Charles. 709'.24
Erte. [1st American ed.] New York, C. N. Potter; distributed by Crown Publishers [1970] ix, 198 p. plates (part col.), ports. 30 cm. Bibliography: p. 192-194. [NK1535.E7S65 1970] 70-125360 15.95
1. Erte BIP

Erwitt, Elliott.

CALLAHAN, Sean. 770'.92'4
The private experience, Elliott Erwitt / text by Sean Callahan, with the editors of Alskog, inc. [New York] : T. Y. Crowell, [1974] 88 p. : ill. (some col.) ; 29 cm. (Masters of contemporary photography) [TR140.E78C34] 74-8232 ISBN 0-690-00623-3 : 7.95. ISBN 0-690-00624-1 pbk. : 3.95
1. Erwitt, Elliott. 2. Photography, Artistic. I. Alskog, inc. II. Erwitt, Elliott. III. Title.

ERWITT, Elliott. 770'.92'4
Recent develoments / Elliott Erwitt ; introd. by Wilfred Sheed. New York : Simon and Schuster, c1978. p. cm. [TR654.E782] 78-17998 ISBN 0-671-24645-3 : 17.95 ISBN 0-671-24646-1 pbk. : 9.95
1. Erwitt, Elliott. 2. Photography, Artistic. I. Title. BIP

Escher, Maurits Cornelis, 1898-1971.

ERNST, Bruno. 769'.92'4
The magic mirror of M. C. Escher / Bruno Ernst ; [translated from the Dutch by John E. Brigham]. 1st American ed. New York : Random House, c1976. 112 p. : ill. (some col.) ; 32 cm. Includes index. [N6953.E82E76 1976] 75-664 ISBN 0-394-49217-X : 15.00
1. Escher, Maurits Cornelis, 1898-1971. I. Title. BIP

ESCHER, Maurits Cornelis, 1898- 760'.0924
The graphic work of M. C. Escher. [New ed.] New York, Meredith Press [1967] 22 p., 69 plates (part col.) illus., port. 32 cm. Translation of Grafiek en tekeningen. Captions in Dutch, English, German, and French. [NE670.E75A43 1967] 67-9321
I. Title.

ESCHER, Maurits Cornelis, 1898- 769'.92'4
The world of M. C. Escher. [Edited by J. L. Locher] New York, H. N. Abrams [1971?] xi, 59 p., 300 illus. (part col.) 29 cm. Bibliography: p. 55-57. [NE670.E75L6] 70-161039 ISBN 0-8109-0107-2
1. Escher, Maurits Cornelis, 1898- I. Locher, J. L., ed. BIP

ESCHER, Maurits Cornelis, 1898- 769'.92'4
The world of M. C. Escher, with texts by M. C. Escher [and] J. L. Locher. [Edited by J. L. Locher] New concise NAL ed. New York, H. N. Abrams; distributed by New American Library [1974, c1971] 151 p. illus. (part col.) 31 cm. [NE670.E75L6 1974] 73-20290
1. Escher, Maurits Cornelis, 1898- I. Locher, J. L. II. Title.

MACGILLAVRY, Caroline Henriette, 1904- 769'.92'4
Fantasy & symmetry : the periodic drawings of M. C. Escher / Caroline H. MacGillavry. New York : H. N. Abrams, [1976] xi, 84 p. : ill. (some col.) ; 27 cm. Reprint of the 1965 ed. published for International Union of Crystallography by A. Oosthoek's Uitgeversmaatschappij, Utrecht under title: Symmetry aspects of M. C. Escher's periodic drawings. Includes index. Bibliography: p. xi, [NC745.M3 1976] 75-39835 ISBN 0-8109-0850-6 : 15.00
1. Escher, Maurits Cornelis, 1898- 2. Symmetry. 3. Colors. I. Title. BIP

SCHATTSCHNEIDER, Doris. 736'.98
M. C. Escher kaleidocycles / by Doris Schattschneider and Wallace Walker. 1st ed. New York : Ballantine Books, 1977. 1 portfolio (iv, 43 p., 16 fold. leaves of plates) : ill. (some col.) ; 30 cm. Includes 16 folded sheets of two-dimensional drawings which can be separated from their surrounding extra paper to form 17 polyhedral forms. Bibliography: p. 38. [QA447.S3] 77-9910 ISBN 0-345-25686-7 pbk. : 8.95
1. Escher, Maurits Cornelis, 1898-1971. 2. Geometrical models. 3. Design, Decorative. 4. Symmetry. I. Escher, Maurits Cornelis, 1898-1971. II. Walker, Wallace, joint author. III. Title. IV. Title: Kaleidocycles. BIP

Escorial.

CABLE, Mary. 914.6'41
El Escorial, by Mary Cable and the editors of the Newsweek Book Division. New York, Newsweek [1971] 172 p. illus. (part col.) 30 cm. (Wonders of man) Bibliography: p. 169. [N3418.C3] 70-154726
1. Escorial. I. Newsweek, inc. Book Division.

DAVIE, John. 726.774
The monastery of El Escorial and the Prince's Lodge; the eight wonder of the world. Edited and supplemented by Herbert W. Serra Williamson. Madrid, New York, British American Pub. Co., 1952. 95p. illus. 18cm. [NA7776.E8D38] 53-23596
1. Escorial. 2. Art-Escorial. I. Title.

LOZOYA, Juan Contreras y Lopez de Ayala, marques de, 1893- 946'.04
The Excorial; the roya at La Granja de San Ildefonso. New York, Meredith Press [1967, c1965] 156 p. illus. (part col.) 28 cm. (Great galleries series) Cover title: The Escorial and San Ildefonso. Translation of Escorial e San Ildefonso. [N3418.L613] 68-31930
1. Escorial. 2. San Ildefonso, Spain. I. Title: The Escorial and San Ildefonso.

LOZOYA, Juan Contreras y Lopez de Ayala, marques de 1893- 708.6
The Escorial; the royal palace at La Granja de San Ildefonso. New York, Meredith [1967, c.1965] 156p. illus. (pt. col.) 28cm. (Great galleries ser.) Cover title: The Escorial and San Ildefonso. Tr. of Escorial e San Ildefonso. [N3418.L613] 68-31930 8.95 bds.,
1. Escorial. 2. San Ildefonso, Spain. I. Title. II. Title: The Escorial and San Ildefonso.

WILLIAMSON-SERRA, Herbert William, 1900- 914.6'41
The eighth wonder of the world : the Monastery of El Escorial and the Prince's Lodge / ed. by Herbert W. Serra Williamson. Madrid ; New York : British American Pub. Co., 1953. 95 p. : ill. ; 17 cm. On cover: A Guide to the Monastery of El Escorial. Includes index. [NA7776.E8W55] 75-315849
1. Escorial. I. Title.

Esherick, Wharton.

ESHERICK, Wharton. 741.9'73
Drawings by Wharton Esherick / compiled, edited, and with an introd. by Gene Rochberg. New York : Van Nostrand Reinhold, c1978. [112] p. : chiefly ill. ; 29 cm. [NC139.E83A4 1978] 77-70383 ISBN 0-442-26967-6 : 15.00
1. Esherick, Wharton. 2. Artists' preparatory studies. I. Rochberg, Gene. II. Title. BIP

Eskimo craft—Juvenile literature.

COMINS, Jeremy. 745.5
Eskimo crafts and their cultural backgrounds / Jeremy Comins. New York : Lothrop, Lee & Shepard Co., [1975] 125 p. : ill. ; 25 cm. Includes index. Bibliography: p. 121-122. Instructions for making sculpture, stencil prints, applique, models, and other objects in the style of Eskimo artists. [TT125.C65] 75-9573 ISBN 0-688-41705-1 : 5.95 ISBN 0-688-51705-6 lib.bdg. : 5.11 5.95
1. Eskimo craft—Juvenile literature. I. Title. BIP

Eskimos—Alaska.

ALASKA. University. 398.2'09701
Alaska native arts and crafts: potential for expansion; final report to Bureau of Indian Affairs, U.S. Department of the Interior. [College, Alaska] 1964. 162 p. illus. 29 cm. "Under contract no. 14-20-06050-1053." Bibliography: p. 121-124. [E98.A7A38] 67-64976
1. Eskimos—Alaska. 2. Eskimos—Alaska—Art. 3. Indians of North America—Alaska—Art. I. United States. Bureau of Indian Affairs. II. Title.

Eskimos—Alaska—Art.

RAY, Dorothy Jean. 709'.701 s
Graphic arts of the Alaskan Eskimo. [Washington, U.S. Indian Arts and Crafts Board; for sale by the Supt. of Docs., U.S. Govt.Print. Off., 1969] 87 p. illus., map, ports. 27 cm. (Native American arts, 2) Cover title. Bibliography: p. 82-83. [E98.A7N36 no. 2] 72-603663 1.00
1. Eskimos—Alaska—Art. I. United States. Indian Arts and Crafts Board. II. Title. III. Series.

Eskimos—Alaska—Art—Exhibitions.

THE Far North; 745'.09701
2000 years of American Eskimo and Indian art [by] Henry B. Collins [and others] Washington, National Gallery of Art, 1973. xxx, 289 p. illus. (part col.) 27 cm. Catalog of an exhibition held at the National Gallery of Art, March 7-May 15, 1973, and others. Includes bibliographical references. [E99.E7F28] 72-97570
1. Eskimos—Alaska—Art—Exhibitions. 2. Indians of North America—Alaska—Art—Exhibitions. I. Collins, Henry Bascom, 1899- II. United States. National Gallery of Art. BIP

THE Far North : 745
2000 years of American Eskimo and Indian art / Henry B. Collins ... [et al.]. Bloomington : Indiana University Press, [1977] p. cm. Catalog of an exhibition held at the National Gallery of Art, March 7-May 15, 1973, and others. Includes bibliographical references. [E99.E7F28 1977] 77-3132 ISBN 0-253-32120-4 : 22.50 ISBN 0-253-28105-9 pbk. : 14.95
1. Eskimos—Alaska—Art—Exhibitions. 2. Indians of North America—Alaska—Art—Exhibitions. I. Collins, Henry Bascom, 1899- II. United States. National Gallery of Art.

Eskimos—Alaska—Art—Exhibitions.

SURVIVAL : 709'.01'1
life and art of the Alaskan Eskimo : [exhibition] / Barbara Lipton, guest curator ; introd. by Froelich Rainey ; annotated bibliography of Allan Chapman. Newark, N.J. : Newark Museum, c1977. 96 p. : ill. (some col.) ; 27 cm. "Published in cooperation with Morgan and Morgan, inc." Sponsored by the Newark Museum and the American Federation of Arts. [E99.E7S87] 76-53613 ISBN 0-87100-121-7 pbk. : 7.95
1. Eskimos—Alaska—Exhibitions. 2. Eskimos—Alaska—Art—Exhibitions. I. Lipton, Barbara. II. Newark Museum Association, Newark, N.J. III. American Federation of Arts.

Eskimos—Art.

ANCHORAGE Historical and Fine Arts Museum. 709'.01'109798
An introduction to the native art of Alaska. Anchorage, 1972. 84 p. illus. 24 cm. Includes bibliographical references. [E99.E7A6 1972] 74-151835
1. Eskimos—Art. 2. Indians of North America—Alaska—Art. I. Title.

BURLAND, Cottie Arthur, 1905- 709'.01'109701
Eskimo art [by] Cottie Burland. London, New York, Hamlyn, 1973. 96 p. illus. (some col.), map (on lining papers). 29 cm. Includes index. Bibliography: p. 96. [E99.E7B915] 74-150445 ISBN 0-600-33083-4 £1.95
1. Eskimos—Art. I. Title.

HOFFMAN, Walter James, 1846-1899. 732'.2'09798
The graphic art of the Eskimos : based upon the collections in the National Museum / by Walter James Hoffman. New York : AMS Press, [1975] p. cm. Reprint of the 1897 ed. published by the U.S. Govt. Print. Off., Washington, which was extracted from the report of the U.S. National Museum for 1895. [E99.E7H6 1975] 74-5846 ISBN 0-404-11651-5 : 35.00
1. Eskimos—Art. 2. Eskimos—Implements. 3. Indians of North America—Sign language. I. United States. National Museum. II. Title. BIP

HOUSTON, James A., 1921- 769'.922
Eskimo prints [by] James Houston. Barre, Mass., Barre Pub., 1967. 110 p. illus. (part col.), col. map. 22 x 27 cm. English and French. [E99.E7H85] 66-23208
1. Eskimos—Art. 2. Eskimos—Baffin Island. I. Title.

MELDGAARD, Jorgen. 730.998
Eskimo sculpture. [1st English ed. Translated by Jytte Lynner and Peter Wait] New York, C. N. Potter [1960] 48 p. illus. 24 cm. Includes bibliography. [E99.E7M493] 61-15110
1. Eskimos — Art. I. Title.

RITCHIE, Carson I. A. 709'.01'1
Art of the Eskimo / Carson I. A. Ritchie. South Brunswick, N.J. : Barnes, 1979, c1978. p. cm. Includes bibliographical references and index. [E99.E7R558] 76-50211 ISBN 0-498-01916-0 : 25.00
1. Eskimos—Art. 2. Eskimos—Social life and customs. I. Title. BIP

Eskimos—Art—Catalogs.

ROCHESTER Museum and Science Center. 736'.6
Eskimo ivory carvings in the Rochester Museum, by Christina Burr. Lilita Bergs, editor. [Rochester, N.Y., 1972] ii, 88 p. illus. 25 cm. Bibliography: p. 86-88. [E99.E7R596] 72-193673
1. Eskimos—Art—Catalogs. 2. Ivories—Rochester, N.Y.—Catalogs. I. Burr, Christina. II. Title.

Eskimos—Art—Directories.

GRAY, Philip Howard, 1926- 730'.92'2
A directory of Eskimo artists in sculpture and prints / Philip Howard Gray. Bozeman, Mont. : Gray, [1974] iv, 264 p. ; 14 x 24 cm. Includes bibliographical references and index. [E99.E7G72] 74-196834
1. Eskimos—Art—Directories. I. Title.

Eskimos—Art—Exhibitions.

CANADIAN Eskimo Arts Council. 732'.2'0740113541
Sculpture/Inuit. Sculpture of the Inuit: masterworks of the Canadian Arctic. La sculpture chez les Inuit: chefs-d'oeuvre de l'Arctique canadien. [Toronto, Published for the Canadian Eskimo Arts Council by the University of Toronto Press, 1971] 493 p. illus. (part col.), col. map. 24 cm. Catalogue of an exhibition organized by the Canadian Eskimo Arts Council for showing at museums throughout the world. Text in English, Eskimo and French. [E99.E7C287] 70-166937 17.50
1. Eskimos—Art—Exhibitions. 2. Sculpture—Canada—Exhibitions. I. Title.

HOUSTON, Tex. Museum of Fine Arts. 709.01'1
The Eskimo. [Exhibition] sponsored by Humble Oil & Refining Co., September 20 to November 23, 1969. Houston, Tex. [1969] 29 p. illus., map. 28 cm. [E98.A7H73] 73-98823
1. Eskimos—Art—Exhibitions. I. Title.

Eskimos—Canada.

CARPENTER, Edmund Snow, 1922- 709'.701
Eskimo realities [by] Edmund Carpenter. Designed by Arnold Skolnick. Photos. by Eberhard Otto, Fritz Spiess [and] Jorgen Meldgaard. [1st ed.] New York, Holt,

Rinehart and Winston [1973] 212 p. illus. 21 x 24 cm. [E99.E7C34] 72-91570 ISBN 0-03-007576-9 12.50
1. Eskimos—Canada. 2. Eskimos—Art. I. Otto, Eberhard, 1913- illus. II. Spiess, Fritz, illus. III. Meldgaard, Jorgen, illus. IV. Title.

Eskimos—Canada—Pictorial works.

ETOOK, Tivi, 1928- 398.2'0971
In the days long past = Autrefois / Tivi Etook ; [translated from the Eskimo]. [Montreal : Federation des Cooperatives du Nouveau-Quebec], 1976. 48 p. : chiefly ill. ; 20 x 28 cm. English and French. [NE543.E88A4613] 77-460056
1. Etook, Tivi, 1928- 2. Eskimos—Canada—Pictorial works. I. Title. II. Title: Autrefois.

KURELEK, William, 1927- 759.11
The last of the Arctic / by William Kurelek. Toronto : Pagurian Press ; Momence, Ill. : distributed by Publishers Marketing Group, c1976. 94 p. : ill. (some col.) ; 31 cm. [ND249.K85A5] 77-352575 ISBN 0-88932-031-4 : 19.95
1. Kurelek, William, 1927- 2. Eskimos—Canada—Pictorial works. 3. Eskimos—Canada—Social life and customs. I. Title. BIP

MARSH, Winifred Petchey. 759.11
People of the willow : the Padlimiut tribe of the Caribou Eskimo / portrayed in watercolours by Winifred Petchey Marsh. Toronto : Oxford University Press, 1976[i.e.1977] 63 p. : chiefly col. ill., map ; 23 x 26 cm. [ND1942.M34A53] 77-353618 ISBN 0-19-540271-5 : 10.95
1. March, Winifred Petchey. 2. Eskimos—Canada—Pictorial works. I. Title.
Distributed by Oxford University Press, New York BIP

MORGAN, Peter, 1951- 769'.92'4
Peter Morgan. [Montreal : Federation des Cooperatives du Nouveau-Quebec], 1976. [20] p. : chiefly ill. ; 26 cm. An exhibition organized by the Canadian Eskimo Art Council. English and French. [NE543.M67C36] 77-465174
1. Morgan, Peter, 1951- 2. Eskimos—Canada—Pictorial works. I. Canadian Eskimo Art Council.

Eskimos—Pictorial works.

LIFE with the 779'.9'97000497
Eskimo : [a photo essay : 50 historic photographs from the early 1900's in the Canadian Arctic and Siberia]. Saanichton, B.C. ; Seattle : Hancock House, c1977. [16] p. : chiefly ill. ; 28 cm. [E99.E7L55] 78-303737 ISBN 0-919654-72-X : 2.00
1. Eskimos—Pictorial works.

Essex Institute, Salem, Mass.

MERRILL, 688.7'2'07401445
Madeline O.
Dolls & toys at the Essex Institute / by Madeline & Richard Merrill ; photographs by Richard Merrill. Salem, Mass. : Essex Institute, c1976. 60 p. : ill. ; 21 cm. (Esses Institute museum booklet series ; 1) Bibliography: p. 60. [NK4892.U6S345] 76-40405 ISBN 0-88389-066-6 : 4.95
1. Essex Institute, Salem, Mass. 2. Dolls—Massachusetts—Salem. 3. Toys—Massachusetts—Salem. I. Merrill, Richard, 1908- joint author. II. Essex Institute, Salem, Mass. III. Title. IV. Series: Essex Institute, Salem, Mass. Essex Institute museum booklet series ; 1. BIP

PAYSON, Huldah Smith. 708'.144'5
Museum collections of the Essex Institute / by Huldah Smith Payson. Salem , Mass. : Essex Institute, c1978. 66 p., [1] leaf of plates : ill. ; 21 cm. (Essex Institute museum booklet series ; 3) Includes bibliographical references. [N6505.P34] 78-67991 ISBN 0-88389-070-4 pbk. : 2.50
1. Essex Institute, Salem, Mass. 2. Americana. I. Title. II. Series: Essex Institute, Salem, Mass. Essex Institute museum booklet series ; no. 3. BIP

Estienne, Robert, 1503?-1559.

ARMSTRONG, Elizabeth 926.55
(Tyler)
Robert Estienne, royal printer; an historical study of the elder Stephanus. Cambridge [Eng.] University Press, 1954. xx, 309p. illus., port., facsim. 27cm. Bibliography. p. 289-297. [Z232.E8A7] 55-1390
1. Estienne, Robert, 1503?-1559. I. Title.

Etchers—Scotland—Biography.

MCBEY, James, 1883- 769'.92'4 B
1959.
The early life of James McBey : an autobiography, 1883-1911 / edited by Nicolas Barker. Oxford [Eng.] ; New York : Oxford University Press, 1977. ix, 131 p., [8] leaves of plates : ill. ; 25 cm. [NE2047.6.M32A24] 77-6395 ISBN 0-19-211738-6 : 12.00
1. McBey, James, 1883-1959. 2. Etchers—Scotland—Biography. I. Barker, Nicolas. II. Title. BIP

Etching.

LUMSDEN, Ernest S., 1883- 767.2
The art of etching; a complete & fully illustrated description of etching, drypoint, soft-ground etching, acquatint & their allied arts, together with technical notes upon their own work by many of the leading etchers of the present time, by E. S. Lumsden. New York, Dover [1962] 376p. illus. 21cm. (T49) 2.50 pap.,
1. Etching. 2. Dry-point. I. Title.

LUMSDEN, Ernest S., 1883- 767.2
The art of etching; a complete & fully illustrated description of etching, drypoint, soft-ground etching, a quatint & their allied arts, together with technical notes upon their own work by many of the leading etchersof the present time. [Gloucester, Mass., Peter Smith 1963] 376p. illus. 21cm. (Dover bk. rebound) 4.50
1. Etching. 2. Dry-point. I. Title. BIP

Etching, American.

BENSON, Frank Weston, 730'.924
1862-1951.
Etchings and drypoints by Frank W. Benson; an illustrated and descriptive catalogue, with an original etching by Mr. Benson and reproductions of all the plates, compiled and arranged by Adam E. M. Paff ... Boston and New York, Houghton Mifflin company, 1917-59. 5v. front., illus. 32cm. Limited edition. 'Biographical summary' v. 1, p.ix-[x] [NE2210.B4A3] 17-5407
I. Paff, Adam Edwin Merriman, 1891- comp. II. Title.

KEELER, Charles Butler, 769'.924
1882-1964.
Charles Butler Keeler, American artist, 1882-1964. Introd. by Vernon Patterson. Newport Beach, Calif., Lithographed by Hendricks Print. Co. [1969] 1 portfolio ([18] l. 1 illus., 12 plates, port.) 32 cm. Title on portfolio: Selected etchings by Charles B. Keeler. "Limited edition of two hundred copies ... Number 60." Each plate is accompanied by a leaf of explanatory comments taken almost entirely from the artist's letters and journals. [NE2210.K38P3] 75-9711
I. Patterson, Vernon.

KOEHLER, Sylvester Rosa, 759.13
1837-1900.
American etchings ; American art / S. R. Koehler. New York : Garland Pub. Co., 1977. p. cm. (The Art experience in late nineteenth-century America) Reprint of the 1886 ed. of the author's American etchings published by Estes and Lauriat, Boston and of the author's American art published by Cassell, New York. [NE2003.7.K63] 75-28876 ISBN 0-8240-2236-X lib.bdg. : 50.00
1. Etching, American. 2. Etching—19th century—United States. 3. Painting, American. 4. Painting, Modern—19th century—United States. I. Koehler, Sylvester Rosa, 1837-1900. American art. 1977. II. Title. III. Series.

STACTTON, Marc, 1923- 769'.92'4
The mushroom pickers [by Marc Stactton]. Oakland, Calif., Limited Editions, 1973. 1 portfolio (chiefly illus.) 36 x 39 cm. "Edition of fifty." No. 3. The illus. are 17 drypoint etchings. [NE2225.S72A5] 74-170378
I. Title.

Etching—Technique.

BANISTER, Manly Miles, 767'.2
1914-
Etching and other intaglio techniques, by Manly Banister. Totowa, N.J., Littlefield, Adams, 1974 [c1969] 128 p. illus. 28 cm. (A Littlefield, Adams quality paperback, no. 286) Reprint of the ed. published by Sterling Pub. Co., New York. [NE2135.B35 1974] 74-10990 ISBN 0-8226-0286-5 4.50 (pbk.)
1. Etching—Technique. 2. Intaglio printing. I. Title.

BRUNSDON, John. 765
The technique of etching and engraving. New York, Reinhold Pub. Corp. [1966, c1965] 152 p. illus., plates. 26 cm. Bibliography: p. 116. [NE2130.B7] 65-25848
1. Etching—Technique. 2. Engraving—Technique. I. Title.

CHAMBERLAIN, Walter. 765
Etching and engraving / Walter Chamberlain. New York : Viking Press, 1973, c1972. 200 p. : ill. (some col.) ; 25 cm. (A Studio book) Published in 1972 under title: The Thames and Hudson manual of etching and engraving. Includes index. Bibliography: p. 182. [NE2130.C47 1973] 72-11102 ISBN 0-670-29827-1 : 12.95
1. Etching—Technique. 2. Prints—Technique. I. Title.

CHAMBERLAIN, Walter. 765
The Thames and Hudson manual of etching and engraving / Walter Chamberlain. London : Thames & Hudson, 1978, c1972. 200 p. : ill. ; 24 cm. (The Thames and Hudson manuals) Includes index. Bibliography: p. 182. [NE2130.C48] 77-82852 ISBN 0-500-68001-9 : 6.95
1. Etching—Technique. 2. Engraving—Technique. I. Title. II. Title: Etching and engraving.
Distributed by W. W. Norton, New York, NY 10036 BIP

COKER, Peter, 1926- 767'.2
Etching techniques / Peter Coker. London : Batsford, 1976. 95 p. : ill. ; 26 cm. [NE2135.C56] 76-359936 ISBN 0-7134-3063-X : £4.95
1. Etching—Technique. I. Title.

EDMONDSON, Leonard, 1916- 767'.2
Etching. New York, Van Nostrand Reinhold Co. [1973] 136 p. illus. (part col.) 29 cm. Bibliography: p. 132. [NE2130.E35] 72-2662 ISBN 0-442-22235-1 14.95
1. Etching—Technique. I. Title. BIP

GROSS, Anthony, 1905- 760
Etching, engraving, & intaglio printing. London, New York, Oxford U.P., 1970. xi, 172 p. illus. 25 cm. Bibliography: p. 166-167. [NE850.G75] 73-19071 70/-
1. Etching—Technique. 2. Engraving—Technique. 3. Intaglio printing. I. Title. BIP

GROSS, Anthony, 1905- 760
Etching, engraving, and intaglio printing. Revised and abridged ed. London, New York, Oxford University Press, 1973. x, 131 p., leaf. illus. 21 cm. (Oxford paperbacks, handbooks for artists no. 13) Includes index. Bibliography: p. 128-129. [NE850.G75 1973] 74-155377 ISBN 0-19-289916-3 5.75
1. Etching—Technique. 2. Engraving—Technique. 3. Intaglio printing. I. Title.

HAMERTON, Philip Gilbert, 767'.2
1834-1894.
The etcher's handbook, giving an account of the old processes, and of processes recently discovered. Illustrated by the author. Freeport, N.Y., Books for Libraries Press [1972] p. "First published 1871." [NE2130.H3 1972] 72-8461 ISBN 0-8369-6976-6
1. Etching—Technique. I. Title.

TREVELYAN, Julian 767.2
Etching; modern methods of intaglio printmaking. New York, Waston-Guptil [1964,c.1963] 96p. illus. (part. col.) 26cm Bibl. 64-14768 6.95
1. Etching—Technique. 2. Engraving—Technique. I. Title.

WOODS, Gerald. 760
The craft of etching and lithography. London, Blandford Pr., 1965. 75p. illus. (pt. col.) 23cm. [NE2130.W6] 66-31987 3.50
1. Etching—Technique. 2. Lithography—Technique. I. Title.
Available from C. T. Branford, Newton, Mass.

Etchings, French—Exhibitions.

WEISBERG, Gabriel 769'.944'074013
P.
The etching Renaissance in France: 1850-1880, by Gabriel P. Weisberg. [Salt Lake City, Utah Museum of Fine Arts, 1971] 104 p. illus. 22 x 27 cm. Catalog of an exhibition held at the Utah Museum of Fine Arts, Febr. 14-Mar. 14, 1971, and at 3 other museums beginning Apr. 12. Bibliography: p. 45-46. [NE2049.25.W4] 74-146407
1. Etchings, French—Exhibitions. I. Utah Museum of Fine Arts. II. Title.

Etchings, Venetian—Exhibitions.

RHODE Island School of 769.945'31
Design, Providence. Museum of Art.
Venice in the eighteenth century; prints and drawings. An exhibition [at the] Museum of Art, Rhode Island School of Design, Providence, Rhode Island, 11 January--5 February 1967. [Providence, 1967] [87] p. illus. 22 cm. Exhibition arranged by Henri Zerner. "Sponsored in part by the Cultural Agency of the State of Rhode Island." [NE661.V4R45] 67-17765
1. Etchings, Venetian—Exhibitions. 2. Drawings, Venetian—Exhibitions. I. Zerner, Henri. II. Title. BIP

Ethiopian magic scrolls.

MERCIER, Jacques, 745.6'7'0963
1946-
Ethiopian magic scrolls / by Jacques Mercier. New York : G. Braziller, [1978] p. cm. Bibliography: p. [ND3285.7.A1M47] 78-9330 ISBN 0-8076-0896-3 : 24.95 ISBN 0-8076-0897-1 pbk. : 11.95
1. Ethiopian magic scrolls. 2. Illumination of books and manuscripts, Ethiopian. I. Title. BIP

Ethnic art.

GRIGSBY, J. Eugene. 709'.73
Art & ethnics : background for teaching youth in a pluralistic society / J. Eugene Grigsby, Jr. Dubuque, Iowa : W. C. Brown Co., c1977. xii, 147 p. : ill. ; 28 cm. (Trends in art education) Includes index. Bibliography: p. 137-140. [N6537.5.G74] 76-12675 ISBN 0-697-03242-6 pbk. : 5.95
1. Ethnic art. 2. Ethnic attitudes in art. 3. Ethnicity. 4. Art—Study and teaching—United States. I. Title.

Ethnic arts—United States—Addresses, essays, lectures.

YARDBIRD lives! / 700'.973
Edited by Ishmael Reed and Al Young. 1st Evergreen ed. New York : Grove Press : distributed by Random House, 1978. 288 p. : ill. ; 20 cm. (An Evergreen book) Compiled from Yardbird reader. [NX512.2.Y37 1978] 77-18321 ISBN 0-394-50159-4 : 10.00. ISBN 0-394-17041-5 pbk. : 4.95
1. Ethnic arts—United States—Addresses, essays, lectures. I. Reed, Ishmael, 1938- II. Young, Al, 1939- III. Yardbird reader. BIP

Ethnology—Africa, West—Juvenile literature.

PRICE, Christine, 731'.75'0966
1928-
Dancing masks of Africa / by Christine Price. New York : Scribner, c1975. [48] p.

: col. ill. ; 27 cm. Rhythmic text and illustrations introduce a variety of West African ceremonial masks and their meaning. [GN652.5.P74] 75-4028 ISBN 0-684-14332-1 : 6.95
1. Ethnology—Africa, West—Juvenile literature. 2. Masks, African—Africa, West—Juvenile literature. I. Title. **BIP**

Ethnology—New Guinea—Pictorial works.

COX, Paul.　　　779'.2'0924
Home of man; the people of New Guinea [by] Paul Cox and Ulli Beier. [Melbourne, Thomas] Nelson [(Australia) 1971] 94 p. illus. 29 cm. [GN671.N5C7] 72-195834 ISBN 0-17-019527-9
1. Ethnology—New Guinea—Pictorial works. I. Beier, Ulli. II. Title.

Ethnology—Oceania—Exhibitions.

BRUNOR, Martin A.　　　709.01'1
Arts & crafts of the Austral Islands; a special exhibition, 17 December 1968, to 30 April, 1969, by Martin A. Brunor. [Salem] Mass., Peabody Museum of Salem, 1969. 21, [18] p. illus. 26 cm. [GN662.B74] 75-90977
1. Ethnology—Oceania—Exhibitions. I. Peabody Museum of Salem, Salem, Mass. II. Title.

Ethnology —Polesie

MASSACHUSETTS.　　　778.9'9'4765
University. Art Gallery.
Yesterday's people: peasants of Polesie; [catalogue of] an exhibition of photographs of rural eastern Poland of the 1930's by Joseph Obrebski, October 3 to October 14, 1973, University Art Gallery. Amherst, [1973?] [16] p. illus. 26 cm. Cover title. Includes bibliographical references. [DK511.P62M37 1973] 75-303505
1. Obrebski, Jozef 2. Ethnology—Polesie—Exhibitions. I. Obrebski, Jozef. II. Title.

Ethnology—Polynesia.

BARROW, Tui Terence,　　　732'.2'0996
1923-
Art and life in Polynesia [by] T. Barrow. [1st ed.] Rutland, Vt., C. E. Tuttle [1973, c1972] 191 p. illus. (part col.) 30 cm. Bibliography: p. 181-184. [GN670.B29] 72-77509 ISBN 0-8048-1059-1 21.50
1. Ethnology—Polynesia. 2. Art, Primitive—Polynesia. I. Title.

Eton College.

TREASURES of Eton　　　700'.74'02296
/ editor, James McConnell ; technical editor, Jeremy M. Potter ; art editor, William Winter. London : Chatto & Windus, 1976. 180 p., [16] leaves of plates : ill. ; 29 cm. Includes index. Bibliography: p. 171-172. [NX544.E86T73] 76-376871 ISBN 0-7011-2162-9 : £8.50
1. Eton College. 2. Arts—Eton, Eng. I. McConnell, James Douglas Rutherford, 1915-　　　**BIP**

Etook, Tivi, 1928—

ETOOK, Tivi, 1928-　　　398.2'0971
In the days long past = Autrefois / Tivi Etook ; [translated from the Eskimo]. [Montreal : Federation des Cooperatives du Nouveau-Quebec], 1976. 48 p. : chiefly ill. ; 20 x 28 cm. Includes index. English and French. [NE543.E88A4613] 77-460056
1. Etook, Tivi, 1928- 2. Eskimos—Canada—Pictorial works. I. Title. II. Title: Autrefois.

Etretat, France—Descr.—Views.

SCHWARTZ, Manfred, 1909-　　　759.13
Etretat; an artist's theme and development. New York, Shorewood [1966] 102p. illus. (pt. col.) 28cm. [ND237.S93A44] 65-23718 9.95
1. Etretat, France—Descr.—Views. I. Title.

Euboian League.

WALLACE, William P　　　737.4
The Euboian League and its coinage. New York, American Numismatic Society, 1956. xi, 180 p. illus., 16 plates, map. 24 cm. (Numismatic notes and monographs, no. 134) Bibliographical footnotes. [DF227.83.W3] 56-14645
1. Euboian League. 2. Numismatics, Greek. I. Title. II. Series.

Europe—Description and travel.

MCCULLOCH, Alan.　　　927.5
Trial by tandem. Illustrated by the author. Melbourne, F. W. Cheshire [1950] 235 p. illus. 22 cm. [ND1105.M35A45] 52-30339
1. Europe—Descr. & trav. I. Title.

Europe—Description and travel—Views.

MCNEAR, Everett, 1904-　　　741.91
Young eye seeing; some letters written in 1932 and 1933. Chicago, P. Theobald, 1956. 94p. illus. 27cm. [NC1075.M33A55] 57-18508
1. Europe—Descr. & trav.—Views. I. Title.

Europe—Description and travel—1971- —Addresses, essays, lectures.

STOCK, Dennis.　　　779'.9'9140455
This land of Europe : a photographic exploration / by Dennis Stock ; introduced by H. R. Trevor-Roper ; with essays by Konrad Lorenz ... [et al.]. 1st ed. Tokyo ; New York : Kodansha International ; New York : distributed by Harper & Row, 1976. 132 p. : col. ill. ; 29 cm. [D923.S83] 76-9360 ISBN 0-87011-276-7 : 25.00
1. Europe—Description and travel—1971- —Addresses, essays, lectures. 2. Man—Influence on nature—Europe—Addresses, essays, lectures. I. Lorenz, Konrad. II. Title.

Europe—Historic houses, etc.

NICOLSON, Nigel.　　　910'.918'21
Great houses of the Western World. Photography by Ian Graham. New York, Putnam [1968] 320 p. illus. (part col.), ports. 32 cm. [NA7325.N5] 68-22255 25.00
1. Europe—Historic houses, etc. 2. United States—Historic houses, etc. I. Graham, Ian, illus. II. Title.

Europe in art.

HARRIS, Kenneth, 1904-　　　759.13
The necessity for nonconformity : selected works of Kenneth Harris ; designed by Edward A. Conner. Norfolk : Donning, c1976. 128 p. : ill. (some col.) ; 28 cm. [N6537.H35A53] 76-28375 ISBN 0-915442-21-3 : 12.95
1. Harris, Kenneth, 1904- 2. Europe in art. 3. Chesapeake Bay in art. I. Title.

European War, 1914-1918—Art and the war.

JONES, Barbara　　　745'.09'041
Mildred, 1912-
Popular arts of the First World War [by] Barbara Jones & Bill Howell. [1st ed.] New York, McGraw-Hill [1972] 175 p. illus. 26 cm. [N9150.J66 1972] 72-1576 ISBN 0-07-033006-9 14.95
1. European War, 1914-1918—Art and the war. 2. Kitsch. I. Howell, Bill, joint author. II. Title.

European War, 1914-1918—Pictorial works.

EBY, Kerr, 1890-1946.　　　760'.0924
War. With a new introd. for the Garland ed., by Charles Chatfield. New York, Garland Pub., 1971. 9, [40] p. illus. 31 cm. (The Garland library of war and peace) Reprint of the 1936 ed. [NE2012.E28A57 1971] 75-147683 ISBN 0-8240-0440-X
1. European War, 1914-1918—Pictorial works. I. Title. II. Series.

European War, 1914-1918—Posters.

DARRACOTT, Joseph.　　　769'.4'99403
The First World War in posters, from the Imperial War Museum, London / selected and edited by Joseph Darracott. New York : Dover Publications, 1974. xxiii p., [37] leaves of plates : 75 ill. ; 31 cm. [D522.25.D36] 73-94348 ISBN 0-486-23027-9. pbk. : 4.95
1. London. Imperial War Museum. 2. European War, 1914-1918—Posters. I. London. Imperial War Museum. II. Title.

FLAGG, James Montgomery,　　　741.9'73
1877-1960.
The James Montgomery Flagg Poster book / with an introd. by Susan E. Meyer. New York : Watson-Guptill Publications, 1975. [47] p. : chiefly col. ill. ; 41 cm. [D522.25.F55 1975] 74-25890 ISBN 0-8230-1836-9 : 6.95
1. European War, 1914-1918—Posters. I. Meyer, Susan E. II. Title.

European War, 1914-1918—Posters—Exhibitions.

NEW Jersey Historical　　　769'.5
Society.
The New Jersey Historical Society collection of World War 1 posters : exhibition, sale & auction at the Museum of the New Jersey Historical Society ; collection appraisal and catalogue preparation by Gallery 9. Newark, N.J. : The Society, c1976. 89 p., [2] leaves of plates : ill. (some col.) ; 25 cm. Includes index. [D522.25.N48 1976] 76-383532 5.00
1. European War, 1914-1918—Posters—Exhibitions. I. New Jersey Historical Society. Museum. II. Gallery 9. III. Title. IV. Title: Collection of World War 1 posters.

Evans, Bob, 1947—

WELSH Arts Council.　　　741.9'429
Bob Evans / [Welsh Arts Council] : The Council, 1976. Folder ([4] p.) : ill. ; 30 cm. Catalogue of an exhibition held at the Welsh Arts Council, Saturday 3 April-Wednesday 21 April 1976. Parallel Welsh and English text. [N6797.E88W44 1976] 76-380831 ISBN 0-905171-08-X
1. Evans, Bob, 1947-

Evans, Frederick H.

NEWHALL, Beaumont,　　　779'.4'0924
1908-
Frederick H. Evans: photographer of the majesty, light, and space of the medieval cathedrals of England and France. [Millerton, N.Y., Aperture, 1973] 1 v. (unpaged) illus. 27 cm. "Published to accompany a major exhibition of British photographers prior to 1915 to be presented by the Alfred Stieglitz Center of the Philadelphia Museum of Art in 1975." Includes bibliographical references. [TR659.N48] 73-85260 ISBN 0-912334-48-7 7.50
1. Evans, Frederick H. 2. Photography, Architectural—Exhibitions. I. Alfred Stieglitz Center.

Evans, Garth, 1934—

WELSH Arts Council.　　　709'.2'4
Garth Evans / [Welsh Arts Council] ; photography by Eileen Tweedy, John Webb]. Cardiff : The Council, 1976. Folder ([4] p.) : ill. ; 30 cm. Catalogue of an exhibition held at the Welsh Arts Council, Friday 19 March-Friday 2 April 1976. Parallel Welsh and English text. Bibliography: p. [4] [N6797.E89W44 1976] 76-380805 ISBN 0-905171-09-8
1. Evans, Garth, 1934-

Evans, J.

SAVAGE, Gail.　　　759.14'074'017311
Three New England watercolor painters : [exhibition] / catalogue by Gail and Norbert H. Savage and Esther Sparks. [Chicago] : Art Institute of Chicago, 1974. 72 p. : ill. (some col.) ; 25 cm. Includes paintings by J. Evans, J. H. Davis, and J. A. Davis. [ND1810.S28] 74-21601

1. Evans, J. 2. Davis, Joseph H. 3. Davis, J. A. 4. Water-colors, American—Exhibitions. 5. Primitivism in art—New England—Exhibitions. I. Savage, Norbert H., joint author. II. Sparks, Esther, joint author. III. Evans, J. IV. Davis, Joseph H. V. Davis, J. A. VI. Chicago. Art Institute. VII. Title.

Evans, Walker, 1903-1975.

EVANS, Walker, 1903-　　　779'.092'4
1975.
Walker Evans, first and last. 1st ed. New York : Harper & Row, c1978. 199 p. : all ill. ; 31 cm. [TR654.E915 1978] 77-11824 ISBN 0-06-011261-1 : 29.95
1. Evans, Walker, 1903-1975. 2. Photography, Artistic. I. Title.

Eveline Lowe Primary School.

GREAT Britain Dept.　　　727'.1'094216
of Education and Science.
Eveline Lowe Primary School, London. London, H.M.S.O., 1967. [5], 93p. illus., plans, tables, diagrs. 30cm. (Its Building bulletin, 36) [LB3219.G7A2 no. 36] 68-114341 2.10
1. Eveline Lowe Primary School. I. Title. II. Series.
Available in New York from British Info.

Evenepoel, Henri Jacques Edouard, 1872-1899.

HYSLOP, Francis Edwin,　　　759.9493
1909-
Henri Evenepoel : Belgian painter in Paris, 1892-1899 / Francis E. Hyslop. University Park : Pennsylvania State University Press, [1975] x, 145 p. : ill. ; 24 cm. Bibliography: p. 143. [ND673.E8H974] 75-2227 ISBN 0-271-01191-2 : 14.50
1. Evenepoel, Henri Jacques Edouard, 1872-1899. 2. Painting—Paris. I. Title. **BIP**

Everdingen, Allart van, 1621-1675.

DAVIES, Alice I.,　　　760'.092'4
1943-
Allart van Everdingen / Alice I. Davies. New York : Garland Pub., 1979 p. cm. (Outstanding dissertations in the fine arts) Originally presented as the author's thesis, Harvard, 1973. Bibliography: p. [N6953.E93D38 1978] 77-94692 ISBN 0-8240-3223-3 lib bdg : 52.50
1. Everdingen, Allart van, 1621-1675. 2. Artists—Netherlands—Biography. I. Everdingen, Allart van, 1621-1675. II. Title. III. Series. **BIP**

Evergood, Philip, 1901—

BAUR, John Ireland Howe,　　　759.13
1909-
Philip Evergood. Text by John I. H. Baur. New York, H. N. Abrams [1974] p. [ND237.E8B32] 72-11790 ISBN 0-8109-0104-8
1. Evergood, Philip, 1901- I. Evergood, Philip, 1901-　　　**BIP**

BAUR, John Ireland Howe,　　　759.13
1909-
Philip Evergood. New York, Published for the Whitney Museum of American Art by Praeger [1960] 116, [9] p. plates (part col.) 24 x 29 cm. (Books that matter) "This monograph is published on the occasion of Philip Evergood's retrospective exhibition at the Whitney Museum of American Art, held in April and May, 1960." "Catalog of the exhibition": p. [119]-[120] "Bibliography ... by ... Rosalinda Irvine": p. [121]-[122] [ND237.E8B3] 60-10691
1. Evergood, Phillip, 1901- I. Irvine, Rosalinda. II. Whitney Museum of American Art, New York.

EVERGOOD, Philip, 1901-　　　760.0924
The graphic work of Philip Evergood: selected drawings and complete prints, by Lucy R. Lippard. Foreword by Abram Lerner. Poem by James A. Michener. New York, Crown Publishers [1966] 159, [1] p. illus. 29 cm. Bibliography: p. 155-[160] [NC1075.E85L5] 65-17022
1. Lippard, Lucy R. I. Title.

EVERGOOD, Philip, 1901- 759.13
Philip Evergood: a painter of ideas, by Alfredo Valente [Exhibition] New York, Gallery of Modern Art, 1969. South Brunswick, N.J., A. S. Barnes [1969] 27 p. illus. 24 cm. [ND237.E8V3] 71-17710 ISBN 0-498-07527-3
I. Valente, Alfredo. II. New York (City). Gallery of Modern Art Including the Huntington Hartford Collection.

EVERGOOD, Philip, 1901- 759.13
Philip Evergood: paintings and drawings. Exhibition, May 10-June 2, 1972. New York, Kennedy Galleries [1972] [32] p. illus. (part col.) 27 cm. [ND237.E8K46] 72-170860
I. Kennedy Galleries, inc., New York.

Everlasting flowers.

CARICO, Nita Cox, 635.966
The dried-flower book; a guide to methods and arrangements [by] Nita Cox Carico [and] Jane Calvert Guynn. All flower arrangements and all sketches by Nita Cox Carico. [1st ed.] Garden City, N. Y., Doubleday, 1962. 128 p. illus. 25 cm. [SB447.C3] 62-7609
1. Everlasting flowers. 2. Flower arrangement. I. Guynn, Jane Calvert, joint author. II. Title.

THOMPSON, Dorothea Schnibben. 745.92
Creative decorations with dried flowers. Drawings by Marion Seiler. Photos. by William Brinkhous. New York, Hearthside Press [1965] 125 p. illus. (part col.) 25 cm. [SB447.T47] 65-15468
1. Everlasting flowers. 2. Flower arrangement. I. Title. BIP

Evers, Carl G.

EVERS, Carl G. 759.13
The marine paintings of Carl G. Evers / introd. by Ian Ballantine. Toronto ; New York : Peacock Press, 1975. [6] p., [45] leaves of plates : 45 col. ill. ; 23 x 28 cm. [ND1839.E93A45] 75-10068 pbk. : 5.95
1. Evers, Carl G. 2. Ships in art. I. Title.

EVERS, Carl G. 759.13
The marine paintings of Carl G. Evers introduction by Ian Ballantine New York, Charles Scribner's Sons [1975] [6] p., [45] leaves of plates 45 col. ill. 23 x 28 cm. [ND1839.E93A45] 10.00.
1. Evers, Carl C. 2. Ships in Art. I. Title.
L.C. card no. for original edition: 75-10068. BIP

Evolution—Pictorial works.

AKSTON, Joseph James, 1902- 759.13
Beginning of the beginning; an unfolding story of how nature and life evolved on our planet, painted and written, by Joseph James Akston. With an introd. by James A. Michener and a commentary by Gordon Brown. New York, H. N. Abrams [1971] 63 p. col. illus. 37 cm. [ND237.A29B7] 70-135656 ISBN 0-8109-0036-X
1. Evolution—Pictorial works. I. Brown, Gordon. II. Title.

Ewing Museum of Nations.

EWING Museum of Nations. 732'.2'0966074017359
African art : permanent collection, Illinois State University Normal-Bloomington, the Ewing Museum of Nations, Illinois State University Foundation / [F. Louis Hoover, editor ; photography, Illinois State University Photographic Services]. [Normal] : Illinois State University, [1974?] [128] p. : chiefly ill. (some col.) ; 22 cm. Errata slip inserted. [N7398.E94 1974] 74-28644 3.00
1. Ewing Museum of Nations. 2. Art—Africa, West—Catalogs. 3. Art, Primitive—Africa, West—Catalogs. I. Hoover, Francis Louis, 1913- II. Title.

Exakta camera.

ABEL, Charles, 1891- 770.2
The Exakta guide, by Kenneth S. Tydings and Charles Abel. 2d ed. New York, Greenberg, 1956. 128p. illus. 20cm. Authors' names in reverse order in 1951 ed. which was published under title: The modern Exakta guide and reference book. [TR263.E9A2 1956] 55-12254
1. Exakta camera. I. Tydings, Kenneth S., joint author. II. Title.

ABEL, Charles, 1891- 770.2
The modern Exakta guide and reference book, by Charles Abel and Kenneth S. Tydings. New York, Greenberg, '1951. 124 p. illus. 20 cm. [TR263.E9A2] 51-12415
1. Exakta camera. I. Title.

ALLINSON, Kenneth Leslie 771.31
Exakta handbook. London, Fountain Pr. [dist. New York, Morgan & Morgan, 1964, c. 1956] 158p. illus. 12x16cm. (Fountain photobk.) 56-14640 2.95bds.,
1. Exakta camera. 2. Photography—Handbooks, manuals, etc. I. Title.

ALLINSON, Kenneth Leslie 770.2
Exakta handbook. London, Fountain Press Philadelphia, Rayelle Publications [1956] 158p. illus. 12x16cm. (A Fountain photobook) [TR263.E9A38] 56-14640
1. Exakta camera. 2. Photography—Handbooks, manuals, etc. I. Title.

BERKOWITZ, George Joseph, 1915- 770.2
A complete guide to the Exakta V. New York, Exakta Camera Co. [1951] 188 p. illus. 15 cm. [TR263.E49B4] 51-25400
1. Exakta camera. I. Title.

BERKOWITZ, George Joseph, 1915- 770.2
A complete guide to the Exakta V [2d print.] New York, Exakta Camera Co. [1951] 195 p. illus. 15 cm. [TR263.E9B4 1951a] 51-7423
1. Exakta camera. I. Title.

DESCHIN, Jacob. 770.2
Exakta photography; a manual of the Exakta-Exa singlelens reflex camera system. [1st ed.] San Francisco, Camera Craft Pub. Co. [1955] 192p. illus. 25cm. [TR263.E9D4] 55-11888
1. Exakta camera. 2. Photography—Handbooks, manuals, etc. I. Title.

DESCHIN, Jacob. 771.31
Exakta photography; a manual of the Exakta-Exa single-lens reflex camera system. [2d ed.] San Francisco, Camera Craft Pub. Co. [1959] 192 p. illus. 25 cm. [TR263.E9D4 1959] 59-14730
1. Exakta camera. 2. Photography—Handbooks, manuals, etc. I. Title.

TYDINGS, Kenneth S 771.31
Advanced Exakta-Exa guide. Philadelphia, Chilton Co., Book Division, c1960. 120 p. illus. 20 cm. (Modern camera guide series, 495) [TR263.E9T8] 60-9224
1. Exakta camera. 2. Photography — Handbooks, manuals, etc. I. Title.

WURST, Werner 771.31
Exakta manual; the complete guide to miniature photography with the Exakta camera. Tr. from German by F. Bradley. London, Fountain Pr. [dist. New York,Morgan & Morgan, 1964, c.1960] xi, 419p. illus., col. plates. 23cm. (Fountain photobk.) 64-3086 9.95
1. Exakta camera. 2. Photography—Handbooks, manuals, etc. I. Title.

Excavations (Archaeology)—Colorado.

SWANNACK, Jervis D. 917.88'27
Big Juniper House, Mesa Verde National Park—Colorado, by Jervis D. Swannack, Jr. Washington, U.S. National Park Service, 1969. 188 p. illus., maps, plans. 30 cm. (Archeological research series, no. 7-C) At head of title: Wetherill Mesa excavations. Bibliography: p. 181-182. [E51.U75 no. 7-C] 77-600350 5.00
1. Excavations (Archaeology)—Colorado. 2. Mesa Verde National Park. 3. Pueblo Indians—Antiquities. 4. Colorado—Antiquities. I. Title. II. Title: Wetherill Mesa excavations. III. Series: U.S. National Park Service. Archeological research series, no. 7-C

Excavations (Archaeology)—Egypt.

†BURTON, Harry, 1879-1940. 779'.9'932010924
The discovery of Tutankhamun's tomb / text by Howard Carter ; photos. by Harry Burton ; edited by Polly Cone. New York : Metropolitan Museum of Art : distributed by Grosset & Dunlap, 1977, c1976. xxvii, 82 p. : ill. ; 28 cm. "Originally published as Wonderful things." Much of the text is abridged and adapted from The tomb of Tut-ankh-Amen, by H. Carter and A. C. Mace. Published on the occasion of the exhibition, Treasures of Tutankhamun, at the National Gallery of Art, Washington. D.C., and other museums, 1976-1979. [DT87.5.B87 1977] 77-84859 ISBN 0-448-14554-5. ISBN 0-448-14546-4 pbk. : 5.95
1. Tutankhamun, King of Egypt—Tomb. 2. Excavations (Archaeology)—Egypt. 3. Egypt—Antiquities. I. Carter, Howard, 1873-1939. II. Cone, Polly. III. Carter, Howard, 1873-1939. The tomb of Tut-ankh-Amen. IV. New York (City). Metropolitan Museum of Art. V. Title. BIP

Excavations (Archaeology)—Florida.

BULLEN, Ripley P 975.9
Excavations on Cape Haze Peninsula, Florida [by] Ripley P. and Adelaide K. Bullen. Gainesville, University of Florida, 1956. 56p. illus., maps. 23cm. (Contributions of the Florida State Museum: social sciences, no. 1) Bibliography: p. [55]-56. [E78.F6B8] 913.759 A56
1. Excavations (Archaeology)—Florida. 2. Florida—Antiq. I. Bullen, Adelalde K., joint author. II. Title. III. Series: Florida. University. Gainesville. State Museum. Contributions: social sciences, no. 1

SEARS, William Hulse, 1920- 913.7591
Excavations on lower St. Johns River, Florida. Gainesville, University of Florida, 1957. v. 53p. illus. map. diagrs., tables. 23cm. (Contributions of the Florida State Museum: social sciences, no.2) [E78.F6S4] A 57
1. Excavations (Archaeology)—Florida. 2. Florida—Antiq. I. Title. II. Series: Florida. University, Gainesville. State Museum. Contributions: social sciences, no.2

Excavations (Archaeology)—Oklahoma—McCurtain Co.

WYCKOFF, Don G. 917.66'64
The archaeological sequence in the Broken Bow Reservoir area, McCurtain County, Oklahoma. Norman, Stovall Museum of Natural History, University of Oklahoma, 1967. x, 211 p. illus., maps. 28 cm. Bibliography: p. 197-211. [E78.O45W9] A 68
1. Excavations (Archaeology)—Oklahoma—McCurtain Co. 2. Oklahoma—Antiquities. 3. Indians of North America—Oklahoma—Antiquities. I. Oklahoma. University. J. Willis Stovall Museum. II. Title.

Excavations (Archaeology)—Utah.

GUNNERSON, James H 979.2
An archaeological survey of the fremont area. [Salt Lake City] University of Utah, Dept. of Anthropology, 1957. vi, 154p. illus., map. 28cm. (University of Utah. Dept. of Anthropology. Anthropological papers, no. 28) Bibliography: p. 147-154. [E51.U8 no. 28] 913.792 58-63002
1. Excavations (Archaeology)—Utah. 2. Utah—Antiq. 3. Fremont River. I. nthropological papers, no. 28) II. Title. III. Series: Dept. of Anthrolopology

Excavations (Archaeology) — Utah — Sevier Co.

TAYLOR, Dee Calderwood, 1922- *979.2
Two Fremont sites and their position in southwestern pre-history. With Appendices by Noel Morss [and] William H. Burt. [Salt Lake City] University of Utah, Dept. of Anthropology, 1957. xi, 185 p. illus., maps. 28 cm. (University of Utah. Dept. of Anthropology. Anthropological papers, no. 29) Bibliography: p. 174-185. [E51.U8 no. 29] [913.792] 58-63003
1. Excavations (Archaeology) — Utah — Sevier Co. 2. Indians of North America — Southwest, New. 3. Southwest, New — Antiq. I. Title. II. Series: Utah. University. Dept. of Anthropology. Anthropological papers, no. 29

Exceptional children—Education.

KATHERINE Lilly Conroy Learning Laboratory. 727'.9
The design of pre-school learning laboratory in a rehabilitation center [by Ronnie Gordon. New York] Institute of Rehabilitation Medicine, New York University Medical Center, 1969. 61 p. illus. 28 cm. (Rehabilitation monograph 39) Cover title. Bibliography: p. 61. [LC4041.K37A5] 72-16968
1. Exceptional children—Education. 2. Architecture and the mentally handicapped children. I. Gordon, Ronnie. II. New York University Medical Center. Institute of Physical Medicine and Rehabilitation. III. Title. IV. Series.

Exchange Bank & Trust Company—Art collections.

JOHNSON, Frank Tenney, 1874-1939. 759.13
Frank Tenney Johnson Western paintings. Text by Harold McCracken. Collection of the Exchange Bank & Trust Company, Dallas. [Dallas?] c1971. [24 p.] illus. 21 x 26 cm. [ND237.J72M3] 76-186380
1. Exchange Bank & Trust Company—Art collections. 2. The West in art. I. McCracken, Harold, 1894-

Exeter Cathedral.

WESTALL, Wilfrid. 914.23'5
Exeter Cathedral, its life and work. [Norwich] Jarrold [1963] [32] p. illus. 25 cm. [NA5471.E9W47] 74-179280
1. Exeter Cathedral. I. Title.

Exoticism in art—Europe.

JULLIAN, Philippe. 759.05
The orientalists : European painters of Eastern scenes / by Philippe Jullian ; [translated from the French by Helga and Dinah Harrison]. Oxford : Phaidon, 1978 210 p. : ill. (some col.), ports. ; 26 x 29 cm. Translation of Les orientalistes. Includes index. Bibliography: p. 198-202. [ND457.J8413] 78-361557 pbk. : 49.95 ISBN 0-7148-1780-5 : £29.95
1. Exoticism in art—Europe. 2. Painting, European. 3. Painting, Modern—19th century—Europe. I. Title.
Distributed by Dutton, New York

Expressionism (Art)

CHENEY, Sheldon, 1886- 759.06
Expressionism in art. Rev. ed. New York, Liveright Pub. Corp., 1958 [c1948] 415p. illus. 25cm. [ND1265.C5 1958] 58-13737
1. Expressionism (Art) I. Title. BIP

GERHARDUS, Maly. 759.06
Expressionism : from artistic commitment to the beginning of a new era / Maly and Dietfried Gerhardus ; [translated by Stephen Crawshaw]. Oxford : Phaidon, 1979. 112 p. : ill. (some col.) ; 27 cm. (Phaidon 20th-century art) Translation of Expressionismus. Bibliography: p. 29. [ND196.E9G4713 1979] 78-74422 ISBN 0-7148-1951-4 : 17.50
1. Expressionism (Art) 2. Painting, Modern—20th century. I. Gerhardus, Dietfried, joint author. II. Title.
Distributed by Dalton, New York

GROHMANN, Will, 1887- 759.06
Expressionists. New York, H. N. Abrams [1957] unpaged. illus. 17cm. (Pocket library of great art, A32) [ND1265.G74] 759.915 58-3731
1. Expressionism (Art) 2. Paintings. I. Title.

HOFMANN, Werner, 1928- 759.06
Expressionist watercolors, 1905-1920. New York, H. N. Abrams [1967] 101 p. plates (part col.), ports. 33 cm. Translation of

Aquarelle des Expressionismus, 1905-1920. [ND1798.H613] 67-25288
1. Expressionism (Art) 2. Water-colors. I. Title.

PEHNT, Wolfgang. 724.9
Expressionist architecture. New York, Praeger [1973] 231 p. illus. 27 cm. Translation of Die Architektur des Expressionismus. Bibliography: p. 219-226. [NA682.E9P4313 1973] 72-81583 27.50
1. Expressionism (Art) 2. Architecture, Modern—20th century. I. Title. BIP

TUCHMAN, Maurice 759.06
Van Goah and epressionism commentary. New York, Solomon R. Guggenheim Mus., 1964]. 1v. (unpaged) (col. illus.) 26x12cm. Bibl. 64-21306 1.50 pap.,
1. Gogh, Vincent van, 1853-1890. 2. Expressionism (Art) 3. Paintings—Exhibitions. I. Solomon R. Guggenheim Museum, New York. II. Title.

WHITFORD, Frank. 760'.0943
Expressionism. London, New York, Hamlyn, 1970. 5-189 p. illus. (some col.), facsims., ports. 22 cm. (Movements of modern art) Illus. (incl. 1 col.), on lining papers. Bibliography: p. 188. [N6494.E9W46] 71-576704 ISBN 0-600-02639-6 35/-
1. Expressionism (Art) I. Title.

WHITNEY Museum of American Art, New York. 709.73
Four American expressionists: Doris Caesar, Chaim Gross, Karl Knaths, Abraham Rattner. Whitney Museum of American Art, Jan. 14 -- Mar. 1, 1959 [and others] Exhibition and catalogue. [New York, 1959] 72 p. illus. 28 cm. [N6512.W47] 59-868
1. Caesar, Doris. 2. Gross, Chaim. 3. Knaths, Karl, 1891- 4. Rattner, Abraham. 5. Expressionism (Art) I. Title.

ZIGROSSER, Carl, 1891- 769.084
The expressionists; a survey of their graphic art. New York, G. Braziller, 1957. 37 p. 123 illus. (part mounted col.) 29 cm. [NE950.Z5] 57-1608
1. Expressionism (Art) 2. Engravings. 3. Printmakers. I. Title. BIP

Expressionism (Art)—Addresses, essays, lectures.

MIESEL, Victor H., comp. 759.3
Voices of German expressionism, edited by Victor H. Miesel. Englewood Cliffs, N.J., Prentice-Hall [1970] x, 211 p. 22 cm. (A Spectrum book) Includes bibliographical references. [NX600.E9M5] 71-90968 5.95
1. Expressionism (Art)—Addresses, essays, lectures. I. Title. BIP

Expressionism (Art)—Austria.

SCHIELE, Egon, 1890-1918. 760'.092'4
The art of Egon Schiele / Erwin Mitsch ; [translated from the German by W. Keith Haughan]. London : Phaidon ; New York : distributed by Praeger, 1975. 267 p. : ill. (some col.) ; 29 cm. Translation of Egon Schiele, 1890-1918. Bibliography: p. 265-267. [ND511.5.S3M5713] 76-12709 ISBN 0-7148-1641-8 : 45.00
1. Schiele, Egon, 1890-1918. 2. Expressionism (Art)—Austria. I. Mitsch, Erwin, 1931- II. Title.

Expressionism (Art)—Exhibitions.

ALLENTOWN, Pa. Art Museum. 709'.43
The Blue Four and German expressionism, March 10-April 21, 1974; a fiftieth anniversary exhibition commemorating the group's founding in Weimar during 1924, plus work by other artists active in Germany between 1905 and 1930. [Catalogue. Allentown, 1974] 42 p. illus. (part col.) 28 cm. Bibliography: p. 38. [N6868.5.E9A44 1974] 74-75202
1. Blaue Vier (Group of artists) 2. Expressionism (Art)—Exhibitions. 3. Expressionism (Art)—Germany. 4. Art, Modern—20th century—Germany. I. Title.

ART Museum of South Texas. 760'.09'04070164113
Expressionism in modern art : [catalogue of an exhibition] December 11, 1974—February 2, 1975, Art Museum of South Texas, Corpus Christi, Texas. [Corpus Christi, Tex. : Golden Banner Press, 1974] [32] p. : ill. ; 21 x 23 cm. Includes bibliographical references. [N6494.E9A7 1974] 75-311349
1. Expressionism (Art)—Exhibitions. 2. Art, Modern—20th century—Exhibitions. I. Title.

KANDINSKY, Wassily, 1866-1944. 760'.0904'07401471
Kandinsky, Franz Marc, August Macke: drawings and watercolors. New York, Hutton-Hutschnecker Gallery [1969] xv, 129 p. plates (part col.) 29 cm. An exhibition held Apr. 16-May 28, 1969, with a catalogue prepared by H. K. Rothel. [N6494.E9K3] 73-25357
1. Expressionism (Art)—Exhibitions. I. Marc, Franz, 1880-1916. II. Macke, August, 1887-1914. III. Rothel, Hans Konrad, 1909- IV. Hutton-Hutschnecker Gallery.

LEONARD Hutton Galleries. 709'.43
German expressionists paintings, drawings, watercolors, sculpture. New York [1972] 48 p. illus. (part col.) 30 cm. Catalog of the exhibition held Nov. 1972-Feb. 1973. [N6868.5.E9L46] 73-170808
1. Expressionism (Art)—Exhibitions. 2. Expressionism (Art)—Germany. 3. Art, Modern—20th century—Germany. I. Title.

SERGE Sabarsky Gallery. 759.06
Expressionists; major paintings, watercolors, drawings and sculptures by 17 German expressionists at the Serge Sabarsky Gallery [shown in three consecutive exhibitions. New York, c1972] 176 p. (chiefly col. illus.) 29 cm. [N6868.5.E9S47] 72-93408
1. Expressionism (Art)—Exhibitions. 2. Expressionism (Art)—Germany. 3. Art, Modern—20th century—Germany. I. Title.

Expressionism (Art)—Germany.

DUBE, Wolf Dieter. 760'.09'04
Expressionism. Translated by Mary Whittall. New York, Praeger Publishers [1973, c1972] 215 p. illus. (part col.) 22 cm. London ed. published under title: The expressionists. Bibliography: p. 208. [N6868.5.E9D8213 1973] 72-79505 10.00
1. Expressionism (Art)—Germany. 2. Art, Modern—20th century—Germany. I. Title.

SELZ, Peter Howard, 1919- 759.915
German expressionist painting. Berkeley, University of California Press, 1957. xx, 379 p. 37 illus., 180 plates (part col.) 29 cm. Bibliographical references included in "Notes" (p. [327]-353) Bibliography: p. [354]-370. [ND568.5.E9S45] 57-10501
1. Expressionism (Art)—Germany. 2. Painting, Modern—20th century—Germany. 3. Paintings, German. I. Title.

VERGO, Peter. 759.3'36
The Blue Rider / Peter Vergo. Oxford : Phaidon Press, 1977. 16 p., [24] leaves of plates : col. ill. ; 31 cm. Bibliography: p. 14. [ND568.5.E9V47] 77-75307 ISBN 0-7148-1749-X : 6.95
1. Blaue Reiter. 2. Expressionism (Art)—Germany. 3. Painting, Modern—20th century—Germany. I. Title.
Distributed by E.P. Dutton, New York

Expressionism (Art)—Germany—Bibliography.

GERMAN expressionism in the fine arts : 016.76'00943 a bibliography / by John M. Spalek ... [et al.] ; index by Bruce M. Broerman. Los Angeles : Hennessey & Ingalls, 1977. 272 p. ; 24 cm. (Art and architecture bibliographies ; 3) Includes indexes. [Z5961.G4G47] [N6868.5.E9] 72-188987 ISBN 0-912158-18-2 : 39.95
1. Expressionism (Art)—Germany—Bibliography. 2. Art, Modern—20th century—Germany—Bibliography. I. Spalek, John M. II. Series. BIP

Expressionism (Art)—Germany—Exhibitions.

DEUTSCHER Expressionismus 700'.943'07401641411 = German expressionism : toward a new humanism : an exhibition of German expressionist graphics and related printed materials in the Sarah Campbell Blaffer Gallery, and in the special collections of the Library, University of Houston, March 3 through April 3, 1977. [Houston, Tex.] : Sarah Campbell Blaffer Gallery, University of Houston, c1977. [142] p. : ill. ; 27 cm. "An introduction to the expressionistic movement": p. [11]-[40] by P. W. Guenther. Includes catalog of the exhibition. Includes bibliographical references. [NX550.A1D48] 77-152287
1. Expressionism (Art)—Germany—Exhibitions. 2. Arts, German—Exhibitions. 3. Arts, Modern—20th century—Germany—Exhibitions. I. Guenther, Peter W. II. Sarah Campbell Blaffer Gallery. III. Houston, Tex. University. Libraries. IV. Title: German expressionism.

Expressionism (Art)—Switzerland—Exhibitions.

EXPRESSIONISMUS in der Schweiz, 1905-1930 v. 12 : Austellung, Kunstmuseum Winterthur, 14. September bis 9. November 1975 : [Katalog / Redaktion, Erika Erni, Rudolf Koella ; Mitarbeiter, Martin Pauli (Biografien), David Simek (Zeittafel)]. Winterthur : Das Museum, c1975. 209 p. : ill. (some col.) ; 21 cm. Includes bibliographical references. [N7148.5.E94E94] 76-453122
1. Expressionism (Art)—Switzerland—Exhibitions. 2. Art, Swiss—Exhibitions. 3. Art, Modern—20th century—Switzerland—Exhibitions. I. Erni, Erika. II. Koella, Rudolf. III. Winterthur. Kunstmuseum.

Exter, Alexandra.

ARTIST of the theatre—Alexandra Exter : 792'.025'0924 B four essays, with an illustrated check list of scenic and costume designs exhibited at the Vincent Astor Gallery, the New York Public Library at Lincoln Center (spring-summer 1974). New York : New York Public Library : distributed by Readex Books, [1974] 40 p. : ill. ; 24 cm. Bibliography: p. 40. [ND2888.E97A89] 74-78230 ISBN 0-87104-250-9 pbk. : 4.50
1. Exter, Alexandra. I. Exter, Alexandra. II. New York Public Library at Lincoln Center.

Extinct animals in art.

EVANS, Larry, 1939- 743'.6
How to draw prehistoric monsters / written and illustrated by Larry Evans. San Francisco : Troubador Press, 1978. p. cm. [NC780.5.E9] 78-26225 ISBN 0-912300-97-3 pbk. : 3.50
1. Extinct animals in art. 2. Drawing—Technique. I. Title. BIP

Eyck, Hubert van, 1366-1426.

ASIHENE, E. V. 709'.669
Understanding the traditional art of Ghana / Emmanuel V. Asihene. Rutherford [N.J.] : Fairleigh Dickinson University Press, c1978. 95 p. : ill. ; 29 cm. Includes index. Bibliography: p. 93. [N7399.G5A74] 77-67 ISBN 0-8386-2130-9 : 12.50
1. Art, Ghanaian. I. Title. BIP

BROCKWELL, Maurice Walter, 1869-1958. 759.9493
The Van Eyck problem. Westport, Conn., Greenwood Press [1971] 102 p. illus. 23 cm. Reprint of the 1954 ed. [ND673.E87B72 1971] 78-138101 ISBN 0-8371-5677-7
1. Eyck, Hubert van, 1366-1426. I. Title. BIP

PHILIP, Lotte Brand. 759.9493
The Ghent altarpiece and the art of Jan van Eyck. Princeton, N.J., Princeton University Press, 1971. xvii, 255, [106] p. illus. 31 cm. Bibliography: p. 227-235. [ND673.E87P5] 73-113007 ISBN 0-691-03870-8 35.00
1. Eyck, Hubert, van, 1366-1426. Adoration of the Mystic Lamb. 2. Eyck, Jan van, 1390-1440. Adoration of the Mystic Lamb. I. Title.

Eyck, Jan van, 1390-1440.

BALDASS, Ludwig von, 1887- [759.9493]
Jan van Eyck. New York, Phaidon Publishers; distributed by Garden City Books [1952] 297 p. (p. [107]-[266] plates (part col.)) illus. (part col.) 31 cm. "The catalogue": p. [267]-291. Bibliographical footnotes. [ND673.E9B33 1952a] 927.5 52-9471
1. Eyck, Jan van, 1390-1440. II. Title.

BOL, L. J. 739.9493
Jan van Eyck [by] L. J. Bol. [Translator: Albert J. Fransella] New York, Barnes & Noble [1965] 89 p. (p. 19-72, illus. (part col.)) 18 cm. (Barnes & Noble art series, 624) [ND673.E9B63] 66-141
1. Eyck, Jan van, 1390-1440. I. Title.

DHANENS, Elisabeth. 759.9493
Van Eyck: the Ghent altarpiece [by] Elisabeth Dhanens. New York, Viking Press [1973] 154 p. illus. (1 col.) 23 cm. (Art in context) Bibliography: p. [143]-146. [ND673.E87D49 1973] 72-78206 ISBN 0-670-74273-2 8.95
1. Eyck, Jan van, 1390-1440. Adoration of the Mystic Lamb. 2. Eyck, Hubert van, 1366-1426. Adoration of the Mystic Lamb. 3. Ghent. Saint Bavon (Cathedral) I. Title.

Eyck, Jan van, 1390-1440—Juvenile literature.

NUGENT, Frances Roberts. 92
Jan van Eyck: master painter. Text and drawings by Frances Roberts Nugent. With reproductions from Van Eyck's paintings. Chicago, Rand McNally [1962] 64p. illus. 24cm. [ND673.E9N8] 62-13168
1. Eyck, Jan van, 1390-1440—Juvenile literature. I. Title.

Eyerly, Ray, 1894—

BLODGETT, Beverley. 760'.092'4
A picture or two : the story of Ray Eyerly / by Beverley Blodgett. ; with forward [sic] by Tom McCall. McMinnville, Or. : Oakwood Press, [1974] ix, 124, [3] p., [8] leaves of plates. : ill. (some col.) ; 23 cm. Bibliography: p. [125]-[127] [ND237.E84B55] 74-13705
1. Eyerly, Ray, 1894- I. Title. BIP

Ezekiel, Moses, Sir, 1844-1917.

EZEKIEL, Moses, Sir, 1844-1917. 730'.92'4 B
Memoirs from the Baths of Diocletian / Moses Jacob Ezekiel ; edited by Joseph Gutmann and Stanley F. Chyet. Detroit : Wayne State University Press, 1975. 509 p. : ill. ; 26 cm. Includes index. Bibliography: p. 490-493. [NB237.E9A35] 74-28009 ISBN 0-8143-1525-9 : 25.00
1. Ezekiel, Moses, Sir, 1844-1917. 2. Sculptors—Virginia—Correspondence, reminiscences, etc. 3. Sculptors—Rome (City)—Correspondence, reminiscences, etc. I. Gutmann, Joseph, ed. II. Chyet, Stanley F., ed. III. Title.

Faberge, Karl Gustavovich, 1846-1920.

CLEVELAND Museum of Art. 739.2
Faberge and his contemporaries; the India Early Minshall Collection of the Cleveland Museum of Art [by] Henry Hawley. [Cleveland] Cleveland Mus. of Art. [1967] 139p. illus. (pt. col.) 24cm. Bibl. [NK7405.C55] 67-28951 7.50
1. Faberge, Karl Gustavovich, 1846-1920. 2. India Early Minshall Collection. I. Hawley, Henry. II. Minshall, India Early. III. Title.

POST, Marjorie Merriweather. 739.27
The art of Karl Faberge and his comtemporaries; Russian imperial portraits and mementoes (Alexander III—Nicholas II) Russian imperial decorations and watches, by Marvin C. Ross. With a

foreword by Marjorie Merriweather Post. [1st ed.] Norman, University of Oklahoma Press [1965] xviii, 238 p. illus., col. plates, ports. (part col.) 24 cm. (Her The Collections of Marjorie Merriweather Post) Bibliography: p. 229-233. [NK7417.F3P6] 65-14804
1. Faberge, Karl Gustavovich, 1846-1920. 2. Crown jewels—Russia. I. Ross, Marvin Chauncey, 1904- II. Title.

-SNOWMAN, Abraham Kenneth, 1919-   739.22747
The art of Carl Faberge. [2d ed.] Boston, Boston Book & Art Shop [1962?] 186 p. plates (part col.) ports., facsims. 26 cm. Bibliography: p. 167. [NK7417.F3S5 1962] 62-20070
1. Faberge, Karl Gustavovich, 1846-1920. I. Title.

SNOWMAN, Abraham Kenneth,   927.39 1919-
The art of Carl Faberge. Boston, Boston Book & Art Shop [1953] 167 p. illus. (part col.) ports., facsims., geneal. table. 26 cm. Bibliography: p. 151. [NK7417.F3S5 1953a] 55-9574
1. Faberge, Karl Gustavovich, 1846-1920.   BIP

Faberge Karl Gustavovich, 1846-1920.

PHOENIX, Ariz. Art Museum.   739.2
Faberge; the M. T. Heller II Collection [exhibition] Phoenix Art Museum, October-November, 1971. [Phoenix, 1971] [20] p. illus. 24 cm. [NK7417.F3P45] 72-175304
1. Faberzhe (Firm) 2. Heller, M. T.—Art collections. 3. Jewelry—Exhibitions. 4. Gold articles—Exhibitions.

Faberzhe, Karl Gustavovich, 1846-1920.

ISAAC Delgado Museum   739.2'272'4 of Art, New Orleans.
Treasures by Peter Carl Faberge and other master jewellers: the Matilda Geddings Gray Foundation Collection. [Catalogue notes by Susan Grady and William A. Fagaly. Exhibition held] Nov. 3 through Dec. 31, 1972. [New Orleans, Matilda Geddings Gray Foundation, 1972] 1 v. (unpaged) illus. (part col.) 25 cm. [NK7301.N45A67] 72-92872
1. Faberzhe, Karl Gustavovich, 1846-1920. 2. Matilda Geddings Gray Foundation—Art collections. 3. Jewelry—Exhibitions. I. Grady, Susan. II. Fagaly, William A. III. Title.

LESLEY, Parker.   739.2'092'4
Faberge : a catalog of the Lillian Thomas Pratt Collection of Russian imperial jewels / by Parker Lesley. Richmond : Virginia Museum, c1976. 160 p. : col. ill. ; 29 cm. Published in 1960 under title: Handbook of the Lillian Thomas Pratt Collection. [NK7417.F3L47 1976] 76-16557 ISBN 0-917046-00-5 : 17.50
1. Faberzhe, Karl Gustavovich, 1846-1920. 2. Pratt, Lillian Thomas—Art collections. 3. Crown jewels—Russia—Catalogs. I. Virginia Museum of Fine Arts, Richmond.   BIP

Fabian, Stephen E., 1930—

FABIAN, Stephen E.,   741.9'73 1930-
Fantasy by Fabian : the art of Stephen E. Fabian / edited by Gerry de la Ree. Saddle River, N.J. : G. de la Ree, 1978. 128 p. : ill. ; 29 cm. [NC975.5.F25A4 1978] 78-103799 15.50
1. Fabian, Stephen E., 1930- 2. Fantasy in art. I. De la Ree, Gerry. II. Title.
Publisher's address : 7 Cedarwood Lane, Saddle River, NJ 07458

Fables.

AESOPUS   743.97
12 fables of Aesop Newly narrated by Glenway Wescott. Lino blocks by Antonio Frasconi Mus. of Mod. Art., dist. Garden City, N.Y., Doubleday, 1964 c195-. 32]p. illus. 22cm. 64-57301 price unreported pap.,
1. Fables. I. Wescott, Glenway, 1901- II. Frasconi, Antonio, illus. III. Title.

Fabric flowers.

ENTREKIN, Dee.   745.59'43
Make your own silk flowers / by Dee Entrekin. New York : Sterling Pub. Co., [1975] 80 p. : ill. ; 24 cm. Includes index. Instructions for making a variety of flowers from silk and other fabrics. [TT890.5.E57] 74-31705 ISBN 0-8069-5318-7 : 7.95 ISBN 0-8069-5319-5 lib.bdg. : 6.89
1. Fabric flowers. I. Title.   BIP

WOODS, Pamela.   745.59'43
Flowers from fabrics / Pamela Woods. Chicago : Regnery, 1976. 120 p. : ill. ; 26 cm. Includes index. [TT890.5.W66 1976b] 76-6295 ISBN 0-8092-8019-1 : 10.00 ISBN 0-8092-7984-3 pbk. : 5.95
1. Fabric flowers. I. Title.

Fabric pictures.

ALEXANDER, Eugenie.   746.445
Fabric pictures. London, Mills & Boon [dist. Newton Centre, Mass., C. T. Branford, 1959, i.e., 1960] 94p. illus. (col. front.) 26cm. 60-2823 5.95
1. Fabric pictures. I. Title.   BIP

SOYAMA, Takehiko.   746.445
Oshi-e; Japanese relief pictures. Tokyo, Toto Shuppan Co.; Rutland, Vt., Japan Pubns. [c.1964] 25p. illus. (pt. col.) mounted col. sample. 31cm. 64-7404 3.75 bds.,
1. Fabric pictures. I. Title.

Facades.

HOFFMANN, Kurt, 1923-   729'.1
Designing architectural facades : an ideas file for architects / Kurt Hoffmann, Helga Griese, Walter Meyer-Bohe. New York : Whitney Library of Design, 1975. 168 p. : ill. ; 30 cm. Translation of Fassaden. Includes index. [NA2840.H6313 1975] 74-20605 ISBN 0-8230-7145-6 : 17.95
1. Facades. 2. Building materials. I. Griese, Helga, joint author. II. Meyer-Bohe, Walter, joint author. III. Title.

Facades—Great Britain.

MACKERTICH, Peter.   725'.2'0941
Facade : a decade of British and American commercial architecture / [compiled by Tony and Peter Mackertich ; photography by Peter Mackertich ; with an introduction by Bevis Hillier. London : Mathews Miller Dunbar Ltd, 1976. [83] p. : chiefly col. ill. ; 21 cm. [NA3543.M3] 77-367506 ISBN 0-903811-20-0
1. Facades—Great Britain. 2. Art deco—Great Britain. 3. Office buildings—Great Britain. 4. Facades—United States. 5. Art deco—United States. 6. Office buildings—United States. I. Mackertich, Tony. II. Title.   BIP

Facades—New York (City)

CUNNINGHAM,   779'.9'3910720973 William J.
Facades / Bill Cunningham. [Harmondsworth, Eng. ; New York : Penguin Books, 1978] 128 p. : chiefly ill. ; 26 cm. Cover title. [NA2840.N4] 78-323629 ISBN 0-14-004948-7 pbk. : 8.95
1. Facades—New York (City) 2. Costume—New York (City)—History. I. Title.

Face.

PERARD, Victor Semon,   743.492 1870-
Drawing faces and expressions. Rev. by Rune Hagman. New York, Pitman Pub. Corp. [1956] 63p. illus. 20x27cm. (Pitman drawing series) [NC770.P4 1956] 55-12077
1. Face. 2. Anatomy, Artistic. 3. Drawing—Instruction. I. Hagman, Rune, ed. II. Title.

ZAIDENBERG, Arthur, 1903-   743.49
How to draw heads and faces. London, New York, Abelard-Schuman [1967, c1966] 64 p. illus. 27 cm. [NC770.Z3 1967] 66-9739
1. Face. 2. Head. 3. Drawing—Instruction. I. Title.   BIP

Face in art.

AMES, Lee J.   743'.49
Draw 50 famous faces / Lee J. Ames. 1st ed. Garden City, N.Y. : Doubleday, c1978. [63] p. : all ill. ; 32 cm. [NC770.A46] 77-15878 ISBN 0-385-13217-4 : 6.95. ISBN 0-385-13218-2 lib.bdg. : 7.90
1. Face in art. 2. Drawing—Technique. 3. Biography—Portraits. I. Title.

EMBERLEY, Ed.   743'.49
Ed Emberley's Drawing book of faces. 1st ed. Boston : Little, Brown, 1975. 32 p. : col. ill. ; 20 x 27 cm. Includes index. Simple step-by-step instructions for drawing a wide variety of faces reflecting various emotions and professions. [NC770.E42] 74-32033 ISBN 0-316-23609-8 lib.bdg. : 4.95
1. Face in art. 2. Drawing—Instruction. I. Title. II. Title: Drawing book of faces.

PERARD, Victor Semon,   743.492 1870-1957.
Drawing faces and expressions. Rev. by Rune Hagman. New York, Pitman Pub. Corp. [1958] 64 p. illus. 20 x 27 cm. [NC770.P4 1958] 58-13037
1. Face in art. 2. Anatomy, Artistic. 3. Drawing—Instruction. I. Title.   BIP

PERARD, Victor Semon,   743.492 1870-1957.
Drawing faces and expressions. Rev. by Rune Hagman. New York, Pitman Pub. Corp. [1956] 63 p. illus. 20 x 27 cm. (Pitman drawing series) [NC770.P4 1956] 55-12077
1. Face in art. 2. Anatomy, Artistic. 3. Drawing—Instruction. I. Hagman, Rune, ed. II. Title.

Face in art—Juvenile literature.

SELLECK, Jack.   704.94'2
Faces / Jack Selleck. Worcester, Mass. : Davis Publications, c1977. 96 p. : ill. (some col.) ; 27 cm. (Insights to art series) Includes index. Presents examples of the use of faces to communicate ideas and emotions. [N7573.S44] 76-50511 ISBN 0-87192-088-3 : 8.95
1. Face in art—Juvenile literature. 2. Art—Juvenile literature. I. Title. II. Series.   BIP

Faces.

BRIDGMAN, George Brant,   743.4 1864-1943
Heads, features, and faces. [Rev., enl. ed.] New York, Sterling [c.1932-1962] 125p. illus. 20cm. (Worthwhile how-to paperbacks, 504) First ed. pub. in 1932 under title: Features and faces. 62-12598 1.00 pap.,
1. Faces. 2. Anatomy, Artistic. I. Title.

Factories.

WILD, Friedemann.   725'.4
Factories. New York, Van Nostrand Reinhold Co. [1972] 136 p. illus. 26 cm. (Design & planning) Translation of Industriebau, Fertigungsbetriebe. [NA6400.W4813] 70-163486
1. Factories. 2. Architecture, Industrial—Designs and plans. I. Title. II. Series.

Factories— Design and construction.

ROYCRAFT, Duane Francis,   725.4 1915-
Industrial building details. 2d ed. New York, F. W. Dodge Corp. [1959] vii, 352p. (chiefly diagrs.) 31cm. First published in 1948 under title: Modern industrial construction, a detail reference. [TH4516.R6 1959] 59-8312
1. Factories— Design and construction. I. Title.

Fairbanks, Avard Tennyson, 1897—

FAIRBANKS, Eugene F.   730'.92'4
A sculptor's testimony in bronze and stone; the sacred sculpture of Avard T. Fairbanks, by Eugene F. Fairbanks. [Salt Lake City, Publishers Press, c1972] 101 p. illus. (part col.) 28 cm. [NB237.F3F34] 73-158695
1. Fairbanks, Avard Tennyson, 1897- I.

Fairbanks, Avard Tennyson, 1897- II. Title.

Fairies in art.

PHILLPOTTS, Beatrice.   753'.7
The book of fairies / Beatrice Phillpotts. New York : Ballantine Books, 1979, c1978. p. cm. First published under title: Fairy paintings. Includes index. [ND237.P47A4 1979] 78-19680 ISBN 0-345-28091-1 : 15.00. ISBN 0-345-28092-X pbk. : 7.95
1. Phillpotts, Beatrice. 2. Fairies in art. I. Title.   BIP

WOHL, Jack.   817'.5'4
Pixies. [1st ed.] New York, Holt, Rinehart and Winston [1967, c1966] 1 v. (unpaged) illus. 21 cm. [NC1429.W595A52] 67-13479
1. Title.

Fairlie, Reginald, 1883-1952.

NUTTGENS, Patrick.   726.50941
Reginald Fairlie, 1883-1952; a Scottish architect. Edinburgh, Oliver and Boyd [1959] 58p. illus. 22cm. [NA997.F3N8] 59-65118
1. Fairlie, Reginald, 1883-1952. I. Title.

Fairy lamps—Catalogs.

ANTHONY, T. Robert.   749'.63
19th century fairy lamps, by T. Robert Anthony. Color photography by Frank L. Forward. 1st ed. Manchester, Vt., Forward's Color Productions, 1969. [42] p. col. illus. 23 cm. [NK5440.F3A5] 74-22741
1. Fairy lamps—Catalogs. I. Forward, Frank L., illus. II. Title.

MACSWIGGAN, Amelia E   749.63
Fairy lamps; evening's glow of yesteryear. With an introd. by Marjorie M. Smith. New York, Fountainhead Publishers [1962] 170p. illus. 24cm. [NK9990.L3M3] 61-14823
1. Lanups— Hist. I. Title.

Falconet, Etienne Maurice, 1716-1791.

LEVITINE, George.   730'.92'4
The sculpture of Falconet. With a translation from the French of Falconet's Reflexions sur la sculpture by Eda Mezer Levitine. Greenwich, Conn., New York Graphic Society [1972] 144 p. illus. 23 cm. Bibliography: p. 141. [NB553.F2L48] 71-181348 ISBN 0-8212-0383-5 17.40
1. Falconet, Etienne Maurice, 1716-1791. I. Title.

Fales, Douglas A., 1929—

FALES, Douglas A., 1929-   741.9'71
Glengarry sketchbook / by Douglas A. Fales. Ottawa : Borealis Press, 1976. [75] p. : ill. ; 25 x 33 cm. [NC143.F3A46] 77-364781 ISBN 0-919594-31-X
1. Fales, Douglas A., 1929- 2. Glengarry Co., Ont., in art. 3. Glengarry Co., Ont. I. Title.

Family in art.

MOHAMED, Ethel Wright.   746.3'92'4
My life in pictures / Ethel Wright Mohamed ; edited by Charlotte Capers and Olivia P. Collins. Jackson : Mississippi Dept. of Archives and History, 1976. 40 p. : col. illus. ; 26 cm. [NK9298.M63A25] 77-356180
1. Mohamed, Ethel Wright. 2. Family in art. 3. Embroidery—Mississippi. I. Title.

Fan (African people)

FERNANDEZ, James W.   720'.967'2
Fang architectonics / J. W. Fernandez. Philadelphia : Institute for the Study of Human Issues, c1977. 41 p. : ill. ; 28 cm. (Working papers in the traditional arts ; no. 1) "The original version of this working paper ... was prepared at the Conference on Traditional African Architecture ... September 24-26, 1970, Smithsonian Conference Center, Maryland."

Bibliography: p. 40-41. [DT546.F39] 76-53553 ISBN 0-915980-65-7 pbk. : 2.95
1. Fan (African people) 2. Architecture, Fan (African people) I. Title. II. Series. BIP

Fancy-work.

ALDRICH, Dot. 745.5
Creating with cattails, cones, and pods, by Dot Aldrich (with Gen Aldrich Young who also did the drawings) Great Neck, N.Y., Hearthside Press [1971] 224 p. illus. 25 cm. [TT880.A57] 79-76152 6.95
1. Fancy work. 2. Nature craft. I. Young, Gen Aldrich, joint author. II. Title. BIP

BOOKE, Ruth Voorhees. 635.966
Pressed flower pictures and citrus-skin decorations. Photos. by Louis Buhle. Sketches by the author. Princeton, N.J., Van Nostrand [1962] 228 p. illus. 22 cm. [SB449.3.D7B6] 62-4481
1. Fancy-work. 2. Flowers—Collection and preservation. 3. Flower arrangement. I. Title.

GRAINGER, Stuart E. 746'.04'71
Creative ropecraft / Stuart E. Grainger. 1st ed. New York : Norton, c1975. 128 p. : ill. ; 24 cm. Includes index. Bibliography: p. 125. [TT840.G63 1975b] 76-49142 ISBN 0-393-08746-8 : 8.95
1. Fancy work. 2. Rope. 3. Knots and splices. I. Title. BIP

HIRST, Irene, ed. 746
The complete book of needlework. [1st American ed.] New York, Taplinger Pub. Co., 1963 [c1962] 320 p. illus. 24 cm. [TT750.H58] 63-15249
1. Fancy work.

JONES, C S Mrs. 747.204
Household elegancies: how to make and restore Victorian art objects; suggestions in household art and tasteful home decorations [by] Henry T. Williams [and] Mrs. C.S. Jones. Watkins Glen, N.Y., Century House [c1967] 300, [5] p. illus. 22 cm. (Library of Victorian culture) On spine: How to make and restore Victorian art objects. Bibliography: p. [303] [TT880.J6] 67-30253
1. Fancy work. 2. Interior decoration. I. Williams, Henry T., joint author. II. Title. III. Title: How to make and restore Victorian art objects.

KREISCHER, Lois. 746.4
Symmography: three-dimensional creative designs with yarn without knotting or knitting. New York, Crown [1971] 62 p. illus. (part col.) 28 cm. (Crown's arts and craft series) [TT840.K74] 78-168314 1.98
1. Fancy work. I. Title.

LAMMER, Jutta. 746.4
The Reinhold book of needlecraft: embroidery, crochet, knitting, weaving, macrame, applique, patchwork, and many other handicraft techniques, old and new. Drawings by Ellen-Ingrid Baumanns and others. Photos by Manfred Bauer and Barbara Schulten. New York, Van Nostrand Reinhold Co. [1973] 296 p. illus. 25 cm. Translation of Das grosse Ravensburger Handarbeitsbuch. [TT750.L2413 1973] 73-1630 ISBN 0-442-24671-4 12.95
1. Fancy work. I. Title.

ROBINSON, Renee. 646.4
Fashion details : decorative tips for home sewers / Renee Robinson. New York : Van Nostrand Reinhold Co., 1977. 112 p. : ill. ; 25 cm. Includes index. [TT750.R59] 76-42285 ISBN 0-442-26971-4 : 10.95
1. Fancy work. 2. Dressmaking. I. Title.

SHORT, Eirian. 746.4'4
Embroidery and fabric collage. New York, Scribner's [1973 c.1971] xiii, 130 p. col. front., illus, 3 col. plates, diagrs. 25 cm. Bibliography: p. 123. [TT750.S57 1973] 77-39840 ISBN 0-684-12923-X. 12.50.
1. Fancy work. 2. Embroidery. I. Title.

TIME-LIFE Books. 746.4
Decorative techniques / by the editors of Time-Life Books. New York : Time-Life Books, c1975. 176 p. : col. ill. ; 30 cm. (The art of sewing) Includes index. [TT750.T55 1975] 75-29597
1. Fancy work. 2. House furnishings. 3. Decoration and ornament. I. Title. BIP

Fans.

CHIBA, Reiko, ed. 736.7
Painted fans of Japan; fifteen Noh-drama masterpieces. Rutland, Vt., Tuttle [1963, c.1962] 41p. col. illus. 13cm. Bibl. 62-20775 4.50
1. Fans. 2. Paintings, Japanese. 3. No (Japanese drama and theater) I. Title. BIP

FLORY, M. A. 736'.7
A book about fans; the history of fans and fan-painting, by M. A. Flory, with a chapter on fan-collecting by Mary Cadwalader Jones. New York, Macmillan. Detroit, Gale Research Co., 1974 [c1895] xiii, 141 p. illus. 22 cm. [NK4870.F5 1974] 72-174940 ISBN 0-8103-4049-6 11.00
1. Fans. 2. Fan painting. I. Jones, Mary Cadwalader Rawle, 1850-1935. II. Title.

FLORY, M. A. 736'.7
A book about fans : the history of fans and fan-painting / by M. A. Flory ; with a chapter on fan-collecting by Mary Cadwalader Jones. Boston : Longwood Press, 1977. p. cm. Reprint of the 1895 ed. published by Macmillan, New York. [NK4870.F5 1977] 77-23572 ISBN 0-89341-204-X lib.bdg. : 20.00
1. Fans. 2. Fan painting. I. Jones, Mary Cadwalader Rawle, 1850-1935. II. Title. BIP

Fans—Collectors and collecting.

GOSTELOW, Mary. 736'.7
The fan / Mary Gostelow. Dublin : Gill & Macmillan, 1976. 151 p. : ill. (some col.) ; 25 cm. Includes index. Bibliography: p. 146-147. [NK4870.G67] 76-380229 ISBN 0-7171-0721-3 : £13.00
1. Fans—Collectors and collecting. I. Title.

Fans—History.

ARMSTRONG, Nancy J. 736'.7'09
A collector's history of fans / Nancy Armstrong. 1st American ed. New York : C. N. Potter : distributed by Crown Publishers, 1974. 208 p. : ill. (some col.) ; 26 cm. Includes index. Bibliography: p. 202-203. [NK4870.A75 1974] 74-78079 ISBN 0-517-51605-5 : 15.00
1. Fans—History. I. Title.

Fantasy in art.

FABIAN, Stephen E., 1930- 741.9'73
Fantasy by Fabian : the art of Stephen E. Fabian / edited by Gerry de la Ree. Saddle River, N.J. : G. de la Ree, 1978. 128 p. : ill. ; 29 cm. [NC975.5.F25A4 1978] 78-103799 15.50
1. Fabian, Stephen E., 1930- 2. Fantasy in art. I. De la Ree, Gerry. II. Title.
Publisher's address : 7 Cedarwood Lane, Saddle River, NJ 07458

FENSCH, Thomas. FIC
Alice in Acidland. South Brunswick, A. S. Barnes [1970] 146 p. ports. 22 cm. "Lewis Carroll Revisited."—Book jacket. Includes text of Alice in Wonderland. [PZ4.F337Al] [PS3556.E5] 813'.5'4 70-92041 5.95
I. Dodgson, Charles Lutwidge, 1832-1898. Alice's adventures in Wonderland. 1970. II. Title.

FINLAY, Virgil. 741.9'73
The third book of Virgil Finlay : the fantasy art of Virgil Finlay / edited and published by Gerry de la Ree ; [graphics by Helen de la Ree]. Saddle River, N.J. : G. de la Ree, 1979. 127 p. : chiefly ill. ; 29 cm. [NC975.5.F5A4 1979] 79-100280 15.50
1. Finlay, Virgil. 2. Fantasy in art. I. De la Ree, Gerry. II. Title. BIP

Fantin-Latour, Ignace Henri Jean Theodore, 1836-1904.

LUCIE-SMITH, Edward. 759.4
Henri Fantin-Latour / Edward Lucie-Smith. New York : Rizzoli, 1977. 167 p. : ill. (some col.) ; 29 cm. Includes index. Bibliography: p. 163. [ND553.F3L82 1977] 77-73363 ISBN 0-8478-0113-6 : 35.00
1. Fantin-Latour, Ignace Henri Jean Theodore, 1836-1904. I. Title.

VERRIER, Michelle. 759.4
Fantin-Latour / Michelle Verrier. New York : Harmony Books, 1978. p. cm. Bibliography: p. [ND553.F3V47 1978] 78-1374 ISBN 0-517-53413-4 pbk. : 6.95
1. Fantin-Latour, Ignace Henri Jean Theodore, 1836-1904. 2. Painters—France—Biography. I. Fantin-Latour, Ignace Henri Jean Theodore, 1836-1904. II. Title. BIP

Farinelli, Carlo Broschi, called, 1705-1782.

SITWELL, Sacheverell, Sir, bart., 1897- 709'.03'2
Southern baroque art; a study of painting, architecture and music in Italy and Spain of the 17th & 18th centuries. Freeport, N.Y., Books for Libraries Press [1971] 319 p. illus. 23 cm. Reprint of the 1924 ed. Contents.Contents.—The serenade at Caserta.—"Les Indes galantes."—The king and the nightingale: Philip V and Farinelli.—Mexico.—Biographical index and bibliography (p. 279-319) [NX552.A1S5 1971] 70-179539 ISBN 0-8369-6668-6
1. Farinelli, Carlo Broschi, called, 1705-1782. 2. The arts, Baroque—Italy. 3. The arts, Baroque—Spain. 4. The arts, Baroque—Mexico. BIP

Farington, Joseph, 1747-1821.

FARINGTON, Joseph, 1747-1821. 759.2 B
The diary of Joseph Farington / edited by Kenneth Garlick and Angus Macintyre. New Haven : Published for the Paul Mellon Centre for Studies in British Art by Yale University Press, 1978- p. cm. (Studies in British art) Contents.Contents.—v. 1. July 1793-December 1794.—v. 2. January 1795-August 1796. [N6797.F37A2 1978] 78-7056 ISBN 0-300-02294-8 : 60.00 set
1. Farington, Joseph, 1747-1821. 2. London. Royal Academy of Art. 3. Artists—England—Biography. 4. Arts, English. 5. England—Civilization—18th century. 6. England—Civilization—19th century. I. Garlick, Kenneth, 1916- II. Macintyre, Angus D. III. Paul Mellon Centre for Studies in British Art. IV. Title. V. Series.

Farm buildings.

CARTER, Deane G 1894- 631.2
Farm buildings. Line drawings by Keith H. Hinchcliff. 4th ed., rewritten. New York, Wiley [1954] 291p. illus. 24cm. First ed., 1922 by W. A. Foster and D. G. Carter. [NA8201.C35 1954] 54-9499
1. Farm buildings. 2. Architecture, Domestic. I. Foster, William Arthur, 1884-1941. Farm buildings. II. Title.

DOANE Agricultural Service, St. Louis. 631.2
Doane designed farm buildings. St. Louis [1951] 1 v. (loose-leaf) illus. 30 cm. [NA8200.D6] 51-7531
1. Farm buildings. I. Title.

NEUBAUER, Loren Wenzel, 1904- 728.9
Farm building design [by] Loren W. Neubauer [and] Harry B. Walker. Englewood Cliffs, N.J., Prentice-Hall, 1961. 611 p. illus. 24 cm. Includes bibliography. [NA8200.N4] 61-8229
1. Farm buildings. 2. Building. I. Walker, Harry Bruce, 1884- joint author. II. Title.

Farm buildings—U.S.

HALSTED, Byron David, 1852-1918. 728'.9
Barns, sheds and outbuildings / edited by Byron D. Halsted. Brattleboro, Vt. : Stephen Greene Press, c1977. 240 p. : ill. ; 21 cm. Reprint of the 1881 ed. published by Orange Judd, New York under title: Barn plans and outbuildings. Bibliography: p. 235-237. [NA8201.H2 1977] 76-50020 ISBN 0-8289-0293-3 : 6.95
1. Farm buildings—United States. 2. Barns—United States. I. Title. BIP

SLOANE, Eric. 728.9
An age of barns. New York, Ballantine Books [1974, c1967] lv. (unpaged) illus. 23 cm. Includes bibliography. [NA8230.S57] 66-26946 4.95 (pbk.)
1. Farm buildings—U.S. I. Title.

Farm life in art.

HAMIL, James R., 1937- 759.13
Farmland, USA / by James R. Hamil and Harold Hamil Kansas City, Mo. : Lowell Press, c1975. 100 p. : col. ill. ; 26 x 33 cm. Includes index. [ND1839.H35H34] 75-18756 ISBN 0-913504-24-6 : 20.00
1. Hamil, James R., 1937- 2. Farm life in art. 3. Farm life—United States—Pictorial works. I. Hamil, Harold, joint author. II. Title. BIP

HARKONEN, Helen B 704.94963
Farms and farmers in art, by Helen B. Harkonen. Designed by Robert Clark Nelson. Minneapolis, Lerner Publications Co., [1965] 64 p. illus. 27 cm. [N8217.F3H3] 64-8204
1. Farm life in art. I. Nelson, Robert Clark. II. Title. BIP

WYETH, Andrew, 1917- 759.13
Wyeth at Kuerners. Boston : Houghton Mifflin, 1976. viii, 324 p. : ill. (some col.) ; 26 x 34 cm. Includes index. [ND237.W93W93 (fol.)] 76-6171 ISBN 0-395-21990-6 : 75.00
1. Wyeth, Andrew, 1917- 2. Kuerner, Karl, 1898- —Portraits, etc. 3. Kuerner, Anna—Portraits, etc. 4. Farm life in art. I. Title.

Farm life—New York (State)

NEW York. Agricultural Experiment Station, Ithaca. 728.67
Farmhouse planning guides, household activity data and space needs related to design. [Ithaca?] 1959. 135p. illus., diagrs., tables. 22 x 28cm. 'A publication of the Cornell University Agricultural Experiment Station and the New York State College of Home Economics, units of the State University of New York at Cornell University, in association with the Cornell University Housing Research Center.' [TH4920.N4] A 61
1. Farm life—New York (State) 2. Farmhouses. 3. Home economics—Equipment and supplies. I. Cornell University. New York State College of Home Economics. II. Title.

Farm life—New York (State)—Pictorial works.

CONSENTINO, Joseph. 779.9'917303924
Farm life today. Photos. by Joseph Consentino. [Introductory statement by Joseph Consentino. New York, New York State Council on the Arts, c1971] [4] p., 50 plates. 37 cm. Issued in a case. "An exhibit portfolio produced by the New York State Council on the Arts for the New York Museums Collaborative." [S521.5.N7C66] 72-171183
1. Farm life—New York (State)—Pictorial works. I. New York (State). State Council on the Arts. II. Museums Collaborative. III. Title.

Farmhouses.

HODGELL, Murlin Ray. 728.6
Contemporary farmhouses: Flexiplan 71204. Prepared by M. R. Hodgell, under the direction of the Farmhouse Technical Committee (NC-9) of the north central region. Urbana, University of Illinois Press, 1956. 22 p., 24 plans. illus. 29 x 45 cm. (North central regional publication 58) Illinois. Agricultural Experiment Station [Urbana] Bulletin 600. [TH4920.H63] 56-63279
1. Farmhouses. I. Title. II. Title: Flexiplan. III. Series.

Farmhouses—England.

COOK, Olive. 728.6084
English cottages and farmhouses, text by Olive Cook; 273 photos. by Edwin Smith New York, Studio Publications [1955] 50p. plates, maps, diagrs. 32cm. Bibliography: p. 17. [NA8202.C6] 55-1516
1. Farmhouses—England. 2. Farm

buildings—England. 3. Cottages. I. Smith, Edwin, photographer. II. Title.

Farmhouses—United States.

KAUFFMAN, Henry J., 1908- 728.67
The American farmhouse / text and photos. by Henry J. Kauffman ; floor plans by Tom Callahan. New York : Hawthorn Books, c1975. xi, 265 p., [8] leaves of plates : ill. (some col.) ; 29 cm. Includes index. Bibliography: p. 259-260. [NA8210.K38 1975] 75-5036 ISBN 0-8015-0220-9 : 16.95
1. Farmhouses—United States. I. Title.

Farnese family.

RABBI Solari, Giovanna. 929.2
The house of Farnese [by] Giovanna R. Solari. Translated by Simona Morini and Frederic Tuten. [1st ed.] Garden City, N.Y., Doubleday, 1968. 310 p. illus., geneal. table (on lining papers), ports. 22 cm. Translation of Storie di casa Farnese. Bibliography: p. 295-298. [DG975.P25.R33] 67-19121
1. Farnese family. I. Title.

Farnsworth, Lizzie Amelia, 1865-1941.

FARNSWORTH, Russell H., 1900- 974.3'6
Over Cram Hill, by Russell H. Farnsworth. With old photos. copied for reproduction by Horace B. Eldred. Burlington, Vt., Offset print. by Queen City Printers, [1967] 79 p. illus. 23 cm. [CT275.F415F3] 67-8081
1. Farnsworth, Lizzie Amelia, 1865-1941. I. Title.

Farny, Henry Francois, 1847-1916.

CARTER, Denny T., 1940- 759.13 B
Henry Farny / by Denny T. Carter. New York : Watson-Guptil Publications, 1978. p. cm. Includes index. Bibliography: p. [ND237.F25C33 1978] 78-17999 ISBN 0-8230-2239-0 : 35.00
1. Farny, Henry Francois, 1847-1916. 2. The West in art. 3. Indians of North America—Pictorial works. I. Farny, Henry Francois, 1847-1916. BIP

Fasanella, Ralph.

WATSON, Patrick, 1929- 759.13
Fasanella's city; the painting of Ralph Fasanella with the story of his life and art, by Patrick Watson. [1st American ed.] New York, Knopf; [distributed by Random House] 1973. ix, 148 p. illus. (part col.) 31 cm. [ND237.F26W37] 73-7269 ISBN 0-394-48823-7 15.00
1. Fasanella, Ralph. I. Fasanella, Ralph. II. Title.

Fashion.

BALLARD, Bettina. 659.152
In my fashion. New York, D. McKay Co. [1960] 312 p. 21 cm. [TT515.B32] 60-9569
1. Fashion. 2. Vogue. I. Title.

BENDER, Marylin. 391
The beautiful people. New York, Coward-McCann [1967] 320 p. illus., ports. 22 cm. [TT507.B43] 67-23143
1. Fashion. 2. Clothing trade. 3. Costume design. I. Title.

BERGEN, Polly, 1930- 646'.34
I'd love to, but what'll I wear? / Polly Bergen [and Kathrin Perutz]. 1st ed. [New York?] : Wyden Books, c1977. vii, 245 p. : ill. ; 24 cm. [TT507.B44] 77-2125 ISBN 0-671-22803-X : 10.95
1. Fashion. 2. Clothing and dress. I. Perutz, Kathrin, 1939- joint author. II. Title. BIP

BERTIN, Celia, 1921- 646.01
Paris a' la mode. Translated from the French by Marjorie Deans. Illustrated by Mariel Deans. New York, Harper [1957] 254p. illus. 22cm. Translation of Haute couture, terre inconnue. [TT502.B453 1957] 56-11070
1. Fashion. I. Title.

BYRNES, Garrett Davis. 070.4454
Fashion in newspapers. [New York] Published for the American Press Institute by Columbia University Press, 1951. 74 p. illus. 28 cm. ([Columbia University. American Press Institute] Handbook for editors, no. 2) Bibliography: p. 74. [TT507.B87] 51-14078
1. Fashion. 2. Photography, Commercial. I. Title. II. Series.

EPSTEIN, Beryl (Williams) 1910- 687
Young faces in fashion. [1st ed.] Philadelphia, Lippincott [c1956] 176 p. illus. 22 cm. [TT505.A1E64] 56-6215
1. Fashion. I. Title.

ESQUIRE. 646.32
Esquire fashion guide for all occasions. Edited by Frederic S. Birmingham. Introd. by Oscar E. Schoeffler. Illustrated by Alvin Pimsler. Rev. ed. New York, Harper & Row [1962] 204 p. illus. 22 cm. [TT618.ES] 62-21134
1. Fashion. 2. Men's clothing. I. Birmingham, Frederic Alexander, 1911- ed. II. Title. III. Title: Fashion guide for all occasions.

FAIRCHILD, John. 746.9
The fashionable savages. [1st ed.] Garden City, N.Y., Doubleday, 1965. viii, 200 p. ports. 24 cm. [TT505.F3A3] 65-19882
1. Fashion. 2. Costume design. I. Title.

HARTNELL, Norman. 9326.40
Silver and gold. New York, Pitman Pub. Corp. [1956] 141p. illus. 26cm. Autobiography. [TT505] 56-7405
I. Title.

INSTANT fashion. 746.9
Designed for you by a team of prominent designers and fashion experts. [New York] Graphic Enterprises [1969] 128 p. illus. 20 cm. "Published in association with Parade magazine". [TT507.I48] 76-80636
1. Fashion. 2. Clothing and dress.

LAMBERT, Eleanor. 746.9'2
World of fashion : people, places, resources / by Eleanor Lambert. New York : R. R. Bowker Co., 1976. xi, 361 p. ; 24 cm. Includes index. Bibliography: p. 345-349. [TT515.L16] 75-43904 ISBN 0-8352-0627-0
1. Fashion. I. Title. BIP

LEVIN, Phyllis Lee 338.4768712
The wheels of fashion. Garden City, N. Y., Doubleday [c.]1965. xix, 244p. illus., ports. 24cm. [TT507.L45] 65-11853 5.95
1. Fashion. 2. Clothing trade—U. S. 3. Costume design. I. Title.

MERRIAM, Eve, 1916- 659.1
Figleaf; the business of being in fashion. With drawings by Burmah Burris. [1st ed.] Philadelphia, Lippincott [1960] 255 p. illus. 22 cm. [TT507.M47] 60-13580
1. Fashion. I. Title.

MILINAIRE, Caterine. 646'.34
Cheap chic / by Caterine Milinaire and Carol Troy ; designed by Bea Feitler. New York : Harmony Books, [1975] 223 p. : ill. ; 29 cm. Includes index. [TT515.M59 1975] 75-25562 ISBN 0-517-52453-8 : 12.95. ISBN 0-517-52368-X pbk. : 5.95
1. Fashion. 2. Clothing and dress. I. Troy, Carol, joint author. II. Title. BIP

MILINAIRE, Caterine. 646'.34
Cheap chic / by Caterine Milinaire and Carol Troy ; designed by Bea Feitler. Rev. ed. / rev. by Carol Troy. New York : Harmony Books, c1978. p. cm. [TT515.M59 1978] 78-4148 ISBN 0-517-53456-8 : 12.95 ISBN 0-517-52368-X pbk. : 5.95
1. Fashion. 2. Clothing and dress. I. Troy, Carol, joint author. II. Title.

NASH, Eleanor Arnett. 646
Beauty is not an age. [1st ed.] New York, Harper [1953] 225 p. 22 cm. [TT507.N27] 52-11693
1. Fashion. 2. Clothing and dress. 3. Beauty, Personal. I. Title.

NAYLOR, Brenda. 646'.34
Fashion sense / [by] Brenda Naylor. London : The author, 1976. 128 p. : ill. (some col.) ; 25 cm. Includes index. [TT507.N29] 77-350766 ISBN 0-9504981-0-6 : £5.00
1. Fashion. 2. Clothing and dress. I. Title.

NEW York Dress Institute. 687.12062747
Report. [New York] v. illus. 28 cm. annual. [TT500.N48] 52-16187
I. Title.

PIERRE, Clara. 646'.34
Looking good : the liberation of fashion / Clara Pierre. New York : Reader's Digest Press : distributed by Crowell, 1976. 295 p. : ill. ; 21 cm. Includes index. [TT507.P52 1976] 76-22191 ISBN 0-88349-093-5 : 8.95
1. Fashion. 2. Clothing and dress. 3. Beauty, Personal. I. Title.

REVSON, Lyn. 646.7
Lyn Revson's world of style : how to join it and live it / by Lyn Revson. 1st ed. [New York] : Wyden Books, c1977. p. cm. [TT507.R47] 77-14945 ISBN 0-671-22954-0 : 8.95
1. Fashion. 2. Beauty, Personal. 3. Entertaining. 4. Women—Conduct of life. I. Title.

ROSHCO, Bernard. 687.12
The rag race; how New York and Paris run the break-neck business of dressing American women. New York, Funk & Wagnalls [1963] 308 p. 22 cm. Includes bibliography. [TT504.R65] 63-10473
1. Fashion. 2. Clothing trade. I. Title.

ROWE, Patricia Lingane. 741.672
Shorthand fashion sketching. [3d ed.] New York, Fairchild Publications [1960] 93 p. illus. 31 cm. [TT509.R68] 60-6848
1. Fashion. 2. Drawing — Instruction. I. Title.

ROWE, Patricia Lingane. 741.67
Shorthand fashion sketching. New York, Fairchild Publications [1953] unpaged. illus. 31cm. [TT509.R68] [TT509.R68] 743 53-9650 53-9650
1. Fashion. 2. Drawing—Instruction. I. Title.

ROWE, Patricia Lingane. *741.67
Shorthand fashion sketching. New York, Fairchild Publications [c1956] unpaged. illus. 31cm. [TT509.R68 1956] [TT509.R68 1956] 743 57-13923 57-13923
1. Fashion. 2. Drawing—Instruction. I. Title. BIP

RYAN, Mildred (Graves) 1905- 646
Dress smartly; a 100 point guide. Illustrated by Shirley Langworthy. New York, Scribner [1956] 128p. illus. 27cm. [TT507.R85] 56-7127
1. Fashion. 2. Clothing and dress. I. Title.

RYAN, Mildred (Graves) 1905- 646
Dress smartly; a 100 point guide. Illustrated by Jacqueline Waterbury Jacobs and Shirley Langworthy. Rev. ed. New York, Scribner [1967] 128 p. illus. 26 cm. [TT507.R875 1967] 68-13007
1. Fashion. 2. Clothing and dress. I. Title.

SCHIAPARELLI, Elsa. 926.46
Shocking life. [1st ed.] New York, Dutton, 1954. 254 p. illus. 22 cm. Autobiography. [TT505.S3A3] 54-109187
I. Title.

TEXAS. University. Division of Extension. Industrial and Business Training Bureau. 646.01
Basic fashion training. Issued by the University of Texas, Division of Extension, Industrial and Business Training [Bureau] in cooperation with Texas Education Agency, Vocational Division, Distributive Education Service. Austin [1952?] viii, 76 l. illus. 28cm. Includes bibliographies. [TT508.T4] 55-62334
1. Fashion. I. Title.

TOLMAN, Ruth. 391
Guide to fashion merchandise knowledge. Bronx, N.Y., Milady Pub. Corp. [1973] xiv, 498 p. illus. 24 cm. "Vol. 1." "Companion to this book, 'Volume II: Guide to fashion merchandising with emphasis on retailing'." Bibliography: p. 469-480. [TT518.T64] 72-92456 10.00
1. Fashion. 2. Costume—History. 3. Decoration and ornament—History. I. Title.
Publisher's Address: 3839 White Plains Rd. N.Y. 10467 BIP

VREELAND, Alida, 1898- 646.069
Opportunities in fashion. New York, Grosset & Dunlap [1951] 112 p. 20 cm. (Vocational guidance manuals) [TT507.V7] 52-235
1. Fashion. 2. Clothing and dress. I. Title.

Fashion—Addresses, essays, lectures.

ADBURGHAM, Alison. 391.008
View of fashion; drawings by Haro. London, Allen & Unwin, 1966. 285p. front., illus. 23cm. [TT519.A3] 67-71098 6.00
1. Fashion—Addresses, essays, lectures. I. Title.
American distributor: Hillary House, New York.

Fashion as a profession.

BERRIEN, Edith (Heal) 1903- 746.9023
Fashion as a career, by Edith Heal. Fashion portfolio by Bob Walker. New York, J. Messner [1966] 191 p. illus. 22 cm. Bibliography: p. 184-185. [TT507.B45] 66-14010
1. Fashion as a profession. I. Title.

BRENNER, Barbara. 646.01069
Careers and opportunities in fashion. [1st ed.] New York, Dutton, 1964. 191 p. illus., port. 21 cm. "Reading list": p. [182]-185. [TT507.B67] 63-20849
1. Fashion as a profession. I. Title.

CURTIS, Frieda Steinmann, 1898-- 646.069
Careers in the world of fashion. New York, Woman's Press, 1953. 268p. 21cm. [TT507.C95] 53-5829
1. Fashion as a profession. I. Title.

FASHION Group. 646.01
Your future in the fashion world. Edited by Olive P. Gately. Contributors: Edith Battles [and others. 1st ed.] New York, R. Rosen Press, 1960. 160 p. 20 cm. (Careers in depth) [TT502.F26] 60-14843
1. Fashion as a profession. 2. Retail trade. 3. Woman—Employment. I. Title.

IRONSIDE, Janey. 646.01069
Fashion as a career. [London] Museum Press stamped: distributed by Sportshelf, New Rochelle, N. Y.] 1962; 150p. illus. 23cm. Includes bibliography. [TT507.I7] 62-6500
1. Fashion as a profession. I. Title.

JABENIS, Elaine. 391'.0023
The fashion director; what she does & how to be one. New York, Wiley [1972] xiv, 407 p. illus. 23 cm. Bibliography: p. 395-396. [TT507.J29] 72-768 ISBN 0-471-43125-7
1. Fashion as a profession. I. Title. BIP

KRIEGER, Murray, 1912- 687'.023
635 exciting careers in the world of fashion and merchandising [New York] LIM Press [1970] 125 p. 18 cm. Cover title. Page 125, blank for "Notes." [TT507.K77] 75-142171
1. Fashion as a profession. I. Title.

MCDERMOTT, Irene Elizabeth. 687'.023
Opportunities in clothing; fashion, merchandising [by] Irene E. McDermott and Jeanne L. Norris. Peoria, Ill., C. A. Bennett Co. [1968] 350 p. illus. 25 cm. Bibliography: p. 337-344. [TT518.M34] 68-10288
1. Fashion as a profession. 2. Clothing trade. 3. Dressmaking. I. Norris, Jeanne L., joint author. II. Title. BIP

MCDERMOTT, Irene Elizabeth. 687'.023
Opportunities in clothing: fashion, merchandising [by] Irene E. McDermott and Jeanne L. Norris. Peoria, Ill., C. A. Bennett Co. [1972] 350 p. illus. 25 cm. Bibliography: p. 337-343. A textbook on the clothing field and its job possibilities. Includes sections on dressmaking techniques, fibers and fabrics, principles of design, selling mechanics, and other pertinent topics. [TT518.M34 1972] 72-197311 ISBN 0-87002-140-0
1. Fashion as a profession. 2. Clothing trade. 3. Dressmaking. I. Norris, Jeanne L., joint author. II. Title.

SETTLE, Alison 646.01069
Fashion as a career. London, Batsford [dist. New Rochelle, N.Y., SportShelf, 1965, c.1963] 128p. illus. 19cm. (Batsford career bks.) Bibl. [TT507.S46] 65-895 4.00 bds.,
1. Fashion as a profession. I. Title.

Fashion as a profession—Juvenile literature.

SIEGEL, Margot. 946.9'2
Fashion. Designed by Don Pulver. Minneapolis, Dillon Press [1970] 93 p. illus., port. 24 cm. (Looking forward to a career) Discusses the necessary qualifications and education for various careers in the fashion field. [TT507.S64] 73-115872 ISBN 0-87518-020-5
1. Fashion as a profession—Juvenile literature.

SIEGEL, Margot. 746.9'2
Fashion. [2d ed.] Minneapolis, Dillon Press [1974, c1970] 90 p. illus. 24 cm. (Looking forward to a career) Bibliography: p. 90. Discusses the necessary qualifications and education for various careers in the fashion field. [TT507.S64 1974] 73-20222 4.95 (library binding.)
1. Fashion as a profession—Juvenile literature. I. Title.

Fashion—Biography.

KEENAN, Brigid, 391'.07'20922
1939-
The women we wanted to look like / by Brigid Keenan. New York : St. Martin's Press, [1978] p. cm. Includes index. Bibliography: p. [TT505.A1K43 1978] 78-4014 ISBN 0-312-88783-3 : 14.95
1. Fashion—Biography. 2. Fashion—History—20th century. I. Title. BIP

Fashion—Dictionaries.

CALASIBETTA, Charlotte 746.9'2'03
Mankey.
Fairchild's dictionary of fashion / by Charlotte Calasibetta ; edited by Ermina Stimson Goble, Lorraine Davis. New York : Fairchild Publications, [1975] xiv, 693 p., [8] leaves of plates : ill. (some col.) ; 25 cm. Includes index. [TT503.C34] 74-84805 ISBN 0-87005-133-4 : 50.00
1. Fashion—Dictionaries. 2. Costume—Dictionaries. I. Title. II. Title: Dictionary of fashion. BIP

Fashion drawing.

DILLEY, Romilda. 741.672
Drawing women's fashions. New York, Watson-Guptill Publications [1959] 149 p. illus. 29 cm. [TT509.D5] 58-13524
1. Fashion drawing. I. Title.

DILLEY, Romilda 741.6'72
Fundamental fashion drawing. [Rev. ed.] New York, Sterling [1967] 128p. illus. 28cm. First ed., 1959, has title: Drawing women's fashions. [TT509.D5 1967] 67-5159 1.95 pap.,
1. Fashion drawing. I. Title.

GIBSON, Mary Richards 741.672
How to do fashion drawing. Fort Lauderdale, Fla., Allied Pubs. [c.]1964. 40p. illus. (pt. col.) 34cm. (Margaret Harold Pubn.) 64-19972 1.95 pap.,
1. Fashion drawing. I. Title.

IRELAND, Patrick John. 746.9'2
Design drawing for menswear / Patrick John Ireland. New York : Wiley, 1976. p. cm. "A Halsted Press book." [TT509.I68] 76-22674 ISBN 0-470-98897-5 : 9.95
1. Fashion drawing. 2. Men's clothing. I. Title.

IRELAND, Patrick John. 746.9'2
Drawing and designing children's and teenage fashions / Patrick John Ireland. New York : Wiley, 1979. p. cm. "A Halsted Press book." [TT640.I73 1979] 79-1265 ISBN 0-470-26592-2 : 12.50
1. Children's clothing—Pattern design. 2. Fashion drawing. I. Title. BIP

IRELAND, Patrick John. 746.9'2
Drawing and designing menswear / Patrick John Ireland. London : Batsford, 1976. 96 p. : chiefly ill. ; 25 cm. [TT509.I68 1976b] 77-370172 ISBN 0-7134-3227-6 : £3.95. ISBN 0-7134-3228-4 pbk.
1. Fashion drawing. 2. Men's clothing. I. Title. BIP

IRELAND, Patrick John. 741.6'72
Fashion design drawing. New York, Wiley [1970] 127 p. illus. 31 cm. [TT509.I7 1970b] 73-134681
1. Fashion drawing. I. Title. BIP

IRELAND, Patrick John. 741.67'2
Fashion drawing for advertising. New York, Wiley [1974] 128 p. illus. 26 cm. "A Halsted Press book." [TT509.I72] 74-3741 ISBN 0-470-42833-3 7.95
1. Fashion drawing. I. Title. BIP

SLOANE, Eunice. 741.6'72
Illustrating fashion [by] E. Sloane. [1st ed.] New York, Harper & Row [1968] 319 p. illus. 32 cm. [TT509.S55] 67-22544
1. Fashion drawing. I. Title. BIP

SLOANE, Eunice. 741.67'2
Illustrating fashion / E. Sloane. Rev. ed. New York : Harper & Row, c1977. 319 p. : ill. ; 31 cm. [TT509.S55 1977] 76-26254 ISBN 0-06-013893-9 : 20.00
1. Fashion drawing. I. Title.

Fashion—Exhibitions.

DEGRAW, Imelda G. 746.9'2
25 years couturiers : [exhibition catalog] Denver Art Museum, September 20-December 7, 1975 / by Imelda G. DeGraw; ill. by Lou Boxwell. Denver : The Museum, 1975. ca. 100 p. : ill. ; 30 x 13 cm. [TT502.D43] 75-21427 ISBN 0-914738-10-0
1. Fashion—Exhibitions. 2. Costume designers. I. Denver. Art Museum. II. Title.

Fashion—History.

BALMAIN, Pierre, 746.90924 B
1914-
My years and seasons. Translated by Edward Lanchberry with Gordon Young. [1st ed.] Garden City, N.Y., Doubleday, 1965. xiv, 216 p. ports. 22 cm. [TT505.B3A313 1965] 65-19913
I. Title.

BEATON, Cecil Walter 391.09
Hardy, 1904-
The glass of fashion [1st ed.] Garden City, N. Y., Doubleday, 1954. 397 p. illus. 24 cm. [TT502.B4] 53-10653
1. Fashion—History. I. Title.

DIOR, Christian. 926.46
Christian Dior and I. Translated from the French by Antonia Fraser. [1st ed.] New York, Dutton, 1957. 251 p. illus., ports. 22 cm. London ed. (Weidenfeld and Nicolson) has title: Dior. [TT505.D5A353 1957a] 57-8971

DIOR, Christian. 646.01
Talking about fashion [by] Christian Dior as told to Elie Rabourdin and Alice Chavane; translated by Eugenia Sheppard. New York, Putnam [1954] 112 p. illus. 20 cm. Translation of Je suis courturier. [TT505.D5A315] 54-5486
I. Title.

GARLAND, Madge. 391'.009
The changing form of fashion. New York, Praeger Publishers [1971, c1970] xiv, 130 p. illus. 26 cm. [TT504.G36] 70-109477 8.95
1. Fashion—History. I. Title.

GOLD, Annalee. 391
75 years of fashion / by Annalee Gold. New York : Fairchild Publications, [1975] 111 p. : ill. ; 29 cm. [TT504.G64] 74-24531 ISBN 0-87005-144-X : 7.95
1. Fashion—History. I. Title.

LATOUR, Anny. 646.01
Kings of fashion. Translated from the German by Mervyn Savill. [1st American ed.] New York, Coward McCann [1958] 270p. illus. 23cm. Translation of Magier dor Mode. [TT504.L313] 58-10379
1. Fashion—Hist. I. Title.

PENN, Irving. 779'.9'74692
Inventive Paris clothes, 1909-1939 : a photographic essay / by Irving Penn ; with text by Diana Vreeland. New York : Viking Press, [1977] p. cm. (A Studio book) [TT507.P38] 77-6622 ISBN 0-670-40067-X : 16.95
1. Fashion—History. 2. Clothing and dress—History. 3. Costume designers—France—Paris. I. Vreeland, Diana. II. Title. BIP

ROBINSON, Julian. 746.9'2
Fashion in the forties / Julian Robinson. London : Academy Editions ; New York : St. Martin's Press, 1976. 103 p. : chiefly ill. (some col.) ; 30 cm. [TT504.R6 1976] 76-17338 pbk. : 12.50
1. Fashion—History. 2. Clothing trade—History. I. Title. BIP

Fashion—History—20th century.

BERNARD, Barbara. 746.9'2
Fashion in the 60's / [compiled and written by] Barbara Bernard. London : Academy Editions ; New York : St. Martin's Press, 1978. 87 p. : chiefly ill., ports. ; 20 cm. [TT504.6.G7B47 1978] 78-60788 ISBN 0-312-28460-8 (St. Martin's) : 4.95
1. Fashion—History—20th century. 2. Costume designers—Great Britain. 3. Costume—Great Britain—History—20th century. I. Title. BIP

GLYNN, Prudence. 391'.009'04
In fashion / Prudence Glynn. New York : Oxford University Press, 1978. p. cm. Includes index. [TT504.G55] 78-56372 ISBN 0-19-520072-1 : 19.95
1. Fashion—History—20th century. 2. Clothing trade—History—20th century. I. Title. BIP

Fashion—Periodicals—Exhibitions.

MANCHESTER Polytechnic. 746.9'2
Library.
Fashion magazines, 1799-1975 : an exhibition / Manchester Polytechnic Library. [Manchester] : [The Library], [1976] [24] p. : chiefly ill. ; 22 cm. Cover title. Bibliography: p. [6]-[7] [TT502.M36 1976] 76-381260 ISBN 0-901276-09-X
1. Fashion—Periodicals—Exhibitions. I. Title.

Fashion photography.

AVEDON, Richard. 779'.9'39100924
Avedon—photographs, 1974-1977. 1st ed. [New York] : Farrar, Straus, & Giroux, 1978. ca. 250 p. : all ill. ; 27 cm. [TR679.A93] 78-50653 ISBN 0-374-23200-8 : 50.00
1. Avedon, Richard. 2. Fashion photography. I. Title. II. Title: Photographs, 1947-1977. BIP

BELSON, Al. 778.9'9'391
Fashion photography techniques. New York, Amphoto [1970] 157 p. illus. (part col.) 27 cm. [TR679.B45] 70-97876 10.00
1. Fashion photography. I. Title. BIP

CRAGIN, Valerie. 778.9'24
Photographic modeling / by Valerie Cragin. Los Angeles : Petersen Pub. Co., c1975. 80 p. : ill. ; 28 cm. (Petersen's how-to photographic library) [TR679.C7] 75-10066 ISBN 0-8227-0102-2 pbk. : 2.95
1. Fashion photography. 2. Glamour photography. 3. Models, Fashion. I. Title. BIP

DE MEYER, Adolf, 770'.92'4 B
1868-1949.
DeMeyer / edited by Robert Brandau ; with a biographical essay by Philippe Jullian. 1st ed. New York : Knopf : distributed by Random House, 1976. 50 p., [51] leaves of plates : ill. ; 33 cm. [TR679.D45 1976] 75-36796 ISBN 0-394-49744-9 : 25.00
1. DeMeyer, Adolf, 1868-1949. 2. Fashion photography. 3. Photography—Portraits. I. Brandau, Robert. II. Jullian, Philippe. BIP

HOYNINGEN-HUENE. 770'.92'4 B
Los Angeles, Friends of the Libraries, University of Southern California, 1970. 20 p. illus. 26 cm. Contents.—Pucciani, O. F. George Hoyningen-Huene, 1900-1968.—Horst, H. P. George Hoyningen-Huene: a sketch.—Bocher, M. R. Hoyningen-Huene and the Paris Vogue.—Lerman, L. The self-education of George Huene.—Israel, C. E. Gene Allen and George Cukor remember a friend.—Blanch, L. A recollection of George Huene.—Clark, A. A bibliographical list (p. 19) [TR140.H69A23] 73-156907
1. Hoyningen-Huene, George, 1900-1968. 2. Fashion photography. I. Hoyningen-Huene, George, 1900-1968. II. Los Angeles. University of Southern California. Friends of the Libraries.

Fashion—Pictorial works.

VECCHIO, Walter. 687'.1'00222
The fashion makers, a photographic record. Text by Robert Riley. New York, Crown Publishers [1968] ix, 277 p. illus., ports. 29 cm. [TT506.V4] 67-27050
1. Fashion—Pictorial works. 2. Clothing trade—Pictorial works. I. Riley, Robert. II. Title.

Fashion shows.

CORINTH, Katherine 659.15'2
(Clary)
Fashion showmanship; everything you need to know to give a fashion show [by] Kay Corinth. New York, Wiley [1970] vii, 280 p. illus., forms, ports. 24 cm. Bibliography: p. 271-272. [TT502.C68] 76-109430
1. Fashion shows. I. Title.

CURTIS, Frieda Steinmann, 659.153
1898-
How to give a fashion show. New York, Fairchild Publications [1950] vi, 90 p. 22 cm. [TT502.C8] 51-9065
1. Fashion shows. I. Title.

CURTIS, Frieda Steinmann, 659.153
1898-
How to give a fashion show. [2d ed.] New York, Fairchild Publications [1957] 98 p. 23 cm. [TT502.C8 1957] 57-6840
1. Fashion shows. I. Title.

SEBASTIAN, Fannie B 659.152
The fashion festival. Boston, Christopher Pub. House [1962] 86 p. 21 cm. [TT502.S4] 62-17838
1. Fashion shows. 2. Beauty, Personal. I. Title.

Fashion—Vocational guidance.

HAMBURGER, Estelle. 746.9'2
Fashion business : it's all yours / Estelle Hamburger ; illustrated by students at Parsons School of Design. San Francisco : Canfield Press, c1976. xiv, 306 p. : ill. ; 23 cm. [TT507.H173] 76-3549 ISBN 0-06-453500-2 : 5.95
1. Fashion—Vocational guidance. I. Parsons School of Design, New York. II. Title. BIP

SERVIAN, Martha S. 677'.0023
Fashion and textiles careers / Martha S. Servian ; consulting editor, Xenia F. Fane. Englewood Cliffs, N.J. : Prentice-Hall, c1977. p. cm. Includes bibliographies and index. [TT507.S43] 76-23389 ISBN 0-13-392779-2. pbk. : 3.25
1. Fashion—Vocational guidance. 2. Clothing trade—Vocational guidance. 3. Textile industry—Vocational guidance. I. Title.

Fashion—Vocational guidance—Juvenile literature.

CASSIDAY, Doris. 687'.023
Fashion industry careers / by Doris and Bruce Cassiday ; photos. by Chuck Freedman. New York : Watts, 1977. 65 p. : ill. ; 24 cm. (A Career concise guide) Includes index. Bibliography: p. 63. Describes the training and duties of various occupations, from designers to sewers, in the fashion industry. [TT507.C36] 77-5351 ISBN 0-531-01303-0 lib.bdg. : 4.47
1. Fashion—Vocational guidance—Juvenile literature. 2. Clothing trade—Vocational guidance—Juvenile literature. I. Cassiday, Bruce, joint author. II. Freedman, Chuck. III. Title. BIP

Fashions.

DAVES, Jessica. 338.4768712
Ready-made miracle; the American story of fashion for the millions. New York, Putnam [1967] 256 p. illus., facsims., ports. 24 cm. Includes bibliographical references. [TT504.4.D3 1967] 67-15106
1. Fashions. 2. Clothing trade—U.S. I. Title.

Faulkner, Barry, 1881-1966.

FAULKNER, Barry, 1881-1966. 759.13
Barry Faulkner; sketches from an artist's life. Dublin, N.H., W. L. Bauhan, 1973. xiv, 208 p. illus. 25 cm. Autobiography. [ND237.F267A22] 70-162875 ISBN 0-87233-023-0 10.00
1. Faulkner, Barry, 1881-1966. 2. Painters—United States—Correspondence, reminiscences, etc.

Fautrier, Jean, 1808-

BUCARELLI, Palma. 759.4
Jean Fautrier; pittura e materia. Pref. di Giuseppe Ungaretti, 16 illustrazioni a sei colori, 32 illustrazioni in nero, catalogo illustrato con 700 riproduzioni. [1. ed. Milano] Il Saggiatore [1960] 413p. illus., plates (part col.) ports. 22cm. (La Cultura, v. 20) Bibliography: p.203-[210] [ND553.F36B8] 60-39987
1. Fautrier, Jean, 1808- I. Title.

Fautrier. Jean, 1897-

RAGON, Michel. 759.4
Fautrier; twelve reproductions. Edited by J. C. Lambert. Photos. by Luc Joubert. Translated by Haakon Chevalier. New York, Golden Griffin Books, Arts, inc. [1958] 50 p. 12 mounted col. illus. (incl. jacket) 19 cm. (The Pocket museum) [ND553.F36R33] 58-13500
1. Fautrier. Jean, 1897- I. Title. II. Series.

Fauvism.

APOLLONIO, Umbro 754.06
Fauves and cubists. New York, Crown Publishers [1959, i.e., 1960] 93p. (Bibl.: p.89-91.) mounted col. illus. 30cm. 60-50355 7.95 bds.,
1. Fauvism. 2. Cubism. 3. Paintings, French. I. Title.

CRESPELLE, Jean Paul. 759.4
The Fauves. [Translated by Anita Brookner] Greenwich, Conn., New York Graphic Society [1962] 351 p. illus., 100 col. plates. 29 cm. Bibliography: p. 349-351. [ND1265.C713] 62-18719
1. Fauvism. 2. Painting, French. I. Title.

LEYMARIE, Jean. 759.06
Fauvism: biographical and critical study Translated by James Emmons. [New York] Skira [1959] 163 p. mounted col. illus. 19 cm. (The Taste of our time, v. 28) Bibliography: p. 149-[152] [ND1265.L52] 59-7255
1. Fauvism. 2. Paintings.

MULLER, Joseph Emile. 759.06
Fauvism. [Translated from the French by Shirley E. Jones] New York, Praeger [1967] 260 p. 216 illus. (part col.), facsim., ports. 22 cm. (Praeger world of art series) Includes bibliographies. [ND1265.M79] 67-27147
1. Fauvism.

Fauvism—Exhibitions.

ELDERFIELD, John. 759.4
The "wild beasts" : Fauvism and its affinities / John Elderfield. New York : Museum of Modern Art : distributed by Oxford University Press, c1976. 167 p. : ill. (some col.) ; 24 cm. Published on the occasion of an exhibition of Fauvist art held at the Museum of Modern Art, March 26-June 1, 1976, at the San Francisco Museum of Modern Art, June 29-Aug. 15, 1976, and at the Kimbell Art Museum, Fort Worth, Sept. 11-Oct. 31, 1976. Bibliography: p. 161-166. [N6494.F3E42] 76-1491 ISBN 0-19-519889-1 15.00. ISBN 0-19-519890-5 pbk.
1. Fauvism—Exhibitions. 2. Art, Modern—20th century—Exhibitions. I. New York (City). Museum of Modern Art. II. San Francisco Museum of Modern Art. III. Kimbell Art Museum. IV. Title. V. Title: Fauvism. BIP

LEONARD Hutton Galleries. 759.06
Fauves and expressionists [exhibition] April 18-June 12, 1968. [New York, 1968] 64 p. illus. (part col.) 31 cm. [ND196.F3L4] 72-279375
1. Fauvism—Exhibitions. 2. Expressionism (Art)—Exhibitions. I. Title.

Fauvism—France.

OPPLER, Ellen C. 759.06
Fauvism reexamined / Ellen C. Oppler. New York : Garland Pub., 1976. 413, [23] leaves of plates : ill. ; 22 cm. (Outstanding dissertations in the fine arts) Originally presented as the author's thesis, Columbia, 1969. Bibliography: p. 386-406. [NX549.A1O66 1976] 75-23805 ISBN 0-8240-1999-7 lib.bdg. : 30.00
1. Fauvism—France. 2. Arts, Modern—20th century—France. I. Title. II. Series. BIP

Fauvism—History.

DIEHL, Gaston. 759.06
The fauves / Gaston Diehl. New York : H. N. Abrams, 1975. 168 p. : ill. (some col.) ; 34 cm. (The Library of great art movements) Includes index. Bibliography: p. 163[164] [ND196.F3D5313] 72-5650 ISBN 0-8109-0114-5 : 25.00
1. Fauvism—History. 2. Painting, Modern—20th century. I. Title. BIP

Feasts at the Valois court (Tapestries)

YATES, Frances Amelia. 746.3'9493'30740551
The Valois tapestries / Frances A. Yates. 2d ed. London : Routledge & K. Paul, 1975. xxvii, 150 p., [28] leaves of plates : ill. ; 28 cm. Includes bibliographical references and index. [NK3055.V3Y3 1975] 76-359541 ISBN 0-7100-8244-4 : 35.00
1. Feasts at the Valois court (Tapestries) 2. Tapestry, Flemish. I. Title.
Distributed by Routledge and Kegan Paul, Boston BIP

Feather flowers.

WOODS, Pamela. 745.59'43
Flowers from feathers. Illustrated by Michael Woods. New York, Drake [1974, c1973] 128 p. illus. 25 cm. [TT891.W66 1974] 73-6842 ISBN 0-87749-557-2 7.95
1. Feather flowers. I. Title. BIP

Federal aid to historic sites—United States.

NATIONAL Trust for Historic Preservation in the United States. Office of Preservation Services. 338.4'7'06953
A guide to Federal programs for historic preservation : 1976 supplement / Office of Preservation Services ; principal consultant, Nancy D. Schultz ; project coordinators, Russell V. Keune, Peter H. Smith ; assistants, Barbara S. Perry, Theresa M. Profilet. Washington : Preservation Press, 1976. 110 p. ; 28 cm. Includes index. [E159.N356 1976b] 76-383340 ISBN 0-89133-039-9 pbk. : 4.50
1. Federal aid to historic sites—United States. 2. Historic buildings—United States—Conservation and restoration. I. Schultz, Nancy D. II. National Trust for Historic Preservation in the United States. A guide to Federal programs. III. Title. BIP

Federal aid to historic sites—United States—Directories.

NATIONAL Trust for Historic Preservation in the United States. 353.008'5
A guide to Federal programs : programs and activities related to historic preservation / a project of the National Trust for Historic Preservation with the cooperation and assistance of the Advisory Council on Historic Preservation and the Legislative Reference Service, Library of Congress ; principal consultant, Nancy D. Schultz. Washington : The Trust, [1974] 398 p. ; 28 cm. Includes index. [E159.N356 1974] 75-305235
1. Federal aid to historic sites—United States—Directories. 2. Historic sites—Conservation and restoration. I. Schultz, Nancy D. II. United States. Advisory Council on Historic Preservation. III. United States. Library of Congress. Legislative Reference Service. IV. Title.

Federal aid to the arts—U.S.

CULTURAL directory 338.4'7'700973
: guide to federal funds and services for cultural activities / research conducted by Linda Coe. New York : Associated Councils of the Arts, [1975] xii, 340 p. : 28 cm. Published in 1971 under title: Washington and the arts. Includes index. Bibliography: p. 311. [NX735.W3 1975] 75-5577 4.00
1. Federal aid to the arts—United States. I. Coe, Linda, 1945- II. Associated Councils of the Arts.

MELTZER, Milton, 1915- 700'.973
Violins and shovels : the WPA arts projects / by Milton Meltzer. New York : Delacorte Press, [1976] p. cm. Includes index. Bibliography: p. Examines art projects run during the 1930's which were funded by the Work Projects Administration. [NX735.M44] 75-32916 ISBN 0-440-09316-3 : 6.95
1. United States. Work Projects Administration. 2. Federal aid to the arts—United States. 3. Arts, Modern—20th century—United States. I. Title. BIP

NETZER, Dick, 1928- 338.4'7'700973
The subsidized muse : public support for the arts in the United States / Dick Netzer. Cambridge ; New York : Cambridge University Press, 1978. ix, 289 p. ; 24 cm. "A Twentieth Century Fund study." Includes index. bibliography: p. 264-280. [NX730.N4] 77-25441 ISBN 0-521-21966-3 : 14.95
1. National Endowment for the Arts. 2. Federal aid to the arts—United States. 3. Arts—Scholarships, fellowships, etc.—United States. 4. Art commissions—United States. I. Title. BIP

NIXON, Richard Milhous, 1913- 338.4'7'7
The arts: a creative partnership. [Washington, 1971] [10] p. ports. 23 cm. "Text of the President's remarks to the Associated Councils of the Arts, Mayflower Hotel, Washington, D.C., May 26, 1971. [NX735.N5] 72-193667
1. Federal aid to the arts—United States. I. Title.

O'CONNOR, Francis V. 338.4'3
Federal support for the visual arts: the New Deal and now; a report on the New Deal art projects in New York City and State with recommendations for present-day Federal support for the visual arts to the National Endowment for the Arts ... By Francis V. O'Connor. 2d ed. Greenwich, Conn., New York Graphic Society, 1971 [c1969] viii, 227 p. illus. 28 cm. Bibliography: p. 209-227. [N8837.O26 1971] 72-175175 ISBN 0-8212-0347-9
1. Federal Art Project. 2. Federal aid to the arts—U.S. I. National Endowment for the Arts. II. Title.

UNITED States. Library of Congress. Education and Public Welfare Division. 338.4'7'7
"Millions for the arts"; Federal & State cultural programs, an exhaustive Senate report. Washington, Washington international arts letter [1972] 58 p. 28 cm. (Arts patronage series) Reprint, with new introd., of pts. 2-3 of its Survey of United States and foreign government support for cultural activities. [NX730.A47] 72-78232
1. Federal aid to the arts—United States. 2. State encouragement of science, literature, and art—United States. I. Title. II. Series.

Federal Art Project.

MCKINZIE, Richard D. 338.4'7'70973
The New Deal for artists [by] Richard D. McKinzie. [Princeton] Princeton University Press [1973] xii, 203 p. illus. 23 x 27 cm. Includes bibliographical references. [N8838.M32] 70-39053 ISBN 0-691-04613-1 17.50
1. Federal Art Project. 2. Federal aid to the arts—United States. I. Title. BIP

THE New Deal art projects; an anthology of memoirs. Edited by Francis V. O'Connor. Washington, Smithsonian Institution, 1972. ix, 339 p. illus. 28 cm. Bibliography: p. 330-331. [N8838.N4] 72-181525 ISBN 0-87474-113-0 12.50 709'.73
1. Federal Art Project. I. O'Connor, Francis V., ed. BIP

O'CONNOR, Francis V. 338.4'3
Federal support for the visual arts: the New Deal and now; a report on the New Deal art projects in New York City and State with recommendations for present-day Federal support for the visual arts to the National Endowment for the Arts ... By Francis V. O'Connor. 2d ed. Greenwich, Conn., New York Graphic Society, 1971 [c1969] viii, 227 p. illus. 28 cm. Bibliography: p. 209-227. [N8837.O26 1971] 72-175175 ISBN 0-8212-0347-9
1. Federal Art Project. 2. Federal aid to the arts—U.S. I. National Endowment for the Arts. II. Title.

O'CONNOR, Francis V. 338.4'7'7
Federal support for the visual arts: the New Deal and now; a report on the New Deal art projects in New York City and State with recommendations for present-day Federal support for the visual arts to the National Endowment for the Arts. By Francis V. O'Connor. Greenwich, Conn., New York Graphic Society, 1969. viii, 226 p. illus. 28 cm. Bibliography: p. 209-226. [N6512.O25] 76-109702
1. Federal Art Project. 2. Art and state—U.S. I. National Endowment for the Arts. II. Title.

Federal Art Project—Exhibitions.

DECORDOVA and Dana Museum and Park, Lincoln, Mass. 709'.74'07401444
By the people, for the people : New England, September 25-November 27, 1977, DeCordova Museum, Lincoln, Massachusetts. Lincoln, Mass. : The Museum, c1977. 92 p. : ill. ; 25 cm. "Catalog and exhibition." Includes bibliographical references. [N8838.D38 1977] 77-88006
1. Federal Art Project—Exhibitions. 2. Art, American—New England—Exhibitions. 3. Art, Modern—20th century—New England—Exhibitions. I. Title.

Federal Art Project. New York (City)

BERMAN, Greta. 751.7'3'097471
The lost years : mural painting in New York City under the Works Progress Administration's Federal Art Project, 1935-1943 / Greta Berman. New York : Garland Pub., [1978] p. cm. (Outstanding dissertations in the fine arts) Originally presented as the author's thesis, Columbia, 1975. Bibliography: p. [ND2638.N4B37 1978] 77-94687 ISBN 0-8240-3216-0 : lib.bdg. : 37.50
1. Federal Art Project. New York (City) 2. Mural painting and decoration—New York (City) 3. Mural painting and decoration, American—New York (City) I. Title. II. Series. BIP

Fei, Paolo di Giovanni, ca. 1345-1411.

MALLORY, Michael. 759.5
The Sienese painter Paolo di Giovanni Fei (c. 1345-1411) / Michael Mallory. New York : Garland Pub., 1976. iii, 248 p., [27] leaves of plates : ill. ; 21 cm. (Outstanding dissertations in the fine arts) Originally presented as the author's thesis, Columbia University, 1965, under the title: Paolo di Giovanni Fei. Includes bibliographies. [ND623.F275M25 1976] 75-23802 ISBN 0-8240-1997-0 lib.bdg. : 27.50

1. Fei, Paolo di Giovanni, ca. 1345-1411. I. Title. II. Series. BIP

Feininger, Andreas, 1906—

FEININGER, Andreas, 1906- 779'.092'4
Andreas Feininger : a retrospective / with an introd. by Bhupendra Karia. New York : International Center of Photography, [1976] p. cm. "Catalogue of an exhibition shown in the International Center of Photography in the fall of 1976." Includes index. Bibliography: p. [TR647.F44 1976] 76-43006 6.00
1. Feininger, Andreas, 1906- 2. Photography, Artistic—Exhibitions. I. Karia, Bhupendra, 1936- II. International Center of Photography.

Feininger, Lyonel Charles Adrian, 1871-1956.

FEININGER, Lyonel Charles Adrian, 1871-1956. 759.13
Lyonel Feininger. Edited by June L. Ness. New York, Praeger [1974] 264 p. illus. (part col.) 23 cm. (Documentary monographs in modern art) Bibliography: p. 257-260. [ND237.F33N47] 72-88673 ISBN 0-275-43570-9 13.50
1. Feininger, Lyonel Charles Adrian, 1871-1956. 2. Painters—United States—Correspondence, reminiscences, etc. I. Ness, June L., ed.

FEININGER, Lyonel Charles Adrian, 1871-1956. 759.13
Lyonel Feininger, 1871-1956 : [exhibition], March 13-April 11, 1976. Palm Beach : Society of the Four Arts, [1976] [20] p. : ill. ; 24 cm. "Lent by the Museum of Modern Art, New York, the Brooklyn Museum, New York, the Whitney Museum of American Art, New York." [N6537.F37S6] 77-357821
1. Feininger, Lyonel Charles Adrian, 1871-1956. I. Society of the Four Arts.

FEININGER, Lyonel Charles Adrian, 1871-1956. 760'.092'4
Lyonel Feininger; a definitive catalogue of his graphic work: etchings, lithographs, woodcuts. Das graphische Werk: Radierungen, Lithographien, Holzschnitte [by] Leona E. Prasse. [German translations by Annegret Janda. Cleveland] Cleveland Museum of Art; [distributed by Press of Case Western Reserve University, 1972] 304 p. illus. 31 cm. On spine: Feininger: his graphic work. Introductory matter in English and German. Errata slip inserted. Bibliography: p. 285-286. [NE539.F44P72] 74-108899 ISBN 0-910386-18-8
1. Feininger, Lyonel Charles Adrian, 1871-1956. I. Prasse, Leona E. II. Title: Feininger: his graphic work.

FEININGER, Lyonel Charles Adrian, 1871-1956. 760'.0924
The ruin by the sea. Introd. by Eila Kokkinen. Selections of drawings and prints edited by William S. Lieberman. [1st ed.] New York, Museum of Modern Art [1968] 32 p. illus. (part col.) 16 cm. [NC139.F4L5] 68-14668
I. Kokkinen, Eila. II. Lieberman, William Slattery, 1924- III. New York (City). Museum of Modern Art. IV. Title.

FEININGER, T. Lux 709.24
Lyonel Feininger: city at the edge of the world. Text by T. Lux Feininger. Photos. by Andreas Feininger. New York, Praeger [c.1965] 121p. illus. (pt. col.) ports. 27cm. [ND237.F33F4] 65-25280 14.95; 11.95 until Dec. 31.
1. Feininger, Lyonel Charles Adrian, 1871-1956. I. Feininger, Andreas, 1906- illus. II. Title.

HESS, Hans. 759.13
Lyonel Feininger. new byork, Abrams [1961] xvi, 354p. illus. (pt. col.) 31cm. Bibl. 61-9389 20.00
1. Feininger(Lyonel Charles Adrian, 1871-1956. I. Title.

NEW York (City) Museum of Modern Art. 759.13
Lyonel Feininger, with essays by Alois J. Schardt and Alfred H. Barr, Jr., and excerpts from the artist's letters. Edited by Dorothy C. Miller. Marsden Hartley, with statements by the artist [and] foreword by Monroe Wheeler. Reprint ed. [New York] Published for the Museum of Modern Art by Arno Press, 1966 [c1944] 95 p. illus. 27 cm. Title on spine: Feininger-Hartley. Includes catalogs of the artists' works exhibited at the Museum of Modern Art, ca. 1944. Includes bibliographies. [ND236] 66-26122
1. Feininger, Lyonel Charles Adrian, 1871-1956. 2. Hartley, Marsden, 1877-1943. I. Schardt, Alois Jakob, 1889- II. Barr, Alfred Hamilton, 1902- III. Miller, Dorothy Canning, 1904- ed.

PASADENA, Calif. Art Museum. 760'.0924
Lyonel Feininger, 1871-1956; a memorial exhibition: Pasadena Art Museum, April 26-May 29, 1966; Milwaukee Art Center, July 10-August 11, 1966; Baltimore Museum of Art, September 7-October 23, 1966. [Alhambra, Calif., Printed by the Cunningham Press for the Pasadena Art Museum. 1966] [64] p. illus. (part col.), port. 27 cm. Bibliography: p. [16]-[17] [N6537.F37P3] 71-4146
1. Feininger, Lyonel Charles Adrian, 1871-1956. I. Baltimore. Museum of Art. II. Milwaukee. Art Center.

SCHEYER, Ernst, 1900- 741.0973
Lyonel Feininger: caricature & fantasy. Detroit, Wayne State University Press, 1964. x, 196 p. illus. (part col.) facsims., ports. 24 cm. Bibliography: p. 189-191. [ND237.F33S3] 64-15880
1. Feininger, Lyonel Charles Adrian, 1871-1956. BIP

Feke, Robert, 1705 (ca.)-1750.

FOOTE, Henry Wilder, 1875- 759.13 B
Robert Feke, colonial portrait painter. New York, Kennedy Galleries, 1969 [c1930] xix, 223 p. illus., geneal. table. 27 cm. (Library of American art) Bibliographical footnotes. [ND237.F35F6 1969] 72-75357
1. Feke, Robert, 1705 (ca.)-1750. BIP

Feldman, Lou.

FELDMAN, Lou. 779'.092'4
Camera eye-deas of Lou Feldman. [Worcester? Mass.] : Feldman, 1978. 124 p. : chiefly ill. ; 28 cm. [TR654.F45] 78-109102 17.95
1. Feldman, Lou. 2. Photography, Artistic. I. Title.

Fell, John Bp. of Oxford, 1625-1686.

CARTER, Harry Graham. 655.2'4
The Fell types; what has been done in and about them [by] Harry Carter. New York, Oxford University Press, 1968. 25 p. illus. 16 cm. [Z250.A2C35] 68-58716
1. Fell, John Bp. of Oxford, 1625-1686. I. Title.

OXFORD University Press. 686'.224
Notes on a century of typography at the University Press, Oxford, 1693-1794, by Horace Hart. [1st ed. reprinted ; with an introduction and additional notes by Harry Carter. Oxford, Clarendon Press, 1970. ix, 16, xvi, 203 p., plate. illus. facsims., port. 33 cm. Includes bibliographical references. [Z232.O98A55] 70-24174 ISBN 0-19-818138-8 £10.00
1. Fell, John, Bp. of Oxford, 1625-1686. 2. Type and type-founding. 3. Printing—Specimens. I. Hart, Horace, 1840-1916. II. Title. BIP

Fellig Arthur, 1900-1968.

FELLIG, Arthur, 1900-1968. 770'.92'4 B
Weegee : an autobiography / by Weegee [i.e. A. Fellig]. New York : Da Capo Press, 1975, c1961. 159 p., [28] leaves of plates : ill. ; 23 cm. Reprint of the ed. published by Ziff-Davis Pub. Co., New York. [TR140.F4A3 1975] 75-4885 ISBN 0-306-70737-3 lib.bdg. : 11.95
1. Fellig, Arthur, 1900-

FELLIG, Arthur, 1900-1968. 779'.092'4
Weegee. Millerton, N.Y. : Aperture, c1978. 95 p. : chiefly ill. ; 21 cm. (The Aperture history of photography series ; 8) Bibliography: p. 95. [TR820.F46] 77-80020 ISBN 0-89381-021-5 : 7.95
1. Fellig, Arthur, 1900-1968. 2. Photography, Journalistic.

FELLIG, Arthur, 1900-1968. 779'.92'4
Weegee / [compiled and edited] by Louis Stettner. New York : Knopf, 1977. p. cm. Bibliography: p. [TR820.F45 1977] 77-75356 ISBN 0-394-40770-9 : 15.00 ISBN 0-394-73322-3 pbk. : 8.95
1. Fellig, Arthur, 1900-1968. 2. Photography, Journalistic. I. Stettner, Louis, 1922-

Felt marker decoration.

TORBET, Laura. 745.7
How to do everything with markers / by Laura Torbet. Indianapolis : Bobbs-Merrill, c1976. 200 p. : ill. ; 29 cm. [TT386.T67] 76-4169 ISBN 0-672-52143-1 : 12.50
1. Felt marker decoration. I. Title. BIP

Felt work.

GOLDMAN, Phyllis W. 746.9
Decorate with felt [by] Phyllis W. Goldman. New York, Crowell [1973] 136 p. illus. 24 cm. [TT880.G63 1973] 73-9848 ISBN 0-690-00084-7 4.95
1. Felt work. 2. Interior decoration—Amateurs' manuals. I. Title.

GOLDMAN, Phyllis W. 745.5
Make it from felt [by] Phyllis W. Goldman. New York, Crowell [1971] 135 p. illus. 27 cm. Instrutions for making various accessories, decorations, and toys from felt. [TT880.G64 1971] 70-170994 ISBN 0-690-51144-2 6.95
1. Felt work. I. Title.

JANVIER, Jacqueline. 746.4
Felt crafting. New York, Sterling Pub. Co. [1970] 48 p. illus. 20 cm. (Little craft book series) Translation of Travaux en feutrine. Directions for making pictures, toys, games, and decorative scenes with felt cut-outs. [TT880.J3513 1970] 79-90805
1. Felt work. I. Title.

LAMMER, Jutta. 746'.04'62
Fun with felt. New York, Watson-Guptill Publications [1969, c1968] 57 p. illus. (part col.) 19 cm. Translation of Alles aus Filz. Instructions for making a variety of useful and decorative items from felt, such as baby shoes, wall hangings, and dolls. [TT880.L3213] 76-118115 ISBN 0-8230-1975-6 3.50
1. Felt work. I. Title.

SOMMER, Elyse. 746'.04'63
A new look at felt : applique, stitchery, and sculpture / by Elyse and Mike Sommer. New York : Crown Publishers, [1975] 120 p. : ill. ; 29 cm. Includes index. Bibliography: p. 115. [TT880.S664 1975] 75-11794 ISBN 0-517-51860-0 : 6.95 ISBN 0-517-51861-9 pbk. : 4.95
1. Felt work. I. Sommer, Mike, joint author. II. Title.

Felt work—Juvenile literature.

*GOLDMAN, Phyllis W. 746.046
Make it from felt [by] Phyllis W. Goldman. New York, Funk & Wagnalls [1974, c1971] 135 p. illus. 26 cm. [TT880] 74-3656 ISBN 0-308-10135-9. 2.50 (pbk.)
1. Felt work—Juvenile literature. I. Title.

NEWSOME, Arden J. 746'.04'632
Make it with felt; an art and craft book, written and illustrated by Arden J. Newsome. New York, Lothrop, Lee & Shepard Co. [1972] 96 p. illus. 25 cm. Directions for making a variety of games, toys, household and personal effects from felt. [TT880.N48] 77-181892 4.25
1. Felt work—Juvenile literature. I. Title.

TEMKO, Florence. 746'.04'63
Felt craft. Illustrated by Steve Madison. [1st ed.] Garden City, N.Y., Doubleday [1973] 64 p. illus. (part col.) 22 cm. (Crafts for children) Instructions for creating a variety of items from felt. [TT880.T46] 73-78675 ISBN 0-385-03464-4 4.95
1. Felt work—Juvenile literature. I. Madison, Steve, illus. II. Title. BIP

Felton, Alfred, 1831-1904.

LINDSAY, Daryl, 1890- 708.994
The Felton bequest, an historical record, 1904-1959. New York, Oxford [1964] x, 105p. illus., plates, ports. 23cm. 64-3451 5.50
1. Felton, Alfred, 1831-1904. 2. Victoria, Australia. National Gallery, Melbourne. I. Title. BIP

Feminism and the arts—Addresses, essays, lectures.

LIPPARD, Lucy R. 704.042
From the center : feminist essays on women's art / Lucy R. Lippard. New York : Dutton, c1976. vi, 314 p., [4] leaves of plates : ill. (some col.) ; 21 cm. Includes bibliographical references and index. [NX180.F4L56 1976] 76-150915 ISBN 0-525-47427-7 : 6.95
1. Feminism and the arts—Addresses, essays, lectures. I. Title. BIP

Femmes fatales in art.

BADE, Patrick. 700'.9'034
The femme fatale / by Patrick Bade. New York : Mayflower Books, 1979. p. cm. [NX650.F46B32] 78-11577 ISBN 0-8317-3250-4 : 14.95
1. Femmes fatales in art. 2. Arts, Modern—19th century. I. Title. BIP

Fences.

SCHMIDT, Carl Frederick, 1894- 717
Fences, gates, and garden houses. Rochester, N. Y., 1963. 106 l. (chiefly illus., diagrs.) 29 cm. [NA8390.S3] 63-24488
1. Fences. 2. Gates. 3. Architecture, Domestic—U. S. I. Title.

SCHULER, Stanley. 717
How to build fences, gates, and walls / by Stanley Schuler. New York : Collier Books, 1976. 182 p. : ill. ; 28 cm. Includes index. [TH4965.S37 1976b] 75-35662 4.95
1. Fences. 2. Gates. 3. Walls. I. Title. BIP

SCHULER, Stanley. 717
How to build fences, gates, and walls / by Stanley Schuler. New York : Macmillan, c1976. 182 p. : ill. ; 28 cm. Includes index. [TH4965.S37 1976] 75-35660 ISBN 0-02-607370-6 : 13.50
1. Fences. 2. Gates. 3. Walls. I. Title.

STONNELL, Richard D 631.2'7
Fences for outdoor living, by Richard D. Stonnell. New York, Simmons-Boardman Pub. Corp. [1964] 96 p. illus. 28 cm. [NA8390.S7] 64-8663
1. Fences. I. Title.

SUNSET. 717.85
How to build fences and gates. [2d ed.] Menlo Park, Calif., Lane Pub. Co. [1958] 112 p. illus. 28 cm. (A Sunset book) [S723.S9 1958] 58-9946
1. Fences. 2. Gates. I. Title.

VON MIKLOS, Josephine (Bogdan) 1900- 717
Good fences make good neighbors. Photos. & text by Josephine von Miklos. New York, Scribner [1972] vii, 117 p. illus. 22 cm. [NA8390.V65 1972] 72-503 ISBN 0-684-12935-3 7.95
1. Fences. I. Title.

Fenderich, Charles

U.S. Library of Congress. Prints and Photographs Division. 769.973
Charles Fenderich, lithographer of American statesmen; a catalog of his work, by Alice Lee Parker and Milton Kaplan. Washington, 1959. ii, 64 p. plates, ports., facsims. 27 cm. [NE2415.F4U5] 59-60089

1. Fenderich, Charles I. Parker, Alice Lee. II. Kaplan, Milton, 1918- III. Title. BIP

Fenderich, Charles—Catalogs.

FENDERICH, Charles. 769'.92'4
Charles Fenderich, lithographer of American statesmen / by Alice Lee Parker and Milton Kaplan ; edited and with a foreword by Lillian B. Miller. Chicago : University of Chicago Press, 1978. ix, 68 p. ; 23 cm. & microfiche (3 sheets : all. ill. ; 11 x 15 cm.) in pocket. (Chicago visual library ; 23) "Adapted from Charles Fenderich, lithographer of American statesmen ... (Washington, D.C. : Library of Congress, 1959)." At head of title: The Library of Congress. [NE2364.5.F46A4 1978] 76-24470 ISBN 0-226-69243-4 : 25.00
1. Fenderich, Charles—Catalogs. I. Parker, Alice Lee. II. Kaplan, Milton. III. United States. Library of Congress. Prints and Photographs Division. Charles Fenderich, lithographer of American statesmen. IV. Title.

Fenollosa, Ernest Francisco, 1853-1908.

CHISOLM, Lawrence W. 709'.2'4 B
Fenollosa : the Far East and American culture / by Lawrence W. Chisolm. Westport, Conn. : Greenwood Press, 1976. p. cm. Reprint of the 1963 ed. published by Yale University Press, New Haven, which was issued as 8 of Yale publications in American studies. Includes index. Bibliography: p. [N7483.F43C47 1976] 76-22680 ISBN 0-8371-8975-6 lib.bdg. : 19.75
1. Fenollosa, Ernest Francisco, 1853-1908. 2. Art, Far Eastern—United States. 3. East and West. I. Series: Yale publications in American studies ; 8.

Ferargil Galleries, New York.

PRICE, Frederic Newlin. 708.147
Goodbye Ferargil. New Hope, Pa., Huffnagle Press [1958] unpaged. illus: 25cm. [N8660.F4P7] 58-30027
1. Ferargil Galleries, New York. 2. Art dealers. 3. Artists— Correspondence, reminiscences, etc. I. Title.

Ferber, Herbert, 1906-

ANDERSEN, Wayne V 730.973
The sculpture of Herbert Ferber, Itinerary: Walker Art Center, Apr. 15 to May 27, 1962 [and others] Minneapolis, Walker Art Center [1962] 64 p. illus. 24 cm. Includes bibliography. [NB237.F43A5] 62-15410
1. Ferber, Herbert, 1906- I. Walker Art Center, Minneapolis. II. Title.

Fernandez, Augustin, 1928—

FERNANDEZ, Agustin, 759.97291
1928-
Agustin Fernandez, by R. C. Kenedy. Joseph A. Novak, editor. [New York, Printed by Rapoport Print. Corp., 1973] 1 v. (unpaged) illus. 28 cm. Includes bibliography. [N6605.F47K46] 73-77897
1. Fernandez, Agustin, 1928- I. Kenedy, R. C.

FERNANDEZ, Armand, 1928- 709'.2'4
Arman; or, four and twenty blackbirds baked in a pie; or, Why settle for less when you can settle for more. Text by Henry Martin. New York, H. N. Abrams [1973?] 200 p. illus. (part col.) 28 x 30 cm. Bibliography: p. 199-200. [N6853.F4M37] 73-101619 ISBN 0-8109-0026-2 35.00
I. Fernandez, Armand, 1928- I. Martin, Henry, fl. 1972- II. Title.

FERNANDEZ, Armand, 1928- 709'.2'4
Arman—selected works, 1958-1974 : an exhibition organized by the La Jolla Museum of Contemporary Art, La Jolla, California, September 15-October 29, 1974. [La Jolla, Calif. : La Jolla Museum of Contemporary Art, 1974] [48] p. : chiefly ill. (some col.) ; 28 cm. Errata slip inserted. Bibliography: p. [45] [N6853.F4L34] 74-18537
1. Fernandez, Armand, 1928- I. La Jolla Museum of Contemporary Art. II. Title.

Ferns.

KRAMER, Jack, 1927- 747'.9
Ferns and palms for interior decoration. Drawings by Michael Valdez (unless otherwise stated) New York, Scribner [1972] xii, 113 p. illus. 28 cm. [SB429.K7] 72-326 ISBN 0-684-12930-2 6.95
1. Ferns. 2. Palms. 3. House plants in interior decoration. I. Title.
Pbk. 3.95, ISBN 0-684-12931-0 BIP

Feron, Louis, 1901—

FERON, Louis, 1901- 739.2'092'4
Louis Feron, goldsmith, jeweler, sculptor. Manchester, N.H. : Currier Gallery of Art, c1977. [38] p. : ill. ; 26 cm. "[Exhibition] February 20-March 20, 1977, the Currier Gallery of Art, Manchester, New Hampshire." "Catalogue" : p. [12]-[22] [NK7198.F37C87] 77-72761
1. Feron, Louis, 1901- 2. Goldwork—United States—Exhibitions. I. Currier Gallery of Art, Manchester, N.H.

Ferrer, Rafael.

FERRER, Rafael. 709'.2'4
Deseo; an adventure [by] Rafael Ferrer. With an essay by Carter Ratcliff, and an autobiography by Rafael Ferrer. Cincinnati, Ohio, Contemporary Arts Center [1973] 56 p. illus. (part col.) 26 cm. Catalog of an exhibition held at the Contemporary Arts Center, Cincinnati, 1973. Bibliography: p. 56. [N6614.F47R37] 73-174154
1. Ferrer, Rafael. I. Ratcliff, Carter. II. Contemporary Arts Center, Cincinnati. III. Title.

FERRER, Rafael. 709'.24
Enclosures. [Exhibition] September 25 to October 30, 1971. Philadelphia, Institute of Contemporary Art, University of Pennsylvania [1971] [22] p. illus. 22 x 28 cm. Label mounted on p. [1]: Supplied by Worldwide Books, inc., Boston. [N6614.F47P4] 70-198438
I. Pennsylvania. University. Institute of Contemporary Art. II. Title.

Ferris, Keith—Catalogs.

FERRIS, Keith. 759.13
The aviation art of Keith Ferris / introd. by Keith Ferris ; [edited by Ian Ballantine]. 1st ed. New York : Peacock Press/Bantam Books, 1978. [95] p. : ill. (some col.) ; 23 x 29 cm. [ND237.F38A4 1978] 78-105758 7.95
1. Ferris, Keith—Catalogs. 2. Airplanes in art—Catalogs. 3. Airplanes—Pictorial works—Catalogs. I. Ballantine, Ian. II. Title. BIP

Feshin, Nikolai Ivanovich, 1881-1955.

BALCOMB, Mary N. 759.13
Nicolai Fechin / by Mary N. Balcomb ; with a foreword by Eya Fechin Branham. 1st ed. [Flagstaff, Ariz.] : Northland Press, c1975. xxiv, 167 p. : chiefly ill. (some col.) ; 32 cm. Bibliography: p. 165-167. [ND699.F43B34] 75-11161 ISBN 0-87358-140-7 : 40.00
1. Feshin, Nikolai Ivanovich, 1881-1955. I. Feshin, Nikolai Ivanovich, 1881-1955. BIP

Festivals—Great Britain.

ARTS Council of Great 700'.25'41
Britain.
A list of festivals in Great Britain with forecast dates / [Arts Council of Great Britain]. 6th ed. London : The Council, 1976. iv, 33 p. ; 30 cm. Cover title. [GT4843.A77 1976] 77-363443 ISBN 0-7287-0104-9 : £0.30
1. Festivals—Great Britain. I. Title.

Fiberwork.

HAMAMURA, John. 746.1'4
Woven works / by John and Susan Hamamura. San Francisco : Chronicle Books, c1978. 95 p. : col. ill. ; 22 x 24 cm. "A Prism edition." Bibliography: p. 93. [N7433.9.H35] 78-17163 ISBN 0-87701-118-4 : 14.95
1. Fiberwork. 2. Weaving. I. Hamamura, Susan, joint author. II. Title. BIP

WALLER, Irene. 730'.92'2 B
Textile sculptures / Irene Waller. New York : Taplinger Pub. Co., 1977. 160 p. : ill. (some col.) ; 29 cm. Bibliography: p. 160. [N6494.F47W34 1977b] 77-71688 ISBN 0-8008-7579-6 : 17.50
1. Fiberwork. 2. Art, Modern—20th century. 3. Artists—Biography. BIP

Field, Saul, 1912—

FIELD, Saul, 1912- 769'.92'4
Bloomsday, by Saul Field and Morton Levitt. Greenwich, Conn., New York Graphic Society [1972] 119 p. illus. (part col.) 41 cm. [NE543.F53L48] 72-80414 ISBN 0-8212-0451-3 27.50
1. Field, Saul, 1912- 2. Joyce, James, 1882-1941. Ulysses—Illustrations. I. Levitt, Morton, joint author. II. Title.

Fiesole, Giovanni da, called Fra Angelico, 1387-1455.

FIESOLE, Giovanni da, [759.5]
called Fra Angelico, 1387-1455.
Fra Angelico, by John Pope-Hennessy. New York, Phaidon Publishers, distributed by Garden City Books, [1952.] 213p. illus., plates (part col.) 31 cm. Addendum slip inserted at p. 203. Catalogue: p. 165-207. Bibliography: p. 164. [ND623.F5P65] 927.5 55-7818
I. Pope-Hennessy, John, 1913- II. Title.

FIESOLE, Giovanni da, 759.5
called Fra Angelico, 1387-1455.
Fra Angelico / John Pope-Hennessy. 2d ed. Ithaca, N.Y. : Cornell University Press, 1974. vi, 242 p., [32] leaves of plates : ill. (some col.) ; 32 cm. "Catalogue": p. 189-239. Includes index. Bibliography: p. 188. [ND623.F5P65 1974] 74-9200 ISBN 0-8014-0855-5 : 42.50
1. Fiesole, Giovanni da, called Fra Angelico, 1387-1455. I. Pope-Hennessy, John Wyndham, Sir, 1913-

Fifty-six Group Wales.

FIFTY-SIX Group Wales. 709'.2'2
The artist and how to employ him / 56 Group Wales. [Cardiff : The Group], 1976. 64 p. : ill. (some col.), ports. ; 30 cm. [N6792.F53 1976] 76-381122 ISBN 0-9505005-0-X : £1.95
1. Fifty-six Group Wales. 2. Art, Modern—20th century—Wales—Exhibitions. I. Title.

Figurative art—Exhibitions.

EXTRAORDINARY realities, 759.13
by Robert Doty. With a pref. by Edward Gorey. New York, Whitney Museum of American Art [1973] 67 p. illus. (part col.) 21 cm. Catalog of an exhibition shown at the Whitney Museum of American Art, Oct. 16-Dec. 2, 1973; the Everson Museum of Art, Syracuse, N.Y., Jan. 15-Feb. 18, 1974; and the Contemporary Arts Center, Cincinnati, Mar. 8-Apr. 27, 1974. [ND212.5.F5E97] 73-85128 4.00 (pbk.)
1. Figurative art—Exhibitions. 2. Figurative art—United States. 3. Painting, Modern—20th century—United States. I. Doty, Robert M. II. Whitney Museum of American Art, New York. III. Everson Museum of Art of Syracuse and Onondaga County. IV. Contemporary Arts Center, Cincinnati.

Figurative art—United States.

AMERICAN Federation of 759.13
Arts.
Painterly realism. [Exhibition selected by Bill Sullivan, circulation consultant] Organized and circulated by the American Federation of Arts. New York [1970] 1 v. (unpaged) illus. 26 cm. Held at the Smith College Museum of Art. [ND212.A52] 71-114435
1. Figurative art—United States. 2. Paintings, American—Exhibitions. I. Sullivan, Bill, 1942- II. Smith College. Museum of Art. III. Title. BIP

GESKE, Norman A. 708.13'0945'3
Venice 34. The figurative tradition in recent American art, by Norman A. Geske. Washington, Published for the National Collection of Fine Arts by the Smithsonian Institution Press [1968] 131 p. illus. (part col.), ports. 27 cm. American exhibition prepared for the XXXIV International Biennial Exhibition of Art, Venice, Italy, 1968. Sponsored by the National Collection of Fine Arts and the Sheldon Memorial Art Gallery of the University of Nebraska at Lincoln. Contents.Contents.—Introduction, by N. A. Geske.—Leonard Baskin.—Byron Burford.—Robert Cremean.—Edwin Dickinson.—Richard Diebenkorn.—Frank Gallo.—Red Grooms.—James McGarrell.—Reuben Nakian.—Fairfield Porter.—Catalog of the exhibition (p. 123-130) Includes bibliographies. [N6512.G4] 68-61295 10.00
1. Figurative art—United States. 2. Figurative art—Exhibitions. I. Smithsonian Institution. National Collection of Fine Arts. II. Nebraska. University. Sheldon Memorial Art Gallery. III. Venice. Biennale d'arte, 34th, 1968. IV. Title. V. Title: The figurative tradition in recent American art.

Figure drawing.

ANTHONY, William 1934- 743.4
A new approach to figure drawing. New York, Crown Publishers [1965] 112 p. illus. 29 cm. [NC765.A62] 65-15841
1. Figure drawing. I. Title.

BLACK, Arthur, 1892- 743.4
How to draw the human figure. New York, McGraw-Hill, 1950. ix, 169 p. illus. 26 cm. [NC765.B55] 50-8295
1. Figure drawing. I. Title.

*BRIDGMAN, George Brant, 743.4
1864-1943
Life drawing. New York, Barnes & Noble [1966.c.1924.1961] 159p. illus. 21cm. (Everyday handbk. no. 304) 1.00 pap.,
I. Title.

DOBKIN, Alexander, 1908- 743'.4
Principles of figure drawing. Rev. ed. New York, Funk & Wagnalls [1975] 258 p. illus. 29 cm. [NC765.D57 1975] 74-16373 ISBN 0-308-10084-0 10.00
1. Figure drawing. I. Title. BIP

GOLDSTEIN, Nathan. 743'.4
Figure drawing : the structure, anatomy, and expressive design of human form / Nathan Goldstein. Englewood Cliffs, N.J. : Prentice-Hall, c1976. x, 293 p. : ill. ; 29 cm. Includes index. Bibliography: p. 285. [NC765.G64] 75-17786 ISBN 0-13-314765-7 : 12.95
1. Figure drawing. I. Title.

HALE, Robert Beverly, 1901- 741.4
Drawing lessons from the great masters. New York, Watson-Guptill [c.1964] 271p. illus. 29cm. [NC765.H15] 64-24246 10.00
1. Figure drawing. 2. Human figure in art. 3. Anatomy, Artistic. I. Title. BIP

HAMM, Jack 743.4
Drawing the head and figure. New York, Grosset [c.1963] 120p. illus. 29cm. 63-8124 1.95; 2.60 pap., lib. ed.,
1. Figure drawing. I. Title.

HOGARTH, Burne. 743'.43
Dynamic figure drawing. New York, Watson-Guptill Publications [1970] 176 p. illus. 29 cm. [NC765.H63] 73-87324 ISBN 0-8230-1575-0 9.95
1. Figure drawing. I. Title. BIP

JELLICO, John. 743'.4
Figure drawing. Serial 6485-1. [Ed. 2] Scranton, International Correspondence Schools [1969] 50 p. illus. 26 cm. [NC760.J4 1969] 74-25979
1. Figure drawing.

KRAMER, Jack. 743'.4
Human anatomy & figure drawing; the integration of structure and form. New York, Van Nostrand Reinhold Co. [1972]

143 p. illus. 29 cm. Bibliography: p. 139. [NC765.K7 1972] 73-162680
1. Figure drawing. 2. Anatomy, Artistic. I. Title. BIP

MORE figures in art. 741.9'24
Introd. by Emanuel Borden. [1st ed.] Alhambra, Calif., Borden Pub. Co. [1968] [48] p. (chiefly illus.) 31 cm. (Master draughtsman series) [NC760.M535] 68-28185
1. Figure drawing. I. Borden Publishing Company. BIP

OLIVER, Charles, 1911- 743'.4
Anatomy and perspective; the fundamentals of figure drawing. New York, Viking Press [1972] 96 p. illus. 25 cm. (A Studio book) Bibliography: p. 95 [NC760.O4] 77-185280 ISBN 0-670-12224-6 7.95
1. Figure drawing. 2. Anatomy, Artistic. 3. Perspective. I. Title.

PERARD, Victor Semon, 1870- 743.4
Figure drawing 2d ed. New York, Pitman [1956] unpaged. illus. 20x 26cm. (Pitman drawing series) [NC765.P4 1956] 56-12128
1. Figure drawing. I. Title. BIP

PERARD, Victor Semon, 1870-1957. 743.4
Figure drawing comes to life; a series of experiments in drawing the figure conducted by Calvin Albert, interpreted in a text by Dorothy Gees Seckler. New York, Pitman [1956] unpaged. illus. 20 x 26 cm. (Pitman drawing series) [NC765.P4 1956] 56-12128
1. Figure drawing.

PITZ, Henry Clarence, 1895- 743.4
How to use the figure in painting and illustration. New York. Reinhold [c.1965] 144p. illus. (pt. col.) 29cm. [NC765.P5] 65-12976 12.50
1. Figure drawing. 2. Figure painting. 3. Human figure in art. I. Title.

PITZ, Henry Clarence, 1895- 743.4
How to use the figure in painting and illustration, by Henry C. Pitz. New York, Reinhold [1965] 144 p. illus. (part col.) 29 cm. [NC765.P5] 65-12976
1. Figure drawing. 2. Figure painting. 3. Human figure in art. I. Title.

RAYNES, John, 1929- 701
Figures. [1st American ed. New York, Watson-Guptill Publications, 1965] 56 p. illus. 18 x 20 cm. (Watson-Guptill drawing books) Cover title: Drawing figures. [NC765.R3] 65-19000
1. Figure drawing. I. Title. II. Title: Drawing figures.

REFREGIER, Anton, 1905- 743.4
Natural figure drawing, with photos. and drawings by the author and many other illus. [2d ed.] New York, Tudor Pub. Co. [1960, c.1948, 1960] 128p. illus. 28cm. 60-15040 3.50; 1.45 pap.,
1. Figure drawing. 2. Anatomy, Artistic. I. Title.

SHEPPARD, Joseph, 1930- 743'.44
Drawing the female figure / by Joseph Sheppard. New York : Watson-Guptill Publications, 1975. 158 p. : chiefly ill. ; 29 cm. Bibliography: p. 158. [NC765.S43 1975] 75-15872 ISBN 0-8230-1370-7 : 13.95
1. Figure drawing. 2. Women in art. 3. Nude in art. I. Title. BIP

SHIMER, Genevieve. 743.4
Drawing children. New York, Pitman [1960] unpaged. illus. 20 x 26 cm. (Pitman art series, 9) [NC765.S45] 60-5771
1. Figure drawing. 2. Children in art. I. Title. BIP

VANDERPOEL, John Henry, 1857-1911. 743.4
The human figure. New York, Dover Publications [1958, c1935] 143 p. illus. 24 cm. [NC765.V3] 57-14883
1. Figure drawing. I. Title. BIP

WIGG, Philip R. 743'.4
Introduction to figure drawing; perceptual and conceptual problems in drawing from life [by] Philip R. Wigg. Dubuque, Iowa, Brown [1967] ix, 147p. illus. (pt. col.) 32cm. (Brown art ser.) [NC765.W5] 67-21324 7.95
1. Figure drawing. I. Title.

YEAGER, Bunny. 743.44
Drawing the human figure using photographs, by Bunny Yeager and Tony Floreani. New York, A. S. Barnes [1965] 181 p. illus. 29 cm. [NC765.Y4] 65-13916
1. Figure drawing. 2. Photography of women. I. Floreani, Tony, joint author. II. Title.

ZAIDENBERG, Arthur, 1903- 743.4
Drawing the human figure. New York, A. S. Barnes [1963] 126 p. illus. 26 cm. [NC765.Z2853] 63-18260
1. Figure drawing. I. Title.

ZAIDENBERG, Arthur, 1903- 743.4
Drawing the human figure in action. London, New York, Abelard-Schuman [1961] 112 p. (chiefly illus.) 26 cm. [NC765.Z286] 61-10528
1. Figure drawing. I. Title.

ZAIDENBERG, Arthur, 1903- 743.4
How to draw athletes in action; step-by-step sequences of figures in action in games and sports, showing uniforms and equipment used. London, New York, Abelard-Schuman [1965] 64 p. illus. 27 cm. [NC785.Z3] 65-23654
1. Figure drawing. 2. Athletes. 3. Action in art. I. Title.

Figure drawing—Catalogs.

BINION, Alice. 741'.092'2
Antonio and Francesco Guardi, their life and milieu : with a catalogue of their figure drawings / Alice Binion. New York : Garland Pub., 1976. 466 p. : ill. ; 21 cm. (Outstanding dissertations in the fine arts) Originally presented as the author's thesis, Columbia University, 1971. Bibliography: p. [333]-348. [NC257.G8B56 1976] 75-23782 ISBN 0-8240-1979-2 lib.bdg. : 32.50
1. Guardi, Francesco, 1712-1793. 2. Guardi, Giovanni Antonio, 1698-1760. 3. Figure drawing—Catalogs. I. Title. II. Series.

Figure drawing—Juvenile literature.

COWELL, Cyril 743.4
Your book of figure drawing. Illus. by the author. London, Faber and Faber [dist. Hollywood-by-the-Sea, Fla., Transatlantic, c.1964] 55p. illus. 22cm. [NC765] 65-7023 3.00
1. Figure drawing—Juvenile literature. I. Title.

Figure painting.

BASSFORD, Wallace, 1900- 704.94'24
Painting the female figure. New York, Reinhold Pub. Corp. [1967] 128 p. illus. (part col.) 29 cm. [ND1290.B33] 67-24850
1. Figure painting. 2. Women in art. I. Title.

BOOK of American figure painters. 757'.0973
New York : Garland, 1977. p. cm. (The Art experience in late nineteenth century America ; no. 11) Each plate excepting the first, accompanied by two leaves, one with title of painting reproduced and name of painter, the other with descriptive poem. Selections from this work published later in 4 volumes, with titles: Gems of American art, Selected pictures by American artists, Choice pictures by American artists, and American art. Reprint of the 1886 ed. published by Lippincott, Philadelphia. [ND210.B6 1977] 75-28875 ISBN 0-8240-2235-1 lib.bdg. : 50.00
1. Figure painting. 2. Painting, American. 3. Painting, Modern—19th century—United States. 4. Painters—United States. I. Title. II. Series. BIP

DE RUTH, Jan, 1922- 757.22
Painting the nude. New York, Watson-Guptill Publications [1967] 197 p. illus. (part col.) 29 cm. [ND1290.D4] 67-13742
1. Figure painting. 2. Nude in art. I. Title. BIP

OLSON, Herbert Vincent, 1905- 757
Painting the figure in watercolor [by] Herb Olsen [pseud.] New York, Reinhold [1958] 166 p. illus. 27 cm. [ND2190.O45] 58-7199
1. Figure painting. 2. Water-color painting—Technique. I. Title.

SCHMID, Richard, 1934- 751.4'5
Richard Schmid paints the figure; advanced techniques in oil. New York, Watson-Guptill Publications [1973] 142 p. illus. (part col.) 29 cm. Bibliography: p. 140. [ND1290.S27] 73-5549 ISBN 0-8230-4865-9 15.00
1. Figure painting. I. Title. BIP

SOYER, Moses, 1899- 751.4
Painting the human figure. Edited by Robert W. Gill. New York, Watson-Guptill Publications [1964] 160 p. illus. (part col.) 27 cm. [ND1290.S6] 64-24247
1. Figure painting. 2. Nude in art. I. Gill, Robert W., ed. II. Title.

WYNNE-MORGAN, John. 704.94'24
The nude and the portrait; how to pose and paint them. New York, Emerson Books [1963] 141 p. illus. (part col.) ports. 23 cm. [ND1290.W9] 63-20235
1. Figure painting. 2. Portrait painting. I. Title. BIP

Figure painting—Exhibitions.

FREER Gallery of Art, Washington, D.C. 709'.5'0740153 s
Chinese figure painting, by Thomas Lawton. Washington, Smithsonian Institution, 1973. x, 236 p. illus. (part col.) 31 cm. (Its fiftieth anniversary exhibition, v. 2) Catalogue. Includes bibliographical references. [N5020.W52F733 1973 vol. 2] [ND1293.C6] 757'.0951 73-87219 ISBN 0-87923-088-6
1. Figure painting—Exhibitions. 2. Figure painting—China. I. Lawton, Thomas, 1931- II. Title. III. Series: Freer Gallery of Art, Washington, D.C. Fiftieth anniversary exhibition, v. 2.

Figureheads of ships.

BREWINGTON, Marion Vernon, 1902- 736'.4
Shipcarvers of North America, by M. V. Brewington. New York, Dover Publications [1972, c1962] xiv, 173 p. illus. 24 cm. Bibliography: p. 147-153. [VM308.B74 1972] 79-187020 3.00 (pbk)
1. Figureheads of ships. 2. Wood-carving, American. 3. Wood-carving, Canadian. 4. Ships, Wooden. I. Title.

PINCKNEY, Pauline A. 736'.4
American figureheads and their carvers, by Pauline A. Pinckney. Port Washington, N.Y., Kennikat Press [1969, c1940] 223 p. illus. 26 cm. Bibliography: p. 204-210. [VM308.P5 1969] 68-8207
1. Figureheads of ships. 2. Wood-carving, American. I. Title.

Fiji Islands—Antiq.

GIFFORD, Edward Winslow, 1887- 301.2'4
Archaeological excavations in Fiji. [Berkeley, University of California Press, 1951] v. 189-288 p. illus., maps, diagrs. 28 cm. (Anthropological records: 13: 3) "Appendix I. Petrography of pottery, by G. H. Curtis": p. 239-241. Bibliography: p. 257-258. [E51.A58 vol. 13, no. 3] A51
1. Fiji Islands—Antiq. 2. Excavations (Archaeology)—Viti Levu. I. Curtis, Garniss H. II. Title. III. Title: Petrography of pottery. IV. Series.

Fillin family—Art collections.

A Family collection; 707'.09747'43
drawings, sculptures and oils by American artists, selected from the Collection of Lucille and Walter Fillin and their children. [Albany, Albany Institute of History and Art? 1962] 1 v. (chiefly illus.) 18 cm. An exhibit shown during 1962-1963 at the Albany Institute of History and Art, and other museums. [N6510.F35] 338.4'3745'10973 75-303517
1. Fillin family—Art collections. 2. Art, American—Exhibitions. 3. Art, Modern—19th century—United States. 4. Art, Modern—20th century—United States. I. Albany Institute of History and Art.

Film posters.

KOBAL, John, comp. 769
50 years of movie posters. Compiled and edited with commentary by John Kobal. Introd. by David Robinson. New York, Bounty Books [1973?] 175 p. (chiefly illus., part col.) 44 x 31 cm. On cover: A Trewin Copplestone production. [PN1995.9.P5K6] 73-87428 ISBN 0-517-51386-2 9.95 (spinal bdg.)
1. Film posters. I. Title.

Film posters, American.

MORELLA, Joe. 769'.4'979143
Those great movie ads, by Joe Morella, Edward Z. Epstein, and Eleanor Clark. New Rochelle, N.Y., Arlington House [1972] 320 p. illus. 29 cm. [PN1995.9.P5M6] 75-189371 ISBN 0-87000-153-1 14.95
1. Film posters, American. I. Epstein, Edward Z., joint author. II. Clark, Eleanor, joint author. III. Title.

Film posters, Russian.

CONSTANTINE, Mildred. 769'.5
Revolutionary Soviet film posters [by] Mildred Constantine and Alan Fern. Baltimore, Johns Hopkins University Press [1974] xi, 97 p. illus. 31 cm. Bibliography: p. 92-93. [PN1995.9.P5C6] 74-6817 ISBN 0-8018-1641-6 12.95
1. Film posters, Russian. I. Fern, Alan Maxwell, 1930- joint author. II. Title. BIP

Filmus, Michael, 1943—

FILMUS, Michael, 1943- 741.9'73
Green River : Berkshire scenes / by Michael Filmus ; with text by Berkshire authors. Lenox, Mass. : Bookstore Press, [1975] [32] p. : ill. ; 16 x 23 cm. [NC139.F453A45] 75-320690
1. Filmus, Michael, 1943- 2. Berkshire Hills, Mass., in art. I. Title.

Fima.

FIMA. 759.95694
Fima. [New York, Jewish Museum, 1972] [24] p. illus. (part col.) 24 cm. Catalog of an exhibition held at the Jewish Museum, Dec. 20, 1972-Mar. 18, 1973. Bibliography: p. [23]-[24] [ND979.F47J48] 72-96379
1. Fima. I. Jewish Theological Seminary of America. Jewish Museum.

Finance—Massachusetts—History—Sources.

DAVIS, Andrew McFarland, 1833-1920, ed.-comp. 769'.569744
Colonial currency reprints, 1682-1751. With an introd. and notes. New York, B. Franklin [1971] 4 v. illus. 26 cm. (Burt Franklin American classics of history and social science series, 2) Reprint of the 1910-11 ed. which was issued as v. 32-35 of the Publications of the Prince Society. [HG506.D3 1971] 72-172475
1. Finance—Massachusetts—History—Sources. 2. Money—Massachusetts—History—Sources. 3. Banks and banking—Massachusetts—History—Sources. I. Title. II. Series: Prince Society, Boston. Publications, v. 32-35. BIP

Finch-Davies, Claude Gibney, 1875-1920.

KEMP, Alan C. 759.941
The biography of Claude Gibney Finch-Davies, 1875-1920 : observer, student and highly skilled illustrator of Southern African birds / text by A. C. Kemp. Pretoria : Transvaal Museum, c1976. 33 p., [30] leaves of plates : ill. (some col.), facsims. ; 36 cm. Includes bibliographical references. [QL31.F52K45] 77-368019 ISBN 0-620-02081-4
1. Finch-Davies, Claude Gibney, 1875-1920. 2. Ornithologists—South Africa—Biography. 3. Birds—Africa, Southern—Pictorial works. I. Title.

Fine arts—Congresses.

THE Arts at the grass   700'.6
roots. Edited by Bruce Cutler. Lawrence,
University Press of Kansas, 1968. xiii, 270
p. 23 cm. Proceedings of the first Kansas
conference on the arts, Wichita, September
29-October 1, 1966. Bibliography: p. 194-
195. [NX50.K3 1966] 68-14433
1. Fine arts—Congresses. I. Cutler, Bruce,
1930-

Fine, Jud.

FINE, Jud.   709'.2'4
Jud Fine : confessions and related work,
1970-1976. [Fullerton] : Art Gallery,
California State University, Fullerton,
c1976. 33, [6] p. : chiefly ill. ; 24 cm.
"[Exhibition held] September 17, 1976,
through October 14, 1976, Art Gallery,
California State University, Fullerton."
Bibliography: p. [36] [N6537.F46C34] 76-
380452
1. Fine, Jud. I. California State University,
Fullerton. Art Gallery.

Finger painting.

BARKER, Elver A.   751.4'9
Finger painting in oils [by] Elver A.
Barker. Foreword by Harold Woodford
Pond. Princeton, N.J., Van Nostrand
[1968] xix, 156 p. illus. (part col.) 25 cm.
Bibliography: p. 149-152. [ND2490.B3] 67-
27984
1. Finger painting. I. Title.

BETTS, Victoria Bedford,   751.49
1913-
Exploring finger paint. Worcester, Mass.,
Davis Publications [1963] 132 p. illus. 28
cm. [ND2490.B4] 63-10497
1. Finger painting. I. Title.

WOLFF, Margaret A.   751.4'9
Finger painting, by Margaret A. Wolff.
New York, Pitman Pub. Corp. [1968] 32 p.
illus. (part col.) 20 x 26 cm. (Pitman art
books, 60) [ND2490.W6] 68-11007
1. Finger painting.   BIP

Fingerprints.

KATZ, Marjorie P.   741.2'6
Fingerprint owls and other fantasies [by]
Marjorie P. Katz. New York, M. Evans;
distributed in association with Lippincott,
Philadelphia [1972] [64] p. illus. 27 cm.
Instructions for creating pictures with
fingerprints. [NC655.K29] 72-85648 3.95
1. Fingerprints. 2. Drawing—Instruction—
Juvenile literature.   I. Title.
   BIP

Fingesten, Peter.

FINGESTEN, Peter.   741.9'73
Obscure departures / by Peter Fingesten.
[New York : Pace University, 1973] 1
portfolio ([1] leaf, 9 leaves of plates : 9 ill.)
; 29 cm. Cover title. [NC139.F46A46] 75-
320265
1. Fingesten, Peter. I. Title.

Finishes and finishing.

SODERBERG, George A   667.6
Finishing materials and methods.
Bloomington, Ill., McKnight & McKnight
Pub. Co. [1952] 320 p. illus. 24 cm.
[TT305.S75] 52-7180
1. Finishes and finishing. I. Title.

SODERBERG, George A.   667.9
Finishing materials and methods.
Bloomington, Ill., McKnight & McKnight
[1959] 382 p. illus. 24 cm. Includes
bibliography. [TT305.S75 1959] 59-16270
1.   Finishes   and   finishing.

SODERBERG, George A.   667'.9
Finishing technology [by] George A.
Soderberg. [3d ed.] Bloomington, Ill.,
McKnight & McKnight [1969] xviii, 308 p.
illus. (part col.) 27 cm. First-2d eds.
published under title: Finishing materials
and methods. Bibliography: p. 297-300.
[TT305.S6 1969] 72-86470
1. Finishes and finishing. I. Title.   BIP

SODERBERG, George A   *684.1
Restoring and maintaining finishes -- spot
finishing [by] George A. Soderberg [and]
Paul W. Karcher. Milwaukee, Bruce Pub.
Co. [1958] 88 p. illus. 26 cm. [TT325.S6]
58-12103
1. Finishes and finishing. 2. Furniture —
Repairing. I. Karcher, Paul W., joint
author. II. Title.

Finishes and finishing — Addresses, essays, lectures.

JOHNSON, Fred D., 1920-   667'.9
Modern finishing methods, by Fred D.
Johnson. [Toronto, Mclean-Hunter Pub.
Co., 1966] 181 p. illus. 29 cm. $5.00 Can.
(C 64-4101) Cover title. A manual
covering all phases of organic finishing,
based on articles that first appeared in
Canadian paint and finishing. [TT305.J62]
67-82000
1. Finishes and finishing — Addresses,
essays, lectures. 2. Painting, Industrial —
Addresses, essays, lectures. I. Title.

Finishes and finishing — Equipment and supplies.

BLUNDELL, Brian F.   621.9
An introduction to industrial finishing
equipment, by Brian F. Blundell. [1st ed.]
Oxford, New York, Pergamon Press [1965]
viii, 188 p. illus. 23 cm. [TT305.B55] 64-
23712
1. Finishes and finishing — Equipment and
supplies. I. Title. II. Title: Industrial
finishing equipment.

Finlay, Virgil.

FINLAY, Virgil.   741'.92'4
The book of Virgil Finlay, being the
drawings of Virgil Finlay (1914-1971) from
the collection of Gerry de la Ree / edited
and published by Gerry de la Ree. [1st ed.]
Saddle River, N.J. : De la Ree, 1975. 128
p. : chiefly ill. ; 29 cm. [NC975.5.F5D4]
76-351180 15.00
1. Finlay, Virgil. 2. De la Ree, Gerry—Art
collections. I. Title: The book of Virgil
Finlay, being the drawings of Virgil Finlay
...

FINLAY, Virgil.   741.9'73
The third book of Virgil Finlay : the
fantasy art of Virgil Finlay / edited and
published by Gerry de la Ree ; [graphics
by Helen de la Ree]. Saddle River, N.J. :
G. de la Ree, 1979. 127 p. : chiefly ill. ; 29
cm. [NC975.5.F5A4 1979] 79-100280
15.50
1. Finlay, Virgil. 2. Fantasy in art. I. De la
Ree, Gerry. II. Title.   BIP

FINLAY, Virgil.   741.9'73
Virgil Finlay : an astrology sketchbook /
[edited by] Beverly C. Finlay. West
Kingdom, R.I. : D. M. Grant, 1975. 148 p.
: ill. (some col.) ; 27 cm. [NC139.F47F54]
76-360965 15.00
1. Finlay, Virgil. 2. Atrology in art. I.
Finlay, Beverly C.

Finlayson, Reginald William, 1907— Art collections.

SHIH, Hsio-Yen, 1933-   759.952
Nanga and Zenga; Japanese paintings in
the Finlayson Collection. [Windsor, Ont.,
Art Gallery of Windsor, 1973] [28] p. illus.
22 x 28 cm. Cover title. Limited ed. of 500
copies. Catalog of an exhibition held at the
Art Gallery of Windsor, Jan. 7-Jan. 31,
1973. Bibliography: p. [27] [ND2071.S45]
74-165581
1. Finlayson, Reginald William, 1907—Art
collections. 2. Nanga—Exhibitions. 3.
Painting, Zen—Exhibitions. 4. Painting,
Japanese—Chinese influences. I. Art
Gallery of Windsor. II. Title.

Finta, Alexander, 1881-

LENGYEL, Alfonz.   730'.92'4
The life and art of Alexander Finta,
Hungarian-American sculptor. Washington,
Hungarian Reformed Federation of
America, 1964. iii, 74 p. illus., port. 20 cm.
(Hungarica Americans, 7) [NB237.F5L4]
66-50145

1. Finta, Alexander, 1881- I. Title. II.
Series.

Fiorentino, Rosso, 1494-1540.

CARROLL, Eugene A.   741'.092'4
The drawings of Rosso Fiorentino /
Eugene A. Carroll. New York : Garland
Pub., 1976. 2 v. (viii, 564, 18, [104] leaves
of plates) : ill. ; 21 cm. (Outstanding
dissertations in the fine arts) Reprint of the
author's thesis, Harvard, 1964. Includes
bibliographical references. [NC257.F52C37
1976] 75-23786 ISBN 0-8240-1982-2
lib.bdg. : 80.00 80.00(2 vols) 80.00
1. Fiorentino, Rosso, 1494-1540. I. Title.
II. Series.   BIP

Fire Heart Creek site.

LEHMER, Donald Jayne,   970.4'84'88
1917-
The Fire Heart Creek site, by Donald J.
Lehmer. Editor: Warren W. Caldwell.
Editorial assistants: Joyce B. Williams,
Jerry L. Livingston [and] Paulette C.
Workman. Lincoln, Neb., 1966. v, 115 p.
illus., plates. 25 cm. (Smithsonian
Institution. River Basin Surveys.
Publications in salvage archeology, no. 1)
Bibliography: p. 77-79. [E78.N75L4] 67-
60628
1. Fire Heart Creek site. 2. Arikara
Indians—Antiquities. I. Series: River Basin
Surveys. Publications in salvage
archeology, no. 1.

Fire Island, N.Y.—Description—Views.

BRAYNARD, Frank Osborn,   741.973
1916-
From Fire Island to Venice; a tugman's
holiday sketchbook, by Frank O. Braynard.
[Tuckahoe, N.Y.] De Graff [1966] 144p.
illus. 29cm. [NC1075.B68A47] 66-19785
8.00
1. Fire Island. N.Y.—Deser.—Views. 2.
Venice—Descr.—Views. I. Title.

Firearms.

BOWMAN, Hank Wieand   623.44
Famous guns from the Winchester
collection. Greenwich, Conn., Fawcett
Publications, c1958. 143 p. illus. 24 cm. (A
Fawcett how-to book, 395) [TS535.B65]
58-59560
1. Firearms. I. Title.   BIP

BRYANT, Will.   623.44
Great American guns and frontier fighters,
written and illustrated by Will Bryant.
New York, Grosset & Dunlap [1961] 160p.
illus. 29cm. [TS535.B74] 61-65174
1. Firearms. 2. Frontier and pioneer life—
U. S. I. Title.

CHAPEL, Charles Edward,   623.44
1904-
The gun collector's handbook of values. 2d
rev. ed. New York, Coward-McCann
[1951] xiii, 403 p. illus. 22 cm.
Bibliography: p. 383-388. [TS535.C47
1951] 51-8922
1. Firearms. 2. Collectors and collecting. I.
Title.

GREENER, William   683'.4
Wellington.
The gun and its development, by W. W.
Greener. 9th ed., rewritten, and with many
additional illus. New York, Bonanza Books
[1967?] xx, 804 p. illus., ports. 23 cm.
Reprint of the 1910 ed. [TS533.G7 1967]
67-274420
1. Firearms. 2. Firearms—History. I. Title.

HATCHER, Julian   623.4
Sommerville, 1888-
Hatcher's notebook, a standard reference
book for shooters, gunsmiths, ballisticians,
historians, hunters, and collectors. [2d ed.]
Harrisburg, Pa., Stackpole Co. [1957]
629p. illus. 24cm. [TS535.H27 1957] 57-
14138
1. Firearms. I. Title.   BIP

HATCHER, Julian   623.44
Sommerville, 1888-
Hatcher's notebook, a standard reference
book for shooters, gunsmiths, ballisticians,
historians, hunters, and collectors. [3d ed.]
Harrisburg, Pa., Stackpole Co. [1962] 640

p. illus. 24 cm. [TS535.H27 1962] 62-
12654
1. Firearms.

HAYWARD, John Forrest,   799.21
1916-
The art of the gunmaker. New York, St.
Martin's Press [1962-1964) 2 v. illus.,
plates (part col.) 25 cm.
Contents.Contents.—v. 1. 1500-1660.—v.
2. Europe and America, 1660-1830.
Includes   bibliographical   references.
[TS535.H35] 62-5869
1. Firearms. I. Title.

KENNEDY, Monty.   736.4
The checkering and carving of gunstocks.
Edited by Thomas G. Samworth. [2d ed.]
Harrisburg, Pa., Stackpole [1962] 343 p.
(p. 337-343 advertisements) illus., diagrs. 29
cm. (Firearms design and assembly, v. 4)
A Samworth book. [NK6904.K4 1962] 62-
6548
1. Firearms. 2. Wood-carving—Technique.
I. Title. II. Series: Firearm design and
assembly, v. 4   BIP

KOLLER, Lawrence R 1912-   623.44
Book of guns. [New York, Maco Magazine
Corp., 1956] 136p. illus. 24cm. (Maco, 49)
[TS535.K58 1956a] 57-2130
1. Firearms. I. Title.

KOLLER, Lawrence R 1912-   623.44
The complete book of guns; every make
and model, all ammunition, scopes, and
sights. [New York, Maco Magazine Corp.,
1954] 144p. illus. 24cm. (Maco, 16)
[SK274.K7] 54-4504
1. Firearms. 2. Shooting. I. Title.

KOLLER, Lawrence R 1912-   623.443
Popular handguns, all newest U. S.,
European models ... Special tips on
collecting old guns, by Herb Glass. [New
York, Maco Magazine Corp., 1957] 136p.
illus. 24cm. (Maco, 57) Cover title.
[TS537.K62] 57-13760
1. Firearms. I. Title.

KOLLER, Lawrence R. 1912-   623.44
1967.
Book of guns. New York, Random House
[1956] 136 p. illus. 25 cm. [TS535.K58]
56-10934
1. Firearms. I. Title.

POPE, Dudley.   623.409
Guns; from the invention of gunpowder to
the 20th century. Drawings by Max Millar.
New York, Delacorte Press [1965] 254 p.
illus. (part col.) ports. 31 cm. [U800.P6]
65-25584
1. Firearms. 2. Ordnance. I. Millar, Max,
illus. II. Title.

RYWELL, Martin, 1905-1972.   623.44
Gun collectors' guide: old guns for profit;
the complete guide to antique gun
collecting. [1st ed.] Harriman, Tenn.,
Pioneer Press [1964] 128 p. illus. 23 cm.
[TS535.R914] 54-8699
1. Firearms. I. Title.

Firearms, American.

MILITARY Arms   683'.4'00973
Research Service.
United States martial & collectors arms.
San Jose, Calif., 1971. iv, 83 p. 19 cm. (its
MARS TM 157) Pages 75-83, blank for
"Notes." [TS533.2.M54] 75-161051 ISBN
0-912370-04-1 2.50
1. Firearms, American. 2. Firearms—
Identification. 3. Firearms—Collectors and
collecting. I. Title. II. Series.

RYWELL, Martin, 1905-   623.44
Fell's collector's guide to American antique
firearms. New York, F. Fell [1963] 215 p.
illus. 24 cm. [NK6912.R92] 63-11395
1. Firearms, American. I. Title. II. Title:
Collector's guide to American antique
firearms.

WEST, Bill.   683'.4'00973
Remington arms & history. [1st ed.] Azusa,
Calif. [1970] 1 v. (various pagings) illus.,
ports. 24 cm. [TS533.2.W46] 71-121899
1. Remington Arms Company, inc. 2.
Firearms, American. I. Title.

Firearms, American—Collectors and collecting.

FLAYDERMAN, E. Norman. 683.4'00973
Flayderman's Guide to antique American firearms and their values / by Norm Flayderman. Northfield, Ill. : DBI Books, c1977. 576 p. : ill. ; 27 cm. Includes bibliographies and indexes. [TS532.4.F58 1977] 75-36418 ISBN 0-695-80650-5 : 12.95
1. Firearms, American—Collectors and collecting. 2. Firearms, American—Prices. I. Title. II. Title: Guide to antique American firearms and their values. BIP

Firearms, American—History.

BUTLER, David F. 683'.4'00973
United States firearms: the first century, 1776-1875 [by] David F. Butler. [New York] Winchester Press [1971] 249 p. illus. 29 cm. [TS533.2.B87] 77-146062 15.00
1. Firearms, American—History. I. Title.

SERVEN, James Edsall, 1899- 683'.4'00973
200 years of American firearms / by James E. serven; edited by Joseph J. Shroeder, Jr. Chicago : Follett Pub. Co., c1975. 224 p. : ill. ; 28 cm. [TS533.2.S47] 74-25251 ISBN 0-695-80599-1 : 7.95
1. Firearms, American—History. 2. Firearms industry and trade—United States—History. I. Title.

Firearms, British.

NEAL, William Keith. 623.4'4
The Mantons, gunmakers [by] W. Keith Neal and D. H. L. Back. New York, Walker [1967, c1966] xv, 300 p. illus. (part col.) facsims., geneal. table., ports. (part col.) 26 cm. Bibliography: p. 294-295. [TS535.M34N4 1967a] 67-12527
1. Manton, John, 1752-1834. 2. Manton, Joseph, 1766-1835. 3. Firearms, British. 4. Firearms industry and trade—Great Britain. I. Back, David Henry Lempriere, joint author. II. Title.

Firearms, British—Exhibitions.

NEW York (City). Metropolitan Museum of Art. 683'.4'00942
Early firearms of Great Britain and Ireland from the collection of Clay P. Bedford. [New York]; distributed by New York Graphic Society, Greenwich, Conn. [1971] 187, [4] p. illus. 29 cm. Bibliography: p. [190]-[191] [TS532.2.U6N43] 77-178856 ISBN 0-87099-112-4 17.50
1. Firearms, British—Exhibitions. I. Title. BIP

Firearms—Catalogs.

AMERICAN antique guns and their current prices. 739.74 1950/51-41Harriaman, Tenn., Pioneer Press. v. illus. 23cm. Compiler: 1950/51- M. Rywell. [NK6912.A5] 56-1817
1. Firearms—Catalogs. 2. Firearms—Collectors and collecting. I. nnual. II. Rywell, Martin, 1905-

BLACKMORE, Howard L. 739.7'4'41
Royal sporting guns at Windsor [by] Howard L. Blackmore. London, H.M.S.O. [for the Ministry of Public Building and Works], 1968. v, 69p. 53 plates, illus. (incl. 1 col.), fascim. 31cm. [NK6903.W5B55] 68-31979 9.54
1. Firearms—Catalogs. 2. Windsor, House of—Art collections. I. Windsor Castle. II. Title.
Available in New York from British Info.

†GUSLER, Wallace B. 739.7'4
Decorated firearms, 1540-1870, from the Collection of Clay P. Bedford / by Wallace B. Gusler and James D. Lavin. Williamsburg, Va. : Colonial Williamsburg Foundation ; Charlottesville : distributed by the University Press of Virginia, c1977. xi, 242 p. : ill. ; 24 x 28 cm. Includes index. Bibliography: p. 239. [NK6903.B4G87] 76-53750 ISBN 0-87935-041-5 : 25.00
1. Bedford, Clay P., 1903- —Art collections. 2. Firearms—Catalogs. 3. Art metal-work—Catalogs. I. Lavin, James D., joint author. II. Title. BIP

PRUDHOMME, Edward C 623.443
Gun engraving review. Shreveport, La., Gun Engraving Review Pub. Co., c1961. 145p. illus. 29cm. [NK6912.P7] 62-506
1. Firearms—Catalogs. I. Title.

REMINGTON arms catalogues, 1877-1899: 338.4'7'6834029 rifles, carbines, muskets, pistols & shotguns, illustrated cartridges, sights, parts & accessories, by Bill West. [Azusa, Calif., 1970] 42, 48, 43 p. illus., facsims. 22 cm. [TS534.7.R4] 79-125420 ISBN 0-911614-09-5 10.00
1. Firearms—Catalogs. I. West, Bill, comp. II. Remington Arms Company, inc. BIP

RYWELL, Martin, 1905- 623.440838
American antique guns and their current prices; catalogue of U. S. pistols and revolvers that list, describes, and gives up-to-date prices on every American make, model, and type from flintlock through automatics; over 2000 firearms. 1953--1954. 5th ed. Harriman, Tenn., Pioneer Press, 1953. 92p. illus. 23cm. [TS535.R9 1953] 53-7146
1. Firearms—Catalogs. I. Title.

RYWELL, Martin, 1905- 623.440838
American antique guns and their current prices, catalogue of U.S. pistols and revolvers that lists, describes and gives up-to-date prices on every American make, model, and type from flintlock through automatics; over 2,000 firearms. 1951-1952 ed. Harriman, Tenn., Pioneer Press, c1951. 58 p. illus. 23 cm. [TS535.R9 1951] 51-4087
1. Firearms — Catalogs. I. Title.

RYWELL, Martin, 1905- 623.440838
American antique guns and their current prices; catalogue of U.S. pistols and and revolvers that lists, describes, and gives up-to-date prices on every American make, model, and type from flintlock through automatics; over 2000 firearms. 1950-1951 ed. Harriman, Tenn. Pioneer Press, c1950. 40 p. illus. 23 cm. Bibliography: p. 30. [TS535.R9] 50-12011
1. Firearms — Catalogs. I. Title.

UNITED States Cartridge Company. 683'.4'0075
Illustrated catalogue of United States Cartridge Company's collection of firearms; the most complete collection in the United States ... Old Greenwich, Conn., WE, inc. [1971] 140 p. illus. 24 cm. Reprint of the 1920 ed. [TS534.7.U54] 76-28148 6.00
1. Firearms—Catalogs. 2. Firearms—Collectors and collecting. I. Title.

[VICTORIA and Albert Museum, South Kensington] 623.44
European firearms, by J. F. Hayward. New York, Philosophical Library [1955] 53p. illus., 34plates. 26cm. 'A guide to the museum collection of firearms.' Bibliography: p. 22 [TS535] 55-14757
I. Hayward, John Forrest, 1916- II. Title.

WEST, Bill. 683'.4'009034
Hartley & Graham catalogues, 1895-1899. Illustrated: rifles, carbines, pistols, shotguns, cannon, cartridges, gun sights, cases, traps, loaders, tools, etc. Other Americana: bicycles, whistles, dog sundries, compasses, knives, cups, decoys, flasks, axes, lanterns, golf equip., leather goods. [1st ed. Azusa, Calif., 1972] 22, 112 p. illus. 28 cm. (His West arms library) Cover title: Hartley & Graham arms and ammunition 1895-1899 sporting goods catalogues. [TS534.7.W47] 72-91046
1. Firearms—Catalogs. 2. Ammunition—Catalogs. I. Hartley & Graham. II. Title.

Firearms—Collectors and collecting.

AMERICAN antique rifles and their current prices. 739.7 Harriman, Tenn., Pioneer Press. v. illus. 23cm. Compiler: M. Rywell. [NK6912.A53] 58-1123
1. Firearms—Collectors and collecting. 2. Rifles. I. Rywell. Martin, 1905-

BIVENS, Frank E 739.7
Half century scrapbook of vari-type firearms, based on the pictorial and descriptive catalog of the Frank E. Bivens, Jr. inspirational collection of varitype firearms and accessories. Catalogued by F. Theodore Dexter. Photography by Orville Logan Snider. [Santa Monica? Calif., 1960] 202p. illus., port. 28cm. [NK6903.B5] 60-41574
1. Firearms—Collectors and collecting. I. Dexter, Fred Theodore, 1885- II. Title.

BOWMAN, Hank Wieand. 683'.4'009
Antique guns from the Stagecoach collection. New York, Arco [1969, c1964] 111 p. illus., ports. 24 cm. [TS532.4.B67 1969] 78-75361 3.50
1. Firearms—Collectors and collecting. I. Shakopee, Minn. Stage Coach Museum. II. Title. BIP

BOWMAN, Hank Wieand. 623.44
Antique guns from the Stagecoach collection; early self-contained cartridge firearms, single and multi-shot pistols, percussion Colts, Allen & Wheelocks, Colt Dragoons, Remingtons, fine cased and one-of-a-kind weapons. [Greenwich, Conn., Fawcett Publications, 1964] 112 p. illus., ports. 24 cm. Cover title. [NK6903.B6] 65-265
1. Firearms — Collectors and collecting. I. Shakopee, Minn. Stage Coach Museum. II. Title.

BOWMAN, Hank Wieand. 623.44
Famous guns from famous collections. New York, Arco Pub. Co. [1957] 143p. illus. 25cm. (The Do-it-yourself series) [NK6912] 57-14778
1. Firearms—Collectors and collecting. 2. Firearms—Hist. I. Title.

BOWMAN, Hank Wieand. B67
Famous guns from famous collections. Greenwich, Conn., Fawcett Publications, c1957. 144p. illus., port. 24cm. (A Fawcett how-to book, 331) [NK6912] 623 57-1833
1. Firearms—Collectors and collecting. 2. Firearms—Hist. I. Title.

BOWMAN, Hank Wieand. 338.4'7'6834029
Famous guns from the Harolds Club collection. Greenwich, Conn., Fawcett Publications, c1962. 144p. illus. 24cm. (A Fawcett book, 518) [NK6903.H3B6] 62-52282
1. Firearms—Collectors and collecting. 2. Harold's Club, Reno, Nev. I. Title.

CHAPEL, Charles Edward, 1904- 623.44075
The complete book of gun collecting. New York, Coward-McCann [1961, c1960] 222p. illus. 21cm. First published in 1939 under title: Gun collecting. [TS535.C45 1961] 60-12482
1. Firearms—Collectors and collecting. I. Title.

CHAPEL, Charles Edward, 1904- 623.44
The gun collector's handbook of values. 3d rev. ed. New York, Coward-McCann [1955] xiii, 398p. illus., 49 plates. 22cm. Bibliography: p. 377-381. [TS535.C47 1955] 55-10077
1. Firearms—Collectors and collecting. I. Title. BIP

CHAPEL, Charles Edward, 1904- 623.44075
The gun collector's handbook of values. 7th rev. ed. New York, Coward-McCann [1966] xii, 398 p. illus. 22 cm. Bibliography: p. 377-381. [TS535.C47 1966] 66-20147
1. Firearms—Collectors and collecting. 2. Firearms—Catalogs. I. Title.

CHAPEL, Charles Edward, 1904-1967. 623.44075
The gun collector's handbook of values. 5th rev. ed. New York, Coward-McCann [1960] 398 p. illus. 22 cm. Includes bibliography. [TS535.C47 1960] 60-14195
1. Firearms—Collectors and collecting. 2. Firearms—Catalogs. I. Title.

CHAPEL, Charles Edward, 1904-1967. 623.44075
The gun collector's handbook of values. 6th rev. ed. New York, Coward-McCann [1963] xii, 398 p. illus. 22 cm. Bibliography: p. 377-381. [TS535.C47 1963] 63-19521
1. Firearms—Collectors and collecting. 2. Firearms—Catalogs. I. Title.

CHAPEL, Charles Edward, 1904-1967. 623.4'4'075
The gun collector's handbook of values. 8th rev. ed., rev. by Mrs. Charles Edward Chapel. New York, Coward-McCann [1968] xiii, 398 p. illus., facsim. 22 cm. Bibliography: p. 377-381. [TS532.4.C47 1968] 69-13547 10.00
1. Firearms—Collectors and collecting. 2. Firearms—Catalogs. I. Chapel, Charles Edward, Mrs., ed. II. Title.

CHAPEL, Charles Edward, 1904-1967. 623.4'4'075
The gun collector's handbook of values. 9th rev. ed., rev. by Mrs. Charles Edward Chapel. New York, Coward-McCann [1970] xiii, 398 p. illus., facsim. 22 cm. Bibliography: p. 377-382. [TS532.4.C47 1970] 71-127415 12.50
1. Firearms—Collectors and collecting. 2. Firearms—Catalogs. I. Chapel, Charles Edward, Mrs., ed. II. Title.

CHAPEL, Charles Edward, 1904-1967. 683'.4'0075
The gun collector's handbook of values / by Charles Edward Chapel. 12th rev. ed. / rev. by Mrs. Charles Edward Chapel. New York : Coward, McCann & Geoghegan, c1977. 462 p. : ill. ; 22 cm. Includes index. Bibliography: p. 441-446. [TS532.4.C47 1977] 76-53035 ISBN 0-698-10825-6 : 17.50
1. Firearms—Collectors and collecting. 2. Firearms—Catalogs. I. Chapel, Charles Edward, Mrs. II. Title.

CHAPEL, Charles Edward, 1904-1967. 683'.4'0075
The gun collector's handbook of values / by Charles Edward Chapel. 11th rev. ed. / rev. by Mrs. Charles Edward Chapel. New York : Coward, McCann & Geoghegan, [1975] 462 p. : ill. ; 22 cm. Includes index. Bibliography: p. 440-445. [TS532.4.C47 1975] 74-18634 ISBN 0-698-10580-X : 17.50
1. Firearms—Collectors and collecting. 2. Firearms—Catalogs. I. Chapel, Charles Edward, Mrs. II. Title.

GUN collector's digest. 683'.4'0075 Edited by Joseph J. Schroeder, Jr. Northfield, Ill., Digest Books [1974] 320 p. illus. 28 cm. Bibliography: p. 303-320. [TS532.4.G85 1974b] 74-173515 6.95
1. Firearms—Collectors and collecting. I. Schroeder, Joseph J., ed. BIP

GUN collector's digest, 683'.4'0075 edited by Joseph J. Schroeder, Jr. Chicago, Follett Pub. Co. [1974] 320 p. illus. 28 cm. "The collector's bookshelf": p. 303-320. [TS532.4.G85] 73-83406 ISBN 0-695-80432-4 6.95
1. Firearms—Collectors and collecting. I. Schroeder, Joseph J., ed.

GUNS of the world; 683'.4'0075 the complete collectors' & traders' guide [by] James E. Serven [and others. Los Angeles, Petersen Pub. Co., 1972] 400 p. illus. (part col.) 28 cm. Cover title. [TS532.4.G88] 72-85969 6.95
1. Firearms—Collectors and collecting. I. Serven, James Edsall, 1899-

LINDSAY, Merrill. 739.7'4'075
The lure of antique arms / by Merrill Lindsay. New York : D. McKay Co., [1975] p. cm. Includes index. Bibliography: p. [TS532.4.L56] 74-25989 ISBN 0-679-20299-4 : 9.95
1. Firearms—Collectors and collecting. I. Title. BIP

LINDSAY, Merrill. 739.7'4'075
The lure of antique arms / Merrill Lindsay. [South Hackensack, N.J.] : Stoeger Pub. Co., [1978] p. cm. (Stoeger sportsman's library) Reprint of the 1976 ed. published by D. McKay Co., New York. Includes index. Bibliography: p. [TS532.4.L56 1978] 77-90759 ISBN 0-88317-044-2 pbk. : 5.95
1. Firearms—Collectors and collecting. I. Title.
5distributed by Follett

MYRUS, Donald, 1927- 623.44075
Collectors' guns. New York, Maco Magazine Corp. [1961] 128 p. illus. 24 cm. (Maco, M97) [NK6903.M9] 62-503
1. Firearms — Collectors and collecting. I. Title.

MYRUS, Donald, 1927- 623.44075
Collectors' guns. New York, Arco Pub. Co. [1962, c1961] 128 p. illus. 24 cm. (The Do -- it -- yourself series) [NK6904.M9] 61-17822
1. Firearms — Collectors and collecting. I. Title.

MYRUS, Donald, 1927- 355.8
Collectors' guns, a fully illustrated history; how to identify all rare and famous arms. New York, Maco Magazine Corp. [1963] 128 p. illus., ports. 24 cm. "M112." Cover title. Bibliography: p. 9. [NK6904.M9] 63-25345
1. Firearms — Collectors and collecting. I. Title.

PALMER, Andy, 1897- 623.44084
Great guns; a photographic catalog of famous guns & their history. from the Andy Palmer collection displayed at the Military Inn, Dearborn, Michigan. [Dearborn? 1956] 80p. illus. 29cm. [NK6902.D4P3] 57-28738
1. Firearms—Collectors and collecting. I. Title.

PETERSON, Harold Leslie, 1922- 623.44'074'0158326
The Fuller collection of American firearms; America's military long arms [by] Harold L. Peterson. [Philadelphia, Eastern National Park & Monument Association, 1967] 63 p. illus. 22 x 28 cm. [TS532.4.P47] 73-171703
1. Fuller, Claud E., 1877-1957. 2. Firearms—Collectors and collecting. 3. Firearms, American. I. Title.

RYWELL, Martin, 1905- 739.74
American antique rifles and their current prices; a reference guide. Comprehensive compilation of all the known American rifles, shotguns, and carbines, of every make, model, and type, in easy-to-consult dictionary form; lists, describes, and gives up-to-date prices. 1956-57 ed. Harriman, Tenn., Pioneer Press, c1956. 52p. illus. 23cm. [NK6912.R9] 56-1817
1. Firearms —Collectors and collecting. 2. Rifles. I. Title.

RYWELL, Martin, 1905-1972. 683'.4'075
Gun collectors' guide: old guns for profit; complete guide to antique gun collecting. Harriman, Tenn., Pioneer Press [1966] 128 p. illus., ports. 24 cm. Bibliography: p. 99-100. [TS535.R914 1966] 67-66342
1. Firearms—Collectors and collecting. I. Title.

SERVEN, James Edsall, 1899- ed. 623.44075
The collecting of guns, edited by James E. Serven. [Authors] William A. Albaugh III [and others] Design and layout by Simon Frankel. [1st ed.] Harrisburg, Pa., Stackpole Co. [1964] 272 p. illus., ports. 29 cm. Bibliography: p. 270-272. [TS535.S445] 64-14890
1. Firearms—Collectors and collecting. 2. Firearms—History. I. Title.

SERVEN, James Edsall, 1899- 683'.4
The rare and valuable antique arms / by James E. Serven. [St. Paul, Minn.] : Pioneer Press, c1976. 106 p. : ill. ; 23 cm. [TS532.4.S47] 77-150021 ISBN 0-913150-37-1 : 4.95
1. Firearms—Collectors and collecting. I. Title.

STEINWEDEL, Louis William. 683'.4'0075
The gun collector's fact book / Louis William Steinwedel. New York : Arco Pub. Co., c1975. 217 p. : ill. ; 24 cm. Includes bibliographical references and index. [TS532.4.S75] 74-77434 ISBN 0-668-03499-8 : 10.00 lib. bdg. ISBN 0-668-03782-2 pbk. : 5.95
1. Firearms—Collectors and collecting. I. Title. BIP

WILKINSON, Frederick John, 1922- 683'.4'009
Antique guns and gun collecting / by Frederick Wilkinson. London ; New York : Hamlyn, 1974. 96 p. : ill. (some col.), facsims. ; 29 cm. Ill. on lining papers. Includes index. Bibliography: p. 93. [TS532.4.W53] 75-328751 ISBN 0-600-33928-9 : £1.95
1. Firearms—Collectors and collecting. I. Title.

Firearms—Dictionaries.

CAREY, Arthur Merwyn, 1890- 683.09
English, Irish, and Scottish firearms makers: when, where, and what they made, from the middle of the sixteenth century to the end of the nineteenth century. New York, Crowell [1954] xv, 121 p. illus. 24 cm. Bibliography: p. 120-121. [TS535.C265] 54-8440
1. Firearms—Dictionaries. 2. Firearms—History. 3. Firearms industry and trade—Gt. Brit. I. Title.

CAREY, Arthur Merwyn, 1890- 338.4'7'683400942
English, Irish, and Scottish firearms makers: when, where, and what they made, from the middle of the sixteenth century to the end of the nineteenth century [by] A. Merwyn Carey. [2d ed.] New York, Arco [1967] xv, 121 p. illus. 25 cm. Bibliography: p. 120-121. [TS535.C265 1967a] 67-18414
1. Firearms—Dictionaries. 2. Firearms, British. 3. Firearms industry and trade—Great Britain. I. Title.

PETERSON, Harold Leslie, 1922- ed. 623.4403
Encyclopedia of firearms, edited by Harold L. Peterson. [1st ed.] New York, Dutton [1964] 367 p. illus. (part col.) 26 cm. Includes bibliographies. [TS535.P43] 64-25937
1. Firearms—Dictionaries. I. Title.

Firearms—Drawings.

MURTZ, Harold A., comp. 683'.4'00223
The Gun digest book of exploded firearms drawings / edited by Harold A. Murtz. 2d ed. Northfield, Ill. : DBI Books, c1977. 320 p. : chiefly ill. ; 28 cm. [TS534.5.M87 1977] 77-156099 ISBN 0-695-80842-7 : 7.95
1. Firearms—Drawings. I. Gun digest. II. Title. III. Title: Exploded firearms drawings. BIP

Firearms—Exhibitions.

PRUDHOMME, Edward C. 739.7'4
E. C. Prudhomme, master gun engraver; a retrospective exhibition: 1946-1973. April 1 to May 13, 1973, the R. W. Norton Art Gallery. [Shreveport, La., R. W. Norton Art Gallery, 1973] 32 p. illus. 29 cm. Catalogue. [TS532.2.U6S563] 73-78704 ISBN 0-913060-01-1
1. Prudhomme, Edward C. 2. Firearms—Exhibitions. I. Norton (R. W.) Art Gallery. II. Title.

Firearms, French.

MASTER French gunsmiths' designs of the XVII-XIX centuries, 739.7'4 reproduced in facsimile. Introd. and notes by Stephen V. Grancsay. New York, Winchester Press, 1970. 208 p. illus., facsims. 26 x 34 cm. The facsimile reproductions are chiefly from pattern books in the library of S. V. Grancsay. "The Cabinet d'armes of Louis XIII": p. 185-208. Bibliography: p. 167-181. [NK6949.F5M3] 74-99752
1. Firearms, French. 2. Art metal-work, French. I. Grancsay, Stephen Vincent, 1897- BIP

Firearms, French—History.

KENNARD, Arthur Norris. 683'.4'00944
French pistols and sporting guns [by] A. N. Kennard. [London, New York, Hamlyn, 1972] 63 p. illus. 19 cm. (Country life collectors' guides) Label mounted on t.p.: Transatlantic Arts, New York, sole distributor for the U.S.A. [TS533.4.F8K45] 73-154221 ISBN 0-600-43594-6
1. Firearms, French—History. I. Title. BIP

Firearms—History.

ABELS, Robert. 683
Early American firearms. Cleveland, World Pub. Co. [1950] 63 p. illus., 7 col. plates. 20 cm. (The American arts library, 1587) Bibliography: p. 63. [TS535.A2] 50-58030
1. Firearms—Hist. 2. Firearms industry and trade—U. S. I. Title.

BLACKMORE, Howard L. 739.7
Firearms [by] Howard L. Blackmore. [London, Studio Vista; New York, Dutton, 1964] 158 p. illus., facsims., ports. 19 cm. (A Dutton Vista pictureback, 2) [NK6906.B53] 64-4417
1. Firearms—Hist. I. Title.

BLACKMORE, Howard L. 623.4409
Guns and rifles of the world New York, Viking [c.1965] x, 134p. illus., plates (1 col.) 31cm. (Studio bk.) Bibl. [TS535.B58] 65-171169 30.00
1. Firearms—Hist. 2. Firearms—Pictorial works. I. Title.

BOWMAN, Hank Wieand 623.4'4
Famous guns from the Smithsonian collection. New York, Arco [1967, c.1966] 112p. illus. 24cm. [TS535.B648 1967] 67-16180 3.50
1. Firearms—Hist. 2. Firearms—Patents. I. Smithsonian Institution. II. Title. BIP

HENDERSON, James, 1905- 623.44
Firearms collecting for amateurs. London, Muller, 1966. 143p. illus., 12 plates, diagrs. 20cm. [TS535.H4] 66-72082 2.50
1. Firearms—Hist. 2. Firearms—Collectors and collecting. I. Title.
Distributed by Barnes & Noble. New York.

JACKSON, Herbert J. 739.7
European hand firearms of the sixteenth, seventeenth & eighteenth centuries, by Herbert J. Jackson, & with a treatise on Scottish hand firearms, by Charles E. Whitelaw. London, Holland Press; Chicago, Quadrangle Books [1960] xvi, 108p. illus. 33cm. 60-980 25.00
1. Firearms—Hist. 2. Firearms—Collectors and collecting. I. Whitelaw, Charles Edward. II. Title. BIP

JACKSON, Herbert J 739.7
European hand firearms of the sixteenth, seventeenth & eighteenth centuries, by Herbert J. Jackson, & with A treatise on Scottish hand firearms, by Charles E. Whitelaw. London, Holland Press; Chicago, Quadrangle Books [1960] xvi, 108p. illus. 33cm. [NK6909.J3 1960] 60-980
1. Firearms—Hist. 2. Firearms—Collectors and collecting. I. Whitelaw, Charles Edward. II. Title.

RICKETTS, Howard. 739.7
Firearms. New York, Putnam [1962] 128p. illus. 22cm. (Pleasures and treasures) [NK6906.R5] 62-13080
1. Firearms—Hist. 2. Firearms—Collectors and collecting. I. Title.

ROGERS, Albert Henry, 1899- 623.44209
Firearms of yesterday. New York, Vantage Press [1953] 52p. 23cm. [TS535.R63] 52-13304
1. Firearms—Hist. I. Title.

SERVEN, James Edsall, 1899- 623.4209
Colt firearms, 1836-1954. Santa Ana, Calif., 1954. ix, 385p. illus., ports., map. 32cm. [TS535.S45] 54-8380
1. Firearms—Hist. I. Title.

WINANT, Lewis. 623.4409
Early percussion firearms; a history of early percussion firearms ignition, from Forsyth to Winchester .44/40. New York, Morrow, 1959. 292 p. illus. 25 cm. Includes bibliography. [TS535.W49] 59-11701
1. Firearms — Hist. 2. Firearms — Locks. I. Title.

WINANT, Lewis. 739.7
Firearms curiosa. New York, St. Martin's Press [1961, c1955] 281 p. illus. 24 cm. Includes bibliography. [TS535.W5 1961] 61-65680
1. Firearms — Hist. I. Title. BIP

Firearms—History.

AKEHURST, Richard. 683'.4'00903
The world of guns. London, New York, Hamlyn, 1972. 127 p. illus. (some col.), ports. 30 cm. Illus. on lining papers. [TS533.A57] 73-153653 ISBN 0-600-39236-8 3.95
1. Firearms—History. I. Title.

BOWMAN, Hank Wieand. 623.44
Famous guns from the Smithsonian collection. Greenwich, Conn., Fawcett Publications, 1966. 112 p. illus., ports. 24 cm. [TS535.B648] 66-9041
1. Firearms—History. 2. Firearms—Patents. I. Smithsonian Institution. II. Title.

CHAPEL, Charles Edward, 1904-1967. 623.44
Guns of the Old West. New York, Coward-McCann [1961] 306 p. illus. 27 cm. Includes bibliography. [TS535.C48] 61-10978
1. Firearms—History. 2. Frontier and pioneer life—The West. I. Title.

HALLS, Christopher. 683'.4'00994
Guns in Australia / by Christopher Halls. Sydney ; New York : Hamlyn, 1974. 173 p. : ill. (part col.), diagrs. ; 29 cm. Includes index. Bibliography: p. 172-173. [TS533.4.A8H34] 76-352681 ISBN 0-600-07291-6 : 6.95
1. Firearms—History. 2. Australia—History. I. Title.

HELD, Robert, 1929- 623'.4'09
The age of firearms; a pictorial history from the invention of gunpower to the advent of the modern breechloader. Research assistance and book design by Nancy Held. Revision edited by Joseph J. Schroeder, Jr. New and rev. ed. Northfield, Ill., Gun Digest Co. [1970] 192 p. illus. 31 cm. Bibliography: p. [188]-[189] [TS533.H44 1970] 70-90430 4.95
1. Firearms—History. I. Title.

LINDSAY, Merrill. 739.7'4'09
One hundred great guns; an illustrated history of firearms. Photos. by Bruce Pendleton. Book designed by Verne Noll. Lock illus. by Peter Parnall. New York, Walker [1967] 379 p. illus. (part col.), facsims. 34 cm. Bibliography: p. 310-365. [TS535.L494] 67-23653
1. Firearms—History. 2. Firearms industry and trade—History. I. Title.

•NEAL, W. Keith 683.4009'42'073
Great British gunmakers, 1740-1790; the history of John Twigg and the Packington guns [by] W. Keith Neal&D.H.L. Back. [Totowa, N.J.] Sotheby Parke Bernet Publications, [1975] 196p. ill(part col.) 30cm. Includes index. [TS532.4] ISBN 0-85667-015-4 70.00
1. Twigg, Jhn, 1732-1790. 2. Firearms-history. I. Back, D.H.L. joint author. II. Title. BIP

PETERSON, Harold Leslie, 1922- 683'.4'009
The great guns, by Harold L. Peterson and Robert Elman. Special photography by J. Barry O'Rourke. New York, Grosset & Dunlap [1971] 252 p. illus. 31 cm. "A Ridge Press book." Bibliography: p. 247. [TS533.P47 1971] 74-143184 ISBN 0-448-02069-6 14.95
1. Firearms—History. I. Elman, Robert, joint author. II. Title.

PETERSON, Harold Leslie, 1922- 623.44075
The treasury of the gun. Technical consultation by Howard L. Blackmore, Claude Blair [and] William Reid. [Special photography by Arie de Zanger] New York, Golden Press [1962] 249 p. illus. (part col.) ports. 31 cm. Bibliography: p. [247]-[248] [NK6906.P4] 62-15426
1. Firearms—History. 2. Firearms—Collectors and collecting. I. Title.

ROSA, Joseph G. 683'.4'009
The pleasure of guns : the intricate and beautiful work of famous gunsmiths / Joseph G. Rosa & Robin May. London : Octopus Books, 1974. 96 p. : chiefly col. ill. ; 33 cm. Distributed in USA by Crescent Books, New York, N.Y. Includes index. [TS533.R67] 75-310078 ISBN 0-517-10559-4 5.95

1. Firearms—History. I. May, Robin, joint author. II. Title.
Available from Outlet Book Co., 419 Park Ave. S., New York, N.Y. 10016.

ROSEBUSH, Waldo Emerson, 1889-1961. 623.44
American firearms and the changing frontier. Written for the Eastern Washington State Historical Society. Drawings by Ronald Kuhler. Spokane, Eastern Washington State Historical Society, 1962. xiv, 99 p. illus., port. 25 cm. (Eastern Washington State Historical Society, Spokane./Publication no.1) Bibliography: p. 89-90. [TS535.R68] 63-3903
1. Firearms—History. 2. U.S. Army—Firearms. 3. U.S.—History, Military. I. Title. II. Series. BIP

WILKINSON, Frederick John, 1922- 683'.4'009
Antique firearms, by Frederick Wilkinson. Garden City, N.Y., Doubleday [1969] [6], 255, x p. illus. (part col.) 25 cm. (Guinness signatures) Bibliography: 6th prelim. page. [TS533.W5 1969b] 71-93202 10.95
1. Firearms—History. I. Title.

WILKINSON, Frederick John, 1922- 683'.4'00903
Antique firearms / by Frederick Wilkinson. San Rafael, Calif. : Presidio Press, 1978,c1969 276 p. : ill. ; 25 cm. Includes index. Bibliography: p. [8] [TS533.W5 1977] 77-86542 ISBN 0-89141-050-3 : 14.95
1. Firearms—History. I. Title. BIP

WILKINSON, Frederick John, 1922- 683'.42
Flintlock guns and rifles; an illustrated reference guide, by F. Wilkinson. [Harrisburg, Pa.] Stackpole Books [1971] 80 p. illus. 23 cm. Bibliography: p. 78-80. [TS533.W52] 77-140740 ISBN 0-8117-0664-8 4.95
1. Firearms—History. 2. Firearms—Locks. I. Title.

WILKINSON-LATHAM, Robert. 683'.4'009
Antique guns in color, to 1865 / Robert Wilkinson-Latham ; special photography by John Searle Austin ; color paintings and line drawings by Peter Sarson and Tony Bryan. New York : Arco Pub. Co., 1978, c1977. 215 p. : ill. (some col.) ; 20 cm. (Arco color series) Includes index. [TS533.W55] 77-26334 ISBN 0-668-04467-5 : 8.95. ISBN 0-668-04478-0 pbk. : 6.95
1. Firearms—History. I. Title.

WINANT, Lewis. 623.4409
Firearms curiosa. [Limited ed.] New York, Greenberg [1955] 281 p. illus. 24 cm. [TS535.W5] 54-7114
1. Firearms—History. I. Title.

Firearms—Maintenance and repair.

LISTER, Ronald. 683.4
Antique firearms: their care, repair, and restoration. New York, Crown Publishers [1964, c1963] 220 p. illus. 25 cm. [TS535.L5 1964] 64-23797
1. Firearms—Maintenance and repair. 2. Firearms—Collectors and collecting. I. Title.

Firearms—Patents.

GT. Brit. Patent Office. 683'.4'00272
Illustrated British firearms patents, 1714-1853, compiled and edited by Stephen V. Grancsay and Merrill Lindsay. New York, Winchester Press, 1969. 1 v. (various pagings) illus. 28 cm. A selection of patents from the original 5 vols. of English patent law published in 1854 under title: Specifications of patents of invention relating to fire-arms, projectiles, &c. ... Includes bibliography. [TS534.5.G7] 77-99750
1. Firearms—Patents. 2. Firearms, British. I. Grancsay, Stephen Vincent, 1897- ed. II. Lindsay, Merrill, ed. III. Title. BIP

Firearms—Private collections—U.S.

DE JARNETTE, Bertrand, 1899- 739.7'4'0740182273
The Dr. M. B. De Jarnette Firearms Collection. Owner and author: Bertrand De Jarnette. Nebraska City, Neb. [1970] 143 p. illus. 28 cm. On cover: The DeJarnette Antique Firearms Collection. [NK6903.D4D4] 70-21401
1. Firearms—Private collections—U.S. I. Title. II. Title: The DeJarnette antique firearms collection.

Firearms, Spanish.

LAVIN, James D. 683.40946
A history of Spanish firearms. New York, Arco [c.1965] 304p. illus., ports. 25cm. (Arco gun lib.) Bibl. [TS535.L35] 65-14456 9.95
1. Firearms, Spanish. 2. Firearms industry and trade—Spain. I. Title.

Firearms—Virginia—History.

SWAYZE, Nathan L. 683'.4'00975526
The Rappahannock Forge / by Nathan L. Swayze. [Dallas] : American Society of Arms Collectors, 1976. 34 p., [1] leaf of plates : ill. ; 28 cm. (An American Society of Arms Collectors publication ; no. 2) [TS533.2.S94] 75-39159
1. Firearms—Virginia—History. I. Title. II. Series: American Society of Arms Collectors. An American Society of Arms Collectors publication ; no. 2.

Fireplaces.

DEBAIGTS, Jacques. 721'.8
The modern fireplace / Jacques Debaigts. New York : Van Nostrand Reinhold Co., [1975] p. cm. [NA3050.D4] 75-10011 ISBN 0-442-22068-5 : 30.00
1. Fireplaces. I. Title. BIP

HOW to build outdoor fireplaces and furniture [by David X. Manners and others. Dan Blue, editor] Larry Eisinger, editor-in-chief. New York, Arco Pub. Co. [c1957] 144p. illus. 25cm. (The Do-it-yourself series) An Arco how-to book, 333. [SB473.5.H62] 57-14217 717.9
1. Fireplaces. 2. Garden ornaments and furniture. 3. Outdoor cookery. I. Manners, David X., 1912- II. Blue, Dan, ed.

HOW to build outdoor fireplaces and lawn furniture. [Greenwich, Conn., Fawcett Publications, 1955] 144p. illus. 24cm. (A Fawcett book, no. 268) [SB473.5.H68 1955a] 55-2566 717.9
1. Fireplaces. 2. Garden ornaments and furniture. 3. Barbecue cookery. I. Fawcett Publications, inc.

HOW to build outdoor fireplaces and lawn furniture. New York, Arco Pub. Co. [1955] 144p. illus. 26cm. (The Do-it-yourself series) Arco handy book for better living. A Fawcett book, no. 268. [SB473.5.H68 1955] 55-8136 717.9
1. Fireplaces. 2. Garden ornaments and furniture. 3. Barbecue cookery.

HOW to build outdoor fireplaces and lawn furniture. Wm. T. McKeown, editor. [Greenwich, Conn., Fawcett Publications, 1953] 144p. illus. 24cm. (A Fawcett book, no. 177) [SB473.5.H68] 53-1701 717.9
1. Fireplaces. 2. Garden ornaments and furniture. 3. Barbeoue cookery. I. McKeown, William T., ed. II. Fawcett Publications, inc.

†WEST, Trudy. 728
The fireplace in the home / [by] Trudy West ; line illustrations by P. C. Young. Newton Abbot ; North Pomfret, Vt. : David and Charles, 1976. 160 p. : ill. ; 22 cm. Includes index. [TH7425.W47] 74-81060 ISBN 0-7153-6751-X : 13.95
1. Fireplaces. I. Title. BIP

Fireplaces—United States.

KAUFFMAN, Henry J., 1908- 749'.62'0973
The American fireplace : chimneys, mantelpieces, fireplaces & accessories / Henry J. Kauffman ; introd. by Joe Kindig III. New York : Galahad Books, c1972. 352 p. : ill. ; 28 cm. Includes index. Bibliography: p. 343-345. [NA3050.K34 1972b] 75-12274 ISBN 0-88365-330-3 : 20.00
1. Fireplaces—United States. I. Title. BIP

KAUFFMAN, Henry J., 1908- 749'.62'0973
The American fireplace: chimneys, mantelpieces, fireplaces & accessories [by] Henry J. Kauffman. Introd. by Joe Kindig III. Nashville, T. Nelson [1972] 352 p. illus. 28 cm. "Fireplace cookery, by Leland Rickard Meyer": p. 325-342. Bibliography: p. 343-345. [NA3050.K34] 79-39775 ISBN 0-8407-4320-3
1. Fireplaces—United States. I. Title.

Fires—Pictorial works.

RUSCHA, Edward. 779
Various small fires and milk. [Los Angeles?] 1964. 1 v. of illus. 18 cm. "400 copies printed." [TR650.R77] 65-2765
1. Fires—Pictorial works. I. Title.

First published in London in 1949 under title: English cottage furniture.

ROE, Frederic Gordon, 1894- 749.22
Antique English cottage furniture. New York, M. McBride Co. [1950] 128 p. illus. 23 cm. Bibliographical references included in "Notes" (p. 119-121) [NK2528.R63 1950] 50-8073
1. First published in London in 1949 under title: English cottage furniture. 2. Furniture — Gt. Brit. I. Title.

Fischer von Erlach, Johann Bernhard, 1656-1723.

AURENHAMMER, Hans. 720'.92'4
J. B. Fischer von Erlach. Cambridge, Mass., Harvard University Press, 1973. 193 p. illus. 26 cm. Includes bibliographical references. [NA1011.5.F57A94 1973b] 73-83421 ISBN 0-674-46988-7 15.95
1. Fischer von Erlach, Johann Bernhard, 1656-1723. I. Fischer von Erlach, Johann Bernhard, 1656-1723. BIP

Fischinger, Oskar, 1900-1967.

LONG Beach, Calif. Museum of Art. 759.3
Bildmusik: art of Oskar Fischinger. [Long Beach, Calif., 1970] 1 v. (unpaged) illus. (part col.) 21 cm. Exhibition held June 28-July 26, 1970. [PN1998.A3F44] 72-132818
1. Fischinger, Oskar, 1900-1967. I. Fischinger, Oskar, 1900-1967. II. Title.

Fish prints.

HIYAMA, Yoshio, 1909- 760
Gyotaku; the art and technique of the Japanese fish print, by Yoshio Hiyama. Seattle, University of Washington Press [1964] 64 p. illus., plates. 21 cm. [NE1340.H5 1964] 64-8398
1. Fish prints. I. Title: The art and technique of the Japanese fish print.

Fisher, Jonathan, 1768-1847.

FISHER, Jonathan, 1768-1847. 759.13
Versatile Yankee; the art of Jonathan Fisher, 1768-1847 [by] Alice Winchester. [1st ed.] Princeton, Pyne Press [1973] 29, [15] p. illus., 40 col. plates. 32 cm. "List of works": p. [34]-[42] [ND237.F44W56] 73-79528 ISBN 0-87861-051-0 35.00
1. Fisher, Jonathan, 1768-1847. I. Winchester, Alice. II. Title.

WILLIAM A. Farnsworth Library and Art Museum, Rockland, Me. 709'.24
The arts and crafts of the versatile Parson Fisher, 1768-1847: 1967 summer [Rockland, Me., c1967] [31] p. illus., facsim., map, plans, port. 16 x 22 cm. [N6537.F5W5] 72-671
1. Fisher, Jonathan, 1768-1847. I. Title.

Fishermen—Chesapeake Bay.

DE GAST, Robert, 1936- 779'.9'6394110975518
The oystermen of the Chesapeake. [Photographed and written by Robert de Gast. Camden, Me., International Marine Pub. Co., 1970] 1 v. (unpaged) illus. 23 x 29 cm. Issued in a case. [SH365.M3D4] 78-125357 ISBN 0-87742-010-6 16.00
1. Fishermen—Chesapeake Bay. 2. Oyster fisheries—Chesapeake Bay. 3. Skipjacks. I. Title. BIP

Fishes in art.

CAPON, Robin. 745.4
Introducing design techniques; 78 variations on a theme. New York, Watson-Guptill [1972] 96 p. illus. 21 cm. [N7430.C33] 72-3267 ISBN 0-8230-2555-1 7.95
1. Fishes in art. 2. Art—Technique. I. Title.

Fishing nets.

DABLEM, Ted, 1931- 746'.0466
How-to book of knots, nets, and smoked fish. Illustrated by the author. 1st ed. St. Petersburg, Fla., Great Outdoors [1968] 84 p. illus. 22 cm. [SH344.8.N4D33] 79-27307
1. Fishing nets. 2. Gray mullets. 3. Coolsery (Fish) I. Title.

Fitchburg, Mass.—History.

KIRKPATRICK, Doris. 974.4'3
The city and the river. Photos. by W. Frederick Lucas. Drawings by Carolyn C. Winslow. [Fitchburg, Mass.] Fitchburg Historical Society, 1971- v. illus. 28 cm. Bibliography: v. 1, p. 429-440. [F74.F5K5] 75-31689
1. Fitchburg, Mass.—History. I. Title.

Flagg, James Montgomery, 1877-1960.

FLAGG, James Montgomery, 1877-1960. 741.973
Celebrity-artist. With biographical portrait by G. L. Freeman. Watkins Glen, N.Y., Century House, c1960. 104 p. illus., port. 27 cm. First published in 1951 under title: Celebrities. [NC1429.F53 1960] 60-15561
I. Title.

FLAGG, James Montgomery, 1877-1960. 741.9'73
James Montgomery Flagg, by Susan E. Meyer. New York, Watson-Guptill Publications [1974] 207 p. illus. 32 cm. [NC975.5.F55M48] 74-9628 ISBN 0-8230-1835-0 27.50
1. Flagg, James Montgomery, 1877-1960. I. Meyer, Susan E.

Flagg, Jared Bradley, 1820-1899.

PERKINS, Helen D. 759.13
An illustrated catalogue of known portraits by Jared B. Flagg, 1820-1899. Compiled by Helen D. Perkins. Hartford, Conn. [Stowe-Day Foundation, 1972] 64 p. illus. 26 cm. On cover: A catalogue of a Connecticut artist. Published for an exhibit of selected Flagg portraits, sponsored by the Stowe-Day Foundation, Mar. 1-June 30, 1972, held at Nook Farm Visitors' Center, Hartford, Conn. [ND1329.F55P46] 72-75449
1. Flagg, Jared Bradley, 1820-1899. 2. Portraits, American—Catalogs. I. Nook Farm Visitors' Center. II. Stowe-Day Foundation. III. Title. BIP

Flagg Tanning Corporation—Art collections.

MILWAUKEE. Art Center. 759.97294
Haiti, the naive tradition: the Flagg Tanning Corporation Collection. Milwaukee [1974] 120 p. illus. (part col.) 26 cm. Catalogue of an exhibition which opened Dec. 6, 1973. [ND306.M54 1974] 74-78457
1. Flagg Tanning Corporation—Art collections. 2. Paintings, Haitian—

1. Floral decoration. I. Title.

CONWAY, John Gregory, 1909- 635.9663
Encyclopedia of flower arrangement. Photography by Julian Hiatt. New York, Knopf [1957] 294 p. illus. 24 cm. [SB449.C67] 57-10304
1. Floral decoration.

CONWAY, John Gregory, 1909- 635.9663
Treasury of flower arrangements. Photography by Julian Hiatt. [1st ed.] New York, Knopf, 1953. 337 p. illus. 28 cm. [SB449.C75] 53-6847
1. Floral decoration. I. Title.

CUTLER, Katherine N 635.9663
Junior flower arranging. Photos. by Roche, drawings by Joan Lucas. New York, M. Barrows [1957] 183p. illus. 21cm. [SB449.C83 1957] 57-1064
1. Floral decoration. I. Title.

CUTLER, Katherine N. 635.9663
Junior flower arranging. Photos. by Roche; drawings by Joan Lucas. New York, M. Barrows [1954] 179 p. illus. 21 cm. [SB449.C83] 54-5374
1. Floral decoration. I. Title.

CYPHERS, Emma Hodkinson. 635.9663
Design and depth in flower arrangement. New York, Hearthside Press [1958] 118 p. illus. 25 cm. [SB449.C88] 58-85360
1. Floral decoration. I. Title.

CYPHERS, Emma Hodkinson. 635.9663
Flower arrangement at the crossroads. Boston, Christopher Pub. House [1953] 219p. illus. 21cm. [SB449.C89] 53-9080
1. Floral decoration. I. Title.

CYPHERS, Emma Hodkinson. 635.9663
Foliage arrangements. New York, Hearthside Press [1956] 126 p. illus. 25 cm. [A Home and garden bookshelf. For flower arrangers] [SB449.3.F6C9] 56-10750
1. Floral decoration. 2. Leaves. I. Title.

CYPHERS, Emma Hodkinson. 635.9665
Giving and getting awards for flower arrangements. New York, Hearthside Press [1956] 56 p. 22 cm. [SB449.C892] 56-7387
1. Floral decoration. 2. Flower shows. I. Title.

CYPHERS, Emma Hodkinson, ed. 635.9663
Holiday flower arrangements. New York, Hearthside Press [1954] 127 p. illus. 24 cm. [SB449.C893] 54-11631
1. Floral decoration. I. Title.

DODSON, Margaret. 635.9663
An easy guide to color for flower arrangers, with arrangements and floral wheel in full color. New York, Hearthside Press [1956] 54 p. illus. 22 cm. [SB449.D6] 56-7385
1. Floral decoration. 2. Color. I. Title.

FISHER, Louise Bang, 1886- 635.9663
An eighteenth-century garland; the flower and fruit arrangements of Colonial Williamsburg. Williamsburg, Va., Colonial Williamsburg, 1951. xiv, 91 p. plates (part col.) ports. 25 cm. "References to the text": p. 79-81. Bibliographical references included in "A note to the curious" (p. 83-86) [SB449.F5] Agr
1. Floral decoration. 2. Horticulturists. I. Title.

FORT, Marie Johnson. 635.9663
Flower arrangements for all occasions; an informal and practical discussion of modern flower arranging. Edited by Robert L. Sommerville. New York, Rinehart [195-] 237 p. illus. 28 cm. [SB449.F6] 52-8079
1. Floral decoration. I. Title.

GANNON, Ruth Tuttle, 1895- 635.9663
Winter bouquets with color; the art of arranging dried flowers. [2d ed.] New York, Studio Publications in association with Crowell [1951] 80 p. illus. 24 cm. [SB449.5.W5G3 1951] 52-887
1. Floral decoration. 2. Everlasting flowers. I. Title.

GOLDSON, Rae L. 745.92
Contemporary flower arrangement; Rev., enlarged with 147 arrangements. New York, Hearthside [c.1955, 1962] 531p. illus. 25cm. 4.95 bds.,
1. Floral decoration. I. Title.

GOLDSON, Rae L. 635.9663
Contemporary flower arrangement: design and technique in modern methods, with text and 103 arrangements. New York, Hearthside Press [1955] 127 p. illus. 25 cm. [Hearthside how-to-do-it books] [SB449.G62] 55-7526
1. Floral decoration. I. Title.

HATTON, Richard George, 1864-1926 745.44
Handbook of plant and floral ornament; selected from the herbals of the finest examples of plant-drawing found in those rare works, whether executed in wood-cuts or in copperplate engravings, arranged for the use of the decorator with supplementary illustrations and with some remarks on the use of plant-form in design. [Gloucester, Mass., Peter Smith, 1961] ix, 539p. illus. 'Formerly titled: The craftman's plant-book; or, Figures of plants.' (Dover bk. rebound) 5.01
I. Title. BIP

HAYES, Naida Gilmore, 1912- 635.9663
Landscape flower arrangements; a new approach to dried materials. New York, Studio Publications in association with Crowell [1953] 96 p. illus. 22 cm. [SB449.3.D7H38] 53-5391
1. Floral decoration. I. Title.

HERRIGEL, Gustie Luise. 635.9663
Zen in the art of flower arrangement; an introduction to the spirit of the Japanese art of flower arrangement. With a foreword by Daisetz T. Suzuki. Translated from the German by R. F. C. Hull. Newton Centre, Mass., C. T. Branford Co. [1958] 124 p. illus. 19 cm. Translation of Der Blumenweg. [SB450.H423] 58-2987
1. Floral decoration. I. Title. BIP

HILL, Amelia Leavitt. 635.9663
Arranging flowers from the roadside, fields, and woods. New York, Studio Publications in association with Crowell [1952] 151 p. illus. (part col.) 25 cm. [SB449.3.W5H5] Agr
1. Floral decoration. I. Title.

ISHIMOTO, Tatsuo. 634.9663
The art of driftwood and dried arrangements. New York, Crown Publishers [1951] 143 p. illus. 24 cm. [SB449.178] 51-12003
1. Floral decoration. I. Title. II. Title: Driftwood and dried arrangements.

ISHIMOTO, Tatsuo. 635.9653
The art of plant and driftwood arrangement. New York, Crown Publishers [1954] 125 p. illus. 24 cm. [SB449.183] 54-11176
1. Floral decoration. I. Title. II. Title: Driftwood arrangement.

IWATA, Michiko, 1893- 635.9663
Japanese flower arrangement [by] Seido Iwata. New York, Studio Publications [1955?] 1 v. illus. 26 cm. Another ed., in English, published in Tokyo by the Seibikai Floral Art Institute, has title: Ohana no hon. [SB449.19 1955] 55-14998
1. Floral decoration. I. Title.

JONES, Ina, 1904- 635.9663
Arranging church flowers. Dallas, B. Upshaw [1950] 112 p. illus. 20 cm. Bibliography: p. [107] [SB449.J6] Agr
1. Floral decoration. I. Title. II. Title: Church flowers.

KITTEL, Mary Badham. 635.9663
Easy ways to good flower arrangement. London, New York, Studio Publications [1957] 120p. illus. 24cm. Includes bibliographies. [SB449.K5] 57-9253
1. Floral decoration. I. Title.

LOUISIANA Garden Club Federation. 635.9663
Louisiana arranges flowers. [Franklin, La., 1956] 64p. illus. 24cm. [SB449.L6] 56-24839
1. Floral decoration. I. Title.

MCCLINTON, Katharine (Morrison) 635.9663
Flower arrangement in the church, [6th print, rev.] New York, Morehouse-Gorham, 1954. 116p. illus. 20cm. [SB449.M27 1954] 55-439
1. Floral decoration. I. Title.

MARCUS, Margaret Fairbanks. 635.9663
Period flower arrangement. Modern adaptations selected or arranged by Mrs. Anson Howe Smith. New York, M. Barrows [1952] 256 p. illus. (part col.) 28 cm. Includes bibliographies. [SB449.M34] 52-13791
1. Floral decoration. 2. Floral decoration—History. 3. Symbolism of flowers. I. Title.

MARSHALL, Virginia Stone. 635.9663
Flower arranging for juniors; written and illustrated by Virginia Stone Marshall. [1st ed.] Boston, Little, Brown [1954] 113p. illus. 22cm. [SB449.M345] 54-5116
1. Floral decoration. I. Title.

ROBERTS, Patricia Easterbrook. 635.9663
How to make flower decorations. New York, Studio Publications [1958] 100 p. illus. 24 cm. [SB449.R56] 58-5669
1. Floral decoration. I. Title.

ROGERS, Matilda, 1894- 635.9663
Flower arrangements anyone can do anywhere; illustrated with photos. and with drawings by Robert Pious. New York, Dodd, Mead, 1954. 190p. illus. 20cm. [SB449.R633] 54-8875
1. Floral decoration. I. Title.

RUTT, Anna Hong. 635.9663
The art of flower and foliage arrangement. All flower arrangements by Anna Hong Rutt. All photos. by Elemore Morgan. New York, Macmillan, 1958. 248 p. illus. 22 cm. [SB449.R8] 58-5464
1. Floral decoration. 2. Leaves. I. Title. II. Title: Flower and foliage arrangement. BIP

RYMER, Grace. 745.92
The art of floral design. New York, Vantage Press [1963] 189 p. illus. 24 cm. [SB449.R9] 63-910
1. Floral decoration. I. Title.

SCHAFFER, Florence M 635.9663
ABC of driftwood for flower arrangers. Photos. by Mol Manley. New York, Hearthside Press [1957] 128p. illus. 24cm. [SB449.S433] 57-11965
1. Floral decoration. 2. Wood. I. Title. II. Title: Driftwood for flower arrangers.

SHOJI, Kane, 1885- 635.9663
The Japanese principles of design in flower arrangement, Senke school, by Kane Shoji and Violet Johnson. [1st ed.] Seattle, Chieftain Press, 1950. 153 p., 7 p. illus., port. 25 cm. English and Japanese; added t. p. in Japanese. Bibliography: p. 15. [SB449.S5] 51-1606
1. Floral decoration. I. Johnson, Violet Mellissia, 1893- joint author. II. Title.

SPRY, Constance, 1886- 635.9663
The art of arranging flowers. With a foreword by Beverley Nichols. New York, Studio Publications in association with T.Y. Crowell [1953] 68p. illus. 22cm. London ed. (Dent) has title: How to do the flowers. [SB449.S615 1953a] 53-12483
1. Floral decoration. I. Title.

SPRY, Constance, 1886- 635.9663
A Constance Spry anthology. With illus. by Rex Whistler and Lesley Blanch. New York, Studio Publications [1954] 112p. illus. 26cm. [SB449] 54-5744
1. Floral decoration. I. Title.

SPRY, Constance, 1886- 635.9663
Party flowers. New York, Studio Publications in association with Crowell [1956] 80 p. illus. 23 cm. [[SB449]] 57-380
1. Floral decoration. I. Title.

SPRY, Constance, 1886- 635.9663
Summer & autumn flowers, arranged by Constance Spry. New York, Studio Publications [1951] 116 p. illus. 26 cm. [SB449.S62 1951a] 52-7384
1. Floral decoration. I. Title.

SPRY, Constance, 1886- 635.9663
Winter & spring flowers, arr. by Constance Spry. Illustrated with 24 hand coloured photos. and 12 monochrome plates. New York, Studio Publications [1952] x, 140 p. illus. (part col.) 26 cm. [SB449.S63] 52-12395
1. Floral decoration. I. Title.

STARKER, Carl, 1892- 635.9663
Album of arrangements. [Compiled by Emma Hale] Seattle, Chieftain Press, 1953. 258 p. illus. 27 cm. [SB449.S68] 54-875
1. Floral decoration. I. Title.

STELLE, Anita. 635.9663
Seven keys to distinction in flower arrangement. With photographic commentary by Margaret Dodson. New York, Hearthside Press [1957] 127 p. illus. 24 cm. [SB449.S714] 56-10751
1. Floral decoration. I. Title.

STEVENSON, Violet W 635.9663
Flower arrangement through the year. London, W. H. & L. Collingridge; New York, Transatlantic Arts [1952] 72p. illus. 25cm. [SB449.S717] 53-1164
1. Floral decoration. I. Title.

STEVENSON, Violet W 635.9663
Flower decoration for the home. London, W. H. & L. Collingridge; New York, Transatlantic Arts [1950] 120 p. illus. 22 cm. [SB449.S72] 51-8108
1. Floral decoration. I. Title.

STOLTZ, Raymond Russ, Mrs. 635.9663
Flower show ribbon-winning arrangements. New York, Scribner [1958] 146 p. illus. 25 cm. [SB449.S75] 57-6070
1. Floral decoration. I. Title.

THE Studio book of 635.9664
flowers and flower arrangements. London, New York, Studio Publications [c1956] 224 p. illus. (part col.) 31 cm. [SB449.S76] 56-8659
1. Floral decoration.

SWIFT, Loret. 635.9663
Flower arranging book. New York, Arco Pub. Co. [1954] 144p. illus. 26cm. (Arco hand-books for better living) A reissue of the author's 'Today's woman book of flower arranging' (a Fawcett book, no.229) [SB449] 54-9241
1. Floral decoration. I. Title. II. Title: Today's woman book of flower arranging.

SWIFT, Loret. 635.9663
Today's woman book of flower arranging. Greenwich, Conn., Fawcett Publications, c1954. 144p. illus. 24cm. (A Fawcett book, no.229) [SB449.S9] 54-31525
1. Floral decoration. I. Title.

UNDERWOOD, Raye Miller. 635.9663
The complete book of dried arrangements. New York, M. Barrows [1952] 193 p. illus. 21 cm. [SB449.3.D7U5] 52-11290
1. Floral decoration. I. Title: Dried arrangements.

VAN REMSSELAER, Eleanor 635.9663
Decorating with pods and cones. With photos. by Blair Stapp. Princeton, N. J., Van Nostrand [1957] 179 p. illus. 21 cm. Includes bibliographies. [SB449.V3] 57-8147
1. Floral decoration. I. Title.

WHEELER, Esther. 635.9663
The complete book of flowers and plants for interior decoration [by] Esther Wheeler and Anabel Combs Lasker, assisted by Barbara Baer. Drawings by Janet Porto. New York, Hearthside Press [c1957] 190 p. illus. 29 cm. [SB449.W49] 57-11964
1. Floral decoration. 2. Interior decoration. 3. House plants. I. Lasker, Anabel (Combs) joint author. II. Title. III. Title: Flowers and plants for interior decoration.

WILSON, Adelaide B 635.9663
Color in flower arrangement. Color photography by Roche. New York, Barrows [1954] 128p. illus. 24cm. Includes bibliography. [SB449.W54] 54-5380
1. Floral decoration. 2. Color. I. Title.

WILSON, Helen Van Pelt, 1901- ed. 635.9663
The joy of flower arranging. New York, M. Barrows [1951] 252 p. illus. (part col.) 21 cm. [SB449.W55] Agr
1. Floral decoration. I. Title.

WOOD, Marie (Stevens) Walker, 1883- 635.9663
Flower arrangements, judged and point

scored. Macon, Ga., Merriewoode Press [1952] 166 p. illus. 22 cm. Includes bibliography. [SB449.W65] 52-14656
1. Floral decoration. I. Title.

Floral decoration, Chinese.

LI, Hui-lin, 1911- 635.9663
Chinese flower arrangement. Philadelphia, Hedera House, 1956. 122p. illus. 24cm. [SB450.L5] 56-58012
1. Floral decoration, Chinese. I. Title.

Floral decoration—Dictionaries.

STEVENSON, Violet W 635.9664
The encyclopaedia of floristry. London, W. H. & L. Collingridge; New York, Translantic Arts [1954] 159p. illus. 23cm. [SB449.S716] 56-4156
1. Floral decoration—Dictionaries. I. Title. II. Title: Floristry.

Floral decoration—History.

BERRALL, Julia S. 635.9663
A history of flower arrangement. London, New York, Studio Publications in association with Crowell [1953] 159, [1] p. illus. (part col.) 29 cm. Bibliographical references included in "A source list of garden flowers" (p. 152-[160]) [SB449.B43] 53-7527
1. Floral decoration—History.

Floral decoration, Japanese.

TESHIGAWARA, Sofu, 1900- 635.9663
Ikebana; Japanese flower arrangements, by Sofu Teshigahara. Sofu Teshigahara: his life and art, by Sumio Mizusawa. Color photos. by Ken Domon. [Translated by Ken Murayama. Edited by Hiroshi Teshigahara [and] Koen Shigemori] New York, Studio Publications [1958] 80 p. illus. (part col.) ports. 35 cm. [SB450.T4] 58-1464
1. Floral decoration, Japanese. I. Mizusawa, Sumio, 1905- II. Title.

Florence. Bigallo.

SAALMAN, Howard. 727.9
The Bigallo; the oratory and residence of the Compagnia del Bigallo e della Misericordia in Florence. New York, Published by New York University Press for the College Art Association of America, 1969. xxvi, 68 p. illus., facsim., plans. 29 cm. (Monographs on archaeology and the fine arts, 19) Includes bibliographical references. [NA5621.F515S2] 69-18285
1. Florence. Bigallo. I. Title. II. Series. BIP

Florence. Campanile.

TRACHTENBERG, Marvin. 726'.597
The Campanile of Florence Cathedral: "Giotto's tower." New York, New York University Press, 1971. 230 p. 348 plates (part col.) 32 cm. Bibliography: p. [209]-216. [NA5621.F52T7] 70-124532 ISBN 0-8147-8151-9
1. Giotto di Bondone, 1266?-1337. 2. Florence. Campanile. I. Title.

Florence—Description—Views.

ZOCCHI, Giuseppe, 1711-1767. 914.5'5'00222
Views of Florence and Tuscany. Seventy-seven drawings from the collection of the Pierpont Morgan Library, New York. [Catalogue] by Elaine Evans Dee. [Meriden, Conn., Produced by the Meriden Gravure Co. and the Stinehour Press, Lunenburg, Vt., 1968] [35] p. illus., 77 plates. 22 x 26 cm. "[Exhibition] circulated by the International Exhibitions Foundation, 1968-1969." [NC1155.Z6A57] 68-59110
1. Florence—Description—Views. 2. Tuscany in art. I. Dee, Elaine Evans. II. Pierpont Morgan Library, New York. III. International Exhibitions Foundation. IV. Title. BIP

Florence—Fountains.

WILES, Bertha Harris, 1896- 731'.722'094551
The fountains of Florentine sculptors and their followers from Donatello to Bernini / by Bertha Harris Wiles. New York : Hacker Art Books, 1975. x, 163 p., [61] leaves of plates : ill. ; 29 cm. Reprint of the 1933 ed. published by Harvard University Press, Cambridge, Mass. Includes index. Bibliography: p. [109]-135. [NA9415.F6W5 1975] 79-143370 ISBN 0-87817-089-8 : 30.00
1. Florence—Fountains. 2. Sculpture—Florence—History. 3. Sculpture, Renaissance—Florence. 4. Sculpture, Baroque—Florence. I. Title: The fountains of Florentine sculptors and their followers ... BIP

Florence. Galleria degli Uffizi.

ROSCI. MARCO 750.740551
The Uffizi and Pitti galleries. Text by Marco Rosci. [Tr. from Italian by Anthony Firmin O'Sullivan] New York, Appleton-Century [dist. Meredith. 1965,c.1963] 160p. illus. (pt. col.) 28cm. (Great galleries ser.) [N2570.R573] 65-21681 8.95 bds.,
1. Florence. Galleria degli Uffi3i 2. Florence. Galleria Palatina. I. Title.

ROSSI, Filippo. 708.5
The Uffizi, Florence. New York, H. N. Abrams [1957] 60p. illus. (part mounted col.) 39cm. (Great paintings of the world) An Abrams art book. In portifollo. [N2570.R6] 57-4024
1. Florence. Galleria degli Uffizi. 2. Paintings—Florence. I. Title.

Florence. Galleria palatina.

FRANCINI Ciaranfi, Anna Maria. 708.5'51
The Pitti Gallery (Galleria Palatina). Visitors' guide and catalogue of paintings ... With 78 plates. [Translated by Evelyn Sandberg Vavala] Florence, Arnaud, 1967. vii, 153 p. 37 plates. 17 cm. Translation of Pitti, Galleria palatina. [N2560.F713] 68-110726 L 750
1. Florence. Galleria palatina. 2. Paintings—Florence—Catalogs. I. Title.

Florence in art.

FINIGUERRA, Tommaso, 1426-1464. 741.9'45
A Florentine picture-chronicle; being a series of ninety-nine drawings representing scenes and personages of ancient history, sacred and profane, by Maso Finiguerra. Reproduced from the originals in the British Museum by the Imperial Press, Berlin. With many minor illus. drawn from contemporary sources and a critical and descriptive text by Sidney Colvin. New York, B. Blom, 1970. vi, 42 p. 117 illus., 99 plates. 41 cm. Reprint of the 1898 ed. [NC257.F5C6 1970] 68-56527
I. Colvin, Sidney, Sir, 1845-1927. II. British Museum. Dept. of Prints and Drawings. III. Title. BIP

WHITNEY, Bill, 1921- 741.9'73
Drawings of Florence. [Olivet, Mich.] Olivet College Press, 1971. 60 p. of illus. 22 x 23 cm. [NC139.W46A43] 79-175100
1. Florence in art. I. Title. BIP

Florence. Palazzo Medici.

HYMAN, Isabelle. 728.8'2'094551
Fifteenth century Florentine studies : the Palazzo Medici and a ledger for the Church of San Lorenzo / Isabelle Hyman. New York : Garland Pub., 1977. p. cm. (Outstanding dissertations in the fine arts) Originally presented as the author's thesis, New York University, 1968. Bibliography: p. [NA7756.F65H93 1977] 76-23631 ISBN 0-8240-2700-0 lib.bdg. : 50.00
1. Florence. Palazzo Medici. 2. Florence. San Lorenzo (Church) I. Title. II. Series. BIP

Florence. Palazzo Pitti.

CAMPBELL, Malcolm, 1934- 759.5
Pietro da Cortona at the Pitti Palace : a study of the planetary rooms and related projects / by Malcolm Campbell Princeton, N.J. : Princeton University Press, c1976. p. cm. (Princeton monographs in art and archaeology ; 41) Includes index. Bibliography: p. [ND623.P56C35] 76-3247 ISBN 0-691-03891-0 : 40.00
1. Pietro da Cortona, 1596-1669. 2. Florence. Palazzo Pitti. I. Title. II. Series. BIP

Florence. San Giovanni (Baptistery)

GHIBERTI, Lorenzo, 1378-1455. 730.9'24
Ghiberti's bronze doors, by Richard Krautheimer. Princeton, N.J., Princeton University Press, 1971. 17, [118] p. 155 illus., 4 col. plates. 29 cm. [NB1287.F6G38 1971] 78-154999 ISBN 0-691-03874-0 7.50
1. Florence. San Giovanni (Baptistery) I. Krautheimer, Richard, 1897- II. Title. III. Title: Bronze doors.

Florence. San Miniato al Monte (Church)

HARTT, Frederick. 726.595094551
The Chapel of the Cardinal of Portugal, 1434-1459, at San Miniato in Florence [by] Frederick Hartt, Gino Corti [and] Clarence Kennedy. Philadelphia, University of Pennsylvania Press [1964] 192 p. 158 plates (part col.) 32 cm. (The Haney Foundation series of studies in English, American and foreign literature; modern history, sociology, and economics; music and art, v. 1) Bibliography: p. 185-188. [NA5621.F8H3] 62-17064
1. Florence. San Miniato al Monte (Church) 2. Jaime de Portugal, Cardinal, 1434?-1459. I. Title. II. Series. BIP

Florence. Santa Maria del Fiore (Cathedral)—Juvenile literature.

ROCKWELL, Anne F. 92 (j)
Filippo's dome [by] Anne Rockwell. [1st ed.] New York, Atheneum, 1967. 82 p. illus. 25 cm. [NA5621.F5R6] 67-3026
1. Florence. Santa Maria del Fiore (Cathedral)—Juvenile literature. 2. Brunelleschi, Filippo, 1377-1446. I. Title.

Florence. Santa Trinita (Church)

SAALMAN, Howard. 726.5'0945'51
The Church of Santa Trinita in Florence. [New York] College Art Association of America, 1966. 42 p. illus., plans (part fold.), plates. 32 cm. (Monographs on archaeology and fine arts, 12) "An earlier version of this report was accepted in ... 1960 by the faculty of the Institute of Fine Arts, New York University, in partial fulfilment of the requirements for the degree of doctor of philosophy." Bibliographical footnotes. [NA5621.S37S2] 66-27568
1. Florence. Santa Trinita (Church) I. Title. II. Series.

Florida—Antiquities.

GRAY, J. Mason. 975.9'004'97
Indian artifact ident.. [Lutz, Fla. : J. M. Gray, 1975] 167 p. : ill. ; 28 cm. Cover title. "Authors edition, copy no. 2 of 50." Imprint stamped on p. [2] of cover. Includes index. Bibliography: p. 158-167. [E78.F6G72] 73-92731
1. Indians of North America—Florida—Antiquities. 2. Florida—Antiquities. I. Title.

Florida. University, Gainesville. Dept. of Architecture.

UNIVERSITY of Florida architecture impressions. 309.2'62
[R. John Clees, editor. Gainesvillle, Architecture Publications Committee, University of Florida Dept. of Architecture, 1970] 36 p. illus. 22 x 28 cm. Cover title. [NA2304.F58U54] 70-633409
1. Florida. University, Gainesville. Dept. of Architecture. I. Clees, R. John, ed.

Florida. University, Gainesville. State Museum. Dept. of Natural Sciences.

FLORIDA. University, Gainesville. State Museum. Dept. of Natural Sciences. 574'.08 s
Catalogue of type specimens in the Department of Natural Sciences, Florida State Museum / Carter R. Gilbert, ed. Gainesville : University of Florida, 1974. p. 102-120 ; 23 cm. (Bulletin of the Florida State Museum : Biological sciences ; v. 18, no. 2) Cover title. [QH1.F6 vol. 18, no. 2] [QH70.U62] 591'.074'015979 75-621767 1.75
1. Florida. University, Gainesville. State Museum. Dept. of Natural Sciences. 2. Type specimens (Natural history) I. Gilbert, Carter Rowell, 1930- II. Title. III. Series: Florida. University, Gainesville. State Museum. Bulletin. Biological sciences ; v. 18, no. 2.

Florida. University, Gainesville. University Gallery.

FLORIDA. University, Gainesville. University Gallery. 738.3
Pre-Columbian pottery of Peru from the collection of the University Gallery / by Elisabeth K. Gordon, photography by Roy C. Craven, Jr. Gainesville : University Gallery, College of Architecture and Fine Arts, University of Florida, 1975. [16] p., [10] leaves of plates : ill. ; 23 cm. (University Gallery bulletin ; 1, no. 1) "This collection is being shown and documented in conjunction with the special photographic exhibition: Machu Picchu of the Inca ... These two exhibitions are being presented to mark the advent of the 25th Annual Latin American Conference." Bibliography: p. [10] [F3429.3.P8F56 1975] 75-624261
1. Florida. University, Gainesville. University Gallery. 2. Indians of South America—Peru—Pottery—Exhibitions. I. Gordon, Elsbeth K. II. Craven, Roy C., 1924- III. Title. IV. Series: Florida. University, Gainesville. University Gallery bulletin ; 1, no. 1.

Florini, Marcel, 1922-

KENTUCKY. UNIVERSITY. ART GALLERY. 730'.973
Graphics '66: Marcel Fiorini [Lexington, University of Kentucky, c1965] 1 v. (unpaged) illus., port. 28 cm. "A centennial publication of the University of Kentucky." Catalogue of an exhibition held Nov. 14-Dec. 19, 1965. French and English. [NE650.F526K4] 66-63792
1. Florini, Marcel, 1922- . I. Title.

Florsheim, Richard, 1924—

FREUNDLICH, August L. 759.13' B
Richard Florsheim / August L. Freundlich. South Brunswick [N.J.] : A. S. Barnes, c1976. p. cm. "This special edition is limited to 112 copies .... This is copy [ND237.F48F73] 74-30724 ISBN 0-498-01636-6 : 15.00. ISBN 0-498-01760-5 (lim. ed.) : 100.00
1. Florsheim, Richard, 1924- I. Florsheim, Richard, 1924- BIP

Flour-mills—Virginia—Pictorial works.

HOLLIS, Jay S. 779'.9'6647209755
Virginia gristmills : a photographic presentation / Jay S. Hollis. McLean, Va. : EPM Publications, c1978. p. cm. [TS2135.U62V53] 78-1094 ISBN 0-914440-22-5 pbk. : 10.00
1. Flour-mills—Virginia—Pictorial works. I. Title. BIP

Flower arrangement.

ALDRICH, Dot. 745.922
For pod happy people, these decorative arrangements. Original drawings by Gen Young. St. Petersburg, Fla., Great Outdoors Pub. Co. [1963] 56 p. illus. 28 cm. [SB449.3D7A42] 63-3878
1. Flower arrangement. 2. Handicraft. I. Title. II. Title: Decorative arrangements.

ALDRICH, Dot 745.922
For pod happy people, these decorative arrangements. Orig. drawings by Gen Young. St. Petersburg, Fla., Great Outdoors [c.1963] 56p. illus. 28cm. 63-3878 1.50 pap.,
1. Flower arrangement. 2. Handicraft. I. Title. II. Title: Decorative arrangements.

AMER, Jean B 635.966
Flower arrangements for special occasions. Nashville, Allied Publications [1962] 128p. illus. 28cm. (A Margaret Harold publication) [SB449.A43] 62-14457
1. Flower arrangement. I. Title.

AMER, Jean B. 635.966
Flower arrangements for special occasions [Reissue] Fort Lauderdale, Fla., Allied Pubns. [1965]c.1962. 128p. illus. 28cm. (Margaret Harold pubn.) [SB449.A43] 62-14457 1.95 pap.,
1. Flower arrangement. I. Title.

AMER, Jean B 635.9663
A picture book of prize-winning flower arrangements, and how to make them. [Nashville? 1959] unpaged. illus. 35cm. (A Margaret Harold publication) [SB449.A443] 59-15500
1. Flower arrangement. I. Title. II. Title: Prize-winning flower arrangements.

ASCHER, Amalie Adler. 745.92'24
The complete flower arranger. New York, Simon and Schuster [1974] 288 p. illus. 25 cm. "A Helen Van Pelt Wilson book." [SB449.A66] 73-17695 ISBN 0-671-21666-X 9.95
1. Flower arrangement. I. Title. **BIP**

BAYLES, Vera Todd. 635.9663
Chrysanthemums indoors. All arrangements by the author except plates 29 and 45. New York, Hearthside Press [1960] 92 p. illus. 24 cm. [SB449.B3] 60-12959
1. Flower arrangement. 2. Chrysanthemums. I. Title.

BENZ, Morris, 1909- 745.92'2
Flowers : abstract form / M. Benz. Houston, Tex. : San Jacinto Pub. Co., c1976. 146 p. : col. ill. ; 29 cm. [SB449.B378] 76-28584 47.50
1. Flower arrangement. 2. Art, Abstract. I. Title. **BIP**

BENZ, Morris, 1909- 635.9663
Flowers: creative designs; geometric analysis. [New ed.,rev.] Houston, Tex., San Jacinto Pub. Co. [1962] 287p. 28cm. First published in 1952 under title: Flowers: their creative designs; descriptive analysis. [SB449.B4 1962] 62-18671
1. Flower arrangement. I. Title. **BIP**

BENZ, Morris, 1909- 745.92
Flowers : abstract form II / M. Benz. 2d ed., rev. Houston, Tex. : San Jacinto Pub. Co., c1979. 225 p. : col. ill. ; 29 cm. [SB449.B378 1979] 78-65678 47.50
1. Flower arrangement. 2. Art, Abstract. I. Title.
Publishers address: P. Box 66254, Houston, Texas 77006

BENZ, Morris, 1909- 635.9663
Flowers: free form-interpretive design. Houston, Tex., San Jacinto Pub. Co. [1960] 247 p. illus. 29 cm. [SB449.B38] 59-15356
1. Flower arrangement. I. Title.

BENZ, Morris, 1909- 745.9224
Flowers: geometric form [by] M. Benz. [3d ed.] Houston, Tex., San Jacinto Pub. Co. [1966] xv, 320 p. illus. (part col.) 28 cm. Published in 1952 under title: Flowers: their creative designs; descriptive analysis. [SB449.B4 1966] 66-25443
1. Flower arrangement. I. Title.

BEST, Margaret. 745.92'2
The miniature flower arrangement book [by] Margaret and Godfrey Best. New York, Scribner [1971, c1970] 164 p. illus. (part col.) 25 cm. [SB449.B433 1971b] 78-154755 ISBN 0-684-12442-4 9.95
1. Flower arrangement. I. Best, Godfrey, joint author. II. Title.

BEST of show in flower arrangements; 635.9663 tri-color, award of distinction and blue ribbon winners from top shows of America. 1961- [Nashville, Allied Publications] v. col. illus., ports. 35cm. annual. Compiler: 1961- M. Harold. [SB449.B435] 61-17988
1. Flower arrangement. I. Harold, Margaret, comp.

**BEST of show in flower arrangements;* 745.920222 bk. 6. Do-it-yourself instructions on how to create Tricolor. Award of Distinction. and Creativity Award winners from top shows of America [Comp. by Margaret Harold. Comments by Peggy G. Feasev. Fort Lauderdale, Fla., Allied Pubns., 1966] 1v. col. illus. 40p. (Margaret Harold pubn.) [SB449.B436] 1.95 pap.,
1. Flower arrangement. I. Harold, Margaret, comp. II. Feasey, Peggy G.

BEST of show in flower 745.920222
arrangements.
A treasury of best of show in flower arrangements. Comp. by Margaret Harold. Fort Lauderdale, Fla., Allied Pubns. [c.1966] 207p. col. illus., ports. 35cm. [SB449.B436] 66-6140 9.95 bds.,
1. Flower arrangement. I. Harold, Margaret, comp. II. Title.

BEST of show in flowers arrangements; 635.9663 bk.7, Comp. by M. Harold. Comments by Peggy G. Feasy. Ft. Lauderdale, Fla Allied Pubns., 1967] v. col. illus. 28cm. annual [SB449.B435] 61-17988 1.95 pap.,
1. Flower arrangement. I. Harold, Margaret, comp.

BETTER homes and gardens 745.922 Better homes and gardens flower arranging [2d ed.] New York, Meredith, c.1965. 160p. illus. (pt. col.) 29cm. [SB449.B437] 65-2704 3.95 bds.,
1. Flower arrangement. I. Title: Flower arranging.

BIELAR, Marie Frances. 745.92
The art of floral desigining and simple rules. [Woodland? Calif., 1963] 92 p. illus. 22 cm. [SB449.B52] 63-5480
1. Flower arrangement. I. Title.

BODE, Frances. 745.92
Creativity in flower arrangement. Photos. by William Bode. New York, Hearthside Press [1967] 160 p. illus. (part col.) 24 cm. Bibliography: p. [154] [SB449.B64] 67-17831
1. Flower arrangement. I. Title.

BODE, Frances. 745.92
New structures in flower arrangement, including assemblages, collages, constructions, combines, mobiles, stabiles, stamobiles and maxim-art. Photos by William Bode. New York, Hearthside Press [1968] 123 p. 89 illus. (part col.) 25 cm. [SB449.B642] 68-20193
1. Flower arrangement. I. Title. **BIP**

BODINE, Lillian Lewis. 745.92'2
The incomplete book of flower arranging. Photos by Dick Voyles. Line drawings by Isabel Jones. [1st ed.] Grandview, Miss., Diversity Books, 1967. 96 p. illus. (part col.) 30 cm. [SB449.B644] 67-21072
1. Flower arrangement. I. Title.

BODINE, Lillian Lewis 745.92'2
The incomplete book of flower arranging. Photos. by Dick Voyles. Line drawings by Isabel Jones [1st ed.] Grandview, Miss., Diversity, 1967. 96p. illus. (pt. col.) 30cm. [SB449.B644] 67-21072 6.95, Loose-leaf ring binder
1. Flower arrangement. I. Title.

BRANDENBURGER, Nelda H. 745.92
Interpretive flower arrangement, by Nelda H. Brandenburger. Photos. by DeWitt Bishop. New York, Hearthside Press [1969] 157 p. illus. (part col.) 25 cm. Bibliography: p. 151-152. [SB449.B7] 72-76153 6.95
1. Flower arrangement. I. Bishop, DeWitt, illus. II. Title.

BUFFET-CHALLIE, 745.92'2
Laurence. buffetchallie laurence
Flower decoration in European homes. Flower arrangements by Jacques Bedat. New York, Morrow [1969] 207 p. illus. (part col.) 25 x 26 cm. Translation of L'art des fleurs en Europe. [SB449.B75513 1969b] 77-80900 14.95
1. Flower arrangement. I. Title.

CLARK, Virginia 745.92'6
(Hickman) 1908-
The new book of wedding flowers, decorations, and etiquette by Virginia Clark. Drawings by Jeanette Westfall. New York, Hearthside Press [1970] 192 p. illus., col. plates. 25 cm. Rev. ed. cf. Dust jacket. First published in 1961 under title: The complete book of wedding flowers and decorations, with a section on etiquette. [SB449.5.W4C5 1970] 79-130540 ISBN 0-8208-0054-6 7.95
1. Flower arrangement. 2. Wedding etiquette. I. Title.

CLARK, Virginia (Hickman) 745.926
1908-
Wedding flowers, decorations, and etiquette, by Virginia Clark. Drawings by Jeanette Westfall. New York, Hearthside Press [1966] 160 p. illus. (part col.) 25 cm. First published in 1961 under title: The complete book of wedding flowers and decorations. [SB449.5.B7C55 1966] 66-15786
1. Flower arrangement. 2. Bridal bouquets. 3. Wedding etiquette. I. Title. **BIP**

CLEMENTS, Julia 745.922
ABC of flower arranging. Princeton, N.J., Van Nostrand [1964, c.1963] 85p. illus. (pt. col.) 26cm. 64-54979 4.95
1. Flower arrangement. I. Title. **BIP**

CLEMENTS, Julia. 745.92'2
ABC of flower arranging / Julia Clements. New York : Quadrangle/New York Times Book Co., c1976. 96 p. : ill. ; 26 cm. [SB449.C578 1976] 76-4132 ISBN 0-8129-0635-7 : 6.95
1. Flower arrangement. I. SB449.c578 1976 II. Title.

CLEMENTS, Julia. 745.92
Colour book of flower arrangements. Princeton, N. J., Van Nostrand [1965, c1964] [96] p. illus. (part col.) 26 cm. [SB449.C579 1965] 65-4186
1. Flower arrangement. I. Title.

CLEMENTS, Julia 745.92'2
Flower arrangements in stately homes. New York, Arco [1967, c.1966] 124p. illus. (pt. col.) 31cm. [SB449.C5797 1967] 67-13853 9.00
1. Flower arrangement. I. Title.

CLEMENTS, Julia. 635.966
Fun without flowers. New York, Van Nostrand [1962?] 128 p. illus. 26 cm. [SB449.C582 1962] 62-4078
1. Flower arrangement. I. Title.

CLEMENTS, Julia. 635.9663
A treasury of rose arrangements. New York, Hearthside Press [c1959] 86p. illus. 24cm. 'American edition of My roses.' [SB449.C583 1959] 59-7987
1. Flower arrangement. 2. Roses. I. Title.

COX, Helen. 745.92'03
The floral art book of reference. Flower arrangements by Barbara Pearce and Stuart McHugh. Oxford, New York, Pergamon Press [1970] x, 103 p. illus. 25 cm. [SB449.C77 1970] 70-91462
1. Flower arrangement. I. Title. **BIP**

CUTLER, Katherine N. 745.92
How to arrange flowers for all occasions [by] Katherine N. Cutler. New York, Doubleday, 1967. 256 p. illus., col. plates. 24 cm. [SB449.C8] 67-12874
1. Flower arrangement. I. Title.

CYPHERS, Emma Hodkinson, 745.926
ed.
Holiday flower arrangements, revised. New York, Hearthside Press [1965] 128 p. illus. (part col.) 25 cm. [SB449.C893 1965] 65-25574
1. Flower arrangement. I. Title.

CYPHERS, Emma Hodkinson. 745.9224
Modern abstract flower arrangements; how to identify, evaluate, and design them. New York, Hearthside Press [1964] 128 p. illus. 25 cm. ([A Home and garden bookshelf]) [SB449.C895] 64-21744
1. Flower arrangement. I. Title.

CYPHERS, Emma Hodkinson. 635.9663
Modern art in flower arrangement. New York, Hearthside Press [1959] 123 p. illus. 25 cm. [SB449.C896] 59-7985
1. Flower arrangement. I. Title.

CYPHERS, Emma Hodkinson. 745.92
Nature, art, and flower arrangement. New York, Hearthside Press [1963] 160 p. illus. 25 cm. [SB449.C897] 63-99283
1. Flower arrangement. I. Title.

CYPHERS, Emma Hodkinson. 745.925
The new book of foliage arrangements. New York, Hearthside Press [1965] 152 p. illus. 25 cm. Revised and enl. ed. of the author's Foliage arrangements with a text on modern designs. [SB449.3.F6C9 1965] 64-21085
1. Flower arrangement. 2. Leaves. I. Title. **BIP**

CYPHERS. EMMA HODKINSON, 745.926
ed.
Holiday flower arrangements, rev. New York, Hearthside [c.1954. 1965] 128p. illus. (pt. col.) 25cm. [SB449.C893] 65-25574 4.95 bds.,
1. Flower arrangement. I. Title.

DUNLOP, Hazel 635.9663
Peckinpaugh.
Flower arranging for fun. New York, Viking Press [1959] 119 p. illus. 21 cm. (A Studio book) [SB449.D78] 59-6593
1. Flower arrangement. I. Title.

EASTERBY, Estelle G. 635.9663
The home book of flower arrangements, using Oriental, European, and colonial containers. [1st ed.] Philadelphia, Chilton Co., Book Division [1960] 156 p. illus. 24 cm. [SB449.E18] 60-6376
1. Flower arrangement. I. Title.

FEASEY, Peggy. 745.92
Rubies & roses; gems portrayed in flowers. Rutland, Vt., C. E. Tuttle Co. [1970, c1969] 128 p. illus. (part col.) 27 cm. Bibliography: p. 123. [SB449.F38] 72-83077 12.50
1. Flower arrangement. 2. Precious stones. I. Title. **BIP**

FIELDS, Nora. 745.92
Flower arranging for parties. South Brunswick, A. S. Barnes [1975] 169 p. illus. 29 cm. [SB449.5.P3F53] 73-109 ISBN 0-498-01316-2 15.00
1. Flower arrangement. 2. Party decorations. I. Title.

FIELDS, Nora. 745.92'24
Flowers and foliage; creative compositions. South Brunswick, A. S. Barnes [1973] 166 p. illus. (part col.) 29 cm. [SB449.F48] 71-39828 ISBN 0-498-01162-3 15.00
1. Flower arrangement. I. Title.

FREEHOF, Lillian B. 745.926
(Simon) 1906-
Flowers and festivals of the Jewish year, by Lillian S. Freehof, Lottie C. Bandman. Drawings, photos. by S William Hinzman. New York, Hearthside [c.1964] 192p. illus. (pt. col.) 25cm. (Home and garden bk.-shelf) Bibl. 64-19655 5.95
1. Flower arrangement. 2. Fasts and feasts—Judaism. I. Bandman, Lottie C., joint author. II. Title.

GLEASON, Dorothy H 745.92'6
Think a theme; an idea workbook for flower arrangers, by Dorothy H. Gleason. Cincinnati, Stratford Press [1965] xvi, 77 p. 22 cm. [SB449.G56] 67-1112
1. Flower arrangement. I. Title.

GODDARD, Helen Snow 745.92
Wilson.
The gardener's book of arrangements. Photos. by Paul Genereux. Wood sculpture and sketches by Carl Goddard. [New York] Macmillan [1970] xii, 192 p. illus. 21 cm. [SB449.G614] 71-96448
1. Flower arrangement. I. Title.

GOLDSON, Rae L 745.922
Contemporary flower arrangement, Rev. and enl., with 147 arrangements. New York, Hearthside Press [1962] 127, S31 p. illus. 25 cm. [SB449.G62 1962] 62-10513
1. Flower arrangement. I. Title.

GOLDSON, Rae L. 745.92
New trends in flower arrangement, by Rae L. Goldson. New York, Hearthside Press [1966] 117 p. illus. 25 cm. [SB449.G625] 66-26477
1. Flower arrangement. I. Title. **BIP**

*GORDON, Robert L. 745.92'2
Professional flower arranging for beginners. New York, Arco Publishing [1974, c1972] 102 p., col. illus. 20 cm. [SB449] 73-89232 ISBN 0-668-03452-1 4.95 (pbk.)
1. Flower arrangement. 2. Flower arrangement, Japanese. I. Title.
Cloth ed. 6.59, ISBN 0-668-03392-4 **BIP**

GREGER, Gustl Mary. 745.92
Beauty in flowers; the Star's flower arrangement book, the best of Mrs. Greger: 52 individual flower arrangements, one for each week of the year, sleected from her columns appearing in the Sunday star, by Mr. Herbert H. Greger. [Washington, 1964] 105 p. illus. 23 cm. Cover title. [SB449.G68] 66-2715
1. Flower arrangement. I. The Sunday star, Washington, D.C. II. Title.

GROVES, Joan. 745.922
Ilford color book of flower decoration. Color photos. by James Adams. New York, McGraw-Hill [1964] 112 p. col. illus. 23 cm. [SB449.G7] 64-20421
1. Flower arrangement. 2. Photography of plants. I. Title.

GUERTNER, Beryl 745.92
The Australian book of flower arrangement. Sydney, K. G. Murray Pub. Co. [New Rochelle, N.Y., Australian Bk. Center, 1965] 127p. illus. (pt. col.) 26cm. [SB449.G8] 65-955 7.50 bds.,
1. Flower arrangement. I. Title.

HAWKES, Frances Ann. 745.92
The gracious art of flower arrangement, edited by Frances Ann Hawkes. Photos. by Michael Plomer. Garden City, N.Y., Doubleday [1969, c1968] 118 p. col. illus. 31 cm. At head of title: Susan Pulbrook; Rosamund Gould. First published in 1968 under title: The Pulbrook and Gould book of flower arrangement. [SB449.H388 1969] 70-79413 12.95
1. Flower arrangement. I. Plomer, Michael, illus. II. Pulbrook, Susan, Lady. III. Pulbrook and Gould Limited. IV. Title.

HEMINGWAY, Beth 745.922
Flower arrangement with antiques. New York. Hearthside [c.1965] 191p. illus. (pt. col.) 25cm. [SB449.H44] 65-14122 5.95 bds.,
1. Flower arrangement. I. Title.

HICKS, David, 1929- 745.92'24
The David Hicks Book of flower arranging / as told to Maureen Gregson ; introd. by Julia Clements. New York : Van Nostrand Reinhold Co., 1976. 87 p. : ill. (some col.) ; 30 cm. Includes index. [SB449.H46] 76-11678 ISBN 0-442-23408-2 : 9.95
1. Hicks, David, 1929- 2. Flower arrangement. 3. Flowers. 4. Interior decorators—England—Biography. I. Gregson, Maureen. II. Title. III. Title: Book of flower arranging.

HILLIER, Florence Bell, 745.92
1916-
Basic guide to flower arranging. New York, McGraw-Hill [1974] vi, 280 p. illus. 25 cm. [SB449.H48] 73-8634 ISBN 0-07-028907-7 14.95
1. Flower arrangement. 2. Gardens, Miniature. 3. Flowers—Drying. I. Title. **BIP**

INMAN, Nancy Aldrich. 745.92'24
Tropical flower arranging; a practical guide. Rutland, Vt., C. E. Tuttle Co. [1973] 116 p. illus. 22 cm. Bibliography: p. 111-112. [SB449.I53] 72-88931 ISBN 0-8048-1093-1 8.25
1. Flower arrangement. 2. Dried flower arrangement. 3. Tropical plants. I. Title. **BIP**

KESTEL, Elizabeth S. 745.92'6
At home with flowers; arrangements featuring improvised containers. [St. Paul, Bruce Pub. Co., 1963] 130 p. illus. (part col.) 21 cm. [SB449.K4] 63-23139
1. Flower arrangement. I. Title.

KLAMKIN, Marian. 745.92
Flower arranging for period decoration. Photos. by Charles Klamkin. New York, Funk & Wagnalls [1969, c1968] vi, 213 p. illus. 22 cm. Bibliography: p. 201-203. [SB449.K55] 68-17479 6.95
1. Flower arrangement. I. Title.

KNIGHT, Mary G. 745.92
Abstract and not-so abstract flower arrangement [by] Mary G. Knight. Photos. by Lewis Henderson. Princeton, N. J., Van Nostrand [1965] xiii, 111 p. illus. (part col.) 23 cm. [SB449.K58] 65-26472
1. Flower arrangement. I. Title.

KNIGHT, Mary G. 745.92'5
Weathered wood with flowers, by Mary G. Knight. New York, Morrow [1968] 127 p. illus. (part col.) 22 cm. [SB449.3.D8K55] 68-20169
1. Flower arrangement. 2. Driftwood arrangement. I. Title.

KOHLER, Julilly House, 745.92
1915-
Plants and flowers to decorate your home / by Julilly H. Kohler ; photographs by Bill Hilms ; drawings by Grambs Miller. New York : Golden Press, c1977. 160 p., [8] leaves of plates : ill. (some col.) ; 28 cm. Includes index. [SB449.K64] 76-19244 ISBN 0-307-49335-0 : 12.95.
1. Flower arrangement. 2. House plants in interior decoration. 3. Plants, Ornamental. I. Helms, Bill. II. Miller, Grambs. III. Title.

KROH, Patricia. 635.9663
Design with flowers, unlimited. [1st ed.] Garden City, N. Y., Doubleday, 1959. 141 p. illus. 24 cm. [SB449.K68] 59-12018
1. Flower arrangement. I. Title.

KROH, Patricia. 745.92
A new world of flower arrangement; designs for our times. Author's flower arrangement photography by Milton B. Freudenheim, Sr. [1st ed.] Garden City, N.Y., Doubleday, 1969. 160 p. 106 illus. (part col.) 27 cm. Bibliography: p. [157] [SB449.K685] 70-84380 7.95
1. Flower arrangement. 2. Flower arrangement, Japanese. I. Title.

LAZIER, Harry A. 745.92'2
Carnations; elegance in floral arrangements [by Harry A. Lazier] Denver, Colorado Flower Growers Association [1968?] 183 p. illus. (part col.) 30 cm. [SB449.L38] 68-9279
1. Flower arrangement. 2. Carnations.

LIM, Bian Yam, 1933- 745.92
Exotic flower arrangements. Introd. and plant notes by Violet Stevenson. New York, Funk & Wagnalls [1969] 144 p. illus. (part col.) 26 cm. First published in London in 1967 under title: The eye of the flower arranger. [SB449.L48 1969] 69-11932 7.95
1. Flower arrangement. I. Stevenson, Violet W. II. Title.

LOVE, Diane. 745.92'2
Flowers are fabulous for decorating. New York, Collier Books [1975] xi, 99 p. illus. (part col.) 21 x 28 cm. [SB449.3.A7L68] 74-14834 ISBN 0-02-575560-9 10.00
1. Flower arrangement. 2. Fabric flowers. I. Title.

LOWRY, Martha Ryan. 745.9224
Floral art for America. Photography by Harold Corsini. New York, M. Barrows [1964] 191 p. plates (part col.) 29 cm. [SB449.L63] 64-22210
1. Flower arrangement. I. Corsini, Harold, illus. II. Title.

MACQUEEN, Sheila. 635.9'66
Flower arranging from your garden / Sheila Macqueen. 1st ed. Radnor, Pa. : Chilton Book Co., 1977. 158 p. : ill. (some col.) ; 27 cm. Includes index. [SB449.M318 1977] 77-2468 ISBN 0-8019-6628-0 : 10.95
1. Flower arrangement. 2. Plants, Ornamental. I. Title. **BIP**

MACQUEEN, Sheila 745.92
Flowers for arrangement. London, W.H. & L. Collingridge dist. Hollywood-by-the-Sea, Fla. transatlantic, 1963,c.1962 104p. illus. (pt. col.) 21x23cm. 63-25572 7.50
1. Flower arrangement. I. Title.

MAIA, Ronaldo. 745.92
Decorating with flowers / by Ronaldo Maia, Denise Otis, Ernst Beadle. New York : H. N. Abrams, [1978] p. cm. Includes index. [SB449.M328] 78-5243 ISBN 0-8109-0808-5 : 35.00
1. Flower arrangement. I. Otis, Denise, joint author. II. Beadle, Ernst, joint author. III. Title. **BIP**

MASSINGHAM, Betty. 745.92'2
Flower arranging in colour. London, New York, Hamlyn [1969] 5-301 p. illus. (some col.). 30 cm. Bibliography: p. 301. [SB449.M3545] 79-28355 30/-
1. Flower arrangement. I. Title.

MAURICE, Grizelda. 745.92
Arranging flowers. London, Studio Vista; New York, Watson-Guptill, 1967. 104p. front., illus. (some col.) 19cm. Bibl. [SB449.M23] 68-10156 2.50
1. Flower arrangement. I. Title.

MILLARD, Nancy. 745.92
Dried flower arrangements, from garden, bush and seashore. Photo. by Gilbert Millard. [2d ed.] Sydney, Melbourne, Murray [1967] Stamped on t.p.: Dist. by Sportshelf, New Rochelle, N.Y. 128p. illus. (pt. col.) diagrs. 25cm. [SB449.D7M5 1967] 68-79450 9.00 bds.,
1. Flower arrangement. 2. Flowers—Drying. I. Title.

MOIR, May. 745.92
Flower sculpture in Hawaii : a handbook / by May Moir. Honolulu : Topgallant Pub. Co., 1977. p. cm. Bibliography: p. [SB449.M56] 77-11874 ISBN 0-914916-24-6 : 15.00. ISBN 0-914916-25-4 pbk. : 3.95
1. Flower arrangement. 2. Flower arrangement—Hawaii. I. Title.

MORRISON, Winifrede. 745.92'6
Flower arrangements for special occasions / Winifrede Morrison ; drawings by Margaret Davies. London : B. T. Batsford, 1976. 87 p., [2] leaves of plates : ill. (some col.) ; 26 cm. [SB449.48.M67] 76-370081 ISBN 0-7134-3088-5 : 8.95
1. Flower arrangement. 2. Holiday decorations. 3. Party decorations. 4. Handicraft. I. Title.
Distributed by Hippocrene Books N.Y. N.Y. **BIP**

MULLINS, Ruth E. 635.9663
Religious themes in flower arrangement. New York, Hearthside Press [1959] 118 p. illus. 25 cm. [SB449.M78] 59-14252
1. Flower arrangement. I. Title.

OHIO Association of 745.92'6
Garden Clubs.
Flower arrangements. Compiled by Mrs. Howard J. Piehler [and] Mrs. Edward R. Ray. [1st ed. Urbana, Ohio, 1962] 72p. illus. 22cm. [SB449.O4] 62-21349
1. Flower arrangement. I. Piehler, Dorothy Maybelle (Rohde) 1907- comp. II. Ray, Grace (Baker) 1910- comp. III. Title.

O'NEILL, Jeanne Lamb. 745.92
Flower arranging without flowers : and hundreds of other garden club secrets that nobody ever tells you / by Jeanne Lamb O'Neill ; illustrated by Jeanne, Sean, and Cyn O'Neill. Indianapolis : Bobbs-Merrill, c1976. xv, 198 p. : ill. ; 27 cm. Includes index. Bibliography: p. [188] [SB449.O58] 74-17675 ISBN 0-672-52008-7 : 14.95
1. Flower arrangement. 2. Design, Decorative—Plant forms. I. Title.

PAGE. PHYLLIS C., comp. 745.92
The handbook for flower arrangers. comp. by Phyllis Page. London. Blandford Pr. [1966] viii; 199p. col. illus. 19cm. [SB449.P23] 66-33065 4.50
1. Flower arrangement. I. Title.
Available from Intl. Pubns. Service. New York. **BIP**

PARKIN, Beverley. 745.92'092'4
The gift of flowers : a personal story and practical guide to flower arranging / by Beverley Parkin ; [photos. by David Alexander ; ill. by Rachel Beckingham]. 1st American ed. Grand Rapids : Eerdmans, 1976, c1975. 60 p. : ill. ; 25 cm. [SB449.P29 1976] 75-38549 ISBN 0-8028-3479-5 : 4.95
1. Flower arrangement. I. Title. **BIP**

PAUTZ, Phyllis. 745.92
How to decorate with natural materials. Garden City, N.Y., Doubleday [1973, c.1971] 239 p. illus. 23 cm. (Dolphin Book, C526) First published in 1971 under title: Decorating with plant crafts and natural materials. [SB449.P35] 70-150912 ISBN 0-385-08327-0 2.95 (pbk.)
1. Flower arrangement. 2. House plants. 3. Decoration and ornament. 4. Handicraft. I. Title.

PETERS, Mary A. 745.92
Permanent beauty; [basic fundamentals in artificial flower arranging] 1st ed. Editing by Hill House, Austin, Tex. Austin, Print. [by] Firm Foundation Pub. House [1963] 84 p. illus. (part col.) port., diagr. 23 cm. [SB449.P37] 63-25350
1. Flower arrangement. I. Title.

PETERSON, Caroline E., 745.922
1875-
The art of flower arrangement in Hawaii [by] Caroline E. Peterson, Kenneth Kingrey. Honolulu, Univ. of Hawaii Pr. [c.] 1962. 101p. illus. (pt. col.) 29cm. 62-16168 15.00; 25.00, limited ed., bxd.
1. Flower arrangement. I. Kingrey, Kenneth, joint author. II. Title.

PETTIT, Rhea Ferne. 704.948'55
The Madonna story. Montezuma, Iowa, Sutherland Print. Co. [1970] 137 p. illus. (part col.), port. 26 cm. Bibliography: p. 135. [N8070.P47] 73-134945 7.95
1. Mary, Virgin—Art. 2. Flower arrangement. I. Title.

POWELL, Myrtis N. 745.92
Candles in flower arrangements, by Myrtis N. Powell. Photos. by Ernest Hardin. New York, Van Nostrand Reinhold Co. [1969] 104 p. illus. (part col.) 24 cm. [SB449.3.C3P6] 77-90329
1. Flower arrangement. 2. Candles. I. Title.

RENDELL, Joan. 745.92
Flower arrangement with a marine theme. New York, Taplinger [1967] 127 p. illus. 22 cm. [SB449.R44] 67-17806
1. Flower arrangement. I. Title. **BIP**

RICHARDSON, Ione. 635.9663
Flower arrangement the American way. New Orleans, Pelican Pub. Co. [1960] 167p. illus. 26cm. [SB449.R5] 61-911
1. Flower arrangement. I. Title.

RIESTER, Dorothy W. 745.92
Design for flower arrangers [by] Dorothy W. Riester. 2d ed. New York, Van Nostrand Reinhold [1971] 191 p. illus. 21 cm. Bibliography: p. 188-189. [SB449.R52 1971] 70-110063 8.95
1. Flower arrangement. 2. Design, Decorative—Plant forms. I. Title.

RITTNER, Carl F. 745.92'2
Vase arrangements for the professional florist, in color, by the Rittners. [n.p., 1966] 100 p. illus. (part col.) 28 cm. Cover title. [SB449.R545] 67-3612
1. Flower arrangement. I. Rittner, Eunice, joint author. II. Title.

ROBERTS, Patricia 745.922
Easterbrook
Flower arrangements through the year. New York, Viking [c.]1963. 90p. illus. (pt. col.) 26cm. (Studio bk.) 63-12362 5.95 bds.,
1. Flower arrangement. I. Title.

ROBERTS, Patricia 635.9663
Easterbrook.
Simplified flower arrangements. New York, Viking Press [1960] 134p. illus. 24cm. (A Studio book) [SB449.R57] 60-14090
1. Flower arrangement. I. Title.

ROCKWELL, Frederick 635.9663
Frye, 1884-
New complete book of flower arrangement [by] F. F. Rockwell and Esther C. Grayson. An American Garden Guild book. [1st ed.] Garden City, N.Y., Doubleday [1960] 336 p. illus. 22 cm. Includes bibliography. [SB449.R624] 59-12429
1. Flower arrangement. I. Grayson, Esther C., joint author. II. Title.

SCHMITT, Mimi Lawrence. 745.92
The complete book of artificial flowers, fruit, and foliage, by Mimi Schmitt. New York, Hearthside Press [1964] 125 p. illus. (part col.) 25 cm. [SB449.3.A7S3] 63-17153
1. Flower arrangement. 2. Artificial flowers. 3. Artificial fruit. I. Title.

SHIELDS, Phyllis G. 745.92'2
A guide to flower arranging; in ten basic lessons, by Phyllis G. Shields. [Newton, Mass.] C. T. Branford Co. [1967] ix, 117 p. plates. 22 cm. Includes bibliographies. [SB449.S47] 67-16025
1. Flower arrangement. I. Title. **BIP**

SHINNO, Tat. 635.9663
Flower arranging by Tat. Cover [by] Tyrus Wong. Los Angeles, Printed for Tat's inc. by Fashion Press [1961] 237 p. illus. 27 cm. [SB449.S48] 62-1099
1. Flower arrangement. I. Title.

SHINNO, Tat 745.922
Flower arranging by Tat; step-by-step instructions showing how to create and use flower arrangements. Menlo Park, Calif., Lane [c.1965] 100p. illus. (pt. col.) 28cm. (Sunset bk.) [SB449.S48] 65-19051 1.95 pap.,
1. Flower arrangement. I. Title. **BIP**

SMITH, George Worsnop, 1934- 745.92
Flower arrangements and their settings [by] George W. Smith. New York, Viking Press [1967] 200 p. illus. (part col.) 26 cm. (A Studio book) [SB449.S548] 67-4611
1. Flower arrangement. I. Title.

SMITH, Georgiana Reynolds. 745.92'24
The flower lover's book of natural arrangements. Drawings by Margaret Philbrick. [1st ed.] Garden City, N.Y., Doubleday, 1972. xiii, 143 p. illus. 22 cm. [SB449.S549] 73-180110 7.95
1. Flower arrangement. I. Title.

SMITH, Mina 745.92
Arranging flowers. Drawings by the author. London, Museum Pr. [dist. New Rochelle, N.Y., SportShelf, 1964, c.1963] 136p. illus. (pt. col.) 23cm. (Step-by-step bk.) Bibl. 64-6236 5.50 bds.,
1. Flower arrangement. I. Title.

SOULES, Ken 745.92
Basic floral designing [Florists' Transworld Delivery. dist. Detroit. Mich. 48226. Mercury House, 900 W. Lafayette. 1966, c.1965] viii, 85p. illus. 23cm. [SB449.S567] 66-2044 1.95, pap., plastic bdg.
1. Flower arrangement. I. Title.

SOUTAR, Merelle. 745.92'5
The driftwood flower arrangement book. New York, Funk & Wagnalls [1969] 163 p. illus. (part col.) 25 cm. [SB449.3.D8S6 1969] 69-11933 7.95
1. Flower arrangement. 2. Driftwood arrangement. I. Title.

SOUTAR, Merelle. 745.922
Flower design with accessories. London, New York, Van Nostrand [1965, c1964] 177 p. illus. (part col.) 24 cm. [SB449.S582 1965] 65-2052
1. Flower arrangement. 2. Flower arrangement—Equipment and supplies. I. Title.

SQUIRES, Mabel. 745.92
A handbook of dried arrangements and decorations, with a simplified introduction to drying plants and flowers. Photos. by Richard E. Green. New York, M. Barrows, 1964. 95 p. illus. (part col.) 21 cm. [SB449.3.D7S7] 64-23574
1. Flower arrangement. 2. Plants—Drying. I. Title.

SQUIRES, Mabel. 745.92'5
New trends in dried arrangements and decorations. Photos. by Richard B. Green. New York, M. Barrows; distributed by Morrow, 1967. 128 p. illus. 21 cm. [SB449.3.D7S75] 67-16369
1. Flower arrangement. I. Title.

STEVENSON, Violet W. 745.922
Decorating with flowers and plants. London, Odhams Pr. [dist. Hollywood-by-the-Sea. Transatlantic, c.1963] 96p. illus., col. plates, 26cm. 63-6598 5.00 bds.,
1. Flower arrangement. I. Title.

STEVENSON, Violet W 635.9663
Flower arrangement in color. New York, Viking Press [1954] 70 p. illus. 22 cm. (A Studio book) [SB449.S7465] 61-8061
1. Flower arrangement. I. Title.

STEVENSON, Violet W. 745.92'2
Flower arrangement made easy [by] Violet Stevenson. London, New York, Hamlyn, 1970. 64 p. illus. (some col.). 25 cm. (A Leisure-plan book in colour) [SB449.S7167] 70-30180 ISBN 0-600-44332-9 £0.40
1. Flower arrangement. I. Title.

STEVENSON, Violet W. 745.92
Flower arranging, by Violet Stevenson. Illustrated by George Thompson, June Baker, and Elsie Wrigley. New York, Grosset & Dunlap [1970] 159 p. 240 col. illus. 22 cm. (A Grosset all-color guide, 6) Bibliography: p. 156. Step by step advice for picking flowers and plants and arranging them in the proper container in an appropriate blending of color, shape, and texture. Includes instructions for drying flowers. [SB449.S718 1969] 76-120434 3.95
1. Flower arrangement. I. Thompson, George, illus. II. Baker, June, illus. III. Wrigley, Elsie, illus. IV. Title.

STEVENSON, Violet W. 745.922
Flower decoration for the table, in color [by] Violet Stevenson. New York, Viking Press [1965, c1964] 70 p. col. illus. 23 cm. (A Studio book) [SB449.S73] 65-10265
1. Flower arrangement. 2. Table setting and decoration. I. Title.

STOCKWELL, Betty 745.92
Flower arrangement. London, I. Pitman [New Rochelle, N.Y., SportShelf, 1966, c.1964] xii, 132p. illus. (pt. mounted col.) 26cm. Bibl. [SB449.S74] 66-3331 11.75
1. Flower arrangement. I. Title.

STOLTZ, Raymond Russ, Mrs. 745.92'2
Interpretive floral designs; theme interpretation in flower arrangement: Chinese, Japanese, traditional, modern, abstraction, assemblage. South Brunswick, A. S. Barnes [1972] 251 p. illus. (part col.) 29 cm. Bibliography: p. 237-244. [SB449.S753] 71-124220 ISBN 0-498-07685-7 15.00
1. Flower arrangement. I. Title.

SUTTER, Anne Bernat. 745.92'24
New approach to design principles; a comprehensive analysis of design elements and principles in floral design. Flower arrangements by the author. [St. Louis, Allied Print. Co., 1967] vi, 196 p. illus. (part col.) 28 cm. [SB449.S88] 67-5753
1. Flower arrangement. I. Title. **BIP**

SVINICKI, Eunice. 745.92
Step-by-step flowercraft / by Eunice Svinicki. New York : Golden Press, c1977. 64 p. : ill. (some col.) ; 29 cm. (Step-by-step craft seris) Bibliography: p. 64. [SB449.S895] 76-55117 ISBN 0-307-42020-5 : 2.95
1. Flower arrangement. 2. Dried flower arrangement. 3. Artificial flowers. 4. Nature craft. I. Title. II. Title: Flowercraft.

TAMPION, John. 635.9'66
Botany for flower arrangers [by] John Tampion & Joan Reynolds. New York, Drake [1972, c1971] 149 p. illus. 23 cm. Includes bibliographical references. [SB449.T34] 72-176588 ISBN 0-87749-184-4 5.95
1. Flower arrangement. 2. Botany. 3. Plants—Collection and preservation. I. Reynolds, Joan, joint author. II. Title.

TANGYE, Enid 745.92
Flowers for all occasions. New York, Hawthorn [1966. c.1964] 150p. illus. (pt. col.) 26cm. [SB449.T35 1966] 66-14517 7.95
1. Flower arrangement. I. Title.

VAN RENSSELAER, Eleanor. 635.9664
Decorating with seed mosaics, chipped glass, and plant materials. Princeton, N. J., Van Nostrand [1960] 214 p. illus. 21 cm. [SB449.V32] 60-15137
1. Flower arrangement. 2. Plants, Decorative. 3. Handicraft. I. Title.

VAN RENSSELAER, Eleanor. 745.925
New decorations with pods, cones, and leaves. Photos. by Doug Morris. Princeton, N.J., Van Nostrand [1966] xx, 199 p. illus. (part col.) 21 cm. Bibliography: p. 187-189. [SB449.3.D7V3] 66-27526
1. Flower arrangement. 2. Decoration and ornament. I. Title.

VON MIKLOS, Josephine (Bogdan) 1900- 745.92'24
Wildflowers in your house. With 227 black and white and 8 full color photos. by the author and 108 bouquets mostly by Anne H. Straus. [1st ed.] Garden City, N.Y., Doubleday, 1968. 176 p. illus. (part col.) 27 cm. Bibliography: p. 172. [SB449.3.W5V65] 68-18101
1. Flower arrangement. 2. Wild flowers. I. Title.

WAY, Marjorie Scott. 745.92
Essential forms for flower arrangement. Brattleboro, Vt., S. Greene Press, 1966. viii, 184 p. illus. 24 cm. [SB449.W32] 66-16672
1. Flower arrangement. I. Title.

WESTLAND, Pamela. 745.92
The art of decorating with flowers / Pamela Westland. London : Ward Lock, 1976. 128 p. : ill. (some col.) ; 27 cm. American ed. published under title: Decorating with wild flowers. Includes index. [SB449.3.W5W47 1976b] 77-364273 ISBN 0-7063-5027-8
1. Flower arrangement. 2. Wild flowers. 3. Plants—Collection and preservation. 4. Nature craft. I. Title.

WESTLAND, Pamela. 745.92
Decorating with wild flowers / Pamela Westland. Emmaus, Pa. : Rodale Press, 1976. 128 p. : ill. (some col.) ; 27 cm. Includes index. [SB449.3.W5W47 1976] 75-45881 ISBN 0-87857-126-4 : 12.95
1. Flower arrangement. 2. Wild flowers. 3. Plants—Collection and preservation. 4. Nature craft. I. Title. **BIP**

WHEELER, Esther. 745.92
The complete book of flowers and plants for interior decoration [by] Esther Wheeler and Anabel Combs Lasker. Rev. by Anabel Combs Lasker, assisted by Barbara Baer. Drawings by Janet Porto. New York, Hearthside Press [1969] 206 p. illus. (part col.) 29 cm. [SB449.W49 1969] 75-92490 10.00
1. Flower arrangement. 2. House plants in interior decoration. I. Lasker, Anabel (Combs) joint author. II. Title.

WILSON, Clarice T. 635.9663
Art principles of flower arrangement. [1st ed.] Philadelphia, National Council Books [1961] 111 p. illus. 24 cm. [SB449.W547] 61-10148
1. Flower arrangement. I. Title.

WILSON, Helen Van Pelt, 1901- ed. 635.966
Flower arrangement; designs for today. Contributors: Freda Case [and others] Princeton, N.J., Van Nostrand [1962] 262 p. illus. 22 cm. [SB449.W549] 62-20142
1. Flower arrangement.

WILSON, Helen Van Pelt, 1901- 745.92
Flowers, space, and motion; new designs in hanging flower arrangements. New York, Simon and Schuster [1971] 127 p. illus. 25 cm. Bibliography: p. 124. [SB449.W5492] 71-159141 ISBN 0-671-20965-5 7.95
1. Flower arrangement. 2. Mobiles (Sculpture) I. Title. **BIP**

WILSON, Lois. 745.92
Miniature flower arrangements and plantings. Color photos. by Lockwood Haight. [Princeton, N.J.] Van Nostrand, c1963. 181 p. illus. 24 cm. Includes bibliography. [SB449.W57] 63-1728
1. Flower arrangement. 2. Gardens, Miniature. I. Title.

WILSON, Lois. 745.92
Miniature flower arrangements and plantings. Color photos. by Lockwood Haight. New York, Hawthorn Books [1970, c1963] xiv, 179 p. illus. (part col.) 24 cm. "A Helen Van Pelt Wilson book." [SB449.W57 1970] 72-107896 6.95
1. Flower arrangement. 2. Gardens, Miniature. I. Title.

Flower arrangement, Chinese.

LI, Hui-lin, 1911- 635.9663
Chinese flower arrangement. Princeton, N. J., Van Nostrand [1959] 125p. illus. 24cm. [SB450.L52] 59-15100
1. Flower arrangement, Chinese. I. Title.

Flower arrangement—Dictionaries.

CONSTANCE Spry Flower School. 745.92'03
Constance Spry's encyclopedia of flower arranging and indoor plant decoration. Compiled by the Constance Spry School, London, with contribution from Anthony Marr [and others] New York, Crown Publishers [1973, c1972] 192 p. illus. 26 cm. [SB449.C66 1973] 73-82929 ISBN 0-517-50578-9 9.95
1. Flower arrangement—Dictionaries. 2. Cut flowers—Dictionaries. 3. House plants—Dictionaries. I. Marr, Anthony. II. Title. III. Title: Encyclopedia of flower arranging and indoor plant decoration.

STEVENSON, Violet W. 745.92'03
The encyclopedia of floristry [by] Violet Stevenson. New York, Drake Publishers [1973] 160, 96 p. illus. 23 cm. Contents.Contents.—The encyclopedia of floristry.—The encyclopedia of Christmas and festival decorations. [SB449.S716 1973] 73-3102 ISBN 0-87749-450-9 9.95
1. Flower arrangement—Dictionaries. I. Stevenson, Violet W. The encyclopaedia of Christmas and festival decorations. 1973. II. Title.

Flower arrangement—History.

BERRALL, Julia S. 745.92'09
A history of flower arrangement [by] Julia S. Berrall. Rev. ed. New York, Viking Press [1968] 175 p. illus. (part col.) 29 cm. (A Studio book) Bibliographical references included in "A source list of garden flowers" (p. 168-175) [SB449.B43 1968] 68-23997 ISBN 0-670-37280-3 12.95
1. Flower arrangement—History. I. Title.

NICHOLS, Beverley, 1899- 745.92'09
The art of flower arrangement. With drawings by William McLaren. New York, Viking Press [1967] 239 p. illus. (part col.), col. facsims. 26 cm. (A Studio book) [SB449] 68-31938
1. Flower arrangement—History. I. Title.

Flower arrangement in churches.

HUNT, Fern Bowers. 635.9663
Floral decorations for your church. [1st ed.] Philadelphia, Chilton Co., Book Division [1960] 223 p. illus. 25 cm. Includes bibliography. [SB449.5.C4H8] 60-8094
1. Flower arrangement in churches. I. Title.

INMAN, Jack. 745.92'6
Floral art in the church. Photos. by Richard T. Lee. Nashville, Abingdon Press [1968] 192 p. illus. (part col.) 27 cm. Bibliography: p. 191. [SB449.5.C4I54] 68-22199
1. Flower arrangement in churches. I. Title.

JONES, Iona Trevor. 745.92'6
Pilgrimage of flowers. Chester (1 Bank Close, Chester, CH2 1PB), J. L. Pearce, 1970. 191 p. illus. (some col.), coats of arms, facsims., map, ports. (some col.) 25 cm. [SB449.5.C4J65] 76-884679 ISBN 0-9501938-0-1 £3.00
1. Charles, Prince of Wales, 1948- 2. Flower arrangement in churches. 3. Churches—Wales. I. Title.

MCCLINTON, Katharine (Morrison) 635.9663
Flower arrangement in the church. [7th print., rev.] New York, Morehouse-Gorman Co., 1958. 122p. illus. 20cm. [SB449.5.C4M3 1958] 58-4277
1. Flower arrangement in churches. I. Title.

MULLINS, Ruth E. 745.92'6
Flowers and symbols for the Christian year, by Ruth E. Mullins. New York, Hearthside Press [1967] 150, [10] p. illus. (part col.) 24 cm. Bibliography: p. [151] [SB449.5.C4M84] 66-26478
1. Flower arrangement in churches. I. Title.

PATTESON-KNIGHT, Francis. 635.9663
Arranging flowers for the sanctuary [by] Francis Patteson-Knight and Margaret McReynolds St. Claire. With drawings by Francis Patteson-Knight. Foreword by Francis B. Sayre, Jr. [1st ed.] New York, Harper [1961] 126 p. illus. 22 cm. Includes bibliography. [SB449.5.C4P3] 61-6455
1. Flower arrangement in churches. I. St.

Bibliography: p. 287. [SB450.S95] 72-12094 10.00
1. Flower arrangement, Japanese. I. Title.

TESHIGAHARA, Wafu, 1911-. 745.92252
Japanese flower arrangement; a new illustrated guide to mastery. With photos, by Kaichi Ushiki. [1st ed.] Tokyo, Palo Alto, Calif., Kodansha International [1966] 158 p. illus. (part col.) 22 cm. Translation of Ikebana dokushu sho) [SB450.T45] 66-27558
1. Flower arrangement, Japanese. I. Title. BIP

TESHIGAWARA, Kasumi, 1932- 745.92'252
Flower arrangements from Japan / by Kasumi Teshigawara ; with a pref. by Sofu Teshigawara ; photos. by Miki Takagi. Tokyo ; New York : Kodansha International, 1974. 128 p. : ill. ; 20 cm. First ed. published in 1964 under title: Space and color in Japanese flower arrangement. [SB450.T39 1974] 75-305001 ISBN 0-87011-238-4 pbk. : 3.95
1. Flower arrangement, Japanese. I. Title.

TESHIGAWARA, Kasumi, 1932- 745.92252
Space and color in Japanese flower arrangement. With a pref. by Sofu Teshigawara. Photos. by Miki Takagi. [1st ed.] Tokyo, Kodansha International; Japan Publications Trading Co., distributors, Rutland, Vt. [1964, c1965] 128 p. illus. (part col.) 21 x 22 cm. [SB450.T39] 64-25790
1. Flower arrangement, Japanese. I. Title.

TESHIGAWARA, Sofu, 1900- 745.92
Sofu: his boundless world of flowers and form, by Sofu Teshigahara. Photos. by Ken Domon. [1st ed.] Tokyo. Palo Alto, Calif., Kodansha Intl. [1966] 116p. illus. (pt. col.) 40cm. [SB450.T414] 66-24835 35.00
1. Flower arrangement, Japanese. I. v8Domon, Ken, 1909- II. Title.

UYEHARA, Allie Marie, 1926- 745.92'252
Ten keys to modern Japanese flower arrangement / Allie Marie Uyehara. 1st ed. New York ; Vantage Press, [1975] 94 p., [4] leaves of plates : ill. ; 21 cm. [SB450.U9] 74-17271 ISBN 0-533-01440-9 : 6.95
1. Flower arrangement, Japanese. I. Title.

WALKER, Linda M. 745.92'252
Ikebana; a guide to Japanese flower arrangement [by] Linda M. Walker. New York, Drake Publishers [1972] 141 p. illus. (part col.) 23 cm. [SB450.W33] 72-2896 ISBN 0-87749-293-X 6.95
1. Flower arrangement, Japanese. I. Title.

WEBB, Lida 745.92252
An easy guide to Japanese flower arrangement styles. Drawings by Larry Keith. New York, Hearthside [c.1963] 159p. illus., plates. 21cm. 63-17150 3.95 bds.,
1. Flower arrangement, Japanese. I. Title. II. Title: Japanese flower arrangement styles.

WEBB, Lida. 634.9663
An easy guide to Japanese flower arrangement styles. Drawings by Larry Keith. New York, Hearthside Press [c1963] 159 p. illus., plates. 21 cm. [SB450.W38] 63-17150
1. Flower arrangement, Japanese. I. Title: Japanese flower arrangement styles. II. Title.

WEBB, Lida. 635.9663
Popular styles of Japanese flower arrangement. Drawings by Larry Keith. New York, Hearthside Press [1959] 124 p. illus. 21 cm. [SB450.W4] 59-7984
1. Flower arrangement, Japanese. I. Title.

WHITAKER, Caroline B. 745.92'252
The bride's book of flower arrangement / by Caroline B. Whitaker : photos. by Miki Takagi. Rutland, Vt. : C. E. Tuttle Co., 1975. 231 p. : ill. (some col.) ; 24 cm. Includes index. Bibliography: p. 225-226. [SB450.W48] 74-83392 ISBN 0-8048-1143-1 : 15.00
1. Flower arrangement, Japanese. I. Title. BIP

Flower arrangement—Juvenile literature.

MUNARI, Bruno. 745.92
A flower with love. Translated by Patricia Tracy Lowe. New York, Crowell [1974] [30] p. illus. (part col.) 22 cm. Instructions for and examples of ikebana, Japanese floral arrangements containing special messages. [SB449.M79] 74-2059 ISBN 0-690-00570-9
1. Flower arrangement—Juvenile literature. I. Title. BIP

TABER, Gladys (Bagg) 1899- 745.92
Flower arranging, by Gladys Taber. Illustrated by Grambs Miller. [1st ed.] New York, Holt, Rinehart and Winston [1969] 46 p. illus. 21 cm. (A Book to begin on) Gives suggestions on where to find various kinds of flowers, how to arrange them, how to make a terrarium, and how to make flower arrangements for special occasions. [PZ10.T22Fl] 69-11816 2.95
1. Flower arrangement—Juvenile literature. I. Miller, Grambs, illus. II. Title.

Flower arrangement shows.

HIRSCH, Sylvia. 745.92
The art of judging and exhibiting flower arrangements. New York, Crowell [1968] 88 p. illus. (part col.) 22 cm. [SB449.15.H57] 68-17073
1. Flower arrangement shows. I. Title. II. Title: Flower arrangements.

Flower language.

GREENAWAY, Kate, 1846-1901. 741.9'42
The complete Kate Greenaway; featuring Language of flowers, and listing all her illustrated books with value guide. Watkins Glen, N.Y., Century House [1967] 64 p. illus. 16 cm. [NC1115.G7] 66-29515
1. Flower language. 2. Flowers in art. I. Title. II. Title: Language of flowers.

Flower painting and illustration.

ARLING, Emanie (Nahm) 759.13
A pot with felling; flower paintings, with a short autobiography. New York, Eriksson-Taplinger Co., [c.]1960. 46p. col. plates. 21cm. 60-6433 4.95 half cloth.,
I. Title.

ARLING, Emanie (Nahm) 759.13
A pot with felling; flower paintings, with a short autobiography. New York, Eriksson-Taplinger Co., [c.]1960. 46p. col. plates. 21cm. 60-6433 4.95 half cloth.,
I. Title.

ARLING, Emanie (Nahm) 759.13
A pot with felling; flower paintings, with a short autobiography. New York, Eriksson-Taplinger Co., [c.]1960. 46p. col. plates. 21cm. 60-6433 4.95 half cloth.,
I. Title.

ASKER, Randi. 745.09781
Rose-painting in Norway. Oslo, Dreyer, 1965. 50p. illus. 28cm. [NK1460.A8] 66-77211 4.50 pap.,
1. Flower painting and illustration. 2. Decoration and ornament—Norway. I. Title.
Distributed by Vanous in New York. BIP

BARNES, Clara (Ernst) 1894- 758.42
Painting flowers for pleasure, oil techniques. New York, Reinhold [1962] 112p. illus. 27cm. [ND1400.B27] 62-19488
1. Flower painting and illustration. I. Title.

COATS, Alice M. 760
The book of flowers; four centuries of flower illustration [by] Alice M. Coats. New York, McGraw-Hill [1973] 208 p. illus. (part col.) 38 cm. Bibliography: p. 201-202. [NC815.C62] 73-556 ISBN 0-07-011480-3 30.00
1. Flower painting and illustration. I. Title.

COATS, Alice M. 741.64
The treasury of flowers / Alice M. Coats. New York : McGraw-Hill, [1975] 30, [164] p. : ill. ; 24 cm. Includes indexes. Bibliography: p. 28-30. [NC815.C63] 75-5599 ISBN 0-07-011482-X : 14.95
1. Flower painting and illustration. I. Title. BIP

COOPER, Mario. 751.422
Flower painting in watercolor. New York, Reinhold Pub. Corp. [1962] 143 p. illus. 27 cm. [ND2300.C6] 62-10718
1. Flower painting and illustration. 2. Water-color painting—Technique.

COOPER, Mario. 751.4'22
Flower painting in watercolor. Rev. ed. New York, Van Nostrand Reinhold Co. [1972] 141 p. illus. (part col.) 27 cm. [ND2300.C6 1972] 72-186773
1. Flower painting and illustration. 2. Water-color painting—Technique. I. Title.

FABRI, Ralph, 1894- 751.4
Complete guide to flower painting. New York, Watson-Guptill Publications [1968] 159 p. illus. (part col.) 29 cm. [ND1400.F3] 68-12343
1. Flower painting and illustration. I. Title. II. Title: Flower painting.

FLOWER painting / 758'.42
[text by] Robin Gibson. Oxford : Phaidon, 1976. 16 p., 48 p. of plates : chiefly col. ill. ; 31 cm. [ND1400.F46] 76-344 ISBN 0-7148-1692-2 : 6.95
1. Flower painting and illustration. 2. Flowers in art. I. Gibson, Robin.
Distributed by E.P.Dutton, N.Y.

KLAVINS, Uldis. 751.4'5
The art of painting wild flowers : paintings / by Uldis Klavins ; designed, edited, and produced by Lester Rossin for M. Grumbacher, inc. New York : M. Grumbacher, c1977. 30 p. : col. ill. ; 32 cm. (The Grumbacher library ; B421) [ND1400.K57] 77-369473 1.95
1. Flower painting and illustration. 2. Painting—Technique. I. Title.

MARCUS, Margaret Fairbanks. 758'.42
Flower painting. New York, H. N. Abrams [1970] 24 p. illus. (part col.) 33 cm. (The Library of great painters. Portfolio ed.) [ND1400.M3 1970] 69-14746
1. Flower painting and illustration. I. Title.

MARCUS, Margaret Fairbanks. 758.42
Flower painting. New York, H. N. Abrams [1953] 24 p. illus. (part mounted col.) 33 cm. (The Library of great painters. Portfolio ed.) An Abrams art book. [ND1400.M3] 53-8465
1. Flower painting.

MARCUS, Margaret Fairbanks. 758.42
Flower painting by the great masters. New York, H. N. Abrams in association with Pocket Books [1954] [74] p. 43 illus. (part col.) 18cm. (The Pocket library of great art, A24) An Abrams art book. Bibliography:p. [74] [ND1400.M32] 55-591
1. Flower painting. I. Title.

MILLS, John FitzMaurice, 1917- 751.4
Flower painting. New York, Pitman Pub. Corp. [1961] 90 p. illus. 26 cm. [ND1400.M5] 61-66469
1. Flower painting and illustration. I. Title.

PARSONS, Joy 751
Painting flowers, written, illus. by Joy Parsons. New York, Warne [1965, c.1964] 64p. illus. (pt. col.) 22cm. [ND1400] 65-10016 2.95 bds.,
1. Flower painting and illustration. I. Title.

PERARD, Victor Semon, 1870-1957. 743.76
Drawing flowers. New York, Pitman Pub. Corp. [1958] unpaged. illus. 20x26cm. (Pitman drawing series) [NC815.P4 1958] 58-6979
1. Flower painting and illustration. I. Title. BIP

REID, Charles, 1937- 751.4'22
Flower painting in watercolor / by Charles Reid. New York : Watson-Guptill Publications, 1979. p. cm. Includes index. Bibliography: p. [ND2300.R44 1979] 78-26535 ISBN 0-8230-1849-0 : 19.50
1. Flower painting and illustration. 2. Water-color painting—Technique. I. Title. BIP

SIMEON, Margaret. 743.76
How to draw garden flowers. London, New York, Studio Publications [1953] 64 p. illus. 18 cm. (The How to draw series) [NC815.S5] 53-11398
1. Flower painting and illustration. I. Title.

SMITH, Marcella. 758.42
Flower painting in water colour. New York, Pitman Pub. Corp. [1955] 79 p. illus. 22 cm. [ND2300.S5] 56-13832
1. Flower painting and illustration. 2. Water-color painting—Technique.

ZAIDENBERG, Arthur, 1903-- 743.7
How to draw flowers, fruit and vegetables. New York, Abelard [c.1964] 63p. illus. 27cm. 64-13158 3.00
1. Flower painting and illustration. 2. Fruit painting and illustration. 3. Drawing—Instruction. I. Title.

ZAIDENBERG, Arthur, 1903- 743.7
How to draw flowers, fruit, vegetables. London, New York, Abelard-Schuman [1964] 63 p. illus. 27 cm. [NC815.Z3] 64-13158
1. Flower painting and illustration. 2. Fruit painting and illustration. 3. Drawing — Instruction. I. Title.

ZICHY, Maria. 751.4
Flower painting, its art and technique. [New York] Watson-Guptill [1961] 109 p. illus. 26 cm. [ND1400.Z5] 60-15710
1. Flower painting and illustration. I. Title.

Flowers—Collection and preservation.

BROWN, Emily L. 745.92
Bouquets that last, by Emily Brown. New York, Hearthside Press [1970] 175 p. illus. (part col.) 27 cm. [SB447.B76] 70-113258 ISBN 8-208-00708- 10.00
1. Flowers—Collection and preservation. 2. Flower arrangement. 3. Dried flower arrangement. I. Title.

CONDON, Geneal. 635.966
The art of flower preservation. [1st ed.] Menlo Park, Calif., Lane Book Co. [1962] 61 p. illus. 28 cm. (A Sunset book, 425) [SB447.C6] 62-12470
1. Flowers—Collection and preservation. I. Title.

CONDON, Geneal. 745.92
The complete book of flower preservation. Englewood-Cliffs, N.J., Prentice-Hall [1970] ix, 210 p. illus. (part col.) 24 cm. [SB447.C63] 70-117008 ISBN 0-13-156802-7 7.95
1. Flowers—Collection and preservation. I. Title. BIP

EVERLASTING flowers. 745.92
1st American ed. New York : Macmillan, 1976. 88 p. : ill. ; 29 cm. [SB447.E93 1976] 76-3361 5.95
1. Flowers—Collection and preservation. 2. Dried flower arrangement. 3. Everlasting flowers. 4. Pressed flower pictures. 5. Nature craft. I. Macmillan Publishing Company. BIP

Flowers—Drying.

AMLICK, Barbara H. 745.92'2
Getting started in dried flower craft [by] Barbara H. Amlick. New York, Bruce Pub. Co. [1971] viii, 70 p. illus. (part col.) 28 cm. (Getting started series) Bibliography: p. 67-68. [SB447.A45] 70-152291 2.95
1. Flowers—Drying. 2. Dried flower arrangement. 3. Pressed flower pictures. I. Title.

BUGBEE, Audrey Steiner. 745.92
How to dry flowers the easy way / Audrey Steiner Bugbee ; with photos. by John Murphy and Timothy Cross. Boston : Houghton Mifflin, 1975. xiii, 95 p. : ill. ; 27 cm. [SB447.B83] 74-30113 ISBN 0-395-20441-0 : 10.95
1. Flowers—Drying. I. Title. BIP

*DERBYSHIRE, Jane 745.92
The Arco Book of dried and pressed flowers [by] Jane Derbyshire & Renee Burgess. New York, Arco Pub. Co. [1975] 96 p. ill. (part col.) 26 cm. Includes index. [SB449] 74-14120 ISBN 0-668-03511-0 7.95
1. Flowers—Drying. I. Burgess, Renee, joint author II. Title. BIP

FOSTER, Laura Louise. 745.92
Keeping the plants you pick. Illustrated by the author. New York, Crowell [1970] 149 p. illus. 24 cm. Bibliography: p. 136-140. [SB449.3.D7F6] 74-101926 4.95
1. Flowers—Drying. 2. Pressed flower pictures. 3. Dried flower arrangement. I. Title. BIP

KAREL, Leonard, 1912- 745.92
Dried flowers: from antiquity to the present; a history and a practical guide to flower drying. Metuchen, N.J., Scarecrow Press, 1973. viii, 184 p. 22 cm. Bibliography: p. 153-157. [SB447.K29] 72-10909 ISBN 0-8108-0512-X 6.00
1. Flowers—Drying. I. Title. BIP

MAXWELL, Cathleen. 745.92
Dried flowers : their preservation and arrangement, also instructions on making pomanders and other conceits / by Cathleen Maxwell and Molly Nicholl ; [illustrations by Judith Maxwell]. Bath : The American Museum, [1976] [20] p. : ill. ; 22 cm. Cover title. [SB447.M39] 76-378216 ISBN 0-9504971-2-6 : £0.25
1. Flowers—Drying. 2. Dried flower arrangement. 3. Nature craft. I. Nicholl, Molly, joint author. II. Title.

SQUIRES, Mabel. 635.9663
The art of drying plants and flowers. New York, M. Barrows, 1958. 258 p. illus. 21 cm. [SB449.S65] 58-8160
1. Flowers—Drying. 2. Plants—Drying. 3. Dried flower arrangement. I. Title.

WHITLOCK, Sarah. 745.5
Dried flowers : how to prepare them / by Sarah Whitlock and Martha Rankin. New York : Dover Publications, 1975, c1962. 31 p. : ill. ; 22 cm. Originally published under title: New techniques with dried flowers. Includes index. [SB447.W45 1975] 75-17126 ISBN 0-486-21802-3 pbk. : 1.00
1. Flowers—Drying. I. Rankin, Martha, joint author. II. Title. BIP

WHITLOCK, Sarah. 745.5
New techniques with dried flowers, by Sarah Whitlock and Martha Rankin. Color photography by Catherine Bishop and Edwin Roseberry. New York, Hearthside Press [1962] 31 p. illus. 21 cm. "Based on a pamphlet, Drying flowers for color, by the same authors." [SB447.W45] 62-10512
1. Flowers—Drying. I. Rankin, Martha, joint author. II. Title.

Flowers in art.

BAZIN, Germain. 758.42
A gallery of flowers. New York, Appleton-Century [1964, c1960] 206 p. 45 col. plates. 26 cm. Translated by Jonathan Griffin from the French version of a work first published in Germany under title: Das Blumenbouquet. [ND1400.B353] 64-24476
1. Flowers in art. 2. Paintings, European. I. Title.

CHEWNING, Emily Blair. 769'.4'34
The illustrated flower / text by Emily Blair Chewning ; designed by Seymour Chwast ; compiled by J. C. Saures ; edited by William E. Maloney ; picture research by Laurie Platt Winfrey. New York : Harmony Books, 1977. 72 p. : ill. (some col.) ; 33 cm. "A Push Pin Press book." [N7680.C45 1977] 76-56449 ISBN 0-517-52876-2 : 10.95 ISBN 0-517-52913-0 pbk. : 5.95
1. Flowers in art. I. Suares, Jean-Claude. II. Chwast, Seymour. III. Title. BIP

DUNTHORNE, Gordon. 769'.4'34
Flower & fruit prints of the 18th and early 19th centuries; their history, makers and uses, with a catalogue raisonne of the works in which they are found. New York, Da Capo Press, 1970. xiv, 275 p. illus. (part col.) 34 cm. (Da Capo Press series in graphic art, v. 6) Reprint of the 1938 ed. Includes bibliographies. [NE953.D8 1970] 67-25443 60.00
1. Flowers in art. 2. Fruit in art. I. Title.

MITCHELL, Peter, 758'.42 B
fl.1968-
Great flower painters; four centuries of floral art. Woodstock, N.Y., Overlook Press [1973] 272 p. illus. (part col.) 29 cm. Bibliography: p. 263-264. [ND2300.M57] 72-95231 ISBN 0-87951-008-0 27.95
1. Flowers in art. 2. Still-life painting. 3. Painters. I. Title. BIP

REID, Charles, 1937- 751.4'5
Flower painting in oil / by Charles Reid. New York : Watson-Guptill Publications, 1976. 167 p. : ill. (some col.) ; 29 cm. Includes index. [ND1400.R45 1976] 75-45423 ISBN 0-8230-1848-2 : 16.95
1. Flowers in art. 2. Painting—Technique. I. Title. BIP

Flowers in art—Exhibitions.

KELLEY, Chapman, 1932- 759.13
An exhibition of wildflower works by Chapman Kelley, April 18-May 26, 1977, Atelier Chapman Kelley ... Dallas, Texas / foreword by Samuel Shannon Blain, Jr. ; photography by Candice Land ; color photography by Doug Handel. Dallas : Kelley, c1977. 35 p. : ill. (some col.) ; 24 cm. [ND1839.K44A93] 77-150941
1. Kelley, Chapman, 1932- 2. Flowers in art—Exhibitions. 3. Landscape architecture—Texas—Dallas—Exhibitions. I. Atelier Chapman Kelley. II. Title: An exhibition of wildflower works by Chapman Kelley ...

Flowers—Pictorial works.

BOSC, Jean Maurice, 741.5944
1924-
Two flowers [by] Bosc. New York, World Pub. Co. [1970] [63] p. of illus. 17 cm. "Originally published ... under the title: La fleur dans tous ses etats." [NC1499.B73A4513 1970] 78-137687
I. Title.

HOLLADAY, Harriett 741.973
MacDonald.
Ravens Creek, MCMLX drawings. [Notes by Carolyn R. Hammer] Lexington, Ky., Anvil Press [c.1960] [9] 1., 6 col., plates. 17cm. (Anvil Press special publication, 4) 60-1233 6.00 pap., lim. ed.
1. Flowers—Pictorial works. I. Title.

MANNERING, Eva, ed. 758.42
Flower portraits. London Ariel Pr. [dist. New York. Taplinger. 1965. c.1961] 14p. illus., 18 col. plates. 41cm. [QK98.M28] 65-29569 12.95
1. Flowers—Pictorial works. I. Title.
Contents omitted.

Flowers—U.S.

ZIM, Herbert Spencer, 581.973
1909-
Flowers; a guide to familiar American wild flowers, by Herbert S. Zim and Alexander C. Martin. Illustrated by Rudolf Freud. 134 paintings in full color. New York, Simon and Schuster [1950] 157 p. col. illus. 16 cm. (A Golden nature guide) "Sponsored by the Wildlife Management Institute." [QK112.Z5] 50-8172
1. Flowers—U.S. 2. Botany—Pictorial works. I. Martin, Alexander Campbell, 1897- joint author. BIP

Fo kuang ssu, Wu-t'ai hsien, China—History.

RHIE, Marylin M. 732'.4
The Fo-kuang ssu : literary evidences and Buddhist images / Marylin M. Rhie. New York : Garland Pub., 1977. xi, 274 p. : ill. ; 21 cm. (Outstanding dissertations in the fine arts) Reprint of the author's thesis, University of Chicago, 1970. "Translation of Tun-huang MS (Stein) 397": p. 47-64. Bibliography: p. 183-194. [BQ6345.W842F67 1977] 76-23690 ISBN 0-8240-2721-3 lib.bdg. : 32.50
1. Fo kuang ssu, Wu-t'ai hsien, China—History. 2. Tun-huang manuscripts. Ms. 397. 3. Sculpture, Buddhist—Wu-t'ai hsien, China. 4. Sculpture—Wu-t'ai hsien, China. I. Tun-huang manuscripts. Ms. 397. English. 1977. II. Title. III. Series. BIP

Folger Shakespeare Library, Washington, D. C.

HARD, Charles Frederick 730.973
The sculptured scenes from Shakespeare; a description of John Gregory's marble reliefs on the Folger Library Building. Washington, Folger Shakespeare; a description of John Gregory's marble reliefs on the Folger Library Building. Washington, Folger Shakespeare Library, [c.]1959. 27p. illus. 22cm. 60-414 apply pap.,
1. Gregory, John, 1879-1958. 2. Folger Shakespeare Library, Washington, D. C. I. Title.

Folger, Walter, 1765-1849.

GARDNER, William Edward, 926.81
1872-
The clock that talks and what it tells; a portrait story of the maker: Hon. Walter Folger, Jr., astronomer, mathematician, navigator, lawyer, judge, legislator, congressman, philosopher; but he called himself: clock and watchmaker ... [Nantucket] Whaling Museum Publications; distributed by the Personal Book Shop, Boston [1954] viii, 143p. illus., ports, facsims. 21cm. [Nantucket, Mass. Whaling Museum. Publications] 'Books used by Walter Folger Jr.': p. 135-136. Bibliography: p. 119-120. [CT275.F652G3] 55-514
1. Folger, Walter, 1765-1849. I. Title. II. Series.

Folk art.

JACOPETTI, Alexandra. 745'.0973
Native funk & flash; an emerging folk art [by] Alexandra Jacopetti. Photos. by Jerry Wainwright. [San Francisco] Scrimshaw Press, 1974. 111 p. col. illus. 23 x 26 cm. [NK789.J32 1974] 74-7073 ISBN 0-912020-37-7 12.95
1. Folk art. I. Wainwright, Jerry, 1926- illus. II. Title.
Pbk. 7.95, ISBN 0-912020-38-5.

SABINE, Ellen S. 745.4
American folk art. Drawings by the author, color photos. by Hilda Borcherding. Princeton, N. J., Van Nostrand [1958] 132 p. illus. 28 cm. [NK1130.S182] 58-13834
1. Folk art. 2. Folk art—U.S. 3. Decoration and ornament—U.S. 4. Design, Decorative. I. Title.

Folk art—America.

SHALKOP, Robert L. 730'.9'171246
Reflections of Spain, by Robert L. Shalkop. [Colorado Springs] Taylor Museum of the Colorado Springs Fine Arts Center [1968] 39 p. illus. 21 x 27 cm. Catalog of a loan exhibition held at the Taylor Museum. Bibliography: p. 37-39. [NK801.S5] 68-7816
1. Folk art—America. 2. Religious articles—Exhibitions. I. Colorado Springs. Fine Arts Center. Taylor Museum. II. Title.

Folk-art—Arroyo Hondo—Catalogs.

SHALKOP, Robert L. 745'.09789'53
The folk art of a New Mexican village, by Robert L. Shalkop. [Colorado Springs] Taylor Museum of the Colorado Springs Fine Arts Center [1969] 48 p. illus. 16 x 23 cm. On cover: Arroyo Hondo. "Catalogue of materials from Arroyo Hondo in the Taylor Museum": p. 34-48. Bibliography: p. 32. [N7911.A7S5] 76-7657
1. Folk-art—Arroyo Hondo—Catalogs. 2. Christian art and symbolism—Catalogs. I. Colorado Springs. Fine Arts Center. Taylor Museum. II. Title.

Folk art—Czechoslovakia.

*HASALOVA, Vera 745.449'437
Folk art of Czechoslovakia [by] Vera Hasalova [and] Jaroslav Vajdis. New York Arco [1975] 293 p. illus. (part col.), maps [1975] Bibliography: p. 291-293. [NK1013.C9] 74-81680 ISBN 0-668-03510-2 20.00
1. Folk art—Czechoslovakia. I. Vajdis, Jaroslav, joint author. II. Title. BIP

Folk art—England.

FLETCHER, Geoffrey S. 745.0942
Popular art in England, Written, illus. by Geoffrey S. Fletcher. London, Harrap [dist. New Rochelle, N.Y. SportShelf, 1963, c.1962] 87p. illus. col. front. 22cm. 63-6054 4.25
1. Folk art—England. I. Title.

HUGHES, Therle. 745
Cottage antiques. New York, Praeger [1967] 219 p. illus., col. plate. 23 cm. [NK928.H8 1967b] 67-24710
1. Folk art—England. 2. Art objects, English. 3. Art objects—Collectors and collecting. I. Title.

Folk art—Europe.

HANSEN, Hans Jurgen, 1921- 745.5
European folk art in Europe and the Americas. General editor: H. J. Hansen. Introd. by Robert Wildhaber. With contributions by Peter Anker [and others] New York, McGraw-Hill [1968] 281 p. illus. (part col.) 31 cm. Translation of Europas Volkskunst und die europaisch beeninflusste Volkskunst Amerikas. [NK925.H313 1968b] 68-16683 25.00
1. Folk art—Europe. 2. Folk art—America. I. Anker, Peter. II. Title.

RITZ, Gislind Maria, 1925- 749.2
The art of painted furniture [by] Gislind M. Ritz. Photos. by Helga Schmidt-Glassner. English translation by Sigrid MacRae. New York, Van Nostrand Reinhold [1971, c1970] 175 p. illus., 52 col. plates. 29 cm. Translation of Alte bemalte Bauernmobel Europa. Bibliography: p. 169-173. [NK925.R513 1971] 76-150509
1. Folk art—Europe. 2. Furniture, European. 3. Decoration and ornament, European. I. Title.

Folk art—Exhibitions.

ABBY Aldrich Rockefeller 709.73
Folk Art Collection, Williamsburg, Va.
American folk art: the exhibition of 1932. American folk art the exhibition of nineteen thirty-two [Williamsburg, Va., 1968?] 19 p. col. illus. 26 cm. Catalogue of an exhibition held Jan. 16-Mar. 3, 1968. "A reassembly of the first exhibition of Abby Aldrich Rockefeller's collection of American folk art held at the Museum of Modern Art from November 30, 1932, until January 15, 1933." [NK807.A36] 77-29251
1. Folk art—Exhibitions. 2. Folk art—U.S. I. Title.

ANGLO- 745'.09763'074016318
AMERICAN Art Museum.
Louisiana folk art. [Baton Rouge, 1972] 44 p. illus. 21 x 26 cm. Catalog of an exhibition held Oct. 1-Dec. 15, 1972. [NK835.L8A84] 72-612156
1. Folk art—Exhibitions. 2. Folk art—Louisiana. I. Title.

FOLK art in 745'.0973'074015
America, a living tradition : selections from the Abby Aldrich Rockefeller Folk Art Collection, Williamsburg, Virginia : [catalogue of] an exhibition organized by the Abby Aldrich Rockefeller Folk Art Collection and the High Museum of Art, Atlanta, Georgia. Atlanta : High Museum of Art, 1974. 96 p. : ill. (some col.) ; 25 cm. Exhibition held at the High Museum of Art, Atlanta, Sept. 14-Oct. 31, 1974, and other museums Nov. 24, 1974-Nov. 15, 1975. Bibliography: p. 96. [NK807.F64] 74-83252
1. Folk art—Exhibitions. 2. Folk art—United States. 3. Primitivism in art—United States. I. Abby Aldrich Rockefeller Folk Art Collection, Williamsburg, Va. II. High Museum of Art. III. Title.

THE Herbert Waide 745'.0973
Hemphill, Jr. Collection of 18th, 19th, and 20th century American folk art : presented at Heritage Plantation of Sandwich in the Arts and Crafts Building, Sandwich, Massachusetts, May 1st through October 15th, 1974, and Columbus Museum of Arts and Crafts, Columbus, Georgia, opening the new Bradley Wing November 9th, 1974, through February 2nd, 1975. [Sandwich, Mass. : Heritage Plantation of

Sandwich, 1974] 48 p. : ill. ; 23 cm. [NK805.H45] 74-186337
1. Hemphill, Herbert Waide—Art collections. 2. Folk art—Exhibitions. 3. Folk art—United States. I. Heritage Plantation of Sandwich. II. Columbus Museum of Arts and Crafts.

JAMINI Roy & 709'.54'14074015979
Bengali folk art; a special exhibition of works in the Collection of Mr. & Mrs. Thomas J. Needham of Jacksonville, Florida. [Gainesville, University Gallery, University of Florida, 1971] [44] p. illus. (part col.) 23 cm. Catalogue of an exhibition held at the University Gallery, University of Florida, Mar. 19-Apr. 25, 1971 and at the Jacksonville Art Museum, May 6-30, 1971. [N7307.B4J3] 76-198197
1. Roy, Jamini, 1887- 2. Needham, Thomas J.—Art collections. 3. Folk art—Exhibitions. 4. Folk art—Bengal. I. Roy, Jamini, 1887- II. Florida. University, Gainesville. University Gallery. III. Jacksonville Art Museum.

KRAMRISCH, Stella, 1898- 709'.54
Unknown India; ritual art in tribe and village. [Philadelphia? 1968] 127 p. illus. (part col.) 31 cm. Cover title. Map on p. [3] of cover. Catalog of an exhibition held Jan. 20 to Feb. 26, 1968, at the Philadelphia Museum of Art, March 28 to June 9, 1968, at the M. H. de Young Memorial Museum, and July 15 to Aug. 20, 1968, at the City Art Museum of St. Louis. Bibliography: p. 124-127. [NK1047.K7] 68-14542
1. Folk art—Exhibitions. 2. Folk art—India. I. Philadelphia Museum of Art. II. De Young Memorial Museum, San Francisco. III. St. Louis. City Art Museum. IV. Title.

NEW York (City). Museum of Modern Art. 709'.73
American folk art; the art of the common man in America, 1750-1900. New York, Museum of Modern Art. Reprint ed. [New York] Published for the Museum of Modern Art by Arno Press, 1969 [c1932] 52 p. plates. 27 cm. Includes catalog of an exhibition. Bibliography: p. 47-52. [NK805.N38 1969] 71-86427
1. Folk art—Exhibitions. 2. Folk art—U.S. I. Title.

SOCIETY of the Four Arts. 745'.0973
American folk art; an exhibition in honor of Edith Gregor Halpert, March 10 to April 8, 1973. Palm Beach, Fla., [1973] [16] p. illus. 23 cm. Selection of American folk art from Mrs. Halpert's estate. [NK805.S62 1973] 74-156572
1. Halpert, Edith—Art collections. 2. Folk art—Exhibitions. 3. Folk art—United States. I. Title.

Folk art—Finland.

RACZ, Istvan, 1908- 745'.009471
Treasures of Finnish folk art. Photos by Istvan Racz. Introd. and notes on the illustrations by Niilo Valonen. Translated from the Finnish by Diana Tullberg. New York, Praeger [1969, c1967] 229 p. (chiefly illus. (part col.), maps) 32 cm. Translation of Suomen Kansantaiteen aarteita. [NK1035.F5R313] 69-18515 15.00
1. Folk art—Finland. 2. Art industries and trade, Finnish. 3. Implements, utensils, etc.—Finland. I. Valonen, Niilo. II. Title.

Folk art—France.

CUISENIER, Jean, 1927- 745'.0944
French folk art / by Jean Cuisenier. 1st ed. Tokyo ; New York : Kodansha International ; New York : distributor, Harper & Row, 1977. 310 p. : ill. (some col.) ; 29 cm. Translation of L'art populaire en France. Includes index. Bibliography: p. 255-296. [NK947.C8313] 76-44158 ISBN 0-87011-297-X : 65.00
1. Folk art—France. I. Title.

Folk art — Gt. Brit.

LAMBERT, Margaret. Hon. 745.1'03
English popular art [by] M. Lambert and Enid Marx. London, Neu York, B.T. Batsford, 1951. viii, 120 p. illus., facsims., plates. (port col.) 22 cm. [NK928.L3] 67-46333
1. Folk art — Gt. Brit. I. Marx, Enid. 1902- joint author. II. Title.

MARX, Enid. 1902- joint author. 745.1'03
English popular art [by] M. Lambert and Enid Marx. London, Neu York, B.T. Batsford, 1951. viii, 120 p. illus., facsims., plates. (port col.) 22 cm. [NK928.L3] 67-46333
1. Folk art — Gt. Brit. I. Title.

Folk art—Hawaiian Islands.

FRANKENSTEIN, Alfred Victor, 1906- 704.9482
Angels over the altar; Christian folk art in Hawaii and the South Seas. Photography: Norman Carlson. Honolulu, Univ. of Hawaii Pr. 1961. viii, 101p. illus. (pt. col.) 28cm. 61-8433 12.00 pap.,
1. Folk art—Hawaiian Islands. 2. Folk art—Oceanica. 3. Christian art and symbolism. I. Carlson, Norman K., illus. II. Title.

Folk art—History.

BOSSERT, Helmuth Theodor, 1889- 600
Folk art of Asia, Africa, and the Americas [by] Helmuth Th. Bossart. New York, Praeger [1964] 23 p., 80 col. plates, 34 cm. "Combined edition of two volumes previously published under the titles Folk art of primitive peoples and Decorative art of Asia and Egypt." "Companion volume to ... Folk art of Europe." -- Dust jacket. [NK600.B583] 64-22922
1. Folk art — Hist. 2. Art Industries and trade — Hist. I. Bossert, Helmuth Theodor, 1889- Folk art of primitive peoples. II. Bossert, Helmuth Theodor, 1889- Decorative art of Asia and Egypt. III. Title.

BOSSERT, Helmuth Theodor, 1889-1961. 745
Folk art of Asia, Africa, and the Americas / Helmuth Th. Bossert. New York : Hastings House, 1975. 23 p., 40, 40 leaves of plates : col. ill. ; 35 cm. "Combined edition of two volumes previously published under the titles Folk art of primitive peoples, and Decorative art of Asia and Egypt." Reprint of the 1964 ed. published by Praeger, New York. Companion volume to the author's Folk art of Europe. Includes indexes. [NK600.B6213 1975] 74-28204 ISBN 0-8038-2306-1 : 49.95
1. Folk art—History. 2. Art industries and trade—History. I. Bossert, Helmuth Theodor, 1889-1961. Decorative art of Asia and Egypt. II. Title.

Folk art—Hungary.

GINK, Karoly. 745'.09439
Folk art and folk artists in Hungary [by] Karoly Gink [and] Ivor Sandor Kiss. [Translated by Eva Racz. 2d ed.] New York, Hastings House [1971, c1968] 108, [32] p. illus. (part col.) 24 cm. Translation of Magyar tajak muveszete. [NK1035.H8G513 1971] 77-165458 ISBN 0-8038-2283-9
1. Folk art—Hungary. 2. Decoration and ornament—Hungary. I. Kiss, Ivor Sandor, joint author. II. Title.

Folk art—India—Exhibitions.

REEVES, Ruth, 1892-1966 745.5'0954
Folk arts of India: metal, ceramics, jewelry, textiles. and wood; an exhibition of the Ruth Reeves Memorial Collection, Syracuse University, and related work loaned by private collectors. Catalog and notes by Ruth Reeves. Ed., introd. by Alexandra K. Schmeckebier. Syracuse, N. Y., Sch. of Art, Syracuse Univ., 1967. 93p. illus., map. 22cm. [NK1047.R4] 67-20393 price unreported pap.,
1. Folk art—India—Exhibitions. 2. Art industries and trade, Indic— Exhibitions. I. Schmeckebier, Alexandra K., ed. II. Ruth Reeves Memorial Collection. III. Syracuse University. IV. Title.

Folk art—Italy.

TOSCHI, Paolo, 1893- 745.0945
Arte popolare italiana, [title translated: Folk art in Italy] Roma, Carlo Bestetti [1960 dist., New York 21, Wittenborn & Co., 1018 Madison Ave.] 451p. Bibl.: p.439-448 (chiefly plates and illus., part col.) 32cm. (Text in Italian) 60-24 27.50
1. Folk art—Italy. I. Title.

Folk art—Japan.

ASIA Society 709.52
Mingei: folk arts of old Japan, by Hugo Munsterberg. [New York] Abrams [c.1965] 143p. illus. (pt. mounted col.) 26cm. (Catalogue of an exhibition sel. by Dr. Hugo Munsterberg shown in Asia House Gallery in spring of 1965.) Bibl. [N7350.A75] 65-19378 9.00 bds.,
1. Folk art—Japan. 2. Folk art—Exhibitions. I. Munsterberg, Hugo, 1916- II. Title.

ASIA Society. 709.52
Mingei: folk arts of old Japan, by Hugo Munsterberg. [New York] Distributed by H. N. Abrams [1965] 143 p. illus. (part mounted col.) 26 cm. "Catalogue of an exhibition selected by Dr. Hugo Munsterberg and shown in Asia House Gallery in the spring of 1965." Bibliography: p. 142. [N7350.A75] 65-19378
1. Folk art — Japan. 2. Folk art — Exhibitions. I. Munsterberg, Hugo. 1916- II. Title.

MUNSTERBERG, Hugo, 1916- 745
The folk arts of Japan. With a pref. by Soetsu Yanagi. [1st ed.] Tokyo, Rutland, Vt., C. E. Tuttle Co. [1958] 168 p. illus., col. map, plates (part col.) 21 x 22 cm. [NK1071.M8] 58-7496
1. Folk art—Japan. **BIP**

Folk art—Kentucky—Exhibitions.

FOLK art of Kentucky 709'.769'074016947
: a survey of Kentucky's self-taught artists : [exhibited at the University of Kentucky Fine Arts Gallery, from November 23, 1975 to December 19, 1975]. [Lexington, Ky. : The Gallery], c1976. [40] p. : ill. (some col.) ; 29 cm. [NK835.K4F64] 76-10444
1. Folk art—Kentucky—Exhibitions. 2. Primitivism in art—Kentucky—Exhibitions. I. Kentucky. University. Art Gallery.

Folk art—Latin America.

GIRARD, Alexander H. 745.5'098
El encanto de un pueblo. The magic of a people; folk art and toys from the collection of the Girard Found. [by] Alexander Girard. Photos. by Charles and Ray Eames. New York, Viking [1968] [73] p. col. illus. 23cm. (Studio bk.) English or Spanish Based on the exhibition at Hemis-Fair in San Antonio in 1968. [NK889.G5 1968] 68-15482 4.95
1. Folk art—Latin America. 2. Toys. I. Girard Foundation. II. San Antonio. Hemis-Fair, 1968. III. Title. IV. Title: The magic of a people.

Folk art—Lithuania.

FELDON, Victoria. 745'.0947'5
Lithuanian folk art. [Los Angeles, 1966?] 77 p. plates. 26 cm. "[A catalog of] an exhibition presented by the Museum and Laboratories of Ethnic Arts and Technology at the University of California, Los Angeles, UCLA Ethnic Art Galleries, November 21, 1966-January 15, 1967." "The exhibition is an outgrowth of Mrs. Feldon's research for her master's thesis in the folklore and mythology group." Bibliography: p. 77. [NK976.L5F4] 78-628298
1. Folk art—Lithuania. 2. Art industries and trade—Lithuania—Exhibitions. I. California. University. University at Los Angeles. Museum and Laboratories of Ethnic Arts and Technology. II. Title.

Folk art—Mexico.

DORNER, Gerd. 745.0972
Folk art of Mexico. Translated by Gladys Wheelhouse. New York, Barnes [1963 c1962] 67 p. mounted col. illus., map. 22 cm. (Metropolis books) Bibliography: p. 66-67. [NK844.D613] 63-6257
1. Folk art — Mexico. I. Title.

SCHMIDT, James Norman, 1912- 381'.45'7450972
A shopper's guide to Mexico: where, what, and how to buy [by] James Norman and Margaret Fox Schmidt. Newly rev. and updated. Garden City, N.Y., Dolphin Books [1973] viii, 272 p. 19 cm. (A Dolphin handbook, C466) First published in 1959 under title: In Mexico; where to look, how to buy Mexican popular arts and crafts. [NK844.S35 1973] 72-85363 ISBN 0-385-02055-4 1.95
1. Folk art—Mexico. 2. Art industries and trade—Mexico. 3. Shopping—Mexico. 4. Mexico—Description and travel—1951-—Guide-books. I. Schmidt, Margaret Fox. II. Title.

TAMPA Bay Art Center. 745'.0972
Folk art of Mexico. [Catalogue by Darrell Bohlsen. Tampa, Fla., 1971] [36] p. illus. 26 cm. "All works shown in this publication were retained from an exhibition of over 350 examples of Mexican folk art that the Tampa Bay Art Center organized and presented in the fall of 1970." [NK844.T3] 77-198445
1. Folk art—Mexico. I. Bohlsen, Darrell. II. Title.

TONEYAMA, Kojin, 1921- 745'.0972
The popular arts of Mexico / by Kojin Toneyama ; with a foreword and notes on modern Mexican folk crafts by Carlos Espejel ; Japanese text translated by Richard L. Gage. 1st English ed. New York : Weatherhill/Heibonsha, 1974. 225 p. : 306 col. ill. ; 38 cm. Translation of Mekishiko no Mingei. [NK844.T5913] 74-76105 ISBN 0-8348-1030-1 : 55.00
1. Folk art—Mexico. 2. Art industries and trade—Mexico. I. Title.

TOOR, Frances, 1890-1956. 745'.0972
Mexican popular arts; being a fond glance at the craftsmen and their handiwork in ceramics, textiles, metals, glass, paint, fibres, and other materials. Illustrated by L. Alice Wilson. Mexico, D. F., F. Toor Studios, 1939. Detroit, Blaine Ethridge—Books, 1973. 107, [14] p. illus. 24 cm. "Added plates": p. [109]-[121] [NK844.T6 1973] 73-78363 10.00
1. Folk art—Mexico. 2. Art industries and trade—Mexico. I. Title. **BIP**

WINN, Robert K. 745'.0972
V. J. M. y J. : Viva Jesus, Maria y Jose : a celebration of the birth of Jesus : Mexican folk art and toys from the Collection of Robert K. Winn / foreword by Everett H. Jones ; photos. by Michael J. Smith. San Antonio : Trinity University Press, c1977. vii, 103 p. : col. ill. ; 23 cm. Bibliography: p. 101. [NK844.W5] 77-89457 ISBN 0-911536-68-X : 10.00
1. Winn, Robert K.—Art collections. 2. Folk art—Mexico. 3. Toys—Mexico. 4. Christian art and symbolism—Mexico. 5. Crib in Christian art and tradition. 6. Christmas—Mexico. I. Smith, Michael Jay, 1946- II. Title. III. Title: Viva Jesus, Maria y Jose. **BIP**

Folk art—Michigan—Exhibitions.

MACDOWELL, Marsha. 745'.09774'074017427
Michigan folk art, its beginnings to 1941 : Kresge Art Gallery, Michigan State University, East Lansing, August 29-October 10, 1976 : exhibition / sponsored by the Museum, Michigan State University and the Michigan Department of State, Michigan Historical Museum ; [catalog, Marsha MacDowell, C. Kurt Dewhurst]. East Lansing : The University, c1976. 104 p. : ill. ; 28 cm. Includes bibliographical references and index. [NK835.M5M32] 76-380461
1. Folk art—Michigan—Exhibitions. I. Dewhurst, C. Kurt, joint author. II. Kresge Art Gallery. III. Michigan. State University, East Lansing. Museum. IV.

Michigan. Historical Museum, Lansing. V. Title.

Folk art—Near East.

CALIFORNIA. University. 745'.0956
University at Los Angeles. Museum and Laboratories of Ethnic Arts and Technology.
The Near East in UCLA collections. [Los Angeles, 1969] 30 p. illus. 19 x 23 cm. Catalog of a loan exhibition held May-June 1969 in the Ethnic Art Galleries, University of California, Los Angeles. Bibliography: p. 30. [NK1038.C34] 75-626540
1. Folk art—Near East. 2. Folk art—Exhibitions. I. Title.

Folk art — New England

LORD, Priscilla Sawyer. 745.00974
The folk arts and crafts of New England. by Priscilla Sawyer Lord and Daniel J. Foley. [1st ed.] Philadelphia, Chilton Books [1965] xix, 282 p. illus. (part col.) ports. 31 cm. Bibliography: p. 253-265. [NK810.L6] 65-23607
1. Folk art — New England 2. Art industries and trade — New England. I. I. Foley, Daniel J. joint author. II. Title.

LORD, Priscilla Sawyer. 745.0974
The folk arts and crafts of New England / Priscilla Sawyer Lord, Daniel J. Foley. New ed. Philadelphia : Chilton Books, [1975] p. cm. Includes index. Bibliography: p. [NK810.L6 1975] 75-18530 ISBN 0-8019-6240-4 : 12.50
1. Folk art—New England. 2. Art industries and trade—New England. I. Foley, Daniel J., joint author II. Title.

Folk art—New Mexico.

HALL, Elizabeth Boyd 745.509789
(White) 1903-
Popular arts of colonial New Mexico, by E. Boyd [pseud.] Santa Fe, Museum of International Folk Art, 1959. 51 p. illus. 23 cm. Includes bibliography. [NK835.N5H3] 59-11399
1. Folk art—New Mexico. I. Title. **BIP**

HALL, Elizabeth Boyd 745'.09789
White, 1903-
Popular arts of Spanish New Mexico [by] E. Boyd. Santa Fe, Museum of New Mexico Press, 1974. viii, 518 p. illus. (part col.) 29 cm. Bibliography: p. 484-485. [NK835.N5H32] 74-76660 ISBN 0-89013-064-7 34.95
1. Folk art—New Mexico. 2. Spanish Americans in New Mexico. I. Title. **BIP**

Folk art—Norway.

GILBERTSON, 745'.09481'0973
Donald E.
A treasury of Norwegian folk art in America / Donald E. Gilbertson, James F. Richards, Jr. ; photography, William Schmid ; foreword, Marion Nelson. Osseo, Wis. : Tin Chicken Antiques, c1975. 96 p. : chiefly ill. (some col.) ; 28 cm. [NK991.G54] 75-34538
1. Folk art—Norway. 2. Folk art—United States. I. Richards, James F., joint author. II. Title.

HAUGLID, Roar. 745
Native art of Norway, by Roar Hauglid [and others] Edited by Roar Hauglid. New York, Praeger [1967, c1965] 175 p. illus. (part col.) 28 cm. Previous ed., 1953, has title: The native arts of Norway. Contents.Contents.—Wood carving, by R. Hauglid.—Rose painting, by R. Asker.—Norwegian art weaving, by H. Engelstad.—Folk costumes, by G. I. Traetteberg. [NK991.H38 1967] 67-21845
1. Folk art—Norway. I. Title.

STEWART, Janice S. 745
The folk arts of Norway. Madison, University of Wisconsin Press, 1953. xvii, 246 p. 152 illus., 5 col. plates, maps (on lining papers) 28 cm. Bibliography: p. [231]-235. [NK991.S8] 53-13050
1. Folk art—Norway.

Folk art—Pennsylvania.

ADAMS, Ruth Constance, 1911- 745
Pennsylvania Dutch art. Cleveland, World Pub. Co. [1950] 64 p. illus., col. plates. 20 cm. (The American arts library, 1582) [NK835.P4A6] 50-58060
1. Folk art—Pennsylvania. 2. Art, Pennsylvania German. I. Title.

LICHTEN, Frances. 745.44
Folk art motifs of Pennsylvania. New York, Hastings House [1954] 95 p. illus. (part col.) 26 x 31 cm. [NK835.P4L48] 54-10701
1. Folk art—Pennsylvania. 2. Design, Decorative. I. Title. **BIP**

LICHTEN, Frances. 745.4'49'748
Folk art motifs of Pennsylvania / Frances Lichten. New York : Dover Publications, 1976, c1954. viii, 71 p., [8] leaves of plates : ill. (some col.) ; 29 cm. (Dover pictorial archive series) [NK835.P4L48 1976] 75-28849 ISBN 0-486-23303-0 pbk. : 2.95
1. Folk art—Pennsylvania. 2. Design, Decorative—Pennsylvania. 3. Art, Pennsylvania German. I. Title.

LICHTEN, Frances 745.09748
Folk art of rural Pennsylvania. New York, Scribners [1963, c.1946] xiv, 276p. illus. (pt. col.) 31cm. 63-4600 17.50
1. Folk art—Pennsylvania. 2. Art industries and trade—Pennsylvania. I. Title.

ROBACKER, Earl Francis. 745.1
Touch of the Dutchland [by] Earl F. Robacker. New York, A. S. Barnes [1965] 240 p. illus. 26 cm. [NK835.P4R62] 65-17211
1. Folk art — Pennsylvania. 2. Art, Pennsylvania German. 3. Art industries and trade — Pennsylvania. I. Title.

Folk art—Pennsylvania—Exhibitions.

ALLENTOWN, 745'.09748'074014827
Pa. Art Museum.
Pennsylvania folk art : [exhibition], October 20 through December 1, 1974, Allentown Art Museum. Allentown, Pa. : The Museum, [1974] 98 p. : ill. ; 28 cm. Bibliography: p. 97. [NK835.P4A44 1974] 74-84402
1. Folk art—Pennsylvania—Exhibitions. I. Title.

Folk art—Peru.

PETTERSON, Richard B. 745.5'0985
Folk art of Peru [by] Richard Petterson. [Claremont, Calif., 1968] 58 p. illus. (part col.), map, ports. 27 cm. [NK916.P4] 76-281802
1. Folk art—Peru. I. Title.

Folk art—Rumania.

BANATEANU, Tancred 745.449498
The ornament in the Rumanian folk art [by] T. Banateanu, M. Focsa. Bucharest, Meridiane Pub. House [dist. New York, Vanous] 1963. [50]p. plates (pt. col.) 23cm. 64-1258 2.50 pap.,
1. Folk art—Rumania. 2. Design, Decorative—Rumania. I. Focsa, Marcela, joint author. II. Title.

Folk art—Russia.

HASEGAWA, Shichiro, 745.44947
1913-
Folk art of the world, form and pattern [dist. Austin, Tex., Perkins Oriental, 1964] 159p. illus. (pt. mounted col.) map, port. 21x22cm. In Japanese: t.p. in English and Japanese. Bibl. [NK975.H3] 65-226 7.50 bds.,
1. Folk art—Russia. 2. Art industries and trade—Russia. I. Title.

Folk art—Russia—History.

PRONIN, Alexander. 745'.0947
Russian folk arts [by] Alexander and Barbara Pronin. South Brunswick, Barnes [1975] 192 p. illus. 32 cm. Bibliography: p. [184] [NK975.P76] 73-117 ISBN 0-498-01276-X
1. Folk art—Russia—History. I. Pronin, Barbara, joint author. II. Title.

Folk art—U.S.

BISHOP, Robert Charles. 730'.973
American folk sculpture / by Robert Bishop. 1st ed. New York : Dutton, 1974. 392 p. : ill. ; 29 cm. Includes index. Bibliography: p. 388-389. [NK805.B56] 74-10477 ISBN 0-525-05350-6 : 28.50
1. Folk art—United States. 2. Sculpture, American. 3. Primitivism in art—United States. I. Title.

CARRAHER, Ronald G. 745.5'0973
Artists in spite of art [by] Ronald G. Carraher. New York, Van Nostrand Reinhold [1970] 112 p. (chiefly illus.) 19 x 26 cm. [NK808.C37] 78-126878
1. Folk art—U.S. I. Title.

COLBY College, Waterville, 759.13
Me.
A group of paintings from the American heritage collection of Edith Kemper Jette and Ellerton Marcel Jette. Waterville, Colby College Press, 1956. 94p. (p. 11-94 illus.) 24cm. [ND210.C67] 57-1572
1. Folk art—U. S. 2. Paintings, American. 3. Paintings—Private collections. I. Jette, Edith Kemper. II. Jette, Ellerton Marcel. III. Title.

COLONIAL Williamsburg, inc. 745.3
inc.
The Abby Aldrich Rockefeller folk art collection: a descriptive catalogue by Nina Fletcher Little. [1st ed. Williamsburg, Va., Published by] Colonial Williamsburg; distributed by Little, Brown, Boston [1957] xvi, 402p. 165col. illus. 27cm. To the reader [includes errata and addendum]' (p. xvii) and 'Supplementary bibliography' (p. 394a) inserted. Includes bibliographies. [N6510.C66] 57-6251
1. Folk art—U. S. 2. Folk art—Williamsburg, Va. I. Rockefeller, Abbey Greene (Aldrich) II. Little, Nina Fletcher, 1903- III. Title.

COLONIAL Williamsburg, inc. 745
American folk art from the Abby Aldrich Rockefeller folk art collection. Williamsburg, Va. [1959] 46 p. illus. (part col.) 24 cm. Catalogue of a traveling exhibition arranged in cooperation with the American Federation of Art. [N6510.C67] 59-11825
1. Folk art—U.S. 2. Folk art—Exhibitions. I. Rockefeller, Abby Greene Aldrich. II. American Federation of Arts. III. Title.

FRIED, Frederick. 745'.0973
America's forgotten folk arts / by Frederick and Mary Fried. 1st ed. New York : Pantheon Books, c1978. p. cm. Bibliogrphy: p. Includes index. [NK805.F74] 78-51790 ISBN 0-394-40714-8 : 15.95
1. Folk art—United States. 2. Primitivism in art—United States. I. Fried, Mary, 1913- joint author. II. Title. **BIP**

GLADSTONE, M. J. 745'.0973
A carrot for a nose : the form of folk sculpture on America's city streets and country roads / M. J. Gladstone. New York : Scribner, [1974] 70 p. : ill. (some col.) ; 27 cm. [NK805.G55] 72-11229 ISBN 0-684-13663-5 : 9.95
1. Folk art—United States. 2. Sculpture, American. 3. Primitivism in art—United States. I. Title. **BIP**

HEMPHILL, Herbert 745'.0973
Waide.
Twentieth-century American folk art and artists / by Herbert W. Hemphill, Jr., Julia Weissman. 1st ed. New York : E. P. Dutton, 1974. 237 p. : ill. (some col.) ; 29 cm. Includes index. Bibliography: p. 232-233. [NK808.H38 1974] 74-12934 ISBN 0-525-22473-4 : 27.50
1. Folk art—United States. 2. Primitivism in art—United States. I. Weissman, Julia, joint author. II. Title.

HORWITZ, Elinor Lander. 745'.0973
The bird, the banner, and Uncle Sam : images of America in folk and popular art / Elinor Lander Horwitz ; J. Roderick Moore, consultant. 1st ed. Philadelphia : Lippincott, c1976. 167 p. : ill. (some col.) ; 26 cm. Includes index. Bibliography: p. 163. Discusses the patriotic symbols and heroes of the American people and their use in past and present art and craft objects. [NK805.H69] 76-16492 ISBN 0-397-31690-9 : 8.95 ISBN 0-397-31691-7 pbk. :
1. Folk art—United States. 2. Symbolism in art—United States. 3. United States in art. I. Title. **BIP**

*LIPMAN, Jean. 745.0973
Provocative parallels; naive early americans/international sophisticates. New York, E. P. Dutton & Co., 1975 144 p. ill., (part col.), 21 cm. [NK807] 7.95 (pbk.)
1. Folk art—United States. I. Title.

LIPMAN, Jean Herzberg, 745'.0973
1909-
The flowering of American folk art, 1776-1876 [by Jean Lipman and Alice Winchester New York, Viking Press, in cooperation with the Whitney Museum of American Art [1974] 288 p. illus. (part col.) 29 cm. (A Studio book) Bibliography: p. 284-287. [NK806.L52 1974] 73-6081 ISBN 0-670-32120-6 19.95
1. Folk art—United States. 2. Primitivism in art—United States. I. Winchester, Alice, joint author. II. Whitney Museum of American Art, New York. III. Title.

LIPMAN, Jean Herzberg, 745'.0973
1909-
The flowering of American folk art, 1776-1876 / Jean Lipman and Alice Winchester Harmondsworth, Eng. ; New York : Penguin Books, 1977, c1974. 288 p. : ill. (some col.) ; 28 cm. "In cooperation with the Whitney Museum of American Art." Bibliography: p. 284-287. [NK806.L52 1977] 77-2237 ISBN 0-14-004500-7 pbk. : 9.95
1. Folk art—United States. 2. Primitivism in art—United States. I. Winchester, Alice, joint author. II. Whitney Museum of American Art, New York. III. Title. **BIP**

NEAL, Avon. 745
Ephemeral folk figures: scarecrows, harvest figures, and snowmen. Photos. by Ann Parker. [1st ed.] New York, C. N. Potter; distributed by Crown [1969] 176 p. illus. (part col.) 29 cm. [NK805.N37 1969] 73-91447 10.00
1. Folk art—U.S. I. Parker, Ann, illus. II. Title.

PENDERGAST, Anthony W., 731.732
1879-
Cigar store figures in American folk art, by A. W. Pendergast and W. Porter Ware. [Chicago, Lightner Pub. Corp., 1953] 73p. illus. 24cm. [NK805.P45] 53-25045
1. Folk art—U.S. 2. Sculpture, American. I. Ware, William Porter, joint author. II. Title.

PHILLIPS, Ammi, 1788-1865. 759.13
Ammi Phillips: portrait painter, 1788-1865. Introd. by Mary Black. Catalog by Barbara C. and Lawrence B. Holdridge. New York, C. N. Potter for the Museum of American Folk Art; distributed by Crown Publishers [1969] 56 p. illus. (part col.), facsims. 29 cm. "Exhibition of the works of Ammi Phillips shown at the Museum of American Folk Art in New York City from October 14 to December 1, 1968, and at the Albany Institute of History and Art from December 9, 1968 to January 7, 1969." Bibliography: p. 56. [ND237.P47A6] 68-58001 6.00
I. Holdridge, Barbara C., 1929- II. Holdridge, Lawrence B. III. Museum of American Folk Art. IV. Albany Institute of History and Art. V. Title.

RHODES, Lynette I. 745'.0973
American folk art from the traditional to the naive / Lynette I. Rhodes. Cleveland : Cleveland Museum of Art ; Bloomington : distributed by Indiana University Press, c1978. 117 p. : ill. (some col.) ; 19 x 22 cm. (Themes in art) "Catalog": p. 110-115. Bibliography: p. 110. [NK805.R46] 79-104017 ISBN 0-910386-42-0 : 7.95
1. Folk art—United States. I. Cleveland Museum of Art. II. Title. III. Series.

SMITHSONIAN 708.155'4252
Institution.
American folk art: The art and spirit of a people; from the Eleanor and Mabel Van Alstyne Collection, by Peter C. Welsh. Catalog entries prepared by Anne Castrodale. Washington, 1965. 1 v. (unpaged) illus. (part col.), col. port. 23 cm. (Smithsonian publication 4615) Bibliography: leaf at end. [NK807.S58] 66-61813

1. Folk art—U.S. I. Van Alstyne, Eleanor Van Ness, 1881- II. Marsh, Mabel Van Alstyne. III. Welch, Peter C. IV. Castrodale, Anne. V. Title. VI. Title: The art and spirit of a people.

SMITHSONIAN Institution. 745.5
American folk art: The art and spirit of a people; from the Eleanor and Mabel Van Alstyne Collection, by Peter C. Welsh. Catalog entries prepared by Anne Castrodale. Washington, 1965. 1 v. (unpaged) illus. (part col.), col. port. 23 cm. (Smithsonian publication 4615) Bibliography: leaf at end. [NK807.S58] 66-61813
1. Folk art—U.S. I. Van Alstyne, Eleanor Van Ness, 1881- II. Marsh, Mabel Van Alstyne. III. Welch, Peter C. IV. Castrodale, Anne. V. Title. VI. Title: The art and spirit of a people.

Folk art—United States—Addresses, essays, lectures.

HOW to know American folk 709'.73
art : eleven experts discuss many aspects of the field / edited by Ruth Andrews. 1st ed. New York : Dutton, c1977. xix, 204 p., [16] leaves of plates : ill. (some col.) ; 21 cm. Includes bibliographies and index. [NK805.H73] 77-72039 ISBN 0-525-47460-9 pbk. : 6.95
1. Folk art—United States—Addresses, essays, lectures. I. Andrews, Ruth. BIP

Folk art—United States—Catalogs.

ABBY Aldrich 709'.73'07401554252
Rockefeller Folk Art Collection, Williamsburg, Va.
The Abby Aldrich Rockefeller Folk Art Collection : a gallery guide / by Beatrix T. Rumford. Williamsburg, Va. : The Collection, c1975. 31 p. : col. ill. ; 26 cm. Bibliography: p. 30-31. [NK807.A35 1975] 75-36926 ISBN 0-87935-033-4 : 2.00
1. Abby Aldrich Rockefeller Folk Art Collection, Williamsburg, Va. 2. Folk art—United States—Catalogs. I. Rumford, Beatrix T.

THE All-American dog 704.94'32
: man's best friend in folk art / [compiled by] Robert Bishop ; designed by Ellen Blissman ; [photography by Joshua Schreier]. New York : Avon, in association with Museum of Americn Folk Art, 1978, c1977. 152 p. : ill. (some col.) ; 23 cm. Bibliography:p. 151. [NK805.A58] 77-84981 ISBN 0-380-01863-2 : 5.95
1. Folk art—United States—Catalogs. 2. Dogs in art—Catalogs. I. Bishop, Robert Charles. II. Museum of American Folk Art.

Folk art—U.S.—Exhibitions.

ALBRIGHT-KNOX Art 707*.4*014797
Gallery.
American folk art from the Shelburne Museum in Vermont. [Exhibition at the] Albright-Knox Art Gallery, Buffalo, December 17, 1965-January 30, 1966. [Buffalo, c1965] 36 p. illus. (part col.) 30 cm. [NK807.Ay] 71-1329
1. Folk art—U.S.—Exhibitions. I. Shelburne, Vt. Museum. II. Title.

DOTY, Robert M. 745'.0973'0740171
American folk art in Ohio collections : Akron Art Institute, Akron, Ohio / by Robert Doty. New York : Distributed by Dodd, Mead, [c1976] [95] p. : ill. (some col.) ; 22 x 23 cm. Catalogue of an exhibition held Sept. 18-Dec. 5, 1976. Includes bibliographical references. [NK805.D67] 76-54374 ISBN 0-396-07360-3 : 10.00
1. Folk art—United States—Exhibitions. 2. Folk art—Collectors and collecting—Ohio—Exhibitions. I. Akron, Ohio. Art Institute. II. Title.

Folk art—United States—History.

AMERICA'S folk art; 745'.00973
treasures of American folk arts and crafts in distinguished museums and collections. General editor: Robert L. Polley. Introd. by James A. H. Conrad. New York, Putnam, [1968] 189 p. illus. (part col.) 32 cm. "In association with Country Beautiful Foundation." [NK805.A65] 68-31615 12.95
1. Folk art—United States—History. 2. Art industries and trade, American—History. I. Polley, Robert L., ed.

Folk art—United States—Juvenile literature.

HORWITZ, Elinor 745'.092'2
Lander.
Contemporary American folk artists / Elinor Lander Horwitz ; J. Roderick Moore, consultant ; with photos. by Joshua Horwitz. 1st ed. Philadelphia : Lippincott, [1975] 143 p. : ill. ; 26 cm. Includes index. Bibliography: p. 139. Briefly discusses the lives and works of twenty-two American folk painters, carvers, and environmentalists. [NK808.H63] 75-14353 ISBN 0-397-31626-7 : 7.95 ISBN 0-397-31627-5 pbk. : 2.95
1. Folk art—United States—Juvenile literature. I. Horwitz, Joshua. II. Title. BIP

Folk art—Virginia.

WUST, Klaus German, 731.5'49
1925-
Folk art in stone, southwest Virginia, by Klaus Wust. Edinburg, Va., Shenandoah History, 1970. [28] p. illus., maps. 27 cm. [NK835.S6W8] 71-131440
1. Folk art—Virginia. 2. Sepulchral monuments—Virginia. I. Title.

Folk-lore—China.

WILLIAMS, Charles 704.94'6'0951
Alfred Speed, 1884-
Outlines of Chinese symbolism and art motives : an alphabetical compendium of antique legends and beliefs, as reflected in the manners and customs of the Chinese / C. A. S. Williams. 3d rev. ed. New York : Dover Publications, 1976. xxi, 472 p. : ill. ; 22 cm. Reprint of the 1941 ed. published by Kelly and Walsh, Shanghai. Includes bibliographical references and index. [GR335.W53 1976] 76-40397 ISBN 0-486-23372-3 : 5.00
*1. Folk-lore—China. 2. Symbolism. 3. China—Social life and customs. I. Title.*BIP

WILLIAMS, Charles 704.94'6'0951
Alfred Speed, 1884-
Outlines of Chinese symbolism and art motives : an alphabetical compendium of antique legends and beliefs, as reflected in the manners and customs of the Chinese / by C. A. S. Williams. With an introd. to the new ed. by Terence Barrow. Rutland, Vt. : C. E. Tuttle Co., 1974. xxix, 472 p., [3] leaves of plates : ill. (some col.) ; 22 cm. Reprint of the 3d rev. ed. published in 1941 by Kelly and Walsh, Shanghai. Includes bibliographical references and index. [GR335.W53 1974b] 73-90237 ISBN 0-8048-1127-X : 12.50
1. Folk-lore—China. 2. Symbolism. 3. China—Social life and customs. I. Title.

Follies.

CASSON, Hugh Maxwell, 914.20485
Sir 1910- ed.
Follies. [1st Amer. ed. New York] Taplinger [1966, c.1965] 124p. illus. (pt. col.) 2 col. maps. 19cm. (Gold leaf Brit. landmarks ser.) Res., design, and illus. by Paul Sharp. Writing by E. M. Hatt. [NA8460.C3] 66-2329 1.50 pap.,
1. Follies. 2. Architecture—Gt. Brit. I. Sharp, Paul. II. Hatt, E. M. III. Title.

LANCASTER, Clay 720.973
Architectural follies in America; or, Hammer, sawtooth & nail. Rutland, Vt., C. E. Tuttle Co [1960] 243p. Bibliographical footnotes illus. (part col.) plans. 28cm. 59-14088 10.00, half cloth, bxd.
1. Follies. 2. Architecture—U.S. I. Title.

Folon, Jean-Michel—Catalogs.

FOLON, Jean-Michel. 769'.92'4
Posters by Folon / introd. by Milton Glaser. New York : H. N. Abrams, [1978] p. cm. [NC1850.F64A4 1978] 78-4392 ISBN 0-8109-2158-8 pbk. : 8.95
1. Folon, Jean-Michel—Catalogs. BIP

Fonseca, Jose Paulo Moreira da.

FONSECA, Jose Paulo 709'.81
Moreira da.
Jose Paulo Moreira da Fonseca, o pintor e o poeta = Jose Paulo Moreira da Fonseca, the painter and the poet / traducao/translation, Kerry Shawn Keys, Kern Krapohl. [Rio de Janeiro] : Spala Editora, [1976?] 213 p. : ill. (some col.), ports. ; 31 cm. On spine: Jose Paulo, o pintor e o poeta, the painter and the poet. Cr$500.00 Includes bibliographical references and index. [NX533.Z9F664] 77-470106
1. Fonseca, Jose Paulo Moreira da. I. Title. II. Title: Jose Paulo, o pintor e o poeta, the painter and the poet.

Fontana, Lucio, 1899-1968.

BALLO, Guido, 1914- 709'.24
Lucio Fontana. New York, Praeger [1971] 268 p. illus. (part col.) 30 cm. Bibliography: p. 263-268. [NB623.F65B3 1971] 78-154353 30.00
1. Fontana, Lucio, 1899-1968.

CIRLOT, Juan Eduardo 730.924
Lucio Fontana. Barcelona. Editorial G. Gili [1966] 59p. illus. (1 mounted col.) 21cm. (Coleccion Nueva orbita) Spanish and English. Bibl. [NB623.F65C5] 66-8776 4.00
1. Fontana. Lucio, 1899- I. Title.
Available from Wittenborn in New York.

Fontana, Lucio, 1899-1968—Exhibitions.

FONTANA, Lucio, 1899- 709'.2'4
1968.
Lucio Fontana, 1899-1968, a retrospective : [exhibition], The Solomon R. Guggenheim Museum, New York City. New York : Solomon R. Guggenheim Foundations, 1977. 112 p. : chiefly ill. ; 26 cm. Bibliography: p. 110-111. [N6923.F6A4 1977] 77-88448 ISBN 0-89207-010-2 pbk. : 6.98
1. Fontana, Lucio, 1899-1968—Exhibitions. I. Solomon R. Guggenheim Museum, New York. II. Title.

Food warmers.

NEWMAN, Harold. 738.3'83
Veilleases. 1750-1860 South Brunswick [N.J.] A. S. Barnes [1967] 258 p. illus. (part col.) 29 cm. "Notes and references": p. 243-254. [NK4695.F6N4] 66-18198
1. Food warmers. I. Title.

NEWMAN, Harold 738.3'83
Veilleuses,1750-1860. South Brunswick [N.J.] A. S. Barnes [1967] 258p. illus. (pt. col.) 29cm. Notes and references: p. 243-254. [NK4695F6N4] 66-18198 20.00
1. Food warmers. I. Title.

Forbes, Edward Waldo, 1873-1969.

EDWARD Waldo Forbes, 708'.00924 B
Yankee visionary. [Cambridge, Mass.] Fogg Art Museum, Harvard University [1971] xi, 161 p. illus., maps, plans, ports. 22 cm. Includes the catalog of the exhibition held Jan. 16-Feb. 22, 1971, at the Fogg Art Museum. Contents.Contents.—Edward Waldo Forbes: art museum director, by J. Coolidge.—Edward Waldo Forbes: city planner, by B. A. Mandelbaum and M. K. Fitzsimons.—Edward Waldo Forbes: herald of conservation, by E. H. Jones.—Gifts and bequests of Edward Waldo Forbes. Includes bibliographical references. [N406.F6E3] 76-145673
1. Forbes, Edward Waldo, 1873-1969. I. Forbes, Edward Waldo, 1873-1969. II. Harvard University. William Hayes Fogg Art Museum.

Forbes, Edwin, 1839-1895.

FORBES, Edwin, 1839- 769'.92'4
1895.
Life studies of the great army / by Edwin Forbes. [1st ed.]. [San Francisco] : Dunderave, 1976, [c1975] 1 portfolio, ([3] leaves, 40 leaves of plates : 40 ill.) ; 38 cm. Cover title. Ed. statement from label mounted on verso of cover. [NE2012.F67A49 1976] 77-151132
1. Forbes, Edwin, 1839-1895. 2. United States—History—Civil War, 1861-1865—Art and the war. I. Title.

Forbes, W. Stanton.

FORBES, W. Stanton. 769'.92'4
Ghosts / by W. Stanton Forbes. Athens, Ga. : Forbes, [1974] 40 p. : all ill. ; 22 cm. "Number 32 of 50 copies." [NE1336.F67A46] 75-314823
1. Forbes, W. Stanton. 2. Ghosts in art. I. Title.

Ford, Henry, 1863-1947.

OLSON, Sidney. 923.373
Young Henry Ford: a picture history of the first forty years. Detroit, Wayne State University Press, 1963. 188 p. illus., ports., facsims. 29 cm. Errata slip inserted. [CT275.F68O4] 63-20162
1. Ford, Henry, 1863-1947. I. Title.

Ford, John Charles, 1929—

SCHWABACHER, Ethel K. 709'.2'4
John Ford, conquistador / Ethel K. Schwabacher ; with an introd. by Naomi Bliven. New York : Published for the Country Art Gallery Locust Valley, L.I., N.Y., by Nadelstein Press, 1974. 39 p. : ill. ; 28 cm. Includes bibliographical references. [N6537.F67S38] 74-84492 5.50
1. Ford, John Charles, 1929-

Ford Theatre, Washington, D.C.

MCCLURE, Stanley William, 975.3
1905-
Ford's Theatre and the House Where Lincoln Died, by Stanley W. McClure. [Rev. Washington, U.S. National Park Service, 1969] 40, [2] p. illus. 24 cm. (National Park Service historical handbook no. 3) Previous editions issued under title: The Lincoln Museum and the House Where Lincoln Died. Bibliography: p. [42] [E457.65.M3 1969] 76-603534 0.50
1. Ford Theatre, Washington, D.C. 2. Lincoln Museum, Washington, D.C. I. Title. II. Series: U.S. National Park Service. Historical handbook series, no. 3

Forde Abbey.

ROPER, John, 1936- 914.3'8
Forde Abbey, near Chard, Somerset: an illustrated survey of the former Cistercian monastery, now the Dorset home of the Roper family; history and description of the contents and gardens written by John Roper. [New ed.]. Derby, English Life Publications, 1968. [32] p. illus., col. coat of arms. 15 x 22 cm. Col. maps on lining papers. [DA690.F68R6] 77-422989 2/6
1. Forde Abbey. I. Title.

Fore-edge painting.

WEBER, Carl Jefferson, 096'.1
1894-1966.
Fore-edge painting; a historical survey of a curious art in book decoration. Irvington-on-Hudson, N.Y., Harvey House, 1966. xiii, 223 p. illus. (part mounted col.) 26 cm. Bibliography: p. 211-212. [ND2370.W37] 66-26931
1. Fore-edge painting. I. Title. BIP

Forester, Russell, 1920—

FORESTER, Russell, 1920- 741.9'73
Drawings / Sheldon Memorial Art Gallery, University of Nebraska, Lincoln, Nebraska, November 2, 1976, to November 28, 1976. Small paintings / Everson Museum of Art, Syracuse, New York, January 21, 1977, to February 20, 1977. [s.l. : s.n., 1976?] [56] p. : ill. (some col.) ; 21 cm. [N6537.F675S53] 76-42184
1. Forester, Russell, 1920- I. Sheldon Memorial Art Gallery. II. Everson Museum of Art of Syracuse and Onondaga County.

SUBJECT INDEX FORTIFICATION—AMERICA—HISTORY—EXHIBITIONS.

Forgery of works of art.

FLEMING, Stuart James. 702'.8
Authenticity in art : the scientific detection of forgery / Stuart J. Fleming ; foreword by S. A. Goudsmit. New York : Crane, Russack, 1976, c1975. 164 p., [6] leaves of plates : ill. (some col.) ; 25 cm. Includes index. Bibliography: p. [155]-157. [N8790.F57 1976] 75-27303 ISBN 0-8448-0752-4 : 14.50
1. Forgery of works of art. 2. Art—Expertising. I. Title. BIP

GOODRICH, David L. 700
Art fakes in America, by David L. Goodrich. New York, Viking Press [1973] 246 p. illus. 22 cm. Bibliography: p. [225]-235. [N8790.G63 1973] 73-4170 ISBN 0-670-13417-1 7.95
1. Forgery of works of art. 2. Art—United States. I. Title.

JEPPSON, Lawrence. 751.5'8
The fabulous frauds; fascinating tales of great art forgeries. New York, Weybright and Talley [1970] xii, 338 p. 25 cm. Bibliography: p. 320-325. [N8790.J4 1970] 78-99004 10.00
1. Forgery of works of art. I. Title.

KILBRACKEN, John Raymond Godley, baron, 1920- 927.5
The master forger; the story of Han van Meegeren. New York, W. Funk [1951?] 223p. illus. 20cm. [ND653.M58K53 1951a] 51-7661
1. Meegeren, Han van, 1889-1947. 2. Vermeer, Johannes, 1632-1675. 3. Hooch, Pieter de, 17th cent. 4. Forgery of works of art. 5. Paintings—Expertising. I. Title.

KURZ, Otto, 1908- 708'.054
Fakes. 2d rev., enl. ed. [Magnolia, Mass., P. Smith, 1968] 348p. illus. 22cm. (Dover bk. rebound) [N8790.K8 1967] 5.00
1. Forgery of works of art. I. Title.

MENDAX, Fritz, pseud. 708.054
Art fakes and forgeries. Translated from the German by H. S. Whitman. New York, Philosophical Library [1956] 222 p. illus. 23 cm. Translation of Aus der Welt der Falscher. [N8790.M413 1956] 57-3443
1. Forgery of works of art. 2. Literary forgeries and mystifications. I. Title.

SAVAGE, George, 1909- 708.054
Forgeries, fakes, and reproductions; a handbook for the art dealer and collector. New York, Praeger [1964, c.1963] xiii, 312p. illus., ports. 23cm. Bibl. 64-25426 8.95
1. Forgery of works of art. 2. Collectors and collecting. I. Title.

SCHMITT, Heinrich, 1894- 708.054
The art of the faker; three thousand years of deception, by Frank Arnau [pseud.] Tr. from German by J. Maxwell Brownjohn. Boston, Little, Brown [1961 c.1959, 1961] 364p. illus. (part col.) 61-5317 7.50
1. Forgery of works of art. I. Title.

SCHULLER, Sepp 708.054
Forgers, dealers, experts; strange chapters in the history of art. Translated from the German by James Cleugh. New York, Putnam [1960] xv, 200p. illus. 23cm. 60-13452 4.50
1. Forgery of works of art. I. Title.

STEIN, Anne-Marie. 751.5'8'0924 B
Three Picassos before breakfast; memoirs of an art forger's wife, by Anne-Marie Stein, as told to George Carpozi, Jr. New York, Hawthorn Books [1973] 192 p. illus. 25 cm. [ND553.S855S83 1973] 72-7784 6.95
1. Stein, David. 2. Forgery of works of art. I. Carpozi, George. II. Title.

YATES, Raymond Francis, 1895- 708.054
Antique fakes and their detection. Photographs and drawings by the author. [1st ed.] New York, Harper [1950] x, 229 p. illus. 22 cm. [N8790.Y3] 50-6925
1. Forgery of works of art. I. Title.

Forgery of works of art — Bibl.

REISNER, Robert George. 016.708054
Fakes and forgeries in the fine arts a bibliography. New York, Special Libraries Association, 1950. iv, 58 p. 28 cm. [Z5939.5.R4] 50-14485
1. Forgery of works of art — Bibl. I. Title.

Forgery of works of art—Exhibitions.

MINNEAPOLIS. Institute of Arts. 707'.4'0176579
Fakes and forgeries : [catalogue of an exhibition] the Minneapolis Institute of Arts, July 11-September 29, 1973. [Minneapolis] : The Institute, c1973. [272] p. : ill. ; 22 cm. Bibliography: p. [264]-[270] [N8790.M56 1973] 73-86977
1. Forgery of works of art—Exhibitions. 2. Reproduction of art objects—Exhibitions. I. Title. BIP

Forging.

SMITH, Robert Ernest, 1879- *671.52
Forging and welding. Bloomington, Ill., McKnight & McKnight Pub. Co. [c1956] 160 p. illus. 27 cm. Previous editions published under title: Units in forging and welding. [TT205.S645 1956] 56-13677
1. Forging. 2. Welding. I. Title. BIP

Forgioli, Attilio, 1933—

FORGIOLI, Attilio, 1933- 759.9493'2
Attilio Forgioli : paintings, pastels, gouaches : [catalogue of an exhibition held at] Fischer Fine Art Limited ... January 1976 / [text by Roberto Tassi]. London : Fischer Fine Art Ltd, 1976. [37] p. : chiefly ill. (some col.), port. ; 26 cm. Text in English and Italian. [ND623.F728T37] 76-367860 ISBN 0-904867-06-4
1. Forgioli, Attilio, 1933- I. Tassi, Roberto. II. Fischer Fine Art Limited.

Form (Aesthetics)

ABELL, Walter. 701.17
Representation and form; a study of aesthetic values in representational art. Introd. by Arthur Pope. Westport, Conn., Greenwood Press [1971, c1936] xviii, 172 p. illus. 27 cm. Includes bibliographical references. [N66.A2 1971] 79-138573 ISBN 0-8371-5772-2
1. Form (Aesthetics) 2. Composition (Art) I. Title. BIP

ANDERSON, John Mueller. 701
The realm of art [by] John M. Anderson. University Park, Penn. State Univ. Pr. 1967. xiv, 190p. 21cm. [N7430.A67] 67-16195 8.75
1. Form (Aesthetics) 2. Creation (Literary, artistic, etc.) I. Title. BIP

BYWATER, William G., 1940- 701'.17
Clive Bell's eye / William G. Bywater, Jr. Detroit : Wayne State University Press, 1975. 249 p. : ill. ; 24 cm. Includes index. "A checklist of the published writings of Clive Bell, by Donald A. Laing": p. [211]-242. [N7445.2.B44B9] 74-23853 ISBN 0-8143-1534-8
1. Bell, Clive, 1881-1964. 2. Form (Aesthetics) 3. Art—Philosophy. I. Title. BIP

COOK, Theodore Andrea, Sir, 1867-1928. 574'.01'516215
The curves of life : being an account of spiral formations and their application to growth in nature, to science, and to art : with special reference to the manuscripts of Leonardo da Vinci / by Theodore Andrea Cook. New York : Dover Publications, 1979. xxx, 479 p. : ill. ; 22 cm. Includes index. [QH351.C66 1979] 78-14678 ISBN 0-486-23701-X pbk. : 5.95
1. Spirals. 2. Morphology. 3. Growth. 4. Spirals in art. I. Title. BIP

DERKATSCH, Inessa I. 701.17
Wassily Kandinsky's theory of the identity of realism and abstraction in his essay: Uber die Formfrage, by Inessa I. Derkatsch. Berkeley, University of California, 1967. 51 l. 29 cm. Bibliography: leaves 49-51. [N7430.K35D4] 68-1532
1. Kandinsky, Wassily, 1866-1944. 2. Form (Aesthetics) I. Title.

HILL, Anthony, 1930- 701.17
Data: directions in art, theory, and aesthetics; an anthology, edited by Anthony Hill. Greenwich, Conn., New York Graphic Society [1969, c1968] 302 p. illus. 26 cm. On spine: Directions in art, theory, and aesthetics. Includes bibliographical references. [N7430.H68 1969] 68-12368 ISBN 0-8212-0294-4 15.00
1. Form (Aesthetics) 2. Composition (Art) I. Title. II. Title: Directions in art, theory, and aesthetics.

MUNRO, Thomas, 1897- 701
Form and style in the arts: an introduction to aesthetic morphology. Cleveland, Press of Case Western Reserve University, 1970. xvii, 467 p. illus., col. plates. 27 cm. Bibliography: p. [460] [N7430.M84] 76-84493 17.50
1. Form (Aesthetics) 2. Composition (Art) I. Title.

SAUNDERS, A. N. W. 701
Imagination all compact: understanding the arts [by] A. N. W. Saunders. London, Methuen, 1967. Dist. in the U. S. A. by Barnes & Noble [New York] 208p. illus. (music), 16 plates. 21cm. (Methuen's gen. studies bks.) Bibl. [N7430.S2] 68-74756 4.00 bds.,
1. Form (Aesthetics) 2. Imaginction. I. Title.

Form (Aesthetics)—Addresses, essays, lectures.

JACOBUS, Lee A. comp. 701.17
Aesthetics and the arts [by] Lee A. Jacobus. New York, McGraw [1968] xii, 315p. 23cm. Bibl. [N7430.J3] 67-26882 prices unreported
1. Form (Aesthetics)—Addresses, essays, lectures. 2. Art—Philosophy—Addresses, essays, lectures. I. Title. BIP

Form perception—Juvenile literature.

PORTER, Albert W. 701'.8
Shape and form / Albert W. Porter. Worcester, Mass. : Davis Publications, [1974] 80 p. : ill. ; 26 cm. (Elements of design) Includes index. Text and photographs explore the art elements of shape and form through observing the qualities of design in and beauty of various shapes found in our environment and studying the effects of light on these shapes. [N7430.5.P67] 75-321022 ISBN 0-87192-064-6
1. Form perception—Juvenile literature. 2. Form (Aesthetics)—Juvenile literature. 3. Visual discrimination—Juvenile literature. I. Title. II. Series. BIP

Formaggio, Dino.

BOTTICELLI, Sandro, 1447?-1510 759.5
Botticelli [by] Dino Formaggio [Tr. from Italian by Paul Colacicchi] London Oldbourne Pr. [dist. Chester Springs, Pa., Dufour, 1965, c.1960] 13p. plates (pt. col.) 32cm. (Gallery of great masters) [ND623] 65-7812 6.95 bds.,
1. Formaggio, Dino. I. Title.

Forner, Raquel, 1902—

CORCORAN Gallery of Art, Washington D.C. 759.982
Raquel Forner: Space mythology. Mythologie spatiale. March 15th to April 7th, 1974. Du 15 mars au 7 avril, 1974. Washington, D.C. [1974] [14] p. illus. 21 x 26 cm. French and English. Catalog of an exhibition. Bibliography: p. [9]-[10]. [ND339.F65C67 1974] 74-166547
1. Forner, Raquel, 1902- I. Forner, Raquel, 1902-

Fort Bowie National Historic Site.

SHEIRE, James W. 725'.18
Ft. Bowie National Historic Sites, by James W. Sheire. [Washington] Division of History, Office of Archeology and Historic Preservation, 1968. 90 (i.e. 128) illus., map. 27 cm. "Historic structures report, part II." Includes bibliographical references. [F819.F6S5] 75-601789
1. Fort Bowie National Historic Site.

Fort Laramie National Historic Site, Wyo.

MCDERMOTT, John Dishon. 725'.18
1874 cavalry barracks, Fort Laramie National Historic Site, by John D. McDermott & James Sheire. [Washington] Office of History and Historic Architecture, Eastern Service Center, 1970. iv, 98, [29] l. illus., plans (3 fold. in pocket) 27 cm. "Historic structures report, historical data section." Includes bibliographical references. [F769.F6M28] 76-612278
1. Fort Laramie National Historic Site, Wyo. I. Sheire, James W., joint author. II. Title.

Fort Laramie, Wyo.—Pictorial works.

WARNER, Robert C. 759.13
The Fort Laramie of Alfred Jacob Miller : a catalogue of all the known illustrations of the first Fort Laramie / by Robert C. Warner. Laramie : University of Wyoming, 1973. v, 163 leaves : ill. ; 29 cm. Thesis (M.A.)—University of Wyoming. Bibliography: leaves [156]-163. [N6537.M54W37] 74-186939
1. Miller, Alfred Jacob, 1810-1874. 2. Fort Laramie, Wyo.—Pictorial works. 3. The West in art. I. Title.

Fort Lauderdale, Fla. Second Presbyterian Church.

BROOKS, Bart. 726.41
The sanctuary, Second Presbyterian Church. Written and illustrated by Bart Brooks. [1st ed.] Fort Lauderdale [Fla.] Second Presbyterian Church [c1962] 59 p. illus. (part col.) ports. 24 x 29 cm. [NA5235.F6B7] 62-22309
1. Fort Lauderdale, Fla. Second Presbyterian Church. I. Title.

Fort Madison, Iowa — Descr. — Views.

EVANS, Lenore. 717.77'99
Our town, Fort Madison, Iowa; a book of sketches. [Fort Madison, Iowa, G. H. Fisher, 1966] 1 v. (chiefly illus.) 22 cm. Cover title. [F629.F7E9] 67-3646
1. Fort Madison, Iowa — Descr. — Views. I. Title.

Fortetsa, Crete.

BROCK, James King. 738.38
Fortetsa; early Greek tombs near Knossos. With line and coloured drawings by Audrey Corbett and Ursula Brock. Cambridge [Eng.] University Press, 1957. xvii, 244p. illus., 174 plates (incl. diagrs., plans, part col.) 26cm. (British School at Athens. Supplementary paper no. 2) [NK685.C8B7] 58-1935
1. Fortetsa, Crete. 2. Art objects, Cretan. 3. Pottery, Cretan. 4. Tombs—Crete. I. Title. II. Series.

Fortification.

TOY, Sidney 728.8109
A history of fortification from 3000 B.C. to A.D. 1700. London Heinemann [dist. Chester Springs, Pa., Dufour. 1964] 262p. illus. 23cm. 55-35812 6.00
1. Fortification. 2. Castles. I. Title.

Fortification—America—History—Exhibitions.

MARSHALL, Douglas W. 711'.4'0973
The city in the new world: the military contribution; by Douglas W. Marshall. [Ann Arbor] William L. Clements Library, University of Michigan, 1973. 20 p. 23 cm. (William L. Clements Library, University of Michigan. Bulletin 78) "A guide to the exhibition arranged for the conference sponsored by the Center for the Coordination of Ancient and Modern Studies." [UG410.M37] 74-166112
1. Fortification—America—History—Exhibitions. 2. Cities and towns—Planning—America—Exhibitions. 3. America—History—To 1810—Exhibitions. I. Michigan. University. Center for the Coordination of Ancient and Modern

Studies. II. Title. III. Series: Michigan. University. William L. Clements Library. Bulletin 78.

Fortification—United States—History.

ROBINSON, Willard 725'.18'0973
Bethurem, 1935-
American forts—architectural form and function / Willard B. Robinson. Urbana : Published for the Amon Carter Museum of Western Art, Fort Worth, by the University of Illinois Press, [1977] c1976. p. cm. Includes index. Bibliography: p. [UG410.R6] 76-25130 ISBN 0-252-00589-9 : 14.95
1. Fortification—United States—History. 2. Military architecture—United States—History. I. Amon Carter Museum of Western Art, Fort Worth, Tex. II. Title.

Fortuny Marsal, Mariano Jose Maria Bernardo, 1838-1874.

MARTI, Jose, 1853-1895. 759.6
Dos cronicas desconocides de Jose Marti; sobre los pintores Mariano Fortuny y Eduardo Zamacois. Traduccion de Carlos Ripoll. New York, Publicaciones de la Revista Cubana, 1968. 68 l. 28 cm. Consists of 2 articles in English and Spanish "Mariano Fortuny" and "One of the greatest modern painters; the career and the works of the Spaniard, Eduardo Zamacois" which first appeared in English in the Sun, New York, v. 47, no. 208 (Mar. 27, 1881), p. 2, columns 3-6, and v. 49, no. 60 (Oct. 30, 1881), p. 3, columns 1-3, respectively. [ND812.M3] 79-208060
1. Fortuny Marsal, Mariano Jose Maria Bernardo, 1838-1874. 2. Zamacois y Zabala, Eduardo, 1842?-1871. I. Title.

Foss, Chris.

FOSS, Chris. 759.2
Science fiction art / illus. by Chris Foss ; introd. by Brian Aldiss. London : Hart-Davis, MacGibbon, 1976. [4] p., [10] leaves of plates : all ill. ; 46 cm. [ND497.F64A57] 76-363978 ISBN 0-246-10937-8 : £1.95
1. Foss, Chris. 2. Science fiction—Illustrations. I. Title.

Fostoria Glass Company, Moundsville, W. Va.

WEATHERMAN, Hazel 748.2'9154'16
Marie, 1920-
The first Fostoria price watch. Springfield, Mo., Weatherman Glassbooks [1974] 136 p. illus. 21 cm. "Keyed to the fully illustrated Fostoria: its first fifty years." [NK5198.F6W39] 74-169182 ISBN 0-913074-31-4 4.00
1. Fostoria Glass Company, Moundsville, W. Va. 2. Glassware, American—Catalogs. I. Fostoria Glass Company, Moundsville, W. Va. II. Weatherman, Hazel Marie, 1920- Fostoria: its first fifty years. III. Title.

WEATHERMAN, Hazel 748.2'9154'16
Marie, 1920-
Fostoria: its first fifty years. [Springfield, Mo., The Weathermans, 1972] xxiv, 320 p. (chiefly illus., part col.) 23 x 28 cm. [NK5198.F6W4] 72-189146 15.00
1. Fostoria Glass Company, Moundsville, W. Va. I. Title.

Fouchet, Max Pol.

FRIEDLAENDER, Johnny, 759.43
1912-
Johnny Friedlaender: oeuvre, 1961-1965. Introd.: Max-Pol Fouchet. [New York] Touchstone Pubs. [1967] 76p. (chiefly illus. (pt. col., part mounted) col. plate (in pocket) port. 33cm. Text in French, English, German [NE2210.F75A25] 67-1439 17.50, bxd.
1. Fouchet, Max Pol. I. Title.

Foucquet, Jean, 1415?-1480?

COX, Trenchard, 1905- 759.4
Jehan Foucquet, native of Tours. Freeport, N.Y., Books for Libraries Press [1972] xiv, 150 p. illus. 22 cm. Reprint of the 1931 ed. Bibliography: p. 137-144. [ND553.F6C6 1972] 72-7072 ISBN 0-8369-6926-X
1. Foucquet, Jehan, 1415?-1480? BIP

FOUCQUET, Jehan, 1415-1480 759.4
Fouquet, by M. Ledivelec. New York, Crown [1965] 36p. chiefly illus. (pt. col.) 18cm. (Little bks. on great artists) Biographical sketch in French, English, and German. [ND553.F6L4] 65-3261 .69 pap.,
I. Ledivelec, Madeleine. II. Title.

Found objects (Art)

CAPON, Robin. 745.5
Art from scrap materials / Robin Capon. London : B. T. Batsford, 1975. 88 p. : ill. ; 21 cm. Bibliography: p. 88. [N7433.7.C35] 75-318212 ISBN 0-7134-2915-1 : 9.50
1. Found objects (Art) 2. Art—Technique. I. Title.
Distributed by Hippocrene Books.

RASMUSEN, Henry N. 735'.29
Sculpture from junk [by] Henry Rasmusen, Art Grant. New York, Reinhold [1967] 102p. illus. (pt. col.) 21cm. (Art horizons bk.) [N690.R34] 67-14160 6.95 bds.,
1. Found objects (Art) 2. Sculpture, Modern—20th cent. I. Grant, Art, joint author. II. Title. III. Series.

REED, Carl. 731.4
Sculpture from found objects [by] Carl Reed [and] Burt Towne. Worcester, Mass., Davis Publications [1974] 96 p. illus. 26 cm. [NB1271.R43] 73-93382 ISBN 0-87192-056-5 8.95
1. Found objects (Art) 2. Sculpture. I. Towne, Burt, joint author. II. Title. BIP

Found objects (Art)—Juvenile literature.

COMINS, Jeremy. 745.5
Art from found objects. New York, Lothrop, Lee & Shepard Co. [1974] 126 p. illus. 24 cm. Instructions for making sculpture, jewelry, mobiles, collages, and other items from various found and mechanical objects. [N7433.C54 1974] 74-8220 ISBN 0-688-41646-2 5.50; 4.81 (lib. bdg.)
1. Found objects (Art)—Juvenile literature. I. Title. BIP

Founding—Amateurs' manuals.

CHOATE, Sharr. 739'.14
Creative casting: jewelry, silverware, sculpture. Drawings by the author; photos. by the author except where otherwise noted. New York, Crown Publishers [1966] x, 213 p. illus. (part col.) 27 cm. Bibliography: p. 209-210. [TS741.C5] 66-26172
1. Founding—Amateurs' manuals. 2. Jewelry. 3. Silversmithing. 4. Sculpture—Technique. I. Title.

Fountain pens.

LAWRENCE, Cliff, 1932- 681.6
Fountain pens : history, repair, & current values / by Cliff Lawrence. Paducah, Ky. : Collector Books, c1977. 94 p. : ill. (some col.) ; 22 cm. Includes bibliographical references. [TS1266.L38] 77-155727 ISBN 0-89145-064-5 : 7.95
1. Fountain pens. I. Title.

Fountains.

AMERICAN Federation of Arts. 729
Fountains in contemporary architecture. Selected by Minor L. Bishop. An exhibition organized by the American Federation of Arts under a grant from the Old Dominion Foundation. Circulated March 1965-March 1967. [2d ed. New York, Distributed by October House, 1965] [76] p. (chiefly illus.) 31 cm. [NA9405.A75 1965] 65-16640
1. Fountains. 2. Architecture, Modern — 20th cent. I. Bishop, Minor L. II. Title.

DUMBARTON Oaks 714'.094
Colloquium on the History of Landscape Architecture, 5th, 1977.
Fons sapientiae : Renaissance garden fountains / [edited by Elizabeth B. MacDougall]. Washington : Dumbarton Oaks, Trustees for Harvard University, 1979. p. cm. Papers presented at the conference. Includes bibliographical references. [NA9400.D85 1977] 78-55012 ISBN 0-88402-080-8 : 25.00
1. Fountains, Renaissance—Congresses. 2. Water in landscape architecture—Congresses. 3. Fountains in literature—Congresses. I. MacDougall, Elisabeth B. II. Title.

PFANNSCHMIDT, Ernst 731.7'22
Erik.
Fountains and springs. [1st American ed.] New York, Universe Books [1969] 208 p. illus. 28 cm. Translation of Wasserspiele; Brunnen, Quellen und Fontanen. Bibliography: p. 208. [NA9406.P4513 1969] 69-11835 15.00
1. Fountains. I. Title.

Fountains—France.

MILLER, Naomi. 731'.722
French Renaissance fountains / Naomi Miller. New York : Garland Pub., 1977. viii, ii, 483 p. : ill. ; 21 cm. (Outstanding dissertations in the fine arts) Originally presented as the author's thesis, New York University, 1966. Bibliography: p. 316-327. [NA9413.F8M54 1977] 76-23645 ISBN 0-8240-2713-2 lib.bdg. : 45.00
1. Fountains—France. 2. Architecture, Renaissance—France. 3. Classicism in architecture—France. I. Title. II. Series. BIP

Fountains in art.

†MACDOUGALL, Elisabeth B. 741.64
Fons sapientiae : garden fountains in illustrated books, 15th-18th centuries : catalogue / by Elisabeth B. MacDougall and Naomi Miller ; with bibliography by Laura Byers. Washington : Dumbarton Oaks, 1977. p. cm. Exhibition, Apr. 30-June 30, 1977, organized for the 5th Dumbarton Oaks Colloquium on the History of Landscape Architecture. Bibliography: p. [NC961.F66M32] 77-76011 ISBN 0-88402-073-8 : 4.00
1. Fountains in art. 2. Illustration of books—Exhibitions. I. Miller, Naomi, joint author. II. Dumbarton Oaks. III. Dumbarton Oaks Colloquium on the History of Landscape Architecture, 5th, 1977. IV. Title. BIP

Fowles, Edward.

FOWLES, Edward. 706'.5 B
Memories of Duveen Brothers / [by] Edward Fowles ; introduction by Sir Ellis Waterhouse. London : Times Books, 1976 [7], 215 p., [16] p. of plates : ill., facsim., ports. ; 24 cm. "Abridged by Michael Glover." Includes index. [N8660.F67A25 1976] 77-359790 ISBN 0-7230-0155-3 : £7.95
1. Fowles, Edward. 2. Duveen Brothers. 3. Duveen, Joseph Duveen, Baron, 1869-1939. 4. Art dealers—Great Britain—Biography. I. Title.

Fowling—Pictorial works.

RIPLEY, Aiden Lassell, 769'.924
1896-1969.
Sporting etchings. Commentary by Dana S. Lamb. Introd. by Guido Perera. Barre, Mass., Barre Publishers, 1970. 91 p. illus. 23 x 29 cm. [NE2012.R5L3] 72-111105 ISBN 0-8271-7005-X 17.50
1. Fowling—Pictorial works. I. Lamb, Dana Storrs, 1901- II. Title.

Fox, Josephine Clardy, 1881-1970.

BURNS, Ruby. 917.64'96 B
Josephine Clardy Fox: traveler, opera-goer, collector of art, benefactor. El Paso, Texas Western Press, 1973. xvi, 143 p. illus. 27 cm. [CT275.F6893B87] 73-83925 ISBN 0-87404-042-6 10.00
1. Fox, Josephine Clardy, 1881-1970.

Fox, Milton S., 1904-1971.

ART studies for an editor : 709
25 essays in memory of Milton S. Fox / edited by Frederick Hartt and Patricia Egan ; designed by Robin Fox. New York : H. N. Abrams, [1975] p. cm. [N7442.2.F692] 74-30303 ISBN 0-8109-0279-6 : 25.00
1. Fox, Milton S., 1904-1971. 2. Art—Addresses, essays, lectures. I. Fox, Milton S., 1904-1971. II. Hartt, Frederick, ed. III. Egan, Patricia, ed.

Fox Talbot Museum of Photography.

NATIONAL Trust for 770'.74'02312
Places of Historic Interest or Natural Beauty.
Fox Talbot Museum, Lacock : an illustrated guide / [text by Robert Lassam]. [London] : National Trust, 1976. [18] p. : ill., ports. ; 15 x 21 cm. [TR6.G72L36] 77-364707 ISBN 0-7078-0076-5 : £0.30
1. Fox Talbot Museum of Photography. I. Lassam, Robert. II. Talbot, William Henry Fox, 1800-1877. III. Title.

Fox, Terry, 1943—

TERRY Fox / 709'.2'4
Brenda Richardson. Berkeley, [Calif.] : University Art Museum, 1973. ca. 150 p. : ill. ; 21 x 26 cm. Includes filmography and bibliography. [TR647.F68A57] 73-620112
1. Fox, Terry, 1943- 2. Photography, Artistic—Exhibitions. I. Richardson, Brenda. II. California. University. Art Museum.

Foxes in art.

VARTY, Kenneth. 704.94'32
Reynard the Fox: a study of the fox in medieval English art. New York, Humanities, 1967. 169p. col. front., 96 plates (incl. facsims.). 29cm. Bibl. [N6763.V3] 67-104025 17.50
1. Foxes in art. 2. Art, Medieval—England. I. Title.

Fragonard, Jean Honore, 1732-1806.

THUILLIER, Jacques. 759.4
Fragonard; biographical and critical study. Translated from the French by Robert Allen. [Geneva] Skira [distributed in the U.S. by the World Pub. Co., Cleveland, 1967] 156 p. col. plates. 19 cm. (The Taste of our time [v. 46]) Bibliography: p. 143-[146] [ND553.F7T413 1967] 66-30307
1. Fragonard, Jean Honore, 1732-1806.

WAKEFIELD, David. 759.4
Fragonard / David Wakefield. New York : Two Continents Pub. Group, c1976. p. cm. Includes index. Bibliography: p. [ND553.F7W34 1976] 77-70919 ISBN 0-8467-0246-0 : 13.95. ISBN 0-8467-0245-2 pbk. : 7.95
1. Fragonard, Jean Honore, 1732-1806. 2. Painters—France—Biography. BIP

France — Antiq.

JEFFERSON, Thomas, Pres. 923.173
U.S. 1743-1826.
Thomas Jefferson among the antiquities of southern France in 1787. A tribute to E. Harold Hugo. Princeton, N.J., 1954. 22 p. plates. 19 cm. "Four hundred copies ... printed." Two letters, one by Jefferson to the Comtesse de Tesse, the other by the comtesse in reply. [DC31.T48] 60-35423
1. Hugo, Everett Harold, 1910- 2. France — Antiq. I. Noailles de Tesse, comtesse de. II. Title.

France—Civilization—1830-1900.

HEMMINGS, Frederick 700'.944
William John.
Culture and society in France, 1848-1898; dissidents and philistines [by] F. W. J. Hemmings. New York, Scribner [1972, c1971] 280 p. illus. 24 cm. Bibliography: p. 264-268. [DC33.6.H43 1972] 73-110683 ISBN 0-684-12578-1
1. France—Civilization—1830-1900. I. Title.

WALDBERG, Patrick. 704.94'2
Eros in la belle epoque. Translation by Helen R. Lane. New York, Grove Press [1969] 191 p. illus., ports. 26 cm. Translation of Eros modern' style.

Bibliographical footnotes. [DC338.W313] 68-22015 10.00
1. France—Civilization—1830-1900. 2. Erotic art. 3. Sex in literature. I. Title.

France—Civilization—1830-1900—Caricatures and cartoons.

DAUMIER, Honore Victorin, 1808-1879. 741.5'944
Daumier : eyewitness of an epoch / J. R. Kist. London : Victoria and Albert Museum, 1976. 26, 96 p. : ill. ; 18 cm. Translation of Daumier, verslaggever van zijn tijd, 1832-1872. At head of title: Victoria and Albert Museum. Bibliography: p. 23. [NC1499.D3K4513] 77-352841 ISBN 0-901486-93-0 : £1.25
1. France—Civilization—1830-1900—Caricatures and cartoons. 2. French wit and humor, Pictorial. I. Kist, J. R. II. Victoria and Albert Museum, South Kensington. BIP

France—Court and courtiers.

SAUNDERS, Edith. 926.46
The age of Worth, couturier to the Empress Eugenie. London, New York, Longmans, Green [1954] 218p. illus. 23cm. [TT505.W58S3] 55-1216
1. Worth, Charles Frederick, 1825-1895. 2. France—Court and courtiers. I. Title.

SAUNDERS, Edith. 926.46
The age of Worth, couturier to the Empress Eugenie. Bloomington, Indiana University Press, 1955. 218p. illus. 23cm. [TT505] 55-8084
1. Worth, Charles Frederick, 1825-1895. 2. France—Court and courtiers. I. Title.

France—History—Revolution, 1789-1799—Pictorial works.

DOWD, David Lloyd. 944.04'0924
Pageant-master of the Republic; Jacques-Louis David and the French Revolution. Freeport, N.Y., Books for Libraries Press [1969, c1948] xiv, 205 p. illus., ports. 24 cm. (Select bibliographies reprint series) Includes bibliographical references. [ND553.D25D6 1969] 72-75507
1. David, Jacques Louis, 1748-1825. 2. France—History—Revolution, 1789-1799—Pictorial works. I. Title. BIP

France—Soc. life & cust.—Illustrations.

LARTIGUE, Jacques H., 1894- 779.949914
Boyhood photos of J. H. Lartigue: the family album of a gilded age. [Lausanne?] A. Guichard [1966] 126p. 162 photos. (incl. ports.) 24x30cm. The captions and text were written by Jean Fondin from interviews with the photographer [TR140.L32F6] 66-8895 19.50
1. France—Soc. life & cust.—Illustrations. I. Fondin, Jean. II. Title.
Available from Time, Inc., New York.

France—Social life and customs.—Pictorial works.

SCHNEIDER, Pierre. 760'.0924
The world of Watteau, 1684-1721, by Pierre Schneider and the editors of Time-Life Books New York, Time, inc. [1967] 191 p. illus. (part col.) 31 cm. (Time-Life library of art) Bibliography: p. 185. [ND553.W3S35] 67-20332
1. Watteau, Jean Antoine, 1684-1721. 2. France—Social life and customs.—Pictorial works. I. Time-Life Books. II. Title. BIP

Franceschi, Pietro di Benedetto dei, 1416?-1492.

BUSIGNANI, Alberto. 759.5
Piero della Francesca; [the life and work of the artist, illustrated with 80 full-color plates. Translated from the Italian by Pearl Sanders. 1st American ed.] New York, Grosset & Dunlap [1968] 39 p. illus., col. plates. 18 cm. (The New Grosset art library, 16) Bibliography: p. 26-27. [ND623.F78B83 1968b] 68-26682
1. Franceschi, Pietro di Benedetto dei, 1416?-1492. I. Title.

CLARK, Kenneth McKenzie, Sir, 1903- 759.5
Piero della Francesca, complete edition [by] Kenneth Clark. [2nd. ed., revised.] London, New York, Phaidon [1969.] 239 p. illus. (part col.), plates (part col.), ports. (part col.) 31 cm. Bibliographical references included in "Notes to the text" (p. 77-81) [ND623.F78C6 1969] 69-19805 25.00
1. Franceschi, Pietro di Benedetto dei, 1416?-1492. I. Title.

FRANCESCHI, Pietro di Benedetto dei, 1416?-1492. 759.5
The complete paintings of Piero della Francesca. Introd. by Peter Murray. Notes and catalogue by Pierluigi de Vecchi. New York, N. H. Abrams [1970, c1967] 111 p. illus. (part col.), ports. 32 cm. (Classics of the world's great art) Translation of L'opera completa di Piero della Francesca. Bibliography: p. 82. [ND623.F78D413 1970b] 79-85176 ISBN 0-8109-5513-X
I. De Vecchi, Pierluigi.

GILBERT, Creighton. 759.5
Change in Piero della Francesca. [New York] Published for the Institute of Fine Arts, New York University [by] J. J. Augustin, Locust Valley, N.Y. [1968] xiv, 116 p. plates. 24 cm. (Walter W. S. Cook alumni lecture) Bibliographical references included in "Notes" (p. 57-116) [ND623.F78G5] 75-3734
1. Franceschi, Pietro di Benedetto dei, 1416?-1492. I. Title. II. Series.

HENDY, Philip, Sir, 1900- 759.5
Piero della Francesca and the early Renaissance [by] Philip Hendy. [1st American ed.] New York, Macmillan [1968] 248 p. illus. (part col.) 26 cm. Bibliographical footnotes. [ND623.F78H4 1968] 68-24113 12.50
1. Franceschi, Pietro di Benedetto dei, 1416?-1492. I. Title.

LAVIN, Marilyn Aronberg. 759.5
Piero della Francesca: The Flagellation. [New York, Viking Press, 1972] 109 p. illus. 23 cm. (Art in context) Includes bibliographical references. [ND623.F78L34 1972] 74-165930 ISBN 0-670-55494-4 7.50
1. Franceschi, Pietro di Benedetto dei, 1416?-1492. Flagellation. I. Title.

PODRO, Michael. 759.5
Piero della Francesca's Legend of the true Cross / by Michael I. Podro. Newcastle upon Tyne : University of Newcastle upon Tyne, 1974. 20 p. : ill. ; 24 cm. (Charlton lecture ; 55th) Includes bibliographical references. [ND623.F78P62] 75-517594 ISBN 0-900565-91-8 : £1.00
1. Franceschi, Pietro di Benedetto dei, 1416?-1492. Legend of the true Cross. 2. Arezzo. San Francisco (Church) I. Title. II. Series.

Franceschi, Pietro di Benedetto del, 1416?-1492.

CLARK, Kenneth McKenzie, Sir 1903- 759.5
Piero delia Francesca. With 219 illus. New York, Phaidon Publishers; distributed by Oxford University Press [1951] 212 p. plates (part col.) 31 cm. [ND623.F78C6] 51-4973
1. Franceschi, Pietro di Benedetto del, 1416?-1492. I. Title.

NEW York. Metropolitan Museum of Art. 759.5
Piero della Francesca; prepared for self-instruction. New York [Distributor: Book-of-the-Month Club, 1954] unpaged. 13 x 18cm. (The Metropolitan library of home art exhibits) [ND623.F78N4] [ND623.F78N4] 927.5 55-31669 55-31669
1. Franceschi, Pietro di Benedetto del, 1416?-1492. I. Title.

Francesco d'Assisi, Saint 1182-1226.

TINTORI, Leonetto, 1908- 704.9486
The painting of the life of St. Francis in Assisi. With notes on the arena chapel, and a 1964 appendix, by Leonetto Tintori, Millard Meiss. New York, Norton, [1967,c.1962] xv, 207p. illus. 20cm. (Norton lib., N393) Bibl. [N8080.T55] 1.95 pap.,
1. Francesco d'Assisi, Saint 1182-1226. 2. Assisi, San Francesco (Church) 3. Padua. Madonna dell' Arena (Chapel) 4. Saints—Art. 5. Mural painting and decoration. I. Meiss, Millard, joint author. II. Title.

TINTORI, Leonetto, 1908- 704.9486
The painting of The life of St. Francis in Assisi, with notes on the Arena Chapel, by Leonetto Tintori and Millard Meiss. [New York] New York University Press, 1962. xv, 205 p. illus. 25 cm. At head of title: Conservation Center, Institute of Fine Arts, New York University. Erratum slip inserted. "Selective list of technical studies": p. 187-188. Includes bibliographical references. [N8080.T55] 62-10308
1. Francesco d'Assisi, Saint, 1182-1226. 2. Saints—Art. 3. Assisi. San Francesco (Church) 4. Padua. Madonna dell'Arena (Chapel) 5. Mural painting and decoration, Italian. I. Meiss, Millard, joint author. II. Title.

Francesco d'Assisi, Saint, 1182-1226 — part.

KUPPERS, Leonhard, 1903- 704.9486
Francis of Assisi. [Translated from the German by Hans Hermann Rosenwald] Recklinghausen [Ger.] A. Bongers; distributed by Taplinger Pub. Co. [New York, c1964] 61 p. col. illus. 18 cm. (The Saints in legend and art, v. 4) [N8080.K813] 67-4426
1. Francesco d'Assisi, Saint, 1182-1226 — part. I. Title.

Franciabigio, 1484-1525.

MCKILLOP, Susan Regan. 708.5'5
Franciabigio / Susan Regan McKillop. Berkeley : University of California Press, c1974. xvii, 322 p., [38] leaves of plates : ill. ; 32 cm. (California studies in the history of art ; 16) Includes indexes. Bibliography: p. 275-290. [ND623.F783M32] 76-107661 ISBN 0-520-01688-2 : 40.00
1. Franciabigio, 1484-1525. I. Title. II. Series. BIP

Francis, Harley, 1940—

FRANCIS, Harley, 1940- 741.9'73
The night blooming delirious : a suite of drawings and poems / by Harley Francis, II. New York : Studio 3000, [1975] [54] p. : ill. ; 21 cm. [NC139.F715A53] 75-1203 ISBN 0-915100-03-7 pbk. : 2.00
1. Francis, Harley, 1940- 2. Unicorns in art. I. Title.

Francis, Sam, 1923—

SELZ, Peter Howard, 1919- 759.13
Sam Francis, by Peter Selz. New York, H. N. Abrams [1976 i.e.,1975] p. cm. [ND237.F67S44] 74-16096 ISBN 0-8109-0265-6 37.50
1. Francis, Sam, 1923- BIP

Franck, Frederick, 1909—

FRANCK, Frederick, 1909- 741'.092'4
The Zen of seeing; seeing/drawing as meditation, drawn and handwritten by Frederick Franck. New York, Vintage Books [1973] xxi, 130 p. illus. 27 cm. [NC139.F72A58] 73-174195 3.45 (pbk.)
1. Franck, Frederick, 1909- 2. Zen Buddhism. I. Title. BIP

FRANCK, Frederick, 1909- 741'.092'4
The Zen of seeing : seeing, drawing as meditation / drawn and handwritten by Frederick Franck. 1st ed. New York : Knopf : distributed by Random House, 1973. xxi, 130 p. : ill. ; 28 cm. [NC139.F72A58 1973b] 74-184817 ISBN 0-394-48804-0 : 7.95
1. Franck, Frederick, 1909- 2. Zen Buddhism. I. Title.

Frankenthaler, Helen, 1928—

FRANKENTHALER, Helen, 1928- 759.13
Helen Frankenthaler. [Text] by E. C. Goossen. [New York, Printed by Rapoport Printing Corp., 1969] 72 p. illus. (part col.), ports. 23 cm. Catalog of an exhibition organized by the Whitney Museum of American Art and the International Council of the Museum of Modern Art, and shown Feb. 20-Apr. 6, 1969 at the Whitney. Bibliography: p. 68-72. [ND237.F675G63] 69-19884
I. Goossen, E. C. II. Whitney Museum of American Art, New York. III. International Council of the Museum of Modern Art, New York.

FRANKENTHALER, Helen, 1928- 759.13
Helen Frankenthaler : paintings 1969-1974 : [exhibitions] : Corcoran Gallery of Art, Washington D. C., April 20-June 1, 1975, Seattle Art Museum, June 26-September 14, 1975, Museum of Fine Arts, Houston, October 10-November 23, 1975. Washington : Corcoran Gallery of Art, c1975. [48] p. : ill. (some col.) ; 21 cm. Bibliography: p. [41]-[47] [ND237.F675C67] 75-7886
1. Frankenthaler, Helen, 1928- I. Corcoran Gallery of Art, Washington, D.C. II. Seattle. Art Museum. III. Houston, Tex. Museum of Fine Arts.

ROSE, Barbara. 759.13
Frankenthaler. Text by Barbara Rose. New York, H. N. Abrams [1971?] 272 p. plates (part col.) 28 cm. Bibliography: p. [265]-272. [ND237.F675R6] 70-141762 ISBN 0-8109-0126-9 25.00
I. Frankenthaler, Helen, 1928-

Frankfurt am Main. Frobenius-Institut.

CERVICEK, Pavel. 016.732'2
Catalogue of the rock art collection of the Frobenius Institute / by Paval Cervicek ; with drawings by Gisela Wittner and photos by Margit Matthews. 1. Aufl. Wiesbaden : Steiner, 1976. xv, 306 p., [99] leaves of plates : ill. ; 24 cm. (Studien zur Kulturkunde ; Bd. 41) Includes bibliographies and index. [GN799.P4C45] 77-356931 ISBN 3-515-01856-5
1. Frankfurt am Main. Frobenius-Institut. 2. Rock paintings—Catalogs. 3. Petroglyphs—Catalogs. I. Frankfurt am Main. Frobenius-Institut. II. Title. III. Series.

Franklin, Benjamin, 1706-1790.

HARRIS, Elizabeth M. 681'.62
The common press : being a record, description, & delineation of the early eighteenth-century handpress in the Smithsonian Institution, with a history & documentation of the press / by Elizabeth Harris ; and drawings & advice on construction by Clinton Sisson. Boston : D. R. Godine, 1978. 62 p. : ill. ; 28 cm. & portfolio (8 fold. leaves of plates : ill. ; 28 cm.) Issued in a case. Includes bibliographical references. [Z249.H28] 77-79005 ISBN 0-87923-211-0 : 20.00
1. Franklin, Benjamin, 1706-1790. 2. Smithsonian Institution. 3. Handpress. 4. Handpress—Drawings. I. Title. BIP

OSWALD, John Clyde, 1872-1938. 973.32'0924 B
Benjamin Franklin, printer. Ann Arbor, Mich., Gryphon Books, 1971. xv, 244 p. facsims., port. 22 cm. "Facsimile reprint of the 1917 edition." [Z232.F8O8 1917a] 71-143632
1. Franklin, Benjamin, 1706-1790.

OSWALD, John Clyde, 1872-1938. 070.5'092'4 B
Benjamin Franklin, printer. Published by Doubleday, Page for the Associated Advertising Clubs of the World, 1917. Detroit, Gale Research Co., 1974. xv, 244 p. illus. 22 cm. [Z232.F8O8 1974] 74-3020 ISBN 0-8103-3642-1 12.50
1. Franklin, Benjamin, 1706-1790.

Franklin, Benjamin, 1706-1790—Portraits.

SELLERS, Charles Coleman, 1903- 704.9423
Benjamin Franklin in portraiture. New Haven, Yale University Press, 1962. xi, 452 p. illus., ports. (part col.) 28 cm. "Published in cooperation with the

American Philosophical Society." Bibliographical footnotes. [N7628.F7S4] 62-8263
1. Franklin, Benjamin, 1706-1790—Portraits. I. Title. BIP

Franklin Mint.

CULVER, Virginia. 737'.0973
Guidebook of Franklin Mint issues / edited by Virginia Culver and Chester L. Krause. [2d ed.] Iola, Wis. : Krause Publications, 1975. 222 p. : ill. ; 28 cm. Includes indexes. [CJ5813.F732C84 1975] 76-364213 ISBN 0-87341-005-X pbk. : 6.50
1. Franklin Mint. 2. Medals—United States. 3. Tokens—United States. I. Krause, Chester L., joint author. II. Title.

KRAUSE, Chester L. 737'.0973
Guidebook of Franklin Mint issues / edited by Chester L. Krause. [3d ed.]. Iola, Wis. : Krause Publications, 1976. 222 p. : ill. ; 28 cm. First-2d ed. written by V. Culver and C. L. Krause. Includes indexes. [CJ5813.F732C84 1976] 76-7254 ISBN 0-87341-009-2 : 6.50
1. Franklin Mint. 2. Medals—United States. 3. Tokens—United States. I. Culver, Virginia. Guidebook of Franklin Mint issues. II. Title.

Franklin Photolettering.

FRANKLIN Photolettering. 686.2'24
Modern display alphabets : 100 complete fonts / selected and arr. by Paul E. Kennedy, from the Franklin Photolettering catalogue. New York : Dover Publications, 1974. 100 p. ; 29 cm. [Z250.K4F7 1974] 74-79330 ISBN 0-486-23097-X pbk. : 2.50
1. Franklin Photolettering. 2. Printing—Specimens. I. Kennedy, Paul E. II. Title. BIP

Franz, Alison.

ROBERTSON, Martin. 733'.3'09385
The Parthenon frieze text, Martin Robertson; photos., Alison Frantz. New York, Oxford University Press, 1975. 16 p., [24] leaves of plates, ill. 32 cm. Bibliography: p. 16. [NB91.A7R62] 74-83716 ISBN 0-19-519783-6 9.50.
1. Franz, Alison. 2. Athens. Parthenon. Frieze. I. Title.

Frary, Michael, 1918—

FRARY, Michael, 1918- 759.13
Impressions of the Texas Panhandle / by Michael Frary. 1st ed. College Station : Texas A&M University Press, c1977. 112 p. : some col. ill. ; 24 x 32 cm. (The Joe and Betty Moore Texas art series ; no. 2) [ND237.F676A45] 77-89515 ISBN 0-89096-037-2 : 24.50
1. Frary, Michael, 1918- 2. Texas Panhandle in art. I. Title. II. Series. BIP

Frasconi, Antonio.

BALTIMORE. Museum of Art. 759.13
The work of Antonio Frasconi, 1952-1963; woodcuts, lithographs, and books. [Exhibition] November 1963. [Baltimore, 1963] 1 v. (unpaged) illus. 23 cm. "Circulated in part by the Smithsonian Institution." [NE1215.F7B3] 66-40636
1. Frasconi, Antonio. I. Title.

FRASCONI, Antonio. 769'.92'4
Frasconi: against the grain; the woodcuts of Antonio Frasconi. With an introd. by Nat Hentoff and an appreciation by Charles Parkhurst. New York, Macmillan [1974] 159 p. illus. 29 cm. [NE1112.F72A45] 74-8805 ISBN 0-02-551100-9. 12.95
1. Frasconi, Antonio. I. Title.
Pbk. 7.95; ISBN 0-02-000600-4.

Fraser, Charles, 1782-1860.

SMITH, Alice Ravenel 759.157
Huger, 1876-
Charles Fraser, by Alice R. Huger Smith and D. E. Huger Smith. Charleston, S.C., Garnier [1967] ix, 58 p. ports. 25 cm. "Unabridged and unaltered republication of the limited edition (325) originally published ... in 1924." [ND1337.U6F71967] 68-23427
1. Fraser, Charles, 1782-1860. I. Smith, Daniel Elliott Huger, joint author.

Fraser, James Earle, 1876-1953.

KRAKEL, Dean Fenton, 730'.92'4
1923-
End of the trail; the odyssey of a statue [by] Dean Krakel. [1st ed.] Norman, University of Oklahoma Press [1973] xvii, 196 p. illus. 26 cm. Includes bibliographical references. [NB237.F67K72] 72-9265 8.95
1. Fraser, James Earle, 1876-1953. End of the trail. 2. Fraser, Laura Gardin, 1889-1966. I. Title.

Fratta Polesine, Italy. Villa Badoer.

PUPPI, Lionello. 945'.35
The Villa Badoer at Fratta Polesine / Lionello Puppi ; translated by Catherine Enggass. University Park : Pennsylvania State University Press, [1975,i.e.1977] p. cm. (Corpus Palladianum ; v. 7) Includes index. Bibliography: p. [NA1123.P2P8313] 75-19403 ISBN 0-271-01203-X : 30.00
1. Fratta Polesine, Italy. Villa Badoer. 2. Palladio, Andrea, 1508-1580. I. Title. II. Series. BIP

Frazetta, Frank.

FRAZETTA, Frank. 741.9'73
The fantastic art of Frank Frazetta / introd. by Betty Ballantine. New York : Rufus Publications, 1975. [12] p., 42 leaves of plates : ill. (some col.) ; 29 cm. [NC975.5.F72A45] 75-11192 5.95
1. Frazetta, Frank. I. Title. BIP

FRAZETTA, Frank. 741.9'73
Frank Frazetta / introd. by Betty Ballantine. 1st U.S. ed. New York : Peacock Press/Bantam Books, 1977. [95] p. : chiefly ill. (some col.) ; 29 cm. "Book two." [NC1850.F7A45 1977] 77-77520 7.95
1. Frazetta, Frank. 2. Science fiction—Illustrations. BIP

FRAZETTA, Frank. 741.9'73
Frank Frazetta / introd. by Betty Ballantine. 1st U.S. ed. New York : Peacock Press/Bantam Books, 1978. [93] p. : chiefly ill. (some col.) ; 29 cm. "Book three." [N6537.F75A4 1978] 78-61114 pbk. : 7.95
1. Frazetta, Frank. 2. Science fiction—Illustrations. I. Ballantine, Betty.

Freas, Frank Kelly, 1922—

FREAS, Frank Kelly, 741.9'73
1922-
Frank Kelly Freas : the art of science fiction / by Frank Kelly Freas ; introd. by Isaac Asimov. Norfolk, Va. : Donning Co., c1977. p. cm. [NC975.5.F74A45] 77-8644 ISBN 0-915442-30-2 collector's ed. : 29.95. ISBN 0-915442-37-X pbk. : 7.95. ISBN 0-915442-38-8 lib. ed. : 12.95
1. Freas, Frank Kelly, 1922- 2. Illustrators—United States—Biography. 3. Science fiction—Illustrations. I. Title. BIP

Frederick's of Hollywood.

GOTTWALD, Laura, comp. 391'.42
Fredericks of Hollywood, 1947-1973; 26 years of mail order seduction. Edited by Laura & Janusz Gottwald. New York, Drake Publishers [1973, i.e. 1974] 255 p. illus. 31 cm. "A Strawberry Hill book." [TT555.G67] 73-17466 ISBN 0-87749-582-3 12.98; 7.95 (pbk.)
1. Frederick's of Hollywood. 2. Clothing and dress—Catalogs. I. Gottwald, Janusz, joint comp. II. Title.

Fredericksburg, Va.—Description—Views.

SHIBLEY, Ronald 779'.9'9755366
E., 1942-
Historic Fredericksburg : a pictorial history / by Ronald E. Shibley. Norfolk, Va. : Donning, c1976. 160 p. : ill. ; 28 cm. [F234.F8S45] 76-25540 ISBN 0-915442-16-7 : 13.95
1. Fredericksburg, Va.—Description—Views. 2. Fredicksburg, Va.—Buildings—Pictorial works. I. Title.

Freehand technical sketching.

KATZ, Hyman H. 744.4
Technical sketching and visualization for engineers [by] Hyman H. Katz. Illustrated by the author. [Chicago?] c1967. 161 p. illus. 28 cm. [T359.K3 1967] 70-6685
1. Freehand technical sketching. I. Title.

Freemasons—Medals.

FREEMASONS. U.S. Scottish 737.4
Rite. Supreme Council for the Southern Jurisdiction. Library. Hanauer Collection.
Masonic chapter pennies. By E. A. King. [Waltham, Mass., Quarterman Pub. [1972] 360 p. illus. 22 cm. [HS433.F7 1972] 73-189167 ISBN 0-88000-000-7
1. Freemasons—Medals. 2. Freemasons. Royal Arch Masons. 3. Freemasons—Symbolism. 4. Coins. I. King, Edward A., 1877- II. Title.

Freemasons—Symbolism—Pictorial works—Exhibitions.

SCOTTISH Rite 745'.0973'07401444
Masonic Museum of Our National Heritage.
Masonic symbols in American decorative arts. Lexington, Mass. : Scottish Rite Masonic Museum of Our National Heritage, c1976. 110 p. : ill. ; 22 cm. "Exhibition: September 1975 to September 1976." "Catalog": p. [55]-[108] [NK805.S34 1976] 76-16690
1. Freemasons—Symbolism—Pictorial works—Exhibitions. 2. Art, Decorative—United States—Exhibitions. 3. Symbolism in art—United States—Exhibitions. I. Title.

Freer, Charles Lang, 1856-1919.

MEYER, Agnes Elizabeth 709'.24
(Ernst) 1887-
Charles Lang Freer and his gallery, by Agnes E. Meyer. Washington, Freer Gallery of Art, 1970. 23 p. col. illus., port. 23 cm. [N857.5.M48] 70-124106
1. Freer, Charles Lang, 1856-1919. 2. Freer Gallery of Art, Washington, D.C.

Freer Gallery of Art, Washington, D.C.

FREER Gallery of 709'.51'0740153
Art, Washington, D.C.
Masterpieces of Chinese and Japanese art : Freer Gallery of Art handbook. Washington : Smithsonian Institution, 1976. v, 142 p. : ill. (some col.) ; 23 cm. [N7336.F7 1976] 76-11656
1. Freer Gallery of Art, Washington, D.C. 2. Art, Chinese—Catalogs. 3. Art, Japanese—Catalogs. 4. Art—Washington, D.C.—Catalogs. I. Title. BIP

Frelinghuysen, George G.—Art collections.

CALIFORNIA. University. 709.01'1
University at Los Angeles. Museum and Laboratories of Ethnic Arts and Technology.
The George G. Frelinghuysen collection at UCLA; objects from Africa, Indonesia, the South Seas, and Asia. [Los Angeles? 1968?] 35 p. illus. 29 cm. Catalog of the collection, part of which was exhibited May 5-June 30, 1968, in the Ethnic Art Galleries, University of California, Los Angeles. [N5311.C25] 68-66150
1. Frelinghuysen, George G.—Art collections. 2. Art, Primitive—Exhibitions. I. Title.

French, Daniel Chester, 1850-1931.

MYERS, Robert 731'.76'0977265
Henry, 1894-
Beneficence; the statue on the campus of Ball State University, Muncie, Indiana. Robert Henry Myers, editor. Muncie, Ind., Ball State University, 1972. 128 p. illus. 26 cm. Bibliography: p. 123-128. [NB237.F7M93] 72-619607
1. French, Daniel Chester, 1850-1931. 2. Indiana. Ball State University, Muncie. 3. Muncie, Ind. Beneficence (Statue) I. Title.

RICHMAN, Michael. 730'.92'4
Daniel Chester French, an American sculptor / Michael Richman ; postscript by Paul W. Ivory. New York : Metropolitan Museum of Art for the National Trust for Historic Preservation, c1976. xi, 208 p. : ill. ; 26 cm. Catalog of the exhibition to be held at the Metropolitan Museum of Art, Nov. 4, 1976-Jan. 10, 1977; the National Collection of Fine Arts, Smithsonian Institution, Feb. 11-Apr. 17, 1977; the Detroit Institute of Arts, June 15-Aug. 28, 1977; Fogg Art Museum, Harvard University, Sept. 30-Nov. 30, 1977. Includes bibliographical references. [NB237.F7R49] 76-40897 ISBN 0-87099-153-1 pbk. 5.95
1. French, Daniel Chester, 1850-1931. I. French, Daniel Chester, 1850-1931. II. New York (City). Metropolitan Museum of Art. III. National Trust for Historic Preservation in the United States.

RICHMAN, Michael 730'.92'4
Tingley.
The early career of Daniel Chester French, 1869-1891. [Newark? Del.] 1974. vii, 353 l. 30 cm. Thesis—University of Delaware. Bibliography: leaves 303-315. [NB237.F7R52] 74-174387
1. French, Daniel Chester, 1850-1931. I. Title.

French literature—20th century—History and criticism.

LEMAITRE, Georges 709'.44
Edouard, 1898-
From cubism to surrealism in French literature [by] Georges Lemaitre. New York, Russell & Russell [1967, c1941] 247 p. illus. 22 cm. Bibliography: p. 219-240. [PQ305.L4 1967] 66-24722
1. French literature—20th century—History and criticism. 2. Cubism—France. 3. Surrealism. I. Title. BIP

French wit and humor, Pictorial.

DAUMIER, Honore 769'.92'4
Victorin, 1808-1879.
Daumier, 120 great lithographs / edited by Charles F. Ramus. New York : Dover Publications, 1978. xx, 138 p. : ill. ; 31 cm. (Dover art collections) Bibliography: p. [137]-138. [NC1499.D3A4 1978] 77-83928 ISBN 0-486-23512-2 : 5.00
1. Daumier, Honore Victorin, 1808-1879. 2. French wit and humor, Pictorial. I. Ramus, Charles F. II. Title.

FRENCH satirical 741.5'944
drawings from "L'Assiette au beurre" : selection, translations, and text / by Stanley Appelbaum. New York : Dover Publications, 1978. 161 p., [4] leaves of plates : chiefly ill. ; 31 cm. English and French. [NC1498.A8F73] 77-84742 ISBN 0-486-23583-1 : 6.50
1. French wit and humor, Pictorial. I. Applebaum, Stanley. II. L'Assiette au beurre. BIP

HOUSE, Brant, pseud., ed. 741.5
Love from France; from the droll pens of leading French cartoonists, edited by Brant House with the assistance of Edna Bennett. New York, A. A. Wyn [1955] 94p. illus. 26cm. [NC1497.H65A47] 55-7641
1. French wit and humor, Pictorial. I. Title.

Frerichs, William C. A., 1829-1905.

NORTH Carolina. Museum 759.9492
of Art, Raleigh.
William C. A. Frerichs, 1829-1905 : a retrospective exhibition September 15-October 20, 1974 Raleigh : North Carolina Museum of Art, 1974. [60] p. : ill. (some col.) ; 18 x 26 cm. Includes bibliographical references. [ND237.F72N67 1974] 75-620603 ISBN 0-88259-075-8
1. Frerichs, William C. A., 1829-1905. BIP

SUBJECT INDEX FULLER, CLAUD E.

Frick Art Museum, Pittsburgh.

FRICK Art Museum, Pittsburgh. 708'.14'886
Treasures of the Frick Art Museum / text by Walter Read Hovey. Pittsburgh : The Museum, 1975. p. cm. Includes index. [N710.5.A87] 75-26681
1. Frick Art Museum, Pittsburgh. 2. Art—Pittsburgh. I. Hovey, Walter Read, 1895- II. Title.

Friedlaender, Walter F., 1873-1966.

ESSAYS in honor of Walter Friedlaender. Edited by Marsyas. [New York] Institute of Fine Arts, New York University; distributed by J. J. Augustin, Locust Valley, N.Y., 1965. xiii, 194 p. 29 cm. (Marsyas; studies in the history of art. Supplement 2) Includes bibliographical references. [N7442.4.F74] 74-168035 709
1. Friedlaender, Walter F., 1873-1966. 2. Art—Addresses, essays, lectures. I. Friedlaender, Walter F., 1873-1966. II. New York University. Institute of Fine Arts. III. Title. IV. Series.

Friedman, Bruce, 1924- —Art collections.

FERBRACHE, Lewis. 759.194'074'019466
The Dr. and Mrs. Bruce Friedman Collection. [San Francisco] California Historical Society [1969?] [31] p. illus. 28 cm. Loan exhibition held at the California Historical Society, Sept. 30-Nov. 15, 1969. [N6530.C2F4] 76-24094
1. Friedman, Bruce, 1924- —Art collections. 2. Friedman, Bruce Mrs.—Art collections. 3. Art, American—Exhibitions. 4. Art, American—California. I. California Historical Society. II. Title.

Friedrich, Caspar David, 1774-1840.

BORSCH-SUPAN, Helmut 759.3
Caspar David Friedrich / Helmut Borsch-Supan ; [translated from the German by Sarah Twohig]. New York : G. Braziller, 1974. 184 p. : ill. (some col.) ; 30 cm. Includes index. Bibliography: p. 181. [ND588.F75B6213] 73-93687 ISBN 0-8076-0747-9 : 35.00
1. Friedrich, Caspar David, 1774-1840. I. Friedrich, Caspar David, 1774-1840.

FRIEDRICH, Caspar David, 1774-1840. 759.3
Caspar David Friedrich / edited by Jorg Traeger. New York : Rizzoli, c1976. 97 p. : ill. (some col.) ; 25 cm. English, German and French. [ND588.F75T7] 76-151002 ISBN 0-8478-0033-4 : 16.50
1. Friedrich, Caspar David, 1774-1840. 2. Painters—Germany—Biography. I. Traeger, Jorg, 1942-

FRIEDRICH, Caspar David, 1774-1840. 759.3
Caspar David Friedrich / hrsg. von Jorg Traeger ; [transl. into Engl. by Gillian Turner ; trad. francaise par Denise Baumann]. Munchen : Bruckmann, 1976. 97 p. : chiefly ill. (some col.) ; 25 cm. English, French, and German. [ND588.F75T7 1976b] 77-484085 ISBN 3-7654-1649-5 : DM35.00
1. Friedrich, Caspar David, 1774-1840. 2. Painters—Germany—Biography. I. Traeger, Jorg, 1942-

SIEGEL, Linda. 759.3
Caspar David Friedrich and the age of German Romanticism / by Linda Siegel ; with a foreword by George Levitine. Boston : Branden Press, c1978. 169 p., [71] leaves of plates : ill. (some col.) ; 23 cm. Bibliography: p. 151-155. [ND588.F75S53] 75-43055 ISBN 0-8283-1659-7 : 25.00
1. Friedrich, Caspar David, 1774-1840—Influence. 2. Romanticism in art—Germany. 3. Landscape painting—19th century—Germany. I. Title. BIP

Friedrich II, Emperor of Germany, 1194-1250.

VALENTINER, Wilhelm Reinhold, 1880- 734.43
The Bamberg rider; studies of mediaeval German sculpture. Los Angeles, Zeitlin & Ver Brugge, 1956. ix, 166p. illus. 27cm. 'Limited edition of 500 copies.'--Dust jacket. Bibliographical references included in 'Notes' (p. 150-157) Bibliography: p. 158-159. [NA5586.B3V3] 56-58361
1. Friedrich II, Emperor of Germany, 1194-1250. 2. Bamberg. Dom. 3. Sculpture, German. 4. Sculpture, Medieval. I. Title.

Friese-Greene, William, 1855-1921.

FORTH, Muriel, 1907- 608'.7'24 B
Friese-Greene; close-up of an inventor [by] Ray Allister. New York, Arno Press, 1972. 192 p. illus. 23 cm. (The Arno Press cinema program. The literature of cinema) Reprint of the 1948 ed. published by Marsland Publications, London. [TR140.F7F6 1972] 71-169339 ISBN 0-405-03908-5
1. Friese-Greene, William, 1855-1921. I. Series: The Arno Press cinema program. II. Series: The Literature of cinema.

Friezes—Greece—Corinth.

STURGEON, Mary Carol, 1943- 938'.7 s
Sculpture : the reliefs from the theater / by Mary C. Sturgeon. Princeton, N.J. : American School of Classical Studies at Athens, 1977. p. cm. (Corinth ; v. 9, pt. 2) A revision of the author's thesis, Bryn Mawr College, 1971. Bibliography: p. [DF261.C65A6 vol. 9, pt. 2] [NB91.C615] 733'.3'09387 77-383 ISBN 0-87661-092-0
1. Corinth, Greece. Odeum. 2. Friezes—Greece—Corinth. 3. Relief (Sculpture)—Greece—Corinth. I. Title. II. Series: American School of Classical Studies at Athens. Corinth ; v. 9, pt. 2.

Frink, Elisabeth, 1930—

FRINK, Elisabeth, 1930- 730'.92'4
The art of Elisabeth Frink. With an introd. by Edwin Mullins. [1st U.S. ed.] Park Ridge, N.J., Noyes Press [1973, c1972] 1 v. (chiefly illus.) 30 cm. Bibliography: p. [20] [NB497.F74A42 1973] 72-85246 ISBN 0-8155-5012-X 20.00
1. Frink, Elisabeth, 1930- I. Title.

Frishmuth, Harriet Whitney, 1880—

ARONSON, Charles N., 1913- 730'.92'4
Sculptured hyacinths [by] Charles N. Aronson. [1st ed.] New York, Vantage Press [1973] 219 p. illus. (part col.) 29 cm. [NB237.F75A89] 73-163947 ISBN 0-533-00550-7 24.95
1. Frishmuth, Harriet Whitney, 1880- I. Title. BIP

Frith, Francis.

JAY, Bill. 779'.4'0924
Victorian cameraman; Francis Frith's views of rural England, 1850-1898. Newton Abbot, David & Charles [1973, i.e.1974] 112 p. illus. 25 cm. [DA667.J39] 73-164057 ISBN 0-7153-5895-2
1. Frith, Francis. 2. England—Description and travel—Views. I. Title.
Distributed by David and Charles, Vermont, 10.50.

Frontier and pioneer life.

PARISH, Peggy. 745.5
Let's be early settlers with Daniel Boone. Drawings by Arnold Lobel. New York, Harper & Row [1967] 96 p. illus. 24 cm. Specific instructions for making many pieces of clothing or items used by an early pioneer, such as powder horns, braided rugs, coonskin hats, or horn books. Includes instructions for small models and dioramas of frontier life. [PZ10.P2545Ld] AC 67
1. Frontier and pioneer life. 2. Handicraft. I. Lobel, Arnold, illus. II. Title. BIP

Frontier and pioneer life in art.

THE Pioneers : 704.94'9'978
images of the frontier : 109 illustrations / selected and introduced by Joseph Czestochowski. Oxford : Phaidon ; New York : Dutton, 1977. 96 p. : chiefly ill. (some col.) ; 42 cm. (Phaidon giant art paperbacks) [N8214.5.U6P56] 77-75400 ISBN 0-7148-1775-9 : 8.95
1. Frontier and pioneer life in art. 2. Frontier and pioneer life—United States—Pictorial works. 3. The West in art. I. Czestochowski, Joseph. BIP

Frost, Arthur Burdett, 1851-1928.

REED, Henry M. 760'.0924
The A. B. Frost book, by Henry M. Reed. With a foreword by Eugene V. Connett. Rutland, Vt., C.E. Tuttle Co. [1967] 149 p. illus. (part col.) 31 cm. "Books illustrated by A. B. Frost": p. 141-146. [NC139.F75R4] 67-21929
1. Frost, Arthur Burdett, 1851-1928. I. Title.

Frost, Robert, 1874-1963—Quotations.

MELVIN, Betsy. 779'.9'974
Robert Frost country / Betsy and Tom Melvin ; foreword by William Meredith. Garden City, N.Y. : Doubleday, 1976. p. cm. [TR654.M455] 76-2806 ISBN 0-385-12180-6 : 14.95. ISBN 0-385-12127-X pbk. : 6.95
1. Frost, Robert, 1874-1963—Quotations. 2. Photography, Artistic. 3. New England—Description and travel—Views. I. Melvin, Tom, joint author. II. Frost, Robert, 1874-1963. III. Title. BIP

Frost, Terry, 1915—

FROST, Terry, 1915- 759.2
Terry Frost, paintings, drawings and collages : [catalogue of an exhibition organised by the] Arts Council [and] South West Arts, 1976-77. [London] : Arts Council of Great Britain, 1976. 48 p. : chiefly ill. (some col.) ; 18 cm. Errata slip inserted. Bibliography: p. 22. [N6797.F74A77] 77-369120 ISBN 0-7287-0117-0 : £1.50
1. Frost, Terry, 1915- I. Arts Council of Great Britain. II. South West Arts.

Froud, Brian.

FROUD, Brian. 759.2
The land of Froud / edited by David Larkin ; introd. by Brian Sanders. 1st ed. New York : Peacock Press / Bantam Books, 1977. [14] p., [41] leaves of plates : chiefly ill. (some col.) ; 29 cm. [NC978.5.F76L37] 77-71731 ISBN 0-553-01055-7 : 7.95
1. Froud, Brian. 2. Grotesque in art. I. Larkin, David. II. Title.

Fruhbeck, Franz Josef, b. 1795.

SMITH, Robert Chester, 1912- 759.36
Franz Fruhbeck's Brazilian journey; a study of some paintings and drawings made in the years 1817 and 1818 and now in the possession of the Hispanic Society of America [by] Robert C. Smith and Gilberto Ferrez. Philadelphia, University of Pennsylvania Press [1960] 128 p. 16 plates, port., map (on lining papers) 29 cm. Bibliographical references included in "Notes." [ND538.F7S6 1960] 58-11748
1. Fruhbeck, Franz Josef, b. 1795. 2. Leopoldina, consort of Pedro I. Emperor of Brazil, 1797-1826. 3. Rio de Janeiro — Descr. — Views. I. Ferrez, Gilberto, joint author. II. Fruhbeck, Franz Josef, b. 1795. Skizze meiner Reise nach Brasilien in Sud-Amerika. III. Title. BIP

Fruit in art.

MANNERING, Eva, ed. 769.434
Fruit prints; Turpin, Poiteau, and Riefel. Princeton, N.J., Van Nostrand [1965] 8p., 22 col. illus. 25cm. (Golden Ariels, no. 5) [NE953.M3] 65-9606 3.95 bds.,
1. Fruit in art. I. Turpin, Pierre Jean Francois, 1775-1840. II. Poiteau, Antoine, 1766-1854. aRiefel, Carlos. III. Riefel, Carlos IV. Title.

Fry, Edwin Maxwell, 1899—

FRY, Edwin Maxwell, 1899- 720'.92'4
Autobiographical sketches / [by] Maxwell Fry ; with twenty-six illustrations by the author. London : Elek, 1975. 167 p. : ill. ; 23 cm. [NA997.F78A22] 76-361717 ISBN 0-236-40010-X : 14.95
1. Fry, Edwin Maxwell, 1899- 2. Architects—Great Britain—Correspondence, reminiscences, etc. I. Title.
Distributed by Technical Impex BIP

Fry, Roger Eliot, 1866-1934.

EDMONTON Art Gallery. 759.2
Roger Fry, artist and critic : March 19-April 18, 1976 : an exhibition / organized by the Edmonton Art Gallery. [Edmonton, Alta. : Edmonton Art Gallery, 1976] 15 p., [6] leaves of plates : ill. ; 24 cm. Includes bibliographical references. [ND497.F83E35 1976] 77-351072
1. Fry, Roger Eliot, 1866-1934. I. Fry, Roger Eliot, 1866-1934. II. Title.

WOOLF, Virginia Stephen, 1882-1941. 709'.2'4 B
Roger Fry : a biography / Virginia Woolf. New York : Harcourt Brace Jovanovich, 1976, c1940. 303 p., [8] leaves of plates : ill. ; 21 cm. (A Harvest book ; HB338) Includes index. [N7483.F79W66 1976] 75-34023 ISBN 0-15-678520-X pbk. : 4.50
1. Fry, Roger Eliot, 1866-1934. BIP

Fuji in art.

KATSUSHIKA, Hokusai, 1760-1849. 759.952
Hokusai; the thirty-six views of Mt. Fuji, by Muneshige Narazaki. English adaptation by John Bester. [1st ed.] Tokyo, Palo Alto, Calif., Kodansha International [1968] 96 p. 2 maps, col. plates. 26 cm. (Masterworks of Ukiyo-E, 3) [NE1325.K3A447] 68-17460 3.50
1. Fuji in art. 2. Fuji—Description and travel—Views. I. Narazaki, Muneshige, 1904- II. Title. III. Title: The thirty-six views of Mt. Fuji. IV. Series.

Fuji—Views.

KATSUSHIKA, Hokusai, 1760-1849. 769.952
Hokusai's views of Mt. Fuji, with poems by Easley Stephen Jones. Rutland, Vt., Tuttle [1965] 61p. (on double leaves col. illus. 10x14cm. Includes reprods. of 24 illustrator's prints of views of Mt. Fuji. Bibl. [NE1325.K3A45] 65-12269 2.95, bxd.
1. Fuji—Views. 2. Fuji—Poetry. 3. Poetry of places—Japan—Fuji. I. Jones, Easley Stephen, 1884-1947. II. Title. III. Title: Views of Mt. Fuji. BIP

Fuller, Alfred Walter Francis, 1882-1961—Art collections.

FORCE, Roland W. 709'.9
The Fuller Collection of Pacific artifacts [by] Roland W. Force and Maryanne Force. New York, Praeger [1971] xvi, 360 p. illus. 32 cm. Bibliography: p. 352-356. [NK1093.A1F6 1971b] 75-131354 35.00
1. Fuller, Alfred Walter Francis, 1882-1961—Art collections. 2. Art objects—Oceanica—Catalogs. I. Force, Maryanne, joint author. II. Title.

Fuller, Claud E., 1877-1957.

PETERSON, Harold Leslie, 1922- 623.44'074'0158326
The Fuller collection of American firearms; America's military long arms [by] Harold L. Peterson. [Philadelphia, Eastern National Park & Monument Association, 1967] 63 p. illus. 22 x 28 cm. [TS532.4.P47] 73-171703
1. Fuller, Claud E., 1877-1957. 2. Firearms—Collectors and collecting. 3. Firearms, American. I. Title.

Fuller, Richard Buckminister, 1895-

MCHALE, John 721.46
R. Buckminster Fuller. New York, Braziller [c.]1962. 127p. illus. 26cm. (Makers of contemporary architecture) Bibl. 62-16263 4.95
1. Fuller, Richard Buckminister, 1895- I. Title.

Fuller, Richard Buckminster, 1895- — Bibliography.

CLOSE, Gloria W. 016.3092'08 s
R. Buckminster Fuller : a selected bibliography of references in the D. H. Hill Library and the Design Library, North Carolina State University / Gloria W. Close. Monticello, Ill. : Council of Planning Librarians, 1977. 34 p. ; 28 cm. (Exchange bibliography - Council of Planning Librarians ; 1349) Cover title. [Z5942.C68 no. 1349] [Z8318.27] [TA140] 016.62 77-153492 pbk. : 3.50
1. Fuller, Richard Buckminister, 1895- — Bibliography. 2. North Carolina. State University, Raleigh. Design Library. 3. Hill (D. H.) Library. I. Series: Council of Planning Librarians. Exchange bibliography ; 1349.

Functionalism (Architecture)

BLAKE, Peter, 1920- 724.9
Form follows fiasco : why modern architecture hasn't worked / by Peter Blake ; designed by Samina Quraeshi. 1st ed. Boston : Little, Brown, c1977. p. cm. "An Atlantic Monthly Press book." Includes index. [NA682.F8B55] 76-54801 ISBN 0-316-09940-6 : 12.95 ISBN 0-316-09939-2 pbk. : 6.95
1. Functionalism (Architecture) 2. Architecture, Modern—20th century. I. Title. BIP

Fundaburk, Emma Lila, 1922—

ART in the environment in the United States 709'.73 : a book of 600 photographs of art in architectural, natural, historic, and modern settings across the nation / compiled by Emma Lila Fundaburk and Mary Douglass Foreman. Luverne, Ala. : Fundaburk, c1975. 223 p. : chiefly ill. ; 28 cm. Includes index. [N6505.A73] 75-24620 ISBN 0-910642-02-8
1. Fundaburk, Emma Lila, 1922- 2. Art—United States. 3. Art—United States—Galleries and museums. I. Foreman, Mary Douglass Fundaburk, 1922-

Funeral rites and ceremonies—Egypt.

NEEDLER, Winifred. 759.932
An Egyptian funerary bed of the Roman period in the Royal Ontario Museum. [Chicago, Printed by the University of Chicago Press, 1963] 67 p. illus. 26 cm. (Art and Archaeology Division, Royal Ontario Museum. Occasional paper 6) Bibliography: p. 49-56. [DT62.T6N37] 78-264756
1. Funeral rites and ceremonies—Egypt. 2. Beds and bedsteads. I. Title. II. Series: Toronto. Royal Ontario Museum. Art and Archaeology Division. Occasional paper 6

Funeral rites and ceremonies—New England.

TASHJIAN, Dickran, 1940- 736'.5'0974
Memorials for children of change; the art of early New England stonecarving, by Dickran and Ann Tashjian. [1st ed.] Middletown, Conn., Wesleyan University Press [1974] xv, 309 p. illus. 26 cm. Bibliography: p. [297]-299. [GT3203.T37] 73-6006 ISBN 0-8195-4061-7 20.00
1. Funeral rites and ceremonies—New England. 2. Stone carving—New England. 3. Puritans—New England. I. Tashjian, Ann, 1942- joint author. II. Title. BIP

Fur.

KAPLAN, David Gordon, 1908- 675
The fur book; a practical guide to fur garment making, maintenance, repairing and remodeling. New York, National Cleaner & Dyer [1950] xvi, 271 p. illus. 22 cm. [TT525.K3] 50-14123
1. Fur. 2. Tailoring.

Fur garments.

CUDLIPP, Edythe. 685'.24
Furs / Edythe Cudlipp. New York : Hawthorn Books, c1978. x, 221 p. : ill. ; 24 cm. Includes index. [TT525.C82 1978] 77-99075 ISBN 0-8015-4310-X : 9.95
1. Fur garments. I. Title. BIP

KAPLAN, David Gordon, 1908- 338.4'7'6753
World of furs / David G. Kaplan ; edited by Ed Kleinman. New York : Fairchild Publications, c1974. ix, 234 p. : ill. ; 24 cm. Includes index. Bibliography: p. 221-223. [TT525.K32] 75-153567 ISBN 0-87005-098-2 : 15.00
1. Fur garments. 2. Fur trade. I. Title. BIP

WILDER, Edna, 1916- 646.1'6
Secrets of Eskimo skin sewing / Edna Wilder. Anchorage : Alaska Northwest Pub. Co., c1976. vii, 125 p. : ill. ; 22 cm. [TT525.W54] 76-3783 pbk. : 4.95
1. Fur garments. 2. Hides and skins. 3. Sewing. 4. Eskimo craft. I. Title. BIP

Fur—History.

WILCOX, Ruth Turner, 1888- 391.09
The mode in furs; the history of furred costume of the world from the earliest times to the present. New York, Scribner, 1951. xi, 257 p. illus. 29 cm. Bibliography: p. 255-257. [GT2070.W5] 51-12491
1. Fur—History. 2. Costume—History. I. Title.

Furness, Frank, 1839-1912.

O'GORMAN, James F. 720'.92'4
The architecture of Frank Furness, by James F. O'Gorman. Catalogue of selected buildings, by George E. Thomas and James F. O'Gorman. Checklist of the architecture and projects of Frank Furness, by George E. Thomas and Hyman Myers. Special photography by Cervin Robinson. [Philadelphia] Philadelphia Museum of Art [1973] 211 p. illus. (part col.) 29 cm. "Published on the occasion of the exhibition at the Philadelphia Museum of Art, April 5 to May 27, 1973." Includes bibliographical references. [NA737.F85O34] 73-77307
1. Furness, Frank, 1839-1912. I. Thomas, George E. II. Myers, Hyman. III. Philadelphia Museum of Art. IV. Title.

Furniture.

ARONSON, Joseph, 1898- 749
The book of furniture and decoration: period and modern. New rev. and augm. ed. New York, Crown Publishers [1952] 242 p. illus. 28 cm. [NK2230.A7 1952] 52-5679
1. Furniture. 2. Interior decoration. I. Title.

BAKER, Bill. 684.1
Furniture you can build. New York, Arco Pub. Co. [1955] 144p. illus. 26cm. (The Do-it-yourself series) Originally published as Fawcett book, no. 281. [TT197] 55-11940
1. Furniture. I. Title.

BICK, Alexander Frederick, 1890- 684.1
Contemporary furniture. Milwaukee, Bruce Pub. Co. [1954] 89 p. illus. 27 cm. [TT197.B52] 54-7782
1. Furniture. 2. Woodwork. I. Title.

BROADBENT, V. E. 1900- 684
Bedroom furniture, period and modern. Milwaukee, Bruce [1950] v, 122 p. illus., diagrs. 31 cm. [TS880.B7] 50-6516
1. Furniture. I. Title.

BRY, Paul. 684
How to build your own furniture. New York, Macmillan, 1951. 138 p. illus. 22 cm. [TT197.B847] 51-4962
1. Furniture. I. Title.

CHERNER, Norman. 684
Make your own modern furniture; working plans and room designs for more comfortable and convenient living. Drawings by Norman Cherner and Frank Stork; photos. by Thomas Yee. New York, McGraw-Hill [1951] 140 p. illus. 26 cm. [TT197.C53] 51-12173
1. Furniture. 2. Interior decoration. I. Title.

CHIPPENDALE, Thomas, 1718-1779. 749.22
The gentleman & cabinet-maker's director. New York, Dover Publications [1966] 1 v. (chiefly illus.) 31 cm. "Unabridged and unaltered republication of the third ed. published by the author in London in 1762." [NK2542.C5A3 1762a] 66-24135
1. Furniture. 2. Decoration and ornament—Chippendale style. I. Title. BIP

CHIPPENDALE, Thomas, 1718-1779 749.22
The gentleman and cabinet-maker's director. Reprint of the third ed. with a biog. sketch and photographic suppl. of Chippendale-type furniture [Magnolia, Mass., P. Smith, 1967, c.1966] 20p. 100p. of plates. photogs. 31cm. (Dover bk. rebound Unabridged, unaltered repubn. of the 3d ed. pub. by the author in London in 1762. This ed. also contains a biog. sketch of Thomas Chippendale by N.I. Bienenstock, ed. of The furniture world and a photographic suppl. showing various styles of Chippendale furniture [NK2542.C5 A3 1762a] 6.75
1. Furniture. I. Title.

COBB, Hubbard H 1917- 684
The Wise practical home furniture builder, by Hubbard Cobb. Designs by Sigman-Ward. New York, W. H. Wise, 1951. xii, 248 p. illus. 22 cm. [TT197.C6] 52-21
1. Furniture. I. Wise (Wm. H.) and Company, Inc., New York. II. Title.

COLLANI, Arthur. 684.2
Build your own modern furniture. New York, Home Craftsman Pub. Corp. [1954] 96 p. illus. 28 cm. (Home craftsman series of woodworking manuals) [TT197.C63] 54-8905
1. Furniture. 2. Cabinet-work. I. Title. II. Title: Modern furniture.

DAL Fabbro, Mario, 1913- 749.245
Furniture for modern interiors. New York, Reinhold [1954] 207 p. (chiefly illus.) 27 cm. (A Progressive architecture book) [TS880.D29] 53-12490
1. Furniture. I. Title.

DAL FABBRO, Mario, 1913- 684.1
How to build modern furniture. 2d ed. New York, F. W. Dodge Corp. [1957] 214 p. illus. 26 cm. [TS880.D312] 57-9273
1. Furniture. I. Title. BIP

DAL FABBRO, Mario, 1913- 684
How to build modern furniture. New York, F. W. Dodge Corp. [1951-52] 2 v. illus. 20 cm. Contents.Contents.—v. 1. Practical construction methods.—v. 2 Designs and assembly. [TS880.D3] 51-14782
1. Furniture. I. Title.

DAL FABBRO, Mario, 1913- 684.08
How to make wood furnishings for your home. New York, McGraw [c.1965] viii, 168p. illus. 26cm. [TT197.D27] 65-22955 5.95 bds.,
1. Furniture. 2. Woodwork. I. Title.

DANIELS, George Emery, 1914- 684
The easy way to make and remodel your own furniture. Illus. by the author. New York, Greystone Press [1952] 304 p. illus. 25 cm. At head of title: Mr. Fix-It. [TT197.D28] 52-10957
1. Furniture. I. Title. II. Title: Mr. Fix-It.

DE CRISTOFORO, R. J. 684.1
How to build your own furniture, by R. J. DeCristoforo. New York, Popular Science Pub. Co. [1965] 176 p. illus. 24 cm. (Popular Science skill book) [TT197.D32] 64-18092
1. Furniture. I. Title. BIP

DECRISTOFORO, R. J. 684.1
How to build your own furniture, by R. J. DeCristoforo. New York, Barnes & Noble [1973, c.1965] 178 p. illus. 21 cm. (Everyday handbooks, EH352) (A Popular science skill book) [TT197.D32] ISBN 0-06-463352-7 1.95 (pbk.)
1. Furniture. 2. Do-it-yourself manuals. I. Title.
L.C. card no. for hardbound edition: 64-18092.

FRIEDMAN-WEISS, Jeffrey 684.1'04'0222
Made with oak / by Jeffrey Friedman-Weiss and Herbert H. Wise, with Andria Alberts. New York : Links : distributed by Quick Fox, c1975. [95] p. : chiefly ill. (some col.) ; 24 cm. [TS885.F68] 75-18143 ISBN 0-8256-3052-5 : 5.95
1. Furniture. 2. Oak. I. Wise, Herbert, joint author. II. Alberts, Andria, joint author. III. Title. BIP

FURNITURE handbook, 684.1'6 1962- ed. [Chicago, Science and Mechanics Pub. Co.] v. illus. 24 cm. (S & M books) Reprint of articles appearing in Science and mechanics. [TT197.F85] 63-4458
1. Furniture. 2. Woodwork. 3. Science and mechanics.

GRABE, Klaus. 684.1
Build your own modern furniture. Greenwich, Conn., Fawcett Publications, c1954. 144p. illus. 24cm. (A Fawcett book, no. 215) [TT197.G68] 54-9190
1. Furniture. I. Title.

GROTZ, George. 698.3
From gunk to glow; or, The gentle art of refinishing antiques and other furniture, by George Grotz, the furniture doctor. [3d ed.] Deep River, Conn., New Era Press [1958, c1955] 64p. illus. 20cm. [TT197.G77 1958] 58-4726
1. Furniture. 2. Wood finishing. I. Title.

GUNERMAN, Milton John, 1906- 684
ed.
Cabinets, bookcases and wall shelves; how to build all types of cabinets, shelving and storage facilities for the modern home. New York, Home Craftsman Pub. Corp. [1950] 126 p. illus., diagrs. 31 cm. (The Home craftsman series of wood-working manuals) [TT197.G84] 50-12259
1. Furniture. 2. Handicraft. I. Title.

HARDY, Kay, 1902- 645.4
How to finish or refinish your furniture. Sketches by the author. New York, Funk & Wagnalls [1951] x, 166 p. illus. 26 cm. "A Kay Hardy home primer." Bibliography: p. 159-161. [TS885.H3] 51-11353
1. Furniture. 2. Wood finishing. I. Title.

HENNESSEY, William James, 1901- 749
Modern furnishings for the home. New York, Reinhold Pub. Corp. [1952-56] 2v. illus. 27cm. Vol. 2 by W. J. Hennessey and E. D. Hennessey, associate. [NK2260.H4] 52-9369
1. Furniture. I. Title.

HEPPLEWHITE (A.) and Co. 684.1
The cabinet-maker & upholsterer's guide [by] George Hepplewhite. The 3d ed. of 1794. New York, Dover Publications [1969] viii, 24 p. 123 illus. 28 cm. "An unabridged and unaltered republication of the third (1794) edition ... A new introduction has been written ... by Joseph Aronson." "From drawings by A. Hepplewhite and Co., cabinet-makers." Bibliography: p. [ix] [TT196.H4 1969] 69-19164 3.00
1. Furniture. I. Hepplewhite, George, d. 1786. II. Title. BIP

HINCKLEY, F. Lewis. 749
A directory of antique furniture; the authentic classification of European and American designs for professionals & connoisseurs. New York, Crown Publishers [1953] xxxiv p., 335 p. of illus. 29 cm. [NK2260.H5] 52-10776
1. Furniture. I. Title. BIP

HINCKLEY, F Lewis. 749
Directory of the historic cabinet woods. New York, Crown Publishers [1960] 186p. illus. 29cm. Bibliography: p. 183. [NK2260.H52] 59-14030
1. Furniture. 2. Cabinet-work. 3. Hardwoods. I. Title. II. Title: Historic cabinet woods.

THE History of furniture 749.2 / introd. by Francis Watson ; [editor, Anne Charlish]. London : Orbis, c1976. 344 p. : ill. (some col.) ; 31 cm. Includes index. Bibliography: p. 332-335.

1. Furniture, American. 2. Decoration and ornament, American. I. Title.

ORMSBEE, Thomas Hamilton, 1890- 749.21
Field guide to American Victorian furniture. Drawings by Ernest Halberstadt. Boston, Little [1964, c.1952] 428p. illus. 19cm. Bibl. 4.95
1. Furniture, American. 2. Furniture—Collectors and collecting. I. Title.

ORMSBEE, Thomas Hamilton, 1890- 749.212
Field guide to American victorian furniture. Drawings by Ernst Halberstadt. [1st ed.] Boston, Little, Brown [1952] 428 p. illus. 19 cm. [NK2407.O7] 52-9095
1. Furniture, American. 2. Furniture—collectors and collecting. I. Title.

SACK, Albert. 749.211
Fine points of furniture: early American. Foreword by Israel Sack; introd. by John Meredith Graham II. New York, Crown Publishers [1950] xvi, 303 p. illus. 26 cm. [NK2406.S29] 50-11156
1. Furniture, American. 2. Furniture—Collectors and collecting. I. Title.

SHEA, John Gerald. 684.1
Colonial furniture making for everybody. Princeton, N.J., Van Nostrand [1964] xiv, 214 p. illus. 29 cm. [TT197.S63] 64-19834
1. Furniture, American. 2. Furniture making—Amateurs' manuals. 3. Woodwork. I. Title. BIP

STICKLEY (L. and J. G.) inc., Fayetteville, N.Y. 749.21
The story of a developing furniture style, its inspiration, its objectives. [50th anniversary ed. Fayetteville, 1950] 52 p. illus. 26 cm. [NK2265.S82] 50-28420
1. Furniture, American. I. Title.

TREVES, Ralph. 684.1
Early American furniture you can build. New York, Arco Pub. Co. [1964, c1963] 112 p. illus. 25 cm. (Arco how-to-library) [TT197.T67 1964] 64-20463
1. Furniture, American. 2. Woodwork. I. Title.

TREVES, Ralph. 684.1'042'0973
Early American furniture you can build / by Ralph Treves. New York : Arco Pub. Co., 1976, c1963. p. cm. [TT195.T73 1976] 76-5410 pbk. : 2.95
1. Furniture, American. 2. Furniture making—Amateurs' manuals. I. Title.

TREVES, Ralph. 684.1'6
Early American furniture you can build, Photos., where not otherwise credited, by Harold Siegried. Greenwich, Conn., Fawcett Publication, 1963. 112 p. illus., diagrs. 24 cm. "547." [TT197.T67] 64-171
1. Furniture, American. 2. Woodwork, I. Title. BIP

WILLIAMS, Henry Lionel. 749.213
Country furniture of early America. New York, Barnes [c1963] 138 p. illus. 29 cm. [NK2406.W5] 63-18264
1. Furniture, American. I. Title. BIP

WILLIAMS, Henry Lionel. 749.2'13
Country furniture of early America / by Henry Lionel Williams. New York : A.S. Barnes, [1979]c1963. 138p. : ill. ; 28 cm. Includes index. [NK2406.W5] ISBN 0-498-02045-2 pbk. : 5.95
1. Furniture, American. I. Title.
L.C. card no. for 1963 A.S. Barnes ed.:63-18264.

Furniture, American — Catalogs.

BOSTON. Museum of Fine Arts 749.213074014461
American furniture in the Museum of Fine Arts Boston [by] Richard H. Randall. Jr. Boston. Author [c.1965] xvii. 276p. illus. 29cm. Catalog. [NK2406.B65] 65-24149 25.00 bds.,
1. Furniture. American—Catalogs. 2. Furniture—Boston—Catalogs. I. Randall, Richard H. II. Title.

BOSTON. Museum of Fine Arts. 749.213074014461
American furniture in the Museum of Fine Arts, Boston [by] Richard H. Randall, Jr. Boston [1965] xvii, 276 p. illus. 29 cm. Catalog. [NK2406.B65] 65-24149
1. Furniture, American — Catalogs. 2. Furniture — Boston — Catalogs. I. Randall, Richard H. II. Title.

HARKNESS, Douglas W 749.211
Catalogue of unrecorded American antique furniture and decoration. by Douglas W. Harkness. Photos. by Edward A. Durling. South Glens Falls, N.Y. [1964] [75] p. illus. 24 cm. Cover title: American antique furniture and decoration. [NK2406.H3] 66-4059
1. Furniture, American — Catalogs. I. Title. II. Title: American antique furniture and decoration.

HENRY Francis du Pont Winterthur Museum. 749.213
American furniture, Queen Anne and Chippendale periods, in the Henry Francis du Pont Winterthur Museum, by Joseph Downs. Foreword by Henry Francis du Pont. New York, Viking Press [1967, c1952] 1 v. (various pagings) illus., col. plates. 31 cm. (A Winterthur book) Includes bibliographies. [NK2406] 67-8132
1. Furniture, American — Catalogs. I. Downs, Joseph. II. Du Pont, Henry Francis, 1880- III. Title.

HENRY Francis du Pont Winterthur Museum. 749.213
American furniture, the Federal period, in the Henry Francis du Pont Winterthur Museum, by Charles F. Montgomery. Foreword by Henry Francis du Pont. With photos. by Gilbert Ask. New York, Viking Press [1966] 497 p. illus. (part col.) 32 cm. (A Winterthur book) Bibliography: p. 484-489. [NK2406.H4] 66-19411
1. Furniture, American—Catalogs. I. Montgomery, Charles F. II. Du Pont, Henry Francis, 1880- III. Title. IV. Series.

NUTTING, Wallace, 1861-1941. 749.213
Checklist of early American reproductions. With an introductory essay on The art-crafts ideology; or, Wallace Nutting's colonial revival, by John Freeman. [Rev. and expanded] Watkins Glen, N.Y., American Life Foundation, 1969. 1 v. (unpaged) illus. 23 cm. (Classic guidebooks to the visual arts) Includes bibliographical references. [NK2406.N68 1969] 73-96940
1. Furniture, American—Catalogs. 2. Ironwork—U.S.—Catalogs. I. American Life Foundation, Watkins Glen, N.Y. II. Title. III. Title: Early American reproductions.

Furniture, American—Collectors and collecting.

ORMSBEE, Thomas Hamilton, 1890- 749.21
Field guide to early American furniture. New York, Bantam [1965, c.1961] 353p. 18cm. (Bantam Home Owner's lib., QH3) [NK2406.O65] 1.25 pap.,
1. Furniture, American—Collectors and collecting. I. Title.

ORMSBEE, Thomas Hamilton, 1890- 749.211
Field guide to early American furniture. [1st ed.] Boston, Little, Brown, 1951. xxxix, 464 p. illus. 19 cm. Bibliography: p. [463]-464. [NK2406.O65] 51-9372
1. Furniture, American—Collectors and collecting. 2. Furniture—Collectors and collecting. I. Title.

Furniture, American—Congresses.

WINTERTHUR Conference on Museum Operation and Connoisseurship, 15th, 1969. 749.2'13
Country cabinetwork and simple city furniture. Edited by John D. Morse. Charlottesville, Published for the Henry Francis du Pont Winterthur Museum, Winterthur, Del. [by] the University Press of Virginia [1970] xiv, 311 p. illus. 23 cm. (Winterthur Conference report, 1969) Includes bibliographical references. [NK2406.W53 1969] 77-114194
1. Furniture, American—Congresses. 2. Cabinet-workers—U.S.—Congresses. I. Morse, John D., 1906- ed. II. Henry Francis du Pont Winterthur Museum. III. Title. IV. Series: Winterthur Conference on Museum Operation and Connoisseurship. Report, 1969 BIP

Furniture, American—Exhibitions.

BALTIMORE. Museum of Art. 749.2152
Maryland Queen Anne and Chippendale furniture of the eighteenth century. [New York] Published by October House for the Baltimore Museum of Art [1968] 128 p. illus., facsims., map. 21 cm. "An exhibition presented at the Baltimore Museum of Art, March 5 to April 14, 1968." [NK2435.M3B3] 68-24479
1. Furniture, American—Exhibitions. 2. Furniture—Maryland. I. Title.

BARNES, Jairus B. 749.2'13'074017132
American furniture in the Western Reserve, 1680-1830. Catalogue by Jairus B. Barnes and Moselle Taylor Meals. [Cleveland, Western Reserve Historical Society, 1972] 133 p. illus. 23 cm. (The Western Reserve Historical Society publication no. 125) Catalogue of a loan exhibition held at the Western Reserve Historical Society, May 22-July 16, 1972. "A triennial presentation of the Women's Advisory Council." [NK2405.B37] 72-80571
1. Furniture, American—Exhibitions. I. Meals, Moselle Taylor, joint author. II. Western Reserve Historical Society, Cleveland. III. Western Reserve Historical Society, Cleveland. Women's Advisory Council. IV. Title. V. Series: Western Reserve Historical Society, Cleveland. Publication no. 125.

THE Dunlaps & their furniture. Manchester, N.H., Currier Gallery of Art [1970] 310 p. illus. 26 cm. Catalogue, by Charles S. Parsons, of an exhibition held at the Currier Gallery of Art, Aug.-13 Sept. 1970. "Transcription of Major John Dunlap's account book": p. [171]-310. Bibliography: p. 67-69. [NK2439.D86P37] 70-129914 749.2'142
1. Dunlap family. 2. Furniture, American—Exhibitions. I. Parsons, Charles Sumner, 1904- II. Dunlap, John, 1746-1792. III. Currier Gallery of Art, Manchester, N.H. BIP

ELDER, William Voss. 749.2'152'6
Baltimore painted furniture, 1800-1840. Introd. and commentary by William Voss Elder, III. [Baltimore] Baltimore Museum of Art [1972] 132 p. illus. 23 x 28 cm. Catalogue of an exhibition held at the Baltimore Museum of Art, April 18-Jan 4, 1972. "Cabinetmakers and allied tradesmen working in Baltimore, 1800-1840": p. 93-129. Bibliography: p. 130-132. [NK2438.B3E4] 72-77869 ISBN 0-912298-25-1
1. Furniture, American—Exhibitions. 2. Furniture, American—Baltimore. 3. Decoration and ornament, American—Baltimore. I. Baltimore. Museum of Art. II. Title. BIP

INDIANAPOLIS Museum of Art. 749.2'13
Indianapolis collects: American furniture, 1700-1850. [Editor: Richard L. Warrum. Indianapolis, Speedway Press, 1972] ii, 28 p. illus. 26 cm. Catolog of the exhibition held Jan. 11-Feb. 27, 1972. [NK2406.I52] 73-170776
1. Furniture, American—Exhibitions. I. Warrum, Richard L., ed. II. Title.

MADIGAN, Mary Jean Smith. 749.2'13
Eastlake-influenced American furniture, 1870-1890; [catalogue of an exhibition] November 18, 1973-January 6, 1974, the Hudson River Museum. [Yonkers, N.Y., Hudson River Museum, 1973] [66] p. illus. 29 cm. Bibliography: p. [64]-[65] [NK2407.M32] 73-90034 ISBN 0-87100-043-1
1. Eastlake, Charles Locke, 1833-1906—Influence. 2. Furniture, American—Exhibitions. 3. Decoration and ornament—Victorian style. I. Hudson River Museum. II. Title. BIP

NOYES, Eliot F. 749.213
Organic design in home furnishings, by Eliot F. Noyes. Reprint ed. [New York] Published for the Museum of Modern Art by Arno Press, 1969 [c1941] 48 p. illus. 27 cm. Bibliography: p. 45-46. [NK2408.N68 1969] 70-86424
1. Furniture, American—Exhibitions. 2. Design, Industrial—U.S. I. New York (City). Museum of Modern Art. II. Title. BIP

POESCH, Jessie J. 749.2'163'074016353
Early furniture of Louisiana; text and catalogue by Jessie J. Poesch. Photos. by Betsy Swanson. [New Orleans] Louisiana State Museum [1972] xviii, 85 p. illus. 28 cm. An exhibition at the Cabildo, Louisiana State Museum, New Orleans, Feb. 27-July 31, 1972. Includes bibliographical references. [NK2435.L6P6] 76-177927
1. Furniture, American—Exhibitions. 2. Furniture, American—Louisiana. 3. Furniture—Louisiana. I. Louisiana State Museum, New Orleans. II. Title.

RENWICK Gallery. 749.2'13'074013
Woodenworks; furniture objects by five contemporary craftsmen: George Nakashima, Sam Maloof, Wharton Esherick, Arthur Espenet Carpenter, Wendell Castle. [St. Paul, Minnesota Museum of Art, 1972] 48 p. illus. 25 cm. Cover title. "An exhibition sponsored jointly by Renwick Gallery of the National Collection of Fine Arts, Smithsonian Institution, Washington, D.C., January 28 through July 19, 1972, and Minnesota Museum of Art, Saint Paul, Minnesota, October 12 through December 31, 1972." Bibliography: p. 47-48. [NK2408.R4] 75-178893
1. Furniture, American—Exhibitions. 2. Furniture workers—United States. I. Minnesota Museum of Art. II. Title.

WRIGHT, Frank Lloyd, 1867-1959. 749.213
Frank Lloyd Wright: vision and legacy. Exhibition, Gallery, Architecture Building, Sept. 15-Oct. 1, 1965. [Urbana] Committee of Architectural Heritage, University of Illinois [1966] [32] p. illus. 22 cm. Published as an undergraduate project at the University of Illinois as part of a campaign to raise funds to assist in the restoration of the F. C. Robie house in Chicago. [NK2408.W7] 67-4528
1. Furniture, American—Exhibitions. I. Illinois. University. Committee of Architectural Heritage.

Furniture—American—History.

DOWNS, Joseph. 749.211
American furniture in the Henry Francis du Pont Winterthur Museum. Foreword by Henry Francis du Pont. New York, Macmillan, 1952- v. illus. (part col.) 31 cm. Contents.[1] Queen Anne and Chippendale periods. Includes bibliographies. [NK2406.D6] 52-8567
1. Furniture, American—Hist. I. Henry Francis Du Pont WinterthurMuseum. II. Du Pont, Henry Francis, 1880- III. Title.

KOVEL, Ralph M. 749.21
American country furniture, 1780-1875 [by] Ralph and Terry Kovel. New York, Crown [c.1965] vi, 248p. illus. 29cm. Bibl. [NK2406.K6] 65-15848 7.50
1. Furniture, American—Hist. I. Kovel, Terry H., joint author. II. Title.

MARGON, Lester 749.213
Masterpieces of American furniture, 1620-1840.Compendium, with photos., measured drawings and descriptive commentary. New York, Architectural Bk. [c.1965] 256p. illus. 28cm. [NK2406.M39] 64-8125 12.50
1. Furniture, American—Hist. I. Title.

NUTTING, Wallace, 1861-1941 749.213
Furniture of the Pilgrim century (of American origin) 1620-1720, with maple and pine to 1800, including colonial utensils and wrought-iron hardware into the 19th century; 2v. Completely rev., enlarged ed. [Gloucester, Mass., P. Smith, 1966] 2v. (714p.) illus. 24cm. (Dover bks. rebound) Unaltered repubn. of the work pub. in 1924 by the Old Amer Co. [NK2406.N71965] 5.00ea.,
1. Furniture, American—Hist. I. Title. BIP

SUBJECT INDEX FURNITURE, COLONIAL—UNITED STATES.

NUTTING, Wallace, 1861-1941. 749.213
Furniture of the Pilgrim century (of American origin) 1620-1720, with maple and pine to 1800, including colonial utensils and wrought-iron house hardware into the 19th century. Completely rev. and greatly enl. New York, Dover Publications [1965] 2 v. (714 p.) illus. 24 cm. "An unabridged and unaltered republication of the revised and enlarged edition published ... in 1924." [NK2406.N7] 65-26030
1. Furniture, American — Hist. I. Title.

OTTO, Celia Jackson 749.213
American furniture of the nineteenth century. New York, Viking [c.1965] 229p. illus., 3 col. plates. 29cm. (studio bk.) [NK2407.O8] 65-21483 12.00 bds.,
1. Furniture, American—Hist. I. Title.

Furniture, American—History.

COMSTOCK, Helen. 749.211
American furniture: seventeenth, eighteenth, and nineteenth century styles. New York, Viking Press [1962] 336 p. illus. 29 cm. (A Studio book) Bibliography: p. 319-324. [NK2406.C58] 62-18074
1. Furniture, American—History. I. Title.

KOVEL, Ralph M. 749.21
American country furniture, 1780-1875 [by] Ralph and Terry Kovel. New York, Crown [1965] vi, 248 p. illus. 29 cm. Bibliography: p. 232. [NK2406.K6] 65-15848
1. Furniture, American—History. I. Kovel, Terry H., joint author. II. Title. BIP

MARGON, Lester. 749.213
Masterpieces of American furniture, 1620-1840. A compendium, with photos, measured drawings and descriptive commentary. New York, Architectural Book Pub. Co. [1965] 256 p. illus. 28 cm. [NK2406.M39] 64-8125
1. Furniture, American—History. I. Title. BIP

MARGON, Lester. 749.213
More American furniture treasures, 1620-1840; an anthology with photographs, measured drawings, and eclectic discussions. New York, Architectural Book Pub. Co. [1971] 256 p. illus. 28 cm. Bibliography: p. 95. [NK2406.M392 1971] 70-150013 ISBN 0-8038-0163-7 15.00
1. Furniture, American—History. I. Title. BIP

NUTTING, Wallace, 1861-1941. 749.213
Furniture of the Pilgrim century with maple and pine to 1800, including colonial utensils and wrought-iron house hardware into the 19th century. Completely rev. and greatly enl. New York, Dover Publications [1965] 2 v. (714 p.) illus. 24 cm. "An unabridged and unaltered republication of the revised and enlarged edition published ... in 1924." [NK2406.N7 1965] 65-26030
1. Furniture. American—History. I. Title.

Furniture, Ancient.

BAKER, Hollis S. 749.201
Furniture in the ancient world; origins & evolution, 3100-475 B.C. [by] Hollis S. Baker. With an introd. by Sir Gordon Russell. New York, Macmillan [1966] 351 p. illus. (part col.) 29 cm. "A Giniger book." Bibliographical references included in "Notes" (p. 322-333) [NK2280.B3] 66-23893
1. Furniture, Ancient. I. Title.

Furniture, Bermuda—Catalogs.

HYDE, Bryden Bordley, 1914- 749.297299
Bermuda's antique furniture & silver. [Hamilton] Bermuda National Trust; [distributor for North America: Maryland Historical Society, Baltimore, 1971] xvii, 198 p. illus. 29 cm. [NK2486.B4H9] 76-157116 15.00
1. Furniture, Bermuda—Catalogs. 2. Silver articles, Bermuda—Catalogs. I. Title. BIP

Furniture, British Hist.

MACDONALD-TAYLOR, M. S. 749.22
Furniture. [New York] Oxford [c.]1961[ ] 95p. illus. (History in pictures) Bibl. 61-4599 2.00
1. Furniture, British Hist. 2. Art industries and trade—Gt. Brit.—Hist. I. Title.

MACDONALD-TAYLOR, Margaret Stephens. 749.22
Furniture. [London] Oxford University Press, 1961. 95p. illus. 24cm. (History in pictures) Includes bibliography. [NK2528.M18] 61-4599
1. Furniture, British— Hist. 2. Art industries and trade—Gt. Brit.—Hist. I. Title.

Furniture, Canadian.

PALARDY, Jean, 1905- 749.21
The early furniture of French Canada. Tr. from French by Eric McLean [2d rev. ed.] Toronto, Macmillan of Canada [dist.] New York, St. Martin s 1965[c.1963] 413p. illus., map, 11 col. plates. 32cm. [NK2442.P313] 65-22627 25.00; 22.50 sFurniture, French-Canadian--Hist.
I. Title.

SYMONS, Scott, 1933- 749.2'11
Heritage; a romantic look at early Canadian furniture. Photos. by John de Visser. [1st ed.] Greenwich, Conn., New York Graphic Society [1971] [220] p. illus., 47 col. plates. 33 cm. Bibliography: p. [213] [NK2441.S96 1971] 71-162721 20.00
1. Furniture, Canadian. I. De Visser, John, illus. II. Title.

Furniture — Catalogs.

FURNITURE forum. 645
[Sarasota, Fla. v. illus. 28 cm. annual. Began publication with 1948/49 vol. Cf. Union list of serials. "Contemporary design source reference." [NK2265.F8] 66-98191
1. Furniture — Catalogs.

SIMPSON, Thomas. 749
Fantasy furniture; design and decoration. New York, Reinhold Book Corp. [1968] 95 p. illus. (part col.) 21 cm. (An Art horizons book) [NK2260.S55] 68-16023
1. Furniture—Catalogs. 2. Decoration and ornament. I. Title.

Furniture—Charleston, S.C.

BURTON, E. Milby. 749.21'5'7915
Charleston furniture, 1700-1825, by E. Milby Burton. Columbia, University of South Carolina Press [1970, c1955] 150 p. illus., facsims. 29 cm. Bibliography: p. 143-145. [NK2438.C5B8 1970] 73-120917 12.50
1. Furniture—Charleston, S.C. 2. Cabinet-workers—Charleston, S.C. I. Title. BIP

BURTON, E Milby. 749.211
Charleston furniture, 1700-1825. Charleston, S. C., Charleston Museum, 1955. 150p. illus., facsims. 29cm. (Catributions from the Charleston Museum, 12) Bibliography: p. 143-145. [NK2438.C5B8] 55-11622
1. Furniture—Charleston, S. C. 2. Cabinet -workers. I. Title. II. Series: Charleston Museum, Charleston, S. C. Contributionsfrom the Charleston Museum, v. 12

Furniture—Chester Co., Pa.

SCHIFFER, Margaret Berwind 749.274813
Furniture and its makers of Chester County, Pennsylvania. Philadelphia, Univ. of Pa. Pr. [1966] 280p. 168 plates (incl. map) 29cm. Pub. under the auspices of the Chester County Hist. Soc., West Chester, Pa. Bibl. [NK2435.P4S3] 65-28609 15.00
1. Furniture—Chester Co., Pa. 2. Furniture, American. 3. Cabinet-workers. I. Title. BIP

Furniture, Chinese.

DRUMMOND, William, 1910- 749.2951
Chinese furniture. Notes prepared by William Drummond. [Photos. by Fritjoff Himmele] New York, Intercultural Arts Press [1969] [35] l. 27 col. slides (film, 2 x 2 in.) 30 cm. (The Sackler collections, ser. 13, lecture 1) The slides are in pockets in 2 transparent leaves. [NK2668.D7] 68-28019
1. Furniture, Chinese. I. Himmele, Fritjoff, illus.

ECKE, Gustav 749.251
Chinese domestic furniture. Rutland, Vt., Tuttle [1963, c.1962] 49p., 161p. of illus. 32cm. Added t. p., in Chinese. Bibl. 62-21540 25.00, bxd.
1. Furniture, Chinese. I. Title. BIP

KATES, George Norbert, 1895- 749.2951
Chinese household furniture, from examples selected and measured by Caroline F. Bieber, Beatrice M. Kates. Photogs. by Hedda Hammer Morrison. New York, Dover [1962, c.1948] 125p. illus. (T958) Bibl. 1.50
1. Furniture, Chinese. I. Bieber, Caroline Frances. II. Morrison, Hedda Hammer. III. Title. BIP

KATES, George Norbert, 1895- 749.2951
Chinese household furniture, from examples selected and measured by Caroline F. Bieber, Beatrice M. Kates. Text by George N. Kates; photos. by Hedda Hammer Morrison. [Gloucester, Mass., Peter Smith, 1962, c.1948] xiii, 125p. illus., 21cm. [Dover bk. rebound] Bibl. 3.50
1. Furniture, Chinese. I. Bieber, Caroline Frances. II. Morrison, Hedda Hammer. III. Title.

Furniture—Collectors and collecting.

BAKER, Mary Gladys Steel, 1892- 708.051
A dictionary of antiques, by Sheila Stuart (Mrs. Howard Baker) Edinburgh, W. & R. Chambers [1953] 263p. illus. 23cm. [NK1125.B33 1953] 54-4571
1. Furniture—Collectors and collecting. 2. Art objects—Collectors and collecting. I. Title.

CURTIS, Tony. 749.2'075
Furniture / compiled by Tony Curtis. [Galashiels] : [Lyle Publications], [1976] 3-125 p. : ill. ; 16 cm. (Antiques and their values) Includes index. [NK2240.C86] 77-352382 ISBN 0-902921-46-0 : £1.50
1. Furniture—Collectors and collecting. 2. Furniture—Prices. I. Title.

GROSS, Leslie, 1927- 749.075
Housewives' guide to antiques; how to get the most for your money when furnishing your home with antiques. Illustrated by the author. [1st ed.] New York, Exposition Press [1959] 180 p. illus. 21 cm. [NK2240.G73] 59-16444
1. Furniture—Collectors and collecting. 2. Art objects—Collectors and collecting. 3. Antiques. I. Title.

HENDERSON, James, 1905- 749.2
Furniture collecting for amateurs. London, Muller, 1967. [9], 134p. 12 plates. 19cm. [NK2240.H45] 67-93549 3.00
1. Furniture—Collectors and collecting. I. Title.
Distributed by Barnes & Noble New York.

HUGHES, George Bernard, 1896- 749'.075
Small antique furniture [by] Bernard and Therle Hughes. New York, Praeger [1968, c1958] 219 p. illus. 23 cm. [NK2240.H8 1968] 68-21581
1. Furniture—Collectors and collecting. I. Hughes, Therle, joint author. II. Title. BIP

MARSH, Moreton. 749.21
The easy expert in collecting and restoring American antiques. Philadelphia, Lippincott [1968,c.1959] 176p. illus. 21cm. (LP4) Bibl. [NK2240.M38] 1.95 pap.,
1. Furniture—Collectors and collecting. 2. Furniture—Repairing. I. Title.

MARSH, Moreton. 749.21
The easy expert in collecting and restoring American antiques. 1st ed. Philadelphia, Lippincott 1960, c1959 176 p. illus. 26 cm. Incudes bibliography. [NK2240.M38] 59-13079
1. Furniture—Collectors and collecting. 2. Furniture—Repairing. I. Title.

PHILP, Peter [Dennis Alfred Peter Philp] 749.075
Antiques today. Chester Springs, Pa., Dufour [1961, c.1960] 157p. 60-3641 3.50 bds.,
1. Furniture—Collectors and collecting. 2. Pottery—Collectors and collecting. I. Title.

THEUS, Will H. 749
How to detect and collect antique furniture / Will H. Theus. 1st ed. New York : Knopf : distributed by Random House, 1978. x, 209 p., [4] leaves of plates : ill. ; 21 cm. Includes index. Bibliography: p.[199]-201. [NK2240.T45 1978] 77-16281 ISBN 0-394-40098-4 : 10.95 ISBN 0-394-73492-0 pbk. : 6.95
1. Furniture—Collectors and collecting. 2. Furniture—Expertising. I. Title. BIP

TOLLER, Jane 749.3
Antique miniature furniture in Great Britain and America. [U.S. ed.] Newton, Mass., Branford [1966] 112p. illus. 23cm. Bibl. [NK2240.T6 1966a] 66-15712 6.95
1. Furniture—Collectors and collecting. 2. Furniture—Models. 3. Furniture, British. 4. Furniture, American. I. Title.

YARMON, Morton. 749.211
Early American antique furniture. New York, Arco Pub. Co. [1954] 144p. illus. 24cm. (Arco handi-books for better living) Originally published as Fawcett book no. 145. [NK2240] 54-9614
1. Furniture—Collectors and collecting. 2. Furniture, American. I. Title.

Furniture, Colonial—Middle Atlantic States.

HUMMEL, Charles F. 748.2'14
A Winterthur guide to American Chippendale : furniture : Middle Atlantic and Southern Colonies / Charles F. Hummel. New York : Crown, 1976. p. cm. "A Winterthur book/Rutledge." Bibliography: p. [NK2410.5.H85 1976] 76-10845 ISBN 0-517-52783-9 : 6.95
1. Henry Francis du Pont Winterthur Museum. 2. Furniture, Colonial—Middle Atlantic States. 3. Furniture—Middle Atlantic States. 4. Furniture, Colonial—Southern States. 5. Furniture—Southern States. 6. Decoration and ornament—Chippendale style. I. Henry Francis du Pont Winterthur Museum. II. Title.

Furniture, Colonial—New England.

FALES, Dean A. 749.2'14'074014422
The furniture of historic Deerfield / Dean A. Fales, Jr. 1st ed. New York : Dutton, 1976. 294 p. : ill. (some col.), map (on lining paper) ; 29 cm. Includes index. [NK2410.F34 1976] 76-25790 ISBN 0-525-11101-8 : 25.00
1. Furniture, Colonial—New England. 2. Furniture—New England. 3. Furniture—Massachusetts—Deerfield. I. Title.

LYON, Irving Whitall, 1840-1896. 749.2'14
The colonial furniture of New England : a study of the domestic furniture in use in the seventeenth and eighteenth centuries / Irving Whitall Lyon ; introd. by Dean A. Fales, Jr. New York : E. P. Dutton, 1977. xxvi, 285 p., [58] leaves of plates : ill. ; 21 cm. A reissue of the 1924 ed. Includes index. [NK2406.L9 1977] 76-52320 ISBN 0-525-47452-8 : 6.95
1. Furniture, Colonial—New England. 2. Furniture—New England. I. Title. BIP

Furniture, Colonial—United States.

CALLAHAN, Kevin. 749.2'13
Early American furniture / by Kevin Callahan. New York : Drake Publishers, 1975. 158 p. : ill. ; 28 cm. [NK2406.C34] 76-4519 ISBN 0-8473-1075-2 : 12.95. ISBN 0-8473-1186-4 pbk. : 5.95
1. Furniture, Colonial—United States. 2. Furniture—United States. I. Title.

Furniture, Colonial—United States—Catalogs.

NEW York 749.2'14'07401471 (City). Metropolitan Museum of Art. *American furniture of the colonial period /* Marvin D. Schwartz. [New York] : Metropolitan Museum of Art, [1976] 93 p. : ill. (some col.) ; 24 cm. Bibliography: p. 93. [NK2406.N37 1976] 76-18763 ISBN 0-87099-149-3 : 6.95
1. New York (City). Metropolitan Museum of Art. 2. Furniture, Colonial—United States—Catalogs. 3. Furniture—United States—Catalogs. I. Schwartz, Marvin D. II. Title. BIP

Furniture, Colonial—Virginia—Exhibitions.

FURNITURE of eastern 749.2'155 *Virginia, the product of mind and hand :* on display at the Virginia Museum, March 14 through April 30, 1978 : an exhibition / co-sponsored by the Virginia Museum and the Colonial Williamsburg Foundation ; exhibition organized by Wallace B. Gusler. Richmond : The Museum, c1978. 31 p. : ill. ; 26 cm. [NK2435.V5F87] 78-3499 ISBN 0-917046-04-8 pbk. : 2.00
1. Furniture, Colonial—Virginia—Exhibitions. 2. Furniture—Virginia—Exhibitions. I. Gusler, Wallace B. II. Virginia Museum of Fine Arts, Richmond. III. Colonial Williamsburg Foundation.

Furniture—Connecticut.

BARBOUR, Frederick K 749.2146 *The stature of fine Connecticut furniture.* [n. p., 1959] unpaged (chiefly illus.) 28cm. [NK2435.C8B3] 59-52932
1. Furniture—Connecticut. I. Title.

BULKELEY, Houghton. 749.2146 *Contributions to Connecticut cabinet making.* [Hartford, Connecticut Historical Society, c1967] 97 p. illus., facsims. 25 cm. On spine: Connecticut cabinet making. "Contains all the articals on Connecticut cabinetmaking written by Houghton Bulkeley for the Connecticut Historical Society Bulletin from 1957-1966." Bibliography: p. 93. [NK2435.C8B8] 68-2357
1. Furniture—Connecticut. 2. Cabinet-workers—Connecticut. I. Title. II. Title: Connecticut cabinet making.

WADSWORTH Atheneum, 749.2746 Hartford. *Connecticut furniture:* seventeenth and eighteenth centuries. Hartford, 1967. xvi, 156 p. illus. 27 cm. "An exhibition organized by the Wadsworth Atheneum for its one hundred and twenty-fifth anniversary celebration [Nov. 3-Dec. 17, 1967]" "Sources and development of styles of Connecticut Furniture" and catalog notes, by John T. Kirk. Bibliography: p. 154-155. [NK2435.C8W3] 67-29632
1. Furnitrue—Connecticut. 2. Furniture, American—Exhibitions. I. Kirk, John T. II. Title.

WADSWORTH Atheneum, 749.2746 Hartford. *Connecticut furniture: seventeenth and eighteenth centuries.* Hartford, 1967. xvi, 156 p. illus. 27 cm. "An exhibition organized by the Wadsworth Atheneum for its one hundred and twenty-fifth anniversary celebration [Nov. 3-Dec. 17, 1967]" "Sources and development of styles of Connecticut Furniture" and catalog notes, by John T. Kirk. Bibliography: p. 154-155. [NK2435.C8W3] 67-29632
1. Furniture—Connecticut. 2. Furniture, American—Exhibition. I. Kirk, John T. II. Title. BIP

Furniture, Danish.

HIORT, Esbjorn. 749.28 *Modern Danish furniture.* [Translation: Eve M. Wendt] L'art mobilier moderne danois. [Traduction: Cecilie Lund] Moderne danische Mobelkunst. [Ubersetzung Anna Kjaorgaard] Moderne danske mobler. New York, Architectural Book Pub. Co., 1956. 133p. plates. 31cm. [NK2585.H52] 56-59182
1. Furniture, Danish. I. Title.

Furniture design.

CAPLAN, Ralph. 338.7'61'749217415 *The design of Herman Miller /* by Ralph Caplan. New York : Whitney Library of Design, 1976. 119 p. : ill. ; 23 cm. [TS880.C36 1976] 76-6489 ISBN 0-8230-7141-3 : 13.50
1. Miller (Herman) Furniture Company, inc., Zeeland, Mich. 2. Furniture design. I. Title.
Available from Watson-Guptill.

HAYWARD, Charles Harold, 749.22 1898- *English period furniture designs,* drawn from the original pieces by the author, Charles H. Hayward. New York, Arco Pub. Co. [1969, c1968] 111 p. illus. 26 cm. [TT196.H3] 69-17871 4.95
1. Furniture design. 2. Furniture, English. I. Title.

KETTLESS, Alonzo 684.1'042 William Percy. *Designs for wood :* how to pan and create your own furniture / Alonzo W. P. Kettless. New York : Scribner, c1978. 128 p. : ill. ; 28 cm. [TT196.K47 1978] 77-87177 ISBN 0-684-15541-9 : 12.95
1. Furniture design. 2. Furniture making. 3. Cabinet-work. I. Title.

LONG Beach, Calif. Museum 749.3 of Art. *Seven decades of design;* a traveling exhibition. [Long Beach, 1967 or 8] 1 v. (unpaged) illus. 26 cm. "Sponsored by the California Arts Commission: organized by the Long Beach Museum of Art." [NK2715.L6] 67-30419
1. Furniture design. 2. Chairs—Exhibitions. I. California. Arts Commission. II. Title.

MEADMORE, Clement. 684.1'3 *The modern chair: classics in production.* New York, Van Nostrand Reinhold Co. [1975] p. cm. [TS886.5.C45M42 1975] 74-18399 ISBN 0-442-25305-2 18.95
1. Furniture design. 2. Chairs. I. Title.

OSBURN, Burl Neff, 1896- 749 *Measured drawings of early American furniture /* Burl N. Osburn and Bernice B. Osburn. New York : Dover Publications, 1974, c1975. 81 p. : ill. ; 28 cm. "Unabridged and corrected republication of the work originally published in 1926." Includes bibliographical references. [TT196.O8 1975] 74-79936 ISBN 0-486-23057-0 pbk. : 3.00
1. Furniture design. 2. Furniture, American. I. Osburn, Bernice B., joint author. II. Title. BIP

PILE, John F. 684.1 *Modern furniture /* John F. Pile. New York : Wiley, c1978. p. cm. "A Wiley-interscience publication." Includes index. Bibliography: p. [TT196.P54] 78-5440 ISBN 0-471-02667-0 : 25.00
1. Furniture design. I. Title. BIP

SHERATON, Thomas, 1751-1806. 749 *The cabinet-maker and upholsterer's drawing-book.* Charles F. Montgomery and Wilfred P. Cole, editors. New York, Praeger [1970] 1 v. (various pagings) illus. 27 cm. (Praeger reprints on arts, crafts, and trades) Reprint of the 1802 ed., with a new introd. by L. O. J. Boynton and new editor's pref. [NK2542.S5A32 1970] 69-19364
1. Furniture design. 2. Furniture, English. I. Title. BIP

SHERATON, Thomas, 1751- 749.2'2 1806. *The cabinet-maker and upholsterer's drawing-book.* With a new introd. by Joseph Aronson. New York, Dover Publications [1972] xxiii, 240 p. illus. 29 cm. "Reproduces material from various early editions ... published by the author in London between 1793 and 1802." Bibliography: p. xiv-xv. [NK2542.S5A354 1972] 72-77998 ISBN 0-486-22255-1 5.95 (pbk)
1. Furniture design. 2. Furniture—England. I. Title.

*SMITH, Nancy A. 749.2 *Old furniture:* understanding the craftsman's art, by Nancy A. Smith. Drawings by Glenna Lang. Photographs by Richard Cheek. Indianapolis, New York, Bobbs-Merrill, [1975] 191 p. ill. 26 cm. Includes index. Bibliography: p. 185. [NK2240] 74-17661 ISBN 0-672-51894-5 12.95
1. Furniture design. 2. Furniture making. 3. Furniture finishing. 4. Furniture—History. I. Title. BIP

*TRIGG, John. 684.1'04 *Fashioning furniture:* beautiful designs that will save you money. Designed, written and illustrated by John Trigg and David Field. Additional illustrations by Marilyn Day. Photography by Richard Sharpe studios. New York, Arco, [1975] 96 p. col. ill. 26 cm. (Leisuretime series) [TT196] 74-19758 ISBN 0-668-03695-8 5.95
1. Furniture design. 2. Implements, Utensils, etc. 3. Furniture making. 4. Furniture design. 5. Woodwork. I. Field, David. joint author. II. Title. BIP

Furniture design—History.

HONOUR, Hugh. 749.2 *Cabinet makers and furniture designers.* [1st American ed.] New York, Putnam [1969] 320 p. illus. (part col.) 29 cm. (Great craftsmen) Bibliography: p. 311-314. [NK2350.H6 1969] 77-77548 22.50
1. Furniture design—History. 2. Furniture workers. 3. Cabinet-workers. I. Title.

Furniture—Dictionaries.

ARONSON, Joseph, 1898- 749.03 *The encyclopedia of furniture.* 3ed ed., completely rev New York. Crown Publishers [1965] ix, 484 p. illus. 29 cm. Bibliography: p. [476]-479. [NK2205.A7 1965] 65-24334
1. Furniture—Dictionaries. I. Title. BIP

ARONSON, Joseph, 1898- 749'.03 *The new encyclopedia of furniture,* New York, Crown Publishers,[1967]Cix, 484 p. illus., 16 col. plates. 29 cm. First-3rd ed. published under title: The encyclopedia of furniture. Bibliography: p. [476]-479. [NK2205.A7 1967] 67-9815
1. Furniture—Dictionaries. I. Title.

GLOAG, John, 1896- 749.03 *A short dictionary of furniture;* containing 1767 terms used in Britain and America. New York, Holt, Rinehart and Winston [1965] 565 p. illus. 22 cm. Bibliography: p. 532-536. [NK2205.G55 1965] 65-22445
1. Furniture—Dictionaries. I. Title. BIP

GLOAG, John, 1896- 749.03 *A short dictionary of furniture;* containing 1764 terms used in Britain and America. With 630 illus. from original sources and by various hands of which 144 were specially drawn by Ronald Escott. New York, Studio Publications [1955?] 565p. illus., ports. 23cm. Includes bibliographical references. [NK2205] 55-14277
1. Furniture—Dictionaries. I. Title.

LOCKWOOD, Luke Vincent, 749'.03 1872-1951. *The furniture collectors' glossary.* New York, Da Capo Press, 1967. viii, 55 p. illus. 24 cm. (Da Capo Press series in architecture and decorative art. v. 8) "A Da Capo Press reprint edition." "An unabridged republication of the first edition published...in 1913 by the Walpole Society." [NK2240.L75 1967] 67-27460
1. Furniture — Dictionaries. I. Walpole Society (United States) II. Title. BIP

SENG Company, Chicago. 749.02 *The Seng handbook:* furniture facts. Commemorating eighty years of service to the furniture industry, 1874-1954. [Garth Bentley, editor. Chicago, 1954] 176p. illus. 18cm. [NK2205.S4] 54-36472
1. Furniture—Dictionaries. I. Title.

SHERATON, Thomas, 1751- 749'.03 1806. *Cabinet dictionary.* With an introd. by Wilford P. Cole and Charles F. Montgomery. New York, Praeger [1970] 2 v. (xviii, viii, 440, 6 p.) illus. 22 cm. (Praeger reprints on arts, crafts, and trades) Reprint of the 1803 ed. [NK2205.S5 1970] 69-19365
1. Furniture—Dictionaries. 2. Cabinet-work—Dictionaries. I. Title.

Furniture—Drawings.

HANDBERG, Ejner. 684.1'04'0222 *Shop drawings of Shaker furniture and woodenware;* measured drawings. Stockbridge, Mass., Berkshire Traveller Press [1973-75] 2 v. illus. 23 cm. [TT196.H27] 73-83797 ISBN 0-912944-09-9 3.00 (v. 1) 3.50 (v. 2)
1. Furniture—Drawings. 2. Furniture, Shaker. I. Title. BIP

SMITH, George, upholder 749 extraordinary to His Royal Highness the Prince of Wales. *Collection of designs for household furniture and interior decoration;* with a new index to the 158 plates. Introd. by Constance V. Hershey. Charles F. Montgomery and Benno M. Forman, editors. New York, Praeger [1970] xxviii, xiv, 33 p., 158 plates. 28 cm. (Praeger reprints on arts, crafts, and trades) Reprint of the 1808 ed., with a new index to the plates. [NK2542.S6 1970] 69-19362
1. Furniture—Drawings. 2. Interior decoration. I. Title.

Furniture—Dublin—Catalogs.

HINCKLEY, F. Lewis. 749.2'9'4183 *A directory of Queen Anne, early Georgian, and Chippendale furniture;* establishing the preeminence of the Dublin craftsmen [by] F. Lewis Hinckley. New York, Crown [1971] 277 p. illus. 29 cm. [NK2538.D8H55 1971] 77-127497 10.00
1. Furniture—Dublin—Catalogs. 2. Decoration and ornament—Queen Anne style. 3. Decoration and ornament—Chippendale style. 4. Decoration and ornament—Georgian style. I. Title.

Furniture—England.

BRACKETT, Oliver, 1875- 749.22 1941. *English furniture illustrated;* a pictorial review of English furniture from Chaucer to Queen Victoria. Rev. and edited by H. Clifford Smith. New York, Macmillan, 1950. 300 p. (p. 29-268 plates) 32 cm. "Originally published under the title of An encyclopaedia of English furniture." [NK2528.B7 1950a] 50-14046
1. Furniture—England. I. Title.

GEFFRYE Museum, 749.2'2'07402144 London. *Geffrye Museum /* [text by Jeffery Daniels]. Derby : English Life Publications [for the Inner London Education Authority], 1975. [2], 30 p. : ill. (some col.), map, ports. ; 14 x 21 cm. [NK2538.L66G43 1975] 76-353159 ISBN 0-85101-091-1 : £0.40
1. Geffrye Museum, London. 2. Furniture—England. 3. Decoration and ornament—England. I. Daniels, Jeffery.

STEPHENSON, Sue H. 717 *Rustic furniture /* Sue H. Stephenson. New York : Van Nostrand Reinhold, [1979] p. cm. Includes index. Bibliography: p. [NK2528.S73] 78-9872 ISBN 0-442-27974-4 : 14.95
1. Furniture—England. 2. Decoration and ornament, Rustic—England. 3. Furniture—United States. 4. Decoration and ornament, Rustic—United States. I. Title. BIP

Furniture—England—Catalogs.

GROTZ, George. 749.2'075 *The current antique furniture style & price guide :* with decorative accessories / edited by George Grotz. 1st ed. Garden City, N.Y. : Doubleday, 1979. p. cm. [NK2547.G7] 77-27673 ISBN 0-385-13165-8 : 9.95
1. Furniture—England—Catalogs. 2. Furniture—France—Catalogs. 3. Furniture—United States—Catalogs. I. Title. BIP

Furniture—England—Exhibitions.

CHELTENHAM Art Gallery 749.2'2 and Museum. *Good citizen's furniture :* the work of Ernest and Sidney Barnsley : [catalogue of an exhibition held at Cheltenham Art

Gallery & Museum 5th November 1976-15th January 1977]. [Cheltenham] : [The Art Gallery and Museum], [1976] [49] p. : ill., ports. ; 15 x 21 cm. Cover title. Errata slip inserted. [TS882.G73C483] 77-364064 ISBN 0-905157-01-X : £0.75
1. Barnsley, Ernest, 1863-1926. 2. Barnsley, Sidney, 1865-1926. 3. Furniture—England—Exhibitions. I. Barnsley, Ernest, 1863-1926. II. Barnsley, Sidney, 1865-1926. III. Title.

Furniture—England—Gloucestershire—Exhibitions.

WELLS-COLE, Anthony. WellsCole Anthony 749.2'423'807402393
Oak furniture from Gloucestershire and Somerset : [catalogue of an exhibition held at] Bristol, St Nicholas Church Museum, 2 April-1 May 1976, Leeds, Stable Court Exhibition Galleries, Temple Newsam, 12 May-12 June 1976 / [catalogue written by Anthony Wells-Cole and Karin Walton]. [Bristol] : [Bristol City Museum and Art Gallery], [1976] xvi, 32 p. : ill. ; 23 cm. Bibliography: p. xvi. [NK2531.G56W44] 77-362880 ISBN 0-900199-05-9 : £0.50
1. Furniture—England—Gloucestershire—Exhibitions. 2. Furniture—England—Somerset—Exhibitions. I. Walton, Karin-M., joint author. II. St. Nicholas Church, Bristol, Eng. Museum. III. Temple Newsam House, Leeds, Eng. IV. Title.

Furniture — England — Hist.

FASTNEDGE, Ralph, 1913- 749.22
English furniture styles from 1500 to 1830 [Harmondsworth, Middlesex] Penguin Books [1955] xxiii, 320p. illus. 18cm. (A Pelican book, A309) Includes bibliographical references. [NK2529.F25] 56-1081
1. Furniture—England—Hist. I. Title.

ROGERS, John Charles. 749.2'2
English furniture. Rev. and enl. by Margaret Jourdain. London, Country Life; New York, Scribner [1950] 244 p. illus. 26 cm. Bibliographical footnotes. [NK2529.R] A52
1. Furniture — England — Hist. I. Title.

ROGERS, John Charles. 749.22
English furniture. Rev. and enl. by Margaret Jourdain. [3d rev. ed.] London, Country Life, ltd.; New York, Sterling Pub. Co. [1959] 244p. illus., diagrs. 26cm. Bibliographical footnotes. [NK2529.R73 1959] 59-3607
1. Furniture— England— Hist. I. Title.

YARWOOD, Doreen. 747.88
The English home; a thousand years of furnishing and decoration. New York, Scribner, 1956. xxix, 393 p. illus. (part col.) 26 cm. [NK25258] 56-14055
1. Furniture — Engliahd — Hist. 2. Interior decoration — England. 3. Art objects — England. I. Title.

Furniture, English.

BIRD, Anthony. 749.22
English furniture for the private collector, including antique clocks. New York, Distributed by Hearthside Press [1962, c1961] 216 p. illus. 23 cm. (A Deerfield book) [NK2529.B43 1962] 62-13156
1. Furniture, English. 2. Furniture—Collectors and collecting.

BRADSHAW, Albert Ernest 749.5
Handmade woodwork of the twentieth century. London, J. Murray [Hollywood-by-the-Sea, Fla., Transalantic, 1963, c.1962] 115p. (Chiefly illus.) 26cm. 63-2904 8.75 bds.,
1. Furniture, English. 2. Wood-carving, English. 3. Cabinet-workers. I. Title.

CESCINSKY, Herbert, 1875- 749.22
English furniture from Gothic to Sheraton; a concise account of the development of English furniture and woodwork from the Gothic of the fifteenth century to the classic revival of the early nineteenth. New York, Dover Publications [1968, c1937] 406 p. illus., facsims. 29 cm. Includes bibliographies. [NK2528.C4 1968] 68-19173
1. Furniture, English. 2. Woodwork—England. I. Title. BIP

CESCINSKY, Herbert, 1875- 749.22
English furniture from Gothic to Sheraton; a concise account of the development of English furniture and woodwork from the Gothic of the fifteenth century to the classic revival of the early nineteenth. [Magnolia, Mass., Peter Smith, 1968,c.1967] 406p. illus., facsims. 29cm. (Dover bk. rebound) Bibl. [NK2528.C4 1968] 68-19173 10.00
1. Furniture, English. 2. Woodwork—England. I. Title.

CESCINSKY, Herbert, 1875- 749.22
The gentle art of faking furniture [Magnolia, Mass., Peter Smith, 1968] ix, 167p. illus. port. 24cm. (Dover bk., rebound) Unabridged, unaltered repubn. of the work orig. pub. in 1931 [NK2529.C42 1967] 6.50
1. Furniture, English. 2. Forgery of works of art. I. Title. BIP

CESCINSKY, Herbert, 1875- 749.22
The gentle art of faking furniture. New York, Dover Publications [1967] ix, 167 p. illus., port. 24 cm. "An unabridged and unaltered republication of the work originally published ... in 1931." [NK2529.C42 1967] 67-28636
1. Furniture, English. 2. Forgery of works in art. I. Title.

CRAWLEY, W. 749.2'2'075
Is it genuine? A guide to the identification of eighteenth-century English furniture [by] W. Crawley. New York, Hart Pub. Co. [1972] 188 p. illus. 26 cm. [NK2529.C75 1972] 70-186672 ISBN 0-8055-1041-9 20.00
1. Furniture, English. 2. Furniture—Expertising. I. Title.

DAVIS, Frank Cecil, 1892- 749.22
The plain man's guide to second-hand furniture [by] Frank Davis [New ed.] London, M. Joseph [1971, c.1961] xvii, 83 p. illus. 21 cm. [NK2528.D3] 62-6941 ISBN 0-7181-0936-8
1. Furniture, English. 2. Furniture—Collectors and collecting. I. Title.
Dist. by Transatlantic Arts for 6.95. BIP

FASTNEDGE, Ralph, 1913- 749.22
Sheraton furniture. New York, Yoseloff [c.1962] 125p. illus. (pt. col.) 26cm. Bibl. 62-10187 12.50
1. Sheraton, Thomas, 1751-1806. 2. Furniture, English. I. Title.

*GILBERT, Christopher. 749.2'2
Late Georgian & Regency Furniture. [London, Hamlyn Publishing Group, 1972] 63 p. illus. 19 cm. (Country Life Collectors' Guides) Label stamped on title page: Transatlantic Arts, Inc., sole distributor for the U.S.A. [NK2529] 2.95
1. Furniture, English. I. Title. BIP

GLOAG, John, 1896- 749.2'2
Guide to furniture styles: English and French, 1450 to 1850. Illustrated by Maureen Stafford. New York, Scribner [1972] 232 p. illus. 24 cm. [NK2529.G55] 72-162 ISBN 0-684-12938-8 14.95
1. Furniture, English. 2. Furniture, French. I. Title.

HARRIS, Eileen 749.22
The furniture of Robert Adam. London, A. Tiranti [dist. Hollywood-by-the-Sea, Fla., Transatlantic, 1964, c.1963] viii, 110p. illus., plates.s 19cm. (Chapters in art ser., v. 38) Bibl. 64-56194 12.00
1. Adam, Robert, 1728-1792. 2. Furniture, English. I. Title.

HARRIS, John, 1931- comp. 749.22
Regency furniture designs from contemporary source books, 1803-1826. A collection of pattern-books, including selections from Thomas Sheraton [and others] With various comparative plates of 1744 to 1812. Chicago, Quadrangle Books, 1961 [c1960] vi, 26, [108]p. (chiefly illus.) 26cm. [NK2529.H22] 61-17156
1. Furniture, English. I. Title.

HARRIS, John Frederick, 1931- comp. 749.22
Regency furniture designs from contemporarv source books, 1803-1826. A collection of pattern-books, including selections from Thomas Sheraton [others] With various comparative plates of 1744 to 1812. Chicago, Quadrangle Books, 1961[c.1960] vi, 26, [108]p. (chiefly illus.) 26cm. 61-17156 10.00 bds.,
1. Furniture, Englis. I. Title.

HAYDEN, Arthur, 1868-1946 749.42
Chats on cottage and farmhouse furniture. Ed. rev. by Cyril G. E. Bunt. London, E. Benn [New York. Dover, 1965] 237p. illus. 21cm. (Chats ser.) [NK2529] 65-29909 3.00
1. Furniture. English. 2. Collectors and collecting. 3. Textile industry and fabrics, English. I. Blunt, Cyril George Edward. 1882- ed. II. Title. III. Series.

HAYWARD, Charles Harold, 1898- 749.22
English period furniture [by] Charles H. Hayward. [Rev. and enl. ed.] New York, Scribner [1971] 270 p. illus. 23 cm. [NK2529.H44 1971] 77-155926 ISBN 0-684-12443-2 10.00
1. Furniture, English. I. Title. BIP

HEWITT, Linda, 1940- 749.2'2
Chippendale and all the rest; some influences on eighteenth-century English furniture. Illus. by Robert G. Hewitt. South Brunswick, A. S. Barnes [1974] 161 p. illus. 26 cm. Bibliography: p. 141-144. [NK2529.H49] 72-6386 ISBN 0-498-01188-7
1. Chippendale, Thomas, 1718-1779. 2. Furniture, English. 3. Cabinet-workers—England. I. Title.

HUGHES, Therle. 749.22
Old English furniture. New York, McBride [1950] 201 p. illus. 23 cm. [NK2529.H77 1950] 51-9330
1. Furniture, English. I. Title. BIP

HUGHES, Therle 749.22
Old English furniture. [Rev. ed.] New York, Macmillan [1963] 201p. illus. (pt. col.) 23cm. 63-5317 9.95
1. Furniture, English. I. Title.

HUGHES, Therle. 749.22
Old English furniture. New York, Praeger [1969, c1963] 201 p. illus. 23 cm. [NK2529.H77 1969] 69-19858 8.95
1. Furniture, English. I. Title.

*HUGHES, Therle. 749.22
The pocket book of furniture. Illus. by the author. [London] [Country Life] [1971, c.1968] 416 p. illus. 16 cm. [NK2528.H77] ISBN 0-600-43067-7
1. Furniture, English. I. Title.
Distributed by Transatlantic Arts, Levittown, N.Y., for 6.95.

JOY, Edward Thomas. 749.2'2
Antique English furniture [by] Edward T. Joy. New York, Drake Publishers [1972] 192 p. illus. 25 cm. Bibliography: p. 191-192. [NK2529.J69 1972b] 73-168240 ISBN 0-87749-275-1 9.95
1. Furniture, English. I. Title.

JOY, Edward Thomas 749.22
The book of English furniture. [Cranbury, N.J.] A. S. Barnes [1966, c.1964] 104p. illus. (pt. col.) 27cm. [NK2528.J66] 65-24845 5.00
1. Furniture, English. I. Title.

MUSGRAVE, Clifford. 749.22
Adam and Hepplewhite and other neo-classical furniture. [1st American ed.] New York, Taplinger Pub. Co. [1966] 223, [96] p. illus. (part col.) 26 cm. Bibliography: 175-178. [NK2542.A3M8 1966] 66-11302
1. Adam, Robert, 1728-1792. 2. Hepplewhite, George, d. 1786. 3. Furniture, English. I. Title.

MUSGRAVE, Clifford. 749.22
Regency furniture, 1800-1830. New York, T. Yoseloff [1962, c1961] 157p. illus. (part col.) 26cm. Bibliography: p. 149-151. [NK2529.M8 1962] 62-10186
1. Furniture, English. I. Title. BIP

NICKERSON, David. 749.22
English furniture of the eighteenth century. New York, Putnam [1963] 128 p. illus. (part col.) 22 cm. (Pleasures and treasures) [NK2529.N5] 63-15528
1. Furniture, English. I. Title.

ROE, Frederic Gordon, 1894- 749.22
English cottage furniture. New ed., rev. and enl. New York, Roy Publishers [1962, c1961] 240 p. illus. 22 cm. [NK2528.R63 1962] 62-9880
1. Furniture, English. I. Title.

ROE, Frederic Gordon, 749.212
Victorian furniture. New York, Roy [1952] 160 p. illus. 23 cm. [NK2530.R58] 52-12451
1. Furniture, English. I. Title.

STAFFORD, Maureen. 749.22
British furniture through the ages, illustrated by Maureen Stafford. With an introd. by Robert Keith Middlemas. [1st American ed.] New York, Coward-McCann [1966] x, 112 p. illus. 26 cm. [NK2528.S7 1966] 66-10846
1. Furniture, English. I. Middlemas, Robert Keith, 1935- II. Title.

TOLLER, Jane. 749.2'2
English country furniture. [1st American ed.] South Brunswick, A. S. Barnes [1973] 176 p. illus. 23 cm. Bibliography: p. 171. [NK2529.T74 1973] 73-46 ISBN 0-498-01366-9 7.95
1. Furniture, English. 2. Decoration and ornament, Rustic. I. Title. BIP

YOUNG, Dennis 749.22
Furniture in Britain today. Meubles en Grande-Bretagne aujourd'hui. Mobel in Grossbritannien Heute. [By] Dennis & Barbara Young. New York, Wittenborn [c.1964] 1v. (unpaged) 310 illus. 30cm. [NK2530.Y6] 65-117 10.50 bds.,
1. Furniture, English. I. Young, Barbara, joint author. II. Title. III. Title: Meubles en Grande-Bretagne aujourd'hui. IV. Title: Mobel in Grossbritannien Heute.

Furniture, English—Handbooks, manuals, etc.

NEGUS, Arthur. 749.2'2
Going for a song; an informal guide to English furniture [by] Arthur Negus as told to Max Robertson. New York, Taplinger Pub. Co. [1972, c1969] 221 p. illus. 25 cm. [NK2578.N4 1972] 72-163886 ISBN 0-8008-3290-6 6.95
1. Furniture, English—Handbooks, manuals, etc. I. Robertson, Maxwell, 1915- II. Title. BIP

Furniture, English—History.

BRETT, Gerard 749.22
English furniture and its setting from the later sixteenth to the early nineteenth century. Illus. from the collection of the Royal Ontario Museum, Univ. of Toronto. [Toronto] Pub. for Royal Ontario Museum by Univ. of Toronto Pr. [1965] x, 117p. illus. 21cm. Bibl. [NK2529.B7] 65-9809 6.50
1. Furniture, English—Hist. I. Toronto. Royal Ontario Museum. II. Title.

CONNOISSEUR. (The) 749.22
The Connoisseur new guide to antique English furniture. Ed. by L. G. G. Ramsey, ed. of the Connoisseur. Introd. by Terence Davis. New York, Dutton [c.1961] 192p. illus. (col. front.) 25cm. (Connoisseur new guides) Bibl. 61-66005 4.95 bds.,
1. Furniture, English—Hist. I. Ramsey, L. G. G., ed. II. Title. III. Title: Antique English furniture.

GLOAG, John, 1896- 749.22
English furniture. 5th ed., rev. and enl. London, A. o-6-8 C. Black [New York, Barnes & Noble, c.1965] xvi, 183p. illus. 23cm. (Lib. of Eng. art) [NK2528.G48] 65-4602 6.00
1. Furniture, English—Hist. I. Title. II. Series.

JOY, Edward Thomas 749.22
English furniture. A.D. 43-1950. New York, Arco [1963, c.1962] xi, 84p. illus. 26cm. (1118) 63-19889 4.00
1. Furniture, English—Hist. I. Title.

MACDONALD-TAYLOR, Margaret Stephens 749.22
English furniture from the Middle Ages to modern times. [1st Amer. ed.] New York,

Putnam [1966. c.1965] 299p. illus., plates (1 col.) 26cm. Bibl. [NK2528.M17] 66-14485 8.95
1. Furniture. English—Hist. I. Title.

SYMONDS, Robert Wemyss, 1889-1958 749.22
Victorian furniture, by R. W. Symonds, B. B. Whineray. London, Country Life [dist. New York, Taplinger, 1963, c.1962] 232p. plates. (col. front.) 29cm. 63-2076 25.00
1. Furniture, English—Hist. I. Whineray, B. B., joint author. II. Title.

VICTORIA and Albert Museum, South Kensington. 749.22
A short history of English furniture. London, H.M.S.O., 1966. [4], 32p. 100 plates 26cm. (Its Large picture book, no. 20). Bibl. [N1150.A752 no. 20] 67-74303 5.00
1. Furniture, English—Hist. I. Title. II. Series.
American distributor: British Info., New York.

WOODFORDE, John 749.22
The observer's book of furniture. Illus. by Roy Spencer. New York, Warne [1964] 224p. illus. 15cm. (Observer's pocket ser., 35) [NK2528.W6] 64-18383 1.25 bds.,
1. Furniture, English—Hist. I. Title. II. Series. BIP

Furniture, English—History.

DEAN, Margery. 749.22
English antique furniture, 1450-1850. New York, Universe Books [1969] 109 p. illus. 21 cm. [NK2528.D4] 69-17308
1. Furniture, English—History. I. Title.

FASTNEDGE, Ralph, 1913- 749.22
English furniture styles from 1500 to 1830. [1st American ed.] New York, Barnes [1964] 320 p. illus. 26 cm. Includes bibliographies. [NK2529.F25 1964] 64-3941
1. Furniture, English—History. I. Title.

GLOAG, John, 1896- 749.22
English furniture 6th ed. London, Adam & Charles Black [1973 c1965] 183 p. illus. 23 cm. (Library of English Art) [NK2528.G48] ISBN 0-713613181
1. Furniture, English—History. I. Title.
Distributed by Charles T. Branford Newton Centre, Mass. for 10.50.

HARRISON, John Kirkbride. 749.2'2
A history of English furniture; written and illustrated by John K. Harrison. London, Mills and Boon, 1972. 184 p. illus. 20 x 26 cm. Bibliography: p. 179-181. [NK2528.H29 1972] 72-171505 ISBN 0-263-05060-2
1. Furniture, English—History. I. Title.
Distributed by Transatlantic Arts; 10.00.

HAYWARD, Helena 749.22
Thomas Johnson and English rococo. London, A. Tiranti [dist. Hollywood-by-the-Sea, Fla., Transatlantic] 1964[c.1963] viii, 45p. 191 illus. 29cm. (Master hands ser.) 64-55935 12.50 bds.,
1. qJohnson, Thomas, Carver. 2. Furniture, English. 3. Decoration and ornament, Rococo. I. Title.

MACQUOID, Percy, d.1925. 749.2'2
A history of English furniture. New York, Dover [1972] 4 v. illus. 28 cm. Reprint of the 1904-08 ed. Contents.Contents.—v. 1. The age of oak, 1500-1660.—v. 2. The age of walnut, 1660-1720.—v. 3. The age of mahogany, 1720-1770.—v. 4. The age of satinwood, 1770-1820. [NK2529.M3232] 76-158732 ISBN 0-486-22203-9 (v. 1) 5.00 per vol.
1. Furniture, English—History. I. Title.

MACQUOID, Percy, d. 1925 749.2'2
A history of English furniture. Magnolia, Mass., Peter Smith [1973 c1972] 4 v. illus 28 cm. (Dover book rebound) Reprint of the 1904-08 ed. Contents.Contents: v. 1. The age of oak, 1500-1660.—v. 2. The age of walnut, 1660-1720.—v. 3. The age of mahogany, 1720-1770.—v. 4. The age of satinwood, 1770-1820. [NK2529.M3232] 76-158732 ISBN 0-8446-4577-X 32.00 set.
1. Furniture, English—History. I. Title.
To order individual volumes: vol. 1: 0-8446-4578-8 vol. 2: 0-8446-4579-6 vol. 3: 0-8446-4580-X vol. 4: 0-8446-4581-8.

WOLSEY, Samuel Wilfred. 749.22
Furniture in England: the age of the joiner, by S. W. Wolsey and R. W. P. Luff. New York, Praeger [1969, c1968] xiv, 104 p. illus. 25 cm. Bibliographical footnotes. [NK2529.W6 1969] 69-17082 10.00
1. Furniture, English—History. 2. Cabinet-workers—Gt. Brit. I. Luff, R. W. P., joint author. II. Title.

Furniture, European.

MARGON, Lester. 749.24
Masterpieces of European furniture, 1300-1840; a compendium, with photographs, measured drawings, and descriptive commentary. New York, Architectural Book Pub. Co. [1968] 288 p. illus., facsims., plans 28 cm. [NK2525.M3] 67-25741
1. Furniture, European. I. Title. BIP

RITZ, Gislind Maria, 1925- 749.2
The art of painted furniture [by] Gislind M. Ritz. Photos. by Helga Schmidt-Glassner. English translation by Sigrid MacRae. New York, Van Nostrand Reinhold [1971, c1970] 175 p. illus., 52 col. plates. 29 cm. Translation of Alte bemalte Bauernmobel Europa. Bibliography: p. 169-173. [NK925.R513 1971] 76-150509
1. Folk art—Europe. 2. Furniture, European. 3. Decoration and ornament, European. I. Title.

Furniture—Exhibitions.

CONTEMPORARY Arts Museum. 749.2'04
International design: new attitudes, new forms. [Houston, Printed by Fidelity Print. Co., 1972] 32 p. illus. (part col.) 26 cm. Catalog of an exhibition organized by the Contemporary Arts Museum, Houston, Tex., and held at the museum Dec. 1, 1972-Jan. 28, 1973. [NK2395.C66] 72-96013
1. Furniture—Exhibitions. 2. Lighting, Architectural and decorative—Exhibitions. I. Title.

LA Jolla Museum of Contemporary Art 749.2'13
Innovations: contemporary home environs; an exhibition organized by the La Jolla Museum of Contemporary Art, La Jolla, California, December 15, 1973-February 3, 1974. [La Jolla, Calif., c1973] 1 v. (chiefly illus., part col.) 22 x 28 cm. [NK2395.L3 1973] 73-93187
1. Furniture—Exhibitions. I. Title.
Publisher's address: 700 Prospect Street, La Jolla, CA 92037

ST. Louis. City Art Museum. 749.204
Product environment; exhibition of new furniture. [St. Louis, 1970] 72 p. (chiefly illus.) 22 cm. "Organized by City Art Museum of Saint Louis. Designed by Terrence Cashen and David Suttle." Exhibited at the City Art Museum of Saint Louis, Apr. 24-June 7, 1970; Dallas Museum of Fine Arts, July 15-Aug. 30, 1970; Philadelphia Museum of Art, Oct. 2-Nov. 10, 1970; and the Albright-Knox Art Gallery, Buffalo, Jan. 6-Feb. 14, 1971. [TS882.S35] 70-16299
1. Furniture—Exhibitions. I. Title.

U. S. National Park Service. 749.211
Catalogue; exhibit of 18th century furniture, May 17, 1952 under the auspices of the National Park Service, Independence National Historical Park Project. [n. p., 1952] iv. 27cm. [NK2210.P5] 53-60933
1. Furniture—Exhibitions. I. Title.

Furniture—Expertising.

WAY, Nelson E., 1908- 749
Antiques don't lie : how to make antique furniture tell everything, including its age / Nelson E. Way and Constance Stapleton. 1st ed. Garden City, N.Y. : Doubleday, 1975. ix, 150 p. : ill. ; 22 cm. [NK2240.W37] 75-20761 ISBN 0-385-07087-X : 7.95
1. Furniture—Expertising. 2. Furniture—Collectors and collecting. I. Stapleton, Constance, 1930- joint author. II. Title.

Furniture finishing.

BROWNING, Elizabeth Lowry. 749
With love and elbow grease; a guide to antiquing, decorating, and finishing almost anything. New York, Simon and Schuster [1968] 124 p. illus. 24 cm. [TT199.4.B7] 68-19938 4.95
1. Furniture finishing. 2. Decoration and ornament. I. Title.

BRUMBAUGH, James E. 684.1'043
Wood furniture, finishing, refinishing, repairing, by James E. Brumbaugh. [1st ed.] Indianapolis, T. Audel [1974] 343 p. illus. 22 cm. [TT199.4.B76] 73-91640 ISBN 0-672-23216-2 6.95
1. Furniture finishing. 2. Furniture—Repairing. I. Title.

FISCHMAN, Walter Ian. 684.1'043
Furniture finishing / by Walter Fischman. Indianapolis : Bobbs-Merrill, [1978] p. cm. Includes index. [TT199.4.F47] 78-55663 ISBN 0-672-52349-3 : 15.00
1. Furniture finishing. I. Title. BIP

GASTON, Desmond. 684.1'044
Care and repair of furniture, including refinishing and upholstering / Desmond Gaston. Garden City, N.Y. : Doubleday, 1978, c1977. 176 p. : ill. ; 25 cm. Includes index. [TT199.G37 1978] 78-55622 ISBN 0-385-14466-0 : 9.95
1. Furniture finishing. 2. Furniture—Repairing. I. Title.

GROTZ, George, 749
Decorating furniture with a little bit of class. [1st ed.] Garden City, N.Y., Doubleday, 1969. ix, 84 p. illus. 21 cm. [TT199.4.G76] 69-12854 1.95
1. Furniture finishing. I. Title.

GROTZ, George. 684.1'0443
From gunk to glow; or, The gentle art of refinishing antiques and other furniture. Chester, Conn., Pequot Press, [1973, c1971] 64 p. 22 cm. [TT199.4.G77 1973] 73-5803 ISBN 0-394-70994-2 1.25 (pbk.)
1. Furniture finishing. I. Title. BIP

HIGGINS, Alfred, 1906- 684.1'0443
Common-sense guide to refinishing antiques. New York, Funk & Wagnalls [1969, c1968] xi, 224 p. illus. 22 cm. [TT199.4.H53] 68-17478 5.95
1. Furniture finishing. I. Title. BIP

HIGGINS, Alfred, 1906- 684.1'0443
Common-sense guide to refinishing antiques / by Alfred Higgins. Rev. ed. New York : Funk & Wagnalls, [1976] p. cm. Includes index. [TT199.4.H53 1976] 76-8913 ISBN 0-308-10252-5 : 7.95
1. Furniture finishing. I. Title.

HOWELL-KOEHLER, Nancy. 684.1'044
Step-by-step furniture finishing / by Nancy Howell-Koehler. New York : Golden Press, 1975. 80 p. : ill. (some col.) ; 29 cm. Bibliography: p. 79. [TT199.4.H68] 74-82072 ISBN 0-307-42014-0 pbk. : 2.95
1. Furniture finishing. I. Title.

JOYNER, Nina Glenn. 684.1'0443
Furniture refinishing at home / Nina Glenn Joyner. Rev. ed. Radnor, Pa. : Chilton Book Co., [1975] 132 p. : ill. ; 27 cm. (Chilton's creative crafts series) Includes index. [TT199.4.J68 1975] 74-28061 ISBN 0-8019-6144-0 : 12.50. ISBN 0-8019-6145-9 pbk. : 5.95
1. Furniture finishing. I. Title.

KUHN, H. W. 684.1
Refinishing furniture, by H. W. Kuhn. New York, Arco Pub. Co. [1964, c1963] 109 p. illus. 24 cm. (Arco how-to library) Previous ed. published under title: How-to refinish furniture. [TT199.K8 1964] 64-15182
1. Furniture finishing. I. Title. BIP

MINNESOTA Mining and Manufacturing Company. Automotive-Hardware Trades Division. 684.1'0443
The home pro furniture refinishing and antiquing guide / [Automotive-Hardware Trades Division, 3M Company]. [St. Paul : The Division, 1975] i, 170 p. : ill. ; 14 x 21 cm. (Its The home pro guide series) "Cat. no. 9745." [TT199.4.M56 1975] 74-82965
1. Furniture finishing. I. Title.

PATTOU, Albert Brace. 684.1'0443
Furniture; furniture finishing, decoration and patching. A new and complete work on furniture of all kinds, with full practical instruction on finishing, patching and decoration—materials, tools and processes, by Albert Brace Pattou and Clarence Lee Vaughn. New York, Drake Publishers [1971, c1970] 551 p. illus. 21 cm. [TS885.P38 1971] 73-24061
1. Furniture finishing. I. Vaughn, Clarence Lee, 1890- joint author. II. Title.

PATTOU, Albert Brace. 684.1'0443
Furniture finishing / by Albert Brace Patton [i.e. Pattou] & Clarence Lee Vaughn. New & rev. ed. New York : Drake Publishers, 1975. 224 p. : ill. ; 23 cm. (A Drake home craftsman's book) Previous editions published under title: Furniture; furniture finishing, decoration and patching. [TT199.4.P37 1975] 76-3147 4.95
1. Furniture finishing. I. Vaughn, Clarence Lee, 1890- joint author. II. Title.

SAVAGE, Jessie D. 684.1'0443
Professional furniture refinishing for the amateur / Jessie D. Savage. 1st ed. New York : Harper & Row, [1975] vi, 202 p. : ill. ; 21 cm. Includes index. [TT199.4.S27 1975] 74-20414 ISBN 0-06-013774-6 : 7.95
1. Furniture finishing. I. Title. BIP

SWEDBERG, Robert W. 684.1'044
Off your rocker / Robert W. and Harriett Swedberg. Des Moines : Wallace-Homestead Book Co., c1976. 89 p. : ill. ; 23 cm. [TT199.4.S93] 75-5494 ISBN 0-87069-126-0 : 3.95
1. Furniture finishing. 2. Furniture—Repairing. I. Swedberg, Harriett, joint author. II. Title. BIP

WICKS, Harry, 1931- 684.1'0443
Furniture refinishing / by Harry Wicks. New York : Grosset & Dunlap, 1977. 96 p. : ill. ; 28 cm. (Grosset good life books) Includes index. [TT199.4.W5] 75-5425 ISBN 0-448-12051-8 : 1.95. ISBN 0-448-13321-0 lib.bdg. : 4.99
1. Furniture finishing. I. Title.

Furniture—France.

FUSCO, Renato de. 749.2'4
Le Corbusier, designer : furniture, 1929 / Renato De Fusco. 1st U.S. ed. Woodbury, N.Y. : Barrons, 1977,c1976. p. cm. [NK2550.J36F8713 1976] 77-81368 ISBN 0-8120-5148-3 : 11.95
1. Jeanneret-Gris, Charles Edouard, 1887-1965. 2. Furniture—France. 3. Furniture—Drawing. I. Title.

OGLESBY, Catharine, 1895- 749.243
French provincial decorative art. New York, Scribner, 1951. viii, 214 p. illus. (part col.) 32 cm. Bibliography: p. 212-214. [NK2548.O34] 51-13137
1. Furniture—France. 2. Art objects—France. I. Title.

Furniture, French.

SOUCHAL, Genevieve. 749.24
French eighteenth-century furniture. Translated from the French by Simon Watson Taylor. Photos. by E. Boudot-Lamotte. New York, Putnam [1961] 129 p. illus. (part col.) ports. 22 cm. (Pleasures and treasures) Bibliography: p. 5. [NK2548.S653] 61-12202
1. Furniture, French. I. Title.

SZABOLCSI, Hedvig 749.24
French furniture in Hungary. [Tr. by Edna Lenart. Budapest] Corvina Pr. [1964] 48p. illus., 48 plates (pt. col.) 19cm. [NK2458.S85] 66-47365 4.95
1. Furniture French. 2. Furniture—Hungary. I. Title.
American distributor: Branden Pr., Boston. BIP

VERLET, Pierre 749.24
French royal furniture; an historical survey followed by a study of forty pieces preserved in Great Britain and the United States [Tr. from the orig. French ms. by Michael Bullock] New York, Potter [dist. Crown, 1964, c.1963] 201p. plates (pt. col.) 25cm. Bibl. [NK2548.V413] 64-20134 12.50

1. Furniture, French. I. Title.

WATSON, Franics John Bagott, 1907- 749.24
Louis XVI furniture. New York, Philosophical Library [1960] vi, 162 p. illus., plates. 19 cm. Bibliography: p. 95. [NK2548.W3] 61-4064
1. Furniture, French. 2. Decoration and ornament — Louis XVI style. I. Title.

Furniture, French—Directories.

HINCKLEY, F. Lewis. 749.24
A directory of antique French furniture, 1735-1800; over 300 illustrations of provincial, Parisian, and other European antique furniture [by] F. Lewis Hinckley. New York, Crown [1967] ix, 214 p. illus. 29 cm. Bibliography: p. 213-214. [NK2548.H57] 67-24767
1. Furniture, French—Directories. 2. Furniture—Dictionaries—French. I. Title.

Furniture, French—History.

APRA, Nietta. 749.2'4
The Louis styles: Louis XIV, Louis XV, Louis XVI. New York, World Pub. [1973] p. (Connoisseur's library) [NK2548.A69] 72-10447 ISBN 0-529-05016-1
1. Furniture, French—History. 2. Decoration and ornament—Louis XIV style. 3. Decoration and ornament—Louis XV style. 4. Decoration and ornament—Louis XVI style. I. Title. II. Series: Connoisseur's library (New York)

FRENCH cabinetmakers of the eighteenth century. 749.24 Foreword by Pierre Verlet [Tr. from French. Paris] Hachette [New York, French & European Pubns., 1965, c.1963] 341p. illus. (pt. col.) 32cm. e(Collection Connaissance des arts 'Grands artisans d'autrefois') Completed under the general direction of Claude Fregnac with the coop. of Conaissance des arts; introd. by Jean Meuvret. [NK2548.E213] 65-28968 27.50
1. Furniture, French—Hist. 2. Cabinet-workers. I. Fregnac, Claude. II. Meuvret, Jean. III. Connaissance des arts.

VIAUX, Jacqueline. 749.24
French furniture. Translated by Hazel Paget. New York, Putnam [1964] 200 p. illus. (part col.) 21 cm. Translation of Le meuble en France. [NK2547.V473] 64-13023
1. Furniture, French—History. I. Title.

Furniture, German.

HUTH, Hans, 1892- 749.2'3
Roentgen furniture : Abraham and David Roentgen, European cabinet-makers / Hans Huth. London ; New York : Sotheby Parke Bernet, 1974 1974. vii, 108 p., 68 leaves of plates : ill. ; 30 cm. Original ed. published in German in 1928 under title: Abraham und David Roentgen und ihre Neuwieder möbelwerkstatt. Includes index. Bibliography: p. 97-99. [NK2554.R6H813] 74-187943 ISBN 0-85667-003-0 : 55.00
1. Roentgen, Abraham, 1711-1793. 2. Roentgen, David, 1743-1807. 3. Furniture, German. I. Title. BIP

Furniture—Germany—Exhibitions.

NEW York (City). Museum of Modern Art. 749.2'3
Ludwig Mies van der Rohe : furniture and furniture drawings from the Design Collection and the Mies van der Rohe Archive, the Museum of Modern Art, New York / by Ludwig Glaeser. New York : The Museum, c1977. 88 p. : ill. ; 26 cm. Bibliography: p. 86. [NK2554.M5N48 1977] 76-24509 ISBN 0-87070-555-5 pbk. : 4.95
1. Mies van der Rohe, Ludwig, 1886-1969. 2. Furniture—Germany—Exhibitions. 3. Furniture—Drawings—Exhibitions. I. Mies van der Rohe, Ludwig, 1886-1969. II. Glaeser, Ludwig. III. Mies van der Rohe Archive.

Furniture—Gt. Brit.

HAYDEN, Arthur, 1868-1946. 749.222
Chats on cottage and farmhouse furniture. Edited and rev. by Cyril G. E. Bunt. [Rev. ed.] New York, Wyn, 1950. 237 p. plates. 21 cm. "Old English chintzes, by Hugh Phillips": p. 216-235. [NK2529.H3 1950] 50-9343
1. Furniture—Gt. Brit. 2. Collectors and collecting. 3. Textile industry and fabrics—Gt. Brit. I. Phillips, Hugh. II. Title.

Furniture, Greek.

ROBSJOHN-GIBBINGS, Terence Harold, 1905- 749.2938
Furniture of classical Greece, by T. H. Robsjohn-Gibbings and Carlton W. Pullin. New York, Knopf [1964, c1963] 122 p. illus. (part col.) 32 cm. [NK2305.R6] 63-17054
1. Furniture, Greek. I. Pullin, Carlton W., joint author. II. Title.

Furniture—Handbooks, manuals, etc.

GAINES, Edith. 749
Dictionary of antique furniture [by] Edith Gaines [and] Dorothy H. Jenkins. Illustrated by Helen Disbrow and Charles Reiger. [1st ed.] Princeton, Pyne Press [1974] 75 p. illus. 28 cm. On cover: Woman's day dictionary of antique furniture. Articles were previously published in Woman's day. [NK2240.G34] 73-91974 ISBN 0-87861-061-8 3.95 (pbk.).
1. Furniture—Handbooks, manuals, etc. 2. Decoration and ornament—Handbooks, manuals, etc. I. Jenkins, Dorothy Helen, 1907- II. Title. III. Title: Woman's day dictionary of antique furniture.

GUERTNER, Beryl. 747
Australian book of furnishing and decorating. Sydney, Melbourne, Murray [1967] Stamped on t.p.: dist. by Sportshelf, New Rochelle, N. Y. 192p. illus. (pt. col.), diagrs., plans. 29cm. [NK2230.G8] 68-78100 17.50
1. Furniture—Handbooks, manuals, etc. 2. Interior decoration. I. Title.

Furniture—History.

DAVIS, Frank, 1892- 749.2
Furniture; a picture history. London, Vista Bks. [Chester Springs, Pa., Dufour, 1966, c.1958] 160p. illus. 29cm. (Picture hist. ser.) First pub. in 1958 by Macmillan under title: A picture history of furniture [NK2270] 65-8376 8.50
1. Furniture—Hist. I. Title.

GREAT styles of furniture: 749.2 English, Italian, French, Dutch, Spanish. New York, Viking [1963] 308p. illus. (pt. col.) 31cm. (Studio bk.) 63-18910 20.00; after Dec. 31, 22.50
1. Furniture—Hist. 2. Interior decoration—Hist.

MACMILLAN, Donald D. 749.203
Great furniture styles, 1660-1830. Illus. by Peter Spier. New York, Odyssey, c.1965. 41p. illus. (pt. col.) col. ports. 11x17cm. (Odyssey lib., 21)) [NK2360.M3] 65-23286 .95 bds.,
1. Furniture—Hist. I. Spier, Peter, illus. II. Title.

PHILP, Peter, [Dennis Alfred Peter Philp] 749.2
Antique furniture for the smaller home. New York, [Arco] [1963, c.1962] 172p. illus. 19cm. (Arc bks., 1025) Bibl. 62-20986 .95 pap.,
1. Furniture—Hist. 2. Furniture—Collectors and collecting. I. Title. BIP

RUSSELL, Gordon, Sir 1892- 749.2
Looking at furniture. [Rev., enl. ed.] London. L Humphries New York, Label mounted on t.p.: Sole dist. for the U.S.A., Transatlantic [1964] 64p. illus. 26cm. Previous eds. pub. under title : Furniture [NK2270.R8 1964] 66-31977 4.50
1. Furniture—Hist. I. Title.

SCHMITZ, Hermann, 1882- 749.09
The encyclopedia of furniture; an outline history of furniture design in Egypt, Assyria, Persia, Greece, Rome, Italy, France, the Netherlands, Germany, England, Scandinavia, Spain, Russia, and in the Near and Far East up to the middle of the nineteenth century. Compiled by authorities in various countries under the general direction of Herman Schmitz, and with an introd. by H. P. Shapland. New York, F. A. Praeger [1957] liii p. 320p. of illus. 30cm. [NK2270.S363 1957] 57-9791
1. Furniture—Hist. I. Title.

WANSCHER, Ole 749.2
The art of furniture; 5000 years of furniture and interiors. Tr. from Danish by David Hohnen. New York, Reinhold. [1967, c.1966] 419p. illus. (pt. col.) 27cm. Tr. of Mobelkunsten. Bibl. [NK2270.W313] 66-25546 25.00
1. Furniture—Hist. I. Title.

Furniture—History.

BOGER, Louise Ade. 749.2
The complete guide to furniture styles. New York, Scribner [1959] x, 438 p. plates, map. 26 cm. Bibliography: p. 423-429. [NK2270.B63] 59-6239
1. Furniture—History. I. Title. BIP

BOGER, Louise Ade. 749.2
The complete guide to furniture styles. Enl. ed. New York, Scribner [1969] xii, 500 p. illus. 26 cm. Bibliography: p. 481-490. [NK2270.B63 1969] 73-85267 17.50
1. Furniture—History. I. Title. II. Title: Furniture styles.

BOGER, Louise Ade. 749.2
Furniture past & present; a complete illustrated guide to furniture styles from ancient to modern. [1st ed.] Garden City, N.Y., Doubleday, 1966. 520 p. illus. 27 cm. Bibliography: p. 506-508. [NK2270.B64] 66-20939
1. Furniture—History. I. Title. BIP

GLOAG, John, 1896- 749.2
A social history of furniture design from B.C. 1300 to A.D. 1960 New York, Crown Publishers [1966] 202 p. illus. (part col.), facsims. 29 cm. Bibliography: p. 192. [NK2270.G55 1966a] 66-20207
1. Furniture—History. I. Title.

HAYWARD, Helena, ed. 749.2
World furniture; an illustrated history [by] Douglas Ash [and others] New York, McGraw-Hill, 1965. 320 p. illus., col. plates. 35 cm. Bibliography: p. 312. [NK2270.H3] 65-18175
1. Furniture—History. I. Ash, Douglas. II. Title.

**THE History of furniture* 684.1009 / introduction by Sir Francis Watson. New York : Morrow, c1976. 344 p. : col. ill. ; 31 cm. Includes index. Bibliography: p. 332-35. [NK2270] 76-7256 ISBN 0-688-03083-1
1. Furniture—History.
Contents omitted.

MOLESWORTH, Hender Delves, 1907- 749.2
Three centuries of furniture in color [by] H. D. Molesworth [and] John Kenworthy-Browne. New York, Viking Press [1972] 328 p. illus. 32 cm. (A Studio book) Bibliography: p. 321-324. [NK2350.M64 1972] 72-81670 ISBN 0-670-70688-4 19.95
1. Furniture—History. I. Kenworthy-Browne, J. A., joint author. II. Title.

PHILP, Peter. 749.2
Antique furniture for the smaller home. New York, Arc Books [1963, c1962] 172 p. illus. 19 cm. [NK2235.P45] 62-20968
1. Furniture—History. 2. Furniture—Collectors and collecting. I. Title. BIP

RIBALTA, Marta. 749.2'04
Los muebles = Furniture = Les meubles / director, Marta Ribalta ; diseno grafico, Estudio Zimmermann. 1. ed. Barcelona : Blume ; distribucion, New York : Universe Books, 1978. 269 p. : ill. (some col.) ; 26 cm. (Habitat ; 6) English, French, and Spanish. Errata slip inserted. [NK2395.R5] 79-339546 ISBN 8-470-31059-3 pbk. : 5.95
1. Furniture—History—20th century. 2. House furnishings—History—20th century. I. Title. II. Title: Furniture. III. Title: Les meubles. IV. Series: Habitat (Barcelona) ; 6.

SYNGE, Lanto. 749.2
Antique furniture / Lanto Synge ; photography, Bob Loosemore. New York : Arco Pub. Co., [1978] c1977. p. cm. Includes index. Bibliography: p. [NK2270.S9] 77-13369 ISBN 0-668-04471-3 : 7.95. ISBN 0-668-04482-9 pbk. : 5.95
1. Furniture—History. I. Title. BIP

WARMAN, Edwin G., 1915- 749.2
Antique furniture guide; a guide to periods and styles from ancient times up to the Victorian era. Edited by Edwin G. Warman. Uniontown, Pa., E. G. Warman Pub., 1971. 153 p. illus. 22 cm. [NK2270.W35] 71-28030 5.00
1. Furniture—History. I. Title. BIP

Furniture in art.

ry Art.
PENNSYLVANIA. University. Institute of Contemporary Art.
Improbable furniture : [exhibition], Institute of Contemporary Art, University of Pennsylvania, Philadelphia, 10 March to 10 April 1977, [La Jolla Museum of Contemporary Art, La Jolla, California, 20 May to 6 July 1977]. Philadelphia : The Institute, c1977. 47 p. : ill. ; 22 x 27 cm. Includes bibliographical references. [N6487.P45P466] 76-58800 ISBN 0-88454-022-7
1. Furniture in art. 2. Art, Modern—20th century—Exhibitions. I. La Jolla Museum of Contemporary Art. II. Title.

Furniture industry and trade—Great Britain—History.

WILLS, Geoffrey. 749.2'2
Craftsmen and cabinet-makers of classic English furniture / Geoffrey Wills. New York : St. Martin's Press, [1976] c1974. p. cm. Includes index. Bibliography: p. [TS810.G7W54 1976] 75-34773 ISBN 0-85152-941-0 pbk. : 13.50
1. Furniture industry and trade—Great Britain—History. 2. Furniture, English. I. Title. BIP

Furniture industry and trade—New England—History.

WATSON, Aldren Auld, 1917- 684.1'04
Country furniture, by Aldren A. Watson. Illus. by the author. New York, Crowell [1974] 274 p. illus. 26 cm. Bibliography: p. 265-267. Describes the history, community, and daily life of the early American furniture maker, the types of wood he chose, his shop, tools, techniques, and business affairs. [TS880.W33 1974] 73-18013 ISBN 0-690-00190-8
1. Furniture industry and trade—New England—History. 2. Furniture making. 3. Furniture, American. I. Title. BIP

Furniture industry and trade—Texas—History.

TAYLOR, Lonn, 1940- 749.2'764
Texas furniture : the cabinetmakers and their work, 1840-1880 / by Lonn Taylor and David B. Warren ; foreword by Ima Hogg. Austin : University of Texas Press, [1975] p. cm. Includes index. Bibliography: p. [TS806.T4T39] 75-20391 ISBN 0-292-73801-3 : 22.50
1. Furniture industry and trade—Texas—History. 2. Furniture, American. I. Warren, David B., 1937- joint author. II. Title. BIP

Furniture, Italian.

DESIGN italiano. 749.2'5
Mobili. Furniture. Meubles. Mobel. A cura di Enrichetta Ritter. Graphic design di Bruno Munari. Introduzione di Gillo Dorfles. [New York, Watson-Guptill Publications, 1974, c1968] p. cm. (Whitney library of design) English, French, German, and Italian. [NK2561.D45 1974] 73-13885 ISBN 0-8230-7144-8 15.00
1. Furniture, Italian. I. Ritter, Enrichetta, ed. II. Dorfles, Gillo, 1910-

ODOM, William Macdougal, 1884-1942. 749.25
A history of Italian furniture from the fourteenth to the early nineteenth century. 2d ed. New York, Archive Press, 1966- v. illus. 37 cm. Contents.-- v. 1. Gothic and Renaissance furniture. Bibliography: v. 1 p. 355-356. [NK2560.O3 1966] 67-10441
1. Furniture, Italian. I. Title.

Furniture—Kentucky—Exhibitions.

SPEED Art Museum, Louisville, Ky. 749.2'169'074016944
Kentucky furniture : an exhibition, May 12 through June 30, 1974, J. B. Speed Art Museum, Louisville, Kentucky. Louisville, Ky. : The Museum, [1974] 86 p. : chiefly ill. ; 26 cm. [NK2435.K4S64 1974] 75-314179
1. Furniture—Kentucky—Exhibitions. I. Title.

Furniture—London.

FASTNEDGE, Ralph, 1913- ed. 749.22
Shearer furniture designs, from the Cabinet-makers' London book of prices, 1788. pref., descriptive notes, by Ralph Fastnedge. London, A. Tiranti [dist. Hollywood-by-the-Sea, Fla., Transatlantic, 1964c.1962] 22p. illus., facism., 17 plates. 26cm. (Master hands ser.) [NK2542.S4F3] 65-1445 6.00 bds.,
1. Shearer, Thomas, fl. 1788. 2. Furniture—London. I. Society of Cabinet-Makers, London. The Cabinet makers'London book of prices. II. Title. BIP

Furniture making.

BUTLER, David F. 684.1
Simplified furniture design and construction [by] David F. Butler. South Brunswick, A. S. Barnes [1970] 118 p. illus. 22 cm. [TS880.B87] 74-88253 5.95
1. Furniture making. I. Title. BIP

DAL FABBRO, Mario, 1913- 684.1'2
Upholstered furniture; design and construction. New York, McGraw-Hill [1969] 215 p. illus. 29 cm. [TS880.D36] 69-13602
1. Furniture making. 2. Upholstery. I. Title. BIP

DANIELE, Joseph William. 68410420974
Building colonial furnishings, miniatures, and folk art / Joseph W. Daniele. Harrisburg, Pa. : Stackpole Books, c1976. p. cm. [TT200.D36] 76-17006 ISBN 0-8117-2052-7 : 14.95
1. Furniture making. 2. Furniture, Colonial—United States. 3. Miniature objects—United States. 4. Folk art—United States. I. Title. BIP

DOUGLASS, James Harvey. 684.1'04
Projects in wood furniture [by] J. H. Douglass [and] R. H. Roberts. Bloomington, Ill., McKnight & McKnight Pub. Co. [1967] 254 p. illus. 24 cm. First published in 1935 under title: Modern projects in woodwork. [TT194.D6 1967] 67-21721
1. Furniture making. 2. Woodwork (Manual training) I. Roberts, Richard Hugh, 1898 or 9-1947, joint author. II. Title.

DOUGLASS, James Harvey. 684.1'04
Units in woodworking [by] J. H. Douglass, Forest L. Penny [and] R. H. Roberts. [5th ed.] Albany, N.Y., Delmar Publishers [1973] 208 p. illus. 27 cm. First published in 1935 under title: Modern projects in woodwork. [TT194.D6 1973] 72-13391
1. Furniture making. 2. Woodwork (Manual training) I. Penny, Forest L., joint author. II. Roberts, Richard Hugh, 1898 or 9-1947, joint author. III. Title. BIP

GOTTSHALL, Franklin H. 684.1042
Furniture of pine, poplar, and maple [by] Franklin H. Gottshall. New York, Bonanza Books [1966] 111 p. illus. 28 cm. [TT197.G58] 66-22924
1. Furniture making. I. Title.

JONES, Michael Owen. 684.1'3
The hand made object and its maker / by Michael Owen Jones. Berkeley : University of California, 1975. xi, 261 p. : ill. ; 25 cm. Includes bibliographical references. [TT194.J66] 73-93055 ISBN 0-520-02697-7 : 14.95
1. Furniture making. I. Title. BIP

JOYCE, Ernest. 684.1
Encyclopedia of furniture making. [New York] Drake Publications [1970] 494 p. illus. 26 cm. Bibliography: p. 490. [TS880.J68] 73-24132
1. Furniture making. I. Title. BIP

MAGUIRE, Byron W., 1931- 684.1'04
The complete book of woodworking and cabinetmaking [by] Byron W. Maguire. Reston, Va., Reston Pub. Co. [1974] xii, 403 p. illus. 24 cm. [TT194.M33] 73-22158 ISBN 0-87909-153-3 17.00
1. Furniture making. 2. Woodwork. I. Title. BIP

MEADMORE, Clement. 684.1'04
How to make furniture without tools / Clement Meadmore. 1st ed. New York : Pantheon Books, [1975] 77 p., 23 leaves of plates : ill. ; 28 cm. [TT194.M4] 74-26203 ISBN 0-394-73063-1 pbk. : 4.95
1. Furniture making. I. Title. BIP

PRAK, Anco L. 684.1'04
Furniture manufacturing processes / by Anco L. Prak and Thomas W. Myers ; under the sponsorship of the Furniture Foundation, inc. and the School of Engineering of North Carolina State University . 1st ed. Raleigh : Dept. of Industrial Engineering, North Carolina State University, c1977. 263 p. in various pagings : ill. ; 28 cm. Includes bibliographical references. [TS880.P65] 77-152730 8.00
1. Furniture making. I. Myers, Thomas W., joint author. II. Furniture Foundation. III. North Carolina. State University, Raleigh. School of Engineering. IV. Title.

SMITH, Nancy A. 684.1'04
Old furniture : understanding the craftsman's art / by Nancy A. Smith ; drawings by Glenna Lang, photos. by Richard Cheek. Boston : Little, Brown, [1976] c1975. 191 p. : ill. ; 26 cm. Includes index. Bibliography: p. 185. [TT200.S55 1976] 76-13035 ISBN 0-316-79932-7 pbk. : 5.95
1. Furniture making. 2. Furniture—Repairing. 3. Furniture finishing. I. Lang, Glenna. II. Cheek, Richard. III. Title.

STAMBERG, Peter S. 684.1'04
Instant furniture : low-cost, well-designed, easy-to-assemble tables, chairs, couches, beds, desks, and storage systems / Peter S. Stamberg. New York : Van Nostrand Reinhold, [1976] p. cm. Includes index. [TT195.S7] 75-40933 ISBN 0-442-27935-3 : 12.95. ISBN 0-442-27934-5 pbk. : 7.95
1. Furniture making. I. Title. BIP

†TRUSSELL, John R. 684.1'04
Introduction to furniture making / John R. Trussell. New York : Drake Publishers, 1976, c1970. 142 p. : ill. ; 23 cm. (A Drake home craftsman's series) First published in 1970 under title: Introducing furniture making. Includes index. [TT194.T78 1976] 76-49687 ISBN 0-8473-1339-5 pbk. : 4.95
1. Furniture making. I. Title. BIP

ZEGEL, Jon, 1948- 684.1'042
Fast furniture : the Zegel system / written & illustrated by Jon M. Zegel. Philadelphia : Running Press, 1978. p. cm. [TT194.Z43] 77-29110 ISBN 0-89471-029-X lib.bdg. : 9.80. pbk. : 4.95
1. Furniture making. I. Title. BIP

Furniture making—Amateurs' manuals.

ALBERS, Vernon Martin, 1902- 684.1
Advanced furniture construction, by Vernon M. Albers. South Brunswick, A. S. Barnes [1972] 110 p. illus. 22 cm. [TT195.A42] 78-37822 ISBN 0-498-01110-0 6.95
1. Furniture making—Amateurs' manuals. I. Title. BIP

ALBERS, Vernon Martin, 1902- 684.104
Amateur furniture construction, by Vernon M. Albers. Large type edition. Brunswick, N.J. A. S. Barnes [1974, c1970] 127 p. illus. 26 cm. Bibliographical references [TT195.A43] 75-88248 ISBN 0-498-01599-8 5.95
1. Furniture making—Amateur's manuals. I. Title. BIP

BLACKBURN, Graham. 684.1'042
Illustrated furniture making / written and illustrated by Graham Blackburn. New York : Simon and Schuster, c1977. 176 p. : ill. ; 29 cm. Includes index. Bibliography: p. 169-170. [TT195.B58] 77-472 ISBN 0-671-22468-9 : 9.95 ISBN 0-671-22807-2 pbk. : 3.95
1. Furniture making—Amateurs' manuals. I. Title. BIP

BLANDFORD, Percy W. 684.1'04'0974
How to make Early American and Colonial furniture / Percy Blandford. Blue Ridge Summit, PA : Tab Books, [1979] p. cm. Includes index. [TT195.B59] 78-26896 ISBN 0-8306-9843-4 : 12.95. ISBN 0-8306-1114-2 pbk. : 7.95
1. Furniture making—Amateurs' manuals. 2. Furniture, Early American. I. Title. BIP

BRANN, Donald R. 684.1'042'0973
How to build colonial furniture / by Donald R. Brann. Briarcliff Manor, N.Y. : Directions Simplified, inc., c1976. 258 p. : ill. ; 23 cm. (Easi-bild home improvement library ; 761) [TT195.B68] 74-24602 ISBN 0-87733-761-6 pbk. : 3.50 ISBN 0-87733-061-1 lib.bdg. :
1. Furniture making—Amateurs' manuals. 2. Furniture, Colonial. I. Title. BIP

BRANN, Donald R. 645'.4'0202
How to build contemporary furniture, by Donald R. Brann. Briarcliff Manor, N.Y., Directions Simplified [1967] c1966. 50 p. (p. 47-50 advertisements) illus., plans. 23 cm. (Easi-bild simplified directions, 667) [TT195.B69] 66-30644 1.00
1. Furniture making—Amateurs' manuals. I. Title. II. Title: Contemporary furniture.

BRANN, Donald R. 684.1'002'02
How to build family room furniture, by Donald R. Brann. Briarcliff Manor, N.Y., Directions Simplified [1967] c1965. 50 p. (p. 48-50 advertisements) illus., plans. 23 cm. (Easi-bild simplified directions, 661) [TT195.B7] 65-27231 1.00
1. Furniture making—Amateurs' manuals. I. Title. II. Title: Family room furniture.

BRANN, Donald R. 684.1'8
How to build outdoor furniture / Donald R. Brann. Briarcliff Manor, N.Y. : Directions Simplified, c1976. 130 p., [1] fold. leaf of plates : ill. ; 23 cm. (Easi-Bild home improvement library ; 754) (Easi-bild simplified directions) [TT197.5.O9B7] 76-14045 ISBN 0-87733-754-3 pbk. : 3.50
1. Furniture making—Amateurs' manuals. 2. Outdoor furniture. I. Title. II. Title: Outdoor furniture. BIP

BRANN, Donald R. 684.08'028
How to build three workbenches, by Donald R. Brann. Briarcliff Manor, N.Y., Directions Simplified [1967] c1966. 50 p. (p. 47-50 advertisements) illus., plans. 23 cm. (Easi-bild simplified directions, 672) On cover: How to build workbenches. Published in 1972 under title: How to build workbenches. [TT197.5.T3B7] 66-30452 1.00
1. Furniture making—Amateurs' manuals. 2. Workbenches. 3. Workshops—Equipment and supplies. I. Title. II. Title: Workbenches.

CLEAVER, Diane. 684.1'042
The box book; the world's cheapest way to build furniture. Written & illustrated by Diane Cleaver. New York, McKay [1974] xiv, 114 p. illus. 24 cm. [TT195.C55] 73-84064 ISBN 0-679-50417-6 4.95
1. Furniture making—Amateurs' manuals. I. Title.

DAL Fabbro, Mario, 1913- 684.1*
How to build modern furniture. 2d ed. New York, F. W. Dodge Corp. [1957] 214 p. illus. 26 cm. [TS880.D312] 57-9273
1. Furniture making—Amateurs' manuals. I. Title.

DAL Fabbro, Mario, 1913- 684.1
How to build modern furniture / Mario Dal Fabbro. 3d. ed. New York : McGraw-Hill, c1976. vii, 211 p. : ill. ; 25 cm. Includes index. [TT195.D34 1976] 75-31916 ISBN 0-07-015185-7 : 7.50
1. Furniture making—Amateurs' manuals. I. Title.

DANIELE, Joseph William. 684.1'042'0973
Building early American furniture [by] Joseph W. Daniele. [Harrisburg, Pa.] Stackpole Books [1974] 253 p. illus. 29 cm. (An Early American society book) [TT195.D36] 74-10953
1. Furniture making—Amateurs' manuals. 2. Furniture, American. I. Title. BIP

DE CRISTOFORO, R. J. 684.1'042
How to build your own furniture / by R. J. DeCristoforo. 2d ed., rev. and updated. New York : Book Division, Times Mirror Magazines : [distributed by] Harper and Row, 1976. 176 p. : ill. ; 23 cm. (Popular science skill book) Includes index. [TT195.D4 1976] 76-382773 ISBN 0-06-011782-6 pbk. : 3.50
1. Furniture making—Amateurs' manuals. I. Title.

DOTY, Roy, 1922- 684.1'04
Wordless workshop, illustrated by Roy Doty. Selected by Harry Walton. New York, Taplinger Pub. Co. [1967] 127 p. (chiefly illus.) 24 cm. "Complete, simple, picture-by-picture instructions for making over 50 household helps." [TT195.D6] 66-12947
1. Furniture making—Amateur's manuals. I. Walton, Harry, ed. II. Title. BIP

GOTTSHALL, Franklin H. 745.213
How to make colonial furniture [by] Franklin H. Gottshall. Photos. by Bruce H. Gottshall. New York, Bruce Pub. Co. [1971] 182 p. illus. 32 cm. [TT195.G67] 77-132460 9.95
1. Furniture making—Amateurs' manuals. 2. Furniture, American. I. Title. BIP

GOTTSHALL, Franklin H. 684.1'042
Masterpiece furniture making / Franklin H. Gottshall. Harrisburg, Pa. : Stackpole Books, c1979. p. cm. (An Early American Society book) Includes index. [TT195.G675 1979] 79-12 ISBN 0-8117-0974-4 : 17.95
1. Furniture making—Amateurs' manuals. I. Title. BIP

GOTTSHALL, Franklin H. 684.1'042
Reproducing antique furniture [by] Franklin H. Gottshall. New York, Crown [1971] xiv, 240 p. illus. (part col.) 31 cm. [TT195.G68 1971] 76-147339 9.95
1. Furniture making—Amateurs' manuals. I. Title. BIP

HAGERTY, Francis W. 749
Make your own antiques / by Francis W. Hagerty. 1st ed. Boston : Little, Brown, [1975] xii, 113 p. : ill. ; 28 cm. Bibliography: p. 113. [TT195.H33] 75-19448 ISBN 0-316-33783-8 pbk. : 5.95
1. Furniture making—Amateurs' manuals. 2. Furniture, Colonial—United States. I. Title. BIP

HEDDEN, Jay W. 684.1'042
Making Mediterranean furniture, by Jay W. Hedden and Monte Burch. Drawings by John Chaisson. New York, Arco [1973] xi, 110 p. illus. 25 cm. [TT195.H43] 72-3336 ISBN 0-668-02654-5 7.50
1. Furniture making—Amateurs' manuals. I. Burch, Monte, joint author. II. Title. BIP

HENNESSEY, James. 684.1
Nomadic furniture 2, by James Hennessey and Victor Papanek, with many easy-to-follow diagrams, photographs & drawings by the authors. [1st ed.] New York, Pantheon Books [1974] 153 p. illus. 28 cm. At head of title: More about how to build and where to buy lightweight furniture that folds, collapses, stacks, knocks down, inflates, or can be thrown away but recycled. Being both a book of instruction and a catalog of access for easy moving. [TT195.H47] 73-18725 ISBN 0-394-48563-7 8.95; 5.95 (pbk.)
1. Furniture making—Amateurs' manuals. 2. Furniture—Catalogs. I. Papanek, Victor J., joint author. II. Title.

HENNESSEY, James. 684.1
Nomadic furniture: how to build and where to buy lightweight furniture that folds, collapses, stacks, knocks-down, inflates or can be thrown away and recycled. Being both a book of instruction and a catalog of access for easy moving, by

James Hennessey & Victor Papanek. [1st ed.] New York, Pantheon Books [1973] 149 p. illus. 28 cm. [TT195.H145] 72-3412 3.95
1. Furniture making—Amateurs' manuals. 2. Furniture—Catalogs. I. Papanek, Victor J., joint author. II. Title.

HODGES, Lewis H. 684.1'042
66 weekend wood furniture projects / by Lewis H. Hodges. 1st ed. Blue Ridge Summit, Pa. : Tab Books, 1978. 373 p. : ill. ; 22 cm. Includes index. [TT195.H6] 77-11402 ISBN 0-8306-7974-X : 10.95. ISBN 0-8306-6974-4 pbk. : 6.95
1. Furniture making—Amateurs' manuals. I. Title.

ISAACS, Ken. 684.1'04
How to build your own living structures / Ken Isaacs. New York : Harmony Books, [1974] 136 p. : ill. ; 21 x 31 cm. [TT195.18 1974] 72-96651 Pbk. : 4.95
1. Furniture making—Amateurs' manuals. 2. House construction—Amateurs' manuals. 3. Woodwork. I. Title. BIP

KRAMER, Jack, 1927- 684.1'042
Fold-away furniture / by Jack Kramer ; designs by Adrian Martinez. New York : Cornerstore Library, c1978. 127 p. : ill. ; 28 cm. [TT195.K72] 78-112289 ISBN 0-346-12341-0 : 4.95
1. Furniture making—Amateurs' manuals. I. Martinez, Adrian. II. Title. BIP

LABARGE, Lura. 684.1'04
Crate craft : easy-to-make furniture and accessories you can build quickly and inexpensively / by Lura LaBarge ; ill. and diagrs. by Lura LaBarge ; projects built by George W. Beierle. New York : Butterick Pub., c1976. 197 p. : ill. ; 23 cm. [TT195.L3] 76-9185 ISBN 0-88421-053-7 : 5.95
1. Furniture making—Amateurs' manuals. I. Title. BIP

MAGUIRE, Byron W., 1931- 684.1'04
Simple furniture making and refinishing / Byron W. Maguire. Reston, Va. : Reston Pub. Co., c1977. xi, 372 p. : ill. ; 24 cm. Includes index. [TT195.M33] 77-503 ISBN 0-87909-765-5 : 13.95
1. Furniture making—Amateurs' manuals. 2. Furniture finishing. I. Title. BIP

MARGON, Lester. 684.1'042
Construction of American furniture treasures : measured drawings of selected museum pieces with complete information on their construction and reproduction ... 38 full-page plates, 344 detail drawings and more than 40 photographs of the work of the most famous early American cabinetmakers / by Lester Margon. Corrected republication. New York : Dover Publications, 1975. 168 p. : ill. ; 29 cm. Includes index. [TT195.M353 1975] 74-79937 ISBN 0-486-23056-2 pbk. : 4.00
1. Furniture making—Amateurs' manuals. 2. Furniture, American. I. Title. BIP

MARLOW, Andrew W. 684.1'04
Classic furniture projects / A. W. Marlow. New York : Stein and Day, 1977. 210 p. : ill. ; 25 cm. [TT195.M359] 76-54800 ISBN 0-8128-2184-X : 12.95
1. Furniture making—Amateurs' manuals. I. Title. BIP

MARLOW, Andrew W. 684.1'04'0973
The early American furniture-maker's manual [by] A. W. Marlow. New York, Macmillan [1973] 130 p. illus. 26 cm. [TT195.M36] 72-91257 7.95
1. Furniture making—Amateurs' manuals. 2. Furniture, American. I. Title. BIP

MARLOW, Andrew W. 684.1'04
Fine furniture for the amateur cabinetmaker / by A. W. Marlow ; photography by I. B. Warner. New York : Stein and Day, 1977, c1955. 200 p. : ill. ; 28 cm. "A Scarborough book." Reprint of the ed. published by Macmillan, New York. [TT195.M364 1977] 77-151252 ISBN 0-8128-2250-1 : 4.95
1. Furniture making—Amateurs' manuals. 2. Cabinet-work. I. Title.

MEILACH, Dona Z. 684.1
Creating modern furniture : trends, techniques; appreciation / by Dona Z. Meilach ; consultant, Lawrence B. Hunter. New York : Crown Publishers, [1975] vii, 310 p. : ill. ; 27 cm. (Crown's arts and crafts series) Includes index. Bibliography: p. 301-303. [TT195.M44 1975] 75-12759 ISBN 0-517-51609-8 : 10.95 ISBN 0-517-52461-9 pbk. : 5.95
1. Furniture making—Amateurs' manuals. I. Title. BIP

MOSER, Thomas. 684.1'042'0974
How to build Shaker furniture / Thos. Moser ; with measured drawings by Christian Becksvoort. New York : Drake, 1977. ix, 209 p. : ill. ; 28 cm. Bibliography: p. 205-[207] [TT195.M67] 76-46809 ISBN 0-8473-1493-6 : 14.95 ISBN 0-8473-1468-5 pbk. : 6.95
1. Furniture making—Amateurs' manuals. 2. Furniture, Shaker. I. Becksvoort, Christian. II. Title. BIP

PETERSON, Franklynn. 684.1'04
The build-it-yourself furniture catalog / Franklynn Peterson ; [line drawings by Jack Hearne]. Englewood Cliffs, N.J. : Prentice-Hall, c1976. 308 p. : ill. ; 24 cm. Includes index. [TT195.P47] 76-6567 ISBN 0-13-085910-9 : 9.95
1. Furniture making—Amateurs' manuals. I. Title. BIP

PROPER, Churchill H. 684.1
Furniture and accessories, by Churchill H. Proper. Illustrated by the author. Charlotteville, N.Y., Story House Corp., 1971. 32 p. illus. 22 cm. (Handicraft series) [TT195.P76] 76-185671
1. Furniture making—Amateurs' manuals. 2. Handicraft. I. Title. BIP

PROVEY, Joseph. 684.1
Systems of living space / Joseph Provey. Chicago : H. Regnery Co., c1976. p. cm. [TT195.P77] 76-6280 ISBN 0-8092-8097-3 : 10.00 pbk. : 4.95
1. Furniture making—Amateurs' manuals. I. Title.

SCHUTZE, Rolf. 684.1'04
Making modern Danish furniture. Rev. ed. New York, Van Nostrand Reinhold Co. [1973] 112 p. illus. 23 cm. Translation of Moderne mobelslojd. [TT195.S3713 1973] 72-9725 ISBN 0-442-29976-1 4.95
1. Furniture making—Amateurs' manuals. 2. Furniture, Danish. I. Title.

SCHUTZE, Rolf. 684.1'04
Making modern furniture. New York, Reinhold [1967] 95 p. illus. 23 cm. ([Reinhold Scandinavian craft series]) [TT197.S42] 66-24548
1. Furniture making—Amateurs' manuals. I. Title.

SHEA, John Gerald. 684.1'042
Anatomy of contemporary furniture [by] John G. Shea. [Rev. ed.] New York, Van Nostrand Reinhold [1973] vii, 191 p. illus. 29 cm. First published in 1965 under title: Contemporary furniture making for everybody. Bibliography: p. 188. [TT195.S5 1973] 73-6684 ISBN 0-442-27543-9 12.95
1. Furniture making—Amateurs' manuals. I. Title.

WINDSOR, Henry Haven, 1859-1924. 684.1'04
Mission furniture : how to make it / H. H. Windsor. Santa Barbara : P. Smith, 1976. 120 p. : ill. ; 28 cm. An abridged version of the ed. first published 1909-1912. [TT195.W56 1976] 76-16090 ISBN 0-87905-064-0 pbk. : 5.95
1. Furniture making—Amateurs' manuals. I. Title. BIP

ZAKAS, Spiros. 684.1
Furniture in 24 hours / Spiros Zakas and his students at Parsons School of Design ; photos. by David Cox and Boguslaw Kapusto. 1st Collier Bks. ed. New York : Collier Books, 1976. xiii, 128 p. : illus. ; 28 cm. [TT195.Z34 1976] 76-21870 ISBN 0-02-633390-2 : 10.00
1. Furniture making—Amateurs' manuals. I. Parsons School of Design, New York. II. Title.

ZAKAS, Spiros. 684.1
More furniture in 24 hours / by Spiros Zakas and his students at Parsons School of Design. New York : St. Martin's Press, [1978] p. cm. [TT195.Z35] 78-3989 ISBN 0-312-54803-6 : 10.95. ISBN 0-312-54804-4 pbk. : 5.95
1. Furniture making—Amateurs' manuals. I. Parsons School of Design, New York. II. Title. BIP

Furniture making and trade—United States—History.

DUNBAR, Michael. 684.1'3
Windsor chairmaking / by Michael Dunbar ; photos. by Eric White. New York : Hastings House, c1976. 153 p. : ill. ; 24 cm. Includes index. Bibliography: p. 149. [TS886.5.C45D86] 75-40499 ISBN 0-8038-8077-4 : 9.95
1. Furniture making and trade—United States—History. 2. Chair-makers—United States. 3. Furniture making—Amateurs' manuals. I. Title. BIP

Furniture—Middle West.

SEMPLE, Marlene. 749.2'17'075
Introductory guide to Midwest antiques / by Marlene Semple. Matteson, Ill. : Greatlakes Living Press, 1977, c1976 192 p. : ill. ; 22 cm. Includes index. Bibliography: p. 185-186. [NK2410.5.S45] 75-41638 ISBN 0-915498-17-0 : 5.95
1. Furniture—Middle West. 2. Antiques—Middle West. I. Title. BIP

Furniture—Models.

GEE, Kenneth F. 745.5923
Make your own dolls' house furniture. [label: Boston, C. T. Branford Co., 1959] 80p. illus. 19cm. 60-116 2.00 bds.,
1. Furniture—Models. 2. Doll-houses. I. Title. II. Title: Dolls' house furniture.

Furniture, Mormon—Utah.

MORNINGSTAR, Connie, 1927- 749.2'192
Early Utah furniture / Connie Morningstar. Logan, Utah : Utah State University Press, 1976. p. cm. Includes index. [NK2435.U8M67] 76-29637 ISBN 0-87421-088-7 : 9.95
1. Furniture, Mormon—Utah. 2. Furniture—Utah. 3. Cabinet-workers—Utah—Directories. I. Title. BIP

Furniture—Netherlands—History—20th century.

BARONI, Daniele. 749.2'9492
The furniture of Gerrit Thomas Rietveld / Daniele Baroni. 1st U.S. ed. Woodbury, N.Y. : Barron's, 1978, c1977. 178 p. : ill. (some col.) ; 23 x 25 cm. Translation of I mobili di Gerrit Thomas Rietveld. Bibliography: p. 175-178. [NK2570.R43B3713 1977] 77-17883 ISBN 0-8120-5201-3 : 13.95
1. Rietveld, Gerrit Thomas, 1888-1964. 2. Furniture—Netherlands—History—20th century. I. Title. BIP

Furniture—New Brunswick.

RYDER, Huia Gwendoline, 1904- 749.2'115
Antique furniture by New Brunswick craftsmen [by] Huia G. Ryder. Toronto, New York, McGraw-Hill Ryerson [1973, c1965] xii, 180 p. illus. 23 cm. Bibliography: p. 172-173. [NK2441.R9 1973] 74-155372 ISBN 0-07-092979-3
1. Furniture—New Brunswick. 2. Furniture—Collectors and collecting. 3. Cabinet-workers—New Brunswick. I. Title.

Furniture—New Brunswick—Saint John—Catalogs.

NEW Brunswick Museum. 749.2'115'074011532
Heritage furniture = Le mobilier traditionnel : a catalogue featuring selected heritage furniture from the collection of the New Brunswick Museum = catalogue de meubles anciens choisis parmi les collections du Musee du Nouveau-Brunswick / edited, with an introd. by A. Gregg Finley ; photography ... by Don Simpson. Saint John, N.B. : New Brunswick Museum, 1976. 63 p. : chiefly ill. (some col.) ; 26 cm. (NBM collection catalogue ; 2) English and French. Bibliography: p. 60-61. [NK2441.N48 1976] 77-559484
1. New Brunswick Museum. 2. Furniture—New Brunswick—Saint John—Catalogs. I. Finley, A. Gregg. II. Title. III. Title: Le mobilier traditionnel. IV. Series: New Brunswick Museum. NBM collection catalogue ; 2.

Furniture—New England.

KETTELL, Russell Hawes. 749.2'14
The pine furniture of early New England / Russell Hawes Kettell. New York : Dover Publications, [1975?] c1929. ca. 500 p. : 284 ill. ; 29 cm. Reprint of the ed. published by Doubleday, New York. Includes bibliography. [NK2410.K4 1975] 75-19008 ISBN 0-486-20145-7
1. Furniture—New England. I. Title. BIP

Furniture—New England—Catalogs.

COLONIAL Williamsburg Foundation. 749.2'1'407401554252
New England furniture at Williamsburg; [catalog] by Barry A. Greenlaw. Abridged ed. Williamsburg, Va. [1974] [20] p. illus. 23 cm. (The Williamsburg decorative arts series) [NK2410.C64 1974] 74-18017 ISBN 0-87935-022-9 1.25
1. Furniture—New England—Catalogs. 2. Furniture—Williamsburg, Va.—Catalogs. I. Greenlaw, Barry A. II. Title. III. Series. BIP

Furniture—New Jersey.

NEWARK Museum Association, Newark, N. J. 749.21
Early furniture made in New Jersey, 1690-1870; an exhibition, October 10, 1958--January 11, 1959, the Newark Museum, Newark, New Jersey. [Newark] c1958. 89p. illus. 26cm. Includes bibliography. [NK2435.N5N4] 58-45883
1. Furniture—New Jersey.SFurniture—Exhibitions. I. Title.

Furniture—New South Wales—History.

CRAIG, Clifford. 749.2'9944
Early colonial furniture in New South Wales and Van Diemen's Land [by] Clifford Craig, Kevin Fahy [and] E. Graeme Robertson. Melbourne, Georgian House, 1972. viii, 220 p. illus. 28 cm. Illus. on lining papers. Bibliography: p. 213-215. [NK2690.N49C72] 73-155736 ISBN 0-85585-486-3 30.00
1. Furniture—New South Wales—History. 2. Furniture—Tasmania—History. I. Fahy, Kevin, joint author. II. Robertson, Edward Graeme, joint author. III. Title.

Furniture—New York (City)

NEW York. Museum of the City of New York. 749.211
Furniture by New York cabinet makers, 1500 to 1860 exhibition] November 15, 1956 to March 3, 1957. V. Isabelle Miller, curator of furniture. [New York, 1956] 84p. illus. 24cm. [NK2438.N4N4] 57-53
1. Furniture—New York (City) 2. Furniture, American—Exhibitions. I. Miller, V. Isabelle. II. Title.

Furniture—New York (State)

ALBANY Institute of History and Art. 749.2147
New York furniture before 1840 in the collection of the Albany Institute of History and Art. [Albany, N.Y., Author, 125 Washington Ave., c.1962] 63p. illus. 26cm. (Cogswell Fund ser., pubn. no. 2) Bibl. 62-1917 2.50 pap.,
1. Furniture—New York (State) I. Title.

Furniture—North Carolina—Exhibitions.

DAY, Thomas, ca.1801-ca.1861. 749.2'13
Thomas Day, cabinetmaker : an exhibition at the North Carolina Museum of History, Raleigh, North Carolina, 1975. Raleigh : [North Carolina Museum of History, Dept. of Cultural Resources], c1975. 75 p. : ill. ;

31 cm. Includes bibliographical references. [NK2439.D38N67] 76-351668
1. Day, Thomas, ca.1801-ca. 1861. 2. Furniture—North Carolina—Exhibitions. I. North Carolina Museum of History.

Furniture—North Carolina—History—18th century—Exhibitions.

NORTH 749.2'156'074015655
Carolina Museum of History.
North Carolina furniture, 1700-1900 : [exhibition, October 17-December 31, 1977 / edited by Robert E. Winters, Jr. Raleigh : North Carolina Museum of History, Division of Archives and History, Dept. of Cultural Resources, c1977. xiii, 77 p. : ill. ; 28 cm. Includes bibliographical references. [NK2435.N8N67 1977] 77-14718
1. Furniture—North Carolina—History—18th century—Exhibitions. 2. Furniture—North Carolina—History—19th century—Exhibitions. I. Winters, Robert E. II. Title.

Furniture—Pennsylvania.

GAMON, Albert T. 749.2148
Pennsylvania country antiques [by] Albert T. Gamon. Englewood Cliffs, N.J., Prentice-Hall [1968] 189 p. illus. 26 cm. Bibliography: p. 185-186. [NK2435.P4G3] 68-14999
1. Furniture—Pennsylvania. 2. Furniture—Collectors and collecting. I. Title.

Furniture—Period.

NEW furniture. 745.058
[v.5] Edited by Gerd Hatje New York, Praeger [1960] 162p. illus. 30cm. 53-35419 10.00
1. Furniture— Period. I. Hatje, Gerd, ed.

NEW furniture. 745.058
Neue Mobel. Meubles nouveaux [v.] 7. New York, Praeger [c.1964] 162p. illus. 30cm. 53-35419 12.50
1. Furniture—Period. I. Hatje, Gerd, ed.

NEW furniture. 745.058
Neue mobel. Meubles nouveaux. Muebles modernos [Text: Michel Mortier. Translator into German: Christine Hereth. Translator into Spanish: Horacio Crespo] New York, Praeger [c.1962] 155p. 30cm. annual. 53-35419 12.50
1. Furniture—Period.

NEW furniture. Neue 745.058
Mobel.
Meublesmodernos. [v.] 8. New York, Praeger [1966] 152p. illus. 30cm. Eds.: v.8-G. Hatje, K. Kaspar. [NK2200.N49] 53-35419 12.50
1. Furniture—Period. I. Hatje, Gerd, ed. II. Kaspar, K., ed. III. Title.

Furniture, Portuguese.

SANDAO, Arthur de 749.269
O movel pintado em Portugal [por] Arthur de Sandao. [Porto], Livraria Civilizacao, [1966] Stamped on t.p.: Amer. dist.: Wittenborn, New York. 249p. plates (pt. col.) facsims., ports. 32cm. Summary in French, English, and German. Bibl. [NK2603.S2 1966] 67-5803 42.50
1. Furniture, Portuguese. 2. Decoration and ornament, Portuguese. I. Title.

Furniture — Repairing.

ALBERS, Vernon Martin, 684.1'044
1902-
The repair and reupholstering of old furniture [by] Vernon M. Albers. Large type ed. South Brunswick, N.J. A. S. Barnes [1974, c1969] 102 p. illus. 22 cm. [TT199.A5] 69-13029 ISBN 0-498-01597-1 5.95
1. Furniture—Repairing. I. Title. BIP

ALBERS, Vernon Martin, 684.1'044
1902-
The repair and reupholstering of old furniture [by] Vernon M. Albers. New York, Barnes & Noble, a divn. of Harper [1972, c.1969] 104 p. illus. 21 cm. (Everyday handbooks, EH336) [TT199.A5] pap., 1.75
1. Furniture—Repairing. I. Title.

ALCOUFFE, Daniel. 684.1'044
The restorer's handbook of furniture / Daniel Alcouffe. New York : Van Nostrand Reinhold Co., [1977] p. cm. Translation of Restauration du mobilier. Includes index. Bibliography: p. [TT199.A5213] 77-5589 ISBN 0-442-20281-4 : 22.50
1. Furniture—Repairing. I. Title. BIP

BERGER, Robert, 684.1'044
1933(July8)-
All about antiquing and restoring furniture. New York, Hawthorn Books [1971] viii, 181 p. illus. 24 cm. [TT199.B47] 77-130711 5.95
1. Furniture—Repairing. 2. Furniture finishing. I. Title.

BRANN, Donald R. 684.1
How to repair and reupholster furniture, by Donald R. Brann. Briarcliff Manor, N.Y., Directions Simplified [1967] c1966. 49, [1] p. (p. 44-[50] advertisements) illus., plans. 23 cm. (Easi-bild simplified directions, 623) [TT199.B6] 66-27694 0.75
1. Furniture—Repairing. 2. Upholstery. I. Title.

BRANN, Donald R. 684.1'044
How to repair, refinish, and reupholster furniture / by Donald R. Brann. 8th print., rev. ed. Braircliff Manor, N.Y. : Directions Simplified, 1976. 97 p. (p. 91-97 advertisements) : ill. ; 23 cm. (Esai-bild simplified directions ; 623) Edition for 1967 (c1966) published under title: How to repair and reupholster furniture. [TT199.B7 1976] 76-362199 ISBN 0-87733-623-7 pbk. : 2.00
1. Furniture—Repairing. 2. Upholstery. I. Title.

CARRELL, Al. 684.1'044
Super handyman's fix and finish furniture guide / Al Carrell. Englewood Cliffs, N.J. : Prentice-Hall, [1975] xi, 180 p. : ill. ; 24 cm. Includes index. [TT199.C37] 74-22216 ISBN 0-13-875997-9 : 7.95
1. Furniture—Repairing. 2. Furniture finishing. I. Title. BIP

DAVIS, Kenneth. 684.1'044
Restoring furniture / Kenneth Davis and Thom Henvey ; [ill., David Parr]. New York : Arco Pub. Co., c1978. 112 p. : col. ill. ; 30 cm. Bibliography: p. 111. [TT199.D38] 77-11401 ISBN 0-668-04545-0 : 16.95
1. Furniture—Repairing. I. Henvey, Thom, joint author. II. Title. BIP

FAREWELL, William Henry, 684.1
1898-
Easy does it furniture restoration, the Vermont way. Rutland, Vt., C. E. Tuttle Co. [1962] 41 p. illus. 23 cm. [TT199.F3] 62-53470
1. Furniture—Repairing. I. Title. BIP

FURNITURE care & refinishing 684.1
/ [editorial director, Allen D. Bragdon ; text editor, Tim Snyder]. Los Angeles : Petersen Pub. Co., c1977. 95 p. : ill. ; 28 cm. (Petersen home repair and maintenance guides) Includes index. [TT199.F77] 77-76139 ISBN 0-8227-8006-2 pbk. : 2.95
1. Furniture—Repairing. 2. Furniture finishing. I. Bragdon, Allen D. II. Snyder, Tim. III. Petersen Publishing Company.

GROTZ, George. 684.1
The furniture doctor, being practical information for everybody about the care, repair, and refinishing of furniture, with easy to follow directions and tricks of the trade that use commonly available materials, all presented with the author's usual hilarious anecdotes in the Yankee manner and more about his infamous Uncle George. [1st ed.] Garden City, N.Y., Doubleday, 1962. 286 p. illus. 22 cm. [TS885.G7] 62-7640
1. Furniture—Repairing. I. Title.

HAYWARD, Charles 684.1'044
Harold, 1898-
Antique furniture repairs / Charles H. Hayward. New York : Scribner, c1976. 128 p. : ill. ; 22 cm. Published in 1967 under title: Furniture repairs. Includes index. [TT199.H3 1976b] 76-5223 ISBN 0-684-14720-3 : 7.95
1. Furniture—Repairing. I. Title. BIP

HAYWARD, Charles 684.1'044
Harold, 1898-
Furniture repairs [by] Charles H. Hayward. Princeton, N.J., Van Nostrand [1967] 191 p. illus. 22 cm. ([A Woodworker handbook]) [TT199.H3 1967b] 70-858
1. Furniture—Repairing. I. Title. II. Series: Woodworker handbooks

HILTS, Leonard Finley. 684.1
Popular Mechanics complete book of furniture / by Len Hilts ; consulting editor, W. Clyde Lammey. New York : Book Division, Hearst Corp., c1976. 320 p. : ill. ; 24 cm. Includes index. [TT199.H54] 75-23587 ISBN 0-910990-62-X : 8.95
1. Furniture—Repairing. 2. Furniture finishing. 3. Upholstery. I. Title. II. Title: Complete book of furniture. BIP

HOCHMAN, Louis. 684.1
How to refinish furniture. Greenwich, Conn., Fawcett Publications, c1954. 144p. illus. 24cm. (A Fawcett book, no. 236) [TT199.H6] 54-39048
1. Furniture—Repairing. I. Title.

HOCHMAN, Louis. 684.1
How to refinish furniture. New York, Arco Pub. Co. [1954] 144p. illus. 26cm. (Arco handi-books for better living) Originally published as Fawcett book no. 236. [TT199] 54-9246
1. Furniture—Repairing. I. Title.

KINNEY, Ralph Parsons. 684
The complete book of furniture repair and refinishing; easy to follow guide with step-by-step methods. New York, Scribner [1950] xii, 240 p. illus. 25 cm. Bibliography: p. 229-230. [TT199.K5] 50-9191
1. Furniture—Repairing. BIP

KUHN, H. W. 645
How-to refinish furniture. Greenwich, Conn., Fawcett Publications, c1963. 112 p. illus. 24 cm. (A Fawcett book, no 550) [TT199.K8] 64-2083
1. Furniture — Repairing. 2. Wood finishing. I. Title. BIP

MEYERS, L. Donald, 684.1'044
1929-
The furniture lover's book : finding, fixing, finishing / L. Donald Meyers. 1st ed. New York : Dutton, c1977. 239 p. : ill. ; 27 cm. "A Sunrise book." Includes index. [TT199.M44 1977] 76-54882 ISBN 0-87690-234-4 : 12.95
1. Furniture—Repairing. 2. Furniture finishing. I. Title.

MEYERS, L. Donald, 684.1'044
1929-
Furniture repair and refinishing [by] L. Donald Meyers [and] Richard Demske. Reston, Va., Reston Pub. Co. [1974] viii, 261 p. illus. 24 cm. [TT199.M45] 74-8485 ISBN 0-87909-273-4 9.95
1. Furniture—Repairing. 2. Furniture finishing. I. Demske, Richard, 1930- joint author. II. Title. BIP

NUNN, Richard V. 684.1'044
Furniture repair & refinishing / by Richard V. Nunn and Beverly J. Nunn. Birmingham, Ala. : Oxmoor House, 1975. 96 p. : ill. ; 28 cm. (Family guidebook series) Includes index. [TT199.N86] 75-2876 1.95
1. Furniture—Repairing. 2. Furniture finishing. I. Nunn, Beverly J., joint author. II. Title. BIP

RODD, John. 684.1
The repair and restoration of furniture. New York, Scribner, 1955. 179p. illus. 26cm. [TS885] 55-13689
1. Furniture—Repairing. I. Title.

RODD, John. 684.1'044
Restoring and repairing antique furniture / John Rodd. New York : Van Nostrand Reinhold Co., 1976. 240 p. : ill. ; 26 cm. Includes index. [TT199.R62] 75-37898 ISBN 0-442-26970-6 : 11.95
1. Furniture—Repairing. 2. Furniture finishing. 3. Furniture—Collectors and collecting. I. Title.

ROWLAND, Tom. 684.1'044
Restoring and renovating antique furniture / [by] Tom Rowland ; with drawings by Ronald Reeves. London : Luscombe, 1976. 172 p. : ill. ; 23 cm. Includes index. [TT199.R68 1976] 76-373167 ISBN 0-86002-085-1 : £4.95
1. Furniture—Repairing. 2. Furniture finishing. I. Title. BIP

SPURLOCK, Julia 749
The homemaker's guide to refinishing and restoring antiques (formerly entitled: Pass thy hand for the finishing touch) New York, Cornerstone [1967, c.1965] 191p. illus. 21cm. (Cornerstone lib., CN131) [TT325.S65] 1.00 pap.,
1. Furniture—Repairing. 2. Wood finishing. I. Title.

SPURLOCK, Julia. 749
The homemaker's guide to refinishing and restoring antiques = formerly entitled Pass thy hand for the finishing touch / by Julia Spurlock. New York : Galahad Books, [1974] c1965. 191 p. : ill. ; 22 cm. Includes index. [TT199.4.S69 1974] 73-91803 ISBN 0-88365-034-7 : 5.00
1. Furniture—Repairing. 2. Furniture finishing. I. Title.

WENN, Leslie. 684.1'044
The complete book of restoring old furniture. New York, Drake Publishers [1973] p. [TT199.W45] 73-5571 ISBN 0-87749-519-X 6.95
1. Furniture—Repairing. 2. Furniture finishing. I. Title.

WENN, Leslie. 684.1'044
Restoring antique furniture / Leslie Wenn ; with an historical introd. by Martin Drury. New York : Watson-Guptill, [1975] c1974. p. cm. Includes index. [TT199.W46 1975] 75-4542 ISBN 0-8230-4546-3 : 9.95
1. Furniture—Repairing. I. Title. BIP

Furniture—Repairing—Amateurs' manuals.

BLANDFORD, Percy W. 684.1'044
Do-it-yourselfer's guide to furniture repair & refinishing / by Percy Blandford. 1st ed. Blue Ridge Summit, Pa. : G. L. Tab Books, c1977 321 p. : ill. ; 22 cm. Includes index. [TT199.B55] 77-5552 ISBN 0-8306-7894-8 : 9.95. ISBN 0-8306-6894-2 pbk. : 5.95
1. Furniture—Repairing—Amateurs' manuals. 2. Furniture finishing—Amateurs' manuals. I. Title. BIP

JOHNSON, Lorraine. 643'7
How to restore, repair, and finish almost everything / Lorraine Johnson. New York : Macmillan, c1977. p. cm. [TT199.J63] 77-8135 13.95
1. Furniture—Repairing—Amateurs' manuals. 2. Furniture finishing—Amateurs' manuals. 3. Repairing—Amateurs' manuals. I. Title.

Furniture — Savannah.

THEUS, Mrs. Charlton 749.2158'724
M.
Savannah furniture, 1735-1825 [by] Mrs. Carlton M. Theus. [Savannah? 1967] xi, 100 p. illus. 21 cm. [NK2406.T45] 67-7031
1. Furniture — Savannah. 2. Cabinet-workers — Savannah. I. Title.

Furniture, Scandinavian.

HARD af Segerstad, Ulf. 749.28
Modern Scandinavian furniture. [English translation by Nancy and Edward Maze] [Totowa, N. J.] Bedminster Press [1963] 131 p. illus. (part col.) 26 cm. ([Svensk library series]) [NK2581.H3A53] 63-11354
1. Furniture, Scandinavian. I. Title.

Furniture, Shaker.

MEADER, Robert F. W. 749.2'14
Illustrated guide to Shaker furniture [by] Robert F. W. Meader. New York, Dover Publications [1972] ix, 128, 15 p. illus. 31 cm. [NK2406.M43] 74-164732 ISBN 0-486-22819-3 4.00
1. Furniture, Shaker. I. Title. BIP

SHEA, John Gerald. 749.213
The American Shakers and their furniture, with measured drawings of museum classics [by] John G. Shea. New York, Van Nostrand Reinhold Co. [1971] xv, 208 p. illus., facsims., maps (on lining papers) 29 cm. [NK2407.S5] 76-27593 12.95

SUBJECT INDEX FURNITURE—VIRGINIA—WILLIAMSBURG—HISTORY—18TH CENTURY.

1. Furniture, Shaker. 2. Shakers. I. Title.

Furniture, Shaker—New Hampshire—Exhibitions.

NEW Hampshire Historical Society. 749.2'2'074014272
True gospel simplicity : Shaker furniture in New Hampshire : an exhibition at the New Hampshire Historical Society, Concord, New Hampshire, 3 July 1974 to 30 September 1974. [Concord] : The Society, c1974. [32] p. : ill. ; 26 cm. [NK2435.N4N48 1974] 75-315617
1. Furniture, Shaker—New Hampshire—Exhibitions. I. Title. BIP

Furniture—Southern States—Hist.

ANTIQUES. 749.211
Southern furniture, 1640-1820; a loan exhibition presented in Richmond at the Virginia Museum of Fine Arts, January 21-March 1, 1952, under the sponsorship of the magazine Antiques, Colonial Williamsburg [and] the Virginia Museum. [New York?, 1952. 64p. illus. 32cm. 'Anniversary edition of Antiques.' [NK2414.A5] 53-2875
1. Furniture—Southern States—Hist. I. Virginia Museum of Fine Arts, Richmond. II. Title.

Furniture, Spanish.

BURR, Grace Hardendorff 749.26
Hispanic furniture, from the fifteenth through the eighteenth century. 2d ed., rev. and enl. New York, Archive Pr., 38 E. 57 St., 1964. xix, 231p. illus. 32cm. Bibl. [NK2599.B8] 64-22364 22.50
1. Furniture, Spanish. 2. Furniture—Spain—Hist. I. Title.

DOMENECH Gallissa, Rafael, 1874-1929. 749.26
Antique Spanish furniture. Muebles antiguos espanoles, by Rafael Domenech (Galissa) & Luis Perez Bueno. Translated from the Spanish by Grace Hardendorff Burr. Bilingual ed. [1st English ed.] New York, Archive Press, 1965. 142 p. 61 plates. 32 cm. [NK2600.D613] 64-25672
1. Furniture, Spanish. I. Perez Bueno, Luis, joint author. II. Title.

Furniture, Spanish American—New Mexico.

VEDDER, Alan C., 1912- 749.2'189
Furniture of Spanish New Mexico / Alan C. Vedder ; photography by David Donoho. 1st ed. Santa Fe, N.M. : Sunstone Press, 1977. 96 p. : ill. ; 29 cm. [NK2435.N6V43] 76-50322 ISBN 0-913270-67-9 : 12.95. ISBN 0-913270-66-0 pbk. : 8.95
1. Furniture, Spanish American—New Mexico. 2. Furniture, Colonial—New Mexico. I. Title. BIP

Furniture—Suffield, Conn.

BISSELL, Charles S 749.211
Antique furniture in Suffield, Connecticut, 1670-1835. [Hartford?] Connecticut Historical Society and Suffield Historical Society, 1956. ix, 128p. 61plates (incl. facsims.) 28cm. [NK2438.S8B5] 56-2826
1. Furniture—Suffield, Conn. 2. Furniture, American. 3. Cabinet-workers. I. Title.

Furniture—U. S.

AMERICAN furniture and its makers / edited by Ian M. G. Quimby. 749.2'13
Chicago : Published for the Henry Francis du Pont Winterthur Museum by the University of Chicago Press, 1979. xi, 244 p. : ill. ; 29 cm. (Winterthur portfolio ; 13) Includes bibliographical references and index. [N9.W52 vol. 13] [NK2405] 79-107207 ISBN 0-226-92139-5 : 20.00
1. Furniture—United States—History. 2. Cabinet-workers—United States—Registers, etc. 3. Furniture industry and trade—United States—History. I. Quimby, Ian M. G. II. Title. III. Series.

ANTIQUE furniture handbook. 749
[Watkins Glen, N. Y., Century House, 1950- v. illus. 22 cm. Title from spine;each vol. has special t. p. Contents.no. 1. Victorian furniture, by R. and L. Freeman. no. 11. Primitive pine furniture, by J. Lazeare. [NK2240.A5] 50-5184
1. Furniture—U. S. 2. Collectors and collecting. I. Freeman, Ruth (Sunderlin)

ANTIQUES. 749.213
The Antiques treasury of furniture and other decorative arts at Winterthur, Williamsburg, Sturbridge, Ford Museum, Cooperstown, Deefield [and] Shelburne. Edited by Alice Winchester and the staff of Antiques magazine. [1st ed.] New York, Dutton, 1959. 320p. illus. (part col.) 31cm. [NK806.A5] 59-12514
1. Furniture—U. S. 2. Art industries and trade—U. S. 3. Art—U. S. 4. Museums—U. S. I. Winchester, Alice, ed. II. Title.

BISHOP, Robert Charles. 749.2'13
Guide to American antique furniture / Robert Bishop. New York : Galahad Books, [1975?] c1973. 224 p., [6] leaves of plates : ill. ; 26 cm. "Formerly published under the title How to know American antique furniture." Includes index. Bibliography: p. 215-218. [NK2405.B57 1975] 75-9452 ISBN 0-88365-305-2 : 12.50
1. Furniture—United States. 2. Furniture—Collectors and collecting. I. Title.

CAMPBELL, Christopher M. 749.2'14'074017433
American Chippendale furniture, 1755-1790 / by Christopher M. Campbell Dearborn, Mich. : Greenfield Village & Henry Ford Museum, c1975. 44 p. : ill. ; 26 cm. Text on p. [3] of cover. [NK2406.C35] 76-353722
1. Furniture—United States. 2. Furniture, Colonial—United States. 3. Decoration and ornament—Chippendale style. I. Edison Institute (Henry Ford Museum and Greenfield Village) Dearborn, Mich. II. Title.

HAGLER, Katharine Bryant. 749.2'13
American Queen Anne furniture, 1720-1755 / by Katharine Bryant Hagler. Dearborn, Mich. : Greenfield Village & Henry Ford Museum, c1976. 52 p. : ill. ; 26 cm. [NK2406.H26] 76-377113
1. Furniture—United States. 2. Furniture, Colonial—United States. 3. Decorration and ornament—Queen Anne style. I. Edison Institute (Henry Ford Museum and Greenfield Village) Dearborn, Mich. II. Title.

JORDAN, Jerard. 749.2'13
The spirit of America : country furniture, 1700-1840 / by Jerard and Pat Jordan. Des Moines : Wallace-Homestead Book Co., c1975. 103 p. : ill. (some col.) ; 23 cm. [NK2406.J67] 75-325036 ISBN 0-87069-119-8 : 7.95
1. Furniture—United States. I. Jordan, Pat, 1942- joint author. II. Title.

LOCKWOOD, Luke Vincent, 1872-1951. 749.211
Colonial furniture in America. Vol. 1 and v. 2 complete. Supplementary chapters and 136 plates of new subjects have been added to this ed., which now includes over 1000 illus. of representative pieces. 3d ed. New York, Castle Books, 1957 [c1926] xxiv, 398, xx, 354p. illus. 29cm. Published by arrangement with Scribner; special t. p. for v. 2 has imprint: New York, Scribner, 1951. [NK2406.L8 1957] 58-2091
1. Furniture—U. S. I. Title.

MCCOBB, Paul. 749.213
Directional designs. [New York? Directional Furniture Showrooms, 1956] 111p. (chiefly illus., port.) 29cm. [NK2408.M2] 56-10272
1. Furniture—U.S. I. Title.

MILLER, Edgar George, 1864-1940. 749.211
The standard book of American antique furniture. New York, Greystone Press [1950] x, 856 p. illus. 29 cm. "Abridgment of the two-volume work, American antique furniture." [NK2406.M56 1950] 50-6480
1. Furniture—U.S. I. Title.

†MORNINGSTAR, Connie, 1927- 749.2'13
American furniture classics / by Connie Morningstar. Des Moines : Wallace-Homestead Book Co., c1976. iv, 180 p. : ill. (some col.) ; 29 cm. Includes index. Bibliography: p. 170-171. [NK2405.M67] 75-21327 ISBN 0-87069-133-3 : 9.95
1. Furniture—United States. I. Title. BIP

NATIONAL Association of Furniture Manufacturers. 749.213
Directory of furniture designers. Chicago [1956] 57p. 28cm. [NK2408.N3] 57-28085
1. Furniture—U. S. I. Title. II. Title: Furniture designers.

NUTTING, Wallace, 1861-1941. 749.21
Furniture treasury (mostly of American origin) All periods of American furniture with some foreign examples in America; also American hardware and household utensils. 5000 illus. with descriptions on the same page. New York, Macmillan, 1954 [c1948] 2 v. in 1. illus. 27 cm. [NK2406.N732 1954] A 55
1. Furniture—U.S. 2. Hardware—U.S. 3. Implements, utensils, etc.—U.S. 4. Clock and watch makers—U.S. 5. Clocks and watches. I. Title. BIP

SHACKLETON, Robert, 1860-1923. 749.213
The quest of the colonial [by] Robert and Elizabeth Shackleton. Illustrated with many photos and with decorations by Harry Fenn. Detroit, Singing Tree Press, 1970. ix, 425 p. illus. 22 cm. Reprint of the 1907 ed. [NK2406.S5 1970] 72-99075
1. Furniture—U.S. 2. Furniture—Collectors and collecting. I. Shackleton, Elizabeth (Fleming) 1871-1936, joint author. II. Title. BIP

SHEA, John Gerald. 749.2'1
Antique country furniture of North America / by John G. Shea. New York : Van Nostrand Reinhold Co., [1975] p. cm. Includes index. Bibliography: p. [NK2405.S47] 75-9118 ISBN 0-442-27544-7 : 16.95
1. Furniture—United States. 2. Antiques—United States. 3. Furniture—Canada. 4. Antiques—Canada. I. Title. BIP

SINGLETON, Esther, d.1930. 749.213
The furniture of our forefathers. With notes on the illus. by Russell Sturgis. Improved ed. New York, B. Blom, 1970. xxvi, 663 p. illus. 27 cm. [NK2406.S6 1970] 68-56505
1. Furniture—U.S. I. Sturgis, Russell, 1836-1909. II. Title. BIP

SPOONER, Ella Brown (Jackson) 1880- 749.21
Way back when; ideas wise and otherwise, and memories about American furniture. [1st ed.] New York, Exposition Press [1953] 118p. illus. 21cm. [NK2405.S66] 52-12347
1. Furniture—U. S. I. Title.

Furniture—United States—Collectors and collecting.

MARSH, Moreton. 749.2'14
The easy expert in American antiques : knowing, finding, buying, and restoring early American furniture / Moreton Marsh. New, rev. ed. Philadelphia : Lippincott, c1978. 282 p. : ill. ; 24 cm. First ed. (c1959) published under title: The easy expert in collecting and restoring American antiques. Includes index. Bibliography: p. 265-272. [NK2406.M395 1978] 78-9050 ISBN 0-397-01287-X : 12.95 ISBN 0-397-01288-8 pbk. : 6.95
1. Furniture—United States—Collectors and collecting. 2. Furniture, Colonial—United States—Collectors and collecting. 3. Furniture—Repairing. I. Title. BIP

Furniture—United States—History.

ORMSBEE, Thomas Hamilton, 1890- 749.211
Early American furniture makers; a social and biographical study. With 122 illus. New York, Archer House [1957] 185p. illus. 22cm. [NK2405.O7 1957] 57-13366
1. Furniture—U. S.—Hist. 2. Cabinet-workers. I. Title. BIP

Furniture—United States—History.

ORMSBEE, Thomas Hamilton, 1890- 749.2'13
Early American furniture makers, a social and biographical study. New York, Crowell. Detroit, Gale Research Co., 1974. p. cm. Reprint of the 1930 ed. Bibliography: p. [NK2405.O7 1974] 70-174089 ISBN 0-8103-4086-0
1. Furniture—United States—History. 2. Furniture workers—United States. I. Title.

Furniture, Victorian.

SWEDBERG, Robert W. 749.2'04
Victorian furniture : styles and prices / by Robert W. and Harriett Swedberg ; photos. by the authors. Des Moines : Wallace-Homestead Book Co., c1976. 139 p. : ill. ; 26 cm. "1876 and 1977 prices." Bibliography: p. 139. [NK2390.S93] 76-6832 ISBN 0-87069-177-5 : 6.95
1. Furniture, Victorian. 2. Furniture—Prices. I. Swedberg, Harriett, joint author. II. Title.

TERRY, Henry. 582'.13'094257
A Victorian flower album : God's floral gems glistening on the verdant face of nature / collected and painted in the summer evenings of 1873 as a pleasing recreation by Henry Terry. New York : Viking Press, 1978. ix, 119 p. : col. ill. ; 23 x 28 cm. (A Studio book) Includes index. [QK306.T47 1978b] 78-62206 ISBN 0-670-74592-8 : 16.95
1. Wild flowers—England—Oxfordshire—Pictorial works. 2. Wild flowers—Pictorial works I. Title. BIP

THE Victorian cabinet-maker's assistant; 749.22
418 original designs with descriptions and details of construction. With a new introd. by John Gloag. New York, Dover Publications [1970] 1 v. (various pagings) illus. 31 cm. Reprint of the anonymous work published in London by Blackie in 1853 under title: The Cabinet-maker's assistant. [NK2530.C3 1970] 73-103140 ISBN 0-486-22353-1 5.00
1. Furniture, Victorian. BIP

Furniture, Victorian—Catalogs.

ANDREWS, John. 749.2'2
The price guide to Victorian furniture / John Andrews. Woodbridge : Antique Collectors' Club, 1973. [11], 339 p. : chiefly ill. ; 21 cm. (Price guide series) "Victorian furniture price revision list, January 1975": 17 p. inserted. Includes index. [NK2390.A53] 75-320951 ISBN 0-902028-18-9 : £4.75
1. Furniture, Victorian—Catalogs. I. Title.

Furniture—Virginia.

HARRIS, Marleine Reader, 1902- 749
Virginia antiques, a history and handbook for the collector. Exposition Press [1953] viii, 183p. illus., facsims. 29cm. [NK2435.V5H3] 52-7651
1. Furniture—Virginia. 2. Furniture—Collectors and collecting. I. Title.

LYNCH, Ernest Carlyle. 749.211
Furniture antiques found in Virginia; a book of measured drawings. Milwaukee, Bruce Pub. Co. [1954] 95 p. illus. 29 cm. Bibliography: p. 93. [NK2435.V5L9] 54-7784
1. Furniture—Virginia. 2. Furniture, American. I. Title.

Furniture—Virginia—Williamsburg—History—18th century.

GUSLER, Wallace B. 749.2'155'4252
Furniture of Williamsburg and eastern Virginia, 1710-1790 / Wallace B. Gusler. Richmond, Va. : Virginia Museum of Fine Arts, [1979] p. cm. Includes index. Bibliography: p. [NK2438.W54G87] 78-27282 ISBN 0-917046-05-6 : 24.00
1. Furniture—Virginia—Williamsburg—History—18th century. 2. Furniture—Virginia—History—18th century. I. Title. BIP

Furniture, Welsh—Hist.

DAVIES, Leonard Twiston, 749.22
Sir 1894-
Welsh furniture; an introduction [by] L. Twiston-Davies and H. J. Lloyd-Johnes. Cardiff, University of Wales Press, 1950. viii, 53 p. 72 plates. 24 cm. [NK2540.D3] 51-50990
1. Furniture, Welsh—Hist. I. Lloyd-Johnes, Herbert Johnes. joint author. II. Title.

Furntiure, American.

ANDREWS, Edward Deming, 749.213
1894-1964.
Religion in wood; a book of Shaker furniture, by Edward Deming Andrews and Faith Andrews. Bloomington, Indiana University Press [1966] xxi, 106 p. illus. 28 cm. Bibliography: p. 105-106. [NK2406.A5] 66-12722
1. Furntiure, American. 2. Shakers — Indus. I. Andrews, Faith, joint author. II. Title. BIP

Fusco, Paul.

MORAN, Tom. 770'.92'2
The photo essay, Paul Fusco & Will McBride / text by Tom Moran, with the editors of Alskog, inc. [New York] : T. Y. Crowell, [1974] 94 p. : ill. (some col.) ; 29 cm. (Masters of contemporary photography) Title on spine: Fusco & Mcbride: the photo essay. [TR139.M58] 74-8231 ISBN 0-690-00621-7 : 7.95 ISBN 0-690-00622-5 pbk. : 4.95
1. Fusco, Paul. 2. McBride, Will, 1931- 3. Photography, Documentary. I. Fusco, Paul. II. McBride, Will, 1931- III. Alskog, inc. IV. Title. V. Title: Fusco & McBride, the photo essay.

Fuseli, Henry, 1741-1825.

POWELL, Nicolas. 759.2
Fuseli: The Nightmare. [New York, Viking Press, 1973, c1972] 120 p. illus. 23 cm. (Art in context) Includes bibliographical references. [ND853.F85P68] 79-180831 ISBN 0-670-33285-2 7.50
1. Fuseli, Henry, 1741-1825. Nightmare. I. Title.

TOMORY, P. A., 1922- 759.2
The life and art of Henry Fuseli [by] Peter Tomory. New York, Praeger [1972] 255 p. illus. (part col.) 30 cm. Bibliography: p. 238-239. [ND853.F87T65] 72-77546 25.00
1. Fuseli, Henry, 1741-1825. I. Title.

Fusible materials in sewing.

HUTTON, Jessie. 646.2'1
Singer magic fusibles in fashion sewing / Jessie Hutton ; book design, art direction, and production supervision, Claire F. Valentine. New York : Golden Press, c1977. vii, 88 p. : ill. ; 28 cm. On spine: Magic fusibles in fashion sewing. Includes index. [TT557.H87] 76-53156 ISBN 0-307-09876-1 : 4.95
1. Fusible materials in sewing. I. Singer Company. II. Title. III. Title: Magic fusibles in fashion sewing. BIP

Future life (Greco-Roman religion) in art—Hindu influences.

ALVAREZ, Octavio J. 704.94'7
The celestial brides : a study in mythology and archaeology / by Octavio Alvarez ; introd. by Marie Delcourt ; pref. by Jan van der Marck. Stockbridge, Mass. : H. Reichner, c1978. xxiii, 275, 152 p., [1] leaf of plates : ill. (some col.) ; 29 cm. Includes index. [N7760.A52] 77-91208 ISBN 0-9601520-0-8 : 30.00
1. Future life (Greco-Roman religion) in art—Hindu influences. 2. Art and mythology—Italy—Etruria. 3. Art and mythology—Rome. 4. Future life—History of doctrines. I. Title.
Publisher's address : Main St., Stockbridge, MA 01262 BIP

Futurism.

CLOUGH, Rosa (Trillo) 709'.04
1906-
Futurism: the story of a modern art movement; a new appraisal. New York, Greenwood Press [1969, c1961] 297 p. illus. 23 cm. Bibliography: p. 283-290. [N6494.F8C56 1969] 71-90487
1. Futurism.

Futurism (Art)

*APPOLLONIO, Umbro, 1911- 759.06
Futurist manifestos, edited and with an introd. by Umbro Appollonio. Translations by Robert Brain [and others] New York, Viking Press [1974, c1973] 232 p. illus. (part col.) 22 cm. (Documents of 20th century art.) Translation of Futurismo. Bibliography: p. 221-227. [ND196.F8] 72-89124 ISBN 0-670-01966-6 12.50
1. Futurism (Art). I. Title. BIP

CLOUGH, Rosa (Trillo) 709.04
1906-
Futurism the story of a modern art movement, a new appraisal. New York, Philosophical Library [1961] 297p. illus. 20cm. Includes bibliography. [N6490.C65] 60-15952
1. Futurism (Art) 2. Futurism. I. Title.

MARTIN, Marianne W. 709.04'1
Futurist art and theory 1909-1915, by Mariane W. Martin. Oxford, Clarendon Pr., 1968 xxx, 228p. 144 plates, illus. (some col.), facsims., ports. 26cm. [N6494.F8M3] 68-114920 17.75
1. Futurism (Art) I. Title.
Available in New York from Oxford Univ. Pr. BIP

MARTIN, Marianne W. 700'.9'041
Futurist art and theory, 1909-1915 / by Marianne W. Martin. New York : Hacker Art Books, 1978, c1968. xxxii, 228 p., [77] leaves of plates : ill. ; 26 cm. Reprint of the ed. published by Clarendon Press, Oxford. Includes index. Bibliography: p. [207]-213. [NX600.F8M38 1978] 75-44910 ISBN 0-87817-192-4 lib. bdg. : 40.00
1. Futurism (Art) 2. Arts, Modern—20th century. I. Title.

TAYLOR, Joshua Charles, 759.06
1917-
Futurism. New York, Museum of Modern Art; distributed by Doubleday, Garden City [1961] 153 p. illus. (part col.) 25 cm. "Biographies and catalogue of the exhibition [May 31-Sept. 5, 1961]": p. 141-[148] "Selected bibliography of futurism, 1905-1961": p. 135-[140] [ND1265.T39] 61-11271
1. Futurism (Art) 2. Paintings—Exhibitions. BIP

Futurism (Art)—Addresses, essays, lectures.

MARINETTI, Filippo 700'.9'04
Tommaso, 1876-1944.
Marinetti; selected writings. Edited, and with an introd., by R. W. Flint. Translated by R. W. Flint and Arthur A. Coppotelli. New York, Farrar, Straus and Giroux [1972] 366 p. illus. 24 cm. Includes selections from the author's Futurist theory and invention, The untamables, and Futurist memoirs. [NX600.F8M37 1972] 71-189338 ISBN 0-374-20290-7 12.95
1. Futurism (Art)—Addresses, essays, lectures. I. Flint, R. W., ed.

Futurism (Art)—Bibliography.

ANDREOLI-DEVILLERS, Jean 709'.04
Pierre, 1940-
Futurism and the arts : a bibliography, 1959-73 = Le futurisme et les arts : bibliographie, 1959-73 = Il futurismo e le arti : bibliografia, 1959-73 / Jean-Pierre Andreoli-deVillers. Toronto ; Buffalo : University of Toronto Press, [1975] xxix, 189 p. ; 21 cm. Includes index. [Z5936.F85A62] 74-79005 ISBN 0-8020-2120-4 : 17.50
1. Futurism (Art)—Bibliography. 2. Arts, Modern—20th century—Bibliography. I. Title. II. Title: Le futurisme et les arts. III. Title: Il futurismo e le arti.

Futurism (Art)—Exhibitions.

ALBERT Loeb & Krugier 709'.45
Gallery.
The futurism: Balla, Boccioni, Carra, Russolo, Severini. [New York, 1968] 1 portfolio (16 p., chiefly illus.) 33 cm. (Tauhus, no. 8) Title from portfolio. Catalog of an exhibition held at Albert Loeb & Krugier Gallery, New York, Nov.-Dec. 1968. [N6918.5.F8A43 1968] 74-151908
1. Futurism (Art)—Exhibitions. 2. Futurism (Art)—Italy. 3. Art, Modern—20th century—Italy. I. Title.

SOLOMON R. Guggenheim 709'.04
Museum, New York.
Futurism: a modern focus; the Lydia and Harry Lewis Winston Collection, Dr. and Mrs. Barnett Malbin. New York [Solomon R. Guggenheim Foundation, 1973] 251 p. illus. (part col.) 27 cm. Catalog of the exhibition held in the fall of 1973 at the Solomon R. Guggenheim Museum, New York. Bibliography: p. 232. [N6494.F8S64 1973] 73-86860 13.75
1. Winston, Lydia, 1897- —Art collections. 2. Winston, Harry Lewis—Art collections. 3. Futurism (Art)—Exhibitions. I. Title.

Gables—Netherlands—Influence.

HITCHCOCK, Henry Russell, 721'.5
1903-
Netherlandish scrolled gables of the sixteenth and early seventeenth centuries / Henry-Russell Hitchcock. New York : Published by New York University Press for the College Art Association of America, 1978. p. cm. (Monographs on archaeology and fine arts ; 34) [NA2920.H57] 77-81905 ISBN 0-8147-3383-2 : 22.50
1. Gables—Netherlands—Influence. 2. Gables—Europe, Northern. 3. Architecture, Renaissance—Netherlands. 4. Architecture, Renaissance—Europe, Northern. I. College Art Association of America. II. Title. III. Series. BIP

Gabo, Naum, 1890—

ALBRIGHT-KNOX Art 709'.24
Gallery.
Naum Gabo. Buffalo [1968] 27 p. illus. 22 cm. Catalog of an exhibition held March 2-April 14, 1968 at the Albright-Knox Art Gallery, Buffalo, New York. [NB699.G3A8] 68-4708
1. Gabo, Naum, 1890-

FIVE European 730'.94'07401471
sculptors: Naum Gabo-Antoine Pevsner, with an introd. by Herbert Read and texts by Ruth Olson and Abraham Chanin; Wilhelm Lehmbruck-Aristide Maillol, with an introd. by Jere Abbott; Henry Moore, by James Johnson Sweeney. Reprinted. New York, Published for the Museum of Modern Art by Arno Press, 1969. 1 v. (various pagings) illus., ports. 29 cm. Reprint of 3 catalogs of exhibitions at the Museum of Modern Art, originally issued separately, 1930-1948. Includes bibliographies. [NB458.F58] 75-86444
1. Gabo, Naum, 1890- 2. Pevsner, Antoine, 1886- 3. Lehmbruck, Wilhelm, 1881-1919. 4. Maillol, Aristide Joseph Bonaventure, 1861-1944. 5. Moore, Henry Spencer, 1898- I. New York (City). Museum of Modern Art. Naum Gabo [and] Antoine Pevsner. 1969. II. New York (City). Museum of Modern Art. Wilhelm Lehmbruck, Aristide Maillol. 1969. III. Sweeney, James Johnson, 1900- Henry Moore. 1969. BIP

NEWMAN, Teresa. 730'.92'4
Naum Gabo, the constructive process / [by] Teresa Newman. London : Tate Gallery Publications, 1976. 63 p. : ill., ports. ; 16 cm. Catalogue of an exhibition held at the Tate Gallery, 13 Nov.-12 Dec. 1976. Bibliography: p. 63. [NB699.N37N48] 77-476468 ISBN 0-905005-65-1 : £1.25
1. Naum, Gabo, 1890- I. Naum Gabo, 1890- II. Tate Gallery, London. III. Title.

NEWMAN, Teresa. 730'.92'4
Naum Gabo, the constructive process / [by] Teresa Newman. London : Tate Gallery Publications, 1976. 63 p. : ill., ports. ; 16 cm. Catalogue of an exhibition held at the Tate Gallery, 13 Nov.-12 Dec. 1976. Bibliography: p. 63. [NB699.N37N48] 77-476468 ISBN 0-905005-65-1 : £1.25
1. Naum, Gabo, 1890- I. Naum Gabo, 1890- II. Tate Gallery, London. III. Title.

Gaddi, Agnolo, d. 1396.

COLE, Bruce, 1938- 759.5
Agnolo Gaddi / Bruce Cole. Oxford [Eng.] ; New York : Clarendon Press, 1977. xiv, 100 p., [26] leaves of plates : ill. ; 30 cm. (Oxford studies in the history of art and architecture).) Includes index. Bibliography: p. 91-95. [ND623.G28C64] 77-365869 ISBN 0-19-817339-3 : 28.75
1. Gaddi, Agnolo, d. 1396. I. Title. II. Series.
Distributed by Oxford University Press, New York BIP

Gadsby's Tavern, Alexandria, Va.

FAUBER, J. Everette. 728.5
Restoration, "Gadsby's Tavern" in Old Town at Alexandria, Virginia / J. Everette Fauber, Jr. Lynchburg, Va. : Fauber, 1976. v, 78 leaves, [35] leaves of plates : ill. ; 29 cm. Cover title. Bibliography: leaves 72-78. [NA7845.A433F38] 76-151664
1. Gadsby's Tavern, Alexandria, Va. 2. Alexandria, Va.—Hotels, motels, etc.—Conservation and restoration. I. Title. II. Title: "Gadsby's Tavern" in Old Town at Alexandria, Virginia.

Gaffney, S.C.—Description—Views.

CALLISON, Helen 779'.9'975742
Vassy.
Cherokee County's first half-century through the lens of June H. Carr, photographer / by Helen Vassy Callison and Bobby Gilmer Moss ; with a foreword by Percy H. Carr. [Gaffney, S.C. : Southern Renaissance Press, 1975] vii, 75 p. : ill. ; 34 cm. Imprint from label mounted on verso of t.p. Bibliography: p. 75. [F279.G14C34] 75-329637
1. Gaffney, S.C.—Description—Views. 2. Cherokee Co., S.C.—Description and travel—Views. I. Moss, Bobby Gilmer, joint author. II. Carr, June H., 1877-1960. III. Title.

Gag, Wanda, 1893-1946—Juvenile literature.

DUIN, Nancy E. 741'.092'4 B
Wanda Gag, author and illustrator of children's books, by Nancy E. Duin. Charlotteville, N.Y., SamHar Press, 1973. 32 p. 22 cm. (Outstanding personalities, no. 57) Bibliography: p. 31-32. A biography of the painter, author, and illustrator, famous for such children's books as Millions of Cats. [NC975.5.G34D84] 92 73-77601 1.98 (lib. bdg.)
1. Gag, Wanda, 1893-1946—Juvenile literature. I. Title. BIP

Gainsborough, Thomas, 1727-1788.

GAINSBOROUGH, Thomas, 1727- 759.2
1788.
Gainsborough : paintings and drawings / [selected by] John Hayes. London : Phaidon, 1975. 232 p. : ill. (some col.) ; 29 cm. Includes index. Bibliography: p. 53-54. [ND497.G2H38] 75-721 ISBN 0-7148-1639-6 : 30.00
1. Gainsborough, Thomas, 1727-1788. I. Hayes, John T.

GAINSBOROUGH, Thomas, 1727- 927.5
1788.
Letters. Edited by Mary Woodall. [Rev. ed.] Greenwich, Conn., New York Graphic Society [c1963] 184 p. illus., ports., facsims. 29 cm. Includes bibliographical references. [ND497.G2A3 1963] 63-25404
I. Woodall, Mary, ed. II. Title.

WARK, Robert R v. 12
Gainsborough's the Blue Boy. San Marino, Calif., Henry E. Huntington Library & Arts Gallery [c1963] 29 p. illus. 16 cm. [ND407.G2W26] 64-2016
1. Gainsborough, Thomas, 1727-1788. I. Title. II. Title: The Blue Boy.

SUBJECT INDEX GARDEN ORNAMENTS AND

WILLIAMSON, Geoffrey. 759.2
The ingenious Mr. Gainsborough; Thomas Gainsborough: a biographical study. New York, St. Martin's Press [1972] 224 p. illus. 23 cm. Bibliography: p. 216-217. [ND497.G2W53 1972b] 72-78435 10.00
1. Gainsborough, Thomas, 1727-1788. I. Title.

WOODALL, Mary. 759.2
Thomas Gainsborough. New York, Barnes & Noble [1970] 90 p. plates (part col.) 18 cm. (Barnes & Noble art series) "No. 629." [ND497.G2W59 1970] 74-16127 0.95
1. Gainsborough, Thomas, 1727-1788.

WORMAN, Isabelle. 759.2 B
Thomas Gainsborough : a biography 1727-1788 / by Isabelle Worman. Lavenham [Eng.] : T. Dalton, 1976. 148 p. : ill. (some col.) ; 24 cm. Includes index. Bibliography: p. 145. [ND497.G2W65] 77-355134 ISBN 0-900963-69-7 : £4.80
1. Gainsborough, Thomas, 1727-1788. 2. Painters—Great Britain—Biography. I. Gainsborough, Thomas, 1727-1788. **BIP**

Galba, Servius Sulpicius, Emperor of Rome, d. 69.

KRAAY, Colin M 737
The aes coinage of Galba. New York, American Numismatic Society, 1956. x, 125p. 37 plates, diagrs. 23cm. (Numismatic notes and monographs, no 133) 'The present study at first formed part of a monograph on the aes coinage of the period A. D. 68-71 and was subsequently, in an enlarged form, submitted as a D. Phil, thesis in the University of Oxford.' Bibliographical footnotes. [CJ1001.K7] 56-
1. Galba, Servius Sulpicius, Emperor of Rome, d. 69. 2. Numismatics, Roman. I. Title. II. Series.

Galdikas, Adomas, 1893-1969.

GALDIKAS, Adomas, 1893-1969. 759.75
Adomas Galdikas : a color odyssey / by Charlotte Willard ; with an essay by Waldemar George. New York : October House, c1973. 171 p. : ill. (some col.) ; 28 cm. Bibliography: p. 171. [ND699.G32W54] 72-93105 ISBN 0-8079-0186-5 : 14.95
1. Galdikas, Adomas, 1893-1969. I. Willard, Charlotte.

Gallardo, Villasenor, Gervasio, 1934-

PERUCHO, Joan, 1920- 659.1323
Caleidoscopio: 4 [i.e. cuatro] graficos. [Bacelona, Editorial Blume: Name stamped on t.p.: Wittenborn, New York,] 1966 lv. (chiefly illus., ports.) 24cm. [NC987.P4] 67-1337 8.50
1. Gallardo, Villasenor, Gervasio, 1934- 2. Giralt, Miracle, R., 1911- 3. Pedragosa, Juan, 1930- 4. Pla Narbona, Jose, 1928- I. Title.

Gallego, Fernando, ca. 1440-ca. 1507.

ARIZONA. University. Kress Collection. 759.6
The retablo of the cathedral of Ciudad Rodrigo by Fernando Gallego, from the Samuel H. Kress collections at the University of Arizona, [Tuscon University of Arizona, 1960] vii, 53p. illus., col. plate. 28cm. Cover title. 'The English text and this catalogue was written by Robert M. Quinn ... and translated into Spanish by Renato I. Rosaldo.' [ND813.G24A9] 61-63545
1. Gallego, Fernando, ca. 1440-ca. 1507. 2. Cludad Rodrigo, Spain. I. Title.

QUINN, Robert MacLean. 759.6
Fernando Gallego and the retablo of Ciudad Rodrigo. Version espanola de Renato Rosaldo. Tucson, University of Arizona Press, 1961. xi, 117p. illus., plates. 29cm. The retablo is now in the Kress Collection at the University of Arizona. Bibliography: p. 116-117. [ND813.G24Q5] 60-15915
1. Gallego, Fernando, ca. 1440-ca. 1507. 2. Cludad Rodrigo, Spain. Catedral. I. Title. **BIP**

Galli da Bibiena family.

PHILADELPHIA Museum of Art. 741.9'45
Drawings by the Bibiena family. [Philadelphia, Printed by the Winchell Co., 1968] [64] p. illus. 19 x 26 cm. Catalog of an exhibition held Jan. 10-Feb. 28, 1968, at the Philadelphia Museum of Art. Includes bibliographies. [NC257.G3P45] 68-30069
1. Galli da Bibiena family. I. Title.

Gallier, James.

GALLIER, James. 720'.92'4 B
Autobiography of James Gallier, architect. With a new introd. by Samuel Wilson, Jr., and a supplement of illus. New York, Da Capo Press, 1973. xi, 150, [42] p. illus. 23 cm. (Da Capo Press series in architecture and decorative art, v. 25) Reprint of the 1864 ed. [NA737.G34A2 1973] 69-13715 ISBN 0-306-71247-4 15.00
1. Gallier, James. **BIP**

Game and game-birds—Pictorial works.

HAGERBAUMER, David. 759.13
Selected American game birds [by] David Hagerbaumer, with Sam Lehman. Caldwell, Idaho, Caxton Printers, 1972. [117] p. 26 col. plates. 27 x 30 cm. [QL674.H2] 74-137773 ISBN 0-87004-213-0 30.00
1. Game and game-birds—Pictorial works. I. Lehman, Sam. II. Title. **BIP**

Games in art.

BRUEGEL, Pieter, the elder, d. 1569 759.9493
Children's games [Text by] Paul Portmann. Berne Switzerland] Hallwag [dist. New York, Taplinger, c. 1964] 1v. (unpaged) 18 col. illus. 19cm. (Crbis pictures, 12) 64-55223 2.50 bds.,
1. Games in art. I. Portmann, Paul Ferdinand. II. Title.

Ganz, Jo Ann—Art collections.

LOS Angeles Co., Calif. Museum of Art, Los Angeles. 760'.0973
Chosen works of American art, 1850-1924, from the Collection of Jo Ann and Julian Ganz, Jr. [1969] [32] p. illus. 19 x 22 cm. Catalog of a loan exhibition held in the Ahmanson Gallery of the museum Oct. 1-Nov. 16, 1969. [N6510.L67] 73-452642
1. Ganz, Jo Ann—Art collections. 2. Ganz, Julian—Art collections. 3. Art, American—Exhibitions. 4. Art, Modern—19th century—U.S. 5. Art, Modern—20th century—U.S. I. Title.

Garages.

BAKER, Geoffrey Harold, 1912- 725.38
Parking [by] Geoffrey Baker & Bruno Funaro. New York, Reinhold [1958] 202 p. illus. 27 cm. [NA8348.B25] 58-13376
1. Garages. 2. Automobile parking. I. Funaro, Bruno, 1911-1957, joint author.

GT. Brit. Ministry of Housing and Local Government. 711.58
Cars in housing. London, H.M.S.O., 1966- v. illus., col. plans, tables. 30cm. (Its Design bulletin 10) Contents.1. Some medium density layouts. Bibl. [TH6010.G7 no.10] 67-71447 2.50 pap.,
1. Garages. 2. Architecture, Domestic—Designs and plans. I. Title. II. Series.
American distributor: British Info., New York.

KLOSE, Dietrich. 725.38
Metropolitan parking structures; a survey of architectural problems and solutions. [Translated into English by E. Rockwell] New York, F. A. Praeger [1965] 247 p. illus., maps, plans. 23 x 29 cm. English and German. [NA8348.K55] 65-19576
1. Garages. 2. Automobile parkings. I. Title.

LECKEY, Wayne Charles, 1912- 728.949
How to build your own garage. Chicago, Popular Mechanics Press [1953] 128 p. illus. 28 cm. At head of title: Popular mechanics. [TH4960.L4] 53-10880
1. Garages. 2. Air raid shelters. I. Title.

Garbisch, Edgar William—Art collections.

CHRYSLER Museum at Norfolk. 759.13'074'0155521
48 masterpieces ; from the Collection of Edgar William & Bernice Chrysler Garbisch Norfolk, Va. : Chrysler Museum at Norfolk, [1975] 68 p. : ill. ; 22 x 28 cm. On cover: The gift of American naive paintings from the collection of Edgar William & Bernice Chrysler Garbisch. [ND207.5.P7C49 1975] 75-13524
1. Garbisch, Edgar William—Art collections. 2. Garbisch, Bernice Chrysler—Art collections. 3. Chrysler Museum at Norfolk. 4. Paintings, America—Catalogs. 5. Primitivism in art—United States—Catalogs. 6. Paintings, Colonial—United States—Catalogs. 7. Painting, Modern—19th century—United States—Catalogs. I. Title.

Garcia Ponce, Juan.

TAMAYO, Rufino, 1900- 759.9'72
Tamayo. Introd. by Juan Garcia Ponce. [Tr. from Spanish by Emma Gutierrez Suarez] New York, Tudor [1967] 1 v. (unpaged) illus. (pt. col.) 41cm. English and Spanish. [ND259.T3G3] 67-31803 30.00
1. Garcia Ponce, Juan. I. Title.

Garden cities.

CREESE, Walter L. 711.40942
The search for environment; the garden city, before and after [by] Walter L. Creese. New Haven, Yale University Press, 1966. xx, 360 p. illus. 28 cm. [HT161.C7] 66-12492
1. Garden cities. I. Title.

MOSS-ECCARDT, John, 1930-3 711'.4'0924 B
Ebenezer Howard, an illustrated life of Sir Ebenezer Howard, 1850-1928. Aylesbury, Shire Publications, 1973. 48 p. illus., facsims., maps, ports. 21 cm. (Lifelines, 18) Includes bibliographical references and index. [HT161.H7M67] 74-155513 ISBN 0-85263-205-3
1. Howard, Ebenezer, Sir, 1850-1928. 2. Garden cities.
Distributed by International Publication Service, 3.00 pbk.

Garden cities—England.

MACFADYEN, Dugald, 1867- 711'.4
Sir Ebenezer Howard and the town planning movement. Cambridge, M.I.T. Press [1970] ix, 199 p. illus., plans, port. 23 cm. [HT161.H7M3 1970] 73-105748 8.95
1. Howard, Ebenezer, Sir, 1850-1928. 2. Garden cities—England. I. Title. **BIP**

Garden Club of Virginia.

WILLIAMS, Dorothy Hunt. 635.9'09755
Historic Virginia gardens; preservations by the Garden Club of Virginia. Charlottesville, Published for the Garden Club of Virginia by the University Press of Virginia [1975] p. cm. Bibliography: p. [SB466.U65V88] 74-19422 ISBN 0-8139-0604-0 :
1. Garden Club of Virginia. 2. Gardens—Virginia. 3. Gardens—Conservation and restoration. 4. Virginia—Historic houses, etc.—Conservation and restoration. I. Garden Club of Virginia. II. Title. **BIP**

Garden lighting.

NIGHTINGALE, Frank B 712.6246
Garden lighting. [Altadena, Calif., Knight Pub. Co., 1958] 224p. illus. 22cm. [SB476.N5] 58-32023
1. Garden lighting. 2. Electric light fixtures. I. Title.

SCHULER, Stanley. 712
Outdoor lighting for your home. Princeton, N. J., Van Nostrand [1962] 192 p. illus. 21 cm. [SB476.S45] 62-20141
1. Garden lighting. 2. Christmas decorations. I. Title.

Garden ornaments and furniture.

AUL, Henry B. 717
How to build garden structures: grills, terraces, shelters, arbors, fences, gates, etc. New York, Sheridan House [1950] 384 p. illus. 22 cm. [SB473.5.A9 1950] 50-10896
1. Garden ornaments and furniture. I. Title.

BRIMER, John Burton. 643.7
Designs for outdoor living. Garden City, N. Y., Doubleday [1959] 401p. illus. 22cm. (An American garden guild book) Includes bibliography. [SB473.5.B7] 59-5291
1. Garden ornaments and furniture. I. Title.

EDWARDS, Paul Francis. 712'.0942
English garden ornament, by Paul Edwards. South Brunswick [N. J.] A. S. Barnes [1967, c 1965] 110 p. illus., col. plates. 28 cm. Bibliography: p. 106-107. [SB473.5.E3 1967] 67-13083
1. Garden ornaments and furniture. I. Title.

FLETCHER, Harry Lutf Verne, 1902- 712.62
The feature garden. Newton, Mass., C. T. Branford Co. [1961, c.1960] 142p. illus. 61-11852 3.50 bds.,
1. Garden ornaments and furniture. I. Title.

FOLEY, Daniel J. 717
The complete book of garden ornaments, complements, and accessories [by] Daniel J. Foley. New York, Crown [1972] viii, 247 p. illus. 27 cm. Bibliography: p. 236-238. [SB473.5.F65 1972] 70-147324 ISBN 0-517-50078-7 9.95
1. Garden ornaments and furniture. I. Title.

GRANT WHITE, John Ernest. 717'.094
Garden art and architecture [by] J. E. Grant White. London, New York [etc.] Abelard-Schumann, 1968. xxxii, 110 p. 163 illus. 30 cm. [NA8450.G68 1968] 68-10341 ISBN 0-200-71574-7 55/-
1. Garden ornaments and furniture. 2. Landscape architecture. I. Title.

HAND, Jackson. 643.7
Projects you can make for living outdoors. Greenwich, Conn., Fawcett Publications, c1958. 144p. illus. 24cm. (Fawcett how-to book 378) [SB473.5.H25] 58-2834
1. Garden ornaments and furniture. I. Title.

HAWKINS, Reginald Robert, 1902- 717
Arbors and trellises, breezeways, fences and gates [and] small buildings, by Reginald R. Hawkins and Charles H. Abbe. New York, Van Nostrand [1951] vi, 151 p. illus. 22 cm. (Their The home mechanic's outdoor library) "Most of the material ... appeared first in the authors' Home mechanic's outdoor handbook." [SB473.5.H29] 51-5139
1. Garden ornaments and furniture. I. Abbe, Charles H., joint author. II. Title.

HAWKINS, Reginald Robert, 1902- 714.3
Garden pools, fountains, swimming pools, sprinkling systems [and] recreation areas, by Reginald R. Hawkins and Charles H. Abbe. New York, Van Nostrand [1951] vi, 139 p. illus. 22 cm. [Their The home mechanic's outdoor library] "Most of the material ... appeared first in the authors' Home mechanic's outdoor handbook." [SB473.5.H3] 51-5138
1. Garden ornaments and furniture. 2. Fountains. 3. Swimming pools. I. Abbe, Charles H., joint author. II. Title.

HAWKINS, Reginald Robert, 1902- 717.9
Outdoor fireplaces and grills, walls and tree wells, terrace [and] incinerators by Reginald R. Hawkins and Charles H. Abbe. New York, Van Nostrand [1951] vi, 149 p. illus. 22 cm. [Their The home mechanic's outdoor library] "Most of the material ... appeared first in the author's

Home mechanic's outdoor handbook."
[SB473.5.H33] 51-5137
*1. Garden ornaments and furniture. I.
Abbe, Charles H., joint author. II. Title.*

HOCHMAN, Louis. 645.8
*How to build patios, terraces, barbecues,
walks, fences, awnings, gates.* Artwork
within the book by Frank Schwarz; cover
terrace photo. by Max Tatch-Shostal,
fireplace photo. by Edwin Lester Smith-
Shostal. Greenwich, Conn., Fawcett
Publications, c1955. 144p. illus. 24cm. (A
Fawcett how-to book, 270) [SB473.5.H62
1955a] 55-3569
*1. Garden Ornaments and furniture. 2.
Masonry. I. Title.*

HOCHMAN, Louis. 645.8
*How to build patios, terraces, barbecues,
walks, fences, awnings, gates.* New York,
Arco Co. [1955] 144 p. illus. 26 cm. (The
Do-it-yourself series) Arco handy books
for better living. Fawcett book 270.
[SB473.5.H62] 55-9430
*1. Garden ornaments and furniture. 2.
Masonry. I. Title.*

MANNERS, David X 1912- 645.8
Projects you can make for outdoor living.
[Greenwich, Conn., Fawcett Publications,
1960] 144p. illus. 24cm. (A Fawcett how-
to-book, 444) [SB473.5.M3] 60-3439
*1. Garden ornaments and furniture. 2.
Outdoor life. I. Title.*

POPULAR mechanics magazine. 645.8
Lawn and patio furnishings. [Chicago]
Popular Mechanics Press [1960] 127p.
illus. 24cm. [SB473.5.P635] 60-5307
*1. Garden ornaments and furniture. I.
Title.*

ROCKWELL Manufacturing 645.8
Company. Delta Power Tool Division.
*Projects for outdoor living; a selection of
delightful projects designed for your
outdoor living.* Pittsburgh [1955] 112p.
illus. 23cm. (Deltacraft
library)
[SB473.5.R6] 55-41312
*1. Garden ornaments and furniture. 2.
Woodwork. I. Title.*

WALKDEN, G B 684.18
Garden carpentry, written and illustrated
by G. B. Walkden. London, W. H. & L.
Collingridge[1960]; label: Hollywood-by-
the-Sea, Fla., Transatlantic Arts. 96 p. illus
21 cm. [SB473.5.W3] 61-886
*1. Garden ornaments and furniture. 2.
Carpentry. I. Title.*

Garden ornaments and furniture—Catalogs.

KENNETH Lynch & Sons. 717
Garden ornaments / by Kenneth Lynch.
Canterbury, Conn. : Canterbury Pub. Co.,
c1974. 768 p., [12] leaves of plates : ill. ;
37 cm. (The Architectural handbook
series) Includes indexes. [SB473.5.K46
1974] 75-326518
*1. Kenneth Lynch & Sons. 2. Garden
ornaments and furniture—Catalogs. 3.
Garden ornaments and furniture—Pictorial
works. I. Lynch, Kenneth. II. Title.*

Garden ornaments and furniture—Pictorial works.

HUNT, Peter Raymond Slater. 717
The book of garden ornament, edited by
Peter Hunt. New York, Architectural Book
Pub. Co. [1974] xxi, 298 p. illus. 29 cm.
[SB473.5.H86 1974] 73-19894 ISBN 0-
8038-0027-4
*1. Garden ornaments and furniture—
Pictorial works. 2. Landscape
architecture—Pictorial works. I. Title.*

Garden—Virginia.

GARDEN Club of Virginia 712.6
Homes and gardens in old Virginia. Ed. by
Frances Archer Christian, Susanne
Williams Massie. Rev. for the Garden Club
of Virginia, by Ella Williams Smith,
Caroline Pickrell Strudwick, Frances
Claiborne Guy. Richmond, Va. Garrett
Massie, 1962. xvi, 544p. illus. (1, col.)
25cm. 62-6935 7.50
*1. Garden—Virginia. 2. Virginia—Historic
houses, etc. I. Christian, Frances Archer,*

ed. II. Massie, Susanne Williams, ed. III.
Title.

Gardening.

CHAPLIN, Mary 712.714
Riverside gardening: design, construction,
planting. London, W. H. & L. Collingridge
[dist. Hollywood-by-the-Sea, Fla.,
Transatlantic, c.1964) 111p. illus. 23cm.
64-6565 7.50 bds.,
1. Gardening. I. Title.

HOUSE & garden's 26 easy 712'.6
little gardens. New York : Penguin Books,
[1979] p. cm. Includes index.
[SB453.H764 1979] 78-26783 pbk. : 7.95
1. Gardening. I. House & garden.

HOUSE & garden. 712.6
The garden book. Editor: Robert Harling.
Garden editor: Peter Coats. Art editor:
Alex Kroll. [London, Conde Nast
Publications; New York St. Martin's Press,
1966] c1965. 256 p. illus. (part col.) 30
cm. [SB453.H76] 66-11856
*1. Gardening. 2. Gardens. I. Harling,
Robert, ed. II. Title.*

MORE, Daphne. 712'.6
Ideas for interesting gardens / with ...
photography and drawings by the author /
Daphne More. Newton Abbot ; North
Pomfret, Vt. : David and Charles, 1974.
160 p. : ill. (some col.), plans ; 23 cm.
Includes index. Bibliography: p. 157-158.
[SB453.M67] 75-302081 ISBN 0-7153-
6445-6 : 8.95
*1. Gardening. 2. Landscape gardening. 3.
Birds, Attracting of. I. Title.* **BIP**

SCOBEY, Joan. 745.92
Gifts from your garden / by Joan Scobey
and Norma Myers ; ill. by Paul Bacon.
Indianapolis : Bobbs-Merrill, [1975] p. cm.
Includes index. [SB454.S38] 75-512 ISBN
0-672-51895-3 : 10.00
*1. Gardening. 2. Handicraft. 3. Gifts. I.
Myers, Norma, joint author. II. Title.* **BIP**

Gardening—Caricatures and cartoons.

THELWELL, Norman, 635'.02'07
1923-
Up the garden path; Thelwell's guide to
gardening. [1st ed.] New York, Dutton
[1967] 128 p. illus. 21 cm.
[NC1479.T54A49 1967b] 66-21300
*1. Gardening—Caricatures and cartoons. I.
Title.*

Gardens.

COATS, Peter. 712
Great gardens of the Western World.
Introd. by Harold Nicolson. New York,
Putnam [1963] 311 p. illus. (part col.)
ports., plans 33 cm. [SB465.C6] 63-7549
1. Gardens. I. Title.

GRANT, John Alexander, 712.6
1913-
Garden design illustrated, by John A.
Grant and Carol L. Grant. Seattle,
University of Washington Press, 1954. 145
p. illus. 27 cm. [SB453.G698] 54-12725
*1. Gardens. I. Grant, Carol Longabaugh,
1906- joint author. II. Title.* **BIP**

HADFIELD, MILES 712
The art of the garden [London. Studio
Vista; New York. Dutton, c.1965] 160p.
illus., plans. 19cm. (Dutton Vista
picturebook, 9) [SB470.5.H2] 65-3593 1.75
pap.,
*1. Gardens. 2. Landscape gardening—Hist.
I. Title.*

HADFIELD, Miles. 712
Gardens. New York, Putnam [1962] 128 p.
illus. (part col.) ports. 22 cm. (Pleasures
and treasures) [SB451.H3] 62-13081
1. Gardens.

PAGE, Russell. 712
The education of a gardener. [New York]
Atheneum, 1962. 381 p. illus. 24 cm.
[SB473.P28] 62-17287
*1. Gardens. 2. Landscape architecture. I.
Title.*

SHEPHEARD, Peter. 712.6
Modern gardens; masterworks of
international garden architecture. New

York, F. A. Praeger [1954] 144p. illus.
29cm. (Books that matter) [SB465.S45] 53-
10486
1. Gardens. I. Title.

Gardens—Australia.

TANNER, Howard. 712.6'0994
The great gardens of Australia / [by]
Howard Tanner, assisted by Jane Begg.
South Melbourne, Vic. : Macmillan, 1976.
198 p. : ill. (some col.) ; 27 cm.
Bibliography: p. 197-198. [SB466.A7T36]
77-350244 ISBN 0-333-21052-2
*1. Gardens—Australia. I. Begg, Jane. II.
Title.*

Gardens, Chinese.

KESWICK, Maggie. 712
The Chinese garden : history, art &
architecture / Maggie Keswick ;
contributions and conclusion by Charles
Jencks. New York : Rizzoli, 1978. 216 p. :
ill. (some col.) ; 32 cm. Includes index.
Bibliography: p. 211-214. [SB457.55.K47
1978] 78-57898 ISBN 0-8478-0193-4 :
35.00
*1. Gardens, Chinese. 2. Gardens—China. I.
Jencks, Charles, joint author. II. Title.* **BIP**

Gardens—England.

DUTTON, Ralph, 1898- 712
The English garden. Illustrated from old
prints, pictures and drawings, and from
photos. by Will F. Taylor and others. [2d
ed., rev.] London, New York, Batsford
[1950] vi, 122 p. illus 23 cm. (The British
heritage series) [SB466.G7D85 1950] 50-
12976
1. Gardens—England. I. Title. II. Series.

Gardens—England—Devon—Guide-books.

SYNGE, Patrick 914.23'5'04857
Millington.
Devon and Cornwall / Patrick M. Synge.
London : Batsford, 1977. 158 p., [10]
leaves of plates : ill. (some col.) ; 23 cm.
(The Gardens of Britain ; 1) Includes
index. [SB466.G75D487] 78-301814 ISBN
0-7134-0927-4 : 12.95
*1. Gardens—England—Devon—Guide-
books. 2. Gardens—England—Cornwall—
Guide-books. I. Title.*
Distributed by Hippocrene Books, New
York, NY 10016

Gardens—England—History.

EASTWOOD, Dorothea, 712'.6'0942
1912-
The story of our gardens. [Bedford, Eng.]
Gordon Fraser [Gallery, 1958] vii, 92 p.
illus. 22 cm. [SB466] 75-602 1.95
*1. Gardens—England—History. I. Title.*BIP

Gardens, English—France.

WIEBENSON, Dora. 712'.0944
The picturesque garden in France / Dora
Wiebenson. Princeton, N.J. : Princeton
University Press, c1978. xviii, 137 p., [44]
leaves of plates : ill. ; 29 cm. Includes
index. Bibliography: p. [123]-132.
[SB466.F8W53] 77-22704 ISBN 0-691-
03930-5 : 30.00
*1. Gardens, English—France. 2. Gardens,
English. 3. Gardens—France.* **BIP**

Gardens—Europe.

MCFADDEN, Dorothy Loa 712.094
(Mausloff) 1902-
Touring the gardens of Europe. Wheel tour
maps by Winfield Barnes. New York,
McKay [c.1965] xiii, 306p. illus., maps.
22cm. [SB466.E9M3] 65-18547 5.95
*1. Gardens—Europe. 2. Europe—Descr. &
trav.—Guide-books. I. Title.*

SIREN, Osvald, 1879- 635.9094
*China and gardens of Europe of the
eighteenth century.* New York, Ronald
Press Co. [1950] xiv, 223. 192 p. illus.
(part col.) 32 cm. Bibliography: p. 215-219.
[SB466.E9S5] Agr

*1. Gardens—Europe. 2. Landscape
gardening—Europe. I. Title.*

Gardens—Europe—Guide-books.

MCFADDEN, Dorothy Loa 914'.04'55
Mausolff, 1902-
*Gardens of Europe; a pictorial tour with
descriptions and directions for visiting
them.* Text by Dorothy Loa McFadden.
Pictures by James L. and Dorothy Loa
McFadden. South Brunswick, A. S. Barnes
[1970] 195 p. illus. (part col.) 29 cm.
[SB466.E9M29] 78-107127 ISBN 0-498-
07576-1 25.00
*1. Gardens—Europe—Guide-books. 2.
Gardens—Pictorial works. I. McFadden,
James L., illus. II. Title.*

Gardens—France—Congresses.

DUMBARTON Oaks 712'.0944
Colloquium on the History of Landscape
Architecture 1973.
The French formal garden / [edited by
Elisabeth B. MacDougall and F. Hamilton
Hazlehurst]. Washington : Dumbarton
Oaks Trustees for Harvard University,
1974. vi, 87 p., [23] leaves of plates : ill. ;
27 cm. Papers presented at the conference.
[SB466.F8D85 1973] 75-318945
*1. Gardens—France—Congresses. I.
MacDougall, Elisabeth B. II. Hazlehurst,
Franklin Hamilton. III. Title.*

Gardens—Gt. Brit.

HADFIELD, Miles. 712.640942
Gardening in Britain. London, Hutchinson
[1960; covered by label] [Newton, Mass.]
[C. T. Branford] 482 p. illus. 24 cm.
Includes bibliography. [SB466.G7H27] 60-
52118
*1. Gardens—Gt. Brit. 2. Landscape
gardening—Gt. Brit. I. Title.*

HADFIELD, Miles. 712'.6'0942
A history of British gardening. London,
New York, Spring Books, 1969. 483 p., 33
plates. illus., plans. 23 cm. Two plans on
lining papers. Rev. ed. Gardening in
Britain, London, Hutchinson, 1960.
Includes bibliographical references.
[SB466.G7H21 1969] 74-467575 30/-
*1. Gardens—Gt. Brit. 2. Landscape
architecture—Gt. Brit. I. Title.*

HELLYER, Arthur 712'.6'0942
George Lee, 1903-
Gardens to visit in Britain [by] Arthur
Hellyer. London, New York, P. Hamlyn
[1970] 160 p. illus. (part col.) maps. 29
cm. [SB453.3.G7H38] 78-20409 ISBN 0-
600-44179-2
1. Gardens—Gt. Brit. I. Title.

HYAMS, Edward S. 635.90942
The English garden [by] Edward Hyams.
Photos. by Edwin Smith. New York, H. N.
Abrams [1964?] 287 p. illus. (part col.) 33
cm. "Bibliographical notes": p. 281-283.
[SB466.G7H9] 64-20202
*1. Gardens—Gt. Brit. 2. Gardens—
Pictorial works. 3. Landscape gardening—
Gt. Brit. I. Title.*

ROPER, Lanning. 712.644
Royal gardens: Buckingham Palace,
Windsor Castle, Sandringham House, the
Palace of Holyroodhouse, Balmoral Castle.
With a foreword by G. A. Jellicoe.
London, W. H. & L. Collingridge; New
York, Transatlantic Arts [1953] 96p. illus.
29cm. [SB466.G7R65] 53-11604
1. Gardens—Gt. Brit. I. Title.

Gardens—Gt. Brit.—Pictorial works.

COATS, Peter. 712'.6
Great gardens of Britain. New York,
Putnam [1967] 286p. illus. (pt. col.) 32cm.
[SB466.G7C65] 67-19973 25.00
*1. Gardens—Gt. Brit.—Pictorial works. I.
Title.* **BIP**

Gardens—History.

BERRALL, Julia S. 712.09
The garden; an illustrated history, by Julia
S. Berrall. New York, Viking Press [1966]
388 p. illus. (part col.) plans. 29 cm. (A
Studio book) Bibliographical references

SUBJECT INDEX

GARDENS—PICTORIAL WORKS.

included in "Notes" (p. 382) [SB451.B47] 66-18845
1. Gardens—History. I. Title. BIP

CRISP, Frank, Sir, bart., 1843-1919. 712'.09
Mediaeval gardens; flowery medes and other arrangements of herbs, flowers, and shrubs grown in the Middle Ages, with some account of Tudor, Elizabethan, and Stuart gardens. Edited by Catherine Childs Paterson, with illus. from original sources collected by the author. New York, Hacker Art Books, 1966. 2 v. in 1. illus., plans. 29 cm. Reprint of the 1924 edition. Bibliography: v. 1, p. 121-130. [SB451.C7 1966] 67-4273
1. Gardens—History. 2. Landscape gardening—History. I. Paterson, Catherine Childs (Crisp) ed. II. Title.

GOTHEIN, Marie Luise (Schroeter) 1863-1931. 712'.09
A history of garden art. Edited by Walter P. Wright. Translated from the German by Mrs. Archer-Hind, with over 600 illus. New York, Hacker Art Books, 1966. 2 v. illus. 29 cm. Reprint of the 1928 edition. Translation of Geschichte der Gartenkunst. Bibliography: v. 2, p. 459-460. [SB451.G62 1966] 67-4274
1. Gardens—History. 2. Landscape architecture—History. I. Wright, Walter Page, 1864-1940, ed. II. Title. BIP

HYAMS, Edward S. 712'.6
A history of gardens and gardening, by Edward Hyams. New York, Praeger Publishers [1971] ix, 345 p. illus. (part col.), ports. 29 cm. Bibliography: p. 334-336. [SB451.H9] 70-109474 25.00
1. Gardens—History. 2. Gardening—History. I. Title.

RANDHAWA, Mohindar Singh, 1909- 712'.09
Gardens through the ages / Mohinder Singh Randhawa. Delhi : Macmillan Co. of India, 1976. xi, 303 p., 23 leaves of plates : ill. ; 23 cm. Includes bibliographical references and index. [SB451.R23] 76-904820 Rs75.00
1. Gardens—History. 2. Landscape architecture—History. I. Title. BIP

Gardens — Iran.

WILBER, Donald Newton. 712.0955
Persian gardens & garden pavilions. Rutland, Vt., C. E. Tuttle Co. [1962] 239 p. illus. (part col., part fold.) map. plans. 27 cm. Bibliography: p. [231]-235. [SB466.I6W5] 62-9360
1. Gardens — Iran. 2. Palaces — Iran. 3. Pavilions. I. Title. BIP

Gardens—Ireland.

HYAMS, Edward S. 712'.6
Irish gardens. Text by Edward Hyams. Photos. by William MacQuitty. With a foreword by Daniel J. Foley. New York, Macmillan [1967] 160 p. illus., col. plates. 31 cm. [SB466.I65H9 1967b] 67-12795
1. Gardens—Ireland. I. MacQuitty, William. II. Title.

Gardens, Islamic—Congresses.

DUMBARTON Oaks Colloquium on the History of Landscape Architecture, 4th, 1974. 712
The Islamic garden / [edited by Elizabeth B. MacDougall and Richard Ettinghausen]. Washington : Dumbarton Oaks, Trustees for Harvard University, 1976. 135 p., [20] leaves of plates : ill. ; 26 cm. Papers presented at the conference. Includes bibliographical references. [SB457.8.D85 1974] 76-468 ISBN 0-88402-064-9 15.00
1. Gardens, Islamic—Congresses. 2. Gardens—Iran—Congresses. 3. Gardens—Spain—Congresses. 4. Gardens—India—Congresses. I. MacDougall, Elizabeth B. II. Ettinghausen, Richard. III. Title.

Gardens—Italy.

MCGUIRE, Frances Margaret (Cheadle) 712.60945
Gardens of Italy. New York, Barrows [dist. Morrow, c.]1964. 223p. illus. 22cm. 64-23575 4.95
1. Gardens—Italy. I. Title.

MASSON, Georgina. 712.0945
Italian gardens. With 211 photogravure plates and 2 color plates. New York, Abrams [1961] 300 p. plates (part col.) maps. 33 cm. Bibliography: p. 293-296. [SB466.I8M3] 61-15925
1. Gardens—Italy. I. Title.

SHEPHERD, John Chiene 712.0945
Italian gardens of the Renaissance [by] J. C. Shepherd, G. A. Jellicoe. [1st Amer. ed.] New York, Architectural Bk. [1966] viii, 118p. 209 illus. (incl. plans) map. 26cm. English, French, & German. [SB466.I8S5 1966] 66-16594 10.95
1. Gardens—Italy. 2. Landscape architecture—Italy. 3. Art, Renaissance. I. Jellicoe, Geoffrey Alan, 1900- joint author. II. Title.

Gardens—Italy—History.

DUMBARTON Oaks Colloquium on the History of Landscape Architecture, 1st., 1971. 712'.6'0945
The Italian garden. [Edited by David R. Coffin] Washington, Dumbarton Oaks, 1972. xi, 114 p. illus. 26 cm. Includes bibliographical references. [SB466.I8D8 1971] 72-93722
1. Gardens—Italy—History. I. Coffin, David R., ed. II. Dumbarton Oaks. III. Title.

Gardens—Italy—Rome.

FAURE, Gariel [Auguste Gabriel Faure] 712.0945632
Gardens of Rome. Fair Lawn, N.J. Essential Books, [dist. New York. Oxford 1960] 200 p. illus., fold. col. map. 23 cm. (Les Beaux pays) 60-50106 bds., 8.50
1. Gardens—Italy—Rome. I. Title.

Gardens—Japan.

HARADA, Jiro, 1878- 712.6
Japanese gardens. Boston, C. T. Branford Co. [1956] 160p. illus. 30cm. 'Successor to [the author's] The gardens of Japan.' [SB466] 56-12490
1. Gardens—Japan. I. Title.

HORIGUCHI, Sutemi, 1895- 712.0952
Tradition of Japanese garden [Tr. from Japanese by Kazuko Okamura, Shigetaka Kaneko, Makoto Kuwabara. 2d ed. Tokyo] Kokusai Buna Shinokai; dist. [Honolulu. Hawaii] East West Ctr. Pr. [1964, c.1962] 185p. illus. (pt. col.) map, plans. 30cm. 64-2824 15.00
1. Gardens—Japan. 2. Landscape gardening—Japan. 3. Gardens—Pictorial works. I. Title.

KASHIKIE, Isamu. 712.62
The ABC of Japanese gardening. Translated by John Nathan. [Tokyo, Rutland, Vt.] Japan Publications Trading Co. [1964] 64 p. illus., plans. 21 cm. [SB466.J3K34] 64-2379
1. Gardens — Japan. 2. Landscape gardening — Japan. I. Title.

KINCAID, Viola W. 712'.0952
Japanese garden and floral art [by] Mrs. Paul Kincaid. New York, Hearthside Press [1966] 189 p. illus. 25 cm. [SB466.J3K5] 66-26674
1. Gardens—Japan. 2. Flower arrangement, Japanese. I. Title.

KUCK, Loraine E. 635.9'0952
The world of the Japanese garden; from Chinese origins to modern landscape art, by Loraine Kuck. With color photos. by Takji Iwamiya. [1st ed.] New York, Walker/Weatherhill [1968] 414 p. illus., 205 plates (part col.) 27 cm. "A Weathermark edition." Bibliography: p. 405-406. [SB466.J3K82] 68-26951 17.50
1. Gardens—Japan. I. Title.

MORI, Osamu 712.0952
Typical Japanese gardens. Tr. by Atsuo Tsuruoka. [Tokyo] Shibata Pub. Co.; [dist.: Rutland, Vt., Japan Pubns. Trading Co., 1963]c.1962. 161p. illus. (pt. col.) maps. 27cm. 62-22391 7.50
1. Gardens—Japan. 2. Landscape gardening—Japan. I. Title.

TAKAKUWA, Gisei, 1894- 712'.0952
Invitation to Japanese gardens. Photos. by Kiichi Asano. Commentary by Gisei Takakuwa. English adaptation by Richard F. Dickinson and Nobunao Matsuyama. [1st English language ed.] Rutland, Vt., Tuttle [1970] 168 p. illus. (part col.), 2 col. maps. 26 cm. Translation of Oniwa haiken. [SB466.J3T25413] 74-87788 ISBN 0-8048-0708-6 12.50
1. Gardens—Japan. 2. Gardens—Pictorial works. I. Asano, Kiichi, 1914- illus. II. Title.

TAKAKUWA, Gisei, 1894- 712'.6'0952
Japanese gardens revisited. Photos. by Kiichi Asano. Commentary by Gisei Takakuwa. English adaptation by Frank Davies & Hirokuni Kobatake. Rutland, Vt., C. E. Tuttle Co. [1973] v, 165 p. illus. 27 cm. Translation of Zoku oniwa haiken. [SB466.J3T25413 1973] 72-88930 17.50
1. Gardens—Japan. 2. Gardens—Pictorial works. 3. Gardens, Japanese—History. I. Asano, Kiichi, 1914- II. Title.

YOSHIDA, Tetsuro, 1894-1956. 635.90952
Gardens of Japan. Translated from the German by Marcus G. Sims. New York, F. A. Praeger [1957] 187 p. illus. (part col.) 28 cm. Bibliography: p. 186. [SB466.J3Y613] 57-12773
1. Gardens—Japan.

Gardens, Japanese.

ISHIMOTO, Tatsuo. 712'.0952
Japanese gardens today; how the Japanese use rocks, water, plants, by Tatsuo and Kiyoko Ishimoto. New York, Crown Publishers [1968] 127 p. illus., map. 24 cm. [SB458.I8] 68-9077 3.95
1. Gardens, Japanese. I. Ishimoto, Kiyoko, joint author. II. Title.

ITO, Teiji, 1922- 712'.0952
The Japanese garden; an approach to nature. Text by Teiji Ito. Photos. by Takeji Iwamiya. Design by Yusaku Kamekura. New Haven, Yale University Press, 1972. 205 p. illus. (part col.) 29 cm. Translation of Nihon no niwa. "English version by Donald Richie." [SB458.I8513] 72-75196 ISBN 0-300-01601-8 25.00
1. Gardens, Japanese. 2. Gardens—Japan. I. Iwamiya, Takeji, 1920- illus. II. Title. BIP

ITO, Teiji, 1922- 712'.2
Space and illusion in the Japanese garden. Text by Teiji Itoh, photos. by Sosei Kuzunishi. Translated and adapted from the Japanese, by Ralph Friedrich and Masajiro Shimamura. New York, Weatherhill [1973] 229 p. illus. 26 cm. Translation of Shakkei to tsuboniwa. [SB458.I8713] 72-89445 ISBN 0-8348-1512-5 8.95
1. Gardens, Japanese. 2. Gardens—Japan. I. Kuzunishi, Sosei, illus. II. Title.

*MINAKAWA, Taizo, 1917- 712.0952
Expressions of Japanese gardens. Kyoto, Japan, Kyoto-Shoin Co. [Berkeley, Calif., Perkins Oriental, 1966] 1v. (unpaged) 16 color prints in portfolio. 37cm. Comes with leaflet, with foreword and article by Donald Keene, The Man and art of Taizo Minakawa. (Collected works of Taizo Minakawa) English and Japanese. 9.00
I. Title.

SAITO, Katsuo, 1893- 712.62
Magic of trees and stones; secrets of Japanese gardening, by Katsuo Saito, Sadaji Wada [Tr. by Richard L. Gage. Rutland, Vt.] JPT Bk. Co. [c.1964] xv, 282p. 31cm. Bibl. [SB466.J3S19] 64-7610 12.50
1. Gardens, Japanese. I. Wada, Sadaji, 1918- II. Title.

Gardens, Japanese—History.

HAYAKAWA, Masao, 1925- 712'.0952
The garden art of Japan. Translated by Richard L. Gage. [1st ed.] New York, Weatherhill [1973] 173 p. illus. 24 cm. (The Heibonsha survey of Japanese art) Translation of Niwa. [SB458.H3813] 72-92257 ISBN 0-8348-1014-X 8.95
1. Gardens, Japanese—History. 2. Gardens—Japan. I. Title. II. Series. BIP

HOLBORN, Mark. 712'.0952
The ocean in the sand : Japan, from landscape to garden / Mark Holborn. Boulder, Colo. : Shambhala ; [New York] : distributed by Random House, 1978. 104 p. : ill. ; 23 x 25 cm. Includes index. Bibliography: p. 102. [SB458.H64] 78-58223 ISBN 0-87773-135-7 pbk. : 6.95
1. Gardens, Japanese—History. 2. Gardens, Japanese—Japan—History. 3. Japan—Civilization. 4. Landscape—Japan. I. Title. BIP

Gardens—Louisiana.

LEBLANC, Joyce Yeldell. 917.63'04
The Pelican guide to gardens of Louisiana. Gretna [La.] Pelican Pub. Co., 1974. 64 p. illus. (part col.) 22 cm. [SB466.U65L684] 74-834 ISBN 0-88289-003-4 2.95 (pbk.)
1. Gardens—Louisiana. I. Title. II. Title: Gardens of Louisiana. BIP

Gardens—Maine—Appeldore Island, Kittery.

THAXTER, Celia Laighton, 1835-1894. 635'.09741'95
An island garden / by Celia Thaxter ; illustrated by Childe Hassam ; with a new introd. by John M. Kingsbury. Bowie, MD : Heritage Books, 1978. xiii, ix, 130 p., [15] leaves of plates : ill. ; 23 cm. Reprint of the 1894 ed. published by Houghton, Mifflin, Boston. Includes index. [SB466.U7T6 1978] 78-3464 ISBN 0-917890-06-X : 15.00
1. Thaxter, Celia Laighton, 1835-1894. 2. Gardens—Maine—Appeldore Island, Kittery. 3. Appledore Island, Kittery, Me.—Description. I. Title. BIP

Gardens—New England.

ZOOK, Nicholas. 712'.6'0974
A guide to gardens of New England open to the public. Barre, Mass., Barre Publishers, 1973. 96 p. illus. 24 cm. [SB466.U65N486] 72-92469 ISBN 0-8271-7251-6 4.95
1. Gardens—New England. I. Title.

Gardens—New York—Westchester Co.

FOX, Helen (Morgenthau) 712.0974727
Adventure in my garden. New York, Crown [1965] 167p. illus., 12 col. plates., ports. 26cm. [SB453.2.N7F6] 65-15832 4.95
1. Gardens—New York—Westchester Co. I. Title.

Gardens—Ohio—Cleveland.

LEDERER, Clara. 712.5
Their paths are peace; the story of Cleveland's Cultural Gardens. [Cleveland] Cleveland Cultural Garden Federation, 1954. 99p. illus. 29cm. [SB466.U6L4] 55-24328
1. Gardens—Ohio—Cleveland. I. Title.

Gardens, Oriental—United States—Guide-books.

MCFADDEN DOROTHY LOA MAUSOLFF 1902- 917.3'04'925
Oriental gardens in America : a visitor's guide / by Dorothy Loa McFadden ; photos by James L. McFadden, Dorothy Loa McFadden, & others. Los Angeles : Douglas-West Publishers, c1976. 248 p., [4] leaves of plates : ill. (some col.) ; 24 cm. Bibliography: p. [241]-248. [SB466.U6M23] 75-46014 ISBN 0-913264-21-0 : 15.95
1. Gardens, Oriental—United States—Guide-books. 2. Gardens, Oriental—Guide-books. 3. Gardens, Japanese—United States—Guide-books. I. Title. BIP

Gardens—Pictorial works.

JELLICOE, Susan. 712'.6'0222
Modern private gardens, by Susan and Geoffrey Jellicoe. London, New York [etc.] Abelard-Schuman, 1968. 127 p. illus.,

plans. 22 x 26 cm. [SB465.J45] 68-10340 ISBN 0-200-71494-5 55/-
1. Gardens—Pictorial works. I. Jellicoe, Geoffrey Alan, 1900- joint author. II. Title.

SCHULER, Elizabeth. 712.084
Gardens around the world: terraces, patios, balconies, window boxes, garden decor, planting, and pools. Text by Elizabeth Schuler. With an introd. and notes by Peter Pesel. New York, H. N. Abrams [1964] 256 p. illus., col. plates. 27 cm. Translation of Mein Garten, mein Paradies; Gartenfreuden aus aller Welt. [SB165.S313] 64-20293
1. Gardens—Pictorial works. I. Title.

Gardens—South Carolina.

SHAFFER, Edward Terry Hendrie, 1880- 712.6
Carolina gardens the history, romance and tradition of many gardens of two States through more than two centuries. Foreword by DuBose Heyward. [3d ed. New York] Devin. 1963[c.1937-1963] 326p. illus. 23cm. 63-15596 6.95
1. Gardens—South Carolina. 2. Gardens—North Carolina. I. Title.

Gardens—South Carolina—Charleston.

BRIGGS, Loutrel Winslow, 1893- 635.909757
Charleston gardens. Photos. by R. Adamson Brown and others. Columbia, University of South Carolina Press [1951] xviii, 156 p. illus., maps. 29 cm. Bibliography: p. 155-156. [SB466.U7C5] Agr
1. Gardens—South Carolina—Charleston. I. Brown, R. Adamson. illus. II. Title. BIP

Gardens—Southern States.

WEDDA, John. 917.5'04'4
Gardens of the American South / John Wedda. New York : Galahad Books, c1971. 255 p., [16] leaves of plates : ill. (some col.) ; 29 cm. [SB466.U65S69 1971b] 73-88994 ISBN 0-88365-105-X : 12.50
1. Gardens—Southern States. I. Title.

WEDDA, John. 917.5'04'4
Gardens of the American South. [1st ed. Richmond, Va.] Westover Pub. Co. [1971] 255 p. illus. (part col.) 29 cm. (A Media general publication) [SB466.U65S69] 73-161080 ISBN 0-87858-008-5 12.50
1. Gardens—Southern States. I. Title.

Gardens—Symbolic aspects.

COMITO, Terry, 1935- 712'.01
The idea of the garden in the Renaissance / Terry Comito. New Brunswick, N.J. : Rutgers University Press, c1977. p. cm. Includes index. Bibliography: p. [SB470.7.C65] 77-12798 ISBN 0-8135-0841-X : 15.00
1. Gardens—Symbolic aspects. 2. Gardens, Renaissance. 3. Gardens, Medieval. 4. Renaissance. I. Title. BIP

Gardens—U.S.

DUTTON, Joan Parry. 635.90973
Enjoying America's gardens. New York, Reynal [1958] 311 p. illus. 22 cm. [SB466.U6D8] 58-12945
1. Gardens—U.S. 2. Botany—U.S. 3. Plant introduction. I. Title.

FITCH, James Marston. 712.62
Treasury of American gardens [by] James M. Fitch & F. F. Rockwell. New York, Harper [1956] 175p. illus. (part col.) diagrs. 34cm. [SB466.U6F5] 56-8496
1. Gardens—U. S. I. Rockwell, Frederick Frye, 1884— joint author. II. Title. III. Title: American gardens.

FROHMAN, Louis H. 712.0973
A pictorial guide to American gardens, by Louis H. Frohman and Jean Elliot. New York, Crown Publishers [1960] xv, 364 p. illus. (part col.) ports. 27 cm. [SB466.U6F7] 60-8622
1. Gardens—U.S. I. Elliot, Jean, joint author. II. Title.

GREAT gardens of America. 635.9'0973 General editor: Carroll C. Calkins. New York, Coward-McCann [1969] 298 p. illus. (part col.) 32 cm. [SB466.U6G7 1969] 71-90381 22.50
1. Gardens—U.S. I. Calkins, Carroll C., ed.

LOGAN, Harry Britton, 1910- 917'.04'53
The traveler's guide to North American gardens. New York, Scribner [1973] p. [SB466.U6L63] 73-1103 ISBN 0-684-13493-4
1. Gardens—United States. 2. Gardens—North America. I. Title.

THE new illustrated encyclopedia of gardening (unabridged). 635'.03, Edited by T. H. Everett with contributions from twenty horticulturists and authorities in the United States and Canada. New and rev. ed. New York, Greystone Press [1972-73] 26 v. (4206 p.), illus, 26 cm. [SB45.N424,] 72-192032 99.50.
1. Gardens—United States. 2. Wild flowers—North America. I. Everett, Thomas H., ed.

ROBERTS, Martha McMillan. 580.744
Public gardens and arboretums of the United States. Text and photos. by Martha McMillan Roberts. [1st ed.] New York, Holt, Rinehart and Winston [1962] 148 p. illus. 29 cm. [SB466.U6R6] 62-16247
1. Gardens—U.S. 2. Arboretums. I. Title.

SCHULER, Stanley. 712'.6'0973
America's great private gardens. New York, Macmillan [1967] 218 p. illus. (part col.) map. 32 cm. [SB466.U6S34] 67-12802
1. Gardens—United States. I. Title.

WILKINSON, Norman B. 712'.6'0922 B
E. I. du Pont, botaniste; the beginning of a tradition [by] Norman B. Wilkinson. Charlottesville, Published for the Eleutherian Mills-Hagley Foundation, University Press of Virginia [1972] xi, 139 p. illus. 27 cm. [SB63.D87W55] 76-171485 ISBN 0-8139-0399-8
1. Du Pont de Nemours, Eleuthere Irenee, 1771-1834. 2. Du Pont family (Pierre Samuel Du Pont de Nemours, 1739-1817) 3. Gardens—United States. I. Eleutherian Mills-Hagley Foundation, Greenville, Del. BIP

Gardens—United States—Directories.

GARDEN Club of America. 917.3'04'926
Guide to public gardens. New York : Garden Club of America, c1976. 122 p. ; 22 cm. Includes bibliographical references. [SB466.U6G32 1976] 77-150630 3.50
1. Gardens—United States—Directories. I. Title.

Gardens—U.S.—Hist.

SLOSSON, Elvenia, comp. 635.90973
Pioneer American gardening. New York, Coward-McCann [1951] xiv, 306 p. illus. 23 cm. "Bibliography and acknowledgments": p. 301-306. [SB466.U6S58] Agr
1. Gardens—U.S.—Hist. I. Title.

Gardens—Virginia.

GARDEN Club of Virginia. 917.55
Homes and gardens in old Virginia, edited by Frances Archer Christian [and] Susanne Williams Massie. Revised for the Garden Club of Virginia by Virginia Christian Claiborne, Ella Williams Smith [and] Caroline Pickrell Strudwick. Richmond, Garrett and Massie [1950] xvi, 544 p. illus. 25 cm. [SB466.U7G33 1950] 51-67
1. Gardens—Virginia. 2. Virginia—Historic houses, etc. I. Christian, Frances Archer. ed. II. Massie, Susanne Williams. ed. III. Title.

GARDEN Club of Virginia. 917.55
Homes and gardens in old Virginia, edited by Frances Archer Christian [and] Susanne Williams Massie. Rev. for the Garden Club of Virginia by Virginia Christian Claiborne, Ella Williams Smith [and] Caroline Pickrell Strudwick. Richmond, Garrett and Massie [c] 1953. xvi, 544p. illus. 25cm. [SB466.U7G33 1953] 53-11461
1. Gardens—Virginia. 2. Virginia—Historic houses, etc. I. Christian, Frances Archer, ed. II. Massie, Susanne Williams, ed. III. Title.

WILLIAMS, Dorothy Hunt. 635.9'09755
Historic Virginia gardens; preservations by the Garden Club of Virginia. Charlottesville, Published for the Garden Club of Virginia by the University Press of Virginia [1975] p. cm. Bibliography: p. [SB466.U65V88] 74-19422 ISBN 0-8139-0604-0 :
1. Garden Club of Virginia. 2. Gardens—Virginia. 3. Gardens—Conservation and restoration. 4. Virginia—Historic houses, etc.—Conservation and restoration. I. Garden Club of Virginia. II. Title. BIP

Gardens—Virginia—Williamsburg.

COLONIAL Williamsburg Foundation. 712.6'09755'4252
The gardens of Williamsburg. Williamsburg, Va., Distributed by Holt, Rinehart and Winston, New York, c1970. 47 p. col. illus. 28 cm. [SB466.U65W53] 70-140635 ISBN 0-910412-90-1 3.95
1. Gardens—Virginia—Williamsburg. 2. Gardens—Pictorial works. I. Title. BIP

Gardens—Virginia—Williamsburg—History.

NOEL Hume, Audrey. 635.9'09755'4252
Archaeology and the colonial gardener. Williamsburg, Va., Colonial Williamsburg Foundation [1974] 93 p. illus. 23 cm. (Colonial Williamsburg archaeological series, no. 7) Includes bibliographical references. [SB466.U65W56] 73-80008 ISBN 0-87935-012-1 1.50 (pbk.)
1. Gardens—Virginia—Williamsburg—History. 2. Gardening—Virginia—Williamsburg—History. 3. Williamsburg, Va.—Antiquities. I. Title. II. Series. BIP

Gardens—Washington, D.C.—History.

THE White House gardens: 712'.6'09753 a history and pictorial record. Pref.: Patricia Nixon. A general survey: Frederick L. Kramer. Concepts & design of the rose garden: Mrs. Paul Mellon. Introd. to the color plates: Lloyd Goodrich. Col. plates: Harold Sterner. New York, Great American Editions [1973] 144 p. illus. (part col.) 25 x 31 cm. Bibliography: p. 141-142. [SB453.2.W35W46] 72-87184 ISBN 0-913826-04-9 19.50
1. Gardens—Washington, D.C.—History. 2. Washington, D.C. White House—History. 3. Flowers—Pictorial works. I. Kramer, Frederick L. II. Mellon, Rachel Lambert (Lloyd) III. Goodrich, Lloyd, 1897- IV. Sterner, Harold, illus.

Gardner, Isabella (Stewart) 1840-1924.

CARTER, Morris, 1877- 708'.1'44610924 B
Isabella Stewart Gardner and Fenway Court. Freeport, N.Y., Books for Libraries Press [1972, c1925] xi, 254 p. illus. 22 cm. [N5220.G26C3 1972] 72-5539 ISBN 0-8369-6901-4
1. Gardner, Isabella (Stewart) 1840-1924. 2. Isabella Stewart Gardner Museum, Boston. I. Title. BIP

PALFFY, Eleanor. 920.7
The lady and the painter; an extravaganza, based on incidents in the lives of the two principal characters: Mrs. John Lowell Gardner of the Isabella Stewart Gardner Museum, and the artist, John Singer Sargent. Decorations by Alanson Hewes. New York, Coward-McCann [1951] 263 p. illus. 21 cm. [N8384.G3P3] 51-13732
1. Gardner, Isabella (Stewart) 1840-1924. 2. Sargent, John Singer, 1856-1924. I. Title.

THARP, Louise (Hall) 1898- 706'.5
Mrs. Jack; a biography of Isabella Stewart Gardner. [1st ed.] Boston, Little, Brown [1965] xii, 365 p. illus., ports. 22 cm. Bibliographical references included in "Chapter notes" (p. [329]-345) [N8384.G3T5] 65-18129
1. Gardner, Isabella (Stewart) 1840-1924. I. Title.

Garment cutting.

KOGOS International Corporation. 6874.103
Efficiency and incentives in the cutting room. Great Neck, N.Y.,Kogos International Corp., c1963. 64 p. illus., ports. 23 cm. [TT498.E45] 63-22666
1. Garment cutting. 2. Clothing trade—Management. I. Title.

MOULTON, Bertha. 687.12
Garment-cutting and tailoring for students. New York, Theatre Arts Books [1968, c1967] 223 p. illus. 31 cm. First published in 1949 under title: The "T & M" system of ladies' garment cutting and practical tailoring. [TT520.M867 1968] 68-8789 16.50
1. Garment cutting. 2. Tailoring (Women's) I. Title.

Garthright House, Va.

JONES, Russell. 728.3'7'09755462
Garthright House. Contributions by James Askins. Washington, Office of History and Historic Architecture, Eastern Service Center, 1971. 73 p., 22 l. illus. 28 cm. At head of title: Richmond National Battlefield Park. "Historic structures report, architectural data." [NA7238.R5J6] 75-613997
1. Garthright House, Va. I. Askins, James. II. Title.

Gaspard, Leon, 1882-1964.

GASPARD, Leon, 1882-1964. 759.13
Leon Gaspard: a retrospective exhibition, July 7-August 5, 1967. [San Francisco, Maxwell Galleries, 1967] 39 p. illus. (part col.) 25 cm. [ND237.G285A48] 73-282521
I. Maxwell Galleries.

WATERS, Frank, 1902- 927.5
Leon Gaspard. Flagstaff, Ariz., Northland Pr. [c.] 1964. 114p. illus. (pt. col.) port. 32cm. [ND237.G285W3] 64-20419 14.50
1. Gaspard, Leon, 1882-1964. I. Title.

Gatch, Lee.

AMERICAN Federation of Arts. 759.13
Lee Gatch, by Perry T. Rathbone. New York, Author [1083 Fifth Ave.] [c.1960] 28p. (Bibl.: p. 224.) plates (part col.) port. 18cm. 60-2193 2.00; .50 pap.,
1. Gatch, Lee. I. Rathbone, Perry Townsend. II. Title.

Gatling, Eva Ingersoll, 1912—

THE Art of the director : 708'.147'25 Eva Gatling's fifteen years at the Heckscher Museum : a loan exhibition from the collection of the Heckscher Museum / organized by Ronald G. Pisano, July 16-September 5, 1977, The Museums at Stony Brook, Stony Brook, New York. Stony Brook : The Museums, c1977. [24] p. : ill. ; 21 cm. [N5020.N7H422] 77-371847
1. Gatling, Eva Ingersoll, 1912- 2. Art—Exhibitions. I. Pisano, Ronald G. II. Heckscher Museum. III. Museums at Stony Brook.

Gaudi y Cornet, Antonio, 1852-1926.

CASANELLES, E 720'.924
Antonio Gaudi; a reappraisal [by] E. Casanelles. Greenwich, Conn., New York Graphic Society [1967 or 8, c1965] 124 p. 128 plates (part col.) facsim., port. 23 cm. Translation of Nueva vision de Gaudi. [NA1313.G3C383] 68-17554
1. Gaudi y Cornet, Antonio, I. Title.

CASANELLES, E. 720'.924
Antonio Gaudi; a reappraisal [by] E. Casanelles. Greenwich, Conn., New York Graphic Society [1967 or 8, c1965] 124 p., 128 plates (part col.) facsim., port. 23 cm.

Translation of Nueva vision de Gaudi. [NA1313.G3C383] 68-17554
1. Gaudi y Cornet, Antonio, 1852-1926.

CIRLOT, Juan Eduardo. 720'.924
The genesis of Gaudian architecture. [Edited by Luis Marsans and the Marquis de Aguilar de Vilahur. English translation by Joyce Wittenborn. 1st ed.] New York, G. Wittenborn [1967] 1 v. (unpaged) illus. (part fold.) 33 cm. Text in English and Spanish; captions in English, French, and Spanish. Translation of Introduccion a la arquitectura de Gaudi. [NA1313.G3C553] 67-29167
1. Gaudi y Cornet, Antonio, 1852-1926. I. Title.

COLLINS, George Roseborough, 1917- 720.946
Antonio Gaudi. New York, G. Braziller, 1960. 136 p. illus., plates (part col.) port. 26 cm. (The Masters of world architecture series) Bibliography: p. 131-134. [NA1313.G3C6] 60-6078
1. Gaudi y Cornet, Antonio, 1852-1926. I. Title. II. Series. BIP

COLLINS, George Roseborough, 1917- 016.72 s
Antonio Gaudi and the Catalan movement, 1870-1930. [Compiled by George R. Collins with the assistance of Maurice E. Farinas] Edited by William B. O'Neal. Charlottesville, Published for the American Association of Architectural Bibliographers [by] the University Press of Virginia, 1973. xxxiv, 173 p. illus. 24 cm. (American Association of Architectural bibliographers. Papers, v. 10) [Z5941.A5 vol. 10] [Z8327.8] 016.720'9467 74-159878 ISBN 0-8139-0477-3 10.00
1. Gaudi y Cornet, Antonio, 1852-1926—Bibliography. 2. Architedture—Catalonia—Bibliography. I. Farinas, Maurice E., joint author. II. Title. III. Series.

DESCHARNES, Robert. 720'.924 B
Gaudi; the visionary [by] Robert Descharnes. [Photos. by] Clovis Prevost. Pref. by Salvador Dali. Translation from the French by Frederick Hill. Followed by "Gaudi's artistic and religious vision" by Francesc Pujols. Introd. by Joan Alavedra. Translation from the Catalan by Judith C. Rohrer. Editor: George R. Collins. New York, Viking Press [1971] 247 p. illus. (part col.), ports. 31 cm. (A Studio book) Translation of La vision artistique et religieuse de Gaudi and La visio artistica i religiosa d'en Gaudi. "Selected bibliography, by George R. Collins": p. 246-247. [NA1313.G3D413] 71-101778 ISBN 0-670-33586-X
1. Gaudi y Cornet, Antonio, 1852-1926. I. Prevost, Clovis, illus. II. Pujols, Francisco, 1882-1962. La visio artistica i religiosa d'en Gaudi. English. 1971.

GAUDI Y CORNET, Antonio, 1852-1926. 720.946
Antonio Gaudi, 1852-1926 [by] Cesar Martinell. [Translated from the Italian by Peter Simmons.] New York. Universe Books [1960] [16]p. 70 plates (6 col.) 17cm. (Universe architecture series) Bibl.: p.[14] 60-12419 1.50 pap.,
I. Martinell, Cesar, 1888- II. Title.

GIEDION-WELCKER, Carola 720.946
Park Guell de A. Gaudi [por] C. Giedion-Welcker.Fotoscop: Gomis-Prats. New York, Wittenborn [1966] 64p. plates (pt. col.) plan. 21cm. Spanish, German, English, and French. [NA1313.G3G5] 66-8743 15.00
1. Gaudi y Cornet, Antonio, 1852-1926. I. Title.

MARTINELL y Brunet, Cesar, 1888-1973. 720'.92'4
Gaudi : his life, his theories, his work / Cesar Martinell ; translated from the Spanish by Judith Rohrer ; edited by George R. Collins. Cambridge, Mass. : MIT Press, [1975] p. cm. Translation of Gaudi: su vida, su teoria, su obra. Includes indexes. Bibliography: p. [NA1313.G3M2813 1975] 74-109 ISBN 0-262-13087-4 : 45.00
1. Gaudi y Cornet, Antonio, 1852-1926. I. Title.

SWEENEY, James Johnson, 1900- 720'.924
Antoni Gaudi [by] James Johnson Sweeney and Josep Lluis Sert. Rev. ed. New York, Praeger [1970, c1960] 191 p. illus. (part col.), facsims., plans, ports. 29 cm. Bibliography: p. 187-191. [NA1313.G3S9 1970] 70-125363 18.50
1. Gaudi y Cornet, Antonio, 1852-1926. I. Sert, Jose Luis, 1902- joint author.

SWEENEY, James Johnson, 1900- 720.946
Antoni Gaudi [by] James Johnson Sweeney and Josep Lluis Sert. New York, Praeger [1961, c1960] 191 p. illus. (part col.) ports., plans. 29 cm. (Books that matter) Bibliographical references included in "Notes" (p. 177-181) Bibliography: p. 187-191. [NA1313.G3S9] 60-15244
1. Gaudi y Cornet, Antonio, 1852-1926. I. Sert, Jose Luis, 1902- joint author.

Gaudi y Cornet, Antonio, 1852-1926—Bibliography.

COLLINS, George Roseborough, 1917- 016.72 s
Antonio Gaudi and the Catalan movement, 1870-1930. [Compiled by George R. Collins with the assistance of Maurice E. Farinas] Edited by William B. O'Neal. Charlottesville, Published for the American Association of Architectural Bibliographers [by] the University Press of Virginia, 1973. xxxiv, 173 p. illus. 24 cm. (American Association of Architectural bibliographers. Papers, v. 10) [Z5941.A5 vol. 10] [Z8327.8] 016.720'9467 74-159878 ISBN 0-8139-0477-3 10.00
1. Gaudi y Cornet, Antonio, 1852-1926—Bibliography. 2. Architedture—Catalonia—Bibliography. I. Farinas, Maurice E., joint author. II. Title. III. Series.

Gaudier-Brzeska, Henri, 1891-1915.

EDE, Harold Stanley, 1895- 730'.92'4
Savage messiah, by H. S. Ede. New York, Outerbridge & Lazard; distributed by Dutton [1972, c1971] 160 p. illus. 22 cm. [NB553.G35E4 1972] 72-84263 ISBN 0-87690-081-3 6.95
1. Gaudier-Brzeska, Henri, 1891-1915. 2. Brzeska, Sophie Suzanne. I. Title. BIP

GAUDIER-BRZESKA, Henri, 1891-1915 741.944
Drawings and sculpture. Introd. by Mervyn Levy. New York, October House [1965] 30, [82]p. plates (pt. mounted col.) 29cm. Bibl. [NC1135.G38L4] 65-17936 15.00
I. Levy, Mervyn. II. Title.

GAUDIER-BRZESKA, Henri, 1891-1915. 760'.092'4
Ezra's bowmen of Shu. [Cambridge? Mass., Adams House & Lowell House Printers, 1965] 1 portfolio ([1] l., 1 plate) 54 cm. Title from label on portfolio. 87 copies. No. 55 Contains a drawing by the author and a leaf with an introd. by Guy Davenport and a letter from the author to John Cournos, dated 27 Dec. 1914. [NC248.G2A45 1965] 68-42550
I. Cournos, John, 1881- II. Davenport, Guy. III. Title.

GAUDIER-BRZESKA, Henri, 1891-1915. 741.9'44
Sixty drawings by Henri Gaudier-Brzeska, 1891-1915 : [catalogue of an exhibition held at the] Mercury Gallery, 26 Cork St., London, W.1., October 15-November 15 1975. London : Mercury Gallery, [1976] [40] p.: ill., facsims., ports. ; 19 cm. Includes extracts from letters by Gaudier-Brzeska. Bibliography: p. [40] [NC248.G2M47] 76-378725 ISBN 0-9501919-1-4 : £0.75
1. Gaudier-Brzeska, Henri, 1891-1915. I. Mercury Gallery. II. Title.

POUND, Ezra Loomis, 1885- 730'.924
Gaudier-Brzeska, a memoir [by] Ezra Pound. [New York, New Directions Pub. Corp., 1970] 147 p. illus., ports. 21 cm. (A New Directions book) Includes bibliographical references. [NB553.G35P6 1970] 78-107490 7.50
1. Gaudier-Brzeska, Henri, 1891-1915. BIP

POUND, Ezra Loomis, 1885- 730.944
Gaudier-Brzeska, a memoir. [New York] New Directions [1961] 147p. illus. 60-9893 8.25
1. Gaudier-Brzeska, Henri, 1891-1915. I. Title.

Gaudy ware.

WILLIAMS, Howard Y. 738.3'7
Gaudy Welsh china / by Howard Y. Williams. Des Moines : Wallace-Homestead Book Co., c1978. 130 p. : ill. ; 20 x 23 cm. Bibliography: p. 124-130. [NK4340.G38W54] 76-15495 ISBN 0-87069-167-8 : 12.95
1. Gaudy ware. 2. Pottery, Welsh. I. Title. BIP

Gauguin, Paul, 1848-1903.

ANDERSEN, Wayne V. 759.4 B
Gauguin's paradise lost [by] Wayne Andersen. With the assistance of Barbara Klein. New York, Viking Press [1971] xii, 371 p. illus. 25 cm. Bibliography: p. 355-362. [ND553.G27A74 1971] 72-135347 ISBN 0-670-33593-2 12.50
1. Gauguin, Paul, 1848-1903. I. Klein, Barbara. II. Title.

BOUDAILLE, Georges 759.4
Gaugin. [Tr. from French by Alisa Jaffa] New York, Tudor [1966, c1964] 274p. illus. (pt. col.) 22cm. [ND553.G27B633] 66-6881 5.95
1. Gauguin, Paul, 1848-1903. I. Title.

CHARMET, Raymond 759.4
Paul Gauguin. [Ed.: Anthony Bosman. Tr.: Havdn Barnes] New York, Barnes & Noble [1966] 90p. illus., facsims., plates (pt. col.) 18cm. (Barnes & Noble art ser., no. 625) [ND553.G27C38] 66-8811 .75 pap.,
1. Gauguin. Paul. 1848-1903. I. Title.

CHICAGO. Art Institute. 709.44
Gauguin: paintings, drawings, prints, sculpture. The Art Institute of Chicago [Feb. 12-Mar. 29, 1959] The Metropolitan Museum of Art [Apr. 21-May 31, 1959. Chicago, 1959] 90p. illus. (part col.) port. 26cm. Bibliography: p. 27. [ND553.G27C45] 59-867
1. Gauguin, Paul, 1848-1908. I. New York. Museum of Modern Art. II. Title.

CHICAGO. Art Institute. 769.944
Gauguin prints [at] the Art Institute of Chicago [and] the Metropolitan Museum of Art. [Prepared by Hugh Edwards, associate curator of prints & drawings. Chicago] 1959. unpaged. illus. 22cm. [NE650.G3C47] 59-1817
1. Gauguin, Paul, 1848-1903. I. New York. Metropolitan Museum of Art. II. Edwards, Hugh L. III. Title.

CINCINNATI. Art Museum. 759.4
The early work of Paul Gauguin; genesis of an artist. [Cincinnati, 1971] 35 p. illus. (part col.), ports. 26 cm. Catalog of the exhibition held Mar. 18-Apr. 26, 1971. Bibliography: p. 13. [ND553.G27C48] 79-24364
1. Gauguin, Paul, 1848-1903. I. Title.

COGNIAT, Raymond, 1896- 759.4
Gauguin. [Tr. from French by Kenneth Martin Leake] New York, Abrams [1963] 79p. col. illus. 19cm. (Students' ser. of great artists) 63-14300 1.95
1. Gauguin, Paul, 1848-1903. I. Title.

DANIELSSON, Bengt 759.4
Gauguin in the South Seas [Tr. from Swedish by Reginald Spink. 1st Amer ed.] Garden City, N. Y., Doubleday, 1966 [c.1964, 1965] 336p. illus. (pt. col.) ports. (pt. col.) 24cm. Bibl. [ND553.G27D33] 65-12363 7.95
1. Gauguin, Paul, 1848-1903. 2. Oceanica—Descr. and trav. Views. I. Title.

DIEHL, Gaston. 759.4
Gauguin. Translated from the French by Anne Ross. New York, Crown Publishers [1967] 46 p. illus. (part col.) 19 cm. (Basic art library) [ND553.G27D53] 68-507
1. Gauguin, Paul, 1848-1903.

FIELD, Richard S. 759.4
Paul Gauguin : the paintings of the first voyage to Tahiti / Richard S. Field. New York : Garland Pub., 1977, i.e.1978 415, [15] p. : [44] leaves of plates : ill. ; 21 cm. (Outstanding dissertations in the fine arts) Originally presented as the author's thesis, Harvard, 1963. Includes bibliographies. [ND553.G27F53 1977] 76-23617 ISBN 0-8240-2688-8 lib.bdg. : 45.00
1. Gauguin, Paul, 1848-1903. 2. Tahiti in art. 3. Tahiti—Description and travel—Views. I. Title. II. Series.

GAUGUIN, Paul, 1848-1903. 741.9'44
The drawings of Gauguin [text by] Ronald Pickvance. Feltham, New York, Hamlyn, 1970. 44 p., 132 plates. illus. (some col.), facsim. 32 cm. Bibliography: p. 44. [NC248.G25P5] 70-587099 ISBN 0-600-02555-1 £2.50
I. Pickvance, Ronald. II. Title.

GAUGUIN, Paul, 1848-1903. 759.4 B
Noa Noa / by Paul Gauguin ; translated from the French by O. F. Theis. Danbury, CT : Archer Editions Press, 1976, c1919. 148 p., [9] leaves of plates : ill. ; 21 cm. Reprint of the ed. published by N. L. Brown, New York. [ND553.G27A25 1976] 76-16128 ISBN 0-89097-006-8 : 15.00
1. Gauguin, Paul, 1848-1903. 2. Tahiti. 3. Painters—France—Correspondence, reminiscences, etc. I. Title. BIP

GAUGUIN, Paul, 1848-1903. 741.9'44
Paul Gauguin: monotypes. By Richard S. Field. [Philadelphia] Philadelphia Museum of Art [1973] 148 p. illus. (part col.) 25 cm. Catalog of the exhibition held at the Philadelphia Museum of Art, March 23-May 13, 1973. Bibliography: p. 144-145. [NE2246.G3F5] 73-77306
1. Gauguin, Paul, 1848-1903. I. Field, Richard S. II. Philadelphia Museum of Art. III. Title.

GAUGUIN, Paul [Eugene Henry Paul Gauguin] 1848-1903 759.4
Intimate journals. [from French] by Van Wyck Brooks. Pref. by Emil Gauguin. With the 29 drawings from the [original] ms. & 25 additional pages of drawings & paintings [Gloucester, Mass., P. Smith, 1966, c.1936, 1949] 254p. illus., ports. facsims. 21cm. (Midland bks, MB13 rebound) [ND553] 4.00
I. Title. BIP

HANSON, Lawrence. 759.4
Noble savage; the life of Paul Gauguin, by Lawrence and Elisabeth Hanson. New York, Random House [1955, c1954] 299p. illus. 24cm. [ND553.G27H33 1955] 927.5 55-5792
1. Gauguin, Paul, 1848-1903. I. Hanson, Elisabeth M., joint author. II. Title.

HANSON, Lawrence. 927.5
The sockers: Gaugin, Van Gogh, Cezanne [by] Lawrence and Elisabeth Hanson. New York, Random House [c1963] xv, 334 p. illus., ports. 25 cm. Bibliography: p. [325]-328. [ND553.G27H34] 63-11619
1. Gaugin, Paul, 1848-1903. 2. Gogh, Vincent van, 1853-1890. 3. Cezanne, Paul, 1839-1906. 4. Post-impressionism (Art) I. Hanson, Elisabeth M., joint author. II. Title.

HUYGHE, Rene. 759.4
Gauguin. [Translated by Helen C. Slonim] New York, Crown Publishers, 1959. 96 p. illus. (part mounted, part col.) 29 cm. Bibliography: p. 93-95. [ND553.G27H813] 59-65053
1. Gauguin, Paul, 1848-1903. BIP

MARCHIORI, Giuseppe. 759.4
Gauguin. [1st American ed. Translated from the Italian by Caroline Beamish] New York, Grosset & Dunlap [1967] 39, [80] p. col. illus. 18 cm. (The New Grosset art library, 11) On cover: Gauguin; the life and work of the artist. [ND553.G27M323 1967] 68-12745
1. Gauguin, Paul, 1848-1903.

PERRUCHOT, Henri, 1917- 927.5
Gauguin. Translated by Humphrey Hare. Edited by Jean Ellsmoor. [1st ed.] Cleveland, World Pub. Co. [1964, c1963] 398 p. illus., ports., facsim. 23 cm. (His Art and destiny, v. 4) Translation of La vie de Gaugin. Bibliography: p. 371-389. [ND553.G27P433] 64-12463
1. Gauguin, Paul, 1848-1903.

SCHNEEBERGER, Pierre Francis 759.4
Gauguin: Tahiti. [Tr. from French by Diana Imber] New York 20. French &European Pubns., 610 Fifth Ave. [1963]

62p. mounted col. illus. 21cm. (Rhythm & colour, 6) Bibl. 63-3616 3.95
1. Gau)uin, Paul, 1848-1903. I. Title.

SCHNEIDER, Bruno F. 759.4
Gauguin. Text by Bruno Schneider. Tr. by Susan Bellamy. New York, Crown [1966] 28p. illus., 10 col. plates. 31cm. (Folio art bks.) [ND553.G27S36] 66-3966 1.45 pap.,
1. Gauguin, Paul, 1848-1903. I. Title.

SOLOMON R. Guggenheim Museum, New York 759.4
Gauguin and the decorative style; [exhibition. New York, 1966] [46]p. illus. (pt. col.) 26cm. (Its Commentary, 1/66) Bibl. [ND553.G27S6] 66-25519 1.75 pap.,
1. Gauguin, Paul, 1848-1903. I. Title.

WERNER, Alfred, 1911- 759'.4
Paul Gauguin. New York, McGraw-Hill [1967] 47 p. illus., 20 col. slides (in pockets) 29 cm. (Color slide program of the great masters) [ND553.G27W4] 67-16265
1. Gauguin, Paul, 1848-1903. 2. Lantern slides. I. Title. II. Series. **BIP**

WILDENSTEIN, Daniel, 1917- 759.4
Gauguin [by] Daniel Wildenstein [and] Raymond Cogniat [in collaboration with the Wildenstein Foundation, Paris. 1st U.S. ed.] Garden City, N.Y., Doubleday [1974] 94 p. illus. (part col.) 34 cm. (The Great impressionists) Translation of Paul Gauguin. Bibliography: p. 94. [ND553.G27W5213] 73-11046 ISBN 0-385-09533-3 9.95
1. Gauguin, Paul, 1848-1903. I. Gauguin, Paul, 1848-1903. II. Cogniat, Raymond, 1896- joint author. III. Wildenstein Foundation.
Library binding 6.95; ISBN 0-385-08363-7.

Gauguin, Paul, 1848-1903—Catalogs.

GAUGUIN, Paul, 1848-1903. 709'.2'4
Gauguin : 116 reproductions / selected & introduced by Nicholas Wadley. Oxford : Phaidon, 1978. [16] p., 96 p. of plates : chiefly ill., (chiefly col.), ports. (some col.) ; 42 cm. [N6853.G34A4 1978] 77-88232 ISBN 0-7148-1793-7 pbk. : 9.95
1. Gauguin, Paul, 1848-1903—Catalogs. I. Wadley, Nicholas.
Distributed by Dutton, N.Y.

Gauguin, Paul, 1848-1903—Juvenile literature.

PETER, Adeline. 759.4 B
Paul Gauguin, by Adeline Peter and Ernest Raboff. Edited by Bradley Smith. Garden City, N.Y., Doubleday [1974] [31] p. illus. (part col.) 29 cm. (Art for children) (A Gemini-Smith book) A brief biography of this nineteenth-century French artist accompanies reproductions and analyses of several of his works. [ND553.G27P45] 73-75360 ISBN 0-385-05012-7 4.95
1. Gauguin, Paul, 1848-1903—Juvenile literature. I. Raboff, Ernest Lloyd, joint author. II. Title.
Library binding; 5.70, ISBN 0-385-06994-4

Gaul, Gilbert William, 1855-1919.

GAUL, Gilbert William, 1855-1919. 759.13
Gilbert Gaul : [exhibition], Tennessee Fine Arts Center, March 9-April 13, 1975, Huntsville Museum of Art, May 1-30, 1975 / by James F. Reeves. Huntsville, [Ala.] : The Museum, [1975] 60 p. : ill. ; 26 cm. Includes catalogue. Bibliography: p. 60. [ND237.G295R43] 75-313958
1. Gaul, Gilbert William, 1855-1919. I. Reeves, James F. II. Tennessee Fine Arts Center. III. Huntsville Museum of Art.

Gaulli. Giovanni Battista, 1639-1709.

ENGGASS, Robert, 1921- 759.5
The painting of Baciccio, Giovanni Battista Gaulli, 1639-1709. University Park, Penn. State Univ. Pr. [c.]1964. xix, 200p. 139 illus. (incl. ports.) 29cm. Bibl. 64-15074 20.00
1. Gaulli. Giovanni Battista, 1639-1709. I. Title.

Gautama Buddha—Art.

COOMARASWAMY, Ananda Kentish, 1877-1947. 732'.4
The origin of the Buddha image, by Ananda K. Coomaraswamy. [1st Indian ed.] New Delhi, Munshiram Manoharlal [1972] 42 p. illus. 29 cm. "Unabridged and unaltered republication of the work first published in Art bulletin, vol. IX, no. 4." Includes bibliographical references. [N8193.2.C66 1972] 72-907857
1. Gautama Buddha—Art. I. Title.
Distributed by Verry; 12.00

Gay, Edward, 1837-1928.

COKER, Richard G. 759.13 B
Portrait of an American painter: Edward Gay, 1837-1928, by Richard G. Coker. [1st ed.] New York, Vantage Press [1973] 115 p. illus. 21 cm. Includes bibliographical references. [ND237.G318C64] 74-157761 ISBN 0-533-00777-1 3.95
1. Gay, Edward, 1837-1928. I. Title.

Gay, John, 1685-1732. The beggar's opera.

HOGARTH, William, 1697-1764 759.2
the beggar's opera' by Hogarth and Blake. Portfolio comp. by Wilmarth Sheldon Blake, Philip Hofer [Pub. by] Harvard and Yale [dist.] New Haven, Conn., Yale [c.] 1965. 15, [15]p. illus. facsims. 24x31cm. and [1]1, 11 plates. 55x69cm. Issued in portfolio. Plates are reprods. of Hogarth's seven versions of his picture which illus. act 3, scene 11, air 5 of John Gay's The beggar's opera, with reprods. of the 1st and 4th states of Blake's engraving after the Duke of Leeds version, and including a mod. restrike of the 4th state. Bibl. [ND497.H7L4] 65-15050 100.00, bxd.
1. Gay, John, 1685-1732. The beggar's opera. I. Blake, William, 1757-1827. II. Lewis, Wilmarth Sheldon, 1895- comp. III. Hofer, Philip, 1898- comp. IV. Title.

Gebauer, Clara—Art collections.

GEBAUER, Paul, 1900- 730'.0967'11
A guide to Cameroon art from the Collection of Paul and Clara Gebauer. [Exhibition] Portland Art Museum, October 30 - December 1, 1968. [Portland, Or., 1968] [43] p. illus., maps, ports. 23 cm. [N7397] 76-5033
1. Gebauer, Clara—Art collections. 2. Art, Cameroon—Exhibitions. I. Portland, Or. Art Museum. II. Title.

Gebelein, George Christian, 1878-1945.

LEIGHTON, Margaretha Gebelein. 739.2'3'724 B
George Christian Gebelein, Boston silversmith, 1878-1945 : a biographical sketch / by Margaretha Gebelein Leighton, in collaboration with Esther Gebelein Swain and J. Herbert Gebelein. Boston : [Gebelein], 1976. xix, 118 p., [4] leaves of plates : ill. ; 25 cm. Includes bibliographical references. [NK7198.G35L44] 76-52871
1. Gebelein, George Christian, 1878-1945. 2. Silversmiths—Massachusetts—Boston—Biography. 3. Silverwork—Massachusetts—Boston. I. Swain, Esther Gebelein, joint author. II. Gebelein, J. Herbert, joint author. III. Title.

Geffrye Museum, London.

GEFFRYE Museum, London. 749.2'2'07402144
Geffrye Museum / [text by Jeffery Daniels]. Derby : English Life Publications [for the Inner London Education Authority], 1975. [2], 30 p. : ill. (some col.), map, ports. ; 14 x 21 cm. [NK2538.L66G43 1975] 76-353159 ISBN 0-85101-091-1 : £0.40
1. Geffrye Museum, London. 2. Furniture—England. 3. Decoration and ornament—England. I. Daniels, Jeffery.

Geishas.

CHANDLER, Billie T 745.92252
The geisha story, with doll-and-flower arrangements. Photos. by Herbert F. Herpolsheimer, Jr. Rutland, Vt., C.E. Tuttle Co. [1963] 56 p. (chiefly illus.) 18 cm. [GV1472.3.C5] 63-8718
1. Geishas. I. Title. **BIP**

Gela, Sicily—Antiquities.

GRIFFO, Pietro. 913.3'7'8
Gela; the Ancient Greeks in Sicily [by] Pietro Griffo [and] Leonard von Matt. Greenwich, Conn., New York Graphic Society [1968] 223 p. illus. (part col.), maps (part col.) 34 cm. Translation of Gela; destin d'une cite grecque de Sicile. Bibliography: p. 213-216. [DG975.G34G693] 68-29116 17.50
1. Gela, Sicily—Antiquities. I. Matt, Leonard von, joint author. II. Title: The Ancient Greeks in Sicily.

Gelatin—Congresses.

SYMPOSIUM on Photographic Gelatin, 2d, Trinity College, Cambridge, Eng., 1970. 771'.53
Photographic gelatin; proceedings of the Second Symposium on Photographic Gelatin held at Trinity College, Cambridge, August-September, 1970. Edited by R. J. Cox. London, New York, Academic Press for The Scientific and Technical Group of the Royal Photographic Society, 1972. xiii, 309 p. illus. 24 cm. Includes bibliographical references. [TR280.S95 1970] 79-170758 ISBN 0-12-194450-6 15.50
1. Gelatin—Congresses. I. Cox, R. J., ed. II. Royal Photographic Society of Great Britain, London. III. Title. **BIP**

Gelee, Claude, called Claude Lorrain, 1600-1682.

COTTE, Sabine. 741.9'44
Claude Lorrain. [Translated by Helen Sebba] New York, G. Braziller [1971, c1970] 96 p. illus. 25 cm. (The Great draughtsmen) Translation of L'univers de Claude Lorrain. [NC248.G3C613 1971] 76-137220 ISBN 0-8076-0594-8 7.95
1. Gelee, Claude, called Claude Lorrain, 1600-1682. **BIP**

KITSON, Michael. 759.4
Claude Lorrain: Landscape with the Nymph Egeria. [Newcastle upon Tyne, Eng.] University of Newcastle upon Tyne, 1968. 20 p. illus. 24 cm. (Charlton lecture, 49) Includes bibliographical references. [ND553.G3K52] 77-488072
1. Gelee, Claude, called Claude Lorrain, 1600-1682. Landscape with the nymph Egeria. I. Title. II. Series.

MANWARING, Elizabeth Wheeler, 1879- 701.17
Italian landscape in eighteenth century England; a study chiefly of the influence of Claude Lorrain and Salvator Rosa on English taste, 1700-1800. New York, Russell & Russell, 1965. vii, 243p. plates, port. 23cm. First pub. in 1925. [BH301.L3M3] 66-10419 8.50
1. Gelee, Claude, called Claude Lorrain, 1600-1682. 2. Rosa, Salvatore, 1615-1673. 3. Landscape. 4. Nature (Asthetics) 5. Landscape painting—Italy. 6. Landscape gardening—England. I. Title. **BIP**

ROTHLISBERGER, Marcel. 759.4
Claude Lorrain: the paintings. New Haven, Yale University Press, 1961. 2v. plates, ports. 28cm. (Yale publications in the history of art. 13) Contents.v. 1. Critical catalogue.--v. 2. Illustrations. Bibliography: v. 1. p.551-558. [ND553.G3R6] 61-6319
1. Gelee, Claude, called Claude Lorrain, 1600-1682. I. Title. II. Series. **BIP**

ROTHLISBERGER, Marcel. 759.4
The Claude Lorrain album in the Norton Simon, inc., Museum of Art. Los Angeles, Los Angeles County Museum of Art [1971] 33 p., 64 l. illus. 25 x 31 cm. [NC248.G3R6] 79-158485 ISBN 0-87587-045-7
1. Gelee, Claude, called Claude Lorrain, 1600-1682. II. Norton Simon, inc. Museum of Art. III. Title.

ROTHLISBERGER, Marcel. 741.9'44
Claude Lorrain: the drawings. Berkeley, University of California Press, 1968. 2 v. plates. 33 cm. (California studies in the history of art, 8) Contents.Contents.—[1] Catalog.—[2] Plates. Bibliography: v. [1], p. 459-462. [NC248.L6A43] 66-24050 110.00
1. Gelee, Claude, called Claude Lorrain, 1600-1682. I. Title. II. Series.

Gem carving.

KENNEDY, Gordon S. 736'.2
The fundamentals of gemstone carving, by Gordon S. Kennedy and others. Compiled and edited by Pansy D. Kraus. Planning and direction by Hugh N. Leiper. San Diego, Calif., Lapidary Journal, Inc., 1967. vi, 128 p. illus. (part col.) 30 cm. [NK5535.K4] 67-7443
1. Gem carving. I. Krauss, Pansy D., ed. II. Leiper, Hugh N. III. Title.

WALTER, Martin. 736'.2
Gemstone carving / Martin Walter. Radnor, Pa. : Chilton Book Co., c1977. xiv, 157 p., [2] leaves of plates : ill. (some col.) ; 27 cm. (Chilton's creative crafts series) Includes index. Bibliography: p. 152-154. [NK5525.W34 1977] 76-27650 ISBN 0-8019-6192-0 : 12.50 ISBN 0-8019-6193-9 pbk. : 6.95
1. Gem carving. I. Title. **BIP**

Gem cutting.

FIRSOFF, Valdemar Axel. 736'.2'028
Working with gemstones / V. A. Firsoff. New York : Arco Pub. Co., c1974. x, 210 p. : ill. (some col.) ; 23 cm. Includes index. Bibliography: p. 203-206. [TS752.5.F57 1974b] 74-90929 ISBN 0-668-03430-0 : 8.95
1. Gem cutting. I. Title. **BIP**

HUTTON, Helen. 736'.2
Practical gemstone craft. New York, Viking Press [1972] 103 p. illus. 25 cm. (A studio book) Bibliography: p. 102-103. [TS752.5.H88] 73-185385 ISBN 0-670-57061-3 8.95
1. Gem cutting. 2. Precious stones. I. Title.

LONG, Frank W. 736'.2'028
The creative lapidary : materials, tools, techniques, design / Frank W. Long. New York : Van Nostrand Reinhold, 1976. 136 p. : ill. ; 25 cm. Includes index. Bibliography: p. 133-134. [TS752.5.L65] 76-21357 ISBN 0-442-24887-3 : 12.95
1. Gem cutting. I. Title. **BIP**

QUICK, Lelande. 736'.2'028
Gemcraft : how to cut and polish gemstones / Lelande Quick and Hugh Leiper. 2d ed. / rev. by Pansy D. Kraus. Radnor, Pa. : Chilton Book Co., c1977. p. cm. (Chilton's creative crafts series) Includes indexes. Bibliography: p. [TS752.Q5 1977] 77-4578 ISBN 0-8019-6242-0 : 13.95. ISBN 0-8019-6243-9 pbk. : 7.95
1. Gem cutting. 2. Gem carving. I. Leiper, Hugh N., joint author. II. Kraus, Pansy D. III. Title.

SCARFE, Herbert. 736'.2
Cutting and setting stones. New York, Watson-Guptill Publications [1972] 95 p. illus. 22 cm. Bibliography: p. 94. [TS752.5.S27] 72-3356 ISBN 0-8230-1150-X
1. Gem cutting. 2. Jewelry making. I. Title.

SCARFE, Herbert. 736'.2'028
Techniques of gem cutting : a lapidary manual / Herbert Scarfe. New York : Watson-Guptill Publications, c1975. 172 p., 4 leaves of plates : ill. ; 27 cm. Includes index. Bibliography: p. 166-167. [TS752.5.S28 1975] 75-6993 ISBN 0-8230-5095-5 : 14.95
1. Gem cutting. I. Title. **BIP**

SHORE, Eric. 736'.2'028
Lapidary for pleasure & profit / Eric Shore. New York : Arco Pub. Co., [1978] p. cm. [TS752.5.S49] 77-25058 ISBN 0-668-04533-7 : 7.95
1. Gem cutting. I. Title. **BIP**

SWEETMAN, Leonard H. 736'.2'028
Cabochon gems today [by] Leonard H.

Sweetman. [Coatesville? Pa., 1971] 68 p. illus. 23 cm. [TS752.5.S96] 70-133939 3.00
1. Gem cutting. I. Title. BIP

VARGAS, Glenn. 736'.2'028
Diagrams for faceting / by Glenn & Martha Vargas ; all ill. by the authors. Thermal, Calif. : Vargas, c1975. xiv, 176 p. : ill. ; 28 cm. A companion vol. to the authors': Faceting for amateurs. Includes index. [TS752.5.V29] 75-21404 12.00
1. Gem cutting. I. Vargas, Martha, joint author. II. Title. BIP

VARGAS, Glenn. 736'.2028
Faceting for amateurs, by Glenn Vargas and Martha Vargas. [Palm Desert, Calif., Printed by Desert Printers, 1969] viii, 330 p. illus. 28 cm. Bibliography: p. 317. [TS752.5.V3] 70-87173
1. Gem cutting. I. Vargas, Martha, joint author. II. Title. BIP

WALTER, Martin. 736'.2
Gem cutting is easy. Photos. by Joe Rothstein. New York, Crown Publishers [1972] 95 p. illus. 29 cm. Bibliography: p. 89. [TS752.5.W34] 72-84318 ISBN 0-517-50020-5 4.95
1. Gem cutting. I. Title. BIP

Gem cutting—Amateurs' manuals.

VARGAS, Glenn. 736'.2'028
Faceting for amateurs / by Glenn Vargas and Martha Vargas ; all ill. by the authors unless otherwise credited. 2d ed. Thermal, Calif. : Vargas, c1977. xii, 345 p. : ill. ; 28 cm. Includes index. Bibliography: p. 330. [TS752.5.V3 1977] 76-57449 ISBN 0-917646-01-0 : 17.50
1. Gem cutting—Amateurs' manuals. I. Vargas, Martha, joint author. II. Title.

Gem cutting—Handbooks, manuals, etc.

SINKANKAS, John. 736'.2'028
Gemstone & mineral data book; a compilation of data, recipes, formulas, and instructions for the mineralogist, gemologist, lapidary, jeweler, craftsman, and collector. [New York] Winchester Press [1972] 346 p. 24 cm. Includes bibliographical references. [TS752.5.S56] 77-188597 ISBN 0-87691-067-3 8.95
1. Gem cutting—Handbooks, manuals, etc. 2. Mineralogy—Handbooks, manuals, etc. I. Title. BIP

SINKANKAS, John. 736'.2'028
Gemstone & mineral data book; a compilation of data, recipes, formulas, and instructions for the mineralogist, gemologist, lapidary, jeweler, craftsman, and collector. New York, Collier Books [1974, c1972] 346 p. 24 cm. Reprint of the ed. published by Winchester Press, New York. [TS752.5.S56 1974] 74-14786 ISBN 0-02-094100-5 3.95
1. Gem cutting—Handbooks, manuals, etc. 2. Mineralogy—Handbooks, manuals, etc. I. Title.

Gemini G. E. L. (Firm)

WALKER Art Center, Minneapolis. 769'.973
Johns, Kelly, Lichtenstein, Motherwell, Nauman, Rauschenberg, Serra, Stella : prints from Gemini G.E.L. : an exhibition organized by Walker Art Center. [Minneapolis : The Center, 1974] 40 p. : ill. ; 28 cm. Held at Walker Art Center, Minneapolis, Aug. 17-Sept. 29, 1974, and at various other institutions through Aug. 1975. [NE508.W34 1974] 74-13773
1. Gemini G. E. L. (Firm) 2. Prints, American—Exhibitions. I. Gemini G. E. L. (Firm) II. Title. III. Title: Prints from Gemini G. E. L.

Gems.

AXON, Gordon V. 553'.8
The wonderful world of gems [by] Gordon V. Axon. New York, Criterion Books [1967] 160 p. illus. 22 cm. Bibliography: p. 157. [TS752.A9] 67-11918
1. Gems. I. Title.

DAKE, Henry Carl, 1896-- 549
The art of gem cutting, complete. 5th ed. Portland, Or., Mineralogist Pub. Co., c1954. 128p. illus. 24cm. [TS752.D3 1954] 54-26977
1. Gems. I. Title. BIP

DAKE, Henry Carl. 1896- 739.27
The art of gem cutting, complete. 6th ed. Portland, Or., Mineralogist Pub. Co., c1956. 128 p. illus. 23 cm. [TS752.D3 1956] 56-35792
1. Gems. I. Title.

DAKE, Henry Carl, 1896- 736.2
The art of gem cutting, including cabochons, faceting, spheres, tumbling, and special techniques. 7th ed. Mentone, Calif., Gembks., c.1963. 96p. illus. 23cm. 63-25894 2.00 pap.,
1. Gems. I. Title.

DESAUTELS, Paul E. 736.2'074'0153
Gems in the Smithsonian, [by] Paul E. Desautels. Washington, Smithsonian Institution Press, 1972. 63 p. illus. (chiefly col.) 27 cm. 1965 ed. issued under title: Gems in the Smithsonian Institution. [NK5510.W3D4 1972] 76-39489 ISBN 0-87474-117-3 6.95
1. Smithsonian Institution. 2. Gems. I. Title.

DESAUTELS, Paul E 736.2
Gems in the Smithsonian Institution, by Paul E. Desautels. Washington, [Smithsonian Institution] 1965. 74 p. illus. (part col.) ports. 23 cm. (Smithsonian Institution. Publication no. 4608) [NK5510.W3D4] 65-60068
1. Gems. I. Title.

MIDDLETON, John Henry, 1846-1896. 736'.2
Ancient gems; the engraved gems of classical times. Chicago, Argonaut, 1969. xvi, 157, xxxvi p. illus. 24 cm. (The Argonaut library of antiquities) Reprint of the 1891 ed. first published under title: The engraved gems of classical times. "Works on antique gems": p. xiii-xv (1st group) "Catalogue of the engraved gems in the Fitzwilliam Museum" ([iii]-xxvi p.) [NK5565.M6 1969] 67-29128
1. Gems. 2. Classical antiquities. I. Cambridge. University. Fitzwilliam Museum. II. Title.

O'BRIEN, Dan, 1904- 739.274
How to cut gems. Photography by Sandy Faber. Drawings by Eve Faber. Hollywood, Calif., D. and M. O'Brien [1953] 50 p. illus. 24 cm. [TS752.O2] 54-36
1. Gems. I. Title.

QUICK, Lelande. 736.2028
Gemcraft; how to cut and polish gemstones [by] Lelande Quick and Hugh Leiper. [1st ed.] Philadelphia, Chilton Co., Book Division [1959] 181 p. illus. 27 cm. [TS752.Q5] 59-13626
1. Gems. 2. Glyptics. I. Leiper, Hugh N., joint author. II. Title.

SEIDLER, Ned. 549
Gems and jewels, written and illustrated by Ned Seidler. New York, Odyssey Press [1964] 44 p. illus. (part col.) col. port. 11 x 17 cm. (The Odyssey library, 11) [NK7650.S4] 64-12883
1. Gems. 2. Jewelry. I. Title.

SINKANKAS, John. 739.274
Gem cutting; a lapidary's manual. Princeton, N.J., Van Nostrand [1955] 413 p. illus. 24 cm. [TS752.S5] 55-10916
1. Gems. I. Title.

SINKANKAS, John. 736.2028
Gem cutting; a lapidary's manual. 2d ed. Princeton, N. J., Van Nostrand [1962] 297 p. illus. 29 cm. [TS752.S5 1962] 63-810
1. Gems. I. Title.

SPERISEN, Francis J 1900- 736.2028
The art of the lapidary. Milwaukee. Bruce Pub. Co. [1961] 390 p. illus. 24 cm. [TS752.S73 1961] 61-17435
1. Gems. I. Title. BIP

SPERISEN, Francis J., 1900- 739.274
The art of the lapidary. Milwaukee, Bruce Pub. Co. [1950] x, 382 p. illus. 25 cm. Bibliography: p. 370-371. [TS752.S73] 50-6533
1. Gems. I. Title.

WEINSTEIN, Michael. 736.2
The world of jewel stones. New York, Sheridan House [1958] 430 p. illus. 25 cm. Includes bibliography. [NK7650.W4] 58-14178
1. Gems. 2. Jewelry. 3. Precious stones. I. Title. BIP

WILLEMS, J Daniel, 1888- 739.274
Gem cutting. [2d ed.] Peoria, Ill., C.A. Bennett Co. [1952] 224 p. illus. 23 cm. [TS752.W64] 52-13981
1. Gems. I. Title.

WILSON, Mab. 553'.8
Gems. New York, Viking Press [1967] 168 p. illus., facsims., 28 col. plates, ports. 25 cm. (A Studio book) [GT2250.W5 1967] 67-19501
1. Gems. I. Title.

Gems—Catalogs.

SINKANKAS, John. 553'.8
Van Nostrand's standard catalog of gems. Princeton, N.J., Van Nostrand [1968] xiii, 286 p. illus. 22 cm. Bibliography: p. 274-[277] [TS752.S53 1968] 68-19369
1. Gems—Catalogs. 2. Precious stones—Catalogs. I. Title. II. Title: Standard catalog of gems. BIP

Gems, Classical—Catalogs.

OXFORD. University. Ashmolean Museum. 736'.2'093807402574
Catalogue of the engraved gems and finger rings / Ashmolean Museum, Oxford ; by John Boardman and marie-Louise Vollenweider. Oxford : Clarendon Press ; New York : Oxford University Press, 1978- v. : ill. ; 29 cm. Includes index. Contents.Contents.—1. Greek and Etruscan. [NK5565.O93 1978] 77-30290 ISBN 0-19-813195-X (v. 1) : 62.50 (vol. 1)
1. Oxford. University. Ashmolean Museum. 2. Gems, Classical—Catalogs. 3. Gems—England—Oxford—Catalogs. 4. Rings, Classical—Catalogs. 5. Rings—England—Oxford—Catalogs. I. Boardman, John, 1927- II. Vollenweider, Marie-Louise. III. Title.

OXFORD. University. Ashmolean Museum. 736'.2'093807402574
Catalogue of the engraved gems and finger rings / Ashmolean Museum, Oxford ; by John Boardman and marie-Louise Vollenweider. Oxford : Clarendon Press ; New York : Oxford University Press, 1978- v. : ill. ; 29 cm. Includes index. Contents.Contents.—1. Greek and Etruscan. [NK5565.O93 1978] 77-30290 ISBN 0-19-813195-X (v. 1) : 62.50 (vol. 1)
1. Oxford. University. Ashmolean Museum. 2. Gems, Classical—Catalogs. 3. Gems—England—Oxford—Catalogs. 4. Rings, Classical—Catalogs. 5. Rings—England—Oxford—Catalogs. I. Boardman, John, 1927- II. Vollenweider, Marie-Louise. III. Title.

Gems, Greek.

BOARDMAN, John, 1927- 736'.2'0938
Archaic Greek gems; schools and artists in the sixth and early fifth centuries B.C. Evanston, Northwestern University Press, 1968. 236 p. illus. (part col.) 26 cm. Includes bibliographical references. [NK5565.B6 1968b] 68-25581
1. Gems, Greek. I. Title. BIP

Gems—Handbooks, manuals, etc.

*FIRSOFF, Val Axel. 553'.8
Working with gemstones, by V. A. Firsoff. New York, Arco [1974] x, 210 p. illus. (part. col.) 23 cm. [TS752] 73-90929 ISBN 0-668-03430-0 8.95
1. Gems—Handbooks, manuals, etc. 2. Precious stones—Handbooks, manuals, etc. I. Title.

Gems—Juvenile literature.

PEARL, Richard Maxwell, 1913- 736
Wonders of gems. New York, Dodd, Mead [1963] 63 p. illus. 24 cm. [NK7650.P4] 63-10336
1. Gems—Juvenile literature. I. Title. BIP

Gems—Private collections.

INDIANA. University. Museum of Art. v. 12
A selection of ancient gems from the collection of Burton Y. Berry. Bloomington, 1965. 67, [1] p. illus. 29 x 14 cm. (Its Publication no. 5) Bibliography: p. [68] [NK5515.B4I5] 67-63588
1. Gems—Private collections. 2. Gems—Bloomington, Ind.—Catalogs. I. Berry, Burton Yost. II. Title. III. Series.

General Motors de Mexico—Art collections.

IMAGE of Mexico; 760'0972
the General Motors of Mexico Collection of Mexican graphic art. Editor: Harry H. Ransom; special editor; Thomas Mabry Cranfill; photographic editor: Hans Beacham [and others] Austin, University of Texas at Austin, 1969. 2 v. illus., ports. 26 cm. (The Texas quarterly, v. 12, no. 3-4) At head of title: A special issue. Articles, captions, and biographical sketches in English and Spanish. [AP2.T269 vol. 12, no. 3-4] [NE44.4] 77-30163 1.50 ea.
1. General Motors de Mexico—Art collections. 2. Prints, Mexican—Catalogs. 3. Drawings, Mexican—Catalogs. I. Cranfill, Thomas Mabry, ed. II. Beacham, Hans, ed. III. Title. IV. Series.

Generalic, Ivan.

GENERALIC, Ivan. 759.9497 B
The magic world of Ivan Generalic / [edited] by Nebojsa Tomasevic ; translated from the Italian by John Shepley. New York : Rizzoli, 1976, c1975. 223 p. : ill. (some col.) ; 31 cm. Translation of Il mondo magico di Ivan Generalic. [ND953.G4T6513 1976] 76-11251 ISBN 0-8478-0044-X : 27.50
1. Generalic, Ivan. 2. Painters—Yugoslavia—Biography. 3. Primitivism in art—Yugoslavia. I. Tomasevic, Nebojsa. II. Title.

Genji monogatari emaki.

THE Tale of Genji scroll. 759.952
[Translated by] Ivan Morris; introd. by Yoshinobu Tokugawa. [Tokyo, Palo Alto, Calif.] Kodansha International [1971] 154 p. col. plates. 31 x 57 cm. Translation of Genji monogatari emaki. Facsimile reproduction of the existing fragments of the scroll. "The tale of Genji scroll is a free visual re-creation in which a number of isolated scenes from Murasaki's novel are represented." [ND1059.6.G4G413] 77-128695
1. Genji monogatari emaki. I. Morris, Ivan I., tr. II. Murasaki Shikibu, b. 978? Genji monogatari. BIP

Genoa—Palaces.

RUBENS, Peter Paul, Sir, 1577-1640. 728.8'2
Palazzi antichi di Genova. Palazzi moderni di Genova. With an introductory essay by Alan A. Tait. New York, Blom, 1968. 2 v. in 1. 139 plates (incl. plans) 40 cm. Reproduction of the 1663 ed., first published in 1622 as two separate works, each having title: Palazzi di Genova. Captions in Italian. [NA7756.G3R8 1968] 68-21226
1. Genoa—Palaces. 2. Architecture—Genoa. 3. Architecture—Designs and plans. I. Title. II. Title: Palazzi moderni di Genova.

Genre painting, American.

HILLS, Patricia. 759.13
The genre painting of Eastman Johnson : the sources and development of his style and themes / Patricia Hills. New York : Garland Pub., 1977. xix, 251 p. : ill. ; 21 cm. (Outstanding dissertations in the fine arts) Thesis—New York University, 1973. Bibliography: p. 179-190. [ND237.J7H53] 76-23627 ISBN 0-8240-2697-7 : 35.00

1. Johnson, Eastman, 1824-1906. 2. Genre painting, American. I. Title. II. Series. BIP

WILLIAMS, Hermann Warner, 1908- 754'.0973
Mirror to the American past; a survey of American genre painting: 1750-1900. Greenwich, Conn., New York Graphic Society [1973] 248 p. illus. (part col.) 27 cm. Bibliography: p. 229-240. [ND2351.W54 1973] 78-154329 ISBN 0-8212-0444-0 17.50
1. Genre painting, American. I. Title.

Genre painting, Japanese.

YAMANE, Yuzo, 1919- 754'.0952
Momoyama genre painting. Translated by John M. Shields. [1st English ed.] New York, Weatherhill [1973] 182 p. illus. (part col.) 24 cm. (The Heibonsha survey of Japanese art, v. 17) Translation of Momoyama no fuzokuga. [ND1452.J3Y3513] 72-92099 ISBN 0-8348-1012-3 8.95
1. Genre painting, Japanese. 2. Japan—History—Azuchi-Momoyama period, 1568-1603. I. Title. II. Series. BIP

Genre paintings, American—Exhibitions.

CRANBROOK Academy of Art, Bloomfield Hills, Mich. Museum. 759.13
Genre, portrait, and still life painting in America; the Victorian Era. Bloomfield Hills, Mich. [1973] 20 p. illus. 26 cm. "Volume 1, number 2." Catalog of an exhibition held at the Museum Aug. 26-Sept. 30, 1973. Bibliography: p. 20. [ND1451.5.C72 1973] 73-88750
1. Genre paintings, American—Exhibitions. 2. Portrait painting, American—Exhibitions. 3. Painting, Victorian—United States. I. Title.

Genre paintings—Exhibitions.

STERLING and Francine Clark Art Institute, Williamstown, Mass. 754'.0944'36
The elegant academics; chroniclers of nineteenth-century Parisian life. [North Adams, Mass., Printed by Lamb Print. Co., 1974] 106 p. illus. 22 cm. Catalogue of an exhibition held Mar. 19-June 2, 1974, at Sterling and Francine Clark Art Institute and June 12-July 31, 1974, at Wadsworth Atheneum. [ND1452.F85S83 1974] 74-176014
1. Genre paintings—Exhibitions. 2. Genre painting—Paris. 3. Paris in art. I. Wadsworth Atheneum, Hartford. II. Title.

Genre paintings, German—Exhibitions.

MILWAUKEE. Art Center. 759.3'074'07595
Paintings from the Von Schleinitz Collection; German genre paintings of the 19th century. Milwaukee [1969?] 1 v. (unpaged) plates (part col.) 20 cm. Catalog of the exhibition held Sept. 13-Oct. 13, 1969 at the Milwaukee Art Center. [ND1452.G3M5] 78-18741
1. Von Schleinitz, Rene—Art collections. 2. Genre paintings, German—Exhibitions. I. Title.

Gent, Thomas, 1693-1778.

GENT, Thomas, 1693-1778. 686.2'092'4 B
The life of Mr. Thomas Gent, printer, of York, written by himself. New York, Garland Pub., 1974. iv, 208 p. 22 cm. (The English book trade, 1660-1853) Reprint of the 1832 ed. printed for T. Thorpe, London. [Z232.G33G46 1974] 74-7445 ISBN 0-8240-0984-3
1. Gent, Thomas, 1693-1778. I. Title. II. Series.

Gentilz, Theodore, ca. 1820-1906.

GENTILZ, Theodore, ca.1820-1906. 759.13 B
Gentilz: artist of the old Southwest; drawings and paintings by Theodore Gentilz. Text by Dorothy Steinbomer Kendall; archival research by Carmen Perry. Austin, University of Texas Press [1974] xiii, 127 p. illus. (part col.) 31 cm. (The Elma Dill Russell Spencer Foundation series, no. 6) Bibliography: p. 121-123. [ND237.G33K46] 74-6495 ISBN 0-292-72705-4 17.50
1. Gentilz, Theodore, ca. 1820-1906. 2. Texas in art. 3. Mexico in art. I. Kendall, Dorothy Steinbomer, 1912- II. Perry, Carmen. III. Title. IV. Series.

Geodesic domes.

DOMEBOOK one[-two, 690'.1'46
by Lloyd Kahn and others. Los Gatos, Calif., Pacific Domes, 1970-71] 2 v. illus., plans. 37 cm. Cover title. Vol. 2 published at Bolinas, Calif., and distributed by Random House, New York. Bibliography: v. 1, p. 54; v. 2, p. 122. [TH2170.D64] 73-27449 3.00 (v. 1.) 4.00 (v. 2)
1. Geodesic domes. I. Kahn, Lloyd. II. Pacific Domes (Organization)

Geodesic domes—Juvenile literature.

HOWELL, Ruth Rea. 690
The dome people. Text by Ruth Howell. Photos. by Arline Strong. [1st ed.] New York, Atheneum, 1974. 57 p. illus. 19 x 24 cm. Follows each step in the building of a geodesic dome by a group of teenagers who, failing to find a suitable building for their activities, decided to build one. [TH2170.H68 1974] 73-84829 ISBN 0-689-30139-1 5.25
1. Geodesic domes—Juvenile literature. I. Strong, Arline, illus. II. Title. BIP

Geoffrey, J. Iqbal, 1939—

GEOFFREY, J. Iqbal, 1939- 759.9549
Geoffrey: power and the image, by E. W. Johnson. Macomb, Western Illinois University, Division of Public Services, 1969. 123 p. illus. (part col.), port. 21 cm. (Western Illinois University monograph series) (Western Illinois University bulletin, v. 48, no. 1.) Bibliography: p. 117-118. [ND1010.G4J6] 68-8398
I. Johnson, Edward Warren, 1941- II. Title. III. Series: Illinois. Western Illinois University, Macomb. Monograph series

J. Iqbal Geoffrey: in search of an ideal landscape. 759.9549
Introd. by Thomas W. Leavitt. Biographical data collected by A. S. Alley. Contributors: Teresa H. Bauer [and others] (the class of advanced painting) Limited ed. Notre Dame, Ind., Dept. of Art, Saint Mary's College [1967] [28] p. illus., ports. 23 cm. Bibliography: p. [22] [ND1010.G4J2] 67-31466
1. Geoffrey, J. Iqbal, 1939- I. Leavitt, Thomas W. II. Alley, A. S. III. Bauer, Teresa H. IV. Saint Mary's College, Notre Dame, Ind. Dept. of Art.

LUISI, David. 759.9549
Re: J. Iqbal Geoffrey; a collection of critical essays. Edited by David Luisi. Ellensburg, Central Washington State College [1971?] 55 p. 23 cm. Includes bibliographical references. [ND1010.73.G4L8] 77-635318
1. Geoffrey, J. Iqbal, 1939- I. Title.

Geometrical drawing.

AMIR-MOEZ, Ali R. 513.1
Ruler, compass, and fun, by Ali R. Amir-Moez. New ed. [Boston] Ginn [1966] 45p. 26cm. (Ginn enrichment program) [QA464.A45 1966] 66-12550 .76 pap.,
1. Geometrical drawing. I. Title.

CRITCHLOW, Keith. 745.4
Order in space; a design source book. New York, Viking Press [1970, c1969] 120 p. illus. 21 x 31 cm. (A Studio book) Bibliography: p. 120. [QA464.C84 1970] 73-120105 ISBN 0-670-52830-7 7.50
1. Geometrical drawing. 2. Design. I. Title. BIP

HOREMIS, Spyros 745.4'49'24
Optical and geometrical patterns and designs: 92 original plates. Introd. by Janet Koch. Magnolia, Mass., Peter Smith [1973, c1970] 92 p. (chiefly illus.) 32 cm. (Dover book rebound) [NK1570.H58 1970] 70-106491 ISBN 0-8446-4557-5 6.00
1. Geometrical drawing. I. Title. BIP

LEWITT, Sol, 1928- 745.4
Arcs, from corners & sides, circles, & grids and all their combinations. [Berne] Kunsthalle Bern & Paul Bianchini, 1972. [208] p. illus. 21 cm. Label mounted on t.p.: "American distributor: Wittenborn and Company, 1018 Madison Ave., New York, N.Y., 10021." [NK1570.L48] 73-160742
1. Lewitt, Sol, 1928- 2. Geometrical drawing. I. Bern. Kunsthalle. II. Title.

PEARSON, George, 1911- 744.42
Geometrical drawing. [London] Oxford University Press, 1957. 128p. illus. 24cm. [QA464.P34] 58-741
1. Geometrical drawing. I. Title.

PEARSON, George, 1911- 744.4'2
Geometrical drawing, by G. Pearson. 2nd ed. London, Oxford Univ. Pr., 1968. 144p. illus. 24cm. [QA464.P34 1968] 68-112700 2.10
1. Geometrical drawing. I. Title.
Available from Oxford Univ. Pr. New York.

SHUPE, Hollie W 744.4
A manual of engineering geometry and graphics for students and draftsmen [by] Hollie W. Shupe [and] Paul E. Machovina. New York, McGraw-Hill, 1956. 347p. illus. 25cm. (The Engineering drawing series) [QA497.S5] 55-11569
1. Geometrical drawing. 2. Graphic methods. I. Machovina, Paul E., joint author. II. Title. III. Title: Engineeringgeometry and graphics.

TURNER, Robert Henry, 1925- 744.422
Engineering geometry [by] R. H. Turner, H. J. Smith. London, Macdonald [1963] 153p. illus. 26cm. [T353.T79] 66-6813 4.85
1. Geometrical drawing. 2. Engineering graphics. I. Smith, Harold John, joint author. II. Title.
Now available from Ginn, Boston.

WOOLVEN, Sydney John 744'.01'515
Practical geometry for technical drawing, by S. J. Woolven. London, Cambridge Univ. Pr., 1967. viii, 256p. 2 tables, diagrs. 26cm. [QA464.W6] 67-15394 3.95
1. Geometrical drawing. 2. Geometry, Descriptive. I. Title.
Available from the publisher's New York office.

Geometrical models.

SCHATTSCHNEIDER, Doris. 736'.98
M. C. Escher kaleidocycles / by Doris Schattschneider and Wallace Walker. 1st ed. New York : Ballantine Books, 1977. 1 portfolio (iv, 43 p., 16 fold. leaves of plates) : ill. (some col.) ; 30 cm. Includes 16 folded sheets of two-dimensional drawings which can be separated from their surrounding extra paper to form 17 polyhedral forms. Bibliography: p. 38. [QA447.S3] 77-9910 ISBN 0-345-25686-7 pbk. : 8.95
1. Escher, Maurits Cornelis, 1898-1971. 2. Geometrical models. 3. Design, Decorative. 4. Symmetry. I. Escher, Maurits Cornelis, 1898-1971. II. Walker, Wallace, joint author. III. Title. IV. Title: Kaleidocycles. BIP

Geometry—Curiosa and miscellany.

BRUNES, Tons. 513.09
The secrets of ancient geometry--and its use. Tr. by Charles M. Napier from the orig. Danish manuscript. Drawings and analyses by the author. Copenhagen, Rhodos, [1967] 2 v. illus., plates. 27cm. Tr. of Den hemmelige oldtidsgeometri og dens anvendelse. [NC740.B713] 67-98822 40.00 set., in slipcase.
1. Geometry—Curiosa and miscellany. 2. Symbolism of numbers. 3. Composition (Art). I. Title.

George, Herbert, 1940—

GEORGE, Herbert, 1940- 730'.92'4
Herbert George : [exhibition] Everson Museum of Art of Syracuse and Onondaga County, Syracuse, New York, February 18 through March 20, 1977. Syracuse : The Museum, 1977. [27] p. : ill. ; 20 x 28 cm. [NB237.G47E93] 76-52568
1. George, Herbert, 1940- I. Everson Museum of Art of Syracuse and Onondaga County.

George, Saint, d. 303 — Art.

KUPPERS, Leonhard, 1903- 704.9486
George. Recklinghausen [Ger.] A. Bongers; distributed by Taplinger Pub. Co. [New York, c1964] 67 p. col. illus. 18 cm. (The Saints in legend and art, v. 6) Translation of Der hellige Georg. [N8080.K8213] 67-16587
1. George, Saint, d. 303 — Art. I. Title.

George, Thomas, 1918—

GEORGE, Thomas, 1918- 741.9'73
Kweilin, Kwangsi Province, People's Republic of China : drawings / by Thomas George. [New York : Betty Parsons Gallery, c1975] 14 leaves : chiefly ill. ; 30 x 41 cm. Cover title. "Exhibition ... sponsored and organized by the Betty Parsons Gallery ... New York." "Edition [of] 500 copies." [NC139.G24B47] 75-34521
1. George, Thomas, 1918- 2. Kuei-lin, China, in art. I. Betty Parsons Gallery. II. Title.

Georgetown, D.C.—Historic houses, etc.

U.S. Commission of Fine Arts. 720'.9753
Georgetown architecture-Northwest; Northwest Washington, District of Columbia. Washington [1970] viii, 661 p. illus., facsims., maps, ports. 29 cm. (Historic American Buildings Survey. Selections, no. 6) Includes bibliographical references. [NA705.A25 no. 6] 71-608955
1. Georgetown, D.C.—Historic houses, etc. 2. Architecture—Washington, D.C. I. Title. II. Series.

U.S. Commission of Fine Arts. 720'.9753
Georgetown architecture, Northwest Washington, District of Columbia. Issued jointly by the Commission of Fine Arts and the Historic American Buildings Survey. Washington, 1970. xxxvii, 291 p. illus., plans. 28 cm. (Historic American Buildings Survey. Selections, no. 10) Includes bibliographical references. [NA705.A25 no. 10] 75-608956
1. Georgetown, D.C.—Historic houses, etc. 2. Architecture—Washington, D.C. I. Title. II. Series.

U.S. Commission of Fine Arts. 720'.9'753
Georgetown architecture: the waterfront; northwest Washington, District of Columbia. Issued jointly by the Commission of Fine Arts and the Historic American Buildings Survey. Washington, 1968. iii, 297 p. illus. 28 cm. (Historic American Buildings Survey. Selections, no. 4) [NA705.A25 no. 4] 79-600486
1. Georgetown, D.C.—Historic houses, etc. 2. Architecture—Washington, D.C. I. Historic American Buildings Survey. II. Title. III. Series.

U.S. Commission of Fine Arts. 728.3'09753
Georgetown residential architecture, northeast: Northwest Washington, District of Columbia. Washington [1969] xiii, 233 p. illus. 28 cm. (Historic American Buildings Survey. Selections, no. 5) [NA705.A25 no. 5] 77-604029
1. Georgetown, D.C.—Historic houses. 2. Architecture, Domestic—Georgetown, D.C. I. Title. II. Series.

Georgia—Antiquities.

WAUCHOPE, Robert, 1909- 975.8
Archaeological survey of Northern Georgia with a test of some cultural hypotheses. Salt Lake City [Society for American Archaeology] 1966. xxxii, 482 p. illus.,

SUBJECT INDEX GHORMLEY, JAMES GRANT

maps. 26 cm. (Memoirs of the Society for American Archaeology, no. 21) "Issued as American antiquity, volume 32, number 5, part 2, July 1966." Bibliography: p. 473-479. [E78.G3W3] 67-5548
1. Georgia—Antiquities. 2. Indians of North America—Georgia—Antiquities. I. Title. II. Series: Society for American Archaeology. Memoirs, 21.

Georgia—Description and travel—Views.

CONGER, Ledlie William. 917.58'03
Sketching and etching Georgia: fifty etchings and drawings, by Ledlie William Conger. With a foreword by the artist. Text by Ruth Dunlop Conger. [Atlanta, Conger Print. Co., 1971] 1 v. (unpaged) illus. 32 cm. [NC139.C6C6] 75-177364 30.00
1. Georgia—Description and travel—Views. I. Conger, Ruth Dunlop. II. Title.

Georgia—Governors—Biography.

ALLEN, Frederick. 779'.9'9739260924 B
Jimmy Carter, a photobiography / written by Frederick Allen. Houston, Tex. : EFP Pub. Co., c1976. [80] p. : ill. ; 28 cm. [F291.3.C37A76] 76-150399 2.95
1. Carter, Jimmy, 1924- 2. Georgia—Governors—Biography. I. Title.

Georgia. Surveyor General.

GEORGIA. Surveyor General. 016.912
Pre-nineteenth century maps in the collection of the Georgia Surveyor General Department : a catalog / compiled by Janice Gayle Blake, Surveyor General Department, Office of the Secretary of State. Atlanta : State Print. Off., 1975. xx, 173 p. ; 28 cm. Includes index. Bibliography: p. 153-157. [Z6022.G46 1975] [GA201] 75-620098
1. Georgia. Surveyor General. 2. Maps, Early—Bibliography—Catalogs. 3. North America—Maps—To 1800—Bibliography—Catalogs. I. Blake, Janice Gayle. II. Title.

Georgia (Transcaucasia)—Bibliography—Catalogs.

OXFORD. University. Bodleian Library. 018'.1
Catalogue of the Wardrop Collection and of other Georgian books and manuscripts in the Bodleian Library [by] David Barrett. [Oxford] Published for the Marjory Wardrop Fund by Oxford University Press, 1973. 354 p. 26 cm. [Z2514.G3O95] 73-161993 ISBN 0-19-920028-9
1. Wardrop, John Oliver, Sir, 1864-1948. 2. Wardrop, Marjory Scott, 1869-1909. 3. Georgia (Transcaucasia)—Bibliography—Catalogs. 4. Manuscripts, Georgian—Bibliography—Catalogs. I. Barrett, David. Distributed by Oxford University Press N.Y. 48.00 BIP

Gerber, Sidney—Art collections.

WASHINGTON (State). University. Museum. 709'.01'1
Crooked beak of heaven; masks and other ceremonial art of the Northwest coast, by Bill Holm. Seattle, Published for the Thomas Burke Memorial Washington State Museum and the Henry Art Gallery by the University of Washington Press [1972] 96 p. illus. 28 cm. (Index of art in the Pacific Northwest, no. 3) "Catalogue of the Sidney Gerber Memorial Collection of Northwest Coast Indian Art in the Thomas Burke Memorial Washington State Museum." Bibliography: p. 95-96. [E78.N78W3] 77-39631 ISBN 0-295-95172-9
1. Gerber, Sidney—Art collections. 2. Indians of North America—Northwest coast of North America—Art—Catalogs. 3. Art—Seattle—Catalogs. I. Holm, Bill, 1925- II. Henry Art Gallery. III. Title. IV. Series. BIP

Gericault, Jean Louis Andre Theodore, 1791-1824.

CLEMENT, Charles, 1821-1887. 760'.092'4 B
Gericault : a biographical and critical study with a catalogue raisonne of the master's works / Charles Clement ; introd. by Lorenz Eitner ; the catalogue of Gericault's work brought up to date by Lorenz Eitner in a new suppl. ; [suppl. translated by Regis Annequin]. New York : Da Capo, 1974. xv, iii, 472 p., [29] leaves of plates : ill. ; 24 cm. Text in French; introd. in English. Reprint of the 1879 ed. published by Didier, Paris. Includes bibliographical references. [ND553.G45C6 1974] 73-83834 ISBN 0-306-70643-1
1. Gericault, Jean Louis Andre Theodore, 1791-1824.

EITNER, Lorenz Edwin Alfred 741.944
Gericault: an album of drawings in the Art Institute of Chicago. Text and catalogue by Lorenz Eitner. [Chicago] University of Chicago Press [c.1960] 48p. [111]p. illus. 23x29cm. 'The Chicago Album': p.[1]-[108] (2d group) bibl.. references included in 'Notes' (p.[43]-48 (1st group) 60-14231 10.00
1. Gericault, Jean Louis Andre Theodore, 1791-1824. I. Chicago. Art Institute. II. Title.

GERICAULT and his work. 759.4
Translated by Winslow Ames. Lawrence, University of Kansas Press, 1955. 92p. plates (part col.) 26cm. Bibliography: p.64-66. [ND553.G45B444] [ND553.G45B444] 927.5 55-6524 55-6524
1. Gericault, Jean Louis Andre Theodore, 1791-1824. I. Berger, Klaus, 1901- BIP

GERICAULT, Jean Louis Andre Theodore, 1791-1824. 741'.092'4 B
Gericault [by] Lorenz Eitner. [Los Angeles, Los Angeles County Museum of Art, c1971] 189 p. illus. 26 cm. Catalog of an exhibition held at the Los Angeles County Museum of Art, Oct. 12-Dec. 12, 1971; the Detroit Institute of Arts, Jan. 23-Mar. 7, 1972; and the Philadelphia Museum of Art, Mar. 30-May 14, 1972. Includes bibliographies. [ND553.G45E33] 70-173255 ISBN 0-87587-046-5
I. Eitner, Lorenz Edwin Albert. II. Los Angeles Co., Calif. Museum of Art. Los Angeles. III. Detroit. Institute of Arts. IV. Philadelphia Museum of Art.

GERICAULT, Jean Louis Andre Theodore, 1791-1824. 769'.92'4
The graphic art of Gericault. [Exhibition] February 5 - March 30, 1969. Catalogue by Kate H. Spencer. New Haven, Conn., Yale University Art Gallery [1969?] 37 p. 53 plates. 19 x 22 cm. Bibliography: p. 19. [NE2349.5.G4S6] 72-180693
I. Spencer, Kate H. II. Yale University. Art Gallery. III. Title.

Gerig, Bruce.

GERIG, Bruce. 741.9'73
European suite : catalogue : an international exhibition tour shown in twenty-two States and seven foreign countries, 1970-1975 : drawings / by Bruce Gerig ; edited by Sharon Rider. New York : Studio 3000, [1975] [52] p. : ill. ; 21 cm. [NC139.G26R52] 75-9889 ISBN 0-915100-04-5 pbk. : 3.00
1. Gerig, Bruce. I. Rider, Sharon, 1936- II. Title. BIP

Germany (Democratic Republic, 1949-)—Intellectual life.

KOHN, Erwin. 700
German Democratic Republic: art and literature. Dresden, Verlag Zeit im Bild [1969] 94 p. illus., map. 14 cm. [DD261.2.K58] 77-498984 1.25
1. Germany (Democratic Republic, 1949-)—Intellectual life. I. Title.

Germany—Description and travel—Views.

KRUSE, Werner. 741.9'43
Touring Germany: Bremen, Hamburg, Hanover, Dusseldorf, Cologne, Bonn, Frankfurt, Stuttgart, Nuremberg, Munich, Berlin. Illustrated by Robinson. New York, Funk & Wagnalls [1967] [64] p. (chiefly illus., maps) 34 cm. [NC1140.K74] 68-13269
1. Germany—Description and travel—Views. I. Title.

Germany—History, Comic, satirical, etc.

LEWIS, Beth Irwin. 741'.0924 B
George Grosz: art and politics in the Weimar Republic. Madison, University of Wisconsin Press [1971] xviii, 328 p. illus., ports. 25 cm. Revision of the author's thesis, University of Wisconsin. Includes bibliographical references. [NC251.G66L48 1971] 79-143764 ISBN 0-299-05901-4 12.50
1. Grosz, George, 1893-1959. 2. Germany—History, Comic, satirical, etc. I. Title.

Gerome, Jean Leon, 1824-1904.

GEROME, Jean Leon, 1824-1904. 759.4
Jean-Leon Gerome (1824-1904) Organized by Bruce H. Evans. Introd. and commentaries by Gerald M. Ackerman. Essay by Richard Ettinghausen. [Dayton? Ohio, 1972] 104 p. illus. 23 cm. Catalog of an exhibition held at the Dayton Art Institute, Nov. 10-Dec. 30, 1972; the Minneapolis Institute of Arts, Jan. 26-Mar. 11, 1973; and the Walters Art Gallery, April 6-May 20, 1973. Bibliography: p. 103-104. [ND553.G5A66] 72-172734
1. Gerome, Jean Leon, 1824-1904. I. Ackerman, Gerald M. II. Dayton Art Institute, Dayton, Ohio. III. Minneapolis. Institute of Arts. IV. Walters Art Gallery, Baltimore.

Gertler, Mark, 1891-1939.

WOODESON, John. 759.2
Mark Gertler; biography of a painter, 1891-1939. [Toronto, Buffalo] University of Toronto Press [1973] xii, 413 p. illus. (part col.) 24 cm. Includes bibliographical references. [ND497.G47W66 1973] 73-79294 ISBN 0-8020-2060-7 15.00
1. Gertler, Mark, 1891-1939.

Gesture in art.

BARASH, Moshe. 709'.45
Gestures of despair in medieval and early Renaissance art / by Moshe Barasch. New York : New York University Press, 1976. p. cm. Includes bibliographical references and index. [N5975.B37] 76-4601 ISBN 0-8147-1006-9 : 35.00
1. Gesture in art. 2. Despair in art. 3. Art, Medieval. 4. Art, Renaissance—Early Renaissance. I. Title. BIP

Gesualdo, Carlo, principe di Venosa, 1560 (ca.)-1613.

ROWLAND, Daniel B. 709.03
Mannerism--style and mood; an anatomy of four works in three art forms. New Haven, Conn., Yale [c.]1964. xii, 136p. illus., music. 23cm. (Yale College ser., 2) Bibl. 64-12658 5.00
1. Gesualdo, Carlo, principe di Venosa, 1560 (ca.)-1613. 2. Donne, John, 1573-1631. An anatomy of the world. 3. Mannerism (Art) 4. Painting, Italian. 5. Madrigal. 6. Part-songs, Italian—To 1800. I. Title. BIP

Getty (J. Paul) Museum.

GETTY (J. Paul) Museum. 681'.113'0944074019493
Clocks in the collection of the J. Paul Getty Museum / Gillian Wilson. Malibu, Calif. : The Museum, [1976] p. cm. Includes bibliographies. [NK7482.M34G473] 76-25150 ISBN 0-89236-004-6 : 3.95
1. Getty (J. Paul) Museum. 2. Clocks and watches—Malibu, Calif.—Catalogs. I. Wilson, Gilliam, 1941- II. Title.

Getty, Jean Paul, 1892- —Art collections.

MINNEAPOLIS. Institute of Arts. 707'.4'176579
The J. Paul Getty Collection. [Minneapolis, 1972] [100] p. illus. (part col.) 26 cm. Catalog of an exhibition held June 29-Sept. 3, 1972. [N5220.G45M5] 72-80295
1. Getty, Jean Paul, 1892- —Art collections. I. Title.

Ghent, Norfolk, Va., in art.

JACKSON, Alexander B., 1925- 760'.092'4
As I see Ghent : a visual essay / by A. B. Jackson. Norfolk, Va. : Donning, c1976. p. cm. [N6537.J28A43] 76-43065 ISBN 0-915442-22-1 : 29.95
1. Jackson, Alexander B., 1925- 2. Ghent, Norfolk, Va., in art. 3. Ghent, Norfolk, Va. 4. Norfolk—Description—Views. I. Title.

Ghermandi, Quinto, 1916-

MARCHIORI, Giuseppe 730.945
Quinto Ghermandi. Bologna, Edizioni ALFA [dist. New York, Wittenborn, 1962] 74p. plates, port. 30cm. (Scultori d'oggi, 1.) Bibl. 63-616 4.50 pap.,
1. Ghermandi, Quinto, 1916- I. Title.

Gheyn, Jacob de, 1565-1629.

JUDSON, Jay Richard. 741.9'492
The drawings of Jacob de Gheyn II, by J. Richard Judson. New York, Grossman Publishers, 1973. 44, [110] p. illus. 26 cm. Includes bibliographical references. [NC263.G48J82 1973] 72-95371 ISBN 0-670-28399-1 14.95
1. Gheyn, Jacob de, 1565-1629. I. Gheyn, Jacob de, 1565-1629. II. Title.

Ghiberti, Lorenzo, 1378-1455.

KRAUTHEIMER, Richard, 1897- 927.3
Lorenzo Ghiberti, by Richard Krautheimer in collaboration with Trude Krautheimer-Hess. Princeton, Princeton University Press, 1956. viii, 457 p. illus., plates. 31 cm. (Princeton monographs in art and archaeology, 31) "Sources [documents]": p. 359-421. Bibliography: p. 425-438. [NB623.G45K7] 734.45 56-8383
1. Ghiberti, Lorenzo, 1378-1455. I. Series. BIP

LORENZO Ghiberti, 734.45
by Richard Krautheimer in collaboration with Trude Krautheimer-Hess. Princeton, Princeton University Press, 1956. viii, 457p. illus., plates. 31cm. (Princeton monographs in art and archaeology, 31) 'Sources [documents]': p. 359-421. Bibliography: p. 425-438. [NB623.G45K7] 927.3 56-8383
1. Ghilberti, Lorenzo, 1378-1455. I. Krautheimer, Richard, 1897- II. Series.

Ghirlandaio, Domenico Bigordi, known as, 1449-1494—Influence.

FAHY, Everett. 759.5
Some followers of Domenico Ghirlandajo / Everett Fahy. New York : Garland, 1976. 230 p., [22] leaves of plates : ill. ; 21 cm. (Outstanding dissertations in the fine arts) Originally presented as the author's thesis, Harvard, 1968. Includes bibliographies. [ND615.F34 1976] 75-23790 ISBN 0-8240-1986-5 lib.bdg. : 27.50
1. Ghirlandaio, Domenico Bigordi, known as, 1449-1494—Influence. 2. Painting, Renaissance—Italy. 3. Painting, Italian. 4. Painters—Italy. I. Title. II. Series. BIP

Ghormley, James Grant, 1925-1967.

GHORMLEY, Ruby Pearl (Foreman) 1901- 686.2'092'4 B
Ghormley and offset; a biography, by Pearl Ghormley. [Austin, Tex., Rupegy Pub. Co., 1972] xvi, 222 p. illus. 24 cm. [Z249.G47] 73-178281 6.95

1. Ghormley, James Grant, 1925-1967. I. Title.

Ghosts in art.

FORBES, W. Stanton. 769'.92'4
Ghosts / by W. Stanton Forbes. Athens, Ga. : Forbes, [1974] 40 p. : all ill. ; 22 cm. "Number 32 of 50 copies." [NE1336.F67A46] 75-314823
1. Forbes, W. Stanton. 2. Ghosts in art. I. Title.

Giacometti, Alberto, 1901-1966.

GIACOMETTI, Alberto, 1901-1966. 730'.92'4
Alberto Giacometti. [New York] Praeger in association with the Solomon R. Guggenheim Museum [1974] p. cm. Catalog of a retrospective exhibition held at the Solomon R. Guggenheim Museum. Includes bibliographical references. [NB553.G4S64] 74-77334 25.00
1. Giacometti, Alberto, 1901-1966. I. Solomon R. Guggenheim Museum, New York.

GIACOMETTI, Alberto, 1901-1966. 709'.2'4
Alberto Giacometti : the Milton D. Ratner Family Collection : [catalog of exhibition] The Art Institute of Chicago, 1974-75. [Chicago] : The Institute, c1974. 59 p. : chiefly ill. ; 31 cm. Pref. by Milton D. Ratner. Exhibition held at the Art Institute of Chicago, Nov. 2, 1974-Jan. 12, 1975, at the Rosary College, River Forest, Ill., Jan. 27-Feb. 17, 1975, at the Joslyn Art Museum, Omaha, Neb., Mar. 1-21, 1975, at the Elvehjem Art Center, University of Wisconsin, Madison, May 1-21, 1975, and at the Israel Museum, Jerusalem. [N6853.G5R38] 74-21618
1. Giacometti, Alberto, 1901-1966. 2. Ratner family—Art collections. I. Ratner, Milton D. II. Chicago. Art Institute. III. Title.

GIACOMETTI, Alberto, 1901-1966. 741.9494
Alberto Giacometti drawings [by] James Lord. Greenwich, Conn., New York Graphic Society [1971] 266 p. illus., 11 col. plates. 32 cm. (A Paul Bianchini book) Bibliography: p. 253-266. [NC248.G46L6 1971] 73-155487 ISBN 0-8212-0381-9 30.00
I. Lord, James. II. Title.

GIACOMETTI, Alberto, 1901-1966 741.9'494
Giacometti; a sketchbook of interpretive drawings. Text by Luigi Carluccio. [Tr. by Barbara Luigia La Penta] New York, Abrams [1967] xxxvi p., 144 plates. 26cm. [NC1135.G44C3] 67-15900 15.00
I. Carluccio, Luigi. II. Title. III. Title: A sketchbook of interpretive drawings.

GIACOMETTI, Alberto, 1901-1966. 769'.924
Giacometti: the complete graphics and 15 drawings, by Herbert C. Lust. Introd. by John Lloyd Taylor. New York, Tudor Pub. Co. [1970] 224 p. 368 illus. 31 cm. Catalogue of an exhibition arr. by the Milwaukee Art Center. First shown there in May 1970, the exhibition later traveled to 6 other galleries throughout the United States. [NE650.G5L8] 73-114205 ISBN 0-8148-0410-1
I. Lust, Herbert C. II. Milwaukee. Art Center.

HOHL, Reinhold. 730'.92'4 B
Alberto Giacometti. New York, H. N. Abrams [1972, c1971] 328 p. illus. (part col.) 31 cm. Translated from German. Bibliography: p. 311-324. [NB553.G4H613] 70-160216 ISBN 0-8109-0139-0 30.00
1. Giacometti, Alberto, 1901-1966.

LORD, James. 709.494
A Giacometti portrait. New York, Museum of Modern Art; distributed by Doubleday, Garden City, N.Y. [1965] 68 p. ports. 21 cm. [ND853.G44L6] 65-23848
1. Giacometti, Alberto, 1901- I. Title.

NEW york. Museum of Modern Art. 927
Alberto Giacometti. Introd. by Peter Selz and an autobiographical statement by the artist [Catalog] Mus. of Mod. Art, New York in collaboration with the Art Inst. of Chicago [others] Dist. Garden City, N.Y., Doubleday [c.1965] 119p. illus. (pt. col.) facsims., port. 27cm. Catalog of a comprehensive exhibition of Giacometti's work org. by the Mus. of Mod. Art, N.Y. in 1965. Bibl. [N7153.G47N4] 65-23847 7.95; 3.75 pap.,
1. Giacometti, Alberto, 1901- I. Selz, Peter. II. Title.

NEW York. Museum of Modern Art. 927
Alberto Giacometti. With an introd. by Peter Selz and an autobiographical statement by the artist. Museum of Modern Art, New York in collaboration with the Art Institute of Chicago [and others] Garden City, N.Y., Distributed by Doubleday [1965] 119 p. illus. (part col.) facsims., port. 27 cm. The catalog of a comprehensive exhibition of Giacometti's work organized by the Museum of Modern Art, New York, in 1965. Bibliography: p. 112-114. [N7153.G47N4] 65-23847
1. Giacometti, Alberto, 1901-1966. I. Selz, Peter Howard, 1919-

SIDNEY Janis Gallery. 709'.2'2
Giacometti & Dubuffet [New York, Sidney Janis Gallery, c1968] [28] p. (incl. cover) illus. 28 cm. Catalog of an exhibition of painting and sculpture, Nov. 6-30, 1968, at Sidney Janis Gallery, New York. [N6853.G5S53] 73-161618
1. Giacometti, Alberto, 1901-1966. 2. Dubuffet, Jean, 1901- I. Giacometti, Alberto, 1901-1966. II. Dubuffet, Jean, 1901- III. Title.

Gibbons, Grinling, 1648-1721.

GREEN, David 730.942
Grinling Gibbons: his work as carver and statuary, 1648-1721. London, Country Life, ltd. [dist. New York, Taplinger, c.1964] 207p. illus., ports. 28cm. Bibl. 64-55741 30.00
1. Gibbons, Grinling, 1648-1721. I. Title.

Gibbs, James, 1682-1754.

FRIEDMAN, Terry. 726'.5'0924
James Gibbs as a church designer: an exhibition celebrating the restoration of the Cathedral Church of All Saints at Derby, 1972 [by Terry Friedman and Peter Burman] Derby, The Chapterhouse Press, 1972. [36] p. illus., ports. 23 cm. Bibliography: p. [30] [NA997.G5F74] 73-154115 ISBN 0-903675-00-5 £0.25
1. Gibbs, James, 1682-1754. I. Burman, Peter, joint author. II. Title.

Gibran, Kahlil, 1883-1931.

GIBRAN, Kahlil, 1883-1931. 741.9'5691
Twenty drawings. With an introductory essay by Alice Raphael. [2d ed.] New York, Knopf, 1974 [c1919] p. cm. [NC319.L43G53 1974] 74-7723 ISBN 0-394-49426-1 10.00
1. Gibran, Kahlil, 1883-1931. I. Raphael, Alice Pearl, 1887- II. Title. BIP

GIBRAN, Kahlil, 1883-1931. 741.9'5691
Twenty drawings. With an introductory essay by Alice Raphael. New York, Vintage Books [1974, c1919] 91 p. illus. (part col.) 31 cm. Reprint of the ed. published by Knopf, New York. [NC319.L43G53 1974b] 74-9154 ISBN 0-394-71123-8 4.95 (pbk.).
1. Gibran, Kahlil, 1883-1931. I. Raphael, Alice Pearl, 1887- II. Title.

GIBRAN, Kahlil, 1922- 730'.924
Sculpture: Kahlil Gibran. With a foreword by Evan H. Turner. [1st ed.] Boston, Bartlett Press [1970] x, 134 p. illus., ports. 29 cm. [NB237.G5A57] 71-130940

Gifford, Sanford Robinson, 1823-1880.

GIFFORD, Sanford Robinson, 1823-1880. 759.13
Sanford Robinson Gifford, 1823-1880 [Austin, University of Texas Art Museum, 1970?] 84 p. illus. 21 x 26 cm. Catalog of an exhibition organized by the University of Texas Art Museum and held at the University of Texas at Austin, Oct. 25-Dec. 13, 1970; the Albany Institute of History and Art, Dec. 28, 1970-Jan. 31, 1971; and the Hirschl & Adler Galleries, New York, Feb. 8-27, 1971. Includes bibliographical references. [ND237.G4T49] 72-198137
I. Texas. University at Austin. Art Museum. II. Texas. University at Austin. III. Albany Institute of History and Art. IV. Hirschl & Adler Galleries.

WEISS, Ila, 1939- 759.13 B
Sanford Robinson Gifford (1823-1880) / Ila Weiss New York : Garland Pub., 1977. ca. 600 p. : ill. ; 21 cm. (Outstanding dissertations in the fine arts) Reprint of the author's thesis, Columbia, 1968; with a new pref. Includes bibliographical references. [ND237.G4W44 1977] 76-23655 lib.bdg. : 57.50
1. Gifford, Sanford Robinson, 1823-1880. 2. Landscape painters—United States—Biography. I. Title. II. Series. BIP

Gift wrapping.

HOME Packaging Company, Los Angeles. 745.54
Gift wrapping. Los Angeles, c1960. 60p. illus. 28cm. (Packaging for progress) [TT870.H57] 60-34930
1. Gift wrapping. I. Title.

LOWRIE, Drucella. 745.54
The art of wrapping gifts. New York, Studio Publications in association with Crowell [1950] 96 p. illus. 25 cm. [TT870.L75] 50-14721
1. Gift wrapping. I. Title.

OKA, Hideyuki, 1905- 745.59
How to wrap five eggs; Japanese design in traditional packaging. Foreword by George Nelson. Photo. by Michikazu Sukai. [Tr., adapted for Western readers by Atsuko Nii, Ralph Friedrich. 1st U.S. ed.] New York, Harper [1967] 203p. illus., plates (pt. col.), map (on lining papers) 30cm. Weathermark ed. Tr. of (romanized) Nihon no dento pakkeji [TT870.O3813] 67-29619 15.00
1. Gift wrapping. 2. Packaging. 3. Decoration and ornament—Japan. 4. Design, Decorative—Japan. I. Sakai, Michikazu. illus. II. Title.

OKA, Hideyuki, 1905- 745.59
How to wrap five more eggs : traditional Japanese packaging / by Hideyuki Oka ; with photos. by Michikazu Sakai. 1st ed. New York : Weatherhill, 1975. 215 p. : chiefly ill. ; 27 cm. Translation of Kokoro no zokei. Issued in conjunction with an exhibition held at the Japan House Gallery, New York, 1975-76. [TT870.O39 1975] 74-23690 ISBN 0-8348-0108-6 : 15.00
1. Gift wrapping. 2. Packaging. 3. Decoration and ornament—Japan. 4. Design, Decorative—Japan. I. Title. BIP

O'SHAUGHNESSY, Marjorie, 1907- 745.54
Gift wrapping; concise simple steps show you how to make beautiful packages for all occasions [by] Adelaide & Josephine Shaw. New York, Arc Books [1965, c1952] 64 p. illus. 19 cm. (A Do-it-yourself guide) First published in 1952 under title: A simplified guide to gift wrapping. [TT870.O4 1965] 65-28111
1. Gift wrapping. I. Clarke, Dorothy Josephine (O'Shaughnessy) 1907- joint author. II. Title.

O'SHAUGHNESSY, Marjorie, 1907- 745.54
A simplified guide to gift wrapping, by Adelaide and Josephine Shaw. New York, Homecrafts Publishers [1952] 64 p. illus. 24 cm. [TT870.O4] 52-4850
1. Gift wrapping. I. Clarke, Dorothy Josephine (O'Shaughnessy) 1907- joint author. II. Title.

SARA, Dorothy 745.54
101 gift wrapping hints. 1st ed. New Augusta. Ind., Editors & Engineers [1966] 96p. illus. 18cm. (Skillfact lib., 655) [TT870.S28] 66-28981 1.00 pap.,
1. Gift wrapping. I. Title.

Gilbert, Arthur, 1913- —Art collections.

LOS Angeles Co., Calif. Museum of Art, Los Angeles. 739.2'3'074019494
Monumental silver : selections from the Gilbert Collection : [catalog] : Los Angeles County Museum, 28 April-10 July 1977 / William Ezelle Jones. Los Angeles : Los Angeles County Museum of Art, c1977. 118 p. : ill. (some col.) ; 26 cm. Bibliography: p. 117-118. [NK7101.L75L674] 76-57976 ISBN 0-87587-077-5 pbk. : 5.50
1. Gilbert, Arthur, 1913- —Art collections. 2. Silverwork—Exhibitions. 3. Hall-marks. I. Jones, William Ezelle. II. Title. BIP

SHERMAN, Anthony C. 759.94'074'019493
The Gilbert Mosaic Collection, by Anthony C. Sherman. Edited by M. Barbara Scheibel. West Haven, Conn., Pendulum Press [1971] 61 p. (chiefly col. plates) 32 cm. [NA3755.B48G57] 71-172497
1. Gilbert, Arthur, 1913-—Art collections. 2. Mosaics—Beverly Hills, Calif.—Catalogs. I. Title.

Gilbert, Arthur, 1913- —Art collections—Exhibitions.

LOS Angeles Co., Calif. Museum of Art, Los Angeles. 738.5'094'074019494
The art of mosaics : selections from the Gilbert Collection, Los Angeles County Museum of Art, 28 April-10 July, 1977 : [catalog] / Alvar Gonzalez-Palacios. Los Angeles : The Museum, c1977. 143 p. : ill. (some col.) ; 26 cm. Bibliography: p. [8] [NA3755.L67L674] 77-75331 ISBN 0-87587-080-5 pbk. : 6.50
1. Gilbert, Arthur, 1913- —Art collections—Exhibitions. 2. Mosaics—Exhibitions. I. Gonzalez-Palacios, Alvar. II. Title.

Gilbert, Cass, 1859-1934.

THOMPSON, Neil B., 1921- 917.76'581
Minnesota's State Capitol: the art and politics of a public building, by Neil B. Thompson. St. Paul, Minnesota Historical Society, 1974. 100 p. illus. 27 cm. (Publications of the Minnesota Historical Society) (Minnesota historic sites pamphlet series, no. 9) Includes bibliographical references. [NA4413.S24T45] 74-4326 ISBN 0-87351-085-2 4.50 (pbk.)
1. Gilbert, Cass, 1859-1934. 2. St. Paul. State Capitol. 3. Politics in art. I. Title. II. Series. III. Series: Minnesota Historical Society. Publications. BIP

Gilbert, J. H. Grenville.

NEW York. Metropolitan Museum of Art. 736.6
American engraved powder horns; a study based on the J. H. Grenville Gilbert collection, by Stephen V. Grancsay, curator emeritus, Dept. of Arms and Armor. New printing. Philadelphia. R. Riling Arms Books Co., 1965 [c1946] viii, 96 p. illus., map, 47 plates, port. 30 cm. Cover title: American powder horns. "Annotated bibliography": p. 89-96 [NK6020.N4 1965] 65-25087
1. Gilbert, J. H. Grenville. 2. Powder flasks. 3. Bone carving. I. Grancsay, Stephen Vincent, 1897- II. Title. III. Title: American powder horns. BIP

Gilcrease, Thomas, 1890-1962.

MILSTEN, David Randolph. 704'.36 B
Thomas Gilcrease. San Antonio, Tex., Naylor Co. [1969] xxii, 468 p. illus., ports. 23 cm. Bibliography: p. 451-458. [CT275.G399M5] 74-84447 12.95
1. Gilcrease, Thomas, 1890-1962.

Gilding.

CHAMBERS, Donald L. 745.7
How to gold leaf antiques and other art objects; techniques of an ancient art explained step by step in how-to-do-it text

SUBJECT INDEX GIORGIONE, GIORGIO BARBARELLI

and pictures [by] Donald L. Chambers. New York, Crown Publishers [1973] 108 p. illus. 27 cm. [TT380.C45 1973] 72-96672 ISBN 0-517-50355-7 7.95
1. Gilding. I. Title. BIP

WAGNER, Charles Louis Henry, 1879- 745.56
Text book of gilding for sign and related arts. Boston, Wagner School of Sign and Commercial Art [1950] 115 p. illus. 23 cm. [TT380.W15] 50-672
1. Gilding. I. Title.

Giles, Alfred, 1853-1920.

JUTSON, Mary Carolyn Hollers. 720'.92'4
Alfred Giles: an English architect in Texas and Mexico. Photography by Joe S. Lawrie. San Antonio, Trinity University Press [1972] xviii, 178 p. illus. 29 cm. (San Antonio Conservation Society series, no. 1) Bibliography: p. 167-172. [NA997.G54J87] 72-75338 ISBN 0-911536-42-6
1. Giles, Alfred, 1853-1920. 2. Architecture—Texas. 3. Architecture—Mexico. I. Title. II. Series: San Antonio Conservation Society. San Antonio Conservation Society series, no. 1.

Gill, Eric, 1882-1940.

BRADY, Elizabeth A., 1914- 686.2'24 B
Eric Gill: twentieth century book designer, by Elizabeth A. Brady. Rev. ed. Metuchen, N.J., Scarecrow Press, 1974. vii, 142 p. illus. 22 cm. Bibliography: p. 127-135. [Z232.G47B7 1974] 73-18453 ISBN 0-8108-0640-1 5.00
1. Gill, Eric, 1882-1940.

BREWER, Roy, 1924- 686.2'24
Eric Gill: the man who loved letters. Totowa, N.J., Rowman and Littlefield [1973] x, 86 p. illus. 26 cm. (The Ars typographica library) [Z250.A2G53] 73-7724 ISBN 0-87471-148-7 15.00
1. Gill, Eric, 1882-1940. 2. Type and type-founding—History. I. Title.

CLARK, Betty. 769'.92'4
A tribute to Eric Gill / Betty Clark. [Oxford] : Studio One Gallery, 1976. [10] p. : port. ; 22 cm. Catalogue of an exhibition held at Studio One Gallery, 22-30 Nov. 1976. [NE1147.6.G55C58] 77-363165 ISBN 0-9505455-0-3 : £0.20
1. Gill, Eric, 1882-1940. I. Gill, Eric, 1882-1940. II. Studio One Gallery. III. Title.

GILL, Eric, 1882-1940. 709'.24 B
Autobiography. New York, Biblo and Tannen, 1968 [c1941] xv, 300, [33] p. illus., ports. 22 cm. "Illustrations": p. [301]-[333] [NB497.G55A3 1968] 68-54231

GILL, Eric, 1882-1940. 686.2'24'0924
The letter forms and type designs of Eric Gill / notes by Robert Harling. [Westerham] : Eva Svensson, 1976. 64 p., [4] p. of plates (4 fold.) : ill. (some col.), facsims., port. ; 19 cm. "Notes ... first published in Alphabet & Image and now, rev. and expanded." [NK3631.G54H37 1976] 77-358363 ISBN 0-903696-05-3. ISBN 0-903696-04-5 pbk.
1. Gill, Eric, 1882-1940. 2. Lettering. 3. Type and type founding. I. Harling, Robert. II. Title. BIP

GILL, Eric, 1882-1940. 686.2'24'0924
The letter forms and type designs of Eric Gill / notes by Robert Harling. 2d rev. ed. U.S. ed. [Westerham, Eng.] : E. Svensson ; Boston : D. R. Godine, 1978. 63 p., [2] fold. leaves of plates : ill. (some col.) ; 20 cm. "These notes were first published in Alphabet & image and now, revised and expanded." [NK3631.G54H37 1978] 76-24232 ISBN 0-87923-200-5 : 15.00 ISBN 0-87923-201-3 pbk. :7.50
1. Gill, Eric, 1882-1940. 2. Lettering. 3. Type and type founding. I. Harling, Robert. II. Title.

KINDERSLEY, David. 730'.924 B
Mr. Eric Gill; recollections of David Kindersley. [San Francisco] Book Club of California, 1967. 24 p. illus., port. 19 cm. [NB497.G55K5] 67-66314
1. Gill, Eric, 1882-1940. I. Book Club of California, San Francisco.

THE Life and works of Eric Gill; 741'.0924 papers read at a Clark Library symposium, 22 April 1967, by Cecil Gill, Beatrice Warde & David Kindersley. Introd. by Albert Sperisen. Los Angeles, William Andrews Clark Memorial Library, University of California, 1968. ix, 67 p. illus., facsims., port. 26 cm. (William Andrews Clark Memorial Library seminar papers) [NB497.G55L5] 77-630232
1. Gill, Eric, 1882-1940. I. Gill, Cecil. II. Warde, Beatrice Lamberton (Becker) 1900- III. Kindersley, David. IV. California. University. University at Los Angeles. William Andrews Clark Memorial Library. V. Title. VI. Series.

SPEAIGHT, Robert, 1904- 730.924
The life of Eric Gill. New York, Kenedy [1966] xvii, 323p. illus., ports. 24cm. Bibl. [NB497.G55S6 1966a] 66-25003 6.95
1. Gill, Eric, 1882-1940. I. Title.

Gill, Eric, 1892-1940—Bibl.

GILL, Evan R., comp. 741
The inscriptional work of Eric Gill; an inventory. London, Cassell [Chester Springs, Pa., Dufour, 1965, c.1964] xvii, 140p. illus., facsims. 26cm. [Z8342.2.G53] 65-7105 12.50
1. Gill, Eric, 1892-1940—Bibl. I. Title. BIP

Gill, Irving John, 1870-1936.

LOS Angeles Co., Calif. Museum, Los Angeles. 720.973
Irving Gill, 1870-1936. Los Angeles County Museum, in collaboration with the Art Center in La Jolla. Photos. by Marvin Rand. Los Angeles] 1958. 59 p. illus. 19 cm. [NA737.G53L6] 59-24456
1. Gill, Irving John, 1870-1936. I. Title.

Giller, Norman M.

GILLER, Norman M. 720'.92'4 B
An adventure in architecture / Norman M. Giller. Miami Beach, Fla. : Virgo Press, c1976. 248 p. : ill. ; 26 cm. Includes index. [NA737.G534A43] 76-28287 12.50
1. Giller, Norman M. 2. Architects—United States—Biography. I. Title. BIP

Gilliam, Sam.

GILLIAM, Sam. 759.13
Sam Gilliam, paintings, 1950-1975, Fendrick Gallery, October 15 through November 8, 1975 : [catalog] Washington : The Gallery, 1975. [12] p. : ill. (some col.) ; 21 x 26 cm. Bibliography: p. [3] of cover. [ND237.G45F46] 75-24116
1. Gilliam, Sam. I. Fendrick Gallery.

WADSWORTH Atheneum, Hartford. 709'.2'2
Gilliam / Edwards / Williams: extensions; [catalogue of an exhibition] Wadsworth Atheneum, Hartford, Connecticut, February 6-March 17, 1974. [Hartford, 1974] 39 p. illus. (part col.) 23 cm. Includes bibliographies. [N6512.W28 1974] 73-94026
1. Gilliam, Sam. 2. Edwards, Melvin E. 3. Williams, William T., 1942- 4. Art, Modern—20th century—United States. I. Title. II. Title: Extensions.

Gillinder and Sons.

SHUMAN, Susan. 748.2'9148'11
"Lion" pattern glass / by Susan W. and John A. Shuman III. Boston : Branden Press, c1977. 29 p., [23] leaves of plates : ill. ; 22 cm. Bibliography: p. 29. [NK5198.G44A4 1977] 77-71739 ISBN 0-8283-1695-3 : 7.50
1. Gillinder and Sons. 2. Pattern glass, Victorian—Pennsylvania. 3. Lions in art. I. Shuman, John A., joint author. II. Title.

Gillon, Joseph Werner, 1905- —Art collections.

FAGG, William Buller. 732
African sculpture from the Tara Collection. Exhibited by Mr. & Mrs. J. W. Gillon. Catalogue by William Fagg. [Notre Dame? Ind., 1971] 60 p. illus. (part col.) 29 cm. Erratum slip inserted. Held at Art Gallery, University of Notre Dame, March 28-May 23, 1971. Bibliography: p. 57-58. [N7398.F3] 72-198259
1. Gillon, Joseph Werner, 1905- —Art collections. 2. Art, African—Exhibitions. 3. Art, Primitive—Africa, West. I. Notre Dame, Ind. University. Art Gallery. II. Title.

Gillray, James, 1757-1815.

GILLRAY, James, 1757-1815. 769'.924
The works of James Gillray: 582 plates and supplement containing the 45 so-called "suppressed plates." Bronx [New York] B. Blom, 1968. 1 v. (chiefly illus.) port. 34 cm. First ed., 1851. Facsim. of original t.p. reads: The works of James Gillray, from the original plates, with the addition of many subjects not before collected. London, Printed for H. G. Bohn by C. Whiting. [NC1479.G5B7 1968] 68-21201
1. Bohn, Henry George, 1796-1884. II. Title. BIP

HILL, Draper 741.5942
Mr. Gillray the caricaturist, a biography. Greenwich, Conn., Phaidon Pubs; dist. N. Y. Graphic [1965] vi, 266p. 147 illus. 26cm. Bibl. [NC1479.G5H5] 65-4471 8.50
1. Gillray, James, 1757-1815. I. Title.

WRIGHT, Thomas, 1810-1877. 741.5942
Historical & descriptive account of the caricatures of James Gillray; comprising a political and humorous history of the latter part of the reign of George the Third [by] Thomas Wright and R. H. Evans. New York, B. Blom, 1968. xv, 496 p. port. 24 cm. First ed., 1851. A descriptive accompaniment to the 582 engravings of v. 1 of The works of James Gillray. [NC1479.G5W8 1968] 68-21202
1. Gillray, James, 1757-1815. 2. Great Britain—History—George III, 1760-1820. I. Evans, Robert Harding, 1778-1857, joint author. II. Gillray, James, 1757-1815. The works of James Gillray. III. Title.

Gilman, James Franklin, 1850-1929.

DAWSON, Adele Godchaux, 1905- 759.13
James Franklin Gilman, nineteenth century painter / by Adele Godchaux Dawson. Canaan, N.H. : Phoenix Pub., c1975. vii, 159 p. : ill. (some col.) ; 32 cm. Includes index. Bibliography: p. 146-147. [ND237.G46D38] 75-20929 ISBN 0-914016-20-2 : 15.00
1. Gilman, James Franklin, 1850-1929. I. Title.

Gilpin, William, 1724-1804.

BARBIER, Carl Paul 709.42
William Gilpin: his drawings, teaching, and theory of the picturesque. Oxford [Eng.] Clarendon Pr. [dist. New York, Oxford, c.] 1963 xiv, 196p. 16 plates. 29cm. Bibl. 63-5975 10.00
1. Gilpin, William, 1724-1804. I. Title.

Gimond, Marcel Antoine, 1804-1961.

LYONS. Musee des beaux-arts. 730'.92'4
Marcel Gimmond [exposition] Musee de Lyon [juillet-septembre] 1962. [Lyon, 1962] 1 v. (unpaged) illus., ports. 22 cm. [NB553.G47L9] 66-44740
1. Gimond, Marcel Antoine, 1804-1961. I. Title.

Gimson, Ernest, 1864-1919.

ERNEST Gimson, his life & work. 749.2'2 B New York : Garland Pub., 1978. vii, 47 v p., [60] leaves of plates : ill. ; 29 cm. (The Aesthetic movement & the arts and crafts movement) Three articles on Gimson, with notes on the 60 plates. Reprint of the 1924 ed. published by the Shakespeare Head Press, Stratford-upon Avon. [NK942.G5E7 1978] 76-17779 ISBN 0-8240-2485-0 : lib.bdg. : 35.00
1. Gimson, Ernest, 1864-1919. 2. Art industries ad trade—England—Biography. I. Title. II. Series.

Gindertael, Roger van, 1899-

SCHNEIDER, Gerard, 1896- 759.9494
Gerard Schneider, Peintures. Par R. V. Gindertael. Preface de Marcel Brion. [Venezia], Alfieri, [1968]. Stamped on t.p.: Amer. dist., Wittenborn. New York. 1v. (unpaged) 85 plates. 23x24cm. English, French and Italian. [ND553.S42G5] 68-131830 15.00
1. Gindertael, Roger van, 1899- I. Title.

Ginger beer bottles—Catalogs.

ADAMS, Tony, fl.1976- 663'.9
Ginger beer collecting : an illustrated price guide / by Tony Adams, Andy Payne and M. Davison ; edited by E. S. Thompson and M. J. Coffin ; photographs by M. J. Coffin. Southampton : Southern Collectors' Publications, [1976] 52 p. : ill. ; 21 cm. Bibliography: p. 3. [NK5440.B6A35] 77-374258 ISBN 0-905438-01-9 : £1.25
1. Ginger beer bottles—Catalogs. 2. Ginger beer bottles—Collectors and collecting. I. Payne, Andy, joint author. II. Davison, Mick, joint author. III. Title.

Giorgione, Giorgio Barbarelli, known as, 1477-1511.

BALDASS, Ludwig von, 1887-1963 759.5
Giorgione. Notes on the plates by Gunther Heinz. [Tr. from from German by J. Maxwell Brownjohn] New York, Abrams [1965] 188p. illus., plates (26 mounted col.) 34cm. Bibl. [ND623.G5B33] 65-23171 25.00
1. Giorgione, Giorgio Barbarelli, known as, 1477-1511. I. Heinz, Gunther. II. Title.

PIGNATTI, Terisio, 1920- 759.5
Giorgione. Complete ed. [New York] Phaidon; [distributors in the U.S.: Praeger Publishers, 1971] 369 p. illus., col. plates. 29 cm. Bibliography: p. [187]-211. [ND623.G5P543] 70-118659 ISBN 0-7148-1457-1 35.00
1. Giorgione, Giorgio Barbarelli, known as, 1477-1511.

STEARNS, Frank Preston, 1846-1917. 759.5
Four great Venetians; an account of the lives and works of Giorgione, Titian, Tintoretto, and Il Veronese. Freeport, N.Y., Books for Libraries Press [1969] xi, 376 p. illus. 23 cm. (Essay index reprint series) Reprint of the 1901 ed. [ND621.V5S8 1969] 76-86786
1. Giorgione, Giorgio Barbarelli, known as, 1477-1511. 2. Tiziano Vecelli, 1477-1576. 3. Tintoretto, Jacopo Robusti, known as, 1512-1594. 4. Veronese, Paolo Cagliari, known as, 1528-1588. 5. Art—Venice. I. Title. BIP

VENTURI, Lionello, 1885- 759
Four steps toward modern art: Giorgione, Caravaggio, Manet, Cezanne. New York, Columbia University Press, 1956. ix, 81 p. 33 plates (incl. ports.) 21 cm. (Bampton lectures in America, no. 8) Bibliographical references included in "Notes" (p. [79]-81) [ND35.V38] 56-8357
1. Giorgione, Giorgio Barbarelli, known as, 1477-1511. 2. Caravaggio, Michelangelo Merist da, 1569?-1600. 3. Manet, Edouard, 1832-1883. 4. Cezanne, Paul, 1839-1906. I. Title. II. Series.

WIND, Edgar, 1900- 759.5
Giorgione's Tempesta with comments on Giorgione's Poetic Allegories. Oxford, Clarendon Press, 1969. xi, 51 p., 48 p. of plates. 30 cm. "Notes and references": p. 17-43. [ND623.G5W5] 79-445918 unpriced
1. Giorgione, Giorgio Barbarelli, known as, 1477-1511. I. Title. BIP

Giotto di Bondone, 1266?-1337.

BATTISTI, Eugenio 759.5
Giotto. biographical and critical study. Translated from the Italian by James Emmons. [Lausanne] Skira; [distributed in the U. S. by World Pub. Co., Cleveland, 1960] 146p. (Bibl: p. 133-[138]) (The Taste of our time, v. 32) 60-8730 5.75
1. Giotto di Bondone, 1266?-1337. 2. ounted col. illus. 19cm. I. Title.

BAXANDALL, Michael. 750'.1
Giotto and the orators: humanist observers of painting in Italy and the discovery of pictorial composition, 1350-1450. Oxford, Clarendon Press, 1971. xii, 185 p., 16 plates; illus., facsim. 25 cm. (Oxford-Warburg studies) Includes texts in Greek and Latin. Bibliography: p. [178]-180. [ND170.B37] 79-851462 ISBN 0-19-817178-1 £3.75
1. Giotto di Bondone, 1266?-1337. 2. Painting, Renaissance. 3. Composition (Art) I. Title. BIP

COLE, Bruce, 1938- 759.5
Giotto and Florentine painting, 1280-1375 / Bruce Cole. 1st ed. New York : Harper & Row, c1976. x, 209 p. : ill. ; 22 cm. (Icon editions) Includes index. Bibliography: p. [195]-197. [ND623.G6C57 1976] 75-7632 ISBN 0-06-430900-2 : 8.50
1. Giotto di Bondone, 1266?-1337. 2. Painting, Florentine. 3. Painting, Gothic—Florence. I. Title. BIP

EIMERL, Sarel. 759.5
The world of Giotto, c. 1267-1337, by Sarel Eimerl and the editors of Time-Life Books New York, Time, inc. [1967] 199 p. illus. (part col.) 31 cm. (Time-Life library of art) Bibliography: p. 193-194. [ND623.G6E35] 67-23024
1. Giotto di Bondone, 1266?-1337. I. Time-Life Books. II. Title.

GIOTTO and his contemporaries. 759.5 Translated by Susan Bellamy. New York, Crown Publishers, 1958. 98p. (chiefly col. plates) 30cm. Bibliography: p. 98. [ND623.G6C273] [ND623.G6C273] 927.5 58-12886 58-12886
1. Giotto di Bondone. 1266?-1337. 2. Paintings, Slenese. 3. Paintings, Florentine. I. Carli, Enzo, 1910-

GIOTTO di Bondone, 1266?-1337. 759.5
The complete paintings of Giotto. Introd. by Andrew Martindale. Notes and catalogue by Edi Baccheschi. New York, H. N. Abrams [1969, c1966] 128 p. illus. (part col.) 32 cm. (Classics of the world's great art) Bibliography: p. 82. [ND623.G6B253 1969b] 69-16901
I. Baccheschi, Edi. II. Title.

GIOTTO di Bondone, 1266?-1337. 759.5
Giotto [by] Mario Bucci. [Translated from the Italian by Caroline Beamish. 1st American ed.] New York, Grosset & Dunlap [1968] 39 p., 80 col. plates. 18 cm. (The New Grosset art library, 18) Bibliography: p. 32-33. [ND623.G6B83 1968b] 68-26684
I. Bucci, Mario.

MEISS, Millard Lazare 759.5
Giotto and Assisi, by Millard Meiss. New York, Norton [1967, c.1960] 28p. supp. of plates. 20cm. (Norton lib., N384) Bibl. [ND623.G6M38] 1.65 pap.,
1. Giotto of Bondone, 1266?-1337. 2. Assisi. San Francesco (Church) I. Title.

MEISS, Millard [Lazare] 759.5
Giotto and Assisi. [New York] New York University Press, [c.]1960 28p. Bibliography: p. 26-28. (Walter W. S. Cook alumni lecture, 1959) 60-9443 lates. 25cm. 5.00
1. Giotto di Bondone, 1266?-1337. 2. Assisi. San Francesco (Church) I. Title. II. Series.

RUSKIN, John, 1819-1900. 759.5
Giotto and his works in Padua : being an explanatory notice of the series of woodcuts executed for the Arundel Society after the frescoes in the Arena Chapel / by John Ruskin. Boston : Longwood Press, 1977. p. cm. Reprint of the 1854 ed. published by Levey, Robson & Franklyn, London. [ND623.G6R8 1977] 77-9344 ISBN 0-89341-207-4 lib.bdg. : 15.00
1. Giotto di Bondone, 1266?-1337. 2. Padua. Madonna dell' Arena (Chapel) I. Title.

SCHNEIDER, Laurie, comp. 759.5
Giotto in perspective. Englewood Cliffs, N.J., Prentice-Hall [1974] xii, 172 p. illus. 21 cm. (The Artists in perspective series) (A Spectrum book) Bibliography: p. 168-169. [ND623.G6S37 1974] 74-8016 ISBN 0-13-356717-6 7.95
1. Giotto di Bondone, 1266?-1337. I. Title. Pbk. 2.95, ISBN 0-13-356709-5.

SEMENZATO, Camillo. 759.5
Giotto. New York, Barnes & Noble [1964] 80 p. illus. (part col.) 18 cm. (Barnes & Noble art series, no. 619) [ND623.G6S453] 64-56937
1. Giotto di Bondone, 1266?-1337. I. Title.

SIREN, Osvald, 1879- 759.5
Giotto and some of his followers / by Osvald Siren ; English translation by Frederic Schenck. New York : Hacker Art Books, 1975. 2 v. (x, 285 p., [110] leaves of plates) in 1 : ill. ; 27 cm. Reprint of the 1917 ed. published in 2 v. by Harvard University Press, Cambridge, Mass. Includes bibliographical references. [ND615.S5 1975] 75-189860 ISBN 0-87817-112-6 : 75.00
1. Giotto di Bondone, 1266?-1337. 2. Painting, Italian. 3. Painting, Gothic—Italy. 4. Painters—Italy. I. Title. BIP

SMART, Alastair, 1922- 759.5
The Assisi problem and the art of Giotto: a study of the Legend of St. Francis in the Upper Church of San Francesco, Assisi. Oxford, Clarendon Press, 1971. xx, 311 p., 111 plates. illus., facsims. 30 cm. Contains the Latin text, and English translation of the Legenda maior by St. Bonaventura. Bibliography: p. [294]-295. [ND623.G6S5] 78-26697 ISBN 0-19-817166-8 £8.00
1. Giotto di Bondone, 1266?-1337. Legend of Saint Francis (Painting) I. Bonaventura, Saint, Cardinal, 1221-1274. Legenda maior S. Francisci. English and Latin. 1971. II. Tit BIP

STUBBLEBINE, James H., comp. 759.5
Giotto: the Arena Chapel frescoes. Edited by James H. Stubblebine. [1st ed.] New York, Norton [1969] xiii, 218 p. 129 illus. 22 cm. (Norton critical studies in art history) Includes an introductory essay, backgrounds and sources, and criticism. Bibliography: p. [215]-218. [ND623.G6S7] 67-17689 6.50
1. Giotto di Bondone, 1266?-1337. 2. Podua. Madonna dell'Arena (Chapel) I. Title.

STUBBLEBINE, James H., comp. 759.5
Giotto: the Arena Chapel frescoes. Edited by James H. Stubblebine. [1st ed.] New York, Norton [1969] xiii, 218 p. 129 illus. 22 cm. (Norton critical studies in art history) Includes an introductory essay, backgrounds and sources, and criticism. Bibliography: p. [215]-218. [ND623.G6S7] 67-17689 6.50
1. Giotto di Bondone, 1266?-1337. 2. Podua. Madonna dell'Arena (Chapel) I. Title.

TINTORI, Leonetto, 1908- 759.5
Giotto: the Peruzzi Chapel [by] Leonetto Tintori and Eve Borsook. With a pref. by Ugo Procacci and photos. by Nadie Tronci. New York, H.N. Abrans [1965] 106 p. 163 illus. (part mounted col.) plans. 31 cm. Included bibliographical references. [ND623.G6T5] 65-3961
1. Giotto di Bondone, 2. Florence. Santa Croce (Church) Cappelia Peruzzi. I. Borsook, Eve, joint author. II. Tronci, Nadir, illus. III. Title.

TRACHTENBERG, Marvin. 726'.597
The Campanile of Florence Cathedral: "Giotto's tower." New York, New York University Press, 1971. 230 p. 348 plates (part col.) 32 cm. Bibliography: p. [209]-216. [NA5621.F52T7] 70-124532 ISBN 0-8147-8151-9
1. Giotto di Bondone, 1266?-1337. 2. Florence. Campanile. I. Title.

Giotto di Bondone, 1266?-1337—Addresses, essays, lectures.

PENNSYLVANIA. State University. Dept. of Art History. 759.5
Seminar one: Giotto and his times; a collection of essays. Edited by Price Amerson [and others] Graphic editor: Jeanne Stevens. University Park, Graduate Students, Dept. of Art History, Pennsylvania State University, 1971. ix, 244 p. illus. 23 cm. Includes bibliographical references. [ND623.G6P37] 72-196256
1. Giotto di Bondone, 1266?-1337—Addresses, essays, lectures. I. Amerson, Price, ed. II. Title.

Giotto di Bondone, 1266?-1337—Juvenile literature.

ROCKWELL, Anne F. 759.5 B
The boy who drew sheep [by] Anne Rockwell. [1st ed.] New York, Atheneum, 1973. 37 p. illus. 25 cm. Based on the biography of Giotto di Bondone as written down by G. Vasari in the sixteenth century. A brief biography of the early Renaissance artist who was the most famous of his time and introduced a new way of painting. [ND623.G6R62 1973] 92 72-86948 4.50
1. Giotto di Bondone, 1266?-1337—Juvenile literature. I. Title. BIP

Gipsies—Pictorial works.

KOUDELKA, Josef, 1938- 779'.2'0924
Gypsies : photographs / by Josef Koudelka. Millerton, New York : Aperture, c1975. [135] p. : chiefly ill. ; 28 x 31 cm. [TR681.G9K68 1975] 75-13611 ISBN 0-912334-74-6 : 22.50. ISBN 0-912334-85-1 pbk. :museum ed. 15.00
1. Gipsies—Pictorial works. I. Title.
Museum edition is available from the Museum of Modern Art, New York.

Gipsies—Spain.

JONES, Jo. 760'.0924
Paintings and drawings of the gypsies of Granada. Text by Augustus John [and others] Detroit, Folklore Associates [1969] 71 p. illus. (part col.), map. 32 cm. [N6797.J6J6 1969b] 78-8842 ISBN 0-901533-00-9 12.50
1. Gipsies—Spain. I. John, Augustus Edwin, 1878-1961. II. Title. III. Title: The gypsies of Granda. BIP

Giraudier, Antonio.

GIRAUDIER, Antonio. 700'.924
Selections from five works. With black & white reproductions from the author's paintings & drawings. [Chicago, Adams Press, 1968] 54 p. illus. 23 cm. "Selections from 5 unpublished works: The branches; Mar-grave; Essential winter; Soul spree; Jade mirrors." [PS3557.I7A6 1968] 68-30966 3.00

GIRAUDIER, Antonio. 811'.5'4
Sheaves / Antonio Giraudier. Rev. Charleston, Ill. : Prairie Poet Books, 1975. xiii, 263 p. : 10 ill. ; 22 cm. "A compilation of nine definitive works ... with ten reproductions from original artworks by the author." "In honor of the Bicentennial." [PS3557.I7S5] 76-352100 ISBN 0-915284-14-6 : 2.50
I. Title.
Contents omitted

GIRAUDIER, Antonio. 759.13
Ten remembrances for Don Quixote and other works / by Antonio Giraudier ; [photos. by Otto E. Nelson]. New York City : Avanti Galleries, c1975. [55] p. : ill. (some col.) ; 23 cm. Cover title: Giraudier. "A Bi-centennial celebration, October 21 through November 7." "A Giraudier—'Ten remembrances for Don Quixote'—program/book." Includes bibliographical references. [N6537.G47A92] 75-330239
1. Giraudier, Antonio. I. Avanti Galleries. II. Title.

Girodet-Trioson, Anne Louis Girodet de Roussy, known as, 1767-1824.

LEVITINE, George. 759.4
Girodet-Trioson : an iconographical study / George Levitine. New York : Garland, [1978] p. cm. (Outstanding dissertations in the fine arts) Originally presented as the author's thesis, Harvard, 1952. [ND553.G6L48 1978] 77-94702 ISBN 0-8240-3235-7 : lib.bdg. : 42.50
1. Girodet-Trioson, Anne Louis Girodet de Roussy, known as, 1767-1824. 2. Neoclassicism (Art)—France. I. Title. II. Series. BIP

Gislebertus, 12th cent.

GRIVOT, Denis. 730.944
Gislebertus, Sculptor of Autun, by Denis Grivot and George Zarnecki. Introd. by T. S. R. Boase. [New York] Orion Press [1961] 180p. illus., maps, plans. 32cm. Bibliographical footnotes. [NB553.G53G7] 61-14186
1. Gislebertus, 12th cent. 2. Autun, France. Saint-Lazare (Cathedral) I. Zarnecki, Jerzy, joint author. II. Title.

GRIVOT, Denis 730.944
Gislebertus sculptor of Autun, by Denis Grivot, George Zarnecki. Introd. by T. S. R. Boase. [New York] Orion Pr. with Trianon Pr. [c.1961] 180p. illus., maps. 32cm. Bibl. 61-14186 13.50
1. Gislebertus, 12th cent. 2. Autun, France. SaintLazare (Cathedral) I. Zarnecki, Jerzy, joint author. II. Title.

Giulio Romano, Giulio Pippi, known as, 1499-1546.

HARTT, Frederick. 927
Giulio Romano. New Haven, Yale University Press, 1958. 2v. plates, plans. 29cm. Contents.v. 1. Text.--v. 2. Illustrations. Bibliography: v. 1, p.331-[339] [ND623.G65H3] 58-5460
1. Giulio Romano, Giulio Pippi, know as, 1492-1546. I. Title. BIP

VERHEYEN, Egon. 945'.28
The Palazzo del Te in Mantua : images of love and politics / Egon Verheyen ; with plans by Diane Finiello Zervas. Baltimore : Johns Hopkins University Press, c1977. xvi, 156 p. : ill. ; 29 cm. Includes index. Bibliography: p. 145-152. [NA7756.M3V47] 76-47365 ISBN 0-8018-1809-5 : 25.00
1. Giulio Romano, Giulio Pippi, known as, 1499-1546. 2. Federigo II Gonzaga. 3. Mantua. Palazzo del Te. 4. Decoration and ornament, Architectural—Italy—Mantua. I. Title. BIP

Giza. Great Pyramid of Cheops.

FIX, William R., 1941- 932
Pyramid odyssey / by William R. Fix. 1st American ed. New York : Mayflower Books, c1978. p. cm. Includes index. Bibliography: p. [DT63.F55] 78-14540 ISBN 0-8317-7160-7 : 10.00
1. Giza. Great Pyramid of Cheops. 2. Atlantis. I. Title. BIP

POCHAN, Andre Pelissier Robert. 932
The mysteries of the great pyramids : the luminous horizons of Khoufou / A. Pochan. New York : Avon, 1978. xv, 288 p., [8] leaves of plates : ill. ; 18 cm. Translation of L'Enigme de la Grande Pyramide. Includes bibliographical references. [DT63.5.P6213] 77-92348 ISBN 0-380-00881-5 pbk. : 2.25
1. Giza.—Great Pyramid of Cheaps—Miscellanea. I. Title. BIP

Giza—Tombs.

BADAWY, Alexander. 932
The tomb of Nyhetep-Ptah at Giza and the tomb of 'Ankhm'ahor at Saqqara / by Alexander Badawy. Berkeley : University of California Press, 1978. ix, 61 p., [57] leaves of plates (12 fold.) : ill. ; 31 cm. (University of California publications : Occasional papers ; no. 11, archaeology) Includes bibliographical references and

index. [DT73.G5B3] 77-73507 ISBN 0-520-09575-8 pbk. : 15.00
1. Nyhetep-Ptah—Tomb. 2. 'Akhm'ahor—Tomb. 3. Giza-Tombs. 4. Sakkara—Tombs. 5. Egypt—Antiquities. I. Title. II. Series: California. University. University of California publications : Occasional papers ; no. 11. BIP

BADAWY, Alexander. 932
The tombs of Iteti, Sekhem'ankh-Ptah, and Kaemnofert at Giza / by Alexander Badawy. Berkeley : University of California Press, 1976. 36 p., [27] leaves of plates (7 fold.) : ill. ; 31 cm. (University of California publications : Occasional papers ; no. 9) Includes bibliographical references and index. [DT73.G5B32] 75-620057 ISBN 0-520-09544-8 : 10.00
1. Giza—Tombs. 2. Tombs—Egypt. I. Title. II. Series: California. University. University of California publications : Occasional papers ; no. 9. BIP

DUNHAM, Dows, 1890- 913.32
The mastaba of Queen Mersyankh III, G7530-7540, by Dows Dunham and William Kelly Simpson. Boston, Dept. of Egyptian and Ancient Near Eastern Art, Museum of Fine Arts, Boston, 1974. v, 26 p., [49] p. of illus. (part fold.) 35 cm. (Giza mastabas, v. 1) "Based upon the excavations and recording of late George Andrew Reisner and William Stevenson Smith, Museum of Fine Arts—Harvard University Expedition." Includes bibliographical references. [DT73.G5D85] 73-88232
1. Meresankh III, Queen of Egypt. 2. Giza—Tombs. I. Simpson, William Kelly. II. Reisner, George Andrew, 1867-1942. III. Smith, William Stevenson. IV. Title. V. Series.

Glacier Bay National Monument—Antiquities.

ACKERMAN, Robert E. 917.98'2
Archeological survey, Glacier Bay National Monument, southeastern Alaska [by] Robert E. Ackerman. Pullman, Laboratory of Anthropology, Washington State University, 1964- v. illus. (part fold.), map. 28 cm. (Laboratory of Anthropology, Washington State University. Report of investigations, no. 28) "A final report to the National Park Service, contract no. 14-10-0434-942." Bibliography: v. 1, p. 33-34. [E78.W3W3 no. 28, etc.] 69-63023
1. Glacier Bay National Monument—Antiquities. I. U.S. National Park Service. II. Title. III. Series: Washington (State) State University, Pullman. Laboratory of Anthropology. Report of investigations, no. 28

ACKERMAN, Robert E. 917.97'03'08 s
The archeology of the Glacier Bay Region, southeastern Alaska; final report of the archeological survey of the Glacier Bay National Monument [by] Robert E. Ackerman. Pullman, Washington State University, Laboratory of Anthropology, 1968. x, 123 p. illus., map. 28 cm. (Washington State University. Laboratory of Anthropology. Report of investigations, no. 44) "Research sponsored by the National Park Service under contracts: 14-10-0434-942, 14-10-0434-1512, and 14-10-0434-1907." Bibliography: p. 113-120. [E78.W3W3 no. 44] 78-626774 3.00
1. Glacier Bay National Monument—Antiquities. 2. Tlingit Indians—Antiquities. I. U.S. National Park Service. II. Title. III. Series: Washington (State). State University, Pullman. Laboratory of Anthropology. Report of investigations, no. 44

Glacier National Park.

WORLD-WIDE Research 917.86'52'043
and Publishing Co. National Parks Division.
A Photographic and comprehensive guide to Glacier & Waterton Lakes National Parks. All photography by Michael D. Yandell. Casper, Wyo. [1974] 73 p. col. illus. 31 cm. (National parkways, v. 7) [F737.G5W67 1974] 74-176168 1.95
1. Glacier National Park. 2. Waterton Lakes National Park, Alta. I. Yandell, Michael D., illus. II. Title. III. Title: Glacier & Waterton Lakes National Parks. IV. Series.

Glackens, William J., 1870-1938.

FLINT, Janet A. 741.9'73
Drawings by William Glackens, 1870-1938. [By] Janet A. Flint. Washington, Published for the National Collection of Fine Arts by the Smithsonian Institution Press, 1972. [22] p. illus. 27 cm. "Catalog of the exhibition [February 25- April 30, 1972, National Collection of Fine Arts, Smithsonian Institution]": p. [9-22]. [NC139.G5F55] 72-81
1. Glackens, William J., 1870-1938. I. Smithsonian Institution. National Collection of Fine Arts. II. Title.

GLACKENS, Ira, 1907- 759.13
William Glackens and the Ashcan group; the emergence of realism in American art. New York, Crown Publishers [1957] 267 p. illus. (part col.) 24 cm. [ND237.G5G55] 927.5 57-8771
1. Glackens, William J., 1870-1938. 2. Painters, American. 3. Realism in art. I. Title.

RUTGERS University, New 760'.0924
Brunswick, N.J. University Art Gallery.
The art of William Glackens. [Exhibition] January 10 through February 10, 1967. [New Brunswick? N.J., 1967] 19 p. illus. 24 cm. (Its Bulletin, v. 1 no. 1) Text by Richard J. Wattenmaker, director, University Art Gallery. "The art of William Glackens; observations at random": viii p. inserted. [N722.A3 vol. 1, no. 1] 67-64461
1. Glackens, William J., 1870-1938. I. Wattenmaker, Richard J. II. Title. III. Series.

ST. Louis. City Art 759.13
Museum.
William Glackens in retrospect. [Saint Louis, City Art Museum, 1966] 1 v. (chiefly illus. (part col.)) 25 cm. Exhibition held at the City Art Museum of Saint Louis, Nov. 19-Dec. 31; National Collection of Fine Arts, Smithsonian Institution, Feb. 1-Apr. 2; Whitney Museum of American Art, Apr. 25-June 11, 1966-1967. Catalog edited by Charles E. Buckley. Text by Leslie Katz. [ND237.G5S3] 66-30341
1. Glackens, William, 1870-1938. I. Buckley, Charles E., ed. II. Katz, Leslie, 1918- III. Smithsonian Institution. National Collection of Fine Arts. IV. Whitney Museum of American Art, New York. V. Title.

Gladys English Memorial Collection of Original Illustrations for Children's Books.

CALIFORNIA Library 741.6'42
Association. Children's and Young People's Section.
Illustrations for children: the Gladys English Collection. [2d ed. Berkeley, California Library Association, 1967] 45 p. illus. 23 cm. (Keepsake series, no. 5) Title page has imprint of original ed.: Berkeley, California Library Association, 1963. [N4030.C3 1967] 67-66384
1. Gladys English Memorial Collection of Original Illustrations for Children's Books. I. Title. II. Series: California Library Association. Keepsake series, no. 5.

Glamour photography.

BROOKS, David, 1933- 779'.24
Glamour photography / by David Brooks. Los Angeles : Petersen Pub. Co., [1974] 80 p. : ill. (some col.) ; 28 cm. (Petersen's how-to photographic library) [TR678.B76] 74-19664 ISBN 0-8227-0087-5 pbk. : 2.95
1. Glamor photography. 2. Photography of the nude. I. Title.

COLMER, Michael. 741.68
Calendar girls / [selected by] Michael Colmer. London : Sphere, 1976. 144 p. : chiefly ill. (some col.) ; 31 cm. Published simultaneously in the U.S. under the title: Glamour calendar art. [TR678.C64 1976b] 77-353215 ISBN 0-7221-2458-9 : £2.50
1. Glamour photography. 2. Calendar art. I. Title.

COLMER, Michael. 741.68
Glamour calendar art / Michael Colmer. Chicago : Regnery, 1976. 144 p. : chiefly ill. (some col.) ; 31 cm. [TR678.C64 1976] 76-6265 ISBN 0-8092-8034-5 : 14.95
1. Glamour photography. 2. Calendar art. I. Title. BIP

GABOR, Mark, 1939- 778.9'24
The pin-up; a modest history. New York, Universe Books [1972] 271 p. illus. 32 cm. Bibliography: p. 263. [TR678.G3] 73-189116 ISBN 0-87663-163-4 20.00
1. Glamour photography. I. Title. BIP

GOWLAND, Peter. 778.9'24
Gowland's guide to glamour photography. New York, Crown [1972] 170 p. illus. (part col.) 26 cm. [TR678.G68 1972] 76-185079 6.95
1. Glamour photography. I. Title. II. Title: Guide to glamour photography. BIP

HURRELL, George. 770'.92'4 B
The Hurrell style : fifty years of photographing Hollywood / photos. by George Hurrell ; text by Whitney Stine. New York : John Day Co., [1976] p. cm. Includes index. [TR678.H87] 76-15396 ISBN 0-381-98293-9 : 14.95
1. Hurrell, George. 2. Glamour photography. I. Stine, Whitney, 1930- II. Title. BIP

LAWTON, Richard, 1943- 779'.2
comp.
Grand illusions, by Richard Lawton. With a text by Hugo Leckey. New York, McGraw-Hill [1973] 255 p. (chiefly illus.) 29 cm. [TR678.L38] 73-492 ISBN 0-07-036783-3 20.00
1. Glamor photography. I. Leckey, Hugo. II. Title.

Glaser, Milton.

GLASER, Milton. 741.9'73
The Milton Glaser poster book. New York : Harmony Books, 1977. p. cm. [NC1850.G55A5 1977] 77-8081 ISBN 0-517-53025-2 pbk. : 5.95
1. Glaser, Milton. I. Title.

Glasgow school of painting.

MARTIN, David, 759.9414'43 B
artist.
The Glasgow School of painting / David Martin. Edinburgh : P. Harris, 1976. [7], 72 p., [12] p. of plates : ill., ports. ; 16 cm. Reprint of the 1897 ed. published by G. Bell & Sons, London. [ND481.G5M4 1976] 77-375308 ISBN 0-904505-15-4 : £2.00
1. Glasgow school of painting. 2. Painting, Modern—19th century—Scotland—Glasgow. 3. Painters—Scotland—Biography. I. Title.

Glasgow—Streets—Pictorial works.

ANNAN, Thomas, 779'.9'9141443
d.1887.
Photographs of the old closes and streets of Glasgow, 1868/1877 : with a supplement of 15 related views / Thomas Annan ; with a new introd. by Anita Ventura Mozley. New York : Dover Publications, 1977. xv, 55 p. : chiefly ill. ; 31 cm. Original ed. published in 1878 or 1879 by the Glasgow City Improvements Trust, Glasgow, under title: Photographs of old closes, streets, &c., taken 1868-1877; supplementary photos. taken from the 1900 ed. published under title: Old closes and streets, a series of photogravures, 1868-1899. [DA890.G5A55 1977] 76-27495 ISBN 0-486-23442-8 : 5.00
1. Glasgow—Streets—Pictorial works. 2. Glasgow—Description—Views. I. Title. BIP

Glasier, Marshall, 1902—

GLASIER, Marshall, 1902- 741.9'73
Recent works by Marshall Glasier : [exhibition], September 29-October 27, 1974. [Binghamton] : University Art Gallery, State University of New York at Binghamton, [1974] 20, [36] p. : chiefly ill. ; 28 cm. Includes reprints of catalogs of exhibitions in 1963 and 1959 presented by the Gallery Committee of Harpur College, which later became SUNY-Binghampton. [N6537.G5N48] 75-622157
1. Glasier, Marshall, 1902- I. New York (State). State University at Binghamton. University Art Gallery.

Glass.

BURTON, John, 1894- 748
Glass: philosophy and method, hand-blown, sculptured, colored. [1st ed.] Philadelphia, Chilton Book Co. [1967] 278 p. 288 illus., facsim., port. 26 cm. Includes bibliographies. [TP857.3.B86] 67-28894
1. Glass I. Title.

BURTON, John, 1894- 748
Glass: philosophy and method, hand-blown, sculptured, colored. [1st ed.] Philadelphia, Chilton Book Co. [1967] 278 p. 288 illus., facsim., port. 26 cm. Includes bibliographies. [TP857.3.B86] 67-28894
1. Glass. 2. Glass blowing and working. I. Title.

CALEY, Earle Radcliffe, 748.2901
1900-
Analyses of ancient glasses, 1790-1957, a comprehensive and critical survey Corning, N. Y., Corning Museum of Glass, 1962. 118 p. tables. 28 cm. (Corning [N.Y.] Museum of Glass Monographs, v. 1) Bibliographical footnotes. [TP857.C3] 62-13805
1. Glass. I. Title. II. Series.

MCMILLAN, Peter Warwick 666
Glass-ceramics, New York, Academic [c.] 1964. viii, 229p.illus. 23cm. (Non-metallic solids, v.1) [TP862.M3] 64-8067 7.50
1. Glass. I. Title. II. Series.

Glass blowing and working.

AMERICAN Scientific 666.1082
Glassblowers Society.
Symposium on the art of glassblowing. 1st-1956- [Wilmington, Del.] v. diagrs. 24cm. Sponsored by the society in cooperation with Corning Glass Works. [TP859.A65] 58-3756
1. Glass blowing and working. I. Corning Glass Works, Corning, N.Y. II. Title.

ANDERSON, Harriette. 748
Kiln-fired glass. [1st ed.] Philadelphia, Chilton Book Co. [1970] xv, 185 p. illus. 27 cm. Bibliography: p. 177. [TP862.A5 1970] 77-116917
1. Glass blowing and working. 2. Glass painting and staining. I. Title. BIP

BERLYE, Milton K. 666'.1
The encyclopedia of working with glass, by Milton K. Berlye. Dobbs Ferry, N.Y., Oceana Publications, 1968. viii, 270 p. illus. 29 cm. Includes bibliographies. [TP859.B5] 67-25903
1. Glass blowing and working. I. Title. BIP

HAMMESFAHR, James E. 666'.1
Creative glass blowing [by] James E. Hammesfahr [and] Clair L. Stong. With a foreword by Charles H. Greene. San Francisco, W.H. Freeman [1968] 196 p. illus. 20 x 24 cm. Bibliography: p. [191]-192. [TP859.H25] 68-14225
1. Glass blowing and working. I. Stong, Clair L., joint author. II. Title. BIP

KINNEY, Kay. 748
Glass craft: designing, forming, decorating. [1st ed.] Philadelphia, Chilton Co., Book Division [1962] 178 p. illus. 27 cm. [TP859.K5] 61-14025
1. Glass blowing and working. I. Title.

KULASIEWICZ, Frank, 1930- 748.2
Glassblowing. New York, Watson-Guptill Publications [1974] 215 p. illus. 29 cm. Bibliography: p. 209-210. [TT298.K84 1974] 74-12446 ISBN 0-8230-2120-3
1. Glass blowing and working. I. Title. BIP

NOKES, Malcolm Cuthbert. 666.1
Modern glass working and laboratory technique. [3d ed.] Brooklyn, Chemical Pub. Co., 1950. xiii, 157 p. illus. 21 cm. [TP859.N63] 50-9174
1. Glass blowing and working. I. Title.

ROGERS, La Verne. 666.122
Working with glass. [Houston, Tex., Nardco Co., Glass Colors Division, 1961] 76p. illus. 28cm. [TP859.R6] 61-4814

1. Glass blowing and working. I. Title.

SCHULER, Frederic. 666'.12
Flameworking; glassmaking for the craftsman. [1st ed.] Philadelphia, Chilton Book Co. [1968] xi, 131 p. illus. 26 cm. [TP859.S32] 68-30863
1. Glass blowing and working. I. Title. BIP

SCHULER, Frederic. 748
Glassforming; glassmaking for the craftsman, by Frederic and Lilli Schuler. [1st ed.] Philadelphia, Chilton Book Co. [1970] xv, 151 p. illus. (part col.) 27 cm. Bibliography: p. 147. [TP859.S33 1970] 71-135056
1. Glass blowing and working. 2. Glass painting and staining. I. Schuler, Lilli, joint author. II. Title. BIP

WHEELER, E. L. 666.1
Scientific glassblowing. With a pref. by G. Ross Robertson. New York, Interscience Publishers, 1958. 478 p. 24 cm. [TP859.W48] 55-12144
1. Glass blowing and working. I. Title.

Glass candlesticks—Catalogs.

ARCHER, Margaret, 1927- 749'.63
Glass candlesticks / by Margaret and Douglas Archer ; [photography by Bruce H. Linker]. 1st ed. Paducah, Ky. : Collector Books, c1975. 108 p. : col. ill. ; 23 cm. [NK5440.C26A72] 76-354211 ISBN 0-89145-001-7 : 7.95
1. Glass candlesticks—Catalogs. 2. Glass candlesticks—Collectors and collecting. I. Archer, Douglas, 1926- joint author. II. Title.

Glass candy containers.

EIKELBERNER, George. 748'.8
American glass candy containers, by George Eikelberner and Serge Agadjanian. Belle Mead, N.J., S. Agadjanian [1967] 1 v. (unpaged) illus. 28 cm. [NK5440.C3E35] 67-22339
1. Glass candy containers. I. Agadjanian, Serge, joint author. II. Title.

EIKELBERNER, George. 748'.8
More American glass candy containers, by George Eikelberner and Serge Agadjanian. Belle Mead, N.J., S. Agadjanian [1970] 1 v. (unpaged) illus., ports. 28 cm. [NK5440.C3E35 1970] 70-120107
1. Glass candy containers. I. Agadjanian, Serge, joint author. II. Title.

Glass candy containers—Catalogs.

MATTHEWS, Robert T. 748'.8
Antiquers' of glass candy containers, by Robert T. Matthews. Glenelg, Md., [1970] 1 v. (various pagings) illus. 29 cm. Includes a bibliography. [NK5440.C3M27] 74-19886
1. Glass candy containers—Catalogs. I. Title. BIP

Glass candy containers—Collectors and collecting.

MATTHEWS, Robert T. 748'.8
A collection of old glass candy containers; things of the past illustrated in glass, by Robert T. Matthews. [1st ed.] Glenelg, Md. [1966] 45 l. (chiefly illus.) 28 cm. Bibliography: leaf 45. [NK5112.M37] 67-2511
1. Glass candy containers—Collectors and collecting. I. Title.

MATTHEWS, Robert T. 748'.8
A collection of old glass candy containers; things of the past, illustrated in glass. With a new suppl.: Later candy containers. By Robert T. Matthews. 2d ed. rev. and enl. Glenelg, Md., c1967. 59, S14, [6] l. illus., port. 28 cm. Bibliography: leaf [S19] [NK5440.C3M28 1967] 68-1707
1. Glass candy containers—Collectors and collecting. I. Title.

MATTHEWS, Robert T. 748'.8
A collection of old glass candy containers; things of the past, illustrated in glass. With a new suppl.: Later candy containers. By Robert T. Matthews. 3d ed., rev. and enl. Glenelg, Md. [1969] 62, S14, [8] l. illus., port. 29 cm. Bibliography: leaf [7] (3d group) [NK5440.C3M28 1969] 78-272484
1. Glass candy containers—Collectors and collecting. I. Title.

MATTHEWS, Robert T. 748.2'075
Old glass candy containers: price guide, by Robert T. Matthews. 2d ed. rev. and enl. Glenelg, Md., c1966. [18] l. illus. 28 cm. Cover title. [NK5440.C3M3 1966b] 68-1618
1. Glass candy containers—Collectors and collecting. 2. Glassware—Prices. I. Title.

Glass Christmas decorations—Collectors and collecting.

ROGERS, Maggie. 748.8
The glass Christmas ornament, old & new : a collector's compendium and price guide / by Maggie Rogers with Judith Hawkins ; [photos. by Edward Gowans ; design by Clyde Van Cleve]. Forest Grove, Or. : Timber Press, c1977. xiii, 126 p. : ill. (some col.) ; 23 cm. [NK5440.C57R63] 77-16741 ISBN 0-917304-07-1 pbk. : 9.95
1. Glass Christmas decorations—Collectors and collecting. I. Hawkins, Judith, joint author. II. Title.
Distributed by ISBS

Glass, Colored.

BEDFORD, John, 1907- 748.592
Bristol and other coloured glass. New York, Walker [1965, c1964] 64 p. illus., col. plates. 19 cm. (His Collectors' pieces, 2) [NK5104.B37 1965] 65-22129
1. Glass, Colored. 2. Glassware—Collectors and collecting. I. Title.

DAVIS, Derek C. 748'.8
Colored glass [by] Derek C. Davis & Keith Middlemas. Photos. by Michael Plomer. New York, C. N. Potter [1968] 119 p. col. illus. 31 cm. ([The Collector's world in color]) [NK5143.D28 1968] 68-31839 10.00
1. Glass, Colored. 2. Glassware, British. I. Middlemas, Robert Keith, 1935- joint author. II. Plomer, Michael, illus. III. Title.

WELKER, Mary. 748.2'9171'92
Cambridge, Ohio, glass in color, by Mary and Lyle Welker and son Lynn. New Concord, Ohio [1969] [32] p. col. illus. 23 cm. [NK5112.W43] 75-8016 4.95
1. Cambridge Glass Company, Cambridge, O. 2. Glass, Colored. I. Welker, Lyle, joint author. II. Welker, Lynn, joint author. III. Title.

Glass, Colored—History.

MIDDLEMAS, Robert Keith, 1935- 748.5'9
Antique glass in color [by] Keith Middlemas. [1st ed. in U.S.A.] Garden City, N.Y., Doubleday [1971] 120 p. col. illus. 31 cm. [NK5106.M53 1971] 71-134442 12.95
1. Glass, Colored—History. I. Title.

Glass construction.

HIX, John, 1938- 721'.044
The glass house. Cambridge, Mass., MIT Press [1974] 208 p. illus. 26 cm. Bibliography: p. 197-198. [NA4140.H59 1974] 74-5201 ISBN 0-262-08076-1 22.50
1. Glass construction. 2. Greenhouses. I. Title.

PETER, John, 1917- 624.18
Design with glass [New York] Reinhold [1965, c.1964] 159p. illus., plans. 19x26cm. (Materials in mod. architecture ser., v.1) Bibl. [NA4140.P4] 65-13506 12.00
1. Glass construction. 2. Architecture, Modern—20th cent. I. Title. II. Series.

SCHEERBART, Paul, 1863-1915. 721'.044
Glass architecture, by Paul Scheerbart; and Alpine architecture, by Bruno Taut. Edited with an introd. by Dennis Sharp. Glass architecture translated by James Palmes. Alpine architecture translated by Shirley Palmer. New York, Praeger [1972] 127 p. illus. 23 cm. Includes bibliographical references. [NA4140.S413 1972] 70-183059 8.50
1. Glass construction. I. Sharp, Dennis, comp. II. Taut, Bruno, 1880-1938. Alpine Architektur. English and German. 1972. III. Title. IV. Title: Alpine architecture.

Glass craft.

DUNCAN, Alastair, 1942- 748.5
Leaded glass : a handbook of techniques / by Alastair Duncan. New York : Watson-Guptill Publications, 1975. 216 p., [2] leaves of plates ; ill. ; 26 cm. Includes index. Bibliography: p. 212. [TT298.D86 1975] 75-1037 ISBN 0-8230-2660-4 : 18.50
1. Glass craft. I. Title. BIP

EPPENS-VAN Veen, Jos H. 748
Colorful glasscrafting, by Jos H. Eppens-van Veen. [Translated by Manly Banister. Adapted by Anne E. Kallem] New York, Sterling [1973] 112 p. illus. (part col.) 29 cm. Translation of Spelen met glas. [TT298.E6613] 72-81044 ISBN 0-8069-5226-1 6.95
1. Glass craft. I. Title.
Library Edition 6.39; ISBN 0-8069-5227-X. BIP

FLAVELL, Ray. 748.2
Studio glassmaking [by] Ray Flavell & Claude Smale. New York, Van Nostrand Reinhold Co. [1974] 108 p. illus. 21 x 22 cm. [TT298.F55] 79-39889 ISBN 0-442-30021-2 7.50
1. Glass craft. I. Smale, Claude, joint author. II. Title.

FRENCH, Jennie, 1947- 748.5
Glass-works; the copperfoil technique of stained glass. New York, Van Nostrand Reinhold Co. [1974] 104 p. illus. (part col.) 28 cm. [TT298.F73] 74-12748 ISBN 0-442-22442-7
1. Glass craft. I. Title. BIP

HAMILTON, Walter J. 748.5
The advanced techniques of making leaded glass projects, by Walter J. Hamilton. [1st ed. Silver Spring, Md.] Hamilton Studio [1972] viii, 178 p. illus. 22 cm. Includes bibliographical references. [TT298.H34] 72-89957
1. Glass craft. 2. Glass painting and staining. I. Title.

HAMMESFAHR, James E. 748.2
Creative glass blowing : scientific and ornamental / by James E. Hammesfahr & Clair L. Stong ; with a foreword by Charles H. Greene. San Francisco : W. H. Freeman, [1978] p. cm. Includes index. Bibliography: p. [TT298.H37] 77-27598 ISBN 0-7167-0088-3 : 7.95.
1. Glass craft. 2. Glass blowing and working. I. Stong, Clair L., joint author. II. Title.

ISENBERG, Anita. 745.59'32
Stained glass lamps; construction and design [by] Anita and Seymour Isenberg. [1st ed.] [Radnor, Pa.] Chilton Book Co. [1974] xiv, 222 p. illus. 26 cm. Includes bibliographies. [TT298.I84] 73-16084 ISBN 0-8019-5839-3 12.50
1. Glass craft. 2. Glass painting and staining. 3. Lampshades, Glass. I. Isenberg, Seymour, joint author. II. Title.
Pbk. 5.95, ISBN 0-8019-5840-7. BIP

LIPS, Claude. 748.5
Art and stained glass. [1st ed.] Garden City, N.Y., Doubleday, 1973. 96 p. illus. 26 cm. [TT298.L56] 72-92255 ISBN 0-385-08286-X 3.95
1. Glass craft. I. Title. BIP

LUCIANO, 1934- 749'.63
Stained glass lamp art / by Luciano & Stan Colson, with Donna Colson. Palo Alto, Ca. : Hidden House/Flash Books ; New York : distribution, Quick Fox, [c1976] 144 p., [2] leaves of plates : ill. (some col.) ; 28 cm. [TT298.L818] 76-12430 ISBN 0-8256-3812-7 : 5.95
1. Glass craft. 2. Lampshades, Glass. I. Colson, Stan, joint author. II. Colson, Donna, joint author. III. Title. BIP

MCKEITHAN, Kent. 748.5
The encyclopedia of stained glass design and construction. Illustrated by Mary Pavlick. New York, Drake Publishers [1974] p. [TT298.M3] 73-18402 12.95
1. Glass craft. I. Title.

O'BRIEN, Vincent, 1919- 748.5
Techniques of stained glass : leaded, faceted, and laminated glass / Vincent O'Brien. New York : Van Nostrand Reinhold, 1977. p. cm. Includes index. Bibliography: p. [TT298.O27] 77-77969 ISBN 0-442-26259-0 : 14.95
1. Glass craft. I. Title. BIP

ROTHENBERG, Polly. 748
The complete book of creative glass art / by Polly Rothenberg. New York : Crown Publishers, [1974] xi, 276 p., [4] leaves of plates : ill. (some col.) ; 27 cm. (Crown's arts and crafts series) Includes index. Bibliography: p. 269. [TT298.R66 1974] 74-80319 ISBN 0-517-51690-X : 9.95
1. Glass craft. I. Title. BIP

ROTHENBERG, Polly. 748.5
Creative stained glass; techniques for unfired and fired projects. New York, Crown Publishers [1973] 96 p. illus. (part col.) 29 cm. Bibliography: p. 92. [TT298.R67] 73-82930 4.95
1. Glass craft. 2. Glass painting and staining—Technique. I. Title. BIP

ROTHENBERG, Polly. 748.6
Decorative glass—painting, embossing, engraving, etching / Polly Rothenberg. New York : Crown, 1977, c1976. 96 p., [4] leaves of plates : ill. (some col.) ; 29 cm. Includes index. [TT298.R68 1977] 76-18967 ISBN 0-517-52391-4 : 6.95 pbk. : 4.95
1. Glass craft. I. Title.

SCOBEY, Joan. 748.5
Stained glass / by Joan Scobey. New York : Dial Press, 1978. p. cm. Bibliography: p. [TT298.S36] 78-17265 ISBN 0-8037-4926-0 : 14.95
1. Glass craft. 2. Glass painting and staining—History. I. Title. BIP

SIBBETT, Ed. 748.5'022'2
Art Nouveau stained glass pattern book : 104 designs for workable projects / Ed Sibbett, Jr. New York : Dover Publications, 1978. 60 p. : chiefly ill. ; 28 cm. (Dover pictorial archive series) [TT298.S48 1978] 77-87497 ISBN 0-486-23577-7 pbk. : 2.00
1. Glasscraft. 2. Art nouveau. I. Stained glass pattern book. II. Title. BIP

SIBBETT, Ed. 748.5'022'2
Stained glass pattern book : 88 designs for workable projects / Ed Sibbett, Jr. New York : Dover Publications, c1976. 62 p. : chiefly ill. ; 28 cm. (Dover pictorial archive series) [TT298.S5 1976] 76-15447 ISBN 0-486-23360-X pbk. : 2.00
1. Glass crafts. 2. Glass painting and staining. I. Title. BIP

STILLMAN, Peter R. 748.5
Stained glass for the amateur, by Peter R. Stillman. Illustrated by the author. Charlotteville, N.Y., SamHar Press, 1973. 32 p. (p. 31-32 blank) illus. 22 cm. (Hand crafts and hobbies) [TT298.S74] 73-76622
1. Glass craft. I. Title. BIP

WOOD, Paul W. 748.5
Artistry in stained glass / by Paul W. Wood. New York : Sterling Pub. Co., c1976. 96 p., [4] leaves of plates : ill. (some col.) ; 26 cm. Includes index. Discusses principles of color and texture helpful in planning stained glass projects and includes complete instructions for creating different objects. [TT298.W65] 76-1185 ISBN 0-8069-5342-X : 7.95 lib.bdg. : 6.89
1. Glass craft. I. Title. BIP

Glass craft—Juvenile literature.

SATTLER, Helen Roney. 748.2
Jar and bottle craft. Written and illustrated by Helen Roney Sattler. New York, Lothrop, Lee & Shepard Co. [1974] 96 p. illus. 23 cm. Directions for making lamps, bookends, vases and other gifts and household items from jars and bottles. [TT298.S27] 73-14799 ISBN 0-688-41536-9 4.25
1. Glass craft—Juvenile literature. I. Title.
Library binding 3.94; ISBN 0-688-51536-3. BIP

Ornamental. 3. Decoration and ornament, Architectural. I. Title.

WOOD, Paul W. 748.5
Stained glass crafting, by Paul W. Wood. New York, Sterling Pub. Co. [1967] 80 p. illus. (part col.) 22 cm. [NK5304.W66 1967] 67-27750
1. Glass painting and staining. I. Title. BIP

WOOD, Paul W. 748.5
Stained glass crafting, by Paul W. Wood. Enl. ed. New York, Sterling [1971] 96 p. illus. (part col.) 22 cm. [TT298.W66 1971] 75-26167 ISBN 0-8069-5094-3
1. Glass painting and staining. I. Title.

WOOD, Paul W. 748.5
Starting with stained glass, by Paul W. Wood. New York, Sterling Pub. Co. [1973] 48 p. illus. 20 cm. (Little craft book series) Introduces the tools, materials, and techniques for making a variety of decorative objects from stained glass. [TT298.W67 1973] 72-95216 2.95
1. Glass painting and staining. 2. Glass craft. I. Title. BIP

YOUNG, Mary E. 748.5
Singing windows, written and illustrated by Mary Young. New York, Abingdon Press [1962] 63 p. illus. 25 cm. Includes bibliography. [NK5304.Y6] 62-7869
1. Glass painting and staining. I. Title.

Glass painting and staining—Cambridge, Eng.

HARRISON, Kenneth. 748.5
The windows of King's College Chapel, Cambridge; notes on their history and design. Cambridge [Eng.] University Press, 1952. 89 p. illus. 22 cm. [NK5344.C27H37] 52-11262
1. Glass painting and staining—Cambridge, Eng. 2. Cambridge. University. King's College. Chapel. I. Title.

Glass painting and staining—Chartres, France.

DIERICK, Alfons 748.594
The stained glass at Chartres. Berne, Hallwag [Dist. New York, Taplinger] [1960] 9p. 19 col. plates. 19cm. (Orbis pictus, 2) 60-4012 2.00 bds.,
1. Glass painting and staining—Chartres, France. 2. Chartres, France. Notre-Dame (Cathedral). I. Title.

JOHNSON, James Rosser. 748.594
The radiance of Chartres; studies in the early stained glass of the cathedral. New York, Random House [1965] xii, 96 p. illus. (part col.) 21 cm. (Columbia University studies in art, history, and archaeology, no. 4) Bibliography: p. 91-94. [NK5349.C5J6 1965] 64-15894
1. Glass painting and staining—Chartres, France. 2. Chartres, France. Notre-Dame (Cathedral) I. Title. II. Series.

Glass painting and staining—Conservation and restoration—Bibliography.

NEWTON, Roy G. 016.7485'028
The deterioration and conservation of painted glass : a critical bibliography and three research papers / R. G. Newton. London : Published for the British Academy by Oxford University Press, 1974. viii, 93 p. : ill. ; 25 cm. (Corpus vitrearum Medii Aevi : Great Britain : Occasional papers ; 1) [Z5956.G5N48] 74-191760 ISBN 0-19-725947-2 pbk. : 13.00
1. Glass painting and staining—Conservation and restoration—Bibliography. 2. Glass painting and staining—Conservation and restoration—Addresses, essays, lectures. I. Title. II. Series.
Distributed by Oxford University Press, New York. BIP

Glass painting and staining—Dictionaries.

DRAKE, Wilfred James, 1879-1948. 748.403
A dictionary of glasspainters and 'glasyers' of the tenth to eighteenth centuries. New York, Metropolitan Museum of Art, 1955. 224p. illus. 29cm. Bibliography: p. 221-224. [NK5304.D7] 56-21114
1. Glass painting and staining—Dictionaries. I. Title.

Glass painting and staining—England.

ARNOLD, Hugh 748
Stained glass of the middle ages in England & France, Fifty plates in colour by Lawrence B. Saint. London, A. & C. Black [New York, Barnes & Noble, 1965] xiv, 269p. col. front., col. plates. 24cm. [NK5308.A7] 40-10700 10.00
1. Glass painting and staining—England. 2. Glass painting and staining—France. 3. Art, Medieval. I. Saint, Lawrence Bradford, 1885-illus. II. Title.

BAKER, John 748.5942
English stained glass. Introduction by [Sir] Herbert Read. Text and comments by John Baker. Photographs by Alfred Lammer. New York, Harry N. Abrams, [1960] 244p. Bibl:: p.242-243. illus. (part col.) mounted col. plates. 29cm. 60-10886 25.00
1. Glass painting and staining—England. 2. Glass painting and staining—Specimens, reproductions, etc. I. Title.

WOODFORDE, Christopher. 748.5
English stained and painted glass. Oxford [Eng.] Clarendon Press, 1954. xvii, 83p. 81plates (1 col.) 25cm. Bibliography: p. 67-69. [NK5343.W75] 54-14660
1. Glass painting and staining—England. 2. Glass painting and staining—Specimens, reproductions, etc. I. Title.

Glass painting and staining, English.

READ, Herbert Edward, Sir, 1893-1968. 748.5'92
English stained glass. London, New York, Putnam's Sons. Millwood, N.Y., Kraus Reprint Co., 1973. xvii, 259 p. illus. 31 cm. Reprint of the 1926 ed. Bibliography: p. 250-253. [NK5343.R4 1973] 72-13755 35.00
1. Glass painting and staining, English. I. Title. BIP

Glass painting and staining — Europe.

HUTTER, Heribert. 748.594
Medieval stained glass. Translated by Margaret Shenfield. New York, Crown Publishers [1964] 62 p. 24 col. plates, 19 cm. (Movements in world art) Bibliography: p. [15] [NK5342.H813] 64-24749
1. Glass painting and staining — Europe. 2. Glass painting and staining — Specimens, reproductions, etc. I. Title.

Glass painting and staining, French.

WITZLEBEN, Elisabeth von, 1905- 748.5'94
Stained glass in French cathedrals. [Translated from the German by Francisca Garvie] New York, Reynal [1968] 264 p. illus., 46 col. plates. 33 cm. Translation of Licht und Farbe aus Frankreichs Kathedralen. Bibliography: p. 260-261. [NK5349.A2W53 1968b] 68-25490 45.00
1. Glass painting and staining, French. I. Title.

Glass painting and staining, Gothic—France—Chartres.

LILLICH, Meredith P., 1932- 748.5'945'1
The stained glass of Saint-Pere de Chartres / by Meredith P. Lillich. Middletown, Conn. : Wesleyan University Press, [1978] p. cm. Includes index. Bibliography: p. [NK5349.C5L54] 77-13926 ISBN 0-8195-5023-X : 40.00
1. Chartres, France. Saint Pierre (Church) 2. Glass painting and staining, Gothic—France—Chartres. 3. Glass painting and staining, French—France—Chartres. I. Title. BIP

Glass Painting and staining—History.

HILL, Robert, 1939- 748.5
Stained glass : music for the eye / Robert & Jill Hill, Hans Halberstadt. [Oakland, Calif.] : Scrimshaw Press, [1976] p. cm. [NK5306.H55] 76-27286 ISBN 0-912020-55-5. ISBN 0-912020-45-8 pbk.
1. Glass Painting and staining—History. 2. Glass painting and staining—Technique. I. Hill, Jill, 1944- II. Halberstadt, Hans. III. Title.

LEE, Lawrence. 748.5'9
Stained glass / Lawrence Lee, George Seddon, Francis Stephens ; with photos. by Sonia Halliday and Laura Lushington. New York : Crown Publishers, 1976. 207 p. : ill. (some col.) ; 38 cm. Bibliography: p. 207. [NK5306.L43 1976] 76-18928 ISBN 0-517-52728-6 : 35.00
1. Glass painting and staining—History. I. Seddon, George, 1927- joint author. II. Stephens, Francis, 1921- joint author. III. Title.

SOWERS, Robert. 748.5
The lost art; a survey of one thousand years of stained glass. With an introd. by Sir Herbert Read. New York, G. Wittenborn [1954] 80 p. illus. (part col.) 26 cm. (Problems of contemporary art, no. 7) Bibliography: p. 80. [NK5304.S68 1954] 54-4418
1. Glass painting and staining—History. 2. Glass painting and staining—Specimens, reproductions, etc. I. Title. II. Series.

Glass painting and staining—Israel.

CHAGALL, Marc, 1887- 748.5'97
The Jerusalem windows / Marc Chagall ; text and notes by Jean Leymarie ; [translated from the French by Elaine Desautels]. 2d ed. New York : G. Braziller, 1975. xix, 89 p. : ill. (some col.) ; 27 cm. Translation of Vitraux pour Jerusalem. [NK5398.C5L433 1975] 75-326569 ISBN 0-8076-0807-6 : 15.00 ISBN 0-8076-0807-6 pbk. : 6.95
1. Chagall, Marc, 1887- 2. Hadassah-University Medical Center, Jerusalem. Synagogue. 3. Glass painting and staining—Israel. I. Leymarie, Jean. II. Title.

Glass painting and staining—Jerusalem.

CHAGALL, Marc, 1887- 748.595694
The Jerusalem windows. Text and notes by Jean Leymarie. [Translated from the French by Elaine Desautels] New York, G. Braziller [1962] 210 p. illus., plates (part col.), port. 24 cm. [NK5398.C5L43] 62-18146
1. Hadassa-University Medical Center, Jerusalem. Synagogue. 2. Glass painting and staining—Jerusalem. I. Leymarie, Jean. II. Title.

CHAGALL, Marc, 1887- 748.5'9'5694
The Jerusalem windows. Text and notes by Jean Leymarie. [Translated from the French by Elaine Desautels. 1st rev. ed.] New York, G. Braziller [1967] xix, 111 p. plates (part col.) 28 cm. Translation of Vitraux pour Jerusalem. [NK5398.C5L433 1967] 67-9083
1. Hadassah-University Medical Center, Jerusalem. Synagogue. 2. Glass painting and staining — Jerusalem. I. Leymarie, Jean. II. Title.

FREUND, Miriam Kottler, 1906- 748.5995694
Jewels for a crown; the story of the Chagall windows. Foreword by Rene d'Harnoncourt. New York, McGraw-Hill [1963] 64 p. illus. (part col.) 26 cm. [NK5398.C5F7] 63-19440
1. Chagall, Marc, 1887- 2. Hadassa-University Medical Center, Jerusalem. Synagogue. 3. Glass painting and staining—Jerusalem. I. Title.

Glass painting and staining—New York (State)

SORACI, Carmelo 748.59747
The convict and the stained glass windows. [New York, Dell, 1962, 1961] 239p. 17cm. (Chapel bk., 1460) .50 pap.,
1. Glass painting and staining—New York (State) 2. Prisons—New York (State) I. Title.

SORACI, Carmelo. 748.59747
The convict and the stained glass windows. New York, John Day Co. [1961] 253 p. illus. 21 cm. Autobiography. [NK5398.S6A2] 61-8285
1. Glass painting and staining—New York (State) 2. Prisons—New York (State) I. Title.

Glass painting and staining — Norwich, Eng.

WOODFORDE, Christopher. 748.4
The Norwich school of glass-painting in the fifteenth century. London, New York, Oxford University Press, 1950. xiv, 233 p. illus., 44 plates. 26 cm. [NK5344.N6W6] 51-7566
1. Glass painting and staining — Norwich, Eng. I. Title.

Glass painting and staining — Oxford, Eng.

WOODFORDE, Christopher. 748.5
The stained glass of New College, Oxford. London, New York, Oxford University Press, 1951. 109 p. illus. 26 cm. [NK5344.O8W6] 51-13386
1. Glass painting and staining — Oxford, Eng. 2. Oxford. University. New College. I. Title.

Glass painting and staining—Patterns.

NERVO, Joanne, comp. 748.5'022'2
Stained glass patterns : panels, fixtures / compiled at Nervo Art Stained Glass Works, Berkeley, California, Joanne Nervo. Enl. ed. [Berkeley, Calif.] : Nervo, 1974, c1972. 244 p. : all ill. ; 22 cm. [TT298.N47 1974] 75-302495 6.95
1. Glass painting and staining—Patterns. I. Nervo Art Stained Glass Works. II. Title.

Glass painting and staining—Phoenix, Ariz.

LINCOLN, Joseph Colville. 748.5'9191'73
The windows of Trinity Cathedral. [1st ed. Flagstaff, Ariz.] Northland Press [1973] vii, 81 p. illus. (part col.) 26 cm. [NK5312.L56] 73-78003 ISBN 0-87358-106-7
1. Trinity Cathedral, Phoenix, Ariz. 2. Glass painting and staining—Phoenix, Ariz. I. Title.

Glass painting and staining, Romanesque—England—Canterbury.

CAVINESS, Madeline Harrison, 1938- 748.5'922'34
The early stained glass of Canterbury Cathedral, circa 1175-1220 / Madeline Harrison Caviness. Princeton, N.J. : Princeton University Press, c1977. p. cm. Includes index. Bibliography: p. [NK5344.C3C38] 77-10419 ISBN 0-691-03927-5 : 35.00
1. Canterbury Cathedral. 2. Glass painting and staining, Romanesque—England—Canterbury. 3. Glass painting and staining, Gothic—England—Canterbury. 4. Glass painting and staining—England—Canterbury. I. Title.

Glass painting and staining—Technique.

BERNSTEIN, Jack W. 748.5
Stained-glass craft [by] Jack W. Bernstein. Historical pref. by Leon Gordon Miller. New York, Macmillan [1973] ix, 118 p. illus. 28 cm. Bibliography: p. 115-116. [TT298.B47] 72-91258 9.95
1. Glass painting and staining—Technique. I. Title.

DUVAL, Jean Jacques, 1930- 748.5
Working with stained glass; fundamental techniques and applications. Photos. by Peter R. Stillman. New York, Crowell [1972] 132 p. illus. 27 cm. [NK5304.D8] 74-184975 ISBN 0-690-89706-5 8.95
1. Glass painting and staining—Technique. I. Title. BIP

FRENCH, Jennie, 1947- 748.5
Design for stained glass / Jennie French. New York : Van Nostrand Reinhold Co.,

SUBJECT INDEX GLASSWARE, AMERICAN.

[1978] p. cm. Includes index. [NK5304.F74] 78-18001 ISBN 0-442-22467-2 : 16.95
1. Glass painting and staining—Technique. I. Title. BIP

ISENBERG, Anita. 748.5
How to work in stained glass [by] Anita & Seymour Isenberg. [1st ed.] Philadelphia, Chilton Book Co. [1972] xvii, 237 p. illus. 26 cm. Bibliography: p. 231-233. [TT298.I83] 70-184138 ISBN 0-8019-5638-2
1. Glass painting and staining—Technique. I. Isenberg, Seymour, joint author. II. Title. BIP

ISENBERG, Anita. 748.5'028
Stained glass, advanced techniques and projects / Anita & Seymour Isenberg. 1st ed. Radnor, Pa. : Chilton Book Co., c1976. xxiii259 p., [4] leaves of plates : ill. ; 27 cm. (Chilton's creative crafts series) Includes index. Bibliography: p. 255-256. [TT298.I835 1976] 75-31848 ISBN 0-8019-6194-7 : 13.95 pbk. : 7.95
1. Glass painting and staining—Technique. I. Isenberg, Seymour, joint author. II. Title.

JUDSON, Walter W. 748.5
Introduction to stained glass; a step-by-step guide [by] Walter W. Judson. Illus. by James R. Gangwer. Los Angeles, Nash Pub. [1972] x, 138 p. illus. 21 cm. [TT298.J8] 72-81852 ISBN 0-8402-8051-3 2.45
1. Glass painting and staining—Technique. I. Title.

LEE, Lawrence 748.5
Stained glass. London, New York, etc. Oxford U.P., 1967. 96 p. front., illus., diagrs. 21 cm. (Oxford paperbacks, handbooks for artists, 4) Bibliography: p. 94. [NK5304.L38 1967] 68-93643 12/6
1. Glass painting and staining—Techniques. I. Title.

LIMBOS, Edouard. 748.5'028
Stained glass windows from paper, by E. Limbos & M. C. Maine. Illus. by Marc Berthier. New York, Drake Publishers [1973] 96 p. illus. 19 cm. Translation of La Ronde des vitraux. [NK5304.L513] 73-3140 ISBN 0-87749-465-7 2.95 (pbk.)
1. Glass painting and staining—Technique. I. Maine, Marie Colette, joint author. II. Title.

Glass painting and staining—Technique—Juvenile literature.

ERIKSON, Erik. 748.5
Step-by-step stained glass : a complete introduction to the craft of stained glass / by Erik Erikson ; conceived and edited by William and Shirley Sayles. New York : Golden Press, [1974] 80 p. : ill. (some col.) ; 29 cm. (The Golden Press step-by-step craft series) Bibliography: p. 79. Introduces the tools, materials, and techniques for making and working with stained glass and suggests a variety of projects. [TT298.E68] 74-76678 2.95
1. Glass painting and staining—Technique—Juvenile literature. I. Title.

Glass painting and staining—United States—Directories.

TIFFANY Studios, New York. 748.5'913
A partial list of windows. [2d ed.] New York [1973] 119 p. 21 cm. [NK5398.T53A56 1973] 74-150411
1. Tiffany Studios, New York. 2. Glass painting and staining—United States—Directories. I. Title.

Glass painting and staining—U.S.—Hist.

LLOYD, John Gilbert 748.5913
Stained glass in America. Jenkintown, Pa., Foundation Bks., 1963. 150p. illus., 12 col. plates. 27cm. Bibl. 63-19543 apply
1. Glass painting and staining—U.S.—Hist. I. Title.

Glass painting and staining, Victorian—Great Britain.

SEWTER, A. C. 748.5'92
The stained glass of William Morris and his circle : a catalogue / A. Charles Sewter. New Haven : Published for the Paul Mellon Centre for Studies in British Art by Yale University Press, 1975. xi, 335 p. ; 32 cm. (Studies in British art) "Volume II." Includes indexes. [NK5343.S482] 75-325961 ISBN 0-300-01836-3 : 70.00
1. Morris, William, 1834-1896. 2. Glass painting and staining, Victorian—Great Britain. 3. Glass painters—Great Britain. I. Title. II. Series.

SEWTER, A. C. 748.5'92
The stained glass of William Morris and his circle [by] A. Charles Sewter. New Haven, Published for the Paul Mellon Centre for Studies in British Art by Yale University Press, 1974. xii, 119 p., [324] p. of illus. (part col.) 32 cm. (Studies in British art) Bibliography: p. 103-107. [ND5343.S48] 72-91307 ISBN 0-300-01471-6 50.00
1. Morris, William, 1834-1896. 2. Glass painting and staining, Victorian—Great Britain. 3. Glass painters—Great Britain. I. Title. II. Series. BIP

Glass painting and staining—Washington, D.C.

BAYLESS, John Hocking. 917.53
Jewels of light : stained glass at Washington Cathedral / by John Hocking Bayless ; edited by Nancy S. Montgomery. Washington : Cathedral Church of Saint Peter and Saint Paul, c1975. 48 p. : ill. (some col.) ; 23 cm. [NK5312.B38] 75-29719
1. Glass painting and staining—Washington, D.C. 2. Washington, D.C. Cathedral of St. Peter and St. Paul. I. Title.

Glass sculpture—Exhibitions.

LOWE Art Museum. 748.2'904
International glass sculpture. [Coral Gables, Fla., 1973] 53 p. illus. 25 cm. Catalog of the exhibition held Apr. 7-May 6, 1973. Bibliography: p. 51-52. [NB1270.G4L68 1973] 74-189757
1. Glass sculpture—Exhibitions. I. Title.

WILLSON, Robert, 1928- 748.2'913
Glass sculpture: international tour, 1968-1971. [Miami, Fla., Mnemosyne Pub. Co., c1969] [50] p. (incl. cover) illus. (part col.), ports. 26 cm. Cover title. Label on cover: Supplied by Worldwide Books, inc., Boston. This catalog is designed for exhibitions at the Museo Correr, Venice and other galleries and museums. Bibliography: p. [47]-[48] [NK5198.W55A43] 75-18672
I. Venice. Museo civico Correr. II. Title.

Glassman, Joel, 1946—

GLASSMAN, Joel, 1946- 709'.2'2
Joel Glassman, Carlos Gutierrez-Solana, Paul Kos; an exhibition organized by the La Jolla Museum of Contemporary Art, La Jolla, California, October 13-December 5, 1973. [La Jolla, Calif., c1973] 24 p. illus. 21 cm. Includes bibliographies. [N6530.C2G552] 73-92614
1. Glassman, Joel, 1946- 2. Gutierrez-Solana, Carlos, 1947- 3. Kos, Paul, 1942- 4. Art, Modern—20th century—San Francisco Bay region. I. Gutierrez-Solana, Carlos, 1947- II. Kos, Paul, 1942- III. La Jolla Museum of Contemporary Art.

Glassware.

[BROTHERS, John Stanley] 1896- 666'.122
Thumbnail sketches. Kalamazoo, Mich., J. S. Brothers, jr. [c1940] 47, [1] p. illus. 27 cm. Chiefly reprints of articles which have appeared in "Hobbies." cf. Foreword. [NK5104.B7] A41
1. Glassware. I. Title.

GROVER, Ray. 748.2'9'22
Contemporary art glass / by Ray and Lee Grover. New York : Crown Publishers, [1975] xvi, 208 p., [16] leaves of plates : ill. (some col.) ; 29 cm. Includes index. Bibliography: p. 199-201. [NK5110.G72 1975] 75-2046 ISBN 0-517-51628-4 : 19.95
1. Glassware. 2. Artists—Biography. I. Grover, Lee, joint author. II. Title.

HELLER, David. 748.6
In search of V. O. C. glass. Cape Town, M. Miller [1951?] 108p. illus. 25cm. [NK5154.H4] 55-32842
1. Glassware. 2. Foregery of works of art. 3. Nederlandsche Oost-Indiache Compagnie. I. Title.

REVI, Albert Christian. 748.2'904
Nineteenth century glass: its genesis and development. Rev. ed. London, Camden, N. J., Nelson, 1967. xviii, 301p. illus. (pt. col.) 28cm. [NK5109.R4 1967] 67-103761 12.50
1. Glassware. 2. Glass manufacture. I. Title.

REVI, Albert Christian. 748.2904
Nineteenth century glass, its genesis and development. New York, Nelson [1959] xviii, 270 p. illus. 28 cm. [NK5109.R4] 59-15032
1. Glassware. 2. Glass manufacture. I. Title.

SAVAGE, George, 1909- 748.2'9
Glass and glassware. London, Octopus Books, 1973, [i.e.1974] 128 p. illus. (chiefly col.) 32 cm. Distributed in U.S.A. by Crescent Books, a division of Crown Publishers, New York. Illus. on lining papers. Includes index. [NK5104.S28] 74-177063 ISBN 0-7064-0143-3 5.98
1. Glassware. I. Title.

SAVAGE, George, 1909- 748.2'9
Glass of the world / George Savage. New York : Galahad Books, 1975, c1973. 128 p. : ill. (some col.) ; 33 cm. Original ed. published under title: Glass and glassware. Includes index. [NK5104.S28 1975] 75-324901 15.00
1. Glassware. I. Title.

STENNETT-WILLSON, Ronald. 748.2
Modern glass / Ronald Stennett-Wilson. New York : Van Nostrand Reinhold Co., [1976, c1975] p. cm. Includes indexes. [NK5110.S83 1976] 75-16913 ISBN 0-442-27958-2 : 25.00
1. Glassware. I. Title. BIP

STEUBEN Glass, inc. 748.2
British artists in crystal. New York [1954] 1v. (unpaged) 20plates. 26cm. [NK5103.S69] 54-8840
1. Glassware. 2. Artists, British. I. Title.

Glassware—Albany, Ind.

BOND, Marcelle. 748.2'9172'65
The beauty of Albany glass, 1893 to 1902. Berne, Ind., Publishers Print. House [1972] 125 p. illus. 23 cm. [NK5112.B57] 72-188385 7.95
1. Glassware—Albany, Ind. 2. Glassware—Collectors and collecting. I. Title.

Glassware, American.

CORNING Glass Works. Steuben Glass 748.2913
Poetry in crystal; interpretations in crystal of thirty one new poems by contemporary American poets. [New York, Author, c.1963] 86p. illus. 28cm. Collaboration with the Poetry Soc. of America. 63-12592 5.00
1. Glassware American. 2. American poetry—20th cent. I. Poetry Society of America. II. Title.

FARRAR, Estelle Sinclaire. 748.2'913
H. P. Sinclaire, Jr., glassmaker. Garden City, N.Y., Farrar Books, 1974-75. 2 v. illus. 26 cm. Contents.Contents.—v. 1. The years before 1920.—v. 2. The manufacturing years. Includes bibliographies. [NK5198.S45F37] 74-168304
1. Sinclaire, Henry Purdon. 2. Glassware, American. I. Title.

*GROSS, Vicki 748.2'973
That collectible McKee in color, by Vicki and Mike Gross. [Hillsboro, Ore., 1973] 34 p. col. illus. 23 cm. Cover title. McKee and Bros. Glass Co. [NK5112.] 4.95 (pbk)
1. Glassware, American. 2. Glassware—Collectors and collecting. I. Gross, Mike, joint author. II. Title.
Available from the authors, P.O. Box 29, Hillsboro, OR 97123. A Price list is also available for 1.00 (pbk)

HARTUNG, Marion T 748.8
Carnival glass; one hundred patterns [by] Marion T. Hartung. [2d ed. Emporia, Kan., c1965- v. illus. 22 cm. [NK5112.H312] 67-2922
1. Glassware, American. I. Title.

HARTUNG, Marion T 748.2913
Carnival glass, one hundred patterns. Sketches by Dick Bulla. [1st ed.] Salisbury? N. C., 1960-61] 2v. illus. 22cm. [NK5112.H3] 60-43280
1. Glassware, American. I. Title.

HOTCHKISS, John F. 748.2
Current cut glass prices, by John F. Hotchkiss. [Rochester? N.Y., 1965] 56 p. illus. 22 cm. [NK5112.H59] 65-9390
1. Glassware, American. 2. Glassware — Prices. 3. Cut glass. I. Title.

HOTCHKISS, John F. 748.2
Current cut glass prices [*rochester, N.Y. 14617, Author, 89 Sagamore Drive, c.1965] 56p. illus. 22cm. [NK5112.H59] 65-9390 2.50 pap.,
1. Glassware, American. 2. Glassware—Prices. 3. Cut glass. I. Title.

KAMM, Minnie Elizabeth (Watson) 1886-1954. 748.2913
The Kamm-Wood encyclopedia of antique pattern glass. Serry Wood [pseud.] editor. Watkins Glen, N.Y., Century House, c1961. 2 v. illus. 24 cm. [NK5112.K284] 61-5439
1. Glassware, American. 2. Pattern glass. I. Freeman, Graydon La Verne, 1904- ed. II. Title: Encyclopedia of antique pattern glass.

LEE, Ruth Webb, 1894- 748.2'913
Current values of antique glass: Victorian glass, Sandwich glass, art glass, cup plates; the blue book of valuations. Rev. ed. Wellesley Hills, Mass., Lee Publications [1969] 339 p. illus. 22 cm. [NK5112.L39 1969] 79-26606
1. Glassware, American. 2. Glassware—Prices. I. Title.

LINDSEY, Bessie M. 748.2913
American historical glass; historical association adds distinction to glassware, by Bessie M. Lindsey. Rutland, Vt., Tuttle [1966] xxviii, 541p. illus. 24cm. First pub. in 1948 under title: Lore of our land pictured in glass. [NK5112.L53 1966] 67-11934 10.00
1. Glassware, American 2. Glassware—Collectors and collecting. I. Title.

PLAUT, James Sachs, 1912- 748.2'9147'83
Steuben glass; a monograph by James S. Plaut. 3d rev. and enl. ed. New York, Dover Publications [1972] xi, 111 p. illus. 29 cm. [NK5112.P56 1972] 72-78376 ISBN 0-486-22892-4 3.50
1. Steuben Glass, inc. 2. Glassware, American. I. Title. BIP

PRESZNICK, Rose M. 748.29771
Carnival & iridescent glass: price guide. Pen and ink drawings made by Rose M. Presznick. [Lodi, Ohio Author, Rt. 1, Box 173. 1963, c.1962] 66p. illus. 21cm. 63-2413 5.00,pap., plastic bdg.
1. Glassware, American. 2. Glassware—Prices. I. Title.

SCHWARTZ, Marvin D. 748.2'973
Collectors' guide to antique American glass, by Marvin D. Schwartz. [1st ed.] Garden City, N.Y., Doubleday, 1969. x, 150 p. illus. 22 cm. [NK5103.S3] 68-27138 4.95
1. Glassware, American. 2. Glassware—Collectors and collecting. I. Title. BIP

STEUBEN Glass, inc. 748'.8
The four seasons. Glass and gold design by Donald Pollard. Engraving design by Alexander Seidel. Engraving executed by Roland Erlacher. Goldwork by Louis Feron. [Special commemorative ed. New York, 1969] 19 p. illus. (part col.) 25 cm. [NK5112.S73] 70-96477

1. Glassware, American. I. Title.

STEUBEN Glass, inc. 748.2913
Islands in crystal. [New York, 1966?] [16] p. (chiefly illus.) 26 cm. [NK5112.S748] 66-28245
1. Glassware, American. 2. Artists, Americans. I. Title.

STUART, Anna Maude. 748.8
Bread plates and platters. [Hillsboro? Calif., 1965] xvi, 163 p. illus. 24 cm. [NK5112.S78] 67-41440
1. Glassware, American. 2. Glassware — Collectors and collecting. I. Title. BIP

WATKINS, Lura (Woodside) 748.2913
American glass and glassmaking. Southampton, N.Y., Cracker Barrel Press [196-?] 103 p. illus. 23 cm. Bibliography: p. 103. [NK5112.W28 1960z] 70-13034 2.25
1. Glassware, American. 2. Glass manufacture—U.S. I. Title.

Glassware, American — Catalogs.

HARTUNG, Marion T 748.2913
Carnival glass price guide 1966 [by] Marion T. Hartung. [1st ed. Emporia, Kan., 1966] 62 p. 22 cm. (Her Carnival glass series) [NK5112.H32] 67-762
1. Glassware, American — Catalogs. 2. Glassware — Prices. I. Title.

HARTUNG, Marion T 748.8
Carnival glass price guide, 1965 [by] Marion T. Hartung. [1st ed. Emporia, Kan., 1965] 56 p. 22 cm. (Her Carnival glass series) [NK5112.H32] 65-67696
1. Glassware, American — Catalogs. 2. Glassware — Prices. I. Title.

MCPEEK, Carole. 748.2'9171'54
Verlys of America decorative glass, 1935-1951 [by] Carole and Wayne McPeek. 1st ed. Newark, Ohio, Printed by Newark Leader Print. Co. [1972] 66 p. illus. 19 x 26 cm. [NK5198.V4M3] 72-189964 7.50
1. Verlys of America, inc. 2. Glassware, American—Catalogs. I. McPeek, Wayne, joint author. II. Title. BIP

MILLER, Robert William, 1922- 748.2'9144'92
Mary Gregory and her glass, by Robert W. Miller. Des Moines, Iowa [Wallace-Homestead Book Co., 1972] 32 p. illus. (part col.) 23 cm. [NK5198.G73M54] 73-152536 4.95
1. Gregory, Mary Alice, 1856-1908. 2. Boston and Sandwich Glass Company. 3. Glassware, American—Catalogs. I. Title.
Publishers Address: 1912 Grand Avenue Des Moines, Iowa 50305.

VAN PELT, Mary. 748.8
Animal kingdom in treasured glass, by Mary Van Pelt and Wanda Huffman. Photography by Roy F. Van Pelt. Line drawings by Buddy C. Van Pelt. [Garden Grove, Calif.] c1972. 48 p. illus. 23 cm. [NK5112.V23] 72-91758 5.50
1. Glassware, American—Catalogs. 2. Animals in art. I. Huffman, Wanda, joint author. II. Title.

WEATHERMAN, Hazel Marie, 1920- 748.2'9154'16
The first Fostoria price watch. Springfield, Mo., Weatherman Glassbooks [1974] 136 p. illus. 21 cm. "Keyed to the fully illustrated Fostoria: its first fifty years." [NK5198.F6W39] 74-169182 ISBN 0-913074-31-4 4.00
1. Fostoria Glass Company, Moundsville, W. Va. 2. Glassware, American—Catalogs. I. Fostoria Glass Company, Moundsville, W. Va. II. Weatherman, Hazel Marie, 1920- Fostoria: its first fifty years. III. Title.

Glassware, American—Exhibitions.

AMERICAN glass now. 748.2'913
[Toledo, Museum of Art, 1972] 64 p. illus. (part col.) 22 cm. Catalogue of a travelling exhibition organized by the Toledo Museum of Art and the Museum of Contemporary Crafts of the American Crafts Council. [NK5104.A43] 72-88951
1. Glassware, American—Exhibitions. I. Toledo. Museum of Art. II. American Crafts Council. Museum of Contemporary Crafts.

DALLAS. Museum of Fine Arts. 748.2'074'013
Air, light, form: new American glass. Exhibition dates: May 3-June 4, 1967. [Dallas, 1967] 20 p. illus. 26 cm. [NK5112.D28] 68-352
1. Glassware, American—Exhibitions. I. Title.

KEEFE, John Webster. 748.2'913
Libby glass a tradition of 150 years, 1818-1968 [Toledo, Ohio] Toledo Museum of Art [1968] 69 p. illus. 22 cm. Catalog of an exhibition in honor of the 150th anniversary of Libbey glass, presented by the Toledo Museum of Art and Owens-Illinois, inc., and held at the Toledo Museum of Art. Bibliography: p. 69. [NK5112.K4] 68-23391
1. The Libbey Glass Co. 2. Glassware, American—Exhibitions. I. Toledo. Museum of Art. II. Owens-Illinois, inc. III. Title.

PERROT, Paul N. 748.2'9147'83
Steuben: seventy years of American glassmaking [by] Paul N. Perrot, Paul V. Gardner [and] James S. Plaut. New York, Praeger [1974] 172 p. illus. (part col.) 26 cm. Catalog of the exhibition held at the Toledo Museum of Art and various other museums throughout the United States beginning Nov. 1974 and lasting two years. [NK5101.T62T647] 74-6730 ISBN 0-275-44320-5 15.00
1. Steuben Glass, inc. 2. Glassware, American—Exhibitions. I. Gardner, Paul Vickers, 1908- II. Plaut, James Sachs, 1912- III. Toledo. Museum of Art. IV. Title.

REFLECTIONS on glass. 748.2'074'019
[Long Beach, Calif., Long Beach Museum of Art, 1971] 1 v. (chiefly illus. (part col.)) 22 cm. Catalog of the exhibition held at Long Beach Museum of Art, Feb.-Mar., 1971, Portland Art Museum, Nov., 1971, and the Phoenix Art Museum, Mar.-Apr., 1972. [NK5104.R4] 73-154447
1. Glassware, American—Exhibitions. I. Long Beach, Calif. Museum of Art. II. Portland, Or. Art Museum. III. Phoenix, Ariz. Art Museum.

Glassware, American—Lancaster, N.Y.

DUNN, Jean W. 917.47'96'0308 s
Glass; Lancaster and Lockport, New York, by Jean W. Dunn. [Buffalo, N.Y.] Buffalo and Erie County Historical Society [1971] 20 p. illus. 25 cm. (Adventures in western New York history, v. 17) Cover title. Bibliography: p. 20. [F116.A45 vol. 17] [NK5112] 75-28669
1. Glassware, American—Lancaster, N.Y. 2. Glassware, American—Lockport, N.Y. I. Title. II. Series.

Glassware, American—New Jersey.

PEPPER, Adeline. 748.2'91'49
The glass gaffers of New Jersey, and their creations from 1739 to the present. New York, Scribner [1971] xvi, 330 p. illus. (part col.) 27 cm. Bibliography: p. 316-320. [NK5112.P45] 70-123831 ISBN 0-684-10459-8 17.50
1. Glassware, American—New Jersey. I. Title.

Glassware, Ancient.

BOSTON. Museum of Fine Arts. 748.2'993
Ancient glass in the Museum of Fine Arts, Boston, by Axel von Saldern. [Greenwich, Conn.] [New York Graphic Society] [1968] 94 p. illus. (part col.) 23 cm. Includes bibliographical references. [NK5107.B6] 67-31751 8.50
1. Glassware, Ancient. 2. Glassware—Boston—Catalogs. I. Saldern, Axel von, 1923- II. Title. BIP

CORNING, N. Y. Museum of Glass. 748
Glass from the ancient world: the Ray Winfield Smith collection; [catalogue of] a special exhibition. Corning, 1957. 298p. illus. 23cm. Bibliography: p. 287-298. [NK5107.C6] 57-11404
1. Glassware, Ancient. 2. Glassware—Private collections. 3. Glassware—Exhibitions. I. Smith, Ray Winfield. II. Title.

Glassware, Ancient — Hist.

NEUBERG, Frederic. 748
Ancient glass. Translated from the German by Michael Bullock and Alisa Jaffa. [Toronto,] University of Toronto Press [1962] ix, 110 p. illus. (part mounted col.) plates, maps (on lining papers) 26 cm. Bibliography: p. 103-107. [NK5107.N463] 63-5593
1. Glassware, Ancient — Hist. I. Title.

Glassware, British—Hist.

WAKEFIELD, Hugh [Hubert George Wakefield] 1915- 748.292
Nineteenth century British glass. New York, Yoseloff [1962, c.1961] 64p. illus. (pt. col.) 26cm. Bibl. 62-10189 8.95
1. Glassware, British—Hist. I. Title.

Glassware—California—San Francisco.

POWELL, Edith Hopps. 748.2'9194'61
San Francisco's heritage in art glass / by Edith Hopps Powell ; photography, by Brian Moran. 1st ed. Seattle : Salisbury Press Book, c1976. [87] p. : ill. (some col.) ; 35 cm. [NK5112.P68] 76-2527 ISBN 0-87564-013-3 : 27.95
1. United Art Glass Company. 2. Glassware—California—San Francisco. 3. Decoration and ornament—Art nouveau. I. Moran, Brian. II. Title. BIP

Glassware, Canadian.

SPENCE, Hilda Jennings. 748.2'911
A guide to early Canadian glass [by] Hilda & Kelvin Spence. [Don Mills, Ont.] Longmans Canada [c1966] 112 p. illus. (part col.) 26 cm. $10.00 Can. (C67-205) [NK5113.S6] 67-92116
1. Glassware, Canadian. 2. Glassware — Collectors and collecting. I. Spence, Kelvin D.M., joint author. II. Title.

Glassware, Canadian—Catalogs.

UNITT, Doris Joyce. 748.2911
Treasury of Canadian glass [by] Doris and Peter Unitt. [2d ed. Peterborough, Ont.] Clock House [1969] 280 p. illus. (part col.) 29 cm. Bibliography: p. 275. [NK5113.U5 1969] 75-480391 25.00
1. Glassware, Canadian—Catalogs. I. Unitt, Peter, 1914- joint author. II. Title.

Glassware—Catalogs.

STEUBEN Glass. 748.2
Steuben crystal. [New York, c1956] unpaged (chiefly illus.) 25 cm. [NK5199.S78] 56-9432
1. Glassware — Catalogs. I. Title.

WHITALL Tatum Company. 666'.19'029
Whitall, Tatum & Co., 1880; flint glassware, blue ware, perfume and cologne bottles, show bottles and globes, green glassware, stoppers, druggists' sundries. Illustrated catalog and historical introd. [1st ed.] Princeton, Pyne Press [1971] 72, [8] p. illus. 23 cm. (American historical catalog collection) Facsim. ed. Original t.p. reads: Whitall, Tatum & Co., glass manufacturers, druggists', chemists', and perfumers' glassware, druggists' sundries. Philadelphia, 1880. Bibliography: p. [79]-[80] [TP865.W5 1880a] 74-146206 ISBN 0-87861-004-9 3.25
1. Glassware—Catalogs. I. Title. II. Series.

Glassware — Collectors and collecting.

AMAYA, Mario. 748'.075
Tiffany glass. New York, Walker [1967] 84 p. illus. (part col.) 22 cm. (Collectors' blue books) [NK5198.T5A8 1967] 67-23092
1. Tiffany, Louis Comfort, 1848-1933. 2. Glassware—Collectors and collecting. I. Title.

BONES, Frances. 748.2'075
Collectibles of the depression. [Houston, c1971] 96 p. illus. 16 x 24 cm. [NK5112.B58] 72-176090 5.50
1. Glassware—Collectors and collecting. 2. Glassware, American—Catalogs. I. Title.

CURTIS, Tony. 748.2'075
Glass / compiled by Tony Curtis. [Galashiels] : [Lyle Publications], 1976. 3-125 p. : ill. ; 16 cm. (Antiques and their values) Includes index. [NK5105.C87] 77-352381 ISBN 0-902921-48-7 : £1.50
1. Glassware—Collectors and collecting. 2. Glassware—Prices. I. Title.

FREEMAN, Graydon La Verne, 1904- 748.4
Iridescent glass. Introd. by Frederick Carder. Watkins Glen, N. Y., Century House [c1956] 128p. illus. 23cm. [NK5112.F7] 56-881
1. Glassware—Collectors and collecting. 2. Glassware—U. S. I. Title. BIP

GROS-GALLINER, Gabriella. 748.2'9
Glass: a guide for collectors. [1st American ed.] New York, Stein and Day [1970] 175 p. illus., facsim., 4 col. plates. 22 cm. Bibliography: p. 163-166. [NK5105.G73 1970b] 78-126973 7.95
1. Glassware—Collectors and collecting. I. Title.

GROVER, Ray. 748.2
Art glass nouveau [by] Ray and Lee Grover. [1st ed.] Rutland, Vt., C. E. Tuttle Co. [1967] 231 p. col. illus. 31 cm. Bibliography: p. 225-226. [NK5105.G75] 67-10197
1. Glassware—Collectors and collecting. 2. Art nouveau. I. Grover, Lee, joint author. II. Title. BIP

LAFFERTY, James R. 748.2'9'04
The forties revisited; a guide, by James R. Lafferty. [Barstow? Calif.] c1968. 80 p. (chiefly illus.) 18 cm. [NK5105.L34] 72-2353
1. Glassware—Collectors and collecting. 2. Pottery—Collectors and collecting. I. Title.

LAGERBERG, Theodore C 666'.122
A color picture guide to over 100 types of collectible glass [by Ted and Vi Lagerberg New Port Richey, Fla., Modern Photographers, 1963- v. (unpaged, chiefly col. illus.) 16 x 23 cm. Cover title. [NK5104.L24] 64-7
1. Glassware — Collectors and collecting. I. Lagerberg, Viola V., joint author II. Title. III. Title: Collectible glass.

MILLS, Flora Rupe. 748.2075
Excursions in old glass. San Antonio, Naylor Co. [1961] 231p. illus. 22cm. [NK5140.M5] 61-10663
1. Glassware—Collectors and collecting. I. Title.

PAYTON, Mary. 748.2'03
The observer's book of glass / [by] Mary and Geoffrey Payton. London ; New York : F. Warne, 1976. 192 p., [8] p. of plates : ill. (some col.) ; 15 cm. (The Observer's pocket series ; 62) Includes index. Bibliography: p. 183-184. [NK5104.P38 1976] 75-8054 ISBN 0-7232-1549-9 : 2.95
1. Glassware—Collectors and collecting. I. Payton, Geoffrey, joint author. II. Title. BIP

ROBERTSON, Richard Austin. 748
Chats on old glass. New York, A. A. Wyn, 1954. 179p. illus. 21cm. [The Chats series] [NK5104] 54-6946
1. Glassware—Collectors and collecting. I. Title. BIP

ROBERTSON, Robert Alexander. 748
Chats on old glass, by R. A. Robertson. Rev., with a new chapter on American glass, by Kenneth M. Wilson. New York, Dover Publications [1969] xiii, 167 p. 77 plates. 22 cm. Bibliography: p. 157-159. [NK5104.R6 1969] 68-14051 2.25
1. Glassware—Collectors and collecting. I. Wilson, Kenneth M. II. Title.

SHUMAN, John A. 748.2
Art glass sampler : a pictorial guide to 57 diversified kinds of collectible glass / by John A. Shuman III. Des Moines : Wallace-Homestead Book. Co., c1978. 142 p. : ill. (some col.) ; 29 cm. Includes index. Bibliography: p. 133-134. [NK5104.S48] 76-15704 ISBN 0-87069-121-X : 12.95

POLAK, Ada Buch. 748.29
Modern glass. [1st American ed.] New York, T. Yoseloff [1962] 94p. illus. 26cm. (Faber monographs on glass) Includes bibliography. [NK5110.P6 1962] 62-10191
1. Glassware—Hist. I. Title.

SAVAGE, George, 1909- 748.29
Glass. New York, Putnam [c.1965] 128p. illus. (pt. col.) 22cm. (Pleasures & treasures) [NK5106.S3] 65-12438 4.95
1. Glassware—Hist. 2. Glass manufacture—Hist. I. Title.

SCHRIJVER, Elka 748.29
Glass and crystal; v.1. [Tr. from Dutch] New York, Universe [c.1964] v. illus. 21cm. Contents.v.1. From earliest times to 1850. Bibl. 64-10342 2.75; 1.95 pap.,
1. Glassware—Hist. I. Title.

SCHRIJVER, Elka 748.29
Glass and crystal v.2. English tr. New York, Universe Bks. [1965, c.1964] 94p. illus. 21cm. Contents.v. 2. From 1850 to the present. [NK5106.S423] 64-10342 2.75; 1.95 pap.,
1. Glassware—Hist. I. Title.

Glassware—History.

CORNING, N.Y. Museum of Glass. 748.2'9
A survey of glassmaking from ancient Egypt to the present / The Corning Museum of Glass ; compiled by Charleen K. Edwards. Chicago : University of Chicago Press, 1977. vii, 59 p. ; 23 cm. & microfiche (2 sheets : col. ill. ; 11 x 15 cm.) in pocket. (A University of Chicago Press text-fiche) Bibliography: p. 53-59. [NK5106.C67 1977] 77-15599 ISBN 0-226-68902-6 : 26.00
1. Glassware—History. I. Edwards, Charleen K. II. Title. BIP

KAMPFER, Fritz. 748.2'9
Glass: a world history; the story of 4000 years of fine glass-making, by Fritz Kampfer and Klaus G. Beyer. Translated and rev. by Edmund Launert. Greenwich, Conn., New York Graphic Society [1967, c1966] 314, [1] p. illus. (part col.) 31 cm. Revised translation of Viertausend Jahre Glas, published 1966. Bibliographical references included in "Glossary" (p. [295]-[315]) [NK5106.K313 1967] 66-26796
1. Glassware—History. I. Beyer, Klaus G., 1922- joint author. II. Launert, Edmund, ed. III. Title.

KATONA, Imre. 748.8
Beakers, cups, goblets : nineteenth century glass in the Budapest Museum of Applied Arts / Imre Katona ; [translation by Lily Halapy ; translation rev. by Elisabeth West]. Budapest : Corvina Kiado ; New York : available from International Publications Service, 1978. 48 p., [24] leaves of plates : 48 col. ill. ; 19 cm. [NK5109.8.K3713 1978] 79-670021 ISBN 9-631-30286-5 pbk. : 5.00
1. Budapest. Szapmuveszeti Muzeum—Catalogs. 2. Glassware—History—19th century—Catalogs. 3. Drinking vessels—History—19th century—Catalogs. I. Budapest. Szapmuveszeti Muzeum. II. Title.
Publisher's adress: 114 E. 32nd St., New York, NY 10016 BIP

LABINO, Dominick. 748.2'9
Visual art in glass. Dubuque, Iowa, W. C. Brown Co. [1967, c1968] xvi, 142 p. illus. 23 cm. (Art horizons series) Bibliography: p. 131-135. [NK5104.L2] 68-14574
1. Glassware—History. I. Title.

WEBBER, Norman W. 748.2'92
Collecting glass, by Norman W. Webber. Melbourne, Lansdowne, 1973. 196 p. ill., diagrs. 25 cm. Includes index. Bibliography: p. [184] [NK5106.W32 1973] 74-155114 ISBN 0-7018-0168-9 rev 9.95
1. Glassware—History. 2. Glassware—Collectors and collecting. I. Title. BIP

WEISS, Gustav, 1922- 748.2'9
The book of glass. Translated by Janet Seligman. New York, Praeger Publishers [1971] 353 p. illus. (part col.), maps. 24 cm. Translation of Ullstein Glaserbuch. Bibliography: p. 346-349. [NK5106.W413] 78-107151
1. Glassware—History. I. Title.

WILKINSON, O. N. 748.2'9
Old glass: manufacture, styles, uses, by O. N. Wilkinson. New York, Philosophical Library [1968] 200 p. illus., map. 22 cm. Bibliography: p. 187-189. [NK5106.W5 1968b] 68-6826 10.00
1. Glassware—History. I. Title.

Glassware—History—20th century.

BEARD, Geoffrey W. 748.2'904
International modern glass / by Geoffrey Beard. New York : Scribner, [1978] c1976. p. cm. Includes index. Bibliography: p. [NK5110.B39 1978] 78-56432 ISBN 0-684-15934-1 : 30.00
1. Glassware—History—20th century. I. Title. BIP

BEARD, Geoffrey W. 748.5'904
International modern glass / Geoffrey Beard. London : Barrie & Jenkins, 1976. 264 p., [3] leaves of col. plates : ill. ; 31 cm. Includes index. Bibliography: p. 254-256. [NK5110.B39] 77-364651 ISBN 0-214-20081-7 : £16.50
1. Glassware—History—20th century. I. Title.

Glassware—History—Outlines, syllabi, etc.

TOLEDO. Museum of Art. 748.2'9
Art in glass; a guide to the glass collections. [Toledo, 1969] 141 p. illus. (part col.) 28 cm. Bibliography: p. 141. [NK5106.T6] 72-108877
1. Glassware—History—Outlines, syllabi, etc. I. Title.

Glassware. Hungarian — Hist.

BORSOS, Bela. 748.2'939'1
Glassmaking in old Hungary, by Bela Borsos. [Translated by Zsuzsanna Horn] Boston, Branden Press [c1963] 56 p. 48 plates (part col.) 18 cm. [NK5148.B6] 67-2277
1. Glassware. Hungarian — Hist. I. Title.

Glassware—Indiana—Greentown—Catalogs.

INDIANAPOLIS Museum of Art.
Greentown glass [exhibition] / by Catherine Beth Lippert ; with an introd. by James S. Measell ; Indianapolis Museum of Art, October 1 - November 9, 1975. Indianapolis : Indianapolis Museum of Art, c1975. 43 p. : ill. ; 26 cm. Bibliography: p. 19. [NK5112.I5 1975] 75-29897
1. Indiana Tumbler and Goblet Company, Greentown. 2. Indianapolis Museum of Art. 3. Glassware—Indiana—Greentown—Catalogs. I. Lippert, Catherine Beth. II. Title.

Glassware — Iowa City.

RIGHTER, Miriam. 748.8
Iowa City glass. [Iowa City, 1963] 55 p. illus. 22 cm. Includes bibliography. [NK5112.R5] 63-3518
1. Glassware — Iowa City. 2. Iowa City Flint Glass Manufacturing Company. I. Title. BIP

Glassware—Iran.

FUKAI, Shinji, 1924- 748.5'9955
Persian glass / by Shinji Fukai ; photos. by Bin Takahashi. 1st English ed. New York : Weatherhill/Tankosha, 1977. p. cm. Translation of Perushia no garasu. [NK5174.A1F8413 1977] 77-23736 ISBN 0-8348-1515-X : 50.00
1. Glassware—Iran. 2. Iran—Antiquities. I. Takahashi, Bin. II. Title. BIP

Glassware, Iranian—Exhibitions.

CORNING, N.Y. Museum of Glass. 748.2'9955'074014783
A tribute to Persia: Persian glass. [Corning, 1972] 18, [1] p. illus. 23 cm. Catalog of a special exhibition, spring-summer 1972, prepared in honor of the 2500th anniversary of the founding of the Persian Empire. Bibliography: p. [19] [NK5174.A1C67] 72-2312 ISBN 0-87290-060-6
1. Glassware, Iranian—Exhibitions. I. Title.

Glassware—Ireland.

BOYDELL, Mary. 748.2'99415
Irish glass / [by] Mary Boydell. Norwich : Jarrold and Sons, 1976. [28] p. (2 fold.) : ill. (some col.), facsim., port. ; 25 cm. (The Irish heritage series ; 5) Bibliography: p. [27] [NK5146.A1B69] 77-362742 ISBN 0-900346-09-4 : £0.70
1. Glassware—Ireland. I. Title. II. Series.

Glassware, Irish.

WARREN, Phelps. 748.2'99415
Irish glass; the age of exuberance. New York, Scribner [1971, c1970] 155 p., [96] p. of illus. 3 col. plates. 26 cm. Bibliography: p. 150-151. [NK5146.W3 1971] 72-152561 ISBN 0-684-12426-2 17.50
1. Glassware, Irish. I. Title.

Glassware, Italian—History.

MARIACHER, Giovanni. 748.295
Italian blown glass, from ancient Rome to Venice. [Translation by Michael Bullock and Johanna Capra] New York, McGraw-Hill [1961] 245 p. illus. (part mounted) 84 col. plates. 31 cm. Translation of Il vetro soffiato de Roma antica a Venezia. Bibliography: p. 61-62. [NK5152.M313] 61-15890
1. Glassware, Italian—History. I. Title.

Glassware, Japanese—History.

BLAIR, Dorothy, 1890- 748.2'952
A history of glass in Japan. [1st ed. New York, Kodansha International/USA, 1973] 479 p. plates (part col.) 30 cm. "A Corning Museum of Glass monograph." Bibliography: p. 461-469. [NK5184.A1B55 1973] 72-94022 ISBN 0-87011-196-5 60.00
1. Glassware, Japanese—History. I. Corning, N.Y. Museum of Glass. II. Title. BIP

Glassware—Ohio—Catalogs.

CAMBRIDGE Glass Company, Cambridge, Ohio. 748.2'9171'92
Catalogue of table glassware, lamps, barware, and novelties manufactured by the Cambridge Glass Company. [1st ed.]. [Cambridge, Ohio : H. Bennett, 1976] 106 p. : chiefly ill. ; 22 x 29 cm. Cover title: 1903 catalog of pressed and blown glass ware manufactured by the Cambridge Glass Co., Cambridge, O. Reprint of the 1903 ed. published by the Cambridge Glass Co., Cambridge, Ohio. Includes index. [NK5198.C28A43 1976] 76-362976
1. Cambridge Glass Company, Cambridge, Ohio. 2. Glassware—Ohio—Catalogs. I. Title: Catalogue of table glassware, lamps, barware, and novelties ... II. Title: 1903 catalog of pressed and blown glass ware ...

Glassware—Patents.

PETERSON, Arthur Goodwin, 1904- 748.2'913
Glass patents and patterns, by Arthur G. Peterson. Sanford, Fla., Celery City Print. Co.; available from the author, DeBary, Fla. [1973] 226 p. illus. 22 cm. Includes bibliographical references. [TP865.P47] 72-91628
1. Glassware—Patents. 2. Glassware—Collectors and collecting. I. Title.

Glassware—Pennsylvania—Catalogs.

PENNSYLVANIA glassware, 1870-1904; 748.2'9148 pressed tumblers, stem ware, patterned sets, cruets, jars; etched and cut glass globes, shades, stalactites, balls; flint glass flasks, brandies, whiskeys, decanters, bitters, condiment bottles, jars; cut glass bowls, celeries, carafes, decanters, jugs, tankards, nappies, bon-bons, goblets, tumblers. Compiled by the editors of the Pyne Press. [1st ed.] Princeton [N.J.] Pyne Press; [distributed by Scribner, New York, 1972] 156 p. illus. 28 cm. (American historical catalog collection) Contains reproductions of the important plates from catalogs of King, Son & Co., early 1870's (Cascade Glassworks); Phoenix Glass Co., 1893; Agnew Co., ltd., 1894; T. B. Clark & Co., 1896; and United States Glass Co., 1904. [NK5112.P44 1972] 72-76872 ISBN 0-87861-023-5 4.95
1. Glassware—Pennsylvania—Catalogs. I. Pyne Press. II. King, Son & Company. III. Title. IV. Series.

Glassware—Pennsylvania—Pittsburgh—History.

INNES, Lowell. 748.2'9148'86
Pittsburgh glass, 1797-1891 : a history and guide for collectors / Lowell Innes. Boston : Houghton Mifflin, 1976. p. cm. Includes index. Bibliography: p. [NK5112.I55] 76-25833 ISBN 0-395-20733-9 : 30.00
1. Glassware—Pennsylvania—Pittsburgh—History. 2. Glassware—Collectors and collecting. I. Title. BIP

Glassware—Pennsylvania—Washington.

KRAUSE, Gail. 748.2'9148'82
The encyclopedia of Duncan glass / Gail Krause. 1st ed. Hicksville, N.Y. : Exposition Press, c1976. viii, 223 p. : ill. (some col.) ; 24 cm. [NK5198.D86K7] 76-366971 ISBN 0-682-48527-6 : 17.50
1. Duncan & Miller Glass Company. 2. Glassware—Pennsylvania—Washington. 3. Glassware—Collectors and collecting. I. Title. BIP

Glassware—Prices.

HOTCHKISS, John F. 748.2'02'9
Art glass prices, by John F. Hotchkiss. [Rochester, N.Y., Hotchkiss House, c.1967] no. 3. illus. 21cm. Bibl. [NK5104.H6] 68-187 3.50 pap.,
1. Glassware—Prices. 2. Glassware—Collectors and collecting. I. Title.
Publisher's address: 89 Sagamore Drive, Rochester, N.Y. 14617.

LEE, Ruth Webb, 1894- 748.2
Price guide to pattern glass. New York, M. Barrows, 1955. 331 p. illus. 21 cm. "The old forms listed...are all taken from [the author's] Early American pressed glass, and the plate numbers refer to that volume." [NK5104.L35 1955] 55-5313
1. Glassware—Prices. I. Title. BIP

LEE, Ruth Webb, 1894- 748.2085
The revised price guide to pattern glass. 3d ed. New York, M. Barrows, 1963. 331 p. illus. 21 cm. "Revisions..by Robert W. Lee." Previous editions published under title: Price guide to pattern glass. [NK5104.L35 1963] 63-17698
1. Glassware—Prices. I. Title. II. Title: Price guide to pattern glass.

WARMAN, Edwin G., 1915- 748.2
Milk glass price guide; a guide to current values on more than 2100 different items. Uniontown, Pa., Warman Pub. Co. [1960] 59 p. 22 cm. [[NK5112]]
1. Glassware—Prices. 2. Glassware—Collectors and collecting. I. Title.

WARMAN, Edwin G. 1915- 748.2
Milk glass price guide, by Edwin G. Warman and T. T. Foley; a guide to current values on more than 2000 different items. 1952-53 ed. Uniontown, Pa., Warman Pub. Co. [1952] 71 p. 22 cm. Prices by plate numbers according to Warman's Milk glass addends, Millard's Opaque glass, and Belknap's Milk glass. [NK5104.W3] 52-24827
1. Glassware — Prices. 2. Glassware — Collectors and collecting. I. Title.

Glassware—Private collections.

CORNING, N.Y. Museum of Glass 748.2075
A decade of glass collecting; selections from the Melvin Billups collection, a special exhibition, 1962. Corning [N.Y., Author, c.1962] 64p. illus. 23cm. Bibl. 62-17708 1.15 pap.,
1. Glassware—Private collections. I. Billups, Melvin P. II. Title.

N., ed. II. Corning, N.Y. Museum of Glass.

Glastonbury Abbey.

KENAWELL, William W.   726.7094238
The quest at Glastonbury, a biographical study of Frederick Bligh Bond. New York, Helix [dist. Taplinger, 1965] xi, 318p. illus., facsims., plans, ports. 24cm. Bibl. [DA690.G45K4] 65-18997 8.50
1. Bond, Frederick Bligh, 1864-1945. 2. Glastonbury Abbey. I. Bond, Frederick Bligh, 1864-1945. II. Title.   **BIP**

Glazes.

FRASER, Harry, 1937-   738.1'44
Glazes for the craft potter [by] H. Fraser. New York, Watson-Guptill Publications [1974] p. [TT922.F7 1974] 73-9589 ISBN 0-8230-2132-7 9.95
1. Glazes. 2. Pottery craft. I. Title.   **BIP**

GREEN, David Burnet,   666'.4'44
1929-
Pottery glazes, by David Green. New York, Watson-Guptill Publications [1973, c1963] 143 p. illus. (part col.) 27 cm. First published in 1963 under title: Understanding pottery glazes. Bibliography: p. 138-140. [TP812.G77 1973] 72-13454 ISBN 0-8230-4217-0 9.95
1. Glazes. I. Title.   **BIP**

GREEN, David Burnet, 1929-   620.14
Understanding pottery glazes. London, Faber and Faber [1963] 128 p. illus. 23 cm. Bibliography: p. 82-84. [TP812.G77] 66-2868
1. Glazes. I. Title.   **BIP**

SANDERS, Herbert H.   738.1'44
Glazes for special effects, by Herbert H. Sanders. New York, Watson-Guptill Publications [1974] 151 p. illus. 29 cm. Bibliography: p. 145. [TT922.S26] 74-6126 ISBN 0-8230-2134-3 13.95
1. Glazes. I. Title.   **BIP**

Glazes—Abstracts.

KOENIG, John Henry.   016.666
Literature abstracts of ceramic glazes [by] J. H. Koenig [and] W. H. Earhart. [Rev. ed. Philadelphia, College Offset Press] 1951. iv, 395 p. 24 cm. [TP812.K63 1951] 51-6532
1. Glazes—Abstracts. I. Earhart, William Henry, 1912- joint author. II. Title.

Glazier Collection of Illuminated Manuscripts.

PIERPONT Morgan Library,   096'.1
New York.
The Glazier Collection of Illuminated Manuscripts, comp. by John Plummer. New York, 1968. 50p. 57 plates (pt col.) 29cm. [ND2895.P5A55] 68-17003 8.75: 4.75 pap.,
1. Glazier Collection of Illuminated Manuscripts. I. Glazier, William S. II. Plummer, John. III. Title.
Publisher's address: 29 E. 36th St., New York. N. Y. 10016.

Glazing (Ceramics)

GREBANIER, Joseph, 1912-   738.1'44
Chinese stoneware glazes / by Joseph Grebanier ; photography of the author's work by Paul E. Grebanier. New York : Watson-Guptill Publications, 1975. 144 p. : ill. ; 27 cm. Includes index. Bibliography: p. 141. [TT922.G73 1975] 74-23115 ISBN 0-8230-0625-5 : 10.95
1. Glazing (Ceramics) 2. Pottery, Chinese. 3. Glazes. I. Title.   **BIP**

TROY, Jack, 1938-   738.1'44
Salt-glazed ceramics / by Jack Troy. New York : Watson-Guptill Publications, 1977. 159 p. : ill. ; 29 cm. Includes index. Bibliography: p. [156]-157. [TT922.T76 1977] 76-53036 ISBN 0-8230-4630-3 : 17.95
1. Glazing (Ceramics) I. Title.   **BIP**

Gleason, Herbert Wendell, 1855-1937.

THOREAU country :   818'.3'09 B
photographs and text selections from the works of H. D. Thoreau / by Herbert W. Gleason ; edited by Mark Silber ; introd. by Paul Brooks. San Francisco : Sierra Club Books, 1975. xv, 143 p. : ill. ; 36 cm. [TR653.T47] 75-8865 ISBN 0-87156-140-9 : 32.50. ISBN 0-87156-144-1 pbk. : 9.95
1. Gleason, Herbert Wendell, 1855-1937. 2. Thoreau, Henry David, 1817-1862—Illustrations. 3. New England—Description and travel—Views. 4. Nature photography. I. Thoreau, Henry David, 1817-1862. Selections. 1975.   **BIP**

Gleizes, Albert, 1881-1953.

SOLOMON R. Guggenheim   759.4
Museum, New York.
Albert Gleizes, 1881-1953; a retrospective exhibition, by Daniel Robbins. The Solomon R. Guggenheim Museum, New York, in collaboration with Musee national d'art moderne, Paris; Museum am Ostwall, Dortmund. [New York, Author, 1964] 131p. illus. (pt. col.) port. 28cm. Catalog of 'Exhibition 64/5, Sept.-Oct., 1964. Bibl. 64-25186 4.95 pap.,
1. Gleizes, Albert, 1881-1953. I. Robbins, Daniel. II. Title.

Glendale, Calif. Forest Lawn Memorial-Park.

FOREST Lawn Memorial-Park   718
Association, inc., Glendale, Calif.
Pictorial Forest Lawn. 2d ed. Glendale, c1953. 70p. (chiefly illus.) 37cm. [F869.G5F73 1953] 53-37767
1. Glendale, Calif. Forest Lawn Memorial-Park. I. Title.

HANCOCK, Ralph, 1903-   718
The Forest Lawn story. Los Angeles, Academy Publishers [1955] 160p. illus. 24cm. [F869.G5H35] 55-7438
1. Glendale, Calif. Forest Lawn Memorial-Park. I. Title.

Glengarry Co., Ont., in art.

FALES, Douglas A., 1929-   741.9'71
Glengarry sketchbook / by Douglas A. Fales. Ottawa : Borealis Press, 1976. [75] p. : ill. ; 25 x 33 cm. [NC143.F3A46] 77-364781 ISBN 0-919594-31-X
1. Fales, Douglas A., 1929-. 2. Glengarry Co., Ont., in art. 3. Glengarry Co., Ont. I. Title.

Gleyre, Marc Charles Gabriel, 1806-1874.

GLEYRE, Marc Charles   759.9493
Gabriel, 1806-1874.
Charles Gleyre : ou, Les illusions perdues : exposition [itinerante, Wander-] Ausstellung, Kunstmuseum Winterthur, Musee Cantini, Marseille, Stadtische Galerie im Lenbachhaus, Munchen, Kunsthalle Kiel, Aagauer Kunsthaus, Aarau, Musee cantonal des beaux-arts, Lausanne, 1974/75 : [catalogue, Katalog] / red., Ursula Sturzinger, Rudolf Koella, Hans A. Luthy.; trad., Lise Siegenthaler-Rioult]. Winterthur : [Kunstmuseum], 1974. 242 p. : ill. (some col.) ; 21 cm. Bibliography: p. 154-155. [ND853.G5S87] 75-509167
1. Gleyre, Marc Charles Gabriel, 1806-1874. I. Sturzinger, Ursula. II. Koella, Rudolf. III. Luthy, Hans A. IV. Winterthur. Kunstmuseum.

Gloucester, Eng.—Antiquities.

HEIGHWAY, Carolyn M.   942.4'14
Ancient Gloucester : the story of the roman and medieval city / by Carolyn Heighway ; designed and illustrated by Richard M. Bryant. [Gloucester] : Gloucester City Museum, 1976. [5], 13 p., 6 leaves of plates : 6 maps (3 col.) ; 30 cm. [DA690.G5H347] 76-383290 ISBN 0-903340-04-6 : £0.35
1. Gloucester, Eng.—Antiquities. I. Title.

Gloucester, Mass. Beauport.

CHAMBERLAIN, Samuel, 1895-   728.37
Beauport at Gloucester, the most fascinating house in America. The pictures by Samuel Chamberlain, the words by Paul Hollister. New York, Hastings House [1951] 84 p. illus., col. plates. 24 cm. [NA7238.G55C5] 51-14687
1. Gloucester, Mass. Beauport. I. Hollister, Paul Merrick, 1890- II. Title.

Gloucester, Mass.—Description—Views—Collected works.

PHOTOGRAPHIC history of   974.4'5
Gloucester. [Gloucester? Mass. : Gloucester Historical Reproductions, c1976- v. : chiefly ill. ; 22 x 29 cm. Cover title. Photos. collected by J. B. Benham, M. J. Horgan, Jr., and G. J. Lafata. [F74.G5P48] 76-151847
1. Gloucester, Mass.—Description—Views—Collected works. I. Benham, James B., 1900-1960. II. Horgan, Martin J. III. Lafata, Gaspar J.

Glove industry.

BECK, S. William.   391.41
Gloves, their annals and associations. A chapter of trade and social history, by S. William Beck. London, Hamilton, Adams, 1883. Detroit, Singing Tree Press, 1969. xvii, 263 p. illus. 22 cm. [GT2170.B4 1969] 75-75801
1. Glove industry. I. Title.

Gloves.

CLOSE, Eunice.   646.48
How to make gloves, with diagrams and photographs illustrating the methods of making gloves in the home. Boston, C. T. Branford Co. [1950] 92 p. illus. 24 cm. [TS2160.C8] 50-8363
1. Gloves.

EMLYN-JONES, Gwen.   646.4'8
Make your own gloves / Gwen Emlyn-Jones. New York : Scribner, [1975] c1974. 109 p. : ill. ; 26 cm. Includes index. Bibliography: p. [86] [TT666.E47 1975] 74-11808 ISBN 0-684-14105-1 : 8.95
1. Gloves. I. Title.

HUMMEL, Edith M.   646.48
You can make your own gloves. [2d ed.] New York, Fairchild Publications [1950] 79 p. illus. 31 cm. [TT290.H8 1950] 50-6175
1. Gloves. I. Title.

WOOLF, Natalie S.   685.4
Glovemaking for beginners. Bloomington, Ill., McKnight & McKnight [1951] 109 p. illus. 27 cm. [TS2160.W6] 51-7780
1. Gloves. I. Title.

Gloves—Hist.

SEVERN, William   391.41
Hand in glove, by Bill Severn, Illus. by Vana Earle. New York, McKay [c.1965] x, 179p. illus. 21cm. Bibl. [TS2160.S48] 65-23673 3.95
1. Gloves—Hist. I. Title.

Glue.

GODARD, Keith.   709'.2'4
Glue glue. [1st ed.] New York, Works, 1973. 1 v. (chiefly illus.) 21 cm. [N6537.G58A46] 73-78390
1. Godard, Keith. 2. Glue. I. Title.

Gluing.

MARRA, Alan A 1915-   674
Manual of gluing, by Alan A. Marra in cooperation with the School of Forestry and Conservation. Chicago, National Association of Furniture Manufacturers [1950- 1 v. (loose-leaf) illus. 30 cm. At head of title: Engineering Research Institute, University of Michigan. "Sponsored by the National Association of Furniture Manufacturers and administered through the Engineering Research Institute of the University of Michigan. The work was carried on in the Wood Technology

Laboratory of the University. Project M 760." [TT200.M28] 50-13406
1. Gluing. 2. Glue. I. Michigan. University. Engineering Research Institute. II. Title.

Glyptics.

SUTHERLAND, Beth Benton.   736.2
The romance of seals and engraved gems. Foreword by A. E. Alexander. New York, Macmillan [1965] xvi, 174 p. illus., ports. 24 cm. Bibliography: p. 167-170. [NK5500.S8] 65-10403
1. Glyptics. 2. Seals (Numismatics) I. Title.

God—Poetry.

CRANE, Ila Hunt, 1918-   811'.5'4
1971.
Poems about God. Paintings by Marie Lang. [Hollwood, Calif., Kaybee Press, 1972] 128 p. col. illus. 29 cm. Fifty poems about God dedicated to the children of each state. [PS3553.R27P6 1972] 71-162851 ISBN 0-87786-002-5 7.50
1. God—Poetry. I. Lang, Marie, illus. II. Title.

Godard, Keith.

GODARD, Keith.   709'.2'4
Glue glue. [1st ed.] New York, Works, 1973. 1 v. (chiefly illus.) 21 cm. [N6537.G58A46] 73-78390
1. Godard, Keith. 2. Glue. I. Title.

GODARD, Keith.   760
Itself. [1st ed.] New York, Works, 1970. [46] p. illus. (part col.) 21 cm. [PS3557.O25I8] 70-136957
I. Title.

Goddard, George Henry, 1817-1906.

SHUMATE, Albert.   709'.24
The life of George Henry Goddard, artist, architect, surveyor, and map maker, written by Albert Shumate. With a pref. by Francis P. Farquhar. [Berkeley] Friends of the Bancroft Library, University of California, 1969. 13 p. fold. map (in pocket) 36 cm. (The Series of keepsakes issued by the Friends of the Bancroft Library, no. 17) Bibliography: p. 11-13. [N6537.G6S5] 79-631610
1. Goddard, George Henry, 1817-1906. I. Title. II. Series: Friends of the Bancroft Library. Keepsakes, no. 17

Godefroy, Maximilian, fl. 1806-1824.

ALEXANDER, Robert L.,   720'.92'4
1920-
The architecture of Maximilian Godefroy [by] Robert L. Alexander. Baltimore, Johns Hopkins University Press [1974] 240 p. illus. 24 cm. (The Johns Hopkins studies in nineteenth-century architecture) Includes bibliographical references. [NA737.G55A78] 74-6810 ISBN 0-8018-1286-0 16.00
1. Godefroy, Maximilian, fl. 1806-1824. I. Title. II. Series.   **BIP**

Gods in art.

MARTIN,   704.94'7'074019478
Carolyn.
Hearst Castle : mythology, legend, history in art / by Carolyn Martin. Cambria, Calif. : Galatea Publications, c1977. 44 p. : ill. ; 22 cm. Bibliography: p. 44. [N7760.M3] 77-152576
1. Hearst-San Simeon State Historical Monument. 2. Gods in art. 3. Legends—Illustrations. 4. History in art. I. Title.

WECHSLER, Herman Joel, 1904-   292
Gods and goddesses in art and legend; great myths as pictured by great masters. New York, Pocket Books [1950] 111, [1] p. 64 plates. 17 cm. (Pocket book 661) Bibliography: p. 111-[112] [N7760.W45] 50-3895
1. Gods in art. 2. Mythology, Classical. I. Title.

WILDENSTEIN and   704.947'094
Company, inc., New York.
Gods & heroes; baroque images of

antiquity. A loan exhibition from North American collections for the benefit of the archaeological exploration of Sardis, October 30, 1968, to January 4, 1969. New York [1968] 24, [52] p., 53 p. of illus. 4 col. plates. 27 cm. Held at the gallery of Wildenstein and Company. Includes bibliographical references. [N7760.W5] 68-59052
1. Gods in art. 2. Heroes in art. 3. Art, Baroque—Exhibitions. I. Title.

Goeritz, Mathias, 1915-

ZUNIGA, Olivia 709.43
Mathias Goeritz. [Tr. from Spanish by Sonia Levy-Spira] Mexico, Editorial Intercontinental [dist. New York, Wittenborn, 1964] 211p. illus., plates (pt. mounted col.) port. 23cm. Bibl. [N6888.G6Z83] 65-17 7.00
1. Goeritz, Mathias, 1915- I. Title.

Goethe, Johann Wolfgang von, 1749-1832—Knowledge—Medals.

GOETHE, Johann Wolfgang von, 1749-1832. 841'.6
Goethe's Italian medals. Introd. and comments by Edward Gans. Translation by Max Knight. Eight plates of original medals owned by Goethe, and eight plates of medals discussed by Goethe and photographed from the collection of the British Museum, London. [San Diego, Calif.] Malter-Westerfield Pub. Co.; [distributed by Argonaut, Chicago, 1969] ix, [22] p. illus., 16 plates. 29 cm. Cover title: Goethe's Italian Renaissance medals, by Edward Gans. Imprint covered by label: Argonaut, Chicago. English and German. "First re-publication of an essay [Beytrage zur Geschichte der Schaumunzen aus neuerer Zeit] in the Jenaische allgemeine Literatur-Zeitung, 1810, by J. W. Goethe and Heinrich Meyer (Weimarer Kunstfreunde)" [CJ5649.G63] 76-85127
1. Goethe, Johann Wolfgang von, 1749-1832—Knowledge—Medals. 2. Medals—Italy. I. Meyer, Hans Heinrich, 1760-1832, joint author. II. Gans, Edward. III. Title.

Goetz, Karl, 1875-1950.

KIENAST, Gunter W. v. 12
The medals of Karl Goetz, by Gunter W. Kienast. [1st ed.] Cleveland, Artus Co., 1967. ii, 284 p. illus., ports. 29 cm. "Limited to 500 numbered copies." Bibliography: p. 276. [NK6398.G6K5] 67-21457
1. Goetz, Karl, 1875-1950. I. Title.

Goff, Bruce, 1904—

COOK, Jeffrey. 720'.92'4
The architecture of Bruce Goff / Jeffrey Cook. 1st U.S. ed. New York : Harper & Row, c1978. 135 p. : ill. (some col.) ; 26 cm. (Icon editions) Includes index. [NA737.G56C66 1978] 78-2135 ISBN 0-06-430950- : 22.50
1. Goff, Bruce, 1904- I. Title. **BIP**

DE LONG, David Gilson, 1939- 720'.92'4
The architecture of Bruce Goff : buildings and projects, 1916-1974 / David Gilson De Long. New York : Garland Pub., 1977. 2 v. : ill. ; 22 cm. (Outstanding dissertations in the fine arts) Originally presented as the author's thesis, Columbia, 1976. vol. 2: illustrations. Bibliography: v. 1, p. 518-531. [NA737.G56D44 1977] 76-23610 ISBN 0-8240-2682-9 : 90.00
1. Goff, Bruce, 1904- 2. Architecture, Modern—20th century—United States. I. Title. II. Series.

GOFF, Bruce, 1904- 720'.924
Bruce Goff: a portfolio of the work of Bruce Goff. Designed and compiled by William Murphy [and] Louis Muller. New York, Architectural League of New York [1970] [5] l., 22 l. of illus. (in portfolio) plans (6 fold.) 28 x 43 cm. "An outcome of the exhibition held at the Architectural League of New York from January 22 to February 11, 1970." [NA737.G56M8] 77-133066
I. Murphy, William, 1940- II. Muller, Louis. III. Architectural League of New York.

Gogh, Vincent van, 1853-1890.

ABELES, Ehvn, 1909- 927.5
The man who painted the sun; the story of Vincent Van Gogh, by Kerwin Bowles [pseud.] Illustrated by Henry Kallem. New York, Stravon Publishers [1951] 31 p. illus. 22 x 28 cm. (A Child's book of great artists) [ND653.G7A6] 51-14728
1. Gogh, Vincent van, 1853-1890. 2. Art—Juvenile literature. I. Title.

BURRA, Peter 759.9492
Van Gogh [by] Peter Burra. New York, Coller [1962] 127p. 18cm. (AS65Y) .95 pap.,
1. Van Gogh, Vincent Willem, 1853-1890. I. Title.

BURRA, Peter 759.9492
Van Gogh [by] Peter Burra. New York, Coller [1962] 127p. 18cm. (AS65Y) .95 pap.,
1. Van Gogh, Vincent Willem, 1853-1890. I. Title.

CABANNE, Pierre. 927.5
Van Gogh. [Translated from the French by Mary I. Martin. 1st American ed.] Englewood Cliffs, N.J., Prentice-Hall [1963] 288 p. illus. (part col.) 22 cm. Bibliography: p. 280. [ND653.G7C33 1963] 63-4334
1. Gogh, Vincent van, 1853-1890. I. Title.

CABANNE, Pierre. 759.9492 B
Van Gogh. [Translated from the French by Daphne Woodward] New York, H. N. Abrams [1971?] 288 p. illus. (part col.) 22 cm. Bibliography: p. 286. [ND653.G7C33 1971] 71-143482 ISBN 0-8109-0523-X
1. Gogh, Vincent van, 1853-1890.

CABANNE, Pierre. 759.9492 B
Van Gogh / Pierre Cabanne; translated from the French by Daphne Woodward New York : Praeger Publishers, 1975, c1963. 288 p. : ill. (some col.) ; 21 cm. (Praeger world of art paperbacks) (A Praeger world of art profile) Includes bibliographical references and index. [ND653.G7C33 1975] 74-8443 ISBN 0-275-71680-5 pbk. : 5.95
1. Gogh, Vincent van, 1853-1890.

CHETHAM, Charles Scott. 759.9492
The role of Vincent van Gogh's copies in the development of his art / Charles Chetham. New York : Garland Pub., 1976. 288 p., [8] leaves of plates : ill. ; 21 cm. (Outstanding dissertations in the fine arts) Originally presented as the author's thesis, Harvard University, 1960. Bibliography: p. 284-288. [ND653.G7C4 1976] 75-23788 ISBN 0-8240-1984-9 lib.bdg. : 27.50
1. Gogh, Vincent van, 1853-1890. 2. Pictures—Copying. I. Title. II. Series. **BIP**

COGNIAT, Raymond, 1896- 759.9492
Van Gogh. [Translated from the French by James by James Cleugh] New York, H. N. Abrams [1959] 88p. col. illus. 19cm. [ND653.G7C483] 59-11865
1. Gogh, Vincent van, 1853-1890. I. Title.

DIEHL, Gaston. 759.9492
Van Gogh. [Translated from the French by Anne Ross] New York, Crown Publishers [1966] 46 p. illus. (part col.) 19 cm. (Basic art library) [ND653.G7D513] 66-26177
1. Gogh, Vincent van, 1853-1890.

ELGAR, Frank. 927.5
Van Gogh, a study of his life and work. [Translated from the French by James Cleugh] New York, Praeger [1958] 256, [60] p. illus. (part col.) 21 cm. Bibliography: p. [35]-[38] (2d group) [ND653.G7E523] 759.9492 58-12092
1. Gogh, Vincent van, 1853-1890.

ELGAR, Frank. 759.9492 B
Van Gogh; a study of his life and work. [Translated from the French by James Cleugh] New York, Praeger [1966, c1958] 239 [55] p. illus. (part col.) 22 cm. (A Praeger world of art profile) Bibliography: p. [33]-[36] (2d group) [ND653.G7E533 1966] 66-9326
1. Gogh, Vincent van, 1853-1890.

ERPEL, Fritz. 759.9492
Van Gogh; the self-portraits. With a pref. by H. Gerson. Translation by Doris Edwards Greenwich, Conn., New York Graphic Society [1969] 66 p. 51 plates (part col.), ports. 28 cm. Translation of Die Selbstbildnisse Vincent van Goghs. [ND653.G7E733] 68-29117 7.50
1. Gogh, Vincent van, 1853-1890. I. Title.

EVANS, Grose. 760'.0924
Van Gogh. New York, McGraw-Hill [1968] 48 p. illus., 20 col. slides (film, 2 x 2 in.) 29 cm. (Color slide program of the great masters) The slides are in pockets inside the front cover. [ND653.G7E9] 68-20386
1. Gogh, Vincent van, 1853-1890. 2. Lantern slides—Catalogs. I. Title. II. Series.

GOGH, Vincent van, 1853-1890. 741.91
Drawings and watercolours; a selection of 32 plates in colour, with notes by Doublas Cooper, including also the essay Colours, by Hugo von Hofmannsthal. New York, Macmillan [1955] 92, [3]p. col. illus. 30cm. 'Bibliographical abbreviations': p. [95] [NC1125.G6C615] 55-3821
I. Cooper, Douglas, 1911- II. Title.

GOGH, Vincent van, 1853-1890. 759.9492 B
My life & love are one : quotations from the letters of Vincent Van Gogh to his brother Theo / edited by Irving and Jean Stone ; selected and arranged by Susan Polis Schutz and Nancy Hoffman ; designed by Stephen Schutz. Boulder, Colo. : Blue Mountain Arts, 1976. 63 p. : ill. ; 22 cm. [ND653.G7A344] 75-37346 ISBN 0-88396-016-8 pbk. : 3.50
1. Gogh, Vincent van, 1853-1890. 2. Gogh, Theo van, 1857-1891. 3. Painters—Netherlands—Correspondence. I. Title.

GOGH, Vincent van, 1853-1890. 759.9492
Van Gogh. [New York] St. Martin's Press [1972] [4] p., 13 col. plates. 34 cm. [ND653.G7A4878] 72-76959 4.95 (pbk.)

GOGH, Vincent van, 1853-1890. 759.9492
Van Gogh. Text and notes by Gerald E. Finley. New York, Tudor Pub. Co. [1966] 36 p. 91 col. plates. 18 cm. Bibliography: p. 15. [ND653.G7F53] 66-10490
I. Finley, Gerald E.

GOGH, Vincent Van, 1853-1890 759.492
Van Gogh. Text by Hermann Jedding. Tr. by Susan Bellamy. New York, Crown [1965] 26p. illus. (10 mounted col.) 30cm. (Folio art bks.) [ND653.G7J363] 65-5030 1.45 pap.,
I. Jedding, Hermann. II. Title.

GOGH, Vincent van, 1853-1890. 759.9492
Van Gogh, by Parker Tyler. Garden City, N.Y., Doubleday, 1968 [i.e. 1969] 141 p. illus. (part col.), 78 col. plates, ports. 25 cm. (World art series) [ND653.G7T9] 68-23387 7.95
I. Tyler, Parker.

GOGH, Vincent van, 1853-1890. 759.9492
Van Gogh. Text by Marco Valsecchi. Greenwich, Conn., New York Graphic Society [1959, c1957] 17, [1] p. illus., 33 col. plates. 36 cm. Bibliography: p. [18] [ND653.G7V333] 59-4520
I. Valsecchi, Marco.

GOGH, Vincent van, 1853-1890. 759.9492
Van Gogh. [Text by Meyer Schapiro.] [New York] [H. N. Abrams] [1952] 6 p. illus., 16 col. plates (incl. cover) 39 cm. (An Abrams art book) In portfolio: title from cover. [ND653.G7S37] 927.5 53-1382
I. Schapiro, Meyer, 1904-

GOGH, Vincent van, 1853-1890. 759.9492
Vincent van Gogh. Text by Meyer Schapiro. New York, H. N. Abrams [1969] 39 p. illus. (part col.) 33 cm. (Great art of the ages) [ND653.G7S377] 69-19718
I. Schapiro, Meyer, 1904-

GOGH, Vincent van, 1853-1890. 759.9492
Vincent van Gogh. Text by Meyer Schapiro. [1st ed.] New York, H. N. Abrams, 1950. 130 p. illus., col. plates. 34 cm. (The Library of great painters) [ND653.G7S38] 50-12714
I. Schapiro, Meyer, 1904- II. Title.

GOGH, Vincent van, 1853-1890. 759.9492
Vincent van Gogh / [compiled by] Richard Shone. New York : St. Martin's Press, 1978. [88] p. : chiefly col. ill. ; 28 cm. [ND653.G7A4 1978a] 77-9210 ISBN 0-312-83674-0 pbk. : 5.95
1. Gogh, Vincent van, 1853-1890. I. Shone, Richard.

GOGH, Vincent van, 1853-1890. 759.9492
Vincent Van Gogh, the late works. Text by Meyer Schapiro. New York, H. N. Abrams [1970?] 24 p. illus. (part col.) 33 cm. (The Library of great painters. Portfolio ed.) [ND653.G7S39] 69-14763 ISBN 0-8109-3071-4
I. Schapiro, Meyer, 1904-

GOGH, Vincent van, 1853-1890. 759.9492
Vincent van Gogh (1853-1890) Text by Robert Gold-water. New York, H. N. Abrams in association with Pocket Books [1953] [74]p. 38 illus. (part col.) 18cm. (The Pocket library of great art. A6) An Abrams art book. Bibliography: p. [74] [ND653.G7G6] 54-15090
I. Goldwater, Robert John, 1907- II. Title.

GOGH, Vincent van, 1853-1890. 759.9492
The works of Vincent van Gogh: his paintings and drawings [by] J.-B. de la Faille. [Rev., augm., and annotated ed. New York] Reynal, in association with Morrow [1970] 701 p. illus., facsims., col. plates, ports. 38 cm. First published in 1928 under title: L'ouvre de Vincent van Gogh, catalogue raisonne; the 2d ed. was published in 1939 under title: Vincent van Gogh. "Van Gogh and the words, by A. H. Hammacher": p. 9-37. Bibliography: p. [699]-701. [ND653.G7L32 1970] 71-128116 55.00
I. Faille, Jacob Baart de la, 1886-1959. II. Hammacher, Abraham Marie, 1897- III. Title.

GRAETZ, H. R. 759.9492
The symbolic language of Vincet van Gogh. New York, McGraw [c.1963] 315p. illus. (pt. mounted col.) ports., facsims. 25cm. Includes quotations, tr. by the author, from Van Gogh's letters. The numbers in the margin of the pages correspond to the numbers given to the letters in the eds. of The collected letters of Vincent van Gogh, Wereldbibliotheek, Amsterdam, 1953/4, and N.Y. Graphic Society, 1958. Bibl. 62-18006 9.95
1. Goh)0gh, Vincent van, 1853-1890. I. Gogh, Vincent van, 1853-1890. II. Title.

HAMMACHER, Abraham Marie, 1897- 759.9492
Genius and disaster; the ten creative years of Vincent van Gogh [by] A. M. Hammacher. New York, H. N. Abrams [1968] 188 p. illus. (part col.) 28 x 30 cm. [ND653.G7H24] 68-11540
1. Gogh, Vincent van, 1853-1890. I. Title.

HANSON, Lawrence. 927.5
Passionate pilgrim; the life of Vincent van Gogh, by Lawrence and Elisabeth Hanson. New York, Random House [1955] 300p. illus. 24cm. [ND653.G7H275] 55-8162
1. Gogh, Vincent van, 1853-1890. I. Hanson, Elisabeth M., joint author. II. Title.

HONOUR, Alan. 759.9492
Tormented genius; the struggles of Vincent van Gogh. New York, Morrow, 1967. 191 p. 6 col. plates. 22 cm. Bibliography: p. [183]-184. [ND653.G7H65 1967] 67-19687
1. Gogh, Vincent van, 1853-1890. I. Title. **BIP**

HUISMAN, Philippe 759.492
Van Gogh: portraits. [Tr. from French by Diana Imber] New York 20 French & European Pubns., 610 Fifth Ave. [1963] 65p. mounted col. illus. 21cm. (Rhythm & colour, 3) Bibl. 63-3614 3.95
1. Gogh, Vincent van, 1853-1890. I. Title.

HUYGHE, Rene. 759.9492
Van Gogh. [Translated by Helen C. Slonim] New York, Crown Publishers, 1958. 95 p. illus. (part mounted col.) plates

(part col.) 29 cm. Bibliography: p. 92-94. [ND653.G7H93] 58-12881
1. Gogh, Vincent van, 1853-1890. BIP

JONES, Jack Raymond. 759.9492 (B)
The man who loved the sun: the life of Vincent Van Gogh. London, Evans Bros., 1966. 176 p. 16 plates. 22 1/3 cm. 21/- Bibliography: p. 172-173. [ND653.G7J6] 66-78334
1. Gogh, Vincent van, 1853-1890. I. Title.

KELLER, Horst. 759.9492
Vincent van Gogh; the final years. [New York, H. N. Abrams, 1970] 81 p. illus. (part col.) 30 cm. Translation of Die Jahre der Vollendung. [ND653.G7K413] 78-125783 ISBN 0-8109-0526-4
1. Gogh, Vincent van, 1853-1890.

KNUTTEL, Gerhardus, 1889- 759.9492
Vincent van Gogh. [Translation: Corry van Alphen] New York, Barnes & Noble [1962, c1961] 89 p. illus. (part col.) 18 cm. (Barnes & Noble art series) [ND653.G7K573] 62-52811
1. Gogh, Vincent van, 1853-1890.

LASSAIGNE, Jacques, 1910- 759.9492
Van Gogh. [1st U.S. ed.] Garden City, N.Y., Doubleday [1973] 95 p. illus. (part col.) 34 cm. (The Great impressionists) Bibliography: p. 94. [ND653.G7L36 1973] 73-82258 ISBN 0-385-08365-3 9.95
1. Gogh, Vincent van, 1853-1890. I. Title.

LEYMARIE, Jean. 759.9492 B
Van Gogh / [text by Jean Leymarie ; translated from the French by James Emmons]. New ed. New York : Rizzoli International Publications, 1977. 210 p. : ill. (some col.) ; 35 cm. (Discovering the nineteenth century) Translation of Qui etait van Gogh? Includes index. Bibliography: p. 199-[200] [ND653.G7L463 1977] 78-100029 ISBN 0-8478-0119-5 : 45.00
1. Gogh, Vincent van, 1853-1890. 2. Painters—Netherlands—Biography. I. Title. II. Series.

LEYMARIE, Jean. 759.9492
Who was van Gogh? [text by Jean Leymarie Geneva, Skira; distributed in the U.S. by World Pub. Co., Cleveland, 1968] 210 p. illus. (part col.) 24 cm. (Who was?) Translation of Qui etait van Gogh? Bibliography: p. 199-[200] [ND653.G7L463] 68-20496
1. Gogh, Vincent van, 1853-1890. I. Title.

LUBIN, Albert J. 759.9492 B
Stranger on the earth; a psychological biography of Vincent van Gogh [by] Albert J. Lubin. [1st ed.] New York, Holt, Rinehart Winston [1972] xxii, 265 p. illus. 24 cm. Bibliography: p. 255-256. [ND653.G7L75 1972] 75-182772 ISBN 0-03-091352-7 8.95
1. Gogh, Vincent van, 1853-1890. I. Title.

MASINI, Lara Vinca. 759.9'492
Van Gogh. [Translated from the Italian by Caroline Moorehead. 1st American ed.] New York, Grosset & Dunlap [1967] 39 [80] p. illus. (part col.) 18 cm. (The New Grosset art library, 2) On cover: Van Gogh; the life and work of the artist. [ND653.G7M333 1967] 67-24229
1. Gogh, Vincent van, 1853-1890.

MEIER-GRAETE, Julius, 1867-1935. 759.9492
Vincent van Gogh; a biographical study. Translated by John Holroyd-Reece. Westport, Conn., Greenwood Press [1970] xvi, 239 p. 61 plates. 23 cm. Reprint of the 1933 ed. [ND653.G7M5 1970] 76-109788 ISBN 8-371-42784-
1. Gogh, Vincent van, 1853-1890.

NAGERA, Humberto. 759.9492
Vincent Van Gogh; a psychological study. Foreword by Anna Freud. New York, International Universities Press [1967] 182 p. illus. (part col.) 23 cm. [ND653.G7N3 1967b] 67-31967
1. Gogh, Vincent van, 1853-1890.

NEW York (City). Museum of Modern Art. 759.9'492
Vincent van Gogh. With an introd. and notes selected from the letters of the artist, edited by Alfred H. Barr, Jr. Westport, Conn., Greenwood Press [1970] 193 p. illus., map. 24 cm. Reprint of the 1935 ed. "Books van Gogh read as cited in his letters": p. 44-46. Bibliography: p. 192-193. [ND653.G7N4 1970] 78-109811 ISBN 0-8371-4302-0
1. Gogh, Vincent van, 1853-1890. I. Barr, Alfred Hamilton, 1902- ed.

NEW York (City) Museum of Modern Art. 760'.0924
Vincent van Gogh: with an introd. and notes selected from the letters of the artist, edited by Alfred H. Barr, Jr. And A bibliography comprising a catalogue of the literature published from 1890 through 1940; with an introductory essay and notes, by Charles Mattoon Brooks, Jr. New York, Published for the Museum of Modern Art by Arno Press, 1966. 193, xviii, 58 p. illus. 27 cm. Reprint of 2 works previously published separately. Includes bibliographies. [ND653.G7N4 1966] 66-26121
1. Gogh, Vincent van, 1853-1890. I. Barr, Alfred Hamilton, 1902- ed. II. Brooks, Charles Mattoon, 1908- Vincent van Gogh, a bibliography. III. Title.

NORDENFALK, Carl Adam Johan, 1907- 927.5
The life and work of van Gogh. New York, Philosophical Library [1953] 206 p. plates (incl. ports.; part col.) 26 cm. Translated by Lawrence Wolfe. Bibliography: p. 198-204. [ND653.G7N614] 53-7906
1. Gogh, Vincent van, 1853-1890.

PACH, Walter, 1883-1958. 759.9492
Vincent van Gogh, 1853-1890; a study of the artist and his work in relation to his times. Freeport, N.Y., Books for Libraries Press [1969] 55 p. 30 plates (incl. ports.) 24 cm. (Select bibliographies reprint series) Reprint of the 1936 ed. [ND653.G7P3 1969] 78-99666
1. Gogh, Vincent van, 1853-1890.

POLLOCK, Griselda. 759.9492 B
Vincent van Gogh, artist of his time / Griselda Pollock and Fred Orton. New York : Dutton, 1978. 80 p. : ill. (some col.) ; 29 cm. Bibliography: p. 6 [ND653.G7P64] 78-56652 ISBN 0-7148-1883-6 : 12.95. ISBN 0-7148-1906-9 pbk : 6.95
1. Gogh, Vincent van, 1853-1890. 2. Painters—Netherlands—Biography. I. Orton, Fred, joint author. II. Gogh, Vincent van, 1853-1890. III. Title.

RIPLEY, Elizabeth, 1906- 927.5
Vincent van Gogh, a biography. With drawings and paintings by Vincent van Gogh. New York, Oxford University Press, 1954. 68 p. illus. 26 cm. [ND653.G7R5] 54-10010
1. Gogh, Vincent van, 1853-1890.

ROSKILL, Mark W., 1933- 759.9492
Van Gogh, Gauguin, and the Impressionist circle [by] Mark Roskill. Greenwich, Conn., New York Graphic Society [1970] 310 p. illus. 26 cm. Bibliography: p. 284-294. [ND547.5.I4R6 1970b] 76-110665 ISBN 0-8212-0388-6 13.50
1. Gogh, Vincent van, 1853-1890. 2. Gauguin, Paul, 1848-1903. 3. Impressionism (Art)—France. I. Title.

TOLEDO. Museum of Art. 759.9492
Van Gogh and his world; observations by Van Gogh on art, by artists on Van Gogh. [Toledo] 1968. [21] l. illus. 28 cm. "Prepared for use in connection with the exhibition at the Toledo Museum of Art, Van Gogh drawings and watercolors, January 14-March 3, 1968." Bibliography: leaf [20] [ND653.G7T6] 79-283517
1. Gogh, Vincent van, 1853-1890. I. Gogh, Vincent van, 1853-1890.

TRALBAUT, Mark Edo. 759.9492
Van Gogh; a pictorial biography. [Translated by Margaret Shenfield] New York, Viking Press [1959] 143 p. illus. (part col.) ports., maps, facsims. 24 cm. (A Studio book) [ND653.G7T673] 60-10086
1. Gogh, Vincent van, 1853-1890.

TRALBAUT, Mark Edo. 759.9492 B
Vincent van Gogh [by] Marc Edo Tralbaut. New York, Viking Press [1969] 350 p. illus. (part col.) 31 cm. (A Studio book) Translation of Van Gogh, le mal aime. Bibliography: p. 350. [ND653.G7T67453 1969] 76-87251 ISBN 6-7074-2783- 40.00
1. Gogh, Vincent van, 1853-1890. I. Title.

TREBLE, Rosemary. 759.9492
Van Gogh and his art / [by] Rosemary Treble. London ; New York : Hamlyn, 1975. 128 p. : ill. (some col.), ports. (some col.) ; 35 cm. Includes index. [ND653.G7T74] 76-354842 ISBN 0-600-36179-9 : £3.95
1. Gogh, Vincent van, 1853-1890. I. Gogh, Vincent van, 1853-1890. II. Title.

TUCHMAN, Maurice 759.06
Van Goah and epressionism commentary. New York, Solomon R. Guggenheim Mus., 1964]. 1v. (unpaged) (col. illus.) 26x12cm. Bibl. 64-21306 1.50 pap.,
1. Gogh, Vincent van, 1853-1890. 2. Expressionism (Art) 3. Paintings—Exhibitions. I. Solomon R. Guggenheim Museum, New York. II. Title.

VINCENT van Gogh in full colour. [927.5] 50 plates. [London] Phaidon Publishers; distributed by Oxford University Press, New York [195] unpaged, illus. 31 cm. [ND653.G7A53] 759.9422 51-14044
I. Gogh, Vincent van, 1853-1890.

VINCENT VAN GOGH STICHTING. 759.9492
Vincent van Gogh: paintings and drawings; [exhibition at] the M. H. de Young Memorial Museum, San Francisco, the Los Angeles County Museum, the Portland Art Museum, the Seattle Art Museum, October 1958 to April 1959. [San Francisco? 1959] [52] p. plates (part col.) 26 cm. [ND653.G7V53] 60-250
1. Gogh, Vincent van, 1853-1890. I. De Young Memorial Museum, San Francisco. II. Title.

WALLACE, Robert, 1919- 759.9492 B
The world of Van Gogh, 1853-1890, by Robert Wallace and the editors of Time-Life Books New York, Time-Life Books [1969] 192 p. illus. (part col.), ports. 32 cm. (Time-Life library of art) Bibliography: p. 184. [ND653.G7W34] 70-78988
1. Gogh, Vincent van, 1853-1890. 2. Time-Life Books. I. Title. BIP

WELSH-OVCHAROV, Bogomila, comp. 759.9492
Van Gogh in perspective. Englewood Cliffs, N.J., Prentice-Hall [1974] x, 178 p. illus. 21 cm. (The Artists in perspective series) (A Spectrum book) Bibliography: p. [177]-178. [ND653.G7W42 1974] 73-19718 ISBN 0-13-940437-6 6.95
1. Gogh, Vincent van, 1853-1890. I. Title.
Pbk. 2.45, ISBN 0-13-940429-5

WELSH-OVHAROV, Bogomila. 759.9492 B
Vincent van Gogh : his Paris period 1886-1888 / Bogomila Welsh-Ovcharov. Utrecht : Editions Victorine, 1976. xi, 302 p. : ill. ; 28 cm. Thesis—Toronto. Includes index. Bibliography: p. 255-261. [ND653.G7W43] 77-465148
1. Gogh, Vincent van, 1853-1890. 2. Painters—Netherlands—Biography. 3. Painters—France—Paris—Biography.

WILDENSTEIN and Company, inc., New York. 759.9492
Van Gogh: loan exhibition; for the benefit of the Public Education Association, March 24-April 30, 1955. New York [1955] 77p. illus. (part col.) 26cm. [ND653.G7W53] 56-4478
1. Gogh, Vincent van, 1853-1890. I. Title.

WILKIE, Kenneth, 1942- 759.9492 B
The van Gogh assignment / Kenneth Wilkie. New York : Paddington Press : distributed by Grosset & Dunlap, c1978. 207 p. : ill. ; 22 cm. [ND653.G7W54] 77-20966 ISBN 0-448-23167-0 : 7.95
1. Gogh, Vincent van, 1853-1890. 2. Painters—Netherlands—Biography. I. Title. BIP

Gogh, Vincent van, 1853-1890—Art collections.

BROOKLYN Institute of Arts and Sciences. Museum. 769'.074'014723
Van Gogh's sources of inspiration; 100 prints from his personal collection. [Brooklyn, 1971] [39] p. illus. 23 cm. "The Brooklyn Museum, a special exhibition/February 1-April 4, 1971." Bibliography: p. [39] [NE59.S7G63] 70-151803
1. Gogh, Vincent van, 1853-1890—Art collections. 2. Prints—Exhibitions. I. Title.

Gogh, Vincent van, 1853-1890—Juvenile literature.

ABELES, Elvin, 1909- 927.5
The man who painted the sun; the story of Vincent Van Gogh, by Kerwin Bowles. Illustrated by Henry Kallem. New York, Stravon Publishers [1951] 31 p. illus. 22 x 28 cm. (A Child's book of great artists) [ND653.G7A6] 51-14728
1. Gogn, Vincent van, 1853-1890 — Juvenile literature. I. Title.

DOBRIN, Arnold. 759.9492 B
I am a stranger on the earth : the story of Vincent Van Gogh / by Arnold Dobrin. New York : F. Warne, c1975. 95 p. : ill. (some col.) ; 22 x 23 cm. Includes index. Bibliography: p. 90. A biography of the nineteenth-century Dutch artist emphasizing the interrelationship of his life and his art. [ND653.G7D56] 92 75-8105 ISBN 0-7232-6121-0 lib.bdg. : 7.95
1. Gogh, Vincent van, 1853-1890—Juvenile literature. I. Gogh, Vincent van, 1853-1890. II. Title.

LUCHNER, Laurin. 759.9492
A child's story of Vincent van Gogh [by] Laurin Luchner and George Kaye. Pictures by Vincent van Gogh. [New York] Scroll Press [1971, c1965] [32] p. illus. (part. col.) 26 cm. Translation of Der Maler Vincent. Describes a day in the life of the artist van Gogh illustrated with many of his paintings. [ND653.G7L7613 1971] 92 71-140318 4.95
1. Gogh, Vincent van, 1853-1890—Juvenile literature. I. Kaye, George, joint author. II. Gogh, Vincent van, 1853-1890. III. Title.

PETER, Adeline. 759.9492 B
Vincent Van Gogh, by Adeline Peter and Ernest Raboff. Garden City, N.Y., Doubleday [1974] [31] p. illus. (part col.) 29 cm. (Art for children) (A Gemini-Smith book) A brief biography of this nineteenth-century Dutch painter accompanies reproductions and analyses of several of his works. [ND653.G7P43] 73-75362 ISBN 0-385-05009-7 4.95
1. Gogh, Vincent van, 1853-1890—Juvenile literature. I. Raboff, Ernest Lloyd, joint author. II. Title.
Library binding, 5.70, ISBN 0-385-06695-5

Gold articles.

RICKETTS, Howard. 738.4
Antique gold and enamelware in color. [1st ed.] Garden City, N.Y., Doubleday [1971] 124 p. col. illus. 31 cm. Bibliography: p. 123. [NK6405.R5] 78-134441 12.95
1. Gold articles. 2. Enameled ware. I. Title.

Gold articles, Chinese—Exhibitions.

GYLLENSVARD, Bo. 739.2
Chinese gold, silver, and porcelain: the Kempe Collection. [New York] Asia Society; distributed by New York Graphic Society [1971] 135 p. illus. 22 cm. "An Asia House Gallery publication." Catalogue of an exhibition circulated by the International Exhibitions Foundation and shown in the Asia House Gallery, and other participating museums, spring 1971. Bibliography: p. 84-85. [NK7183.A1G9] 79-152378 ISBN 0-87848-036-6
1. Kempe, Carl—Art collections. 2. Gold articles, Chinese—Exhibitions. 3. Silver articles, Chinese—Exhibitions. 4. Porcelain, Chinese—Exhibitions. I. Asia House Gallery, New York. II. International Exhibitions Foundation. III. Title.

SINGER, Paul, 1904- 739.2'074'01471
Early Chinese gold & silver. New York, China House Gallery, China Institute in America [1971] 72 p. illus. 23 cm. Catalogue of an exhibition at the China

SUBJECT INDEX
GOLDSMITHING, MEDIEVAL.

House Gallery, New York City, Oct. 21, 1971-Jan. 30, 1972. [NK7183.A1S5] 76-30948
1. Gold articles, Chinese—Exhibitions. 2. Silver articles, Chinese—Exhibitions. I. China House Gallery. II. China Institute in America. III. Title.

Gold boxes—New York (City)—Catalogs.

NEW York 739.2'274'07401471 (City). Metropolitan Museum of Art.
Gold boxes : the Wrightsman collection / text by Clare Le Corbeiller ; photos. by Malcolm Varon. New York : Metropolitan Museum of Art, c1977. p. cm. Catalog of a permanent exhibit at the Metropolitan Museum of Art, New York. [NK7102.N4N476 1977] 77-23592 ISBN 0-87099-166-3 pbk. : 4.95
1. Wrightsman, Charles B.—Art collections. 2. New York (City). Metropolitan Museum of Art. 3. Gold boxes—New York (City)—Catalogs. 4. Goldwork, Rococo—New York (City)—Catalogs. I. Le Corbeiller, Clare. II. Varon, Malcolm. III. Title.

Gold coins.

DURST, Sanford J. 737.4'09
Contemporary world gold coins, 1934-74 / by Sanford J. Durst. 1st ed. New York : Durst, [1975] 98 p. : ill. ; 25 cm. [CJ1545.D87] 74-24558 ISBN 0-915262-01-0 : 8.95
1. Gold coins. I. Title. BIP

FRIEDBERG, Robert, 1912- 737.4
Gold coins of the world, complete from 600 A.D. to 1958; illus. standard catalogue with valuations. Coin & Currency Inst. [Chicago, Dist. Follett, 1962, c.1958] 384p. facsims. 29cm. Pref. in English, French, German, Italian, and Spanish. 15.00
1. Gold coins. I. Title.

FRIEDBERG, Robert, 737.40216 1912-
Gold coins of the world, complete from 600 A. D. to the present; an illustrated standard catalogue with valuations. 2d ed., rev. and edited by Jack Friedberg. New York, Coin and Currency Institute [1965] 415 p. illus. 29 cm. Preface in English, German, Italian, and Spanish. Includes bibliographical references. [CJ113.F7 1965] 65-27635
1. Gold coins. I. Friedberg, Jack, ed. II. Title.

FRIEDBERG, Robert, 737.4'021'6 1912-
Gold coins of the world : complete from 600 A.D. to the present : an illustrated standard catalogue with valuations / by Robert Friedberg. 4th ed., rev. and edited / by Jack and Arthur Friedberg. New York : Coin and Currency Institute, c1976. 467 p. : ill. ; 29 cm. Preface in English, French, German, Italian, and Spanish. Includes bibliographical references and index. [CJ1545.F74 1976] 75-36702 ISBN 0-87184-304-8 : 22.50
1. Gold coins. I. Friedberg, Jack. II. Friedberg, Arthur. III. Title.

FRIEDBERG, Robert, 737.4'021'6 1912-
Gold coins of the world, complete from 600 A.D. to the present: an illustrated standard catalogue with valuations, by Robert Friedberg. Rev. and edited by Jack Friedberg. 3d ed. New York, Coin and Currency Institute [1971] 428 p. illus. 29 cm. Preface in English, French, German, Italian, and Spanish. Includes bibliographical references. [CJ113.F7 1971] 70-157937 ISBN 0-87184-303-X
1. Gold coins. I. Friedberg, Jack, ed. II. Title.

HARRIS, Robert P. 737.4
Gold coins of the Americas; a catalogue of gold coins of the Western Hemisphere from 1750 to date, by Robert P. Harris. With special assistance from Davis H. Carr. 1st ed. Florence, Ala., ANCO [1971] iv, 280 p. illus. 24 cm. [CJ1808.H37] 75-168568
1. Gold coins. 2. Coins, American. 3. Coins, Canadian. 4. Coins, Latin American. I. Title.

HOBSON, Burton. 737.4
Historic gold coins of the world. Foreword by Howard Linecar. Photos. by Michael V. DiBiase. Garden City, N.Y., Doubleday [1971] 192 p. col. illus. 29 cm. [CJ113.H6] 70-28263 25.00
1. Gold coins. I. Title.

HOPPE, Donald J. 737.4
How to invest in gold coins [by] Donald J. Hoppe. New Rochelle, N.Y., Arlington House [1970] 304 p. illus. 24 cm. Bibliography: p. [293]-295. [CJ113.H64] 70-115342 8.95
1. Gold coins. I. Title. BIP

HOPPE, Donald J. 737.4
How to invest in gold coins. New York, Arco [1973, c.1970] 295 p. illus. 20 cm. Bibliography: p. [293]-295. [CJ113.H64] ISBN 0-668-02999-4 2.95 (pbk.)
1. Gold coins. I. Title.
L.C. card no. for hardbound edition: 70-115342.

MASON, Don Walter. 332.4'52
Intrinsic values of gold coins. Long Beach, Calif., D. Mason and Associates [1973] 2 v. 28 cm. Contents.Contents.—[v. 1] For bullion ranges of $50-$800 per ounce.—v. 2. For bullion ranges of $300-$1050 per ounce. Bibliography: v. 1, p. 165. [CJ113.M37] 73-76082 9.99 (pbk.)
1. Gold coins. I. Title. BIP

SCHLUMBERGER, Hans. 737.4
Gold coins of Europe since 1800; a catalogue with valuations New York, Sterling Pub. Co. [1968] 352 p. illus. 26 cm. Translation of Goldmunzen Europas seit 1800. [CJ1545.S313 1968] 68-18787 15.00
1. Gold coins. I. Title.

TURNER, William Wesley, 737.4 1910-
Double eagles of the world; a study of the U.S.A. $20.00 gold piece and its equivalent in other monies of the world, by W. W. Turner. [Nashville? 1967] 47 p. illus. 28 cm. Cover title. [CJ113.T8] 67-4437
1. Gold coins. I. Title.

TURNER, William Wesley, 332.4'222 1910-
Gold coins for financial survival [by] W. W. Turner. Nashville, Turner Publications [1971] 240 p. illus. 24 cm. Bibliography: p. [225]-227. [CJ113.T82] 73-179024
1. Gold coins. I. Title.

TURNER, William Wesley, 737.4 1910-
Turner's Simplified pricing system for USA and world gold coins / by W. W. Turner. Leesburg, Fla. : Turner Publications, c1976- v. : ill. ; 25 cm. Contents.Contents.—v. 1. Popular world gold coins and sets. [CJ1545.T87] 76-8077
1. Gold coins. 2. Coins, American. 3. Coins—Prices. I. Title. II. Title: Simplified pricing system for USA and world gold coins.

VERBANEC, William R. 737.4'021'6
Handbook of gold coin technology : buyers' guide for gold coins / by William R. Verbanec. Santa Clara, Calif. : W. R. Verbanec Enterprises, 1974. 1 v. ; 22 cm. Loose-leaf for updating. Bibliography: leaves 240-241. [CJ1545.V47] 74-79215
1. Gold coins. I. Title.

Gold figurines, Classical—Catalogs.

VERMEULE, Cornelius Clarkson, 733 1925-
Greek and Roman sculpture in gold and silver [by] Cornelius Vermeule. Boston, Museum of Fine Arts [1974] 43 p. illus. 22 cm. Includes bibliographical references. [NK7107.3.V47] 74-80074 ISBN 0-87846-081-0
1. Gold figurines, Classical—Catalogs. 2. Silver figurines, Classical—Catalogs. 3. Classical antiquities—Catalogs. 4. Gods in art. 5. Animals in art. I. Boston. Museum of Fine Arts. II. Title. BIP

Gold-leaf.

RASMUSSEN, W. E. 739.2'27794'96 H.
The goldbeaters of Orange, California [by] W. E. H. Rasmussen. Orange, Calif., Rasmussen Press [1974] 15 p. illus. 23 cm. "Limited edition of about 125. No. 126". [TS725.R37] 74-181639
1. Gold-leaf. 2. Goldsmithing—California—Orange. I. Title.

Gold mines and mining—Victoria, Australia—History.

GILL, Samuel Thomas, 741.9'94 1818-1880.
The goldfields illustrated: the sketches of S. T. Gill. Melbourne, Lansdowne, 1972. 108 p. illus. 23 x 29 cm. Bibliography: p. 108. [TN428.V6G54] 73-159195 ISBN 0-7018-0155-7 8.50
1. Gold mines and mining—Victoria, Australia—History. 2. Gold mines and mining—Victoria, Australia—Pictorial works. 3. Victoria, Australia—Industries—History. I. Title.

Gold—Standards of fineness.

BADCOCK, William. 739.2
A new touchstone for gold and silver wares. Introd. by William O'Sullivan. New York, Praeger Publishers [1971, c1970] x, 218 [151] p. illus. 23 cm. "Photolithographic facsimile of the second edition [1679]." Original t.p. reads: A new touch-stone for gold and silver wares ... the second edition, corrected and much enlarged, by W. B. of London, goldsmith. To which is likewise added, The useful and easie tables of Mr. John Reynolds ... London: printed for J. Bellinger in Cliffords-Inn-lane, and T. Basset at the George near Cliffords-Inn-gate in Fleetstreet, 1679. [HD9747.A2B26 1679a] 75-122452 18.00
1. Gold—Standards of fineness. 2. Silver—Standards of fineness. I. Reynolds, John, assay-master of the mint, fl. 1651. Brief and easie way by tables. 1971. II. Title. III. Title: Brief and easie way by

Goldberg, Howard Ellner.

GOLDBERG, Howard Ellner. 741.9'73
Howard Ellner Goldberg. [Hastings-on-Hudson, N.Y., Printed by the Morgan Press, 1973] [22] l. illus. (part col.) 35 cm. [NC139.G58A47] 73-75290
1. Goldberg, Howard Ellner.

Goldberg, Reuben Lucius, 1883-1970.

DO it the hard way; 741.5973
Rube Goldberg and modern times. [Washington] National Museum of History and Technology, [1970] [32] p. illus., port. 21 cm. Cover title. Articles written by D. J. Boorstin, A. C. Golovin, and R. Goldberg for an exhibition at the National Museum of History and Technology. [NC1429.G46D6] 79-144126
1. Goldberg, Reuben Lucius, 1883-1970. I. Boorstin, Daniel Joseph, 1914- II. Golovin, Anne Castrodale. III. Goldberg, Reuben Lucius, 1883-1970. IV. National Museum of History and Technology.

MARZIO, Peter C. 741'.092'4 B
Rube Goldberg; his life and work [by] Peter C. Marzio. [1st ed.] New York, Harper & Row [1973] xiii, 322 p. illus. 22 x 26 cm. Bibliography: p. 307-315. [NC1429.G46M3 1973] 73-4108 ISBN 0-06-012830-5 12.50
1. Goldberg, Reuben Lucius, 1883-1970.

Golden, William, 1911-1959.

GOLDEN, Cipe Pineles, ed. 741.6
The visual craft of William Golden. Eds.: Cipe Pineles Golden, Kurt Weihs, Robert Strunsky. New York, Braziller [c.]1962. 156p. illus. 22x28cm. 62-9694 12.50
1. Golden, William, 1911-1959. 2. Commercial art. 3. Columbia Broadcasting System, inc. CBS Television. I. Title.

Goldschneider, Ludwig, 1896-

THEOTOCOPULI, Dominico, 759.6 called El Greco, d. 1614.
El Greco; paintings, drawings, and sculptures, by Ludwig Goldscheider. [3d ed.] New York, Phaidon Publishers; distributed by Garden City Books 1954. 223p. (chiefly illus.(part mounted col.))31cm Bibliography: p. 219. [ND813.T4G5 1954a] 927.5 54-38500
1. Goldschneider, Ludwig, 1896- I. Title.

Goldsmithing.

CELLINI, Benvenuto, 1500-1571 730
The treatises of Benvenuto Cellini on goldsmithing and sculpture. Tr. from Italian by E. R. Ashbee [Magnolia, Mass., P. Smith, 1968] xiv, 164p. illus. 24cm. (Dover bk. rebound) Unabridged, unaltered repubn. of the lim. ed. orig. pub. in 1888 [i.e. 1898] [NK7104.C443 1967] 4.50
1. Goldsmithing. 2. Sculpture. I. Title.

CELLINI, Benvenuto, 1500- 730 1571.
The treatises of Benvenuto Cellini on goldsmithing and sculpture. Translated from the Italian by C. R. Ashbee. New York, Dover Publications [1967] xiv, 164 p. illus. 24 cm. "Unabridged republication of the limited edition originally published ... in 1888 [i.e. 1898]" [NK7104.C443 1967] 66-13829
1. Goldsmithing. 2. Sculpture. I. Title. BIP

STATON-BEVAN, William 739.22 Norman, 1912-
The goldsmith's and silversmith's handbook; a practical manual for all workers in gold, silver, platinum, and palladium, based on the well-known handbooks by George E. Gee. Completely rev. and rewritten by Staton Abbey [pseud.] New York, Van Nostrand [c1952] 105 p. illus. 23 cm. [[TS725]] 53-6153
1. Goldsmithing. 2. Silversmithing. I. Title.

Goldsmithing—Bulgaria—Panagyurishte.

VENEDIKOV, Ivan 739.2274977
The Panagyurishte gold treasure. [Tr.: Alexander Risov. New York, Vanous, 1961] 27p. 31 plates (pt. col.) 32cm. 62-424 8.90
1. Goldsmithing—Bulgaria—Panagyurishte. 2. Goldsmithing, Ancient. 3. Drinking vessels. I. Title.

Goldsmithing—Handbooks, manuals, etc.

SCHWAHN, Christian 739.2
Workshop methods for gold-and silversmiths. Translated from the German by W. Jacobsohn. New York, Chemical Pub. Co., 1960[ ] 144p. 19cm. 60-4705 4.00
1. Goldsmithing—Handbooks, manuals, etc. 2. Silversmithing—Handbooks, manuals, etc. I. Title.

Goldsmithing—History.

BLAKEMORE, Kenneth. 739.2'27
The book of gold. New York, Stein and Day [1971] 224 p. illus. 26 cm. Bibliography: p. 219. [NK7106.B55] 73-160347 ISBN 0-8128-1413-4 20.00
1. Goldsmithing—History. I. Title.

Goldsmithing—Italy.

ROSSI, Filippo, 739.22
Italian jeweled arts. [Translated by Elisabeth Mann Borgese] New York, H. N. Abrams [1957, c1954] 233p. (p. [59]-[221] col. plates) illus. (An abrams art book) Translation of capolavori di oreficerin italiana dall'xi al xviii secolo. (part mounted part col.) 31cm. Bibliographical references included in 'Notes' (p. 53-[56]) Bibliography: p. 223. [NK7152.R613] 58-3307
1. Goldsmithing—Italy. 2. Art objects, italian I. Title. II. Series.

Goldsmithing, Medieval.

BELLI Barsali, Isa. 739.2'27'4
Medieval goldsmith's work; [translated by Margaret Crosland from the Italian]. London, New York, Hamlyn, 1969. 3-157 p. col. illus. 20 cm. (Cameo) Originally published as L'oreficeria medioevale. Milano, Fratelli Fabbri Editori, 1966. [NK7108.B413] 77-481903 15/-

1. Goldsmithing, Medieval. I. Title.

Goldsmithing — U.S.

BOHAN, Peter J. 739.22773
American gold, 1700-1860; a monograph based on a loan exhibition, April 2-June 28, 1963 Yale University, Art Gallery. [By] Peter J. Bohan. [New Haven c1963] 52 p. illus. 18 cm. "Catalogue": p. [25]-50. Bibliography: p. 51-52. [NK7112.B56] 63-20055
1. Goldsmithing — U.S. 2. Goldsmithing — Exhibitions. I. Yale University. Art Gallery. II. Title.

Goldsmiths—Australia.

ALBRECHT, Kurt. 739.2'0994
19th century Australian gold and silversmiths. [Richmond, Vic.] Hutchinson Australia [1969] 69 p. facsims., tables. 24 cm. Vol. contains 69 p. of text and 40 p. of plates. [NK7190.A1A75] 71-107337 5.40
1. Goldsmiths—Australia. 2. Silversmiths, Australian. 3. Hall-marks. I. Title. II. Title: Australian gold and silver smiths.

Goldsmiths—Biography.

HONOUR, Hugh. 739.2'0922
Goldsmiths & silversmiths. [1st American ed.] New York, Putnam [1971] 320 p. illus. 29 cm. (Great craftsmen) Includes bibliographical references. [NK7197.H6 1971] 77-142221 25.00
1. Goldsmiths—Biography. 2. Silversmiths—Biography. I. Title.

Goldsmiths—England.

LEVER, Christopher, 1932- 739.2'092'2 B
Goldsmiths and silversmiths of England / Christopher Lever. London : Hutchinson, 1975. 256 p., leaf of plate, [32] p. of plates : ill., facsim., geneal. tables, ports. ; 25 cm. Includes index. Bibliography: p. [243]-248. [NK7143.L48] 75-314072 ISBN 0-09-121220-0 : 12.00
1. Goldsmiths—England. 2. Silversmiths—England. I. Title.
Distributed by Humanities Press BIP

Goldsmiths—England—London—Registers.

GRIMWADE, Arthur. 739.2'09421
London goldsmiths, 1697-1837 : their marks and lives from the original registers at Goldsmiths' Hall and other sources / by Arthur G. Grimwade. London : Faber, 1975 ix, 728 p. : ill. ; 26 cm. [NK7144.L66G74] 76-358285 ISBN 0-571-10550-5 : 79.95
1. Goldsmiths—England—London—Registers. 2. Hall-marks. I. Title.
Distributed by Rowman & Littlefield BIP

Goldsmiths, French.

FRENCH master goldsmiths and silversmiths from the seventeenth to the nineteenth century. 739.2 Pref. by Jacques Helft. New York, French & European Publications [1966] 333 p. illus. (part col.) 32 cm. (The Connaissance des arts collection "Grands artisans d'autrefois") "Conceived and executed by Claude Fregnac." Translation of Les Grands orfevres de Louis XIII a Charles X. Bibliography: p. 333. [NK7149.G73] 66-9055
1. Goldsmiths, French. 2. Silversmiths, French. I. Fregnac, Claude.

Goldstone, Lafayette Anthony, 1876-1958.

GOLDSTONE, Aline May (Lewis) 1878- comp. 720'.924
Lafayette A. Goldstone; a career in architecture, a record compiled by Aline Lewis Goldstone and Harmon H. Goldstone. New York, 1964. 148 p. illu;., port. 22 cm. "Limited to 200 copies ... Number 175." [Na737.G58G6] 64-3364
1. Goldstone, Lafayette Anthony, 1876-1958. I. Goldstone, Harmon Hendricks, 1911- joint comp. II. Title.

Goldthwaite, Anne, 1875?-1944.

GOLDTHWAITE, Anne, 1875?-1944. 760'.092'4
Anne Goldthwaite, 1869-1944 : [exhibition], March 22 through May 1, 1977, Montgomery Museum of Fine Arts, Montgomery, Alabama. Montgomery : The Museum, c1977. 70 p. : ill. ; 25 cm. [N6537.G617M66] 77-74790 ISBN 0-89280-006-2 pbk. : 5.00
1. Goldthwaite, Anne, 1875?-1944. I. Montgomery Museum of Fine Arts. BIP

Goldwater, Barry Morris, 1909- —Art collections.

HEARD Museum of Anthropology and Primitive Art, Phoenix, Ariz. 745.59'22'09701
The Goldwater Kachina Doll Collection. Presented to the Heard Museum by Barry M. Goldwater. Tempe, Published for the Heard Museum by the Arizona Historical Foundation, 1969. 27 p. illus. (part col.), port. 26 cm. Contents.Contents.—Building the collection, by B. Goldwater.—Hopi kachinas, by B. Harvey. Bibliography: p. 23. [E99.H7H4] 71-15590
1. Goldwater, Barry Morris, 1909- —Art collections. 2. Katcinas. 3. Hopi Indians. I. Goldwater, Barry Morris, 1909- II. Harvey, Byron. III. Title.

WRIGHT, Barton. 745.59'22
Kachinas : the Barry Goldwater collection at the Heard Museum / text by Barton Wright ; photography by Jerry Jacka ; design by Gary Avey. 1st ed. Phoenix, Ariz. : W. A. Krueger Co., c1975. xii, 60 p. : col. ill. ; 23 x 29 cm. Includes index. Bibliography: p. 53. [E99.H7W733] 75-34541
1. Goldwater, Barry Morris, 1909- —Art collections. 2. Katcinas. 3. Hopi Indians—Religion and mythology. I. Jacka, Jerry D. II. Heard Museum of Anthropology and Primitive Art, Phoenix, Ariz. III. Title. BIP

Goldweights, Ashanti—Catalogs.

DE KOLB, Eric. 739.2'27'6
Ashanti goldweights. New York, Gallery d'Hautbarr [1968] 83 p. illus. 25 cm. [NK7889.A8D4] 68-3925
1. Goldweights, Ashanti—Catalogs. I. Title.

PLASS, Margaret Webster. 732'.2'0966074017289
African miniatures; goldweights of the Ashanti. New York, Praeger [1967] 26 p. 166 illus., maps. 26 cm. Bibliography: p. 6. [NK7889.A8P5 1967b] 739
1. Goldweights, Ashanti—Catalogs. I. Title.

PLASS, Margaret Webster. 739.2'27'667
African miniatures; goldweights of the Ashanti. New York, Praeger [1967] 26 p. 166 illus., maps. 26 cm. Bibliography: p. 6. [NK7889.A8P5 1967b] 67-29603
1. Goldweights, Ashanti—Catalogs. I. Title.

Goldweights, Ashanti—Exhibitions.

NOTRE Dame, Ind. University. Art Gallery. 732'.2'0966074017289
Ashanti goldweights and Senufo bronzes; Collection of Mr. and Mrs. Eric de Kolb. [Notre Dame, 1970] [32] p. illus. 22 x 29 cm. Cover title. Exhibition, Art Gallery, University of Notre Dame, Sept. 6-Nov. 15, 1970. [NK7889.6.G5N67] 73-299002
1. De Kolb, Eric—Art collections. 2. Goldweights, Ashanti—Exhibitions. 3. Bronzes, Senufo—Exhibitions. I. Title.

Goldwork—History.

WILLSBERGER, Johann, 1941- 739.2'27
Gold / by Johann Willsberger ; translated from German by Joachim Neugroschel. Garden City, N.Y. : Doubleday, 1976. 178 p. : ill. (some col.) ; 29 cm. [NK7106.W5613] 76-9636 ISBN 0-385-12266-7 : 24.95
1. Goldwork—History. I. Title. BIP

Goldwork—Italy.

CARDUCCI, Carlo. 739.22737
Gold and silver treasures of ancient Italy. Greenwich, Conn., New York Graphic Society [1964, c1963] xxxiii, 85 p. illus., plates (part col.) 31 cm. "The antique Italian gold and silver exhibition opened on June 16, 1961, at the Palazzo Chiablese in Turin. In September of the same year the exhibition was moved to the Castello Svevo in Bari and later still, to the Museo Nazionale in Naples, where it remained open to the public until its appearance in the Palazzo Reale in Milan. The exhibition was thus conceived as a travelling showpiece. It was organized by the Direzione General alle Antichita e Belle Arti, assisted by the superintendents and directors of Italian state and communal museums." "This book is not meant to replace the exhibition's official catalogue...but is aimed at complementing it with a somewhat more specialized description of the objects on show; it draws attention to technical details in certain objects." Bibliography: p. xxxi-xxxiii. [NK7152.C283] 63OGold an
1. Goldwork—Italy. 2. Goldwork—Ancient. 3. Silverwork—Italy. 4. Silverwork, Ancient. I. Italy. Direzione generale per le antichita e belle arti. II. Title.

Goldwork, Renaissance.

HAYWARD, John Forrest, 1916- 739.2'094
Virtuoso goldsmiths and the triumph of mannerism, 1540-1620 / J. F. Hayward. London : Sotheby Parke Bernet ; Totowa, N.J. : available from Biblio Distribution Center for Sotheby Parke Bernet Publications, c1976. 751 p. : ill. (some col.) ; 34 cm. Includes indexes. Bibliography: p. [729]-731. [NK7109.3.H38 1976b] 77-365238 ISBN 0-85667-005-7 : 100.00
1. Goldwork, Renaissance. 2. Mannerism (Art) I. Title. BIP

Goldwork—United States—Exhibitions.

FERON, Louis, 1901- 739.2'092'4
Louis Feron, goldsmith, jeweler, sculptor. Manchester, N.H. : Currier Gallery of Art, c1977. [38] p. : ill. ; 26 cm. "[Exhibition] February 20-March 20, 1977, the Currier Gallery of Art, Manchester, New Hampshire." "Catalogue" : p. [12]-[22] [NK7198.F37C87] 77-72761
1. Feron, Louis, 1901- 2. Goldwork—United States—Exhibitions. I. Currier Gallery of Art, Manchester, N.H.

Golf-links.

JONES, Rees L. 333.7'7'0973 s
Golf course developments, by Rees L. Jones [and] Guy L. Rando. [Washington] ULI [1974] 105 p. illus. 28 cm. (Urban Land Institute. Technical bulletin 70) [NA9000.U67 no. 70] [GV975] 711'.558 73-86554 17.50 (pbk.)
1. Golf-links. I. Rando, Guy L., joint author. II. Title. III. Series. BIP

Goltzius, Hendrik, 1558-1617.

CONNECTICUT. University. Museum of Art. 769'.9492
Hendrik Goltzius & the printmakers of Haarlem. [Storrs, 1972] 100 p. illus. 22 cm. Catalog, prepared by F. den Broeder, of the exhibition held Apr. 22-May 21, 1972. Includes bibliographical references. [NE670.G65C6] 72-184258
1. Goltzius, Hendrik, 1558-1617. 2. Prints, Dutch—Exhibitions. I. Goltzius, Hendrik, 1558-1617. II. den Broeder, Frederick. III. Title.

Goltzius, Hendrik, 1558-1617—Catalogs.

GOLTZIUS, Hendrik, 1558-1617. 769'.92'4
Hendrik Goltzius, 1558-1617 : the complete engravings and woodcuts / edited by Walter L. Strauss. New York : Abaris Books, 1977- v. : ill. ; 32 cm. Errata slip inserted. Includes index. Contents.Contents.— —v. 2. The years 1586-1600. Bibliography: p. 769-[772] [NE670.G65A4 1977] 76-22304 120.00 (2 vol. set)
1. Goltzius, Hendrik, 1558-1617—Catalogs. I. Strauss, Walter L.

Gonzalez, Julio, 1876-1942.

WITHERS, Josephine. 730'.92'4 B
Julio Gonzalez : sculpture in iron / by Josephine Withers. New York : New York University Press, 1977. p. cm. Includes index. Bibliography: p. [NB813.G6W57] 76-26798 ISBN 0-8147-9171-9 : 40.00
1. Gonzalez, Julio, 1876-1942. 2. Sculptors—Spain—Biography. BIP

Good Samaritan shilling.

NEWMAN, Eric P 737.49744
The secret of the Good Samaritan shilling. Supplemented with notes on other genuine and counterfeit Massachusetts silber coins. New York, American Society, 1959. xi, 71p. 9plates. 23cm. *Numismatic Numismatic notes and monographs, no. 142) Bibliographical footnotes. [CJ1841.N4] 59-16304
1. Good Samaritan shilling. I. Title. II. Series. BIP

Goodhue, Bertram Grosvenor, 1869-1924.

WHITAKER, Charles Harris, 1872-1938, ed. 720'.92'4
Bertram Grosvenor Goodhue : architect and master of many arts / text by Hartley Burr Alexander ... [et al.] ; edited by Charles Harris Whitaker. New York : Da Capo Press, 1976, c1925. p. cm. (Da Capo Press series in architecture and decorative art) Reprint of the ed. published by Press of the American Institute of Architects, New York. [NA737.G6W5 1976] 76-22484 ISBN 0-306-70826-4 : 65.00
1. Goodhue, Bertram Grosvenor, 1869-1924. I. Alexander, Hartley Burr, 1873-1939.

Goodnough, Robert, 1917-

BUSH, Martin H. 759.13
Goodnough, by Martin H. Bush and Kenworth Moffett. Wichita, University Art Museum, Wichita State University; [distributed by McCormick-Armstrong Co., 1973] 112 p. illus. (part col.) 24 cm. "A McKnight Fine Arts Center book." Pages [108]-112 blank. Bibliography: p. 102-104. [ND237.G612B87] 73-620039 7.50
1. Goodnough, Robert, 1917- I. Moffett, Kenworth, joint author.

EVERSON Museum of Art of Syracuse and Onondaga County. 759.13
Robert Goodnough : Andre Emmerich Gallery, New York, October 26-November 13, 1974 : Everson Museum of Art of Syracuse and Onondaga County, December 6, 1974-January 26, 1975. [Syracuse, N.Y. : Everson Museum of Art of Syracuse and Onondaga County, 1974] [16] p. : ill. (some col.) ; 23 cm. Text on p. [3] of cover. Includes bibliography. [ND237.G612E93 1974] 74-14372
1. Goodnough, Robert, 1917- I. Goodnough, Robert, 1917- II. Andre Emmerich Gallery, New York.

GUEST, Barbara 759.13
Goodnough [by] Barbara Guest, B. H. Friedman. Paris, G. Fall [dist. New York, Efron, 1963, c.1962] 63p. illus. (pt. ol.) 19cm. (Pocket museum) 63-5300 1.95 pap.,
1. Goodnough, Robert, 1917- I. Friedman, Bernard Harper, 1926- joint author. II. Title.

Goodrich, Lloyd, 1897-

DICKINSON, Edwin Walter 1891- 741.943063-13961
The drawings of Edwin Dickinson Essay by Lloyd Goodrich. New Haven, Conn., Yale [c.1963. 18p., 58 plates. 31cm. (Drawings Soc. pubn.) 12.50; after Jan. 1, 15.00
1. Goodrich, Loyd, 1897- I. Title.

SUBJECT INDEX

GOTHIC REVIVAL (ARCHITECTURE)—UNITED

WYETH, Andrew, 1917- 751.422
The four seasons: paintings and drawings. Pref. by Lloyd Goodrich. New York, Art in America [dist. McGraw, 1963] [4]p. 12 plates (pt. col.) in portfolio. 44cm. 63-1943 45.00, bxd.
1. Goodrich, Lloyd, I. Title.

Goodwin, Arthur Clifton, 1866?-1929.

EMERSON, Sandra. 759.13
A. C. Goodwin, 1864-1929 [by Sandra Emerson, Lucretia H. Giese and Laura C. Luckey. Exhibition: July 15- August 25, 1974 Boston, Museum of Fine Arts [1974] [22] p. illus. 27 cm. Includes catalog of the exhibition and bibliographical references. [ND237.G6124E43] 74-83566 ISBN 0-87846-084-5
1. Goodwin, Arthur Clifton, 1866?-1929. I. Giese, Lucretia H. II. Luckey, Laura C. III. Boston. Museum of Fine Arts. IV. Title. BIP

Gore, Art, 1926—

GORE, Art, 1926- 779'.92'4
Images of yesterday / by Art Gore. Palo Alto, Calif. : American West Pub. Co., [1975] [103] p. : chiefly ill. ; 24 x 32 cm. [TR140.G65A32] 75-6322 ISBN 0-910118-67-1 : 12.95
1. Gore, Art, 1926- 2. Photographers—Correspondence, reminiscences, etc. 3. Country life—United States. I. Title. BIP

Gorey, Edward St. John.

GOREY, Edward St. John. 741.9'73
Amphigorey; fifteen books by Edward Gorey. New York, Putnam [1972] 1 v. (unpaged) illus. 29 cm. Contents.Contents.—The unstrung harp.—The listing attic.—The doubtful guest.—The object-lesson.—The bug book.—The fatal lozenge.—The hapless child.—The curious sofa.—The willowdale handcar.—The gashly-crumb tinies.—The insect god.—The west wing.—The wuggly ump.—The sinking spell.—The remembered visit. [PS3513.O614A8] 72-80859 ISBN 0-399-11003-8 12.95
I. Title. BIP

GOREY, Edward St. John. 741.9'73
Amphigorey too / Edward Gorey. [New York] : Putnam, c1975. ca. 300 p. : chiefly ill. ; 29 cm. [PS3513.O614A84] 75-27316 ISBN 0-399-11565-X : 15.00
I. Title. BIP

GOREY, Edward St. John. 741.9'73
The Awdrey-Gore legacy [by] Edward Gorey. New York, Dodd, Mead [1972] [64] p. illus. 16 x 24 cm. "A ... shorter version of this book appeared in National lampoon." [PS3513.O614A95] 72-478 ISBN 0-396-06598-8 3.95
I. Title. BIP

GOREY, Edward St. John. 741.9'73
The broken spoke / Edward Gorey. New York : Dodd, Mead, c1976. [30] leaves of plates : chiefly ill. ; 14 x 20 cm. [NC1879.G67A43] 76-13327 ISBN 0-396-07375-1 : 6.95
1. Gorey, Edward St. John. 2. Bicycles and tricycles in art. I. Title. BIP

GOREY, Edward St. John. 741.9'73
Leaves from a mislaid album. [1st ed.] New York, Gotham Book Mart, 1972. [17] plates (in portfolio) 18 cm. Title from portfolio. Issued in an envelope. [NC975.5.G6A52] 72-192457
I. Title.

Gorham Manufacturing Company.

RAINWATER, Dorothy T., comp. 739.2'3'773
Sterling silver holloware: tea and coffee service, pitchers and ewers, bookmarks, ash trays, candelabra, salts and peppers, desk sets and dressing sets, berry bowls, napkin rings, cups, tea balls and bells, trays, flasks, match safes. Edited, with an historical introd. by Dorothy T. Rainwater. [1st ed. Princeton, N.J., Pyne Press; Distributed by Scribner, New York, 1973] 1 v. (various pagings) illus. 29 cm. (American historical catalog collection) Reprint of three catalogs: Gorham Manufacturing Company, 1888 and Gorham Martele, 1900, published in New York; Unger Brothers, 1904, published in Newark, N.J. Bibliography: p. 16. [NK7198.G76R34 1973] 72-95726 ISBN 0-87861-040-5 6.95
1. Gorham Manufacturing Company. 2. Unger Brothers. 3. Silverware, American—Catalogs. I. Gorham Manufacturing Company. II. Unger Brothers. III. Title. IV. Series.

Gorky, Arshile, 1904-1948.

ACQUISITION 759.13'074'01471
priorities : aspects of postwar painting in America, including Arshile Gorky, works 1944-1948 : [exhibition] the Solomon R. Guggenheim Museum, New York. New York : Solomon R. Guggenheim Foundation, 1976. 119 p. : ill. (some col.) ; 28 cm. "Exhibition 76/3." [ND212.5.A25A25] 76-29096 ISBN 0-89207-005-6
1. Gorky, Arshile, 1904-1948. 2. Painting, American—Exhibitions. 3. Painting, Abstract—United States—Exhibitions. 4. Painting, Modern—20th century—United States—Exhibitions. I. Solomon R. Guggenheim Museum, New York. II. Title: Aspects of postwar painting in America. III. Title: Arshile Gorky, works 1944-1948.

GORKY, Arshile, 1904-1948. 759.13
Arshile Gorky. Text by Julien Levy. New York, H. N. Abrams [1966] 235 p. 208 illus. (part col.), facsim., ports. (part col.) 28 x 30 cm. Bibliography: p. 234-235. [ND237.G613L4] 66-18827
I. Levy, Julien.

GORKY, Arshile, 1904-1948. 741.9'73
Drawings. New York, Walker [1970] [4] p., 22 plates (part col.) 29 cm. [NC139.G64A44 1970] 73-101627 6.95

GORKY, Arshile, 1904-1948. 741.9'73
Gorky: drawings [by] Jim M. Jordan. New York, M. Knoedler [1969] 62 p. illus. (part col.), ports. 22 cm. Catalog of an exhibition at the M. Knoedler & Co., inc., New York, Nov. 25-Dec. 27, 1969. Includes bibliographical references. [NC139.G64J6] 73-109179
I. Jordan, Jim M. II. Knoedler (M.) and Company, inc. III. Title.

GORKY, Arshile, 1904-1948. 759.13
Murals without walls : Arshile Gorky's aviation murals rediscovered / Ruth Bowman, guest curator. Newark, N.J. : Newark Museum, 1978. 96 p. : ill. (some col.) ; 27 cm. "Exhibition at the Newark Museum, November 15, 1978-March 11, 1979; the American Federation of Arts tour, July 1979-December 1980." Bibliography: p. 93-95. [ND237.G613A4 1978] 78-13898 ISBN 0-932828-01-9 : 7.95
1. Gorky, Arshile, 1904-1948—Exhibitions. 2. Newark Airport. 3. Mural painting and decoration—20th century—New Jersey—Newark—Exhibitions. 4. Aeronautics in art—Exhibitions. I. Bowman, Ruth. II. Newark Museum Association, Newark, N.J. III. American Federation of Arts. IV. Title. BIP

REIFF, Robert F., 1918- 759.13
A stylistic analysis of Arshile Gorky's art from 1943-1948 / Robert F. Reiff. New York : Garland Pub., 1977. xi, 372 p. : ill. ; 21 cm. (Outstanding dissertations in the fine arts) Reprint of the author's thesis, Columbia University, 1961. Bibliography: p. 266-277. [ND237.G613R43] 76-23679 ISBN 0-8240-2719-1 lib.bdg. : 37.50
1. Gorky, Arshile, 1904-1948. 2. Composition (Art) 3. Influence (Literary, artistic, etc.) I. Title. II. Series. BIP

ROSENBERG, Harold 759.13
Arshile Gorky: the man, the time, the idea. New York, Grove [1963, c.1962] 144p. illus. 21cm. (E-365) 2.95 pap.,
1. Gorky, Arshile, 1904-1948. I. Title.

ROSENBERG, Harold. 759.13
Arshile Gorky: the man, the time, the idea. New York, Horizon Press [1962] 144 p. illus. 22 cm. [ND237.G613R6] 62-11237
1. Gorky, Arshile, 1904-1946.

SCHWABACHER, Ethel. 759.13
Arshile Gorky. With a pref. by Lloyd Goodrich, and an introd. by Meyer Schapiro. New York, Published for the whitney Museum of American Art by Macmillan, 1957. 159p. illus., col. plates. 29cm. Bibliography: p. 153-155. [ND237G613S36] [ND237G613S36] 927.5 57-12946 57-12946
1. Gorky, Arshile, 1904-1948. I. Title.

SEITZ, William Chapin 759.9566
Arshile Gorky: paintings, drawings, studies. Foreword by Julien Levy. Mus. of Modern Art; dist. Doubleday, Garden City, N. Y. [1963,c.1962] 56p. illus. (pt. col.) ports. 24cm. Exhibitions: the Mus. of Modern Art, New York, Dec. 17, 1962;the Washington Gallery of Modern Art, March 12, 1962. Bibl. 62-22083 7.50 pap.,
1. Gorky, Arshile, 1904-1948. I. New York. Museum of Modern Art. II. Title.

SEITZ, William Chapin. 759.13
Arshile Gorky: paintings, drawings, studies, by William C. Seitz. With a foreword by Julien Levy. The Museum of Modern Art in collaboration with the Washington Gallery of Modern Art. Reprint ed. [New York] Published for the Museum of Modern Art by Arno Press, 1972 [c1962] 56 p. illus. 25 cm. Bibliography: p. 52. [ND237.G613S4 1972] 75-169313 ISBN 0-405-01571-2 11.00
1. Gorky, Arshile, 1904-1948. I. New York (City). Museum of Modern Art. II. Washington, D.C. Gallery of Modern Art.

Gorman, Rudolph Carl, 1932—

MONTHAN, Doris Born, 1924- 769'.92'4 B
R. C. Gorman : the lithographs / by Doris Monthan ; with a foreword by Jules Heller. 1st ed. Flagstaff [Ariz.] : Northland Press, c1978. xix, 170 p., [1] leaf of plates : ill. (some col.) ; 32 cm. Includes bibliographies and index. [NE2312.G67M67] 78-58469 ISBN 0-87358-179-2 : 35.00
1. Gorman, Rudolph Carl, 1932- 2. Lithographers—United States—Biography. 3. Navaho Indians—Biography. I. Gorman, Rudolph Carl, 1932- BIP

Gorse, France.

GORSE, France. 730'.92'4
Sculptor France Gorse [by] John A. Arnez [and] Rudy Vecerin. New York, Studia Slovenica, 1971. xvi, 72 p. illus. 24 cm. (Studia Slovenica 8) [NB953.G6A89] 73-156911 10.00
1. Gorse, France. I. Arnez, John A. II. Vecerin, Rudy. III. Title. IV. Series.

Goss China Company Ltd.

GALPIN, John. 738.2'7
A handbook of Goss china. Portsmouth, J. Galpin (18 Lodge Ave., East Cosham), 1972. [2], 82 p. illus. 19 cm. Cover title: Goss china. [NK4210.G58G36] 73-168256 ISBN 0-9502548-0-0 £1.10
1. Goss China Company Ltd. 2. Porcelain, English. I. Title. II. Title: Goss china. BIP

REES, Diana. 738.2'7
A pictorial encyclopaedia of Goss china, by Diana Rees and Marjorie G. Cawley. Newport, Ceramic Book Company, 1970. viii, 29 p., 65 plates. illus. (1 col.), coat of arms, facsim., port. 30 cm. [NK4210.G58R42] 74-164439 ISBN 0-900272-01-5 £4.00
1. Goss China Company Ltd. 2. Pottery, English. 3. Porcelain, English. I. Cawley, Marjorie G., joint author. II. Title.

Goss, William Henry.

WARD, Roland. 738.2'7
The price guide to the models of W. H. Goss / by Roland Ward. Woodbridge [Eng.] : Antique Collectors' Club, c1975. 189 p., 4 leaves of plates : chiefly ill. (some col.) ; 28 cm. Includes index. [NK4210.G583W37] 76-358880 ISBN 0-902028-20-0 : £6.95
1. Goss, William Henry. 2. Goss China Company Ltd. 3. Miniature heraldic porcelain—Catalogs. I. Title.

Gothic revival (Architecture)

*CLARK, Kenneth, Sir 1903- 724.3
The Gothic revival; an essay in the history of taste [Baltimore] Penguin [1964, c.1962] 218p. illus. 18cm. (Pelican bk. A687) Bibl. 1.45 pap.,
I. Title. BIP

CLARK, Kenneth McKenzie, Baron Clark, 1903- 720'.942
The Gothic revival; an essay in the history of taste [by] Kenneth Clark. New York, Humanities Press, 1970 [c1962] xii, 236 p. illus. 23 cm. "First published 1928." Includes bibliographical references. [NA610.C5 1970] 73-14966 ISBN 0-391-00027-6 7.50
1. Gothic revival (Architecture) I. Title.

GARRIGAN, Kristine Ottesen, 1939- 720'.9
Ruskin on architecture: his thought and influence. [Madison] University of Wisconsin Press [1973] xv, 220 p. illus. 25 cm. Includes bibliographical references. [NA610.G37] 73-2045 ISBN 0-299-06460-3 20.00
1. Ruskin, John, 1819-1900—Influence. 2. Gothic revival (Architecture) 3. Architecture, Victorian. I. Title.

HERSEY, George L. 724'.3
High Victorian Gothic; a study in associationism [by] George L. Hersey. Baltimore, Johns Hopkins University Press [1972] xx, 234 p. illus. 19 x 26 cm. (The Johns Hopkins studies in nineteenth-century architecture) Bibliography: p. [212]-224. [NA610.H47] 71-172880 ISBN 0-8018-1285-2 15.00
1. Gothic revival (Architecture) I. Title. II. Series. BIP

STANTON, Phoebe B. 726'.5'0973
The Gothic revival & American church architecture; an episode in taste, 1840-1856 [by] Phoebe B. Stanton. Baltimore, Johns Hopkins Press [1968] xxiv, 350 p. illus. 24 cm. (The Johns Hopkins studies in nineteenth-century architecture) Bibliographical footnotes. [NA5210.S7] 68-16273 12.95
1. Gothic revival (Architecture) 2. Church architecture—United States. I. Title. II. Series. BIP

Gothic revival (Architecture)—England.

DAVIS, Terence, 1924- 720'.942
The Gothick taste / Terence Davis. 1st American ed. Rutherford, [N.J.] : Fairleigh Dickinson University Press, 1975. 168 p. : ill. (some col.) ; 31 cm. Includes index. Bibliography: p. 165-166. [NA966.D38 1975] 75-10733 ISBN 0-8386-1746-8 : 30.00
1. Gothic revival (Architecture)—England. 2. Architecture, Modern—17th-18th centuries—England. I. Title. BIP

Gothic revival (Architecture) - History.

GERMANN, Georg. 724.'3'094
Gothic revival in Europe and Britain : Sources, influences and ideas / Georg Germann ; Translated by Gerald Onn. Cambridge, MA : M.I.T. Press, 1978. 263p. : ill. ; 27 cm. Includes bibliographical references. [NA610.G4713] ISBN 0-262-57050-5 pbk. : 12.95
1. Gothic revival (Architecture) — History. I. Title.
L.C. card no. for 1973 MIT Press ed. : 72-9999. BIP

GERMANN, Georg. 724'.3'094
Gothic revival in Europe and Britain: sources, influences, and ideas. Translated by Gerald Onn. [1st American ed.] Cambridge, Mass., MIT Press [1973, c1972] 263 p. illus. 28 cm. Includes bibliographical references. [NA610.G4713 1973] 72-9999 ISBN 0-262-07059-6 25.00
1. Gothic revival (Architecture)—History. I. Title.

Gothic revival (Architecture)—United States.

ANDREWS, Wayne. 720'.973
American gothic : its origins, its trials, its triumphs / text and photos. by Wayne Andrews. 1st ed. New York : Random

House, c1975. 154 p. : ill. ; 29 cm. Includes index. Bibliography: p. 148-149. [NA710.A53 1975] 75-10250 ISBN 0-394-49760-0
1. Gothic revival (Architecture)—United States. 2. Architecture, Modern—19th century—United States. I. Title.

LOTH, Calder, 1943- 720'.973
The only proper style : Gothic architecture in America / Calder Loth, Julius Trousdale Sadler, Jr. 1st ed. Boston : New York Graphic Society, c1975. p. cm. Includes index. Bibliography: p. [NA705.L67 1975] 75-9094 ISBN 0-8212-0693-1 : 19.95
1. Gothic revival (Architecture)—United States. 2. Architecture—United States. I. Sadler, Julius Trousdale, joint author. II. Title. BIP

Gotsch, Friedrich Karl, 1900—

FLEMING, Hanns Theodor. 741.973
F. K. Gotsch, eine Monographie. Geleitwort von Alfred Hentzen. Hamburg, H. Christian, 1963. 135 p. illus., plates (part col.) port 25 cm. Bibliography: p. 128-133. [ND588.G635F5] 66-48336
1. Gotsch, Friedrich Karl, 1900- I. Title.

GOTSCH, Friedrich Karl, 709'.2'4
1900-
F. K. Gotsch : Holzschnitte, Radierungen, Lithographien, Monotypien : zum 75. Geburtstag : [Ausstellung] 26. November 1975 bis 18. Januar 1976, Altonaer Museum in Hamburg, Norddeutsches Landesmuseum / [Katalog und Einfuhrung, Christine Knupp]. [Hamburg : Altonaer Museum, 1975] [56] p. : ill. ; 24 cm. Bibliography: p. [9] [NE654.G68K58] 76-454139
1. Gotsch, Friedrich Karl, 1900- I. Knupp, Christine. II. Altonaer Museum in Hamburg.

Gottlieb, Adolph, 1903-

GOTTLIEB, Adolph, 1903- 759.13
Adolph Gottlieb, by Robert Doty and Diane Waldman. [New York] Whitney Museum of American Art [1968] 121 p. illus. (part col.), port. 24 cm. Catalog of an exhibition held Feb. 14 to March 31, 1968, at the Whitney Museum of American Art, and other museums. Bibliography: p. 116-121. [ND237.G614D6] 68-2316
I. Doty, Robert M. II. Waldman, Diane. III. Whitney Museum of American Art, New York.

GOTTLIEB, Adolph, 1903- 759.13
Adolph Gottlieb, by Robert Doty and Diane Waldman. New York, Published for the Whitney Museum of American Art and the Solomon R. Guggenheim Museum by F. A. Praeger [1968] 121 p. illus. (part col.), port. 25 cm. Catalog of an exhibition held Feb. 14 to Mar. 31, 1968, at the Whitney Museum of American Art, and other museums. Bibliography: p. 116-121. [ND237.G614D6 1968] 68-3250
I. Doty, Robert M. II. Waldman, Diane. III. Whitney Museum of American Art, New York. IV. Solomon R. Guggenheim Museum, New York.

GOTTLIEB, Adolph, 1903- 759.13
Adolph Gottlieb, by Robert Doty and Diane Waldman. New York, Published for the Whitney Museum of American Art and the Solomon R. Guggenheim Museum by F. A. Praeger [1968] 121 p. illus. (part col.), port. 25 cm. Catalog of an exhibition held Feb. 14 to Mar. 31, 1968, at the Whitney Museum of American Art, and other museums. Bibliography: p. 116-121. [ND237.G614D6 1968] 68-19542
I. Doty, Robert M. II. Waldman, Diane. III. Whitney Museum of American Art, New York. IV. Solomon R. Guggenheim Museum, New York.

GOTTLIEB, Adolph, 1903- 730'.924
Gottlieb: sculpture. [College Park, Md., University Press, 1970] [9], [11] p. (incl. cover. chiefly illus.) 22 cm. Cover title. "Marca-Relli: collage" ([11] p. (2d group)) has special title. Label mounted on p. [3] (1st group): Supplied by Worldwide Books, Boston. Contents.Contents.—Catalogue of an exhibition held at the University of Maryland Art Gallery, Oct. 15-Nov. 22, 1970. [NB237.G65M3] 75-635694
I. Marca-Relli, Conrad, 1913- II. Maryland. University. Art Gallery. III. Title. IV. Title: Marca-Relli: collage.

WALKER Art Center, 759.13
Minneapolis.
Adolph Gottlieb. Text by Martin Friedman. An exhibition org. by the Walker Art Center, April 28 through June 9, 1963, and shown in the Amer. sect. of the VII Bienal de Sao Paulo, September through December 1963 [Minneapolis, Author. 1710 Lyndale; 1963] unpaged. illus. 28cm. Bibl. 63-4849 price unreported
1. Gottlieb, Adolph, 1903- I. Friedman, Martin L. II. Title.

Gould, John, 1804-1881.

SAUER, Gordon C. 769'.92
John Gould bird print reproductions / Gordon C. Sauer. 1st ed. Kansas City, Mo. : Distributed by Richland Enterprises, 1977. v, 76 p. : ill. ; 24 cm. [QL674.S23] 77-367544
1. Gould, John, 1804-1881. 2. Birds—Pictorial works. I. Gould, John, 1804-1881. II. Title.

Gould, Mary Earle—Art collections.

GOULD, Mary Earle. 643
Early American wooden ware & other kitchen utensils. Rutland, Vt., C. E. Tuttle Co. [1962] xii, 243 p. illus. 24 cm. [NK9712.G68 1962] 69-13499 ISBN 0-8048-0153-3 9.35
1. Gould, Mary Earle—Art collections. 2. Treenware—United States. 3. Implements, utensils, etc.—United States. I. Title.

Goulet, Lorrie, 1925—

GOULET, Lorrie, 1925- 730'.92'4
Recent sculpture by Lorrie Goulet. New York, Kennedy Galleries [1973] [24] p. illus. 28 cm. Catalog of an exhibition held at the Kennedy Galleries, Oct. 4-20, 1973. [NB237.G67K46] 73-179271
1. Goulet, Lorrie, 1925- I. Kennedy Galleries, inc., New York. II. Title.

Goundie, George, 1913—

GEORGE Goundie, 709'.73'074017595
sculpture—Joseph Friebert, paintings, professors emeritus, Department of Art : two retrospective exhibitions : with an exhibition of the work of their selected former students, University of Wisconsin-Milwaukee, Fine Arts Galleries, 7 March through 1 April 1977. [Milwaukee] : The Galleries, c1977. [28] p. : ill. ; 16 x 23 cm. [N6512.G36] 77-371307
1. Goundie, George, 1913- 2. Friebert, Joseph, 1908- 3. Art, American—Exhibitions. 4. Art, Modern—20th century—United States—Exhibitions. I. Goundie, George, 1913- II. Friebert, Joseph, 1908- III. Wisconsin. University-Milwaukee. School of Fine Arts. Galleries.

Gourd craft.

MORDECAI, Carolyn. 745.5
Gourd craft : growing, designing, and decorating ornamental and hardshelled gourds / by Carolyn Mordecai. New York : Crown Publishers, c1978. x, 212 p., [4] leaves of plates : ill. ; 26 cm. Includes index. Bibliography: p. 204-206. [TT880.M65 1978] 77-25870 ISBN 0-517-52830-4 : 12.95 ISBN 0-517-52831-2 pbk. : 6.95
1. Gourd craft. 2. Gourds. I. Title. BIP

Gourds—Peru.

MENZIE, Eleanor. 736
Hand carved and decorated gourds of Peru / by Eleanor Menzie ; illustrated with photos. by Sidney Karneke ... [et al.]. Santa Monica, Calif. : Karneke Publishers, c1976. 73 p. : ill. ; 24 cm. Bibliography: p. 71. [NK6075.M46] 76-383555 6.95
1. Gourds—Peru. 2. Decoration and ornament—Peru. 3. Carving (Art industries)—Peru. I. Karneke, Sidney. II. Title.
Publisher's Address : P.O. Box 3371, Santa Monica, Ca.9040 BIP

Goya y Lucientes, Francisco Jose de, 1746-1828.

ABBRUZZESE, Margherita. 759.6
Goya. [Translated from the Italian by Caroline Beamish]. [1st American ed.] New York, Grosset & Dunlap [1967] 39, [80] p. illus. (part col.) 18 cm. (The New Grosset art library, 6) On cover: Goya; the life and work of the artist. Bibliography: p. 31. [ND813.G7A62 1967] 67-25790
1. Goya y Lucientes, Francisco Jose de, 1746-1828.

CHABRUN, Jean Francois, 759.6 (B)
1920-
Goya. [Translated from the French by J. Maxwell Brownjohn] New York, Tudor Pub. Co. [c1965] 278 p. illus. (part col.) ports. (part col.) 22 cm. Bibliography: p. 273. [[ND813]] 66-8622
1. Goya y Lucientes, Francisco Jose de, 1746-1828. I. Title.

DESCARGUES, Pierre. 759.6 B
Goya / Pierre Descargues. New York : Putnam, [1975] p. cm. Translated from the French. Includes index. Bibliography: p. [ND813.G7D4213] 75-6584
1. Goya y Lucientes, Francisco Jose de, 1746-1828.

DIEHL, Gaston. 759.6
Goya. [Translated from the French by Anne Ross] New York, Crown Publishers [1966] 45 p. illus. (part col.) 19 cm. (Basic art library) [ND813.G7D513] 66-26179
1. Goya y Lucientes, Francisco Jose de, 1746-1828.

GASSIER, Pierre comp. 741.092
The drawings of Goya: the sketches, studies and individual drawings New York, Harper & Row [1975] 581 p. 407 plate (incl. 9 col) 30 cm. Bibliography: p. 573-578. [NC287] 75-6337 ISBN 0-06-011469-X 60.00.
1. Goya y Lucientes, Francisco Jose de, 1746-1828 II. Title.

GASSIER, Pierre. 927.5
Goya; [biographical and critical study. Translated by James Emmons. New York] Skira [1955?] 139 p. 57 mounted col. illus. 19 cm. (The Taste of our time, v. 13) Bibliography: p. 127-129. [ND813.G7G324] 759.6 55-10594
1. Goya y Lucientes, Francisco Jose de, 1746-1828.

GERSON, Noel Bertram, 1914- 759.6
The double lives of Francisco de Goya, by Samuel Edwards. New York, Grosset & Dunlap [1973] 248 p. illus. 22 cm. Bibliography: p. 243. [ND813.G7G47] 73-6901 ISBN 0-448-01377-0 7.95
1. Goya y Lucientes, Francisco Jose de, 1746-1828. I. Title.

GLENDINNING, Oliver Nigel 759.6
Valentine.
Goya and his critics / Nigel Glendinning. New Haven : Yale University Press, 1977. xii, 340 p. : ill. ; 26 cm. Includes bibliographical references and index. [ND813.G7G53] 76-49693 ISBN 0-300-02011-2 : 30.00
1. Goya y Lucientes, Francisco Jose de, 1746-1828. I. Title. BIP

GOYA, a biography. 759.6
With drawings, etchings, and paintings by Goya. New York, Oxford University Press, 1956. 68p. illus. 27cm. (Oxford books for boys and girls) [ND813.G7R5] 927.5 56-10458
1. Goya y Lucientes, Francisco Jose de, 1746-1828. I. Ripley, Elizabeth.

GOYA y Lucientes, Francisco 759.6
Jose de 1746-1826
Goya. Text by Jose Gudiol [Tr. from Spanish by Priscilla Muller] New York, Abrams [1965] 168p. illus. (pt. col.) ports. (pt. col.) 33cm. (Lib. of great painters) Bibl. [ND813.G7G773] 64-10760 15.00
I. Goya y Lucientes, Francisco Jose de, II. Title.

GOYA y Lucientes, 769'.924
Francisco Jose de, 1746-1828.
The disparates; or, The proverbios. New York, Dover Publications [1969] 2 p., 26 plates. 28 x 35 cm. Reprint of the 1864 ed., which was published under title Los proverbios, with a new introd. by P. Hofer and 8 additional reproductions. Captions in English and Spanish. [NE702.G7A45 1969] 68-28063 2.75
I. Hofer, Philip, 1898- II. Title. BIP

GOYA y Lucientes, 741.9'46
Francisco Jose de, 1746-1828.
Drawings; the complete albums. [Reconstruction] by Pierre Gassier. [Translated by James Emmons and Robert Allen] New York, Praeger [1973] 656 p. illus. 31 cm. Translation of Les dessins de Goya: les albums. Bibliography: p. 649-654. [NC287.G65G37] 72-81582 42.50
1. Goya y Lucientes, Francisco Jose de, 1746-1828. I. Gassier, Pierre. II. Title.

GOYA y Lucientes, Francisco 759.6
Jose de, 1746-1828
Goya [by] Dino Formaggio. New York, Yoseloff [1961, c.1960] 12p. plates (part col.) 32cm. (Gallery of great masters) 61-13931 5.95 bds.,
I. Formaggio, Dino. II. Title.

GOYA y Lucientes, 759.46
Francisco Jose' de, 1746-1828
Goya, by M. Ledivelec. New York, Crown [1965] 36p. (chiefly illus. pt. col.) 18cm. (Little bks. on great artists) [ND813.G7L48] 65-5029 .69 bds.,
I. Ledivelec, Madeleine. II. Title.

GOYA y Lucientes, Francisco 759.6
Jose de, 1746-1828.
Goya, by Keizo Kanki. Tokyo, Palo Alto, Calif., Kodansha International, [1969] 154 p. illus. (part col.) 19 cm. (This beautiful world, v. 10) Bibliography: p. 153-154. [ND813.G7K28] 78-82652 1.95
I. Kanki, Keizo. II. Title.

GOYA y Lucientes, 709.46
Francisco Jose de, 1746-1828
Goya, his complete etchings, acquatints, and lithographs. Text by Enrique Lafuente Ferrari. [Tr. from Spanish by Raymond Rudorff] New York, Abrams [1962] xxxiv, p., 288p. (chiefly illus.) 34cm. 62-11623 17.50
I. Lafuente Ferrari, Enrique. II. Title.

GOYA y Lucientes, Francisco 759.6
Jose de, 1746-1828.
Goya. Introd. by Enrique Lafuente Ferrari. New York, New Amer. Lib., by arr. with UNESCO [1966] 24p. 30 col. plates. 17cm. (Mentor-Unesco art bk.) MQ696. Bibl. [ND813.G7L366] 66-31775 .95 pap.,
I. Lafuenta Ferrari, Enrique. II. United Nations Educational, Scientific and Cultural Organization. III. Title.

GOYA y Lucientes, 741.9'46
Francisco Jose de, 1746-1828.
Goya: 67 drawings Introd. and comments by A. Hyatt Mayor. [New York] Metropolitan Museum of Art; distributed by New York Graphic Society [1974] p. [NC287.G65M39] 74-1474 ISBN 0-87099-091-8
1. Goya y Lucientes, Francisco Jose de, 1746-1828. I. Mayor, Alpheus Hyatt, 1901- II. Title.

GOYA y Lucientes, Francisco 759.6
Jose de, 1746-1828.
Goya (Francisco Jose de Goya y Lucientes) Text by Frederick S. Wight. New York, H. N. Abrams [1969] 39 p. illus. (part col.) 33 cm. (Great art of the ages) [ND813.G7W535 1969] 72-192322
I. Wight, Frederick Stallknecht, 1902-

GOYA y Lucientes, Francisco 759.6
Jose de, 1746-1828.
Goya (Francisco Jose de Goya y Lucientes) Text by Frederick S. Wight. New York, H. N. Abrams [1970] 24 p. illus. (part col.) 33 cm. (The Library of great painters. Portfolio ed.) [ND813.G7W535 1970] 69-14748
I. Wight, Frederick Stallknecht, 1902-

GOYA y Lucientes, 709.46
Francisco Jose de, 1746-1828.
Goya, his complete etchings, aquatints, and lithographs. Text by Enrique Lafuente Ferrari. [Translated from the Spanish by Raymond Rudorff.] New York, Abrams [1962] xxxiv, p., 288 p. of plates. 34 cm. [NE702.G7L253] 62-11623
I. Lafuente Ferrari, Enrique.

HARRIS, Enriqueta. 759.6
Goya. [New York] Phaidon; [distributed in the U.S. by F. A. Praeger, 1969] 92 p.

illus., 50 col. plates. 31 cm. Bibliography: p. 91. [ND813.G7H3] 69-12788 5.95
1. Goya y Lucientes, Francisco Jose de, 1746-1828.

HOLLAND, Vyvyan Beresford, 1886- 927.5
Goya, a pictorial biography. New York, Viking Press [1962, c1961] 144 p. illus., 3 col. plates, facsim. 22 cm. (A Studio book) [ND813.G7H6] 61-15436
1. Goya y Lucientes, Francisco Jose de, 1746-1828.

HORWITZ, Sylvia L. 759.6 B
Francisco Goya, painter of kings and demons / by Sylvia L. Horwitz ; pref. by Elizabeth Borton de Trevino. 1st ed. New York : Harper & Row, [1974] xii, 194 p. : ill. ; 22 cm. Includes index. Bibliography: p. 189-191. [ND813.G7H64 1974] 74-2613 ISBN 0-06-022594-7 : 5.95. ISBN 0-06-022595-5 lib.bdg. : 5.79
1. Goya y Lucientes, Francisco Jose de, 1746-1828. I. Title.

KLINGENDER, Francis Donald. 709'.24
Goya in the democratic tradition [by] F. D. Klingender. Introd. by Herbert Read. New York, Schocken [1968] xvi, 235p. 122 illus. 20cm. Bibl. footnotes [ND813.G7K6 1968] 68-16658 7.50; 2.95 pap.,
1. Goya y Lucientes, Francisco Jose de, 1746-1828. I. Title.

LEWIS, Dominic Bevan Wyndham, 1894-1969. 759.6 B
The world of Goya. [1st American ed.] New York, C. N. Potter [1968] 256 p. illus. (part col.), col. plates, ports. (part col.) 26 cm. Bibliography: p. 249. [ND813.G7L55 1968b] 67-20542 10.00
1. Goya y Lucientes, Francisco Jose de, 1746-1828. I. Title.

LICHT, Fred, 1928- comp. 759.6
Goya in perspective. Englewood Cliffs, N.J., Prentice-Hall [1973] x, 180 p. illus. 22 cm. (The Artists in perspective series) (A Spectrum book) [ND813.G7L562 1973] 73-6932 ISBN 0-13-361964-8 6.95
1. Goya y Lucientes, Francisco Jose de, 1746-1828. I. Title.
Contents Omitted. Pbk. 2.45; ISBN 0-13-361956-7.

MALRAUX, Andre, 1901- v. 12
Saturn, an essay on Goya. [Translated by C. W. Chilton] New York, Phaidon Publishers; distributed by Garden City Books [1957] 184p. illus. (part mounted col.) 32cm. [NE702.G7M] A58
1. Goya y Lucientes, Francisco Jose de, 1746-1828. I. Title.

SALAS, Xavier de 759.6
Francisco Jose de Goya y Lucientes. New York, Barnes & Noble [c.1961] 89p. illus. (pt. col.) ports. 18cm. (Barnes & Noble art ser.) 62-52816 .75 pap.,
1. Goya y Lucientes, Francisco Jose de, 1746-1828. I. Title.

SANCHEZ CANTON, Francisco Javier, 1891- 759.6
Goya [1st Eng. lang. ed. tr. by Henry Mins] NewYork, Reynal [dist. Morrow, 1964] 95p. 137 illus. (pt. mounted, pt. col.) 56 col. plates. 41cm. (Grand monographs of art) Plates are reproductions of the 14 murals in Goya's country house Quinto del Sordo. Bibl. 64-57495 100.00
1. Goya y Lucientes, Francisco Jose de, 1746-1828. I. Title.

SAYRE, Eleanor. 760'.092'4
The changing image : prints by Francisco Goya : [exhibition, Museum of Fine Arts, Boston, October 24-December 29, 1974, The National Gallery of Canada, Ottawa, January 24-March 14, 1975] / Eleanor A. Sayre and the Department of Prints and Drawings. Boston : Museum of Fine Arts, 1974, [i.e.1975] xii, 325 p. : ill. ; 28 cm. Errata slip inserted. Includes bibliographical references. [NE2062.5.G6S29] 74-19964 ISBN 0-87846-085-3 : 30.00
1. Goya y Lucientes, Francisco Jose de, 1746-1828. I. Goya y Lucientes, Francisco Jose de, 1746-1828. II. Boston. Museum of Fine Arts. Dept. of Prints and Drawings. III. Boston. Museum of Fine Arts. IV. Ottawa. National Gallery of Canada. V. Title. BIP

SAYRE, Eleanor. 769'.92'4
Late Caprichos of Goya : fragments from a series : commentary & notes / by Eleanor Sayre. New York : Walker : in association with the Dept. of Printing and Graphic arts, Harvard College Library [Cambridge, Mass.], 1971. 46, [33] p. : ill. ; 30 cm. & portfolio ([6] leaves of plates : ill.) "Philip Hofer books." The portfolio contains 6 etchings printed from the original copper plates. Issued in a case. Bibliography: p. 45-46. [NE2062.5.G6S3] 75-308294
1. Goya y Lucientes, Francisco Jose de, 1746-1828. Caprichos. I. Goya y Lucientes, Francisco Jose de, 1746-1828. Caprichos. II. Goya y Lucientes, Francisco Jose de, 1746-1828. Caprichos. III. Title.

SCHICKEL, Richard. 760'.0924
The world of Goya, 1746-1828, New York, Time-Life Books [1968] 192 p. illus. (part fold., part col.), map, ports. (part col.) 32 cm. (Time-Life library of art) Bibliography: p. 187. [ND813.G7S35] 68-56432
1. Goya y Lucientes, Francisco Jose de, 1746-1828. I. Time-Life Books. II. Title. III. Title: ..by Richard Schickel and the editors of Time-Life Books BIP

STEADMAN, David W. 769.92'4
The graphic art of Francisco Goya : [exhibition] from the Norton Simon Foundation, the Norton Simon, Inc. Museum of Art and the Pomona College collections / David W. Steadman. [Claremont, Calif.] : Galleries of the Claremont Colleges, Pomona College, Scripps College, c1975. 65 p. : ill. ; 24 cm. Includes bibliographical references. [NE2062.5.G6S83] 74-33051
1. Goya y Lucientes, Francisco Jose de, 1746-1828. I. Goya y Lucientes, Francisco Jose de, 1746-1828. II. Claremont College, Claremont, Calif. Galleries. III. Title.

STEARNS, Monroe 759.6
Goya and his times. New York, Watts [1966] 276 p. illus. 25 cm. [Immortals of mankind] Immortals of mankind. Immortals of mankind. Bibl. [ND813.G7S67] 66-12123 5.95 4.46 lib. ed.,
1. Goya y Lucientes, Francisco Jose de, 1746-1828. I. Title.

THOMAS, Hugh, 1931- 759.6
Goya: The Third of May 1808. [New York, Viking Press, 1973, c1972] 112 p. illus. 23 cm. (Art in context) Bibliography: p. [103]-104. [ND813.G7T47] 72-185279 ISBN 0-670-34712-4 7.50
1. Goya y Lucientes, Francisco Jose de, 1746-1828. I. Title.

TRAPIER, Elizabeth Du Gue, 1893- 759.6
Goya and his sitters; a study of his style as a portraitist. New York, Printed by order of the Trustees, Hispanic Soc. of Amer. *c.]1964. 66p. illus., geneal. tables, ports. 26cm. (Hispanic notes & monographs; peninsular ser.) 64-4672 10.00
1. Goya y Lucientes, Francisco Jose de, 1746-1828. I. Title. BIP

UNITED States. National Gallery of Art. 759.6
Goya in the Prado : [exhibition]. Washington : National Gallery of Art, 1976. [23] p. : ill. ; 22 x 23 cm. Bibliography: p. [23] [ND813.G7U54 1976] 76-371311
1. Goya y Lucientes, Francisco, Jose de, 1746-1828. I. Goya y Lucientes, Francisco Jose de, 1746-1828. II. Madrid. Museo Nacional de Pintura y Escultura. III. Title.

VALLENTIN, Antonina, 1893-1957. 759.6 B
This I saw; the life and times of Goya. Translated from the French by Katherine Woods. Westport, Conn., Greenwood Press [1971, c1949] 371 p. illus. 23 cm. Translation of Goya. Bibliography: p. 361-363. [ND813.G7V2913 1971] 78-152612 ISBN 0-8371-6047-2
1. Goya y Lucientes, Francisco Jose de, 1746-1828. I. Title. BIP

VIRCH, Claus, 1927- 709.46
Francisco Goya. New York, McGraw [c1967] 48p. illus., port., 20 col. slides (film, 2 x 2 in.) in pockets. 29cm. (Color slide program of the great masters) [ND813.G7V57] 67-29890 7.95 bds.,
1. Goya y Lucientes, Francisco Jose de, 1746-1828. 2. Lantern slides—Catalogs. I. Title. II. Series. BIP

VIRGINIA Museum of Fine Arts, Richmond. 769'.92'4
Francisco Goya: portraits in paintings, prints and drawings; an exhibition organized by the Virginia Museum, May 8 through June 11, 1972. [Richmond, 1972] 43 p. illus. 26 cm. Bibliography: p. 42. [N7113.G68V5] 72-80484
1. Goya y Lucientes, Francisco Jose de, 1746-1828. I. Title.

WILDENSTEIN and company, inc., new york. [927.5]
A loan exhibition of Goya, for the benefit of the Institute of Fine Arts, New York University, November 9-December 16, 1950 at Wildenstein New York. [New York, 1950] 51 p. illus. 29 cm. The exhibition has been organized by Vladimir Visson and David Wildenstein, with the collaboration of Ima N. Ebin." "On Goya's legend and life, by Jose Lopez-Rey": p.9-16. [ND813.G7W55] 759.6 50-58316
1. Goya y Lucientes, Francisco Jose de, 1745-1828. 2. Art, Spanish—Exhibitions. I. Title.

WILLIAMS, Gwyn A. 760'.092'4
Goya and the impossible revolution / Gwyn A. Williams. 1st American ed. New York : Pantheon Books, c1976. 194 p. : ill. ; 24 cm. Includes index. Bibliography: p. 185-186. [NE2062.5.G6W55 1976] 76-5945 ISBN 0-394-49304-4 : 12.95
1. Goya y Lucientes, Francisco Jose de, 1746-1828. I. Title. BIP

Goya y Lucientes, Francisco Jose, de, 1746-1828. Caprichos.

GOYA y Lucientes, Francisco Jose de, 1746-1828. 769'.924
Los caprichos, by Francisco Goya y Lucientes. With a new introd. by Philip Hofer. New York, Dover Publications [1969] 9 p. 87 plates (incl. port.) 24 cm. Captions in English and Spanish. [NE2195.G78C34] 69-14996 2.75
I. Hofer, Philip, 1898- II. Title. BIP

LOPEZ-REY, Jose. 767.2
Goya's Caprichos: beauty, reason & caricature. [Princeton] Princeton University Press, 1953. 2v. plates. 23cm. Contents.v. 1. Text.--v.2. Plates. Bibliography: v. 1. p. 215-220. [NE2195.G78C35] 52-13143
1. Goya y Lucientes, Francisco Jose, de, 1746-1828. Caprichos. I. Title. BIP

Goya y Lucientes, Francisco Jose de, 1746-1828—Catalogs.

GOYA y Lucientes, Francisco Jose de, 1746-1828. 759.6
Francisco Goya / [selected by] Eric Young. New York : St. Martin's Press, 1978. [8] p., 40 leaves of plates : 40 col. ill. ; 28 cm. [ND813.G7A4 1978a] 77-95304 ISBN 0-312-30319-X : 5.95
1. Goya y Lucientes, Francisco Jose de, 1746-1828—Catalogs. I. Young, Eric. II. Title.

Goya y Lucientes, Francisco Jose de, 1746-1828.

DESPARMET FITZ-GERALD, Xaviere. 759.6
goya. New York, Scribner, 1956. 44[1] p. 36col. plates. 38cm. (The Gallery of masterpieces) Bibliography: p. 0--[45] [ND813.G7D43] 57-539
1. Goya y Luctentes, Francisc0 Jose de. 1746-1828. I. Title.

Gozzoli, Benozzo, 1420-1497.

STOKES, Hugh, 1875-1932. 759.5
Benozzo Gozzoli / [by Hugh Stokes]. New York : AMS Press, [1976] p. cm. Reprint of the 1904 ed. published by G. Newnes, London; F. Warne, New York, in series: Newnes' art library. "List of Gozzoli's principal works: p. [ND623.G8S7 1976] 75-41264 ISBN 0-404-14612-0 : 16.00
1. Gozzoli, Benozzo, 1420-1497. I. Series: Newnes' art library. BIP

Graffiti.

DEKORNE, James B., 1936- 730'.9789
Aspen art in the New Mexico highlands; a photo essay, by James B. DeKorne. Santa Fe, Mueseum of New Mexico Press, 1970. 12, [43] p. 69 illus. 27 cm. Includes bibliographical references. [NK9712.D4] 71-127640
1. Graffiti. 2. Folk art—New Mexico. 3. Wood-carving—New Mexico. I. Title. BIP

PRITCHARD, Violet. 741.9'42
English medieval graffiti, by V. Pritchard. Cambridge, Cambridge U. P., 1967. xii, 196 p. front., illus., map, facsims. 25 1/2 cm. 70/- (B 67-22401) Bibliography: p. [184]-189. [CN960.P7] 66-11034
1. Graffiti. I. Title. BIP

Graffiti—California—Los Angeles.

†ROMOTSKY, Jerry. 745.6'197'0979494
Los Angeles barrio calligraphy / by Jerry Romotsky and Sally R. Romotsky. Los Angeles : Dawson's Book Shop, 1976. 78 p. : ill. ; 25 cm. (Los Angeles miscellany ; 6) "300 copies printed." Bibliography: p. 77-78. [GT3913.C22L677] 76-150103 ISBN 0-87093-170-9 : 15.00
1. Graffiti—California—Los Angeles. 2. Calligraphy—California—Los Angeles. 3. Mexican Americans—Los Angeles. I. Romotsky, Sally R., joint author. II. Title.

Graffito decoration.

CURRAN, C. P. 693.6
Dublin decorative plasterwork of the seventeenth and eighteenth centuries [by] C. P. Curran. [1st American ed.] New York, Transatlantic Arts, 1967. x, 124 p. illus. (part col.), plans. 26 cm. Bibliography: p. 113-115. [NK1440.C8 1967b] 68-439
1. Graffito decoration. 2. Decoration and ornament—Dublin. I. Title.

Graham, Anne, 1925—

GRAHAM, Anne, 1925- 741.9'94
Australian outlines : drawings / by Anne Graham ; introd. by Bruce Petty. Melbourne : Lansdowne, 1976. [115] p. : chiefly ill. ; 21 x 27 cm. [NC371.G7A58] 76-370346 ISBN 0-7018-0520-X
1. Graham, Anne, 1925- 2. Australia—Biography—Portraits. I. Title.

GREENAWAY, Ronald. 759.994
Anne Graham paintings; a critical evaluation. Melbourne, Aldine Press, 1969. 24 p. illus. (part col.) 21 cm. [ND1105.G67G7] 73-514582
1. Graham, Anne, 1925- I. Title.

Granada (City) Cathedral.

ROSENTHAL, Earl E., 726.6094682
The Cathedral of Granada; a study in the Spanish Renaissance. Princeton, N. J., Princeton Univ. Press [c.]1961. xiii, 235p. illus. 31cm. Bibl. 61-6908 20.00
1. Granada (City) Cathedral. I. Title.

Granaries.

RICKMAN, Geoffrey. 725'.35'0937
Roman granaries and store buildings. Cambridge [Eng.] University Press, 1971. xxiii, 349 p. illus., plans. 24 cm. Bibliography: p. 336-338. [NA8240.R5] 76-116843 ISBN 0-521-07724-9
1. Granaries. 2. Warehouses—Rome. I. Title. BIP

Grandee, Joe Ruiz, 1929—

SCHULTZ, Joy. 709'.24
The West still lives; a book based on the paintings and sculpture of Joe Ruiz Grandee. [Dallas, Printed by Heritage Press, 1970] iii, 54, [80] p. illus. (part col.), ports. (part col.) 32 cm. [N6537.G68S3] 72-12689
1. Grandee, Joe Ruiz, 1929- I. Title.

Grandville, Jean Ignace Isidore Gerard, called, 1803-1847.

GRANDVILLE, Jean Ignace 741.9'44
Isidore Gerard, called, 1803-1847.
Bizarreries and fantasies of Grandville; 266 illustrations from Un autre monde and Les animaux. Introd. and commentary by Stanley Appelbaum. New York, Dover Publications [1974] xix, 165 p. (chiefly illus.) 29 cm. Bibliography: p. xix. [NC1499.G66A85] 73-76962 ISBN 0-486-22991-2 4.00 (pbk.)
1. Grandville, Jean Ignace Isidore Gerard, called, 1803-1847. Autre monde—Illustrations. 2. Grandville, Jean Ignace Isidore Gerard, called, 1803-1847. Animaux—Illustrations. I. Appelbaum, Stanley, ed. II. Grandville, Jean Ignace Isidore Gerard, called, 1803-1847. Un autre monde. III. Hetzel, Pierre Jules, 1814-1886. Scenes de la vie privee et publique des animaux. IV. Title. BIP

Grant, Earle W., 1890- —Art collections.

SAN Diego, Calif. Fine 708.194'98
Arts Gallery.
Grant-Munger Collection: American and European 19th & 20th century art and Asiatic art. [San Diego] 1970. xi, 123 p. illus. (part col.) 26 cm. Catalog by M. E. Petersen and C. M. Skinner. [N5220.G75] 70-129015
1. Grant, Earle W., 1890- —Art collections. 2. Munger, Pliny, 1890-1962—Art collections. I. Petersen, Martin E. II. Skinner, Carl M. III. Title.

Grant Lake site, N.W.T.

WRIGHT, James Vallier, 971.9'4
1932-
The Grant Lake site, Keewatin district, N.W.T. / J. V. Wright. Ottawa : National Museums of Canada, 1976. v, 122 p. : ill. ; 28 cm. (Mercury series ISSN 0316-1854s) (Paper - Archaeological Survey of Canada ; no. 47 ISSN 0317-2244s) Summary in French.IBibliography: p. 98-100. [E78.C2W933] 77-368332
1. Grant Lake site, N.W.T. I. Title. II. Series: National Museum of Man. Archaeological Survey of Canada. Paper ; no. 47 III. Series: Mercury series.

Graphic arts.

ACHILLEOS, Chris, 1947- 759.2
Beauty and the beast : a collection of heroic fantasy illustrations / Chris Achilleos. New York : Simon and Schuster, c1978. 92 p. : chiefly col. ill. ; 30 cm. (A Fireside book) [NC978.5.A25.A4 1978] 78-4394 ISBN 0-671-24297-0 : 19.95
1. Achilleos, Chris, 1947- I. Title. BIP

AMERICAN Institute of 655.06273
Graphic Arts.
The American Institute of Graphic Arts. [Report] New York. v. illus. 24cm. annual. Title varies: 19 The story of the American Institute of Graphic Arts. [NC1.A5] 53-37338
I. Title.

BALLINGER, Raymond A., 655.2'5
1907-
Layout and graphic design [by] Raymond A. Ballinger. New York, Van Nostrand Reinhold [1970] 96 p. illus. (part col.) 28 cm. 1956 ed. published under title: Layout. [Z253.5.B28 1970] 72-90309
I. Title.

ELDREDGE, David C. 811'.5'4
Salomouse : a true tail : from an original story by Dionyos M. Kuhcyntos / adapted by David C. Eldredge ; translated by Kuhcyntos M. Dnomyar ; designed and illustrated by Raymond Michael Sotnychuk, assisted by Jozef Csoresony ; inspired by Yoj Siztalot. [Philadelphia : Tyler School of Art, c1976] [39] p. : ill. ; 32 cm. "54 copies." No. 21. [PS3555.L35S2 1976] 76-372267
I. Sotnychuk, Raymond Michael, 1954- II. Title.

HAMILTON, Edward A. 760
Graphic design for the computer age; visual communication for all media [by] Edward A. Hamilton. New York, Van Nostrand Reinhold [1970] 191 p. illus. (part col.), col. maps, ports. (part col.) 28 cm. Bibliography: p. 187-188. [NC997.H23] 69-16379
1. Graphic arts. 2. Communication. I. Title.

KAGY, Frederick D. 655.3
Graphic arts. Chicago, Goodheart-Willcox Co. [1961] 112 p. illus. 27 cm. (Goodheart-Willcox's build-a-course series) [Z244.K25] 61-5338
1. Graphic arts. BIP

KAGY, Frederick D. 686.2'2
Graphic arts / by Frederick D. Kagy ; Walter C. Brown, consulting editor. South Holland, Ill. : Goodheart-Willcox Co., c1978. p. cm. (Goodheart-Willcox's build-a-course series) Includes index. [Z244.K25 1978] 78-5456 ISBN 0-87006-252-2 : 4.40
1. Graphic arts. 2. Printing, Practical. I. Brown, Walter Charles, 1918- II. Title.

KAUFFMANN, Desire, 1901- 760
Graphic arts & crafts. 2d ed. Princeton, N. J., Van Nostrand [1962] 260 p. illus. 22 cm. [NE860.K27 1962] 62-52238
1. Graphic arts.

SELAME, Joe. 769'.924
So we spin. [Creation and graphics by Joe Selame. Verse by Elinor Selame. 1st ed. Newton, Mass., Selame Design Associates, 1971] 59 p. illus. 28 cm. [NC1429.S46S4] 77-26355 2.95
I. Selame, Elinor. II. Title.

STEVENSON, George A ed. 655.303
Graphic arts handbook and products manual. [1st ed.] Torrance, Calif., Pen and Press Publications [1960] 364 p. illus. 24 cm. [Z244.3.S84] 60-30277
1. Graphic arts. I. Title.

Graphic arts, American—Catalogs.

HAROLD, Margaret, comp. 760
Prize-winning graphics. [Ft. Lauderdale, Fla., Allied Pubns.] 1966. 37p. illus., ports. 34cm. 63-14993 1.95 pap.,
1. Graphic arts, American—Catalogs. I. Title.

PRIZE-WINNING graphics. 760
Comp. by Margaret Harold. Fort Lauderdale, Fla., Allied Pubns., c.1964. 39p. illus. ports. 34cm. 63-14993 1.95 pap.,
1. Graphic arts, American—Catalogs. I. Harold, Margaret, comp.

WEITENKAMPF, Frank, 760'.0973
1866-1962.
American graphic art. With a new introd. by E. Maurice Bloch. New York, Johnson Reprint Corp., 1970. ix, xiii, 328 p. illus., ports. 23 cm. (Series in American studies) Reprint of the 1924 ed. "Frank Weitenkampf: a selective list of publications relating to American graphic art, 1927-1959": p. viii-ix (1st group) [NE505.W4 1970] 78-111388
1. Graphic arts, American. II. Title. III. Series.

Graphic arts, British.

LAMBERT, Frederick. 741.6
Graphic design Britain. London, Owen [1968, c.1967] 1v. (unpaged) facsims. 32cm. [NC978.L3] 67-103899 15.00
1. Graphic arts, British. 2. Commercial art. I. Title.
Available from Dufour, Chester Springs, Pa.

Graphic arts—History.

CLEAVER, James 760
A history of graphic art. New York, Philosophical [c.1963] 282p. illus. 23cm. Bibl. 63-6423 12.00
1. Graphic arts—Hist. 2. Engraving—Hist. I. Title. BIP

CLEAVER, James. 769'.9
A history of graphic art. New York, Greenwood Press [1969, c1963] 282 p. illus., facsims., port. 23 cm. Bibliography: p. 261-267. [NE400.C6 1969] 73-95115
1. Graphic arts—History. 2. Engraving—History. I. Title.

GOWANS, Alan. 760
The unchanging arts; new forms for the traditional functions of art in society. [1st ed.] Philadelphia, Lippincott, 1971 [c1970] x, 433 p. illus., facsims., ports. 24 cm. Includes bibliographical references. [NC998.G6] 70-96839 12.95
1. Graphic arts—History. 2. Art and society. I. Title.

NEUMANN, Eckhard. 760'.09
Functional graphic design in the 20's. New York, Reinhold [1967] 96p. illus. (pt. col.) 21cm. [NC95.N4] 67-14159 6.95 bds.,
1. Graphic arts—Hist. 2. Commercial art—Hist. I. Title.

STUBBE, Wolf. 372.52
Graphic arts in the twentieth century. New York, Praeger [1963] 318 p. illus. (part col.) 31 cm. "Biographies, compiled by Kurt Sternelle": p. [251]-306. [NC95.S813] 63-20968
1. Graphic arts — Hist. 2. Artists. I. Title.

Graphic arts — New York (City) — Direct.

NEW York art directors 655.3
buying guide. 1961- [New York, Contempo Pub. Corp.] v. 20 cm. annual. [NC997.A1N4] 63-5962
1. Graphic arts — New York (City) — Direct. 2. Commercial art — Direct.

Graphic arts—Period.

GRAPHIS annual. 741.67'058
International annual of advertising graphics. Zurics, Walter Herdeg, The Graphis Pr. The '68/69 edition is now available from Hastings House, New York, for $19.50. L.C. card order no.: 56-24907.

GRAPHIS annual : 741.67'058
the international annual of advertising and editorial graphics. Zurich, Switzerland : Graphics Press.
The 1977-78 ed.,c1977, edited by Walter Herdeg, is available from Hastings House for 37.50. ISBN 0-8038-2687-7. L.C. card no.:56-24907.

PRATT Institute, Brooklyn. 760.5
Art School.
ADLIB no. 1- 1953- [Brooklyn] v. chiefly illus. (part col.) 23-33cm. annual. Issued by the students and faculty of the Art School, Pratt Institute. [NC1.A4] 60-499
1. Graphic arts—Period. I. Title.

Graphic arts, Rumanian.

MILITANT graphic art in 769.9498
Rumania. Bucharest, Meridiane Pub. House [New York, Vanous, 1964] 336p. (chiefly illus. (pt. mounted, pt. col.)) 32cm. Pub. under the edship. of Jules Perahim [others] Bibl. [NC1200.R8G73] 64-57168 10.00, bxd.
1. Graphic arts, Rumanian. I. Perahim, Jules, ed.

Graphic arts, Spanish.

GRAFISTAS, 659.13'23'0946
Agraupacion FAD, Barcelona
Grafistas. Agrupacion FAD; seleccion de obras del arte grafico espanol creadas y realizadas por miembos de la entidad Grafistas, Agrupacion FAD. Barcelano (Espana) [Barcelona, Editorial Blume, c.1964] xix, 143p. (chiefly illus., ports.) 31cm. Spanish & English. [NC987.G7] 67-38435 15.00
1. Graphic arts, Spanish. 2. Illustrators, Spanish. I. Title.
American distributor: Wittenborn, New York.

Graphic arts—Study and teaching.

BARANSKI, Matthew. 760.7
Graphic design; a creative approach. Scranton, International Textbook Co. [1960] 208 p. illus. 27 cm. (International textbooks in art education) Includes bibliography. [NE970.B3] 59-14753
1. Graphic arts—Study and teaching. 2. Design—Study and teaching. I. Title.

EMERGING patterns; 760'.071
academic and industrial approaches to education, training, and manpower development in graphic communications. Pittsburgh, Graphic Arts Technical Foundation [1969?] vi, 90 p. ports. 16 x 23 cm. Addresses given at the 1969 GATF general education meeting. Includes bibliographical references. [NE970.E5] 76-96930
1. Graphic arts—Study and teaching. I. Graphic Arts Technical Foundation.

Graphic arts—Study and teaching—Addresses, essays, lectures.

NASH, Ray, 1905- 760'.071
Education in the graphic arts; a symposium held in the Wiggin Gallery, Boston Public Library, on May 5, 1967. The speakers: Ray Nash, Fritz Eichenberg [and] Frederick Walkey. Boston, 1969. 43 p. 23 cm. [NE970.N37] 77-85398
1. Graphic arts—Study and teaching—Addresses, essays, lectures. I. Eichenberg, Fritz, 1901- joint author. II. Walkey, Frederick, 1922- joint author. III. Boston. Public Library. IV. Title. BIP

Graphic arts. Swiss.

BANGERTER, Walter 741.609494
Offizielle Schweizer Grafik. Arts graphiques officiels en Suisse. Official graphic art in Switzerland [Autoren: Walter Bangerter, Armin Tschanen. Geleitwort: H. P. Tschudi. Einfuhrungstext: W. Kampfen. Mitarbeiter: M. Altdorfer. et al. Ubersetzungen: Franzosisch. A. Moneda; Englisch, M. J. Wynne]Zurich, ABC Verlag [dist. New York, Hastings, 1965, c.1964] 1v. (unpaged) illus. (pt. col.) 26cm. German. French, and English [NC291.B3] 65-2266 15.00 bds.,
1. Graphic arts. Swiss. 2. Government publicity, Switzerland. I. Tschanen, Armin, joint author. II. Title. III. Title: Arts graphiques officiels en Suisse. IV. Title: Official graphic art in Switzerland.

NEUBURG, Hans, 1904- 769.91494
Schweizer Industrie Grafik. Grdphisme industriel en Suisse. (Graphic design in Swiss industry. Zurich, ABC Verlag New York Hastings, 1966 200p. illus. (pt. col.) 26cm. German, French, and English [NC997.N39] 66-3372 19.50
1. Graphic arts, Swiss. I. Title. II. Title: Graphisme industriel en Suisse. III. Title: Graphic design in Swiss industry.

Graphic arts—Technique.

BOWMAN, William J. 741.4
Graphic communication [by] William J. Bowman. New York, Wiley [1967, c1968] xi, 210 p. illus. 29 cm. (Wiley series on human communication) [NC730.B63] 67-29931
1. Graphic arts—Technique. 2. Communication—Audio-visual aids. I. Title. BIP

BRUNNER, Felix, 1929- 760
A handbook of graphic reproduction processes ... Handbuch der Druckgraphik ... Manuel de la gravure ... [French version: Albert Flocon. English version: Dennis Qu. Stephenson] New York, Hastings-House [1962] 379 p. illus. (part col.) 21 x 23 cm. (Visual communication books) Bibliography: p. 378-379. [NE850.B7] 62-13981
1. Graphic arts—Technique. I. Title. II. Title: Handbuch der Druckgraphik. III. Title: Manuel de la gravure. IV. Title: Graphic reproduction processes. BIP

BURTT, George, 1914- 760'.28
Putting yourself across with the art of graphic persuasion. West Nyack, N.Y., Parker Pub. Co. [1972] 242 p. illus. 24 cm. [NC997.B74] 78-168582 ISBN 0-13-744672-1
1. Graphic arts—Technique. I. Title.

CATALDO, John W 760
Graphic design & visual communication. Text & graphic design by John W. Cataldo. Scranton, International Textbook Co. [1966] xiii, 203 p. illus. (part col.) facsims.

(part col.) 25 cm. (International textbooks in art and art education) Bibliography: p. 293. [NC730.C3] 65-23804
1. Graphic arts — Technique. 2. Design. 3. Communication — Audio-visual aids. I. Title.

CROY, Peter. 760'.028
Graphic design and reproduction techniques. [Translated by G. P. Burden. 1st American ed.] New York, Hastings House [1968] 282 p. illus. 23 cm. (Visual communication books) Translation of Grafik, Form und Technik. [NC730.C713 1968] 68-16002
1. Graphic arts—Technique. 2. Printing, Practical—Make-up. I. Title. BIP

GARRETT, Lillian. 745.4
Visual design: a problem-solving approach. New York, Reinhold Pub. Corp. [1967] 215 p. illus. 29 cm. Bibliography: p. 215. [NC730.G29] 66-14433
1. Graphic arts—Technique. 2. Design. I. Title. BIP

GARRETT, Lillian. 745.4
Visual design : a problem-solving approach / Lillian Garrett. Huntington, N.Y. : R. E. Krieger Pub. Co., 1975, c1967. 215 p. : ill. ; 29 cm. Reprint of the ed. published by Van Nostrand Reinhold Co., New York. Bibliography: p. 215. [NC730.G29 1975] 75-12638 ISBN 0-88275-332-0
1. Graphic arts—Technique. I. Title.

HOFMANN, Armin, 1920- 760.28
Graphic design manual: principles and priactice[English version tr. from German: D. Q. Stephenson. New York] Reinhold [c.1965] 172p. (chiefly illus.) 26cm. [NC730.H54] 65-7866 10.00
1. Graphic arts—Technique. 2. Design. I. Title. BIP

HOFMANN, Armin, 1920- 760.28
Graphic design manual: principles and practice. [English version: D. Q. Stephenson] [New York] Reinhold [1965] 172 p. (chiefly illus.) 26 cm. Translation of Methodik der Form- und Bildgestaltung. [NC730.H54] 65-7866
1. Graphic arts—Technique. 2. Design. I. Title.

*SPRINGER, Richard D. 744.422
Problems for basic graphics; drawing and descriptive geometry, series A [by] R. D. Springer [others. Boston, Allyn, c.1963] various p. (in pockets) illus. 30cm. 3.75, pap., unbound
1. Title.

STANKOWSKI, Anton, 1906- 769
Funktion und ihre Darstellung in der Werbegrafik; die Sichtbarmachung unsichtbarer Vorgange. Visual presentation of invisible processes; how to illustrate invisible processes in graphic design. La fonction et sa representation dans le dessin publicitaire; concretisation des processus invisibles. New York, Hastings [1967] 127p. illus. (pt. col.) 31cm. English version: D. Q. Stephnson; version francaise: Madeleine Wolf. [NC997.S82 1967] 67-7097 16.50
1. Graphic arts—Technique. 2. Commercial art—Printing. I. Title. II. Title: Visual presentation of invisible processes. III. Title: La fonction et sa representation dans le dessin publicitaire.

VAN UCHELEN, Rod. 741.6
Say it with pictures / Rod van Uchelen. New York : Van Nostrand Reinhold, [1978] p. cm. Includes index. [NC730.V36] 78-8670 ISBN 0-442-28642-2 : 12.95 ISBN 0-442-28644-9 pbk. : 7.95
1. Graphic arts—Technique. I. Title. BIP

ZAIDENBERG, Arthur, 1903- 741.4
New Encyclopedia of drawing, painting, and the graphic arts; a complete, fundamental book of instruction for hobbyists, art students, and professional artists. New York, Barnes [1961] 222 p. illus. 26 cm. [NC730.Z38 1961] 60-9866
1. Graphic arts — Technique. 2. Drawing — Instruction. I. Title.

Graphic Arts (television).

*HURREL, Ron 770.28
Van Nostrand Reinhold manual of television graphics. New York, Van Nostrand Reinhold Co. [1974, c1973] 136 p. illus. 25 cm. [TR690.4] 73-14118 ISBN 0-442-23601-8 9.95
1. Graphic Arts (television). 2. Photography. I. Title.

Graphic arts, Yugoslav.

KRZISNIK, Zoran 769.9497
Contemporary Yugoslav graphic art. Text by Zoran Krzisnik [Eds.: Oto Bihalji-Merin, Jara Ribnikar] New York, Shorewood, [c.]1964. xxi, 144p. chiefly illus. (pt. col.) 34cm. 64-22282 19.50 bds.,
1. Graphic arts, Yugoslav. I. Title.

Graphic cameras.

KINGSBURY, Richard. 770.2
The Graphic 35 guide. New York, Greenberg [1956] 123p. illus. 20cm. (The Modern camera guide series) [TR263.G7K5] 56-9281
1. Graphic cameras. 2. Photography—Handbooks, manuals, etc. I. Title.

THE Speed Graphic guide. 770.2
including Crown and Century cameras. New York, Greenberg, c1952. 128p. illus. 20cm. (The Modern camera guide series) 7T9 [TR263.]
1. Graphic cameras. 2. Photography—Handbooks, manuals, etc. I. Tydings, Kenneth S

Graphicstudio—Exhibitions.

BARO, Gene. 769'.9759'65
Graphicstudio U.S.F. : an experiment in art and education / by Gene Baro. [Brooklyn], N.Y. : Brooklyn Museum, c1978. 208 p. (p. 208 blank) : ill. (some col.) ; 31 cm. "Published for the exhibition Graphicstudio U.S.F.: an experiment in art and education, the Brooklyn Museum, New York, May 13-July 16, 1978." [NE539.G69A4 1978] 78-6796 ISBN 0-87273-068-9 : 8.95
1. Graphicstudio—Exhibitions. 2. Prints—20th century—Florida—Tampa—Exhibitions. 3. Group work in art—Florida—Tampa—Exhibitions. I. Brooklyn Institute of Arts and Sciences. Museum. II. Title. BIP

Grass, Gunter, 1927—

GRASS, Gunter, 1927- 741.9'43
Inmarypraise [by] Gunter Grass. Photos: Maria Rama. Layout: P. J. Wilhelm. [English translation by Christopher Middleton] New York, Harcourt Brace Jovanovich [1974] 87 p. illus. (part col.) 25 cm. "A Helen and Kurt Wolff book." Translation of Mariazuehren. Poem in English and German. [NC251.G63R3513] 74-180420 ISBN 0-15-144406-4 15.00
1. Grass, Gunter, 1927- I. Rama, Maria. II. Title. BIP

Grassi, Giovannino de, d. 1398.

GRASSI, Giovannino de', 091
d.1398.
The Visconti hours, National Library, Florence. [Introductions and commentary by] Millard Meiss and Edith W. Kirsch. New York, G. Braziller [1972] 262 p. col. illus. 26 cm. Reproductions of illuminations by Giovannino de' Grassi and Luchino Belbello from the Visconti hours ms. Bibliography: p. 262. [ND3363.V57G72] 72-75371 ISBN 0-8076-0651-0
1. Grassi, Giovannino de, d. 1398. 2. Belbello, Luchino, 15th century. 3. Florence. Biblioteca nazionale centrale. 4. Hours, Books of. I. Belbello, Luchino, 15th century, joint author. II. Meiss, Millard. III. Kirsch, Edith W. IV. Catholic Church. Liturgy and ritual. Hours. (Ms. Visconti)

Gratianus, the canonist.

TWO essays on the 262.9'23
Decretum of Gratian, by Hellmut Lehmann-Haupt and Charles McCurry. Together with an original leaf printed on vellum by Peter Schoeffer at Mainz in 1472. Los Angeles, Zeitlin & Ver Brugge, 1971. [17] p. 51 cm. "193 copies printed by Saul & Lillian Marks at the Plantin Press, Los Angeles." Unnumbered copyright deposit copy, without an original leaf. Contents.Contents.—Peter Schoeffer of Gernsheim, printer of the Decretum at Mainz in 1472, by H. Lehmann-Haupt.—The Decretum of Gratian, by C. McCurry. [Z241.G73T95] 73-164721
1. Gratianus, the canonist. Decretum. 2. Schoffer, Peter, ca. 1425-ca. 1502. I. Lehmann-Haupt, Hellmut, 1903- Schoeffer of Gernsheim. 1971. II. McCurry, Charles. The Decretum of Gratian. 1971.

Graubner, Gotthard, 1930—

GRAUBNER, Gotthard, 1930- v. 12
Gotthard Graubner : [Ausstellung] : Hamburger Kunsthalle, 28. November 1975 bis 18. Januar 1976 : [Katalog / Herausgeber, Werner Hofmann]. Hamburg : Hamburger Kunsthalle, [1975?] 115 p. : ill. (some col.) ; 24 cm. Bibliography: p. 92-93. [ND488.G652H64] 76-458207
1. Graubner, Gotthard, 1930- I. Hofmann, Werner, 1928- II. Hamburg. Kunsthalle.

Graves, Morris, 1910—

FINE Arts Patrons of 759.13
Newport Beach.
Morris Graves, retrospective. Organized by the Fine Arts Patrons of Newport Harbor, co-sponsored by the Newport Harbor Service League, for exhibit in the Pavilion Gallery, Balboa, California, March 1 to March 31, 1963. [Catalogue of the exhibition. Balboa? 1963] unpaged. illus. 23 cm. "Text adapted from 'Morris Graves,' by Frederick S. Wight, John I. H. Baur, and Duncan Phillips, published by the University of California Press." [ND237.G615F5] 63-41072
1. Graves, Morris, 1910- I. Balboa, Calif. Pavilion Gallery. II. Title.

GRAVES, Morris, 1910- 741.9'73
The drawings of Morris Graves : with comments / by the artist ; John Cage, Series re Morris Graves ; David Daniels, pref. ; edited by Ida E. Rubin. Boston : Published for the Drawing Society by New York Graphic Society, 1974. 159 p., [8] leaves of plates : ill. (some col.) ; 29 cm. Bibliography: p. 157. [NC139.G69C33] 73-89952 ISBN 0-316-19305-4 : 22.50
1. Graves, Morris, 1910- I. Cage, John. Series re Morris Graves. 1974. II. Title. BIP

MORRIS Graves; 707.4
a retrospective. [Eugene? Or., 1966?] 63 p. illus. (part col.) 23 cm. Catalogue of a loan exhibition held at the University of Oregon Museum of Art Feb. 8-Mar. 13, 1966, and sponsored by the Friends of the Museum. Bibliography: p. 62-63. [ND237.G615M6] 70-278715 2.00
1. Graves, Morris, 1910- I. Oregon. University. Museum of Art.

Graves, Nancy Stevenson, 1940—

GRAVES, Nancy Stevenson, 759.13
1940-
Nancy Graves. [Catalog of] an exhibition organized by the La Jolla Museum of Contemporary Art, La Jolla, California, August 25-October 7, 1973 [and] Art Museum of South Texas, Corpus Christi, Texas, October 18-November 29, 1973. [La Jolla, Calif., 1973] 40 p. illus. (part col.) 22 x 28 cm. Bibliography: p. 39. [ND237.G616L34] 73-87278
1. Graves, Nancy Stevenson, 1940- I. La Jolla Museum of Contemporary Art. II. Art Museum of South Texas.

GRAVES, Nancy Stevenson, 709'.2'4
1940-
Nancy Graves: sculpture and drawing 1970-1972. [Philadelphia, Institute of Contemporary Art, University of Pennsylvania, 1973, c1972] [20] p. illus. 22 x 28 cm. Catalogue of an exhibition held at the Philadelphia Institute of Contemporary Art, Sept. 22-Nov. 1, 1972 and the Cincinnati Contemporary Arts Center, Nov. 30, 1972-Jan. 9, 1973. Bibliography: p. [19] [NB237.G74P46 1973] 73-173344
1. Graves, Nancy Stevenson, 1940- I. Pennsylvania. University. Institute of Contemporary Art. II. Contemporary Arts Center, Cincinnati.

Gray, Percy, 1869-1952.

WHITTON, Donald C. 759.13
Percy Gray, 1869-1952, by Donald C. Whitton and Robert E. Johnson. Pref. by Joseph A. Baird, Jr. With an introd. by Thomas Albright and a concluding essay by Lewis Ferbrache. San Francisco, 1970. 94 p. illus. (part col.), geneal. table, ports. 21 x 23 cm. Includes the catalog of an exhibition held at the California Historical Society, San Francisco, Dec. 1, 1970-Jan. 23, 1971. Bibliography: p. 89. [ND1839.G7W48] 70-141825
1. Gray, Percy, 1869-1952. I. Johnson, Robert E., joint author. II. California Historical Society.

Gray, Thomas, 1716-1771—Illustrations.

BLAKE, William, 1757-1827. 759.2
Water-colours illustrating the poems of Thomas Gray. With an introd. and commentary by Sir Geoffrey Keynes. Chicago, J. P. O'Hara, 1972. xx, 72 p. port. 30 cm. Each water-color contains the text illustrated. All 116 are reproduced in monochrome, 16 also in color. Originally published in 1922 under title: William Blake's designs for Gray's poems. [ND1942.B55G72 1972] 70-186889 ISBN 0-87955-600-5 25.00
1. Gray, Thomas, 1716-1771—Illustrations. I. Gray, Thomas, 1716-1771. II. Keynes, Geoffrey Langdon, Sir, 1887- III. Title.

Grayson site, Calif.

OLSEN, William H. 970.4'94'58
Archeology of the Grayson Site Merced County, California, by William H. Olsen and Louis A. Payen. Sacramento, State of California, Dept. of Parks and Recreation, Archeological Resources Section, 1969. viii, 46 p. illus., maps. 28 cm. (Archeological report 12) Bibliography: p. 43. [E78.C15A27 no. 12] 75-637309
1. Grayson site, Calif. I. Payen, Louis A., joint author. II. California. Archeological Resources Section. III. Title. IV. Series.

Great Britain—Antiquities, Roman—Bibliography.

STAMAS, Joan D. 016.3092 s
Roman towns in Britain : a bibliography / Joan Stamas. Monticello, Ill. : Council of Planning Librarians, 1978. 21 p. ; 28 cm. (Exchange bibliography - Council of Planning Librarians ; 1473) Cover title. [Z5942.C68 no. 1473] [DA145] 016.361'04 78-103355 2.00
1. Great Britain—Antiquities, Roman—Bibliography. 2. Romans—Great Britain—Bibliography. 3. Great Britain—History—Roman period, 55 B.C.-449 A.D.—Bibliography. 4. Cities and towns, Ancient—Great Britain—Bibliography. I. Title. II. Series: Council of Planning Librarians. Exchange bibliography ; 1473.

Gt. Brit.—Historic houses, etc.

SORRELL, Alan 720.942
Living history. London, B. T. Batsford [New Rochelle, N.Y., Leisure Time, c.1965] 95p. illus., map. 23x30cm. [DA660.S66] 65-6417 6.75
1. Gt. Brit.—Historic houses, etc. 2. Gt. Brit.—Antiq. I. Title.

Great Britain—History—Charles II, 1660-1685.

WAYLAND, Virginia. 741.5'942
Francis Barlow's sketches for the Meal Tub Plot playing cards. With introductory notes and an account of the Plot in relation to its times, by Virginia and Harold Wayland. Pasadena, Calif., H. & V. Wayland, 1971. 40 p. illus. 20 x 26 cm. (The Wayland playing card monographs, no. 2) "Two hundred copies have been printed." Bibliography: p. 39. [DA448.W38] 72-188910
1. Great Britain—History—Charles II, 1660-1685. 2. Popish Plot, 1678. I. Wayland, Harold, joint author. II. Barlow, Francis, 1626?-1702, illus.

Great Britain—History—Elizabeth, 1558-1603.

STRONG, Roy C. 757'.0942
The cult of Elizabeth : Elizabethan portraiture and pageantry / Roy Strong. London : Thames and Hudson, 1977. 227 p. : ill. (some col.) ; 26 cm. Includes bibliographical references and index. [DA356.S83] 77-378494 ISBN 0-500-23263-6 : 24.95
1. Elizabeth, Queen of England, 1533-1603. 2. Great Britain—History—Elizabeth, 1558-1603. I. Title.
Distributed by W.W. Norton. BIP

Great Britain—History—George III, 1760-1820.

WRIGHT, Thomas, 1810-1877. 741.5942
Historical & descriptive account of the caricatures of James Gillray; comprising a political and humorous history of the latter part of the reign of George the Third [by] Thomas Wright and R. H. Evans. New York, B. Blom, 1968. xv, 496 p. port. 24 cm. First ed., 1851. A descriptive accompaniment to the 582 engravings of v. 1 of The works of James Gillray. [NC1479.G5W8 1968] 68-21202
1. Gillray, James, 1757-1815. 2. Great Britain—History—George III, 1760-1820. I. Evans, Robert Harding, 1778-1857, joint author. II. Gillray, James, 1757-1815. The works of James Gillray. III. Title.

Gt. Brit.—Indus.

WYMER, Norman. 338.4'7'68
Rural crafts. Illustrated by photos. by the author. London. Oxford University Press. 1952. 127p. illus. 19cm. (The Story of the countryside, ser. 2, book 6) [TT57.W93] 54-29837
1. Gt. Brit.—Indus. 2. Handicraft. I. Title. II. Series.

Gt. Brit.—Intellectual life.

THE Times, London. Literary supplement. 914.2
The British imagination; a critical survey from the Times Literary supplement. With an introd. by Arthur Crook. New York, Atheneum, 1961. 203 p. 22 cm. [DA566.4.T5] 61-12783
1. Gt. Brit.—Intellectual life. 2. Creation (Literary, artistic, etc.) I. Title.

Great Britain—Kings and rulers—Art patronage.

PLUMB, John Harold, 1911- 941'.00992 B
Royal heritage : the treasures of the British crown / by J. H. Plumb. 1st American ed. New York : Harcourt Brace Jovanovich, c1977. 360 p. : ill. (some col.) ; 31 cm. "Published in association with the television series written by Huw Wheldon and J. H. Plumb." Includes index. [N5245.P54 1977] 77-3832 ISBN 0-15-179011-6 : 25.00
1. Great Britain—Kings and rulers—Art patronage. 2. Great Britain—Kings and rulers—Art collections. 3. Great Britain—History. I. Wheldon, Huw P., 1916- II. Title. BIP

Great Britain—Kings and rulers—Portraits—Exhibitions.

HAPPY and glorious : six reigns of royal photography / Colin Ford. 1st American ed. New York : Macmillan, 1977. p. cm. Catalog of an exhibition marking Queen Elizabeth's Silver Jubilee, held at the National Portrait Gallery in London from, March to October, 1977. [DA28.1.H23 1977] 77-2297 ISBN 0-02-539590-4 : 11.95 779'.9'94100992074
1. Great Britain—Kings and rulers—Portraits—Exhibitions. I. Ford, Colin John, 1934- II. London. National Portrait Gallery. BIP

ORLEANS House Gallery. 760'.07'4021795
Princes and palaces; 800 years of royal associations with Richmond upon Thames [catalogue of an exhibition held at] Orleans House Gallery, Twickenham, 20 October 1973 to 21 April 1974. Richmond, London Borough of Richmond upon Thames [Amenities Committee] 1973. 31 p. 23 cm. [DA28.1.O67 1973] 74-162445 ISBN 0-903704-15-3 £0.20
1. Great Britain—Kings and rulers—Portraits—Exhibitions. 2. Richmond, Eng. (Surrey)—Palaces—Exhibitions. I. Title.

Great Britain. Parliament (The buildings)

THE Houses of Parliament / edited by M. H. Port. New Haven : Published for the Paul Mellon Centre for Studies in British Art (London) by Yale University Press, 1976. xxi, 347 p., [1] leaf of plates : ill. (some col.) ; 31 cm. (Studies in British art) Includes bibliographical references and index. [NA4415.G72L664] 76-3374 ISBN 0-300-02022-8 : 35.00 725'.11'0942132
1. Great Britain. Parliament (The buildings) 2. Gothic revival (Architecture)—London. I. Port, Michael Harry. II. Paul Mellon Centre for Studies in British Art. III. Series. BIP

Great Britain—Social life and customs—20th century—Pictorial works.

THE Angry 30's / [compiled by Julian Symons.] London : Eyre Methuen, 1976. ca. 150 p. : chiefly ill. ; 24 cm. (Picture file) [DA566.4.A66] 77-351008 ISBN 0-413-32990-9 : £1.95 941.083'022'2
1. Great Britain—Social life and customs—20th century—Pictorial works. 2. United States—Social life and customs—1918-1945—Pictorial works. I. Symons, Julian, 1912-

Great Britain—Social life and customs—Pictorial works.

GEORGE, Mary Dorothy (Gordon) 914.2'03
Hogarth to Cruikshank: social change in graphic satire [by] M. Dorothy George. New York, Walker [1967] 224 p. illus. (part col.) 31 cm. Includes bibliographical references. [NC1470] 67-13227 20.00
1. Great Britain—Social life and customs—Pictorial works. 2. Caricatures and cartoons—Great Britain. I. Title.

Great Casterton, Eng.—Antiquities, Roman.

THE Roman town and villa at Great Casterton, Rutland; report by members of the summerschools in Romano-British archaeology held at Great Casterton. [1st]-1950- [Notingham] University of Nottingham. v. illus., plans. 25cm. Title varies slightly. Editor: 1950- P. Corder. [DA690.G823R6] 52-40345 914.22'9
1. Great Casterton, Eng.—Antiquities, Roman. I. Corder, Philip, ed.

Great Falls, Potomac River.

REBER, James Quinter, 1911- 779'.36'09752
Potomac portrait, by James Q. Reber. With an introd. by William C. Everhart. [New York, Liveright, 1974] 95 p. (chiefly illus.) 29 cm. [F187.M7R42] 73-93128 ISBN 0-87140-585-7 10.00
1. Great Falls, Potomac River. I. Title.
Pbk. 4.95

Great Lakes region—Antiq.

QUIMBY, George Irving, 1913- 970.47
Indian culture and European trade goods; the archaeology of the historic period in the western Great Lakes region. Madison, University of Wisconsin Press, 1966. xiv, 217 p. illus., map. 25 cm. Bibliography: p. 203-209. [E78.G7Q49] 66-13805
1. Great Lakes region—Antiq. 2. Indians of North America—Great Lakes region—Antiq. 3. Indians of North America—Implements. I. Title. BIP

Great Plains — Antiq.

WEDEL, Waldo Rudolph, 1908- 571
Prehistoric man on the Great Plains. Norman, University of Oklahoma Press [1961] xviii, 355 p. illus., maps 24 cm. Bibliography: p. 312-340. [E78.W5W4] 61-9002
1. Great Plains — Antiq. 2. Indians of North America — Antiq. 3. Indians of North America — Great Plains. I. Title. BIP

Greater St. Louis Arts and Education Council.

NEWTON, Michael. 338.4'7'7
Persuade and provide; the story of the Arts and Education Council in St. Louis, by Michael Newton and Scott Hatley. With an introd. by Nancy Hanks. [New York] Associated Councils of the Arts [1970] 249 p. illus. 24 cm. [NX26.S2N4] 73-124435 7.50
1. Greater St. Louis Arts and Education Council. I. Hatley, Scott, joint author. II. Title.

Greece—Antiquities.

HAFNER, German. 709'.38
Art of Crete, Mycenae, and Greece. New York, H. N. Abrams [1969, c1968] 264 p. illus. (part col.), maps. 23 cm. (Panorama of world art) Translation of Kreta und Hellas. Bibliography: p. 258-260. [DF77.H31513] 68-28392
1. Greece—Antiquities. 2. Crete—Antiquities. I. Title.

Greece—Descr. & trav.—Views.

SASEK, Miroslv 914.95
This is Greece [New York] Macmillan, c.1966. 60p. col. illus. 32cm. [ND1946.S2A522] 66-10844 3.50; 3.74 bds., lib. ed.,
1. Greece—Descr. & trav.—Views. I. Title.

Greece, Modern—Description and travel—Views.

LEAR, Edward, 1812-1888. 741.9'42
Edward Lear in Greece; a loan exhibition from the Gennadius Library, Athens. Circulated by the International Exhibitions Foundation, 1971-1972. [Meriden, Conn., Printed by Meriden Gravure Co., 1971] 87 p. (chiefly illus.) 22 x 26 cm. Participating museums: Amherst College and others. [NC242.L4A45] 72-154602
1. Greece, Modern—Description and travel—Views. I. American School of Classical Studies at Athens. Gennadius Library. II. International Exhibitions Foundation. III. Amherst College. IV. Title.

MILLER, Henry, 1891- 914.95
Greece. Drawings by Anne Poor. New York, Viking Press [1964] 55 p. illus. (part col.) port. 27 cm. (A Studio book) [NC1075.P65M5] 64-15057
1. Greece, Modern — Descr. & trav. — Views. I. Poor, Anne, illus. II. Title.

MOORE, Roy, 1924- 779'.9'91450924
Reflections on Greece. Photos. by Roy Moore. With quotations from Nikos Kazantzakis. New York, Walker [1971] 1 v. (chiefly illus., part col.) 34 cm. [DF719.M66 1971] 73-166182 30.00
1. Greece, Modern—Description and travel—Views. 2. Greece—Antiquities. I. Kazantzakes, Nikos, 1883-1957. II. Title.

WILCZYNSKI, Katerina. v. 12
Homage to Greece. Edited by H. M. Andrews. London, Macmillan; New York, St. Martin's Press, 1964. xiv, 125 p. illus., mounted col. plates, map. 32 cm. Includes bibliography. [NC1157.W49] 65-9605
1. Greece, Modern — Descr. & trav. — Views. I. Andrews, Henry Maxwell, ed. II. Title.

Greek drama (Comedy) — Illustrations.

WEBSTER, Thomas Bertram Lonsdale, 1905- 703
Monuments illustrating old and middle comedy, by T. B. L. Webster. [London, Institute of Classical Studies; distributed by International University Booksellers] 1960. viii, 80 p. plates. 28 cm. (University of London. Institute of Classical Studies. Bulletin supplement no. 9) [N7760.W414] 67-8890
1. Greek drama (Comedy) — Illustrations. I. Title. II. Series: London. University. Institute of Classical Studies. Bulletin supplement no. 9

Greek revival (Architecture)—History—Sources.

*HAMLIN, Talbot 720.973
Greek revival architecture in America: being an account of important trends in American architecture and American life prior to the war between the States. Together with a list of articles on architecture in some Amer. periodicals prior to 1850 by Sarah Hull Jenkins Simpson Hamlin, 1887-1930. Introd. by Leopold Arnaud. New York, Dover [1964, c.1944] 439p. illus. 22cm. Reprint of the ed. pub. in 1944 by Oxford. (T1148) Bibl. 3.00 pap.,
I. Title. BIP

*HAMLIN, Talbot 724.973
Greek revival architecture in America: being an account of important trends in American architecture and American life prior to the war between the States. Together with a list of articles on architecture in some Amer. periodicals prior to 1850, by Sarah Hull Jenkins Simpson Hamlin, 1887-1930. Introd. by Leopold Arnaud [Gloucester, Mass., P. Smith, 1964, c.1944] 439p. illus. 22cm. Reprint of the ed. pub. in 1944 by Oxford (Dover bk. T1148 rebound) Bibl. 5.00
I. Title.

WIEBENSON, Dora. 724'.23
Sources of Greek revival architecture. University Park, Pennsylvania State University Press [1969] 136 p. 59 plates. 26 cm. Bibliographical footnotes. [NA600.W5 1969b] 76-75000 10.50
1. Greek revival (Architecture)—History—Sources. I. Title. BIP

Green, Michael, 1943—

[GREEN, Michael], 1943- 741.9'73
A hobbit's travels : being hitherto unpublished travel sketches of Sam Gamgee. Philadelphia : Running Press, c1978. p. cm. Sketches based on the places in J. R. R. Tolkien's The hobbit. [NC975.5.G73A4 1978] 78-15318 ISBN 0-89471-041-9 lib. bdg. : 9.80. ISBN 0-89471-040-0 pbk. : 3.95
1. Green, Michael, 1943- 2. Tolkien, John Ronald Reuel, 1892-1973—Illustrations. I. Tolkien, John Ronald Reuel, 1892-1973. The hobbit. II. Title. BIP

Greenaway, Kate, 1846-1901.

ENGEN, Rodney K. 759.2
Kate Greenaway / Rodney K. Engan. London : Academy Editions ; New York : Harmony Books, 1976. 68 p. : ill. (some col.) ; 30 cm. Pages [9]-60 consist of reproductions of K. Greenaway's work. "List of works illustrated by Kate Greenaway": p. 61-68. [ND1942.G8E53 1976] 75-37388 9.95
1. Greenaway, Kate, 1846-1901.

GREENAWAY, Kate, 1846-1901. 741.9'42
Drawings by Kate Greenaway, verses by Laura E. Richards : from the Ladies' home journal, 1895 and 1896 / compiled and arranged by Lucile Rasmussen. [Berkeley?] : Rasmussen Press, 1974. 81 p. : ill. ; 75 mm. "Limited edition of 200 numbered copies." Contents.Contents.—April children.—Maidie's dance.—The picnic tea.—Off for dancing school.—In springtime. [NC139.G7A57 1974] 75-324761
1. Greenaway, Kate, 1846-1901. I. Richards, Laura Elizabeth Howe, 1850-1943. II. Rasmussen, Lucile. III. Title.

[1968] 142 p. illus. 26 cm. [NC1860.C35] 68-27548
1. Greeting cards. I. Title.

CHASE, Ernest Dudley, 741.6'8
1878-
The romance of greeting cards; an historical account of the origin, evolution, and development of the Christmas card, valentine, and other forms of engraved or printed greetings from the earliest days to the present time. With an introd. by Harry W. Brown. Cover design by Marjorie Wallingford and hand lettering by William P. Havican. Cambridge, Mass., Printed by University Press, 1926. Detroit, Tower Books, 1971 [c1927] xv, 255 p. illus., ports. 22 cm. [NC1860.C5 1971] 76-159914
1. Greeting cards. I. Title. BIP

HALLMARK Cards, inc. 817.54082
Greetings, dearie! A connoisseur's collection of humor from Hallmark contemporary cards ... [Garden City, N. Y., Doubleday. 1962] 190p. (chiefly illus.) 26cm. [NC1860.H3] 62-19027
1. Greeting cards. 2. American wit and humor, Pictorial. I. Title.

HOLTJE, Adrienne. 745.59'4
Cardcraft : twenty-two techniques for making your own greeting cards and notepaper / Adrienne and Bert Holtje. Radnor, Pa. : Chilton Book Co., c1978. v, 178 p., [4] leaves of plates : ill. ; 26 cm. (Chilton's creative crafts series) [TT872.H64 1978] 78-17266 ISBN 0-8019-6655-8 : 10.95. ISBN 0-8019-6656-6 pbk. : 6.95
1. Greeting cards. 2. Stationery. I. Holtje, Herbert, joint author. II. Title. III. Title: Notepaper. BIP

LEEMING, Joseph, 1897- 741.68
Fun with greeting cards. Illustrated by Jessie Robinson. [1st ed.] Philadelphia, Lippincott [1960] 95p. illus. 24cm. [NC1860.L38] 60-11355
1. Greeting cards. I. Title.

MAKE your own greeting 741.67
cards [by] Charles Francis [pseud.] New York, Studio Publications in Association with Crowell [1955] 154p. illus. 21cm. [NC1860.H6] 741.68 55-11110
1. Greeting cards. I. Holme, Bryan, 1913-

PURDY, Susan Gold, 1939- 745.54
Holiday cards for you to make. Philadelphia, Lippincott [1967] 64 p. col. illus. 27 cm. [GV1218.P3P8] 67-5101
1. Greeting cards. 2. Handicraft. I. Title.

PURDY, Susan Gold, 1939- 745.54
Holiday cards for you to make. Philadelphia, Lippincott [1967] 64 p. col. illus. 27 cm. Instructions for making greeting cards for fun or profit. [GV1218.P3P8] AC 67
1. Greeting card. 2. Handicraft. I. Title. BIP

THE romance of greeting 741.67
cards; an historical account of the origin, evolution and development of Christmas cards, valentines and other forms of greeting cards from the earliest days to the present time. [Rev. ed.] edited by James D. Chamberlain with an introd. by Stephen Q. Shannon. Decorations adapted from Kate Greenaway designs. In commemoration of the fiftieth anniversary of Rust Craft greeting cards, 1906-1956. [Dedham, Mass., Rust Craft, 1956] x, 252p. illus. 24cm. [NC1860.C5 1956] [NC1860.C5 1956] 741.68 A57 57-3053
1. Greeting cards. I. Chase, Ernest Dudley, 1878-

SNOW, Maria. 745.59'4
Greetings! / By Maria and Peter Snow. Indianapolis : Bobbs-Merrill, [1976] p. cm. Includes index. [TT872.S66] 76-10083 ISBN 0-672-52237-3 : 10.00
1. Greeting cards. 2. Paper work. I. Snow, Peter, joint author. II. Title.

Greeting cards—Juvenile literature.

BARISH, Matthew. 760
The kid's book of cards and posters. Illustrated by Erika Wallace and others. Englewood Cliffs, N.J., Prentice-Hall [1973] 96 p. illus. (part col.) 22 cm. Bibliography: p. 93-94. Lists appropriate holidays and occasions throughout the year

for greeting cards and posters and discusses the necessary materials and techniques for creating them. [TT872.B37] 72-13859 ISBN 0-13-515114-7 5.95
1. Greeting cards—Juvenile literature. 2. Posters—Juvenile literature. I. Wallace, Erika, illus. II. Title. BIP

KOVASH, Emily. 745.59'4
How to have fun making cards. Illustrated by Nancy Inderieden. [Mankato, Minn., Creative Education; distributed by Childrens Press, Chicago, 1974] 31 p. illus. (part. col.) 25 cm. (Creative education craft series) Briefly traces the history of greeting card messages and gives suggestions for making original cards for all occasions. [TT872.K68] 74-10532 ISBN 0-87191-360-7
1. Greeting cards—Juvenile literature. I. Inderieden, Nancy, illus. II. Title. BIP

Gregorius Nazianzenus, Saint, Patriarch of Constantinople.

GALAVARIS, George. 745.6'7
The illustrations of the liturgical homilies of Gregory Nazianzenus. Princeton, N.J., Princeton University Press, 1969. xiii, 269, cxii p. illus. (part col.), facsims. 31 cm. (Studies in manuscript illumination, no. 6) Includes bibliographies. [ND3385.G7G3] 69-12138 ISBN 6-910386-00- 30.00
1. Gregorius Nazianzenus, Saint, Patriarch of Constantinople. Orationes theologicae—Illustrations. I. Title. II. Series. BIP

Gregory, John, 1879-1958.

HARD, Charles Frederick 730.973
The sculptured scenes from Shakespeare; a description of John Gregory's marble reliefs on the Folger Library Building. Washington, Folger Shakespeare; a description of John Gregory's marble reliefs on the Folger Library Building. Washington, Folger Shakespeare Library, [c.]1959. 27p. illus. 22cm. 60-414 apply pap.,
1. Gregory, John, 1879-1958. 2. Folger Shakespeare Library, Washington, D. C. I. Title.

Gregory, Mary Alice, 1856-1908.

MILLER, Robert 748.2'9144'92
William, 1922-
Mary Gregory and her glass, by Robert W. Miller. Des Moines, Iowa [Wallace-Homestead Book Co., 1972] 32 p. illus. (part col.) 23 cm. [NK5198.G73M54] 73-152536 4.95
1. Gregory, Mary Alice, 1856-1908. 2. Boston and Sandwich Glass Company. 3. Glassware, American—Catalogs. I. Title. Publishers Address: 1912 Grand Avenue Des Moines, Iowa 50305.

Greuze, Jean-Baptiste, 1725-1805.

BROOKNER, Anita. 759.4
Greuze: the rise and fall of an eighteenth-century phenomenon. Greenwich, Conn., New York, Graphic Society [1972] xvi, 176 p. 121 illus. (part col.) 26 cm. Appendix in English and French. Includes bibliographical references. [ND553.G8B76 1972b] 72-80422 ISBN 0-8212-0483-1 22.50
1. Greuze, Jean-Baptiste, 1725-1805. I. Title.

Griffin, Walter Burley, 1876-1937.

BIRRELL, James 720.924
Walter Burley Griffin [St. Lucia] Univ. of Queens-land Pr. [dist. San Francisco, Tri-Ocean, 1965. c.1964] 203p. illus., plans, ports. 26cm. Bibl. [NA1605.G7B5] 65-29760 14.75
1. Griffin, Walter Burley, 1876-1937. I. Title.

GRIFFIN, Walter Burley, 720'.924
1876-1936.
Walter Burley Griffin, selected designs. Edited by David T. Van Zanten. Palos Park, Ill., Prairie School Press, 1970. 113 p. illus. 31 x 35 cm. Bibliography: p. 108-111. [NA737.G75A58] 70-126770
I. Title.

Griggs, Frederick Landseer Maur, 1876-1938.

COMSTOCK, Francis Adams 769.924
A Gothic vision; F. L. Griggs and his work. [Boston] Boston Public Lib., 1966. xi, 364p. illus., port. 29cm. Bibl. [NE2210.G7C6] 66-12131 15.00
1. Griggs, Frederick Landseer Maur, 1876-1938. I. Title.

OXFORD. University. 760'.092'4
Ashmolean Museum. Dept. of Western Art.
Centenary exhibition of the etchings and drawings of F. L. Griggs, R.A., R.E. (1876-1938) : McAlpine Gallery, 13 March-30 May 1976. [Oxford, Eng.] : Ashmolean Museum, Department of Western Art, [1976] 23 p. ; 26 cm. [NE2047.6.G74O95 1976] 76-372585
1. Griggs, Frederick Landseer Maur, 1876-1938. I. Griggs, Frederick Landseer Maur, 1876-1938. II. McAlpine Gallery. III. Title.

Grimm, Jakob Ludwig Karl, 1785-1863.

CHILDREN from many lands 760
illustrate Grimm's fairy tales. Sponsored by the Follett Pub. Co. Circulated by the American Federation of Arts. [New York, 1968] 30 p. illus. (part col.) 21 cm. "Catalog ... prepared by the American Federation of Arts for the Follett Publishing Company." [N352.C53] 68-21567
1. Grimm, Jakob Ludwig Karl, 1785-1863. Kinder- und Hausmarchen. 2. Children as artists. 3. Fairy tales—Illustrations—Catalogs. I. American Federation of Arts. II. Follett Publishing Company, Chicago.

Grimshaw, John Atkinson, 1836-1893.

ALEXANDER 759.2'074'02842
Galleries.
The paintings of Atkinson Grimshaw & his followers. Harrogate : Alexander Galleries, 1976. [43] p. : chiefly ill. ; 26 cm. Cover title. [ND497.G74A8] 76-380890 £2.25
1. Grimshaw, John Atkinson, 1836-1893. 2. Paintings, English—Exhibitions. 3. Influence (Literary, artistics, etc.) I. Grimshaw, John Atkinson, 1836-1893. II. Title.

Grinter, Neville, 1930—

GRINTER, Neville, 1930- 759.9931
Hamilton and the Waikato / Neville Grinter. Wellington : A. H. & A. W. Reed, 1976. 32 p. : ill. (some col.) ; 25 cm. [ND1108.G74A45] 77-370661 ISBN 0-589-00971-0
1. Grinter, Neville, 1930- 2. Hamilton, N. Z., in art. 3. Hamilton, N. Z.—Description. 4. Waikato Valley in art. 5. Waikato Valley—Description and travel. I. Title.

Gris, Juan, 1887-1927.

GAYA Nuno, Juan Antonio 759.6
Juan Gris / Juan Antonio Gaya-Nuno ; [translated by Kenneth Lyons]. 1st U.S. ed. Boston : New York Graphic Society, c1975. 267 p. : chiefly ill. (some col.) ; 27 cm. Includes indexes. Bibliography: p. 256-263. [ND813.G75G3713 1975b] 76-360310 ISBN 0-8212-0667-2 : 47.50
1. Gris, Juan, 1887-1927. I. Gris, Juan, 1887-1927.

JUAN Gris, 759.6
by James Thrall Soby [director of the exhibition] The Museum of Modern Art, New York, in collaboration with the Minneapolis Institute of Arts, San Francisco Museum of Art [and] Los Angeles County Museum. [New York, 1958] 128p. illus. (part col.) port. 25cm. 'Selected bibliography by Bernard Karpel': p. 120-124. [ND813.G75N4] 927.5 58-8632
1. Gris, Juan, 1887-1927. I. New York. Museum of Modern Art. II. Soby, James Thrall, 1906-

KAHNWEILER, Daniel Henry, 759.6
1884-
Juan Gris; his life and work. Translated by Douglas Cooper. [Rev. ed.] New York, H.

N. Abrams [1969, c1946] 347 p. illus. (part col.), facsims, plates. 31 cm. Translation of Juan Gris, sa vie, son oevre, ses ecrits. "Bibliography by Bernard Karpel": p. 331-341. [ND813.G75K3 1969b] 69-11532
1. Gris, Juan, 1887-1927. I. Title.

Grisaille painting—Exhibitions.

WILLIAM Marsh Rice 750
University, Houston, Tex. Institute for the Arts.
Gray is the color : [catalogue of] an exhibition of grisaille painting, XIIIth-XXth centuries, Rice Museum, Houston, Texas, October 19, 1973, to January 19, 1974, organized by the Institute for the Arts, Rice University. Houston : The Institute, 1974. 171 p. : ill. ; 23 cm. Includes bibliographical references and index. [ND1489.W54 1974] 73-92776 ISBN 0-914412-08-6
1. Grisaille painting—Exhibitions. I. Houston, Tex. Rice Museum. II. Title.

Griswold, Florence, 1850-1937.

HEMING, Arthur Henry 704'.361
Howard, 1870-1940.
Miss Florence and the artists of Old Lyme. Illustrated by James Stevenson. Foreword by Nelson C. White. Essex, Conn., Pequot Press [1971] 69 p. illus., facsims., col. port. 28 cm. [ND235.O4H4] 78-124471
1. Griswold, Florence, 1850-1937. 2. Painting—Old Lyme, Conn. I. Title. BIP

Grogan, Tony.

GROGAN, Tony. 759.968
Tony Grogan's vanishing Cape Town / text by Brian Barrow. Cape Town : D. Nelson, 1976. [39] p. : ill. (some col.) ; 25 x 33 cm. [NC368.6.S63G76] 77-357819 ISBN 0-909238-21-9
1. Grogan, Tony. 2. Cape Town in art. 3. Cape Town—Description. I. Barrow, Brian. II. Title. III. Title: Vanishing Cape Town.

Grohmann, Will, 1887-

KLEE, Paul, 1879-1940. 741.943
Paul Klee drawings. text by Will Grohmann. Translated from the German by Norbent Guterman New York, H. N. Abrams [1960] 176p. illus., plates. 29cm. 60-11598 15.00 bds.,
1. Grohmann, Will, 1887- I. Title.

Grooms, Red.

TULLY, Judd. 709'.2'4
Red Grooms and Ruckus Manhattan / Judd Tully. 1st ed. New York : G. Braziller, c1977. 31 p., [30] leaves of plates : ill. (some col. ; 29 cm. Bibliography: p. 28. [NB237.G84T84] 76-55130 ISBN 0-8076-0849-1 pbk. : 8.95 ISBN 0-8076-0848-3 : 17.50
1. Grooms, Red. Ruckus Manhattan. I. Title.

Gropius, Walter, 1883-1969.

ALDEN, Richard, 1942- 720'.92'4
Unity and diversity : on Gropius' problem of unity in diversity / by Richard Alden. [State College? Pa.] : s.n., [1974] iv, 17 p. : ill. ; 28 cm. Cover title. Includes bibliographical references. [NA1088.G85A79] 74-84643
1. Gropius, Walter, 1883-1969. 2. Architectural design. 3. Architecture—Composition, proportion, etc. I. Title.

FITCH, James Marston. 720.943
Walter Gropius. New York, G. Braziller, 1960. 128 p. plates, plans. 26 cm. (The Masters of world architecture series) "Selected bibliography of books and articles written by Walter Gropius": p. 120-121. "Selected bibliography on Walter Gropius": p. 122-123. [NA1088.G85F5] 60-13308
1. Gropius, Walter, 1883- I. Title. II. Series. BIP

FOUR great makers of modern 724.9
architecture: Gropius, Le Corbusier, Mies van der Rohe, Wright. Verbatim record of a symp. held at the Sch. of Architecture from March to May 1961. New York,

SUBJECT INDEX

GROUNDS MAINTENANCE.

Columbia Univ. [dist. Wittenborn, 1964, c.1963] vii, 296p. illus. 28cm. Ed. papers orig. presented at the Four great makers prog. 64-3191 7.50 pap.,
1. Gropius, Walter, 1883- 2. Jeanneret-Gris, Charles Edouard, 1887- 3. Mies van der Rohe, Ludwig, 1886- 4. Wright, Frank Lloyd, 1869-1959. 5. Architecture, Modern—20th cent.—Congresses. I. Columbia University. School of Architecture. II. Title: Four great makers program.

FOUR great makers of modern architecture: Gropius, Le Corbusier, Mies van der Rohe, Wright. 720'.922
The verbatim record of a symposium held at the School of Architecture, Columbia University, March-May, 1961. New York, Da Capo Press, 1970. vii, 296 p. illus., plans. 24 cm. (Da Capo Press series in architecture and decorative art, v. 37) Reprint of the 1963 ed. [NA21.F6 1970] 78-130312 ISBN 0-306-70065-4
1. Gropius, Walter, 1883-1969. 2. Jeanneret-Gris, Charles Edouard, 1887-1965. 3. Mies van der Rohe, Ludwig, 1886-1969. 4. Wright, Frank Lloyd, 1867-1959. 5. Architecture, Modern—20th century—Congresses. I. Columbia University. School of Architecture. BIP

FRANCISCONO, Marcel. 707'.1
Walter Gropius and the creation of the Bauhaus in Weimar: the ideals and artistic theories of its founding years. Urbana, University of Illinois Press [1971] xvi, 336 p. illus. 24 cm. Bibliography: p. 298-322. [N70.F69] 73-126519 ISBN 0-252-00128-1 11.95
1. Gropius, Walter, 1883-1969. 2. Bauhaus. 3. Art—Philosophy. I. Title.

GIEDION, Sigfried, 1888- 927.2
Walter Gropius, work and teamwork. New York, Reinhold Pub. Corp. [1954] 249 p. illus., ports., plans. 26 cm. Bibliography: p. 237-243. [NA1088.G85G52] 54-14245
1. Gropius, Walter, 1883-1969.

Gropius, Walter, 1883-1969—Bibliography.

GROPIUS, Wren, Latrobe, Wright. 016.72 s
Charlottesville, Published for the American Association of Architectural Bibliographers [by the] University Press of Virginia [1972] 132 p. 24 cm. (American Association of Architectural Bibliographers. Papers, v. 9) [Z5941.A5 vol. 9] [Z8369.43] 016.72'092'2 72-195645 ISBN 0-8139-0391-2 7.50
1. Gropius, Walter, 1883-1969—Bibliography. 2. Wren, Christopher, Sir, 1632-1723—Bibliography. 3. Latrobe, Benjamin Henry, 1764-1820—Bibliography. 4. Wright, Frank Lloyd, 1867-1959—Bibliography. I. American Association of Architectural Bibliographers. II. Title. III. Series.

Gross, Chaim, 1904—

GROSS, Chaim, 1904- 730'.92'4
Chaim Gross, by Frank Getlein. New York, H. N. Abrams [1974] 235 p. illus. (part col.) 28 x 30 cm. Bibliography: p. 233-235. [NB237.G85G47] 73-13807 ISBN 0-8109-0160-9
1. Gross, Chaim, 1904- I. Getlein, Frank. BIP

GROSS, Chaim, 1904- 709'.2'4
Chaim Gross : sculpture and drawings : [exhibition], January 23-March 27, 1977, Montclair Art Museum, Montclair, N.J. [Montclair, N.J : The Museum], c1977. [19] p. : ill. ; 26 cm. [N6537.G74M65] 77-151858
1. Gross, Chaim, 1904- I. Montclair, N.J. Art Museum.

GROSS, Chaim, 1904- 730'.92'4
Chaim Gross: sculpture and drawings. Washington, Published for National Collection of Fine Arts by Smithsonian Institution Press; [for sale by the Supt. of Docs., U.S. Govt. Print Off.] 1974. 47 p. illus. 26 cm. ([Smithsonian Institution Press publication, no. 5243]) Text by J. Flint. Catalog of an exhibition held Sept. 13-Nov.24, 1974, at the National Collection of Fine Arts Smithsonian Institution. Bibliography: p. 43-45. [NB237.G85F55] 74-18237
1. Gross, Chaim, 1904- 2. Artists' preparatory studies—United States. I. Flint, Janet A. II. Smithsonian Institution. National Collection of Fine Arts. III. Title.

MOWSHOWITZ, Israel. 730'.92'4
The sculpture reliefs of the Ten commandments by Chaim Gross at International Synagogue, John F. Kennedy International Airport, New York / introd. and text by Israel Mowshowitz. Jamaica, N.Y. : International Synagogue, 1973. [38] p. : col. ill. ; 29 cm. Half title: The Ten commandments. [NB237.G85M68] 73-83023
1. Gross, Chaim, 1904- Ten commandments. 2. International Synagogue, Jamaica, N.Y. I. Gross, Chaim, 1904- II. Title. III. Title: The Ten commandments.

TARBELL, Roberta K. 709'.2'4
Chaim Gross : retrospective exhibition : sculpture, paintings, drawings, prints, the Jewish Museum, New York, May 26-October 24, 1977 / Roberta K. Tarbell. New York : The Museum, c1977. 40 p. : ill. ; 25 cm. [N6537.G74T37] 77-75406
1. Gross, Chaim, 1904- I. Gross, Chaim, 1904- II. Jewish Theological Seminary of America. Jewish Museum.

Grosz, George, 1893-1959.

BAUR, John Ireland Howe, 1909- 759.13
George Grosz. [Research by Rosalind Irvine] New York, Published for the Whitney Museum of American Art by Macmillan, 1954. 67p. illus. (part col.) port. 26cm. 'The result of a retrospective exhibition of the work of George Grosz held by the Whitney Museum of American Art in January and February 1954.'--p. 67. 'Catalogue of the exhibition': p. 60-63. Bibliography: p. 65-67. [ND237.G68B3] 54-802 927 54-802
1. Grosz, George, 1893- 2. Paintings. American—Exhibitions. I. Whitney Museum of American Art, New yYork. II. Title.

GROSZ, George, 1893-1959. 741.973
Der Spiesser-Spiegel. Image of the German Babbit. With an autobiographical sketch by the artist, and additional remarks by Walter Mehring. New York, Arno Press [1968] x, 14 p., 60 illus. 27 cm. (Arno series of contemporary art, no. 17) Includes a reprint of the 1932 German ed. with an English translation by Alfred Werner. [NC1075.G88A57] 68-9232
I. Title. II. Title: Image of the German Babbit. BIP

GROSZ, George, 1893-1959 741.943
Ecce homo. New York 10003, J. Brussel [United Bk. Guild, 100 4th Ave., c.]1965. 1v. (unpaged) plates (16 col.) 37 cm. [NC1145.G7343] 65-9191 35.00, bds., lim. ed.
I. Title.

GROSZ, George, 1893-1959 741.943
Ecce homo. Introd. by Henry Miller. New York, Grove [1966, c.1965] iv. (unpaged) plates (16 col.) 33 cm. [NC1145.G7343] 15.00
I. Title.
First published in Berlin in 1923. Published in New York in 1965 by J. Brussel and distributed by United Book Guild without the introductory material.

GROSZ, George, 1893-1959. 741.5'943
Ecce homo / by George Grosz. New York : Dover Publications, 1976. 84 p. : chiefly ill. (some col.) ; 29 cm. (Dover art collections) "An unabridged republication of the work originally published by the Malik-Verlag, Berlin, in 1923 ... Ausgabe C. ... The text has been newly translated specially for the present edition." English and German. [NC251.G66A4413] 76-26191 ISBN 0-486-23410-X : 4.00
1. Grosz, George, 1893-1959. I. Title.

GROSZ, George, 1893-1959. 741.943
George Grosz, [Einfuhrung von Ruth Berenson und Norbert Muhlen und ein Essay des Kunstlers. Herbert Bittner, Herausgeber. New York, Arts, inc., 1961] 52p. 108p. of illus. col. plates, port. 29cm. Bibliography: p. 36-45. [ND237.G68B43] 61-38005
I. Title.

GROSZ, George, 1893-1959. 759.3
George Grosz : works in oil : Heckscher Museum, Huntington, New York, July 1-September 4, 1977 / text by Eva Ingersoll Gatling. New York : The Museum, c1977. 35 p. : ill. (some col.) ; 28 cm. Bibliography: p. 23. [ND588.G698A45] 77-82076 ISBN 0-89062-054-7
1. Grosz, George, 1893-1959. I. Gatling, Eva Ingersoll. II. Heckscher Museum.

GROSZ, George, 1893-1959. 741.943
George the artist. Edited by Herbert Butter New York, Arts, inc., 1960] 51p. 108p. of illus. col. plates, port. 29cm. (A Golden griffin book) Bibliography: p. [33]-43. [ND237.G68B4] 59-15105
I. Title.

GROSZ, George, 1893-1959. 741.943
Grosz : October 2-November 14, 1974. Washington : Lunn Gallery/Graphics International Ltd., [1974] [16] p. : chiefly ill. ; 24 cm. & price list. [NC251.G66L86] 74-19132
1. Grosz, George, 1893-1959. I. Lunn Gallery.

GROSZ, George, 1893-1959. 741.9'43
Love above all, and other drawings; 120 works. New York, Dover Publications [1971] 119 p. (chiefly illus.) 28 cm. A republication of the author's Uber alles die Liebe (1930) and Die Gezeichneten (1930), with English and German captions. [NC139.G74A54 1971] 78-121583 ISBN 0-486-22675-1 2.50
I. Grosz, George, 1893-1959. Die Gezeichneten. English and German. 1971. II. Title. BIP

HESS, Hans, art curator. 741.5'943
George Grosz. [1st American ed.] New York, Macmillan [1974] 272 p. illus. (part col.) 29 cm. Bibliography: p. 266-270. [NC1509.G78H47 1974] 74-7414 ISBN 0-02-551270-6 22.50
1. Grosz, George, 1893-1959. 2. Politics in art. 3. German wit and humor, Pictorial.

LEWIS, Beth Irwin. 741'.0924 B
George Grosz: art and politics in the Weimar Republic. Madison, University of Wisconsin Press [1971] xviii, 328 p. illus., ports. 25 cm. Revision of the author's thesis, University of Wisconsin. Includes bibliographical references. [NC251.G66L48 1971] 79-143764 ISBN 0-299-05901-4 12.50
1. Grosz, George, 1893-1959. 2. Germany—History, Comic, satirical, etc. I. Title.

Grotesque.

DANIEL, Howard, 1911- 704.946
Devils, monsters, and nightmares; an introduction to the grotesque and fantastic in art. New York, Abelard [1965, c.1964] 67p., 298 illus., 299-304p. 29cm. Bibl. [N8217.G8D3] 64-19637 12.50
1. Grotesque. I. Title.

DOTY, Robert M. 709'.73
Human concern/personal torment; the grotesque in American art, by Robert Doty. New York, Published for the Whitney Museum of American Art by Praeger [1969] [81] p. illus. (part col.) 26 cm. Catalogue of an exhibition held at the Whitney Museum of American Art, New York, Oct. 14-Nov. 30, 1969, and at the Art Museum, University of California, Berkeley, Jan. 20-Mar. 1, 1970. Bibliography: p. [79-80] [N6512.D6] 79-89621 7.95
1. Grotesque. 2. Art, American—Exhibitions. 3. Art, Modern—20th century—U.S. I. Whitney Museum of American Art, New York. II. California. University. Art Museum. III. Title.

KAYSER, Wolfgang Johannes, 1906-1960. 704.94
The grotesque in art and literature. Translated by Ulrich Weisstein. Bloomington, Indiana University Press [1963] 224 p. illus. 24 cm. Translation of Das Groteske: seine Gestaltung in Malerei und Dichtung. [N8217.G8K33] 63-9719
1. Grotesque. 2. Grotesque in literature. I. Title.

WILDRIDGE, Thomas Tindall. 704.948
The grotesque in church art, by T. Tindall Wildridge. London, W. Andrews, 1899. Detroit, Gale Research Co., 1969. vii, 228 p. illus. 23 cm. [N8180.W4 1969] 68-30633
1. Grotesque. 2. Christian art and symbolism. 3. Church decoration and ornament. I. Title. BIP

Grotesque in art.

BASKIN, Leonard, 1922- 769'.922
Five addled etchers. Hanover, N.H., Dartmouth Publications [1969] 52 p. illus. (part fold.) 32 cm. (Hamilton B. Mitchell lecture on printing and graphic arts, 1) [NE2150.B3] 70-78030 10.00
1. Grotesque in art. 2. Etchings. I. Title. II. Series. BIP

KAYSER, Wolfgang Johannes, 1906-1960. 704.94
The grotesque in art and literature. Translated by Ulrich Weisstein. Gloucester, Mass., P. Smith, 1968 [c1963] 224 p. illus. 24 cm. Translation of Das Grotske: seine Gestaltung in Malerei und Dichtung. Bibliographical references included in "Notes" (p. 190-201) [N8217.G8K33 1968] 78-3767
1. Grotesque in art. 2. Grotesque in literature. I. Title. BIP

PETAJA, Emil, 1915- comp. 741.64'092'2
The Hannes Bok memorial showcase of fantasy art. Compiled & edited by Emil Petaja. San Francisco, SISU Publishers [1974] 166 p. illus. (part col.) 28 cm. [NC960.P467] 73-92462 10.00
1. Bok, Hannes, 1914-1964. 2. Grotesque in art. 3. Illustration of books. I. Bok, Hannes, 1914-1964. II. Title. III. Title: Showcase of fantasy art.

THE Waking dream : 769'.4
fantasy and the surreal in graphic art, 1450-1900 / introd. and commentaries by Edward Lucie-Smith ; notes on the plates by Aline Jacquiot ; [translated from the French by Nicholas Fry]. 1st American ed. New York : Knopf, 1975. 224 p. : chiefly ill. ; 31 cm. Translation of Quatre siecles de surrealisme. Includes index. [NE962.G7Q3713 1975] 74-21775 ISBN 0-394-49758-9 : 17.50
1. Grotesque in art. 2. Prints. 3. Surrealism. I. Lucie-Smith, Edward. II. Jacquiot, Aline.

WOODROFFE, Patrick, 1940- 760'.092'44
"Mythopoeikon" : fantasies, monsters, nightmares, daydreams : the paintings, book-jacket illustrations, and record-sleeve designs of Patrick Woodroffe / with a commentary by the artist. [Limpsfield, Eng. : Dragon's World, c1976] 155 p. : chiefly col. ill. ; 30 cm. [NC1883.3.W66A55] 77-363167 ISBN 0-905071-09-3. ISBN 0-905071-08-5 pbk. : £3.95
1. Woodroffe, Patrick, 1940- 2. Grotesque in art. I. Title.

Grotesque in art—Juvenile literature.

BARR, Beryl. 704 (j)
Wonders, warriors, and beasts abounding. Foreword by Thomas P. F. Hoving. [1st ed.] Garden City, N.Y., Doubleday [1967] 128 p. illus. (part col.) 29 cm. [N8217.G8B33] 67-9679
1. Grotesque in art—Juvenile literature. I. Title.

Grounds maintenance.

CONOVER, Herbert S. 712
Grounds maintenance handbook. 2d ed. New York, F. W. Dodge Corp. [1958] 501 p. illus. 24 cm. [SB476.C6 1958] 58-6360
1. Grounds maintenance.

CONOVER, Herbert S. 635.9
Grounds maintenance handbook / Herbert S. Conover. 3d ed. New York : McGraw-Hill, [1976] p. cm. Includes index. [SB476.C6 1976] 76-18901 ISBN 0-07-012412-4 : 22.50
1. Grounds maintenance. I. Title. BIP

ORAVETZ, Jules A. 635.9
Grounds maintenance, by Jules Oravetz, Sr. [1st ed.] Indianapolis, T. Audel [1971] 374 p. illus. 22 cm. Published in 1975 under title: Gardening and landscaping. [SB472.O65] 72-153447
1. Grounds maintenance. 2. Landscape gardening.

Group of Seven.

HUNKIN, Harry. 759.11
A story of the Group of Seven / Harry Hunkin. Toronto ; New York : McGraw-Hill Ryerson, c1976. 160 p. : ill. (some col.), ports. ; 21 x 22 cm. Originally published 1971 under title: There is no finality. [N6545.5.S4H8 1976] 77-364169 ISBN 0-07-082418-5 : 10.95
1. Group of Seven. 2. Art, Modern—20th century—Canada. I. Title.

Group work in architecture.

CAUDILL, William Wayne. 720'.28
Architecture by team; a new concept for the practice of architecture. New York, Van Nostrand Reinhold [1971] xvi, 346 p. illus., ports. 16 x 24 cm. [NA737.C3C3] 75-157696
1. Caudill, Rowlett, Scott. 2. Group work in architecture. I. Title.

GRIFFIN, Charles William, 1925- 711 .12
Development building: the team approach. by C. W. Griffin. Illustrated by Charles D. Stokes. [Washington, American Institute of Architects]; distributed by Halsted Press Division, Wiley, New York [1972] 130 p. illus. 29 cm. [NA2540.G65] 72-79441 15.00
1. Group work in architecture. I. American Institute of Architects. II. Title.

Groves, William E., 1906- —Art collections.

WIESENDANGER, Martin. 759.13'074'016318
19th century Louisiana painters and paintings from the Collection of W. E. Groves. [By Martin and Margaret Wiesendanger. Gretna [La.] Pelican Pub. Co., 1971. 118 p. illus. 24 cm. [ND230.L8W53] 73-156076 ISBN 0-911116-52-4
1. Groves, William E., 1906- —Art collections. 2. Paintings, American—Exhibitions. 3. Painting, Modern—19th century—Louisiana. 4. Painters—Louisiana. I. Wiesendanger, Margaret, joint author. II. Title.

Grum, Zeljko.

MESTROVIC, Ivan, 1883-1962 730.9497
Ivan Mestrovic [by] Zeljko Grum. Photos. by Toso Dabac. Zagreb, Matica Hrvatska [dist. New York, Vanous, 1963] xxxvi, 189p. chiefly illus. 29cm. 63-3936 14.90
1. Grum, Zeljko. I. Title.

Grundy, John Hull.

EXHIBITION of works by John Hull Grundy : [catalogue of an exhibition held] 6th December 1976 to 28 January 1977, 10am to 4pm, in the Study Centre of the Royal Army Medical College / [compiled by N. R. H. Burgess]. [London] : [Royal Army Medical College], [1976] [11] p. : ill. ; 25 cm. Cover title. "Notes for the souvenir catalogue were compiled by Mr. J. H. Grundy and Mrs. A. Grundy, and the catalogue was composed by Dr. Burgess and the staff of the Department of Medical Illustration, Royal Army Medical College." [NC242.G78B87] 77-372932 ISBN 0-9505525-0-X 760'.092'4
1. Grundy, John Hull. I. Grundy, John Hull. II. Grundy, A. III. Burgess, N. R. H. IV. Royal Army Medical College. V. Royal Army Medical College. Dept. of Medical Illustration.

Grunewald, Mathias, 16th cent.

BURKHARD, Arthur. 759.3
Matthias Grunewald : personality and accomplishment / by Arthur Burkhard. New York : Hacker Art Books, 1976. x, 123 p., [90] leaves of plates : ill. ; 28 cm. Reprint of the 1936 ed. published by Harvard University Press, Cambridge, Mass. Bibliography: p. [95]-111. [ND588.G7B9 1976] 75-10712 ISBN 0-87817-186-X : 35.00
1. Grunewald, Mathias, 16th cent. BIP

GRUNEWALD, Mathias, 16thcent. 759.3
Grunewald / with an essay by J.-K. Huysmans ; [translated from the French by Robert Baldick]. Oxford : Phaidon, 1977 16 p., [48] p. of plates : chiefly col. ill. ; 31 cm. [ND588.G7H88 1976] 76-388 ISBN 0-7148-1751-1 : 6.95
1. Grunewald, Mathias, 16th cent. I. Huysmans, Joris Karl, 1848-1907.
Distributed by E.P.Dutton, N.Y.

SCHMITT, Pierre 759.3
Mathias Grunewald and other old masters in Colmar. Introd. by Pierre Schmitt. [Tr. from German by Gladys Wheelhouse] With 28 color plates by E. Ohresser. New York, A. S. Barnes [1963, c.1961] 67p. mounted col. illus. 22cm. [Metropolis bks.] 63-61336 4.95
1. Grunewald, Mathias, 16th cent. 2. Painters, German—Colmar. I. Title.

Gual, Enrique F.

ALFARO SIQUEIROS, David, 1896- 759.12
Siqueiros. Introd. de Enrique Gual; traduccion al ingles por Emma Gutierrez Suarez. Mexico, Ediciones Galeria de Arte Misrachi [New York, Heinman, c.1965] 46p. illus., col. plates. 38cm. [ND259.A4G823] 66-36205 25.00
1. Gual, Enrique F. I. Title.

Guanajuato, Mexico (City)—Antiquities—Pictorial works.

THE Mummies of Guanajuato / photography, Archie Lieberman ; story, Ray Bradbury. New York : H. N. Abrams, 1978. [96] p. : ill. ; 31 cm. The next in line, by Ray Bradbury: p. [20]-[58] [F1219.1.G86M85] 813'.5'4 77-16022 ISBN 0-8109-2150-2 pbk. : 9.95 FIC
1. Guanajuato, Mexico (City)—Antiquities—Pictorial works. 2. Mummies—Pictorial works. 3. Mexico—Antiquities—Pictorial works. I. Lieberman, Archie. II. Bradbury, Ray, 1920- The next in line. 1978. BIP

Guardi, Francesco, 1712-1793.

BINION, Alice. 741'.092'2
Antonio and Francesco Guardi, their life and milieu : with a catalogue of their figure drawings / Alice Binion. New York : Garland Pub., 1976. 466 p. : ill. ; 21 cm. (Outstanding dissertations in the fine arts) Originally presented as the author's thesis, Columbia University, 1971. Bibliography: p. [333]-348. [NC257.G8B56 1976] 75-23782 ISBN 0-8240-1979-2 lib.bdg. : 32.50
1. Guardi, Francesco, 1712-1793. 2. Guardi, Giovanni Antonio, 1698-1760. 3. Figure drawing—Catalogs. I. Title. II. Series.

Guerrero, Mexico (State)—Antiquities.

GAY, Carlo T. E. 730.972'7
Mezcala stone sculpture; the human figure, by Carlo T. E. Gay. Greenwich, Conn., Distributed by the New York Graphic Society, 1967. 39 p. illus., maps. 28 cm. (Museum of Primitive Art. Studies, no. 5) Bibliography: p. 39. [F1219.1.G93G3] 66-28587
1. Guerrero, Mexico (State)—Antiquities. 2. Indians of Mexico—Guerrero (State)—Antiquities. 3. Indians of Mexico—Sculpture. I. Title. II. Series: New York. Museum of Primitive Art. Studies, no. 5.

Guggenheim, Marguerite, 1898- —Art collections.

CALAS, Nicolas. 708.5
The Peggy Guggenheim collection of modern art. Text by Nicolas Calas and Elena Calas. New York, H. N. Abrams [1966] 263 p. plates (part col.) 36 cm. [N5220.G889] 66-26654
1. Guggenheim, Marguerite, 1898- —Art collections. 2. Art, Modern—20th century. I. Calas, Elena, joint author. II. Title.

Guido da Siena, 13th cent.

STUBBLEBINE, James H 759.5
Guido da Siena, by James H. Stubblebine. Princeton, N.J., Princeton University Press, 1964. xv, 121 p. 128 illus. 31 cm. Bibliography: p. 110-116. [ND623.G95S8] 63-23395
1. Guido da Siena, 13th cent. I. Title.

Guild of handicraft, London.

ASHBEE, Charles Robert, 1863-1942. 338.6'32'0942
Craftmanship in competitive industry / C. R. Ashbee. New York : Garland Pub., 1977, i.e.1978 258 p. : ill. ; 24 cm. (The Aesthetic movement & the arts and crafts movement) Reprint of the 1908 ed. published by Essex House Press, Campden, England. [NK1149.G8A8 1977] 76-17772 ISBN 0-8240-2477-X lib.bdg. : 35.00
1. Guild of handicraft, London. 2. Arts and crafts movement. I. Title. II. Series.

Guilford Courthouse National Military Park.

U.S. National Park Service. 712'.5'0975662
Guilford Courthouse National Military Park, North Carolina; master plan. [Washington] 1969. 69 p. illus., maps., plans (both part fold.) 28 cm. [E241.G9U52] 71-603139
1. Guilford Courthouse National Military Park.

Guilfoyle, William Robert, 1840-1912.

PESCOTT, Richard Thomas Martin, 1905- 712'.5 B
W. R. Guilfoyle, 1840-1912 : the master of landscaping / [by] R. T. M. Pescott. Melbourne ; New York : Oxford University Press, 1974. xvii, 153 p., 13 p. of plates : ill., facsims., front., map on lining papers ; 25 cm. Includes index. Bibliography: p. 143-145. [SB470.G84P47] 75-320160 ISBN 0-19-550454-2 : 9.75
1. Guilfoyle, William Robert, 1840-1912. 2. Melbourne. Botanic Garden. 3. Landscape gardening—Australia—Melbourne.

Guimard, Hector, 1867-1942.

GRAHAM, F. Lanier. 709'.24
Hector Guimard [by] F. Lanier Graham. New York, Museum of Modern Art [1970] 36 p. illus. 26 cm. Catalog of the exhibition held Mar. 10-May 10, 1970, at the Museum of Modern Art, New York. [NA1053.G8G7] 69-11451
1. Guimard, Hector, 1867-1942. I. New York (City). Museum of Modern Art.

GUIMARD, Hector, 1867-1942. 720'.92'4
Hector Guimard / [text by Gillian Naylor and Yvonne Brunhammer]. New York : Rizzoli, 1978. 112 p. : ill. ; 30 cm. (Architectural monographs ; 2) Resumes in French, German, Italian, and Spanish. Bibliography: p. 104. [NA1053.G8A4 1978] 78-58779 13.95
1. Guimard, Hector, 1867-1942. I. Naylor, Gillian. II. Brunhammer, Yvonne. III. Series: Architectural monographs (New York) ; 2.

GUIMARD, Hector, 1867-1942. 720'.92'4
Hector Guimard : [1867-1942] : Landesmuseum Munster, 16. Marz-27. April 1975 / [Ausstellung u. Katalog, Yvonne Brunhammer, Klaus Bussmann, Roswitha Kock ; Ubers., Susanne Schmidt ; Photogr., Laurent Sully Jaulmes ; Hrsg., Landesmuseum f. Kunst u. Kulturgeschichte Munster d. Landschaftsverb. Westfalen-Lippe]. Munster : Landesmuseum Munster, 1975. 139 p., [7] leaves of plates : ill. ; 23 cm. Bibliography: p. 122-128. [NA1053.G8B79] 75-522783 DM10.00
1. Guimard, Hector, 1867-1942. I. Brunhammer, Yvonne. II. Bussmann, Klaus. III. Kock, Roswitha. IV. Landesmuseum fur Kunst und Kulturgeschichte Munster.

GUIMARD, Hector, 1867-1942. 720'.92'4
Hector Guimard : Architektur in Paris um 1900 : Museum Villa Stuck, Munchen, 27. Mai-17. August 1975 / [Ausstellung und Katalog, Yvonne Brunhammer, Klaus Bussmann, Roswitha Kock ; Ubersetzungen, Susanne Schmidt]. Munster : Landesmuseum fur Kunst und Kulturgeschichte, [1975?] 139 p., [7] leaves of plates : ill. ; 23 cm. Introductory essay by Yvonne Brunhammer in French and German. Bibliography: p. 122-128. [NA1053.G8B78] 75-521089
1. Guimard, Hector, 1867-1942. 2. Architecture—Paris—Exhibitions. 3. Decoration and ornament—Art nouveau—Exhibitions. I. Brunhammer, Yvonne. II. Bussmann, Klaus. III. Kock, Roswitha. IV. Stuck-Villa (Museum) V. Landesmuseum fur Kunst- und Kulturgeschichte Munster.

Gulf coast (United States) in art.

STOCKFLETH, Julius, 1857-1935. 759.13
Julius Stockfleth, Gulf Coast marine and landscape painter / by James Patrick McGuire ; introduction by Eric Steinfeldt. San Antonio : Trinity University Press, 1976. xii, 161 p. : chiefly ill. (some col.) ; 23 x 27 cm. "Published in conjunction with an exhibition of paintings and drawings by Julius Stockfleth in December, 1976 at the Rosenberg Library, Galveston, Texas." Bibliography: p. 15-16. [N6537.S75M32 1976] 76-29876 ISBN 0-911536-67-1 pbk. : 10.00
1. Stockfleth, Julius, 1857-1935. 2. Gulf coast (United States) in art. I. McGuire, James Patrick. II. Rosenberg Library, Galveston. III. Title.

Gulick, Henry Thomas, 1872-1964.

GULICK, Henry Thomas, 1872-1964. 759.13
Henry Thomas Gulick, 1872-1964. [Exhibition] Montclair Art Museum, Montclair, New Jersey, April 21-June 23, 1974. [Montclair, N.J., Montclair Art Museum, 1974] [36] p. illus. (part col.) 18 x 26 cm. [ND237.G77M66] 74-171049
1. Gulick, Henry Thomas, 1872-1964. 2. Primitivism in art—United States. I. Montclair, N.J. Art Museum.

Gulls—Pictorial works.

BRODATZ, Phil. 779'.32
Gulls in flight. [Coral Gables, Fla.] c1973. [4] l., [12] l. of plates. 27 x 35 cm. Signed ed. of 25 copies printed. [QL696.C46B76] 73-89871
1. Gulls—Pictorial works. I. Title.

Gunn, Gordon, 1916—

RHIND, Neil. 759.941
A Scottish painter and his world—Gordon Gunn. Aberdeen, Impulse Publications Ltd, 1972. [2], 30, [36] p., 8 leaves. illus. (incl. 8 col.) 22 x 30 cm. [ND1942.G86R48] 73-160898 ISBN 0-901311-25-1 £5.50
1. Gunn, Gordon, 1916- I. Gunn, Gordon, 1916- II. Title.

Gunsmithing.

ACKLEY, Parker O. 683'.4
Home gun care & repair, by Parker O. Ackley. Harrisburg, Pa., Stackpole Books [1969] 191 p. illus. 20 cm. [TS535.A26] 69-16147 5.95
1. Gunsmithing. 2. Firearms—Maintenance and repair. I. Title. BIP

BAKER, Clyde. 683.4
Modern gunsmithing; a manual of firearms design, construction, and remodeling for

amateurs & professionals. Harrisburg, Pa., Stackpole Co. [c1959] 535 p. illus., port. 23 cm. (Samworth books on firearms) [TS535.B23] 64-5437
1. Gunsmithing. 2. Firearms. I. Title.

BASIC gun repair. 683'.403
Los Angeles : Petersen Pub. Co., [1973] 240 p. : ill. ; 28 cm. Cover title: Petersen's basic gun repair. [TS535.B317] 72-96583 3.95
1. Gunsmithing. I. Petersen Publishing Company. II. Title: Petersen's basic gun repair.

BISH, Tommy L. 683'.4
Home gunsmithing digest, by Tommy L. Bish. Northfield, Ill., Gun Digest Pub. Co. [1970] 319 p. illus. 28 cm. [TS535.B54] 71-118931 4.95
1. Gunsmithing. I. Title. BIP

BROWNELL, Frank,. comp. 683'.4
Gunsmith kinks; a fascinating and widely varied accumulation of shop kinks, short cuts, techniques and comments sent by practicing gunsmiths from all over the world to F. R. "Bob" Brownell. Edited and compiled by his son Frank Brownell. Montezuma, Iowa, F. Brownell, 1969. viii, 496 p. illus. 23 cm. [TS535.B67] 77-90353 9.95
1. Gunsmithing. I. Brownell, Frank Royce, 1911- II. Title.

BUCHELE, William. 683'.4
Recreating the Kentucky rifle. [n.p., 1966] 83 p. illus. (2 fold. in pocket) 24 cm. On spine: Kentucky rifle. [TS535.B8] 67-2303
1. Gunsmithing. 2. Kentucky rifles. I. Title. II. Title: Kentucky rifle.

BUCHELE, William. 683'.4
Recreating the Kentucky rifle, by William Buchele. 2d ed., rev. & edited by George Shumway. York, Pa., G. Shumway [1970] vii, 189 p. illus. (2 fold. in pocket) 22 cm. [TS535.B8 1970] 70-105321
1. Gunsmithing. 2. Kentucky rifle. I. Shumway, George, ed. II. Title.

DUNLAP, Roy F., 1914- 683.4
Gunsmithing; a manual of firearms design, construction, alteration, and remodeling. For amateur and professional gunsmiths, and users of modern firearms. Drawings by Paul Webb. 2d ed. Harrisburg, Pa., Stackpole Co. 1963 ix, 742 p. illus., ports. (1 col.) 23 cm. Bibliography: p.37-39. [TS535.D8 1963] 63-21755
1. Gunsmithing.

DUNLAP, Roy F, 1914- 683
Gunsmithing; a manual of firearms design, construction, alteration, and remodeling. For amateur and professional gunsmiths and users of modern firearms. Drawings by Paul Webb. Georgetown, S. C., Small-Arms Technical Pub. Co., 1950. ix, 714 p. illus., ports. 23 cm. (A Samworth book on Firearms) "Reference books and sources of supply": p. 37-64. [TS535.D8] 51-128
1. Gunsmithing. I. Title.

HOWE, James Virgil. 683
The amateur guncraftsman [a practical handbook for those who like guns] New York, Funk & Wagnalls [1967,c.1953] xii, illus. 304p. (F2) [TS535.H57 1953] 53-6988 1.50 pap.,
1. Gunsmithing. 2. Firearms. I. Title.

HOWE, James Virgil. 683
The modern gunsmith; a guide for the amateur and professional gunsmith in the design and construction of firearms, with practical suggestions for all who like guns. Rev. ed., with suppl. giving latest developments up to 1941. New York, Funk & Wagnalls [c1941-54] 2v. illus., ports., diagrs. 27cm. Bibliography: v. 1, p. 424. [TS535.H62] 53-6989
1. Gunsmithing. 2. Firearms. I. Title.

KAUFFMAN, Henry. 683
Early American gunsmiths, 1650-1850: illustrated and documented. Harrisburg, Pa., Stackpole Co. [1952] xx, 94 p. illus., port., map. 27 cm. [TS535.K3] 52-6593
1. Gunsmithing. 2. Firearms industry and trade—U. S. I. Title.

MACFARLAND, Harold E. 683
Gunsmithing simplified. Drawings by Forrest Christensen. [1st ed.] Washington, Combat Forces Press [1950]Cxv, 802 p. illus. 26 cm. (A National Rifle Association library book) "A Sportman's Press book." [TS535.M3] 50-11303
1. Gunsmithing. I. Title.

MACFARLAND, Harold E. 683.403
Introduction to modern gunsmithing. Drawings by Thomas E. Wessel. Harrisburg, Pa., Stackpole [c.1965] 320p. illus. 23cm. [TS535.M32] 65-21622 6.95
1. Gunsmithing. I. Title. II. Title: Modern gunsmithing. BIP

MACFARLAND, Harold E. 683'.4
Introduction to modern gunsmithing / Harold E. MacFarland ; drawings by Thomas E. Wessel. New York : Barnes & Noble Books, 1974, c1965. 319 p. : ill. ; 21 cm. Reprint of the ed. published by Stackpole Books, Harrisburg, Pa. Includes index. [TS535.M32 1974] 75-310935 ISBN 0-06-463426-4 : 2.95 ($3.25 Can.)
1. Gunsmithing. I. Title.

NONTE, George C. 683'.43
Pistolsmithing [by] George C. Nonte, Jr. [Harrisburg, Pa.] Stackpole Books [1974] 560 p. illus. 24 cm. Bibliography: p. 524-525. [TS535.N58] 74-10783 ISBN 0-8117-1133-1
1. Gunsmithing. 2. Pistols. I. Title. BIP

STELLE, James Parish. 683'.4
The gunsmith's manual; a complete handbook for the American gunsmith, being a practical guide to all branches of the trade, by J. P. Stelle and Wm. B. Harrison. New York, Excelsior Pub. House. [Highland Park, N.J., Gun Room Press, 1972] xv, 376 p. illus. 22 cm. Reprint of the 1883 ed. [TS535.S7 1972] 72-187111 ISBN 0-88227-002-8
1. Gunsmithing. I. Harrison, William B., fl. 1868-1883, joint author. II. Title.

STELLE, James Parish. 683
How to be a gunsmith or, Gunsmith's manual a complete handbook for the American gunsmith, being a practical guide to all branches of the trade. By J. P. Stelle and Wm. B. Harrison. Authoritative text reproduced by Columbia Research Reprints; Martin Rywell, editor. Harriman, Tenn., Pioneer Press [c1955] 376p. illus. 18cm. First published in 1883 under title: The gunsmith's manual. [TS535.S7 1955] 56-535
1. Gunsmithing. I. Harrison, William B., joint author. II. Title.

SWINNEY, Holman J 1919- 683
New York State gunmakers; a partial checklist. Cooperstown, N.Y., Freeman's Journal Press, 1951. 59 p. illus. 23 cm. "Originally ... published in ... the January and April, 1951, issues of New York history, the quarterly of the New York State Historical Association." [TS535.S9] 51-39166
1. Gunsmithing. I. Title.

WALKER, Ralph T., 1931- 683'.4
Hobby gunsmithing, by Ralph T. Walker. Edited by Jack Lewis. Chicago, Follett [1972] 320 p. illus. 28 cm. [TS535.W23] 72-86644 ISBN 0-695-80361-1 5.95
1. Gunsmithing. I. Title. BIP

WOLFF, Eldon G. 683'.42
Wyatt Atkinson: riflesmith, by Eldon G. Wolff. [Milwaukee, Milwaukee Public Museum, 1963?] 38-51 p. illus., ports. 23 cm. (Milwaukee. Public Museum. Publications in history, no. 6) Cover title. "Reprinted from Lore, Spring, 1964, vol. 14, no. 2." [TS535.W62] 73-16439
1. Atkinson, Wyatt. 2. Gunsmithing. I. Title. II. Series.

Gunsmithing—Amateurs' manuals.

BURCH, Monte. 683'.4
Gun care and repair / Monte Burch. New York : Winchester Press, c1978. ix, 191 p. : ill. ; 26 cm. Includes index. [TS535.B87] 78-2338 ISBN 0-87691-256-0 : 10.95
1. Gunsmithing—Amateurs' manuals. I. Title.

CARMICHEL, Jim. 683'.403
Do-it-yourself gunsmithing / by Jim Carmichel ; with photos by the author. New York : Outdoor Life, c1977. x, 372 p. : ill. ; 25 cm. Includes index. [TS535.C27] 77-12450 ISBN 0-06-010638-7 : 13.95
1. Gunsmithing—Amateurs' manuals. I. Title. BIP

Gunsmithing—Dictionaries.

SATTERLEE, Leroy De Forest, 1891- 683
American gun makers by Arcadi Gluckman and L.D. Satterlee. 2d rev ed including supplement of American gun makers Harrisburg, Pa., Stackpole Co. [1953] 243, [3]p. 25cm. Authors' names in reverse order in previous ed. Bibliography: p. [245]--[246] [TS535.S29 1953] 53-5668
1. Gunsmithing—Dictionaries. 2. Firearms industry and trade—U. S. 3. Firearms—Hist. I. Gluckman, Arcadi, 1896- joint author. II. Title.

Gunsmithing — Direct.

GARDNER, Robert Edward. 623.44
Small arms makers: a directory of fabricators of firearms, edged weapons, crossbows, and polearms. New York, Crown Publishers [1963] 378 p. illus. 29 cm. Bibliography: p. 375-378. [TS535.G32] 62-20058
1. Gunsmithing — Direct. 2. Arms and armor — Direct. I. Title.

Gunsmiths, American—Perry County, Pa.

CHANDLER, Roy F. 683'.4'0097845
A history of early Perry County guns and gunsmiths, by Roy F. Chandler & Donald L. Mitchell. [New Bloomfield, Pa.] 1969. 128 p. illus., facsim., geneal. tables, maps, ports. 29 cm. "Copy number 251 of 300." [TS533.3.P4C5] 74-7694
1. Gunsmiths, American—Perry County, Pa. 2. Kentucky rifle. I. Mitchell, Donald L., joint author. II. Title.

Gunsmiths—Bedford Co., Pa.

HETRICK, Calvin. 683'.42'0974871
The Bedford County rifle and its makers. York, Pa., G. Shumway [1973] 39 p. illus. 28 cm. "First published in 1959 as an addition to the fourth edition of J. G. W. Dillin's book The Kentucky rifle." [TS533.3.P4H37] 73-163367 ISBN 0-87387-063-8
1. Gunsmiths—Bedford Co., Pa. 2. Kentucky rifle. 3. Bedford Co., Pa.—History. I. Title. BIP

Gunsmiths—Maine.

DEMERITT, Dwight B. 683'.4'09741
Maine made guns and their makers, by Dwight B. Demeritt Jr. Hallowell, Maine, Published for the Maine State Museum by P. S. Plumer, Jr. [1973] vii, 209 p. illus. 29 cm. (Maine heritage series, 2) Bibliography: p. 191-196. [TS533.3.M2D45] 73-91769 ISBN 0-913764-04-3
1. Gunsmiths—Maine. 2. Firearms industry and trade—Maine. 3. Firearms, American. I. Maine State Museum. II. Title. III. Series. BIP

Gunsmiths—Maryland—Biography.

HARTZLER, Daniel D., 1941- 338.4'7'68409752
Arms makers of Maryland / by Daniel D. Hartzler. 1st ed. York, Pa. : G. Shumway, 1977. 310 p. : ill. ; 32 cm. (Longrifle series) [TS533.3.M3H37] 74-24434 ISBN 0-87387-054-9 : 29.50
1. Gunsmiths—Maryland—Biography. 2. Firearms industry and trade—Maryland—History. 3. Maryland—Industries. I. Title. BIP

Gunsmiths—Ohio.

HUTSLAR, Donald A. 338.7'68'340025771
Gunsmiths of Ohio, 18th & 19th centuries, by Donald A. Hutslar. Edited by Nancy Bagby. York, Pa., G. Shumway [1973- v. illus. 32 cm. (Longrifle series) Contents.Contents.—v. 1. Biographical data. Bibliography: v. 1, p. 417-426. [TS533.3.O3H87] 72-87114 ISBN 0-87387-026-3 (v. 1) 29.50 (v. 1)
1. Gunsmiths—Ohio. I. Title.

Gunsmiths—Vermont.

HORN, Warren R. 683.4'009743
Gunsmiths and gunmakers of Vermont : a partial checklist from the early years through 1900 / by Warren R. Horn. Burlington, Vt. : Horn Co., c1975. iii, 75 p. : ill. ; 23 cm. Bibliography: p. 73-75. [TS533.3.V5H67] 75-21180
1. Gunsmiths—Vermont. 2. Vermont—Biography. I. Title.

Gunstocks.

ARTHUR, Robert, 1919- 739.7'4'425
The shotgun stock; design, construction and embellishment. South Brunswick [N.J.] A. S. Barnes [1971] 175 p. illus. 27 cm. Includes bibliographical references. [TS535.A73] 73-107107 ISBN 0-498-07621-0 12.00
1. Gunstocks. 2. Shot-guns. I. Title.

LINDEN, Alvin. 683'.4
Alvin Linden tells about restocking a rifle. [Harrisburg, Pa.] Stackpole Books [1969] 3 v. in 1. illus. (3 fold. in pocket) 29 cm. (A Samworth book) Reissue in 1 v. of the texts and patterns previously published as books 1-3 of the Firearms design and assembly series. Contents.Contents.—Inletting.—Shaping the inletted blank.—Gunstock finishing. [TS535.L486 1969] 69-16152 9.95
1. Gunstocks. I. Title. II. Title: Restocking a rifle.

NEWELL, A. Donald. 683.4
Gunstock, finishing & care, a text-book covering the various means and methods by which modern protective and decorative coatings may be applied in the correct and suitable finishing of gun and rifle stocks. For amateur and professional use. Georgetown, S.C., Small-Arms Technical Pub. Co., 1954 [c1949] 473 p. illus. (part col.) 23 cm. (Samworth books on firearms) [TS535.N395] 64-2108
1. Gunstocks. 2. Wood finishing. I. Title. BIP

Gupta dynasty.

HARLE, James C. 732'.4
Gupta sculpture : Indian sculpture of the fourth to the sixth centuries A.D. / J. C. Harle. Oxford [Eng.] : Clarendon Press, 1974. xii, 57 p., [40] leaves of plates : ill. ; 29 cm. Bibliography: p. [32]. [NB1002.H33] 75-306296 ISBN 0-19-817322-9 : 19.25
1. Gupta dynasty. 2. Sculpture, Hindu. I. Title.
Distributed by Oxford University Press New York. BIP

Gustaf VI Adolf, King of Sweden, 1882- —Art collections.

GUSTAV V I ADOLF King of Sweden, 1882. 709.51
Chinese art from the collection of H. M. King Gustaf VI Adolf of Sweden byBo Gyllensvard and John Alexander Pope. [New York] Asia Society; distributed by H. N. Abrams [1966] 147 p. illus., col. plates. 28 cm. ("An Asia House gallery publication") "Exhibition ... assembled by Bo Gyllensvard in cooperation with John A. Pope for a tour of American museums organized by the International Exhibitions Foundation, Washington, D.C." Bibliography: p. 147. [NK550.G8] 66-22367
1. Gustaf VI Adolf, King of Sweden, 1882- —Art collections. 2. Art objects, Chinese. I. Title.

Guston, Philip.

ASHTON, Dore 759.13
Philip Guston. New York, Grove Press [c.1960] 63p. (Bibl.) illus. (part col.) 21cm. (Evergreen gallery book 10--E-196) 59-14404 3.95; 1.95 pap.,
1. Guston, Philip. I. Title.

ASHTON, Dore. 759.13
Yes, but ... : a critical study of Philip Guston / by Dore Ashton. New York :

Viking Press, 1976. xvi, 206 p., [2] leaves of plates : ill. (some col.) ; 26 cm. Includes index. Bibliography: p. 193-197. [ND237.G8A82 1976] 75-43993 ISBN 0-670-79388-4 : 14.95
1. Guston, Philip, 1913- I. Title.

GUSTON, Philip, 1913- 759.13
Philip Guston. [Catalogue of paintings and drawings] October 1970. New York, Marlborough Gallery [1970] 44 p. illus. (part col.), port. 30 cm. Label mounted on t.p.: Supplied by Worldwide Books, Boston. [ND237.G8A55] 79-199787
I. Marlborough Gallery.

SOLOMON R. Guggenheim 759.13
Museum, New York.
Philip Guston. New York, [1962] Catalog of "Exhibition '62/4, the Solomon R. Guggenheim Museum, New York, May 2-July 1, 1962; Los Angeles County Museum, May 15-June 23, 1963." Bibliography: p. 120-123. [ND237.G8S6] 62-16504
1. Guston, Philip, 1913- I. Los Angeles County Museum, Los Angeles. II. Title.

Gutenberg, Johann, 1397?-1468.

GEKLER, Mary E. 655.1'43
Johannes Gutenberg, Father of Printing; commemorating the fifth centenary of his death, 1468-1968. [Text and research by Mary E. Gekler. Chicago, Franciscan Herald Press, 1968] 23 p. illus. (part col.) maps, port. 28 cm. [Z126.Z7G4] 68-5971
1. Gutenberg, Johann, 1397?-1468.

GOFF, Frederick 686'.1'0924
Richmond, 1916-
Johann Gutenberg and the Scheide Library at Princeton / by Frederick R. Goff. [Princeton, N.J.] : Princeton University Press, 1976. p. 72-84, [2] leaves of plates : ill. ; 26 cm. Caption title. Extracted from v. 37, no. 2, winter 1976 issue of the Princeton University Library chronicle. Bibliography: p. 83-84. [Z126.Z7G59] 76-377522
1. Gutenberg, Johann, 1397?-1468. 2. Scheide Library. 3. Printing—History—Origin and antecedents. I. Title.

GOFF, Frederick 686.1'0924
Richmond, 1916-
The permanence of Johann Gutenberg [by] Frederick R. Goff. [Austin] Humanities Research Center, University of Texas at Austin; [distributed by University of Texas Press, 1971, c1970] 29 p. 22 cm. (Bibliographical monograph series, no. 3) (Lew David Feldman lectureship in bibliography, 1968) "500 copies." Includes bibliographical references. [Z126.Z7G6] 78-89558
1. Gutenberg, Johann, 1397?-1468. I. Title. II. Series. III. Series: Texas. University at Austin. Humanities Research Center. Bibliograpical monograph, 3 BIP

LEHMANN-HAUPT, Hellmut, 655.11
1903-
Gutenberg and the Master of the Playing Cards. New Haven, Yale University Press, 1966. xii, 83 p. illus., facsims. (part col.) 29 cm. Bibliographical footnotes. [Z126.A3L4] 66-21527
1. Gutenberg, Johann, 1397?-1468 2. Master of the Playing Cards, 15th century. I. Title.

MCMURTRIE, Douglas 686'.1'0924 B
Crawford, 1888-1944.
Wings for words; the story of Johann Gutenberg and his invention of printing. With the collaboration of Don Farran. Illustrated by Edward A. Wilson. New York, Rand McNally, 1940. Detroit, Tower Books, 1971. 175 p. illus. 24 cm. A biography of the man who developed the process of printing from moveable type in the fifteenth century. [Z126.Z7M32 1971] 92 78-167061
1. Gutenberg, Johann, 1397?-1468. 2. Printing—History—Origin and antecedents. I. Wilson, Edward Arthur, 1886- illus. II. Title. BIP

THORPE, James Ernest, 220'.47
1915-
The Gutenberg Bible, landmark in learning / by James Thorpe. San Marino, Calif. : Huntington Library, 1975. 23 p. : facsims. ; 24 cm. [Z241.B58T47] 75-324777
1. Gutenberg, Johann, 1397?-1468. 2. Bible. Latin. ca.1454-55. Mainz. Gutenberg (42 lines) I. Title.

Gutenberg, Johann, 1397?-1468—Bibliography.

STILLWELL, Margaret 016.093
Bingham, 1887-
The beginning of the world of books, 1450 to 1470; a chronological survey of the texts chosen for printing during the first twenty years of the printing art, with a synopsis of the Gutenberg documents. New York, Bibliographical Society of America, 1972. xxviii, 112 p. 26 cm. Appendixes (p. [73]-106): A. The Gutenberg documents: notes on the manuscript records, 1420-1468. The Gutenberg tradition as stated in the printed books of the fifteenth century, 1468-1499.—B. Undated imprints assigned to the Netherlands. Bibliography: p. xxi-xxv. [Z240.S816] 79-185917
1. Gutenberg, Johann, 1397?-1468—Bibliography. 2. Incunabula—Bibliography. I. Title. BIP

Gutenberg, Johann, 1397?-1468—Juvenile literature.

HARRIS, Brayton. 686.1'092'4 B
Johann Gutenberg and the invention of printing. New York, Watts, 1972. xv, 144 p. illus. 22 cm. (A Franklin Watts biography) Bibliography: p. 141-142. A biography of the man who developed printing from moveable type in the fifteenth century. [Z126.Z7H37] 92 73-150377 ISBN 0-531-00967-X
1. Gutenberg, Johann, 1397?-1468—Juvenile literature. 2. Printing—Invention—Juvenile literature. I. Title.

Gutierrez-Solana, Jose, 1886-1945.

BARRIO-GARAY, Jose L. 759.6 B
Jose Gutierrez Solana : painting and writings / Jose Luis Barrio-Garay. Lewisburg [Pa.] : Bucknell University Press, [1975] p. cm. Includes index. Bibliography: p. [ND813.G8B33 1976] 72-3524 ISBN 0-8387-1228-2 : 40.00
1. Gutierrez-Solana, Jose, 1886-1945. BIP

Guttag, Julius—Coin collections.

GUTTAG, Julius. 737.4'9'8
The Julius Guttag collection of Latin American coins / arr. by Edgar H. Adams. Lawrence, Mass. : Quarterman Publications, [1974] 527 p. : ill. ; 24 cm. Published in 1929 under title: Catalogue of the collection of Julius Guttag. Includes index. [CJ1803.2.G87G87 1974] 74-80921 ISBN 0-88000-027-9 : 35.00
1. Guttag, Julius—Coin collections. 2. Coins, American. 3. Coins, Latin American. I. Title. BIP

Gwathmey, Charles, 1938—

BRESLOW, Kay. 728.3
Charles Gwathmey & Robert Siegel : residential works, 1966-1977 / text by Kay and Paul Breslow ; introd. by Philip Johnson. New York : Architectural Book Pub. Co., [1977] p. cm. English, Japanese, French, and German. [NA737.G94B73] 77-8643 ISBN 0-8038-0045-2 : 35.00
1. Gwathmey, Charles, 1938- 2. Siegel, Robert, 1939- 3. Dwellings—New England. 4. Dwellings—Middle Atlantic States. I. Breslow, Paul, joint author. II. Title.

Gymnasiums—Apparatus and equipment.

DRESSING rooms & related 725'.85
service facilities for physical education, athletics, and recreation. Washington, Council on Facilities, Equipment, and Supplies, American Association for Health, Physical Education, and Recreation [1972] iii, 41 p. illus. 23 cm. Bibliography: p. 41. [GV409.D7] 72-189457
1. Gymnasiums—Apparatus and equipment. I. American Association for Health, Physical Education, and Recreation. Council for Facilities, Equipment, and Supplies.

. H. Glenister.

GLENISTER, S. H. 745.51
Contemporary design in woodwork. 3 [by] London, Murray [1968] Label on t.p.: dist. Transatlantic, New York, 89, [1] p. illus. 26cm. [NK9604.G5 1968] 68-115087 6.95
1. . H. Glenister. 2. Woodwork. 3. Furniture design. I. Title.

Haagensen, Frederick Hans, 1877-1943.

HAAGENSEN, Frederick 769'.92'4
Hans, 1877-1943.
Catalogue, Frederick Hans Haagensen, 1877-1943 ... [Maldon, Essex] : Audrey M. Haagensen, 1976. 87 p. : ill., ports. ; 18 x 23 cm. Catalogue of an exhibition arranged by Audrey Haagensen at the Haagensen Gallery, with text by Louise Dawson. [NE2047.6.H3H3] 77-361140 ISBN 0-9505398-0-5 : £1.50
1. Haagensen, Frederick Hans, 1877-1943. I. Haagensen, Audrey M. II. Dawson, Louise. III. Haagensen Gallery.

Haarlem. Frans Hals-Museum der Gemeinte Haarlem.

BOARD, Henricus Petrus, 759.9492
1906-
Frans Hals Museum Haarlem: Dutch painting. Tr. from Dutch by J. J. Kliphuis. Munich, Ahrbeck/Hannover, Knorr & Hirth [1967] 79p. col. illus. 18cm. (Little art bk.) [N2470.B213] 68-73571 4.50
1. Haarlem. Frans Hals-Museum der Gemeinte Haarlem. I. Title.
American distributor: Heinman, New York.

Habsburg, House of—Art patronage.

TREVOR-ROPER, Hugh. 709'.03'1
Princes and artists : patronage and ideology at four Habsburg courts, 1517-1633 / Hugh Trevor-Roper. With 123 ill. London : Thames and Hudson, c1976. 176 p. : ill. ; 25 cm. "Lectures ... delivered at the State University of New York, College at Purchase, New York, in October 1974, being the first of the annual Yaseen Lectures." Includes index. Bibliography: p. 165-167. [N6805.T73] 77-362465 ISBN 0-500-23232-6 : £6.50
1. Habsburg, House of—Art patronage. 2. Art, Renaissance—Austria. 3. Art, Modern—17th-18th centuries—Austria. 4. Art—Austria. I. Title. BIP

Hadassah-University Medical Center, jerusalem. Synagogue.

CHAGALL, Marc, 1887- 748.595694
The Jerusalem windows. Text and notes by Jean Leymarie. [Translated from the French by Elaine Desautels] New York, G. Braziller [1962] 210 p. illus., plates (part col.), port. 24 cm. [NK5398.C5L43] 62-18146
1. Hadassa-University Medical Center, Jerusalem. Synagogue. 2. Glass painting and staining—Jerusalem. I. Leymarie, Jean. II. Title.

CHAGALL, Marc, 1887- 748.5'9'5694
The Jerusalem windows. Text and notes by Jean Leymarie. [Translated from the French by Elaine Desautels. 1st rev. ed.] New York, G. Braziller [1967] xix, 111 p. plates (part col.) 28 cm. Translation of Vitraux pour Jerusalem. [NK5398.C5L433 1967] 67-9083
1. Hadassah-University Medical Center, Jerusalem. Synagogue. 2. Glass painting and staining — Jerusalem. I. Leymarie, Jean. II. Title.

Haddelsey, Vincent, 1934—

HADDELSEY, Vincent, 1934- 759.2
Haddelsey's horses / paintings by vincent Haddelsey ; text by Caroline Silver, with Vincent Haddelsey. New York : St. Martin's Press, 1978. 62 p. : col. ill. ; 27 x 30 cm. [ND497.H28A4 1978] 78-438 ISBN 0-312-35642-0 : 10.00
1. Haddelsey, Vincent, 1934- 2. Horses in art. I. Silver, Caroline, 1938- II. Title. BIP

Hadley, Paul, 1880-1971.

HARDIN, Becky. 759.13 B
The Indiana State flag, its designer : biography of Paul Hadley with anthology of his paintings / [by Becky Hardin]. [Mooresville, IN : Hardin, c1976] 40 p. : ill. (some col.) ; 28 cm. Cover title. Includes bibliographical references and index. [ND1839.H3H37] 76-12963 4.00
1. Hadley, Paul, 1880-1971. 2. Painters—United States—Biography. I. Title.

Hafif, Marcia, 1929—

HAFIF, Marcia, 1929- 759.13
Marcia Hafif : an exhibition organized by the La Jolla Museum of Contemporary Art, April 5-May 18, 1975. La Jolla, Calif. : The Museum, [1975] [16] p. : ill. (some col.) ; 21 cm. Bibliography: p. [15] [ND237.H17L34] 75-7793
1. Hafif, Marcia, 1929- I. La Jolla Museum of Contemporary Art.

Haftmann, Werner.

NOLDE, Emil [Emil Hansen] 749.943
Emil Nolde. Text by Werner Haftmann. [Translated from the German by Norbert Guterman] New York, H. N. Abrams [1959] 44, [96] p. (bibliography) illus. (part mounted col.) 33cm. (The Library of great painters) 59-8845 15.00
1. Haftmann, Werner. I. Title.

Hague. Gemeentemuseum.

CAVALIERE, Alik, 1926- 730'.924
Alik Cavaliere. [Tentoonstelling] Haags Gemeentemuseum 17 juni t. m. 30 juli, 1967. 's-Gravenhage, 1967. 1 v. (unpaged) 23cm. Bibl. [NB623.C245A42] 67-68416 15.00
1. Hague. Gemeentemuseum. I. Title.

Hague. Kabinet van Schilderijen.

TOTH-UBBENS, Magdi. 759.9492
Mauritshuis, The Hague; Dutch painting [by] Magdi Toth-Ubbens; tr. from Dutch by J. J. Kliphuis. Munich, Ahrbeck, Knorr & Hirth [1967] Label mounted on t. p.: W. S. Heinman, New York. 79p. col. plates. 18cm. (Little art bk.) [ND646.T6713] 68-8612 4.50
1. Hague. Kabinet van Schilderijen. 2. Paintings, Dutch—Catalogs. I. Title.

Hahn, Karl Wilhelm, 1829-1887.

ARKELIAN, Marjorie Dakin. 759.13
William Hahn : genre painter, 1829-1887 : exhibition, June 15-August 29, the Oakland Museum, Low Bay / by Marjorie Dakin Arkelian ; introd. by George W. Neubert. [Oakland, Calif.] : Oakland Museum, Art Dept., 1976. 81 p. : ill. (some col.) ; 28 cm. Includes index. Bibliography: p. 74-79. [ND588.H25A74] 76-15880
1. Hahn, Karl Wilhelm, 1829-1887. I. Oakland Museum. Art Dept. II. Title.

Hahn. Otto.

MASSON, Andre, 1896- 759.4
Masson. [by] Otto Hahn [Tr. from French by Robert Erich Wolf] New York, Abrams. [c.1965] 77p. illus. (pt. col) 21x23cm. (Mod artists) Bibl. [ND553.M336H33] 65-19564 5.95
1. Hahn. Otto. I. Title. BIP

Haiku.

ATWOOD, Ann. 779'.3
Haiku: the mood of earth. New York, Scribner [1971] [32] p. col. illus. 24 x 26 cm. A collection of haiku about nature each illustrated with two related color photographs. [PZ8.3.A922Hai] 70-162737 ISBN 0-684-12494-7 5.95
1. Haiku. I. Title.

LESSING, Janel. 741.973
Drawings and haiku. [Los Angeles, Ankrum Gallery, 1965] 1 v. (unpaged) illus. 31 cm. [NC1075.L37A44] 65-29335
1. Title.

STEWART, Harold. 759.952
A net of fireflies; Japanese haiku and haiku paintings, with verse translations and an essay by Harold Stewart. [1st ed.] Rutland, Vt., Tokyo, Japan, C. E. Tuttle Co. [1960] 180 p. (on double leaves) col. illus. 20 cm. Bibliography: p. [171]-172. [ND1055.S75] 60-15603
1. Haiku. 2. Japanese poetry — Translations into English. 3. English poetry — Translations from Japanese. 4. Paintings, Japanese. I. Title. BIP

Hairpin lace.

FISH, Harriet U. 746.2
Creative lace-making with thread and yarn, by Harriet U. Fish. New York, Sterling Pub. Co. [1972] 48 p. illus. (part col.) 20 cm. (Little craft book series) Instructions for making lace from thread and yarn for decorating items ranging from wall decorations and flat flowers to wardrobe items and Afghans. [TT805.F57 1972] 72-81039 ISBN 0-8069-5216-4 2.95
1. Hairpin lace. I. Title.
Library Edition 2.69, ISBN 0-8069-5217-2

Hajji Baba Club, New York.

FOSTER, Olive 746.7'5'08
Olmstead.
Fine arts, including folly; a history of the Hajji Baba Club, 1932-1960. [New York] Hajji Baba Club [1966] 57 p. 22 cm. 500 copies. Bibliography: p. 57. [NK11.H3F63] 67-2594
1. Hajji Baba Club, New York. I. Title.

Hale, Eng. (Cheshire)—Description—Views.

HALE and around : its past in pictures. Altrincham : Sherratt for Hale Civic Society, 1976. [90] p. : chiefly ill., facsims., maps ; 18 x 21 cm. [DA690.H15H34] 77-370976 ISBN 0-85427-051-5 : £1.80
1. Hale, Eng. (Cheshire)—Description—Views. 2. Hale, Eng. (Cheshire)—Social life and customs—Pictorial works. I. Hale Civic Society.

Hale, Philip Leslie, 1865-1931.

HALE, Nancy, 1908- 759.13
The life in the studio. [1st ed.] Boston, Little, Brown [1969] xiv, 209 p. 21 cm. Autobiographical. [ND236.H3] 69-16965 5.95
1. Hale, Philip Leslie, 1865-1931. 2. Hale, Lillian Westcott, 1881-1963. I. Title.

Halesowen, Eng. St. John Baptist (Church)

LAY, Walter Edwin. 914.24'7'0485
Hales Owen Parish Church, St. John Baptist: a guide and historical sketch, by W. E. Lay. 3d ed. Gloucester, British Publishing Co., [1967] 21 p. front., illus., tables. 18 1/2 cm. unpriced (B67-9182) [NA5471.H246L3] 67-86504
1. Halesowen, Eng. St. John Baptist (Church) I. Title.

Half-cent.

COHEN, Roger S. 737.49'73
American half cents, the "little half sisters"; a reference book on the United States half cent coined from 1793 to 1857, by Roger S. Cohen, Jr. With the assistance of Ray Munde and Paul Munson. [Bethesda? Md., 1971] ix, 105 p. illus. 29 cm. Bibliography: p. 105. [CJ1836.C64] 78-183786
1. Half-cent. I. Munde, Ray, joint author. II. Munson, Paul, joint author. III. Title.

Half-dime.

VALENTINE, Daniel 737.4'9'73
Webster, 1863-
The United States half dimes / Daniel W.

Valentine ; with additional material by Kamal M. Ahwash ... [et al.]. Lawrence, Mass. : Quarterman Publications, [1975] xi, 273 p. : ill. ; 24 cm. Reproduction of previously published articles. [CJ1835.V3 1975] 74-80917 ISBN 0-88000-049-X 25.00
1. Half-dime. 2. Coins, American. 3. Silver coins. I. Ahwash, Kamal M. II. Title.
Contents omitted. BIP

Half-dollar.

OVERTON, Al C. 737.49'73
Early half dollar die varieties, 1794-1836, by Al C. Overton. Colorado Springs, Colo., 1967. xiv, 349 p. illus. 24 cm. [CJ1835.O8 1967] 67-28456
1. Half-dollar. I. Title.

OVERTON, Al C. 737.49'73
Early half dollar die varieties, 1794-1836, by Al C. Overton. Rev. ed. Colorado Springs, Colo., 1970. xii, 274 p. illus. 24 cm. [CJ1835.O8 1970] 74-128567 15.00
1. Half-dollar. I. Title.

Hall, Frederick Garrison, 1879-1946.

HALL, Frederick 769'.92'4
Garrison, 1879-1946.
Frederick Garrison Hall: etchings, bookplates, designs. [Edited] by Elton Wayland Hall. With a biographical sketch by Ariel Hall & a personal memoir by Henry P. Rossiter. Boston, Boston Public Library, 1972. 130 p. illus. 29 cm. "500 copies." Bibliography: p. 111. [NE2012.H34H34] 72-86025
1. Hall, Frederick Garrison, 1879-1946. I. Hall, Elton Wayland, ed.

Hall, John Hancock, 1781-1841.

HUNTINGTON, Roy Theodore, 683'.42 1916-
Hall's breechloaders; John H. Hall's invention and development of a breechloading rifle with precision-made interchangeable parts and its introduction into the United States service, by R. T. Huntington. Edited by Nancy Bagby. York, Pa., G. Shumway [1972] xiv, 369 p. illus. 24 cm. Bibliography: p. 365. [TS533.2.H85] 71-91843 ISBN 0-87387-025-5 15.00
1. Hall, John Hancock, 1781-1841. 2. Hall's rifle. I. Title. BIP

Hall-marks.

BANISTER, Judith. 739.2'3'742
English silver hall-marks: with lists of English, Scottish and Irish hall-marks and makers marks; edited by Judith Banister. London, New York, Foulsham, 1970. 96 p. illus. 16 cm. [NK7210.B36] 73-165732 ISBN 0-572-00674-8 £0.50
1. Hall-marks. 2. Silver articles, British. I. Title.

DIVIS, Jan. 739.2'3'0278
Silver marks of the world / [by] Jan Divis ; [illustrations by Jaromir Knotek ; translated from the Czech by Joy Moss-Kohoutova]. London ; New York : Hamlyn, 1976. 246 p. : ill. ; 20 cm. Includes bibliographies and indexes. [NK7210.D5813] 77-355268 ISBN 0-600-38156-0 : 5.95
1. Hall-marks. I. Title.

LORIE, Douglas. 736.8
Collectors pocket digest of hall-marks on English, Scottish, & Irish silver from the 16th century to the year 1900. New York [1950] 61 p. illus. 16 cm. Magnifying glass attached. [NK7210.L6] 51-580
1. Hall-marks. I. Title.

MACDONALD-TAYLOR, 745'.02'78
Margaret.
A dictionary of marks : metalwork, furniture, ceramics / compiled and edited by Margaret Macdonald-Taylor. Revised ed. / with an introduction by Bevis Hillier. London : Connoisseur, 1976. 319 p., plate : ill. (incl 1 col.) ; 22 cm. Includes indexes. Bibliography: p. 311-[312]. [NK7210.M25 1976] 77-362741 ISBN 0-900305-11-8 : £3.95
1. Hall-marks. 2. Pottery—Marks. 3. Marks of origin. I. Title.

MACDONALD-TAYLOR, 704.987
Margaret Stephens
A dictionary of marks: metalwork, furniture, ceramics; the identification handbook for antique collectors. Introd. by L. G. G. Ramsey. New York, Hawthorn [c.1962] 318p. illus. (pt. col.) 22cm. Bibl. 62-17114 5.95
1. Hall-marks. 2. Pottery—Marks. 3. Marks of origin. I. Title. BIP

TICHER, Kurt. 739.2'3'74183
Hall-marks on Dublin silver, 1730-72 [by] Kurt Ticher, Id Delamer, and William O'Sullivan Dublin, National Museum of Ireland, 1968. [31] p. illus. 22 cm. At head of title: Ard-Mhusaem no h-Eireann An Roinn Oideachais. [NK7210.T54] 72-285216
1. Hall-marks. 2. Silversmithing—Ireland—Dublin. I. Delamer, Ida, joint author. II. O'Sullivan, William, joint author. III. Title.

Halloween decorations—Juvenile literature.

GIBBONS, Gail. 394.2'683
Things to make and do for Halloween / by Gail Gibbons. New York : F. Watts, 1976. 48 p. : col. ill. ; 23 cm. (Things to make and do book) A collection of games, jokes, and instructions on how to make costumes, party foods, makeup, and puppets, all on a Halloween theme. [TT900.H32G5] 75-19396 ISBN 0-531-01103-8 : 2.95
1. Halloween decorations—Juvenile literature. 2. Halloween—Juvenile literature. I. Title. BIP

GLOVACH, Linda. 394.2'683
The little witch's Halloween book / by Linda Glovach. Englewood Cliffs, N.J. : Prentice-Hall, [1975] 48 p. : col. ill. ; 24 cm. Includes index. Step-by-step instructions for a variety of Halloween activities, foods, costumes, and festivities. [TT900.H32G56] 75-11713 ISBN 0-13-537985-7 lib.bdg. : 4.95
1. Halloween decorations—Juvenile literature. 2. Cookery—Juvenile literature. I. Title.

Hall's rifle.

HUNTINGTON, Roy Theodore, 683'.42 1916-
Hall's breechloaders; John H. Hall's invention and development of a breechloading rifle with precision-made interchangeable parts and its introduction into the United States service, by R. T. Huntington. Edited by Nancy Bagby. York, Pa., G. Shumway [1972] xiv, 369 p. illus. 24 cm. Bibliography: p. 365. [TS533.2.H85] 71-91843 ISBN 0-87387-025-5 15.00
1. Hall, John Hancock, 1781-1841. 2. Hall's rifle. I. Title. BIP

Halper, Roe.

HALPER, Roe. 741.9'73
Tears of the Prophets / by Roe Halper ; with an introd. by Alexander M. Schindler. 1st ed. Westport, Conn. : Bayberry Press, [1975] [110] p. : chiefly ill. ; 29 cm. [NC139.H23B5] 75-33530 ISBN 0-916326-01-2
1. Halper, Roe. 2. Judaism and social problems in art. I. Bible. O.T. Prophets. English. Jewish Publication Society. Selections. 1975. II. Title.

Halpern, Lea Henny, 1901—

BALTIMORE. Museum of 738'.092'4 Art.
Lea Halpern : dates of the exhibition, January 27-March 21, 1976. [Baltimore] : Baltimore Museum of Art, [1976?] [24] p., [8] leaves of plates : ill. (8 col. in pocket) ; 26 cm. "Catalogue of the exhibition": p. [11]-[24] [NK4210.H3B34 1976] 76-359580
1. Halpern, Lea Henny, 1901- 2. Pottery, Dutch—Exhibitions. I. Halpern, Lea Henny, 1901-

Halpert, Edith.

CONNECTICUT. University. 709'.73
Museum of Art.
Edith Halpert and the Downtown Gallery. [Exhibition. Storrs, Conn.] 1968. [41] p. 58 illus. 21 cm. [N6512.C5816] 68-65427
1. Halpert, Edith. 2. New York (City). Downtown Gallery. 3. Art, American—Exhibitions. I. Title.

Halpert, Edith—Art collections.

SOCIETY of the Four 745'.0973 Arts.
American folk art; an exhibition in honor of Edith Gregor Halpert, March 10 to April 8, 1973. Palm Beach, Fla., [1973] [16] p. illus. 23 cm. Selection of American folk art from Mrs. Halpert's estate. [NK805.S62 1973] 74-156572
1. Halpert, Edith—Art collections. 2. Folk art—Exhibitions. 3. Folk art—United States. I. Title.

Hals, Frans, 1584-1666.

BEEREN, Willem A. L. 759.9492
Frans Hals. [Tr.: Albert J. Fransella] New York, Barnes &Noble [1963, c.1962] 90p. illus. (pt. col.) 18cm. (Barnes & Noble art ser., 609) 63-5387 .75 pap.
1. Hals, Frans, 1584-1666. I. Title.

DESCARGUES, Pierre. 759.9492
Hals. Biographical and critical study. Translated from the French by James Emmons. Skira, 1968. 145 p. col. plates. 19 cm. (The Taste of our time) "Distributed in the United States by the World Publishing Company,... Cleveland." Bibliography: p. 134-[136] [ND653.H2D393] 68-20497 unpriced
1. Hals, Frans, 1584-1666.

WRIGHT, Christopher, 759.9492 1945-
Frans Hals / Christopher Wright. Oxford [Eng.] : Phaidon, 1977. 15, 48 p. of plates : col. ill. ; 31 cm. Bibliography: p. 15. [ND653.H2W74] 77-73887 ISBN 0-7148-1750-3 : 6.95
1. Hals, Frans, 1584-1666. I. Hals, Frans, 1584-1666.
Distributed by E.P. Dutton

Hamada, Shoji, 1894—

LEACH, Bernard 738.3'092'4 B Howell, 1887-
Hamada, potter / Bernard Leach. London : Thames and Hudson, 1976. 306 p. : ill. (some col.), ports. ; 31 cm. Text in form of dialogue between the author and Hamada. Includes index. [NK4210.H32L4 1976] 76-377126 ISBN 0-500-23222-9 : £20.00
1. Hamada, Shoji, 1894- 2. Potters—Japan—Biography. I. Hamada, Shoji, 1894-II. Title. BIP

Hamblett, Theora, 1895—

HAMBLETT, Theora, 1895- 759.13
Theora Hamblett paintings / by Theora Hamblett, in collaboration with Ed Meek and William S. Haynie. Jackson : University Press of Mississippi, 1975. 96 p. : col. ill. ; 31 cm. [ND237.H258M43] 74-25674 ISBN 0-87805-069-8 : 15.00
1. Hamblett, Theora, 1895- I. Meek, Ed, joint author. II. Haynie, William S., joint author. III. Title. BIP

Hamburg—Description—Views.

HAMBURG. 760'.074'03515
Kunsthalle.
Views of Hamburg. [Translation: Suzan Meves.] (Hamburg, Hamburger Kunsthalle, 1967]) [11] p., 35 p. of illus. 21 cm. Exhibition held at Knoedler & Co., inc., N.Y., from June 20th to July 7th 1967. [N5070.H29K7713] 78-409068 3.00
1. Hamburg—Description—Views. 2. Art—Exhibitions. I. Knoedler (M.) and Company, inc. II. Title.

Hamil, James R., 1937—

HAMIL, James R., 1937- 759.13
Farmland, USA / by James R. Hamil and

Harold Hamil Kansas City, Mo. : Lowell Press, c1975. 100 p. : col. ill. ; 26 x 33 cm. Includes index. [ND1839.H35H34] 75-18756 ISBN 0-913504-24-6 : 20.00
1. Hamil, James R., 1937- 2. Farm life in art. 3. Farm life—United States—Pictorial works. I. Hamil, Harold, joint author. II. Title. BIP

Hamilton, James, 1819-1878.

BROOKLYN, Institute of Arts and Sciences. Museum. 759.13
James Hamilton, 1819-1878, American marine painter. by Arlene Jacobowitz [Brooklyn, N.Y., Author, 1966] 99p. illus., facsims., ports. 23cm. Catalog of a special exhibition held March 28 to May 22, 1966, at the Brooklyn Mus. Bibl. [ND237.H26B7] 66-21098 2.00 pap.,
1. Hamilton, James, 1819-1878. I. Jacobwitz, Arlene. II. Title.

Hamilton, N. Z., in art.

GRINTER, Neville, 1930- 759.9931
Hamilton and the Waikato / Neville Grinter. Wellington : A. H. & A. W. Reed, 1976. 32 p. : ill. (some col.) ; 25 cm. [ND1108.G74A45] 77-370661 ISBN 0-589-00971-0
1. Grinter, Neville, 1930- 2. Hamilton, N. Z., in art. 3. Hamilton, N. Z.—Description. 4. Waikato Valley in art. 5. Waikato Valley—Description and travel. I. Title.

Hamilton, Richard.

HAMILTON, Richard. 769'.92'4
The prints of Richard Hamilton. An exhibition organized by Wesleyan University in conjunction with Petersburg Press, London and New York. Catalogue prepared by Richard S. Field. Middletown, Conn., Davison Art Center, Wesleyan University, 1973. 63 p. illus. 20 x 24 cm. "Participating institutions: 28 September-4 November 1973, Davison Art Center, Wesleyan University, Middletown, Connecticut [and others]" Includes bibliographical references. [NE642.H32F54] 73-88175 3.50
1. Hamilton, Richard. I. Field, Richard S. II. Davison Art Center.

HAMILTON, Richard. 709'.2'4
Richard Hamilton. New York, Solomon R. Guggenheim Museum [1973] 100 p. illus. (part col.) 25 cm. Catalog of the exhibition held in the fall of 1973 at the Solomon R. Guggenheim Museum, New York. Bibliography: p. 96-97. [N6797.H3S64] 73-85377 7.50
1. Hamilton, Richard. I. Solomon R. Guggenheim Museum, New York.

Hamilton, Va. Minor Bartlow House.

LEWIS, John G. 917.55'28
The Minor Bartlow House, Loudoun County, Hamilton, Virginia, 1744-1970 [by] John G. Lewis [and] Elisabeth D. Lewis. Hamilton, Va., 1970. iv, 55 p. illus., facsim., maps, plans. 23 cm. Bibliography: p. 55. [NA7238.Z9H355] 76-23606
1. Hamilton, Va. Minor Bartlow House. I. Lewis, Elisabeth D., joint author. II. Title.

Hammer, Armand, 1897- —Art collections.

THE Armand Hammer Collection. 750'.74'019494
A loan exhibition for the benefit of the Smithsonian Institution, National Endowment for the Arts, American Association of Museums. Exhibited at the Smithsonian Institution [and elsewhere] Washington [1970] [136] col. illus. 28 cm. [N5220.H26A7] 72-22632
1. Hammer, Armand, 1897- —Art collections. 2. Art—Exhibitions. I. Smithsonian Institution.

BROOKS Memorial Art Gallery, Memphis, Tenn. 750'.74'019494
The Armand Hammer Collection. Exhibition] October 2 - December 30, 1969, Brooks Memorial Art Gallery. [Memphis, 1969] 1 v. (unpaged) 82 plates. 23 cm. [N5220.H26B7] 73-22580
1. Hammer, Armand, 1897- —Art collections. 2. Paintings—Exhibitions. I. Title.

Hammer, Victor Karl, 1882—

HAMMER, Carolyn Reading. 745.6'1
Notes on the two-color initials of Victor Hammer / by Carolyn Reading Hammer. [Lexington, Ky. : Stamperia del Santuccio, 1966] 9 p. : col. ill. ; 21 cm. "125 copies printed." [Z276.H265] 75-302347
1. Hammer, Victor Karl, 1882- 2. Initials. I. Hammer, Victor Karl, 1882- II. Title.

HAMMER, Victor Karl, 1882- 759.13
Victor Hammer. [Lexington, Ky., 1970] 27 p. illus. 23 cm. An exhibition of a selection from the artist's works, Transylvania University, Morlan Gallery, Sept. 27-Oct. 11, 1970. [N6537.H34M6] 72-200021
I. Morlan Gallery.

NORTH Carolina. Museum of Art, Raleigh. 759.13
Victor Hammer, a retrospective exhibition, April 4-25, 1965, North Carolina Museum of Art, Raleigh. [Raleigh, 1965?] 91 p. illus. 26 cm. Bibliography: p. 90. [ND237.H28N6] 66-64855
1. Hammer, Victor Karl, 1882- I. Title.

Hammocks.

ANDREWS, Denison, 1935- 746.9
Hammock : how to make your own and lie in it / by Denison Andrews. New York : Workman Pub. Co., c1978. 120 p. : ill. ; 21 cm. [TT849.2.A5 1978] 77-28517 ISBN 0-89480-028-0 pbk. : 2.95
1. Hammocks. I. Title. BIP

Hamon, Rei Paul F.

HAMON, Rei Paul F. 741.9'931
Rei Hamon : artist of the New Zealand bush : second collection. Auckland : Collins, 1976. 93 p. : ill. ; 38 cm. [NC374.H3A55] 77-465035 ISBN 0-00-216912-6
1. Hamon, Rei Paul F. 2. New Zealand in art. I. Title: Artist of the New Zealand bush.

Hampshire, Eng.—Churches.

GREEN, Margaret Joan, 1922- 914.42'704'85
Hampshire churches [by] Margaret Green. Winchester, Winton Publications [1967] 172 p. front., illus., maps. 23 cm. Bibliography: p. 145-146. [NA5471.H28G7] 67-90735
1. Hampshire, Eng.—Churches. 2. Church architecture—Hampshire, Eng. I. Title.

Hampton Court.

MARILLER, Henry Currie, 1865-1951 746.394219
The tapestries at Hampton Court Palace. [Rev. ed.] London, pub. for the Ministry of Works by H. M. Stationary Off. dist. New York, British Info. 1962. 31p. illus., 18x25cm. 62-53092 1.05 pap.,
1. Hampton Court. 2. Tapestry—Hampton, Eng. (Middlesex)—Catalogs. I. Gt. Brit. Ministry of Works. II. Title.

Hampton, James, 1909-1964.

HARTIGAN, Lynda Roscoe. 709'.2'4
The Throne of the Third Heaven of the Nations Millenium General Assembly : James Hampton : March 8 through June 19, 1977, Montgomery Museum of Fine Arts, Montgomery, Alabama. [Montgomery, Ala.] : The Museum, c1977. 20, [1] p. : ill. ; 25 cm. Exhibition catalog by L. R. Hartigan. Bibliography: p. [31] [NB237.H24H37] 77-72659 ISBN 0-89280-005-4
1. Hampton, James, 1909-1964. Throne of the Third Heaven of the Nations Millenium General Assembly. I. Montgomery Museum of Fine Arts. II. Title. BIP

Hand in art.

BORDEN, Emanuel. 704.94962913
The hand in art. [1st ed.] Los Angeles, Borden Pub. Co. [1963] unpaged (chiefly illus.) 31 cm. (Master draughtsman series) [N8217.H3B6] 63-3937
1. Hand in art. 2. Drawings. I. Title. BIP

BRIDGMAN, George Brant, 1864-1943. 704.94'2
The book of a hundred hands. New York, Dover Publications [1971, c1920] 173 p. illus. 24 cm. [NC774.B7 1971] 78-182099 ISBN 0-486-22709-X 2.00
1. Hand in art. I. Title.

*BRIDGMAN, George Brant, 1864-1943 743.49
Book of 100 hands. New York, Barnes & Noble [1966, c.1920] 128p. illus. 21cm. (Everyday handbks., no. 299) 1.00 pap.,
I. Title.

HENNINGER, Joseph M., 1906- 743'.49
Drawing of the hand, and its anatomy, by Joseph M. Henninger. [1st ed.] Alhambra, Calif., Borden Pub. Co., 1973. 132 p. illus. (part col.) 24 x 32 cm. [NC774.H46] 73-78839 6.50
1. Hand in art. 2. Anatomy, Artistic. I. Title. BIP

HOGARTH, Burne. 743'.49
Drawing dynamic hands / by Burne Hogarth. New York : Watson-Guptill Publications, 1977. 144 p. : ill. ; 29 cm. Includes index. Bibliography: p. 142. [NC774.H63 1977] 76-50016 ISBN 0-8230-1367-7 : 12.95
1. Hand in art. 2. Drawing—Instruction. I. Title.

Hand—Pictorial works—Juvenile literature.

BAER, Edith. 779'.2
The wonder of hands. Photos. by Tana Hoban. New York, Parents' Magazine Press [1970] [47] p. (chiefly illus.) 27 cm. Describes in verse, accompanied by photographs, the many things hands can do. [PZ10.B14Wo] 77-93852 3.95
1. Hand—Pictorial works—Juvenile literature. I. Hoban, Tana, illus. II. Title. BIP

Hand spinning.

CASTINO, Ruth A. 1929- 746.1'2
Spinning & dyeing the natural way [by] Ruth A. Castino. Photos. by Marjorie Pickens. New York, Van Nostrand Reinhold [1974] 104 p. illus. (part col.) 24 cm. Includes information about spinning with spindles and spinning wheels, yarn preparation, dyeing with plants, various fibers, and weaving. Bibliography: p. 103. [TT847.C37] 73-11758 ISBN 0-442-21482-0
1. Hand spinning. 2. Dyes and dyeing, Domestic. I. Pickens, Marjorie, 1931- illus. II. Title. BIP

CHANNING, Marion L. 746.1'2
The magic of spinning: how to do it yourself, with the emphasis on wool, the history of spinning and other facts, by Marion L. Channing. Illustrated by Walter E. Channing. [4th ed.] Marion, Mass. [1971] 48 p. illus. 23 cm. Bibliography: p. ix. [TT847.C47 1971] 72-180769
1. Hand spinning. I. Title.

CHAPIN, Doloria. 746.1'2
International handspinning directory and handbook. [Fabius? N.Y.] 1971. 91 p. illus., music, ports. 28 cm. On cover: Let's go spinning. [TT847.C5] 71-26671
1. Hand spinning. 2. Hand spinning—Directories. I. Title. II. Title: Let's go spinning.

CROCKETT, Candace, 1945- 746.1'2
The complete spinning book / by Candace Crockett. New York : Watson-Guptill Publications, 1977. 215 p. : ill. ; 29 cm. Includes index. Bibliography: p. 212-213. [TT847.C76] 77-2712 ISBN 0-8230-0860-6 : 18.50
1. Hand spinning. I. Title. BIP

DUNCAN, Molly. 746.1
Spin, dye & weave your own wool. New York, Sterling Pub. Co. [1973] 72 p. illus. 22 cm. First published in 1968 under title: Spin your own wool and dye it and weave it. [TT847.D85 1973] 72-95215 ISBN 0-8069-5238-5
1. Hand spinning. 2. Hand weaving. 3. Dyes and dyeing—Wool. I. Title.

THE Handspun project book / edited by Deborah Kahn. 746.1
Tarzana, CA : Select Books, c1978. vii, 88 p, [2] leaves of plates : ill. ; 29 cm. Includes index. Bibliography: p. 84. [TT847.H36] 78-64613 ISBN 0-910458-13-8 pbk. : 7.95
1. Hand spinning. 2. Hand weaving. 3. Textile crafts. I. Kahn, Deborah. BIP

HOCHBERG, Bette. 746.1'2
Handsprindles / written and illustrated by Bette Hochberg. Santa Cruz, Calif. : B. and B. Hochberg ; Oakland, Calif. : wholesale distributor, Straw Into Gold, c1977. 73 p. : ill. ; 22 cm. Includes bibliographical references. [TT847.H6] 76-62721 ISBN 0-9600990-2-6 : 3.95
1. Hand spinning. 2. Spindle-whorls. I. Title.

HOPPE, Elisabeth, 1915- 746
Carding, spinning, dyeing : an introduction to the traditional wool and flax crafts / Elisabeth Hoppe, Ragnar Edberg ; [translated from the Swedish by Marianne Turner]. New York : Van Nostrand Reinhold, [1975] 75 p. : ill. ; 21 cm. Translation of Karda, spinna, farga. Includes bibliographical references. [TT847.H6613] 74-6790 ISBN 0-442-30072-7 : 6.95 ISBN 0-442-30073-5 pbk. : 3.50
1. Hand spinning. 2. Carding. 3. Dyes and dyeing. I. Edberg, Ragnar, 1931- joint author. II. Title. BIP

KLUGER, Marilyn. 746.1'2
The joy of spinning. Illustrated by Nanene Queen Jacobson. New York, Simon and Schuster [1971] 187 p. illus. 24 cm. [TT847.K58] 72-139634 ISBN 0-671-20859-4 6.95
1. Hand spinning. I. Title. BIP

SEAGROATT, Margaret. 746.1
A basic textile book / Margaret Seagroatt. New York : Van Nostrand Reinhold Co., [1975] 96 p. : ill. (some col.) ; 23 cm. Includes bibliographical references and index. [TT847.S4 1975] 75-12165 ISBN 0-442-25064-9 : 9.95 ISBN 0-442-25066-5 pbk. : 5.95
1. Hand spinning. 2. Hand weaving. 3. Dyes and dyeing—Textile fibers. I. Title. BIP

SIMMONS, Paula. 746.1
Spinning and weaving with wool / by Paula Simmons. Seattle : Pacific Search Press, c1977. p. cm. Continues the author's Raising sheep the modern way. Includes index. Bibliography: p. [TT847.S57] 77-76137 ISBN 0-914718-28-2 : 12.95. 7.95
1. Hand spinning. 2. Hand weaving. I. Title. BIP

SPINNING around the world : 746.1'2
international handspinning directory and handbook, 1975. [Fabius?, N.Y. : D. M. Chapin], c1975. 191 p. : ill., music ; 28 cm. The 1971 ed., by D. Chapin, had title: International handspinning directory and handbook. [TT847.C5 1975] 76-356545
1. Hand spinning. 2. Hand spinning—Directories. I. Chapin, Doloria. II. Chapin, Doloria. International handspinning directory and handbook. III. Title: International handspinning directory and handbook, 1975.

SVINICKI, Eunice. 746.1'2
Step-by-step spinning & dyeing / by Eunice Svinicki. New York : Golden Press, [1974] 64 p. : ill. (some col.) ; 29 cm. (Step-by-step craft series) Bibliography: p. 64. [TT847.S9] 74-76679 2.95
1. Hand spinning. 2. Dyes and dyeing—Textile fibers. I. Title. II. Title: Spinning & dyeing.

THRESH, Christine. 746.1'2
Spinning with a drop spindle. [Rev. ed. Santa Rosa, Calif.] Thresh Publications [1974, c1972] 24 p. illus. 21 cm. Bibliography: p. 24. [TT847.T45 1974] 74-169150 ISBN 0-9600572-3-4 1.00
1. Hand spinning. I. Title. BIP

Hand spinning—England—Lancashire.

BLAKE, Marguerite. 338.6'34
Revival of spinning and weaving in Langdale (1883-1901) / by Marguerite Blake. Langdale : The author, 1976. 15 p. : ill., 2 ports. ; 22 cm. (The Langdale series) [TT847.B57] 77-358988 ISBN 0-9505124-0-0 : £0.48
1. Hand spinning—England—Lancashire. 2. Hand weaving—England—Lancashire. I. Title. II. Series.

Hand weaving.

ALEXANDER, Marthann. 746.1
Simple weaving. New York, Taplinger Pub. Co. [1969] vii, 112 p. illus. 24 cm. [TT848.A65] 68-17470
1. Hand weaving. I. Title. BIP

ALEXANDER, Marthann. 746.1'4
Weaving on cardboard; simple looms to make & use. New York, Taplinger Pub. Co. [1972] 88 p. illus. 24 cm. Instructions for making sixteen simple cardboard looms with suggestions for a variety of projects to make on them. [TT848.A67] 70-164416 ISBN 0-8008-8120-6 5.95
1. Hand weaving. I. Title. BIP

ATWATER, Mary Meigs, 1878- 745.52
Byways in hand-weaving. New York Macmillan, 1954. 128 p. illus. 24 cm. [TT848.A77] 54-7961
1. Hand weaving. I. Title. BIP

BECHER, Lotte. 745.52
Handweaving: designs and instructions. London, New York, Studio Publications [1954] 96 p. illus. 26 cm. (The How to do it series, no. 52) [TT848.B38] 55-365
1. Hand weaving.

BELFER, Nancy. 746.1'4
Weaving : design and expression / Nancy Belfer. Worcester, Mass. : Davis Publications, [1975] 160 p., [4] leaves of plates : ill. (some col.) ; 26 cm. Includes index. Bibliography: p. 156-157. [TT848.B384] 74-27624 ISBN 0-87192-068-9 : 12.95
1. Hand weaving. I. Title.

BENNETT, Noel, 1939- 746.7'2
Designing with the wool : advanced techniques in Navajo weaving / Noel Bennett. 1st ed. Flagstaff, [Ariz.] : Northland Press, c1979. x, 118 p. : ill. ; 25 cm. Bibliography: p. 111-114. [TT848.B39] 78-51842 ISBN 0-87358-171-7 : 7.50
1. Hand weaving. 2. Navaho Indians—Textile industry and fabrics. 3. Indians of North America—Southwest, New—Textile industry and fabrics. I. Title. BIP

BERNSTEIN, Marion H. 746.4'1
Off-loom weaving, by Marion H. Bernstein. Diagrams by Susan Henderson. New York, Sterling Pub. Co. [1971] 48 p. illus. (part col.) 20 cm. (Little craft book series) Describes the techniques used in weaving such items as a collar, doll, tunic, picture, lamp shade, and room divider without a loom. [TT848.B43 1971] 79-167667 ISBN 0-8069-5172-9
1. Hand weaving. I. Henderson, Susan, illus. II. Title.

BOWEN, Kernochan. 746.1'4
Four-harness weaving / by Kernochan Bowen. New York : Watson-Guptill Publications, 1978. 160 p. : ill. ; 31 cm. Includes index. Bibliography: p. 157. [TT848.B66 1978] 78-88 ISBN 0-8230-1889-X : 18.50
1. Hand weaving. I. Title.

BROSTOFF, Laya. 746.1'4
Professional handweaving on the fly-shuttle loom / Laya Brostoff. New York : Van Nostrand Reinhold, [1978] p. cm. Includes index. Bibliography: p. [TT848.B734] 77-15070 ISBN 0-442-20948-7 : 16.50
1. Hand weaving. I. Title. BIP

BROWN, Rachel. 746.1
The Weaving, spinning, and dyeing book / Rachel Brown ; illustrated by Rachel Brown and Cheryl McGowen. 1st ed. New York : Knopf : distributed by Random House, 1978. xiv, 366 p., [4] leaves of plates : ill. ; 29 cm. Includes index. Bibliography: p. [356]. [TT848B75] 77-1653 ISBN 0-394-49801-1 : 17.50 ISBN 0-394-73383-5 pbk. : 9.95
1. Hand weaving. 2. Hand spinning. 3. Dyes and dyeing—Textile fibers. I. Title. BIP

CHERRY, Eve. 745.52
Teach yourself handweaving. New York, Roy Publishers [1957] 191p. illus. 19cm. (The Teach yourself books) [TT848.C42] 57-5052
1. Hand weaving. I. Title.

CHRISTOPHER, Frederick John. 745.52
Handloom weaving; edited by Lili Blumenau. New York, Dover Publications [1954] 128p. illus. 19cm. (Dover-Foyle handbook) [TS1490.C5 1954] 55-3547
1. Hand weaving. I. Title.

COLLINGWOOD, Peter, 1922- 746.7'2
The techniques of rug weaving. New York, Watson-Guptill Publications [1969, c1968] 527 p. illus. (part col.) 26 cm. Bibliography: p. 514-516. [TT850.C6 1968] 68-24486 17.50
1. Hand weaving. 2. Rugs. I. Title. BIP

CREAGER, Clara. 746.1'4
Weaving; a creative approach for beginners. [1st ed.] Garden City, N.Y., Doubleday, 1974. 192 p. illus. 26 cm. [TT848.C64] 73-16503 ISBN 0-385-02901-2 3.95 (pbk.)
1. Hand weaving. I. Title. BIP

DAVISON, Marguerite Porter, ed. 745.52
A handweaver's source book; a selection of 224 patterns from the Laura M. Allen collection. Drawings by Charles C. Denzler. Swarthmore, Pa. [1953] 228 p. illus. 28 cm. [TT848.D33] 54-21564
1. Hand weaving. I. Allen, Laura M. II. Title. BIP

DENDEL, Esther Warner, 1910- 746.1'4
The basic book of fingerweaving. With photos. and drawings by Jo Dendel. New York, Simon and Schuster [1974] 128 p. illus. 24 cm. [TT848.D45] 73-17697 ISBN 0-671-21697-X 7.95
1. Hand weaving. 2. Braid. I. Title. BIP

DENDEL, Esther Warner, 1910- 746.1'4
The basic book of twining / by Esther Warner Dendel ; with photos. and drawings by Jo Dendel. New York : Van Nostrand Reinhold Co., 1978. 100 p. : ill. ; 28 cm. Includes index. [TT848.D453] 77-27428 ISBN 0-442-22076-6 : 12.95
1. Hand weaving. I. Title. II. Title: Twining. BIP

DENDEL, Esther Warner, 1910- 746.1'4
Needleweaving ... easy as embroidery. Philadelphia, Countryside Press; distributed by Doubleday, Garden City, N.Y. [1972] 128 p. illus. 29 cm. [TT848.D46 1972] 77-187033 ISBN 0-385-07686-X 7.95
1. Hand weaving. I. Title.

DENDEL, Esther Warner, 1910- 746.1'4
Needleweaving ... easy as embroidery. Philadelphia, Countryside Press [1971] 94 p. illus. 24 cm. (A Farm journal countryside craft book) [TT848.D46] 77-31589
1. Hand weaving. I. Title. BIP

DUCHEMIN, Mad. 746.1'4
Hand weaving : an introduction to weaving on 2, 3, and 4 harnesses / Mad Duchemin. New York : Van Nostrand Reinhold, 1975. 93 p. : ill. ; 26 cm. Translation of Le tissage a la main sur 2, 3, et 4 lames. [TT848.D7613] 75-7142 ISBN 0-442-22183-5 : 9.95
1. Hand weaving. I. Title.

FANNIN, Allen. 746.1'4
Handloom weaving technology / Allen A. Fannin. New York : Van Nostrand Reinhold Co., 1979. p. cm. Includes index. Bibliography: p. [TT848.F24] 76-4447 ISBN 0-442-22370-6 : 19.95
1. Hand weaving. I. Title. BIP

FREY, Berta. 746.1'4
Designing and drafting for handweavers : basic principles of cloth construction / Berta Frey. New York : Collier Books, 1975, c1958. xii, 225 p. : ill. ; 21 cm. Includes index. [TT848.F7 1975] 75-6739 ISBN 0-02-011400-1 pbk. : 5.95
1. Hand weaving. I. Title.

GARRETT, Cay. 746.1'4
Warping, all by yourself. Illustrated by Dorothy M. Beebee. [Santa Rosa, Calif.] Thresh Publications [1974] 160 p. illus. 19 x 20 cm. Bibliography: p. 159-160. [TT848.G34] 74-9515 ISBN 0-913664-03-0 2.95 (pbk.).
1. Hand weaving. I. Title.

GILBY, Myriam. 746.1'4
Free weaving / Myriam Gilby. New York : Pitman, 1976. 156 p., [4] leaves of plates : ill. ; 29 cm. Includes index. Bibliography: p. 152-153. [TT848.G55] 76-355152 ISBN 0-273-00495-6
1. Hand weaving. I. Title. BIP

GILBY, Myriam. 746.1'4
Free weaving / Myriam Gilby. New York : Scribner, c1976. 156 p., [4] leaves of plates : ill. ; 29 cm. Includes index. Bibliography: p. 152-153. [TT848.G55 1976b] 76-358257 ISBN 0-684-14515-4 : 14.95
1. Hand weaving. I. Title.

HALSEY, Mike. 746.1'4
Foundations of weaving [by] Mike Halsey and Lore Youngmark. Photos. by Edwina Ferguson. Drawings by Mike Halsey. New York, Watson-Guptill Publications [1975] 205 p. illus. 25 cm. Bibliography: p. 198-199. [TT848.H28 1975b] 73-14777 ISBN 0-8230-1916-0 10.95
1. Hand weaving. I. Youngmark, Lore, joint author. II. Title. BIP

HARTUNG, Rolf. 746.1
Creative textile design: thread and fabric. [Translator: Brian Battershaw] New York, Reinhold Pub. Corp. [1964, c1963] 96 p. illus. (part col.) 21 cm. Translation of Textiles Werken: Faden und Gewebe. [TT848.H3713] 64-13650
1. Hand weaving. I. Title.

HELD, Shirley E. 746.1'4
Weaving : a handbook of the fiber arts / Shirley E. Held. 2d ed. New York : Holt, Rinehart and Winston, c1978. xii, 388 p. : ill. ; 29 cm. Includes index. Bibliography: p. 373-376. [TT848.H43 1978] 77-24219 ISBN 0-03-042821-1 : 21.95
1. Hand weaving. I. Title.

HINDSON, Alice. 745.52
Designer's drawloom; an introduction to drawloom weaving and repeat pattern planning. Boston, C. T. Branford Co. [1958] 236 p. illus. 23 cm. [TT848.H5] 58-2221
1. Hand weaving. 2. Looms. 3. Textile design. I. Title.

HOLLAND, Nina, 1934- 746.1'4
Inkle loom weaving. New York, Watson-Guptill Publications [1973] 143 p. illus. (part col.) 27 cm. Bibliography: p. 139. [TT848.H58 1973] 73-5758 ISBN 0-8230-2551-9 10.50
1. Hand weaving. I. Title. BIP

HOLLAND, Nina, 1934- 746.1'4
The weaving primer : a complete guide to inkle, backstrap, and frame looms / Nina Holland. Radnor, Pa. : Chilton Book Co., c1978. viii, 201 p., [4] leaves of plates : ill. ; 27 cm. (Chilton's creative crafts series) Includes index. Bibliography: p. 190. [TT848.H59 1978] 77-14743 ISBN 0-8019-6624-8 : 13.95 ISBN 0-8019-6625-6 pbk. : 7.95
1. Hand weaving. I. Title. BIP

*HOOPER, Luther. 746.1'4
Hand-loom weaving : plain and ornamental / by Luther Hooper ; with line drawings by the author and Noel Rooke ; also several illustrations from ancient and modern textiles. London : Pitman ; New York : Taplinger, 1979. xxii, 338p., [8] leaves of plates : ill. ; 19 cm. (A Pentalic book) Includes index. [TT848] ISBN 0-8008-3805-X pbk. : 9.95
1. Handweaving. I. Title.

*HOOPER, Luther. 746.1'4
Hand-loom weaving : plain and ornamental / by Luther Hooper ; with line drawings by the author and Noel Rooke ; also several illustrations from ancient and modern textiles. London : Pitman ; New York : Taplinger, 1979. xxii, 338p., [8] leaves of plates : ill. ; 19 cm. (A Pentalic book) Includes index. [TT848] ISBN 0-8008-3805-X pbk. : 9.95
1. Handweaving. I. Title.

HOPPE, Elisabeth, 1915- 746.1'4
Free weaving on frame and loom [by] Elisabeth Hoppe, Estine Ostund [and] Lisa Melen. New York, Van Nostrand Reinhold [1974] p. Translation of Vava fritt i ram och vavstol. [TT848.H613] 73-16707 ISBN 0-442-30038-7 5.95
1. Hand weaving. I. Ostund, Estine, 1924- II. Melen, Lisa, 1917- III. Title.
Pbk. 3.50, ISBN 0-442-30039-5.

HOWER, Virginia G. 746.1
Weaving, spinning, and dyeing : a beginner's manual / Virginia G. Hower ; with drawings by the author. Englewood Cliffs, N.J. : Prentice-Hall, c1976. xiii, 169 p. : ill. ; 24 cm. (The Creative handcrafts series) (A Spectrum book) Includes index. [TT848.H67] 75-33120 ISBN 0-13-947812-4 : 10.95 ISBN 0-13-947804-3 pbk. :
1. Hand weaving. 2. Hand spinning. 3. Dyes and dyeing—Textile fibers. I. Title.

ICKIS, Marguerite, 1897- 746.1
Weaving as a hobby. New York, Sterling Pub Co. [1968] 72 p. illus. (part col.) 22 cm. (Sterling crafts books) An introduction to weaving as a hobby, including choosing and dressing a loom and suggestions for patterns on two- and four-harness looms. [TT848.I25] 67-27752
1. Hand weaving. I. Title. BIP

ICKIS, Marguerite, 1897- 746.1'4
Weaving as a hobby. Totowa, N.J., Littlefield, Adams, 1974 [c1968] 72 p. illus. 21 cm. (A Littlefield, Adams quality paperback, no. 287) Reprint of the ed. published by Sterling Pub. Co., New York, in series: Sterling crafts books. An introduction to weaving as a hobby, including choosing and dressing a loom and suggestions for patterns on two- and four- harness looms. [TT848.I25 1974] 74-11262 ISBN 0-8226-0287-3 2.95 (pbk.).
1. Hand weaving.

KREVITSKY, Nik. 746.9'2
Shaped weaving; making garments and accessories with simple needle- and finger-weaving techniques [by] Nik Krevitsky [and] Lois Ericson. New York, Van Nostrand Reinhold [1974] 104 p. illus. 28 cm. Bibliography: p. 104. [TT848.K68] 73-16704 ISBN 0-442-22324-2
1. Hand weaving. 2. Clothing and dress. 3. Dress accessories. I. Ericson, Lois, joint author. II. Title.

KRONCKE, Grete. 746.1'4
Simple weaving; designs, material, technique [by] Grete Kroncke. [Translated from the Danish by Christine Hauch] New York, Van Nostrand Reinhold Co. [1973] 95 p. illus. 21 cm. (A Reinhold craft paperback) Translation of the author's Sjove vaveformer, and Sjov med tov. [TT848.K713] 72-7846 ISBN 0-442-29972-9 5.50
1. Hand weaving. I. Kroncke, Grete. Sjov med tov. English. 1973. II. Title.
Pbk. 2.95; ISBN 0-442-29981-8.

LEWIS, Alfred Allan. 746.1'4
Everybody's weaving book / by Alfred Allan Lewis, with Julienne Krasnoff ; black-and-white photography by Julienne Krasnoff, color photography by Ronald Frank, line drawings by Tamara Heslen. New York : Macmillan, c1976. 190 p. : ill. ; 29 cm. Includes index. Bibliography: p. 185. [TT848.L48] 75-31512 ISBN 0-02-571270-5 : 14.95
1. Hand weaving. I. Krasnoff, Julienne, joint author. II. Title. BIP

MAREIN, Shirley. 746.1'4
Off the loom; creating with fibre. New York, Viking Press [1972] 96 p. illus. 25 cm. (A Studio book) Bibliography: p. 94. [TT848.M37] 72-79479 ISBN 0-670-52053-5 8.95
1. Hand weaving. I. Title.

MATTERA, Joanne, 1948- 746.1'4
Navajo techniques for today's weaver / by Joanne Mattera. New York : Watson-Guptill Publications, 1975. 160 p. : ill. ; 26 cm. Includes index. Bibliography: p. 157-158. [TT848.M38] 75-12648 ISBN 0-8230-3153-5
1. Hand weaving. 2. Indians of North

America—Textile industry and fabrics. 3. Navaho Indians—Industries. I. Title. BIP

MEILACH, Dona Z. 746.1'4
Weaving off-loom [by] Dona Z. Meilach and Lee Erlin Snow. Chicago, Regnery [1973] 202 p. illus. (part col.) 29 cm. Bibliography: p. 199. [TT848.M45] 72-11198 12.95
1. Hand weaving. I. Snow, Lee Erlin, joint author. II. Title. BIP

MOORMAN, Theo. 746.3'92'4
Weaving as an art form : a personal statement / Theo Moorman ; black and white photography by Nicholas Large, color photography by John Walling. New York : Van Nostrand Reinhold Co., [1975] 104 p. : ill. ; 24 cm. Includes index. [TT848.M66] 74-18908 ISBN 0-442-25370-2 : 8.95
1. Moorman, Theo. 2. Hand weaving. I. Title. BIP

MORRISON, Phylis, 1927- 746.1'4
Spiders' games : a book for beginning weavers / by Phylis Morrison. Seattle : University of Washington Press, c1979. p. cm. [TT848.M675] 78-21754 ISBN 0-295-95620-8 : 14.95
1. Hand weaving. I. Title.

MORRISON, Phylis, 1927- 746.1'4
Spiders' games : a book for beginning weavers / by Phylis Morrison. Seattle : University of Washington Press, c1979. p. cm. [TT848.M675] 78-21754 ISBN 0-295-95620-8 : 14.95
1. Hand weaving. I. Title. BIP

MURRAY, Rosemary. 746.1'4
Practical modern weaving / Rosemary Murray. New York : Van Nostrand Reinhold, [1975] 112 p. : ill. ; 27 cm. Includes index. Bibliography: p. 110. [TT848.M87] 74-9189 ISBN 0-442-30077-8 : 9.95 ISBN 0-442-30078-6 pbk. : 5.95
1. Hand weaving. I. Title. BIP

NAUMANN, Rose. 746.1'4
The off-loom weaving book [by] Rose Naumann and Raymond Hull. New York, Scribner [1973] 190 p. illus. 26 cm. [TT848.N38] 72-11139 ISBN 0-684-13303-2 8.95
1. Hand weaving. I. Hull, Raymond, 1919- joint author. II. Title.

OVERMAN, Ruth. 745.5202824
Contemporary handweaving [by] Ruth Overman [and] Lula Smith. Ames, Iowa State College Press [1955] 180 p. illus. 26 cm. [TT848.O9] 55-9960
1. Hand weaving. I. Smith, Lula Edna, joint author. II. Title.

PARKER, Xenia Ley. 746.1'4
Creative handweaving / Xenia Ley Parker ; drawings by the author. New York : Dial Press, 1976. vii, 179 p., [2] leaves of plates : ill. ; 18 x 26 cm. Includes index. [TT848.P35] 75-38751 ISBN 0-8037-1405-X : 12.95
1. Hand weaving. I. Title. BIP

PLATH, Iona. 746.1'4
The craft of handweaving. Photos. by the author. New York, Scribner [1972] 128 p. illus. 28 cm. (The Scribner library. Emblem editions) Published in 1964 under title: Handweaving. [TT848.P5 1972] 74-39006 ISBN 0-684-12742-3 3.95
1. Hand weaving. I. Title.

PLATH, Iona. 746.1
Handweaving. Photos. by the author. New York, Scribner [1964] 163 p. illus. (part col.) 27 cm. [TT848.P5] 64-20518
1. Hand weaving.

POWNALL, Glen. 746.1
Spinning and weaving. New York, Drake Publishers [1973] 80 p. illus. (part col.) 26 cm. (His Creative leisure series) [TT848.P68 1973] 72-10515 ISBN 0-87749-324-3 3.95
1. Hand weaving. 2. Hand spinning. I. Title.

RAINEY, Sarita R. 746.1
Weaving without a loom [by] Sarita R. Rainey. Worcester, Mass., Davis Publications [1966] 132 p. illus. (part col.) ports. 24 x 25 cm. Bibliography: p. 132. [TT848.R25] 65-15254
1. Hand weaving. I. Title. BIP

RAINEY, Sarita R. 746.1'4
Weaving without a loom / Sarita R. Rainey. Englewood Cliffs, N.J. : Prentice-Hall, c1977. xviii, 136 p., [4] leaves of plates : ill. ; 24 cm. (A Spectrum book : The Creative handcrafts series) Bibliography: p. 135-136. [TT848.R25 1977] 77-5437 ISBN 0-13-947796-9 : 7.95
1. Hand weaving. I. Title. BIP

REDMAN, Jane. 746.1'4
Frame-loom weaving / Jane Redman. New York : Van Nostrand Reinhold, 1976. 144 p. : ill. ; 24 cm. Includes index. Bibliography: p. 136-137. [TT848.R35] 75-20693 ISBN 0-442-26860-2 : 13.50
1. Hand weaving. 2. Looms. I. Title. BIP

REGENSTEINER, Else, 1906- 746.1
The art of weaving. New York, Van Nostrand Reinhold Co. [1970] 184 p. illus. (part col.) 29 cm. Bibliography: p. 181-182. [TT848.R43] 76-110062
1. Hand weaving. I. Title. BIP

RUSSELL, Elfleda. 746.1'4
Off-loom weaving : a basic manual / Elfleda Russell ; diagrams by Elfleda Russell. 1st ed. Boston : Little, Brown, [1975] 180 p. : ill. ; 22 cm. (The Crafts series) [TT848.R86] 74-23685 ISBN 0-316-76295-4 : 7.95. ISBN 0-316-76296-2 pbk. : 3.95
1. Hand weaving. 2. Card weaving. I. Title.

RYALL, Pierre. 746.1'4
Weaving, technique for the multi-harness loom / by Pierre Ryall. New York : Van Nostrand Reinhold, [1979] p. cm. Translation of v. 2 of Le tissage a la main, by P. and F. Ryall. Includes index. [TT848.R913] 78-26327 ISBN 0-442-27085-2 pbk. : 8.95
1. Hand weaving. I. Ryall, Francoise, joint author. II. Title.

SEAGROATT, Margaret. 746.7
Rug weaving for beginners. New York, Watson-Guptill [1972, c1971] 104 p. illus. 24 cm. Bibliography: p. 103. [TT848.S39 1972] 73-190517 ISBN 0-8230-4616-8 7.95
1. Hand weaving. 2. Rugs. I. Title. BIP

SELANDER, Malin 746.109485
Swedish handweaving. Translated [from the Swedish] by Karin Haakonsen-Melander. [dist. Big Sur, Cal., Craft & Hobby Bk. Service] [1959] 128p. illus. (pt. col.) 26cm, 59-65219 6.95 bds.,
1. Hand weaving. I. Title.

SHORT, Jacqueline. 746.1'4
Imaginative weaving / Jacqueline Short. London : Pitman, 1976. viii, 120 p., [4] p. of plates : ill. (some col.) ; 26 cm. Includes index. [TT848.S52] 77-364686 ISBN 0-273-00490-5 : £3.95
1. Hand weaving. I. Title.

SMITH, Joyce Ronald, 1930- 746.1'4
Taaniko : Maori hand-weaving / by Joyce Ronald Smith. New York : Scribner, [1975] 96 p. : ill. ; 29 cm. Includes index. Bibliography: p. 94. [TT848.S6] 74-28907 ISBN 0-684-14204-X
1. Hand weaving. 2. Textile fabrics, Maori. I. Title.

STRAUB, Marianne. 746.1'4
Hand weaving and cloth design / Marianne Straub. New York : Viking Press, [1976] p. cm. (A Studio book) Includes index. Bibliography: p. [TT848.S75] 76-16558 ISBN 0-670-36037-6 : 14.95
1. Hand weaving. 2. Textile design. I. Title. BIP

SWANSON, Karen, 1940- 746.1'4
Rigid heddle weaving / by Karen Swanson. New York : Watson-Guptill Publications, [1975] p. cm. Includes index. Bibliography: p. [TT848.S94 1975] 75-16265 ISBN 0-8230-4555-2 : 17.50
1. Hand weaving. I. Title. BIP

TABER, Barbara, 1939- 746.1'4
Backstrap weaving / by Barbara Taber and Marilyn Anderson. New York : Watson-Guptill Publications, 1975. 160 p. : ill. ; 26 cm. Includes index. Bibliography: p. 157-158. [TT848.T23 1975] 74-31203
1. Hand weaving. I. Anderson, Marilyn, 1937- joint author. II. Title. BIP

TACKER, Harold, 1910- 746.1'4
Band weaving; the techniques, looms, and uses for woven bands [by] Harold and Sylvia Tacker. New York, Van Nostrand Reinhold Co. [1974] 104 p. illus. 25 cm. Bibliography: p. 102. [TT848.T25] 73-1633 ISBN 0-442-28404-7
1. Hand weaving. I. Tacker, Sylvia, 1919- joint author. II. Title. BIP

THOMAS, Diane. 746.9
The regional creative ojo book / by Diane Thomas. Phoenix, Ariz. : Hunter Pub. Co., c1976. 52 p. : ill. ; 28 cm. [TT848.T423] 75-44654 pbk. : 2.95
1. Hand weaving. 2. Ojo de Dios (Talisman) I. Title. BIP

THORPE, Azalea Stuart. 746.1
Elements of weaving: a complete introduction to the art and techniques, by Azalea Stuart Thorpe and Jack Lenor Larsen. Edited by Mary Lyon. [1st ed.] Garden City, N.Y., Doubleday, 1967. 257 p. illus. 27 cm. Bibliography: p. 245-247. [TT848.T43] 67-11164
1. Hand weaving. I. Larsen, Jack Lenor, joint author. II. Title.

THORPE, Azalea Stuart. 746.1'4
Elements of weaving : a complete introduction to the art and techniques / by Azalea Stuart Thorpe and Jack Lenor Larsen ; edited by Mary Lyon. Rev. ed. Garden City, N.Y. : Doubleday, c1978. 257 p. : ill. ; 26 cm. Includes index. Bibliography: p. 247-[248] [TT848.T43 1978] 78-104983 ISBN 0-385-12540-2 : 5.95
1. Hand weaving. I. Larsen, Jack Lenor, joint author. II. Lyon, Mary. III. Title.

THORPE, Heather G. 745.52
A handweaver's workbook. Illus. by Virginia L. Cummings. New York, Macmillan, 1956. 179 p. illus. 22 cm. [TT848.T45] 56-7668
1. Hand weaving. I. Title.

THORPE, Heather G. 745.52
A handweaver's workbook. New York, Collier Books, [1974, c1956] x, 179 p. illus 21 cm. [TT848.T45] 2.95 (pbk.)
1. Hand weaving. I. Title.
L.C. card number for original ed.: 56-7668. BIP

TIDBALL, Harriet. 745.52
The handloom weaves; an analysis and classification of the 52 most important harness controlled weaves for the handloom, with illustrations, drafts, tie-ups, treadling orders, selvage threadings, and explanations. Monterey, Calif., Distributed by Craft and Hobby Book Service, c1957. 38 p. illus. 25 cm. [TT848.T53] 57-49779
1. Hand weaving. I. Title. BIP

TIDBALL, Harriet. 746.1
The weaver's book; fundamentals of handweaving. New York, Macmillan, 1961. 173 p. illus. 25 cm. [TT848.T55] 60-13222
1. Hand weaving. I. Title. BIP

TOD, Osma (Palmer) Gallinger, 1895- 746.1
The joy of hand weaving [by] Osma Gallinger Tod. 2d ed. Princeton, N. J., D.Van Nostrand Co. [1964] xiii, 326 p. illus (part col.) port. 26 cm. Bibliography:p. 320-322. [TT848.T68] 64-4620
1. Hand weaving. I. Title.

TOD, Osma Palmer Gallinger, 1895- 746.1'4
The joy of hand weaving / by Osma Gallinger Tod. New York : Dover Publications, 1977, c1964. xiii, 326 p. : ill. ; 26 cm. Reprint of the ed. published by Bonanza Books, New York. Includes index. Bibliography: p. 320-322. [TT848.T68 1977] 76-42959 ISBN 0-486-23458-4 : 4.50
1. Hand weaving. I. Title. BIP

TOVEY, John. 677.02824
The technique of weaving. London, B.T. Batsford; New York, Reinhold Pub. Corp. [1965] 128 p. 26 cm. Bibliography: p. 125. [TT848.T78] 66-14430
1. Hand weaving. I. Title.

TOVEY, John. 746.1'4
The technique of weaving / John Tovey. New York : Scribner, [1975] 128 p., [4] leaves of plates : ill. (some col.) ; 26 cm. Includes index. Bibliography: p. 9. [TT848.T78 1975b] 74-32605 ISBN 0-684-14322-4 : 8.95
1. Hand weaving. I. Title.

TROTZIG, Liv. 746.1'4
Weaving bands [by] Liv Trotzig and Astrid Axelsson. [Translated from the Swedish by Marianne Turner] New York, Van Nostrand Reinhold Co. [1974] p. Translation of Band. [TT848.T8513] 73-16714 ISBN 0-442-30032-8 5.95
1. Hand weaving. 2. Braid. I. Axelsson, Astrid, joint author. II. Title.
Pbk. 3.50, ISBN 0-442-30033-6.

TURNER, Alta R. 746.1'4
Finger weaving: Indian braiding, by Alta R. Turner. New York, Sterling Pub. Co. [1973] 48 p. illus. (part col.) 20 cm. (Little craft book series) Bibliography: p. 46. Directions for using finger weaving, or flat braiding, to make belts, hair ties, collars, neck-ties, and other items with designs created by North American Indians and ancient Peruvians. [TT848.T88 1973] 72-95200 2.95
1. Hand weaving. 2. Braid. 3. Indians of North America—Textile industry and fabrics. 4. Indians of South America—Peru—Textile industry and fabrics. I. Title.
Library binding 2.69.

WEAVING; techniques & projects, by the editors of Sunset Books. 746.1'4
[Edited by Alyson Smith Gonsalves. 1st ed.] Menlo Park, Calif., Lane Books [1974] 80 p. illus. (part col.) 28 cm. (Sunset hobby & craft books) (A Sunset book) [TT848.W37] 74-89580 ISBN 0-376-04751-8 1.95 (pbk.)
1. Hand weaving. I. Gonsalves, Alyson Smith, ed.

WEIGLE, Palmy, 1920- 746.1'4
Color exercises for the weaver / by Palmy Weigle. New York : Watson-Guptill Publications, 1976. 160 p. : col. ill. ; 27 cm. Includes index. Bibliography: p. 128. [TT848.W377] 76-3733 ISBN 0-8230-0727-8 ISBN 0-8230-0728-6 pbk. : 7.95
1. Hand weaving. 2. Color in the textile industries. I. Title. BIP

WEIGLE, Palmy, 1920- 746.1'4
Double weave / by Palmy Weigle. New York : Watson-Guptill Publications, 1978. p. cm. Includes index. Bibliography: p. [TT848.W378] 78-9653 ISBN 0-8230-1355-3 : 12.95
1. Hand weaving. I. Title. BIP

WEST, Virginia M. 746.1
Finishing touches; a study of finishing details for handwoven articles [by] Virginia M. West. [Newton, Mass.] C. T. Branford Co. [1967, c1968] vii, 102 p. illus. 22 cm. Title on spine: Finishing touches for the handweaver. [TT848.W4] 68-12793
1. Hand weaving. I. Title. II. Title: Finishing touches for the handweaver.

WHITE, Alice Violet. 746.4'1
Weaving is fun / by A. V. White. New York : Dover Publications, 1975, c1959. 94 p. : ill. ; 22 cm. Reprint of the ed. published by Mills & Boon, London. Includes index. [TT848.W45 1975] 74-27568 ISBN 0-486-22724-3 pbk. : 1.75 1.50
1. Hand weaving. I. Title.

WILSON, Jean Verseput. 746.1'4
The pile weaves / by Jean Wilson. New York : Scribner, 1979. p. cm. Bibliography: p. [TT848.W479] 78-24100 ISBN 0-684-16085-4 pbk. : 9.95
1. Hand weaving. I. Title. BIP

*WILSON, Jean Verseput 646.4
The pile weaves; twenty-six techniques and how to do them. New York Van Nostrand Reinhold [1974] 96 p. illus. (part col.) 22 cm. Bibliograph: p. 95-96. [TT848] 72-2665 ISBN 0-442-29519-7 5.95
1. Hand weaving. 2. Clothing and dress. I. Title.
Pbk. 2.95; ISBN 0-442-29520-0

WILSON, Jean Verseput. 746.1
Weaving is for anyone [by] Jean Wilson. New York, Reinhold [1967] 144 p. illus. 26 cm. Bibliography: p. 143. [TT848.W5] 66-24552
1. Hand weaving. I. Title. BIP

WILSON, Jean Verseput. 746.1'4
Weaving is fun; a guide for teachers, children & beginning weavers, about yarns, baskets, cloth & tapestry [by] Jean Wilson. New York, Van Nostrand Reinhold Co. [1971] 140 p. illus. (part col.) 27 cm. Bibliography: p. 138. [TT848.W52] 74-126877 ISBN 0-289-70196-1
1. Hand weaving. I. Title.

WILSON, Jean Verseput. 746.1'4
Weaving you can use / Jean Wilson. New York : Van Nostrand Reinhold, [1975] 136 p., [4] leaves of plates : ill. (some col.) ; 28 cm. Includes index. Bibliography: p. 134. [TT848.W526] 74-7778 ISBN 0-442-29547-2 pbk. : 6.95
1. Hand weaving. I. Title. BIP

WILSON, Jean Verseput. 646.4
Weaving you can wear [by] Jean Wilson with Jan Burhen. New York, Van Nostrand Reinhold Co. [1973] 128 p. illus. 28 cm. [TT848.W53] 73-1634 ISBN 0-442-29511-1 8.95
1. Hand weaving. 2. Clothing and dress. I. Title.
Pbk. 4.95; ISBN 0-442-29514-6 BIP

WINDEKNECHT, Margaret B. 746.1'4'08 s
Creative monk's belt / Margaret B. Windeknecht. Santa Ana, Calif. : HTH Publishers, c1976. 40 p. : ill. ; 27 cm. (Monograph - Shuttle Craft Guild ; 30) Bibliography: p. 40. [TS1490.S54 no. 30] [TT848] 746.1'4 76-57344 ISBN 0-916658-33-3
1. Hand weaving. 2. Weaving—Patterns. I. Title. II. Title: Monk's belt. III. Series: Shuttle Craft Guild. Monograph ; 30. BIP

WORST, Edward Francis, 1874- 746.1'4
Weaving with foot-power looms / Edward F. Worst. New York : Dover Publications, 1974. 275 p. : ill. ; 17 x 23 cm. Reprint of the 1924 ed. published by Bruce Pub. Co., Milwaukee, under title: Foot-power loom weaving. Includes index. [TT848.W67 1974] 74-75270 ISBN 0-486-23064-3 pbk. : 4.00
1. Hand weaving. 2. Weaving—Patterns. I. Title. BIP

ZIELINSKI, Stanislaw A 746.103
Encyclopaedia of hand-weaving. New York, Funk & Wagnalls [1959] 190 p. illus. 24 cm. [TT848.Z5] 59-11308
1. Hand weaving. I. Title.

ZNAMIEROWSKI, Nell. 746.1
Step-by-step weaving; a complete introduction to the craft of weaving, including photographs in full color. Designed by and produced under the supervision of William and Shirley Sayles. New York, Golden Press [1967] 96 p. illus. (part col.) 31 cm. [TT848.Z6] 67-13490
1. Hand weaving. I. Title.

Hand weaving—Africa, West.

LAMB, Venice. 746.1'4'0966
The Lamb collection of West African narrow strip weaving : exhibited at the Textile Museum, March 7 to September 20, 1975 : [catalogue] / by Venice and Alastair Lamb ; edited by Patricia Fiske. Washington : The Museum, c1975. 48 p. : ill. (some col.) ; 26 cm. Bibliography: p. 32. [TT848.L35] 75-326523
1. Hand weaving—Africa, West. 2. Textile fabrics—Africa, West. I. Lamb, Alastair, 1930- joint author. II. Washington, D.C. Textile Museum. III. Title. IV. Title: West African narrow strip weaving.

Hand weaving—Bolivia.

CASON, Marjorie. 746.1'4
The art of Bolivian Highland weaving / by Marjorie Cason and Adele Cahlander New York : Watson-Guptill Publications, 1976. p. ; cm. Bibliography: p. [TT848.C3] 76-41703 ISBN 0-8230-0264-0 : 17.95
1. Hand weaving—Bolivia. I. Cahlander, Adele, joint author. II. Title. BIP

Hand weaving—Dictionaries.

ZIELINSKI, Stanislaw A. 746.1'4'03
Encyclopedia of hand-weaving / Stanislaw A. Zielinski. New York : Funk & Wagnalls, [1976] c1959. ix, 190 p. : ill. ; 23 cm. [TT848.Z5 1976] 75-45519 ISBN 0-308-10072-7 pbk. : 4.50
1. Hand weaving—Dictionaries. I. Title. BIP

Hand weaving—Guatemala.

ANDERSON, Marilyn, 1937- 746.1'4'097281
Guatemalan textiles today / by Marilyn Anderson. New York : Watson-Guptill Publications, 1978. 200 p. : ill. ; 29 cm. Includes index. Bibliography: p. 197-198. [TT848.A7435] 78-782 ISBN 0-8230-2158-0 : 24.50
1. Hand weaving—Guatemala. 2. Textile fabrics—Guatemala. 3. Textile crafts—Guatemala. I. Title. BIP

BJERREGAARD, Lena. 746.124
Techniques of Guatemalan weaving / Lena Bjerregaard. New York : Van Nostrand Reinhold, 1977. p. cm. Translation of Indianervaevning fra Guatemala. Includes index. Bibliography: p. [TT848.B4913] 77-7184 12.95
1. Hand weaving—Guatemala. 2. Design, Decorative—Guatemala. 3. Indians of Central America—Textile industry and fabrics. I. Title. BIP

DE RODRIGUEZ, Judy Ziek. 746.1'4
Weaving on a backstrap loom : pattern designs from Guatemala / Judy Ziek de Rodriguez and Nona M. Ziek ; photos. by Roberta Forest ; drawings and figures by Kathy Ryan ; graphs by Judith Ziek de Rodriguez. New York : Hawthorn Books, c1978. xii, 188 p., [4] leaves of plates : ill. (some col.) ; 29 cm. Includes index. Bibliography: p. 182-183. [TT848.D47 1978] 77-72809 ISBN 0-8015-3187-X : 14.95
1. Hand weaving—Guatemala. 2. Weaving—Guatemala—Patterns. I. Ziek, Nona, joint author. II. Title. BIP

Hand weaving—History.

THE Art of the weaver / 746.1'4
edited by Anita Schorsch. 1st ed. New York : Universe Books, c1978. 255 p. : ill. ; 29 cm. (Antiques magazine library) "A Main Street Press book." Consists of articles which were originally published in the magazine Antiques, taken from issues 1925 through 1976. Includes bibliographical references and index. [TT848.A763] 77-91925 ISBN 0-87663-297-5 : 12.95 ISBN 0-87663-982-1 pbk. : 8.95
1. Hand weaving—History. 2. Textile fabrics—History. 3. Rugs—History. I. Schorsch, Anita. II. Antiques.

Hand weaving—Juvenile literature.

CREATIVE Educational Society, Mankato, Minn. 746.1'4
How to have fun weaving, by editors of Creative [Educational Society] Illustrated by Betty Sievert. Mankato, Minn. ;[distributed by Childrens Press, Chicago, 1973, c1974] 31 p. illus. (part col.) 25 cm. (Creative craft book) On spine: Weaving. A brief history of weaving, instructions for basic weaving steps and making a loom, and directions for three simple projects. [TT848.C65] 73-12467 ISBN 0-87191-272-4
1. Hand weaving—Juvenile literature. I. Sievert, Betty. II. Title. III. Title: Weaving. BIP

FISHER, Leonard Everett. 746.1
The weavers, written & illustrated by Leonard Everett Fisher. New York, F. Watts [1966] 45 p. illus. 23 cm. (Colonial American craftsmen) [TT848.F55] 66-10581
1. Hand weaving — Juvenile literature. 2. Weaving — U.S. — Juvenile literature. I. Title. BIP

GILBREATH, Alice Thompson. 746.1'4
Fun with weaving / Alice Gilbreath ; illustrated by Judith Hoffman Corwin. New York : Morrow, 1976. 94 p. : ill. ; 24 cm. Instructions for making some twenty gift or household items using different weaving techniques. [TT848.G54] 75-34006 ISBN 0-688-22063-0 : 5.50 ISBN 0-688-32063-5 lib.bdg. : 4.81
1. Hand weaving—Juvenile literature. I. Corwin, Judith Hoffman. II. Title. BIP

HARVEY, Virginia I. 746.1'4
Split-ply twining / Virginia I. Harvey. Santa Ana, CA : HTH Publishers, c1976. 46 p. : ill. ; 27 cm. (Threads in action monograph series ; issue 1) Describes the textile technique of split-ply twining with diagrammed directions for weaving some samples. [TT848.H38] 75-46510 ISBN 0-916658-32-5 pbk. : 5.00
1. Hand weaving—Juvenile literature. I. Title. BIP

HETZER, Linda. 746'.04'71
Yarn crafts / crafts by Linda Hetzer ; photos. by Steven Mays, ill. by Sally Shimizu and Lynn Matus. Milwaukee : Raintree, c1978. p. cm. Easy-to-follow instructions for a selection of projects involving weaving, string craft, and stitchery. [TT848.H47] 77-29052 ISBN 0-8172-1176-4 lib.bdg. : 7.93
1. Hand weaving—Juvenile literature. 2. Needlework—Juvenile literature. 3. String craft—Juvenile literature. 4. Yarn—Juvenile literature. I. Mays, Steven. II. Shimizu, Sally. III. Matus, Lynn. IV. Title. BIP

KELLY, Karin. 746.1'4
Weaving. Pictures by George Overlie. Minneapolis, Lerner Publications Co. [1973] 32 p. illus. 19 cm. (An Early craft book) Simple instructions for making several kinds of looms and weaving on them, with suggestions for various projects. [TT848.K44] 72-13336 ISBN 0-8225-0861-3 3.95 (Lib. bdg.)
1. Hand weaving—Juvenile literature. I. Overlie, George, illus. II. Title.

LIGHTBODY, Donna M. 746.2'7
Braid craft / by Donna M. Lightbody. New York : Lothrop, Lee & Shepard Co., c1976. p. cm. Includes index. Bibliography: p. Explains the basic techniques of braiding and includes a variety of projects with complete instructions and materials suggestions. [TT848.L52] 76-19079 ISBN 0-688-41769-8 : 5.95 ISBN 0-688-51769-2 lib.bdg. :
1. Hand weaving—Juvenile literature. 2. Braid—Juvenile literature. I. Title. BIP

LIGHTBODY, Donna M. 746.1'4
Easy weaving [by] Donna M. Lightbody. Illustrated with photos. New York, Lothrop, Lee, & Shepard Co. [1974] 143 p. illus. 24 cm. Bibliography: p. 141. Introduces the basic techniques and materials of weaving without a loom, including instructions for making weaving frames and for weaving many projects. Includes information on the history of weaving. [TT848.L53] 74-9823 ISBN 0-688-40057-4
1. Hand weaving—Juvenile literature. I. Title. BIP

PARKER, Zenia Ley. 746.4
A beginner's book of off-loom weaving / Xenia Ley Parker. New York : Dodd, Mead, c1978. 224 p. : ill. ; 25 cm. Includes index. Introduces various off-loom weaving techniques including macrame, fingerweaving, braiding, and coiling. [TT848.P34] 77-16880 ISBN 0-396-07558-4 : 6.95
1. Hand-weaving—Juvenile literature. I. Title. BIP

RUBENSTONE, Jessie. 746.1'4
Weaving for beginners / by Jessie Rubenstone ; photos. by Charles Forbes Ward, Jr. 1st ed. Philadelphia : Lippincott, [1975] 80 p. : ill. ; 23 cm. An introduction to the equipment and techniques of weaving with instructions for making such items as a shag rug, shoulder bag, scarf, and a pillow. [TT848.R8] 75-16309 ISBN 0-397-31635-6 : 5.95 ISBN 0-397-31636-4 pbk. : 2.95
1. Hand weaving—Juvenile literature. I. Ward, Charles Forbes. II. Title.

Hand weaving—Mexico.

HALL, Joanne. 746.1'4
Mexican tapestry weaving / Joanne Hall. Helena, MT. : J. Arvidson Press, c1976. 156 p. : 242 ill. ; 29 cm. Bibliography: p. 155-156. [TT848.H25] 77-351132 sprial bdg. : 8.50
1. Hand weaving—Mexico. 2. Indians of Mexico—Textile industry and fabrics. I. Title. BIP

Hand weaving — Patterns.

LUNDBACK, Maja. 746.1
Small webs, by Maja Lundback and Marta Rinde-Ramsback. Translated from the Swedish by Gerda M. Andersen. [Vasteras, Sweden, ICA-Pub. Co. [1959; covered by label: Big Sur, Calif., Craft & Hobby Book Service] 104 p. illus. 22 cm. [[TT848]] A62
1. Hand weaving — Patterns. I. Rinde-Ramsback, Marta, 1920- joint author. II. Title.

PYYSALO, Helvi 746.1
Hand weaving patterns from Finland; 122 useful projects for the home and studio [by] Helvi Pyysalo [and] Viivi Merisalo. Translated [from the Finnish] by Bertha B. Needham [and] Aili J. Marsh. Newton, Mass., C. T. Branford Co. [1960, i.e., 1961] 48p. illus. (part col.) 30cm. 58-14228 5.00 bds.,
1. Hand weaving—Patterns. 2. Weaving—Finland. I. Merisalo, Viivi, joint author. II. Title.

Hand weaving—Study and teaching (Elementary)

ROMBERG, Jenean. 746.1'4
Let's discover weaving / Jenean Romberg. New York : Center for Applied Research in Education, [1975] 64 p. : ill. ; 28 cm. (Her Arts and crafts discovery units) [TT848.R63] 75-16263 ISBN 0-87628-532-9 : 3.95
1. Hand weaving—Study and teaching (Elementary) 2. Creative activities and seat work. I. Title. BIP

Handbags.

ERICSON, Lois. 646.48
The bag book / Lois Ericson & Diane Ericson. New York : Van Nostrand Reinhold, 1976. 112 p., [2] leaves of plates : ill. ; 27 cm. Includes index. Bibliography: p. 110. [TT667.E74] 75-36117 ISBN 0-442-22326-9 : 10.50 ISBN 0-442-22327-7 pbk. : 6.95
1. Handbags. 2. Textile crafts. 3. Leather work. 4. Basket making. I. Ericson, Diane, joint author. II. Title. BIP

FRAGER, Dorothy. 646.4'8
Cloth hats, bags 'n baggage / Dorothy Frager. Radnor, Pa. : Chilton Book Co., c1977. p. cm. (Chilton's creative crafts series) [TT667.F69] 77-6116 ISBN 0-8019-6367-2 : 12.50. ISBN 0-8019-6368-0 pbk. : 6.95
1. Handbags. 2. Hats. 3. Luggage. I. Title. BIP

FRAGER, Dorothy. 646.4'8
Start off in making cloth handbags / Dorothy Frager ; photos. and line drawings by Dorothy Frager. Radnor, Pa. : Chilton Book Co., c1975. 29 p. : ill. (some col.) ; 27 cm. (Chilton's basic crafts series) Provides complete instructions for making five different cloth handbags and gives tips for selecting suitable fabrics for each project. [TT667.F7] 76-373758 ISBN 0-8019-6184-X pbk. : 1.95
1. Handbags. I. Title. II. Title: Cloth handbags.

HOUCK, Carter. 646.4'8
The big bag book / Carter Houck and Myron Miller. New York : Scribner, c1977. 150 p., [4] leaves of plates : ill. ; 28 cm. [TT667.H68] 77-7163 ISBN 0-684-15180-4 : 14.95. ISBN 0-684-15179-0 pbk. : 6.95
1. Handbags. 2. Tote bags. I. Miller, Myron, 1918- joint author. II. Title. BIP

Handcraft.

AMON, Martha Ruth 745.5
Handcrafts simplified [by] Martha Ruth Amon, Ruth Holtz Rawson. Bloomington, Ill., McKnight & McKnight Pub. Co. [c.1961] 210p. Bibl. illus. 21x27cm. 61-16023 4.40; 2.80 pap.,

1. Handcraft. I. Rawson, Ruth Holtz, joint author. II. Title.

PARISI, Tony. 680
Craftsman's instruction handbook. [New enl. ed.] New York, Educational Materials [1951] 96 p. illus. 28 cm. [TT157.P3 1951] 51-4610
1. Handcraft. I. Title.

Handcrafts—Juvenile literature.

*ARNOLD, Wesley F. 745.5
Fun with next to nothing, handcraft projects for boys and girls. Written, illus. by Wesley F. Arnold, Wayne C. Cardy. New York, Scholastic [1964, c.1962] 80p. illus. 21cm. (TW 525) .45 pap.,
1. Handcrafts—Juvenile literature. I. Title. BIP

Handel, Georg Friedrich, 1685-1759.

FROST, Miriam. 779'.092'4
Messiah : a photographic meditation on Handel's Messiah / by Miriam Frost and Keith McCormick. Minneapolis, MN : Winston Press, c1978. 60 p., [1] leaf of plates : ill. ; 20 x 22 cm. [TR654.F78] 78-59409 ISBN 0-03-045721-1 pbk. : 5.95
1. Handel, Georg Friedrich, 1685-1759. Messiah. 2. Photography, Artistic. I. McCormick, Keith, joint author. II. Handel, Georg Friedrich, 1685-1759. Messiah. III. Title. BIP

Handicraft

BUILD it. 694.024
Greenwich, Conn., Fawcett Publications, c1956. 144p. illus. 24cm. (A Fawcett how-to book. 312) [TT153.B8 1958] 58-4888
1. Handicaraft. 2. Workshop receipts. I. Fawcett Publications, inc.

Handicraft.

ABELES, Kim Victoria, 1952- 745.5
Crafts, cookery, and country living / Kim Victoria Abeles. New York : Van Nostrand Reinhold Co., c1976. 163 p. : ill. ; 28 cm. Includes index. Bibliography: p. 160-161. [TT157.A2 1976] 76-6914 ISBN 0-442-20236-9 pbk. : 7.95
1. Handicraft. 2. Cookery. I. Title. BIP

ABELL, Vivian. 745.5
Don't throw it away! [New York] Creative Home Library, [1973] 180 p. illus. (part col.) 26 cm. [TT157.A23] 73-7844 ISBN 0-696-19100-8 7.95
1. Handicraft. I. Title.

ALKEMA, Chester Jay. 745.5
Alkema's scrap magic : how to turn your trash can into a treasure chest / by Chester Jay Alkema ; photos by the author. New York : Sterling Pub. Co., c1976. 120 p. : ill. ; 25 cm. Includes index. [TT157.A44] 76-19769 ISBN 0-8069-5352-7 : 12.95. lib.bdg. : 11.29
1. Handicraft. 2. Waste products. I. Title. II. Title: Scrap magic. BIP

ALLEN, Opal Beebe. 745.5
Through the year with crafts [by] Opal Beebe Allen and Naomi Morris Ready. Milwaukee, Bruce Pub. Co. [1958] 120p. illus. 24cm. [TT160.A45] 58-6222
1. Handicraft. I. Ready, Naoml Morris, joint author. II. Title.

THE American home. 643.7
The American home basic manual of how-to-do-it's. [Garden City? N. Y., 1955?] 179p. illus. 32cm. [TT155.A5] 55-4117
1. Handicraft. 2. Dwellings—Maintenance and repair. I. Title. II. Title: Basic manual of how-to-do-it's.

ANDERSEN, Gretchen Mann, 1933- 745.5
Creative exploration in crafts / Gretchen Mann Andersen. Reston, Va. : Reston Pub. Co., c1976. xvi, 284 p. : ill. ; 24 cm. Includes index. Bibliography: p. 267-277. [TT157.A55] 75-38762 ISBN 0-87909-169-X : 12.95 ISBN 0-87909-168-1 pbk. : 8.95
1. Handicraft. I. Title. BIP

ARNOLD, Arnold. 745.5'02'4054
The Crowell book of arts and crafts for children / by Arnold Arnold. New York : Crowell, [1975] xxii, 437 p. : ill. ; 24 cm. Includes index. Bibliography: p. [429]-437. [TT157.A76 1975] 75-2333 ISBN 0-690-00567-9 : 10.00
1. Handicraft. I. Title. BIP

THE Art of acrylic crafts. 745.5
[Designed and edited by Walter Brooks. New York, Western Pub. Co., 1971] 48 p. illus. 32 cm. (A Grumbacher library book) [TT157.A77] 73-139156 1.00
1. Handicraft. 2. Acrylic resins. I. Brooks, Walter, 1921- ed.

AUDELS do-it-yourself encyclopedia; 643.7
comprehensive how-to-series for the entire family; containing material from the Illustrated do-it-yourself encyclopedia written in simple language with fill step-by-step instructions ... [Prepared and edited by How-To Assocites] Illustrated ed. New York, T. Audel [c1959] 2 v. (1012 p.) illus. 23cm. [TT155.A8] 60-338
1. Handicraft. 2. Dwellings. 3. Building—Repair and reconstruction. I. How-To Associates. II. Title: Do-it-yourself encyclopedia.

AUDELS do-it-yourself encyclopedia; 643'.03
comprehensive how-to series for the entire family containing material from the Illustrated do-it-yourself encyclopedia, written in simple language with full step-by-step instructions and profusely illustrated. [Prepared and edited by How-To Associates] Indianapolis, T. Audel [1968] 2 v. (1012 p.) illus., plans. 23 cm. [TT155.A83] 68-8893 4.50 (per vol.)
1. Handicraft. 2. Dwellings—Maintenance and repair. 3. Dwellings—Remodeling. I. How-To Associates. II. Title: Do-it-yourself encyclopedia.

BACON, Richard M. 630
The Yankee magazine book of forgotten arts / Richard M. Bacon. New York : Simon and Schuster, c1978. 219 p. : ill. ; 29 cm. Collection of articles previously published in the Yankee magazine. Includes bibliographies. [TT157.B2] 77-28761 ISBN 0-671-22824-2 : 9.95
1. Handicraft. 2. Cookery. 3. Livestock. 4. Building. I. Yankee. II. Title. BIP

BAILLIE, Eugene Kenneth, 1901- 745.5
Homespun crafts. Milwaukee, Bruce Pub. Co. [1952] 159 p. illus. 23 cm. [TT157.B32] 680 52-8173
1. Handicraft. 2. Salvage (Waste, etc.) I. Title.

BALE, Robert O. 745.5
Creative nature crafts. Minneapolis, Burgess Pub. Co. [1959] 120 p. illus. 21 cm. Includes bibliography. [TT160.B32] 59-8291
1. Handicraft. I. Title.

BALE, Robert O 745.5
Stepping stones to nature. Minneapolis, Burgess Pub. Co. [1960] 141p. illus. 22cm. (Burgess camping series) [TT160.B324] 60-8275
1. Handicraft. 2. Nature study. I. Title.

THE Beautiful crafts book. 745.5
New York : Sterling Pub. Co., 1976. 128 p. : ill. (some col.) ; 26 cm. Includes index. [TT157.B357 1976] 76-150393 ISBN 0-8069-5366-7 : 14.95 ISBN 0-8069-5367-5 lib.bdg. :
1. Handicraft. BIP

BENSON, Kenneth R. 745.5
Arts and crafts for home, school, and community / Kenneth R. Benson and Carl E. Frankson, with Thomas Buttery. Saint Louis : Mosby, 1975. viii, 136 p. : ill. ; 28 cm. [TT157.B379] 75-322666 ISBN 0-8016-0615-2 : 7.50
1. Handicraft. I. Frankson, Carl E., joint author. II. Buttery, Thomas, joint author. III. Title. BIP

BENSON, Kenneth R. 745.5
Creative nature crafts [by] Kenneth R. Benson [and] Carl E. Frankson. Mildred Kaiser, illustrator. Englewood Cliffs, N.J., Prentice-Hall [1968] xiii, 97 p. illus. 28 cm. [TT157.B38] 68-21476
1. Handicraft. I. Frankson, Carl E., joint author. II. Title. BIP

BERMAN, Norman. 745.5
Art from clutter / Norman Berman, Andrew Pinto. 1st ed. New York : R. Rosen Press, 1976. p. cm. Describes basic design concepts for a number of handicraft projects. All projects utilize materials which can be easily collected. [TT157.B43] 76-8500 ISBN 0-8239-0341-9 : 9.66
1. Handicraft. I. Pinto, Andrew, joint author. II. Title. BIP

†*BETTER homes and gardens creative crafts and stitchery.* 745.5
1st ed. [Des Moines] : Meredith Corp., c1976. 288 p. : ill. (some col.) ; 32 cm. (Better homes and gardens books) Includes index. [TT157.B447] 76-19163 ISBN 0-696-00381-3 : 12.95
1. Handicraft. 2. Needlework. I. Title: Creative crafts and stitchery. BIP

†*BETTER homes and gardens treasures from throwaways.* 745.5
1st ed. Des Moines : Meredith Corp., c1976. 256 p. : ill. ; 29 cm. (Better homes and gardens books) Includes index. [TT157.B459] 75-38246 ISBN 0-696-45000-3 : 9.95
1. Handicraft. 2. Waste products. I. Title: Treasures from throwaways.

BIDDLE, Dorothy, 1887- 394.268
Christmas idea book [by] Dorothy Biddle and Dorothea Blom. New York, M. Barrows [1953] 221 p. illus. 21 cm. Includes bibliography. [TT157.B5] 53-8669
1. Handicraft. 2. Floral decoration. I. Blom, Dorothea Johnson, 1911- joint author. II. Title.

BIRMINGHAM, Lloyd. 745.5
Handy Family. New York, New American Library, [1972] 95 p. illus. (A Signette, P5259) Pap. .60
1. Handicraft. I. Title.

BLUE Mountain Crafts Council. 745.5
The joy of crafts / Blue Mountain Crafts Council. [New York] : Holt, Rinehart and Winston, 1975. p. cm. [TT157.B65] 74-24777 ISBN 0-03-014481-7 : 19.95
1. Handicraft. I. Title.

BODKIN, Cora. 745.5'02'40565
Crafts for your leisure years / Cora Bodkin, Helene Leibowitz, Diana Wiener. Boston : Houghton Mifflin, 1976. p. cm. Bibliography: p. [TT157.B663] 76-29636 ISBN 0-395-24767-5 : 12.95. ISBN 0-395-24837-X pbk. : 6.95
1. Handicraft. I. Leibowitz, Helene. II. Wiener, Diana. III. Title. BIP

BOHM, Hansi. 745.5
Making simple constructions. New York, Watson-Guptill [1972, c1971] 104 p. illus. (part col.) 24 cm. Bibliography: p. 102. [TT910.B64] 70-190516 ISBN 0-8230-2995-6 7.95
1. Handicraft. 2. Assemblage (Art) I. Title. II. Title: Constructions.

THE Book of crafts, 745.5
edited by Henry Pluckrose. Chicago, H. Regnery Co. [1971] viii, 248 p. illus. 29 cm. [TT157.B68] 76-163268 8.95
1. Handicraft. I. Pluckrose, Henry Arthur, ed.

BRITTON, Dorothea S. 745.5
The complete book of bazaars [by] Dorothea S. Britton. New York, Coward, McCann & Geoghegan [1973] 254 p. illus. 22 cm. [TT880.B75 1973] 72-76683 ISBN 0-698-10467-6 7.95
1. Handicraft. 2. Bazaars, Charitable. I. Title.

*BROWN, Opal. 745.5
Fun with handcraft; 44 creative projects for everyone. Grand Rapids, Baker Book House [1975] 59 p. ill. 18 cm. [TT157] ISBN 0-8010-0628-7 1.25 (pbk.)
1. Handicraft. I. Title. BIP

BUILD it. 680
Greenwich, Conn., Fawcett Publications, '1950. 143 p. illus. 24 cm. (A Fawcett book, no. 101) [TT153.B8] 50-14264
1. Handicraft. 2. Workshop receipts. I. Fawcett Publications, inc.

BUILD it. 680
Greenwich, Conn., Fawcett Publications, c1956. 144p. illus. 24cm. (A Fawcett how-to book, 312) [TT153.B8 1956] 56-58111
1. Handicraft. 2. Workshop receipts. I. Fawcett Publications. inc.

BUILD it yourself. 684
Chicago, Science and Mechanics Pub. Co. [19 v. illus. 24cm. 'A selected group of the most popular articles which appeared first in Science and mechanics magazine. [TT157.B8] 55-2231
1. Handicraft. I. Science and mechanics.

CARDOZO, Peter. 790'.1
The second whole kids catalog / created by Peter Cardozo ; designed by Ted Menten ; senior writer Joyce Siat. Toronto ; New York : Bantam Books, c1977. v, 250 p. : ill. ; 28 cm. A source book for handicrafts, amusements, and hobbies. Includes bibliographies and addresses for a variety of free materials. [TT157.C23] 78-313775 ISBN 0-553-01084-0 : 7.50
1. Handicraft. 2. Amusements. 3. Hobbies. 4. Handicraft—Bibliography. 5. Amusements—Bibliography. 6. Hobbies—Bibliography. 7. Free material. I. Menten, Theodore. II. Title. BIP

CARLSON, Bernice Wells. 680
Make it yourself! Handicraft for boys and girls; illustrated by Aline Hansens. New York, Abingdon-Cokesbury Press [1950] 160 p. illus. 24 cm. [TT157.C27] 50-6501
1. Handicraft. I. Title.

CASSELMAN, B. J. 745.5
Crafts from around the world / B. J. Casselman. [New York] : Creative Home Library, [1975] 256 p. : ill. ; 27 cm. Includes index. Bibliography: p. 252-253. [TT145.C37] 75-952 ISBN 0-696-17900-8 : 12.95
1. Handicraft. I. Title.

CHAMBERLAIN, Marcia. 746
Beyond weaving, by Marcia Chamberlain and Candace Crockett. Photos. by David Donoho. New York, Watson-Guptill Publications [1974] 191 p. illus. 29 cm. Bibliography: p. 185-187. [TT699.C47 1974] 74-1110 ISBN 0-8230-0486-4 14.95
1. Handicraft. I. Crockett, Candace, 1945- joint author. II. Title. BIP

CHERNER, Norman. 684.1
How to build children's toys and furniture. Drawings by the author. New York, McGraw-Hill [1954] 144 p. illus. 26 cm. [TT157.C42] 53-12441
1. Handicraft. 2. Toys. 3. Furniture. I. Title.

CHEW AND SONS, Salisbury, Md. 745.5922
Artcrafting little people, by the Chews. Photos. by Photo-lite, inc. Illus. by Mrs. H. Lewis Chew. Salisbury, Md., Chew & Sons, Bx. 1125, c.1962. 109p. 29cm. 62-46364 2.95
1. Handicraft. I. Chew, Sallie B., illus. II. Title.

CHRISMAN, Irma Brown. 394.268
Christmas trees, decorations, and ornaments. Drawings by Ann Harris Strachan. New York, Hearthside Press [1956] 96p. illus. 25cm. [TT157.C47] 56-10752
1. Handicraft. 2. Christmas decorations. I. Title.

CHRISMAN, Irma Brown. 394.268
Christmas trees, decorations, and ornaments. Drawings by Ann Haris Strachan. New York, Hearthside Press [1956] 96 p. illus. 25 cm. [TT157.C47] 56-10752
1. Handicraft. 2. Christmas decorations. I. Title.

CLAPPER, Edna. 745.5
Pack-o-fun craft projects; make it yourself with odds and ends, by Edna and John Clapper. New York, Hawthorn Books [1972] 256 p. illus. 22 cm. [TT157.C48 1972] 72-88528 4.95
1. Handicraft. I. Clapper, John, joint author. II. Title.

COFFEY, Ernestine Sabrina. 684
A leader's guide to nature and garden fun, by Ernestine Sabrina Coffey and Dorothy Fitch Minton. Drawings by Jane Reynolds Crow. New York, Hearthside Press [1957] 127p. illus. 21cm. [TT157.C528] 57-8287
1. Handicraft. 2. Floral decoration. 3. Decoration and ornament. I. Minton,

Dorothy Fitch, joint author. II. Title. III. Title: Nature and garden fun.

COFFEY, Ernestine Sabrina. 684
A leader's guide to nature and garden fun, by Ernestine Sabrina Coffey and Dorothy Fitch Minton. Drawings by Jane Reynolds Crow. New York, Hearthside Press [1957] 127p. illus. 21cm. [TT157.C528] 57-8287
1. Handicraft. 2. Floral decoration. 3. Decoration and ornament. I. Minton, Dorothy Fitch, joint author. II. Title. III. Title: Nature and garden fun.

COFFEY, Ernestine Sabrina. 680
Your own book of nature and garden fun, by Ernestine Sabrina Coffey and Dorothy Fitch Minton. Drawings by Jane Reynolds Crow. New York, Hearthside Press [1957] 63p. illus. 22cm. [TT157.C53] 57-8286
1. Handicraft. 2. Floral decoration. 3. Decoration and ornament. I. Minton, Dorothy Fitch, joint author. II. Title.

COLBY, Carroll B. 680
Early American crafts; tools, shops, and products, by C. B. Colby. New York, Coward-McCann [1967] 48 p. illus. 28 cm. A survey of colonial American crafts as practiced today in restored historic villages and towns in the U.S. [TT23.C64] AC 67
1. Handicraft. 2. United States—Industries—History. I. Title.

COLE, Judy Slaughter. 745.5
A pioneer workshop / by Judy Slaughter Cole and Mary Mitchell Minturn ; illustrated by Grayson Slaughter. 1st ed. Kansas City, Mo. : Lowell Press, 1975. x, 112 p. : ill. ; 22 cm. Includes bibliographical references. [TT157.C54] 75-24614 ISBN 0-913504-26-2
1. Handicraft. 2. Cookery. 3. United States—Social life and customs—19th century. I. Minturn, Mary Mitchell, joint author. II. Title.

COLORADO Occupational Therapy Association. 680
At your fingertips. [Rev. Denver] '1952. 1 v. (loose-leaf) illus. 25 cm. [TT157.C55] 52-43010
1. Handicraft. 2. Occupational therapy—Handbooks, manuals, etc. I. Title.

THE Compleat craftsman : 745.5
yesterday's handicraft projects for today's family / compiled by Martin Lawrence. New York : Universe Books, 1977. 251 p. : ill. ; 29 cm. " A Main Street Press book." Includes index. [TT157.L32] 77-70473 ISBN 0-87663-300-9 : 14.95 14.95. ISBN 0-87663-968-6 pbk. : 7.95
1. Lawrence, Martin. 2. Handicraft. BIP

CONNORS, Dorsey. 680
Dorsey Connors' book; gadgets galore! [Chicago] Popular Mechanics Press [1953] 238p. illus. 23cm. [TT157.C64] 53-9418
1. Handicraft. I. Title. II. Title: Gadgets galore!

COWBOURNE, Donald 745.5
Creative crafts for beginners. London. Blandford Pr. [Newton Centre, Mass., Branford, 1966,c.1965] 96p. illus. 23cm. [NK70] 66-4922 ISBN CD 3.95 bds.,
1. Handicraft. 2. Paper work. I. Title.

COX, Doris E. 1904- 745
Creative hands, an introduction to craft techniques [by] Doris Cox and Barbara Warren. 2d ed. New York, Wiley [1951] xiii, 381 p. illus. 26 cm. Bibliography: p. 359-373. [TT171.C6 1951] 51-11326
1. Handicraft. I. Warren, Barbara Kate, 1915- joint author. II. Title.

CRAFTS jamboree / 745.5
edited by Yvonne Deutch. New York : Van Nostrand Reinhold Co., [1977] p. cm. Includes index. [TT157.C685] 77-6403 ISBN 0-442-21351-4 : 14.95
1. Handicraft. I. Deutch, Yvonne. BIP

CREATIVE crafts / 745.5
[chief advisory editor Angela Jeffs, advisory editors Wendy Martensson, Patsy North]. Oxford : Elsevier-Phaidon, 1977. 432 p. : ill. (chiefly col.), col. ports ; 27 cm. Includes index. Bibliography: p. 427. [TT157.C717 1977a] 78-306392 ISBN 0-7290-0054-0 : 11.95
1. Handicraft. I. Jeffs, Angela. II. Martensson, Wendy. III. North, Patsy.

CREATIVE crafts / 745.5
[advisory editors, Angela Jeffs, chief, Wendy Martensson, Patsy North]. New York : Sterling Pub. Co., c1977. 432 p. : ill. ; 27 cm. Includes index. [TT157.C717] 77-151390 ISBN 0-8069-5378-0 : 25.00. ISBN 0-8069-5379-9 lib.bdg. : 24.89
1. Handicraft. I. Jeffs, Angela. II. Martensson, Wendy. III. North, Patsy. IV. Sterling Publishing Company, inc., New York.

CREATIVE handicrafts course 745.5
a step-by-step guide to popular handicrafts / edited by Linda Olsheim. New York : Bounty Books, 1976. p. cm. Includes index. [TT157.C724] 76-7412 ISBN 0-517-52631-X
1. Handicraft. I. Olsheim, Linda. BIP

CREEKMORE, Betsey Beeler. 745.5
Making gifts from oddments & outdoor materials, by Betsey B. Creekmore. New York, Hearthside Press [1970] 224 p. illus. (part col.) 25 cm. [TT157.C73] 78-113260 7.95
1. Handicraft. 2. Design, Decorative—Plant forms. I. Title. BIP

CROSS, Linda. 745.5
Kitchen crafts, by Linda and John Cross. Illustrated by Burt Blum. Photos. by John Retallack. New York, Macmillan [1974] 120 p. illus. 30 cm. [TT157.C75] 73-8351 ISBN 0-02-528940-3 3.95 (pbk.)
1. Handicraft. I. Cross, John, 1936- joint author. II. Title. BIP

D'AMATO, Janet. 745.5'09701
American Indian craft inspirations, by Janet and Alex D'Amato. Illus. by Janet D'Amato. New York, M. Evans [1972] 224 p. illus. 25 cm. [TT157.D34] 72-83734 7.95
1. Handicraft. 2. Indians of North America—Costume and adornment. 3. Indians of North America—Art. 4. Indians of North America—Industries. I. D'Amato, Alex, joint author. II. Title. BIP

D'AMATO, Janet. 745.5
Gifts to make for love or money; a how-to book of imaginative ideas for fun-giving or fund-raising, by Janet and Alex D'Amato. New York, Golden Press [1973] viii, 184 p. illus. (part col.) 26 cm. (The Betty Crocker home library) [TT157.D343] 72-87344 2.50
1. Handicraft. 2. Gifts. I. D'Amato, Alex, joint author. II. Title.

DANK, Michael Carlton. 745.5
Scrap craft; 105 projects, written and illustrated by Michael Carlton Dank. New York, Dover Publications [1969] xii, 376 p. illus. 22 cm. First published in 1946 under title: Adventures in scrap craft. [TT157.D35 1969] 69-17471 2.50
1. Handicraft. I. Title. BIP

DARMAN, Marion, 1937- 745.5
Making treasures from trash / Marion Darman ; ill. by William Darman. South Brunswick : A. S. Barnes, [1975] 112 p. : ill. ; 27 cm. [TT157.D37 1975] 74-9280 ISBN 0-498-01609-9 : 9.95
1. Handicraft. 2. Waste products. I. Title.

THE Deltagram. 680
Home workshop projects. Greenwich, Conn., Fawcett Publications [1953] c1952. 143p. illus. 24cm. (A Fawcett book, no.173) 'Material ... is reprinted from the Deltagram.' [TT157.D43] 53-19587
1. Handicraft. I. Title.

THE Deltagram. 680
Home workshop projects. New York, Arco Pub. Co. [1954, c1952] 143p. illus. 24cm. (The Do-it-yourself series) An Arco how-to book. Originally published as Fawcett book no.173. 'Material ... is reprinted from the Deltagram.' [TT157.D43 1954] 55-10823
1. Handicraft. I. Title.

THE Deltagram. 680
Home workshop projects. Greenwich, Conn., Fawcett Publications, c1955. 143p. illus. 24cm. (A Fawcett how-to book, 291) Cover title: New home workshop projects. 'Material ... is reprinted from The Deltagram.' [TT157.D43 1955] 56-696
1. Handicraft. I. Title. II. Title: New home workshop projects. III. Series.

DERENDINGER, Gertrud 745.5
It's fun making things. Tr. from German by Jeremy Hamand Burgdorf, Switzerland, RIA Pubs., [New York, Heinman, 1966] 55p. illus. (pt. col.) 30cm. Patterns on both sides of a sheet, 58x80cm. fold. 20x29cm., in pocket. [TT157.D4713] 66-5529 4.00 pap.,
1. Handicraft. I. Title. BIP

DOLE, Hilary, 1945- 745.5
Craft digest, edited by Hilary Dole. Northfield, Ill., Digest Books [1974] 288 p. illus. 28 cm. Includes bibliographical references. [TT157.D62] 73-91586 5.95
1. Handicraft. I. Title.

DOUGHERTY, Bob. 680
The Dremel handbook of hobbies, crafts and projects. [New York] Benjamin Co. [1967] 160 p. illus. 21 cm. Bibliography: p. 158. [TT157.D64] 67-29004
1. Handicraft. 2. Models and modelmaking. I. Dremel Manufacturing Company. II. Title. III. Title: Hobbies, crafts and projects.

DOW, Emily R., 1904- 745.5
Crafts for fun & fairs [by] Emily R. Dow. Illustrated by the author. New York, M. Barrows, 1964. 271 p. illus. 22 cm. Bibliography: p. [261]-262. [TT157.D65] 64-22511
1. Handicraft. I. Title.

DUVALL, Carol. 745.5
Wanna make something out of it? Illus. by Joyce Martin. Photos. by Mike Duvall. Los Angeles, Nash Pub. [1972] 205 p. illus. 15 x 23 cm. [TT157.D85 1972] 72-81831 ISBN 0-8402-1277-1 6.95
1. Handicraft. I. Title.

ECKSTEIN, Artis Aleene. 745.5
How to make treasures from trash, by Artis Aleene Eckstein in collaboration with Alice R. Shannon. Great Neck, N.Y., Hearthside Press [1972] 223 p. illus. 25 cm. [TT157.E35] 72-79086 8.95
1. Handicraft. I. Title. BIP

EDWARDS, Jeanne, 1895- 745.5
Creative crafts. Grand Rapids, Zondervan Pub. House [1970] 62 p. illus. 28 cm. [TT157.E38] 72-106446
1. Handicraft. I. Title.

EGGE, Ruth Stearns. 745.5
How to make something from nothing. New York, Coward-McCann [1968] 224 p. illus. 22 cm. [TT157.E43] 68-23371 5.95
1. Handicraft. I. Title.

EPPLE, Anne Orth. 745.5
Nature crafts. [1st ed.] Radnor, Pa., Chilton Book Co. [1974] 149 p. illus. 27 cm. [TT157.E66 1974] 73-20367 ISBN 0-8019-5939-X
1. Handicraft. I. Title.

EPPLE, Anne Orth. 745.5
Something from nothing crafts / Anne Orth Epple ; [photos. by Lewis E. Epple]. 1st ed. Radnor, Pa. : Chilton Book Co., c1976. xiv, 203 p., [6] leaves of plates : ill. ; 27 cm. (Chilton's creative crafts series) Includes index. [TT157.E67 1976] 75-42111 ISBN 0-8019-6369-9. ISBN 0-8019-6370-2 pbk.
1. Handicraft. 2. Waste products. I. Title. BIP

ERDAHL, Berlyn J., 1934- 745.5
Cyclopedic treasury of arts and crafts activities using scrap materials / Berlyn J. Erdahl. West Nyack, N.Y. : Parker Pub. Co., c1977. p. cm. Includes index. [TT157.E7] 77-7056 ISBN 0-13-196600-6 : 14.95
1. Handicraft. 2. Creative activities and seat work. 3. Waste products. I. Title. BIP

FELLMAN, Barbara C. 745.59'2
Fun with baskets, by Barbara C. Fellman. New York, Scribner [1975] xi, 110 p. illus. 24 cm. [TT157.F44] 74-12226 ISBN 0-684-13992-8 9.95
1. Handicraft. 2. Baskets. I. Title.

*FIAROTTA, phyllis. 745.5
101 gifts you can make at home / by Phyllis and Noel Ficarotta. [New York, Bantam, 1968] 96p. illus. 14cm. (Minibk., FX4349) .50 pap.,
1. Handicraft. I. Ficarotta, Noel. joint author. II. Title.

FIAROTTA, Phyllis. 745.5
Phyllis Fiarotta's Nostalgia crafts book. New York : Workman Pub. Co., 1974. 232 p. : ill. (some col.) ; 28 cm. [TT157.F48] 75-8812 ISBN 0-911104-43-7 : 10.95 ISBN 0-911104-44-5 pbk. : 5.95
1. Handicraft. I. Title. II. Title: Nostalgia crafts book. BIP

FIAROTTA, Phyllis. 745.5
Treasury of craft designs. Toronto, New York, Bantam Books [1973] xi, 179 p. illus. 18 cm. [TT857.F4] 72-13744 1.95 (pbk.)
1. Handicraft. I. Title.

FLEMING, Gerry. 745.5
Scrap craft for youth groups. New York, John Day Co. [1969] 216 p. illus. 29 cm. [TT160.F55] 68-24143 6.95
1. Handicraft. I. Title. BIP

FOBEL, Jim. 745.59'41
The big book of fabulous, fun-filled celebrations and holiday crafts / by Jim Fobel and Jim Boleach, with Virginie Elbert. 1st ed. New York : Holt, Rinehart, and Winston, c1978. 223 p. : ill. ; 29 cm. "A Gladstone book." [TT157.F588] 78-4698 14.95
1. Handicraft. 2. Cookery. 3. Holidays. I. Boleach, Jim, joint author. II. Elbert, Virginie, joint author. III. Title. BIP

FOULSHAM (W.) Company, ltd. 745.5
The bumper book of things a boy can make / W. Foulsham & Co. Ltd. Blue Ridge Summit, Pa. : Tab Books, [1978] p. cm. Includes index. Presents step-by-step instructions for projects such as kites, rafts, airplane models, bows and arrows, and stilts to make with basic household supplies and materials. [TT157.F68 1978a] 78-12278 ISBN 0-8306-9881-7 : 8.95. ISBN 0-8306-1090-1 pbk. : 4.95
1. Handicraft. I. Title. BIP

FOULSHAM (W.) Company, ltd. 745.5
The bumper book of things a girl can make / W. Foulsham & Co. Ltd. Blue Ridge Summit, Pa. : TAB Books, [1978] p. cm. Includes index. Provides instructions for over 200 alphabetically arranged craft projects of interest to girls including bookends, Christmas cards, glove puppets, and a tobacco pouch. [TT157.F68 1978] 78-12537 ISBN 0-8306-9880-9 : 8.95. ISBN 0-8306-1091-X pbk. : 4.95
1. Handicraft. I. Title. BIP

FRANKEL, Lillian Berson. 745.5
Creating from scrap, by Lillian and Godfrey Frankel. With drawings by Shizu. New York, Sterling Pub. Co. [1962] 127 p. illus. 21 cm. [TT160.F64] 62-12593
1. Handicraft. I. Frankel, Godfrey, joint author. II. Title.

FREER, Marjorie Mueller. 745
Gifts to make at home; illustrated by Howard Freer. New York, Studio Publications in association with Crowell [1952] 96 p. illus. 25 cm. [TT157.F74] 52-10375
1. Handicraft. I. Title.

FURRELL, A. Wyburd 745.5
East-west handicrafts for amateur craftsmen, students teachers, artists, interior decorators, occupational therapists, and handicapped persons, by A. Wyburd Furrell. Dorothy L. Furrell. St. Louis. Mo. 63138 [East-West Handicrafts, Box 13430. North County Stn., c.1965] 130p. illus. 29cm. Bibl. [TT157.F86] 65-3992 5.95; 4.95 pap.,
1. Handicraft. I. Furrell, Dorothy L., joint author. II. Title.

GEROULD, Christopher. 690
119 easy-to-do home improvement projects; a guide for the week-end handyman. Illus. by Sigman-Ward. New York, Universal Pub. and Distributing Corp. [1950] 112 p. illus. 24 cm. [TT155.G46] 50-12643
1. Handicraft. 2. Dwellings—Maintenance and repair. I. Title.

GIANT book of crafts / 745.5
compiled by Anne E. Kallem, assisted by Louisa B. Hellegers and Steven Morgenstern. New York : Sterling Pub. Co., c1975. 480 p., [16] leaves of plates : ill. (some col.) ; 29 cm. Includes index. [TT157.G44] 75-14517 20.00
1. Handicraft. I. Kallem, Anne E. II.

Hellegers, Louisa Bumagin. III. Morgenstern, Steven. BIP

GICK, James E. 745.5
Modern American handicrafts. [Fort Worth. Tex., Pacific Arts & Crafts, P.O. Box 1479, c.1960] 1 v. (various pagings) illus. (part col.) 23x29cm. 60-51291 9.95 lea. cl.,
1. Handicraft. I. Title. II. Title: American handicrafts.

GILBERT, Dorothy. 745.5
Can I make another one? More craft ideas for the pre-school child. London, Faber and Faber [1973] 61 p. illus. 22 cm. Label mounted on t.p.: "Transatlantic Arts, Inc., Levittown, N.Y., sole distributor for the U.S.A." Directions for making such things as octopuses, letter holders, bracelets, and forts from egg cartons, beads, feathers, and other easily obtainable materials. [TT160.G44] 73-175612 ISBN 0-571-10102-X 6.95
1. Handicraft. 2. Models and modelmaking. I. Title.

GIRL Scouts of the United States of America. 745
Exploring the hand arts [by Corinne Murphy, arts and crafts adviser, Program Development Division] New York [1955] 118 p. illus. 24 cm. [NK70.G5] 56-1994
1. Handicraft. I. Title. BIP

GODA, Sawako. 745.5
Fun with junk; making funny figures out of odds and ends. Photos by Yoshikatsu Saeki. New York, Crown Publishers [1966] 40 p. col. illus. 21 x 22 cm. [TT157.G55] 66-18456
1. Handicraft. I. Title.

GORMAN, Robert, 1917- 680
Hobby tools and how to use them. Prepared under the direction of X-Acto, inc. Long Island City, N. Y., 1956. 95p. illus. 23cm. [TT157.G58] 56-45526
1. Handicraft. I. Title.

GOSS, Mary, 1909- 680
Do-it fun for boys and girls, by Mary and Dale Goss. Peoria, Ill., C. A. Bennett Co. [1950] 128 p. illus. 24 cm. [TT157.G6] 50-11170
1. Handicraft. I. Goss, Dale, 1910- joint author. II. Title.

GOTTSHALL, Franklin H 745.5
Craftwork in metal, wood, leather, plastics. Milwaukee, Bruce Pub. Co. [1954] 144p. illus. 29cm. [TT157.G62] 54-7891
1. Handicraft. I. Title.

GOULD, Elaine. 745.5'02'40816
Arts and crafts for physically and mentally disabled : the how, what, and why of it / by Elaine Gould and Loren Gould. Springfield, Ill. : Thomas, c1978. xix, 348 p. : ill. ; 29 cm. Includes index. [TT149.G58] 77-27853 ISBN 0-398-03783-3 spiral : 34.50
1. Handicraft for the physically handicapped. 2. Handicraft for the mentally handicapped. I. Gould, Loren, joint author. II. Title. BIP

GOULD, Elaine. 745.5'024'0565
Crafts for the elderly, by Elaine Gould and Loren Gould. Springfield, Ill., Thomas [1971] vii, 210 p. illus. 24 cm. [TT157.G63] 76-135932
1. Handicraft. 2. Aged—Recreation. I. Gould, Loren, joint author. II. Title. BIP

GREEN, Marjorie Canfield. 745.5
Gifts, gadgets, and glamour; craft projects for gift-giving. Milwaukee, Bruce Pub. Co. [1961] 96 p. illus. 25 cm. [TT157.G64] 61-8172
1. Handicraft. 2. Gifts. I. Title.

GREER, Rita. 745.5
An introduction to arts and crafts / Rita Greer. New York : Viking Press, 1975, c1974. vi, 122 p., [2] leaves of plates : ill. (some col.) ; 16 x 22 cm. (A Studio book) [TT149.G67 1975] 74-9260 ISBN 0-670-40048-3 : 6.95
1. Handicraft. I. Title.

GRIFFIS, Martha Hughes, 1907- 745.5
Fun with shapes in space; how to make 3-dimensional "things" useful in home, school, and community recreation, including techniques of string construction in addition to other skills and materials, by Toni Hughes [pseud.] All constructions and drawings created by Toni Hughes [pseud.] [1st ed.] New York, Dutton, 1960. 221 p. illus. 26 cm. [TT157.G665] 60-5996
1. Handicraft. I. Title.

GRIFFIS, Martha Hughes, 1907- 745
How to make shapes in space; a recreational craft book with instructions, diagrams, and photographs, for making three-dimensional greeting cards, posters, garlands, masks, ornaments, toys, and decorations of all kinds [by] Toni Hughes [pseud.] [1st ed.] New York, Dutton, 1955. 217 p. illus. 26 cm. [TT157.G67] 55-5353
1. Handicraft. I. Title.

GRIFFIS, Martha Hughes, 1907- 745.5
Toni Hughes' book of party favors and decorations. [1st ed.] New York, Dutton [1960] 124p. illus. 26cm. 'A junior edition of material compiled from [the author's] How to make shapes in space and Fun with shapes in space.' [TT157.G6652] 60-11871
1. Handicraft. I. Title. II. Title: Party favors and decorations.

GRIFFIS, Martha Hughes [Toni Hughes, pseud.] 745.5
Toni Hughes book of party favors and decorations. New York, Dutton [c.1960] 124p. illus. 26cm. 'A junior edition of material compiled from [the author's] How to make shapes in space and Fun with shapes in space.' 60-11871 3.75
1. Handicraft. I. Title. II. Title: Party favors and decorations.

GRIMM, Gretchen, 1912- 745.5
Crafts for school and home, by Gretchen Grimm and Catherine Skeels. Illus. by Edward Seth Fish, and others. Milwaukee, Bruce Pub. Co. [1955] 128p. illus. 24cm. [TT160.G87] 680 55-12387
1. Handicraft. I. Skeels, Catherine, joint author. II. Title.

GRIMM, Gretchen, 1912- 745.5
Creative adventures in arts and crafts. Milwaukee, Bruce Pub. Co. [1962] 96p. illus. 24cm. [TT157.G68] 62-10342
1. Handicraft. I. Title.

GRIMM, Gretchen, 1912- 745.5
An introduction to basic crafts. Minneapolis, Burgess Pub. Co. [1968] viii, 115 p. illus. 26 cm. (Burgess education series) Bibliography: p. 109-114. [TT157.G683] 68-15376
1. Handicraft. I. Title. II. Title: Basic crafts.

GRISWOLD, Lester Everett. 680
Handicraft; simplified procedure and projects. 9th ed. [Colorado Springs, 1951] 480 p. illus. 24 cm. [TT157.G73 1951] 51-8356
1. Handicraft. I. Title.

GRISWOLD, Lester Everett. 680
Handicraft; simplified procedure and projects. 9th ed. New York, Prentice-Hall [c1952] 480p. illus. 24cm. [TT157.G73 1952] 52-14542
1. Handicraft. I. Title.

GRISWOLD, Lester Everett. 745.5
The new handicraft: processes and projects, by Lester & Kathleen Griswold. New York, Van Nostrand Reinhold [1972, c.1969] v, 462 p. illus. 23 cm. First-ninth eds. pub. under title: Handicraft. "References & sources of supply": p. 452-457. [TT157G73 1969] ISBN 0-442-22862-7 pap., 4.95
1. Handicraft. I. Griswold, Kathleen, joint author. II. Title. BIP

GRISWOLD, Lester Everett. 745.5
The new handicraft, processes and projects, by Lester and Kathleen Griswold. 10th ed. Minneapolis, Burgess Pub. Co. [1969] v, 462 p. illus. 23 cm. First-9th editions published under title: Handicraft. "References and sources of supply": p. 452-457. [TT157.G73 1969] 68-59213
1. Handicraft. I. Griswold, Kathleen, joint author. II. Title.

HAINES, Ray Edward, ed. 745.5
The home crafts handbook. 2d ed. New York, Princeton, N.J., Van Nostrand [c.1948, 1960] xiv, 1008p. illus. 21cm. 60-2746 7.50
1. Handicraft. I. Title.

HAMMETT, Catherine Tilley. 745.5
Creative crafts for campers, by Catherine T. Hammett and Carol M. Horrocks. Illus. by Carol M. Horrocks. New York, Association Press [1957] 431 p. illus. 23 cm. [TT160.H35] 57-5045
1. Handicraft. I. Horrocks, Carol M., joint author. II. Title.

HANAUER, Elsie V. 745.5
A handbook of crafts, by Elsie V. Hanauer. South Brunswich [N. J.] Barnes [1966] 112 p. (chiefly illus.) 22 cm. [TT157.H32] 66-25027
1. Handicraft. I. Title.

HANDY man's home manual. 680
[Greenwich, Conn., Fawcett 1968] v. illus. 24cm. (654) Issues for 19 pub. by Modern Mechanix Pub. Co. [TT155.H3] 34-32010 .95 pap.,
1. Handicraft. 2. Repairing—Amateurs' manuals.

HARRIS, Kit. 745.5
Handcrafts. Dee Why West, N.S.W., New York, Hamlyn, 1972. 144 p. col. illus. 28 cm. [TT157.H34] 73-152489 ISBN 0-600-07058-1 3.95
1. Handicraft. I. Title.

HAUTZIG, Esther Rudomin. 745.5
Let's make presents; 100 gifts for less than $1.00. Illustrated by Ava Morgan. New York, Crowell [1962] 191 p. illus. 23 cm. [TT157.H355] 61-14532
1. Handicraft. I. Title. BIP

HAWKINS, Reginald Robert, 1902- 684
Easy-to-make outdoor play equipment. New York, Macmillian, 1957. 99 p. illus. 25 cm. [TT155.H35] 57-5773
1. Handicraft. 2. Toys. I. Title. II. Title: Outdoor play equipment.

HELFMAN, Harry Carmozin, 1910- 745.5
Fun with your fingers; working with sticks, paper, and string [by] Harry Helfman. Illustrated by Robert Bartram. New York, W. Morrow [1968] 47 p. col. illus. 23 cm. Directions for making God's Eyes, color wheels, paper mobiles, and newspaper pine trees as well as instructions on weaving and string painting. [TT160.H395] AC 68
1. Handicraft. I. Bartram, Robert, illus. II. Title.

HELLEGERS, Louisa Bumagin, comp. 745.5
Family book of crafts, compiled by Louisa B. Hellegers and Anne E. Kallem, assisted by Eric Smith and the editors of Sterling. New York, Sterling Pub. Co. [1973] 576 p. illus. 29 cm. Bibliography: p. 565-568. [TT145.H4 1973] 72-95199 ISBN 0-8069-5250-4 20.00
1. Handicraft. I. Kallem, Anne E., joint comp. II. Title.
Library binding 16.79; ISBN 0-8069-5251-2. BIP

HELLER, Louis. 745
Guide to arts and crafts: drawing, painting, pottery, metal work, and other interesting handicrafts. Chicago, J. G. Ferguson [c1954] 180p. illus. 2icm. [NK1130.H4] 55-24569
1. Handicraft. 2. Drawing—Technique. 3. Painting—Technique. I. Title.

HENNESSEY, William James, 1901- 680
Things for boys and girls to make. Diagrs. and pictures by the author. New York, Harper [1954] 117 p. illus. 24 cm. [TT160.H4] 54-8958
1. Handicraft. I. Title.

HERSHOFF, Evelyn Glantz. 745.5
It's fun to make things from scrap materials. Illustrated by the author. New York, Dover Publications [1964, c1944] 373 p. illus. 22 cm. First published in 1944 under title: Scrap fun for everyone. [TT157.H45 1964] 64-25093
1. Handicraft. I. Title. BIP

HERSHOFF, Evelyn Glantz. 680
Scrap fun for everyone; 401 things anyone can make [by] Evelyn Glantz...illustrated by the author. New York city, Larch book co. [1944] 384 p. illus. 21 cm. [TT157.H45] 44-46825
1. Handicraft. I. Title.

HERTZBERG, Robert Edward, 1905- 684
How to build with plywood. Greenwich, Conn., Fawcett Publications, c1956. 144p. illus. 24cm. (A Fawcett how-to book, 317) [TT200.H4] 56-58619
1. Handicraft. 2. Plywood. I. Title.

HILL, Arthur M. 745.5
Making do; basic things for simple living [by] Arthur M. Hill. New York, Ballantine Books [1972] 148 p. illus. 28 cm. [TT157.H46] 72-197315 ISBN 0-345-02812-0 3.95
1. Handicraft. I. Title.

HILS, Karl. 745.5
Crafts for all; a natural approach to crafts. Foreword by Herbert Read. Newton Centre, Mass., C. t. Branford Co. [1960] 168 p. illus. 25 cm. Translation of Werken fur alle. [TT145.H513] 60-815
1. Handicraft. I. Title. BIP

HILS, Karl. 745.59
Creative crafts. [1st English language ed.] London, B. T. Batsford; New York, Reinhold Pub. Corp. [1966, c1965] 127 p. illus. (part col.) 24 cm. Translation of Werkbuch fur die Familie. [TT157.H47] 66-13732
1. Handicraft. I. Title.

HOBBY Industry Association of America. 745.5'06'01
Silver anniversary convention and trade show, Hobby Industry Association of America, celebrating 25 years of progress, 1940-1965; convention, January 29 and 30, trade show, January 31-February 4, Sherman House, Chicago, Illinois. [New York, 1965] 62 p. illus., plan, ports, 22 cm. Cover title. [TT1.H553A52] 66-42635
I. Title.

HOLLANDER, Annette. 745.59'3
Bookcraft: how to construct note pad covers, boxes, and other useful items. Text prepared by Maureen Hollander. Black and white photos. by Charles S. Koch and Richard Suavez. New York, Van Nostrand Reinhold [1974] 101 p. illus. 27 cm. Bibliography: p. 101. [TT157.H547] 74-5946 ISBN 0-442-23467-8
1. Handicraft. 2. Bookbinding. I. Title.

HOME craftsman. 684.1
Book of garden furniture, barbecues, and fences; a complete illustrated manual on making accessories for outdoor living... Edited by Arthur Wakeling. New York, Home Craftsman Pub. Corp. [1953] 95p. illus. 29cm. (The Home craftsman series of woodworking manuals) [TT157.H575] 53-10746
1. Handicraft. 2. Garden ornaments and furniture. I. Wakeling, Arthur, ed. II. Title. III. Title: Garden furniture, barbecues, and fences

*HOOGEWEGEN, Annelike, comp. 745.5
The house and crafts book; over 100 ideas in full color, comp. by Annelike Hoogewegen [and others], Trans. by Patricia Crampton. New York, Dial, 1974 [c1971] 159 p. illus. (part. col.) 25 cm. [TT155] 73-17945 ISBN 0-8037-3786-6 8.95
1. Handicraft. I. Title.

HORTH, Arthur Cawdron, 1874- ed. 680
101 things for a boy to make / by L. B. & A. C. Horth; rev. by P. Yabsley. 9th ed., rev. and re-illustrated. Philadelphia, Lippincott [1954] 181p. illus. 19cm. Previous editions edited by A. C. Horth. [TT160] 54-8658
1. Handicraft. 2. Woodwork (Manual training) I. Horth, Lillie B., joint ed. II. Title.

HORTH, Lillie B 680
101 things for girls to do / by L. B. & A. C. Horth; rev. by M. Metcalfe. 8th ed., rev. and re-illustrated. Philadelphia, Lippincott [1954] 180p. illus. 19cm. [TT171] 54-8659
1. Handicraft. I. Horth, Arthur Cawdron, 1874- joint author. II. Title.

HOW-TO Associates. 643.7
Audels do-it-yourself encyclopedia; comprehensive how-to series for the entire

League of New Hampshire arts and Crafts in collaboration with robert Scharff. New York, Arco Pub. Co. [1954] 144p. illus. 25cm. (Arco handl-books for better living) Originally published as Fawcett book no. 152. [TT155] 54-11133
1. Handicraft. I. Title.

LEEMING, Joseph, 1897- 745.56
Fun with wire. [1st ed.] Philadelphia, Lippincott [c1956] 96p. illus. 24cm. [TE205.L43] 55-11809
1. Handicraft. 2. Wire. I. Title.

LEEMING, Joseph, 1897-1968. 680
Fun with fabrics; amusing, interesting and useful things to make of cloth and felt. Illustrated by Jessie Robinson. [1st ed.] Philadelphia, Lippincott [1950] 96 p. illus. 26 cm. [TT160.L372] 50-5422
1. Handicraft. I. Title.

LEFEVRE, Gregg. 731
Junk sculpture. New York, Sterling Pub. Co. [1973] 48 p. illus. 20 cm. (Little craft book series) Suggestions for projects of varying difficulty using discarded articles to make a variety of sculpture. [TT910.L43 1973] 72-95204 ISBN 0-8069-5258-X 2.95
1. Handicraft. 2. Found objects (Art) I. Title.

LEHNUS, Opal Hull. 745.5
Creative artcrafts for churches. Anderson, Ind., Warner Press [1963] 64 p. illus. 28 cm. Bibliography: p. 2. [TT157.L35] 63-10215
1. Handicraft. 2. Creative activities and seat work. I. Title.

LEHNUS, Opal Hull. 745
Creative crafts for churches. Anderson, Ind., Warner Press [1958] 63 p. illus. 28 cm. [TT155.L43] 58-6419
1. Handicraft. 2. Creative activities and seat work. I. Title.

LEVINE, Nancy. 745.5
Hardcore crafts / Nancy Levine. 1st ed. New York : Ballantine Books, 1976. p. cm. "Tree Communications edition." [TT157.L43] 76-8938 ISBN 0-345-24997-6 pbk. : 6.95
1. Handicraft. 2. Erotica. I. Title. BIP

LEWIS, Griselda, ed. 745.5
Handbook of crafts. [London] E. Hulton [dist. Newton Centre, Mass., Charles T. Branford, 1960] 371p. (Bibls.) illus. 23cm. 60-50564 6.95
1. Handicraft. 2. Art industries and trade. I. Title.

LINCOLN, Martha. 680
The workshop book for parents and children, by Martha Lincoln and Katharine Torrey. Boston, Houghton Mifflin, 1955. 214 p. illus. 27 cm. Includes bibliography. [TT160.L49] 54-6820
1. Handicraft. I. Torrey, Katharine, joint author. II. Title.

LINDBECK, John Robert. 745
Basic crafts [by] John R. Lindbeck, Lester G. Duenk [and] Marc F. Hansen. John L. Feirer, editor. Peoria, Ill., C. A. Bennett Co. [1968, c1969] 274 p. illus. (part col.) 24 cm. [TT160.L495] 68-10286
1. Handicraft. I. Duenk, Lester G., joint author. II. Hansen, Marc F., joint author. III. Title. BIP

LINSLEY, Leslie. 745.5
The art of creative acrylic (Hyplar) crafts / by Leslie Linsley ; designed, edited, and produced by Lester Rossin for M. Grumbacher, inc. ; photography by Jon Aron. New York : M. Grumbacher, c1976. 30 p. : col. ill. ; 32 cm. (The Grumbacher library ; B435) [TT857.L55] 77-369194 1.95
1. Handicraft. 2. Polymer painting. I. Title.

LINSLEY, Leslie. 745.5
Custom made / by Leslie Linsley ; photos. by Jon Aron. 1st ed. New York : Harper & Row, c1979. p. cm. Includes index. [TT157.L484 1979] 78-69623 ISBN 0-06-012633-7 : 12.95
1. Handicraft. I. Title. BIP

LINSLEY, Leslie. 745.5
Wildcrafts / Leslie Linsley ; photography by Jon Aron. 1st ed. Garden City, N.Y. : Doubleday, 1977. 192 p., [8] leaves of plates : ill. ; 27 cm. Includes index. [TT157.L485] 76-50777 ISBN 0-385-12687-5 : 12.95
1. Handicraft. 2. Nature craft. I. Title. BIP

LOGAN, Elizabeth D. 745.59'41
Scrap craft; ideas for holidays and parties, by Elizabeth D. Logan. With diagrs. by June K. Ciancio. New York, Scribner [1973] x, 246 p. illus. 28 cm. [TT157.L56 1973] 72-7730 ISBN 0-684-13206-0 12.50
1. Handicraft. 2. Party decorations. 3. Children's parties. 4. Gifts. I. Title.

LUCIE-SMITH, Edward. 745.5'092'2 B
World of the makers : today's master craftsmen and craftswomen : text and photography / by Edward Lucie-Smith. New York : Paddington Press, [1975] 223 p. : ill. ; 28 cm. [TT149.L82 1975] 74-15916 ISBN 0-8467-0037-9 pbk. : 7.95
1. Handicraft. 2. Artisans. I. Title.

MCCALL'S golden do-it book. 745.5
Adapted by Joan Wyckoff. Edited by Nan Comstock. Illustrated by William Dugan. New York, Golden Press, c1960. 156 p. illus. 29 cm. [NK70.M25] 60-51403
1. Handicraft. 2. Art—Study and teaching. I. Wyckoff, Joan.

MCCANN, Karen Carlson. 745.5
Creative home decorations you can make; low-cost ways to beautify your home, by Karen Carlson McCann, with Sue T. Garmon. Drawings and photos. by Karen Carlson McCann. [1st ed.] Garden City, N.Y., Doubleday, 1968. 142 p. illus. 24 cm. [TT157.M32] 68-22511 4.95
1. Handicraft. 2. Decoration and ornament. I. Garmon, Sue T. II. Title.

MCLEISH, Minnie. 372.5
Beginnings: teaching art to children, by Minnie McLeish and Ella Moody. Entirely Newed. London, New York, Studio Publications [1953] 96 p. illus. 26 cm. (The How to do it series, no. 28) [NK70.M3 1953] 53-1954
1. Handicraft. I. Moody, Ella, joint author. II. Title. III. Title: Teaching art to children.

MCNEICE, William C. 745.5
Crafts for retarded: through their hands they shall learn. [By] William C. McNeice [and] Kenneth R. Benson. Illustrated by Albert Mackevich. [1st ed.] Bloomington, Ill., McKnight & McKnight Pub. Co. [1964] 134 p. illus. 27 cm. Bibliography: p. 130-131. [TT157.M34] 64-22301
1. Handicraft. 2. Mentally handicapped children—Education. I. Benson, Kenneth R., joint author. II. Title.

MADDEN, Ira C 680
Creative handicraft, teaches students to think and to plan Chicago, Goodheart-Willcox Co. [1955] 224p. illus. 29cm. Includes bibliography. [TT160.M27] 55-6459
1. Handicraft. I. Title.

MAKE it and use it; 745.5
handicraft for boys and girls. Illustrated by Aline Hansens. New York, Abingdon Press [1958] 160p. illus. 24cm. [TT157.C26] [TT157.C26] 680 58-14640 58-14640
1. Handicraft. I. Carlson, Bernice (Wells)

MALCOLM, Dorothea C. 745.5
Art from recycled materials [by] Dorothea C. Malcolm. Worcester, Mass., Davis Publications [1974] 128 p. illus. 26 cm. Bibliography: p. 128. [TT157.M347] 73-93381 ISBN 0-87192-059-X 9.95
1. Handicraft. I. Title. BIP

MANLEY, Seon. 745.5
Adventures in making: the romance of crafts around the world. New York, Vanguard Press [1959] 180 p. illus. 27 cm. Includes bibliography. [TT149.M3] 59-12397
1. Handicraft. I. Title. BIP

MASON, Bernard Sterling, 1896-1953. 796.54 s
Crafts of the woods. Illus. by Frederic H. Kock. South Brunswick, A. S. Barnes [1973] 208 p. illus. 22 cm. (His Woodcrafts library, pt. 3) First published in 1939 as pt. 3 (p. 371-569) of the author's Woodcraft. [TT7.M37 pt. 3] [SK601] 745.5'09701 72-9064 ISBN 0-498-01297-2 5.95
1. Handicraft. 2. Indians of North America—Industries. I. Title. II. Series.

MECHANIX illustrated. 680
How to build it; easy-to-build projects for workshop fans. [Greenwich, Conn., Fawcett Publications, 1951] 144 p. illus. 24 cm. (A Fawcett book, no. 124) [TT155.M4] 51-31286
1. Handicraft. I. Title.

MEHTA, Rustam Jehangir 745.50954
The handicrafts and industrial arts of India; a pictorial and descriptive survey of Indian craftsmanship as seen in masterpieces . . Bombay, Taraporevala's Treasure House of Books [dist. New York, International Publications Service 1960, i.e.1961] 157p. illus., 154 plates (part col.) 29cm. Bibl.: p.[153]-[154] 61-213 18.50 decorated cloth,
1. Handicraft. 2. India—Indus. I. Title.

MEILACH, Dona Z. 745.5
Accent on crafts, by Dona Z. Meilach. [Edited by Judy Martin and others. Lake Zurich, Illinois Bronze Powder & Paint Co., c1970] 50 p. col. illus. 26 cm. Cover title. [TT157.M45] 70-136460 2.00
1. Handicraft. I. Title.

MEILACH, Dona Z. 745.5
How to create your own designs; an introduction to color, form & composition [by] Dona Z. Meilach, Jay Hinz [and] Bill Hinz. [1st ed.] Garden City, N.Y., Doubleday, 1975. 216 p. illus. 27 cm. Bibliography: p. 214. [TT149.M46] 74-130 ISBN 0-385-01877-0 12.50
1. Handicraft. 2. Design. I. Hinz, Jay, joint author. II. Hinz, Bill, joint author. III. Title. BIP

MERAS, Phyllis. 745.5
Vacation crafts / Phyllis Meras. Boston : Houghton Mifflin, 1978. 160 p. : ill. ; 24 cm. [TT157.M458] 78-2774 ISBN 0-395-26498-7 : 11.95 pbk. : 6.95
1. Handicraft. 2. Nature craft. I. Title. BIP

MERCER, Eileen. 745.5
Let's make it from junk / by Eileen Mercer ; photos. by Ed Bievenour ; drawings by Kevin Franklin. Harrisburg, Pa. : Stackpole Books, c1976. 160 p. : ill. ; 24 cm. Includes index. [TT157.M46] 76-3551 ISBN 0-8117-0939-6 : 8.95
1. Handicraft. 2. Waste products. I. Bievenour, Ed. II. Franklin, Kevin. III. Title.

METCALF, Harlan G. 745.59'2
Whittlin', whistles, and thingamajigs; the pioneer book of nature crafts and recreation arts, by Harlan G. Metcalf. [Harrisburg, Pa.] Stackpole Books [1974] 190 p. illus. 29 cm. Bibliography: p. 183-187. [TT157.M47] 74-8630
1. Handicraft. 2. Nature study. 3. Games. I. Title.

MILES, Bebe. 745.59'4
Designing with natural materials. New York: Van Nostrand Reinhold, [1975] 131 p. illus 24 cm. [TT857.M54 1975] 74-7780 ISBN 0-442-25370-2 9.95
1. Handicraft. I. Title. BIP

MOLONEY, Joan. 745.5
Book of boutique crafts / Joan Moloney. 1st U.S. ed. New York : Harper and Row, c1974. 192 p. in various pagings, [8] leaves of plates : ill. from ; 29 cm. [TT145.M64 1974] 73-22774 ISBN 0-06-012996-4 : 9.95
1. Handicraft. I. Title.

MOORE, Frank C., 1892- 372.5
Handcrafts for elementary schools; a handbook of practical suggestions for teachers [by] Frank C. Moore, Carl H. Hamburger [and] Anna-Laura Kingzett. Illustrated by Anna-Laura Kingzett. Boston, Heath [1953] 324 p. illus. 26 cm. [TT165.M6] 53-12282
1. Handicraft. 2. Manual training. I. Title.

MOORE, William, 1914- 684
Fun with tools, by William Moore and Robert Cynar. New York, Random House [1957] 64p. illus. 27cm. [TT160.M63] 57-7528
1. Handicraft. 2. Tools. I. Cynar, Robert, joint author. II. Title.

*MORRIS, Jill 745.5
Gifts galore! gifts to make for everyone. Illustrated by Hildegarde Bone. New York, Arco Pub. Co. [1975] 96 p. col. ill. 26 cm. (Leisuretime) [TT157] 74-19758 5.95
1. Handicraft. 2. Gift. I. Title. BIP

NAGLE, Avery (Leeming) 745.59
Fun with naturecraft, by Avery Nagle and Joseph Leeming. Illustrated by Jessie Robinson. [1st ed.] Philadelphia, Lippincott [1964] 80 p. illus. 24 cm. [TT157.N23] 64-11447
1. Handicraft. I. Lemming, Joseph, 1897- joint author. II. Title.

NAGLE, Avery (Leeming) 745.5
Kitchen table fun, by Avery Nagle & Joseph Leeming. Illustrated by Jessie Robinson. [1st ed.] Philadelphia, Lippincott [1961] 95p. illus. 24cm. [TT160.N3] 61-11741
1. Handicraft. I. Leeming, Joseph, 1897- joint author. II. Title.

NEWKIRK, Louis Vest, 1901- 680
Crafts for everyone, by Louis V. Newkirk and La Vada Zutter. Scranton, International Textbook Co. [1950] viii, 210 p. illus. 28 cm. (Arts and industries series) Includes bibliographies. [TT157.N4] 50-7245
1. Handicraft. I. Zutter, La Vada, 1905- joint author.

NEWMAN, Thelma R. 745.59'3
The container book : basic processes for making bags, baskets, boxes, bowls, and other container forms with fibers, fabrics, leather, wood, plastics, metal, clay, glass, and natural materials / by Thelma R. Newman and Jay Hartley Newman. New York : Crown Publishers, c1977. xiii, 304 p., [4] leaves of plates : ill. ; 27 cm. Includes index. Bibliography: p. [297]-298. [TT157.N43 1977] 77-401 14.95 pbk. : 7.95
1. Handicraft. 2. Containers. I. Newman, Jay Hartley, joint author. II. Title.

NICHOLE, Louis. 745.5
Designer accessories to make for your home : 35 easy, inexpensive ways to complement any room / by Louis Nichole ; [ill. by Mel Klapholtz]. New York : Butterick Pub., c1978. 200 p. : ill. ; 25 cm. Includes indexes. [TT857.N52] 77-20530 ISBN 0-88421-043-X : 7.95
1. Handicraft. I. Title. BIP

NOON, Elizabeth F., 1914- ed. 372.5
The new handcraft book. Contributors: Evelyn Civerolo [and others] Dansville, N. Y., F. A. Owen Pub. Co. [1950] 80 p. illus. 34 cm. (The Instructor activity guide series) [TT157.N6] 50-6824
1. Handicraft.

NOON, Elizabeth F 1914- ed. 372.5
The new handcraft book. Contributors: Evelyn Civerolo [and others. Rev.] Dansville, N. Y., F. A. Owen Pub. Co. [1956] 80p. illus. 33cm. (The Instructor activity guide series) [TT157] 57-2726
1. Handicraft. I. Title. II. Title: Handcraft book.

*OLMAN, Alexandra Eames. 745.5
Mother Nature's craft book. Illus. by Lauren Rosen. New York, Pyramid Books [1975] 96 p. illus. 18 cm. [TT157] 74-15280 ISBN 0-515-03570-X 0.95 (pbk.)
1. Handicraft. I. Rosen, Lauren, illus. II. Title.

1001 how-to ideas. 684.8
New 1965 ed. New York, Sci. & Mechanics, c.1965. 96p. illus. 24cm. (Sci. & Mech annual, no 747) [TT155.05] 61-1959 .75 pap.,
1. Handicraft. 2. Workshop receipts. 3. Dwellings, Maintenance and repair. I. Science and mechanics.

OSTRANDER, Sheila 745.5
Gadgets and gifts for girls to make, written, illus. by Sheila Ostrander. New York, Sterling [c.1962] 124p. 21cm. 62-12595 2.50
1. Handicraft. I. Title.

OSTRANDER, Sheila. 745.5
Nick-nacks for neatness, written and illustrated by Sheila Ostrander. New York, Sterling Pub. Co. [c1963] 125 p. illus. 21 cm. [TT157.O8] 63-19158
1. Handicraft. I. Title.

1. Handicraft. 2. Metal-work. I. Shirley, Alfred Frank, joint author. II. Title.

SLADE, Richard. 745.5
Clever hands; a book of arts and crafts for boys and girls. With photos. by John Watts. London, Faber and Faber [1959; label: Transatlantic Arts, Hollywood-by-the-Sea, Fla.] 62 p. illus. 26 cm. [[NK70]] 59-4784
1. Handicraft. I. Title.

SNOOK, Barbara. 745.59'4
Making birds, beasts, and insects / Barbara Snook. New York : Scribner, [1974] 96 p. : chiefly ill. ; 22 cm. [TT157.S57] 74-4815 ISBN 0-684-14034-9 : 5.95
1. Handicraft. 2. Birds. 3. Insects. 4. Animals. I. Title.

SOKOL, Camille. 745.5
How to be mother's helper. Pictures by Bill Sokol. New York, Platt & Munk [1968] 67 p. col. illus. 23 cm. Simple instructions on knitting, cooking, gardening, making collages and other things for the home from available household articles. [PZ10.S7168Ho] AC 68
1. Handicraft. 2. Cookery. 3. Gardening. I. Sokol, Bill, illus. II. Title.

SPORTS craft 680
v.1- [Chicago, Science and Mechanics Pub. Co., 1953- v. illus. 24cm. (A Science and mechanics handbook) [TT157.S68] 54-19447
1. Handicraft.

STIERI, Emanuele, 1891- 745.56
Aluminum projects for your home. Englewood Cliffs, N.J., Prentice-Hall [1957] 208 p. illus. 26 cm. [TT242.S8] 57-5231
1. Handicraft. 2. Aluminum. I. Title.

STILES, David R. 745.5
Fun projects for dad and the kids. Illus. by the author. New York, Arco [c.1963] 96p. (chiefly illus., diagrs.) 28cm. 63-9634 3.50; 1.95 pap.,
1. Handicraft. 2. Toys. 3. Woodwork. I. Title. BIP

SUNSET 745.5
Gifts you can make, by the eds. of Sunset bks. and Sunset magazine. Menlo Park, Calif., Lane [c.1965] 96p. illus. 28cm. (Sunset bk. 428) [TT157.S85] 65-22743 1.95 pap.,
1. Handicraft. I. Title.

SYMONS, Arthur, 1909- 643
The fix-it book. New York, Sterling Pub. Co. [1967] 128 p. illus. 21 cm. "Revised from 101 things a boy can do around the house [published in 1961]" An introduction to do-it-yourself projects for the home, including painting; using tools; caring for the automobile, garden, and house; understanding household electricity, plumbing, and heating; and practicing home safety. [TT160.S94 1967] AC 67
1. Handicraft. 2. Dwellings—Maintenance and repair. 3. Repairing. I. Title. BIP

SYMONS, Arthur, 1909- 643.7
101 things a boy can do around the house. Illus. by Dwight Dobbins. New York, Sterling Pub. Co. [1961] 128 p. illus. 21 cm. [TT160.S94] 61-10409
1. Handicraft. 2. Dwellings — Maintenance and repair. I. Title.

THINGS to do in a day. 745.5
New York : Collier Books, 1976. p. cm. Originally published in 1975 under title: The Do-it-yourself book of things to do in a day. [TT157.T48 1976b] 76-1991 ISBN 0-02-011870-8 pbk. : 5.95
1. Handicraft. BIP

THINGS to do in a day. 745.5
1st American ed. New York : Macmillan, 1976. 64 p. : ill. ; 29 cm. London ed. (M. Cavendish Publications) has title: The do-it-yourself book of things to do in a day. [TT157.T48 1976] 76-2035 ISBN 0-02-578240-1 : 8.95
1. Handicraft. BIP

A Treasury of things to make / by the editors of Sphere magazine. 745.5
New York : Platt & Munk, c1977. 223 p. : ill. ; 29 cm. [TT157.T73] 77-80345 ISBN 0-8228-7720-1 : 12.95
1. Handicraft. I. Sphere (Chicago)

TURNER, G. Alan. 745.5
Creative crafts for everyone. New York, Viking Press, 1959. 263 p. illus. 24 cm. (A Studio book) [TT155.T84] 59-12828
1. Handicraft. I. Title.

VAN ZANDT, Eleanor. 745.5
Crafts for fun and profit. Garden City, N.Y., Doubleday, 1974 [c1973] 144 p. illus. 27 cm. Bibliography: p. 143-144. [TT157.V28 1974] 73-82239 ISBN 0-385-08882-5 6.95
1. Handicraft. I. Title.

VON MIKLOS, Josephine (Bogdan) 1900- 680
Make-it yourself. Pictures, text, and original designs by the author. New York, Maco Magazine Corp., e1956. 144 p. illus. 24 cm. (Maco 39) [TT157.V6] 56-2051
1. Handicraft. I. Title.

VON MIKLOS, Josephine (Bogdan) 1900- 680
Make-it yourself, Pictures, text, and original designs by Von Miklos. New York, Random House [1956] 144 p. illus. 25 cm. [TT157.V6 1956a] 56-6338
1. Handicraft. I. Title.

VOSS, Gunther. 745.5
Reinhold craft and hobby book. Translated by Thomas E. Burton. New York, Reinhold Pub. Corp. [c1963] 360 p. illus. (part col.) 23 cm. Translation of Knaurs Bastelbuch. [TT145.V613] 63-19223
1. Handicraft. I. Title.

WAGNER, Glenn A. 680
The book of hobby craft; with photos, and drawings by the author. New York, Dodd, Mead [1952] 95 p. illus. 25 cm. [TT160.W3] 52-11732
1. Handicraft. I. Title.

WAGNER, Glenn A. 680
Hobbycraft for everybody; with photos. and drawings by the author. New York, Dodd, Mead [1954] 96 p. illus. 25 cm. [TT157.W26] 54-13279
1. Handicraft. 2. Hobbies. I. Title.

WAGNER, Glenn A *745.5 680
Things to make yourself. With photos, and drawings by the author. New York, Dodd, Mead [1957] 96 p. illus. 24 cm. [TT157.W28] 57-12132
1. Handicraft. I. Title.

WALTER, Fritz, 1899- 745.5
Practical handicraft. New York, Taplinger Pub. Co. [1968- c1967- v. illus. 26 cm. Translation of Wir werken [von] Fritz und Hanspeter Walter. Contents.Contents.—1. Working in metal, leather, clay, and other media.—2. Working with wood. [TT153.W3432] 68-25516 5.95
1. Handicraft. I. Walter, Hanspeter, 1926- II. Title.

WALTNER, Willard 745
Hobbycraft around the world [by] Willard & Elma Waltner. New York, Lantern [c.1966] 139p. illus. 24cm. [TT157.W3515] 66-11074 4.95; 5.60 lib. ed.,
1. Handicraft. I. Waltner, Elma, joint author. II. Title. BIP

WALTNER, Willard. 745.5
Hobbycraft for juniors [by] Willard & Elma Waltner. New York, Lantern Press [1967] 138 p. illus. 24 cm. Simple directions for making easily assembled handicrafts, for gifts or for fun. [TT160.W43] AC 67
1. Handicraft. I. Waltner, Elma, joint author. II. Title. BIP

WALTNER, Willard. 745.5
Holiday hobbycraft [by] Willard & Elma Waltner. New York, Lantern Press [1964] 142 p. illus., diagrs. 24 cm. [GV1201.W225] 64-10341
1. Handicraft. I. Waltner, Elma, joint author. II. Title. BIP

WALTNER, Willard. 745.5
The new hobbycraft book, by Willard and Elma Waltner. New York, Lantern Press [1963] 144 p. illus. 24 cm. [GV1201.W226] 63-17987
1. Handicraft. I. Waltner, Elma, joint author. II. Title. BIP

WALTNER, Willard. 745.5
A new look at old crafts [by] Willard and Elma Waltner. Mount Vernon, N.Y., Lantern Press [1971] 142 p. illus. 24 cm. [TT157.W353 1971] 70-143700
1. Handicraft. I. Waltner, Elma, joint author. II. Title. BIP

WALTNER, Willard. 745.5
Wonders of hobbycraft, by Willard and Elma Waltner. New York, Lantern Press [1962] 144 p. illus. 24 cm. [GV1201.W23] 62-9534
1. Handicraft. I. Waltner, Elma, joint author. II. Title.

WALTNER, Willard. 745.5'028
Year round hobbycraft, by Willard and Elma Waltner. New York, Lantern Press [1968] 144 p. illus. 24 cm. [TT157.W355] 68-23984 4.95
1. Handicraft. I. Waltner, Elma, joint author. II. Title. BIP

WALTNER, Willard. 745.5
Year round hobbycraft, by Willard and Elma Waltner. New York, Lantern Press [1968] 144 p. illus. 24 cm. Simple directions for creating toys, gifts, and decorations, many especially suited for a particular month or season. Explains the origin of the name of each month and significant associations. [TT157.W355] AC 68
1. Handicraft. I. Waltner, Elma, joint author. II. Title.

WALTON, Harry. 745.59
Plastics for the home craftsman. New York, McGraw-Hill [1951] 191 p. illus. 24 cm. [TT297.W3] 51-5162
1. Handicraft. 2. Plastics. I. Title.

WARDWELL, Jane 745.5
10 crafts for kids. New York, Association Press [c.1961] 128p. 61-7108 2.95 bds.,
1. Handicraft. I. Title.

WARDWELL, Jane. 745.5
10--cent crafts for kids. New York, Association Press [1961] 128 p. illus. 23 cm. [GV1203.W3] 61-7108
1. Handicraft. I. Title.

*WATSTEIN, Esther. 745.5
Pillow talk. [New York, Bantam Books [1974] 89 p. 16 cm. (A Bantam minibook) [TT157] 0.60 (pbk.)
1. Handicraft. I. Title.

WESTLAND, Pamela. 745.5
The complete book of home crafts / edited by Pamela Westland. New York : Viking Press, 1974. 296 p. : ill. (some col.) ; 29 cm. (A Studio book) Includes index. [TT157.W47 1974] 74-5604 ISBN 0-670-23401-X : 16.95
1. Handicraft. I. Title.

WHEELER, Geoffrey, 1936- comp. 745.5
How to succeed in crafts. Compiled and edited by Geoffrey Wheeler. [1st ed.] New York, Hobby Publications [1973] 320 p. illus. 28 cm. [TT145.W45] 73-173405 9.95
1. Handicraft. 2. Business. I. Title. Publisher's address: 229 W. 28 St. N.Y. 10001.

WILLIAMS, Guy R. 745.5
Instructions in handicrafts. London, Museum Pr. [dist. New Rochelle, N.Y., SportShelf, 1965, c.1964] 128p. illus. 23cm. (Brompton lib.) Bibl. [TT157.W55] 65-893 4.25 bds.,
1. Handicraft. I. Title.

WILLIAMS, Guy R. 745.5
Teach your child to be handy. London, Pearson [dist. Hollywood-by-the-Sea, Fla., Transatlantic, c.1964] 94p. illus. 21cm. [TT157.W56] 65-153 3.00
1. Handicraft. I. Title.

WILLIAMS, Hazel Pearson. 745.5
Making things from discards : beautiful and practical creations with bottles, bread dough, tin cans, egg cartons, plastics, and folded magazines / by Hazel Pearson Williams. New York : Bounty Books, [1974] 180 p. : ill. (some col.) ; 29 cm. Includes index. [TT157.W57] 74-76681 ISBN 0-517-51616-0 : 6.98 ISBN 0-517-51617-9 pbk. : 4.95
1. Handicraft. 2. Waste products. I. Title.

WILLOUGHBY, George Alonzo. 1894- 745.5
General crafts. Consulting specialists, Raymond La Bounty [and others] Peoria, Ill., C. A. Bennett [1959] 144 p. illus. 26 cm. [NK1130.W5] 58-59812
1. Handicraft. 2. Art industries and trade. I. Title. BIP

WINTER, Garry, ed. 745.5
Crafts & hobbies. New York, Arco Pub. Co. [1964, c1962] 156 p. illus. 24 cm. (Arco hobby library) [TT157.W58 1964] 64-21342
1. Handicraft. 2. Hobbies. I. Title. BIP

WIRTENBERG, Patricia Z. 745.5
All-around-the-house art and craft book, by Patricia Z. Wirtenberg. Photos. by Patricia Z. Wirtenberg. Boston, Houghton Mifflin Co., 1968. 103 p. illus. 27 cm. Fifty "recipes" using common household items for projects in painting, printing, collage, assemblage and sculpture. [TT157.W59] 68-28058 5.00
1. Handicraft. I. Title. BIP

WOLVERTON, Ruth. 745.59'2
The build-it book of learning playthings / by Ruth Wolverton. 1st ed. Blue Ridge Summit, Pa. : G/L Tab Books, 1977. 323 p. : ill. ; 22 cm. "No. 915." Includes index. Bibliography: p. 313-319. [TT157.W595] 77-154165 9.95
1. Handicraft. 2. Educational toys. I. Title.

THE Woman's day book of Weekend crafts : more than 100 quick-to-finish projects / by the editors of Woman's day. 745.5
Boston : Houghton Mifflin, 1978. 176 p., [4] leaves of plates : ill. (some col.) ; 25 cm. [TT157.W613 1978] 77-15496 ISBN 0-395-26284-4 : 11.95
1. Handicraft. I. Woman's Day. BIP

WOOD, Katharine Marie, 1910- 745.5
Here's how ... to use odds and ends for fun and profit. Written and illustrated by Katharine Wood. New York, McKay [1968] vii, 88 p. illus. 21 cm. Instructions for making toys and other objects from tin, paper, cloth, glass, wood, plastics and items found around the house. [TT160.W62] AC 68
1. Handicraft. I. Title.

**WORKING with odds and ends.* 745'.5
New York, Franklin Watts, [1974 c1972] 176 p. col. illus. 30 cm. [TT160] ISBN 0-531-02678-7 5.95
1. Handicraft. BIP

WORKSHOP ideas; tool techniques, projects to make. 684'.08
New York, Arco, 1973 [c1972] 112 p. illus. 25 cm. [TT157.W64] 72-95384 3.95
1. Handicraft.

WORKSHOP projects. 394.268
no. 1- [Greenwich, Conn., Fawcett Publications, 1954?- v. illus. 29cm. At head of title. v. 1- True, the man's magazine. [TT157.W65] 55-23556
1. Handicraft.

YATES, Raymond Francis, 1895- 745
Early American crafts & hobbies; a treasury of skills, avocations, handicrafts, and forgotten pastimes and pursuits from the golden age of the American home, by Raymond F. & Marguerite W. Yates. Edited by Mary Lyon. New York, W. Funk, 1954. 221 p. illus. 24 cm. [TT157.Y28] 54-9613
1. Handicraft. 2. Hobbies. I. Yates, Marguerite W., joint author. II. Title.

YATES, Raymond Francis, 1895- *745.5
How to make beautiful gifts at home, by Raymond F. Yates and Marguerite W. Yates. New York, W. Funk [1952] 233 p. illus. 20 cm. [TT157.Y3] 680 52-8016
1. Handicraft. I. Title.

YOUNG, Jean. 745.5
Woodstock craftsman's manual. Provoked by Jean Young. New York, Praeger [1972-73] 2 v. illus. 29 cm. [TT157.Y58] 76-185655 10.00 per vol.
1. Handicraft. I. Title. BIP

YOUNG, Jean. 745.5
Woodstock craftsman's manual / edited by Jean Young. New York : Penguin Books, [1978] p. cm. (A Penguin handbook) Reprint of the 1973 ed. published by Praeger, New York. [TT157.Y58 1978] 78-8559 ISBN 0-14-046340-2 pbk. : 8.95
1. Handicraft. I. Title.

produced by Ted Smart. New Malden : Colour Library International Ltd, 1976. 63 p. : ill. (chiefly col.), col. ports. ; 29 cm. Includes index. [TT57.G52] 77-360709 ISBN 0-904681-06-8 : £3.95
1. Handicraft—Great Britain. 2. Artisans—Great Britain. I. Title.

JENKINS, John Geraint. 745.50942
Traditional country craftsmen [by] J. Geraint Jenkins. Illustrated by Winifred Mumford. New York, Praeger [1966, c1965] xix, 236 p. illus., ports. 23 cm. Bibliography: p. 222-228. [TT57.L4] 66-15841
1. Handicraft—Gt. Brit. I. Title. BIP

JENKINS, John Geraint. 680
Traditional country craftsmen / J. Geraint Jenkins ; drawings by Winifred Mumford. Rev. ed. London ; Boston : Routledge & Kegan Paul, 1978. xix, 253 p., [24] leaves of plates : ill. ; 23 cm. Includes index. Bibliography: p. 240-245. [TT57.J4 1978] 77-30381 ISBN 0-7100-8726-8 : 15.00
1. Handicraft—Great Britain. I. Title.

JONES, John L. 581.6'1
Crafts from the countryside / John L. Jones. Newton Abbot [Eng.] ; North Pomfret, Vt. : David & Charles, c1975. 96 p. : ill. ; 22 cm. Includes index. Bibliography: p. 95. [TT57.J66] 75-10516 ISBN 0-7153-7049-9 : 10.95
1. Handicraft—Great Britain. 2. Nature craft. I. Title. BIP

MANNERS, John. 680
Country crafts in pictures / J. E. Manners. Newton Abbot ; North Pomfret, Vt. : David and Charles, 1976. 108 p. : chiefly ill. ; 24 cm. Includes index. [TT57.M35] 75-43205 ISBN 0-7153-7147-9 : 9.95
1. Handicraft—Great Britain. I. Title. BIP

MANNERS, John. 745.5'0942
Country crafts today [by] J. E. Manners. Detroit, Gale 1974. 208 p. illus. 22 cm. Bibliography: p. 201-202. [TT57.M36] 74-4355 ISBN 0-8103-2013-4 9.00
1. Handicraft—Great Britain. I. Title. BIP

WISEMAN, E. J. 680
Victorian do-it-yourself : handicrafts and pastimes of the 1880s / E. J. Wiseman. Newton Abbot [Eng.] ; North Pomfret, Vt. : David & Charles, c1976. 168 p. : ill. ; 26 cm. Includes extracts from Amateur work, illustrated (1881-1891). [TT57.W57] 77-355037 ISBN 0-7153-7307-2 : 11.95
1. Handicraft—Great Britain. 2. Great Britain—Social life and customs—19th century. I. Amateur work, illustrated. II. Title. BIP

Handicraft—Handbooks, manuals, etc.

SWEZEY, Kenneth M. 745.5'02'02
Formulas, methods, tips, and data for home and workshop, by Kenneth M. Swezey. New York, Popular Science Pub. Co. [1969] xvii, 691 p. 19 cm. [TT153.S88] 68-54377 7.95
1. Handicraft—Handbooks, manuals, etc. 2. Workshop receipts. I. Title. BIP

Handicraft—Handbooks, manuals—Woodstock, N.Y.

*YOUNG, Jean. 745.5
Woodstock craftsman's manual 2 New York, Praeger Publishers [1973] 288 p. illus., 28 cm. [TT157] 72-92472 10.00; 4.95 (pbk.)
1. Handicraft—Handbooks, manuals—Woodstock, N.Y. I. Title.

Handicraft—Hist.

WHITAKER, Irwin 745.5
Crafts and craftsmen. Dubuque, Iowa, W. C. Brown [1967] vii, 109p. illus. 23cm. (Art horizons ser.) Bibl. [NK600.W54] 67-22710 1.95 pap.,
1. Handicraft—Hist. 2. Handicraft—U.S. 3. Artists' materials. I. Title.

Handicraft—India—Juvenile literature.

SOLEILLANT, Claude. 745.5'0954
India in color : activities & projects / by Claude Soleillant ; [translated by Steven Morgenstern ; photos. by Christian Murtin]. New York : Sterling Pub. Co., c1977. 96 p. : ill. ; 20 cm. Translation of L'Inde. Includes index. Suggests activities, foods, and handicrafts with an Indic theme. [TT103.S6413] 77-79499 ISBN 0-8069-4550-8 : 7.95 ISBN 0-8069-4551-6 lib. bdg. : 7.49
1. Handicraft—India—Juvenile literature. 2. Cookery, Indic—Juvenile literature. I. Murtin, Christian. II. Title.

Handicraft — Iran — Hist.

WULFF, Hans E. 745.5'0955
The traditional crafts of Persia: their development, technology, and influence on Eastern and Western civilizations [by] Hans E. Wulff. Cambridge, M. I. T. Press [c1966] xxiv, 404 p. illus. (part col.), map. 27 cm. Bibliography: p. 305-314. [TT107.W8] 66-22642
1. Handicraft — Iran — Hist. 2. Technology — Iran — Hist. I. Title. BIP

Handicraft—Israel.

DAYAN, Ruth. 745.5'095694
Crafts of Israel [by] Ruth Dayan with Wilburt Feinberg. New York, Macmillan [1974] 174 p. 26 cm. [TT113.175D38] 73-10787 ISBN 0-02-534420-X 14.95
1. Handicraft—Israel. I. Feinberg, Wilburt, joint author. II. Title. BIP

Handicraft—Italy.

D'AMATO, Janet. 745.5'0945
Italian crafts : inspirations from folk art / Janet and Alex D'Amato. New York : M. Evans, c1977. 160 p. : ill. ; 24 cm. Includes index. Bibliography: p. 156-157. [TT79.D35] 76-30523 ISBN 0-87131-227-1 : 7.95
1. Handicraft—Italy. 2. Folk art—Italy. I. D'Amato, Alex, joint author. II. Title. BIP

Handicraft—Japan—Okinawa (Prefecture)

SUGIMURA, Tsune, 1926- 745.5'0952'81
Living crafts of Okinawa. Photos. by Tsune Sugimura, with text by Hisao Suzuki. [1st ed.] New York, Weatherhill [1973] 235 p. (chiefly illus., part col.) 30 cm. Sugimura's photos. were originally published in Okinawa no te (Hands of Okinawa) in 1972. Suzuki's new text was translated and adapted into English by Patricia Murray and the staff of Weatherhill. [TT106.O4S83 1973] 72-78603 ISBN 0-8348-0073-X 19.50
1. Handicraft—Japan—Okinawa (Prefecture) I. Suzuki, Hisao, 1926- II. Title.

Handicraft—Juvenile literature.

ABISCH, Roz. 745.5
Easy-to-make holiday fun things. Written and illustrated by Roz Abisch and Boche Kaplan. [Middletown, Conn.] Xerox Education Publications [1973] 92 p. illus. 21 cm. Directions for easy-to-make handicraft projects appropriate for the various seasons, months, and holidays of the year. [TT160.A15] 72-91772 0.75 (pbk.)
1. Handicraft—Juvenile literature. 2. Holidays—Juvenile literature. I. Kaplan, Boche, joint author. II. Title. BIP

ALBRECTSEN, Lis. 745.5'09701
Tepee and moccasin; Indian craft for young people. New York, Van Nostrand Reinhold [1972] 94 p. illus. 22 cm. Translation of Med tipi og mokkasiner. Instructions for making Indian costumes, necklaces, and drums are accompanied by advice on Indian cooking and a discussion of smoke signals. [TT160.A413] 76-183492
1. Handicraft—Juvenile literature. 2. Indians of North America—Industries—Juvenile literature. 3. Indians of North America—Art. I. Title.

ALLEN, Judy. 745.5
Exciting things to do with nature materials / by Judy Allen ; illustrated by Barbara Firth. Philadelphia : Lippincott, 1977. p. cm. (Look and make books) Instructions for making a variety of decorative and useful objects from twigs, seeds, feathers, leaves, and other things found in woods, fields, and on the seashore. [TT160.A44 1977] 76-39960 ISBN 0-397-31743-3 : 4.95
1. Handicraft—Juvenile literature. 2. Nature craft—Juvenile literature. I. Firth, Barbara. II. Title. BIP

†BOWMAN, Bruce. 745.51
Toothpick sculpture & ice-cream stick art / by Bruce Bowman. New York : Sterling Pub. Co., c1976. 64 p., [4] leaves of plates : ill. (some col.) ; 21 cm. Includes index. Directions for making a variety of handicraft items using white glue and toothpicks or ice-cream sticks. [TT880.B68] 76-19808 ISBN 0-8069-5373-X : 5.95 lib.bdg. : 5.69
1. Handicraft—Juvenile literature. 2. Toothpicks—Juvenile literature. 3. Staffs (Sticks, canes, etc.)—Juvenile literature. I. Title. II. Title: Ice-cream stick art. BIP

CANEY, Steven. 649'.51
Steven Caney's playbook / by Steven Caney. New York : Workman Pub. Co., [1975] p. cm. Projects, constructions, games, puzzles, and other activities for children organized according to the spaces where they play. [TT160.C34] 75-9816 ISBN 0-911104-37-2 : 9.95. ISBN 0-911104-38-0 pbk. : 4.95
1. Handicraft—Juvenile literature. 2. Games—Juvenile literature. I. Title. II. Title: Playbook. BIP

CHERNOFF, Goldie Taub. 745.5
Just a box? Pictures by Margaret Hartelius. New York, Walker [1973] [24] p. col. illus. 20 x 24 cm. Simple directions for making a basket, hat, zoo, totem pole, puppet, plane, and other objects from discarded cardboard boxes. [TT160.C52 1973] 72-95762 ISBN 0-8027-6138-0 2.95
1. Handicraft—Juvenile literature. 2. Boxes—Juvenile literature. I. Hartelius, Margaret A., illus. II. Title.

CHOATE, Judith. 745.5
Scrapcraft; 50 easy-to-make handicraft projects, by Judith Choate and Jane Green. [1st ed.] Garden City, N.Y., Doubleday [1973] 64 p. illus. 22 cm. Instructions for projects made from paper, tin, pasta, and seed and other materials found around the house. [TT160.C53] 72-89814 ISBN 0-385-09413-2 4.95
1. Handicraft—Juvenile literature. I. Green, Jane, joint author. II. Title.

CHRISTIAN, Mary Blount. 745.5
The Gooshill Gang craft book / written by Mary Blount Christian ; illustrated by Betty Wind. St. Louis : Concordia Pub. House, c1978. 32 p. : ill. ; 23 cm. Directions for eighteen simple crafts with an explanation of how four children use them in practicing Christian principles. [TT160.C54] 77-28950 ISBN 0-570-07362-6 : 0.95
1. Handicraft—Juvenile literature. I. Wind, Betty. II. Title. BIP

CONAWAY, Judith, 1948- 745.5
City crafts from secret cities / by Judith Conaway. Chicago : Follett Pub. Co., c1978. 95 p. : ill. ; 21 x 26 cm. Suggests numerous handicraft projects that introduce the dress, transportation, communication, housing, and recreation from the cities of several ancient civilizations. [TT160.C65] 77-88640 ISBN 0-695-40874-7 lib.bdg. : 8.97
1. Handicraft—Juvenile literature. 2. Cities and towns, Ruined, extinct, etc.—Juvenile literature. I. Title. BIP

COOPER, Michael, 1943- 745.59'41
Things to make and do for George Washington's birthday / by Michael Cooper. New York : Watts, 1979. p. cm. (A Things to make and do book) A collection of games, recipes, and craft projects suitable for George Washington's birthday celebrations. Includes a brief account ofWashington's life. [TT160.C67] 78-11709 ISBN 0-685-65724-8 lib. bdg. : 6.90
1. Washington, George, Pres. U.S., 1732-1799—Juvenile literature. 2. Handicraft—Juvenile literature. 3. Cookery—Juvenile literature. 4. Games—Juvenile literature. 5. Presidents—United States—Biography—Juvenile literature. 6. Washington's Birthday—Juvenile literature. I. Title. BIP

*CREATIVE crafts for children. 745.5
Lees Summit. Mo., Unity Bks. [c.] 1966 64p. illus. (pt. col.) 26cm. 2.00 pap.,

CUTLER, Katherine N. 745.5
From petals to pinecones; a nature art and craft book [by] Katherine N. Cutler. Illustrated by Giulio Maestro. New York, Lothrop, Lee & Shepard Co. [1969] 128 p. illus. 25 cm. Bibliography: p. [124] Instructions for making gifts and decorations using such natural objects as pine cones, nuts, flowers, driftwood, stones, and others. Includes a chapter on school projects. [TT160.C9] 79-81753 4.50
1. Handicraft—Juvenile literature. 2. Nature study. I. Maestro, Giulio, illus. II. Title.

D'AMATO, Janet. 745.5'096
African crafts for you to make, by Janet and Alex D'Amato. New York, J. Messner [1969] 65 p. col. illus., maps (on lining papers) 26 cm. Bibliography: p. 65. Instructions for making replicas of household items, houses, musical instruments, ceremonial objects, clothing, and personal effects of various African tribes. Includes a brief explanation of the origin, use, and significance of each object. [TT160.D26] 70-75690 4.95
1. Handicraft—Juvenile literature. 2. Handicraft—Africa. I. D'Amato, Alex, joint author. II. Title. BIP

D'AMATO, Janet. 745.5'0973
Colonial crafts for you to make, by Janet and Alex D'Amato. New York, Messner [1975] 64 p. illus. 26 cm. Introduces various crafts that flourished during the colonial era and gives instructions for making replicas of many representative items. [TT160.D263] 74-19005 ISBN 0-671-32705-4 6.95
1. Handicraft—Juvenile literature. 2. Handicraft—United States—Juvenile literature. 3. United States—Social life and customs—Colonial period, ca. 1600-1775—Juvenile literature. I. D'Amato, Alex, joint author. II. Title.
Lib. bdg. 6.29, ISBN 0-671-32706-2. BIP

D'AMATO, Janet. 745.59
Handicrafts for holidays, by Janet and Alex D'Amato. Foreword by Morton Thompson. New York, Lion Press [1967] 65 p. col. illus. 26 cm. Simple instructions for making gifts, greeting cards, and costumes for holidays throughout the year. [TT160.D27] 67-27108
1. Handicraft—Juvenile literature. 2. Holidays—Juvenile literature. I. D'Amato, Alex, joint author. II. Title. BIP

D'AMATO, Janet. 745.5'0973
More colonial crafts for you to make / by Janet and Alex D'Amato. New York : J. Messner, c1977. p. cm. Introduces various crafts that flourished during the colonial era and gives instructions for making replicas of many representative items. [TT160.D28] 77-6333 ISBN 0-671-32841-7 lib.bdg. : 7.79
1. Handicraft—Juvenile literature. 2. Handicraft—United States—Juvenile literature. 3. United States—Social life and customs—Colonial period, ca. 1600-1775—Juvenile literature. I. D'Amato, Alex, joint author. II. Title. BIP

DE PAOLA, Thomas Anthony. 394.2'683
Things to make and do for Valentine's Day / by Tomie de Paola. New York : F. Watts, 1976. 48 p. : col. ill. ; 23 cm. (Things to make and do books) A collection of crafts, projects, recipes, jokes, and games on a St. Valentine's Day theme. [TT160.D37] 75-38974 ISBN 0-531-01187-9 lib.bdg. : 4.90
1. Handicraft—Juvenile literature. 2. Cookery—Juvenile literature. 3. Games—Juvenile literature. 4. St. Valentine's Day—Juvenile literature. I. Title. BIP

*DEWING, Mary, comp. 745.5
Modelling is easy when you know how, edited by Mary Dewing and Kathleen Douet New York, Arco, [1974] 48 p. col. illus., 31 cm. [TT160] 74-76266 4.95
1. Handicraft—Juvenile literature. I. Douet, Kathleen, joint comp. II. Title.

DOBRIN, Arnold. 745.59'41
Make a witch, make a goblin : a book of Halloween crafts / by Arnold Dobrin. New

York : Four Winds Press, c1977. vii, 120 p. : ill. ; 24 cm. Instructions for making costumes, party decorations, trick-or-treat bags, puppets, and party food, all on a Halloween theme. [TT160.D63] 77-177 ISBN 0-590-07450-4 : 6.95
1. Handicraft—Juvenile literature. 2. Cookery—Juvenile literature. 3. Halloween decorations—Juvenile literature. I. Title. BIP

EASY crafts book / 745.5
by the editors of Sterling. New York : Sterling Pub. Co., c1975. 96 p. : ill. (some col.) ; 22 x 25 cm. Includes index. Instructions for over sixty craft projects arranged by medium such as cardboard, newspaper, and yarn, which need only simple tools and materials. [TT160.E18] 76-358054 ISBN 0-8069-5328-4 : 8.95 ISBN 0-8069-5329-2 lib.bdg. :
1. Handicraft—Juvenile literature. I. Sterling Publishing Company, inc., New York. BIP

EDWARDS, Brian, 1936- 745.59
Busy fingers book of games to make and play / written and designed by Brian Edwards. Chicago : Rand McNally, 1974. 93 p. : col. ill. ; 30 cm. On spine: Games to make and play. Step-by-step instructions for a variety of projects to make from inexpensive materials. [TT160.E38] 74-193304 ISBN 0-528-82183-0 3.95
1. Handicraft—Juvenile literature. 2. Games—Juvenile literature. I. Title. II. Title: Games to make and play.

EDWARDS, Brian, 1936- 745.59
Busy fingers book of toys to make / written and designed by Brian Edwards. Chicago : Rand McNally, 1974. 93 p. : col. ill. ; 30 cm. On spine: Toys to make. Step-by-step instructions for making such toys as flowers, a castle, kite, clock, airplane and such useful items as a pencil holder, bookends, and a candy dish. [TT160.E39 1974] 74-193305 ISBN 0-528-82184-9 : 3.95
1. Handicraft—Juvenile literature. 2. Toys—Juvenile literature. I. Title. II. Title: Toys to make.

ELLISON, Elsie C. 746.4
Fun with lines and curves, by Elsie C. Ellison. With illus. adapted from the author's drawings by Susan Stan. New York, Lothrop, Lee and Shepard Co. [1972] 95 p. illus. 24 cm. Directions for geometric designs made with ruler, compass, and protractor and embellished with thread. [TT160.E44] 72-1095 ISBN 0-688-40012-4 4.25
1. Handicraft—Juvenile literature. 2. Geometrical drawing—Juvenile literature. I. Stan, Susan, illus. II. Title. BIP

ENDICOTT, Robert F. 745.51
Scrap wood fun for kids; 100 easy-to-make projects for boys and girls. New York, Association [c.1961] 223p. illus. 23cm. 61-14181 4.95 bds.,
1. Handicraft—Juvenile literature. I. Title.

ESHMEYER, Reinhart Ernest. 745.5
Ask any vegetable / R. E. Eshmeyer ; illustrated with photos. and drawings by the author. Englewood Cliffs, N.J. : Prentice-Hall, [1975] 151 p. : ill. (some col.) ; 24 cm. Includes index. Instructions for making various animals and scenes using vegetables. [TT160.E75] 74-20969 ISBN 0-13-049759-2 : 7.95
1. Handicraft—Juvenile literature. 2. Vegetables—Juvenile literature. I. Title. BIP

FIAROTTA, Phyllis. 745.5
Be what you want to be craft book / by Phyllis Fiarotta and Noel Fiarotta. New York : Workman Pub. Co., [1977] p. cm. Includes index. More than two hundred crafts projects to make props for role playing many occupations. Includes instruments for the musician, disguises for the private eye, and equipment for the photographer. [TT160.F47] 76-52860 ISBN 0-911104-94-1 : 10.95. ISBN 0-911104-95-X pbk. : 5.95
1. Handicraft—Juvenile literature. 2. Occuptions—Juvenile literature. I. Fiarotta, Noel, joint author. II. Title.

FIAROTTA, Phyllis. 790.19'22
Confetti : the kids' rainbow party book / by Phyllis Fiarotta & Noel Fiarotta. New York : Workman Pub., [1978] p. cm. Instructions for twenty-two parties, including birthday, holiday, Mother's Day, and new baby, with details for making invitations, decorations, favors, and food. [TT160.F472] 78-7121 ISBN 0-89480-049-3 : 10.95 ISBN 0-89480-050-7 pbk. : 5.95
1. Handicraft—Juvenile literature. 2. Cookery—Juvenile literature. 3. Children's parties—Juvenile literature. I. Fiarotta, Noel, joint author. II. Title. BIP

FIAROTTA, Phyllis. 745.5
Pin it, tack it, hang it : the big book of kids' bulletin boards / by Phyllis Fiarotta, with Noel Fiarotta. New York : Workman Pub. Co., [1975] p. cm. Step-by-step instructions for constructing bulletin boards from different materials with suggestions for using them either as an activity center or a standing scrapbook reflecting the user's experiences or interests. [TT160.F48] 75-20211 ISBN 0-911104-61-5 : 7.95. ISBN 0-911104-63-1 pbk. : 3.95
1. Handicraft—Juvenile literature. 2. Bulletin boards—Juvenile literature. I. Fiarotta, Noel, joint author. II. Title. BIP

FIAROTTA, Phyllis. 745.5
Sticks & stones & ice cream cones; the craft book for children, by Phyllis Fiarotta with Noel Fiarotta. New York, Workman Pub. Co. [1973] 320 p. illus. 21 x 23 cm. Instructions for a wide variety of handicraft projects from casting footprints to making puppets. [TT160.F5] 74-160843 ISBN 0-911104-29-1 9.95
1. Handicraft—Juvenile literature. I. Fiarotta, Noel. II. Title.
Pbk. 4.95; ISBN 0-911104-30-5 BIP

FIAROTTA, Phyllis. 745.5
The you and me heritage tree : children's crafts from 21 American traditions / by Phyllis Fiarotta and Noel Fiarotta. New York : Workman Pub. Co., c1976. 283 p. : ill. ; 22 x 24 cm. Step-by-step instructions for more than 100 craft projects drawn from twenty-three different ethnic traditions in the United States and using easily available materials. [TT160.F52 1976] 75-44133 ISBN 0-911104-74-7 10.95 ISBN 0-911104-73-9 pbk. 4.95
1. Handicraft—Juvenile literature. I. Fiarotta, Noel, joint author. II. Title. BIP

FRIEDRICHSEN, Carol S. 745.59'24
The Pooh craft book : inspired by Winnie-the-Pooh and The house at Pooh Corner by A. A. Milne, illustrations by E. H. Shepard / by Carol S. Friedrichsen. [New York] : Dutton, [1976] p. cm. Directions for handicrafts inspired by Winnie-the-Pooh including a felt picture, hunny pot, snow scene, and stuffed animals. [TT160.F73] 76-10711 ISBN 0-525-37410-8 : 5.95
1. Handicraft—Juvenile literature. 2. Soft toy making—Juvenile literature. I. Title. BIP

GHINGER, Judith. 745.59'41
Hooray days : New Year's to Christmas : things to make and do / by Judith Ghinger ; illustrated by Marina Givotovsky. New York : Golden Press, c1977. 48 p. : col. ill. ; 26 cm. (A Kid's paperback) Includes instructions for games and decorations to make for various holidays throughout the year. [TT160.G415] 76-39651 ISBN 0-307-12355-3 pbk.: 1.95
1. Handicraft—Juvenile literature. 2. Games—Juvenile literature. 3. Holiday decorations—Juvenile literature. I. Givotovsky, Marina. II. Title. BIP

GIBBONS, Gail. 745.59'41
Things to make and do for Columbus Day / by Gail Gibbons. New York : F. Watts, 1977. [48] p. : col. ill. ; 27 cm. (Things to make and do book) Describes the reasons Columbus Day is celebrated and gives suggestions for celebrating by making and doing various things. [TT160.G42] 76-30781 ISBN 0-531-01274-3 lib. bdg. : 6.90
1. Handicraft—Juvenile literature. 2. Cookery—Juvenile literature. 3. Games—Juvenile literature. 4. Columbus Day—Juvenile literature. I. Title. BIP

GIBBONS, Gail. 745.59'41
Things to make and do for your birthday / by Gail Gibbons. New York : F. Watts, 1978. 48 p. : col. ill. ; 27 cm. (A Things to make and do book) Includes projects, games, jokes, and party foods for use in celebrating birthdays. [TT160.G425] 77-15109 ISBN 0-531-01462-2 lib.bdg. : 6.90
1. Handicraft—Juvenile literature. 2. Cookery—Juvenile literature. 3. Games—Juvenile literature. 4. Birthdays—Juvenile literature. I. Title. BIP

GIFTS for everybody / 745.5
Cameron and Margaret Yerian, editors. Chicago : Childrens Press, [1975] 47 p. : ill. ; 24 cm. (Fun time activities) Includes index. Instructions for making useful and ornamental objects for oneself or for gifts. Includes link belts, etched fungus, spice shakers, cork coasters, matchbox furniture, a hammock, and many more. [TT160.G43] 75-16386 ISBN 0-516-01329-7 lib.bdg. : 6.60
1. Handicraft—Juvenile literature. I. Yerian, Cameron John. II. Yerian, Margaret. BIP

GILBREATH, Alice Thompson. 745.5
Beginning crafts for beginning readers [by] Alice Gilbreath. Illustrated by Joe Rogers. Chicago, Follett Pub. Co. [1972] 31 p. col. illus. 23 cm. (Wonderland books) Easy-to-read instructions for making such items as a totem pole, book mark, and puppet from easily accessible materials. [TT160.G45] 71-184461 ISBN 0-695-80317-4 2.95
1. Handicraft—Juvenile literature. I. Rogers, Joe, illus. II. Title. BIP

GILBREATH, Alice Thompson. 745.5
More beginning crafts for beginning readers / Alice Gilbreath ; illustrated by Joe Rogers. Chicago : Follett Pub. Co., 1976. 32 p. : col. ill. ; 23 cm. Continues Beginning crafts for beginning readers. Easy-to-read instructions for making such items as an alligator, a kite, a charm bracelet, and a race car. [TT160.G455] 76-367145 ISBN 0-695-80635-1 : 4.95 ISBN 0-695-40635-3 lib.bdg. :
1. Handicraft—Juvenile literature. I. Rogers, Joe. II. Title.

GILBREATH, Alice Thompson. 745.5
Spouts, lids, and cans; fun with familiar metal objects [by] Alice Gilbreath. Illustrated by Pamela Carroll. New York, Morrow, 1973. 48 p. illus. 24 cm. Instructions for making a variety of toys and gifts from common household items such as salt-box spouts and metal lids. [TT160.G46] 72-10255 ISBN 0-688-20064-8 3.95
1. Handicraft—Juvenile literature. I. Carroll, Pamela, illus. II. Title.
Library edition 3.78; ISBN 0-688-25064-5.

GLOVACH, Linda. 745.59'41
The Little Witch's Thanksgiving book / by Linda Glovach. Englewood Cliffs, N.J. : Prentice-Hall, c1976. 48 p. : col. ill. ; 24 cm. Includes index. Handicrafts, a puppet play, and recipes related to the celebration of Thanksgiving Day. [TT160.G55] 76-9847 ISBN 0-13-537993-8 lib.bdg. : 5.95
1. Handicraft—Juvenile literature. 2. Cookery—Juvenile literature. 3. Thanksgiving Day—Juvenile literature. I. Title. BIP

GUTH, Phyllis. 745.5'02'40544
Crafts for kids / by Phyllis Guth ; illustrated by the author. 1st ed. Blue Ridge Summit, Pa. : G/L Tab Books, 1975. 182 p. : ill. ; 22 cm. Includes index. Based on the author's column of the same title, first published in the Evening chronicle, Allentown, Pa. [TT160.G94] 75-4287 ISBN 0-8306-5766-5 : 7.95. ISBN 0-8306-4766-X pbk. : 3.95
1. Handicraft—Juvenile literature. I. Title. BIP

HAUTZIG, Esther (Rudomin) 745.5
Let's make more presents; easy and inexpensive gifts for every occasion, by Esther Hautzig. Illustrated by Ray Skibinski. New York, Macmillan [1973] 150 p. illus. 24 cm. Instructions for making a variety of gifts from easily available materials. Included are puppets, candies, tie dye shirts, candles, and others. [TT160.H368] 72-92445 ISBN 0-02-743490-7 5.95
1. Handicraft—Juvenile literature. 2. Gifts—Juvenile literature. I. Skibinski, Ray, illus. II. Title. BIP

HELFMAN, Harry Carmozin, 1910- 745.5
Creating things that move : fun with kinetic art / Harry Helfman ; illustrated with photos. by the author. New York : Morrow, 1975. 48 p. : ill. ; 24 cm. Explains the principles of kinetic or movable art with instructions for nine projects. [TT160.H394] 75-11719 ISBN 0-688-22038-X : 4.95 ISBN 0-688-32038-4 lib.bdg. : 4.59
1. Handicraft—Juvenile literature. 2. Kinetic art—Juvenile literature. I. Title.

HELFMAN, Harry Carmozin, 1910- 745.5
Making pictures without paint [by] Harry Helfman. Illustrated with photos. by the author. New York, Morrow, 1973. 47 p. illus. 24 cm. Instructions for projects using the techniques of collage, mosaic, applique, stitchery, rubbing, and others. [TT160.H396] 72-4234 ISBN 0-688-20068-0 3.75
1. Handicraft—Juvenile literature. I. Title. BIP

HORN, George F. 745.5
Crafts for today's schools [by] George F. Horn. Worcester, Mass., Davis Publications [1972] 144 p. illus. 27 cm. Bibliography: p. 141. Describes the tools, materials, and techniques for making a variety of objects from wire, wood, glass, clay, and cloth. [TT160.H56] 79-181784 ISBN 0-87192-045-X
1. Handicraft—Juvenile literature. I. Title.

HOWIE, Olive. 745.5 (j)
Handy crafts from scraps; a collection of illustrated how-to-make articles from scrap and inexpensive materials. Photos contributed by Vickie Gale, Oscar Faulk, and Frank Howman. Minneapolis, Denison [1967] 77 p. illus. (part col.) 29 cm. [TT160.H68] 67-19670
1. Handicraft—Juvenile literature. I. Title.

HSIAO, Pia. 745.5
Superbook of things to make / Pia Hsiao, Neil Lorimer. New York : Platt & Munk, c1976. 127 p. : col. ill. ; 28cm. Includes index. [TT160.H74] 75-24622 ISBN 0-8228-8989-7 : 4.95
1. Handicraft—Juvenile literature. I. Lorimer, Neil, joint author. II. Title.

INOUYE, Carol. 745.5
Naturecraft / Carol Inouye. 1st ed. Garden City, N.Y. : Doubleday, [1975] 64 p. : ill. ; 22 cm. Instructions for a number of handicraft projects using beans, stones, shells, driftwood, flowers, corn, fruits, cones, nuts, and other natural materials. [TT160.I58] 74-33681 ISBN 0-385-01164-4 : 5.95
1. Handicraft—Juvenile literature. I. Title. BIP

JANVIER, Jeannine. 745.5
Fabulous birds you can make / by Jeannine Janvier ; photos. by Jean-Pierre Tesson ; [translated by Maxine Hobson]. New York : Sterling Pub. Co., c1976. 32 p. : ill. (some col.) ; 22 cm. (Easy craft series) Translation of Merveilleux oiseaux. Includes index. Directions for making a puppet, letter and newspaper pouch, and other craft representations of birds. [TT160.J3613] 76-19818 ISBN 0-8069-5404-3 : 3.95 ISBN 0-8069-5405-1 lib.bdg. : 3.99
1. Handicraft—Juvenile literature. 2. Zoological models—Juvenile literature. I. Title. II. Title: Birds you can make. III. Series. BIP

JANVIER, Jeannine. 745.5
Fantastic fish you can make / by Jeannine Janvier ; photos. by Boris Teplitzky ; [translated by Maxine Hobson]. New York : Sterling Pub. Co., c1976. 32 p. : col. ill. ; 22 cm. (Easy craft series) Translation of Merveilleux poissons. Includes index. Instructions for making a trivet, jigsaw puzzle, jewelry, and other craft items inspired by creatures from the sea. [TT160.J3713] 76-19819 ISBN 0-8069-5406-X : 3.95 ISBN 0-8069-5407-8 lib.bdg. : 3.99
1. Handicraft—Juvenile literature. 2. Fishes—Juvenile literature. I. Title. II. Series. BIP

KINNEY, Jean Brown. 745.5
22 famous painters and illustrators tell how they work : invaluable advice from the guiding faculty of Famous Artists School, Westport, Conn. c6 by Jean and Cle Kinney. New York :

Atheneum, 1976. p. cm. Explains the contributions to American culture of many different ethnic groups and provides instructions for making folk art for each group. [TT160.K48] 76-5409 ISBN 0-689-30541-9
1. Handicraft—Juvenile literature. 2. Folk art—Juvenile literature. I. Kinney, Cle, joint author. II. Title.

KINSER, Charleen. 745.5
Outdoor art for kids / written and illustrated by Charleen Kinser. Chicago : Follett, [1975] 96 p. : ill. (some col.) ; 23 cm. Directions for things that can be made outdoors such as effigies, cages, mosaics, musical instruments, mud art, and ice molds. [TT160.K5] 74-18133 ISBN 0-695-80533-9 : 5.95 ISBN 0-695-40533-0 lib.bdg. : 5.97
1. Handicraft—Juvenile literature. 2. Art—Juvenile literature. I. Title. BIP

KLIMO, Joan Fincher. 745.5
What can I do today? A treasury of crafts for children. [New York] Pantheon Books [1971] 58 p. col. illus. 29 cm. Directions for sixteen sculpting, printing, pasting, stitching, and decorating projects for rainy days. [TT160.K56] 72-153979 ISBN 0-394-92309-X (library ed.)
1. Handicraft—Juvenile literature. I. Title.

KUEHNEMANN, Ursula. 745.5
Presents for Dad. New York, Taplinger Pub. Co. [1967, c 1966] v. (unpaged) illus. 21 cm. Translation of Geschenke fur Vatl selbatgemacht. [TT160.K763] 67-11512
1. Handicraft — Juvenile literature. I. Title.

KUEHNEMANN, Ursula. 745.5
Presents for Mother. New York, Taplinger Pub. Co. [1967, c1966] 1 v. (unpaged) illus. 21 cm. Translation of Geschenke fur Muttl selbatgemacht. [TT160.K753] 67-11513
1. Handicraft — Juvenile literature. I. Title.

KUEHNEMANN, Urusla. 745.5 (j)
Presents for Mother. New York, Taplinger Pub. Co. [1967, c1966] 1 v. (unpaged) illus. 21 cm. Translation of Geschenke fur Mutti selbstgemacht. [TT160.K753] 67-11513
1. Handicraft—Juvenile literature. I. Title.

LAMARQUE, Colette. 745.59'28
A world of models. New York, Drake Publishers [1973] 60 p. col. illus. 23 cm. Translation of Autour du monde. Instructions for craft projects depicting scenes from many different countries. [TT160.L3213] 73-3197 ISBN 0-87749-479-7 3.95
1. Handicraft—Juvenile literature. 2. Models and modelmaking—Juvenile literature. I. Title.

LAW, Felicia. 745.5
Something to make; illustrated by Gunvor Edwards. Harmondsworth, Penguin, 1971. 137 p. illus. 20 cm. (A Young Puffin original) [TT160.L33] 70-27073 ISBN 0-14-030473-8 £0.25 ($0.95 U.S.)
1. Handicraft—Juvenile literature. I. Title.

LEE, Tina. 745.5
Things to do. Pictures by Manning Lee. [1st ed.] Garden City, N. Y., Doubleday [1965] 64 p. illus. (part col.) 27 cm. [TT157.L33] 64-10514
1. Handicraft—Juvenile literature. I. Lee, Manning De Villeneuve, 1894- illus. II. Title. BIP

LOPSHIRE, Robert. 745.5
The beginner book of things to make : fun stuff you can make yourself = formerly published as How to make flibbers, etc. / By Robert Lopshire. New York : Beginner Books, [1977?] c1964. 61 p. : col. ill. ; 24 cm. Step-by-step instructions for making such handicraft items as a huffel hat, flibbers, and limp lamps. [TT160.L66 1977] 77-150284 ISBN 0-394-83493-3 : 3.50 lib.bdg. : 4.39
1. Handicraft—Juvenile literature. I. Title. II. Title: Things to make. BIP

MCCALL'S book of paper, wood, and paint crafts; 745.5 based on McCall's giant golden make-it book. Designed, arr. by John Peter. Illus. by Corinne Malvern, Bob Riley. 1965 ed. New York, Golden [1965] 48p. col. illus. 26cm. (Golden hobby bk.) [TT160.M24] 65-7702 .50
1. Handicraft—Juvenile literature. I. McCall's giant golden make-it book.

MCCALL'S make-your-own decorations and gifts book, 745.5 Based on the McCall's golden do-it book. Adap. by Joan Wyckoff. Ed. by Nan Comstock. Illus. by William Dugan. 1965 ed. New York, Golden [1965] 48p. col. illus. 26cm. (Golden hobby bk.) [TT160.M255] 65-3553 .50
1. Handicraft—Juvenile literature. I. Wycoff, Joan. II. Title: McCall's golden do-it book. III. Title: Decorations and gifts book.

MELL, Howard. 745.5
Making things from odds and ends, written and illustrated by Howard Mell & Eric Fisher. New York, Drake Publishers [1971] 80 p. illus. (part col.) 26 cm. (I can do it, 4) Instructions for creating toys, puppets, and other items from newspapers, wire, straws, pipe cleaners, and other readily available materials. [TT160.M43] 70-29162 ISBN 0-87749-072-4
1. Handicraft—Juvenile literature. I. Fisher, Eric, joint author. II. Title.

MELL, Howard. 372.5'3
Modelling, building & carving, written and illustrated by Howard Mell & Eric Fisher. New York, Drake Publishers [1971] 80 p. illus. (part col.) 26 cm. (I can do it, 3) Explains techniques for modelling with dough, clay, and wire, building with cardboard, balsa wood, and polystyrene, and carving candles, soap, and plaster. [TT165.M44 1971] 72-27340 ISBN 0-87749-071-6
1. Handicraft—Juvenile literature. I. Fisher, Eric, joint author. II. Title.

THE Mickey Mouse make-it book. 745.5 New York, Random House [1974] [42] p. col. illus. 25 cm. (Disney's wonderful world of reading) Easy-to-read, step-by-step instructions for ten things to make and do with bands, soda pop cans, aluminum foil, crayons, scissors and other common items. [TT160.M47] 74-5241 ISBN 0-394-82555-1
1. Handicraft—Juvenile literature. BIP

MILLER, Jay. 745.5
Making gifts / by Jay and Frank Miller ; pictures by George Overlie. Minneapolis : Lerner Publications Co., [1975] p. cm. (An Early craft book) Directions for making practical and attractive gifts from readily available and inexpensive materials. Includes decorated stationery, crepe paper flowers, planters, wind chimes, picture albums, checkerboards, and games. [TT160.M48] 74-33532 ISBN 0-8225-0867-2 lib.bdg. : 3.95
1. Handicraft—Juvenile literature. 2. Gifts—Juvenile literature. I. Miller, Frank, 1919- joint author. II. Overlie, George, ill. III. Title. BIP

MILLER, Jay. 745.5
Nature crafts / by Jay and Frank Miller ; pictures by George Overlie. Minneapolis : Lerner Publications Co., [1975] p. cm. (An Early craft book) Instructions for making various projects using seeds, nuts, leaves, weeds, and flowers and for making dolls from corn husks and apples. [TT160.M49] 74-33535 ISBN 0-8225-0866-4 lib.bdg. : 3.95
1. Handicraft—Juvenile literature. I. Miller, Frank, 1919- joint author. II. Overlie, George, ill. III. Title.

MILLER, Lynne. 745.5'02'40544
Make your own thing ... : games, puzzles, gimmicks & gifts / by Lynne Miller ; illustrated by William Hogarth. New York : J. Messner, c1979. p. cm. Instructions for making things for yourself and gifts for others. Includes games, puzzles, and handicraft. [TT157.M49] 78-27729 ISBN 0-671-32906-5 : 7.29
1. Handicraft—Juvenile literature. 2. Games—Juvenile literature. 3. Puzzles—Juvenile literature. 4. Gifts—Juvenile literature. I. Hogarth, William, 1926- II. Title.

MILLER, Lynne. 745.5'02'40544
Make your own thing ... : games, puzzles, gimmicks & gifts / by Lynne Miller ; illustrated by William Hogarth. New York : J. Messner, c1979. p. cm. Instructions for making things for yourself and gifts for others. Includes games, puzzles, and handicraft. [TT157.M49] 78-27729 ISBN 0-671-32906-5 : 7.29
1. Handicraft—Juvenile literature. 2. Games—Juvenile literature. 3. Puzzles—Juvenile literature. 4. Gifts—Juvenile literature. I. Hogarth, William, 1926- II. Title. BIP

MOBLY, June Rose. 745.5'02'4054
Year 'round crafts for children / by June Rose Mobly ; illustrated by Mildred Ward. Cincinnati : Standard Pub., c1974. 64 p. : ill. ; 29 cm. Instructions for making a variety of holiday decorations, gifts, masks, puzzles, and other items from easily obtainable materials. [TT160.M54] 74-82557
1. Handicraft—Juvenile literature. I. Ward, Mildred. II. Title. III. Title: Crafts for children.

NEWSOME, Arden J. 745.5
Crafts and toys from around the world, by Arden J. Newsome. New York, J. Messner [1971, c1972] 95 p. illus. 27 cm. Step-by-step directions for reproducing thirty-three toys, games, and handicrafts introduced to America by immigrants from twenty foreign countries. [PZ10.N56Cr3] 78-180532 ISBN 0-671-32489-6 5.95
1. Handicraft—Juvenile literature. 2. Toy making—Juvenile literature. I. Title. BIP

NEWSOME, Arden J. 745.51
Spoolcraft [by] Arden J. Newsome. Illus. by Kathleen McGee and Arden J. Newsome. New York, Lothrop, Lee & Shepard Co. [1970] 158 p. illus. 25 cm. Describes handicraft projects for both boys and girls using wooden thread spools. [TT160.N49] 70-101476 4.95
1. Handicraft—Juvenile literature. I. McGee, Kathleen, illus. II. Title. BIP

NICOL, Linda. 745.5'02'40544
What can I do today? : [Over 100 projects for girls, age 6-12] / projects designed by Linda Nicol and David Clark ; col. ill. by Brian Edwards. Chicago : Rand McNally, 1973. 127 p. : col. ill. ; 30 cm. Gives instructions for creating a variety of toys, gifts, decorations, and costumes. [TT171.N52 1973] 74-195097 ISBN 0-528-82197-0 : 3.95
1. Handicraft—Juvenile literature. I. Clark, David, 1937- joint author. II. Edwards, Brian, 1936- ill. III. Title.

PARISH, Peggy. 745.59
Sheet magic; games, toys and gifts from old sheets. Illusrated by Lynn Sweat. New York, Macmillan [1971] 96 p. illus. 24 cm. Ideas for games, toys, and gifts that can be made from old sheets. [PZ10.P2545Sh] 78-155263
1. Handicraft—Juvenile literature. 2. Amusements—Juvenile literature. I. Sweat, Lynn, illus. II. Title. BIP

PEAKE, Miriam Morrison. 745.5
101 glamorous gifts to make. Illustrated by Ethel Gold. New York, Four Winds Press [1968, c1967] 96 p. illus. 23 cm. [TT171.P4] 68-27280 3.50
1. Handicraft—Juvenile literature. 2. Gifts. I. Title.

PLOQUIN, Genevieve. 745.5
From wheelbarrows to rockets. New York, Drake Publishers [1973] 62 p. col. illus. 23 cm. Translation of De la brouette au module. Instructions for making craft projects such as carts, boats, planes, space ships, and other transportation vehicles. [TT160.P61513] 73-3196 ISBN 0-87749-478-9 3.95
1. Handicraft—Juvenile literature. 2. Models and modelmaking—Juvenile literature. I. Title.

*PLOQUIN, Genevieve. 745.5
What to make with pine cones / by Genevieve Ploquin ; photographs by Boris Teplitzky. New York : Sterling Pub. Co., c1976. 32p. : ill. (some col.) ; 22 cm. (Easy craft series) Includes index. Summary: Easy step by step directions for making many crafts projects out of pine cones. [TT874] 76-19823 ISBN 0-8069-5412-4 : 3.95 ISBN 0-8069-5413-2 lib.bdg. : 3.99
1. Handicraft-Juvenile literature. I. Title.

POUNTNEY, Kate. 745.5
Creative crafts for children / Kate Pountney. London : Faber and Faber, 1977. 64 p. : ill. ; 26 cm. [TT160.P76] 78-305323 ISBN 0-571-10948-9 : 5.95
1. Handicraft—Juvenile literature.
Distributed by Faber and Faber, Salem, NH BIP

PRATSON, Frederick John. 745.5
The special world of the artisan [by] Frederick J. Pratson. Boston, Houghton Mifflin, 1974. 119 p. illus. 24 cm. Describes the creative processes of five different artisans: the potter, wood sculptor, glass-blower, weaver, and musical instrument maker. [TT160.P77] 73-21724 ISBN 0-395-18510-6 5.95
1. Handicraft—Juvenile literature. I. Title. BIP

PRICE, Lowi. 745.5
Concoctions : recipes for creeping crystals, invisible ink, self-stick plastic, grease paint, playdough, and other inedibles / by Lowi Price and Marilyn Wronsky. New York : Dutton, [1976] p. cm. Recipes, using around-the-house ingredients, for making a variety of silly and sensible things such as cosmetics, inks, pastes, fake plastic, blender paper, and a silver-plated twig. [TT160.P8] 76-25842 ISBN 0-52528137-1 : 5.95
1. Handicraft—Juvenile literature. I. Wronsky, Marilyn, joint author. II. Title. BIP

A Pumpkin in a pear tree : 745.59'41 creative ideas for twelve months of holiday fun / by Ann Cole ... [et al.] ; illustrated by Debby Young. 1st ed. Boston : Little, Brown, [1975] p. cm. Bibliography: Suggestions for simple projects, games, and crafts, using common household materials, for holidays throughout the year. [TT160.P85] 75-17645 ISBN 0-316-15110-6 lib.bdg. : 7.95 ISBN 0-316-15111-4 pbk. : 3.95
1. Handicraft—Juvenile literature. 2. Holiday decorations—Juvenile literature. 3. Cookery—Juvenile literature. 4. Games—Juvenile literature. I. Cole, Ann. II. Young, Debby.

PURDY, Susan Gold, 1939- 745.59'41
Christmas gifts for you to make / by Susan Purdy. 1st ed. Philadelphia : Lippincott, c1976. 96 p. : ill. (some col.) ; 26 cm. Directions for making a wide variety of useful and decorative gifts suitable for any occasion. [TT160.P87] 76-10160 ISBN 0-397-31695-X : 7.95 pbk. : 4.95
1. Handicraft—Juvenile literature. I. Title. BIP

QUINN, Gardner. 394.2'683
Valentine crafts and cookbook / by Gardner Quinn ; with illus. by Madeline Grossman. New York : Harvey House, c1977. 46 p. : ill. ; 24 cm. Includes instructions for Valentine's Day cards, boxes, gifts, and a party. Relates superstitions and customs of the day. [TT160.Q56] 77-78093 ISBN 0-8178-5592-0 lib.bdg. : 3.99
1. Handicraft—Juvenile literature. 2. Cookery—Juvenile literature. 3. St. Valentine's Day—Juvenile literature. I. Grossman, Madeline. II. Title. BIP

RAZZI, James. 745.5
Bag of tricks! Fun things to make and do with the groceries. Edited by Thomas S. Roberts. New York, Parents' Magazine Press [1971] 61 p. col. illus. 19 x 26 cm. Instruction for making toys, jewelry, party favors, mobiles, and other objects from common household items. [TT160.R36] 75-136996 ISBN 0-8193-0449-2
1. Handicraft—Juvenile literature. I. Title. BIP

RAZZI, James. 745.5
Just for Kids! Things to make, do, and see: easy as 1-2-3. New York, Parents' Magazine Press [1974] 61 p. col. illus. 20 x 27 cm. Magic tricks, puzzles, games, and things to make from ordinary materials such as cereal boxes and plastic wrap, for children from four to eight. [TT160.R37] 73-13521 ISBN 0-8193-0723-8
1. Handicraft—Juvenile literature. 2. Games—Juvenile literature. I. Title. BIP

RAZZI, James. 745.5
Star-spangled fun! : Things to make, do, and see from American history / by James Razzi ; edited by Rugh Craig. New York : Parent's Magazine Press, c1976. 61 p. : ill. (some col.) ; 20 x 27 cm. Instructions for

SUBJECT INDEX HANDICRAFT—JUVENILE LITERATURE.

games and activities which reflect historical and cultural aspects of American life. [TT160.R38] 74-30397 ISBN 0-8193-0817-X : 5.50 ISBN 0-8193-0818-8 lib.bdg. : 4.96
1. Handicraft—Juvenile literature. 2. Games—Juvenile literature. 3. United States—Social life and customs—Juvenile literature. I. Title. BIP

ROCKWELL, Harlow. 745.5
I did it. New York, Macmillan [1974] 56 p. col. illus. 23 cm. (Ready-to-read) Simple instructions for making a variety of things from easily available materials. Included are a paper bag disguise, a papier mache fish, and bread. [TT160.R58] 73-19059 ISBN 0-02-777550-X. 4.95 (lib. bdg.)
1. Handicraft—Juvenile literature. I. Title. BIP

ROCKWELL, Harlow. 745.5
Look at this / Harlow Rockwell. New York : Macmillan, c1978. 64 p. : ill. ; 23 cm. (Ready-to-read handbook) Easy-to-read text gives instructions for three craft projects: a dancing frog, homemade applesauce, and a noisemaker. [TT160.R59] 77-12716 ISBN 0-02-777590-9 : 6.95
1. Handicraft—Juvenile literature. I. Title. BIP

ST. Tamara. 745.5'095
Asian crafts. Written & illustrated by St. Tamara. New York, Lion Press [1970] 63 p. illus. 27 cm. Instructions for making masks, flowers, jewelry, pottery, and other items associated with various Asian countries. [TT160.S25 1970] 71-86983 ISBN 0-87460-073-1
1. Handicraft—Juvenile literature. 2. Handicraft—Asia. I. Title. BIP

SATTLER, Helen Roney. 745.59
Sock craft: toys, gifts, and other things to make. New York, Lothrop, Lee & Shephard Co. [1972] 160 p. illus. 24 cm. Numerous items to make from nylons and socks include stuffed animals, puppets, toys, hats, purses, travel bags, and covered clothes hangers. [TT160.S27] 72-1102 ISBN 0-688-40004-3 4.95
1. Handicraft—Juvenile literature. I. Title.

SAUNDERS, Everett E. 745.5
Constructing. Racine, Wis., Whitman Pub. Co. [1967- v. (unpaged) col. illus. 30 cm. (A Whitman creative art book) [TT160.S28] 67-5984
1. Handicraft—Juvenile literature. I. Title.

SCARRY, Richard. 745.54
Richard Scarry's best rainy day book ever : more than 500 things to color and make. New York : Random House, c1974. 176 p. : chiefly ill. (some col.) ; 28 cm. Includes such activities as connecting-the-dots, making holiday decorations and cards, coloring, and making paper models. [TT160.S293 1974] 75-24158 ISBN 0-394-83018-0 : 2.95
1. Handicraft—Juvenile literature. 2. Painting books—Juvenile literature. 3. Amusements—Juvenile literature. I. Title. II. Title: Best rainy day book ever.

SCIENCE and mechanics. 372.5'045
High-school mechanics. [New York, Science & Mechanics Pub. Co.] 1963. 144 p. illus., diagrs. 24 cm. (A Science and mechanics handbook, no. 656) Cover title. [TT160.S33] 63-23711
1. Handicraft—Juvenile literature. I. Title.

SEIDELMAN, James E. 745.5
Shopping cart art [by] James E. Seidelman and Grace Mintonye. Illustrated by Kaye Sherry. [New York] Crowell-Collier Press [1969, c1970] 56 p. col. illus. 30 cm. Directions for sculpture, painting, printing, and puppet projects using materials easily available in the supermarket. [TT160.S36] 78-93279
1. Handicraft—Juvenile literature. I. Mintonye, Grace, joint author. II. Sherry, Kaye, illus. III. Title. BIP

SEIDELMAN, James E. 745.5
Shopping cart art [by] James E. Seidelman & Grace Mintonye. Illus. by Kaye Sherry. Abridged edition. New York, Collier Books [1973, c.1970] 46 p. illus. (pt. col.) 23 cm. (Collier juvenile paperbacks) Directions for sculpture, painting, printing, and puppet projects using materials easily available in the supermarket. [TT160.S36] 78-93279 0.95 (pbk.)
1. Handicraft—Juvenile literature. I. Mintonye, Grace, joint author. II. Sherry, Kaye, illus. III. Title.

SIMONS, Robin. 745.5
Recyclopedia : games, science equipment, and crafts from recycled materials / written and illustrated by Robin Simons ; developed at the Boston Children's Museum. Boston : Houghton Mifflin, 1976. x, 118 p. : ill. ; 24 cm. Suggestions for games, crafts, and scientific equipment that can be made from recycled materials. [TT160.S46] 76-17132 ISBN 0-395-24734-9 : 6.95 ISBN 0-395-24380-7 pbk. :
1. Handicraft—Juvenile literature. 2. Games—Juvenile literature. 3. Scientific apparatus and instruments—Juvenile literature. 4. Recycling (Waste, etc.)—Juvenile literature. I. Boston. Children's Museum. II. Title. BIP

STAPLETON, Marjorie. 745.5
Make things grandma made / Marjorie Stapleton. New York : Taplinger Pub. Co., 1975. 63 p. : ill. ; 22 cm. Instructions for making some popular and traditional Victorian crafts and foods including toffee apples, peg dolls, and silhouettes. [TT160.S68 1975] 74-21672 ISBN 0-8008-5052-1 : 6.95
1. Handicraft—Juvenile literature. I. Title. BIP

STAPLETON, Marjorie. 745.5
Make things sailors made / Marjorie Stapleton. New York : Taplinger Pub. Co., 1975. 63 p. : ill. ; 22 cm. Gives instructions for creating a variety of items made by sailors in the past including samplers, straw boxes, scrimshaw, and ship models. [TT160.S69 1975] 74-33171 ISBN 0-8008-5053-X : 6.95
1. Handicraft—Juvenile literature. 2. Seamen—Juvenile literature. I. Title. BIP

STRING, raffia and material. 746.4
New York, F. Watts [1971, c1970] 183 p. illus. 31 cm. (Color crafts) First published in 1970 under title: Working with string, raffia and material. Illustrated instructions of graded difficulty for making puppets, wigs, pillows, and other decorative items from material, string, raffia, and wool. [TT880.W67 1971] 77-158979 ISBN 0-531-02004-5 5.95
1. Handicraft—Juvenile literature. I. Title. II. Title: Working with string, raffia and material. III. Series. BIP

SUNSET crafts for children, 745.5
by the Sunset editorial staff. Book ed.: Marian May. [1st ed.] Menlo Park, Calif., Lane Books [1968] 96 p. illus. 27 cm. [TT160.S9] 68-28153 1.95
1. Handicraft—Juvenile literature. I. May, Marian, ed. II. Sunset. III. Title: Crafts for children.

SYMONS, Arthur, 1909- 643'.7
The fix-it book. New York, Sterling Pub. Co. [1967] 128 p. illus. 21 cm. "Revised from 101 things a boy can do around the house [published in 1961]" [TT160.S94 1967] 67-3608
1. Handicraft—Juvenile literature. 2. Dwellings—Maintenance and repair—Juvenile literature. I. Title.

TEMKO, Florence. 745.5
The big felt burger : and 27 other crafts projects to relish / Florence Temko ; illustrated by Linda Winchester. 1st ed. Garden City, N.Y. : Doubleday, c1977. vi, 138 p. : ill. ; 22 cm. Includes indexes. Instructions for creating and decorating a variety of items with easily available materials. [TT160.T34] 75-14843 ISBN 0-385-09899-5 : 5.95. lib.bdg. : 6.70
1. Handicraft—Juvenile literature. I. Winchester, Linda. II. Title. BIP

TEMKO, Florence. 745.59'41
Folk crafts for world friendship / Florence Temko ; illustrated by Yaroslava. 1st ed. Garden City, N.Y. : Doubleday, c1976. p. cm. Describes celebrations and crafts of many countries. Instructions call for materials such as paper, fabric, and clay. [TT160.T35] 76-4215 ISBN 0-385-11115-0 : 4.95.
1. Handicraft—Juvenile literature. 2. Festivals—Juvenile literature. 3. Holidays—Juvenile literature. I. Yaroslava, pseud. II. Title. BIP

THOMSON, Neil, 1948- 745.59'2
Fairground games to make and play / by Neil and Ruth Thomson ; illustrated by Chris McEwan. 1st American ed. Philadelphia : Lippincott, c1978. 45 p. : ill. ; 27 cm. Illustrated instructions for constructing toys, games, and other amusements that recreate the fun of country fairs. [TT160.T37 1978] 77-23593 ISBN 0-397-31770-0 : 4.95
1. Handicraft—Juvenile literature. 2. Games—Juvenile literature. I. Thomson, Ruth, joint author. II. McEwan, Chris. III. Title.

TUTHILL, Marge. 745.5'02'40544
Arts and crafts for children : 52 projects for children to create on their own / Marge Tuthill. New York : Paulist Press, c1978. 110 p. : ill. ; 23 cm. Instructions for a variety of projects that can be done alone or with friends including straw painting, collages, macaroni necklaces, sock puppets, and stamp pictures. [TT160.T87] 78-51588 ISBN 0-8091-2114-X pbk. : 5.95
1. Handicraft—Juvenile literature. 2. Creative activities and seat work—Juvenile literature. I. Title. BIP

VAN ZANDT, Eleanor 745.5
More crafts for fun / by Eleanor Van Zandt and Ann Dunn. Garden City, N.Y. : Doubleday, 1975, c1974. 144 p. : ill. (some col.) ; 26 cm. "A Doubleday Dolphin book." Bibliography: p. 142-143. Step-by-step instructions with photos and diagrams for making such craft projects as a patchwork shoulder bag, glove puppets, hand-printed stationery, and embroidered zodiac designs. [TT160.V34 1975] 74-29181 ISBN 0-385-01277-2 pbk. : 5.95
1. Handicraft—Juvenile literature. I. Dunn, Ann, joint author. II. Title.

*VERMEER, Jackie. 745.5
The little kid's Americana craft book / Jackie Vermeer ; photography by Duane D. Davis. New York : Taplinger, 1976c1975. 128p. : ill. ; 25 cm. Includes index. A variety of American folk crafts are explored using contemporary materials. [TT160] 74-21698 ISBN 0-8008-4927-2 : 9.95
1. Summary: 2. Handicraft-Juvenile literature. I. Title. BIP

VERMEER, Jackie. 745.5
The little kid's craft book [by] Jackie Vermeer and Marian Lariviere. [1st ed.] New York, Taplinger Pub. Co. [1973] 128 p. illus. (part col.) 25 cm. Ideas and instructions for craft activities involving clay, mosaics, mobiles, puppets, nature study, and much more. [TT160.V47] 72-8324 8.95
1. Handicraft—Juvenile literature. I. Lariviere, Marian, joint author. II. Title. BIP

VERMEER, Jackie. 745.59
The little kid's four seasons craft book / Jackie Vermeer and Marian Lariviere. 1st ed. New York : Taplinger Pub. Co., 1974. 128 p., [4] leaves of plates : ill. (some col.) ; 25 cm. Includes index. Ideas and instructions for using natural materials in craft activities commemorating the seasons and their holidays. [TT160.V48 1974] 73-18791 ISBN 0-8008-4926-4 : 9.95
1. Handicraft—Juvenile literature. I. Lariviere, Marian, joint author. II. Title.

WEISS, Harvey. 745.5
The gadget book. New York, Crowell [1971] 60 p. illus. (part col.) 24 cm. Lists the necessary equipment and gives instructions for making such items as a weather vane, sunbeam alarm clock, hand-held sail, and other useful and useless gadgets. [TT160.W43] 70-132307 ISBN 0-690-32124-4 4.50
1. Handicraft—Juvenile literature. I. Title.

WEISS, Harvey. 745.5
Sticks, spools, and feathers. New York, Young Scott Books [1962] 64 p. illus. 29 cm. [NK70.W4] 62-51701
1. Handicraft—Juvenile literature. I. Title.

WILLIAMS, Barbara. 745.59
Pins, picks, & popsicle sticks : a straight-line crafts book / Barbara Williams and Susan Arnold ; ill. by Susan Arnold. New York : Holt, Rinehart and Winston, c1977. 142 p. : ill. ; 24 cm. Illustrated directions for making household, party, and Christmas decorations, gifts, party favors, and toys from common materials such as pins, toothpicks, dowel rods, fabric scraps, and paint. [TT160.W5724] 76-41164 ISBN 0-03-017786-3 lib. bdg. : 5.95
1. Handicraft—Juvenile literature. I. Arnold, Susan, joint author. II. Title. III. Title: A straight-line crafts book. BIP

*WILLIAMS, Peter H. M. 372.5'5.
Lively craftwork [by] Peter H. M. Williams. Illus. by the author. London, Mills & Boon [1971, c.1969] 192 p. illus., col. plates. 2 fold. charts. 22 cm. "Suggestions for further reading": p. 191. [TT160] 0-263
1. Handicraft—Juvenile literature. 2. Creative activities. I. Title.
Available from Transatlantic Arts, Levittown, N.Y., for $9.95.

WISEMAN, Ann. 745.5
Making things; the hand book of creative discoveries. [1st ed.] Boston, Little, Brown [1973] 159 p. illus. 28 cm. Bibliography: p. 156-159. Instructions for making over 100 items from paper, potatoes, leaves, rope, bread, clay, and other easily available materials. [TT160.W5733] 73-760 6.95
1. Handicraft—Juvenile literature. I. Title. BIP

WISEMAN, Ann 745.5
Making things; the handbook of creative discoveries [1st ed.] Boston, Little, Brown and Co. [1975] 161 p. ill. (part col.) 27 cm. Includes indexes. Contents.Contents: Book 2 Includes bibliographies. Summary: instructions for making over 100 items from paper, string, bread, wire, clay, and other easily available materials. [TT160.W5733] 75-7789 8.95
1. Handicraft—Juvenile literature. I. Title.
Pbk; 4.95. BIP

WOODSIDE, John JUV
Boden's beasts. Designed by Arthur Boden. New York, Obolensky [1965] 1v. (unpaged) illus. (pt. col.) 24cm. (Astor bks.) [PZ10.W749Bo] 745.54 64-23777 3.95
1. Handicraft—Juvenile literature. 2. Animals—Juvenile literature. I. Boden, Arthur, illus. II. Title.

WOODSIDE, John. 745.59'2
Boden's beasts, by John Woodside. Designed by Arthur Boden. [New York] Two Continents Pub. Group [1975, c1964] p. cm. Instructions in verse for making animals from various household materials such as egg boxes, clothespins, and pill boxes. [TT160.W638 1975] 74-17281 ISBN 0-8467-0042-5 4.95
1. Handicraft—Juvenile literature. 2. Animals—Juvenile literature. I. Boden, Arthur, illus. II. Title. BIP

WOODSIDE, John. 745.59'2
Boden's birds, by John Woodside. Designed by Arthur Boden. [New York] Two Continents Pub. Group [1975, c1974] p. cm. Instructions in verse for making birds from various household materials—egg boxes, clothespins, pill boxes, etc. [TT160.W64 1975] 74-17282 ISBN 0-8467-0043-3 4.95
1. Handicraft—Juvenile literature. 2. Birds—Juvenile literature. I. Boden, Arthur, illus. II. Title.

WOODSIDE, John. 745.59
Boden's bugs, by John Woodside. Designed by Arthur Boden. [New York] Two Continents Pub. Group [1975] p. cm. Instructions in verse for making insects from such household materials as egg boxes, tape dispensers, and pill boxes. [TT160.W65] 74-17229 ISBN 0-8467-0044-1
1. Handicraft—Juvenile literature. 2. Insects—Juvenile literature. I. Boden, Arthur, illus. II. Title.

WYCKOFF, Joan. j745.5
Twist presents 34 selections from McCall's golden do-it book and the make-it book. Adapted by Joan Wyckoff. Edited by Nan Comstock New York, Golden Press, c1961. 64 p. illus. 28 cm. [NK70.T85] 62-463
1. Handicraft — Juvenile literature. I. Title.

Y4 Design (Group) 745.5
Creative activities ... program / [prepared and produced by Y4 Design for Regensteiner Publishing Enterprises].

[Chicago] : Childrens Press, c1974. 20 v. : col. ill. ; 25 cm. Contents.Contents.—1. Making.—2. Playing.—3. Discovering.—4. Performing.—5. Creating.—6. Collecting.—7. Communicating.—8. Producing.—9. Fooling.—10. Organizing.—11. Growing.—12. Caring.—13. Building.—14. Searching.—15. Foraging.—16. Traveling.—17. Exploring.—18. Sewing.—19. Cooking.—20. Finding, index and guide. [TT160.Y23 1974] 75-325669
1. Handicraft—Juvenile literature. 2. Games—Juvenile literature. I. Regensteiner Publishing Enterprises. II. Title.

YOUNG, Jean. 745.5
Woodstock kid's crafts / dreamed up by Jean Young. Indianapolis : Bobbs-Merrill, c1974. 125 p. : ill. ; 29 cm. Introduces the tools, materials, and techniques of tie dyeing, basket weaving, rock tumbling, and other crafts and projects. [TT160.Y64] 73-13223 ISBN 0-672-51906-2 : 7.95 ISBN 0-672-52027-3 pbk. : 3.95
1. Handicraft—Juvenile literature. I. Title.

ZECHLIN, Katharina. 745.59'2
Games you can build yourself / by Katharina Zechlin ; [translated by Manly Banister ; adapted by Burton Hobson]. New York : Sterling Pub. Co., [1975] 80 p. : ill. ; 24 cm. (Little craft book series) Translation of Dekorative Spiele zum Selbermachen. Includes index. Instructions for making and playing unusual and colorful games which can be enjoyed solo, with groups, or even as wall hangings. [TT160.Z3713] 74-82327 ISBN 0-8069-5308-X : 5.95
1. Handicraft—Juvenile literature. 2. Games—Juvenile literature. I. Title. BIP

Handicraft—Juvenile works.

LINCOLN, Martha. 684.8
A workshop of your own, by Martha Lincoln and Katharine Torrey. Boston, Houghton Mifflin, 1959. 148 p. illus. 15 x 20 cm. [TT160.L494] 59-5194
1. Handicraft—Juvenile works. I. Torrey, Katharine, joint author. II. Title.

Handicraft—Kentucky.

ROYCE, Craig Evan. 745'.092'2 B
Country miles are longer than city miles / by Craig Evan Royce ; photographs by Jeffrey Gitlin. Pasadena, Calif. : W. Ritchie Press, c1976. 125 p. : ill. ; 26 cm. [TT24.K4R68] 75-18098 ISBN 0-378-07897-6 ISBN 0-378-07892-5 pbk. : 6.95
1. Handicraft—Kentucky. 2. Artisans—Kentucky—Biography. I. Gitlin, Jeffrey. II. Title.

Handicraft—Latin America—Juvenile literature.

COMINS, Jeremy. 745.5'098
Latin American crafts and their cultural backgrounds. New York, Lothrop, Lee & Shepard Co. [1974] 128 p. illus. 25 cm. Bibliography: p. 124. Instructions for making sculpture, jewelry, and other objects in the style of ancient and modern Latin American craftsmen. [TT27.5.C65] 73-17704 ISBN 0-688-41582-2 4.50
1. Handicraft—Latin America—Juvenile literature. I. Title.
Library binding; 4.14, ISBN 0-688-51582-7.

Handicraft—Mexico.

HARVEY, Marian. 745.5'0972
Crafts of Mexico. Photos. by Ken Harvey. New York, Macmillan [1973] viii, 248 p. illus. 28 cm. Bibliography: p. 243-245. [TT28.M6H37] 72-86037 12.95
1. Handicraft—Mexico. I. Title.

SAYER, Chloe. 745.5'0972
Crafts of Mexico / Chloe Sayer ; photographed by Marcos Ortiz. Garden City, N.Y. : Doubleday, 1977. 142, [2] p. : ill. (chiefly col.) ; 27 cm. (Crafts of the world) Bibliography: p. [144] [TT28.S28] 76-51863 ISBN 0-385-13118-6 : 9.95
1. Handicraft—Mexico. I. Title. II. Series.

Handicraft—Mexico—Juvenile literature.

SOLEILLANT, Claude. 745.5
Activities & projects : Mexico in color / by Claude Soleillant ; [translated by Steven Morgenstern ; photos by Christian Murtin] . New York : Sterling Pub. Co., c1977. 96 p. : ill. (some col.) ; 20 cm. Translation of Activites aux couleurs du ... Mexique. Includes index. Presents instructions for costumes, games, food, handicraft items, decorations, dances, and a play which can be used as part of a party or festival with a Mexican theme. [TT28.S6413] 77-81955 ISBN 0-8069-4552-4 : 7.95 ISBN 0-8069-4553-2 lib.bdg. : 7.49
1. Handicraft—Mexico—Juvenile literature. 2. Cookery, Mexican—Juvenile literature. I. Murtin, Christian. II. Title. III. Title: Mexico. BIP

Handicraft—Minnesota.

CRAFTS in Minnesota. 680
[Minneapolis : Magazine Production Class, School of Journalism and Mass Communication, University of Minnesota, 1976] 48 p. : ill. ; 28 cm. [TT24.M6C7] 76-383821 1.50
1. Handicraft—Minnesota. I. Minnesota. University. School of Journalism and Mass Communication. Magazine Production Class.

Handicraft—New Jersey—History.

VAN HOESEN, Walter Hamilton, 1897- 745.5'0949
Crafts and craftsmen of New Jersey. Rutherford [N.J.] Fairleigh Dickinson University Press [1973] 251 p. illus. 21 cm. Bibliography: p. 242-243. [TT24.N5V35] 72-421 ISBN 0-8386-1080-3 11.00
1. Handicraft—New Jersey—History. 2. Artisans—New Jersey. I. Title. BIP

Handicraft—New York (City)—Equipment and supplies—Directories.

GLASSMAN, Judith. 338.4'7'7455028
New New York guide to craft supplies / Judith Glassman. 2d ed. New York : Workman Pub. Co., 1974. 244 p. ; 21 cm. Previous ed. published under title: New York guide to craft supplies. Includes index. Bibliography: p. 197-234. [TT12.G57 1974] 75-8809 ISBN 0-911104-48-8 pbk. : 2.95
1. Handicraft—New York (City)—Equipment and supplies—Directories. I. Title. II. Title: New York guide to craft supplies.

Handicraft—Nigeria.

FAGG, William Buller. 745.5'09669
The living arts of Nigeria. Edited by William Fagg. Photos. by Peccinotti. Illustrated by Michael Foreman. [1st American ed.] New York, Macmillan [1972, c1971] [106] p. (chiefly col. illus.) 26 cm. Bibliography: p. [106] [TT119.N54F34 1972] 72-77278 12.95
1. Handicraft—Nigeria. I. Title.

Handicraft—Ontario—Directories.

HIMEL, Susan. 745'.025'713
Handmade in Ontario : a guide to crafts and craftsmen / Susan Himel and Elaine Lambert. Toronto ; New York : Van Nostrand Reinhold, c1976. iv, 154 p. : ill. ; 19 cm. Includes index. Bibliography: p. 148-149. [TT27.O6H55] 75-43064 ISBN 0-442-29931-1 pbk. : 5.95
1. Handicraft—Ontario—Directories. 2. Artisans—Ontario—Directories. I. Lambert, Elaine, joint author. II. Title. BIP

Handicraft—Period.

MCCALL'S Christmas make-it ideas. v. 1- 394.268
[New York] [McCall Corp.] 1958- v. illus. (part col.) 19 cm. [TT1.M25] 58-4545
1. Handicraft—Period. 2. Christmas decorations—Period.

Handicraft—Scotland.

MACKAY, James Alexander. 745'.09411
Rural crafts in Scotland / James A. Mackay. London : R. Hale & Co., 1976. 188 p., [8] leaves of plates : ill., ports. ; 23 cm. [TT61.M3] 76-377191 ISBN 0-7091-5460-7 : £4.00
1. Handicraft—Scotland. I. Title. BIP

Handicraft—Scotland—Highlands of Scotland.

MANNERS, John. 680
Crafts of the Highlands and Islands / John Manners. Newton Abbot [Eng.] ; North Pomfret, Vt. : David & Charles, c1978. 128 p. : ill. ; 22 cm. Includes index. Bibliography: p. 125. [TT61.M35] 77-91719 ISBN 0-7153-7485-0 : 11.95
1. Handicraft—Scotland—Highlands of Scotland. I. Title. BIP

Handicraft—South America—Juvenile literature.

CONAWAY, Judith, 1948- 745.5
Manos : South American crafts for children / Judith Conaway. Chicago : Follett Pub. Co., c1978. 96 p. : ill. ; 21 x 26 cm. Suggests numerous craft projects that introduce handwork, such as brickmaking, weaving, and tooling, that is part of the South American culture. [TT34.C66] 78-3228 ISBN 0-695-41189-6 lib. bdg. : 8.97
1. Handicraft—South America—Juvenile literature. I. Title. BIP

Handicraft—Southwest, New.

MILLER, Marjorie Ann. 745.5'09701
Indian arts and crafts [by] Marjorie Miller. Illus. by Ann Bruce Chamberlain. Los Angeles, Nash Pub. [1972] 118 p. illus. 22 cm. [E78.S7M55] 78-167526 ISBN 0-8402-8006-8 2.45
1. Handicraft—Southwest, New. 2. Indians of North America—Southwest, New—Industries. 3. Indians of North America—Southwest, New—Art. I. Title.

MILLER, Marjorie Ann. 745.5'09701
Indian arts and crafts / Marjorie Miller ; ill. by Ann Bruce Chamberlain. New York : Galahad Books, [1974] c1972. 118 p. : ill. ; 22 cm. Originally published by Nash Pub., Los Angeles. [TT23.9.M54 1974] 73-90678 ISBN 0-88365-233-1 : 4.95
1. Handicraft—Southwest, New. 2. Indians of North America—Southwest, New—Industries. 3. Indians of North America—Southwest, New—Art. I. Title.

Handicraft—Southwest, New—Juvenile literature.

KRENZ, Nancy, 1937- 745.5
Southwestern arts and crafts projects, ages 5-12 / by Nancy Krenz and Patricia Byrnes. 2d. ed., rev. and enl. Santa Fe, N.M. : Sunstone Press, 1978. p. cm. Includes index. Includes instructions for a variety of projects with a Southwestern theme. [TT23.9.K73 1978] 77-18988 ISBN 0-913270-62-8 pbk. : 8.95
1. Handicraft—Southwest, New—Juvenile literature. I. Byrnes, Patricia, 1937- joint author. II. Title.

Handicraft—Study and teaching.

†ARANGIS, Louise M. 745.5
Treasury of creative handcraft activities for elementary teachers / Louise M. Arangis. West Nyack, N.Y. : Parker Pub. Co., c1976. 233 p. : ill. ; 26 cm. Includes index. [TT157.A69] 75-29278 ISBN 0-13-930545-9 : 12.95
1. Handicraft—Study and teaching. 2. Creative activities and seat work. I. Title. BIP

HAWS, Robert W. 670
Manufacturing in the school shop [by] Robert W. Haws [and] Carl J. Schaefer. 2d ed. Chicago, American Technical Society [1972] x, 126 p. illus., forms. 26 cm. [TT165.H38 1972] 70-175284 ISBN 0-8269-3626-1
1. Handicraft—Study and teaching. 2. Manufactures. I. Schaefer, Carl J., 1920- joint author. II. Title.

KAMPMANN, Lothar. 745.5
Creating with found objects. New York, Van Nostrand Reinhold [1973] 72 p. col. illus. 21 cm. (Art media series) Translation of Zufalliges und Gefundenes. Suggestions for making pictures, sculpture, and constructions out of such "found" objects as string, boxes, bottle tops, stones, and crumpled paper. [TT169.K3513] 72-2792 ISBN 0-442-24249-2 5.95
1. Handicraft—Study and teaching. 2. Found objects (Art) 3. Handicraft. I. Title.

LAXTON, Mike. 745.5'07
Using constructional materials. New York, Van Nostrand Reinhold [1974] p. cm. [TT168.L34] 73-14360 ISBN 0-442-29999-0 4.95
1. Handicraft—Study and teaching. I. Title.

LINDERMAN, Earl W. 372.5'5
Crafts for the classroom / Earl W. Linderman, Marlene M. Linderman. New York : Macmillan, c1977. xxiii, 497 p. : ill. ; 26 cm. Includes bibliographies and index. [TT150.L56] 74-3798 ISBN 0-02-370780-1 : 12.95
1. Handicraft—Study and teaching. I. Linderman, Marlene M., joint author. II. Title. BIP

LINSE, Barbara Bucher, 1924- 372.5'5
Arts and crafts for all seasons. Palo Alto, Calif., Fearon Publishers [1969] 66 p. illus. 29 cm. (A Fearon teacher-aid book) [TT165.L55] 68-57698 2.00
1. Handicraft—Study and teaching. I. Title. BIP

LYON, Jean, 1913- 745.5
Arts and crafts objects children can make for the home / Jean Lyon. West Nyack, N.Y. : Parker Pub. Co., c1976. p. cm. Includes index. [TT150.L94] 76-16781 ISBN 0-13-047068-6 : 12.95
1. Handicraft—Study and teaching. I. Title.
Distributed by Prentice Hall. BIP

ONTARIO. Sports and Fitness Division. 745.5
Arts & crafts : a manual for leaders / [prepared by Maggie Miles for the Sports and Fitness Division, Ministry of Culture and Recreation]. [Toronto] : Ministry of Culture and Recreation, [1976?] 108 p. : ill. ; 22 cm. Cover title. [TT150.O57 1976] 77-364685
1. Handicraft—Study and teaching. I. Miles, Maggie. II. Title.

THE Reinhold book of art and craft techniques, for parents, teachers, and children 745.5
/ [translation from the German by Alba Lorman] New York : Van Nostrand Reinhold, 1976. 190 p., [4] leaves of plates : ill. ; 19 cm. Translation of Basteln mit Kindern. Includes index. [TT157.B3513 1976] 75-38619 ISBN 0-442-26875-0. ISBN 0-442-26876-9 pbk.
1. Handicraft—Study and teaching.

ROBBINS, Ireene. 372.5'5
Arts and crafts from across the Nation : a 50-State treasury of classroom projects / Ireene Robbins. West Nyack, NY : Parker Pub. Co., 1977,c1978 p. cm. Includes index. [TT150.R6] 77-23875 ISBN 0-13-048819-4 : 12.95
1. Handicraft—Study and teaching. 2. United States—Study and teaching. I. Title.

SHIVERS, Jay Sanford, 1930- 745.5'07
Recreational crafts: programming and instructional techniques [by] Jay S. Shivers [and] Clarence R. Calder. New York, McGraw-Hill [1974] xiii, 440 p. illus. 25 cm. (McGraw-Hill series in health education, physical education, and recreation) Bibliography: p. 425-428. [TT168.S53] 73-18437 ISBN 0-07-056980-0 10.95
1. Handicraft—Study and teaching. I. Calder, Clarence R., joint author. II. Title.

WAGNER, Lee. 371.9'28
Teaching crafts to the mentally retarded. Minneapolis, T. S. Denison [1974] 115 p. illus. 29 cm. [TT169.W33] 73-92313 ISBN 0-513-01334-2 4.98 (lib. ed.)
1. Handicraft—Study and teaching. 2. Mentally handicapped—Education. I. Title.

SUBJECT INDEX HANDICRAFT — YEARBOOKS.

Handicraft—Study and teaching—Directories.

COYNE, John. 745.5
By hand; a guide to schools and careers in crafts [by] John Coyne & Tom Hebert. [1st ed.] New York, E. P. Dutton, 1974. 255 p. 22 cm. "A Sunrise book." Bibliography: p. [221]-223. [TT12.C69 1974] 73-18022 8.95
1. Handicraft—Study and teaching—Directories. 2. Artisans. I. Hebert, Tom, joint author. II. Title.

Handicraft—Study and teaching (Elementary)

ROGERS, Donald, 1923- 372.5'044
The Donald Rogers illustrated handbook of arts and crafts lesson plans for the elementary teacher : an innovative classroom-tested approach / Donald Rogers. West Nyack, N.Y. : Parker Pub. Co., 1977,c1976. 240 p. : ill. ; 26 cm. Includes index. [TT150.R63] 76-24823 12.95
1. Handicraft—Study and teaching (Elementary) I. Title. BIP

Handicraft—Sweden—History.

NYLEN, Anna-Maja, 1912- 746'.09485
Swedish handcraft / by Anna-Maja Nylen ; translated by Anne-Charlotte Harvey. New York : Van Nostrand Reinhold, [1976] p. cm. Translation of Hemslojd. Includes indexes. Bibliography: p. [TT89.N9513] 75-28331 ISBN 0-442-26090-3 : 35.00
1. Handicraft—Sweden—History. I. Title. BIP

Handicraft—Sweden—Juvenile literature.

LOFGREN, Ulf. 745.5'09485
Swedish toys, dolls, and gifts you can make yourself : traditional Swedish handcrafts / by Ulf Lofgren. New York : Collins + World in cooperation with the U.S. Committee on UNICEF, c1978. p. cm. (A Unicef storycraft book) Presents brief discussions of and easy-to-follow instructions for such traditional Swedish handicrafts as an Advent calendar, an Easter witch, and the Lapp four-wind hat. [TT89.L63] 78-8619 ISBN 0-529-05448-5 : 5.95. ISBN 0-529-05449-3 lib. bdg. : 5.91
1. Handicraft—Sweden—Juvenile literature. I. Title. II. Series. BIP

Handicraft—Tennessee.

KRECHNIAK, Helen Bullard, 1902- 745'.09768
Crafts and craftsmen of the Tennessee mountains / Helen Bullard. Falls Church, Va. : Summit Press, 1976. viii, 213 p. : ill. ; 23 cm. Includes index. Bibliography: p. 208. [TT24.T2K73] 76-11688
1. Handicraft—Tennessee. 2. Artisans—Tennessee. I. Title.

Handicraft. Toys.

PETTON, B W 1895- 633.7
How to build games and toys. New York, Van Nostrand 1951] 264 p. illus. 22 cm. [TT157.P36] 51-12772
1. Handicraft. Toys. I. Title.

Handicraft—United States.

KINNEY, Jean Brown. 745.5'0973
How to make 19 kinds of American folk art from masks to TV commercials [by] Jean and Cle Kinney. [1st ed.] New York, Atheneum, 1974. 121 p. illus. 26 cm. [TT23.K53 1974] 73-91014 7.95
1. Handicraft—United States. I. Kinney, Cle, joint author. II. Title. BIP

KINNEY, Jean Brown. 745.5'0973
21 kinds of American folk art and how to make each one [by] Jean and Cle Kinney. [1st ed. New York, Atheneum, 1972. 121 p. illus. 26 cm. [TT23.K56 1972] 70-175556 6.95
1. Handicraft—United States. 2. Folk art—United States. I. Kinney, Cle, joint author. II. Title.

NATIONAL Geographic Society, Washington, D.C. Special Publications Division. 680
The craftsman in America / prepared by the Special Publications Division, National Geographic Society, Washington, D.C. Washington : The Society, [1975] 199 p. : ill. ; 27 cm. Includes bibliographical references and index. [TT23.N37 1975] 74-28804 ISBN 0-87044-176-0 : 4.25
1. Handicraft—United States. 2. Artisans—United States. I. Title. BIP

PETTIT, Florence Harvey. 745.5'0973
How to make whirligigs and whimmy diddles and other American folkcraft objects, by Florence H. Pettit. Illustrated by Laura Louise Foster. New York, Crowell [1972] xvi, 349 p. illus. 24 cm. Bibliography: p. 334-335. [TT23.P47 1972] 78-175108 ISBN 0-690-41389-0 6.95
1. Handicraft—United States. I. Title. BIP

RAFFAELLI, Roberta. 745.5'0973
Early American crafts. [Des Moines] Creative Home Library [1974] 288 p. illus. 26 cm. Bibliography: p. 286. [TT23.R33] 74-13359 ISBN 0-696-19990-4 9.95
1. Handicraft—United States. I. Title.

WALTNER, Willard. 745.5
Heritage hobbycraft / Willard and Elma Waltner. Mount Vernon, N.Y. : Lantern Press, c1977. 128 p. : ill. ; 24 cm. Presents directions for American Indian baskets, a Pilgrim spool puppet, Appalachian cornhusk dolls, and other craft items representative of various cultures in America. [TT23.W34 1977] 77-19087 ISBN 0-8313-0105-8 : 7.95
1. Handicraft—United States. I. Waltner, Elma, joint author. II. Title. BIP

YATES, Raymond Francis, 1895- 745.5'0973
Early American crafts & hobbies; a treasury of skills, avocations, handicrafts, and forgotten pastimes and pursuits from the golden age of the American home, by Raymond F. & Marguerite W. Yates. Edited by Mary Lyon. New York, Funk & Wagnalls [1974, c1954] 221 p. illus. 23 cm. [TT23.Y37 1974] 74-166238 ISBN 0-308-10097-2 2.95
1. Handicraft—United States. 2. Hobbies. I. Yates, Marguerite W., joint author. II. Title.

Handicraft—United States—Appalachian region.

CRUTCHFIELD, James Andrew, 1938- 745.5'0974
A primer of handicrafts of the southern Appalachians / by James A. Crutchfield. Nashville : Williams Press, c1976. [63] p. : ill. ; 29 cm. Bibliography: p. [62]-[63] [TT23.2.C78] 77-372213
1. Handicraft—United States—Appalachian region. I. Title.

Handicraft—United States—Catalogs.

THE Goodfellow catalog of wonderful things : traditional & contemporary crafts / [edited by] Christopher Weills. New York : Berkley Pub. Corp., 1977. xi, 418 p. : ill. ; 28 cm. (A Berkley Windhover book) Includes indexes. Bibliography: p. 378-380. [TT23.G66] 77-153935 ISBN 0-425-03402-X : 7.95 680
1. Handicraft—United States—Catalogs. 2. Artisans—United States—Directories. I. Weills, Christopher. BIP

Handicraft—United States—Directories.

COLIN, Paul, 1946- 745.5'07
Craft sources : the ultimate catalog for craftspeople / Paul Colin and Deborah Lippman. New York : M. Evans, [1975] 242 p. : ill. ; 29 cm. Includes bibliographical references and index. [TT12.C64] 75-12543 ISBN 0-87131-183-6 : 12.50 ISBN 0-87131-184-4 pbk. 5.95
1. Handicraft—United States—Directories. 2. Handicraft—Bibliography. I. Lippman, Deborah, joint author. II. Title. BIP

FEINMAN, Jeffrey. 745.5'025'73
The catalog of kits / by Jeffrey Feinman. New York : Morrow, 1975. 251 p. : ill. ; 29 cm. Includes index. [TT12.F44] 75-12590 ISBN 0-688-05283-5 pbk. : 6.95
1. Handicraft—United States—Directories. 2. Handicraft—United States—Catalogs. I. Title. BIP

GOUSHA (H. M.) Company. 338.4'7'745502573
American crafts guide; a comprehensive directory to craft shops, galleries, crafts schools, museums, and studios of individual craftsmen across the United States. [Editor: Marian May. 1st ed.] San Jose, Calif., Gousha Publications [1973] 222 p. illus. 21 cm. On spine: Gousha American crafts guide. [TT12.G68 1973] 72-97826 ISBN 0-913040-19-3 3.95 (pbk.)
1. Handicraft—United States—Directories. I. May, Marian, ed. II. Title. III. Title: Gousha American crafts guide.

Handicraft—United States—Equipment and supplies—Directories.

ROSENBLOOM, Joseph. 381'.45'7455028
Craft supplies supermarket / Joseph Rosenbloom. Willits, Calif. : Oliver Press, 1974. x, 214 p. (p. 206-212 advertisements) : ill. ; 22 cm. (Finder's guide ; no. 2) A directory. Pages 213-214 blank for "Notes." Includes index. [TT12.R64] 74-84298 ISBN 0-914400-01-0 pbk. : 3.95
1. Handicraft—United States—Equipment and supplies—Directories. I. Title.

Handicraft—United States—History.

BOWLES, Ella (Shannon) 1886- 746
Homespun handicrafts. With 60 illus. New York, B. Blom, 1972. 251 p. illus. 21 cm. Reprint of the 1931 ed. [TT23.B68 1972] 75-183343 15.75
1. Handicraft—United States—History. I. Title. BIP

TRUPP, Philip Zbar. 973
The art of craftsmanship : an examination of the historical values which have shaped the American spirit / written by Philip Trupp ; illustrated by Hugh Frost. Washington : Acropolis Books, c1976. p. cm. Originally printed in 1969 for the members of the National Tool, Die, and Precision Machining Association. [TT23.T78] 76-25595 ISBN 0-87491-043-9 pbk. : 3.95
1. Handicraft—United States—History. I. Title. BIP

Handicraft—United States—History—Juvenile literature.

HOOPLE, Cheryl G. 745.5'0973
The heritage sampler : a book of colonial arts & crafts / by Cheryl G. Hoople ; pictures and diagrs. by Richard Cuffari. New York : Dial Press, [1975] x, 132 p. : ill. ; 25 cm. Bibliography: p. 131-132. Discusses the practical necessity of the crafts employed by the American colonists. Includes instructions for duplicating the crafts today. [TT23.H66] 75-9203 ISBN 0-8037-5414-0 : 5.95. ISBN 0-8037-5430-2 lib. bdg. : 5.47
1. Handicraft—United States—History—Juvenile literature. 2. United States—History—Colonial period, ca. 1600-1775—Juvenile literature. 3. Cookery—Juvenile literature. I. Cuffari, Richard, 1925- II. Title. BIP

Handicraft—United States—Juvenile literature.

COLBY, Carroll B. 670
Early American crafts; tools, shop, and products, by C. B. Colby. New York, Coward-McCann [1967] 48 p. illus. 28 cm. [TT23.C64] 67-24212
1. Handicraft—U.S.—Juvenile literature. I. Title.

FISHER, Leonard Everett. 640
The homemakers. Written & illustrated by Leonard Everett Fisher. New York, Franklin Watts, 1973. 48 p. illus. 22 cm. (Colonial Americans) Describes how four staples—candles, soap, brooms, and cider—were made in colonial times. [TT23.F56] 73-5692 ISBN 0-531-01047-3 3.95
1. Handicraft—United States—Juvenile literature. I. Title. BIP

MEYER, Carolyn. 745.5'0973
People who make things : how American craftsmen live and work / Carolyn Meyer. 1st ed. New York : Atheneum Publishers, 1975. 200 p. : ill. ; 22 cm. "A Margaret K. McElderry book." Traces the history of spinning and weaving, patchwork and quilting, silversmithing, jewelry making, glassblowing, pottery, woodworking, and bookbinding and examines the lives of two or three artisans working in each craft. [TT23.M48 1975] 74-18189 ISBN 0-689-50012-2 lib.bdg. : 6.50
1. Handicraft—United States—Juvenile literature. 2. Artisans—United States—Juvenile literature. I. Title. BIP

Handicraft—Vocational guidance.

SOMMER, Elyse. 338.4'7'7455023
Career opportunities in crafts / by Elyse Sommer. New York : Crown Publishers, c1977. viii, 280 p. : ill. ; 23 cm. Includes index. Bibliography: p. 255-260. [TT149.S58 1977] 76-40322 ISBN 0-517-52873-8 : 10.95 pbk. : 5.95
1. Handicraft—Vocational guidance. I. Title. BIP

Handicraft—Vocational guidance—Juvenile literature.

BRENT, Patricia Jenkins. 745.5'023
Crafts careers / Patricia Jenkins Brent ; photos. by Daniel Arthur. New York : Watts, 1977. 66 p. : ill. ; 24 cm. (A Career concise guide) Includes index. Considers various aspects of a career in crafts, such as training, licensing, professional organizations, and marketing, and discusses ten crafts in detail. [TT160.B818] 77-6479 ISBN 0-531-01304-9 lib.bdg. : 4.47
1. Handicraft—Vocational guidance—Juvenile literature. I. Arthur, Daniel. II. Title. BIP

Handicraft—Wales.

JOHN, Brian Stephen. 680
Rural crafts of Wales / [by] Brian S. John. Newport, Dyfed : Greencroft Books, 1976. [1], 37 p. : ill., ports. ; 21 cm. Bibliography: p. 37. [TT63.J63] 77-361663 ISBN 0-9504014-9-8 : £0.65
1. Handicraft—Wales. I. Title.

JONES, Mary Eirwen. 670'.09429
Welsh crafts : an account of the historic Welsh crafts and as they exist today / Mary Eirwen Jones. London : Batsford, 1978. 160 p., [8] leaves of plates : ill. ; 23 cm. Includes index. [TT63.J66] 78-314639 ISBN 0-7134-1087-6 : 11.50
1. Handicraft—Wales. I. Title.
Distributed by Hippoirene Books BIP

Handicraft—Wisconsin.

WHYTE, Bertha Kitchell, 1890- 745.5'09775
Craftsmen of Wisconsin. [1st ed.] Racine, Wis., Western Pub. Co. [1971] 222 p. illus. (part col.), map (on lining paper), ports. (part col.) 29 cm. Includes bibliographical references. [NK835.W6W5] 79-150495 15.00
1. Handicraft—Wisconsin. I. Title.

Handicraft — Yearbooks.

HOUSE & garden crafts guide. [New York, Conde Nast Publications] v. illus. (part col.) 32 cm. annual. [TT159.H6] 64-4263 v. 12
1. Handicraft — Yearbooks. I. Title: Crafts guide.

SCIENCE and mechanics. 745.5'06'01
Toys and games you can make. Chicago. Science and Mechanics Pub. Co. v. illus. 24cm. (Science and mechanics handbook annual) [TT1.S35] 58-45055
1. Handicraft—Yearbooks. 2. Toys—Yearbooks. I. Title.

Handicrafts.

*BURNS, Elena G. 745.5
Recycling with imagication; mix a little "magic" with imagination and you have imagication: the formula for recycling paper and plastic containers into exciting decorative gifts, even furniture, by Elena. Woodland Hills, Calif. [1973 c.1972] v. illus. 22 cm. [TT160] 1.95 (pbk)
1. Handicrafts. 2. Paper work. I. Title.
Order from the author, P.O. Box 851, Woodland Hills, CA 91364.

*JORDAN, Eve. 745.5
Arts & crafts at home. New York, House of Collectibles [1973] 191 p. illus. 18 cm. Cover title: Step by step arts & crafts at home. [TT160] ISBN 0-87637-148-9 1.95 (pbk.)
1. Handicrafts. I. Title.
Publisher's address: 17 Park Ave., New York, NY 10016 BIP

*SAWYER, Ruth Bassette 745.5
Diversional therapy; arts and crafts for the hospital patient. New York, Exposition [1967] 68p. illus. 21cm. Bibl. 4.00
1. Handicrafts. I. Title.

Handicrafts—Juvenile literature.

**WIRE, wood and cork.* 745.5
New York, Franklin Watts [1972] 171 p., color illus., 31 cm. This is a book of projects that can be made with wire, wood and cork. [TT160] 71-187310 ISBN 0-531-02556-X 5.95
1. Handicrafts—Juvenile literature. BIP

Handkerchiefs.

BRAUN-RONSDORF, Margarete. 391.'4
The history of the handkerchief. by Dr. M. Braun-Ronsdorf. Leigh-on-Sea (Ex.) F. Lewis. 1967. 39p. 56 plates. 30cm. Bibl. [GT2350.B7] 67-77035 35.00
1. Handkerchiefs. I. Title.
Available from Textile Book Service, P. O. Box 656, Metuchen, N. J. 08840. BIP

Handpress.

HARRIS, Elizabeth M. 681'.62
The common press : being a record, description, & delineation of the early eighteenth-century handpress in the Smithsonian Institution, with a history & documentation of the press / by Elizabeth Harris ; and drawings & advice on construction by Clinton Sisson. Boston : D. R. Godine, 1978. 62 p. : ill. ; 28 cm. & portfolio (8 fold. leaves of plates : ill. ; 28 cm.) Issued in a case. Includes bibliographical references. [Z249.H28] 77-79005 ISBN 0-87923-211-0 : 20.00
1. Franklin, Benjamin, 1706-1790. 2. Smithsonian Institution. 3. Handpress. 4. Handpress—Drawings. I. Title. BIP

Handpress—Handbooks, manuals, etc.

ALLEN, Lewis M. 655.3'12
Printing with the handpress. Herewith a definitive manual by Lewis M. Allen to encourage fine printing through hand-craftsmanship. Kentfield, Calif., Allen Press, 1969. 75 p. illus. 31 cm. "Edition limited to 140 copies." Bibliography: p. 75. [Z249.A48] 71-6534
1. Handpress—Handbooks, manuals, etc. I. Title. BIP

ALLEN, Lewis M. 686.2'253
Printing with the handpress : herewith a definitive manual by Lewis M. Allen to encourage fine printing through hand-craftsmanship. Huntington, N.Y. : R. E. Krieger Pub. Co., 1976, c1969. 75 p. : ill. ; 29 cm. Reprint of the ed. published by Van Nostrand Reinhold, New York. Includes index. Bibliography: p. 75. [Z249.A48 1976] 75-42044 ISBN 0-88275-379-7 : 11.50
1. Handpress—Handbooks, manuals, etc. I. Title.

Handspinning.

KLUGER, Marilyn. 746.1'2
The joy of spinning : the first complete book on handspinning for the hobbyist and craftsman, from choosing a wheel to carding, spinning, and dyeing the handspun yarns with native plant dyes / by Marilyn Kluger ; illustrated by Nanene Queen Jacobson. New York : Simon and Schuster, [1978] c1971. 187 p. : ill. ; 24 cm. (A Fireside book) Includes index. Bibliography p. 157. [TT847.K58 1978] 78-103173 ISBN 0-671-24213-X pbk. : 4.95
1. Handspining. I. Title.

Haniwa.

MIKI, Fumio, 1911- 730'.952
Haniwa / by Fumio Miki ; translated and adapted with an introd. by Gina Lee Barnes. 1st ed. New York : Weatherhill, 1974. 151 p. : ill. (some col.) ; 23 cm. (Arts of Japan ; 8) Includes index. Bibliography: p. 147-148. [NB159.J3M5413] 73-88477 ISBN 0-8348-2714-X. ISBN 0-8348-2715-8 pbk. : 7.95
1. Haniwa. BIP

Hansegger, John Konstantin, 1908-

LARSEN, Erik 759.9494
Hansegger, a contribution to a critical study of his art. Hpsg. von A. Eric Scotoni [Dust. New York, Heinman, 1962, c.1961] 100p. illus. (pt. col.) 29cm. German, French, English. Bibl. 62-3991 8.00 bds.,
1. Hansegger, John Konstantin, 1908- I. Title.

Hanson, Joseph Mellor, 1900-

ZIFF, Paul. 759.2
J. M. Hanson. Ithaca, N.Y., Cornell University Press [1962] 51 p. 33 plates. 28 cm. [ND497.H334Z5] 62-14826
1. Hanson, Joseph Mellor, 1900- I. Title. BIP

Hanukkah decorations.

ROCKLAND, Mae Shafter. 745.59'41
The Hanukkah book / Mae Shafter Rockland. New York : Schocken Books, 1975. xii, 174 p. : ill. ; 24 cm. Includes index. [TT900.H34R6] 75-10609 ISBN 0-8052-3590-6 : 10.00
1. Hanukkah decorations. I. Title. BIP

Happening (Art)

HENRI, Adrian. 709'.04
Environments and happenings. New York, Praeger [1974] p. cm. (World of art) Bibliography: [PN3203.H4] 72-79509 10.00
1. Happening (Art) I. Title.

KAPROW, Allan. 700.8
Assemblage, environments & happenings. Text and design by Allan Kaprow. With a selection of scenarios by: 9 Japanese of the Gutai Group, Jean-Jacques Lebel [and others] New York, H. N. Abrams [1966] 341 p. illus., ports. 32 cm. Title on p. [146] and [147]; false title on p. [1] and [2]: Step right in. Scenarios selected complement those published in M. Kirby's Happenings, an illustrated anthology, 1965. Cf. p. 210. [NX458.K3] 65-17018
1. Happening (Art) 2. Environment (Art) 3. Assemblage (Art) I. Gutai Bijutsu Kyokai. II. Lebel, Jean Jacques. III. Title. IV. Title: Step right in.

VOSTELL, Wolf, 1932- 709'.24
Miss Vietnam, and texts of other happenings. Translated by Carl Weissner. San Francisco, Nova Broadcast Press, 1968. 39 p. illus. 20 cm. (Nova broadcast, 2) [PN3205.V62] 74-229938 1.65
1. Happening (Art) I. Title.

WHITECHAPEL Art 700'.92'4
Gallery, London.
Leopoldo Maler, mortal issues, a sanctuary with flames & figures : [catalogue of an exhibition held in the] Main Gallery [of Whitechapel Art Gallery], 26 February-4 April 1976. London : Whitechapel Art Gallery, [1976] 12 p. : ill., ports. ; 30 cm. Bibliography: p. 10-11. [PN3206.W438 1976] 76-364247
1. Maler, Leopoldo, 1937- 2. Happening (Art) I. Maler, Leopoldo, 1937- II. Title.

Harari, Michael—Art collections.

HILLIER, Jack Ronald. 759.952'074
The Harari Collection of Japanese paintings and drawings. Catalogue compiled by J. Hillier. [1st ed.] Boston, Boston Book and Art [1970- v. illus., plates (part col.) 32 cm. Contents.Contents.—v. 1. Genre and Ukiyo-e school (excluding Hokusai and his school and Hiroshige)—v. 2. Hokusai and his school and Hiroshige. Bibliography: v. 2, p. 353-354. [N7352.H54] 73-120286
1. Harari, Michael—Art collections. 2. Art, Japanese—Catalogs. I. Title.

Harding, Helen Mary—Art collections.

MINNESOTA Museum of 707.4'0176581
Art.
Adventure with art: the Helen Mary Harding Collection. Saint Paul [1972] [32] p. illus. (1 col.) 24 cm. (Minnesota Museum of Art. Catalog. 115) "Paintings, drawings, sculpture, prints, by major twentieth century artists, 15 June-17 September 1972, Minnesota Museum of Art." [N6487.S18M52] 72-86125
1. Harding, Helen Mary—Art collections. 2. Art, Modern—20th century—Exhibitions. I. Title. II. Series.

Hardingstone—Antiquities.

WOODS, Peter John, 1936- 913.3'6
Excavations at Hardingstone, Northants, 1967-8, by P. J. Woods; a report to Northamptonshire County Council. Northampton, Northamptonshire County Council, 1969. [1], iii, 91 (i.e. 123 p.) (13 fold.), plate. illus. 26 cm. Cover title. [DA690.H24W6] 75-488156 free
1. Hardingstone—Antiquities. I. Northamptonshire, Eng. County Council. II. Title.

Hare, Chauncey, 1934-

HARE, 779'.9'30917309240924
Chauncey, 1934-
Interior American / Chauncey Hare ; designed by Marvin Israel and Kate Morgan. Millerton, N.Y. : Aperture, inc., c1978. 174 p., [1] leaf of plates : chiefly ill. ; 24 x 30 cm. [TR820.5.H37] 78-66663 ISBN 0-89381-028-2 : 20.00
1. Hare, Chauncey, 1934- 2. Photography, Documentary. 3. United States—Social life and customs—Pictorial works. I. Title.

Hare, James H., 1856-1946.

GOULD, Lewis L. 770'.92'4 B
Photojournalist : the career of Jimmy Hare / by Lewis L. Gould & Richard Greffe. Austin : University of Texas Press, c1977. 157 p. : ill. ; 26 cm. Includes bibliographical references and index. [TR140.H37G68] 76-52920 ISBN 0-292-74004-2 : 12.95
1. Hare, James H., 1856-1946. 2. Photography, Journalistic. 3. Photographers—United States—Biography. I. Greffe, Richard, 1947- joint author. II. Title. BIP

Harlequin—Art.

THE disguises of 759.5
Harlequin; a series of paintings by Giovanni Domenico Ferretti (1692-1768) belonging to the John and Mable Ringling Museum of Art, Sarasota, Florida. An exhibition organized and presented by the University of Kansas Museum of Art, in Lawrence, with loans of supplementary works by the artist from the Samuel J. Bloomingdale collection of New York, November-December, 1956. [Lawrence, 1956?] 1v. (unpaged) illus., port. 25cm. [ND623.F35K3] 927.5 57-62639
1. Harkquin—Art. I. Kansas. University. Museum of Art. II. Ferretti, Giovanni Domenico, 1692-1768. III. John and Mable Ringling Museum of Art, Sarasota, Fla.

Harlem, New York (City)—History.

SCHOENER, Allon, comp. 974.71
Harlem on my mind; cultural capital of Black America, 1900-1968, edited by Allon Schoener. Pref. by Thomas P. F. Hoving. Introd. by Candice Van Ellison. New York, Random House [1969, c1968] 255 p. illus., ports. 29 cm. Supplements an exhibition held at the Metropolitan Museum of Art in 1969 and organized by the museum in association with the New York State Council on the Arts. [F128.68.H3S3] 68-28558 12.95
1. Harlem, New York (City)—History. 2. Negroes—New York (City) I. New York (City) Metropolitan Museum of Art. II. New York (State) State Council on the Arts. III. Title. BIP

Harmsen, William—Art collections—Catalogs.

HARMSEN, Dorothy. 704.94'9'978
American Western art : a collection of one hundred twenty-five Western paintings and sculpture with biographies of the artists / by Dorothy Harmsen ; foreword by Bill Harmsen. [Denver] : Harmsen Pub. Co., c1977. xiii, 256 p. : col. ill. ; 31 cm. On spine: Harmsen Collection, v. 2. Bibliography: p. 254-256. [N8214.5.U6H28] 77-80017 ISBN 0-9601322-1-X : 40.00
1. Harmsen, William—Art collections—Catalogs. 2. Harmsen, Dorothy—Art collections—Catalogs. 3. The West in art—Catalogs. 4. Art, Modern—19th century—Catalogs. 5. Art, Modern—20th century—Catalogs. 6. Artists—Biography. I. Title.
Available from Two Continents BIP

Harnett, William Michael, 1848-1892.

FRANKENSTEIN, Alfred 927.5
Victor, 1906-
After the hunt; William Harnett and other American still life painters, 1870-1900. Berkeley, University of California Press, 1953. xiii, 189 p. plates (1 col.) 29 cm. Bibliographical footnotes. [ND237.H315F7] 759.13 53-11237
1. Harnett, William Michael, 1848-1892. 2. Painters, American. 3. Still-life painting. 4. Painting, American. I. Title. BIP

FRANKENSTEIN, Alfred 759.13
Victor, 1906-
After the hunt; William Harnett and other American still life painters, 1870-1900 [by] Alfred Frankenstein. Rev. ed. Berkeley, University of California Press, 1969. xix, 200 p. illus., col. front. 29 cm. (California studies in the history of art, 12) Bibliographical footnotes. [ND237.H315F7 1969] 68-31417 16.50
1. Harnett, William Michael, 1848-1892. 2. Painters—United States. 3. Still-life painting, American. I. Title. II. Series.

Harold Warp Pioneer Village, Minden, Neb.

WARP, Harold. 973'.074'0182394
A history of man's progress, from 1830 to the present; a complete and historical description in chronological order of items on display at the Harold Warp Pioneer Village ... Rev. issue. Minden, Neb., Harold Warp Pioneer Village, 1967. 415 p. illus., ports. 32 cm. [GN37.M53W3 1967] 67-8671
1. Harold Warp Pioneer Village, Minden, Neb. I. Title.

Harpers Ferry, W. Va.—Description—Views.

REBER, James 779'.9'9754990924
Quinter, 1911-
Harpers Ferry / photography by James Q. Reber ; with narrative by James V. Murfin. Chevy Chase, Md. : J. Q. Reber Photo Publications, c1975. 89 p., [2] leaves of plates : ill. ; 29 cm. [F249.H2R42] 75-26366 ISBN 0-9600892-1-7 : 10.95. ISBN 0-9600892-2-5 pbk.
1. Harpers Ferry, W. Va.—Description—Views. I. Murfin, James V. II. Title.

Harris, Allen, 1924-1970.

PENNSYLVANIA Academy of 730'.92'4
the Fine Arts, Philadelphia.
Allen Harris memorial exhibition. Philadelphia [1972] 1 v. (unpaged) illus. 27

cm. Catalog of the exhibition held Mar. 14-Apr. 9, 1972. [NB237.H26P4] 76-190479
1. Harris, Allen, 1924-1970. I. Title.

Harris, Kenneth, 1904—

HARRIS, Kenneth, 1904- 759.13
The necessity for nonconformity : selected works of Kenneth Harris ; designed by Edward A. Conner. Norfolk : Donning, c1976. 128 p. : ill. (some col.) ; 28 cm. [N6537.H35A53] 76-28375 ISBN 0-915442-21-3 : 12.95
1. Harris, Kenneth, 1904- 2. Europe in art. 3. Chesapeake Bay in art. I. Title.

Harris, Lawren Stewart, 1885-1970.

HARRIS, Lawren Stewart, 1885-1970. 759.11
Lawren Harris / edited by Bess Harris and R. G. P. Colgrove ; and with an introd. by Northrop Frye. Toronto : Macmillan of Canada, 1976, c1969. xii, 146 p. : ill. (some col.) ; 22 x 28 cm. [ND249.H28H3 1976] 77-368957 ISBN 0-7705-1453-7 : 14.95
1. Harris, Lawren Stewart, 1885-1970. 2. Painters—Canada—Biography. I. Harris, Bess, ed. II. Colgrove, R. G. P., ed.

Harris, Paul, 1925—

LEON, Dennis. 709'.2'4
Paul Harris / Dennis Leon. New York : H. N. Abrams, [1975] p. cm. (Modern artists) Bibliography: p. [N6537.H36L46] 75-1480 ISBN 0-8109-0359-8 : 7.95
1. Harris, Paul, 1925- **BIP**

Harrison, Liz, 1947—

HARRISON, Liz, 1947- 709'.2'4
Liz Harrison, 24 days in the life of a papaver : an environment [at the] Ideas gallery, 13 January-8 February 1976. London : White-chapel Art Gallery, [1976] . Folder ([4] p.) : ill., port. ; 30 cm. Bibliography: p. [4] [N6797.H33W47] 76-366728 ISBN 0-85488-028-3 : £0.22
1. Harrison, Liz, 1947- I. Whitechapel Art Gallery, London. II. Title: 24 days in the life of a papaver.

Harrison, Thomas, 1744-1829—Exhibitions.

GROSVENOR Museum, Chester, Eng. 720'.22'2
The modest genius : [catalogue of] an exhibition of drawings and works of Thomas Harrison / [editor Margaret Gillison]. [Chester] : [Grosvenor Museum], [1977] 26 p. : ill. ; 21 x 30 cm. Cover title. "The exhibition ... made possible through the joint co-operation of the Grosvenor Museum, the Cheshire County Museum Service and the North-West Museums and Art Gallery Service." [NA997.H27G76 1977] 77-375628 £0.40
1. Harrison, Thomas, 1744-1829—Exhibitions. I. Harrison, Thomas, 1744-1829. II. Cheshire County Museum Service. III. North-West Museums and Art Gallery Service. IV. Title.

Harry Northwood Glass Company.

EDWARDS, Bill. 748.2'9148'89
Northwood, king of carnival glass / by Bill Edwards. Paducah, Ky. : Collector Books, c1978. 132 p. : col. ill. ; 22 cm. [NK5439.C35E35] 78-113418 ISBN 0-89145-070-X : 8.95
1. Harry Northwood Glass Company. 2. Carnival glass. I. Title. **BIP**

HARTUNG, Marion T. 748.2
Northwood pattern glass: clear, colored, custard, and carnival, by Marion T. Hartung. [1st ed. Emporia? Kan., 1969] 101 p. illus. (part col.) 28 cm. Cover title: Northwood pattern glass in color. [NK5112.H34] 72-11038 9.95
1. Harry Northwood Glass Company. I. Title.

Hart, Joel Tanner, 1810-1877.

COLEMAN, John Winston, 1898- 709'.2'2
Three Kentucky artists—Hart, Price, Troye / J. Winston Coleman, Jr. Lexington : University Press of Kentucky, [1974] 76 p., [4] leaves of plates : ill. ; 21 cm. (The Kentucky bicentennial bookshelf) "Partial list of portraits by Samuel Price": p. 44-[48] [N6530.K4C64] 74-7873 ISBN 0-8131-0202-2 pbk. : 3.95
1. Hart, Joel Tanner, 1810-1877. 2. Price, Samuel Woodson, 1828-1918. 3. Troye, Edward, 1808-1874. 4. Art—Kentucky. I. Title. II. Series.

Hartley, Marsden, 1877-1943.

*AMES, Polly Scribner. 759.13
Marsden Hartley in Maine (through the eyes of Katie Young of Corea, Maine) by (Polly) Scribner Ames. With illus. by the author, a foreword by Elizabeth McCausland and an afterword by Carl Sprinchorn. Edited by Richard S. Sprauge. Orono, Me., Univ. of Maine Pr., 1972. 36 p. illus. 16 x 23 cm. (Maine studies, 94)
1. Hartley, Marsden, 1943. I. Young, Katie. II. Sprague, Richard S., ed. III. Title. **BIP**

AMES, Polly Scribner. 759.13 B
Marsden Hartley in Maine (through the eyes of Katie Young of Corea, Maine) by (Polly) Scribner Ames, with illus. by the author. A foreword by Elizabeth McCausland, and an afterword by Carl Sprinchorn. Edited by Richard S. Sprague. Orono, University of Maine Press, 1972. 36 p. illus. 16 x 24 cm. (Maine studies, 94) [ND237.H3435A84] 73-153218 2.95
1. Hartley, Marsden, 1877-1943. I. Young, Katie. II. Title. III. Series.

HARTLEY, Marsden, 1877-1943. 769'.92'4
Marsden Hartley: lithographs and related works. [Lawrence? Kan., 1972] [40] p. illus. 23 cm. ([Kansas. University. Museum of Art] Miscellaneous publications, no. 85) Catalogue of an exhibition held at the University of Kansas Museum of Art, March 19-Apr. 16, 1972. Includes bibliographical references. [NE2312.H3K3] 72-611425
I. Kansas. University. Museum of Art. II. Title. III. Series.

HARTLEY, Marsden, 1877-1943. 769'.92'4
Marsden Hartley: lithographs and related works. [Lawrence? Kan., 1972] [40] p. illus. 23 cm. ([Kansas. University. Museum of Art] Miscellaneous publications, no. 85) Catalogue of an exhibition held at the University of Kansas Museum of Art, March 19-Apr. 16, 1972. Includes bibliographical references. [NE2312.H3K3] 72-611425
I. Kansas. University. Museum of Art. II. Title. III. Series.

MCCAUSLAND, Elizabeth, 1899- 759.13
Marsden Hartley. Minneapolis, University of Minnesota Press [1952] xi, 80 p. illus. 26 cm. Bibliography: p. 76-80. [ND237.H3435M3] 52-7483
1. Hartley, Marsden, 1877-1943. I. Title.

Hartmann, Sadakichi, 1867-1944.

FOWLER, Gene, 1890-1960. 927
Minutes of the last meeting. New York, Viking Press, 1954. 277 p. illus. 22 cm. [N8375.H34F6] 54-6425
1. Hartmann, Sadakichi, 1867-1944. I. Title.

HARTMANN, Sadakichi, 1867-1944. 770
The vailant knights of Daguerre : selected critical essays on photography and profiles of photographic pioneers / by Sadakichi Hartmann ; edited by Harry W. Lawton and George Knox, with the collaboration of Wistaria Hartmann Linton ; foreword by Thomas F. Barrow ; bibliography compiled by Michael Elderman. Berkeley : University of California Press, c1978. xiii, 364 p. : ill. ; 28 cm. Includes index. Bibliography: p. 335-358. [TR642.H37 1978] 76-47987 ISBN 0-520-03356-6 : 25.00
1. Hartmann, Sadakichi, 1867-1944. 2. Photography, Artistic—History and criticism. I. Lawton, Harry W. II. Knox, George. III. Linton, Wistaria Hartmann. IV. Title.

Hartung, Hans, 1904—

GIBSON, Michael, 1929- 759.3
Hans Hartung. [New York, Lefebre Gallery, c1971] [12] p. illus. 19 cm. Caption title. Catalog of an exhibition, Feb. 2-Mar. 6, 1971, Lefebre Gallery, New York. [ND588.H34G5] 72-198422
1. Hartung, Hans, 1904- I. Lefebre Gallery.

GINDERATAEL, Roger van, 1899- 759.3
Hans Hartung. Tr. by W. J. Stachan. New York, Universe Bks. [c.1961] 125, [3]p. illus. (col.) ports. 29cm. Bibl. 61-14584 12.00
1. Hartung, Hans, I. Title.

HARTUNG, Hans, 1904- 759.3
Hans Hartung. Text by Umbro Apollonio. Translated by John Shepley. New York, H. N. Abrams [1972, c1966] 1 v. (unpaged) 202 illus. (79 col.) 32 cm. Includes a bibliography. [ND588.H34A813] 72-4459 ISBN 0-8109-0163-3 35.00
I. Apollonio, Umbro, 1911-

HARTUNG, Hans, 1904- 759.3
Hans Hartung. [Houston, Tex., Museum of Fine Arts, 1969] 55 p. (chiefly plates (part col.), port.) 29 cm. Cover title: Hartung. Catalog of the exhibition held Apr. 24-July 6, 1969, in the Museum of Fine Arts, Houston. Exhibition also held Sept. 10-Oct. 6, 1969, in the Musee du Quebec, Quebec, and Oct. 14-Dec. 7, 1969, in the Musee d'art contemporain, Montreal. [ND588.H34A45] 75-85542
I. Houston, Tex. Museum of Fine Arts. II. Quebec (City). Musee de la province de Quebec. III. Museum of Contemporary Art, Montreal.

NEW York (City). Metropolitan Museum of Art. 759.3
Hans Hartung : paintings, 1971-1975 : [exhibition], October 16, 1975-January 4, 1976 : [catalogue]. New York : Metropolitan Museum of Art, 1975. p. cm. Bibliography: p. [ND588.H34N48 1975] 75-31609 ISBN 0-87099-145-0 : 4.95
1. Hartung, Hans, 1904- I. Hartung, Hans, 1904-

Harunobu, 1725?-1770.

HILLIER, Jack Ronald. 769'.924
Suzuki Harunobu; an exhibition of his colour-prints and illustrated books on the occasion of the bicentenary of his death in 1770. Catalogue by Jack Hillier. [Philadelphia] Philadelphia Museum of Art; distributed by Boston Book and Art [Boston, 1970] 239 p. illus. (part col.) 32 cm. Held at the Philadelphia Museum of Art Sept. 18 to Nov. 22, 1970. "The colour-prints of Suzuki Harunobu by Jack Hillier": p. 7-21; also in Japanese: p. 22-32. Captions in English and Japanese. Bibliography: p. 236-238. [NE1325.S85H5] 77-125547 ISBN 0-8435-2005-1 25.00
I. Suzuki, Harunobu, 1725?-1770. II. Philadelphia Museum of Art.

KONDO, Ichitaro, 1910-1961. 761.283
Suzuki Harunobu, 1725?-1770. Text by Ichitaro Kondo. Translated and adapted by Kaoru Ogimi. [1st English ed.] Tokyo, Rutland, Vt., C. E. Tuttle Co. [1956] 1 v. (unpaged) illus. (part col.) 18 cm. (Kodansha library of Japanese art, no. 7) Title also in Japanese on t. p. Bibliography: [1] p. at end. [NE1325.H3K6] 56-11124
1. Harunobu, 1725?-1770. I. Series.

Harvard University. Graduate School of Design. Library.

HARVARD University. Graduate School of Design. Library. 019'.1
Catalogue of the Library of the Graduate School of Design, Harvard University. Boston, Mass., G. K. Hall, 1968. 44 v. 37 cm. [Z5945.H28 1968] 73-169433
1. Harvard University. Graduate School of Design. Library. 2. Architectural design—Bibliography—Catalogs. 3. Engineering design—Bibliography—Catalogs. I. Title.

Harvard University. Library.

ACKERMAN, James S. 016.72'0945
A bibliography of Italian Renaissance and baroque architecture, with classification numbers of volumes in the Harvard University collections / compiled by James S. Ackerman and John A. Pinto. Cambridge, Mass. : [s.n.], 1974. 31 p. ; 28 cm. Cover title. [Z5944.I8A35] [NA1115] 75-321160
1. Harvard University. Library. 2. Architecture—Italy—Bibliography. 3. Architecture, Renaissance—Italy—Bibliography. 4. Architecture, Baroque—Italy—Bibliography. 5. Classification—Books—Architecture. I. Pinto, John A., joint author. II. Title: A bibliography of Italian Renaissance and baroque architecture ...

Harvard University. Library. Houghton Library.

HARVARD University. Library. Houghton Library. 016.296
Hebrew manuscripts in the Houghton Library of the Harvard College Library : a catalogue / prepared by Mordechai Glatzer ; edited by Charles Berlin and Rodney Gove Dennis. Cambridge, Mass. : Harvard University Library, 1975. 68 p. : ill. ; 23 cm. Includes indexes. [Z6621.H34H44] [BM495] 75-329641
1. Harvard University. Library. Houghton Library. 2. Manuscripts, Hebrew—Cambridge, Mass.—Catalogs. 3. Manuscripts, Hebrew—Facsimiles. I. Glatzer, Mordechai. II. Title.

Harvard University. Peabody Museum of Archaeology and Ethnology.

BREW, John Otis, 1906- 913.03'1'07401444
Early days of the Peabody Museum at Harvard University. Cambridge, Mass., The Museum, 1966. 18 p. illus., ports. 24 cm. [GN37.C333B7] 68-3604
1. Harvard University. Peabody Museum of Archaeology and Ethnology. I. Title.

BREW, John Otis, 1906- 913.03'1'07401444
People and projects of the Peabody Museum, 1866-1966, by J. O. Brew. Cambridge, Peabody Museum of Harvard University, 1966. iv, 59 p. illus. (on cover) 24 cm. "The Peabody Museum Library, by Margaret Currier, librarian": p. 57-59. [GN37.C353B72] 75-9817
1. Harvard University. Peabody Museum of Archaeology and Ethnology. I. Title.

Hasidism—Pictorial works.

MOSKOWITZ, Ira. 760'.092'4
The Hasidim. Paintings, drawings, and etchings by Ira Moskowitz. Text by Isaac Bashevis Singer and the artist. New York, Crown Publishers [1973] 31, [122] p. illus. (part col.) 29 cm. [ND237.M79S56 1973] 72-84288 ISBN 0-517-50047-7 10.00
1. Moskowitz, Ira. 2. Hasidism—Pictorial works. I. Singer, Isaac Bashevis, 1904- II. Title.

Haskell, Ernest, 1876-1925.

MOORE, Russell J. 760'.092'4
Ernest Haskell, 1876-1925, a retrospective exhibition : a portfolio of selected work / introd. by Ruth Fine Lehrer ; catalogue by Russell J. Moore ; organized by the Bowdoin College Museum of Art. Brunswick, Me. : The Museum, 1976. 1 portfolio (26 p., [8] leaves of plates) : ill. ; 28 cm. Includes bibliographical references. [N6537.H365M66] 76-382184
1. Haskell, Ernest, 1876-1925. I. Haskell, Ernest, 1876-1925. II. Lehrer, Ruth Fine. III. Bowdoin College. Museum of Art. IV. Title.

Hasselblad camera.

BARRY, Les. 771.31
Hasselblad photography. New York,

Universal Photo Books [1959] 128p. illus. 24cm. [TR263.H3B3] 59-12541
1. Hasselblad camera. 2. Photography—Handbooks, manuals, etc. I. Title.

FREYTAG, Heinrich.　　　　　771.3'1
The Hasselblad way: the Hasselblad photographer's companion [by] H. Freytag; translated [from the German] and adapted by L. A. Mannheim. London, New York, Focal P., 1968. 419 p. illus. (incl 12 col.) 22 cm. Translation of Das Hasselblad-Buch. [TR263.H3F713] 71-377662 63/-
1. Hasselblad camera. 2. Photography—Handbooks, manuals, etc. I. Title.　　**BIP**

FREYTAG, Heinrich Walter　771.3'1
The Hasselblad way; the Hasselblad photographer's companion [by] H. Freytag. 4th ed. London, New York, Focal Press; distributed in the U.S.A. by Amphoto, New York [1972] 423 p. illus. 22 cm. "Translated and adapted by L. A. Mannheim from Das Hasselblad-Buch." [TR263.H3F713 1972] 75-82670 ISBN 0-8174-0620-4 16.95 (U.S.)
1. Hasselblad camera. 2. Photography—Handbooks, manuals, etc. I. Title.

Hastings, Warren, 1732-1818—Fiction.

BRAUTLACHT, Erich, 1902-　709.43
Versuchung in Indien; der Fall Warren Hastings: Roman. Hamburg, P. Zsolnay, 1958. 298 p. 21 cm. [PT2603.R393V4] 58-47506
1. Hastings, Warren, 1732-1818—Fiction. I. Title.

Hatch, John Davis—Art collections.

HATCH, John　741.9'73'0740941835
Davis.
100 American drawings : loan exhibition from the collection of John Davis Hatch ... [autumn exhibition] National Gallery of Ireland, Dublin, 7th September-8th October 1976 .. / [catalogue entries by Gary Burger Dublin : National Gallery of Ireland, [1976] [74] p., [50] leaves of plates : ill. ; 25 cm. (Heim exhibition catalogues ; no. 26) On spine: American drawings. Includes index. Bibliography: p. [72] [NC105.H26 1976] 77-363055
1. Hatch, John Davis—Art collections. 2. Drawing, American—Exhibitions. I. Burger, Gary. II. Dublin. National Gallery of Ireland. III. Heim Gallery. IV. Title. V. Title: American drawings. VI. Series: Heim exhibition catalogues (Dublin) ; no. 26.

HATCH, John Davis.　708'.21'32 s
100 American drawings : loan exhibition from the collection of John Davis Hatch ... [autumn exhibition] National Gallery of Ireland, Dublin, 7th September-8th October, 1976 / [catalogue entries by Gary Burger] London : Heim Gallery (London), [1976] [74] p., [50] leaves of plates : ill. ; 25 cm. (Heim exhibition catalogues ; no. 26) On spine: American drawings. Includes index. Bibliography: p. [72] [N8640.H4 no. 26] [NC105] 741.9'73'07402132 77-363084
1. Hatch, John Davis—Art collections. 2. Drawing, American—Exhibitions. I. Burger, Gary. II. Dublin. National Gallery of Ireland. III. Heim Gallery. IV. Title. V. Title: American drawings. VI. Series.

Hatchett, Duayne, 1925—

HATCHETT, Duayne, 1925-　730'.92'4
Duayne Hatchett: recent paintings and sculpture. [Buffalo, N.Y., Buffalo Fine Arts Academy, 1974] 36 p. illus. 22 cm. Exhibition held at the Albright-Knox Art Gallery, Buffalo, N.Y., Mar. 1-31, 1974. Bibliography: p. 33. [N6537.H37A74] 74-166174
1. Hatchett, Duayne, 1925- I. Albright-Knox Art Gallery.

Hatpins.

MEYER, Florence E.　739.27'8
Pins for hats and cravats worn by ladies and gentlemen / by Florence E. Meyer. [Des Moines : Wallace-Homestead Book Co., 1974] [52] p. : ill. ; 23 cm. Bibliography: p. [51]-[52] [NK7695.M48] 75-303169 5.95
1. Hatpins. 2. Stickpins. I. Title.

Hatpins—Collectors and collecting.

BAKER, Lillian.　739.27'8
The collector's encyclopedia of hatpins and hatpin holders / by Lillian Baker. Paducah, Ky. : Collector Books, c1976. viii, 216 p. : ill. (some col.) ; 29 cm. Includes indexes. Bibliography: p. 177-179. [NK7695.B34] 77-357307 ISBN 0-89145-016-5 : 19.95
1. Hatpins—Collectors and collecting. 2. Hatpin holders—Collectors and collecting. I. Title. II. Title: Hatpins and hatpin holders.　　**BIP**

Hats.

FELDMAN, Annette.　746.9'2
The hat book / Annette Feldman. New York : Van Nostrand Reinhold, c1978. 96 p., [2] leaves of plates : ill. ; 28 cm. Includes index. [TT655.F45] 78-7877 ISBN 0-442-21559-2 : 11.95
1. Hats. I. Title.　　**BIP**

KILGOUR, Ruth Edwards.　391.4
A pageant of hats, ancient and modern. [1st ed.] New York, R. M. McBride Co. [1958] 389 p. illus. 26 cm. Bibliography: p. 385-386. [GT2110.K5] 58-10648
1. Hats. I. Title.

SEVERN, William.　391.4
Here's your hat. Illustrated by Vana Earle. New York, D. McKay Co. [1963] x, 209 p. illus. 23 cm. Bibliography: p. 202-205. [GT2110.S4] 63-18873
1. Hats. I. Title.

WILCOX, Ruth Turner, 1888-　391.4
The mode in hats and headdress, including hair styles, cosmetics, and jewelry. New York, Scribner [1959] xiii, 348 p. illus. 26 cm. Bibliography: p. 345-348. [GT2110.W5 1959] 59-14064
1. Hats. I. Title.

Hats—History.

DE COURTAIS, Georgine.　391'.2
Women's headdress and hairstyles in England from AD 600 to the present day. London, B. T. Batsford [1973] 183 p. illus. 25 cm. Bibliography: p. 176-177. [GT2110.D42] 73-331251 ISBN 0-7134-0858-8
1. Hats—History. 2. Hairdressing—Great Britain—History. 3. Veils—History. I. Title.
Distributed by Rowman and Littlefield, 10.00.

Hats—Juvenile literature.

KENWORTHY, Leonard Stout, 1912-　391'.43
Hats, caps, and crowns / Leonard S. Kenworthy. New York : J. Messner, c1977. p. cm. Includes index. Depicts headgear of people all over the world. [GT2110.K44] 77-23800 ISBN 0-671-32874-3 : 6.64
1. Hats—Juvenile literature. I. Title.　　**BIP**

Haughton, Benjamin, 1865-1924.

PORTSMOUTH City Museum and　759.2
Art Gallery.
Benjamin Haughton R.B.A., 1865-1924 : paintings presented to Portsmouth City Museum by Miss B. Haughton : [catalogue of an exhibition held from] 21st Sept. to 20th Oct. 1974. [Portsmouth Eng.] : Portsmouth City Museum and Art Gallery, [1974] 29 p. : ill. ; 30 cm. Cover title. Bibliography: p. 29 [ND497.H39P67 1974] 75-329027
1. Haughton, Benjamin, 1865-1924.

Haussmann, Georges Eugene, Baron, 1809-1891.

SAALMAN, Howard.　711'.4'0944361
Haussmann: Paris transformed. New York, G. Braziller [1971] 128 p. illus. 25 cm. (Planning and cities) Bibliography: p. 121-122. [HT169.F72P367 1971] 76-143399 ISBN 0-8076-0583-2 5.95
1. Haussmann, Georges Eugene, Baron, 1809-1891. 2. Cities and towns—Planning—Paris. I. Title.

Havasupai Indians—Basket making.

MCKEE, Barbara.　746.4'1
Havasupai baskets and their makers, 1930-1940 / by Barbara and Edwin McKee and Joyce Herold; basket photos by E. Tad Nichols. [Flagstaff, Ariz.] : Northland Press, [1975] xvii, 142 p. : ill. ; 25 cm. Bibliography: p. 141-142. [E99.H3M32] 74-82364 ISBN 0-87358-134-2 : 8.50
1. Havasupai Indians—Basket making. 2. Indians of North America—Southwest, New—Basket making. I. McKee, Edwin Dinwiddie, 1906- joint author. II. Herold, Joyce, joint author. III. Title.　　**BIP**

Havell, William, 1782-1857.

READING, Eng. Museum and　759.2
Art Gallery.
William Havell, 1782-1857; [catalogue of an exhibition held at Reading Museum and Art Gallery, February 20th-March 21st 1970] Reading, Reading Museum and Art Gallery, 1970. [56] p. illus. 26 cm. Includes bibliographical references. [N6797.H35R4] 77-487091 10/8
1. Havell, William, 1782-1857.

Haverlin, Carl.

KATCHAMAKOFF, Atanas,　709.24
1898-
Atanas Katchamakoff: Leskovetz, La Quinta. Los Angeles 90069. Zeitlin & Ver Brugge. 815 North La Cienega. 1965. 100p. (chiefly illus. (pt. col.) ports 29cm. Includes a brief biog. by Carl Haverlin. [N6537.K3H3] 66-564 12.50
1. Haverlin, Carl. I. Title.

Haviland china.

SCHLEIGER, Arlene, 1907-　738.2'7
Two hundred patterns of Haviland china. Illus. by Richard R. Schleiger. [3d rev. ed. Omaha, 1967- v. illus. 22 cm. [NK4399.H4S34] 67-6751
1. Haviland china. I. Title.　　**BIP**

SCHLEIGER, Arlene, 1907-　738.27
Two hundred patterns of Haviland china. Illus. by Richard R. Schleiger. [Omaha, 1950-55] 3v. illus. 22cm. [NK4399.H4S3] 50-14180
1. Haviland china. I. Schleiger, Richard R., illus. II. Title.

SCHLEIGER, Arlene, 1907-　738.27
Two hundred patterns of Haviland china. [Rev. ed.] Illus. by Richard R. Schleiger. [Omaha, 1953- v. illus. 22cm. [NK4399.H4S32] 53-386570
1. Haviland china. I. Schleiger, Richard R., illus. II. Title.

YOUNG, Harriet (Gallagher)　738.27
1910-
Grandmother's Haviland. Chicago, c1962. 99 p. illus. 22 cm. Includes bibliography. [NK4399.H4Y6] 62-53507
1. Haviland china. I. Title.

YOUNG, Harriet　738.2'7
(Gallagher) 1910-
Grandmother's Haviland [by] Harriet Young. [2d rev. ed. Des Moines, Wallace-Homestead Book Co., c1970] 200 p. illus. (part col.), facsims., port. 26 cm. [NK4399.H4Y6 1970] 78-22994
1. Haviland china. I. Title.

Hawaii Co., Hawaii—Description and travel.

WENKAM, Robert,　779'.9'9196910924
1920-
The Big Island, Hawaii / by Robert Wenkam. Chicago : Rand McNally, 1975. 117 p. : ill. (some col.) ; 36 cm. [DU628.H28W46] 75-21313 ISBN 0-528-81020-0 : 25.00
1. Wenkam, Robert, 1920- 2. Hawaii Co., Hawaii—Description and travel. I. Title.

Hawken rifle.

BAIRD, John D., 1928-　683'.42
Fifteen years in the Hawken Lode, by John D. Baird. 1st ed. Chaska, Minn., Buckskin Press, 1971. ix, 120 p. illus.,

facsims., ports. 29 cm. [TS535.B17] 77-26197
1. Hawken rifle. 2. Shooting. I. Title.　**BIP**

BAIRD, John D., 1928-　623.4'425
Hawken rifles, the mountain man's choice, by John D. Baird. 1st ed. Franklin, Ind., Printed by Franklin Printing Service [1968] xvii, 95 p. illus. ports. 29 cm. [TS535.B18] 68-5344
1. Hawken, Samuel T., 1792-1884. 2. Hawken, Jacob, 1786-1849. 3. Hawken rifle. I. Title.

Hawken, Samuel T., 1792-1884.

BAIRD, John D., 1928-　623.4'425
Hawken rifles, the mountain man's choice, by John D. Baird. 1st ed. Franklin, Ind., Printed by Franklin Printing Service [1968] xvii, 95 p. illus., ports. 29 cm. [TS535.B18] 68-5344
1. Hawken, Samuel T., 1792-1884. 2. Hawken, Jacob, 1786-1849. 3. Hawken rifle. I. Title.

Hawkins, Irene, fl. 1942-1947.

SITWELL, Sacheverell,　741'.092'4
Sir, bart., 1897-
A note for bibliophiles / by Sacheverell Sitwell. [Badby] : [The author], [1976] [15] p. : facsims. ; 22 cm. Limited ed. of 30 signed copies. No. 21. [NC1883.3.H38S58] 76-379262 ISBN 0-903591-24-3
1. Hawkins, Irene, fl. 1942-1947. 2. Book jackets—Great Britain. I. Title.

Hawksmoor, Nicholas, 1661-1736.

DOWNES, Kerry.　720'.924
Hawksmoor. New York, Praeger [1970, c1969] 216 p. illus., plans, plates, port. 22 cm. Based on the author's thesis, 1959. Bibliography: p. 212-213. [NA997.H3D62 1970] 72-100032 8.50
1. Hawksmoor, Nicholas, 1661-1736.

Hawthorne, Charles Webster, 1872-1930.

CONNECTICUT. University.　759.13
Museum of Art.
The paintings of Charles Hawthorne. [Intro. by Marvin S. Sadik, director. Storrs, Conn.] 1968. [88] p. illus. (1 col.), ports. 28 cm. Catalogue of an exhibition held at the University of Connecticut Museum of Art, Storrs, Oct. 12-Nov. 17, 1968; Hirschl & Adler Galleries, New York, Dec. 5-31, 1968. [ND237.H37C6] 72-625360
1. Hawthorne, Charles Webster, 1872-1930. I. Sadik, Marvin S. II. Hirschl & Adler Galleries. III. Title.

Hawthorne, Nathaniel, 1804-1864. The marble faun.

BARNETT, Gene Austin.　330.9'73 s
Art as setting in The marble faun [by] Gene A. Barnett. (In Wisconsin Academy of Sciences, Arts and Letters. Transactions. Madison. 23 cm. v. 54 (1965) p. 231-247) Bibliographical footnotes. [[AS36.W7 vol.54]] A68
1. Hawthorne, Nathaniel, 1804-1864. The marble faun. I. Title.

Haydon. Benjamin Robert. 1786-1846.

GEORGE, Eric.　759.2
The life and death of Benjamin Robert Haydon, historical painter, 1786-1846. 2nd ed. with additions by Dorothy George. Oxford, Clarendon Pr., 1967. xiii, 400p. front., 20 plates (incl. ports.). 23cm. Bibl. [ND497.H4G4 1967] 67-113552 7.20
1. Haydon. Benjamin Robert. 1786-1846. I. George, Mary Dorothy (Gordon) II. Title. Available from Oxford Univ. Pr., New York.

HAYDON, Benjamin Robert,　927.5
1786-1846.
Diary. Edited by Willard Bissell Pope. Cambridge, Harvard University Press, 1960-63. 5 v. illus., ports., facsims. 25 cm. Contents.CONTENTS. -- v. 1. 1808-1815. -- v. 2. 1816-1824. -- v. 3. 1825-1832. -- v. 4. 1832-1840. -- v. 5. 1840-1846.

SUBJECT INDEX HEFZI-BAH. ISRAEL. BETH

Bibliographical footnotes. [ND497.H4A37] 60-5394
I. Title. BIP

OLNEY, Clarke, 1901- 927.5
Benjamin Robert Haydon, historical painter. Athens, University of Georgia Press [1952] xiv, 309 p. illus., ports. 24 cm. Bibliography: p. 272-280. [ND497.H4O43] 52-14773
1. Haydon, Benjamin Robert, 1786-1846. I. Title.

Hayter, Stanley William, 1901-

CORCORAN Gallery of Art, Washington, D.C. 760'.092'4
Stanley William Hayter: paintings, drawings, and prints, 1928-1950; [exhibition,] May 12-June 16, 1973. Washington [1973] [20] p. illus. 18 x 23 cm. Catalog. Introd. by J. Kainen. [NE642.H35C67] 73-81800
1. Hayter, Stanley William, 1901- I. Kainen, Jacob.

LIMBOUR, Georges, 1902- 759.2
Hayter. [Paris, G. Fall, dist. New York, Efron] c.1962. 77p. col. illus. 19cm. (Le Musee de poche) 62-52313 1.50 pap.,
1. Hayter, Stanley William, 1901- I. Title.

Head.

LOOMIS, Andrew, 1892- 743.491
Drawing the head and hands. New York, Viking Press, 1956. 154p. illus. 32cm. [NC770.L6] 55-9640
1. Head. 2. Hand. 3. Drawing—Instruction. I. Title. BIP

Head in art.

GORDON, Louise. 743'.49
How to draw the human head : techniques and anatomy / Louise Gordon. New York : Viking Press, 1977. 120 p. : ill. ; 26 cm. (A studio book) Includes index. [NC770.G67] 77-832 ISBN 0-670-38328-7 : 7.95
1. Head in art. 2. Anatomy, Artistic. 3. Drawing—Instruction. I. Title. BIP

LOW, Joseph, 1911- 759.13
Heads. [Newtown, Conn. Eden Hill Press [c1960] [54]p. (on double leaves) col. illus. 16 x 22cm. 'Printed by the artist from his original cuts in an edition of 450 copies ... Number 89.' [NE1215.L65A46] 62-3687
I. Title.

LUCCHESI, Bruno, 1926- 731'.74
Modeling the head in clay / sculpture by Bruno Lucchesi ; text and photos. by Margit Malmstrom. New York : Watson-Guptill Publications, c1979. p. cm. Includes index. Bibliography: p. [NB1932.L8 1979] 79-350 ISBN 0-8230-3098-9 : 17.95
1. Head in art. 2. Modeling. 3. Sculpture—Technique. I. Malmstrom, Margit. II. Title.

LUCCHESI, Bruno, 1926- 731'.74
Modeling the head in clay / sculpture by Bruno Lucchesi ; text and photos. by Margit Malmstrom. New York : Watson-Guptill Publications, c1979. p. cm. Includes index. Bibliography: p. [NB1932.L8 1979] 79-350 ISBN 0-8230-3098-9 : 17.95
1. Head in art. 2. Modeling. 3. Sculpture—Technique. I. Malmstrom, Margit. II. Title. BIP

MILLS, John W. 731'.82
Head and figure modelling / John W. Mills. London : B. T. Batsford, 1977. 137 p. : ill. ; 26 cm. Includes index. [NB1930.M5] 77-364247 ISBN 0-7134-3258-6 : 10.95
1. Head in art. 2. Human figure in art. 3. Modeling. I. Title.
Distributed by Hippocrene Books, New York.

Heade, Martin Johnson, 1819-1904.

STEBBINS, Theodore E. 759.13
The life and works of Martin Johnson Heade / Theodore E. Stebbins, Jr. New Haven : Yale University Press, 1975. xix, 303 p., [4] leaves of plates : ill. (some col.) ; 29 cm. (Yale publications in the history of art ; 26) Includes index. Bibliography: p. 198-201. [ND237.H39S68] 74-83794 ISBN 0-300-01808-8 : 30.00
1. Heade, Martin Johnson, 1819-1904. I. Title. II. Series. BIP

Health facilities—Design and construction.

AMERICAN Hospital Association. 725'.5
Directory of architects for health facilities. Chicago : American Hospital Association, c1975. vi, 49 p. : forms ; 28 cm. [RA967.A47 1975a] 75-325772 ISBN 0-87258-170-5 pbk. : 6.50
1. Health facilities—Design and construction. 2. Architects—United States—Directories. I. Title. BIP

AMERICAN Hospital Association. 658.2
Selection of architects for health facility projects / American Hospital Association. Chicago : The Association, c1975. p. cm. [RA967.A47 1975] 75-26726
1. Health facilities—Design and construction. 2. Architects—Selection and appointment. I. Title.

Health facilities—Design and construction—Directories.

AMERICAN Hospital Association. 725'.5'0922
Directory of architects for health facilities. 1977 ed. Chicago : American Hospital Association, c1977. v, 51 p. : forms ; 28 cm. [RA967.A47 1977] 77-22270 ISBN 0-87258-217-5 : 6.50
1. Health facilities—Design and construction—Directories. 2. Architects—United States—Directories. I. Title.

Health facilities—Design and construction—Estimates—United States.

HOSPITAL/HEALTHCARE 658.1'54
building costs / J. H. Farley, chief editor ; L. D. Varela, editorial assistant. 2d ed. New York : Dodge Building Cost Services, McGraw-Hill Information Systems Co., c1977. ii, 125 leaves ; 29 cm. (Dodge research report) [RA967.H587 1977] 77-152936
1. Health facilities—Design and construction—Estimates—United States. 2. Health facilities—United States—Design and construction—Costs. I. Farley, J. H. II. Varela, L. D. III. McGraw-Hill Information Systems Company. Dodge Building Cost Services.

Health facilities—Design and construction—Exhibitions.

A Portfolio of 725'.5'0973
architecture for health. Chicago : American Hospital Association, c1977. v, 160 p. : ill. ; 28 cm. "Represents 77 health facility design projects that were exhibited at the 1976 American Hospital Association convention." "AHA catalog no. 2300." Includes indexes. [RA967.P63] 77-23782 ISBN 0-87258-219-1 : 17.50
1. Health facilities—Design and construction—Exhibitions. 2. Health facilities—United States—Design and construction—Exhibitions. I. American Hospital Association.

Health facilities—United States—Design and construction.

UNITED States. Congress. House. Committee on Interstate and Foreign Commerce. Subcommittee on Public Health and Welfare. 690.5'51'0973
Hospital and health facility construction and modernization. Hearings, Ninety-first Congress, first session, on H.R. 6797...H.R. 7059...[and] H.R. 3783 ... Washington, U.S. Govt. Print. Off., 1969. vii, 368 p. illus., forms, map. 23 cm. Hearings held Mar. 25-28, 1969. "Serial no. 91-8." [RA967.U453] 77-601583
1. Health facilities—United States—Design and construction. I. Title.

Healy, Anne.

HEALY, Anne. 730'.92'4
Monumenta '76 : Newport, Rhode Island, August 1 through September 5, 1976 / Anne Healy. Newport, R.I. : Monumenta Newport, 1976. 24 p. : ill. ; 29 cm. [NB237.H37M66] 76-29179
1. Healy, Anne. I. Monumenta Newport Inc. II. Title.

Healy, George Peter Alexander, 1813-1894.

DE MARE, Marie. 927.5
G. P. A. Healy, American artist; an intimate chronicle of the nineteenth century. Introd. by Eleanor Roosevelt. New York, McKay [1954] 304 p. illus. 24 cm. [ND237.H4D4] 759.13 53-11377
1. Healy, George Peter Alexander, 1813-1894.

VIRGINIA Museum of Fine Arts, Richmond. 757.9
A souvenir of the exhibition entitled Healy's sitters; or, A portrait panorama of the Victorian Age, being a comprehensive collection of the likenesses of some of the most important personages of Europe & America, as portrayed by George Peter Alexander Healy between the years 1837 and 1899, supplemented with documents relating to the artist's life and furnishings of the period, on view at the Virginia Museum of Fine Arts ... 24 January-5 March 1950. [Richmond] 1950 94 p. illus., map. 26 cm [ND237.H4V5] 50-58174
1. Healy, George Peter Alexander, 1813-1894. 2. Portraits — Exhibitions. I. Title.

Hearst-San Simeon State Historical Monument.

MARTIN, Carolyn. 704.94'7'074019478
Hearst Castle : mythology, legend, history in art / by Carolyn Martin. Cambria, Calif. : Galatea Publications, c1977. 44 p. : ill., ; 22 cm. Bibliography: p. 44. [N7760.M3] 77-152576
1. Hearst-San Simeon State Historical Monument. 2. Gods in art. 3. Legends—Illustrations. 4. History in art. I. Title.

Heart in art.

DELPIRE, Robert. 704.94'2
The book of hearts / Robert Delpire et Andre Martin. New York : Warner Books, 1977. 76 p. : all col. ill. ; 21 cm. [N8217.H53D44] 77-154466 ISBN 0-446-87495-7 pbk. : 5.50
1. Heart in art. 2. Art. I. Martin, Andre, photographer, joint author. II. Title. BIP

Heartfield, John, 1891-1968.

HEARTFIELD, John, 1891-1968. 779'.9'320943085
Photomontages of the Nazi period / John Heartfield ; [essay by Wieland Herzfelde translated by Eva Bergoffen, all other translations from German by Nancy Reynolds]. New York : Universe Books, 1977. 143 p. : ill. ; 26 cm. Translation of Krieg im Frieden. Bibliography: p. 142. [TR685.H4213] 76-41663 ISBN 0-87663-281-9 : 10.00 ISBN 0-87663-954-6 pbk. : 5.95
1. Heartfield, John, 1891-1968. 2. Photography, Composite. 3. National socialism—Caricatures and cartoons. 4. German wit and humor, Pictorial. I. Herzfelde, Wieland. II. Title. BIP

Heaven—Art.

HUGHES, Robert, 1936- 704.948'4
Heaven and hell in Western art. New York, Stein and Day [1968] 288 p. illus. (part col.) 29 cm. Bibliographical references included in "Notes" (p. 283-284) [N8150.H8] 68-27617 17.50
1. Heaven—Art. 2. Hell—Art. I. Title.

Heaven in art.

CAVENDISH, Richard. 704.948
The visions of heaven and hell / by Richard Cavendish. New York : Harmony Books, 1977. p. cm. [N7793.H4C38 1977] 77-5402 ISBN 0-517-53097-X : 12.00 ISBN 0-517-53098-8 pbk. : 6.95
1. Heaven in art. 2. Hell in art. 3. Art—Themes, motives. I. Title.

Hebald, Milton.

GETLEIN, Frank. 730'.924
Milton Hebald. New York, Viking Press [1971] 156 p. illus., ports. 24 cm. (A Studio book) [NB237.H38G4 1971] 79-151007 ISBN 0-670-47624-2 12.50
1. Hebald, Milton.

Hebrew language—Alphabet.

KATZ, Alexander Raymond, 1895- [492.411]
A new art for an old religion. Introd. by C. J. Bulliet; explanatory notes by Shlomo Marenof. Rev. ed. New York, R. F. Moore Co. [1952] unpaged. illus. 24 cm. First ed. published in 1945 under title: Prelude to a new art for an old religion. [PJ4589.K3 1952] 745.44 52-8564
1. Hebrew language—Alphabet. I. Title.

PODWAL, Mark H., 1945- 741.9'73
A book of Hebrew letters / Mark Podwal. 1st ed. Philadelphia : Jewish Publication Society of America, 1978. [64] p. : chiefly ill. ; 23 cm. [NC139.P59A4 1978] 78-70076 ISBN 0-8276-0117-4 : 12.50 ISBN 0-8276-0118-2 pbk. : 5.95
1. Podwal, Mark H., 1945- 2. Hebrew language—Alphabet—Illustrations. I. Title. BIP

Heckett, Eric H, Mrs.—Art collections.

PITTSBURGH. Carnegie Institute. Museum of Art.
Ancient bronzes; a selection from the Heckett Collection, Heckmeres Highlands, Valencia, Pennsylvania. Pittsburgh, 1964. [84] p. illus. 23 cm. Catalog of the exhibition held Nov. 5, 1964-Jan. 10, 1965. [NK7907.P5] 73-172084
1. Heckett, Eric H, Mrs.—Art collections. 2. Bronzes, Ancient—Exhibitions. I. Title.

Heeramaneck, Nasli M.—Art collections.

KUWAYAMA, George. 738'.0951
Chinese ceramics: the Heeramaneck Collection, a gift from Nasli M. Heeramaneck. [Los Angeles, Los Angeles County Museum of Art, c1973] 48 p. illus. 26 cm. Catalog of an exhibition held at the Los Angeles County Museum of Art, Dec. 18, 1973-Mar. 3, 1974. Bibliography: p. 47-48. [NK4165.K9] 73-89351 ISBN 0-87587-057-0
1. Heeramaneck, Nasli M.—Art collections. 2. Pottery, Chinese—Exhibitions. 3. Porcelain, Chinese—Exhibitions. I. Los Angeles Co., Calif. Museum of Art, Los Angeles. II. Title. BIP

LOS Angeles Co., Calif. Museum of Art, Los Angeles. 709'.17'67
Islamic art: the Nasli M. Heeramaneck Collection, gift of Joan Palevsky. Edited by Pratapaditya Pal. [Los Angeles, c1973] 232 p. illus. 26 cm. Bibliography: p. 230-231. [N6263.L6L64 1973] 73-88144 ISBN 0-87587-056-2 7.50 (pbk.)
1. Heeramaneck, Nasli M.—Art collections. 2. Los Angeles Co., Calif. Museum of Art, Los Angeles. 3. Art, Islamic—Catalogs. 4. Art—Los Angeles—Catalogs. I. Pal, Pratapaditya, ed. II. Title.

Hefzi-Bah. Israel. Beth Alpha Synagogue.

GOLDMAN, Bernard Marvin, 1922- 726.3
The sacred portal; a primary symbol in ancient Judaic art [Detroit. Wayne State Univ. Pr., c.1966] 215p. illus. 26cm. Bibl. [NA5978.H4G6] 65-16836 10.00
1. Hefzi-Bah. Israel. Beth Alpha Synagogue. 2. Synagogue art—Hefzi-Bah, Israel. 3. Mosaics—Hefzi-Bah. Israel. I. Title.

GOLDMAN, Bernard Marvin, 1922- 726.3
The sacred portal; a primary symbol in ancient Judaic art, by Bernard Goldman. [Detroit] Wayne State University Press [1966] 215 p. illus. 26 cm. Bibliography: p. 191-206. [Na5978.G4G6] 64-16836
1. Hefzi-Bah, Israel, Beth Alpha Synagogue. 2. Synagogue art — Hefzi-Bah, Israel. 3. Mosaics — Hefzi-Bah, Israel. I. Title.

Hegel, Georg Wilhelm Friedrich, 1770-1831. Aesthetik.

KAMINSKY, Jack, 1922- 701.17
Hegel on art; an interpretation of Hegel's aesthetics. [Albany] State Univ. of N.Y. [dist., New York, University Pubs., c.1962] ix, 207p. 22cm. Bibl. 61-14335 6.00
1. Hegel, Georg Wilhelm Friedrich, 1770-1831. Aesthetik. I. Title. BIP

Hegel, Georg Wilhelm Friedrich. 1770-1831. Schopenhauer, Arthur, 1788-1860.

KNOX, Israel, 1904- 701
The aesthetic theories of Kant, Hegel, and Schopenhauer. New York, Humanities Press, 1958. 219 p. 23 cm. Issued in 1966 as thesis, Columbia University. [[B2799]] A63
1. Hegel, Georg Wilhelm Friedrich. 1770-1831. Schopenhauer, Arthur, 1788-1860. 2. Kant, Immanuel—Aesthetics. 3. Aesthetics. I. Title. BIP

Heinemann, Lore—Art collections.

STAMPFLE, Felice. 741.9'4
Drawings from the Collection of Lore and Rudolf Heinemann. Catalogue by Felice Stampfle and Cara D. Denison. With an introd. by James Byam Shaw. New York, Pierpont Morgan Library, 1973. 189 p. 120 plates. 28 cm. Catalog of an exhibition. Includes bibliographical references. [NC15.N56P537] 73-79034 ISBN 0-87598-040-6 7.50
1. Heinemann, Lore—Art collections. 2. Heinemann, Rudolf—Art collections. 3. Drawings—Exhibitions. I. Denison, Cara D., joint author. II. Pierpont Morgan Library, New York. III. Title. BIP

Heisey (A. H.) & Co.

BRADLEY, Stephen H. 748.8
Heisey stemware / by Stephen H. Bradley, Constance S. Ryan, Robert R. Ryan. Newark, Ohio : Spencer Walker Press, 1976. 238 p. : ill. ; 29 cm. Includes index. [NK5198.H4B7] 76-370469
1. Heisey (A. H.) & Co. 2. Stemware, American—Catalogs. I. Ryan, Constance S., joint author. II. Ryan, Robert R., joint author. III. Title. BIP

CUDD, Viola N. 748.2'9171'54
Heisey glassware, by Viola N. Cudd. [1st ed.] Brenham, Tex., Herrmann Print Shop; [sold by] The Antique Barn [1969] xi, 242 p. illus., facsims., plates (part col.), ports. 23 cm. [NK5198.H4C8] 73-284928
1. Heisey (A. H.) & Co. I. Title.

EMANUELE, Concetta. 748.2
Heisey gems. [2d ed. Sunol, Calif., 1969] 2 v. illus. 28 cm. Cover title. Vol. 2 of 1st ed. Includes bibliographies. [NK5198.H4E4 1969] 79-21433
1. Heisey (A. H.) & Co. I. Title.

VOGEL, Clarence W., 1908- 748.2'9'171
[Heisey reference books. 1st ed. Plymouth, Ohio, Heisey Publications, 1969- v. illus. (part col.) 14 x 23 cm. Contents.Contents.— —book 2. Heisey's colonial years, 1906-1922.—book 3. Heisey's art and colored glass, 1922-1942.—book 4. Heisey's early and late years, 1896-1958. [NK5198.H4V6] 75-22070 10.00 (v. 2) varies
1. Heisey (A. H.) & Co. I. Title. II. Title: Heisey's colonial years, 1906-1922. III. Title: Heisey's art and colored glass, 1922-1942.

WILLEY, Harold E. 748.2'9171'54
Heisey's cut handmade glassware / by Harold E. Willey. [Newark? Ohio] : Willey, c1974. 147 p. : ill. ; 23 cm. Cover title. Includes index. [NK5198.H4W54] 75-308357
1. Heisey (A. H.) & Co. 2. Willey, Harold E.—Art collections. 3. Cut glass, American—Catalogs. I. Title.

YEAKLEY, Virginia. 748.2'91'7154
Heisey glass in color, by Virginia and Loren Yeakley. Newark, Ohio [1970] [32] p. (incl. covers) 15 col. plates. 23 cm. [NK5198.H4Y43] 73-291762 5.95
1. Heisey (A.H.) & Co. I. Yeakley, Loren, joint author. II. Title.

Heizer, Dorothy Wendell, 1881—

KRECHNIAK, Helen Bullard, 1902- 745.59'22
Dorothy Heizer, the artist and her dolls [by] Helen Bullard. New York, National Institute of American Doll Artists, 1972. v, 78 p. illus. 23 cm. Bibliography: p. 76. [NK4894.2.H34K73] 71-190747
1. Heizer, Dorothy Wendell, 1881- I. Title.

Held, Al, 1928—

HELD, Al, 1928- 759.13
Al Held / by Marcia Tucker. New York : Whitney Museum of American Art, 1974. 108 p. : ill. (some col.) ; 24 cm. "Al Held: catalogue of the exhibition, Whitney Museum of American Art, October 11-December 1, 1974" (1 leaf) inserted at end. Bibliography: p. 105-108. [ND237.H43T82] 74-15524
1. Held, Al, 1928- I. Tucker, Marcia. II. Whitney Museum of American Art, New York.

HELD, Al, 1928- 759.13
Al Held. San Francisco Museum of Art, San Francisco, California, January 9-February 25, 1968. The Corcoran Gallery of Art, Washington, D.C., March 16-April 21, 1968. [San Francisco, 1968] 24 p. illus. (part col.) 24 x 21 cm. Introductory text by Eleanor Green. Bibliography: p. 23-24. [ND237.H43A42] 68-19953
I. Green, Eleanor, 1929- II. San Francisco. Museum of Art. III. Corcoran Gallery of Art, Washington, D.C.

Held, John, 1889-1958.

HELD, John, 1889-1958. 741.5'973
The wages of sin and other Victorian joys and sorrows. As seen and engraved by that old sentimentalist, John Held, Jr. New York, Dover Publications [1972, c1964] vi, 168 p. illus. 29 cm. Reprint of the 1931 ed. published by J. Washburn, New York under title: The works of John Held, Jr. [NC1429.H38A57 1972] 75-188950 ISBN 0-486-22861-4 2.50
1. Held, John, 1889-1958. 2. American wit and humor, Pictorial. I. Title. BIP

Held, Julius Samuel, 1905-

RUBENS, Peter Paul Sir 1577-1640. 741.9'45
Rubens: selected drawings. With an introd. and a critical catalogue by Julius S. Held. [New York] Phaidon Publishers; distributed by Doubleday, Garden City [1959] 2 v. illus. (part mounted col.) 31 cm. Contents.v. 1. The text. -- v. 2. The plates. Bibliography: v. 1, p. 169-170. [NC1055.R8H4] 60-2275
1. Held, Julius Samuel, 1905- I. Title.

Helena, Mont. — Hist. — Pictorial works.

GRAFF, James R comp. 978.66
Historic Helena; an early-day photographic history of Montana's scenic capital city, 1864-1964. Compiled for Home Building and Loan Association by James R. Graff, in cooperation with other Helena residents and institutions, for publication during Montana's Centennial Year, and the 100th anniversary of the discovery of gold in Last Chance Gulch, now present-day Helena, Montana. Limited 1st ed. Helena, Mont., Printed by Thurber Print. Co., 1964. 1 v. (unpaged) illus., facsims., ports. 28 cm. [F739.H4G7] 64-55839
1. Helena, Mont. — Hist. — Pictorial works. I. Home Building and Loan Association, Helena, Mont. II. Title.

Heliker, John, 1909—

GOODRICH, Lloyd, 1897- 760'.0924
John Heliker, by Lloyd Goodrich and Patricia FitzGerald Mandel. New York, Published for the Whitney Museum of American Art by F. A. Praeger [1968] 48 p. illus. (part col.), ports. 21 x 22 cm. "Published on the occasion of the first full-scale retrospective exhibition of John Heliker's works, organized by the Whitney Museum of American Art in the spring of 1968." "Catalogue": p. 45-47. Bibliography: p. 17-18. [ND237.H44G6] 68-25639
1. Heliker, John, 1909- I. Mandel, Patricia FitzGerald, joint author. II. Whitney Museum of American Art, New York.

Hells Canyon—Antiquities.

CALDWELL, Warren Wendell. 970.4'795
Hells Canyon archeology, by Warren W. Caldwell and Oscar L. Mallory. Editor: Jerome E. Petsche. Lincoln, Neb., 1967. iii, 153 p. illus., maps (1 fold.) 25 cm. (River Basin Surveys. Publication in salvage archeology, no. 6) At head of title: River Basin Surveys, Museum of Natural History, Smithsonian Institution. Bibliography: p. 97-101. [E78.N77C29] 68-60368
1. Hells Canyon—Antiquities. 2. Northwest, Pacific—Antiquities. 3. Indians of North America—Northwest, Pacific—Antiquities. 4. Excavations (Archaeology)—Northwest, Pacific. I. Mallory, Oscar L., joint author. II. Title. III. Series.

Helmets.

CHAPPELL, Gordon. 355.8'1
Summer helmets of the U.S. Army, 1875-1910. [Cheyenne] Wyoming State Archives and Historical Dept., 1967. 35 p. illus., ports. 23 cm. (Wyoming State Museum monograph no. 1) Bibliographical references included in "Notes and sources" (p. 30-31) [AM101.W915 no. 1] 68-64313 1.25
1. U.S. Army—Uniforms—History. 2. Helmets. I. Title. II. Series: Wyoming. State Museum, Cheyenne. Monograph no. 1

HENCKEN, Hugh O'Neill, 1902- 623.4'41
The earliest European helmets; Bronze Age and early Iron Age [by] Hugh Hencken. Cambridge, Mass., Peabody Museum of Archaeology and Ethnology, Harvard University, 1971. xiv, 199 p. illus. 28 cm. (Peabody Museum, Harvard University. American School of Prehistoric Research. Bulletin no. 28) Bibliography: p. [191]-199. [U825.H45] 78-152525
1. Helmets. I. Title. II. Series: Harvard University. American School of Prehistoric Research. Bulletin no. 28. BIP

RANKIN, Robert H. 355.14
Helmets and headdress of the Imperial German Army, 1870-1918. Drawings by the author [New Milford, Conn.] N. Flayderman, R.F.D. 2, Squash Hollow [c.] 1965. vi, 152p. illus., ports. 23cm. Bibl. [U825.R3] 65-23502 9.50
1. Helmets. 2. Head-gear. I. Title.

RANKIN, Robert H 355.14
Helmets and headdress of the Imperial German Army, 1870-1918 by Robert H. Rankin. Drawings by the author. [New Milford, Conn.] N. Flayderman, 1965. vi, 152 p. illus., ports. 23 cm. Bibliography: p. 149-152. [U825.R3] 65-23502
1. Helmets. 2. Head-gear. I. Title.

Helmets—Europe—History.

CURTIS, Howard M. 739.7'5
2,500 years of European helmets, 800 B.C.-1700 A.D. / Howard M. Curtis. 1st ed. North Hollywood, Calif. : Beinfeld Pub., c1978. xiii, 346 p. : ill. (some col.) ; 19 x 23 cm. Bibliography: p. 344-346. [U825.C87] 76-20423 ISBN 0-917714-06-7 : 19.95
1. Helmets—Europe—History. I. Title.

Helmle & Helmle.

RUSSO, Edward J. 338.7'61'72
Helmle & Helmle, architects / Edward J. Russo. Srpingfield, Ill. : Sangamon County Historical Society, 1974. vii, 32 p. : ill. ; 22 cm. (Bicentennial studies in Sangamon history) Bibliography: p. 31-32. [NA737.H38R87] 75-305234 1.40
1. Helmle & Helmle. 2. Architecture—Springfield, Ill. I. Title. II. Series.

Hemenway, Nancy.

HEMENWAY, Nancy. 746.3'92
Textures of our Earth : Bayetage tapestries, 1972-1977 / by Nancy Hemenway. Brunswick, Me. : Bowdoin College Museum of Art, 1977. [47] p. : ill. (some col.) ; 28 cm. Cover title: Hemenway, textures of our Earth. Catalogue of an exhibition organized by the Bowdoin College Museum of Art; participating museums: Bowdoin College Museum of Art, Aug. 5-Sept. 25, 1977; Virginia Museum of Fine Arts, Oct. 18-Nov. 20, 1977; Seattle Art Museum, May 18-June 25, 1978; Textile Museum, Sept. 15-Oct. 28, 1978. [NK3012.A3H45] 77-89623
1. Hemenway, Nancy. I. Bowdoin College. Museum of Art. II. Title. III. Title: Hemenway, textures of our Earth.

Hemphill, Herbert Waide—Art collections.

THE Herbert Waide 745'.0973
Hemphill, Jr. Collection of 18th, 19th, and 20th century American folk art : presented at Heritage Plantation of Sandwich in the Arts and Crafts Building, Sandwich, Massachusetts, May 1st through October 15th, 1974, and Columbus Museum of Arts and Crafts, Columbus, Georgia, opening the new Bradley Wing November 9th, 1974, through February 2nd, 1975. [Sandwich, Mass. : Heritage Plantation of Sandwich, 1974] 48 p. : ill. ; 23 cm. [NK805.H45] 74-186337
1. Hemphill, Herbert Waide—Art collections. 2. Folk art—Exhibitions. 3. Folk art—United States. I. Heritage Plantation of Sandwich. II. Columbus Museum of Arts and Crafts.

Henri, Robert, 1865-1929.

CENTURY Association, New York. 759.13'074'01471
Robert Henri & five of his pupils: George Bellows, Eugene Speicher, Guy Pene Du Bois, Rockwell Kent [and] Edward Hopper. Loan exhibition of paintings, April 5 to June 1, 1946. Freeport, N.Y., Books for Libraries Press [1971] [61] p. illus. 27 cm. (Biography index reprint series) Text signed: Helen Appleton Read. Reprint of the 1946 ed. [ND212.C4 1971] 74-160918 ISBN 0-8369-8081-6
1. Henri, Robert, 1865-1929. 2. Bellows, George Wesley, 1882-1925. 3. Speicher, Eugene Edward, 1883-1962. 4. Du Bois, Guy Pene, 1884-1958. 5. Kent, Rockwell, 1882- 6. Hopper, Edward, 1882-1967. 7. Paintings, American—Exhibitions. 8. Ashcan School. I. Read, Helen Appleton. II. Title. BIP

HENRI, Robert, 1865-1929. 759.13
Robert Henri (1865-1929) : paintings and drawings in the collection of the University of Nebraska and the Nebraska Art Association: Sheldon Memorial Art Gallery, University of Nebraska, Lincoln, 1971. Lincoln : Nebraska Art Association, [1971?] 56 p. : ill. ; 26 cm. [ND237.H5N36] 75-623169
1. Henri, Robert, 1865-1929. I. Sheldon Memorial Art Gallery. II. Nebraska Art Association.

HOMER, William Innes. 759.13 B
Robert Henri and his circle, by William Innes Homer with the assistance of Violet Organ. Ithaca, Cornell University Press [1969] xvii, 308 p. illus., facsims., 4 col. plates, ports. 27 cm. Bibliography: p. 291-300. [ND237.H5H6] 75-81594 17.50
1. Henri, Robert, 1865-1929. I. Organ, Violet. II. Title. BIP

Hans Heysen, including drawings from his sketchbooks selected by David Heysen. Adelaide : Rigby, 1976. 63 p. : ill. (some col.) ; 24 cm. [N7405.H4T45] 76-379632 ISBN 0-7270-0066-7
1. Heysen, Hans, Sir, 1877-1968. 2. Artists—Australia—Biography. 3. Hahndorf, Australia, in art. I. Title.

Hibbard, Aldro Thompson, 1886—

COOLEY, John L. 760'.0924
A. T. Hibbard, N.A.; artist in two worlds [by] John L. Cooley. With a commentary by Aldren A. Watson. [1st ed.] Concord, N.H., Rumford Press [1968] 174 p. illus. 27 cm. [ND237.H57C6] 68-7465
1. Hibbard, Aldro Thompson, 1886- I. Title: Artist in two worlds.

Hicks, David, 1929—

HICKS, David, 1929- 745.92'24
The David Hicks Book of flower arranging / as told to Maureen Gregson ; introd. by Julia Clements. New York : Van Nostrand Reinhold Co., 1976. 87 p. : ill. (some col.) ; 30 cm. Includes index. [SB449.H46] 76-11678 ISBN 0-442-23408-2 : 9.95
1. Hicks, David, 1929- 2. Flower arrangement. 3. Flowers. 4. Interior decorators—England—Biography. I. Gregson, Maureen. II. Title. III. Title: Book of flower arranging.

Hicks, Edward, 1780-1849.

A.C.A. Galleries. 759.13'0740147'1
Four American primitives: Edward Hicks, John Kane, Anna Mary Robertson Moses, Horace Pippin. New York, [1972] [65] p. (incl. cover) illus. 28 cm. "February 22-March 11, 1972." [ND236.A14] 72-180613
1. Hicks, Edward, 1780-1849. 2. Kane, John, 1860-1934. 3. Moses, Anna Mary (Robertson) 1860-1961. 4. Pippin, Horace, 1888-1946. 5. Primitivism in art.

ANDREW Crispo Gallery. 759.13
Edward Hicks, a gentle spirit : [catalog of an exhibition, May 16 thru June 28, 1975]. New York : A. Crispo Gallery, c1975. [67] p. : ill. (some col.) ; 23 x 26 cm. Includes bibliographical references. [ND237.H58A52 1975] 75-15072 pbk. : 10.00
1. Hicks, Edward, 1780-1849. 2. Primitivism in art—United States. I. Title.
Publisher's address: 41 E. 57th St., N.Y., N.Y. 10022.

FORD, Alice Elizabeth, 1906- [759.13]
Edward Hicks, painter of the Peaceable Kingdom. Philadelphia, University of Pennsylvania Press, 1952. xvi, 161 p. plates (part col.) porta, geneal. table. 29 cm. Bibliography: p. 123-126. [ND237.H58F6] 927.5 52-13392
1. Hicks, Edward, 1780-1849. I. Title.

FORD, Alice Elizabeth, 1906- 759.13
Edward Hicks, painter of the Peaceable Kingdom, by Alice Ford. Philadelphia, University of Pennsylvania Press, 1952. Millwood, N.Y., Kraus Reprint Co., 1973. xvii, 161 p. illus. 29 cm. Bibliography: p. 123-[126] [ND237.H58F6 1973] 73-10195 ISBN 0-527-30400-X
1. Hicks, Edward, 1780-1849. I. Title. BIP

HICKS, Edward, 1780-1849. 759.13
A peaceable season. Introd. by Eleanore Price Mather. Princeton, Pyne Press; [distributed by Scribner, New York, 1973] [60] p. col. illus. 21 cm. Passages from the artist's memoirs and reproductions on his paintings, with descriptive legends. [ND237.H58M32] 73-79523 ISBN 0-87861-052-9 4.95
1. Hicks, Edward, 1780-1849. I. Mather, Eleanore Price. II. Title.

MATHER, Eleanore Price, 1910- 759.13
Edward Hicks, primitive Quaker; his religion in relation to his art. [Wallingford, Pa., Pendle Hill Publications, 1970] 35 p. illus., port. 19 cm. (Pendle Hill pamphlet, 170) Bibliography: p. 34-35. [ND237.H58M3] 75-110287 0.55
1. Hicks, Edward, 1780-1849.

PULLINGER, Edna S. 759.13
A dream of peace; Edward Hicks of Newtown, by Edna S. Pullinger. Philadelphia, Dorrance [1973] 93 p. illus. 22 cm. Bibliography: p. 91-93. [ND237.H58P84] 73-76215 ISBN 0-8059-1848-5 3.95
1. Hicks, Edward, 1780-1849. I. Title. BIP

THREE self-taught 759.148
Pennsylvania artists; Hicks, Kane and Pippin : Exhibition at the Museum of Art, Carnegie Institute, Pittsburgh, Oct. 21-Dec. 4,1966, and the Corcoran Gallery of Art, Washington, Jan.6-Feb.10,1967. Pittsburgh, Printed by Carnegie Institute Press, 1966?] 1 v. (unpaged) 121 plates (part col.) 29 cm. Cover title. [ND236.T45] 67-68114
1. Hicks, Edward, 1780-1849. 2. Kane, John, 1860-1934. 3. Pippin, Horace, 1888-1946. I. Pittsburgh. Carnegie Institute. Museum of Art. II. Corcoran Gallery of Art, Washington, D.C.

Hicks, Sheila, 1934—

LEVI-STRAUSS, Monique. 746.3'973
Sheila Hicks. New York, Van Nostrand Reinhold Co. [1974] p. [NK3012.A3H524] 74-4529 ISBN 0-442-24766-4 15.00
1. Hicks, Sheila, 1934- 2. Tapestry, American.

Hidcote Manor, Eng. Garden.

SACKVILLE-WEST, Victoria Mary, Hon., 1892-1962. 914.24'17
Hidcote Manor Garden, Gloucestershire. [Revised ed.] / [written by V. Sackville-West, G.S.T., G.H.B.]. [London] : National Trust, 1976. 33 p., [8] p. of plates : col. ill., plan ; 22 cm. "Adapted from an article published in the Journal of the Royal Horticultural Society, vol. LXXIV, part 11, November 1949." [SB466.G8H546 1976] 77-360249 ISBN 0-7078-0057-9 : £0.25
1. Hidcote Manor, Eng. Garden. I. National Trust for Places of Historic Interest or Natural Beauty. II. Title.

Hiding-places (Secret chambers, etc.)

KROTZ, David. 643
How to hide almost anything / by David Krotz ; illustrated by Nina Sklansky. New York : Morrow, 1975. 157 p. : ill. ; 24 cm. [TT200.K76] 74-30320 ISBN 0-688-02894-2
1. Hiding-places (Secret chambers, etc.) 2. Woodwork. I. Title. BIP

KROTZ, David. 643
How to hide almost anything : or, Come home, America, and find your treasures where you stashed them / by David Krotz ; illustrated by Nina Sklansky. New York : Collier Books, 1978, c1975. 157 p. : ill. ; 24 cm. [TT200.K76 1978] 77-17528 ISBN 0-02-080590-X : 3.95
1. Hiding-places (Secret chambers, etc.) 2. Woodwork. I. Title.

Higgins, Victor, 1884-1949.

HIGGINS, Victor, 1884-1949. 759.13
The Art Gallery of the University of Notre Dame and the Indianapolis Museum of Art present Victor Higgins, an Indiana born artist working in Taos, New Mexico, University of Notre Dame, October 26-December 31, 1975, Indianapolis Museum of Art, March 2-March 30, 1976 : [exhibition]. [Notre Dame, Ind.] : The Gallery, c1975. 87 p. : ill. (some col.) ; 26 cm. Cover title: Victor Higgins, 1884-1949. Bibliography: p. 19. [ND237.H584N68] 75-34941
1. Higgins, Victor, 1884-1949. I. Notre Dame, Ind. University. Art Gallery. II. Indianapolis Museum of Art.

High-rise apartment buildings.

JENSEN, Rolf. 728.2
High density living. New York, Praeger [1966] 245 p. illus., plans. 31 cm. Includes bibliographies. [NA7860.J45] 66-12527
1. High-rise apartment buildings. 2. Architecture, Domestic—Europe. I. Title.

SCHMITT, Karl Wilhelm 728.2
Multistory housing. Mehrgeschossiger Wohnbau. [Tr. by E. Rockwell] New York, Praeger [1966] 215p. illus., plans. 26cm. English and German. [NA7860.S3313] 66-12990 18.50
1. High-rise apartment buildings. I. Title. II. Title: Mehrgeschossiger Wohnbau.

High-rise apartment buildings—Juvenile literature.

TANNENBAUM, Beulah. 728.3'1
High rises, by Beulah Tannenbaum and Myra Stillman. Illustrated by Marta Cone. New York, McGraw-Hill [1974] 64 p. illus. 24 cm. (Science in the city) Text and drawings describe the steps in the design and construction of high-rise apartments. [TH4820.T3] 73-17762 4.33
1. High-rise apartment buildings—Juvenile literature. I. Stillman, Myra, joint author. II. Cone, Marta, illus. III. Title.

High-voltage photography.

DAKIN, H. S. 778.3
High-voltage photography [by] H. S. Dakin. San Francisco [1974] 65 p. illus. 28 cm. Cover title. Includes bibliographical references. [TR760.D34] 74-77233
1. High-voltage photography. BIP

PARKER, Don H. 778.3
Photopsychography ... new image of man, by Don H. Parker. Monterey, Calif., Eikon Gallery Press [1974] 1 portfolio ([27] p., 6 col. plates) 22 x 28 cm. "A work published in coordination with the first international exhibition of Kirlian high frequency photopsychography organized and presented by the Eikon Gallery." [TR760.P37] 74-186333 10.00
1. High-voltage photography. I. Eikon Gallery. II. Title.

High-voltage photography—Congresses.

WESTERN Hemisphere Conference on Kirlian Photography, Acupuncture, and the Human Aura, 1st, New York, 1972. 133
The Kirlian aura: photographing the galaxies of life. Edited by Stanley Krippner and Daniel Rubin. [1st ed.] Garden City, N.Y., Anchor Books, 1974. 208 p. illus. 21 cm. (Social change series) Published in 1973 under title: Galaxies of life. Bibliography: p. 200-204. [TR760.W47 1972] 73-10733 ISBN 0-385-06574-4 3.95
1. High-voltage photography—Congresses. 2. Psychical research—Congresses. 3. Acupuncture—Congresses. I. Krippner, Stanley, 1932- ed. II. Rubin, Daniel, ed. III. Title.

Highway law—U.S.

UNITED States. Congress. House. Committee on Public Works. Subcommittee on Roads. 713'.0973
Review of highway beautification, 1967. Hearings, Ninetieth Congress, first session, on H.R. 7797. Washington, U.S. Govt. Print. Off., 1967. viii, 1097 p. illus., map. 24 cm. Hearings held Apr. 5-May 3, 1967. "90-1." [LAW] 67-61878
1. Highway law—United States. 2. Advertising, Outdoor—Law and legislation—United States. I. Title.

U.S. Dept. of Commerce. 625.7'7
1967 highway beautification program. Report together with additional correspondence to the United States Congress, pursuant to Public law 89-285, Highway beautification act of 1965. Washington, U.S. Govt. Print. Off., 1967. vii, 61 p. 24 cm. (90th Congress, 1st session. Senate. Document no. 6) Bibliography: p. 55-61. [TE177.U45] 67-60989 0.25
1. Highway law—U.S. 2. Advertising, Outdoor—Law and legislation—U.S. 3. Roadside improvement. I. Title. II. Series: U.S. 90th Congress, 1st session, 1967. Senate. Document no. 6

Hill, David Octavius, 1802-1870.

BRUCE, David, 1939- comp. 779'.2'0922
Sun pictures; the Hill-Adamson calotypes. Greenwich, Conn., New York Graphic Society [1974, c1973] 247 p. illus. 30 cm. Bibliography: p. 243. [TR651.B78 1974] 73-87361 ISBN 0-8212-0588-9 17.50
1. Hill, David Octavius, 1802-1870. 2. Adamson, Robert, 1821-1848. 3. Photography, Artistic. 4. Calotype. I. Hill, David Octavius, 1802-1870. II. Adamson, Robert, 1821-1848. III. Title.

HILL, David Octavius, 1802-1870. 779'.092'4
An early Victorian album : the photographic masterpieces (1843-1848) of David Octavius Hill and Robert Adamson / edited and with an introd. by Colin Ford ; and an essay by Roy Strong. 1st American ed. New York : Knopf, 1975, c1974. p. cm. London ed. (J. Cape) has subtitle: the Hill/Adamson collection. Includes bibliographical references and index. [TR651.H53 1974b] 74-21315 ISBN 0-394-49733-3 : 17.50
1. Hill, David Octavius, 1802-1870. 2. Adamson, Robert, 1821-1848. 3. Photography, Artistic. 4. Photography—Portraits. 5. Calotype. I. Adamson, Robert, 1821-1848. II. Ford, Colin John, 1934- III. Title. BIP

Hill, James Jerome, 1905—

SAINT Paul Art Center. 759.13
Jerome Hill; painter, film maker, collector. Saint Paul [1965] 47 p. illus. (part col.) 23 cm. Catalog of an exhibition held Apr. 29-Oct. 3, 1965. [ND237.H597S2] 68-7150
1. Hill, James Jerome, 1905-

Hill, John, 1770-1850.

KOKE, Richard J 769.973
A checklist of the American engravings of John Hill (1770-1850) master of aquatint, together with a list of prints colored by him and a list of his extant original drawings. New York, New York Historical Society, 1961. 87p. illus., port., facsim. 24cm. [NE539.H5K6] 61-66305
1. Hill, John, 1770-1850. I. Title. BIP

TOLEDO. Museum of Art. 704.94'9'978
Art of the American West : from the Collection of John and Margaret Hill, the Toledo Museum of Art, July 6-August 10, 1975 : [exhibition]. Toledo : The Museum, [1975] 16 p. : ill. ; 18 cm. Catalog. [N8214.5.U6T64 1975] 75-16064
1. Hill, John A., 1970- —Art collections. 2. Hill, Margaret M.—Art collections. 3. The West in art—Exhibitions. 4. Art, American—Exhibitions. I. Title.

Hilliard, Nicholas, 1537 (ca.)-1619.

AUERBACH, Erna. 751.7'7'0954074
Nicholas Hilliard. Boston, Boston Book & Art Shop [1964, c1961] xxiv, 352 p. illus. (part col.), facsims., ports. (part col.) 25 cm. "Catalogue": p. 287-335. Bibliography: p. 336-338. [ND1337.G8H52 1964] 64-66312
1. Hilliard, Nicholas, 1537 (ca.)-1619. I. Title.

Hillotype.

HILL, Levi L., b.1816. 778.6'3
A treatise on heliochromy; or, The production of pictures, by means of light, in natural colors. Embracing a full, plain, and unreserved description of the process known as the hillotype, including the author's newly discovered collodio-chrome, or natural colors on collodionized glass, by L. L. Hill. Facsim. ed. with an introd. by William B. Becker. State College, Pa., Carnation Press, 1972. xii, 175 p. 23 cm. Half title: Heliochromy. Original t.p. has imprint: N.Y., Robinson & Caswell, 1856. Includes bibliographical references. [TR510.H64 1856a] 71-173025 ISBN 0-87601-005-2
1. Hillotype. I. Title. II. Title: Heliochromy. BIP

SUBJECT INDEX HISTORIC BUILDINGS—GREAT BRITAIN.

Hilton, John W.

AINSWORTH, Katherine, 1908- 759.13 B
The man who captured sunshine : episodes in the life of John W. Hilton, botanist, gemologist, zoologist, and gifted painter of the desert scene / as garnered during long years of friendship by Katherine Ainsworth. Palm Springs, Calif. : ETC Publications, c1978. xiv, 274 p., [8] leaves of plates : ill. (some col.) ; 24 cm. Includes index. [CT275.H59914A46] 77-21823 ISBN 0-88280-054-X : 15.00
1. Hilton, John W. 2. United States—Biography. I. Title. BIP

Himmelfarb, John, 1946—

HIMMELFARB, John, 1946- 741.9'73
The family dog : drawings / by John Himmelfarb. [Chicago] : Himmelfarb, c1973. 40 leaves : chiefly ill. ; 21 x 27 cm. "A Darryl Licht transport document." Includes index. [NC139.H54A44] 75-314182
1. Himmelfarb, John, 1946- I. Title.

Hinchey, William James, 1829-1893.

SPRINGER, Lynn E. 741.9'73
The rediscovered work of William J. Hinchey : [exhibition held at the St. Louis Art Museum, 28 June-Sept., 1974 / catalogue by Lynn E. Springer ; introd. by Katherine Hinchey Cochran. St. Louis : St. Louis Art Museum, [1974] 35 p. : ill. ; 25 cm. [NC139.H55S67] 74-14581
1. Hinchey, William James, 1829-1893. I. Hinchey, William James, 1829-1893. II. St. Louis Art Museum. III. Title.

Hind, William George Richardson, 1833-1888.

HARPER, J. Russell. 759.11
William G. R. Hind / J. Russell Harper. Ottawa : National Gallery of Canada, 1976. 91 p. : chiefly ill. (some col.) ; 24 cm. (Canadian artists series ; no. 2) Bibliography: p. 91. [ND1843.H56H37] 77-366096 ISBN 0-88884-273-2
1. Hind, William George Richardson, 1833-1888. 2. Canada in art. I. Hind, William George Richardson, 1833-1888. II. Title. III. Series.

HARPER, J. Russell. 759.11
William G. R. Hind (1833-1888); a Confederation painter in Canada. [Catalogue: by J. Russell Harper. Hamilton, Ont., 1967] [33] p. illus. (1 col.) map. 22 x 25 cm. "An exhibition organized and circulated by Willistead Art Gallery of Windsor of Centennial Year, 1967." Bibliography: p. [30]. [ND249.H5H3] 68-113332 1.00 Can.
1. Hind, William George Richardson, 1833-1888. I. Willistead Art Gallery of Windsor.

Hindson, Mark T.—Art collections.

DAVEY, Neil K. 736'.68
Netsuke : a comprehensive study based on the M. T. Hindson Collection / Neil K. Davey ; pref. by W. W. Windworth. New York : Sotheby Parke Bernet, 1974. 564 p., [2] leaves of plates : ill. ; 31 cm. "Catalogue of the M. T. Hindson Collection": p. [13]-275; catalog of other netsuke: p. 276-439. Includes index. [NK6050.D38 1974] 74-187939 ISBN 0-85667-013-8 : 70.00
1. Hindson, Mark T.—Art collections. 2. Netsukes—Catalogs. I. Title.

Hine, Lewis Wickes, 1874-1940.

GUTMAN, Judith Mara. 770'.924
Lewis W. Hine, and the American social conscience. New York, Walker [1967] 156 p. illus., ports. 25 cm. Bibliography: p. 52-60. [TR140.H52G8] 67-23089
1. Hine, Lewis Wickes, 1874-1940. 2. United States—Social conditions—Pictorial works. I. Title.

HINE, Lewis Wickes, 1874-1940. 779'.092'4
America & Lewis Hine : photographs 1904-1940 : [exhibition] / foreword by Walter Rosenblum ; biographical notes by Naomi Rosenblum ; essay by Alan Trachtenberg ; design by Marvin Israel. New York : Aperture, inc., c1977. 142 p. : ill. ; 25 x 30 cm. Published in conjunction with an exhibition organized by the Brooklyn Museum. [TR820.5.H56 1977] 77-70068 ISBN 0-89381-008-8 : 22.50.
1. Hine, Lewis Wickes, 1874-1940. 2. Photography, Documentary. 3. Photographers—United States—Biography. I. Trachtenberg, Alan. II. Brooklyn. Institute of Arts and Sciences. Museum. III. Title. BIP

HINE, Lewis Wickes, 1874-1940. 770'.92'4
Lewis W. Hine, 1874-1940 : two perspectives / by Judith Mara Gutman; [editors; Cornell Kapa, Judith Mana Gutman,Bhupendra Kania]. New York : Grossman Publishers, 1974. 84 p. : ill. ; 23 cm. (ICP library of photographers ; v. 4) Bibliography: p. 82-83. [TR140.H52G82 1974] 72-11010 ISBN 0-670-42742-X : 10.00. ISBN 0-670-42743-8 pbk. : 5.95
1. Hine, Lewis Wickes, 1874-1940. 2. United States—Social conditions—Pictorial works. I. Gutman, Judith Mara. II. Series: International Fund for Concerned Photography. ICP library of photographers ; v. 4.

Hippodrome Theater.

CLARKE, Norman, 1935- 792.097'471
The mighty Hippodrome. South Brunswick [N.J.] A. S. Barnes [1968] 144 p. illus. (part col.), ports. 29 cm. Bibliography: p. 142. [F128.8.H5C55] 67-19466
1. Hippodrome Theater. I. Title.

Hiquily, Philippe, 1925-

JOUFFROY, Alain 730.944
Hiquily. [Paris] G. Fall [dist. New York, Efron. c.1962] 89p. illus. (pt. col.) 23cm. French and English. 62-52235 4.50
1. Hiquily, Philippe, 1925- I. Title.

Hirsch, Joseph, 1910—

HIRSCH, Joseph, 1910- 769'.924
The graphic work of Joseph Hirsch, compiled and edited by Sylvan Cole, Jr. New York, Associated American Artists, 1970. [11] p., 66 plates, port. 26 cm. Bibliography: p. [9] [NE2312.H5C6] 76-124389
I. Cole, Sylvan, comp. II. Title.

HIRSCH, Joseph, 1910- 759.13
Joseph Hirsch : recent paintings : [catalogue of the exhibition] April 7-24, 1976. N[ew] Y[ork] : Kennedy Galleries, c1976. [8] p. : ill. ; 28 cm. [ND237.H64K46] 76-361637
1. Hirsch, Joseph, 1910- I. Kennedy Galleries, inc., New York.

Hirschvogel, Augustin, 1503-1553.

SCHWARZ, Karl, 1885- 741'.092'4
Augustin Hirschvogel. New York, Collectors Edition [1971] 2 v. illus. 26 cm. "The text volume [(in German)] is a reprint of the 1917 Berlin edition, pp. i-xi and 1-215. All the works illustrated in the Berlin edition are to be found in the plate volume accompanying this new edition." Plate volume contains new English text by B. A. Rifkin. Vol. 2 has title: Plates accompanying Augustin Hirschvogel. Bibliography: v. 1, p. [209]-215. [NC251.H5S3 1971] 741.9'43 78-130958 ISBN 0-87681-052-0
1. Hirschvogel, Augustin, 1503-1553.

Hirshhorn Museum and Sculpture Garden.

THE Hirshhorn 709'.04'0740153
Museum & Sculpture Garden, Smithsonian Institution. Foreword by S. Dillon Ripley. Edited and with an introd. by Abram Lerner. Essays by Linda Nochlin [and others] New York, H. N. Abrams [1974] 770 p. illus. (part col.) 30 cm. "Inaugural publication of the Hirshhorn Museum and Sculpture Garden." Includes bibliographies. [N857.6.H57] 74-5454 ISBN 0-8109-0165-X
1. Hirshhorn Museum and Sculpture Garden. 2. Art, Modern—19th century—Washington, D.C.—Catalogs. 3. Art, Modern—20th century—Washington, D.C.—Catalogs. I. Lerner, Abram, ed. II. Nochlin, Linda. III. Hirshhorn Museum and Sculpture Garden.

HORWITZ, Elinor Lander. 735'.29'0740153
A child's garden of sculpture : photographed at the Hirshhorn Museum and Sculpture Garden, Smithsonian Institution / by Elinor Lander Horwitz ; photos. by Joshua Horwitz ; foreword by S. Dillon Ripley. Washington : Washingtonian Books, c1976. [79] p. : ill. ; 26 cm. An introduction to appreciating and understanding sculpture, with examples from the Hirshhorn Museum. [NB198.H67] 75-44630 ISBN 0-915168-17-0 : 5.50 ISBN 0-915168-15-4 pbk. : 2.50
1. Hirshhorn Museum and Sculpture Garden. 2. Sculpture, Modern—20th century—Juvenile literature. I. Horwitz, Joshua. II. Title. BIP

Historic American Buildings Survey.

HISTORIC American Buildings Survey. 720'.973
Documenting a legacy; 40 years of the Historic American Buildings Survey. [Washington, Library of Congress, 1973] 269-294 p. illus. 26 cm. Reprint from the Quarterly journal of the Library of Congress, Oct. 1973. Issued in conjunction with an exhibition held Nov. 1, 1973 to Jan. 31, 1974, in the Library of Congress. [NA705.H56 1973] 73-17422 ISBN 0-8444-0103-X
1. Historic American Buildings Survey. 2. Architecture—United States. 3. United States—Historic houses, etc. I. United States. Library of Congress. II. Title.

Historic buildings—Conservation and restoration.

UNITED States. Dept. of the Army. 623'.08 s
Historic preservation maintenance procedures. [Washington] : Headquarters, Dept. of the Army, 1977. 55 p. in various pagings : ill. ; 28 cm. (Technical manual - Department of the Army ; TM5-801-2) Cover title. Includes bibliography. [U408.3.A13TM5-801-2] [TH3401] 721'.028 77-601851
1. Historic buildings—Conservation and restoration. I. Title. II. Series: United States. Dept. of the Army. Training publication ; TM 5-801-2.

Historic buildings—Conservation and restoration—Economic aspects—United States—Congresses.

ECONOMIC Benefits of Preserving Old Buildings Conference, Seattle, 1975. 338.4'3
Economic benefits of preserving old buildings : papers from the Economic Benefits of Preserving Old Buildings Conference / sponsored by the National Trust for Historic Preservation, Seattle, Wash., July 31-August 2, 1975, cosponsors, City of Seattle, Historic Seattle Preservation and Development Authority, endorsing sponsors, American Institute of Architects ... [et al.]. Washington : Preservation Press, National Trust for Historic Preservation, 1976. 164 p. : ill. ; 27 cm. [E159.E26 1975] 76-5086 pbk. : 5.50
1. Historic buildings—Conservation and restoration—Economic aspects—United States—Congresses. I. National Trust for Historic Preservation in the United States. BIP

Historic buildings—England.

COLLINSON, Hugh. 942
County monuments : their families and houses / Hugh Collinson. Newton Abbot ; North Pomfret, Vt. : David and Charles, 1975. 176 p. : ill., ports. ; 23 cm. Includes index. Bibliography: p. 169-170. [DA660.C6] 75-323477 ISBN 0-7153-6742-0 : £3.95
1. Historic buildings—England. 2. Monuments—England. 3. England—Civilization. I. Title.

HOGG, Garry. 914.2
A guide to English country houses. New York, Arco Pub. Co. [1970, c1969] 160 p. illus. (part col.), map (on lining papers) 26 cm. [DA660.H67 1970] 70-90891 ISBN 0-668-02080-6 6.95
1. Historic buildings—England. I. Title. BIP

INNESS-SMITH, Robert. 942.5'2
The Dukeries and Sherwood Forest / Robert Innes-Smith. Derby : English Life Publications, [1974] [2], 26 p. : ill. (incl. 3 col.), coats of arms, geneal. table, ports. ; 14 cm. Cover title. [DA660.156] 75-302704 ISBN 0-85101-081-4 : £0.20
1. Historic buildings—England. I. Title.

Historic buildings—England—Ashford.

ASHFORD Local History Group. 942.2'392
Ashford's past at present / [compiled by the Ashford Local History Group ; illustrations by W. R. Briscall]. Ashford, Kent : L.R.B. Historical Publications, 1976. 20 p. : ill., maps ; 31 cm. Cover title. [DA690.A8027A8 1976] 77-351166 ISBN 0-905511-00-X : £0.75
1. Historic buildings—England—Ashford. 2. Ashford, Eng.—Buildings. 3. Ashford, Eng.—Description. I. Title.

Historic buildings—England—London.

HALL, Martin. 942.1'00992 B
The blue plaque guide to London homes / [by] Martin Hall. London : Queen Anne Press, 1976. 159 p. : ill., facsims., ports. ; 25 cm. Includes index. Bibliography: p. 153. [DA689.H48H34 1976] 76-372190 ISBN 0-362-00287-8 : £5.95
1. Historic buildings—England—London. 2. London—Dwellings. 3. England—Biography. I. Title.

Historic buildings—Great Britain.

FEDDEN, Henry Romilly, 1908- 914.2'04'85
The National Trust guide to England, Wales and Northern Ireland / compiled by Robin Fedden and Rosemary Joakes. 1st American ed. New York : Knopf, 1974, c1973. 688 p. : ill., maps ; 24 cm. First published in 1973 under title: The National Trust guide. Includes index. [DA660.F33 1974] 74-1679 ISBN 0-394-49384-2 : 15.00
1. Historic buildings—Great Britain. 2. Historic sites—Great Britain. 3. Great Britain—History. I. Joekes, Rosemary, joint author. II. National Trust for Places of Historic Interest or Natural Beauty. III. Title. BIP

HADFIELD, Miles. 914.2'03
A book of country houses; edited by Miles Hadfield; with contributions by Alec Clifton-Taylor [and others] London, New York, Country Life Books, 1969. 272 p. illus., plan, ports. 26 cm. Bibliography: p. 262-263. [DA660.H14] 71-852303 ISBN 0-600-43027-8 55/-
1. Historic buildings—Great Britain. I. Clifton-Taylor, Alec. II. Title.

HARLING, Robert. 914.2
The great houses and finest rooms of England. Conversations in stately homes between their owners and Robert Harling. New York, Viking Press [1969] 208 p. illus. (part col.), ports. 32 cm. (A Studio book) [DA660.H25 1969] 77-87254 16.95
1. Historic buildings—Great Britain. 2. Art—Great Britain. I. Title.

STURDY, David. 942
Historic monuments of England and Wales / David and Fiona Sturdy. London : Dent, 1977. 218 p. : ill., maps ; 25 cm. Includes index. [DA660.S87] 77-369345 ISBN 0-460-04158-4 : 14.50
1. Historic buildings—Great Britain. 2. Historic sites—Great Britain. 3. Great Britain—History. I. Sturdy, Fiona, joint author. II. Title.
Dist. by Biblio Distribution Centre, Totowa, NJ

Historic buildings—Great Britain—Alderney—Conservation and restoration.

BRETT, Charles 720'.9423'43
Edward Bainbridge, 1928-
Buildings of the island of Alderney / compiled for the Alderney Society, August 1975-March 1976, by C. E. B. Brett. [Belfast] : Ulster Architectural Heritage Society for the Alderney Society, 1976. 50 p., [2] fold. leaves of plates : ill., maps, plans ; 30 cm. Bibliography: p. 5. [DA670.A5B73] 77-350703 ISBN 0-9504668-3-2 : £1.75
1. Historic buildings—Great Britain—Alderney—Conservation and restoration. 2. Alderney—History. I. Alderney Society. II. Ulster Architectural Heritage Society. III. Title.

Historic buildings—Iowa.

HISTORIC American Buildings 977.7
Survey.
The Iowa catalog : a list of measured drawings, photographs, and written documentation in the Survey, 1977 / Historic American Buildings Survey ; compiled by Wesley I. Shank. Iowa City : University of Iowa Press, 1979. p. cm. Includes index. Bibliography: p. [F622.H57 1979] 79-11666 ISBN 0-87745-091-9 : 8.95. ISBN 0-87745-092-7 pbk. : 5.95
1. Historic buildings—Iowa. 2. Iowa—History, Local. 3. Architecture—Iowa. I. Shank, Wesley I. II. Title. BIP

MACY, Harriet P., 1883- 741.9777
1968.
Sketches of historic Iowa, by Harriet P. Macy. [Ames, Iowa, Carter Press, 1969] viii, 92 p. illus., port. 29 cm. [F622.M24] 78-98930
1. Historic buildings—Iowa. I. Title.

Historic buildings—Massachusetts.

MASSACHUSETTS. Bureau of 711'.4
Transportation Planning and Development.
Historic sites study; report. Boston [1967] 40 p. illus. 28 cm. (Massachusetts. Dept. of Public Works. Publication no. 748) Demonstration city: Boxford, Mass. [TA24.M4A27 no. 748] 68-64506
1. Historic buildings—Massachusetts. 2. Boxford, Mass. 3. Cities and towns—Planning—Massachusetts. I. Title. II. Series.

Historic buildings—Massachusetts—Andover—Conservation and restoration.

HISTORICAL agencies and 974.4'5
public policy : opportunities for humanists in Massachusetts. [North Andover, Mass. : Merrimack Valley Textile Museum], c1976. 44 p. : ill. ; 22 cm. Cover title. [F74.A6H57] 76-362224
1. Historic buildings—Massachusetts—Andover—Conservation and restoration. 2. Historic buildings—Massachusetts—Lawrence—Conservation and restoration. 3. Andover, Mass.—Buildings. 4. Lawrence, Mass.—Buildings. 5. Historical societies—Massachusetts. I. Merrimack Valley Textile Museum, North Andover, Mass.

Historic buildings—Massachusetts—Hanover.

BARKER, Barbara 974.4'82
Underhill.
Houses of the Revolution in Hanover, Massachusetts / by Barbara Underhill Barker, Lucy Josselyn Bonney, Anne Bonney Henderson. [Hanover, Mass.] : Hanover Historical Society, c1976. vii, 151 p. : ill., fold. map (in pocket) ; 23 cm. Bibliography: p. 151. [F74.H2B19] 77-355853
1. Historic buildings—Massachusetts—Hanover. 2. Hanover, Mass.—Dwellings. I. Bonney, Lucy Josselyn, joint author. II. Henderson, Anne Bonney, joint author. III. Hanover Historical Society. IV. Title.

Historic buildings—Massachusetts—Newton.

PRE-1855 Newton houses 974.4'4
remaining in 1976 : Newton's Corner and Nonantum. Newton, Mass. : Friends of the Jackson Homestead, c1976. 84 p. : ill. ; 22 cm. (Publication of the Jackson Homestead ; no. 11) Cover title: Newton Corner-Nonantum, Newton's older houses. [F74.N56P68] 76-151113
1. Historic buildings—Massachusetts—Newton. 2. Newton, Mass.—Dwellings. I. Jackson Homestead. Newton, Mass. Friends. II. Title: Newton's older houses. III. Series: Jackson Homestead, Newton, Mass. Publication of the Jackson Homestead ; 7.

Historic buildings—Massachusetts—North Falmouth—Guide-books.

DUNKLE, William M. 917.44'92
North Falmouth Bicentennial guide : colonial homes and sites from 1677 to 1880 : with notes on the men who fought during the Revolutionary period, 1775-1783, historic weather events, and a brief history of the area / compiled by William M. Dunkle, Jr. 1st ed. [North Falmouth, Mass.] : North Falmouth Bicentennial Subcommittee ; Woods Hole, Mass. : distribution by Woods Hole Press, 1975. 29 p., [1] fold. leaf of plates : ill. ; 22 cm. Includes bibliographical references. [F74.N814D86] 75-45781 ISBN 0-915176-12-2 : 1.75
1. Historic buildings—Massachusetts—North Falmouth—Guide-books. 2. North Falmouth, Mass.—Buildings. I. North Falmouth Bicentennial Subcommittee. II. Title.

Historic buildings—Massachusetts—Pictorial works.

HISTORIC American 779'.9'9744
Buildings Survey.
Historic buildings of Massachusetts : photographs from the Historic American Buildings Survey. New York : Scribner, [1976] p. cm. (Scribner historic buildings series) [F65.H64 1976] 76-12600 ISBN 0-684-14567-7 : 12.50. ISBN 0-684-14560-X pbk. : 5.95
1. Historic buildings—Massachusetts—Pictorial works. 2. Massachusetts—History, Local—Pictorial works. I. Title. BIP

Historic buildings—Mexico.

SHIPWAY, Verna (Cook) 728'.0972
1890-
Houses of Mexico; origins and traditions, by Verna Cook Shipway and Warren Shipway. New York, Architectural Book Pub. Co. [1970] xx, 249 p. (chiefly illus.) 29 cm. [NA7244.S44 1970] 72-133125 ISBN 0-8038-0104-1 13.95
1. Historic buildings—Mexico. 2. Architecture, Domestic—Mexico. I. Shipway, Warren, joint author. II. Title. BIP

Historic buildings—Montana.

LUCKE, Robert C. 978.6'03
Historic homes of north central Montana / by Robert C. Lucke. 1st ed. [Havre, Mont. : Hill County Print.], 1977- v. : ill. ; 18 x 25 cm. [F732.L82] 77-365503
1. Historic buildings—Montana. 2. Montana—History, Local. I. Title.

Historic buildings—Montana—Helena.

BAUCUS, Jean. 978.6'615
Helena, her historic homes / text by Jean Baucus ; ill. by Gayle Shanahan. Helena, Mont. : Baucus and Shanahan, c1976- v. : ill. ; 18 x 24 cm. Bibliography: v. 1, p. [68] [F739.H4B38] 76-373130
1. Historic buildings—Montana—Helena. 2. Helena, Mont.—Dwellings. I. Shanahan, Gayle. II. Title.

Historic buildings—New England.

CHAMBERLAIN, Samuel, 1895- 917.4
A small house in the sun; the visage of rural New England. [Special anniversary ed.] New York, Hastings House [1971, c1936] 96 p. (chiefly illus.) 32 cm. [NA715.C45 1971] 77-154657 ISBN 0-8038-6704-2 12.50
1. Historic buildings—New England. 2. Architecture—New England. 3. Architecture, Colonial—New England. I. Title. BIP

ROLLESTON, Sara Emerson. 974.6
Heritage houses : the American tradition in Connecticut 1660-1900 / Sara Emerson Rolleston ; foreword by David W. Dangremond. New York : Viking Press, [1979] p. cm. (A Studio book) [F95.R64] 79-14854 ISBN 0-670-36880-6 : 15.00
1. Historic buildings—Connecticut—Guide-books. 2. Connecticut—History, Local. 3. Architecture, Domestic—Connecticut. I. Title. BIP

Historic buildings—New York (City)

ROSEBROCK, Ellen 974.7'1
Fletcher.
Counting-house days in South Street : New York's early brick seaport buildings / by Ellen Fletcher Rosebrock. New York : South Street Seaport Museum, [1975] 48 p. : ill. ; 22 cm. Bibliography: p. 43-44. [F128.7.R67] 75-310617 ISBN 0-913344-18-4 pbk. : 2.50
1. Historic buildings—New York (City) 2. Warehouses—New York (City) 3. New York (City)—Buildings. 4. New York (City)—Streets—South Street. I. Title. BIP

Historic buildings—New York (City)—Guide-books.

GOLDSTONE, Harmon 917.47'1'044
Hendricks, 1911-
History preserved : a guide to New York City landmarks and historic districts / by Harmon H. Goldstone and Martha Dalrymple. New York : Schocken Books, 1976, c1974. 576 p. : ill. ; 23 cm. Reprint of the ed. published by Simon and Schuster, New York. Includes index. Bibliography: p. [530]-532. [F128.7.G64 1976] 76-9142 ISBN 0-8052-0544-6 pbk. : 8.95
1. Historic buildings—New York (City)—Guide-books. 2. New York (City)—Buildings. 3. New York (City)—Description—1951- —Guide-books. I. Dalrymple, Martha, joint author. II. Title.

Historic buildings—New York (City) region, N.Y.

RIFKIND, Carole. 917.47'1'044
Mansions, mills, and main streets / Carole Rifkind and Carol Levine. New York : Schocken Books, [1975] viii, 248 p. : ill. ; 20 cm. Includes index. [F128.7.R53] 74-26915 ISBN 0-8052-3584-1 : 12.50. ISBN 0-8052-0473-3 pbk. : 5.75
1. Historic buildings—New York (City) region, N.Y. 2. New York (City) region, N.Y.—Description and travel—Guide-books. I. Levine, Carol, joint author. II. Title. BIP

Historic buildings—Texas—Gillespie Co.

WHITE, J. Roy. 741.9'73
Hill country revisited / by J. Roy White ; introd. by Joe B. Frantz. San Antonio : Trinity University Press, c1977. xix 51 p. : ill. ; 22 x 25 cm. [F392.G5W47] 77-89818 ISBN 0-911536-70-1 : 10.95
1. Historic buildings—Texas—Gillespie Co. 2. Historic buildings—Texas—Blanco Co. 3. Gillespie Co.—History, Local. 4. Blanco Co.—History, Local. I. Title. BIP

Historic buildings—Texas—Rio Grande Valley—Pictorial works.

BAILEY, Ben P. 741.9'73
Border lands sketchbook = Libro de bosquejos fronterizos / Ben P. Bailey, Jr. ; translated by Channing Horner and Louise Bailey Horner. [Waco? Tex.] : Bailey, c1976. v, 170 p. : ill. (some col.) ; 29 cm. English and Spanish. Includes bibliographical references. [NC139.B28A42] 76-39665
1. Bailey, Ben P. 2. Historic buildings—Texas—Rio Grande Valley—Pictorial works. 3. Buildings in art. I. Title. II. Title: Libro de bosquejos fronterizos.

Historic buildings—United States.

BEINKE, Nancy K. 917.3'03
A list of furnished historic houses in the United States. Compiled by Nancy K. Beinke. [Washington?] U.S. Office of Archeology and Historic Preservation, 1970. iv, 173 p. 27 cm. [E159.B4] 77-609305
1. Historic buildings—United States. I. United States. Office of Archeology and Historic Preservation. II. Title.

DANIEL, Jean Houston. 725'.1
Executive mansions and capitols of America, by Jean Houston Daniel and Price Daniel. Waukesha, Wis., Country Beautiful; distributed by Putnam, New York [1969] 290 p. col. illus. 32 cm. "All Governors and First Ladies have contributed photographs or articles, or both. Each Governor's wife has either furnished or personally written the description and history of her State's mansion". Bibliography: p. 286-[288] [E159.D3] 71-77604 25.00
1. Historic buildings—United States. 2. Capitols—United States. I. Daniel, Price. II. Title.

DAVIDSON, Marshall B. 728'.0973
The American Heritage history of notable American houses. Author and editor in charge, Marshall B. Davidson. Biographical essays, Margot P. Brill. New York, American Heritage Pub. Co. [1971] 383 p. illus. 29 cm. [NA7205.D3] 75-149724 ISBN 0-07-015467-8 19.95
1. Historic buildings—United States. 2. Architecture, Domestic—United States. I. Title. II. Title: Notable American houses.

HAAS, Irvin. 917.3'03
America's historic villages & restorations / by Irvin Haas. New York : Arco Pub. Co., [1974] 149 p. : ill. ; 26 cm. [E159.H122] 74-77712 ISBN 0-668-03354-1 : 8.95
1. Historic buildings—United States. 2. United States—History. I. Title. II. Title: Villages & restorations. BIP

HOUSES of great 973'.099'2
Americans. Fort Atkinson, Wis. : Home Library Pub. Co., c1976. 96 p. : ill. (some col.) ; 32 cm. [E159.H79] 76-370700 ISBN 0-87294-089-6 : 4.98
1. Historic buildings—United States. I. Home Library Publishing Company.

LEVIN, Phyllis Lee. 917.3'03
Great historic houses of America. New York, Coward-McCann [1970] 296 p. illus. (part col.) 32 cm. [E159.L48 1970] 79-127409 22.50
1. Historic buildings—United States. I. Title.

REIF, Rita. 917.3'03
Treasure rooms of America's mansions, manors and houses. New York, Coward-McCann [1970] 297 p. illus. (part col.) 32 cm. [NA7205.R43 1970] 73-127410 22.50
1. Historic buildings—United States. 2. Architecture, Domestic—United States—Conservation and restoration. 3. Decoration and ornament—United States. I. Title.

WILLIAMS, Henry Lionel. 917.3'03
A treasury of great American houses, by Henry Lionel Williams and Ottalie K. Williams. [1st ed.] New York, Putnam [1970] 295 p. illus. (part col.), plans. 32 cm. [NA7610.W5 1970] 70-116993
1. Historic buildings—United States. 2. Architecture, Domestic—United States. I. Williams, Ottalie Kroeber, 1901- joint author. II. Title.

Historic buildings—United States—Conservation and restoration.

INFORMATION from the 069'.53
National Trust for Historic Preservation. Washington : The Trust, c1976- v. ; 28 cm. Contents.Contents.—[1] Factors affecting valuation of historic property.—[2] Economic analyses of adaptive use projects, Butler Square.—[3] Economic analyses of adaptive use projects, Guernsey Hall.—[4] Economic analyses of adaptive use projects, Long Wharf.—[5] Economic

analyses of adaptive use projects, Stanford Court.—[6] Economic analyses of adaptive use projects, Trolley Square. Includes bibliographical references. [E159.I53] 76-380534
1. Historic buildings—United States—Conservation and restoration. I. National Trust for Historic Preservation in the United States.

NATIONAL Trust for Historic Preservation in the United States. 720'.28
America's forgotten architecture / National Trust for Historic Preservation, Tony P. Wrenn, and Elizabeth D. Mulloy. New York : Pantheon Books, c1976. 311 p. : ill. ; 28 cm. Includes index. Bibliography: p. [297]-[300] [E159.N356 1976a] 76-9467 ISBN 0-394-49692-2 : 20.00. ISBN 0-394-73228-6 pbk. : 8.95
1. Historic buildings—United States—Conservation and restoration. 2. Cities and towns—Planning—United States. I. Wrenn, Tony P. II. Mulloy, Elizabeth D. III. Title. BIP

NATIONAL Trust for Historic Preservation of the United States. Office of Preservation Services. 069'.53
A guide to State historic preservation programs : a project of the Office of Preservation Services of the National Trust for Historic Preservation under the auspices of a grant from the National Endowment for the Humanities, with the cooperation and assistance of the State Historic Preservation officers and staffs ; researched and compiled by Betts Abel ; edited by Jennie B. Bull. Bicentennial ed. Washington : Preservation Press, 1976. 533 p. ; 28 cm. [E159.N356 1976] 75-44561 ISBN 0-89133-031-3 pbk. : 8.00
1. Historic buildings—United States—Conservation and restoration. 2. Historic sites—United States—Conservation and restoration. 3. Federal aid to historic sites—United States. I. Abel, Betts. II. Bull, Jennie B. III. Title.

STANFORTH, Deirdre. 069'.53
Restored America / by Deirdre Stanforth and Louis Reens. New York : Praeger, [1975] p. cm. [E159.S72] 74-5573 ISBN 0-275-49740-2 : 25.00
1. Historic buildings—United States—Conservation and restoration. I. Reens, Louis, joint author. II. Title.

UNITED States. Advisory Council on Historic Preservation. 069'.53
The national historic preservation program today / prepared by the Advisory Council on Historic Preservation, at the request of Henry M. Jackson, chairman, Committee on Interior and Insular Affairs, United States Senate. Washington : U.S. Govt. Print. Off., 1976. vii, 111 p. ; 24 cm. At head of title: 94th Congress, 2d session. Committee print. Includes bibliographical references. [E159.U5 1976] 76-600713
1. Historic buildings—United States—Conservation and restoration. 2. Historic buildings—Conservation and restoration. I. United States. Congress. Senate. Committee on Interior and Insular Affairs. II. Title.

ZIEGLER, Arthur P. 711'.59
Historic preservation in inner city areas; a manual of practice, by Arthur P. Ziegler, Jr. [1st ed.] Pittsburgh, Allegheny Press [1971] vi, 77 p. illus. 22 cm. [E159.Z5] 72-171721
1. Historic buildings—United States—Conservation and restoration. 2. Cities and towns—Planning—United States. I. Title.

ZIEGLER, Arthur P. 338.4'3
Revolving funds for historic preservation : a manual of practice / by Arthur P. Ziegler, Jr., Leopold Adler, II, Walter C. Kidney ; with assistance from Frances Edmunds ... [et al.] ; pref. by James Biddle. 1st ed. Pittsburgh : Ober Park Associates, [1975] 111 p. : ill. ; 22 cm. [E159.Z52] 74-79208
1. Historic buildings—United States—Conservation and restoration. I. Adler, Leopold, 1923- joint author. II. Kidney, Walter C., joint author. III. Title.

Historic buildings—United States—Conservation and restoration—Handbooks, manuals, etc.

SEALE, William. 069.53
Recreating the historic house interior / William Seale. Nashville, Tenn. : American Association for State and Local History, c1978. p. cm. Includes index. Bibliography: p. [E159.S49] 78-14361 ISBN 0-910050-32-5 : 22.00
1. Historic buildings—United States—Conservation and restoration—Handbooks, manuals, etc. 2. United States—History, Local. 3. Interior decoration—United States. I. Title. BIP

Historic buildings—United States—Guide-books.

HECHTLINGER, Adelaide. 917.4'04'4
The Pelican guide to historic homes and sights of Revolutionary America / by Adelaide Hechtlinger. Gretna, La. : Pelican Pub. Co., 1976- v. : ill. ; 22 cm. Includes index. Contents.Contents.—v. 1. New England. [E159.H42] 76-20434 ISBN 0-88289-090-5 : 2.95 (v. 1)
1. Historic buildings—United States—Guide-books. 2. United States—Description and travel—1960- —Guide-books. I. Title. BIP

Historic buildings—United States—Juvenile literature.

HAMMOND Incorporated. 917.3'03
Landmarks of liberty. [Maplewood, N.J., 1970] 93 p. illus. (part col.), col. maps, ports. 27 cm. The histories of twenty-two shrines and monuments throughout the Nation. [E159.H24] 77-114691 3.50
1. Historic buildings—United States—Juvenile literature. 2. Monuments—United States—Juvenile literature. I. Title. BIP

Historic buildings—United States—Pictorial works.

GILBERT, Eugene. 917.3'04'925
America's past in pencil : a sketchbook of historic homes / sketches by Eugene Gilbert ; research, text, editing, Olive Fielding Marrical. Santa Ana, Calif. : First American Title Insurance Co., c1976. 115 p. : ill. ; 28 cm. Bibliography: p. 114. [E159.G52] 75-35420 3.50
1. Historic buildings—United States—Pictorial works. I. Marrical, Olive Fielding. II. Title.

GREIFF, Constance M. 973'.074
Lost America: from the Atlantic to the Mississippi. Edited by Constance M. Greiff. With a foreword by James Biddle. [1st ed.] Princeton, N.J., Pyne Press, 1971. x, 244 p. illus. 29 cm. A companion volume to Lost America: from the Mississippi to the Pacific. [E159.G7] 75-162363 ISBN 0-87861-008-1 17.95
1. Historic buildings—United States—Pictorial works. I. Title.

TONDREAU, Bill. 973.92'022'2
Images of early America / designed and produced by the office of Charles and Ray Eames for Herman Miller, inc. ; photos. by Bill Tondreau, Alex Funke, Charles Eames. [s.l.] : C. and R. Eames, 1976. 47 p. : chiefly col. ill. ; 23 cm. [E159.T65] 76-29108
1. Historic buildings—United States—Pictorial works. 2. Historic sites—United States—Pictorial works. 3. United States—Description and travel—1960- —Views. I. Funke, Alex, joint author. II. Eames, Charles. III. Eames, Ray. IV. Herman Miller, inc. V. Title.

Historic gardens—Conservation and restoration.

FAVRETTI, Rudy J. 712'.6'0973
Landscapes for historic buildings : a handbook for reproducing and creating authentic landscape settings / Rudy J. Favretti and Joy P. Favretti. Nashville : American Association for State and Local History, 1978. p. cm. Includes index. Bibliography: p. [SB467.F38] 78-17200 ISBN 0-910050-34-1 : 10.00
1. Historic gardens—Conservation and restoration. 2. Historic sites—Conservation and restoration. 3. Landscape gardening. 4. Landscape architecture—United States—History. I. Favretti, Joy P., joint author. II. Title.

Historic Hill District, St. Paul.

OLD Town Restorations, inc. 720'.28
Building the future from our past : a report on the Saint Paul Historic Hill District planning program. Saint Paul : Old Town Restorations, inc., c1975. p. cm. [NA108.S24O42 1975] 75-34194 ISBN 0-87518-127-9
1. Historic Hill District, St. Paul. 2. Architecture—St. Paul—Conservation and restoration. I. Title.

Historic houses, etc.—Conservation and restoration—Congresses.

HISTORIC Towns and Cities Conference, York, Eng., 1968. 711'.4'0942
Conservation and development in historic towns and cities, edited by Pamela Ward. Newcastle upon Tyne, Oriel Press, 1968. x, 275 p. illus., facsims., maps, plans. 31 cm. Held in association with the Institute of Advanced Architectural Studies at the University of York. [CC135.H5 1968c] 68-55979 ISBN 0-85362-046-6 75/-
1. Historic houses, etc.—Conservation and restoration—Congresses. 2. Cities and towns—Planning—Congresses. I. Ward, Pamela, ed. II. York, Eng. University. Institute of Advanced Architectural Studies. III. Title.

Historic houses—Massachusetts—Merrimack Valley.

HOWELLS, John Mead, 1868-1959. 728'.09744'5
The architectural heritage of the Merrimack / by John Mead Howells. Bowie, Md. : Heritage Books, 1978. p. cm. Reprint of the 1941 ed. published by Architectural Book Pub. Co., New York. [NA7235.M4H6 1978] 78-16093 ISBN 0-917890-13-2 : 18.95
1. Historic houses—Massachusetts—Merrimack Valley. 2. Architecture, Domestic—Massachusetts—Merrimack Valley. 3. Architecture, Colonial—Massachusetts—Merrimack Valley. 4. Gardens—Massachusetts—Merrimack Valley. I. Title. BIP

Historic sites—Delaware—Conservation and restoration—Bibliography.

DAVIS, Lenwood G. 016.3092 s
Preserving historic landmarks and the human scale in towns and cities in Delaware / Lenwood G. Davis. Monticello, Ill. : Council of Planning Librarians, 1978 [c1977] 11 p. ; 28 cm. (Exchange bibliography - Council of Planning Librarians ; 1438) Cover title. [Z5942.C68 no. 1438] [Z1267] [F165] 016.9751 78-100286 pbk. : 1.50
1. Historic sites—Delaware—Conservation and restoration—Bibliography. I. Title. II. Series: Council of Planning Librarians. Exchange bibliography ; 1438.

Historic sites—England.

BAILEY, Bernadine Freeman, 1901- 942
American shrines in England / Bernadine Bailey. South Brunswick : A. S. Barnes, c1976. p. cm. Includes index. [DA660.B15 1976] 75-20586 ISBN 0-498-01727-3 : 15.00
1. Historic sites—England. 2. Historic buildings—England. 3. United States—History. 4. Great Britain—History. I. Title. BIP

Historic sites—Great Britain—Conservation and restoration.

DOBBY, Alan. 069'.53
Conservation and planning / Alan Dobby. London : Hutchinson, 1978. 173 p., [2] leaves of plates : ill. ; 23 cm. (The Built environment series) Includes bibliographical references and index. [DA655.D6] 78-313494 ISBN 0-09-132270-7 : 15.95 ISBN 0-09-132271-5 pbk. : 7.95
1. Historic sites—Great Britain—Conservation and restoration. 2. Historic sites—Conservation and restoration. I. Title.
Distributed by Hutchinson, Salem,NH BIP

Historic sites—Ohio—Conservation and restoration—Bibliography.

DAVIS, Lenwood G. 016.3092 s
Preserving historic landmarks and the human scale in Columbus and Ohio / Lenwood G. Davis. Monticello, Ill. : Council of Planning Librarians, 1978, c1977. 20 p. ; 28 cm. (Exchange bibliography - Council of Planning Librarians ; 1538) Cover title. [Z5942.C68 no. 1538] [Z1323] [F492] 016.069'53'09771 78-105707 pbk. : 2.00
1. Historic sites—Ohio—Conservation and restoration—Bibliography. 2. Ohio—History, Local—Bibliography. 3. Historic sites—Ohio—Columbus—Conservation and restoration—Bibliography. 4. Columbus, Ohio—Buildings—Conservation and restoration—Bibliography. 5. Ohio—History—Societies, etc—Directories. I. Title. II. Series: Council of Planning Librarians. Exchange bibliography ; 1538.

Historic sites—United States.

ALEGRE, Mitchell R. 917.3'04'92
A guide to museum villages : the American heritage brought to life / Mitchell R. Alegre. New York : Drake, 1978. 160 p. : ill. ; 23 cm. Includes index. [E159.A367] 77-72399 ISBN 0-8473-1656-4 : 5.95
1. Historic sites—United States. 2. Historical museums—United States. 3. United States—History, Local. 4. Villages—United States. I. Title. BIP

NATIONAL Register of Historic Places. 353.008'6
Historic preservation grants-in-aid (as of October 31, 1972) ... Washington, 1972. iv, 42 p. 27 cm. [E159.N342 1972] 73-602445
1. Historic sites—United States. 2. United States—Historic houses, etc. 3. Grants-in-aid—United States. I. Title.

Historic sites—United States—Conservation and restoration.

GREIFF, Constance M. 069'.53
The historic property owner's handbook / Constance M. Greiff. Washington : Preservation Press, 1977. [92] p. in various pagings : ill. ; 30 cm. "Prepared for the National Trust for Historic Preservation." [E159.G697] 77-88407 ISBN 0-89133-059-3 : 7.50
1. Historic sites—United States—Conservation and restoration. 2. Historic buildings—United States—Conservation and restoration. 3. Federal aid to historic sites. I. National Trust for Historic Preservation in the United States. II. Title. BIP

KING, Thomas F. 069'.53
Anthropology in historic preservation : caring for culture's clutter / Thomas F. King, Patricia Parker Hickman, Gary Berg. New York : Academic Press, c1977. xi, 344 p. : ill. ; 24 cm. (Studies in archeology) Includes index. Bibliography: p. 321-328. [E159.K56] 77-75574 ISBN 0-12-408250-5 : 15.00
1. Historic sites—United States—Conservation and restoration. 2. Historic buildings—United States—Conservation and restoration. 3. United States—Antiquities—Collection and preservation. 4. Anthropology—United States. I. Hickman, Patricia Parker, joint author. II. Berg, Gary, joint author. III. Title. BIP

TRAVIS, Richard W. 309.2'5'0973
Regional components of the recognition of historic places / by Richard W. Travis. [Urbana] : Geography Graduate Student Association, University of Illinois at Urbana-Champaign, 1972. 15 p. ; 28 cm. (Occasional publications of the Dept. of Geography ; paper no. 3) Cover title. Bibliography: p. 13-15. [E159.T79] 73-623486
1. Historic sites—United States—Conservation and restoration. I. Title. II.

Series: Illinois. University at Urbana-Champaign. Dept. of Geography. Occasional publications ; paper no. 3.

Historic sites—United States—Conservation and restoration—Bibliography.

CLINE, William Erich. 016.3092 s
Historic preservation literature, 1969-1977 : selected references / by William Erich Cline. Monticello, Ill. : Council of Planning Librarians, 1978. 51 p. ; 28 cm. (Exchange bibliography - Council of Planning Librarians ; no. 1457) [Z5942.C68 no. 1457] [Z1251.A2] [E159] 016.069'53 78-103477 5.00
1. Historic sites—United States—Conservation and restoration—Bibliography. 2. United States—History, Local—Bibliography. I. Title. II. Series: Council of Planning Librarians. Exchange bibliography ; no. 1457.

Historic sites—United States—Guide-books.

LORD, Suzanne. 917.3'04'926
American travelers' treasury : a guide to the nation's heirlooms / by Suzanne Lord. New York : Morrow, 1977. 588 p. ; 21 cm. (Americans-discover-America series) [E159.L67] 77-292 ISBN 0-688-03130-7 : 5.95
1. Historic sites—United States—Guide-books. 2. Historic buildings—United States—Guide-books. 3. Historical museums—United States—Guide-books. I. Title. BIP

Historic sites—United States—Pictorial works.

FRIEDLANDER, Lee. 779'.9'973
The American monument / Lee Friedlander. New York : Eakins, c1976. [83] leaves : chiefly ill. ; 31 x 44 cm. [E159.F74] 76-6715 ISBN 0-87130-043-5 : 65.00
1. Historic sites—United States—Pictorial works. 2. Monuments—United States—Pictorial works. I. Title. BIP

Historical markers—Idaho.

IDAHO. Dept. of Highways. Public Information Section. 979.6
The historical sign program in the State of Idaho. [Boise] 1966. 40 p. illus. (part col.), maps. (part col.) 14 x 22 cm. Cover title. [F747.A45] 68-64061
1. Historical markers—Idaho. I. Title.

Historical markers—New York (City)

WILLENSKY, Elliot. 069'.15
Guide to developing a neighborhood marker system. [New York, c1972] 63 p. illus. 25 cm. "Prepared for the Museum of the City of New York." [F128.37.W54] 73-176525
1. Historical markers—New York (City) I. New York (City). Museum of the City of New York. II. Title.

Historical museums—U.S.

ZOOK, Nicholas. 973'.074'013
Museum villages, U.S.A. Barre, Mass., Barre Publishers, 1971 [c1970] 136 p. illus. 26 cm. [E159.Z56] 71-111102 ISBN 0-8271-7008-4 8.95
1. Historical museums—U.S. I. Title.

History, Modern—20th century—Pictorial works.

NEW York, Press Photographers Association 909.820222
New York Press Photographers; golden anniversary 1915-1965. [Ed., William N. Jacobellis. New Rochelle, N.Y., SportShelf, 1966 c.1965] 259p. (chiefly illus., facsims., ports) 29cm. [D426.N18] 66-3289 5.00
1. History, Modern—20th cent.—Pictorial works. I. Jacobellis, William, ed. II. Title.

History, Modern—20th century—Pictorial works.

COHN, Lawrence, 1932- 909.82
Movietone presents the 20th century / by Lawrence Cohn ; introd. by Lowell Thomas. New York : Saint Martin's Press, c1976. p. cm. [D426.C63] 75-26177 17.95
1. History, Modern—20th century—Pictorial works. I. Twentieth Century-Fox Film Corporation. II. Title. BIP

RICKARDS, Maurice, 1919- 769'.5
Posters of protest and revolution. Selected and reviewed by Maurice Rickards. New York, Walker [1970] 30 p. 80 illus. (part col.) 26 cm. [D426.R5 1970] 78-84212 12.50
1. History, Modern—20th century—Pictorial works. 2. Political posters. I. Title.

SALOMON, Erich. 779'.9'90194
Portrait of an age. Selected by Han de Vries and Peter Hunter-Salomon. Biography and notes by Peter Hunter-Salomon. Photographic layout by Han de Vries. Translated by Sheila Tobias. New York, Collier Books [1975, c1967] xiv, 221 p. illus. 28 cm. Translation of Portrat einer Epoche. Bibliography: p. 218. [D426.S213 1975] 74-9749 ISBN 0-02-000820-1 4.95
1. History, Modern—20th century—Pictorial works. I. Vries, Han de, ed. II. Hunter-Salomon, Peter, ed. III. Title.

History—Philosophy.

GAY, Peter, 1923- 759.4
Art and act : on causes in history—Manet, Gropius, Mondrian / by Peter Gay. 1st ed. New York : Harper & Row, [1975], c1976 p. cm. (Icon editions) Originated as 7 lectures delivered at Cooper Union in Mar. and Apr. of 1974. Includes index. Bibliography: p. [ND553.M3G38] 75-12291 ISBN 0-06-433248-9 : 15.00
1. Manet, Edouard, 1832-1883. 2. Gropius, Walter, 1883-1969. 3. Mondriaan, Pieter Cornelis, 1872-1944. 4. History—Philosophy. I. Title. BIP

Hitchcock, Lambert, 1795-1852.

BLANCHARD, Roberta Ray. 749.31
How to restore and decorate chairs. Drawings by the author. New York, Avenel Books [1952] 128 p. illus. 28 cm. [NK2715.B57] 52-11241
1. Hitchcock, Lambert, 1795-1852. 2. Chairs. 3. Stencil work. I. Title.

KENNEY, John Tarrant. 338.7'68'41
The Hitchcock chair; the story of a Connecticut Yankee—L. Hitchcock of Hitchcocks-ville—and an account of the restoration of his 19th-century manufactory. [1st ed.] New York, C. N. Potter; distributed by Crown Publishers [1971] x, 339 p. illus. 29 cm. Bibliography: p. 333-334. [NK2439.H5K4 1971] 79-150696 12.50
1. Hitchcock, Lambert, 1795-1852. I. Title.

Hitchell site.

JOHNSTON, Richard B 917.83'382
The Hitchell site, by Richard B. Johnston. Lincoln, Neb., 1967. v, 113 p. illus., maps, plan. 25 cm. (River Basin Surveys. Publications in salvage archeology, no. 3) Bibliography: p. 86-89. [E78.S63J63] 67-61450
1. Hitchell site. I. Title. II. Series.

Hitler, Adolf, 1889-1945.

ROXAN, David. 133.4'4
The jackdaw of Linz; the story of Hitler's art thefts, by David Roxan and Ken Wanstall. London, Cassell [1964] xii, 195 p. illus., map, ports. 22 cm. [N6492.2.R65] 65-6389
1. Hitler, Adolf, 1889-1945. 2. World War, 1939-1945 — Art and the war. 3. World War, 1939-1945 — Destruction and pillage — Europe. 4. Art — Europe. I. Wanstall, Ken, joint author. II. Title.

ROXAN, David 940.53187
The rape of art; the story of Hitler's plunder of the great masterpueces of Europe, by David Roxan, Ken Wanstall [1st Amer. ed.] New York, Coward [1965, c.1964] 195p. illus., map, plans, ports. 22cm. [N6492.2.R65] 65-14195 5.00
1. Hitler, Adolf, 1889-1945. 2. World War, 1939-1945—Art and the war. 3. World War, 1939-1945—Destruction and pillage—Europe. 4. Art—Europe. I. Wanstall, Ken, joint author. II. Title.

Hittorff, Jacob Ignaz, 1792-1867.

SCHNEIDER, Donald David, 1935- 720'.92'4
The works and doctrine of Jacques Ignace Hittorff, 1792-1867 / Donald David Schneider. New York : Garland Pub., 1977, i.e.1978 2 v. : ill. ; 22 cm. (Outstanding dissertations in the fine arts) Reprint of the author's thesis, Princeton, 1970. Bibliography: v. 2, p. 360-393. [NA1053.H5S33 1977] 76-23721 ISBN 0-8240-2727-2 lib.bdg. : 100.00 (2 vols)
1. Hittorff, Jacob Ignaz, 1792-1867. I. Title. II. Series.

Hnizdovsky, Jacques, 1915—

TAHIR, Abe M. 769'.92'4
Hnizdovsky : woodcuts, 1944-1975 : a catalogue raisonne / by Abe M. Tahir, Jr. ; with a foreword by Peter A. Wick. Gretna, La. : Pelican Pub. Co., 1976. p. cm. Includes index. [NE1112.H54T33] 76-12461 ISBN 0-88289-072-7 : 25.00. ISBN 0-88289-150-2 handprinted ed. : 95.00. ISBN 0-88289-149-9 handcol. ed. : 350.00
1. Hnizdovsky, Jacques, 1915- I. Hnizdovsky, Jacques, 1915-

Hockney, David.

HOCKNEY, David. 759.2 B
David Hockney / by David Hockney ; edited by Nikos Stangos ; introductory essay by Henry Geldzahler. New York : H. N. Abrams, 1977, c1976. 312 p. : ill. (some col.) ; 28 cm. Includes index. [N6797.H57A42 1977] 76-11721 ISBN 0-8109-1058-6 : 35.00
1. Hockney, David. 2. Artists—Great Britain—Biography. BIP

HOCKNEY, David. 759.2 B
David Hockney / by David Hockney ; edited by Nikos Stangos ; introductory essay by Henry Geldzahler. London : Thames & Hudson, c1976. 312 p. : with 414 ill. ; 27 cm. Includes index. [N6797.H57S7 1976] 77-354409 ISBN 0-500-09108-0 : £10.00
1. Hockney, David. 2. Artists—Great Britain—Biography. I. Stangos, Nikos.

HOCKNEY, David. 760'.0924
Paintings, prints, and drawings, 1960-1970. Boston, Boston Book and Art [1970] 100 p. illus. (part col.) 29 cm. A corr. version of the catalog of the exhibition held Apr. 2-May 3, 1970, at the Whitechapel Art Gallery, London. Bibliography: p. 100. [N6797.H57A56] 78-129451 7.95
I. Whitechapel Art Gallery, London.

Hodgkin, Howard, 1932—

HODGKIN, Howard, 1932- 759.2
Forty-five paintings, 1949-1975 : [catalog of an exhibition held at the] Museum of Modern Art, Pembroke Street, Oxford, 14 March-18 April 1976 ... [et al.] / Howard Hodgkin. [London] : Arts Council of Great Britain, [1976] 76 p. : col. ill. ; 21 cm. Bibliography: p. 73-74. [ND497.H665M87] 76-383864 £2.00
1. Hodgkin, Howard, 1932- I. Museum of Modern Art, Oxford. II. Title.

Hodgkins, Frances, 1869-1947.

DUNEDIN, N.Z. University of Otago. Library. Hocken Collection. 759.9931
The origins of Frances Hodgkins; an exhibition of paintings in the centennial year of her birth. [Dunedin, N.Z.] Hocken Library, University of Otago, 1969. 27, [1] p. illus., ports. 25 cm. Catalogue and selection of the paintings by Una Platts. Bibliography: p. [28] [ND1108.H6D8] 75-546405
1. Hodgkins, Frances, 1869-1947. I. Platts, Una. II. Title.

Hodgson, Thomas Sherlock, 1924—

HODGSON, Thomas Sherlock, 1924- 709'.2'4
Creativity is change / Tom Hodgson. [s.l. : s.n., 1976] [33] p. : ill. (some col.) ; 19 x 20 cm. [N6549.H63A43] 77-465888 7.50
1. Hodgson, Thomas Sherlock, 1924- I. Title.

Hodin, Josef Paul.

KERN, Walter, 1898- 759.9494
Walter Kern; Introd. by J. P. Hodin and original texts by Walter Kern. (Translated by Diana Imber from the German) Neuchatel, Ed. du Griffon; American distributor: Wittenborn, New York [1966] 101 p. illus. 31 cm. (Plastic arts of the 20th century) sfr 60.-(SW 67-A2-319) [ND853.K43H6] 67-76627
1. Hodin, Josef Paul. I. Title.

Hodler, Ferdinand, 1853-1918.

SELZ, Peter Howard, 1919- 759.9494
Ferdinand Hodler [by] Peter Selz with contributions by Jura Bruschweiler, Phyllis Hattis [and] Eva Wyler. [Berkeley, University Art Museum, 1972] 140 p. illus. (part col.) 26 cm. Catalogue of an exhibition held at the University Art Museum, Berkeley, Nov. 22, 1972-Jan. 7, 1973, at the Solomon R. Guggenheim Museum, New York, Feb. 2-Apr. 8, 1973, and at the Busch-Reisinger Museum, Harvard University, May 1-June 22, 1973. Bibliography: p. 129-130. [ND853.H6S44] 72-619599
1. Hodler, Ferdinand, 1853-1918. I. California. University. Art Museum. II. Solomon R. Guggenheim Museum, New York. III. Harvard University. Busch-Reisinger Museum of Germanic Culture.

Hofer, Carl, 1878-1955.

RIGBY, Ida Katherine. 759.3
Karl Hofer / Ida Katherine Rigby. New York : Garland Pub., 1976. xiv, 369 p. : ill. ; 22 cm. (Outstanding dissertations in the fine arts) Appendices (p. 333-346): I. Hofer's poems.—II. Chronology.—III. Selected exhibitions. Bibliography: p. 347-369. [ND588.H58R53] 75-23811 ISBN 0-8240-2005-7 lib.bdg. : 30.00
1. Hofer, Carl, 1878-1955. I. Title. II. Series. BIP

Hofer, Philip, 1898- —Art collections.

ROSENFIELD, John M. 709'.52'07401444
The courtly tradition in Japanese art and literature: selections from Hofer and Hyde collections [by] John M. Rosenfield, Fumiko E. Cranston [and] Edwin A. Cranston. [Cambridge] Fogg Art Museum, Harvard University, 1973. 316 p. illus. (part col.) 22 x 28 cm. [NX584.A1R67] 73-85473
1. Hofer, Philip, 1898- —Art collections. 2. Hyde, Donald Frizell, 1909-1966—Art collections. 3. Hyde, Mary Morley Crapo—Art collections. 4. Arts, Japanese. I. Cranston, Fumiko E., joint author. II. Cranston, Edwin A., joint author. III. Harvard University. William Hayes Fogg Art Museum. IV. Title.

Hoffbauer, Charles, 1875-1957.

HOFFBAUER, Charles, 1875-1957. 759.4
Charles Hoffbauer (1875-1957) : drawings, temperas & oil paintings. W. Sommerville, Mass. : Gropper Art Gallery, [1977] [29] p. : ill. ; 21 x 27 cm. "Research, text, and catalog design [by] Joseph Gropper." Bibliography: p. [28]-[29] [N6853.H63G76] 77-377189
1. Hoffbauer, Charles, 1875-1957. I. Gropper, Joseph. II. Gropper Art Gallery.

Hofmann, Hans, 1880-1966.

HOFMANN, Hans, 1880-1966. 759.13
Hans Hofmann: the Renate series. New York, Metropolitan Museum of Art [1972] 39 p. illus. 22 cm. Text by H. Geldzahler.

Bibliography: p. 39. [ND237.H667G44] 72-81727 ISBN 0-87099-119-1
I. Geldzahler, Henry.

HOFMANN, Hans, 1880-1966. 759.13
Hans Hofmann : a retrospective exhibition, cosponsored by the Hirshhorn Museum and Sculpture Garden, October 14, 1976-January 2, 1977, and the Museum of Fine Arts, Houston, February 4-April 3, 1977 / by Walter Darby Bannard. [Houston : Museum of Fine Arts], c1976. 128 p. : ill. (some col.) ; 27 cm. Bibliography: p. 123-128. [ND237.H667B36] 76-27637
1. Hofmann, Hans, 1880-1966. I. Bannard, Walter Darby, 1934- II. Hirshhorn Museum and Sculpture Garden. III. Houston, Tex. Museum of Fine Arts.

HOFMANN, Hans, 1880-1966. 759.13
Hans Hofmann, paintings of the '40s, '50s, and '60s. [Exhibition at the] Andre Emmerich Gallery, inc., Jan. 3d through 22, 1970. [New York, Andre Emmerich Gallery, 1970] 10 col. plates, port. 26 cm. [ND237.H667A45] 73-21950
I. Andre Emmerich Gallery, New York.

HOFMANN, Hans, 1880-1966. 759.13
Hans Hofmann: ten major works. New York, Andre Emmerich Gallery [1973] [13] p. (chiefly col. illus.) 31 cm. Catalog of an exhibition held Jan. 6-24, 1973, at the Andre Emmerich Gallery. [ND588.H59A82] 73-171501
1. Hofmann, Hans, 1880-1966. I. Andre Emmerich Gallery, New York.

HOFMANN, Hans, 1880-1966. 759.13
Hans Hofmann: ten major works. [New York, Andre Emmerich Gallery, 1969?] [21] p. plates (part col.), port. 31 cm. Label mounted on t.p.: Supplied by Worldwide Books, inc., Boston. Exhibition held Jan. 11-30, 1969 at the Andre Emmerich Gallery. [ND237.H667A57] 73-199843
I. Andre Emmerich Gallery, New York.

SEITZ, William Chapin. 759.13
Hans Hofmann; with selected writings by the artist. New York, Museum of Modern Art; distributed by Doubleday, Garden City, N. Y. [1963] 64 p. illus. (part col.) ports. 26 cm. "Selected bibliography, by Inga Forslund": p. 60-62. Bibliographical references included in "Notes" (p. 54) [ND237.H667S4] 63-21551
1. Hofmann, Hans, 1880- I. Title.

SEITZ, William Chapin. 759.13
Hans Hofmann, by William C. Seitz. With selected writings by the artist. New York, Museum of Modern Art. Reprint ed. [New York] Published for the Museum of Modern Art by Arno Press, 1972 [c1963] 64 p. illus. 26 cm. Bibliography: p. 60-62. [ND237.H667S4 1972] 79-169314 ISBN 0-405-01572-0 11.00
1. Hofmann, Hans, 1880-1966. I. New York (City). Museum of Modern Art.

WIGHT, Frederick Stallknecht, 1902- 927.5
Hans Hofmann. Berkeley, University of California Press, 1957. 66 p. illus. (part col.), port. 28 cm. Bibliography: p. 64-65. [ND237.H667W5] 57-7593
1. Hofmann, Hans, 1880-1966.

Hogarth, William, 1697-1764.

ANTAL, Frederick. 759.2
Hogarth and his place in European art. New York, Basic Books [1962] xxi, 270p. 152 plates. 26cm. Bibliographical references included in 'Notes' (p. 218-257) [ND497.H7A63] 62-13871
1. Hogarth, William, 1697-1764. I. Title.

FORREST, Ebenezer, fl.1774. 759.2
Hogarth's peregrination; edited with an introd. by Charles Mitchell. Oxford, Clarendon Press, 1952. xxxi, 51, [3]p. illus. 24cm. First published in 1782 under title: An account of what seemed most remarkable in the five days' peregrination of the five following persons, viz. Messieurs Tothall, Scott, Hogarth, Thornhill, and Forrest.Includes a version in Hudibrastic verse by W. Gosting. 'Bibliographical note': p. [53] [ND497.H7F6 1952] [ND497.H7F6 1952] 927.5 A 53 A 53
I. Hogarth, William, 1697-1764. II. Gosting, William, 1696-1777. III. Mitchell, Charles, ed. IV. Title.

HOGARTH, William, 1697-1764. 769'.92'4
Engravings by Hogarth. Edited by Sean Shesgreen. New York, Dover [1973] xxxiii, 205 p. 101 illus. 35 cm. Bibliography: p. [xxxi]-xxxiii. [NE642.H6S47 1973] 72-96411 ISBN 0-486-22479-1 6.00
1. Hogarth, William, 1697-1764. I. Shesgreen, Sean, 1939- ed. II. Title. BIP

HOGARTH, William, 1697-1764. 759.2
Hogarth [by] R. B. Beckett. Boston, Boston Book & Art Shop [1955] vii, 80p. 142plates. 26cm. (English master painters) 'Catalogue of Hogarth's paintings': p. [35]-75. [ND497] 927.5 55-9578
I. Beckett, Ronald Brymer. II. Title. III. Series.

HOGARTH, William, 1697-1764. 769'.924
Hogarth; the complete engravings [by] Joseph Burke and Colin Caldwell. New York, H. N. Abrams [196-] 30 p., [250] p. of illus., [36] p. 34 cm. Bibliography: p. 30. [NE642.H6B8] 68-26785
I. Burke, Joseph. II. Caldwell, Colin. III. Title.

HOGARTH, William, 1697-1764. 760'.0924
William Hogarth; a loan exhibition of paintings, drawings, and prints at the Virginia Museum, 30 January through 5 March, 1967. [Edited by William Francis.] Richmond, Virginia Museum, 1967] 43 p. illus. 31 cm. "Morals and mime: the essential Hogarth, by Sir John Summerson": p. 5-13. Bibliography: p. 42. [N6797.H6F7] 67-63035
I. Francis, William Rummel, ed. II. Summerson, John Newenham, Sir, 1904- III. Virginia Museum of Fine Arts, Richmond.

JARRETT, Derek. 760'.092'4 B
The ingenious Mr Hogarth / Derek Jarrett. London : M. Joseph, 1976. 223 p., [12] leaves of plates : ill. ; 24 cm. Includes index. Bibliography: p. [214]-217. [ND497.H7J37] 76-380637 ISBN 0-7181-1489-2 : £7.00
1. Hogarth, William, 1697-1764. 2. Painters—Great Britain—Biography. I. Title.

LICHTENBERG, Georg Christoph, 1742-1799. 769'.924
Hogarth on high life. The Marriage a la mode series, from George Christoph Lichtenberg's commentaries. Translated and edited by Arthur S. Wensinger with W. B. Coley. [1st ed.] Middletown, Conn., Wesleyan University Press [1970] lii, 150 p. illus., 6 fold. plates. 39 cm. Translation of pt. 4 of the author's Ausfuhrliche Erklarung der Hogarthischen Kupferstiche. Appendices (p. 115-147): I. Lichtenberg on the Hogarth commentaries: extracts from certain of his letters.—II. Jean-Andre Rouquet's Explanation of the prints entitled Marriage a la mode.—III. Marriage a-la-mode: an humorous tale, in six cantos in hudibrastic verse. Bibliography: p. 148-150. [NE642.H6L466325 1970] 79-82541 ISBN 0-8195-4009-9
1. Hogarth, William, 1697-1764. I. Wensinger, Arthur S., 1926- ed. II. Coley, W. B., 1923- ed. III. Title. IV. Title: The Marriage a la mode series. BIP

LICHTENBERG, Georg Christoph, 1742-1799. 769.924
The world of Hogarth; Lichtenberg's commentaries on Hogarth's engravings. Translated from the German and with an introd. by Innes and Gustav Herdan. Boston, Houghton Mifflin, 1966. xxiii, 297 p. illus. 26 cm. Translation of Lfg. 1-4 of Ausfuhrliche Erklarung der Hogarthischen Kupferstiche, an enl., rev. version of a series of commentaries which appeared originally in the Gottinger Taschenkalender, 1784-96. [NE642.H6L53 1966a] 66-27492
1. Hogarth, William, 1697-1764. I. Title.

LINDSAY, Jack, 1900- 760'.092'4 B
Hogarth : his art and his world / Jack Lindsay. New York : Taplinger Pub. Co., 1979, c1977. p. cm. Includes index. Bibliography: p. [ND497.H7L77 1979] 78-21289 ISBN 0-8008-3916-1 : 14.95
1. Hogarth, William, 1697-1764. 2. Painters—England—Biography. BIP

MOORE, Robert Etheridge, 1920- 759.2
Hogarth's literary relationships. New York, Octagon Books, 1969 [c1948] viii, 202 p. illus. 24 cm. Bibliographical footnotes. [ND497.H7M6 1969] 70-76001
1. Hogarth, William, 1697-1764. 2. Fielding, Henry, 1707-1754. 3. Art and literature. 4. English literature—18th century—History and criticism. I. Title. BIP

PAULSON, Ronald. 759.2 B
Hogarth: his life, art, and times [by] Ronald Paulson. Abridged by Anne Wilde. [Abridged ed.] New Haven, Yale University Press, 1974. xiii, 461 p. illus. 24 cm. Bibliography: p. 443-444. [ND497.H7P39] 73-91338 ISBN 0-300-01766-9 20.00
1. Hogarth, William, 1697-1764. I. Wilde, Anne.
Pbk. 8.95, ISBN 0-300-01763-4. BIP

QUENNELL, Peter, 1905- 927.5
Hogarth's progress. New York, Viking Press, 1955. 318p. 25cm. [ND497.H7Q4 1955a] 55-7378
1. Hogarth, William, 1696-1764. I. Title.

QUENNELL, Peter, 1905- 759.2
Hogarth's progress. Freeport, N.Y., Books for Libraries Press [1973] p. (Biography index reprint series) Reprint of the 1955 ed. [ND497.H7Q4 1973] 72-13187 ISBN 0-8369-8145-6
1. Hogarth, William, 1697-1764. I. Title.

Hogen monogatari emaki (Paintings)

MASON, Penelope E., 1935- 759.952
A reconstruction of the Hogen-Heiji monogatari emaki / Penelope E. Mason. New York : Garland Pub., 1977. vii, 279 p., [38] leaves of plates : ill. ; 21 cm. (Outstanding dissertations in the fine arts) Reprint of the author's thesis, New York University, 1970. Bibliography: p. 268-279. [ND1059.6.H63M37 1977] 76-23639 ISBN 0-8240-2709-4 : 35.00
1. Hogen monogatari emaki (Paintings) 2. Heiji monogatari emaki (Paintings) I. Title. II. Series. BIP

Hohlwein, Ludwig, 1874—

HOHLWEIN, Ludwig, 1874- 759.3
Hohlwein posters in full color / Ludwig Hohlwein. New York : Dover Publications, 1976. 48 p. : all col. ill. ; 37 cm. [NC1850.H6A46 1976] 76-24055 ISBN 0-486-23408-8 : 6.00
1. Hohlwein, Ludwig, 1874- I. Title. BIP

Holbein, Hans, the younger. 1497-1543.

ART Association of Indianapolis, Indiana. John Herron. Art Institute. 759.0838
Holbein and his contemporaries, a loan exhibition of painting in France, the Netherlands, Germany, and England, October 22-December 24, 1950. [Rev. ed. Indianapolis, 1950] unpaged. illus. 25cm. [N5020.I49 1950] 57-19946
1. Holbein, Hans, the younger. 1497-1543. 2. Paintings, Renaissance— Exhibitions. I. Title.

HOLBEIN, Hans the Younger, 1497-1543 741.943
The drawings of Holbein. Text-notes on the plates by Marguerite Kay. London, P. Hamlvn [1966] 42p. 57 plates (pt. col.) 31cm. [Masterpieces of graphic art] [NC1055.H7K3] 68-71630 12.50
I. Kay, Marguerite. II. Title.
Distributed by Tudor, New York

HOLBEIN, Hans, the Younger, 1497-1543. 759.3
Holbein / [by] Helen Langdon. Oxford : Phaidon, 1976. 16 p., [48] p. of plates : col. ill., col. ports. ; 31 cm. [ND588.H7L28] 77-352859 ISBN 0-7148-1748-1 : 6.95
1. Holbein, Hans, the Younger, 1497-1543. I. Langdon, Helen.
Distributed by E.P. Dutton, New York

HOLBEIN, Hans, the Younger, 1497-1543. 769'.92'4
Images from the Old Testament = Historiarum Veteris Testamenti icones / by Hans Holbein (the Younger). New York : Paddington Press, c1976. p. cm. (Masterpieces of the illustrated book) Reprint of the 1543 ed. published by Trechsel and Frellon, Lyons; with new introd. French and Latin. [NE1150.5.H64A4714 1976] 76-3813 ISBN 0-8467-0147-2 pbk. : 4.95
1. Holbein, Hans, the Younger, 1497-1543. 2. Bible. O.T.—Pictures, illustrations, etc. I. Title. II. Title: Historiarum Veteris Testamenti icones. BIP

Holgate, Edwin H.

REID, Dennis R. 759.11
Edwin Holgate / Dennis Reid. Ottawa : National Gallery of Canada, 1976. 87 p. : chiefly ill. (some col.) ; 24 cm. (Canadian artists series ; no 4) Bibliography: p. 85 [ND249.H7R44] 77-358365 ISBN 0-88884-314-3
1. Holgate, Edwin H. 2. Painters—Canada—Biography. I. Holgate, Edwin H. II. Title. III. Series.

Holiday decorations.

BENNETT, Maggi. 745.59
Holiday ideas [by] Maggi Bennett, Sarajean Capua [and] Jeanette McArthur. Hollywood, Fla., Dukane Press [1971, c1970] 32 p. col. illus. 32 cm. Directions for making a ghost mobile, pinata, manger scene, valentine box, Easter bunny, and other holiday decorations. [TT900.H6B4] 78-127623 ISBN 0-87800-031-3
1. Holiday decorations. 2. Handicraft. I. Capua, Sarajean, joint author. II. McArthur, Jeanette, 1919- joint author. III. Title.

BERRY, Jane. 745.59'41
How to make party and holiday decorations / Jane Berry. 1st ed. Radnor, Pa. : Chilton Book Co., c1976. x, 181 p., [6] leaves of plates : ill. ; 27 cm. (Chilton's creative crafts series) [TT900.H6B43 1976] 75-46508 ISBN 0-8019-6230-7 : 10.95 ISBN 0-8019-6231-5 pbk. : 6.95
1. Holiday decorations. 2. Party decorations. I. Title. BIP

SATTLER, Helen Roney. 745.59'41
Holiday gifts, favors, and decorations that you can make, written and illustrated by Helen Roney Sattler. New York, Lothrop, Lee & Shepard Co. [1971] 188 p. illus. 24 cm. [TT900.H6S27] 74-155751 4.95
1. Holiday decorations. 2. Gifts. I. Title. BIP

STEPHAN, Barbara B. 745.59'41
Decorations for holidays & celebrations : ideas, inspirations, and techniques for making festival objects from natural materials, decorated eggs, kitchen crafts, fabric, wood, paper, metal, and glass / by Barbara B. Stephan. New York : Crown Publishers, c1978. 344 p., [4] leaves of plates : ill. ; 27 cm. (Crown's arts and crafts series) Includes index. Bibliography: p. 333-334. [TT900.H6S73] 77-13228 ISBN 0-517-51593-8 : 15.95 ISBN 0-517-51594-6 pbk. : 8.95
1. Holiday decorations. I. Title. BIP

Holiday decorations—Juvenile literature.

PARISH, Peggy. 745.59'41
December decorations : a holiday how-to book / by Peggy Parish ; illustrated by Barbara Wolff. New York : Macmillan, [1975] p. cm. (A ready-to-read handbook) Directions very young readers can follow for making Christmas and Chanukah decorations for home and school from inexpensive household materials. [TT900.H6P37] 75-14285 ISBN 0-02-769920-X
1. Holiday decorations—Juvenile literature. I. Wolff, Barbara. II. Title. BIP

PARISH, Peggy. 745.59'41
Let's celebrate : holiday decorations you can make / by Peggy Parish ; illustrated by Lynn Sweat. New York : Greenwillow Books, c1976. 56 p. : ill. (some col.) ; 22 cm. (Greenwillow read-alone) Instructions

for making decorations for holidays throughout the year. Includes an Easter bush, a log cabin, and a valentine mobile. [TT900.H6P38] 76-2726 ISBN 0-688-80050-5 : 5.95 ISBN 0-688-84050-7 lib.bdg. :
1. Holiday decorations—Juvenile literature. I. Sweat, Lynn. II. Title. **BIP**

WAGNER, Lee. 745.59'41
How to have fun making holiday decorations. Illustrated by Nancy Inderieden. [Mankato, Minn., Creative Education, 1974] p. cm. (Creative Education craft series) Instructions for creating decorations for Easter, Christmas, Valentine's Day, Fourth of July, and other holidays throughout the year. [TT900.H6W33] 74-12308 ISBN 0-87191-362-3 4.45
1. Holiday decorations—Juvenile literature. I. Inderieden, Nancy, illus. II. Title. **BIP**

Holland, Henry, 1745-1806.

STROUD, Dorothy. 720'.924
Henry Holland; his life and architecture. South Brunswick [N.J.] A. S. Barnes [1967, c1966] 159 p. illus., plans, ports. 26 cm. Bibliographical footnotes. [NA997.H6S79 1966a] 67-13085
1. Holland, Henry, 1745-1806.

Hollar, Wenceslaus, 1607-1677.

HIND, Arthur Mayger, 769'.92'4
1880-1957.
Wenceslaus Hollar and his views of London and Windsor in the seventeenth century. New York, B. Blom, [1973 c1972] xiv, 92 p., lxiv p. of illus. 26 cm. Reprint of the 1922 ed. published by J. Lane, London. Bibliography: p. 26-27. [NE642.H7H5 1972] 68-56500 13.75
1. Hollar, Wenceslaus, 1607-1677. 2. London in art. I. Title.

VAN EERDE, Katherine S., 769'.924
1920-
Wenceslaus Hollar: delineator of his time [by] Katherine S. Van Eerde. Charlottesville, Published for Folger Shakespeare Library [by] University Press of Virginia [1970] ix, 122 p. illus. (2 fold.), facsims., maps, plans, ports. 28 cm. "Bibliographical essay": p. [111]-115. [NE642.H7V3] 70-110753 ISBN 8-13-902975- 15.00
1. Hollar, Wenceslaus, 1607-1677. I. Folger Shakespeare Library, Washington, D.C.

Holman, James Henry, 1821-1891.

NEW Brunswick Museum, St. 759.11
John.
Exhibition of portraits by James Henry Holman, 1821-1891; presented by the New Brunswick Museum, February 10th, 1959. [St. John?] Printed by Lingley Print. Co. [1959] unpaged. illus. 22cm. [ND249.H6N4] 59-30619
1. Holman, James Henry, 1821-1891. I. Title.

Holmes, Burton, 1870—

HOLMES, Burton, 779'.9'910924
1870-
Burton Holmes : the man who photographed the world : travelogues, 1892-1938 / photos. and text by Burton Holmes ; selected and edited by Genoa Caldwell ; introd. by Irving Wallace. New York : Abrams, [1977] p. cm. Includes index. [G226.H6A32] 77-8075 ISBN 0-8109-1059-4 : 25.00
1. Holmes, Burton, 1870- 2. Travelers—United States—Biography. I. Caldwell, Genoa. II. Title. **BIP**

Holography.

CAULFIELD, Henry John, 1936- 770
The applications of holography [by] H. J. Caulfield [and] Sun Lu. New York, Wiley-Interscience [1970] xiii, 138 p. illus. 24 cm. (Wiley series in pure and applied optics) Includes bibliographies. [QC449.C37] 77-107585 ISBN 0-471-14080-5
1. Holography. I. Lu, Sun, 1938- joint author. II. Title. **BIP**

COLLIER, Robert Jacob, 535'.4
1926-
Optical holography [by] Robert J. Collier, Christoph B. Burckhardt [and] Lawrence H. Lin. New York, Academic Press, 1971. xvii, 605 p. illus. (part col.) 24 cm. Includes bibliographical references. [QC449.C64] 74-137619
1. Holography. I. Burckhardt, Christoph B., joint author. II. Lin, Lawrence H., joint author. III. Title. **BIP**

DOWBENKO, George. 535'.4
Homegrown holography / written and illustrated by George Dowbenko. Garden City, N.Y. : Amphoto, c1978. 160 p. : ill. ; 29 cm. Includes index. Bibliography: p. 157-158. [QC449.D68] 76-16450 ISBN 0-8174-2113-0 : 13.95 ISBN 0-8174-2406-7 pbk. : 7.95
1. Holography. I. Title. **BIP**

KOCK, Winston E. 770
Lasers and holography; an introduction to coherent optics [by] Winston E. Kock. [1st ed.] Garden City, N.Y., Doubleday, 1969. xiv, 103 p. illus. 22 cm. (Science study series) Edition for 1975 published under title: Engineering applications of lasers and holography. Bibliography: p. [98] [QC449.K6] 69-15174 4.50
1. Holography. 2. Lasers. 3. Optics. I. Title. II. Series.

LEHMANN, Matt. 774
Holography; technique and practice. London, New York, Focal Press, 1970. 148 p. illus. 25 cm. Bibliography: p. 145-146. [QC449.L44] 70-577977 ISBN 0-240-50718-5 £4.00
1. Holography. I. Title.

SMITH, Howard Michael, 1938- 770
Principles of holography [by] Howard M. Smith. New York, Wiley-Interscience [1969] xii, 239 p. illus. 23 cm. Includes bibliographies. [QC449.S6] 69-16129
1. Holography. I. Title. **BIP**

SMITH, Howard Michael, 1938- 774
Principles of holography / Howard M. Smith. 2d ed. New York : Wiley, [1975] xiv, 279 p. : ill. ; 23 cm. "A Wiley-Interscience publication." Includes bibliographical references and index. [QC449.S6 1975] 75-5631 ISBN 0-471-80341-3 : 16.50
1. Holography. I. Title.

YURA, Harold T. 774
Holography in a spatially inhomogeneous medium [by] H. T. Yura. [Santa Monica, Calif.] 1970. 20 p. illus. 28 cm. ([Rand Corporation. Paper] P-4394) Cover title. Includes bibliographical references. [AS36.R28 no. 4394] 72-26193
1. Holography. I. Title. II. Series.

Holography—Congresses.

UNITED States-Japan Seminar 774
on Information Processing by Holography, 2d, Washington, D.C., 1969. Applications of holography; proceedings. Edited by Euval S. Barrekette [and others] New York, Plenum Press, 1971. viii, 396 p. illus. 26 cm. Includes bibliographical references. [QC449.U5 1969] 76-148415 ISBN 0-306-30526-7 16.00
1. Holography—Congresses. I. Barrekette, Euval Salomon, 1931- ed. II. Title. **BIP**

Holy sepulcher in art.

FORSYTH, William H. 730'.944
The entombment of Christ: French sculptures of the fifteenth and sixteenth centuries [by] William H. Forsyth. Cambridge, Mass., Published for the Metropolitan Museum of Art by Harvard University Press, 1970. xx, 216 p. 273 illus., map. 30 cm. Bibliography: p. 203-209. [N8053.5.F63] 70-99523 ISBN 0-674-25775-8
1. Holy sepulcher in art. 2. Sculpture, French. 3. Sculpture, Renaissance—France. I. New York (City). Metropolitan Museum of Art. II. Title.

Holyfield, Frank.

HOLYFIELD, Frank. 741.9'73
The southern mountains; a collection of

drawings. Chapel Hill, University of North Carolina Press [1973] 1 portfolio ([1] l., 9 plates) 51 cm. Title from portfolio. [NC139.H58A55] 73-8001 ISBN 0-8078-1215-3 17.50
1. Holyfield, Frank. 2. Bald Mountains, N.C. and Tenn., in art. I. Title.

Homburger, Freddy—Art collections.

HARVARD University. 707'.4'014461
William Hayes Fogg Art Museum.
Selections from the collections of Freddy and Regina T. Homburger; a loan exhibition. [Cambridge, Mass.] Harvard University, Fogg Art Museum [1971] ix, 190 p. illus. 22 cm. Held Apr, 2-24, 1971. [N5220.H63H3] 75-152744
1. Homburger, Freddy—Art collections. 2. Homburger, Regina T.—Art collections. 3. Art—Exhibitions. I. Title.

MAINE State Museum. 707'.4'01416
Freddy and Regina T. Homburger Art Collection; [loan exhibition. Augusta, 1971] 1 v. (unpaged) illus. 21 x 27 cm. Cover title. [N5220.H63M34] 73-156895
1. Homburger, Freddy—Art collections. 2. Homburger, Regina T.—Art collections. 3. Art—Exhibitions. I. Title.

Home.

GANNETT, William Channing, 728
1840-1923
The house beautiful . . . in a setting designed by Frank Lloyd Wright and printed by hand by William Herman Winslow, Frank Lloyd Wright. River Forest, Auvergne Press, 1896-97. [Park Forest, Ill., W. R. Hasbrouck, Prairie School Pr., 117 Fir St., 1963] [1]l., facsim.: [55]p. illus. 36cm. Folio of 12 plates is attached to front lining paper. 63-16073 22.50, ltd. ed.
1. Home. I. Wright, Frank Lloyd, 1869-1959,illus. II. Title.

Home economics.

BRADFORD, Barbara Taylor, 747
1933-
The complete encyclopedia of homemaking ideas. [Prepared with the cooperation of the National Design Center] New York, Meredith Press [1968] 624 p. illus. (part col.) 26 cm. "An Edward Ernest book." [TX301.B63] 68-15013
1. Home economics. 2. Interior decoration. I. National Design Center. II. Title. III. Title: Encyclopedia of homemaking ideas.

Home economics—Utah—History.

PAXMAN, Shirley 745.5'09792
Brockbank.
Homespun : domestic arts & crafts of Mormon pioneers / Shirley B. Paxman. Salt Lake City : Desert Book Co., 1976. 134 p. : ill. ; 21 x 23 cm. Includes index. Bibliography: p. 130-131. [TX24.U8P38] 76-369984 ISBN 0-87747-584-9 pbk. : 3.95
1. Home economics—Utah—History. 2. Handicraft—Utah—History. 3. Arts, Mormon. I. Title. **BIP**

Home workshops.

*MANNERS, David X. 684.08
How to design and build a home workshop [by] David X. Manners. Indianapolis, Theodore Audel [1975] 127 p. ill. 19 cm. (Popular science mini-guide) [TT152] ISBN 0-672-23812-8 2.50 (pbk.)
1. Home workshops. I. Title.

Homer Laughlin China Company.

BERKOW, Nancy Pratt. 738.3'7
Fiesta ware / by Nancy Berkow. Des Moines : Wallace-Homestead Book Co., c1978. i, 124 p. (p. 124 blank) : ill. (some col.) ; 21 cm. [NK4210.H65B47] 76-23908 ISBN 0-87069-200-3 pbk. : 8.95
1. Homer Laughlin China Company. 2. Pottery, American. I. Title. **BIP**

HUXFORD, Sharon. 738.3'7
The collectors encyclopedia of Fiesta, with Harlequin and Riviera / by Sharon & Bob

Huxford. Rev. 2d ed. Paducah, Ky. : Collector Books, c1976. 142 p. : col. ill. ; 22 cm. First ed. published in 1974 under title: The story of Fiesta. [NK4210.H65H89 1976] 77-361290 ISBN 0-89145-010-6 : 7.95
1. Homer Laughlin China Company. 2. Pottery, American. I. Huxford, Bob, joint author. II. Title.

Homer, Winslow, 1836-1910.

HANNAWAY, Patti. 759.13
Winslow Homer in the tropics. Foreword by Hereward Lester Cooke. Richmond, Va., Westover Pub. Co. [1973] 296 p. illus. (part col.) 24 x 32 cm. Bibliography: p. 283-286. [ND1839.H6H36] 73-79127 ISBN 0-87858-038-7 29.95
1. Homer, Winslow, 1836-1910. 2. Homer, Winslow, 1910. 3. Caribbean area in art. I. Title.

SMITH College. Museum of 761.2
Art.
Winslow Homer: illustrator. Catalogue of the exhibition, with a checklist of wood engravings and a list of illustrated books, prepared by Mary Bartlett Cowdrey. Smith College, February 1951: Williams College, March 1951. Northampton, Mass., 1951. 66 p. plates. 23 cm. [NE1215.H58S5] 51-3173
1. Homer, Winslow, 1830-1910. 2. Wood-engravings, American. 3. Art, American—Exhibitions. I. Cowdrey, Mary Bartlett, 1910- II. Williams College. Lawrence Art Museum. III. Title.

Homer, Winslow, 1836-1910—Bibliography.

DAVIS, Melinda 016.75913
Dempster, 1950-
Winslow Homer : an annotated bibliography of periodical literature / by Melinda Dempster Davis. Metuchen, N.J. : Scarecrow Press, 1975. viii, 130 p. ; 22 cm. [Z8414.83.D38] [ND237.H7] 75-29243 ISBN 0-8108-0876-5 : 6.00
1. Homer, Winslow, 1836-1910—Bibliography.

Homer, Winslow, 1836-1910—Juvenile literature.

HYMAN, Linda. 759.13
Winslow Homer: America's old master. [1st ed.] Garden City, N.Y., Doubleday [1973] 95 p. illus. (part col.) 25 cm. A biography and analysis of the major works of the nineteenth-century American painter often called America's "Old Master." [ND237.H7H95 1973] 92 72-92225 ISBN 0-385-03488-1 4.95
1. Homer, Winslow, 1836-1910—Juvenile literature. I. Title.

Homerus. Ilias—Illustrations.

FRIIS JOHANSEN, 738.3/82/0938
Knud, 1887-
The Iliad in early Greek art, by K. Friis Johansen. Copenhagen, Munksgaard, 1967. 287p. illus. 26cm. Rev. & tr. of Iliaden i tidlig groesk Kunst. [NK4646.F713] 67-89433 10.00
1. Homerus. Ilias—Illustrations. 2. Vasepainting, Greek. I. Title.
American distributor: Humanities, New York.

Honami, Koetsu, 1558-1637.

LEACH, Bernard Howell, 709.52
1887-
Kenzan and his tradition: the lives and times of Koetsu, Sotatsu, Korin and Kenzan. New York, Transatlantic Arts [1967] 3-173p. col. front., illus., 108 plates (incl. ports., facsims.) table, diagr. 26cm. [corrected entry] [ND1059.035 L4] 27.50
1. Honami, Koetsu, 1558-1637. 2. Ogata, Korin, 1658-1716. 3. Ogata, Kenzam, 1663-1743. 4. Tawaraya, Sotatsu, d. 1643. I. Title.

Honduras — Antiq.

STONE, Doris (Zemurray)   913.7283
1909-
The archaeology of central and southern Honduras. Cambridge, Mass., Peabody Museum, 1957. xii, 135 p. illus., plates (part col.) maps (2 fold.) 27 cm. (Papers of the Peabody Museum of Archaeology and Ethnology, Harvard University, v. 49, no. 3) (Harvard University. Peabody Museum of Archaeology and Ethnology. Papers v. 49, no. 3) "References": p. 131-135. [E51.H337 vol. 49, no. 3] A58
1. Honduras — Antiq. 2. Indians of Central America — Honduras. I. Title. II. Series.

Honeyman, Robert B.—Art collections.

BAIRD, Joseph   760'.0973'074019467
Armstrong.
Catalogue of original paintings, drawings, and watercolors in the Robert B. Honeyman, Jr. Collection [Bancroft Library, University of California, Berkeley] Compiled by Joseph Armstrong Baird, Jr. Berkeley, The Friends of the Bancroft Library, University of California, 1968. vii, 196 p. 28 cm. Bibliography: p. vii. [N5220.H64B3] 70-25367
1. Honeyman, Robert B.—Art collections. 2. California—Description and travel—Views. I. California. University. Bancroft Library. II. Title.

Hong Kong—Descrs.—Views.

SASEK, Miroslav   915.125
This is Hong Kong. [New York] Macmillan, c.1965. 60p. col. illus. 32cm. [ND1946.S2A523] 65-19787 2.95; 3.52 bds., lib. ed.,
1. Hong Kong—Descrs.—Views. I. Title.   BIP

Honolulu—Description.

WENKAM, Robert,   779'.9'9969304
1920-
Honolulu is an island / photos. and text by Robert Wenkam. Chicago : Rand McNally, 1978. 126 p., [1] leaf of plates : col. ill. ; 36 cm. [DU629.H7W46] 78-56260 ISBN 0-528-81075-8 : 25.00
1. Honolulu—Description. 2. Oahu—Description and travel. I. Title.   BIP

Honolulu. Executive Building.

IOLANI Palace Restoration   725'.17
Project.
Iolani Palace restoration. [Written, designed, and produced by the Iolani Palace Restoration Project staff and special consultants. Project director: George Moore. Honolulu, Friends of Iolani Palace, 1970] 203 p. illus., plans. 22 x 28 cm. Cover title. Bibliography: p. 199-203. [NA4443.H6I55] 72-124274
1. Honolulu. Executive Building. I. Moore, George, 1929- II. Title.

Hood, Mount, Or.

LOWE, Don.   779'.9'9179561
Mount Hood : portrait of a magnificent mountain / by Don and Roberta Lowe. Caldwell, Idaho : Caxton Printers, 1975. xiii, 119 p. : ill. ; 39 cm. Includes index. [F882.H85L68] 74-150818 ISBN 0-87004-226-2 : 25.00
1. Hood, Mount, Or. I. Lowe, Roberta, joint author. II. Title.

Hood, Mount, Or.—Description—Views.

ATKESON, Ray.   779'.9'9179561
Beautiful Mt. Hood / photography by Ray Atkson ; text by Robin Carey. Portland, Or. : Beautiful West Pub. Co., c1977. 71 p. : col. ill. ; 29 cm. [F882.H85A87] 78-102323 ISBN 0-915796-27-9 : 12.95.
1. Hood, Mount, Or.—Description—Views. I. Carey, Robin. II. Title.   BIP

Hood, Raymond Mathewson, 1881-1934.

KILHAM, Walter   720'.92'4
Harrington, 1904-
Raymond Hood, architect; form through function in the American skyscraper, by Walter H. Kilham, Jr. New York, Architectural Book Pub. Co. [1974, c1973] 200 p. illus. 26 cm. Bibliography: p. 193-195. [NA737.H57K54] 73-12395 ISBN 0-8038-0218-8
1. Hood, Raymond Mathewson, 1881-1934.

Hooking.

CUYLER, Susanna.   746.7'4
The high-pile rug book. [1st ed.] New York, Harper & Row [1974] xi, 140 p. illus. 27 cm. Bibliography: p. 135. [TT850.C88 1974] 73-4074 ISBN 0-06-010936-X 10.00
1. Hooking. 2. Rugs, Hooked. 3. Rya rugs. I. Title.

WISEMAN, Ann.   746.7'4
Rag tapestries and wool mosaics. New York, Van Nostrand Reinhold Co. [1969] 108 p. illus. (part col.) 22 cm. [TT850.W49] 69-17634
1. Hooking. I. Title.

Hooking—Juvenile literature.

WISEMAN, Ann.   746.7'5
Rags, rugs, and wool pictures; a first book of rug hooking. New York, Scribner [1968] 32 p. illus. (part col.) 27 cm. Simple instructions for creating craft items with a hook and easily obtainable cloth material. [TT850.W5] 68-29368 3.95
1. Hooking—Juvenile literature. 2. Rugs, Hooked—Juvenile literature. I. Title.   BIP

Hoover Dam.

HANSEN, Oskar J. W. F.,   730'.924
1892-
Sculptures at Hoover Dam [by Oskar J. W. Hansen. Washington, U.S. Dept. of the Interior, Bureau of Reclamation, 1968] 20 p. illus., port. 24 cm. Cover title. [NB237.H25A49 1968] 79-600218
1. Hoover Dam. I. Title.

Hoover, Herbert Clark, Pres. U. S., 1874— Cartoons, satire, etc.

DARLING, Jay Norwood, 1876-   741.5
As Ding saw Hoover. Edited by John M. Henry. With introd. by W. W. Waymack. Ames, Iowa State College Press [1954] 138p. illus. 24cm. [NC1429.D237H4] 54-11723
1. Hoover, Herbert Clark, Pres. U. S., 1874— Cartoons, satire, etc. I. Title.

Hope diamond.

PATCH, Susanne Steinem.   736'.23
Blue mystery : the story of the Hope diamond / Susanne Steinem Patch. Washington : Smithsonian Institution Press, 1976. 64 p. : ill. ; 26 cm. Bibliography: p. 64. [NK7663.P37] 76-619404 ISBN 0-87474-165-3 pbk : 3.95
1. Hope diamond. I. Title.   BIP

Hope, James, 1819-1892.

FREEMAN, Graydon La Verne,   759.13
1904-
The Hope paintings. Watkins Glen, N. Y., Century House [c.1961] 96p. illus. 60-13415 8.50
1. Hope, James, 1819-1892. I. Title.

Hopewell culture.

DEUEL, Thorne, 1890-   914.22'5
Hopewellian dress in Illinois. Springfield, 1952. 165-175p. illus. 30cm. (Illinols. State Museum, Springfield. Report of investigations no.3) 'Reprinted from Cole anniversary volume, The archeology of eastern United States (Griffln, ed.) the University of Chicago Press, 1952.' Bibliography: 2p. inserted at end. [AM101.I374 no.3] A54

1. Hopewell culture. 2. Indians of North America—Costume and adornment. I. Title. II. Series.

Hopfer, Daniel, 1493-1536, fl.

GRUNWALD Graphic Arts   760'.0922
Foundation.
The Hopfers of Augsburg; sixteenth century etchers. [An exhibition] presented by the Grunwald Graphic Arts Foundation, Print Gallery, UCLA Dickson Art Center, November 14 to December 11, 1966. [Los Angeles? 1966?] 30 p. illus. 22 cm. Bibliography: p. 10. [NE2165.H63G7] 67-68161
1. Hopfer, Daniel, 1493-1536, fl. 2. Hopfer family. I. Dickson Art Center. II. Title.

Hopi Indians—Art.

MORI, John.   739.2'3'7701
Hopi silversmithing, by John & Joyce Mori. Los Angeles, Southwest Museum, 1971. 20 p. illus. 20 cm. (Southwest Museum leaflets, no. 35) Cover title. Bibliography: p. 20. [E99.H7M66] 72-187611
1. Hopi Indians—Art. 2. Indians of North America—Silversmithing. I. Mori, Joyce, joint author. II. Title. III. Series: Los Angeles. Southwest Museum. Leaflets, no. 35.

Hopi Indians—Art—Exhibitions.

KOENIG, Seymour H.   709'.01'1
Hopi clay, Hopi ceremony : an exhibition of Hopi art, the Katonah Gallery, Katonah, New York, March 28-May 21, 1976 : [catalog] / organized by Seymour and Harriet Koenig. Katonah, N.Y. : The Gallery, c1976. 116 p. : ill. ; 21 x 26 cm. Bibliography: p. 69-71. [E99.H7K63] 75-43463
1. Hopi Indians—Art—Exhibitions. 2. Indians of North America—Arizona—Art—Exhibitions. I. Koenig, Harriet, joint author. II. Katonah Gallery. III. Title.

Hopi Indians—Biography.

KABOTIE, Fred.   759.13 B
Fred Kabotie, Hopi Indian artist : an autobiography told with Bill Belknap. 1st ed. Flagstaff : Museum of Northern Arizona, c1977. xv, 149 p. : ill. (some col.) ; 24 x 27 cm. Includes index. [E99.H7K32] 77-79071 ISBN 0-87358-164-4 : 35.00
1. Kabotie, Fred. 2. Hopi Indians—Biography. 3. Artists—Arizona—Biography. I. Belknap, Bill, 1920- joint author. II. Title.

Hopi Indians—Biography—Juvenile literature.

FOWLER, Carol.   730'.092'4 B
Daisy Hooee Nampeyo / by Carol Fowler. Minneapolis : Dillon Press, c1977. 74 p. : ill. ; 24 cm. (The Story of an American Indian) A biography of the Hopi Indian artist famous for her pottery, sculpture, and jewelry. [E99.H7F64] 92 76-54809 ISBN 0-87518-141-4 : 4.95
1. Nampeyo, Daisy Hooee, 1910— Juvenile literature. 2. Hopi Indians—Biography—Juvenile literature. 3. Artists—Arizona—Biography—Juvenile literature. I. Title.   BIP

Hopi Indians—Painting.

BRODER, Patricia   759.191'35
Janis.
Hopi painting : the world of the Hopis / by Patricia Janis Broder. [1st ed.] New York : Dutton, [1978] 319 p. : ill. (some col.) ; 29 cm. "A Brandwine Press book." Includes index. Bibliography: p. 305-311. [E99.H7B84 1978] 78-68404 ISBN 0-525-12711-9 : 25.00
1. Hopi Indians—Painting. 2. Indians of North America—Painting. I. Title.   BIP

Hopi Indians—Pottery.

FEWKES, Jesse Walter,   738.3'7
1850-1930.
Designs on prehistoric Hopi pottery. New

York, Dover Publications [1973] 181, [1] p. illus. 24 cm. Pt. 1 reprinted from the 17th Annual report (1898) of the Bureau of American Ethnology; pt. 2 reprinted from the 33d Annual report (1919) Contents.Contents.—Sikyatki and its pottery.—Designs on prehistoric Hopi pottery.—Bibliography (p. [182]) [E99.H7F324 1973] 73-81507 ISBN 0-486-22959-9 3.50 (pbk.)
1. Hopi Indians—Pottery. 2. Indians of North America—Southwest, New—Pottery. I. Title.   BIP

SIKORSKI, Kathryn A.   738.3'09701
Modern Hopi pottery, by Kathryn A. Sikorski. Logan, Utah State University Press, 1968. 92 p. illus. 23 cm. (Utah State University. Monograph series, v. 15, no. 2) Bibliography: p. 91-92. [E99.H7S53] 68-65938
1. Hopi Indians—Pottery. 2. Indians of North America—Arizona—Pottery. I. Title. II. Series: Utah. State University of Agriculture and Applied Science, Logan. Monograph series, v. 15, no. 2

Hopi Indians—Social life and customs—Pictorial works.

HARVEY, Byron.   759.01'1
Ritual in Pueblo art; Hopi life in Hopi painting. New York, Museum of the American Indian, Heye Foundation, 1970. vii, 81 p. illus. (part col.) 26 cm. (Contributions from the Museum of the American Indian, Heye Foundation, v. 24) Bibliography: p. 79-81. [E51.N42 vol. 24] [E99.H7] 67-30973 10.00
1. Hopi Indians—Social life and customs—Pictorial works. 2. Hopi Indians—Art. I. Title. II. Series: New York (City). Museum of the American Indian, Heye Foundation. Contributions, v. 24

Hopkins, Budd, 1931—

HOPKINS, Budd, 1931-   759.13
Retrospective exhibition, 1957-1972. Huntington, W.Va., Huntington Galleries [1973] [39] p. illus. (part col.) 21 cm. Held at Huntington Galleries Jan. 28-Feb. 25, 1973. [ND237.H745H86] 73-157922
1. Hopkins, Budd, 1931- I. Huntington Galleries.

Hopper, Edward, 1882-1967.

HOPPER, Edward, 1882-1967.   759.13
Edward Hopper / text by Lloyd Goodrich. New concise ed. New York : H. N. Abrams, 1976, i.e.1977 158 p. : ill. (some col.) ; 24 x 28 cm. Includes index. [ND237.H75G6 1976] 76-23494 ISBN 0-8109-2058-1 : 17.50
1. Hopper, Edward, 1882-1967. I. Goodrich, Lloyd, 1897-   BIP

HOPPER, Edward, 1882-1967.   759.13
Edward Hopper; selections from the Hopper bequest to the Whitney Museum of American Art, by Lloyd Goodrich. Exhibition and catalogue by the Whitney Museum of American Art. [New York, Whitney Museum of American Art, 1971] 66 p. illus. (part col.) 24 cm. [ND237.H75G63] 79-171022
1. Goodrich, Lloyd, 1897- II. Whitney Museum of American Art, New York.

HOPPER, Edward, 1882-   760'.0924
1967.
Edward Hopper, 1882-1967: oils, watercolors, etchings. [Rockland, Me., Printed by Courier-Gazette, 1971] [29] p. illus. 25 x 35 cm. "An exhibition presented by the William A. Farnsworth Library and Art Museum, Rockland, Maine, July 9 through September 5, 1971, and by the Pennsylvania Academy of the Fine Arts, Philadelphia, Pennsylvania, September 24 through October 31, 1971." "Catalogue": p. [25]-[28] [N6537.H6A45] 75-27286
1. William A. Farnsworth Library and Art Museum, Rockland, Me. II. Pennsylvania Academy of the Fine Arts, Philadelphia.

WHITNEY Museum of American   759.13
Art, New York.
Edward Hopper, exhibition and catalogue. [Text] by Lloyd Goodrich. New York [1964] 72 p. illus. (part col.) port. 24 cm. Exhibition held at the Whitney Museum of American Art, Sept. 29-Nov. 29, 1964; the

Art Institute of Chicago, Dec. 18, 1964-Jan. 31, 1965; the Detroit Institute of Arts, Feb. 18-Mar. 21, 1965; the City Art Museum of St. Louis, Apr. 7-May 9, 1965. Bibliography: p. 69-71. [ND237.H75W49] 65-66986
1. Hopper, Edward, 1882- I. Goodrich, Lloyd, 1897- II. Title.

WHITNEY Museum of American Art, New York. 759.13
Edward Hopper retrospective exhibition. Text by Lloyd Goodrich. Whitney Museum of American Art, New York, February 11-March 26, 1950. Museum of Fine Arts, Boston, April 13-May 14, 1950. Detroit Institute of Arts, Detroit, June 4-July 2, 1950. [New York, 1950] 60 p. 32 plates (part col.) 18 x 23 cm. "The text and illustrations of this catalogue are from a book on Edward Hopper by Lloyd Goodrich published by Penguin Books, ltd." Bibliography: p. 50-52. [ND237.H75W5] 51-4601
1. Hopper, Edward, 1882- 2. Paintings, American—Exhibitions. I. Goodrich, Lloyd, 1897- II. Title.

Hopson, William Fowler, 1849-1935.

ALLEN, Francis Wilbur. 097
The bookplates of William Fowler Hopson; a descriptive check list. [New Haven] Yale University Library, 1961. 65p. illus., ports. 21cm. [Z996.H7A63] 61-3218
1. Hopson, William Fowler, 1849-1935. 2. Book-plates. I. Title.

Hornsey, Eng. (Middlesex). College of Art—Riot, 1968 (May-July)

THE Hornsey affair 378.42'188
[by] students and staff of Hornsey College of Art. Harmondsworth, Penguin, 1969. 220 p. illus. 19 cm. (Penguin education special) [N346.5.G72H66] 72-170210 ISBN 0-14-080096-4 £0.30
1. Hornsey, Eng. (Middlesex). College of Art—Riot, 1968 (May-July) 2. Art—Study and teaching (Higher)—Great Britain.

Horowitz, Raymond J.—Art collections.

PILGRIM, Dianne H. 759.13'074'01471
American Impressionist and realist paintings & drawings from the collection of Mr. & Mrs. Raymond J. Horowitz, exhibited at the Metropolitan Museum of Art, 19 April through 3 June 1973. Introd. by John K. Howat [and] Dianne H. Pilgrim. Catalogue by Dianne H. Pilgrim. [New York, Metropolitan Museum of Art, 1973] p. Includes bibliographies. [ND210.5.I4P54] 73-4242 ISBN 0-87099-122-1 pap. 4.95
1. Horowitz, Raymond J.—Art collections. 2. Paintings, American—Exhibitions. 3. Drawings, American—Exhibitions. 4. Impressionism (Art)—United States. 5. Realism in art. I. New York (City). Metropolitan Museum of Art. II. Title.

Horror tales—Illustrations.

HAINING, Peter. 741.65
Terror! : A history of horror illustrations from the pulp magazines / Peter Haining ; designed by Christopher Scott. [s.l.] : A & W Visual Library, c1976. 176 p. : chiefly ill. (some col.) ; 28 cm. [NC968.5.H6H34] 76-53975 ISBN 0-89104-071-4. ISBN 0-89104-067-6 pbk. : 12.50
1. Horror tales—Illustrations. 2. Magazine illustration. I. Title. BIP

TERROR! : 741.65
a history of horror illustrations from the pulp magazines / [compiled by] Peter Haining ; designed by Christopher Scott. London : Souvenir Press, 1976. 176 p. : chiefly ill. (some col.) ; 28 cm. [NC968.5.H6T47 1976] 77-354236 ISBN 0-285-62257-9 : £4.95
1. Horror tales—Illustrations. 2. Magazine illustration. I. Haining, Peter.

Horse and rider (Sculpture)

HALL, Michael D. 730'.92'4
Reconsiderations of sculpture by Leonardo da Vinci: a bronze statuette in the J. B. Speed Art Museum, MCMLXXIII, by Michael Hall. Louisville, Ky., 1973. 59 p. illus. 28 cm. (J. B. Speed Art Museum bulletin, v. 29) Includes bibliographical references. [NB623.L6H34] 73-88457
1. Leonardo da Vinci, 1452-1519. 2. Speed Art Museum, Louisville, Ky. 3. Horse and rider (Sculpture) 4. Sculpture—Attribution. I. Title. II. Series: Speed Art Museum, Louisville, Ky. Bulletin — J. B. Speed Art Museum, v. 29.

Horse brasses.

HARTFIELD, George. 739.52
Horse brasses. London, New York, Abelard-Schuman [1965] 62 p. illus. 23 cm. [GT5888.H3] 65-17014
1. Horse brasses.

Horses—France—Camargue, Ile de la—Pictorial works.

SILVESTER, Hans Walter. 779'.32
Horses of the Camargue / photos. and text by Hans Silvester ; pref. by Konrad Lorenz ; [translated by Jill Hugh-Jones]. New York : Viking, 1976. [24] p., [36] leaves of plates : col. ill. ; 27 x 31 cm. (A Studio book) Translation of Chevaux de Camargue. [SF284.F7S4913 1976] 75-29957 ISBN 0-670-37956-5 : 27.50
1. Horses—France—Camargue, Ile de la—Pictorial works. 2. Camargue, Ile de la—Description and travel—Views. I. Title. BIP

Horses in art.

ANDERSON, C. W. 758.3
The look of a thoroughbred. New York, Harper [c.1963] 4p. various 1. chiefly col. illus. 40cm. 5.00, bxd.,
1. Horses in art. I. Title.

HADDELSEY, Vincent, 1934- 759.2
Haddelsey's horses / paintings by vincent Haddelsey ; text by Caroline Silver, with Vincent Haddelsey. New York : St. Martin's Press, 1978. 62 p. : col. ill. ; 27 x 30 cm. [ND497.H28A4 1978] 78-438 ISBN 0-312-35642-0 : 10.00
1. Haddelsey, Vincent, 1934- 2. Horses in art. I. Silver, Caroline, 1938- II. Title. BIP

HAINES, Francis. 758.3
Appaloosa, the spotted horse in art and history. Austin, Published for the Amon Carter Museum of Western Art, Fort Worth by the University of Texas Press [1963] xii, 103 p. illus., col. plates. 29 cm. Bibliography: p. 101-103. [N7660.H25] 63-11191
1. Horses in art. 2. Appaloosa horse. I. Amon Carter Museum of Western Art, Fort Worth, Tex. II. Title.

HAINES, Francis. 758.3
Appaloosa, the spotted horse in art and history. East Lansing, Mich. Published by Caballus Publishers with the cooperation of the Amon Carter Museum of Western Art, Fort Worth, Texas, and the Appaloosa Horse Club of Moscow, Idaho [1972, c1963] xii, 103 p. illus., col. plates. 29 cm. Bibliography: p. 101-103. [N7660.H25] 63-11191
1. Horses in art. 2. Appaloosa horse. I. Amon Carter Museum of Western Art, Fort Worth, Tex.

HARLAN, Harold Coffman, 1890- 743.69725
Let's draw horses. [New Madison, Ohio] Blenis Pub. Co. [1950] [62] p. 40 plates. 28 cm. [NC780.H25] 50-13497
1. Horses in art. I. Title.

THE Horse in art. 704.9432
Introd. by Stephen Longstreet. [1st ed.] Alhambra, Calif., Borden Pub. Co. [1966] 1 v. (chiefly illus.) 31 cm. (Master draughtsman series) [NC780.H68] 66-4030
1. Horses in art. 2. Action in art. I. Longstreet, Stephen, 1907-

THE Horse in art: paintings-sculpture, 17th-20th century, graphics, 15th-20th century. 704.94'32'074019491
Santa Barbara, Calif., Santa Barbara Museum of Art, [1974] [40] p. illus. 26 cm. Loan exhibition selected and organized by Margaret Mallory and held at the Santa Barbara Museum of Art, June 22-July 21, 1974. "Catalogue of the exhibition [by Shelley Ruston]": p. [32]-[39] [N7668.H6H67] 74-82298
1. Horses in art. 2. Art—Exhibitions. I. Mallory, Margaret. II. Santa Barbara, Calif. Museum of Art.

LIVINGSTONE-LEARMONTH, David. 704.9432
The horse in art. London, New York, Studio Publications [1958] 48, [96] p. illus. (part mounted col.) 30 cm. [N7660.L55] 58-3863
1. Horses in art. I. Title.

ORCHARD, Vincent. 758.3
The British thoroughbred; reproducing sixteen original paintings by the masters of horse portraiture, with detailed biographical commentaries on the horses. New York, Taplinger Pub. Co. [1966, c1962] 1 v. (various pagings) col. illus. 42 cm. Cover title: The British thoroughbred, 1700-1850. [ND466.O7 1966] 66-25570
1. Horses in art. 2. Paintings, British. I. Title.

SUARES, Jean-Claude. 760
The illustrated horse : a poster book / by Jean-Claude Suares and Charles Stephen. New York : Harmony Books, c1979. p. cm. [NC1810.S83 1979] 78-25722 ISBN 0-517-53633-1 pbk. : 6.95
1. Horses—Posters. 2. Horses in art. I. Stephen, Charles, 1954- II. Title.

Horses in art—Juvenile literature.

BEHRENS, June. 704.94'32
Looking at horses / by June Behrens ; illustrated with art reproductions. Chicago : Childrens Press, [1976] p. cm. "A Golden Gate junior book." An illustrated history of the artistic representation of horses from the works of cave men to early twentieth-century painters. [N7668.H6B43] 76-14939 ISBN 0-516-08814-9 lib.bdg. : 6.60
1. Horses in art—Juvenile literature. 2. Art—Juvenile literature. I. Title. BIP

BOLOGNESE, Don. 743'.69'725
Drawing horses and foals / by Don Bolognese. New York : F. Watts, 1977. p. cm. (How to draw) Instructions for beginning sketches and following through to the finished drawing. [NC780.B58] 77-3688 ISBN 0-531-00379-5 lib.bdg. : 5.90
1. Horses in art—Juvenile literature. 2. Drawing—Instruction—Juvenile literature. I. Title. II. Series. BIP

ZUELKE, Ruth. 704.94 (j)
The horse in art. Designed by Robert Clark Nelson. Minneapolis, Lerner Publications Co. [1965] 64 p. illus., ports. 27 cm. [N7660.Z8] 64-22378
1. Horses in art—Juvenile literature. I. Title. BIP

Horses—Pictures, illustrations, etc.

ANDERSON, Clarence William, 1891-1971. 743.69725
Horse show. New York, Harper [1951] unpaged. illus. 27 cm. [NC1075.A5A43] 51-12781
1. Horses—Pictures, illustrations, etc. I. Title.

ANDERSON, Clarence Williams, 1891- 759.13
The look of a thoroughbred. New York, Harper & Row, 1963. [3] p., 8 plates (in portfolio) 42 cm. [ND237.A64A5] 63-5043
1. -horses — Pictures, illustrations, etc. I. Title.

DENNIS, Wesley 758.3
Portfolio of horse paintings, Commentary by Marguerite Henry. Chicago, Rand McNally, c.1964. [20] 1. col. illus., 16 col. plates. 38cm. Pub. in 1952 1nder title: Portfolio of horses. 64-22279 3.95 pap.,
1. Horses—Pictures, illustrations, etc. 2. Horse breeds. I. Henry, Marguerite, 1902- II. Title.

HOLME, Bryan, 1913- ed. 704.9432
Horses. Introd. by Alleine E. Dodge. New York, Studio Publications in association with Crowell [1951] 98 p. illus. 28 cm. [SF303.H6] 51-7117
1. Horses—Pictures, illustrations, etc. 2. Horses in art.

MORRIS, George Ford. 704.9432
Portraitures of horses, a few people, some dogs & other animals; with autobiographical comment, and narrative. Being a collection of more than five hundred reproduction of the artist's and author's work... accompanied by numerous photographic illustrations, and works of other artists. [Shrewsbury, N. J., Fordacre Studios, c1952] 280p. (chiefly illus.) 28x36cm. [N7660.M67] 53-28866
1. Horses—Pictures, illustrations, etc. I. Title.

Horsham, Eng.—History—Pictorial works.

A picture of Horsham. 942.2'64
[Chichester] : West Sussex County Council, Library and Archives Service, 1976. [30] p. : of ill., facsim., ports. ; 22 cm. [DA690.H78P52] 77-367189 ISBN 0-905139-02-X : £0.50
1. Horsham, Eng.—History—Pictorial works. I. West Sussex, Eng. County Council. Library and Archives Service.

Horticulture—Dictionaries.

BAILEY, Liberty Hyde, 1858-1954, ed. 635'.0973
Cyclopedia of American horticulture : comprising suggestions for cultivation of horticultural plants, descriptions of the species of fruits, vegetables, flowers, and ornamental plants sold in the United States and Canada, together with geographical and biographical sketches and a synopsis of the vegetable kingdom / by L. H. Bailey, assisted by Wilhelm Miller and many expert cultivators and botanists. New York : Gordon Press, 1975,i.e.1976 6 v. (xlii, 2016 p., [140] leaves of plates) : ill. ; 27 cm. Reprint of the 4th ed. published in 1906 by Doubleday, Page, New York. Includes index. [SB45.B17 1975] 72-98055 ISBN 0-87968-247-7 : 500.00
1. Horticulture—Dictionaries. 2. Gardening—Dictionaries. 3. Horticulture—United States—Dictionaries. 4. Horticulture—Canada—Dictionaries. I. Miller, Wilhelm, 1869- joint ed. II. Title.

Horticulture—Dictionaries—Polyglot.

ELSEVIER'S Dictionary of horticulture in nine languages: 635'.03
English, French, Dutch, German, Danish, Swedish, Spanish, Italian, Latin. Amsterdam, New York, Elsevier Pub. Co., 1970. xvi, 561 p. 23 cm. Compiled under the auspices of the Ministry of Agriculture and Fisheries at The Hague, The Netherlands. [SB45.E43] 72-103349 ISBN 0-444-40812-6 26.00
1. Horticulture—Dictionaries—Polyglot. 2. Dictionaries, Polyglot. I. Netherlands (Kingdom, 1815-). Mistrie Ministrie van Landbouw en Visserij. II. Title: Dictionary of horticulture.

Horticulture—Terminology.

A Technical glossary of horticultural and landscape terminology. 635'.03
[1st ed.] Washington, D.C., Horticultural Research Institute [1971] viii, 109 p. 24 cm. Compiled by Dept. of Landscape Architecture, Pennsylvania State University, and others for the Horticultural Research Institute. Bibliography: p. 109. [SB45.T4] 78-165521
1. Horticulture—Terminology. 2. Landscape architecture—Terminology. I. Horticultural Research Institute. II. Pennsylvania. State University. Dept. of Landscape Architecture.

Horwitz, Joseph B.—Art collections.

TRADITIONAL ceremonial objects and Jewish folk art from the Joseph B. and Olyn Horwitz Judaica Collection, Cleveland Ohio. 745.5
[Exhibition] Klutznick Exhibit Hall, B'nai B'rith Building, Washington, D.C. [Washington, 1969?] 46 p. illus., ports. 22 cm. [N7417.T7] 79-275288
1. Horwitz, Joseph B.—Art collections. 2. Horwitz, Olyn—Art collections. 3. Jewish art and symbolism—Exhibitions. I. B'nai B'rith.

SUBJECT INDEX HOTELS, TAVERNS, ETC.

Hory, Elmyr de.

IRVING, Clifford. 759.39'1
Fake: the story of Elmyr de Hory, the greatest art forger of our time. [1st ed.] New York, McGraw-Hill [1969] x, 243 p. illus., facsims., col. plates, ports. 23 cm. [N8791.H617] 72-86087
1. Hory, Elmyr de. I. Title.

Hosiery.

FELKIN, William 687'.32'09
Felkin's History of the machine-wrought hosiery and lace manufactures. Centenary ed., introduced by an essay on the life and work of William Felkin by Stanley D. Chapman; comprehensive index comp. by Sheila M. Uppadine. Newton Abbot (Devon), David & Charles, 1967. lix, 596p. 20 plates (incl. diagrs., port.) 22cm. Bibl. [TT685.F3 1967] 67-89041 13.50 bds.,
1. Hosiery. 2. Lace and lace making. I. Title. II. Title: History of the machine-wrought hosiery and lace manufactures.
American distributor: Kelley, New York.

Hosiery—Hist.

HASKELL, Ira Joseph, 1883- 687.309
Hosiery thru the years. Lynn, Mass., Printed by Carole Mailing Service, c1956. 124 l. illus. 29cm. [TT681.H3] 56-26582
1. Hosiery—Hist. I. Title.

Hosiery industry—Hist.

GRASS, Milton N 687.309
History of hosiery. [Limited 1st ed. New York, Fairchild Publications, 1955 [i.e.1956] 283p. illus. 24cm. Includes bibliographies. [TT681.G7 1956a] 56-4641
1. Hosiery industry—Hist. 2. Costume—Hist. I. Title.

GRASS, Milton N 687.309
History of hosiery, from the piloi of ancient Greece to the nylons of modern America. [1st ed. New York] Fairchild Publications, 1955 [c1956] 283p. illus. 24cm. Includes bibliography. [TT681.G7] 55-11807
1. Hosiery industry—Hist. 2. Costume—Hist. I. Title.

Hosking, Eric John.

HOSKING, Eric John. 770'.92'4 B
An eye for a bird; the autobiography of a bird photographer [by] Eric Hosking, with Frank W. Lane. Foreword by Prince Philip, Duke of Edinburgh. [1st American ed.] New York, P. S. Eriksson [1973, c1970] xviii, 302 p. illus. 24 cm. [TR140.H67A3 1973] 72-93312 ISBN 0-8397-0290-6 10.00
1. Hosking, Eric John. 2. Photography of birds. I. Lane, Frank Walter. II. Title.

Hosoe, Eiko, 1933—

NEBRASKA. University. Sheldon Memorial Art Gallery. 779'.074'078229
Five photographers; an international invitational exhibition shown at the Sheldon Memorial Art Gallery, University of Nebraska Art Galleries, May 7 through June 2, 1968. [Lincoln, 1968] [48] p. illus. 22 x 23 cm. Preparation of the exhibition and the catalogue by Michael McLoughlin, exhibition director. [TR6.N36] 70-81
1. Hosoe, Eiko, 1933- 2. Meatyard, Ralph Eugene, 1925- 3. Sudek, Josef, 1896- 4. Winogrand, Garry, 1928- 5. Wood, John, 1922- 6. Photography—Exhibitions. I. McLoughlin, Michael. II. Title.

Hospital de Tavera.

WILKINSON, Catherine, 1941- 725'.51'094643
The Hospital of Cardinal Tavera in Toledo / Catherine Wilkinson. New York : Garland Pub., 1977, i.e.1978 xx, 467, 135 p. : ill. ; 22 cm. (Outstanding dissertations in the fine arts) Originally presented as the author's thesis, Yale, 1968. Bibliography: p. [453]-467. [RA989.S74T748 1977] 76-23660 ISBN 0-8240-2739-6 lib.bdg. : 45.00
1. Hospital de Tavera. 2. Bustamente Herrera, Bartolome de, 1501-1570. 3. Covarrubias, Alonso de, ca. 1488-1570. 4. Hospitals—Spain—Design and construction—History. 5. Architecture, Renaissance—Spain. I. Title. II. Series. BIP

Hospitals — Construction.

AMERICAN Hospital Association. 711.555
Manual of hospital planning procedures. Chicago [1959] 72p. illus. 23cm. (Its Publications. M41-59) [RA967.A47] 59-2136
1. Hospitals construction. I. Title. II. Title: Hospital planning procedures.

ARCHITECTURAL record. 725.51
Hospitals, clinics, and health centers. [New York, F. W. Dodge Corp., 1960] viii, 264p. illus., plans. 30cm. 'Discussions and presentations ... [which] originally appeared in the pages of Architectural record.' [RA967.A7] 60-15663
1. Hospitals—Construction. 2. Clinics. 3. Medical centers. I. Title. BIP

CARNER, Donald C. 658'.91'36211
Planning for hospital expansion and remodeling, by Donald C. Carner. With a foreword by Ray E. Brown. Springfield, Ill., C. C. Thomas [1968] xvi, 112 p. illus. 23 cm. [RA967.C33] 67-12018
1. Hospitals—Construction. 2. Hospitals—Administration. I. Title.

DELON, Gerald L. 725'.51
Quantitative methods for evaluating hospital design [by] Gerald L. Delon and Harold E. Smalley. Rockville, Md., National Center for Health Services Research and Development [1970] xiv, 239 p. illus., plans. 26 cm. "Final report." "Report NCHS-RD-70-1." Bibliography: p. 219-233. [RA967.D45] 71-608939
1. Hospitals—Construction. I. Smalley, Harold Eugene, 1921- joint author. II. Title.

HUDENBURG, Roy. 725'.51
Planning the community hospital. New York, McGraw-Hill [1967] viii, 438 p. illus. 23 cm. Includes bibliographies. [RA967.H8] 67-12627
1. Hospitals—Construction. 2. Hospitals—Administration. I. Title. BIP

NUFFIELD Provincial Hospitals Trust. 362.11
Studies in the functions and design of hospitals, the report of an investigation sponsored by the Nuffield Provincial Hospitals Trust and the University of Bristol. London, New York, Oxford University Press, 1955. xx, 191p. illus., maps, plans. 25x31cm. Includes bibliographies. [RA967.N8] 56-1806
1. Hospitals—Construction. I. Bristol, Eng. University. II. Title.

ROSENFIELD, Isadore. 725'.51
Hospital architecture; integrated components [by] Isadore Rosenfield, in collaboration with Zachary Rosenfield. New York, Van Nostrand Reinhold Co. [1971] xii, 324 p. illus., plans. 29 cm. Includes bibliographical references. [RA967.R597] 79-152544
1. Hospitals—Construction. I. Rosenfield, Zachary, 1925- joint author. II. Title.

ROSENFIELD, Isadore. 725'.5
Hospital architecture and beyond [by] Isadore Rosenfield in collaboration with Zachary Rosenfield. New York, Van Nostrand Reinhold Co. [1969] viii, 310 p. illus., plans. 29 cm. Bibliographical footnotes. [RA967.R595] 78-6131
1. Hospitals—Construction. I. Rosenfield, Zachary, 1925- joint author. II. Title. BIP

ROSENFIELD, Isadore. 362.1
Hospitals, integrated design. 2d ed., completely rev. New York, Reinhold [1951] 398 p. illus., maps, plans. 31 cm. (Progressive architecture library. [1]) Includes bibliographies. [RA967.R6 1951] 51-11306
1. Hospitals — Construction. I. Title. II. Series.

SOUDER, James J 725.51
Planning for hospitals; a systems approach using computer-aided techniques, by James J. Souder [and others] Chicago, American Hospital Association, 1964. viii, 167 p. illus. 29 cm. "This study was supported by the U.S. Public Health Service under research project W-59." Includes bibliographies. [RA967.S63] 64-56469
1. Hospitals—Construction. I. American Hospital Association. II. Title.

WHEELER, Edward Todd, 1906- 725'.51
Hospital modernization and expansion [by] E. Todd Wheeler. New York, McGraw-Hill [1971] xv, 261 p. illus. 28 cm. [RA967.W48] 71-116673
1. Hospitals—Construction. I. Title. BIP

Hospitals—Constructions.

INTERNATIONAL Symposium on Hospital and Medical School Design, Dundee, Scot., 1961. 725.5
Hospital and medical school design. [2v.] international symposium held at Queen's College, Dundee, July, 1961. Chairman: Malcolm Knox. Ed. by George H. Bell [Dist. Baltimore, Williams & Wilkins, c.1962] 134; 129p. illus. (pt. col.) 21x30cm. Contents.v.1. Papers and discussion.--v.2. Architectural plans and diagrams. Bibl. 62-6929 16.00. plastic bdg., bxd.
1. Hospitals—Constructions. 2. Medical colleges—Construction. 3. Medical centers. I. Bell, George Howard, ed. II. Dundee, Scot. Queen's College. III. Title.

Hospitals—Design and construction.

AMERICAN Hospital Association. 658.4'51
Signs and graphics for health care facilities. Chicago : American Hospital Association, c1977. p. cm. "AHA catalog no. 1262." Includes index. Bibliography: p. [RA967.A47 1977a] 77-26180 ISBN 0-87258-179-9 : write for info.
1. Hospitals—Design and construction. 2. Signs and sign-boards. I. Title. BIP

ROSENFIELD, Isadore. 725'.51
Hospital architecture : integrated components / Isadore Rosenfield in collaboration with Zachary Rosenfield. Huntington, N.Y. : R. E. Krieger Pub. Co., 1976, c1971. p. cm. Reprint of the ed. published by Van Nostrand Reinhold, New York. Includes bibliographical references and index. [RA967.R597 1976] 76-7994 ISBN 0-88275-417-3 : 29.50
1. Hospitals—Design and construction. I. Rosenfield, Zachary, 1925- joint author. II. Title.

Hospitals—Design and construction—Data processing.

HAWKES, Dean. 725'.51'0184
The development of an environmental model / Dean Hawkes. Cambridge : University of Cambridge, Department of Architecture, 1971. [7], 55 p. : ill. ; 30 cm. (Land use and built from studies : Working paper ; no. 55) Bibliography: p. 55. [RA967.H35] 75-318334 ISBN 0-903248-53-0
1. Hospitals—Design and construction—Data processing. 2. Hospitals—Design and construction—Mathematical models. 3. Environmental engineering (Buildings) I. Title. II. Series: Land use and built form studies : Working papers ; no. 55.

Hospitals—Design and construction—History.

THOMPSON, John D. 725'51'09
The hospital : a social and architectural history / John D. Thompson and Grace Goldin. New Haven : Yale University Press, 1975. xxvii, 349 p. : ill. ; 29 cm. Includes index. Bibliography: p. 339-342. [RA967.T5] 74-19574 ISBN 0-300-01829-0 : 25.00
1. Yale-New Haven Hospital. 2. Hospitals—Design and construction—History. 3. Hospital wards. 4. Hospitals—Sociological aspects. 5. Hospital care. I. Goldin, Grace, joint author. II. Title. BIP

Hospitals, Gynecologic and obstetric—Design and construction.

ROSS Laboratories, Columbus, Ohio. 725'.57
Planning and design for perinatal and pediatric facilities / Ross Laboratories. Columbus, Ohio : The Laboratories, [1977] vi, 100 p. : ill. ; 29 cm. Includes bibliographies. [RG500.R67 1977] 77-82725 12.95
1. Hospitals, Gynecologic and obstetric—Design and construction. 2. Hospitals—Nurseries—Design and construction. 3. Children—Hospitals—Design and construction. I. Title.

Hospitals, Military—U.S.—Design and construction.

U.S. General Accounting Office. 725'.59
Need for Veterans Administration to acquire hospital sites before developing working drawings and specifications for construction of hospitals; report to the Congress by the Comptroller General of the United States. [Washington, 1969] 36 p. illus. 27 cm. Cover title. [UH473.A54 1969] 79-602220
1. U.S. Veterans Administration. 2. Hospitals, Military—U.S.—Design and construction. I. Title.

Hospitals—Spain—Design and construction—History.

WILKINSON, Catherine, 1941- 725'.51'094643
The Hospital of Cardinal Tavera in Toledo / Catherine Wilkinson. New York : Garland Pub., 1977, i.e.1978 xx, 467, 135 p. : ill. ; 22 cm. (Outstanding dissertations in the fine arts) Originally presented as the author's thesis, Yale, 1968. Bibliography: p. [453]-467. [RA989.S74T748 1977] 76-23660 ISBN 0-8240-2739-6 lib.bdg. : 45.00
1. Hospital de Tavera. 2. Bustamente Herrera, Bartolome de, 1501-1570. 3. Covarrubias, Alonso de, ca. 1488-1570. 4. Hospitals—Spain—Design and construction—History. 5. Architecture, Renaissance—Spain. I. Title. II. Series. BIP

Hospitals—Specifications.

UNITED States. General Accounting Office. 725'.51
Need to improve reviews of drawings and specifications prepared by architect-engineers before solicitation of hospital construction bids; report to the Congress [on the] Veterans Administration, by the Comptroller General of the United States. [Washington, 1968] 47 p. 27 cm. Cover title. [RA967.5.U6U54 1968] 68-62737
1. United States. Veterans Administration. 2. Hospitals—Specifications. 3. Hospitals, Military—United States—Design and construction. I. Title.

Hostetler, David, 1926—

ADAMS, Phillip D. 730'.924
David Hostetler, the carver from Coolville Ridge, by Phillip D. Adams. Kalamazoo, School of Graduate Studies, Western Michigan University, 1967. 52 p. 36 illus. 23 cm. (Western Michigan University, Kalamazoo. School of Graduate Studies. Faculty contributions, ser. 10, no. 1) Bibliographical footnotes. [LB5.M56 ser. 10, no. 1] 68-2654
1. Hostetler, David, 1926- I. Title. II. Series: Michigan. Western Michigan University, Kalamazoo. School of Graduate Studies. Faculty contributions, ser. 10, no. 1

Hotels, taverns, etc.

ABRABEN, E 647.94
Resort hotels: planning and management [by] E. Abraben. New York, Reinhold Pub. Co. [1965] viii, 98 p. illus., maps, plans. 22 x 27 cm. [NA7820.A3] 65-7520
1. Hotels, taverns, etc. 2. Architecture — Designs and plans. I. Title.

END, Henry, 1915- 728.5
Interiors 2nd book of hotels / by Henry

End. New York : Whitney Library of Design, 1978. 223 p. : ill. ; 32 cm. Includes index. Bibliography: p. 220. [NA7800.E53] 77-25036 ISBN 0-8230-7281-9 : 26.50
1. Hotels, taverns, etc. I. Title.

END, Henry, 1915- 728.5
Interiors book of hotels & motor hotels. With an introd. by Lawson A. Odde. New York, Whitney Library of Design [1963] x, 252 p. illus. (part col.) plans. 32 cm. Bibliography: p. 245-246. [NA7800.E5] 62-18474
1. Hotels, taverns, etc. 2. Interior decoration. I. Title.

HATTRELL (W. S.) and Partners 728.5
Hotels, restaurants, bars. New York, Reinhold [c.1962] xiv, 146p. illus. 30cm. 62-9164 16.00
1. Hotels, taverns, etc. 2. Restaurants, lunch rooms, etc. 3. Architecture—Designs and plans. I. Title.

KOCH, Alexander 728.5
Hotelbauten, Motels, Ferienhauser. [dist. New York, W. S. Heinman] [1958, i.e., 1959] 315p. (chiefly illus., plans) 31cm. In German, English, and French. 59-24188 20.00
1. Hotels, taverns, etc. 2. Tourist camps, hostels, etc. 3. Architecture—Designs and plans. 4. Interior decoration. I. Title.

SMITH, Douglas Henry. 728.5
Hotel and restaurant design / Douglas Smith. New York : Van Nostrand Reinhold, 1978. 137 p. : ill. (some col.) ; 21 x 22 cm. Bibliography: p. 133. [NA7800.S6 1978] 77-90841 ISBN 0-442-27795-4 : 15.95
1. Hotels, taverns, etc. I. Title.

WEISSKAMP, Herbert. 728.5
Hotels: an international survey. New York, Praeger [1968] 209 p. illus. 29 cm. English and German. [NA7800.W42] 68-31525 20.00
1. Hotels, taverns, etc. I. Title.

Hotels, taverns, etc.—Bibliography.

†PENNER, Richard H. 016.3092 s
Hotel design and development : an introduction and bibliography / Richard H. Penner. Monticello, Ill. : Council of Planning Librarians, 1977. 32 p. ; 28 cm. (Exchange bibliography - Council of Planning Librarians ; 1399) Cover title. [Z5942.C68 no. 1399] [Z6250] [NA7800] 016.7285 78-304892 3.00
1. Hotels, taverns, etc.—Bibliography. 2. Hotel management—Bibliography. I. Title. II. Series: Council of Planning Librarians. Exchange bibliography ; 1399.

Hotels, taverns, etc.—Great Britain.

LINDLEY, Kenneth Arthur, 1928- 914.2
Seaside architecture, [by] Kenneth Lindley. London, H. Evelyn, 1973. 160, [4] p. illus. (some col.). 25 cm. (Excursions into architecture) [NA7850.G7L54] 73-166921 ISBN 0-8277-2830-1
1. Hotels, taverns, etc.—Great Britain. 2. Seaside resorts—Great Britain. I. Title.
Distributed by British Book Center, New York, 25.00.

Hotels, taverns, etc. Great Britain.

*ROULSTONE, Alan 725.72
Taverns in towns a pictorial anthology by Alan Roulstone with descriptive text by Michael Roulstone 1st ed. Huntingdon, England, Balfour Books, [1973] 96 p col. illus., 25 cm. [NA7845] ISBN 0-85944-001-X
1. Hotels, Taverns, etc—GreatBritain I. Title.
Distributed by Tranatlantic Arts. Levittown, N.Y. for 6.95

Houdon, Jean Antoine, 1741-1828.

HEATON, Ronald E., 1898- 730'.924
The image of Washington; the history of the Houdon statue, by Ronald E. Heaton. Norristown? Pa. [1971] 31 p. illus., facsim. 23 cm. Includes bibliographical references. [F234.R5H4] 75-25222
1. Houdon, Jean Antoine, 1741-1828. 2. Richmond. Washington statue (Houdon's) I. Title.

WORCESTER, Mass. Art Museum. 730'.92'4
Sculpture by Houdon; a loan exhibition, Worcester Art Museum, January 16 through February 23, 1964, by H. H. Arnason. [Worcester, 1964] 144 p. illus. 23 cm. Includes bibliographies. [NB553.H8W6] 64-5245
1. Houdon, Jean Antoine, 1741-1828. I. Arnason, H. H. II. Title.

Houghton, Arthur Amory, 1906- — Library.

HOUGHTON, Arthur Amory, 1906- 016.091
A checklist of manuscripts in the library of Arthur A. Houghton, Jr. Compiled by Robert F. Metzdorf. New York, 1969. 52 p. 23 cm. A revision and extension of the 1953 checklist which was based on a detailed catalog of Houghton's library prepared by William H. Bond. [Z6623.H68H68 1969] 74-172422
1. Houghton, Arthur Amory, 1906- — Library. 2. Manuscripts, English—Catalogs. I. Metzdorf, Robert Frederic, 1912- II. Title.

Hours, Books of.

THE Book of hours : 745.6'7'094
illuminated pages from the world's most precious manuscripts / with a historical survey and commentary by John Harthan. New York : Crowell, [1977] p. cm. Includes index. Bibliography: p. [ND3363.A1B66] 77-620 ISBN 0-690-01504-6 : 29.95
1. Hours, Books of. 2. Illumination of books and manuscripts. I. Harthan, John P. II. Catholic Church. Liturgy and ritual. Hours. BIP

FOUCQUET, Jehan, 1415?-1480? 091
The Hours of Etienne Chevalier [by] Jean Fouquet. Pref. by Charles Sterling. Introd. and legends by Claude Schaefer. [Translated from the French by Marianne Sinclair] New York, G. Braziller [1971] 128 p. col, plates. 28 cm. Translation of Les heures d'Etienne Chevalier. Reproduction of 47 miniatures, 40 of which are in the Musee Conde, Chantilly. Bibliography: p. 126-127. [ND3363.C55F613] 78-160131 ISBN 0-8076-0618-9
1. Hours, Books of. 2. Illumination of books and manuscripts. I. Chevalier, Etienne, d. 1474. II. Chantilly. Musee Conde. III. Title. BIP

THE Grandes heures of 745.6'7
Jean, Duke of Berry; Bibliotheque nationale, Paris. Introd. and legends by Marcel Thomas. [Translated from the French by Victoria Benedict and Benita Eisler (Introduction)] New York, G. Braziller [1971] 183 p. 110 col. plates. 44 cm. "Reproduced from the illuminated manuscript (ms. lat. 919) belonging to the Bibliotheque nationale, Paris, France." Includes a full color facsimile reproduction of the text. Translation of Les Grandes heures de Jean de France duc de Berry. [ND3363.B5G713] 75-167761 45.00
1. Hours, Books of. 2. Illumination of books and manuscripts. I. Thomas, Marcel, 1917- ed. II. Berry, Jean de France, duc de, 1340-1416. III. Paris. Bibliotheque nationale. Mss. (Latin 919) BIP

GRASSI, Giovannino de', d.1398. 091
The Visconti hours, National Library, Florence. [Introductions and commentary by] Millard Meiss and Edith W. Kirsch. New York, G. Braziller [1972] 262 p. col. illus. 26 cm. Reproductions of illuminations by Giovannino de' Grassi and Luchino Belbello from the Visconti hours ms. Bibliography: p. 262. [ND3363.V57G72] 72-75371 ISBN 0-8076-0651-0
1. Grassi, Giovannino de, d. 1398. 2. Belbello, Luchino, 15th century. 3. Florence. Biblioteca nazionale centrale. 4. Hours, Books of. I. Belbello, Luchino, 15th century, joint author. II. Meiss, Millard. III. Kirsch, Edith W. IV. Catholic Church. Liturgy and ritual. Hours. (Ms. Visconti)

MASTER of Mary of Burgundy, fl.1475-1490. 091
A book of hours for Engelbert of Nassau, the Bodleian Library, Oxford. Introd. and legends by J. J. G. Alexander. New York, G. Braziller [1970] [193] p. 115 col. plates. 14 cm. The plates, except 1, are reproductions of illuminated pages from the MS. Douce 219-220. Bibliography: p. [32]-[33] [ND3174.M3A65] 78-128576 ISBN 0-8076-0578-6 25.00
1. Alexander, Jonathan James Graham. II. Catholic Church. Liturgy and ritual. Hours. (MS. Engelbert of Nassau) III. Engelbrecht II, Count of Nassau-Dillenberg-Dietz, 1451-1504. IV. Oxford University. Bodleian Library. MSS. (Douce 219-220) V. Title.

MAXIMILIAN I, Emperor of Germany, 1459-1519 091
The book of hours of the Emperor Maximilian the First. Decorated by Albrecht Durer ... and other artists [and] printed in 1513 by Johannes Schoensperger at Augsburg. Edited and with a detailed commentary by Walter L. Strauss. New York, Abaris Books, 1974. v, 344 p. illus. 31 cm. In Latin, with marginal translations and notes in English. This ed. consists of a reproduction of the 62 folios in the Staatsbibliothek, Munich, and the 57 folios preserved at the Bibliotheque Municipale, Besancon, with the lacking signatures substituted from the undecorated copy of the Prayer Book at the Oesterreichische Nationalbibliothek, Vienna. Bibliography: p. 338-340. [ND3363.M3M39 1974] 73-81346 ISBN 0-913870-01-3
1. Hours, Books of. 2. Illumination of books and manuscripts, German. I. Durer, Albrecht, 1471-1528, illus. II. Strauss, Walter L., ed. III. Title. BIP

STERLING, Charles, 1901- 091
The Master of Claude, Queen of France, a newly defined miniaturist / by Charles Sterling ; with 101 ill. New York : H. P. Kraus, 1975. 71 p. : ill. (some col.) ; 27 cm. (Rare books monograph[s] series ; v. 5) Includes bibliographical references. [ND3363.C58S8] 74-22065 18.00
1. Master of Claude of France. 2. Claude, Queen Consort of Francis I, King of France, 1499-1524. 3. Hours, Books of. 4. Prayer-books. 5. Illumination of books and manuscripts, Medieval. I. Title. II. Series.

THE Tres riches heures of 096'.1
Jean, Duke of Berry. Musee Conde, Chantilly. Introd. and legends by Jean Longnon and Raymond Cazelles. Pref. by Millard Meiss. [Translated from the French by Victoria Benedict] New York, G. Braziller [1969] 26, [2] p., 139 col. plates. 30 cm. Miniatures from MS. 65 in the Bibliotheque of the Musee Conde, Chantilly, by the brothers Jean, Herman, and Pol de Limbourg, under the direction of Pol; the work was completed by Jean Colombe. Bibliography: p. [27]-[28] [ND3363.B5T713 1969b] 70-79776
1. Hours, Books of. I. Limbourg, Pol de, ca. 1385-ca. 1416. II. Colombe, Jean, d. 1529, illus. III. Longnon, Jean, 1887- ed. IV. Cazelles, Raymond, ed. V. Berry, Jean de France, duc de, 1340-1416. VI. Chantilly. Musee Conde. Bibliotheque. MSS. (65) VII. Catholic Church. Liturgy and ritual. Hours. (MS. Tres riches heures de Jean, duc de Berry) BIP

House-boats.

ALLYN, Rubert Royce, 1901- 728.7
How to build a houseboat for $900, by Rube Allyn. Illustrated by the author.]1st ed.] St. Petersburg, Fla., Great Outdoors Pub. Co. [1964] 82 p. illus., plans. 22 cm. [VM335.A4] 64-55908
1. House-boats. I. Title.

House construction.

TUTTLE, Edward X. 728.6
With benefit of architect: a manual for those about to build [by] Edward X. Tuttle, Jr. New York, Mcamillan [1968] 277p. illus., facsims., plans. 24cm. [TH4811.T8] 68-19826 7.95
1. House construction. 2. Architecture, Domestic. I. Title. BIP

House construction—Handbooks, manuals, etc.

SCHMIDT, John L. 728
Construction lending guide; a handbook of homebuilding design and construction [by] John L. Schmidt, Walter H. Lewis [and] Harold Bennett Olin. [1st ed.] Chicago, American Savings and Loan Institute [1966] 1 v. (various pagings) illus., maps, plans. 29 cm. Prepared for the United States Savings and Loan League. A revision of v. 3 [i.e. pt. 3] "Construction," was published in 1970 under title: Construction: principles, materials & methods. [TH4813.S3] 66-23400
1. House construction—Handbooks, manuals, etc. 2. Architecture, Domestic—Handbooks, manuals, etc. I. Olin, Harold Bennett, joint author. II. United States Savings and Loan League. III. Title. IV. Title: A handbook of homebuilding design and construction.

House decoration—U. S.

BRAZER, Esther (Stevens) 1898-1945 747
Early American decoration; a comprehensive treatise revealing the technique involved in the art of early American decoration of furniture, walls, tinware, etc. An invaluable reference book and a complete course of instruction for the student of early design and restoration. Illus. with drawings, natural-color photogs. by the author. Springfield, Mass., Pond Ekberg, State & Andrew St. [1962, c.1940, 1947] 265p. 29cm. 16.50
1. House decoration—U. S. 2. Furniture—U. S. 3. Tinware. 4. Design, Decorative. I. Title.

House funishings industry and trade — U.S.

MERCHANDISE Mart, inc., Chicago. *747 658.945
Market facts, a guidebook to the international homefurnishings market. [1st ed.] Chicago [1952] unpaged. illus. 23 cm. [HD9773.U5M4] 52-413905
1. House funishings industry and trade — U.S. I. Title.

House furnishings.

BRADFORD, Barbara Taylor, 1933- 747'.8'8
Decorating ideas for casual living / Barbara Taylor Bradford. New York : Simon and Schuster, c1977. 237 p. : ill. ; 26 cm. Includes index. [TX311.B68] 74-34023 ISBN 0-671-21969-3 : 12.95
1. House furnishings. 2. Interior decoration. I. Title.

THE Complete basic book 747'.8'8
of home decorating / edited by William E. Hague. Garden City, N.Y. : Doubleday, c1976. xiv, 523 p., [38] leaves of plates : ill. ; 24 cm. Includes index. [TX311.C58] 75-21616 ISBN 0-385-11562-8 : 12.95
1. House furnishings. 2. Interior decoration. I. Hague, William E. BIP

FRIEDMANN, Arnold. 747'.8'831
Commonsense design : a complete guide to good interior design on a budget / by Arnold Friedmann ; ill. and collaboration by Philip F. Farrell, Jr. New York : Scribner, [1976] p. cm. [TX311.F74] 76-15179 ISBN 0-684-14685-1 : 10.95. ISBN 0-684-14688-6 pbk. : 5.95
1. House furnishings. 2. Interior decoration. I. Farrell, Philip F. II. Title. BIP

LINDAHL, Judy. 747'.9
Decorating with fabric : hundreds of exciting and creative fabric ideas for decorating your home quickly and inexpensively / by Judy Lindahl. New York : Butterick Pub., c1977. 223 p., [6] leaves of plates : ill. (some col.) ; 26 cm. Includes index. [TT387.L56] 77-89712 ISBN 0-88421-037-5 : 9.95
1. House furnishings. 2. Textile fabrics. I. Title. BIP

MALINO, Emily. 747'.75
Super living rooms / Emily Malino ; ill. by Sally Andrews. 1st ed. New York : Random House, c1976. xii, 143 p. : ill. ; 24 cm. [TX311.M26] 75-40558 ISBN 0-394-

49901-8 : 10.00 ISBN 0-394-73103-4 pbk. :
1. House furnishings. 2. Interior decoration. 3. Living rooms. I. Title. BIP

PHILLIPS, Barty. 747
How to decorate your home without going broke / by Barty Phillips ; projects and question and answer section by Eleanor Van Zandt. Garden City, N.Y. : Doubleday, 1975, c1974. 144 p. : ill. ; 26 cm. Bibliography: p. 144. [TX311.P45 1975] 74-10420 ISBN 0-385-07043-8 : 4.95
1. House furnishings. 2. Interior decoration. I. Title. BIP

WILSON, Jose. 747'.8'8
The dollar-saving decorating book / by Jose Wilson & Arthur Leaman. 1st ed. Garden City, N.Y. : Doubleday, 1976. p. cm. [TX311.W538] 76-2832 ISBN 0-385-03245-5 : 9.95
1. House furnishings. 2. Interior decoration. I. Leaman, Arthur, joint author. II. Title. BIP

House furnishings—Catalogs.

WILSON, Jose. 747'.8'802573
The first complete home decorating catalogue / by Jose Wilson & Arthur Leaman. 1st ed. New York : Holt, Rinehart and Winston, [1975] p. cm. Includes index. [TX311.W54] 75-5474 ISBN 0-03-014646-1 pbk. : 10.00
1. House furnishings—Catalogs. I. Leaman, Arthur, joint author. II. Title. BIP

House furnishings—Juvenile literature.

ALLEN, Phyllis Sloan. 747
The young decorator : a textbook for high schools and a guide for all home decorators / Phyllis Sloan Allen. Provo, Utah : Brigham Young University Press, [1975] xviii, 219 p. : ill. (some col.) ; 28 cm. Includes index. Bibliography: p. 215-216. A high school textbook introducing basic principles and techniques of interior decorating and furnishing. [TX311.A43] 74-23449 ISBN 0-8425-0162-2 pbk. : 6.95
1. House furnishings—Juvenile literature. 2. Interior decoration—Juvenile literature. I. Title. BIP

House painting.

CHLYSTYK, Walter 698.1
Painting and decorating. New York, McGraw [c.1965] 104p. illus. (pt. col.) 25cm. (McGraw found. ser.) [TT320.C5] 65-6456 4.50
1. House painting. 2. Paper-hanging. I. Title.

COMPLETE home decorator (The) 747
an illus. guide to modern methods of painting and decorating for the amateur and the craftsman. Contribs.: John Charles [others] London, Odhams Pr. [dist. Hollywood-by-the-Sea, Fla., Transatlantic, 1964, c.1960] 2 pts. (416p.) in 1 v. illus. (pt. col.) diagrs., plans. 26cm. 64-3274 8.00
1. House painting. I. Charles, John.

CONTI, Evelyn. 747'.213
Add a touch of heritage decoration to your home / by Evelyn Conti and Pat Plaxico. New York : Popular Library, [1975] 94 p., [16] leaves of plates : ill. (some col.) ; 20 cm. At head of title: Sherwin Williams. [TT320.C67] 74-25999 2.50
1. House painting. 2. Interior decoration. I. Plaxico, Pat, joint author. II. Sherwin-Williams Company. III. Title.

DAY, Richard, 1928- 698.1
Guide to painting your home. Greenwich, Conn., Fawcett Publications [1967] 112 p. illus. 24 cm. [TT320.D28] 67-7679
1. House painting. I. Title. II. Title: Painting your home.

DEVOE Home Decorating 698.1
Institute, New York.
Do-it-yourself guide to successful home painting and decorating. New York, Simon and Schuster, 1954. 224 p. illus. 24 cm. [TT320.D492] 54-9806
1. House painting. 2. Interior decoration. I. Title.

GOODHEART-WILCOX'S painting 698
and decorating encyclopedia; a complete library of Professional know-how on painting, decorating, and wood finishing in one easy-to-use volume. Edited by William Brushwell. Homewood, Ill., Goodheart-Willcox Co. [1964] 288 p. illus. (part col.) map. 28 cm. [TT320.G6 1964] 64-22379
1. House painting. I. Brushwell, William, ed.

GOODHEART-WILLCOX'S 698.1
painting and decorating encyclopedia; a complete library of professional know-how on painting, decorating, and wood finishing in one easy-to-use volume. Edited by William Brushwell. South Holland, Ill., Goodheart-Willcox Co. [1973] 272 p. illus. 29 cm. [TT320.G6 1973] 72-90782 ISBN 0-87006-160-7
1. House painting. I. Brushwell, William, ed.

HARDY, Kay, 1902- 698
How to paint and wall-paper. Sketches by the author. New York, Funk & Wagnalls [1950] x, 166 p. illus. 26 cm. "A Kay Hardy home primer." [TT320.H28] 50-8937
1. House painting. 2. Paper-hanging.

HOLLOWAY, John Gifford 698
Everett, 1894-
The modern painter and decorator. [5th ed.] London, New York, Caxton Pub. Co. [1961] 3 v. illus. (part col.) 25 cm. Previous editions by A. S. Jennings. Bibliography: v. 3, p. 267-270. [TT320.H72 1961] 62-5870
1. House painting. 2. Interior decoration. I. Jennings, Arthur Seymour, b. 1860. The modern painter and decorator. II. Title.

MANLY, Harold Phillips, 1887- 698
Painting and paperhanging; a practical guide for everyone on the correct use of paint, varnish, enamel, lacquer, shellac, stain, calcimine, and even whitewash, and up-to-date methods of wallpaper and wall fabric hanging. Wilmette, Ill., F. J. Drake [1953] 129p. illus. 21cm. (Drake's handyman series) [TT320.M36] 53-2885
1. House painting. 2. Paper-hanging. I. Title.

MORGAN, Alfred Powell, 1889- 698
Handyman's painting and paper hanging guide. [Greenwich, Conn., Fawcett Publications, 1952, c1951] 144 p. illus. 24 cm. (A Fawcett book, no. 138) [TT320.M84] 52-26043
1. House painting. 2. Paper hanging. I. Title.

NUNN, Richard V. 698.1
Home paint book / Richard V. Nunn ; [ill., John Anderson]. Birmingham, Ala. : Oxmoor House, 1976. 96 p. : ill. ; 28 cm. (Family guidebook series) Includes index. [TT320.N86] 75-32260 pbk. : 1.95
1. House painting. I. Title. BIP

PAINTING and Decorating 698.1
Contractors of America.
Painting and decorating craftsman's manual and textbook. Rev. ed. Chicago, 1957. 417p. illus. 20cm. [TT320.P28 1957] 57-10693
1. House painting. 2. Paper-hanging. I. Title.

PAINTING and Decorating 698.1
Contractors of America.
Painting and decorating craftsman's manual and textbook. 4th ed. Chicago, 1965. xvi, 526 p. illus. 21 cm. [TT320.P28] 65-24763
1. House painting. 2. Paper-hanging. I. Title.

PAINTING and Decorating 698.1
Contractors of America.
Painting and decorating craftsman's manual and textbook / prepared by Painting and Decorating Contractors of America. 5th ed. Falls Church, Va. : Painting and Decorating Contractors of America, 1975. xviii, 686 p. : ill. ; 21 cm. Includes index. [TT320.P28 1975] 74-22956
1. House painting. 2. Paper-hanging. I. Title.

REID, Maurice H 698.1
Do your own painting; how to get best results, inside and out. New York, Crowell, c1956. 62p. illus. 20cm. [TT320.R4] 56-4812
1. House painting. I. Title.

TATTERSALL, Robert. 698
Decorating / [by] Bob Tattersall. London : Pelham, 1978. 125 p. : ill. ; 21 cm. (Tricks of the trade) Includes index. [TT323.T37 1978] 78-321190 ISBN 0-7207-1036-7 : 7.95
1. House painting. 2. Paper-hanging. I. Title.
Distributed by Transatlantic Arts, Levittown, N.Y. BIP

TIME-LIFE Books. 698
Paint and wallpaper / by the editors of Time-Life Books. New York : Time-Life Books, c1976. 128 p. : ill. ; 28 cm. (Home repair and improvement) Includes index. [TT320.T55 1976] 76-3377 7.95
1. House painting. 2. Paper-hanging. I. Title. BIP

House painting—Amateurs' manuals.

BANOV, Abel. 698.1
Book of successful painting / by Abel Banov, with Marie-Jeanne Lytle. Farmington, Mich. : Structures Pub. Co., 1975. 114 p. : ill. (some col.) ; 29 cm. Includes index. [TT320.B28] 74-21836 ISBN 0-912336-11-0 : 12.00 ISBN 0-912336-12-9 pbk. : 4.95
1. House painting—Amateurs' manuals. 2. Interior decoration—Amateurs' manuals. I. Lytle, Marie-Jeanne, joint author. II. Title. BIP

HAND, Jackson. 698.1
How to do your own painting and wallpapering. [New York] Popular Science Pub. Co. [1968] v, 170 p. illus. 24 cm. ([A Popular science skill book]) [TT320.H26] 68-31230 3.95
1. House painting—Amateurs' manuals. 2. Paper-hanging—Amateurs' manuals. I. Title.

HAND, Jackson. 698.1
How to do your own painting and wallpapering. New York, Barnes & Noble [1974, c1968] 170 p. illus. 21 cm. (A Popular Science Skill book) [TT320.H26] ISBN 0-06-463414-0 1.95 (pbk.)
1. House painting—Amateurs' manuals. 2. Paper-hanging. I. Title.
L.C. card no. for original ed.: 68-31230 BIP

HAND, Jackson. 698.1
How to do your own painting and wallpapering / [by Jackson Hand]. 2d ed., rev. and updated. New York : Book Division, Times Mirror Magazines : [distributed by] Harper & Row, 1976. 170 p. : ill. ; 23 cm. (Popular science skill book) Includes index. [TT320.H26 1976] 76-382774 ISBN 0-06-011782-6 pbk. : 4.95
1. House painting—Amateurs' manuals. 2. Paper-hanging—Amateurs' manuals. I. Title.

LANDSMANN, Leanna. 698.1'4
Painting & wallpapering / by Leanna Landsmann. New York : Grosset & Dunlap, c1975. 79 p. : ill. ; 28 cm. (Grosset good life books) Includes index. [TT320.L25 1975] 74-33760 ISBN 0-448-11954-4 pbk. : 1.95.
1. House painting—Amateur's manuals. 2. Paper-hanging—Amateurs' manuals. I. Title.

LIBIEN, Lois. 645'.2
Paint it yourself : the complete indoor house-painting book / by Lois Libien & Margaret Strong. 1st ed. New York : Morrow, 1978. 223 p. ; 24 cm. Includes index. [TT323.L5] 78-6692 ISBN 0-688-03289-3 : 9.95
1. House painting—Amateurs' manuals. 2. Interior decoration—Amateurs' manuals. I. Strong, Margaret, joint author. II. Title.

SCHERER, John Louis. 698.1
Complete handbook of home painting / by John L. Scherer. 1st ed. Blue Ridge Summit, Pa. : G/L Tab Books, 1975. 210 p. : ill. ; 22 cm. Includes index. [TT320.S33] 74-33625 ISBN 0-8306-5762-2 : 7.95. ISBN 0-8306-4762-7 pbk. : 4.95
1. House painting—Amateurs' manuals. I. Title. BIP

SCHULTZ, Morton J. 698.1
The practical handbook of painting and wallpapering, by Morton S[c]hultz. New York, Arco Pub. Co. [1969] 128 p. illus. (part col.) 24 cm. [TT320.S37] 75-9222 ISBN 0-668-02059-8
1. House painting—Amateurs' manuals. 2. Paper-hanging—Amateurs' manuals. I. Title.

WHEELER, Gershon J. 698
Interior painting, wallpapering, and paneling; a beginner's approach [by] Gershon Wheeler. Reston, Va., Reston Pub. Co. [1974] xiii, 171 p. illus. 24 cm. [TT323.W47] 74-5135 ISBN 0-87909-363-3 7.95
1. House painting—Amateurs' manuals. 2. Paper-hanging—Amateurs' manuals. 3. Paneling—Amateurs' manuals. I. Title.

House plants in interior decoration.

ALLEN, Oliver E. 747'.9
Decorating with plants / by Oliver E. Allen and the editors of Time-Life Books. Alexandria, Va. : Time-Life Books, c1978. 160 p. : ill. ; 28 cm. (The Time-Life encyclopedia of gardening) Includes index. Bibliography: p. 154-155. [SB419.A44] 78-95146 ISBN 0-8094-2579-3 : 8.95
1. House plants in interior decoration. 2. Flower arrangement. 3. Indoor gardening. 4. Interior decoration. I. Time-Life Books. II. Title. BIP

DECORATING with plants and 747'.9
flowers. [New York] Creative Home Library [1972] 125 p. col. illus. 27 cm. [SB449.D35] 72-80747 ISBN 0-696-18900-3 4.95
1. House plants in interior decoration. 2. Flower arrangement.

ELBERT, Virginie. 747'.9
The house plant decorating book / by Virginie F. and George A. Elbert. 1st ed. New York : Dutton, c1976. p. cm. "A Sunrise book." Includes index. Bibliography: p. [SB419.E45 1976] 76-7411 13.95
1. House plants in interior decoration. I. Elbert, George, 1911- joint author. II. Title. BIP

GAINES, Richard L., 1949- 729
Interior plantscaping : building design for interior foliage plants / Richard L. Gaines. 1st ed. New York : McGraw-Hill, c1977. p. cm. Includes index. Bibliography: p. [SB419.G27] 77-9350 ISBN 0-07-022678-4 : 28.50
1. House plants in interior decoration. 2. House plants. I. Title. BIP

HAWKEY, William S. 747'.9
Living with plants; a book of home decorating & plant care, by William S. Hawkey. Illustrated by Tim Shortt. Photography by Norman McGrath and Douglas Mesney. New York, Morrow [1974] 192 p. illus. 29 cm. Bibliography: p. 187. [SB419.H34] 74-7079 ISBN 0-688-00277-3 15.95
1. House plants in interior decoration. I. Title. BIP

KRAMER, Jack, 1927- 747'.9
How to use houseplants indoors for beauty and decoration [by] Jack Kramer and Andrew R. Addkison. [1st ed.] Garden City, N.Y., Doubleday, 1974. x, 129 p. illus. 27 cm. [SB419.K713] 74-1771 ISBN 0-385-01415-5 9.95
1. House plants in interior decoration. I. Addkison, Andrew R., joint author. II. Title.

SKELSEY, Alice Fulton, 747.9
1926-
Every room a garden / by Alice Skelsey and Cecile Mooney. New York : Workman Pub. Co., [1975] p. cm. [SB419.S52] 75-20176 ISBN 0-911104-26-7 pbk. : 5.95
1. House plants in interior decoration. I. Mooney, Cecile, joint author. II. Title. BIP

WALLACH, Carla. 747'.9
Interior decorating with plants / Carla Wallach. New York : Macmillan, c1976. 239 p., [8] leaves of plates : ill. ; 29 cm. Includes index. Bibliography: p. [234]-236. [SB419.W23 1976] 76-14892 12.95
1. House plants in interior decoration. I. Title.

WALLACH, Carla. 747'.9
Interior decorating with plants / by Carla Wallach. New York : Collier Books, 1976. p. cm. Includes index. Bibliography: p.

[SB419.W23 1976b] 76-15019 ISBN 0-02-012000-1 pbk. : 8.95
1. House plants in interior decoration. I. Title. BIP

House plants in interior decoration—Congresses.

SYMPOSIUM on the Use of Living Plants in the Interior Environment, Kansas City, Mo., 1975. 747'.9
From the plants point of view : a Symposium on the Use of Living Plants in the Interior Environment, June 22-24, 1975 : [proceedings / symposium coordinator, John H. Blake III ; assistant and editor, Maria T. Estevez]. [Alexandria, Va. : Society of American Florists, c1976] 83 p. : ill. ; 26 cm. [SB419.S96 1975] 76-365706
1. House plants in interior decoration—Congresses. I. Blake, John H. II. Estevez, Maria T. III. Title.

House plants in interior decoration—Pictorial works.

WESTON, Marybeth Little. 747'.9
Decorating with plants / writer, Marybeth Little Weston ; editor, Barbara Plumb ; designer, Albert T. Hamowy. 1st ed. New York : Pantheon Books, c1978. 160 p. : ill. ; 28 cm. "A House & garden book." [SB419.W286] 77-16138 ISBN 0-394-42680-0 : 12.95
1. House plants in interior decoration—Pictorial works. I. Title. BIP

Household linens.

ROBINSON, Renee. 746.9
Streamlined curtains and covers [by] Renee Robinson and Julian Robinson. New York, St. Martin's Press [1971, c1968] 128 p. illus. 20 cm. [TT387.R6 1971] 71-153507 2.95
1. Household linens. 2. Slip covers. I. Robinson, Julian, joint author. II. Title. BIP

Housing.

BAUER, Catherine, 1905- 301.5'4
Modern housing. New York, Arno Press, 1974 [c1934] xvi, 330, 48 p. illus. 22 cm. (Metropolitan America) Reprint of the ed. published by Houghton Mifflin, Boston. Bibliography: p. 305-[325] [NA7550.B3 1974] 73-11908 ISBN 0-405-05386-X 19.00
1. Housing. 2. Labor and laboring classes—Dwellings—United States. I. Title. II. Series. BIP

Housing—Gt. Brit.

PEPPER, Simon. 711'.58
Housing improvement: goals and strategy. [1st ed.] New York, Wittenborn [1971] 135 p. illus. 30 cm. (Architectural Association. Paper no. 8) Bibliography: p. 132-135. [HD7332.A3P4] 72-172702 ISBN 0-8150-0180-0 (pbk) 9.50
1. Housing—Gt. Brit. 2. Urban renewal—Gt. Brit. I. Title. II. Series: Architectural Association, London. Paper no. 8.

Housing—U. S.

PRATT Institute, Brooklyn. School of Architecture. 728.0973
Methods of reducing the cost of public housing; research report. Brooklyn [1960] 139p. illus., plans. 24x36cm. [NA7540.P7] 60-51136
1. Housing—U. S. 2. Architecture, Domestic—Designs and plans. 3. Apartment houses—U. S. I. Title.

Houston Antique Museum.

MILLER, Robert William, 1922- 745.1'074'016882
The fabulous Houston; a museum of fine antiques, Chattanooga, Tenn., by Robert W. Miller. [Des Moines, Wallace-Homestead Book Co., c1971] 1 v. (unpaged) col. illus. 23 cm. [NK460.C45H65] 72-176962
1. Houston Antique Museum. 2. Houston, Anna Safely, 1876-1951—Art collections. I. Title.

Houston, Tex. Museum of Fine Arts.

ERDMAN, Donnelley. 720'.8 s
The museums of fine arts, Houston: fifty years of growth, 1922-1972 [by] Donnelley Erdman with Peter C. Papademetriou. [Houston, Tex., 1972] 40 p. illus. (3 fold. in pocket) 23 cm. (Architecture at Rice 28) [NA1.A785 no. 28] [N576.H7] 727'.7'097641411 72-80057 ISBN 0-8150-0532-6
1. Houston, Tex. Museum of Fine Arts. I. Title. II. Series: Architecture at Rice University, 28.

Houvling, Ronald—Art collections.

HOLT, Don, 1940- 666'.19
Avon bottles: identification and price guide, by Don Holt and Beverly Craig. Photos. by Modern Studio. [Hudson, N.H., 1969] 43 p. illus. 22 cm. "Avon bottle collection owned by Mr. & Mrs. Roland Houvling." [NK5440.B6H6] 76-21829 2.00
1. Houvling, Ronald—Art collections. 2. Houvling, Ronald Mrs.,—Art collections. 3. Bottles, American—Catalogs. I. Craig, Beverly, joint author. II. Avon Products, inc. III. Title.

Hoving, Thomas Pearsall Field, 1931—

HESS, John L. 069'.092'4
The grand acquisitors [by] John L. Hess. Boston, Houghton Mifflin, 1974. 178 p. illus. 22 cm. [N610.H47] 73-22021 ISBN 0-395-18013-9 5.95
1. Hoving, Thomas Pearsall Field, 1931- 2. New York (City). Metropolitan Museum of Art. I. Title.

Howald, Ferdinand—Art collections.

COLUMBUS Gallery of Fine Arts, Columbus, O. 750'.74'017157
From the Collection of Ferdinand Howald: 19th and 20th century paintings—School of Paris, Renaissance paintings, Italian and Middle Eastern ceramics; given to the Columbus Gallery of Fine Arts, 1931. [Columbus, 1969] [28] p. illus., port. 22 x 27 cm. Pref. signed: Mahonri Sharp Young. Catalogue of an exhibition held Oct. 10-Dec. 31, 1969. [N5220.H67] 70-277663
1. Howald, Ferdinand—Art collections. 2. Art—Exhibitions. I. Young, Mahonri Sharp, 1911- II. Title.

COLUMBUS Gallery of Fine Arts, Columbus, Ohio. 759.13'074'017157
American paintings in the Ferdinand Howald Collection. Catalogue prepared by Marcia Tucker, with research assistance and biographies by Kasha Linville. Introd. by Edgar P. Richardson. [Columbus, c1969] 119 p. illus., col. plates. 28 cm. Includes bibliographical references. [ND212.C65] 72-95250
1. Howald, Ferdinand—Art collections. 2. Paintings, American—Catalogs. 3. Painting, Modern—20th century—U.S. I. Tucker, Marcia. II. Title.

SELECTIONS from the Ferdinand Howald Collection, the Columbus Gallery of Fine Arts, Columbus, Ohio. 759.06 New York, American Federation of Arts [1970] 1 v. (unpaged) illus. 21 cm. Catalog of the exhibition circulated 1970-71 by the American Federation of Arts. "AFA exhibition number 70-1." [ND195.S39] 77-134911
1. Howald, Ferdinand—Art collections. 2. Paintings, Modern—20th century—Exhibitions. I. Columbus Gallery of Fine Arts, Columbus, Ohio. II. American Federation of Arts.

Howard, David, 1948—

HOWARD, David, 1948- 779'.092'4
Realities / David Howard. [San Francisco] : San Francisco Center for Visual Studies, c1976. [49] p. : chiefly ill. ; 28 cm. [TR656.H68] 76-47802 4.95
1. Howard, David, 1948- 2. Photography, Abstract. I. Title. BIP

Howard, Ebenezer, Sir, 1850-1928.

MACFADYEN, Dugald, 1867- 711'.4
Sir Ebenezer Howard and the town planning movement. Cambridge, M.I.T. Press [1970] ix, 199 p. illus., plans, port. 23 cm. [HT161.H7M3 1970] 73-105748 8.95
1. Howard, Ebenezer, Sir, 1850-1928. 2. Garden cities—England. I. Title. BIP

MOSS-ECCARDT, John, 1930-3 711'.4'0924 B
Ebenezer Howard, an illustrated life of Sir Ebenezer Howard, 1850-1928. Aylesbury, Shire Publications, 1973. 48 p. illus., facsims., maps, ports. 21 cm. (Lifelines, 18) Includes bibliographical references and index. [HT161.H7M67] 74-155513 ISBN 0-85263-205-3
1. Howard, Ebenezer, Sir, 1850-1928. 2. Garden cities.
Distributed by International Publication Service, 3.00 pbk.

Howard, Joel T.—Art collections.

DALLAS. Museum of Fine Arts. 758.1'0973'07401642812
The Joel T. and Kathryn Howard Collection of American painting. Dallas : Museum of Fine Arts, [1951] [15] p. : ill. ; 26 cm. Cover title. [ND1351.5.D34 1951] 75-313578
1. Howard, Joel T.—Art collections. 2. Howard, Kathryn—Art collections. 3. Dallas. Museum of Fine Arts. 4. Landscape painting, American—Catalogs. 5. Landscape painting—Dallas—Catalogs. I. Title.

Howard, Loretta Hines—Art collections.

THE Nativity; 704.948'55'07401471 the Christmas creche at the Metropolitan Museum of Art; the Loretta Hines Howard Collection, photographed by Lee Boltin. Commentary by Olga Raggio. [1st ed.] Garden City, N.Y., Doubleday [1969] [62] p. col. illus. 29 cm. [N8065.B6] 75-81519 7.95
1. Howard, Loretta Hines—Art collections. 2. Crib in Christian art and tradition. I. Raggio, Olga, 1926- II. New York (City). Metropolitan Museum of Art.

Howe, George, 1886-1955.

STERN, Robert A. M. 720'.92'4
George Howe : toward a modern American architecture / Robert A. M. Stern. New Haven : Yale University Press, 1975. xiii, 273 p., [40] leaves of plates : ill. ; 26 cm. "Writings by George Howe": p. 253-259. Includes bibliographical references and index. [NA737.H65S83] 73-86918 ISBN 0-300-01642-5 : 25.00.
1. Howe, George, 1886-1955. BIP

WEST, Helen Howe. 720'.92'4 B
George Howe, architect, 1886-1955; recollections of my beloved father. [Philadelphia, Produced by W. Nunn Co., 1973] 114 p. illus. 27 cm. Includes bibliographical references. [NA737.H65W47] 73-88249
1. Howe, George, 1886-1955.

Howe, Oscar, 1915—

PENNINGTON, Robert. 759.13
Oscar Howe. artist of the Sioux. [Sioux Falls, S. D.] Dakota Territory Centennial Commission, 1961. 61p. illus. 21cm. [ND237.H79P4] 62-4299
1. Howe, Oscar, 1915- I. Title.

Howe, Oscar, 1915-—Juvenile literature.

MILTON, John R. 759.13 B
Oscar Howe, by John R. Milton. Minneapolis, Dillon Press [1972] 56 p. illus. 24 cm. A biography of the Yanktonai Sioux who despite many obstacles became a prominent artist and teacher. [E99.Y26H65] 92 74-172870 ISBN 0-87518-043-4
1. Howe, Oscar, 1915-—Juvenile literature. I. Title.

Howell, Charles Augustus, d. 1890.

ANGELI, Helen (Rossetti) 704'.09
Pre-Raphaelite twilight; the story of Charles Augustus Howell. London, Richards Press, 1954. St. Clair Shores, Mich., Scholarly Press, 1971. xiii, 256 p. illus., ports. 22 cm. [PR466.A8 1971] 72-158494 ISBN 0-403-01312-7
1. Howell, Charles Augustus, d. 1890. 2. Preraphaelitism. I. Title. BIP

Howell, Claude, 1915—

HOWELL, Claude, 1915- 759.13
Claude Howell : a retrospective exhibition of paintings organized by the North Carolina Museum of Art, Raleigh, N.C., January 19-February 16, 1975, with the collaboration of the Southeastern Center for Contemporary Art, Winston-Salem, N.C., March 7-March 28, 1975, and the participation of the Mint Museum of Art, Charlotte, N.C., April 6-May 4, 1975. Raleigh : The Museum, [1975] 84 p. : chiefly ill. ; 23 cm. [ND237.H795N67] 74-31996 ISBN 0-88259-077-4
1. Howell, Claude, 1915- I. North Carolina. Museum of Art, Raleigh. II. Southeastern Center for Contemporary Art. III. Mint Museum of Art.

Howland, John Dare, 1843-1914.

HOWLAND, John Dare, 1843-1914. 759.13
The art and activities of John Dare (Jack) Howland: painter, soldier, Indian trader, and pioneer, by Nolie Mumey. Boulder, Colo., Johnson Pub. Co., 1973. xix, 237 p. illus. (part col.) 29 cm. Includes bibliographical references. [ND237.H82M85] 73-166334
1. Howland, John Dare, 1843-1914. I. Mumey, Nolie, 1891- II. Title. III. Title: John Dare Howland.

Hoxie, Vinnie (Ream) 1847-1914.

HALL, Gordon Langley. j92
Vinnie Ream; the story of the girl who sculptured Lincoln. [1st ed.] New York, Holt, Rinehart and Winston [1963] 149 p. 22 cm. Includes bibliography. [NB237.H7H3] 63-12746
1. Hoxie, Vinnie (Ream) 1847-1914. I. Title.

Hoyem, Andrew.

HOYEM, Andrew. 741.9'73
Picture/poems : an illustrated catalogue of drawings and related writings, 1961-1974, prepared by the artist and poet, published on the occasion of an exhibition, January 18 through March 16, 1975, the Fine Arts Museums of San Francisco, California Palace of the Legion of Honor / Andrew Hoyem. San Francisco : Arion Press, 1975. [60] p. : ill. ; 29 cm. "Limited to 500 copies." [NC139.H68C34] 76-350133
1. Hoyem, Andrew. I. California Palace of the Legion of Honor, San Francisco. II. Title.

Hoyningen-Huene, George, 1900-1968.

HOYNINGEN-HUENE. 770'.92'4 B
Los Angeles, Friends of the Libraries, University of Southern California, 1970. 20 p. illus. 26 cm. Contents.Contents.—Pucciani, O. F. George Hoyningen-Huene, 1900-1968.—Horst, H. P. George Hoyningen-Huene: a sketch.—Bocher, M. R. Hoyningen-Huene and the Paris Vogue.—Lerman, L. The self-education of George Huene.—Israel, C. E. Gene Allen and George Cukor remember a friend.—Blanch, L. A recollection of George Huene.—Clark, A. A bibliographical list (p. 19) [TR140.H69A23] 73-156907
1. Hoyningen-Huene, George, 1900-1968. 2. Fashion photography. I. Hoyningen-Huene, George, 1900-1968. II. Los Angeles. University of Southern California. Friends of the Libraries.

SUBJECT INDEX HUMAN FIGURE IN

Hsia-shan-t'u (Scroll)

FONG, Wen. 758'.1'0951
Summer mountains : the timeless landscape / Wen Fong. [New York] : Metropolitan Museum of Art, 1975. [74] p. : ill. ; 35 cm. Includes bibliographical references. [ND1049.F66] 75-23008 ISBN 0-87099-135-3 : 25.00
1. Hsia-shan-t'u (Scroll) 2. Painting, Chinese—Sung-Yuan dynasties, 960-1368. 3. Painting, Chinese—Ming-Manchu (Ch'ing) dynasties, 1368-1912. 4. Landscape in art. 5. Mountains in art. 6. Paintings—Attribution. I. Title.

Hubbard, Elbert, 1856-1915.

HAMILTON, Charles Franklin, 1915- 808'.00924 B
As bees in honey drown; Elbert Hubbard and the Roycrofters [by] Charles F. Hamilton. South Brunswick, A. S. Barnes [1973] 253 p. illus., facsims. 24 cm. Includes bibliographical references. [Z232.R8H35] 77-37811 ISBN 0-498-01052-X 10.00
1. Hubbard, Elbert, 1856-1915. 2. Roycroft Shop, East Aurora, N.Y. I. Title. BIP

LEVULIS, Stanley, 1924- 700'.924
The story of Elbert Hubbard and the Roycrofters of East Aurora, by Stanley and Dorothy Levulis. [Blasdell, N.Y., 1971] v, 31 p. illus. 22 cm. Cover title. [NK1149.R6L4] 79-27950 3.95
1. Hubbard, Elbert, 1856-1915. 2. Roycroft Shop, East Aurora, N.Y. I. Levulis, Dorothy, joint author. II. Title.

Hubbard, Elbert, 1856-1915—Biography.

CHAMPNEY, Freeman. 700'.924 B
Art & glory; the story of Elbert Hubbard. New York, Crown Publishers [1968] v. 248 p. illus., facsims., ports. 24 cm. Includes bibliographical references. [PS2043.C47] 68-20472
1. Hubbard, Elbert, 1856-1915—Biography. I. Title.

STOTT, Mary Roelofs, 1918- 700'.92'4 B
Elbert Hubbard, rebel with reverence : a granddaughter's tribute by Mary Roelofs Stott. Watkins Glen, N.Y. : Century House Americana Publishers, 1974 96 p. : ill. ; 26 cm. Includes index. [PS2043.S8] 74-21057 4.95
1. Hubbard, Elbert, 1856-1915—Biography. I. Title.

Huber, Wolfgang, 1485 (ca.)-1553.

ROSE, Patricia, 1929- 759.3
Wolf Huber studies : aspects of Renaissance thought and practice in Danube School painting / Patricia Rose. New York : Garland Pub., 1977. iii, 540 p. : ill. ; 21 cm. (Outstanding dissertations in the fine arts) Reprint of the author's thesis, Columbia University, 1973. Bibliography: p. 524-540. [ND588.H8R67 1977] 76-23711 ISBN 0-8240-2725-6 : 45.00
1. Huber, Wolfgang, 1485 (ca.)-1553. 2. Donauschule. 3. Painting, Renaissance—Germany. I. Title. II. Series. BIP

Hudson, Grace Carpenter, 1865-1937.

BAIRD, Joseph Armstrong. 759.13
Grace Carpenter Hudson (1865-1937): oil paintings and sketches, including works on loan from C. Frederick Faude. [Catalog of an exhibition] May 22-August 1, 1962, California Historical Society, San Francisco. [San Francisco, California Historical Society, 1962?] [13] p. illus. 28 cm. Bibliography: p. [7] [ND237.H87B34] 74-184891
1. Hudson, Grace Carpenter, 1865-1937. 2. Indians of North America—Pictorial works. I. California Historical Society.

Hudson River School.

HOWAT, John K. 758'.1'097473
The Hudson River and its painters, by John K. Howat. Pref. by James Biddle. Foreword by Carl Carmer. New York, Viking Press [1972] 207 p. illus. (part col.) 32 cm. (A Studio book) [ND1351.5.H6 1972] 73-184065 ISBN 0-670-38558-1 25.00
1. Hudson River School. 2. Landscape painting, American. 3. Hudson Valley—Description and travel—Views. I. Title.

HOWAT, John K. 758'.1'097473
The Hudson River and its painters / by John K. Howat ; pref. by James Biddel, foreword by Carl Carmer. New York : Penguin Books, [1978] p. cm. Includes index. Bibliography: p. [ND1351.5.H6 1978] 78-12734 ISBN 0-14-005080-9 pbk. : 14.95
1. Hudson River School. 2. Landscape painting, American. 3. Landscape painting—19th century—United States. 4. Hudson Valley—Description and travel—Views. I. Title. BIP

LASSITER, Barbara Babcock. 758'.1'0973
American wilderness : the Hudson River school of painting / Barbara Babcock Lassiter. 1st ed. Garden City, N.Y. : Doubleday, c1977. p. cm. [ND1351.5.L37] 73-13089 ISBN 0-385-08192-8 : 4.95 ISBN 0-385-04376-7 lib. bdg. : 5.70
1. Hudson River School. 2. Landscape painting, American. 3. United States in art. I. Title. BIP

NORTON (R. W.) Art Gallery. 758'.1'0973
The Hudson River school: American landscape paintings from 1821-1907. A loan exhibition, October 14-November 25, 1973, the R. W. Norton Art Gallery, Shreveport, Louisiana. [Shreveport, La., 1973] 106 p. illus. (part col.) 28 cm. Catalog of the exhibition. Bibliography: p. 104-106. [ND1351.5.N67 1973] 73-81399 ISBN 0-913060-03-8 7.25 (pbk.)
1. Hudson River School. 2. Landscape painting, American—Exhibitions. I. Title.

Hudson, Robert, 1938—

ROBERT Hudson/Richard 739.2'092'4
Shaw, work in porcelain. [Catalogue of an exhibition] May 11-July 1, 1973, San Francisco Museum of Art. [San Francisco, 1973] 35 p. illus. 26 cm. Bibliography: p. 34. [NK4210.H82R62] 73-164556
1. Hudson, Robert, 1938- 2. Shaw, Richard, 1941- 3. Porcelain, American. I. Hudson, Robert, 1938- II. Shaw, Richard, 1941- III. San Francisco. Museum of Art.

Hudson Valley — Descr. & trav. — Views.

LEWIS, Jack, 1912- 759.13
The Hudson River. Albany? 1964 272 p. illus. (part col.) 31 cm. [ND1839.L45A447] 65-2636
1. Hudson Valley — Descr. & trav. — Views. I. Title.

Hudson's Bay Company.

GINGRAS, Larry. 769'.559'71
Paper money of the Hudson's Bay Company. [Richmond, B.C., Author, P.O. Box 15] 1969. 22 p. illus. 23 cm. "Published under the auspices of the Canadian Numismatic Research Society." [HG657.G54] 71-512629 2.00
1. Hudson's Bay Company. 2. Paper money—Canada. I. Canadian Numismatic Research Society. II. Title.

Huebler, Douglas.

HUEBLER, Douglas. 741.9'73
Douglas Huebler. New York, S. Siegelaub [1968] [19] p. 15 illus. 20 cm. Exhibition held at Seth Siegelaub during November 1968. [NC139.H8A45] 75-696
I. Seth Siegelaub (Art gallery)

HUEBLER, Douglas. 709'.2'4
Douglas Huebler: location pieces, site sculpture, duration works, drawings, variable pieces. [Exhibition dates: Oct. 3-Nov. 12, 1972. Boston, Museum of Fine Arts, c1972] [38] p. illus. 23 cm. "Presented cooperatively by the Museum of Fine Arts, Boston, and the Institute of Contemporary Art, Boston." Bibliography: p. [37]-[38] [N6537.H75B64] 73-161978
1. Huebler, Douglas. I. Boston. Museum of Fine Arts. II. Boston. Institute of Contemporary Art.

HUEBLER, Douglas. 709'.2'4
Location pieces, site sculpture, duration works, drawings, variable pieces. [Boston, Museum of Fine Arts, c1972] [36] p. illus. 23 cm. Catalog of an exhibition presented cooperatively by the Museum of Fine Arts, Boston, and the Institute of Contemporary Art, Boston, Oct. 3-Nov. 12, 1972. Bibliography: p. [35]-[36] [N6537.H75B67] 73-159346
1. Huebler, Douglas. I. Boston. Museum of Fine Arts. II. Boston. Institute of Contemporary Art. III. Title.

Huge, Jurgan Frederick, 1809-1878.

LIPMAN, Jean (Herzberg) 1909- 759.13
Rediscovery: Jurgan Frederick Huge (1809-1878) by Jean Lipman. New York, Archives of American Art [1973] 32 p. illus. 23 cm. [ND1839.H76L56] 72-93428
1. Huge, Jurgan Frederick, 1809-1878. I. Title.

Hugh Stubbins and Associates.

†STUBBINS, Hugh, 1912- 720'.6'57444
Architecture, the design experience / Hugh Stubbins ; editing by Susan Braybrooke ; book design by Hugh Stubbins and Merle Westlake ; foreword by Marcel Breuer ; introd. by Mildred Schmertz. New York : Wiley, c1976. xv, 190 p. : ill. ; 29 cm. "A Wiley-Interscience publication." Includes index. [NA2750.S88] 75-42173 ISBN 0-471-83482-3 : 18.95
1. Hugh Stubbins and Associates. 2. Architectural design. 3. Architecture, Modern—20th century—United States—Case studies. I. Title.

Hugo, Everett Harold, 1910-

JEFFERSON, Thomas, Pres. U.S. 1743-1826. 923.173
Thomas Jefferson among the antiquities of southern France in 1787. A tribute to E. Harold Hugo. Princeton, N.J., 1954. 22 p. plates. 19 cm. "Four hundred copies ... printed." Two letters, one by Jefferson to the Comtesse de Tesse, the other by the comtesse in reply. [DC31.T48] 60-35423
1. Hugo, Everett Harold, 1910- 2. France — Antiq. I. Noailles de Tesse, comtesse de. II. Title.

Huichol Indians—Art—Exhibitions.

THE Huichol creation of the 746.3
world / yarn tablas by Jose Benitez Sanchez and Tutukila Carrillo ; essay and catalogue by Juan Negrin ; [edited by Roger D. Clisby]. Sacramento, Calif. : E. B. Crocker Art Gallery, 1975. 122 p. : ill. (some col.) ; 21 x 23 cm. Exhibition held at the E. B. Crocker Art Gallery, Dec. 6, 1975-Jan. 18, 1976; the San Jose Museum of Art, May 5-June 6, 1976. [F1221.H9H84] 75-25217
1. Benitez Sanchez, Jose, 1938- 2. Carrillo, Tutukila, 1949- 3. Huichol Indians—Art—Exhibitions. 4. Huichol Indians—Religion and mythology—Exhibitions. I. Benitez Sanchez, Jose, 1938- II. Carrillo, Tutukila, 1949- III. Negrin, Juan, 1945- IV. Crocker Art Gallery, Sacramento, Calif. V. San Jose Museum of Art.

Hulings, Clark, 1922—

HULINGS, Clark, 1922- 759.13
Hulings : a collection of oil paintings / by Clark Hulings. 1st ed. Kansas City, Mo. : Lowell Press, c1976. [88] p. : col. ill. ; 22 x 28 cm. [ND237.H88A47] 76-21158 ISBN 0-913504-37-8 pbk. : 9.95
1. Hulings, Clark, 1922-

Hull, Eng.—Description—Views.

HULL old and new / 942.8'37'08
[compiled by] Terence Suthers. Wakefield : EP Publishing, 1975. [5], 99 p. : of ill. ; 18 x 24 cm. [DA690.H9H84] 75-323615 ISBN 0-7158-1080-4 : £1.95
1. Hull, Eng.—Description—Views. I. Suthers, Terence. BIP

Hull, Marie Atkinson, 1890—

NORWOOD, Malcolm M. 759.13
The art of Marie Hull / by Malcolm M. Norwood, Virginia McGehee Elias, and William S. Haynie. Jackson : University Press of Mississippi, 1975. 95 p. : ill. (some col.) ; 32 cm. [ND237.H89N67] 74-25675 ISBN 0-87805-068-X : 15.00
1. Hull, Marie Atkinson, 1890- I. Elias, Virginia McGehee, joint author. II. Haynie, William S., joint author. III. Hull, Marie Atkinson, 1890- IV. Title. BIP

Hull Pottery Company.

FELKER, Sharon Loraine. 738.3'7
Lovely Hull pottery / by Sharon L. Felker. [Des Moines, Iowa : Wallace-Homestead Book Co., 1974] [50] p. : ill. (some col.) ; 23 cm. Cover title. [NK4210.H84F44] 74-75949 5.95
1. Hull Pottery Company. 2. Pottery, American. I. Title.

Human figure in art.

AGNIEL, Marguerite. 943
Body sculpture. [Completely rev. and enl.] Mays Landing, N. J., Sunshine Pub. Co., 1958. 95p. illus. 29cm. (Sunshine books) [NC765.A4 1958] 58-12187
1. Human figure in art. 2. Beauty, Personal. I. Title.

ALBERT, Calvin, 1918- 743.4
Figure drawing comes to life; a series of experiments in drawing the figure conducted by Calvin Albert, interpreted in a text by Dorothy Gees Seckler. New York, Reinhold Pub. Corp. [1957] 160p. illus. 27cm. [NC765.A43] 57-9460
1. Human figure in art. 2. Drawing—Instruction. I. Seckler, Dorothy Gees, 1910- II. Title.

BERRY, William A. 743'.4
Drawing the human form : methods, sources, concepts : a guide to drawing from life / William A. Berry. New York : Van Nostrand Reinhold, 1977. 256 p. : ill. ; 29 cm. Includes index. Bibliography: p. 250-251. [NC765.B39] 76-48736 ISBN 0-442-20718-2 : 16.95 ISBN 0-442-20717-4 pbk. : 7.95
1. Human figure in art. 2. Drawing—Instruction. I. Title. BIP

BROPHY, John, 1899-1965. 704.94'21
The face of the nude; a study in beauty. New York, Tudor Pub. Co. [1968] 160 p. illus., 102 col. plates. 30 cm. [N73.B7 1968] 68-57797
1. Human figure in art. 2. Nude in art. I. Title.

COCHIN, Charles Nicolas, 1715-1790. 743.4
A course in drawing, by Nicolas Cochin the Younger and Denis Diderot;being the plates and notes on figure drawing in the Encyclopedie, ou Dictionnaire raisonne des sciences, des arts et des metiers of 1751. Edited and translated by Philipp P. Fehl. Chicago, University of Chicago Press [1954] x, 73p. illus. 31cm. At head of title: The University of Chicago. University College. [NC765.C58] 54-4223
1. Human figure in art. 2. Drawing—Instruction. I. Diderot, Denis, 1713-1784, joint uathor. II. Chicago. University. University College. III. Title.

DUKE University, Durham, N.C. Art Museum. 730'.74'0156563
Paintings by Rosemarie Beck. Sculpture by Richard A. Miller. Durham, Duke University Museum of Art [1971] 48 p. illus., facsims. 22 cm. On cover: The human form in contemporary art. Catalog of the exhibition held Mar. 21-Apr. 23, 1971. Bibliography: p. 22-29. [N6536.D8] 71-27486
1. Beck, Rosemarie. 2. Miller, Richard A., 1922- 3. Human figure in art. I. Title. II. Title: Sculpture by Richard A. Miller. III. Title: The human form in contemporary art.

DURER, Albrecht, 1471- 741.9'43
1528.
The human figure; the complete "Dresden sketchbook." Edited, with an introd., translations, and commentary by Walter L. Strauss. [Magnolia, Mass.] [Peter Smith] [1973, c1972] xviii, 354 p. illus. 29 cm. (Dover paperback rebound) "The illustrations have been reproduced from those in the portfolio Das Skizzenbuch von Albrecht Durer in der koniglichen offentlichen Bibliothek zu Dresden, edited by Robert Bruck." Bibliography: p. 345-347 [NC251.D8575] 70-184686 ISBN 0-486-21042-1 10.00
1. Durer, Albrecht, 1471-1528 2. Human figure in art. I. Strauss, Walter L. II. Durer, Albrecht, 1471-1528 Das Skizzenbuch von Albrecht Durer in der koniglichen offentlichen Bibliothek zu Dresden. 1972 III. Title.

ELSEN, Albert Edward, 731.8'2
1927-
The partial figure in modern sculpture; from Rodin to 1969, by Albert E. Elsen. The Baltimore Museum of Art [exhibition: 2 December 1969 through 1 February 1970. Baltimore, 1969] 114 p. illus. 22 x 28 cm. Bibliography: p. 105-107. [NB198.E47] 73-106903
1. Human figure in art. 2. Sculpture, Modern—20th century—Exhibitions. I. Baltimore. Museum of Art. II. Title.

GORDON, Louise. 743'.4
How to draw the human figure : an anatomical approach / Louise Gordon. New York : Viking Press, [1979] p. cm. (A Studio book) Includes index. [NC765.G67] 78-12863 ISBN 0-670-38329-5 : 12.95
1. Human figure in art. 2. Anatomy, Artistic. 3. Drawing—Technique. I. Title. BIP

HATTON, Richard George, 743.4
1864-1926
Figure drawing [Gloucester, Mass., P. Smith, 1965] xi. 350p. illus. 21cm. (Dover bk. T1377 rebound) First pub. in 1904 [NC765.H2] 4.00
1. Human figure in art. I. Title. BIP

HATTON, Richard George, 743.4
1864-1926
Figure drawing. New York, Dover [1965] xi, 350p. illus. 21cm. (T1377) Unabridged, unaltered repubn. of the work first pub. in 1904 [NC765.H2] 64-15502 2.00 pap.,
1. Human figure in art. I. Title. BIP

HICKEY, Helen. 730'.9416'3
Images of stone / [by] Helen Hickey ; photographs by Bill Porter. Belfast : Blackstaff Press [for] the Arts Council of Northern Ireland, 1976. 119 p. : ill., 2 maps ; 20 cm. Includes bibliographies. [NB482.H5] 77-363173 ISBN 0-85640-110-2 : £1.95
1. Human figure in art. 2. Art and religion—Ireland. 3. Stone carving—Ireland. I. Porter, Bill. II. Title.

HOGARTH, Paul, 1917- 743'.4
Drawing people. New York, Watson-Guptill Publications [1971] 167 p. illus. (part col.) 27 cm. [NC760.H65] 73-125850 ISBN 0-8230-1425-8 10.95
1. Human figure in art. 2. Anatomy, Artistic. I. Title.

JELLICO, John. 701
The figure in repose and motion. Serial 6486. [Ed. 1] Scranton, International Correspondence Schools [1964] 67, 2 p. illus. 28 cm. [NC765.J4] 66-5764
1. Human figure in art. 2. Animal locomotion. I. International Correspondence Schools, Scranton, Pa. II. Title.

LADNER, Gerhart Burian, 704.948'2
1905-
Ad imaginem Dei; the image of man in mediaeval art, by Gerhart B. Ladner. Latrobe, Pa., Archabbey Press [c1965] xiv, 165 p. illus. 20 cm. (Wimmer lecture. 1962) Bibliographical references included in "Notes" (p. 69-115) [N7832.L283] 65-28205
1. Human figure in art. 2. Christian art and symbolism. 3. Art, Medieval. I. Title. II. Series.

LHOTE, Andre, 1885- 757
Theory of figure painting. Translated by W. J. Strachan. New York, Praeger [1954] xv, 168 p. illus. (part col.) 26 cm. (Books that matter) "First American edition."—Dust jacket. Translation of Traite de la figure. [N7570.L513] 54-8512
1. Human figure in art. I. Title.

MARSHALL, Francis. 743.44
Drawing the female figure. London, New York, Studio Publications [1957] 96p. illus. 26cm. (How to do it series, no. 69) [NC765.M35] 57-3417
1. Human figure in art. 2. Drawing—Instruction. I. Title.

MARTIN, Alvin. 731'.82'074014
Recent figure sculpture. [Chronological summary of the criticism by Alvin Martin. Cambridge] Fogg Art Museum, Harvard University [1972] 48 p. illus. 27 cm. Catalog of a loan exhibition at the Fogg Art Museum, Harvard University, and other institutions, Sept. 15, 1972, to Mar. 17, 1973. Bibliography: p. 44-47. [NB212.M33] 72-89851
1. Human figure in art. 2. Sculpture, American—Exhibitions. 3. Sculpture, Modern—20th century—United States. I. Harvard University. William Hayes Fogg Art Museum. II. Title.

NAPPER, John. 743.4
Life drawing, by John Napper and Nicholas Mosley. London, New York, Studio Publications [1954] 95 p. illus. 26 cm. (The How to do it series, no. 54) [NC765.N35] 54-14935
1. Human figure in art. 2. Anatomy, Artistic. I. Mosley, Nicholas, 1923- joint author. II. Title. III. Series.

NICHOLS, Dale, 1904- 743.4
Figure drawing; a system of drawing and design. [New York] Watson-Guptill Publications [1957] 63p. illus. 31cm. [NC765.N5] 57-7107
1. Human figure in art. 2. Drawing—Instruction. I. Title.

PLANT, Margaret. 760'.092'4
Paul Klee, figures and faces / Margaret Plant. London : Thames and Hudson, 1978. 208 p. : ill. (some col.) ; 27 cm. Includes bibliographical references and index. [N6888.K55P55] 77-92270 ISBN 0-500-23274-1 : 27.50
1. Klee, Paul, 1879-1940. 2. Human figure in art. 3. Head in art. I. Klee, Paul, 1879-1940. II. Title.
Distributed by W. W. Norton, New York, NY 10036

REID, Charles, 1937- 751.4'22
Figure painting in watercolor. New York, Watson-Guptill Publications [1972] 158 p. illus. (part col.) 22 x 29 cm. Bibliography: p. 155. [ND2190.R45] 74-175245 ISBN 0-8230-1710-9 15.00
1. Human figure in art. 2. Water-color painting—Technique. I. Title. BIP

ROSWELL, J. Harrison 743.92
The world's greatest figure drawings, a compilation with commentary and biographical sketches. New York, Atlantis Books Inc., 260 West 36th Street, New York 18 [c.1964] 267p. 120 plates. 35cm. 64-56356 25.00
1. Human figure in art. 2. Nude in art. 3. Drawings. I. Title.

RUBINS, David K. 743.4
The human figure; an anatomy for artists. New York, Studio Publications, in association with Crowell [1953] 94 p. illus. 29 cm. [NC760.R9] 53-10710
1. Human figure in art. I. Title. BIP

RUBINS, David K. 743'.4
The human figure : an anatomy for artists / David K. Rubins. New York : Viking Press, 1975, c1953. 94 p. : ill. ; 28 cm. (A Studio book) (A Viking compass book) Includes index. [NC760.R9 1975] 75-17693 ISBN 0-670-00607-6 pbk. : 3.50
1. Human figure in art. I. Title.

SCHORR, Harry Dreve. 743
Figure indication for the artist, art director, and layout man; an easy, thorough way to learn to indicate the human figure. [1st ed.] New York, Watson-Guptill Publications [1952] 94p. illus. 23x31cm. [NC765.S36] 52-11334
1. Human figure in art. 2. Drawing—Instruction. I. Title.

SELZ, Peter 704.942
New images of man. With statements by the artists. New York, Museum of Modern Art; distributed by Doubleday, Garden City, N.Y. [1960, c.1959] 159p. ('Selected bibliography by Ilse Falk'. p. 155-159.) illus. (part col.) 25cm. 59-14221 5.00 bds.,
1. Human figure in art. 2. Art, Modern—20th cent. I. Title.

SHEPHERD 760'.0944'07401471
Gallery.
Ingres & Delacroix through Degas & Puvis de Chavannes : the figure in French art, 1800-1870 : Shepherd Gallery, May-June, 1975 : catalog / by Martin L. H. Reymert ... [et al.], with the assistance of Gary Koehler ... [et al.]. New York : The Gallery, c1975. vii, 392 p. : ill. ; 22 cm. Includes index. Bibliography: p. 383-390. [N6847.S45 1975] 76-359210
1. Human figure in art. 2. Art, French—Exhibitions. 3. Art, Modern—19th century—France—Exhibitions. I. Reymert, Martin L. H. II. Title.

SINGER, Joe, 1923- 741.2'35
How to paint figures in pastel / by Joe Singer. New York : Watson-Guptill Publications, 1976. 167 p. : ill. (some col.) ; 29 cm. Includes index. Bibliography: p. 165. [NC880.S48] 75-42410 ISBN 0-8230-2460-1 : 16.95
1. Human figure in art. 2. Pastel drawing. I. Title. BIP

STICH, Sidra. 757
Alfred Leslie, Philip Pearlstein, Wayne Thiebaud: contemporary views of man. [Exhibition] Hayden Gallery, Massachusetts Institute of Technology, Cambridge, Massachusetts, September 28 through October 31, 1971. [Cambridge? Mass., MIT Committee on the Visual Arts, 1971] 1 v. (unpaged) illus. 22 x 23 cm. [ND212.S7] 73-30564
1. Leslie, Alfred, 1927- 2. Pearlstein, Philip, 1924- 3. Thiebaud, Wayne. 4. Human figure in art. I. Hayden Gallery. Committee on the Visual Arts. II. Massachusetts Institute of Technology. Committee on the Visual Arts. Contemporary Views of man. III. Title: Contemporary views of man.

WENTINCK, Charles. 704.94'2
The human figure in art from prehistoric times to the present day. Translated from the French by Eva Cooper. Wynnewood, Pa., Livingston Pub. Co. [1971] 160 p. col. illus. 32 cm. [N7570.W413] 72-167747 ISBN 0-87098-037-8 18.50
1. Human figure in art. I. Title. BIP

ZAIDENBERG, Arthur, 1903- 743.4
Drawing the figure from top to toe. [1st ed.] Cleveland, World Pub. Co. [1966] xiv, 153 p. illus. 28 cm. [NC760.Z3] 66-22550
1. Human figure in art. I. Title. BIP

ZAIDENBERG, Arthur, 1903- 743'.4
Drawing the figure from top to toe. New York, Funk & Wagnalls [1974] xiv, 153 p. illus. 27 cm. [NC760.Z3 1974] 73-21206 ISBN 0-308-10107-3 3.50 (pbk.)
1. Human figure in art. I. Title.

Humanism in art.

VON BLUM, Paul. 701
The art of social conscience / Paul Von Blum. New York : Universe Books, 1976. xii, 243 p. : ill. ; 24 cm. Includes index. Bibliography: p. 229-234. [N8217.H78V66] 76-2127 ISBN 0-87663-228-2 : 10.00. ISBN 0-87663-934-1 pbk. : 5.95
1. Humanism in art. 2. Politics in art. 3. Art. I. Title. BIP

Humanities.

DUDLEY, Louise 701.17
The humanities; applied aesthetics [by] Louise Dudley and Austin Faricy. 3d ed. rev. by Louise Dudley. New York, McGraw-Hill, 1960[c.1940-1960] xvii, 466p. (17p. bibl.) illus., diagrs. 24cm. 701.17 62-5663 59-15048 6.95
1. Humanities. 2. Art. 3. Aesthetics. 4. Music—Philosophy and aesthetics. I. Faricy, Austin. II. Faricy, Austin III. Title.

DUDLEY, Louise, 1884- 701.17
The humanities; applied aesthetics [by] Louise Dudley and Austin Faricy. 2d ed. New York, McGraw-Hill, 1951. 518 p. illus. 24 cm. [N7425.D8 1951] 51-14258
1. Humanities. 2. Aesthetics. 3. Music—Philosophy and aesthetics. I. Title. BIP

Hummel art—Collectors and collecting.

HOTCHKISS, John F. 738.8
Hummel art / by John F. Hotchkiss. 1st ed. Des Moines : Wallace-Homestead Book Co., 1978. 240 p. (p. 239-240 blank) : ill. (some col.) ; 28 cm. Includes index. Bibliography: p. 225-227. [NK1125.H665] 78-107922 ISBN 0-87069-184-8 : 17.95. ISBN 0-87069-249-6 pbk. : 13.95
1. Hummel art—Collectors and collecting. 2. Hummel figurines—Collectors and collecting. I. Title. BIP

Hummel figurines—Collectors and collecting—Catalogs.

LUCKEY, Carl F. 738.8
Hummel figurines : a collectors identification and value guide / by Carl F. Luckey. rev. Florence, Ala. : Books America, c1978. v, 300 p., [4] leaves of plates : ill. (some col.) ; 22 cm. Includes index. [NK4660.L8 1978] 78-110696 ISBN 0-89689-000-7 : 8.95
1. Hummel figurines—Collectors and collecting—Catalogs. I. Title.

Hundertwasser, pseud.

CHIPP, Herschel Browning. 759.36
Hundertwasser, by Herschel B. Chipp and Brenda Richardson. Berkeley, University Art Museum, University of California; distributed by New York Graphic Society, Greenwich, Conn. [1968] 144 p. illus. (part col.), port. 22 cm. Catalog of a loan exhibition held at the University Art Museum, University of California, Berkeley, October 8-November 10, 1968, and others. Bibliography: p. 141-143. [ND538.H83C45] 68-65709
I. Richardson, Brenda, joint author. II. Hundertwasser, pseud. III. California. University. Art Museum.

HUNDERTWASSER, pseud. 759.36
Hundertwasser / Werner Hofmann. New York : Rizzoli, 1976. 30 p., 48 leaves of plates : col. ill. ; 18 cm. [ND511.5.H8H613] 76-13778 ISBN 0-8478-0055-5 : 6.50
1. Hundertwasser, pseud. I. Hofmann, Werner, 1928-

HUNDERTWASSER, pseud. 759.436
Rainy day [by] Hundertwasser. Idea, photography and design: Manfred Bockelmann. [Translation into English by Leslie Owen, translation into French by Denise Baumann. Greenwich, Conn.] New York Graphic Society [1974, c1972] 88 p. illus. (part col.) 25 cm. English, French, and German. First published in 1972 under title: Regentag. [ND511.5.H8B6 1974] 73-89947 15.00
1. Hundertwasser, pseud. I. Bockelmann, Manfred, illus. II. Title.

Hundt, Ferdinand.

BEYLO, Frank, comp. 741'.0922
Of times forgotten and men remembered; nineteenth century drawings by Nepomuk Hundt [and] Ferdinand Hundt. Research compiled and text written by Frank Beylo. Discovery data offered by Santi Egitto. Johnson City, N.Y., Johnson City Pub. Co. [1968] [74] p. illus., map. 28 cm. [NC249.B48] 76-2843 2.98
1. Hundt, Ferdinand. 2. Hundt, Nepomuk. I. Title.

Hunt of the unicorn tapestries.

NEW York (City). 746.3'94
Metropolitan Museum of Art. Cloisters.
The unicorn tapestries : the set of late Gothic tapestries at The Cloisters / Margaret B. Freeman, Curator Emeritus. New York : Metropolitan Museum of Art, [1976] p. cm. Includes bibliographical references and index. [NK3049.U5N43 1976] 76-2466 ISBN 0-87099-147-7 : 50.00
1. New York (City). Metropolitan Museum

of Art. Cloisters. 2. Hunt of the unicorn tapestries. 3. Tapestry, Gothic—France. 4. Tapestry—France. I. Freeman, Margaret Beam, 1899- II. Title. BIP

Hunt, Peter, of Provincetown, Mass.

DU Pont de Nemours (E.I.)   747.6 and Company.
Transformagic, a gay adventure in restyling old furniture. [Wilmington, Del., 1944] 61 p. illus. (part col.) port. 21 cm. Cover title. "This is the second book we have published about Peter Hunt, the noted provincetown artist." [NK2137D85] 44-29620
1. Hunt, Peter, of Provincetown, Mass. 2. Interior decoration. 3. Furniture. I. Title.

Hunt, Richard Howard, 1935—

NEW York (City). Museum   730'.924 of Modern Art.
The sculpture of Richard Hunt. New York [1971] 24 p. illus. 22 cm. Catalogue of an exhibition held at the Museum of Modern Art, New York, March 23-June 7, 1971 and at the Art Institute of Chicago, Aug. 21-Oct. 4, 1971. "Bibliography, by Judy Goldman": p. 21-24. [NB237.H79N4] 71-150083 ISBN 0-87070-376-5
1. Hunt, Richard Howard, 1935- I. Chicago. Art Institute. II. Title.

QUINCY Art Club.   709'.2'4
Richard Hunt: small sculpture, drawings, lithographs. An exhibition organized by the Quincy Art Club. [Quincy, Ill., 1972] 15 p. illus. 23 cm. Catalog of the exhibition held Feb. 6-27, 1972 at the Quincy Art Center, Quincy, Ill., and Apr. 1-30, 1972 at the Civic Fine Arts Association, Sioux Falls, S.D. Bibliography: p. 13. [N6537.H8Q5] 76-189437
1. Hunt, Richard Howard, 1935- I. Quincy Art Center. II. Civic Fine Arts Association. III. Title.

Hunt, William Morris, 1824-1879.

KNOWLTON, Helen Mary,   759.13 1832-1918.
Art-life of William Morris Hunt. New York, B. Blom, 1971. xii, 219 p. illus. 21 cm. Reprint of the 1899 ed. [ND237.H9K5 1971] 75-173172
1. Hunt, William Morris, 1824-1879. I. Title. BIP

LANDGREN, Marchal E.   759.13
The late landscapes of William Morris Hunt : [exhibition] : Department of Art, /University of Maryland Art Gallery, College Park, Maryland, 16 January-22 February 1976, Albany Institute of History and Art, Albany, New York, 13 March-25 April 1976 / selected and introduced by Marchal E. Landgren ; chronology and catalogue by Sharman Wallace McGurn. [College Park : Art Gallery, University of Maryland, 1976] p. cm. "University of Maryland Department of Art, museum training program, 1975." Bibliography: p. [ND237.H9L36] 75-40173 8.00
1. Hunt, William Morris, 1824-1879. I. Hunt, William Morris, 1824-1879. II. McGurn, Sharman Wallace. III. Maryland. University. Dept. of Art. IV. Maryland. University. Art Gallery. V. Albany Institute of History and Art. VI. Title.

Hunter, Sam, 1923-

HOFMANN, Hans, 1880-   759.13
Hans Hofmann. Introd. by Sam Hunter and five essays by Hans Hofmann. New York, Abrams [1963] 227p. illus. (pt. mounted col.) group port. 28cm. 63-12457 25.00
1. Hunter, Sam, 1923- I. Title.

Hunting.

SCHALDACH, William   760'.092'4 Joseph, 1896-
The wind on your cheek; or, More chips from the log of an artist sportsman [by] William J. Schaldach. With an introd. by Arnold Gingrich. New York, Freshet Press [1972] 157 p. illus., col. plates. 29 cm. [SK33.S353] 72-81480 17.50

1. Hunting. 2. Fishing. 3. Outdoor life. I. Title. BIP

Hunting guns—History.

AKEHURST, Richard.   739.7'4'425
Sporting guns. New York, Putnam [1968] 120 p. illus. (part col.) 22 cm. ([Pleasures and treasures]) bibliography: p. 120. [SK274.A35 1968b] 68-12220 5.95
1. Hunting guns—History. I. Title.

Hunting—Posters.

GREAT sporting posters   769'.4'32 of the golden age / Sid Latham. Harrisburg, Pa. : Stackpole Books, c1978. [4] p., [22] leaves : ill. (some col.) ; 41 cm. [SK36.9.G7 1978] 78-7623 ISBN 0-8117-2115-9 pbk. : 8.95
1. Hunting—Posters. 2. Fishing—Posters. I. Latham, Sidney. BIP

Huntley, Va.

WRENN, Tony P.   917.55'291'03
Huntley: a Mason Family country house, by Tony P. Wrenn. Fairfax, Va., Fairfax County Division of Planning, 1971. viii, 56 p. illus. 23 cm. Cover title: Huntley, Fairfax County, Virginia. "This study was undertaken at the request of the Fairfax County History Commission in 1969." Bibliography: p. 55-56. [NA7235.V52H88] 76-183058 1.50
1. Huntley, Va. I. Fairfax Co., Va. Planning Division. II. Fairfax Co., Va. History Commission. III. Title.

Huq, Anwarul, 1918—

HUQ, Anwarul, 1918-   759.9549'2
Anwarul Huq / [edited by Muhammad Sirajul Islam]. [Dacca] [Bangladesh Shilpakala Academy, 1976. [6], 22, [2] p. : chiefly ill. ; 20 cm. (Contemporary art series of Bangladesh ; 4) Imprint date in ms. [ND1010.H78168] 77-900887 Tk20.00
1. Huq, Anwarul, 1918- I. Islam, Mohd. Sirajul, 1939- II. Title. III. Series.

Hurd, Jacob, 1703-1758.

FRENCH, Hollis, 1868-   739.2'3722 1940.
Jacob Hurd and his sons Nathaniel & Benjamin, silversmiths, 1702-1781. Foreword by Kathryn C. Buhler. New York, Da Capo Press, 1972 [c1939] xvi, 147, 8 p. illus. 26 cm. (Da Capo Press series in architecture and decorative art, v. 39) Includes bibliographical references. [NK7198.H8F7 1972] 70-175722 ISBN 0-306-70406-4
1. Hurd, Jacob, 1703-1758. 2. Hurd, Nathaniel, 1730-1777. 3. Hurd, Benjamin, 1739-1781. I. Title.

Hurd, Peter, 1904-

HORGAN, Paul, 1903-   927.5
Peter Hurd: a portrait sketch from life. Austin, Published for the Amon Carter Museum of Western Art, Fort Worth, by the University of Texas Press [1965] 68 p. illus. (part col.) 29 cm. "[Issued on the occasion of a retrospective exhibition of the artist's work at the Amon Carter Museum in Fort Worth and the California Palace of the Legion of Honor in San Francisco." [ND237.H94H6] 65-13519
1. Hurd. Peter, 1904- I. Amon Carter Museum of Western Art, Fort Worth, Tex. II. California Palace of the Legion of Honor, San Francisco. III. Title.

HURD, Peter, 1904-   769'.924
Peter Hurd; the lithographs. Introd. by Andrew Wyeth. Editor, John Meigs. [Lubbock, Tex.] Baker Gallery Press, 1968. 23 p., 58 plates. illus., ports. 31 cm. [NE2415.H87A49] 68-9683 16.95
I. Title.

HURD, Peter, 1904-   759.13
Peter Hurd sketch book. Chicago, Sage Books [1971] 121 p. illus. (part col.) 31 x 37 cm. [ND1839.H8A54] 70-150751 ISBN 0-8040-0531-1 30.00
I. Title.

HURD, Peter, 1904-   769'.924
Peter Hurd: the lithographs. Introd. by Andrew Wyeth. Editor: John Meigs. 2d ed. [Lubbock, Tex.] Baker Gallery Press, 1969. 23 p., 60 plates. illus., ports. 32 cm. [NE2415.H87A49 1969] 70-224666 15.00 I. Title. BIP

Hurley, Wilson, 1924- —Exhibitions.

HURLEY, Wilson, 1924-   759.13
Wilson Hurley : an exhibitions of oil paintings. 1st ed. Kansas City, Mo. : The Lowell Press, c1978. [38] p., [24] leaves of plates : color ill. ; 24 x 26 cm. The paintings reproduced in this book were prepared for a one-man exhibition and sale at the National Cowboy Hall of Fame and Western Heritage Center, Oklahoma City, Dec. 3, 1977 through Jan. 9, 1978. [ND237.H944A4 1978] 77-15342 ISBN 0-913504-41-6 : 9.95
1. Hurley, Wilson, 1924- —Exhibitions. I. National Cowboy Hall of Fame and Western Heritage Center.

Hurrell, George.

HURRELL, George.   770'.92'4 B
The Hurrell style : fifty years of photographing Hollywood / photos. by George Hurrell ; text by Whitney Stine. New York : John Day Co., [1976] p. cm. Includes index. [TR678.H87] 76-15396 ISBN 0-381-98293-9 : 14.95
1. Hurrell, George. 2. Glamour photography. I. Stine, Whitney, 1930- II. Title. BIP

Hurschler, J. L.—Art collections.

SAN Diego,   746.3'94'074019498 Calif. Fine Arts Gallery.
Contemporary tapestries: the Hurschler Collection. [San Diego, Calif., 1973] [25] p. (incl. p. [3] of cover) illus. (part col.) 22 x 28 cm. Catalogue of an exhibition held Jan. 17-Feb. 18, 1973. [NK3007.S36] 73-80324
1. Hurschler, J. L.—Art collections. 2. Tapestry—Exhibitions. I. Title.

Husserl, Edmund, 1859-1938.

KAELIN, Eugene Francis,   700'.1 1926-
Art and existence: a phenomenological aesthetics [by] Eugene F. Kaelin. Lewisburg [Pa.] Bucknell University Press [1971, c1970] 357 p. col. illus. 22 cm. Bibliography: p. 340-347. [BH201.K34 1971] 74-101236 ISBN 0-8387-7582-9 12.00
1. Husserl, Edmund, 1859-1938. 2. Heidegger, Martin, 1889- 3. Aesthetics, Modern—20th century. 4. Phenomenology. I. Title. BIP

Hutton, Addison, 1834-1916.

YARNALL, Elizabeth   720'.92'4 B Biddle.
Addison Hutton: Quaker architect, 1834-1916. Introd. by George B Tatum Philadelphia, Art Alliance Press [1974] 78 p., [32] p. of illus. 29 cm. Includes bibliographical references. [NA737.H87Y37] 73-13082 ISBN 0-87982-013-6 10.00
1. Hutton, Addison, 1834-1916.

Ibaugh site.

KINSEY, W Fred, 1929-   917.8963044
Archaeologist at work; a story in pictures, by W. Fred Kinsey, III. Photography by Karl Rath. Harrisburg, Pennsylvania Historical and Museum Commission, 1964. [32] p. illus. 28 cm. Bibliography: p. [32] [E78.P4K5] 68-5389
1. Ibaugh site. 2. Archaeology—Methodology. I. Pennsylvania. Historical and Museum Commission. II. Title.

Ibo tribe—Rites and ceremonies.

OTTENBERG, Simon.   731'.75'096694
Masked rituals of Afikpo, the context of an African art : [published in connection with

an exhibition shown at the Henry Art Gallery, University of Washington, May 24-June 21, 1975]. Seattle : Published for the Henry Art Gallery by the University of Washington Press, [1975] 229 p., [8] leaves of plates : ill. ; 29 cm. (Index of art in the Pacific Northwest ; no. 9) Includes index. Bibliography: p. 223-225. [DT515.42.O89] 74-26954 ISBN 0-295-95391-8 : 19.50
1. Ibo tribe—Rites and ceremonies. 2. Masks (Sculpture)—Nigeria. I. Henry Art Gallery. II. Title. III. Series.

Ibsen, Henrik, 1828-1908.

PLEKHANOV, Georgii   709'.44 Valentinovich, 1856-1918.
Art and society & other papers in historical materialism / George V. Plekhanov. New York : Oriole Editions, [1974] 187 p. ; 23 cm. Contents.Contents.—Art and society.—Historical materialism and the arts.—Ibsen, petty bourgeois revolutionist.—French drama and painting of the 18th century. Includes bibliographical references. [N72.S6P5713] 74-79551 ISBN 0-88211-069-1 : 8.50
1. Ibsen, Henrik, 1828-1908. 2. Art and society. 3. Arts, French. I. Title.

Icart, Louis.

SCHNESSEL, S. Michael.   769'.92'4
A collector's guide to Louis Icart, by S. Michael Schnessel. (Princeton, N.J., distributed by The Exhumation, 1973] 48 p. (chiefly illus.) 28 cm. [NE2049.5.I25S36] 74-161988 5.95
1. Icart, Louis. 2. Women in art. I. Icart, Louis. II. Title.

SCHNESSEL, S. Michael.   760'.092'4
Icart / by S. Michael Schnessel. 1st ed. New York : Potter : distributed by Crown, 1976. p. cm. Includes index. Bibliography: p. [N6853.I22S36 1976] 76-14478 ISBN 0-517-52498-8 : 19.95
1. Icart, Louis. 2. Art deco—France. BIP

Ice carving.

AMENDOLA, Joseph.   736.94
Ice carving made easy. [New Haven?] [1960] 128 p. illus. 23 cm. [NK6030.A55] 60-3795
1. Ice carving. BIP

FORSTER, August Ernst,   731.254 1898-
Fancy ice carving. New York, Ahrens Pub. Co. [1955] 95p. illus. 22cm. Published in 1947 under title: Fancy ice-carving in 30 lessons. [NK6030.F6 1955] 55-11151
1. Ice carving. I. Title.

Icon painting—Balkan Peninsula.

CHATZEDAKES,   755'.2'09496 Manoles.
Etudes sur la peinture postbyzantine / Manolis Chatzidakis. London : Variorum, 1976. 247 p. in various pagings, [180] p. of plates : ill., facsims., ports. ; 23 cm. (Variorum reprint ; CS 52) Reprint of 8 articles in English, French, German, or Modern Greek, originally published between 1940 and 1974. Includes bibliographical references and indexes. [N8189.B28C5] 77-457151 ISBN 0-902089-96-X : £25.00
1. Icon painting—Balkan Peninsula. 2. Mural painting and decoration, Medieval—Balkan Peninsula. 3. Mural painting and decoration—Balkan Peninsula. I. Title.

Icon painting—History.

TAYLOR, John, 1945-   755'.2
Icon painting / by John Taylor. New York : Mayflower Books, [1979] p. cm. (In the history of art) [N8187.T38] 78-25925 ISBN 0-8317-4813-3 : 12.50 ISBN 0-8317-4814-1 pbk. : 6.95
1. Icon painting—History. 2. Orthodox Eastern Church and art—History. I. Title. II. Series. BIP

Icons.

CAVARNOS, Constantine.   704.948'2
Orthodox iconography : four essays ... /

by Constantine Cavarnos. Belmont, Mass. : Institute for Byzantine and Modern Greek Studies, c1977. 76 p., [12] leaves of plates : ill. ; 21 cm. Includes index. Bibliography: p. 67-68. [N8187.C38] 77-74606 ISBN 0-914744-36-4 : 6.50. ISBN 0-914744-37-2 pbk. : 3.95
1. Icons. 2. Orthodox Eastern Church and art. I. Title.

ICONS. 755'.2
[New York] St. Martin's Press [1972] 1 v. (unpaged) 21 col. plates. 34 cm. Compiled by copyright holder, Susan Miller? [N8187.I26] 72-76958
1. Icons. I. Miller, Susan, comp.

OUSPENSKY, Leonide. 704.948
The meaning of icons, by Leonid Ouspensky and Vladimir Lossky. Edited by Urs Graf-Verlag. [Translated by G. E. H. Palmer and E. Kadloubovsky] Boston, Boston Book and Art Shop [1956] 222p. illus., plates (part col.) 32cm. [N7956.O882 1956] 55-11394
1. Icons. 2. Painting, Russian. 3. Christian art and symbolism. I. Lossky, Vladimir, 1903- II. Title.

RICE, David Talbot, 1903- 755
The icons of Cyprus. With chapters by Rupert Gunnis, Tamara Talbot Rice. London, Allen & Unwin [Mystic, Conn., Verry, 1964] 287p. col. front., illus., plates (pt. col.) 29cm. (Half-title: Courtauld Inst. pubns. on Near Eastern art, 2) Pub. with collaboration of the Univ. of London and Univ. of Edinburgh (Moray fund) Bibl. 38-15944 22.50
1. Icons. 2. Cyprus. 3. Painting—Cyprus. 4. Painting, Byzantine. I. Gunnis, Rupert. II. Rice, Tamara (Abelson) Talbot. III. Title.

SAVITSCH, Eugene de, 1903- 704.9482
Russian ecclesiastical art; a descriptive catalogue of the De Savitsch collection, compiled by Nathalie Scheffer Photos. by Dimitri Wolkonsky and M. de Agustin. Washington, 1951. xi, 89p. illus. 24cm. Bibliography: p. [87]-89. [N7956.S385] 53-15215
1. Icons. 2. Christian art and symbolism. 3. Art objects, Russian. 4. Art objects—Private collections. I. Scheffer, Nathalie, comp. II. Title.

SCHWEINFURTH, Philipp, 1887- 704.948
Russian icons. New York, Oxford University Press [1953] 60p. 26 illus. (part mounted, part col.) 26cm. (Iris books) Bibliography: p. [8] [M7956.S35] 53-4515
1. Icons. 2. Christian art and symbolism. I. Title. II. Series.

SKROBUCHA, Heinz. 755.5
Icons [by] Heinz Skrobuche [sic] Translated by M. v. Herzfeld and R. Gaze. Philadelphia, Dufour Editions, 1965 [c1963] vi, 125 p. col. plates. 19 cm. (Realms of art, 1) Translation of Die Botschaft der Ikonen. "Notes and sources": p. 30-31. [N7832.S5313 1965] 64-15191
1. Icons. I. Title.

SKROBUCHA, Heinz 709.94
Introduction to icons. Tr. by Giovanni Rossetti, Marguerite Buchloh. Recklinghausen, A. Bongers; dist. Taplinger [New York, 1961] 73p. illus. (pt. col.) 18cm. (Pictorial lib. of Eastern Church art, v. 10) Tr. of Von Geist und Gestalt der Ikonen. [N8080.S5613] 67-16578 2.50 bds.,
1. Icons. I. Title.

UNITED Nations Educational, Scientific and Cultural Organization. 759.7
Russian icons from the twelfth to the fifteenth century. Introd. by Victor Lasareff. [New York] New Amer. Lib. [c.1958, 1962] 24, [5]p. illus. 28 col. plates. 17cm. (Mentor-Unesco art bk., MQ455) Bibl. 62-53159 .95 pap.,
1. Icons. 2. Painting, Russian. I. Lazarev, Viktor Nikitich, 1896- II. Title.

WEITZMAN, Kurt, 1904- 704.948'2
The icon : holy images, 6th to 14th century / by Kurt Weitzmann. New York : G. Braziller, [1978] p. cm. Bibliography: p. [N8187.W44] 78-6495 ISBN 0-8076-0892-0 : 24.95. ISBN 0-8076-0893-9 pbk. : 11.95
1. Icons. 2. Icon painting. 3. Votive offerings in art. 4. Christian art and symbolism. I. Title. BIP

WILD, Doris 704.9482
Holy icons in the religious art of the Eastern Church. New York, Taplinger [c.1961] 11p. 22 col. plates (Orbis pictus, 5) 61-65183 2.00 bds.,
1. Icons. I. Title.

WINKLER, Martin, 1893- 704.9485
Holidays of the Church. Translated by Marguerite Buchloh and Igor Rosimirow. Recklinghausen, A. Bongers; distributed by Taplinger Pub. Co. [New York, 1958) 80 p. 16 col. plates 18 cm. (Pictorial library of Eastern Church art, v. 8) Translation of Festtage. [N8050.W5313] 67-16576
1. Jesus Christ — Art. 2. Mary, Virgin — Art. 3. Icons. I. Title.

WINKLER, Martin, 1893- 704.948/6
The saints on icons. [Tr. from German by Hans Hermann Rosenwald] Recklinghausen, Aurel Bongers; dist. Taplinger [New York, 1967] 80p. col. plates. 18cm. (Pictorial lib. of Eastern Church art. v. 11) Tr. of Heilige und Heiligenleben. [N8080.W5613] 67-16580 2.50 bds.,
1. Icons. 2. Saints—Art. I. Title.

Icons—Athos, Mount—Catalogs.

HUBER, Paul, writer on icons. 704.948'2'094956
Athos: miraculous icons; introduction [by] Peter Sutermeister [English translation by John L. McHale]. Berne, Hallwag [1968] [7] p. 19 col. plates. 19 cm. (Orbis pictus (Bern) 21) [N8080.H7613] 68-122344
1. Icons—Athos, Mount—Catalogs. 2. Art—Athos, Mount—Catalogs. I. Title.

Icons, Bulgarian—Catalogs.

SOFIA. Natsionalna khudozhestvena galeriia. Branch for Medieval Bulgarian Pictorial Art. 704.948'2
Old Bulgarian art / K. Paskaleva ; [translator, Marguerite Alexieva]. [Sofia] : Sofia Press, 1976. 57 p. : chiefly col. ill. ; 20 x 22 cm. On cover: National Art Gallery. Plan of gallery: [1] leaf inserted. [N8189.B8S63 1976] 77-458444
1. Sofia. Natsionalna khudozhestvena galeriia. 2. Icons, Bulgarian—Catalogs. 3. Icons—Bulgaria—Sofia—Catalogs. I. Paskaleva, Kostadinka Georgieva. II. Title.

Icons, Byzantine.

A Treasury of icons, 704.948'2
sixth to seventeenth centuries; from the Sinai Peninsula, Greece, Bulgaria, and Yugoslavia [by] Kurt Weitzmann, Manolis Chatzidakis, Krsto Miatev, Svetozar Radojcic. [Translated by Robert Erich Wolf] New York, Abrams [1968, c1966] civ p., 220 p. of illus. (part col.) map. 33 cm. Translation of Ikone sa Balkana. Includes bibliographical references. [N8080.I413 1968b] 67-12687
1. Icons, Byzantine. 2. Art, Early Christian. I. Weitzmann, Kurt, 1904-

Icons, Byzantine—Sinai—Catalogs.

WEITZMANN, Kurt, 1904- 755'.2
The Monastery of Saint Catherine at Mount Sinai, the icons / photos. by John Galey. Princeton, N.J. : Princeton University Press, [1975- p. cm. Includes index. Contents.Contents.—1. Weitzmann, K. From the sixth to the tenth century. [N8189.E32S558] 75-3482 ISBN 0-691-03543-1 : 75.00
1. Sinai. Saint Catharine (Basilian monastery) 2. Icons, Byzantine—Sinai—Catalogs. 3. Icons—Sinai—Catalogs. I. Galey, John. II. Title.

Icons—Catalog.

ECKHARDT, Thorvi. 704.948/4
Icons of angels and prophets. [Tr. from the German by Hans Hermann Rosenwald] Recklinghausen, Aurel Bongers; dist. Taplinger [New York, 1967] 82p. col. plates. 18cm. (Pictorial lib. of Eastern Church art, v. 13) Tr. of Engel und Phopheten. [N8080.E3913] 67-16582 2.50 bds.,
1. Icons—Catalog. 2. Angels—Art. 3. Prophets—Art. I. Title.

Icons—Cyprus.

PAPAGEORGIOU, Athanasios. 755'.2'095645
Icons of Cyprus [by] Athanasius Papageorgiou. Pref. by Monsignor Makarios. Translation by James Hogarth. New York, Cowles Book Co. [1970] 131 p. col. illus., map. 35 cm. Bibliography: p. 127-128. [N8189.C9P313] 70-18152 29.50
1. Icons—Cyprus. 2. Icon painting—Cyprus. I. Title.

Icons—Czechoslovak Republic—Catalogs.

SKROBUCHA, Heinz. 755'.2
Icons in Czechoslovakia; photography by Ladislav Neubert; [translated from the Czech MS by Neil Morris and Simon Pleasance]. London, New York, Hamlyn, 1971. xxiv, [131] p. col. illus. tipped in, maps. 29 cm. Bibliography: p. [125]-[127] [N8189.C95S5713] 72-175377 ISBN 0-600-02005-3 £2.75
1. Icons—Czechoslovak Republic—Catalogs. I. Title.

Icons—Dublin—Catalogs.

DUBLIN. National Gallery of Ireland. 704.948'4'074094183
Icons; the Natasha Allen Collection, catalogue [by] David Talbot Rice [and] Tamara Talbot Rice. 1968. 62 p. illus. (some col.) 26 cm. Label on t.p.: Supplied by Worldwide Books, Inc. New York. Bibliography: p. 62. [N7827.D78] 68-30495 unpriced
1. Allen, Natasha—Art collections. 2. Icons—Dublin—Catalogs. I. Rice, David Talbot, 1903- II. Rice, Tamara (Abelson) Talbot.

Icons, Greek.

MCKENZIE, A Dean. 704.948'4'074094183
Greek and Russian icons and other liturgical objects in the Collection of Mr. Charles Bolles Rogers [by] A. Dean MacKenzie. Milwaukee, University of Wisconsin [1965] 44, 35 p. illus. (part col.) 28 cm. Catalog of an exhibition held Nov. 15 to Dec. 10, 1965, Dept. of Art History Gallery, University of Wisconsin, Milwaukee. Bibliography: p. 22. [N7827.M3] 66-65270
1. Rogers, Charles Bolles—Art collections. 2. Icons, Greek. 3. Icons, Russian. I. Wisconsin. University, Milwaukee. Dept. of Art History. II. Title.

Icons—History.

RICE, David Talbot, 1903-1972. 755'.2
Icons and their history / David and Tamara Talbot Rice. Woodstock, N.Y. : Overlook Press, 1974. 192 p., [4] leaves of plates : ill. (some col.) ; 29 cm. Includes index. Bibliography: p. 6. [N8187.R52 1974] 74-78136 ISBN 0-87951-021-8 : 35.00
1. Icons—History. I. Rice, Tamara Abelson Talbot, joint author. II. Title. BIP

Icons—Madison, Wis.—Catalogs.

ELVEHJEM Art Center. 704.948'2
Icons from the Elvehjem Art Center, by George Galavaris. [Madison, Wis., 1973] xxii, 127 p. illus. 27 cm. Bibliography: p. xv-xxii. [N8186.U6E454 1973] 74-167272
1. Elvehjem Art Center. 2. Icons—Madison, Wis.—Catalogs. I. Galavaris, George. II. Title.

Icons, Romanian—Catalogs.

IRIMIE, Cornel. 755'.2'09498
Romanian icons painted on glass [by] Cornel Irimie [and] Marcela Focsa. [1st American ed.] New York, Norton [1971, c1970] 34 p. illus., 149 col. plates. 30 cm. Translation of Icoane pe sticla. Bibliography: p. 23-[26] [N8189.R8I713 1971] 75-28484 25.00
1. Icons, Romanian—Catalogs. 2. Glass painting and staining, Romanian. I. Focsa, Marcela, joint author. II. Title. BIP

Icons, Russian.

ONASCH, Konrad. 755'.2
Russian icons / [compiled by] Konrad Onasch ; [translated from the German by I. Grafe]. Oxford : Phaidon, 1977. 19 p., 48 p. of plates : col. ill. ; 31 cm. Translation of Altrussische Ikonen. [N8189.R9O4913] 77-75399 ISBN 0-7148-1792-9 : 7.95
1. Icons, Russian. I. Title.
Distributed by E.P. Dutton BIP

SOLOUKHIN, Vladimir Alekseevich. 704.9484
Searching for icons in Russia [by] Vladimir Soloukhin. Translated from the Russian by P. S. Falla. [1st American ed.] New York, Harcourt Brace Jovanovich [1972, c1971] 191 p. illus. 22 cm. "A Helen and Kurt Wolff book." [N8186.R9S613 1972] 76-174515 ISBN 0-15-179917-2
1. Icons, Russian. 2. Icons—Private collections—Russia. I. Title.

Icons, Russian—Catalogs.

ZAGORSK, Russia. Gosudarstvennyi istoriko-khudozhestvennyi muzei. 755'.2'09496
Zagorsk : ancient Russian painting in the collection of the Zagorsk Historical and Art Museum / [compiled by Tatiana Nikolajevna Manushina]. Moscow : Pub. House "Soviet Russia", 1976. 64 p. : col. ill. ; 20 cm. [N8189.R92Z349 1976] 77-474499 0.93rub
1. Zagorsk, Russia. Gosudarstvennyi istoriko-khudozhestvennyi muzei. 2. Icons, Russian—Catalogs. 3. Icons—Russian Republic—Zagorsk—Catalogs. I. Manushina, Tat'iana Nikolaevna. II. Title.

Idaho — Antiq. — Collected works.

SWANSON, Earl Herbert, 1927- 917.8963044
Birch Creek papers. [Pocatello, Idaho, 1964- v. illus., map. 28 cm. (Occasional papers of the Idaho State University Museum, no. 13) "Errata for artifact figure references": leaf inserted in v. 1. Contents. -- An archaeological reconnaissance in the Birch Creek Valley of eastern Idaho, by E. H. Swanson, Jr., and A. L. Bryan. Bibliography: v. 1, p. 19-20. [E78.I18I4 no. 13, etc.] 64-64269
1. Idaho — Antiq. — Collected works. 2. Indians of North America — Idaho — Antiq. — Collected works. I. Bryan, Alan Lyle, joint author. II. Title. III. Series: Idaho. State University. Pocatello. Museum. Occasional papers, no. 13

Ihle, John, 1925—

IHLE, John, 1925- 769'.92'4
Ihle : survey of work, 1957-1976. Grand Forks : University of North Dakota Art Galleries, c1977. [48] p. : ill. (some col.) ; 18 cm. Prepared in conjunction with an exhibition organized by the University of North Dakota Art Galleries and shown Oct. 12, 1976-June 19, 1977 at University of North Dakota Art Galleries, Grand Forks, N.D. and other galleries. Catalog: p. [45]-[47] [NE539.I48N67] 77-79251
1. Ihle, John, 1925- I. North Dakota. University. Art Galleries.

Ikeda, Masuo, 1934—

CASTILE, Rand. 769'.92'2
Ikeda & Ida : two new Japanese printmakers / Rand Castile. [New York] : Japan Society, [1974] 45 p. : ill. ; 21 x 22 cm. "Catalogue of the exhibition of Japan House Gallery shown in the fall of 1974 as an activity of the Japan Society, inc." [NE773.I4C37] 74-13776 ISBN 0-913304-03-4
1. Ikeda, Masuo, 1934- 2. Ida, Shoichi, 1940- I. Ikeda, Masuo, 1934- II. Ida, Shoichi, 1940- III. Japan Society of New York. IV. Title.

SUBJECT INDEX ILLUMINATION OF BOOKS

Ikoflex camera.

TYDINGS, Kenneth S 770.2
A guide to the Ikoflex. New York, Greenberg, c1954. 128p. illus. 20cm. (The Modern camera guide series) [TR263.I29T9] 53-12838
1. Ikoflex camera. 2. Photography—Handbooks, manuals, etc. I. Title.

Ikonta camera.

EMANUEL, Walter Daniel, 1908- 770.2
Ikonta guide; how to make the most of the roll film Ikonta (and Nettar) and Super Ikonta cameras. 1st American ed. Hollywood-by-the-Sea, Fla., Transatlantic Arts, '1952. 72 p. illus. 17 cm. "A Focal Press book." [TR263.I 3E5] 52-35686
1. Ikonta camera. 2. Photography—Handbooks, manuals, etc. I. Title.

Il Bacchiacca, Francesco Ubertini, known as, 1494 or 5-1557.

NIKOLENKO, Lada. 759.5
Francesco Ubertini called Il Bacchiacca. Locust Valley, N.Y., J. J. Augustin [1966] 108 p. plates. 24 cm. Contents.Contents.—Stylistic analysis and chronology of paintings by Bacchiacca.—Catalogue raisonne of the authentic paintings.—Attributed paintings.—False attributions.—Lost paintings.—Copies after Bacchiacca.—Bibliography (p. 95-101) [ND623.B13N5] 66-23724
1. Il Bacchiacca, Francesco Ubertini, known as, 1494 or 5-1557. I. Title.

Ilford Photographic Exhibition.

OUTSTANDING 779'.074'09945
Australian and New Zealand photographers show their concern: the Ilford Photographic Exhibition; edited by Harry Marks. Melbourne, Thomas Nelson (Australia) 1972. 92 p. chiefly illus. 28 cm. Cover title: Concern. [TR646.A74V556] 73-163133 ISBN 0-17-001976-4 3.50
1. Ilford Photographic Exhibition. I. Marks, Harry, ed. II. Title: Concern.

Illinois. Arts Council.

ILLINOIS. Arts Council. 338.4'7'7009773
Seven year report / Illinois Arts Council. [s.l.] : The Council, [1973?] [39] p. : ill. ; 28 cm. [NX24.I3I44 1973] 74-623632
1. Illinois. Arts Council.

Illinois. University at Urbana-Champaign. Air Photo Repository.

ILLINOIS. University at Urbana-Champaign. Committee on Aerial Photography. 016.779'9'77835
University of Illinois Air Photo Repository; catalog. Urbana, 1967. 1 v. (various pagings) map, photos. 28 cm. [TR810.I47 1967] A 68
1. Illinois. University at Urbana-Champaign. Air Photo Repository. 2. Aerial photographs—Catalogs.

Illumination of books.

FRENCH and Flemish 745.6'7
illuminated manuscripts from Chicago collections. [Chicago] Division of the Humanities of the University of Chicago [1969] [57] p. illus. (part col.) 28 cm. "[Catalog prepared for a loan exhibition held at] the Newberry Library April 9 to May 30, 1969 ... in honor of the 44th annual meeting of the Mediaeval Academy of America held at the University of Chicago, April 17, 18, and 19." Includes bibliographies. [ND2990.F7] 71-82870
1. Illumination of books. 2. Illumination of books and manuscripts, Flemish—Exhibitions. 3. Illumination of books and manuscripts, Renaissance—Exhibitions. 4. Illumination of books and manuscripts—Chicago. I. Chicago. University. Division of the Humanities. II. Newberry Library, Chicago. III. Mediaeval Academy of America.

Illumination of books and manscripts, Gothic.

RANDALL, Lilian M. C. 096.1
Images in the margins of Gothic manuscripts [by] Lilian M. C. Randall. Berkeley, Univ. of Calif. Pr., 1966. viii, 235p., [156] p. of illus. 29cm. (Calif. studies in the hist. of art, 4) Bibl. [ND2980.R3] 65-18561 22.50 bds.,
1. Illumination of books and manscripts, Gothic. I. Title. II. Series. BIP

Illumination of books and manuscripts.

HERBERT, John Alexander, 1862- 096
Illuminated manuscripts. New York, B. Franklin [1958] xiii, 355 p. plates. 25 cm. (Burt Franklin bibliographical series, 11) Bibliography: p. 331-340. [ND3310.H4 1958] 61-38371
1. Illumination of books and manuscripts. I. Title. BIP

OLD Testament 755'.4
miniatures: a medieval picture book with 283 paintings from the Creation to the story of David. Introd. and legends by Sydney C. Cockerell. Pref. by John Plummer. New York, G. Braziller [1969] 208 p. col. illus. 40 cm. Reproduction of 46 leaves of an imperfect manuscript of Old Testament illustrations now in the Morgan Library, with additional reproductions of 2 leaves in the Bibliotheque nationale, Paris, and another now in the possession of Dr. and Mrs. Peter Ludwig, Aachen, Germany. Previously published in 1927 for the Roxburghe Club under the title: A Book of Old Testament illustrations of the middle of the thirteenth century. The descriptive pages have been inserted between the plates and pertinent Biblical passages have been supplied. Bibliography: p. 4. [ND3356.B6 1969] 75-82000 50.00
1. Bible. O.T.—Pictures, illustrations, etc. 2. Illumination of books and manuscripts. I. Cockerell, Sydney Carlyle, Sir, 1867-1962. II. Plummer, John. III. Bible. O.T. English, Douai. Selections. 1969.

Illumination of books and manuscripts, Anglo-Saxon—Catalogs.

TEMPLE, Elzbieta. 745.6'7'0942 s
Anglo-Saxon manuscripts, 900-1066 / by Elzbieta Temple. London : Harvey Miller, c1976. 243 p. : ill. (some col.) ; 34 cm. (A Survey of manuscripts illuminated in the British Isles ; v. 2) Includes bibliographical references and indexes. [ND3128.K35 vol. 2] [ND2940] 745.6'7'0942 76-373399 ISBN 0-85602-016-8 : £28.50
1. Illumination of books and manuscripts, Anglo-Saxon—Catalogs. I. Title. II. Series.

Illumination of books and manuscripts—Armenia.

DURNOVE, Libiia Aleksandrovna. 759.9566
Armenian miniatures. Text and notes by Lydia A. Dournovo. Pref. by Sirarpie Der Nersessian. [Text translated from the French by Irene J. Underwood] New York, H. N. Abrams [1961] 181 p. mounted illus. (part col.) col. map (on lining paper) 31 cm. [ND3239.A7D83] 61-15292
1. Erivan. Matenadaran. 2. Illumination of books and manuscripts—Armenia. I. Title.

Illumination of books and manuscripts, Armenian.

WALTERS Art Gallery, Baltimore. 745.6'7'095662
An introduction to Armenian manuscript illumination : selections from the collection in the Walters Art Gallery / by Sirarpie Der Nersessian. Baltimore : The Gallery, 1974. [12] p., [18] leaves of plates : ill. (some col.) ; 27 cm. (A Walters Art Gallery picture book) [ND3245.A7W34 1974] 75-309486
1. Walters Art Gallery, Baltimore. 2. Illumination of books and manuscripts, Armenian. I. Der Nersessian, Sirarpie, 1896- II. Title. III. Series. BIP

Illumination of books and manuscripts, Armenian—Catalogs.

DER NERSESSIAN, Sirarpie. 091'.09752'6
Armenian manuscripts in the Walters Art Gallery. Baltimore, The Trustees, 1973. x, 111 p., 243 p. of illus. 8 col. plates. 39 cm. Bibliography: p. 93-97. [ND3245.A7D47] 74-177384
1. Walters Art Gallery, Baltimore. 2. Illumination of books and manuscripts, Armenian—Catalogs. 3. Illumination of books and manuscripts—Baltimore—Catalogs. I. Walters Art Gallery, Baltimore. II. Title. BIP

Illumination of books and manuscripts, Byzantine.

STUDIES in East Christian 709'.37
and Roman art, by Walter Dennison and Charles R. Morey. New York, Macmillan, 1918. [New York, Johnson Reprint Corp., 1972] xiii, 175 p. illus., col. plates. 23 cm. Original ed. issued as v. 12 of University of Michigan studies, Humanistic series. Contents.Contents.—pt. 1. East Christian paintings in the Freer collection, by C. R. Morey.—pt. 2. A gold treasure of the late Roman period from Egypt, by W. Dennison. Includes bibliographical references. [ND2930.S8 1972] 78-39137
1. Illumination of books and manuscripts, Byzantine. 2. Painting, Byzantine. 3. Jewelry, Roman. I. Freer, Charles Lang, 1856-1919. II. Dennison, Walter, 1869-1917. A gold treasure of the late Roman period. 1972. III. Morey, Charles Rufus, 1877-1955. East Christian paintings in the Freer collection. 1972. IV. Series: Michigan. University. University of Michigan studies. Humanistic series, v. 12. BIP

Illumination of books and manuscripts, Byzantine—Addresses, essays, lectures.

THE Place of book 745.6'7'09495
illumination in Byzantine art / Kurt Weitzmann ... [et al.]. Princeton, N.J. : Art Museum, Princeton University : distributed by Princeton University Press, c1975. 184 p. : ill. ; 27 cm. Papers of a symposium held Apr. 14, 1973, in connection with an exhibition honoring K. Weitzmann at the Art Museum, Princeton University. Includes bibliographical references and index. [ND2930.P56] 74-84574 ISBN 0-691-03910-0 : 28.50
1. Illumination of books and manuscripts, Byzantine—Addresses, essays, lectures. I. Weitzmann, Kurt, 1904- II. Princeton University. Art Museum.

Illumination of books and manuscripts, Byzantine—History.

WEITZMANN, Kurt, 1904- 745'.6'7
Studies in classical and Byzantine manuscript illumination. Edited by Herbert L. Kessler. With an introd. by Hugo Buchthal. Chicago, University of Chicago Press [1971] xxii, 346 p. illus. 27 cm. "Bibliography of Kurt Weitzmann": p. [335]-339. [ND2930.W43] 77-116381 ISBN 0-226-89246-8 22.50
1. Illumination of books and manuscripts, Byzantine—History. I. Title. BIP

Illumination of books and manuscripts—Canterbury. Eng.

DODWELL, Charles Reginald. v. 12
The Canterbury school of illumination, 1066-1200. Cambridge [Eng.] University Press, 1954. xv, 139p. illus., 73plates. 32cm. 'Substantially the same as the dissertation submitted ... for a Ph. D. Degree at Cambridge in August 1950.' 'A hand-list of manuscripts illuminated at Canterbury between 1050 and 1200 : p. 120-123. Bibliography: p. 125- 129. [ND3132.C3D6] 55-1223
1. Illumination of books and manuscripts—Canterbury. Eng. 2. Illumination of books and manuscripts—Specimens, reproductions, etc. I. Title.

DODWELL, Charles Reginald. 755.4
The great Lambeth Bible. With introd. and notes by C. R. Dodwell. New York, T. Yoseloff [1959] 38 p. mounted col. illus. 29 cm. [The Library of illuminated manuscripts] Bibliographical references included in "Notes" (p. 37-38) [ND3355.L3] 59-16875
1. Bible. Manuscripts, Latin. Lambeth Bible. 2. Illumination of books and manuscripts—Canterbury, Eng. 3. Miniature painting—Canterbury, Eng. I. Title. II. Series.

Illumination of books and manuscripts, Carlovingian.

CAROLINGIAN painting 745.6'7'094
/ introduction by Florentine Mutherich ; commentaries by J. E. Gaehde. New York : G. Braziller, 1977. p. cm. Bibliography: p. [ND2950.C37] 76-15908 ISBN 0-8076-0851-3 : 17.50 ISBN 0-8076-0852-1 pbk. :
1. Illumination of books and manuscripts, Carlovingian. I. Mutherich, Florentine. II. Gehde, J. E.

Illumination of books and manuscripts, Carlovingian—France—Tours.

KESSLER, Herbert L., 1941- 745.6'7
The illustrated Bibles from Tours / by Herbert L. Kessler. Princeton, N.J. : Princeton University Press, c1977. p. cm. (Studies in manuscript illumination ; no. 7) Based on the author's thesis, Princeton, 1965. Includes bibliographical references and index. [ND3355.K47] 76-45902 ISBN 0-691-03923-2 : 42.50
1. Bible—Pictures, illustrations, etc. 2. Illumination of books and manuscripts, Carlovingian—France—Tours. 3. Illumination of books and manuscripts—France—Tours. I. Title. II. Series.

Illumination of books and manuscripts, Celtic.

THE Book of Kells 745.6'7'0941822
: reproductions from the manuscript in Trinity College, Dublin / with a study of the manuscript by Francoise Henry. 1st American ed. New York : Knopf, 1974. 226 p. : ill. ; 35 cm. "126 colour plates, 75 monochrome illustrations." Issued in a slipcase. Includes bibliographical references. [ND3359.B7B65] 74-194761 ISBN 0-394-49475-X : 65.00
1. Bible. Manuscripts, Latin. N.T. Gospels. Book of Kells—Illustrations. 2. Illumination of books and manuscripts, Celtic. I. Henry, Francoise.

NORDENFALK, Carl Adam Johan, 1907- 745.6'7'0941
Celtic painting : Hiberno-Saxon book illumination / by Carl Nordenfalk. New York : G. Braziller, 1977. p. cm. Bibliography: p. [ND2940.N67] 76-16443 ISBN 0-8076-0825-4 : 17.50. ISBN 0-8076-0826-2 : 9.95
1. Illumination of books and manuscripts, Celtic. I. Title.

Illumination of books and manuscripts—Czechoslovak Republic.

KVET, Jan, 1896- 096
Czechoslovakian miniatures from Romanesque and Gothic manuscripts. Introd. by Jan Kvet [New York] Pub. by the New Amer. Lib. of World Lit. by arrangement with UNESCO [c.1959, 1964] 24p. [4]p. (on fold. l.) illus., 28 col. plates (pt. fold.) 17cm. (Mentor-Unesco art bk., MQ588) Bibl. [ND3144.C9K8] 65-267 .95 pap.,
1. Illumination of books and manuscripts—Czechoslovak Republic. I. United Nations Educational, Scientific and Cultural Organization. II. Title.

UNITED Nations Educational, Scientific and Cultural Organization. 759.9437
Czechoslovakia: Romanesque and Gothic illuminated manuscripts. Pref. [by] Hanns Swarzenski. Introd. [by] Jan Kvet. [Greenwich, Conn.] New York Graphic Society [1959] 20, [2] p. illus., 32 col. plates. 48 cm. (UNESCO world art series 12) Material compiled by experts from UNESCO and the New York Graphic

Society. Bibliography: p. [21]-[22] [ND3144.C9U5] 59-3963
1. Illumination of books and manuscripts—Czechoslovak Republic. 2. Illumination of books and manuscripts—Specimens, reproductions, etc. I. New York Graphic Society. II. Title. III. Series.

Illumination of books and manuscripts, Dutch.

DELAISSE, L. M. J. 091
A century of Dutch manuscript illumination by L. M. J. Delaisse. Berkeley, Univ. of Calif. Pr., 1968. xii, 102p. [79]p. of illus. (pt. col.) 33cm. (Calif. studies in the hist. of art. 6) Bibl. refs. [ND3167.D4 1968] 65-10577 25.00
1. Illumination of books and manuscripts, Dutch. 2. Illumination of books and manuscripts, Gothic—Netherlands. I. Title. II. Series. BIP

THE Hours of Catherine of 096.1
Cleves. Introd. and commentaries by John Plummer. New York, G. Braziller [1966] 359 p. 160 col. facsims. 21 cm. "Reproduced from the illuminated manuscript belonging to the Guennol Collection and the Pierpont Morgan Library." Bibliography: p. 358-359. [ND3363.C3P55 1966] 66-23096
1. Illumination of books and manuscripts, Dutch. 2. Hours, Books of. I. Catharina van Kleef, Duchess of Gelderland, 1417-1476. II. Plummer, John. BIP

PLUMMER, John. 759.9492
The book of hours of Catherine of Cleves. Foreword by Frederick B. Adams, Jr. Incorporating comments by Harry Boder [and others] New York, Pierpont Morgan Library, 1964. 83 p. 32 plates (part col.) 24 cm. Bibliography: p. 83. [ND3363.C3P55] 65-4021
1. Illumination of books and manuscripts, Dutch. 2. Hours, Books of. I. Catharina van Kleef, duchess of Gelderland, 1417-1476. II. Title. BIP

Illumination of books and manuscripts, Early Christian.

WEITZMANN, Kurt, 745.6'7'09495
1904-
Late antique-early Christian painting / by Kurt Weitzmann. New York : G. Braziller, 1977. p. cm. Bibliography: p. [ND2930.W42] 76-16444 ISBN 0-8076-0830-0 : 17.50. ISBN 0-8076-0831-9 pbk. : 9.95
1. Illumination of books and manuscripts, Early Christian. I. Title. BIP

Illumination of books and manuscripts — England.

PACHT, Otto, 1962- v. 12
The rise of pictorial narrative in twelfth-century England. Oxford, Clarendon Press, 1962. xii, 63 p. 12 plates. 28 cm. Bibliographical footnotes. [ND3128.P3] 62-6403
1. Illumination of books and manuscripts — England. 2. Art, English. 3. Art, Medieval. I. Title.

Illumination of books and manuscripts, English.

MITCHELL, W. J. Thomas, 821'.7
1942-
Blake's composite art : a study of the illuminated poetry / W. J. T. Mitchell. Princeton, N.J. : Princeton University Press c1978. xix, 230 p., [27] leaves of plates : ill. ; 25 cm. Includes bibliographical references and index. [PR4147..M5] 77-7116 16.50
1. Blake, William, 1757-1827—Criticism and interpretation. 2. Blake, William, 1757-1827—Aesthetics. 3. Illumination of books and manuscripts, English. I. Title. BIP

SAUNDERS, O. Elfrida. 745.6'7
English illumination, by O. Elfrida Saunders. New York, Hacker Art Books, 1969. 132, [258] p. (chiefly illus.) 29 cm. Reprint of the 1933 ed. Bibliography: p. [121]-124. [ND2940.S3 1969] 71-78356
1. Illumination of books and manuscripts, English. I. Title.

TURNER, D. H. 096.1
Early Gothic illuminated manuscripts in England [London] Trustees of the Brit. Mus. [New York, Brit. Info., c.1965] 32p. 20 plates (4 col.) 22cm. Based mainly on ms. located in the Dept. of Mss. of the Brit. Mus. Bibl. [ND3128.T8] 66-169 1.00 pap.,
1. Illumination of books and manuscripts, English. 2. Illumination of books and manuscripts, Gothic. I. British, Museum. Dept. of Manuscripts. II. Title.

Illumination of books and manuscripts, Ethiopian.

LEROY, Jules. 759.963
Ethiopian painting, in the late Middle Ages and during the Gondar dynasty. [Translation by Claire Pace] New York, F. A. Praeger [1967] 60 p. col. plates. 15 illus. (part col.) 32 cm. Bibliography: p. 43-45. [ND3286.E8L43] 67-20403
1. Illumination of books and manuscripts, Ethiopian. 2. Mural painting and decoration, Ethiopian. I. Title.

LEROY, Jules. 759.963
Ethiopian painting, in the late Middle Ages and during the Gondar dynasty. [Translation by Claire Pace] New York, F. A. Praeger [1967] 60 p., 60 col. plates. 15 illus. (part col.) 32 cm. Bibliography: p. 43-45. [ND3286.E8L43 1967] 67-20403
1. Illumination of books and manuscripts, Ethiopian. 2. Mural painting and decoration, Ethiopian. I. Title.

Illumination of books and manuscripts—Exhibitions.

GABRIEL, 745.6'7'094074017289
Astrik Ladislas, 1907-
The Ambrosiana Collection at the University of Notre Dame : the Frank M. Folsom Ambrosiana Microfilm and Photographic Collection, a project of the Samuel H. Kress Foundation : an exhibition of selected manuscript leaves and miniatures from the 9th to the 16th century, master drawings from the 15th to the 17th century, a photographic documentation : catalogue / by Astrik L. Gabriel. [Chicago] : Sears Bank and Trust Co., c1976. 64 p. : ill. (some col.) ; 26 cm. Exhibition of material from the Medieval Institute of the University of Notre Dame, held at the Sears Bank and Trust Co., Nov. 29, 1976-Jan. 28, 1977, and at the Art Gallery, University of Notre Dame, Apr. 17-June 12, 1977. [N4010.N67N673] 76-53846
1. Notre Dame, Ind. University—Photograph collections—Exhibitions. 2. Illumination of books and manuscripts—Exhibitions. 3. Miniature painting—Exhibitions. 4. Drawing, Renaissance—Exhibitions. 5. Drawing, Baroque—Exhibitions. I. Milan. Biblioteca ambrosiana. II. Sears Bank and Trust Company. III. Notre Dame, Ind. University. Mediaeval Institute. IV. Notre Dame, Ind. University. Art Gallery. V. Title.

PENNSYLVANIA Farm Museum 745.6'7
of Landis Valley.
Pennsylvania German Fraktur and color drawings, exhibited at Pennsylvania Farm Museum of Landis Valley, Lancaster, Pennsylvania, May 19-June 30, 1969. [Lancaster, Pa., 1969] [72] p. illus., facsims. (both part col.) 28 cm. Contents.Contents.—Introduction, by D. Yoder.—Fraktur types; an interpretation, by V. S. Gunnion and C. J. Hopf. Includes bibliographical references. [ND3035.P4P4] 72-82719
1. Illumination of books and manuscripts—Exhibitions. 2. Pennsylvania Germans. 3. Folk art—Pennsylvania. I. Title.

Illumination of books and manuscripts—France.

MORAND, Kathleen 745.67
Jean Pucelle. Oxford, Clarendon Pr. [dist. New York, Oxford, 1963, c.1962] xiv, 49p. 33 plates. 29cm. Based on thesis, University of London. Bibl. 63-1388 7.20
1. Pucelle, Jean, fl. 1320. 2. Illumination of books and manuscripts—France. I. Title.

Illumination of books and manuscripts, French.

AVRIL, Francois. 745.6'7'0944
Manuscript painting at the court of France : the fourteenth century, 1310-1380 / Francois Avril ; [translated from the French by Ursule Molinaro, with the assistance of Bruce Benderson]. New York : G. Braziller, 1978. 118 p. : ill. (some col.) ; 29 cm. Bibliography: p. 31-[33]. [ND3147.A8813] 77-78721 ISBN 0-8076-0878-5 : 20.00. ISBN 0-8076-0879-3 pbk. : 9.95
1. Illumination of books and manuscripts, French. 2. Illumination of books and manuscripts, Gothic—France. I. Title.

MEISS, Millard. 016.09
French painting in the time of Jean de Berry : the Limbourgs and their contemporaries / by Millard Meiss, with the assistance of Sharon Off Dunlap Smith and Elizabeth Home Beatson. New York : G. Braziller, 1974. 2 v. : ill. (some col.) ; 32 cm. (The Franklin Jasper Walls lectures) Includes indexes. Bibliography: v. 1, p. 482-505. [ND3147.M38 1974] 73-90120 ISBN 0-8076-0734-7 : 70.00
1. Limbourg, Pol de, ca. 1385-ca. 1416. 2. Limbourg, Hermann de, ca. 1385-ca. 1416. 3. Limbourg, Hennequin de, ca. 1385-ca. 1416. 4. Berry, Jean de France, duc de, 1340-1416. 5. Illumination of books and manuscripts, French. 6. Illumination of books and manuscripts, Gothic—France. 7. Hours, Books of. I. Smith, Sharon Off Dunlap, joint author. II. Beatson, Elizabeth Home, joint author. III. Title. IV. Series.
Contents omitted.

Illumination of books and manuscripts, French—France—Paris.

BRANNER, Robert. 745.6'7'0944361
Manuscript painting in Paris during the reign of Saint Louis : a study of styles / by Robert Branner. Berkeley : University of California Press, c1977. xxiv, 270 p., [75] leaves of plates : ill. (some col.) ; 31 cm. (California studies in the history of art ; 18) Includes index. Bibliography: p. 145-149. [ND3149.P5B72] 73-78541 ISBN 0-520-02462-1 : 48.50
1. Illumination of books and manuscripts, French—France—Paris. 2. Illumination of books and manuscripts, Gothic—France—Paris. 3. Artists' studios—France—Paris. I. Title. II. Series.

Illumination of books and manuscripts, German.

GOLDSCHMIDT, Adolph, 745.6'7
1863-1944.
German illumination. New York, Hacker Art Books, 1970. 1 v. (various pagings) illus. 32 cm. Reprint of the 1928 ed. Translation of Die deutsche Buchmalerei. Contents.Contents.—v. 1. Carolingian period.—v. 2. Ottonian period. Includes bibliographies. [ND3151.G613 1970] 72-78359
1. Illumination of books and manuscripts, German. 2. Illumination of books and manuscripts, Carlovingian—Germany. 3. Illumination of books and manuscripts, Ottonian—Germany. I. Title.

Illumination of books and manuscripts—Germany (Democratic Republic, 1949-)

ROTHE, Edith. 096'.1'0943
Mediaeval book illumination in Europe; the collections of the German Democratic Republic. [Translated from the German by Mary Whittall] New York, Norton [1968] 306 p. illus. (part col.), facsims. (part col.) 29 cm. Translation of Buchmalerei aus zwolf Jahrhunderten. Bibliography: p. [285]-[296] [ND2894.G4R613] 68-31992 17.50
1. Illumination of books and manuscripts—Germany (Democratic Republic, 1949-) I. Title.

Illumination of books and manuscripts, Gothic.

PIRANI, Emma. 745.6'7'094
Gothic illuminated manuscripts; [translated from the Italian by Margaret Crosland]. Feltham, Hamlyn, 1970. 158 p. col. illus., col. facsim. 20 cm. (Cameo) Translation of La miniatura gotica. [ND2980.P5713] 72-195617 ISBN 0-600-01250-6 £0.90
1. Illumination of books and manuscripts, Gothic. I. Title.

UNTERKIRCHER, Franz. 745.6'7'0944
King Rene's book of love = le cueur d'amours expris / introd. and commentaries by F. Unterkircher ; [translated from the German by Sophie Wilkins]. New York : G. Braziller, 1975. 14 p., [16] leaves of plates : col. ill. ; 28 cm. Text on versos of plates. Includes bibliography. [ND3399.R4U58] 75-7957 ISBN 0-8076-0788-6 : 15.00
1. Rene I, d'Anjou, King of Naples and Jerusalem, 1409-1480. Livre du cuer d'amours espris—Illustrations. 2. Vienna. Nationalbibliothek. Mss. (2597) 3. Illumination of books and manuscripts, Gothic. I. Rene I, d'Anjou, King of Naples and Jerusalem, 1409-1480. Livre du cuer d'amours espris. English. Selections. 1975. II. Title. III. Title: Le cueur d'amours esp BIP

Illumination of books and manuscripts, Gothic—Acre, Israel.

FOLDA, Jaroslav. 016.091
Crusader manuscript illumination at Saint-Jean d'Acre, 1275-1291 / Jaroslav Folda Princeton, N.J. : Princeton University Press, [1975] p. cm. [ND3240.A27F64] 75-2991 ISBN 0-691-03907-0 : 35.00
1. Illumination of books and manuscripts, Gothic—Acre, Israel. 2. Illumination of books and manuscripts—Acre, Israel. I. Title. BIP

Illumination of books and manuscripts, Gothic—Germany—Handbooks, manuals, etc.

GOTTINGEN. 745.6'7'028
Niedersachsische Staats- und Universitatsbibliothek. MSS. (Cod. Ms./Uffenb. 51)
The Gottingen model book : a facsimile edition and translations of a fifteenth-century illuminators' manual / edited, with commentary, by Hellmut Lehmann-Haupt ; based in part on the studies of the late Dr. Edmund Will. Columbia : University of Missouri Press, 1979, c1972. p. cm. English or German. Bibliography: p. [ND2980.G6 1978] 78-62289 ISBN 0-8262-0261-6 : 35.00
1. Illumination of books and manuscripts, Gothic—Germany—Handbooks, manuals, etc. 2. Illumination of books and manuscripts, German—Handbooks, manuals, etc. I. Lehmann-Haupt, Hellmut, 1903- II. Will, Edmund, 1884- III. Title.

Illumination of books and manuscripts, Gothic—Handbooks, manuals, etc.

GOTTINGEN. Niedersachsische 091
Staats- und Universitatsbibliothek. MSS. (Cod. Ms./Uffenb. 51)
The Gottingen model book; a facsimile edition and translations of a fifteenth-century illuminators' manual. Edited, with commentary, by Hellmut Lehmann-Haupt. Columbia, University of Missouri Press [1972] 102 p. illus. (part col.) 21 x 27 cm. "Based in part on the studies of the late Dr. Edmund Will." Original text in Rhenish Franconian dialect, translations into modern German and English. Includes bibliographical references. [ND2980.G6 1972] 72-155843 ISBN 0-8262-0102-4 25.00
1. Illumination of books and manuscripts, Gothic—Handbooks, manuals, etc. I. Lehmann-Haupt, Hellmut, 1903- ed. II. Title. BIP

Illumination of books and manuscripts, Greek—Exhibitions.

ctions;
ILLUMINATED Greek manuscripts from American collections; an exhibition in honor of Kurt Weitzmann. Edited by Gary Vikan. [Princeton, N.J.] Art Museum, Princeton University; distributed by Princeton University Press [1973] 231 p. illus. (part col.) 27 cm. Catalog of an exhibition held at the Princeton University

Art Museum Apr. 14-May 20, 1973. Includes bibliographies. [ND3155.I4 1973] 72-92151 ISBN 0-691-03889-9 18.00 (Lib. bdg.)
1. Illumination of books and manuscripts, Greek—Exhibitions. 2. Illumination of books and manuscripts—United States. I. Weitzmann, Kurt, 1904- II. Vikan, Gary, ed. III. Princeton University. Art Museum.

Illumination of books and manuscripts—Hanover, N.H.—Catalogs.

DARTMOUTH College. Library. 091
Illuminated manuscripts in the Dartmouth College Library. Compiled by Georgia G. Cook [and others] Edited by Robert L. McGrath. Hanover, N.H., 1972. 35 p. illus. 29 cm. Edition limited to 500 copies. Includes bibliographical references. [ND2895.H36D33] 72-91192
1. Illumination of books and manuscripts—Hanover, N.H.—Catalogs. I. Cook, Georgia G., comp. II. McGrath, Robert L., 1935- ed. III. Title.

Illumination of books and manuscripts—History.

MITCHELL, Sabrina 745.6709
Medieval manuscript painting. New York, Viking [c.1965] 45, 167p. of plates (pt. col.) 20cm. (Compass hist. of art, Compass bks., CA7) [ND2920.M55] 64-21645 2.25 pap.,
1. Illumination of books and manuscripts—Hist. 2. Illumination of books and manuscripts—Specimens, reproductions, etc. I. Title.

Illumination of books and manuscripts—History.

DIRINGER, David, 1900- 745.67
The illuminated book, its history and production. New York, Philosophical Library [1958] 524 p. illus. (some col.) 26 cm. Includes bibliographies. [ND2920.D55] 58-3435
1. Illumination of books and manuscripts—History. I. Title.

DIRINGER, David, 1900- 745.6'7'09
The illuminated book: its history and production. Rev. ed. New York, Praeger [1967] 514 p. illus. (part col.) 27 cm. Includes bibliographies. [ND2920.D55 1967] 66-12525
1. Illumination of books and manuscripts—History. I. Title.

ROBB, David Metheny, 1903- 745.6'7'09
The art of the illuminated manuscript [by] David M. Robb. [Philadelphia] Philadelphia Art Alliance [1973] 356 p. illus. 32 cm. Bibliography: p. 337-345. [ND2900.R63] 78-37830 ISBN 0-87982-001-2
1. Illumination of books and manuscripts—History. I. Title. **BIP**

ROBB, David Metheny, 1903- 745.6'7'09
The art of the illuminated manuscript [by] David M. Robb. South Brunswick, A. S. Barnes [1973] 356 p. illus. (part col.) 32 cm. Bibliography: p. 337-345. [ND2900.R63 1973b] 73-14782 ISBN 0-498-01118-6 40.00
1. Illumination of books and manuscripts—History. I. Title.

WEITZMANN, Kurt, 1904- 096.1
Illustrations in roll and codex; a study of the origin and method of text illustration. [2d. print., with addenda] Princeton [N.J.] Princeton University Press, 1970. x, 261 p. illus., 56 plates. 31 cm. (Studies in manuscript illumination, no. 2) Includes bibliographical references. [ND2900.W4 1970] 70-22791 ISBN 0-691-03865-1 17.50
1. Illumination of books and manuscripts—History. I. Title. II. Series. **BIP**

Illumination of books and manuscripts, Hungarian.

BERKOVITS, Ilona. 745.6'7
Illuminated manuscripts in Hungary, XI-XVI centuries. Translated by Zsuzsanna Horn. Rev. by Alick West. New York, Praeger [1969] 110 p. illus., facsims. (part col., 1 fold. col. in pocket), 44 col. plates. 33 cm. Translation of Magyar kodexek a XI-XVI szazadban. Bibliography: p. 97-100. [ND3144.H8B413 1969b] 69-11964 27.50
1. Illumination of books and manuscripts, Hungarian. 2. Illumination of books and manuscripts, Medieval—Hungary. I. Title.

Illumination of books and manuscripts, Indic—Exhibitions.

BINNEY, Edwin. 745.6'7'0954s
Indian miniature painting from the Collection of Edwin Binney 3rd : an exhibition at the Portland Art Museum, December 2, 1973-January 20, 1974 : catalogue and text / by Edwin Binney 3rd. Portland, Or. : The Museum, 1974-c1973- v. : ill. (some col.) ; 20 x 22 cm. Contents.Contents.—1. The Mughal and Deccani schools with some related Sultanate material. Bibliography: v. 1, p. 198-202. [ND3247.B5] 75-322917
1. Binney, Edwin—Art collections. 2. Illumination of books and manuscripts, Indic—Exhibitions. 3. Miniature painting, Indic—Exhibitions. I. Portland, Or. Art Museum. II. Title.

MCNEAR, Ann. 759.95
Persian and Indian miniatures from the Collection of Everett and Ann McNear : [Museum of Art, University of Iowa, Iowa City, Art Institute of Chicago, Chicago, Illinois, the Walters Art Gallery, Baltimore, Maryland, 1974-1975] / [text, Ann McNear ; design, Everett McNear]. Chicago : Art Institute of Chicago, 1974. 63 p. : ill. (some col.) ; 23 cm. Catalog of the exhibition. [ND3247.M28] 74-23038
1. McNear, Everett, 1904- —Art collections. 2. McNear, Ann—Art collections. 3. Illumination of books and manuscripts, Indic—Exhibitions. 4. Miniature painting, Indic—Exhibitions. 5. Illumination of books and manuscripts, Iranian—Exhibitions. 6. Miniature painting, Iranian—Exhibitions. I. McNear, Everett, 1904- II. Iowa. University. Museum of Art. III. Chicago. Art Institute. IV. Walters Art Gallery, Baltimore. V. Title.

Illumination of books and manuscripts—Iran.

GRAY, Basil, 1904- 759.955
Persian painting. [New York] Skira; [distributed by World Pub. Co., Cleveland, 1961] 191 p. mounted col. illus., map. 29 cm. (Treasures of Asia) "Bibliography, a select list of Western authorities": p. 173-[174] [ND980.G72] 61-10169
1. Illumination of books and manuscripts—Iran. 2. Painting—Iran. I. Title. II. Series.

Illumination of books and manuscripts, Iranian.

WELCH, Anthony. 745.6'7'0955
Artists for the Shah : late sixteenth-century painting at the Imperial Court of Iran / Anthony Welch. New Haven : Yale University Press, 1976. xvi, 233 p., [8] leaves of plates : ill. (some col.) ; 25 cm. Large parts of work appeared in the author's 1972 doctoral dissertation for Harvard University. Includes index. Bibliography: p. 221-223. [ND3241.W43] 75-18188 ISBN 0-300-01915-7 : 25.00
1. Illumination of books and manuscripts, Iranian. 2. Illumination of books and manuscripts, Islamic—Iran. 3. Art patronage—Iran. I. Title.

†WELCH, Stuart Cary. 745.6'7'0955
Persian painting : five royal Safavid manuscripts of the sixteenth century / Stuart Cary Welch. New York : G. Braziller, 1976. 127 p. : ill. (some col.) ; 28 cm. "Plates and commentaries": p. [33]-127. Bibliography: p. 28. [ND3241.W44] 75-38508 ISBN 0-8076-0812-2 : 17.50
1. Illumination of books and manuscripts, Iranian. 2. Miniature painting, Iranian. I. Title. **BIP**

WELCH, Stuart Cary. 745.6'7'0955
Royal Persian manuscripts / Stuart Cary Welch. London : Thames and Hudson, 1976. 127 p. : ill. (some col.); 28 cm. Bibliography: p. 28. [ND3241.W45 1976] 76-369197 ISBN 0-500-27074-0 : £4.50
1. Illumination of books and manuscripts, Iranian. 2. Illumination of books and manuscripts, Islamic—Iran. 3. Safavids—Art collections. I. Title.

Illumination of books and manuscripts, Iranian—Catalogs.

INDIA Office Library. 745.6'7'095507402132
Persian paintings in the India Office Library : a descriptive catalogue / B. W. Robinson. London : Sotheby Parke Bernet, 1976. xiii, 271 p., [16] leaves of plates : ill. (some col.) ; 26 cm. Includes indexes. [ND3241.I53 1976] 76-378764 ISBN 0-85667-026-X : 55.00
1. India Office Library. 2. Illumination of books and manuscripts, Iranian—Catalogs. 3. Illumination of books and manuscripts, Islamic—Iran—Catalogs. 4. Miniature painting, Iranian—Catalogs. 5. Miniature painting, Islamic—Iran—Catalogs. I. Robinson, Basil William. II. Title.
Available from publisher: 81 Adams Drive, Totowa, N.J. **BIP**

Illumination of books and manuscripts, Iranian—Exhibitions.

BINNEY, Edwin. 016.091
Persian and Indian miniatures: from the Collection of Edwin Binney, 3rd. [Text and catalog by Edwin Binney, 3rd.] Exhibited at the Portland Art Museum Sept. 28-Nov. 29, 1962. [Portland, Ore., Portland Art Association, 1962] 47 p. illus. (part. col.) 20 cm. [ND3241.B49] 74-159780
1. Binney, Edwin—Art collections. 2. Illumination of books and manuscripts, Iranian—Exhibitions. 3. Illumination of books and manuscripts, Indic—Exhibitions. 4. Miniature painting, Iranian—Exhibitions. 5. Miniature painting, Indic—Exhibitions. I. Portland, Or. Art Museum. II. Title.

BINYON, Laurence, 1869-1943. 751.7'7'0955
Persian miniature painting, including a critical and descriptive catalogue of the miniatures exhibited at Burlington House, January-March, 1931, by Laurence Binyon, J. V. S. Wilkinson and Basil Gray. New York, Dover Publications [1971] xiv, 212 p. 225 illus. (part col.) 24 cm. Reprint of the 1933 ed. Bibliography: p. 193-195. [ND3241.B5 1971] 68-19989 ISBN 0-486-22054-0 6.00
1. Illumination of books and manuscripts, Iranian—Exhibitions. 2. Miniature painting, Iranian—Exhibitions. I. Wilkinson, James Vere Stewart, joint author. II. Gray, Basil, 1904- joint author. III. London. Royal Academy of Arts. IV. Title. **BIP**

Illumination of books and manuscripts, Islamic.

PINDER-WILSON, Ralph H. 745.6'7
Paintings from Islamic lands. Editor: R. Pinder-Wilson. Columbia, University of South Carolina Press [1969] 204 p. illus., facsims., plates. 25 cm. (Oriental studies, 4) Includes bibliographical references. [ND2955.P55 1969b] 69-17154 ISBN 8-7249-1382- 7.95
1. Illumination of books and manuscripts, Islamic. I. Title. **BIP**

Illumination of books and manuscripts, Islamic—Catalogs.

GRUBE, Ernst J. 745.6'7
Islamic paintings from the 11th to the 18th century in the Collection of Hans P. Kraus [by] Ernst J. Grube. New York, H. P. Kraus [1972?] 291 p. illus., 54 [i.e. 55] col. plates. 36 cm. On spine: Islamic paintings: the Kraus Collection. Bibliography: p. 17-[21] [ND2955.G7] 72-187217
1. Kraus, Hans Peter, 1907- —Art collection. 2. Illumination of books and manuscripts, Islamic—Catalogs. 3. Paintings, Islamic—Catalogs. I. Title. II. Title: The Kraus Collection.

Illumination of books and manuscripts—Italy.

FORMAGGIO, Dino. 759.5
A book of miniatures, edited by Dino Formaggio and Carlo Basso. Translated by Peggy Craig. New York, Tudor Pub. Co. [1962] 143 p. 132 mounted col. illus. 34 cm. Translation of La miniatura. [ND3159.F613] 62-53225
1. Illumination of books and manuscripts—Italy. 2. Illumination of books and manuscripts—Specimens, reproductions, etc. I. Basso, Carlo, joint author.

Illumination of books and manuscripts—Italy—Hist.

MEISS, Millard. 745.67
Andrea Mantegna as illuminator; an episode in Renaissance art, humanism, and diplomacy. New York, Columbia University Press, 1957. xi, 114p. illus. (part col.) ports. 22cm. Bibliography: p. 82-83. [ND3162.M3M4] 57-2308
1. Mantegua, Andrea, 1431-1506. 2. Illumination of books and manuscripts—Italy—Hist. 3. Initials. I. Title.

SALMI, Mario, 1889- 759.5
Italian miniatures. [2d ed., rev. and enl. Translated by Elisabeth Borgese-Mann; Milton S. Fox, editor] New York, H. N. Abrams [1956] 214p. 176 illus. (77 mounted col.) 31cm. [An Abrams art book] First published in 1954, in a private edition by the Banca Nazionale del Lavoro.' Bibliography: p. 199-202. [ND3159.S] A 57
1. Illumination of books and manuscripts—Italy —Hist. 2. Illumination of books and manuscripts—Specimens, reproductions, etc. 3. Miniature painting—Italy. 4. Miniature painting—Reproductions, facsimiles, etc. I. Title.

Illumination of books and manuscripts, Jewish.

GUTMANN, Joseph. 745.6'7
Hebrew manuscript painting / Joseph Gutmann. 1st ed. New York : G. Braziller, 1978. p. cm. Bibliography: p. [ND2935.G79] 78-3643 ISBN 0-8076-0890-4 : 22.95 ISBN 0-8076-0891-2 pbk. : 10.95
1. Illumination of books and manuscripts, Jewish. 2. Illumination of books and manuscripts, Medieval. I. Title. **BIP**

GUTMANN, Joseph. 745.6'7'09174924
Images of the Jewish past; an introduction to medieval Hebrew miniatures. New York, Society of Jewish Bibliophiles, 1965. [76] p. 22 plates (incl. facsims.) 31 cm. Bibliography: p. [23]-[25] [ND2935.G8] 68-3320
1. Illumination of books and manuscripts, Jewish. 2. Illumination of books and manuscripts, Medieval. I. Title.

Illumination of books and manuscripts, Medieval.

MINER, Dorothy Eugenia. 745.6'7
Anastaise and her sisters : women artists of the Middle Ages / Dorothy Miner. Baltimore : Walters Art Gallery, 1974. 24 p. : ill. ; 22 cm. Includes bibliographical references. [ND2920.M54] 75-309852
1. Anastaise. 2. Illumination of books and manuscripts, Medieval. 3. Women painters. I. Title.

MUNBY, Alan Noel Latimer. 091
Connoisseurs and medieval miniatures, 1750-1850 [by] A. N. L. Munby. Oxford, Clarendon Press, 1972. x, 170, [17] p. illus., facsims., ports. 25 cm. Includes bibliographical references. [ND2920.M78] 73-152046 ISBN 0-19-818148-5 £4.50
1. Illumination of books and manuscripts, Medieval. 2. Illumination of books and manuscripts—Collectors and collecting—Great Britain. I. Title.

MUNBY, Alan Noel Latimer. 091
Connoisseurs and medieval miniatures, 1750-1850 [by] A. N. L. Munby. Oxford, Clarendon Press, 1972. x, 170, [17] p. illus., facsims., ports. 25 cm. Includes bibliographical references. [ND2920.M78] 73-152046 ISBN 0-19-818148-5 15.25
1. Illumination of books and manuscripts,

Medieval. 2. Illumination of books and manuscripts—Collectors and collecting—Great Britain. I. Title.
Distributed by Oxford University Press N.Y.

Illumination of books and manuscripts, Medieval—Catalogs.

ANCONA, Paolo d', 1878- 759.02
The art of illumination; an anthology of manuscripts from the sixth to the sixteenth century, by P. d'Ancona & E. Aeschlimann. [Translated from the Italian by Alison M. Brown. With additional notes on the plates by M. Alison Stones. London, New York] Phaidon; [distributed by F. A. Praeger, New York, 1969] 235 p. 145 illus., (part col.) 32 cm. Bibliography: p. 233-234. [ND2920.A513] 68-27421 25.00
1. Illumination of books and manuscripts, Medieval—Catalogs. I. Aeschlimann, Erardo, joint author. II. Title.

KUP, Karl, 1903- 745.6'7
The Christmas story in medieval and Renaissance manuscripts from the Spencer Collection. [New York] New York Public Library, 1969. [121] p. 55 facsims. 26 cm. (Spencer Publication Fund publication no. 1) [ND3355.K8] 70-98680
1. Bible—Pictures, illustrations, etc. 2. Illumination of books and manuscripts, Medieval—Catalogs. 3. Illumination of books and manuscripts, Renaissance—Catalogs. I. New York (City). Public Library. Spencer Collection. II. Title. III. Series.

OXFORD. 016.7456'7'07402574
University. Bodleian Library.
Illuminated manuscripts : an index to selected Bodleian Library color reproductions / compiled and edited by Thomas H. Ohlgren. New York : Garland Pub., 1977. p. cm. (Garland reference library of humanities ; v. 89) [ND2920.O9 1977] 76-52689 ISBN 0-8240-9884-6 lib.bdg. : 75.00
1. Oxford. University. Bodleian Library. 2. Illumination of books and manuscripts, Medieval—Catalogs. 3. Illumination of books and manuscripts, Medieval—Indexes. 4. Illumination of books and manuscripts—Slides—Indexes. 5. Illumination of books and manuscripts—England—Oxford—Catalogs. 6. Illumination of books and manuscripts—England—Oxford—Indexes. I. Ohlgren, Thomas H., 1941- II. Title.

PIERPONT Morgan 745.6'7'094
Library, New York.
Mediaeval & Renaissance manuscripts. New York [1974] xvi, 106 p. facsims. 30 cm. (Its Major acquisitions, 1924-1974) Errata slip inserted. Bibliography: p. 105-106. [ND2920.P53 1974] 73-92929 8.00 (pbk.).
1. Pierpont Morgan Library, New York. 2. Illumination of books and manuscripts, Medieval—Catalogs. 3. Illumination of books and manuscripts, Renaissance—Catalogs. 4. Illumination of books and manuscripts—New York (City)—Catalogs. I. Title.

UNITED States. National 016.09
Gallery of Art.
Medieval & Renaissance miniatures from the National Gallery of Art : [catalogue] / compiled by Carra Ferguson, David S. Stevens Schaff, Gary Vikan ; under the direction of Carl Nordenfalk ; edited by Gary Vikan. [Washington] : The Gallery, 1975. xxvi, 196 p., 5 leaves of plates : ill. (some col.) ; 28 cm. Fourth exhibition from the Lessing J. Rosenwald collection, held Jan. 26-June 1, 1975. Includes bibliographical references and index. [ND2920.U54 1975] 74-28397
1. United States. National Gallery of Art. 2. Illumination of books and manuscripts, Medieval—Catalogs. 3. Illumination of books and manuscripts, Renaissance—Catalogs. 4. Illumination of books and manuscripts—Washington, D.C.—Catalogs. I. Nordenfalk, Carl Adam Johan, 1907- II. Rosenwald, Lessing Julius, 1891- III. Title. BIP

Illumination of books and manuscripts, Medieval—France.

MEISS, Millard. 096'.1'0944
French painting in the time of Jean De Berry; the late Fourteenth century and the patronage of the Duke. London, Phaidon, 1967. U. S. dist.: Praeger, New York. 2v. illus., plates (1 col.) 31cm. (Natl. Gallery of Art: Kress Found. studies in the hist. of European art no. 2) Bibl. [ND3147.M37 1967] 67-29885 30.00 set,
1. Berry, Jean de France, duc de, 1340-1416. 2. Illumination of books and manuscripts, Medieval—France. 3. Miniature painting, French. I. Title. II. Series: Kress Foundation studies in the history of European art, no. 2 BIP

Illumination of books and manuscripts, Mogul.

WELCH, Stuart Cary. 745.6'7'0954
Imperial Mughal painting / Stuart Cary Welch. New York : George Braziller, 1977,i.e.1972 p. cm. Bibliography: p. [ND3247.W44] 77-4049 ISBN 0-8076-0870-X : 19.95. ISBN 0-8076-0871-8 pbk. : 9.95
1. Illumination of books and manuscripts, Mogul. 2. Miniature painting, Mogul. I. Title. BIP

Illumination of books and manuscripts, Mughal.

BINNEY, Edwin. 745.6'7'0954 s
The Mughal and Deccani schools with some related Sultanate material : catalogue and text / by Edwin Binney 3rd. Portland, Or. : Portland Art Museum, 1974, c1973. 203 p. : ill. (some col.) ; 20 x 22 cm. (His Indian miniature painting from the collection of Edwin Binney 3rd ; 1) Bibliography: p. 198-202. [ND3247.B5 no. 1] [ND3248] 745.6'7'0954074 75-322918
1. Illumination of books and manuscripts, Mughal. 2. Miniature painting, Mughal. 3. Illumination of books and manuscripts—Deccan, India. 4. Miniature paintings—Deccan, India. I. Title.

Illumination of books and manuscripts — Oxford.

HASSALL, A. G. 745.6'7'07402574
Treasures from the Bodleian Library / A. G. and W. O. Hassall ; introd. by R. W. Hunt. New York : Columbia University Press, 1976. 160 p. : col. ill. ; 37 cm. Includes bibliographical references and index. [ND2897.O93H37 1976] 75-33231 ISBN 0-231-04060-1 : 60.00
1. Oxford. University. Bodleian Library. 2. Illumination of books and manuscripts—Oxford. I. Hassall, William Owen, joint author. II. Title. BIP

OXFORD. University. 745.67
Bodleian Library.
Illuminated manuscripts in the Bodleian Library, Oxford [compiled by] Otto Pacht and J. J. G. Alexander. Oxford, Clarendon P., 1966- v. col. front., plates. 22 cm. v. 1:6/6/- (B 66-19149) Contents.1. German, Dutch, Flemish, French and Spanish schools. [ND2897.O9] 66-76339
1. Illumination of books and manuscripts — Oxford. 2. Illumination of books and manuscripts, Medieval. I. Pacht, Otto, 1902- II. Alexander, Jonathan James Graham. III. Title.

Illumination of books and manuscripts—Paris.

PORCHER, Jean. 096
The Rohan book of hours; with an introd. and notes. New York, T. Yoseloff [1960, c1959] 32 p. 8 mounted col. illus. 29 cm. [the Library of illuminated manuscripts] The illuminated designs reproduced are from the ms., Heures de Rohan, in the Bibliotheque nationale. [ND3363.R6P62 1960] 60-16082
1. Illumination of books and manuscripts—Paris. 2. Miniature painting—Paris. 3. Hours, Books of. I. Title. II. Series.

Illumination of books and manuscripts, Pennsylvania German.

BORNEMAN, Henry Stauffer, 016.091
1870-1955.
Pennsylvania German illuminated manuscripts; a classification of fraktur-schriften and an inquiry into their history and art. New York, Dover Publications [1973] 59 p., [32] p. of illus. (part col.) 21 x 29 cm. "A corrected republication of the work originally published in 1937 by the Pennsylvania German Society as volume 46 of its Proceedings and papers." [ND3035.P4B6 1973] 72-95047 ISBN 0-486-22926-2 4.50 (pbk.)
1. Illumination of books and manuscripts, Pennsylvania German. I. Title. II. Series: Pennsylvania-German Society. Proceedings and addresses, v. 46. BIP

Illumination of books and manuscripts, Pennsylvania German—Catalogs.

PHILADELPHIA. Free 974.8'004'31 s
Library.
The Pennsylvania German Fraktur of the Free Library of Philadelphia : an illustrated catalogue / compiled by Frederick S. Weiser & Howell J. Heaney ; [photography by William B. Daub & Robert G. Hostetter ; translations by Larry M. Neff & Frederick S. Weiser]. Breinigsville : Pennsylvania German Society, 1976. 2 v. : ill. (some col.) ; 25 x 27 cm. (Publications of the Pennsylvania German Society ; v. 10-11) Includes bibliographical references and indexes. [GR110.P4A372 vol. 10-11] [ND3035.P4] 745.6'7'09748074014811 76-13357 ISBN 0-911122-32-X (v. 1). ISBN 0-911122-33-8 (v. 2)
1. Philadelphia. Free Library. 2. Illumination of books and manuscripts, Pennsylvania German—Catalogs. 3. Illumination of books and manuscripts—Pennsylvania—Philadelphia—Catalogs. I. Weiser, Frederick Sheely, 1935- II. Heaney, Howell J. III. Title. IV. Series: Pennsylvania-German Society. Publications ; v. 10-11. BIP

Illumination of books and manuscripts, Renaissance—Italy.

ALEXANDER, Jonathan 745.6'7'0945
James Graham.
Italian Renaissance illuminations / J. J. G. Alexander. New York : Braziller, 1977. p. cm. Bibliography: p. [ND3159.A4 1977] 77-2841 ISBN 0-8076-0863-7 : 19.95 pbk. : 9.95
1. Illumination of books and manuscripts, Renaissance—Italy. 2. Illumination of books and manuscripts, Italian. I. Title. BIP

Illumination of books and manuscripts, Romanesque—Belgium—Meuse Valley.

DYNES, Wayne. 745.6'7'094934
The illuminations of the Stavelot Bible / Wayne Dynes. New York : Garland, 1979 p. cm. (Outstanding dissertations in the fine arts) Bibliography: p. [ND3355.D96] 77-94693 ISBN 0-8240-3225-X lib bdg : 30.00
1. Bible. Latin. Stavelot Bible—Illustrations. 2. Illumination of books and manuscripts, Romanesque—Belgium—Meuse Valley. 3. Illumination of books and manuscripts—Belgium—Meuse Valley. I. Title. II. Series. BIP

Illumination of books and manuscripts, Spanish.

DOMINGUEZ Bordona, 745.6'7'096
Jesus.
Spanish illumination, by J. Dominguez Bordona. New York, Hacker Art Books, 1969. 2 v. in 1. 160 plates. 32 cm. "First printed in 1929." Issued also under title: La miniatura espanola. Bibliography: v. 2, p. 78-[85] [ND3199.D59 1969] 77-78360
1. Illumination of books and manuscripts, Spanish. I. Title. BIP

WILLIAMS, John, 745.6'7'0946
1928-
Early Spanish manuscript illumination / John Williams. New York : G. Braziller, 1977. p. cm. Bibliography: p. [ND3199.W54] 77-4042 ISBN 0-8076-0866-1 : 19.95. ISBN 0-8076-0867-X pbk. : 9.95
1. Illumination of books and manuscripts, Spanish. 2. Illumination of books and manuscripts, Medieval—Spain. I. Title. BIP

Illumination of books and manuscripts—Specimens, reproductions, etc.

BRIEGER, Peter H., 1898- 745.6'7
Illuminated manuscripts of the Divine comedy, by Peter Brieger, Millard Meiss [and] Charles S. Singleton. [Princeton, N.J.] Princeton University Press [1969] 2 v. facsims. (part col.), plates (part col.) 32 cm. (Bollingen series, 81) Contents.Contents.—v. 1. Text.—v. 2. Plates. Bibliography: v. 1, p. [341]-350. [PQ4366.B7] 68-20867 45.00
1. Dante Alighieri, 1265-1321—Illustrations. 2. Illumination of books and manuscripts—Specimens, reproductions, etc. I. Meiss, Millard. II. Singleton, Charles Southward, 1909- III. Title. IV. Series. BIP

BRUSSELS. Bibliotheque royale 096
de Belgique. Section des manuscrits
Medieval miniatures from the Department of Manuscripts (formerly the "Library of Burgundy") the Royal Lib. of Belgium. Commentaries by L. M. J. Delaisse. Foreword by H. Liebaers; introd. by F. Masai. New York, Abrams [1965] 216p. mounted col. illus. 31cm. [ND2898.B7A5213] 65-12094 25.00
1. Illumination of books and manuscripts—Specimens, reproductions, etc. I. Delaisse, L. M. J. II. Title.

MARTIN, John Rupert. 745.67
The illustration of The heavenly ladder of John Climacus. Princeton, Princeton University Press, 1954. vii, 198p. 112 plates. 31cm. (Studies in manuscript illumination, no. 5) Bibliographical footnotes. [ND3385.J6M3] 54-6078
1. Joannes Climacus. Saint, 6th cent. Scals paradist. 2. Illumination of books and manuscripts—Specimens, reproductions, etc. 3. Minature painting—Reproductions, facsimiles, etc. I. Title. II. Title: The heavenly ladder. III. Series.

NEW York (City) 096.1
Metropolitan Museum of Art.
The Hours of Jeanne d'Evreux, Queen of France, at the Cloisters, the Metropolitan Museum of Art. [New York] [Metropolitan Museum of Art] 1957. 28 p, 48 facsims. (part col.) 14 cm. "Of the 209 folios comprising the original Book of Hours, forty-eight characteristic pages, including all the full-page pictures, are here illustrated." [ND3363.J42N4] 57-9363
1. Illumination of books and manuscripts—Specimens, reproductions, etc. 2. Hours, Books of. I. Jeanne d'Evreux, consort of Charles IV, King of France, d. 1371. II. Catholic Church. Liturgy and ritual. Hours.

Illumination of books and manuscripts, Turkish.

ETTINGHAUSEN, Richard 759.9561
Turkish miniatures from the thirteenth to the eighteenth century. Introd. by Richard Ettinghausen. [New York] New Amer. Lib. by arrangement with UNESCO [c.1965] 24p., [4]p. (on fold leaf) illus., 28 col. plates (pt. fold.) 17cm. (Mentor-Unesco art bk. MQ646) [ND3271] 65-29967 .95 pap.,
1. Illumination of books and manuscripts, Turkish. I. United Nations Educational, Scientific and Cultural Organization. II. Title.

Illumination of books and manuscripts, Turkish—Exhibitions.

BINNEY, Edwin. 745.6'7'09561
Turkish miniature paintings and manuscripts from the collection of Edwin Binney, 3rd, by Edwin Binney, 3rd. [New York] The Metropolitan Museum of Art [1973] 139 p. illus. 22 cm. Catalog of an exhibition held in the Metropolitan Museum of Art, New York and the Los Angeles County Museum of Art.

Bibliography: p. 135-137. [ND3211.B56] 73-11016 ISBN 0-87099-077-2 4.95 (pbk.)
1. Binney, Edwin—Art collections. 2. Illumination of books and manuscripts, Turkish—Exhibitions. 3. Miniature painting, Turkish—Exhibitions. I. New York (City). Metropolitan Museum of Art. II. Los Angeles Co., Calif. Museum of Art, Los Angeles. III. Title.

Illumination of books and manuscripts—Vienna—Catalogs.

VIENNA. 096'.1'0943613
Nationalbibliothek.
A treasury of illuminated manuscripts; a selection of miniatures from manuscripts in the Austrian National Library [by] Franz Unterkircher. [Translated from the German by J. Maxwell Brownjohn. 1st American ed.] New York, Putnam [1967] 264 p. 60 col. facsims. 39 cm. Translation of Abendlandische Buchmalerei; Miniaturen aus Handschriften der Osterreichischen Nationalbibliothek. London ed. (Thames & Hudson) has title: European illuminated manuscripts in the Austrian National Library. Contents.Contents.—Pre-Romanesque illumination, eighth-eleventh centuries.—Illumination in Austria, twelfth century.—Early Gothic illumination in Austria and Germany, thirteenth-fourteenth centuries.—Illumination in Bohemia and Moravia, fourteenth-fifteenth centuries.—Illumination in the service of the rulers of Austria, thirteenth-fourteenth centuries.—Italian illumination, thirteenth - sixteenth centuries.—Illumination in France and England, thirteenth-fifteenth centuries.—Illumination in the OA treasury of illuminated manuscripts; a selection of miniatures from manuscripts in the Austrian Nationa
1. Illumination of books and manuscripts—Vienna—Catalogs. I. Unterkircher, Franz. II. Title.

Illumination of books and manuscripts—Virginia.

WUST, Klaus German, 1925- 745.6'7
Virginia fraktur; penmanship as folk art, by Klaus Wust. Edinburgh, Va., Shenandoah History, Publishers, 1972. 28 p. illus. (part col.) 27 cm. Bibliography: p. 28. [ND3035.V8W8] 79-189313
1. Illumination of books and manuscripts—Virginia. 2. Art, Pennsylvania German—Virginia. I. Title.

Illumination of books and manuscripts—Winchester, Eng.

WORMALD, Francis. 096
The Benedictional of St. Ethelwold; with an introd. and notes. New York, T. Yoseloff [1960, c1959] 30 p. 8 mounted col. illus. 29 cm. (The Library of illuminated manuscripts) The illuminated miniatures reproduced are from the ms. in the British Museum. [ND3362.5.W6] 60-1239
1. Aethelwold, Saint, Bp. of Winchester. 2. Illumination of books and manuscripts—Winchester, Eng. 3. Benedictionals. I. Title. II. Series.

Illusmination of books and manuscripts—Specimens, reproductions, etc.

KARLSRUHE. Badische 755.55
Landesbibliothek.
Miniatures of the life of Our Lady, from the collection of medieval manuscripts in the Baden State Library, Karlsruhe, West Germany, with notes by Franz Schmitt. Westminster, Md., Newman Press, 1960[ ] [28]p. mounted col. illus. 60-14824 1.75
1. Illusmination of books and manuscripts—Specimens, reproductions, etc. 2. Mary, Virgin—Art. 3. Mary, Virgin—Poetry. I. Schmitt, Franz, 1908- II. Title.

Illustrated books.

CRANE, Walter, 1845-1915. 741.6'4
Of the decorative illustration of books old and new. London, New York, G. Bell, 1905. Detroit, Gale Research Co., 1968. xiv, 341 p. facsims. 20 cm. Half title: The decorative illustration of books. [Z1023.C89 1968] 68-30611
1. Illustrated books. I. Title. II. Title: The decorative illustration of books. BIP

Illustrated books—19th century.

MUIR, Percival 741.6'4'0942
Horace, 1894-
Victorian illustrated books [by] Percy Muir. New York, Praeger Publishers [1971] xv, 287 p. illus. 26 cm. Includes bibliographies. [Z1023.M92 1971] 70-138245 20.00
1. Illustrated books—19th century. 2. Illustration of books—Gt. Brit. I. Title.

Illustrated books—19th century—Catalogs.

GARVEY, Eleanor M. 741.6'4
The turn of a century, 1885-1910; art nouveau-Jugendstil books. [Catalogue by Eleanor M. Garvey, Anne B. Smith, and Peter A. Wick. Cambridge] Dept. of Printing and Graphic Arts, Harvard University, 1970. 124 p. illus., facsims. 24 cm. Exhibition held at Houghton Library. Bibliography: p. 115-117. [NC960.G37] 73-122903
1. Illustrated books—19th century—Catalogs. 2. Illustrated books—20th century—Catalogs. 3. Decoration and ornament—Art nouveau. I. Smith, Anne Blake, joint author. II. Wick, Peter A., joint author. III. Harvard University. Library. Houghton Library. IV. Title.

Illustrated books—20th cent.

CULVER, Roy. 810.54
Continents of vapor; a collection of twenty-one poems and eight etchings, accomplished entirely by the hand processes. Poems by Roy Culver. Prints by Louise A. Moss. Kansas City, Mo., Excalibur Press, 1965. i v. (unpaged) plates. 31 cm. 50 copies printed. [PS3553.U4C6] 66-5336
I. Moss, Louise A., illus. II. Title.

ENSLIN, Theodore. 818'.5'403
The July book / Theodore Enslin ; illustrated by Chuck Miller. Berkeley, Calif. : Sand Dollar, c1976. [47] p. : ill. ; 23 cm. [PS3555.N76J8] 77-370923
I. Title. BIP

FOREMAN, Kenneth Joseph, FIC
1891-
Methuselah; fantasy on a moral theme, by Kenneth J. Foreman. With 12 line drawings by Doyle Robinson. Richmond, John Knox Press [1968] 125 p. illus. 21 cm. [PZ4.F717Me] [PS3556.O72] 813'.5'4 68-30860 1.95
I. Title.

HONEGGER, Warja. 808.88
Folded story. [Re-told and drawn by Warja Honegger-Lavater. 1st American ed.] New York 19 v. vol. illus. 19 cm. Cover title Each vol. consists of a continuous folded strip (19 x 166 cm.) with illus. on one side and text on the reverse. English, French, and German. [NE2415.H65A45] 67-5642
I. Title.
Contents omitted

*LAVATER, Warja Honegger 741
Folded stories; nos. 6-10. Basle, Basilius Pr. [dist. New York, Wittenborn, 1964] unpaged. illus. (pt. col.) Contents.6. Rape of the Sabine women.--7. Passion and reason.--8. The good intention is blue.--9. Night and day and night.--10. Extra . . . ordinary Lemuel. 6-9, 3.75; 10, 4.50 bds.(nos.
I. Title.

LEWIS, John Noel Claude, 741.6'4
1912-
The twentieth century book, its illustration and design [by] John Lewis. [New York] Reinhold [1967] 272p. illus. (pt. col.) 30cm. [NC95.L4] 67-14165 25.00
1. Illustrated books—20th cent. 2. Illustration of books. I. Title.

SIMPSON, Joyce Tillery. 920
Ladder to the sky; illustrated by Kurt Werth. New York, Crowell [1950] 239 p. illus. 21 cm. [CT275.S52167A3] 50-6731
I. Title.

Illustrated books, Children's.

CIANCIOLO, Patricia J. 741.64'2
Illustrations in children's books / Patricia Cianciolo. 2d ed. Dubuque, Iowa : W. C. Brown Co. Publishers, c1976. xiii, 210 p. : ill. ; 23 cm. (Literature for children) Includes bibliographies and index. [NC965.C5 1976] 75-13194 ISBN 0-697-06208-2 pbk. : 3.95
1. Illustrated books, Children's. I. Title.

STEPHENS, Henry Louis, 741.6'42
1824-1882.
A frog he would a wooing go, from original designs by H. L. Stephens. New York, Walker [1967] [20] p. (chiefly illus.) 26 cm. Originally published in 1864. [NC1075.S74A44] 67-23095
I. Title. BIP

WHALLEY, Joyce Irene. 028.5
Cobwebs to catch flies : illustrated books for the nursery and schoolroom, 1700-1900 / Joyce Irene Whalley. Berkeley : University of California Press, 1975, c1974. 163 p. : ill. (some col.) ; 26 cm. Includes index. Bibliography: p. 136-149. [NC965.W47 1975] 74-27298 ISBN 0-520-02931-3 : 14.95
1. Illustrated books, Children's. 2. Illustration of books—Themes, motives. I. Title. BIP

Illustrated books, Children's—History and criticism.

BADER, Barbara. 741.6'42
American picturebooks : from Noah's ark to The beast within. New York : Macmillan, [1975] p. cm. Includes index. Bibliography: p. [NC965.B32] 72-93304 ISBN 0-02-708080-3 : 40.00
1. Illustrated books, Children's—History and criticism. 2. Illustrators, American. 3. Picture books for children. 4. Children's literature, American—History and criticism. I. Title.

KLEMIN, Diana. 741.9
The art of art for children's books; a contemporary survey. [1st ed.] New York, C. N. Potter [1966] 128 p. illus. (part col.) 26 cm. Bibliography: p. 125. [NC965.K55] 66-20220
1. Illustrated books, Children's—History and criticism. 2. Illustrators. I. Title.

MACCANN, Donnarae. 741.64'2
The child's first books; a critical study of pictures and texts, by Donnarae MacCann & Olga Richard. New York, Wilson, 1973. 135 p. illus. 30 cm. Bibliography: p. 125-128. [Z1023.M25] 73-3224 ISBN 0-8242-0501-4 10.00
1. Illustrated books, Children's—History and criticism. 2. Picture-books for children. 3. Children's literature—History and criticism. I. Richard, Olga, joint author. II. Title. BIP

PIERPONT Morgan Library, 741.64'2
New York.
Early children's books and their illustration / the Pierpont Morgan Library, New York. Boston : D. R. Godine, c1975. xxx, 263 p., [11] leaves of plates : ill. (some col.) ; 31 cm. Includes index. Bibliography: p. 255-258. [PN1009.A1P52 1975] 75-15020 ISBN 0-87923-158-0 : 35.00
1. Illustrated books, Children's—History and criticism. I. Title. BIP

PITZ, Henry Clarence, 741.642
1895-
Illustrating children's books: history, technique, production. New York, Watson-Guptill Publications [1963] 207 p. illus. (part col.) ports., diagrs., facsims. 29 cm. Bibliography: p. 204-205. [NC965.P5] 63-18772
1. Illustrated books, Children's—History and criticism. 2. Illustration of books. I. Title.

Illustrated periodicals.

HOGARTH, Paul, 1917- 741.6'5
The artist as reporter London: Studio Vista. New York Reinhold [1967] 96 p. front., illus., facsims. 20 1/2 cm. 251-(B67-9689) Bibliography: p. 5. [NC968.H6 1967] 67-14166
1. Illustrated periodicals. 2. History in art. 3. Wit and humor. Pictorial. I. Title.

LARNED, William 741.65
Livingston, 1880-
Magazine illustrating. Serial 6432. [Ed. 1] Scranton, International Correspondence Schools, c1959. 70p. illus. 19cm. [NC968.L3] 60-24337
1. Illustrated periodicals. I. International Correspondence Schools, Scranton, Pa. II. Title.

MARSHALL, Francis 741.65
Magazine illustration. London, New York, Studio [dist. Viking, 1960] 96p. illus. 26cm. 60-2293 6.95
1. Illustrated periodicals. I. Title.

Illustrated periodicals—Indexes.

ELLIS, Jessie (Croft) 741.6'01'6
Index to illustrations. Boston, F. W. Faxon Co., 1966 [c1967] xi, 682 p. 25 cm. (Useful reference series no. 95) "Books and periodicals used in the index": p. xi. [NC996.E62] 66-11619
1. Illustrated periodicals—Indexes. 2. Illustrated books—Indexes. I. Title. II. Series.

Illustration of books.

BUTSCH, Albert Fidelis. 745.6'7
comp.
Handbook of Renaissance ornament; 1290 designs from decorated books. With a new introd. and captions by Alfred Werner. New York, Dover Publications [1969] xv, 226 plates (incl. facsims.), 229-231 p. 31 cm. (Dover pictorial archive series) The designs appeared originally in the author's Die Bucherornamentik der Renaissance. [NE905.B87 1969] 68-13685 ISBN 0-486-21998-4 4.50
1. Illustration of books. 2. Decoration and ornament, Renaissance. I. Werner, Alfred, 1911- II. Title. BIP

THE Fantastic 741.64'2'09041
kingdom / edited by David Larkin ; with biographical notes by Margaret Maloney. New York : Ballantine Books, 1974, 1975 printing. [16] p., 40 leaves of plates : chiefly col. ill. ; 30 cm. [NC960.F28 1975] 76-352905 ISBN 0-345-24468-0 pbk. : 5.95
1. Illustration of books. 2. Fairy tales—Illustrations. I. Larkin, David. II. Maloney, Margaret.

GILL, Bob, 1931-. 741.6
Illustration: aspects and directions [by] Bob Gill & John Lewis. New York, Reinhold Pub. Corp. [1964] 96 p. illus. (part col.) 20 cm. (Reinhold paperbacks) [NC960.G5] 64-175538
1. Illustration of books. I. Lewis, John Noel Claude, 1912- joint author. II. Title.

KLEMIN, Diana. 741'.0922
The illustrated book: its art and craft. [1st ed.] New York, distributed by Crown [1970]. 159 p. illus., (part col.) 27 cm. Bibliography: p. [152]-153. [NC960.K55 1970] 69-13402
1. Illustration of books. I. Title.

LAMB, Lynton 741.64
Drawing f0r illustration. New York, Oxford [c.]1962[ ] 211p. illus. 26cm. 62-2771 7.20
1. Illustration of books. 2. Photomechanical processes. I. Title.

LAMB, Lynton. 741.64
Drawing for illustration. London, New York, Oxford University Press, 1962. 211p. illus. 26cm. [NC960.L23] 62-2771
1. Illustration of books. 2. Photomechanical processes. I. Title.

THE Pen & ink and cross 741.64
hatch styles of the early illustrators / compiled by Dick Sutphen. New York : Art Direction Book Co., c1976. 191 p. : chiefly ill. ; 29 cm. Spine title: The early illustrators. "A copyright free handbook." [NC960.P36] 76-27145 ISBN 0-910158-21-5 : 19.50
1. Illustration of books. 2. Magazine illustration. I. Sutphen, Richard. II. Title: The early illustrators.

PEPPIN, Brigid. 741.64
Fantasy : the golden age of fantastic illustration / Brigid Peppin. New York : Watson-Guptill, [1975] 191 p. : ill. (some

col.) ; 32 cm. Includes index. Bibliography: p. 23. [NC960.P463 1975] 75-9622 ISBN 0-8230-1635-8 : 25.00
1. Illustration of books. 2. Grotesque in art. 3. Decoration and ornament—Victorian style. I. Title. BIP

SIMON, Howard, 1903- 741.64'09
Five hundred years of art in illustration, from Albrecht Durer to Rockwell Kent / by Howard Simon. New York : Hacker Art Books, 1978. xvii, 476 p. : ill. ; 27 cm. First published in 1942 under title: 500 years of art & illustration. Reprint of the 2d ed., 1945 published by World Pub. Co., Cleveland. Includes index. [NC960.S5 1978] 77-73730 ISBN 0-87817-212-2. : 40.00
1. Illustration of books. 2. Illustrators. 3. Engravers. I. Title.

STANILAND, Lancelot Norman, 1899- 741.44
The principles of line illustration; with emphasis on the requirements of biological and other scientific workers. Cambridge, Harvard University Press, 1953. 212p. illus. 22cm. [NC960.S75 1953] 53-7829
1. Illustration of books. 2. Drawings—Instruction. I. Title.

WYATT, Joan. 759.2
A middle-Earth album : paintings / by Joan Wyatt, inspired by Tolkien's Lord of the rings ; introd. and commentaries by Jessica Yates. New York : Simon and Schuster, c1979. p. cm. (A Fireside book) [ND1942.W9A4 1979] 79-3948 ISBN 0-671-24954-1 : 14.95 ISBN 0-671-24928-2 pbk. : 7.95
1. Wyatt, Joan—Catalogs. 2. Tolkien, John Ronald Reuel, 1892-1973. Lord of the rings—Illustrations—Catalogs. I. Yates, Jessica. II. Title. BIP

ZAIDENBERG, Arthur, 1903- 741.64
Illustrating and cartooning. [1st ed.] Garden City, N.Y., Doubleday, 1959. 190 p. illus. 27 cm. [NC960.Z33] 59-6379
1. Illustration of books. 2. Caricature. 3. Commercial art. I. Title.

Illustration of books—Addresses, essays, lectures.

THE Illustrator's notebook / edited by Lee Kingman. Boston : The Horn Book, 1978. xvii, 153 p. : ill. (some col.) ; 28 cm. Essays originally appeared in The Horn book magazine. Includes index. Bibliography: p. 143-144. [NC960.I44] 77-20028 ISBN 0-87675-013-7 : 25.00 741.64
1. Illustration of books—Addresses, essays, lectures. 2. Illustrators—Addresses, essays, lectures. I. Kingman, Lee. II. The Horn book magazine.

Illustration of books—Bibliography—Catalogs.

EASSON, Roger R. 769'.92'4
William Blake: book illustrator; a bibliography and catalogue of the commercial engravings, by Roger R. Easson and Robert N. Essick. Normal, American Blake Foundation at Illinois State University, 1972- v. plates. 28 cm. Contents.Contents.—v. 1. Plates designed and engraved by Blake. [NE642.B5E2] 72-82993 ISBN 0-913130-01-X
1. Blake, William, 1757-1827. 2. Illustration of books—Bibliography—Catalogs. I. Essick, Robert N., joint author. II. Blake, William, 1757-1827. III. Title.

Illustration of books—England.

NYMPHETS & fairies : three Victorian children's illustrators / Graham Ovenden. London : Academy Editions ; New York : St. Martin's Press, 1976. 88 p. : chiefly ill. (some col.) ; 20 cm. Includes ill. "reproduced from early editions of works [in the collection of G. Ovenden] illustrated by" W. S. Coleman, R. Doyle, and E. V. Boyle. [NC978.N9 1976] 76-44580 ISBN 0-85670-229-3 : 3.95 741.9'42
1. Illustration of books—England. 2. Illustrated books, Children's. 3. Illustrators—England. I. Ovenden, Graham. II. Coleman, William Stephen. III. Doyle, Richard, 1824-1883. IV. Boyle, Eleanor Vere Gordon, Hon., 1825-1916. BIP

Illustration of books—England—Catalogs.

RAY, Gordon Norton, 1915- 741.64'0942
The illustrator and the book in England from 1790 to 1914 / Gordon N. Ray; formal bibliographical descriptions by Thomas V. Lange; photography by Charles V. Passela New York : Pierpont Morgan Library, c1976. xxxiii, 336 p., [1] leaf of plates : ill. ; 31 cm. Includes indexes. Bibliography: p. 317-325. [NC978.R37] 76-10042 ISBN 0-19-519883-2 : 59.95
1. Illustration of books—England—Catalogs. 2. Illustrators—England. I. Lange, Thomas V. II. Passela, Charles V. III. Pierpont Morgan Library, New York. IV. Title. BIP

Illustration of books—Exhibitions.

BALTIMORE. Museum of Art. 096'.1'074015271
French illustrated books of the 19th and 20th century: [exhibition] the Baltimore Museum of Art, October 15 through January 14. Baltimore [1967?] [24] p. illus. 22 cm. Bibliography: p. [24] [NC980.B32] 79-288485
1. Illustration of books—Exhibitions. 2. Illustration of books—France. I. Title.

BROOKLYN Institute of Arts and Sciences. Museum. 741.64'0973'074014723
A century of American illustration. [Brooklyn] Brooklyn Museum [1972] 155 p. illus. 23 cm. Catalog of the exhibition held Mar. 22-May 14, 1972 in the Brooklyn Museum. Bibliography: p. 154-155. [NC975.B76] 78-189826
1. Illustration of books—Exhibitions. 2. Illustration of books—United States. I. Title.

DELAWARE Art Museum. 741.64'0973'07401512
The golden age of American illustration, 1880-1914 [Catalog of the exhibition] September 14-October 15, 1972. [Wilmington, 1972] 67 p. illus. 22 x 28 cm. [NC975.D44] 72-88906
1. Illustration of books—Exhibitions. 2. Illustration of books—United States. I. Title.

HENRY Clay Frick Fine Arts Library. 741.44
An informal catalogue for an exhibition of eighty-six books selected from the Henry Clay Frick Fine Arts Library and held in memory of John Gabbert Bowman, 1879-1963 [i.e. 1877-1962], chancellor of the University of Pittsburgh, 1921-1945. Spring 1964. Pittsburgh, University of Pittsburgh [1964] 52 p. illus., port. 28 cm. On cover: None can see the limits of its reach. John Gabbert Bowman. Introd. signed: Walter Read Hovey. [NC961.P54A6] 75-296433
1. Illustrations of books—Exhibitions. I. Bowman, John Gabbert, 1877-1962. II. Hovey, Walter Read, 1895- III. Title. IV. Title: None can see the limits of its reach.

NEW York (City). Public Library. Berg Collection. 741.942
Pen & brush: the author as artist; an exhibition in the Berg Collection of English and American literature [by] Lola L. Szladits and Harvey Simmonds. [New York] New York Public Library, Astor, Lenox, and Tilden Foundations [1969] 59 p. illus. 27 cm. Contents.Contents.—William Makepeace Thackeray.—William Blake to Denton Welch. [NC15.N43N47] 71-92623 ISBN 0-87104-142-1
1. Illustration of books—Exhibitions. 2. Illustration of books—Great Britain. 3. Illustration of books—United States. 4. Authors as artists—Biography. I. Szladits, Lola L. II. Simmonds, Harvey. III. Title.

Illustration of books—France.

HOLLOWAY, Owen E. 741.6'4
French Rococo book illustration [by] Owen E. Holloway. [1st American ed.] New York, Transatlantic Arts, 1969. vi, 115, [131] p. 283 illus. 26 cm. [NC980.H6 1969b] 79-88659
1. Illustration of books—France. 2. Illustrated books—18th century. 3. Decoration and ornament, Rococo—France. I. Title. BIP

STRACHAN, Walter John, 1903- 741.6'4
The artist and the book in France; the 20th century livre d'artiste [by] W. J. Strachan. [1st ed.] New York, G. Wittenborn [1969] 368 p. 181 illus., 8 col. plates. 30 cm. Bibliography: p. 350-353. [NC980.S78] 68-29813 45.00
1. Illustration of books—France. 2. Illustrated books—20th century. I. Title. BIP

Illustration of books — France — Exhibitions.

GARVEY, Eleanor M. 741.6
The arts of the French book, 1900-1965; illustrated books of the school of Paris, by Eleanor M. Garvey and Peter A. Wick. Dallas, Pub. for the Friends of the Dallas Public Lib. by Southern Methodist Univ. Pr., 1967. 119p. illus. (pt. col.) 24cm. Catalogue of an exhibition sponsored by The Friends of the Dallas Public Library at the Dallas Public Library, March 28-May 6, 1967 . . . [and] at the Sterling Memorial Library, Yale University, New Haven, Connecticut, May 22-June 27, 1967. Bibl. [NC980.G3] 67-16782 12.50
1. Illustration of books — France — Exhibitions. 2. Illustrated books — 20th cent. I. Wick, Peter A., joint author. II. Dallas. Public Library. III. Yale University. Library. IV. Title.

Illustration of books—Germany.

LANG, Lothar. 741.64'0943
Expressionist book illustration in Germany, 1907-1927 / Lothar Lang translated by Janet Seligman Boston : New York Graphic Society, 1976. 245 p. : ill. (some col.) ; 28 cm. Translation of Expressionistische Buchillustration in Deutschland, 1907-1927. Bibliography: p. 212-239. [NC981.L2513] 74-21732 ISBN 0-8212-0617-6 : 27.50
1. Illustration of books—Germany. 2. Expressionism (Art)—Germany. I. Title. BIP

LANG, Lother. 741.64'0943
Expressionist book illustration in Germany, 1907-1927 / [by] Lother Lang ; translated [from the German] by Janet Seligman. London : Thames and Hudson, 1976. 246 p. : chiefly ill. (some col.), facsims. ; 28 cm. Translation of Expressionistische Buchillustration in Deutschland, 1907-1927. Includes index. Bibliography: p. 212-239. [NC981.L2513 1976b] 76-380390 ISBN 0-500-23219-9 : £12.00
1. Illustration of books—Germany. 2. Expressionism (Art)—Germany. I. Title.

Illustration of books—Great Britain.

HOFER, Philip, 1898- comp. 741.64
Eighteenth- century book illustrations. Los Angeles, William Andrews Clark Memorial Library, University of California, 1956. xi p., [48] p. of illus. 21cm. (Augustan Reprint Society. Publication no. 58) Bibliography: p. xi. [NC978.H58] 56-58330
1. Illustration of books—Gt. Brit. I. Title. II. Series.

ONCE upon a time : some contemporary illustrators of fantasy / edited and introduced by David Larkin. 1st U.S. ed. New York : Peacock Press, 1976. [14] p., [42] leaves of plates (2 fold.) : col. ill. ; 28 cm. [NC978.O5] 76-15477 6.95 741.64'0941
1. Illustration of books—Great Britain. 2. Grotesque in art. 3. Surrealism. I. Larkin, David.

SALAMAN, Malcolm Charles, 1855-1940. 096'.1'0942
British book illustration yesterday and today, with commentary by Malcolm C. Salaman. Edited by Geoffrey Holme. London, The Studio, 1923. Detroit, Gale Research Co., 1974. viii, 175 p. illus. 23 cm. [NC978.S25 1974] 73-175758 ISBN 0-8103-3977-3
1. Illustration of books—Great Britain. I. Title.

Illustration of books—Handbooks, manuals, etc.

PENNELL, Joseph, 1857-1926. 745.6'7
The illustration of books; a manual for the use of students, notes for a course of lectures at the Slade School, University College. Ann Arbor, Mich., Gryphon Books, 1971. xii, 166 p. 22 cm. "Facsimile reprint of the 1896 edition." [NC960.P43 1896a] 78-146921
1. Illustration of books—Handbooks, manuals, etc. I. Title. BIP

Illustration of books—History.

ELLIS, Richard Williamson, 1895- 741.64
Book illustration; a survey of its history & development shown by the work of various artists, together with critical comments. Kingsport, Tenn., Kingsport Press, 1952. 76 p. illus. 28 cm. [NC960.E4] 52-1988
1. Illustration of books—Hist. 2. Illustrators. I. Title.

Illustration of books—History.

BENESCH, Otto, 1896-1964. 741.64'094
Artistic and intellectual trends from Rubens to Daumier as shown in book illustration. New York, Walker, 1969 [c1943] xvi, 91 p. illus. 25 cm. Includes bibliographical references. [NC960.B4 1969] 76-88626
1. Illustration of books—History. 2. Illustration of books—Themes, motives. I. Title.

BLAND, David. 741.64
A history of book illustration; the illuminated manuscript and the printed book. [1st ed.] Cleveland, World Pub. Co. [1958] 448 p. illus. (part mounted col.) facsims. (part mounted col.) 28 cm. Bibliography: p. [429]-432. [NC960.B62] 58-10061
1. Illustration of books—History. 2. Illumination of books and manuscripts—History.

BLAND, David. 745.6'7
A history of book illustration; the illuminated manuscript and the printed book. [2d rev. ed.] Berkeley, University of California Press, 1969. 459 p. facsims. (part col.) 29 cm. Bibliography: p. [437]-441. [NC960.B62 1969b] 69-12472 25.00
1. Illustration of books—History. 2. Illumination of books and manuscripts—History. I. Title.

BLAND, David. 741.64
The illustration of books. [1st ed.] New York, Pantheon Books [1952] 160 p. illus. 21 cm. [Z1023.B63] 52-7926
1. Illustration of books—History.

Illustration of books—United States.

THE Edgar Rice Burroughs library of illustration / [conceived, designed, and edited by Russ Cochran] Limited Centennial ed. West Plains, Mo. : Cochran, 1976- v. : ill. (some col.) ; 32 cm. Most of the ill. by J. A. St. John. [NC975.E24] 77-150518 741.64'0973
1. Burroughs, Edgar Rice, 1875-1950—Illustrations. 2. Illustration of books—United States. I. Burroughs, Edgar Rice, 1875-1950. II. Cochran, Russ. III. St. John, James Allen, 1872-1957.

GAMMELL, Robert Hale Ives, 1893- 759.13
A pictorial sequence, painted by R. H. Ives Gammell, based on The Hound of heaven by Francis Thompson. Cambridge, Mass., University Press, 1956. 55p. illus. 23cm. [ND237.G25A52] 56-42024
I. Thompson, Francis, 1859-1907. The Hound of heaven. II. Title.

LAWSON, Robert, 1892-1957. 741'.092'4
Robert Lawson, illustrator; a selection of his characteristic illustrations. With introd. and comment by Helen L. Jones. Boston, Little, Brown [1972] vi, 121 p. illus. 27 cm. "Books illustrated by Robert Lawson": p. 119-120. [NC975.5.L3J6] 73-129912 ISBN 0-316-47281-6 7.95

SUBJECT INDEX ILLUSTRATORS—UNITED STATES—BIOGRAPHY.

I. Jones, Helen L. II. Title.

Illustration of books—United States—Exhibitions.

FREEMAN, Judy. 741.64'2'074014942
Contemporary American illustrators of children's books : [exhibition] Rutgers University Art Gallery ... New Brunswick, New Jersey, October 6-November 17, 1974 ... / [compiled by Judy Freeman] ; with an essay by A. Hyatt Mayor. [New Brunswick] : Rutgers, State University, c1974. 72 p. : ill. ; 28 cm. [NC975.F73] 74-620110
1. Illustration of books—United States—Exhibitions. 2. Illustrated books, Children's—Exhibitions. I. Rutgers University, New Brunswick, N.J. Art Gallery. II. Title.

Illustration of books—U.S.—Period.

**ILLUSTRATORS 64* 741.64058
the annual of illustration. Ed.: Bernard Fuchs. Designer: Robert Geismann. New York. Pub. for soc. of Illustrators [by] Hastings [c.1964] 252p. illus. (pt. col.) 31cm. 59-10849 15.00
1. Illustration of books—U.S.—Period. I. Society of Illustrators, New York.

ILLUSTRATORS; 741.64058
the annual of American illustrations. 1961. New York Pub. for the Soc. of Illustrators by Hastings, c.1961. unpaged. illus. (pt. col.) 31cm. 59-10849 14.00
1. Illustration of books—U.S.—Period. I. Society of Illustratorss, New York

ILLUSTRATORS; 741.64058
the annual of American illustration. 1st-1959- New York, Published for the Society of Illustrators by Hastings House. v. illus. (part col.) 31cm. [NC975.A1 I5] 59-10849
1. Illustration of books—U. S.—Period. I. Society of Illustrators, New York.

ILLUSTRATORS; 741.64/058
the annual of American illustration. 9th 1967-1968. New York, pub. for the Soc. of Illustrators by Hastings. v. illus. (pt. col.) 31cm. [NC975.A1 I5] 59-10849 16.50
1. Illustration of books—U.S.—Period. I. Society of Illustrators, New York.

ILLUSTRATORS 741.64058
the annual of American illustration. Ed.: Harry Carter. Designer: Suren Ermoyan. New York, Pub. for Soc. of Illustrators [by] Hastings [c.1963] 233p. illus. (pt. col.) 31cm. 59-10849 15.00
1. Illustration of books—U.S.—Period. I. Society of Illustrators, New York.

ILLUSTRATORS 741.64058
the annual of American illustration. Ed.: Robert Peak. Designer: John Van Zwienen. New York. Pub. for Soc. of Illustrators [by] Hastings [c.1965] (various p.) illus. (pt. col.) 31cm. 59-10849 15.00
1. Illustration of books—U.S.—Period. I. Society of Illustrators, New York.

ILLUSTRATORS 741.64058
the annual of American illustration. Ed.: Austin Briggs. Designer: William H.b Buckley. New York, Pub. for The Society of Illustrators [by] Hastings [c.1962] 223p. illus. (pt. col.) 31cm. 59-10849 14.00
1. Illustration of books—U. S.—Period. I. Society of Illustrators, New York.

ILLUSTRATORS 741.64058
the annual of American illustration. New York, Hastings, 1966. 245p. illus. (pt. col.) 30cm. Pub. for the Soc. of Illustrators. Ed.: 1966-67- Harry J. Schaare. Designer: H. Kurt Stoessel. 59-10849 16.00
1. Illustration of books—U.S.—Period. I. Society of Illustrators, New York.

ILLUSTRATORS. 741.64058
the annual of American illustration. Editor: Howard Munce. Designer: Lester Beall. New York, Published for the Society of Illustrators by Hastings House. [c.1960] 254p. illus. (part col.) 31cm. 59-10849 12.95
1. Illustration of books—U. S.—Period: I. Society of Illustrators, New York.

Illustrators.

DODD, Loring Holmes 741.6
A generation of illustrators and etchers. Boston, Chapman & Grimes [c.1960] 214p. illus. 21cm. 60-12275 5.00
1. Illustrators. 2. Etchers. I. Title.

KINGMAN, Lee, comp. 016.7416'42'0922
Illustrators of children's books, 1957-1966, compiled by Lee Kingman, Joanna Foster [and] Ruth Giles Lontoft. Boston, Horn Book, 1968. xvii, 295 p. illus. (part col.) 28 cm. A supplement to Illustrators of children's books, 1744-1945, by B. E. Mahony, L. P. Latimer, and B. Folmsbee and Illustrators of children's books, 1946-1956, by R. H. Viguers, M. Dalphin, and B. M. Miller. Includes bibliographies. [NC965.K54] 76-4001 20.00
1. Illustrators. 2. Illustrated books, Children's—Bibliography. I. Foster, Joanna, joint comp. II. Lontoft, Ruth Giles, joint comp. III. Miller, Bertha E. (Mahony) Illustrators of children's books, 1744-1945. IV. Title.

VIGUERS, Ruth Hill, comp. 741.6'42'0922
Illustrators of children's books, 1946-1956, compiled by Ruth Hill Viguers, Marcia Dalphin [and] Bertha Mahony Miller. Boston, Horn Book, 1958. xvii, 299 p. illus. 28 cm. A supplement to Illustrators of children's books, 1774-1945, by B. E. Mahony. Includes bibliographies. [NC965.V5] 79-4034
1. Illustrators. 2. Illustrated books, Children's—Bibliography. I. Dalphin, Marcia, 1882- joint comp. II. Miller, Bertha E. (Mahony), joint comp. III. Miller, Bertha E. (Mahony). Illustrators of children's books, 1744-1945. IV. Title.

Illustrators, American.

AMERICAN Federation of Arts. 741.6058
Official directory, American illustrators and advertising artists. [Washington, Americal Federation of Arts] v. 23 cm. [NC975.O33] 50-3549
1. Illustrators, American. I. Title.

HALSEY, Ashley. 741.65
Illustrating for magazines. [Rev. ed.] New York, Sterling Pub. Co. [c1964] 96 p. illus., ports. 28 cm. (A Bridgman giant) First published in 1951 under title: Illustrating for The Saturday evening post. [NC975.H3] 64-24681
1. Illustrators, American. 2. The Saturday evening post. I. Title.

HALSEY, Ashley. 741.65
Illustrating for the Saturday evening post; with a foreword by Kenneth Stuart. Boston, Arlington House [1951] xii, 160 p. illus., ports. 32 cm. Much of the content first appeared in Inside information, a Post publication. [NC975.H3] 51-10267
1. Illustrators, American. 2. The Saturday evening post. I. Title.

ROHLFS, Christian, 1849-1938. 759.3
The best of Christian Rohlfs. [By] Paul Vogt; English translation by Hans Rosenwald. New York, Atlantis Books [1964] 89 p. illus., col. plates, port. 27 cm. [ND588.R57V57 1964] 68-5803 10.00
I. Vogt, Paul, 1926- ed. II. Title.

STROZZI, Bernardo, 1581-1644. 759.5
Bernardo Strozzi: paintings and drawings. Dedication exhibition of the University Art Gallery, October 8 to November 5, 1967. [Catalogue] by Michael Milkovich. Binghamton, University Art Gallery, State University of New York at Binghamton [1968?] 102 p. illus. 26 cm. Stamped on t.p.: [Supplied by] Worldwide Books, New York. Bibliography: p. 101-102. [ND623.S7M5] 68-63947
I. Milkovich, Michael. II. New York (State). State University at Binghamton. University Art Gallery. III. Title.

Illustrators—Biography.

ILLUSTRATORS of children's books, 1967-1976 / compiled by Lee Kingman, Grace Allen Hogarth, Harriet Quimby. Boston : Horn Book, 1978. xiv, 290 p. : ill. (some col.) ; 28 cm. A supplement to Illustrators of children's books, 1744-1945, compiled by B. E. Mahony, L. P. Latimer, and B. Folmsbee, Illustrators of children's books, 1946-1956, by R. H. Viguers, M. Dalphin, and B. M. Miller, and Illustrators of children's books, 1957-1966, by L. Kingman, J. Foster, and R. G. Lontoft. Cumulative index of artists listed in all above mentioned volumes: p. 268-285. [NC965.I44] 78-13759 ISBN 0-87675-018-8 : 32.50 741'.092'2 B
1. Illustrators—Biography. 2. Illustration of books—20th century. 3. Illustrated books, Children's—Bibliography. I. Kingman, Lee. II. Hogarth, Grace Allen, 1905- III. Quimby, Harriet B. IV. Miller, Bertha E. Mahony. Illustrators of children's books, 1744-1945.

MILLER, Bertha E. Mahony, comp. 741'.092'2 B
Contemporary illustrators of children's books / compiled by Bertha E. Mahony and Elinor Whitney. Detroit : Gale Research Co., 1978, c1930. p. cm. [NC965.M58 1978] 78-17018 ISBN 0--8103-4308-8 : 22.00
1. Illustrators—Biography. 2. Illustration of books—20th century. 3. Illustrated books, Children's. 4. Children's literature—Bibliography. I. Whitney, Elinor, joint author. II. Title. **BIP**

Illustrators—Biography—Dictionaries.

WARD, Martha Eads. 741'.092'2 B
Illustrators of books for young people / by Martha E. Ward and Dorothy A. Marquardt. 2d ed. Metuchen, N.J. : Scarecrow Press, 1975. 223 p. ; 22 cm. Includes index. [NC45.W3 1975] 75-9880 ISBN 0-8108-0819-6 : 8.00
1. Illustrators—Biography—Dictionaries. 2. Illustrated books, Children's—Dictionaries. I. Marquardt, Dorothy A., joint author. II. Title.

Illustrators, British.

HOGARTH, Paul, 1917- 741.6'0922
Artists on horseback; the Old West in illustrated journalism, 1857-1900. New York, Watson-Guptill Publications [1972] 288 p. illus. 31 cm. Includes bibliographical references. [NC978.H59] 77-190518 ISBN 0-8230-0350-7 17.50
1. Illustrators, British. 2. Journalism, Pictorial. 3. The West in art. 4. Northwest, Canadian, in art. I. Title.

Illustrators—Dictionaries.

WARD, Martha Eads. 741'.0922
Illustrators of books for young people, by Martha E. Ward and Dorothy A. Marquardt. Metuchen, N.J., Scarecrow Press, 1970. 166 p. 22 cm. [NC45.W3] 78-15380
1. Illustrators—Dictionaries. 2. Illustrated books, Children's—Dictionaries. I. Marquardt, Dorothy A., joint author. II. Title. **BIP**

Illustrators—England—Biography.

HAMMELMANN, Hanns A. 741'.092'2 B
Book illustrators in eighteenth-century England / Hanns Hammelmann ; edited and completed by T. S. R. Boase. New Haven : Published for the Paul Mellon Centre for Studies in British Art (London) by Yale University Press, 1975. xiv, 120 p., [20] leaves of plates : ill. ; 26 cm. (Studies in British art) Includes indexes. [NC978.H28] 75-2770 ISBN 0-300-01895-9 : 27.50
1. Illustrators—England—Biography. 2. Illustration of books—England. 3. Illustrated books—18th century. I. Boase, Thomas Sherrer Ross, 1898-1974. II. Title. III. Series. **BIP**

ROBINSON, Charles. 741'.092'4
Charles Robinson / text by Leo deFreitas. London : Academy Editions ; New York : St.Martins Press, 1976 87p. : ill.(some col.) ; 29 cm. Bibliography:p.83-87. [NC978.5.R6D43] 76-11424 ISBN 0-85670-277-3 : 12.50 ISBN 0-85670-282-X pbk. : 7.95
1. Illustrators-England-Biography. I. De Freitas, Leo. II. Robinson, Charles.

Illustrators—France—Biography.

WHITE, Colin. 741'.092'4 B
Edmund Dulac / Colin White. New York : Scribner, c1976. 205 p. : ill. (some col.) ; 29 cm. Includes bibliographical references and index. [NC980.5.D84W47] 76-9562 ISBN 0-684-14791-2 : 25.00
1. Dulac, Edmund, 1882-1953. 2. Illustrators—France—Biography. **BIP**

WHITE, Colin. 741'.092'4 B
Edmund Dulac / [by] Colin White. London : Studio Vista, 1976. 208 p. : ill. (some col.), facsims., map, music, plan, ports. ; 29 cm. Includes bibliographical references and index. [NC980.5.D84W47 1976b] 77-364635 ISBN 0-289-70751-X : £10.50
1. Dulac, Edmund, 1882-1953. 2. Illustrators—France—Biography.

Illustrators—Great Britain.

REID, Forrest, 1876-1947. 741.64'0941
Illustrators of the eighteen sixties : an illustrated survey of the work of 58 British artists / Forrest Reid. New York : Dover Publications, 1975. xv, 295 p. : ill. ; 24 cm. Reprint of the 1928 ed. published by Faber & Gwyer, London under title: Illustrators of the sixties. Includes index. "A list of first editions of books illustrated by artists of the sixties": p. 271-282. [NC978.R4 1975] 74-12539 ISBN 0-486-23121-6 pbk. : 5.00
1. Illustrators—Great Britain. 2. Illustration of books—Great Britain. I. Title. **BIP**

Illustrators—Great Britain—Correspondence.

CALDECOTT, Randolph, 1846-1886. 741'.092'4 B
Yours pictorially : illustrated letters of Randolph Caldecott / edited by Michael Hutchins. London : F. Warne, 1976, i.e.1977 x, 284 p., [8] p. of plates : ill., facsims. (some col.), port. ; 24 cm. Includes index. [NC978.5.C3A347 1976] 76-2923 ISBN 0-7232-1981-8 : 15.00
1. Caldecott, Randolph, 1846-1886. 2. Illustrators—Great Britain—Correspondence. I. Hutchins, Michael. II. Title.

Illustrators—United States.

REED, Walt, ed. 741.60973
the illustrator in America, 1900-1960's New York, Reinhold Pub. Corp. [1967, c1966] 271, [1] p. illus. (part col.) 33 cm. Bibliography: p. 271-[272] [NC975.R4] 66-24545
1. Illustrators—United States. 2. Illustration of books—United States. I. Title.

WATSON, Ernest William, 1884-1969. 741.6'0922
Forty illustrators and how they work, by Ernest W. Watson. With chapters by Matlack Price, Norman Kent, and Guy Rowe. Freeport, N.Y., Books for Libraries Press [1970, c1946] xv, 318 p. illus., plates (part col.), ports. 31 cm. (Essay index reprint series) [NC975.W3 1970] 76-121510 ISBN 0-8369-1899-1
1. Illustrators—United States. 2. Illustration of books—United States. I. Title.

Illustrators—United States—Biography.

BLEGVAD, Erik. 741'.092'4 B
Self-portrait—Erik Blegvad / written and illustrated by Erik Blegvad. Reading, Mass. : Addison-Wesley, c1979. p. cm. A well-known illustrator discourses on himself, his life, and his work. [NC975.5.B55A2 1979] 92 78-23765 ISBN 0-201-00498-4 lib.bdg. : 7.95
1. Blegvad, Erik. 2. Illustrators—United States—Biography. I. Title.

FREAS, Frank Kelly, 1922- 741.9'73
Frank Kelly Freas : the art of science

fiction / by Frank Kelly Freas ; introd. by Isaac Asimov. Norfolk, Va. : Donning Co., c1977. p. cm. [NC975.5.F74A45] 77-8644 ISBN 0-915442-30-2 collector's ed. : 29.95. ISBN 0-915442-37-X pbk. : 7.95. ISBN 0-915442-38-8 lib. ed. : 12.95
1. Freas, Frank Kelly, 1922- 2. Illustrators—United States—Biography. 3. Science fiction—Illustrations. I. Title. BIP

GREENE, Douglas G. 741'.092'4 B
W. W. Denslow / by Douglas G. Greene and Michael Patrick Hearn ; with an introd. by Patricia Denslow Eykyn. [Mount Pleasant] : Clarke Historical Library, Central Michigan University, c1976. vii, 225 p. : ill. ; 24 cm. (Juvenile series ; no. 2) "A bibliography of the work of W. W. Denslow": p. 168-211. [NC975.5.D46G73] 77-353964
1. Denslow, William Wallace, 1856-1915. 2. Illustrators—United States—Biography. I. Hearn, Michael Patrick, joint author. II. Series: Juvenile series (Mount Pleasant, Mich.) ; no. 2.

HUTCHINSON, William Henry, 1910- 741'.092'4 B
The world, the work, and the West of W. H. D. Koerner / W. H. Hutchinson. 1st ed. Norman : University of Oklahoma Press, 1979, c1978 p. cm. Includes index. Bibliography: p. [NC975.5.K63H87] 78-58125 ISBN 0-8061-1471-1 : 35.00
1. Koerner, William Henry Dethlef. 2. Illustrators—United States—Biography. 3. The West in art. I. Title. BIP

KENT, Rockwell, 1882-1971. 741.9'73 B
It's me, O Lord : the autobiography of Rockwell Kent. New York : Da Capo Press, 1977, c1955. x, 617 p., [23] leaves of plates : ill. ; 24 cm. (Da Capo Press series in graphic art) Reprint of the ed. published by Dodd, Mead, New York. [NC975.5.K46A25 1977] 77-5590 ISBN 0-306-77412-7 : 39.50
1. Kent, Rockwell, 1882-1971. 2. Illustrators—United States—Biography. I. Title.

Image, Selwyn, 1849-1930.

†IMAGE, Selwyn, 1849-1930. 709'.2'4 B
Selwyn Image letters / A. H. Mackmurdo, editor. New York : Garland Pub., 1977. 219 p., [2] leaves of plates : ill. ; 23 cm. (The Aesthetic movement & the arts and crafts movement) Reprint of the 1932 ed. published by G. Richards, London. Includes index. [N7483.I45A37 1977] 76-17780 ISBN 0-8240-2486-9 : 35.00
1. Image, Selwyn, 1849-1930. 2. Art historians—England—Correspondence. I. Title. II. Series.

Images, Photographic.

DAINTY, J. C. 621.36
Image science : principles, analysis and evaluation of photographic-type imaging processes / J. C. Dainty and R. Shaw. London ; New York : Academic Press, 1974. xiv, 402 p. : ill. ; 24 cm. Includes bibliographical references and indexes. [TR222.D34] 74-5667 ISBN 0-12-200850-2
1. Images, Photographic. I. Shaw, Rodney, 1937- joint author. II. Title. BIP

FRIESER, Hellmut, 1901- 621.36'7
Photographic information recording = Photographische Informationsaufzeichnung / H. Frieser ; with a contribution by Klaus Biedermann. New York : Wiley, [1975] p. cm. "A Halsted Press book." German and English. Includes indexes. Bibliography: p. [TR222.F74] 75-20097 ISBN 0-470-28117-0 : 67.00
1. Images, Photographic. I. Title. II. Title: Photographische Informationsaufzeichnung. BIP

JACOBSOHN, Kurt, 1906- 770
Imaging systems / Kurt I. Jacobson and Ralph E. Jacobson. 1st ed. New York : Wiley, 1976. p. cm. "A Halsted Press book." [TR222.J3] 76-23144 ISBN 0-470-98905-X : 27.50
1. Images, Photographic. 2. Photography, Applied. 3. Imaging systems. I. Jacobson, R. E., joint author. II. Title. BIP

JACOBSON, Kurt, 1906- 770'.28
Imaging systems : mechanisms and applications of established and new photosensitive processes / [by] Kurt I. Jacobson and Ralph E. Jacobson. London ; New York : Focal Press, 1976. 319 p. : ill. ; 25 cm. Includes bibliographical references and index. [TR222.J3 1976b] 77-370170 ISBN 0-240-50790-8 : £11.95
1. Images, Photographic. 2. Photography, Applied. 3. Imaging systems. I. Jacobson, R. E., joint author. II. Title.

Images, Photographic—Congresses.

IMAGE assessment & specification : seminar-in-depth, May 20-22, 1974, Rochester, New York / editor, David Dutton ; co-sponsor, The Optical Society of America, in cooperation with the International Commission on Optics, Sira Institute. Palos Verdes Estates, Calif. : Society of Photo-Optical Instrumentation Engineers, c1974. xii, 311 p. : ill. ; 29 cm. (Proceedings of the Society of Photo-Optical Instrumentation Engineers ; v. 46) Includes bibliographical references and index. [TR222.I45] 75-330494 621.36'7
1. Images, Photographic—Congresses. I. Dutton, David. II. Optical Society of America. III. Society of Photo-Optical Instrumentation Engineers. IV. Series: Society of Photo-Optical Instrumentation Engineers. Proceedings ; v. 46.

SOCIETY of Photographic Scientists and Engineers. 152.1'423
Advances in the psychophysical and visual aspects of image evaluation : a summary of the proceedings of an SPSE technical section conference, October 24-25, 1977, Rochester, New York / edited by Roger P. Dooley. Washington : Society of Photographic Scientists and Engineers, c1977. 133 p. : ill. ; 28 cm. Includes bibliographies and index. [TR222.S63 1977] 77-85177 ISBN 0-89208-092-2 pbk. : 15.00
1. Images, Photographic—Congresses. 2. Visual perception—Congresses. 3. Psychology, Physiological—Congresses. I. Dooley, Roger P. II. Title. BIP

SPSE International Conference on Image Analysis and Evaluation, Toronto, Canada, 1976. 621.36'7
Image analysis and evaluation : SPSE Conference proceedings, July 19-23, 1976, Toronto, Canada / edited by Rodney Shaw. Washington : [Society of Photographic Scientists and Engineers], c1977. 538 p. : ill. ; 29 cm. Includes bibliographical references and index. [TR222.S2 1976] 77-73670 ISBN 0-89208-089-2 : 39.95
1. Images, Photographic—Congresses. I. Shaw, Rodney, 1937- II. Society of Photographic Scientists and Engineers. III. Title.

Imaging systems.

UNCONVENTIONAL imaging processes / Eric Brinckman ... [et al.]. 1st ed. London ; New York : Focal Press, 1978. 150 p. : ill. ; 25 cm. Includes bibliographical references and index. [TR147.U53] 78-315322 ISBN 0-8038-7505-3 : 34.95 770'.28
1. Imaging systems. I. Brinckman, Eric.
Distributed by Hastings House BIP

WADE, Kent E. 770
Alternative photographic processes : a resource manual for the artist, photographer, craftsperson / Kent E. Wade. Dobbs Ferry, N.Y. : Morgan & Morgan, c1978. 179 p., [8] leaves of plates : ill. ; 24 cm. Bibliography: p. [175]-179. [TR147.W25] 77-83836 ISBN 0-87100-136-5 : 11.95
1. Imaging systems. I. Title. BIP

Imitation (in art)

MAISON, K. E. 704.94
Art themes and variations; five centuries of interpretations and re-creations. With an introd. by Michael Ayrton. New York, H. N. Abrams [1960] 224 p. mounted col. illus., plates (part col.) 33 cm. [N7428.M28] 60-15637
1. Imitation (in art) 2. Paintings. I. Title.

Immerman, Irene.

TOULOUSE-LAUTREC MONFA, Henri Marie Raymond de, 1864-1901 759.4
Toulouse-Lautrec, by Andre Leclerc[pseud.] New York, Crown [1963] 36p. chiefly illus. 18cm. (Little bks. on great artists) First pub. in 1948? under the title: Lautrec. Biographical sketch in French, English, German. Biographical sketch in French, English, German. 63-5635 .69
1. Immerman, Irene. I. Title.

Implements, utensils, etc.—Collectors and collecting.

LANTZ, Louise K. 683'.82
Old American kitchenware 1725-1925 [by] Louise K. Lantz. Camden, T. Nelson [1970] 289 p. illus., facsims. 26 cm. Bibliography: p. 283-285. [NK806.L29] 75-101527
1. Implements, utensils, etc.—Collectors and collecting. 2. Art industries and trade, American. I. Title. BIP

Implements, utensils, etc.—The West—Collectors and collecting.

BRESSIE, Wesley. 745.5
101 ghost town relics : how to display, price guide / by Wes and Ruby Bressie; cover and photos by Wes and Ruby Bressie. 1st ed. Yreka, Calif., Printed by Nolan's News-Journal Litho, 1967. 72 p. (chiefly illus., part col.) 22 cm. Bibliography: p. 70. [NK807.B7] 68-888
1. Implements, utensils, etc.—The West—Collectors and collecting. I. Bressie, Ruby, joint author. II. Title.

TURNER, Thomas Edward. 745.1'0978
Ole timey stuff; a compilation of historical facts, illustrations, and classifications of iron, wire, guns, and glass, etc. from the old American West. [1st ed.] Mesquite, Tex., 1968] 176 p. illus., facsims., ports. 26 cm. Bibliography: p. 175-176. [NK807.T8] 68-6309
1. Implements, utensils, etc.—The West—Collectors and collecting. I. Title.

Impressionism (Art)

ACQUA, Gian Alberto dell', 1909- 759.05
The French impressionists. Translated by Susan Bellamy. New York, Crown Publishers, 1958. 102p. (chiefly col. plates) 30cm. Bibliography: p.100-102. [ND547.A2513] [ND547.A2513] 759.914 58-12885 58-12885
1. Impressionism (Art) 2. Paintings, French. I. Title.

BOWNESS, Alan, ed. 709.034
Impressionists and post-impressionists. New York, Watts [1965] 296p. illus. (pt. col.) ports. (pt. col.) 25cm. (Great art and artists of the world) Bibl. [ND1265.B67] 65-10269 12.95
1. Impressionism (Art) 2. Post-impressionism (Art) 3. Art, French. I. Title. II. Series.

COGNIAT, Raymond, 1896- 759.05
The century of the impressionists. [Translated by Graham Snell] New York, Crown Publishers [1960] 206p. illus. (part mounted col.) col. plates. 33cm. Bibliography: p. 203-204. [ND1265.C5463] 60-50321
1. Impressionism (Art) 2. Paintings. I. Title. BIP

COGNIAT, Raymond, 1896- 759.914
French painting at the time of the impressionists. [Edited by Andre Gloeckner] Translated from the French by Lucy Norton. New York, Hyperion Press; distributed by Macmillan [1951] 163 p. col. illus. 37 cm. "Impressionism general works": p. 153-154. "Selected works on each artist": p. 155-163. [ND1265.C544] 51-11006
1. Impressionism (Art) 2. Painting, French. 3. Painters, French. I. Title.

COURTHION, Pierre. 759'.05
Impressionism. Text by Pierre Courthion. Translated by John Shepley. New York, H. N. Abrams [1972] 205 p. illus. (part col.) 33 cm. (The Library of great art movements) Bibliography: p. 203-204. [N6465.I4C6813] 79-142740 ISBN 0-8109-0202-8
1. Impressionism (Art) I. Title.

COURTHION, Pierre. 759.05
Impressionism / Pierre Courthion ; translated by John Shepley. New York : H. N. Abrams, 1977. 160 p. : ill. (some col.) ; 30 cm. Includes index. Bibliography: p. 156-157. [N6465.I4C6813 1977] 76-50479 ISBN 0-8109-2067-0 pbk. : 7.95
1. Impressionism (Art) 2. Art, Modern—19th century. I. Title. BIP

DUNSTAN, Bernard, 1920- 759.05
Painting methods of the Impressionists / by Bernard Dunstan. New York : Watson-Guptill Publications, 1976. p. cm. Includes index. Bibliography: p. [ND192.I4D86 1976] 76-25552 ISBN 0-8230-3710-X : 17.95
1. Impressionism (Art) 2. Painting, Modern—19th century. 3. Painting—Technique. I. Title.

GAUNT, William, 1900- 759.4
Impressionism: a visual history. New York, Praeger [1970] 296 p. 108 col. plates. 31 cm. "Biographies": p. 273-284. Bibliography: p.285-287. [ND192.I4G38] 76-100033 20.00
1. Impressionism (Art) I. Title.

HANSON, Lawrence. 759.4
Impressionism: golden decade [by] Lawrence and Elisabeth Hanson. [1st ed.] New York, Holt, Rinehart and Winston [1961] 268 p. illus. 22 cm. Includes bibliography. [ND547.H36] 61-110373
1. Impressionism (Art) 2. Painters, French. I. Lawrence, Elisabeth M., joint author.

THE impressionists and their world. Introd. by Basil Taylor. [Rev. ed.] London, Phoenix House [Chester Springs, Pa., Dufour, c.1957] 29, 96p. 96 plates (pt. col.) 32cm. Bibl. [ND1265] 66-31451 6.95 759.05
1. Impressionism (Art) I. Taylor, Basil.

JAFFE, Hans Ludwig C. 759.4
The world of the impressionists; the artists who painted with delight in being alive, by Hans L. C. Jaffe and the editors of Hammond. [Maplewood, N.J.] Hammond Incorporated, 1969] 256 p. illus. (part col.), ports. 32 cm. [ND192.I4J3] 69-18893 14.95
1. Impressionism (Art) I. Hammond Incorporated. II. Title.

LASSAIGNE, Jacques, 1910- 759.05
Impressionism. [Translated from the French by Paul Eve] New York, Funk & Wagnalls [1970, c1969] 207 p. illus. (part col.) 28 cm. (History of painting) Bibliography: p. [204] [ND192.I4L313 1970] 79-100539 7.95
1. Impressionism (Art) 2. Painting, Modern—19th century. I. Title.

LEYMARIE, Jean. 759.05
Impressionism; biographical and critical study. Translated by James Emmons. [Lausanne] Skira [1955] 2v. mounted col. illus. 19cm. (The Taste of our time, v. 11-12) Bibliography: v. 2, p. 127-[129] [ND547.L54] [ND547.L54] 759.914 55-7701 55-7701
1. Impressionism (Art) 2. Paintings, French. 3. Painters, French. I. Title.

MATHEY, Francois. 759.05
The impressionists. Translated by Jean Steinberg. New York, Praeger [1961] 289 p. illus. 21 cm. (Books that matter) Praeger paperbacks, PPS-50. [ND547.M343] 61-5759
1. Impressionism (Art) 2. Painting, French—History.

NOCHLIN, Linda, ed. 759.05
Impressionism and post-impressionism, 1874-1904; sources and documents Englewood Cliffs, N.J., Prentice-Hall [1966] ix, 222 p. facsim. 23 cm. (Sources and documents in the history of art series) Bibliographical footnotes. [ND1265.N58] 66-23610
1. Impressionism (Art) 2. Post-impressionism (Art) 3. Art, Modern—19th century—Sources. I. Title. II. Series. BIP

POOL, Phoebe. 759.05
Impressionism. New York, Praeger [1967] 287 p. illus. (part col.) 28 cm. (Praeger

Impressionism (Art)—Juvenile literature.

GREENFELD, Howard. 759.05
The Impressionist revolution. [1st ed.] Garden City, N.Y., Doubleday [1972] 111 p. illus. (part col.) 25 cm. Details the Impressionist "revolution" by which such artists as Renoir, Monet, and Pissarro protested the materialistic emphasis of nineteenth-century French society. [ND192.I4G73] 72-76163 ISBN 0-385-04131-4 5.95
1. Impressionism (Art)—Juvenile literature. 2. Painting—Juvenile literature. I. Title.

Impressionism (Art)—United States.

BOYLE, Richard J. 759.13
American impressionism / Richard J. Boyle. Boston : New York Graphic Society, 1974. 236 p. : ill. (some col.) ; 30 cm. Includes index. Bibliography: p. 233-236. [ND210.5.I4B68] 73-89951 ISBN 0-8212-0597-8 : 29.50
1. Impressionism (Art)—United States. 2. Painting, American. 3. Painting, Modern—19th century—United States. I. Title. BIP

BROOKLYN Institute of Arts and Sciences. Museum. 759.13
Leaders of American impressionism: Mary Cassatt, Childe Hassam, John H. Twatchman [and] J. Alden Weir. New York, Arno Press, 1974. 43 p. illus. 22 cm. Reprint of the 1937 ed. published by the Brooklyn Museum, Brooklyn, N.Y. Catalog of an exhibition. [ND210.5.I4B76 1974] 75-128385 ISBN 0-405-00876-7 6.50
1. Cassatt, Mary, 1844-1926. 2. Hassam, Childe, 1859-1935. 3. Twachtman, John Henry, 1853-1902. 4. Weir, Julian Alden, 1852-1919. 5. Impressionism (Art)—United States. 6. Paintings, American—Exhibitions. I. Title.

HOOPES, Donelson F. 759.13
The American impressionists, by Donelson F. Hoopes. New York, Watson-Guptill Publications [1972] 159 p. illus. 29 cm. Bibliography: p. 155-157. [ND210.5.I4H6] 72-190522 ISBN 0-8230-0212-8 25.00
1. Impressionism (Art)—United States. 2. Painting, Modern—19th century—United States. I. Title.

Includes bibliographies.

ADAMS, Ansel Easton, 1902- 917.3
My camera in the national parks; 30 photographs with interpretative text and informative material on the parks and monuments, and photographic data. Yosemite National Park, V. Adams and Houghton Mifflin, Boston, 1950. 97 p. 30 plates. 37 cm. [E160.A3] 50-10356
1. Includes bibliographies. 2. National parks and reserves—U. S. 3. Photography, Artistic. I. Title.

Incunabula.

BUHLER, Curt Ferdinand, 1905- 093
The fifteenth-century book: the scribes, the printers, the decorators. Philadelphia, University of Pennsylvania Press [1960] 195p. illus. 24cm. Bibliographical references included in 'Notes' (p. 94-183) [Z240.B924 1960] 60-8542
1. Incunabula. I. Title.

HAEBLER, Konrad, 1857- 093
The study of incunabula, by Konrad Haebler; tr. from German by Lucy Eugenia Osborne. Foreword by Alfred W. Pollard. New York, Grolier, 1933; New York, Kraus Reprint, 1967. xvip. 1 l., 241p. 25cm. Tr. from the German ed. of 1925, but embodies also certain revs. of the text made by the author in 1932. Tr's. note [Z240.H132E] 33-31237 25.00
1. Incunabula. 2. Printing—Hist.—Origin and antecedents. I. Osborne. Lucy Eugenia. tr. II. Grolier Club, New York. III. Title. IV. Title: Translation of Handbuch der inkunabeikunde BIP

PROCTOR, Robert George Collier, 1868-1903. 094
Bibliographical essays. New York, B. Franklin [1969] xlviii, 243 p. illus., facsims., port. 23 cm. (Burt Franklin bibliography and reference series, 60) Reprint of the 1905 ed. Contents.Contents.—Robert Proctor [memoir]—Report of Proctor memorial fund.—Accipies woodcut.—On two plates in Sotheby's Principia typographica.—Marcus Reinhard and Johann Gruninger.—Incunabula at Grenoble.—The Gutenberg Bible.—A short view of Berthelet's editions of the statutes of Henry VIII.—On two Lyonnese editions of the Ars moriendi.—Ulrich von Ellenbog and the press of S. Ulrich at Augsburg.—The French royal Greek types and the Eton Chrysostom.—The early printers of Koln.—Tracts on early printing: List of the founts of type and woodcut devices used by the printers of the southern Netherlands in the fifteenth century. A note on Eberhard Frommolt of Basel, printer. Additions to Campbell's Annales de la typographie neerlandaise au 15e siecle.—Table of supplements to Campbell.—Author-registerOBibliographical essays. New
1. Incunabula. 2. Printing—History. 3. Bibliography. I. Title. BIP

STILLWELL, Margaret Bingham, 1887- 093
Incunabula and Americana, 1450-1800; a key to bibliographical study. [2d ed.] New York, Cooper Square Publishers, 1961 [c1930] xviii, 483 p. facsims. 27 cm. Includes bibliographies. [Z240.A1S8] 61-13271
1. Incunabula. 2. Printing — Hist. — Bibl. 3. Printing — Hist. — America. 4. Bibliography — Bibl. — Incunabula. 5. Bibliography — Bibl. — America. 6. America — Bibl. I. Title.

TYPENREPERTORIUM der wiegendrucke., von Konrad Haebler. Leipzig. 1905-1924. Nendeln, Liechtenstein, Kraus-Thomson Org., 1968. 3v. in 1. facsims. (pt. fold.) tables. 24cm. Imprint varies . . . [Z1009. D99] [Z240.H133] 5-30281 94.50 093
1. Incunabula. 2. Type and type-founding. 3. Printing—Hist.—Origin and antecedents. I. Haebler, Konrad, 1857-
Order from Kraus-Thomson, 9491 Nendeln, Liechtenstein.

Incunabula — Bibl. — Catalogs.

BRYN Mawr College Library. 016.016093
Fifteenth-century books in the library of Howard Lehman Goodhart. With a description and check list by Phyllis Walter Goodhart Gordan. Stamford, Conn. Overbrook Press, 1955. 160 p. 27 cm. "Two hundred and fifty copies." [Z240.B9] A56
1. Incunabula — Bibl. — Catalogs. I. Goodhart, Howard Lehman, 1884?-1951. II. Gordan, Phyllis Walter (Goodhart) III. Title.
contents omitted

BUHLER, Curt Ferdinand 1905- 016.0941
Fifteenth century books and the twentieth century: an address by Curt F. Buhler, and a catalogue of an exhibition of fifteenth century books held at the Grolier Club, April 15-June 1, 1952. New York, Grolier Club, 1952. 57p. facsims. 23cm. [Z240.B925] 52-14618
1. Incunabula—Bibl.—Catalogs. I. Grolier Club, New York. II. Title.

CAMBRIDGE. University. Library. 016.093
A catalogue of the fifteenth-century printed books in the University Library, Cambridge, compiled by J. C. T. Oates, under-librarian. Cambridge [Eng.] University Press, 1954. xii, 898p. illus., facsims., plan. 27cm. Includes bibliographical references. [Z240.C167] 55-2525
1. Incunabula—Bibl.—Catalogs. I. Oates, John Claud Trewhard. II. Title.

GOFF, Frederick Richmond, 1916- ed. 016.093
Incunabula in American libraries; a third census of fifteenth-century books recorded in North American collections, compiled and edited by Frederick R. Goff. New York, Bibliographical Society of America, 1964. ixiii, 798 p. 26 cm. The second census, edited by Margaret B. Stillwell, was published in 1940 under the same title. [Z240.G58] 65-1485
1. Incunabula — Bibl. — Catalogs. 2. Catalogs, Union. I. Stillwell, Margaret Bingham, 1887- ed. Incunabula in American libraries. II. Title.

NORTH Carolina. University. Library. 016.093
Incunabula in the Hanes collection of the Library of the University of North Carolina. Enl. ed. Compiled by Olan V. Cook, associate librarian. Chapel Hill, University of North Carolina Press, 1960. xvii, 180p. 24cm. (Hanes Foundation publications, no. 2) [Z240.N86 1960] 60-51499
1. Incunabula— Bibl.—Catalogs. I. Cook, Olan Victor. II. Title. III. Series: North Carolina. University. Library. Hanes Foundation for the Study of the Origin and Development of the Book. Hanes Foundation publications, no. 2

YALE University. Library. 016.093
Incunabula in the Yale University libraries, by Thomas E. Marston, curator of classics, with the collaboration of Leon Nemoy. New Haven, 1955. 82 p. 22 cm. Includes the Stillwell numbers and locations of holdings of the Yale libraries, and describes the incunabula unlisted in Stillwell. [Z240.Y23] 58-978
1. Incunabula — Bibl. — Catalogs. I. Marston, Thomas E. II. Stillwell, Margaret Bingham, 1887- III. Title. IV. Title: Incunabula in American libraries.

Incunabula—Bibliography.

DUFF, Edward Gordon, 1863-1924. 016.093
Fifteenth century English books; a bibliography of books and documents printed in England and of books for the English market printed abroad. [Folcroft, Pa.] Folcroft Library Editions, 1974. p. cm. Reprint of the 1917 ed. printed for the Bibliographical Society at the Oxford University Press, which was issued as no. 18 of the Society's Illustrated monographs. [Z240.D852 1974] 74-14846 ISBN 0-8414-3779-3 (lib. bdg.)
1. Incunabula—Bibliography. 2. Printing—History—Great Britain. 3. Great Britain—Imprints. I. Title. II. Series: Bibliographical Society, London. Illustrated monographs, no. 18.

LONE, Emma Miriam, 1872-1953. 016.093
Some noteworthy firsts in Europe during the fifteenth century / by E. Miriam Lone. New York : B. Franklin, 1971. xiv, 72 p. : facsims. ; 18 cm. (Selected essays in history, economics & social science ; 317) (Burt Franklin research & source works series ; 871) On spine: Noteworthy firsts in Europe. Reprint of the 1930 ed. published by L. C. Harper, New York. Includes index. [Z240.L85 1971] 77-172189 ISBN 0-8337-2138-0
1. Incunabula—Bibliography. 2. Books—History—1400-1600. 3. Bibliography—First editions. 4. Printing—History—Origins and antecedents. I. Title. II. Title: Noteworthy firsts in Europe. BIP

STILLWELL, Margaret Bingham, 1887- 016.093
The beginning of the world of books, 1450 to 1470; a chronological survey of the texts chosen for printing during the first twenty years of the printing art, with a synopsis of the Gutenberg documents. New York, Bibliographical Society of America, 1972. xxviii, 112 p. 26 cm. Appendixes (p. [73]-106): A. The Gutenberg documents: notes on the manuscript records, 1420-1468. The Gutenberg tradition as stated in the printed books of the fifteenth century, 1468-1499.—B. Undated imprints assigned to the Netherlands. Bibliography: p. xxi-xxv. [Z240.S816] 79-185917
1. Gutenberg, Johann, 1397?-1468—Bibliography. 2. Incunabula—Bibliography. I. Title. BIP

Incunabula—Bibliography—Catalogs.

DUBLIN. University. Library. 018'.1
Catalogue of fifteenth-century books in the Library of Trinity College, Dublin, and in Marsh's Library, Dublin, with a few from other collections (with illustrations) by T. K. Abbott. New York, B. Franklin [1970] vi, 225 p. illus., facsims. 24 cm. (Burt Franklin bibliography and reference series, 360) Reprint of the 1905 ed. Bibliography: p. [v]-vi. [Z240.D81 1970] 70-128846
1. Incunabula—Bibliography—Catalogs. I. Abbott, Thomas Kingsmill, 1829-1913. II. Marsh's Library, Dublin. III. Title.

FINGER, Frances L. 016.7595
Catalogue of the incunabula in the Elmer Belt Library of Vinciana, by Frances L. Finger. Los Angeles, Friends of the UCLA Library, 1971. xvii, 80 p. facsim. 27 cm. "250 copies." Bibliography: p. xv-xvii. [Z240.F47] 79-149086 ISBN 0-378-06151-8
1. Leonardo da Vinci, 1452-1519—Sources. 2. Belt, Elmer, 1893- —Library. 3. Incunabula—Bibliography—Catalogs. I. California. University. University at Los Angeles. Art Library. II. Title.

KRAUS, H. P., firm, booksellers, New York. 093
Monumenta xylographica et typographica. The cradle of printing part II. New York [1971] 167 p. illus. facsims. (part col.) 36 cm. (Its Catalogue 131) "Price list" ([1] l.) inserted. [Z240.Z9K7] 73-159518
1. Kraus, H. P., firm, booksellers, New York. 2. Incunabula—Bibliography—Catalogs. 3. Incunabula—Facsimiles. I. Title. II. Title: The cradle of printing part II. III. Series.

LENKEY, Susan V. 016.093
Stanford incunabula, 1975 : a descriptive catalog / compiled by Susan V. Lenkey. [Stanford, Calif. : Leland Stanford Junior University, 1975] 92 p. : ill. ; 28 cm. [Z240.L455] 75-321801
1. Stanford University. Libraries. 2. Incunabula—Bibliography—Catalogs. I. Stanford University. II. Title.

PIERPONT Morgan Library, New York. 093
Early printed books. New York [1974] xvi, [105] p. facsims. 30 cm. (Its Major acquisitions, 1924-1974) Errata slip inserted. [Z240.P62 1974] 73-92930 8.00
1. Pierpont Morgan Library, New York. 2. Incunabula—Bibliography—Catalogs. I. Title.

WAHLERT Memorial Library. 016.093'074'017739
Printed books, 1471-1500; an exhibition commemorating the UNESCO International Book Year. Dubuque, Iowa [1972] viii, 71 p. illus. 22 cm. Number 55 of 300 copies printed. [Z240.W216] 72-92807
1. Wahlert Memorial Library. 2. Incunabula—Bibliography—Catalogs. I. Title.

Incunabula—Bibliography—Union lists.

GOFF, Frederick Richmond, 1916- ed. 016.093
Incunabula in American libraries; a third census of fifteenth-century books recorded in North American collections. Reproduced from the annotated copy maintained by Frederick R. Goff, compiler and editor. Millwood, N.Y., Kraus Reprint Co., 1973 [c1964] lxiii, 798 p. 29 cm. Reprint of the ed. published by the Bibliographical Society of America, New York; annotated and corrected, with new introd. and list of dealers. [Z240.G58 1973] 72-10463 35.00
1. Incunabula—Bibliography—Union lists. 2. Catalogs, Union. 3. Books—Prices. 4. Antiquarian booksellers—Directories. I. Title. BIP

Incunabula—Facsimiles.

KRAUS, H. P., firm, booksellers, New York. 655.24
The cradle of printing, from Mainz and Bamberg to Westminster and St. Albans; one hundred incunabula and manuscripts important for the development of early printing. New York [1954] 99p. illus. (part mounted) facsims. (part col.) 36cm. 'Price list' ([2] p.) inserted. 'The first book of a living author ever printed, 'Johannes Brunner's' Grammatica rhythmica, by Hans Nachod. (Rare books; notes on the history of old book sand manuscripts ... volume VII, no. 4, May, 1954)' ([3]p.) inserted. [Z241.K75] 55-605
1. Incunabula—Facsimiles. I. Title.

SUBJECT INDEX INDIANS—ART—CATALOGS.

MORISON, Stanley, 1889-1967. 093
German incunabula in the British Museum : one hundred ifty-two facsimile plates of fine book-pages from presses of Germany. New York : Hacker Art Books, 1975. 26 p., [76] leaves of plates : ill. ; 40 cm. Reprint of the 1928 ed. published by V. Gollancz Limited, London. [Z240.M86 1975] 73-143358 ISBN 0-87817-077-4 : 100.00
1. Incunabula—Facsimiles. 2. Type and type-founding. 3. Printing—History—Germany. 4. Printing—Specimens. I. British Museum. Dept, of Printed Books. II. Title.

Index of American Design.

CHRISTENSEN, Erwin Ottomar, 1890- 745
The Index of American Design. Introd. by Holger Cahill. New York, Macmillan, 1950. xviii, 229 p. 378 illus. (part col.) 31 cm. Bibliography: p. 219-221. [NK1403.C5] 50-10215
1. Index of American Design. I. Title. BIP

India Early Minshall Collection.

CLEVELAND Museum of Art. 739.2
Faberge and his contemporaries; the India Early Minshall Collection of the Cleveland Museum of Art [by] Henry Hawley. [Cleveland] Cleveland Mus. of Art. [1967] 139p. illus. (pt. col.) 24cm. Bibl. [NK7405.C55] 67-28951 7.50
1. Faberge, Karl Gustavovich, 1846-1920. 2. India Early Minshall Collection. I. Hawley, Henry. II. Minshall, India Early. III. Title.

India—History—1765-1947—Pictorial works.

THE Last Empire : 779'.9'954035
photography in British India, 1855-1911 / pref. by the Earl Mountbatten of Burma ; with texts by Clark Worswick and Ainslie Embree. Millerton, N.Y. : Aperture, c1976. 146, [2] p. : ill. ; 26 x 30 cm. "Accompanies an exhibition organized by the Asia House Gallery of the Asia Society for the summer of 1976." Bibliography: p. [148]-[149] [DS479.L28 1976] 76-21208 ISBN 0-912334-86-X : 19.95
1. India—History—1765-1947—Pictorial works. I. Worswick, Clark. II. Embree, Ainslie Thomas. III. Asia House Gallery, New York.

India Office Library.

INDIA Office Library. 745.6'7'095507402132
Persian paintings in the India Office Library : a descriptive catalogue / B. W. Robinson. London : Sotheby Parke Bernet, 1976. xiii, 271 p., [16] leaves of plates : ill. (some col.) ; 26 cm. Includes indexes. [ND3241.I53 1976] 76-378764 ISBN 0-85667-026-X : 55.00
1. India Office Library. 2. Illumination of books and manuscripts, Iranian—Catalogs. 3. Illumination of books and manuscripts, Islamic—Iran—Catalogs. 4. Miniature painting, Iranian—Catalogs. 5. Miniature painting, Islamic—Iran—Catalogs. I. Robinson, Basil William. II. Title.
Available from publisher: 81 Adams Drive, Totowa, N.J. BIP

Indian craft.

HUNT, Walter Bernard, 1888- 745.5'09701
The complete how-to book of Indiancraft, by W. Ben Hunt. [1st Collier Books ed.] New York, Collier Books [1973] 187 p. illus. 26 cm. First published in 1969 under title: Ben Hunt's big Indiancraft book. Bibliography: p. 183. [TT157.H75 1973] 73-162087 2.95
1. Indian craft. 2. Indians of North America—Industries. I. Title. BIP

MINOR, Marz. 745
The American Indian craft book / Marz and Nono Minor ; ill. and photos. by the authors. Lincoln : University of Nebraska Press, 1978, c1972. 416 p. : ill. ; 21 cm. Includes index. [TT22.M56 1978] 77-14075 ISBN 0-8032-0974-6 : 15.00 ISBN 0-8032-5891-7 pbk. : 4.95
1. Indian craft. 2. Indians of North America—Industries. 3. Indians of North America—Social life and customs. I. Minor, Nono, joint author. II. Title.

NORBECK, Oscar E. 745.5
Book of authentic Indian life crafts / by Oscar E. Norbeck ; illustrated by John B. Eves. Rev. ed. North Plainfield, N.J. : Galloway Corp., 1974. 260 p. : ill. ; 24 cm. Previous editions published under title: Book of Indian life crafts. Includes bibliographical references. [TT22.N67 1974] 74-81910 ISBN 0-87874-012-0 : 8.95
1. Indian craft. I. Title. BIP

STRIBLING, Mary Lou. 745.5
Crafts from North American Indian arts : techniques, designs, and contemporary applications / Mary Lou Stribling. New York : Crown Publishers, [1975] xi, 308 p., [4] leaves of plates : ill. (some col.) ; 27 cm. (Crown's arts and crafts series) Includes index. Bibliography: p. 297-299. [TT22.S84 1975] 75-12842 ISBN 0-517-51612-8 : 10.95 ISBN 0-517-51613-6 pbk. : 5.95
1. Indian craft. 2. Indians of North America—Industries. I. Title. BIP

Indian craft—Juvenile literature.

GOGNIAT, Maurice, 1934- 745.5
Indian toys you can make / by Maurice Gogniat ; photos. by Jean-Pierre Tesson ; [translated by Maxine Hobson]. New York : Sterling Pub. Co., c1976. 32 p. : ill. (some col.) ; 22 cm. (Easy craft series) Translation of Jeux d'Indiens. Includes index. Instructions for making craft items and toys with an Indian theme. [TT23.G6313] 76-19820 ISBN 0-8069-5408-6 : 3.95 ISBN 0-8069-5409-4 lib.bdg. : 3.99
1. Indian craft—Juvenile literature. 2. Toy making—Juvenile literature. I. Title. II. Series. BIP

Indiana Tumbler and Goblet Company, Greentown.

BOYD, Ralph. 748'.8
Greentown, by Ralph and Louise Boyd. Photography by Tom Tucker. 1st ed. Lagro, Ind., Printed by Commercial Print. [1969] [44] p. col. illus. 23 cm. Cover title. [NK5112.B6] 73-9251 6.50
1. Indiana Tumbler and Goblet Company, Greentown. 2. Glassware—Greentown, Ind.—Catalogs. I. Boyd, Louise, joint author. II. Tucker, Tom, illus.

INDIANAPOLIS Museum of Art.
Greentown glass [exhibition] / by Catherine Beth Lippert ; with an introd. by James S. Measell ; Indianapolis Museum of Art, October 1 - November 9, 1975. Indianapolis : Indianapolis Museum of Art, c1975. 43 p. : ill. ; 26 cm. Bibliography: p. 19. [NK5112.I5 1975] 75-29897
1. Indiana Tumbler and Goblet Company, Greentown. 2. Indianapolis Museum of Art. 3. Glassware—Indiana—Greentown—Catalogs. I. Lippert, Catherine Beth. II. Title.

Indianapolis. Children's Museum—History.

KENNY, David H. 069'.09772'52
Fifty years young : the Children's Museum / David H. Kenny. New York : Newcomen Society in North America, 1975. 32 p. : ill. ; 23 cm. (Newcomen publication ; no. 1035) "Delivered at the 1975 Indiana Dinner of the Newcomen Society in North America, held at Indianapolis." [AM101.I5K46] 75-36874
1. Indianapolis. Children's Museum—History. I. Title. II. Series.

Indianapolis Museum of Art.

INDIANAPOLIS Museum of Art. 708'.172'52 s
40 master-works; a selection of paintings in the Indianapolis Museum of Art, honoring the inaugural year of the Museum, 1970-71 [Indianapolis, 1970] 41 p. (chiefly illus. (part col.)) 26 cm. (Its Bulletin/catalogue, v. 57, no. 1) [N577.A4 vol. 57, no. 1] [N577] 750'.74'01252 74-160767
1. Indianapolis Museum of Art. 2. Paintings—Indianapolis—Catalogs. I. Title. II. Series.

WRIGHTSON, Priscilla. 708'.172'52 s
The English picturesque: villa and cottage, 1760-1860. Introd., catalogue, and notes by Priscilla Wrightson. Pref. by Carl J. Weinhardt. [Indianapolis, Indianapolis Museum of Art, 1973] 136-205 p. illus. 26 cm. (Indianapolis Museum of Art. Bulletin/catalogue, v. 1, no. 3 (new ser.)) Errata slip inserted. [N577.A4 n.s. vol. 1, no. 3] [NE628] 769'.4'40942 74-152795
1. Indianapolis Museum of Art. 2. Architecture, Domestic, in art. 3. Prints, English—Catalogs. 4. Prints—Indianapolis—Catalogs. I. Title. II. Series: Indianapolis Museum of Art. Bulletin/catalogue. New ser., v. 1, no. 3.

Indians—Architecture—Juvenile literature.

BALDWIN, Gordon Cortis, 1908- 722'.91
Pyramids of the New World, by Gordon C. Baldwin. New York, Putnam [1971] 224 p. illus. 22 cm. Bibliography: p. 210-212. Summary: Describes the New World's Pre-Columbian pyramids and their significance in the social, political, and religious life of long-vanished civilizations. [E59.A67B35 1971] 76-113517 4.86
1. Indians—Architecture—Juvenile literature. 2. Pyramids—Juvenile literature. I. Title.

Indians—Art.

APPLETON, Le Roy H. 970.67
Indian art of the Americas. New York, Scribner [1950] xii, [4], 279 p. 79 col. plates, maps. 32 cm. Errata slip mounted on p. [xiii] Bibliography: p. 265-270. [E59.A7A6] 50-14584
1. Indians—Art. 2. Indians—Religion and mythology. I. Title.

APPLETON, LeRoy H. 970.1
American Indian design and decoration [by] Le Roy H. Appleton. New York, Dover Publications [1971] viii, 277 p. illus. (part col.), maps. 29 cm. (The Dover pictorial archive series) First published 1950 under title: Indian art of the Americas. Bibliography: p. 264-269. [E59.A7A6 1971] 74-151421 ISBN 0-486-22704-9
1. Indians—Art. 2. Indians—Religion and mythology. I. Title.

BECKER-DONNER, Etta, 1911- 970.65717
Ancient American painting. Translated by Margaret Shenfield. New York, Crown Publishers [1963] 64 p. 24 col. plates. 19 cm. (Movements in world art) Translation of Prakolumbische Malerei. Bibliography: p. 64. [E59.A7B413] 63-5828
1. Indians — Art. I. Title.

BUSHNELL, Geoffrey Hext Sutherland. 709.17498
Ancient arts of the Americas [by] G. H. S. Bushnell. New York, F. A. Praeger [1965] 287 p. illus. (part col.) maps. 22 cm. (Praeger world of art series) Bibliography: p. 267-268. [E59.A7B97] 65-20077
1. Indians—Art. 2. America—Antiquities. 3. Indians—Antiquities. I. Title.

ESSAYS in pre-Columbian 970.67
art and archaeology, by Samuel K. Lothrop and others. Cambridge, Harvard University Press, 1961. 507 p. illus., maps. 25 cm. "Bibliographies": p. [449]-483. [E59.A7E8] 61-18531
1. Indians—Art. 2. Latin America—Antiquities. 3. Art—Spanish America. I. Lothrop, Samuel Kirkland, 1892-

GREY, Michael. 709'.01'1
Pre-Columbian art / Michael Grey. New York : St. Martin's Press, 1978. [88] p. : col. ill. ; 28 cm. [E59.A7G73] 77-95302 ISBN 0-312-63580-X pbk. : 5.95
1. Indians—Art. I. Title. BIP

KELEMEN, Pal. 709'.7
Art of the Americas, ancient and Hispanic, with a comparative chapter on the Philippines. New York, Crowell [1969] xiii, 402 p. illus., maps. 24 cm. Bibliography: p. 359-361. [N6502.K38] 72-87163 10.00
1. Indians—Art. 2. Art, Colonial—Latin America. 3. Art—Latin America. 4. Art—Philippine Islands. I. Title.

KELEMEN, Pal. 970.6571
Medieval American art; masterpieces of the New World before Columbus. New York, Macmillan, 1956. xxii, 414, 33p. 308plates, map (on lining papers) 29cm. Bibliography: p.385-406. [E59.A7K4 1956] 57-335
1. Indians—Art. 2. Indians—Antiq. 3. America— Antiq. I. Title.

KELEMEN, Pal. 709.7
Medieval American art; masterpieces of the New World before Columbus. 3d rev. ed. New York, Dover Publications [1969] 2 v. (xli, 418 p.) illus., map. 28 cm. Bibliography: p. 387-408. [E59.A7K4 1969] 68-28248 3.75 per vol.
1. Indians—Art. 2. Indians—Antiquities. 3. America—Antiquities. I. Title.

KUBLER, George, 1912- 970.67
The art and architecture of ancient America; the Mexican, Maya, and Andean peoples. Baltimore, Penguin Books [1962] xxxv, 396p. illus., 168 plates, maps. 27cm. (The Pelican history of art, Z21) Bibliography: p. 365-378. [E59.A7K8] 62-5022
1. Indians—Art. 2. Spanish America—Antiq. 3. Art—Spanish America. I. Title. II. Series. BIP

KUBLER, George, 1912- 709'.01'1
The art and architecture of ancient America : the Mexican, Maya, and Andean peoples / George Kubler. 2d ed. Harmondsworth [Eng.] ; Baltimore : Penguin, 1975. xliii, 420 p., [97] leaves of plates : ill. ; 27 cm. (The Pelican history of art) Includes index. Bibliography: p. 385-402. [E59.A7K8 1975] 77-352362 ISBN 0-14-056021-1 : 29.50
1. Indians—Art. 2. Indians—Architecture. 3. Indians—Antiquities. 4. Latin America—Antiquities. I. Title. II. Series.

SCHUSTER, Alfred B 709
The art of two worlds; studies in pre-Columbian and European cultures. New York, Praeger [1959] 188p. illus., 32 plates. 26cm. (Books that matter) 'A publication of the Ibero-Amerikanische Bibliothek, Berlin.' Bibliographical references included in 'Notes' (p. 157-[164]) [N6501.5.S35] 59-7723
1. Indians—Art. 2. Art—Europe. 3. Art—Near East. I. Title.

WUTHENAU, Alexander von. 738.3
The art of terracotta pottery in pre-Columbian Central and South America. [Translated by the author and Irene Nicholson] New York, Crown Publishers [1970, c1969] 203 p. illus. (part col.) 24 cm. (Art of the world; the historical, sociological, and religious backgrounds) Translation of Altamerikanische Tonplastik. Bibliography: p. 192-195. [E59.A7W813] 75-103627 6.95
1. Indians—Art. I. Title. II. Series: Art of the world. BIP

Indians—Art—Addresses, essays, lectures.

PRE-COLUMBIAN art 709'.01'1
history : selected readings / [edited by] Alana Cordy-Collins, Jean Stern. Palo Alto, Calif. : Peek Publications, c1977. vi, 519 p. : ill. ; 26 cm. Includes bibliographies. [E59.A7P66] 78-100680 ISBN 0-917962-41-9 pbk. : 4.95
1. Indians—Art—Addresses, essays, lectures. 2. Indians—Antiquities—Addresses, essays, lectures. 3. America—Antiquities—Addresses, essays, lectures. I. Cordy-Collins, Alana. II. Stern, Jean, 1946-

Indians—Art—Catalogs.

HARVARD University. 709'.01'1
Robert Woods Bliss Collection of Pre-Columbian Art, Washington, D.C.
Pre-Columbian art / edited by Elizabeth P. Benson. Chicago : University of Chicago Press, c1976. p. cm. (A University of

Chicago Press text/fiche) At head of title: Dumbarton Oaks collections. [E59.A7H34 1976] 76-8176 ISBN 0-226-68981-6
1. Bliss, Robert Woods, 1875-1962—Art collections. 2. Indians—Art—Catalogs. 3. Indians—Antiquities—Catalogs. 4. America—Antiquities—Catalogs. I. Benson, Elizabeth P. II. Title. III. Title: Dumbarton Oaks collections.

MINT Museum of Art. 732.2
The Pre-Columbian Collection; [catalog] Research, text, and introd. by M. Keating Griffiss. [Charlotte, N.C., 1970] 20, [55] p. illus. 23 cm. [E59.A7M56 1970] 71-137507
1. Mint Museum of Art. 2. Indians—Art—Catalogs. I. Griffiss, M. Keating.

Indians—Art—Congresses.

ART and environment in 709'.01'1 *native America* / edited by Mary Elizabeth King and Idris R. Traylor, Jr. Lubbock : Texas Tech Press, 1974. 169 p. : ill. ; 26 cm. (Special publications - The Museum, Texas Tech University ; no. 7) Papers presented at a symposium held at The Museum, Texas Tech University on Oct. 29, 1971, sponsored by the International Center for Arid and Semi-arid Land Studies. Includes bibliographies. [E59.A7A68] 74-623588 5.00
1. Indians—Art—Congresses. 2. Man—Influence of environment—Congresses. I. King, Mary Elizabeth. II. Traylor, Idris R. III. International Center for Arid and Semi-arid Land Studies. IV. Series: Texas Tech University. Museum. Special publications ; no. 7.

Indians—Art—Exhibitions.

BLISS, Robert Woods, 970.65717 1875-
Pre-Columbian art. Text and critical analyses by S. K. Lothrop, W. F. Foshag [and] Joy Mahler. New York, Phaidon Publishers; distributed by Garden City Books, 1957. 285 p. illus., plates (part col.) maps. 35 cm. At head of title: Robert Woods Bliss collection. Catalog of the collection which is now in the National Gallery of Art. [E59.A7B63] 57-14181
1. Indians—Art—Exhibitions. 2. Latin America—Antiquities. I. Lothrop, Samuel Kirkland, 1892- II. U.S. National Gallery of Art. III. Title.

CORNELL University. 709.01'1 Andrew Dickson White Museum of Art.
Pre-Columbian art of Latin America, 10th century B.C.-16th century A.D. [Ithaca, N.Y., Cornell University, Office of University Publications, 1966] 47 p. illus., map. 25 cm. An exhibition prepared in association with the Cornell Latin American Year and held May 14-June 26, 1966 at the Andrew Dickson White Museum of Art. Bibliography: p. 47. [E59.A7C6] 66-23112
1. Indians—Art—Exhibitions. 2. Latin America—Antiquities. I. Title.

EASBY, Elizabeth 730'.9701 Kennedy.
Before Cortes, sculpture of Middle America; a centennial exhibition at the Metropolitan Museum of Art from September 30, 1970 through January 3, 1971. Catalogue by Elizabeth Kennedy Easby and John F. Scott. Foreword by Thomas P. F. Hoving. Pref. by Dudley T. Easby, Jr. [New York] Metropolitan Museum of Art; distributed by New York Graphic Society [1970] 322 p. illus. (part col.), col. maps. 29 cm. Bibliography: p. 319. [E59.A7E17] 74-123875 16.95
1. Indians—Art—Exhibitions. I. Scott, John Frederik, 1936- joint author. II. New York (City). Metropolitan Museum of Art. III. Title.

HARVARD University. Robert 709'.8 Woods Bliss Collection of Pre-Columbian Art, Washington, D.C.
Handbook. Washington, Dumbarton Oaks, Trustees for Harvard University [c1963] xi, 78 [103] p. illus., maps, plates. 23 cm. Bibliography: p. 77 (2d group) [E59.A7H34] 66-8021
1. Indians — Art — Exhibitions. I. Title.

NEW York (City). Museum 709.01'1 of Modern Art.
American sources of modern art, May 10 to June 30, 1933, the Museum of Modern Art ... New York. Reprint ed. [New York] Published for the Museum of Modern Art by Arno Press, 1969 [c1933] 50 p., [54] p. of illus. 27 cm. "American sources of modern art" (p. 5-21) signed: Holger Cahill. Bibliography: p. 23-28. [E59.A7N4 1969] 78-86426
1. Indians—Art—Exhibitions. I. Cahill, Holger, 1893-1960. II. Title. BIP

NEW York (City) Museum of 732'.2 Primitive Art.
Precolumbian art in New York; selections from private collections. [New York]; Distributed by New York Graphic Society, Greenwich, Conn. [1969] [68] p. illus. 31 cm. Exhibition shown Sept. 12 - Nov. 9, 1969. Bibliography: p. [67]-[68] [E59.A7N43] 70-93956
1. Indians—Art—Exhibitions. 2. Art—Private collections—New York (City) I. Title.

NEW York (City). Museum 709'.01'1 of the American Indian, Heye Foundation.
Indian art of the Americas : [a touring exhibition] / text by Frederick J. Dockstader ; photography by Carmelo Guadagno. New York : Museum of the American Indian, Heye Foundation, 1973. 304 p., [12] leaves of plates : ill. (some col.) ; 28 cm. Catalog of the exhibition. Bibliography: p. 297-304. [E59.A7N46 1973a] 73-89979
1. Indians—Art—Exhibitions. I. Dockstader, Frederick J. II. Title.

NEW York (City). 709'.01'109701 Museum of the American Indian, Heye Foundation.
Masterworks from the Museum of the American Indian, Heye Foundation. Introd. by Frederick J. Dockstader. [New York] Metropolitan Museum of Art [1973] 63 p. illus. 27 cm. Catalog of an exhibition held at the Metropolitan Museum of Art, New York, Oct. 18 to Dec. 31, 1973. Bibliography: p. 63. [E59.A7N46 1973] 73-16278 ISBN 0-87099-082-9 2.50 (pbk.)
1. New York (City). Museum of the American Indian, Heye Foundation. 2. Indians—Art—Exhibitions. I. New York (City). Metropolitan Museum of Art. II. Title.

THOMSON, Charlotte. 732'.2
Ancient art of the Americas from New England collections; exhibition and catalogue by Charlotte Thomson. Boston, Museum of Fine Arts [1971] 141 p. illus. (part col.) 24 cm. Exhibition held at the Museum of Fine Arts, Boston, Dec. 2, 1971-May 28, 1972. Bibliography: p. 140. [E59.A7T5] 70-183709 ISBN 0-87846-062-4
1. Indians—Art—Exhibitions. I. Boston. Museum of Fine Arts. II. Title.

Indians—Basket making.

MASON, Otis Tufton, 1838- 746.4'1 1908.
Aboriginal American basketry : studies in a textile art without machinery / Otis Tufton Mason. Santa Barbara, [Calif.] : P. Smith, 1976. ix, 137-548 p., 248 [i.e. 124] leaves of plates : ill. ; 23 cm. Reprint of the 1904 ed. published by Govt. Print. Off., Washington, which was issued as Annual report of the Board of Regents of the Smithsonian Institution for the year ending June 30, 1902 and also as Document no. 484 of House of Representatives, 57th Congress, 2d session. Bibliography: p. 545-548. [E59.B3M3 1976] 76-11828 ISBN 0-87905-034-9 pbk. : 8.50
1. Indians—Basket making. I. Title. II. Series: Smithsonian Institution. Annual report of the Board of regents.

MASON, Otis Tufton, 1838- 746.4'1 1908.
Aboriginal Indian basketry. [Glorieta, N.M., Rio Grande Press, 1970] 169-548 p. illus., plates (part col.) 29 cm. (Annual report of the Board of Regents of the Smithsonian Institution) (57th Congress, 2d session. House of Representatives. Document no. 484.) (A Rio Grande classic.) Cover title. Reprint of the 1902 ed., published under title: Aboriginal American basketry: studies in a textile art without machinery. Bibliography: p. 545-548. [E59.B3M3 1970] 71-112623
1. Indians—Basket making. I. Title. II. Series: Smithsonian Institution. Annual report of the Board of Regents. III. Series: U.S. 57th Cong., 2d sess., 1902-1903. House. Document no. 484

Indians—Bibliography—Catalogs.

UNIVERSITY of 016.91'0039'69881 Guyana. Library.
A catalogue of the Roth collection in the University of Guyana Library. Compiled by Carol Collins. Georgetown, 1971. ii, 32 l. 28 cm. (University of Guyana Library series, no. 4) "Select bibliography of the published works of W. E. Roth": leaf ii. [Z1209.U584 1971] 74-160789
1. Roth, Walter Edmund, 1861?-1933—Library. 2. Indians—Bibliography—Catalogs. 3. Australian aborigines—Bibliography—Catalogs. I. Title. II. Series: University of Guyana. Library. University of Guyana Library series, no. 4.

Indians—City planning.

HARDOY, Jorge Enrique. 711'.4'098
Urban planning in pre-Columbian America [by] Jorge Hardoy. New York, Braziller [1968] 128 p. illus., maps, plans. 25 cm. (Planning and cities) Bibliography: p. 121-123. [E59.C55H3] 68-24700 5.95
1. Indians—City planning. 2. Cities and towns—Planning—Latin America. 3. Latin America—Antiquities. I. Title. BIP

Indians—Costume and adornment.

WELCH, Frankie. 739.27'09701
Indian jewelry; how to wear, buy, and treasure America's first fashion pieces. McLean, Va., EMP Publications, 1973. 77 p. illus. 19 cm. [E59.C6W44] 73-89560
1. Indians—Costume and adornment. 2. Jewelry. I. Title.

Indians—Dwellings—Juvenile literature.

LAVINE, Sigmund A. 392'.36'0097
The houses the Indians built / Sigmund A. Lavine. Illustrated with photos. and old prints. New York : Dodd, Mead, [1975] 89 p. : ill. ; 24 cm. Includes index. Text and illustrations survey the homes built by various North and South American Indian tribes. [E59.D9L38] 74-25524 ISBN 0-396-07076-0 lib.bdg. 4.95
1. Indians—Dwellings—Juvenile literature. I. Title. BIP

Indians—Goldsmithing.

EMMERICH, Andre. 980.6739
Sweat of the sun and tears of the moon: gold and silver in pre-Columbian art. Seattle, University of Washington Press, 1965. xxiii, 216 p. illus., facsims., col. map (on lining papers) 4 col. plates. 25 cm. Bibliography: p. 193-206. [E59.A7E6] 65-10819
1. Indians—Goldsmithing. 2. Indians—Silversmithing. 3. Latin America—Antiquities. 4. Indians—Art. I. Title. BIP

Indians—Money.

TAXAY, Don. 332.49'701
Money of the American Indians and other primitive currencies of the Americas. New York, Nummus Press [1970] 158 p. illus. 25 cm. Includes bibliographical references. [E59.M7T3] 78-141349 5.95
1. Indians—Money. I. Title.

Indians of Central America—Collected works.

HANDBOOK of Middle 970.4'2 *American Indians.* Robert Wauchope, general editor. Austin, University of Texas Press [1964-76] 16 v. illus., maps, plans. 28 cm. Contents.Contents.—v. 1. Natural environment and early cultures, R. C. West, vol. editor.—v. 2-3. Archaeology of southern Mesoamerica, G. R. Willey, vol. editor.—v. 4. Archaeological frontiers and external connections, G. F. Ekholm and G. R. Willey, vol. editors.—v. 5. Linguistics, N. A. McQuown, vol. editor.—v. 6. Social anthropology, M. Nash, vol. editor.—v. 7-8. Ethnology, E. Z. Vogt, vol. editor.—v. 9. Physical anthropology, T. D. Stewart, vol. editor.—v. 10-11. Archae[o]logy of northern Mesoamerica, G. F. Elkholm and I. Bernal, vol. editors.—v. 12-15. Guide to ethnohistorical sources, H. F. Cline, vol. editor.—v. 16. Sources cited and artifacts illustrated, M. A. L. Harrison, vol. editor. Includes bibliographies. [F1434.H3] 64-10316 ISBN 0-292-70014-8 (v. 9) 15.00 (v. 9) varies
1. Indians of Central America—Collected works. 2. Indians of Mexico—Collected works. I. Wauchope, Robert, 1909- ed. BIP

Indians of Central America—Guatemala—Industries.

OSBORNE, Lilly de 745.09728 Jongh.
Indian crafts of Guatemala and El Salvador. [1st ed.] Norman, University of Oklahoma Press [1965] xxvi, 278 p. maps (part fold.) plates (part col.) 24 cm. (The Civilization of the American Indian series, 79) Bibliography: p. 252-257. [F1465.3.I5O8] 65-11242
1. Indians of Central America—Guatemala—Industries. 2. Indians of Central America—Salvador—Industries. 3. Indians of Central America—Costume and adornment. 4. Indians of Central America—Textile industry and fabrics. I. Title. II. Series. BIP

OSBORNE, Lilly de 746'.097281 Jongh.
Indian crafts of Guatemala and El Salvador / by Lilly de Jongh Osborne ; foreword by J. Eric S. Thompson ; paintings by Julia Ayau de Lopez Escobar. 2d printing, with revisions, changes, additions. Norman : University of Oklahoma Press, 1975. xxvi, 385 p., [2] leaves of plates : ill. (some col.) ; 24 cm. (The Civilization of the American Indian series ; v. 79) Includes index. Bibliography: p. 358-363. [F1465.3.I5O8 1975] 76-351424 15.00
1. Indians of Central America—Guatemala—Industries. 2. Indians of Central America—Salvador—Industries. 3. Indians of Central America—Costume and adornment. 4. Indians of Central America—Textile industry and fabrics. I. Title. II. Series.

Indians of Central America—Nicaragua—Pottery.

WYCKOFF, Lydia L. 738.3'097285
A suggested Nicaraguan pottery sequence based on the museum collection, by Lydia L. Wyckoff. New York, Museum of the American Indian, Heye Foundation, 1971. x, 42, [45] p. illus. 17 cm. (Indian notes and monographs. Miscellaneous series, no. 58) Bibliography: p. 39-42 (2d group) [F1525.3.P6W9] 75-139868
1. Indians of Central America—Nicaragua—Pottery. I. New York (City). Museum of the American Indian, Heye Foundation. II. Title. III. Series: New York (City). Museum of the American Indian, Heye Foundation. Indian notes and monographs. Miscellaneous series, no. 58. BIP

Indians of Central America—Panama—Antiquities.

SAPIR, Olga Linares de. 970 s
Ecology and the arts in ancient Panama : on the development of social rank and symbolism in the central provinces / Olga F. Linares. Washington : Dumbarton Oaks, Trustees for Harvard University, 1977. 86 p. : ill. ; 27 cm. (Studies in pre-Colombian art and archaeology ; no. 17) Bibliography: p. 80-86. [E51.S85 no. 17] [F1565] 972.87 77-86627 pbk. : 6.00
1. Indians of Central America—Panama—Antiquities. 2. Panama—Antiquities. 3. Sitio Conte site, Panama. 4. Indians of Central America—Panama—Art. 5. Cocle, Panama (Province)—Antiquities. I. Title. II. Series. BIP

(chiefly illus.) 24 cm. (Dover pictorial archives) [F1219.3.A7E497 1971] 73-168905 ISBN 0-486-22794-4 1.50
1. Indians of Mexico—Art. 2. Spindle-whorls. I. Title. BIP

FIELD, Frederick Vanderbilt, 1905- 761
Pre-Hispanic Mexican stamp designs / by Frederick V. Field. New York : Dover Publications, 1974. xiv, 208 p. : chiefly ill. ; 29 cm. (Dover pictorial archive series) Bibliography: p. [207]-208. [F1219.3.A7F45] 73-89751 ISBN 0-486-23039-2 pbk. : 4.00
1. Indians of Mexico—Art. 2. Indians of Mexico—Antiquities. 3. Mexico—Antiquities. 4. Design, Decorative—Mexico. I. Title. BIP

GRIFFITH, James S. 709'.72'1
Legacy of conquest; the arts of Northwest Mexico [by] James S. Griffith. [Colorado Springs] Taylor Museum of the Colorado Springs Fine Arts Center, c1967. 32 p. illus. 21 cm. Bibliography: p. 32. [F1219.3.A7G68] 68-4582
1. Indians of Mexico—Art. I. Colorado Springs Fine Arts Center. Taylor Museum. II. Title.

GROTH-KIMBALL, Irmgard. 972.01
The art of ancient Mexico. 109 photos. by Irmgard Groth-Kimball; text and notes by Franz Feuchtwanger. London, New York, Thames and Hudson [1954] 125p. illus., map. 32cm. [F1219.3.A7G713] 913.72 54-4625
1. Indians of Mexico—Art. 2. Mexico—Antiq. 3. Art—Mexico. I. Feuchtwanger, Franz. II. Title.

HELFRITZ, Hans, 1902- 970.4'2
Mexican cities of the gods; an archaeological guide. New York, Praeger [1970] 180 p. illus., maps, plans. 22 cm. Translation of Die Gotterburgen Mexikos. Bibliography: p. 178. [F1219.3.A7H413] 75-85518 6.95
1. Indians of Mexico—Art. 2. Indians of Mexico—Antiquities. 3. Mexico—Description and travel—1951- I. Title.

KLEIN, Cecelia F. 709'.01'1
The face of the earth : frontality in two-dimensional Mesoamerican art / Cecelia F. Klein. New York : Garland Pub., 1976. 366 p. : ill. ; 21 cm. (Outstanding dissertations in the fine arts) Originally presented as the author's thesis, Columbia University, 1972, under the title: Frontality in postclassic Mexican two-dimensional art. Bibliography: p. 264-293. [F1219.3.A7K44 1976] 75-23799 ISBN 0-8240-1994-6 lib.bdg. : 27.50
1. Indians of Mexico—Art. 2. Indians of Mexico—Religion and mythology. I. Title. II. Series. BIP

LOS Angeles Co., Calif. Museum of Art, Los Angeles. 732'.2'09723
Sculpture of ancient west Mexico, Nayarit, Jalisco, Colima; the Proctor Stafford Collection. [Articles by] Michael Kan, Clement Meighan [and] H. B. Nicholson. [Los Angeles, 1970] 116 p. illus. (part col.), col. map. 28 cm. Exhibition held July 7-Aug. 30, 1970 at the Los Angeles County Museum of Art. Bibliography: p. 112-114. [F1219.3.A7L6] 72-130462
1. Indians of Mexico—Art. I. Kan, Michael. II. Meighan, Clement Woodward, 1925- III. Nicholson, Henry B. IV. Title.

PRECOLUMBIAN art of North America and Mexico; 709'.01'10972
general editor Francesco Abbate; translated [from the Italian] by Elizabeth Evans. London, New York, Octopus Books, 1972. 159 p., chiefly 98 col. illus. 20 cm. Translation of Arte precolumbiana. Bibliography: p. 154. [F1219.3.A7P7213] 73-151904 ISBN 0-7064-0030-5 2.95
1. Indians of Mexico—Art. 2. Indians of North America—Art. I. Abbate, Francesco, ed.

PREHISPANIC Mexican art [by] Paul Westheim [and others] 709'.01'1
Translated under the direction of Lancelot C. Sheppard. New York, Putnam [1972] 447 p. illus. (part col.) 34 cm. "A Ginger book." Bibliography: p. 397-398. [F1219.3.A7P7313] 70-142463 37.50
1. Indians of Mexico—Art. I. Westheim, Paul.

SHAO, Paul, 1940- 709'.01'1
Asiatic influence in Pre-Colombian American art / Paul Shao. 1st ed. Ames : Iowa State University Press, 1976. p. cm. Includes bibliographies. [F1219.A7S52] 76-22631 ISBN 0-8138-1855-9 : 25.00
1. Indians of Mexico—Art. 2. Indians of Central America—Art. 3. Indians—Transpacific influences. 4. Indians—Chinese influences. I. Title.

VON WINNING, Hasso. 732.2
Pre-Columbian art of Mexico and Central America. Text and notes by Hasso Von Winning Selection of plates by Alfred Stendahl New York, Abrams [1968] xv, 388 p. illus. (part col.), maps. 34 cm. Bibliography: p. 386-388. [F1219.3.A7V6] 68-13065
1. Indians of Mexico—Art. 2. Indians of Central America—Art. I. Title. BIP

WESTHEIM, Paul 970.67
The art of ancient Mexico. Tr. from Spanish by Ursula Bernard. Garden City, N.Y., Doubleday [c.]1965. xvii, 260p. illus., plans, plates. 19cm. (First pub. in Spanish, tr. from the orig. German by Mariana Frenk, as Arte antiguo de Mexico in 1950) Bibl. (Anchor bk., A416) [F1219.3.A7W413] 64-19224 1.95 pap.,
1. Indians of Mexico—Art. 2. Mexico—Antiq. I. Title.

Indians of Mexico—Art—Bibliography.

KENDALL, Aubyn. 016.972
The art and archaeology of pre-Columbian middle America : an annotated bibliography of works in English / Aubyn Kendall. Boston : G. K. Hall, c1977. p. cm. (Reference publications in Latin American studies) Includes index. [Z1208.M4K45] [F1219.3.A7] 77-14146 ISBN 0-8161-8093-8 : 25.00
1. Indians of Mexico—Art—Bibliography. 2. Indians of Central America—Art—Bibliography. 3. Indians of Mexico—Antiquities—Bibliography. 4. Indians of Central America—Antiquities—Bibliography. 5. Mexico—Antiquities—Bibliography. 6. Central America—Antiquities—Bibliography. I. Title. II. Series. BIP

KENDALL, Aubyn. 016.709'72
The art of pre-Columbian Mexico: an annotated bibliography of works in English. Austin, Institute of Latin American Studies, University of Texas at Austin, 1973. x, 115 p. illus. 23 cm. (Guides and bibliographies series, 5) [Z1208.M4K46] 72-96193
1. Indians of Mexico—Art—Bibliography. I. Title. II. Series. BIP

Indians of Mexico—Art—Congresses.

ORIGINS of religious art & iconography in preclassic Mesoamerica 709'.01'1
/ edited by H. B. Nicholson. [Los Angeles] : UCLA Latin American Center Publications, 1976. vii, 181 p., [1] fold. leaf of plates : ill. ; 29 cm. (UCLA Latin American studies series ; v. 31) Consists of some of the papers presented at a conference held at the University of California Los Angeles, Feb. 25-26, 1973, sponsored by the Ethnic Arts Council of Los Angeles, and others. Includes bibliographies and index. [F1219.3.A7O75] 75-620028 ISBN 0-87903-031-3 : 17.50
1. Indians of Mexico—Art—Congresses. 2. Indians of Central America—Art—Congresses. 3. Indians of Mexico—Religion and mythology—Congresses. 4. Indians of Central America—Religion and mythology—Congresses. I. Nicholson, Henry B. II. Ethnic Arts Council of Los Angeles.

Indians of Mexico—Art—Exhibitions.

EDWARD H. Merrin Gallery. 732'.2
Works of art from pre-Columbian Mexico and Guatemala. New York [1971] 1 v. (chiefly illus.) 28 cm. Catalog of an exhibition held in the autumn, 1971. [F1219.3.A7E3] 74-198534
1. Indians of Mexico—Art—Exhibitions. 2. Indians of Central America—Guatemala—Art—Exhibitions. I. Title.

LINDUFF, Katheryn M. 732'.2'09701
Ancient art of middle America : selections from the Jay C. Leff Collection : Huntington Galleries, February 17 through June 9, 1974 / Katheryn M. Linduff. [Huntington? W. Va. : s.n., 1974] 124 p. : ill. ; 21 x 26 cm. Bibliography: p. 121-122. [F1219.3.A7L48] 74-76892
1. Leff, Jay C.—Art collections. 2. Indians of Mexico—Art—Exhibitions. 3. Indians of Central America—Art—Exhibitions. I. Huntington Galleries. II. Title.

Indians of Mexico—Baja California.

MEIGHAN, Clement Woodward, 1925- 970.4'2
Indian art and history; the testimony of prehispanic rock paintings in Baja California [by] Clement W. Meighan. Los Angeles, Dawson's Book Shop, 1969. 79 p. illus. (part col.), map, col. plates. 23 cm. (Baja California travels series, 13) Bibliography: p. 77-79. [F1219.3.A7M42] 79-82462
1. Indians of Mexico—Baja California. 2. Indians of Mexico—Art. I. Title. II. Series.

Indians of Mexico—Baja California—Antiquities.

CROSBY, Harry, 1926- 972'.2'00497
The cave paintings of Baja California : the great murals of an unknown people / written and photographed by Harry Crosby ; other ill. by Joanne Haskell Crosby ; commissioned by Helen K. Copley ; edited by Richard F. Pourade. [La Jolla, Calif.] : Copley Books, c1975. p. cm. Sequel to The King's Highway in Baja California. Bibliography: p. [F1219.1.B3C76] 75-18265
1. Indians of Mexico—Baja California—Antiquities. 2. Rock paintings—Mexico—Baja California. 3. Petroglyphs—Baja California. 4. Baja California—Antiquities. I. Title. BIP

GRANT, Campbell, 1909- 732'.2'09701
Rock art of Baja California. With Notes on the pictographs of Baja California by Leon Diguet (1895), translated by Roxanne Lapidus. Los Angeles, Calif., Dawson's Book Shop, 1974. 146 p. illus., maps, col. plates. 23 cm. (Baja California travels series, 33) Diguet's article was originally published in Paris in L'anthropologie, v. 6 (1895), p. 160-175. Bibliography: p. 129-135. [F1219.1.B3G72] 73-89732 ISBN 0-87093-233-0 24.00
1. Indians of Mexico—Baja California—Antiquities. 2. Baja California—Antiquities. 3. Rock paintings—Mexico—Baja California. 4. Petroglyphs—Baja California. I. Diguet, Leon. Note sur la pictographie de la Basse-Californie. English. 1974. II. Title. III. Series.

MASSEY, William C. 970.4'2'2
The Castaldi collection from central and southern Baja California [by] William C. Massey. [Berkeley, University of California, Dept. of Anthropology, 1966] vii, 76 p. illus., map. 28 cm. (Contributions of the University of California Archaeological Research Facility, no. 2) Bibliography: p. 74-76. [E51.C2 no. 2] 67-64781
1. Indians of Mexico—Baja California—Antiquities. I. Title. II. Series: California. University. Archaeological Research Facility. Contributions, no. 2

SEVEN rock art sites in Baja, California 972.2
/ by Clement W. Meighan ... [et al.] ; edited by Clement W. Meighan and V. L. Pontoni. Socorro, N.M. : Ballena Press, c1978. v, 236 p. : ill. ; 27 cm. (Ballena Press publications on North American rock art ; no. 2) Bibliography: p. 231-236. [F1219.1.B3S48] 79-108547 8.95
1. Indians of Mexico— Baja California—Antiquities. 2. Petroglyphs—Mexico—Baja California. 3. Rock paintings—Mexico—Baja California. 4. Baja California—Antiquities. 5. Mexico—Antiquities. I. Meighan, Clement Woodward, 1925- II. Pontoni, V. L. III. Title. IV. Series. BIP

Indians of Mexico — Congresses.

SYMPOSIUM on Middle American Anthropology, Boston, 1955. 970.42
Antropologia de Mesoamerica. [Symposium de la American Anthropological Association] Ed. de Gordon R. Willey, Evon Z. Vogt y Angel Palerm. Washington, Union Panamericana, 1960. 2 v. 25 cm. (Estudios monograficos, 5 y 10) Issued also in English. Contents.Contents. -- v. La Argueologia mesoamericana desde 1906, por A. Kidder. Las secuencias regionales en Mesoamerica y sus relaciones, por G. F. Ekholm. Estudios sobre arte mesoamericano, por T. Proskouriakoff. Investigaciones sobre la escritura jeroglifica Maya, por J. E. S. Thompson. -- v. Linguistica mesoamericana: 1955, por N. A. McQuown. Etnografia mesoamericana, por P. Carrasco. Antropologia aplicada en Mexico, por A. Caso y G. Aguirre Beltran. Teoria en etnologia mesoamericana, por J. Guillin. El problema de la subsistencia en la historia mesonamericana, por H. Aschmann. Includes bibliographies. [F1434.S95 1955a] P A
1. Indians of Mexico — Congresses. 2. Indians of Central America — Congresses. 3. Mexico — Antiq. — Congresses. 4. Central America — Antiq. — Congresses. I. Willey, Gordon Randolph, 1913- ed. II. American Anthropological Association. III. Title. IV. Series: Pan American Union. Social Science Section. Estudios monograficos, 5 [etc.]

Indians of Mexico—Durango, Mexico (State)—Pottery.

KELLEY, J. Charles, 1913- 972 s
An introduction to the ceramics of the Chalchihuites culture of Zacatecas and Durango, Mexico / by J. Charles Kelley, Ellen Abbott Kelley ; ill. by Sandra Rife. Carbondale : University Museum, Southern Illinois University, c1971- v. : ill. ; 28 cm. (Research records - University Museum, Southern Illinois University : Mesoamerican studies ; no. 5) Contents.Contents.—pt. 1. The decorated wares. Bibliography: pt. 1, p. 181-182. [F1219.M57 no. 5] [F1219.1.D86] 972'.4 74-146048
1. Indians of Mexico—Durango, Mexico (State)—Pottery. 2. Indians of Mexico—Zacatecas, Mexico (State)—Pottery. 3. Chalchihuites, Mexico. 4. Indians of Mexico—Antiquities. 5. Mexico—Antiquities. I. Kelley, Ellen Abbott, joint author. II. Title: An introduction to the ceramics of the Chalchihuites culture ... III. Series: Mesoamerican studies ; no. 5.

Indians of Mexico—Durango (State)—Implements.

SPENCE, Michael W. 970.1'08 s
Some lithic assemblages of Western Zacatecas and Durango, Mexico, by Michael W. Spence. Carbondale, University Museum, Southern Illinois University [1971] v, 50 l. illus. 28 cm. (Mesoamerican studies, no. 8) Bibliography: leaves 27-30. [F1219.M57 no. 8] [F1219.3.I4] 972'.1 70-170332
1. Indians of Mexico—Durango (State)—Implements. 2. Indians of Mexico—Zacatecas (State)—Implements. 3. Durango, Mexico (State)—Antiquities. 4. Zacatecas, Mexico (State)—Antiquities. I. Title. II. Series.

Indians of Mexico—Hist.

GARTH, Charles Meredith. 972.01
The flower weavers; builders of old Mexico. With 24 photos.[1st ed.] New York, Exposition Press [1954] 119p. illus. 21cm. (A Banner book) Includes bibliography. [F1219.G37] 54-10974
1. Indians of Mexico—Hist. 2. Mexico—Antiq. 3. Mexico—Descr. & trav. 4. Art—Mexico. I. Title.

Indians of Mexico—Masks—Exhibitions.

MEXICAN masks. 731'.75
[Essay by Donald Cordry. Fort Worth, Amon Carter Museum of Western Art, c1973] 32 p. illus. 25 cm. Cover title.

Catalog of an exhibition from the collection of Mr. and Mrs. Donald Cordry, presented at Witte Memorial Museum, San Antonio, Jan. 6—Mar. 3, 1974, and other museums. [F1219.3.M4M48] 73-92100 ISBN 0-88360-004-8
1. Indians of Mexico—Masks—Exhibitions. I. Cordry, Donald Bush. II. Amon Carter Museum of Western Art, Fort Worth, Tex. III. Witte Memorial Museum, San Antonio. **BIP**

Indians of Mexico — Oaxaca [State]

WILLIAMS, Gerald. 970.6746
Textiles of Oaxaca. [Photos. of exhibition textiles by Gerda Peterich, others by the author] Manchester, N.H., Currier Gallery of Art [c1964] 63 p. maps, plates. 23 cm. At head of title: Hopkins Center, Dartmouth College, Hanover, N.H. "Exhibiting institutions: Syracuse University [and others]" "Catalogue": p. 39-43. Bibliography: p. 37-38. [F1219.1.O11W5] 65-2825
1. Indians of Mexico — Oaxaca [State] 2. Indians of Mexico — Textile industry and fabrics. I. Dartmouth College. Hopkins Center. II. Currier Gallery of Art. Manchester, N.H. III. Title.

Indians of Mexico—Pottery.

BRENNER, Anita, 1905- 738
The influence of technique on the decorative style in the domestic pottery of Culhuacan. New York, AMS Press [1969] 94, [1] p. illus. 24 cm. (Columbia University contributions to anthropology, v. 13) At head of title: Publicacion de la Escuela internacional de acqueologia y etnologia americanas. Reprint of the 1931 ed. Bibliography: p. [95] [F1219.3.P8B84 1969] 78-82356
1. Indians of Mexico—Pottery. 2. Culhuacan, Mexico (Federal District)—Antiquities. I. Title. II. Title: The domestic pottery of Culhuacan. III. Series: Columbia University. Columbia University contributions to anthropology, v. 13 **BIP**

MATHENY, Ray T. 970.4 s
The ceramics of Aguacatal, Campacha, Mexico, by Ray T. Matheny. Provo, Utah, New World Archaeological Foundation, Brigham Young University, 1970. xiii, 155 p. illus. 27 cm. (Papers of the New World Archaeological Foundation, no. 27) A revision of the author's thesis, University of Oregon. Bibliography: p. 153-155. [F1219.N475 no. 27] [F1435.3.P8] 970.4'26 72-189439
1. Indians of Mexico—Pottery. 2. Aguacatal site, Mexico. I. Title. II. Series: New World Archaeological Foundation. Papers, no. 27.

THE Natalie Wood 732'.2
collection of pre-Columbian ceramics from Chupicuaro, Guanajuato, Mexico, at UCLA. Edited by Jay D. Frierman. Los Angeles, Museum & Laboratories of Ethnic Arts & Technology, University of California, 1969. xv, 92 p. illus. (part col.), maps. 29 cm. (University of California, Los Angeles. Museum and Laboratories of Ethnic Arts & Technology. Occasional papers, no. 1) Contents.Contents.—A reappraisal of Chupicuaro, by M. P. Weaver.—West Mexican radiocarbon dates of archaeologic significance, by R. E. Taylor [and others]—The extent of the Chupicuaro tradition, by H. W. McBride.—Photographic catalog of the Natalie Wood collection at UCLA.—Appendix: Inventory of burials and associated objects excavated in 1946-47 by the Instituto Nacional de Antropologia e Historia at Chupicuaro, Guanajuato, Mexico. Includes bibliographies. [F1219.1.C54N3] 68-66110
1. Wood, Natalie—Art collections. 2. Indians of Mexico—Pottery. 3. Chupicuaro, Mexico—Autiquities. I. Frierman, Jay D., ed. II. Weaver, Muriel Porter. III. California. University. University at Los Angeles. Museum and Laboratories of Ethnic Arts and Technology. IV. Series: California. University. University at Los Angeles. Museum and Laboratories of Ethnic Arts and Technology. Occasional papers, no. 1

Indians of Mexico—Pyramids.

TOMPKINS, Peter. 972
Mysteries of the Mexican pyramids / by Peter Tompkins ; with historic ill. from many sources, and original drawings by Hugh Harleston, Jr. 1st ed. New York : Harper & Row, c1976. p. cm. Includes index. Bibliography: p. [F1219.3.P9T58 1976] 74-15857 ISBN 0-06-014324-X : 18.50
1. Indians of Mexico—Pyramids. 2. Mexico—Antiquities. 3. Occult sciences—Mexico. I. Title. **BIP**

Indians of Mexico—Sculpture—Congresses.

THE Iconography of 732'.2'0972
Middle American sculpture. Texts by Ignacio Bernal [and others] [New York] Metropolitan Museum of Art [1973] 167 p. illus. 25 cm. "The papers in this volume, a companion to the exhibition catalogue, Before Cortes, were presented at a symposium held at the Metropolitan Museum during October 1970." Includes bibliographies. [F1219.3.A7I25] 73-4975 ISBN 0-87099-075-6 12.50
1. Indians of Mexico—Sculpture—Congresses. 2. Indians of Central America—Sculpture—Congresses. 3. Mexico—Antiquities—Congresses. 4. Central America—Antiquities—Congresses. I. Bernal, Ignacio. II. New York (City). Metropolitan Museum of Art. III. Easby, Elizabeth Kennedy. Before Cortes, sculpture of Middle America.

Indians of Mexico—Sculpture—Exhibitions.

DWYER, Jane Powell. 730
Fire, earth, and water : sculpture from the Land Collection of Mesoamerican Art : [exhibited at the Fine Arts Museums of San Francisco, California Palace of the Legion of Honor, July 4, 1975-September 14, 1975, Honolulu Academy of Arts, January-March, 1976, Seattle Art Museum, April-June, 1976] / by Jane P. Dwyer and Edward B. Dwyer ; [photos. by James Medley ; ill. by Wendy Kitamata]. [San Francisco] : Fine Arts Museums of San Francisco, c1975. 141 p. : ill. (some col.) ; 28 cm. Bibliography: p. 138-139. [F1219.3.A7D98] 75-14770 ISBN 0-88401-006-6 pbk. : 7.95
1. Land, Lewis K.—Art collections. 2. Indians of Mexico—Sculpture—Exhibitions. 3. Indians of Central America—Sculpture—Exhibitions. I. Dwyer, Edward Bridgman, joint author. II. California Palace of the Legion of Honor, San Francisco. III. Honolulu Academy of Arts. IV. Seattle. Art Museum. V. Title.

Indians of Mexico—Seals (Numismatics)

FIELD, Frederick 929.8
Vanderbilt, 1905-
Thoughts on the meaning and use of pre-Hispanic Mexican sellos, by Frederick V. Field. Washington, Dumbarton Oaks, Trustees for Harvard University, 1967. 48 p. illus. 28 cm. (Studies in pre-Columbian art and archaeology, no. 3) Bibliography: p. 48. [E51.S85 no. 3] 67-31521 2.00
1. Indians of Mexico—Seals (Numismatics) I. Title. II. Series. **BIP**

Indians of Mexico—Sonora—Dwellings.

FAY, George Emory, 1927- 728
An Indian-Mexican house type in Sonora, Mexico, by George E. Fay. Greeley, Colorado State College, Museum of Anthropology, 1969. 9 l. illus., plan. 28 cm. (Museum of Anthropology miscellaneous series, no. 5) Cover title. Bibliography: leaf 9. [GN4.U53 no. 5] 75-630805
1. Indians of Mexico—Sonora—Dwellings. 2. Dwellings—Sonora, Mexico. I. Title. II. Series: Colorado. State College, Greeley. Museum of Anthropology. Miscellaneous series, no. 5

Indians of Mexico—Textile industry and fabrics.

GOODMAN, Frances 746.4'4'0972
Schaill.
The embroidery of Mexico and Guatemala / by Frances Schaill Goodman. New York : Scribner, c1976. 81 p. : ill. ; 28 cm. Includes index. [F1219.3.T4G66] 75-29325 ISBN 0-684-14498-0 : 14.95
1. Indians of Mexico—Textile industry and fabrics. 2. Indians of Central America—Guatemala—Textile industry and fabrics. 3. Embroidery—Mexico. 4. Embroidery—Central America. I. Title. **BIP**

Indians of Mexico—Veracruz—Art.

ANCIENT art of Veracruz, 732'.2
February 23, 1971-June 13, 1971; an exhibit sponsored by the Ethnic Arts Council of Los Angeles at the Los Angeles County Museum of Natural History. [Los Angeles, Ethnic Arts Council of Los Angeles, 1971] 92 p. illus. (part col.), map (p. [2] of cover) 28 cm. Bibliography: p. 92 and p. [3] of cover. [F1219.1.V47A8] 76-26955
1. Indians of Mexico—Veracruz—Art. I. Ethnic Arts Council of Los Angeles. II. Los Angeles Co., Calif. Museum of Natural History, Los Angeles.

Indians of North America—Alabama—Antiquities—Exhibitions.

HUNTINGDON College, 976.1
Montgomery, Ala. Art Gallery.
Huntingdon College bicentennial exhibition of pre-Columbian art and culture, November 3-December 13, 1975, Huntingdon College Art Gallery / [text by David Chase]. Montgomery, Ala. : The Gallery, c1975. [48] p. : ill. ; 18 x 23 cm. [E78.A28H86 1975] 76-350297
1. Indians of North America—Alabama—Antiquities—Exhibitions. 2. Alabama—Antiquities—Exhibitions. 3. Indians—Antiquities—Exhibitions. 4. America—Antiquities—Exhibitions. I. Chase, David W. II. Title. III. Title: Exhibition of pre-Columbian art and culture.

Indians of North America—Alabama—Art—Exhibitions.

MELLOWN, Robert O. 709'.01'1
The art of the Alabama Indians / Robert O. Mellown. [University] : University of Alabama Art Gallery, 1976. 43 p. : ill. ; 21 cm. Catalog of an exhibition. Bibliography: p. 43. [E78.A28M44] 76-47796
1. Indians of North America—Alabama—Art—Exhibitions. 2. Indians of North America—Alabama—Antiquities—Exhibitions. 3. Alabama—Antiquities—Exhibitions. I. Alabama. University. Art Gallery. II. Title.

Indians of North America—Alaska—Basket making.

PAUL, Frances (Lackey) 970.674558
1889-
Spruce root basketry of the Alaska Tlingit. Edited by Willard W. Beatty. [Lawrence, Kan.] Dept. of the Interior, Bureau of Indian Affairs [1954] 80 p. illus., fold. map. 25 cm. (Indian handicrafts, 8) Bibliography: p. 71. [E98.I5U73 no. 8] 56-61492
1. Indians of North America—Alaska—Basket making. 2. Tlingit Indians—Basket making. I. Title. II. Series: United States. Bureau of Indian Affairs. Indian handicrafts, 8.

Indians of North America—Antiquities.

ROGERS, Hugh C 1889- 970.6571
Indian relics and their story, a handbook for collectors. Fort Smith, Ark., Printed by Franklin Print. Co., c1954. 134p. illus. 24cm. [E98.A6R6] 54-27350
1. Indians of North America—Antiq. 2. Collectors and collecting. I. Title.

STEEGE, Louis C 970.6571
Stone artifacts of the Northwestern Plains, [by Louis C. Steege and Warren W. Welch. Colorado Springs, Northwestern Plains Pub. Co., 1961] 131 p. illus. 23 cm. Includes bibliography. [E98.A6S7] 62038630
1. Indians of North America — Antiq. 2. Indians of North America — Implements. 3. Indians of North America — Northwestern States. I. Welch, Warren W joint author. II. Title.

Indians of North America—Antiquities.

BRENNAN, Louis A. 732'.2
Artifacts of prehistoric America / by Louis A. Brennan. Harrisburg, Pa. : Stackpole Books, [1975] p. cm. Includes index. [E77.9.B72] 75-20386 ISBN 0-8117-0174-3 : 14.95
1. Indians of North America—Antiquities. 2. Indians of North America—Implements. 3. North America—Antiquities. I. Title.

MARTINEAU, LaVan. 970.1
The rocks begin to speak. [1st ed.] Las Vegas, Nev., KC Publications [1973] xiv, 210 p. illus. 27 cm. Bibliography: p. 197-199. [E98.P6M37] 72-85137 8.95
1. Indians of North America—Antiquities. 2. North America—Antiquities. 3. Rock paintings—North America. 4. Petroglyphs—North America. I. Title.
P.O. Box 14883 Las Vegas, Nev. 89114. **BIP**

Indians of North America—Antiquities—Congresses.

SYMPOSIUM on Primitive 930'.1
Technology and Art, Calgary, Alta., 1974.
Primitive technology and art / edited by J. S. Raymond ... [et al.]. Calgary, Alta. : Archaeological Association, Dept. of Archaeology, University of Calgary, [1976] ii, 181 p. : ill. ; 22 cm. A slip mounted on t.p. changes title to: Primitive art and technology. Papers presented at a symposium sponsored by the University of Calgary Archaeological Association with the assistance of the Dept. of Archaeology. Includes bibliographies. [E98.I5S95 1974] 77-370764
1. Indians of North America—Antiquities—Congresses. 2. Industries, Primitive—Congresses. 3. Archaeology—Methodology—Congresses. 4. North America—Antiquities—Congresses. I. Raymond, James Scott. II. University of Calgary Archaeological Association. III. Calgary University. Dept. of Archaeology. IV. Title. V. Title: Primitive art and technology.

Indians of North America—Arizona—Antiquities.

DE OER, Warren R. 979.1'0004'97
Archaeological explorations in northern Arizona : NA10754, a Sinagua settlement of the Rio de Flag phase / Warren R. De Boer. Flushing, N.Y. : Queens College Press, 1976. 69p. : ill. ; 28 cm. (Queens College Publications in anthropology ; no. 1) Bibliography:p.67-69. [E78.A7D4] 76-150615 5.00
1. Indians of North America-Arizona-Antiquities. 2. Sinagua culture. I. rizona-Antiquities. II. Title. III. Series:Queens College, Flushing N.Y.

MARTIN, Paul Sidney, 970.4'91
1899-
The archaeology of Arizona; a study of the southwest region [by] Paul S. Martin [and] Fred Plog. [1st ed.] Garden City, N.Y., Published for the American Museum of Natural History [by] Natural History Press, 1973. xx, 422 p. illus. 27 cm. Bibliography: p. 387-416. [E78.A7M298] 72-76192 ISBN 0-385-07075-6 16.95
1. Indians of North America—Arizona—Antiquities. 2. Arizona—Antiquities. 3. Indians of North America—Southwest, New—Antiquities. 4. Southwest, New—Antiquities. I. Plog, Fred. II. American Museum of Natural History, New York. III. Title.

Indians of North America—Arizona—Grand Canyon—Antiquities—Collected works.

GRAND Canyon 979.1'32
archaeological series / Douglas W. Schwartz ... [et al.]. Santa Fe : School of

American Research Press, c1979- p. cm. Includes bibliographical references. [E78.A7G69] 79-11920 ISBN 0-933452-00-4 (v. 1) pbk. : 4.95
1. Indians of North America—Arizona—Grand Canyon—Antiquities—Collected works. 2. Grand Canyon—Antiquities—Collected works. I. Schwartz, Douglas Wright, 1929-

Indians of North America—Arms and armor.

MASON, Otis Tufton, 1838-1908. 355.8'2
North American bows, arrows, and quivers, by Otis Tufton Mason. Chipped arrow heads, by Gerard Fowke. Introd. and front. drawings by Ernest Berke. Page decorations by Carl J. Pugliese. Yonkers, N.Y., C. J. Pugliese, 1972. 216 p. illus. 29 cm. Reprint of O. T. Mason's work, published in 1894 in the Smithsonian report from 1893, and of S. Fowkes excerpt (Smaller chipped implements) from his Stone art, issued in the 13th Annual report of the U.S. Bureau of American Ethnology, 1891-92. [E98.A65M3 1972] 72-171901
1. Indians of North America—Arms and armor. 2. Bow and arrow. 3. Indians of North America—Implements. I. Fowke, Gerard, 1855-1933. Stone art. Smaller chipped implements. 1972. II. Title. III. Title: Chipped arrow heads.

Indians of North America—Art.

AMERICAN 709'.01'1097010740176579
Indian art: form and tradition. [Minneapolis, 1972] 154 p. illus. (part col.) 26 cm. Issued in connection with the exhibition organized by the Walker Art Center, Minneapolis Institute of Arts, and Indian Art Association, and held Oct. 22-Dec. 31, 1972, at the 1st two institutions. "Catalogue of the exhibition": p. 117-145. Bibliography: p. 148-151. [E98.A7A44] 72-90701
1. Indians of North America—Art. I. Walker Art Center, Minneapolis. II. Minneapolis. Institute of Arts. III. Indian Art Association.

AUTHENTIC Indian designs 745.4
: 2500 illustrations from Reports of the Bureau of American Ethnology / edited by Maria Naylor. New York : Dover Publications, c1975. xxii, 219 p. : chiefly ill. ; 28 cm. (Dover pictorial archive series) [E98.A7A97] 74-17711 ISBN 0-486-23170-4 pbk. : 5.00
1. Indians of North America—Art. 2. Design, Decorative—North America. I. Naylor, Maria. II. United States. Bureau of American Ethnology. Annual report.

BRODY, J. J. 759.9'701
Indian painters & white patrons, by J. J. Brody. Albuquerque, University of New Mexico Press [1971] xvii, 238 p. illus. (part col.), maps. 27 cm. A revision of the author's thesis, University of New Mexico. Bibliography: p. 223-229. [E98.A7B7 1971] 79-129805 ISBN 0-8263-0192-4 15.00
1. Indians of North America—Art. 2. Art patronage—U.S. I. Title. **BIP**

COVARRUBIAS, Miguel, 1904-1957. 970.67
The eagle, the jaguar, and the serpent; Indian art of the Americas: North America: Alaska, Canada, the United States. [1st ed.] New York, Knopf, 1954. xviii, 314, xi p. illus., plates (part col.) maps. 28 cm. Bibliography: p. 297-314. [E98.A7C63] 52-6415
1. Indians of North America—Art. 2. Indians—Art. 3. Indians—Origin. I. Title.

DOCKSTADER, Frederick J. 970.67
Indian art in America; the arts and crafts of the North American Indian. Greenwich, Conn., New York Graphic Society [1961] 224 p. illus. (part mounted col.), map. 29 cm. Bibliography: p. 222-224. [E98.A7D57] 60-8921
1. Indians of North America—Art. 2. Indians of North America—Industry. I. Title.

DOCKSTADER, Frederick J. 709'.01'1
Indian art in America : the arts and crafts of the North American Indian / Frederick J. Dockstader. New York : Promontory Press, [1974?] 223, [1] p. : ill. (some col.) ; 29 cm. Bibliography: p. 222-[224] [E98.A7D57 1974] 73-89243 ISBN 0-88394-008-6 : 12.98
1. Indians of North America—Art. 2. Indians of North America—Industries. I. Title.

DOUGLAS, Frederic Huntington, 1897-1956. 709'.73
Indian art of the United States, by Frederic H. Douglas and Rene d'Harnoncourt. New York, Museum of Modern Art. Reprint ed. [New York] Published for the Museum of Modern Art by Arno Press, 1969 [c1941] 204 p. illus. 27 cm. "Based on an exhibition which was sponsored by the Indian Arts and Crafts Board of the United States Department of the Interior." Bibliography: p. 195-203. [E98.A7D6 1969] 74-86425
1. Indians of North America—Art. I. Harnoncourt, Rene d', 1901- joint author. II. U.S. Indian Arts and Crafts Board. III. New York (City). Museum of Modern Art. IV. Title.

EXPOSITION of Indian Tribal Arts, inc. 709.01'1
Introduction to American Indian art; to accompany the first exhibition of American Indian art selected entirely with consideration of esthetic value. Glorieta, N.M., Rio Grande Press; [distributed by MacRae's Indian Book Distributors, Santa Rosa, Calif., 1970] 219 p. illus. 29 cm. (A Rio Grande classic) Title on spine: American Indian art. "First published in 1931." Bibliography: p. 205-217. [E98.A7E95 1970] 70-119862 ISBN 0-87380-047-8 10.00
1. Indians of North America—Art. I. Title. II. Title: American Indian art. **BIP**

FEDER, Norman. 709.01'1
American Indian art. New York, Harry N. Abrams [1971] 445, [2] p. illus., 60 col. plates. 28 x 30 cm. Bibliography: p. 439-[446] [E98.A7F38] 69-12484 ISBN 0-8109-0014-9
1. Indians of North America—Art. I. Title. **BIP**

FEDER, Norman. 709'.01'1
American Indian art. New shorter ed. New York, H. N. Abrams; distributed by New American Library [1973] 147, [4] p. illus. (part col.) 30 cm. Bibliography: p. [149]-[151] [E98.A7F38 1973] 73-4857
1. Indians of North America—Art. I. Title.

GLUBOK, Shirley. 709
The art of the North American Indian. Designed by Oscar Krauss. New York, Harper & Row [1964] [48] p. illus. (part col.) 26 cm. Shows the influence of nature and natural materials in the handcrafting of masks, totems, beaded and quill-designed clothing, kachinas, pottery, weapons, and other objects by the North American Indian. [E98.A7G55] AC 68
1. Indians of North America—Art. I. Title. **BIP**

HABERLAND, Wolfgang. 398.2'09701
The art of North America. New York, Crown Publishers [1964] 251 p. illus. (part col.), maps. 24 cm. (Art of the world) Translation of Nordamerika; Indianer, Eskimo, Westindien. Bibliography: p. 212-220. [E98.A7H243] 68-15660
1. Indians of North America—Art. I. Title. II. Series.

HABERLAND, Wolfgang. 709'.011'097
The art of North America. [Rev. ed.] New York, Greystone Press [1968, c1964] 257 p. illus. (part col.) 24 cm. (Art of the world) Rev. translation of Nordamerika; Indianer, Eskimo, Westindien. Bibliography: p. 218-226. [E98.A7H243 1968] 73-158141
1. Indians of North America—Art. I. Title. II. Series.

HOLM, Oscar William. 709.17497
Northwest coast Indian art; an analysis of form, by Bill Holm. Seattle, University of Washington Press, 1965. xvii, 115 p. illus., map. 25 cm. (Thomas Burke Memorial Washington State Museum. Monograph no. 1) Bibliography: p. 105-108. [E78.N78H6] 65-10818
1. Indians of North America — Art. 2. Indians of North America — Northwest coast of North America. I. Title. II. Series: Washington (State) University. Museum. Monograph no. 1

HOTZ, Gottfried. 970.1
Indian skin paintings from the American Southwest; two representations of border conflicts between Mexico and the Missouri in the early eighteenth century. Translated by Johannes Malthaner. [1st ed.] Norman, University of Oklahoma Press [1970] xiv, 248 p. illus., maps, port. 24 cm. (The Civilization of the American Indian series, v. 94) Translation of Indianische Ledermalereien. Includes bibliographical references. [E98.A7H7213] 69-10625 9.95
1. Indians of North America—Art. 2. Pawnee Indians—Wars. 3. Apache Indians—Wars. I. Title. II. Series.

INVERARITY, Robert Bruce, 1909- 970.67
Art of the Northwest Coast Indians. Berkeley, University of California Press, 1950. xiv, 243 p. illus. (part col.) map (on lining papers) 29 cm. Bibliography: p. 237-243. [E98.A7 I 5] 50-62872
1. Indians of North America—Art. 2. Indians of North America—Northwest, Pacific. I. Title. **BIP**

OGLESBY, Catharine, 1895- 745'.09791'3
Modern primitive arts of Mexico, Guatemala, and the Southwest. Freeport, N.Y., Books for Libraries Press [1969] 226 p. illus. 23 cm. (Essay index reprint series) Reprint of the 1939 ed. Bibliography: p. 219-222. [E98.A7O5 1969] 75-90670
1. Indians of North America—Art. 2. Indians of Mexico—Art. 3. Indians of Central America—Art. 4. Pueblo Indians. 5. Navaho Indians. 6. Indians of Central America—Guatemala. I. Title. **BIP**

SETON, Julia (Moss) 1889- 970.67455
American Indian arts, a way of life. New York, Ronald Press Co. [1962] 246 p. illus. 24 cm. Includes bibliography. [E98.A7S4] 62-15439
1. Indians of North America — Art. 2. Handicraft. I. Title.

SIDES, Dorothy (Smith) 970.6745
Decorative art of the southwestern Indians. With annotations by Clarice Martin Smith, and a foreword by Frederick Webb Hodge. New York, Dover Publications [1961] xviii p., 50 plates. 22 cm. Annotations for each plate on verso of preceding plate. "An unabridged and corrected republication of the work first published in portfolio format ... in 1936." Bibliography: p. xiii-xviii. [E98.A7S53 1961] 62-353
1. Indians of North America—Art. 2. Indians of North America—New Mexico. 3. Indians of North America—Arizona. I. Smith, Clarice Martin. II. Title.

TANNER, Clara Lee. 970.675
Southwest Indian painting. Tucson, University of Arizona Press [1957] xvii, 157 p. illus. (part col.) maps (on lining papers) 31 cm. Bibliography: p. 150-153. [E98.17T3] 57-59199
1. Indians of North America — Art. 2. Indians of North America — Southwest, New. I. Title.

TOWNSEND, Earl C 970.657173
Birdstones of the North American Indian; a study of these most interesting stone forms, the area of their distribution, their cultural provenience, possible uses, and antiquity. Indianapolis, 1959. x, 719 p. illus., col. plates, map. 29 cm. Bibliography: p. 705-714. [E98.A7T65] 59-4606
1. Indians of North America — Art. 2. Indians of North America — Antiq. 3. Sculpture, Primitive. I. Title.

VAILLANT, George Clapp, 1901-1945. 709'.701
Indian arts in North America. New York, Cooper Square Publishers, 1973. xiii, 63 p. 96 plates, 29 cm. Reprint of the 1939 ed. published by Harper, New York. Bibliography: p. 55-63. [E98.A7V25 1973] 72-97071 ISBN 0-8154-0469-7 12.50 (lib. bdg.)
1. Indians of North America—Art. I. Title. **BIP**

Indians of North America—Art—Bibliography.

DAWDY, Doris Ostrander. 016.75913
Annotated bibliography of American Indian painting. New York, Museum of the American Indian, Heye Foundation, 1968. 27 p. 26 cm. (Contributions from the Museum of the American Indian, Heye Foundation, v. 21, pt. 2) [E51.N42 vol. 21, pt. 2] 78-8195
1. Indians of North America—Art—Bibliography. I. Title. II. Series: New York. Museum of the American Indian, Heye Foundation. Contributions, v. 21, pt. 2

U.S. Indian Arts and Crafts Board. 016.9701
Bibliography of contemporary American Indian and Eskimo arts and crafts. Washington [1964] 4 p. 27 cm. (Its Bibliography no. 1) [Z1209.U496 no. 1] 016.9701 74-291556
1. Indians of North America—Art—Bibliography. 2. Indians of North America—Industries—Bibliography. I. Title. II. Series.

UNITED States. 016.7455'0973
Indian Arts and Crafts Board.
Bibliography of contemporary American Indian and Eskimo arts and crafts. Washington [1964?] [4] l. 27 cm. (Its Bibliography no. 4/6-64) At head of title: Fact sheet. [Z1209.U496 no. 4/6-64] 72-600523
1. Indians of North America—Art—Bibliography. 2. Indians of North America—Industries—Bibliography. I. Title. II. Series.

Indians of North America—Art—Exhibitions.

AMON Carter Museum of Western Art, Fort Worth, Tex. 709'.701
The Institute of American Indian Arts alumni exhibition. [Fort Worth, Tex., 1973?] 67 p. illus. 23 x 26 cm. Catalogue of an exhibition to be held at the Museum of the Institute of American Indian Arts, Dec. 17, 1973-Jan. 28, 1974; Amon Carter Museum, Feb. 14-Mar. 31; New Orleans Museum of Art, Apr. 27-June 10; and Oklahoma Art Center, July 21-Sept. 5. [E98.A7A46 1973] 73-92099 ISBN 0-88360-003-X
1. Institute of American Indian Arts. 2. Indians of North America—Art—Exhibitions. I. Institute of American Indian Arts. Museum. II. New Orleans Museum of Art. III. Oklahoma Art Center. IV. Title. V. Title: Alumni exhibition. **BIP**

COE, Ralph T. 709'.01'1
Sacred circles : two thousand years of North American Indian art : exhibition organized by the Arts Council of Great Britain with the support of the British-American Associates, [held at the] Hayward Gallery, London, 7 October 1976-16 January 1977 : catalogue / by Ralph T. Coe. [London] : Arts Council of Great Britain, 1976. 236 p. : ill. (some col.), ports. ; 28 cm. Bibliography: p. 29-31. [E98.A7C54] 77-363447 ISBN 0-7287-0095-6 : £5.00. ISBN 0-7287-0096-4 pbk.
1. Indians of North America—Art—Exhibitions. I. Arts Council of Great Britain. II. British-American Associates. III. Hayward Gallery. IV. Title. **BIP**

DESIGNER/CRAFTSMAN Guild.
The spirit and the hand; an exhibition of contemporary native American crafts formed by the Designer/Craftsman Guild, April 15 through May 13, 1972. [Fort Wayne, Ind.] Fort Wayne Public Library [1972] [28] p. illus. 20 x 25 cm. Bibliography: p. [26]-[27] [E98.A7D4] 72-79123
1. Indians of North America—Art—Exhibitions. 2. Indians of North America—Industries—Exhibitions. I. Fort Wayne. Public Library. II. Title.

*DUFF, Wilson 732'.2
Images: stone b.c., thirty centuries of northwest coast Indian sculpture photographs and drawings by Hilary Stewart. Seattle, University of Washington Press [1975] 191 p. chiefly ill. 24 cm. "An exhibition originating at the Art Gallery of

SUBJECT INDEX INDIANS OF NORTH

Greater Victoria" [E59] ISBN 0-295-95421-3 17.50.
1. Indians of North America—Art—Exhibitions. I. Title.

FEDER, Norman. 759.1
North American Indian painting. New York, Museum of Primitive Art; distributed by the New York Graphic Society, Greenwich, Conn. [1967] 1 v. (unpaged) illus. 28 cm. Prepared in conjunction with an exhibition held at the Museum of Primitive Art, New York. Bibliography: p. [iii] of cover. [E98.A7F4] 67-25276
1. Indians of North America—Art—Exhibitions. I. New York. Museum of Primitive Art. II. Title.

FEDER, Norman. 709.01'1
Two hundred years of North American Indian art. New York, Praeger [1972] xxxi, 128 p. illus. (part col.) 26 cm. Catalog of an exhibition held at the Whitney Museum of American Art. Bibliography: p. 121-124. [E98.A7F43 1972] 70-176395 12.50
1. Indians of North America—Art—Exhibitions. I. Whitney Museum of American Art, New York. II. Title.

SCHNEIDER, Mary Jane. 709'.73
Contemporary Indian crafts : [a special exhibit sponsored by the Museum of Anthropology, University of Missouri-Columbia and the National Endowment for the Arts, February 1, 1972, to June 30, 1972 : catalog ...] / by Mary Jane Schneider. [Columbia : Museum of Anthropology, University of Missouri-Columbia, 1975?] 51 p. : ill. ; 28 cm. [E98.A7S36] 75-326254
1. Indians of North America—Art—Exhibitions. 2. Indians of North America—Industries—Exhibitions. I. University of Missouri—Columbia. Museum of Anthropology. II. National Endowment for the Arts. III. Title. BIP

SEATTLE. Century 21 Exposition, 1962. 709.011
Northwest coast Indian art, by Erna Gunther. [Seattle] [1962?] 101 p. illus. (part col.) maps. 23 cm. Catalog of an exhibit in the Fine Arts Pavilion at the Seattle World's Fair, Apr. 21-Oct. 21, 1962. [E78.N78S4] 66-42763
1. Indians of North America—Art—Exhibitions. 2. Indians of North America—Northwest coast of North America. I. Gunther, Erna, 1896- II. Title.

TRITON Museum of Art. 709'.701
Arts of the American Indian. [Exhibition at the] Triton Museum of Art, Santa Clara, California, April 9 - May 15, 1972. [Santa Clara, 1972] [19] p. illus. 27 cm. Catalog. [E98.A7T74] 74-160779
1. Indians of North America—Art—Exhibitions. I. Title.

Indians of North America—Art—Juvenile literature.

GLUBOK, Shirley. 970.67
The art of the North American Indian. Designed by Oscar Krauss. New York, Harper & Row [1964] [48] p. illus. (part col.) 26 cm. [E98.A7G55] 64-11829
1. Indians of North America — Art — Juvenile literature. I. Title.

GLUBOK, Shirley. 709'.01'1
The art of Woodland Indians / by Shirley Glubok ; designed by Gerard Nook. New York : Macmillan, c1976. p. cm. A survey of the art and crafts of the forest-dwelling Indians of the Atlantic seaboard. [E98.A7G56] 76-12434 ISBN 0-02-736440-2 : 7.95
1. Indians of North America—Art—Juvenile literature. 2. Indians of North America—Industries—Juvenile literature. I. Title. BIP

Indians of North America—Art—Northwest coast of North America—Exhibitions.

SIEBERT, Erna. 709'.7
North American Indian art: masks, amulets, wood carvings and ceremonial dress from the North-West coast; [by] Erna Siebert, Werner Forman, tr. by Philippa Heniges. London, Hamlyn [1967] 43p. col. front., illus., 81 col. plates. 31cm. Tr. of Indianskeument. Bibl. [E78.N78S513] 67-108263 12.50
1. Indians of North America—Art—Northwest coast of North America—Exhibitions. I. Forman, Werner. joint author. II. Title.
Distributed by Tudor, New York.

Indians of North America—Basket making.

JAMES, George Wharton, 1858-1923. 746.4'1
Indian basketry. New York, Dover Publications [1972] 271 p. illus. 24 cm. Reprint of the 1909 ed. Includes bibliographical references. [E98.B3J29 1972] 72-81280 3.50 (pbk)
1. Indians of North America—Basket making. I. Title. BIP

JAMES, George Wharton, 1858-1923. 746.4'1
Indian basketry, and How to make Indian and other baskets. 3d ed., rev. and enl. Glorieta, N.M., Rio Grande Press [1970] 271, 136 p. illus. 29 cm. (A Rio Grande classic) Reprint of the 1903 ed., with new introductory matter. Includes bibliographies. [TS910.J27 1970] 73-119863
1. Indians of North America—Basket making. 2. Basket making. I. James, George Wharton, 1858-1923. How to make Indian and other baskets. 1970. II. Title. III. Title: How to make Indian and other baskets.

JONES, Joan Megan. 746.4'1
Northwest coast basketry and culture change. [Seattle] Thomas Burke Memorial Washington State Museum [University of Washington, 1968] viii, 60 l. illus. 28 cm. (Thomas Burke Memorial Washington State Museum. Research report no. 1) Cover title. Thesis (M.A.)—University of Washington. Bibliography: p. 60. [E78.N78J6] 78-632185
1. Indians of North America—Basket making. 2. Indians of North America—Northwest coast of North America. I. Title. II. Series: Washington (State). University. Museum. Research report no. 1

LAMB, Frank W. 746.4'1
Indian baskets of North America, by Frank W. Lamb. [1st ed.] Riverside, Calif., Riverside Museum Press [1972] 155 p. illus. 29 cm. Bibliography: p. 153-155. [E98.B3L34] 72-189529 8.50
1. Indians of North America—Basket making. I. Title.

MILES, Charles, 1894- 746.4'1
American Indian and Eskimo basketry: a key to identification. Written and compiled by Charles Miles and Pierre Bovis. [Deluxe ed.] San Francisco, Calif., P. Bovis [1969] 144 p. illus., map. 24 cm. Bibliography: p. 19. [E98.B3M5] 70-9044
1. Indians of North America—Basket making. I. Bovis, Pierre, 1943- joint author. II. Title.

NAVAJO School of Indian Basketry, Los Angeles. 746.4'1
Indian basket weaving. New York, Dover Publications [1971] 103 p. illus. 24 cm. Reprint of the 1903 ed. [E98.B3N3 1971] 72-179789 ISBN 0-486-22616-6 1.75
1. Indians of North America—Basket making. 2. Basket making. I. Title. BIP

Indians of North America—Basket making—Exhibitions.

FALLON, Carol. 746.4'1
The art of the Indian basket in North America : [exhibition], August 24-October 5, 1975, the University of Kansas Museum of Art, Lawrence, Kansas / introd. and catalogue by Carol Fallon. Lawrence : The Museum, c1975. 56 p. : ill. ; 23 x 26 cm. (Miscellaneous publication of the Museum of Art ; no. 99) Bibliography: p. 53-54. [E98.B3F34] 75-21766
1. Indians of North America—Basket making—Exhibitions. I. Kansas. University. Museum of Art. II. Title. III. Series: Kansas. University. Museum of Art. Miscellaneous publications ; no. 99.

Indians of North America—Bibliography.

THOMAS Gilcrease Institute of American History and Art, Tulsa, Okla. Library. 016.9703
The Gilcrease-Hargrett catalogue of imprints. Compiled by Lester Hargarett. Prepared for publication and with an introd. by G. P. Edwards. Foreword by John C. Ewers. [1st ed.] Norman, University of Oklahoma Press [1972] xviii, 400 p. 24 cm. [Z1209.2.U5T48] 72-859 ISBN 0-8061-1020-1
1. Indians of North America—Bibliography. 2. Five Civilized Tribes—Bibliography. 3. The West—History—Bibliography. I. Hargrett, Lester, 1902-1962, comp. II. Title. BIP

Indians of North America—Biography—Directories.

SNODGRASS, Jeanne O., 1927- 759.13
American Indian painters; a biographical directory. Compiled by Jeanne O. Snodgrass. New York, Museum of the American Indian, Heye Foundation, 1968. xi, 269 p. 26 cm. (Contributions from the Museum of the American Indian, Heye Foundation, v. 21, pt. 1) Bibliography: p. 264-269. [E51.N42 vol. 21, pt. 1] 67-27949 7.50
1. Indians of North America—Biography—Directories. 2. Indians of North America—Art. I. Title. II. Series: New York. Museum of the American Indian, Heye Foundation. Contributions, v. 21, pt. 1 BIP

Indians of North America—British Columbia—Antiquities.

SMITH, Harlan Ingersoll, 1872-1940. 971.1
Cairns of British Columbia and Washington / by Harlan Ingersoll Smith and Gerard Fowke. New York : AMS Press, 1975. p. 55-75, [6] leaves of plates : ill. ; 24 cm. Reprint of the 1901 ed. published in New York, which was issued as v. 4 of Memoirs of the American Museum of Natural History, Anthropology, v. 3, pt. 2, and as v. 2, pt. 2 of Publications of the Jesup North Pacific Expedition. [E78.B9S64 1975] 73-3517 ISBN 0-404-58118-8 : 27.50
1. Indians of North America—British Columbia—Antiquities. 2. Indians of North America—Washington (State)—Antiquities. 3. British Columbia—Antiquities. 4. Washington (State)—Antiquities. I. Fowke, Gerard, 1855-1933, joint author. II. Title. III. Series: American Museum of Natural History, New York. Memoirs ; v. 4. IV. Series: The Jesup North Pacific Expedition. Publications ; v. 2, pt. 2.

SMITH, Harlan Ingersoll, 1872-1940. 971.1'2
Shell-heaps of the lower Fraser River, British Columbia / by Harlan Ingersoll Smith. New York : AMS Press, 1975. p. 133-191, [2] leaves of plates : ill. ; 24 cm. Reprint of the 1903 ed. published by E. J. Brill, Leiden, and G. E. Stechert, New York, which was issued as v. 4 of Memoirs of the American Museum of Natural History, Anthropology, v. 3, pt. 4, and as v. 2, pt. 4 of Publications of the Jesup North Pacific Expedition. Includes bibliographical references. [E78.B9S65 1975] 73-3519 ISBN 0-404-58120-X : 27.50
1. Indians of North America—British Columbia—Antiquities. 2. British Columbia—Antiquities. 3. Kitchen-middens—British Columbia. 4. Frasier Valley, B.C.—Antiquities. I. Title. II. Series: American Museum of Natural History, New York. Memoirs ; v. 4. III. Series: The Jesup North Pacific Expedition. Publications ; v. 2, pt. 4. BIP

Indians of North America—British Columbia—Art—Pictorial works.

STELTZER, Ulli. 709'.711
Indian artists at work / Ulli Steltzer. Vancouver : J. J. Douglas, c1976. 163 p. : ill. ; 26 cm. [E78.B9S75] 77-363119 ISBN 0-88894-116-1 : 13.95
1. Indians of North America—British Columbia—Art—Pictorial works. 2. Indians of North America—British Columbia—Portraits. 3. Artists—British Columbia—Portraits. I. Title. BIP

Indians of North America—British Columbia—Costume and adornment.

BOAS, Franz, 1858-1942. 391'.6
Facial paintings of the Indians of northern British Columbia / by Franz Boas. New York : AMS Press, 1975. 24 p., [7] leaves of plates : ill. ; 24 cm. Reprint of the 1898 ed. published in New York, which was issued as v. 2 of the Memoirs of the American Museum of Natural History, Anthropology, v. 1, pt. 1, and as v. 1, pt. 1 of the Jesup North Pacific Expedition publications. [E78.B9B62 1975] 73-3509 ISBN 0-404-58101-3 : 20.00
1. Indians of North America—British Columbia—Costume and adornment. I. Title. II. Series: American Museum of Natural History, New York. Memoirs ; v. 2. III. Series: The Jesup North Pacific Expedition. Publications ; v. 1, pt. 1. BIP

Indians of North America—California—Alameda Co.—Antiquities.

PHEBUS, George. 979.4'65'00497
Contributions to Costanoan archaeology : archaeological investigations at 4-ALA-330 and 4-SMA-22 / by George Phebus, Jr. [San Francisco : San Francisco State University, Treganza Anthropology Museum], 1973. 75 p., [11] leaves of plates : ill. ; 28 cm. (Treganza Anthropology Museum papers ; no. 12) Bibliography: p. 74-75. [E78.C15P44] 75-622268
1. Indians of North America—California—Alameda Co.—Antiquities. 2. Alameda Co., Calif.—Antiquities. 3. California—Antiquities. I. Title. II. Series: Treganza Anthropology Museum. Papers ; no. 12.

Indians of North America—California—Antiquities.

HEIZER, Robert Fleming, 1915- 732'.2'09701
Prehistoric rock art of California [by] Robert F. Heizer and C. W. Clewlow, Jr. Ramona, Calif., Ballena Press, 1973. 2 v. illus. 27 cm. Contents.Contents.—v. 1. Text and plates.—v. 2. Figures. Bibliography: v. 1, p. 122-148. [E78.C15H44] 74-161869 12.50
1. Indians of North America—California—Antiquities. 2. Rock paintings—California. 3. Petroglyphs—California. 4. California—Antiquities. I. Clewlow, C. William, joint author. II. Title.

TURNER, Wilson G. 917.94'95'008 s
3 essays on petroglyphology, by Wilson G. Turner with Eva Fopiano and Bob Reynolds. Illus. by Wilson G. Turner [Bloomington, Calif., San Bernardino County Museum Association, 1971] 34 p. illus. 28 cm. (San Bernardino County Museum Association. Quarterly, v. 19, no. 1) [E78.C15S2 vol. 19, no. 1] 732'.2'09701 73-170226 2.00
1. Indians of North America—California—Antiquities. 2. California—Antiquities. 3. Rock paintings. 4. Petroglyphs. I. Fopiano, Eva. II. Reynolds, Bob. III. Title. IV. Series.

Indians of North America—California—Basket making—Exhibitions.

CYPRESS College. Fine Arts Gallery. 746.4'1
California Indian basketry : an artistic overview : exhibition, November 15 through December 10, 1976, Cypress College Fine Arts Gallery, Cypress, California / exhibit annotations, Arthur M. Silva and William C. Cain. Cypress, Calif. : The Gallery, c1976. 84 p. : ill. ; 28 cm. [E78.C15C95 1976] 77-353859
1. Indians of North America—California—Basket making—Exhibitions. I. Silva, Arthur M. II. Cain, William C. III. Title.

Indians of North America—California—Fresno Valley—Antiquities.

WALLACE, William James. 970.4'94 s
Archaeological investigations at Hidden Reservoir, Madera County, California [by] William J. Wallace. Los Angeles, 1970. iii, 45 l. illus. 28 cm. (Contributions to California archaeology, no. 7) Bibliography: l. 36-39. [E78.C15C685 no. 7] 917.94'81 74-153657
1. Indians of North America—California—Fresno Valley—Antiquities. 2. Fresno Valley, Calif.—Antiquities. I. Title. II. Series.

Indians of North America—California—Glenn Co. — Antiquities.

THE Archaeology of the Black Butte Reservoir region, Glenn and Tehama Counties, California. 917.94'31 Pt. 1: Salvage archaeology in the Black Butte area, Glenn County, California, by Adan Treganza and Martin Heickson. Pt. 2: A study of 4-Glenn-10: the Brownell Indian Cemetery, by Wallace Woolfenden. [San Francisco] San Francisco State College, Anthropology Museum, 1969. 59, 100 p. illus. 28 cm. (San Francisco State College, Anthropology Museum. Occasional paper no. 2) Includes bibliographies. [E78.C15A74] 73-623199
1. Indians of North America—California—Glenn Co. —Antiquities. 2. Indians of North America—California—Tehama Co.—Antiquities. 3. Black Butte Lake, Calif.—Antiquities. 4. California—Antiquities. I. Heickson, Martin. II. Treganza, Adan Eduardo, 1916-1968. Salvage archaeology in the Black Butte area, Glenn County, California. 1969. III. Woolfenden, Wallace. A study of 4-Glenn-10: the Brownell Indian Cemetery. 1969. IV. Series: California. State College, San Francisco. Anthropology Museum. Occasional papers, no. 2.

Indians of North America—California—Marin Co.—Antiquities.

CONTRIBUTIONS to the archaeology of Point Reyes National Seashore; 917.94'62 a compendium in honor of Adan E. Treganza. Edited by Robert E. Schenk. [San Francisco, Treganza Anthropology Museum] 1970. xvii, 321 p. illus. 28 cm. (Treganza Museum. Papers, no. 6) Contents.Contents.—Kawahara, S. A survey of the physical setting of the Point Reyes Peninsula area, Marin County, California.—Mannion, L. and Mannion, M. C. Abstracts from the Kelly manuscript: Coast Miwok material culture.—Moratto, M. J. A history of archaeological research at Point Reyes, California.—Edwards, R. L. A settlement pattern hypothesis for the Coast Miwok based on an archaeological survey of Point Reyes Seashore.—King, T. F. and Upson, W. F. Protohistory on Limantour Sandspit: archaeological investigations at 4-Mrn-216 and 4-Mrn-298.—Henn, W. G. Faunal analysis of 4-Mrn-216, a seasonal site on Limantour Sandspit, Point Reyes National Seashore.—Wilson, S. C. Faunal analysis of 4-Mrn-298W: a perspective of 4-Mrn-216.—Von der Porten, E. P. The porcelains and terra cottas of Drakes Bay.—a compendium in honor of Adan E. Treganza. Edited by Robert E. Schenk. [San Francisco, Treganza Anthropology Museum] 1970. xvii, 321 p. illus. 28 cm. (Treganza Museum. Papers, no. 6) Contents.Contents.—Kawahar
1. Treganza, Adan Eduardo, 1916-1968. 2. Indians of North America—California—Marin Co.—Antiquities. 3. Point Reyes National Seashore—Antiquities. I. Treganza, Adan Eduardo, 1916-1968. II. Schenk, Robert E., 1944-1970, ed. III. Series: Treganza Anthropology Museum. Papers, no. 6.

Indians of North America—California—Pictorial works.

DRAWN from life : 760
California Indians in pen and brush / [compiled] by Theodora Kroeber, Albert B. Elsasser, Robert F. Heizer. Socorro, N.M. : Ballena Press, c1977. 295 p. : ill. ; 24 cm. Bibliography: p. 285-294. [N8217.I5D73] 78-100278 ISBN 0-87919-068-X : 8.95
1. Indians of North America—California—Pictorial works. I. Kroeber, Theodora. II. Elsasser, Albert B. III. Heizer, Robert Fleming, 1915-

Indians of North America—California—Tuolumne Valley—Antiquities.

MORATTO, Michael J. 917.94'45
A study of prehistory in the Tuolumne River Valley, California. Edited by Michael J. Moratto. [San Francisco, Treganza Anthropology Museum] 1971. vi, 177 l. illus. 28 cm. (Treganza Anthropology Museum. Papers, no. 9) "Prepared in partial fulfillment of contract 4970P10605 between the U.S. National Park Service and the Frederic Burk Foundation for Education of San Francisco State College." Bibliography: leaves 146-159. [E78.C15M68] 73-623194
1. Indians of North America—California—Tuolumne Valley—Antiquities. 2. Tuolumne Valley, Calif.—Antiquities. 3. Miwok Indians—Antiquities. I. Title. II. Series.

Indians of North America—Costume and adornment.

HOFSINDE, Robert. 391
Indian costumes, written and illustrated by Robert Hofsinde (Gray-Wolf) New York, W. Morrow [1968] 94 p. illus. 21 cm. Describes everyday, wartime, and ceremonial dress characteristic of the tribal groups of North America: Apache, Blackfoot, Crow, Iroquois, Navaho, Northwest Coast Indians, Ojibwa, Pueblo, Seminole, Sioux, and Indians of today. [E98.C8H6] AC 68
1. Indians of North America—Costume and adornment. I. Title. BIP

HUNT, Walter Bernard, 1888-1970. 970.1
The golden book of Indian crafts and lore. New York, Simon and Schuster [1954] 111 p. illus. 29 cm. [E98.C8H83] 54-12821
1. Indians of North America—Costume and adornment. 2. Indians of North America—Dances. I. Title. II. Title: Indian crafts and lore.

ORCHARD, William C. 745.5
Beads and beadwork of the American Indians : a study based on specimens in the Museum of the American Indian, Heye Foundation / by William C. Orchard. 2d ed. New York : The Museum, 1975. 168 p., [8] leaves of plates : ill. (some col.) ; 26 cm. (Contributions from the Museum of the American Indian, Heye Foundation ; v. 11) Includes bibliographical references. [E98.C8O7 1975] 75-16030
1. Indians of North America—Costume and adornment. 2. Beadwork. 3. Indians—Costume and adornment. 4. Indians—Art. I. Title. II. Series: New York (City). Museum of the American Indian, Heye Foundation. Contributions ; v. 11.

Indians of North America—Costume and adornment—Exhibitions.

CONN, Richard. 746.9'2
Robes of white shell and sunrise : personal decorative arts of the native American : [catalog of an exhibition] Denver Art Museum, November 9, 1974-January 19, 1975 / by Richard Conn. Denver : Denver Art Museum, [1974] 150 p. : ill. (some col.) ; 22 x 28 cm. Bibliography: p. 150. [E98.C8C66] 74-16739 ISBN 0-914738-04-6
1. Denver. Art Museum. 2. Indians of North America—Costume and adornment—Exhibitions. I. Denver. Art Museum. II. Title. BIP

Indians of North America—Costume and adornment—Juvenile literature.

HOFSINDE, Robert. 391'.0091'7597 (j)
Indian costumes, written and illustrated by Robert Hofsinde (Gray-Wolf) New York, W. Morrow [1968] 94 p. illus. 21 cm. [E98.C8H6] 68-11895
1. Indians of North America—Costume and adornment—Juvenile literature. I. Title.

Indians of North America—Culture.

VIDLER, Virginia, 1928- 974'.004'97
American Indian antiques : arts and artifacts of the Northeast / Virginia Vidler. South Brunswick : A. S. Barnes, c1975. 156 p. : ill. ; 32 cm. Includes index. Bibliography: p. 152-153. [E78.E2V53 1976] 74-9302 ISBN 0-498-01495-9 : 20.00
1. Indians of North America—Culture. 2. Indians of North America—Implements. 3. Antiquities—United States. I. Title. BIP

Indians of North America—Dwellings.

LAUBIN, Reginald. 970.657186
The Indian tipi; its history, construction, and use, by Reginald and Gladys Laubin (Tatanka Wanjila na Wiyaka Wastewin) With a history of the tipi by Stanley Vestal. Norman, University of Oklahoma Press [1957] 208 p. illus. 24 cm. [E98.D9L3] 57-5958
1. Indians of North America—Dwellings. I. Laubin, Gladys, joint author. II. Title. BIP

LAUBIN, Reginald. 301.5'4
The Indian tipi : its history, construction, and use / by Reginald and Gladys Laubin (Tatanka Wanjila na Wiyaka Wastewin). With a history of the tipi / by Stanley Vestal. 2d ed. Norman : University of Oklahoma Press, 1977. p. cm. [E98.D9L3 1977] 77-23039 ISBN 0-8061-1433-9 : 12.50
1. Indians of North America—Dwellings. I. Laubin, Gladys, joint author. II. Vestal, Stanley, 1887-1957. The history of the tipi. 1977. III. Title.

Indians of North America—Embroidery.

ORCHARD, William C. 970.1 s
The technique of porcupine-quill decoration among the North American Indians, by William C. Orchard. 2d ed. New York, Museum of the American Indian, Heye Foundation, 1971. 82 p. illus. 25 cm. (Contributions from the Museum of the American Indian, Heye Foundation, v. 4, no. 1) [E51.N42 vol. 4, no. 1, 1971] [E98.E5] 746.4'4 79-170009 3.50
1. Indians of North America—Embroidery. I. Title. II. Series: New York (City). Museum of the American Indian, Heye Foundation. Contributions, v. 4, no. 1. BIP

Indians of North America—Florida—Antiquities.

GRAY, J. Mason. 975.9'004'97
Indian artifact ident.. [Lutz, Fla. : J. M. Gray, 1975] 167 p. : ill. ; 28 cm. Cover title. "Authors edition, copy no. 2 of 50." Imprint stamped on p. [2] of cover. Includes index. Bibliography: p. 158-167. [E78.F6G72] 73-92731
1. Indians of North America—Florida—Antiquities. 2. Florida—Antiquities. I. Title.

Indians of North America—Florida—Implements.

BULLEN, Ripley P. 681'.763
A guide to the identification of Florida projectile points / Ripley P. Bullen. Rev. ed. Gainesville, Fla. : Kendall Books, 1975. 62 p. : ill. ; 28 cm. Bibliography: p. 58-62. [E78.F6B82 1975] 75-2972 pbk. : 2.00
1. Indians of North America—Florida—Implements. 2. Florida—Antiquities. 3. Projectile points. 4. Indians of North America—Florida—Antiquities. I. Title.

BULLEN, Ripley P. 970.4759
A guide to the identification of Florida projectile points, by Ripley P. Bullen. Gainesville, Florida State Museum, University of Florida, 1968. 50 p. illus. 28 cm. Cover title. "References cited": p. 7-10. [E78.F6B82] A 68
1. Indians of North America—Florida—Implements. 2. Florida—Antiquities. 3. Projectile points. 4. Indians of North America—Florida—Antiquities. I. Florida. University, Gainesville. State Museum. II. Title.

Indians of North America—Great Basin—Antiquities.

FOUR Great Basin petroglyph studies. 930'.1 s Berkeley : University of California, Dept. of Anthropology, 1974. 130 p. : ill. ; 28 cm. (Contributions of the University of California Archaeological Research Facility ; no. 20) Contents.Contents.—Heizer, R. F., and Hester, T. R. Two petroglyph sites in Lincoln County, Nevada.—Nissen, K. M. The record of a hunting practice at petroglyph site NV-LY-1.—Bard, J. C., and Busby, C. I. The manufacture of a petroglyph: a replicative experiment.—Pori, M., and Heizer, R. F. An attempt at computer analysis determination of California rock art styles. Includes bibliographies. [E51.C2 no. 20] [E78.G67] 732'.2'0979 75-620910
1. Indians of North America—Great Basin—Antiquities. 2. Great Basin—Antiquities. 3. Petroglyphs—Great Basin. I. Series: California. University. Archaeological Research Facility. Contributions ; no. 20.

Indians of North America—Great Lakes region—Art—Exhibitions.

FLINT Institute of Arts. 745'.09701
The art of the Great Lakes Indians. [Flint, Mich., 1973] xxxviii, 114 p. illus. (part col.) 28 cm. Catalog of an exhibition organized by the Flint Institute of Arts; held March 25-July 1, 1973. Bibliography: p. 112-113. [E78.G7F54] 72-97819
1. Indians of North America—Great Lakes region—Art—Exhibitions. I. Title.

Indians of North America—Great Lakes region—Costume and adornment—Exhibitions.

BEADS : 746.5
their use by Upper Great Lakes Indians : an exhibition / produced by the Grand Rapids Public Museum and the Cranbrook Academy of Art/Museum. Grand Rapids : The Museum, c1977. 81 p. : ill. ; 29 cm. (Grand Rapids Public Museum publication ; no. 3) Cover title. Includes bibliographies. [E78.G7B4] 77-89533
1. Indians of North America—Great Lakes region—Costume and adornment—Exhibitions. 2. Beadwork—Great Lakes region—Exhibitions. I. Grand Rapids Public Museum. II. Cranbrook Academy of Art, Bloomfield, Mich. Museum. III. Series: Grand Rapids Public Museum. Grand Rapids Public Museum publication ; no. 3.

Indians of North America—Great Plains.

WIED-NEUWIED, Maximilian Alexander Philipp, Prinz von, 1782-1867. 978'.004'97
People of the first man : life among the Plains Indians in their final days of glory : the firsthand account of Prince Maximilian's expedition up the Missouri River, 1833-34 / edited and designed by Davis Thomas and Karin Ronnefeldt ; watercolors by Karl Bodmer. New York : Dutton, 1976. 256 p. : ill. ; 31 cm. Includes index. [E78.G73W5 1976] 76-16577 29.95
1. Indians of North America—Great Plains. 2. Missouri Valley—Description and travel. I. Thomas, Davis. II. Ronnefeldt, Karin. III. Bodmer, Karl, 1809-1893. IV. Title.

Indians of North America—Great Plains—Art.

DUNN, Dorothy, 1903- 759.01'1
American Indian painting of the Southwest and Plains areas. [1st ed. Albuquerque] University of New Mexico, 1968. xxvii, 429 p. illus. (part col.) 29 cm. Includes

Greater Victoria" [E59] ISBN 0-295-95421-3 17.50.
1. Indians of North America—Art—Exhibitions. I. Title.

FEDER, Norman.   759.1
North American Indian painting. New York, Museum of Primitive Art; distributed by the New York Graphic Society, Greenwich, Conn. [1967] 1 v. (unpaged) illus. 28 cm. Prepared in conjunction with an exhibition held at the Museum of Primitive Art, New York. Bibliography: p. [iii] of cover. [E98.A7F4] 67-25276
1. Indians of North America—Art—Exhibitions. I. New York. Museum of Primitive Art. II. Title.

FEDER, Norman.   709.01'1
Two hundred years of North American Indian art. New York, Praeger [1972] xxxi, 128 p. illus. (part col.) 26 cm. Catalog of an exhibition held at the Whitney Museum of American Art. Bibliography: p. 121-124. [E98.A7F43 1972] 70-176395 12.50
1. Indians of North America—Art—Exhibitions. I. Whitney Museum of American Art, New York. II. Title.

SCHNEIDER, Mary Jane.   709'.73
Contemporary Indian crafts : [a special exhibit sponsored by the Museum of Anthropology, University of Missouri-Columbia and the National Endowment for the Arts, February 1, 1972, to June 30, 1972 : catalog ...] / by Mary Jane Schneider. [Columbia : Museum of Anthropology, University of Missouri-Columbia, 1975?] 51 p. : ill. ; 28 cm. [E98.A7S36] 75-326254
1. Indians of North America—Art—Exhibitions. 2. Indians of North America—Industries—Exhibitions. I. University of Missouri—Columbia. Museum of Anthropology. II. National Endowment for the Arts. III. Title.   BIP

SEATTLE. Century 21   709.011
   Exposition, 1962.
Northwest coast Indian art, by Erna Gunther. [Seattle] [1962?] 101 p. illus. (part col.) maps. 23 cm. Catalog of an exhibit in the Fine Arts Pavilion at the Seattle World's Fair, Apr. 21-Oct. 21, 1962. [E78.N78S4] 66-42763
1. Indians of North America—Art—Exhibitions. 2. Indians of North America—Northwest coast of North America. I. Gunther, Erna, 1896- II. Title.

TRITON Museum of Art.   709'.701
Arts of the American Indian. [Exhibition at the] Triton Museum of Art, Santa Clara, California, April 9 - May 15, 1972. [Santa Clara, 1972] [19] p. illus. 27 cm. Catalog. [E98.A7T74] 74-160779
1. Indians of North America—Art—Exhibitions. I. Title.

Indians of North America—Art—
   Juvenile literature.

GLUBOK, Shirley.   970.67
The art of the North American Indian. Designed by Oscar Krauss. New York, Harper & Row [1964] [48] p. illus. (part col.) 26 cm. [E98.A7G55] 64-11829
1. Indians of North America — Art — Juvenile literature. I. Title.

GLUBOK, Shirley.   709'.01'1
The art of Woodland Indians / by Shirley Glubok ; designed by Gerard Nook. New York : Macmillan, c1976. 48 p. : col. ill. A survey of the art and crafts of the forest-dwelling Indians of the Atlantic seaboard. [E98.A7G56] 76-12434 ISBN 0-02-736440-2 : 7.95
1. Indians of North America—Art—Juvenile literature. 2. Indians of North America—Industries—Juvenile literature. I. Title.   BIP

Indians of North America—Art—
   Northwest coast of North
   America—Exhibitions.

SIEBERT, Erna.   709'.7
North American Indian art: masks, amulets, wood carvings and ceremonial dress from the North-West coast; [by] Erna Siebert, Werner Forman, tr. by Philippa Heniges. London, Hamlyn [1967] 43p. col. front., illus., 81 col. plates. 31cm.

Tr. of Indianskeument.   Bibl.
[E78.N78S513] 67-108263 12.50
1. Indians of North America—Art—Northwest coast of North America—Exhibitions. I. Forman, Werner. joint author. II. Title.
Distributed by Tudor, New York.

Indians of North America—Basket
   making.

JAMES, George Wharton,   746.4'1
   1858-1923.
Indian basketry. New York, Dover Publications [1972] 271 p. illus. 24 cm. Reprint of the 1909 ed. Includes bibliographical references. [E98.B3J29 1972] 72-81280 3.50 (pbk)
1. Indians of North America—Basket making. I. Title.   BIP

JAMES, George Wharton,   746.4'1
   1858-1923.
Indian basketry, and How to make Indian and other baskets. 3d ed., rev. and enl. Glorieta, N.M., Rio Grande Press [1970] 271, 136 p. illus. 29 cm. (A Rio Grande classic) Reprint of the 1903 ed., with new introductory matter. Includes bibliographies. [TS910.J27 1970] 73-119863
1. Indians of North America—Basket making. 2. Basket making. I. James, George Wharton, 1858-1923. How to make Indian and other baskets. 1970. II. Title. III. Title: How to make Indian and other baskets.

JONES, Joan Megan.   746.4'1
Northwest coast basketry and culture change. [Seattle] Thomas Burke Memorial Washington State Museum [University of Washington, 1968] viii, 60 l. illus. 28 cm. (Thomas Burke Memorial Washington State Museum. Research report no. 1) Cover title. Thesis (M.A.)—University of Washington. Bibliography: p. 60. [E78.N78J6] 78-632185
1. Indians of North America—Basket making. 2. Indians of North America—Northwest coast of North America. I. Title. II. Series: Washington (State). University. Museum. Research report no. 1

LAMB, Frank W.   746.4'1
Indian baskets of North America, by Frank W. Lamb. [1st ed.] Riverside, Calif., Riverside Museum Press [1972] 155 p. illus. 29 cm. Bibliography: p. 153-155. [E98.B3L34] 72-189529 8.50
1. Indians of North America—Basket making. I. Title.

MILES, Charles, 1894-   746.4'1
American Indian and Eskimo basketry: a key to identification. Written and compiled by Charles Miles and Pierre Bovis [Deluxe ed.] San Francisco, Calif., P. Bovis [1969] 144 p. illus., map. 24 cm. Bibliography: p. 19. [E98.B3M5] 70-9044
1. Indians of North America—Basket making. I. Bovis, Pierre, 1943- joint author. II. Title.

NAVAJO School of Indian   746.4'1
   Basketry, Los Angeles.
Indian basket weaving. New York, Dover Publications [1971] 103 p. illus. 24 cm. Reprint of the 1903 ed. [E98.B3N3 1971] 72-179789 ISBN 0-486-22616-6 1.75
1. Indians of North America—Basket making. 2. Basket making. I. Title.   BIP

Indians of North America—Basket
   making—Exhibitions.

FALLON, Carol.   746.4'1
The art of the Indian basket in North America : [exhibition], August 24-October 5, 1975, the University of Kansas Museum of Art, Lawrence, Kansas / introd. and catalogue by Carol Fallon. Lawrence : The Museum, c1975. 56 p. : ill. ; 23 x 26 cm. (Miscellaneous publication of the Museum of Art ; no. 99) Bibliography: p. 53-54. [E98.B3F34] 75-21766
1. Indians of North America—Basket making—Exhibitions. I. Kansas. University. Museum of Art. II. Title. III. Series: Kansas. University. Museum of Art. Miscellaneous publications ; no. 99.

Indians of North America—
   Bibliography.

THOMAS Gilcrease   016.9703
   Institute of American History and Art, Tulsa, Okla. Library.
The Gilcrease-Hargrett catalogue of imprints. Compiled by Lester Hargarett. Prepared for publication and with an introd. by G. P. Edwards. Foreword by John C. Ewers. [1st ed.] Norman, University of Oklahoma Press [1972] xviii, 400 p. 24 cm. [Z1209.2.U5T48] 72-859 ISBN 0-8061-1020-1
1. Indians of North America—Bibliography. 2. Five Civilized Tribes—Bibliography. 3. The West—History—Bibliography. I. Hargrett, Lester, 1902-1962, comp. II. Title.   BIP

Indians of North America—
   Biography—Directories.

SNODGRASS, Jeanne O.,   759.13
   1927-
American Indian painters; a biographical directory. Compiled by Jeanne O. Snodgrass. New York, Museum of the American Indian, Heye Foundation, 1968. xi, 269 p. 26 cm. (Contributions from the Museum of the American Indian, Heye Foundation, v. 21, pt. 1) Bibliography: p. 264-269. [E51.N42 vol. 21, pt. 1] 67-27949 7.50
1. Indians of North America—Biography—Directories. 2. Indians of North America—Art. I. Title. II. Series: New York. Museum of the American Indian, Heye Foundation. Contributions, v. 21, pt. 1 BIP

Indians of North America—British
   Columbia—Antiquities.

SMITH, Harlan Ingersoll,   971.1
   1872-1940.
Cairns of British Columbia and Washington / by Harlan Ingersoll Smith and Gerard Fowke. New York : AMS Press, 1975. p. 55-75, [6] leaves of plates : ill. ; 24 cm. Reprint of the 1901 ed. published in New York, which was issued as v. 4 of Memoirs of the American Museum of Natural History, Anthropology, v. 3, pt. 2, and as v. 2, pt. 2 of Publications of the Jesup North Pacific Expedition. [E78.B9S64 1975] 73-3517 ISBN 0-404-58118-8 : 27.50
1. Indians of North America—British Columbia—Antiquities. 2. Indians of North America—Washington (State)—Antiquities. 3. British Columbia—Antiquities. 4. Washington (State)—Antiquities. I. Fowke, Gerard, 1855-1933, joint author. II. Title. III. Series: American Museum of Natural History, New York. Memoirs ; v. 4. IV. Series: The Jesup North Pacific Expedition. Publications ; v. 2, pt. 2.

SMITH, Harlan Ingersoll,   971.1'2
   1872-1940.
Shell-heaps of the lower Fraser River, British Columbia / by Harlan Ingersoll Smith. New York : AMS Press, 1975. p. 133-191, [2] leaves of plates : ill. ; 24 cm. Reprint of the 1903 ed. published by E. J. Brill, Leiden, and G. E. Stechert, New York, which was issued as v. 4 of Memoirs of the American Museum of Natural History, Anthropology, v. 3, pt. 4, and as v. 2, pt. 4 of Publications of the Jesup North Pacific Expedition. Includes bibliographical references. [E78.B9S65 1975] 73-3519 ISBN 0-404-58120-X : 27.50
1. Indians of North America—British Columbia—Antiquities. 2. British Columbia—Antiquities. 3. Kitchen-middens—British Columbia. 4. Frasier Valley, B.C.—Antiquities. I. Title. II. Series: American Museum of Natural History, New York. Memoirs ; v. 4. III. Series: The Jesup North Pacific Expedition. Publications ; v. 2, pt. 4.   BIP

Indians of North America—British
   Columbia—Art—Pictorial works.

STELTZER, Ulli.   709'.711
Indian artists at work / Ulli Steltzer. Vancouver : J. J. Douglas, c1976. 163 p. : ill. ; 26 cm. [E78.B9S75] 77-363119 ISBN 0-88894-116-1 : 13.95
1. Indians of North America—British Columbia—Art—Pictorial works. 2.

Indians of North America—British Columbia—Portraits. 3. Artists—British Columbia—Portraits. I. Title.   BIP

Indians of North America—British
   Columbia—Costume and
   adornment.

BOAS, Franz, 1858-1942.   391'.6
Facial paintings of the Indians of northern British Columbia / by Franz Boas. New York : AMS Press, 24 p., [7] leaves of plates : ill. ; 24 cm. Reprint of the 1898 ed. published in New York, which was issued as v. 2 of the Memoirs of the American Museum of Natural History, Anthropology, v. 1, pt. 1, and as v. 1, pt. 1 of the Jesup North Pacific Expedition publications. [E78.B9B62 1975] 73-3509 ISBN 0-404-58101-3 : 20.00
1. Indians of North America—British Columbia—Costume and adornment. I. Title. II. Series: American Museum of Natural History, New York. Memoirs ; v. 2. III. Series: The Jesup North Pacific Expedition. Publications ; v. 1, pt. 1. BIP

Indians of North America—
   California—Alameda Co.—
   Antiquities.

PHEBUS, George.   979.4'65'00497
Contributions to Costanoan archaeology : archaeological investigations at 4-ALA-330 and 4-SMA-22 / by George Phebus, Jr. [San Francisco : San Francisco State University, Treganza Anthropology Museum], 1973. 75 p., [11] leaves of plates : ill. ; 28 cm. (Treganza Anthropology Museum papers ; no. 12) Bibliography: p. 74-75. [E78.C15P44] 75-622268
1. Indians of North America—California—Alameda Co.—Antiquities. 2. Alameda Co., Calif.—Antiquities. 3. California—Antiquities. I. Title. II. Series: Treganza Anthropology Museum. Papers ; no. 12.

Indians of North America—
   California—Antiquities.

HEIZER, Robert   732'.2'09701
   Fleming, 1915-
Prehistoric rock art of California [by] Robert F. Heizer and C. W. Clewlow, Jr. Ramona, Calif., Ballena Press, 1973. 2 v. illus. 27 cm. Contents.Contents.—v. 1. Text and plates.—v. 2. Figures. Bibliography: v. 1, p. 122-148. [E78.C15H44] 74-161869 12.50
1. Indians of North America—California—Antiquities. 2. Rock paintings—California. 3. Petroglyphs—California. 4. California—Antiquities. I. Clewlow, C. William, joint author. II. Title.

TURNER, Wilson G.   917.94'95'008 s
3 essays on petroglyphology, by Wilson G. Turner with Eva Fopiano and Bob Reynolds. Illus. by Wilson G. Turner [Bloomington, Calif., San Bernardino County Museum Association, 1971] 34 p. illus. 28 cm. (San Bernardino County Museum Association. Quarterly, v. 19, no. 1) [E78.C15S2 vol. 19, no. 1] 732'.2'09701 73-170226 2.00
1. Indians of North America—California—Antiquities. 2. California—Antiquities. 3. Rock paintings. 4. Petroglyphs. I. Fopiano, Eva. II. Reynolds, Bob. III. Title. IV. Series.

Indians of North America—
   California—Basket making—
   Exhibitions.

CYPRESS College. Fine   746.4'1
   Arts Gallery.
California Indian basketry : an artistic overview : exhibition, November 15 through December 10, 1976, Cypress College Fine Arts Gallery, Cypress, California / exhibit annotations, Arthur M. Silva and William C. Cain. Cypress, Calif. : The Gallery, c1976. 84 p. : ill. ; 28 cm. [E78.C15C95 1976] 77-353859
1. Indians of North America—California—Basket making—Exhibitions. I. Silva, Arthur M. II. Cain, William C. III. Title.

Indians of North America—California—Fresno Valley—Antiquities.

WALLACE, William James. 970.4'94 s
Archaeological investigations at Hidden Reservoir, Madera County, California [by] William J. Wallace. Los Angeles, 1970. iii, 45 l. illus. 28 cm. (Contributions to California archaeology, no. 7) Bibliography: l. 36-39. [E78.C15C685 no. 7] 917.94'81 74-153657
1. Indians of North America—California—Fresno Valley—Antiquities. 2. Fresno Valley, Calif.—Antiquities. I. Title. II. Series.

Indians of North America—California—Glenn Co. —Antiquities.

THE Archaeology of the Black Butte Reservoir region, Glenn and Tehama Counties, California. 917.94'31
Pt. 1: Salvage archaeology in the Black Butte area, Glenn County, California, by Adan Treganza and Martin Heickson. Pt. 2: A study of 4-Glenn-10: the Brownell Indian Cemetery, by Wallace Woolfenden. [San Francisco] San Francisco State College, Anthropology Museum, 1969. 59, 100 p. illus. 28 cm. (San Francisco State College, Anthropology Museum. Occasional paper no. 2) Includes bibliographies. [E78.C15A74] 73-623199
1. Indians of North America—California—Glenn Co. —Antiquities. 2. Indians of North America—California—Tehama Co.—Antiquities. 3. Black Butte Lake, Calif.—Antiquities. 4. California—Antiquities. I. Heickson, Martin. II. Treganza, Adan Eduardo, 1916-1968. Salvage archaeology in the Black Butte area, Glenn County, California. 1969. III. Woolfenden, Wallace. A study of 4-Glenn-10: the Brownell Indian Cemetery. 1969. IV. Series: California. State College, San Francisco. Anthropology Museum. Occasional papers, no. 2.

Indians of North America—California—Marin Co.—Antiquities.

CONTRIBUTIONS to the archaeology of Point Reyes National Seashore; 917.94'62
a compendium in honor of Adan E. Treganza. Edited by Robert E. Schenk. [San Francisco, Treganza Anthropology Museum] 1970. xvii, 321 p. illus. 28 cm. (Treganza Museum. Papers, no. 6) Contents.Contents.—Kawahara, S. A survey of the physical setting of the Point Reyes Peninsula area, Marin County, California.—Mannion, L. and Mannion, M. C. Abstracts from the Kelly manuscript: Coast Miwok material culture.—Moratto, M. J. A history of archaeological research at Point Reyes, California.—Edwards, R. L. A settlement pattern hypothesis for the Coast Miwok based on an archaeological survey of Point Reyes Seashore.—King, T. F. and Upson, W. F. Protohistory on Limantour Sandspit: archaeological investigations at 4-Mrn-216 and 4-Mrn-298.—Henn, W. G. Faunal analysis of 4-Mrn-216, a seasonal site on Limantour Sandspit, Point Reyes National Seashore.—Wilson, S. C. Faunal analysis of 4-Mrn-298W: a perspective of 4-Mrn-216.—Von der Porten, E. P. The porcelains and terra cottas of Drakes Bay.—a compendium in honor of Adan E. Treganza. Edited by Robert E. Schenk. [San Francisco, Treganza Anthropology Museum] 1970. xvii, 321 p. illus. 28 cm. (Treganza Museum. Papers, no. 6) Contents.Contents.—Kawahar
1. Treganza, Adan Eduardo, 1916-1968. 2. Indians of North America—California—Marin Co.—Antiquities. 3. Point Reyes National Seashore—Antiquities. I. Treganza, Adan Eduardo, 1916-1968. II. Schenk, Robert E., 1944-1970, ed. III. Series: Treganza Anthropology Museum. Papers, no. 6.

Indians of North America—California—Pictorial works.

DRAWN from life : 760
California Indians in pen and brush / [compiled] by Theodora Kroeber, Albert B. Elsasser, Robert F. Heizer. Socorro, N.M. : Ballena Press, c1977. 295 p. : ill. ; 24 cm. Bibliography: p. 285-294. [N8217.I5D73] 78-100278 ISBN 0-87919-068-X : 8.95
1. Indians of North America—California—Pictorial works. I. Kroeber, Theodora. II. Elsasser, Albert B. III. Heizer, Robert Fleming, 1915-

Indians of North America—California—Tuolumne Valley—Antiquities.

MORATTO, Michael J. 917.94'45
A study of prehistory in the Tuolumne River Valley, California. Edited by Michael J. Moratto. [San Francisco, Treganza Anthropology Museum] 1971. vi, 177 l. illus. 28 cm. (Treganza Anthropology Museum. Papers, no. 9) "Prepared in partial fulfillment of contract 4970P10605 between the U.S. National Park Service and the Frederic Burk Foundation for Education of San Francisco State College." Bibliography: leaves 146-159. [E78.C15M68] 73-623194
1. Indians of North America—California—Tuolumne Valley—Antiquities. 2. Tuolumne Valley, Calif.—Antiquities. 3. Miwok Indians—Antiquities. I. Title. II. Series.

Indians of North America—Costume and adornment.

HOFSINDE, Robert. 391
Indian costumes, written and illustrated by Robert Hofsinde (Gray-Wolf) New York, W. Morrow [1968] 94 p. illus. 21 cm. Describes everyday, wartime, and ceremonial dress characteristic of the tribal groups of North America: Apache, Blackfoot, Crow, Iroquois, Navaho, Northwest Coast Indians, Ojibwa, Pueblo, Seminole, Sioux, and Indians of today. [E98.C8H6] AC 68
1. Indians of North America—Costume and adornment. I. Title. BIP

HUNT, Walter Bernard, 1888-1970. 970.1
The golden book of Indian crafts and lore. New York, Simon and Schuster [1954] 111 p. illus. 29 cm. [E98.C8H83] 54-12821
1. Indians of North America—Costume and adornment. 2. Indians of North America—Dances. I. Title. II. Title: Indian crafts and lore.

ORCHARD, William C. 745.5
Beads and beadwork of the American Indians : a study based on specimens in the Museum of the American Indian, Heye Foundation / by William C. Orchard. 2d ed. New York : The Museum, 1975. 168 p., [8] leaves of plates : ill. (some col.) ; 26 cm. (Contributions from the Museum of the American Indian, Heye Foundation ; v. 11) Includes bibliographical references. [E98.C8O7 1975] 75-16030
1. Indians of North America—Costume and adornment. 2. Beadwork. 3. Indians—Costume and adornment. 4. Indians—Art. I. Title. II. Series: New York (City). Museum of the American Indian, Heye Foundation. Contributions ; v. 11.

Indians of North America—Costume and adornment—Exhibitions.

CONN, Richard. 746.9'2
Robes of white shell and sunrise : personal decorative arts of the native American : [catalog of an exhibition] Denver Art Museum, November 9, 1974-January 19, 1975 / by Richard Conn. Denver : Denver Art Museum, [1974] 150 p. : ill. (some col.) ; 22 x 28 cm. Bibliography: p. 150. [E98.C8C66] 74-16739 ISBN 0-914738-04-6
1. Denver. Art Museum. 2. Indians of North America—Costume and adornment—Exhibitions. I. Denver. Art Museum. II. Title. BIP

Indians of North America—Costume and adornment—Juvenile literature.

HOFSINDE, Robert. 391'.0091'7597 (j)
Indian costumes, written and illustrated by Robert Hofsinde (Gray-Wolf) New York, W. Morrow [1968] 94 p. illus. 21 cm. [E98.C8H6] 68-11895
1. Indians of North America—Costume and adornment—Juvenile literature. I. Title.

Indians of North America—Culture.

VIDLER, Virginia, 1928- 974'.004'97
American Indian antiques : arts and artifacts of the Northeast / Virginia Vidler. South Brunswick : A. S. Barnes, c1975. 156 p. : ill. ; 32 cm. Includes index. Bibliography: p. 152-153. [E78.E2V53 1976] 74-9302 ISBN 0-498-01495-9 : 20.00
1. Indians of North America—Culture. 2. Indians of North America—Implements. 3. Antiquities—United States. I. Title. BIP

Indians of North America—Dwellings.

LAUBIN, Reginald. 970.657186
The Indian tipi; its history, construction, and use, by Reginald and Gladys Laubin (Tatanka Wanjila na Wiyaka Wastewin) With a history of the tipi by Stanley Vestal. Norman, University of Oklahoma Press [1957] 208 p. illus. 24 cm. [E98.D9L3] 57-5958
1. Indians of North America—Dwellings. I. Laubin, Gladys, joint author. II. Title. BIP

LAUBIN, Reginald. 301.5'4
The Indian tipi : its history, construction, and use / by Reginald and Gladys Laubin (Tatanka Wanjila na Wiyaka Wastewin). With a history of the tipi / by Stanley Vestal. 2d ed. Norman : University of Oklahoma Press, 1977. p. cm. [E98.D9L3 1977] 77-23039 ISBN 0-8061-1433-9 : 12.50
1. Indians of North America—Dwellings. I. Laubin, Gladys, joint author. II. Vestal, Stanley, 1887-1957. The history of the tipi. 1977. III. Title.

Indians of North America—Embroidery.

ORCHARD, William C. 970.1 s
The technique of porcupine-quill decoration among the North American Indians, by William C. Orchard. 2d ed. New York, Museum of the American Indian, Heye Foundation, 1971. 82 p. illus. 25 cm. (Contributions from the Museum of the American Indian, Heye Foundation, v. 4, no. 1) [E51.N42 vol. 4, no. 1, 1971] [E98.E5] 746.4'4 79-170009 3.50
1. Indians of North America—Embroidery. I. Title. II. Series: New York (City). Museum of the American Indian, Heye Foundation. Contributions, v. 4, no. 1. BIP

Indians of North America—Florida—Antiquities.

GRAY, J. Mason. 975.9'004'97
Indian artifact ident.. [Lutz, Fla. : J. M. Gray, 1975] 167 p. : ill. ; 28 cm. Cover title. "Authors edition, copy no. 2 of 50." Imprint stamped on p. [2] of cover. Includes index. Bibliography: p. 158-167. [E78.F6G72] 73-92731
1. Indians of North America—Florida—Antiquities. 2. Florida—Antiquities. I. Title.

Indians of North America—Florida—Implements.

BULLEN, Ripley P. 681'.763
A guide to the identification of Florida projectile points / Ripley P. Bullen. Rev. ed. Gainesville, Fla. : Kendall Books, 1975. 62 p. : ill. ; 28 cm. Bibliography: p. 58-62. [E78.F6B82 1975] 75-2972 pbk. : 2.00
1. Indians of North America—Florida—Implements. 2. Florida—Antiquities. 3. Projectile points. 4. Indians of North America—Florida—Antiquities. I. Title.

BULLEN, Ripley P. 970.4759
A guide to the identification of Florida projectile points, by Ripley P. Bullen. Gainesville, Florida State Museum, University of Florida, 1968. 50 p. illus. 28 cm. Cover title. "References cited": p. 7-10. [E78.F6B82] A 68
1. Indians of North America—Florida—Implements. 2. Florida—Antiquities. 3. Projectile points. 4. Indians of North America—Florida—Antiquities. I. Florida. University, Gainesville. State Museum. II. Title.

Indians of North America—Great Basin—Antiquities.

FOUR Great Basin petroglyph studies. 930'.1 s
Berkeley : University of California, Dept. of Anthropology, 1974. 130 p. : ill. ; 28 cm. (Contributions of the University of California Archaeological Research Facility ; no. 20) Contents.Contents.—Heizer, R. F., and Hester, T. R. Two petroglyph sites in Lincoln County, Nevada.—Nissen, K. M. The record of a hunting practice at petroglyph site NV-LY-1.—Bard, J. C., and Busby, C. I. The manufacture of a petroglyph: a replicative experiment.—Pori, M., and Heizer, R. F. An attempt at computer analysis determination of California rock art styles. Includes bibliographies. [E51.C2 no. 20] [E78.G67] 732'.2'0979 75-620910
1. Indians of North America—Great Basin—Antiquities. 2. Great Basin—Antiquities. 3. Petroglyphs—Great Basin. I. Series: California. University. Archaeological Research Facility. Contributions ; no. 20.

Indians of North America—Great Lakes region—Art—Exhibitions.

FLINT Institute of Arts. 745'.09701
The art of the Great Lakes Indians. [Flint, Mich., 1973] xxxviii, 114 p. illus. (part col.) 28 cm. Catalog of an exhibition organized by the Flint Institute of Arts; held March 25-July 1, 1973. Bibliography: p. 112-113. [E78.G7F54] 72-97819
1. Indians of North America—Great Lakes region—Art—Exhibitions. I. Title.

Indians of North America—Great Lakes region—Costume and adornment—Exhibitions.

BEADS : 746.5
their use by Upper Great Lakes Indians : an exhibition / produced by the Grand Rapids Public Museum and the Cranbrook Academy of Art/Museum. Grand Rapids : The Museum, c1977. 81 p. : ill. ; 29 cm. (Grand Rapids Public Museum publication ; no. 3) Cover title. Includes bibliographies. [E78.G7B4] 77-89533
1. Indians of North America—Great Lakes region—Costume and adornment—Exhibitions. 2. Beadwork—Great Lakes region—Exhibitions. I. Grand Rapids Public Museum. II. Cranbrook Academy of Art, Bloomfield, Mich. Museum. III. Series: Grand Rapids Public Museum. Grand Rapids Public Museum publication ; no. 3.

Indians of North America—Great Plains.

WIED-NEUWIED, Maximilian Alexander Philipp, Prinz von, 1782-1867. 978'.004'97
People of the first man : life among the Plains Indians in their final days of glory : the firsthand account of Prince Maximilian's expedition up the Missouri River, 1833-34 / edited and designed by Davis Thomas and Karin Ronnefeldt ; watercolors by Karl Bodmer. New York : Dutton, 1976. 256 p. : ill. ; 31 cm. Includes index. [E78.G73W5 1976] 76-16577 29.95
1. Indians of North America—Great Plains. 2. Missouri Valley—Description and travel. I. Thomas, Davis. II. Ronnefeldt, Karin. III. Bodmer, Karl, 1809-1893. IV. Title.

Indians of North America—Great Plains—Art.

DUNN, Dorothy, 1903- 759.01'1
American Indian painting of the Southwest and Plains areas. [1st ed. Albuquerque] University of New Mexico, 1968. xxvii, 429 p. illus. (part col.) 29 cm. Includes

Exhibitions. I. United States. Museum of the Plains Indian, Browning, Mont. II. Title.

Indians of North America—Nevada—Pictorial works.

CAPLES, Robert Cole. 741.9'73
People of the silent land; a portfolio of Nevada Indians [by] Robert Caples. Reno, University of Nevada Press, 1972. 1 portfolio ([4] p., 9 plates) 56 cm. "Text excerpted from Survival arts of the primitive Paiutes, by Margaret M. Wheat." [NC139.C33A53] 74-131004
1. Indians of North America—Nevada—Pictorial works. I. Title.

Indians of North America—New Mexico.

UFER, Walter, 1876-1936. 759.13
Ufer in retrospective. [Phoenix? Ariz., 1970] [22] p. illus., port. 26 cm. Catalog of the exhibition organized by the Phoenix Art Museum and the Western Art Associates, Oct.-Dec. 1970. [ND237.U37A58] 71-18750
1. Indians of North America—New Mexico. 2. Indians of North America—Pictorial works. I. Phoenix, Ariz. Art Museum. II. Western Art Associates. III. Title.

Indians of North America—New Mexico—Antiquities.

SCHAAFSMA, Polly. 732'.2
Rock art in New Mexico / by Polly Schaafsma ; photography by Karl Kernberger and Curtis Schaafsma. Albuquerque : Published for the Cultural Properties Review Committee, in cooperation with the State Planning Office, by the University of New Mexico Press, 1972, t.p. 1975. xii, 209 p. : ill. (some col.) ; 28 cm. Bibliography: p. 205-209. [E78.N65S34 1975] 75-5496 ISBN 0-8263-0372-2 : 8.50
1. Indians of North America—New Mexico—Antiquities. 2. New Mexico—Antiquities. 3. Rock paintings—New Mexico. 4. Petroglyphs—New Mexico. I. Kernberger, Karl. II. Schaafsma, Curtis. III. New Mexico. Cultural Properties Review Committee. IV. New Mexico. State Planning Office. V. Title.

Indians of North America—New Mexico—Pottery.

BARNETT, Franklin. 738
Birds on Rio Grande pottery; bird, birdling, and bird tail motifs found on Rio Grande glaze pottery vessels from ancient Tonque Indian ruin in New Mexico. [Yuma, Ariz., Printed by Southwest Printers, c1968] v, 22 p. illus. 22 cm. Bibliography: p. 22. [E98.P8B3] 74-8301
1. Indians of North America—New Mexico—Pottery. 2. Birds in art. 3. Tonque Pueblo. 4. New Mexico—Antiquities. I. Title.

Indians of North America—New York (State)

BEAUCHAMP, William Martin, 1830-1925. 081 s
Metallic ornaments of the New York Indians, by William M. Beauchamp. [East Berlin, Pa., Buffalo Enterprise, 1973?] 120 p. 37 plates. 24 cm. (New York State Museum. Bulletin 73. Archaeology 8) (University of the State of New York. Bulletin 305) Caption title. Facsims. reprint of the 1903 ed. published by the University of the State of New York, Albany. [Q11.N82 no. 73, 1973] [E78.N7] 745'.09701 73-76734
1. Indians of North America—New York (State) 2. Indians of North America—Metal-work. 3. Indians of North America—Costume and adornment. I. Title. II. Series: New York (State). State Museum and Science Service. Bulletin 73. BIP

Indians of North America—New York (State)—Metal-work.

BEAUCHAMP, William Martin, 1830-1925. 745.56
Metallic ornaments of the New York Indians / by William M. Beauchamp. New York : AMS Press, 1976. 120 p., [19] leaves of plates : ill. ; 23 cm. Reprint of the 1903 ed. published by the University of the State of New York, Albany, which was issued as Bulletin 73, Archaeology 8 of the New York State Museum and as Bulletin 305 of the University of the State of New York. Includes index. [E78.N7B36 1976] 74-7928 ISBN 0-404-11814-3 : 12.50
1. Indians of North America—New York (State)—Metal-work. 2. Indians of North America—New York (State)—Costume and adornment. 3. Indians of North America—New York (State)—Antiquities. 4. New York (State)—Antiquities. I. Title. II. Series: New York (State). State Museum and Science Service. Bulletin ; 73.

Indians of North America—North Carolina—Antiquities.

BIERER, Bert W. 739.7'2
Indian arrowheads and spearheads in the Carolinas; a field guide. 170 natural size photos. compiled chronologically by Bert W. Bierer. Columbia, S.C., Carolina Indian Lore Publications [1974] 83 p. illus. 22 cm. [E78.N74B53] 74-75803 4.95
1. Indians of North America—North Carolina—Antiquities. 2. Indians of North America—South Carolina—Antiquities. 3. North Carolina—Antiquities. 4. South Carolina—Antiquities. 5. Projectile points. I. Title.

Indians of North America — Northwest coast of North America.

HARNER, Michael J 709.01'1
Art of the Northwest Coast. An exhibition at the Robert H. Lowie Museum of Anthropology of the University of California, Berkeley, March 26-October 17, 1965. Catalogue by Michael J. Harner and Albert B. Elsasser. [Berkeley University of California, c1965] 112 p. illus., map. 23 cm. Bibilography: p. 111-112. [E78.N78H3] 65-21473
1. Indians of North America — Northwest coast of North America. 2. Indians of North America — Art — Exhibitions. I. Elsasser, Albert B. II. California. University. Robert H. Lowie Museum of Anthropology. III. Title.

Indians of North America—Northwest coast of North America—Art.

BOAS, Franz, 1858-1942. 709'.01'1
The decorative art of the Indians of the north Pacific coast / by Franz Boas. New York : AMS Press, [1976] p. 123-176 : ill. ; 23 cm. Reprint of the 1897 ed. published by order of the Trustees of the American Museum of Natural History, New York, which was issued as v. 9 of its Bulletin. [E78.N78B62 1976] 74-7936 ISBN 0-404-11823-2 : 7.00
1. Indians of North America—Northwest coast of North America—Art. I. Title. II. Series: American Museum of Natural History, New York. Bulletin ; v. 9. BIP

DAVIS, Starr. 709'.01'1
Tongues & totems: comparative arts of the Pacific Basin; a comparison of Northwest coast Indian art with art forms of other cultures around the Pacific Basin, with special reference to the collection of the Alaska International Art Institute, by Starr & Richard Davis. [Anchorage] Alaska International Art Institute [1974] 127 p. illus. 26 cm. Bibliography: p. 124-127. [E78.N78D38] 74-82243
1. Indians of North America—Northwest coast of North America—Art. 2. Art—Pacific area. I. Davis, Richard D., joint author. II. Alaska International Art Institute. III. Title.

HOLM, Bill, 1925- 709'.01'1
A dialogue on form and freedom : Northwest coast Indian art / Bill Holm, William Reid. Houston, Tex. : Institute for the Arts, Rice University, c1975. 260 p. : ill. (some col.) ; 23 cm. On spine: Form and freedom. "Published in conjunction with a Northwest Coast Indian art exhibition, organized by the Institute for the Arts, Rice University, Houston, with the cooperation of the Metropolitan Museum of Art, New York, and participated in by the Art Gallery of Ontario, Toronto, and the Seattle Art Museum." Includes bibliographical references. [E78.N78H59] 75-21395 ISBN 0-914412-09-4
1. Indians of North America—Northwest coast of North America—Art. I. Reid, William, 1920- joint author. II. William Marsh Rice University, Houston, Tex. Institute for the Arts. III. New York (City). Metropolitan Museum of Art. IV. Title. V. Title: Form and freedom.

•HOLM, Bill. 709'.01'1
Indian art of the Northwest Coast : a dialogue on craftmanship and aesthetics / [by] Bill Holm [and] Bill Reid. Houston, Tex. : Institute for the arts, Rice University ; Seattle : distributed by the University of Washington Pr., 1976c197 63]p. : ill., [50] col.plates ; 24 cm. Originally published as : Form and freedom: a dialogue on Northwest Coast Indian art. Includes bibliographical references. [E78.N78H59] 76-15041 ISBN 0-295-95531-7 : 20.00
1. Indians of North America-Northwest Coast of North America-At. I. Reid, Bill, joint author. II. Title. BIP

HOLM, Bill, 1925- 709.17497
Northwest coast Indian art; an analysis of form, by Bill Holm. Seattle, University of Washington Press, 1965. xvii, 115 p. illus., map. 25 cm. (Thomas Burke Memorial Washington State Museum. Monograph no. 1) Bibliography: p. 105-108. [E78.N78H6] 65-10818
1. Indians of North America—Northwest coast of North America—Art. I. Title. II. Series: Washington (State). University. Museum. Monograph no. 1

STEWART, Hilary. 769'.9795
Looking at Northwest Coast Indian art / Hilary Stewart. Seattle : University of Washington Press, 1979. p. cm. [E78.N78S764] 78-73988 ISBN 0-295-95645-3 pbk. : 6.95
1. Indians of North America—Northwest coast of North America—Art. 2. Prints, Indian—Northwest coast of North America. I. Title.

Indians of North America—Northwest coast of North America—Art—Catalogs.

WASHINGTON (State). University. Museum. 709'.01'1
Crooked beak of heaven; masks and other ceremonial art of the Northwest coast, by Bill Holm. Seattle, Published for the Thomas Burke Memorial Washington State Museum and the Henry Art Gallery by the University of Washington Press [1972] 96 p. illus. 28 cm. (Index of art in the Pacific Northwest, no. 3) "Catalogue of the Sidney Gerber Memorial Collection of Northwest Coast Indian Art in the Thomas Burke Memorial Washington State Museum." Bibliography: p. 95-96. [E78.N78W3] 77-39631 ISBN 0-295-95172-9
1. Gerber, Sidney—Art collections. 2. Indians of North America—Northwest coast of North America—Art—Catalogs. 3. Art—Seattle—Catalogs. I. Holm, Bill, 1925- II. Henry Art Gallery. III. Title. IV. Series. BIP

Indians of North America—Northwest coast of North America—Art—Exhibitions.

DUFF, Wilson. 709'.174'97
Arts of the raven: masterworks by the northwest coast Indian; an exhibition in honour of the one hundredth anniversary of Canadian Confederation. Catalogue text by Wilson Duff, with Contributory articles by Bill Holm and Bill Reid. [Vancouver, 1967] 1 v. (unpaged) illus. (part col.), map. 28 cm. (C 67-3540) Held at the Vancouver Art Gallery, 15 June-24 September 1967. [E78.N78D8] 68-81854
1. Indians of North America—Northwest coast of North America—Art—Exhibitions. I. Vancouver, B.C. Art Gallery. II. Title.

LELOOSKA; Shona-Hah, 730'.92'4
Tsungani, Patty Fawn. [Exhibition dates: January 26 to April 7, 1974, Pasadena Museum of Modern Art. Pasadena? Calif., Design World Productions, 1974] 64 p. (chiefly col. illus.) 24 cm. [E78.N78L44] 74-81621 12.00 (pbk.)
1. Lelooska, 1934- 2. Indians of North America—Northwest coast of North America—Art—Exhibitions. I. Lelooska, 1934- II. Pasadena Museum of Modern Art.
Publisher's address: 222 Glenarm, Pasadena, Calif. 91105.

PRINCETON University. Art Museum. 709.01'1
Art of the Northwest coast [Exhibition] Jan. 22 throught [sic] Mar. 2, 1969. [Princeton, N.J., Princeton Print. Co., 1969] 45 p. illus., map. 26 cm. Catalogue edited and designed by Hedy Backlin-Landman. Bibliographical references included in "Notes" (p. [24]) Bibliography: p. 25. [E78.N78P7] 70-8001
1. Indians of North America—Northwest coast of North America—Art—Exhibitions. I. Backlin-Landman, Hedy, ed. II. Title.

REX W. Wignall Museum Gallery. 730
Tribal arts of the Pacific Northwest : [exhibition], June 2-July 2, 1976. Alta Loma, Calif. : Rex W. Wignall Museum Gallery, c1976. 35 p. : ill. ; 28 cm. Bibliography: p. 30-32. [E78.N78R48 1976] 76-372430
1. Indians of North America—Northwest coast of North America—Art—Exhibitions. 2. Indians of North America—Northwest coast of North America—Industries—Exhibitions. I. Title.

WHATCOM Museum of History and Art. 709'.795
Arts of a vanished era. Text by Susan H. L. Barrow and Garland F. Grabert. Photography by Jack Carver and Mr. and Mrs. Mark Flanders. [Bellingham, Wash., 1968] 63 p. (chiefly illus., map (on lining papers)) 24 cm. Catalogue of an exhibition of the Whatcom Museum of History and Art, June 12-Oct. 31, 1968. Bibliography: p. 14. [E78.N78W48] 68-9204
1. Indians of North America—Northwest coast of North America—Art—Exhibitions. I. Barrow, Susan H. L. II. Grabert, Garland F. III. Title. BIP

Indians of North America—Northwest coast of North America—Art—Juvenile literature.

GLUBOK, Shirley. 709'.01'1
The art of the Northwest Coast Indians / by Shirley Glubok ; designed by Gerard Nook. New York : Macmillan, [1975] 48 p. : ill. (some col.) ; 26 cm. Text and photographs examine the artistic heritage of the Indian tribes inhabiting the Pacific coast of the United States and Canada. [E78.N78G58] 74-22384 ISBN 0-02-736150-0 : 7.95
1. Indians of North America—Northwest coast of North America—Art—Juvenile literature. I. Nook, Gerard, ill. II. Title. BIP

Indians of North America—Northwest Coast of North America—Basket making.

INDIAN baskets of the Northwest Coast / by Allan Lobb ; photography by Art Wolfe ; drawings by Barbara Paxson. Portland, Or. : C. H. Belding, c1978. 119 p. : chiefly ill. (some col.) ; 27 cm. Includes index. [E78.N78I53] 78-51216 ISBN 0-912856-37-8 : 19.50. 746.4'1
1. Indians of North America—Northwest Coast of North America—Basket making. I. Lobb, Allan. II. Wolfe, Art.

Indians of North America—Northwest coast of North America—Masks.

MALIN, Edward. 731'.75
World of faces : masks of the northeast

coast Indians / Edward Malin. Portland, Or. : Timber Press, c1978. p. cm. [E78.N78M34] 77-26786 ISBN 0-917304-03-9 : 11.95 ISBN 0-917304-05-5 pbk. : 9.95
1. Indians of North America—Northwest coast of North America—Masks. I. Title. BIP

Indians of North America—Northwest coast of North America—Sculpture.

WINGERT, Paul Stover, 1900- 732'.2
American Indian sculpture : a study of the Northwest coast / Paul S. Wingert. New York : Hacker Art Books, 1976. xii, 144 p., [38] leaves of plates : ill. ; 26 cm. Reprint of the 1949 ed. published by J. J. Augustin, New York, which was originally presented as the author's thesis, Columbia. Bibliography: p. [124]-129. [E78.N78W6 1976] 75-11063 ISBN 0-87817-168-1 lib.bdg. : 20.00
1. Indians of North America—Northwest coast of North America—Sculpture. 2. Salishan Indians—Sculpture. I. Title. BIP

Indians of North America—Northwest coast of North America—Wood-carving.

REID, William. 732'.2
Out of the silence. Photos. by Adelaide De Menil. Text by William Reid. New York, Published for Amon Carter Museum, Fort Worth, by Outerbridge & Dienstfrey [1971] 120 p. illus., map. 25 cm. [E78.N78R4] 74-137008 ISBN 0-87690-043-0 7.95
1. Indians of North America—Northwest coast of North America—Wood-carving. I. De Menil, Adelaide, illus. II. Amon Carter Museum of Western Art, Fort Worth, Tex. III. Title. BIP

Indians of North America—Northwest Pacific—Art.

*HILL, Beth 709.011'795
Indian petroglyphs of the Pacific Northwest [by] Beth and Ray Hill. Seattle, University of Washington Press [1975 c1974] 320 p. illus. 24 cm. Bibliography: p. 299-309. [NK5595] 74-78344 ISBN 0-295-95412-4 19.95.
1. Indians of North America—Northwest Pacific—Art. 2. Petroglyphs. I. Hill, Ray, joint author. II. Title.

Indians of North America—Northwest, Pacific—Pictorial works.

KANE, Paul, 1810-1871. 917.11'04'2
Paul Kane, the Columbia wanderer, 1846-7; sketches and paintings of the Indians and his lecture, "The Chinooks." Edited with an introd. by Thomas Vaughan. [Portland] Oregon Historical Society, 1971. viii, 54, [11] p. illus. 28 cm. Includes a reproduction of "A comprehensive, explanatory, correct pronouncing dictionary, and jargon vocabulary," by F. N. Blanchet, 2d ed., 1853 ([11] p.) at end. Includes bibliographical references. [N6549.K3V3] 74-176250
1. Indians of North America—Northwest, Pacific—Pictorial works. 2. Chinook Indians. I. Vaughan, Thomas, 1924- ed. II. Blanchet, Francis Norbert, Abp., 1795-1883. A comprehensive, explanatory, correct pronouncing dictionary, and jargon vocabulary. 1971. III. Title. BIP

Indians of North America—Pictorial works.

BAIRD, Joseph Armstrong. 759.13
Grace Carpenter Hudson (1865-1937): oil paintings and sketches, including works on loan from C. Frederick Faude. [Catalog of an exhibition] May 22-August 1, 1962, California Historical Society, San Francisco. [San Francisco, California Historical Society, 1962?] [13] p. illus. 28 cm. Bibliography: p. [7] [ND237.H87B34] 74-184891
1. Hudson, Grace Carpenter, 1865-1937. 2. Indians of North America—Pictorial works. I. California Historical Society.

CATLIN, George, 1796-1872. 759.13
George Catlin : painter of the Indians of the Americas : opening exhibition, Sordoni Art Gallery, Wilkes College, Wilkes-Barre, Pennsylvania / introd. and catalogue by Vivian Varney Guyler. [Wilkes-Barre, Pa. : Sordoni Art Gallery?, 1973] [28] p. : ill. (some col.) ; 26 cm. [ND237.C35G89] 75-315758
1. Catlin, George, 1796-1872. 2. Indians of North America—Pictorial works. I. Guyler, Vivian Varney. II. Sordoni Art Gallery.

CATLIN, George, 1796-1872. 759.13
George Catlin book of American Indians / Royal Hassrick. New York : Watson-Guptill, 1977. p. cm. Includes index. Bibliography: p. [ND237.C35H36] 77-7930 ISBN 0-8230-2111-4 : 25.00
1. Catlin, George, 1796-1872. 2. Indians of North America—Pictorial works. I. Hassrick, Royal B. BIP

CURTIS, Edward S., 1868-1952. 779'.9'97000497
Edward Sheriff Curtis : visions of a vanishing race / by Florence Curtis Graybill and Victor Boesen ; photos. prepared by Jean-Anthony du Lac. New York : Crowell, [1976] p. cm. [E77.5.C78 1976] 76-16579 ISBN 0-690-01162-8 : 35.00
1. Crutis, Edward S., 1868-1952. 2. Indians of North America—Pictorial works. I. Graybill, Florence Curtis. II. Boesen, Victor. BIP

CURTIS, Edward S., 1868-1952. 779'.9'9730497
Portraits from North American Indian life / Edward S. Curtis ; introductions by A. D. Coleman and T. C. McLuhan. [New York] A & W Visual Library, [1975], c1972 xvi, 176 p. : chiefly ill. ; 23 x 31 cm. A selection of plates from the author's The North American Indian, supplemental vols. Reprint of the ed. published by Outerbridge & Lazard, New York. [E77.C982 1972b] 74-33775 ISBN 0-89104-003-X : 7.95
1. Indians of North America—Pictorial works. I. Title. BIP

DAWLEY, Joseph. 751.4'5
Painting western character studies : techniques in oil / by Joseph Dawley ; as told to Gloria Dawley and Robert Kolbe. New York : Watson-Guptill, 1975. 160 p. : ill. (some col.) ; 29 cm. Includes index. [ND1302.D37 1975] 75-17889 ISBN 0-8230-3877-7 : 15.95
1. Indians of North America—Pictorial works. 2. Cowboys in art. 3. Painting—Technique. I. Dawley, Gloria. II. Kolbe, Robert, 1931- III. Title.

FARBER, Joseph C., 1903- 779.9'9'9730497
Native Americans : 500 years after / photos. by Joseph C. Farber ; text by Michael Dorris. New York : Crowell, [1975] 333 p. : ill. ; 29 cm. Includes index. Bibliography: p. 325-326. [E77.5.F37 1975] 75-15994 ISBN 0-690-00728-0 : 14.95
1. Indians of North America—Pictorial works. I. Dorris, Michael. II. Title.

GRIDLEY, Marion Eleanor, 1906- comp. 731.8'9
America's Indian statues, compiled by Marion E. Gridley. Chicago, The Amerindian [1966] 104 p. illus., ports. 23 cm. [NB205.G7] 66-31997
1. Indians of North America—Pictorial works. 2. Sculpture, American. I. Title.

KANE, Paul, 1810-1871. 759.11
Paul Kane's frontier; including Wanderings of an artist among the Indians of North America, by Paul Kane. Edited with a biographical introd. and a catalogue raisonne by J. Russell Harper. Austin, Published for the Amon Carter Museum, Fort Worth, and the National Gallery of Canada by the University of Texas Press [1971] xviii, 350 p. illus. (part col.), ports. (part col.) 30 cm. Bibliography: p. 341-342. [ND249.K3H3] 79-146522 ISBN 0-292-70110-1 27.50
1. Indians of North America—Pictorial works. I. Harper, J. Russell, ed. II. Amon Carter Museum of Western Art, Fort Worth, Tex. III. Ottawa. National Gallery of Canada. IV. Kane, Paul, 1810-1871. Wanderings of an artist among the Indians of North America. 1971. V. Title.

MILLER, Alfred Jacob, 1810-1874. 759.13
Braves and buffalo; Plains Indian life in 1837. Water-colours of Alfred J. Miller, with descriptive notes by the artist. Introduced by Michael Bell. [Toronto] University of Toronto Press [1973] 176 p. illus. (part col.) 24 x 31 cm. (The Public Archives of Canada series, 3) [ND1839.M54A42] 73-85088 15.00
1. Miller, Alfred Jacob, 1810-1874. 2. Indians of North America—Pictorial works. I. Title. II. Series: Canada. Public Archives. The Public Archives of Canada series, 3. BIP

MILLICHAP, Joseph R. 759.13
George Catlin / by Joseph R. Millichap. Boise, Idaho : Boise State University, c1977. 48 p. ; 21 cm. (Boise State University Western writers series ; no. 27) Bibliography: p. 47-48. [ND237.C35M54] 77-76200 ISBN 0-88430-051-X : 2.00
1. Catlin, George, 1796-1872. 2. Indians of North America—Pictorial works. I. Title. II. Series: Boise State University. Boise State University Western writers series ; no. 27. BIP

REMINGTON, Frederic, 1861-1909. 759.13
Remington's frontier sketches. New York, B. Franklin [1969] [7] p. 15 plates. 24 x 31 cm. (Art history and art reference series, 25) (Burt Franklin research & source works series, 398.) Reprint of the 1898 ed. [E83.866.R38 1969] 70-101992
1. Indians of North America—Pictorial works. I. Title. BIP

SAMPSON, Frank, 1923- 759.13
Frank Sampson, recent works : [exhibition] , Denver Art Museum, January 18-March 2, 1975. Denver : Denver Art Museum, [1975] [20] p. : chiefly ill. ; 31 cm. [ND237.S266D46] 75-309091 ISBN 0-914738-07-0
1. Sampson, Frank, 1923- 2. Indians of North America—Pictorial works. I. Denver. Art Museum.

SCHOONOVER, Frank Earle, 1877-1972. 760'.092'4 B
Frank Schoonover, illustrator of the North American frontier / by Cortlandt Schoonover. New York : Watson-Guptill Publications, 1976. p. cm. Includes index. [ND237.S4338S37] 76-16509 ISBN 0-8230-4655-9 : 35.00
1. Schoonover, Frank Earle, 1877-1972. 2. Indians of North American—Pictorial works. 3. The West in art. 4. Indians of North America—Canada, Northern—Pictorial works. 5. Canada, Northern, in art. I. Schoonover, Cortlandt. II. Title.

Indians of North America—Pictorial works—Exhibitions.

CURTIS, Edward S., 1868-1952. 779'.9'97010924
The North American Indians: a selection of photographs by Edward S. Curtis. Text compiled with an introd. by Joseph Epes Brown. New York [Aperture] 1972. 94 p. (chiefly illus.) 26 cm. Published in conjunction with an exhibition held Sept. 7-Oct. 15, 1972, in Philadelphia Museum of Art. Includes bibliographical references. [E77.5.C82] 72-87367 ISBN 0-912334-34-7 10.00
1. Indians of North America—Pictorial works—Exhibitions. I. Brown, Joseph Epes. II. Title.
Publisher's Address: Elm Street, Millerton, New York, 12546

MCGREW, Ralph Brownell, 1916- 759.13
R. Brownell McGrew : Laguna Beach Museum of Art, presented by the Thunderbird Foundation, August, 1978. 1st ed. Kansas City : Lowell Press, c1978. xvii, 128 p. : ill. (some col.) ; 23 x 29 cm. [N6537.M334A4 1978] 78-53113 ISBN 0-913504-43-2 : 25.00.
1. McGrew, Ralph Brownell, 1916- —Exhibitions. 2. Indians of North America—Pictorial works—Exhibitions. 3. The West in art—Exhibitions. I. Laguna Beach Museum of Art. II. Thunderbird Foundation. BIP

Indians of North America—Pictorial works—Juvenile literature.

COEN, Rena Neumann. 757
The Red man in art. Designed by Vicki Hall. Minneapolis, Lerner Publications Co. [1972] 71 p. illus. (part col.) 26 cm. (Fine art books for young people) Examines paintings of Indian subjects by such well-known painters as Remington, Catlin, etc., as well as some of the art and artifacts by North American Indians. [N8217.I5C63 1972] 72-267 ISBN 0-8225-0171-6 4.50
1. Indians of North America—Pictorial works—Juvenile literature. I. Title. BIP

Indians of North America—Pictures, illustrations, etc.

MCDERMOTT, John Francis, 1902- 759.13
Seth Eastman, pictorial historian of the Indian. [1st ed.] Norman, University of Oklahoma Press [1961] x, 270 p. plates (part col.) ports. 27 cm. "Checklist of works [by S. Eastman]": p. 228-255. Bibliography: p. 256-261. [ND237.E35M33] 61-15145
1. Eastman, Seth, 1808-1875. 2. Indians of North America—Pictures, illustrations, etc.

Indians of North America—Portraits.

CYBIS, Boleslaw, 1895-1957. 741.9'438
Folio one; American Indian drawings. [Trenton, N.J., Cybis, c1970] 1 portfolio ([1] l., 9 plates, part col.) 62 cm. Title from portfolio. Each plate in folder with descriptive letterpress. [NC312.P63C94 (fol.)] 72-171633
1. Indians of North America—Portraits. I. Title.

REISS, Winold, 1886-1953. 759.3
Winold Reiss: Plains portraits. Exhibition October 4 through October 28, 1972, Kennedy Galleries, Inc. New York, [Kennedy Galleries, c1972] 32 p. illus. (part col.) 27 cm. [ND1329.R34K46] 73-170565
1. Reiss, Winold, 1886-1953. 2. Indians of North America—Portraits. I. Kennedy Galleries, inc., New York. II. Title.

REYNOLDS, Charles R., comp. 778.9'2'09701
American Indian portraits; from the Wanamaker expedition of 1913, chosen and with an introd. by Charles R. Reynolds, Jr. Brattleboro, Vt., S. Greene Press [1971] 123 p. ports. 32 cm. The pictures may have been taken by Joseph Kossuth Dixon, who led the expedition or by members of his staff, Rollin Lester Dixon, W. B. Cline, and John D. Scott. [E89.R4] 76-173404 ISBN 0-8289-0146-5 12.50
1. Indians of North America—Portraits. I. Dixon, Joseph Kossuth. II. Title.

RINEHART, Frank A. 779'.9'9701
The face of courage; the Indian photographs of Frank A. Rinehart. Cover illus.: Harley Brown. Introd. by: Royal Sutton. Illus.: Derek Fitz James. [Fort Collins, Colo.] Old Army Press [1972] [30] p., 90 plates. illus. 31 cm. [E89.R56] 70-184828
1. Indians of North America—Portraits. 2. Indians of North America—Great Plains. I. Title.

VIOLA, Herman J. 759.13
The Indian legacy of Charles Bird King / Herman J. Viola. 1st ed. Washington : Smithsonian Institution Press, c1976. 152 p. : ill. (some col.) ; 29 cm. (Smithsonian Institution Press publication ; no. 6256) "Catalog of War Department Indian Gallery": p. 143-145. Includes index. Bibliography: p. 146-148. [ND237.K53V56] 76-15022 19.95
1. King, Charles Bird, 1785-1862. 2. Indians of North America—Portraits. 3. Indians of North America—Government relations—1789-1869. I. Title. BIP

Indians of North America — Pottery.

FONTANA, Bernard L. 970.67383
Papago Indian pottery, by Bernard L. Fontana [and others] Seattle, University of

Washington Press, 1962 [i. e. 1963] 163 p. illus. 23 cm. At head of title: The American Ethnological Society. Includes bibliography. [E98.P8F54 1963] 62-9271
1. Indians of North America—Pottery. 2. Papago Indians—Art. I. American Ethnological Society. II. Title.

HEIMLICH, Marion Dunlevy. 970.657155
Guntersville Basin pottery. University, Geological Survery of Alabama, 1952. 69p. tables. 23cm. (Geological Survey of Alabama. Musum paper. 32) [E98.P8H4] 55-62184
1. Indians of North America—Pottery. 2. Pottery—Guntersville Basin. I. Title. II. Series: Alabama. State Geologist. Museum. Museum paper, 32

WIMBERLY, Steve Boynton, 1916- 970.65715
Indian pottery from Clarke County and Mobile County, Southern Alabama. With The geographic and historic background, by Christine Wimberly; The lithic material, by Daniel W. Josselyn; and A study of Indian skeletal material from Clarke and Mobile Counties, by Marshall T. Newman. University, Ala., Geological Survey of Alabama, 1960. viii, 262 p. illus., maps. 24 cm. (Alabama Museum of Natural History. Museum paper 36) Bibliography: p. 258-262. [E78.A28W5] 62-62668
1. Indians of North America — Pottery. 2. Indians of North America — Alabama. 3. Mobile Co., Ala. — Antiq. 4. Clarke Co., Ala. — Antiq. I. Title. II. Series: Alabama. Geological Survey. Museums. Museum paper 36

Indians of North America—Silversmithing.

MERA, Harry Percival, 1875-1951. 970.673923
Indian silverwork of the Southwest, illustrated. [2d ed.] Globe, Ariz., D. S. King, 1960- v. illus. 23cm. [E98.S55M43] 61-1677
1. Indians of North America—Silversmithing. 2. Indians of North America—Southwest, New. 3. Silversmithing—Southwest, New. I. Title. BIP

Indians of North America—Silverwork.

HUNT, Walter Bernard, 1888-1970. 970.673923
Indian silversmithing. Milwaukee, Bruce Pub. Co. [1960] 160 p. 27 cm. [E98.S55H85 1960] 60-4298
1. Indians of North America—Silverwork. 2. Silverwork—Southwest, New. I. Title. BIP

HUNT, Walter Bernard, 1888-1970. 970.1
Indian silversmithing. Milwaukee, Bruce Pub. Co. [1952] 160 p. illus. 27 cm. [E98.S55H85] 970.673923 52-11328
1. Indians of North America—Silverwork. 2. Silverwork—Southwest, New. I. Title.

Indians of North America—Social life and customs.

NORBECK, Oscar E. 745.5
Indian crafts for campers; a condensation of Book of Indian life crafts, by Oscar E. Norbeck. Illustrated by John B. Eves. New York, Association Press [1967] 128 p. illus. 16 cm. (The Camp and trail pocket library) Includes bibliographies. [E77.N6 1967] 67-11533
1. Indians of North America—Social life and customs. 2. Indians of North America—Industries. I. Title.

Indians of North America—Southern States—Juvenile literature.

GLUBOK, Shirley. 709'.01'1
The art of the southeastern Indians / by Shirley Glubok ; designed by Gerard Nook ; special photography by Alfred Tamarin. New York : Macmillan, c1978. 48 p. : ill. ; 26 cm. A survey of the art and history of the various Southeastern Indian tribes from 5000 B.C. to the present. [E78.S65G58 1978] 77-20850 ISBN 0-02-736480-1 : 7.95
1. Indians of North America—Southern States—Juvenile literature. 2. Indians of North America—Southern States—Art—Juvenile literature. I. Title. BIP

Indians of North America—Southern States—Pictorial works.

FUNDABURK, Emma Lila, 1922- ed. 760
Southeastern Indians: life portraits; a catalogue of pictures, 1564-1860. Metuchen, N.J., Scarecrow Reprint Corp., 1969. 135 p. illus., maps, ports. 28 cm. Reprint of the 1958 ed. Includes bibliographical references. [E78.S65F8 1969] 76-6022
1. Indians of North America—Southern States—Pictorial works. 2. Art—United States. I. Title.

Indians of North America—Southwest, New.

BENNETT, Edna Mae. 739.27
Turquoise and the Indian. Denver, Sage Books [1966] 152 p. illus. (part col.) map, port. 22 cm. Bibliography: p. 142-149. [E78.S7B4] 66-25963
1. Indians of North America—Southwest, New. 2. Indians of North America—Costumes and adornment. 3. Turquoise—Southwest, New. I. Title. BIP

Indians of North America—Southwest, New—Art.

JACKA, Jerry D. 739.27
Turquoise treasures : the splendor of Southwest Indian art / photography by Jerry Jacka ; text by Spencer Gill. Portland, Or. : Graphic Arts Center Pub. Co., c1975. [96] p. : chiefly col. ill. ; 27 cm. [E78.S7J18] 75-7141 ISBN 0-912856-21-1 : 19.50
1. Indians of North America—Southwest, New—Art. 2. Indians of North America—Southwest, New—Costume and adornment. 3. Turquoise. I. Gill, Spencer. II. Title. BIP

MONTHAN, Guy. 709'.2'2
Art and Indian individualists : the art of seventeen contemporary Southwestern artists and craftsmen / by Guy and Doris Monthan ; foreword by Lloyd Kiva New. 1st ed. Flagstaff, Ariz. : Northland Press, c1975. xviii, 197 p. : ill. (some col.) ; 32 cm. Includes index. Bibliography: p. 189-191. [E78.S7M66] 74-31544 ISBN 0-87358-137-7 : 35.00
1. Indians of North America—Southwest, New—Art. 2. Art—Southwest, New. I. Monthan, Doris Born, 1924- joint author. II. Title. BIP

TANNER, Clara Lee. 759.979
Southwest Indian painting; a changing art. 2d ed. Tucson, University of Arizona Press [1973] xvii, 477 p. illus. (part col.) 32 cm. Bibliography: p. 453-458. [E78.S7T32 1973] 74-160812 ISBN 0-8165-0309-5 35.00
1. Indians of North America—Southwest, New—Art. I. Title. BIP

Indians of North America—Southwest, New—Art—Juvenile literature.

GLUBOK, Shirley. 709.01'1
The art of the Southwest Indians. Photos. by Alfred Tamarin. Designed by Gerard Nook. New York, Macmillan [1971] 48 p. illus. 25 x 26 cm. Describes and discusses wall and sand paintings, Katchina dolls, pottery, and other forms of Southwest Indian art. Illustrated with black and white photographs. [E78.S7G45] 78-133558
1. Indians of North America—Southwest, New—Art—Juvenile literature. I. Title.

Indians of North America—Southwest, New—Arts.

TANNER, Clara Lee. 745
Prehistoric southwestern craft arts / Clara Lee Tanner. Tucson : University of Arizona Press, c1976. xiii, 226 p. : ill. (some col.) ; 31 cm. Includes index. Bibliography: p. 219-222. [E78.S7T29] 75-19865 ISBN 0-8165-0582-9 : 17.50. ISBN 0-8165-0416-4 pbk. : 8.95
1. Indians of North America—Southwest, New—Arts. 2. Indians of North America—Southwest, New—Industries. I. Title. BIP

Indians of North America—Southwest, New—Basket making.

NEWMAN, Sandra Corrie. 746.4'1
Indian basket weaving : how to weave Pomo, Yurok, Pima, and Navajo baskets / by Sandra Corrie Newman. 1st ed. Flagstaff [Ariz.] : Northland Press, [1974] xvi, 91 p. : ill. ; 23 cm. Bibliography: p. 89-90. [E98.B3N48] 73-79779 ISBN 0-87358-112-1 : 4.95
1. Indians of North America—Southwest, New—Basket making. 2. Basket making. I. Title.

Indians of North America—Southwest, New—Basket making—Exhibitions.

HOULIHAN, Patrick T. 746.4'1
Indian basket designs of the Greater Southwest : Utah Museum of Fine Arts, University of Utah, 18 April-30 May, 1976 / by Patrick T. Houlihan. Salt Lake City : Utah Museum of Fine Arts, University of Utah, c1976. [48] p. (incl. cover) : ill. ; 21 cm. "The exhibition ... is the fifth in a series commemorating the American Revolution Bicentennial." [E78.S7H75] 76-5655
1. Indians of North America—Southwest, New—Basket making—Exhibitions. 2. Indians of North America—Southwest, New—Art—Exhibitions. I. Utah Museum of Fine Arts. II. Title.

JETT, Stephen C., 1938- 746.4'1
Interwoven heritage : a bicentennial exhibition of Southwestern Indian basketry and textile arts, featuring the C. Hart Merriam collection of baskets and the Stephen C. Jett collection of Navajo weaving, January 9-February 8, 1976 : [catalogue] / Stephen C. Jett. Davis : University of California, Davis, Memorial Union Art Gallery, c1976. 44 p., [2] leaves of plates : ill. ; 28 cm. Bibliography: p. 41-44. [E78.S7J47] 76-359672
1. Merriam, Clinton Hart, 1855-1942—Art collections. 2. Jett, Stephen C., 1938- —Art collections. 3. Indians of North America—Southwest, New—Basket making—Exhibitions. 4. Navaho Indians—Textile industry and fabrics—Exhibitions. 5. Indians of North America—Southwest, New—Textile industry and fabrics—Exhibitions. I. California. University, Davis. Art Gallery. II. Title.

Indians of North America—Southwest, New—Costume and adornment.

BENNETT, Edna Mae. 739.27'09701
Turquoise jewelry of the Indians of the Southwest [by] Edna Mae and John F. Bennett. [Colorado Springs, Turquoise Books, 1973] 148 p. illus. 29 cm. Bibliography: p. 147-148. [E78.S7B42] 74-152738 15.00
1. Indians of North America—Southwest, New—Costume and adornment. 2. Indians of North America—Southwest, New—Industries. 3. Turquoise—Southwest, New. I. Bennett, John F., joint author. II. Title. BIP

BRANSON, Oscar T. 739.27
Indian jewelry making / by Oscar T. Branson. Tucson, Ariz. : Treasure Chest Publications, c1977. 64 p. : col. ill. ; 31 cm. [E98.C8B7] 77-369474 ISBN 0-442-21418-9 : 12.95
1. Indians of North America—Southwest, New—Costume and adornment. 2. Jewelry making—Amateurs' manuals. 3. Indian craft. I. Title. BIP

CONROY, Kathleen. 739.27'09789
What you should know about authentic Indian Jewelry / by Kathleen Conroy ; ill. Diane M. Smucny. 1st ed. Denver, Colo. : Gro-Pub Group, c1975. 111 p. : ill. (some col.) ; 21 cm. Bibliography: p. 109-111. [E78.S7C64] 75-27722 ISBN 0-914990-01-2 pbk. : 3.75
1. Indians of North America—Southwest, New—Costume and adornment. 2. Jewelry—Southwest, New. I. Smucny, Diane M. II. Title.

FRAZIER, Gloria. 739.27
Navajos call it hard goods / by Gloria Frazier. [s.l. : s.n., c1976] (Tombstone? Ariz. : Tombstone Printers) 66 p. : ill. ; 22 cm. Cover title. Bibliography: p. 65-66. [E78.S7F75] 76-51101
1. Indians of North America—Southwest, New—Costume and adornment. 2. Indians of North America—Southwest, New—Silverwork. 3. Turquoise—Southwest, New. I. Title.

JACKA, Jerry D. 736
Indian jewelry of the prehistoric Southwest / photos. by Jerry D. Jacka ; text by Nancy S. Hammack. Tucson : University of Arizona Press, c1975. [48] p. : col. ill. ; 23 cm. [E78.S7J17] 75-8017 ISBN 0-8165-0515-2 : 4.95
1. Indians of North America—Southwest, New—Costume and adornment. 2. Southwest, New—Antiquities. 3. Indians of North America—Southwest, New—Antiquities. I. Hammack, Nancy S., joint author. II. Title. BIP

LUND, Marsha Mayer, 1939- 739.27
Indian jewelry : fact and fantasy / by Marsha Mayer Lund. Boulder, Colo. : Paladin Press, c1976. 159 p. : ill. ; 22 cm. Bibliography: p. 157-159. [E78.S7L86] 76-5401 ISBN 0-87364-052-7 pbk. : 6.95
1. Indians of North America—Southwest, New—Costume and adornment 2. Indians of North America—Southwest, New—Industries 3. Jewelry—Directories. I. Title. BIP

ROSNEK, Carl, 1926- 739.27'0979
Skystone and silver : the collector's book of Southwest Indian jewelry / by Carl Rosnek and Joseph Stacey. Englewood Cliffs, N.J. : Prentice-Hall, c1976. ix, 166 p., [40] leaves of plates : ill. ; 31 cm. Includes index. [E78.S7R67] 76-29060 ISBN 0-13-812834-0 : 39.95
1. Indians of North America—Southwest, New—Costume and adornment. 2. Jewelry—Southwest, New. 3. Jewelry—Collectors and collecting. I. Stacey, Joseph, joint author. II. Title. BIP

Indians of North America—Southwest, New—Industries.

TANNER, Clara Lee. 745.5'09791
Southwest Indian craft arts. Tucson, University of Arizona Press [1968] 206 p. illus. (part col.), map. 32 cm. Bibliography: p. 199-202. [E78.S7T3] 66-24299
1. Indians of North America—Southwest, New—Industries. 2. Indians of North America—Southwest, New—Art. I. Title. BIP

Indians of North America—Southwest, New—Pictorial works.

VROMAN, Adam Clark, 1856-1916. 970.4'9
Dwellers at the source; Southwestern Indian photographs of A. C. Vroman, 1895-1904, by William Webb and Robert A. Weinstein. New York, Grossman Publishers, 1973. 213 p. illus. 24 x 28 cm. "From the A. C. Vroman Collection at the Natural History Museum of Los Angeles County." Bibliography: p. 212-213. [E78.S7V76 1973] 72-77703 ISBN 0-670-28671-0 25.00
1. Indians of North America—Southwest, New—Pictorial works. I. Webb, William, 1919- II. Weinstein, Robert A. III. Los Angeles Co., Calif. Museum of Natural History, Los Angeles. IV. Title. BIP

Indians of North America—Southwest, New—Pottery.

BENNETT, M. Ann. 738.3
Basic ceramic analysis / M. Ann Bennett. [Portales : Eastern New Mexico University], 1974. xi, 183 p. : ill. ; 27 cm. (Technical series - San Juan Valley Archaeological Project ; no. 1) (Contributions in anthropology ; v. 6, no. 1) [E78.S7B43] 75-621756
1. Indians of North America—Southwest, New—Pottery. 2. Pueblo Indians—Pottery. 3. Pottery—Analysis. I. Title. II. Series. III. Series: San Juan Valley Archaeological Project. Technical series — San Juan Valley Archaeological Project ; no. 1.

Translation of Kunstgeschichte des alten Peru. Reprint of the 1924 ed. published by E. Benn, London. "Publication of the Ethnological Institute of the Ethnographical Museum, Berlin." Bibliography: p. 66-68 (1st group) [F3429.3.A7L3313 1975] 72-87767 ISBN 0-87817-119-3 : 60.00
1. Indians of South America—Peru—Art. 2. Indians of South America—Peru—Antiquities. 3. Peru—Antiquities. I. Doering, Heinrich, joint author. II. Title.
BIP

Indians of South America—Peru—Art—Exhibitions.

ANDRE Emmerich Gallery, New York. 709'.701
Sun gods and saints, art of pre-Columbian and colonial Peru; an exhibition organized in cooperation with Alan C. Lapiner, December 6 to 31, 1969. New York [1969?] 1 v. (chiefly illus., part col.) map (p. [2] of cover) 28 cm. On cover: Peru. Includes bibliography. [F3429.3.A7A674] 78-21256
1. Indians of South America—Peru—Art—Exhibitions. 2. Art—Peru—Exhibitions. I. Lapiner, Alan C. II. Title.

SAWYER, Alan Reed, 1919- 709'.174'98
Master craftsmen of ancient Peru. [by] Alan R. Sawyer. [New York, Solomon R. Guggenheim Foundation, 1968] 101 p. illus. (part col.), col. maps. 28 cm. "Exhibition 68/6." Catalogue of an exhibition organized by and presented at the Solomon R. Guggenheim Museum. [F3429.3.A7S26] 68-56627
1. Indians of South America—Peru—Art—Exhibitions. 2. Peru—Antiquities. I. Solomon R. Guggenheim Museum, New York. II. Title.

Indians of South America—Peru—Goldwork.

LECHTMAN, Heather. 301.2'4
Seven matched hollow gold jaguars from Peru's early horizon / Heather Lechtman, Lee A. Parsons, William J. Young. Washington : Dumbarton Oaks, Trustees for Harvard University, 1975. 46 p. : ill. (some col.) ; 27 cm. (Studies in pre-Columbian art and archaeology ; no. 16) Bibliography: p. 45-46. [E51.S85 no. 16] [F3429.3.G5] 615'.89 75-21192 3.00
1. Indians of South America—Peru—Goldwork. 2. Chauvin, Peru. 3. Peru—Antiquities. I. Parsons, Lee Allen, 1932- joint author. II. Young, William Jonathan, 1906- joint author. III. Title. IV. Series. BIP

Indians of South America—Peru—Ica (Dept.)—Pottery.

MENZEL, Dorothy. 738.3'7
Pottery style and society in ancient Peru : art as a mirror in the Inca Valley, 1350-1570 Dorothy Menzel. Berkeley : University of California Press, c1976. xiii, 275 p., [32] leaves of plates : ill. ; 29 cm. Bibliography: p. [257]-260. [F3429.1.I24M46] 74-29797 ISBN 0-520-02970-4 : 25.00
1. Indians of South America—Peru—Ica (Dept.)—Pottery. 2. Ica, Peru (Dept.)—Antiquities. 3. Peru—Antiquities. I. Title.
BIP

Indians of South America—Peru—Pottery—Exhibitions.

FLORIDA. University, Gainesville. University Gallery. 738.3
Pre-Columbian pottery of Peru from the collection of the University Gallery / by Elisabeth K. Gordon, photography by Roy C. Craven, Jr. Gainesville : University Gallery, College of Architecture and Fine Arts, University of Florida, 1975. [16] p., [10] leaves of plates : ill. ; 23 cm. (University Gallery bulletin ; 1, no. 1) "This collection is being shown and documented in conjunction with the special photographic exhibition: Machu Picchu of the Inca ... These two exhibitions are being presented to mark the advent of the 25th Annual Latin American Conference." Bibliography: p. [10] [F3429.3.P8F56 1975] 75-624261
1. Florida. University, Gainesville. University Gallery. 2. Indians of South America—Peru—Pottery—Exhibitions. I. Gordon, Elsbeth K. II. Craven, Roy C., 1924- III. Title. IV. Series: Florida. University, Gainesville. University Gallery bulletin ; 1, no. 1.

WITEK, Joan. 738.3'0985
Mochica, Paracas, and Nazca : one thousand years of ancient Peruvian ceramics, June 14-July 27. Flushing, N.Y. : Queens Museum, c1975. [24] p. : ill. ; 22 cm. "This exhibition has been selected from the collection of the Metropolitan Museum of Art." [F3429.3.P8W57] 76-357699
1. New York (City). Metropolitan Museum of Art. 2. Indians of South America—Peru—Pottery—Exhibitions. I. Queens Museum. II. Title.

Indians of South America—Pottery—Exhibitions.

BALTIMORE. Museum of Art. 738
Myths of ancient Peru; [exhibition, Oct. 7-Nov. 30, 1969. Baltimore, Md., 1969] 32 p. illus., map (on lining paper) 22 cm. Includes essays by H. Bruce Greene and William L. Hommel. [F3429.3.P8B3] 77-100497
1. Indians of South America—Pottery—Exhibitions. I. Title.

Indians of the West Indies—Antiquities—Bibliography.

CHEVRETTE, Valerie. 016.709'01'1
Annotated bibliography of the precolumbian art and archaeology of the West Indies. New York, Library, Museum of Primitive Art, 1971. 18 p. 28 cm. (Primitive art bibliographies, no. 9) [Z1208.W45C48] 74-186728
1. Indians of the West Indies—Antiquities—Bibliography. 2. Indians of the West Indies—Art—Bibliography. I. Title. II. Series.

Industrial arts.

BIZLEWICZ, George. 736.2028
Industrial arts: guide for teaching the lapidary arts. New Brunswick, N. J., Vocational Division, Curriculum Laboratory, New Brunswick. [TS752.B5] A59
I. Title.

CURRY, Estell H. 600
General industrial arts [by] Estell H. Curry, Rolland H. Pardonnet [and] Russell W. Symes. Princeton, N.J., Van Nostrand [1967] vi, 234 p. illus. 27 cm. [TT165.C8] 67-1505
1. Industrial arts. 2. Manual training. I. Pardonnet, Rolland H., joint author. II. Symes, Russell W., joint author. III. Title.

INDUSTRIAL arts 600
[by] William D. Wolansky [and others] Toronto, New York [etc.] McGraw-Hill [1968] xi, 372 p. illus. 25 cm. Includes bibliographical references. [TT165.I5] 68-115426
1. Industrial arts. I. Wolansky, William D.

LAUSTRUP, Jes. 607'.1'2
Exploring industrial education [by] Jes Laustrup, Chris H. Groneman [and] John L. Feirer. Toronto, New York, McGraw-Hill Co. of Canada [1968] xvi, 248 p. illus. (part col.) 25 cm. [TT165.L38] 75-31461
1. Industrial arts. I. Groneman, Chris Harold, 1906- joint author. II. Feirer, John Louis, joint author. III. Title.

LINDBECK, John Robert. 745.5
Basic crafts / John R. Lindbeck, Lester G. Duenk, Marc F. Hansen ; John L. Feirer, editor. 2d ed. Peoria, Ill. : C. A. Bennett Co., c1979. 331 p. : ill. ; 24 cm. Includes index. [TT165.L48 1979] 77-84989 ISBN 0-87002-275-X : 9.28
1. Industrial arts. I. Duenk, Lester G., joint author. II. Hansen, Marc F., joint author. III. Feirer, John Louis. IV. Title. BIP

STEINMETZ, Rollin C. 745.5
Vanishing crafts and their craftsmen [by] Rollin C. Steinmetz [and] Charles S. Rice. New Brunswick, N. J., Rutgers University Press, 1959. 160 p. illus. 24 cm. [T139.S7] 59-7515
1. Industrial arts. 2. Handicraft. I. Rice, Charles Scott, 1910- joint author. II. Title.

Industrial arts—Early works to 1800.

MOXON, Joseph, 1627-1700. 684.08
Mechanick exercises; or, The doctrine of handy-works, applied to the arts of smithing, joinery, carpentry, turning, bricklaying, to which is added, Mechanick dyalling: shewing how to draw a true sun-dyal on any given plane, however scituated; only with the help of a straight ruler and a pair of compasses, and without any arithmetical calculation. With an introd., table of contents, and captions explaining the 26 plates by Benno M. Forman. Charles F. Montgomery, editor. New York, Praeger [1970] xxxvii, 352 p. illus. 21 cm. (Praeger reprints on arts, crafts, and trades) Originally published in 1703. [TT144.M93 1970] 69-19363
1. Industrial arts—Early works to 1800. 2. Sun-dials. I. Title.

Industrial arts—Examinations, questions, etc.

ARCO Publishing Company, New York. 607'.36
Apprentice, mechanical trades; the complete study guide for scoring high, by the Arco editorial board. New York, Arco [1966, c1965] 128, [52] p. illus. 26 cm. [TT149.A68] 64-24632
1. Industrial arts—Examinations, questions, etc. I. Title. BIP

ARCO Publishing Company, New York. 607'.36
Apprentice, mechanical trades, by the Arco editorial board. [5th ed.] New York [1973] 192 p. illus. 26 cm. (Arco civil service test tutor) "The complete study guide for scoring high." [TT169.A7 1973] 73-89227 ISBN 0-668-00571-8 4.00
1. Industrial arts—Examinations, questions, etc. I. Title.

†ARCO Publishing Company, New York. 607'.36
Apprentice, mechanical trades : the complete study guide for scoring high / by the Arco editorial board. 6th ed. New York : Arco, c1977. 192 p. : ill. ; 26 cm. (Arco civil service test tutor) [TT169.A7 1977] 77-21217 ISBN 0-668-00571-8 : 6.00
1. Industrial arts—Examinations, questions, etc. I. Title.

COWLES Education Corporation. 607
How to pass NTE teaching area examination: industrial arts education. New York [1968] 1 v. (unpaged) 28 cm. [TT149.C6] 67-26828
1. Industrial arts—Examinations, questions, etc. 2. National teacher examinations. I. Title. II. Title: NTE teaching area examination: Industrial arts education.

GRUBER, Edward C. 607
Teacher of industrial arts; high school and junior high school, by Edward C. Gruber. [New York, Arco Pub. Co., 1970] 1 v. (various pagings) 26 cm. (Arco teacher license series) [TT149.G7 1970] 75-18814 6.00
1. Industrial arts—Examinations, questions, etc. 2. Industrial arts—Study and teaching (Secondary) I. Title.

GRUBER, Edward C. 607.73
Teacher of industrial arts; high school and junior high school. [New York, Arco, 1965] 1 v. (various pagings) forms. 27cm. (Arco teacher license ser.) [TT149.G7] 65-22179 3.00 pap.,
1. Industrial arts—Examinations, questions, etc. 2. Industrial arts—Study and teaching (Secondary) I. Arco Publishing Company, New York. II. Title.

Industrial arts—Juvenile literature.

GRONEMAN, Chris Harold, 1906- 600
General industrial education / Chris H. Groneman, John L. Feirer. 6th ed. New York : McGraw-Hill, c1979. xi, 564 p. : ill. ; 25 cm. (McGraw-Hill publications in industrial education) Includes index. A junior high industrial arts textbook introducing the basics of drafting, graphic art, woodworking, electronics, metalworking, plastics, leather, electricity, power mechanics, and home maintenance and providing information of careers in each of these areas. [TT165.G74 1979] 78-17517 ISBN 0-07-024991-1 : 14.00
1. Industrial arts—Juvenile literature. 2. Manual training—Juvenile literature. I. Feirer, John Louis, joint author. II. Title.

GRONEMAN, Chris Harold, 1906- 600
General industrial education [by] Chris H. Groneman [and] John L. Feirer. 5th ed. New York, McGraw-Hill [1974] xi, 564 p. illus. 25 cm. (McGraw-Hill publications in industrial education) First-4th editions published under title: General shop. A junior high industrial arts textbook featuring industrial careers, drafting, graphic arts, woodworking, metalworking, plastics, leather, electricity, electronics, power mechanics, and home maintenance. [TT165.G74 1974] 73-9827 ISBN 0-07-024965-2 9.24
1. Industrial arts—Juvenile literature. 2. Manual training—Juvenile literature. I. Feirer, John Louis, joint author. II. Title.
BIP

OLSON, Delmar Walter, 1909- 607
Industrial arts for the general shop [by] Delmar W. Olson. 3d ed. Englewood Cliffs, N.J., Prentice-Hall [1968] 404 p. illus. 24 cm. (Prentice-Hall industrial arts series) Includes bibliographies. [TT165.O45 1968] 68-3451
1. Industrial arts—Juvenile literature. I. Title. BIP

OLSON, Delmar Walter, 1909- 600
Industrial arts for the general shop [by] Delmar W. Olson. 4th ed. Englewood Cliffs, N.J., Prentice-Hall [1972, c1973] 470 p. illus. 24 cm. (Prentice-Hall industrial arts series) Includes bibliographies. A textbook outlining the techniques of technical drawings, woodworking, metalworking, electronics, graphic arts, ceramics, plastics, and leatherwork. [TT165.O45 1973] 73-159424 ISBN 0-13-459131-3 8.12
1. Industrial arts—Juvenile literature. I. Title.

Industrial arts—Study and teaching.

AMERICAN Industrial Arts Association. Environmental Education Committee. 301.31'07
Environmental education; role of industrial arts education. Edited by Donald P. Lauda. Washington [1973] viii, 27 p. illus. 23 cm. Cover title: Growing together to insure the future. Bibliography: p. 25-27. [TT169.A45 1973] 74-157830
1. Industrial arts—Study and teaching. 2. Ecology—Study and teaching. I. Lauda, Donald P., ed. II. Title. III. Title: Growing together to insure the future.

BAIRD, Ronald J. 607'.1
Contemporary industrial teaching; solving everyday problems, by Ronald J. Baird. South Holland, Ill., Goodheart-Willcox Co. [1972] 200 p. illus. 27 cm. Bibliography: p. 193-197. [TT168.B25] 78-185957 ISBN 0-87006-130-5
1. Industrial arts—Study and teaching. I. Title. BIP

CHARNECO Babilonia, Efrain. 607
Metodologia para la ensenanza de las artes industriales y la educacion vocacional industrial / Efrain Charneco Babilonia, Amalia Llabres de Charneco. 1. ed. [Rio Piedras] : Universidad de Puerto Rico, Editorial Universitaria, 1976. p. cm. Bibliography: p. [TT168.C45] 76-3715 ISBN 0-8477-2722-X
1. Industrial arts—Study and teaching. I. Llabres de Charneco, Amalia, joint author. II. Title. BIP

GIACHINO, Joseph William, 1906- 607
Course construction in industrial arts, vocational and technical education / Joseph W. Giachino, Ralph O. Gallington. 4th ed. Chicago : American Technical Society, c1977. 355 p. : ill. ; 23 cm. Includes bibliographies and index. [TT150.G53 1977] 77-73214 ISBN 0-8269-4065-X 8.95
1. Industrial arts—Study and teaching. 2. Vocational education. 3. Technology—

PACH, Walter, 1883-1958. 759.4
Ingres. New York, Hacker Art Books, 1973. xii, 290 p. illus. 27 cm. Reprint of the 1939 ed. published by Harper, New York. [ND553.I5P3 1973] 77-143359 ISBN 0-87817-078-2 25.00
1. Ingres, Jean Auguste Dominique, 1780-1867. BIP

PICON, Gaetan. 759.4
Ingres; biographical and critical study. Tr. from French by Stuart Gilbert. [Geneva] Skira [1967] 128p. 19cm. (Taste of our time, v.47) [ND553.I5P513] 67-25117 7.50
1. Ingres, Jean Auguste Dominique, 1780-1867. II. Title.
American distributor: World, Cleveland.

Initials.

ALEXANDER, Jonathan James Graham. 745.6'7
The decorated letter / by J. J. G. Alexander. New York : G. Braziller, [1978] p. cm. Bibliography: p. [ND3335.A43] 78-6487 ISBN 0-8076-0894-7 : 24.95. ISBN 0-8076-0895-5 pbk. : 11.95
1. Initials. 2. Decoration and ornament—Themes, motives. 3. Illumination of books and manuscripts. I. Title. BIP

HAMMER, Carolyn Reading. 745.6'1
Notes on the two-color initials of Victor Hammer / by Carolyn Reading Hammer. [Lexington, Ky. : Stamperia del Santuccio, 1966] 9 p. : col. ill. ; 21 cm. "125 copies printed." [Z276.H265] 75-302347
1. Hammer, Victor Karl, 1882- 2. Initials. I. Hammer, Victor Karl, 1882- II. Title.

PLANTIN, Christophe, ca.1520-1589. 686.2'09493'2
Ornamental initials : the woodcut initials of Christopher Plantin : a complete catalogue / by Stephen Harvard. New York : American Friends of the Plantin-Moretus Museum, 1974. xiii, 26, [169] p. : chiefly ill. ; 32 cm. Includes bibliographical references. [NK3631.P52H37] 74-75791
1. Plantin, Christophe, ca. 1520-1589. 2. Initials. I. Harvard, Stephen. II. Antwerp. Musee Plantin-Moretus. III. Title.

Initiations (in religion, folk-lore, etc.)

CORY, Hans. 572.9678
African figurines: their ceremonial use in puberty rites in Tanganyika. New York, Grove Press [1956] 176p. illus. 26cm. [GN483] 56-10956
1. Initiations (in religion, folk-lore, etc.) 2. Puberty. 3. Terracottas—Tanganyika Territory. I. Title.

Ink bottles—Catalogs.

COVILL, William E. 748'.8
Ink bottles and inkwells, by William E. Covill, Jr. [1st ed.] Taunton, Mass., W. S. Sullwold [1971] 431 p. illus. 26 cm. [NK5440.B6C66] 72-165308 17.50
1. Ink bottles—Catalogs. 2. Inkwells—Catalogs. I. Title. BIP

Ink bottles—Collectors and collecting.

TANSLEY, June. 745.1
The collectors 2nd book of ink bottles : a further 140 varieties, drawn full-size : text and price guide / by June Tansley. Bembridge, [Eng.] : J. Tansley, c1976. 67 p. : ill. ; 22 cm. Cover title. [NK5440.B6T28] 77-360400 £0.90
1. Ink bottles—Collectors and collecting. 2. Ink bottles—Catalogs. I. Title.

TANSLEY, June. 745.1
The collectors book of ink bottles : with 100 fullsize illustrations, information and price guide / by June Tansley. Rev. ed. Isle of Wight : Tansley, 1976. 63 p. : ill. ; 22 cm. Cover title. Includes bibliographical references. [NK5440.B6T27 1976] 77-360252 £0.90
1. Ink bottles—Collectors and collecting. I. Title.

Inkle weaving.

BRESS, Helene. 746.1'4
Inkle weaving. New York, Scribner [1974] p. cm. [TT848.B72] 74-8426 ISBN 0-684-13870-0 8.95
1. Inkle weaving. I. Title. BIP

NEHER, Evelyn. 746.1'4
Inkle / by Evelyn Neher. Guilford, Conn. : Neher, [1974] xviii, 314 p. : ill. ; 24 cm. Bibliography: p. [311]-314. [TT848.N43] 75-304939
1. Inkle weaving. I. Title.

SMITH, Frances B. 746.1'4
Inkle loom weaving / Frances B. Smith. New York : Sterling Pub. Co., c1976. 48 p. : ill. (some col.) ; 20 cm. (Little craft book series) Includes index. Discusses techniques and materials used for inkle weaving, a form of weaving originating in Scotland. [TT848.S59] 76-1179 ISBN 0-8069-5348-9 : 3.75 lib.bdg. : 3.75
1. Inkle weaving. I. Title.

Inkstands—Collectors and collecting.

RIVERA, Betty. 745.1
Inkstands & inkwells: a collector's guide, by Betty and Ted Rivera. New York, Crown Publishers [1973] vii, 216 p. illus. 24 cm. Bibliography: p. 206-210. [NK6035.R58 1973] 72-96655 ISBN 0-517-50419-7 7.95
1. Inkstands—Collectors and collecting. 2. Inkwells—Collectors and collecting. I. Rivera, Ted, joint author. II. Title.

Inkwells—Catalogs.

MCGRAW, Vincent D. 745.1
McGraw's book of antique inkwells. [1st ed. Minneapolis, 1972- v. illus. 22 cm. [NK6035.M32] 73-153234
1. Inkwells—Catalogs. I. Title.

Inkwells—Prices.

WALTER, Leo G. 745.1
Walter's inkwells of 1885, by Leo G. Walter, Jr. [Akron, Ohio, 1968- v. illus. 23 cm. 1968 price supplement ([3] p.) inserted in v. 1. [NK6035.W3] 68-6123
1. Inkwells—Prices. I. Title.

Inness, George, 1825-1894.

CIKOVSKY, Nicolai. 759.13
George Inness. New York, Praeger [1971] 159 p. illus. (part col.), port. 27 cm. (American art & artists) Bibliography: p. 155-156. [ND1839.Z8I55] 79-117471 15.00
1. Inness, George, 1825-1894. I. Title. II. Series.

CIKOVSKY, Nicolai. 759.13 B
The life and work of George Inness / Nicolai Cikovsky, Jr. New York : Garland Pub., 1977. xxv, 380 p., [65] leaves of plates : ill. ; 21 cm. (Outstanding dissertations in the fine arts) Originally presented as the author's thesis, Harvard, 1965. Bibliography: p. 371-380. [ND237.I5C55 1977] 76-23605 ISBN 0-8240-2679-9 lib.bdg. : 50.00
1. Inness, George, 1825-1894. 2. Landscape painters—United States—Biography. I. Title. II. Series. BIP

INNESS, George, 1854-1926. 759.13 B
Life, art, and letters of George Inness. Introd. by Elliott Daingerfield. New York, Kennedy Galleries [and] Da Capo Press, 1969. xxviii, 290 p. illus., ports. 24 cm. (Library of American art) Reprint of the 1917 ed. [ND237.I5I6 1969] 76-87444
1. Inness, George, 1825-1894. I. Title. BIP

IRELAND, LeRoy. 759.13
The works of George Innes; an illustrated catalogue raisonne Pref. by Donald B. Goodall. Foreword by Robert G. McIntyre. Austin, University of Texas Press [1965] xxiii, 476 p. illus., port. 29 cm. Bibliography: p. 455-459. [ND237.I517] 65-16467
1. 1. Inness, George, 1825-1894. I. Title.

IRELAND, LeRoy 759.13
The works of George-Inness; an illustrated catalogue raisonne. Pref. by Donald B. Goodall. Foreword by Robert G. MacIntyre. Austin, Univ. of Tex. Pr. [c.1965] xxiii, 476p. illus., port. 29cm. Bibl. [ND237.I517] 65-16467 17.50
1. Inness, George, 1825-1894. I. Title.

WERNER, Alfred, 1911- 759.13
Inness landscapes. New York, Watson-Guptill Publications [1973] 87 p. col. illus. 29 cm. Bibliography: p. 9. [ND237.W443I56] 73-4559 ISBN 0-8230-2553-5 17.50
1. Inness, George, 1825-1894. I. Inness, George, 1825-1894. II. Title. BIP

Inness, George, 1825-1894—Exhibitions.

MCCAUSLAND, Elizabeth, 1899-1966. 759.13
George Inness : an American landscape painter, 1825-1894 / by Elizabeth McCausland. New York : AMS Press, [1978] xvi, 87 p. : ill. ; 24 cm. Reprint of the 1946 ed. published by American Artists Group, New York. Bibliography: p. 84-87. [ND237.I5M3 1978] 76-42705 ISBN 0-404-15365-8 : 26.00
1. Inness, George, 1825-1894—Exhibitions. BIP

Inscriptions, Greek.

GREEK numismatic epigraphy [by] John E. Hartmann [and] George Macdonald. Chicago, Argonaut, 1969. 92 p. illus. 22 cm. "Articles by John E. Hartmann published in the North American journal of epigraphy plus three articles by George Macdonald [two of which were first published in the Numismatic chronicle]" Includes bibliographical references. [CJ385.G69] 66-19184 737.49'38
1. Inscriptions, Greek. 2. Coins, Greek. I. Hartmann, John E. II. Macdonald, George, Sir, 1862-1940.

[PHOROS (romanized form)]; tribute to Benjamin Dean Meritt. Edited by Donald William Bradeen and Malcolm Francis McGregor. Locust Valley, N.Y., J. J. Augustin, 1974. 187 p. illus., 27 plates. 29 cm. Includes bibliographical references. [CN350.P5] 73-90280 18.00 729'.3'0938
1. Inscriptions, Greek. I. Bradeen, Donald William, 1918-1973, ed. II. McGregor, Malcolm Francis, 1910- ed. III. Meritt, Benjamin Dean, 1899-

Inscriptions, Greek—Athens.

BRADEEN, Donald William, 1918-1973. 938'.5 s
Inscriptions : the funerary monuments / by Donald W. Bradeen. Princeton, N.J. : American School of Classical Studies at Athens, 1974. xi, 240 p., [43] leaves of plates : ill. ; 32 cm. (The Athenian Agora ; v. 17) Includes indexes. Bibliography: p. [ix]-xi. [DF287.A23A5 vol. 17] [CN384] 938'.5 75-332165
1. Inscriptions, Greek—Athens. 2. Epitaphs—Athens. 3. Athens. Agora. I. Title. II. Series: American School of Classical Studies at Athens. The Athenian Agora ; v. 17.

Inscriptions, Greek—Curium, Cyprus.

MITFORD, Terence Bruce. 481'.7'093937
The inscriptions of Kourion [by] T. B. Mitford. Philadelphia, American Philosophical Society, 1971. xvi, 422 p. illus., map, plans, port. 26 cm. (Memoirs of the American Philosophical Society, v. 83) Bibliography: p. xv. [Q11.P612 vol. 83] 78-121295 20.00
1. Inscriptions, Greek—Curium, Cyprus. 2. Cypriote syllabary. I. Title. II. Series: American Philosophical Society, Philadelphia. Memoirs, v. 83 BIP

Inscriptions, Greek—Kharga, Egypt (Oasis)

NEW York (City). Metropolitan Museum of Art. Egyptian Expedition. 913.32
The Temple of Hibis in El Khargeh oasis. [New York] Arno Press, 1973 [c1941] 2 v. in 1. illus. 32 cm. Reprint of pt. 1 (1941) and pt. 2 (1938) of the 3 vol. ed. published by the expedition. Parts 1 and 2 originally issued as v. 13-14 of the expedition's Publications. Contents.Contents.—pt. 1. Winlock, H. E. The excavations.—pt. 2. Evelyn White, H. G. and Oliver, J. H. Greek inscriptions. Includes bibliographies. [DT73.K5N48 1973] 76-168414 ISBN 0-405-02252-2
1. Kharga, Egypt (Oasis). Temple of Hibis. 2. Inscriptions, Greek—Kharga, Egypt (Oasis) I. Winlock, Herbert Eustis, 1884-1950. II. Evelyn-White, Hugh Gerard, d. 1924- III. Oliver, James Henry, 1905- IV. Title. V. Series: New York (City). Metropolitan Museum of Art. Egyptian Expedition. Publications, v. 13-14. BIP

Inscriptions, Meroitic.

TRIGGER, Bruce G. 932*.01
The Meroitic funerary inscriptions from Arminna West, by Bruce G. Trigger, with comments and indexes by Andre Heyler and pref. by Wm. K. Simpson. Based on field work by the director and Aubrey S. Trik [and others] New Haven, Peabody Museum of Natural History of Yale University, 1970. xii, 71 p. illus., maps. 35 cm. (Publications of the Pennsylvania-Yale Expedition to Egypt, no. 4) English or French. Bibliography: p. v-vii. [DT73.M6T7] 72-123644
1. Inscriptions, Meroitic. I. Title. II. Series: Pennsylvania-Yale Expedition to Egypt, 1961-1962. Publications, no. 4 BIP

Inscriptions, Mycenaean.

BENNETT, Emmett Leslie, 1918- ed 481.7
The Mycenae tablets II. With an introd. by Alan J. B. Wace and Elizabeth B. Wace. Translation and commentary by John Chadwick. Philadelphia, American Philosophical Society, 1958. 122p. illus., map, plans. 30cm. (Transactions of the American Philosophical Society, new ser., v. 48, pt. 1) Includes bibliographical references. [Q11.P6 n.s., vol. 48, pt.1] 58-7023
1. Inscriptions, Mycenaean. I. Wace. Alan John Bayard, 1879—1957. II. Wace, Elizabeth B. III. Chadwick, John. IV. Title. V. Series: American Philosophical Society, Philadelphia. Transactions, new ser., v. 48, pt. 1

Inscriptions, Runic.

THALBITZER, William Carl, 1873- 439.617
Two runic stones, from Greenland and Minnesota. Washington, Smithsonian Institution, 1951, 71 p. illus. 25 cm. (Smithsonian miscellaneous collections, v. 116, no. 3) Publication 4021. Bibliography: p. 67-71. [Q11.S7] 51-61361
1. Inscriptions, Runic. I. Title. II. Series: Smithsonian Institution. Smithsonian miscellaneous collections, v. 116, no. 3

Insects.

BURNS, A N 1899- 579
Notes on collecting and mounting insects. Melbourne, N. H. Seward [1953;] 55p. illus 21cm. sInsects-Collection and preservation. [QL465.B93] 54-29353
I. Title.

FANNING, Eleanor Ivanye. 595.7
Insects from close up. Photos. by Harry F. Brevoort. Text by Eleanor Ivanye Fanning. New York, Crowell [1965] viii, 150 p. illus. 28 cm. [QL467.F355] 65-15228
1. Insects. 2. Photography of insects. I. Brevoort, Harry F., illus. II. Title.

ROSS, Edward Shearman, 1915- 595.7
Insects close up; a pictorial guide for the photographer and collector featuring 125 photographs and drawings. Berkeley, Published for the California Academy of Sciences by the University of California Press, 1953. 79 p. illus. 24 cm. [QL466.R6] 53-11246
1. Insects. 2. Insects—Pictorial works. I. Title.

WEAVER, Norman. 743.657
How to draw insects. London, New York,

SUBJECT INDEX INTERIOR DECORATION.

Studio Publications [1958] 64 p. illus. 17 cm. (How to draw, 42) [NC783.W4 1958] 59-9040
1. Insects. 2. Drawing—Instruction. I. Title.

Insects—Pictorial works.

PARENTI, Umberto. 595.7'0022'2
Insects; world of miniature beauty. With an introd. by Michael Tweedie. New York, Golden Press [1972, c1971] 110 p. illus. 31 cm. (New dimensions) Translation of Alla scoperta degli insetti. [QL466.P3713 1972] 72-167720 2.95
1. Insects—Pictorial works. I. Title.

SEGUY, E. A. 745.4
Seguy's Decorative butterflies & insects in full color / E. A. Seguy. New York : Dover Publications, 1977. 40 p. : chiefly col. ill. ; 32 cm. Reprint of 2 portfolios by Seguy: Papillons, published by Tolmer Editeur, Paris; and, Insectes, published by Editions Ducharte et Van Buggenhoudt, Paris. [QL466.S46 1977] 77-83361 ISBN 0-486-23552-1 : 5.00
1. Insects—Pictorial works. 2. Butterflies—Pictorial works. I. Seguy, E. A. Papillons. 1977. II. Seguy, E. A. Insects. 1977. III. Title. IV. Title: Decorative butterflies & insects in full color. BIP

STANEK, V. J. 595.7'0022'2
The pictorial encyclopedia of insects [by] V. J. Stanek. London, New York, P. Hamlyn [1969] 543 p. illus. (part col.) 23 cm. Translation of Das grosse Bilderlexikon der Insekten. [QL466.S7713] 76-481367
1. Insects—Pictorial works. I. Title.

Instamatic camera.

KEMP, Weston D., 1936- 771.3'1
Better pictures with your Kodak Instamatic / Weston Kemp. Englewood Cliffs, N. J. : Prentice-Hall, [1975] v, 90 p. : ill. ; 23 cm. (Modern photo guide) (A Spectrum book) [TR263.I57K45] 75-17860 ISBN 0-13-075994-5 : 10.95 ISBN 0-13-075978-3 pbk. : 3.95
1. Instamatic camera. 2. Photography—Handbooks, manuals, etc. I. Title.

Institute of American Indian Arts.

AMON Carter Museum of Western Art, Fort Worth, Tex. 709'.701
The Institute of American Indian Arts alumni exhibition. [Fort Worth, Tex., 1973?] 67 p. illus. 23 x 26 cm. Catalogue of an exhibition to be held at the Museum of the Institute of American Indian Arts, Dec. 17, 1973-Jan. 28, 1974; Amon Carter Museum, Feb. 14-Mar. 31; New Orleans Museum of Art, Apr. 27-June 10; and Oklahoma Art Center, July 21-Sept. 5. [E98.A7A46 1973] 73-92099 ISBN 0-88360-003-X
1. Institute of American Indian Arts. 2. Indians of North America—Art—Exhibitions. I. Institute of American Indian Arts. Museum. II. New Orleans Museum of Art. III. Oklahoma Art Center. IV. Title. V. Title: Alumni exhibition. BIP

Intaglio printing.

LEAF, Ruth. 765
Intaglio printmaking techniques / by Ruth Leaf. New York : Watson-Guptill Publications, 1976. 232 p. : ill. (some col.) ; 31 cm. Includes index. Bibliography: p. 229. [NE1625.L4 1976] 76-16089 ISBN 0-8230-2554-3 : 22.50
1. Intaglio printing. I. Title. BIP

ROSS, John, 1921- 765'.028
The complete intaglio print; the art and technique of the intaglio print, the collagraph, photographic intaglio, care of prints, the dealer and the edition, collecting prints, print workshop, sources, and charts [by] John Ross [and] Clare Romano. New York, Free Press [1974] xiii, 121 p. illus. (part col.) 31 cm. Bibliography: p. 117-118. [NE1625.R67] 74-2697 6.95 (pbk.)
1. Intaglio printing. I. Romano, Clare, joint author. II. Title. BIP

Intaglio printing—Exhibitions.

CONTEMPORARY intaglios 769'.904'7
: the etching process : an exhibition organized by the Printmaking Workshop and the American Federation of Arts. New York : American Federation of Arts, [1974] [16] p. : ill. ; 26 cm. "AFA exhibition no. 73-3 circulated from March 1974 through January 1977." [NE1952.N48A432] 74-76426
1. Intaglio printing—Exhibitions. 2. Etching—Technique. I. American Federation of Arts. II. Printmaking Workshop. BIP

Interdisciplinary Model Programs in the Arts for Children and Teachers (Project)

PENNSYLVANIA. State University. Arts Impact Evaluation Team. 709'.73
IMPACT: Interdisciplinary Model Programs in the Arts for Children and Teachers; a summary report. Submitted to the Arts and Humanities Program, Office of Education, the U.S. Dept. of Health, Education, and Welfare. University Park, 1973. 47 p. 28 cm. Cover title: Arts impact: curriculum for change. [NX304.P46 1973] 74-185053
1. Interdisciplinary Model Programs in the Arts for Children and Teachers (Project) 2. Arts—Study and teaching—United States. 3. Curriculum enrichment. I. United States. Office of Education. Arts and Humanities Program. II. Title: Arts impact: curriculum for change.

Interferometer.

VEST, Charles M. 774
Holographic interferometry / Charles V. West. New York : Wiley, 1979, c1978 p. cm. (Wiley series in pure and applied optics) Includes bibliographical references and index. [TA1555.V47] 78-14883 ISBN 0-471-90683-2 : 25.00
1. Interferometer. 2. Holography. I. Title. BIP

Interior decorating.

*TODAY'S home decorating 747'.058
Guide; no. 11. Greenwich, Conn., Fawcett, 1968. v. illus. (pt. col.) 28cm. (Fawcett serv. ser.) .95 pap.,
1. Interior decorating. I. Title.

**TODAY'S home decorationg* 747.058
guide; no. 9. Greenwich, Conn., Fawcett, c.1966. 128p. illus. (pt. col.) 29cm. (Fawcett service ser.) .75 pap.,
1. Interior decorating.

Interior decoration.

ALEXANDER, Mary Jean. 747.88
Decorating begins with you. Foreword by Harold W. Grieve. [1st ed.] Garden City, N. Y., Doubleday, 1958. 165p. illus. 22cm. [NK2115.A58] 58-12028
1. Interior decoration. I. Title.

ALEXANDER, Mary Jean 747.88
Decorating begins with you. Foreword by Harold W. Grieve. Garden City, N. Y., Doubleday [1961, c.1958] 159p. illus. (Dolphin handbk., C354) .95 pap.,
1. Interior decoration. I. Title.

ALEXANDER, Mary Jean. 747
Decorating made simple. Drawings by Lyman Maring. [1st ed.] Garden City, N.Y., Doubleday, 1964. vii, 182 p. illus. 26 cm. (Made simple books) [NK2115.A584] 64-13823
1. Interior decoration. I. Title. BIP

ALEXANDER, Mary Jean. 747
Designing interior environment. New York, Harcourt Brace Jovanovich [1972] xv, 236 p. illus. (part col.) 27 cm. Includes bibliographies. [NK2110.A5] 77-187041 ISBN 0-15-517372-3
1. Interior decoration. 2. Design. I. Title. BIP

AMERICAN Institute of Decorators. 747.069
Manual of professional practice. [New York, c1955] 239p. illus. 31cm. [NK2113.A6] 56-1281
1. Interior decoration. 2. Interior decoration as a profession. I. Title.

AMERICAN Institute of Interior Designers. 747.069
Manual of professional practice. [New York 1955] 239 p. illus. 31 cm. Published by the institute under its earlier name: American Institute of Decorators. [NK2113.A6] 56-1281
1. Interior decoration. 2. Interior decoration as a profession. I. Title.

ARMSTRONG Cork Company. 747
The Armstrong book of interior decoration. New York, Macmillan [1962] 191p. illus. (part col.) plans. 28cm. [NK2130.A7] 62-16671
1. Interior decoration. I. Title.

ARTISTIC homes : 747'.8'83
or how to furnish with taste. New York : Garland Pub., 1978. p. cm. (The Aesthetic movement & the arts and crafts movement ; 15) Reprint of the 1881 ed. published by Ward, Lock, London. [NK2110.A69 1978] 76-17759 ISBN 0-8240-2464-8 : lib.bdg. : 35.00
1. Interior decoration. 2. Aesthetic movement (British art) I. Series.

AUSTIN, Ruth Erma, 1905- 747
Furnishing your home [by] Ruth E. Austin [and] Jeanhette O. Parvis. Edited by Ivol Spafford. Boston. Houghton Mifflin [c1961] 282p. illus. 22cm. [NK2110.A8 1961] 61-3792
1. Interior decoration. 2. House furnishings. I. Parvis, Jeannette O., joint author. II. Title.

BALL, Victoria (Kloss) 747
The art of interior design; a text in the aesthetics of interior design, by Victoria Kloss Ball with the help of Mary Louise Shipley. New York, Macmillan [1960] 343 p. illus. 29 cm. Includes bibliography. [NK2110.B33] 60-5407
1. Interior decoration. I. Title.

BARNES, Joanna. 747
Starting from scratch; a guide to home decorating. [1st ed.] New York, Hawthorn Books [1968] 192 p. illus. 24 cm. Bibliography: p. 185-186. [NK2115.B3 1968] 68-30709 5.95
1. Interior decoration. I. Title.

BETTER homes and gardens. 747.88
Decorating book [New ed. Des Moines, Meredith 1962, c.1956, 1961] 400p. (loose-leaf) illus. (pt. col.) 26cm. 62-3486 3.95, ring binder.
1. Interior decoration. 2. Furniture.

BETTER Homes and Gardens. 747.88
Decorating ideas. New room-by-room decorating tips. [Des Moines, Ia., Meredith Pub. Co., c.1960] 160p. illus. (part col) 29cm. 56-4826 2.95 bds.,
1. Interior decoration. 2. Furniture. I. Title.

BETTER homes and gardens 747'.8'8
decorating book. [Rev. ed. Des Moines, Meredith Press, 1968] 400 p. illus. (part col.) 25 cm. [NK2115.B383 1968] 73-5898
1. Interior decoration. 2. Furniture. BIP

BISHOP, Carolyn. 747'.8'8
25 decorating ideas under $100. Garden City, N.Y., N. Doubleday [1968] 72 p. illus. (part col.) 24 cm. (The Doubleday home decorating program) [NK2115.B48] 78-801
1. Interior decoration. I. Title.

BJERKOE, Ethel Hall. 747.213
Antiques for your home. Garden City, N. Y., N. Doubleday [1966] 72 p. illus. (part col.) 24 cm. (The Amy Vanderbilt success program for women) [NK2115.B5] 66-4550
1. Interior decoration. I. Title.

BLOHM, Carl C. 1909- 747
A guide to home decorating; all phases of decorating, from selecting color schemes to the arrangement of furniture, and including a guide to careful buying. [1st ed.] New York, Citadel Press [1953] 155 p. illus. 24 cm. [NK2110.B55] 53-11128
1. Interior decoration. I. Title: Home decorating.

BLONDIN, Catherine, 1901- 747
Dress up your home. Scranton, Laurel Publishers; distributed by Grosset & Dunlap, New York, 1952. 120 p. illus. 23 cm. [Books for better living] [NK2115.B6] 52-10734
1. Interior decoration. I. Title.

BONELLIE, Helen-Janet. 747
Introduction to interior design. South Brunswick [N.J.] A. S. Barnes [1969, c1968] 86 p. illus. (part col.) 29 cm. [NK2115.B64] 68-27196 8.95
1. Interior decoration. I. Title. II. Title: Interior design.

BOWERS, Mabel Goode. 747
Decorate your way. New York, Scribner [1968] 158 p. illus. (part col.) 27 cm. [NK2115.B67] 68-12496 7.95
1. Interior decoration. I. Title.

BRADFORD, Barbara Taylor, 1933- 747'.028
Easy steps to successful decorating. New York, Simon and Schuster [1971] 286 p. illus. (part col.) 25 cm. [NK2110.B67] 72-154093 ISBN 0-671-20998-1 12.50
1. Interior decoration. I. Title.

BRADFORD, Barbara Taylor, 1933- 747'.8'83
Making space grow / Barbara Taylor Bradford. New York : Simon and Schuster, 1979. p. cm. [NK2113.B7] 78-10767 ISBN 0-671-22473-5 : 12.95
1. Interior decoration. 2. Room layout (Dwellings) I. Title. BIP

BRAGDON, Lillian J ed. 747.88
Color guide to home decoration, by 20 of America's foremost interior decorators, including Elizabeth Whitney [and others] Editors: Lillian J. Bragdon, Sylvia E. Link, Peggy S. Boehm. New York, Sterling Pub. Co. [1956] 191p. illus. 36cm. [NK2115.B68] 56-11132
1. Interior decoration. I. Whitney, Elizabeth. II. Title.

BRANDT, Mary L. 747.88
Decorate your home for better living. With decorative spots by Marylin Hafner. New York, Scribner, 1950. x, 269 p. illus. (part col.) 25 cm. Bibliography: p. 257-258. [NK2110.B7] 50-5348
1. Interior decoration. I. Title.

BRANDT, Mary L 747.88
Good housekeeping book of home decoration [by] Mary L. Brandt. Prepared under the supervision of Mary Kraft. New York, McGraw-Hill [1957] 312p. illus. 29cm. [NK2115.B69] 57-13182
1. Interior decoration. I. Title.

BROWN, Effa. 747
Color in home decoration; designs for living. Chicago, Wilcox and Follett [1951] 128 p. illus. (part col.) 31 cm. Includes descriptive panels from the author's newspaper column "Designs for living." [NK2115.B828] 51-9987
1. Interior decoration. I. Title. II. Title: Designs for living.

CARNEY, Clive. 747
Furnishing art and practice. Line drawings by June Carney. London, New York, Oxford University Press [1950] xv, 359 p. illus., plates (part col.) 29 cm. [NK2110.C25] 51-2712
1. Interior decoration. 2. Silversmithing. 3. Pottery. I. Title.

†*CELEBRITY homes :* 747'.8'80922
Architectural digest presents the private worlds of thirty international personalities / edited by Paige Rense. 1st ed. Los Angeles : Knapp Press, 1977. 255 p. : col. ill. ; 31 cm. On spine : Architectural digest celebrity homes. [NK1980C4] 77-84047 ISBN 0-89535-001-7 : 25.00
1. Interior decoration. I. Rense, Paige. II. Architectural digest. III. Title: Celebrity homes. BIP

CHAMBERLAIN, Narcissa G. 747
Old rooms for new living, being a collection of early American interiors, authentic in design, various in period, and suitable for today's living; this is a treasury of tradition for the home decorator. Photos. by Samuel Chamberlain. New York, Hastings House [1953] 130 p. illus. 25 cm. [NK2115.C47] 53-11684
1. Interior decoration. I. Title. BIP

CHESKIN, Louis, 1907- 747.88
How to color-tune your home. New York, Macmillan [1954] 203 p. illus. 22 cm. [NK2115.C48] 53-13461
1. Interior decoration. I. Title.

CHESKIN, Louis, 1907- 747.88
How to color-tune your home. Rev. ed. Chicago, Quadrangle Books, 1962. 206 p. illus. 22 cm. [NK2115.C48 1962] 62-22017
1. Interior decoration. 2. Color. I. Title.

CLARK, Duvie. 747
The not so terrible move; or, What do you do with the bed? [1st ed.] New York, Harper & Row [1975] ix, 224 p. 21 cm. [NK2115.C58 1975] 73-4071 ISBN 0-06-010786-3 6.95
1. Interior decoration. I. Title.

COMMERY, E. W. 747.88
How to decorate and light your home, by E. W. Commery and C. Eugene Stephenson. New York, Coward-McCann [1955] 256 p. illus. 26 cm. [NK2110.C55] 55-10429
1. Interior decoration. 2. Lighting. I. Stephenson, C. Eugene, joint author. II. Title.

CRAIG, Hazel Thompson, 1904- 747
Homes with character, by Hazel Thompson Craig and Ola Day Rush. Boston, Heath [1952] 351 p. illus. 24 cm. [NK2115.C92] 52-7312
1. Interior decoration. I. Title.

CRAIG, Hazel Thompson, 1904- 747
Homes with character. 3d ed. Lexington, Mass., D. C. Heath [1970] 482 p. illus. (part col.) 25 cm. Includes bibliographies. [NK2115.C92 1970] 77-106072
1. Interior decoration. I. Title.

CRAIG, Hazel Thompson, 1904- 747
Homes with character, by Hazel Thompson Craig, Ola Day Rush. Rev. ed. Boston, Heath [c.1962] 351p. illus. (pt. col.) Bibl. (T)62 4.80
1. Interior decoration. I. Rush, Ola Day, 1890- joint author. II. Title.

CRAIG, Hazel Thompson, 1904- 747
Homes with character, by Hazel ThompsonCraig and Ola Day Rush. Rev. ed. Boston, Heath [1966] 352 p. illus. 24 cm. Bibliography: p. 352. [NK2115.C92 1966] 66-3825
1. Interior decoration. I. I. Rush, Ola Day, 1800- joint author. II. Title.

CRAIG. HAZEL THOMPSON, 1904- 747
Homes with character. by Hazel Thompson Craig. Ola Dav Rush. Rev. ed. Boston. Heath [c.1962. 1966] 351p. illus. 24cm. Bibl. [NK2115.C92] 62-9969 5.32
1. Interior decoration. I. Rush, Ola Day, 1890- joint author. II. Title.

D'ARCY, Barbara. 747'.213
Bloomingdale's book of home decorating. [1st ed.] New York, Harper & Row [1973] 264 p. illus. 26 cm. [NK2115.D26] 73-4064 ISBN 0-06-010948-3 10.95
1. Interior decoration. I. Bloomingdale Brothers, inc., New York. II. Title. BIP

DAVIS, Deering. 747.8571
Contemporary decor: restaurants, lounges, bars. With special articles by Dorothy Draper [and others] New York, Architectural Book Pub. Co. [1950] 158 p. illus. 28 cm. [The "Designing for business" series] [NK2117.D3] 50-14087
1. Interior decoration. I. Title.

DECORATING handbook, 747
edited by Miriam B. Reichl. [New York, c1951] 255p. illus. 21cm. (The Homemaker's encyclopedia) [TX311.H7] 645 58-28599
1. Interior decoration. I. Homemaker's Encyclopedia, inc., New York. II. Reichl, Miriam Brudno, 1909- ed.

DECORATION, 747
v.1. Planned, produced by the staffot Conaissance des arts, directed by Pierre Levallois. Tr. from French. New York, French & European Pubns. [c.1962, 1963] 322p. illus., col. plates, diagrs., plans. 32cm. 63-22835 27.50; 24.50 until Dec. 1
1. Interior decoration. I. Levallois, Pierre. II. Connaissance des arts.

DECORATION 747
[v.8. Prepd. by a team at Realites, led by Pierre Levallois, others] and a team at Connaissance led by its chief ed., Francis Spar. Commentary by Robert Joffet. Paris, Librairie Hachett, New York, French & European Pubns., 1966] 271p. illus., col. plates. 32cm. Contents.[v.8] Gardens and flowers, their design and arrangement. The Connaissance des Arts Collection [NK2120.D423] 63-22835 27.50
1. Interior decoration. 2. Gardens. 3. Landscape gardening I. Levallois, Pierre. II. Spar, Francis. III. Connaissance des arts.

DEMACHY, Alain. 747
Interior architecture and decoration / Alain Demachy. New York : Morrow, c1974. 163 p. : ill. (some col.) ; 27 cm. Translation of Architecture d'interieur et decoration. [NK2110.D3913 1974] 74-11646 ISBN 0-688-00281-1 : 27.50
1. Interior decoration. I. Title.

DERIEUX, Mary, 1886- 747
The complete book of interior decorating, by Mary Derieux. Isabelle Stevenson. New. rev. ed. New York, Greystone [dist.] Hawthorn [c.1964] x, 466p. illus. (pt. col.) 28cm. 64-13281 8.95 bds.,
1. Interior decoration. I. Stevenson, Isabelle, 1915- joint author. II. Title.

DEWOLFE, Elsie, 1865-1950 747'.8'8
The house in good taste / by Elsie de Wolfe. New York : Arno Press, 1975 [c1913] p. cm. (The Leisure class in America) Reprint of the ed. published by Century Co., New York. [NK2115.D6 1975] 75-1839 ISBN 0-405-06908-1 : 19.00
1. Interior decoration. I. Title. II. Series.

DO it yourself home 747
decorating ideas; favorites from home economics teachers. [Mary Anne Richards, editor. Montgomery, Ala., Favorite Recipes Press, 1970] 254 p. illus. (part col.) 26 cm. [NK2115.D7] 75-113376
1. Interior decoration. I. Richards, Mary Anne, 1919- ed. II. Title: Home decorating ideas.

DRAPER, Dorothy (Tuckerman) 747
365 shortcuts to home decorating. New York, Dodd [c.1965] 313p. 22cm. [NK2115.D82] 65-14622 4.50
1. Interior decoration. I. Title.

DRAPER, Dorothy (Tuckerman) 747
1889-
Decorating is fun! Foreword by Benjamin Sonnenberg. Illus. by Gary Pizzarelli. [1st ed.] Garden City, N.Y., Doubleday [1962] 188 p. illus. 27 cm. Includes bibliography. [NK2115.D8 1962] 62-11374
1. Interior decoration. I. Title.

DRAPER, Dorothy (Tuckerman) 747
1889-
365 shortcuts to home decorating, by Dorothy Draper. New illustrated. New York, Dodd, Mead [1968] 313 p. illus. 22 cm. [NK2115.D82 1968] 68-26158 5.50
1. Interior decoration. I. Title.

DU Pont de Nemours (E.I.) 747.6
and Company.
Transformagic, a gay adventure in restyling old furniture. [Wilmington, Del., 1944] 61 p. illus. (part col.) port. 21 cm. Cover title. "This is the second book we have published about Peter Hunt, the noted provincetown artist." [NK2137D85] 44-29620
1. Hunt, Peter, of Provincetown, Mass. 2. Interior decoration. 3. Furniture. I. Title.

EASTLAKE, Charles Locke, 747
1833-1906.
Hints on household taste in furniture, upholstery and other details. 3d ed. (rev.) London, Longmans, Green, 1872. New York, B. Blom, 1971. xviii, 306 p. illus. 24 cm. [NK2115.E3 1971] 73-177519
1. Interior decoration. I. Title. BIP

EASTLAKE, Charles Locke, 749
1833-1906.
Hints on household taste in furniture, upholstery, and other details. New York, Dover Publications [1969] xxx, 304 p. illus. (part col.), front. 21 cm. Reprint of the 1878 ed., with a new introd. by John Gloag. [NK2115.E3 1969] 69-16924 ISBN 0-486-22307-8 4.00
1. Interior decoration. I. Title: Household taste in furniture, upholstery, and other details.

EUSTIS, Marjorie H (Gelm) 747.88
The home decorator's guide. New York, Studio Publications [1955] 142p. illus. 21cm. [NK2110.E9] 55-5845
1. Interior decoration. I. Title.

FAULKNER, Ray Nelson, 747.88
1906-
Inside today's home [by] Ray Faulkner in collaboration with Sarah Faulkner. New York, Holt [1954] 653 p. illus. 25 cm. [NK2110.F38] 54-6601
1. Interior decoration. I. Title. BIP

FAULKNER, Ray Nelson, 747.88
1906-
Inside today's home [by] Ray Faulkner [and] Sarah Faulkner. Rev. ed. New York, Holt, Rinehart and Winston [1960] 583 p. illus. 25 cm. [NK2110.F38 1960] 60-10134
1. Interior decoration. I. Faulkner, Sarah, joint author. II. Title.

FAULKNER, Ray Nelson, 747'.8'8
1906-
Inside today's home [by] Ray Faulkner [and] Sarah Faulkner. 3d ed. New York, Holt, Rinehart and Winston [1968] vii, 552 p. illus. (part col.), plans. 29 cm. [NK2110.F38 1968] 68-11356
1. Interior decoration. I. Faulkner, Sarah, joint author. II. Title.

FAULKNER, Ray Nelson, 747'.8'8
1906-
Inside today's home / Ray Faulkner, Sarah Faulkner. 4th ed. New York : Holt, Rinehart and Winston, [1975] p. cm. [NK2110.F38 1975] 74-11832 ISBN 0-03-089714-9. ISBN 0-03-089480-8 college ed. : 17.50
1. Interior decoration. I. Faulkner, Sarah, joint author. II. Title.

FLOYD, Wayne. 747
Decorating with photographs. Philadelphia, Chilton Books [1965] 128 p. illus. 24 cm. [NK2113.F55] 65-17121
1. Interior decoration. 2. Photographs — Trimming, mounting, etc. 3. Picture frames and framing. I. Title.

FLOYD, Wayne. 747
Decorating with photographs. New York, American Photographic Book Co. [1965] 128 p. illus. 24 cm. [NK2113.F55 1965a] 66-253
1. Interior decoration. 2. Photographs — Trimming, mounting, etc. 3. Picture frames and framing. I. Title.

FRANKL, Paul Theodore, 747'.204
1886-
Form and re-form; a practical handbook of modern interiors, by Paul T. Frankl. New York, Hacker Art Books, 1972. xiii, 203 p. illus. 24 cm. Reprint of the 1930 ed. Bibliography: p. 193-199. [NK2110.F67 1972] 72-143347 ISBN 0-87817-067-7
1. Interior decoration. 2. Decoration and ornament. I. Title. BIP

FREEMAN, John Crosby, 749.204
comp.
Furniture for the Victorian home; from A. J. Downing, American: County houses (1850) and J. C. Loudon, English: Encyclopedia (1833) New introd. and index by John C. Freeman. [Watkins Glen, N.Y.] American Life Foundation; [distributed by Century House] 1968. 212 p. illus. 24 cm. (Library of Victorian culture) [NK2115.F67] 68-55040
1. Interior decoration. 2. Furniture design. I. Downing, Andrew Jackson, 1815-1852. The architecture of country houses. II. Loudon, John Claudius, 1783-1843. An encyclopaedia of cottage, farm, and villa architecture and furniture. III. Title.

FRIEDMANN, Arnold. 747
Interior design; an introduction to architectural interiors [by] Arnold Friedmann, John F. Pile [and] Forrest Wilson. New York, American Elsevier [1970] xii, 303 p. illus. 27 cm. Bibliography: p. 289-292. [NK2110.F678] 77-75527
1. Interior decoration. I. Pile, John F., joint author. II. Wilson, Forrest, 1918- joint author. III. Title.

FRIEDMANN, Arnold. 747
Interior design : an introduction to architectural interiors / Arnold Friedmann, John F. Pile, Forrest Wilson. Rev. [i.e. 2d.] ed. New York : Elsevier, c1976. xv, 432 p. : ill. (some col.) ; 26 cm. Includes index. Bibliography: p. 417-423. [NK2110.F678 1976] 75-26331 ISBN 0-444-00178-6 : 17.00
1. Interior decoration. I. Pile, John F., joint author. II. Wilson, Forrest, 1918- joint author. III. Title.

GATZ, Konrad, ed. 747
Decorative design for contemporary interiors: color, decoration, painting. New York, Architectural Book Pub. Co., 1956. 239 p. (chiefly illus. (part col.)) 31 cm. English and German. [NK2110.G3] 56-4169
1. Interior decoration. 2. Design, Decorative. I. Title.

GECK, Francis Joseph, 747.02
1900-
Interior design and decoration: an outline. Dubuque, Iowa, Brown [c.1962] 249p. illus. 28cm. 4.50, pap., spiral bdg.
I. Title.

GECK, Francis Joseph, 1900- 747
Introduction to interior decoration, an outlins. Dubuque, Iowa, W. C. Brown Co., 1955. 249p. illus. 23cm. [NK2115.G34] 55-12838
1. Interior decoration. I. Title.

GILLIATT, Mary. 747.22
English style in interior decoration [by] Mary Gilliatt [and] Michael Boys. New York, Viking Press [1967] 144 p. illus. (part col.) 29 x 37 cm. (A Studio book) Photos. by M. Boys. [NK2043.G5] 67-28280
1. Interior decoration. 2. Decoration and ornament, English. I. Boys, Michael, illus. II. Title.

GOODALL, Ann. 747
Anyone for decorating? [1st ed.] Birmingham, Ala., Banner Press [1964] 67 p. illus. 22 cm. [NK2115.G6] 64-24924
1. Interior decoration. I. Title.

GRANT, Ian. 747.2
Great interiors, edited by Ian Grant. Photos. by Edwin Smith. New York, Dutton, 1967. 288 p. illus., col. plates. 32 cm. Contents.Contents.—Preface, by C. Beaton.—Introduction, by I. Grant.—Early classical, by R. Dutton.—Baroque and rococo, by H. Hayward.—Neo-classical, by T. Davis.—Romantic revival, by P. Fleetwood-Hesketh.—High Victorian, by D. Hinton.—Fin-de-siecle, by A. Barker.—Modern, by R. F. Jordan. [NK2130.G7] 67-18098
1. Interior decoration. I. Smith, Edwin, 1912- illus. II. Title.

GREEN, Charles, 1919- 747.07
Sketching and design for upholsterers. Prepared by Charles Green [and] William O'Reilly. New Brunswick, N.J., Vocational Division, Curriculum Laboratory, 19 v. illus. 28 cm. [NK3195.G7] A 59
1. Interior decoration. 2. Furniture. 3. Upholstery. 4. Drawing—Instruction. I. O'Reilly, William F., joint author. II. New Jersey. Division of Vocational Education. Curriculum Laboratory, New Brunswick. III. Title.

GREEN, Lois Wagner, ed. 747.8523
Interiors book of offices, edited, with introd. New York, Whitney Library of Design [1959] xi, 163p. illus. (part col.) plans. 31cm. [NK2113.G7] 59-15427
1. Interior decoration. 2. Office furniture. I. Title.

GREER, Michael. 747
Inside design. [1st ed.] Garden City, N.Y., Doubleday, 1962. 254 p. illus. 29 cm. [NK2110.G68] 62-7639
1. Interior decoration. I. Title.

GRUEN, Gerry. 747
Modern home decorating. New York, Arco Pub. Co. [1955] 144 p. illus. 26 cm. (The Do-it-yourself series) Arco handy books for better living. A Fawcett book, no. 266. [NK2115.G77] 55-9120
1. Interior decoration. I. Title.

SUBJECT INDEX INTERIOR DECORATION.

HALSEY, Elizabeth T. 747.88
Ladies' home journal book of interior decoration, by Elizabeth T. Halsey, with the co-operation of Ladies' home journal interior decoration editor, Henrietta Murdock, architectural & garden editor, Richard Pratt, contributing editor, Gladys Taber, and designer-contributor, H. T. Williams. Philadelphia, Curtis Pub. Co. [1954] 237 p. illus. (part col.) 36 cm. [NK2110.H24] 53-10654
1. Interior decoration. I. Title.

HALSEY, Elizabeth T 747.88
Ladies' home journal book of interior decoration, by Elizabeth T. Halsey, with the co-operation of Ladies' home journal former interior decoration editor, Henrietta Murdock, interior decoration editor, Cynthia McAdoo Wheatland, architectural and graden editor, Richard Pratt, homemaking editor, Margaret Davidson, contributing editor, Gladys Taber [and] designer contributor, H. T. Williams. Philadelphia, Curtis Pub. Co. [1957] 256p. illus. 26cm. [NK2110.H24 1957] 57-9700
1. Interior decoration. I. Title.

HARDY, Kay, 1902- 747.88
Harmonize your home; a practical guide for home decorators. New York, Funk & Wagnalls, 1955. 127 p. illus. 23 x 28 cm. [NK2115.H27] 54-9736
1. Interior decoration. I. Title.

HARDY, Kay, 1902- 747
Room by room; a guide to wise buying. New York, Funk & Wagnalls [1959] 232 p. illus. 22 cm. [NK2115.H273] 58-11360
1. Interior decoration. I. Title.

HARTLEY, Paul. 747.88
How to beautify your home with color. New York, McGraw-Hill [1952] 80 p. illus. 26 cm. [NK2115.H3] 51-12663
1. Interior decoration. 2. Color. I. Title.

HATJE, Gerd. 747
Design for modern living; a practical guide to home furnishing and interior decoration, by Gerd and Ursula Hatje. New York, H. N. Abrams [1962] 318 p. 550 illus. (part col.) plans. 29 cm. Translation of Knaurs Wohnbuch. [NK2130.H313] 62-13661
1. Interior decoration. I. Hatje, Ursula, joint author. II. Title.

HAWEIS, Mary Eliza Joy, 1852-1898. 747
The art of decoration / Mrs. H. R. Haweis. New York : Garland, 1977. p. cm. (The Aesthetic movement & the arts and crafts movement) Reprint of the 1881 ed. published by Chatto and Windus, London. [NK2110.H325 1977] 76-17761 ISBN 0-8240-2466-4 lib.bdg. : 35.00
1. Interior decoration. 2. Furniture. I. Title. II. Series. BIP

HAWKINS, Reginald Robert, 1902- 643.3
The kitchen book, planning and remodeling. New York, Van Nostrand [1953] 345 p. illus. 24 cm. [NK2117.H38] 53-10095
1. Interior decoration. I. Title.

HEARD, Frances. 747'.204
Founders guide to modern decorating / by Frances Heard, Harriet Burket and JoAnn Francis Gray. New York : Popular Library, [1974] 96 p., [16] leaves of plates : ill. ; 21 cm. Includes index. [NK1980.H42] 74-82309 pbk. : 2.00
1. Interior decoration. 2. Furniture. I. Burket, Harriet, joint author. II. Gray, JoAnn Francis, joint author. III. Title.

HENDERS, Charles H 747
Home decorating guide. New York, Published by Fawcett for Sterling Pub. Co., c1952. 144p. illus. 25cm. Published in 1951 under title: Today's woman home decorating guide. [NK2110.H38 1952] 52-14352
1. Interior decoration. I. Title.

HENDERS, Charles H. 747
Today's woman home decorating guide. [Greenwich, Conn., Fawcett Publications, 1951] 144 p. illus. 24 cm. (Fawcett book, 122) [NK2110.H38] 51-6498
1. Interior decoration. I. Title. II. Title: Home decorating guide.

HICKS, David. 747
David Hicks on home decoration. [1st American ed. New York] World Pub. [1972] 168 p. illus. 32 cm. [NK2135.H5A44 1972] 72-76413 ISBN 0-529-04700-4 15.00
I. Title.

HICKS, David. 747
David Hicks on living—with taste. [1st American ed. New York] Macmillan [1969, c1968] 150 p. illus. (part col.) 31 cm. [NK2115.H47 1969] 69-16266
1. Interior decoration. I. Title. II. Title: On living—with taste. BIP

HICKS, David. 747
On decoration; [text collaboration by Gwen Robyns] New York, Macmillan [1967, c1966] 152 p. (chiefly illus. (part col.)) 33 cm. [NK2135.H5 1967] 67-25299
1. Interior decoration. 2. Colors. I. Title. II. Title: David Hicks on decoration.

HOMEMAKER'S Encyclopedia, inc., New York. 747.88
Decorating handbook, edited by Miriam B. Reichl. [New York, 1952, c1951] 235p. illus. 21cm. (The Homemaker's encyclopedia) Published in 1951 under title: Your decorating handbook. [NK2110.H56 1952] 58-28599
1. Interior decoration. I. Reichl, Miriam Brudno, 1909- ed. II. Title.

HOMEMAKER'S Encyclopedia, inc., New York. 645
Your decorating handbook, edited by Nancy Daggett [pseud. New York, 1951] 255p. illus. 21cm. (The Homemaker's encyclopedia) [NK2110.H56] 51-8500
1. Interior decoration. I. Reichl, Miriam Brudno, 1909- ed. II. Title.

HOUSE & garden. 747
Complete guide to interior decoration, edited by Richardson Wright. New York, Simon and Schuster, 1942. 304p. illus. (part col.) 33cm. [NK2110.H59 1942] 42-4888
1. Interior decoration. I. Wright, Richardson Little, 1887- ed. II. Title.

HOUSE & garden. 747
Decorating book. [Greenwich, Conn., Fawcett Publications, 1964] 112 p. illus. 24 cm. Cover title. "574" [NK2115.H53] 64-56509
1. Interior decoration. I. Title.

INTRODUCTION to home furnishings / Dorothy Stepat-Devan ... [et al.]. 3d ed. New York : Macmillan, c1979. p. cm. Previous editions by D. Stepat-De Van. Includes index. Bibliography: p. [TX311.S76 1979] 78-17412 ISBN 0-02-417090-9 : 14.50 645
1. House furnishings. 2. Interior decoration. I. Stepat-De Van, Dorothy, 1916- Introduction to home furnishings.

KETCHAM, Howard, 1902- 747.88
Paint it yourself; how to use color and decorating designs in the home. New York, Greystone Press [1954] 283 p. illus. 26 cm. [A Mr. Fix-it book] First published in 1949 under title: How to use color and decorating designs in the home. [NK2115.K48 1954] 53-11689
1. Interior decoration. 2. Handicraft. 3. Decoration and ornament. I. Title.

KETTELL, Russell Hawes. 747.213
Early American rooms; a consideration of the changes in style between the arrival of the Mayflower and the Civil War in the regions originally settled by the English and the Dutch. Articles by Frederick Lewis Allen [others] Russell Hawes Kettell, ed. New York, Dover [1967] xvii, 200p. illus. (pt. col.;, facsims., plans. 29cm. Reprint of the 1936 ed. [NK2003.K4 1967] 67-14251 3.50 pap.,
1. Interior decoration. 2. Furniture, American—Hist. 3. U.S.—Soc. life & cust.—Illustrations. I. Allen, Frederick Lewis, 1890-1954. II. Title.

KETTELL, Russell Hawes. 747.213
Early American rooms; a consideration of the changes in style between the arrival of the Mayflower and the Civil War in the regions originally settled by the English and the Dutch. With articles by Frederick Lewis Allen [others Russell Hawes Kettell, ed. [Magnolia, Mass., P. Smith, 1967] xvii, 200p illus. (pt. col.) facsims., plans. 29cm. (Dover bk. reprint) Reprint of the 1936 ed. [NK20003.K4 1967] 6.00
1. Interior decoration. 2. Furniture, American—Hist. 3. U.S.—Soc. life & cust.—Illustrations. I. Allen Frederick Lewis, 1890-1954. II. Title. BIP

KORNFELD, Albert. 747
The Doubleday book of interior decorating. Garden City, N.Y., Doubleday [1965] 216 p. illus. (part col.) forms, plans. 29 cm. [NK2110.K67] 65-16142
1. Interior decoration. I. Title.

KORNFELD, Albert. 747
The Doubleday book of interior decorating and encyclopedia of styles. Garden City, N. Y., Doubleday [1965] 360 p. illus. (part col.) forms, plans. 29 cm. Contents.Partial contents.—Do-it-yourself handbook.—Encyclopedia of styles. [NK2110.K67 1965a] 65-9118
1. Interior decoration. 2. Furniture. I. Title. II. Title: Encyclopedia of styles. III. Title: Interior decorating and encyclopedia of styles. BIP

KOUES, Helen. 747
The American woman's new encyclopedia of home decorating. Chicago, Consolidated Book Publishers [1954] 976 p. illus. 23 cm. Published in 1948 under title: The American woman's encyclopedia of home decorating. [TX311.K68 1954] 54-2155
1. Interior decoration. 2. Furniture. 3. Dwellings. I. Title.

LIMAN, Ellen. 747'.8'8
The spacemaker book / Ellen Liman ; drawings by Nancy Stahl. New York : Viking Press, 1977. 117 p. : ill. ; 22 x 29 cm. (A Studio book) [NK2113.L55 1977] 77-714 ISBN 0-670-66012-4 : 8.95
1. Interior decoration. 2. Personal space. 3. Room layout (Dwellings) I. Stahl, Nancy. II. Title. BIP

L'OEIL; revue d'art, no. 1. 747
The best in European decoration; pictures and text chosen from L'Deil, the international art review. Ed. by Georges and Rosamond Bernier. Tr. from French best in European decoration pictures and text chosen fromL'Oeil New York, Reynal [dist. Morrow, 1963] 157p. chiefly illus. (pt. col.) 32cm. 15.00 bds.,
1. Interior decoration. I. Bernier, Georges, ed. II. Bernier, Rosamond, joint ed. III. Title.

LOFTIE, William John, 1839-1911. 700
A plea for art in the house / by W. J. Loftie. Suggestions for house decoration / by Rhoda and Agnes Garrett. Dress / by Margaret Oliphant. Music in the house / by John Hullah. New York : Garland Pub., 1978. 401 p. in various pagings : ill. ; 19 cm. (The Aesthetic movement & the arts and crafts movement) Reprint of the 1876 ed. of A plea for art in the house; of the 2d ed. (1877) of Suggestions for house decoration in painting, woodwork, and furniture; of the 1878 ed. of Dress, all published by Macmillan, London; and of the 1877 ed. of Music in the house, published by Porter & Coates, Philadelphia, which were all issued in series: Art at home series. On spine: Art in the house. [NK2115.L83 1978] 76-18320 ISBN 0-8240-2460-5 : lib.bdg. : 35.00
1. Interior decoration. 2. Furniture. 3. Collectors and collecting. 4. Clothing and dress. 5. Music in the house. I. Garrett, Rhoda, 1841-1882. Suggestions for house decoration in painting, woodwork, and furniture. 1978. II. Oliphant, Margaret Oliphant Wilson, 1828-1897. Dress. 1978. III. Hullah, John Pyke, 1812-1884. Music in the house. 1978. IV. Title. V. Series. VI. Series: Art at home series.

MCCALL'S magazine 747
McCall's decorating book, by the decorating eds. of McCall's [New York] Random [1965] xiii, 302p. illus. (pt. col.) 33cm. [KN2110.M28] 64-17939 12.95
1. Interior decoration.

MACMILLAN, Donald D 747.88
Good taste in home decoration. With illus. by Marvin Culbreth. [1st ed.] New York, Holt [1954] 372p. illus. 24cm. [NK2110.M325] 53-5269
1. Interior decoration. I. Title.

MAGNANI, Franco. 747'.8'83
Living spaces : 150 design ideas from around the world / edited [and text] by Franco Magnani ; translated by Bobbi Mitchell. London : Studio Vista ; New York : Whitney Library of Design, c1978. 120 p. : col. ill. ; 29 cm. [NK2130.M34 1978] 78-52968 ISBN 0-8230-7356-4 (Whitney) : 22.50
1. Interior decoration. I. Title.

MASSEE, William Edman. 747
The art of comfort; illustrated by Dorothy Ivens. [1st ed.] Indianapolis, Bobbs-Merrill [1952] 253 p. illus. 22 cm. [NK2110.M34] 52-10281
1. Interior decoration. 2. Human engineering. I. Title.

MAYABB, James E 747.88
The complete book of home decorating. New York, W. H. Wise, 1955. 372p. illus. 27cm. [NK2110.M38] 55-13684
1. Interior decoration. I. Title.

MEYER, Genevieve 747
Today's woman decorating ideas. Greenwich, Conn., Fawcett, c.1965. 112p. illus. 23cm. (595) [NK2115.M43] 66-239 .75 pap.,
1. Interior decoration. I. Title. II. Title: Decorating ideas.

MEYER, Genevieve. 747
Today's woman small home decorating guide. Greenwich, Conn. Fawcett Publications [1966] 112 p. illus. 24 cm. [NK2113.M4] 66-5631
1. Interior decoration. I. Title.

MODERN furniture and decoration. Edited by Robert Harling. New York, Viking Press [1971] 205 p. col. illus. 32 cm. (A Studio book) [NK2130.M6 1971] 747 77-162665 ISBN 0-670-48290-0 25.00 747
1. Interior decoration. I. Harling, Robert, ed.

MORTON, Ruth. 747
The home and its furnishings. Illustrator and collaborator, Erna Karolyi. New York, McGraw-Hill [1953] 463 p. illus. 24 cm. (American home and family series) [NK2115.M63] 52-11516
1. Interior decoration. I. Title.

NATIONAL Design Center. 747
Guide to home decorating ideas. [New York, Meredith Press, c1965] 97 p. illus. (part col.) 28 cm. [NK2115.N3] 66-6407
1. Interior decoration I. Title.

NEW York (City) Museum of Modern Art. 747
What is modern interior design? By Edgar Kaufmann, Jr. New York [1953] 32 p. illus. 26 cm. (Its Introductory series to the modern arts, 4) "A companion and supplement to a booklet issued earlier by the Museum of Modern Art, What is modern design?" [NK2110.N38] 53-4059
1. Interior decoration. I. Kaufmann, Edgar, 1910- II. Title.

OBST, Frances Melanie. 747
Art and design in home living. New York, Macmillan [1963] 332 p. illus. 31 cm. Includes bibliography. [NK2110.O2] 62-8565
1. Interior decoration. 2. Architecture, Domestic—Designs and plans. I. Title. BIP

OGG, Elizabeth. 747.88
Decorating on a budget. New York, M. Barrows [1954] 246 p. illus. 22 cm. [NK2115.O37] 54-5379
1. Interior decoration. I. Title.

OSTROW, Albert A. 747.79
Planning your home for play. Drawings by Anthony Lombardo. Atlanta, Tupper & Love [1954] 132 p. illus. 27 cm. [NK2117.O8] 54-6406
1. Interior decoration. 2. Recreation. I. Title.

PAHLMANN, William. 747
The Pahlmann book of interior design. New York, Crowell [1955] 256 p. illus. 26 cm. (A Studio book) [NK2110.P15] 55-10206
1. Interior decoration. I. Title: Interior design.

PAHLMANN, William. 747
The Pahlmann book of interior design. [Rev. ed.] New York, Viking Press [1960] 252 p. illus. 26 cm. [NK2110.P15 1960] 60-15156

1. Interior decoration. I. Title: Interior design.

PAHLMANN, William. 747
The Pahlmann book of interior design. [3d ed., newly rev.] New York, Viking Press [1968] 252 p. illus. (part col.) 26 cm. (A Studio book) [NK2110.P15 1968] 68-16447
1. Interior decoration. I. Title. II. Title: Interior design.

PANERO, Julius. 747
Anatomy for interior designers [by] Julius Panero. 3d ed. New York, Whitney Library of Design 1962 146 p. illus., diagrs., tables. 27 cm. Third ed. of Francis de N. Schroeder's Anatomy for interior designers. [NK2113.P32] 62-18472
1. Interior decoration. 2. Interior decoration as a profession. I. Schroeder, Francis de Neufville, 1901- Anatomy for interior designers. II. Title.

PAULEY, Sylvia P 747.88
Let's decorate. Pen and ink sketches by Ralph Wehrenberg. New York, Comet Press Books, 1958. 164p. illus. 29cm. [NK2115.P37] 58-3115
1. Interior decoration. 2. Furniture. I. Title.

PELUZZI, Giulio. 747
Living the modern way; form and color in interior decoration. Edited by Giulio Peluzzi & Rivista dell'arredamento. [Translated into English by Babette Bettina Honig. Adaptation for the American ed. by Elizabeth Earl] New York, Universe Books [c1963] 250 p. (chiefly col. illus.) 30 cm. Translation of Forma e clore nell'arredamento moderno. [NK2130.P383] 63-18340
1. Interior decoration. 2. Furniture. I. Rivista dell'arredamento, II. Title. III. Title: Form and color in interior decoration.

PELUZZI, Giulio 747
The modern room. [Ed. by Giulio Peluzzi. Tr. into English by Ruth A. Marsden] New York, Universe Bks. [1967] 210p. (chiefly col. illus.) 30cm. Tr. of Forma e colore nell'arredamento moderno. [NK2130.P383 1967] 67-12504 15.00
1. Interior decoration. 2. Furniture. I. Title.

PEPIS, Betty. 747.88
Guide to interior decoration. New York, Reinhold Pub. Corp. [1957] 215p. illus. 27cm. [NK1980.P4] 57-9463
1. Interior decoration. I. Title.

PEPIS, Betty 747
Home decorating made easy, by Betty Pepis, Harry Walton. New York Popular Lib. [1966] 221p. illus. (pt. col.) 18cm. [NK2115.P442] 67-1817 .75 pap.,
1. Interior decoration. I. Walton, Harry, joint author. II. Title.

PLUMB, Barbara. 747
Young designs in living. New York, Viking Press [1969] 159 p. illus. (part col.) 29 cm. (A Studio book) [NK2130.P55 1969] 78-87249 14.95
1. Interior decoration. I. Title.

RACZ, Rhonda. 747
101 great decorating ideas [New York, Bantam Books, 1969] 95 p. illus. 14 cm. (A Bantam minibook) [NK2115.R27] 71-98974 0.50
1. Interior decoration. I. Title.

*RATCLIFF, Harry. 645
Home decorating; a craftsman's approach. With drawings by Susan Hitchės. [2d ed.] London, Mills & Boon [1972, c.1971] 93 p. illus., col. plates. 22 cm. [NK2115] ISBN 0-263-51395-5
1. Interior decoration. 2. Buildings—Repair and construction. I. Title.
Available from Transatlantic Arts, Levittown, N.Y., for 6.95.

RECKOW, Hazel Marcia (Kory) 747
1909-
Creative home decorating, by Hazel Kory Rockow and Julius Rockow; illustrated by Robert J. Curry. New York, H. S. Stuttman Co.; distributed by Garden City Books, Garden City, N. Y. [1953] 420p. illus. (part col.) 28cm. 'Creative home decorating trends' (p. [327]--420) has special t. p. [NK2110.R6 1953] 53-2370
1. Interior decoration. I. Rockow, Julius, 1912- joint author. II. Title.

REILLY, Esther Huntington. 747
At home with decorating. [1st ed.] Philadelphia, Chilton Book Co. [1971] viii, 107 p. illus. 28 cm. [NK2115.R37 1971] 71-145803 ISBN 0-8019-5616-1
1. Interior decoration. I. Title.

REIST, Janet Aston. 747
Elegant decorating on a limited budget; have an attractive setting now and quality pieces for the future. New York, Macmillan [1965] xi, 172 p. illus. 22 cm. [NK2115.R4] 65-17822
1. Interior decoration. I. Title. BIP

RIES, Estelle H. 747
Home design for modern living. [Cranbury. N. J.] A. S. Barnes [c.1966] 483p. illus. 25cm. [NK2113.R5] 65-24831 6.95
1. Interior decoration. I. Title.

RIES, Estelle H 747
Home design for modern living [by] Estelle H. Ries. South Brunswick [N.J.] A. S. Barnes [1966] 483 p. illus. 25 cm. [NK2113.R5] 65-24831
1. Interior decoration. I. Title.

ROCKOW, Hazel Marcia 747.88
(Kory) 1909-
New creative home decorating, by Hazel Kory Rockow and Julius Rockow. Illustrated by Robert J. Curry. New York, H. S. Stuttman [1957] 294p. illus. 27cm. Previous editions published under title: Creative home decorating. [NK2110.R6 1957] 57-4222
1. Interior decoration. I. Rockow, Julius, 1912- joint author. II. Title. III. Title: Creative home decorating.

RODGERS, Dorothy F. 1909- 747
My favorite things; a personal guide to decorating & entertaining [by] Dorothy Rodgers. [1st ed.] New York, Atheneum, 1964. xvi, 282 p. illus., col. plates, col. port. 30 cm. [NK2110.R62] 64-22105
1. Interior decoration. 2. Entertaining. 3. Cookery. I. Title. BIP

RUTT, Anna Hong. 747
Home furnishing. Corr. 2d ed. New York, Wiley [1961, c1948] 508 p. illus. 24 cm. Includes bibliography. [NK2110.R8 1961] 61-160982
1. Interior decoration. I. Title.

SARA, Dorothy. 747
Interior decorating ideas. [1st ed.] New Augusta, Ind., Editors and Engineers [1966] 96 p. illus. 18 cm. (Skillfact library, 645) On spine: Interior decorating. [NK2115.S32] 66-27397
1. Interior decoration. I. Title.

SAVAGE, George, 1909- 747.2
A concise history of interior decoration. New York, Grosset & Dunlap [1967, c1966] 285 p. illus. (part col.) 22 cm. Bibliography: p. 265-266. [NK1710.S3 1967] 66-20646
1. Interior decoration. I. Title.

SCHROEDER, Francis de 747
Neufville, 1901-
Anatomy for interior designers; and How to talk to a client. Illus. by Nino Repetto, Henry Stahlhut, and Mario Carreno. 2d ed. New York, Whitney Publications [c1951] 96p. illus. 26cm. [NK2113.S35 1951] 51-14376
1. Interior decoration. 2. Interior decoration as a profession. I. Title. II. Title: How to talk to a client.

SCHULER, Josef Egon, ed. 7447.204
Interiors for contemporary living; an international survey in color.Introd. by Cathrin Seifert. With text by Franz Bauer. [New York, Architectural Bk. Pub. Co., [151 E. 50 St.] [1961, c.1960] 204p. col. illus. 27cm. 61-19719 15.95
1. Interior decoration. I. Bauer, Franz, 1901- II. Title.

SHERWIN-WILLIAMS Company. 747.88
Paint and color style guide; authentic color styling by the Sherwin Williams decorative studios. [Cleveland] [1951] 100 p. (chiefly col. illus.) 43 x 49 cm. [NK2137.S475] 51-23895
1. Interior decoration. 2. House painting. I. Title.

SKURKA, Norma. 747'.204
Underground interiors : decorating for alternate life styles / by Norma Skurka and Oberto Gili. New York : Galahad Books, c1972. 121 p. : ill. ; 32 cm. [NK2130.S55 1972b] 75-9456 ISBN 0-88365-307-9 : 12.50
1. Interior decoration. I. Gili, Oberto. II. Title. BIP

SKURKA, Norma. 747'.204
Underground interiors; decorating for alternate life styles, by Norma Skurka and Oberto Gili. [New York] Quadrangle Books [1972] 121 p. illus. 31 cm. [NK2130.S55 1972] 72-85241 ISBN 0-8129-0293-9 14.95
1. Interior decoration. I. Gill, Oberto. II. Title.

STIER, Olga. 747
Decorating small apartments. Text and captions by Olga Stier. Edited by J. E. Schuler. New York, W. Morrow [1969] 217 p. illus. (part col.), plans. 27 cm. Translation of Mein eigenes Reich. [NK2115.S6913] 79-7202 12.95
1. Interior decoration. I. Schuler, Josef Egon, ed. II. Title.

STIERI, Emanuele, 1891- 728
How to make your home worth more. New York, Prentice-Hall, 1953. 204 p. illus. 24 cm. [NK2115.S695] 53-12735
1. Interior decoration. 2. Building. I. Title.

STODDARD, Alexandra. 747'.213
Style for living; how to make where you live you. Illustrated by Bill Goldsmith. [1st ed.] Garden City, N.Y., Doubleday, 1974. x, 304 p. illus. 27 cm. [NK2115.S698] 73-82250 ISBN 0-385-08252-5 12.50
1. Interior decoration. I. Title. BIP

STRAMESI, Annette. 747'.8'8
Creative home decorating : the inside story / Annette Stramesi. New York : Dorison House, c1977. 144 p., [4] leaves of plates : ill. (some col.) ; 24 cm. Includes index. [NK2115.S74] 77-71482 ISBN 0-916752-14-3 : 7.95
1. Interior decoration. I. Title.

SULAHRIA, Julie. 747
Inside design : creating your own environment / Julie Sulahria, Ruby Diamond. San Francisco : Canfield Press, c1977. 321 p. : ill. ; 24 cm. Includes bibliographies and index. [NK2110.S9] 77-129 12.95
1. Interior decoration. I. Diamond, Ruby, joint author. II. Title. BIP

TERHUNE, Florence B 747
Decorate with charm, by Florence B. Terhune. [New York] Emily Post Institute [1964, c 1963] 113 p. 24 cm. (Emily Post's guidebooks for homemakers) [NK2115.T39] 63-9022
1. Interior decoration. 2. Color. I. Title.

TERHUNE, Florence B 747
Interior decorating for you; illustrated by Jessie Robinson. [New ed.] New York, M. Barrows [1952] 284p. illus. 26cm. First published in 1944 under title: Decorating for you. [NK2115.T4 1952] 52-14752
1. Interior decoration. I. Title.

**TODAY'S home decorating* 747.058
guide [1965 ed.] no. 8. Greenwich, Conn., Fawcett, c.1965. 125p. illus. (pt. col.) 28cm. (Fawcett serv. ser.) .75 pap.,

TODAY'S home decorating 747
guide;no. 6. 1963 ed. Greenwich, Conn., Fawcett, c.1963. 144p. illus. (pt. col.) 28cm. (Fawcett service ser.) .75 pap.,
1. Interior decoration.

TODAY'S woman. 747.88
Small home decorating. [Greenwich, Conn., Fawcett Publications, 1953] 144p. illus. 24cm. (A Fawcett book, no. 197) [NK2110.T58] 53-3765
1. Interior decoration. I. Title.

**TODAY'S woman small home* 747.213
decorating guide, by Genevieve Meyer. Greenwich, Conn., Fawcett, c.1966. 112p. illus. 24cm. (no. 620) .95 pap.,
1. Interior decoration. 2. Furniture. I. Myer, Genevieve.

TODD, Dorothy. 747'.204
The new interior decoration : an introduction to its principles, and international survey of its methods / by Dorothy Todd and Raymond Mortimer. New York : Da Capo Press, 1977. vii, 42 p., [49] leaves of plates : ill. ; 29 cm. (Da Capo Press series in architecture and decorative art) Reprint of the 1929 ed. published by Scribner, New York. Includes index. [NK2110.T6 1977] 77-4444 35.00
1. Interior decoration. I. Mortimer, Raymond, 1895- joint author. II. Title. BIP

TRILLING, Mabel Barbara. 747
Design your home for living [by] Mabel B. Trilling [and] Florence Williams Nicholas. Philadelphia, Lippincott [1953] 408p. illus. 23cm. [NK2110.T693] 53-1001
1. Interior decoration. I. Nicholas, Florence (Williams) 1893- joint author. II. Title.

VAN DOMMELEN, David B. 747
Designing and decorating interiors [by] David B. Van Dommelen, New York, Wiley [1965] xiv, 277 p. illus., plans. 26 cm. Includes bibliographies. [NK2110.V36] 65-24298
1. Interior decoration. I. Title.

VAN DOMMELEN, David B. 745.9
New uses for old cannonballs, and other novel decorative arrangements [by] David B. Van Dommelen. [New York] Funk & Wagnalls [1966] vii, 152p. illus. 14 x 21cm. Bibl. [NK2115.V24] 66-15368 4.95
1. Interior decoration. I. Title.

VARNEY, Carleton. 747
Book of decorating ideas. Indianapolis, Bobbs-Merrill [1971] xv, 195 p. illus. 24 cm. [NK2115.V317] 70-142474 7.95
1. Interior decoration. 2. House furnishings. I. Title.

VARNEY, Carleton. 747
The family decorates a home. Indianapolis, Bobbs-Merrill Co. [1969] 210 p. illus. (part col.), plans. 29 cm. [NK2115.V32] 69-13102 10.00
1. Interior decoration. 2. Architecture, Domestic—Designs and plans. I. Title.

*WAUGH, Alice 747
Interior design; a laboratory manual for house furnishing. Minneapolis, Burgess, 1967, c.1961. 77p. illus. 28cm. The opposing side of each p. is blank. Bibl. 3.00 pap.,
1. Interior decoration. I. Title. BIP

WETZLAR, Elisabeth. 748'.8'8
Rustic interiors; for town and country. New York, Universe Books [1969] 130 p. (chiefly col. illus., part col.) 30 cm. Translation of Rustikale Raume. [NK2117.W3813 1969] 76-90937 ISBN 0-87663-105-7 12.50
1. Interior decoration. 2. Country homes. I. Title.

WHARTON, Edith Newbold 747'.8'8
Jones, 1867-1937.
The decoration of houses / Edith Wharton and Ogden Codman, Jr. New York : Arno Press, 1975. p. cm. (The Leisure class in America) Reprint of the 1897 ed. published by Scribner, New York. Bibliography: p. [NK2110.W5 1975] 75-932 ISBN 0-405-06938-3 : 21.00
1. Interior decoration. I. Codman, Ogden, joint author. II. Title. III. Series. BIP

WHITON, Augustus Sherrill 747
1887-
Elements of interior design and decoration. Philadelphia, Lippincott [1951] xvii, 829, xxviii p. illus. 24 cm. Previous editions published under title: Elements of interior decoration. Includes bibliographies. [NK2110.W55] 51-4395
1. Interior decoration. 2. Interior decoration—Hist. 3. Furniture. 4. Decoration and ornament. I. Title.

WHITON, Augustus Sherrill, 747
1887-1961.
Elements of interior design and decoration. Chicago, Lippincott [1957] 829, xxviii p. illus. 24 cm. First published in 1937 under title: Elements of interior decoration. [NK2110.W55] 58-6124
1. Interior decoration. 2. Interior decoration — Hist. 3. Furniture. 4. Decoration and ornament. I. Title.

WHITON, Augustus 330.9'73 s
Sherrill, 1887-1961.
Elements of interior design and decoration. [3d ed.] Philadelphia, Lippincott [1963] xviii, 852, xxviii p. illus., ports., diagrs. 24 cm. Editions for 1937-1944 published under title: Elements of interior decoration;

GILLIATT, Mary. 747'.8'83
Decorating a realistic guide to interior design / by Mary Gilliatt. 1st ed. New York : Pantheon Books, c1977. p. cm. Includes index. [NK2115.G425] 77-4769 ISBN 0-394-40700-8 : 25.00
1. Interior decoration—Handbooks, manuals, etc. I. Title. BIP

GILLIATT, Mary. 747'.8'83
How to decorate without a decorator : a realistic guide to interior design / by Mary Gilliatt ; book design by Janet Odgis ; photos by Michael Dunne with Michael Nicholson and others. London : Thames and Hudson, 1977. 268 p. : ill. (some col.) ; 29 cm. American ed. published under title: Decorating. Includes index. [NK2115.G425 1977b] 78-305884 ISBN 0-500-01189-3 : 25.00
1. Interior decoration—Handbooks, manuals, etc. I. Title.
Distributed by Pantheon, New York, NY

GOLD, Frances Joslin. 747'.8'83
The instant decorator / by Frances Joslin Gold. 1st ed. New York : C. N. Potter : distributed by Crown Publishers, c1976. xiii, 104 p. : ill. ; 30 x 38 cm. [NK2115.G56 1976] 76-26584 ISBN 0-517-50396-4 : 27.50
1. Interior decoration—Handbooks, manuals, etc. I. Title. BIP

HATJE, Gerd. 747'.204
Decorating for modern living / Gerd Hatje, Peter Kaspar. New York : H. N. Abrams, [1977] p. cm. Abridged version of the authors' 1601 decorating ideas for modern living, originally published in 1974. Includes index. [NK2115.H34] 76-48806 pbk. : 8.95
1. Interior decoration—Handbooks, manuals, etc. I. Kaspar, Peter, joint author. II. Title.

HATJE, Gerd. 747'.204
1601 decorating ideas for modern living; a practical guide to home furnishing and interior design, [by] Gerd Hatje and Peter Kaspar New York, H. N. Abrams [1974] 296 p. illus. (part col.) 29 cm. [NK2115.H33] 73-19988 ISBN 0-8109-0129-3
1. Interior decoration—Handbooks, manuals, etc. I. Kaspar, Peter, joint author. II. Title.

HOUSE & home book of 747'.8'8
interior design / by the editors of House & home. New York : H & H Housing Press, c1978. p. cm. Editors: J. Robinson and S. Cymes. Includes index. [NK2110.H595] 77-10867 ISBN 0-07-030473-4 : 14.95
1. Interior decoration—Handbooks, manuals, etc. I. Robinson, Jeremy (author not established pending further info.) II. Cymes, Sue. III. House and home. IV. Title: Book of interior design.
Publisher's address : 1221 Ave. of America, New York, NY 10020

KATZ, Marjorie P. 747
Instant-effect decorating; hundreds of easy, inexpensive ways to make your home exciting and livable, by Marjorie P. Katz. Drawings by the author. Photos. by David Sagarin. New York, M. Evans; distributed in association with Lippincott, Philadelphia [1972] 320 p. illus. 25 cm. [NK2115.K25] 76-168690 8.95
1. Interior decoration—Handbooks, manuals, etc. I. Title.

LIND, Louise T. 747'.213
The home you love to live in [by] Louise T. Lind. [Babson Park, Mass., 1972] xiv, 169 p. illus. 28 cm. [NK2115.L57] 73-183790
1. Interior decoration—Handbooks, manuals, etc. I. Title.

MUNFORD, Lois. 747'.8'83
Learn overnight how to interior decorate like a professional with Two-seasons design / by Lois Munford. Irvine, CA : Jemco Co., c1976. 97 p. : ill. (some col.) ; 22 cm. Cover title. [NK2115.M76] 76-19119
1. Interior decoration—Handbooks, manuals, etc. I. Title.

O'CONNELL, C. B. 747
Home furnishing self help, by C. B. O'Connell. Metuchen, N.J., Scarecrow Press, 1968. 181 p. illus. 22 cm. [NK2115.O25] 68-12618
1. Interior decoration—Handbooks, manuals, etc. I. Title. BIP

PARKER, Dorothy, 1922- 747
Ms. Pinchpenny's book of interior design / by Dorothy Parker. New York : Van Nostrand Reinhold Co., [1978] p. cm. Includes index. [NK2115.P287] 78-17732 ISBN 0-442-26558-1 : 9.95
1. Interior decoration—Handbooks, manuals, etc. I. Title. BIP

RUEDISUELI, Kevin. 643'.7
Making your place a home / by Kevin Ruedisueli. New York : Quick Fox, c1977. vii, 184 p. : ill. ; 28 cm. [NK2115.R83] 76-56574 ISBN 0-8256-3068-1 : 6.95
1. Interior decoration—Handbooks, manuals, etc. I. Title. BIP

VARNEY, Carleton. 747'.8'83
Be your own decorator / Carleton Varney. 1st ed. New York : Playboy Press : distribution by Simon and Schuster, c1978. p. cm. [NK2115.V316] 78-10242 ISBN 0-87223-514-9 : 15.95
1. Interior decoration—Handbooks, manuals, etc. I. Title. BIP

WILSON, Forrest, 1918- 729'.2
Graphic guide to interior design / written and drawn by Forrest Wilson. New York : Van Nostrand Reinhold, c1977. v, 128 p. ; ill. ; 21 x 28 cm. Includes index. [NK2113.W54] 76-45280 ISBN 0-442-29549-9 : 10.95 ISBN 0-442-29552-9 pbk. : 4.95
1. Interior decoration—Handbooks, manuals, etc. 2. Design—Handbooks, manuals, etc. I. Title. BIP

Interior decoration—Hist.

JONES, David Thomas. v. 12
Architectural interiors. Serial 6411-1. [Ed. 2] Scranton, International Correspondence Schools, c1962. 72 p. illus. 19 cm. [NK1860.J6] 63-2070
1. Interior decoration—Hist. 2. Furniture—Hist. I. International Correspondence Schools, Scranton, Pa. II. Title.

PRAZ, Mario, 1896- 747.203
An illustrated history of furnishing, from the Renaissance to the 20th century [Tr. from Italian by William Weaver] New York, Braziller [1964] 396p. illus. (pt. col.) 31cm. Bibl. 64-21020 25.00; 20.95 before Jan. 1,
1. Interior decoration—Hist. 2. Genre (Art) I. Title.

Interior decoration—Hollywood, Calif.

KNIGHT, Arthur. 747'.09794'93
The Hollywood style. Photos. by Eliot Elisofon. [New York] Macmillan [1969] 216 p. illus. (part col.), map (on lining papers) 32 cm. [NK2002.K6] 69-12942 22.50
1. Interior decoration—Hollywood, Calif. 2. Moving-picture actors and actresses, American—Homes and haunts—Hollywood, Calif. I. Elisofon, Eliot, illus. II. Title.

Interior decoration—Japan.

JAPANESE interiors, 747.2952
by the Edit. Bd., Gakuyo Shobo. [Tr. by Donald L. Philippi. Photogs. by Sadaaki Kimura, Tatsuzo Sato] Tokyo, Gakuyo Shobo [dist. Rutland, Vt., Japan Pubns. Trading Co., 1963, c.1962] 88p. illus. (pt. col.) 27cm. 62-18109 3.95 bds.,
1. Interior decoration—Japan. 2. Art industries and trade—Japan. I. Kimura, Sadaaki, 1910- illus. II. Sato, Tatsuzo, 1904- illus. III. Gakuyo Shobo, Tokyo.

Interior decoration—Juvenile literature.

ALEXANDER, Mary Jean. 747'.77
Designing your own room / by Mary Jean Alexander ; illustrated by Barbara Fiore. New York : F. Watts, 1977. 64 p. : ill. ; 24 cm. (A Concise guide) Includes index. An introduction to basics of interior design, including tips on coordinating decorating ideas with individual personalities. [NK2115.A585] 76-46636 ISBN 0-531-00091-5 lib. bdg. : 4.47
1. Interior decoration—Juvenile literature. I. Fiore, Barbara. II. Title.

BARKIN, Carol. 747'.77
Slapdash decorating / Carol Barkin and Elizabeth James ; illustrated by Rita Folden Leydon. New York : Wanderer Books, [1979] c1977. p. cm. Reprint of the ed. published by Lothrop, Lee & Shepard Co., New York. Includes index. Quick, easy, and inexpensive ways to create or improvise with furniture, windows, walls, floors, and accessories to give your room a new look. [NK2115.B28 1979] 78-32134 ISBN 0-671-33027-6 : 2.95
1. Interior decoration—Juvenile literature. 2. Handicraft—Juvenile literature. I. James, Elizabeth, joint author. II. Leydon, Rita Floden. III. Title.

MOORE, Mary (Furlong) 747
Your own room; the interior decorating guide for girls. Illustrated by Laura Jean Allen. New York, Grosset & Dunlap [c.1960] vii, 80p. col. illus. 24cm. 60-2486 2.95 bds.,
1. Interior decoration—Juvenile literature. I. Title.

MOORE, Mary (Furlong) 1910- 747
Your own room; the interior decorating guide for girls. Illustrated by Laura Jean Allen. New York, Grosset & Dunlap [1960] 80p. illus. 24cm. [NK2117.M6] 60-2486
1. Interior decoration—Juvenile literature. I. Title.

SILVIAN, Leonore. 747'.77
Slapdash decorating / by Leonore Silvian. New York : Lothrop, Lee & Shepard Co., c1977. p. cm. Quik, easy, and inexpensive ways to create or improvise with furnitue, windows, walls, floors, and accessories to give your room a new look. [NK2115.B28] 77-22241 ISBN 0-688-41813-9 : 5.95 ISBN 0-688-51813-3 lib.bdg. : 5.49
1. Interior decoration—Juvenile literature. 2. Handicraft—Juvenile literature. I. James, Elizabeth, joint author. II. Leydon, Rita Floden. III. Title. BIP

Interior decoration—Los Angeles—Directories.

FAULKNER, Suzanne. 747'.025'79493
The L.A. home furnishing decorating & accessory buying guide. Los Angeles, J. P. Tarcher [1973] vi, 153 p. 14 x 21 cm. (A Tarcher/Southern California guide) [NK1705.F38] 73-76664 ISBN 0-87477-010-6 2.95
1. Interior decoration—Los Angeles—Directories. 2. Art objects—Los Angeles—Directories. I. Title.

Interior decoration—Mexico.

SHIPWAY, Verna (Cook) 1890- 728.60972
Mexican homes of today, by Verna Cook Shipway, Warren Shipway. New York, Architectural Bk. [dist. Hastings. c.1964] xxi, 248p. illus., plans. 28cm. [NK2014.S49] 64-8118 12.95
1. Interior decoration—Mexico. 2. Architecture, Domestic—Mexico. I. Shipway, Warren, joint author. II. Title. BIP

SHIPWAY, Verna (Cook) 1890- 747.2972
Mexican interiors, by Verna Cook Shipway and Warren Shipway. New York, Architectural Book Pub. Co. 1962 xiii, 257 p. illus. 29 cm. [NK2014.S5] 62-16187
1. Interior decoration—Mexico. 2. Furniture, Mexican. 3. Art industries and trade—Mexico. I. Shipway, Warren, joint author. II. Title. BIP

Interior decoration—New England.

CHAMBERLAIN, Samuel, 1895- 917.4
The Chamberlain selection of New England rooms, 1639-1863, by Samuel Chamberlain and Narcissa G. Chamberlain. New York, Hastings House [1972] 192 p. illus. 29 cm. [NK2005.C45] 72-6160 ISBN 0-8038-1176-4 20.00
1. Interior decoration—New England. 2. Historic buildings—New England. I. Chamberlain, Narcissa G., joint author. II. Title. BIP

Interior decoration—Period.

BUDGET decorating; 747.7
ed. by Jo Ann Francis and the eds. of Maco Mag. Corp. [New York, Maco Mag. Corp. [New York, Maco Mag. Corp., dist.] S. & S. [c. 1964, 1965] 95p. illus. (pt. col.) 28cm. [NK1700.B77] 64-66274 3.95 bds.,
1. Interior decoration—Period.

HOUSE & garden. 747.05
Decorating guide. [Greenwich, Conn., Conde Nast Publications] v. illus. (part col.) 33 cm. Annual -1962; semiannual, fall/winter 1962/63 -- Title varies: Book of decorating. -- -1962, Book of decorating and entertaining. Vol. for fall/winter 1962/63 issued jointly by Living for young homemakers. [NK1700.H76] 58-845
1. Interior decoration — Period. I. Living for young homemakers. II. Title.

INTERIOR design. 747.05
[East Stroudsberg, Pa., etc., Interior Design Division of Whitney Communications Corp., etc.] v. in illus. (part col.) ports. 24-31cm. monthly Began publication with Apr. 1932 issue. Publication suspended May 1942-Mar. 1949. Title varies: -Dec. 1936, The Decorators digest.--Jan. 1937-Nov. 1950, Interior design and decoration. Editor: H. V. Anderson. [NK1700.D55] 60-50565
1. Interior decoration—Period. I. Anderson, Harry Vernon, 1902- ed.

Interior decoration—Practice.

SIEGEL, Harry. 747
A guide to business principles and practices for interior designers, with actual examples of the specialized procedural forms to be used in the office. New York, Whitney Library of Design [1968] 202 p. forms. 32 cm. [NK2116.S5] 68-57364 13.95
1. Interior decoration—Practice. I. Title. BIP

SIEGEL, Harry. 658'.91'747213
This business of interior design : a practical checklist for analyzing the various conditions of a design project and the related clauses for a letter of agreement / Harry Siegel. New York : Whitney Library of Design, 1976. 63 p. ; 26 cm. Includes index. [NK2116.2.S5] 76-2469 ISBN 0-8230-7460-9 pbk. : 4.95
1. Interior decoration—Practice. I. Title.

Interior decoration—Psychological aspects.

FRANKEL, Virginia. 747'.01'9
What your house tells about you. Illustrated by Loretta Trezzo. New York, Trident Press [1972] 156 p. illus. 21 cm. [NK2113.F67] 78-182265 ISBN 0-671-27089-3 5.95
1. Interior decoration—Psychological aspects. I. Title. BIP

HARMON, Margaret H. 747'.01'9
Psycho-decorating : what homes reveal about people / Margaret H. Harmon. 1st ed. New York : Wyden Books, c1977. p. cm. Bibliography: p. [NK2113.H29] 77-16282 ISBN 0-671-22951-6 : 9.95
1. Interior decoration—Psychological aspects. I. Title.

ST. Marie, Satenig S. 747'.01'9
Homes are for people [by] Satenig S. St. Marie. New York, Wiley [1973] x, 400 p. illus. (part col.) 25 cm. Includes bibliographies. [NK2113.S25] 72-10244 ISBN 0-471-82635-9 10.95
1. Interior decoration—Psychological aspects. I. Title. BIP

VARNEY, Carleton. 747
You and your apartment. Indianapolis, Bobbs-Merrill [1967] xiii, 178 p. illus. (part col.), plans. 29 cm. [NK2115.V33] 67-27228
1. Interior decoration—Psychological aspects. 2. Architecture, Domestic—Designs and plans. I. Title.

Interior decoration—Spain.

BYNE, Arthur, 1883-1935. 747.26
Spanish interiors and furniture; photographs and drawings. With a brief text by Mildred Stapley. Magnolia, Mass. Peter Smith 1973 [c1969] 3 v. in one (306 p.), illus., 31 cm. (Dover bk rebound) [NK2062.B8] 70-97502 ISBN 0-8446-4522-2 10.00
1. Interior decoration—Spain. 2. Furniture, Spanish. I. Byne, Mildred (Stapley) 1875-1941. II. Title.

Interior decoration—Study and teaching.

YABLONSKI, Winifred, 747'.8'83
1941-
Designing home interiors : a study guide / by Winifred Yablonski and Carolyn Breedon. Provo, Utah : Brigham Young University Press for Coast Community College District and Rancho Santiago Community College District, c1978. p. cm. Includes bibliographical references. [NK2116.4.Y3] 78-18004 ISBN 0-8425-1317-5 pbk. : 4.50
1. Interior decoration—Study and teaching. I. Breedon, Carolyn, 1944- joint author. II. Coast Community College District. III. Rancho Santiago Community College District. IV. Title. BIP

Interior decoration—Study and teaching—United States.

GERALD, John D. 747
Interior decoration and design / by John D. Gerald and Marguerite Rittenhouse. Scranton, Pa. : School of Interior Design, International Correspondence Schools, [1975- v. : ill. ; 27 cm. "4901A-B-Contents.Contents.—v. A, sect. 1. Principles of interior design. [NK2116.5.G47] 75-307546
1. Interior decoration—Study and teaching—United States. I. Rittenhouse, Marguerite, joint author. II. International Correspondence Schools, Scranton, Pa. III. Title.

INTERIOR Design 747'.071'173
Educators Council. Curriculum Research Project.
A critical study of interior design education; final report. Arnold Friedmann, chairman, curriculum research. [Kew Gardens, N.Y.] 1968. iii, 134 p. illus. 28 cm. "Addendum [to the project's Directory, institutions offering interior design education]": p. [32]-[34] [NK2116.5.I5] 71-289204
1. Interior decoration—Study and teaching—U.S. 2. Universities and colleges—U.S.—Directories. I. Friedmann, Arnold. II. Title.

Interior decoration—Study and teaching—U.S.—Directories.

INTERIOR Design 747'.071'173
Educators Council. Curriculum Research Project.
Directory, institutions offering interior design education. [Kew Gardens, N.Y.] 1968. 29 p. 28 cm. [NK2116.5.I52] 75-289631
1. Interior decoration—Study and teaching—U.S.—Directories. 2. Universities and colleges—U.S.—Directories. I. Title. II. Title: Institutions offering interior design education.

Interior decoration—U. S.

AMERICAN Builder 747.88
Book of modern home decoration. New York, Simmons-Boardman Pub. Corp. [c.1959] 91p. illus. 29cm. 59-15676 2.95
1. Interior decoration—U.S. I. Title. II. Title: Modern home decoration.

AMERICAN interiors 747'.8'80973
: Architectural digest presents a decade of imaginative residential design / edited by Paige Rense. 1st ed. Los Angeles : Knapp Press, 1978. 287 p. : ill. ; 31 cm. Title on spine: Architectural digest American interiors. [NK2004.A45] 77-23652 ISBN 0-89535-002-5 : 29.95
1. Interior decoration—United States. I. Rense, Paige. II. Architectural digest. III. Title: Architectural digest. American interiors.

BAKER, Theresa Chalmers. 747.0973
A decorator's dizzy decade; the fun and foibles of a decorator in the twenties. Foreword by Gerard Harrington. [1st ed.] New York, Exposition Press [1961] 245p. 21cm. (An Exposition-banner book) [NK2002.B3] 61-616
1. Interior decoration—U. S. I. Title.

BALDRIGE, Letitia. 747'.213
Home; the Burlington House awards: American interiors. New York, Viking Press [1972] 172 p. illus. 23 cm. (A Studio book) [NK2004.B3] 70-184355 ISBN 0-670-37665-5 12.50
1. Interior decoration—United States. I. Burlington Industries, inc. II. Title.

BALDWIN, Billy. 747'.213
Billy Baldwin decorates. [1st ed.] New York, Holt, Rinehart and Winston [1972] 219 p. illus. (part col.) 30 cm. "A House & Garden book." [NK2135.B34A42 1972] 74-161814 ISBN 0-03-001021-7 15.00
1. Baldwin, Billy. 2. Interior decoration—United States. I. Title.

BJERKOE, Ethel Hall. 747.21
Decorating for and with antiques; with drawings by Lyn Watson. [1st ed.] Garden City, N.Y., Doubleday, 1950. 250 p. illus. 27 cm. Bibliography: p. [231]-236. [NK2113.B6] 50-9147
1. Interior decoration—U.S. 2. Furniture—U.S. I. Title.

BJERKOE, Ethel Hall. 747.21
How to decorate for and with antiques. With drawings by Lyn Watson. Garden City, N. Y., Doubleday, 1959. 256 p. illus. 27 cm. First ed. published in 1950 under title: Decorating for and with antiques. Includes bibliography. [NK2113.B6 1959] 59-8256
1. Interior decoration—U. S. 2. Furniture—U. S. I. Title.

BROOKLYN Institute of 747.2'3
Arts and Sciences. Museum.
American interiors, 1675-1885; a guide to the American period rooms in the Brooklyn Museum [by] Marvin D. Schwartz. [Brooklyn, 1968] vi, 114 p. illus. (part col.) 23 cm. Bibliography: p. 107. [NK2002.B7] 68-57682
1. Interior decoration—United States. 2. Historic buildings—United States. I. Schwartz, Marvin D. II. Title.

CHICAGO. Art Institute. 747
American rooms in miniature by Mrs. James Ward Thorne. [5th ed.] Chicago, Author, 1962[c.1942] unpaged. illus. 20x23cm. This group of miniature rooms [was] . . . presented to the Art Inst. of Chic. in 1942. 62-6432 1.00 pap.,
1. Interior decoration—U. S. 2. Architectural models. I. Thorne, Narcissa (Niblack) II. Title.

COMSTOCK, Helen. 747.88
100 most beautiful rooms in America New York, Studio Publications [1958] 210 p. illus. (part col.) 31 cm. [NK2002.C57] 58-12294
1. Interior decoration—U.S. 2. Furniture—U.S. I. Title.

COMSTOCK, Helen. 747.88
100 most beautiful rooms in America. Rev. ed New York, Viking Press [1965] 210 p. illus. (part col.) 32 cm. (A Studio book) [NK2002.C57 1965] 65-20811
1. Interior decoration—United States. 2. Furniture—United States. I. Title.

DOWNS, Joseph. 974
A selection of American interiors, 1640-1840, in the Henry Francis du Pont Winterthur Museum, Winterthur, Delaware / by Joseph Downs and Alice Winchester New York : Magazine Antiques, 1951. 48 p. : chiefly ill. ; 32 cm. [NK2002.D68] 75-304383
1. Henry Francis du Pont Winterthur Museum. 2. Interior decoration—United States. 3. Antiques in interior decoration. I. Winchester, Alice, joint author. II. Henry Francis du Pont Winterthur Museum. III. Title: A selection of American interiors ...

FRANKEL, Virginia. 747'.213
Interior space, interior design; livability and function with flair. [1st ed.] Garden City, N.Y., Doubleday, 1973. 191 p. illus. (part col.) 29 cm. [NK2004.F72] 72-83140 ISBN 0-385-06255-9 14.95
1. Interior decoration—United States. I. Title.

FRIEDMAN-WEISS, 747'.213 B
Jeffrey.
Good lives / by Jeffrey Weiss and Herbert H. Wise. New York : Quick Fox, c1977. [94] p. : col. ill. ; 24 cm. [NK2004.F74] 77-78527 ISBN 0-8256-3080-0 : 6.95 ISBN 0-8256-3083-5 : 12.95
1. Interior decoration—United States. I. Wise, Herbert H., joint author. II. Title. BIP

GILBERT, Rose Bennett. 747'.8'83
The you-do-it book of early American decorating / Rose Bennett Gilbert, Patricia Hart McMillan. 1st ed. Garden City, N.Y. : Doubleday, c1978. p. cm. Includes index. [NK2003.G54] 77-15150 ISBN 0-385-12711-1 : 12.95
1. Interior decoration—United States. 2. Decoration and ornament, Early American. I. McMillan, Patricia Hart, joint author. II. Title. BIP

NELSON, George, 1908- ed. 747
Living spaces. [New York] Whitney Publications, 1952] 145p. (chiefly illus., plans) 31cm. (Interiors library, 1) [NK2110.N35] 52-14781
1. Interior decoration—U. S. 2. Furniture—U. S. I. Title.

PETERSON, Harold Leslie, 917.3'03
1922-
Americans at home: from the Colonists to the Late Victorians; a pictorial source book of American domestic interiors with an appendix on inns and taverns [by] Harold L. Peterson. New York, Scribner [1971] xviii p. 205 plates. 29 cm. Each plate accompanied by descriptive text. [NK2002.P4] 75-143956 ISBN 0-684-12344-4 14.95
1. Interior decoration—U.S. 2. U.S.—Social life and customs—Pictorial works. I. Title.

RAND, Marcia. 747.213
Be your own decorator. Illustrated with photos., and with drawings by Helen Forbes. New York, Dodd, Mead, 1959. 176 p. illus. 24 cm. [NK2110.R35] 59-7977
1. Interior decoration—U.S. I. Title.

ROGERS, Meyric Reynold, 747'.213
1893-
American interior design / Meyric R. Rogers. New York : Arno Press, 1976 [c1947] 309 p. ; 29 cm. (America in two centuries, an inventory) Reprint of the 1st ed. published by Norton, New York. Includes index. Bibliography: p. 297-302. [NK2002.R64 1976] 75-22838 ISBN 0-405-07709-2 : 23.00
1. Interior decoration—United States. 2. Furniture—United States. I. Title. II. Series. BIP

SKURKA, Norma. 747'.8'83
The New York times book of interior design and decoration / Norma Skurka. New York : Quadrangle/New York Times Book Co., c1976. p. cm. Includes index. Bibliography: p. [NK2004.S57 1976] 76-9690 ISBN 0-8129-0653-5 : 20.00
1. Interior decoration—United States. I. Title. BIP

SWEENEY, John A H 747.213
The treasure house of early American rooms. Photos by Gilbert Ask. Introd. by Henry Francis du Pont. New York, Viking Press [1963] 179 p. illus. (part col.) facsims. 29 cm. (A Winterthur book) Collection housed in Henry Francis duPont Winterthur Museum. [NK2003.S9] 63-15585
1. Interior decoration — U.S. 2. Furniture, American. 3. Art industries and trade — U.S. I. DuPont, Henry Francis, 1890- II. Henry Francis DuPont Winterthur Museum. III. Title. IV. Series: Winterthur series

SWEENEY, John A H 747.213
Winterthur illustrated. Photos. by Gilbert Ask. Introd. by Henry Francis DuPont. [New Castle? Del.] 1963. 179 p. illus. (part col.) facsims. 28 cm. (A Winterthur book) Collection housed in Henry Francis duPont Winterthur Museum. Issued also under title: The treasure house of early American rooms. [NK460.W5S9 1963] 64-9912
1. Interior decoration — U.S. 2. Furniture, American. 3. Art industries and trade — U.S. I. DuPont, Henry Francis, 1890- II. Henry Francis DuPont Winterthur Museum. III. Title.

TWEE, Katharine, ed. 747.213
The finest rooms, by America's great decorators. Introd. by Russell Lynes. New York, Viking Press [1964] 168 p. illus. (part col.) 33 cm. (A Studio book) [NK2002.T9] 64-20859
1. Interior decoration — U.S. 2. Interior decorators — U.S. I. Title.

VARNEY, Carleton. 747'.8'83
Carleton Varney decorates from A to Z : an encyclopedia of home decoration / by Carleton Varney. Indianapolis : Bobbs-Merrill, [1977] p. cm. [NK2004.3.V37A43] 77-76890 ISBN 0-672-51863-5 : 17.50
1. Varney, Carleton. 2. Interior decoration—United States. I. Title. BIP

WILLIAMS, Henry Lionel. 747.0973
America's small houses and city apartments; the personal homes of designers and collectors, by Henry Lionel Williams and Ottalie K. Williams. With an introd. by J. A. Lloyd Hyde. New York, Barnes [1964] 255 p. illus. (part col.) 35 cm. [NK2002.W49] 64-21363
1. Interior decoration—U.S. 2. Collectors and collecting—U.S. 3. Architecture, Domestic—U.S. I. Williams, Ottalie Kroeber, 1901- joint author. II. Title.

WILSON, Jose. 747'.213
Decorating American style / Jose Wilson & Arthur Leaman. 1st ed. Boston : New York Graphic Society, c1975. 200 p. : ill. (some col.) ; 29 cm. Bibliography: p. 199-200. [NK2002.W52] 75-363 ISBN 0-8212-0603-6
1. Interior decoration—United States. 2. Furniture—United States. I. Leaman, Arthur, joint author. II. Title. BIP

WILSON, Jose. 747.213
Decoration U.S.A. By Jose Wilson and Arthur Leaman. New York, Macmillan [1965] 278 p. illus. (part col.) 31 cm. [NK2002.W53] 65-22666
1. Interior decoration—United States. 2. Furniture—United States. I. Leaman, Arthur, joint author. II. Title.

Interior decoration—United States—History.

SEALE, William. 747'.213
The tasteful interlude : American interiors through the camera's eye, 1860-1917 / William Seale. New York : Praeger, 1975. 256 p. : ill. ; 26 cm. (American decorative arts series) Includes index. [NK2003.5.S42] 74-1724 ISBN 0-275-43840-6 : 20.00
1. Interior decoration—United States—History. 2. Furniture—United States. 3. Art industries and trade, American—History. 4. United States—Social life and customs—1865-1918. I. Title.

Interior decoration—Vocational guidance.

BALL, Victoria Kloss. 729
Opportunities in interior design / Victoria Kloss Ball. Rev. ed. Louisville, Ky. : Vocational Guidance Manuals, c1977. v, 122 p. : ill. ; 21 cm. First ed. published in 1963 under title: Opportunities in interior design and decoration. Includes index. Bibliography: p. [118]-119. [NK2116.B3 1977] 76-51706 ISBN 0-89022-228-2 : 4.95 ISBN 0-89022-229-0 pbk. : 2.95
1. Interior decoration—Vocational guidance. I. Title. BIP

Interior decoration—Vocational guidance—Juvenile literature.

SCHNEIDER, Rita Marie. 747'.023
Interior design careers / Rita Marie Schneider ; consulting editor, Xenia F. Fane. Englewood Cliffs, N.J. : Prentice-Hall, c1977. v, 122 p. : ill. ; 24 cm. Includes bibliographies and index. Describes the opportunities and the preparation required for careers in various areas of interior design. [NK2116.S36] 76-

Interior decoration—Yearbooks.

40120 ISBN 0-13-392795-4 : 5.95 pbk. : 3.32
1. Interior decoration—Vocational guidance—Juvenile literature. I. Title. **BIP**

AMERICAN Institute of   747.058
Interior Designers.
The A.I.D. annual. 1942- New York. v. illus. 31 cm. Vols. for 1942- issued by the institute under its earlier name: American Institute of Decorators. [NK9.A55] 42-23036
1. Interior decoration — Yearbooks. 2. Art industries and trade — Yearbooks. 3. Art, Decorative — Yearbooks. I. Title.

DECORATIVE art 50...   747.058
the studio year book 1960-61. International furnishing & decoration. Golden jubilee issue. Editor: Terrence Davis. New York, Viking Press [1960] 172p. illus., plates (part col.) 29cm. Editor 1906-Geoffrey Holme 60-36913 9.50
1. Interior decoration—Yearbooks. 2. Art industries and trade—Yearbooks. 3. Art, Decorative—Yearbooks. I. Holme, Geoffrey, 1887- ed. II. The Studio.

DECORATIVE art in modern   745.05
interiors, 1966/67. Ed. by Ella Moody. New York, Viking [c.1966] 161, xiip. illus., plates (pt. col.) 29cm. (Studio bk.) [NK9.D4] 63-6913 14.00
1. Interior decoration—Yearbooks. 2. Art industries and trade—Yearbooks. I. Moody, Ella, ed.

DECORATIVE art in modern   747.058
interiors v.52;the Studio yearbook of international furnishing and decoration 1962 63. New York, Viking, c.1962] 158p. illus. (pt. col.) 29cm. 6-36913 10.95
1. Interior decoration—Yearbooks. 2. Art industries and trade—Yearbooks. 3. Art, Decorative—Yearbooks. I. Moody, Ella, ed.

DECORATIVE art in modern   745.05
interiors; 1967-1968 Yearbook of international furnishing and decoration v.57. New York, Viking [1967] v. illus., plates (pt. col.) 29cm. (Studio bk.) Ed.: 1966- E. Moody. [NK9.D4] 63-6913 14.00
1. Interior decoration—Yearbooks. 2. Art industries — and trade — Yearbooks. I. Moody, Ella. ed.

DECORATIVE art in modern   747.058
interiors; v.54, 1964/5. Art ed.: Ella Moody. New York, Viking [c.1964] 159p. illus. (pt. col.) 29cm. (Studio year bk. of intl. furnishing & decoration, v.54) annual. 64-36913 12.00
1. Interior decoration—Yearbooks. 2. Art industries and trade—Yearbooks. 3. Art, Decorative—Yearbooks. I. Moody, Ella, Ed.

DECORATIVE art in modern   747.058
interiors, 1961/2 [dist. New York, Viking, c.1961] 160p. illus. (part col.) 29cm. (Studio bk.) Title varies. 6-36913 9.50
1. Interior decoration—Yearbooks. 2. Art industries and trade—Yearbooks. 3. Art, Decorative—Yearbooks.

DECORATIVE art in modern   747.05
interiors, 1965/6. Ed.: Ella Moody. New York, Viking [c.1965] 159, xvp. illus. plates (pt. col.) 29cm. (Studio year book of intl. furnishing and decoration, v.55) [NK9.D4] 63-6913 12.50
1. Interior decoration—Yearbooks. 2. Art industries and trade—Yearbooks. I. Moody, Ella, ed.

HOUSE beautiful's   747.05
portfolio of home decorating. v. 1- [New York, Hearst Corp.] 1963 v. illus. (part col.) 32 cm. annual. [NK1700.H8] 63-490
1. Interior decoration — Yearbooks.

I. D. & D.;   747.2205
interior design and decoration. 1966- [New York] October House. v. illus. (part col.) 33 cm. Each vol. carries also in the title the year of issue, i.e. I. D. & D. '66. [NK1700.I 2] 65-23428
1. Interior decoration — Yearbooks. 2. Art industries and trade—Yearbooks. I. Title: Interior design and decoration.

L. D. & D.; interior   747.2205
design and decoration. 1966 [New York]

October House [c.1965] 319p. illus. (pt. col.) 33cm. [NK1700.I2] 65-23428 27.50
1. Interior decoration—Yearbooks. 2. Art industries and trade—Yearbooks. I. Title: Interior design and decoration.

1,001 decorating ideas.   747.05
[New York, Conso Products, 19 v. illus. 28 cm. annual. Began publication in Jan. 1940. [NK1700.O5] 63-11127
1. Interior decoration — Yearbooks.

Interior decorators—Direct.

AMERICAN Institute of   747.06273
Decorators.
Membership directory. New York, 1954. 160p. 20cm. [NK1700.A54] 56-1632
I. Title.

AMERICAN Institute of   747.06273
Interior Designers.
Membership directory. New York. v. 20 cm. Vols. for   issued by the institute under its earlier name: American Institute of Decorators. [NK1700.A54] 56-1632
Title.

ANDERSON, Harry Vernon,   747.058
1902- ed.
The national register of interior designers, 1951 ed. New York, National Register Pub. Co., 1951. 164 p. 24 cm. [NK1705.A5] 52-36742
1. Interior decorators—Direct. I. Title.

Interior decorators—United States—Correspondence, reminiscences, etc.

BALDWIN, Billy.   747'.21'3
Billy Baldwin remembers. New York, Harcourt Brace Jovanovich [1974] 232 p. illus. 29 cm. [NK2004.3.B34A22] 74-8712 ISBN 0-15-112070-6 19.95
1. Baldwin, Billy. 2. Interior decorators—United States—Correspondence, reminiscences, etc. I. Title.

International Association of Printing House Craftsmen.

CHRISTENSEN, Edward   655.2'062'7
H.
Fifty golden years of craftsmanship; a history of the International Association of Printing House Craftsmen, Inc., 1919-1969, by Edward H. Christensen. [Ephrata, Pa., Printing: Science Press, 1969 or 70] xvi, 157 p. illus., ports. 24 cm. [Z120.159C5] 74-83998
1. International Association of Printing House Craftsmen. I. Title.

International style (Architecture)

PEARSON, Paul David,   720'.92'4 B
1936-
Alvar Aalto and the international style / by Paul David Pearson. New York : Whitney Library of Design, 1978. 240 p. : ill. ; 29 cm. Includes index. Bibliography: p. 236. [NA1455.F53A255] 77-20029 ISBN 0-8230-7023-9 : 27.50
1. Aalto, Alvar, 1898-1976. 2. International style (Architecture) I. Title. Distributed by Watson Guptill. **BIP**

International style (Architecture)—South Africa.

HERBERT, Gilbert.   720'.92'4 B
Martienssen and the international style : the modern movement in South African architecture / Gilbert Herbert. Cape Town : Balkema (A.A.), 1976 xi, 283 p. : ill. ; 29 cm. Includes index. Bibliography: p. 271-278. [NA1596.M37H47] 76-350259 ISBN 0-86961-038-4 : 36.00
1. Martienssen, Rex Distin, 1905-1942. 2. International style (Architecture)—South Africa. 3. Architecture, Modern—20th century—South Africa. I. Title. Distributed by Wittenborn

Inverness, Scot.—Description—Views.

DELAVAULT, Pierre.   914.12'1
Old Inverness: a collection of prints in colour and black and white. [Revised ed.] Inverness, Robert Carruthers & Sons, 1967.

[112] p. illus. (some col.), ports. 29 cm. Bibliography: p. [6] [NE215.S4I5 1967] 68-74716 63/-
1. Inverness, Scot.—Description—Views. I. Title.

Iowa—Antiq.

MCKUSICK, Marshall   970.477
Bassford, 1930-
Men of ancient Iowa, as revealed by archeological discoveries. Ames, Iowa State Univ. Pr. [c.1964] xix, 260p. illus., famsim., maps, plans, ports. 26cm. Bibl. [E78.I6M3] 64-13376 6.50
1. Iowa—Antiq. 2. Indians of North America—Iowa. I. Title.

Iowa—Description and travel—1951- —Views.

ZIELINSKI, John   917.77'03'30222
M.
Portrait of Iowa. Introd. by Paul Engle. Photos. by John M. Zielinski and others. Minneapolis, Adams Press [1974] 173 p. illus. 29 cm. [F622.Z53] 74-17265 ISBN 0-914828-01-0 14.95
1. Iowa—Description and travel—1951- Views. I. Title. **BIP**

Iowa—Historic houses, etc.

WAGNER, William   977.7'0022'2
John, 1915-
Sixty sketches of Iowa's past and present; an illustrated guide and narrative to some of Iowa's past and present, by William J. Wagner. Drawings and narrative by the author unless otherwise credited. Edited by Donna M. Brown. With a foreword by John M. Henry. [1st ed West Des Moines, Iowa, Brown and Wagner, 1967] xiii, 179 p. illus., map (on lining paper) 23 x 29 cm. [F622.W29] 68-21074
1. Iowa—Historic houses, etc. I. Title.

Iowa—Maps—Bibliography—Catalogs.

UNITED States.   016.911'777
National Archives.
Cartographic records relating to the Territory of Iowa, 1838-1846. Compiled by Laura E. Kelsay and Frederick W. Pernell. Washington, 1971. vii, 27 p. 27 cm. (Its Special list no. 27) [Z6027.U5U6 1971a] 70-175627
1. United States. National Archives. 2. Iowa—Maps—Bibliography—Catalogs. I. Kelsay, Laura E. II. Pernell, Frederick W. III. Title. IV. Series.

Iowa. State University of Science and Technology, Ames.

RAYNESS, Velma Wallace, 1896-   916
Campus sketches of Iowa State University. [2d ed.] Ames, Iowa State University Press [1962] 53 p. illus. 18 x 22 cm. [NC1075.R36A43] 62-22410
1. Iowa. State University of Science and Technology, Ames. I. Title.

Ireland — Civilization.

BRIGHAM, Gertrude   700'.9415
Richardson.
The road to the Western Isle. Drawings by Frederic Rockwell and Palmer Hayden. Photos. by G. R. Brigham. Boothbay Harbor, Me., Printed by the Boothbay register [1963] 180 p. illus., ports. 20 cm. [DA959.1.B7] 63-47829
1. Ireland — Civilization. 2. Ireland — Descr. & trav. — 1951- I. Title.

Ireland—Description and travel.

SASEK, Miroslav.   914.15
This is Ireland [by] M. Sasek. [New York] Macmillan [1965, c1964] 59 p. col. illus., col. map. 32 cm. Drawings and text introduce the history, geography, major sights, and traditions of the Emerald Isle. [ND1946] AC 68
1. Ireland—Description and travel. I. Title. **BIP**

Ireland—Description and travel—1951- —Views.

REILLY, Cyril A.,   779'.9'91415
1920-
An Irish blessing : a photographic interpretation / by Cyril A. Reilly and Renee Travis Reilly. Minneapolis : Winston Press, c1977. 59 p. : chiefly col. ill. ; 20 x 22 cm. [DA978.R36] 77-71936 ISBN 0-03-021271-5 pbk. : 5.95
1. Ireland—Description and travel—1951- Views. I. Reilly, Renee Travis, joint author. II. Title. **BIP**

Ireland—Description and travel—Views.

SASEK, Miroslav.   914.15
This is Ireland [New York] Macmillan [1965, c.1964] 59p. col. illus., col. map. 32cm. [ND1946.S2A525] 65-1419 2.95; 3.52 bds., lib. ed.,
1. Ireland—Descr. & trav.—Views. I. Title.

SASEK, Miroslav.   914.15
This is Ireland [by] M. Sasek. [New York] Macmillan [1965, c1964] 59 p. col. illus., col. map. 32 cm. [ND1946.S3] 65-7296
1. Ireland—Description and travel—Views. I.   Title.

Iron age—India—South India.

SOUNDARA Rajan, K. V.,   573'.08 s
1925-
Megalithic architecture in southern India / by K. V. Soundara Rajan. Columbia : [Museum of Anthropology, University of Missouri—Columbia], c1975. iii, 14 p. : ill. ; 28 cm. (Museum brief ; no. 12) "Expanded version of the lecture by the author delivered on the 17th of June 1971 at the Department of Anthropology, University of Missouri, Columbia." Bibliography: p. 14. [E151.M87 no. 12] [GN780.32.I4] 722'.4 76-352339 ISBN 0-913134-97-X pbk. : 2.50
1. Iron age—India—South India. 2. Megalithic monuments—India—South India. 3. South India—Antiquities. I. Title. II. Series: Museum briefs ; no. 12. **BIP**

Iron Gate site.

LEONHARDY, Frank C.   500.9'08 s
The archaeology of a late prehistoric village in northwestern California, by Frank C. Leonhardy. Eugene, Museum of Natural History, University of Oregon, 1967. 41 p. illus. 27 cm. (Bulletin of the Museum of Natural History, University of Oregon, no. 4) Bibliography: p. 41. [QH1.O7 no. 4] 68-64901
1. Iron Gate site. I. Title. II. Series: Oregon. University. Museum of Natural History. Bulletin no. 4

Iron-on transfers.

†PARSONS School of   646.4'8
Design, New York.
The Parsons iron-on-book / Parsons School of Design. New York : Pantheon Books, [1977] p. cm. Yearbook of Parsons School of Design for 1977-78, resulting from a senior seminar in publication design. Forty-eight student-produced iron-on designs for T-shirts with complete transferring instructions. [TT852.7.P37 1977] 77-13700 ISBN 0-394-83713-4 pbk. : 5.95
1. Iron-on transfers. 2. T-shirts. I. Title.

Ironstone china.

WETHERBEE, Jean.   738.3
A handbook on white ironstone, with text and drawings by Jean Wetherbee. Canajoharie, N.Y. [1974] 100 p. illus. 23 cm. Cover title: White ironstone. Bibliography: p. 86. [NK4367.17W47] 74-166330 5.00
1. Ironstone china. I. Title. II. Title: White ironstones.

Ironwork.

HOVER, Otto, 1889-   739.4
Wrought iron; encyclopedia of ironwork. [Translated from the German by Ann C.

Weaver.] [2d American ed.] [New York] Universe Books [1962] xxxiii p. illus., 320 plates. 30 cm. Translation of Das Eisenwerk. [NK8205.H573 1962] 62-12006
1. Ironwork. I. Title: Encyclopedia of ironwork.

MEILACH, Dona Z. 739'.4
Decorative and sculptural ironwork : tools, techniques, inspiration / by Dona Z. Meilach ; consultants, George Martin, E. A. Chase, Theodore Davidson. New York : Crown Publishers, c1977. vii, 312 p., [4] leaves of plates : ill. ; 27 cm. Includes index. Bibliography: p. [302]-306. [TT220.M4 1977] 76-45762 ISBN 0-517-52319-1 : 14.95 ISBN 0-517-52658-1 pbk. : 7.95
1. Ironwork. I. Title. BIP

UNDERWOOD, Austin. 739.4
Creative wrought ironwork. Princeton, N.J. Van Nostrand [1966 c1965] 96 p. illus. 22 cm. Bibliography: p. 94. [NK8205.U5 1966] 66-7031
1. Ironwork. I. Title.

ZIMELLI, Umberto. 739'.4
Decorative ironwork [by] Umberto Zimelli and Giovanni Vergerio. London, New York, P. Hamlyn [1969] 159 p. col. illus. 20 cm. (Cameo) Translation of Il ferro battuto. [NK8205.Z513] 75-20652 ISBN 0-600-01228-X
1. Ironwork. I. Vergerio, Giovanni, joint author. II. Title.

Ironwork—Cambridge, Eng.

LISTER, Raymond. 739'.47'4259
Hammer and hand: an essay on the ironwork of Cambridge; with drawings by Richard Bawden. Cambridge, R. Lister, 1969. [5], 42 p. illus. 22 x 26 cm. "500 copies printed." [NK8244.C3L5] 79-498833
1. Ironwork—Cambridge, Eng. I. Bawden, Richard, illus. II. Title.

Ironwork—Catalogs.

JANES, Kirtland & Company. 739'.47'73
Ornamental ironwork; fountains, statuary, vases, urns, lawn furniture, pedestals, baptismal fonts, animals veranda, summer house. Janes, Kirtland & Co., 1870, illustrated catalog and historical introduction. [1st ed.] Princeton [N.J.] Pyne Press [1971] 1 v. (unpaged) illus. 28 cm. (American historical catalog collection) Includes bibliography. [NK8299.J35] 72-162357 3.25
1. Ironwork—Catalogs. I. Title. II. Series.

Ironwork—England.

GARDNER, John Starkie, 1844-1930. 739'.4742
English ironwork of the XVIIth & XVIIIth centuries; an historical & analytical account of the development of exterior smithcraft. [New York] B. Blom [1972] xxxvi, 336 p. illus. 24 cm. Reprint of the 1911 ed. [NK8243.G3 1972] 69-16319 27.50
1. Ironwork—England. 2. Decoration and ornament, English. 3. Architecture—Details. I. Title.

HARRIS, John, comp. 739.4742
English decorative ironwork from contemporary source books, 1610-1836; a collection of drawings and pattern books. . . Chicago, Quadrangle Books [1960] vi, 18p. 172 illus. 26cm. 60-6625 10.00 bds.,
1. Ironwork—England. 2. Architectural ironwork. I. Title.

Ironwork—England—History.

GARDNER, John Starkie, 1844-1930. 739'.4742
English ironwork of the XVIIth and XVIIIth centuries; an historical & analytical account of the development of exterior smithcraft. With 88 collotype plates from photographs chiefly by Horace Dan, architect and upwards of 150 other illustrations. Boston, Milford House [1973] p. Reprint of the 1911 ed. published by B. T. Batsford, London and W. Helburn, New York. [NK8243.G3 1973] 73-4894 ISBN 0-87821-125-X
1. Ironwork—England—History. 2. Decoration and ornament, English. 3. Architecture—Details. I. Title.

Ironwork—Exhibitions.

MADE of iron. 739.4
Houston, Texas, September-December 1966. [Houston, 1966?] 288 p. illus. 23 cm. At head of title: University of St. Thomas Art Department. "This exhibition was assembled as a contribution to the Arts Festival of Houston, October 1966, held in honor of the inauguration of Jones Hall for the Performing Arts." Includes bibliographies. [NK8201.H6] 67-26420
1. Ironwork—Exhibitions. I. Houston, Tex. University of St. Thomas. Art, Dept.

Ironwork—France.

FRANK, Edgar Block, 1882- 739.4
Old French ironwork; the craftsman and his art. Cambridge, Harvard University Press, 1950. xiv, 221 p. illus., 96 plates. 25 cm. Translation of Petite ferronnerie ancienne. Bibliography: p. 217-218. [NK8249.F713] 50-9903
1. Ironwork—France. I. Title.

Ironwork—Great Britain.

LISTER, Raymond. 739'.47'42
Decorative wrought ironwork in Great Britain. [1st Tuttle ed.] Rutland, Vt., C. E. Tuttle Co. [1970] xii, 267 p. illus. 23 cm. [NK8243.L5 1970] 72-113903 ISBN 0-8048-0902-X 7.50
1. Ironwork—Great Britain. I. Title.

Ironwork—Louisiana.

CHRISTIAN, Marcus Bruce, 1900- 682'.09763
Negro ironworkers in Louisiana, 1718-1900, by Marcus Christian. Gretna [La.] Pelican Pub. Co., 1972. vii, 61 p. illus. 22 cm. Bibliography: p. 37-43. [NK8212.A1C57] 72-85953 ISBN 0-911116-74-5 2.50
1. Ironwork—Louisiana. 2. Negroes—Employment—Louisiana. I. Title. BIP

Ironwork—Melbourne.

ROBERTSON, Edward Graeme. 739'.47'945
Ornamental cast iron in Melbourne, by E. Graeme Robertson. Melbourne, Georgian House [1967] x, 229 p. (chiefly illus.) maps (on lining papers) 31 cm. [NK8291.R57] 67-96312
1. Ironwork—Melbourne. 2. Melbourne—Dwellings. I. Title.

Ironwork—Philadelphia.

WALLACE, Philip B. 739'.47'74811
Colonial ironwork in old Philadelphia; the craftsmanship of the early days of the Republic [by] Philip B. Wallace. Measured drawings by William Allen Dunn. Introd. by Fiske Kimball. New York, Dover Publications [1970] 147 p. (chiefly illus.) 28 cm. Reprint of the 1930 ed., with new index. [NK8212.P4W3 1970] 73-104811 ISBN 4-86220-796- 4.00
1. Ironwork—Philadelphia. 2. Decoration and ornament, Architectural—Philadelphia. 3. Architecture—Details. I. Title. BIP

Ironwork—U.S.

HORST, Melvin. 739'.47'73
Early iron ware. Photography by Mel Horst. Text by Elmer L. Smith. Lebanon, Pa., Applied Arts Publishers [1971] 32 p. illus. 28 cm. [NK8212.A1H6] 78-30497 1.25
1. Ironwork—U.S. I. Smith, Elmer Lewis. II. Title. BIP

KAUFFMAN, Henry J., 1908- 739.4773
Early American ironware, cast and wrought. Rutland, Vt., Tuttle [1966] 166p. illus., facsims, 28cm. Bibl. [NK8212.A1K3] 65-16743 10.00
1. Ironwork—U. S. I. Title.

Irony in art.

NEW York (City). New School for Social Research. New School Art Center. 709'.04
Humor, satire, and irony; an international exhibition of sculpture, paintings, drawings, and prints, October 25-December 19, 1972. New York [1972] 40 p. illus. 23 cm. (The Artistic thinking of our time) [N6487.N4N483] 73-171835
1. Irony in art. 2. Art, Modern—20th century—Exhibitions. I. Title. II. Series.

Iroquois Indians—Art—Catalogs.

ROCHESTER Museum and Science Centers. 739.27'8
Iroquois silver brooches (as-ne-as-ga) in the Rochester Museum, by Elizabeth H. Van Horn. Geno Paesano, editor. Rochester, N.Y. [1971] v, 70 p. illus. 25 cm. Bibliography: p. 70. [E99.I7R58] 72-178204
1. Iroquois Indians—Art—Catalogs. 2. Indians of North America—Silversmithing—Catalogs. I. Van Horn, Elizabeth H. II. Title.

Irvine, Sadie.

ORMOND, Suzanne. 738.3'7
Louisiana's art nouveau : the crafts of the Newcomb style / Suzanne Ormond and Mary E. Irvine ; with a foreword by John Canaday. Gretna [La.] : Pelican Pub. Co., 1976. p. cm. Includes index. [NK4340.N47O75] 76-44471 ISBN 0-88289-112-X : 25.00
1. Irvine, Sadie. 2. Tulane University of Louisiana. H. Sophie Newcomb Memorial College for Women. Dept. of Art. 3. Newcomb pottery. 4. Decoration and ornament—Art nouveau. 5. Pottery—Louisiana. I. Irvine, Mary E., joint author. II. Title. BIP

Irwin, Robert, 1928—

LOS Angeles Co., Calif. Museum of Art, Los Angeles. 730'.922
Robert Irwin—Kenneth Price; an exhibition organized by the Los Angeles County Museum of Art in cooperation with the museum's Contemporary Art Council. [Los Angeles, 1966] [32] p. illus. (part col.) 21 cm. Catalog of the exhibition held July 7-Sept. 4, 1966. Includes bibliographical references. [N6536.L65] 76-19447
1. Irwin, Robert, 1928- 2. Price, Kenneth, 1935- I. Los Angeles Co., Calif. Museum of Art, Los Angeles. Contemporary Art Council. II. Title.

Isaacs, Walter F.

MOSELEY, Spencer. 759.13 B
Walter F. Isaacs, an artist in America, 1886-1964 : [catalogue for an exhibition held at the Henry Art Gallery, University of Washington, April 1975] / by Spencer Moseley and T. Gervais Reed. Seattle : Published for the Henry Art Gallery by the University of Washington Press, [1975] p. cm. (Index of art in the Pacific Northwest ; no. 8) Bibliography: p. [ND237.I75M67] 74-28489 ISBN 0-295-95389-6 : 15.00 ISBN 0-295-95390-X pbk. : 7.50
1. Isaacs, Walter F. I. Reed, Truman Gervais, joint author. II. Henry Art Gallery. III. Title. IV. Series.

Isabella d'Este, consort of Francis II, Marquis of Mantua, 1474-1539.

VERHEYEN, Egon. 759.5'28
The paintings in the studiolo of Isabella d'Este at Mantua. New York, Published by New York University Press for the College Art Association of America, 1971. xiii, 105 p. illus. 29 cm. (Monographs on archaeology and the fine arts, 23) Bibliography: p. 105. [ND621.M3V4] 76-164021 ISBN 0-8147-8751-7
1. Isabella d'Este, consort of Francis II, Marquis of Mantua, 1474-1539. 2. Paintings—Mantua. 3. Mantua. Palazzo ducale. Studiolo. I. Title. II. Series. BIP

Isabella Stewart Gardner Museum, Boston.

ISABELLA Stewart Gardner Museum, Boston. 750'.074'014461
European and American paintings in the Isabella Stewart Gardner Museum, by Philip Hendy. Boston, Trustees of the Isabella Stewart Gardner Museum [1974] 316 p. illus. (part col.) 29 cm. Includes bibliographies. [N521.I7A52] 74-79188 ISBN 0-914660-00-4
1. Isabella Stewart Gardner Museum, Boston. 2. Paintings—Boston—Catalogs. I. Hendy, Philip, Sir, 1900- II. Title. BIP

ISABELLA Stewart Gardner Museum, Boston. 708'.144'61
Guide to the collection / Isabella Stewart Gardner Museum. 2d ed. Boston : The Trustees, 1976. 116 p. : ill. ; 18 cm. First ed. published in 1959 under title: Selective guide to the collection. Includes index. [N521.I7A53 1976] 76-4176 ISBN 0-914660-02-0
1. Isabella Stewart Gardner Museum, Boston. 2. Art—Massachusetts—Boston—Catalogs. BIP

ISABELLA Stewart Gardner Museum, Boston. 709'.5'074014461
Oriental and Islamic art in the Isabella Stewart Gardner Museum / Yasuko Horioka, Marylin Rhie, Walter B. Denny. Boston : Trustees of the Museum, 1974. p. cm. Bibliography: p. [N7262.I82] 74-22427 ISBN 0-914660-01-2 pbk. : 3.50.
1. Isabella Stewart Gardner Museum, Boston. 2. Art, Oriental—Catalogs. 3. Art, Islamic—Catalogs. 4. Art—Boston—Catalogs. I. Horioka, Yasuko. II. Rhie, Marylin. III. Denny, Walter B. IV. Title. BIP

ISABELLA Stewart Gardner Museum, Boston. 759.4'074'014461
A selection of paintings, drawings, and watercolors / Isabella Stewart Gardner Museum. Chicago : University of Chicago Press, [1976] p. cm. [ND615.I77 1976] 76-21230 ISBN 0-226-69181-0 : 15.00
1. Isabella Stewart Gardner Museum, Boston. 2. Paintings, Italian—Catalogs. 3. Paintings, Renaissance—Italy—Catalogs. 4. Paintings—Boston—Catalogs. I. Title. BIP

STOUT, George Leslie, 1897- 708.1344'61
Treasures from the Isabella Stewart Gardner Museum [by] George L. Stout. New York, Crown Publishers [1969] 218 p. illus. (part col.), facsim., ports. 29 cm. [N521.I7S7] 79-75084 10.00
1. Isabella Stewart Gardner Museum, Boston. II. Title.

Isabey, Eugene, 1803-1886.

HARVARD University. William Hayes Fogg Art Museum. 760'.0924
Eugene Isabey; paintings, watercolors, drawings, lithographs. Cambridge, Mass. [1967?] 1 v. (unpaged) illus. 22 cm. Catalog of an exhibition held Nov. 22-Dec. 29, 1967. Includes bibliography. [ND553.I8H35] 68-4704
1. Isabey, Eugene, 1803-1886.

Ise Daijingu.

ASAHI SHIMBUN SHA 726.19
Ise, prototype of Japanese architecture [by] Kenzo Tange,Noboru Kawazoe, Photos, by Yoshio Watanabe. Layout, bk. design by Yusaku Kamekura. Cambridge Mass., M.I.T. Pr. [c.1965] 212p. illus., plans. 29cm. Bibl. [NA6057.I8A83] 64-7970 17.50
1. Ise Daijingu. I. Tange, Kenzo, 1913- II. Kawazoe, Noboru, 1908- III. Title.

Isenberg, Arnold.

ISENBERG, Arnold. 111.8'5
Aesthetics and the theory of criticism; selected essays of Arnold Isenberg. Edited by William Callaghan [and others] With an introd. by Mary Mothersill and a biographical sketch by William Callaghan. Chicago, University of Chicago Press

[1973, i.e.1974] xxxix, 322 p. port. 24 cm. Includes bibliographical references. [BH39.I83] 73-77133 ISBN 0-226-38511-6 12.50
1. Isenberg, Arnold. 2. Aesthetics—Collected works. 3. Criticism—Collected works. I. Title.
Contents omitted. BIP

Isleta Indians—Art.

ISLETA paintings. 759.01'1'09701 With introd. and commentary by Elsie Clews Parsons. Edited, and with a new foreword, by Esther S. Goldfrank. [Rev. ed.] Washington, Smithsonian Institution [1970] xxii, 170 p. illus. (part col.), facsims. 29 cm. Bibliography: p. 159-160. [E99.I8 1970] 70-113424 ISBN 0-87474-102-5 13.95
1. Isleta Indians—Art. 2. Isleta Indians—Social life and customs. 3. Indians of North America—Pictures, illustrations, etc. I. Parsons, Elsie Worthington (Clews) 1875-1941. II. Goldfrank, Esther Schiff, ed.

Israel—Description and travel.

SASEK, Miroslav. 915.694
This is Israel. [New York] Macmillan [1962] 60 p. illus. 32 cm. A pictorial tour of the "promised land" presenting drawings of the historic sights and modern city and town life in Israel. [ND1946.S2A526] AC 68
1. Israel—Description and travel. I. Title. BIP

Israel—Description and travel—Views.

JACOBY, Hilla. 779'.9'9569405
The land of Israel / introd. by Heinrich Boll ; wtih 174 photos. in full colour by Hilla and Max Jacoby. London : Thames and Hudson, 1978. 14, 174 [i.e. 213] p. : chiefly col. ill. ; 34 cm. Translation of Shalom, Impressionen aus dem Heiligen Land. [DS108.5.J3213] 78-398816 ISBN 0-500-24101-5 : 35.00
1. Israel—Description and travel—Views. I. Jacoby, Max, 1919- II. Title.
Avail. from W. W. Norton, NYC. BIP

LEVINE, Gemma. 779'.9'95694
Israel, faces and places / presented by Golda Meir ; photos. by Gemma Levine. 1st American ed. New York : Putnam, 1978. [175] p. : chiefly ill. (some col.) ; 28 cm. [DS108.5.L47 1978] 78-53457 ISBN 0-399-12195-1 : 17.50
1. Israel—Description and travel—Views. I. Meir, Golda Mabovitz, 1898- II. Title.

Israel in art.

STERN, Alec, 1904- 769'.92'4
Etchings of Israel, land of the Bible / [Alec Stern]. Studio ed. San Mateo, Calif. : Studio of Alec Stern, [1974] 175 p. : ill. ; 29 cm. [NE2012.S73A45] 74-191739
1. Stern, Alec, 1904- 2. Israel in art. I. Title.

Israels, Isaac La_arus, 1865-1934.

REISEL, Jacob Hirsch. 759.9492
Isaac Israels. Portret van een Hollandse impressionist. [Door] Jacob H. Reisel. Amsterdam, Menno Hertzberger [1966] 208p. with illus. 32cm. Issued also as thesis, Amsterdam. Summary in English. Bibl. [ND653.I8R4 1966] 67-96529 8.50
1. Israels, Isaac Lazarus, 1865-1934. I. Title.
American distributor: Abner Schram, 1860 Bway, New York, N.Y. 10023.

Istanbul. Ayasofya Muzesi.

UNDERWOOD, Paul Atkins, 1902- 246
The mosaics of Hagia Sophia at Istanbul, the portrait of the Emperor Alexander; a report on work done by the Byzantine Institute in 1959 and 1960[by] Paul A. Underwood and Ernest J. W. Hawkins. Cambridge, Mass. 30 cm. no. 15 (1961) p. [187]-217. illus., plates) (In Dumbarton Oaks papers. Bibliographical footnotes. [N5970.D8 no. 15] A65
1. Alexander the Great, 356-323 v. c. 3. Mosaics. 2. Istanbul. Ayasofya Muxesi. I. Bysantine Institute of America. II. Hawkins, Enrest J. W., joint author. III. Title.

Istanbul. Ayasofya Muzesi.

KAHLER, Heinz. 726'.5'094961
Hagia Sophia. With a chapter on the mosaics by Cyril Mango. Translated by Ellyn Childs. New York, Praeger [1967] 74 p. 103 illus. (part col.), fold. plans. 31 cm. Bibliography:p. 70-[72] [NA5870.A9K33] 67-29605
1. Istanbul. Ayasofya Muzesi. 2. Mosaics—Istanbul. I. Title.

KINROSS, John 727'.7'094961
Patrick Douglas Balfour, Baron, 1904-
Hagia Sophia, by Lord Kinross and the editors of the Newsweek Book Division. New York, Newsweek [1972] 172 p. illus. (part col.) 30 cm. (Wonders of man) Bibliography: p. 168. [NA5870.A9K5] 72-163362
1. Istanbul. Ayasofya Muzesi. I. Newsweek, inc. Book Division.

MANGO, Cyril A. 729.72
Materials for the study of the mosaics of St. Sophia at Istanbul. Washington, Dumbarton Oaks Research Library and Collection, 1962. xvii, 145 p. illus. 30 cm. (Dumbarton Oaks studies, 8) Bibliographical footnotes. [NA5870.A9M3] 62-17509
1. Istanbul. Ayasofya Muzesi. 2. Mosaics—Istanbul. I. Title. II. Title: The mosaics of St. Sophia at Istanbul. III. Series. BIP

Istanbul. Church of the Holy Apostles.

NIKOLAOS, Mesarites, 726.5
b.A.D.1163or4.
Description of the Church of the Holy Apostles at Constantinople. Greek text edited with translation, commentary, and introd. by Glanville Downey. Philadelphia, American Philosophical Society, 1957. 855-924p. 30cm. (Transactions of the American Philosophical Society, new ser., v. 47, pt. 6) (American Philosophical Society, Philadelphia. Transcriptions, new ser., v. 47, pt. 6) Bibliographical footnotes. [Q11.P6 vol.47, pt.6] 57-14857
1. Istanbul. Church of the Holy Apostles. I. Title. II. Series.

Istanbul—Churches—Pictorial works.

MATHEWS, Thomas F. 726'.5'094961
The Byzantine churches of Istanbul : a photographic survey / Thomas F. Mathews. University Park : Pennsylvania State University Press, 1976 c1975 p. cm. Includes index. [NA5870.A1M37] 75-27173 ISBN 0-271-01210-2 : 50.00
1. Istanbul—Churches—Pictorial works. 2. Architecture, Byzantine—Istanbul. 3. Church architecture—Istanbul. I. Title. BIP

Istanbul. Kariye Camii.

UNDERWOOD, Paul Atkins, 1902- 246
Fourth preliminary report on the restoration of the frescoes in the Kariye Camii at Istanbul by the Bysantine Institute, 1957-1958 [by] Paul A. Underwood. Cambridge, Mass. 30 cm. no. 13 (1959) p. [185]-212. plates) (In Dumbarton Oaks papers. Bibliographical footnotes. [N5970.D8 no. 13] A65
1. Istanbul. Kariye Camii. I. Byzantine Institute of America. II. Title.

UNDERWOOD, Paul Atkins, 759.94961
1902-
The Kariye Djami [by] Paul A. Underwood. [New York, Bollingen Found.; dist.] Pantheon [c.1966] 3v. plans, plates (pt. col.) 33cm. (Bollingen ser., 70) Issued in a case. Contents.v. 1. Historical introduction and description of the mosaics and frescoes.--v. 2. Plates 1-334. The mosaics.--v. 3. Plates 335-553. The frescoes. [NA5870.K3U5] 65-10404 55.00 bxd. set,
1. Istanbul. Kariye Camii. 2. Mosaics—Istanbul. 3. Mural painting and decoration—Istanbul. I. Title. II. Series. BIP

UNDERWOOD, Paul Atkins, 759.94961
1902-
The Karive Djami [by] Paul A. Underwood. [New York, Bollingen Foundation; distributed by] Pantheon Books [c1966] 3 v. plans, plates (part col.) 33 cm. (Bollingen series, 70) Issued in a case. Contents.-- v. 1. Historical introduction and description of the mosaics and frescoes. -- v. 2. Plates 1-334. The mosaics, -- v. 3. Plates 335-553. The frescoes. Bibliography: v. 1, p. 313. [NA5870.K3U5] 65-10404
1. Istanbul. Kariye Camil. 2. Mosaics — Istanbul. 3. Mural painting and decoration — Istanbul. I. Title. II. Series.

Istanbul. Topkapi Sarayi Muzesi.

DAVIS, Fanny (Ellsworth) 914.96'1
1904-
The Palace of Topkapi in Istanbul, by Fanny Davis. New York, Scribner [1970] xiii, 306 p. illus. (part col.), plans, ports. 27 cm. Bibliography: p. 287-298. [N3690.T817713] 75-113613 14.95
1. Istanbul. Topkapi Sarayi Muzesi. I. Title.

Italian imprints—Union lists.

SHORT-TITLE catalog of 015'.45 *books printed in Italy and of books in Italian printed abroad, 1501-1600,* held in selected North American libraries. [Robert G. Marshall, editor] Boston, G. K. Hall, 1970. 3 v. 27 cm. Contents.Contents.—v. 1. A-F.—v. 2. G-P.—v. 3. Q-Z. Index of printers and publishers. [Z2342.S56] 71-15897
1. Italian imprints—Union lists. 2. Bibliography—Early printed books—16th century—Union lists. 3. Libraries—U.S. I. Marshall, Robert G., ed.

Italy—Descr. & trav.—Views.

BERMAN, Eugene, 1899- 741.91
Imaginary promenades in Italy. [New York] Pantheon Books [1956] [80] p. (chiefly illus.) 29cm. Issued in a case. [NC1075.B524A46] 56-10417
1. Italy—Descr. & trav.—Views. I. Title.

BRADSHAW, John, 1782-1809 759.2
Italian sketchbook; paintings. Introd. by Thomas Yoseloff. [Cranbury, N. J.] A. S. Barnes [c.1966] 102p. (chiefly illus.) 32cm. [ND497.B677Y6] 64-21366 10.00
I. Title.

Italy—History—1492-1559.

COUGHLAN, Robert, 1914- 709.24
The world of Michelangelo, 1475-1564, by Robert Coughlan and the editors of Time-Life Books New York, Time, inc. [1966] 202 p. illus. (part fold., part col.), coats of arms, geneal. tables, maps, plans, ports. (part col.) 31 cm. (Time-Life library of art) Bibliography: p. 198-199. [NB623.B9C6] 66-16540
1. Buonarroti, Michel Angelo, 1475-1564. 2. Italy—History—1492-1559. I. Time-Life Books. II. Title. BIP

Italy—History—15th century—Pictorial works.

BAXANDALL, Michael. 759.5
Painting and experience in fifteenth century Italy; a primer in the social history of pictorial style. London, Oxford University Press, [1974, c1972] 165 p. illus., (part. col.), 20 cm. Bibliography: p. 155-161. [ND615.B32] ISBN 0-19-881329-5
1. Italy—History—15th century—Pictorial works. 2. Painting, Renaissance—Italy. 3. Painting, Italian—History. 4. Painting—Psychological aspects. I. Title.
L.C. card no. for hardcover: 73-156125. Distributed by Oxford University Press, N.Y. for 3.50 (pbk.) BIP

Italy-History-Fiction.

*WOODHOUSE, Martin. FIC
The Medici emerald / Martin Woodhouse and Robert Ross 1st American ed. New York : E.P. Dutton, c1976. 224p. ; 25 cm [PZ4] 759.5 DG 678 76-11873 ISBN 0-525-15458-2 : 8.95
1. Leonardo da Vinci, 1452-1519-Juvenile literature. 2. Italy-History-Fiction. I. Ross, Robert, joint author. II. Title. BIP

Itchkawich, David.

MATTINGLY, John R. 769'.92'4
When men were animals and animals were men : a study of the graphic work of David Itchkawich / John R. Mattingly. New York : Angelica Press, 1976. xvi, 92 p. : ill. ; 23 x 29 cm. [NE2012.I86M37] 77-150459
1. Itchkawich, David. I. Title.

Ivanov, Viacheslav Ivanovich, 1866-1949.

WEST, James D. 891.7'09'003
Russian symbolism; a study of Vyacheslav Ivanov and the Russian symbolist aesthetic [by] James West. London, Methuen [1972, c.1970] vii, 250 p. port. 22 cm. (University paperbacks, UP 453) Bibliography: p. 231-245. [BH221.R93W47] 79-139834 ISBN 0-416-19350-1 pap., 4.50
1. Ivanov, Viacheslav Ivanovich, 1866-1949. 2. Aesthetics, Russian. 3. Symbolism in art. I. Title.
Dist. by Barnes & Noble, New York.

Ivories.

MASKELL, Alfred 736.6
Ivories. Rutland, Vt., Tuttle [c.1966] 551p. plates. 27cm. Reprint of the 1905 ed. Bibl. [NK5825.M4] 66-20572 17.50
1. Ivories. I. Title.

RAY, Dorothy Jean. 736.6
Artists of the tundra and the sea. Seattle, University of Washington Press, 1961. 170 p. illus. 23 cm. [E99.E7R25] 61-14648
1. Ivories. 2. Eskimos—Art. I. Title.

WILLS, Geoffrey. 736'.6
Ivory. [1st American ed.] South Brunswick [N.J.] A. S. Barnes [1969, c1968] 94 p. illus. 22 cm. [NK5825.W52 1969] 68-27235 ISBN 4-9806866-8- 5.00
1. Ivories. I. Title.

Ivories—China.

EASTHAM, Barry Caulfield. 736'.6
Chinese art ivory / by Barry C. Eastham. Rev. and enl., with an introd. / by William C. Hu. Ann Arbor : Ars Ceramica, 1976. xvii, 86 p., [24] leaves of plates : ill. ; 24 cm. Includes index. [NK5983.E3 1976] 76-23710 ISBN 0-89344-003-5 : 17.50
1. Ivories—China. 2. Art objects, Chinese. I. Hu, William Chao-chung. II. Title. BIP

Ivories—Collectors and collecting.

WOODHOUSE, Charles 736'.6
Platten.
Ivories : A history and guide / Charles Platten Woodhouse. New York : Van Nostrand Reinhold Co., 1976. 128 p. : ill. ; 24 cm. Includes index. Bibliography: p. 123. [NK5825.W66 1976] 76-5441 ISBN 0-442-29536-7 : 10.00
1. Ivories—Collectors and collecting. I. Title.

Ivories—History.

BEIGBEDER, Olivier. 736.6
Ivory [by] O. Beigbeder. New York, Putnam [1965] 128 p. illus. (part col.) 23 cm. (Pleasures and treasures) [NK5850.B38] 64-16768
1. Ivories — Hist. I. Title.

Ivories—History.

CUST, Anna Maria 736'.6
Elizabeth.
The ivory workers of the Middle Ages, by A. M. Cust. London, G. Bell, 1902. [New York, AMS Press, 1973] xix, 169 p. illus. 19 cm. Original ed. issued in series: Handbooks of the great craftsmen. Bibliography: p. xvii-xix. [NK5870.C8

accompanied by guard sheets with descriptive letterpress. The Mrs. T. B. Blackstone expedition. Bibl. [GN2.F4 vol.10] 42-15552 20.00 pap.,
1. Jade. 2. China—Antiq. 3. China—Religion. I. Title.

NOTT, Stanley Charles, 1902- 736.24
Chinese jade throughout the ages, a review of its characteristics, decoration, folklore, and symbolism. [2d ed.] Tokyo, Rutland, Vt., C. E. Tuttle Co. [1962] xx, 193 p. illus., plates (part col.) map. 28 cm. "A list of Chinese writings referred to in the text": p. 166-169. "Bibliography chiefly of European and American works relating to China and its arts": p. 170-174. [NK5750.N65 1962] 62-8839
1. Jade. 2. Art objects, Chinese. 3. China—Antiquities. 4. Symbolism in art. 5. Folklore, Chinese. I. Title. BIP

SALMONY, Alfred, 1890-1958. 736.24
Chinese jade through the Wei dynasty. NewYork, Ronald Press Co. [1963] v. 287 p. 46 plates. 27 cm. Bibliographical references included in "Notes." [NK5750.S32] 62-17538
1. Jade. 2. Art objects, Chinese. I. Title. BIP

SAVAGE, George, 1909- 736.24
Chinese jade, a concise introduction. New York, October House [1965, c1964] vi, 72 p. illus. (part col.) 21 cm. (Collectors guidebooks) Bibliography: p. 69. [NK5750.S38 1965] 65-11507
1. Jade. 2. Art objects, Chinese. I. Title. II. Series.

SMITH College. Museum of Art. 736.240838
Archaic Chinese jades, Mr. and Mrs. Ivan B. Hart collection. Catalogue by Elizabeth Lyons. Ed. by Robert J. Poor. Introd. by Charles MacSherry. Northampton, Mass., Author 22cm. Bibl. 63-16261 2.50 pap.,
1. Jade. I. Hart, Ivan B. II. Lyons, Elizabeth. III. Title.

SMITH College, Museum of Art. 549.66
Archaic Chinese jades, Mr. and Mrs. Ivan B. Hart Collection. Catalogue by Elizabeth Lyons. Edited by Robert J. Poor. With an introd. by Charles MacSherry. Northampton, Mass 1963. 70 p. illus. 22 cm. Includes bibliography. [NK5750.S6] 63-16261
1. Jade. I. Hart, Ivan B. II. Lyons, Elizabeth. III. Title.

WILLS, Geoffrey. 736.24
Jade; a collector's guide. South Brunswick [N.J.] A.S. Barnes [1966, c1964] 121 p. illus., plates. 22 cm. Bibliography: p. 104-105. [NK5750.W58] 66-14786
1. Jade. I. Title.

ZARA, Louis, 1910- 736'.24
Jade. New York, Walker [1969] 82, [2] p. illus. 22 cm. (Collectors' blue books) Bibliography: p. [84] [NK5750.Z3] 69-15722 4.50
1. Jade.

Jade art objects.

HEMRICH, Gerald I. 549.6'6
The handbook of jade, by Gerald I. Hemrich. Mentone, Calif., Gembooks [1966] 81 p. illus. 21 cm. [NK5750.H4] 68-1952
1. Jade art objects. I. Title. BIP

LUZZATTO-BILITZ, Oscar. 736'.24'0951
Antique jade; [translated from the Italian by Francis Koval]. London, New York, Hamlyn, 1969. 158 p. 71 col. illus. 20 cm. (Cameo) Originally published as Antiche giade. Millano, Febbri, 1966. [NK5750.L813] 76-437471 ISBN 0-600-01220-4 15/-
1. Jade art objects. I. Title.

Jade art objects—Asia.

WILLS, Geoffrey. 736'.24'095
Jade of the East. [1st ed.] New York, Weatherhill [1972] 196 p. illus. (part col.) 32 cm. Bibliography: p. 191-192. [NK5750.W59] 72-78589 ISBN 0-8348-1854-X 25.00
1. Jade art objects—Asia. 2. Jade art objects—New Zealand. I. Title. BIP

Jade art objects—China.

GOETTE, John Andrew, 1896- 736'.24'0951
Jade lore / by John Goette. 2d ed. / with an introd. by William C. Hu. Ann Arbor, Mich. : Ars Ceramica, 1976. xvii, 321 p. : ill. ; 27 cm. Includes index. Bibliography: p. 300-310. [NK5750.G6 1976] 76-21489 ISBN 0-89344-009-4 : 25.00
1. Jade art objects—China. 2. China—Civilization. I. Title. BIP

HANSFORD, S. Howard. 736'.24'0951
Chinese carved jades, by S. Howard Hansford. Greenwich, Conn., New York Graphic Society [1968] 131 p., 96 plates. illus. (part col.), map. 26 cm. Bibliography: p. 112-120. [NK5750.H28 1968b] 68-11278
1. Jade art objects—China. I. Title.

HARTMAN, Joan M. 736'.24'0951
Chinese jade of five centuries [by] Joan M. Hartman. Rutland, Vt., C. E. Tuttle Co. [1969] 172 p. illus. (part col.) 26 cm. Bibliography: p. 165-167. [NK5750.H34] 69-12077 12.50
1. Jade art objects—China. I. Title. BIP

LAUFER, Berthold, 1874-1934. 736'.24'0951
Jade : a study in Chinese archaeology and religion / Berthold Laufer. New York : Dover Publications, 1974. xiv, 370 p., [42] leaves of plates : ill. ; 22 cm. Reprint of the 1912 ed. issued as publication no. 154 of the Field Museum of Natural History, Chicago, and Anthropological series, v. 10. Includes index. Bibliography: p. 355-360. [NK5750.L38 1974] 74-81085 ISBN 0-486-23123-2 pbk. : 5.00
1. Jade art objects—China. 2. China—Antiquities. 3. China—Religion. I. Title. II. Series: Field Museum of Natural History, Chicago. Publication ; 154. III. Series: Fieldiana : Anthropology ; v. 10.

Jade art objects—China—Catalogs.

MINNEAPOLIS. Institute of Arts.
Chinese jades : archaic and modern from the Minneapolis Institute of Arts / foreword by Samuel Sachs II ; introd. by Na Chih-liang ; [Harold Peterson, editor, Nancy Akre, associate editor ; Vera Shu-Ning Sun-Bailey, translator and researcher ; Gary Mortensen, photographer]. 1st ed. Rutland, Vt. : C. E. Tuttle Co., 1977. 176 p. : ill. (some col.) ; 28 cm. Bibliography: p. 171-174. [NK5750.M54 1977b] 78-102346 25.00
1. Minneapolis. Institute of Arts—Catalogs. 2. Jade art objects—China—Catalogs. 3. Jade art objects—Minnesota—Minneapolis—Catalogs. I. Sachs, Samuel. II. Na, Chih-liang. III. Peterson, Harold, 1935- IV. Title. BIP

SCHEDEL, J. J. 736'.24'0951
The splendor of jade; four thousand years of the art of Chinese jade carving, by J. J. Schedel. With an introd. by Na Chih-liang. [1st ed.] New York, Dutton, 1974. 221 p. col. illus. 32 cm. (A Dutton visual book) Bibliography: p. 221. [NK5750.S39 1974] 74-9855 35.00
1. Schedel, J. J.—Art collections. 2. Jade art objects—China—Catalogs. I. Title. BIP

SCHNEEBERGER, Pierre Francis. 736'.24
Chinese jades and other hardstones / by Pierre-F. Schneeberger ; [translated by Katherine Watson]. Geneva : Baur Collection ; [Boston : distributed by Routledge & K. Paul], c1976. 52 p., [90] p., [38] leaves of plates : ill. (some col.) ; 30 cm. English and French. Bibliography: p. [84]-[85] [NK5750.S394] 77-363000 85.00
1. Jade art objects—China—Catalogs. I. Title. BIP

Jade art objects—China—Exhibitions.

HARTMAN, Joan M. 736'.24'0931074014797
Ancient Chinese jades from the Buffalo Museum of Science : [catalog of the exhibition held] April 3 through June 15, 1975 / by Joan M. Hartman. New York : China House Gallery, China Institute in America, [1975] 80 p. : ill. (some col.) ; 24 cm. Bibliography: p. 80. [NK5750.H33] 75-1619
1. Jade art objects—China—Exhibitions. 2. China—Antiquities. I. Buffalo. Museum of Science. II. China House Gallery. III. Title.

KUWAYAMA, George. 736'.24'0951074019494
Chinese jade from southern California collections : Los Angeles County Museum of Art, October 26, 1976-February 6, 1977 / George Kuwayama. Los Angeles : Far Eastern Art Council of the Los Angeles County Museum of Art, c1976. 74 p. : ill. ; 27 cm. Exhibition catalog. Bibliography: p. 72-74. [NK5750.K88] 76-43233 ISBN 0-87587-074-0
1. Jade art objects—China—Exhibitions. 2. Jade art objects—Collectors and collecting—United States—California, Southern—Exhibitions. I. Los Angeles Co., Calif. Museum of Art, Los Angeles. II. Title. BIP

Jade art objects—Collectors and collecting.

CHU, Arthur. 736'.24'075
The collector's book of jade / by Arthur and Grace Chu. New York : Crown Publishers, c1978. p. cm. Includes index. Bibliography: p. [NK5750.C477 1978] 78-16762 ISBN 0-517-53150-X : 10.95
1. Jade art objects—Collectors and collecting. I. Chu, Grace, joint author. II. Title. BIP

Jaeckel, Willi, 1888-1944.

JAECKEL, Willi, 1888-1944. 741.973
Jaeckel / [Anneliese Markisch]. Dresden : Verlag der Kunst, 1974. 31 p. : ill. (some col.) ; 17 cm. (Maler und Werk) Cover title. Bibliography: p. 31. [ND588.J3M33] 76-456648 2.00M
1. Jaeckel, Willi, 1888-1944. I. Markisch, Anneliese.

Jaggard, William, 1569-1623.

WILLOUGHBY, Edwin Eliott, 1899-1959. 655'.00924
A printer of Shakespeare; the books and times of William Jaggard. New York, Haskell House, 1970. 303 p. illus., facsims., ports. 23 cm. Reprint of the 1934 ed. [Z232.J24W7 1970] 77-92993
1. Jaggard, William, 1569-1623. 2. Shakespeare, William, 1564-1616—Bibliography. I. Title. BIP

Jaguer, Edouard.

BAJ, Enrico, 1924- 759.9493'2
Enrico Baj, by Edouard Jaguer. Milan, New York, Schettini [1956] 123p. (chiefly illus., plates (part col.) port.) 30cm. Bibliography: p. 109-115. [ND623.B17J3] 62-26168
1. Jaguer, Edouard. I. Title.

Jamaica—Descr.& trav.—Views.

KAPPEL, Philip 769.973
Jamaica gallery; a documentary of the island of Jamaica, West Indies. Text, drawings &designs by Philip Kappel. Introd. by John P. Marquand. Boston, Little, Brown [1961, c.1960] unpaged. illus. 29cm. 61-5755 7.50
1. Jamaica—Descr.& trav.—Views. 2. Jamaica—Soc. life & cust. I. Title.

Jamesone, George, 1589 or 90-1644.

THOMSON, Duncan. 759.941
The life and art of George Jamesone / Duncan Thomson. Oxford : Clarendon Press, 1974. xix, 164 p., [33] leaves of plates : ill. ; 25 cm. (Studies in the history of art and architecture) Includes bibliographical references and indexes. [ND1329.J33T48] 74-189857 ISBN 0-19-817337-7 : 41.00
1. Jamesone, George, 1589 or 90-1644. I. Title. II. Series: Oxford studies in the history of art and architecture.
Distributed by Oxford University Press, New York. BIP

Janel, Emil, 1896—

SEAL, Thomas C. 736'.4
The life and works of Emil Janel; an illustrated essay, by Thomas C. Seal. [San Francisco? 1973] viii, 81 p. illus. 32 cm. Bibliography: p. 81. [NK9798.J36S42] 73-166410
1. Janel, Emil, 1896- 2. Wood-carving, American.

Janis, Sidney, 1897- —Art collections.

NEW York (City). Museum of Modern Art. 708.14'71
The Sidney and Harriet Janis Collection; a gift to the Museum of Modern Art. [New York, 1968] 21 p. illus. (part col.) 23 cm. [N5220.J33] 68-19232
1. Janis, Sidney, 1897- —Art collections. 2. Janis, Harriet (Grossman)—Art collections.

NEW York (City). Museum of Modern Art. 709'.04'07401471
Three generations of twentieth-century art; the Sidney and Harriet Janis Collection of the Museum of Modern Art. With a foreword by Alfred H. Barr, Jr. Introd. by William Rubin. New York; distributed by New York Graphic Society, Greenwich, Conn. [1972] xv, 231 p. illus. (part col.) 29 cm. Includes bibliographical references. [N6487.N4M87] 68-17123 ISBN 0-87070-400-1 22.50
1. Janis, Sidney, 1897- —Art collections. 2. Janis, Harriet (Grossman)—Art collections. 3. Art, Modern—20th century—Catalogs. 4. Art—New York (City)—Catalogs. I. Title. BIP

Janus Press.

LEHRER, Ruth Fine. 011
The Janus Press, 1955-75 : an exhibition at the Robert Hull Fleming Museum at the University of Vermont in Burlington, 1975 / catalogue raisonne / by Ruth Fine Lehrer. [Burlington] : Robert Hull Fleming Museum, University of Vermont, c1975. 43 p. : ill. ; 22 cm. "Essay and entries were originally prepared for the Private library." [Z121.L216] 76-356713
1. Janus Press. 2. Printing—Exhibitions. I. Vermont. University. Robert Hull Fleming Museum. II. Title.

Japan.

SEIDENSTICKER, Edward G 1921- 728.810952
Japan, by Edward Seidensticker and the editors of Life. New York, Time, inc. [1962] 159 p. illus. (part col.) col. maps. 28 cm. (Life world library) Bibliography: p. 153-154. [DS806.S4] 65-4565
1. Japan. I. Life (Chicago) II. Title.

Japan—Description and travel—Views.

LEVINE, Jack, 1915- 741.9'73
Facing East. Text by James A. Michener. Original lithographs and woodcuts by Jack Levine. Sketchbook by Jack Levine. New York, Maecenas Press, 1970. 2 portfolios (in case) 51 cm. [NC139.L47M5] 73-28411
1. Japan—Description and travel—Views. I. Michener, James Albert, 1907- II. Title.

OBATA, Chiura. 759.13
Through Japan with brush & ink. Rutland, Vt., C. E. Tuttle Co. [1968] 166 p. illus., map (on lining papers) 18 x 20 cm. [ND1059.O23A54] 68-29545 5.00
1. Japan—Description and travel—Views. I. Title.

Japan—History—Allied occupation, 1945-1952—Collectibles.

KLAMKIN, Marian. 680
Made in Occupied Japan : a collector's guide / by Marian Klamkin. New York : Crown, c1976. p. cm. Includes index.

SUBJECT INDEX JEANNERET-GRIS, CHARLES EDOUARD

[NK1071.K6 1976] 76-17007 ISBN 0-517-52660-3 : 9.95 ISBN 0-517-52661-1 pbk. :
1. Japan—History—Allied occupation, 1945-1952—Collectibles. 2. Art industries and trade—Japan. I. Title. BIP

Japan—History—Allied occupation, 1945-1952—Collectibles—Catalogs.

SIELOFF, Judie Ludwig. 738'.0952
Collectibles of occupied Japan / Judie Ludwig Sieloff. Des Moines : Wallace-Homestead Book Co., c1978. 54 p. : ill. (some col.) ; 26 cm. [NK1071.S48] 78-59870 ISBN 0-87069-207-0 : 8.95 ISBN 0-87069-288-7 price guide : 1.50
1. Japan—History—Allied occupation, 1945-1952—Collectibles—Catalogs. 2. Art industries and trade—Japan—History—20th century—Catalogs. I. Title. BIP

Japanese Americans—Evacuation and relocation, 1942-1945—Pictorial works.

CONRAT, Maisie, comp. 779'.9'940547273
Executive order 9066; the internment of 110,000 Japanese Americans, by Maisie & Richard Conrat. With an introd. by Edison Uno and an epilogue by Tom C. Clark. Photos. by Dorothea Lange, and others. [San Francisco] California Historical Society; [distributed by Serimshaw Press] 1972. 120 p. illus. 23 x 24 cm. (California Historical Society. Special publication no. 51) [D769.8.A6C6 1972b] 70-178278 12.50
1. Japanese Americans—Evacuation and relocation, 1942-1945—Pictorial works. I. Conrat, Richard, joint comp. II. Lange, Dorothea, illus. III. Title. IV. Series.

Japanese in the United States—Pictorial works.

CONRAT, Maisie, comp. 779'.9'940547273
Executive order 9066: the internment of 110,000 Japanese Americans [by] Maisie & Richard Conrat. With an introd. by Edison Uno and an epilogue by Tom C. Clark. Photos. by Dorothea Lange and others. Cambridge, Mass., MIT Press for the California Historical Society [1972] 120 p. illus. 22 x 23 cm. [D769.8.A6C6] 72-9024 3.95
1. Japanese in the United States—Pictorial works. 2. World War, 1939-1945—Evacuation of civilians—Pictorial works. 3. Concentration camps—United States—Pictorial works. I. Conrat, Richard, joint comp. II. Lange, Dorothea, illus. III. California Historical Society. IV. Title.

Japanese Literature—History and criticism.

UEDA, Makoto, 1931- 700'.1'0952
Literary and art theories in Japan. Cleveland, Press of Western Reserve University [1967] xiii, 274 p. illus., ports. 24 cm. Bibliography: p. 252-269. Bibliographical footnotes. [PL708.U33] 67-14521
1. Japanese Literature—History and criticism. 2. Aesthetics, Japanese. I. Title.

Japanese tea ceremony—Utensils.

FUJIOKA, Ryoichi, 1909- 738.2'0952
Tea ceremony utensils, by Ryoichi Fujioka, with Masaki Nakano, Hirokazu Arakawa, and Seizo Hayashiya. Translated and adapted with an introd. by Louise Allison Cort. [1st ed.] New York, Weatherhill [1973] 142 p. illus. (part col.) 24 cm. (Arts of Japan, 3) Translation of Chadogu, v. 22 in the series, Nihon no bijutsu. [GT2915.F8413] 72-11149 ISBN 0-8348-2702-6 7.95
1. Japanese tea ceremony—Utensils. I. Title.
Pbk. 4.95; 0-8348-2705-0 BIP

Japanese wit and humor, Pictorial.

A Cure for gloom; 741.5952
being the full set of "Fan-target Toba pictures" as first published at Osaka, Japan, in 1720 plus fables with & without morals. Edited by Meredith Weatherby. [1st U.S. ed.] New York, Walker/Weatherhill [1968] 68 p. col. illus. 24 cm. "A Weathermark edition." [NC1703.3.T65C8 1968] 68-15700 2.95
1. Tobae ogi no mato (Cartoons) 2. Japanese wit and humor, Pictorial. I. Weatherby, Meredith. II. Title: Fan-target Toba pictures.

Jaques, Francis Lee, 1887-1969.

JAQUES, Florence (Page) 1890-1972. 759.13 B
Francis Lee Jaques: artist of the wilderness world [by] Florence Page Jaques. Foreword by Roger Tory Peterson. A treasury of prose writings from the six Jaques books. Three new appraisals of the artist's work. Memorials to Francis Lee Jaques by Sigurd F. Olson and to Florence Page Jaques by Harriet Buchheister. With 64 paintings and dioramas in full color [and] 100 drawings in scratchboard, pen and ink, and pencil. [1st ed.] Garden City, N.Y., Doubleday, 1973. xxi, 370 p. illus. (part col.) 30 cm. [QH31.J36J36] 72-94561 ISBN 0-385-02239-5 25.00
1. Jaques, Francis Lee, 1887-1969. 2. Natural history—Pictorial works. I. Jaques, Francis Lee, 1887-1969.

Jarrold & Sons Limited.

JARROLD, 1770-1970: 769'.065'4261
a book of East Anglian prints and documents. Norwich, Jarrold & Sons [1970] [5] p., 30 plates (2 fold.). illus., facsims. 38 cm. Cover title. Plate size varies. [NE642.J3J3] 73-596287
1. Jarrold & Sons Limited. 2. Prints, English.

Jarves, James Jackson, 1818-1888.

STEEGMULLER, Francis, 1906- 927
The two lives of James Jackson Jarves. New Haven, Yale University Press, 1951. x, 331 p. illus., ports. 25 cm. "Bibliography of writings by James Jackson Jarves": p. [309]-313. "Sources and acknowledgements": p. [315]-318. [N8384.J3S8] 51-10488
1. Jarves, James Jackson, 1818-1888. I. Title.

Jarves, James Jackson, 1818-1888—Art collections.

YALE University. Art Gallery. 755'.4'094507401468
Italian primitives; the case history of a collection and its conservation. [Contributors for the catalogue: David Arnheim and others. New Haven, 1972] 56 p. illus. 28 cm. Cover title. "An exhibition celebrating the centenary of Yale University's acquisition of the Jarves Collection, April—September, 1972." [ND1651.U6N47] 73-172477
1. Jarves, James Jackson, 1818-1888—Art collections. 2. Paintings, Italian—Exhibitions. 3. Paintings—Conservation and restoration—New Haven. I. Arnheim, David. II. Title.

Jawadeva, son of Bhojadeva. Gitagovinda.

SINHA, Rajeshwar Prasad Narain. 759.954
Geeta govind in Basohli school of Indian painting. Foreword by Rajendra Prasad. Introd. by R. P. N. Sinha. New Delhi, [India] Oxford Book & Stationery Co. [dist., S. Pasadena, Calif., Hutchins Oriental Books, 1958, i.e., 1960] 15p. 9 pages (part col. and part-mounted) 34cm. 60-51363 4.00 pap.,
1. Jawadeva, son of Bhojadeva. Gitagovinda. 2. Painting, Basoli. I. Title.

Jawlensky, Alexej von, 1864-1941.

PASADENA, Calif. Art Museum 759.7
Alexei Jawlensky; a centennial exhibition. Catalog by James T. Demetrion. Organized by the Pasadena Art Museum, April 14-May 19, 1964 [Pasadena] Author [1964] 80p. illus. (pt. col.) port. 27cm. Bibl. 64-6294 3.50 pap.,
1. Jawlensky, Alexej von, 1864-1941. I. Demetrion, James T. II. Title.

WEILER, Clemens, 1909- 759.3
Jawlensky: heads, faces, meditations. [Translated from the German by Edith Kustner and J. A. Underwood] New York, Praeger [1971] 140 p. illus., facsim., col. plates. 39 cm. Translation of Alexej Jawlensky: Kopfe, Gesichte, Meditationen. Bibliography: p. 118. [ND699.J3W3913] 76-122928 45.00
1. Jawlensky, Alexej von, 1864-1941. I. Title.

Jazz musicians—Portraits.

GOTTLIEB, William P. 779'.2
The golden age of jazz : on-location portraits, in words and pictures, of more than 200 outstanding musicians from the late '30s through the '40s / text and photographs by William P. Gottlieb. New York : Simon and Schuster, c1979. p. cm. Includes index. [ML3561.J3G63] 78-31288 ISBN 0-671-24375-1 : 14.95 ISBN 0-671-24730-1 pbk. : 7.95
1. Jazz musicians—Portraits. 2. Jazz music—Pictorial works. I. Title.

Jean sans Peur, Duke of Burgundy, 1371-1419.

MEISS, Millard. 091
The Master of the Breviary of Jean Sans Peur and the Limbourgs. London, Oxford University Press for the British Academy, 1971. [2], 19 p., 17 plates; illus. (some col.) 25 cm. (Lecture on aspects of art, Henriette Hertz Trust of the British Academy, 1970) Includes bibliographical references. [ND3365.A1M4] 70-867616 ISBN 0-19-725658-9 £0.50
1. Jean sans Peur, Duke of Burgundy, 1371-1419. 2. Limbourg, Pol de, ca. 1385-ca. 1416. 3. Breviaries. 4. Illumination of books and manuscripts, French. I. Title. II. Series: British Academy, London (Founded 1901). Annual lecture on aspects of art, Henriette Hertz trust, 1970.

Jeanneret-Gris, Charles Edouard, 1887-1965.

BESSET, Maurice. 720'.924
Who was Le Corbusier? (Translated from the French by Robin Kemball. Geneva, Skira; Distributed in the United States by The World Publishing Company, Cleveland, 1968) 230 p. illus. 24 cm. (Who was?) Translation of Qui etait Le Corbusier? Bibliography: p. 215-[218] [NA1053.J4B43] 68-59085 36.00
1. Jeanneret-Gris, Charles Edouard, 1887-1965. I. Title.

BLAKE, Peter, 1920- 724.9
The master builders : Le Corbusier, Mies van der Rohe, Frank Lloyd Wright / by Peter Blake. New York : Norton, c1976. p. cm. (The Norton library) Includes index. [NA680.B52 1976] 76-7067 ISBN 0-393-00796-0 pbk. : 5.95
1. Jeanneret-Gris, Charles Edouard, 1887-1965. 2. Mies van der Rohe, Ludwig, 1886-1969. 3. Wright, Frank Lloyd, 1867-1959. 4. Architecture, Modern—20th century. I. Title.

BLAKE, Peter, 1920- 724.9
The master builders. [1st ed.] New York, Knopf, 1960. 399 p. illus. 25 cm. [NA1053.J4B55] 60-10276
1. Jeanneret-Gris, Charles Edouard, 1887-2. Mies van der Rohe, Ludwig, 1886- 3. Wright, Frank Lloyd, 1867-1959. 4. Architecture, Modern—20th century. I. Title. BIP

BOUDON, Philippe. 728.3
Lived-in architecture: Le Corbusier's Pessac revisited. Translated by Gerald Onn. With a pref. by Henri Lefebvre. [1st English language ed.] Cambridge, Mass., MIT Press [1972] 200 p. illus. (part col.) 21 cm. Translation of Pessac de Le Corbusier. Bibliography: p. 199-200. [NA1053.J4B613] 70-155321 ISBN 0-262-02083-1 7.95
1. Jeannert-Gris, Charles Edouard, 1887-1965. 2. Pessac, France. Quartiers modernes Fruges. I. Title. BIP

CHOAY, Francoise. 720.9494
Le Corbusier. New York, G. Braziller, 1960. 126 p. plates, port. 26 cm. (The Masters of world architecture series) Bibliography: p. 113-114. [NA1053.J4C5] 60-6079
1. Jeanneret-Gris, Charles Edouard, 1887- I. Title. II. Series.

CRESTI, Carlo. 720'.92'4
Le Corbusier [translated from the Italian]. London, New York, Hamlyn, 1970. 96 p. (chiefly illus. (some col.), plan, ports.). 32 cm. (Twentieth-century masters) Distributed in the U.S. by Crown Publishers. "Writings by Le Corbusier": p. 96. [NA1053.J4C713] 72-177770 ISBN 0-600-35403-2 £1.75
1. Jeanneret-Gris, Charles Edouard, 1887-1965. I. Title.

EVENSON, Norma. 711'.0924
Le Corbusier: the machine and the grand design. New York, G. Braziller [1970, c1969] 128 p. illus., maps, plans. 25 cm. (Planning and cities) Bibliography: p. 125-127. [NA9085.J4E9] 74-87063 5.95
1. Jeanneret-Gris, Charles Edouard, 1887-1965. I. Title.

FUSCO, Renato de. 749.2'4
Le Corbusier, designer : furniture, 1929 / Renato De Fusco. 1st U.S. ed. Woodbury, N.Y. : Barrons, 1977,c1976. p. cm. [NK2550.J36F8713 1976] 77-81368 ISBN 0-8120-5148-3 : 11.95
1. Jeanneret-Gris, Charles Edouard, 1887-1965. 2. Furniture—France. 3. Furniture—Drawing. I. Title.

GARDINER, Stephen. 720'.92'4 B
Le Corbusier / Stephen Gardiner. New York : Viking Press, [1975] c1974. xxiii, 135 p. : ill. ; 19 cm. (Modern masters) Includes index. Bibliography: p. [127]-128. [NA1053.J4G26 1975] 74-6853 ISBN 0-670-42261-4 5.95
1. Jeanneret-Gris, Charles Edouard, 1887-1965.
U Pbk. 2.25; ISBN 0-670-01985-2.

JEANNERET-GRIS, Charles Edouard. 1887- 720.9494
Le Corbusier, 1910-60. New York, G. Wittenborn [1960] 334p. Bibl.: p.18-19. illus. (part col.) diagrs. (part col.) plans. maps (part col.) 24x28cm. (text in French. English and German) 60-51658 15.00
I. Title.

JEANNERET-GRIS, Charles Edouard 1887-1965. 720'.924
Four compositions of Le Corbusier. [Prepared by] John Pettit West III. [New York?] 1967. [2] l., 27 plans. 28 cm. "Prepared in connection with a seminar on Le Corbusier ... given at the Princeton School of Architecture." Based on drawings and photos. from the author's Oeuvre complete. Contents.Contents.—Villa a Garches, 1927.—Villa Savoye a Poissy, 1929, 1930.—Villa Shodan a Ahmedabad, 1952.—Millowner's building a Ahmedabad, 1954. [NA1053.J4W4] 70-11556
I. West, John Pettit. II. Princeton University. School of Architecture. III. Title.

JEANNERET-GRIS, Charles Edouard, 1887-1965. 720'.92'4
Le Corbusier. Edited by Willy Boesiger. New York, Praeger [1972] 254 p. (chiefly illus.) 21 cm. Based on the author's Le Corbusier, 1910-1965 and The complete architectural works of Le Corbusier, edited by Boesiger. [NA1053.J4B5813] 79-166162 8.50
I. Boesiger, Willy, ed. II. Title.

JEANNERET-GRIS, Charles Edouard, 1887-1965. 720'.924
Le Corbusier, 1910-65. [Edited by] W. Boesiger [and] H. Girsberger. New York, Praeger [1967] 351 p. illus. (part col.), facsims., plans (part col.), ports. 23 x 29

cm. English, French and German. Bibliography: p. 18. [NA1053.J4A49] 67-25150
I. Boesiger, Willy, ed. II. Girsberger, Hans, 1898- ed. III. Title.

JEANNERET-GRIS, Charles Edouard, 1887-1965. 720'.924
Le Corbusier. Introd. and notes by Martin Pawley. With 75 photos. by Yukio Futagawa. New York, Simon and Schuster [1970] 136 p. illus. (part col.), plans, port. 27 cm. (Library of contemporary architects) Bibliography: p. 133. [NA1053.J4P34] 70-119716 7.50
I. Pawley, Martin. II. Futagawa, Yukio, 1932- illus.

JEANNERET-GRIS, Charles Edouard, 1887-1965. 720'.924
Le Corbusier: last works. Edited by Willy Boesiger. [English translation by Henry A. Frey] New York, Praeger Publishers [1970] 208 p. illus. (part col.), plans (part col.) 24 x 29 cm. English, French, and German. Forms the eighth volume of Le Corbusier et P. Jeanneret, Ouvres completes. [NA1053.J4A497] 72-109665
I. Boesiger, Willy, ed. II. Title.

JENCKS, Charles. 720'.92'4
Le Corbusier and the tragic view of architecture. Cambridge, Mass., Harvard University Press, 1973. 198 p. illus. 23 cm. Includes bibliographical references. [NA1053.J4J46 1973b] 73-83422 ISBN 0-674-51860-8 13.95
1. Jeanneret-Gris, Charles Edouard, 1887-1965. I. Title. BIP

JORDAN, Robert Furneaux. 720'.92'4
Le Corbusier. New York, L. Hill [1972] xii, 224 p. illus. 26 cm. Bibliography: p. 215-220. [NA1053.J4J67] 72-75903 10.00
1. Jeanneret-Gris, Charles Edouard, 1887-1965. BIP

MOOS, Stanislaus von. 720'.92'4
Le Corbusier, elements of a synthesis / Stanislaus von Moor. Cambridge, Mass. : MIT Press, c1979. p. cm. Translation of Le Corbusier, Elemente einer Synthese. Includes bibliographical references. [NA1053.J4M613] 78-25940 ISBN 0-262-22023-7 : 30.00
I. Jeanneret-Gris, Charles Edouard, 1887-1965. II. Title.

SEKLER, Eduard Franz. 727'.4'7
Le Corbusier at work : the genesis of the Carpenter Center for the Visual Arts / Eduard F. Sekler, William Curtis ; with contributions by Rudolph Arnheim and Barbara Norfleet. Cambridge : Harvard University Press, 1977. p. cm. Includes index. Bibliography: p. [NA1053.J4S44] 77-7315 ISBN 0-674-52059-9 : 35.00
1. Jeanneret-Gris, Charles Edouard, 1887-1965. 2. Harvard University. Carpenter Center for the Visual Arts. I. Curtis, William, 1948- joint author. II. Title. BIP

SEKLER, Mary Patricia May. 741'.092'4
The early drawings of Charles-Edouard Jeanneret (Le Corbusier) 1902-1908 / Mary Patricia May Sekler. New York : Garland Pub., 1977. xviii, 647 p. : ill. ; 21 cm. (Outstanding dissertations in the fine arts) Originally presented as the author's thesis, Harvard, 1973. Bibliography: p. 611-617. [NC248.J4S44 1977] 76-23726 ISBN 0-8240-2728-0 lib.bdg. : 57.50
1. Jeanneret-Gris, Charles Edouard, 1887-1965. I. Title. II. Series. BIP

SERENYI, Peter, 1931- comp. 720'.92'4
Le Corbusier in perspective / edited by Peter Serenyi. Englewood Cliffs, N.J. : Prentice-Hall, [1974] c1975. xii, 166 p., [6] leaves of plates : ill. ; 24 cm. (Artists in perspective series) (A Spectrum book) Bibliography: p. 158-164. [NA1053.J4S47] 74-22451 ISBN 0-13-527291-2 : 8.95 ISBN 0-13-527283-1 pbk. : 2.95
1. Jeanneret-Gris, Charles Edouard, 1887-1965. I. Title. BIP

Jeanneret-Gris, Charles Edouard, 1887-1965—Addresses, essays, lectures.

THE Open hand : 720'.92'4
essays on Le Corbusier / edited by Russell Walden. Cambridge : MIT Press, c1977. xiv, 484 p. : ill. ; 24 cm. Includes bibliographical references and index. [NA1053.J4O63] 76-40046 ISBN 0-262-23074-7 24.95
1. Jeanneret-Gris, Charles Edouard, 1887-1965—Addresses, essays, lectures. 2. Architecture, Modern—20th century—Addresses, essays, lectures. I. Walden, Russell.

Jeanneret-Gris, Charles Edouard, 1887-1965—Bibliography.

GLAGOLA, John. 016.3092 s
Le Corbusier : a bibliography of monographs / John Glagola. Monticello, Ill. : Council of Planning Librarians, 1976. 21 p. ; 28 cm. (Exchange bibliography ; 1041) Cover title. [Z5942.C68 no. 1041] [NA1053.J4] 016.72'092'4 76-480214 pbk. : 2.00
1. Jeanneret-Gris, Charles Edouard, 1887-1965—Bibliography. I. Title. II. Series: Council of Planning Librarians. Exchange bibliography ; 1041.

Jeanneret-Gris, Charles Edouard, 1887-1965—Knowledge and learning.

TURNER, Paul V. 720'.92'4 B
The education of Le Corbusier / Paul Venable Turner. New York : Garland Pub., 1977. p. cm. (Outstanding dissertations in the fine arts) Thesis—Harvard, 1971. Bibliography: p. [NA1053.J4T87] 76-23658 ISBN 0-8240-2732-9 lib.bdg. : 35.00
1. Jeanneret-Gris, Charles Edouard, 1887-1965—Knowledge and learning. 2. Architects—Education—France. I. Title. BIP

Jeans (Clothing)

AMERICAN denim : 746.4'4
a new folk art / presented by Richard M. Owens & Tony Lane ; text by Peter Beagle ; photos. by Baron Wolman and the denim artists. New York : H. N. Abrams, [1975] 156 p. : ill. (some col.) ; 29 cm. [NK4890.J4A43] 74-31430 ISBN 0-8109-0291-5
1. Jeans (Clothing) 2. Decoration and ornament, American. I. Beagle, Peter S. II. Wolman, Baron.

FEHR, Barbara. 391
Yankee denim dandies / written by Barbara Fehr ; designed by Jane Eschweiler. 1st ed. Blue Earth, MN : Piper, c1974. 96 p. : ill. ; 29 cm. Bibliography: p. 94. [TT605.F29] 74-79127 ISBN 0-87832-014-8 : 9.95
1. Jeans (Clothing) 2. Denim. I. Title.

Jeans (Clothing)—Juvenile literature.

ROSENBLOOM, Jonathan. 687'.1
Blue jeans / by Jonathan Rosenbloom. New York : Messner, c1976. 63 p. : ill. ; 23 cm. Includes index. Follows the manufacturing of a pair of jeans from the cotton field which provides cotton for yarn to the store where you buy the finished product. [TT605.R67] 76-20739 ISBN 0-671-32798-4 : 6.29
1. Jeans (Clothing)—Juvenile literature. I. Title. BIP

Jeffers petroglyph site, Minn.

LOTHSON, Gordon A., 1939- 732'.2
The Jeffers petroglyphs site : a survey and analysis of the carvings / by Gordon Allan Lothson. St. Paul : Minnesota Historical Society, 1976. x, 52 p. : ill. ; 28 cm. (Minnesota prehistoric archaeology series ; 12) Bibliography: p. 50-52. [E78.M7L66] 76-10320 ISBN 0-87351-100-X pbk. : 3.95
1. Jeffers petroglyph site, Minn. I. Minnesota Historical Society. II. Title. III. Series. BIP

LOTHSON, Gordon A., 1939- 917.76'28
Jeffers petroglyphs walking tour: a journey through time, by Gordon A. Lothson and Nancy Eubank. St. Paul, Minnesota Historical Society, 1974. vi, 26 p. illus. 15 x 22 cm. (Minnesota historic sites pamphlet series, no. 8) [E78.M7L67] 73-21720 ISBN 0-87351-084-4 1.00 (pbk.)
1. Jeffers Petroglyph site, Minn. I. Eubank, Nancy, joint author. II. Title. III. Series.

Jefferson Co., Wis.—Antiq.

HALL, Robert L 970.47585
The archeology of Carcaudu Point, with an interpretation of the development of Oneota culture in Wisconsin. Madison, University of Wisconsin Press, 1962. 2v. illus., maps, plans, tables. 25cm. Vol. 2: illus. and tables. Bibliography: v. 1, p. 178-191. [E78.W8H3] 62-8165
1. Jefferson Co., Wis.—Antiq. 2. Indians of North America—Wisconsin. 3. Mississippi Valley—Antiq. I. Title.

Jefferson, Thomas, Pres. U.S., 1743-1826.

GUINNESS, Desmond. 720'.92'4
Mr. Jefferson, architect [by] Desmond Guinness & Julius Trousdale Sadler, Jr. New York, Viking Press [1973] 177 p. illus. 29 cm. (A Studio book) [NA737.J4G84 1973] 72-12057 ISBN 0-670-49261-2 14.95
1. Jefferson, Thomas, Pres. U.S., 1743-1826. 2. Architecture, Colonial—United States. I. Sadler, Julius Trousdale, joint author. II. Title.

MUMFORD, Lewis, 1895- 720'.975
The South in architecture. New York, Da Capo Press, 1967. 147 p. 21 cm. (Da Capo Press series in architecture and decorative art, v. 6) (The Dancy lectures, 1941.) Reprint of the 1941 ed. Contents.Contents.—The basis for American form.—The universalism of Thomas Jefferson.—The regionalism of H. H. Richardson.—The social task of architecture. [NA705.M78 1967] 67-27462 6.50
1. Jefferson, Thomas, Pres. U.S., 1743-1826. 2. Richardson, Henry Hobson, 1838-1886. 3. Architecture—U.S. 4. Architecture—Southern States. I. Title. II. Series: Alabama College, Montevallo. Dancy lectures, 1941 BIP

NICHOLS, Frederick Doveton. 720'.92'4
Thomas Jefferson, landscape architect / Frederick Doveton Nichols and Ralph Griswold. Charlottesville : University Press of Virginia, 1977. p. cm. (Monticello monograph series) Includes index. Bibliography: p. [E332.2.N53] 77-10601 ISBN 0-8139-0603-2 : 9.75
1. Jefferson, Thomas, Pres. U.S.—1743-1826. 2. Landscape architecture—United States—History. 3. Architecture, American—History. I. Griswold, Ralph E., joint author. II. Title. BIP

Jefferson, Thomas, Pres. U.S. — Portraits, etc.

VIRGINIA. UNIVERSITY. MUSEUM OF FINE ARTS. 757'.9'0973
The life portraits of Thomas Jefferson, by Alfred L. Bush. Catalogue of an exhibition at the University of Virginia Museum of Fine Arts, 12 through 26 April, 1962. Charlottesville, Va., Thomas Jefferson Memorial Foundation, 1962. 101 p. ports. 28 cm. Includes bibliographical references. [N7628.J4V58] 62-15594
1. Jefferson, Thomas, Pres. U.S. — Portraits, etc. I. Bush, Alfred L. II. Title.

Jeffords, Walter M.—Art collections.

PORTLAND Museum of Art. 759.141'074'014191
Fifty-eight Maine paintings : selections from the Collection of Mr. and Mrs. Walter M. Jeffords, Jr.: catalogue of an exhibition 20 May-20 June 1976, Portland Museum of Art Portland, Me. : The Museum, c1976. 19 p. : ill. (some col.) ; 23 cm. [ND210.P67 1976] 76-372285
1. Jeffords, Walter M.—Art collections. 2. Maine in art. 3. Paintings, American—Exhibitions. 4. Paintings, Modern—19th century—United States—Exhibitions. 5. Paintings, Modern—20th century—United States—Exhibitions. I. Title.

Jenkins, Paul, 1923—

JENKINS, Paul, 1923- 759.13
Jenkins [by] Jean Cassou. New York, Abrams [1964, c.1963] 67p. illus. (pt. col.) port. 21x23cm. (Mod. artists) 64-17174 5.95
I. Cassou, Jean, 1897- II. Title.

JENKINS, Paul, 1923- 759.13
Paintings. Excerpt by James Fitzsimmons. Texts by Kenneth B. Sawyer, Pierre Restany. [dist. New York, Wittenborn, c.1961] 35p. illus. (part col.) port. 31cm. 61-3694 2.50
I. Sawyer, Kenneth B. II. Restany, Pierre. III. Title.

JENKINS, Paul, 1923- 759.13
Paul Jenkins. Text by Albert Elsen. New York, H. N. Abrams [1973] 284 p. (p. [86]-[271] illus., part col.) 28 x 30 cm. Bibliography: p. 281-284. [ND237.J43E47] 75-101622 ISBN 0-8109-0215-X 35.00
1. Jenkins, Paul, 1923- I. Elsen, Albert Edward, 1927- BIP

NORDLAND, Gerald. 759.13
Paul Jenkins retrospective. Text and catalogue by Gerald Nordland, with acknowledgments by Philippe de Montebello. The Museum of Fine Arts, Houston, October 12-December 12, 1971; San Francisco Museum of Art, January 6-February 27, 1972. [Houston, Tex., Museum of Fine Arts; distributed by Universe Books, New York, 1971] 69 p. illus. (part col.) 28 cm. Errata slip inserted. Bibliography: p. 68-69. [ND237.J43N6] 78-172524
1. Jenkins, Paul, 1923- I. Houston, Tex. Museum of Fine Arts. II. San Francisco. Museum of Art. III. Title.

Jensen, Alfred, 1903 (Dec. 11)—

JENSEN, Alfred, 1903(Dec.11)- 759.13
Alfred Jensen, recent paintings, the Pace Gallery, October 27-24 November, 1973. [New York, Pace Editions, 1973] [20] p. illus. (part col.) 28 cm. Catalog of an exhibition. [ND237.J45P32] 73-88815
1. Jensen, Alfred, 1903 (Dec. 11)- I. Pace Gallery.

Jensen, Jens, 1860-1951.

EATON, Leonard K. 712.0973
Landscape artist in America; the life and work of Jens Jensen, by Leonard K. Eaton. Chicago, University of Chicago Press [1964] x, 240 p. illus., plans (1 fold.) ports. 28 cm. "Bibliographical essay": p. 237-240. [SB470.J4E2] 64-23422
1. Jensen, Jens, 1860-1951. I. Title. BIP

Jerusalem. Church of the Holy Sepulcher.

COUASNON, Charles. 726'.5'0956944
The Church of the Holy Sepulchre in Jerusalem. Translated from the original French by J.-P. B. and Claude Ross. London, Oxford University Press for the British Academy, 1974. xi, 64 p., xxviii p. of plates. ill., plans. 25 cm. (The Schweich lectures of the British Academy, 1972) Includes bibliographical references. [DS109.4.C6813] 74-169245 ISBN 0-19-725938-3
1. Jerusalem. Church of the Holy Sepulcher. I. Series: The Schweich lectures, 1972.
Distributed by Oxford University Press, New York, 9.75. BIP

Jerusalem—Description—Views.

CAPA, Cornell. 779'.9'91569440924
Jerusalem: city of mankind, edited by Cornell Capa. Introd. by Teddy Kollek with J. Robert Moskin. New York, Grossman Publishers, 1974. 127 p. (chiefly illus.) 29 cm. [DS109.2.C36 1974] 73-16594 ISBN 0-670-40649-X 15.00
1. Jerusalem—Description—Views. I. Title.
Pbk. 5.95; ISBN 0-670-40645-7.

SCHILLER, Gertrud. 704.948'2
Iconography of Christian art. Translated by Janet Seligman. [1st American ed.] Greenwich, Conn., New York Graphic Society [1971- v. illus. 26 cm. Translation of the 2d ed. of Ikonographie der christlichen Kunst. Contents.—v. 1. Christ's incarnation, childhood, baptism, temptation, transfiguration, works, and miracles.—v. 2. The Passion of Christ. Bibliography: v. 1, p. 467-470. [N7830.S35132] 76-132965 ISBN 0-8212-0365-7 (v. 1.) 25.00 (v. 1) varies
1. Jesus Christ—Art. I. Title. BIP

SHEK, Kai-nung 755.5
Sketches of Christ from a Chinese brush, from the brush of Shek Kai-nung (Johnny Shek) in collaboration with Olaf K. Skinsnes. [Minneapolis, Augsburg Pub. House, 1956] 79 p. illus. 28 cm. [N8050.S45] 56-14543
1. Jesus Christ — Art. 2. Paintings, Chinese. I. Skinsnes, Olaf K. II. Title.

SHORR, Dorothy C 704.9485
The Christ Child in devotional images in Italy during the XIV century. New York, G. Wittenborn, 1954. xi, 203p. illus. 31cm. Bibliography: p.192. 'Photographic sources': p.193. [N8050.S48] 54-1138
1. Jesus Christ—Art. 2. Art—Italy—Hist. I. Title.

TIEPOLO, Giovanni 769'.92'4
Domenico, 1726?-1804.
Picturesque ideas on the flight into Egypt. Etched by Giovanni Domenico Tiepolo. Introd. and captions by Colta Feller Ives. [New York] Metropolitan Museum of Art [1972] [67] p. 27 illus. 23 x 29 cm. On spine: Flight into Egypt. Originally issued under title: Idee pittoresche sopra la fugga in Egitto di Giesu, Maria e Gioseppe. [NE2052.5.T5I9313] 72-90171 ISBN 0-87099-121-3
1. Jesus Christ—Art. 2. Jesus Christ—Nativity. I. Ives, Colta Feller. II. Title. III. Title: Flight into Egypt. BIP

WINKLER, Martin, 1893- 704.9485
Holidays of the Church. Translated by Marguerite Buchloh and Igor Rosimirow. Recklinghausen, A. Bongers; distributed by Taplinger Pub. Co. [New York, 1958] 80 p. 16 col. plates 18 cm. (Pictorial library of Eastern Church art, v. 8) Translation of Festtage. [N8050.W5313] 67-16576
1. Jesus Christ — Art. 2. Mary, Virgin — Art. 3. Icons. I. Title.

WINKLER, Martin, 1893- 704.9485
Holidays or the Church. Tr. by Marguerite Buchloh, Igor Rosimirow. Recklinghausen, A. Bongers; dist. by Taplinger [New York, 1958] 80p. 16 col. plates. 18cm. (Pictorial lib. of Eastern Church art, v. 8) Tr. of Festtage. [N8050.W5313] 67-16576 2.50 bds.,
1. Jesus Christ —Art. 2. Mary, Virgin—Art. 3. Icons. I. Title.

Jesus Christ—Biography.

CONVERSE, Gordon N. 779'.9'2209
Come see the place : the Holy Land Jesus knew / photos. by Gordon N. Converse ; text by Robert J. Bull and B. Cobbey Crisler. Englewood Cliffs, N.J. : Prentice-Hall, c1978. [DS108.5.C65] 78-7054 ISBN 0-13-152538-7 : 12.95
1. Jesus Christ—Biography. 2. Palestine—Description and travel—Views. 3. Christian biography—Palestine. I. Bull, Robert J. II. Crisler, B. Cobbey, 1933- III. Title. BIP

Jesus Christ—Crucifixion—Art.

BROWN, Stephanie. 755'.4
Religious painting : Christ's passion and crucifixtion in the history of art / by Stephanie Brown. New York : Mayflower Books, [1979] p. cm. [ND1430.B76] 78-24454 ISBN 0-8317-7370-7 : 12.95 ISBN 0-8317-7371-5 pbk. : 6.95
1. Jesus Christ—Passion—Art. 2. Jesus Christ—Crucifixion—Art. 3. Painting, Medieval. 4. Painting, Renaissance. 5. Painting, Baroque. I. Title.

HENKES, Robert. 755'.4
The crucifixion in American painting : 80 American painters and the crucifixion theme / by Robert Henkes. New York : Gordon Press, 1977. p. cm. Includes index. [ND205.H4] 77-12369 ISBN 0-8490-1370-4 lib.bdg. : 44.95
1. Jesus Christ—Crucifixion—Art. 2. Painting, American. 3. Painters—United States. I. Title. BIP

VACHON, Andrew William. 759.13
This Man, by Andrew Wm. Vachon. Idaho Falls, Idaho, Western Arts, 1965. 1 v. (unpaged) illus. (part col.) 28 cm. Reproduced from ms. copy. [ND237.V12A57] 65-18195
1. Jesus Christ—Crucifixion—Art. I. Title.

Jesus Christ—Nativity.

RISTOW, Gunter. 704.948/55
The nativity. [Tr. from German by Hans Hermann Rosenwald] Recklinghausen, Aurel Bongers; dist. by Taplinger [New York, c.1967] 68p. illus., plates (pt. col.) 18cm. (Pictorial lib. of Eastern Church art. v. 12) Tr. of Die Geburt Christ. [N8050.R513] 67-16581 2.50 bds.,
1. Jesus Christ—Nativity. 2. Jesus Christ—Art. I. Title.

WEBB, Willard, 1903- 769'.924
Nativity; the story as told by St. Luke and St. Matthew. Presented in block prints by Willard and Margaret Webb. Clifton, Va., 1966. [33] p. (on double leaves) illus. (part col.) 31 cm. [NE1217.W38A5] 68-3597
1. Jesus Christ—Nativity. 2. Jesus Christ—Art. I. Webb, Margaret, 1902- joint author. II. Title.

Jesus Christ—Passion—Art.

BROWN, Stephanie. 755'.4
Religious painting : Christ's passion and crucifixtion in the history of art / by Stephanie Brown. New York : Mayflower Books, [1979] p. cm. [ND1430.B76] 78-24454 ISBN 0-8317-7370-7 : 12.95 ISBN 0-8317-7371-5 pbk. : 6.95
1. Jesus Christ—Passion—Art. 2. Jesus Christ—Crucifixion—Art. 3. Painting, Medieval. 4. Painting, Renaissance. 5. Painting, Baroque. I. Title. BIP

Jesus People—Pictorial works.

LEVI, Hans. 779'.9'26920222
Street Jesus. Photos. by Hans Levi. [San Francisco] H. Levi; [distributed by Scrimshaw Press, 1972] [64] p. photos. 31 cm. [BV4531.2.L48] 72-85937 ISBN 0-912020-27-X 4.95
1. Jesus People—Pictorial works. I. Title.

Jewelry.

ART nouveau jewellery & fans 739.27
[by] Gabriel Mourey, Aymer Vallance, et al. New York, Dover Publications [1973] x, 149 p. illus. 28 cm. Published in 1902 under title: Modern design in jewellery and fans. [NK7309.85.A7A77 1973] 73-75871 ISBN 0-486-22961-0 3.50 (pbk.)
1. Jewelry. 2. Fans. 3. Decoration and ornament—Art nouveau. I. Mourey, Gabriel, 1865-1943.

BAERWALD, Marcus. 739.27
The story of jewelry; a popular account of the lure, lore, science, and value of gems and noble metals in the modern world [by] Marcus Baerwald [and] Tom Mahoney. London, New York, Abelard-Schuman [1960] 221 p. illus. 24 cm. [NK7304.B25] 59-11647
1. Jewelry. I. Mahoney, Tom, joint author.

BAXTER, William Thomas. 739.27
Jewelry, gem cutting, and metalcraft. 3d ed., rev. and enl. New York, Whittlesey House [1950] xiv, 334 p. illus. 21 cm. "Identification of gem stones and gem minerals," by H. C. Dake: p. [295]-321. Bibliography: p. 327. [TS725.B35 1950] 50-7176
1. Jewelry. 2. Gems. 3. Metal-work. 4. Handicraft. BIP

BLAKEMORE, Kenneth. 739.27
The retail jeweller's guide / Kenneth Blakemore ; technical adviser G. F. Andrews. 3rd ed. London ; Boston : Newnes-Butterworths, 1977 323 p. : ill. ; 23 cm. Includes index. [TS725.B53 1976] 77-355278 ISBN 0-408-00266-2 : 25.00
1. Jewelry. 2. Clocks and watches. I. Title.
Distributed by Transatlantic BIP

BOVIN, Murray. 739.27
Jewelry making, for schools, tradesmen [and] Craftsmen. [Reprinted and enl.] Forest Hills, N.Y. [1953] 132p. illus. 28cm. [TS740.B78 1953] 54-215
1. Jewelry. I. Title.

BOVIN, Murray. 739.27
Jewelry making, for schools, tradesmen [and] craftsmen. [Reprinted and enl.] Forest Hills, N. Y. [1955] 147p. illus. 28cm. [TS740.B78 1955] 55-4132
1. Jewelry. I. Title.

BOVIN, Murray. 739.27
Jewelry making, for schools, tradesmen [and] craftsmen. [Reprinted and enl.] Forest Hills, N. Y. [1959] 159p. illus. 26cm. [TS740.B78 1959] 59-16198
1. Jewelry. I. Title.

BOVIN, Murray. 739.27
Jewelry making, for schools, tradesmen [and] craftsmen. Forest Hills, N. Y. [1952] 128 p. illus. 27 cm. [TS740.B78] 52-13978
1. Jewelry. I. Title. BIP

BOVIN, Murray. 739.27
Jewelry making, for schools, tradesmen [and] craftsmen. [Reprinted and rev.] Forest Hills, N. Y. [1964] 159 p. illus. 27 cm. [TS740.B78] 64-54199
1. Jewelry. I. Title.

BRADFORD, Ernie Dusgate 739.27
Selby
Four centuries of European jewellery. New York, Philosophical Library [1953] 226p. illus. 26cm. [NK7142] 53-7921
1. Jewelry. I. Title.

BRADFORD, Ernle Dusgate 739.2
Selby.
Contemporary jewellery and silver design. New York, Pitman Pub. Corp. [1951] 134p. illus. 30cm. [NK7343.B7 1951] 53-1449
1. Jewelry. 2. Silversmithing—Gt. Brit. I. Title.

CHATT, Orville K., 1924- 739.27
Design is where you find it [by] Orville K. Chatt. [1st ed.] Ames, Iowa State University Press [1972] 124 p. illus. (part col.) 18 x 26 cm. Bibliography: p. 124. [TS729.C48] 79-146932 ISBN 0-8138-0415-9
1. Jewelry. I. Title. BIP

CLEGG, Helen. 739.27
Jewelry making for fun and profit, by Henel Clegg and Mary Larom; introd. by Lawrence L. Jarvie, drawings by Mary Larom, photos. by Bernard M. Acosta. [1st ed.] New York, McKay [1951] xi, 162 p. illus. 21 cm. [TS725.C6] 51-11325
1. Jewelry. I. Larom, Mary, joint author. II. Title.

CLIFFORD, Anne. 739.27
Cut-steel and Berlin iron jewellery. [1st American ed.] South Brunswick, A. S. Barnes [1971] 95 p. (p. 36-95 illus., col. plates) 22 cm. Bibliography: p. 33. [NK7305.C55 1971] 75-148455 ISBN 0-498-07907-4 6.95
1. Jewelry. 2. Art metal-work. I. Title.

CURRAN, Mona 739.27
A treasury of jewels and gems. New York, Emerson [c.1961, 1962] 152p. illus.21cm. First pub. in England under title: Jewels and gems. 62-14812 4.50
1. Jewelry. 2. Gems. I. Title. BIP

DARLING, Ada W., 1880- 739.27
Antique jewelry. Watkins Glen, N. Y., Century House [1953] 200 p. illus. 25 cm. [NK7312.D3] 53-2222
1. Jewelry. I. Title.

FLOWER, Margaret Cameron 739.27
Coss.
Victorian jewellery; with a foreword by Margaret J. Biggs and a chapter on collecting by Doris Langley Moore. New York, Duell, Sloan, and Pearce [1951] xxviii, 271 p. illus. 26 cm. Bibliography: p. [257]-260. [NK7109.F55] 51-9606
1. Jewelry. I. Title.

FLOWER, Margaret Cameron 739.27
Coss.
Victorian jewellery, by Margaret Flower. With a foreword by Margaret J. Biggs and a chapter on collecting by Doris Langley Moore. South Brunswick [N.J.] A. S. Barnes [1967] xxviii, 271 p. illus. (part col.) facsim., ports. 26 cm. Bibliography: p. [257]-260. [NK7109.F55 1967] 66-25035
1. Jewelry. I. Title.

FRANK, Joan. 739.27
The jewelry book. New York, Drake Publishers [1975] p. cm. [NK7304.F72] 74-6216 ISBN 0-87749-691-9
1. Jewelry. I. Title.

FRANKE, Lois E 739.27
Handwrought jewelry. Photography by William L. Udell. Bloomington, Ill,. McKnight & McKnight Pub. Co. [1962] 222 p. illus. 27 cm. [TS740.F83] 62-53256
1. Jewelry. I. Title. BIP

GEOFFROY-DECHAUME, Claude. 739.27
Simple craft jewellery adapted for occupational therapy, written and illustrated by Claude Geoffroy-Dechaume. New York, Pitman Pub. Co. [1950?] 63 p. illus. 25 cm. "Issued under the auspices of the Worshipful Company of Goldsmiths of London." [TS741.G4 1950] 51-4053
1. Jewelry. 2. Handicraft. I. Title.

HABERLANDT, Michael, 1860- 739.27
1940.
Primitive and folk jewelry. Ed. by Martin Gerlach. Introd. & captions by Michael Haberlandt. [Magnolia, Mass.] [Peter Smith] [1973 c.1971] xv, 219 p. illus. 29 cm. (Dover bk. rebound) Trans. of Volkerschmuck, mit besonder Berucksichtigung des metallischen Schmuckes. [NK7405.H313] 70-125624 ISBN 0-8446-0107-1 9.50
1. Jewelry. I. Gerlach, Martin, ed. II. Title. BIP

HUGHES, Graham. 739.27
The art of jewelry. New York, Viking Press [1972] 248 p. illus. (part col.) 32 cm. (A Studio book) Bibliography: p. 243. [NK7304.H83] 70-186743 ISBN 0-670-13480-5 25.00
1. Jewelry. I. Title.

JOACHIM, E. E. 739.27'4
Jewelry making step by step; for amateur craftsmen, by E. E. Joachim. Atlanta, Precision Press [1967] A-G, 263 p. illus. (part col.) 22 cm. [TS741.J6] 67-4749
1. Jewelry. I. Title.

LAMMER, Jutta 745.59
Make your own costume jewelry [Tr. from German] New York, Watson-Guptill [1966] c. 1964.,1965. 56p. illus. (pt. col.) 20cm. [TS741.L313] 65-21603 3.50 bds.,
1. Jewelry. I. Title.

LEWES, Klares 739.27
Jewelry making for the amateur. Illus. by Karin Ann Lewes. London. B. T. Batsford; New York. Reinhold [1966, c.1965] 164p. illus. 23cm. Bibl. [TS741.L45] 65-28050 8.00
1. Jewelry. I. Title.

MARTIN, Charles James. 737.27
How to make modern jewelry, by Charles J. Martin in collaboration with Victor D'Amico. New York, Museum of Modern Art; distributed by Doubleday, Garden City, N. Y. [c1960] 96p. illus. 26cm. (Art for beginners series) Includes bibliography. [TS725.M28 1960] 60-15503
1. Jewelry. I. New York. Museum of Modern Art. II. Title.

MORTON, Philip. 739.27
Contemporary jewelry; a studio handbook. New York, Holt, Rinehart and Winston [1970] xii, 308 p. illus. (part col.) 26 cm. Bibliography: p. 300-302. [TS740.M67] 69-16080 9.95
1. Jewelry. 2. Jewelry making. I. Title. BIP

NEWBLE, Brian. 939'.15
Practical enamelling and jewelry work. New York, Viking Press [1967] 96 p. illus. (part col.) 26 cm. (A Studio book) Bibliography: p. 94. [TS740.N4 1967a] 67-4923

; 25 cm. Includes index. Bibliography: p. 267-271. [NK7302.5.G7L63 1976] 77-353071 ISBN 0-7141-0054-4 : £5.50. ISBN 0-7141-0055-2 pbk.
1. British Museum. 2. Jewelry—England—London—Catalogs. I. Title. BIP

Jewelry, English.

BRADFORD, Ernle Dusgate Selby. 739.270942
English Victorian jewellery. [1st American ed.] New York, McBride, 1959. 141 p. illus. 26 cm. [NK7343.B72 1959a] 59-8875
1. Jewelry, English. I. Title.

CURRAN, Mona. 739.270942
Collecting antique jewellery. New York, Emerson Books [1964] 153 p. illus. 21 cm. Bibliography: p. 149. [NK7343.C8] 64-12988
1. Jewelry, English. 2. Jewelry—Collectors and collecting. I. Title. BIP

Jewelry engraving.

HARDY, Richard Allen. 739.27'5
The jewelry engravers manual / R. Allen Hardy and John J. Bowman ; ill. by R. Allen Hardy. Rev. ed. New York : Van Nostrand Reinhold Co., [1976] p. cm. Edition for 1954 by J. J. Bowman. Includes index. [TS729.H34 1976] 75-43139 ISBN 0-442-20965-7 pbk. : 4.95
1. Jewelry engraving. 2. Lettering. 3. Monograms. I. Bowman, John J., joint author. II. Title. BIP

Jewelry, European.

MOUREY, Gabriel, 1865-1943. 739.27'094
European art nouveau jewelry, by G. Mourey and A. Vallance. Watkins Glen, N.Y., Century House [1969] 1 v. (various pagings) illus. 23 cm. Contents.Contents.—Modern British jewellery, by A. Vallance.—Modern French jewellery, by G. Mourey.—Modern Belgian jewellery, by F. Khnopff. [NK7342.M6 1969] 78-96944
1. Jewelry, European. 2. Decoration and ornament—Art nouveau. I. Vallance, Aymer, 1862-1943. II. Khnopff, Fernand, 1858-1921. III. Title.

STEINGRUBER, Erich. 739.27
Antique jewelry. New York, F. A. Praeger [1957] 191 p. illus. (part col.) 20 cm. Bibliography: p. 185-186. [NK7342.S813] 57-12655
1. Jewelry, European. I. Title.

Jewelry—Exhibitions.

ELECTRUM Gallery. 739.27'094
Aspects of jewellery, by contributors from Electrum Gallery, London; [catalogue of an exhibition held at the] Aberdeen Art Gallery, 29 April - 19 May. Aberdeen, Aberdeen Art Gallery and Museum, 1973. [21] p. illus. 30 cm. [NK7310.E44] 73-174624 ISBN 0-900017-04-X
1. Jewelry—Exhibitions. I. Aberdeen Art Gallery, Aberdeen, Scot. II. Title.

IOWA. State University of Science and Technology, Ames. Design Center. 739.27
Jewelry and hollowware; invitational: 72. [Exhibition, February 1-29. Ames, 1972?] [24] p. illus. 21 x 26 cm. Cover title. [NK7310.I68] 73-170799
1. Jewelry—Exhibitions. 2. Silverware—Exhibitions. I. Title.

ISAAC Delgado Museum of Art, New Orleans. 739.2'272'4
Treasures by Peter Carl Faberge and other master jewellers: the Matilda Geddings Gray Foundation Collection. [Catalogue notes by Susan Grady and William A. Fagaly. Exhibition held] Nov. 3 through Dec. 31, 1972. [New Orleans, Matilda Geddings Gray Foundation, 1972] 1 v. (unpaged) illus. (part col.) 25 cm. [NK7301.N45A67] 72-92872
1. Faberzhe, Karl Gustavovich, 1846-1920. 2. Matilda Geddings Gray Foundation—Art collections. 3. Jewelry—Exhibitions. I. Grady, Susan. II. Fagaly, William A. III. Title.

PHOENIX, Ariz. Art Museum. 739.2
Faberge; the M. T. Heller II Collection [exhibition] Phoenix Art Museum, October-November, 1971. [Phoenix, 1971] [20] p. illus. 24 cm. [NK7417.F3P45] 72-175304
1. Faberzhe (Firm) 2. Heller, M. T.—Art collections. 3. Jewelry—Exhibitions. 4. Gold articles—Exhibitions.

Jewelry, French.

WALLY F. Galleries. 739.27'092'4
The prestigious collection, Bijoux de Braque, executed by Heger de Lowenfeld. New York [1963] [24] p. illus. (part col.) 26 cm. Catalog of an exhibition. [NK7398.B7W34 1963] 74-152197
1. Braque, Georges, 1882-1963. 2. Jewelry, French. I. Braque, Georges, 1882-1963. II. Heger de Lowenfeld, Henri Michel. III. Title.

Jewelry—Great Britain—Exhibitions.

CRAFTS Advisory Committee. 739.27'0941'07403
On tour = Auf Tournee : 10 British jewellers in Germany and Australia = Zehn britische Goldschmiede in Deutschland und Australien / [Crafts Advisory Committee]. [London] : [The Committee], [1976] 52 p. : ill. (some col.), ports. ; 20 x 21 cm. Catalogue of an exhibition organised by the Crafts Advisory Committee in conjunction with the British Council, London, 1975-76. English and German. [NK7343.C65 1976] 77-364715
1. Jewelry—Great Britain—Exhibitions. 2. Jewelry—History—20th century—Great Britain—Exhibitions. I. Great Britain. British Council. II. Title. III. Title: Auf Tournee.

Jewelry—History.

EVANS, Joan, 1893- 739.2709
A history of jewellry, 1100-1870. New York, Pitman Pub. Corp. [c1953] 240p. illus., 186 plates (part col.) 26cm. Bibliography: p.204-214. [NK7306.E8] 53-1820
1. Jewelry—Hist. I. Title.

FREGNAC, Claude 739.2709
Jewelry from the Renaissance to art nouveau. Tr. from French by Donald Law de Lauriston. New York, Putnam [c.1965] 127p. illus. (pt. col.) ports. (pt. col.) 22cm. (Pleasures and treasures) [NK7309.F713] 65-12434 4.95 bds.,
1. Jewelry—Hist. I. Title.

GILTAY-NIJSSEN, L. 739.27
Jewelry [Tr. from Dutch] Illus.: Pieter Pouwels. New York, Universe Bks. [c.1964] 112p. illus., plates. maps. 21cm. Bibl. 64-10345 2.75; 1.95 pap.,
1. Jewelry—Hist. I. Title.

HUGHES, Graham. 739.27'09
Jewelry. London, Studio Vista; New York, Dutton, [1966, i.e., 1968] 167p. front., illus. (some col.). 19cm. (Dutton Vista pictureback) Bibl. [NK7306.H8 1966] 68-105206 2.45 pap.,
1. Jewelry—Hist. I. Title.

Jewelry—History.

BLACK, J. Anderson. 739.27'09
The story of jewelry / by J. Anderson Black ; with an introd. by Edward Lucie-Smith. New York : Morrow, 1974. 400 p. : ill. (some col.) ; 31 cm. Includes index. Bibliography: p. 384-385. [NK7306.B56 1974] 74-5504 ISBN 0-688-00321-4 : 29.95
1. Jewelry—History. I. Title. BIP

BURGESS, Frederick William, 1855-1945. 739.27'09
Antique jewellery and trinkets. New York, Putnam. Detroit, Singing Tree Press, 1972. xiii, 399 p. illus. 19 cm. Reprint of the 1919 ed., which was issued as no. 3 of The Home connoisseur series. [NK7106.B8 1972] 74-178622 17.00
1. Jewelry—History. I. Title. II. Series: The Home connoisseur series.

EVANS, Joan, 1893- 739.27'09
A history of jewellery, 1100-1870. [2d ed.] Boston, Mass., Boston Book and Art [1970] 224 p. illus., 204 plates (12 col.) 26 cm. Bibliography: p. 185-200. [NK7306.E8 1970b] 72-124160 22.50
1. Jewelry—History. I. Title.

GREGORIETTI, Guido. 739.27'09
Jewelry through the ages. Foreword by Erich Steingraber. Translated from the Italian by Helen Lawrence. New York, American Heritage [1969] 319 p. illus. (part col.), ports. (part col.) 31 cm. Translation of Il gioiello nei secoli. Bibliography: p. 314-[316] [NK7306.G713] 74-83809 ISBN 0-8281-0007-1 14.95
1. Jewelry—History. I. Title.

HUGHES, Graham. 739.270904
Modern jewelry, an international survey, 1890-1963. New York, Crown Publishers [1963] 256 p. (chiefly illus. (part col.)) 28 cm. Bibliography: p. 253-255. [NK7310.H8] 63-21128
1. Jewelry—History. 2. Art, Modern—20th century. I. Title.

JEWELRY / 739.27'09
under the general editorship of Harold H. Hart ; text by Nancy Goldberg. New York : Hart Pub. Co., c1977. 144 p. : ill. ; 32 cm. (Hart picture archives) Includes index. Bibliography: p. 142. [NK7306.J48] 76-54049 ISBN 0-8055-1210-1 : 12.95. ISBN 0-8055-0303-X pbk. : 5.95
1. Jewelry—History. I. Hart, Harold H., 1903- II. Goldberg, Nancy.

Jewelry—History—20th century.

TURNER, Ralph. 739.27'09'04
Contemporary jewelry : a critical assessment 1945-75 / Ralph Turner. New York : Van Nostrand Reinhold Co., 1976. 208 p. : ill. ; 27 cm. Includes index. Bibliography: p. 203-204. [NK7310.T87 1976] 75-37375 ISBN 0-442-28639-2 : 30.00
1. Jewelry—History—20th century. I. Title.

Jewelry—History—20th century—Exhibitions.

ZAHN, Helga. 739.27'092'4
Helga Zahn : a retrospective assessment, 1960-1976 : jewellery, prints, and drawings, 14 April-12 June 1976 / photography Ray Carpenter ... [et al.]. London : Crafts Advisory Committee, 1976. [25] p. : chiefly ill., port. ; 26 cm. [NK7398.Z33C37] 76-378314 £1.00
1. Zahn, Helga. 2. Jewelry—History—20th century—Exhibitions. I. Carpenter, Ray. II. Crafts Advisory Committee.

Jewelry—History—20th century—United States—Exhibitions.

ELECTRUM Gallery. 739.27'0973'07402132
6 contemporary American jewellers : [catalogue of an exhibition held at the Electron Gallery, June 2-26, 1976.] London : The Gallery, [1976] 1 portfolio ([5] leaves : ill. ; 22 cm. [NK7312.E43 1976] 76-380533 ISBN 0-9505105-0-5
1. Jewelry—History—20th century—United States—Exhibitions. I. Title.

Jewelry—Juvenile literature.

THOMPSON, Brenda. 739.27
Gold and jewels / [original text] by Brenda Thompson and [revised text by] Rosemary Giesen ; illustrated by Caroline Austin and Rosemary Giesen. Minneapolis : Lerner Publications Co., 1977, c1975. [24] p. : ill. (some col.) ; 23 cm. (A First fact book) An introduction to gold, precious gems, and jewelry. Includes information about cutting gems. [TS729.T49 1977] 76-22437 ISBN 0-8225-1356-0 lib.bdg. : 3.95
1. Jewelry—Juvenile literature. 2. Gold—Juvenile literature. I. Giesen, Rosemary, joint author. II. Austin, Caroline. III. Title. BIP

Jewelry making.

BOVIN, Murray. 739.27'4
Centrifugal or lost wax jewelry casting for schools, tradesmen, craftsmen. Forest Hills, N.Y. [1970] 99 p. illus. 27 cm. Title on spine: Jewelry casting for schools, tradesmen, craftsmen. [TS729.B68] 71-135667
1. Jewelry making. 2. Precision casting. I. Title. II. Title: Jewelry casting for schools, tradesmen, craftsmen. BIP

BOVIN, Murray. 739.27'4
Centrifugal or lost wax jewelry casting for schools, tradesmen, craftsmen. Forest Hills, L.I., N.Y. [1971] 103 p. illus. 28 cm. Cover title: Jewelry casting for schools, tradesmen, craftsmen. [TS729.B68 1971] 73-27840 ISBN 0-910280-05-3
1. Jewelry making. 2. Precision casting. I. Title. II. Title: Jewelry casting for schools, tradesmen, craftsmen.

BOVIN, Murray. 739.27
Jewelry making for schools, tradesmen [and] craftsmen. [Enl. and rev.] Forest Hills, N.Y. [1967] 175p. illus. 27cm. [TS740.B78 1967] 67-20040 5.75; 4.20 pap.,
1. Jewelry making. I. Title.
Order from the author, 68-36 108th Street, Forest Hills, New York, N.Y. 11375.

COYNE, John. 739.27
The Penland School of Crafts book of jewelry making / edited by John Coyne ; with photography by Evon Streetman. Indianapolis : Bobbs-Merrill, [1975] p. cm. "A Rutledge book." [TT212.C68] 74-31333 ISBN 0-672-51967-4 : 12.95
1. Jewelry making. I. Penland School of Handicrafts, Penland, N.C. II. Title. BIP

CRAFT Training Institute. 739.27
Handbook of jewelry metalcrafting, by the faculty, CTI. Mercer Island, Wash. [1969] vi, 98 p. illus. 24 cm. [TS741.C67] 72-178314
1. Jewelry making. 2. Art metal-work. I. Title.

EDWARDS, Rod. 739.27
The technique of jewelry / Rod Edwards. New York : Scribner, c1977. 240 p., [3] leaves of plates : ill. (some col.) ; 26 cm. Includes index. [TS725.E37 1977] 77-77547 ISBN 0-684-15309-2 : 17.50
1. Jewelry making. I. Title. BIP

GARRISON, William E. 739.27
Handcrafting jewelry; designs & techniques [by] William E. Garrison and Merle E. Dowd. Chicago, H. Regnery Co. [1972] 204 p. illus. 29 cm. [TS741.G3] 71-183815 12.95
1. Jewelry making. I. Dowd, Merle E., joint author. II. Title.

GRANDO, Michael D. 739.27
Jewelry: form and technique [by] Michael D. Grando. New York, Van Nostrand Reinhold [1970, c1969] 80 p. illus. 21 cm. [TS752.G67 1970] 77-90302 5.95
1. Jewelry making. 2. Jewelry. I. Title.

MEYEROWITZ, Patricia. 739.27
Jewelry and sculpture through unit construction; line drawings by Jacob Meyerowitz. London, Studio Vista; New York, Reinhold Publishing Corporation [1967] 96 p. illus. 26 cm. unpriced. (B***) Bibliography: p. 93. [TS740.M4] 67-20232
1. Jewelry making. 2. Unit construction. 3. Sculpture — Technique. I. Title.

MEYEROWITZ, Patricia. 739.27'4
Making jewelry and sculpture through unit construction / by Patricia Meyerowitz. 2d ed. New York : Dover Publications, 1978. 96 p. : ill. ; 26 cm. Published in 1967 under title: Jewelry and sculpture through unit construction. Includes index. Bibliography: p. 92-93. [TT212.M483 1978] 78-53257 ISBN 0-486-23678-1 pbk. : 2.75
1. Jewelry making. 2. Unit construction. 3. Sculpture—Technique. I. Title. BIP

ROSE, Augustus Foster, 1873-1946. 739.27
Jewelry making and design; an illustrated textbook for teachers, students of design and craft workers, by Augustus F. Rose and Antonio Cirino. 4th rev. ed. New York, Dover [1967] xvi, 306 p. illus. 22 cm. Bibliography: p. [297]-304. [TS740.R6 1967] 66-29501
1. Jewelry making. 2. Design, Decorative. I. Cirino, Antonio, 1889- joint author. II. Title. BIP

York, Association Press [1975] 128 p. illus. 28 cm. [TT212.W34] 74-18098 ISBN 0-8096-1885-0
1. Jewelry making—Amateurs' manuals. 2. Precision casting—Amateurs' manuals. I. Title. BIP

WHARTON, Marshall. 739.27'4
How to make jewelry like a pro / by Marshall Wharton. 1st ed. Blue Ridge Summit, Pa. : G/L Tab Books, 1977. 196 p. : ill. ; 22 cm. Includes index. [TT212.W45] 77-1766 ISBN 0-8306-7775-5 : 7.95. ISBN 0-8306-6775-X pbk. : 4.95
1. Jewelry making—Amateurs' manuals. I. Title.

WOOD, Louise. 739.27
Make your own jewelry : for beginner, hobbyist, and craftsman / by Louise and Orvelo Wood. New York : Grosset & Dunlap, c1975. 192 p. : ill. ; 28 cm. Includes index. Bibliography: p. 180-181. [TT212.W66] 73-18530 ISBN 0-448-11505-0 : 12.95. ISBN 0-448-12143-3 pbk. : 7.95
1. Jewelry making—Amateurs' manuals. I. Wood, Orvelo, joint author. II. Title.

Jewelry making—Amateurs' manuals—Juvenile literature.

MEYER, Carolyn. 736'.2'028
Rock tumbling : from stones to gems to jewelry / by Carolyn Meyer with Jerome Wexler ; 90 photos. by Jerome Wexler. New York : Morrow, 1975. 96 p. : ill. ; 25 cm. Includes index. Describes the equipment, stones, and procedures used in rock tumbling and gives instructions for making the polished stones into jewelry and other items. [TT212.M48] 74-22346 ISBN 0-688-22022-3 : 5.95 ISBN 0-688-32022-8 lib.bdg. : 5.11.
1. Jewelry making—Amateurs' manuals—Juvenile literature. 2. Stone polishing machinery—Juvenile literature. I. Wexler, Jerome, joint author. II. Title.

Jewelry making—Handbooks, manuals, etc.

O'CONNOR, Harold. 739.27'4
The jeweler's bench reference / Harold O'Connor. Crested Butte, Colo. : Dunconor Books, c1977. 68 p. : ill. ; 18 cm. Includes index. Bibliography: p. 4-6. [TS729.O23] 76-53236 12.95
1. Jewelry making—Handbooks, manuals, etc. I. Title. BIP

Jewelry making—Juvenile literature.

DEACON, Eileen. 745.59'42
Making jewelry / words by Eileen Deacon ; illustrations by Grahame Corbett. Milwaukee : Macdonald-Raintree, c1977. p. cm. Includes index. Step-by-step instructions for making original jewelry from available household objects. [TT212.D43] 77-7942 ISBN 0-8393-0116-2 lib. bdg. : 7.99
1. Jewelry making—Juvenile literature. I. Corbett, Grahame. II. Title.
Publisher's address:205West Highland Ave.,Milwaukee Wi.53203 BIP

HETZER, Linda. 745.5
Designer crafts / by Linda Hetzer ; photos. by Steven Mays [; illustrators, Lynn Matus and Sally Shimizu ; text editor, Jill Munves]. Milwaukee : Raintree, c1978. 48 p. : ill. (some col.) ; 26 cm. Introduces various techniques in making jewelry, mosaics, and patchwork and includes step-by-step instructions for a selection of projects involving each craft. [TT212.H47] 77-28784 ISBN 0-8172-1188-8 lib.bdg. : 7.93
1. Jewelry making—Juvenile literature. 2. Mosaics—Technique—Juvenile literature. 3. Patchwork—Juvenile literature. I. Mays, Steven. II. Matus, Lynn. III. Shimizu, Sally. IV. Munves, Jill. V. Title. BIP

LERNER, Sharon. 745.59'42
Making jewelry / by Sharon Lerner ; pictures by George Overlie. Minneapolis : Lerner Publications Co., c1977. 32 p. : ill. ; 19 cm. (An Early craft book) Instructions for using wire and sheet metal to make and decorate necklaces, rings, barrettes, earrings, and other jewelry. [TT212.L47 1977] 76-13066 ISBN 0-8225-0862-1 lib.bdg. : 3.95
1. Jewelry making—Juvenile literature. I. Overlie, George. II. Title. BIP

SATTLER, Helen Roney. 745.59'42
Jewelry from junk. Written and illustrated by Helen Roney Sattler. New York, Lothrop, Lee & Shepard [1973] 95 p. illus. 25 cm. Directions for making jewelry from seeds, chicken bones, branches, bread, washers, and other things easily available in the home. [TS741.S33] 72-88103 ISBN 0-688-40048-5 4.25
1. Jewelry making—Juvenile literature. I. Title.
Library edition 3.94; ISBN 0-688-50048-X. BIP

VILLIARD, Paul. 739.27
Jewelrymaking. [1st ed.] Garden City, N.Y., Doubleday [1973] 96 p. illus. 22 cm. Describes the tools and techniques for making simple necklaces, earrings, bracelets, and pins from leather, wire and beads, and other materials. [TT212.V54] 72-92248 4.95
1. Jewelry making—Juvenile literature. I. Title.

YERIAN, Cameron John. 745.59
Jewelry, candles & papercraft. Cameron and Margaret Yerian, editors. Chicago, Children's Press [1974] 46 p. col. illus. 25 cm. "Fun time." Instructions for making a variety of jewelry items, candles, and paper objects. [TT212.Y47] 74-8339 ISBN 0-516-01301-7
1. Jewelry making—Juvenile literature. 2. Paper work—Juvenile literature. 3. Candlemaking—Juvenile literature. I. Yerian, Margaret, joint author. II. Title. BIP

Jewelry, Mexican—Hist.

DAVIS, Mary L. 739.270972
Mexican jewelry [by] Mary L. Davis, Greta Pack. Drawings by Mary L. Davis. Austin, Univ. of Tex. Pr. [c.1963] 262p. illus. 22cm. Bibl. 63-7435 6.50
1. Jewelry, Mexican—Hist. I. Pack, Greta, joint author. II. Title. BIP

Jewelry—Private collections.

YOUNG, Sheila. 739.27'074'021
The Queen's jewellery; the jewels of H.M. Queen Elizabeth II. New York, Taplinger Pub. Co. [1969] 119 p. illus. (part col.), ports. (part col.) 26 cm. [NK7303.Y6 1969] 71-86660 8.95
1. Elizabeth II, Queen of Great Britain, 1926- 2. Jewelry—Private collections. I. Title.

Jewelry—Repairing.

HARDY, Richard Allen. 739.27
The jewelry repair manual [by] R. Allen Hardy and John J. Bowman. Princeton, N. J., Van Nostrand [1956] 160p. illus. 24cm. [TS740.H3] 56-8397
1. Jewelry—Repairing. I. Bowman, John J., joint author. II. Title.

HARDY, Richard Allen. 739.27
The jewelry repair manual, [by] R. Allen Hardy. With illus. by the author. 2d ed. Princeton, N. J., Van Nostrand [1967] ix, 253 p. illus. 24 cm. [TS740.H3 1967] 67-18068
1. Jewelry—Repairing. I. Title. BIP

JACKSON, William Alexander, 1885- 739.27
Jewelry repairing. Brooklyn, Chemical Pub. Co., 1950. 143 p. illus. 23 cm. [TS740.J3 1950] 50-12772
1. Jewelry—Repairing.

Jewelry trade—Vocational guidance—Juvenile literature.

BAKER, Eugene H. 739.27'023
I want to be a jeweler, by Eugene Baker. Illustrated by Richard Wahl. Chicago, Childrens Press [1973] 30 p. col. illus. 25 cm. While visiting a jewelry store, two children learn about the trade of a jeweler. [HD9747.A2B28] 73-6687 ISBN 0-516-01743-8 3.50
1. Jewelry trade—Vocational guidance—Juvenile literature. I. Wahl, Richard, 1939- illus. II. Title. BIP

Jewelry—United States—Exhibitions.

CALIFORNIA 739.27'0973'074019496
State University, Fullerton. Art Gallery.
Jewelers, U.S.A. : an exhibition / organized by Dextra Frankel ; with catalogue introd. by Arline M. Fisch. [Fullerton] : Art Gallery, California State University, Fullerton, c1976. 37 p. : ill. ; 22 x 31 cm. Exhibition held at the Art Gallery, California State University, Fullerton, Feb. 27-Mar. 25, 1976. [NK7312.C34 1976] 76-361285
1. Jewelry—United States—Exhibitions. 2. Jewelry—History—20th century. I. Title.

Jewelry, Victorian.

ARMSTRONG, Nancy J. 739.27'09'034
Victorian jewelry / by Nancy Armstrong. New York : Macmillan, c1976. p. cm. "A Studio Vista book." Includes index. [NK7309.8.A75] 76-12573 ISBN 0-02-503220-8 : 19.95
1. Jewelry, Victorian. I. Title. BIP

COOPER, Diana. 739.27'0942
Victorian sentimental jewellery [by] Diana Cooper & Norman Battershill. [1st American ed.] South Brunswick, A. S. Barnes [1973] 127 p. illus. 22 cm. [NK7309.8.C66 1973] 72-5877 ISBN 0-498-01261-1 7.95
1. Jewelry, Victorian. I. Battershill, Norman, joint author. II. Title.

FLOWER, Margaret Cameron Coss. 739.27'09'034
Jewellery, 1837-1901 [by] Margaret Flower. New York, Walker [1969, c1968] 64 p. illus. (part col.) 20 cm. (Collectors' pieces, 15) [NK7310.F55] 69-10394 2.95
1. Jewelry, Victorian. I. Title.

FLOWER, Margaret Cameron Coss. 739.27'0942
Victorian jewellery, by Margaret Flower. With a foreword by Margeret J. Biggs and a chapter on collecting by Doris Langley Moore. New and rev. ed. South Brunswick, A. S. Barnes [1973, c1951] xxviii, 271 p. illus. 26 cm. Bibliography: p. 259-260. [NK7109.F55 1973] 72-6463 ISBN 0-498-01265-4 15.00
1. Jewelry, Victorian. I. Title.

GERE, Charlotte. 739.27'0942
Victorian jewelry design. Chicago, H. Regnery Co. [1973, c1972] 285 p. illus. 25 cm. Bibliography: p. [277] [NK7309.8.G4 1973] 72-11941 12.50
1. Jewelry, Victorian. I. Title.

PETER, Mary. 739.27'0942
Collecting Victorian jewellery. New York, Emerson Books [1971, c1970] 100 p. 63 illus., port. 23 cm. [NK7109.P4 1971] 78-137400 ISBN 0-87523-174-8 5.95
1. Jewelry, Victorian. 2. Jewelry—Collectors and collecting. I. Title. BIP

Jewelry, Victorian—Exhibitions.

JANSON, Dora Jane, 1916- 739.27'09'034074015656
From slave to siren: the Victorian woman and her jewelry, from neoclassic to art nouveau. [Durham? N.C., 1971] xi, 111 p. illus. (part col.) 28 cm. Catalog of an exhibition held at Duke University Art Museum, May 1971. Bibliography: p. [107] -111. [NK7309.8.J35] 77-26363
1. Jewelry, Victorian—Exhibitions. I. Duke University, Durham, N.C. Art Museum. II. Title.

Jewish art and symbolism.

GUTMANN, Joseph. 704.94896
Jewish ceremonial art. New York, T. Yoseloff [1964] 37 p., [60] p. of illus. (part col.) 29 cm. Bibliography: p. 36-37. [N8197.G813] 64-12891
1. Jewish art and symbolism. I. Title.

GUTMANN, Joseph, comp. 704.948
No graven images: studies in art and the Hebrew Bible. New York, Ktav Pub. House [1971] lxiii 599 p. illus. 23 cm. English, German, or French. Includes bibliographical references. [N7416.G8] 70-107000
1. Bible—Pictures, illustrations, etc. 2. Jewish art and symbolism. I. Title.

KANOF, Abram, 1903- 296.4
Jewish ceremonial art and religious observance. New York, Abrams [1970] 253 p. 270 illus. (25 col.) 30 cm. Includes bibliographical references. [NK1672.K34] 69-12798
1. Jewish art and symbolism. I. Title.

Jewish art and symbolism—Exhibitions.

TRADITIONAL ceremonial 745.5
objects and Jewish folk art from the Joseph B. and Olyn Horwitz Judaica Collection, Cleveland Ohio. [Exhibition] Klutznick Exhibit Hall, B'nai B'rith Building, Washington, D.C. [Washington, 1969?] 46 p. illus., ports. 22 cm. [N7417.T7] 79-275288
1. Horwitz, Joseph B.—Art collections. 2. Horwitz, Olyn—Art collections. 3. Jewish art and symbolism—Exhibitions. I. B'nai B'rith.

Jewish crafts.

BECKER, Joyce. 745.5
Hanukkah crafts / by Joyce Becker. New York : Bonim Books, [1978] p. cm. (A Bonim activity book) Includes index. [BM729.H35B4] 78-16744 ISBN 0-88482-763-1 : 9.95. ISBN 0-88482-765-8 pbk. : 6.95
1. Jewish crafts. 2. Hanukkah (Feast of lights) I. Title. BIP

BECKER, Joyce. 745.5'02'4296
Jewish holiday crafts / by Joyce Becker. New York : Bonim Books, c1977. 179 p. : ill. ; 29 cm. (Bonim activity book) Includes index. [BM729.H35B42] 77-7478 ISBN 0-88482-755-0 : 6.95
1. Jewish crafts. 2. Fasts and feasts—Judaism. I. Title.

Jewish way of life in art.

OPPENHEIM, Moritz, d.1882. 759.3
Pictures of traditional Jewish family life / by Moritz Daniel Oppenheim ; with an introd. by Alfred Werner. New York : Ktav Pub. House, 1976. p. cm. (The Library of Jewish art) Translation of Bilder aus dem altjudischen Familienleben. [ND588.O58A4313] 76-41250 ISBN 0-87068-472-8 : 25.00
1. Oppenheim, Moritz, d. 1882. 2. Jewish way of life in art. I. Title.

Jewitt, Thomas Orlando Sheldon, 1799-1869.

CARTER, Harry Graham 761.2
Orlando Jewitt. [New York] Oxford [c.] 1962. 48p. illus. 22cm. Bibl. 63-1345 3.40
1. Jewitt, Thomas Orlando Sheldon, 1799-1869. 2. Architecture, Gothic. I. Title.

Jews—Biography.

JUDAIC Heritage Society. 956.94
An epic in sculpture : the medallic history of the Jewish people / conceived and directed by Robert Weber : text by Fred Bertram ; [photography, Alastair Finlay]. New York : Judaic Heritage Society, 1974. 179 p. : ill. ; 29 cm. Bibliography: p. 178-179. [CJ5793.J4J82 1974] 75-308832
1. Jews—Biography. 2. Medals, Jewish. I. Weber, Robert, 1927- II. Bertram, Fred. III. Title. IV. Title: The medallic history of the Jewish people. BIP

Jews in art.

LANDSBERGER, Franz, 1883- 759.9492
Rembrandt, the Jews and the Bible. Tr. from German by Felix N. Gerson. [2d ed.] Philadelphia, Jewish Publication Society of America, 1961 [c.1946] xviii, 190p. illus. 27cm. Bibl. 61-12367 3.50
1. Rembrandt Hermanszoon van Rijn, 1606-1669. 2. Jews in art. 3. Bible—Pictures, illustrations, etc. I. Title.

STEINBERG, Leo 759.1
Jasper Johns. New York, Wittenborn [1963] 45p. (chiefly illus., pt. col., pt. fold.) port. 33cm. Bibl. 63-23478 2.50 pap.,
1. Johns, Jasper, 1930- I. Title.

Johnson, Eastman, 1824-1906.

HILLS, Patricia. 759.13
The genre painting of Eastman Johnson : the sources and development of his style and themes / Patricia Hills. New York : Garland Pub., 1977. xix, 251 p. : ill. ; 21 cm. (Outstanding dissertations in the fine arts) Thesis—New York University, 1973. Bibliography: p. 179-190. [ND237.J7H53] 76-23627 ISBN 0-8240-2697-7 : 35.00
1. Johnson, Eastman, 1824-1906. 2. Genre painting, American. I. Title. II. Series. BIP

JOHNSON, Eastman, 1824-1906. 759.13
Eastman Johnson; [retrospective exhibition] by Patricia Hills. [1st ed.] New York, C. N. Potter, in association with the Whitney Museum of American Art; distributed by Crown Publishers [1972] xxiii, 126 p. illus. (part col.) 25 cm. Catalog of the exhibition held Mar. 28-May 14, 1972, at the Whitney Museum of American Art, New York; June 7-July 22, 1972, at the Detroit Institute of Arts; Aug. 15-Sept. 30, 1972, at the Cincinnati Art Museum; and Oct. 20-Dec. 3, 1972, at the Milwaukee Art Center. Bibliography: p. 124-126. [ND237.J7H5] 70-186696
I. Hills, Patricia. II. Whitney Museum of American Art, New York.

Johnson, Frank Tenney, 1874-1939.

MCCRACKEN, Harold, 1894- 759.13
The Frank Tenney Johnson book; a master painter of the Old West. [1st ed.] Garden City, N.Y., Doubleday, 1974. 207 p. illus. (part col.) 35 cm. Includes bibliographical references. [ND237.J72M28] 74-2373 ISBN 0-385-00094-4 30.00
1. Johnson, Frank Tenney, 1874-1939. I. Johnson, Frank Tenney, 1874-1939. II. Title. BIP

Johnson, Lester, 1919—

JOHNSON, Lester, 1919- 759.13
The kaleidoscopic crowd : [Lester Johnson paintings, 1970-1974 / introd. by Burt Chernow ; with a statement by Harold Rosenberg]. [New York] : D. Anderson, [1975]. 67, [4] p. : ill. (some col.) ; 22 x 22 cm. Bibliography: p. [71] [ND237.J724C47] 74-34550
1. Johnson, Lester, 1919- 2. Crowds in art. I. Chernow, Burt. II. Title.

Johnson, Philip Cortelyou, 1906-

JACOBUS, John M 720.973
Philip Johnson. New York, G. Braziller, 1962. 127p. illus., port. 26cm. (Makers of contemporary architecture) Bibliography: p. [123]-124. [NA737.J6J3] 62-16264
1. Johnson, Philip Cortelyou, 1906- I. Title. II. Series.

Johnson, Raymond Edward, 1927—

JOHNSON, Raymond Edward, 1927- 700'.92'4
Correspondence : an exhibition of the letters of Ray Johnson : North Carolina Museum of Art, 31 October-5 December, 1976. [Raleigh] : The Museum, [1976?] 1 portfolio (84 leaves : ill.) ; 30 cm. Title from portfolio. [N6537.J63A33] 77-360309 ISBN 0-88259-085-5 pbk. : 5.00
1. Johnson, Raymond Edward, 1927- 2. Artists—United States—Correspondence—Exhibitions. I. North Carolina. Museum of Art, Raleigh. BIP

Johnson, William J., 1860-1942—Art patronage.

CHILCOTT, Nicholas. 704'.75 B
A champion of American art / by Nicholas Chilcott. 1st ed. Chicago : Adams Press, c1975. x, 101 p. : ill. ; 18 cm. [N5220.J73C47] 75-20784
1. Johnson, William J., 1860-1942—Art patronage. 2. Paintings, American. 3. Paintings, Modern—19th century—United States. 4. Paintings, Modern—20th century—United States. I. Title.

Johnston, David Claypoole, 1797-1865.

JOHNSON, Malcolm, 1939- 709.24
David Claypool Johnston, American graphic humorist, 1798-1865; [catalog. Lunenburg, Vt., Printed at the Stinehour Press, 1970] 47 p. illus. 23 cm. "An exhibition held jointly by the American Antiquarian Society ... [and others] in March, 1970." [NC1429.J63J6] 77-19841
1. Johnston, David Claypoole, 1797-1865. I. American Antiquarian Society, Worcester, Mass. II. Title. BIP

TATHAM, David. 769'.924
A note about David Claypoole Johnston with a check list of his book illustrations. [Syracuse? N.Y.] 1970. 16 p. illus., 3 ports. 23 cm. Cover title. "First published in 1970 at Syracuse University in the Courier, nos. 34 and 35 ... Reprinted with addenda to the check list and with additional reproductions of Johnston's illustrations." [NC975.5.J6T3] 79-281685
1. Johnston, David Claypoole, 1797-1865. 2. Johnston, David Claypoole, 1797-1865—Bibliography. I. Title.

Johnston, Edward, 1872-1944.

JOHNSTON, Priscilla, 1910- 745.6'1'0924 B
Edward Johnston / by Priscilla Johnston. 2nd ed. London : Barrie and Jenkins, 1976. 316 p., [20] p. of plates : ill., facsims., ports. ; 23 cm. Text on lining papers. Includes index. Bibliography: p. [14] [NK3631.J63J63 1976] 76-377127 ISBN 0-214-20253-4 : £5.25. ISBN 0-214-20295-X pbk.
1. Johnston, Edward, 1872-1944. 2. Calligraphers—Great Britain—Biography. BIP

Johnston, Frances Benjamin, 1864-1952.

JOHNSTON, Frances Benjamin, 1864-1952. 779'.092'4 B
A talent for detail: the photographs of Miss Frances Benjamin Johnston, 1889-1910 / by Pete Daniel and Raymond Smock. New York : Harmony Books, [1974] 182 p. : chiefly ill. ; 22 x 28 cm. "All photographs ... from the Prints and Photographs Division of the Library of Congress." Includes index. [TR140.J64A34 1974] 74-79780 ISBN 0-517-51642-X : 15.00
1. Johnston, Frances Benjamin, 1864-1952. 2. Photography—Portraits. 3. Photography, Documentary. I. Daniel, Pete. II. Smock, Raymond. III. United States. Library of Congress. Prints and Photographs Division. IV. Title.

Johnston, Henrietta (Deering)

MIDDLETON, Margaret Simons. 741'.0924
Henrietta Johnston of Charles Town, South Carolina; America's first pastellist. Columbia, University of South Carolina Press, 1966. xvi, 88 p. illus., ports. 24 cm. Map on lining paper. Includes music. "Notes and references": p. 75-77. [NC139.J6M5] 66-25276
1. Johnston, Henrietta (Deering) BIP

Johnston, James, 1738-1808.

LAWRENCE, Alexander A 1906- 655.4758
James Johnston, Georgia's first printer. With decorations & remarks on Johnston's work by Ray Dilley. Savannah, Pigeonhole Press, 1956. 54p. illus. facsims. 24cm. Bibliographical references included in 'Notes' (p. [45]-54) [Z232.J7L3] 57-18403
1. Johnston, James, 1738-1808. I. Title.

Johnston, Mary Elizabeth, 1890—Art collections.

CINCINNATI. Art Museum. 759.06'074'017178
The Mary E. Johnston Collection. [Cincinnati] 1972. 86 p. illus. (part col.) 26 cm. [N6447.C56 1972] 73-170354
1. Johnston, Mary Elizabeth, 1890—Art collections. 2. Cincinnati. Art Museum. 3. Art, Modern—19th century—Catalogs. 4. Art, Modern—20th century—Catalogs. 5. Art—Cincinnati—Catalogs. I. Title.

Johnston, Randolph Wardell, 1904—

JOHNSTON, Randolph Wardell, 1904- 730'.92'4 B
Artist on his island : a study in self-reliance / by Randolph W. Johnston ; with notes by Denny Johnston. Park Ridge, N.J. : Noyes Press, [1976] c1975. 186 p. : ill. ; 23 cm. [N6537.J66A22] 75-34929 ISBN 0-8155-5042-1 : 8.95
1. Johnston, Randolph Wardell, 1904- 2. Artists—United States. 3. Artists—Bahamas—Great Abaco Island. I. Title.

Jones, David Michael, 1895—

BLAMIRES, David Malcolm. 760'.092'4
David Jones: artist and writer [by] David Blamires. [Toronto] University of Toronto Press, 1972. viii, 220 p. illus. 23 cm. Bibliography: p. 207-213. [PR6019.O53Z6 1972] 77-190341 ISBN 0-8020-1877-7 10.00
1. Jones, David Michael, 1895-

Jones, Herschel Vespasian, 1861-1928—Art collections.

MINNEAPOLIS. Institute of Arts. 760'.074'0176579
The Jones Collection; the bequests of Herschel V. and Tessie Jones [exhibited at] the Minneapolis Institute of Arts, December 12, 1968-February 9, 1969. [Minneapolis, c1968] 1 v. (chiefly illus.) 28 cm. [N5220.J74M5] 68-59312
1. Jones, Herschel Vespasian, 1861-1928—Art collections. 2. Jones, Tessie—Art collections. 3. Art—Exhibitions. I. Title.

Jones, Howard W., 1922—

ST. Louis Art Museum. 730'.92'4
Mid-America invitational: Howard Jones and Arthur Osver. St. Louis exhibition dates: June 26 to July 29, 1973; Kansas City exhibition dates: August 14 to September 16, 1973. St. Louis, Mo., [1973] [32] p. illus. 24 cm. Title from p. [2] of cover. "Co-sponsored by the Nelson Gallery-Atkins Museum, Kansas City, Missouri." [NB237.J58S25] 74-151287
1. Jones, Howard W., 1922- 2. Osver, Arthur, 1912- I. Jones, Howard W., 1922- II. Osver, Arthur, 1912- III. William Rockhill Nelson Gallery of Art and Mary Atkins Museum of Fine Arts, Kansas City, Mo. IV. Title.

Jones, Inigo, 1573-1652.

GOTCH, John Alfred, 1882-1942. 720'.924 B
Inigo Jones. New York, B. Blom, 1968. xi, 271 p. illus., port. 24 cm. Reprint of the 1928 ed. "References and notes": p. 237-245. [NA997.J7G6 1968] 68-20224
1. Jones, Inigo, 1573-1652.

SUMMERSON, John Newenham, Sir 1904- 720.924 (B)
Inigo Jones, by John Summerson. [Baltimore] Penguin, 1966. [i.e. 1967] 149p. illus. (incl. port.) plans. 20cm. (Architect and society) Pelican bk. A839. Bibl. [NA997.J7.S8 1966] 2.25 pap.,
1. Jones, Inigo, 1573-1652. I. Title.

Jones, John Paul, Nov. 18, 1924-

BROOKLYN Institute of Arts and Sciences. Museum. 769.973
John Paul Jones: prints and drawings, 1948-1963 [Text by Una E. Johnson, curator of prints and drawings. Brooklyn, Author, 1963] 62p. illus., port. 23cm. (Amer. graphic artists of the twentieth cent. Monograph no. 1) Bibl. 63-5886 2.00
1. Jones, John Paul, Nov. 18, 1924- I. Johnson, Una E. II. Title. III. Series.

Jones, Lois Mailou.

JONES, Lois Mailou. 759.13
Reflective moments; retrospective 1930-1972. [Boston, 1973] [43] p. illus. 24 cm. Exhibition held Mar. 11-Apr. 15, 1973 at the Museum of the National Center of Afro-American Artists and museum of Fine Arts, Boston. Bibliography: p. [43] [ND237.J76N37] 75-307999
1. Jones, Lois Mailou. I. National Center of Afro-American Artists. Museum. II. Boston. Museum of Fine Arts.

Jong, Hans de, 1932—

ACHTERBERGH, J. W. N. van. 738.2'0924
Omtrent bakbeesten en vuurlanders : overzichtstentoonstelling ceramiek van Hans de Jong, Museum Boymans-Van Beuningen, Rotterdam 10.10-21.11.76 / [tekst, J. W. N. van Achterbergh ; foto's, Dick Wolters]. [Rotterdam : Museum Boymans-Van Beuningen], 1976. 42 p. : ill. ; 25 cm. Bibliography: p. 24. [NK4210.J615A25] 77-461946
1. Jong, Hans de, 1932- 2. Pottery, Dutch—Exhibitions. I. Jong, Hans de, 1932- II. Rotterdam. Museum Boymans-Van Beuningen.

Jongkind, Johan Barthold, 1819-1891.

CUNNINGHAM, Charles Crehore. 759.4'22
Jongkind and the Pre-Impressionists : painters of the Ecole Saint-Simeon : Smith College Museum of Art, Northampton, Massachusetts, October 15-December 5, 1976, Sterling and Francine Clark Art Institute, Williamstown, Massachusetts, December 17, 1976-February 13, 1977 / Charles C. Cunningham, with Susan D. Peters and Kathleen Zimmerer. [Williamstown, Mass.] : The Institute, c1977. 167 p. : ill. ; 26 cm. Bibliography: p. 163-167. [ND547.5.S24C86] 77-73073
1. Jongkind, Johan Barthold, 1819-1891. 2. Saint-Simeon school of painting. 3. Painting, French—Exhibitions. 4. Painting, Modern—19th century—France—Exhibitions. I. Peters, Susan D., joint author. II. Zimmerer, Kathleen, joint author. III. Smith College. Museum of Art. IV. Sterling and Francine Clark Art Institute, Williamstown, Mass. V. Title.

Jonson, Raymond, 1891—

GARMAN, Ed. 759.13
The art of Raymond Jonson, painter / Ed Garman ; foreword by Elaine de Kooning. 1st ed. Albuquerque : University of New Mexico Press, c1976. xx, 199 p., [4] leaves of plates : ill. (some col.) ; 27 cm. Includes bibliographical references and index. [ND237.J77G37] 75-21185 ISBN 0-8263-0404-4 : 15.00
1. Jonson, Raymond, 1891- I. Title. BIP

Jonzen, Karin, 1914—

JONZEN, Karin, 1914- 730'.92'4
Karin Jonzen, sculptor / foreword by Norman St John-Stevas ; introduction by Carel Weight. London : Bachman and Turner, 1976 80 p. : chiefly ill., ports. ; 26 cm. [NB497.J63A48] 77-363177 ISBN 0-85974-055-2 : £4.50
1. Jonzen, Karin, 1914- I. Title.

Jordaens, Jakob, 1593-1678.

HULST, roger Adolf d' 741.9'493
Jordaens drawings / [text by] R. A. d'Hulst ; [translated from the Dutch MS. by P. S. Falla]. London ; New York : Phaidon Press, 1974 [i.e.,1975] 4 v. (3-687 p. [644] p. of plates) : ill. ; 27 cm. (Monographs of the Nationaal Centrum voor de Plastische Kunsten van de XVIde en XVIIde Eeuw ; 5) Based on the author's De tekeningen van Jakob Jordaens. Includes bibliographical references and indexes. [NC266.J67H84]

Heinz Ronner, Sharad Jhaveri, Alessandro Vasella. Boulder, Colo. : Westview Press, [1977] p. cm. Bibliography: p. [NA737.K32R66] 76-41392 ISBN 0-89158-648-2 : 39.50
1. Kahn, Louis I., 1901-1974. I. Jhaveri, Sharad, joint author. II. Vasella, Alessandro, joint author.

SCULLY, Vincent Joseph, 1920- 720.973
Louis I. Kahn. New York, G. Braziller, 1962. 127 p. illus., port., plans. 27 cm. (Makers of contemporary architecture) Bibliography: p. [122]-127. [NA737.K32S38] 62-16265
1. Kahn, Louis I., 1901- I. Title. II. Series. BIP

Kairwan, Mosque of Sidi Okba.

SEBAG, Paul 726.209611
The Great Mosque of Kairouan. Tr. from French by Richard Howard. Photos. by Andre Martin. London, Collier-Macmillan; New York, Macmillan, c.1965. 125p. illus. (pt. col.) plans. 24x26cm [NA6089.K2S43] 64-12211 9.95
1. Kairwan, Mosque of Sidi Okba. I. Martin, Andre, photographer. II. Title.

Kaish, Luise.

KAISH, Luise. 730'.92'4
Sculpture. New York, Jewish Museum [1973] 24 p. illus. 25 cm. Text by A. Kampf. Catalogue of an exhibition held Oct. 2-Dec. 2, 1973 at the Jewish Museum, New York. Includes bibliographical references. [NB237.K27K35] 73-87735
1. Kaish, Luise. I. Kampf, Avram. II. Jewish Theological Seminary of America. Jewish Museum.

Kalish, Max, 1891-1945.

KALISH, Alice. 730'.924
Max Kalish as I knew him. Los Angeles, 1969. 91 l. illus., ports. 28 cm. [NB237.K3K3] 75-285206
1. Kalish, Max, 1891-1945. I. Title.

Kamara, Kadiato.

REINHARDT, Loretta. 301.2'08 s
Mrs. Kadiato Kamara, an expert dyer in Sierra Leone / Loretta Reinhardt. [Chicago] : Field Museum of Natural History, 1976. p. 11-33 : ill. ; 24 cm. (Fieldiana : Anthropology ; v. 66, no. 2 ISSN 0071-4739s) (Publication - Field Museum of Natural History ; 1230) Caption title. Bibliography: p. 33. [GN2.F4 vol. 66, no. 2] [TT853] 667'.3'09664 76-11369
1. Kamara, Kadiato. 2. Dyes and dyeing—Sierra Leone. I. Title. II. Series: Field Museum of Natural History, Chicago. Publication ; 1230. III. Series: Fieldiana : Anthropology ; v. 66, no. 2.

Kamekura, Yusaku, 1915—

KAMEKURA, Yusaku, 1915- 741.6'092'4
The graphic design of Yusaku Kamekura. With a foreword by Herbert Bayer, an essay by Masaru Katsumi, and comments by the designer. [1st ed.] New York, Weatherhill [1973] 188 p. (chiefly illus., part col.) 25 x 26 cm. Translation of Kamekura Yusaku sakuhinshu. [NC999.6.J3K3413] 72-89446 ISBN 0-8348-1704-7 19.50
1. Kamekura, Yusaku, 1915- I. Title.

Kaminaljuyu, Guatemala—Addresses, essays, lectures.

TEOTIHUACAN and 972.81
Kaminaljuyu : a study in prehistoric culture contact / edited by William T. Sanders and Joseph W. Michels. [University Park] : Pennsylvania State University Press, c1977. 467 p. : ill. ; 29 cm. (Pennsylvania State University Press monograph series on Kaminaljuyu) Includes bibliographies. [F1435.1.K3T46] 77-21061 ISBN 0-271-00529-7 : 12.95
1. Kaminaljuyu, Guatemala—Addresses, essays, lectures. 2. Teotihuacan, Mexico—Addresses, essays, lectures. 3. Indians of Central America—Guatemala—Antiquities—Addresses, essays, lectures. I. Sanders, William T. II. Michels, Joseph W. III. Title. IV. Series. BIP

Kaminaljuyu, Guatemala—Antiquities—Addresses, essays, lectures.

THE Ceramics of 738.3'7
Kaminaljuyu, Guatemala / edited by Ronald K. Wetherington. University Park : Pennsylvania State University Press, [1978] p. cm. (The Pennsylvania State University Press monograph series on Kaminaljuyu) [F1435.1.K3C47] 77-14661 ISBN 0-271-00537-8 : 12.95
1. Kaminaljuyu, Guatemala—Antiquities—Addresses, essays, lectures. 2. Guatemala—Antiquities—Addresses, essays, lectures. 3. Mayas—Pottery—Addresses, essays, lectures. 4. Indians of Central America—Pottery—Addresses, essays, lectures. I. Wetherington, Ronald K.

Kandinsky, Wassily, 1866-1944.

BOVI, Arturo. 759.4
Kandinsky [translated from the Italian] London, New York, Hamlyn, 1971. 94 p. illus. (chiefly col.), ports. 32 cm. (Twentieth century masters) Translation of Vassilij Kandinskij. "Distributed in the U.S. by Crown Publishers Inc." Bibliography: p. 93-94. [ND699.K3B613] 73-330994 ISBN 0-600-35303-6 £2.25
1. Kandinsky, Wassily, 1866-1944. I. Kandinsky, Wassily, 1866-1944.

BRION, Marcel, 1895- 759.7
Kandinsky. New York, Abrams [1962] 94p. col. illus. (Student5s ser. of great artists) 61-11937 1.95
1. Kandinsky, Wassili, 1866-1944. I. Title.

DERKATSCH, Inessa I. 701.17
Wassily Kandinsky's theory of the identity of realism and abstraction in his essay: Uber die Formfrage, by Inessa I. Derkatsch. Berkeley, University of California, 1967. 51 l. 29 cm. Bibliography: leaves 49-51. [N7430.K35D4] 68-1532
1. Kandinsky, Wassily, 1866-1944. 2. Form (Aesthetics) I. Title.

DOELMAN, Cornelius 759.7
Wassily Kandinsky. [Tr.: Albert J. Fransella] New York, Barnes & Noble [c.1964] 90p. illus. (pt. col.) port. 18cm. (Barnes & Noble art ser., no. 617) 64-56936 .75 pap.,
1. Kandinsky, Wassily, 1866-1944. I. Title.

GROHMANN, Will, 1887-1968. 759.7
Wassily Kandinsky. New York, H. N. Abrams [1971] 24 p. illus. (part col.) 38 cm. (The Library of great painters. Portfolio ed.) [ND699.K3G683] 71-130285 ISBN 0-8109-3039-0
1. Kandinsky, Wassily, 1866-1944.

GROHMANN, Will, 1887-1968. 759.7
Wassily Kandinsky: life and work. [Translated from the German by Norbert Guterman] New York, H. N. Abrams [1958] 428 p. illus. (part mounted col.) ports. 30 cm. Bibliography: p. 413-425. [ND699.K3G693] 58-13479
1. Kandinsky, Wassily, 1866-1944.

KANDINSKY, Wassily, 1866-1944. 769'.92'4
The graphic work of Kandinsky; a loan exhibition. Introd. and catalogue by Hans Konrad Roethel. Pref. by Thomas M. Messer. Foreword by Michael Petzet. [Washington, International Exhibitions Foundation, c1973] 87 p. illus. (part col.) 28 x 27 cm. Participating museums: The Solomon R. Guggenheim Museum and others. Includes bibliographical references. [NE678.K25R62] 73-92745 8.95 (pbk.)
1. Kandinsky, Wassily, 1866-1944. I. Rothel, Hans Konrad, 1909- II. International Exhibitions Foundations. III. Solomon R. Guggenheim Museum, New York. IV. Title. BIP

KANDINSKY, Wassily, 1866-1944. 759.7
Kandinsky (1866-1944) With an introd. and notes by Herbert Read New York, G. Wittenborn [1959] 24 p. illus. (part mounted col.) 31 cm. [ND699.K3R5] 59-4378
I. Read, Herbert Edward, Sir, 1893-1968.

KANDINSKY, Wassily, 1866-1944. 759.7
Kandinsky: Parisian period, 1934-1944. Essays by Gaetan Picon, Rose-Carol Washton, and Nina Kandinsky. [New York] M. Knoedler [1969] 59 p. illus. (part col.), ports. 22 cm. Catalog of an exhibition at the M. Knoedler & Co., inc., New York, Oct. 21-Nov. 22, 1969. Includes bibliographical references. [ND699.K3P49] 78-105559
I. Picon, Gaetan. II. Washton, Rose-Carol. III. Kandinsky, Nina. IV. Knoedler (M.) and Company, inc. V. Title.

KANDINSKY, Wassily, 1866-1944. 759.7
Vasily Kandinsky, 1866-1944, in the collection of the Solomon R. Guggenheim Museum, New York. [New York, Solomon R. Guggenheim Foundation, 1972] 1 v. (unpaged) illus. (part col) 28 cm. On spine: Kandinsky at the Guggenheim Museum. "Exhibition 72/4." Includes bibliography. [ND699.K3S65] 72-77738
I. Solomon R. Guggenheim Museum, New York. II. Title: Kandinsky at the Guggenheim Museum.

KANDINSKY, Wassily, 1866-1944. 759.7
Watercolors, drawings, writings. With an essay by Jean Cassou. [Translated by Norbert Guterman] New York, Abrams [1961] 51 p. illus., col. plates. 33 cm. The plates are detachable, and two slip-in frames are provided in pocket. [ND1978.K3A53] 61-13854

LASSAIGNE, Jacques, 1910- 759.7
Kandinsky; biographical and critical study. Tr. from French by H. S. B. Harrison [Geneva] Skira [dist. Cleveland, World, c.1964] 131p. mounted col. illus. 19cm. (Taste of our time, v.41) Bibl. 63-23078 6.75
1. Kandinsky, Wassily, 1866-1944. I. Title.

OVERY, Paul. 759.7
Kandinsky: the language of the eye. New York, Praeger Publishers [1969] 192 p. illus., plates (part col.) 29 cm. Bibliography: p. 187. [ND699.K3O9 1969] 70-83261 20.00
1. Kandinsky, Wassily, 1866-1944. I. Title.

SOLOMON R. Guggenheim Museum, New York. 759.7
Vasily Kandinsky, 1866-1944. a retrospective exhibition. Loan exhibition organized by the Solomon R. Guggenheim Museum. New York [1962] 105 p. illus. (part col.) port. 28 cm. Catalog of the exhibition which opened in Pasadena, January 1963, and is to be circulated to 10 American citites. Bibliography: p. 103-105. [ND699.K3S63] 62-22344
1. Kandinsky, Wassily, 1866-1944. I. Title.

SOLOMON R. Guggenheim Museum, New York. 759.7
Vasily Kandinsky, 1866-1944; a retrospective exhibition, The Solomon R. Guggenheim Museum, New York in collaboration with Musee national d'art moderne, Paris; Gemeente Museum, den Haag; Kunsthalle, Basel. [New York, Solomon R. Guggenheim Foundation, 1962] 126 p. illus. (part col.) port. 28 cm. Catalog of the exhibition at the Guggenheim Museum, Jan.-Apr. 1963, later to be circulated in Europe. Bibliography: p. 121-123. [ND699.K3S64] 62-19253
1. Kandinsky, Wassily, 1866-1944. I. Title.

SOLOMON R. Guggenheim Museum, New York. 759.7
Vasily Kandinsky: painting on glass; Hinterglasmalerei Anniversary exhibition [at] the Solomon R. Guggenheim Museum, New York. [New York, S. R. Guggenheim Foundation, 1966] 15, [33] p. illus. (part col.) port. 26 cm. Cover title: Kandinsky, painting on glass. Catalogue of exhibition 66/6 held Dec. 1966 through Feb. 1967. An exhibit of works belonging chiefly to the Stadtische Galerie in Munich. Text by Hans Konrad Rothel, translated by Alfred Werner. Bibliographical references included in "Notes" (p. 15) [NK5398.K25S6] 66-30562
1. Kandinsky, Wassily, 1866-1944. I. Rothel, Hans Konrad, 1909- II. Munich. Stadtische Galerie. III. Title: Painting on glass.

WEISS, Peg. 759.7
Kandinsky in Munich : the formative Jugendstil years / by Peg Weiss. Princeton, N.J. : Princeton University Press, c1978. p. cm. [ND699.K3W43] 78-51203 ISBN 0-691-03934-8 : 30.00
1. Kandinsky, Wassily, 1866-1944. 2. Art nouveau—Germany, West—Munich. I. Title. BIP

Kane, John, 1860-1934.

ARKUS, Leon Anthony, 1915- comp. 759.13
John Kane, painter. [Pittsburgh] University of Pittsburgh Press [1971] xi, 343 p. illus. (part col.), ports. 29 cm. Contents.Contents.—Sky hooks; the autobiography of John Kane, as told to M. McSwigan.—A catalogue raisonne of Kane's paintings, by L. A. Arkus.—Bibliography (p. 337-338) [ND237.K16A8] 72-134488 ISBN 0-8229-3217-2 19.95
1. Kane, John, 1860-1934. I. McSwigan, Marie. II. Kane, John, 1860-1934. Sky hooks. 1971. III. Arkus, Leon Anthony, 1915- A catalogue raisonne of Kane's paintings. 1971. IV. Title: Sky hooks. V. Title: A catalogue raisonne of Kane's paintings. BIP

Kano, Eitoku, 1543-1590.

KANO, Eitoku, 1543-1590. 759.952
Kano Eitoku / Tsuneo Takeda ; translated and adapted by H. Mack Horton and Catherine Kaputa. 1st ed. Tokyo ; New York : Kodansha International, 1977. 178 p. : ill. (some col.) ; 27 cm. (Japanese arts library ; v. 3) Includes index. Bibliography: p. [169]-174. [ND1059.K17T3413] 76-44155 ISBN 0-87011-295-3 : 15.00
1. Kano, Eitoku, 1543-1590. 2. Painters—Japan—Biography. I. Takeda, Tsuneo, 1925- II. Title. III. Series. BIP

Kansas. University. Museum of Art.

CURRY, David Park. 746.3'074'018165
Stitches in time : samplers in the Museum's collection : [an exhibition] March 2-April 6, 1975 / introd. and catalogue by David Park Curry. [Lawrence] : University of Kansas, Museum of Art, [1975] [48] p. : ill. ; 38 x 15 cm. (Miscellaneous publication of the Museum of Art ; no. 98) Bibliography: p. [46]-[47] [NK9101.L38K362] 75-4278
1. Kansas. University. Museum of Art. 2. Samplers—Lawrence, Kan.—Exhibitions. I. Kansas. University. Museum of Art. II. Title. III. Series: Kansas. University. Museum of Art. Miscellaneous publications ; no. 98.

KANSAS. University. Museum of Art. 746.9'7
150 years of American guilts. [Lawrence] 1973. [56] p. illus. 26 cm. (Its Miscellaneous publications, no. 90) Bibliography: p. [52]-[54] [NK9102.L42K364 1973] 73-622705
1. Kansas. University. Museum of Art. 2. Coverlets, American—Catalogs. 3. Coverlets—Lawrence, Kan.—Catalogs. I. Title. II. Series.

Kant, Immanuel—Aesthetics.

KNOX, Israel, 1904- 701
The aesthetic theories of Kant, Hegel, and Schopenhauer. New York, Humanities Press, 1958. 219 p. 23 cm. Issued in 1966 as thesis, Columbia University. [[B2799]] A63
1. Hegel, Georg Wilhelm Friedrich. 1770-1831. Schopenhauer, Arthur, 1788-1860. 2. Kant, Immanuel—Aesthetics. 3. Aesthetics. I. Title. BIP

Catharina, 1741-1807. 2. Painters—Switzerland—Biography. I. Williamson, George Charles, 1858-1942, joint author.

Kaufman, Paul, 1920—

KAUFMAN, Paul, 1920—   779'.092'4
Double exposure / by Paul Kaufman and Ruth Lisa Schechter. 1st ed. New York : Barlenmir House, c1978. [48] p. : ill. ; 29 cm. [TR654.K367] 78-58414 ISBN 0-87929-066-8 : 12.95
1. Kaufman, Paul, 1920- 2. Photography, Artistic. I. Schechter, Ruth Lisa, joint author. II. Title.

Kautzky, Theodore, 1896-1953.

KINGHAN, Charles R   741.973
Ted Kautzky, master of pencil and watercolor, by Charles R. Kinghan, assisted by Kenneth Reid. New York, Reinhold Pub. Corp. [1959] 112p. illus. 27cm. [NC1075.K32K5] 59-14903
1. Kautzky, Theodore, 1896-1953. I. Title.

Kawabata, Minoru, 1911—

KAWABATA, Minoru, 1911-   759.952
Kawabata. [Syracuse, N.Y.] Everson Museum of Art [1974] 20 p. illus. (part col.) 23 cm. Cover title. Catalogue of an exhibition held at the Everson Museum of Art, Syracuse, N.Y., in 1974. Bibliography: p. 18-19. [ND1059.K257E83] 74-77423
1. Kawabata, Minoru, 1911- I. Everson Museum of Art of Syracuse and Onondaga County.

Kay, John, 1742-1826.

*EVANS, Hilary.   709.2
John Kay of Edinburgh; barber, miniaturist and social commentator 1742-1826, [by] Hilary and Mary Evans. Aberdeen, Impulse, 1973. 53 p. illus. 26 cm. [N44]
1. Kay, John, 1742-1826. 2. Artists—Biography and works. I. Evans, Mary, joint author. II. Title.
Distributed by International Publications Service, N.Y., for 22.50.

EVANS, Hilary, 1929-   769'.92'4
John Kay of Edinburgh: barber, miniaturist and social commentator, 1742-1826 [by] Hilary and Mary Evans. Aberdeen, Impulse Publications Ltd, 1973. 53, [97] p. illus., ports. (1 col.) 27 cm. Illus. on lining papers. "Bibliography and iconography": p. 51-53 (1st group). [NE642.K39E92 1973] 74-152868 ISBN 0-901311-28-6 £6.00
1. Kay, John, 1742-1826. 2. Portrait prints—Edinburgh. I. Evans, Mary, 1890- joint author. II. Title.

Keely, Patrick Charles, 1816-1896.

KERVICK, Francis William   927.2
Wynn.
Patrick Charles Keely, architect; a record of his life and work. [South Bend, Ind., Priv. print., 1953] 63p. illus. 26cm. [NA737.K43K4] 53-26750
1. Keely, Patrick Charles, 1816-1896. I. Title.

Keirstead, James Lorimer, 1932—

KEIRSTEAD, James Lorimer,   759.11
1932-
Keirstead; [paintings, edited by Wentworth Henry Smith] Kingston, Ont. [s.n.] c1973. 127 p. chiefly ill. (part col.) 23 cm. [ND249.K4S64] 74-180718
1. Keirstead, James Lorimer, 1932- I. Smith, Wentworth Henry, ed.

Keith, Elizabeth.

OREGON. University.   769'.92'4
Museum of Art.
Elizabeth Keith (1887-1956) : the Orient through Western eyes : an exhibition of works from the Murray Warner Collection in the Museum of Art, University of Oregon, Eugene, Oregon, September 22-November 3, 1974. [Eugene] : The Museum, 1974. [24] p. : ill. ; 22 cm. Bibliography: p. [24] [NE1300.8.G72K446 1974] 74-195089

1. Keith, Elizabeth. 2. Warner, Murray—Art collections. 3. East (Far East) in art. I. Title: The Orient through Western eyes.

Keller, George W., 1842-1935.

RANSOM, David F.   720'.92'4
George Keller, architect / David F. Ransom ; introd. by Barry Hannegan. Hartford, Conn. : Stowe-Day Foundation, c1978. xxxiii, 218 p. : ill. (some col.) ; 28 cm. Includes index. Bibliography: p. 208-210. [NA737.K44R36] 77-14060 ISBN 0-917482-14-X pbk. : 9.95
1. Keller, George W., 1842-1935. 2. Architects—United States—Biography. I. Title.   BIP

Keller, Henry George, 1869-1949.

THE Henry G. Keller   [759.13]
memorial exhibition; catalogue of an exhibition of works by Henry G. Keller, sponsored by the Cleveland Institute of Art and the Cleveland Museum of Art. Held at the Cleveland Museum of Art, February first through March nineteenth, 1950. [Cleveland] Cleveland Museum of Art, 1950. Cleveland [1952] 56 p. 48 plates (incl. port.) 23 cm. [ND237.K44C6] 927.5 50-13110
1. Keller, Henry George, 1869-1949. 2. Paintings, American—Exhibitions. 3. After-dinner speeches. I. Cleveland. Institute of Art. II. Cleveland Museum of Art. III. Title: Friendly speeches.

Kelley, Chapman, 1932—

KELLEY, Chapman, 1932-   759.13
An exhibition of wildflower works by Chapman Kelley, April 18-May 26, 1977, Atelier Chapman Kelley ... Dallas, Texas / foreword by Samuel Shannon Blain, Jr. ; photography by Candice Land ; color photography by Doug Handel. Dallas : Kelley, c1977. 35 p. : ill. (some col.) ; 24 cm. [ND1839.K44A93] 77-150941
1. Kelley, Chapman, 1932- 2. Flowers in art—Exhibitions. 3. Landscape architecture—Texas—Dallas—Exhibitions. I. Atelier Chapman Kelley. II. Title: An exhibition of wildflower works by Chapman Kelley ...

Kelley, Ramon, 1939—

KELLEY, Ramon, 1939-   751.4
Ramon Kelley paints portraits and figures / by Ramon Kelley and Mary Carroll Nelson. New York : Watson-Guptill, [1977]   p.   cm. Includes index. [ND237.K442N44] 77-9919 ISBN 0-8230-4505-6 : 17.50
1. Kelley, Ramon, 1939- 2. Painting—Technique. 3. Portrait painting—Technique. 4. Human figure in art. I. Nelson, Mary Carroll, joint author. II. Title.   BIP

Kelly, Edward, 1854-1880.

MELVILLE, Robert.   759.994
The legend of Ned Kelly, Australia's outlaw hero. Paintings by Sidney Nolan. Text by Robert Melville. Introd. by Alan Moorehead. New York, Viking Press [1964] xiii, 60 p. 27 col. plates. 21 cm. (A Studio book) [ND1105.N6M4] 64-25702
1. Kelly, Edward, 1854-1880. I. Nolan, Sidney, 1917- illus. II. Title.

Kelly, Ellsworth, 1923—

GOOSSEN, E. C.   759.13
Ellsworth Kelly [by] E. C. Goossen. New York, Museum of Modern Art; distributed by New York Graphic Society, Greenwich, Conn. [1973] 127 p. illus. (part col.) 29 cm. Bibliography: p. 117-122. [ND237.K444G66] 72-95077 ISBN 0-87070-414-1 12.50
1. Kelly, Ellsworth, 1923- I. Kelly, Ellsworth, 1923-

KELLY, Ellsworth, 1923-   759.13
Ellsworth Kelly. Text by John Coplans. New York, H. N. Abrams [1972, i.e. 1973] 299 p. illus. (part col.) 28 x 30 cm. Bibliography: p.   295-299.

[ND237.K444C66] 71-101621 ISBN 0-8109-0217-6 28.50
1. Kelly, Ellsworth, 1923- I. Coplans, John.   BIP

KELLY, Ellsworth, 1923-   759.13
Ellsworth Kelly; [an exhibition of paintings & sculpture. New York, Sidney Janis Gallery, 1968] [19] p. (incl. cover) illus. (part col.) 28 cm. Catalogue of an exhibition held Oct. 7-Nov. 2, 1968, at Sidney Janis Gallery, New York. [ND237.K444S52] 73-159593
1. Kelly, Ellsworth, 1923- I. Sidney Janis Gallery.

KELLY, Ellsworth, 1923-   769'.92'4
Ellsworth Kelly; drawings, collages, prints [by] Diane Waldman. Greenwich, Conn., New York Graphic Society [1971] 288 p. illus. (part col.) 32 cm. (A Paul Bianchini book) Bibliography: p. 284-287. [N6537.K38W3 1971] 70-155489 ISBN 0-8212-0382-7 30.00
1. Waldman, Diane.

Kelly, Harold Osman, 1884-1956.

JOHNSON, William Weber,   927.5
1909-
Kelly blue. Foreword by Tom Lea. [1st ed.] Garden City, N. Y., Doubleday, 1960. 263 p. illus. 22 cm. [ND237.K445J6] 60-8875
1. Kelly, Harold Osman, 1884-1956. I. Title.   BIP

JOHNSON, William Weber,   927.5
1909-
Kelly Blue. Foreword by Tom Lea. Lincoln, University of Nebraska Press [1974, c1960] 263 p. 21 cm. (A Bison book) [ND237.K445J6] ISBN 0-8032-5795-3. 2.95 (pbk.)
1. Kelly, Harold Osman, 1884-1956. I. Title.
L.C. card number for original ed.: 60-8875.

JOHNSON, William Weber,   759.13 B
1909-
Kelly blue / William Weber Johnson ; foreword by Tom Lea. College Station : Texas A&M University Press, [1979]   p.   cm. Reprint of the 1960 ed. published by Doubleday, Garden City, N.Y. [ND237.K445J6 1979] 78-21773 ISBN 0-89096-073-9 : 14.95
1. Kelly, Harold Osman, 1884-1955. 2. Painters—United States—Biography. I. Title.

Kelmscot Press.

BROWN University.   655.14213
Library.
William Morris and the Kelmscott Press; an exhibition held in the Library of Brown University, Providence, Rhode Island, from October 9 to December 31, 1959. To which is appended an address by Philip C. Duschnes before the friends of the Library of Brown University, December 7, 1959. Providence, 1960. 44p. 16plates (incl. facsims.) 27cm. 'Some references and acknowledgments': p. 49. [Z232.M87B7] 60-4517
1. Morris, William, 1834-1896. 2. Kelmscot Press. I. Title.

Kemp-Welch, Lucy, 1869-1958.

MESSUM, David.   759.2 B
The life and work of Lucy Kemp-Welch / by David Messum ; edited by Laura Wortley. [Woodbridge] : Antique Collectors' Club, 1976. 111 p. : ill. (some col.), ports. ; 29 cm. Includes catalogue of the L. Kemp-Welch Studio Collection exhibited at the David Messum Gallery, Spring 1976. Ill. on lining papers. [ND497.K446M47] 77-360045 ISBN 0-902028-43-X : 30.00
1. Kemp-Welch, Lucy, 1869-1958. 2. Painters—Great Britain—Biography. 3. Animals in art. I. Kemp-Welch, Lucy, 1869-1958. II. David Messum Gallery. The Lucy Kemp-Welch studio collection. 1976. III. Title.
Distributed by Antique Collectors' Club 1515 Broadway, New York

Kempe, Carl—Art collections.

GYLLENSVARD, Bo.   739.2
Chinese gold, silver, and porcelain: the Kempe Collection. [New York] Asia Society; distributed by New York Graphic Society [1971] 135 p. illus. 22 cm. "An Asia House Gallery publication." Catalogue of an exhibition circulated by the International Exhibitions Foundation and shown in the Asia House Gallery, and other participating museums, spring 1971. Bibliography: p. 84-85. [NK7183.A1G9] 79-152378 ISBN 0-87848-036-6
1. Kempe, Carl—Art collections. 2. Gold articles, Chinese—Exhibitions. 3. Silver articles, Chinese—Exhibitions. 4. Porcelain, Chinese—Exhibitions. I. Asia House Gallery, New York. II. International Exhibitions Foundation. III. Title.

Ken-Amun.

DAVIES, Norman de   913.32'03'1
Garis, 1865-1941.
The tomb of Ken-Amun at Thebes. With plates in color by Norman de Garis Davies, H. R. Hopgood, and Nina de Garis Davies. New York, 1930. [New York] Arno Press, 1973. 2 v. in 1 illus. 32 cm. Reprint of the ed. published by the Museum, which was issued as v. 5 of the Publications of the Metropolitan Museum of Art Egyptian Expedition. At head of title: The Metropolitan Museum of Art Egyptian Expedition. All the plates in this reprint are in black and white. Includes bibliographical references. [DT73.T3D29 1973] 78-168401 ISBN 0-405-02235-2 39.00
1. Ken-Amun. 2. Thebes, Egypt—Tombs. I. Title. II. Series: New York (City). Metropolitan Museum of Art. Egyptian Expedition. Publications, v. 5.

Kennebunkport, Me.—Description—Views.

LOWRY, Lois.   779'.9'974195
Here in Kennebunkport / photos. by Lois Lowry ; text by Frederick H. Lewis. 1st ed. [Kennebunkport, Me.] : Durrell Publications ; Brattleboro, Vt. : distributed by the S. Greene Press, c1978. [95] p. : chiefly ill. ; 23 cm. [F29.K32L68] 78-108790 ISBN 0-911764-20-8 : 4.95
1. Kennebunkport, Me.—Description—Views. 2. Historic buildings—Maine—Kennebunkport—Pictorial works. I. Lewis, Frederick H. II. Title.   BIP

Kennedy Galleries, inc., New York.

KENNEDY   758'.2'07401471
Galleries, inc., New York.
Important marine paintings. New York : Kennedy Galleries, 1976. 24 p. : chiefly ill. ; 24 cm. Cover title. [ND1370.K4 1976] 77-353308
1. Kennedy Galleries, inc., New York. 2. Marine painting—Catalogs. I. Title.

KENNEDY Galleries,   769'.074'01471
inc., New York.
The Kennedy Galleries collection of fine graphics; [catalogue] New York [1974] 47 p. illus. 28 cm. [NE53.N7K464 1974] 74-178222
1. Kennedy Galleries, inc., New York. 2. Prints—New York (City)—Catalogs. I. Title.

Kennedy, John Fitzgerald, Pres. U.S., 1917-1963.

KELEN, Emery, 1896-   769
Stamps tell the story of John F. Kennedy. New York, Meredith Press [1968] 122 p. illus., ports. 24 cm. Bibliography: p. 120. The life of the thirty-fifth President of the United States, as commemorated in stamps issued in countries around the world. Includes description of the stamps. [HE6183.K44] AC 68
1. Kennedy, John Fitzgerald, Pres. U.S., 1917-1963. 2. Postage stamps—Topics—Kennedy, John Fitzgerald, Pres. U.S. 1917-1963. I. Title.

NEW York. Museum of Modern Art 779
A. Kertesz, photographer. Introd. essay by John Szarkowski. [Dist. Garden City, N.Y., Doubleday, c.1964] 63p. illus. 23cm. Bibl. [TR140.K4N4] 64-66100 2.95 pap.,
1. Kertesz, Andre. 2. Photography, Artistic. I. Szarkowski, John. II. Title. III. Title: A. Kertesz, photographer.

Kestner (Firm)

SMITH, Patricia R. 688.7'22
Kestner and Simon & Halbig dolls, 1804-1930 / by Patricia R. Smith ; edited by Tyral Jane Weiss ; photos. by Dwight F. Smith. Paducah, Ky. : Collector Books, c1976. 96 p. : col. ill. ; 22 cm. Bibliography: p. 96. [NK4894.2.K47S64] 76-150225 ISBN 0-89145-022-X : 7.95
1. Kestner (Firm) 2. Simon und Halbig. 3. Dolls—Germany—Catalogs. 4. Dolls—Collectors and collecting—United States. I. Title. BIP

Kevin Roche, John Dinkeloo and Associates.

KEVIN Roche, John 720'.973
Dinkeloo and Associates, 1962-1975 / pref. by J. Irwin Miller ; introd. by Henry-Russell Hitchcock ; edited and photographed by Yukio Futagawa. New York : Architectural Book Pub. Co., 1977, c1975. p. cm. English, French, and German. [NA737.K46K48 1977] 76-30849 ISBN 0-8038-0123-8 : 49.95
1. Kevin Roche, John Dinkeloo and Associates. 2. Architecture, Modern—20th century—United States. I. Roche, Kevin. II. Dinkeloo, John. III. Futagawa, Yukio, 1932-

Keystone View Company.

GARAI, Bernhard, 1891- 770'.924 (B)
The man from Keystone, by Bert Garai. New York, Living Books [1966] 247 p. illus., ports. 23 cm. Autobiographical. [TR140.G3A3 1966] 66-26818
1. Keystone View Company. I. Title.

Khairaho. India—Descr.

LAL, Kanwar 726.15
Immortal Khajuraho. Delhi. Asia Pr., [Mystic, Conn., Verry, 1966] 253p. 234 plates. 32cm. [NS486.K5L29] SA65 48.50
1. Khairaho. India—Descr. I. Title.

Kharga, Egypt (Oasis). Temple of Hibis.

NEW York (City). Metropolitan Museum of Art. Egyptian Expedition. 913.32
The Temple of Hibis in El Khargeh oasis. [New York] Arno Press, 1973 [c1941] 2 v. in 1. illus. 32 cm. Reprint of pt. 1 (1941) and pt. 2 (1938) of the 3 vol. ed. published by the expedition. Parts 1 and 2 originally issued as v. 13-14 of the expedition's Publications. Contents.Contents.—pt. 1. Winlock, H. E. The excavations.—pt. 2. Evelyn White, H. G. and Oliver, J. H. Greek inscriptions. Includes bibliographies. [DT73.K5N48 1973] 76-168414 ISBN 0-405-02252-2
1. Kharga, Egypt (Oasis). Temple of Hibis. 2. Inscriptions, Greek—Kharga, Egypt (Oasis) I. Winlock, Herbert Eustis, 1884-1950. II. Evelyn-White, Hugh Gerard, d. 1924- III. Oliver, James Henry, 1905- IV. Title. V. Series: New York (City). Metropolitan Museum of Art. Egyptian Expedition. Publications, v. 13-14. BIP

Khmers—Antiq.

BRIGGS, Lawrence Palmer. 959.6
The ancient Khmer Empire. Philadelphia, American Philosophical Society, 1951. 295 p. illus., maps. 30 cm. (Transactions of the American Philosophical Society, new ser., v. 41, pt. 1) Bibliography: p. 262-273. [Q11.P6 n.s., vol. 41, pt. 1] 51-2328
1. Khmers—Antiq. 2. Cambodia—Hist. I. Title. II. Series: American Philosophical Society, Philadelphia. Transactions, new ser., v. 41, pt. 1 BIP

Khrushchev, Nikita Sergeevich, 1894-1971.

JOHNSON, Priscilla. 701.1
Khrushchev and the arts; the politics of Soviet culture, 1962-1964. Documents selected and edited by Priscilla Johnson and Leopold Labedz. Cambridge [Mass.] M. I. T. Press [1965] xv, 300 p. illus. 25 cm. [DK276.J6] 64-8311
1. Khrushchev, Nikita Sergeevich, 1894-1971. 2. Russia—Intellectual life. I. Title. BIP

Kibel, Wolf, 1903-1938.

SOUTH African National Gallery, Cape Town. 760'.092'4
Wolf Kibel : retrospective exhibition = oorsig-tentoonstelling : 1976 : [catalogue / compiled by the South African National Gallery]. [Cape Town : The Gallery], 1976. [24] p. : ill. (some col.) ; 19 x 26 cm. English and Afrikaans. [N7396.K5S68] 77-364650
1. Kibel, Wolf, 1903-1938. I. Kibel, Wolf, 1903-1938.

Kierkegaard, Soren Aabye, 1813-1855—Aesthetics.

GEORGE, Arapura Ghevarghese, 1928- 701.17
The first sphere; a study in Kierkegaardian aesthetics. New York, Asia Pub. [dist. Taplinger, 1966,c.1965] x, 80p. 19cm. Bibl. [B4378.E75G4] 66-5738 5.25
1. Kierkegaard, Soren Aabye, 1813-1855—Aesthetics. I. Title. BIP

Kilns.

GREGORY, Ian, 1942- 738.1'3
Kiln building / by Ian Gregory. New York : Watson-Guptill Publications, 1977. p. cm. (Ceramic skillbooks) Includes bibliographical references and index. [TT924.G73 1977] 77-2321 ISBN 0-8230-0590-9 : 7.95
1. Kilns. I. Title. II. Series. BIP

RHODES, Daniel, 1911- 666'.4'3
Kilns; design, construction, and operation. [1st ed.] Philadelphia, Chilton Book Co. [1968] viii, 240 p. illus., plans. 26 cm. Bibliography: p. [233]-234. [TP841.R] 68-575
1. Kilns. I. Title. BIP

RHODES, Daniel, 1911- 666'.4'3
Kilns; design, construction, and operation. [1st ed.] Philadelphia, Chilton Book Co. [1968] viii, 240 p. illus., plans. 26 cm. Bibliography: p. [233]-234. [TP841.R48] 68-57512
1. Kilns. I. Title.

Kilns—Design and construction.

FOURNIER, Robert L., 1915- 681'.7666
Electric kiln construction for potters / Robert Fournier ; photos. by John Anderson ; diagrams by Sheila Fournier. New York : Van Nostrand Reinhold, 1977. 144 p. : ill. ; 24 cm. Includes index. Bibliography: p. 141. [TT924.F68 1977] 76-54001 ISBN 0-442-30134-0 : 10.95
1. Kilns—Design and construction. I. Title. BIP

Kilns, Rotary.

AZBE, Victor J 666.3
Rotary kiln, its performance evaluation and development. St. Louis. Azbe Publications, 1956?] 89p. illus. 29cm. [TP841.A9] 56-3093
1. Kilns, Rotary. I. Title.

Kimball, Charles Frederick, 1831-1903.

KIMBALL, Charles Frederick, 1831-1903. 769'.92'4
Etchings. [Waterville? Me., 1965?] [10] l. illus. 21 x 28 cm. Cover title. Catalog of exhibitions held in May and July 1965, Colby College of Art Museum and Portland Museum of Art. [NE2012.K56C64] 74-166152
1. Kimball, Charles Frederick, 1831-1903. I. Colby College, Waterville, Me. Art Museum. II. Portland Museum of Art. III. Title.

Kimball, Fiske, 1888-1955.

ROBERTS, George, June26,1900- 927
Triumph on Fairmount. Fiske Kimball and the Philadelphia Museum of Art, by George and Mary Roberts. [1st ed.] Philadelphia, Lippincott [1959] 321p. illus. 22cm. [N8375.K5R6] 59-9327
1. Kimball, Ss094n5y 9sk5(0, 1888-1955. 2. Philadelphia Museum of Art. I. Roberts, Mary (Howland) joint author. II. Title.

Kindergartens—Bibliography.

BARTHOLOMEW, Robert. 016.3092'08 s
Indoor and outdoor space for children in nursery-kindergarten programs. Monticello, Ill. [Council of Planning Librarians] 1973. 15 p. 29 cm. (Council of Planning Librarians. Exchange bibliography, 502) Cover title. [Z5942.C68 no. 502] [Z5814.K5] 016.725'57 74-185020 1.50
1. Kindergartens—Bibliography. 2. Nursery schools—Bibliography. 3. School facilities—Bibliography. I. Title. II. Series.

Kinetic art.

BRETT, Guy. 709.04
Kinetic art. London, Studio-Vista; New York, Rienhold 1968. 96p. illus. 20 x 17cm. Bibl. [N6494.K5B7] 68-16035 5.50
1. Kinetic art. I. Title.

ROUKES, Nicholas. 702'.8
Plastics for kinetic art. New York, Watson-Guptill Publications, [1974] 175 p. illus. (part col.) 29 cm. Bibliography: p. 172-173. [N6494.K5R68] 73-21607 ISBN 0-8230-4029-1 15.95
1. Kinetic art. 2. Plastics as art materials. I. Title. BIP

Kinetic art—Exhibitions.

CINCINNATI. Art Museum. 700
Laser light; a new visual art. [Exhibition] organized by the Cincinnati Art Museum and the Laser Laboratory of the University of Cincinnati Medical Center, Cincinnati Art Museum, November 12 through December 14, 1969. [Cincinnati, 1969] 32 p. illus. (part col.), ports. 28 cm. Bibliography: p. 13. [N6494.K5C5] 76-11150
1. Kinetic art—Exhibitions. 2. Light in art. I. Cincinnati. University. Laser Laboratory. II. Title.

HULTEN, Karl Gunnar Pontus, 1924- 709'.22
The machine, as seen at the end of the mechanical age [by] K. G. Pontus Hulten. New York, Museum of Modern Art; distributed by New York Graphic Society, Greenwich, Conn. [1968] 216 p. illus. (part col.) 25 cm. Catalogue of an exhibition to be held at the Museum of Modern Art, Nov. 25, 1968-Feb. 9, 1969; University of St. Thomas, Houston, Mar. 25-May 18, 1969; and San Francisco Museum of Art, June 23-Aug. 24, 1969. Includes bibliographical references. [N6494.K5H8] 68-17130
1. Kinetic art—Exhibitions. 2. Machinery—Exhibitions. I. New York. Museum of Modern Art. II. Houston, Tex. University of St. Thomas. III. San Francisco. Museum of Art. IV. Title.

MILWAUKEE. Art Center. 709.04
Options. [Exhibition] Milwaukee Art Center, June 22 through August 18, 1968 [and] Museum of Contemporary Art, Chicago, September 14 through October 20, 1968. [Milwaukee, Printed by the E. F. Schmidt Co., 1968] 85 p. illus. 28 cm. (Directions 1) "[Exhibition] organized by the Milwaukee Art Center and sponsored by the Jos. Schlitz Brewing Company, in conjunction with the Friends of Art for The Lakefront Festival of the Arts." [N6494.K5M5] 72-454
1. Kinetic art—Exhibitions. I. Museum of Contemporary Art, Chicago. II. Title. III. Series.

Kinetic art—Juvenile literature.

MARKS, Mickey Klar. 702'.8
Op-tricks; creating kinetic art. Kinetics by Edith Alberts. Photographed by David Rosenfeld. [1st ed.] Philadelphia, Lippincott [1972] 40 p. illus. 21 x 26 cm. Step-by-step instructions, accompanied by photographs, for creating art that "tricks" the eye and gives the illusion of movement in painting. [N6494.K5M37] 79-38550 ISBN 0-397-31217-2 (lib. bdg.)
1. Kinetic art—Juvenile literature. I. Alberts, Edith, illus. II. Rosenfeld, David, 1907- illus. III. Title.

Kinetic sculpture.

CHICHURA, Diane B., 1932- 735'.29
Super sculpture; using science, technology, and natural phenomena in sculpture [by] Diane B. Chichura and Thelma K. Stevens. New York, Van Nostrand Reinhold [1974] 79 p. illus. 28 cm. Bibliography: p. 79. [NB1272.C49] 73-16703 ISBN 0-442-21542-8
1. Kinetic sculpture. I. Stevens, Thelma K., 1932- joint author. II. Title. BIP

King, Charles Bird, 1785-1862.

VIOLA, Herman J. 759.13
The Indian legacy of Charles Bird King / Herman J. Viola. 1st ed. Washington : Smithsonian Institution Press, c1976. 152 p. : ill. (some col.) ; 29 cm. (Smithsonian Institution Press publication ; no. 6256) "Catalog of War Department Indian Gallery": p. 143-145. Includes index. Bibliography: p. 146-148. [ND237.K53V56] 76-15022 19.95
1. King, Charles Bird, 1785-1862. 2. Indians of North America—Portraits. 3. Indians of North America—Government relations—1789-1869. I. Title. BIP

King County Rural Library District.

VEBLEN, Marthanna E. 727'.8
Giant strides since Andrew Carnegie : creative architecture in the King County Library System / by Marthanna E. Veblen. 1st ed. Seattle, Wash. : Shorey Book Store, 1974, c1975. 81 p., [4] fold. leaves of plates : ill. ; 22 cm. Limited to 200 copies. Bibliography: p. 81. [Z679.V35 1975] 76-350140 ISBN 0-8466-0309-8 : 6.00
1. King County Rural Library District. 2. Library architecture—King Co., Wash. I. Title. BIP

King, Heath.

KING, Heath. 730'.92'4
Sculpture. [Winston-Salem, N.C., Hunter Pub. Co., 1973] [89] p. illus., 56 plates. 24 cm. [NB237.K52A56] 74-153435
1. King, Heath.

Kings and rulers in art.

LEVEY, Michael. 759.9'4
Painting at court. [New York] New York University Press [1971] 228 p. 177 illus., 7 col. plates. 28 cm. (Wrightsman lectures, 5) "Based on lectures given at the Metropolitan Museum, New York, in 1968." Includes bibliographical references. [ND1140.L46 1971b] 75-124528 ISBN 0-8147-4950-X 15.00
1. Kings and rulers in art. 2. Painting—Psychological aspects. I. Title. II. Series. BIP

Kings and rulers in art—Juvenile literature.

COEN, Rena Neumann 704.94
Kings and queens in art. Designed by Robert Clark Nelson. Minneapolis, Lerner [c.1965] 61p. illus., (pt. col.) ports. 26cm. [N8219.K5C6] 64-8042 3.79 bds.,
1. Kings and rulers in art—Juvenile literature. I. Title. BIP

King's Inns, Dublin. Library.

DE BRUN, Padraig, 1889- 016.091
Catalogue of Irish manuscripts in the King's Inn Library, Dublin. Dublin, Dublin

SUBJECT INDEX KITCHENS—REMODELING.

Institute for Advanced Studies, 1972. xviii, 105 p. 22 cm. Includes bibliographical references. [Z6621.K4753173] 74-157738
1. King's Inns, Dublin. Library. 2. Manuscripts, Irish—Catalogs. I. Title.

King's Lynn, Eng.—Description—Views.

VINTAGE King's Lynn / 942.6'13
[compiled] by Michael Winton. Nelson : Hendon Publishing Co., 1976. 44 p. : chiefly ill., ports. ; 21 x 29 cm. [DA690.K5V56] 77-360767 ISBN 0-86067-008-2 : £1.40
1. King's Lynn, Eng.—Description—Views. 2. King's Lynn, Eng.—Social life and customs—Pictorial works. I. Winton, Michael J., 1939-

Kino, Eusebio Francisco, 1644-1711.

LOS Angeles. Southwest Museum. 701
Padre Kino, memorable events in the life and times of the immortal priest-colonizer of the Southwest depicted in drawings by DeGrazia. With commentaries on the artist and his work by noted authorities on southwestern history and art. Los Angeles, 1962. 54 p. illus., map. 27 cm. [NC139.D4L6] 62-53443
1. Kino, Eusebio Francisco, 1644-1711. 2. DeGrazia, Ted Ettore, 1909- I. Title.

Kinsey, Darius, 1869-1945.

†BOHN, Dave. 770'.92'2
Kinsey, photographer : a half century of negatives by Darius and Tabitha May Kinsey, with contributions by son and daughter, Darius, Jr., and Dorothea / produced by Dave Bohn and Rodolfo Petschek. San Francisco : Chronicle Books, 1977, c1975. p. cm. Contents.Contents.—v. 1. The family album & other early work.—v. 2. The magnificent years. Bibliography: p. [TR140.K45B64 1977] 78-1029 ISBN 0-87701-107-9 : 19.95
1. Kinsey, Darius, 1869-1945. 2. Kinsey, Tabitha May, 1875-1963. 3. Photographers—United States—Biography. 4. Lumbering—Washington (State)—Pictorial works. I. Petschek, Rodolfo, joint author. II. Title. BIP

BOHN, Dave. 770'.92'4
Kinsey, photographer : a half century of negatives by Darius and Tabitha May Kinsey, with contributions by son and daughter, Darius, Jr. and Dorothea / produced by Dave Bohn and Rodolfo Petschek. San Francisco : Scrimshaw Press, 1975. 2 v. (319 p.) : ill. ; 34 cm. Contents.Contents.—v. 1. The family album & other early work.—v. 2. The magnificent years. Bibliography: p. 312-314. [TR140.K45B64] 74-32263 ISBN 0-912020-35-0(v.1) 150.00(boxed set) ISBN 0-912020-36-9(v.2) : 150.00 (boxed set)
1. Kinsey, Darius, 1869-1945. 2. Kinsey, Tabitha May, 1875-1963. 3. Lumbering—Washington (State)—Pictorial works. I. Petschek, Rodolfo, joint author. II. Title.

Kirchner. Ernst Ludwig, 1880-1938.

DUBE-HEYNIG, Annemarie. 769.924
Kirchner, his graphic art. Greenwich, Conn., New York Graphic Society [1966, c1961] 160 p. 96 illus. (part col.) 33 cm. Based on thesis, Gottingen University. Bibliography: p. 156. [NE654.K4D813] 65-26842
1. Kirchner, Ernst Ludwig, 1880-1938. I. Title.

GORDON, Donald E. 759.3
Ernst Ludwig Kirchner [by] Donald E. Gordon. Cambridge, Mass., Harvard University Press, 1968. 475 p. illus., plates (part col.) 30 cm. Bibliography: p. [441]-447. [ND588.K47G62] 68-25610 40.00
1. Kirchner, Ernst Ludwig, 1880-1938. BIP

GROHMANN, Will, 1887- 759.3
E. L. Kirchner. [English translation by Ilse Falk] New York, Arts, inc. [1961] 163p. illus. (part mounted col.) plates (part col.) 30cm. Bibliography: p. 159-163. [ND588.K47G73] 61-15347
1. Kirchner. Ernst Ludwig, 1880-1938. I. Title.

KIRCHNER, 769.924
his graphic art. Greenwich, Conn., New York Graphic Society [1966, c1961] 160 p. 96 illus. (part col.) 33 cm. Based on thesis, Gottingen University. Bibliography: p. 156. [NE654.K4D813] 65-26842
1. Kirchner, Ernst Ludwig, 1880-1938.

KIRCHNER, Ernst Ludwig, 1880-1938. 760'.0924
Ernst Ludwig Kirchner; a retrospective exhibition. By Donald E. Gordon. [Boston, Museum of Fine Arts]; distributed by New York Graphic Society, Greenwich, Conn. [1968] 174 p. 148 illus. (part col.) 26 cm. Exhibitions held at Seattle Art Museum, Pasadena Art Museum, and Museum of Fine Arts, Boston. Bibliography: p. 168-174. [ND588.K47G6] 68-27633 12.50
I. Gordon, Donald E. II. Seattle. Art Museum. III. Pasadena, Calif. Art Museum. IV. Boston. Museum of Fine Arts.

NORTH Carolina. Museum of Art, Raleigh. 759.3
E. L. Kirchner, German expressionist; a loan exhibition, January 10th through February 9th, 1958. Catalogue by W. R. Valentiner. Raleigh [1958] 131p. illus. (part col.) 27cm. Bibliography: p. 51- 52. [ND588.K47N6] 59-2148
1. Kirchner, Ernst Ludwig, 1880-1938. I. Valentiner, Wilhelm Reinhold 1880- II. Title.

Kirlian photography.

DAVIS, Mikol. 778.3
Rainbows of life : the promise of Kirlian photography / Mikol Davis, Earle Lane. 1st Harper colophon ed. New York : Harper & Row, 1978. 93 p., [8] leaves of plates : ill. ; 21 cm. (Harper colophon books ; CN 624) Includes index. Bibliography: p. 83-85. [TR760.D38 1978] 78-110969 ISBN 0-06-090624-3 : 6.95
1. Kirlian photography. I. Lane, Earle, joint author. II. Title. BIP

JOHNSON, Kendall. 778.3
The living aura : radiation field photography and the Kirlian effect / Kendall Johnson ; with a foreword by Thelma Moss. New York : Hawthorn Books, c1975. x, 178 p., [4] leaves of plates : ill. (some col.) ; 29 cm. Includes bibliographical references and index. [TR760.J63 1975] 73-19377 ISBN 0-8015-4312-6 : 15.00
1. Kirlian photography. I. Title.

JOHNSON, Kendall. 778.3
Photographing the nonmaterial world / Kendall Johnson ; with a foreword by Thelma Moss. New York : Hawthorn Books, 1977, c1975 x, 178 p. : ill. ; 29 cm. Includes bibliographical references and index. [TR760.J64 1977] 77-151106 ISBN 0-8015-5871-9 pbk. : 7.95
1. Kirlian photography. I. Title.

Kirlian photography—Congresses.

WESTERN Hemisphere Conference on Kirlian Photography Acupuncture and the Human Aura 2d New York 1973. 778.3
The energies of consciousness : explorations in acupuncture, auras, and Kirlian photography / edited by Stanley Krippner and Daniel Rubin. New York : Gordon and Breach, c1975. xvi, 244 p., [2] leaves of plates : ill. ; 24 cm. (Social change series) "An Interface book." Bibliography: p. 235-243. [TR760.W47 1973] 74-29390 ISBN 0-677-05190-5 : 12.95
1. Kirlian photography—Congresses. 2. Acupuncture—Congresses. 3. Aura—Congresses. I. Krippner, Stanley, 1932- II. Rubin, Daniel. III. Title. BIP

Kissing in art.

THE Kiss / 704.94'9'392
[picture research by Miriam Friedman]. New York : Universe Books, 1976. 95 p. : chiefly col. ill. ; 21 x 22 cm. [N8219.K57K58] 76-5091 ISBN 0-87663-238-X : 7.95 ISBN 0-87663-947-3 pbk. : 4.95
1. Kissing in art. 2. Art. I. Friedman, Miriam, 1951- II. Universe Books.

Kitagawa, Utamaro, 1753?-1806.

HILLIER, Jack Ronald. 769.952
Utamaro: colour prints and paintings. [New York] Phaidon Publishers; distributed by New York Graphic Society, Greenwich, Conn. [1961] 161 p. illus. (part mounted col.) 31 cm. Bibliography: p. 160-161. [NE1325.K5H5] 61-65605
1. Kitagawa, Utamaro, 1753?-1806.

KITAGAWA, Utamaro, 1753?-1806 769'.924
Utamaro, by Muneshige Narazaki. Sadao Kikuchi. Tr. by John Bester. [1st ed.] Tokyo, Palo Alto, Calif., Kodansha Intl. [c.1968] 96p. illus. (pt. col.) 27cm. (Masterworks of Jkiyo-e, 4) [NE1325.K5N33] 68-26556 4.75; 3.50 pap.,
I. Narazaki, Muneshige, 1904- II. Kikuchi, Sadao, Sadao, 1924- III. Title. IV. Series. BIP

Kitchen cabinets.

BRANN, Donald R. 684.1'6
How to build kitchen cabinets, by Donald R. Brann. Briarcliff Manor, N.Y., Directions Simplified [1967] c1966. 67 p. illus., plans. 23 cm. (Easi-bild simplified directions, 658) Published in 1972 under title: How to build kitchen cabinets, room dividers, and cabinet furniture. Page 50, blank for "Notes." [TT197.B765] 65-27708 1.00
1. Kitchen cabinets. I. Title.

BRANN, Donald R. 684.1'6
How to build kitchen cabinets, room dividers, and cabinet furniture / Donald R. Brann. Rev. ed. Briarcliff Manor, N.Y. : Directions Simplified, c1978. 98 p. : ill. ; 23 cm. (Easi-bild ; 658) [TT197.B765 1978] 78-104640 ISBN 0-87733-658-X : 2.50
1. Kitchen cabinets. 2. Cabinet-work. I. Title.

BRANN, Donald R. 645'.4
How to build kitchen cabinets, room dividers, and cabinet furniture, by Donald R. Brann. Briarcliff Manor, N.Y., Directions Simplified, c1972. 96 p. illus. 23 cm. (East-bild, 658/667) First published in 1967 under title: How to build kitchen cabinets. [TT197.B765 1972] 78-129277 1.50
1. Kitchen cabinets. 2. Cabinet-work. I. Title. BIP

GUNERMAN, Milton John, 1906- 684
How to build modern kitchen cabinets; complete instructions, working drawings, and lists of materials for the eleven most popular styles in sizes to suit any kitchen ... [3d ed.] New York, Home Craftsman Pub. Corp., 1952. unpaged. illus. 29 cm. [TT197.G85 1952] 52-2408
1. Kitchen cabinets. I. Title.

STEVENSON, Robert Presley. 684.1'6
How to build and buy cabinets for the modern kitchen, by Robert P. Stevenson. Working drawings by Richard J. Meyer. Rev. [and enl.] ed. New York, Arco Pub. Co. [1974] 262 p. illus. 27 cm. Previous editions published under title: How to build cabinets for the modern kitchen. [TT197.S73 1974] 72-85680 ISBN 0-668-03454-8 10.00
1. Kitchen cabinets. I. Title. BIP

STEVENSON, Robert Presley. 684
How to build cabinets for the modern kitchen. Working drawings by Richard Meyer. New York, Simmons-Boardman Pub. Corp. [1954] 246 p. illus. 27 cm. [TT197.S73] 54-12444
1. Kitchen cabinets. I. Title.

STEVENSON, Robert Presley. 684.16
How to build cabinets for the modern kitchen, by R. P. Stevenson. Working drawings by Richard J. Meyer. [Rev. ed.] New York, Arco Pub. Co. [1966] 256 p. illus. 28 cm. [TT197.S73] 66-15142
1. Kitchen cabinets. I. Title.

Kitchens.

AMERICAN builder. 747.7
Book of modern kitchens, compiled from the pages of American builder magazine. New York, Simmons-Boardman Pub. Corp., 1958. 120p. illus. 29cm. [NA8330.A5] 58-10983
1. Kitchens. 2. Interior decoration. I. Title. II. Title: Modern kitchens.

BRETT, James, 1927- 728
The kitchen : 100 solutions to design problems / by James Brett. New York : Whitney Library of Design, 1977. 207 p. : ill. ; 32 cm. Includes index. [NA8330.B77] 77-22240 ISBN 0-8230-7320-3 : 25.00
1. Kitchens. I. Title. BIP

CONRAN, Terence. 643'.3
The kitchen book / by Terence Conran. New York : Crown Publishers, 1977. p. cm. Includes index. [NK2117.K5C66] 77-7059 ISBN 0-517-53131-3 : 30.00
1. Kitchens. 2. Kitchen utensils. 3. Interior decoration. I. Title. BIP

CONWAY, Charlotte. 747.7
How to plan your kitchen. New York, Greenberg, c1955. 96 p. illus. 21 cm. (Room-by-room decorating series) [NK2117.C6] 55-9036
1. Kitchens. 2. Interior decoration. I. Title.

GALVIN, Patrick J. 728.3
Kitchen planning guide for builders and architects, by Patrick J. Galvin. [1st ed.] Farmington, Mich., Structures Pub. Co., 1972. 199 p. illus. 29 cm. [TX653.G35] 72-86396 ISBN 0-912336-03-X 20.00
1. Kitchens. I. Title.

GALVIN, Patrick J. 728
Kitchen planning guide for builders, designers, and architects / by Patrick J. Galvin. 2d ed. Farmington, Mich. : Structures Pub. Co., c1978. p. cm. First ed. published in 1972 under title: Kitchen planning guide for builders and architects. Includes index. [NA8330.G35 1978] 77-25423 ISBN 0-912336-57-9 : 24.95
1. Kitchens. I. Title.

GILLIATT, Mary. 747'.797
Kitchens and dining rooms [by] Mary Gilliatt. Photos. by Brian Morris [and others] New York, Viking Press [1970] 120 p. illus. (part col.) 24 x 25 cm. (A Studio book) [NK2117.K5G5 1970b] 75-125245 ISBN 0-670-41413-1 12.95
1. Kitchens. 2. Dining rooms. 3. Interior decoration. I. Morris, Brian, illus. II. Title.

HAYES, Babette, 1938- 747'.797'0994
Kitchen design for Australian homes / [by] Babette Hayes. Sydney ; New York : Hamlyn, 1975. 96 p. : ill. ; 27 cm. [NA8330.H37] 76-355688 ISBN 0-600-07351-3
1. Kitchens. 2. Architecture, Domestic—Australia. I. Title.

PRIZEMAN, John. 643.3
Kitchens: design, layout and equipment. London, Macdonald & Co., in association with the Council of Industrial Design, 1966. [1], 65 p. illus., table, diagrs. 21 cm. 7/6 (B 66-2434) "A Design Centre publication." Bibliography: p. 64. [NA8330.P7] 66-74521
1. Kitchens. I. Title.

SALM, Walter G. 643'.7
Remodeling your kitchen or bathroom, by Walter G. Salm. Greenwich, Fawcett [c1967] 112p. illus. 24cm. (Fawcett bk., 653) [TH4816.S25] 68-2130 .95 pap.,
1. Kitchens. 2. Bathrooms. 3. Dwellings—Remodeling. I. Title. BIP

Kitchens—Remodeling.

BRANN, Donald R. 643'.3
How to modernize a kitchen, by Donald R. Brann. Briarcliff Manor, N.Y., Directions Simplified [1967] 80 p. illus., plans. 23 cm. (Easi-bild simplified directions, 608) [TH4816.B7] 67-16947 1.50
1. Kitchens—Remodeling. I. Title. BIP

NUNN, Richard V. 643'.3
Easy kitchen remodeling / by Richard V. Nunn. Birmingham, Ala. : Oxmoor House, 1975. 96 p. : ill. ; 28 cm. (Family guidebook series) Includes index. [TH4816.N86] 75-12124 pbk. : 1.95
1. Kitchens—Remodeling. I. Title. BIP

SALM, Walter G. 643'.7
Remodeling your kitchen or bathroom [by] Walter G. Salm. New York, Arco, [1968, c1967] 112 p. illus., plans. 24 cm. (Library edition) [TH4816.S25 1968] 68-7669 3.50
1. Kitchens—Remodeling. 2. Bathrooms—Remodeling. 3. Dwellings—Remodeling. I. Title.

Kites.

NEWMAN, Lee Scott. 745.59'2
Kite craft; the history and processes of kitemaking throughout the world [by] Lee Scott Newman [and] Jay Hartley Newman. New York, Crown Publishers [1974] vi, 214 p. illus. 27 cm. Bibliography: p. 211. [TL759.N48 1974] 73-91154 ISBN 0-517-51470-2 8.95
1. Kites. I. Newman, Jay Hartley, joint author. II. Title. BIP

STREETER, Tal. 730'.92'4
Kites: red line in the sky [exhibition] April 30 - May 28, 1972. [Lawrence] University of Kansas Museum of Art [1972] [12] p. illus. 24 cm. ([Kansas. University. Museum of Art] Miscellaneous publication, no. 86) [NB237.S76K36] 72-611767
1. Streeter, Tal. 2. Kites. I. Kansas. University. Museum of Art. II. Title. III. Series: Kansas. University. Museum of Art. Miscellaneous publications, no. 86.

Kites—Juvenile literature.

STOKES, Jack. 745.59'2
Let's make a kite! / By Jack Stokes. New York : H. Z. Walck, c1976. [32] p. : col. ill. ; 26 cm. Directions for making and flying a simple kite. [TL759.5.S77] 75-35476 ISBN 0-679-20325-7 6.95
1. Kites—Juvenile literature. I. Title. BIP

Kitsch.

CELEBONOVIC, Aleksa. 759.05
Some call it Kitsch: masterpieces of bourgeois realism. New York, H. N. Abrams [1974] 197 p. illus. (part col.) 32 cm. The text of the original French manuscript, Chefs-d'oeuvre du realisme bourgeois, was adopted and edited by S. Tolstoi. Bibliography: p. 192-194. [ND192.K54C44] 74-8396 ISBN 0-8109-0233-8
1. Kitsch. 2. Paintings, Modern—19th century. I. Title.

DORFLES, Gillo, 1910- 701.17
Kitsch; the world of bad taste. With special contributions by John McHale [and others] and essays by Clement Greenberg and Hermann Broch. [Editorial assistance on the English-language ed. by Vivienne Menkes. New York, Universe Books [1969] 311 p. illus. (part col.), ports. (part col.) 25 cm. Translation of Il Kitsch. [NX210.D6] 78-93950 ISBN 0-87663-106-5 10.00
1. Kitsch. I. McHale, John. II. Title.

Kitsch—United States.

BROWN, Curtis F. 709'.73
Star-spangled kitsch : an astounding and tastelessly illustrated exploration of the bawdy, gaudy, shoddy mass-art culture in this grand land of ours / Curtis F. Brown. New York : Universe Books, 1975. 202 p. : ill. (some col.) ; 29 cm. Bibliography: p. 200. [NX503.B76] 75-330118 ISBN 0-87663-256-8 : 15.00
1. Kitsch—United States. 2. United States—Popular culture. I. Title. BIP

Kivas.

KING, Patrick. 726
Pueblo Indian religious architecture; a photographic study ... [Salt Lake City, Printed by Planning and Research Associates, 1971] 108 p. illus., map, plans. 22 x 28 cm. "Limited printing of 250 copies." Thesis (M.Arch.)—University of Utah. Bibliography: p. 105-107. [E99.P9K5] 76-27952
1. Kivas. 2. Pueblos. I. Title.

SMITH, Watson, 1897- 913'.008 s
Prehistoric kivas of Antelope Mesa, northeastern Arizona. Cambridge, Mass., Peabody Museum of Archaeology and Ethnology, Harvard University, 1972. x, 162 p. illus. 27 cm. (Papers of the Peabody Museum of Archaeology and Ethnology, Harvard University, v. 39, no. 1. Reports of the Awatovi Expedition, no. 9) Bibliography: p. [161]-162. [E51.H337 vol. 39, no. 1] [E99.P9] 970.4'91'3 72-92005 ISBN 0-87365-115-4
1. Kivas. 2. Pueblo Indians—Art. 3. Antelope Mesa, Ariz.—Antiquities. I. Title. II. Series: Harvard University. Peabody Museum of Archaeology and Ethnology. Papers, v. 39, no. 1. III. Series: Harvard University. Peabody Museum of Archaeology and Ethnology. Awatovi Expedition. Reports, no. 9. BIP

VIVIAN, Gordon. 970.4789
The great kivas of Chaco Canyon and their relationships, by Gordon Vivian and Paul Reiter. Santa Fe, N.M., School of American Research, 1960. v, 112 p. illus., mpas. 28 cm. (Monographs of the School of American Research and the Museum of New Mexico, no. 22) Includes bibliography. [E78.N65V5] 61-62948
1. Kivas. 2. Chaco Canyon, N.M. 3. New Mexico — Antiq. I. Reiter, Paul, 1909-1953, joint author. II. Title. III. Title: (Series: Santa Fe, N.M. Schools of American Research. Monographs, no. 22)

Klee, Paul, 1879-1940.

ARMITAGE, Merle, 1893- 759.9494
5 essays on Klee / by Merle Armitage and others. New York, Distributed by Duell, Sloan & Pearce ['1950] 121 p. illus. 19 cm. On cover: A Merie Armitage book. [ND588.K5A7] 50-10565
1. Klee, Paul, 1879-1940. I. Title.

GILVARRY, James. 741.973
Klee: paintings, drawings and prints by Paul Klee from the James Gilvarry collection. An exhibition at the Krannert Art Museum, College of Fine and Applied Arts, University of Illinois, Champaign, 27 September-25 October 1964. [Champaign] 1964?] 1 v. (unpaged) illus. (part col.) 21 cm. [ND588.K5G54] 64-8500
1. Klee, Paul, 1879-1940. I. Illinois. University. Krannert Art Museum. II. Title.

GROHMANN, Will, 1887- 75.9/494
Paul Klee. [Tr. by Norbert Gutermann] New York, Abrams [1967] 167p. illus. (pt. col.), facsim., ports. 23cm. (Lib. of great painters) Bibl. [ND588.K5G763] 67-14056 15.00
1. Klee, Paul, 1879-1940. I. Title.

GROHMANN, Will, 1887- 741.973
Paul Klee. New York, H. N. Abrams [1954] 441p. illus. (part col.) ports. 30cm. 'Paul Klee: a bibliography, compiled by Hannah Muller Applebaum': p. 428-441. [ND588.K] A 55
1. Klee, Paul, 1879-1940. I. Title. BIP

GROHMANN, Will, 1887-1968. 927.5
Paul Klee. New York, H. N. Abrams [1954?] 448 p. illus., plates (part col.), ports, facsim. 31 cm. Bibliography: p. 432-445. [ND588.K5G75] [ND588] 759.9494 55-3209
1. Klee, Paul, 1879-1940.

HAFTMANN, Werner. 927.5
The mind and work of Paul Klee. New York, Praeger [1954] 213 p. illus. (part col.) 22 cm. (Books that matter) Translation of Paul Klee; Wege bildnerischen Denkens. Bibliography: p. 207-208. [ND588.K5H314 1954a] 759.9494 54-11543
1. Klee, Paul, 1879-1940. I. Title.

JAFFE, Hans Ludwig C. 759.9494
Klee; [text by] Hans L. Jaffe; [translated from the Italian] London, New York, Hamlyn, 1972. 94 p. illus. (chiefly col.), ports. 32 cm. (Twentieth-century masters) Distributed in the USA by Crown Publishers. Includes bibliographical references. [ND588.K5J313] 72-183698 ISBN 0-600-35304-4 £2.25
1. Klee, Paul, 1879-1940.

KLEE, Paul, 1879-1940. 704.9425
Drawings. Introd. by Max Huggler. [1st ed.] Alhambra, Calif., Borden Pub. Co. [1965] (Master draughtsman series) [NC1145.K48A43] 65-9303
1. v. (unpaged) illus. (part col.) 31 cm. I. Title.

KLEE, Paul, 1879-1940. 704.9425
Drawings. Introd. by Max Huggler. [1st ed.] Alhambra, Calif., Borden Pub. Co. [1965] (Master draughtsman series) [NC1145.K48A43] 65-9303
1. v. (unpaged) illus. (part col.) 31 cm. I. Title.

KLEE, Paul, 1879-1940. 759.9494
The inward vision; watercolors, drawings, writings. [Translated from the German by Norbert Guterman] New York, H. N. Abrams [1958] 61 p. (p. 31-61 illus.) 16 col. plates. 33 cm. The plates, inserted in individual framing mats, are removable; 2 additional framing mats in pocket. Translation of Im Zwischenreich. [ND1954.K5A483] 58-9035
I. Title.

KLEE, Paul, 1879-1940. 759.9494
Klee. Text by Robert Fisher. Edited by Theodore Reff. New York, Tudor Pub. Co. [1966] 36 p. 91 col. plates. 18 cm. [ND588.K5R43] 66-10559
1. Fisher, Robert, 1931- II. Reff, Theodore, ed.

KLEE, Paul, 1879-1940. 759.9494
Paul Klee. Text by Will Grohmann. New York, Abrams [1970] 24 p. illus. (part. col.) 33 cm. (The Library of great painters. Portfolio ed.) [ND588.K5G75 1970] 69-14751
I. Grohmann, Will, 1887-

KLEE, Paul, 1879-1940. 759.9494
Paul Klee. Text by Will Grohmann. New York, H. N. Abrams [1969] 40 p. illus. (part col.) 33 cm. (Great art of the ages) [ND588.K5G753] 69-19710 ISBN 0-8109-5121-5
I. Grohmann, Will, 1887-1968.

KLEE, Paul, 1879-1940. 759.9'494
Paul Klee. Text by Werner Schmalenbach. Translated from the German by Susan Bellamy. New York, Crown Publishers [1969] 26 p. illus., 10 col. plates. 30 cm. (The Folio art books) [ND588.K5S2913] 70-92486
I. Schmalenbach, Werner, 1917-

KLEE, Paul, 1879-1940. 760'.092'4
Paul Klee, 1879-1940, in the collection of the Solomon R. Guggenheim Museum, New York. New York : Solomon R. Guggenheim Foundation, 1977. 84 p. : ill. (some col.) ; 29 cm. Cover title: Klee at the Guggenheim Museum. "Publication was prepared by Dr. Louise Averill Svendsen." Bibliography: p. 83-84. [N6888.K55S95] 77-78148 ISBN 0-89207-006-4
1. Klee, Paul, 1879-1940. 2. Solomon R. Guggenheim Museum, New York. I. Svendsen, Louise Averill. II. Solomon R. Guggenheim Museum, New York. III. Title: Paul Klee, 1879-1940, in the collection of the Solomon R. Guggenheim Museum ... IV. Title: Klee at the Guggenheim Museum.

*KLEE, Paul, 1879-1940. 759'.9494
Paul Klee notebooks: volume 2: The nature of nature. Translated by Heinz Norden. New York, George Wittenborn [1973 c1970] 454 p. illus. 23 cm. (Documents of Modern Art Series, vol. 17) Originally published under title: Unendliche Naturgeschichte. [ND588] 73-80771 ISBN 0-8150-0040-5 37.50
1. Klee, Paul, 1879-1940 2. Composition (Art) I. Spiller, Jurg, 1913- ed. II. Title.

KLEE, Paul, 1879-1940. 759.9494
Paul Klee: paintings and watercolors from the Bauhaus years, 1921-1931; [catalog of an exhibition] Des Moines Art Center, September 18-October 28, 1973. Introd by Marianne L. Teuber. [Des Moines, Iowa, Des Moines Art Center, 1973] 1 v. (unpaged) 61 plates (part col.) 22 cm. Includes bibliography. [ND1954.K5D47] 73-86308
1. Klee, Paul, 1879-1940. I. Des Moines Art Center. II. Title.

KLEE, Paul, 1879-1940. 760'.0924
Paul Klee; watercolors, drawings, writings. [Translated from German by Norbert Guterman. 2d ed.] New York, H. N. Abrams [1969] 29 p., 31-62 l. of illus. (part col.) 30 cm. Translation of Im Zwischenreich. [ND1954.K5A483 1969] 69-17498
I. Title. II. Title: Watercolors, drawings, writings.

MESSER, Thomas M. 709'.494
Paul Klee exhibition at the Guggenheim Museum: a post scriptum, by Thomas M. Messer. New York, Solomon R. Guggenheim Museum [1968] viii, 40 p. illus. (part. col.) 22 cm. Bibliography: p. [35] [ND588.K5M38] 68-3293
1. Klee, Paul, 1879-1940. I. Solomon R. Guggenheim Museum, New York. II. Title.

METZGER, Michael M. 438.6'42
Paul Klee [by] Michael M. Metzger. Erika A. Metzger. Boston, Houghton [1967] 87p. illus., port. 22cm. (German cultural readers) In German. Bibl. [ND588.K5M4] 67-2746 1.75 pap.,
1. Klee, Paul, 1879-1940. I. Metzger, Erika A., joint author. II. Title.

PAUL Klee. 759.9494
Translated by Alexander Gode. [A Lee Ault ed.] New York, Viking Press, 1952. 156 p. illus., port. 28 cm. Bibliography: p. 151-156. [ND588.K5G5] 927.5 52-13848
1. Klee, Paul, 1879-1940. I. Giedion-Welcker, Carola.

PIERCE, James Smith. 759.9494
Paul Klee and primitive art / James Smith Pierce. New York : Garland Pub., 1976. 192 p. ; 21 cm. (Outstanding dissertations in the fine arts) Originally presented as the author's thesis, New York University. Bibliography: p. 189-192. [ND588.K5P53 1976] 75-23807 ISBN 0-8240-2001-4 lib.bdg. : 20.00
1. Klee, Paul, 1879-1940. 2. Art, Primitive. I. Title. II. Series. BIP

PLANT, Margaret. 760'.092'4
Paul Klee, figures and faces / Margaret Plant. London : Thames and Hudson, 1978. 208 p. : ill. (some col.) ; 27 cm. Includes bibliographical references and index. [N6888.K55P55] 77-92270 ISBN 0-500-23274-1 : 27.50
1. Klee, Paul, 1879-1940. 2. Human figure in art. 3. Head in art. I. Klee, Paul, 1879-1940. II. Title.
Distributed by W. W. Norton, New York, NY 10036

PONENTE, Nello. 759.3
Klee: biographical and critical study. Translated from the Italian by James Emmons. [Lausanne] Skira; [distributed by World Pub. Co., Cleveland, 1960] 140 p. mounted col. illus. 19 cm. (The Taste of our time, v. 31) Bibliography: p. 123-[129] [ND588.K5P63] 60-8729
1. Klee, Paul, 1879-1940.

RABOFF, Ernest Lloyd. 709
Paul Klee, by Ernest Raboff. Garden City, N.Y., Doubleday, 1968. [28] p. illus. (part col.) 29 cm. (Art for children) (A Gemini-Smith book.) One of a series which explains and includes reproductions of the work of artists. Here text explains purpose, symbolism, and technique in fifteen color works and sixteen black and white sketches of Paul Klee. [ND588.K5R3] AC 68
1. Klee, Paul, 1879-1940. I. Title.

SAN Lazzaro, Gualtieri di. 927.5
Klee; a study of his life and work. Translated from the Italian by Stuart Hood. New York, Praeger [1957] 304 p. illus. (part col.) 22 cm. "Klee's writings [books illustrated by him, and principal exhibitions of his works]": p. 281-284. Bibliography: p. 284-286. [ND588.K5S26] 759.9494 57-11232
1. Klee, Paul, 1879-1940.

SPILLER, Jurg. 759.9494
Paul Klee. New York, Barnes & Noble [1962, c1961] 90 p. illus. (part col.) port. 18 cm. (Barnes & Noble art series) [ND588.K5S63] 62-52818
1. Klee, Paul, 1879-1940. I. Title.

Klee, Paul, 1879-1940—Catalogs.

KLEE, Paul, 1879-1940. 759.9494
Klee / [text by] Douglas Hall. Oxford : Phaidon, 1977. 16 p., [48] p. of plates : col. ill. ; 31 cm. Bibliography: p. 16. [ND588.K5A4 1977a] 77-80140 ISBN 0-7148-1803-8 : 7.95

SUBJECT INDEX KNATHS, KARL, 1891

1. Klee, Paul, 1879-1940—Catalogs. I. Hall, Douglas, 1926-

Klee, Paul, 1879-1940—Exhibitions.

KLEE, Paul, 1879-1940 760'.0924
Paul Klee; oils, watercolors, gouaches, drawings, prints from the James Gilvarry Collection. Presented at the Art Gallery, Univ. of Calif., Santa Barbara, October 5 to Nov. 12, 1967. [Santa Barbara, Calif. 1967] 64p. illus. (pt. col.) 26cm. Text by Ala Story. Bibl. [ND588.K5S7] 67-65563 pap., price unreported.
I. Story, Ala. II. Gilvarry, James. III. California. University, Stanta Barbara. Art Gallery. IV. Title.

KLEE, Paul, 1879-1940. 759.9494
Paul Klee; three exhibitions: 1930, introd. by Alfred H. Barr, Jr.; 1941, statements by the artist, articles by Alfred H. Barr, Jr. [and others] edited by Margaret Miller; 1949, introd. by James Thrall Soby. Reprint ed., with a new pref. by Monroe Wheeler. New York, Published for the Museum of Modern Art by Arno Press, 1968. 1 v. (various pagings) illus., port. 27 cm. This volume combines the catalogues of three of the five Klee exhibitions held at the museum; the 1941 exhibition is a reprint of the 9145, 2d rev. and enl. ed. Includes bibliographies. [ND588.K5A49 1968] 68-57298
I. New York. Museum of Modern Art.

KLEE, Paul, 1879-1940. 759.9'494
Paul Klee, 1879-1940; a retrospective exhibition [n.p., Printed by Sterlip Press for the Trustees of the Solomon R. Guggenheim Foundation, New York, 1967] 126 p. (chiefly illus., part col., port.) 28 cm. "Organized by the Solomon R. Guggenheim Museum in collaboration with the Pasadena Art Museum." "Participating institutions: Pasadena Art Museum [and others]" [ND588.K5S613 1967b] 67-19740
I. Solomon R. Guggenheim Museum, New York. II. Pasadena, Calif. Art Museum.

KLEE, Paul, 1879-1940. 759.9494
Paul Klee, 1879-1940, a retrospective exhibition. The Solomon R. Guggenheim Museum, New York, [2nd and rev. ed. New York, 1967] 146 p. (chiefly illus., part col.) 28 cm. "Exhibition 67/1. February-April 1967." [ND588.K5S613 1967] 67-17810
I. Solomon R. Guggenheim Museum, New York. II. Title.

†KLEE, Paul, 1879-1940. 759.9494
Paul Klee, the late years, 1930-1940 : an exhibition at the Serge Sabarsky Gallery, fall 1977. New York : The Gallery, c1977. 92 p. : ill. (some col.) ; 25 cm. [ND588.K5A4 1977] 77-80395 8.00
1. Klee, Paul, 1879-1940—Exhibitions. I. Serge Sabarsky Gallery. II. Title.
Publisher's address : 987 Madison Ave., New York, NY 10021

Klee, Paul, 1879-1940—Juvenile literature.

RABOFF, Ernest Lloyd. 760'.0924 (j)
Paul Klee, by Ernest Raboff. Garden City, N.Y., Doubleday, 1968. 1 v. (unpaged) illus. (part col.) 29 cm. (Art for children) (A Gemini-Smith book.) [ND588.K5R3] 68-26550 3.95
1. Klee, Paul, 1879-1940—Juvenile literature.

Kleiber, Hans, 1887-1967.

FORREST, James Taylor, 1921- 760'.0924
Hans Kleiber; artist of the Big Horns [by James T. Forrest] Big Horn, Wyo., Bradford Brinton Memorial, 1968. 14 p. illus., group port. 23 cm. [N6537.K55F6] 73-243389
1. Kleiber, Hans, 1887-1967. I. Title.

MYGATT, Emmie D. 709'.73
Hans Kleiber, artist of the Big Horn Mountains / by Emmie D. Mygatt and Roberta Cheney. Caldwell, Idaho : Caxton Printers, 1975. p. cm. [N6537.K55M94] 741.9'73 75-12294 ISBN 0-87004-247-5 : 17.95
1. Kleiber, Hans, 1887-1967. I. Cheney, Roberta Carkeek, joint author. II. Kleiber, Hans, 1887-1967. III. Title.

Klein, Yves, 1928-1962.

JEWISH Theological Seminary of America. Jewish Museum. 709'.44
Yves Klein. [Exhibition held at] the Jewish Museum, New York, January 25 through March 12, 1967. Texts by Kynaston McShine, Pierre Descargues [and] Pierre Restany. Wtih extracts from Yves Klein's The monochrome adventure. [New York, 1967] 63 p. illus., ports. 24 cm. Bibliography: p. 59-60. [ND553.K55.J4] 67-17222
1. Klein, Yves, 1928-1962. I. McShine, Kynaston. II. Descargues, Pierre. III. Restany, Pierre. IV. Title.

Kleiner, Bell and Company—Art collections.

NEW York (City). Museum of Modern Art. 760'.74'01471
Tamarind; homage to lithography. Pref. by William S. Lieberman. Introd. by Virginia Allen. New York, Distributed by New York Graphic Society, Greenwich, Conn. [1969] 64 p. illus. (part col.) 25 cm. "Catalog of the exhibition, April 29-June 30, 1969." "All works are ... from the Kleiner, Bell and Company Collection of Tamarind impressions." [NE2272.N4M8] 77-77513 6.95
1. Kleiner, Bell and Company—Art collections. 2. Lithographs—Exhibitions. I. Tamarind Lithography Workshop. II. Title.

Kleinholz, Frank, 1901—

FREUNDLICH, August L. 759.13
Frank Kleinholz: the outsider, by August L. Freundlich. Coral Gables, Fla., University of Miami Press [1969] 127 p. illus. (part col.) 29 cm. Bibliography: p. 115-121. [ND237.K555F7] 73-75849 10.00
1. Kleinholz, Frank, 1901- BIP

*KLEINHOLZ, Frank, 1901- 759.1747
Frank Kleinholz: a self portrait. Introd. by Philip Evergood. New York. Garland Pr., 63 E. 57 [c.1964] 95p. illus. (pt. col.) 27cm. 12.50, lim. ed., bxd.
I. Title.

KLEINHOLZ, Frank, 1901- 759.13
Frank Kleinholz: a self portrait. Introd. by Philip Evergood. New York, Shorewood Publishers [1964] 95 p. plates (part col.) 27 cm. [ND237.K555A2] 64-14859
I. Title.

KLEINHOLZ, Frank, 1901- 707.4'097471
Frank Kleinholz: paintings, drawings, 1942-1972; [exhibition held January 30th through February 17th, 1973. New York, ACA Galleries, 1973, c1972] [56] p. (chiefly illus.) 29 cm. Bibliography: p. [10] [ND237.K555A12 1973] 759.13 74-157565
1. Kleinholz, Frank, 1901- I. A. C. A. Galleries. II. Title.

KLEINHOLZ, Frank, 1901- 769'.92'4
Kleinholz graphics : catalogue raisonne, 1940-1975 / compiled and edited by Sylvan Cole, Jr. ; with a foreword by Ralph G. Martin. Coral Gables, Fla. : University of Miami Press, [1975] 125 p. : chiefly ill. ; 26 cm. Includes index. Bibliography: p. 119-120. [NE539.K55A53] 74-31266 ISBN 0-87024-274-1 : 10.00
1. Kleinholz, Frank, 1901- I. Cole, Sylvan, ed. II. Title.

Klimsch, Karl, 1812-1890.

KLIMSCH, Karl, 1812-1890. 745.4'49'24
Florid Victorian ornament / Karl Klimsch. New York : Dover Publications, 1977. [52] leaves of plates : all ill. ; 29 cm. (Dover pictorial archive series) Reprint of the 1877? ed. published by Asher, London, under title: Ornaments invented & designed by Charles Klimsch. [NK1535.K55A52 1977] 76-58573 ISBN 0-486-23490-8 pbk. : 3.50
1. Klimsch, Karl, 1812-1890. 2. Design, Decorative—Plant forms. 3. Decoration and ornament—Victorian style. I. Title. BIP

Klimt, Gustav, 1862-1918.

HOFMANN, Werner, 1928- 759.36
Gustav Klimt. [Translated by Inge Goodwin] Greenwich, Conn., New York Graphic Society [1972, c1971] 60 p. illus. (part col.) 28 x 31 cm. Translation of Gustav Klimt und die Wiener Jahrhundertwende. Bibliography: p. 56-57. [M6811.5.K55H613 1972b] 70-186455 ISBN 0-8212-0452-1 27.50
1. Klimt, Gustav, 1862-1918. BIP

KLIMT, Gustav, 1862-1918. 759.36
Gustav Klimt : [a poster book]. New York : Harmony Books, 1976. 47 p. : chiefly col. ill. ; 39 cm. [ND511.5.K55A45] 76-20350 ISBN 0-517-52648-4 : 5.95
1. Klimt, Gustav, 1862-1918. I. Title.

KLIMT, Gustav, 1862-1918. 741.9'436
Gustav Klimt : drawings and paintings / [compiled by] Alice Strobl ; [translated from the German by Inga Hamilton]. New York : Rizzoli, 1976. 119 p. : ill. (some col.) ; 18 cm. [NC245.K553S8313] 76-150895 ISBN 0-8478-0053-9 : 6.50
1. Klimt, Gustav, 1862-1918. I. Strobl, Alice.

KLIMT, Gustav, 1862-1918. 759.36
Gustav Klimt / Alessandra Comini. New York : G. Braziller, 1975. 29, 80 p. : ill. (some col.) ; 28 cm. Includes bibliographical references. [ND511.5.K55C65] 75-10965 ISBN 0-8076-0805-X : 15.00 ISBN 0-8076-0806-8 pbk. : 8.95
1. Klimt, Gustav, 1862-1918. I. Comini, Alessandra.

KLIMT, Gustav, 1862-1918. 741.9'436
Gustav Klimt, 1862-1918: drawings. [Exhibition] March - April 1970, the Galerie St. Etienne, New York. [New York, Galerie St. Etienne, 1970] 23 p., 43 plates. port. 21 cm. Bibliography: p. 12. [NC245.K553A46] 70-24994
I. Galerie St. Etienne, New York.

KLIMT, Gustav, 1862-1918. 741.9'436
One hundred drawings. With an introd. by Alfred Werner. New York, Dover Publications [1972] xv p., 100 plates. 32 cm. [NC245.K553A55] 78-157434 ISBN 0-486-22446-5 3.00
I. Title. BIP

NOVOTNY, Fritz, 1902- 759.436
Gustav Klimt; with a catalogue raisonne of his paintings [by] Fritz Novotny [and] Johannes Dobai. [Translated from the German by Karen Olga Philippson] New York, Praeger [1968, c1967] 424 p. illus., 115 plates (part col.), port. 31 cm. Contents.Contents.—Introduction, by F. Novotny.—The paintings.—Catalogue raisonne of the paintings, by J. Dobai.—Biography, by J. Dobai.—Bibliography, by J. Dobai (p. [395]-410) [ND538.K57N613] 68-19809
1. Klimt, Gustav, 1862-1918. I. Dobai, Johannes.

SOLOMON R. Guggenheim Museum, New York. 759.36
Gustav Klimt and Egon Schiele [Exhibition 65/1, February-April 1965] New York, Author [1965] 119p. illus. (pt. col.) ports. 28cm. Bibl. [ND538.K57S6] 65-16678 5.50 pap.,
1. Klimt, Gustav, 1862-1918. 2. Schiele, Egon, 1890-1918. 3. Paintings, Austrian—Exhibitions. 4. Drawings, Austrian—Exhibitions. I. Title.

Kline, Franz, 1910-1962.

DAWSON, Fielding, 1930- 759.13
An emotional memoir of Franz Kline. New York, Pantheon [1967] 147p. 22cm. [ND237.K56D3] 67-23964 4.95
1. Kline, Franz. 1910-1962. I. Title.

GORDON, John, 1912- 759.13
Franz Kline, 1910-1962. New York, Published for the Whitney Museum of American Art by F. A. Praeger [1969] 67 p. 57 illus. (4 col.) 24 cm. A review of Kline's work based on an exhibition of his paintings held at the Whitney Museum of American Art, Oct. 1-Nov. 24, 1968. "Catalogue of the exhibition": p. 61-62. Bibliography: p. 64-67. [ND237.K56G6 1969] 68-57219 4.95
1. Kline, Franz, 1910-1962. I. Whitney Museum of American Art, New York.

KLINE, Franz, 1910-1962. 759.13
Franz Kline, 1910-1962, by John Gordon Franz Kline nineteen ten--nineteen sixty-two New York, Whitney Museum of American Art [1968] 67 p. illus. (part col.), ports. 23 cm. Catalog of an exhibition held Oct. 1-Nov. 24, 1968, at the Whitney Museum of American Art; Dec. 17, 1968-Jan. 26, 1969, at the Dallas Museum of Fine Arts; Feb. 21-Mar. 30, 1969, at the San Francisco Museum of Art; and Apr. 12-May 25, 1969, at the Museum of Contemporary Art, Chicago. Bibliography: p. 64-67. [ND237.K56G62] 68-57217
I. Gordon, John, 1912- II. Whitney Museum of American Art, New York.

WASHINGTON, D.C. Gallery of Modern Art. 707.4
Franz Kline memorial exhibition. Washington, D.C., Author [1963] 59p. illus. 19x22cm. Bibl. 62-21626 apply
1. Kline, Franz I. Title.

Klinger, Max, 1857-1920.

KLINGER, Max, 1857-1920. 769'.924
A glove, and other images of reverie and apprehension; the graphic suites of Max Klinger, loaned by the Staatliche Graphische Sammlung, Munich. [Wichita? Kan., 1971] [24] p. (incl. cover) illus. 23 cm. Catalogue and commentary by Jan von Adlmann. A loan exhibition, organized by the Wichita Art Museum, Aug. 6-Sept. 19, and participating University Art Museum, Berkeley, Oct. 26-Nov. 28, Busch-Reisinger Museum, Harvard University, Dec.-Jan. 1971-1972. Bibliography: p. [23] [NE2050.5.K55V6] 71-170906
I. Von Adlmann, Jan. II. Wichita Art Museum. III. California. University. Art Museum. IV. Harvard University. Busch-Reisinger Museum of Germanic Culture. V. Title.

KLINGER, Max, 1857-1920. 769'.92'4
Graphic works of Max Klinger / introd., notes, and bibliography by J. Kirk T. Varnedoe, with Elizabeth Streicher ; foreword by Dorothea Carus ; technical note by Elizabeth Sahling. New York : Dover Publications, 1977. xxv, 99 p. : ill. ; 31 cm. (Dover art collections) Bibliography: p. 99. [NE2050.5.K55V37 1977] 76-26380 ISBN 0-486-23437-1 : 5.00
1. Klinger, Max, 1857-1920. I. Varnedoe, J. Kirk T. II. Streicher, Elizabeth. III. Title. BIP

Kluth, Karl, 1898-1972.

KLUTH, Karl, 1898-1972. 741.973
Karl Kluth : mit unveroff. Aufzeichnungen d. Kunstlers / Heinz Spielmann. Hamburg : Christians, [1975] 88 p. : chiefly ill. (some col.) ; 23 cm. (Hamburger Kunstler-Monographien zur Kunst des 20. Jahrhunderts ; Bd. 1) [ND588.K66S64] 76-458747 ISBN 3-7672-0388-X : DM24.00
1. Kluth, Karl, 1898-1972. I. Spielmann, Heinz. II. Series: Hamburger Kunstler-Monographien zur Kunst des zwanzigsten Jahrhunderts ; Bd. 1.

Knaresborough, Eng.—Description—Guide-books.

BOYES, Malcolm. 914.28'42
Knaresborough : a practical guide for visitors / compiled by Malcolm Boyes ; illustrated by J. J. Thomlinson. Clapham, N. Yorkshire : Dalesman Books, 1976. 32 p. : ill., maps ; 19 cm. (A Dalesmen mini-book) [DA690.K6B69] 77-367671 ISBN 0-85206-353-9 : £0.35
1. Knaresborough, Eng.—Description—Guide-books. I. Title.

Knaths, Karl, 1891-

KNATHS, Karl, 1891- 759.13
Exhibition of recent paintings by Karl Knaths, 1966 to 1968, January 13 to

February 8, 1969. New York, P. Rosenberg [1969?] 1 v. (unpaged) illus. 26 cm. (Paul Rosenberg & Co. Catalogue no. 161) [ND237.K59A44] 79-243377
1. Title. II. Series: Rosenberg (Paul) and Company, New York. Catalogue no. 161

KNATHS, Karl, 1891- 759.13
Karl Knaths, five decades of painting; a loan exhibition. Introd. by Charles Edward Eaton. Catalogue by Isabel Patterson Eaton. [Washington, International Exhibitions Foundation, c1973] 151 p. illus. (part col.) 28 cm. Participating museums: The William Hayes Ackland Memorial Art Center and others. Bibliography: p. 147-150. [ND237.K59E27] 73-82318
1. Knaths, Karl, 1891- I. Eaton, Isabel Patterson. II. International Exhibitions Foundation. III. North Carolina. University. William Hayes Ackland Memorial Art Center.

MOESANYI, Paul. 759.13
Karl Knaths. Introd. by Duncan Phillips. An appreciation by Emanuel Benson. Commentary by Karl Knaths. Washington, Phillips Gallery, 1957. 101p. illus. (part col.) port. 27cm. [ND237.K59M6] 927.5 57-13428
1. Knaths, Karl, 1891- I. Title.

Knickerbocker, Frances Wentworth Cutler.

KNICKERBOCKER, Frances Wentworth Cutler. 917.44'4'0340924
The minister's daughter: a time-exposure photograph of the years 1903-04, by Frances Wentworth Cutler. Edited and annotated by Charles H. Knickerbocker. Philadelphia, Dorrance [1974] 148 p. port. 22 cm. [CT275.K6575A35] 73-90091 ISBN 0-8059-1969-4 6.95
1. Knickerbocker, Frances Wentworth Cutler. I. Knickerbocker, Charles H., ed. II. Title. BIP

Knife coins—China.

COOLE, Arthur Braddan, 1900- 737.4'9'51
State of Ming knife coins and minor knife coins / Arthur Braddan Coole. Lawrence, Mass. : Quarterman Publications, 1977,c1976 512 p. : chiefly ill. ; 24 cm. (His Encyclopedia of Chinese coins ; v. 6) [CJ3496.C62 vol. 6] [CJ1367] 72-86802 ISBN 0-88000-013-9 : 30.00
1. Knife coins—China. I. Title. II. Series.

Knifemakers Guild—Directories.

A Guide to handmade knives and The official directory of the the Knifemakers Guild / edited by Mel Tappan. 1st ed. Rogue River, Ore. : Janus Press, c1977. 301 p. : ill. ; 21 cm. [TS380.G84] 77-9199 ISBN 0-916172-03-1 pbk. : 9.95 739.7'2
1. Knifemakers Guild—Directories. 2. Knives—Collectors and collecting—United States. I. Tappan, Mel. II. Knifemakers Guild. The official directory of the Knifemakers Guild. 1977. BIP

Knights and knighthood—Juvenile literature.

OAKESHOTT. R. EWART 623
A knight and his castle. Illus. by the author [Chester Springs.Pa.] Dufour [c.] 1966. 107p. illus. 21cm. [U800.O325] 64-25448 2.95 bds.,
1. Knights and knighthood—Juvenile literature. 2. Castles—Juvenile literature. I. Title.

Knitted lace—Patterns.

ABBEY, Barbara, 1903- 746.2
Knitting lace. New York, Viking Press [1974] 143 p. illus. 25 cm. [TT805.A2 1974] 72-12478 ISBN 0-670-41463-8 8.95
1. Knitted lace—Patterns. I. Title.

WALKER, Barbara G. 746.2
The craft of lace knitting [by] Barbara G. Walker. New York, Scribner [1971] 128 p. illus. 28 cm. (The Scribner library. Emblem editions) "Originally published as part of [the author's] A treasury of knitting patterns and A second treasury of knitting patterns." [TT825.W342] 72-165166 ISBN 0-684-12503-X 2.95
1. Knitted lace—Patterns. 2. Lace and lace making—Patterns. I. Title.

Knitting.

ABBEY, Barbara, 1903- 746.4'3
The complete book of knitting. New York, Viking Press [1971] 239 p. illus. 26 cm. (A Studio book) [TT820.A19] 79-168526 ISBN 0-670-23399-4 12.95
1. Knitting. I. Title. BIP

ABBEY, Barbara, 1903- 746.43
Susan Bates presents 101 ways to improve your knitting. [Rev. ed.] New York, Viking Press [1962] 61p. illus. 19cm. (A Studio book) [TT820.A2 1962] 62-11679
1. Knitting. I. Bates, Susan. II. Title. III. Title: 101 ways to improve your knitting.

AYTES, Barbara. 746.4'3
Knitting made easy. [1st ed.] Garden City, N.Y., Doubleday, 1970. xiii, 175 p. illus. 22 cm. [TT820.A94] 79-97648 4.95
1. Knitting. I. Title. BIP

BELLAMY, Virginia Woods. 646.26
Number knitting, the new all-way stretch method. Photos. by Douglas Armsden. New York, Crown Publishers [1952] 274 p. illus. 24 cm. [TT820.B45] 51-12015
1. Knitting. I. Title.

BOEHM, Peggy. 746.4
Knitting without needles. Illustrated by Shizu Matsuda. New York, Sterling Pub. Co. [1963] 124 p. illus. 21 cm. [TT825.B6] 63-19155
1. Knitting. I. Title.

BOYD, Elaine. 746.4'3
Learn to knit the easiest way. [1st ed.] New Augusta, Ind., Editors and Engineers [1967] 96 p. illus. 18 cm. (Skillfact library, 649) [TT820.B717] 66-27401
1. Knitting. I. Title.

BRAY, Bonita. 746.9
Afghans : traditional and modern / by Bonita Bray. New York : Crown, c1977. 96 p. : ill. ; 29 cm. Includes index. [TT825.B7 1977] 77-8641 ISBN 0-517-53104-6 : 14.95
1. Knitting. 2. Crocheting. BIP

CARLSON, Rosalin. 746.4'3
Creative knitting and crocheting. New York, Hearthside Press [1969] 192 p. illus. 24 cm. [TT820.C25] 70-92489 6.95
1. Knitting. 2. Crocheting. I. Title.

CARR, Caroline. 746.4'32
Knitting for the family / [by] Caroline Carr. Sydney ; New York : Hamlyn, 1973. 166 p. : ill. (part col.), diagrs. ; 30 cm. Includes index. [TT820.C257] 74-192971 ISBN 0-600-07121-9 : 3.95
1. Knitting. I. Title.

COLLINS, Marjorie. 746.4'3
Knitting. New York, Drake Publishers [1974, c1973] 96 p. illus. 26 cm. [TT820.C7] 73-10899 ISBN 0-87749-568-8 6.95
1. Knitting.

CONE, Ferne Geller. 746.4'3
Knit art / Ferne Geller Cone. New York : Van Nostrand Reinhold Co., [1975] 104 p. : ill. ; 28 cm. Includes index. Bibliography: p. 101. [TT820.C783] 74-16736 ISBN 0-442-21655-6 : 10.50 ISBN 0-442-21656-4 pbk. : 5.95
1. Knitting. 2. Soft sculpture. I. Title. BIP

CORNELL, Betty. 746.43
Teen-age knitting books, by Betty Cornell in collaboration with the Institute for Hand Knitting, inc. New York, Prentice-Hall [1953] 148 p. illus. 29 cm. [TT825.C7] 53-6366
1. Knitting. I. Title.

CURTIS, Carol, pseud. 746.43
Carol Curtis' complete book of knitting and crocheting. With an introd. by Eloise Davison. New York, Pocket Books [1954] 236p. illus. 16cm. (A Cardinal edition, C-125) [TT820.C96] 54-21565
1. Knitting. 2. Crocheting. I. Title.

DREIBLATT, Martha. 746.43
Knitting for everyone, by Martha Dreiblatt (Marti) With illus. by Eva Melady. [1st ed.] Garden City, N.Y., Dolphin Books, 1964. xi, 337 p. illus., diagrs. 18 cm. (A Dolphin handbook original) "C425." [TT820.D763] 64-11314
1. Knitting. I. Title.

DUNCAN, Ida Riley. 746.43
The complete book of progressive knitting. [Rev. ed.] New York, Liveright Pub. Corp. [1966] x, 387 p. illus. 21 cm. 8th printing. [TT820.D77 1966] 67-645
1. Knitting. I. Title. BIP

DUNCAN, Ida Riley. 746.4'3
The complete book of progressive knitting. New York, Liveright [1971, c1966] x, 387 p. illus. 21 cm. "Liveright L-43." [TT820.D77 1971] 70-149630 ISBN 0-87140-048-0 2.75
1. Knitting. I. Title.

DUNCAN, Ida Riley. 746.43
Knit to fit; a comprehensive guide to hand and machine knitting. New York, Liveright Pub. Corp. [1963] 301 p. illus. 22 cm. [TT820.D78] 63-11969
1. Knitting. 2. Knitting, Machine. I. Title.

DUNCAN, Ida Riley. 746.4'3
Knit to fit; a comprehensive guide to hand and machine knitting and crochet. 2d ed. New York, Liveright [1970] 254 p. illus. 22 cm. [TT820.D78 1970] 75-131267 6.95
1. Knitting. 2. Knitting, Machine. I. Title.

*EDITORS of Sunset Books. 7464'3
Knitting : techniques and projects / editors of Sunset Books. Mnlo Park, Calif. : Lane, c1976. 80p. : ill. (some ed.) ; 28 cm. Includes index. [TT820] 76-7659 ISBN 0-376-04431-4 pbk. : 2.45
1. Knitting. I. Title.

FAMILY fashions to knit & crochet / by the editors of McCall's needlework & Crafts ; editorial director and publisher, Rosemary McMurtry. New York : McCall Pattern Co., c1978. 48 p. : ill. (some col.) ; 28 cm. Cover title: McCall's family fashions to knit & crochet. On cover: vol. 1. Includes index. [TT820.F19] 78-113317 pbk. : 1.35 746.4'3
1. Knitting. 2. Crocheting. I. McMurtry, Rosemary. II. McCall's needlework & crafts. III. Title: McCall's family fashions to knit & crochet.

FELDMAN, Annette. 746.4'3
Knit, purl, and design! [1st ed.] New York, Harper & Row [1972] 146 p. illus. 27 cm. [TT820.F44] 72-79662 ISBN 0-06-011219-0 7.95
1. Knitting. I. Title.

FELDMAN, Annette. 746.4'32
Knit, purl, and design! / Annette Feldman. New York : Galahad Books, c1972. 146 p. : ill. ; 27 cm. Includes index. [TT820.F44 1972] 75-12261 ISBN 0-88365-314-1 : 8.95
1. Knitting. I. Title.

FOUGNER, Dave. 746.4'3
The manly art of knitting. Photography by Marlene Nordstrom Dassett. [Santa Rosa, Calif.] Threshold [1972] 64 p. illus. 21 cm. Bibliography: p. 64. [TT820.F7] 72-13532 ISBN 0-9600572-4-2 1.95
1. Knitting. I. Title.

GILCHRIST, Lee. 746.4'3
Twice-knit knitting. New York, Grosset & Dunlap [1970] 92 p. illus. 21 cm. [TT820.G54 1970] 70-122570 1.95
1. Knitting. I. Title.

GUILD, Vera P 746.4
Knitting, crocheting, and embroidery, by Vera P. Guild. [New York] Emily Post Institute [1964, c1963] viii, 113 p. illus. (part col.) 24 cm. (Emily Post's guidebooks for homemakers) [TT820.G88] 63-9017
1. Knitting. 2. Crocheting. 3. Embroidery. I. Title.

HORNE, Patience. 746.4'3
Patons book of knitting and crochet, by Patience Horne and Stephen Bowden. [1st American ed.] Boston, Little, Brown [1973] vii, 296 p. illus. 24 cm. Bibliography: p. 290. [TT820.H79 1973] 73-11466 8.95
1. Knitting. 2. Crocheting. I. Bowden, Stephen, joint author. II. Patons & Baldwins Limited. III. Title. IV. Title: Book of knitting and crochet.

HUBERT, Margaret. 746.4'32
One-piece knits that fit : how to knit and crochet one-piece garments / by Margaret Huber. New York : Van Nostrand Reinhold Co., [1978] p. cm. Includes index. [TT825.H8] 78-17516 ISBN 0-442-23567-4 : 15.00
1. Knitting. 2. Crocheting. I. Title.

HURLBURT, Regina. 746.4'32
Left-handed knitting / Regina Hurlburt ; drawings by Prue Campbell-Smith. New York : Van Nostrand Reinhold, [1977] p. cm. Includes index. [TT820.H87] 77-77972 ISBN 0-442-23585-2 : 5.95
1. Knitting. I. Title. BIP

JAY, Edith. 646.26
Child's book of knitting. Illus. [by] Lucile Newman, diagrs. [by] Jerry Jay. New York, Greenberg [1952] 92 p. illus. 23 cm. [TT820.J3] 52-8123
1. Knitting. I. Title.

MACDONALD, James, 1923- 646.26
Elementary circular knitting. 1st ed. [Atlanta! Ga.] c1952 221 p. illus. 22 cm. [TT820-M18] 52-40207
1. Knitting. I. Title. II. Title: Circular knitting.

MCELWAIN, Charlotte. 746.4'3
Knitting with stop and go needles; basic and fashion stitches. New York, Reinhold Book Corp. [1968] 143 p. illus. (part col.) 26 cm. [TT820.M19] 66-24554
1. Knitting. I. Title.

PALMER, Cherie. 646.4'3
The perfect fit; charting and fitting knitted and crocheted garments. Illus. by Michael Faye. New York, Scribner [1975] 174 p. illus. 28 cm. Bibliography: p. [169] [TT820.P2] 74-8427 ISBN 0-684-13990-1
1. Knitting. 2. Crocheting. 3. Clothing and dress measurements. I. Title. BIP

PARKER, Xenia Ley. 746.4'3
A beginner's book of knitting and crocheting. New York, Dodd, Mead [1974] 154 p. illus. 25 cm. Describes yarns, wools, fibers, needles, tools, and basic stitches for both crocheting and knitting. Includes patterns in both arts for several useful items. [TT820.P26] 73-11990 ISBN 0-396-06862-6 4.95
1. Knitting. 2. Crocheting. I. Title. BIP

†PARKINSON, Francesca. 746.4'3
Knit and crochet your own original designs / by Francesca Parkinson. New York : Arco Pub. Co., c1977. p. cm. [TT825.P37] 76-41163 ISBN 0-668-04126-9 : 14.95
1. Knitting. 2. Crocheting. I. Title.

PEAKE, Miriam Morrison. 646.26
The Wise handbook of knitting and crocheting. New York, W. H. Wise, 1953 [c1952] 306p. illus. 21cm. [TT820.P37 1953] 53-940
1. Knitting. 2. Crocheting. I. Wise (Wm. H.) and Company, inc., New York. II. Title.

PHILLIPS, Mary Walker. 746.4'3
Creative knitting; a new art form. Edited by William Shirley Sayles. New York, Van Nostrand Reinhold Co. [1971] 119 p. illus. 29 cm. Bibliography: p. 116-117. [TT820.P44] 72-110061
1. Knitting. I. Title.

PHILLIPS, Mary Walker. 746.4'3
Step-by-step knitting; a complete introduction to the craft of knitting, including photos. in full color. Designed by and produced under the supervision of William and Shirley Sayles. New York, Golden Press [1967] 95 p. illus. (part col.) 29 cm. Bibliography: p. 94. [TT820.P45] 67-21709
1. Knitting. I. Title.

RATTNER, Joan. 746.4'3
The official knit-a-dress-a-day knitting book. New York, Grosset [1968] 128p. illus. 21cm. Pub. in assn. with This week magazine. [TT820.R37] 68-19194 1.00 pap.,
1. Knitting. I. This week magazine. II. Title. III. Title: Knit-a-dress-a-day knitting book.

SCHACHENMAYR, Mann & Cie., Salach, Ger. 746.4'3
The book of knitting and crochet. Edited by Thelma M. Nye. [1st English ed. Newton Centre, Mass.] C. T. Branford Co. [1973] 300 p. illus. 26 cm. Translation of Das neue Strick- und Hakelbuch. [TT820.S2713] 74-158961
1. Knitting. 2. Crocheting. I. Nye, Thelma M., ed. II. Title. BIP

SELFRIDGE, Gail. 746.4'32
Patchwork knitting / by Gail Selfridge. New York : Watson-Guptill, 1977. 216 p. : ill. (some col.) ; 29 cm. Includes index. [TT820.S45] 76-51400 ISBN 0-8230-3929-3 : 16.95
1. Knitting. 2. Patchwork. I. Title.

SOMMER, Elyse. 746.4'32
A new look at knitting : an easier and more creative approach / by Elyse and Mike Sommer, text and designs, Elyse Sommer ; photography, Mike Sommer. New York : Crown Publishers, c1977. p. cm. Includes index. Bibliography: p. [TT820.S63 1977] 77-7121 ISBN 0-517-52860-6 : 12.95. ISBN 0-517-52861-4 pbk. : 6.95
1. Knitting. I. Sommer, Mike, joint author. II. Title. BIP

THOMAS, Mary (Hedger) 1889- 746.4'3
Mary Thomas's knitting book. New York, Dover Publications [1972] xiii, 256 p. illus. 22 cm. Reprint of the 1938 ed. published by Hodder and Stoughton, London. [TT820.T47 1972] 72-188814 ISBN 0-486-22817-7 2.50
1. Knitting. I. Title. BIP

THOMPSON, Gladys. 746.4'32
Patterns for guernseys, jerseys, and arans : fishermen's sweaters from the British Isles / Gladys Thompson. 3d rev. ed. New York : Dover Publications, c1979. 172 p. : ill. ; 21 cm. [TT825.T45 1979] 79-102434 ISBN 0-486-22703-0 pbk. : 3.50
1. Knitting—Great Britain—Patterns. 2. Sweaters. I. Title. II. Title: Fishermen's sweaters from the British Isles.

TREXLER, Pat. 746.4'3
Knit and crochet ideas. New York, Arco [1968, c1967] 112 p. illus. 24 cm. [TT820.T74] 67-25017
1. Knitting. 2. Crocheting. I. Title.

*TREXLER, Pat 745.43
Knit and crochet ideas. Greenwich, Conn., Hall House, 1967. 112p. illus. 24cm. (Hall House bk. no. 10) .95 pap.,
1. Knitting. 2. Crochet. I. Title.
Available from Fawcett, Greenwich, Conn.

VON WARTBURG, Ursula. 746.4'3
The workshop book of knitting. [1st ed.] New York, Atheneum, 1973. 148 p. illus. 25 cm. [TT820.V63 1973] 71-157313 ISBN 0-689-20696-8 8.95
1. Knitting. I. Title.

VON WARTBURG, Ursula. 746.4'3
The workshop book of knitting / Ursula von Wartburg. New York : Atheneum, 1978, c1973. 148p. : ill. ; 24 c. Includes index. [TT820.V63] pbk. : 4.95
1. Knitting. I. Title.
L.C. card no. for 1973 hardcover ed.: 71-157313. BIP

WALKER, Barbara G. 746.4'32
Mosaic knitting / Barbara G. Walker. New York : Scribner, c1976. ix, 262 p., [4] leaves of plates : ill. ; 24 cm. [TT825.W345] 75-22311 ISBN 0-684-14243-0 : 12.50
1. Knitting. I. Title. BIP

WARTBURG, Ursula von. 746.4'3
The workshop book of knitting / Ursula von Wartburg. New York : Atheneum, 1978. 148p. : ill. ; 24 cm. [TT820.V63] ISBN 0-689-70564-6 pbk. : 4.95
1. Knitting. I. Title.
L.C. card no. for 1973 Atheneum hardcover ed.: 71-157313

Knitting—Bibliography.

GIFFORD, Virginia Snodgrass. 016.7464'3
An annotated bibliography on hand knitting with an historical introduction. Washington, c1969. 38 l. 29 cm. [Z5956.L2G53] 75-243384
1. Knitting—Bibliography. 2. Knitting—History. I. Title.

Knitting—History.

KIEWE, Heinz Edgar. 746.4'32'09
History of knitting : is it earlier than weaving? / by Heinz Edgar Kiewe. [Oxford : Art Needlework Industries Ltd], 1976. 19 p. : ill. ; 21 cm. (Textile design anthropology) Includes the catalogue of an exhibition. [TT820.K49] 77-358503 ISBN 0-900081-06-6 : £0.20
1. Knitting—History. 2. Knitting—History—Exhibitions. I. Title.

Knitting—Juvenile literature.

CONE, Ferne Geller. 746.4'32
Knutty knitting for kids / Ferne Geller Cone. Chicago : Follet Pub. Co., c1977. 159 p. : ill. 22 cm. Includes index. Presents basic knitting instructions and emphasizes creating original designs by using needles of various sizes and materials such as string, rope, strips of fabric, and seashells. [TT820.C784] 76-50323 ISBN 0-695-80739-0 : 6.95. ISBN 0-695-40739-2 lib.bdg. : 6.99
1. Knitting—Juvenile literature. I. Title. BIP

CREATIVE Educational Society, Mankato, Minn. 746.4'3
How to have fun knitting, by editors of Creative. Illustrated by Nancy Inderieden. [Mankato, Minn., Creative Education; distributed by Childrens Press, Chicago, 1973, c1974] 31 p. illus. (part col.) 25 cm. (Creative craft book) A brief history of knitting, instructions for basic stitches and patterns, and directions for three easy projects. [TT820.C86] 73-12471 ISBN 0-87191-274-0 4.45 (lib. bdg.).
1. Knitting—Juvenile literature. I. Inderieden, Nancy, illus. II. Title. BIP

MEYER, Carolyn. 746.4'3
Yarn—the things it makes and how to make them. Illustrated by Jennifer Perrott. [1st ed.] New York, Harcourt Brace Jovanovich [1972] 128 p. illus. 24 cm. Instructions and patterns for making a number of items by crocheting, knitting, weaving, and by macrame. [TT820.M498] 72-76367 ISBN 0-15-299713-X 5.50
1. Knitting—Juvenile literature. 2. Crocheting—Juvenile literature. 3. Hand weaving—Juvenile literature. 4. Macrame—Juvenile literature. I. Perrott, Jennifer, illus. II. Title. BIP

PHILLIPS, Mary Walker. 746.4'32
Knitting / by Mary Walker Phillips ; illustrated with photographs and drawings. New York : F. Watts, 1977. 87 p. : ill. ; 27 cm. Includes index. Bibliography: p. 85. An introduction to knitting including discussions of yarn, equipment, stitches, and complete directions for several project. [TT820.P445] 76-41717 ISBN 0-531-00837-1 lib.bdg. : 5.20
1. Knitting—Juvenile literature. I. Title.

RUBENSTONE, Jessie. 746.4'3
Knitting for beginners. Photos. by Edward Stevenson. [1st ed.] Philadelphia, Lippincott [1973] 64 p. illus. 23 cm. Explains the use of appropriate materials and techniques for knitting headbands, belts, scarves, afghans, and other articles. [TT820.R78] 73-6755 4.95
1. Knitting—Juvenile literature. I. Stevenson, Edward, illus. II. Title.
Pbk. 1.95 BIP

YERIAN, Cameron John. 746.4
Macrame, knitting, & weaving. Cameron and Margaret Yerian, editors. Chicago, Children's Press [1974] 43 p. col. illus. 25 cm. "Fun time." Introduces tools, techniques, and projects in knitting, hand weaving, and macrame. [TT820.Y47] 74-8451 ISBN 0-516-01302-5
1. Knitting—Juvenile literature. 2. Hand weaving—Juvenile literature. 3. Macrame—Juvenile literature. I. Yerian, Margaret, joint author. II. Title.

Knitting, Machine.

FAUST, Regine. 746.9'2
Fashion knit course outline for hand knitting machines / Regine Faust ; Ewa Lavoy, ill. and layout. Minneapolis : Burgess Pub. Co., Customized Pub. Division, c1978. ix, 265 p. : ill. ; 28 cm. [TT680.F38] 78-100956 ISBN 0-8087-0647-0 pbk. : 6.22
1. Knitting, Machine. I. Lavoy, Ewa. II. Title.

HOLBOURNE, David. 746.4'32
The basic book of machine knitting / David Holbourne. New York : Van Nostrand Reinhold, [1979] p. cm. Includes index. Bibliography: p. [TT680.H58] 78-10763 ISBN 0-442-23482-1 : 13.00
1. Knitting, Machine. I. Title. BIP

MOYER, Earl D. 677'.02824
Principles of double knitting, by Earl D. Moyer. Brooklyn, N.Y., Montrose Supply & Equipment Co. [1972] 121 p. illus. 29 cm. [TT680.M68] 72-180293
1. Knitting, Machine. I. Title.

REICHMAN, Charles, ed. 677.661
Advanced knitting principles. New York, National Knitted Outerwear Association [1964] 224 p. illus. 23 cm. (Knit goods technology manuals) [TT680.R38] 66-1468
1. Knitting, Machine. 2. Knitting-machines. I. Title.

WIGNALL, Harry. 687'3
Knitting. Foreword by J. C. H. Hurd. London, Pitman [1967,c.1964] Stamped on t.p.: Dist. by SportShelf, New Rochelle, N.Y. xi, 132p. illus. 23cm. (Pitman's common commodities and industries) [TT680.W5 1967] 68-967 5.50 bds.,
1. Knitting, Machine. 2. Knitting-machines. I. Title. BIP

Knitting, Machine—Dictionaries.

REICHMAN, Charles. 677'.661'03
Knitting dictionary, edited by Charles Reichman. New York, National Knitted Outerwear Association [c1966] 131 p. illus. 23 cm. [TT679.5.R4] 68-3737
1. Knitting. Machine—Dictionaries. 2. Knitting-machines—Dictionaries. I. Title.

REICHMAN, Charles. 677'.02824
Knitting encyclopedia. Edited by Charles Reichman. New York, National Knitted Outerwear Association [1972] 388 p. illus. 30 cm. [TT679.5.R42] 72-77093
1. Knitting, Machine—Dictionaries. 2. Knit goods—Dictionaries. I. Title.

Knitting—Patterns.

*BOEHM, Peggy 746.4
Knitting without needles. Illus. by Shizu Matsuda. New York, Cornerstone Lib. [1964, c.1963] 124p. 20cm. (CN 85) 1.00 pap.,
I. Title.

CARROLL, Alice, 1908- 746.4'3
Knitting and crocheting your own fashions of the forties. New York, Dover Publications [1973] vii, 327 p. illus. 22 cm. Cover title: Knit & crochet your own fashions of the forties. Published in 1942 and 1949 under title: Complete guide to modern knitting and crocheting. [TT820.C27 1973] 73-80202 ISBN 0-486-21360-9 3.50 (pbk.)
1. Knitting—Patterns. 2. Crocheting—Patterns. I. Title. II. Title: Knit & crochet your own fashions of the forties. BIP

HEILMAN, Joan Rattner. 746.4'3
Large-type knitting book of babies' & children's clothes. Photographed by Kathryn Abbe. New York, World Pub. Co. [1971] 96 p. illus. 28 cm. [TT825.H44 1971] 76-149585 4.95
1. Knitting—Patterns. 2. Children's clothing. I. Title.

HOLLIS, Nesta. 746.4'32
Knitted outfits for teenage dolls / by Nesta Hollis with Winifred Rickwood : photographs by Alphalpus Ltd. London : Faber, 1974. 3,, 134 p., A-G leaves of plates : ill. (some col.) ; 25 cm. Label mounted on t.p.: Sole distributor for the U.S.A.: Transatlantic Arts, Levittown, New York. [TT829.H64] 75-314600 ISBN 0-571-10453-3 : 9.50
1. Knitting—Patterns. 2. Crocheting—Patterns. 3. Doll clothes. I. Rickwood, Winfred, joint author. II. Title. BIP

MCCALL'S super-book of knit & crochet / by the editors of McCall's needlework & crafts. 746.4'3 New York : McCall Pattern Co., c1978. 160 p. : ill. ; 28 cm. Includes index. [TT820.M17] 78-109482 pbk. : 2.95
1. Knitting—Patterns. 2. Crocheting—Patterns. I. McCall's needlework & crafts.

MARIANO, Linda. 746.4'3
The encyclopedia of knitting and crochet stitch patterns / by Linda Mariano. 1st ed. New York : Service Communications, 1977, c1976. 319 p. : ill. ; 29 cm. [TT825.M27] 76-29142 ISBN 0-442-25117-3 : 14.95
1. Knitting—Patterns. 2. Crocheting—Patterns. I. Title. BIP

NEIGHBORS, Jane. 746.4'3
Reversible two-color knitting. New York, Scribner [1974] xv, 200 p. illus. 28 cm. [TT820.N43] 73-1106 ISBN 0-684-13905-7 12.50
1. Knitting—Patterns. I. Title.

NORBURY, James, 1904- 746.4'3
Traditional knitting patterns, from Scandinavia, the British Isles, France, Italy, and other European countries. New York, Dover Publications [1973] 240 p. illus. 24 cm. "An unabridged republication of the work first published in 1962." [TT820.N86 1973] 73-79490 ISBN 0-486-21013-8 3.95 (pbk.).
1. Knitting—Patterns. I. Title.

*POWNALL, Glen. 746.4'3
Knotting crafts. Wellington, N.Z., Seven Seas, [1975 c1974] 84 p. ill. (part col.) 25 cm. (His creative leisure series.) [TT771] ISBN 0-85467-020-3
1. Knitting—Patterns. 2. Lace and Lacemaking. 3. Macrame. 4. Tatting. 5. Crocheting. 6. Netting. I. Title.
Distributed by Int'l Publications Service, Collings for 5.50. BIP

THOMPSON, Gladys. 746.4'3
Patterns for guernseys and jerseys. [Rev. ed.] New York, Dover Publications [1969] 167 p. illus., ports. 22 cm. On spine: Guernsey & jersey patterns. 1955 ed. published under title: Guernsey and jersey patterns. [TT825.T45 1969] 78-77567 8.00
1. Knitting—Patterns. I. Title. II. Title: Guernsey & jersey patterns.

THOMPSON, Gladys. 746.4'3
Patterns for guernseys, jerseys, and arans; fishermen's sweaters from the British Isles. 2d rev. ed. New York, Dover Publications [1971] 170 p. illus. 21 cm. 1955 ed. published under title: Guernsey and jersey patterns; 1969 ed. published under title: Patterns for guernseys and jerseys. [TT825.T45 1971] 71-136140 ISBN 0-486-22703-0 3.00
1. Knitting—Patterns. I. Title. BIP

WALKER, Barbara G. 746.4'3
Barbara Walker's learn-to-knit afghan book, by Barbara G. Walker. Photography by Werner P. Brodde. Artwork by John E. Bradley. New York, Scribner [1974] xiii, 161 p. illus. 20 cm. [TT820.W13] 73-10906 ISBN 0-684-13681-3 7.95
1. Knitting—Patterns. I. Title. II. Title: Learn-to-knit afghan book. BIP

WALKER, Barbara G. 746.4'3
The craft of cable-stitch knitting [by] Barbara G. Walker. New York, Scribner [1971] 128 p. illus. 28 cm. (The Scribner library, SL294 Emblem editions) Originally published as part of the author's A treasury of knitting patterns and A second treasury of knitting patterns issued in 1968 and 1970, respectively. [TT825.W34] 79-165165 ISBN 0-684-12500-5 2.95
1. Knitting—Patterns. I. Title.

WALKER, Barbara G. 746.4'3
The craft of multicolor knitting [by] Barbara G. Walker. Photography by William J. Williams. New York, Scribner [1973] 128 p. illus. (part col.) 28 cm. (The Scribner library. Emblem editions) Originally published as part of the author's A treasury of knitting patterns and A second treasury of knitting patterns. [TT820.W153] 73-3008 ISBN 0-684-13405-5 4.95
1. Knitting—Patterns. I. Title.

WALKER, Barbara G. 746.4'3
Knitting from the top, by Barbara G. Walker. With photos, by Werner P. Brodde. New York, Scribner [1972] 160 p. illus. 27 cm. [TT825.W343] 72-504 ISBN 0-684-12907-8 9.95
1. Knitting—Patterns. I. Title.

WALKER, Barbara G. 746.4'3
Sampler knitting [by] Barbara G. Walker. Photography by Werner P. Brodde. New York, Scribner [1973] xiv, 178 p. illus. 27 cm. [TT820.W158] 72-9771 ISBN 0-684-13263-X 9.95
1. Knitting—Patterns. I. Title.

WALKER, Barbara G. 746.4'3
A second treasury of knitting patterns [by] Barbara G. Walker. Photography by William J. Williams. New York, Scribner [1970] xxxiii, 398 p. illus. (part col.) 27 cm. Bibliography: p. 389. [TT820.W16 1970] 75-102725 15.00
1. Knitting—Patterns. I. Title.

WALKER, Barbara G. 746.4'3
A treasury of knitting patterns [by] Barbara G. Walker. Photography by William J. Williams. New York, Scribner's Sons [1968] xvi, 301 p. illus. (part col.) 27 cm. Bibliography: p. 292. [TT820.W17] 67-24064
1. Knitting—Patterns. I. Title. BIP

WALLER, Jane, comp. 746.4'3
A stitch in time: knitting and crochet patterns of the 1920s, 1930s & 1940s. Introduced & edited by Jane Waller. Abridged ed. Radnor, Pa., Chilton Book Co. [1973] 224 p. illus. 29 cm. (Chilton's creative crafts series) Consists chiefly of reprints of illus. and instructions selected from British women's magazines. [TT825.W35 1973] 73-3327 ISBN 0-8019-5889-X 7.95
1. Knitting—Patterns. 2. Crocheting—Patterns. I. Title.

WESTFALL, Fran. 746.4'3
New Idea encyclopaedia of knitting and crochet stitches. [Melbourne] Lansdowne [1971] x, 123 p. illus. 29 cm. [TT820.W38] 70-861530 ISBN 0-7018-0373-8
1. Knitting—Patterns. 2. Crocheting—Patterns. I. Title. II. Title: Encyclopaedia of knitting and crochet stitches.

ZIMMERMANN, Elizabeth. 746.4'3
Knitter's almanac. Photos. by Tom Zimmermann. Drawings by the author. New York, Scribner [1974] 152 p. illus. 24 cm. [TT820.Z54] 74-8425 ISBN 0-684-14018-7
1. Knitting—Patterns. I. Title.

Knitting—Patterns—Indexes.

HALEVY, Robyne. 746.4'3
Knitting & crocheting pattern index / by Robyne Halevy. Metuchen, N.J. : Scarecrow Press, 1977. 190 p. ; 22 cm. [TT825.H34] 76-50550 ISBN 0-8108-0998-2 : 7.50
1. Knitting—Patterns—Indexes. 2. Crocheting—Patterns—Indexes. I. Title. BIP

Knitting—Scandinavia—Patterns.

CHATTERTON, Pauline. 746.4'32
Scandinavian knitting designs / Pauline Chatterton. New York : Scribner, c1977. vii, 264 p. : ill. ; 28 cm. Includes index. [TT819.S26C48] 76-27879 ISBN 0-684-14817-X : 7.95
1. Knitting—Scandinavia—Patterns. I. Title. BIP

Knives—Collectors and collecting—United States.

A Guide to handmade 739.7'2
knives and The official directory of the the Knifemakers Guild / edited by Mel Tappan. 1st ed. Rogue River, Ore. : Janus Press, c1977. 301 p. : ill. ; 21 cm. [TS380.G84] 77-9199 ISBN 0-916172-03-1 pbk. : 9.95
1. Knifemakers Guild—Directories. 2. Knives—Collectors and collecting—United States. I. Tappan, Mel. II. Knifemakers Guild. The official directory of the Knifemakers Guild. 1977. BIP

Knorr, Hans.

KNORR, Hans. 730'.92'4
Sculpture of Hans Knorr / introd. by Bianca McCullough ; arranged and annotated by Hilde Knorr. Richmond [Australia] : Spectrum Publications, 1976. [84] p. : chiefly ill. ; 25 cm. [NB1105.K58K59] 77-369116 ISBN 0-909837-47-3
1. Knorr, Hans. I. Knorr, Hilde. II. Title.

Knots and splices.

BLANDFORD, Percy W. 746
Knots & splices [by] Percy W. Blandford. New York, Arc Books [1965] 79 p. illus. 18 cm. [VM533.B54 1965] 65-25270
1. Knots and splices. BIP

GRAUMONT, Raoul, 1896- 745.52
Encyclopedia of knots and fancy rope work, by Raoul Graumont and John Hensel. 4th ed., completely rev. and enl. by Raoul Graumont. Cambridge, Md., Cornell Maritime Press, 1952. 690p. illus. 26cm. [TT880.G7 1952] 677.7 53-693
1. Knots and spllces. I. Hensel, John, joint author. II. Title. BIP

OTSUKA, Sueko, 1902- 745.9
Fancy ribbon tying [Tr. from Japanese by Masatsugu Tsuzawa, Donald C. Mann. Rutland, Vt.] Japan Pubns. [1965, c.1964] 64p. illus. 21cm. [TT880] 63-7380 1.00 pap.,
1. Knots and splices. I. Title.

SHAW, George Russell, 746
b.1848.
Knots, useful and ornamental, by George Russell Shaw. New York, Collier Books [1972, c1933] 194 p. illus. 26 cm. [VM533.S4 1972] 78-175593 2.95
1. Knots and splices. I. Title.

WALLER, Irene. 746.4
Knots & netting / Irene Waller. New York : Taplinger Pub. Co., 1977, c1976. 95 p. : ill. ; 26 cm. Includes index. Bibliography: p. 92-94. [TT840.W33 1977] 76-55911 ISBN 0-8008-4484-X : 8.95
1. Knots and splices. 2. Netting. 3. Soft sculpture. I. Title. BIP

Knowles, Charles, 1939-1958.

BIBLE. O.T. Psalms. English. 761
Selections. 1962.
The Psalm book of Charles Knowles. New York, Pinnacle Pr. [dist.] Viking [c.1959,1962] 42p. col. illus. 29cm. Pages 17-35 are a facsimile reproduction of Knowles' orig. 1957 pubn. 62-17941 7.50 bds.,
1. Knowles, Charles, 1939-1958. I. Title.

Knox, Archibald, 1864-1933.

TILBROOK, Adrian J. 739.2'3'724
The designs of Archibald Knox for Liberty & Co. / by A. J. Tilbrook ; jointly edited with Gordon House. 1st ed. London : Ornament Press, 1976. 283 p. : ill., port. ; 22 cm. Includes index. Bibliography: p. 279-280. [NK1535.K58T54] 77-368961 ISBN 0-905464-00-1 : £10.60
1. Knox, Archibald, 1864-1933. 2. Liberty & Co. 3. Decoration and ornament—Art nouveau. 4. Design—England. I. Knox, Archibald, 1864-1933. II. Title.

Knoxville, Tenn.—History.

ISENHOUR, Judith 779'.9'976885
Clayton, 1946-
Knoxville : a pictorial history / by Judith Clayton Isenhour ; introd. by Carson Brewer. Norfolk, Va. : Donning Co., c1978. p. cm. Includes index. Bibliography: p. [F444.K7I83] 78-1489 ISBN 0-915442-46-9 : 16.95
1. Knoxville, Tenn.—History. I. Title. BIP

Koch, John, 1909—

KOCH, John, 1909- 759.13
John Koch. [New York, New York Cultural Center, 1973] 80 p. illus. 18 x 23 cm. Exhibition held at the New York Cultural Center in association with Fairleigh Dickinson University, Feb. 21 to Apr. 1, 1973. Bibliography: p. 80. [ND237.K593N48] 73-75990
1. Koch, John, 1909- I. New York Cultural Center. II. Fairleigh Dickinson University.

KOCH, John, 1909- 759.13
John Koch in New York, 1950-1963; [cataloque of an exhibition] New York, Museum of the City of New York [1963?] 62 p. illus. (part col.) 28 cm. [ND237.K593N47] 74-184377
1. Koch, John, 1909- I. New York (City). Museum of the City of New York. II. Title.

Kochavi, Nora, 1934—

KOCHAVI, Nora, 1934- 730'.92'4
Nora & Naomi: impressions from Sinai. [Catalogue of exhibition] Jewish Museum, New York, April 11, 1973-September 3, 1973. [New York, Jewish Museum, 1973] [12] p. illus. 24 cm. [NK4210.K55B57] 73-78652
1. Kochavi, Nora, 1934- 2. Bitter, Naomi, 1936- 3. Pottery, Israeli—Exhibitions. I. Bitter, Naomi, 1936- II. Jewish Theological Seminary of America. Jewish Museum. III. Title. IV. Title: Impressions from Sinai.

Kocsis, James Paul, 1936—

COLUMBIA, S.C. Museum of 759.13
Art.
Igneous man : [catalog of an exhibition] Columbia Museum of Art, November 10/December 1 / James Paul Kocsis. [s.l. : s.n., 1974] (Northampton, Pa. : R. & S. Printers) [8] leaves : ill. ; 31 cm. [ND237.K594C64 1974] 74-16177
1. Kocsis, James Paul, 1936- I. Kocsis, James Paul, 1936- II. Title.

Kodak camera.

COOPER, Joseph David, 771.31
1917-
Guide to Kodak automatic cameras. New York, Universal Photo Bks. [dist. Amphoto, c. 1962] 128p. illus. 21cm. 61-14250 1.95pap.,
1. Kodak camera. 2. Photography—Handbooks, manuals, etc. I. Title. II. Title: Automatic cameras.

NOLTING, Johannes. 771.3'1
Kodak pocket instamatic camera guide / Johannes Nolting, Georg Blitz ; [English version by Rolf Fricke and Harvey V. Fondiller ; drawings by Heinz Bauer]. New York : Morgan & Morgan, c1974. 74 p. : ill. (some col.) ; 19 cm. Translation of Fototips. [TR263.K54N6413] 74-76641 ISBN 0-87100-076-8 pbk. : 2.95
1. Kodak camera. 2. Miniature cameras. 3. Photography—Handbooks, manuals, etc. I. Blitz, Georg, joint author. II. Title. BIP

Kodak camera—Catalogs.

FEINBERG, Olan R. 338.4'3'7713
The Kodak collector [by Alan R. Feinberg. Winnetka, Ill., 1972] 44 p. 28 cm. Cover title. [TR263.K54F45] 72-178578
1. Kodak camera—Catalogs. I. Title.

Kodak instant camera.

EASTMAN Kodak Company. 771.3'1
Better instant pictures with Kodak instant cameras. [Rochester, N.Y. : Eastman Kodak Co.], c1976. 100 p. : col. ill. ; 22 cm. (Kodak publication ; no. AC-86) Cover title. Includes index. [TR263.K54E2 1976] 76-375586 ISBN 0-87985-181-3 pbk. : 2.95
1. Kodak instant camera. 2. Photography—Handbooks, manuals, etc. I. Title.

Kodiak, Alaska—Antiq.

HEIZER, Robert Fleming, 301.2'4
1915-
Archaeology of the Uyak site, Kodiak Island, Alaska. [Berkeley, University of California Press, 1956] vi, 199p. illus., maps, tables. 28cm. (Anthropological records, v. 17, no. 1) Bibliography: p. 98-102. [E51.A58 vol. 17, no. 1] A56
1. Kodiak, Alaska—Antiq. 2. Eskimos—Antiq. 3. Excavations (Archaeology)—Alaska. I. Title. II. Series.

Koerner, William Henry Dethlef.

HUTCHINSON, William 760'.0924
Henry, 1910-
W. H. D. Koerner: illustrating the Western myth. [Fort Worth, Tex.] Amon Carter Museum of Western Art [1969] [16] p. illus. 26 cm. "Exhibition dates: 24 January through 16 March 1969." [ND237.K5953H8] 70-77084
1. Koerner, William Henry Dethlef. I. Amon Carter Museum of Western Art, Fort Worth, Tex.

HUTCHINSON, William 741'.092'4 B
Henry, 1910-
The world, the work, and the West of W. H. D. Koerner / W. H. Hutchinson. 1st ed. Norman : University of Oklahoma Press, 1979, c1978 p. cm. Includes index. Bibliography: p. [NC975.5.K63H87] 78-58125 ISBN 0-8061-1471-1 : 35.00
1. Koerner, William Henry Dethlef. 2. Illustrators—United States—Biography. 3. The West in art. I. Title. BIP

Kohn, Gabriel, 1910-1975.

KOHN, Gabriel, 1910- 730'.92'4
1975.
Gabriel Kohn, 1910-1975 : The Corcoran Gallery of Art, Washington, D.C., June 4-July 17, 1977. [Washington] : The Gallery, [1977?] 36 p. : ill. ; 21 cm. Introductory essay by J. Livingston. Includes bibliographical references. [NB237.K596L58] 77-77612
1. Kohn, Gabriel, 1910-1975. I. Livingston, Jane. II. Corcoran Gallery of Art, Washington, D.C.

Kokoschka, Oskar, 1886-

BOSMAN, Anthony. 759.3
Oskar Kokoschka. [Translation by Albert J. Fransella] New York, Barnes & Noble [1964] 90 p. illus. (part col.) port. 18 cm. (Barnes & Noble art series, no. 620) [ND538.K62B583] 64-56935
1. Kokoschka, Oskar, 1886- I. Title.

BULTMANN, Bernhard 759.37
Oskar Kokoschka. [Tr. from the German by Michael Bullock] New York, Abrams [1961] 132p. illus. (part col.) 34cm. Bibl. 61-9881 20.00
1. Kokoschka, Oskar, 1886- I. Title.

HODIN, Josef Paul. 759.2 (B)
Oskar Kokoschka; the artist and his time; a biographical study by J. P. Hodin. [Greenwich, Conn.] New York, Graphic Society [1966] xii, 251 p. illus. (part col.) ports. 25 cm. Bibliography: p. 235-245. [ND538.K62H583] 66-15797
1. Kokoschka, Oskar, 1886- I. Title.

KOKOSCHKA, Oskar, 1886- 759.36
Kokoschka, by Ludwig Goldscheider, in collaboration with the artist. [London] Phaidon Publishers, distributed by New York Graphic Society Publishers, Greenwich, Conn. [1963] 78 p. 1 illus., 51 col. plates. 31 cm. [ND538.K62G6] 63-25595
I. Goldscheider, Ludwig, 1896-

KOKOSCHKA, Oskar, 1886- 759.2
Kokoschka [by] Giuseppe Gatt; [translated from the Italian]. London, New York, Hamlyn, 1971. 90 p. chiefly illus. (some col.), music, port. 32 cm. (Twentieth-century masters) "Distributed in the United States of America by Crown Publishers, Inc." Translation of Oskar Kokoschka. Bibliography: p. 90. [ND511.5.K6G313] 72-177840 ISBN 0-600-35305-2 £2.25
I. Gatt, Giuseppe.

KOKOSCHKA, Oskar, 1886- 759.2 B
My life / Oskar Kokoschka ; translated by David Britt. 1st American ed. New York : Macmillan, 1974. 240 p., [8] leaves of plates : ill. ; 24 cm. Translation of Mein Leben. Includes index. [ND511.5.K6A213 1974] 74-2645 10.00
1. Kokoschka, Oskar, 1886- 2. Painters—Austria—Correspondence, reminiscences, etc. I. Title.

KOKOSCHKA, Oskar, 1886- 760'.0924
Oskar Kokoschka. [London, Printed by Tillotsons (Bolton)] 1966. 131 p. (chiefly illus. (part col.), port.) 23 cm. "Cat[alogue] no. 200." Exhibition held at Marlborough-Gerson Gallery, inc., New York, Oct.-Nov. 1966. "Oskar Kokoschka, by E. H. Gombrich": p. 7-9. [ND538.K62A45] 67-4314
I. Marlborough-Gerson Gallery. II. Gombrich, Ernst Hans Josef, 1909- Oskar Kokoschka. 1966.

KOKOSCHKA, Oskar, 1886- 759.2
Oskar Kokoschka : cityscapes and landscapes, a 90th birthday tribute : [catalogue of a] loan exhibition in aid of the Save the Children Fund [held at] Marlborough Fine Art (London) Ltd, March-April 1976. London : Marlborough Fine Art (London) Ltd, [1976] 56 p. : chiefly ill. (some col.), ports. ; 30 cm. [ND511.5.K6M37] 76-370633 ISBN 0-900955-18-X : £2.00
1. Kokoschka, Oskar, 1886- 2. Landscape in art. I. Marlborough Fine Art, ltd., London. II. Title: Cityscapes and landscapes, a 90th birthday tribute.

KOKOSCHKA, Oskar, 1886- 760'.092'4
Oskar Kokoschka : Gemalde und Aquarelle seit 1953 ; Zeichnungen, Druckgrafik, Mosaiken seit 1971 ; das schriftliche Werk : 20. Februar bis 4. Mai 1975, 59. BAT-Ausstellung im BAT-Haus Hamburg, Ausstellung der Lichtwark-Gesellschaft im Kunsthaus Hamburg / [Katalog-Bearbeitung, Heinz Spielmann]. [Hamburg] : BAT Cigaretten-Fabriken GmbH, Presse und Information, [1975] 96 p. : numerous ill. (some col.) ; 26 cm. [N6811.5.K59S68] 75-507311
1. Kokoschka, Oskar, 1886- I. Spielmann, Heinz. II. BAT Cigaretten-Fabriken. III. Lichtwark-Gesellschaft. IV. Hamburg. Kunsthaus.

KOKOSCHKA, Oskar, 1886- 741.9'42
Oskar Kokoschka drawings, 1906-1965. Edited by Ernest Rathenau in collaboration with the artist. [Translated by Heinz Norden] Coral Gables, Fla., University of Miami Press [1970] 285 p. illus. 31 cm. Translation of Handzeichnungen 1906-1965. [NC245.K568A563] 76-129665 17.50 201. (part col.) 31 cm. I. Title.

KOKOSCHKA, Oskar, 1886- 709.436
Watercolours, drawings, writings. With an introd. by John Russell. New York, Abrams [1963] 24 p. 32 plates (part col.) 33 cm. The colored plates are "detachable, and two slip-in frames have been provided" in pocket. [ND1946.K6R8] 63-8921
I. Russell, John, 1919-

SCHMALENBACH, Fritz, 1909- 759.2
Oskar Kokoschka. [Translated by Violet M. Macdonald] Greenwich, Conn., New York Graphic Society [1967] 80 p. illus. (part col.) 27 cm. [ND538.K62S313] 68-18965
1. Kokoschka, Oskar, 1886- I. Title.

VICTORIA and Albert 760'.092'4
Museum, South Kensington.
Homage to Kokoschka : prints and drawings lent by Reinhold, Count Bethusy-Huc / Victoria and Albert Museum. London : [H.M. Stationery Off.], 1976. 64 p. : ill. ; 21 cm. Catalog of an exhibition. Includes bibliographical references. [NE2348.5.K64V5 1976] 76-374847 ISBN 0-901486-94-9 : £1.00
1. Kokoschka, Oskar, 1886- I. Kokoschka, Oskar, 1886- II. Bethusy-Huc, Reinhold, Graf. III. Title.

Kolar, Jiri, 1914—

KOLAR, Jiri., 1914- 759.37
Jiri Kolar : [exhibition]. New York : Solomon R. Guggenheim Museum, 1975. 139 p. : ill. (some col.) ; 26 cm. Errata slip inserted. Bibliography: p. [N6834.5.K6S64] 75-27338
1. Kolar, Jiri, 1914- I. Solomon R. Guggeheim Museum, New York.

Kolb, Leon, 1890—Art collections.

STANFORD 769'.4'2094074019473
University. Libraries. Division of Special Collections.
Portraits: a catalog of the engravings, etchings, mezzotints, and lithographs presented to the Stanford University Library by Dr. and Mrs. Leon Kolb. Compiled by Susan V. Lenkey. [Stanford, Calif.] Stanford University, 1972. 373 p. port. 28 cm. On cover: Collection of Dr. and Mrs. Leon Kolb. [NE240.K64S72] 73-150724
1. Kolb, Leon, 1890—Art collections. 2. Stanford University. Libraries. 3. Portrait prints—Stanford, Calif.—Catalogs. I. Lenkey, Susan V., comp. II. Title.

Kolbe, Georg, 1877-1947.

KOLBE, Georg, 1877- 730'.92'4
1947.
Sculpture from the Collection of B. Gerald Cantor. Drawings from the Georg Kolbe Museum, Berlin. [Ithaca, N.Y., Office of University Publications, Cornell University, 1972] 1 v. (unpaged) illus. 26 cm. Catalog of a traveling exhibition of Kolbe's sculpture and drawings shown at the Andrew Dickson White Museum of Art, Cornell University, and at other museums. [NB588.K6C67] 72-9043
1. Kolbe, Georg, 1877-1947. 2. Cantor, B. Gerald, 1916—Art collections. I. Cornell University. Andrew Dickson White Museum of Art.

Kolin, Sacha, 1911—

KOLIN, Sacha, 1911- 759.13
Sacha Kolin, Everson Museum of Art, Syracuse, New York. [Syracuse, N.Y., Everson Museum of Art, 1973] [16] p. illus. (part col.) 21 x 24 cm. Cover title. Catalogue of an exhibition held Sept. 4-26, 1973. [ND237.K597E93] 73-87422
1. Kolin, Sacha, 1911- I. Everson Museum of Art of Syracuse and Onondaga County.

Kollwitz, Kathe (Schmidt) 1867-1945.

CONNECTICUT. 760'.0924
University. Museum of Art.
Kathe Kollwitz: prints & drawings; the Landauer Collection. [Storrs, Conn.] 1968. [105] p. 31 illus. 22 cm. [NE654.K6C6] 78-626033
1. Kollwitz, Kathe (Schmidt) 1867-1945. 2. Landauer, Walter, 1896- —Art collections. I. Title.

KEARNS, Martha. 769'.92'4 B
Kaethe Kollwitz / by Martha Kearns. Old Westbury, N.Y. : Feminist Press, 1974. p. cm. (Feminist Press biography ; no. 5) Bibliography: p. [NE654.K6K42] 74-26743 ISBN 0-912670-15-0
1. Kollwitz, Kathe Schmidt, 1867-1945. BIP

KLEIN, Mina C. 709'.2'4 B
Kathe Kollwitz; life in art [by] Mina C. Klein [and] H. Arthur Klein. [1st ed.] New York, Holt, Rinehart and Winston [1972] xvi, 183 p. illus. 27 cm. Bibliography: p. 171-172. [NC251.K6K55] 72-150027 ISBN 0-03-086362-7 11.95
1. Kollwitz, Kathe (Schmidt) 1867-1945. I. Klein, H. Arthur, joint author. II. Title.

KLEIN, Mina C. 709'.2'4 B
Kathe Kollwitz, life in art / Mina C. Klein, H. Arthur Klein. New York : Schocken Books, 1975, c1972. xvi, 183 p. : ill. ; 26 cm. Reprint of the ed. published by Holt, Rinehart and Winston. Includes index. Bibliography: p. 171-172. [NC251.K6K55 1975] 75-10858 ISBN 0-8052-0504-7 pbk. : 6.95
1. Kollwitz, Kathe Schmidt, 1867-1945. I. Klein, H. Arthur, joint author. II. Title.

KLIPSTEIN, August, d1951. 769.2
The graphic work of Kathe Kollwitz; complete illustrated catalogue. New York, Galerie St. Etienne, 1955. xix, 359p. illus., facsims. 31cm. '200 copies with English title page.' Text in German. 'The section ... covering the years 1890-1912 is based on the descriptive catalogue by Professor Johannes Sievers, published in 1913.' Bibliography: p. xvi-xviii. [NE654.K6K512] 56-3165
1. Kollwitz, Kathe (Schmidt) 1867-1945. I. Sievers, Johannes. 1880- Die Radlerungen und Steindrucke von Kathe Kollwitz. II. Title.

KOLLWITZ, Kathe 741'.943
(Schmidt) 1867-1945.
The drawings of Kaethe Kollwitz. Introd. by Stephen Longstreet. [1st ed.] Alhambra, Calif., Borden Pub. Co. [1967] 1 v. (chiefly illus.) 31 cm. (Master draughtsman series) [NC1145.K63L6] 68-934
I. Longstreet, Stephen, 1907- II. Title.

KOLLWITZ, Kathe (Schmidt) 741.943
1867-1945.
Kaethe Kollwitz, drawings. [By] Herbert Bittner. New York, T. Yoseloff [1959] 35, [130] p. of plates. illus., port. 29cm. Bibliography: p. 17-18 [NC1145.K63B5] 59-8230
I. Bittner, Herbert. II. Title.

KOLLWITZ, Kathe 769'.92'4
(Schmidt) 1867-1945.
Kollwitz; an exhibition of graphic works by Kathe Kollwitz from the permanent collection of the Minnesota Museum of Art ... 26 September-10 November 1973. [Saint Paul, Minnesota Museum of Art, 1973] 64 p. illus. 24 cm. (Minnesota Museum of Art. Catalog 121) Bibliography: p. 64. [NE654.K6M56] 73-89221
1. Kollwitz, Kathe (Schmidt) 1867-1945. I. Minnesota Museum of Art. II. Title. III. Series.

NAGEL, Otto, 1894-1967. 769'.924
Kathe Kollwitz. [Translated by Stella Humphries] Greenwich, Conn., New York Graphic Society [1971] 261, [1] p. illus. 28 cm. Bibliography: p. [262] [NC251.K6N213] 79-137655 ISBN 0-8212-0401-7 13.50
1. Kollwitz, Kathe (Schmidt) 1867-1945.

PETER Deitsch Fine Arts, 769'.924
inc.
Kathe Kollwitz: rare prints and drawings. New York, 1970. [47] p. illus. 16 x 23 cm. (Its Stock catalogue no. 14, new ser. no. 2) Label on t.p.: Supplied by Worldwide Books, inc., Boston, Mass. [NE654.K6P4] 78-24231
1. Kollwitz, Kathe (Schmidt) 1867-1945.

A Selection of prints 769'.92'4
by Kathe Kollwitz from the Landauer Collection of the William Benton Museum of Art, the University of Connecticut, Storrs. Storrs : William Benton Museum of Art, University of Connecticut, c1975. [53] p. : ill. ; 22 cm. [NE654.K6S44] 75-326801
1. Kollwitz, Kathe Schmidt, 1867-1945. 2. Landauer, Walter, 1896- —Art collections. I. Kollwitz, Kathe Schmidt, 1867-1945. II. William Benton Museum of Art.

Komar, Vitali.

KOMAR, Vitali. 759.7
Komar/Melamid, two Soviet dissident artists / edited by Melvyn B. Nathanson ; with an introd. by Jack Burnham. Carbondale : Southern Illinois University Press, c1979. xxxix, 59 p. : ill. ; 29 cm. Bibliography: p. xiii. [ND699.K557A4 1979] 78-14254 ISBN 0-8093-0887-8 : 15.00
1. Komar, Vitali. 2. Melamid, Aleksandr. 3. Dissident art—Russia. I. Melamid, Aleksandr, joint author. II. Nathanson, Melvyn B., 1944- III. Title.

Konarak, India. Temple.

ELISOFON, Eliot. 731.8'8'945
Erotic spirituality : the vision of Konarak / photos., Eliot Elisofon ; comment, Alan Watts. New York : Collier Books, 1974, c1971. 125 p. ; 28 cm. [NB1008.K6E4 1974] 74-192529 pbk. : 3.95
1. Konarak, India. Temple. 2. Sculpture—Konarak, India. 3. Erotic art—Konarak, India. I. Watts, Alan Wilson, 1915-1973. II. Title.

Kongelige Porcelainsfabrik & Fajancefabriken Aluminia a/s, Copenhagen.

NEWMAN, Earl Nelson. 738.2'7
The Danish Royal Copenhagen plaquettes, 2010 series. [1st ed. Edmond? Okla., 1973] xiii, 123 p. illus. 23 cm. [NK4210.K58N48] 73-154713
1. Kongelige Porcelainsfabrik & Fajancefabriken Aluminia a/s, Copenhagen. 2. Plaquettes—Denmark—Catalogs. I. Title.

Konica camera.

HERZ, Nat. 771.31
Konica pocket handbook; an introduction to better photography. New York, Verlan Books 1960. 186p. illus. 11x15cm. (A Universal photo book) Includes bibliography. [TR263.K55H4] 60-10803
1. Konica camera. 2. Photography—Handbooks, manuals, etc. I. Title.

JACOBS, Lou. 771.3'1
Konica autoreflex manual [by] Lou Jacobs, Jr. New York, American Photographic Book Pub. Co. [1972] 175 p. illus. (part col.) 24 cm. [TR263.K55J33] 72-77135 ISBN 0-8174-0551-8 8.95
1. Konica camera. 2. Photography—Handbooks, manuals, etc. I. Title. BIP

JACOBS, Lou. 771.3'1
The Konica guide / Lou Jacobs, Jr. Garden City, N.Y. : Amphoto, c1978. 120 p., [4] leaves of plates : ill. (some col.) ; 26 cm. (A Modern camera guide series) Includes index. [TR263.K55J34] 78-18816 ISBN 0-8174-2501-2 : 10.95. ISBN 0-8174-2121-1 pbk. : 5.95
1. Konica camera. 2. Photography—Handbooks, manuals, etc. I. Title. II. Series: The Modern camera guide series. BIP

Konti, Isidore, 1862-1938.

KONTI, Isidore, 1862- 730'.92'4
1938.
The sculpture of Isidore Konti, 1862-1938 : [exhibition], January 26-March 30, 1975, the Hudson River Museum. Yonkers, N.Y. : The Museum, c1974. [125] p. : ill. ; 28 cm. Bibliography: p. [122] [NB237.K58H82] 74-33142
1. Konti, Isidore, 1862-1938. I. Hudson River Museum. II. Title. BIP

Koran—Illustrations.

LINGS, 745.6'0917'67107402142
Martin.
The Qur'an : catalogue of an exhibition of Qur'an manuscripts at the British Library, 3 April-15 August 1976 / [by] Martin Lings, Yasin Hamid Safadi. [London] : World of Islam Publishing Co. Ltd for the British Library, 1976. 98 p., xxiv p. of plates : facsims. (some col.), map ; 26 cm. Includes index. Bibliography: p. 95-96. [ND1457.I82L64] 76-378960 ISBN 0-905035-20-8. ISBN 0-905035-21-6 pbk.
1. Koran—Illustrations. 2. Calligraphy, Islamic—Exhibitions. 3. Illumination of books and manuscripts—Exhibitions. I. Safadi, Yasin Hamid, joint author. II. British Library. III. Title.

Kormendi, Elizabeth.

KORMENDI, Eugene. 735.73
The art of Eugene and Elizabeth Kormendi; with an appreciation by Dudley C. Watson. New York, International Press Associates Psychological Library, 1951. unpaged. illus. 24 cm. [NB237.K6W3] 51-40304
1. Kormendi, Elizabeth.

Kottler, Moses, 1896—

SCHOLTZ, Johannes Du 730'.92'4 B
Plessis.
Moses Kottler : his Cape years / J. du P. Scholtz. 1st ed. Cape Town : Tafelberg, 1976. 134 p. : ill. ; 29 cm. Includes catalogue illustrations and catalogue of paintings and sculptures. Includes bibliographical references and index. [N7396.K67S36] 77-355339 ISBN 0-624-00956-4
1. Kottler, Moses, 1896- 2. Artists—South Africa—Biography. I. Kottler, Moses, 1896-

Kovalevsky, Olga.

KOVALEVSKY, Olga. 741.9'47
Studies in movement of Doris Niles and Serge Leslie, drawn by Olga Kovalevsky. Los Angeles [United Printing and Lithograph Co.] 1951. 1 portfolio (iv p. 18 plates (part col.)) 29 cm. "The American edition of this folio is limited to two hundred and fifty numbered copies of which this is number 123." [NC269.K673N54] 75-318291
1. Kovalevsky, Olga. 2. Niles, Doris. 3. Leslie, Serge. 4. Dancing in art. 5. Movement, Aesthetics of. I. Title.

Krakel, Dean Fenton, 1923—

KRAKEL, Dean Fenton, 1923- 069'.9'70924 B
Adventures in Western art / by Dean Krakel. Kansas City, Mo. : Lowell Press, [1977] p. cm. Bibliography: p. [N654.K7] 76-21136 ISBN 0-913504-35-1 : 11.95
1. Krakel, Dean Fenton, 1923- 2. National Cowboy Hall of Fame and Western Heritage Center. 3. Museum directors—United States—Biography. 4. The West in art. I. Title. BIP

Krannert Center for the Performing Arts.

KRANNERT Center for the Performing Arts. 790.2'06'277366
Krannert Center for the Performing Arts: the concept and the design. [Urbana, Ill., 1969 or 70] 75 p. illus. 31 cm. [NA6813.U6U73 1969] 74-172944
1. Krannert Center for the Performing Arts. 2. Theaters—Illinois—Urbana—Construction.

THE Story and facts about the Krannert Center for the Performing Arts. 725'.81'0977366 [Urbana] University of Illinois at Urbana-Champaign [1969?] 30 p. plans. 28 cm. Cover title. [NA6813.U6U77] 74-627876
1. Krannert Center for the Performing Arts.

Krans, Olof, 1838-1916.

SWANK, George. 759.13
Painter Krans of Bishop Hill Colony / by George Swank. Galva, Ill. : Galvaland Press, 1976. 176 p. : ill. (some col.) ; 29 cm. [ND237.K67S9] 76-375114
1. Krans, Olof, 1838-1916. 2. Painters—United States—Bishop Hill, Ill.—Biography. 3. Bishop Hill, Ill.—History. I. Title.

Kranz, Kurt.

KRANZ, Kurt. 741.973
Kurt Kranz : early form sequences, 1927-1932 = Kurt Kranz : fruhe Form-Reihen, 1927-1932 / Hans Richter, Werner Haftmann, Werner Hofmann. Cambridge, Mass. : MIT Press, c1975. 228 p. : ill. (some col.) ; 27 cm. English and German. Includes bibliographical references and indexes. [N6888.K74R52] 75-27384 ISBN 0-262-11060-1
1. Kranz, Kurt. I. Richter, Hans, 1888- II. Haftmann, Werner. III. Hofmann, Werner, 1928-

KRANZ, Kurt. 709'.2'4
Kurt Kranz : early form sequences, 1927-1932 = Kurt Kranz : fruhe form-reihen, 1927-1932 / Hans Richter, Werner Haftmann, Werner Hofmann. Hamburg : H. Christians, c1975. 228 p. : ill. (some col.) ; 27 cm. English and German. Includes index. Bibliography: p. 220-221. [N6888.K74R52 1975b] 76-358047 ISBN 0-262-11060-1 (U.S.A.)
1. Kranz, Kurt. I. Richter, Hans, 1888- II. Haftmann, Werner. III. Hofmann, Werner, 1928-

Krasner, Lenore.

KRASNER, Lenore. 759.13
Lee Krasner : collages and works on paper, 1933-1974 : Corcoran Gallery of Art, January 11 through February 16, 1975 : Pennsylvania State University Museum of Art, March 23 through April 27, 1975 : [catalogue / compiled, edited, and designed by Randall deLeeuw]. Washington : Corcoran Gallery of Art, c1975. 63 p. : ill. (some col.) ; 21 cm. Bibliography: p. 58-63. [N6537.K69D44] 74-33734
1. Krasner, Lenore. I. DeLeeuw, Randall. II. Corcoran Gallery of Art, Washington, D.C. III. Pennsylvania. State University. Museum of Art.

KRASNER, Lenore. 759.13
Lee Krasner: large paintings, by Marcia Tucker. [Catalog of the exhibition at the] Whitney Museum of American Art. New York [1973] 43 p. illus. 20 x 23 cm. Bibliography: p. 41-43. [ND237.K68T82] 73-88962
1. Krasner, Lenore. I. Tucker, Marcia. II. Whitney Museum of American Art, New York. III. Title.

Kraus, H. P., firm, booksellers, New York.

KRAUS, H. P., firm, booksellers, New York. 093
Monumenta xylographica et typographica. The cradle of printing part II. New York [1971] 167 p. illus. facsims. (part col.) 36 cm. (Its Catalogue 131) "Price list" ([1] l.) inserted. [Z240.Z9K7] 73-159518
1. Kraus, H. P., firm, booksellers, New York. 2. Incunabula—Bibliography—Catalogs. 3. Incunabula—Facsimiles. I. Title. II. Title: The cradle of printing part II. III. Series.

Kraus, Hans Peter, 1907- —Art collection.

GRUBE, Ernst J. 745.6'7
Islamic paintings from the 11th to the 18th century in the Collection of Hans P. Kraus [by] Ernst J. Grube. New York, H. P. Kraus [1972?] 291 p. illus., 54 [i.e. 55] col. plates. 36 cm. On spine: Islamic paintings: the Kraus Collection. Bibliography: p. 17-[21] [ND2955.G7] 72-187217
1. Kraus, Hans Peter, 1907- —Art collection. 2. Illumination of books and manuscripts, Islamic—Catalogs. 3. Paintings, Islamic—Catalogs. I. Title. II. Title: The Kraus Collection.

Krebs, Patsy, 1940—

FOUR Californians 709'.794'074019498 : Christopher Georgesco, Patsy Krebs, Andrew Spence, Robert Therrien : [exhibition, La Jolla Museum of Contemporary Art, July 16-September 6, 1977]. [La Jolla, Calif.] : The Museum, c1977. [44] p. : ill. (some col.) ; 18 cm. [N6530.C2F65] 77-82831
1. Krebs, Patsy, 1940- 2. Spence, Andrew, 1947- 3. Therrien, Robert, 1947- 4. Art, Modern—20th century—California—Exhibitions. I. Georgesco, Christopher, 1950- II. La Jolla Museum of Contemporary Art.

Krebs, Rockne, 1938—

WOOD, James N. 730'.924
Rockne Krebs, by James N. Wood. [Buffalo, Printed by Holling Press, 1971] 24 p. illus. 27 cm. Exhibition held at Albright-Knox Art Gallery, Buffalo, Feb. 14-Apr. 30, 1971. Bibliography: p. 22. [NB237.K72W6] 72-25110
1. Krebs, Rockne, 1938- I. Albright-Knox Art Gallery.

Kreeger, David Lloyd, 1909- —Art collections.

THE Collection of Mr. and Mrs. David Lloyd Kreeger 708'.153 / edited by Margy P. Sharpe ; introductions by Charles W. Millard ... [et al.]. Washington : [s.n.], 1976 (Richmond, Va. : W. M. Brown) 303 p. : ill. (some col.) ; 26 cm. Cover title: The Kreeger Collection. Includes index. [N5220.K69C64] 75-40815
1. Kreeger, David Lloyd, 1909- —Art collections. 2. Kreeger, Carmen Felicia Matanzo—Art collections. I. Sharpe, Margy P. II. Title: The Kreeger collection.

DORRA, Henri, 1924- 750'.74'0153
The Kreeger Collection, by Henri Dorra, with the assistance of Anne Betty Weinshenker and Cynthia J. Jaffee. Washington, D.C., 1970. 173 p. illus. 26 cm. [N5220.K69D6] 71-105375
1. Kreeger, David Lloyd, 1909- —Art collections. 2. Kreeger, Carmen Felicia Matanzo—Art collections. I. Weinshenker, Anne Betty, joint author. II. Jaffee, Cynthia J., joint author. III. Title.

Krenkel, Roy G., 1918—

KRENKEL, Roy G., 1918- 741.9'73
Cities & scenes from the ancient world, by Roy G. Krenkel. Pref. by Sanford Zane Meschkow. Philadelphia, Owlswick Press [1974] 82 p. (chiefly illus.) 34 cm. [NC139.K73A43] 74-77464 ISBN 0-913896-02-0 16.00
1. Krenkel, Roy G., 1918- I. Title. BIP

Krenov, James.

KRENOV, James. 684.1'04'0924 B
A cabinetmaker's notebook / James Krenov. New York : Van Nostrand Reinhold Co., 1976. 132 p. : ill. ; 28 cm. Includes index. [TT140.K73A33] 75-30233 ISBN 0-442-24551-3 : 13.50
1. Krenov, James. 2. Cabinet-work. I. Title. BIP

Kriensky, Morris.

KRIENSKY, Morris. 759.13
The way is peace, the road is love. Art and poetry by Kriensky. Norwalk, Conn., C. R. Gibson Co. [1973] [40] p. illus. (part col.) 23 cm. [ND1839.K74A57] 72-92719 ISBN 0-8378-1760-9 3.95
1. Kriensky, Morris. I. Title.

Krimpen, Jan van, 1892-1958.

KRIMPEN, Jan van, 1892-1958. 686.2'24
A letter to Philip Hofer on certain problems connected with the mechanical cutting of punches. A facsim. reproduction, with an introd. and commentary by John Dreyfus. Cambridge, Mass., Dept. of Print. and Graphic Arts, Harvard College Library, 1972. 101 p. illus. 26 cm. (Studies in the history of calligraphy and printing, 4) Facsim. of the Harvard College Library Ms. Typ 410. Includes bibliographies. [Z250.K67 1972a] 73-104909 15.00
1. Krimpen, Jan van, 1892-1958. 2. Hofer, Philip, 1898- 3. Type and type founding. I. Hofer, Philip, 1898- II. Dreyfus, John, ed. III. Title. IV. Series.

Krishna—Art.

ARCHER, William George, 1907- 755.945211
The loves of Krishna in Indian painting and poetry. New York, Grove Press [1960?] 127 p., 40 plates. 20 cm. (An Evergreen book, E-124) Bibliography: p. 121. [BL1220.A7 1960] 58-8584
I. Title.

SPINK, Walter M. 704.948'9'45
Krishnamandala, a devotional theme in Indian art [by] Walter M. Spink. Ann Arbor, Center for South and Southeast Asian Studies, University of Michigan [1971] ix, 133 p. illus. (part col.) 28 cm. (University of Michigan. Center for South and Southeast Asian Studies. Special publications, no. 2) Bibliography: p. 125-126. [N8195.3.K7S6] 79-632669
1. Krishna—Art. 2. Art, Indic. I. Title. II. Series: Michigan. University. Center for South and Southeast Asian Studies. Special publication no. 2.

SPINK, Walter M. 759.954
The quest for Krishna : paintings and poetry of the Krishna legend / Walter Spink. Ann Arbor, Mich. : Spink, c1972. 24, [2] p. : ill. (some col.) ; 28 cm. Bibliography: p. [26] [NX694.K74S64] 72-86697
1. Krishna—Art. 2. Arts, Indic. I. Title.

Kruse, Werner, fl. 1959—

KRUSE, Werner, fl.1959- 741.9'43
New York [by] Robinson. New York, Funk & Wagnalls [1967] [64] p. (chiefly illus., map, ports.) 34 cm. [NC251.K78A5313] 68-13266
1. Kruse, Werner, fl. 1959- 2. New York (City) in art. I. Title.

Ku kung po wu yuan, Peking.

FOURCADE, Francois. 708.951156
Art treasures of the Peking Museum. [Translated from the French by Norbert Guterman] New York, H. N. Abrams [1965] 177 p. 87 mounted col. illus. 33 cm. Translation of Le musee de Pekin. [N3750.P3F63] 65-15981
1. Ku kung po wu yuan, Peking. 2. Art—Peking. I. Title.

Kubin, Alfred, 1877-1959.

KUBIN, Alfred, 1877-1959. 741.9436
Alfred Kubin [by] Wieland Schmied. Prepared with the help of the Albertina Museum, Vienna, and the State Museum of Upper Austria, Linz. Catalogue by Alfred Marks. New York, F. A. Praeger [1969] 445 p. illus., plates (part col.), ports. 29 cm. Translation of Der Zeichner Alfred Kubin. Bibliography: p. 441-443. [NC245.K8S413] 69-13707 65.00
I. Schmied, Wieland, 1929- II. Marks, Alfred, writer on Upper Austria. III. Vienna. Albertina. IV. Linz, Austria. Oberosterreichisches Landesmuseum.

KUBIN, Alfred, 1877-1959. 741.9'436
Alfred Kubin, 1877-1959: an exhibition of drawings and watercolors, December 1970 through January 1971. With an introd. by Alfred Werner New York, Serge Sabarsky Gallery [1970] 1 v. (unpaged) 55 illus. (part col.), port. 25 cm. [NC245.K8A4] 74-143910
I. Serge Sabarsky Gallery.

KUBIN, Alfred, 1877-1959. 760'.092'4 B
Alfred Kubin's autobiography. [New York, Galerie St. Etienne, 196-?] lxxviii p. illus. 21 cm. Translation of Aus meinem Leben. [NC245.K8A2213] 73-170145
1. Kubin, Alfred, 1877-1959.

KUBIN, Alfred, 1877-1959. 741.9'436
Kubin's Dance of death, and other drawings. 83 works, by Alfred Kubin. With a new introd. by Gregor Sebba. New York, Dover Publications [1973] xii p., 83 plates. 29 cm. Includes Die Blatter mit dem Tod originally published in 1918, and Funfzig Zeichnungen originally published in 1923, with captions in German and English. [NC245.K8A52] 72-81285 ISBN 0-486-22884-3 2.50 (pbk.)
1. Kubin, Alfred, 1877-1959. 2. Dance of death. I. Kubin, Alfred, 1877-1959. Die Blatter mit dem Tod. 1973. II. Kubin, Alfred, 1877-1959. Funfzig Zeichnungen. 1973. III. Title. IV. Title: Dance of death. BIP

RAABE, Paul, ed. 704.9425
Alfred Kubin: Leben, Werk, Wirkung. Im Auftrage von Kurt Otte, Kubin-Archiv in Hamburg, zusammengestellt. Hamburg, Rowohlt, 1957. 295p. illus., plates (4 col.) ports., facsim. 25cm. 'Chronologisches Werkverzeichnis : p. 68-189. 'Bibliographischer Lebensbericht': p. 190-249. [NC1145.K825R2] A57
1. Kubin, Alfred, 1877- 2. Kubin, Alfred, 1877- -Bibl. I. Title.

Kuei-lin, China, in art.

GEORGE, Thomas, 1918- 741.9'73
Kweilin, Kwangsi Province, People's Republic of China : drawings / by Thomas George. [New York : Betty Parsons Gallery, c1975] 14 leaves : chiefly ill. ; 30 x 41 cm. Cover title. "Exhibition ... sponsored and organized by the Betty Parsons Gallery ... New York." "Edition [of] 500 copies." [NC139.G24B47] 75-34521
1. George, Thomas, 1918- 2. Kuei-lin, China, in art. I. Betty Parsons Gallery. II. Title.

Kuhn, Walt. 1877-1949.

ADAMS, Philip Rhys, 1908- 759.13
Walt Kuhn, painter : his life and work / by Philip Rhys Adams. Columbus : Ohio State University Press, [1978] p. cm. Includes index. [ND237.K8A84] 78-3502 ISBN 0-8142-0258-6 : 30.00
1. Kuhn, Walt, 1877-1949. 2. Painters—United States—Biography. I. Title. BIP

ARIZONA. University. Art Gallery. 759.13
Painter of vision; a retrospective exhibition of oils, watercolors, and drawings, by Walt Kuhn, 1877-1949, February 6 through March 31. Tucson [1966] 128 p. (chiefly plates (part col.) port.) 27 cm. "Walt Kuhn [by] Philip Rhys Adams": p. 13-35. [ND237.K8A9] 66-63333
1. Kuhn, Walt. 1877-1949. I. Title.

KUHN, Walt, 1877-1949. 741.9'73
Walt Kuhn. [New York, Kennedy Galleries, 1968] [48] p. illus. 28 cm. Catalog of the exhibition held at the Kennedy Galleries, New York, Dec. 3-31, 1968. [ND237.K8A57] 71-18813
I. Kennedy Galleries, inc., New York.

KUHN, Walt, 1877-1949. 759.13
Walt Kuhn, 1877-1949. New York, Kennedy Galleries [1972] [3] p., 29 plates. 28 cm. Catalog of an exhibition held at the Kennedy Galleries, New York, Mar. 1-18, 1972. [ND237.K8K46] 73-157912
1. Kuhn, Walt, 1877-1949. I. Kennedy Galleries, inc., New York.

KUHN, Walt, 1877-1949. 759.13
Walt Kuhn, 1877-1949. New York, Kennedy Galleries [1967] [75] p. illus. 28 cm. Catalogue of an exhibition, Oct. 10th-Nov. 7th, 1967, with introductory text by Frank Getlein. [ND237.K8G4] 67-9301
I. Getlein, Frank. II. Kennedy Galleries, inc., New York. III. Title.

Kuniyoshi, Yasuo, 1893-1953.

KUNIYOSHI, Yasuo, 1893-1953. 759.13
A special loan retrospective exhibition of works by Yasuo Kuniyoshi. [Gainesville, University Gallery, University of Florida, 1969?] [56] p. illus. (part col.) 23 cm. Catalogue of the exhibition held at the University Gallery, University of Florida, February 7-March 30, 1969 and at the National Collection of Fine Arts, Smithsonian Institution, May 9-June 29, 1969. [ND237.K83A47] 71-627626
I. Florida. University, Gainesville. University Gallery. II. Smithsonian Institution. National Collection of Fine Arts. III. Title.

YASUO Kuniyoshi, 1889-1953 : a retrospective exhibition, February 9-March 23, 1975, University Art Museum, the University of Texas at Austin, U.S.A.... Austin : University of Texas Art Museum, [1975] 71 p. : ill. (some col.) ; 22 cm. [N6537.K83Y37] 74-620196 760'.092'4
1. Kuniyoshi, Yasuo, 1893-1953. I. Texas. University at Austin. Art Museum.

Kunkel, Jerry.

KUNKEL, Jerry. 709'.2'4
Jerry Kunkel : [catalog of an exhibition] May 5-June 2. Denver : Denver Art Museum, [1974] [28] p. : chiefly ill. : 23 cm. [N6537.K85D45] 74-80285 ISBN 0-914738-01-1
1. Kunkel, Jerry. I. Denver. Art Museum.

Kupka, Frantisek, 1871-1957.

KUPKA, Frantisek, 1871-1957. 760'.092'4
Frantisek Kupka, 1871-1957 : a retrospective, The Solomon R. Guggenheim Museum, New York. New York : Solomon R. Guggenheim Foundation, 1975. 327 p. : ill. (some col.) ; 28 cm. Cover title: Kupka. "Exhibition 75/5." "Catalogue of the exhibition, by Margit Rowell": p. 81-304. "Addenda to the catalogue": leaf inserted. Bibliography: p. 323-325. [N6834.5.K8R68] 75-27339
1. Kupka, Frantisek, 1871-1957. I. Rowell, Margit. II. Solomon R. Guggenheim Museum, New York.

KUPKA, Frantisek, 1871-1957. 759.4
Kupka: gouaches and pastels [by] Jean Cassou and Denise Fedit. [Translated from the French by Robert Erich Wolf] New York, H. M. Abrahms [1965, c1964] 68 p. illus. (part col.) port. 21 x 23 cm. Bibliography: p. 66-68. [ND1950.K86C33] 65-12091
I. Cassou, Jean, 1897- II. Fedit, Denise.

VACHTOVA, Ludmila. 759.37
Frank Kupka; pioneer of abstract art. Introd. by J. P. Hodin. [Translated from the Czech by Zdenek Lederer] New York, McGraw-Hill [1968] 317 p. illus. (part col.), port. 28 cm. Bibliography: p. 289-290. [ND538.K687V33 1968b] 68-24606 15.95
1. Kupka, Frantisek, 1871-1957.

Kurelek, William, 1927—

KURELEK, William, 1927- 759.11
Kurelek country / William Kurelek. Boston : Houghton Mifflin, 1975. p. cm. [ND249.K85A49 1975] 75-17697 ISBN 0-395-21971-X : 20.00
1. Kurelek, William, 1927- 2. Canada in art. I. Title.

KURELEK, William, 1927- 759.11
The last of the Arctic / by William Kurelek. Toronto : Pagurian Press ; Momence, Ill. : distributed by Publishers Marketing Group, c1976. 94 p. : ill. (some col.) ; 31 cm. [ND249.K85A5] 77-352575 ISBN 0-88932-031-4 : 19.95
1. Kurelek, William, 1927- 2. Eskimos—Canada—Pictorial works. 3. Eskimos—Canada—Social life and customs. I. Title. BIP

Kurokawa, Noriaki, 1934—

KUROKAWA, Noriaki, 1934- 720'.92'4
Metabolism in architecture / Kisho Kurakawa [i.e. N. Kurokawa]. Boulder, Colo. : Westview Press, 1977. 208 p. : ill. ; 26 cm. Includes index. Bibliography: p. 205-207. [NA1559.K83A5 1977] 77-1042 ISBN 0-89158-734-9 lib.bdg. : 22.50
1. Kurokawa, Noriaki, 1934- 2. Metabolism in architecture (movement) I. Title.

Kwakiutl Indians—Art—Exhibitions.

HAWTHORN, Audrey. 730'.09701
Art of the Kwakiutl Indians and other Northwest coast tribes. Vancouver, Univ. of British Columbia; Seattle, London, Univ. of Wash. Pr. [1967] xxx, 410p. illus. (pt. col.) map. 29cm. Bibl. [E99.K9H3] 67-13111 25.00
1. Kwakiutl Indians—Art—Exhibitions. 2. Indians of North America—Northwest coast of North America—Art—Exhibitions. 3. British Columbia. University. Museum of Anthropology. I. Title.

Kyle site.

JELKS, Edward B v. 12
The Kyle site; a stratified central Texas aspect site in Hill County, Texas. With appendices by Thomas W. McKern and Ernest L. Lundelius, Jr. Austin, Dept. of Anthropology, University of Texas, 1962. x, 115 p. illus., maps. 23 cm. (University of Texas. Dept. of Anthropology. Archaeology series, no. 5) Includes bibliographies. [F388.T4 no. 5] 64-63210
1. Kyle site. I. Title. II. Series. III. Series: Texas. University. Dept. of Anthropology. Archaeology series, no. 5

Kyoto, Katsura Rikyu.

ISHIMOTO, Yasuhiro, 1921- 728.8'2
Katsura; tradition and creation in Japanese architecture. Text by Kenzo Tange. Photos. by Yasuhiro Ishimoto. Design by Yusaku Kamekura. [English translation by Charles S. Terry] Redesigned ed. New Haven [Conn.] Yale University Press, 1972 [c1971] 195 p. illus. 30 cm. [NA7758.K94I813 1972] 72-75194 ISBN 0-300-01599-2 22.50
1. Kyoto. Katsura Rikyu. I. Tange, Kenzo, 1913- II. Title.

ISHIMOTO, Yasuhiro. 1921- 720.952
Katsura: tradition and creation in Japanese architecture. Architecture in Japan [by] Walter Gropius. Tradition and creation in Japanese architecture [by] Kenzo Tange. Photos [by] Yasuhiro Ishimoto [Translated from the Japanese. Charles S. Terrv.] New Haven. Conn., Yale University Press. 1960[ ] vi, 36p. text [148]p. plates & plans (part col.) 29cm. 60-51016 15.00
1. Kyoto, Katsura Rikyu. 2. Architecture—Japan. I. Gropius, Walter, 1883- II. Tange, Kenzo. 1913- III. Title.

OKAWA, Naomi, 1929- 722'.1
Edo architecture, Katsura and Nikko / by Naomi Okawa ; with photos. by Chuji Hirayama ; translated by Alan Woodhull and Akito Miyamoto. 1st English ed. New York : Weatherhill, 1975. 162 p., [2] fold. leaves of plates : ill. (some col.) ; 24 cm. (The Heibonsha survey of Japanese art ; v. 20) Translation of Katsura to Nikko. [NA1553.5.O3713] 74-23786 ISBN 0-8348-1027-1 : 12.50
1. Kyoto. Katsura Rikyu. 2. Nikko, Japan (Torhigi Prefecture). Toshogu. 3. Architecture—Japan—Edo period, 1600-1868. I. Title. II. Series.

[SATO, Tatsuzo, 1904-] 728.84
the Katsura Imperial villa. New York 1, Perkins Oriental Bks., 225 Seventh Ave., 1962] 80p. illus. (pt. col.) maps. 22cm. Japanese text, with summary in English. J62 3.50 bds.,
1. Kyoto, Katsura Rikyre. I. Umesao, Tadao, 1920- II. Title.

YANAGI, Ryo 712.095219
Katsura Imperial Palace. Japanese volume written and prepared from a translation by George Saito [dist. Los Angeles, Perkins Oriental Bks., c.1961] 14p.; 179p. illus., plates (mounted col.) 37cm. Added t.p.: La villa imperiale Katsura, par R. Yanagui. Photo., S. Foujimoto. 80.00, bound in silk-bound portfolio.
1. Kyoto. Katsura Rikyu. 2. Gardens—Japan. I. Foujimoto, Shihachi, 1911- illus. II. Saito, George, tr. III. Title.

La Farge, John, 1835-1910.

CORTISSOZ, Royal, 1869-1948. 759.13 B
John La Farge; a memoir and a study. New York, Kennedy Graphics, 1971 [c1911] xii, 268 p. illus., ports. 24 cm. (Library of American art) [ND237.L2C6 1971] 70-87508
1. La Farge, John, 1835-1910.

WEINBERG, Helene Barbara, 1942- 759.13
The decorative work of John La Farge / H. Barbara Weinberg. New York : Garland Pub., 1977. viii, 686 p. : ill. ; 21 cm. (Outstanding dissertations in the fine arts) Originally presented as the author's thesis, Columbia, 1972. Bibliography: p. 471-517. [ND237.L2W44 1977] 76-23654 ISBN 0-8240-2736-1 : 60.00
1. La Farge, John, 1835-1910. I. Title. II. Series. BIP

La Roche site.

HOFFMAN, John Jacob, 1931- 970.4'83'55
The La Roche sites, by J. J. Hoffman. Editor: Jerome E. Petsche. Lincoln, Neb., 1968. iv, 123 p. illus., maps, plans. 25 cm. (River Basin Surveys. Publications in salvage archeology, no. 11) Bibliography: p. 94-97. [E78.S63H59] 79-600250
1. La Roche site. I. Title. II. Series.

La Touche, Rose.

RUSKIN, John, 1819-1900. 826.8
The letters of John Ruskin to Lord and Lady Mount-Temple. Edited, and with an introd., by John Lewis Bradley. [Columbus] Ohio State University Press [1964] xiii, 399 p. 24 cm. Bibliographical footnotes. [PR5263.A32] 64-20414
1. La Touche, Rose. I. Mount-Temple, William Francis Cowper-Temple, 1st baron, 1811-1888. II. Mount-Temple, Georgiana (Tollemache) Cowper-Temple, baroness, 1822-1901. III. Bradley, John Lewis, ed. IV. Title. BIP

La Tour, Georges du Mesnil de, 1593-1652.

LA TOUR, Georges du Mesnil de, 1593-1652. 759.4
Georges de La Tour / Christopher Wright. Oxford : Phaidon ; New York : E. P. Dutton, 1977. 16 p., 48 p. of plates : chiefly col. ill. ; 31 cm. Bibliography: p. 14. [ND553.L28W74 1977] 78-307278 ISBN 0-7148-1807-0 : 7.95
1. La Tour, Georges du Mesnil de, 1593-1652. I. Wright, Christopher, 1945-

NICOLSON, Benedict. 759.4
Georges de La Tour / by Benedict Nicolson and Christopher Wright. London : Phaidon Press, 1974. [1], vi, 234 p., [62] p. of plates, [3] leaves of plates : ill. (some col.), facsims. ; 31 cm. Distributed by Praeger, New York. Includes indexes. Bibliography: p. 221-231. [ND553.L28N52] 73-5154 ISBN 0-7148-1595-0 : 45.00
1. La Tour, Georges du Mesnil de, 1593-1652. I. Wright, Christopher, joint author. BIP

Labels.

HUMBERT, Claude. 741.6'9
Label design; evolution, function, and structure of label. With 1000 illus. chosen and introduced by Claude Humbert. [English translation by Nicholas Fry. German translation by R. M. Ostheimer] New York, Watson-Guptill Publications [1972] 252 p. illus. 29 cm. English, French, and German. [NC1003.H8513] 72-183913 ISBN 0-8230-2586-1 20.00
1. Labels. I. Title.

Labino, Dominick.

LABINO, Dominick. 748.2'913
Dominick Labino; a decade of glass craftsmanship, 1964-1974. [Exhibition organized jointly by the] Pilkington Glass Museum, Victoria and Albert Museum [and] the Toledo Museum of Art, 1974-1975. [Catalogue. Toledo, Toledo Museum of Art, 1974] [59] p. illus. 18 cm. [NK5198.L32P54] 74-79538
1. Labino, Dominick. 2. Glassware—United States. I. Pilkington Glass Museum. II. Victoria and Albert Museum, South Kensington. III. Toledo. Museum of Art.

Labor and laboring classes in art.

BAYNES, Ken. 704.94'9'331
Work [by] Ken Baynes and Alan Robinson. [1st ed.] Boston, Boston Book and Art [1970] 95 p. illus. (part col.) 23 x 27 cm. (Art and society, 2) Exhibition organized by Ken Baynes for the Welsh Arts Council and held at the National Museum of Wales in 1970. [N8219.L2B37] 73-136469 9.50
1. Labor and laboring classes in art. I. Robinson, Alan D., joint author. II. Welsh Arts Council. III. Cardiff, Wales. National Museum of Wales. IV. Title. V. Series: Art and society (Boston) 2

Labor and laboring classes in art—Juvenile literature.

SHISSLER, Barbara Johnson. 704.94'9'331
The worker in art. Designed by Patricia Koskey. Minneapolis, Lerner Publications Co., 1970. 72 p. illus. (part col.), facsim., ports. 27 cm. (Fine art books for young people) Briefly discusses and gives examples of well-known paintings immortalizing working women, laborers, craftsmen, merchants, businessmen, writers, and representatives of six other professions. [N8219.L2S5 1970] 72-84409
1. Labor and laboring classes in art—Juvenile literature. I. Title. BIP

Laboratories.

NUFFIELD Foundation. 727.5
Division for Architectural Studies.
The design of research laboratories, the report of a study. London, New York, Oxford University Press, 1961. xx, 211p. illus., diagrs., plans, tables. 31cm. Includes bibliographies. [NA6751.N8 1961] 61-3907
1. Laboratories. I. Title.

Laboratories—Design and construction.

EVERETT, Kenneth. 727'.5
A guide to laboratory design / K. Everett, D. Hughes. London ; Boston : Butterworths, 1975. 154 p. : ill. ; 22 cm. Includes bibliographical references and index. [TH4652.E9] 75-331675 ISBN 0-408-70682-1 : 9.50
1. Laboratories—Design and construction. 2. Laboratories—Safety measures. I. Hughes, Donald, joint author. II. Title.

FERGUSON, William Rex. 727'.5
Practical laboratory planning [by] W. R. Ferguson. New York, Wiley [1973] xvi, 147 p. illus. (part col.) 26 cm. "A Halsted Press book." [TH4652.F47] 72-10256 ISBN 0-470-25750-4 14.95
1. Laboratories—Design and construction. I. Title.

PURVIS, Marion Joy. 727'.5
Laboratory planning [by] M. J. Purvis. [London] Bailliere Tindall [1973] ix, 97 p. illus. 22 cm. (Laboratory monographs) Imprint covered by label: The Williams & Wilkins Company, Baltimore. Includes bibliographical references. [TH4652.P87 1973] 73-175615 ISBN 0-7020-0424-3 9.75
1. Laboratories—Design and construction. I. Title.

Laboratories—U. S.

ARCHITECTURAL record. 727.5
Buildings for research. [New York] F. W. Dodge, c1958. 224p. illus., diagrs., plans. 31cm. (An Architectural record book) Articles published since 1950. [NA6751.A7] 58-11658
1. Laboratories—U. S. 2. Architecture—Designs and plans. 3. Architecture—U. S. I. Title.

Laboureur, Jean Emile, 1877-1943.

LABOUREUR, Jean Emile, 769'.92'4
1877-1943.
Jean-Emile Laboureur, 1877-1943 : prints, drawings, and books. New York : French Institute/Alliance Francaise, c1977. 62 p. : ill. ; 25 cm. "Catalogue of the exhibition": p. 59-62. [NE650.L3A48] 77-71276
1. Laboureur, Jean Emile, 1877-1943. I. Title: Prints, drawings, and books.

Labyrinths.

MATTHEWS, William Henry, 712
1882-
Mazes and labyrinths; a general account of their history and developments, by W. H. Matthews. London, New York, Longmans, Green, 1922. Detroit, Singing Tree Press, 1969. xviii, 253 p. illus. 22 cm. Bibliography: p. 215-235. [SB475.M3 1969] 70-75946
1. Labyrinths. I. Title. BIP

MATTHEWS, William Henry, 712
1882-
Mazes and labyrinths; their history and development, by W. H. Matthews. New York, Dover Publications [1970] xviii, 253 p. illus. 22 cm. Reprint of the 1922 ed. Bibliography: p. 215-235. [SB475.M3 1970] 70-107665 ISBN 0-486-22614-X 2.50
1. Labyrinths. 2. Maze gardens. I. Title. BIP

Lace and lace making.

BATH, Virginia Churchill. 746.2
Lace. Chicago, H. Regnery Co. [1974] 320 p. illus. 29 cm. Bibliography: p. 313-316. [TT800.B25] 73-20671 ISBN 0-8092-8926-1 20.00
1. Lace and lace making. I. Title.

BATH, Virginia Churchill. 746.2
Lace / Virginia Churchill Bath. New York : Penguin Books, [1979] p. cm. Reprint of the 1974 ed. published by Regnery, Chicago. Includes index. Bibliography: p. [TT800.B25 1979] 78-23354 ISBN 0-14-046378-X pbk. : 8.95
1. Lace and lace making. I. Title.

BROOKLYN Institute of Arts 746.2
and Sciences. Museum.
The lace with the delicate air, Brooklyn Museum, May 1956. [Brooklyn, 1956?] 1v. (unpaged) chiefly illus. 31cm. Cover title. [NK9402.B7A58] 57-47806
1. Lace and lace making. I. Title.

FELDMAN, Annette. 746.2
Handmade lace & patterns / Annette Feldman. 1st ed. New York : Harper & Row, [1975] xiv, 208 p. : ill. ; 27 cm. Includes index. Bibliography: p. 203-204. [TT800.F44 1975] 74-1806 ISBN 0-06-011231-X : 8.95
1. Lace and lace making. 2. Lace and lace making—Patterns. I. Title.

JONES, Mary Eirwen. 746.2
The romance of lace. London, New York, Staples Press [1951] 171 p. illus. 29 cm. [NK9404.J78] 52-3545
1. Lace and lace making. I. Title.

KINMOND, Jean, ed. 746.43
Anchor book of lace crafts [Dist. Newton Centre, Mass., Branford, 1962, c.1961] 192p. illus. 28cm. 62-1097 9.95
1. Lace and lace making. I. Title.

KINZEL, Marianne, 1908- 746.43
First book of modern lace knitting. [2d ed.] London, Mills & Boon [1960; covered by label: Newton, Mass., C. T. Branford Co.] 95 p. illus. 27 cm. [TT800.K53 1960] 61-4629
1. Lace and lace making. I. Title. BIP

KINZEL, Marianne, 1908- 746.2
Second book of modern lace knitting. [Dist. Newton Centre, Mass., Branford, 1962, c.1961] 118p. illus. 27cm. 62-4852 4.95
1. Lace and lace making. I. Title. BIP

KLIOT, Jules. 746.2
Battenberg and point lace : techniques, stitches, and designs from Victorian needlework / edited by Jules & Kaethe Kliot. Berkeley, Calif. : Some Place Publications, [c1978] 32 p. : ill. ; 28 cm. Cover title. [TT805.K55] 78-100828 ISBN 0-916896-12-9 pbk. : 3.50
1. Lace and lace making. 2. Needlework, Victorian. 3. Battenberg lace. I. Kliot, Kaethe, joint author. II. Title. III. Title: Point lace. BIP

LAURY, Jean Ray. 746.2
New uses for old laces. Photos. by Gayle Smalley. [1st ed.] Garden City, N.Y., Doubleday, 1974. xvii, 109 p. illus. 27 cm. [TT800.L17] 73-81439 ISBN 0-385-07592-8 8.95
1. Lace and lace making. 2. Fancy work. I. Title.

MAIDMENT, Margaret. 677.653
A manual of hand-made bobbin lace work. Boston, C. T. Branford Co. [1954] 183p. illus. 26cm. [TT800.M] A55
1. Lace and lace making. I. Title. II. Title: Bobbin lace work. BIP

NIEUWHOFF, Constance. 746.2'2
Contemporary lace making / Constance Nieuwhoff ; [translated from the Dutch by Danielle Adkinson ; photography by Henk Beukers, line drawings by Annet Spruyt]. New York : Van Nostrand Reinhold, [1974] p. cm. Translation of Vrij kantklossen. Bibliography: p. [TT800.N513] 74-6794 ISBN 0-442-30071-9 : 8.95
1. Lace and lace making. I. Title. BIP

PFANNSCHMIDT, Ernst 746.2'2'0904
Erik.
Twentieth-century lace / Ernst-Erik Pfannschmidt. New York : Scribner, c1975. 216 p., [2] leaves of plates : ill. ; 26 cm. Includes bibliographical references and index. [NK9410.P42] 75-4398 ISBN 0-684-14375-5 : 10.00
1. Lace and lace making. I. Title.

POWYS, Marian, 1882- 746.2
Lace and lace-making. Drawings by the author. Boston, C. T. Branford Co., 1953. 219 p. illus. 26 cm. [NK9404.P75] 52-14187
1. Lace and lace making.

SHARP, Mary. 746.2
Point and pillow lace; a short account of various kinds, ancient and modern, and how to recognise them. New York, Dutton. Detroit, Tower Books, 1971. xv, 202 p. illus. 21 cm. "Facsimile reprint of the 1905 edition." Bibliography: p. xiii. [NK9404.S5 1905a] 72-141752
1. Lace and lace making. I. Title. BIP

WARDLE, Patricia. 746.2'094
Victorian lace. New York, F. A. Praeger [1969, c1968] 286 p. illus., ports. 24 cm. Bibliography: p. 267-270. [NK9410.W3 1969] 69-11863 10.00
1. Lace and lace making. 2. Civilization, Modern—19th century. I. Title.

WRIGHT, Doreen. 746.2'2
Bobbin lace making. London, Bell, 1971. 105 p. illus. 26 cm. Dist. in the U.S. by C. T. Branford, Newton Centre, Mass. Bibl: p. 105. [TT800.W75 1972] 72-176889 ISBN 0-7135-1792-1 9.25
1. Lace and lace making. I. Title. BIP

Lace and lace making—Collectors and collecting.

HEAD, R. E., Mrs. 746.2
The lace & embroidery collector; a guide to collectors of old lace and embroidery, by Mrs. Head. Ann Arbor, Mich., Gryphon Books, 1971. 252 p. illus. 22 cm. "This is a facsimile reprint of the 1922 ed." Bibliography: p. 245-246. [NK9404.H4 1971] 78-149781
1. Lace and lace making—Collectors and collecting. 2. Embroidery—Collectors and collecting. I. Title. BIP

HEAD, R. E, Mrs. 746.2
The lace & embroidery collector; a guide to collectors of old lace and embroidery, by Mrs. Head. London, H. Jenkins, 1922. Detroit, Gale Research Co., 1974. 252 p. illus. 18 cm. (The Collectors series) [NK9404.H4 1974] 74-2031 ISBN 0-8103-3663-4 12.00
1. Lace and lace making—Collectors and collecting. 2. Embroidery—Collectors and collecting. I. Title.

Lace and lace making—History.

MEULEN-NULLE, L. W. van 746.22
der
Lace. New York, Universe Books [1964] 79 p. illus. 22 cm. Translation of Kant, met naald en kios en speldenbos. Bibliography: p. 70-71. [NK9406.M413] 64-10343
1. Lace and lace making — Hist. I. Title.

SCHWAB, David E 746.2
The story of lace and embroidery. New York, Fairchild Publications [1951] [95] p. illus. 24 cm. [NK9406.S35] 51-10366
1. Lace and lace making — Hist. 2. Embroidery — Hist. I. Title.

Lace and lace making—History.

HUETSON, T. L. 746.2'2
Lace and bobbins; a history and collector's guide [by] T. L. Huetson. [1st American ed.] South Brunswick, A. S. Barnes [1973] 187 p. illus. 23 cm. Bibliography: p. 184. [TT800.H66 1973] 73-5105 ISBN 0-498-01398-7 6.95
1. Lace and lace making—History. 2. Lace and lace making—Collectors and collecting. 3. Lace bobbins—Collectors and collecting. I. Title.

JACKSON, Emily, 1861- 746.2'09
A history of hand-made lace. Dealing with the origin of lace, the growth of the great lace centres, the mode of manufacture, the methods of distinguishing and the care of various kinds of lace. With supplementary information by Ernesto Jesurum. Detroit, Tower Books, 1971. x, 245 p. illus. 24 cm. "Facsimile reprint of the 1900 edition." Bibliography: p. 98-105. [NK9406.J3 1900a] 70-136558
1. Lace and lace-making—History. I. Title.

PALLISER, Fanny 746.2'09
(Marryat) 1805-1878.
A history of lace. 3d ed. Detroit, Tower Books, 1971. x, 454 p. illus. 23 cm. "Facsimile reprint of the 1875 edition." Bibliography: p. 405-443. [NK9406.P25 1875a] 75-78219
1. Lace and lace making—History. I. Title.

*POND, Gabrielle 746.2
An introduction to lace New York, Charles Scribner's Sons [1975 c1973] 72 p. ill. 22 cm. [NK9404] 75-7882 ISBN 0-684-13830-1 4.95.
1. Lace and lacemaking. I. Title. BIP

SCHWAB, David E. 746.2
The story of lace and embroidery and handkerchiefs. New York, Fairchild Publications [1957] 80, [35] p. illus. 24 cm. [NK9406.S35 1957] 57-2947
1. Lace and lace making—History. 2. Embroidery—History.

Lace and lace making—Patterns.

MELEN, Lisa, 1917- 746.4
Knotting & netting; the art of filet work [by] Lisa Melen. [Translated from Swedish by Joan Bulman] New York, Van Nostrand Reinhold [1973, c1972] 88 p. illus. 23 cm. Translation of Knutet tratt. [TT800.M3813] 72-1857 ISBN 0-442-29958-3 4.95
1. Lace and lace making—Patterns. 2. Netting. I. Title.

VINCIOLO, Federico. 746.2
Renaissance patterns for lace and embroidery; an unabridged facsimile of the 'Singuliers et nouveaux pourtraicts' of 1587. [Translated by Stanley Appelbaum] New York, Dover Publications [1971] xiii, 93 p. illus. 22 cm. (The Dover pictorial archives series) "Republication [with English translation] of a 1909 facsimile edition ... based on a 1606 printing of the third edition (the first printing of this edition was ... in 1587)" Bibliography: p. [ix] [TT800.V55 1971] 79-121586 ISBN 0-486-22438-4 2.00
1. Lace and lace making—Patterns. 2. Embroidery—Patterns. I. Title. BIP

Lacquer and lacquering.

HUTH, Hans, 1892- 745.7'2
Lacquer of the West; the history of a craft and an industry, 1550-1950. Chicago, University of Chicago Press [1971] x, 158, [200] p. illus. (part col.), facsims. 28 cm. Bibliography: p. [136]-138. [NK9900.H87] 73-130185 ISBN 0-226-36315-5
1. Lacquer and lacquering. I. Title. BIP

Lacquer and lacquering, Chinese.

BEDFORD, John, 1907- 745.7'2
Chinese and Japanese lacquer. New York, Walker [1969] 63, [1] p. illus. (part col.) 20 cm. (Collectors' pieces, 16) "Some artists' signatures on Japanese lacquer": p. [64] [NK9900.B4] 69-16051 3.50
1. Lacquer and lacquering, Chinese. 2. Lacquer and lacquering, Japanese. I. Title.

Lacquer and lacquering—East (Far East)

LEE, Yu-kuan. 745.7'2
Oriental lacquer art. [1st ed.] New York, Published for Oriental House Limited, Tokyo [by] Weatherhill [1972, c1971] 394 p. illus. (part col.) 27 cm. Bibliography: p. 360-361. [NK9900.7.E15L4] 74-157275 ISBN 0-8348-0061-6 27.50
1. Lacquer and lacquering—East (Far East) 2. Lacquer and lacquering, Oriental. I. Title.

Lacquer and Lacquering—Japan.

JAHSS, Melvin, 1921- 745.7'2
Inro and other miniature forms of Japanese lacquer art, by Melvin and Betty Jahss. Rutland, Vt., C. E. Tuttle Co. [1971] 488 p. 256 illus. (76 col.) 28 cm. Bibliography: p. 479-482. [NK9900.7.J3J3] 76-109406 ISBN 0-8048-0263-7 27.50
1. Lacquer and Lacquering—Japan. 2. Inro. 3. Miniature objects—Japan. 4. Artists,

Japanese. I. Jahss, Betty, joint author. II. Title.
BIP

RAGUE, Beatrix von. 745.7'2'0952
A history of Japanese lacquerwork / Beatrix von Rague ; translated from the German by Annie R. de Wassermann. Toronto : University of Toronto Press, [1975] p. cm. Translation of Geschichte der japanischen Lackkunst. Includes index. Bibliography: p. [NK9900.7.J3R3313] 73-92299 ISBN 0-8020-2135-2 : 35.00
1. Lacquer and lacquering—Japan. I. Title.
BIP

Lacquer and lacquering—Japan—Exhibitions.

STERN, Harold P. 745.7'2
The magnificent three: lacquer, netsuke, and tsuba; selections from the Collection of Charles A. Greenfield [by] Harold P. Stern. [New York] Japan Society [1972] 141 p. illus. (part col.) 21 x 22 cm. "Catalogue of the exhibition of Japan House Gallery shown in the fall of 1972 as an activity of the Japan Society, inc." Bibliography: p. 137-139. [NK9900.7.J3S83] 72-86696 ISBN 0-913304-00-X
1. Greenfield, Charles A.—Art collections. 2. Lacquer and lacquering—Japan—Exhibitions. 3. Netsukes—Exhibitions. 4. Sword guards, Japanese—Exhibitions. I. Japan House Gallery. II. Japan Society of New York. III. Title.

Lacquer and lacquering, Oriental.

HERBERTS, Kurt. 745.59
Oriental lacquer; art and technique. [Translated from the German by Brian Morgan] New York, H. N. Abrams [1962?] 513 p. illus., plates (part col.) 2 maps. 32 cm. Translation of Das Buch der ostasiatischen Lackkunst. "Notes on the Japanese lacquer artists": p. 394-500. Bibliography: p. 502-513. [NK9900.H413] 63-12456
1. Lacquer and lacquering, Oriental. I. Title.

HERBERTS, Kurt. 745.59
Oriental lacquer: art and technique. [Translated from the German by Brian Morgan] New York, H. N. Abrams [1962?] 513 p. illus., plates (part col.), 2 maps. 32 cm. Translation of Das Buch der ostasiatischen Lackkunst. "Notes on the Japanese lacquer artists": p. 394-500. Bibliography: p. 502-513. [NK9900.H413] 63-12456
1. Lacquer and lacquering, Oriental. I. Title.

LUZZATTO-BILITZ, Oscar. 745.7'2
Oriental lacquer, by Oscar Luzzatto-Bilitz; translated by Pauline L. Phillips from the Italian. London, New York, Hamlyn, 1969. 3-158 p. col. illus. 20 cm. (Cameo) Translation of Lacche orientali. [NK9900.L813] 77-457134 15/-
1. Lacquer and lacquering, Oriental. I. Title.

Ladell, Edward, 1821-1886.

LADELL, Edward, 1821-1886. 759.2
Edward Ladell, 1821-1886 / by Frank Lewis. Leigh-on-Sea : F. Lewis, 1976. 47 p., [48] leaves of plates : ill., geneal. table, port. ; 30 cm. Limited ed. of 500 copies. Includes a catalogue of paintings. [ND497.L14L48] 76-378651 ISBN 0-85317-043-6 : £12.50
1. Ladell, Edward, 1821-1886. I. Lewis, Frank.

Lafever, Minard.

LANDY, Jacob. 720'.924 B
The architecture of Minard Lafever. New York, Columbia University Press, 1970. xii, 313 p. illus., facsim., plans, port. 26 cm. Bibliography: p. 291-296. [NA737.L27L3] 69-19461 17.50
1. Lafever, Minard. I. Title.
BIP

Lafrery, Antoine, 1512-1577.

COLUMBIA 769'.4'36094563207401471
University. Libraries. Avery Architectural Library.
Catalogue of the Earl of Crawford's "Speculum Romanae magnificentiae," now in the Avery Architectural Library / by Lawrence R. McGinniss, with the assi[s]tance of Herbert Mitchell. New York : The Library, Columbia University, c1976. v, 75 p. ; 23 cm. Includes bibliographical references and index. [NE954.3.I8C64 1976] 77-362421
1. Lafrery, Antoine, 1512-1577. Speculum Romanae magnificentiae. 2. Crawford, David Alexander Robert Lindsay, 28th earl of, 1900- —Library. 3. Columbia University. Libraries. Avery Architectural Library. 4. Rome (City) in art. 5. Prints—Catalogs. I. McGinniss, Lawrence R. II. Mitchell, Herbert. III. Crawford, David Alexander Robert Lindsay, 28th earl of, 1900- IV. Title: Catalogue of the Earl of Crawford's "Speculum Romanae magnificentiae" ... V. Title: Speculum Romanae magnificentiae.

Lahore. Central Museum.

MINIATURE paintings on 745.6'7
display in Lahore Museum : Mughal and Rajasthani schools. Lahore : Lahore Museum, 1976. 24 p., [6] leaves of plates : ill. ; 21 cm. (Publication – Lahore Museum ; series 13) [ND1337.I5M56] 77-930123 Rs2.50
1. Lahore. Central Museum. 2. Miniature painting, Indic—Catalogs. 3. Painting, Mogul—Catalogs. 4. Rajput painting—Catalogs. 5. Miniature painting—Pakistan—Lahore—Catalogs. I. Lahore. Central Museum. II. Series: Lahore. Central Museum. Silsilah-yi intisharat-i Lahur 'Aja'ib Ghar ; 13.

Laing Art Gallery, Newcastle-upon-Tyne.

LAING Art 759.941'074'02876
Gallery, Newcastle-upon-Tyne.
British water-colours in the Laing Art Gallery. [Newcastle-upon-Tyne : The Gallery], c1976. 48 p. : chiefly ill. (some col.) ; 20 x 21 cm. [ND1928.L28 1976] 77-368316 £1.00
1. Laing Art Gallery, Newcastle-upon-Tyne. 2. Water-color painting, British—Catalogs. 3. Water-color painting—England—Newcastle-upon-Tyne—Catalogs. I. Title.

Laing, David, 1793-1878—Art collections.

EDINBURGH. 741.9'4'074094134
National Gallery of Scotland.
Old master drawings from the David Laing Bequest : [catalogue of an exhibition held] 14 June-24 July 1976 [at the National Gallery of Scotland]. Edinburgh : The Gallery, [1976] 43 p., leaf of plate, [20] p. of plates : ill., port. ; 24 cm. Errata slip inserted. [NC80.E33 1976] 77-358845 ISBN 0-903148-05-6 : £1.00
1. Laing, David, 1793-1878—Art collections. 2. Drawing, Renaissance—Exhibitions. 3. Drawing, Baroque—Exhibitions. 4. Drawing, Rococo—Exhibitions. I. Title.

Lake Linden, Mich.—Description—Views.

†MONETTE, Clarence 779'.9'9774993
J.
Lake Linden's yesterday : a pictorial history / [by Clarence J. Monette]. Lake Linden, Mich.: Monette, c1977- v. : ill. ; 22 cm. (Local history series ; 10-) [F574.L14M67] 77-155819 1.50 (v. 1)
1. Lake Linden, Mich.—Description—Views. I. Title.

Lalanne, Francois Xacier.

WHITECHAPEL Art 730'.944'0740215
Gallery, London.
Les Lelanne, domesticated beasts & other creatures : [catalogue of an exhibition held in the] Main Gallery [of Whitechapel Art Gallery] 2 June-4 July 1976. London : The

Gallery, 1976. 12 p. : ill., ports. ; 30 cm. Bibliography: p. 5. [NB553.L247W48 1976] 76-381318 ISBN 0-85488-033-X : £0.50
1. Lalanne, Francois Xacier. 2. Lalanne, Claude. 3. Animals in art. I. Lalanne, Francois Xavier. II. Lalanne, Claude. III. Title.

Lalique, Rene, 1860-1945.

MCCLINTON, Katharine 748.2'94
Morrison.
Introduction to Lalique glass / Katharine Morrison McClinton. Des Moines : Wallace-Homestead Book Co., c1978. 112 p. : ill. (some col.) ; 29 cm. [NK5198.L44M3] 77-87949 ISBN 0-87069-238-0 : 14.95
1. Lalique, Rene, 1860-1945. 2. Glassware—France. 3. Decoration and ornament—Art nouveau. 4. Art deco. I. Title.

MCCLINTON, Katharine 748.2'94
Morrison.
Introduction to Lalique glass / Katharine Morrison McClinton. Des Moines : Wallace-Homestead Book Co., c1978. 112 p. : ill. (some col.) ; 29 cm. [NK5198.L44M3] 77-87949 ISBN 0-87069-238-0 : 14.95
1. Lalique, Rene, 1860-1945. 2. Glassware—France. 3. Decoration and ornament—Art nouveau. 4. Art deco. I. Title.
BIP

MCCLINTON, Katharine 748.2'94
Morrison.
Lalique for collectors / Katharine Morrison McClinton. New York : Scribner, [1975] 152 p., [4] leaves of plates : ill. (some col.) ; 24 cm. Bibliography: p. 152. [NK5198.L44.M32] 74-14015 ISBN 0-684-14101-9 : 17.50
1. Lalique, Rene, 1860- 2. Glassware, French. 3. Decoration and ornament—Art nouveau. 4. Art deco. I. Title.
BIP

Lam, Wifredo.

LAM, Wifredo. 759.97291 B
Wifredo Lam / Max-Pol Fouchet. New York : Rizzoli, 1976. 266 p. : chiefly ill. (some col.) ; 30 cm. Includes index. Bibliography: p. 261-266. [ND305.L3F6813] 76-11245 ISBN 0-8478-0032-6 : 50.00
1. Lam, Wifredo. 2. Painters—Cuba—Biography. I. Fouchet, Max Pol.
BIP

Lamaism.

GORDON, Antoinette K. 294.3'4'21
The iconography of Tibetan Lamaism by Antoinette K. Gordon. Rev. (i.e. 2d. ed.) New York, Paragon Book Reprint Corp. 1967 [c.1959] xxxi, 131 p. illus. plates (part col.) 31 cm. Bibliography: p. 111-118. [NB1046.T5G6 1967] 67-7111
1. Lamaism. 2. Idols and images. 3. Art, Buddhist. 4. Art, Tibetan. I. Title.

Lamb, Charles, 1775-1834.

BARNETT, George Leonard. 824.7
Charles Lamb: The evolution of Elia. Bloomington, Indiana University Press, 1964. xi, 286 p. ports., facsims. 23 cm. (Indiana University humanities series, no. 53) Bibliography: p. 270-271. [AS36.I385] [PR4863.B33] 64-63001
1. Lamb, Charles, 1775-1834. I. Title. II. Title: The evolution of Elia. III. Series: Indiana. University. Indiana University humanities series, no. 53
BIP

Lamberti, Niccolo.

GOLDNER, George R., 730'.92'2 B
1943-
Niccolo and Piero Lamberti / George R. Goldner. New York : Garland Pub., [1978] p. cm. (Outstanding dissertations in the fine arts) Originally presented as the author's thesis, Princeton, 1972. Bibliography: p. [NB623.L25G64 1978] 77-94697 ISBN 0-8240-3229-2 lib. bdg. : 40.00

1. Lamberti, Niccolo. 2. Lamberti, Pietro, 1393-1435. I. Title.
BIP

Lambeth Palace. Library.

LAMBETH Palace. Library. 016.091
A catalogue of manuscripts in Lambeth Palace Library, MSS. 1907-2340 / E. G. W. Bill. London : Oxford, 1976. xi, 379 p. ; 23 cm. Includes index. [Z6621.L8194] 77-358094 ISBN 0-19-920079-3 : 55.00
1. Lambeth Palace. Library. 2. Manuscripts—England—Catalogs. 3. Great Britain—Church history—19th century—Sources—Bibliography—Catalogs. 4. Great Britain—Church history—20th century—Sources—Bibliography—Catalogs. 5. Great Britain—History—Sources—Bibliography—Catalogs. I. Bill, Edward Geoffrey Watson. II. Title.
Distributed by Oxford University Press, N.Y.
BIP

Laminated plastics.

WARNER Electric Company, 668.41
inc., Chicago.
How to do plastic laminating for pleasure and profit. [Chicago, 1952] 117 l. illus. 28cm. [TT297.W36] 53-38625
1. Laminated plastics. I. Title.

Laminated wood.

CAPRON, J. Hugh. 674.835
Wood laminating. Bloomington, Ill., McKnight & McKnight Pub. Co. [1963] 94 p. illus., diagrs. 26 cm. [TT200.C33] 63-24463
1. Laminated wood. 2. Woodwork (Manual training) I. Title.
BIP

Lamp shades.

CHRISTOPHER, Frederick 749.63
John.
Lampshade making; edited by Adelaide Shaw [pseud. New York] Dover Publications [1953, c1952] 122p. illus. 20cm. (Dover Foyle handbook) [TT897.C5] 53-10030
1. Lamp shades. I. Title.

Lamps.

FREEMAN, Graydon, La 745.7'2
verne, 1904-
Light on old lamps, by Larry Freeman. [Newly rev. & enl. ed.] Watkins Glen, N. Y., Century House [c1955] 128p. illus., facsims. 22cm. [NK9900.L] A56
1. Lamps. I. Title.

FREEMAN, Graydon La 749'.63
Verne, 1904-
New light on old lamps, by Larry Freeman. Watkins Glen, N.Y., Century House [1968] 220, [2] p. illus. 24 cm. (Library of Victorian culture) Rev. and enl. ed. of the author's Light on old lamps, originally published in 1944. Bibliography: p. [221]-[222] [NK6196.F73 1968] 68-12854
1. Lamps. I. Title.
BIP

GREGUIRE, Helen. 749'.63
Carnival in lights / by Helen Greguire. [Hilton, N.Y.] : Greguire, [1975] 91 p. : col. ill. ; 23 cm. Includes index. [NK6196.G73] 75-312703 11.95
1. Lamps. 2. Lighting, Architectural and decorative. I. Title.
BIP

LITTLE, Ruth. 749.63
Old lamps and new; restoring and decorating. Lubbock, Tex., Brack Publications [1964] 189 p. illus. (part col.) col. ports. 21 cm. [NK9990.L3L5] 64-17394
1. Lamps. I. Title.
BIP

MENKE, H. A. 745.51
28 table lamp projects. Bloomington, Ill., McKnight & McKnight Pub. Co., 1953. 78p. illus. 24cm. [TP746.M5] 53-71907
1. Lamps. I. Title. II. Title: Table lamp projects.

MITTON, Bruce H., 1950- 745.59'32
How to make your own lamps & lampshades / Bruce Mitton. Blue Ridge

Summit, Pa. : Tab Books, [1979] p. cm. Includes index. [TT897.2.M57] 78-26320 ISBN 0-8306-9842-6 : 9.95. ISBN 0-8306-1112-6 pbk. : 5.95
1. Lamps. 2. Lampshades. I. Title. BIP

MURPHY, Bruce W. 745.59'3
Lampmaking : the ancient craft of making lamps / Bruce W. Murphy, Ana G. Lopo. New York : Drake Publishers, [1976] p. cm. Includes index. Bibliography: p. [TT897.2.M87] 76-16360 ISBN 0-8473-1253-4 : 9.95
1. Lamps. I. Lopo, Ana G., joint author. II. Title. BIP

Lamps—Catalogs.

RUSHLIGHT Club. 749'.63
Early lighting; a pictorial guide, compiled and published by the Rushlight Club. [Boston, 1972] x, 129 p. illus. 29 cm. Bibliography: p. 125-126. [NK6196.R87] 72-81882
1. Lamps—Catalogs. 2. Lighting, Architectural and decorative—Catalogs. I. Title. BIP

SZENTLELEKY, Tihamer. 738.8
Ancient lamps. [Rev. by B. E. Bonis and J. Gy. Szilagyi. Translated by Arpad Debreceni. Translation rev. by D. M. Bailey] Chicago, Argonaut, 1969. 158, [77] p. illus., plates. 25 cm. Bibliographical footnotes. [NK4680.S9513] 72-4532
1. Lamps—Catalogs. 2. Pottery, Ancient—Catalogs. I. Title.

Lamps—Egypt—Kom Aushim.

SHIER, Louise Adele, 1906- 738.3'83
Terracotta lamps from Karanis, Egypt : excavations of the University of Michigan / by Louise A. Shier. Ann Arbor : University of Michigan Press, c1978. p. cm. (Studies - The University of Michigan, The Kelsey Museum of Archaeology ; 3) (Monograph publishing on demand : Imprint series) Includes indexes. Bibliography: p. [DT62.L34S53] 78-12501 ISBN 0-472-02702-6 : 19.50
1. Lamps—Egypt—Kom Aushim. 2. Terracotta sculpture, Greco-Roman—Egypt—Kom Aushim. 3. Kom Aushim, Egypt. I. Title. II. Series: Michigan. University. Kelsey Museum of Archaeology. Studies ; 3.
Available from University Microfilms International, Ann Arbor, MI 48106 BIP

Lamps—Greece.

HOWLAND, Richard Hubbard. 938'.5 s
Greek lamps and their survivals / by Richard Hubbard Howland. Princeton, N.J. : American School of Classical Studies at Athens, 1958. ix, 252 p., [29] leaves of plates : ill. ; 32 cm. (The Athenian Agora ; v. 4) Includes indexes. Bibliography: p. ix. [DF287.A23A5 vol.4] [NK4680] 738.3'83 75-322661
1. Lamps—Greece. 2. Athens. Agora. I. Title. II. Series: American School of Classical Studies at Athens. The Athenian Agora ; v. 4. BIP

Lamps—Rome.

PERLZWEIG, Judith. 938'.5 s
Lamps of the Roman period, first to seventh century after Christ / by Judith Perlzweig. Princeton, N.J. : American School of Classical Studies at Athens, 1961. xiv, 240 p., [27] leaves of plates : ill. ; 31 cm. (The Athenian Agora ; v. 7) Includes indexes. Bibliography: p. [x]-xiv. [DF287.A23A5 vol. 7] [NK4675] 738.3'83 75-322654
1. Lamps—Rome. 2. Athens. Agora. I. Title. II. Series: American School of Classical Studies at Athens. The Athenian Agora ; v. 7. BIP

Lampshades.

FISHBURN, Angela. 745.59'32
Making lampshades / Angela Fishburn. New York : Drake Publishers, 1975. 94 p. [4] leaves of plates : ill. ; 26 cm. Includes index. [TT897.F57] 75-316084 ISBN 0-87749-844-X : 10.95
1. Lampshades. I. Title. BIP

FISHBURN, Angela. 745.59'32
Making lampshades : lampshades technique and design / Angela Fishburn. New York : Drake Publishers, 1977. 94 p. : ill. ; 26 cm. Includes index. [TT897.F57 1977] 77-7729 ISBN 0-8473-1560-6 : 5.95
1. Lampshades. I. Title.

Lampshades, Glass—Catalogs.

ROBERTS, Darrah L. 749'.63
Art glass shades, by Darrah L. Roberts. [Des Moines, Iowa, 1968] 31 p. (incl. cover) 15 x 24 cm. [NK5440.L3R6] 70-1792
1. Roberts, Darrah L., Mrs.—Art collections. 2. Lampshades, Glass—Catalogs. 3. Art nouveau. I. Title. BIP

Lampshades, Glass—Collectors and collecting.

ROBERTS, Darrah L. 749'.63
Collecting art nouveau shades / by Darrah L. Roberts. Des Moines : Wallace-Homestead Book Co., [1972] 120 p. : ill. (some col.) ; 24 cm. Includes index. Bibliography: p. 119. [NK5440.L3R62] 76-188606
1. Lampshades, Glass—Collectors and collecting. 2. Decoration and ornament—Art nouveau. I. Title.

Lampshades—Juvenile literature.

LAMPSHADES to make / 745.59'32
[edited by Linda Doeser]. London ; New York : M. Cavendish, c1976. p. cm. Includes index. Step-by-step instructions for making lampshades in a variety of designs from easily available materials. [TT897.L35] 76-3573 ISBN 0-85685-193-0
1. Lampshades—Juvenile literature. I. Doeser, Linda.

LAn-2 site.

JOHNSON, Keith L. 917.94'93
Site LAn-2; a late manifestation of the Topanga complex in southern California prehistory, by Keith L. Johnson. [Berkeley, University of California Press, 1966] viii, 36 p. illus., maps. 28 cm. (Anthropological records, v. 23) Bibliography: p. 23-24. [E51.A58 vol. 23] 67-65372
1. LAn-2 site. I. Title. II. Title: Topanga complex. III. Series.

Lancaster, Mass.—Hist.—Pictorial works.

TYMESON, Mildred McClary. 917.44'3'03
The Lancastrin towns. Photos. by Katherine Knowles. Barre, Mass., Barre, 1967. [F74.L2T9] 67-14591 6.50 bds.,
1. Lancaster, Mass.—Hist.—Pictorial works. 2. Worcester Co., Mass.—Hist.—Pictorial works. I. Knowles, Katherine, illus. II. Title.

Land, Edwin Herbert, 1909—

OLSHAKER, Mark, 1951- 338.7'68'14180924 B
The instant image : Edwin Land and the Polaroid experience / Mark Olshaker. New York : Stein and Day, 1978. xii, 277 p., [5] leaves of plates : ill. ; 24 cm. Includes index. Bibliography: p. 268-270. [TR140.L28O47] 77-15965 ISBN 0-8128-2442-3 : 10.00
1. Land, Edwin Herbert, 1909- 2. Polaroid Corporation, Cambridge, Mass. I. Title.

Land—Illinois—Chicago.

CHICAGO. Dept. of Urban Renewal. 711'.4'0977311
Land use study; staff report. Chicago, 1968- v. illus. 28 cm. Contents.Contents.—[1] Austin study area.—[2] 67th [Street] Stony Island study area.—[3] 63rd [Street] Ashland.—[4] 79th [Street] Racine study area. [HD268.C4A4] 71-3733
1. Land—Illinois—Chicago. 2. Urban renewal—Chicago. I. Title.

Land, Lewis K.—Art collections.

DWYER, Jane Powell. 730
Fire, earth, and water : sculpture from the Land Collection of Mesoamerican Art : [exhibited at the Fine Arts Museums of San Francisco, California Palace of the Legion of Honor, July 4, 1975-September 14, 1975, Honolulu Academy of Arts, January-March, 1976, Seattle Art Museum, April-June, 1976] / by Jane P. Dwyer and Edward B. Dwyer ; [photos. by James Medley ; ill. by Wendy Kitamata]. [San Francisco] : Fine Arts Museums of San Francisco, c1975. 141 p. : ill. (some col.) ; 28 cm. Bibliography: p. 138-139. [F1219.3.A7D98] 75-14770 ISBN 0-88401-006-6 pbk. : 7.95
1. Land, Lewis K.—Art collections. 2. Indians of Mexico—Sculpture—Exhibitions. 3. Indians of Central America—Sculpture—Exhibitions. I. Dwyer, Edward Bridgman, joint author. II. California Palace of the Legion of Honor, San Francisco. III. Honolulu Academy of Arts. IV. Seattle. Art Museum. V. Title.

Landauer, Bella Clara, 1874-1960—Art collections.

AMERICAN advertising 769.5
posters of the nineteenth century : from the Bella C. Landauer Collection of the New-York Historical Society / Mary Black. New York : Dover Publications, 1976. vii, 119 p. : chiefly ill. ; 37 cm. Includes indexes. [HF5843.A68] 76-20834 ISBN 0-486-23356-1 : 6.95
1. Landauer, Bella Clara, 1874-1960—Art collections. 2. New York Historical Society. 3. Posters, American—Private collections. I. Black, Mary C.

Landress, M. M.

LANDRESS, M. M. 364.1'33'0924 B
I made it myself, by M. M. Landress, with Bruce Dobler. New York, Grosset & Dunlap [1973] x, 276 p. 22 cm. [HG336.U5L35] 72-90844 ISBN 0-448-02206-0 6.95
1. Landress, M. M. 2. Counterfeits and counterfeiting—United States. I. Dobler, Bruce. II. Title.

Landsberger, Franz, 1883-1964—Bibliography.

LANDSBERGER, Franz, 1883-1964. 709
A history of Jewish art. Port Washington, N.Y., Kennikat Press [1973, c1946] 369 p. illus. 23 cm. Original ed. issued in series: Commission on Jewish Education of the Union of American Hebrew Congregations and the Central Conference of American Rabbis. Union adult series. Bibliography: p. 341-353. [N7415.L32 1973] 72-85324 ISBN 0-8046-1741-4 17.50
1. Landsberger, Franz, 1883-1964—Bibliography. 2. Art, Jewish—History. I. Title. II. Series: Commission on Jewish Education of the Union of American Hebrew Congregations and the Central Conference of American Rabbis. Union adult series.

Landscape.

BRODATZ, Phil. 779'.36
The elements of landscape; a photographic handbook for artists [by] Phil Brodatz & Dori Watson. New York, Reinhold Book Corp. [1968] 137 p. chiefly illus. 32 cm. [TR660.B75] 68-16019
1. Landscape. 2. Photography—Landscapes. I. Watson, Dori, joint author. II. Title.

DALZELL, Lynne. 016.3092'08 s
Environmental aesthetics, preferences, and assessments : a selected bibliography / Lynne Dalzell. Monticello, Ill. : Council of Planning Librarians, 1978. 16 p. ; 28 cm. (Exchange bibliography — Council of Planning Librarians ; 1488) Cover title. [Z5942.C68 no. 1488] [Z58.L35] [GF90] 016.30131 78-105922 pbk. : 1.50
1. Landscape assessment—Bibliography. I. Title. II. Series: Council of Planning Librarians. Exchange bibliography ; 1488

HUSSEY, Christopher, 1899- 701.17
The picturesque; studies in a point of view. With a new pref. by the author. [Hamden, Conn.] Archon Books, 1967. xv, 307 p. illus. 23 cm. [BH301.L3H8 1967] 68-147
1. Landscape. 2. Nature (Aesthetics) I. Title. BIP

MANWARING, Elizabeth Wheeler, 1879- 701.17
Italian landscape in eighteenth century England; a study chiefly of the influence of Claude Lorrain and Salvator Rosa on English taste, 1700-1800. New York, Russell & Russell, 1965. vii, 243p. plates, port. 23cm. First pub. in 1925. [BH301.L3M3] 66-10419 8.50
1. Gelee, Claude, called Claude Lorrain, 1600-1682. 2. Rosa, Salvatore, 1615-1673. 3. Landscape. 4. Nature (Asthetics) 5. Landscape painting—Italy. 6. Landscape gardening—England. I. Title. BIP

OGDEN, Henry Vining Seton, 1905- 704.943
English taste in landscape in the seventeenth century, by Henry V. S. Ogden and Margaret S. Ogden. Ann Arbor, University of Michigan Press, 1955. xi, 224p. illus. 29cm. Includes bibliographical references. [BH301.L3O3] 55-8649
1. Landscape. 2. Nature (Aesthetics) 3. Landscape painting—England. 4. England—Civilization. I. Ogden, Margaret Sinclair, 1909- joint author. II. Title.

TUNNARD, Christopher. 111.8'5
A world with a view : an inquiry into the nature of scenic values / Christopher Tunnard. New Haven : Yale University Press, 1978. xii, 196 p. : ill. ; 24 cm. Includes bibliographical references and index. [BH301.L3T86 1978] 77-13729 ISBN 0-300-02157-7 : 15.00
1. Landscape. 2. Nature (Aesthetics) I. Title. BIP

Landscape architects—United States—Biography.

STEVENSON, Elizabeth, 1919- 712'.092'4 B
Park maker : a life of Frederick Law Olmstead / by Elizabeth Stevenson. New York : Macmillan, c1977. xxv, 484 p., [8] leaves of plates : ill. ; 25 cm. Includes index. Bibliography: p. 453-469. [SB470.O5S73] 76-52942 ISBN 0-02-614440-9 : 17.95
1. Olmsted, Frederick Law, 1822-1903. 2. Landscape architects—United States—Biography. I. Title. BIP

Landscape architects—United States—Correspondence.

OLMSTED, Frederick Law, 1822-1903. 712'.08 s
The formative years, 1822 to 1852 / Charles Capen McLaughlin, editor, Charles E. Beveridge, associate editor. Baltimore : Johns Hopkins University Press, c1977. xx, 423 p. : ill. ; 25 cm. (The Papers of Frederick Law Olmstead ; v. 1) Includes bibliographical references and indexes. [SB470.O5A2 1977 vol. 1] 712'.08 76-47378 ISBN 0-8018-1798-6 : 20.00
1. Olmsted, Frederick Law, 1822-1903. 2. Landscape architects—United States—Correspondence. 3. Landscape architects—United States—Biography. I. Title.

Landscape architects—United States—Correspondence—collected works.

OLMSTED, Frederick Law, 1822-1903. 712'.08
The papers of Frederick Law Olmstead / Charles Capen McLaughlin, editor, Charles E. Beveridge, associate editor. Baltimore : Johns Hopkins University Press, c1977- v. : ill. ; 25 cm. Contents.Contents.—v. 1. The formative years, 1822 to 1852. Includes bibliographical references and index. [SB470.O5A2 1977] 77-741 ISBN 0-8018-1798-6 (v.1) : 20.00
1. Olmsted, Frederick Law, 1822-1903—Collected works. 2. Landscape architects—United States—Correspondence—collected

works. 3. Landscape architects—United States—Biography—Collected works.

Landscape architecture.

BRAINERD, John W., 1918- 333.7'2
Working with nature; a practical guide [by] John W. Brainerd. New York, Oxford University Press, 1973. 517 p. illus. 24 cm. Bibliography: p. 474-496. [SB472.B68] 73-76907 ISBN 0-19-501667-X 15.00
1. Landscape architecture. 2. Landscape protection. I. Title. BIP

BRIMER, John Burton. 717
Homeowner's complete outdoor building book. Illus. by the author. [Rev., expanded, updated] New York, Popular Science Pub. Co. [1971] 470 p. illus. (part col.) 25 cm. First published in 1959 under title: Designs for outdoor living. [SB473.2.B75 1971] 78-115431 8.95
1. Landscape architecture. 2. Patios. I. Title. II. Title: Complete outdoor building book. BIP

CLEVELAND, Horace William Shaler, b1814 1814 712
Landscape architecture, as applied to the wants of the West. Ed. by Roy Lubove [Pittsburgh] Univ. of Pittsburgh Pr. [c.1965] xxi, 59, [2]p. 21cm. [SB471.C6] 65-12905 2.95
1. Landscape architecture. I. Lubove, Roy, ed. II. Title.

CLEVELAND, Horace William Shaler, b.1814. 712
Landscape architecture, as applied to the wants of the West, by H. W. S. Cleveland. Edited by Roy Lubove. [Pittsburgh] University of Pittsburgh Press [1965] xxi, 59, [2] p. 21 cm. "Bibliographical note": p. [61] Bibliographical footnotes. [SB471.C6 1965] 65-12095
1. Landscape architecture. I. Lubove, Roy, ed, II. Title.

ECKBO, Garrett. 712
The landscape we see. New York, McGraw-Hill [1969] xiv, 223 p. illus., maps, plans. 29 cm. Bibliography: p. 213-218. [SB472.E223] 67-20657 16.00
1. Landscape architecture. I. Title. BIP

ECKBO, Garrett. 712
Urban landscape design. New York, McGraw-Hill Book Co. [1964] vii, 248 p. illus., plans. 29 cm. Bibliography: p. 240-241. [SB472.E23] 63-14578
1. Landscape architecture. 2. Cities and towns—Planning. I. Title. BIP

[ELIOT, Charles William] 1834-1926. 712'.0924 B
Charles Eliot, landscape architect; a lover of nature and of his kind, who trained himself for a new profession, practised it happily and through it wrought much good. Freeport, N.Y., Books for Libraries Press [1971] xxiv, 770 p. illus., maps (part fold.), plans (part fold.), ports. 23 cm. Reprint of the 1902 ed. [SB470.E6E6 1971] 72-160971 ISBN 0-8369-5839-X
1. Eliot, Charles, 1859-1897. 2. Landscape architecture. I. Title. BIP

FAIRBROTHER, Nan. 712
The nature of landscape design: as an art form, a craft, a social necessity. With a foreword by F. Fraser Darling. [1st American ed.] New York, Knopf, 1974. xii, 252 p. illus. 25 cm. [SB472.F3 1974] 73-20758 ISBN 0-394-47046-X 10.00
1. Landscape architecture. I. Title.

GRANT WHITE, John Ernest 712.6
Designing a garden today. New York, Abelard [c.1966] 184p. illus. 22cm. [SB472.G7] 66-17678 6.50
1. Landscape architecture I. Title.

GRANT WHITE, John Ernest. 712.6
Designing a garden today [by] J. E. Grant White. New York, Abelard-Schuman [1966] 184 p. illus. 22 cm. [SB472.G7] 66-17678
1. Landscape architecture. I. Title.

INGELS, Jack E. 712
Landscaping : principles and practices / Jack E. Ingels ; consulting editor, H. Edward Reiley. New York : Van Nostrand Reinhold Co., 1978. v, 210 p., [8] leaves of plates : ill. ; 23 x 28 cm. Includes index. [SB472.I53] 77-26087 ISBN 0-442-23634-4 : 10.95
1. Landscape architecture. 2. Landscape gardening. I. Reiley, H. Edward. II. Title. BIP

INGELS, Jack E. 712
Landscaping, principles and practices / Jack E. Ingels ; consulting editor, H. Edward Reiley. Albany, N.Y. : Delmar Publishers, c1978. v, 210 p., [8] leaves of plates : ill. ; 22 x 28 cm. (Delmar's agriculture series) Includes index. [SB472.I53 1978] 76-51686 ISBN 0-8273-1634-8 pbk. : 9.00
1. Landscape architecture. 2. Landscape gardening. I. Reiley, H. Edward. II. Title. III. Series. BIP

JELLICOE, Geoffrey Alan 712
Studies in landscape design. New York, Oxford University Press, 1960[ ] xvi, 111p. illus., plates. 24cm. 60-1523 4.00
1. Landscape architecture. I. Title.

JELLICOE, Geoffrey, Alan, 1900- 712
Studies in landscape design. London, New York, Oxford University Press, 1960-1966. 2 v. illus., plates, 24 cm. v. 1:25/-; v. 2:50/- (v. 1: B60-4271; v. 2: B66-0126) [SB476.J4] 60-1523
1. Landscape architecture. I. Title.

KASSLER, Elizabeth (Bauer) 1911- 712
Modern gardens and the landscape, by Elizabeth B. Kassler. New York, Museum of Modern Art; distributed by Doubleday, Garden City, N.Y. [c1964] 96 p. illus. (part col.) 25 cm. [SB472.M6] 64-18333
1. Landscape architecture. I. New York. Museum of Modern Art. II. Title.

LAURIE, Michael. 712
An introduction to landscape architecture / Michael Laurie. New York : American Elsevier Pub. Co., [1975] ix, 214 p. : ill. ; 22 x 28 cm. Includes index. Bibliography: p. 203-206. [SB472.L38] 75-35441 ISBN 0-444-00146-8 : 25.00 ISBN 0-444-00171-9 pbk. : 12.00
1. Landscape architecture. I. Title. BIP

LOHMANN, Karl Baptiste, 1887-1963. 712
Fundamentals of landscape architecture / by Karl B. Lohmann. Ed. 4. Scranton, Pa. : International Correspondence Schools, c1974. 100, 3 p., [2] leaves of plates : ill. ; 27 cm. "6417-4." [SB472.L67 1974] 75-306252
1. Landscape architecture. 2. Landscape gardening. I. International Correspondence Schools, Scranton, Pa. II. Title.

LOVEJOY, Derek. 712
Land use and landscape planning. Edited by Derek Lovejoy. With a foreword by the Duke of Edinburgh. New York, Barnes & Noble [1973] xii, 308 p. illus. 29 cm. Includes bibliographical references. [SB472.L73 1973] 74-157862 ISBN 0-06-494372-0 35.00
1. Landscape architecture. 2. Land. I. Title.

THE Man-made landscape / 712
prepared in co-operation with the International Federation of Landscape Architects. Paris : Unesco, 1978. 178 p. : ill. ; 22 cm. (Museums and monuments ; 16) Includes bibliographies. [SB472.M336] 78-360504 pbk. : 13.50
1. Landscape architecture. 2. Reclamation of land. 3. Man—Influence on nature. I. International Federation of Landscape Architects. II. Title. III. Series.
Distributed by Unipub in New York City. BIP

MARLOWE, Olwen C. 712
Outdoor design : a handbook for the architect and planner / Olwen C. Marlowe. New York : Whitney Library of Design, 1977. xiii, 301 p. : ill. ; 25 cm. Includes index. Bibliography: p. [276]-289. [SB472.M345 1977] 77-3706 ISBN 0-8230-7405-6 : 37.50
1. Landscape architecture. I. Title. BIP

MICHEL, Timothy M. 712'.6
Homeowner's guide to landscape design; Timothy M. Michel; illustrated by the author. Taftsville, Vt. : Countryman, Press, c1978. ix, 149 p. : ill. ; 26 cm. Includes index. Bibliography: p. 142-143. [SB473.M46] 78-17262 ISBN 0-914378-32-5 : 9.95. ISBN 0-914378-27-9 pbk. : 7.95
1. Landscape architecture. 2. Landscape gardening. I. Title. BIP

[MOCK, Elizabeth (Bauer)] 1911- 712
Modern gardens and the landscape, by Elizabeth B. Kassler. Mus. of Mod. Art, dist. Garden City, N. Y., Doubleday [c.1964] 96p. illus. (pt. col.) 25cm. [SB472.M6] 64-18333 5.95
1. Landscape architecture. I. New York. Museum of Modern Art. II. Title.

*MORRIS, Philip. 712'.6
Landscaping your home. [Birmingham, Ala., Oxmoor House, 1974] 112 p. illus. 28 cm. (A Southern Living book) [SB473] 73-91440 1.95 (pbk.)
1. Landscape architecture. I. Title. BIP

MUIRHEAD, Desmond. 712
Green days in garden and landscape. [1st ed.] Los Angeles, Miramar Pub. Co. [1961] 272 p. illus. 24 cm. [SB472.M8] 61-18884
1. Landscape architecture. 2. Landscape gardening. I. Title.

MUNSON, Albe E. 624'.15
Construction design for landscape architects [by] Albe E. Munson. New York, McGraw-Hill [1975, c1974] x, 212 p. illus. 24 cm. [SB472.M84 1974] 74-13526 12.50
1. Landscape architecture. 2. Civil engineering. 3. Building sites. I. Title. BIP

NATHAN, Kurt. 624
Basic site engineering for landscape designers. New York, MSS Information Corp. [1973] 150 p. illus. 28 cm. Bibliography: p. 137. [SB472.N3] 73-13518 ISBN 0-8422-0354-0 5.75
1. Landscape architecture. 2. Building sites. 3. Surveying. I. Title. BIP

OLDALE, Adrienne. 712'.6
Garden construction in pictures [by] Adrienne and Peter Oldale. New York, Drake Publishers [1974] 158 p. illus. 29 cm. [SB473.O544 1974] 73-10925 ISBN 0-87749-357-X 10.95
1. Landscape architecture. 2. Gardening. 3. Garden ornaments and furniture. I. Oldale, Peter, joint author. II. Title.

ORTLOFF, Henry Stuart, 1896- 712
The book of landscape design / by H. Stuart Ortloff and Henry B. Raymore. New York : Morrow, 1975, c1959. 316 p., [3] leaves of plates : ill. ; 22 cm. Includes index. Bibliography: p. 309-310. [SB472.O7 1975] 75-307047 3.25
1. Landscape architecture. I. Raymore, Henry Bond, joint author. II. Title. BIP

REPTON, Humphry, 1752-1818. 712'.2
The art of landscape gardening / by Humphry Repton ; edited and with an introd. by John C. Nolen. Sakonnet [R.I.] : Theophrastus, 1977. p. cm. Reprint of the 1907 ed. published by Houghton Mifflin, Boston. Includes index. [SB471.R46 1977] 76-51839 ISBN 0-913728-20-9 : 25.00
1. Landscape architecture. 2. Landscape gardening. I. Title. BIP

ROSE, James C. 712'.6
Modern American gardens, designed by James Rose. Text by Marc Snow. [Photos. by William Barksdale, and others] New York, Reinhold [1967] 224 p. (chiefly illus.) 31 cm. [SB466.U6R65] 66-24556
1. Landscape architecture. 2. Gardens—United States. I. Snow, Marc. II. Title.

RUBENSTEIN, Harvey M. 712'.5
A guide to site and environmental planning [by] Harvey M. Rubenstein. New York, Wiley [1969] 190 p. illus., maps (part col.), plans. 29 cm. Bibliography: p. 181. [SB472.R857] 68-26851
1. Landscape architecture. I. Title. BIP

SIMONDS, John Ormsbee. 712
Landscape architecture; the shaping of man's natural environment. New York, F. W. Dodge Corp. [1961] 244 p. illus. 31 cm. [SB472.S58] 60-53454
1. Landscape architecture. BIP

SMITH, Alice Upham. 712'.6
A distinctive setting for your house: landscaping to enhance a house's style and make the most of its site. [1st ed.] Garden City, N.Y., Doubleday [1973] viii, 184 p. illus. 25 cm. [SB473.S55] 72-84944 ISBN 0-385-01178-4 8.95
1. Landscape architecture. 2. Landscape gardening. I. Title.

STEEL, Fletcher, 1885- 712
Gardens and people. Boston, Houghton [c.] 1964. ix, 221p. 22cm. 64-10265 4.00
1. Landscape architecture. I. Title.

STEELE, Fletcher, 1885- 712
Gardens and people. Boston, Houghton Mifflin, 1964. ix, 221 p. 22 cm. [SB472.S73] 64-10265
1. Landscape architecture. I. Title.

TECHNIQUES of landscape architecture. 712'.3
Edited for the Institute of Landscape Architects by A. E. Weddle. New York, American Elsevier Pub. Co., 1967. xx, 226 p. illus., maps, plans. 29 cm. Includes bibliographies. [SB472] 67-25058
1. Landscape architecture. I. Weddle, A. E., ed. II. Institute of Landscape Architects, London.

WAUGH, Frank Albert, 1869-1943. 635.9
Landscape gardening; treatise on the general principles governing outdoor art; with sundry suggestions for their application in the commoner problems of gardening. New York, O. Judd Co., 1899. viii, 152 p. illus. 19 cm. [SB472.W4] 99-3313
1. Landscape architecture. I. Title.

WEBER, Nelva M. 712'.6
How to plan your own home landscape : how to organize your outdoor space and how to utilize it for maximum pleasure and minimum maintenance all year round / by Nelva M. Weber ; photos. by Molly Adams, drawings by Joseph M. Sammataro. Indianapolis : Bobbs-Merrill, [1976] p. cm. Includes index. [SB473.W4] 75-33535 ISBN 0-672-51890-2 : 11.95
1. Landscape architecture. 2. Landscape gardening. I. Adams, Molly. II. Title. BIP

WEDDLE, A. E., ed. 712'.3
Techniques of landscape architecture. Edited for the Institute of Landscape Architects by A. E. Weddle. New York, American Elsevier Pub. Co., 1967. xx, 226 p. illus., maps, plans. 29 cm. Includes bibliographies. [SB472] 67-25058
1. Landscape architecture. I. Institute of Landscape Architects, London. II. Title.

Landscape architecture — Addresses, essays, lectures.

ROSE, James C 712.082
Gardens make me laugh, by James Rose. Illus. by Osborn. Norwalk, Conn., Silvermine Publishers [1965] 151 p. illus. 22 cm. [SB476.R7] 65-15140
1. Landscape architecture — Addresses, essays, lectures. I. Title.

Landscape architecture as a profession.

FEIN, Albert. 712'.023
A study of the profession of landscape architecture; technical report. [McLean, Va., American Society of Landscape Architects Foundation, 1972] 1 v. (various pagings) 28 cm. "Sponsored by the American Society of Landscape Architects Foundation [and] the Ford Foundation." [SB469.4.A2F45] 72-97051
1. Landscape architecture as a profession. I. American Society of Landscape Architects Foundation. II. Ford Foundation.

FRAZIER, John B. 712'.023
Your future in landscape architecture [by] John B. Frazier and Richard J. Julin. [1st ed.] New York, R. Rosen Press [1967] 124 p. 22 cm. (Careers in depth, 71) Bibliography: p. 113-114. [SB469.4.A2F7] 67-14523
1. Landscape architecture as a profession. I. Julin, Richard J., joint author. II. Title. BIP

GRISWOLD, Ralph E 712.7
Opportunities in landscape architecture. New York, Vocational Guidance Manuals[1961] 80p. 21cm. [SB476.G7] 61-19381

1. Landscape architecture as a profession. I. Title. BIP

GRISWOLD, Ralph E. 712'.023
Opportunities in landscape architecture, by Ralph E. Griswold. New York, Educational Books Division of Universal Pub. and Distributing Corp. [1970] 102 p. illus. 20 cm. (Vocational guidance manuals) (VGM career series, V171.) Bibliography: p. 69-72. [SB476.G7 1970] 71-134958
1. Landscape architecture as a profession. I. Title.

Landscape architecture—Bibliography.

KULP, Kenneth K. 016.3092'08 s
Environmental site planning / Kenneth K. Kulp. Monticello, Ill. : Council of Planning Librarians, 1976. 10 p. ; 28 cm. (Exchange bibliography ; 1030) Cover title. [Z5942.C68 no. 1030] [Z5996.A1] [SB472] 016.712 77-372626 1.50
1. Landscape architecture—Bibliography. 2. Building sites—Bibliography. 3. Land use—Planning—Bibliography. I. Title. II. Series: Council of Planning Librarians. Exchange bibliography ; 1030.

Landscape architecture—Brazil.

BARDI, Pietro Maria, 1900- 712.0981
The tropical gardens of Burle Marx. Photos. by M. Gautherot. New York, Reinhold [c.1964] 155p. illus. (pt. col.) 30cm. English, German, and Italian. Bibl. 63-19224 15.00
1. Marx, Robert Burle, 1909- 2. Landscape architecture—Brazil. 3. Tropical plants—Pictorial works. I. Title.

Landscape architecture — Congresses.

MIDWEST Regional 712'.023
Workshop Research in Landscape Architecture, Ohio State University, Columbus, 1960.
Living in the landscape; proceedings. Columbus, Engineering Experiment Station, Ohio State University, 1961. vi, 53 p. map. 28 cm. (Ohio. State University, Columbus. Engineering Experiment Station. Special report 18) [SB469.M5] A62
1. Landscape architecture — Congresses. I. Ohio. State University, Colubmus. II. Title. III. Series.

Landscape architecture—Contracts and specifications—Great Britain.

DEREK Lovejoy and Partners. 712
Spon's landscape handbook; specifications and prices. London, E & F. N. Spon [1972] xv, 397 p. illus. 22 cm. Bibliography: p. 358-373. [SB476.5.D47] 73-156665 ISBN 0-419-10660-X
1. Landscape architecture—Contracts and specifications—Great Britain. 2. Landscape architecture—Prices—Great Britain. I. Title.
Distributed by Halsted Press, 15.95 ISBN 0-470-54825-8

Landscape architecture—Designs and plans.

LANDSCAPE architectural site 717
construction details : prepared for the Center for Landscape Architectural Education and Research / collected and organized by Gary O. Robinette. Reston, Va. : Environmental Design Press, 1977c1976 385 p. : chiefly ill. ; 28 cm. Bibliography: p. 8. [SB476.4.L36] 76-55519 ISBN 0-918436-01-X pbk. : 20.00
1. Landscape architecture—Designs and plans. 2. Building sites. 3. Building. I. Robinette, Gary O. II. Center for Landscape Architectural Education and Research.

LANDSCAPING for flats: 712.7
the treatment of ground space on high density housing estates. London. H. M. Stationery Off. [dist. New York, British Info., c.]1963. 67p. illus. 30cm. (Design bulln. 5) 1.70 pap.,

Landscape architecture—England.

BLOMFIELD, Reginald Theodore, Sir, 1856-1942. 712'.6'0942
The formal garden in England. With illus. by F. Inigo Thomas. London, New York, Macmillan, 1901. [New York, AMS Press, 1972] xvi, 250 p. illus. 23 cm. Reprint of the 3d ed. Bibliography: p. [242]-244. [SB461.B56 1972] 77-181912 ISBN 0-404-00898-4
1. Landscape architecture—England. 2. Gardens—England. I. Title. BIP

Landscape architecture—Examinations, questions, etc.

ARCO Publishing Company, New York. 712'.076
Landscape architect, all grades, all jurisdictions. [1st ed.] New York [1970] 192 p. illus., plans. 26 cm. (ARCO civil service test tutor) At head of title: The complete study guide for scoring high. [SB469.4.A2A72] 65-27813 5.00
1. Landscape architecture—Examinations, questions, etc. I. Title.

Landscape architecture—Gt. Brit.—History.

HYAMS, Edward S. 712'.0922 B
Capability Brown and Humphry Repton, by Edward Hyams. New York, Scribner [1971] vii, 248 p. illus., facsims., port. 26 cm. Bibliography: p. 238-239. [SB470.B7H9 1971b] 71-123850 ISBN 0-684-10273-0 7.95
1. Brown, Lancelot, 1716-1783. 2. Repton, Humphry, 1752-1818. 3. Landscape architecture—Gt. Brit.—History. I. Title. BIP

Landscape architecture—Handbooks, manuals, etc.

†THE Landscape 712'.021
architects reference manual : illustrated for desk & field use. Orange, Calif. : Basic Information Services, c1976. 384 p., [8] leaves of plates : ill. (some col.) ; 23 cm. Includes bibliographical references. [SB472.L36] 75-32955 ISBN 0-916408-01-9 : 15.50
1. Landscape architecture—Handbooks, manuals, etc.

Landscape architecture—History.

CLIFFORD, Derek Plint. 712.09
A history of garden design. New York, Praeger [1963] 232 p. illus. 26 cm. (Books that matter) [SB470.5.C55] 63-10931
1. Landscape architecture — Hist. I. Title. II. Title: Garden design.

CLIFFORD, Derek Plint. 712.09
A history of garden design, by Derek Clifford. Rev. ed. New York, Praeger [1966, c1963] 252 p. illus. 26 cm. Bibliography: p. 239-244. [SB470.5.C55 1966a] 66-21774
1. Landscape architecture—History. I. Title.

DUMBARTON Oaks 712'.0942
Colloquium on the History of Landscape Architecture, 2d, 1972.
The picturesque garden and its influence outside the British Isles / [edited by Nikolaus Pevsner]. Washington : Dumbarton Oaks, Trustees for Harvard University, 1974. vii, 121 p., [26] leaves of plates : ill. ; 26 cm. Includes bibliographical references. [SB470.5.D85 1972] 74-196954 10.00(v.2)
1. Landscape architecture—History. 2. Gardens—England—History. 3. Gardens—Europe—History. I. Pevsner, Nikolaus, Sir, 1902- ed. II. Dumbarton Oaks. III. Title.

JELLICOE, Geoffrey Alan, 1900- 712'.09
The landscape of man : shaping the environment from prehistory to the present day / Geoffrey and Susan Jellicoe. New York : Viking Press, 1975. 383 p. : ill. ; 30 cm. (A Studio book) Includes index. Bibliography: p. 378-380. [SB470.5.J44] 75-13510 ISBN 0-670-41775-0 : 35.00
1. Landscape architecture—History. 2. Man—Influence on nature—History. I. Jellicoe, Susan, joint author. II. Title.

NEWTON, Norman T., 1898- 712'.09
Design on the land; the development of landscape architecture [by] Norman T. Newton. Cambridge, Mass., Belknap Press of Harvard University Press, 1971. xxiv, 714 p. illus., maps, plans. 26 cm. Bibliography: p. 677-689. [SB470.5.N47] 70-134955 ISBN 0-674-19870-0 25.00
1. Landscape architecture—History. I. Title. BIP

TOBEY, George B. 712'.09
A history of landscape architecture: the relationship of people to environment [by] G. B. Tobey. New York, American Elsevier Pub. Co. [1973] xiv, 305 p. illus. 29 cm. Bibliography: p. 243-245. [SB470.5.T6] 72-87211 ISBN 0-444-00131-X 18.50
1. Landscape architecture—History. 2. Civilization—History. I. Title.

Landscape architecture—History—Study and teaching—United States.

TEACHING landscape 712'.09
architectural history. [McLean, Va. : American Society of Landscape Architects Foundation, 1974?] [287] p. : ill. ; 28 cm. Cover title. Includes bibliographies. [SB469.4.U5T4] 74-83630 14.00
1. Landscape architecture—History—Study and teaching—United States. 2. Landscape architecture—Bibliography. I. American Society of Landscape Architects Foundation.

Landscape architecture—Ireland—History.

MALINS, Edward Greenway. 712'.6'09415
Lost demesnes : Irish landscape gardening, 1660-1845 / Edward Malins & the Knight of Glin ; foreword by Desmond Guinness. London : Barrie & Jenkins, 1976. xvi, 208 p. : ill. ; 31 cm. Errata slip inserted. Includes index. Bibliography: p. 198-200. [SB477.173M34] 77-358772 ISBN 0-214-20275-5 : £15.00
1. Landscape architecture—Ireland—History. 2. Landscape gardening—Ireland—History. 3. Gardens—Ireland—History. I. Fitz-Gerald, Desmond John Villiers, 1937- joint author. II. Title.

Landscape architecture—Mexico.

KIRBY, Rosina Greene. 712'.0972
Mexican landscape architecture from the street and from within. Tucson, University of Arizona Press [1972] 167 p. illus. 24 x 32 cm. Bibliography: p. 161-164. [SB477.M6K57] 72-83818 ISBN 0-8165-0327-3 27.50
1. Landscape architecture—Mexico. I. Title. BIP

Landscape architecture—New York (State)—New York (City)

OLMSTED, Frederick Law, 1822-1903. 712'.5'097471
Landscape into cityscape; Frederick Law Olmsted's plans for a greater New York City. Edited with an introductory essay and notes by Albert Fein. Ithaca, N. Y., Cornell University Press [1968, c1967] x, 490 p. illus., maps (part fold.), plans, ports. 22 cm. (Cornell reprints in urban studies) Twelve documents, of which nine are reports to governmental bodies, five prepared jointly with Calvert Vaux and two with J. James R. Croes. Contents.Contents.—The beginning of Central Park; a fragment of autobiography. ca. 1877.—Description of a plan for the improvement of the Central Park: "Greensward". 1858; 1868 reprint.—Preliminary report to the Commissioners for laying out a park in Brooklyn, New York, 1866.—Report of the lanscape architects and superintendents to the President of the Board of Commissioners of Prospect Park, Brooklyn. 1968.—Report to the Staten Island Improvement Commission of a preliminary scheme of improvements. 1871.—Report of a preliminary survey of RockaOLandscape into cityscape; Frederick Law Olmsted's plans for a greater New York City. Edited with an introductory essay and notes by Albert Fein. Ithaca, N. Y., Cornell University Press [1968, c1967] x, 490 p. illus., maps (part fold.), plans, ports. 22 cm. (Cornell reprints in urban studies) Twelve documents, of which nine are reports to governmental bodies, five prepared jointly with Calvert Vaux and two with J. James R. Croes. Contents.Contents.—The beginning of Central Park; a fragment of autobiography. ca. 1877.—Description of a plan for the improvement of the Central Park: "Greensward". 1858; 1868 reprint.—Preliminary report to the Commissioners for laying out a park in Brooklyn, New York, 1866.—Report of the lanscape architects and superintendents to the President of the Board of Commissioners of Prospect Park, Brooklyn. 1968.—Report to the Staten Island Improvement Comm
1. Landscape architecture—New York (State)—New York (City) 2. New York (City)—Parks. I. Fein, Albert, comp. II. Vaux, Calvert, 1824-1895. III. Croes, John James Robertson, 1834-1906. IV. Title. V. Title: Frederick Law Olmsted's plans for a greater New York City. VI. Series. BIP

Landscape architecture—Northwest, Pacific.

SUNSET. 712'.6'0979
Landscaping for Western living, by the eds. of Sunset bks. and Sunset mag. [3d ed.] Menlo Park. Calif., Lane [1968] 160p. illus. 28cm. [SB473.S87 1968] 68-13533 2.95 pap.,
1. Landscape architecture—Northwest, Pacific. I. Title.

Landscape architecture—Saudi Arabia.

KELLY, Kathleen, 1942- 712'.0953'8
Landscaping the Saudi Arabian desert / Kathleen Kelly, R. T. Schnadelbach. Philadelphia : Delancey Press, c1976. 182 p. : ill. ; 29 cm. Bibliography: p. 180-182. [SB477.S33K44] 76-6678 22.50
1. Landscape architecture—Saudi Arabia. 2. Deserts—Saudi Arabia. 3. Building—Saudi Arabia. 4. Botany—Saudi Arabia. 5. Desert Flora. I. Schnadelbach, R. T., 1939- joint author. II. Title.

Landscape architecture—Study and teaching.

ROBINETTE, Gary O. 712'.07'1173
Landscape architectural education [by] Gary O. Robinette. Dubuque, Iowa, Kendall/Hunt Pub. Co. [1973] 2 v. 29 cm. [SB469.4.A2R62] 72-90767 ISBN 0-8403-0657-1 (v. 1)
1. Landscape architecture—Study and teaching. I. Title.

Landscape architecture—Study and teaching (Internship)—United States.

INTERNSHIP programs 712'.07'1173
in landscape architectural education. [McLean, Va. : American Society of Landscape Architects Foundation, 1974?] [61] p. : ill. ; 28 cm. Cover title. [SB469.4.U5I57] 74-83634 5.00
1. Landscape architecture—Study and teaching (Internship)—United States. I. American Society of Landscape Architects Foundation.

Landscape architecture—Study and teaching—United States.

LANDSCAPE 712'.07'1173
architectural faculty teaching responsibilities and research interests. [McLean, Va. : American Society of Landscape Architects Foundation, 1974?] [60] p. ; 28 cm. Cover title. A collection of answers from various institutions to questionnaire of Council on Education, American Society of Landscape Architects. [SB469.4.U5L36] 74-83636 4.00
1. Landscape architecture—Study and teaching—United States. 2. Landscape

architecture—Research—United States. 3. Universities and colleges—United States—Faculty. I. American Society of Landscape Architects. Council on Education.

Landscape architecture—Study and teaching—United States—Congresses.

NATIONAL Council of Instructors in Landscape Architecture. 712'.07
Proceedings. Edited & assembled by William H. Tishler. Madison, Dept. of Landscape Architecture, University of Wisconsin [1966?] vii, 144 p. illus. 28 cm. Fourteenth NCILA conference held at the University of Wisconsin, June 29-July 2, 1966. [SB469.4.U5N38] 712'.023 78-298783
1. Landscape architecture—Study and teaching—United States—Congresses. I. Tishler, William H., ed. II. Wisconsin. University.

Landscape architecture—Technical.

MARSH, Warner L. 712.014
Landscape vocabulary. Los Angeles, Miramar [c.1964] 316p. illus., maps, diagrs., plan 23cm. Bibl. 64-15420 8.50
1. Landscape architecture—Technical. I. Title.

Landscape architecture—United States.

ROPER, Laura Wood. 712'.092'4 B
Flo: A biography of Frederick Law Olmsted. Baltimore, Johns Hopkins University Press [1973] xvii, 555 p. illus. 25 cm. Includes bibliographical references. [SB470.O5R66] 73-8125 ISBN 0-8018-1508-8 15.00
1. Olmsted, Frederick Law, 1822-1903. 2. Landscape architecture—United States. I. Title.

Landscape architecture—United States—History.

NICHOLS, Frederick Doveton. 720'.92'4
Thomas Jefferson, landscape architect / Frederick Doveton Nichols and Ralph Griswold. Charlottesville : University Press of Virginia, 1977. p. cm. (Monticello monograph series) Includes index. Bibliography: p. [E332.2.N53] 77-10601 ISBN 0-8139-0603-2 : 9.75
1. Jefferson, Thomas, Pres. U.S.—1743-1826. 2. Landscape architecture—United States—History. 3. Architecture, American—History. I. Griswold, Ralph E., joint author. II. Title. BIP

Landscape architecture—United States—History—Sources—Bibliography—Catalogs.

UNITED States. Library of Congress. Manuscript Division. 016.712'092'4
Frederick Law Olmsted : a register of his papers in the Library of Congress. Rev. ed. Washington : Manuscript Division, Research Dept., Library of Congress, 1977. p. cm. (Registers of papers in the Manuscript Division of the Library of Congress ; no. 28A) [Z6616.O5U53 1977] [SB470.O5] 76-608382 ISBN 0-8444-0229-X
1. Olmsted, Frederick Law, 1822-1903—Archives. 2. United States. Library of Congress. Manuscript Division. 3. Landscape architecture—United States—History—Sources—Bibliography—Catalogs. I. Series: United States. Library of Congress. Manuscript Division. Registers of papers in the Manuscript Division of the Library of Congress ; no. 28A.

Landscape architecture—Washington, D.C.

WALLACE, McHarg, Roberts and Todd. 712'.09753
Toward a comprehensive landscape plan for Washington, D.C.; a report prepared for the National Capital Planning Commission. [Washington, U.S. Govt. Print. Off., 1967] ii, 40 p. illus., plans (part col.) 25 x 29 cm. [SB477.U7D55] 68-61137
1. Landscape architecture—Washington, D.C. 2. Washington, D.C.—Description. I. United States. National Capital Planning Commission. II. Title.

Landscape drawing.

BLACK, Arthur, 1892- 741.42
Landscape sketching. New York, McGraw-Hill, 1950. xiii, 109 p. illus. 26 cm. [NC795.B59] 50-9407
1. Landscape drawing. I. Title.

DOUST, Len A 741.42
Sketching the countryside. London, New York, F. Warne [1957] ix, 62p. illus. 22cm. (Doust sketch books) [NC795.D6] 57-4507
1. Landscape drawing. I. Title.

HAMM, Jack. 743'.8'36
Drawing scenery: landscapes and seascapes. New York, Grosset & Dunlap [1972] 120 p. illus. 28 cm. [NC795.H35] 78-183029 ISBN 0-448-01508-0 2.95
1. Landscape drawing. 2. Sea in art. I. Title.

PERARD, Victor Semon, 1870-1957. 741.72
Sketching landscape. New York, Pitman Pub. Corp. [1957] unpaged (chiefly illus.) 20x26cm. (Pitman drawing series) [NC795.P4 1957] 57-10743
1. Landscape drawing. I. Title. BIP

SHEAKS, Barclay. 743'.8'36
Drawing and painting the natural environment. Worcester, Mass., Davis Publications [1974] 135 p. illus. (part col.) 26 cm. [NC790.S45] 74-78390 ISBN 0-87192-060-3 10.95
1. Landscape drawing. 2. Landscape painting. I. Title.

Landscape drawing—Exhibitions.

BAER, Curtis O. 743'.9'36
Landscape drawings [by] Curtis O. Baer. New York, H. N. Abrams [1973] 360 p. illus. (part col.) 28 x 34 cm. "Published in association with the Drawing Society." Bibliography: p. 357. [NC800.B29] 77-135655 ISBN 0-8109-0255-9 35.00
1. Landscape drawing—Exhibitions. I. Title.

Landscape drawing—Technique.

O'CONNOR, John, 1913- 743'.8'36
Landscape drawing and painting / John O'Connor. New York : Viking Press, 1978, c1977. 96 p. : ill. ; 26 cm. (A Studio book) Includes index. [NC795.O37 1978] 77-4849 ISBN 0-670-41772-6 : 9.95
1. Landscape drawing—Technique. 2. Landscape painting—Technique. I. Title. BIP

Landscape drawing—United States—Exhibitions.

IN praise of space : the landscape in American art : [exhibition] organized by Robert Godfrey. New Wilmington, Pa. : Art Dept. of Westminster College, c1976. 68 p. : ill. ; 23 cm. Includes catalogues of 2 exhibitions: "Nineteenth century American landscape drawings" and "Recent American landscape art," held at the Westminster College Art Gallery, Dec. 1975 and Jan.-Feb. 1976, respectively. [NC790.I5] 75-32608 758'.1'0973074014893
1. Landscape drawing—United States—Exhibitions. 2. Landscape painting, American—Exhibitions. I. Godfrey, Robert, 1941- II. Westminster College, New Wilmington, Pa. Art Gallery.

Landscape gardening.

ADDKISON, Andrew R. 712'.6
100 garden plans / by Andrew R. Addkison with Jack Kramer ; botanical drawings by Robert Johnson ; perspective and plan drawings by Michael Valdez. 1st ed. New York : Random House, c1977. p. cm. [SB472.K65] 77-6006 ISBN 0-394-41171-4 : 9.95. ISBN 0-394-73400-9 pbk. : 5.95
1. Landscape gardening. 2. Gardening. 3. Gardens. I. Kramer, Jack, 1927- joint author. II. Title. III. Title: Garden plans.

AJAY, Betty. 712'.6
Betty Ajay's guide to home landscaping. Illus. by Abe Ajay. [1st ed.] New York, McGraw-Hill [1970] xi, 208 p. illus. 22 cm. [SB473.A36] 70-118392
1. Landscape gardening. I. Title. II. Title: Guide to home landscaping.

ATKINSON, Robert E 635.9
Landscaping for outdoor living. [Los Angeles, Trend Books, 1958] 128p. illus. 25cm. (Trend book, 170) [SB472.A75] 58-35853
1. Landscape gardening. I. Title.

ATKINSON, Robert E. 712'.6
Spot gardens; a guide for creating and planting miniature gardens, indoors and outdoors, by Robert E. Atkinson. New York, McKay [1973] viii, 277 p. illus. 27 cm. [SB473.A75] 72-92641 9.95
1. Landscape gardening. 2. Container gardening. I. Title. BIP

AUL, Henry B. 712.62
How to plan modern home grounds; illus. and plans by the author. New York, Sheridan House [1959] 312 p. illus. 22 cm. [SB473.A815] 59-8330
1. Landscape gardening. I. Title.

AUL, Henry B. 712.64
How to plant your home ground. New York, Sheridan House [1953] 383 p. illus. 23 cm. [SB473.A82] 53-7670
1. Landscape gardening. I. Title.

BAILEY, Leo L. 635
A step-by-step guide to landscaping and gardening / Leo L. Bailey. 1st ed. Hicksville, N.Y. : Exposition Press, [1974] xii, 212 p. : ill. ; 24 cm. (An Exposition-banner book) Bibliography: p. 211-212. [SB473.B29] 74-84421 ISBN 0-682-48084-3 : 10.00
1. Landscape gardening. 2. Gardening. 3. Plant propagation. I. Title. BIP

BAILEY, Ralph, 1904- ed. 712.62
Landscaping plans for small homes. Plans by Nelva M. Weber; illus. by Sigman-Ward. [1st ed.] [New York] American Garden Guild [1954] 128 p. illus. 22 cm. [SB473.B32] 54-7133
1. Landscape gardening. I. Title.

BISGROVE, Richard. 712'.6
Making the most of your garden / [by] Richard Bisgrove. London : Ward Lock, 1976. 176 p. : ill. (some col.) ; 26 cm. Includes index. [SB473.B54 1976] 77-355401 ISBN 0-7063-5136-3 : £3.95
1. Landscape gardening. 2. Gardening. I. Title.

BRETT, William Samuel. 712.6
Planning your garden: how to design and construct it. London, Ward, Lock [1957; stamped: distributed by Sportshelf, New Rochelle, N. Y.] 192p. illus. 23cm. [SB473.B7] 58-3210
1. Landscape gardening. 2. Garden ornaments and furniture. I. Title. BIP

BRETT, William Samuel. 712'.09173'2
Small city gardens [by] William S. Brett and Kay Grant. London. New York, Abelard-Schuman [1967] 159 p. illus., plans. 24 cm. [SB473.B72] 66-25010
1. Landscape gardening. I. Grant, Hilda Kay, 1910- joint author. II. Title.

BROOKES, John, 1933- 712'.6
Room outside; a plan for the garden. New York, Viking Press [1970, c1969] 191 p. illus. (part col.) 24 cm. (A Studio book) [SB473.B73 1970] 72-99580 6.95
1. Landscape gardening. I. Title.

BROOKES, John, 1933- 712'.6
Room outside : a new approach to garden design / John Brookes. New York : Penguin Books, [1979] p. cm. Edition of 1970 has subtitle: A plan for the garden. Includes index. Bibliography: p. [SB473.B73 1979] 78-15387 ISBN 0-14-005077-9 pbkk. : 6.95
1. Landscape gardening. I. Title. BIP

BROOKES, John, 1933- 712'.6
The small garden / John Brookes. New York : Macmillan, c1978. 256 p. : ill. ; 30 cm. Includes indexes. Bibliography: p. 248. [SB473.B732] 77-10325 ISBN 0-02-516700-6 : 19.95
1. Landscape gardening. I. Title. BIP

BUSHEY, Donald J 712.6
A guide to home landscaping. With illus. by the author. New York, McGraw-Hill [c1956] 293p. illus. 24cm. [SB473.B75] 55-9536
1. Landscape gardening. I. Title. II. Title: Home landscaping.

CARPENTER, Philip Lee, 1933- 712
Plants in the landscape / Philip L. Carpenter, Theodore D. Walker, Frederick O. Lanphear. San Francisco : W. H. Freeman, [1975] vii, 481 p. : ill. ; 22 x 29 cm. Includes bibliographies and indexes. [SB472.C27] 74-32292 ISBN 0-7167-0778-0 : 15.00
1. Landscape gardening. 2. Plants, Ornamental. I. Walker, Theodore D., joint author. II. Lanphear, Frederick O., joint author. III. Title. BIP

CASSIDAY, Bruce. 635.9
Home guide to lawns and landscaping / by Bruce Cassiday ; drawings by Frank Schwarz. New York : Book Division, Times Mirror Magazines : [distributed by] Harper & Row, c1976. 210 p. : ill. ; 24 cm. "A Popular science book." Includes index. [SB473.C34] 75-40601 ISBN 0-06-010689-1 : 6.95
1. Landscape gardening. 2. Lawns. I. Schwarz, Frank. II. Title. BIP

CHURCH, Thomas Dolliver. 712.62
Gardens are for people; how to plan for outdoor living. New York, Reinhold Pub. Corp. [1955] 248 p. illus. (part col.), diagrs. 33 cm. [SB473.C5] 55-9945
1. Landscape gardening. I. Title.

CHURCH, Thomas Dolliver. 712'.6
Your private world; a study of intimate gardens, by Thomas Church. San Francisco, Chronicle Books [1969] 202 p. illus. 30 cm. [SB473.C52] 74-99220 9.95
1. Landscape gardening. 2. Patios. 3. Swimming pools. I. Title. BIP

CROCKETT, James Underwood. 712'.6
Landscape gardening, by James Underwood Crockett and the editors of Time-Life Books. Watercolor illus. by Rebecca A. Merrilees and Barbara Wolff. New York, Time-Life Books [1971] 160 p. illus. (part col.), col. plan. 28 cm. (The Time-Life encyclopedia of gardening.) [SB473.C76] 77-26564
1. Landscape gardening. I. Time-Life Books. II. Title. BIP

DIETZ, Marjorie J. 712'.6
Landscaping and the small garden, by Marjorie J. Dietz. Garden City, N.Y., Doubleday [1973] 170 p. illus. 25 cm. Bibliography: p. 164-165. [SB473.D5] 72-84907 ISBN 0-385-03884-4 7.95
1. Landscape gardening. 2. Gardening. I. Title.

DOWNING, Andrew Jackson, 1815-1852. 712
A facsimile edition of a treatise on the theory and practice of landscape gardening. With the 1859 sixth ed. suppl. by Henry Winthrop Sargent. And a special appreciation by John O. Simonds, Jr. New York, Funk & Wagnalls [1967] 576 p. illus., port. 22 cm. [SB471.D7 1859a] 67-28078
1. Landscape gardening. I. Sargent, Henry Winthrop, 1810-1882. II. Title. III. Title: A treatise on the theory of landscape gardening.

DOWNING, Andrew Jackson, 1815-1852. 712'.6'0973
A treatise on the theory and practice of landscape gardening / by Andrew Jackson Downing. Little Compton, R.I. : Theophrastus Publishers, 1977. p. cm. Reprint of the 1875 ed., containing a supplement (1859) and a second supplement (1875) by H. W. Sargent, published by Orange Judd Co., New York. Includes index. [SB471.D7 1977] 77-228 ISBN 0-913728-23-3 : 20.00
1. Landscape gardening. 2. Landscape gardening—United States. 3. Ornamental trees—United States. I. Sargent, Henry Winthrop, 1810-1882. II. Title.

DUSTAN, Alice L. 712.62
Landscaping your own home. Drawings by Henry H. Wiss. New York, Macmillan, 1955. 248 p. illus. 22 cm. [SB473.D8] 55-14603
1. Landscape gardening. I. Title.

ECKBO, Garrett. 712.64
The art of home landscaping. New York, F. W. Dodge Corp. [1956] 278 p. illus. 26 cm. Includes bibliography. [SB473.E25] 56-8103
1. Landscape gardening. I. Title. BIP

ECKBO, Garrett. 635.9
Home landscape : the art of home landscaping / Garrett Eckbo. Rev. and enl. ed. New York : McGraw-Hill, c1978. vii, 340 p. : ill. ; 25 cm. Published in 1956 under title: The art of home landscaping. Includes index. Bibliography: p. [327]-331. [SB473.E25 1978] 77-16621 ISBN 0-07-018879-3 : 12.95
1. Landscape gardening. I. Title.

ECKBO, Garrett. 712
Landscape for living. [New York] Architectural Record with Duell, Sloan, & Pearce [1950] 262 p. illus., plans. 28 cm. Bibliography: p. 255-262. [SB472.E22] 50-13528
1. Landscape gardening. 2. Cities and towns—Planning. I. Title.

EVERETT, Thomas H. 712'.6
Lawns & landscapping / by T. H. Everett. New York : Grossett & Dunlap, c1975. 95 p. : ill. ; 28 cm. (Grossett good life books) Revised and updated ed. of the author's Flower garden guide and Lawns and landscaping handbook. Includes index. [SB473.E93 1975] 74-33752 ISBN 0-448-11952-8 pbk. : 1.95
1. Landscape gardening. 2. Lawns. I. Title.

FAVRETTI, Rudy J. 712'.6'0973
For every house a garden : a guide for reproducing period gardens / by Rudy J. Favretti and Joy P. Favretti. 1st ed. Chester, Conn. : Pequot Press, c1977. 137 p. : ill. ; 23 cm. Includes index. [SB473.F38] 76-51128 ISBN 0-87106-080-9 pbk. : 4.95
1. Landscape gardening. 2. Gardens—United States—History. 3. Gardens—Conservation and restoration. 4. Plants, Cultivated—United States—History. I. Favretti, Joy P., joint author. II. Title. BIP

†FELICE, Raymond. 635.9
Successful landscaping / by Raymond Felice. Farmington, Mich. : Structures Pub. Co., 1977. p. cm. [SB473.F44] 77-16624 ISBN 0-912336-55-2 : 12.00. ISBN 0-912336-56-0 pbk. : 4.95
1. Landscape gardening. 2. Gardening. I. Title. BIP

FIEGLER, Ralph H. 712.3
Care and preservation of shade and ornamental plants, by Ralph H. Fiegler. [York? Pa.] 1968. [28] p. illus. 28 cm. A companion publication to the author's How to landscape your home and grounds. [SB473.F5042]
1. Landscape gardening. 2. Ornamental shrubs. 3. Ornamental trees. 4. Garden pests. I. Title.

FOSTER, Ruth S. 635.9
Homeowner's guide to landscaping that saves energy dollars / by Ruth S. Foster ; ill. by James Lombardy. New York : McKay, [1978] p. cm. Includes index. [SB473.F67] 78-2506 ISBN 0-679-50863-5 : 11.95. ISBN 0-679-50866-X pbk. : 5.95
1. Landscape gardening. 2. Dwellings—Energy conservation. I. Title. BIP

GARLAND, Madge. 712'.6
The small garden in the city. New York, G. Braziller [1974, c1973] 136 p. illus. 25 cm. [SB473.G29 1974] 74-76646 ISBN 0-8076-0752-5 12.50
1. Landscape gardening. I. Title. BIP

GIVENS, Harold D. 712'.6
Landscape it yourself / by Harold D. Givens. New York : Harcourt Brace Jovanovich, c1976. p. cm. Includes index. Bibliography: p. [SB469.3.G57] 76-14436 14.95
1. Landscape gardening. I. Title. BIP

GRASBY, Nancy. 712.62
Imaginative small gardens. New York, Hearthside Press [1963] 256 p. illus. 24 cm. Includes bibliography. [SB473.G64] 63-9930
1. Landscape gardening. I. Title.

HACKETT, Brian. 715
Planting design / by Brian Hackett. New York : McGraw-Hill, [1979] c1978. p. cm. Includes bibliographical references and index. [SB472.H17 1979] 78-26625 ISBN 0-025402-8 : 16.95
1. Landscape gardening. 2. Landscape architecture. 3. Plants, Ornamental. I. Title. BIP

HARRIS, John H. 635.9
Keep 'em growing [by] John H. Harris and R. Gordon Halfacre. Raleigh, N.C., Litho Industries [1972] 157 p. illus. 24 cm. [SB473.H37] 71-189492 6.95
1. Landscape gardening. 2. Gardening—Southern States. I. Halfacre, R. Gordon, 1941- joint author. II. Title.

HAWKINS, Reginald Robert, 1902- 713.7
Walks and paths, driveways, steps, curbs, and edgings, by Reginald R. Hawkins and Charles H. Abbe. New York, Van Nostrand [1951] v, 164 p. illus. 22 cm. [Their The home mechanic's outdoor library] "Most of the material ... appeared first in the authors' Home mechanic's outdoor handbook." [SB476.H3] 51-5230
1. Landscape gardening. 2. Roads. I. Abbe, Charles H., joint author. II. Title.

HILL, Amelia Leavitt. 712.62
The homeowner's guide to landscaping. Illustrated by Alfred F. Muscari. New York, Putnam [1954] 205 p. illus. 20 cm. [SB473.H5] 54-10497
1. Landscape gardening. I. Title.

HOBHOUSE, Penelope. 635.9'0941
The country gardener / Penelope Hobhouse. Oxford : Phaidon, 1976. xi, 190 p., [16] leaves of plates : ill. ; 24 cm. Includes index. Bibliography: p. [183]-184. [SB472.H5] 76-379040 ISBN 0-7148-1703-1 : £4.95
1. Landscape gardening. 2. Plants, Ornamental. I. Title.

HOOVER, Norman Kurtz, 1913- 635.9
Approved practices in beautifying the home grounds, by Norman K. Hoover. Edited by Elwood M. Juergenson. [3d ed.] Danville, Ill., Interstate Printers & Publishers [1966] 285 p. illus. 22 cm. [SB473.H57 1966] 66-13963
1. Landscape gardening. 2. Gardening. I. Juergenson, Elwood M., ed. II. Title. BIP

HOOVER, Norman Kurtz, 1913- 635.9
Approved practices in beautifying the home grounds, by Norman K. Hoover. Edited by Elwood M. Juergenson. [4th ed.] Danville, Ill., Interstate Printers & Publishers [1973] 292 p. illus. 22 cm. [SB473.H57 1973] 72-89590 5.50
1. Landscape gardening. 2. Landscape architecture. 3. Gardening. I. Title.

HUBBARD, Henry Vincent, 1875-1947. 712
An introduction to the study of landscape design, by Henry Vincent Hubbard and Theodora Kimball. Rev. ed. Boston, 1967, c1945. 419 p. illus. [SB472.H8 1967]
1. Landscape gardening. I. Hubbard, Theodora Kimball, 1887-1935, joint author.

IREYS, Alice Recknagel. 712'.6
How to plan and plant your own property. Planting plans by the author. Photos by Molly Adams except as noted. New York, Morrow [1975, c1967] 182 p., illus., 28 cm. [SB473I72] ISBN 0-688-06831-6 4.50 (pbk.)
1. Landscape gardening. I. Title. BIP

IREYS, Alice Recknagel. 712'.6
How to plan and plant your own property. Planting plans by the author. Photos. by Molly Adams except as noted. New York, M. Barrows; distributed by M. Morrow, 1967. 182 p. illus. (part col.) 29 cm. [SB473.I72] 67-19689
1. Landscape gardening. I. Title.

IREYS, Alice Recknagel. 712'.6
How to plan and plant your property Photos. by Molly Adams except as noted. New York, M. Barrows; distributed by W. Morrow, 1967. 182 p. illus. (part col.) 29 cm. [SB473 I 72] 67-19689
1. Landscape gardening. I. Title.

IREYS, Alice Recknagel. 712'.6
Small gardens for city and country : a guide to designing and planting your green spaces / Alice Recknagel Ireys. Englewood Cliffs, N.J. : Prentice-Hall, c1977. p. cm. (A Spectrum book) (Home gardening handbooks) Includes index. [SB473.I73] 77-5427 ISBN 0-13-813063-9 : 14.95. ISBN 0-13-813055-8 pbk. 8.95
1. Landscape gardening. I. Title. II. Series. BIP

JENSEN, Jens, 1860-1951. 710.4
Siftings, the major portion of The clearing, and collected writings. Chicago, R. F. Seymour [1956] 145p. illus. 24cm. [SB63.J43A32 1956] 56-14465
1. Landscape gardening. 2. Landscape. I. Title. II. Title: The clearing.

JOHNSON, Loyal Robert, 1904- 635.9
How to landscape your grounds. [2d ed.] New York, De La Mare [1950] ix, 257 p. illus., map. 24 cm. [SB473.J6 1950] Agr
1. Landscape gardening. I. Title.

KENFIELD, Warren G., 1917- 719
The wild gardener in the wild landscape; the art of naturalistic landscaping, by Warren G. Kenfield. Photography by Happy Kitchel Hamilton. New York, Hafner Pub. Co., 1966. xi, 232 p. illus. (part col.), plans. 26 cm. Bibliography: p. 222-223. [SB473.K53] 66-19582
1. Landscape gardening. I. Title. BIP

KILVERT, B. Cory. 712'.6
Informal gardening: the new homeowner's guide to planting his property [by] B. Cory Kilvert, Jr. [New York] Macmillan [1969] 286 p. illus. 21 cm. [SB473.K56] 69-12179
1. Landscape gardening. I. Title.

KORBOBO, Raymond P. 712.62
Complete home landscaping and garden guide. Editorial consultant: E. L. D. Seymour. New York, W. H. Wise, 1954. 368 p. illus. 22 cm. [SB473.K6] 54-11504
1. Landscape gardening. 2. Gardening. I. Title.

KRAMER, Jack, 1927- 712'.6
Garden planning for the small property. Drawings by Charles Hosppner with Frank Chin Loy. New York, Scribner [1972] 137, [10] p. illus. 28 cm. Bibliography: p. [141] [SB473.K7] 78-162771 ISBN 0-684-12517-X 6.95
1. Landscape gardening. I. Title.

KRAMER, Jack, 1927- 635.9
Gardening and home landscaping; a complete illustrated guide. [1st ed.] New York, Harper & Row [1971] viii, 336 p. illus. 29 cm. [SB473.K72] 77-138744 ISBN 0-06-012466-0 9.95
1. Landscape gardening. 2. Landscape architecture. I. Title.

KRAMER, Jack, 1927- 635.9'0973
Gardening and home landscaping : a complete illustrated guide / by Jack Kramer. New York : Galahad Books, [1976?] c1971. viii, 336, 31 p. : ill. ; 29 cm. Includes index. Bibliography: p. [329]-331. [SB473.K72 1976] 76-360 ISBN 0-88365-349-4 : 9.95
1. Landscape gardening. 2. Landscape architecture. I. Title.

KRAMER, Jack, 1927- 712'.6
Gardening and home landscaping guide. New York, Arco [1970, c1968] 112 p. illus. 25 cm. [SB473.K73] 79-88048 3.50
1. Landscape gardening. I. Title. BIP

KRAMER, Jack, 1927- 712'.6
Landscaping your vacation place. New York, Scribner [1974, c1975] viii, 132 p. illus. 29 cm. (The Scribner garden library) [SB473.K74] 74-11228 ISBN 0-684-13959-6 6.95.
1. Landscape gardening. 2. Summer homes. I. Title.
Pbk. 3.95; ISBN 0-684-13966-9.

LEES, Carlton B. 712.62
Budget landscaping. Illustrated by Patricia Maglott. [1st ed.] New York, Holt [1960] 152 p. illus. 22 cm. Includes bibliography. [SB473.L4] 60-6544
1. Landscape gardening. I. Title.

LOHMANN, Karl Baptiste, 1887- 635.9
Fundamentals of landscape architecture. Serial 6417. [Ed. 1] Scranton, International Correspondence Schools, c1961. 67p. illus. 19cm. [SB472.L67] 61-4890
1. Landscape gardening. 2. Plants, Ornamental. I. International Correspondence Schools, Scranton, Pa. II. Title.

LOHMANN, Karl Baptiste, 1887-1963. 712
Fundamentals of landscape architecture. Serial 6417-2. [Ed. 3] Scranton, International Correspondence Schools [1966] 86, 2 p. illus., col. plates. 19 cm. [SB472.L67 1966] 66-7209
1. Landscape gardening. 2. Plants, Ornamental. 3. International Correspondence Schools, Scranton, Pa. I. Title.

MCDONALD, Elvin. 712'.6
The low-upkeep book of lawns and landscape, by Elvin McDonald and Lawrence Power. New York, Hawthorn Books [1971] viii, 152 p. illus. (part col.) 25 cm. "A Helen Van Pelt Wilson book." [SB473.M24 1971] 70-130704 6.95
1. Landscape gardening. 2. Lawns. 3. Landscape architecture. I. Power, Lawrence, joint author. II. Title.

MCKENNA, Patrick J 1897- 712.6
Small home landscaping, by P. J. and Anna B. McKenna. [Greenwich, Conn., Fawcett Publications, 1953] 144p. illus. 24cm. (A Fawcett book, no. 178) [SB473.M255] 53-8207
1. Landscape gardening. I. McKenna, Anna Brohmer, joint author. II. Title.

MALKIN, Robert Samuel. 712.6
How to landscape your own home. Illustrated with 514 sketches by the author. New York, Harper [1955] 432 p. illus. 25 cm. [SB473.M27] 55-6588
1. Landscape gardening. I. Title.

MELADY, John Hayes. 635.9
Better landscaping for your home; illustrated by Eva Melady. New York, Grosset & Dunlop [1953] 184 p. illus. 20 cm. (His The Melady garden books) [SB473.M4] 53-1255
1. Landscape gardening. 2. Plants, Ornamental—U.S. I. Title.

MIDGLEY, Kenneth. 712.6
Garden design; prepared in conjunction and collaboration with the Royal Horticultural Society. Harmondsworth, Penguin, 1966. 223 p. front., illus., plans, tables, diagrs. 18 1/2 cm. (A Penguin handbook, PH127) 12/ ISSN (B66-22681))o[SB473.M48]e67-70344
1. Landscape gardening. I. Royal Horticultural Society, London. II. Title. BIP

MINNESOTA Mining and Manufacturing Company. Automotive-Hardware Trades Division. 635.9
The home pro landscape and lawn care guide / [Automotive-Hardware Trades Division, 3M Company]. [St. Paul : The Division, 1975] i, 172 p. : ill. ; 14 x 21 cm. (Its The home pro guide series) "Cat. no. 9725." [SB475.M5 1975] 74-82961
1. Landscape gardening. 2. Lawns. I. Title.

MOSSMAN, Tam. 712
Gardens that care for themselves : how to grow neater, healthier plants and cut your outdoor chores in half / Tam Mossman ; drawings by Dann Jacobus. 1st ed. Garden City, N.Y. : Doubleday, 1978. xvii, 315 p., [4] leaves of plates : ill. ; 22 cm. Includes index. [SB473.M74] 77-76256 ISBN 0-385-11171-1 : 10.95
1. Landscape gardening. I. Title. BIP

NELSON, William R. 712'.6
Landscaping your home / William R. Nelson, Jr. Rev. ed. Urbana : University of Illinois Press, c1975. 246 p. : ill. ; 29 cm. [SB473.N36 1975] 75-6052 ISBN 0-252-00559-7 : 8.95
1. Landscape gardening. 2. Landscape architecture. I. Title.

NELSON, William R. 712.6
Landscaping your home. [Urbana, University of Illinois College of Agriculture, Cooperative Extension Service, c1963] 151 p. illus. 28 cm. (University of Illinois, College of Agriculture, Cooperative Extension Service. Circular 858) [SB472.N4] 63-62887

SUBJECT INDEX LANDSCAPE GARDENING—FLORIDA.

1. Landscape gardening. I. Title.

NEWCOMB, Duane G. 684.1'8
Mobile home gardening guide. [Beverly Hills, Calif., Trail-R-Club of America, 1963] 154 p. illus. 21 cm. [SB473.N4] 63-23789
1. Landscape gardening. 2. Mobile home living. I. Title.

NEWTON, Patricia. 712'.6
Planning your new garden, by Patricia Newton and Edna Pollard. Melbourne, Sydney [etc.] Lothian [1968] 40 p. illus., diagrs. 22 cm. (Gardening with a purpose books, no. 5) [SB473.N42] 68-131127 1.05 Aust.
1. Landscape gardening. I. Pollard, Edna, joint author. II. Title.

ORTLOFF, Henry Stuart, 1896- 712
The book of landscape design, by H. Stuart Ortloff and Henry B. Raymore. New York, M. Barrows, 1959. 316p. illus. 22cm. Includes bibliography. [SB472.O7] 59-12871
1. Landscape gardening. 2. Landscape gardening—Hist. I. Raymore, Henry Bond, joint author. II. Title. III. Title: Landscape design.

ORTLOFF, Henry Stuart, 1896- 712.62
Color and design for every garden, by H. Stuart Ortloff and Henry B. Raymore. New York, M. Barrows [1951] 301 p. illus. 21 cm. [SB473.O74] Agr
1. Landscape gardening. 2. Plants, Ornamental—U.S. I. Raymore, Henry Bond, joint author. II. Title.

PRATT, Richard. 712.62
Ladies' home journal book of landscaping and outdoor living; the homescaper's guide to good looks and good living on his grounds. [1st ed.] New York, Published by M. Evans and distributed in association with Lippincott, Philadelphia [1963] 225 p. illus. 27 cm. [SB473.P7] 63-8488
1. Landscape gardening. I. Title. II. Title: Landscaping and outdoor living.

RHODES, Peter C. 635.9
Beautify your home grounds; a complete guide to small plot landscaping and ground improvement. With illus. by Leo Soretsky. New York, Homecrafts Publishers [1952] 90p. illus. 28cm. [SB473.R49] 52-11136
1. Landscape gardening. I. Title.

RIES, Estelle H. 712'.6
Garden hobbies [by] Estelle H. Ries. South Brunswick [N.J.] A. S. Barnes [1970] 291 p. illus. 25 cm. [SB473.R53] 77-101234 ISBN 0-498-07359-9 8.50
1. Landscape gardening. 2. Gardens. I. Title.

ROBERTS, Irving, 1915- 712'.6
Home landscaping you can design yourself. Drawings by Gerry Myers. New York, Hawthorn Books [1972] ix, 166 p. illus. 24 cm. "A Helen Van Pelt Wilson book." [SB473.R55] 74-179114 6.95
1. Landscape gardening. I. Title.

ROBINSON, Florence Bell. 715
Palette of plants; sequel to Planting design. Champaign, Ill., Garrard Press [1950] vii, 214 p. illus., map. 21 cm. Bibliography: p. 207-209. [SB472.R65] Agr50
1. Landscape gardening. 2. Plants, Ornamental. I. Title.

RODALE, Jerome Irving, 1898- 712.6
How to landscape your own home, by J. I. Rodale and staff. Supervised by Dorothy Patton Franz. Emmaus, Pa., Rodale Books [1963] 1544 p. illus., maps, tables. 23 cm. [SB473.R57] 63-25959
1. Landscape gardening. 2. Plants, Ornamental. 3. Organic gardening. 4. Gardening. I. Title.

ROSE, James C. 712
Creative gardens. New York, Reinhold Pub. Corp. [1958] 208 p. illus. (part col.) diagrs., facsim., plans. 33 cm. [SB473.R6] 58-7198
1. Landscape gardening. 2. Gardens. I. Title.

SCHERY, Robert W 635.9
The householder's guide to outdoor beauty. Over 300 illus. by Edward J. Brundage. New York, Pocket Books [1963] xii, 337 p. illus., maps. 18 cm. (A Permabook edition) "M-5049." [SB473.S36] 63-6204
1. Landscape gardening. I. Title. II. Title: Outdoor beauty.

SCHULER, Stanley. 712'.6
How to redesign your yard and garden = previously published as Make your garden new again / Stanley Schuler. New York : Hawthorn Books, [1977] c1975. 255 p. : ill. ; 24 cm. Includes index. [SB473.S38 1977] 76-20851 ISBN 0-8015-3746-0 : 4.95
1. Landscape gardening. I. Title.

SCHULER, Stanley. 712'.6
Make your garden new again : how to relandscape, replant, and develop your property / Stanley Schuler. New York : Simon and Schuster, [1975] 255 p. : ill. ; 25 cm. Includes index. [SB473.S38] 74-26793 ISBN 0-671-21949-9 : 9.95
1. Landscape gardening. I. Title. BIP

SCHULER, Stanley. 712'.6
Planning and planting the small garden plot; a practical guide. New York, Dial Press, 1972. 255 p. illus. 24 cm. [SB473.S39] 71-37464 6.95
1. Landscape gardening. 2. Landscape architecture. 3. Gardening. I. Title. BIP

SECOR, Arthur J 712.62
Beautiful homes. [Clear Rapids, Iowa, 1959] 88p. illus. 23cm. Includes bibliography. [SB473.S45] 59-52203
1. Landscape gardening. I. Title.

SITWELL, George Reresby, bart., 1860-1943. 712
on the making of gardens. With an introd. by Sir Osbert Sitwell. New York, Scribner [1951] xix, 76 p. illus. 23 cm. First ed. published in 1909 under title: An essay on the making of gardens. [SB472.S64 1951] 51-12298
1. Landscape gardening. I. Title.

SMALL-SPACE gardens / 712'.6
by the editors of Sunset Books and Sunset magazine ; [edited by Kathryn L. Arthurs]. 1st ed. Menlo Park, Calif. : Lane Pub. Co., 1978. 80 p. : ill ; 28 cm. Cover title: Sunset ideas for small-space gardens. Includes index. [SB473.S54] 77-82874 ISBN 0-376-03701-6 pbk. : 2.95
1. Landscape gardening. 2. Patio gardening. I. Arthurs, Kathryn. II. Sunset. III. Title: Sunset ideas for small-space gardens. BIP

SMITH, Ken, 1927- 712
Western home landscaping / by Ken Smith. Tucson, AZ : H.P. Books, c1978.. 184 p. : ill. ; 29 cm. Includes index. [SB473.S56] 71-52897 pbk. : 7.95
1. Landscape gardening. 2. Landscape architecture. 3. Landscape gardening—The West. I. Title. II. Title: Home landscaping. Publisher's address : P.O. Box 5367, Tucson, AZ 85703 BIP

STEVENSON, Violet W. 717
Gardening with stone / [by] Violet Stevenson. London : Pelham, 1976. [7], 116, [8] p. of plates : ill. ; 23 cm. Includes index. [SB476.S762 1976] 76-376037 ISBN 0-7207-0910-5 : 11.00
1. Landscape gardening. 2. Stone. 3. Rock gardens. I. Title.
Distributed by Transatlantic Arts, Levittown, N.Y.

STOFFEL, Robert J. 712'.6
Do's and don'ts of home landscape design, by Robert J. Stoffel. New York, Hearthside Press [1968] 192 p. illus., plans. 24 cm. [SB473.S844] 68-20197 6.95
1. Landscape gardening. I. Title.

SUNSET. 712.62
Garden & patio building book; five complete Sunset books in one volune to cover your basic outdoor building needs.[1st ed.] Menlo Park, Calif., Lane Book Co. [1960] 1 v. illus. 28 cm. [sB476.S78] 60-9427
1. Landscape gardening. 2. Patios. 3. Greenhouses. 4. Fences. I. Title. BIP

SUNSET. 712.62
Landscaping for modern living; by the editors of Sunset magazine, under the direction of Walter I. Doty [and] Paul C. Johnson. [1st ed.] Memlo Park, Calif., Lane Pub. Co. [1958] 190 p. illus. 28 cm. [SB473.S86] 58-597405
1. Landscape gardening. I. Title.

SUNSET 635.96
Sunset ideas for garden color, by the eds. of Sunset magazine and Sunset bks. 2d rev. ed. Menlo Park, Calif., Lane, c.1965. 80p. illus. (pt. col.) 28cm. (Sunset bks., 315) [SB473.S882] 65-15207 1.95 bds.,
1. Landscape gardening. 2. Color of plants. I. Title.

SUNSET. 712.6
Sunset ideas for landscaping your home; ideas compiled from Sunset magazine. San Francisco, Lane Pub. Co., [1950] 63 p. illus. 28 cm. [SB473.S89] 98Su7 Agr
1. Landscape gardening. I. Title.

SUNSET ideas for 712'.6
landscaping & garden remodeling / by the editors of Sunset books and Sunset magazine / [edited by Robert G. Bander ; ill., Joe Seney, E. D. Bills]. 4th ed. Menlo Park, Calif. : Lane Pub. Co., c1978. 80 p. : ill. ; 28 cm. (A Sunset book) Third ed. published in 1972 under title: Sunset ideas for landscaping. Includes index. [SB473.S896 1978] 77-82872 ISBN 0-376-03454-8 pbk. : 2.95
1. Landscape gardening. 2. Landscape architecture. I. Bander, Robert G. II. Sunset. III. Title: Ideas for landscaping & garden remodeling.

SWENSON, Allan A. 712'.6
Plan your own landscape / by Allan A. Swenson ; designs by Peter J. Swenson ; ill. by Jeff Fallon. New York : Grosset & Dunlap, c1978. vii, 120 p. : ill. ; 28 cm. Includes index. [SB473.S93] 77-77295 ISBN 0-448-14382-8 : 12.95 ISBN 0-448-14383-6 pbk. : 6.95
1. Landscape gardening. I. Swenson, Peter J. II. Fallon, Jeff. III. Title. BIP

TARANTINO, Rhoda Specht. 712'.6
Small gardens are more fun. New York, Simon and Schuster [1972] 159 p. illus. 25 cm. [SB473.T328] 70-188335 ISBN 0-671-21142-0 8.95
1. Landscape gardening. 2. Gardening. I. Title. BIP

TREND Books, inc., Los Angeles. 712.6
15 basic ways to landscape your home. [Los Angeles, 1954] 128p. illus. 24cm. (Trend book, no. 113) [SB473.T7] 54-1805
1. Landscape gardening. 2. Gardening. I. Title.

WILSON, Scott. 624
Landscape construction / by Scott Wilson ; [illustrator, Elizabeth Thurber]. San Luis Obispo : Vocational Education Productions, California Polytechnic State University, 1976. 99 p. : ill. ; 28 cm. [SB472.W58] 76-29123
1. Landscape gardening. 2. Landscape architecture. I. Title.

WOLGENSINGER, Bernard. 712'.6
The personal garden, its architecture and design / Bernard Wolgensinger, Jose Daidone ; [English translation, J. A. Underwood]. New York : Van Nostrand Reinhold, 1975. 160 p. : ill. ; 27 cm. Translation of Votre jardin. Includes index. [SB473.W5813] 74-27200 ISBN 0-442-29569-3 : 30.00
1. Landscape gardening. 2. Landscape architecture. I. Daidone, Jose, joint author. II. Title.

WYMAN, Donald, 1903- 635.9
Easy gardens / by Donald Wyman and Curtis Prendergast, and the editors of Time-Life Books. Alexandria, Va. : Time-Life Books, [1978] p. cm. (Time-Life encyclopedia of gardening) Includes index. Bibliography: p. [SB473.W95] 78-23434 ISBN 0-8094-2637-4 : 9.95
1. Landscape gardening. I. Prendergast, Curtis, joint author. II. Time-Life Books. III. Title. BIP

YATES, Raymond Francis, 1895- 712.6
Living in the back yard, by Borden Hall [pseud.] New York, Harper [1955] 289p. illus. 22cm. [SB473.Y3] 54-12180
1. Landscape gardening. 2. Garden ornaments and furniture. I. Title.

Landscape gardening—Australia.

WILSON, Glen. 715'.0994
Landscaping with Australian plants / [by] Glen Wilson. Melbourne : Thomas Nelson (Australia), 1975. 89 p. : col. ill. ; 29 cm. Includes index. [SB477.A8W5] 76-355326 ISBN 0-17-001991-8
1. Landscape gardening—Australia. 2. Wild flower gardening—Australia. I. Title.

Landscape gardening—Charts, diagrams, etc.

ROBINETTE, Gary O. 712
Off the board, into the ground : techniques of planting design implementation / compiled and collected by Gary O. Robinette. Dubuque, Iowa : Kendall/Hall Pub. Co., c1968. 367 p. : ill. ; 29 cm. [SB472.R6] 75-310936 ISBN 0-8403-0136-7
1. Landscape gardening—Charts, diagrams, etc. 2. Landscape architecture—Charts, diagrams, etc. I. Title. BIP

Landscape gardening—Early works to 1800.

GILPIN, William, 1724-1804. 712'.6'0942593
A dialogue upon the gardens of the right honourable the Lord Viscount Cobham at Stow in Buckinghamshire / William Gilpin ; introd. by John Dixon Hunt. [Los Angeles] : William Andrews Clark Memorial Library, University of California, Los Angeles, 1976. ix, 60 p. ; 22 cm. (Publicaton - Augustan Reprint Society ; no. 176) On cover: A dialogue upon the gardens at Stow. [SB466.G8S764 1976] 76-622992
1. Stowe House. Gardens. 2. Cobham, Richard Temple, 1st Viscount, 1669?-1749. 3. Landscape gardening—Early works to 1800. I. Title: A dialogue upon the gardens of the right honourable the Lord Viscount Cobham ... II. Title: A dialogue upon the gardens at Stow. III. Series: Augustan Reprint Society. Publication ; no. 176.

Landscape gardening—Estimates and costs.

ERNST and Ernst. 658.1'512
1969 operating cost survey [Washington] 1970. 13, [6] l. 29 cm. Compiled for the Associated Landscape Contractors of America. [SB476.8.E75] 79-25101
1. Landscape gardening—Estimates and costs. I. Associated Landscape Contractors of America. II. Title.

Landscape gardening—Examinations, questions, etc.

ARCO Publishing Company, New York. 712'.076
Gardener, assistant gardener; complete study guide to pass high on your civil service test, by the Arco Editorial Board. [2d ed.] New York, Arco [1967] 256 p. illus. 26 cm. (Arco civil service test tutor) [SB469.4.A2A7 1967] 65-26719
1. Landscape gardening—Examinations, questions, etc. 2. New York (City)—Officials and employees—Examination. I. Title. BIP

ARCO Publishing Company, New York. 635.9'076
Gardener, assistant gardener : the complete study guide for scoring high / by the Arco Editorial Board. 3d ed. New York : Arco, c1975. 224 p. : ill. ; 26 cm. (Arco civil service test tutor) [SB469.4.A2A7 1975] 75-27588 ISBN 0-668-01340-0 : 6.00
1. Landscape gardening—Examinations, questions, etc. 2. New York (City)—Officials and employees—Examinations. I. Title.

Landscape gardening—Florida.

PERRY, Mac. 712'.6'09759
Landscape your Florida home. With a special chapter on landscaping mobile homes. Miami, E. A. Seemann Pub. [1972] 174 p. illus. (part col.) 27 cm. [SB473.P45] 72-82922 ISBN 0-912458-08-9 9.95
1. Landscape gardening—Florida. 2.

Landscape architecture—Florida. I. Title.
BIP

STEWART, Hazel, 1905- 712.62
Landscaping your south Florida home. Coral Gables, Fla., F & N Pub. Co. [1956] 144 p. illus. 24 cm. [SB477.U6S8] 56-4102
1. Landscape gardening — Florida. 2. Plants, Ornamental — Florida. I. Title.

Landscape gardening—Gt. Brit.

GREEN, David. 927.12
Gardener to Queen Anne; Henry Wise (1653-1738) and the formal garden. London, New York, Oxford University Press, 1956. xx, 232p. illus., ports., facsims., plans, 28cm. Bibliography: p. [222]-225. [SB470.W5G7] 56-4101
1. Wise, Henry, 1653-1738. 2. Landscape gardening—Gt. Brit. I. Title.

WHITEHEAD, George Edward, 1895- 712.60942
Garden design and construction: an illustrated guide, by George E. Whitehead. London, Faber, 1966. 3-252p. 16 plates (incl. 1 col.) plans. diagrs. 23cm. Bibl. [SB473.W5] 66-76238 11.50
1. Landscape gardening—Gt. Brit. 2. Gardening— Gt. Brit. I. Title.
American distributor: Transatlantic, Levittown, N. Y.

Landscape gardening—Japan.

CONDER, Josiah, 1852-1920. 712.0952
Landscape gardening in Japan. Supplement of 40 plates, new pref. by Clay Lancaster. New York, Dover [c.1964] xv, 251p. illus., plans. 29cm. Unabridged, corrected repubn. of the 2d rev. (1912) ed. of Landscape gardening in Japan, and the Supplement to landscape gardening in Japan, both orig. pub. by Kelly & Walsh in 1893. [SB477.J2C6] 64-18846 2.75 pap.,
1. Landscape gardening—Japan. 2. Gardening—Japan. I. Title.

CONDER, Josiah, 1852-1920 712.0952
Landscape gardening in Japan. With the Supplement of 40 plates & a new preface by Clay Lancaster [Magnolia., Mass., P. Smith, 1966, c.1964] xv, 251p. illus., plans. 29cm. (Dover bk rebound) Repubn. of the 2d rev (1912) ed. of Landscape gardening in Japan, and the Supplement to landscapegardening in Japan, both orig. pub. by Kelly & Walsh in 1893 [SB477.J2C6 1964] 5.50
1. Landscape gardening—Japan. 2. Gardening—Japan. I. Title.

ENGEL, David Harris. 712.0952
Japanese gardens for today. With a foreword by Richard Neutra. [1st ed.] Tokyo, Rutland, Vt., C. E. Tuttle Co. [1959] xvi, 270 p. illus. (part col.) 28 cm. [SB466.J3E5] 59-8191
1. Landscape gardening—Japan. 2. Gardening—Japan. I. Title. BIP

ISHIMOTO, Tatsuo. 712.6
The art of the Japanese garden. New York, Crown Publishers [1958] 128 p. illus. 24 cm. [SB466.J318] 58-8314
1. Landscape gardening—Japan. 2. Gardens—Pictorial works. I. Title.

Landscape gardening-Northwest, Pacific.

SUNSET. 712.6
Landscaping for western living, by the editors of Sunset magazine, under the direction of Walter L. Doty [and] Paul C. Johnson. [1st ed.] Menlo Park, Calif., Lane Pub. Co. [1956] c.192 p. illus. 28 cm. [SB473.S87] 56-7617
1. Landscape gardening-Northwest, Pacific. I. Title.

Landscape gardening—Pictorial works.

MCDONALD, Elvin. 712'.6
Garden ideas A to Z. Garden City, N.Y., Doubleday [1970] 196 p. illus. (part col.) 27 cm. "An American Garden Guild book." [SB473.M23] 74-89092 7.95
1. Landscape gardening—Pictorial works. I. Title.

Landscape gardening—Study and teaching.

WHITE, Stanley, 1891- ed. 712.07
The teaching of landscape architecture, with special referance to the teaching of design; a report to the National Conference on Instruction in Landscape Architecture, by a committee of writers and editors under the general direction of Stanley White. East Lansing, Michigan, 25 June 1953. [Auburn, Ala., S. P. Snow, 1953] xii, 97p. illus. 28cm. Errata leaf inserted. Bibliography: p. 97. [SB469.4.A2W45] 53-2551
1. Landscape gardening—Study and teaching. 2. Landscape gardening—Congresses. I. National Conference on Instruction in Landscape Architecture, East Lansing, Mich., 1953. II. Title.

Landscape gardening—Tropics.

FORTUNE, Maxine 712.0913
A guide to landscaping; a plant selector for the tropics and sub-tropics. St. Petersburg, Fla., Great Outdoors [c.1963] 123p. illus., port. 22cm. 64-472 1.00 pap.,
1. Landscape gardening—Tropics. 2. Plants, Ornamental—Tropics. I. Title. BIP

FORTUNE, Maxine. 712.0913
A guide to landscaping: a plant selector for the tropics and sub-tropics. [1st ed.] ed.] St. Petersburg, Fla., Great Outdoors Pub. Co., [c1963] 123 p. illus., port. 22 cm. [SB473.F66] 64-472
1. Landscape gardening — Tropics. 2. Plants, Ornamental — Tropics. I. Title.

Landscape in art.

ADAMS, Eric. 759.9429
Francis Danby: varieties of poetic landscape. New Haven, Published for the Paul Mellon Centre for Studies in British Art by Yale University Press, 1973. xviii, 207, [96] p. 166 illus. (part col.) 32 cm. (Studies in British art) Bibliography: p. 164-168. [ND497.D32A65] 72-75185 ISBN 0-300-01538-0 27.50
1. Danby, Francis, 1793-1861. 2. Landscape in art. I. Title. II. Series.

APPLETON, Jay. 701
The experience of landscape. London, New York, Wiley [1974] p. Bibliography: p. [N8213.A66] 73-20899 ISBN 0-471-03256-5 22.50
1. Landscape in art. I. Title. BIP

BARCHAM, William L. 759.5
The imaginary view scenes of Antonio Canaletto / William L. Barcham. New York : Garland Pub., 1977. xxix, 345, xiv p. : ill. ; 21 cm. (Outstanding dissertations in the fine arts) Originally presented as the author's thesis, New York University, 1974. Bibliography: p. i-xiv (3d group). [ND623.C2B37 1977] 76-23603 ISBN 0-8240-2677-2 lib.bdg. : 45.00
1. Canal, Antonio, called Canaletto, 1697-1768. 2. Landscape in art. 3. Venice in art. I. Title. II. Series. BIP

BIERSTADT, Albert, 1830-1902 759.13
Albert Bierstadt, 1830-1902 : [exhibition], September 15-October 10, 1972 / Gordon Hendricks New York : M. Knoedler, [1972] 26 p. : ill. (some col.) ; 22 cm. Includes index. [ND237.B585H415] 75-316284
1. Bierstadt, Albert, 1830-1902. 2. Landscape in art. I. Hendricks, Gordon. II. Knoedler (M.) and Company, inc.

BORGMAN, Harry. 743'.8'36
Landscape painting with markers / by Harry Borgman. New York : Watson-Guptill, 1977. 150 p. : ill. (some ill.) ; 29 cm. Includes index. Bibliography: p. 147. [NC878.B67 1977] 77-9345 ISBN 0-8230-2635-3 : 17.50
1. Landscape in art. 2. Dry marker drawing—Technique. I. Title. BIP

DOUGHTY, Thomas, 1793-1856. 759.13
Thomas Doughty, 1793-1856; an American pioneer in landscape painting. Selection and catalogue by Frank H. Goodyear, Jr. Philadelphia, Pennsylvania Academy of the Fine Arts [1973] 33 p. 52 plates. 22 x 27 cm. Catalog of the exhibition held at the Pennsylvania Academy of the Fine Arts, Oct. 19-Dec. 2, 1973, the Corcoran Gallery of Art, Dec. 14, 1973-Jan. 27, 1974, and the Albany Institute of History and Art, Feb. 14-Apr. 7, 1974. Includes bibliographical references. [ND237.D66G66] 73-89435
1. Doughty, Thomas, 1793-1856. 2. Landscape in art. I. Goodyear, Frank Henry, 1944- II. Pennsylvania Academy of the Fine Arts, Philadelphia. III. Corcoran Gallery of Art, Washington, D.C. IV. Albany Institute of History and Art. V. Title.

FREE, Renee. 759.994
Lloyd Rees [by] Renee Free. General editor John Henshaw. Melbourne, Lansdowne, 1972. 107 p. illus., col. plates. 32 cm. (Australian art library) Bibliography: p. 106-107. [ND1105.R4F69] 73-164917 ISBN 0-7018-0133-6 12.95
1. Rees, Lloyd Frederic, 1895- 2. Landscape in art. I. Rees, Lloyd Frederic, 1895-

GALERIE von Loeper. 709'.43
Neue Landschaften bis 1975 : Gerda Ebert ... [et al.]. Hamburg : Galerie von Loeper, [1975] [45] leaves : col. ill. ; 15 x 22 cm. Exhibition catalog. [N6868.G32 1975] 75-507912
1. Landscape in art. 2. Art, German—Exhibitions. 3. Art, Modern—20th century—Germany (Federal Republic, 1949-)—Exhibitions. I. Ebert, Gerda, 1947- II. Title.

GRUNWALD Graphic Arts Foundation. 760
Landscape: the artist's view; a loan exhibition of drawings and prints 16th-20th century. The Grunwald Graphic Arts Foundation Print Gallery, Dickson Art Center, University of California, Los Angeles, April 22 to May 26, 1968. [Los Angeles, 1968] [23] p. illus. 22 x 28 cm. [NC790.G78 1968] 75-309470
1. Landscape in art. 2. Drawings—Exhibitions. 3. Prints—Exhibitions. I. Title.

HENDRICKS, Gordon. 759.13
ABierstadt; an essay and catalogue to accompany a retrospective exhibition of the work of Albert Bierstadt. Fort Worth, Amon Carter Museum [1972] 48 p. illus. (part col.) 22 cm. Exhibition presented at Amon Carter Museum, Fort Worth, Texas, Jan. 27-Mar. 19, 1972, and elsewhere. Includes bibliographical references. [ND237.B585H4] 70-184170
1. Bierstadt, Albert, 1830-1902. 2. Landscape in art. I. Amon Carter Museum of Western Art, Fort Worth, Tex.

HOUSTON, Tex. Museum of Fine Arts. 758'.1'09730740164235
Nature and focus; looking at American painting in the 19th century. [Exhibition] January 21-April 2, 1972. [Houston, 1972] 24 p. illus. 21 cm. Catalogue essay by E. A. Carmean, Jr. Bibliography: p. 22-24. [N6510.H6] 71-189137
1. Landscape in art. 2. Art, American—Exhibitions. 3. Art, Modern—19th century—U.S. I. Carmean, E. A. II. Title.

KOKOSCHKA, Oskar, 1886- 759.2
Oskar Kokoschka : cityscapes and landscapes, a 90th birthday tribute : [catalogue of a] loan exhibition in aid of the Save the Children Fund [held at] Marlborough Fine Art (London) Ltd, March-April 1976. London : Marlborough Fine Art (London) Ltd, [1976] 56 p. : chiefly ill. (some col.), ports. ; 30 cm. [ND511.5.K6M37] 76-370633 ISBN 0-900955-18-X : £2.00
1. Kokoschka, Oskar, 1886- 2. Landscape in art. I. Marlborough Fine Art, ltd., London. II. Title: Cityscapes and landscapes, a 90th birthday tribute.

KOSCHATZKY, Walter. 759.3
Albrecht Durer: the landscape water-colours. [Translated from the German by Philippa McDermott] New York, St. Martin's Press [1973] 111 p. illus. (part col.) 31 x 42 cm. Translation of Albrecht Durer: Die Landschaftsaquarelle. Bibliography: p. 107-109. [ND1954.D8K613 1973] 73-85310 45.00
1. Durer, Albrecht, 1471-1528. 2. Landscape in art. I. Durer, Albrecht, 1471-1528.

NEW American 704.94'36'0973
landscapes; [exhibition] Vassar Art Gallery, May 13 through June 17, 1973. [Poughkeepsie, N.Y., Printed by Hamilton Reproductions, 1973] [36] p. illus. 18 x 26 cm. Includes bibliographical references. [N6512.N343] 73-164553
1. Landscape in art. 2. Art, American—Exhibitions. 3. Art, Modern—20th century—United States. I. Vassar College. Art Gallery.

SANTINI, Pier Carlo. 758'.1'0904
Modern landscape painting; [translated from the Italian by P. S. Falla]. London, Phaidon Press, 1972. 350 p. chiefly illus. (some col.). 29 cm. Translation of Il paesaggio nella pittura contemporanea. Distributed in the U.S.A. by Praeger Publishers. Bibliography: p. [61] [ND195.S2513] 79-165863 ISBN 0-7148-1504-7
1. Landscape in art. 2. Painting, Modern—20th century. I. Title.
35.00

Landscape painters, Australian.

BRACK, John. 759.9'94
Four contemporary Australian landscape painters. Melbourne, New York [etc.] Oxford University Press [1968] 32 p. illus. 22 cm. (National Gallery booklets) Bibliography: p. 32. [ND2089.B7] 76-356990 0.70
1. Landscape painters, Australian. I. Title. II. Series: Victoria, Australia. National Gallery, Melbourne. Booklets

Landscape painters—Great Britain—Biography—Dictionaries.

BEREA, T. B. 758'.1'0942
Handbook of 17th, 18th, and 19th century British landscape painters & watercolorists [by] T. B. Berea. [Chattanooga? Tenn., 1970] 72 p. 22 cm. [ND496.B4] 78-13623
1. Landscape painters—Great Britain—Biography—Dictionaries. I. Title.

Landscape painters—United States—Biography.

CIKOVSKY, Nicolai. 759.13 B
The life and work of George Inness / Nicolai Cikovsky, Jr. New York : Garland Pub., 1977. xxv, 380 p., [65] leaves of plates : ill. ; 21 cm. (Outstanding dissertations in the fine arts) Originally presented as the author's thesis, Harvard, 1965. Bibliography: p. 371-380. [ND237.I5C55 1977] 76-23605 ISBN 0-8240-2679-9 lib.bdg. : 50.00
1. Inness, George, 1825-1894. 2. Landscape painters—United States—Biography. I. Title. II. Series. BIP

TALBOT, William S. 759.13 B
Jasper F. Cropsey, 1823-1900 / William S. Talbot. New York : Garland Pub., 1977. xviii, 578 p., [56] leaves of plates : ill. ; 21 cm. (Outstanding dissertations in the fine arts) Originally presented as the author's thesis, New York University, 1972. Bibliography: p. 570-578. [ND237.C819T342 1977] 76-23652 ISBN 0-8240-2731-0 lib.bdg. : 60.00
1. Cropsey, Jasper Francis, 1823-1900. 2. Landscape painters—United States—Biography. I. Title. II. Series.

WEISS, Ila, 1939- 759.13 B
Sanford Robinson Gifford (1823-1880) / Ila Weiss New York : Garland Pub., 1977. ca. 600 p. : ill. ; 21 cm. (Outstanding dissertations in the fine arts) Reprint of the author's thesis, Columbia, 1968; with a new pref. Includes bibliographical references. [ND237.G4W44 1977] 76-23655 lib.bdg. : 57.50
1. Gifford, Sanford Robinson, 1823-1880. 2. Landscape painters—United States—Biography. I. Title. II. Series. BIP

Landscape painting.

*[HUTT, Wolfgang] 758.40
The living country-side. New York, St. Martin's Press [1974, c1973] 60 p. illus. (part col.) 25 cm. [ND1340] 74-83589 4.95
1. Landscape painting. 2. Still-life painting. I. Title.
BIP

BRIGANTI, Giuliano. 758'.7
The view painters of Europe. [Translated from the Italian by Pamela Waley. New York] Phaidon [1970] 318 p. illus. (part col.) 29 cm. Translation of I vedutisti. Bibliography: p. [311]-312. [ND1349.4.B7413] 75-112770 35.00
1. Landscape painting. 2. Landscape in art. I. Title.

CARLSON, John Fabian, 1875- 1945. 700
Guide to landscape painting. New York, Sterling Pub. Co. [1953] 144p. illus. (part col.) 30cm. (A Bridgman art book) New edition, enlarged and revised.'--Dust jacket. Previous editions published under title: Elementary principles of landscape painting. [ND1340.C] A54
1. Landscape painting. I. Title.

CLARK, Kenneth McKenzie, Baron Clark, 1903- 758'.1'094
Landscape into art / Kenneth Clark. New ed. London : J. Murray, 1976. xvi, 248 p., [8] leaves of plates : ill. (some col.) ; 26 cm. Includes index. [ND1340.C55 1976b] 76-378539 ISBN 0-7195-3171-3 : £9.50
1. Landscape painting. I. Title.

CLARK, Kenneth McKenzie, Baron Clark, 1903- 758'.1
Landscape into art / Kenneth Clark. 1st U.S. ed. New York : Harper & Row, c1976. xv, 248 p., [8] leaves of plates : ill. (some col.) ; 26 cm. "Based on lectures given ... to the University of Oxford." Includes index. [ND1340.C55 1976] 75-23876 ISBN 0-06-010781-2 : 17.50
1. Landscape painting. I. Title.

CLARK, Kenneth McKenzie, Sir 1903- 758.1
Landscape painting. New York, Scribner, 1950. xix, 147 p. 104 plates. 24 cm. "Based on lectures given during ... [the author's] first year as Slade professor to the University of Oxford." [ND1340.C552] 50-6065
1. Landscape painting. I. Title.

FRIEDLANDER, Max J, 1867- 758.1
Landscape, portrait, still-life; their origin and development. [Translated from the German original by R. F. C. Hull] New York, Philosophical Library [1950?] 288 p. 41 plates. 22 cm. [ND1140.F7] 49-50136
1. Landscape painting. 2. Portrait painting. 3. Still-life painting. I. Title.

FRIEDLANDER, Max J., 1867- 1958. 750.13
Landscape, portrait, still-life; their origin and development. [Tr. from German by R. F. C. Hull] New York, Schocken [1963] 288p. illus. 21cm. (SB43) 63-13344 2.45 pap.,
1. Landscape painting. 2. Portrait painting. 3. Still-life painting. I. Title.

HAINES, Frederick Merlin. 758.1
Tone and colour in landscape painting; a simple explanation of the principles deciding the apparent tones and colours of objects in the open air. With a foreword by Stephen Bone. New York, Pitman Pub. Corp. [1955?] 93p. illus. 23cm. [ND1340] 55-10185
1. Landscape painting. I. Title.

JACOBS, Michel, 1877- 758.1
Colour in landscape painting. New York, Citadel Press [1956] 95p. illus., col. plates. 28cm. [ND1340.J3] 56-882
1. Landscape painting. 2. Color. I. Title.

**LANDSCAPES by the masters* 758.1
[Comp. by Margaret Harold. Commentaries by Gus Baker. Fort Lauderdale, Fla., Allied Pubns., c.1964] 40p. col. illus. 34cm. 63-21287 1.95 pap.,
1. Landscape painting. I. Harold, Margaret, comp.

LEITH-ROSS, Harry, 1886 758.1
The landscape painter's manual. New York, Watson-Guptill Publications [1956] 64p. illus. 27cm. [ND1342.L4] 56-13049
1. Landscape painting. 2. Painting—Technique. I. Title.

MCGEE, Lloyd R., 1897- 758.1
You can paint landscapes in oil colors; written, illustrated, and published by Lloyd R. McGee. Rev., 2d ed. Malibu, Calif. [c1953- v. illus. 23cm. [ND1340.M353] 53-16487
1. Landscape painting. I. Title.

RUSKIN, John, 1819-1900. 758'.1
Modern painters, vol. II. "Of ideas of beauty" and "Of the imaginative faculty." Rearranged in two volumes, and rev. by the author. With an introd. by Charles Eliot Norton. Brantwood ed. New York, Merrill, 1893. St. Clair Shores, Mich., Scholarly Press, 1972. p. (The works of John Ruskin) [ND1340.R8 1972] 72-8220 ISBN 0-403-02066-2
1. Landscape painting. 2. Aesthetics. 3. Imagination. I. Title.

SLIVE, Seymour, 1920- 758'.1
Great landscapes. Text by Seymour Slive. New York, H. N. Abrams [1971] 22 p. illus. (part col.) 33 cm. (The Library of great painters. Portfolio ed.) [ND1349.S55 1971] 75-124299 ISBN 0-8109-3032-3
1. Landscape painting. I. Title.

SZABO, Zoltan, 1928- 751.4'22
Landscape painting in watercolor. New York, Watson-Guptill Publications [1971] 183 p. illus. (part col.) 29 cm. Bibliography: p. 179. [ND2435.S9] 79-141045 ISBN 0-8230-2620-5 15.00
1. Landscape painting. 2. Water-color painting—Technique. I. Title. BIP

VALSECCHI, Marco. 758'.1'09034
Landscape painting of the 19th century. [Translated from the Italian by Arthur A. Coppotelli] Greenwich, Conn., New York Graphic Society [1971, c1969] 387 p. illus. (part col.) 29 cm. Bibliography: p. 377-382. [ND1349.5.V3416] 70-134333 ISBN 0-8212-0395-9 30.00
1. Landscape painting. I. Title.

Landscape painting—Addresses, essays, lectures.

CONSTABLE, John, 1776- 1837. 758'.1'09
John Constable's discourses; compiled and annotated by R. B. Beckett. Ipswich, Suffolk Records Society, 1970. iii, ix, 114 p., 4 plates. 1 illus., facsims. 26 cm. (Suffolk Records Society. [Publications] v. 14) "Constable's books and pictures": p. 90-91. [ND1340.C555] 74-580265 ISBN 0-900716-01-0 30/-
1. Landscape painting—Addresses, essays, lectures. I. Beckett, Ronald Brymer, ed. II. Series: Suffolk Records Society, Ipswich. Publications, v. 14

Landscape painting, American.

BORN, Wolfgang, 1893- 758'.1'0973
American landscape painting; an interpretation. Westport, Conn., Greenwood Press [1970, c1948].xiii, 228 p. illus. 27 cm. Includes bibliographical references. [ND1351.B6 1970] 71-100222 ISBN 0-8371-3253-3
1. Landscape painting, American. I. Title. BIP

GUSSOW, Alan, 1931- 758.1'0973
A sense of place: the artist and the American land. With an introd. by Richard Wilbur. Foreword by David R. Brower. San Francisco, Friends of the Earth [1972] 160 p. illus. (part col.) 36 cm. (The Earth's wild places, 6) [ND1351.5.G8] 79-154250 ISBN 0-8415-0135-1 27.50
1. Landscape painting, American. I. Title. II. Series.

HOWAT, John K. 758'.1'097473
The Hudson River and its painters / by John K. Howat ; pref. by James Biddel, foreword by Carl Carmer. New York : Penguin Books, [1978] p. cm. Includes index. Bibliography: p. [ND1351.5.H6 1978] 78-12734 ISBN 0-14-005080-9 pbk. : 14.95
1. Hudson River School. 2. Landscape painting, American. 3. Landscape painting—19th century—United States. 4. Hudson Valley—Description and travel—Views. I. Title. BIP

KENNEDY Galleries, inc., New York. 760'.922
In search of the picturesque; 19th century American painters on their favorite sketching grounds. New York, 1966. 64 p. illus. 24 cm. (The Kennedy quarterly, v. 6, no. 1) [N8640.K4 vol. 6, no. 1] 68-5809
1. Landscape painting, American. 2. Paintings, American—Catalogs. I. Title. II. Series.

LASSITER, Barbara Babcock. 758'.1'0973
American wilderness : the Hudson River school of painting / Barbara Babcock Lassiter. 1st ed. Garden City, N.Y. : Doubleday, c1977. p. cm. [ND1351.5.L37] 73-13089 ISBN 0-385-08192-8 : 4.95 ISBN 0-385-04376-7 lib. bdg. : 5.70
1. Hudson River School. 2. Landscape painting, American. 3. United States in art. I. Title. BIP

LINDQUIST-COCK, Elizabeth. 758'.1'0973
The influence of photography on American landscap painting, 1839-1880 / Elizabeth Lindquist-Cock. New York : Garland Pub., 1977. ix, 205 p., [28] leaves of plates : ill. ; 21 cm. (Outstanding dissertations in the fine arts) Originally presented as the author's thesis, New York University, 1967. Bibliography: p. 181-198. [ND1351.5.L56 1977] 76-23608 ISBN 0-8240-2680-2 lib.bdg. : 35.00
1. Landscape painting, American. 2. Painting from photographs. 3. Art and photography. I. Title. II. Series.

PLEASANTS, Jacob Hall, 1873-1957. 759.1
Four late eighteenth century Anglo-American landscape painters. Freeport, N.Y., Books for Libraries Press [1970] 146 p. illus. 24 cm. (Essay index reprint series) "Proceedings of the American Antiquarian Society for October, 1942." Reprint of the 1943 ed. Includes bibliographical references. [ND1351.4.P55 1970] 78-128288
1. Beck, George, 1748 or 9-1812. 2. Groombridge, William, 1748-1811. 3. Guy, Francis, 1760-1820. 4. Winstanley, William, fl. 1793-1806. 5. Landscape painting, American. I. Title. BIP

Landscape painting, American—Catalogs.

DALLAS. Museum of Fine Arts. 758.1'0973'07401642812
The Joel T. and Kathryn Howard Collection of American painting. Dallas : Museum of Fine Arts, [1951] [15] p. : ill. ; 26 cm. Cover title. [ND1351.5.D34 1951] 75-313578
1. Howard, Joel T.—Art collections. 2. Howard, Kathryn—Art collections. 3. Dallas. Museum of Fine Arts. 4. Landscape painting, American—Catalogs. 5. Landscape painting—Dallas—Catalogs. I. Title.

Landscape painting, American—Exhibitions.

BERMINGHAM, Peter. 758'.1'0973
American art in the Barbizon mood : National Collection of Fine Arts / edited by Peter Bermingham. Chicago : Text/Fiche Publication Division, University of Chicago Press, [1976] p. cm. [ND1351.5.B47 1976] 76-14950 ISBN 0-226-69413-5 12.50
1. Landscape painting, American—Exhibitions. 2. Barbizon school—Influence. I. Smithsonian Institution. National Collection of Fine Arts. II. Title.

BERMINGHAM, Peter. 758'.1'0973
American art in the Barbizon mood / Peter Bermingham. Washington : Published for the National Collection of Fine ARts by the Smithsonian Institution Press, 1975. 191 p. : ill. (some col.) ; 26 cm. "Published on the occasion of an exhibition at the National Collection of Fine Arts, Smithsonian Institution, January 23-April 20, 1975." Bibliography: p. 177-182. [ND1351.5.B47] 74-26664
1. Landscape painting, American—Exhibitions. 2. Barbizon school—Influence. I. Smithsonian Institution. National Collection of Fine Arts. II. Title. BIP

BROCKTON Art Center-Fuller Memorial. 758'.1'0973
Landscape & life in 19th century America, September 12-November 10, 1974, the Brockton Art Center-Fuller Memorial. Brockton, Mass. : Brockton Art Center-Fuller Memorial, [1974] 68 p. : ill. ; 22 cm. Catalogue of an exhibition. Bibliography: p. 66-68. [ND1351.5.B76 1974] 74-18014
1. Landscape painting, American—Exhibitions. 2. United States in art. I. Title.

CALIFORNIA. Arts Commission. 758'.1'09794
Horizons: a century of California landscape painting; [traveling exhibition. Sacramento, 1970?] 32 p. illus. 21 cm. [ND1351.5.C23] 77-633435
1. Landscape painting, American—Exhibitions. 2. Landscape painting—California. I. Title.

HIGH Museum of Art. 758'.1'0973
The beckoning land; nature and the American artist: a selection of nineteenth century paintings. Atlanta [Supplied by Worldwide Books, Boston, 1971] 94 p. illus. (part col.) 25 cm. Catalogue of an exhibition held Apr. 17-June 13, 1971 at the High Museum of Art, Atlanta, with an introductory essay by D. F. Hoopes. [ND1351.5.H5] 77-154212
1. Landscape painting, American—Exhibitions. 2. United States in art. I. Hoopes, Donelson F. II. Title.

KANSAS. University. Museum of Art. 758'.1'0945
The Arcadian landscape; nineteenth-century American painters in Italy. [Lawrence, 1972] 1 v. (unpaged) illus. 26 cm. (Its Miscellaneous publication no. 89) Catalog of the exhibition held Nov. 4-Dec. 3, 1972. Includes bibliography. [ND1351.5.K36 1972] 73-621296
1. Landscape painting, American—Exhibitions. 2. Italy in art. I. Title. II. Series.

NEW York (City). Museum of Modern Art. 759.13'074'01471
The natural paradise : painting in America, 1800-1950 : [exhibition], the Museum of Modern Art, New York / edited by Kynaston McShine ; essays by Barbara Novak, Robert Rosenblum, John Wilmerding. New York : The Museum ; Boston : distributed by New York Graphic Society, c1976. 178 p. : ill. (some col.) ; 24 x 29 cm. Bibliography: p. 171-178. [ND1351.5.N48 1976] 76-23513 ISBN 0-87070-505-9 : 19.95.
1. Landscape painting, American—Exhibitions. 2. Romanticism in art—United States—Exhibitions. 3. United States in art—Exhibitions. I. McShine, Kynaston. II. Title. BIP

NORTON (R. W.) Art Gallery. 758'.1'0973
The Hudson River school: American landscape paintings from 1821-1907. A loan exhibition, October 14-November 25, 1973, the R. W. Norton Art Gallery, Shreveport, Louisiana. [Shreveport, La., 1973] 106 p. illus. (part col.) 28 cm. Catalog of the exhibition. Bibliography: p. 104-106. [ND1351.5.N67 1973] 73-81399 ISBN 0-913060-03-8 7.25 (pbk.)
1. Hudson River School. 2. Landscape painting, American—Exhibitions. I. Title.

STEIN, Roger B. 758'.1'0973
The view and the vision; landscape painting in nineteenth-century America [by] Roger B. Stein. [Exhibition] Henry Gallery, University of Washington, January 2 through February 4, 1968. [Seattle, Henry Gallery, 1968] 32 p. illus. 22 cm. [ND1351.5.S73] 74-184701
1. Landscape painting, American—Exhibitions. 2. United States in art. I. Henry Art Gallery. II. Title.

Landscape painting, Australian (Aboriginal)

BATTARBEE, Reginald Ernest, 1893- 758'.1'0994
Modern aboriginal paintings, with text by Rex & Bernice Battarbee. Adelaide, Rigby, 1971. 32 p. col. illus. 26 cm. [ND1367.A8B3] 76-148545 ISBN 0-85179-269-3
1. Landscape painting, Australian (Aboriginal) 2. Aranda tribe. I. Battarbee, Bernice, joint author. II. Title.
Available from Verry, Mystic, Conn. 4.00. BIP

Landscape painting, British.

HERRMANN, Luke. 758'.1'0942
British landscape painting of the eighteenth century. New York, Oxford University Press, 1974 [c1973] 151 p. illus. (part col.) 29 cm. Bibliography: p. 133-134. [ND1354.4.H47 1974] 73-88405 ISBN 0-19-519757-7 35.00
1. Landscape painting, British. I. Title. BIP

Landscape painting, Canadian—Exhibitions.

HUBBARD, Robert 758.1'0971'074013
Hamilton, 1916-
Canadian landscape painting, 1670-1930; the artist and the land. Text and catalogue by R. H. Hubbard. Essay by Northrop Frye. [Madison, Wis., Elvehjem Art Center]; distributed by the University of Wisconsin Press [1973] 196 p. illus. (part col.) 27 cm. Catalogue of an exhibition held at Elvehjem Art Center, University of Wisconsin, Madison; Hopkins Center Art Galleries, Dartmouth College, Hanover; and University Art Museum, University of Texas, Austin. Bibliography: p. 31. [ND1352.C3H8] 72-11461 ISBN 0-299-97007-8 15.00
1. Landscape painting, Canadian—Exhibitions. I. Elvehjem Art Center. II. Dartmouth College. Hopkins Center. Art Galleries. III. Texas. University at Austin. Art Museum. IV. Title. BIP

Landscape painting—China.

MUNSTERBERG, Hugo, 1916- 758.1
The landscape painting of China and Japan. [1st ed.] Rutland, Vt., C. E. Tuttle Co. [1955] xv, 144 p. col. front., 101 plates. 27 cm. Bibliography: p. 135-138. [ND1366.M8] 55-10622
1. Landscape painting—China. 2. Landscape painting—Japan.

Landscape painting, Chinese.

CONTAG, Victoria. 759.951
Chinese masters of the 17th century. Translated by Michael Bullock. Rutland, Vt., Tuttle [1970, c1969] 53, [96] p. plates. 31 cm. [ND1366.C5713 1970] 79-8940 ISBN 0-8048-0747-7 17.50
1. Landscape painting, Chinese. 2. Landscape painters—China. 3. China—History—Ming dynasty, 1368-1644. I. Title.

DE SILVA, Anil. 758'.1'0951
The art of Chinese landscape painting; in the caves of Tun-huang. Photos by Dominique Darbois. New York, Crown Publishers [1967] 240 p. illus. (part col.), map. 24 cm. (Art of the world; non-European cultures; the historical, sociological, and religious backgrounds) Bibliography: p. 225-228. [ND1366.D4] 67-19591
1. Landscape painting, Chinese. 2. Tun-huang, Kansu. I. Title. II. Series: Art of the world; the historical, sociological, and religious backgrounds

LEE, Sherman E 758.1
Chinese landscape painting. Cleveland, Cleveland Museum of Art [1954] 169p. illus. 26cm. Based on an exhibition sponsored by the Cleveland Museum of Art. 'Catalog [of the exhibition]': p. 144-160. Bibliography: p.142-143. [ND1366.L43] 54-14708
1. Landscape painting, Chinese. 2. Paintings, Chinese—Exhibitions. I. Cleveland Museum of Art. II. Title. BIP

LEE, Sherman E. 759.951
Chinese landscape painting. [2d ed., extensively rev. Cleveland] Cleveland Mus. of Art; dist. Abrams [New York, 1962] 158p. illus. (pt. col., pt. fold.) 26cm. The first edition was a book-catalogue of a loan exhibition held at Cleveland in 1954. Bibl. 62-11141 7.50 bds.,
1. Landscape painting, Chinese. 2. Paintings, Chinese—Exhibitions. I. Title.

SULLIVAN, Michael, 1916- 759.951
The birth of landscape printing in China. Berkeley, University of California Press, 1962. xvii, 213 p. illus., plates 28 cm. Bibliographical references included in "Notes" (p. [183]-207) [ND1366.S9] 60-16863
1. Landscape painting, Chinese. 2. Nature (Aesthetics) 3. Symbolism in art. I. Title.

WANG, Chi-ch'ien. 759.951
Mountains of the mind; the landscape painting of Wang Chi-ch'ien. Edited by Meredith Weatherby. With an appreciation and commentaries by Hsu Hsiao-hu, and critiques by James Cahill, Alfred Frankenstein, and Michael Chacko Daniels. [1st ed.] New York, Walker/Weatherhill [1970] 77 p. (p. [25]-[70] illus., part col.) 31 cm. "A Weatherhill book." [ND1049.W18W4] 70-102914 12.50
I. Weatherby, Meredith, ed. II. Hsu, Hsiao-hu. III. Title.

WANG, Chi-yuan, 1895- 759.951
Landscapes in water-ink painting. New York, School of Chinese Brushwork [1965] [2] p. 5 plates. 45 cm. [ND2070.W3A45] 65-5027
I. Title.

Landscape painting, Chinese—Exhibitions.

BARNHART, 758'.1'095107401471
Richard.
Wintry forests, old trees: some landscape themes in Chinese painting. [New York, China Institute in America, 1972] 64 p. illus. 24 cm. Catalog of an exhibition held at the China House Gallery, Oct. 26, 1972, through Jan. 28, 1973. [ND1366.7.B37] 72-88902
1. Landscape painting, Chinese—Exhibitions. 2. Trees in art. I. China House Gallery. II. Title.

THE Restless 758'.1'0951074013
landscape: Chinese painting of the Late Ming period. James Cahill, editor. Berkeley, University Art Museum [1971] 180 p. illus. (part col.) 28 cm. Catalog of an exhibition held at University Art Museum, Berkeley, Nov. 9, 1971-Jan. 2, 1972, and at Fogg Art Museum, Harvard University, Feb. 12-Apr. 2, 1972, which grew out of a graduate seminar at the Dept. of Art History, University of California, Berkeley. Includes essays by seminar participants. Bibliography: p. 169. [ND1366.72.R47] 77-171043
1. Landscape painting, Chinese—Exhibitions. I. Cahill, James Francis, 1926-ed. II. California. University. Art Museum. III. Harvard University. William Hayes Fogg Art Museum. IV. California. University. Dept. of Art and History of Art.

Landscape painting, Chinese—Sung-Yuan dynasties, 960-1368.

TWO Sung texts on 758'.1'0951
Chinese painting and the landscape styles of the 11th and 12th centuries / [edited by] Robert Junji Maeda. New York : Garland Pub. Co., [1978] p. cm. (Outstanding dissertations in the fine arts) Texts in Chinese with English translations; commentary in English. Originally presented as the editor's thesis, Harvard, 1969. Contents.Contents.—Han, C. Shan shui Ch'un-ch'uan chi (A.D. 1121).—Teng, C. Hua-chi, chapters nine and ten. Bibliography: p. [ND1366.7.T87 1978] 77-94706 ISBN 0-8240-3238-1 lib. bdg. : 22.50
1. Landscape painting, Chinese—Sung-Yuan dynasties, 960-1368. I. Maeda, Robert J. II. Han, Cho, fl. 1119-1125. Shan shui Ch'un-ch'uan chi. English & Chinese. 1978. III. Teng, Ch'un, fl. 1127-1167. Hua chi. Chapters 9-10. English & Chinese. 1978. IV. Title. V. Series. BIP

Landscape painting, Dutch.

BUDAPEST. 758'.1'09492
Szepmuveszeti Muzeum.
Dutch landscapes, by Agnes Czobor. New York, Taplinger Pub. Co. [1968, c1967] 22 p., 48 col. plates. 24 cm. Paintings in the Budapest Museum of Fine Arts. Translation of Holland tajkepek. Bibliography: p. 19. [ND646.B7513 1968] 68-15853 6.95
1. Landscape painting, Dutch. 2. Paintings, Dutch—Catalogs. I. Czobor, Agnes. II. Title.

MICHIGAN. 758'.1'09492
University. Museum of Art.
Italy through Dutch eyes: Dutch seventeenth century landscape artists in Italy. [Exhibition] April 22 through May 24, 1964. Ann Arbor [1964] 1 v. (unpaged) illus. 28 cm. [ND1359.M5] 65-63189
1. Landscape painting. Dutch. 2. Landscape painting — Italy. 3. Paintings, Dutch — Exhibitions. I. Title.

STECHOW, Wolfgang, 1896- 759.9492
Dutch landscape painting of the seventeenth century. [London] Phaidon [Greenwich, Conn., N. Y. Graphic, 1966] ix, 494p. 369 illus. 28cm. (Natl. Gallery of Art, Kress Found. studies in the hist. of European art, no.1) Series: Kress Foundation studies in the history of European art, no.1) Bibl. [ND1359.S8] 66-2795 12.50
1. Landscape painting, Dutch. 2. Landscape painting—Technique. I. Title. II. Series.

Landscape painting, English.

STALEY, Allen. 758'.1'0942
The pre-Raphaelite landscape. Oxford, Clarendon Press, 1973. xxvi, 193, [108] p. illus. (some col.). 30 cm. (Oxford studies in the history of art and architecture) Based on the author's thesis, Yale University, 1965. Includes bibliographical references and index. [ND1354.5.S72] 73-169702 ISBN 0-19-817307-5 £12.50
1. Landscape painting, English. 2. Preraphaelitism—England. I. Title. II. Series. BIP

STALEY, Allen. 758'.1'0942
The Pre-Raphaelite landscapes. Oxford, Clarendon Press, 1973. xxvi, 193, [108] p. illus. (some col.). 30 cm. (Oxford studies in the history of art and architecture) Based on the author's thesis, Yale University, 1965. Includes bibliographical references and index. [ND1354.5.S72] 73-169702 ISBN 0-19-817307-5
1. Landscape painting, English. 2. Preraphaelitism—England. I. Title. II. Series.
Distributed by Oxford University Press, New York, 40.00.

Landscape painting, European—Exhibitions.

BROWN University. 758'.1'07401452
Dept. of Art.
To look on nature: European and American landscape, 1800-1874. An exhibition by the Dept. of Art, Brown University, at the Museum of Art, Rhode Island School of Design, Feb. 3 through Mar. 5, 1972. Providence [1972] 265 p. illus. 26 cm. Bibliography: p. 259-265. [ND1353.5.B7] 71-189468
1. Landscape painting, European—Exhibitions. 2. Landscape painting, American—Exhibitions. I. Rhode Island School of Design, Providence. Museum of Art. II. Title.

Landscape painting—Exhibitions.

SEAVER, Esther 758'.1'074017173
Isabel.
The city by the river and the sea : five centuries of skylines : loan exhibition, April 18 to June 3, 1951, the Dayton Art Institute / by Esther Isabel Seaver. Dayton : Dayton Art Institute, [1951] 38 p., [3] leaves of plates : ill. ; 23 cm. [ND1340.S43] 75-316854
1. Landscape painting—Exhibitions. 2. Cities and towns in art. I. Dayton Art Institute, Dayton, Ohio. II. Title.

Landscape painting, French—Exhibitions.

ITTMANN, John. 758'.1'0944
The forest of Fontainbleau, refuge of reality: French landscape 1800 to 1870. Introd. by John Minor Widsom, Jr. Catalog by John Ittmann, Robert Kashey [and] Martin L. H. Reymert. Corot entries by Victor Carlson. [New York, Shepherd Gallery, 1972] 1 v. (unpaged) illus. (1 col.) 22 cm. "Organized and presented by Shepherd Gallery ... April 22 through June 10 [1972]" Errata sheet inserted. Includes bibliography. [ND1356.5.I8] 72-198371
1. Landscape painting, French—Exhibitions. I. Kashey, Robert, joint author. II. Reymert, Martin L. H., joint author. III. Wisdom, John Minor. IV. Shepherd Gallery. V. Title.

MANNING, Robert L. 758'.1'0944
French landscape painters from four centuries. Loan exhibition, October 20, 1965-January 9, 1966, Finch College Museum of Art. [Catalogue prepared by Robert L. Manning] New York [Finch College Museum of Art, 1965?] [10] p., 61 illus. 23 cm. [ND1356.M33] 70-280412
1. Landscape painting, French—Exhibitions. I. Finch College, New York. Museum of Art. II. Title.

Landscape painting—History.

JEFFARES, Bo. 758'.1
Landscape painting / by Bo Jeffares. New York : Mayflower Books, [1979] p. cm. (In the history of art) [ND1343.J43] 78-25573 ISBN 0-8317-5413-3 : 12.95 ISBN 0-8317-5414-1 pbk.
1. Landscape painting—History. I. Title. II. Series.

JEFFARES, Bo. 758'.1
Landscape painting / by Bo Jeffares. New York : Mayflower Books, [1979] p. cm. (In the history of art) [ND1343.J43] 78-25573 ISBN 0-8317-5413-3 : 12.95 ISBN 0-8317-5414-1 pbk.
1. Landscape painting—History. I. Title. II. Series.

Landscape painting—Hungary.

*TELEPY, Katalin. 704.9436'439
Landscapes in the Hungarian National Gallery [Budapest] Corvina Press [1973] 34 p. 36 col. plates 24 cm. [N3690]
1. Budapest—Hungarian National Gallery. 2. Landscape painting—Hungary. I. Title.
Distributed by International Publications Service, N.Y. for 9.00 BIP

Landscape painting, Italian.

TURNER, Almon Richard. 758.10945
The vision of landscape in Renaissance Italy, by A. Richard Turner. Princeton, N.J., Published for the Dept. of Art and Archaeology, Princeton University [by] Princeton University Press, 1966. xviii, 219 p. illus. 25 cm. Includes bibliographical references. [ND1358.T8] 66-11977
1. Landscape painting, Italian. 2. Painting, Renaissance. I. Princeton University. Dept. of Art and Archaeology. II. Title.

Landscape painting, Japanese.

COVELL, Jon Etta 758.10952
Hastings (Carter) 1910-
Japanese landscape painting. New York, Crown [1963, c.1962] 24p. plates (pt. col.) 18x19cm. (Art of the East lib.) Bibl. 63-3272 1.45 bds.,
1. Landscape painting, Japanese. I. Title. II. Series.

Landscape painting—Norwich, Eng.

GOLDBERG, Norman L 758'.1'094261
Landscapes of the Norwich School; an American debut, 1967. Essay, chronology, and catalogue by Norman L. Goldberg. [Exhibition] organized by the Cummer Gallery of Art, Jacksonville, Fla., with the participation of the Tennessee Fine Arts Center, Nashville, and the Isaac Delgado Museum of Art, New Orleans. [Jacksonville, Fla., Printed by Convention Press, 1967] 157 p. illus. (part col.) map, port. 26 cm. Exhibition held at Cummer Gallery of Art, Feb. 22-Apr. 2, 1967; Tennessee Fine Arts Center, Apr. 11-May 7, 1967; Isaac Delgado Museum of Art, May 16-June 11, 1967. Bibliography: p. 57-59. [ND467.G6] 67-20504
1. Landscape painting—Norwich, Eng. 2. Paintings, English—Exhibitions. I. Cummer Gallery of Art. II. Tennessee Fine Arts Center. III. Isaac Delgado Museum of Art, New Orleans. IV. Title.

SUBJECT INDEX LANGE, DOROTHEA.

Landscape painting—Technique.

BALLINGER, Harry Russell, 1892- 758.1
Painting landscapes [by] Harry R. Ballinger. New York, Watson-Guptill Publications [1965] 175 p. illus. (part col.) 27 cm. [ND1340.B3] 65-15947
1. Landscape painting—Technique. I. Title. BIP

BALLINGER, Harry Russell, 1892- 758'.1
Painting landscapes [by] Harry R. Ballinger. A new, enl. ed. New York, Watson-Guptill Publications [1973, c1965] 192 p. illus. (part col.) 27 cm. [ND1342.B28 1973] 72-8335 ISBN 0-8230-3651-0 14.95
1. Landscape painting—Technique. I. Title.

BETTS, Edward H., 1920- 751.4'5
Creative landscape painting / by Edward Betts. New York : Watson-Guptill Publications, 1978 151 p. : ill. (some col.) ; 28 cm. Includes index. Bibliography: p. 149. [ND1340.B42 1978] 77-16772 ISBN 0-8230-1080-5 : 16.95
1. Landscape painting—Technique. I. Title. BIP

BLAKE, Wendon. 751.4'5
Landscape painting in oil / by Wendon Blake ; paintings by George Cherepov. New York : Watson-Guptill Publications, 1976. 151 p. : ill. (some col.) ; 29 cm. Includes index. Bibliography: p. 149. [ND1342.B55 1976] 75-34024 ISBN 0-8230-2609-4 : 16.95
1. Landscape painting—Technique. I. Cherepov, George, 1909- II. Title. BIP

BRANDT, Rexford Elson, 1914- 758.1
The composition of landscape painting; the dynamic integration of graphic elements from land and sea for expression. Corona del Mar, Calif., Press of the Rex Brandt School, 1959. 108p. illus. 27cm. [ND1342.B7] 59-9295
1. Landscape painting— Technique. I. Title.

BROOKS, Walter, 1921- ed. 751.4
The art of landscape painting; oils, water color, casein, polymer. [Designed and edited by Walter Brooks.] [New York] [Odyssey] [1965] 1 v. (unpaged) illus. (part col.) 32 cm. (A Grumbacher library book) [ND1340.B75] 65-15431
1. Landscape painting—Technique. I. Title.

CADDELL, Foster. 751.4'5
Keys to successful color / by Foster Caddell. New York : Watson-Guptill Publications, 1979. p. cm. Includes index. [ND1342.C26 1979] 78-27779 ISBN 0-8230-2580-2 : 19.50
1. Landscape painting—Technique. 2. Color in art. I. Title.

CADDELL, Foster. 751.4'5
Keys to successful color / by Foster Caddell. New York : Watson-Guptill Publications, 1979. p. cm. Includes index. [ND1342.C26 1979] 78-27779 ISBN 0-8230-2580-2 : 19.50
1. Landscape painting—Technique. 2. Color in art. I. Title. BIP

CADDELL, Foster. 751.4'5
Keys to successful landscape painting / Foster Caddell. New York : Watson-Guptill Publications, 1976. 159 p. : ill. (some col.) ; 29 cm. Includes index. [ND1342.C27 1976] 75-38901 ISBN 0-8230-2579-9 : 15.95
1. Landscape painting—Technique. I. Title. BIP

CARLSON, John Fabian, 1875-1945. 758.1
Guide to landscape painting. [Rev. and enl. ed.] New York, Sterling Pub. Co [1958] 144 p. illus. 29 cm. (A Bridgman art book) First published in 1929 under title: Elementary principles of landscape painting. [ND1340.C34 1958] 58-12555
1. Landscape painting—Technique.

CARRINGTON, Joanna. 751.4'5
Landscape painting for beginners. New York, Watson-Guptill [1971] 102 p. illus. (part col.) 24 cm. Bibliography: p. 100-101. [ND1342.C33] 70-136208 ISBN 0-8230-2605-1 7.95
1. Landscape painting—Technique. I. Title. BIP

DE REYNA, Rudy, 1914- 758'.1
Magic realist landscape painting / by Rudy de Reyna. New York : Watson-Guptill Publications, 1976. 167 p. : ill. (some col.) ; 29 cm. Includes index. Bibliography: p. 165. [ND1342.D47 1976] 76-2720 ISBN 0-8230-2955-7 : 16.95
1. Landscape painting—Technique. 2. Magic realism (Art) I. Title. BIP

HARMON, Donald W. 751.4'5
Landscapes in oils : the natural way / by Harmon. 1st ed. Downey, Calif. : Harmon, 1975. vii, 194 p. : ill. ; 28 cm. [ND1342.H37] 75-30284 ISBN 0-916314-01-4
1. Landscape painting—Technique. I. Title.

JOHNSTON, F. C. 751.45
Starting to paint in oils; an introduction to landscape painting in oil colours. London. Macmillan: New York, St. Martin's. 1966 [c.]1965. vii, 70p. illus. (pt. col.) 26cm. [ND1340.J6] 65-21373 5.95 bds.,
1. Landscape painting—Technique. 2. Color. I. Title.

JOHNSTON, F. C. 751.45
Starting to paint in oils; an introduction to landscape painting in oil colours, by F. C. Johnston. London, Macmillan; New York, St. Martin's Press, 1965 [i.e. 1966] vii, 70 p. illus. (part col.) 26 cm. [ND1340.J6] 65-21373
1. Landscape painting — Technique. 2. Color. I. Title.

O'CONNOR, John, 1913- 751.4
Landscape painting. London, Studio Vista; New York, 92 p. front., illus. (some col.), diagrs. 25 1/2 cm. 35/- (B 67-20823) Watson-Guptill Publications, 1967. (SBN 289 27929 1) Bibliography: p. 89. [ND1340.O3] [67-20823] 68-10228
1. Landscape painting—Technique. I. Title.

OI, Motoi, 1910- 758'.1'07
Instruction in Suiboku landscape. [1st ed.] New York, Japan House of Art [1968] [7] p., 13 plates. illus. 35 cm. [ND1342.O4] 68-1951
1. Landscape painting—Technique. 2. Sumie—Technique. I. Title. II. Title: Suiboku landscape.

PAINTING the West: 758'.1
mountains, by the editors of Beckbar and Lester Tinker. Milwaukee, Beckbar Books of Milwaukee [1968] 29 p. col. illus. 31 cm. (Artist's source book series, no. 1) Cover title. [ND1340.P25] 77-423
1. Landscape painting—Technique. 2. Mountains in art. I. Tinker, Lester. II. Beckbar Books of Milwaukee.

PELLEW, John C., 1903- 758'.1
Acrylic landscape painting [by] John C. Pellew. New York, Watson-Guptill Publications [1968] 158 p. illus. (part col.) 29 cm. [ND1340.P43 1968] 68-27551 12.50
1. Landscape painting—Technique. I. Title. BIP

PELLEW, John C., 1903- 751.4'5
Oil painting outdoors [by] John C. Pellew. New York, Watson-Guptill Publications [1971] 158 p. illus. 29 cm. [ND1342.P4] 70-150143 ISBN 0-8230-3282-5 12.95
1. Landscape painting—Technique. I. Title. BIP

RICHMOND, Leonard. 751.45
Landscape painting in oils. New York, Pitman Pub. Corp. [c1962] 1 v. (unpaged) illus. (part col.) 20 cm. (Pitman art books 37) [ND1340.R54] 62-9137
1. Landscape painting — Technique. I. Title. BIP

RICHMOND, Leonard. 758'.1'028
Landscape painting step-by-step. Rev. and enl. ed. New York, Watson-Guptill Publications [1969, c1958] 143 p. illus. (part col.) 29 cm. 1927 and 1947 editions published under title: The art of landscape painting. [ND1340.R5 1969] 77-82747 15.00
1. Landscape painting—Technique. I. Title. BIP

SCHMID, Richard, 1934- 751.4'5
Richard Schmid paints landscapes / by Richard Schmid. New York : Watson-Guptill Publications, 1975. 143 p. : ill. (some col.) ; 29 cm. Includes index. Bibliography: p. 141. [ND1342.S35 1975] 74-20955 ISBN 0-8230-4862-4 : 15.95
1. Landscape painting—Technique. I. Title. BIP

TAUBES, Frederic 751.45
The art & technique of landscape painting. [New York] Watson-Guptill [c.1960] 80p. illus. (col. front) 27cm. 60-8414 5.50
1. Landscape painting—Technique. I. Title.

TAUBES, Frederic 1900- 751.45
The art & technique of landscape painting. [New York] Watson-Guptill [1960] 80 p. illus. 27 cm. [ND1340.T35] 60-8414
1. Landscape painting — Technique. I. Title.

TAUBES, Frederic, 1900- 758.1028
The technique of landscape painting. New York, Watson-Guptill Publications [1966] 175 p. illus. (part col.) 29 cm. [ND1340.T36] 66-24383
1. Landscape painting—Technique. I. Title.

WAUGH, Coulton, 1896-1973. 751.4'5
Landscape painting with a knife. New York, Watson-Guptill Publications [1974] 191 p. illus. (part col.) 29 cm. Bibliography: p. 190. [ND1342.W37 1974] 74-11148 ISBN 0-8230-2632-9
1. Landscape painting—Technique. 2. Palette knife painting. I. Title. BIP

WOOD, Paul W. 758'.1
Painting abstract landscapes [by] Paul W. Wood. New York, Sterling Pub. Co. [1969] 110 p. illus. (part col.) 29 cm. [ND1340.W6] 69-19485
1. Landscape painting—Technique. 2. Art, Abstract. I. Title.

Landscape painting—Technique—Juvenile literature.

HOLLMANN, Eckhard. 758'.1
Looking at landscapes / Eckhard Hollmann and Helmar Penndorf ; [translated by Neil Jones]. New York : St. Martin's Press, 1976. 59 p. : ill. (some col.) ; 25 cm. (Through artists' eyes) Translation of Wie Maler die Landschaft sehen. A survey of landscape paintings from the Roman Empire to today, including notes on famous artists and brief descriptions and reproductions of selected paintings. [ND1342.H6413 1976] 75-4102 4.95
1. Landscape painting—Technique—Juvenile literature. I. Penndorf, Helmar, joint author. II. Title.

Landscape protection—Great Britain.

THOMAS, Roger, 1938(Oct.)- 711'.0941
Future landscapes / Roger Thomas. London : Cassell, 1976. 64 p. : ill., maps, plan ; 25 cm. (Future environments in Britain) Includes index. Bibliography: p. 63. [QH77.G7T48] 76-384001 ISBN 0-304-29553-1 : £1.10
1. Landscape protection—Great Britain. I. Title.

Landscape protection—U.S.

HUBBARD, Alice Harvey. 719
This land of ours; community and conservation projects for citizens. New York, Macmillan, 1960. 272 p. 22 cm. [QH77.U6H76] 60-6163
1. Landscape protection—U.S. 2. Soil conservation—U.S. 3. Water conservation—U.S. I. Title.

Landscaping gardening.

BUSHEY, Donald J. 712.6
How to landscape your home (Orig title: A guide to home landscaping) Illus. by the author. New York, McGraw [1964, c.1956] 293p. illus., diagrs. 21cm. (09301) 2.95 pap.,
1. Landscaping gardening. I. Title.

SUNSET. 635.9
Sunset ideas for color in your garden; selected articles from Sunset magazine. 1st ed. Menlo Park, Calif., Lane Pub. Co., c1958. c.80 p. illus. 28 cm. [SB473.S88] 58-8216
1. Landscaping gardening. 2. Color of plants. I. Title.

Landseer, Edwin Henry, Sir, 1802-1873.

LENNIE, Campbell, 1926- 759.2 B
Landseer : the Victorian paragon / [by] Campbell Lennie. London : Hamilton, 1976. [10], 259 p., 16 p. of plates : ill., ports. ; 24 cm. Includes index. Bibliography: p. 250-252. [ND497.L2L46 1976] 76-375309 ISBN 0-241-89432-8 : £6.95
1. Landseer, Edwin Henry, Sir, 1802-1873. 2. Painters—Great Britain—Biography. BIP

Lane, Fitz Hugh, 1804-1865.

LANE, Fitz Hugh, 1804-1865. 759.13
Fitz Hugh Lane, 1804-1865. An exhibition of oils, drawings, watercolors, and prints presented by the William A. Farnsworth Library and Art Museum, July 12 through Sept. 15, 1974 [Rockland, Me., William A. Farnsworth Library and Art Museum, 1974] [30] p. illus. (part col.) 22 x 28 cm. [ND237.L27W46] 74-177316
1. Lane, Fitz Hugh, 1804-1865. I. William A. Farnsworth Library and Art Museum.

WILMERDING, John. 759.13
Fitz Hugh Lane. New York, Praeger [1971] 203 p. illus. (part col.), ports. 27 cm. (American art & artists) Bibliography: p. 196-198. [ND237.L27W48] 75-159501
1. Lane, Fitz Hugh, 1804-1865. I. Title. II. Series.

WILMERDING, John 759.13
Fitz Hugh Lane, 1804-1865, American marine painter. Salem, Mass., Essex Inst., 1964. x, 100p. illus. 24cm. Bibl. 64-55222 4.50
1. Lane, Fitz Hugh, I. Title. BIP

WILMERDING, John. 759.13
Fitz Hugh Lane, 1804-1865, American marine painter. Gloucester, Mass., P. Smith [1967] x, 100 p. illus., port. 24 cm. "Checklist of Lane works": p. 53-87. Bibliography: p. 90-92. [ND237.L27W5 1967] 67-4526
1. Lane, Fitz Hugh, 1804-1865.

Lane, Hugh Perry, Sir, 1875-1915

BODKIN, Thomas, 1887- 927
Hugh Lane and his pictures. Dublin, Published by the Stationery Office for an Chomhairle Ealaion (the Arts Council) 1956. xv, 96p. 51 illus. 22cm. [N8386.L3B6 1956] 57-42308
1. Lane, Hugh Percy, Sir 1875-1915. 2. Paintings—Private collections. I. Title.

Lane, Hugh Perry, Sir, 1875-1915.

GREGORY, Isabella Augusta (Persse), Lady, 1852-1932. 704'.7 B
Sir Hugh Lane: his life and legacy. With a foreword by James White. New York, Oxford University Press, 1973. 324 p. illus. 23 cm. (Coole edition, 10) [N5247.L3G73 1973] 73-164508 19.25
1. Lane, Hugh Perry, Sir, 1875-1915. 2. Dublin. Municipal Gallery of Modern Art. 3. Dublin. National Gallery of Ireland.

Lang, Gerhard, 1916—

LANG, Gerhard, 1916- 686.2'2
The word so visual. [Clarks Green, Pa.] Apricot Press [1973] viii, 64 p. (chiefly illus.) 29 cm. "First edition limited to one hundred numbered copies. [No.] 99." [NK1535.L33A57] 73-77101
1. Lang, Gerhard, 1916- 2. Visual perception. I. Title.

Lange, Dorothea.

LANGE, Dorothea. 779'.9'9739170924
Living witness : selected F.S.A. photographs of Dorothea Lange / edited by A. J. Marks ; introd. by William Stott. New York : East River Press, 1976, i.e.1978 p. cm. [TR820.5.L36] 76-972 ISBN 0-89172-004-9 : 29.50

1. Lange, Dorothea. 2. United States. Farm Security Administration. 3. Photography, Documentary. I. United States. Farm Security Administration. II. Title.

MELTZER, Milton, 1915- 770'.92'4 B
Dorothea Lange : a photographer's life / Milton Meltzer. New York : Farrar Straus Giroux, c1978. xii, 399 p. : ill. ; 24 cm. Includes index. Bibliography: p. 385-391. [TR140.L3M44 1978] 78-5509 ISBN 0-374-14323-4 : 15.00
1. Lange, Dorothea. 2. Photographers—United States—Biography.

NEW York (City). Museum of Modern Art. 779.0924
Dorothea Lange. With an introductory essay by George P. Elliott. New York; Distributed by Doubleday, Garden City, N. Y. [1966] 111, [1] p. illus., port. 23 cm. Catalog of an exhibition held at the Museum of Modern Art, New York. Bibliography: p. 108-[112] [TR140.L3N4] 66-17304
1. Lange, Dorothea. I. Elliott, George P., 1918-

Lantern projection.

HARTSELL, Horace Clay 778.2
Overhead projection, by Horace C. Hartsell, W. L. Veenedaal. Buffalo, N. Y., Henry Stewart, 210 Ellicott St. [1961, c.1960] 75p. illus. (part col.) 28cm. 60-16751 2.95 pap.,
1. Lantern projection. 2. Transparencies. I. Veenendaal, Wilfred L., joint author. II. Title.

HEPWORTH, Thomas Cradock. 778.2
The book of the lantern / Thomas Cradock Hepworth. New York : Arno Press, 1978. p. cm. (Aspects of film) Reprint of the 1899 ed. published by Hazell, Watson and Viney, London. Includes index. [TR505.H45 1978] 77-11376 ISBN 0-405-11132-0 lib bdg : 25.00
1. Lantern projection. I. Title. II. Series. BIP

KRAUSE, Earl E 778.45
Three dimensional projection. New York, Greenberg, c1954. 125p. illus. 20cm. (Modern camera guide series) [Q186.K77] 54-11249
1. Lantern projection. 2. Photography, Stereoscopic. I. Title.

Lantern slides.

EASTMAN Kodak Company. 778.2
Photographic production of slides and filmstrips; Kodak audio-visual data book. [2d ed. Rochester, N. Y., author] [c.1955, 1960] 52p. illus., diagrs. 22cm. (Kodak publication no. S-8) 60-2904 .50 pap.,
1. lantern slides. 2. Filmstrips. I. Title.

HEPWORTH, Thomas Cradock. 770'.28
Evening work for amateur photographers, by T. C. Hepworth. New York, Arno Press, 1973. iv, 217 p. illus. 23 cm. (The Literature of Photography) Reprint of the 1890 ed. [TR505.H46 1973] 72-9207 ISBN 0-405-04916-1. 11.00.
1. Lantern slides. 2. Photography—Artificial light. I. Title. II. Series. BIP

KINNEY, Jean Brown. 778.8
97 special effects for your home slide shows, by Jean and Cle Kinney. [1st ed.] New York, R. Rosen Press [1964] 127 p. illus. 20 cm. [TR730.K52] 64-10080
1. Lantern slides. 2. Photography, Trick. I. Kinney, Cle, joint author. II. Title.

KINNEY, Jean Brown. 778.2
How to tell a living story with home slides, by Jean and Cle Kinney. [1st ed.] New York, Richards Rosen Press [1963] 127 p. illus. 20 cm. [TR730.K5] 63-7212
1. Lantern slides. 2. Lantern projection. I. Kinney, Cle, joint author. II. Title. III. Title: Home slides.

MILNER, Cyril Douglas. 778.25
Making lantern slides and filmstrips; technique and practice of the transparency. 3d ed. London, New York, Focal Press [1957] 223p. illus. 19cm. [TR730.M54 1957] 58-24674
1. Lantern slides. 2. Filmstrips. I. Title.

ROTHSCHILD, Norman. 778.2
Mounting, projecting & storing slides, by Norman Rothschild and George B. Wright. 2d ed., rev. New York, Universal Photo Books [1961] 119p. illus. 21cm. (A Universal photo guide) [TR730.R6 1961] 61-19112
1. Lantern slides. 2. Lantern projection. I. Wright, George Benjamin, 1913- joint author. II. Title.

ROTHSCHILD, Norman. 778.2
Mounting, projecting & storing slides, by Norman Rothschild and George B. Wright. [1st ed.] New York, Universal Photo Books [1956] 119 p. illus. 21 cm. (A Universal photo guide) [TR730.R6] 56-13422
1. Lantern slides. 2. Lantern projection. I. Wright, George Benjamin, 1913-1958, joint author. II. Title.

WERNER, Alfred, 1911- 759'.4
Paul Gauguin. New York, McGraw-Hill [1967] 47 p. illus., 20 col. slides (in pockets) 29 cm. (Color slide program of the great masters) [ND553.G27W4] 67-16265
1. Gauguin, Paul, 1848-1903. 2. Lantern slides. I. Title. II. Series. BIP

WOHL, Hellmut. 709'.45
Leonardo da Vinci. New York, McGraw-Hill [1967] 48 p. illus., 20 col. slides (in pockets) 29 cm. (Color slide program of the great masters) [ND623.L5W6] 67-16266
1. Leonardo da Vinci, 1452-1519. 2. Lantern slides. I. Title. II. Series.

Lantern slides — Catalogs.

AMERICAN Library Color Slide Company, inc., New York. 381'.45'7
American Library integrated sets. New York [c1958- v. 22cm. Contents.[1] Color slide groups of architecture, sculpture, painting, and the minor art. compiled by the Art History Dept. [N4040.A47] 59-3926
1. Lantern slides—Catalogs. I. Title.

AMERICAN Library Color Slide Company, inc., New York. 016.709
Art history surveys of architecture, sculpture, painting, and the minor arts from paleolithic times to the present; color slide manual including historical maps and documents, religious iconography, and thematic sets. International ed. New York [c1965] xii. 61 p. illus. 22 cm. Cover title. [N4040.A52] 66-30725
1. Lantern slides — Catalogs. I. Title.

EVANS, Grose. 760'.0924
Van Gogh. New York, McGraw-Hill [1968] 48 p. illus., 20 col. slides (film, 2 x 2 in.) 29 cm. (Color slide program of the great masters) The slides are in pockets inside the front cover. [ND653.G7E9] 68-20386
1. Gogh, Vincent van, 1853-1890. 2. Lantern slides—Catalogs. I. Title. II. Series.

GILBERT, Creighton. 709'.45
Michelangelo. New York, McGraw-Hill [1967] 48 p. illus., 20 col. slides (in pockets) 29 cm. [ND623.B9G5] 67-16264
1. Buonarroti, Michel Angelo, 1475-1564. 2. Lantern slides—Catalogs.

NEW York. Museum of Modern Art. Library. 381'.45'7
Slide catalog. New York, 19 v. 27cm. Black and white slides and negatives in the Museum of Modern Art Library. [N4040.N4] 55-33238
1. Lantern slides— Catalogs. I. Title.

SPENCER, John Richard. 759.5
Titian [by] John R. Spencer. New York, McGraw-Hill [1968] 48 p. illus., 20 col. slides (in pockets), port. 29 cm. (Color slide program of the great masters) [ND623.T7S65] 68-26568
1. Tiziano Vecelli, 1477-1576. 2. Lantern slides—Catalogs. I. Title. II. Series.

VIRCH, Claus, 1927- 709.46
Francisco Goya. New York, McGraw-Hill [c1967] 48p. illus., port., 20 col. slides (film, 2 x 2 in.) in pockets. 29cm. (Color slide program of the great masters) [ND813.G7V57] 67-29890 7.95 bds.,
1. Goya y Lucientes, Francisco Jose de, 1746-1828. 2. Lantern slides—Catalogs. I. Title. II. Series. BIP

Lanyon, Ellen.

LANYON, Ellen. 769'.92'4
Wonder production. [Chicago, Landfall Press] 1971- v. (chiefly plates, part col.) 40 x 52 cm. Vol. 1: "This book is #1X of a limited edition of twelve. Each contains twelve lithographs in one, two or four colors." [NE2312.L36A57] 73-162032 1000.00 (v. 1)
1. Lanyon, Ellen. I. Title.

Lao-tzu.

CHANG, I-t'iao. 720.1
The existence of intangible content in architectonic form based upon the practicality of Laotzu's philosophy, by Amos Ih Tiao Chang. Princeton [Princeton University Press] 1956. 72p. illus. 26cm. [NA2500.C45] 56-6543
1. Lao-tzu. 2. Architecture. I. Lao-tzu. Tao te ching. II. Title.

Lapidus, Morris.

LAPIDUS, Morris. 720'.92'4 B
An architecture of joy / Morris Lapidus. Miami, Fla. : E. A. Seemann, [1977] p. cm. Includes index. [NA737.L32A42] 77-9090 ISBN 0-912458-96-8 : 14.95
1. Lapidus, Morris. 2. Architects—United States—Biography. I. Title. BIP

Lapinski, Tadeusz, 1928—

LAPINSKI, Tadeusz, 1928- 769'.92'4
Tadeusz Lapinski: recent lithographs. New York, Kennedy Graphics [1973] [12] p. illus. 28 cm. Catalog of the exhibition held at the Kennedy Galleries, New York, Apr. 25-May 19, 1973. [NE2371.P6L37] 73-166101
1. Lapinski, Tadeusz, 1928- I. Kennedy Galleries, inc., New York. II. Title.

Larcher, Jean, 1947—

LARCHER, Jean, 1947- 686.2'17
Fantastic alphabets / by Jean Larcher. New York : Dover Publications, 1976. 72 p. : chiefly ill. ; 29 cm. (Dover pictorial archive series) [NK3631.L37A45] 76-24153 ISBN 0-486-23412-6 pbk. : 3.00
1. Larcher, Jean, 1947- 2. Alphabets. I. Title. BIP

Lardera, Berto, 1911—

HAFTMANN, Werner. 730'.924
Lardera: la rose des vents. [New York] M. Knoedler [1968] 24 p. illus., ports. 22 cm. Text in English. Bibliography: p. 23. [NB623.L28H27] 70-75805 1.95
1. Lardera, Berto, 1911- I. Title.

Larsson, Carl Olof, 1853-1919.

LARSSON, Carl Olof, 1853-1919. 759.85
The paintings of Carl Larsson / edited by David Larkin ; introd. by Brian Sanders ; picture research by Celestine Dars. New York : Scribner, 1976. [96] p. : chiefly col. ill. ; 24 x 28 cm. "An Original Peacock Press/Bantam book." [ND793.L27L37] 75-38076 ISBN 0-684-14588-X : 12.00
1. Larsson, Carl Olof, 1853-1919. I. Larkin, David. II. Title.

Larsson, Carl Olof, 1853-1919—Juvenile literature.

LARSSON, Carl Olof, 1853-1919. 759.85
A home / Carl Larsson, with paintings by Carl Larsson ; and a text by Lennart Rudstrom ; translated by Lone Thygesen-Blecher. 1st American ed. New York : Putnam, 1974. [31] p. : col. ill. ; 24 x 32 cm. Translation of Ett hem. Sixteen of Larsson's watercolors of his home and family are accompanied by text explaining the pictures and something of the life of this great Swedish artist. [ND1998.L3R82] 73-91718 ISBN 0-399-20400-8 : 5.95.
1. Larsson, Carl Olof, 1853-1919—Juvenile literature. 2. Sweden—Social life and customs—Pictorial works—Juvenile literature. I. Rudstrom, Lennart. II. Title.

Lasansky, Mauricio, 1914—

AMERICAN Federation of Arts. 769.982
Mauricio Lasansky, by Carl Zigrosser. New York, Author [1083 Fifth Ave.] [c.1960] 19p. (Bibl.: p.15, 17-18.) illus. (part col.) 18cm. 60-2728 2.00; .50 pap.,
1. Lasansky, Mauricio. I. Zigrosser, Carl. II. Title.

LASANSKY, Mauricio, 1914- 769'.92'4
Lasansky, printmaker. Iowa City : University of Iowa Press, c1975. 166 p. ill. (some col.) ; 30 cm. "Catalogue of Lasansky prints: 1933-1973", compiled by J. Thein and P. Lasansky under the direction of M. Lasansky: p. 51-141. Bibliography: p. 164-166. [NE594.L3T44] 75-12633 ISBN 0-87745-057-9 : 45.00
1. Lasansky, Mauricio, 1914- I. Thein, John. II. Lasansky, Phillip. III. Title.

LASANSKY, Mauricio, 1914- 741.9'73
The Nazi drawings / by Mauricio Lasansky. Rev. ed. Iowa City : University of Iowa, 1976. [16] p., 30, [2] leaves of plates : col. ill. ; 32 cm. Catalog of the exhibitions held at Philadelphia Museum of Art, Jan. 17-Feb. 19, 1967 and at three other institutions. Text, The Nazi drawings of Mauricio Lasansky, by E. Honig. [NC139.L36H66 1976] 75-41656 ISBN 0-87745-065-X : 14.95
1. Lasansky, Mauricio, 1914- I. Honig, Edwin. II. Philadelphia Museum of Art. III. Title. BIP

PHILADELPHIA Museum of Art. 741.092
The Nazi drawings by Mauricio Lasansky [exhibition. Philadelphia? c1966] 1 v. (unpaged) 31 col. plates. 31 cm. Held at Philadelphia Museum of Art, Jan. 17-Feb. 19, 1967 and at three other institutions. Text, The Nazi drawings of Mauricio Lasansky, by Edwin Honig. [NC1075.L26P5] 916 68-990
1. Lasansky, Mauricio, 1914- I. Honig, Edwin. II. Title.

Lasers—Congresses.

APPLICATIONS of lasers to photography and information handling; 774 [proceedings, two-day seminar] Editor: Richard D. Murray. [Washington, Society of Photographic Scientists and Engineers] c1968. xi, 293 p. illus. 22 cm. Seminar held April 25-26, 1968. Includes bibliographical references. [TK7871.3.A66] 79-287689
1. Lasers—Congresses. 2. Holography—Congresses. I. Murray, Richard D., 1937- ed. II. Society of Photographic Scientists and Engineers.

Lasers in art.

FINCH College, New York. Museum of Art. Contemporary Study Wing. 770
N dimensional space. Prepared by Ted McBurnett. Introd. by Elayne H. Varian. New York [1970] [24] p. illus., ports. 22 x 28 cm. Catalog of an exhibition held Apr. 22-June 15, 1970, in the Contemporary Wing, Finch College Museum of Art. [N6494.L3F5] 70-122326
1. Lasers in art. 2. Art, Modern—20th century—Exhibitions. 3. Holography. I. McBurnett, Ted. II. Varian, Elayne H. III. Title.

Lassaw, Ibram, 1913—

HECKSCHER Museum. 730'.92'4
Ibram Lassaw; [exhibition] June 9-July 22, 1973, Heckscher Museum, Huntington, New York. [Catalogue. Huntington, N.Y., 1973] 16 p. illus. 29 cm. Errata slip inserted. [NB237.L273H42] 73-84463
1. Lassaw, Ibram, 1913- I. Lassaw, Ibram, 1913-

Last, Clifford, 1918—

DIMMACK, Max. 730'.92'4
Clifford Last. Melbourne, Hawthorn Press, 1972. 90 p. plates. 25 cm. Bibliography: p. 88-89. [NB1105.L37D55] 73-151182 ISBN 0-7256-0052-7 7.50
1. Last, Clifford, 1918-

Latham, John, 1921—

LATHAM, John, 1921- 709'.2'4
John Latham [text by] Terry Measham. London : Tate Gallery Publications, 1976. 2-48 p. : ill., 2 maps, port. ; 16 cm. Distributed in France and Italy by Idea Book, Paris. Includes catalogue of an exhibition held at the Tate Gallery, 18 June-25 July 1976. Bibliography: p. 46-47. [N6797.L36M42] 76-383865 ISBN 0-905005-30-9 : £1.00
1. Latham, John, 1921- I. Measham, Terry. II. Tate Gallery, London.

Lathes.

KRAR, Stephen F. 621.9'42
Turning technology; engine & turret lathes [by] Stephen F. Krar [and] J. William Oswald. Albany, N.Y., Delmar Publishers [1971] vi, 281 p. illus. 26 cm. [TT201.K7] 78-153723
1. Lathes. 2. Turning. I. Oswald, James William, joint author. II. Title. BIP

KRAR, Stephen F. 621.9'42
Turning technology : engine & turret lathes / Stephen F. Krar, J. William Oswald. New York : Van Nostrand Reinhold, 1977, c1971. p. cm. Reprint of the ed. published by Delmar Publishers, Albany. Includes index. [TT201.K7 1977] 77-24997 ISBN 0-442-24244-1 : 11.95
1. Lathes. 2. Turning. I. Oswald, James William, joint author. II. Title.

Latin America—Antiquities.

LEFF, Jay C. 730.098
Ancient art of Latin America from the collection of Jay C. Leff [by] Elizabeth Kennedy Easby. [New York, Brooklyn Museum, 1966] 139 p. illus., maps. 28 cm. "A special exhibition, November 22, 1966-March 5, 1967, the Brooklyn Museum." Bibliography: p. 137. [E59.A7L37] 66-30193
1. Latin America—Antiquities. 2. Indians—Art—Exhibitions. I. Easby, Elizabeth Kennedy. II. Brooklyn Institute of Arts and Sciences. Museum. III. Title.

Latin America—Civilization—Addresses, essays, lectures.

SOUTHEASTERN Conference on Latin American Studies. 700'.98
Artists and writers in the evolution of Latin America. Edited by Edward Davis Terry. University, Published for the Latin American Studies Program, University of Alabama, by University of Alabama Press [1969] x, 191 p. 24 cm. Based on papers given at the 15th annual meeting of the Southeastern Conference on Latin American Studies, held at the University of Alabama, April 4-6, 1968. Includes bibliographical references. [F1408.3.S57] 69-16097 6.00
1. Latin America—Civilization—Addresses, essays, lectures. 2. Art and society—Addresses, essays, lectures. 3. Literature and society—Addresses, essays, lectures. I. Terry, Edward Davis, ed. II. Alabama. University. III. Title. BIP

Latin America—Description and travel.

VAZQUEZ DE ESPINOSA, Antonio d.1630. 918
Description of the Indies, c. 1620. Translated by Charles Upson Clark Washington, Smithsonian Institution Press [1968] xii, 862 p. 24 cm. (Smithsonian miscellaneous collections, v. 102) (Smithsonian publication 3646.) Reprint of the 1942 ed. published under title: Compendium and description of the West Indies. Translation of Compendio y descripcion de las Indias Occidentales, from the Vatican Library manuscript Barberinianus Latinus 3584. [Q11.S7 vol. 102 1968] 68-25124 12.50
1. Latin America—Description and travel. 2. Spain—Colonies—America. 3. Indians. 4. Philippine Islands—Description and travel. I. Title. II. Series: Smithsonian Institution. Smithsonian miscellaneous collections, v. 102

Latin language—Alphabet.

CATICH, Edward M. 741
The origin of the serif; brush writing & Roman letters [by] Edward M. Catich. Davenport, Iowa, Catfish Press [1968] xi, 310 p. illus. (part col.), facsims., port. 29 cm. Bibliographical references included in "Notes" (p. 286-287) [NK3605.C33] 67-30089
1. Latin language—Alphabet. 2. Lettering. I. Title.

Latrobe, Benjamin Henry, 1764-1820.

CARTER, Edward Carlos, 1928- 720'.92'4
The guide and index to the Microfiche edition to the papers of Benjamin Henry Latrobe / Edward C. Carter II, editor in chief ; Thomas E. Jeffrey, microfiche editor. Clifton, N.J. : Published for the Maryland Historical Society by J. T. White, 1976. 129 p. ; 28 cm. [NA737.L34C34] 77-153169
1. Latrobe, Benjamin Henry, 1764-1820. I. Jeffrey, Thomas E. II. Latrobe, Benjamin Henry, 1764-1820. Microfiche edition to the papers of Benjamin Henry Latrobe. III. Maryland Historical Society. IV. Title.

HAMLIN, Talbot Faulkner, 1889- 927.2
Benjamin Henry Latrobe. New York, Oxford University Press, 1955. xxxvi, 633p. illus., ports., facsims., plans. 24cm. Bibliography: p. 605. Bibliographical footnotes. [NA737.L34H3] 55-8117
1. Latrobe, Benjamin Henry, 1764-1820. I. Title.

LATROBE, Benjamin Henry, 1764-1820. 720'.92'4 B
The Virginia journals of Benjamin Henry Latrobe, 1795-1798 / Edward C. Carter II, editor, Angeline Polites, associate editor ; Lee W. Formwalt and John C. Van Horne, editorial assistants. New Haven : Published for the Maryland Historical Society by Yale University Press, 1977. p. cm. (The papers of Benjamin Henry Latrobe : Series I, Journals) Includes index. Contents.Contents.—v. 1. 1795-1797.—v. 2. 1797-1798. [NA737.L34C37] 77-12101 ISBN 0-300-02198-4 : 60.00
1. Latrobe, Benjamin Henry, 1764-1820. 2. Architects—United States—Biography. 3. Virginia—Social life and customs—Colonial period. I. Carter, Edward Carlos, 1928- II. Maryland Historical Society. III. Title. IV. Series. BIP

NORTON, Paul F. 725'.11'09753
Latrobe, Jefferson, and the National Capitol / Paul F. Norton. New York : Garland Pub., 1977. 362, 68 p. : ill. ; 21 cm. (Outstanding dissertations in the fine arts) Originally presented as the author's thesis, Princeton, 1952. Bibliography: p. 353-356. [NA4413.W37N67 1977] 76-23662 ISBN 0-8240-2716-7 lib.bdg. : 40.00
1. Latrobe, Benjamin Henry, 1764-1820. 2. Jefferson, Thomas, Pres. U.S., 1743-1826. 3. Washington, D.C. Capitol. I. Title. II. Series. BIP

Lattice windows—China.

DYE, Daniel Sheets. 729'.38
Chinese lattice designs / Daniel Sheets Dye. New York : Dover Publications, 1974. 469 p. : ill. ; 24 cm. Previous editions published under title: A grammar of Chinese lattice. Reprint of the 1949 ed. published by Harvard University Press, Cambridge as vols. 5-6 of the Harvard-Yenching Institute monograph series. Includes bibliographical references. [NA3583.A1D9 1974] 74-82205 ISBN 0-486-23096-1 pbk. : 5.00
1. Lattice windows—China. 2. Design, Decorative—China. I. Title. II. Series: Harvard-Yenching Institute. Monograph series ; v. 5-6. BIP

Laughlin, Clarence John.

LAUGHLIN, Clarence John. 779'.092'4
Clarence John Laughlin: the personal eye. Introd. by Jonathan Williams. Stories by Lafcadio Hearn. Captions by the photographer. [Millerton, N.Y., Aperture, c1973] 132 p. illus. 28 cm. Catalogue of an exhibition held at the Philadelphia Museum of Art from Nov. 1973 to Jan. 1974. Bibliography: p. 130-131. [TR654.L36] 73-85263 ISBN 0-912334-53-3 12.50
1. Laughlin, Clarence John. 2. Photography, Artistic. I. Hearn, Lafcadio, 1850-1904. II. Philadelphia Museum of Art. BIP

Laurence, Sydney, 1868-1940.

LAURENCE, Jeanne. 759.13
My life with Sydney Laurence. [1st ed.] Seattle, Wash., Salisbury Press Book [1974] 159 p. illus. (part col.) 29 cm. "One hundred six selected paintings from the brush of Sydney Laurence": p. [63]-159. [ND237.L285L38] 74-75661 ISBN 0-87564-010-9 30.00
1. Laurence, Sidney, 1868-1940. 2. Laurence, Jeanne. 3. Painters—United States—Correspondence, reminiscences, etc. I. Laurence, Sidney, 1868-1940. II. Title. BIP

LAURENCE, Sydney, 1868-1940. 759.13
Sydney Laurence (1865-1940), an Alaskan impressionist : [exhibition] February 28-March 30, 1975. [Anchorage] : Anchorage Historical and Fine Arts Museum, [1975] 48 p. : chiefly ill. (some col.) ; 23 cm. Includes bibliographical references. [ND237.L285A6] 75-316046
1. Laurence, Sydney, 1868-1940. I. Anchorage Historical and Fine Arts Museum.

Laurencin, Marie, 1885-1956.

LAURENCIN, Marie, 1885-1956. 760'.092'4
Marie Laurencin / Charlotte Gere. New York : Rizzoli, 1977. 95 p. : ill. (some col.) ; 30 cm. Includes index. Bibliography: p. 28. [ND553.L315A4 1977] 77-74340 ISBN 0-8478-0105-5 : 13.95 ISBN 0-8478-0104-7 pbk. : 7.95
1. Laurencin, Marie, 1885-1956. I. Gere, Charlotte. BIP

Laurens, Henri, 1885-1954.

LAURENS & Braque; 730'.924
les donations Laurens et Braque a l'Etat francais. Edited by Donald H. Karshan. [New York] New York Cultural Center [1971] 63 p. illus., group port. 22 x 28 cm. Catalogue of an exhibition held in New York, and organized under sponsorship of the Minister of State for Cultural Affairs and the Ministry of Foreign Affairs through the French Association for Promotion of Cultural Activities. Bibliography: p. 18-20. [N6852.L38] 72-151304
1. Laurens, Henri, 1885-1954. 2. Braque, Georges, 1882-1963. I. Karshan, Donald H., ed. II. New York Cultural Center. III. France. Ministere d'Etat charge des affaires culturelles.

LAURENS, Henri, 1885-1954. 730'.924
The sculpture of Henri Laurens. Introd. by Werner Hofmann. Recollections of Henri Laurens by Daniel-Henry Kahnweiler. New York, H. N. Abrams [1970] 227 p. illus. (part col.), port. 31 cm. Bibliography: p. 222-225. [NB553.L3H6] 69-14194
I. Hofmann, Werner, 1928- II. Title.

Lauterbach, August W.—Art collections.

KANSAS. University. Museum of Art. 760'.074'08165
The August W. Lauterbach Collection of prints and drawings; an exhibition from the collection of the late Senator August W. Lauterbach, given to the University of Kansas in honor of Dr. Franklin D. Murphy, 1960. Lawrence, Kan. [1966?] 16 p. illus. 23 cm. (Miscellaneous publication of the Museum of Art, no. 50) [NE42.L3K3] 66-65085
1. Lauterbach, August W.—Art collections. 2. Prints—Exhibitions. 3. Drawings—Exhibitions. I. Title. II. Series: Kansas. University. Museum of Art. Miscellaneous publications, no. 50

Lawrence, David Herbert, 1885-1930.

PAINTINGS of D. H. 759.2
Lawrence, edited by Mervyn Levy, with essays by Harry T. Moore, Jack Lindsay and Herbert Read. New York, Viking Press [1964] 104 p. illus. (part col.) 30 cm. (A Studio book) [ND497.L37P3] 64-20860
1. Lawrence, David Herbert, 1885-1930. I. Levy, Mervyn, ed. II. Moore, Harry Thornton.

Lawrence, Jacob, 1917—

LAWRENCE, Jacob, 1917- 759.13
Jacob Lawrence, by Milton W. Brown, with the assistance of Louise A. Parks. New York, Whitney Museum of American Art [1974] 64 p. illus. (part col.), port. 25 cm. "Compiled for the Jacob Lawrence exhibition held at the Whitney Museum of American Art, May, 1974." Errata slip inserted. Bibliography: p. 61-64. [ND1839.L36B76] 74-78123
1. Lawrence, Jacob, 1917- I. Brown, Milton Wolf, 1911- II. Whitney Museum of American Art, New York.

TODD, Ruthven, 1914- 760
Tracks in the snow : studies in English science and art / Ruthven Todd. Brooklyn, N.Y. : Haskell House Pub., 1977. 133 p. : ill. ; 21 cm. Reprint of the 1946 ed. published by Grey Walls Press, London. Includes bibliographical references and index. [PR6039.O26T7 1977] 76-51349 ISBN 0-8383-2159-3 lib.bdg. : 14.95
I. Title.
Contents omitted BIP

Lawrence, Martin.

THE Compleat craftsman : 745.5
yesterday's handicraft projects for today's family / compiled by Martin Lawrence. New York : Universe Books, 1977. 251 p. : ill. ; 29 cm. " A Main Street Press book." Includes index. [TT157.L32] 77-70473 ISBN 0-87663-300-9 : 14.95 14.95. ISBN 0-87663-968-6 pbk. : 7.95
1. Lawrence, Martin. 2. Handicraft. BIP

Lawrence, Mass.—Description—Views—Exhibitions.

MERRIMACK Valley Textile Museum, North Andover, Mass. 917.44'5
New city on the Merrimack; prints of Lawrence, 1845-1876. [North Andover, Mass.] 1974. [32] p. illus. 21 cm. (Its Occasional reports, no. 2) [F74.L4M53 1974] 74-78796
1. Lawrence, Mass.—Description—Views—Exhibitions. I. Title. II. Series.

Lawrence, Sir Thomas,

WORCESTER, Mass. Art Museum. 759.2
Sir Thomas Lawrence, regency painter; a loan exhibition of his portraits. Edited by Kenneth Garlick. Worcester Art Museum, April 27 through June 6, 1960. [Catalogue. Worcester, Mass., 1960?] 58. [3] p. illus. 23 cm. Bibliography: p. [61] [ND497.L4W8] 66-46653
1. Lawrence, Sir Thomas, 1769-1830. I. Garlick, Kenneth, 1916- ed. II. Title.

Lawrence, Thomas Edward, 1888-1935—Portraits, etc.

GROSVENOR, Charles. 704.94'9'9404150924
The portraits of T. E. Lawrence / by Charles Grosvenor. Hillsdale, N.J. : Otterden Press, c1975. 82 p. : ports. ; 28 cm. "200 copies ... number 12." [D568.4.L45G76] 76-359281
1. Lawrence, Thomas Edward, 1888-1935—Portraits, etc. I. Title. BIP

Lawrence, Thomas, Sir, 1796-1830.

ARMSTRONG, Walter, Sir, 1850-1918. 759.2 B
Lawrence. New York, AMS Press [1969] xi, 199 p. ports. 23 cm. Reprint of the 1913 ed. "Catalogue of pictures": p. 107-193. [ND497.L4A7 1969] 70-100531
1. Lawrence, Thomas, Sir, 1796-1830. BIP

Lax, David, 1910—

LAX, David, 1910- 759.13
David Lax, 1970: 60 selected paintings since "Denunciation." [New York] Washington Irving Gallery [1970] 44 p. illus. 26 cm. Cover title. [ND237.L35A42] 76-19778

LAX, David, 1910- 759.13 B
One man show / David Lax. New York : Washington Irving Gallery, c1976. xiv, 353 p. : ill. ; 24 cm. Includes index. Bibliography: p. 333-334. [ND237.L35A447] 76-47850
1. Lax, David, 1910- 2. Painters—United States—Biography. I. Title.

Lazzari, Mary Clifford.

LAZZARI, Mary Clifford. 759.13
Mary Clifford Lazzari paints Victorian Galveston / pref. by Peter Brink. Houston, Tex. : Oleander Enterprises, c1975- v. : ill. (some col.) ; 29 cm. [ND237.L37A54] 75-26389
1. Lazzari, Mary Clifford. 2. Architecture, Victorian, in art. 3. Architecture, Victorian—Galveston—Pictorial works. I. Title.

Le Bateau-Lavoir, Paris.

WARNOD, Jeanine. 759.4
Washboat days. Translated from the French by Carol Green. New York, Grossman, 1972. xi, 241 p. illus. 21 cm. (An Orion Press book) [NX549.P2W3613 1972] 70-157868 ISBN 0-670-75005-0 16.95
1. Le Bateau-Lavoir, Paris. 2. Cubism—Paris—History. I. Title.

Le Brocquy, Louis, 1916—

LE BROCQUY, Louis, 1916- 759.9415
Louis le Brocquy: a retrospective selection of oil paintings 1939-1966. Dublin, Municipal Gallery of Modern Art, 8, XI, 66 - 11, XII, 66. Belfast, Ulster Museum, 19, XII, 66 - 14, I, 67. [Dublin? 1962?] 71 p. illus. 28 cm. Cover title. [ND497.L485D82] 74-187189
1. Le Brocquy, Louis, 1916- I. Dublin. Municipal Gallery of Modern Art. II. Ulster Museum, Belfast.

Le Notre, Andre, 1613-1700.

FOX, Helen (Morgenthau) 712.5
Andre Le Notre, garden architect to kings. New York, Crown [1962] 176p. illus., port., plans (pt. col.) 26cm. Bibl. 62-17518 7.50
1. Le Notre, Andre, 1613-1700. I. Title.

Le Pautre, Antoine, 1614-1691.

BERGER, Robert W. 720'.924
Antoine Le Pautre; a French architect of the era of Louis XIV [by] Robert W. Berger. New York, New York University Press for the College Art Association of America, 1969. xvi, 182 p. illus., plans. 29 cm. (Monographs on archaeology and the fine arts, 18) Originally presented as the author's thesis, Harvard University. Includes bibliographical references. [NA1053.L46B4 1969] 69-18276
1. Le Pautre, Antoine, 1614-1691. I. Title. II. Series. BIP

Le Thoronet, France (Cistercian abbey)

CALI, Francois 726.7712
Architecture of truth; the Cistercian abbey of Le Thoronnet in Provence, photographed by Lucien Herve and arr. with quotations and notes by Francois Cali. With a text by Rayner Heppenstall, and a pref. by La Corbusier. [1st American ed.] New York, G. Braziller [1957] 164p. illus. 28cm. Translation of La plus gremete adventure du monde (with the commission of Cali's introductory text) by R. Heppenstall. [NA5551.L46C313] 57-12839
1. Le Thoronet, France (Cistercian abbey) I. Herve, Lucien, illus. II. Title.

CALI, Francois. 726.7712
Architecture of truth; the Cistercian abbey of Le Thoronnet in Provence, photographed by Lucien Herve and arr. with quotations and notes by Francois Cali. With a text by Rayner Heppenstall, and a pref. by La Corbusier. [1st American ed.] New York, G. Braziler [1957] 164p. illus. 28cm. Translation of La plus grande aventure du monde (with the omission of Call's introductory text) by R. Heppenstall. [NA5551.L46C313] 57-4420
1. Le Thoronet, France (Cistercian abbey) I. Herve, Lucien, illus. II. Title.

Lea, Tom, 1907—

EL Paso, Tex. Public Library. 741'.092'4
A bibliography of writings and illustrations by Tom Lea. An illustrated catalog of the exhibit: El Paso Public Library, December, 1971 - January, 1972. Compiled by Glennis Hinshaw and Lisabeth Lovelace. [El Paso, Tex., 1971] x, 54 p. 19 x 26 cm. 19x26 cm. [NX93.L4E4] 76-178810
1. Lea, Tom, 1907- I. Hinshaw, Glennis. II. Lovelace, Lisabeth. III. Title.

LEA, Tom, 1907- 760'.0924
A picture gallery; paintings and drawings, by Tom Lea, with text by the artist. [1st ed.] Boston, Little, Brown [1968] xiii, 160 p. illus. 29 cm. and portfolio (35 plates (part col)) 40 cm. Issued in a case. [ND237.L4A56] 68-13879
I. Title. BIP

Leach, Bernard Howell, 1887—

LEACH, Bernard Howell, 1887- 738'.092'4
The art of Bernard Leach / edited by Carol Hogben. New York : Watson-Guptill Publications, 1978. 192 p. : ill. (some col.) ; 32 cm. "Based on the retrospective exhibition 'The art of Bernard Leach' held at Victoria and Albert Museum, London, in 1977." Bibliography: p. 185. [NK4210.L35A4 1978a] 78-53889 ISBN 0-8230-0263-2 : 32.50
1. Leach, Bernard Howell, 1887- 2. Pottery—20th century—England. I. Hogben, Carol. II. Victoria and Albert Museum, South Kensington. III. Title. BIP

LEACH, Bernard Howell, 1887- 738'.092'4 B
Beyond East and West : memoirs, portraits, and essays / Bernard Leach. London ; Boston : Faber, 1978. 320 p., [12] leaves of plates : ill. ; 26 cm. Includes index. [NK4210.L35A2 1978] 78-315916 ISBN 0-571-11138-6 : 15.95
1. Leach, Bernard Howell, 1887- 2. Potters—England—Biography. I. Title.
Distributed by Watson Publishing Co., 6608 Hesperia Ave. Reseda, CA 91335 BIP

LEACH, Bernard Howell, 1887- 741.9'42
Drawings, verse & belief [by] Bernard Leach. [Park Ridge, N.J.] Noyes Press [1974, c1973] 111 p. illus. 25 cm. [NC242.L37A44 1974] 73-76368 ISBN 0-8155-5020-0 12.00
1. Leach, Bernard Howell, 1887- I. Title.

Lead-work—England.

WEAVER, Lawrence, Sir, 1876- 739'.54'0942
English leadwork: its art & history [by] Lawrence Weaver. London, B. T. Batsford, 1909. New York, B. Blom, [1973 c1972] xv, 268 p. illus. 26 cm. Bibliography: p. [251]-257. [NK8350.W4 1972] 68-57195 22.50
1. Lead-work—England. 2. Lead-work—England—Bibliography. I. Title.

Leadership in art.

LOWE Art Museum. 730'.0967
Images of authority, from Benin to Gabon : [exhibition] Lowe Art Museum, University of Miami, October 18-November 25, 1973. Coral Gables, Fla. : The Museum, [1973] 55 p. : ill. (some col.) ; 26 cm. Bibliography: p. 55. [N7398.L68 1973] 75-331058
1. Leadership in art. 2. Art, African—Exhibitions. 3. Art, Primitive—Africa, West—Exhibitions. I. Title.

Lear, Edward, 1812-1888.

†BYROM, Thomas. 760'.092'4 B
Nonsense and wonder : the poems and cartoons of Edward Lear / by Thomas Byrom. 1st ed. New York : Dutton, c1977. 244 p. : ill. ; 24 cm. "A Brandywine Press book." Includes index. Bibliography: p. 239-242. [PR4879.L2Z59] 77-14560 ISBN 0-525-16835-4 : 12.95
1. Lear, Edward, 1812-1888. 2. Poets, English—19th century—Biography. 3. Artists—England—Biography. I. Lear, Edward, 1812-1888. Nonsense and wonder. 1977. II. Title. BIP

DAVIDSON, Angus, 1898- 759.2 B
Edward Lear; landscape painter and nonsense poet, 1812-1888. New York, Barnes & Noble [1968] xv, 280 p. illus. 23 cm. Bibliography: p. 273. [ND497.L48D3 1968c] 75-3497 6.00
1. Lear, Edward, 1812-1888.

DAVIDSON, Angus, 1898- 759.2
Edward Lear, landscape painter and nonsense poet (1812-1888). Port Washington, N.Y., Kennikat Press [1968, c1938] xv, 280 p. illus., facsims., ports. 22 cm. "Published works": p. 273. [ND497.L48D3 1968] 68-16282
1. Lear, Edward, 1812-1888.

GARVEY, Eleanor M. 760'.092'4 B
Edward Lear, painter, poet, and draughtsman; an exhibition of drawings, watercolors, oils, nonsense and travel books, Worcester Art Museum [April 18-June 2, 1968. Prepared by Eleanor M. Garvey. Worcester, Mass., Worcester Art Museum] 1968. 88 p. illus. 16 x 23 cm. Includes bibliographical references. [N6797.L42G37] 74-151308
1. Lear, Edward, 1812-1888. I. Worcester, Mass. Art Museum. II. Title.

HOFER, Philip, 1898- 741.9'42
Edward Lear as a landscape draughtsman. Cambridge, Mass., Belknap Press of Harvard University Press, 1967. x, 79, 109 p. illus. (part col.), port. 19 x 26 cm. Bibliography: p. [72]-75. [ND497.L48H6 1967] 67-22865
1. Lear, Edward, 1812-1888. I. Title. BIP

LEAR, Edward, 1812-1888. 760'.0924
Later letters of Edward Lear: to Chichester Fortescue (Lord Carlingford), Lady Waldegrave, and others. Edited by Lady Strachey. Freeport, N.Y., Books for Libraries Press [1971] xi, 366 p. illus., ports. 23 cm. Reprint of the 1911 ed. [NC242.L4A33 1971] 75-175702 ISBN 0-8369-6617-1
I. Strachie, Constance (Braham) Strachey, Baroness, d. 1936, ed.

LEAR, Edward, 1812-1888. 760'.092'4
Lear in the original : drawings and limericks by Edward Lear for his Book of nonsense, now first printed in facsimile, together with other unpublished nonsense drawings / with an introd. and notes by Herman W. Liebert. New York : H. P. Kraus, 1975. p. cm. Includes index. [PR4879.L2L4 1975] 75-2375 20.00
I. Liebert, Herman W. II. Lear, Edward, 1812-1888. Book of nonsense. III. Title.

LEAR, Edward, 1812-1888. 821'.8
Letters of Edward Lear to Chichester Fortescue, Lord Carlingford and Frances, Countess Waldegrave. Edited by Lady Strachey. Freeport, N.Y., Books for Libraries Press [1970] xl, 327 p. illus., plates, ports. 23 cm. Reprint of the 1907 ed. [NC242.L4A3 1970] 70-107812
I. Strachie, Constance (Braham) Strachey, Baroness, d. 1936, ed.

LEAR, Edward, 1812-1888. 741.9'42
Ye long nite in ye wonderfull bedde: a bread-and-butter letter with reservations? Cambridge, Friends of the Fitzwilliam Museum, (1972). (20) p.; chiefly illus. 18 x 22 cm. [NC242.L4A49] 72-195073 ISBN 0-9502286-0-5 £0.25
I. Title.

LEHMANN, John, 1907- 760'.092'4 B
Edward Lear and his world / John Lehmann. New York : Scribner, c1977. 128 p. : ill. ; 25 cm. Includes index. Bibliography: p. 118. [ND497.L48L44 1977] 77-73133 ISBN 0-684-15173-1 : 9.95
1. Lear, Edward, 1812-1888. 2. Painters—England—Biography. 3. Authors, English—19th century—Biography. I. Title. BIP

NOAKES, Vivien, 1937- 760'.0924 B
Edward Lear; the life of a wanderer. [1st American ed.] Boston, Houghton Mifflin, 1969 [c1968] 359 p. illus., facsims., map, ports. 23 cm. Bibliography: p. 343-346. [ND497.L48N6 1969] 69-15024 8.95
1. Lear, Edward, 1812-1888. I. Title.

Lear, Edward, 1812-1888—Juvenile literature.

KELEN, Emery, 1896- 760'.092'4 B
Mr. Nonsense: a life of Edward Lear. With illus. by Edward Lear. [1st. ed.] Nashville, T. Nelson [1973] 128 p. illus. 22 cm. Bibliography: p. [121] Biography of a nineteenth-century Englishman known for his nonsense verse and limericks. [PR4879.L2Z67] 92 73-2672 ISBN 0-8407-6278-X 4.95
1. Lear, Edward, 1812-1888—Juvenile literature. I. Title.

Leather.

BAIRD, Floyd Oliver, 1897- 745.53
Leather secrets. [Manitou Springs? Colo., 1951] 86 p. illus. 63 cm. [TS965.B3] 51-32013
1. Leather. I. Title.

WATERER, John William, 1892- 745.53'1
Leather craftsmanship, by John W. Waterer. New York, Praeger [1968] 121 p. illus. 26 cm. Bibliography: p. [117]-118. [TS965.W28 1968] 68-25991 10.00
1. Leather. 2. Leather work. I. Title.

Leather carving.

GRONEMAN, Chris Harold, 1906- 745.53'1
Leather tooling and carving / by Chris H. Groneman. New York : Dover Publications, 1974, c1950. x, 111 p. : ill. ; 27 cm. Reprint of the ed. published by Laurel Publishers, Scranton. Includes index. Bibliography: p. [107] [TT290.G86 1974] 74-75258 ISBN 0-486-23061-9 pbk. : 2.50
1. Leather carving. I. Title. BIP

Leather garments.

GOLDSWORTHY, Maureen. 646.1'5
Dressmaking with leather / Maureen Goldsworthy. London : Batsford, 1976. 119 p., [2] leaves of plates : ill. (some col.) ; 26 cm. Includes index. [TT524.G64] 77-361722 ISBN 0-7134-3240-3 : 11.50
1. Leather garments. 2. Dressmaking. I. Title.
Distributed by Hippocrene Books, N.Y.,N.Y.

JoRGENSEN, Kirsten. 646.4
Making leather clothes. New York, Van Nostrand Reinhold Co. [1974] p. Translation of Skindsyning. [TT524.J613] 73-16710 ISBN 0-442-30036-0 7.50
1. Leather garments. 2. Leather work. I. Title.

KROHN, Margaret B 646.4
How to sew; leather, suede [and] fur [by] Margaret B. Krohn [and] Phyllis W. Schwebke. Milwaukee Bruce Pub. Co. [1966] viii, 148 p. illus. 26 cm. Includes bibliographies. [TT525.K73] 66-25268
1. Leather garments. 2. Fur garments. I. Schwebke, Phyllis W., joint author. II. Title.

KROHN, Margaret B. 646.4
How to sew; leather, suede [and] fur [by] Margaret B. Krohn [and] Phyllis W. Schwebke. Milwaukee, Bruce Pub. Co. [1966] viii, 148 p. illus. 26 cm. Includes bibliographies. [TT525.K73] 66-25268
1. Leather garments. 2. Fur garments. I. Schwebke, Phyllis W., joint author. II. Title.

LEATHER, Kate. 646.1'5
Fashion with leather / Kate Leather. London : Batsford, 1977. 119 p., [2] leaves of plates : ill. (some col.) ; 26 cm. Includes index. [TT524.L4] 78-309696 ISBN 0-7134-1015-9 : 11.50
1. Leather garments. I. Title.
Distributed by Hippocrene Books, New York, NY **BIP**

MORRIS, Ben, 1943- 646.4'3'04
Making clothes in leather / Ben and Elizabeth Morris. New York : Taplinger Pub. Co., 1976, c1975. 95 p. : ill. ; 26 cm. Includes index. [TT524.M67 1976] 75-21619 ISBN 0-8008-5063-7 : 10.95
1. Leather garments. I. Morris, Elizabeth, 1944- joint author. II. Title. **BIP**

SCHWEBKE, Phyllis W. 646.1'5
How to sew leather, suede, fur [by] Phyllis W. Schwebke [and] Margaret B. Krohn. Rev. ed. New York, Collier Books [1974, c1970] 151 p. illus. 25 cm. Edition for 1966 by M. B. Krohn and P. W. Schwebke. Bibliography: p. 64. [TT524.S38 1974] 74-162866 2.95 (pbk.)
1. Leather garments. 2. Fur garments. I. Krohn, Margaret B., joint author. II. Title.

Leather industry and trade—Bibliography—Catalogs.

NORTHAMPTON Central Reference Library. 016.685
Catalogue of the leather and footwear collections in the Northampton Central Reference Library and the Library of the Northampton Central College of Further Education; [compiled by David Powell and Victor A. Hatley]. Northampton, County Borough of Northampton (Public Libraries, Museums & Art Gallery Committee), 1968. 53 p. 25 cm. [Z7914.L27N66] 70-416930 5/-
1. Leather industry and trade—Bibliography—Catalogs. 2. Boots and shoes—Bibliography—Catalogs. I. Powell, David, Librarian. II. Hatley, Victor A. III. Northampton Central College of Further Education. Library. IV. Title.

Leather work.

ALDRIDGE, Joan. 745.53
Leather animals. [London, New York] Studio Publications [1950] 63 p. illus. 18 cm. (Make it yourself) [TT290.A48] 51-479
1. Leather work. I. Title. II. Series: "Make it yourself" series

ALLER, Doris, 1909- 745.53
Sunset leather craft book. [1st ed.] Menlo Park, Calif., Lane Pub. Co. [1952] 94 p. illus. 28 cm. [TT290.A49] 52-9768
1. Leather work. I. Title.

ARGENT, Jeanne. 745.53'1
Imaginative leatherwork / Jeanne Argent. 1st American ed. South Brunswick, [N.J.] : A. S. Barnes, 1976, c1975. 172 p. : ill. ; 26 cm. [TT290.A73 1976] 75-21691 ISBN 0-498-01831-8 : 8.95
1. Leather work. 2. Leather garments. I. Title.

CHERRY, Raymond. 745.53
General leathercraft. [4th ed.] Bloomington, Ill., McKnight & McKnight Pub. Co. [1955] 144 p. illus. 27 cm. [NK6200.C5 1955] 55-3539
1. Leather work. **BIP**

DEAN, John W. 745.53
Leathercraft techniques and designs. Bloomington, Ill., McKnight & McKnight Pub. Co. [1950] 251 p. illus., col. plate. 26 cm. --107 leathercraft designs in actual size. Bloomington, McKnight & McKnight Pub. Co., '1950. 50 plates. 26 x 41 cm. fold. to 26 x 20 cm. Cover title. [TT290.D38] 50-5415
1. Leather work. I. Title.

DELANO, Joseph. 745.53'1
The new book of leatherwork; projects for today's craftsperson. New York, Drake Publishers [1974] p. [TT290.D43] 74-6076 ISBN 0-87749-681-1 9.95
1. Leather work. I. Title. **BIP**

DIVALENTIN, Maria (Messuri) 1911- 745.53'1
Getting started in leathercraft [by] Maria M. di Valentin. Illustrated by Louis di Valentin. New York, Collier Books [1972] 96 p. illus. (part col.) 28 cm. (Getting started series) Bibliography: p. 94. Introduces the materials, tools, and techniques for making various items from leather. [TT290.D48] 71-183405 2.95
1. Leather work. I. DiValentin, Louis, illus. II. Title. **BIP**

DORNE, David. 745.53'1
Easy-to-do leathercraft projects, with full-size templates / David Dorne. New York : Dover Publications, 1976. 32 p., [16] leaves of plates : ill. ; 28 cm. [TT290.D59 1976] 75-41869 ISBN 0-486-23319-7 pbk. : 2.00
1. Leather work. I. Title. **BIP**

EDWARDS, Steven M. 685
The art of working with leather [by] Steven M. Edwards. [1st ed.] Radnor, Pa., Chilton Book Co. [1974] 152 p. illus. 26 cm. (Chilton's creative crafts series) Bibliography: p. 141. [TT290.E38 1974] 74-7145 ISBN 0-8019-5831-8
1. Leather work. I. Title.

ERVIN, Jonathon. 745.53'1
Jonathon Ervin's leather notebook. Philadelphia : Running Press, c1973. 86 p. : ill. ; 28 cm. [TT290.E78] 74-187856 3.95
1. Leather work. I. Title.

FAULKNER, Jan. 646.1'5
Leathercraft by hand / Jan Faulkner. New York : Walker, 1973. 217 p. : ill. ; 27 cm. [TT290.F38 1973] 73-83316 ISBN 0-8027-0428-X : 8.95
1. Leather work. I. Title. **BIP**

*FAULKNER, Jan. 745.531
Leathercraft by hand. New York, Barnes & Noble [1974, c1973] 217 p. illus. 21 cm. (A Barnes & Noble craft book EH 403) [TT290] ISBN 0-06-463403-5 2.50 (pbk.)
1. Leather work. I. Title.

FURST, Ronald Kenneth. 745.53'1
Soft suede, supple leather; craft and design. New York, Simon and Schuster [1974] 96 p. illus. 24 cm. Introduces the history of leather, the different varieties of this material, and the tools and techniques for working with it to make belts, bags, clothing, and other objects. [TT290.F87] 73-18112 ISBN 0-671-21706-2 7.95
1. Leather work. I. Title. **BIP**

GENFAN, Herb. 745.53'1
Latigo leather / by Herb Genfan and Lyn Taetzsch. New York : Watson-Guptill, 1976. 157 p. : ill. ; 26 cm. Includes index. [TT290.G46] 75-35620 ISBN 0-8230-2650-7 : 12.95 ISBN 0-8230-2651-5 pbk. : 6.95
1. Leather work. I. Taetzsch, Lyn, joint author. II. Title.

GRANT, Bruce, 1893- 745.53'1
Encyclopedia of rawhide and leather braiding. Cambridge, Md., Cornell Maritime Press [1972] xxviii, 528 p. illus. 23 cm. Incorporates material from the author's Leather braiding, and How to make cowboy horse gear. Bibliography: p. 521-522. [TS1040.G75] 72-10407 ISBN 0-87033-161-2 10.00
1. Leather work. 2. Braid. I. Title. **BIP**

GRANT, Bruce, 1893- 745.53
Leather braiding; illustrated by Larry Spinelli. Cambridge, Md., Cornell Maritime Press [1950] xviii, 173 p. illus. 23 cm. [TT290.G77] 50-7746
1. Leather work. I. Spinelli, Larry, illus. II. Title. **BIP**

GRONEMAN, Chris Harold, 1906- 745.53
Applied leathercraft. [2d ed.] Peoria, Ill., C. A. Bennett Co. [1952] 210 p. illus. 22 cm. [TT290.G84 1952] 52-1861
1. Leather work. I. Title.

GRONEMAN, Chris Harold, 1906- 745.53
Leather tooling and carving. Scranton, International Textbook Co. [1950] x, 111 p. illus. 27 cm. Bibliography: p. [107] [TT290.G86] 50-7707
1. Leather work. 2. Handicraft.

GRONEMAN, Chris Harold, 1906- 745.53
Leathercraft. Peoria, Ill., C. A. Bennett Co. [1958] 158 p. illus. 26 cm. [TT290.G863] 58-5509
1. Leather work.

GRONEMAN, Chris Harold, 1906- 745.53
Leathercraft. [Rev.] Peoria, Ill., C. A. Bennett [c.1958, 1963] 160p. illus. 26cm. Bibl. 63-1309 4.20
1. Leather work. I. Title.

HANAUER, Elsie V. 745.53'1
Creating with leather, by Elsie Hanauer. South Brunswick, A. S. Barnes [1970] 135 p. illus. 27 cm. [TT290.H35] 73-107115
1. Leather work. I. Title. **BIP**

HAYES, M. Vincent. 745.53'1
Making it in leather, by M. Vincent Hayes. New York, Drake Publishers [1972] 104, [1] p. illus. 24 cm. Includes glossary. Bibliography: p. [105] A comprehensive look at the craft of leather work. Defines tooling, carving, and embossing, and discusses leather garments, footwear, bookbinding, dyeing and finishing, and tools of the trade. [TT290.H38] 73-159719 5.95
1. Leather work. I. Title.

HELLEGERS, Louisa Bumagin. 745.53'1
Leather tooling / by Charles G. Leland ; [adapted by Louisa Hellegers from the original work entitled "Leather work."] New York : Sterling Pub. Co., [1975] 112 p. : ill. ; 22 cm. "A Discovery House book." Includes index. A guide to the art of tooling leather with drawings of designs suitable for use in decorating a wide variety of objects. [TT290.H44] 74-31707 ISBN 0-8069-8004-4 : 4.95 ISBN 0-8069-8005-2 lib.bdg. : 4.89
1. Leather work. I. Leland, Charles Godfrey, 1824-1903. Leather work. II. Title.

HELLEGERS, Louisa Bumagin. 745.53'1
Leathercrafting, by Grete Petersen. [Translated by Elisabeth D'Altilia. Adapted by Louisa Bumagin Hellegers] New York, Sterling Pub. Co. [1973] 48 p. illus. 20 cm. (Little craft book series) Adaptation of G. Petersen's Skonne ting i skind. Directions for making items in leather, such as sandals, hats, handbags, jewelry, and belts. [TT290.P462H413 1973] 72-95205 ISBN 0-8069-5236-9 2.95
1. Leather work. I. Petersen, Grete. Skonne ting i skind. II. Title.
Library binding 2.69; ISBN 0-8069-5237-7.

HEMARD, Larry. 685'.22
Leathercraft; creative technique and design. Garden City, N.Y., Doubleday, 1972. 143 p. illus. 26 cm. [TT290.H45] 71-175413 3.95
1. Leather work.

HILLS, Pat, 1924- 745.53'1
The leathercraft book [by] Pat Hills, with Joan Wiener. [1st ed.] New York, Random House [1973] vi, 132 p. illus. 28 cm. [TT290.H54] 73-163948 ISBN 0-394-47416-3 8.95
1. Leather work. I. Wiener, Sita, joint author. II. Title.
Pbk. 3.95; ISBN 0-394-70621-8.

KLINGENSMITH, Willey P 745.53
Leatherwork procedure and designs. Milwaukee, Bruce Pub. Co. [1958] 136p. illus. 26cm. Includes bibliography. [TT290.S] 57-13412
1. Leather work. I. Title.

KOECHLIN-SCHWARTZ-BIZEMONT, Dorothee. 745.53'1
Leather craft for today. New York, Drake [1973] 96 p. illus. (part col.) 19 cm. Translation of Fantaisies en cuir. [TT290.K613] 73-3717 ISBN 0-87749-467-3 2.95
1. Leather work. I. Title.

LATHAM, Sidney. 745.53'1
Leathercraft / Sid Latham. New York : Winchester Press, c1977. 182 p. : ill. ; 29 cm. Includes index. [TT290.L36 1977] 76-52410 ISBN 0-87691-227-7 : 10.00
1. Leather work. I. Title.

LATHAM, Sidney. 745.53'1
Leathercraft / Sid Latham. [South Hackensack, N.J.] : Stoeger Pub. Co., 1978. p. cm. (Stoeger sportsman's library) Reprint of the 1977 ed. published by Winchester Press, New York. Includes index. [TT290.L36 1978] 77-90768 ISBN 0-88317-049-3 pbk. : 6.95
1. Leather work. I. Title.
Distributed by Follett

LOEB, Jo, 1944- 745.53'1
The leather book : leather clothes and furniture you can make yourself / by Jo Loeb ; photos. by Terry Clough. Englewood Cliffs, N.J. : Prentice-Hall, [1975] p. cm. Includes index. [TT290.L58] 75-8629 ISBN 0-13-527705-1 : 14.95
1. Leather work. 2. Leather garments. I. Title.

MCCOY, Robert A. 745.53
Basic leathercraft; a worktext in creative design and craftsmanship. Austin, Tex., Steck [c.1961] 136p. illus. 28cm. (Steck industrial arts ser.) 1.20 pap.,
I. Title.

MALESON, Benjamin. 745.53'1
Leatherwork; a basic manual. [1st ed.] Boston, Little, Brown [1974] 178 p. illus. 22 cm. (The crafts series) Bibliography: p. 154. [TT290.M28] 74-11079 ISBN 0-316-54450-7 (pbk.)
1. Leather work. I. Title. **BIP**

MANNEL, Elise. 745.53
Leathercraft is fun. Milwaukee, Bruce Pub. Co. [1952] 92 p. illus. 23 cm. [TT290.M3] 52-8930
1. Leather work. 2. Handicraft. I. Title.

MEILACH, Dona Z. 745.53'1
Contemporary leather; art and accessories, tools and techniques [by] Dona Z. Meilach. Chicago, Regnery [1971] 186 p. illus. (part col.) 30 cm. "Supply sources": p. 182-184. [TT290.M45] 79-163266 10.00
1. Leather work. I. Title.

NEWMAN, Thelma R. 745.53'1
Leather as art and craft [by] Thelma R. Newman. New York, Crown [1973] xiv, 302 p. illus. 27 cm. Bibliography: p. 285-286. [TT290.N48 1973] 73-79849 ISBN 0-517-50574-6 8.95
1. Leather work. I. Title. **BIP**

PARKER, Xenia Ley. 745.53'1
Working with leather. New York, Scribner [1972] 159 p. illus. (part col.) 27 cm. [TT290.P3] 77-37227 ISBN 0-684-12760-1 8.95
1. Leather work. I. Title.

PATTON, Mary. 745.53
Designing with leather and fur. Great Neck, N.Y., Hearthside Press [1972] 254 p. illus. 25 cm. [TT290.P33] 70-185809 8.95
1. Leather work. 2. Fur. I. Title.

PETERSEN, Grete. 745.53
Creative leathercraft. [Translated by Barbara Evans Zimmer] New York, Sterling Pub. Co. [1960] 92 p. illus. 22 cm. (Sterling craft 0ooks) Translation of Laaederarbejde som hobby. [TT290.P443] 60-10378
1. Leather work. I. Title.

PROPER, Churchill H. 685'.51
Bags, cases, purses, by Churchill H. Proper. Illustrated by the author. Charlotteville, N.Y., Story House Corp., 1971. 31 p. illus. 22 cm. (Hand crafts) Describes basic tools for use in working with leather and gives patterns with instructions for making several items. [TT290.P76] 72-185670
1. Leather work. 2. Luggage. 3. Handbags. I. Title.

PROPER, Churchill H. 646.4
Footwear: leathercraft, by Churchill H. Proper. Illustrated by the author. Charlotteville, N.Y., Story House Corp., 1971. 32 p. illus. 22 cm. (Hand crafts) Describes the techniques and the necessary tools and materials for making sandals, moccasins, and boots. [TT290.P77] 78-185669

1. Leather work. 2. Boots and shoes. I. Title.

RUNK, David, 1948- 685'.3103
Shoes for free people / by David Runk ; ill. by Inger Runk. Santa Cruz, Calif. : Unity Press, 1975. p. cm. Includes index. [TT290.R85] 75-25805 pbk. : 2.95
1. Leather work. 2. Boots and shoes. I. Title. **BIP**

SHAW, Gladys J. 745.53'1
Leathercraft, by Gladys J. Shaw. Leicester, Dryad Handicrafts. [Kentfield, Calif., N. K. Gregg, 1971] 62 p. illus. (1 fold. in pocket) 21 cm. (Gregg series of reprints on crafts and hobbies) Reprint of the 2d rev. ed. of 1927. [TT290.S47 1971] 70-163525 ISBN 0-912318-09-0
1. Leather work. I. Title.

SMITH, Brendan. 745.53'1
Brendan's leather book. Written & illustrated by Brendan Smith. [Cotati, Calif.] Outer Straubville Press, 1972. 168 p. illus. 21 cm. [TT290.S58] 72-81867 3.50
1. Leather work. I. Title. **BIP**

TAETZSCH, Lyn. 745.53'1
Leather decoration / by Lyn Taetzsch and Herb Genfan. New York : Watson-Guptill, 1975. 158 p. : ill. ; 29 cm. Includes index. [TT290.T3 1975] 74-32390 ISBN 0-8230-2710-4 : 13.50
1. Leather work. I. Genfan, Herb, joint author. II. Title.

TORBET, Laura. 646.1'5
Leathercraft, you can wear : a complete basic course in leathercraft and 36 projects you can wear with step-by-step instructions / Laura Torbet & John Thamm. New York : Ballantine Books, 1974. 128 p. : ill. ; 28 cm. Bibliography: p. 127. [TT290.T67] 75-302504 ISBN 0-345-24219-X pbk. : 3.95
1. Leather work. 2. Leather garments. I. Thamm, John, ill. II. Title.

VILLIARD, Paul. 745.53'1
A first book of leatherworking. With 62 photos. by the author. New York, Abelard-Schuman [1972] 126 p. illus. 21 cm. [TT290.V54] 74-141557 7.95
1. Leather work. I. Title.

WILLCOX, Donald J. 745.53'1
Leather [by] Donald J. Willcox and James Scott Manning. Chicago, H. Regnery Co. [1973, c1972] 229 p. illus. 29 cm. Translation of Laeder. Includes bibliographical references. [TT290.W4713 1973] 72-11202 14.95
1. Leather work. I. Manning, James Scott, joint author. II. Title.

WILLCOX, Donald J., 1933- 685
Modern leather design. New York, Watson-Guptill Publications [1969] 159 p. illus. 29 cm. Bibliography: p. 154. [TT290.W48] 69-17667 12.50
1. Leather work. I. Title. **BIP**

WILLIAMS, Guy R. 745.53'1
Working with leather [by] Guy R. Williams. New York, Emerson Books [1967] 128 p. illus. 21 cm. [TT290.W5] 67-27693
1. Leather work. I. Title. **BIP**

YOUNT, John T. 745.53'1
Leathercraft handbook, by John T. Yount. San Angelo, Tex., Educator Books, c1971. 104 p. illus. 22 cm. [TT290.Y68] 78-180260 ISBN 0-912092-43-2 6.95
1. Leather work. I. Title. **BIP**

ZARCHY, Harry. 745.53
Leathercraft; a family activity book, written and illustrated by Roger Lewis [pseud.] [1st ed.] New York, Knopf [1953] 44 p. illus. 22 cm. [TT290.Z25] 52-12221
1. Leather work.

ZIMMERMAN, Fred W 745.53
Leathercraft. Chicago, Goodheart-Willcox Co. [1961] 96 p. illus. 27 cm. (Goodheart-Willcox's build-a-course series) [TT290.Z5] 61-5341
1. Leather work. I. Title. **BIP**

ZIMMERMAN, Fred W. 754.53'1
Leathercraft, by Fred W. Zimmerman. Homewood, Ill., Goodheart-Willcox Co. [1969] 96 p. illus. 27 cm. (Goodheart-Willcox's build-a-course series) Bibliography: p. 93. [TT290.Z5 1969] 76-9635
1. Leather work.

ZIMMERMAN, Fred W. 745.53'1
Leathercraft / by Fred W. Zimmerman ; Walter C. Brown, consulting editor. South Holland, Ill. : Goodheart-Willcox Co., 1977. 120 p. : ill. ; 27 cm. (Goodheart-Willcox's build-a-course series) Includes index. Bibliography: p. 115. [TT290.Z5 1977] 77-8007 ISBN 0-87006-234-4 : 4.45
1. Leather work. I. Title.

Leather work—Conservation and restoration.

WATERER, John William, 1892- 685
A guide to the conservation and restoration of objects made wholly or in part of leather [by] John W. Waterer. New York, Drake Publishers [1972] x, 60 p. illus. 26 cm. Title on spine: Conservation and restoration of leather. Bibliography: p. [59]-60. [NK6200.W27 1972b] 70-180136 ISBN 0-87749-180-1 11.95
1. Leather work—Conservation and restoration. I. Title. II. Title: Conservation and restoration of leather.

Leather work—Juvenile literature.

ANDERSON, Lorraine. 745.53'1
Leathercraft / by Lorraine Anderson ; pictures by George Overlie. Minneapolis : Lerner Publications Co., [1975] p. cm. (An Early career book) Describes the tools, materials, and techniques needed to make chokers, headbands, belts, key holders, medallions, leather pouches, Indian dolls, and other items out of leather. [TT290.A56] 74-33529 ISBN 0-8225-0872-9 lib.bdg. : 3.95
1. Leather work—Juvenile literature. I. Overlie, George, ill. II. Title.

GRAINGER, Sylvia, 1942- 745.53'1
Leatherwork / Sylvia Grainger. 1st ed. Philadelphia : Lippincott, c1976. 128 p. : ill. ; 26 cm. Bibliography: p. 128. Discusses the materials, equipment, and techniques of leather work and gives instruction for twenty-two projects. [TT290.G76] 76-21871 ISBN 0-397-31692-5. pbk. : 3.95
1. Leather work—Juvenile literature. I. Title. **BIP**

HETZER, Linda. 745.5
Decorative crafts / by Linda Hetzer; photos. by Steven Mays ; [illustrators, Lynn Matus and Sally Shimizu ; text editor, Jill Munves]. Milwaukee : Raintree, c1978. 48 p. : ill. (some col.) ; 27 cm. Instructions for a selection of projects involving leather, stenciling, and knot-tying and macrame. [TT290.H47] 77-28702 ISBN 0-8172-1178-0 lib. bdg. : 7.93
1. Leather work—Juvenile literature. 2. Stencil work—Juvenile literature. 3. Macrame—Juvenile literature. I. Mays, Steven. II. Shimizu, Sally. III. Matus, Lynn. IV. Munves, Jill. V. Title. **BIP**

PAPIER mache, dyeing & leatherwork. 745.5
[Translated by Nicholas Fry. 1st English ed.] New York, Watts [1973] 175 p. col. illus. 31 cm. (Color crafts) Discusses the basic techniques of papier mache, tie dyeing, batik, and leatherwork and gives directions for projects of five grades of difficulty using these techniques. [TT290.P2813 1973] 73-2303 ISBN 0-531-02632-9 5.95
1. Leather work—Juvenile literature. 2. Papier-mache—Juvenile literature. 3. Tie-dyeing—Juvenile literature. 4. Batik—Juvenile literature. I. Title. II. Series.

Leather work.

*POWNALL, Glen. 745.53'1
Leathercraft. Wellington, N.Z., Seven Seas, [1975 c1974] 76 p. ill. (part col.) 25 cm. (His creative leisure series.) [TT290] ISBN 0-85467-019-X
1. Leatherwork. I. Title.
Distributed by Int'l Publications Service, Collings for 5.50.

Lebanon in art.

THE splendor of Lebanon : eighteenth- and nineteenth-century artists and travellers / [edited] by Marwan R. Buheiry and Leila Ghantus Buheiry. New York : Caravan Books, 1978- v. : ill. ; 49 cm. Bibliography: v. 1, p. [245]. [NE954.3.L4S68] 77-13169 ISBN 0-88206-018-X : 300.00 769'.4'995692
1. Lebanon in art. 2. Prints—18th century. 3. Prints—19th century. I. Buheiry, Marwan R., 1934- II. Buheiry, Leila Ghantus, 1940- **BIP**

Lebenstein, Jan, 1930-

GALERIE Chalette, New York. v. 12
New York.
Jan Lebenstein. New York [1962] 70 p. illus. 24 cm. Exhibition held March-April 1962. Text by Jean Cassou in English and French. [ND600.L343G3] 62-14894
1. Lebenstein, Jan, 1930- I. Cassou, Jean, 1897- II. Title.

L'Ecluse, Charles de, 1526-1609.

PLANT and floral woodcuts for designers and craftsmen : 419 illustrations from the Renaissance herbal of Carolus Clusius / selected and arr. by Theodore Menten. New York : Dover Publications, 1974. 184 p. : chiefly ill. ; 29 cm. (Dover pictorial archive series) [QK41.L423P55 1974] 74-77285 ISBN 0-486-20722-6 pbk. : 4.00 769'.4'34
1. L'Ecluse, Charles de, 1526-1609. Rariorum plantarium historia. 2. Design, Decorative—Plant forms. 3. Botany—Pictorial works. 4. Botany—Pre-Linnean works. I. Menten, Theodore. II. L'Ecluse, Charles de, 1526-1609. Rariorum plantarium historia. **BIP**

Lecythi.

FAIRBANKS, Arthur, 738.3'82'0938
1864-1944.
Athenian lekythoi. New York, Johnson Reprint Corp., 1972. ix, 371, ix, 275 p. illus. 23 cm. Reprint of 2 separate works published in 1907 and 1914 as v. 6 and 7 of University of Michigan studies, Humanistic series. Contents.Contents.—Athenian lekythoi with outline drawing in glaze varnish on a white ground.—Athenian lekythoi with outline drawing in matt color on a white ground. Includes bibliographical references. [NK4650.L5F3 1972] 73-39133
1. Lecythi. I. Fairbanks, Arthur, 1864-1944. Athenian lekythoi with outline drawing in matt color on a white ground. 1972. II. Title. III. Series: Michigan. University. University of Michigan studies. Humanistic series, v. 6-7.

KURTZ, Donna C. 738.3'82'09385
Athenian white lekythoi : patterns and painters / by Donna Carol Kurtz. Oxford [Eng.] : Clarendon Press, 1975. xxi, 254 p., [36] leaves of plates : ill. ; 28 cm. (Oxford monographs on classical archaeology) Includes bibliographical references and indexes. [NK4650.L5K87] 76-379413 ISBN 0-19-813214-X : 90.00
1. Lecythi. 2. Painters—Greece. I. Title. II. Series.
Distributed by Oxford, New York **BIP**

Ledivelec, Madeleine.

DEGAS, Hilaire Germain 759.4
Edgar, 1834-1917.
Degas. by Madeleine Ledivelec. New York, Crown [1963] 36p. chiefly illus. 18cm. (Little bks. on great artistes) Biographical sketch in French, English, German) 63-5632 .69
1. Ledivelec, Medeleine. I. Title.

FIESOLE, Giovanni da, 759.5
called Fra Angelico, 1387-1455.
Fra Angelico, by Madeleine Ledivelec. New York, Crown [1963] 36p. chiefly illus. (pt. col.) 18cm. (Little bks. on great artists) Biographical sketch and list of paintings in French, English, and German. 63-25405 .69 bds.,
1. Ledivelec, Madeleine. I. Title.

MANET, Edouard, 1832-1883 759.4
Manet, by Madeleine Ledivelec. New York, Crown [1963] 36p. chiefly illus. 18cm. (Little bks. on great artists) Biographical sketch in French, English, German. 63-5630 .69
1. Ledivelec, Madeleine. I. Title.

Ledoux, Claude Nicolas, 1736-1806.

CHRIST, Yvan, 1919- 720.944
Projets et divagations de Claude-Nicolas Ledoux, architecte du roi etude. [dist. New York, Wittenborn, 1961] 153p. illus. 26cm. (Cabinet fantastique, v.1) Bibl. 61-65552 9.00
1. Ledoux, Claude Nicolas, 1736-1806. I. Title.

Ledoux, Louis Vernon, 1880-1948—Art collections.

JENKINS, Donald. 769'.952
The Ledoux heritage: the collecting of Ukiyo-e master prints; [catalogue] [New York] Japan Society [1973] 163 p. illus. (part col.) 22 cm. The exhibition was shown at the Japan House Gallery in the fall of 1973 as an activity of the Japan Society, Inc. Bibliography: p. 158-161. [NE1314.N52J364] 73-82970 ISBN 0-913304-02-6 6.00
1. Ledoux, Louis Vernon, 1880-1948—Art collections. 2. Color prints, Japanese—Exhibitions. 3. Ukiyoe—Exhibitions. I. Japan House Gallery. II. Japan Society of New York. III. Title.

Lee, Arthur Tracy, d. 1879.

LEE, Arthur Tracy, 759.13
d.1879.
Fort Davis and the Texas frontier : paintings : from the collections of the Rochester Historical Society, Rush Rhees Library of the University of Rochester, Rochester Museum and Science Center, Kennedy Gallery, inc. / by Arthur T. Lee ; text by W. Stephen Thomas. 1st ed. College Station : Published for the Amon Carter Museum of Western Art, Fort Worth, by the Texas A & M University Press, c1976. x, 109 p. : ill. (some col.) ; 24 x 32 cm. Includes index. Bibliography: p. 105-106. [ND1839.L38T46] 75-40896 ISBN 0-89096-012-7 : 20.00
1. Lee, Arthur Tracy, d. 1879. 2. Texas in art. 3. Fort Davis, Tex. (Fort) I. Thomas, William Stephen. II. Title. **BIP**

Lee, Ian.

LEE, Ian. 709'.2'4
*The third wor*d war* / Ian Lee. New York : A & W Visual Library, 1978. 127 p. : chiefly ill. ; 28 cm. "*Apostrophe theory." [N7433.4.L43A4 1978] 78-55111 ISBN 0-89104-115-X pbk. : 4.95
1. Lee, Ian. 2. Artists' books—England. I. Title.

Lee-Johnson, Eric, 1908-

MCCORMICK, Eric Hall, 759.9931
1906-
Eric Lee-Johnson, with a biographical introduction / by E. H. McCormick ; edited by Janet Paul. Hamilton, N.Z. : Paul's Book Arcade, 1956. 52 p., [16] leaves of plates : ill. (some col.) ; 22 cm. [ND2092.Z8L435] 75-317978
1. Lee-Johnson, Eric, 1908- 2. New Zealand in art.

Lee, Russell, 1903—

LEE, Russel, 1903- 779'.92'4
Russell Lee, photographer / F. Jack Hurley ; introd. by Robert Coles. Dobbs Ferry, N.Y. : Morgan & Morgan, c1978. 206 p. : ill. ; 24 x 30 cm. Bibliography: p. 204-206. [TR820.5.L42] 78-61494 ISBN 0-87100-151-9 : 25.00
1. Lee, Russell, 1903- 2. Photography, Documentary. 3. Photographers—United States—Biography. I. Hurley, Forrest Jack. II. Title.

Leech, John, 1817-1864.

FRITH, William Powell, 741.5942
1819-1909.
John Leech: his life and work. 2d ed. London, R. Bentley, 1891. Detroit, Singing

SUBJECT INDEX

LEICA CAMERA.

Tree Press, 1969. 2 v. illus., port. 22 cm. [NC1479.L47F7 1969] 69-17491
1. Leech, John, 1817-1864.

Leeds, Eng.—Buildings.

LINSTRUM, Derek. 720'.9427'4
Historic architecture of Leeds. Newcastle upon Tyne, Oriel P., 1969. 96 p. (chiefly illus., plans). 25 cm. Maps and index on lining papers. "Sponsored by Leeds Civic Trust." [DA690.L4L5] 68-55976 ISBN 0-85362-056-3 21/-
1. Leeds, Eng.—Buildings. I. Leeds Civic Trust. II. Title.

Leeds, Eng.—Description—Views.

LEEDS old and new / 942.8'19
[compiled by] Patrick Nuttgens and Agnes Rutherford. Wakefield : EP Publishing, 1976. [5], 99 p. : of ill. ; 18 x 24 cm. [DA690.L4L42] 77-355895 ISBN 0-7158-1186-X : £2.25
1. Leeds, Eng.—Description—Views. I. Nuttgens, Patrick. II. Rutherford, Agnes.

Leeds, Eng.—History.

ROBINSON, Percy. 914.27'46
Leeds, old and new. [1st ed. reprinted]; with a new introduction by Joseph Hiley. Wakefield, S.R. Publishers, 1971. vi, xvi, 151 p., 22 leaves. illus. 23 cm. Reprint of the 1st ed., Leeds, Jackson, 1926. [DA690.L4R6 1971] 72-195043 ISBN 0-85409-725-2 £2.25
1. Leeds, Eng.—History. 2. Leeds, Eng.—Buildings. I. Title. BIP

Lees-Milne, James.

LEESMILNE, James 828'.9'1403 B
Ancestral voices / James Lees-Milne. New York : Scribner, 1978. x, 301 p. ; 23 cm. Autobiographical. Continued by: Prophesying peace. Includes bibliographical references and index. [NA2599.8.L43A2 1975] 77-92997 ISBN 0-684-15647-4 : 10.95
1. Lees-Milne, James. 2. Architectural historians—Great Britain—Biography. I. Title. BIP

LEES-MILNE, James. 720'.924 B
Another self. With a wood engraving by Reynolds Stone. [1st American ed.] New York, Coward-McCann [1970] vii, 157 p. illus., ports. 22 cm. Autobiographical. [N7483.L4A3] 70-129177 4.95
I. Title.

LEES-MILNE James. 828'.9'1403 B
Prophesying peace / James Lees-Milne. New York : Scribner, 1978. 253 p. : port. ; 23 cm. Includes index. [NA2599.8.L43A2 1977b] 77-92996 ISBN 0-684-15646-6 : 10.95
1. Lees-Milne, James. 2. Architectural historians—Great Britain—Biography. I. Title. BIP

Leeteg, Edgar William, 1904-1953.

DAVIS, Bernard, 1911- 759.13 B
Leeteg of Tahiti; masterpieces on black velvet. [1st ed. Honolulu, 1969] 266 p. illus. (part col.) 23 cm. [ND237.L53D3] 69-13510 15.00
1. Leeteg, Edgar William, 1904-1953. I. Title.

Lefevre Gallery.

LEFEVRE Gallery. 707'.4'02132
Alex Reid & Lefevre 1926-1976. [London] : Lefevre Gallery, c1976. 175 p. : chiefly ill. (some col.) ; 26 cm. [N8660.L43L43 1976] 77-368956 £11.00
1. Lefevre Gallery. 2. Art dealers—England—Biography. I. Title.

Leff, Jay C.—Art collections.

AFRICAN tribal art from 709'.6
the Jay C. Leff Collection. [Gainesville? Fla., 1967?] 1 v. (unpaged) illus., map. 23 cm. Cover title. Introduction by Jack D. Flam. Catalog of an exhibition at University Gallery, University of Florida, Gainesville, March 5-26, 1967 and Division of Fine Arts, University of South Florida, Tampa, April 11-May 10, 1967. Includes bibliography. [N7397.W4A65] 74-626339
1. Leff, Jay C.—Art collections. 2. Art, African—Exhibitions. 3. Art—Africa, West. I. Flam, Jack D. II. Florida. University, Gainesville. University Gallery. III. Florida. University of South Florida, Tampa. Division of Fine Arts.

THE Art of Black 730'.967'097471
Africa; Collection of Jay C. Leff. [Pittsburgh? 1970] [90] p. illus., map. 24 cm. Catalog of an exhibition at Museum of Art, Carnegie Institute, October 24, 1969—January 18, 1970. [NB1080.A76] 74-13622
1. Leff, Jay C.—Art collections. 2. Sculpture, African—Exhibitions. I. Pittsburgh. Carnegie Institute. Museum of Art.

LINDUFF, Katheryn M. 732'.2'09701
Ancient art of middle America : selections from the Jay C. Leff Collection : Huntington Galleries, February 17 through June 9, 1974 / Katheryn M. Linduff. [Huntington? W. Va. : s.n., 1974] 124 p. : ill. ; 21 x 26 cm. Bibliography: p. 121-122. [F1219.3.A7L48] 74-76892
1. Leff, Jay C.—Art collections. 2. Indians of Mexico—Art—Exhibitions. 3. Indians of Central America—Art—Exhibitions. I. Huntington Galleries. II. Title.

Left-and right-handedness—Caricatures and cartoons.

DE KAY, James T. 741.5973
The left-handed book, by James T. de Kay. New York, M. Evans, distributed in association with J. B. Lippincott Co., Philadelphia [1966] [64] p. illus. 19 cm. [NC1763.L4D4] 66-23271
1. Left-and right-handedness—Caricatures and cartoons. I. Title. BIP

Left and right (Symbolism)—Addresses, essays, lectures.

NEEDHAM, Rodney, comp. 301.2'1
Right & left; essays on dual symbolic classification. Edited and with an introd. by Rodney Needham. Foreword by E. E. Evans-Pritchard. Chicago, University of Chicago Press [1973, i.e.1974] xxxix, 449 p. illus. 24 cm. Essays by Hertz, Granet and Kruyt translated by R. Needham; one by Chelhod translated by J. J. Fox. Includes bibliographies. [GN470.N43] 73-82982 ISBN 0-226-56995-0 19.50
1. Left and right (Symbolism)—Addresses, essays, lectures. 2. Classification, Primitive—Addresses, essays, lectures. I. Title. BIP

Legends, Chinese, in art.

DOMJAN, Joseph, 1907- 769'.92'4
The artist and the legend : a visit to China is remembered and the legends unfold : text and woodcuts / by Joseph Domjan. Tuxedo Park, N.Y. : Opus, c1974. [70] p. : ill. (some col.) ; 29 cm. [NE1300.6.D65A42] 74-81927
1. Domjan, Joseph, 1907- 2. Legends, Chinese, in art. I. Title. BIP

Leger, Fernand, 1881-1955.

DELEVOY, Robert L. 759.1
Leger: biographical and critical study. Tr. from French by Stuart Gilbert. [Geneva] Skira; [dist. World, Cleveland, c.1962] 141p. mounted col. illus. 19cm. (Taste of our time, 38) Bibl. 62-21022 6.75
1. Leger, Fernand, 1881-1955. I. Title.

GOLDING, John. 759.4
Fernand Leger : The mechanic = Le mecanicien / by John Golding. Ottawa : National Gallery of Canada : obtainable from National Museums of Canada, 1976. 27 p. : ill. (some col.) ; 26 cm. (Masterpieces in the National Gallery of Canada ; no. 6) Parallel text in English and French. Bibliography: p. 27. [ND553.L58G64] 76-380106 ISBN 0-88884-308-9
1. Leger, Fernand, 1881-1955. Mechanic. I. Leger, Fernand, 1881-1955. II. Title. III. Title: The mechanic. IV. Title: Le mecanicien. V. Series.

GREEN, Christopher, 1943- 759.4
Leger and the avant-garde / Christopher Green. New Haven : Yale University Press, 1976. xv, 350 p. : ill. (some col.) ; 26 cm. Includes index. Bibliography: p. 316. [ND553.L58G7] 75-11499 ISBN 0-300-01800-2 : 35.00
1. Leger, Fernand, 1881-1955. 2. Avant-garde (Aesthetics) 3. Arts, Modern—20th century. I. Leger, Fernand, 1881-1955. II. Title. BIP

KUH, Katharine. 759.4
Leger. Urbana, University of Illinois Press, 1953. 121p. illus. (part col.) port. 27cm. the first section of this book [is] borrowed from the catalogue prepared for the exhibition [organized in 1953 by the Art Institute of Chicago in collaboration with the San Francisco Museum of Art and the Museum of Modern Art in New York]' 'A selected bibliography, compiled by Hannah B. Muller: p. 108-116. [ND553.L58K8] 927.5 53-13028
1. Leger, Fernand, 1881- I. Title.

LEGER. 759.4
[Catalogue of the exhibition organized by] the Art Institute of Chicago in collaboration with the Museum of Modern Art, New York [and] the San Francisco Museum of Art. By Katharine Kuh. [Chicago, 1953] 90p. illus. (part col.), port. 26cm. 'A selected bibliography, complied by Hannah B. Muller': p. 77-83. [ND553.L58C47] [ND553.L58C47] 927.5 53-1501 53-1501
1. Leger, Fernand, 1881- 2. Paintings, French—Exhibitions. 3. Drawings, French—Exhibitions. I. Chicago. Art Institute. II. Kuh, Katharine.

LEGER, Fernand, 1881- 741.9'44
1955.
Fernand Leger: drawings and gouaches [by] Jean Cassou and Jean Leymarie. Greenwich, Conn., New York Graphic Society [1973] 208 p. illus. (part col.) 32 cm. Bibliography: p. 207. [NC248.L42C3713 1973b] 73-77666 ISBN 0-8212-0532-3 30.00
1. Leger, Fernand, 1881-1955. I. Cassou, Jean, 1897- II. Leymarie, Jean.

SCHMALENBACH, Werner, 1917- 759.4
Fernand Leger / text by Werner Schmalenbach ; translated by Robert Allen with James Emmons. New York : H. N. Abrams, 1976. 173 p. : ill. (some col.) ; 33 cm. (Library of great painters) Errata slip inserted. Includes index. Bibliography: p. 169-170. [ND553.L58S35] 75-5520 ISBN 0-8109-0252-4 : 22.50
1. Leger, Fernand, 1881-1955. I. Leger, Fernand, 1881-1955. II. Title.

SOLOMON R. Guggenheim 759.4
Museum, New York.
Fernand Leger: five themes and variations; [exhibition '62/2, February 28-April 29, 1962] New York [1962] 111 pl (chiefly illus. (part col.) port.) 29 cm. (Master series, no. 1) Bibliography: p. 103-111. [ND553.L58S6] 62-13861
1. Leger, Fernand, 1881-1955. I. Title.

Legibility (Printing)

MCNALLY, Harold Joseph, 686.2'24
1913-
The readability of certain type sizes and forms in sight-saving classes. New York, Bureau of Publications, Teachers College, Columbia University, 1943. [New York, AMS Press, 1972, i.e. 1973] vi, 71 p. 22 cm. Reprint of the 1943 ed., issued in series: Teachers College, Columbia University. Contributions to education, no. 883. Originally presented as the author's thesis, Columbia. Bibliography: p. 67-71. [Z250.A4M25 1972] 71-177040 ISBN 0-404-55883-6 10.00
1. Legibility (Printing) 2. Reading—Physiological aspects. 3. Visually handicapped children. 4. Sight-saving books. I. Title. II. Series: Columbia University. Teachers College. Contributions to education, no. 883. BIP

SPENCER, Herbert, 1924- 655
The visible world. [2d ed., rev.] New York, Hastings House [1969] 107 p. illus. 31 cm. (Visual communication books) Bibliography: p. 85-107. [Z250.A4S5 1969b] 73-5358 7.95
1. Legibility (Printing) I. Title.

Lehman, Robert, 1892-1969—Art collections.

NEW York (City). 708'.147'1
Metropolitan Museum of Art.
The Robert Lehman Collection : a guide / by George Szabo. 1st ed. New York : Metropolitan Museum of Art, 1975. 310 p. : col. ill. ; 23 cm. [N611.L43N48 1975] 74-34207 ISBN 0-87099-127-2 pbk. : 7.50
1. Lehman, Robert, 1892-1969—Art collections. 2. New York (City). Metropolitan Museum of Art. I. Szabo, George. II. Title. BIP

Lehman, Robert, 1892-1969—Art Collections.

CINCINNATI. Art Museum. 708.17177
The Lehman collection, New York. The Cincinnati Art Museum [exhibition] May 8 to July 5, 1959. [Cincinnati, 1959] 343 p. (p. [45]-[338] illus. (part col.)) 26 cm. "Catalog": p. [13]-43. [N5220.L39] 60-570
1. Lehman, Robert, 1892- —Art collections. 2. Art—Exhibitions. I. Title.

COLORADO Springs. 707.4'0188'56
Fine Arts Center.
Paintings and bronzes from the Collection of Mr. Robert Lehman. [Catalog of the exhibition] Colorado Springs Fine Arts Center, Colorado Springs, Colorado, 1951-52. [Colorado Springs, 1951?] [38] p. illus. 28 cm. Cover title: The Robert Lehman Collection. [N5220.L39C6] 73-9050
1. Lehman, Robert, 1892-—Art collections. 2. Paintings—Exhibitions. 3. Bronzes—Exhibitions. I. Title.

Lehmbruck, Wilhelm, 1881-1919.

HOFF, August, 1892- 730'.924
Wilhelm Lehmbruck: life and work. New York, Praeger [1969] 160 p. plates (part col.) 29 cm. [NB588.L45H613] 71-89603 16.00
1. Lehmbruck, Wilhelm, 1881-1919. I. Title.

LEHMBRUCK, Wilhelm, 730'.92'4
1881-1919.
The art of Wilhelm Lehmbruck [By] Reinhold Heller. Washington, National Gallery of Art, 1972. 200 p. illus. 29 cm. Held from May 20, 1972 to Mar. 15, 1973, at the National Gallery of Art, Washington [and others] Bibliography: p. 186-197. [NB588.L45H4] 72-76727
I. Heller, Reinhold. II. United States. National Gallery of Art. III. Title. BIP

LEHMBRUCK, Wilhelm, 1881- 769.943
1919
Die Druckgraphik. Verzeichnis [von] Erwin Petermann. New York, ,wittenborn [c. 1964] xxxvi, p., 200 plates. 31cm. Bibl. 64-55345 45.00
I. Petermann, Erwin. II. Title.

PORTSMOUTH City Museum 709'.2'4
and Art Gallery.
Wilhelm Lehmbruck, 1881-1919 : [catalogue of an exhibition of sculpture, painting, graphic work on loan from the Lehmbruck family and the Wilhelm Lehmbruck Museum, Duisburg held at Portsmouth City Museum and Art Gallery, 27 April-23 June 1974] Portsmouth ([Museum Rd., Old Portsmouth P01 2LJ]) : Portsmouth City Museum and Art Gallery, 1974. [1], 24 p. : ill., ports. ; 25 cm. "Portsmouth Festival 1974." Bibliography: p. 15. [N6888.L35P67 1974] 74-185899 ISBN 0-904316-00-9 : £0.55
1. Lehmbruck, Wilhelm, 1881-1919. I. Lehmbruck, Wilhelm, 1881-1919. II. Wilhelm-Lehmbruck-Museum der Stadt Duisburg.

Leica camera.

BOMBACK, R H 770.2
Basic Leica technique. London, Fountain

Press; Philadelphia, Rayelle Publications [1957, c1954] 254p. illus. 23cm. (A Fountain photobook) [TR263.L4B6 1957] 57-3425
1. Leica camera. 2. Photography—Handbooks, manuals, etc. I. Title.

COOPER, Joseph David, 1917- 771.31
Leica pocket companion. [New York] Universal Photo Bks. [dist. Amphoto., c. 1962] 94p. illus. 15cm. 62-14418 1.95, wire bdg.
1. Leica camera. 2. Photography—Handbooks, manuals, etc. I. Title.

EMANUEL, Walter Daniel, 1908- 770
Leica guide; how to work the Leica and how to work with the Leica. 8th rev. American ed. Hollywood-by-the-Sea, Fla., Transatlantic Arts, c1953. 112p. illus. 17cm. (The Camera guide) A Focal Press book.' [TR263.L4E5 1953] 54-16880
1. Leica camera. I. Title.

EMANUEL, Walter Daniel, 1908- 770
Leica guide; how to work the Leica and how to work with the Leica. 7th rev. American ed. Hollywood-by-the-Sea, Fla., Transatlantic Arts, '1952. 112 p. illus. 17 cm. (The Camera guide) "A Focal Press book." [TR263.L4E5 1952] 52-25261
1. Leica camera. I. Title. BIP

EMANUEL, Walter Daniel, 1908- 771.3'1
Leica guide; how to work with any Leica, by W. D. Emanuel. 42d ed. London, New York, Focal Press; distributed in the U.S.A. by Amphoto, New York, 1972. 136 p. illus. 17 cm. (A Focal camera guide, 695) Distributed in the U.S.A. by Amphoto, New York. [TR263.L4E5 1972] 73-107001 ISBN 0-8174-0695-6 2.50 (U.S.)
1. Leica camera. 2. Photography—Handbooks, manuals, etc. I. Title.

LAGER, James L. 771.3'1
Leica illustrated guide II : lenses, accessories & special models / by James L. Lager. Dobbs Ferry, N.Y. : Morgan & Morgan, c1978. 256 p. : ill. ; 28 cm. Includes index. [TR263.L4L34] 78-54092 ISBN 0-87100-138-1 : 18.95.
1. Leica camera. I. Title.

MATHESON, Andrew. 771.3'1
The Leica and Leicaflex way: the Leica and Leicaflex photographer's companion. 10th ed. London, New York, Focal Press, 1972. 540 p. illus. 22 cm. Sixth ed. published in 1963 under title: The Leica way. [TR263.L4M3 1972] 73-152626 ISBN 0-240-50670-7 £4.50
1. Leica camera. 2. Leicaflex camera. 3. Photography—Handbooks, manuals, etc. I. Title.

MATHESON, Andrew. 770.2
The Leica way; the Leica photographer's companion. 2d ed. London, New York, Focal Press [1954] 415p. illus. 22cm. [TR263.L4M3 1954] 54-4508
1. Leica camera. 2. Photography—Handbooks, manuals, etc. I. Title.

TYDINGS, Kenneth S 770.2
Guide to Leica cameras. New York, Greenberg, c1954. 127p. illus. 20cm. (The Modern camera guide series) [TR263.L4T9] 54-11250
1. Leica camera. 2. Photography—Handbooks, manuals, etc. I. Title.

Leicaflex camera.

FITZIG, Irving. 771.3'1
Leicaflex and Leicaflex SL guide. New York, Amphoto [1969] 96 p. illus. 19 cm. (An Amphoto camera guide) [TR263.L4F57] 68-16455 1.95
1. Leicaflex camera. 2. Photography—Handbooks, manuals, etc. I. Title. BIP

GRANDE, Frank D. 771.3'1
The Leicaflex system of photography, by Frank D. Grande and Simon Nathan. New York, Amphoto [1972] 174 p. illus. 24 cm. [TR263.L4G7] 77-160802 ISBN 0-8174-0539-9 7.95
1. Leicaflex camera. 2. Photography—Handbooks, manuals, etc. I. Nathan, Simon, joint author. II. Title. BIP

Leicester, Eng.—Description—Views.

LEICESTER old and new / [compiled by] William Kidd. 942.5'42'08022 Wakefield : EP Publishing, 1975. [5], 99 p. : chiefly ill. ; 18 x 24 cm. [DA690.L5L43] 76-351467 ISBN 0-7158-1105-3 pbk. : 8.50
1. Leicester, Eng.—Description—Views. I. Kidd, William.
Distributed by British Book Center.

Leigh, William Robinson, 1866-1955.

DUBOIS, June, 1927- 709'.2'4 B
William R. Leigh, artist of frontiers / by June DuBois. Kansas City, Mo. : Lowell Press, [1977] p. cm. [N6537.L423D8] 77-15343 ISBN 0-913504-42-4 : 40.00
1. Leigh, William Robinson, 1866-1955. 2. Artists—United States—Biography. 3. The West in the art. I. Title.

Leighton, Clare, 1899—

LEIGHTON, Clare, 1899- 769'.92'4
Growing new roots : an essay with fourteen wood engravings / by Clare Leighton. San Francisco : Book Club of California, 1976. [50] p. : ill. ; 23 cm. (Publication - Book Club of California ; no. 151) "500 copies ... printed and signed." No. 257. "A Clare Leighton bibliography," compiled by W. J. Fletcher: p. [38]-[48] [NE1112.L43A44] 77-359040
1. Leighton, Clare, 1899- I. Title. II. Series: Book Club of California, San Francisco. Publication ; no. 151.

Leighton, Clare, 1899- —Exhibitions.

FLETCHER, William Dolan. 769'.92'4
Clare Leighton : an exhibition : American sheaves, English seed corn. [Boston : Boston Public Library, c1978] 28 p. : ill. ; 26 cm. Cover title. Catalogue of the exhibition held at Boston Public Library written by W. D. Fletcher. [N6537.L424A4 1978] 78-106570 3.00
1. Leighton, Clare, 1899- —Exhibitions. I. Leighton, Clare, 1899- II. Boston. Public Library.

Leighton, Frederic Leighton, Baron, 1830-1896.

BARRINGTON, Emilie Isabel (Wilson) d.1933. 759.2 B
The life, letters and work of Frederic Leighton, by Mrs. Russell Barrington. New York, Macmillan, 1906. [New York, AMS Press, 1973] 2 v. illus. 24 cm. Bibliography: v. 2, p. 381-392. [ND497.L6B3 1973] 70-140032 ISBN 0-404-00659-0 95.00
1. Leighton, Frederic Leighton, baron, 1830-1896.
Two volumes 47.50 ea.

BAYLISS, Wyke, Sir, 1835-1906. 759.2
Five great painters of the Victorian era: Leighton, Millais, Burne-Jones, Watts, Holman Hunt. New York, AMS Press [1971] vii, 159 p. illus., ports. 19 cm. Reprint of the 1902 ed. [ND467.B4 1971] 72-129384 ISBN 0-404-00696-5
1. Leighton, Frederic Leighton, Baron, 1830-1896. 2. Millais, John Everett, Sir, bart., 1829-1896. 3. Burne-Jones, Edward Coley, Sir, bart., 1833-1898. 4. Watts, George Frederick, 1817-1904. 5. Hunt, William Holman, 1827-1910.

GAUNT, William, 1900- 759.2
Victorian Olympus. New York, Oxford University Press, 1952. 199 p. illus. 21 cm. [ND497.L6G3 1952a] 53-7021
1. Leighton, Frederic Leighton, baron, 1830-1896. 2. Painting—England—Hist. I. Title. BIP

ORMOND, Leonee. 759.2 B
Lord Leighton / Leonee and Richard Ormond. New Haven : Published for the Paul Mellon Centre for Studies in British Art (London) by Yale University Press, 1975. xv, 200 p., [48] leaves of plates : ill. (some col.) ; 30 cm. (Studies in British art) "Catalogue of oil paintings, frescoes, and life-size statues": p. 149-180. Includes bibliographical references and index. [ND497.L6O75] 75-2773 ISBN 0-300-01896-7 : 45.00
1. Leighton, Frederic Leighton, Baron, 1830-1896. I. Leighton, Frederic Leighton, Baron, 1830-1896. II. Ormond, Richard, joint author. III. Paul Mellon Centre for Studies in British Art. IV. Title. V. Series. BIP

Leiris, Michel. Picasso and the human comedy.

PICASSO, Pablo 741.946
A suite of 180 drawings, November 28, 1953--Feb-3, 1954. Pref. by Teriade. Picasso and the human comedy. by Michel Leiris. With an appreciation by Rebecca West. New York, Random House [c.1954] xi, 30p. plates. 19cm. (Modern library paperbacks, P52) 'The original . . . constituted the double number 29/30 of Verve, published in Paris . . . September 15, 1954.' 60-2979 1.95 pap.,
1. Leiris, Michel. Picasso and the human comedy. I. Title.

Leirner, Nelson.

LEIRNER, Nelson. 741.9'81
"The rebellion of the animals" : a series of drawings = "A rebeliao dos animais" : uma serie de desenhos / Nelson Leirner. [Washington: Brazilian-American Cultural Institute?, 1974] [52] p. : chiefly ill. ; 21 cm. An exhibition held at the University Art Museum, University of Texas at Austin, Feb.-Mar.; the Art Gallery of the Brazilian-American Cultural Institute, Washington, D.C., Mar.-Apr.; and Museu de Arte de Sao Paulo, May-June 1974. Includes index. [NC200.L45T49] 75-310103
1. Leirner, Nelson. I. Texas. University at Austin. Art Museum. II. Brazilian American Cultural Institute. Art Gallery. III. Sao Paulo, Brazil (City). Museu de Arte. IV. Title. V. Title: "A rebeliao dos animais."

Leisure—Caricatures and cartoons.

THELWELL, Norman, 1923- 790'.02'07
Thelwell's book of leisure. New York, Dutton, 1969 [c1968] 80 p. (chiefly illus.) 26 cm. [NC1479.T54A423 1969] 69-17224 3.95
1. Leisure—Caricatures and cartoons. I. Title. II. Title: Book of leisure.

Lelooska, 1934-

LELOOSKA; Shona-Hah, Tsungani, Patty Fawn. 730'.92'4 [Exhibition dates: January 26 to April 7, 1974, Pasadena Museum of Modern Art. Pasadena? Calif., Design World Productions, 1974] 64 p. (chiefly col. illus.) 24 cm. [E78.N78L44] 74-81621 12.00 (pbk.)
1. Lelooska, 1934- 2. Indians of North America—Northwest coast of North America—Art—Exhibitions. I. Lelooska, 1934- II. Pasadena Museum of Modern Art.
Publisher's address: 222 Glenarm, Pasadena, Calif. 91105.

Lenart, Harry—Art collections—Exhibitions.

PAL, Pratapaditya. 732'.4'074019494
The divine presence : Asian sculptures from the collection of Mr. and Mrs. Harry Lenart / by Pratapaditya Pal. Los Angeles : Los Angeles County Museum of Art, c1978. 58 p. : ill. ; 26 cm. Catalog of an exhibition held at the Los Angeles County Museum of Art, Aug. 15-Oct. 15, 1978. Bibliography: p. 57. [NB1000.P33] 78-59792 ISBN 0-87587-086-4 pbk. : 4.50
1. Lenart, Harry—Art collections—Exhibitions. 2. Sculpture, South Asian—Exhibitions. 3. Sculpture, Southeast Asian—Exhibitions. 4. Gods in art—Exhibitions. I. Los Angeles Co., Calif. Museum of Art, Los Angeles. II. Title. BIP

L'Enfant, Pierre Charles, 1755-1825.

CAEMMERER, Hans Paul, 1884-1962. 975.3
The life of Pierre Charles L'Enfant, planner of the city beautiful, the city of Washington. Based on original sources. Washington, National Republic Pub. Co., 1950. xxvi, 480 p. illus., ports., maps, 24 cm. Bibliography: p. 472-473. [F195.L53] 51-804
1. L'Enfant, Pierre Charles, 1755-1825. 2. Washington, D. C.—L'Enfant plan. I. Title. BIP

CAEMMERER, Hans Paul, 1884-1962. 711'.0924 B
The life of Pierre Charles L'Enfant. New York, Da Capo Press, 1970 [c1950] xxvi, 480 p. illus., facsims., maps, plans, ports. 24 cm. (Da Capo press series in architecture and decorative art, v. 33) Bibliography: p. 472-473. [F195.L53 1970] 71-87546
1. L'Enfant, Pierre Charles, 1755-1825. 2. Washington, D.C.—L'Enfant plan.

KITE, Elizabeth Sarah, 1864-1954, comp. 711'.4'09753
L'Enfant and Washington, 1791-1792. New York, Arno Press, 1970 [c1929] xi, 182 p. facsim., map, port. 24 cm. (Historical documents, Institut francais de Washington. Cahier 3) (The Rise of urban America) Bibliography: p. 182. [F195.K62 1970] 79-112554 ISBN 0-405-02460-6
1. L'Enfant, Pierre Charles, 1755-1825. 2. Cities and towns—Planning—Washington, D.C. 3. Washington, D.C.—History. 4. Washington, D.C.—L'Enfant plan. I. L'Enfant, Pierre Charles, 1755-1825. II. Washington, George, Pres. U.S., 1732-1799. III. Jefferson, Thomas, Pres. U.S., 1743-1826. IV. Title. V. Series. VI. Series: Institut francais de Washington, Washington, D.C. Historical documents, cahier 3 BIP

Leningrad. Ermitazh.

DESCARGUES, Pierre. 759.074
The Hermitage Museum, Leningrad. New York, H. N. Abrams [1961] 320 p. plates (part col.) 22 cm. [N3350.D4] 61-14628
1. Leningrad. Ermitazh. 2. Paintings—Leningrad.

LENINGRAD. Ermitazh. 759.06'074'0745
Western European painting on the nineteenth and twentieth centuries / the Hermitage ; [introd. and notes by A. Kostenevich ; translated by N. Johnstone and H. Perham]. Leningrad : Aurora Art Publishers, 1976. 306 p. : col. ill. ; 29 cm. [ND457.L4613] 76-378101
1. Leningrad. Ermitazh. 2. Paintings, European—Catalogs. 3. Paintings, Modern—19th century—Europe—Catalogs. 4. Paintings, Modern—20th century—Europe—Catalogs. 5. Paintings—Leningrad—Catalogs. I. Kostenevich, Al'bert Grigor'evich. II. Title.

Leningrad. Gosudarstvennyi russkii muzei.

LENINGRAD. Gosudarstvennyi russkii muzei. 745'.0947'0740745
Russian applied art : eighteenth to early twentieth century / Russian Museum, Leningrad ; [compiled and introd. by E. Ivanova ; edited by V. Pushkariov ; photos. by V. Stukalov ; translated by Yu. Nemetsky]. Leningrad : Aurora, 1976. 199 p. : chiefly col. ill. ; 29 cm. [NK975.L42 1976b] 77-364357 25.00
1. Leningrad. Gosudarstvennyi russkii muzei. 2. Art industries and trade—Russia—Catalogs. 3. Art industries and trade—Russia—Leningrad—Catalogs. I. Ivanova, Elena Aleksandrovna. II. Title.
Distributed by H.N. Abrams, New York

Lenses, Photographic.

BRANDT, Hans Martin. 771.3'52
The photographic lens; tr. from German by L. A. Mannheim. London, New York, Focal Pr., 1968. 260p. illus. 25cm. (Focal lib.) Tr. of Das Photo-Objektiv; Aufbau und Wirkungsweise der wichtigsten Markenobjektive der Weltproduktion. [TR270.B8313] 68-114252 35.00
1. Lenses, Photographic. I. Title.

library of world art, v. 2) Bibliography: p. 57-58. [ND623.L5B323] 61-14139
I. Baroni, Costantino. II. Title. III. Series.

LEONARDO DA VINCI, 1452- 1519. 759.5
Notebooks. Abridged from the translation by Edward MacCurdy; edited, with an introd., by Robert N. Linscott. New York, Modern Library [1957] 455 p. 19 cm. (The Modern library of the world's best books, 156) [ND623.L5A5 1957] [ND623.L5A5 1957] 927.5 57-11170 57-11170
I. Linscott, Robert Newton, 1886- ed. II. Title.

LEONARDO DA VINCI 1452- 1519. 927.5
Selections from the notebooks of Leonardo da Vinci, edited with commentaries by Irma A. Richter. London, New York, Oxford University Press, 1953. xiii, 417 p. illus. 13 cm. (The World's classics, 530) 'Most of the material has been taken from Jean Paul Richter's Literary works of Leonardo da Vinci, the second edition of which was published . . . in 1939.' [ND623.L5A5 1952] 52-4475
I. Title. BIP

LEONARDO'S legacy; 709'.24
an international symposium. Edited by C. D. O'Malley. Berkeley, Calif., University of California Press, 1969. viii, 225 p. illus., facsims. 29 cm. (UCLA Center for Medieval and Renaissance Studies. Publication no. 2) Bibliographical footnotes. [ND623.L5L43] 68-14976 15.00
1. Leonardo da Vinci, 1452-1519. I. O'Malley, Charles Donald, ed. II. Series: California. University. University at Los Angeles. Center for Medieval and Renaissance Studies. Publications, no. 2

LEVINGER, Elma (Ehrlich) 1887- 759.5
Leonardo da Vinci, Who followed the sinking star. Illustrated with photos. and with sketches from da Vinci's notebooks. New York, J. Messner [1954] 192p. illus. 22cm. [ND623.L5L46] [ND623.L5L46] 927.5 54-10591 54-10591
1. Leonardo da Vinci, 1452-1519. I. Title.

LOS Angeles Co., Calif. Museum, Los Angeles. 759.5
Leonardo da Vinci loan exhibition, June 3 to July 1, 1949. [Catalogue prepared by W. R. Valentiner in collaboration with William E. Suida and others] Los Angeles [1949] xvi, 144 p. 67 plates (part col.) 26 cm. Contents.Partial Contents. -- Two sixteenth-century biographies of Leonardo. -- Leonardo's early life, by W. R. Valentiner. -- Selected list of books and articles (p. 65-67) [ND623.L5L6] 49-49132
1. Leonardo da Vinci, 1452-1519. 2. Art, Italian — Exhibitions. I. Title.

MCLANATHAN, Richard B. K. 741.0924
Images of the universe; Leonardo da Vincc: the artist as scientist, by Richard McLanathan. [1st ed. in the U. S. A.] Garden City. N. Y., Doubleday, 1966. 192p. facsims. 29cm. Bibl. [NC1055.L5M25] 66-8249 4.50 bds.,
1. Leonardo da Vinci, I. Title.

MCLANATHAN, Richard B K 741.0924
Images of the universe; Leonardo da Vinci: the artist as scientist. by Richard McLanathan. [1st ed. in the U.S.A.] Garden City, N.Y., Doubleday, 1966. 192 p. facsims. 29 cm. "List of books": p. 187-188. [NC1055.L5M25] 66-8249
1. Leonardo da Vinci, 1452-1519. I. Title.

MCMULLEN, Roy. 759.5
Mona Lisa : the picture and the myth / Roy McMullen. Boston : Houghton Mifflin, 1975. 273 p. : ill. ; 25 cm. Includes index. Bibliography: p. [253]-257. [ND623.L57M32] 75-17837 ISBN 0-395-20734-7 : 12.95
1. Leonardo da Vinci, 1452-1519. Mona Lisa. I. Title. BIP

MCMULLEN, Roy. 759.5
Mona Lisa : the picture and the myth / Roy McMullen. New York : Da Capo Press, 1977, c1975. 273 p. : ill. ; 24 cm. (A Da Capo paperback) Includes index. Bibliography: p. [253]-257. [ND623.L57M32 1977] 77-23574 ISBN 0-306-80067-5 pbk. : 7.95

1. Leonardo da Vinci, 1452-1519. Mona Lisa. I. Title.

MONTI, Raffaele. 759.5
Leonardo da Vinci. [Translated from the Italian by Pearl Sanders. 1st American ed.] New York, Grosset & Dunlap [1967] 39, [81] p. illus. (part col.) 18 cm. (The New Grosset art library, 1) On cover: Leonardo da Vinci; the life and work of the artist. [ND623.V63M63] 67-24227
1. Leonardo da Vinci, 1452-1519.

NEWCOMB, Covelle, 1908- 759.5
Leonardo da Vinci, prince of painters. New York, Dodd, Mead [1965] xv, 265 p. illus. 21 cm. Bibliography: p. 257-260. [ND623.L5N46] 65-23290
1. Leonardo da Vinci, 1452-1519. I. Title.

OST, Hans. 759.9493'2
Leonardo-Studien / von Hans Ost. Berlin ; New York : de Gruyter, 1975. xi, 149 p., [31] leaves of plates : ill. ; 26 cm. (Beitrage zur Kunstgeschichte ; Bd. 11) Includes index. Bibliography: p. 140-144. Habilitationsschrift—Bonn. [ND623.L5O77] 75-512074 ISBN 3-11-005727-1 : DM128.00
1. Leonardo da Vinci, 1452-1519. I. Leonardo da Vinci, 1452-1519. II. Title. BIP

PAINTINGS. 759.5
Introd. by Giorgio Castelfranco. Translated by Ben Johnson and Liana Macellari. New York, Random House [1956] 62 p. plates (part col.) 18 cm. (Library of art) [ND623.L5C35] [ND623.L5C35] 927.5 56-13420 56-13420
1. Leonardo da Vinci, 1452-1519.

PANOFSKY, Erwin, 1892-1968. 701
The Codex Huygens and Leonardo da Vinci's art theory; the Pierpont Morgan Library, Codex M.A. 1139. Westport, Conn., Greenwood Press [1971] 138, [90] p. 117 illus. 24 cm. Reprint of the 1940 ed. Includes bibliographical references. [N65.L4P3 1971] 79-109814 ISBN 0-8371-4306-3
1. Leonardo da Vinci, 1452-1519. 2. Huygens, Constantijn, heer van Zuilichem, 1628-1697. 3. Anatomy, Artistic. 4. Proportion (Art) 5. Perspective. I. Pierpont Morgan Library, New York. Mss. (M.A. 1139) II. Title. BIP

PAYNE, Pierre Stephen Robert, 1911- 759.5 B
Leonardo / Robert Payne. 1st ed. Garden City, N.Y. : Doubleday, 1978. xix, 344 p., [36] leaves of plates : ill. ; 24 cm. Includes index. Bibliography: p. [321]-326. [ND623.L5P37] 78-869 ISBN 0-385-04154-3 : 12.95
1. Leonardo da Vinci, 1452-1519. 2. Painters—Italy—Biography. I. Title.

PEDRETTI, Carlo. 759.5
Leonardo; a study in chronology and style. Berkeley, University of California Press, 1973. 192 p. illus. 25 cm. Bibliography: p. 175-177. [ND623.L5P413] 72-97746 ISBN 0-520-02420-6 10.95
1. Leonardo da Vinci, 1452-1519.

PEDRETTI, Carlo. 728.8'2
Leonardo da Vinci: the royal palace at Romorantin [by] Carlo Pedretti. Cambridge, Belknap Press of Harvard University Press, 1972. xvii, 354 p. illus., facsims. 29 cm. "Index of Leonardo's manuscripts and drawings": p. 333-337. Includes bibliographical references. [NA1123.L4P42 1972] 76-102673 ISBN 0-674-52455-1 20.00
1. Leonardo da Vinci, 1452-1519. 2. Romorantin, France. Palais royal (Proposed) I. Title: The royal palace at Romorantin.

PHILIPSON, Morris H., 1926- ed. 759.5
Leonardo da Vinci, aspects of the Renaissance genius. Selected, edited and introduced by Morris Philipson. New York, G. Braziller [1966] x, 438 p. illus. 24 cm. Bibliographical references included in "Notes" (p. 401-433) [ND623.L5P46] 66-12907
1. Leonardo da Vinci, 1452-1519. I. Title.

LEONARDO da Vinci, 1452- 1519. 759.5
Notebooks. A new selection by Pamela Taylor. [New York] New American Library [c.1960] 253p. illus. 18cm. (A Mentor classic, MT312) Bibl. 60-14724 .75 pap.,
I. Title.

RIPLEY, Elizabeth. [759.5] 927.5
Leonardo da Vinci, a biography. With drawings and paintings by Leonardo. New York, Oxford University Press, 1952. 67 p. illus. 26 cm. [Oxford books for boys and girls] [ND623.L5H56] 52-9432
1. Leonardo da Vinci, 1452-1519. I. Title.

RIPLEY, Elizabeth, 1906- 759.5
Leonardo da Vinci, a biography. With drawings and paintings by Leonardo. New York, Oxford University Press, 1952. 67 p. illus. 26 cm. [Oxford books for boys and girls] [ND623.L5R56] 52-9432
1. Leonardo da Vinci, 1452-1519.

RITCHIE-CALDER, Peter Richie Baron, 1906- 759.5 B
Leonardo & the age of the eye [by] Ritchie Calder. New York, Simon and Schuster [1970] 288 p. illus. (part col.) 27 cm. Bibliography: p. 278. [ND623.L5R62] 71-124472 12.95
1. Leonardo da Vinci, 1452-1519. I. Title.

SHIRLEY, Jean. 92
Leonardo da Vinci. Pictures by Raymond Renard. Adapted by Jean Shirley from the original text. St. Louis, Webster Division, McGraw-Hill [1967] [28] p. col. illus., port. 19 x 21 cm. (Men of genius books) (Around the world library) A short biography of one of the greatest representatives of the Italian Renaissance. [ND623.L5S493] AC 67
1. Leonardo da Vinci, 1452-1519. I. Renard, Raymond, illus. II. Title.

STITES, Raymond Somers. 759.5
The sublimations of Leonardo da Vinci, with a translation of the Codex Trivulzianus, by Raymond S. Stites with M. Elizabeth Stites and Pierina Castiglione. Washington, Smithsonian Institution Press, 1970. x, 422 p. illus., facsims. 29 cm. Includes bibliographical references. [ND623.L5S75] 70-104774 14.95
1. Leonardo da Vinci, 1452-1519. I. Leonardo da Vinci, 1452-1519. Codice trivulziano. English & Italian. 1970. II. Title.

THOMAS, John, 1914- [759.5] 927.5
Leonardo da Vinci. With illus. from the sketchbook of Leonardo da Vinci. New York, Criterion Books [c1957] 191 p. illus. 22 cm. (A Criterion book for young people) [ND623.L5T64] 57-6244
1. Leonardo da Vinci, 1452-1519. I. Title.

VERLEYEN, Cyriel. 759.5
The theft of the Mona Lisa. Illustrated by Henry Branton. New York, Crowell [1971, c1970] [23] p. col. illus. 19 x 21 cm. (His Tales from history) "Also published as Le vol de la Joconde." Describes Leonardo da Vinci's efforts to get the Mona Lisa to smile, the trouble the smile caused him, and the speculation it aroused in the Louvre for three centuries until the painting was mysteriously stolen. [ND623.L5V513 1971] 74-94799 ISBN 0-690-81292-2 2.95
1. Leonardo da Vinci, 1452-1519. Mona Lisa—Juvenile literature. I. Branton, Henry, illus. II. Title.

WILLIAMS, Jay, 1914- 759.5
Leonardo daVinci, by the eds. of Horizon magazine. Author: Jay Williams. Consultant: Bates Lowry. New York, Amer. Heritage; dist. Harper, c.1965. 153p. illus. (pt. col.) col. map. ports. 27cm. (Horizon caravel bk.) Bibl. [ND623.L5W5] 65-20599 3.95; 3.99 bds., lib. ed.,
1. Leonardo da Vinci, 1452-1519. I. Horizon (New York, 1958-) II. Title.

WOHL, Hellmut. 709'.45
Leonardo da Vinci. New York, McGraw-Hill [1967] 48 p. illus., 20 col. slides (in pockets) 29 cm. (Color slide program of the great masters) [ND623.L5W6] 67-16266
1. Leonardo da Vinci, 1452-1519. 2. Lantern slides. I. Title. II. Series.

ZUBOV, Vasilii Pavlovich. 709'.45 B
Leonardo da Vinci [by] V. P. Zubov. Translated from the Russian by David H. Kraus. Cambridge, Harvard University Press, 1968. xviii, 335 p. illus., facsims., port. 25 cm. Translation of Leonardo da Vinchi (romanized form) Includes bibliographical references. [ND623.L5Z83] 67-27096
1. Leonardo da Vinci, 1452-1519. BIP

Leonardo da Vinci, 1452-1519—Juvenile literature.

NOBLE, Iris. 927.5
Leonardo da Vinci: the universal genuis. [1st ed.] New York, Norton [1965] 224 p. illus., port. 21 cm. [ND623.L5N6] 64-17534
1. Leonardo da Vinci, 1452-1519 — Juvenile literature. I. Title.

RABOFF, Ernest Lloyd. 759.5
Leonardo da Vinci, by Ernest Raboff. Garden City, N.Y., Doubleday [1971] [31] p. illus. (part col.) 29 cm. (Art for children) (A Gemini Smith book) Explains some basic techniques of Da Vinci by analyzing a few of his better known paintings. [ND623.L5R28] 78-139054 3.95
1. Leonardo da Vinci, 1452-1519—Juvenile literature. I. Title.

*WOODHOUSE, Martin. FIC
The Medici emerald / Martin Woodhouse and Robert Ross 1st American ed. New York : E.P. Dutton, c1976. 224p. ; 25 cm [PZ4] 759.5 DG 678 76-11873 ISBN 0-525-15458-2 : 8.95
1. Leonardo da Vinci, 1452-1519-Juvenile literature. 2. Italy-History-Fiction. I. Ross, Robert, joint author. II. Title. BIP

Leonardo da Vinci, 1452-1519—Sources.

FINGER, Frances L. 016.7595
Catalogue of the incunabula in the Elmer Belt Library of Vinciana, by Frances L. Finger. Los Angeles, Friends of the UCLA Library, 1971. xvii, 80 p. facsim. 27 cm. "250 copies." Bibliography: p. xv-xvii. [Z240.F47] 79-149086 ISBN 0-378-06151-8
1. Leonardo da Vinci, 1452-1519—Sources. 2. Belt, Elmer, 1893- —Library. 3. Incunabula—Bibliography—Catalogs. I. California. University. University at Los Angeles. Art Library. II. Title.

Leoni, Pompeo, d. 1610?

PROSKE, Beatrice Irene (Gilman) 1899- 735.46
Pompeo Leoni; work in marble and alabaster in relation to Spanish sculpture. New York, Hispanic Society of America, 1956. 49p. illus. 23cm. (Hispanic notes & monographs; essays, studies, and brief biographies) [NB813.L4P7] 927.3 56-14493
1. Leoni, Pompeo, d. 1610? 2. Leoni, Leone, 1509-1590. 3. Sculpture, Spanish. I. Title. BIP

Leslie, Alfred, 1927—

STICH, Sidra. 757
Alfred Leslie, Philip Pearlstein, Wayne Thiebaud: contemporary views of man. [Exhibition] Hayden Gallery, Massachusetts Institute of Technology, Cambridge, Massachusetts, September 28 through October 31, 1971. [Cambridge? Mass., MIT Committee on the Visual Arts, 1971] 1 v. (unpaged) illus. 22 x 23 cm. [ND212.S7] 73-30564
1. Leslie, Alfred, 1927- 2. Pearlstein, Philip, 1924- 3. Thiebaud, Wayne. 4. Human figure in art. I. Hayden Gallery. Committee on the Visual Arts. II. Massachusetts Institute of Technology. Committee on the Visual Arts. Contemporary Views of man. III. Title: Contemporary views of man.

Lesser, Robert—Art collections.

LESSER, Robert. 790.13'2
A celebration of comic art and memorabilia / Robert Lesser ; photos. by Stefan Congrat-Butlar. New York : Hawthorn Books, [1975] 292 p., [8] leaves of plates : ill. (some col.) ; 29 cm. Includes index. [NK808.L47 1975] 74-22928 ISBN 0-8015-1456-8 : 24.50

SUBJECT INDEX LETTERING.

1. Lesser, Robert—Art collections. 2. Comic art paraphernalia—Collectors and collecting. 3. Comic art paraphernalia—United States. I. Title.

Lessing, Carl Friedrich, 1808-1880.

CINCINNATI. Art Museum. 741.9'43
Drawings by Carl Friedrich Lessing, 1808-1880, in the collection of the Cincinnati Art Museum. [Cincinnati, 1972] 31 p. illus. 26 cm. Includes bibliographical references. [NC251.L46C5] 72-178319
1. Lessing, Carl Friedrich, 1808-1880.

Lester and Joan Avnet Collection.

FIGURES and faces; 19th 741.9'24
& 20th century European master drawings from the Lester and Joan Avnet Collection. Selected by William S. Lieberman. New York [1968] 1 v. (chiefly illus.) 23 cm. "Organized and circulated by the American Federation of Arts." [NC30.F5] 68-20084
1. Lester and Joan Avnet Collection. 2. Drawings, European—Exhibitions. I. Lieberman, William Slattery, 1924- II. American Federation of Arts.

Letchworth, Eng. First Garden City Limited, Letchworth, Eng.

PURDOM, Charles 711.4094258
Benjamin, 1883-
The Letchworth achievement. London, Dent. [New York, Hillary House, 1966, c.1963] viii, 150p. illus., maps, plans, ports. 19cm. [HT165.L5P83] 64-54952 3.00
1. Letchworth, Eng. First Garden City Limited, Letchworth, Eng. I. Title.

Letter-pictures.

DAMASE, Jacques 759.06
Revolution typographique depuis Stephane Mallarme. Geneve, Galerie Motte (1966) xxviii, 139p. illus. 27cm. Bibl. [ND1265.D25] 67-87972 12.50 pap.,
1. Letter-pictures. 2. Painting—Hist.—20th cent. I. Title.
American distributor: Hacker Art Bks., New York.

Lettering.

ANDERSON, Charles Roger 1928- 741
Lettering [by] Charles R. Anderson. With illus. by the author and Anita L. Anderson. New York, Van Nostrand Reinhold Co. [1969] 174 p. illus., facsims. 29 cm. Bibliography: p. 171. [NK3600.A67] 69-15894
1. Lettering.

BALLINGER, Raymond A, 1907- 745.6
Lettering art in modern use. New York, Reinhold Pub. Corp. [1952] 246 p. illus. 30 cm. [NK3620.B3] 52-10524
1. Lettering. 2. Alphabets. I. Title. BIP

BALLINGER, Raymond A., 745.6
1907-
Lettering art in modern use [by] Raymond A. Ballinger. Student ed. New York, Reinhold Pub. Corp. [1965] 96 p. illus. (part col.) 27 cm. Bibliography: p. 96. [NK3620.B3 1965] 65-13372
1. Lettering. I. Title.

BASTIEN, Alfred. 744.43
Lettering alphabets for draughtman, advertisement designers, architects, artists, and all craftsman in letters. 7th rev. ed. arr. in the new classification. West Drayton, Middlesex, Typographical Centre [1955] 344p. 25cm. [NK3600.B3 1955] 55-40262
1. Lettering. 2. Alphabets. I. Title.

BASTIEN, Alfred. 744.43
Lettering alphabets for draughtsmen, advertisement designers, architects, artists, and all craftsmen in letters. 5th rev. ed. West Drayton, Middlesex, Typographical Centre [1951] 187 p. 26 cm. [NK3600.B3 1951] 52-13277
1. Lettering. 2. Alphabets. I. Title.

BENSON, John Howard, 1901- 745.6
The elements of lettering, by John Howard Benson and Arthur Graham Carey. [2d ed.] New York, McGraw-Hill, 1950. x, 135 p. illus. 26 cm. Bibliography: p. 130-131. [NK3600.B4 1950] 50-7382
1. Lettering. I. Carey, Arthur Graham. joint author. II. Title. BIP

BIANCO, Yvonne, 745.6'1'0924
1930-1976.
Every dawn is first, Yvonne Bianco, 1930-1976 : [catalogue] / [edited by Callum MacColl]. [s.l. : s.n.], c1976 ([Portland?] : J. Y. Hollingsworth Co.) [32] p. : chiefly ill. (some col.) : 29 cm. Cover title: Yvonne. [NK3631.B47A45] 76-151852
1. Bianco, Yvonne, 1930-1976. 2. Lettering. I. Title. II. Title: Yvonne.

BIEGELEISEN, Jacob Israel, 745
1910-
The ABC of lettering. 2d ed. New York, Harper [c1958] 239p. illus. 24 x 34 cm. [NK3600.B5 1958] 57-13202
1. Lettering. I. Title. BIP

BIEGELEISEN, Jacob Israel, 745.6
1910-
The ABC of lettering [by] J. I. Biegeleisen. 3d ed. New York, Harper & Row [1965] xiii, 248 p. illus. 24 x 34 cm. [NK3600.B5 1965] 65-14683
1. Lettering. I. Title.

BIEGELEISEN, Jacob 745.6'1
Israel, 1910-
The ABC of lettering [by] J. I. Biegeleisen. 4th ed. New York, Harper & Row [1971] xiii, 266 p. illus. 24 x 34 cm. [NK3600.B5 1971] 70-141659 12.50
1. Lettering. I. Title.

BIEGELEISEN, Jacob 745.6'1
Israel, 1910-
The ABC of lettering / J. I. Biegeleisen. 5th ed. New York : Harper & Row, c1976. xvi, 255 p. : ill. ; 24 x 32 cm. [NK3600.B5 1976] 76-5165 ISBN 0-06-010329-9 : 15.00
1. Lettering. I. Title.

BIGGS, John R. 745.6
The craft of lettering. London, Blandford Pr. [New York, Pitman, 1962, c.1961] 64p. illus. 23cm. (Craft ser. 19) 62-53226 2.95 bds.,
1. Lettering. I. Title.

BIGGS, John R. 745.6
The craft of script [London] Blandford Pr. [Chapel Hill, Univ. of N. C., c.1964] 64p. illus. (pt. col.) 23cm. Bibl. 64-55873 2.95 bds.,
1. Lettering. I. Title.

BOLEY, Bill, 1915- 745.6
Bill Boley basiks of lettering. Cincinnati, Signs of the Times Pub. Co. [1952] 192 p. illus. 21 x 29 cm. [NK3620.B63] 52-67707
1. Lettering. I. Title.

BOSTOCK, James. 745.6
Roman lettering for students. London, New York, Studio Publications [1959] 96p. illus. 20cm. [NK3625.R65B6] 59-65232
1. Lettering. I. Title.

BRINKLEY, John, ed. 741.6
Lettering today, a survey and reference book. New York, Reinhold Pub. Corp. [1965, c1964] 143 p. illus. (part col.) 28 cm. [NK3620.B7 1965] 64-7681
1. Lettering. I. Title.

BUCKLEY, Robert D. 745.6
A basic guide to lettering. New York, Greenberg, 1951. 95 p. illus. 28 cm. [NK3600.B85] 51-13930
1. Lettering. 2. Alphabets. I. Title.

BURKE, Arthur Edward, 744.43
1909-
Architectural lettering for plans and ornamental design, by Arthur E. Burke with the collaboration of Truman C. Buss. Chicago, American Technical Society, 1953. 187p. illus. 28cm. [NA2725.B87] 53-446
1. Lettering. I. Title.

CATALDO, John W 745.6
Lettering; a guide for teachers. Worcester, Mass, Davis Publications [c1958] 80p. illus. (part col.) 21x29cm. Bibliography: p.80. [NK3600.C33] 58-13613
1. Lettering. I. Title. BIP

CATICH, Edward M. 745.6'197
The Trajan inscription; an essay, by Edward M. Catich, together with an original rubbing from the inscription. Boston, Society of Printers, 1973. 13 p. illus. 29 cm. "Two hundred and thirty copies ... printed." [NK3605.C35] 74-171005
1. Lettering. 2. Rome (City). Colonna Trajana. I. Society of Printers, Boston. II. Title.

CAVANAGH, John Albert, 745.6
1888-
Lettering and alphabets. New York, Dover Publications [1955, c1946] 121 p. illus. 21 x 26 cm. "Unabridged and unaltered republication of the work first published in 1946 under the title Lettering"; originally published in 1939 as A handbook on lettering. [NK3600] 56-3226
1. Lettering. BIP

DEGERING, Hermann, 1866- 745.61
1942.
Lettering; modes of writing in western Europe from antiquity to the end of the 18th century. New York, Universe Books [1965] xxxvii, 240 p. of illus., facsims. 30 cm. [NK3600.D4 1965] 65-24561
1. Lettering. 2. Writing. I. Title.

DOUGLASS, Ralph 745.6
Calligraphic lettering with wide pen & Bruch. [3d ed., completely rewritten and enl.] New York, Watson [c.1962] 72p. illus. 26cm. Bibl. 62-3990 4.50, bds., spiral bdg.
1. Lettering. I. Title.

DOUGLASS, Ralph. 745.6
Calligraphic lettering with wide pen & brush. New York, Watson-Guptill [1950] 56 p. illus. 26 cm. Bibliography: p. 53. [NK3600.D68] 50-5720
1. Lettering. I. Title.

DOUGLASS, Ralph. 741
Calligraphic lettering with wide pen & brush. 3d ed., rev. & enl. New York] Watson-Guptill Publications [1967] 111 p. illus. 27 cm. Bibliography: p. 65-66. [NK3600.D68 1967] 67-23532
1. Lettering. I. Title.

DURER, Albrecht, 1471-1528 745.6
Of the just shaping of letters. from the Applied geometry of Albrecht Durer, bk. 3 [Tr. from the Latin text of 1535. Gloucester. Mass., P. Smith. 1965] 40p. illus. 28cm. (Dover bk. T1305 rebound) Unabridged, unaltered repubn. of the work first pub. by the Grolier Club in 1917 [NK3615.D733] 3.50
1. Lettering. I. Title.

DURER, Albrecht, 1471-1528 745.6
Of the just shaping of letters, from the Applied geometry of Albrecht Durer, bk.3 [Tr. by R. T. Nichol from the Latin text of the ed. of 1935] New York, Dover [1965] 40p. illus. 28cm. (T1305) Unabridged, unaltered repubn. of work first pub. by Grolier Club in 1917 [NK3615.D733] 64-18848 1.25 pap.,
1. Lettering. I. Title.

DURER, Albrecht, 1471-1528. 411
Of the just shaping of letters, from the Applied geometry of Albrecht Durer, book III. [Translated by R. T. Nichol from the Latin text of the edition of 1935] New York, Dover Publications [1965] 40 p. illus. 28 cm. "Unabridged and unaltered republication of the work first published by the Grolier Club in 1917." [NK3615.D733] 64-18848
1. Lettering. I. Title.

FARRELL, Clayton J. 745.6'1
Pencil practice and layout, by Clayton J. Farrell and Jean Gallagher. [Ed. 1] Scranton, Pa., International Correspondence Schools [1969] 33, 7 p. illus. 23 cm. "Serial 6401-2." [NK3600.F3 1969] 79-22595
1. Lettering. I. Gallagher, Jean, joint author. II. Title.

FRENCH, Thomas Ewing, 744.43
1871-1944.
Lessons in lettering, a series of practice books with text, examples and exercises, by Thomas E. French and William D. Turnbull. 3d ed. [revised by A. J. Philby] New York, McGraw-Hill, '1950. v. illus. 16 x 23 cm. Cover title. [T371.F85 1950] 50-11057
1. Lettering. I. Turnbull, William Davis, 1883- joint author. II. Title.

GATES, David, 1927- 745.6'1
Lettering for reproduction. New York, Watson-Guptill Publications [1969] 191 p. illus. 29 cm. [NK3600.G3] 69-17878
1. Lettering. I. Title.

GILL, Eric, 1882- 686.2'24'0924
1940.
The letter forms and type designs of Eric Gill / notes by Robert Harling. [Westerham] : Eva Svensson, 1976. 64 p., [4] p. of plates (4 fold.) : ill. (some col.), facsims., port. ; 19 cm. "Notes ... first published in Alphabet & Image and now, rev. and expanded." [NK3631.G54H37 1976] 77-358363 ISBN 0-903696-05-3. ISBN 0-903696-04-5 pbk.
1. Gill, Eric, 1882-1940. 2. Lettering. 3. Type and type founding. I. Harling, Robert. II. Title. BIP

GILL, Eric, 1882- 686.2'24'0924
1940.
The letter forms and type designs of Eric Gill / notes by Robert Harling. 2d rev. ed. U.S. ed. [Westerham, Eng.] : E. Svensson ; Boston : D. R. Godine, 1978. 63 p., [2] fold. leaves of plates : ill. (some col.) ; 20 cm. "These notes were first published in Alphabet & image and now, revised and expanded." [NK3631.G54H37 1978] 76-24232 ISBN 0-87923-200-5 : 15.00 ISBN 0-87923-201-3 pbk. :7.50
1. Gill, Eric, 1882-1940. 2. Lettering. 3. Type and type founding. I. Harling, Robert. II. Title.

GORDON, Maggie. 745.6'1
Alphabets and images : inspiration from letterforms / Maggie Gordon. New York : Scribner, [1975] c1974. 96 p. : chiefly ill. ; 21 cm. [NK3600.G63 1975] 74-7805 ISBN 0-684-14083-7 : 7.95
1. Lettering. 2. Letters in art. I. Title.

GRAY, Milner 745.6
Lettering for architects and designers [by] Milner Gray, Ronald Armstrong. New York, Reinhold [c.1962] 160p. illus. 26cm. 62-9163 12.75
1. Lettering. 2. Architectural inscriptions. 3. Signs and signboards. I. Armstrong, Ronald, joint author. II. Title.

GRAY, Nicolete, 1911- 741
Lettering as drawing: contour and silhouette. London, New York, Oxford University Press, 1970. 88 p. illus. 21 cm. (Oxford paperbacks, handbooks for artists, 7) Includes bibliographical references. [NK3600.G82] 70-514584 15/-
1. Lettering. I. Title.

GREER, Alan. 745.6'1
An introduction to lettering / Alan & Rita Greer. New York : Penguin Books, [1978, c1972] p. cm. Includes bibliographical references. [NK3600.G86 1978] 77-16285 ISBN 0-14-046329-1 pbk. : 3.50
1. Lettering. I. Greer, Rita, joint author. II. Title. BIP

GREER, Alan. 745.6'1
An introduction to lettering [by] Alan & Rita Greer. New York, Viking Press [1973, c1972] 121 p. illus. 17 x 22 cm. (A Studio book) $5.95 Includes bibliographical references. [NK3600.G86 1973] 72-81674 ISBN 0-670-40064-5
1. Lettering. I. Greer, Rita, joint author. II. Title.

HAAB, Armin. 745.6
Lettera; a standard book of fine lettering. New York Hastings 1960- v. 24cm. Introd. in English, German & French [MK3600.H2] 60-50012 11.95
1. Lettering. 2. Alphabets. I. Title. BIP

HAAB, Armin 745.6
Lettera; a standard book of fine lettering. Standard-buch guter Gebrauchsschrifen. Recueil de lettres et caracteres. [By] Armin Haab [and] Alex Stocker. [3d ed.] New York, Hastings House [1960, 1954] 128p. 25cm. (Visual communication books) 60-50012 8.50 bds.,
1. Lettering. 2. Alphabets. I. Stocker, Alex, joint author. II. Title.

HAAB, Armin 745.6
Lettera 2; a standard book of fine lettering. Standard-buch guter Gebrauchsschriften. Recueil de lettres et caracteres. [By] Armin

Haab, Walter Haettenschweiler. New York, Hastings House [c.1961] 128p. (Visual communication bks.) 9.50
1. Lettering. 2. Alphabets. I. Title.

HOLME, Rathbone, ed. 745.6
Modern lettering and calligraphy; a sequel to Lettering of today, edited by Rathbone Holme & Kathleen M. Frost. London, New York, Studio Publications [1954] 144 p. illus. 30 cm. [NK3620.H66] 54-2354
1. Lettering. I. Frost, Kathleen M., joint ed. II. Title.

HOLUB, Rand, 1905- 745.6
Lettering simplified, a manual for beginners. New York, Watson-Guptill Publications [1957] 63 p. illus. 26 cm. [NK3600.H632] 57-12739
1. Lettering.

HOLUB, Rand, 1905- 745.6
Scripts. [1st ed.] New York [Watson-Guptill] 1950. 59 p. illus. 20 x 27 cm. (Library of lettering) [NK3600.H633] 50-12671
1. Lettering. I. Title.

HORN, Frederick A., ed. 745.6
Lettering at work; a reference book of modern lettering for the building of business and promotion of sales. London, New York, Studio Publications [1955] 128 p. illus. 30 cm. [NK3620.H68] 55-14838
1. Lettering. I. Title.

HORNUNG, Clarence Pearson. 745.6
Lettering from A to Z. With an introd. by Frederic W. Goudy, and a foreword by Louis Grudin. New York, Wm. Penn Pub. Corp. [c1954] xx, 153p. illus., typog. specimens. 29cm. [NK3600.H65 1954] 61-4159
1. Lettering. 2. Alphabets. I. Title.

LAKER, Russell 745.61
Anatomy of lettering. [Rev. ed.] New York, Viking [1966. c.1965] 96p. illus. 26cm. (Studio bk.) [NK3620.L3] 66-1131 6.95 bds.,
1. Lettering 2. Alphabets. I. Title.

LAKER, Russell. 745.6
Anatomy of lettering. [2d ed.] London, New York, Studio Publications [1960] 94 p. illus. 25 cm. (How to do it series. New ed.) [NK3620.L3 1960] 60-2292
1. Lettering. 2. Alphabets. I. Title.

LARCHER, Jean, 1947- 760'.092'4
Propositions pour une typographie nouvelle = About typography, for a new one = Proposiciones para una tipografia nueva / Jean Larcher. Paris (13, Av. Theophile-Gautier, 75016) : la Noria, 1976. 63 p. : ill. ; 22 x 27 cm. On spine: Ecritures. English, French, and Spanish. [NK3631.L37A534] 77-454017 ISBN 2-85721-005-1 : 30.00F
1. Lettering. 2. Graphic arts. I. Title. II. Title: About typography, for a new one. III. Title: Proposiciones para una tipografia nueva. IV. Title: Ecritures.

LEACH, Mortimer. 745.6
Lettering for advertising. New York, Reinhold Pub. Corp. [c1956] xi, 227p. illus. (part col.) port. 31cm. [NK3630.L4] 56-10596
1. Lettering. I. Title.

LEACH, Mortimer. 745.6
Lettering for advertising. New York, Van Nostrand Reinhold [1975, c1956] xi, 227 p. illus. 29 cm. [NK3630L4] 56-10596 ISBN 0-442-24718-4 8.95 (pbk.)
1. Lettering. I. Title.

LEHNER, Ernest, 1895- 745.6
Alphabets & ornaments [Magnolia, Mass., Peter Smith, 1968,c.1952] 256p. (chiefly illus., facsims.) 29cm. (Rebound) ed. of the unabridged repubn. by Dover of the work orig. pub. in 1952 Bibl. [NK3600.L36 1968] 6.00
1. Lettering. 2. Alphabets. 3. Decoration and ornament. I. Title. BIP

LEHNER, Ernst, 1895- 745.6
Alphabets & ornaments. [1st ed.] Cleveland, World Pub. Co. [1952] 256 p. (chiefly illus., part col.) 32 cm. Bibliography: p. 247-256. [NK3600.L36] 52-5177
1. Lettering. 2. Alphabets. 3. Decoration and ornament. I. Title.

LEHNER, Ernst, 1895- 745.6
Alphabets & ornaments. New York, Dover Publications [1968, c1952] 256 p. (chiefly illus., facsims.) 29 cm. "An unabridged republication of the work originally published ... 1952." Bibliography: p. 247-256. [NK3600.L36 1968] 68-19170
1. Lettering. 2. Alphabets. 3. Decoration and ornament. I. Title.

LESIAK, Michaeline 745.61
The art of fine lettering: basic skills and techniques. Notre Dame [Ind.] Univ. of Notre Dame Pr. [c.1965] 286p. illus. 27cm. Bibl. [NK3620.L47] 65-23520 6.95
1. Lettering. I. Title. BIP

LETTERA. 745.6
A standard book of fine lettering. Standardbuch guter Gebranchsschriften. Recucil de letters et caracteres. [1]- New York, Hastings House [19 v. 21cm. (Visual communication books) No. 1 issued in rev. editions. Prepared by A. Haab (with A. Stocker, 19 W. Harttenschweiler, 19 [NK3600.L43] 60-50012
1. Lettering. 2. Alphabets. I. Haab, Armin.

MACDONALD, Byron J. 745.61
The art of lettering with the broad pen [by] Byron J. Macdonald. New York, Reinhold Pub. Corp. [1966] 63 p. illus. (part col.) 19 x 26 cm. Title on spine: The broad pen. [NK3625.B7M3] 66-24555
1. Lettering. I. Title. II. Title: The broad pen.

MATTHEWS, Eric Christian, 1892- 741.67
Florida signtific advertising. St. Louis, New Era Studio [1956] 125p. illus. 23cm. [TT360.M28] 56-33193
1. Lettering. 2. Sign painting. 3. Advertising cards. I. Title.

MATTHEWS, Eric Christian, 1892- 741.67
Modern signs and show cards. St. Louis, New Era Studio, c1951. 76 p. illus. 29 cm. [NK3620.M36] 51-4711
1. Lettering. 2. Alphabets. 3. Commercial art. I. Title.

MEIJER, M 745.6
Script lettering. [New York] Pitman Pub. Corp., 1956. 54p. illus. 28cm. [NK3630.M4] 57-2476
1. Lettering. I. Title.

MITCHELL, Frederick James, 1902- 745.6
Practical lettering and layout, an approach to good construction and design. 22 full-page illus. by the author. 2d ed. [rev., re-set] London, A. & C. Black [dist. Chester Springs, Pa., Dufour, 1964] 44p. illus. 24cm. [NK3620.M5] 65-342 2.95 bds.,
I. Title. BIP

NESBITT, Alexander, 1901- 745.6
The history and technique of lettering. [New Dover ed.] New York, Dover Publications [1957] 300p. illus. 24cm. First published in 1950 under title: Lettering: the history and technique of lettering as design. Includes bibliography. [NK3600.N4 1957] 57-13116
1. Lettering. I. Title. BIP

NESBITT, Alexander, 1901- 745.6
Lettering; the history and technique of lettering as design. [1st ed.] New York, Prentice-Hall [1950] xvii, 300 p. illus. 28 cm. Bibliography: p. 288-293. [NK3600.N4] 50-13108
1. Lettering. I. Title.

PEN and brush lettering and practical alphabets. 744.43 [New York] Pitman Pub. Corp. [1956] 62p. 25cm. [NK3630.P4] 57-3083
1. Lettering. 2. Alphabets.

PHOTO-LETTERING, inc., New York. 745.6
Alphabet thesaurus; a treasury of letter designs. New York, Reinhold Pub. Corp. [1960- v. illus. 32 cm. Edited by Edward Rondthaler and the staff of Photo-lettering, inc. Design [by] Edward Benguiat, Victor Caruso [and] Wilford Griffin. [NK3630.P5] 60-10826
1. Lettering. I. Rondthaler, Edward, ed. II. Title.

PHOTO-LETTERING, inc., New York. 745.6'1
Alphabet thesaurus. Edited by Edward Rondthaler and the staff of Photo-lettering, inc. Collaborators: Charles Carnival [and others] New York, Van Nostrand Reinhold Pub. Co. [1971- v. illus. 32 cm. "Reference edition." [NK3630.P512] 71-31759 15.00 (v. 3)
1. Lettering. I. Rondthaler, Edward, ed. II. Title.

PHOTO-LETTERING, inc., New York. 745.6
Alphabet thesaurus nine thousand Professional ed. New York, c1960. 740p. illus. 32cm. Issued also as Reference ed. under title: Alphabet thesaurus. [NK3630.P52] 60-26610
1. Lettering. I. Title.

RICHARDSON, H Wilmont. 745.6
Freehand lettering. New York, Sterling Pub. Co. [1960] 112p. illus. 29cm. [NK3600.R5] 60-10379
1. Lettering. I. Title.

RIGAST, Adolph K 744.43
Single stroke draft lettering; a greded series of lessons with explanatory text, lettering models, and exercises. Milwaukee, Bruce Pub. Co. [1954] 96p. illus. 15x24cm. [NK3620.R5] 54-7785
1. Lettering. I. Title.

SCHWANDNER, Johann Georg von, 1716-1791. 745.6
Calligraphy; Calligraphia Latina. New York, Dover Publications [1958] xiv p., facsim.: 14 p. plates. 34 cm. "An unabridged republication of Calligraphia Latina published in 1756 with the introduction translated into English for the first time by E. F. Bleiber." Original t. p. reads: Joannis Georgii Schwandneri, Austriaci stadelkirchensis. Dissertatio epistolaris de calligraphiae: nomenclatione, cultu, prastantia, utilitate. Vienna Austria, Ex typographeo Kaliwodiano, A. O. R. M.DCC.LVI. Bibliographical references included in "Footnotes" (p. xiii-xiv) [NK3615.S3 1756a] 58-4948
1. Lettering. 2. Alphabets. 3. Penmanship. I. Title: Calligraphia Latina. II. Title: Dissertatio epistolaris de calligraphiae.

SHAHN, Ben, 1898- 745.6
Love and joy about letters. New York, Grossman Publishers, 1963. 79 p. illus. (part col.) facsims. 26 x 35 cm. Half title: About letters and lettering. [NK3600.S528] 63-22225
1. Lettering. I. Title.

SHAW, Robert, 1908- 745.6
Practical lettering; a self-instruction guide for beginners and professionals in the commercial and applied arts. New York, Wm. Penn Pub. Corp. [1956, 1955] 96 p. illus. 29 cm. [NK3600.S53] 55-12012
1. Lettering. 2. Alphabets. I. Title. BIP

SHAW, Robert, 1908- 745.6
Practical lettering; a self-instruction guide for beginners and professionals in the commercial and applied arts. New York, Wm. Penn Pub. Corp. [1956, c1955] 96 p. illus. 29 cm. [NK3600.S53] 55-12012
1. Lettering. 2. Alphabets. I. Title.

STUART, A. F. 745.6'197
Lettering for brush and pen / by A. F. Stuart & Quentin Crisp. 4th ed. London : F. Warne, 1976. 47 p., plate : ill. ; 23 cm. [NK3600.S85 1976] 77-361078 ISBN 0-7232-1880-3 : £1.50
1. Lettering. I. Crisp, Quentin, joint author. II. Title.

SWITKIN, Abraham. 745.6'1
Hand lettering today / Abraham Switkin. 1st ed. New York : Harper & Row, c1976. xi, 212 p. : ill. ; 28 cm. [NK3600.S98 1976] 75-25067 ISBN 0-06-014204-9 : 12.50
1. Lettering. I. Title. BIP

THOMPSON, Samuel Winfield, 1906- 745.6
The script letter: its form, construction, and application, by Tommy Thompson. [Rev. ed.] London, New York, Studio Publications [1955] 128p. illus. 26cm. (The How to do it series, no. 21) [NK3600.T5 1955] 55-3822
1. Lettering. 2. Alphabets. I. Title. BIP

WADE, Cecil, 1896- 745.6
Modern lettering and layout. New York, Pitman Pub. Corp. [1950] x, 155 p. illus. 26 cm. [NK3600.W29] 51-2217
1. Lettering. 2. Alphabets. I. Title.

WEEKS, Edward M. 1866- 745.6
Letters analyzed and spaced. Text in collaboration with Esther A. Richards, plates by Edward M. Weeks. [1st ed.] New York, Exposition Press [1952] 109 p. illus. 15 x 23 cm. [T371.W37] 51-12349
1. Lettering. I. Title.

WELO, Samuel. 745.6
Studio handbook: lettering. Over 250 pages lettering, design and layouts, new alphabets. [Rev. ed.] Chicago, F.J. Drake [1960] 282 p. illus. 19 cm. Cover title: Studio handbook: letter and design for artists and advertisers. [NK3620.W4 1960] 60-16189
1. Lettering. 2. Alphabets. I. Title.

WOTZKOW, Helm. 745.6/1
The art of hand-lettering, its mastery and practice [Magnolia, Mass., P. Smith, 1968] x, 320p. illus. 22cm. (Dover bk. rebound) Unabridged, unaltered repubn. of the work orig. pub. in 1952 [NK3620.W68 1967]
1. Lettering. 2. Alphabets. I. Title. BIP

WOTZKOW, Helm, 1898- 745.6
The art of hand- lettering, its mastery & practice. [1st ed.] New York, Watson-Guptill Publications [1952] 320p. illus. 24cm. (Watson-Guptill library of type and lettering) [NK3620.W68] 53-275
1. Lettering. 2. Alphabets. I. Title.

WOTZKOW, Helm, 1898- 745.6'1
The art of hand-lettering, its mastery & practice. New York, Dover Publications [1967, c1952] xv, 320 p. illus. 22 cm. "Unabridged and unaltered republication of the work originally published in 1952." [NK3620.W68 1967] 67-18095
1. Lettering. 2. Alphabets. I. Title.

WRIGHT, Harry Bernard, 1896- 745.6
Lettering; sixty plates in a variety of alphabets. New York, Pitman Pub. Corp. [1950] [64] p. 20 x 26 cm. [NK3600.W7] 50-10424
1. Lettering. 2. Alphabets. I. Title.

WRIGHT, Harry Bernard, 1896- 745.6
Lettering; in a variety of alphabets. New York, Pitman Pub. Corp. [1957] 59 p. 20 x 26 cm. (Pitman drawing series) [NK3600.W7 1957] 57-9371
1. Lettering. 2. Alphabets. I. Title.

Lettering—Bibliography.

BRANSTATOR, Robin. 016.7456
A bibliography of lettering. [Ypsilanti, Eastern Michigan University Library] 1971. 11 l. 29 cm. ([Eastern Michigan University. Library] Bibliography series, no. 13) [Z5956.L45B7] 72-610233
1. Lettering—Bibliography. I. Title. II. Series.

Lettering—History.

GRAY, Nicolete, 1911- 745.6'1'09
Lettering as drawing. London, New York, Oxford University Press, 1971. [8], 193 p. illus., facsims. 25 cm. The two parts of this book were originally published separately in 1970 under titles: Lettering as drawing: the moving line; and Lettering as drawing: contour and silhouette. Includes bibliographical references. [NK3600.G819] 72-190951 ISBN 0-19-211437-9 £6.50
1. Lettering—History. I. Title. BIP

*MANN, William. 745.6'1'09
Lettering and lettering display. New York, Van Nostrand Reinhold [1974] 96 p. illus. (part col.) 19 x 26 cm. [NK3630] 73-18921 ISBN 0-442-30040-9 7.95
1. Lettering—History. I. Title. BIP

Lettering—Juvenile literature.

GOURDIE, Tom 745.6
The Puffin book of lettering. [Baltimore, Penguin, 1962, c.1961] 31p. illus. 18x23cm. (Puffin picture bk. 117) 62-2375 .65 pap.,

1. Lettering—Juvenile literature. I. Title.

GOURDIE, Tom.   745.6
The Puffin book of lettering. [Baltimore, Penguin Books, 1975 c1961] 31 p. ill. 18 cm. by 22 cm. (Puffin picture book) [NK3600.G62Pu2] ISBN 0-14-049117-1 1.95 (pbk.)
1. Lettering—Juvenile literature. I. Title.
L.C. card no. for original edition: 62-2375.

HART, Norman Antony,   745.6 (j)
1925-
The young letterer; a how-it-is-done book of lettering, by Tony Hart. New York, F. Warne [1966, c1965] 63 p. illus. (part col.) 29 cm. [NK3620:H3] 66-13792
1. Lettering—Juvenile literature. I. Title.

Letters in art.

LEYMARIE, Jean.   754
The spirit of the letter in painting. Translated from the French by James Emmons. [Kansas City? Mo.] Hallmark Cards [1961] 90 p. mounted col. illus. 29 cm. [N8219.L4L43] 61-17379
1. Letters in art. 2. Paintings. I. Title.

Leutze, Emanuel, 1816-1868.

HUTTON, Ann (Hawkes)   759.13
Portrait of patriotism: Washington crossing the Delaware. [1st ed.] Philadelphia, Chilton Co. [1959] 190p. illus. 22cm. Includes bibliography. [ND237.L6H8] 59-13779
1. Leutze, Emanuel, 1816-1868. 2. Washington, George, Pres. U. S.—Portraits. 3. Trenton, Battle of, 1776. I. Title.

STEHLE, Raymond L.   759.13
The life and works of Emanuel Leutze, by Raymond L. Stehle. [Washington] 1972. 161, 124 l. 30 cm. "Annotated list of the works of Emanuel Leutze": 124 leaves at end. [ND237.L6S73] 72-194995
1. Leutze, Emanuel, 1816-1868. I. Title.

LeVan, Susan, 1947—

LEVAN, Susan, 1947—   741.9'73
Vegetable parade / Susan LeVan. Ann Arbor : Street Fiction Press, c1977. p. cm. [NC139.L466A56] 77-8078 ISBN 0-914908-90-1 pbk. : 4.95
1. LeVan, Susan, 1947- I. Title.   BIP

Levant—Description and travel.

SEDDON, Thomas, 1821-   759.2 B
1856.
Memoir and letters of the late Thomas Seddon, artist. By his brother, John P. Seddon London, J. Nisbet, 1858. [New York, AMS Press, 1972] vi, 208 p. illus. 19 cm. [ND497.S42S4 1972] 72-148300 ISBN 0-404-05668-7 10.00
1. Levant—Description and travel. 2. Painters, British—Correspondence, reminiscences, etc. I. Seddon, John Pollard, 1827-1906, ed.

Levi Strauss and Company—Art collections.

SAN Francisco. Museum of   709'.73
Art.
The Levi Strauss Collection. [San Francisco, c1974] [16] p. (chiefly illus.) 18 x 23 cm. Catalog of an exhibition held Mar. 15-Apr. 14, 1974. [N6487.S2S257 1974] 74-75999
1. Levi Strauss and Company—Art collections. 2. Art, American—Exhibitions. 3. Art, Modern—20th century—United States. I. Title.

Levine, David, 1926—

LEVINE, David, 1926-   741.5'973
The arts of David Levine / by David Levine ; foreword by Thomas S. Buechner. New York : Knopf, [1978] p. cm. Includes index. [NC1429.L47A4 1978] 78-16309 ISBN 0-394-50265-5 : 25.00
1. Levine, David, 1926- I. Title.   BIP

Levy, Benjamin, 1786-1860.

KORN, Bertram   655.1763355
Wallace.
Benjamin Levy: New Orleans printer and publisher, with a bibliography of Benjamin Levy imprints, 1817-1841. Portland, Me., Anthoensen Press, 1961. 78p. port., facsims. 24cm. 'Reprinted, in an edition of three hundred numbered copies, from The papers of the Bibliographical Society of America (copyright 1960)...Number 40.' Bibliographical footnotes. [Z232.L66K6] 61-11265
1. Levy, Benjamin, 1786-1860. 2. Printing—Hist.—New Orleans. I. Title.

Levy, Julien.

LEVY, Julien.   706'.5 B
Memoir of an art gallery / by Julien Levy. New York : Putnam, c1977. 320 p., [18] leaves of plates : ill. ; 22 cm. Includes index. [N8660.L47A53 1977] 76-24793 8.95
1. Levy, Julien. 2. Art dealers—United States—Correspondence, reminiscences, etc. I. Title.   BIP

Lewis and Clark Expedition.

MUENCH, David.   779'.9'91780420922
Lewis and Clark : voyages of discovery / photography by David Muench ; text by Dan Murphy ; edited by Gweneth DenDooven. Las Vegas, Nev. : KC Publications, c1977. [64] p. : col. ill. ; 31 cm. Includes reproductions of photo-murals which are on permanent display at the Museum of Westward Expansion in St. Louis. [F592.7.M8] 76-57451 7.95 ISBN 0-916122-50-6 pbk. : 3.95
1. Lewis and Clark Expedition. 2. Lewis, Meriwether, 1774-1809. 3. Clark, William, 1770-1838. 4. The West—Description and travel—1951-—Views. I. Murphy, Dan. II. Museum of Westward Expansion. III. Title.

Lewis, Lucy M.—Exhibitions.

A Tribute to Lucy M.   738.3'7
Lewis, Acoma potter / commentary by John E. Collins ; foreword by Frederick J. Dockstader. Fullerton, Calif. : Museum of North Orange County, c1975. 75 p. : ill. (some col.) ; 27 cm. "This catalog was published in conjunction with the Lucy M. Lewis show, September 27-November 30, 1975." Bibliography: p. 73. [E99.A16T75] 75-26373
1. Lewis, Lucy M.—Exhibitions. 2. Acoma Indians—Pottery—Exhibitions. 3. Pueblo Indians—Pottery—Exhibitions. 4. Indians of North America—Southwest, New—Pottery—Exhibitions. I. Lewis, Lucy M. II. Collins, John E. III. Museum of North Orange County.

Lewis, Martin, 1881-1962.

KENNEDY Galleries,   769'.92'4
inc., New York.
Martin Lewis: the graphic work; a catalogue raisonne of the artist's prints published in conjunction with a retrospective exhibition of the artist's work at Kennedy Galleries, April 11-28, 1973. New York [1973] [24] p. illus. 23 cm. Bibliography: p. [24] [NE2012.L48K46] 73-164580
1. Lewis, Martin, 1881-1962. I. Lewis, Martin, 1881-1962.

LEWIS, Martin.   759.13
Martin Lewis; retrospective exhibition: April 11-28, 1973, Kennedy Galleries, New York. [Catalogue. New York, Kennedy Galleries, 1973] 24 p. illus. (part col.) 28 cm. [ND237.L623K46] 74-173461
1. Lewis, Martin. I. Kennedy Galleries, inc., New York.

Lewis, Sydney—Art collections.

DELAWARE Art Museum.   759.13
Contemporary American paintings from the Lewis Collection : [exhibition] Delaware Art Museum, September 13-October 27, 1974. Wilmington, Del. : The Museum, [1974] 44 p. : ill. (some col.) ; 21 cm. [ND212.D44 1974] 74-193211
1. Lewis, Sydney—Art collections. 2.

Paintings, American—Exhibitions. 3. Painting, Modern—20th century—United States. I. Title.

Lewis, Wyndham, 1882-1957.

MICHEL, Walter, 1922-   759.2
Wyndham Lewis: paintings and drawings [by] Walter Michel. With an introductory essay by Hugh Kenner. Berkeley, University of California Press, 1971. 455 p. illus., col. plates, port. 29 cm. Bibliography: p. 453-454. [ND497.L72M5 1971b] 69-11616 ISBN 0-520-01612-2 35.00
1. Lewis, Wyndham, 1882-1957. I. Lewis, Wyndham, 1882-1957.

Lewisohn, Sam Adolph, 1884-

NEW York. Metropolitan   708.147
Museum of Art.
The Lewisohn collection; a catalogue of the paintings, water colors and drawings, prints, and sculpture shown in a special exhibition, November 2 -- December 2, 1951, before the dispersal of bequests to various museums and galleries. New York [1951] 86 p. illus. 19 x 26 cm. [N5020.N432] 52-1035
1. Lewisohn, Sam Adolph, 1884- 2. Art — Exhibitions. I. Title.

Lewitt, Jan, 1907-

LEWITT, Jan, 1907-   759.2
Jan Le Witt; a selection of poems and aphorisms from the artist's notebooks; [with essays] by Sir Herbert Read, Jean Cassou [and] John Smith. Pref. by Pierre Emmanuel. New York, Library Press [1972, c1971] 172 p. illus. 31 cm. Bibliography: p. 171. [ND497.L73R4 1972] 70-173633 ISBN 0-912050-17-9
1. Lewitt, Jan, 1907- I. Read, Herbert Edward, Sir, 1893-1968. II. Cassou, Jean, 1897- III. Smith, John, 1924-

Lewitt, Sol, 1928—

LEWITT, Sol, 1928-   745.4
Arcs, from corners & sides, circles, & grids and all their combinations. [Berne] Kunsthalle Bern & Paul Bianchini, 1972. [208] p. illus. 21 cm. Label mounted on t.p.: "American distributor: Wittenborn and Company, 1018 Madison Ave., New York, N.Y., 10021." [NK1570.L48] 73-160742
1. Lewitt, Sol, 1928- 2. Geometrical drawing. I. Bern. Kunsthalle. II. Title.

Lexington, Mass.—Description—Views.

CHAMBERLAIN, Samuel,   917.44'4
1895-
Lexington and Concord in color. With an introductory text and notes on the illus. by Stewart Beach. A collection of color photos. by Samuel Chamberlain. New York, Hastings House [1970] 94 p. col. illus. 25 cm. (Profiles of America) [F74.L67C52 1970] 78-119796 ISBN 8-03-842694- 4.95
1. Lexington, Mass.—Description—Views. 2. Concord, Mass.—Description—Views. I. Beach, Stewart, 1899- II. Title.

Lexington, Va.—Monuments—Exhibitions.

WASHINGTON   730'.973'0740155852
and Lee University, Lexington, Va.
American sculpture in Lexington : selected examples from public collections : an exhibition / presented by Washington and Lee University, January 4-21, 1977. Lexington : The University, c1977. 47 p. : ill. ; 28 cm. Bibliography: p. 47. [F234.L5W37 1977] 77-356183
1. Washington, George, Pres. U.S., 1732-1799—Monuments, etc.—Exhibitions. 2. Lee, Robert Edward, 1807-1870—Monuments, etc.—Exhibitions. 3. Jackson, Thomas Jonathan, 1824-1863—Monuments, etc.—Exhibitions. 4. Lexington, Va.—Monuments—Exhibitions. 5. Portrait sculpture—United States—Exhibitions. I. Title.

Leyendecker, J. C., 1874-1951.

LEYENDECKER, J. C.,   741.9'73
1874-1951.
J. C. Leyendecker, by Michael Schau. New York, Watson-Guptill Publications [1974] 207 p. illus. 29 cm. [NC975.5.L4S32] 74-7125 ISBN 0-8230-2757-0 27.50
1. Leyendecker, J. C., 1874-1951. I. Schau, Michael, 1945-

LEYENDECKER, J. C.,   741.9'73
1874-1951.
The J. C. Leyendecker Poster book / with an introd. by Norman Rockwell. New York : Watson-Guptill Publications, 1975. [47] p. : chiefly col. ill. ; 41 cm. [NC1850.L45R62 1975] 74-25889 ISBN 0-8230-2758-9 pbk. : 6.95
1. Leyendecker, J. C., 1874-1951. I. Rockwell, Norman, 1894- II. Title.

Li, Ti, 12th cent.

EDWARDS, Richard, 1916-   759.951
Li Ti. Washington, Smithsonian Institution, 1967. xii, 50 p. 33 plates. 24 cm. (Freer Gallery of Art. Occasional papers, v. 3, no. 3) Smithsonian Institution. Publication 4679. Bibliographical footnotes. [ND1049.L717E3] 68-60135
1. Li, Ti, 12th cent. I. Title. II. Series: Freer Gallery of Art, Washington, D.C. Occasional papers, v. 3, no. 3   BIP

Liardet, Wilbraham Frederick Evelyn, 1799-1878.

LIARDET, Wilbraham   759.994
Frederick Evelyn, 1799-1878.
Liardet's water-colours of early Melbourne. Introduction and captions by Susan Adams, edited by Weston Bate. Carlton, Vic., Melbourne University Press on behalf of the Library Council of Victoria, [1972, i.e. 1973] xi, 101 p. illus., maps, col. plates. 24 x 31 cm. Bibliography: p. 99-101. [ND1942.L46A65] 73-165144 25.00
1. Liardet, Wilbraham Frederick Evelyn, 1799-1878. 2. Melbourne—Description—Views. I. Adams, Susan. II. Bate, Weston Arthur, ed. III. Library Council of Victoria. IV. Title.
Distributed by International Scholarly Book Service.   BIP

The Libbey Glass Co.

KEEFE, John Webster.   748.2'913
Libby glass a tradition of 150 years, 1818-1968 [Toledo, Ohio] Toledo Museum of Art [1968] 69 p. illus. 22 cm. Catalog of an exhibition in honor of the 150th anniversary of Libbey glass, presented by the Toledo Museum of Art and Owens-Illinois, inc., and held at the Toledo Museum of Art. Bibliography: p. 69. [NK5112.K4] 68-23391
1. The Libbey Glass Co. 2. Glassware, American—Exhibitions. I. Toledo. Museum of Art. II. Owens-Illinois, inc. III. Title.

Liberia.

STEGMULLER, Camille   966.6'203
Mirepoix.
Liberia in pictures. New York, Sterling Pub. Co. [1971] 64 p. illus., ports. 27 cm. (Visual geography series) Describes the land, climate, history, government, economy, culture, and people of the west African country settled by freed American slaves. [DT624.S68 1971] 73-151709 ISBN 0-8069-1140-9
1. Liberia. I. Title.

Liberia—Social life and customs—Pictorial works.

OWEN, Harrison,   916.6'6'0300222
1936-
When the devil dances. [Los Angeles, Mara Books, 1970] [78] p. illus., port. 29 cm. "Photographic essay." [DT629.O9] 79-134889 ISBN 0-87787-003-9
1. Liberia—Social life and customs—Pictorial works. I. Title.   BIP

Libraries, Special.

JOHNS, Ada Winifred. 026
Special libraries: development of the concept, their organizations, and their services. Metuchen, N.J., Scarecrow Press, 1968. 245 p. 23 cm. Includes bibliographies. [Z675.A2J57] 68-12628
1. Libraries, Special. 2. Engineering libraries.

LEWIS, Chester M., ed. 026
Special libraries: how to plan and equip them. A project of the New York Chapter. [New York] Special Libraries Association, 1963. vi, 117 p. illus. 28 cm. (SLA monograph no. 2) Bibliography: p. 92-102. [Z675.A2L4] 63-18560
1. Libraries, Special. 2. Library architecture. 3. Library fittings and supplies. I. Special Libraries Association. New York Chapter. II. Title. III. Series: Special Libraries Association. Monograph no. 2

Library architecture.

AMERICAN Library Association. Buildings Committee. 022.3
Planning a library building: the major steps; proceedings of the institute sponsored by the American Library Association Buildings Committee at St. Paul, Minnesota, June 19-20, 1954. Hoyt R. Galvin, editor; Kathryn A. Devereaux, assistant editor. Chicago, American Library Association, 1955. 80 p. illus. 28 cm. [Z679.A517 1954] 55-8852
1. Library architecture. I. Galvin, Hoyt Rees, 1911- ed. II. Title.

AMERICAN Library Association. Committee on Library Architecture and Building Planning. 022.314
Buildings for small public libraries, remodeled and adapted, including new designs for branches, prepared for the A. L. A. Committee on Library Architecture and Building Planning by Ernest I. Miller, chairman. Chicago, 1950. 39 p. illus., plans. 28 cm. "Bibliography [by] Helen T. Geer": p. 37-38. [Z679.A52] 50-7478
1. Library architecture. I. Miller, Ernest I.

BAUMANN, Charles H., 1924- 727'.8
The influence of Angus Snead MacDonald and the Snead bookstack on library architecture, by Charles H. Baumann. Metuchen, N.J., Scarecrow Press, 1972. 307 p. illus. 22 cm. A revision of the author's thesis, University of Illinois. Bibliography: p. 285-304. [Z679.B3 1972] 74-171928 ISBN 0-8108-0390-9
1. MacDonald, Angus Snead, 1883-1961. 2. Library architecture. 3. Shelving (for books) 4. Modular coordination (Architecture) I. Title. BIP

BRAWNE, Michael. 727'.8
Libraries: architecture and equipment. [Translated into German by Antje Pehnt] New York, Praeger Publishers [1970] 187 p. illus., plans. 29 cm. English and German. Bibliography: p. 184. [Z679.B83] 73-89609 21.50
1. Library architecture. 2. Library fittings and supplies. I. Title.

COBURN, Morton, 1921- comp. 027.7418'35
A survey of seven recently constructed public library buildings in the United States and Canada. Edmonton, Alta., 1963. 93 p. illus., plans. 29 cm. Bibliography: p. 2. [Z679.C69] 66-40085
1. Library architecture. I. Title.

DOBRAS, Darryl. 727'.8
Research report: a library program outline, by Darryl Dobras [and] Randy Emerson. [Tucson? Ariz.] c1972. 29 p. illus. 22 x 28 cm. [Z679.D62] 73-168155
1. Library architecture. I. Emerson, Randy, joint author. II. Title.

EASTLICK, John T 027.7418'35
The librarian's greatest challenge. [Albany] University of the State of New York, New York State Education Dept., New York State Library, Library Extension [1962] iv. 23 p. 22 cm. Cover title: A library building program. "Based on a speech given as part of the Building Committee's program at the New York Library Association's Annual Conference in October, 1961 at The Laurels, Monticello, New York." "The building program of the East Delavan Branch Library and Erie County Public Library," by M.W. Proctor: p. 17-23. [Z679.E17] A63
1. Library architecture. I. Proctor, Margia W. The building program of the East Delavan Branch Library of the Buffalo and Erie County Public Library. II. Title. III. Title: A library building program.

ELLSWORTH, Ralph Eugene, 1907- 727'.8
Planning manual for academic library buildings, by Ralph E. Ellsworth. Metuchen, N.J., Scarecrow Press, 1973. 159 p. illus. 22 cm. Bibliography: p. 154-155. [Z679.E42] 73-14896 ISBN 0-8108-0680-0
1. Library architecture. 2. Libraries, University and college. I. Title. BIP

ELLSWORTH, Ralph Eugene, 1907- 727'.8
Planning manual for academic library buildings, by Ralph E. Ellsworth. Metuchen, N.J., Scarecrow Press, 1973. 159 p. illus. 22 cm. Bibliography: p. 154-155. [Z679.E42] 73-14896 ISBN 0-8108-0680-0 5.00
1. Library architecture. 2. Libraries, University and college. I. Title.

INSTITUTE on Public Library Architecture, University of Southern California, 1957. 022.3082
A living library, planning public library buildings for cities of 100,000 or less; papers. Martha Boaz, editor. Los Angeles, University of Southern California Press, 1957. vi, 84 p. illus., plans. 26 cm. Bibliography: p. 81-84. [Z679.I5 1957] 58-8970
1. Library architecture. I. Boaz, Martha Terosse, 1913- ed. II. Title. BIP

METCALF, Keyes DeWitt, 1889- 022
Planning academic and research library buildings [by] Keyes D. Metcalf. New York, McGraw-Hill [1965] xv, 431 p. illus. 29 cm. "Sponsored by the Association of Research Libraries and the Association of College and Research Libraries under a grant by the Council on Library Resources." "Selective annotated bibliography": p. 403-411. [Z679.M38] 64-7868
1. Library architecture. 2. Libraries, University and college. I. Association of Research Libraries. II. Association of College and Research Libraries. III. Title. BIP

MYLLER, Rolf. 727.824
The design of the small public library. Illus. by Lewis Silverstein. New York, R. R. Bowker Co., 1966. 95 p. illus. 23 x 28 cm. Bibliography: p. 94-95. [Z679.M98] 66-20401
1. Library architecture. I. Title.

PUBLIC library architecture. 727'.8 [Philadelphia] Drexel Press, 1967. 99 p. illus., plans. 29 cm. (Drexel Library School series no. 20) Contents.Contents.—Twenty-five years of public library architecture, 1941-1966; principles and trends, by J. A. McDonald, Jr.—Public library architecture; proceedings of a conference, edited by D. H. Hunt. Bibliography: p. 31-34. [Z674.D7 no. 20] 66-28586
1. Library architecture. I. McDonald, Joseph Andrew, 1942- Twenty five years of public library architecture, 1941-1966. II. Hunt, Donald H., ed. III. Title. IV. Series.

TATE, Vernon Dale, 1909- 022
Books in libraries, architect vs. librarian; two rounds to a decision. [Papers read at the Club of Odd Volumes, March 21, 1951, by Vernon D. Tate and Ralph Walker. Boston? 1951] 38p. 18cm. [Z679.T3] 56-32514
1. Library architecture. I. Walker, Ralph, 1889- II. Title.

THOMPSON, Godfrey, 1921- 727'.8
Planning and design of library buildings. New York, Van Nostrand Reinhold [1974] 183 p. illus. 31 cm. Bibliography: p. 175-179. [Z679.T53] 73-10843 ISBN 0-9998846-3-8 24.50
1. Library architecture. 2. Library planning. I. Title. BIP

THOMPSON, Godfrey, 1921- 727'.8
Planning and design of library buildings / Godrey Thompson. 2d ed. London : Architectural Press ; New York : Nichols Pub. Co., 1977. 189 p. : ill. ; 31 cm. Includes index. Bibliography: p. 180-185. [Z679.T53 1977] 77-137 ISBN 0-89397-019-0 : 25.00
1. Library architecture. 2. Library planning. I. Title.

WILD, Friedemann. 727'.8
Libraries for schools and universities. New York, Van Nostrand Reinhold Co. [1972] 136 p. illus. 26 cm. (Design & planning) Translation of Bibliotheken fur Forschung und Lehre. [Z679.W6713] 73-163487
1. Library architecture. I. Title. II. Series.

YENAWINE, Wayne Stewart, 1911- ed. 027.7418'35
Contemporary library design. [Syracuse, N.Y.] Syracuse University Press, 1958. vi, 26 p. 23 cm. (Frontiers of librarianship, no. 1) "Three papers which were read at a symposium on contemporary library design held at ... [Syracuse] University on July 18, 1957." Bibliographical footnotes. [Z679.Y45] 38-11800
1. Library architecture. I. Title.

Library architecture—Congresses.

ASSOCIATION of College and Research Libraries. Buildings Committee. 727.8
Proceedings of the meetings [of the] library building plans institute. 1st- 1952- Chicago. no. illus., plans. 28cm. (ACRL monographs) (ACRL monograph) Issued 1952- under an earlier name of the association: Association of College and Reference Libraries. Editors: 1st. D. Jolly.- -2d- D. C. Davidson. Proceedings of the 4th meeting for 1954 in American Library Association. Building Committee. Planning a library building: the major steps. Chicago, 1955. [Z674.A75] [Z674.A75] 022.317 53-2932 53-2932
1. Library architecture—Congresses. I. Jolly, David, 1913- ed. II. Davidson, Donald Curtis, 1911- ed. III. Title. IV. Title: Library building plans institute. V. Series.

DESIGN for reading; 727'.8 papers given at the Annual Weekend Conference of the South Western Branch of the Library Association, held at Cheltenham, May 1969. [Dorchester (Dorset), South Western Branch of the Library Association, 1969] 37 p. illus. 25 cm. [Z679.D47] 73-165152 ISBN 0-85365-491-3 £1.25
1. Library architecture—Congresses. I. Library Association. South-Western Branch.

JOLLY, David, 1913- ed. 777.8
Proceedings of the meetings of the Library Building Plans Institute 1st- 1952- Chicago, Association of College and Reference Libraries. Chicago, 1955. no. illus., plans. 28cm. (ACRL monographs) Editors: 1st D. Jolly.--2d- D. C. Davidson. Proceedings of the 4th meeting for 1954 in American Library Association. Buliding Committee. Planning a library building: the major steps. [Z674.A75] [Z674.A75] 022.317 33-2932 33-2932
1. Library architecture—Congresses. I. Davidson, Donald Curtis, 1911- ed. II. Title. III. Title: Library building plans institute. IV. Series: Association of College and Reference Libraries. ACRL monographs

LIBRARY Architecture Preconference Institute, New York, 1974. 022'.3
An architectural strategy for change : remodeling and expanding for contemporary public library needs : proceedings of the Library Architecture Preconference Institute held at New York, New York, 4-6 July 1974, under the sponsorship of the Architecture for Public Libraries Committee, Buildings and Equipment Section, Library Administration Division, American Library Association / Raymond M. Holt, editor. Chicago : American Library Association, 1976. xii, 149 p. : ill. ; 28 cm. Includes bibliographical references. [Z679.L5 1974] 76-7965 ISBN 0-8389-0210-3 : 12.50
1. Library architecture—Congresses. I. Holt, Raymond M., 1921- II. American Library Association. Architecture for Public Libraries Committee. III. Title. BIP

THE Library building 022'.3 *consultant, role and responsibility.* Edited by Ernest R. DeProspo, Jr. New Brunswick, N.J., Rutgers University Press, 1969. vi, 110 p. 23 cm. "Report of a seminar, Graduate School of Library Service," Rutgers University, June 3-6, 1968. Includes bibliographical references. [Z679.L546] 72-90778
1. Library architecture—Congresses. 2. Library consultants—Congresses. I. DeProspo, Ernest R., 1937- ed. II. Rutgers University, New Brunswick, N.J. Graduate School of Library Service.

LIBRARY Buildings and Equipment Institute, Kent State University, 1961. 022.3
Planning library buildings for service; proceedings. Edited by Harold L. Roth. Chicago, American Library Association, 1964. 127 p. illus., plans. 28 cm. "Sponsored by the Section on Buildings and Equipment, Library Administration Division, American Library Association." Bibliographical footnotes. [Z679.L55 1961] 64-17057
1. Library architecture—Congresses. 2. Architecture—United States. I. Roth, Harold L., ed. II. American Library Association. Library Administration Division. Buildings and Equipment Section. III. Ohio. State University, Kent. IV. Title.

LIBRARY Buildings and Equipment Institute, University of Maryland, 1959. 022.3
Guidelines for library planners; proceedings. To which is added To remodel or not to remodel; papers presented at the Washington A.L.A. conference. Edited by Keith Doms and Howard Rovelstad. Chicago, American Library Association, 1960. 128 p. illus., plans. 28 cm. [Z679.L55 1959] 60-14701
1. Library architecture—Congresses. I. Doms, Keith, ed. II. Rovelstad, Howard, ed. III. Title.

LIBRARY Buildings Institute, Chicago, 1963. 022.082
Problems in planning library facilities: consultants, architects, plans, and critiques; proceedings. Edited by William A. Katz and Roderick G. Swartz. Chicago, American Library Association, 1964. 208 p. illus., plans. 28 cm. "Sponsored by the Library Administration Division, American Library Association." Bibliography: p. 182. [Z679.L56 1963] 64-19851
1. Library architecture—Congresses. I. Katz, William Armstrong, 1924- ed. II. Swartz, Roderick G., ed. III. American Library Association. Library Administration Division. IV. Title.

LIBRARY Buildings Institute, Detroit, 1965. 727'.8
Libraries, building for the future: proceedings of the Library Buildings Institute, and the ALTA workshop conducted at Detroit, Michigan, July 1-3, 1965. Edited by Robert J. Shaw. Chicago, American Library Association, 1967. x, 208 p. illus., plans. 28 cm. Sponsored by the Library Administration Division and the American Library Trustee Association of the American Library Association. Bibliographical footnotes. [Z679.L56 1965] 67-23001
1. Library architecture—Congresses. I. Shaw, Robert J., ed. II. American Library Association. Library Administration Division. III. American Library Trustee Association. IV. Title.

LIBRARY Buildings Institute, San Francisco, 1967. 727'.8
Library buildings: innovation for changing needs; proceedings. Edited by Alphonse F. Trezza. Chicago, American Library Association, 1972. ix, 293 p. illus. 28 cm. Sponsored by the Library Administration Division of the American Library Association. Includes bibliographical references. [Z679.L56 1967] 73-39011 ISBN 0-8389-3132-4 10.00
1. Library architecture—Congresses. 2. Library planning—Congresses. I. Trezza, Alphonse F., ed. II. American Library Association. Library Administration Division. III. Title. BIP

SUBJECT INDEX LIGHTING.

Library architecture—Gt. Brit.

BERRIMAN, Sidney George 727.8240942
British public library buildings, by S. G. Berriman, K. C. Harrison. London. Deutsch [New York. London House, c.1966] 260p. illus., plans. 30cm. (Grafton bk.) At head of title: BPLB. [Z679.B48] 66-2357 25.00
1. Library architecture—Gt. Brit. I. Harrison. Kenneth Cecil, joint author. II. Title. BIP

Library architecture—Ireland—Dublin.

CROOKSHANK, Anne. 027.7418'35
The long room / Anne Crookshank. [Dublin : Gifford & Craven, c1976] 16 p. : ill. ; 25 cm. (Gatherum ; 6) Caption title. Includes bibliographical references. [Z679.C84] 77-351766 £0.45
1. Dublin. University. Library. 2. Library architecture—Ireland—Dublin. 3. Architecture, Modern—17th-18th centuries—Ireland—Dublin. I. Title.

Library architecture—King Co., Wash.

VEBLEN, Marthanna E. 727'.8
Giant strides since Andrew Carnegie : creative architecture in the King County Library System / by Marthanna E. Veblen. 1st ed. Seattle, Wash. : Shorey Book Store, 1974, c1975. 81 p., [4] fold. leaves of plates : ill. ; 22 cm. Limited to 200 copies. Bibliography: p. 81. [Z679.V35 1975] 76-350140 ISBN 0-8466-0309-8 : 6.00
1. King County Rural Library District. 2. Library architecture—King Co., Wash. I. Title. BIP

Library architecture—Lighting.

METCALF, Keyes DeWitt, 1889- 022'.7
Library lighting [by] Keyes D. Metcalf. Washington, Association of Research Libraries, 1970. viii, 99 p. 23 cm. Bibliography: p. 94-95. [Z680.M44] 76-141351
1. Library architecture—Lighting. I. Association of Research Libraries. II. Title.

Library architecture—Terminology.

AMERICAN Library Association. Ad Hoc Committee on the Physical Facilities of Libraries. 022'.3'014
Measurement and comparison of physical facilities for libraries. Chicago, American Library Association, 1970. 23 p. 23 cm. Bibliography: p. 23. [Z679.A512] 76-138670 ISBN 0-8389-3121-9
1. Library architecture—Terminology. I. Title.

Library planning.

BLUEPRINT for the '70s: a Seminar on Library Planning, New York, 1971. 022'.3
Planning the special library; a project of the New York Chapter, SLA. Edited by Ellis Mount. New York, Special Libraries Association, 1972. vi, 122 p. illus. 28 cm. (SLA monograph no. 4) Contains papers presented at the seminar and others which were either obtained especially for this vol. or are reprinted. Bibliography: p. 80-94. [Z679.5.B58 1971] 72-85956 ISBN 0-87111-205-1 Pap. 7.50
1. Library planning. 2. Libraries, Special. I. Mount, Ellis, ed. II. Special Libraries Association. New York Chapter. III. Title. IV. Series: Special Libraries Association. Monograph no. 4. BIP

ELLSWORTH, Ralph Eugene, 1907- 022'.3
Planning the college and university library building; a book for campus planners and architects [by] Ralph E. Ellsworth. [2d ed.] Boulder, Colo., Pruett Press [1968] 145 p. illus. 23 cm. Includes bibliographical references. [Z679.5.E4 1968] 68-56373
1. Library planning. I. Title.

MARPLES, David Leonard. 022'.31'7
Circulation and library design : the influence of 'movement' on the layout of libraries / D. L. Marples, K. A. Knell. Cambridge : D. L. Marples, 1971. [2], 16 leaves : plans ; 30 cm. "An extension to, or a revision of, points made in Appendix II (Standard brief to architects on the planning of departmental libraries) of the First report of the General Board's Committee on Libraries." "Appendix: Standard specification for a library service." [Z679.5.M38] 75-325629 Free
1. Library planning. I. Knell, K. A., joint author. II. Title.

METCALF, Keyes DeWitt, 1889- 022'.31'7
Planning the academic library: Metcalf and Ellsworth at York; edited by Harry Faulkner Brown. Newcastle upon Tyne, Oriel, 1971. [6], 97 p. 21 cm. Contributions made at the course on Academic Library Planning, York Institute of Advanced Architectural Studies, in 1966. [Z679.5.M48] 70-112723 ISBN 0-85362-121-7 £1.50
1. Library planning. 2. Libraries, University and college. 3. Research libraries. I. Ellsworth, Ralph Eugene, 1907- II. Faulkner-Brown, Harry, 1920- ed. III. Title.

TAPPE, A. Anthony. 022'.3
Guide to planning a library building, by A. Anthony Tappe. [Prepared for the Massachusetts Bureau of Library Extension. Boston, Huygens and Tappe, inc., 1968] 48 p. col. illus. 22 x 29 cm. Bibliography: p. 45-47. [Z679.5.T3] 72-626159 3.95
1. Library planning. 2. Public libraries—Massachusetts. I. Title.

Library planning—Addresses, essays, lectures.

READER on the library building / edited by Hal B. Schell. 022'.3
Englewood, Colo. : Microcard Editions Books, 1975. xi, 359 p. : ill. ; 27 cm. (Reader series in library and information science) Includes bibliographical references and index. [Z679.5.R4] 73-93967 ISBN 0-910972-43-5 : 18.95
1. Library planning—Addresses, essays, lectures. 2. Library architecture—Addresses, essays, lectures. I. Schell, Hal B. BIP

Library planning—Handbooks, manuals, etc.

LUSHINGTON, Nolan, 1929- 022'.3
Libraries designed for users : a library planning handbook / by Nolan Lushington & Willis Mills, Jr. Syracuse, N.Y. : Gaylord Professional Publications, 1978 p. cm. Includes index. Bibliography: p. [Z679.5.L87] 78-27114 ISBN 0-915794-29-2 : 20.00
1. Library planning—Handbooks, manuals, etc. I. Mills, Willis, 1933- joint author. II. Title. BIP

Lich-gates.

MESSENT, Claude John Wilson. 726'.591'09426
Lych-gates and their churches in eastern England: South Lincolnshire, Norfolk, Suffolk, North Essex and East Cambridgeshire, their environments described and mention made of others of interest in many parts of England [by] Claude J. W. Messent; with a foreword by William Launcelot Scott Fleming. Norwich, C. J. W. Messent, The Gable, Brundall Road, Blofield, 1970. 238 p. illus. 23 cm. Bibliography: p. 41. [NA5461.M46] 70-515826 40/-
1. Lich-gates. 2. Churches—England. I. Title.

Lichtenstein, Roy, 1923—

CONTEMPORARY Arts Museum. 759.13
Roy Lichtenstein; an exhibition organized by the Contemporary Arts Museum, Houston, Texas, June 21-August 20, 1972. [Houston, Tex., 1972] 23 p. illus. (part col.) 22 cm. Includes bibliographical references. [ND237.L627C6] 72-85939
1. Lichtenstein, Roy, 1923-

LICHTENSTEIN, Roy, 1923- 709'.24
Roy Lichtenstein [by] Diane Waldman. New York, H. N. Abrams [1971] 248 p. 183 illus. (part col.) 31 cm. Bibliography: p. [240]-241. [N6537.L5W32] 74-146825 ISBN 0-8109-0256-7
I. Waldman, Diane.

LICHTENSTEIN, Roy, 1923- 709'.24
Roy Lichtenstein, by Diane Waldman. [Exhibition, the Solomon R. Guggenheim Museum, New York. New York, Solomon R. Guggenheim Foundation, 1969] 112 p. illus. (part col.), port. 26 cm. Bibliography: p. 104-112. [N6537.L5W3] 70-95575
I. Waldman, Diane. II. Solomon R. Guggenheim Museum, New York.

LICHTENSTEIN, Roy, 1923- 760'.0924
Roy Lichtenstein. Organized by John Coplans. [Pasadena, Calif., Pasadena Art Museum, 1967] 64 p. illus. (part col.) 24 cm. Exhibition held at the Pasadena Art Museum April 18-May 28, 1967, and at the Walter Art Center, June 23-July 30, 1967. Bibliography: p. 56-62. [N6537.L5C6] 67-4918
I. Coplans, John. II. Pasadena, Calif. Art Museum. III. Walker Art Center, Minneapolis.

LICHTENSTEIN, Roy, 1923- 709'.2'4
Roy Lichtenstein at CalArts : [exhibition] : drawings and collages from the artist's collection, April 19, 1977, to May 22, 1977, California Institute of the Arts, Valencia, California. Valencia : The Institute, c1977. 112 p. : ill. ; 28 cm. [N6537.L5C3] 77-308
1. Lichtenstein, Roy, 1923- I. California Institute of the Arts. II. Title.

LICHTENSTEIN, Roy, 1923- 741.9'73
Roy Lichtenstein, drawings and prints. With an introd. by Diane Waldman. New York, Chelsea House Publishers [1971] 256 p. illus. (part col.), plates, port. 32 cm. (A Paul Bianchini book) Bibliography: p. 247-254. [NC139.L48A57] 73-90344 30.00

LICHTENSTEIN, Roy, 1923- 709'.73
Roy Lichtenstein [exhibition held at] the Tate Gallery, 6 January--4 February 1968. London, Tate Gallery, 1968. Dist. in U. S. A. by Arno Pr., New York. Bibl. [N6537.L5T3] 68-107803 6.00
I. Tate Gallery, London. II. Title.

LICHTENSTEIN, Roy, 1923- 760'.0924
Roy Lichtenstein: graphics, reliefs & sculpture, 1969-1970. Irvine, University of California [1970] 66 p. illus. (part col.), port. 27 cm. Catalog of the exhibition held Oct. 27-Dec. 6, 1970, at the Art Gallery, University of California, Irvine. Bibliography: p. 66. [N6537.L5A63] 72-140310
I. California. University, Irvine. Art Gallery.

Light in art.

BELLAMY, Richard. 707.4'0149'66
Focus on light; [exhibition] organized by Richard Bellamy, Lucy R. Lippard, and Leah P. Sloshberg. [Trenton, 1967] [70] p. illus. (part col.) 23 cm. Exhibition held at the New Jersey State Museum Cultural Center, Trenton, May 20-Sept. 10, 1967. [N8219.L5B4] 71-631083
1. Light in art. 2. Art—Exhibitions. I. Lippard, Lucy R., joint author. II. Sloshberg, Leah P., joint author. III. New Jersey. State Museum, Trenton. IV. Title.

HESS, Thomas B., comp. 701.8
Light in art. Edited by Thomas B. Hess and John Ashbery. New York, Collier Books [1971, c1969] v, 154 p. illus. 18 cm. (Art news series) "Selected from Art news and Art news annual, XXXV." Contents.Contents.—In the light of dreams, by N. Calas and E. Calas.—The eye of Ra, by K. Levin.—Generation of light, 1945-70, by S. Burton.—Gothic glass, by F. Deuchler.—Byzantium, by J. Beckwith.—The outer light, by G. Laderman.—What color is divine light? By P. Reutersward.—Literal light, by J. Perreault.—Dan Flavin: fiat lux, by W. S. Wilson. Includes bibliographical references. [N8219.L5H47 1971] 71-29109 1.95
1. Light in art. 2. Art—Psychology—Addresses, essays, lectures. I. Ashbery, John, joint comp. BIP

PIENE, Otto, 1928- 701.8
Rainbows. Cambridge, Mass., Migrant Apparition, inc., 1971. 31 p., 32-109 l. illus. 28 cm. Contents.Contents.—Part 1: Lecture.—Part 2: People people. [N8219.L5P5] 71-158073
1. Light in art. I. Title.

ROSS, Charles, 1937- 709'.2'4
The substance of light : sunlight dispersion, the solar burns, point source/star space : selected work of Charles Ross : an exhibition organized by the La Jolla Museum of Contemporary Art, February 6-March 14, 1976. La Jolla, Calif. : The Museum, c1976. 36 p. : ill. (some col.) ; 21 x 25 cm. [N6537.R584L34] 76-3296
1. Ross, Charles, 1937- 2. Light in art. I. La Jolla Museum of Contemporary Art. II. Title.

VALENTINE, DeWain, 1936- 709'.2'4
DeWain Valentine : an exhibition organized by the La Jolla Museum of Contemporary Art, June 28-August 3, 1975 / [photography, DeWain Valentine, full color photos., Michael Arthur, mechanical photography]. [La Jolla, Calif. : The Museum], c1975. [26] p. : ill. (some col.) ; 22 x 28 cm. Bibliography: p. [25] [NC139.V34L3] 75-29802
1. Valentine, DeWain, 1936- 2. Light in art. 3. Space (Art) I. La Jolla Museum of Contemporary Art.

WALKER Art Center, Minneapolis. 709.04
Light, motion, space. Minneapolis [1967] 36 p. illus. 21 cm. An exhibition organized by Walker Art Center in cooperation with the Howard Wise Gallery, New York. Held Walker Art Center, Apr. 8-May 21, 1967; Milwaukee Art Center, June 24-July 30, 1967. Bibliographical references included in "Notes" (p. 10-11) [N5020.M695] 67-23973
1. Light in art. 2. Art, Modern—20th century—Exhibitions. I. Howard Wise Gallery. II. Milwaukee Art Center. III. Title.

Light—Psychological aspects—Bibliography.

BARTHOLOMEW, Robert. 016.3092 s
Human response to the luminous environment in physical facility planning / Robert Bartholomew. Monticello, Ill. : Council of Planning Librarians, 1976. 9 p. ; 28 cm. (Exchange bibliography ; 1051) Cover title. [Z5942.C68 no. 1051] [Z7204.L48] [BF789.L53] 016.62132 76-373533 ISBN pbk. : 1.50
1. Light—Psychological aspects—Bibliography. 2. Light in architecture—Bibliography. 3. Environmental psychology—Bibliography. I. Title: Human response to the luminous environment in physical facility ... II. Series: Council of Planning Librarians. Exchange bibliography ; 1051.

Lighthouses—Pacific States—Views.

BACHE, Hartman. 916
Early west coast lighthouses; eight drawings and paintings, 1855-1859. San Francisco, Book Club of California, 1964. 9 folders. 8 mounted illus. (part col.) 28 cm. (Series of keepsakes) In portfolia. "The texts accompanying the drawings were written by authorities on the histories of the lighthouse depicted." [NC1075.B13A44] 65-2267
1. Lighthouses—Pacific States—Views. 2. Lighthouses—Pacific States. I. Title.

Lighting.

ALLPHIN, Willard. 621.32'2
Primer of lamps and lighting. 3d ed. Reading, Mass., Addison-Wesley Pub. Co. [1973] xi, 228 p. illus. 25 cm. Bibliography: p. 221. [TH7703.A43 1973] 72-12250
1. Lighting. 2. Electric lamps. I. Title.

ALLPHIN, Willard. 621.32
Primer of lamps and lighting. [2d ed.] Salem, Mass., Sylvania Electric Products [c1965] xi, 241 p. illus. 25 cm. Lighting calculation slide rule in pocket.

Bibliography: p. 235. [TH7703.A43] 66-3128
1. Lighting. 2. Electric lamps. I. Title. BIP

COLBY, Carroll B. 621.32
Modern light new usesin protecting and improving life by C. B. Colby. New York, Coward-McCann [1967] 48 p. illus. 28 cm. Many examples of new uses or new types of lighting, as used in sports, safety, airports, photography or science. [TH7703.C63] AC 67
1. Lighting. I. Title.

GLADSTONE, Bernard. 621.32
The complete book of garden and outdoor lighting. Drawings by Richard Stasio. New York, Hearthside Press [1956] 120 p. illus. 21 cm. [TH7725.G55] 56-7386
1. Lighting. I. Title: Garden and outdoor lighting. BIP

HOLMES, John 621.32'2'08
Guyscliffe, 1909-
Essays on lighting / J. G. Holmes. New York : Crane, Russak, 1975. xii, 175 p. : ill. ; 22 cm. "The twenty essays were published over the period January 1972 to April 1974 in the journal Light and lighting, under the general heading, 'Let's keep it simple.'" [TH7703.H62 1975] 75-21733 ISBN 0-8448-0771-0 : 14.50
1. Lighting. I. Title.

HOPKINSON, Ralph 729'.28
Galbraith, 1913-
The lighting of buildings [by] R. G. Hopkinson and J. D. Kay. New York, Praeger [1969] 318 p. illus. 23 cm. Bibliography: p. 311-313. [TH7703.H65 1969b] 69-19889 10.00
1. Lighting. I. Kay, John Davenport, joint author. II. Title.

LARSON, Leslie, 1925- 729.2
Lighting and its design. Drawings by Donald Hanson. New York, Whitney Library of Design [1964] x, 228 p. illus. 29 cm. Bibliography: p. 224-225. [TH7703.L3] 63-11889
1. Lighting. 2. Lighting, Architectural and decorative. I. Title.

MOON, Parry Hiram, 1898- 621.32
The scientific basis of illuminating engineering. Rev. ed. New York, Dover Publications [1961] 608p. illus. 22cm. Includes bibliography. [TH7703.M65 1961] 61-19883
1. Lighting. I. Title.

NATIONAL Research Council. 691.92
Building Research Institute.
Plastics in building illumination. A report on the fifth meeting of the BRI Plastics Study Group, held at the University of Houston, Houston, Texas March 5-6, 1958. Washington, 1958. 99p. illus. 23cm. Includes bibliography. [TH7725.N35] 59-752
1. Lighting. 2. Plastics. 3. Building research. I. Title.

NIGHTINGALE, Frank B 621.32
Lighting as an art. [Skyforest, Calif., Knight pub. Co., 1962] 320p. illus. 22cm. [TH7703.N5] 62-5851
1. Lighting. I. Title.

PHILLIPS, Derek 729.2
Lighting in architectural design. Tech. assistant to the author: John Howard. New York, McGraw [1964, c.1963] ix, 310p. illus., diagrs., plans. 26cm. Bibl. 62-15524 17.50
1. Lighting. 2. Lighting, Architectural and decorative. I. Title.

PRITCHARD, David 621.32
Christopher, 1928-
Lighting [by] D. C. Pritchard. New York, American Elsevier Pub. Co., 1969. 96 p. illus. (part col.) 25 cm. (Environmental physics) Bibliography: p. 93. [TH7703.P69 1969b] 70-75107
1. Lighting. I. Title. II. Series. BIP

PRITCHARD, David 621.32'2
Christopher 1928-
Lighting / D. C. Pritchard. 2d ed. London ; New York : Longman, 1978. 111 p., [1] leaf of plates : ill. ; 24 cm. (Environmental physics series) Includes index. Bibliography: p. [108]-109. [TH7703.P69 1978] 77-21745 ISBN 0-582-41083-5 pbk. : 8.75
1. Lighting. I. Title. II. Series.

STEVENS, Wallace Roberts. 621.32
Building physics: lighting; seeing in the artificial environment [by] W. R. Stevens. [1st ed.] Oxford, New York, Pergamon Press [1969] viii, 235 p. illus. 20 cm. (The Commonwealth and international library. Physics division) Includes bibliographies. [TH7703.S84 1969] 79-77472
1. Lighting. I. Title.

WALDRAM, Percy John. 729.3 721.84
A measuring diagram for daylight illumination for the measurement, predetermination and representation of natural lighting. London, New York, Batsford [1950] 19 p. diagrs. 25 cm. Bibliography: p. 4. [TH7791.W3] 52-32842
1. Lighting. I. Title. II. Title: Daylight illumination.

WEITZ, Charles Earl, 621.32'1
1895-
Illumination principles / by C. E. Weitz. [Ed. 2] / rev. by Willard Allphin. Scranton, Pa. : International Correspondence Schools, c1976. 95, 4 p. : ill. ; 27 cm. "6646-3." [TH7703.W4 1976] 76-150338
1. Lighting. I. Allphin, Willard. II. International Correspondence Schools, Scranton, Pa. III. Title.

Lighting, Architectural and decorative.

KCHLER, Walter, writer on 729.2
electric lighting.
Lighting in architecture (Lichtarchitektur--Architecture in light) Light and color as stereoplastic elements. Pictorial narrative conceived and arranged by Wassili Luckhardt. [Translated from the German by Bertrand Languages, inc.] New York, Reinhold Pub. Corp. [1959] 223p. illus. (part col.) diagrs. 28cm. [TH7725.K613] 59-8034
1. Lighting, Architectural and decorative. 2. Color. I. Luckhardt. Wassili., ed. II. Title.

*POWNALL, Glen. 738.8
Lighting crafts. Wellington, N.Z., Seven Seas, [1975 c1974] 84 p. ill. (part col.) 25 cm. (His creative leisure series.) [NK3685] ISBN 0-85467-022-X
1. Lighting, Architectural and Decorative. I. Title.
Distributed by Int'l Publications Service, Collings for 5.50. BIP

Lighting, Architectural and decorative—History.

DUNCAN, Alastair, 747'.92'0904
1942-
Art nouveau and art deco lighting / Alastair Duncan. New York : Simon and Schuster, c1978. p. cm. Includes index. [TH7725.D86] 78-3632 ISBN 0-671-24307-1 : 25.00
1. Lighting, Architectural and decorative—History. 2. Decoration and ornament—Art nouveau—History. 3. Art deco—History. Congresses. I. Title. BIP

Lighting—History.

HAYWARD, Arthur H. 747.92
Colonial lighting. 3d enl. ed. New introd., suppl., 'Colonial chandeliers,' by James R. Marsh. [Gloucester, Mass., Peter Smith, c.1923-1962] 198p. illus. 21cm. (Dover bk. rebound) 4.00
1. Lighting—Hist. I. Title. BIP

HEBARD, Helen Brigham, 749.630974
1897-1961.
Early lighting in New England, 1620-1861. With sketches by Ellen Hatch Brewster. Rutland, Vt., C. E. Tuttle Co. [1964] 88 p. illus., port. 22 cm. Bibliography: p. 83-84. [NK8360.H34 1964] 64-16175
1. Lighting — Hist. I. Title.

HEBARD, Helen Brigham, 749.630974
1897-1961
Early lighting in New England, 1620-1861. Sketches by Ellen Hatch Brewster. Rutland, Vt., Tuttle [c.1964] 88p. illus., port. 22cm. Bibl. 64-16175 3.50 bds.,
1. Lighting—Hist. I. Title.

Lighting—History.

HAYWARD, Arthur H. 747.92
Colonial lighting. 3d enl. ed. With a new introd. and suppl., "Colonial chandeliers," by James R. Marsh. New York, Dover Publications [1962] 198 p. illus. 21 cm. [NK8360.H3 1962] 62-6720
1. Lighting—History. I. Title.

SMITH, Elmer Lewis. 621.32'3'0973
Early lighting : from tallow to oil in early America / compiled and edited by Elmer L. Smith ; photography by Melvin J. Horst. Lebanon, Pa. : Applied Arts Publishers, c1975. 32 p. : ill. ; 28 cm. [TH7703.S56] 75-322560 1.50
1. Lighting—History. 2. Lamps—History. I. Horst, Melvin. II. Title.

Lighting—Juvenile literature.

COLBY, Carroll B. 621.32
Modern light; new uses in protecting and improving life, by C. B. Colby. New York, Coward-McCann [1967] 48 p. illus. 28 cm. [TH7703.C63] 67-24215
1. Lighting—Juvenile literature. I. Title.

Lighting—Special effects.

†EDMUND Scientific Co. 770'.28
The Edmund unique lighting handbook. Barrington, N.J. : Edmund Scientific Co., c1977. v, 77 p. : ill. ; 28 cm. (The Edmund library of science and hobby books ; no. 9100) [TR590.E35 1977] 77-18409 8.95
1. Lighting—Special effects. 2. Photography—Apparatus and supplies. 3. Electric lighting—Equipment and supplies. I. Title.
Publisher's address : Edscork Building, Barrington, NJ 08007

Lightweight construction.

DREW, Philip, 1943- 720'.92'4
Frei Otto : form and structure / Philip Drew. Boulder, Colo. : Westview Press, [1976] p. cm. Includes bibliographical references and index. [TA663.D73] 76-178 ISBN 0-89158-535-4 : 32.75
1. Otto, Frei, 1925- 2. Lightweight construction. BIP

DREW, Philip, 1943- 720'.92'4
Frei Otto : form and structure / [by] Philip Drew. London : Crosby Lockwood Staples, 1976. 159 p. : ill., port. ; 26 cm. Bibliography: p. 156-159. [TA663.D73 1976b] 76-373202 ISBN 0-258-97053-7 : £15.00
1. Otto, Frei, 1925- 2. Lightweight construction.

SEBESTYEN, Gyula, 1921- 693
Lightweight building construction / Gyula Sebestyen. London : George Godwin ; New York : Wiley, 1977. vii, 382 p. : ill. ; 21 cm. Rev. and updated translation of Konnyuszerkezetes epites. Includes bibliographical references and index. [TH153.S4613 1977] 77-21902 ISBN 0-470-99166-6 : 35.00
1. Lightweight construction. I. Title. BIP

Lilien, Ephraim Mose, 1874-1925.

LILIEN, Ephraim Mose, 769'.92'4
1874-1925.
Jerusalem / by Ephraim Moses Lilien ; with an introd. by Joseph Gutmann. New York : Ktav Pub. House, 1976- p. cm. (The Library of Jewish art) [NE2050.5.L5A46] 76-10755 ISBN 0-87068-471-X (v. 1) : 25.00
1. Lilien, Ephraim Mose, 1874-1925. 2. Jerusalem in art. 3. Palestine in art. I. Title.

Limbourg, Pol de, ca. 1385-ca. 1416.

MEISS, Millard. 016.09
French painting in the time of Jean de Berry : the Limbourgs and their contemporaries / by Millard Meiss, with the assistance of Sharon Off Dunlap Smith and Elizabeth Home Beatson. New York : G. Braziller, 1974. 2 v. : ill. (some col.) ; 32 cm. (The Franklin Jasper Walls lectures) Includes indexes. Bibliography: v. 1, p. 482-505. [ND3147.M38 1974] 73-90120 ISBN 0-8076-0734-7 : 70.00
1. Limbourg, Pol de, ca. 1385-ca. 1416. 2. Limbourg, Hermann de, ca. 1385-ca. 1416. 3. Limbourg, Hennequin de, ca. 1385-ca. 1416. 4. Berry, Jean de France, duc de, 1340-1416. 5. Illumination of books and manuscripts, French. 6. Illumination of books and manuscripts, Gothic—France. 7. Hours, Books of. I. Smith, Sharon Off Dunlap, joint author. II. Beatson, Elizabeth Home, joint author. III. Title. IV. Series.
Contents omitted.

Limerick miter (Silverwork)

HUNT, John, 1900- 739.2'3'741945
The Limerick mitre and crozier. Dublin, Hodges, Figgis [1953] 22, [2] p. illus. 19 cm. Bibliography: p. [24] [NK7233.H86] 75-507291
1. Limerick miter (Silverwork) 2. Limerick crozier (Silverwork) I. Title.

Lincoln, Abraham, Pres. U.S., 1809-1865.

BARTLETT, David 973.7'0924 B
Vandewater Golden, 1828-1912.
Life and public services of Hon. Abraham Lincoln, with a portrait on steel, to which is added a biographical sketch of Hon. Hannibal Hamlin. Freeport, N.Y., Books for Libraries Press [1969] vi, 354 p. port. 23 cm. (Select bibliographies reprint series) "Speeches of Abraham Lincoln": p. [153]-348. [E457.B29 1969] 78-95064
1. Lincoln, Abraham, Pres., U.S., 1809-1865. 2. Hamlin, Hannibal, 1809-1891. I. Lincoln, Abraham, Pres., U.S., 1809-1865. II. Title.

HERNDON, William Henry, 923.173
1818-1891
Herndon's life of Lincoln, the history and personal recollections of Abraham Lincoln as originally written by William H. Herndon, Jesse W. Weik; introd., notes by Paul M. Angle. Illus. with photos. from the Meserve Collection. Cleveland, World [1965, c.1930, 1949] xlvi, 511p. illus., ports. 21cm. (Lincoln centennial lib.) [E457.H576] 49-4258 4.50 bds.,
1. Lincoln, Abraham, Pres., U.S., 1809-1865. I. Weik, Jesse William, 1857-1930, joint author. II. Title.

KOMROFF, Manuel, 973.7'0924 B
1890-
Abraham Lincoln. Illustrated by Charles Beck. New York, Putnam [1959] 127 p. illus. 21 cm. (Lives to remember) Biography of the backwoods boy whose dedication to education, honesty, and equality, made him yesterday's hero, today's legend. [E457.905.K59] 92 AC 68
1. Lincoln, Abraham, Pres. U.S., 1809-1865. I. Beck, Charles, illus. II. Title.

LORANT, Stefan, 1901- 923.173
The life of Abraham Lincoln, a short, illustrated biography. New York, McGraw-Hill [1954] 256 p. illus., ports., facsims. 21 cm. [E457.L87] 54-7674
1. Lincoln, Abraham, Pres. U.S., 1809-1865.

LORANT, Stefan, 1901- 923.173
The life of Abraham Lincoln: a short, illustrated biography. [New York] New American Library [1955, c1954] 256p. illus., ports., facsims. 19cm. (Signet key books, KD319) [E457.L87 1955] 56-27706
1. Lincoln, Abraham, Pres, U. S. 1809-1865. I. Title.

LORANT, Stefan 1901- 923.173
The life of Abraham Lincoln; a short illustrated biography. New York, Bantam Books [1976 c1954] 256 p. illus., ports. facsims. 18 cm. [E457.L87] 1.95 (pbk.)
1. Lincoln, Abraham, Pres. U.S., 1809-1865. I. Title.
L.C. card no. of 1954 McGraw Hill edition: 54-7674.

LOWITZ, Sadyebeth. 973.7'0924 B
Barefoot Abe; a really truly story by Sadyebeth and Anson Lowitz, with illus. by the latter. [Rev. ed.] Minneapolis, Lerner Publications Co. [1967] [56] p. illus. 19 x 22 cm. A simple biography of Lincoln which concentrates on his experiences as a child and young man. [E457.905.L69 1967] 92 AC 68

1. Lincoln, Abraham, Pres. U.S., 1809-1865. I. Lowitz, Anson, joint author. II. Title. BIP

MIERS, Earl Schenck, 1910- 973.7'0924 B
That Lincoln boy. Illustrated by Kurt Werth. Cleveland, World Pub. Co. [1968] 141 p. illus. 24 cm. A portrait of the youth who grew to be sixteenth President of the United States, telling of his family, various homes and jobs, and experiences, through his first campaign for political office. [E457.905.M53] 92 AC 68
1. Lincoln, Abraham, Pres. U.S. 1809-1865. I. Werth, Kurt, illus. II. Title.

MILLER, Francis Trevelyan, 1877-1959. 973.7'0924 B
Portrait life of Lincoln; life of Abraham Lincoln, the greatest American, told from original photographs taken with his authority during the great crisis through which he led his country—treasured among the 7000 Secret Service war negatives in the Brady-Gardner Collection at Springfield, Massachusetts, and in private collections, valued at $150,000, collected by Edward Bailey Eaton. Freeport, New York, Books for Libraries Press [1970] 164 p. illus., ports. 27 cm. Reprint of the 1910 ed. "Hundred greatest books on Abraham Lincoln": p. 161-164. [E457.6.M64 1970] 76-133528
1. Lincoln, Abraham, Pres. U.S., 1809-1865. 2. Lincoln, Abraham, Pres. U.S., 1809-1865—Portraits. I. Title. BIP

MUSCALUS, John Anthony, 1909- 769'.55973
Lincoln portraits on State bank notes, college currency, and scrip, by John A. Muscalus. Bridgeport, Pa., Historical Paper Money Research Institute [1967] 11 p. (chiefly illus.) 23 cm. Cover title. [HG622.M816] 67-31869
1. Lincoln, Abraham, Pres. U.S., 1809-1865. 2. Paper money—United States. 3. Bank-notes—United States. I. Title.

NORTH, Sterling, 1906- 923.173
Abe Lincoln, log cabin to White House. Illustrated by Lee Ames. New York, Random House [c1956] 184p. illus. 22cm. (Landmark books [61]) [E457.N659] 56-5450
1. Lincoln, Abraham, Pres. U. S., 1809-1865. I. Title. BIP

SANDBURG, Carl, 1878-1967. 973.7'092'4 B
Abe Lincoln grows up. With illus. by James Daugherty. New York, Harcourt Brace Jovanovich [1975, c1928] p. cm. (A Voyager book, AVB 92) Reprint of the ed. published by Harcourt Brace & World, New York. [E457.3.S23 1975] 74-17180 1.95 (pbk.)
1. Lincoln, Abraham, Pres. U.S., 1809-1865. I. Title. BIP

U.S. Library of Congress. 923.173
Abraham Lincoln; an exhibition at the Library of Congress in honor of the 150th anniversary of his birth. Washington, 1959. 94 p. illus. 26 cm. [E457.65.U635] 59-60260
1. Lincoln, Abraham, Pres. U.S. — Anniversaries, etc. 2. Lincoln, Abraham, Pres. U.S. — Bibl. — Catalogs. 3. Lincoln, Abraham, Pres. U.S. — Museums, relics, etc. I. Title.

Lincoln, Abraham, Pres. U.S., 1809-1865—Assassination.

CIVIL War times illustrated. 364.1524
Album of the Lincoln murder: illustrating how it was planned, committed, and avenged. A new kind of pictorial history from the editors of Civil War times illustrated. Text by Robert H. Fowler. Harrisburg, Pa., Stackpole Books [1965] 64 p. illus., facsims., maps, ports. 30 cm. [E457.5C59] 65-24689
1. Lincoln, Abraham, Pres. U.S., 1809-1865 — Assassination. I. Fowler, Robert H. II. Title.

CIVIL War times 364.1524
illustrated Album of the Lincoln murder: illustrating how it was planned. committed, and avenged. A new kind of pictorial history from the eds. of Civil War times illustrated. Text by Robert H. Fowler. Harrisburg, Pa., Stackpole [c.1965] 64p. illus., facsims., maps, ports. 30cm. [E457.5.C59] 65-24689 2.95 bds.,
1. Lincoln, Abraham, Pres. U.S., 1809-1865—Assassination. I. Fowler, Robert H.

HAYMAN, LeRoy. 364.15
The death of Lincoln; a picture history of the assassination. New York, Scholastic Book Services [1968] 127 p. illus., facsims., ports. 20 cm. Issued also under title: O captain! The death of Abraham Lincoln. An account of the events leading to the assassination of Lincoln as well as the arrest, trial and punishment of the accused. [E457.5.H33 1968b] AC 68
1. Lincoln, Abraham, Pres. U.S., 1809-1865—Assassination. I. Title.

KUNHARDT, Dorothy (Meserve) 1901- 973.70924
Twenty days; a narrative in text and pictures of the assassination of Abraham Lincoln and the twenty days and nights that followed -- the Nation in mourning, the long trip home to Springfield, by Dorothy Meserve Kunhardt and Philip B. Kunhardt, Jr. Foreword by Bruce Catton. [1st ed.] New York, Harper & Row [1965] 312 p. illus., facsims., ports. 31 cm. [E457.5.K8] 62-15660
1. Lincoln, Abraham, Pres. U.S., 1809-1865 — Assassination. 2. Lincoln, Abraham, Pres. U.S. 1809-1865 — Funeral journey to Springfield. I. Kunhardt, Philip B., joint author. II. Title.

Lincoln, Abraham, Pres. U.S., 1809-1865—Autographs.

NEFF, Ray A. 091
Research report on Lincoln lithography, by Ray A. Neff. [Terre Haute, Ind.] 1968. 17 l. illus., port. 28 cm. Cover title. Report of tests conducted on behalf of Mrs. Linda Goodman, New York, which states that the inscription "Yours truly A. Lincoln" on a lithograph of A. Lincoln was written with pen and ink. "Copy number 7 of ten." [E457.2.N5] 70-2804
1. Lincoln, Abraham, Pres. U.S., 1809-1865—Autographs. I. Goodman, Linda. II. Title.

Lincoln, Abraham, Pres. U.S., 1809-1865—Iconography.

FRAZIER, Carl 917.73
The Lincoln country in pictures, by Carl and Rosalie Frazier. New York, Hastings House [1963] 96 p. illus. 21 cm. [E457.64.F7] 63-19173
1. Lincoln, Abraham, Pres. U.S. — Iconography. I. Frazier, Rosalie, joint author. II. Title. BIP

LORANT, Stefan, 1901- 923.173
Lincoln, a picture story of his life. New York, Harper [1952] 256 p. illus. ports., facsims. 33 cm. "Contents and bibliography": p. 251-256. [E457.6.L78] 52-8481
1. Lincoln, Abraham, Press. U. S. 1809-1865—Inconography. I. Title.

LORANT, Stefan, 1901- 923.173
Lincoln, a picture story of his life. Rev. and enl. ed. New York, Harper [1957] 304 p. illus., ports., facsims. 33 cm. "Contents and bibiliography": p. 299-304. [E457.6.L78 1957] 57-11110
1. Lincoln, Abraham, Pres. U.S., 1809-1865—Iconography.

LORANT, Stefan, 1901- 973.7'0924
Lincoln; a picture story of his life. Rev. and enl. ed. New York, Norton [1969] 336 p. illus., facsims., ports. 33 cm. "Contents and bibliography": p. 329-334. [E457.6.L78 1969] 69-11484 7.95
1. Lincoln, Abraham, Pres. U.S., 1809-1865—Iconography. I. Title.

LOWE, James L. 769'.4'997370924
Lincoln postcard catalog; a check list of Lincoln postcards, old and new [by] James L. Lowe. 1st ed. Folsom, Pa., Better Postcard Collectors' Club [1967] 65 p. illus. 28 cm. [E457.6.L83] 68-1365
1. Lincoln, Abraham, Pres. U.S., 1809-1865—Iconography. 2. Postal cards—Catalogs. I. Title.

LOWE, James L. 016.769'4'997370924
Lincoln postcard catalog; a check list of Lincoln postcards, old and new [by] James L. Lowe. Revised by Dean and Mrs. Charles W. Brennan. 1st revision. Folsom, Pa., Deltiologists of America [1973] 144 p. illus. 29 cm. [E457.6.L83 1973] 73-83549 ISBN 0-913782-05-X
1. Lincoln, Abraham, Pres. U.S., 1809-1865—Iconography. 2. Postal cards—Catalogs. I. Brennan, Charles W. II. Brennan, Charles W., Mrs. III. Title.
Publisher's address: 318 Roosevelt Ave., Folsom, PA. 19033.

WHITE, Clara Lily, ed. 973'.074'016971
Lincoln heritage trail; official souvenir book and tour guide: Illinois, Indiana, Kentucky. Clara Lily White, editor; Ray E. White, photographic editor. Moline, Ill., Desaulniers, 19 -- , [52] p. illus. (part col.) maps (1 fold col.) ports. (part col.) 29 cm. "Approved by the Lincoln Heritage Trail Foundation." [E457.64.L53] 65-53579
1. Lincoln, Abraham, Pres. U.S., 1809-1865 — Iconography. I. White, Ray H., ed. and illus. II. Lincoln Heritage Trail Foundation. III. Title.

Lincoln, Abraham, Pres. U.S., 1809-1865—Medals.

KING, Robert P 973'.074'016971
Lincoln in numismatics, by Robert P. King. [Waynesboro? Va.] Reprinted by Token and Medal Society, 1966. 145 p. illus. 24 cm. Reprinted from issues of the Numismatist, Feb. 1924, Apr. 1927, and Aug. 1933. [E457.65.K5] 67-66272
1. Lincoln, Abraham, Pres. U.S., 1809-1865—Medals. I. Heyl, Edgar G. II. Title.

Lincoln, Abraham, Pres. U.S., 1809-1865—Monuments, etc.

THE Lincoln heritage trail. 973.7'0924
[Chicago, Keepsake Press, 1967?] [39] album l. 28 cm. Caption title. Leaf [1] with text; leaves [2]-[19] each with 2 mounted post cards, postage stamps affixed, some commemorative, cancelled on Lincoln's birthday, Feb. 12, 1967. One card was cancelled in each of 36 places associated with him in Kentucky, Indiana, and Illinois. The post cards have illustrative text and an outline drawing of the particular state. Leaves [20]-[39] blank for additions. [E457.6.L74] 71-223605 27.50
1. Lincoln, Abraham, Pres. U.S., 1809-1865—Monuments, etc. 2. Postage-stamps—Topics—Lincoln, Abraham, Pres. U.S., 1809-1865. 3. Postal cards—United States.

MILLER, Edward, 1905- 973.7'0924
The halls of Lincoln's greatness. Narration, decoration by Edward Miller, Betty Jean Mueller. New York, Meredith [1968] 144p. illus., facsims., map, ports. 24cm. (Halls of greatness bk.) Bibl. [E457.65.M5] 67-24423 3.95
1. Lincoln, Abraham, Pres. U. S., 1809-1865—Museums, relics, etc. 2. Lincoln, Abraham, Pres. U. S., 1809-1865—Monuments, etc. I. Mueller, Betty Jean. joint author. II. Title.

Lincoln, Abraham, Pres. U.S., 1809-1865—Museums, relics, etc.

MILLER, Edward, 1905- 973.7'0924
The halls of Lincoln's greatness. Narration, decoration by Edward Miller, Betty Jean Mueller. New York, Meredith [1968] 144p. illus., facsims., map, ports. 24cm. (Halls of greatness bk.) Bibl. [E457.65.M5] 67-24423 3.95
1. Lincoln, Abraham, Pres. U. S., 1809-1865—Museums, relics, etc. 2. Lincoln, Abraham, Pres. U. S., 1809-1865—Monuments, etc. I. Mueller, Betty Jean. joint author. II. Title.

PETZ, Weldon. 973.7'074'0168944
In the presence of Abraham Lincoln. 1st ed. Harrogate, Tenn., Lincoln Memorial University, 1973. 104 p. illus. 29 cm. "A select view of some of the vast and rare collections of Lincoln and Civil War materials at the Lincoln Memorial University, Cumberland Gap, Harrogate, Tennessee." [E457.65.P47] 73-86603 ISBN 0-914148-00-1 15.00; 10.00 (pbk.)
1. Lincoln, Abraham, Pres. U.S., 1809-1865—Museums, relics, etc. 2. Lincoln Memorial University, Harrogate, Tenn. I. Lincoln Memorial University, Harrogate, Tenn. II. Title.

STERN, Alfred Whital. 973'.074'016971
Scrap book. [n.p., n.d.] 7 v. illus. 31 cm. Binder's title. Consists of clippings from newspaper and periodicals, letters, facsimiles, and photographs, relating chiefly to t e Alfred Whital Stern collection of Lincolniana, and dating from 1928 to 1960. [E457.65.S8] 61-30889
1. Lincoln, Abraham, Pres. U.S. — Museum, relics. etc. I. Title.

Lincoln, Abraham, Pres. U.S., 1809-1865—Portraits.

THE Face of Lincoln / 779'.23
edited and compiled by James Mellon. New York : Viking Press, 1978. p. cm. (A Studio book) [E457.6.F33] 78-13684 ISBN 0-670-30433-6 : 35.00
1. Lincoln, Abraham, Pres. U.S., 1809-1865—Portraits. I. Mellon, James. BIP

HAMILTON, Charles, 1913- 923.173
Lincoln in photographs; an album of every known pose, by Charles Hamilton and Lloyd Ostendorf. [1st ed.] Norman, University of Oklahoma [c1963] x, 409 p. illus., ports., facsims. 26 cm. "Bibliography of Lincoln photograph books": p. 398. [E457.6.H23] 62-16476
1. Lincoln, Abraham, Pres. U.S.—Portraits. I. Ostendorf, Lloyd, joint author. II. Title. BIP

KNOX, Katharine (McCook) 973'.074'016971
'Healy's Lincoln no. 1.' [Enl. version. Washington, 1959] unpaged. illus. 23x11cm. [E457.6.K55 1959] 59-14887
1. Lincoln. Abraham, Pres. L. S.—Portraits. 2. Healy, George Peter Alexander. 1813-1894. 3. Postage-stamps—Topies—Lincoln, Abraham, Pres. U. S., 1809-1865. I. Title.

Lincoln, Abraham, Pres. U.S., 1809-1865—Portraits—Addresses, essays, lectures.

OSTENDORF, Lloyd. 770'.92'2
Lincoln and his photographers; address at annual meeting, Lincoln Fellowship of Wisconsin, Madison, 1971. [Madison] 1972. 14 p. ports. 26 cm. ([Historical Fellowship of Wisconsin] Historical bulletin no. 27) Cover title. [TR681.F3O8] 73-151399
1. Lincoln, Abraham, Pres. U.S., 1809-1865—Portraits—Addresses, essays, lectures. 2. Photographers, American—Addresses, essays, lectures. I. Title. II. Series.

Lincoln, Abraham, Pres. U.S., 1809-1865—Portraits—Exhibitions.

WOOD, Harry, 1910- 704.94'2
The faces of Abraham Lincoln; paintings, sculptures, drawings, and photomontages. With an introductory essay and notes by the artist. Tempe, University of Art Collections, Arizona State University [1970] 88 p. illus. (part col.), ports. (part col.) 28 cm. Catalogue of an exhibition, Arizona State University, Sept. 13-Nov. 1, 1970. Bibliography: p. 84. [E457.6.W6] 75-27854
1. Lincoln, Abraham, Pres. U.S., 1809-1865—Portraits—Exhibitions. 2. Lincoln, Abraham, Pres. U.S., 1809-1865—Cartoons, satire, etc.—Exhibitions. I. Arizona. State University, Tempe. University Art Collections. II. Title.

Lincoln, Abraham, Pres. U.S., 1809-1865—Quotations.

LINCOLN, Abraham, Pres. U.S., 1809-1865. 973.7'092'4 B
An album of Lincoln photographs and words. [New York] : Eakins Press Foundation, c1976. [16] p. (on double leaves) : ill. ; 16 cm. (Eakins pocket album

; 3) Cover title. Folding book. [E457.92 1976] 77-152770 1.95
1. Lincoln, Abraham, Pres. U.S., 1809-1865—Quotations. 2. Lincoln, Abraham, Pres. U.S., 1809-1865—Portraits. 3. Presidents—United States—Portraits. I. Title.

Lincoln, Abraham, Pres. U.S., 1809-1865—Tomb.

CASHMAN, Dorothy 917.73'56
Moline.
The Lincoln tomb. [Springfield? Ill., 1968?] 24 p. port. 22 cm. [E457.52.C37] 68-7378
1. Lincoln, Abraham, Pres. U.S., 1809-1865—Tomb. I. Title.

Lincoln, Abraham, Pres. U.S., 1809-1865—Autographs.

MADIGAN, Thomas F 1891-1936. 012
A catalogue of Lincolniana, with an essay on Lincoln autographs by William E. Barton. New York [19--] x, 88 p. facsims. 29 cm. [Z42.5.L5M3] 51-31797
1. Lincoln, Abraham, Pres. U. S.—Autographs. I. Barton, William Eleazar. 1861-1930. II. Title.

Lincoln, Abraham, Pres. U.S., 1809-1865—Cartoons, satire, etc.

WILSON, Rufus Rockwell, 923.173
1765-1949.
Lincoln in caricature; a historical collection, with descriptive and biographical commentaries by Rufus Rockwell Wilson. Introd. by R. Gerald McMurtry. New York, Horizon Press, 1953. xix, 327p. 163 illus. 26cm. [E457.63.W752 1953] 53-3939
1. Lincoln, Abraham, Pres. U. S.—Cartoons, satire, etc. I. Title.

Lincoln, Abraham, Pres. U.S., 1809-1865—Homes.

REDWAY, Maurine Whorton. 923.173
Marks of Lincoln on our land [by] Maurine Whorton Redway and Dorothy Kendall Bracken. New York, Hastings House [1957] 121p. illus. 26cm. Includes bibliography. [E457.64.R4] 57-8642
1. Lincoln, Abraham, Pres. U. S.—Museums, relics, etc. 2. Lincoln, Abraham, Pres. U. S.—Homes. 3. Lincoln, Abraham, Pres. U. S.—Monuments. etc. I. Bracken, Dorothy Kendall, joint author. II. Title.

Lincoln Back Country Wilderness (Proposed)

U.S. Congress. 719.32'09786
Senate. Committee on Interior and Insular Affairs. Subcommittee on Public Lands.
Lincoln Back Country Wilderness area, Montana. Hearing, Ninety-first, Congress, first session ... March 7, 1969. Washington, U.S. Govt. Print. Off., 1969. v, 64 p. map. 23 cm. "S. 412, a bill to authorize and direct the Secretary of Agriculture to classify as wilderness the national forest lands known as the Lincoln Back Country, and parts of the Lewis and Clark and Lolo National Forests, in Montana, and for other purposes." [KF26.I547 1969a] 70-601296
1. Lincoln Back Country Wilderness (Proposed) I. Title.

Lincoln Cathedral.

ANDERSON, Mary Desiree, 726.5
1902-
The choir-stalls of Lincoln Minster. [Lincoln] Friends of Lincoln Cathedral, 1951. 51p. illus. 24 cm. [NA5471.L7A6] 726.6 53-35117
1. Lincoln Cathedral. 2. Choir-stalls. I. Title.

ANDERSON, Mary Desiree, 729'.93
1902-
The choir stalls of Lincoln Minster, by M. D. Anderson. 2nd ed. Lincoln, Friends of Lincoln Cathedral, 1967. 2-51 p. illus., plans. 24 cm. [NA5471.L7A6 1967] 76-547622 7/6
1. Lincoln Cathedral. 2. Choir-stalls—Lincoln, Eng. I. Title.

CATHEDRAL 690'.66'0942532
craftsman - past and present. [Lincoln, Lincoln Cathedral Fabric Fund, 1973] [16] p. illus., ports. 26 cm. Cover title. Guide to a display designed by Lincoln College of Art in the Cathedral. [NA5471.L7C35] 74-179637 ISBN 0-9502690-1-8 Free.
1. Lincoln Cathedral. 2. Church maintenance and repair. I. Lincoln College of Art.

COOK, George Henry. 726.6
Portrait of Lincoln Cathedral. New York, Chanticleer Press [1950] 65 p. illus., plates, plans. 29 cm. (His The English cathedrals) [NA5471.L7C] A 51
1. Lincoln Cathedral. I. Title.

ZARNECKI, George. 726'.59
Romanesque sculpture at Lincoln Cathedral. Lincoln, Friends of Lincoln Cathedral, 1968. 24 p. 36 plates, illus. 22 cm. (Lincoln Minster pamphlets. Second series no. 2) Bibliographical references included in "Notes" (p. 22-24) [NB471.L5Z3] 79-458153 7/6
1. Lincoln Cathedral. 2. Sculpture, Romanesque—Lincoln, Eng. I. Friends of Lincoln Cathedral. II. Title. III. Series.

Lincoln Cathedral in art.

USHER Gallery. 758'.7'0942253
The cathedral in art: an exhibition of significant paintings depicting Lincoln Cathedral arranged in connection with the cathedral's 900th anniversary celebrations, 8th July to 20th August, 1972; [compiled by Richard H. Wood]. Lincoln, Usher Gallery, [1972]. 16 p. 28 cm. [ND1412.G74U83 1972] 73-173625
1. Lincoln Cathedral in art. 2. Paintings, English—Exhibitions. I. Wood, Richard H., 1908- II. Title.

Lincoln, Eng.—City planning.

LINCOLN, Eng. 711'.58'0942534
Dept. of Planning and Architecture.
Nettleham Glebe development design brief / [City of Lincoln Department of Planning and Architecture]. Lincoln : [The Department], 1976. 30 p. : 2 ill., maps, plans ; 30 cm. [HT169.G72L494] 77-366280 ISBN 0-902092-09-X : £0.50
1. Lincoln, Eng.—City planning. 2. City planning—England. I. Title.

Lincoln, Mary (Todd) 1818-1882—Portraits, caricatures, etc.

OSTENDORF, Lloyd. 973.7'0924
The photographs of Mary Todd Lincoln. [Springfield, Illinois State Historical Society, 1969] 64 p. ports. 25 cm. Reprinted from the Journal of the Illinois State Historical Society, vol. 61, no. 3, autumn 1968. Bibliographical footnotes. [E457.25.O8 1969] 77-7440
1. Lincoln, Mary (Todd) 1818-1882—Portraits, caricatures, etc. I. Title. BIP

Lindenmeier site, Colo.

WILMSEN, Edwin N. 917.88
Lindenmeier: a Pleistocene hunting society [by] Edwin N. Wilmsen. New York, Harper & Row [1974] xiv, 126 p. illus. 24 cm. (Harper's case studies in archaeology) Includes bibliographies. [E78.C6W54] 73-13205 ISBN 0-06-047153-0 3.95 (pbk.).
1. Lindenmeier site, Colo. I. Title.

Lindner, Ernest A.

THE Ernest A. Lindner 681'.62'09
Collection of antique printing machinery. Pasadena [Calif.] V. Gerry, 1971. 44, [6] p. illus. 20 x 23 cm. Bibliography: p. [46] [Z249.E735] 72-31995
1. Lindner, Ernest A. 2. Printing machinery and supplies—History.

Lindner, Richard, 1901—

LINDNER, Richard, 1901- 759.13
Lindner. [Exhibition] University Art Museum, University of California, Berkeley, 17 June/27 July 1969 [and] Walker Art Center, Minneapolis, Minnesota, 11 August/30 August 1969. [San Francisco, California Print Co., 1969] 51 p. illus. (part col.) 21 cm. Bibliography: p. 49. [N6537.L55A48] 73-626868
I. California. University. Art Museum. II. Walker Art Center, Minneapolis.

LINDNER, Richard, 1901- 759.3
Richard Lindner. [Text by] Dore Ashton. New York, H. N. Abrams [1970] 217 p. (chiefly illus., part col.) 28 x 30 cm. Bibliography: p. 215-217. [N6537.L55A9] 69-12799 ISBN 0-8109-0246-X
I. Ashton, Dore.

LINDNER, Richard, 1901- 759.13
Richard Lindner / [text by] Hilton Kramer. Boston : New York Graphic Society, 1975. 255 p. : chiefly ill. (some col.) ; 29 cm. (A Paul Bianchini book) Bibliography: p. 253-255. [ND1839.L56K72 1975b] 74-78458 ISBN 0-8212-0513-7 : 37.50
1. Lindner, Richard, 1901- I. Kramer, Hilton.

Lindsay, Norman, 1879-1969.

HETHERINGTON, John 709'.2'4 B
Aikman, 1907-
Norman Lindsay: the embattled olympian [by] John Hetherington. Melbourne, New York, Oxford University Press, 1973. xiv, 272 p. ill., plates (1 col.) 25 cm. Aus Index. Bibliography: p. 259-262. [N7405.L5H47] 74-160531 ISBN 0-19-550388-0 14.00
1. Lindsay, Norman, 1879-1969. BIP

LINDSAY, Norman, 1879- 709'.2'4
1969.
Siren and satyr : the personal philosophy of Norman Lindsay / [Norman Lindsay] ; introduced by A. D. Hope. South Melbourne : Sun, 1976. 80 p. : chiefly ill. ; 29 cm. (Sun-academy series) [N7405.L5H66] 77-364283 ISBN 0-7251-0226-8
1. Lindsay, Norman, 1879-1969. I. Hope, Alec Derwent, 1907- II. Title.

LINDSAY, Rose. 760'.0924
Model wife; my life with Norman Lindsay. Sydney, London, Ure Smith [1967] 257p. illus., ports. 23cm. [N7405.L5L5] 67-16129 7.50 bds.,
1. Lindsay, Norman. 1879- 2. Models, Artists'—Correspondence, reminiscences, etc. I. Title.
American distributor: Taplinger, New York.

Lindsay, Sir Daryl, 1890-

PHILIPP, Franz Adolf, ed. 759
In honour of Daryl Lindsay; essays and studies, ed. by Franz Phillipp, June Stewart. Melbourne, New York, Oxford [1965] xxi, 246p. plates, port. 28cm. Bibl. [N3948.P45] 65-3245 16.40
1. Lindsay, Sir Daryl, 1890- 2. Victoria, Australia. National Gallery. Melbourne. 3. Art—Galleries and museums. 4. Art—Australia—Addresses, essays, lectures. I. Stewart, June, joint ed. II. Lindsay, Daryl, Sir 1890- III. Title.

Line (Art)

ERNST, James A. 741.4
Drawing the line, fine and commercial art. New York, Reinhold [c.1962] 160p. illus. 27cm. 62-10719 10.00
1. Line (Art) 2. Drawing—Instruction. 3. Commercial art. I. Title.

GENDRON, Adelard A 1901- 701.8
The artist and the line; a lexicon of lineology. [1st ed.] New York, Exposition Press [1954] 164p. 21cm. [N33.G45] 53-8506
1. Line (Art) 2. Art—Terminology. I. Title.

LA Jolla Museum of 759.13
Contemporary Art.
Robert Mangold; an exhibition organized by the La Jolla Museum of Contemporary Art, La Jolla, California, March 23-May 12, 1974. [La Jolla, Calif., 1974] [32] p. illus. (part col.) 19 x 26 cm. Catalog of the exhibition. Bibliography: p. [26]-[27] [ND237.M234J64 1974] 74-77793
1. Mangold, Robert, 1937- 2. Line (Art) I. Mangold, Robert, 1937-

SAMSON, Anne Stringer. 741
Lines, spines, and porcupines, written and illustrated by Anne Stringer Samson. [1st ed.] Garden City, N.Y., Doubleday [1969] [64] p. illus. (part col.) 25 cm. Describes in verse many of the objects and pictures composed of lines. [PZ8.3.S2Li] AC 68
1. Line (Art) I. Title.

STACY, Don, 1925- JUV
The runaway dot. [1st ed.] Indianapolis, Bobbs-Merrill [1969] [31] p. illus. 20 x 21 cm. When the rebellious dot decides to move, he suddenly discovers that a moving dot becomes a line that can be shaped into a picture of almost anything. [PZ7.S7757Ru] 741 Fic 69-12437 3.95
I. Title.

Line (Art)—Juvenile literature.

SELLECK, Jack. 701'.8
Line / Jack Selleck. Worcester, Mass. : Davis Publications, [1974] 80 p. : ill. ; 26 cm. (Elements of design) Includes index. Text and photographs explore "line" in nature, architecture, clothing, food, and all of our environment and demonstrate its uses in art works. [NK1570.S44] 75-321019 ISBN 0-87192-063-8
1. Line (Art)—Juvenile literature. 2. Visual perception—Juvenile literature. I. Title. II. Series. BIP

Lingerie—Hist.

CRAWFORD, Morris De Camp, 391.2
1882-1949.
The history of lingerie in pictures, by M. D. C. Crawford & Elizabeth G. Crawford. New York, Fairchild Publications [1952] 81 p. illus. 22 cm. [GT2073.C7] 52-1838
1. Lingerie—Hist. I. Title. II. Title: Lingerie in pictures.

Linhoff cameras.

TYDINGS, Kenneth S 771.31
Graphic & Linhof press camera guide. Philadelphia, Chilton Co., Book Division, 1961. 127 p. illus. 20 cm. (Modern camera guide series, 678) [TR263.L5T9] 61-8134
1. Linhoff cameras. 2. Photography — Handbooks, manuals, etc. I. Title.

Links, Marty.

LINKS, Marty. 741.9'73
Happy talk : bright thoughts on friendship, love, joy, happiness, and beauty / illustrated by Marty Links. Kansas City, Mo. : Hallmark Cards, c1976. [48] p. : col. ill. ; 24 cm. (Hallmark crown editions) [ND1839.L57A47] 75-20701 ISBN 0-87529-469-3 : 5.00
1. Links, Marty. I. Title.

Linoleum block-printing.

KAFKA, Francis J 761.3
Linoleum block printing. Bloomington, Ill., McKnight & McKnight [1955] 84p. illus. 26cm. [NE1330.K3] 55-35813
1. Linoleum block-printing. I. Title. BIP

KAFKA, Francis J. 761'.3
Linoleum block printing [by] Francis J. Kafka. New York, Dover Publications [1972, c1955] 84 p. illus. 28 cm. Bibliography: p. 82. [NE1330.K3 1972] 72-79299 ISBN 0-486-20308-5 2.00
1. Linoleum block-printing.

ROTHENSTEIN, Michael, 1908- 761
Frontiers of printmaking: new aspects of relief printing. London, Studio Vista; New York, Reinhold [1966] 144p. illus. (some col.) 26cm. Bibl. [NE1330.R6] 66-24551 13.50 bds.,
1. Linoleum block-printing. 2. Wood-engraving—Technique. I. Title.

Lipchitz, Jacques, 1891-

CALIFORNIA. University. 730'.92'4
University at Los Angeles. Art Council.
Jacques Lipchitz; a retrospective selected by the artist. An exhibition sponsored by

the UCLA Art Council, in collaboration with the UCLA Art Galleries, 1963-1964. [Los Angeles, 1963] 72 p. illus. 28 cm. [NB553.L55C3] 63-62858
1. Lipchitz, Jacques, 1891- I. Title.

HAMMACHER, Abraham Marie, 730.947 1897-
Jacques Lipchitz: his sculpture. With an introductory statement by Jacques Lipchitz. New York, H. N. Abrams [1961] 176p. illus., ports., facsims. 31cm. Bibliography: p. 82-85. [NB553.L55H3] 60-10889
1. Lipchitz, Jacques, 1891- I. Title.

HOPE, Henry Radford, 1905- 735.44
The sculpture of Jacques Lipchitz. New York, Museum of Modern Art; [distributed by Simon and Schuster, 1954] 95p. illus., plates, ports. 26cm. 'Catalog of the exhibition': p.90-92. Bibliography: p.93-95. [NB237.L55H6] 54-10937
1. Lipchitz, Jacques, 1891- 2. Sculpture, American—Exhibitions. I. New York. Museum of Modern Art. II. Title.

LIPCHITZ, Jacques, 730'.92'4 B 1891-
Jacques Lipchitz. Text by A. M. Hammacher. New York, Abrams [1975] p. Bibliography: p. [NB553.L55H297] 74-11331 ISBN 0-8109-0238-9 35.00
1. Lipchitz, Jacques, 1891- I. Hammacher, Abraham Marie, 1897-

LIPCHITZ, Jacques, 1891- 730'.924
Jacques Lipchitz: sketches in bronze. Text: H. H. Arnason. Photos. of the maquettes: James Moore. Consulting designer: Bob Cato. New York, Praeger [1969] 195 p. illus. 28 cm. Bibliography: p. 30-32. [NK7998.L56A8] 75-83347 16.50
I. Arnason, H. Harvard. II. Title.

LIPCHITZ, Jacques, 1891- 730'.924
The sculpture of Jacques Lipchitz. [Exhibition] presented by the Dept. of Art and the Dept. of Art History [at the] Art History Gallery and School of Fine Arts Galleries, Apr. 1 through Apr. 30; Herron Museum of Art, Indianapolis, June 8th-29th, 1969. Organized by Jack Wasserman. [Milwaukee, 1969] [66] p. (chiefly illus., port.) 15 x 21 cm. At head of title: The University of Wisconsin-Milwaukee. Includes bibliographical references. [NB553.L55W35] 70-632309
I. Wasserman, Jack, 1921- II. Wisconsin. University, Milwaukee. Dept. of Art and Art Education. III. Wisconsin. University, Milwaukee. Dept. of Art History. IV. Wisconsin. University, Milwaukee. Dept. of Art History. Gallery. V. Wisconsin. University, Milwaukee. School of Fine Arts. Galleries. VI. Art Association of Indianapolis, Indiana. John Herron Art Institute. VII. Title.

PATAI, Irene. 730.944
Encounters; the life of Jacques Lipchiz. Foreword by Andrew C. Ritchie. New York, Funk & Wagnalls Co. [1961] 438 p. illus. 24 cm. Includes bibliography. [NB553.L55P3] 61-16858
1. Lipchitz, Jacques, 1891- I. Title.

VAN BORK, Bert. 730.924
Jacques Lipchitz: the artist at work. With a critical evaluation by Alfred Werner. New York, Crown Publishers [1966] 220 p. illus., ports. 32 cm. [NB553.L55V3] 66-15120
1. Lipchitz, Jacques, 1871-

Lippi, Filippino, d. 1504.

NEILSON, Katharine Bishop. 759.5
Filippino Lippi, a critical study, by Katharine B. Neilson. Westport, Conn., Greenwood Press [1972, c1938] xiv, 235 p. illus. 24 cm. Original ed. issued in series: Harvard-Radcliffe fine arts series. Bibliography: p. [ND623.L67N4 1972] 77-138168 ISBN 0-8371-5625-4
1. Lippi, Filippino, d. 1504. I. Title. II. Series: Harvard-Radcliffe fine arts series. BIP

Lippi, Filippo, Fra, 1412?-1469.

STRUTT, Edward C. 759.5
Fra Filippo Lippi, by Edward C. Strutt. London, G. Bell, 1901. [New York, AMS Press, 1972] xxiii, 202 p. front., 55 plates. 24 cm. "Catalogue of the works of Fra Filippo Lippi": p. 193-198. Bibliography: p. [xix]-xx. [ND623.L7S75 1972] 78-176460 ISBN 0-404-06299-7
1. Lippi, Filippo, Fra, 1412?-1469. BIP

Liquor bottles—Collectors and collecting—United States.

HUGGINS, Phillip Kenneth, 666'.19 1932-
The South Carolina dispensary; a bottle collector's atlas and history of the system. [1st ed. Columbia, S.C.] Sandlapper Press [1971] v, 215 p. illus. 27 cm. "History of the system, adapted from Ben Tillman's baby, by John Evans Eubank[s]" p. [103]-215. Bibliography: p. 213-215. [NK5440.B6H8] 75-177908 ISBN 0-87844-006-2 12.50
1. Liquor bottles—Collectors and collecting—United States. 2. Liquor laws—South Carolina. 3. Liquor problem—South Carolina. I. Eubanks, John Evans. Ben Tillman's baby. II. Title. BIP

Liquor bottles—Europe.

FLETCHER, Edward, 663'.19 fl.1970-
A bottle collectors' guide : European seals, case gins and bitters / [by] Edward Fletcher. London : Latimer New Dimensions, 1976. 144 p. : ill., facsims. ; 20 cm. Includes indexes. Bibliography: p. [137] [NK5440.B6F5325] 77-359495 ISBN 0-901539-47-3 : £3.50
1. Liquor bottles—Europe. 2. Liquor bottles—Collectors and collecting. 3. Trade-marks. I. Title.

Lisboa, Antonio Francisco, 1730-1814.

MANN, Hans. 730.924
The 12 prophets of Aleijadinho. Photos. by Hans Mann. Text by Graciela Mann. Austin, University of Texas Press [1967] 131 p. illus. 29 cm. Bibliography: p. 131. [NB359.L5M32] 66-15700
1. Lisboa, Antonio Francisco, 1730-1814. I. Mann, Graciela. II. Title.

Lisht, Egypt—Antiquities.

GOEDICKE, Hans. 708'.147'1 s
Re-used blocks from the pyramid of Amenemhet I at Lisht. [New York] Metropolitan Museum of Art Egyptian Expedition [1972, c1971] ix, 162 p. illus. 29 cm. (Publications of the Metropolitan Museum of Art, Egyptian Expedition, v. 20) Includes bibliographical references. [DT57.N5 vol. 20] [DT73.L6] 913.2'01 75-159406 ISBN 0-87099-107-8
1. Amenemhat I, King of Egypt. 2. Lisht, Egypt—Antiquities. 3. Relief (sculpture) I. Title. II. Series: New York. Metropolitan Museum of Art. Egyptian Expedition. Publications, v. 20. BIP

Lisht, Egypt—Tombs.

MACE, Arthur 913.32'03'1 Crittenden, 1874-1928.
The tomb of Senebtisi at Lisht, by Arthur C. Mace and Herbert E. Winlock. New York, 1916. [New York] Arno Press, 1973. xxii, 132 p., 35 plates. illus. 32 cm. At head of title: The Metropolitan Museum of Art Egyptian Expedition. Reprint of the ed. which was issued as v. 1 of Publications of the Metropolitan Museum of Art Egyptian Expedition. Bibliography: p. 127-128. [DT73.L6M3 1973] 73-168408 ISBN 0-405-02241-7
1. Senebtisi. 2. Lisht, Egypt—Tombs. I. Winlock, Herbert Eustis, 1884-1950, joint author. II. New York (City). Metropolitan Museum of Art. Egyptian Expedition. III. Title. IV. Series: New York (City). Metropolitan Museum of Art. Egyptian Expedition. Publications, v. 1.

Lissim, Simon, 1900—

DREAMS in the theatre : 759.13
designs of Simon Lissim : three essays and a check list of designs exhibited at the Vincent Astor Gallery, the New York Public Library at Lincoln Center, October 24-December 31, 1975, and at the Columbus (Ohio) Gallery of Fine Arts, March 11-April 4, 1976. New York : The Library : distributed by Readex Books, c1975. 39 p. : ill. ; 18 x 23 cm. "Chronology & bibliography": p. 36-39. [PN2096.L5D7] 75-31917 ISBN 0-87104-261-4 pbk. : 5.00
1. Lissim, Simon, 1900- I. Lissim, Simon, 1900- II. Vincent Astor Gallery. III. Columbus Gallery of Fine Arts, Columbus, Ohio. BIP

Literature and art.

HUNT, John Dixon. 700'.8
Encounters: essays on literature and the visual arts; edited by John Dixon Hunt. London, Studio Vista, 1971. 176 p. illus., facsims., map. 26 cm. Includes bibliographical references. [PR403.H8] 72-189827 ISBN 0-289-70026-4
1. Literature and art. 2. English literature—Addresses, essays, lectures. 3. Art—Addresses, essays, lectures. I. Title.
Available from Norton, 10.00, ISBN 0-393-04355-X

Literature and science.

TODD, Ruthven, 1914- 760
Tracks in the snow : studies in English science and art / Ruthven Todd. Norwood, Pa. : Norwood Editions, 1976. p. cm. Reprint of the 1946 ed. published by the Grey Walls Press, London. Contents.Contents.—Tracks in the snow.—William Blake and the eighteenth-century mythologists.—The reputation and prejudices of Henry Fuseli.—The imagination of John Martin. Includes bibliographical references and index. [PR6039.O26T7 1976] 76-9070 ISBN 0-8482-2600-3 : 20.00
1. Blake, William, 1757-1827. 2. Fuseli, Henry, 1741-1825. 3. Martin, John, 1789-1854. 4. Literature and science. I. Title.

Literature—Dictionaries—Polyglot.

PEI, Mario Andrew, 1901- ed. 703
Liberal arts dictionary in English, French, German [and] Spanish; edited by Mario A. Pei and Frank Gaynor. New York, Philsophical Library [1952] x, 307 p. 24 cm. Bibliography: p. ix-x. [PB333.P4] 52-13716
1. Literature—Dictionaries—Polyglot. 2. Art—Dictionaries—Polyglot. 3. Philosophy—Dictionaries—Polyglot. 4. English language—Dictionaries—Polyglot. I. Gaynor, Frank, 1911- joint author. II. Title.

Literature—Illustrations.

OLD masters' 769'.4'98
reproductions, collectors' items : character sketches of romance, fiction, poetry, and the drama. Oklahoma City : J. Nagy, c1975- v. : ill. ; 28 cm. [N8215.O43] 75-331911
1. Literature—Illustrations. I. Nagy, Joseph.

Literature, Medieval—History and criticism.

PICKERING, Frederick 701.18 Pickering, 1909-
Literature & art in the Middle Ages [by] F. P. Pickering. Coral Gables, Fla., University of Miami Press [1970] xxii, 362 p. illus. 24 cm. Translation of Literatur und darstellende Kunst im Mittelalter. Includes bibliographical references. [PN674.P513] 79-102698 ISBN 0-87024-152-4
1. Literature, Medieval—History and criticism. 2. Art and literature. 3. German literature—Middle High German, 1050-1500—History and criticism. 4. Symbolism. I. Title. BIP

Literature, Modern—Addresses, essays, lectures.

HOWE, Irving, comp. 700'.8
The idea of the modern in literature and the arts. Edited, with an introd. and commentary, by Irving Howe. New York, Horizon Press [1968, c1967] 317 p. 22 cm. Bibliographical footnotes. [PN771.H5895] 68-54188 6.50
1. Literature, Modern—Addresses, essays, lectures. 2. The arts, Modern—20th century—Addresses, essays, lectures. 3. Modernism—Addresses, essays, lectures. I. Title. BIP

READ, Herbert Edward, 700'.9 Sir, 1893-1968.
In defence of Shelley & other essays. Freeport, N.Y., Books for Libraries Press [1968] 282 p. 22 cm. (Essay index reprint series) Reprint of the 1936 ed. [PN710.R37 1968] 68-26470
1. Shelley, Percy Bysshe, 1792-1822. 2. Literature, Modern—Addresses, essays, lectures. 3. Art—Addresses, essays, lectures. I. Title. BIP

Lithographers—United States—Biography.

MONTHAN, Doris Born, 769'.92'4 B 1924-
R. C. Gorman : the lithographs / by Doris Monthan ; with a foreword by Jules Heller. 1st ed. Flagstaff [Ariz.] : Northland Press, c1978. xix, 170 p., [1] leaf of plates : ill. (some col.) ; 32 cm. Includes bibliographies and index. [NE2312.G67M67] 78-58469 ISBN 0-87358-179-2 : 35.00
1. Gorman, Rudolph Carl, 1932- 2. Lithographers—United States—Biography. 3. Navaho Indians—Biography. I. Gorman, Rudolph Carl, 1932- BIP

Lithographic workshops.

KNIGIN, Michael. 763
The contemporary lithographic workshop around the world [by] Michael Knigin and Murray Zimiles. New York, Van Nostrand Reinhold Co. [1974] 318 p. illus. (part col.) 36 cm. [NE2298.K64] 77-149257 ISBN 0-442-24480-0
1. Lithographic workshops. I. Zimiles, Murray, joint author. II. Title.

Lithographs, American.

CONNINGHAM, Frederic Arthur, 763 1890-
Currier & Ives. Cleveland, World Pub. Co. [1950] 63 p. illus., col. plates, port. 20 cm. (The American arts library, 1583) Bibliography: p. 63. [NE2415.C7C616] 50-58061
1. Currier & Ives. 2. Lithograph, American. 3. Lithographers, American.

CURRIER, and Ives 763.084
Currier and Ive's America; a panorama of the mid-nineteenth century scene; eighty prints in full color, with an introd. and commentary by the editor, Colin Simkin [Reissue] New York, Crown [1965, c.1952] 1v. (unpaged) col. plates. 32x42cm. [NE2415.C7S55] 52-10768 10.95 bds.,
1. Lithographs, American. I. Simkin, Colin, ed. II. Title.

FAIRCHILD, Hurlstone. 759.13
La tierra encantada. By William E. Steadman. Tucson, Ariz. [Printed by Walker Lithocraft Printing, c1969] 160 p. (chiefly col. illus.) 29 cm. [ND237.F22S7] 70-13518
I. Steadman, William E. II. Title.

JOHNSON, Lucas. 811'.5'4
Moon shots. Lithographs by Lucas Johnson. Poems by C. W. Truesdale. [New York] Mexican Art Annex, 1968. [35] p. 10 plates. 20 x 28 cm. "Originally published ... in a limited, portfolio edition under the title of El hombre: la guerra." "Published in a first edition of 350 copies." [NE2415.J57M4 1968] 68-23773
I. Truesdale, Calvin William, 1929- II. Title.

KEELER, Harold E 741.973
Waterfront; a sketch book: lithographs drawn on and printed from the stone. Artist, printer: Harold E. Keeler. [n.p., Foliate Press, 1964] 1 v. (chiefly illus.) 19 x 27 cm. No. 52 of 95 copies signed by the artist. [NE2415.K3A56] 64-7014
I. Title.

LANDAU, Jacob 1917- 769'.924 1917-
Kingdom of dreams: E. T. A. Hoffmann;

20 lithographs [by] Jacob Landau. New York, Associated American Artists [1969] [7] p., 20 col. plates., [1] p. (in case) 40 cm. "There are 100 suites (1/100 to 100/100) printed on Rives BFK, and boxed in paper over boards [and other suites]." No. 15/100. [NE2312.L3A5] 70-244633
I. Title.

PETERS, Harry Twyford, 1881-1948. 769'.92'4
Currier & Ives, printmakers to the American people / Harry T. Peters. New York : Arno Press, 1976, c1929-1931. p. cm. (America in two centuries, an inventory) Reprint of the ed. published by Doubleday, Doran, Garden City, N.Y. [NE2312.C8P47 1976] 75-22834 ISBN 0-405-07741-6 : 300.00
1. Currier and Ives. 2. Lithographs, American. I. Title. II. Series.

REPS, John William. 769'.973'07401645315
Cities on stone : nineteenth century lithographic images of the urban West : accompanying exhibition presented at Amon Carter Museum of Western Art, Fort Worth, August 27-October 10, 1976 ... [et. al] / by John W. Reps. Fort Worth [Tex.] : Amon Carter Museum, c1976. 99 p. : ill. (some col.) ; 22 x 28 cm. Bibliography: p. 36-38. [NE2454.R46] 76-12313 ISBN 0-88360-051-X pbk. : 4.95
1. Lithographs, American. 2. The West in art. I. Amon Carter Museum of Western Art, Fort Worth, Tex. II. Title. BIP

SPRUANCE, Benton, 1904-1967. 763
Moby Dick, the passion of Ahab; twenty-six lithographs by Benton Spruance. Text by Lawrance Thompson. [Barre, Mass., Barre Publishers, 1968] 1 portfolio ([10], 26 l., 26 plates) 58 cm. [NE2415.S73T54] 68-29793
I. Thompson, Lawrance Roger, 1906- II. Melville, Herman, 1819-1891. Moby Dick. III. Title.

Lithographs, American—Catalogs.

KING, Roy. 769'.922
The world of Currier & Ives, by Roy King & Burke Davis. New York, Random House [1968] 140 p. 60 col. illus. 37 x 49 cm. The 60 prints reproduced were selected from the Roy King Collection as representative of the work of Currier & Ives. "A selected list of two hundred [and fifty] Currier & Ives prints with their values": p. 136-140. [NE2415.C7K5] 68-28542 30.00
1. Currier and Ives. 2. Lithographs, American—Catalogs. 3. Lithographs—Private collections. I. Currier and Ives. II. Davis, Burke joint author. III. Title.

MARYLAND Historical Society. 769'.074'01526
A. Hoen on stone; lithographs of E. Weber & Co. and A. Hoen & Co., Baltimore, 1835-1969. [Baltimore, 1969] 52 p. illus. 23 cm. Catalogue of an exhibition, Maryland Historical Society, Baltimore, May 5-June 30, 1969, prepared by Lois B. McCauley, curator of graphics. Bibliography: p. 51-52. [NE2415.H58M3] 79-87284
I. McCauley, Lois B. II. Edward Weber & Co. III. Hoen (A.) and Company, inc., Baltimore. IV. Title.

WARMAN, Edwin G., 1915- 769'.973
Fourth print price guide : a check-list and price guide to N. Currier, Currier & Ives, and Currier & Ives reproductions, including Audubon, Icart, Nutting, Parrish, Prang, and other printmakers / Edwin G. Warman. Rev. and enl. ed. Uniontown, Pa. : E. G. Warman Pub., c1976. 145 p. ; 22 cm. Edition of 1955 published under title: Print price guide; 1959 ed. under title: New print price guide; 1969 ed. under title: Third print price guide. [NE2303.7.W3 1976] 76-356023 7.95
1. Currier and Ives. 2. Lithographs, American—Catalogs. 3. Printmakers—United States. 4. Prints, American—Catalogs. I. Title. BIP

Lithographs, American—Exhibitions.

FLINT, Janet A. 769'.973
The way of good and evil: popular religious lithographs of nineteenth-century America. [Exhibition] September 15-November 12, 1972 [by] Janet A. Flint. Washington, National Collection of Fine Arts, Smithsonian Institution [1972] [11] p. 27 cm. [NE2303.7.F54] 73-600519
1. Lithographs, American—Exhibitions. 2. Good and evil in art. I. Smithsonian Institution. National Collection of Fine Arts. II. Title.

MADE in California. 769'.973'074019494
[Los Angeles? 1971?] iv, 41 p. illus., ports. 22 x 29 cm. Catalog of an exhibition of five workshops held at the Grunwald Graphic Arts Foundation, Dickson Art Center, University of California, Los Angeles, from April 19 to May 16, 1971. [NE2310.C2M3] 70-198163
1. Lithographs, American—Exhibitions. 2. Lithography—California. I. Grunwald Graphic Arts Foundation. II. Dickson Art Center.

NEW Mexico. University. Art Museum. 769'.973'074018961
Lithography 1 : first biennial exhibition of contemporary lithography, University Art Museum, University of New Mexico, Albuquerque, March 2-April 13, 1975. Albuquerque : The Museum, c1975. 20 p. : ill. ; 24 cm. [NE2304.N48 1975] 75-4100
1. Lithographs, American—Exhibitions. I. Title.

Lithographs—Catalogs.

CONNINGHAM, Frederic Arthur, 1890- 769'.02'9
Currier & Ives prints; an illustrated check list, by Frederic A. Conningham. Updated by Colin Simkin. [Rev. ed.] New York, Crown Publishers [1970] xx, 300 p. illus. 24 cm. [NE2415.C7C62 1970] 77-105958 12.50
1. Currier and Ives. 2. Lithographs—Catalogs. I. Simkin, Colin. II. Title.

SCHURRE, Jacques. 769'.02'9
Currier & Ives prints; a checklist of unrecorded prints produced by Currier & Ives, N. Currier, and C. Currier. [New York, 1970] [23] p. 22 cm. "The checklist ... is a complete compilation of prints not listed in the recently published revised edition of Conningham's." [NE2312.C8S39] 72-25031
1. Currier and Ives. 2. Lithographs—Catalogs. I. Conningham, Frederic Arthur, 1890- Currier & Ives prints. II. Title. BIP

Lithographs—Collectors and collecting.

NEWMAN, Ewell L. 769'.92'4
A guide to collecting Currier & Ives / by Ewell L. Newman in collaboration with Ladd MacMillan. New York : Pyramid Books, 1975. 158, [2] p. : ill. (some col.) ; 14 x 21 cm. "A Pyramid prestige edition." Includes index. Bibliography: p. [159] [NE2312.C8N48] 76-351422 pbk. : 4.95
1. Currier and Ives. 2. Lithographs—Collectors and collecting. 3. United States in art. I. Macmillan, Ladd. II. Title. BIP

Lithographs—Exhibitions.

CALIFORNIA. University. University at Los Angeles. Art Galleries. 760'.74'01471
Lithographs from the Tamarind Workshop. A circulating exhibition organized by The UCLA Art Galleries, 1962-63; catalogue Los Angeles, 1962] 31 p. (chiefly illus.) 28 cm. [NE2275.L85C3] 63-1606
1. Lithographs—Exhibitions. I. Tamarind Lithography Workshop. II. Title.

INTERNATIONAL biennial of contemporary color lithography. 763
1st- 1950- [Cincinnati] v. illus. (part col.) 31cm. Superseded in 1960 by the museum's International biennial of prints. [NE2275.C5A2] 764 54-16214
1. Lithographs—Exhibitions. I. Cinciannati. Art Museum.

NEW York (City). Museum of Modern Art. 760'.74'01471
Tamarind; homage to lithography. Pref. by William S. Lieberman. Introd. by Virginia Allen. New York, Distributed by New York Graphic Society, Greenwich, Conn. [1969] 64 p. illus. (part col.) 25 cm. "Catalog of the exhibition, April 29-June 30, 1969." "All works are ... from the Kleiner, Bell and Company Collection of Tamarind impressions." [NE2272.N4M8] 77-77513 6.95
1. Kleiner, Bell and Company—Art collections. 2. Lithographs—Exhibitions. I. Tamarind Lithography Workshop. II. Title.

TAMARIND Lithography Workshop. 769'.973'074013
Tamarind: a renaissance of lithography; a loan exhibition from the Tamarind Lithography Workshop. Introd. by E. Maurice Bloch. [Baltimore, Printed by Garamond/Pridemark Press, 1971] 95 p. illus. 21 cm. "Circulated by the International Exhibitions Foundation, 1971-1972." Bibliography: p. 93-95. [NE2272.L6T3] 79-158627
1. Lithographs—Exhibitions. I. Bloch, E. Maurice. II. International Exhibitions Foundation. III. Title.

Lithographs, French.

*[JEANNERET-GRIS, Charles Edward] 1887-1965 763
Oeuvre lithographique by Le Corbusier. Zeurich, Heidi Weber [1967] lv. unpaged. illus. (pt. col.) 30cm. 9.50 pap.,
1. Lithographs, French. I. Title.
American distributor: Wittenborn, New York.

Lithographs, Norwegian—Exhibitions.

MUNCH, Edvard. 1863-1944. 769.2
Edvard Munch, a selection of his prints from American collections [by] William S. Lieberman. New York, Museum of Modern Art; distributed by Simon and Schuster [1957] 39p. illus., plates (1 col.) 25cm. [NE2415.M8L5] 57-7371
1. Lithographs, Norwegian—Exhibitions. 2. Engravings, Norwegian— Exhibitions. 3. Wood-engravings, Norwegian—Exhibitions. I. Lieberman. William Slattery, 1921 II. Title.

Lithographs—Prices.

ART Reference Gallery. Art Appraisal Information Division. 760'.092'4
Price profile on lithographs by James Abbott McNeill Whistler. Montclair, N.J. [1973] vi, 45 p. 22 cm. Includes bibliographical references. [NE2312.W45A89] 73-159630 20.00
1. Whistler, James Abbott McNeill, 1834-1903. 2. Lithographs—Prices. I. Title.

WARMAN, Edwin G., 1915- 769'.029
Third print price guide; a check-list and price guide to N. Currier, Currier & Ives, Kellogg and other printmakers. [Rev. ed.] Uniontown, Pa., E. G. Warman [1969] 139 p. 22 cm. First published in 1955 under title: Print price guide; in 1959, under title: New print price guide. [NE2303.7.W3 1969] 70-17679 4.75
1. Currier (N.) (firm) 2. Lithographs—Prices. 3. Lithographers—United States. I. Title.

Lithographs—United States—Catalogs.

SCHURRE, Jacques. 769'.92'4
Currier & Ives : a checklist of unrecorded prints produced by Currier & Ives, N. Currier, and C. Currier / compiled by Jacques Schurre. Rev. ed. [New York : s.n.], c1976. ii, 28 p. ; 22 cm. Cover title. [NE2312.C8S34 1976] 76-383236
1. Currier and Ives. 2. Lithographs—United States—Catalogs. I. Title.

Lithography.

EICHENBERG, Fritz, 1901- 763
Lithography and silkscreen : art and technique / Fritz Eichenberg. New York : Abrams, 1978. 160 p. : ill. (some col.) ; 30 cm. Six chapters of the author's The art of the print. Includes index. Bibliography; p. [155]-157. [NE2425.E352 1978] 77-20263 ISBN 0-8109-2095-6 pbk. : 7.95
1. Lithography. 2. Serigraphy. I. Title. BIP

FAUX, Ian. 686.2'325
Modern lithography. London, Macdonald & Evans, 1973, [i.e.1974] xviii, 318 p. illus. 23 cm. Includes index. Bibliography: p. [314]-315. [Z252.5.L5F38] 74-181152 ISBN 0-7121-1362-2
1. Lithography. I. Title.
Distributed by Transatlantic Arts; 11.50. BIP

HARTSUCH, Paul Jackson, 1902- 763
Chemistry of lithography. [2d ed.] New York, Lithographic Technical Foundation [1961] 358p. illus. 22cm. [NE2425.H37 1961] 60-13797
1. Lithography. 2. Chemistry, Technical. I. Title.

HARTSUCH, Paul Jackson, 1902- 763
Chemistry of lithography. New York, Lithographic Technical Foundation [1952] 254p. illus. 22cm. ([Lithographic Technical Foundation, inc.] Foundation publications, 401) [NE2425.H37] 53-23541
1. Lithography. 2. Chemistry, Technical. I. Title.

HIRSCH, S. Carl. 763
Printing from a stone; the story of lithography [by] S. Carl Hirsch. New York, Viking Press [1967] 111 p. illus. 25 cm. [NE2295.H5] 67-13605
1. Lithography. I. Title.

REED, Robert Findley, 1890- 763.1
Formulary; formulas for solutions used in lithography. New York, Lithographic Technical Foundation [1956] 87p. illus. 22cm. ([Foundation publications] 602) [TR925.R4] 57-2711
1. Lithography. 2. Chemistry, Technical—Formulae, receipts, prescriptions. I. Title.

†SENEFELDER, Alois, 1771-1834. 763'.22
A complete course of lithography / by Alois Senefelder ; with an introduction by A. Hyatt Mayor and a supplement of thirty-one plates from the first German and French editions. New York : Da Capo Press, 1977. xxviii, 342 p., [29] leaves of plates : ill. ; 26 cm. (A Da Capo paperback) Reprint of the 1819 ed. originally published under title: Vollstandiges Lehrbuch der Steindruckerey. [NE2420.S513 1977] 76-30519 ISBN 0-306-80053-5 pbk. : 7.95
1. Lithography. 2. Lithography—Technique. I. Title.

SENEFELDER, Alois, 1771-1834. 763
The invention of lithography. Translated from the original German by J. W. Muller. [Limited ed.] New York, Fuchs & Lang Manufacturing Co., 1911. [New York, Sun Chemical Corp., 1969] xii, 228 p. illus. 26 cm. [NE2420.S53 1969] 70-108977
1. Lithography. I. Title.

*SORLIER, Charles. 709.04
The lithographs of Chagall, [vol. 4], 1969-1973. Notes and catalogue by Charles Sorlier [and] Fernand Mourlot. New York, Crown Publishers [1974] 180 p. col. illus. 32 cm. [NE2298] 60.00
1. Chagall, Marc, 1887- 2. Lithography. I. Title.

Lithography, American—Exhibitions.

VON GROSCHWITZ, Gustave. 769'.973'074018961
Tamarind : suite fifteen / Clinton Adams ... [et al.] ; text by Gustave Von Groschwitz ; [edited and designed by Clinton Adams]. [Albuquerque] : Tamarind Institute, c1977. 56 p. : ill. (some col.) ; 28 cm. Lithography II, presented by the University Art Museum, the University of New Mexico, Oct. 9 to No. 13, 1977; the second in a series of biennial exibitions. [NE2304.V66] 77-85045
1. Lithography, American—Exhibitions. 2. Lithography—20th century—United States—Exhibitions. I. Adams, Clinton, 1918- II. Tamarind Institute. III. New Mexico. University. Art Museum. IV. Title.

Lithography — Apparatus and supplies.

REED, Robert Findley, 1890- 763
Instruments for quality control in lithography. New York, Lithographic Technical Foundation [1963] 102 p. illus. 22 cm. "321." [NE2490.R4] 62-21197

SUBJECT INDEX LITURGY AND ARCHITECTURE.

1. Lithography — Apparatus and supplies. I. Title.

Lithography—California.

PETERS, Harry 769'.4'99794
Twyford, 1881-1948.
California on stone / Harry T. Peters. New York : Arno Press, 1976, c1935. p. cm. (America in two centuries, an inventory) Reprint of the ed. published by Doubleday, Doran, Garden City, New York. [NE2310.C2P4 1976] 75-22833 ISBN 0-405-07704-1 : 150.00
1. Lithography—California. 2. Lithographers—California. 3. Lithographs, American. 4. Lithographs—California. 5. California in art. I. Title. II. Series. BIP

Lithography—Congresses.

SEMINAR on Lithographic 621.56
Dampening Systems, Chicago, 1962.
Proceedings. Co-sponsors: Lithographic Technical Foundation and Research and Engineering Council of the Graphic Arts Industry. [n. p., 1962] 52 p. illus., diagrs. 28 cm. [NE2250.S4 1962] 67-4533
1. Lithography—Congresses. 2. Lithography—Technique. I. Lithographic Technical Foundation, inc. II. Graphic Arts Research and Engineering Council. III. Title.

Lithography—Handbooks, manuals, etc.

JONES, Stanley. 763'.028
Lithography for artists. London, New York [etc.] Oxford U. P., 1967. 78 p. illus., diagrs. 20 1/2 cm. (Oxford paperbacks, handbooks for artists, 3) (B 67-21940) Bibliography: p. 75. [NE2430.J6] 68-71156
1. Lithography—Handbooks, manuals, etc. I. Title. BIP

Lithography—History.

SENEFELDER, Alois, 1771- 763'.22
1834.
A complete course of lithography. With a new introd. by A. Hyatt Mayor, and a suppl. of thirty-one plates from the first German and French editions. New York, Da Capo Press, 1968. vi, xxviii, 342 p. illus., facsims., ports. 27 cm. (Da Capo Press series in graphic art v. 8) Reprint of the 1819 ed. originally published under title: Vollstandiges Lehrbuch der Steindrukerey. [NE2420.S5 1968] 68-27721 20.00
1. Lithography—History. 2. Lithography—Technique. I. Title. BIP

WEBER, Wilhelm, 1918- 769'.9
A history of lithography. New York, McGraw-Hill [1966] 259 p. illus. (part col.) facsims., ports. 29 cm. Translation of Saxa loquuntur. Bibliography: p. 252-255. [NE2295.W413 1966] 65-26115
1. Lithography—History. I. Title.

Lithography — Metal plate processes.

HALPERN, Bernard R 655.32
Color correction for offset lithography. [1st ed.] New York, Lithographic Technical Foundation [1956] 206p. illus. 22cm. (Lithographic Technical Foundation, inc. Foundation publications, 510/1) On cover: Tone and color correcting for offset lithography: retouching & dot etching. 'A revision of the original two volumes, Tone and color correction--dot etching [by Edward Olownia, and] Tone and color correction--retouching [by Lawrence Brehm] published in 1945.' [NE2540.H29 1956] 57-1287
1. Lithography—Metal plate processes. 2. Chromolithography. I. Title. II. Title: Tone and color correcting for offset lithography.

LATHAM, Charles W 655.314
Advanced pressmanship; sheet-fed presses. New York, Lithographic Technical Foundation [1963] 296 p. illus. 22 cm. [NE2540.L25] 62-22237
1. Lithography — Metal plate processes. I. Title.

LATHAM, Charles W 655.31
Lithographic offset press operating. [Rev. ed.] New York, Lithographic Technical Foundation [1956] 261p. illus. 22cm. ([Lithographic Technical Foundation, inc.] Foundation publications, 505/6) [NE2540.L27 1956] 57-22887
1. Lithography—Metal plate processes. I. Title.

LATHAM, Charles W 655.31
Lithographic offset press operating. [1st ed.] New York, Lithographic Technical Foundation [1955] 261p. illus. 22cm. ([Lithographic Technical Foundation, inc.] Foundation publications, 505/6) 'A revision of the original texts [by D. J. MacDonald and C. W. Latham] published in 1945.' [NE2540.L27 1955] 55-13842
1. Lithography—Metal plate processes. I. MacDonald, David James, 1875- Lithographic offset press operating. II. Title.

REED, Robert Findley, 655.31
1890-
Offset press troubles: sheet-fed presses. New York, Lithographic Technical Foundation [1962] xii, 108 p. illus., diagrs. 22 cm. "Essentially a revision and expansion of the publication Offset press troubles by D. J. MacDonald." [NE2540.R4] 62-21198
1. Lithography — Metal plate processes. I. MacDonald, David James, 1875- Offset press troubles. II. Title.

ROBINSON, Karl Davis. 655.325
Line photography for the lithographic process. Rev. [New York] Lithographic Technical Foundation [1956] 123 p. illus. 22 cm. [TR940] A62
1. Lithography—Metal plate processes. I. Title.

TORY, Bruce E 655.31
Offset lithography. Sydney, Horwitz Publications; Chicago, Graphic Arts Monthly, inc. [1957] 331 p. illus. 30 cm. Includes bibliography [TR940.T59] 58-2815
1. Lithography — Metal plate processes. I. Title.

Lithography — Philadelphia — Hist.

WAINWRIGHT, Nicholas B 763
Philadelphia in the romantic age of lithography; an illustrated history of early lithography in Philadelphia, with a descriptive list of Philadelphia scenes made by Philadelphia lithographers before 1866. Philadelphia, Historical Society of Pennsylvania, 1958. 261 p. illus. 32 cm. [NE2311.P5W3] 58-11725
1. Lithography — Philadelphia — Hist. 2. Lithographs, American. 3. Philadelphia — Descr. — Views. I. Title. BIP

Lithography—Safety measures.

SAFETY and fitness for 613.6'2
the art of lithograph. [Los Angeles, Calif., Tamarind Lithography Workshop, 1970] 33 p. illus. 28 cm. [Z252.5.L5S3] 72-180818 1.50
1. Lithography—Safety measures. I. Tamarind Lithography Workshop.

Lithography—Technique.

ANTREASIAN, Garo Z., 1922- 763
The Tamarind book of lithography: art & techniques [by] Garo Z. Antreasian with Clinton Adams. Los Angeles, Tamarind Lithography Workshop, 1971. 463 p. illus. (part col.) 30 cm. Bibliography: p. 449-[453] [NE2425.A5] 76-121328 ISBN 0-8109-0496-9
1. Lithography—Technique. I. Adams, Clinton, 1918- joint author. II. Tamarind Lithography Workshop. III. Title.

ARNOLD, Grant, 1904- 763
Creative lithography and how to do it. New York, Dover [1964,c.1941] xiv, 214p. illus., plates, port. 22cm. (T1208) Unaltered repubn. of bk. pub. by Harper in 1961. Bibl. 64-20878 1.65 pap.,
1. Lithography—Technique. I. Title. BIP

BANISTER, Manly Miles, 1914- 763
Lithographic prints from stone and plate, by Manly Banister. New York, Sterling Pub. Co. [1972] 128 p. illus. 29 cm. [NE2425.B36 1972] 72-81045 ISBN 0-8069-5228-8 6.95
1. Lithography—Technique. I. Title.
PLB 6.39, ISBN 0-8069-5229-6.

BANISTER, Manly Miles, 1914- 763
Lithographic prints from stone and plate, by Manly Banister. Totowa, N.J., Littlefield, Adams, 1974 [c1972] 128 p. illus. 28 cm. (A Littlefield, Adams quality paperback, no. 285) Reprint of the ed. published by Sterling Pub. Co., New York. [NE2425.B36 1974] 74-10971 ISBN 0-8226-0285-7 4.50 (pbk.)
1. Lithography—Technique. I. Title.

CLIFFE, Henry 763
Lithography; a complete handbook of modern techniques of lithography. New York, Wabton-Guptill [c.1965] 96p. illus. (pt. col.) 26cm. Bibl. [NE2425.C55] 65-15948 6.95
1. Lithography—Technique. I. Title.

DEHN, Adolf Arthur, 1895- 763
How to draw and print lithographs. Drawing on the stone, by Adolf Dehn; Printing from the stone, by Lawrence Barrett. New York, American Artists Group [1950] 119 p. illus. 32 cm. [NE2425.D4] 50-10658
1. Lithography—Technique. I. Barrett, Lawrence Louis, 1897- II. Title.

KNIGIN, Michael. 763
The technique of fine art lithography [by] Michael Knigin and Murray Zimiles. New York, Van Nostrand Reinhold [1970] 143 p. illus. (part col.), plan. 29 cm. [NE2425.K57] 76-90318
1. Lithography—Technique. I. Zimiles, Murray, joint author. II. Title.

KNIGIN, Michael. 763
The technique of fine art lithography / Michael Knigin and Murray Zimiles ; [line drawings by Patrick S. Kennedy]. Rev. ed. New York : Van Nostrand Reinhold Co., 1977. 128 p. : ill. ; 28 cm. Includes index. [NE2425.K57 1977] 76-54289 ISBN 0-442-24479-7 7.95
1. Lithography—Technique. I. Zimiles, Murray, joint author. II. Title.

LOCHE, Renee. 763
Lithography. [English version by Julian Snelling and Claude Namy] New York, Van Nostrand Reinhold Co. [1974, c1971] 127 p. illus. (part col.) 18 x 21 cm. (Craft and art) Bibliography: p. 121-122. [NE2425.L5813 1974] 73-8466 ISBN 0-442-29991-5 7.95
1. Lithography—Technique. I. Title.

TWYMAN, Michael. 763'.09
Lithography, 1800-1850: the techniques of drawing on stone in England and France and their application in works of topography. Lithography eighteen hundred-eighteen fifty London, New York, Oxford U.P., 1970. xxi, 304 p., 88 plates. illus., facsims. 28 cm. Bibliography: p. 255-277. [NE2425.T85] 70-460065 6/-/-
1. Lithography—Technique. I. Title.

VICARY, Richard. 763
Manual of advanced lithography / Richard Vicary. New York : Scribner, c1977. 192 p. : ill. (some col.) ; 25 cm. Includes index. Bibliography: p. 186-189. [NE2425.V5] 76-56890 ISBN 0-684-14937-0 : 12.50
1. Lithography—Technique. I. Title. BIP

VICARY, Richard. 763
Manual of lithography / Richard Vicary. New York : Scribner, c1976. 152 p. : ill. (some col.) ; 25 cm. Errata slip inserted. Includes index. Bibliography: p. 137-138. [NE2425.V52] 76-9656 ISBN 0-684-14748-3 : 9.95
1. Lithography—Technique. I. Title. BIP

VICARY, Richard. 763
The Thames and Hudson manual of lithography / Richard Vicary. London : Thames and Hudson, c1976. 152 p. : ill. (some col.) ; 25 cm. (The Thames and Hudson manuals) Includes index. Bibliography: p. 137-138. [NE2425.V53] 76-378720 ISBN 0-500-67009-9 : £4.00
1. Lithography—Technique. I. Title.

WEAVER, Peter. 763
The technique of lithography. New York, Reinhold Pub. Corp. [1965, c1964] 176 p. illus. (part col.) plan. 23 cm. Bibliography: p. 169-170. [NE2425.W37] 64-8613
1. Lithography—Technique. I. Title.

WEDDIGE, Emil, 1907- 763
Lithography. Scranton, Pa., International Textbook Co. [1966] xx, 221 p. illus., col. plates, ports. 29 cm. (International textbooks in art and art education) Bibliography: p. 215-216. [NE2425.W38] 65-13159
1. Lithography — Technique. I. Title.

Lithography—U.S.

COMSTOCK, Helen. 763
American lithographs of the nineteenth century. New York, Barrows [1950] 170 p. 75 illus. 15 cm. (Collectors' little-book library) [NE2303.C65] 50-11130
1. Lithography—U.S. 2. Lithograph, American. I. Title.

PETERS, Harry Twyford, 769'.92'2
1881-1948.
America on stone : the other printmakers to the American people / Harry T. Peters. New York : Arno Press, 1976, c1931. p. cm. (America in two centuries, an inventory) Reprint of the ed. published by Doubleday, Doran and Co., Garden City, N.Y. Bibliography: p. [NE2303.7.P47 1976] 75-22832 ISBN 0-405-07703-3 : 150.00
1. Lithography—United States. 2. Lithographers—United States. 3. Lithographs, American. I. Title. II. Series. BIP

Little Tennessee River watershed—Antiquities.

SALO, Lawr V. 917.68'85'03
Archaeological investigations in the Tellico Reservoir, Tennessee, 1967-1968; an interim report. Edited by Lawr V. Salo. Contributions by: Duane H. King [and others] Knoxville, Dept. of Anthropology, University of Tennessee, 1969. 1 v. (various pagings) illus. 29 cm. National Park Service contracts nos. 14-10-1-910-20 and 14-10-7:911-12. Includes bibliography. [E78.T3S2] 70-630553
1. Little Tennessee River watershed—Antiquities. 2. Indians of North America—Tennessee. I. King, Duane H. II. Tennessee. University. Dept. of Anthropology. III. Title.

Liturgical objects.

KING, Bucky. 745.5
Ecclesiastical crafts / Bucky King and Jude Martin. New York : Van Nostrand Reinhold, 1978. p. cm. Includes index. Bibliography: p. [NK1650.K47] 77-25033 ISBN 0-442-22966-6 : 16.95
1. Liturgical objects. 2. Church vestments. 3. Christian art and symbolism. 4. Church decoration and ornament. I. Martin, Jude, joint author. II. Title. BIP

Liturgical objects—Judaism—Exhibitions.

KANOF, 704.948'9'6074015655
Abram, 1903-
Ceremonial art in the Judaic tradition : an exhibition organized by the North Carolina Museum of Art, Raleigh, April 27 through June 15, 1975 / introd. and catalogue notes by Abram Kanof. Raleigh : North Carolina Museum of Art, [1975] 92 p. : ill. (some col.) ; 26 cm. Includes bibliographical references. [NK1672.K32] 75-12632 ISBN 0-88259-078-2 pbk. : 3.00
1. Liturgical objects—Judaism—Exhibitions. I. North Carolina. Museum of Art, Raleigh. II. Title. BIP

Liturgy and architecture.

BOUYER, Louis, 1913- 726'.5
Liturgy and architecture. Notre Dame, Ind.] University of Notre Dame Press, 1967. 127 p. plans. 21 cm. Translation of Architecture et liturgie. Bibliographical footnotes. [NA4605.B613] 67-25644
1. Liturgy and architecture. 2. Art and religion. BIP

BRUGGINK, Donald J. 726'.5'0973
When faith takes form; contemporary churches of architectural integrity in America [by] Donald J. Bruggink [and] Carl H. Droppers. Grand Rapids, Mich., W. B. Eerdmans Pub. Co. [1971] 126 p. illus., plans. 22 cm. [NA5212.B78] 70-142904 3.95
1. Liturgy and architecture. 2. Church architecture—U.S. 3. Architecture, Modern—20th century—U.S. I. Droppers, Carl H., joint author. II. Title. BIP

SOVIK, E. A. 726'.5'0904
Architecture for worship [by] E. A. Sovik. Minneapolis, Augsburg Pub. House [1973] 128 p. illus. 20 cm. [NA4825.S64] 73-78254 ISBN 0-8066-1320-3 3.50
1. Liturgy and architecture. 2. Church architecture. 3. Architecture, Modern—20th century. I. Title. BIP

Liturgy and architecture—Addresses, essays, lectures.

DEBUYST, Frederic, 1922- 726'.5
Modern architecture and Christian celebration. Richmond, John Knox Press [1968] 80 p. illus., plans. 22 cm. (Ecumenical studies in worship, no. 18) Lectures with some minor changes originally given by the author at the Institute for the Study of Worship and Religious Architecture, University of Birmingham, Nov. 1966. Bibliographical footnotes. [NA4605.D4] 68-26166 1.95
1. Liturgy and architecture—Addresses, essays, lectures. I. Title. II. Series.

LOOKING to the future : 246'.9
papers read at an international symposium on prospects for worship, religious architecture and socio-religious studies, 1976 / editor J. G. Davies. [Birmingham] : University of Birmingham, Institute for the Study of Worship and Religious Architecture, [1976] [6], 171 p. : map ; 30 cm. Includes bibliographical references. [NA4605.L66] 77-369107 ISBN 0-7044-0234-3 : £1.35
1. Liturgy and architecture—Addresses, essays, lectures. 2. Christian art and symbolism—Addresses, essays, lectures. 3. Worship—Addresses, essays, lectures. I. Davies, John Gordon, 1919- II. Birmingham, Eng. University. Institute for the Study of Worship and Religious Architecture.

Liu, Shang, 8th cent.

EIGHTEEN songs of a nomad 759.951
flute: the story of Lady Wen-chi; a fourteenth-century handscroll in the Metropolitan Museum of Art. Introd., commentary, and translation of poems by Robert A. Rorex and Wen Fong. [New York] Metropolitan Museum of Art; distributed by New York Graphic Society [Greenwich, Conn., 1974] 1 v. (unpaged) illus. (part col.) 25 x 28 cm. The text of the poems on the scroll reproduced here is by Liu Shang; the paintings are by an unknown artist. Includes bibliographical references. [ND3399.L55E37] 74-11140 ISBN 0-87099-095-0 18.50
1. Liu, Shang, 8th cent. Hu chia shih pa p'ai—Illustrations. 2. New York (City). Metropolitan Museum of Art. 3. Ts'ai, Yen, ca. 177-ca. 239—Art. 4. Painting, Chinese—Sung-Yuan dynasties, 960-1368. I. Rorex, Robert A., ed. II. Fong, Wen, ed. III. New York (City). Metropolitan Museum of Art. IV. Liu, Shang, 8th cent. Hu chia shih pa p'ai. English. 1974.

Liverpool.

CHANNON, Howard. 914.27'2
Portrait of Liverpool. 2nd ed. London, Hale, 1972. 224, (24) p. illus., map. 23 cm. [DA690.L8C48 1972] 72-169848 ISBN 0-7091-3025-2
1. Liverpool. I. Title.
Distributed by International Publications Service 7.50. BIP

Liverpool Amateur Photographic Association.

GOOD, George. 016.77
The history of the Liverpool Amateur Photographic Association, from 1853 to 1953. [Liverpool? 1953] 63p. illus. 23cm. [TR1.G57] 57-16208
1. Liverpool Amateur Photographic Association. I. Title.

Liverpool and Manchester Railway.

BURY, Thomas Talbot, 769'.92'4
1811-1877.
Coloured views on the Liverpool and Manchester railway / T. T. Bury ; with an historical introd. to the railway by George Ottley. Oldham [Eng.] : H. Broadbent, c1976. ix, 8 p., [16] leaves of plates (3 fold.) : ill. (some col.) ; 35 cm. A reprint of the original edition published in 1831 by R. Ackermann. Bibliography: p. vi. [TF64.L7B8 1976] 77-353374 ISBN 0-904848-02-7 : £16.50
1. Liverpool and Manchester Railway. I. Title.

Liverpool—Description.

CHANNON, Howard. 942.7'53
Portrait of Liverpool / [by] Howard Channon. 3rd ed. London : Hale, 1976. 231 p., [24] p. of plates : ill., map ; 23 cm. Includes index. [DA690.L8C48 1976] 76-382112 ISBN 0-7091-5575-1 : £4.00
1. Channon, Howard. 2. Liverpool—Description. I. Title.

Liverpool—Description—Views.

LIVERPOOL old and new 942.7'53'08
/ [compiled by] Thomas Lloyd-Jones. Wakefield : EP Publishing, 1975. [5], 98 p. : of ill. ; 18 x 24 cm. [DA690.L8L854] 75-323616 ISBN 0-7158-1104-5 : £1.95
1. Liverpool—Description—Views. I. Lloyd-Jones, Thomas.

Livery buttons—Catalogs.

SQUIRE, Gwen. 391'.45
Livery buttons : the Pitt Collection / [by] Gwen Squire. Pulborough : Leghorn Co., 1976. lxix p., 100 leaves of plates : chiefly ill., port. ; 28 cm. Leaves printed on both sides. Includes indexes. Bibliography: p. lxix. [NK3670.S67 1976] 77-373031 ISBN 0-9504748-0-0 : £10.00
1. Pitt, Ronald—Art collections. 2. Livery buttons—Catalogs. I. Title.

Living room furniture.

POPULAR homecraft. 684
Living room furniture; 35 chairs, tables, odd pieces. Edited by Perry S. Graffam. [Chicago, General Pub. Co., 1950] 88 p. illus., diagrs. 28 cm. (The Home workshop library) Hobby books. Cover title. Reprints of articles from Popular homecraft magazine. [TT197.5.L5P6] 50-14576
1. Living room furniture. I. Graffam, Perry S., 1890- ed. II. Title.

Living rooms.

BRANDT, Mary L. 747.75
How to plan your living room. New York, Greenberg, c1955. 96 p. illus. 21 cm. (Room-by-room decorating series) [NK2117.B66] 55-10658
1. Living rooms. 2. Interior decoration. I. Title.

MILLS, Nancy. 747'.75
Decorating your living room. Garden City, N.Y., N. Doubleday [1968] 72 p. illus. (part col.) 24 cm. (The Doubleday home decorating program) 71-679
1. Living rooms. 2. Interior decoration. I. Title.

RADFORD, Penny. 747'.75
Rooms for living / [by] Penny Radford. London : Design Council, 1976. 70 p. : ill. (chiefly col.) ; 21 x 22 cm. (A Design Centre book) [NK2117.L5R33] 77-355553 ISBN 0-85072-028-1 : £3.25. ISBN 0-85072-029-X pbk.
1. Living rooms. 2. Interior decoration. I. Title. BIP

Livingston Co., N. Y.—Antiq.

RITCHIE, William 913.747
Augustus, 1903-
Dutch Hollow, an early historic period Seneca site in Livingston County, New York. Albany, New York State Archeological Association, 1954. iv, 98p. illus., tables. 26cm. (Researches and transactions of the New York State Archeological Association, v. 13, no. 1) 'Sponsored by Lewis H. Morgan Chapter.' Bibliography: p. 75-79 [E78.N7R478 1954] 54-14929
1. Livingston Co., N. Y.—Antiq. 2. Seneca Indians—Antiq. I. Title. II. Series: New York State Archeological Association. Lewis H. Morgan Chapter, Rochester. Researches and transactions, v. 13. no. 1

Lloyd, Reginald J., 1926—

LLOYD, Reginald J., 760'.092'4
1926-
Paintings, drawings and monotypes in private collections / [by] R. J. Lloyd ; [compiled by Louise MacMillan]. [Barnstaple] : [Porcupines], [1976] [105] p. : of ill., ports. ; 30 cm. [N6797.L58M3] 77-364177 ISBN 0-85531-010-3 : £2.50
1. Lloyd, Reginald J., 1926- 2. Art—Private collections—Great Britain. I. MacMillan, Louise. II. Title.

Loccum. Ger. (Abbey)

KARPA, Oskar. 734.43
Kloster Loccum; 800 Jahre Zisterzienser Abtei in Niedersachsen. Mit Bildern von Edgar Lieseberg. Hannover, H. Feesche [1963] 124 p. plans, plates. 24 cm. Bibliography: p. 122. [NA5586.L57K3] 66-87536
1. Loccum. Ger. (Abbey) I. Title.

Locke, William M., 1894-1972.

THE William M. 683'.43'074017178
Locke Collection; [catalogue. By Frank M. Sellers and others. 1st ed.] East Point, Ga., Antique Armory Inc. [1973] 541 p. chiefly illus. (part col.) 29 cm. Bibliography: p. 538. [TS532.4.W56] 73-91748
1. Locke, William M., 1894-1972. 2. Pistols—Collectors and collecting. I. Locke, William M., 1894-1972. II. Sellers, Frank M. III. The Antique Armory Inc.

Locker, Thomas, 1937—

LOCKER, Thomas, 1937- 759.13
Thomas Locker; the new American realism. Introd. by Joshua C. Taylor. [Chicago, 1972?] 15 p. illus. (part col.) 25 cm. Exhibition held at R. S. Johnson-International Gallery, Spring, 1972. [ND237.L695J63] 72-77758
1. Locker, Thomas, 1937- I. Johnson (R. S.)-International Gallery.

Lockhart, James Haldane Stewart, Sir, 1858-1937—Coin collections.

LOCKHART, James 737.4'9'51
Haldane Stewart, Sir, 1858-1937.
The Lockhart collection of Chinese copper coins / James H. Stewart Lockhart. Lawrence, Mass. : Quarterman Publications, [1975] xv, 174, [62] p. : ill. ; 32 cm. Reprint, with new forward, price guide, and commentary, of the 1915 ed., published by Kelly & Walsh, Shanghai, under title: The Stewart Lockhart collection Chinese copper coins; and issued as Extra volume no. 1 of the Journal of the Royal Asiatic Society, North China Branch. Includes bibliography. [CJ3500.L7 1975] 74-27610 ISBN 0-88000-056-2 : 30.00
1. Lockhart, James Haldane Stewart, Sir, 1858-1937—Coin collections. 2. Coins, Chinese. 3. Copper coins. I. Title. II. Series: Royal Asiatic Society of Great Britain and Ireland. North China Branch, Shanghai. Journal : Extra volume ; no. 1. BIP

Locks and keys—Collectors and collecting.

ZARA, Louis, 1910- 683'.32'075
Locks and keys. New York, Walker [1969] 82, [2] p. illus. 22 cm. (Collectors' blue books) Bibliography: p. [84] [NK8204.Z3 1969] 79-86410 4.50
1. Locks and keys—Collectors and collecting. I. Title.

Lockwood, Ward.

ELDREDGE, Charles C. 759.13
Ward Lockwood, 1894-1963 / Charles C. Eldredge. Lawrence : University of Kansas Museum of Art, 1974. 142 p. : ill. (some col.) ; 27 cm. (Miscellaneous publications of the University of Kansas Museum of Art ; no. 95) Includes bibliographical references. [ND237.L698E42] 74-17874
1. Lockwood, Ward. I. Lockwood, Ward. II. Series: Kansas. University. Museum of Art. Miscellaneous publications ; no. 95.

Locsin, Leandro.

POLITES, Nicholas. 720'.92'4
The architecture of Leandro V. Locsin / by Nicholas Polites ; with a foreword by Fernando Zobel ; photos. by Akio Kawasumi and visual presentation by Norio Ishiguro. 1st ed. New York : Weatherhill, 1977. p. cm. [NA1529.L6P64] 77-1441 ISBN 0-8348-0129-9 : 50.00
1. Locsin, Leandro. 2. Architecture, Modern—20th century—Philippine Islands. I. Kawasumi, Akio, 1923- II. Title. BIP

Loewy, Raymond Fernand, 1893—

THE designs of 745.2'092'4
Raymond Loewy : [an exhibition at the Renwick Gallery of the National Collection of Fine Arts, Smithsonian Institution, Washington, D.C., August 1-November 16, 1975]. Washington : Published for the Renwick Gallery of the National Collection of Fine Arts by the Smithsonian Institution Press : for sale by the Supt. of Docs., U.S. Govt. Print. Office, 1975. 55 p. : ill. ; 30 cm. [T180.W3R464] 75-619164
1. Loewy, Raymond Fernand, 1893- 2. Design, Industrial—Exhibitions. I. Loewy, Raymond Fernand, 1893- II. Renwick Gallery.

Log cabins.

ANGIER, Bradford 728.74
How to build your home in the woods. Illus. by Vena Angier. New York, Hart [1965, c.1952] 310p. illus. 21cm. (House & home) [NA8470.A55] 1.95 pap.,
1. Log cabins. I. Title.

ANGIER, Bradford. 728.74
How to build your home in the woods; illustrated by Vena Angier. New York, Sheridan House [1952] 310 p. illus. 22 cm. [NA8470.A55] 52-13865
1. Log cabins. I. Title. BIP

BROWNLEE Company. 728.74
Brownlee sectional log cabins. Detroit [1951] unpaged. illus. 28 cm. [NA8470.B72] 51-32666
1. Log cabins. I. Title. II. Title: Sectional log cabins.

DUNCAN, S. Blackwell. 694'.2
How to build your own log home & cabin from scratch / S. Blackwell Duncan. Blue Ridge Summit, Pa. : Tab Books, [1978] p. cm. Includes index. [TH4840.D85] 78-10468 ISBN 0-8306-9874-4 : 9.95. ISBN 0-8306-1081-2 pbk. : 5.95
1. Log cabins. I. Title. BIP

HUNT, Walter Bernard, 690'.8'7
1888-1970.
How to build and furnish a log cabin; the easy-natural way using only hand tools and the woods around you [by] W. Ben Hunt. New York, Macmillan [1974] x, 166 p. illus. 25 cm. Reprint of the author's Rustic construction and Building a log cabin published in 1939 and 1947, respectively. [TH4840.H86] 74-12010 ISBN 0-02-557440-X 7.95
1. Log cabins. 2. Rustic woodwork. I.

Hunt, Walter Bernard, 1888-1970. Rustic construction. 1974. II. Hunt, Walter Bernard, 1888-1970. Building a log cabin. 1974. III. Title.
BIP

LEITCH, William C.   694'.2
Hand-hewn : the art of building your own cabin / by William C. Leitch. San Francisco : Chronicle Books, c1976. 122 p. : ill. ; 23 cm. Includes bibliographical references and index. [TH4840.L44] 75-45418 ISBN 0-87701-079-X : 5.95
1. Log cabins. I. Title.
BIP

RITCHIE, James D.   690'.8'7
Successful log houses : planning & building, renovating & repairing. Farmington, Mich. : Structures Pub. Co., [1978] p. cm. Includes index. Bibliography: p. [TH4840.R57] 78-15308 ISBN 0-912336-71-4 : 12.00. ISBN 0-912336-72-2 pbk. : 5.95
1. Log cabins. I. Title.

RUTSTRUM, Calvin.   728.7
The wilderness cabin. Illustrated by Les Kouba. New York, Macmillan, 1961. 169 p. illus. 24 cm. [NA8470.R8] 61-9730
1. Log cabins. I. Title.
BIP

RUTSTRUM, Calvin.   690.8'7
The wilderness cabin. Illustrated by Les Kouba. Rev. ed. New York, Macmillan [1972] 194 p. illus. 22 cm. [TH4835.R87 1972] 73-171992 5.95
1. Log cabins. I. Title.

SPORTS afield.   728.74
Cabin building annual. [New York, Hearst Corp.] v. illus. 29cm. [NA8470.S66] 54-927
1. Log cabins. 2. Cottages. 3. Architecture, Domestic—Designs and plans. I. Title.

SUNSET.   728.7
Cabins and vacation houses, by the editorial staffs of Sunset books & Sunset magazine. Menlo Park, Calif., Lane Book Co. [1960] 128 p. illus. 28 cm. (A Sunset book) [NA8470.S78] 60-5087
1. Log cabins. 2. Cottages. 3. Architecture, Domestic—Designs and plans. 4. Interior decoration. I. Title.
BIP

TIME-LIFE Books.   690'.8'7
Cabins and cottages / by the editors of Time-Life Books. Alexandria, Va. : Time-Life Books, 1978. p. cm. (Home repair and improvement ; 15) Includes index. [TH4840.T55 1978] 78-24577 ISBN 0-8094-2410-X : 7.95
1. Log cabins. 2. Cottages. I. Title.
BIP

WALTON, Harry.   693
How to build your cabin or modern vacation home. New York, Popular Science Pub. Co. [1964] 160 p. illus. 24 cm. (Popular science skill book) [TH4835.W3] 64-13134
1. Log cabins. 2. Summer homes. 3. Building—Amateurs' manuals. I. Title.

Log cabins—Design and construction.

HARD, Roger, 1931-   690'.8'1
Build your own low-cost log home / by Roger Hard ; ill. by Kathryn Hard. Charlotte, Vt. : Garden Way Pub., c1977. iv, 200 p. : ill. ; 28 cm. Includes bibliographies and index. [TH4840.H37] 77-3577 ISBN 0-88266-098-5 : 9.95. ISBN 0-88266-097-7 pbk. : 5.95
1. Log cabins—Design and construction. I. Title.
BIP

MCRAVEN, Charles.   690'.8'64
Building the hewn log house / by Charles McRaven ; paintings by James Burkhart ; photos. by Linda Moore McRaven ; author ; ill. by Chandis Ingenthron and the author. Hollister, Mo. : Mountain Pub. Services, c1978. 208 p. : ill. ; 22 cm. (Arkansas College folklore monograph series ; no. 1) Includes index. [TH4840.M33] 77-85768 ISBN 0-931158-00-1 : 7.95
1. Log cabins—Design and construction. I. Title. II. Series: Arkansas College, Batesville, Ark. Arkansas College folklore monograph series ; no. 1.
BIP

PFARR, Paul.   694'.2
Build your own log cabin / Paul and Karyn Pfarr. New York : Winchester Press, c1978. 191 p. : ill. ; 27 cm. Includes index.

[TH4840.P43] 77-17456 ISBN 0-87691-249-8 : 12.50
1. Log cabins—Design and construction. I. Pfarr, Karyn, joint author. II. Title.
BIP

Log cabins—Texas.

JORDAN, Terry G.   720'.9764
Texas log buildings, a folk architecture / Terry G. Jordan. Austin : University of Texas Press, c1978. 230 p. : ill. ; 25 cm. Includes index. Bibliography: p. 211-222. [NA8470.J67] 77-24559 ISBN 0-292-78023-0 : 15.95
1. Log cabins—Texas. 2. Architecture, Anonymous—Texas. I. Title.

Log cabins—United States.

BEALER, Alex W.   728'.7
The log cabin : homes of the North American wilderness / text and drawings by Alex W. Bealer ; photos. by John O. Ellis. 1st ed. Barre, Mass. : Barre Pub. ; New York : distributed by Crown Publishers, [c1978] 191 p. : ill. (some col.) ; 23 x 26 cm. Includes index. Bibliography: p. [185]-187. [NA8470.B35 1978] 77-26316 ISBN 0-517-52892-4 : 17.95 6.95 ISBN 0-517-53379-0 pbk. : 6.95
1. Log cabins—United States. 2. Log cabins—Canada. I. Ellis, John O. II. Title.
BIP

WESLAGER, Clinton Alfred, 1909-   917.3
The log cabin in America; from pioneer days to the present [by] C. A. Weslager. New Brunswick, N.J., Rutgers University Press [1969] xxv, 382 p. illus., maps, ports. 25 cm. [NA7206.W4] 69-13554 ISBN 0-8135-0596-8 12.50
1. Log cabins—United States. 2. Architecture, Domestic—United States. I. Title.
BIP

Log-end houses.

ROY, Robert L.   694
How to build log-eng houses / by Robert L. Roy. New York : Drake Publishers, [1977] p. cm. [TH4818.W6R69] 77-72392 ISBN 0-8473-1608-4 : 12.95. ISBN 0-8473-1551-7 pbk. : 6.95
1. Log-end houses. I. Title.

Lombardo, Tullio.

WILK, Sarah.   730'.92'4
The sculpture of Tullio Lombardo : studies in sources and meaning / Sarah Wilk. New York : Garland Pub., 1978. a. p. cm. (Outstanding dissertations in the fine arts) Bibliography: p. [NB623.L74W54] 77-94723 ISBN 0-8240-3256-X : lib.bdg. : 37.50
1. Lombardo, Tullio. 2. Sculpture, Renaissance—Italy—Venice. I. Title. II. Series.
BIP

London.

PRITCHETT, Victor Sawdon, 1900-   914.212
London perceived. Photos. by Evelyn Hofer. [1st American ed.] New York, Harcourt, Brace & World [1962] 116 p. illus. 29 cm. [DA677.P7] 62-14471
1. London. I. Hofer, Evelyn. II. Title.
BIP

London—Amusements.

RALPH, James, d.1762.   700
The touch-stone. New York, Garland Pub., 1970. xxviii, 237 p. 22 cm. Facsimile of the Yale University Library copy with imprint: London, Printed and sold by the booksellers of London and Westminster, 1728. [DA688.R17 1728a] 79-112215
1. London—Amusements. I. Title.
BIP

London—Antiquities.

MERRIFIELD, Ralph.   936.2'2
The archaeology of London / by Ralph Merrifield. Park Ridge, N.J. : Noyes Press, [1975], c1974. viii, 95 p. : ill. ; 22 cm. (Regional archaeologies) Includes index. Bibliography: p. 93. Describes archaeological finds in the London area

and their importance in reconstructing the history of the area from the first appearance of man to the seventh century A.D. [DA677.1.M444 1975b] 74-83860 ISBN 0-8155-5033-2 : 9.95
1. London—Antiquities. 2. London region, Eng.—Antiquities. I. Title.
BIP

London—Antiquities—Addresses, essays, lectures.

THE Archaeology of the   942.1
London area : current knowledge and problems / Desmond Collins ... [et al.]. London : London and Middlesex Archaeological Society, 1976. [4], 28 p. : ill., map ; 25 cm. (Special paper - London and Middlesex Archaeological Society ; no. 1) Includes bibliographical references. [DA677.1.A78] 76-376842 ISBN 0-903290-14-6 : £1.00
1. London—Antiquities—Addresses, essays, lectures. I. Collins, Desmond. II. Series: London and Middlesex Archaeological Society. Special paper — London and Middlesex Archaeological Society ; no. 1.

London—Antiquities, Roman.

GRIMES, William Francis.   913.3'6
The excavation of Roman and mediaeval London [by] W. F. Grimes. New York, Praeger [1968] xxi, 261 p. illus., maps, plans, 102 plates. 26 cm. [DA677.1.G75] 68-15431
1. London—Antiquities, Roman. 2. London—History—To 1500. I. Title.

LETHABY, William Richard, 1857-1931.   913.362
Londinium, architecture and the crafts. New York, B. Blom, 1972. 248 p. illus. 21 cm. Reprint of the 1923 ed. [DA677.1.L58 1972] 72-83273
1. London—Antiquities, Roman. 2. Romans in London. I. Title.

MERRIFIELD, Ralph   914.21
The Roman city of London. London. E. Benn [New York, Dover, c1965] xvii, 344p. illus., maps (pt. fold., 1 fold. col. in pocket) plans, plates. 23cm. Bibl. [DA677.1.M45] 66-2309 10.00
1. London—Antiquities, Roman. I. Title.

MERRIFIELD, Ralph.   914.21'2
Roman London. New York, F. A. Praeger [1969] [12], 212 p. illus., maps. 24 cm. Bibliography: 11th-12th prelim. pages. [DA677.1.M46] 75-75111 9.50
1. London—Antiquities, Roman. 2. London—History—To 1500. 3. England—Antiquities, Roman. 4. Romans—England—London. I. Title.

SORRELL, Alan.   942.1'01
Roman London. New York, ARCO [1969] 71 p. illus. 23 x 30 cm. [DA677.1.S655 1969b] 69-12148 6.50
1. London—Antiquities, Roman. I. Title.

London—Antiquities, Roman—Juvenile literature.

ANTHONY, Ilid E.   913.362
Roman London [by] Ilid E. Anthony. Drawings by Isabella Whitworth. With a foreword by Norman Cook. New York, Putnam [1972, c1971] 113 p. illus. 23 cm. (The Young archaeologist books) Bibliography: p. 109-110. Describes what archaeological excavations in and around London have revealed about the Roman town of Londinium with particular attention given to the problems of excavating in a crowded city. [DA677.1.A73 1972] 70-146107 ISBN 0-298-79122-6 3.86
1. London—Antiquities, Roman—Juvenile literature. 2. Romans—Great Britain—London—Juvenile literature. I. Whitworth, Isabella, illus. II. Title.

London—Biography—Portraits.

LADY Ottoline's   779'.9'9421082
album : snapshots and portraits of her famous contemporaries (and of herself), photographed for the most part by Lady Ottoline Morrell : from the collector of her daughter, Julian Vinogradoff / with an introd. by Lord David Cecil ; edited by

Carolyn G. Heilbrun. 1st ed. New York : Knopf, 1976. vii, 117 p. : ill. ; 24 cm. Includes index. [DA676.8.A1L3 1976] 76-13678 ISBN 0-394-48758-3 : 12.50
1. Morrell, Ottoline Violet Anne Cavendish-Bentinck, Lady, 1873-1938—Portraits, etc. 2. London—Biography—Portraits. I. Morrell, Ottoline Violet Anne Cavendish-Bentinck, Lady, 1873-1938. II. Heilbrun, Carolyn G., 1926-

London Bridge.

ELMER, Carlos   914.21
London Bridge in pictures. 1st ed. Scottsdale, Ariz., 1971. 1 v. (unpaged) illus. 31 cm. [DA689.B8E43] 77-177272 2.00
1. London Bridge. I. Title.

London—Buildings.

HOBHOUSE, Hermione.   720'.9421
Lost London. [1st American ed.] Boston, Houghton Mifflin, 1972 [c1971] 250 p. illus. 29 cm. [DA689.H48H62 1972] 71-132787 ISBN 0-395-13521-4 20.00
1. London—Buildings. I. Title.

London—Clubs.

TIMBS, John, 1801-1875.   366'.9'421
Clubs and club life in London; with anecdotes of its famous coffeehouses, hostelries, and taverns, from the seventeenth century to the present time. Detroit, Gale Research Co., 1967. xiv, 544 p. illus. 23 cm. Title page includes original imprint: London, Chatto and Windus [1872] First published under title: Club life of London. Bibliographical footnotes. [DA686.T5 1967] 66-28045
1. London—Clubs. 2. London—Bars, saloons, etc. 3. Literary landmarks—London. I. Title.
BIP

London—Descr.

RASMUSSEN, Steen Eiler, 1898-   914.21
London, the unique city. Introd. by James Bone. Cambridge, M.I.T. Pr. [1967, c.1934] 440p. illus., maps, plans. 25cm. Reprint of the 3d ed., 1948. Bibl. [DA677.R273 1967] 67-14528 12.50; 3.45 pap.,
1. London—Descr. 2. London—Public works. I. Title.

London—Description—Views.

HOGARTH, Paul, 1917-   741.5942
London a la mode. Drawings and captions by Paul Hogarth. Text by Malcolm Muggeridge. New York, Hill and Wang [1966] 141 p. (chiefly illus.) 26 cm. [NC1479.H6M8 1966a] 66-26483
1. London—Description—Views. I. Muggeridge, Malcolm, 1903- II. Title.

London. Dominican Priory.

ADAMS, Joseph Quincy, 1881-1946.   725'.822
The conventual buildings of Blackfriars, London, and the playhouses constructed therein. New York, AMS Press, 1970. 25 p. illus. 24 cm. Reprint of the 1917 ed. Includes bibliographical references. [NA5470.L6A3 1970] 76-113537 ISBN 0-404-00289-7
1. London. Dominican Priory. 2. London. Blackfriars Theatre. I. Title.
BIP

London—Dwellings.

RICKARDS, Maurice, 1919-   914.21'04
Where they lived in London. New York, Taplinger [1972] 104 p. illus. 22 cm. [DA676.H48R5 1972b] 72-145542 ISBN 0-8008-8245-8 7.95
1. London—Dwellings. 2. Biography. I. Title.
BIP

London. Foundling Hospital.

NICOLSON, Benedict.   709'.421
The treasures of the Foundling Hospital.
With a catalogue raisonne based on a draft
catalogue by John Kerslake. Oxford,
Clarendon Press, 1972. xiv, 98 p. illus. 26
cm. (Studies in the history of art and
architecture) Bibliography: p. [92]-95.
[N5208.5.L6N5] 72-192246 ISBN 0-19-
817186-2
1. London. Foundling Hospital. 2. Art—
London—Catalogs. 3. Aesthetics, British. I.
Kerslake, John F. II. London. Foundling
Hospital. III. Title. IV. Series: Oxford
studies in the history of art and
architecture.
Available from Oxford University Press
N.Y. 11.25.   **BIP**

London—Galleries and museums.

BOUMPHREY, Geoffrey   914.21
  Maxwell, 1894-
Open on Sunday. London, New York,
Staples Press [1951] 163 p. illus. 19 cm.
[DA687.G3B6] 52-33513
1. London—Galleries and museums. 2.
London—Parks. I. Title.

London—History.

ODLE, Francis   914.21
The picture story of London, by Francis
Odle, Gerald Howston. London, World
Distributors [dist. New York, Heinman,
1965, c.1964] illus., facsims., maps, ports.
28cm. [DA677.O3] 65-9455 5.00 bds.
1. London—Hist. 2. London—Descr.—
Views. I. Howson, Gerald. II. Title.

London—History.

EHRLICH, Blake, 1917-   942.1
London on the Thames. [1st ed.] Boston,
Little, Brown [1966] xii, 435 p. illus. 25
cm. [DA677.E4] 66-10979
1.   London—History.   2.   London—
Description. I. Title.

London. Home House.

WHINNEY, Margaret   728.8'3
  Dickens.
Home House: no. 20 Portman Square [by]
Margaret Whinney; with a preface by Sir
Anthony Blunt. Feltham, Country Life,
1969. 80 p., 81-128 p. of illus. 23 cm.
[NA7332.W45] 79-469829 15/-
1. London. Home House. I. Title.

London. Imperial War Museum.

DARRACOTT, Joseph   769'.4'99403
*The First World War in posters, from the
Imperial War Museum, London* / selected
and edited by Joseph Darracott. New York
: Dover Publications, 1974. xxiii p., [37]
leaves of plates : 75 ill. ; 31 cm.
[D522.25.D36] 73-94348 | pbk. 4.95
1. London. Imperial War Museum. 2.
European War, 1914-1918—Posters. I.
London. Imperial War Museum. II. Title.

London in art.

DE MARE, Eric   914.21'03'81
  Samuel, 1910-
*The London Dore saw: a Victorian
evocation* [by] Eric de Mare. New York,
St. Martin's Press [1973] 228 p. illus. 31
cm.   Bibliography: p.   221-225.
[NC248.D6D45 1973b] 72-93928 15.00
1. Dore, Gustave, 1832-1883. 2. London in
art. I. Title.

HIND, Arthur Mayger,   769'.92'4
  1880-1957.
*Wenceslaus Hollar and his views of
London and Windsor in the seventeenth
century.* New York, B. Blom, [1973 c1972]
xiv, 92 p., lxiv p. of illus. 26 cm. Reprint
of the 1922 ed. published by J. Lane,
London.   Bibliography: p.   26-27.
[NE642.H7H5 1972] 68-56500 13.75
1. Hollar, Wenceslaus, 1607-1677. 2.
London in art. I. Title.

HOWGEGO, James L.   914.21'2'0222
The city of London through artists' eyes,

by J. L. Howgego. With introd. by
Nikolaus Pevsner. Foreword by Sir Gilbert
Inglefield. New York, Walker [1969] 64 p.
(chiefly illus., part col.) 29 cm.
[N8213.H6] 69-12780 5.95
1.   London   in   art.   2.   London—
Description—Views. I. Title.

KOKOSCHKA, Oskar, 1886-   759.2
London views, British landscapes. Introd.
by Jan Tomes. [Translated from the
German by Christine Cope] New York,
Praeger Publishers [1973, c1972] 84 p.
illus. (part col.) 26 x 33 cm. Translation of
*Londoner Ansichten, englische
Landschaften.* [ND511.5.K6A6213 1973]
72-81918 13.50
1. London in art. 2. Great Britain in art. I.
Tomes, Jan. II. Title.

PHILLIPS, John F. C.,   760'.092'2
  1943-
Shepherd's London / [by] J. F. C. Phillips.
London : Cassell, 1976. 116 p. : ill. (some
col.), geneal. table, map ; 29 cm. Contains
reproductions of works by Thomas Hosmer
Shepherd and other members of the
Shepherd family. Includes index.
Bibliography: p. 110-111. [NC242.S48P48]
77-361079 ISBN 0-304-29675-9 : £5.95
1. Shepard family. 2. London in art. I.
Shepherd, Thomas Hosmer. II. Title. **BIP**

TAMBURI, Orfeo, 1910-   741.9'45
London by Orfeo Tamburi. Verona,
Edizione d'arte Ghelfi, 1972. 16, [45] p.
illus. (part col.) 15 cm. Introduction by
Vera Lindsay. [NC257.T35L56] 73-167826
1. Tamburi, Orfeo, 1910- 2. London in art.
I.   Lindsay,   Vera.   II.   Title.

London—Intellectual life—Exhibitions.

NATIONAL Book League,   700'.92'2
  London.
Bloomsbury group : [catalogue of] an
exhibition arranged by the National Book
League, 1976. London : N.B.L. in
association with the Hogarth Press, [1976]
38 p., [16] p. of plates : ill., ports. ; 25 cm.
(The   Word   and   the   image   ;   7)
[DA688.N28 1976] 76-377498 ISBN 0-
85353-243-5 : £2.00
1. London—Intellectual life—Exhibitions.
2.   London—Biography—Portraits—
Exhibitions. I. Title. II. Series: Word and
image ; 7.

London. International Exhibition, 1862.

DRESSER, Christopher.   745.4'44
*Development of ornamental art in the
International Exhibition* / Christopher
Dresser. New York : Garland Pub., 1978.
192 p. ; 19 cm. (The Aesthetic movement
& the arts and crafts movement) Reprint of
the 1862 ed. published by Day and Son,
London. [NK1378.D73 1978] 76-17750
ISBN 0-8240-2452-4 : 35.00
1. London. International Exhibition, 1862.
2. Decoration and ornament, Victorian—
Exhibitions. I. Title. II. Series.   **BIP**

London. National Gallery.

LONDON. National   759.94'074'02132
  Gallery.
A guide to the National Gallery / [by]
Homan Potterton ; with a foreword by
Michael Levey .... London : The Gallery,
[1976] 168, [2] p. (2 fold.) : ill., general.
table, plans, ports. ; 21 cm. Includes
indexes. [N1070.A67] 76-382243 ISBN 0-
901791-60-1 : £0.50
1.   London.   National   Gallery.   2.
Paintings—England—London—Catalogs. I.
Potterton, Homan. II. Title.

POTTERTON,   759.94'074'02132
  Homan.
The National Gallery, London / Homan
Potterton ; with a preface by Michael
Levey and a complete catalogue of the
paintings. London : Thames & Hudson,
1977. 216 p. : ill. (some col.) ; 21 cm. (The
World of art library) Bibliography: p. [24]
[N1070.P57] 77-375645 ISBN 0-500-
20161-7 pbk. : 7.95
1. London. National Gallery. 2. Painting—
England—London—Catalogs. I. Title.
Distributed by W.W. Norton   **BIP**

London National Gallery—Catalogs.

*THE National Gallery.   708.21
  London.
The Illustrated general catalogue [by] the
National Gallery. London National Gallery
1973. 842 p. illus. 25 cm. [N1070] ISBN
0-8277-2838-7.
1. London National Gallery—Catalogs. I.
Title.
Distributed by the British Book Centre,
Elmsford, N.Y. for 17.50.

London. New London Synagogue.

QUEST.   705
1, 1965 London, Paul Hamlyn for the New
London Synagogue [New York, Tudor,
1966. c.1965] 92p. illus. (pt. col.) ports.
33cm. annual [AP4.Q49] 66-5855 4.95
bds.
1. London. New London Synagogue.

London. No. 10 Downing Street.

MINNEY, Rubeigh James,   354.42038
  1895-
No. 10 Downing Street, a house in history.
[1st American ed.] Boston, Little, Brown
[1963] xvii, 483 p. illus., ports., maps,
plans. 22 cm. Bibliography: p. 445-[452]
[DA687.D7M5 1963] 63-8315
1. London. No. 10 Downing Street. I.
Title.

London—Office buildings.

COWAN, Peter, 1929-   711'.552
The office; a facet of urban growth, by
Peter Cowan, and Daniel Fine [and others]
Foreword by Lord Llewelyn-Davies.
[American ed.] New York, American
Elsevier Pub. Co., 1969. xi, 280 p. illus.,
maps. 23 cm. Bibliography: p. [272]-275.
[NA9053.O3C68 1969] 69-18137 ISBN 0-
444-19772-9 10.75
1. London—Office buildings. 2. Cities and
towns—Planning—London. I. Title.

London—Parks.

THURSTON, Hazel.   914.21
Royal parks for the people; London's ten.
Newton Abbot, North Pomfret, Vt., David
& Charles [1974] 163 p. illus. 22 cm.
Bibliography: p. 150-152. [SB485.L84T48]
74-179387 ISBN 0-7153-6454-5 10.50
1. London—Parks. I. Title.   **BIP**

London—Parks—Regent's Park.

PENNICK, Rupert.   133.3'33
Regent's Park : town planning-or
geomancy? / by Rupert Pennick & Nigel
Pennick. Cambridge : Fenris-Wolf, 1977.
[1], 8 p. : ill., map, plans ; 30 cm.
(Megalithic visions antiquarian papers ; no.
13) [DA685.R43P46] 77-379273
1. London—Parks—Regent's Park. I.
Pennick, Nigel, joint author. II. Title. III.
Series.

SAUNDERS, Ann, 1930-   711'.558
Regent's Park; a study of the development
of the area from 1086 to the present day,
by Ann Saunders (Ann Cox-Johnson) New
York, A. M. Kelley [1969] 244 p. illus.
(part col.), plans. 23 cm. Includes
bibliographical   references.
[DA685.R43S25] 69-11238
1. London—Parks—Regent's Park. I. Title.
                                        BIP

London—Parks—Syon Park.

GARDENING Centre   914.21'82
  Limited.
The guide to Syon Park. [Brentford] : [The
Centre], [1976] [1], 42 p. : ill. (incl. 1 col.),
map ; 21 cm. [DA685.S97G37 1976] 77-
372968 ISBN 0-9505026-0-X
1. London—Parks—Syon Park. I. Title.

London—Parks—Victoria Park.

POULSEN, Charles.   942.1'5
Victoria Park : a study in the history of
East London / by Charles Poulsen.
London : Stepney Books : Journeyman
Press, 1976. [8], 120 p. : ill., plans ; 21 cm.

Bibliography: p. 119. [DA685.V5P68] 77-
373009 ISBN 0-904526-15-1 : £1.20
1. London—Parks—Victoria Park. I. Title.
                                        BIP

London— playgrounds.

TREVELYAN, Janet Penrose   942.3'74
  (Ward) 1879-
Two stories, by Janet Trevelyan (Mrs. G.
M. Trevelyan) London, New York,
Longmans, Green [1954] 222p. illus. 23cm.
[CT788.T78T7] 54-3999
1. Trevelyan, Theodore Macaulay, 1906-
1911. 2. London— playgrounds. I. Title.
Contents omitted.

London-Plazas-Trafalgar Square.

MACE, Rodney.   942.1'32
Trafalgar Square : emblem of empire /
Rodney Mace. London : Lawrence and
Wishart, 1976. 338 p., [20] leaves of plates
: ill. ; 24 cm. Includes index. Bibliography:
p. 323-338. [DA685.T84M32] 76-378564
ISBN 0-85315-368-X : £8.00. ISBN 0-
85315-367-1 pbk.
1. Nelson, Horatio Nelson, 1758-1805—
Monuments, etc. 2. London—Plazas—
Trafalgar Square. I. Title.   **BIP**

*MACE, Rodney.   712.5'09421
Trafalgar Square : Emblem of empire /
[by] Rodney Mace. London : Lawrence
and Wishart, 1976. 338,[40]p. : ill. ; 24 cm.
Includes index. Label mounted on
t.p.:Distributed in U.S.A. by Humanties
Press. [NA9070] ISBN 0-85315-368-X :
16.00
1. London-Plazas-Trafalgar Square. I. Title.

London. Royal Academy of Arts.

GRAVES,   709'.42'07402132
  Algernon.
The Royal Academy of Arts; a complete
dictionary of contributors and their work
from its foundation in 1769 to 1904. New
York, B. Franklin [1972- v. ports. 23
cm. (Burt Franklin bibliography &
reference series, 320. Art history & art
reference, 27) Reprint of the 1905-06 ed.
[N5054.G72] 76-118750 ISBN 0-8337-
1425-2 189.50 (8 vols.)
1. London. Royal Academy of Arts. 2.
Artists, British.   **BIP**

HUTCHISON, Sidney C.   707'.1'1421
*The history of the Royal Academy, 1768-
1968* [by] Sidney C. Hutchison. New
York, Taplinger Pub. Co. [1968] 268 p.
illus. (part col.), facsims., ports. 24 cm.
Bibliographical footnotes. [N1100.H78
1968b] 68-21819 12.95
1. London. Royal Academy of Arts. I.
Title.   **BIP**

LESLIE, George Dunlop,   706.2'42
  1835-1921.
*The inner life of the Royal Academy, with
an account of its schools and exhibitions,
principally in the reign of Queen Victoria.*
New York, B. Blom, 1971. xvi, 286 p.
illus. 22 cm. [N12.R7L4 1971] 72-172552
1. London. Royal Academy of Arts. I.
Title.

ROSSETTI, William   759.2'074'02132
  Michael, 1829-1919.
*Notes on the Royal Academy exhibition,
1868.* Part I. By Wm. Michael Rossetti.
Part II. By Algernon C. Swinburne.
London, J. C. Hotten. [New York, AMS
Press, 1973] p. Reprint of the 1868 ed.
[N5054.R47 1973] 75-144681 ISBN 0-404-
05418-8 5.00
1. London. Royal Academy of Arts. 2.
Art—Exhibitions. I. Swinburne, Algenon
Charles, 1837-1909. II. Title.

London. St. Paul's Cathedral.

LANG, Jane.   726.6
*Rebuilding St. Paul's after the great fire of
London.* London, New York, Oxford
University Press, 1956. xi, 269p. illus.,
ports. 26cm. Bibliography: p. [257]- 261.
[NA5470.S5L3] 56-14474
1. Wren, Christopher, Sir 1632-1723. 2.
London. St. Paul's Cathedral. I. Title.

SUBJECT INDEX LOUD-SPEAKERS.

SHEPHERD, Cecil William. 726.65094212
Everyone's St. Paul's [by] C. W. Shepherd; with thirty-two plates in colour and black-and-white, photographed by A. Ronald Traube and Richard Traube. London, New York, F. Warne [1966] viii, 126 p. 32 plates (some col.) 22 1/2 cm. 25/- Illus., col. plan on endpapers. [DA687.S14S47] 66-15685
1. London. St. Paul's Cathedral. I. Title.

London. Tower.

CARKEET-JAMES, Edward Hamilton, 1893- 914.212
His Majesty's Tower of London. London, New York, Staples Press [1950] 147 p. illus., plan (on lining papers) 19 cm. [DA687.T7O3] 51-400
1. London. Tower. I. Title.

GT. Brit. Ministry of Public Building and Works. 942.1'25
The Tower of London. London, H.M.S.O., 1967. 56p. illus., 5 plates (4 col.), plan. 20cm. (1ts Guide bk.) [DA687.T7A52 1967b] 67-107959 .50 pap.,
1. London. Tower. I. Title. II. Series.
Available from British Info., New York.

HIBBERT, Christopher, 1924- 914.21'2
Tower of London, by Christopher Hibbert and the editors of the Newsweek Book Division. New York, Newsweek [1971] 172 p. illus. (part col.), facsims., plan, ports. 30 cm. (Wonders of man) Bibliography: p. 169. [DA687.T7H5] 70-136436
1. London. Tower. I. Newsweek, inc. Book Division.

MINNEY, Rubeigh James, 1895- 942.1'2
The Tower of London [by] R. J. Minney. Englewood Cliffs, N.J., Prentice-Hall [1970] 230 p. illus. (part col.), maps, ports. 29 cm. Bibliography: p. 225. [DA687.T7M55 1970] 72-123084 ISBN 0-13-925768-3 12.95
1. London. Tower. I. Title.

London. Tower—Juvenile literature.

SHUTTLESWORTH, Dorothy Edwards, 1907- 943
The Tower of London: grim and glamorous, by Dorothy E. Shuttlesworth. Photos. by Camilla Jessel. Drawings by Floyd James Torbert. New York, Hastings House [1970] 88 p. illus., ports. 24 cm. (Famous museum series) Bibliography: p. 84. Traces the history of the Tower of London and describes some of the most famous and unusual exhibits and ceremonies that can be seen there by visitors today. [DA687.T7S54 1970] 79-102158 4.95
1. London. Tower—Juvenile literature. 2. Gt. Brit.—History—Juvenile literature. I. Jessel, Camilla, illus. II. Torbert, Floyd James, illus. III. Title.

London. Vauxhall Gardens.

SCOTT, Walter Sidney, 1900- 942.1
Green retreats; the story of Vauxhall Gardens, 1661-1859. London, Odhams Press [1955; label: Fair Lawn, N. J., Essential Books] 128p. illus. 26cm. [DA689.G3S35] 56-105
1. London. Vauxhall Gardens. I. Title.

Long Island — Hist. — Societies, etc.

LONG Island Historical Society. 706.273
The century book of the Long Island Historical Society. Edited by Walton H. Rawls. [New York, c1964] viii, 206 p. illus. 26 cm. [F116.L952] 64-17238
1. Long Island — Hist. — Societies, etc. I. Rawls, Walton H., ed. II. Title.

Long Island — Historic houses, etc.

LEWIS, Cyril A 759.13
Historical Long Island; paintings and sketches, by Cyril A. Lewis. Text by Charles J. McDermott, Assisted by Jayne Coles. Westhampton Beach, N. Y., Long Island Forum [1964] 109 p. illus., map, port. 29 cm. [ND1839.L44M3] 65-4106
1. Long Island — Historic houses, etc. 2. Long Island — Descr. & trav. — Views. I. McDermott, Charles J. II. Title.

Long rifle.

SHUMWAY, George. 739.7'4'425
Longrifles of note, Pennsylvania. York, Pa. [1968] 74 p. illus. 22 cm. [NK6997.S5] 68-14241
1. Long rifle. 2. Gunsmiths, American—Pennsylvania. 3. Art, Rococo—Pennsylvania. I. Title.

Longcase clocks.

BRUTON, Eric. 681'.113
The longcase clock / [by] Eric Bruton. 2nd ed. London : Hart-Davis MacGibbon, 1976, i.e.1977 246 p. : ill., facsims., ports. ; 23 cm. Includes index. Bibliography: p. [238]-239. [NK7500.L65B78 1976] 77-372953 ISBN 0-246-10881-9 : 29.95
1. Longcase clocks. I. Title.
Distributed by Granada, Suite 3468, 1221 Ave. of the Americas, New York, NY 10020

Longo, Vincent, 1923—

LONGO, Vincent, 1923- 769'.92'4
Eight etchings. Washington, D.C., Graphics International, 1972. 1 portfolio ([3] l., 8 plates (part col.)) 53 cm. "31 copies, including ... 25 portfolios numbered 1 through 25." No. 2. [NE2012.L64A43] 72-171443
1. Longo, Vincent, 1923-

LONGO, Vincent, 1923- 769'.973
Vincent Longo print retrospective, 1954-1970. Washington, D.C. [Corcoran Gallery of Art, 1970] [49] p. illus., port. 24 cm. Catalog of the exhibition held Apr. 3-May 17, 1970, at the Corcoran Gallery of Art, Washington, D.C. Bibliography: p. [49] [NE539.L6A58] 70-121147
1. Corcoran Gallery of Art, Washington, D.C. II. Title.

Looby, Keith Ronald, 1940—

LOOBY, Keith Ronald, 1940- 741.9'94
The history of Australia / drawings by Keith Looby, songs and poems by David Campbell. Sydney : Macleay Museum, University of Sydney, 1976. [57] leaves : chiefly ill. ; 24 x 31 cm. [NC371.L66C35] 77-363175 ISBN 0-909635-06-4
1. Looby, Keith Ronald, 1940- 2. Australia in art. I. Campbell, David Watt Ian. II. Title.

Looms.

HOFFMANN, Marta, 1913- 746.1
The warp-weighted loom; studies in the history and technology of an ancient implement [Oslo?] Universitetsforlaget [New York. Textile Bk. Serv., 257 Park Ave. S., 1965, c.1964] 425p. illus., map. 23cm. (Studia Norvegica, no. 14) Pub. under the auspices of Norsk folkemuseum. Bibl. [GR1.S85 no.14] 65-5567 9.00 pap.,
1. Looms. 2. Hand weaving. 3. Weaving—Europe—Hist. I. Oslo. Norsk folkemuseum. II. Title. III. Series.

MCCREARY, Carol Fillips, 1945- 746.1'4
The traditional Moroccan loom : its construction and use / by Carol Fillips McCreary. Santa Rosa, Calif. : Thresh Publications, [1975] p. cm. [TS1493.M18] 75-23247 ISBN 0-913664-32-4 pbk. : 2.50
1. Looms. 2. Hand weaving. I. Title.

Looney, Ben Earl.

LOONEY, Ben Earl. 759.13
Watercolors of Dixie / by Ben Earl Looney. Baton Rouge : Claitor's Pub. Div., c1974. 90 p. : ill. (some col.) ; 23 x 29 cm. [ND1839.L63A57] 74-21848 13.95
1. Looney, Ben Earl. 2. Southern States in art. I. Title. BIP

Loos, Adolf, 1870-1933.

MUNZ, Ludwig, 1889-1957 720.924
Adolf Loos, pioneer of modern architecture [by] Ludwig Munz, Gustav Kunstler. Introd. by Nikolaus Pevsner. Appreciation by Oskar Kokoschka. [Tr. from German by Harold Meek] New York, Praeger [c.1964, 1966] 234p. illus., plans, port. 24cm. Bibl. [NA1038.L6M83] 66-12528 20.00
1. Loos, Adolf, 1870-1933. I. Kunstler, Gustav, joint author. II. Title.

Loran, Erle, 1905- —Art collections.

AFRICAN and ancient Mexican art : the Loran Collection 732'.2'0966074019461
[exhibited at the M. H. de Young Memorial Museum, October 12, 1974-January 12, 1975 : catalogue] / by Erle Loran ... [et al.]. [San Francisco] : Fine Arts Museums of San Francisco, c1974. 95 p., [3] leaves of plates : ill. (some col.) ; 28 cm. Bibliography: p. 92-95. [N7398.A34] 74-84681 ISBN 0-88401-004-X
1. Loran, Erle, 1905- —Art collections. 2. Art, African—Exhibitions. 3. Art, Primitive—Africa, West—Exhibitions. 4. Indians of Mexico—Art—Exhibitions. I. Loran, Erle, 1905- II. Fine Arts Museums of San Francisco. III. De Young Memorial Museum, San Francisco.

Lord's Supper—Art.

ELLIS, Howard W. 759.5
The Last Supper; the story of the Leonardo da Vinci masterpiece. Nashville, Upper Room [c.1963] 63p. col. illus. 20cm. 63-19190 1.00
1. Leonardo da Vinci, 1452-1519. 2. Lord's Supper—Art. I. Title.

WESSEL, Klaus 704.9484
The Last Supper. Tr. by Giovanni Rossetti, Marguerite Buchloh. Recklinghausen, A. Bongers; dist. by Taplinger [New York, 1964.] 83p. illus. (pt. col.) 18cm. (Pictorial lib. of Eastern Church art, v. 6) Tr. of Abendmahl und Apostelkommunion. [N8054.W413] 67-3866 2.50 bds.,
1. Lord's Supper—Art. I. Title.

Lorenzetti, Ambrogio, 14th cent.

ROWLEY, George. 759.5
Ambrogio Lorenzetti. Princeton, N. J., Princeton University Press, 1958. 2v. plates (part col.) 31cm. (Princeton monograph in art and archaeology, 32) Contents.v. 1. Text.--v. 2. Illustrations. Bibliography: v. 1, p. 143-150. [ND623.L75R59] 927.5 57-10320
1. Lorenzetti, Ambrogio, 14th cent. I. Title. II. Series: Princeton monographs in art and archaeology, 32

Los Angeles Co., Calif. Museum of Art, Los Angeles.

CORPUS vasorum antiquorum. United States of America. The Los Angeles County Museum of Art. 738.3'82'093 s
Berkeley : University of California Press, 1977- v. : ill. ; 34 cm. (Corpus vasorum antiquorum : United States of America ; fasc. 18) At head of title: Union academique internationale. Vol. 1. edited by P. M. Packard and P. A. Clement. Issued in portfolio. Includes bibliography and index. [NK4640.C6U5 fasc. 18] 738.3'82'093074019494 74-84142 ISBN 0-520-02850-3 : 30.00
1. Los Angeles Co., Calif. Museum of Art, Los Angeles. 2. Vases, Ancient—California—Los Angeles—Catalogs. 3. Vases—California—Los Angeles—Catalogs. I. Packard, Pamela M. II. Los Angeles Co., Calif. Museum of Art, Los Angeles. III. Series.

LEBRUN, Federico, 1900-1964 709/.45
Rico Lebrun (1900-1964); an exhibition of drawings, paintings, and sculpture organized for the Los Angeles County Museum of Art by Henry J. Seldis. With catalog essays by Seldis and Peter Selz. [Los Angeles? 1967] 82p. illus. (pt. col.), port. 23cm. Catalog of an exhibition shown at the Los Angeles County Museum of Art, Dec. 5, 1967 to Jan. 14, 1968, and other museums. Bibl. [NC139.L4A56] 67-31098 3.50 pap.,
1. Los Angeles Co., Calif. Museum of Art, Los Angeles. I. Seldis, Henry J. II. Title.

LOS Angeles Co., Calif. Museum, Los Angeles. 759.4
Catalogue of paintings. [Los Angeles] Los Angeles County Museum [1954?- v. plates. 26 cm. Cover title. Contents.Contents.—1. A catalogue of Italian, French, and Spanish paintings, 14-18 century.—2. A catalogue of Flemish, German, Dutch, and English paintings, 15-18 century. [N582.L7A59] 74-154215
1. Los Angeles Co., Calif. Museum, Los Angeles. 2. Paintings—Los Angeles—Catalogs.

LOS Angeles Co., Calif. Museum of Art, Los Angeles. 708'.194'94
Los Angeles County Museum of Art report, July 1, 1973, to June 30, 1975. Los Angeles : The Museum, c1976. 100 p. : ill. ; 28 cm. [N582.L7A32] 75-41910 ISBN 0-87587-066-X
1. Los Angeles Co., Calif. Museum of Art, Los Angeles. I. Title.

LOS Angeles County Museum, Los Angeles. 069.09794
Report. [Los Angeles] v. 28 cm. annual. Report year ends June 30. [AM101.L7223] 52-21811
I. Title.

Los Angeles Co., Calif. Otis Art Institute, Los Angeles.

JARRETT, Mary. 707'.11'79494
The Otis story of Otis Art Institute since 1918 / by Mary Jarrett. Los Angeles : Alumni Association of Otis Art Institute, 1975. 80 p. : ill. ; 28 cm. [N582.L75J37] 75-322026
1. Los Angeles Co., Calif. Otis Art Institute, Los Angeles. I. Los Angeles Co., Calif. Otis Art Institute, Los Angeles. Alumni Association. II. Title.

Los Angeles. Simon Rodia Towers—Juvenile literature.

MADIAN, Jon. 725'.97'0979494
Beautiful junk; a story of the Watts Towers. With photos. by Barbara and Lou Jacobs, Jr. [1st ed.] Boston, Little, Brown [1968] 44 p. illus. 26 cm. A young boy learns how an old man came to build three towers out of "beautiful junk" in the Watts section of Los Angeles, California. [NA2930.M22] 68-21170 3.95
1. Los Angeles. Simon Rodia Towers—Juvenile literature. I. Jacobs, Barbara, illus. II. Jacobs, Lou, illus. III. Title. BIP

Loud-speaker cabinets.

BADMAIEFF, Alexis. 621.3841'361
How to build speaker enclosures, by Alexis Badmaieff & Don Davis. [1st ed.] Indianapolis, H. W. Sams [1966] 144 p. illus. 22 cm. (A Howard W. Sams photofact publication, SEB-1) [TT197.5.L6B3] 66-29405
1. Loud-speaker cabinets. I. Davis, Donald Bast, 1928- joint author. II. Title. BIP

Loud-speaker cabinets — Catalogs.

SYLVANIA ELECTRIC PRODUCTS, inc. 645.4
Folio of fine furniture. [New York? 1965] [54] p. (incl. cover) illus. (part col.) 49 x 72 cm. Cover title. [TT197.S95] 65-21322
1. Loud-speaker cabinets — Catalogs. 2. High-fidelity sound systems. I. Title.

Loud-speakers.

BUCKWALTER, Len. 621.38'0282
Easy speaker projects. [1st ed.] Indianapolis, H. W. Sams [1974] 96 p. illus. 22 cm. [TT197.5.L6B8] 74-79352 ISBN 0-672-21104-1 3.95
1. Loud-speakers. 2. High-fidelity sound systems. I. Title. BIP

Loudon, John Claudius, 1783-1843.

GLOAG, John, 1896- 720'.924 B
Mr. Loudon's England: the life and work of John Claudius Loudon, and his influence on architecture and furniture design. Newcastle upon Tyne, Oriel P., 1970. 224 p., 8 plates. illus., facsims., maps, plans, ports. 25 cm. Includes bibliographical references. [NA997.L63G55] 68-55974 ISBN 8-536-20423- 50/-
1. Loudon, John Claudius, 1783-1843. I. Title.

Louis and Charlotte Bergman Collection.

LA Jolla, Calif. Museum of Art. 708.194
Louis and Charlotte Bergman Collection. [Exhibition] La Jolla Museum of Art, July 15 through September 24, 1967. [La Jolla, 1967] [60] p. illus. (part col.) 31 cm. [N5220.B454] 67-27479
1. Louis and Charlotte Bergman Collection. 2. Art—Exhibitions. I. Bergman, Louis. II. Bergman, Charlotte. III. Title.

Louis, Morris, 1912-1962.

LOUIS, Morris, 1912-1962. 759.13
Bronze veils: first exhibition of a series of paintings from 1958. [New York, Andre Emmerich Gallery, 1969?] [24] p. (incl. cover) illus. (part col.) 22 x 28 cm. Catalogue of an exhibition held at the Andre Emmerich Gallery, New York, Feb. 22-Mar. 13, 1969. [ND237.L75A42] 73-161192
1. Louis, Morris, 1912-1962. I. Andre Emmerich Gallery, New York. II. Title.

LOUIS, Morris, 1912-1962 759.13
Morris Louis,1912-1962. Boston, Mus. of Fine Arts, 1967. 82p. 22cm. Exhibition held at Los Angeles County Mus. of Art, Feb. 15-Mar. 26, 1967; Mus. of Fine Arts, Boston, April 13-May 24, 1967 [and] City Art Mus. of St. Louis, June 16-Aug. 6, 1967. Introd. by Michael Fried: p. 7-24. Bibl. [ND237.L75F7] 67-17663 7.50
I. Fried, Michael. II. Los Angeles Co., Calif. Museum of Art, Los Angeles. III. Boston. Museum of Fine Arts. IV. St. Louis. City Art Museum. V. Title.

MORRIS Louis : 759.13
the veil cycle : an exhibition / organized by Walker Art Center. [Minneapolis] : The Center, c1977. 44 p. : ill. (some col.) ; 25 cm. Catalog of the exhibition held at Walker Art Center, Minneapolis, and others, Feb. 6, 1977-Jan. 22, 1978. Bibliography: p. 43. [ND237.L75M67] 76-50434
1. Louis, Morris, 1912-1962. I. Louis, Morris, 1912-1962. II. Walker Art Center, Minneapolis.

Louisiana—Antiq.

MCINTIRE, William G 976.3
Prehistoric Indian settlements of the changing Mississippi River Delta. Baton Rouge, Louisiana State University Press [1958] x, 128p. illus., fold. maps. 28cm. (Louisiana State University studies. Coastal studies series, no. 1) 'This study was conducted under the auspices of the Office of Naval Research (Project number N7, onr35608, NR388002) through the School of Geology, Louisiana State University.' Bibliography: p.108-113. [E78.L8M3] 913.763 58-5065
1. Louisiana—Antiq. 2. Indians of North America—Louisiana. 3. Mounds—Louisiana. I. Title. II. Series.

Louisiana—Capital and capitol.

GULF South Research Institute. 711'.45
Capitol complex; final report. Baton Rouge, La., 1967. xiii, 191, [43] l. illus. (part. col.), maps. 28 cm. "GSRI Project AS-134, prepared for the Louisiana State Science Foundation." [JK1651.L65G8] 68-63369
1. Louisiana—Capital and capitol. I. Louisiana State Science Foundation. II. Title.

Louisiana—Historic houses, etc.

COOPER, J. Wesley. 728.809763
Louisiana, a treasure of plantation homes. Natchez, Miss., Southern Historical Publications, 1961. 183 p. illus., 44 col. plates. 35 cm. Bibliography: p. 183. [F370.C6] 61-10678
1. Louisiana—Historic houses, etc. I. Title.

Louisiana in art.

ANGLO-AMERICAN Art Museum. 709.763
The Louisiana landscape, 1800-1969. [Baton Rouge, 1969] [52] p. illus. 21 x 26 cm. "[Loan exhibition] September 14-November 15, 1969, Anglo-American Art Museum, Louisiana State University, Baton Rouge, Louisiana." [N6530.L8A82] 73-629571
1. Louisiana in art. 2. Art, American—Exhibitions. 3. Artists, American—Louisiana. I. Title.

Louisiana—Social life and customs—Pictorial works.

MUGNIER, George Francois, 1855-1936. 779'.9'976306
Louisiana images, 1880-1920 a photographic essay / by George Francois Mugnier ; edited with an introd. by John R. Kemp and Linda Orr King. Baton Rouge : Published for the Louisiana State Museum by Louisiana State University, c1975. ix, 130 p. : chiefly ill. ; 28 cm. Bibliography: p. 5-6. [F369.M84 1975] 74-27199 ISBN 0-8071-0151-6 pbk. : 6.95
1. Louisiana—Social life and customs—Pictorial works. I. Louisiana State Museum, New Orleans. II. Title. BIP

Louisiana superdome.

*CHAFIN, Andrew 725.827
The super fans. Lebanon, Va., Sharon [1974] 79 p. illus. 23 cm. [NA6880] 5.95
1. Louisiana superdome. I. Title.
Publisher's address: P.O. Box 1028 Lebanon, Va. 24266

Louisville, Ky.—Description—Views.

WILLIAMS, Caroline. 741.9'73
Louisville scenes. [1st ed.] Garden City, N.Y., Doubleday, 1970. 142 p. illus. 27 cm. [F459.L8W55] 78-113985 8.95
1. Louisville, Ky.—Description—Views. 2. Kentucky—Description and travel—Views. I. Title.

Love in art.

LOVE and marriage. 704.94'9'30142
[1st ed.] Greenwich, Conn., New York Graphic Society [1968] 64 p. illus. (part col.) 31 cm. (Man through his art, v. 5) "Endorsed by the World Confederation of Organizations of the Teaching Profession." Includes bibliographies. [N8220.L6 1968] 68-11207 ISBN 0-7158-0324-7
1. Love in art. 2. Marriage in art. I. World Confederation of Organizations of the Teaching Profession. II. Title. III. Series.

WHITTET, George Sorley, 1913- 704.94'2
Lovers in art [by] G. S. Whittet. London, Studio Vista, 1972. 158 p. illus. 19 cm. (Studio Vista/Dutton picture-back) [N8220.W47 1972] 72-169903 ISBN 0-289-70247-X
1. Love in art. I. Title.
Distributed by Dutton pap. 2.25

Love, Jim, 1927—

LOVE, Jim, 1927- 730'.92'4
Jim Love: in pursuit of the bear. [Houston, Contemporary Arts Museum, 1973] 24 p. illus. 22 cm. Cover title. Exhibition held at Contemporary Arts Museum, Houston, Jan. 17-Feb. 25, 1973; Fort Worth Art Center, Fort Worth, Tex., Mar. 7-Apr. 1, 1973; and Tyler Museum of Art, Tyler, Tex., Apr. 22-May 31, 1973. [NB237.L64C66] 73-75006
1. Love, Jim, 1927- I. Contemporary Arts Museum. II. Fort Worth Art Center-Museum. III. Tyler Museum of Art.

Love poetry, American.

FARABEE, Barbara, 1944- 811'.5'4
A young woman's secret book of erotic love poems. Illustrated by Claudia Ricketts. Millbrae, CA, Celestial Arts [1974] 1 v. (unpaged) illus. 22 cm. [PS3556.A57Y6] 74-9755 ISBN 0-912310-72-3
1. Love poetry, American. I. Title.

Lovet-Lorski, Boris, 1894-

BUSH, Martin H. 730'.924
Boris Lovet-Lorski; the language of time, by Martin H. Bush. With an introd. by Salvatore Quasimodo. An exhibition of sculpture and paintings presented by the School of Art, Syracuse University and held at the Joseph I. Lubin House, Syracuse University, New York City, April 27-May 26, 1967. [Syracuse] [Syracuse University] [1967] 95 p. illus. 23 cm. Bibliography: p. 92-94. [NB237.L65B8] 67-24885
1. Lovet-Lorski, Boris, 1894- I. Syracuse University. School of Art. II. Title.

Low, Will Hicok, 1853-1932.

LOW, Will Hicok, 1853-1932. 759.13
A painter's progress, being a partial survey along the pathway of art in America and Europe ... / by Will H. Low. New York : Garland Pub., 1976, c1910. p. cm. (The Art experience in late nineteenth-century America) Reprint of the ed. published by Scribner, New York, which was issued as the 1910 Scammon lectures. [ND237.L8A56 1976] 75-28889 ISBN 0-8240-2246-7 lib.bdg. : 25.00
1. Low, Will Hicok, 1853-1932. 2. Painters—United States—Biography. 3. Art, American. 4. Art, Modern—19th century—United States. 5. Art, European. 6. Art, Modern—19th century—Europe. I. Title. II. Series. III. Series: Scammon lectures ; 1910.

Lowenfeld, Viktor.

BARKAN, Manuel. 707
Viktor Lowenfeld: his impact on art education. Washington, National Art Education Association, 1966. iii, 24 p. 23 cm. (Research monograph 2) "Delivered as a Viktor Lowenfeld memorial lecture at the 1965 National Art Education Association Conference." "Response to Barkan's paper [by] W. Lambert Brittain": p. [20]-24. Includes bibliographical references. [N70.B24] 79-265878
1. Lowenfeld, Viktor. 2. Art—Philosophy. I. Brittain, W. Lambert. II. Series: National Art Education Association. Research monograph 2

Lowestoft porcelain.

GODDEN, Geoffrey A. 738.2'7
The illustrated guide to Lowestoft porcelain [by] Geoffrey A. Godden. New York, Praeger [1969] xix, 164 p. illus. (part col.) 26 cm. (The Illustrated guides to pottery and porcelain) Bibliography: p. 157-159. [NK4399.L7G6 1969b] 77-88897 15.00
1. Lowestoft porcelain. I. Title.

Lowestoft porcelain—Catalogs.

LEVINE, George Jacob. 738.2'7
Inscribed Lowestoft porcelain [by George J. Levine]. [Norwich, G. J. Levine, The Gable, Brundall] 1968. [3], 13 leaves. 25 x 33 cm. [NK4399.L7L4] 76-488088 10/-
1. Lowestoft porcelain—Catalogs. 2. Porcelain—Marks. I. Title.

Lowry, Laurence Stephen, 1887-1976.

LOWRY, Laurence Stephen, 1887- 741.942
Drawings of L. S. Lowry. Introd., notes 2y Mervyn Levy. [London] Cory, Adams & Mackay [dist. New York. Taplinger, 1965,c.1963,54 22p. 64 plates. 30cm. [NC1115.L6L4] 65-3605 10.00
I. Levy, Mervyn. II. Title.

LOWRY, Laurence Stephen, 1887-1976. 741.9'42
The drawings of L. S. Lowry : public and private / with an introd. and notes by Mervyn Levy. London : Jupiter Books, 1976. 31, 282 p., 9 leaves of col. plates : chiefly ill. ; 30 cm. Bibliography: p. 31. [NC242.L68A44] 77-364484 ISBN 0-904041-69-7 : £12.50
1. Lowry, Laurence Stephen, 1887-1976. I. Title.

LOWRY, Laurence Stephen, 1887-1976. 759.2
L. S. Lowry RA, 1887-1976 : [catalogue of an exhibition held at the Royal Academy], 4 September to 14 November [1976]. [London] : Royal Academy of Arts, 1976. 98 p. : ill. (some col.), facsims., ports. (some col.) ; 24 cm. Bibliography: p. 98 [N6797.L68L66] 77-354410 ISBN 0-900946-28-8 : £1.80
1. Lowry, Laurence Stephen, 1887-1976. I. London. Royal Academy of Arts. II. Title.

Ludecke, Heinz.

DURER, Albrecht, 1471-1528. 769'.92'4
Albrecht Durer [by] Heinz Ludecke. [Translated from the German by Richard Rickett] New York, Putnam [1972] 168 p. illus. 32 cm. Bibliography: p. 168. [ND588.D9L74313 1972] 70-170079 ISBN 0-399-11013-5 16.95
1. Ludecke, Heinz.

Ludington, Wright S.—Art collections.

CALIFORNIA. University. University at Los Angeles. Art Galleries. 708.1794'94
From the Ludington Collection; an exhibition, sponsored by the UCLA Art Council in collaboration with the UCLA Art Galleries, Dickson Art Center, University of California, Los Angeles, March 16 to April 12, 1964. [Los Angeles, 1964] 43 p. illus. (part col.) 28 cm. [N5220.L77C3] 73-271763
1. Ludington, Wright S.—Art collections. 2. Art—Exhibitions. I. California. University. University at Los Angeles. Art Council. II. Dickson Art Center. III. Title.

Luger pistol.

JONES, Harry E 623.443
Luger variations. [Torrance? Calif., 1959- v. illus. 24cm. [TS537.J6] 60-25026
1. Luger pistol. I. Title.

MARVIN, Robert Burrell, 1932- 623.4'43
The identification and pricing of Luger pistols by Robert B. Marvin. Plantation, Fla., Luger journal [1968] 58 p. illus., port. (on p. [4] of cover) 22 cm. "Pricing supplement, June, July, August 1968" ([4] p.) inserted. [TS537.M37] 68-5937
1. Luger pistol. 2. Pistols—Collectors and collecting. I. Title.

Luggage.

ABARSI Casecraft, Los Angeles. 745.59'22'075
Course of instruction: case making, luggage making, case and luggage repairing. [Stamped: Los Angeles, 1953] 73p. illus. 29cm. [TS2301.L8A3] 54-31381
1. Luggage. 2. Leather work. I. Title.

Lugt, Frits, 1884-1970—Art collections—Exhibitions.

REMBRANDT and his century : 741.9'492'07401471
Dutch drawings of the seventeenth century : from the collection of Frits Lugt, Institut neerlandais, Paris, New York-Paris, 1977-1978. [New York : Pierpont Morgan Library, 1978] xxi, 251 p., [68] leaves of plates : ill. ; 26 cm. "Exhibitions: New York, the Pierpont Morgan Library ... 8th December 1977-19th February 1978 ...; Paris, Institut neerlandais ... 16th March-30th April 1978." Includes indexes. Bibliography: p.

223-244. [NC261.R46] 78-107157 pbk. : 15.95
1. Lugt, Frits, 1884-1970—Art collections—Exhibitions. 2. Drawing, Dutch—Exhibitions. 3. Drawing—17th century—Netherlands—Exhibitions. I. Pierpont Morgan Library, New York. II. Institut neerlandais, Paris.

Luiken, Jan, 1649-1712.

LUIKEN, Jan, 1649-1712. 769'.92'4
The drama of the martyrs : from the death of Jesus Christ up to the recent times / drawn and engraved on copper by Jan Luyken ; with an introductory essay by Jan Gleysteen. Lancaster, Pa. : Mennonite Historical Associates, [1975] 141 p. : chiefly ill. ; 19 x 25 cm. Illustrations originally published in the 2d ed., 1685, of Het bloedig tooneel ... by T. J. van Bracht, and subsequently published separately under title: Theatre des martyrs ... [NE670.L8A43] 75-12518 pbk. : 5.95
1. Luiken, Jan, 1649-1712. 2. Christian martyrs in art. I. Bracht, Tieleman Janszoon van, 1625-1664. Het bloedig tooneel. II. Title.

Lukacs, Gyorgy, 1885-1971.

BAHR, Ehrhard. 199'.439
Georg Lukacs [by] Ehrhard Bahr and Ruth Goldschmidt Kunzer. New York, Ungar [1972] x, 162 p. 20 cm. (Modern literature monographs) Rev. and enl. ed. of Georg Lukacs, by E. Bahr, translated by R. G. Kunzer. Bibliography: p. 147-153. [BH221.H84L84213] 70-190350 ISBN 0-8044-2014-9 5.00
1. Lukacs, Gyorgy, 1885-1971. I. Kunzer, Ruth Goldschmidt, joint author. BIP

KIRALYFALVI, Bela, 111.8'5 1937-
The aesthetics of Gyorgy Lukacs / Bela Kiralyfalvi. Princeton, N.J. : Princeton University Press, [1975] ix, 164 p. ; 23 cm. (Princeton essays in literature) Includes index. Bibliography: p. 149-155. [BH221.H84L865] 74-22401 ISBN 0-691-07205-1 : 9.00
1. Lukacs, Gyorgy, 1885-1971. I. Title. BIP

Luke, Saint — Art.

EMMINGHAUS, Johannes H. 704.948'6
Luke [by] Johannes H. Emminghaus. Text of story and legend by Leonhard Kuppers. [Translated from the German by Hans Hermann Rosenwald] Recklinghausen [Ger.] A Bongers; distributed by Taplinger Pub. Co. [New York, c1966] 78 p. col. illus. 18 cm. (The Saints in legend and art, v. 8) [N8080.E4313] 67-4501
1. Luke, Saint — Art. I. Kuppers, Leonhard, 1903- II. Title.

Luks, George Benjamin, 1867-1933.

LUKS, George Benjamin, 759.13 1867-1933.
George Luks, 1866-1933; an exhibition of paintings and drawings dating from 1889-1931. Utica, N.Y., Munson-Williams-Proctor Institute, Museum of Art [1973] 58 p. illus. 24 cm. Catalog of the exhibition held Apr. 1-May 20, 1973 at Munson-Williams-Proctor Institute, Museum of Art, Utica, New York. [ND237.L85M86] 73-160578
1. Luks, George Benjamin, 1867-1933. I. Munson-Williams-Proctor Institute, Utica, N.Y. Museum of Art.

Lumbering—Washington (State)—Pictorial works.

BOHN, Dave. 770'.92'4
Kinsey, photographer : a half century of negatives by Darius and Tabitha May Kinsey, with contributions by son and daughter, Darius, Jr. and Dorothea / produced by Dave Bohn and Rodolfo Petschek. San Francisco : Scrimshaw Press, 1975. 2 v. (319 p.) : ill. ; 34 cm. Contents.Contents.—v. 1. The family album & other early work.—v. 2. The magnificent years. Bibliography: p. 312-314. [TR140.K45B64] 74-32263 ISBN 0-912020-35-0(v.1) 150.00(boxed set) ISBN 0-912020-36-9(v.2) : 150.00 (boxed set)

1. Kinsey, Darius, 1869-1945. 2. Kinsey, Tabitha May, 1875-1963. 3. Lumbering—Washington (State)—Pictorial works. I. Petschek, Rodolfo, joint author. II. Title.

Luminescent postage-stamps—United States.

BOERGER, Alfred G. 769'.56
Handbook on U.S. luminescent stamps [by] Alfred G. Boerger. 1972-73 ed. [Fort Lauderdale, Fla., 1972] 129 p. illus. 20 cm. Cover title. "This handbook is a composite of a bulletin series on tags." [HE6184.L8B63] 72-189746
1. Luminescent postage-stamps—United States. I. Title. II. Title: U.S. luminescent stamps.

Lummi Indians—Art.

WHATCOM Museum of History 736'.4 and Art.
A report: master carvers of the Lummi and their apprentices. Master carvers: Morrie Alexander and Al Charles. Apprentices: Dale James, Israel James, Al Noland [and] Floyd Noland. Photographer: Mary Randlett. [Bellingham, Wash., 1971] 31 p. illus., ports. 24 cm. [E99.L95W5] 72-157750
1. Lummi Indians—Art. 2. Indians of North America—Wood-carving. I. Randlett, Mary, illus. II. Title.

Luster-ware.

BEDFORD, John, 1907- 738.15
Old English lustre ware. New York, Walker [1966] 66 p. illus. (part col.) 19 cm. (Collectors' pieces, 5) [NK4399.L9B4 1966] 66-22379
1. Luster-ware. 2. Pottery—Collectors and collecting. 3. Pottery, English. I. Title.

FROTHINGHAM, Alice Wilson. 738.34
Lustreware of Spain. Printed by order of the trustees. New York [Hispanic Society of America] 1951. xi, 310 p. 221 illus. 26 cm. (Hispanic notes & monographs; essays, studies, and brief biographies. Peninsular series) Bibliographical references included in "Notes" (p. 281-291) Bibliography: p. 291-297. [NK4399.L9F7] 51-10259
1. Luster-ware. 2. Pottery—Spain. I. Title. II. Series.

Lutyens, Edwin Landseer, Sir, 1869-1944.

HUSSEY, Christopher, 1899- 927.2
The life of Sir Edwin Lutyens. London, Country Life; New York, Scribner, 1950. xxii, 602p. illus., ports., map, plans. 26cm. (The Lutyens memorial) [NA997.L8H8 1950] 57-22239
1. Lutyens, Sir Edwin Landseer, 1869-1944. I. Title. II. Series.

LUTYENS, Robert. 720'.924
Notes on Sir Edwin Lutyens: two sets of notes for a lecture to the Art Workers Guild, June 18th 1969. Newcastle upon Tyne, Published for the Art Workers Guild by Oriel, 1970. [2], 13 p. 22 cm. Includes bibliographical references. [NA997.L8L78] 73-516300 5/-
1. Lutyens, Edwin Landseer, Sir, 1869-1944. I. Art Workers Guild, London. II. Title.

Luxardo Girolamo, s.p.a.

AVERY, Constance. 738.3'83
Luxardo bottles; identification and price guide, by Constance Avery and Al Cembura. Photos. by Leslie Avery. [Portland, Or., Metropolitan Printing; distributed by Al Cembura, Berkeley, Calif., c1968] 201 p. illus. (part col.), ports. 21 cm. [NK5440.B6A95] 72-1829 4.75
1. Luxardo Girolamo, s.p.a. I. Title. BIP

Luzwick, Dierdre.

LUZWICK, Dierdre. 741.9'73
The surrealist's Bible : a collection of charcoal drawings / by Dierdre Luzwick. Middle Village, N.Y. : Jonathan David, c1976. 118 p. : ill. ; 29 cm.

[NC139.L89A58] 75-44001 ISBN 0-8246-0206-4 : 12.95
1. Luzwick, Dierdre. 2. Bible—Pictures, illustrations, etc. 3. Surrealism. I. Title. BIP

Lvov. Ukrains'kyi derzhavnyi muzei etnografii ta khudozhn'oho promyslu.

LVOV. 745.5'0947'7107407718
Ukrains'kyi derzhavnyi muzei etnografii ta khudozhn'oho promyslu.
State Museum of Ethnography and Crafts under the UKR.SSR Academy of Sciences = [Derzhavnyi muzei etnohrafii ta khudozhn'oho promyslu AN URSR (romanized form)] / [translated from the Ukrainian by Anatole Bilenko]. Kiev : Mistetstvo, 1976. ca. 250 p. : chiefly ill. (some col.) ; 25 cm. Catalogue of "articles of decorative and applied art" from the museum's collections. English and Ukranian. [NK976.U5L89 1976] 77-474693 6.07rub
1. Lvov. Ukrains'kyi derzhavnyi muzei etnografii ta khudozhn'oho promyslu. 2. Art industries and trade—Ukraine—Catalogs. I. Title. II. Title: Derzhavnyi muzei etnohrafii ta khudozhn'oho promyslu AN URSR.

Lydney, Eng. St. Mary's Church.

BELL, R A Jack. 726.5094241
Parish church of St. Mary, Lydney; by R. A. J. Bell. Foreword by Viscount Bledisloe. 1st ed. Gloucester, British Pub. Co., 1966. 52 p. illus., plan, tables. 18 1/2 cm. unpriced. (B66-13157) [NA5471.L95B4] 66-73443
1. Lydney, Eng. St. Mary's Church. I. Title.

Lymburner, Francis.

LYMBURNER, Francis. 741.9'94
Lymburner; with an introduction by George Molnar. [Melbourne] Lansdowne [1970] 95 p. (chiefly illus.) 32 cm. [NC371.L94M64 1970] 73-173023 ISBN 0-7018-0453-X
1. Lymburner, Francis. I. Molnar, George, 1910-

Lysippus, sculptor.

JOHNSON, Franklin 730'.924 Plotinus, 1896-
Lysippos, by Franklin P. Johnson. New York, Greenwood Press, 1968 [c1927] xii, 334 p. illus. 24 cm. Includes bibliographical references. [NB98.J7 1968] 68-29743
1. Lysippus, sculptor. BIP

SJOQVIST, Erik, 1903- 730'.924
Lysippus. [Cincinnati] University of Cincinnati, 1966. 31 p. illus., ports. 24 cm. (Lectures in memory of Louise Taft Semple, 2d ser.) Lectures delivered Apr. 11-12, 1966 at the request of the University of Cincinnati and its Dept. of Classics. Includes bibliographical references. [NB98.S55] 70-268864
1. Lysippus, sculptor. I. Series: Cincinnati. University. Lectures in memory of Louise Taft Semple

McAdoo, Donald, 1929—

MCADOO, Donald, 1929- 759.13
Reflections of the Outer Banks / through the brush of Donald McAdoo and the pen of Carol McAdoo. Manteo, N.C. : Island Pub. House, c1976. p. cm. "A Commemorative bicentennial publication." Includes index. Bibliography: p. [ND237.M13M32] 75-23489 14.95
1. McAdoo, Donald, 1929- 2. Outer Banks, N.C., in art. 3. Outer Banks, N.C.—History. I. McAdoo, Carol, 1938- II. Title. BIP

McAdory art test.

SICELOFF, Margaret 707'.24 (McAdory) Mrs., 1890-
The construction and validation of an art test. New York, Bureau of Publications, Teachers College, Columbia University, 1929. [New York, AMS Press, 1972, ie 1973] 35 p. illus. 22 cm. Reprint of the

1929 ed., issued in series: Teachers College, Columbia University. Contributions to education, no. 383. Originally presented as the author's thesis, Columbia. Bibliography: p. 35. [N340.S47 1972] 76-177785 ISBN 0-404-55383-4 10.00
1. McAdory art test. I. Title. II. Series: Columbia University. Teachers College. Contributions to education, no. 383.

MacAgy, Douglas, 1913-

BOYNTON, James 759.13
James Boynton. Introd. by Douglas MacAgy. New York, Distributed by Wittenborn [1959] [8] p., 14 plates (part col.) port. 26cm. (Barone Gallery, Inc. New York. Art book series, no. 1) 59-4477 3.95 pap.,
1. MacAgy, Douglas, 1913- I. Title. II. Series: Barone Gallery, in., New York. Art book series, no. 1

Macaroni craft—Juvenile literature.

MERGELER, Karen. 745.5
Noodle doodle! : The art of creating with pasta / by Karen Mergeler ; introd. by Joseph Montell. El Toro, Calif. : Folk-Art Studios, [1975] 104 p., [1] leaf of plates : ill. ; 21 cm. Instructions for making projects from macaroni and other pasta with historical notes on the medium. [TT880.M46] 75-325505 pbk. : 5.95
1. Macaroni craft—Juvenile literature. I. Title. BIP

McBey, James, 1883-1959.

MCBEY, James, 1883- 769'.92'4 B 1959.
The early life of James McBey : an autobiography, 1883-1911 / edited by Nicolas Barker. Oxford [Eng.] ; New York : Oxford University Press, 1977. ix, 131 p., [8] leaves of plates : ill. ; 25 cm. [NE2047.6.M32A24] 77-6395 ISBN 0-19-211738-6 : 12.00
1. McBey, James, 1883-1959. 2. Etchers—Scotland—Biography. I. Barker, Nicolas. II. Title. BIP

McCann, Helena Woolworth—Art collections.

LE CORBEILLER, 382'.45'73820951 Clare.
China trade porcelain: patterns of exchange; additions to the Helena Woolworth McCann Collection in the Metropolitan Museum of Art. Foreword by John Goldsmith Phillips. [New York] Metropolitan Museum of Art; distributed by New York Graphic Society, [1974] 134 p. illus. (part col.) 28 cm. Includes bibliographical references. [NK4565.5.L43] 74-2097 ISBN 0-87099-089-6
1. McCann, Helena Woolworth—Art collections. 2. China trade porcelain—Catalogs. I. Title.

McCarthy, Frank C., 1924—

MCCARTHY, Frank C., 1924- 759.13
The western paintings of Frank C. McCarthy. Edited by Frank Storz. New York, Ballantine Books [1974] 1 v. (chiefly 45 col. plates) 23 x 29 cm. [ND237.M16A57] 74-164377 ISBN 0-345-23844-3 4.95 (pbk.)
1. McCarthy, Frank C., 1924- 2. The West in art. I. Title.

McClusky, John, 1914—

MCCLUSKY, John, 1914- 760.092'4
John McClusky—a retrospective exhibition, August 18-September 29, 1974. Shreveport, La., R. W. Norton Art Gallery [1974] 58 p. illus. (part col.) 28 cm. Cover title. Catalog of an exhibition. [N6537.M32N67] 74-14946 ISBN 0-913060-05-4
1. McClusky, John, 1914- I. Norton (R. W.) Art Gallery.

McCurdy, John Derrickson, 1940-1974.

MCCURDY, John 741.9'73 Derrickson, 1940-1974. *John Derrickson McCurdy (1940-1974) : a* memorial exhibition, 17 April-29 May, 1977, North Carolina Museum of Art. Raleigh : North Carolina Museum of Art, c1977. 54 p. : ill. ; 22 x 23 cm. [N6537.M33N67] 77-6329 ISBN 0-88259-088-X pbk. : 3.50 *1. McCurdy, John Derrickson, 1940-1974.* I. North Carolina. Museum of Art, Raleigh. **BIP**

MacDonald, Angus Snead, 1883-1961.

BAUMANN, Charles H., 1924- 727'.8 *The influence of Angus Snead MacDonald and the Snead bookstack on library architecture,* by Charles H. Baumann. Metuchen, N.J., Scarecrow Press, 1972. 307 p. illus. 22 cm. A revision of the author's thesis, University of Illinois. Bibliography: p. 285-304. [Z679.B3 1972] 74-171928 ISBN 0-8108-0390-9 *1. MacDonald, Angus Snead, 1883-1961. 2. Library architecture. 3. Shelving (for books) 4. Modular coordination (Architecture)* I. Title. **BIP**

Macdonald, Malcolm, 1901- —Art collections.

GULBENKIAN Museum of 738'.0951 Oriental Art and Archaeology. *A descriptive and illustrated catalogue of the Malcolm Macdonald collection of Chinese ceramics in the Gulbenkian Museum of Oriental Art and Archaeology, School of Oriental Studies, University of Durham,* by Ireneus Laszlo Lageza; with a foreword by Malcolm Macdonald. London, Oxford University Press, 1972. lxxxiii, 112, cxlvi p. illus. (some col.), map. 29 cm. Bibliography: p. 101-112. [NK4165.G8] 72-193708 ISBN 0-19-713135-2 £15.00 *1. Macdonald, Malcolm, 1901- —Art collections. 2. Pottery, Chinese—Catalogs. 3. Porcelain, Chinese—Catalogs.* I. Lageza, Ireneus Laszlo. II. Title.

MacDonald, Thoreau, 1901—

MACDONALD, Thoreau, 741.9'71 1901- *Thoreau MacDonald; a catalogue of design and illustration [by] Margaret E. Edison.* [Toronto, Buffalo] University of Toronto Press [1973] ix, 190 p. illus. 28 cm. Bibliography: p. [179]-184. [NC143.M3E34 1973] 72-95462 ISBN 0-8020-1959-5 15.00 *1. MacDonald, Thoreau, 1901-* I. Edison, Margaret E. **BIP**

Maces, Ceremonial—Exhibitions.

HECKSCHER, William S. 378 *Maces; an exhibition of American ceremonial academic scepters in honor of the inauguration of President Terry Sanford, October 18, 1970, the Duke University Museum of Art, continuing through November 13, 1970.* [Catalogue by] William S. Heckscher. [Raleigh, N.C., Printed by Litho Industries, 1970] 55 p. illus. 26 cm. Bibliography: p. 19-26. [NK7425.H4] 72-180695 *1. Maces, Ceremonial—Exhibitions. 2. Art objects, American.* I. Duke University, Durham, N.C. Art Museum. II. Title.

McGowan, Harold, 1909—

MCGOWAN, Harold, 1909- 730'.92'4 *The spirit of Christmas in words and sculpture :* Christmas cards / by Harold McGowan ; introd. by Lee Marc Stein. 1st ed. Central Islip, N.Y. : Metaprobe Institute, [1974] 96 p. (p. 95-96 advertisements) : col. ill. ; 26 cm. [NC1868.M32A56] 74-81246 ISBN 0-682-48082-7 : 35.00 *1. McGowan, Harold, 1909- 2. Christmas cards.* I. Title. Publisher's address: 900 S. Oyster Bay Rd. Hicksville, New York 11801.

McGrew, Ralph Brownell, 1916- — Exhibitions.

MCGREW, Ralph Brownell, 759.13 1916- *R. Brownell McGrew :* Laguna Beach Museum of Art, presented by the Thunderbird Foundation, August, 1978. 1st ed. Kansas City : Lowell Press, c1978. xvii, 128 p. : ill. (some col.) ; 23 x 29 cm. [N6537.M334A4 1978] 78-53113 ISBN 0-913504-43-2 : 25.00 *1. McGrew, Ralph Brownell, 1916- — Exhibitions. 2. Indians of North America— Pictorial works—Exhibitions.* I. Laguna Beach Museum of Art. II. Thunderbird Foundation. **BIP**

McGugan, Ian, 1932—

IAN McGugan and Ed Perera 759.06 : paintings : [catalogue of an exhibition held] 9 October to 9 November 1976 [at] Woodlands Art Gallery. London : London Borough of Greenwich, [1976] [11] p. : ill. ; 21 cm. "Ed Perera": [1] leaf inserted. [ND195.I2] 77-369106 ISBN 0-9504033-5-0 *1. McGugan, Ian, 1932- 2. Perera, Ed, 1936- 3. Painting, Modern—20th century—Exhibitions.* I. McGugan, Ian, 1932- II. Perera, Ed, 1936- III. Woodlands Art Gallery.

Mach, Lee.

MACH, Lee. 730'.92'4 *Collected works of Lee Mach.* [Larchmont, N.Y., Matu Publishers, 1973] [116] p. (chiefly illus.) 32 cm. [NB237.M275A43] 73-172830 *1. Mach, Lee.*

Machetanz, Frederick, 1908—

MACHETANZ, Frederick, 759.13 1908- *The Alaskan paintings of Fred Machetanz* / introd. by Russ Riemann. 1st U.S. ed. New York : Peacock Press/Bantam Book, 1977. [16] p., [40] leaves of plates : ill. (some col.) ; 23 x 28 cm. [ND237.M2125A42 1977] 76-54104 ISBN 0-553-01061-1 : 6.95 *1. Machetanz, Frederick, 1908- 2. Alaska in art.* I. Title. **BIP**

Machine quilting.

STECKEL, Leon R. 746.4'6 *How to do machine quilting for pleasure and profit; a complete instruction and business guide plus hand quilting supplement* [by] Leon R. Steckel. Kansas City, Mo.] c1966. 87 p. illus. 22 cm. Bibliography: p. 84. [TT835.S7] 67-23724 *1. Machine quilting.* I. Title.

Machine sewing.

FANNING, Robbie. 746.4'4 *Decorative machine stitchery :* design, techniques, and projects for every sewing machine / by Robbie Fanning ; ill. and photos by Tony and Robbie Fanning. New York : Butterick Pub., c1976. 191 p. : ill. ; 26 cm. Includes index. Bibliography: p. 186. [TT713.F36] 76-4396 ISBN 0-88421-050-2 : 9.95 *1. Machine sewing. 2. Embroidery, Machine.* I. Title. **BIP**

Machine-tools.

LAMMEY, W. Clyde. 621.9 *Power tools and how to use them.* Chicago, Popular Mechanics Press [1950] 144 p. illus. 24 cm. (Popular mechanics craftsman's library) [TT153.L3] 51-9760 *1. Machine-tools. 2. Handicraft.* I. Title.

Machinery—Drawing.

HAYES, Joseph Trus, 1891- 744.4 *Shop sketching and blue print reading made easy,* by J. T. Hayes and H. W. Paine. [Rev. ed.] Cincinnati, Distributed by the Technology Text Book co., 1951. iv l.,

137 p. 138-155 l. illus. 25 x 36 cm. [T379.H35 1951] 51-4816 *1. Machinery—Drawing. 2. Biue-prints.* I. Paine, Harry Warren, 1890- joint author. II. Title.

PEARSON, George, 1911- 744.422 *Engineering drawing.* [London] Oxford University Press, 1960[ ] 104p. illus. 60-3310 2.00 *1. Machinery—Drawing.* I. Title.

Machinery—Drawings.

INTERNATIONAL 744.4'22'2181 Correspondence Schools, Scranton, Pa. *Machine sketching,* by ICS staff. Serial 5807-5. [Ed. 5] Scranton, [1968] 117, 6 p. illus. 19 cm. [TJ230.I55 1968] 68-3705 *1. Machinery—Drawings.* I. Title.

PEARSON, George, 1911- 744.422 *Engineering drawing* [2d ed. New York] Oxford [c.]1965. 164p. illus. 25cm. [TJ230.P36] 66-567 3.40 bds., *1. Machinery—Drawings.* I. Title.

YANKEE, Herbert W 744.422219 *Machine drafting and related technology* [by] Herbert W. Yankee. St. Louis, Webster Divison, McGraw-Hill [1966] xi, 516 p. illus. 25 cm. Bibliography: p. 501-506. [TJ230.Y26] 64-66272 *1. Machinery—Drawings.* I. Title.

Machinery—Drawings—Juvenile literature.

ZAIDENBERG, Arthur, 743'.8'96218 1903- *How to draw motors, machines and tools.* London, New York, Abelard-Schuman [1970] 63 p. illus. 27 cm. Beginning with explanations of perspective and basic shapes, gives step-by-step instructions for drawing simple and complex motors, machines, and tools. [NC825.M3Z3 1970] 73-122501 ISBN 0-200-71688-3 3.75 (U.S.) *1. Machinery—Drawings—Juvenile literature. 2. Tools—Drawings—Juvenile literature. 3. Drawing—Instruction— Juvenile literature.* I. Title.

McIlhenny, Henry P.—Art collections— Exhibitions.

ALLENTOWN, Pa. 709'.44'074014827 Art Museum. *French masterpieces of the 19th century from the Henry P. McIlhenny Collection :* May 1 through September 18, 1977, Allentown Art Museum. [Allentown, Pa.] : The Museum, c1977. 100 p. : ill. (some col.) ; 28 cm. Includes bibliographies. [N6847.A44 1977] 77-74177 *1. McIlhenny, Henry P.—Art collections— Exhibitions. 2. Art, French—Exhibitions. 3. Art, Modern—19th century—France— Exhibitions.* I. Title.

McIntire, Samuel, 1757-1811.

COUSINS, Frank, 1851- 720'.924 B *The wood-carver of Salem;* Samuel McIntire, his life and work, by Frank Cousins and Phil M. Riley. New York, AMS Press [1970] xx, 168 p. illus., facsims., plans. 23 cm. Reprint of the 1916 ed. [NA737.M25C6 1970] 74-119649 *1. McIntire, Samuel, 1757-1811.* I. Riley, Phil Madison, 1882- joint author. II. Title. **BIP**

KIMBALL, Sidney 720.97445 B Fiske, 1888-1955. *Mr. Samuel McIntire, carver, the architect of Salem.* [Salem, Mass.] Essex Institute of Salem, 1940. Gloucester, Mass., P. Smith, 1966. xiii, 157 p. illus., fold. map, plans, ports. 28 cm. [NA737.M25K5 1966] 67-297 *1. McIntire, Samuel, 1757-1811.* I. Essex Institute, Salem, Mass. II. Title. III. Title: The architect of Salem. **BIP**

MacIver, Loren, 1909—

BAUR, John Ireland Howe, 927.5 1909- *Loren MacIver.* I. Rice Pereira. New York, Published for the Whitney Museum

of American Art by Macmillan, 1953. 71 p. illus. (part col.) ports. 27 cm. "This book is the result of a retrospective exhibition...held by the Whitney Museum of American Art in January and February 1953." Includes bibliographies. [ND237.M214B38] 53-6459 *1. MacIver, Loren, 1909- 2. Pereira, Irene Rice, 1907- 3. Paintings, American— Exhibitions.* I. Whitney Museum of American Art, New York.

MACIVER, Loren, 1909- 759.13 *Loren MacIver; recent paintings.* [New York, 1970?] [24] p. illus., col. plate. 26 cm. Catalog of an exhibition held in November and December, 1970, at the Pierre-Matisse Gallery, New York. [ND237.M214A5] 70-198242 *1. Pierre Matisse Gallery, New York.* II. Title.

Macke, August, 1887-1914.

MACKE, August, 1887- 760'.0924 1914. *Tunisian watercolors and drawings.* New York, H. N. Abrams [1969] 85 p. illus. (part col.), port. 30 cm. Includes Diary of trip to Tunisia, by Paul Klee. Translation of Die Tunisreise; Aquarelle und Zeichnungen. [ND1954.M28B713 1969] 69-17497 *1. Macke, August, 1887-1914. 2. Tunisia in art.* I. Klee, Paul, 1879-1940. Diary of trip to Tunisia. II. Title.

McKean, Hugh—Art collections.

TIFFANY, Louis Comfort, 748.2'913 1848-1933. *Beauty fixed in many mediums;* an exhibition of the works of Louis Comfort Tiffany from the Collection of Hugh and Jeannette McKean. Text by Bruce Dempsey. Catalogue by Mary Ann Colado. [Tallahassee? 1972] [56] p. illus. (part col.) 24 cm. "University Art Gallery, the Florida State University, Tallahassee, Florida, February 15-March 10, 1972." Bibliography: p. [11] [N6537.T5D4] 72-198300 *1. McKean, Hugh—Art collections. 2. McKean, Jeannette—Art collections.* I. Dempsey, Bruce. II. Colado, Mary Ann. III. Florida. State University, Tallahassee. Art Gallery. IV. Title.

Mackennal, Edgar Bertram, Sir, 1863-1931.

HUTCHISON, Noel. 730'.92'4 *Bertram Mackennal /* [by] Noel Hutchison. Melbourne ; New York : Oxford University Press, 1973. 30 p. : ill. ; 19 cm. (Great Australians) Bibliography: p. 30. [NB1105.M32H87] 74-189330 ISBN 0-19-550429-1 : 0.40 *1. Mackennal, Edgar Bertram, Sir, 1863-1931.*

McKenzie, Robert Tait, 1867-1938.

KOZAR, Andrew J. 730'.92'4 *R. Tait McKenzie, the sculptor of athletes* / by Andrew J. Kozar ; with a foreword by Francis S. Grubar. 1st ed. [Knoxville] : University of Tennessee Press, [1975] xxii, 118 p. : ill. ; 27 cm. Includes bibliographical references and index. [NB237.M277K69] 74-34421 ISBN 0-87049-168-7 : 12.95 *1. McKenzie, Robert Tait, 1867-1938. 2. Athletes in art.* I. Title.

McKim, Charles Follen, 1847-1909.

GRANGER, Alfred Hoyt, 720'.92'4 B 1867-1939. *Charles Follen McKim; a study of his life and work.* New York, B. Blom, 1972. xii, 145 p. illus. 24 cm. Reprint of the 1913 ed. [NA737.M3G7 1972b] 79-152623 15.75 *1. McKim, Charles Follen, 1847-1909.* **BIP**

GRANGER, Alfred Hoyt, 720'.92'4 B 1867-1939. *Charles Follen McKim: a study of his life and work.* Boston, Houghton Mifflin, 1913. [New York, AMS Press, 1972] xii, 145 p. illus. 24 cm. [NA737.M3G7 1972] 70-168178 ISBN 0-404-02890-X 7.00

SUBJECT INDEX MACRAME.

1. McKim, Charles Follen, 1847-1909.

MOORE, Charles, 1855- 720'.924 B 1942.
The life and times of Charles Follen McKim. New York, Da Capo Press, 1970 [c1929] xii, 356 p. illus., ports. 24 cm. (Da Capo Press series in architecture and decorative art, v. 32) (A Da Capo Press reprint edition.) [NA737.M3M6 1970] 70-99857
1. McKim, Charles Follen, 1847-1909. I. Title. BIP

McKim, Mead & White.

MCKIM, Mead & White. 720'.6'57471
A monograph of the works of McKim, Mead & White, 1879-1915. With an essay by Leland Roth. New ed. [New York] B. Blom, 1973. p. Includes bibliographical references. [NA737.M4A5 1973] 72-152624
1. McKim, Mead & White. I. Title.

REILLY, Charles 720'.6'57471 Herbert, Sir, 1874-1948.
McKim, Mead & White. New York, B. Blom, 1972. 23 p. illus. 26 cm. Reprint of the 1924 ed., issued in series: Masters of architecture. [NA737.M4R4 1972] 71-180028 12.75
1. McKim, Mead & White. I. Title. II. Series: Masters of architecture. BIP

McKim, Mead & White—Catalogs.

ROTH, Leland M. 720'.6'57471
The architecture of McKim, Mead & White, 1870-1920 : a building list / Leland M. Roth. New York : Garland Pub., 1978. p. cm. (Garland reference library of the humanities ; v. 114) Includes index. Bibliography: p. [NA737.M4A4 1978] 77-83368 ISBN 0-8240-9850-1 : lib.bdg. : 40.00
1. McKim, Mead & White—Catalogs. 2. Architecture, Modern—19th century—Catalogs. 3. Architecture, Modern—20th century—Catalogs. I. Title. BIP

Mackintosh, Charles Rennie, 1868-1928.

HOWARTH, Thomas, 1914- 927.2
Charles Rennie Mackintosh and the modern movement. [New York] Wittenborn Publications [1953] xxviii, 329p. illus., 96 plates (incl. ports.) 26cm. Bibliography: p. 309-314. [NA997.M3H6 1953] 53-13143
1. Mackintosh, Charles Rennie, 1868-1928. I. Title.

HOWARTH, Thomas, 1914- 720'.92'4
Charles Rennie Mackintosh and the modern movement / Thomas Howarth. 2d ed. London : Routledge & Kegan Paul, 1977. 1, 335 p., [48] leaves of plates : ill. ; 26 cm. Includes index. Bibliography: p. 311-320. [N6797.M23H68 1977b] 77-72348 ISBN 0-7100-8538-9 : 26.50
1. Mackintosh, Charles Rennie, 1868-1928. 2. Art nouveau—Great Britain. I. Title.
Distributed by Routledge & Kegan Paul, Boston

HOWARTH, Thomas, 1914- 720'.92'4
Charles Rennie Mackintosh and the modern movement / Thomas Howarth. New York : Garland Pub., 1977. p. cm. (The Aesthetic movement & the arts and crafts movement ; 38) Reprint of the 1952 ed. published by Routledge and K. Paul, London. Includes index. Bibliography: p. [N6797.M23H68 1977] 76-17782 ISBN 0-8240-2487-7 lib.bdg. : 35.00
1. Mackintosh, Charles Rennie, 1868-1928. 2. Art nouveau—Great Britain. I. Title. II. Series.

MACKINTOSH, Charles 720'.22'2 Rennie, 1868-1928.
Architectural sketches & flower drawings by Charles Rennie Mackintosh / Roger Billcliffe. New York : Rizzoli, 1977. 96 p. : ill. (some col.) ; 31 cm. Includes bibliographical references. [NA997.M3B54 1977] 76-62546 ISBN 0-8478-0074-1 : 13.95. ISBN 0-8478-0084-9 pbk. : 7.95
1. Mackintosh, Charles Rennie, 1868-1928. I. Billcliffe, Roger. II. Title. BIP

Mackintosh, Charles Rennie, 1868-1928—Catalogs.

MACKINTOSH, Charles 759.9411 Rennie, 1868-1928.
Mackintosh watercolours / Roger Billcliffe. New York : Taplinger Pub. Co., 1978. 144 p. : ill. (Some col.) ; 31 cm. "A Carter Nash Cameron book." Includes index. Bibliography: p. 22-23. [ND1942.M227A4 1978a] 78-53795 ISBN 0-8008-5044-0 : 20.00
1. Mackintosh, Charles Rennie, 1868-1928—Catalogs. I. Billcliffe, Roger. II. Title.

McLaren, Norman, 1914—

MCLAREN, Norman, 1914- 741.9'41
The drawings of Norman = Les dessins de Norman McLaren / text by Norman McLaren ; edited from taped interviews by Michael White ; [French translation by Rene Chicoine]. Montreal : Tundra Books, c1975. 192 p. : ill. ; 32 cm. English and French parallel text. Bibliography: p. 182. [NC143.M32W45] 76-358769 ISBN 0-912766-28-X (Tundra Books of Northern New York) : 25.00
1. McLaren, Norman, 1914- I. White, Michael.
Distributed by Tundra Books of Northern New York, Plattsburgh, NY

McLaughlin, John, 1898—

MCLAUGHLIN, John, 1898- 759.13
John McLaughlin, recent paintings—1970/1971. Irvine, University of California [1972] 26 p. illus. (part col.) 23 x 24 cm. Catalogue of an exhibition held at the University of California, Irvine, Apr. 7-May 3, 1971. [ND237.M2155C34] 73-634770 3.50
I. California. University, Irvine.

MCLAUGHLIN, John, 1898- 759.13
John McLaughlin: retrospective exhibition. Organized by the La Jolla Museum of Contemporary Art, La Jolla, California, July 7-August 12, 1973. [La Jolla, 1973] 32 p. illus. (part col.) 23 cm. Errata slip inserted. Bibliography: p. 30-31. [ND237.M2155L32] 73-85270
1. McLaughlin, John, 1898- I. La Jolla Museum of Contemporary Art. II. Title.

MCLAUGHLIN, John, 1898- 759.13
John McLaughlin: retrospective exhibition, 1946-1967, November 16, 1968-January 5, 1969, Washington, Corcoran Gallery of Art. [Washington, Printed by H. K. Press, 1968] 30 p. illus. (part col.), port. 25 cm. Bibliography: p. 28. [ND237.M2155A5] 68-57153
I. Corcoran Gallery of Art, Washington, D.C.

McManus, James W., 1942—

MCMANUS, James W., 730'.92'4 1942-
James W. McManus sculpture : new sculpture, Allrich Gallery, Two Embarcadero Center, San Francisco, California, April 29 to May 31, 1977 : a survey of selected works, 1967-1977, De Saisset Museum, University of Santa Clara, Santa Clara, California, May 7 to June 30, 1977. [s.l. : s.n., 1977] ([Sacramento : Graphic Center]) [36] p. : ill. (some col.) ; 24 cm. [NB237.M278A79] 77-152328
1. McManus, James W., 1942- I. Allrich Gallery. II. De Saisset Museum.

McMurtry, John, 1812-1890.

LANCASTER, Clay. 720.81
Back streets and pine trees; the work of John McMurtry, nineteenth century architect-builder of Kentucky. Lexington [Ky.] Bur Press. 1956. viii, 122p. illus., plans. 25cm. (Kentucky monographs, no. 4) 'Two hundred and fifty copies printed. No. 176. abBibliographical references included in Notes (p. 110-122) [NA737.M42L3] 56-4570
1. McMurtry, John, 1812-1890. I. Title. II. Series.

McNay, Marion Koogler.

BURKHALTER, Lois 704'.36'0924 B (Wood)
Marion Koogler McNay; a biography, 1883-1950. San Antonio, Marion Koogler McNay Art Institute [1968] 97 p. illus. (part col.), ports. 28 cm. [N8410.B8] 68-26507
1. McNay, Marion Koogler. I. Marion Koogler McNay Art Institute, San Antonio.

McNear, Everett, 1904- —Art collections.

MCNEAR, Ann. 759.95
Persian and Indian miniatures from the Collection of Everett and Ann McNear : [Museum of Art, University of Iowa, Iowa City, Art Institute of Chicago, Chicago, Illinois, the Walters Art Gallery, Baltimore, Maryland, 1974-1975] / [text, Ann McNear ; design, Everett McNear]. Chicago : Art Institute of Chicago, 1974. 63 p. : ill. (some col.) ; 23 cm. Catalog of the exhibition. [ND3247.M28] 74-23038
1. McNear, Everett, 1904- —Art collections. 2. McNear, Ann—Art collections. 3. Illumination of books and manuscripts, Indic—Exhibitions. 4. Miniature painting, Indic—Exhibitions. 5. Illumination of books and manuscripts, Iranian—Exhibitions. 6. Miniature painting, Iranian—Exhibitions. I. McNear, Everett, 1904- II. Iowa. University. Museum of Art. III. Chicago. Art Institute. IV. Walters Art Gallery, Baltimore. V. Title.

Macpherson, Duncan Ian, 1924—

MACPHERSON, Duncan Ian, 741.5'971 1924-
Macpherson editorial cartoons, 1976. Toronto : Star Reader Service, 1976. [130] p. : all ill. ; 24 cm. Cover title. [NC1449.M3A52] 77-374600
1. Macpherson, Duncan Ian, 1924- 2. Canadian wit and humor, Pictorial. I. Title.

Macrame.

ALFERS, Betty. 746.4
Macrame. New York, Grosset & Dunlap [1971] 85 p. illus. 21 cm. "Published in association with Parade magazine." [TT840.A43] 78-156323 ISBN 0-448-02090-4 (comb-bound) 1.95
1. Macrame.

ANDES, Eugene. 746.4
Far beyond the fringe; three-dimensional knotting techniques using macrame & nautical ropework [by] Eugene Andes. All articles pictured are the work of Gene & Ellen Andes. New York, Van Nostrand Reinhold Co. [1973] 160 p. illus. 28 cm. Bibliography: p. 158. [TT840.A52] 72-7845 ISBN 0-442-20351-9 9.95
1. Macrame. I. Title. BIP

BOGEN, Constance. 746.4
Macrame. With photos by Tom Gartner. New York, Trident Press [1973] 91 p. illus. 28 cm. [TT840.B63] 73-82867 ISBN 0-671-27108-3 7.95
1. Macrame. BIP

BOGEN, Constance. 746.4
Macrame. With photos by Tom Gartner. New York, Pocket Books [1974, c1973] 189 p. illus. 18 cm. [TT840.B63] ISBN 0-671-78696-2 1.50 (pbk.)
1. Macrame. I. Title.
L.C. card no. for original edition: 73-82867.

BRESS, Helene. 746.4
The craft of macrame / Helene Bress. New York : Scribner, 1977c1972 144 p. : ill. ; 28 cm. (The Scribner library ; SL 671 : Emblem editions) "Originally published as part of The macrame book by the same author." [TT840.B67] 76-40748 ISBN 0-684-14723-8 pbk. : 5.95
1. Macrame. I. Title. BIP

BRESS, Helene. 746.4
The macrame book. New York, Scribner [1972] xi, 274 p. illus. 29 cm. Bibliography: p. 267-268. [TT840.B68] 79-37222 ISBN 0-684-12756-3 12.50
1. Macrame. I. Title. BIP

CLOSE, Eunice. 746.4
Macrame made easy. New York, Collier Books [1973] 88 p. illus. 25 cm. [TT840.C543] 73-4055 3.95
1. Macrame. I. Title. BIP

DEPAS, Spencer. 746.4
Macrame, weaving, and tapestry; art in fiber. New York, Macmillan [1973] xv, 144 p. illus. 26 cm. Bibliography: p. 135. [TT840.D45] 72-80912 8.95
1. Macrame. 2. Hand weaving. I. Title.

HARVEY, Virginia I. 746.4
Color and design in macrame [by] Virginia I. Harvey. New York, Van Nostrand Reinhold [1971] 104 p. illus. (part col.) 21 x 26 cm. Bibliography: p. 103. [TT840.H322] 70-163313
1. Macrame. I. Title.

HARVEY, Virginia I. 746.4
Macrame; the art of creative knotting [by] Virginia I. Harvey. New York, Reinhold Pub. Corp. [1967] 128 p. illus. (part col.) 27 cm. Bibliography: p. 127. [TT840.H323] 66-24539
1. Macrame. I. Title.

HENSEL, John. 746.4
The book of ornamental knots; a new form of the macrame art. New York, Scribner [1973] 176 p. illus. 29 cm. [TT840.H45] 73-2270 ISBN 0-684-13409-8 9.95
1. Macrame. I. Title.

LABARGE, Lura. 746.4
Do your own thing with macrame. New York, Watson-Guptill [1973] 150 p. illus. (part col.) 29 cm. Bibliography: p. 148. [TT840.L3 1973] 73-644 ISBN 0-8230-1354-5 11.95
1. Macrame. I. Title. BIP

LASSNER, Jane. 746.4
Big-knot macrame [by] Nils Strom and Anders Enestrom. [Translated by Kenneth T. Dutfield. Adapted by Jane Lassner] New York, Sterling Pub. Co. [1971] 48 p. illus. 19 cm. (Little craft book series) "Originally published under the title: Knopar; sjomanstradition som hobby." Instructions for making or decorating napkin rings, candle holders, mats, and handbags in macrame. [TT840.L3713 1971] 74-167655
1. Macrame. I. Strom, Nils, 1912- Knopar; sjomanstradition som hobby. II. Title. BIP

MEILACH, Dona Z. 746.4
Macrame; creative design in knotting [by] Dona Z. Meilach. New York, Crown Publishers [1971] xii, 212 p. illus. (part col.) 27 cm. Bibliography: p. 202. [TT840.M4 1971] 73-147330 7.95
1. Macrame.

MILAM, Betsy. 746.4'4
Macrame / by Betsy Milam. New York : Grosset & Dunlap, c1977. 96 p. : ill. ; 28 cm. (Grosset good life books) Includes index. Bibliography: p. 94. [TT840.M54] 76-28633 ISBN 0-448-12736-9 : 1.95 ISBN 0-448-13414-4 lib. bdg. : 1.95
1. Macrame. I. Title.

PESCH, Imelda Manalo. 746.4
Macrame; creative knotting, braiding, twisting: threads, cords, yarns. Photos. by John Pesch. New York, Sterling Pub. Co. [1970] 48 p. illus. (part col.) 20 cm. (Little craft book series) Gives directions for tying basic knots and using them to make functional and decorative objects out of cord, twine, yarn, and similar materials. [TT840.P38] 76-126848
1. Macrame. I. Title.

PESCH, Imelda Manalo. 746.4
Macrame plus / by Imelda Manalo Pesch. New York : Sterling Pub. Co., c1976. 80 p., [5] leaves of plates : ill. (some col.) ; 27 cm. Includes index. Discusses craft projects which incorporate other forms of yarn and needle crafts with macrame. [TT840.P39] 76-1186 ISBN 0-8069-5350-0 : 8.95 ISBN 0-8069-5351-9 lib.bdg. :
1. Macrame. I. Title.

PHILLIPS, Mary Walker. 746.4
Step-by-step macrame; a complete introduction to the craft of creative knotting. Conceived and edited by William and Shirley Sayles. New York, Golden Press [1970] 77, [3] p. illus. (part col.) 29 cm. (The Golden Press step-by-step craft

series) Bibliography: p. [79] [TT840.P46] 75-100337 2.50
1. Macrame. I. Title. II. Title: Macrame.

*PILCHER, Ann Mary. 746.4
Macrame; a practical introduction to knotting. [By] Ann Mary Pilcher. Newton, Mass., Charles C. Branford [1972] 95 p. 21 cm. Bibliography p. 94. [TT840] 72-75067
1. Macrame. I. Title.

RACK, Norman. 746.4
Macrame: advanced technique and design [by] Norman and Lilian Rack. [1st ed.] Garden City, N.Y., Doubleday, 1972. 143 p. illus. 27 cm. (Crafts and hobbies, 014) Bibliography: p. [142] [TT840.R2] 72-175416 3.95 (pbk)
1. Macrame. I. Rack, Lilian, joint author.

SCHMID-BURLESON, Bonny. 746.4
The technique of macrame. Newton Centre, Mass., C. T. Branford Co. [1974] p. Includes bibliographies. [TT840.S36] 73-17335 ISBN 0-8231-7034-9
1. Macrame. I. Title. BIP

SCMID-BURLESON, Bonny. 746.4
Fun with macrame. Text by Claus Peter Schmid. New York, Watson-Guptill Publications [1972, c1971] p. [TT840.S35] 75-190512 ISBN 0-8230-1990-X
1. Macrame. I. Schmid-Burleson, Bonny. II. Title.

SIMPLY macrame; 746.4
an introduction to an exciting new craft, by Mary F. Singleton [and others. Berkeley, Calif., Webton Enterprises, 1971] 19 p. illus. 29 cm. [TT840.S56] 78-164035
1. Marcrame. I. Singleton, Mary F.

TORBET, Laura. 746.4
Macrame you can wear; a complete basic course in macrame and 25 brand-new wearable projects with full instructions. Color photos by Mort Engel; black and white photos by Mark Stein. Book design by Katherine Wendel. New York, Ballantine Books [1972] x, 115 p. illus. 28 cm. Bibliography: p. 112. [TT840.T67] 72-189949 3.95
1. Macrame. I. Title.

WALKER, Louisa. 746.4
Graded lessons in macrame, knotting and netting. New York, Dover Publications [1971] xiv, 254 p. illus. 21 cm. Originally published in 1896 under title: Varied occupations in string work: comprising knotting, netting, looping, plaiting, and macrame. [TT840.W28 1971] 73-158734 ISBN 0-486-22754-5 2.00
1. Macrame. 2. Netting. I. Title. BIP

Macrame—Juvenile literature.

CREATIVE Educational Society, Mankato, Minn. 746.4
How to have fun with macrame, by the editors of Creative. Illustrated by Nancy Inderieden. [Mankato, Minn., Creative Education; distributed by Childrens Press, Chicago, 1974] 31 p. illus. (part col.) 25 cm. (Creative craft book) A simple introduction to macrame with instructions for a variety of projects. [TT840.C73 1974] 73-19667 ISBN 0-87191-290-2 4.95
1. Macrame—Juvenile literature. I. Inderieden, Nancy, illus. II. Title.

Macrame—Patterns.

BARNES, Charles. 746.4
Macrame fashions and furnishings, by Charles Barnes and David P. Blake. In collaboration with William Baker. Great Neck, N.Y., Hearthside Press [1972] 256 p. illus. 25 cm. [TT840.B35] 75-185810 ISBN 0-8208-0342-1 8.95
1. Macrame—Patterns. I. Blake, David P., joint author. II. Title.

*BOBERG, Anne-Marie 746.4
Macrame. [By] Anne-Marie Boberg [and] Elsie Svennas. New York, Arco Pub., [1975 c1972] 104 p. ill. 22 cm. Includes index. [TT840] 74-14199 ISBN 0-668-03753-9 7.95 (lib. bdg.)
1. Macrane. I. Svennas, Elsie, joint author II. Title.
Pbk, 3.95; ISBN 0-668-03623-0.

MEILACH, Dona Z. 746.4
Macrame accessories: patterns and ideas for knotting [by] Dona Z. Meilach. New York, Crown Publishers [1972] 96 p. illus. 29 cm. (Crown's arts and crafts series) [TT840.M39 1972] 78-185074 4.95
1. Macrame—Patterns. I. Title.

Macrophotography.

CROY, Otto R., 1902- 778.3'24
Camera close up; same-size and larger than life photography, by O. R. Croy. [English translation by L. A. Mannheim] New York, Amphoto [1970, c1961] 227 p. illus. (part col.) 24 cm. Translation of Alles uber Nahaufnahmen. [TR683.C713 1970] 70-119724 11.95
1. Macrophotography. I. Title.

PAPERT, Jean. 778.3'24
Photomacrography: art and techniques. New York, Amphoto [1971] x, 117 p. illus. (part col.) 27 cm. [TR684.P35] 78-134240 ISBN 0-8174-0536-4 7.95
1. Macrophotography. I. Title.

TOLKE, Arnim. 778.3'24
Macrophoto and cine methods [by] Arnim and Ingeborg Tolke [translated from the German by E. F. Linssen] London, New York, Focal Press, 1971. 270 p. illus. (some col.) 22 cm. Translation of Makrofoto, Makrofilm. [TR684.T6413 1971b] 72-583951 ISBN 0-240-50693-6 £3.00
1. Macrophotography. I. Tolke, Ingeborg, joint author. II. Title.

Macrophotography—Juvenile literature.

LOSS, Joan. 778.3'1
What is it? A book of photographic puzzlers. [1st ed.] Garden City, N.Y., Doubleday [1974] 46 p. illus. 29 cm. The reader is challenged to identify close-up photographs of familiar objects found in most homes shown here from ten to thirty times larger than their real size. [TR684.L67] 73-9038 ISBN 0-385-00396-X 4.50
1. Macrophotography—Juvenile literature. I. Title. BIP

Maddox, Conroy.

MADDOX, Conroy. 759.2
Conroy Maddox : gouaches of the 1940's : [catalogue of an] exhibition open 13 February-12 March 1976 [at] Fischer Fine Art Limited, London. London : Fischer Fine Art Limited, [1976] Folder (4 p.) : ill. (incl. 1 col.) ; 26 cm. Cover title. [ND1942.M23F57] 76-368177 ISBN 0-904867-05-6 : £0.15
1. Maddox, Conroy. I. Fischer Fine Art Limited.

Maderno, Carlo, 1556-1629.

HIBBARD, Howard, 1928- 720'.92'4
Carlo Maderno and Roman architecture, 1580-1630. London, Zwemmer, 1971. xvi, 404 p. illus., geneal. tables, plans. 31 cm. (Studies in architecture, v. 10) Sole distributor in the U.S.A.; Pennsylvania State University Press, University Park, Pa. English or Italian. "Catalogue": p. 107-234. Bibliography: p. 380-390. [NA1123.M3H5 1971] 72-195351 ISBN 0-302-02161-2
1. Maderno, Carlo, 1556-1629. 2. Architecture—Rome (City) I. Title.
39.50 BIP

Madison Art Association, Madison, Wis.

ELA, Janet Smith, 1910- 706.2775
The Madison Art Association, 1901-1951. Madison Art Association nineteen one-nineteen fifty-one [Madison, Wis.] Madison Art Association, '1951. 109 p. 21 cm. [N11.M3E4] 51-33973
1. Madison Art Association, Madison, Wis. I. Title.

Madrid. Museo Nacional de Pintura y Escultura.

LORENTE, Manuel 750.7404641
The Prado, Madrid; v. 1 & 2. [Tr. from Italian by Paul Colacicchi] New York, Appleton-Century [dist. Meredith. 1965, c.1962] 2v. (156;160p.) (chiefly illus. (pt. col.)) 28cm. Great galleries ser.) Great galleries ser.) [N3450.L63] 65-5769 8.95 bds., ea.,
1. Madrid. Museu Nacional de Pintura y Escultura. I. Title.

PRADO, Madrid. 759.9'4'094641
[Texts by Anna Pallucchini, Carlo Ludovicio [sic] Ragghianti and Licia Ragghianti Collobi] New York, Newsweek [1968] 171 p. illus. (part col.) 30 cm. (Great museums of the world) Bibliography: p. [1968] [N3450.A6843] 68-20028
1. Madrid. Museo Nacional de Pintura y Escultura. I. Pallucchini, Anna. II. Ragghianti, Carlo Ludovico. III. Ragghianti Collobi, Licia. IV. Series: Great museums of the world (New York, Newsweek)

WEHLE, Harry Brandeis, 1887- 708.6
The Prado, Madrid. Text by Harry B. Wehle. New York, H. N. Abrams [1956] 60 p. illus., 24 col. plates (part fold.) 39 cm. (Great paintings of the world) An Abrams art book. [N3450.W43] 57-538
1. Madrid. Museo Nacional de Pintura y Escultura. 2. Paintings — Madrid I. Title.

Maekawa, Kunio, 1905—

ALTHERR, Alfred, 1911- 720.922
Three Japanese architects. Drei japanische Architekten; Mayekawa, Tange, Sakakura. [English version by D. Q. Stephenson] New York, Architectural Book Pub. Co. [1968] 179 p. illus., plans. 23 x 29 cm. English and German. [NA1559.M3A78 1968] 68-5228
1. Maekawa, Kunio, 1905- 2. Tange, Kenzo, 1913- 3. Sakakura, Junzo. 4. Architecture, Modern—20th century—Japan. I. Title. II. Title: Drei japanische Architekten.

Magazine design.

HURLBURT, Allen, 1910- 686'.2252
Publication design; a guide to page layout, typography, format and style. [New York] Van Nostrand Reinhold [1971] 138 p. illus. (part col.) 25 cm. Bibliography: p. 132. [Z253.5.H85] 72-163484 15.00
1. Magazine design. I. Title.

HURLBURT, Allen, 1910- 686.2'252
Publication design : a guide to page layout, typography, format, and style / by Allen Hurlburt. Rev. ed. New York : Van Nostrand Reinhold Co., 1976. 134 p. : ill. ; 24 cm. Includes index. Bibliography: p. 128. [Z253.5.H85 1976] 75-33846 ISBN 0-442-23592-5 pbk. : 8.95
1. Magazine design. I. Title.

MCLEAN, Ruari. 655.5'3
Magazine design. London, New York [etc.] Oxford U.P., 1969. 354 p. illus. (some col.), facsims., ports. (some col.) 26 cm. [Z253.5.M22] 68-59646 5/5/-
1. Magazine design.

WHITE, Jan V. 1928- 070.5'72
Designing covers, contents, flash forms departments, editiorials, openers, products for magazines. New York : R. R. Bowker, 1976. xiii, 176p. : ill. ; 29 cm. Continues Editing by design. Includes index. [Z253.5W46] 76-3692 ISBN 0-8352-0900-8 : 16.95
1. Magazine design. I. Title.

WHITE, Jan V., 1928- 070.5'72
Designing covers, contents, flash forms, departments, editorials, openers, products for magazines / by Jan V. White. New York : R. R. Bowker, 1976. xiii, 176 p. : ill. ; 29 cm. On spine: Designing ... for magazines. Continues Editing by design. Includes index. [Z253.5.W46] 76-3692 ISBN 0-8352-0900-8
1. Magazine design. I. Title. II. Title: Designing ... for magazines.

WHITE, Jan V., 1928- 070.5'72
Editing by design; word-and-picture communication for editors and designers, by Jan V. White. New York, R. R. Bowker, 1974. xv, 230 p. illus. 28 cm. [Z253.5.W47] 73-18167 ISBN 0-8352-0692-0 17.50
1. Magazine design. I. Title. BIP

Magazine illustration—England.

THORPE, James, 1876-1949. 741.65'0942
English illustration, the nineties / James Thorpe. New York : Hacker Art Books, 1975. xx, 267 p., [24] leaves of plates : ill. ; 25 cm. Reprint of the 1935 ed. published by Faber and Faber, London. Includes index. [NC978.T5 1975] 72-95117 ISBN 0-87817-128-2 : 25.00
1. Magazine illustration—England. 2. Illustrated periodicals—England. I. Title.

Magi—Art.

BECKWITH, John, 1918- 736'.6
The adoration of the Magi in whalebone. London, H.M.S.O., 1966. [7], 40 p. front., illus. 24 1/2 cm. (B66-17403) (Victoria and Albert Museum [South Kensington] Museum monograph no. 28) Bibliographical references included in "Notes" (p. 31-34) [N8063.B4] 67-78496
1. Magi — Art. I. Title. II. Series.

BIBLE. N. T. Matthew II. English. 1964. Revised standard. 730.9444
The story of the wise men, according to the Gospel of Saint Matthew. New York, Holt, c.1964. 38, [5]p. illus., maps. 29cm. Illus., which include the story as carved on four stone capitals in the Cathedral of Autun, the definitive study by Denis Grivot, George Zarnecki. Gislebertus of Autun; notes on his work and the role of the cathedral in the everyday life of the Middle Ages, by Regine Pernoud and Canon Grivot 4.95
1. Magi—Art. I. Gislebertus, 12th cent. II. Pernoud, Regine, 1909-Gislebertus of Autun. III. Title.

KUPPERS, Leonhard, 1903- 704.948'4
The three kings (Magi). [Tr. from German by Hans Hermann Rosenwald] Recklinghausen, Aurel Bongers; dist. Taplinger [New York, 1967] 68p. col. plates. 18cm. (Saints in legend & art, v. 1) [N8063.K813] 67-112368 2.50 bds.,
1. Magi—Art. I. Title.

Magic in art.

SCHWARTZ, Paul Waldo. 700'.1
Art and the occult / Paul Waldo-Schwartz. New York : G. Braziller, c1975. vii, 168 p. : ill. ; 26 cm. Bibliography: p. 167-168. [N8222.M3S38 1975] 75-7655 ISBN 0-8076-0784-3 : 17.50. ISBN 0-8076-0785-1 pbk. : 7.95
1. Magic in art. 2. Art—Psychology. I. Title. BIP

Magic realism (Art)

DE REYNA, Rudy, 1914- 751.4'2
Magic realist painting techniques. New York, Watson-Guptill Publications [1973] 158 p. illus. (part col.) 29 cm. Bibliography: p. 155. [ND1505.D47 1973] 73-6929 ISBN 0-8230-2956-5 15.00
1. Magic realism (Art) 2. Painting—Technique. I. Title. BIP

Magic realism (Art)—Austria—Vienna.

COMINI, Alessandra. 759.36'13
The fantastic art of Vienna / by Alessandra Comini. 1st ed. New York : Knopf, 1978. p. cm. Includes index. [N6808.5.M3C65 1978] 78-54886 ISBN 0-394-50263-9 : 20.00
1. Magic realism (Art)—Austria—Vienna. 2. Art, Austrian—Austria—Vienna. 3. Art, Modern—20th century—Austria—Vienna. I. Title. BIP

Magnolia Gardens, S.C.

LASHLEY, Dolores C. 712'.6'09757915
Legacy of beauty, by Dolores C. Lashley.

SUBJECT INDEX MAJOLICA.

Columbia, S.C., State Print. Co., 1969. 139 p. illus. (part col.), map (on lining papers) 23 cm. Bibliography: p. 133-139. [SB466.U7M34] 77-23633
1. Drayton, John Grimke, 1815-1891. 2. Magnolia Gardens, S.C. I. Title. BIP

Magritte, Rene, 1898-1967.

GABLIK, Suzi. 759.9493
Magritte. Greenwich, Conn., New York Graphic Society [1970] 208 p. illus. (part col.), ports. 26 cm. "Texts by Magritte": p. 194-195. [ND673.M35G3 1970] 77-125894 ISBN 5-00-490031- 13.50
1. Magritte, Rene, 1898-1967.

MAGRITTE, Rene, 1898- 759.9493
1967.
Magritte, edited by David Larkin. Introd. by Eddie Wolfram. New York, Ballantine Books [1972] [96] p. 40 col. plates. 30 cm. [ND673.M35L3] 72-189948 ISBN 0-345-02692-6 4.95
1. Magritte, Rene, 1898-1967.

MAGRITTE, Rene, 1898- 759.9493
1967.
Rene Magritte. [Catalogue of an exhibition] November 19-December 21, 1968, Byron Gallery, New York. [New York, Byron Gallery, c1968] 94 p. illus. (part col.) 22 cm. On spine: Magritte. [ND673.M35B97] 74-173313
1. Magritte, Rene, 1898-1967. I. Byron Gallery.

MAGRITTE, Rene, 1898- 759.9493
1967.
Rene Magritte. Text by A. M. Hammacher. New York, H. N. Abrams [1974] p. cm. (The Library of great painters) Bibliography: p. [ND673.M35H35] 73-13789 ISBN 0-8109-0278-8 22.50
1. Magritte, Rene, 1898-1967. I. Hammacher, Abraham Marie, 1897-

MAGRITTE, Rene, 1898- 759.9493
1967.
Rene Magritte. Conceived by Jean Saucet. Text by Rene Passeron. Translated from the French by Elisabeth Abbott. Chicago, J. P. O'Hara [1972] 93 p. illus. (part col.) 31 cm. "A Howard Greenfeld book." Bibliography: p. 90-91. [ND673.M35P313] 72-189278 ISBN 0-87955-601-3 15.00
1. Magritte, Rene, 1898-1957. I. Passeron, Rene, 1920-

MAGRITTE, Rene, 1898- 759.9493
1967.
Secret affinities : words and images / by Rene Magritte. Houston, Tex. : Institute for the Arts, Rice University, 1976. 32 p. : ill. ; 23 cm. "Exhibition dates: October 1, 1976-January 2, 1977." Includes bibliographical references. [ND673.M35W54] 76-45518 ISBN 0-914412-12-4 : 2.00
1. Magritte, Rene, 1898-1967. I. William Marsh Rice University, Houston, Tex. Institute for the Arts. II. Title. BIP

NEW York. Museum of 759.9493
Modern Art.
Rene Magritte, by James Thrall Soby. New York; Distributed by Doubleday, Garden City, N.Y. [c1965] 80 p. illus. (part col.) port. 25 cm. Catalog of an exhibition held at the Museum of Modern Art, New York; the Rose Art Museum, Brandeis University, the Art Institute of Chicago; the University Art Museum, University of California, Berkeley; and the Pasadena Art Museum. Bibliography: p. 71-78. [ND673.M35N4] 65-28610
1. Magritte, Rene, 1898- I. Soby, James Thrall, 1906- II. Title.

NOEL, Bernard, 1930- 759.9493
Magritte / by Bernard Noel. New York : Crown Publishers, 1977c1976 p. cm. Bibliography: p. [ND673.M35N613] 76-57235 ISBN 0-517-53009-0 : 4.95
1. Magritte, Rene, 1898-1967.

SYLVESTER, David. 759.4
Magritte. New York, Praeger [1969] 126 p. illus. (part col.) 24 cm. "Revised version ... of the catalogue of the retrospective exhibition presented by the Arts Council of Great Britain at the Tate Gallery, London, in the spring of 1969." Includes bibliographical references. [ND673.M35S92] 77-84094 12.50
1. Magritte, Rene, 1898-1967. I. Arts Council of Great Britain. II. Tate Gallery, London.

TORCZYNER, Harry. 759.9493
Magritte, ideas and images / Harry Torczyner ; translated by Richard Miller. New York : H. N. Abrams, [1977] p. cm. Translation of Rene Magritte, signes et images. Includes index. Bibliography: p. [ND673.M35T6713] 77-79323 ISBN 0-8109-1300-3 : 45.00
1. Magritte, Rene, 1898-1967. I. Title.

Mahabharata—Illustrations.

VEQUAUD, Yves. 755'.9'45095412
Women painters of Mithila / Yves Vequaud. London : Thames and Hudson, 1977. 112 p. : chiefly ill. (some col.) ; 28 cm. Translation of L'art du Mithila. [ND1007.M55V4613 1977b] 78-308556 ISBN 0-500-27093-7 : 8.95
1. Valmiki. Ramayana—Illustrations. 2. Mahabharata—Illustrations. 3. Painting, Indic—India—Mithila. 4. Painting—India—Mithila. 5. Painting, Hindu—India—Mithila. 6. Hindu symbolism. 7. Symbolism in art—India—Mithila. I. Title.
Distributed by W. W. Norton, New York, NY 10036 BIP

Mahabharata. Nalopakhyana.

EASTMAN, Alvan Clark. 741.954
The Nala-Damayanti drawings A study of a portfolio of drawings made for Raja Samsar Cand of Kangra (1774-1823), illustrating an early Indian romance; twenty-nine drawings now in the Museum of Fine Arts, Boston, with the addition of nineteen drawings from other American museums and from a private collection. Boston, Museum of Fine Arts, 1959. xix, 119 p. 47 plates. 23 x 28 cm. Bibliography: p. 113-115. [NC1250.E25] 59-14357
1. Mahabharata. Nalopakhyana. 2. Drawings, Indic. 3. Drawing—Kangra (District) Punjab. I. Boston, Museum of Fine Arts. II. Title.

Mahayana Buddhism in art.

DOHANIAN, Diran Kavork, 732'.4
1931-
The Mahayana Buddhist sculpture of Ceylon / Diran Kavork Dohanian. New York : Garland Pub., 1977. x, 167 p., [38] leaves of plates : ill. ; 21 cm. (Outstanding dissertations in the fine arts) Originally presented as the author's thesis, Harvard, 1964. Bibliography: p. 159-166. [NB1010.6.D64 1977] 76-23613 ISBN 0-8240-2685-3 : 35.00
1. Mahayana Buddhism in art. 2. Sculpture, Buddhist—Sri Lanka. 3. Sculpture, Sinhalese. I. Title. II. Series. BIP

Mahboubian, Benyamin, 1868-1969—Art collections.

TEXAS. 709'.55'07401643
University at Austin. Art Museum.
Treasures of Persian art after Islam: the Mahboubian Collection. [New York, Printed by Plantin Press, c1970] 1 v. (unpaged) illus., map, plates. 23 x 28 cm. Catalog of an exhibition held at the University Art Museum of the University of Texas, at Austin. [N7280.T4] 79-198160
1. Mahboubian, Benyamin, 1868-1969—Art collections. 2. Art, Iranian—Exhibitions. I. Title.

Mai-chi Shan Caves.

SULLIVAN, 731.8'8'943095145
Michael, 1916-
The cave temples of Maichishan. Photos. by Dominique Darbois. With an account of the 1958 expedition to Maichishan by Anil de Silva. Berkeley, University of California Press, 1969. xiv, 77 p. illus., map. 104 plates (part col.) 29 cm. Bibliography: p. 59-63. [NB1043.S77] 69-15829 21.50
1. Mai-chi Shan Caves. 2. Art, Buddhist—Kansu (Province) 3. Sculpture—Kansu (Province) I. De Silva, Anil. II. Title. BIP

Maidstone Museum and Art Gallery.

MAIDSTONE 759.94'074'022375
Museum and Art Gallery.
Foreign paintings catalogue [of the] Maidstone Museum and Art Gallery / [compiled by] Susan Legouix. Maidstone : Maidstone Borough Council for the Maidstone Museum and Art Gallery, 1976. 52 p. : ill., ports. ; 20 x 22 cm. Includes index. [ND454.M3 1976] 77-366201 ISBN 0-905567-00-5 : £0.80
1. Miadstone Museum and Art Gallery. 2. Painting, European—catalogs. 3. Painting, Modern—Europe—Catalogs. 4. Painting—England—Maidstone—Catalogs. I. Legouix, Susan. II. Title.

Mail order antiques business.

LAESTAR, Martha E. 658.8'72
Successful buying and selling of antiques by mail—for both collectors and dealers / by Martha E. Laestar. Rev. ed. New York : Vantage Press, c1975. 97 p. ; 22 cm. [NK1133.3.L33] 76-357676 ISBN 0-533-01620-7 : 3.95
1. Mail-order antique business. I. Title. II. Title: Successful buying and selling of antiques by mail.

Mail-order antiques business.

BAILEY, Robert C., 658.89'7451
fl.1951-
How to start and operate a mail-order antiques business, by Robert C. Bailey. Spring City, Tenn., Hillcrest Shop [1972] 72 p. illus. 28 cm. [NK1133.3.B3] 72-192992 6.95
1. Mail-order antiques business. 2. Art objects—Catalogs. I. Title.

Maillol, Aristide Joseph Bonaventure, 1861-1944.

BUFFALO Fine Arts 730'.92'4
Academy.
Aristide Maillol, with an introd. and survey of the artist's work in American collections, edited by Andrew C. Ritchie. Westport, Conn., Greenwood Press [1972, c1945] 128 p. illus. 26 cm. Bibliography: p. 119-128. [NB553.M3B8 1972] 71-184839 ISBN 0-8371-6329-3 12.00
1. Maillol, Aristide Joseph Bonaventure, 1861-1944. 2. Sculpture, French—United States. I. Ritchie, Andrew Carnduff, ed.

CHEVALIER, Denys. 709'.24
Maillol. [Translated from the French by Eileen B. Hennessy] New York, Crown Publishers [1970] 96 p. illus. (part col.), col. port. 29 cm. Bibliography: p. 95. [NB553.M3C513] 78-108088 3.95
1. Maillol, Aristide Joseph Bonaventure, 1861-1944. BIP

MAILLOL, Aristide 730'.92'4
Joseph Bonaventure, 1861-1944.
Aristide Maillol, 1861-1944. [Texte par] John Rewald. Paris, Braun; agent pour U. S. A.; E. S. Herrmann, New York [1950] [63] p. 60 illus. 17 cm. (Collection des maitres) Text in French, English and German. Bibiliography: p. [63] [NB553.M3R44] 52-37671
I. Rewald, John, 1912- II. Title. III. Series: Collection "Les Maltres

MAILLOL, Aristide Joseph 730'.924
Bonaventure, 1861-1944.
Aristide Maillol (1861-1944) [New York, Perls Galleries, 1970] 44 p. illus., port. 24 cm. Catalog of the exhibition held Mar. 18-Apr. 18, 1970, at the Perls Galleries, New York. [NB553.M3A42] 73-18397
I. Perls Galleries.

MAILLOL, Aristide 730'.92'4
Joseph Bonaventure, 1861-1944.
Aristide Maillol, 1861-1944 : [exhibition], the Solomon R. Guggenheim Museum, New York. New York : Solomon R. Guggenheim Foundation, 1975. 140 p. : ill. ; 22 x 28 cm. Errata sheet inserted. "Exhibition 75/6." Bibliography: p. 136-138. [NB553.M3S64] 75-42576 ISBN 0-89207-000-5 pbk. : 9.50
1. Maillol, Aristide Joseph Bonaventure, 1861-1944. I. Solomon R. Guggenheim Museum, New York.

WALDEMAR-GEORGE, pseud. 730.944
Aristide Maillol. Biography by Dina Vierny. [Tr. from French by Diana Imber] Greenwich, Conn., N. Y. Graphic [1965] 235p. illus. (pt. mounted col.) 29cm. Bibl. [NB553.M3W313] 65-14124 25.00
1. Maillol, Aristide Joseph Bonaventure, 1861-1944. I. Title.

Maine—Capital and capitol.

MAINE. Capitol 711'.551'097416
Planning Commission.
Report of the Capitol Planning Commission, including A master plan for the State Capitol complex, Augusta, Maine, prepared by Frank Grad & Sons. [Augusta] 1969. 26 p. illus., plans. 22 x 28 cm. At head of title: State of Maine. [JK1651.M26A55 1969] 73-628278
1. Maine—Capital and capitol. I. Grad (Frank) and Sons, Newark, N.J.

Maine — Descr. & trav. — Views.

BOWDOIN College. Museum 741.974
of Fine Arts.
As Maine goes: photographs by John McKee. Introd. by William O. Douglas. [Brunswick, Me., Bowdoin College Museum of Art, 1966] 1 v. (unpaged) illus. (part col.) 29 cm. Catalogue of an exhibition held at the Bowdoin College Museum of Art. [F20.B6] 66-9687
1. Maine — Descr. & trav. — Views. 2. Natural resources — Maine. I. Title.

MERRITT, Norman, 1916- 741.974
Maine sketchbook; an artist's impressions of Maine's scenic highlights. Boothbay Harbor, Me., N. Merritt Studio-Gallery [1955- v. (chiefly illus.) 26cm. [NC1075.M62A48] 55-34800
1. Maine—Descr. & trav.—Views. I. Title.

Maine in art.

PORTLAND 759.141'074'014191
Museum of Art.
Fifty-eight Maine paintings : selections from the Collection of Mr. and Mrs. Walter M. Jeffords, Jr.: catalogue of an exhibition 20 May-20 June 1976, Portland Museum of Art Portland, Me. : The Museum, c1976. 19 p. : ill. (some col.) ; 23 cm. [ND210.P67 1976] 76-372285
1. Jeffords, Walter M.—Art collections. 2. Maine in art. 3. Paintings, American—Exhibitions. 4. Paintings, Modern—19th century—United States—Exhibitions. 5. Paintings, Modern—20th century—United States—Exhibitions. I. Title.

Maine—Pol. & govt.—Caricatures and cartoons.

EASTMAN, Joel W. 741.5973
The Maine thing; some of our best friends are Republicans [by] Joel W. Eastman. Freeport, Me., Bond Wheelwright Co. [1964] 1 v. (chiefly illus.) 14 cm. "Full text of 1964 Maine Democratic Party platform": [3] p. at end. [NC1429.E2A5] 64-5337
1. Maine—Pol. & govt.—Caricatures and cartoons. I. Title. II. Title: Some of our best friends are Republicans.

Maison, K. E.

DAUMIER, Honore Victorin 744.944
Drawings. [Text by] K. E. Maison. New York, T. Yoseloff [c.1960] 30p. 150 illus. 29cm. 60-7495 10.00
1. Maison, K. E. I. Title.

DAUMIER, Honore 016.760'0924
Victorin, 1808-1879
Honore Daumier; catalogue raisonne of the paintings, watercolours, and drawings [by] K. E. Maison. [Greenwich, Conn.] N. Y. Graphic [1968] 2v. illus., port. Contents.v. 1. The paintings.--v. 2. The watercolours and drawings. [ND553.D24M3] 67-25493 157.50 set,
1. Maison, K. E. I. Title.

Majolica.

LIVERANI, Giuseppe 738.37
Five centuries of Italian majolica. [tr. from

the Italian]. New York, McGraw-Hill, 1960 [ ] 258p. Bibl.: p.73-[74] (chiefly illus., plates (part col.)) 31cm. 59-13206 28.50 bds.,
1. Majolica. 2. Pottery, Italian. I. Title.

SCAVIZZI, Giuseppe. 738.3
Majolica, Delft and Faience. [translated from the Italian by Peter Locke] Feltham, Hamlyn, 1970. 157 p. col. illus., col. map. 20 cm. (Cameo) Translation of Maioliche dal Rinascimento ad oggi. [NK4315.S3813] 78-861500 ISBN 0-600-35919-0 £0.90
1. Majolica. 2. Delft ware. I. Title.

WALTERS Art Gallery, 738.37
Baltimore.
Catalogue of the Itliaa majolica in the Walters Art Gallery, by Joan Prentice von Erdberg and Marvin C. Ross. Baltimore, 1952. viii, 58p. 64 plates. 26cm. Bibliography: p.47-51. [NK4315.W195] 53-185
1. Majolica. 2. Pottery—Baltimore—Catalogs. I. Van Erdberg, Joan Prentice, 1908- II. Title.

Majolica—America.

GOGGIN, John Mann. 738.3'7
Spanish majolica in the New World; types of the sixteenth to eighteenth centuries [by] John M. Goggin. New Haven, Dept. of Anthropology, Yale University, 1968. xix, 240 p., 18 plates (part col.) illus. 25 cm. (Yake University publications in anthropology, no. 72) On spine: Majolica in the New World. Bibliography: p. 230-240. [GN2.Y3 no. 72] 68-24636
1. Majolica—America. I. Title. II. Title: Majolica in the New World. III. Series: Yale University. Dept. of Anthropology. Yale University publications in anthropology, no. 72 **BIP**

Majolica—Collectors and collecting.

RICKERSON, Wildey C. 738.3'7
Majolica; collect it for fun and profit [by] Wildey C. Rickerson. [2d ed.] Chester, Conn., Pequot Press [1972] 70 p. illus. 23 cm. [NK4315.R5 1972] 72-190530 ISBN 0-87106-111-2
1. Majolica—Collectors and collecting. I. Title.

Majolica, Italian.

SCOTT-TAGGART, John. 738.3'7
Italian maiolica. [London] [Hamlyn] 1972. 63 p. illus., facsims., map. 19 cm. (Country life collectors' guides) Caption title. Bibliography: p. 3. [NK4315.S43] 73-155656 ISBN 0-600-43184-3
1. Majolica, Italian. I. Title.
Distributed by Transatlantic Arts 2.95. **BIP**

Make-up, Theatrical.

KEHOE, Vincent J R 778.92
Photographic make-up for stills and movies; color and black-and-white. Philadelphia, Chilton Books, c1963. 96 p. illus., ports. 21 cm. (Modern camera guide series) [PN2068.K38] 63-23357
1. Make-up, Theatrical. I. Title. II. Series.

Makowski, Tadeusz, 1882-1932.

JAWORSKA, Wladyslawa. 759.71
Tadeusz Makowski : e. poln. Maler in Paris / Wladyslawa Jaworska ; [Übers. d. poln. Ms. von Anna Jankowska]. Dresden : Verlag der Kunst, 1975. 276 p. : ill. (some col.) ; 28 cm. Includes indexes. Bibliography: p. [274] [ND955.P63M3124] 75-522494 54.00M
1. Makowski, Tadeusz, 1882-1932.

Malbone, Edward Greene, 1777-1807.

TOLMAN, Ruel [759.13] 927.5
Pardee, 1878-
The life and works of Edward Greene Malbone, 1777-1807. With an introd. by Theodore Bolton, and a foreword by John Davis Hatch, Jr. New York, New-York Historical Society, 1958. xxiii, 322 p. illus., col. ports., facsims. 25 cm. (The John Divine Jones Fund series of histories and memoirs, 13) Bibliography: p. 280-288. [ND1337.U6M32] 58-2879
1. Malbone, Edward Greene, 1777-1807. 2. U.S. — Biog. — Portraits. I. Title. II. Series: New York Historical Society. The John Divine Jones Fund series of histories and memoirs, 13 **BIP**

Maldarelli, Oronzio, 1892-

ROSENBERG (Paul) and 730'.92'4
Company, New York.
An exhibition of sculpture (1948-1958) by Cronzio Maldarelli, March 9-April 4, 1959 New York [1959] unpaged. illus. 26cm. (Its Catalogue no. 115. 1959) [NB237.M28R6] 59-12001
1. Maldarelli, Oronzio, 1892- I. Title. II. Series.

Maler, Leopoldo, 1937—

WHITECHAPEL Art 700'.92'4
Gallery, London.
Leopoldo Maler, mortal issues, a sanctuary with flames & figures : [catalogue of an exhibition held in the] Main Gallery [of Whitechapel Art Gallery], 26 February-4 April 1976. London : Whitechapel Art Gallery, [1976] 12 p. : ill., ports. ; 30 cm. Bibliography: p. 10-11. [PN3206.W438 1976] 76-364247
1. Maler, Leopoldo, 1937- 2. Happening (Art) I. Maler, Leopoldo, 1937- II. Title.

Malone, Blondelle Octavia Edwards, 1877-1951.

DU BOSE, Louise Jones. 927.740
Enigma; the career of Blondelle Malone in art and society, 1879-1951, as told in her letters and diaries. [Columbia] University of South Carolina Press, 1963. xii, 164 p. illus., ports., map. 24 cm. Bibliography: p. 159-160. [ND237.M232D8] 63-12539
1. Malone, Blondelle Octavia Edwards, 1877-1951. I. Title.

Malory, Thomas, Sir, 15th cent.

BEARDSLEY, Aubrey 741.9'42
Vincent, 1872-1898.
Illustrations for Le morte d'Arthur. Reproduced in facsimile from the Dent ed. of 1893-94; arr. by Edmund V. Gillon, Jr. New York, Dover Publications [1972] ix, 171 p. 28 cm. (Dover pictorial archive series) [NC978.5.M34B42] 71-166432 Pap. 3.00
1. Malory, Thomas, Sir, 15th cent. Le marte d'Arthur—Illustrations. I. Gillon, Edmund Vincent, ed. II. Malory, Thomas, Sir, 15th cent. Le morte d'Arthur. III. Title. **BIP**

Malraux, Andre, 1901-1976.

FLANNER, Janet, 1892- 709.22 B
Men and monuments. Freeport, N.Y., Books for Libraries Press [1970, c1957] xxi, 297 p. illus. 23 cm. (Essay index reprint series) [N7445.F55 1970] 73-121468
1. Malraux, Andre, 1901- 2. Matisse, Henri, 1869-1954. 3. Braque, Georges, 1882-1963. 4. Picasso, Pablo, 1881- 5. World War, 1939-1945—Art and the war. I. Title.

FLANNER, Janet, 1892- 704.91
Men and monuments. New York, Harper [1957] 297 p. illus. 22 cm. [N7445.F55] 55-8021
1. Malraux, Andre, 1901-1976. 2. Matisse, Henri, 1869-1954. 3. Braque, Georges, 1882- 4. Picasso, Pablo, 1881-1973. 5. World War, 1939-1945—Art and the war. I. Title. **BIP**

Mamiya camera.

COOPER, Joseph David, 771.31
1917-
Mamiya-16 camera guide. New York, Universal Photo Bks. [dist. Amphoto, c. 1961] 128p. illus. 61-14251 1.95 pap.,
1. Mamiya camera. 2. Photography—Handbooks, manuals, etc. I. Title.

EMANUEL, Walter Daniel, 771.3'1
1908-
Mamiya Sekor guide; how to use the Mamiya Sekor 2000DTL, 1000DTL, 500DTL, 1000TL, 500TL and 528TL cameras, by W. D. Emanuel. [1st ed.] London, New York, Focal Press; distributed in the U.S.A. by Amphoto, New York [1970] 70 p. illus. 17 cm. (The Camera guide) [TR263.M3E46] 75-144054 ISBN 0-8174-0612-3 2.50 (U.S.)
1. Mamiya camera. 2. Photography—Handbooks, manuals, etc. I. Title. **BIP**

SMITH, Robb. 771.3'1
Mamiya professional systems handbook. Garden City, N.Y., American Photographic Book Pub. Co. [1974] 256 p. illus. (part col.) 27 cm. [TR263.M3S55] 72-91031 15.00
1. Mamiya camera. 2. Photography—Handbooks, manuals, etc. I. Title. **BIP**

TYDINGS, Kenneth S 771.3
New Mamiya C series twin lens reflex guide. Philadelphia, Chilton Co., Book Division, c1961. 127 p. illus. 20 cm. (Modern camera guide series, 828) [TR263.M3T9] 61-11276
1. Mamiya camera. 2. Photography — Handbooks, manuals, etc. I. Title.

Mammals.

HUXLEY, Julian Sorell, 779.32
1887-
Kingdom of the beasts. Photos. by W. Suschitzky. New York, Vanguard Press [1956] 79p. 175illus. (part col.) 31cm. [QL705] 56-12043
1. Mammals. 2. Animal pictures. I. Title.

Man, Felix H., 1893—

MAN, Felix H., 1893- 779'.2'0924
Felix H. Man : reportage portraits, 1929-76 : [catalogue of an exhibition held at the] National Portrait Gallery [1 October 1976 to 2 January 1977]. London : The Gallery, 1976. [19] p. : chiefly ports. ; 24 cm. Bibliography: p. [8] [TR681.F3M36] 77-364176 ISBN 0-904017-10-9 : £0.30
1. Man, Felix H., 1893- 2. Photography—Portraits. I. London. National Portrait Gallery.

Man o'War (Race horse)—Pictorial works.

ANDERSON, Clarence 759.13
William, 1891-
Horse of the century, Man o' War, by C. W. Anderson. New York, Macmillan [1970] [4] p., 8 col. plates (in portfolio) 42 cm. [SF355.M3A52] 74-99109
1. Man o'War (Race horse)—Pictorial works. I. Title. II. Title: Man o'War.

Man, Prehistoric—England—Derbyshire.

KITCHING, James William 571.10942
Bone, tooth & horn tools of palaeolithic man; an account of the osteodontokeratic discoveries in Pin Hole Cave. Derbyshire [Manchester] Manchester Univ. Pr. [dist. New York, Humanities, 1964, c.1963] xiv, 55p. illus., port. 22cm. Bibl. [GN446.K5] 65-601 4.50 bds.,
1. Man, Prehistoric—England—Derbyshire. 2. Implements, utensils, etc. I. Title.

Man, Prehistoric—New England.

FOWLER, William Smith. 573.3
Ten thousand years in America. Illustrated by the author from authentic artifacts. [1st ed.] New York, Vantage Press [1957] 160p. illus. 21cm. Includes bibliography. [E78.N5F6] 56-10566
1. Man, Prehistoric—New England. 2. New England—Antiq. 3. Indians of North America—New England. I. Title.

Man, Prehistoric—Siberia, Western.

CHERNETSOV, Valerii 930'.1 s
Nikolaevich, 1905-1970.
Prehistory of western Siberia / V. N. Chernetsov and W. Moszynska ; edited by Henry N. Michael. Montreal : [Published for] Arctic Institute of North America [by] McGill-Queen's University Press, 1974. xxv, 377 p. : ill. ; 26 cm. (Anthropology of the North : Translations from Russian sources ; no. 9) Includes bibliographical references and index. [GN4.A65 no. 9] [GN855.R9] 957'.3 73-79092 ISBN 0-7735-9074-9 : 25.00
1. Man, Prehistoric—Siberia, Western. 2. Siberia, Western—Antiquities. I. Moszynska, W., joint author. II. Arctic Institute of North America. III. Title. IV. Series.
Distributed by McGill-Queen's University Press, Irvington, N.Y. **BIP**

Man, Prehistoric—Tools—Addresses, essays, lectures.

LITHICS and 930'.1'028
subsistence : the analysis of stone tool use in prehistoric economies / edited by Dave D. Davis ; with contributions by T. Douglas Price ... [et al.]. Nashville : Vanderbilt University, 1978. iii, 198 p. : ill. ; 28 cm. (Vanderbilt University publications in anthropology ; no. 20) Includes bibliographies. [GN799.T6L57] 78-104501 8.50
1. Man, Prehistoric—Tools—Addresses, essays, lectures. 2. Stone implements—Addresses, essays, lectures. I. Davis, Dave D. II. Price, Theron Douglas. III. Series: Vanderbilt University, Nashville. Vanderbilt University publications in anthropology ; no. 20

Manchester, Eng. Art Gallery.

MANCHESTER, 759.941'074'02733
Eng. Art Gallery.
Concise catalogue of British paintings / Manchester City Art Gallery. Manchester : City of Manchester Cultural Services, 1976- v. : ill., ports. ; 21 cm. Errata slip inserted in v. 1. Includes indexes. Contents.Contents.—v. 1. British artists born before 1850. [ND461.M36 1976] 77-352258 ISBN 0-901673-07-2 : £2.50
1. Manchester, Eng. Art Gallery. 2. Painting, British—Catalogs. 3. Painting—England—Manchester—Catalogs. I. Title.

MANCHESTER, Eng. Art 708.2
Gallery.
Report of the Art Galleries Committee. [Manchester!] v. illus. 25 cm. annual. [N1430.A3] 50-57275
I. Title.

MANCHESTER, Eng. Art 738.2'7
Gallery.
Transfer-printed Worcester porcelain at Manchester City Art Gallery : a catalogue / by Emmeline Leary and Peter Walton. [Manchester] : City of Manchester Cultural Services, [1976] 52 p. : ill., port. ; 20 x 21 cm. Includes index. Bibliography: p. 50-51. [NK4395.M33 1976] 77-361624 ISBN 0-901673-08-0 : £1.50
1. Manchester, Eng. Art Gallery. 2. Worcester porcelain—Catalogs. 3. Blue and white transfer ware—Catalogs. I. Leary, Emmeline. II. Walton, Peter, 1944- III. Title.

Manchester, Eng. Art Gallery. Heaton Hall, Heaton Park.

CLEVELAND, Sydney 708'.27'38
Dyson.
Heaton Hall : an illustrated survey of the Lancashire home of the Wilton family, now the property of the Manchester Corporation / [by S. D. Cleveland]. Derby : English Life Publications, [1953] 30 p. : ill. ; 14 x 22 cm. [N1430.C54] 75-331059
1. Manchester, Eng. Art Gallery. Heaton Hall, Heaton Park. I. Title.

Manchester, Eng.—Description—Views.

MANCHESTER old and 942.733080222
new / [compiled by] Frank Mullineux. Wakefield : EP Publishing, 1975. [5], 74 p. : chiefly ill. ; 18 x 25 cm. With the exception of two, photos. from the collection of the City of Manchester Central Library. [DA690.M4M445] 76-351468 ISBN 0-7158-1080-4 pbk. : 8.50
1. Manchester, Eng.—Description—Views.

civilization) (Pelican book, A808.) Bibliography: p. 207-208. [N6370.S78 1967] 67-98470 15/-
1. Mannerism (Art) I. Title. BIP

SHEARMAN, John K. G. 709.03'1
Mannerism. [Baltimore] Penguin Books [1973, c.1967] 215 p. illus. 20 cm. (Pelican books, A808)bBibliography: p. 207-208. (Style and civilization) [N6370.S48] 67-98470 ISBN 0-14-020808-9 3.85 (pbk.)
1. Mannerism (Art) 2. Art—History. I. Title. II. Series.

SMYTH, Craig Hugh. 759.5
Mannerism and maniers. Locust Valley, N.Y., J.J. Augustin [1963] xi, 88 p. plates. 24 cm. "Comprises a paper read in the session on 'Recent concepts of mannerism' at the Twentieth International Congress of Art Historians in September, 1961, and footnotes to it." Bibliographical references included in "Notes" (p. 81-88) [ND615.S59] 64-4828
1. Mannerism (Art) 2. Painting, Italian. I. Title.

WURTENBERGER, Franzsepp, 1909- 709.03
Mannerism, the European style of the sixteenth century. Translated from the German by Michael Heron. [1st ed.] New York, Holt, Rinehart and Winston [1963] 246 p. illus., plates (part col.) ports. (part col.) 34 cm. Bibliography: p. 241-246. [N6370.W813] 63-18066
1. Mannerism (Art) 2. Art, European. I. Title.

Mannerism (Art)—Addresses, essays, lectures.

THE Meaning of mannerism. 700'.9'031 Edited by Franklin W. Robinson and Stephen G. Nichols, Jr. Hanover, N.H., University Press of New England, 1972. 134 p. illus. 24 cm. "Six papers ... read at the New England Renaissance conference, sponsored by the New England Renaissance Society and held at Dartmouth College, October 3 and 4, 1970." Includes bibliographical references. [NX450.6.M3M4] 71-189512 7.50
1. Mannerism (Art)—Addresses, essays, lectures. I. Robinson, Franklin Westcott, ed. II. Nichols, Stephen G., ed. III. New England Renaissance Society. IV. Dartmouth College. BIP

Mannerism (Art)—Catalogs.

BUDAPEST. Szepmuveszeti Muzeum. 759.94
The masters of mannerism, by Marianne Haraszti-Takacs. [Translated by Eva Racz. Rev. by Bertha Gaster] New York, Taplinger Pub. Co. [1969, c1968] 29 p., 48 col. plates. 24 cm. Reproductions of paintings in the Budapest Museum of Fine Arts. Text on versos of plates. Bibliography: p. 27. [ND172.M3B813 1969] 69-15912 7.95
1. Mannerism (Art)—Catalogs. 2. Paintings—Budapest—Catalogs. I. Haraszti, Marianna (Takacs) II. Title.

Mannerism (Art)—Exhibitions.

COHEN (B.) and Sons Trafalgar Galleries. 759.04
In the light of Caravaggio : [catalogue of an exhibition]. London : Trafalgar Galleries, 1976. 61 p. : ill. (some col.) ; 31 cm. Errata slip: [1] leaf inserted. Bibliography: p. 53-61. [ND172.M3C64 1976] 77-359600 £4.00
1. Caravaggio, Michelangelo Merisi da, 1573-1610—Influence. 2. Mannerism (Art)—Exhibitions. 3. Painting, Renaissance—Exhibitions. I. Title.

FORT Worth, Tex. Art Center. v. 12
The School of Fontainebleau; an exhibition of paintings, drawings, engravings, etchings, and sculpture, 1530-1619, Forth Worth Art Center, 15 September-24 October [and] University Art Museum, the University of Texas, 1 November-5 December, 1965. [Austin, Printed by the Print. Division of the University of Texas] 1965. 80 p. illus. (part col.) 22 cm. Bibliography: p. 73-78. [N6375.M3F6] 68-6326
1. Mannerism (Art)—Exhibitions. 2. Art—Fontainebleau. I. Texas. University. Art Museum. II. Title.

Mannerism (Art)—Italy.

JAFFE, Andrew Michael. 759.9493 B
Rubens and Italy / Michael Jaffe. Ithaca, N.Y. : Cornell University Press, 1977. 128 p., [103] leaves of plates : ill. (some col.) ; 29 cm. Includes index. Bibliography: p. 121-123. [ND673.R9J27] 76-20065 ISBN 0-8014-1064-9 : 55.00
1. Rubens, Peter Paul, Sir, 1577-1640. 2. Mannerism (Art)—Italy. 3. Art, Italian. I. Rubens, Peter Paul, Sir, 1577-1640. II. Title. BIP

Mannerism (Art)—Netherlands.

DUTCH mannerism; 759.9492 apogee and epilogue. [Exhibition] April 15-June 7, 1970, Vassar College Art Gallery, Poughkeepsie, New York. [Poughkeepsie, N.Y., 1970] 73 p. 61 plates. 23 cm. Bibliography: p. 13-14. [N6945.D8] 79-124379
1. Mannerism (Art)—Netherlands. 2. Art, Modern—Exhibitions. I. Vassar College. Art Gallery.

Manning, Reg, 1905—

MANNING, Reg, 1905- 748.2'913
Reg Manning's desert in crystal; photographs of the artist's copper wheel engravings on crystal glass and the brief story of how he became involved in the rare and ancient art. [1st ed.] Phoenix, Ariz., Reganson [1973] 63 p. illus. 23 cm. [NK5198.M36A54 1973] 73-91157 3.00 (pbk.)
1. Manning, Reg, 1905- 2. Engraved glass—United States. I. Title. II. Title: Desert in crystal.
Publisher's address: 5724 E. Cambridge Ave., Scottsdale, Az. 85251.

Manors—Durham, Eng. (County)

WHITTAKER, Neville. 942.8'6
The old halls and manor houses of Durham / by Neville Whittaker. Newcastle upon Tyne : Graham, 1975. 96 p. : ill., facsim., plan ; 22 cm. Includes index. [NA7621.D87W45] 75-333074 ISBN 0-85983-047-0 : £1.20
1. Manors—Durham, Eng. (County) 2. Castles—England—Durham (County) I. Title.

Manors—England—History.

COOK, Olive. 942
The English country house : an art and a way of life / Olive Cook ; photos. by A. F. Kersting. New York : Putnam, [1974] 240 p. : ill. (some col.) ; 27 cm. Includes index. [NA7620.C58 1974b] 74-80029 ISBN 0-399-11404-1 : 14.95
1. Manors—England—History. 2. Country homes—England—History. 3. England—Social life and customs—History. I. Title.

Manors—Great Britain.

THE destruction of the country house, 1875-1975 914.2 / Roy Strong...et al.. London : Thames & Hudson, [1974] 192 p. : ill. ; 26 cm. [NA7620.D37] 74-192706 ISBN 0-500-24094-9 : 15.00
1. Manors—Great Britain. 2. Country homes—Great Britain. 3. Great Britain—Historic houses, etc.—Conservation and restoration. I. Strong, Roy C.
Distributed by Transatlantic Arts.

Mansbendel, Peter, 1883-1940—Exhibitions.

MANSBENDEL, Peter, 1883-1940. 730'.92'4
Peter Mansbendel : a Swiss woodcarver in Texas : an exhibit / prepared by the University of Texas at San Antonio, Institute of Texan Cultures, 1977-1978. 1st ed. San Antonio : The Institute, c1977. [47] p. : ill. ; 25 cm. [NK9798.M35A4 1977] 77-154122
1. Mansbendel, Peter, 1883-1940—Exhibitions. 2. Wood-carving—Texas—Exhibitions. I. Institute of Texan Cultures.

Manso, Blanche—Art collections.

SANTA Barbara, Calif. Museum of Art. 759.94
Tantra from the Collection of Blanche Manso. [Santa Barbara, 1970] 40 p. facsims. (part col.), plates (part col.) 24 cm. Catalog of the exhibition held Feb. 8-Mar. 23, 1970. [N8193.Z7T38] 75-116989
1. Manso, Blanche—Art collections. 2. Art, Tantric-Buddhist—Exhibitions. I. Title.

Mansoor, M. A., 1881- —Art collections.

BECKER-COLONNA, Andieina Leanza. 732'.8'074019461
Ancient Egypt : an exhibition of el-Amarna sculptures and reliefs of the M. A. Mansoor Collection / Andreina Leanza Becker-Colonna ; sponsored by the Department of Classical Archaeology of San Francisco State University and by the Marie Stauffer Sigall Foundation. [San Francisco] : The Department?, c1975. 54 p. : ill. ; 28 cm. Cover title. Bibliography: p. 53-54. [NB75.B35] 75-323831
1. Mansoor, M. A., 1881- —Art collections. 2. Sculpture, Egyptian—Exhibitions. 3. Sculpture—Tell el-Amarna—Exhibitions. 4. Egypt—Antiquities. I. San Francisco State University. Dept. of Classical Archaeology. II. Marie Stauffer Sigall Foundation. III. Title.

Mantegna, Andrea, 1431-1506.

MANTEGNA, Andrea, 1431-1506. 759.5
All the paintings of Mantegna, by Renata Cipriani. Translated from the Italian by Paul Colacicchi. New York, Hawthorn Books [1964, c1963] 2 v. [119 p.) col. illus., 184 plates. 18 cm. (The Complete library of world art, v. 20-21) [ND623.M3C5] 63-20693
I. Cipriani, Renata. II. Title. III. Series.

MANTEGNA, Andrea, 1431-1506. 759.5
The complete paintings of Mantegna. Introd. by Andrew Martindale. Notes and catalogue by Niny Garavaglia. New York, H. N. Abrams [1970 or 1, c1967] 128 p. illus., col. plates. 32 cm. (Classics of the world's great art) Originally published in Italy under title: L'opera completa del Mantegna. [ND623.M3B4213 1970] 72-92259 ISBN 0-8109-5510-5
I. Garavaglia, Niny. II. Title.

MANTEGNA, Andrea, 1431-1506. 759.5
Mantegna [by] Franca Zava Boccazzi. [Translated from the Italian by Pearl Sanders. 1st American ed.] New York, Grosset & Dunlap [1971] 39 p., 80 col. plates. 18 cm. (The New Grossett art library, 35) [ND623.M3Z313 1971] 70-110102
I. Zava Boccazzi, Franca. BIP

MANTEGNA, Andrea, 1431-1506. 759.5
Paintings. Text by Giuseppe Fiocco. New York, H. N. Abrams [1963?] 42 p. illus (1 mounted col.) 30 col. plates. 38 cm. Bibliography: p. 42. [ND623.M3F46] 62-19664
I. Fiocco, Giuseppe, 1884-

MEISS, Millard. 745.67
Andrea Mantegna as illuminator; an episode in Renaissance art, humanism, and diplomacy. New York, Columbia University Press, 1957. xi, 114p. illus. (part col.) ports. 22cm. Bibliography: p. 82-83. [ND3162.M3M4] 57-2308
1. Mantegua, Andrea, 1431-1506. 2. Illumination of books and manuscripts—Italy—Hist. 3. Initials. I. Title.

Manton, John, 1752-1834.

NEAL, William Keith. 623.4'4
The Mantons, gunmakers [by] W. Keith Neal and D. H. L. Back. New York, Walker [1967, c1966] xv, 300 p. illus. (part col.) facsims., geneal. table., ports. (part col.) 26 cm. Bibliography: p. 294-295. [TS535.M34N4 1967a] 67-12527
1. Manton, John, 1752-1834. 2. Manton, Joseph, 1766-1835. 3. Firearms, British. 4. Firearms industry and trade—Great Britain. I. Back, David Henry Lempriere, joint author. II. Title.

Mantua. Palazzo del Te.

VERHEYEN, Egon. 945'.28
The Palazzo del Te in Mantua : images of love and politics / Egon Verheyen ; with plans by Diane Finiello Zervas. Baltimore : Johns Hopkins University Press, c1977. xvi, 156 p. : ill. ; 29 cm. Includes index. Bibliography: p. 145-152. [NA7756.M3V47] 76-47365 ISBN 0-8018-1809-5 : 25.00
1. Giulio Romano, Giulio Pippi, known as, 1499-1546. 2. Federigo II Gonzaga. 3. Mantua. Palazzo del Te. 4. Decoration and ornament, Architectural—Italy—Mantua. I. Title. BIP

Mantua. Sant' Andrea (Basilica)

JOHNSON, Eugene J., 1937- 914.5'28
S. Andrea in Mantua : the building history / Eugene J. Johnson. University Park : Pennsylvania State University Press, [1975] p. cm. Bibliography: p. [NA5621.M34J63] 74-30085 ISBN 0-271-01186-6 : 30.00
1. Mantua. Sant' Andrea (Basilica) I. Title. BIP

Manual painting and decoration, Egyptian.

UNITED Nations Education, Scientific and Cultural Organization. 751.730932
Egyptian wall paintings from tombs and temples. Introd. by Christiane Desroches-Nonlecourt. [New York] New Amer. Lib. [c.1954, 1962] 24, [6]p. illus., 28 col. plates. 17cm. (Mentor-Unesco art bk., MQ457) Bibl. 62-53089 .95 pap.,
1. Manual painting and decoration, Egyptian. I. Desroches-Noblecourt, Christiane, 1913- II. Title.

Manual training.

ANDREWS, Robert Charles, 1937- 607'.12'73
Teaching industrial education : principles and practices / by Robert C. Andrews. Peoria, Ill. : C. A. Bennett Co., c1976. 258 p. ; 24 cm. "A revision of Teaching and industrial arts, by Emanuel E. Ericson." Includes bibliographies and index. [TT168.E72 1976] 75-15361 ISBN 0-87002-079-X : 6.60
1. Manual training. 2. Industrial arts—Study and teaching. I. Ericson, Emanuel E., 1888-1959. The teaching the industrial arts. II. Title. BIP

BAUER, Carlton E., ed. 373.2467
Comprehensive general shop. Authors: John Adams [and others] Milwaukee, Bruce Pub. Co. [1959-65] 3 v. illus. 26 cm. General editors: v. 1, Carlton E. Bauer and Robert L. Thompson; v. 2-3, John Miller. [TT165.C6] 59-4616
1. Manual training. I. Thompson, Robert Long, 1908- ed. II. Miller, John Guthrie, 1912- ed. III. Title.

ERICSON, Emanuel E 1888- 371.426
Teaching the industrial arts. [2d ed.] Peoria, Ill., C. A. Bennett Co. [1956] 384p. illus. 22cm. [TT168.E72 1956] 56-13230
1. Manual training. 2. Industrial arts—Study and teaching. I. Title.

GRONEMAN, Chris Harold, 1906- 371.426
General shop by Chris H. Groneman [and] John L. Feirer. New York, McGraw-Hill [c1954] 307p. illus. 25cm. (McGraw-Hill publications in industrial arts) [TT165.G74] 53-8006
1. Manual training. I. Feirer, John Louis, joint author. II. Title.

GRONEMAN, Chris Harold, 1906- 371.426
General shop [by] Chris H. Groneman [and] John L. Feirer. Vincent A. Roy, consultant on ceramics. 2d ed. New York, McGraw-Hill [1956] 342p. illus. 25cm. (McGraw-Hill publications in industrial arts) [TT165.G74 1956] 56-11784
1. Manual training. I. Feirer, John Louis, joint author. II. Title.

GRONEMAN, Chris Harold, 1906- 371.426
General shop [by] Chris H. Groneman and John L. Feirer. Vincent A. Roy, consultant in ceramics. 3d ed. New York, McGraw-Hill [1963] 470 p. illus. 25 cm. (McGraw-Hill publications in industrial arts) [TT165.G74 1963] 62-19245
1. Manual training. I. Feirer, John Louis, joint author. II. Title.

GRONEMAN, Chris Harold, 1906- 373.2'46
General shop [by] Chris H. Groneman [and] John L. Feirer. 4th ed. New York, McGraw-Hill [1969] x, 534 p. illus. (part col.) 24 cm. (McGraw-Hill publications in industrial education) Beginning with 5th ed. (1974) published under title: General industrial education. [TT165.G74 1969] 68-21844
1. Manual training. I. Feirer, John Louis, joint author. II. Title.

KLEHM, Walter Allen, 1903- 371.42688
Crafts for the elementary school: tools and techniques, by Walter A. Klehm and Glenn S. Duncan. Charleston, Eastern Illinois State College, c1953. 1v. (various pagings) illus. 28cm. Bibliography: 5 leaves at end. [TT168.K55] 53-62560
1. Manual training. I. Duncan, Glenn Spenser, 1900- joint author. II. Title.

LINDBECK, John Robert. 600
General industry [by] John R. Lindbeck and Irvin T. Lathrop. John L. Feirer, editor. Peoria, Ill., C. A. Bennett Co. [1968, c1969] 332 p. illus. (part col.) 24 cm. [TT165.L5] 68-10287
1. Manual training. 2. Industrial arts. I. Lathrop, Irvin T., joint author. II. Title. BIP

LINDBECK, John Robert. 600
General industry / John R. Lindbeck and Irvin T. Lathrop ; [John L. Feirer, ed.]. 2d ed. Peoria, Ill. : C. A. Bennett Co., c1977. 605 p. : ill. ; 27 cm. Includes index. [TT165.L5 1977] 76-12711 ISBN 0-87002-185-0 : 13.28
1. Manual training. 2. Industrial arts. I. Lathrop, Irvin T., joint author. II. Title.

MILLER, Wilbur R. 602'.3
Exploring careers in industry. 2d ed. / Wilbur R. Miller, Marion E. Maddox, Lavon B. Smith. Bloomington, Ill. : McKnight Pub. Co., [1975] xiv, 412 p. : ill. ; 24 cm. (A McKnight career publication) First ed. by L. B. Smith and M. E. Maddox published in 1966 under title: Elements of American industry. Includes index. [TT165.S56 1975] 74-14422 ISBN 0-87345-108-2 : 10.64
1. Manual training. 2. Industry. I. Maddox, Marion Errol, 1910- joint author. II. Smith, Lavon Benson, joint author. III. Title.

NEWKIRK, Louis Vest, 1901- 371.426
General shop for everyone; a basal text for industrial arts. Boston, Heath [1952] 261 p. illus. 24 cm. [TT165.N4] 52-7514
1. Manual training. 2. Electric engineering. I. Title.

NEWKIRK, Louis Vest, 1901- 371.426
General shop for everyone; a basal text for industrial arts. Boston, Heath [1959] 280p. illus. 24cm. [TT165.N4 1959] 59-3957
1. Manual training. 2. Electric engineering. I. Title.

NEWKIRK, Louis Vest, 1901- 600
General shop for everyone; a basal text for industrial arts [by] Louis V. Newkirk. Boston, Heath [1966, c1967] 280 p. illus. 24 cm. Includes bibliographies. [TT165.N4 1967] 67-2958
1. Manual training. I. Title.

O'BRIEN, Michael, 1918- 371.426
Shopwork teaching tricks and other aids for shop teachers, by Michael O'Brien, Elwood M. Juergenson [and] Ernest A. Tarone. 2d ed. [Danville, Ill., Interstate Printers and Publishers, 1956] 256p. illus. 22cm. [TT168.O25 1956] 56-58068
1. Manual training. I. Title.

O'BRIEN, Michael, 1918- 373.2'467
Shopwork teaching tricks and other aids for shop teachers, by Michael O'Brien, Elwood M. Juergenson [and] Ernest A. Tarone. [3d ed.] Danville, Ill., Interstate Printers & Publishers [1971] xiv, 342 p. illus. 22 cm. [TT168.O25 1971] 72-121631
1. Manual training. I. Juergenson, Elwood M., joint author. II. Tarone, Ernest A., joint author. III. Title.

SMITH, Lavon Benson. 602.8
Elements of American industry [by] Lavon Benson Smith [and] Marion E. Maddox. Bloomington, Ill., McKnight & McKnight Pub. Co. [1966] 280 p. illus. (part col.) 27 cm. Second ed. by W. R. Miller, M. E. Maddox, and L. B. Smith published in 1975 under title: Exploring careers in industry. [TT165.S56] 66-18388
1. Manual training. I. Maddox, Marion Errol, 1910- joint author. II. Title.

WILLOUGHBY, George Alonzo, 1894- 371.426
General shop handbook; instruction units for beginners, by George A. Willoughby and Duane G. Chamberlain. [New rev. ed.] Peoria, Ill., C. A. Bennett Co. [1958] 100 p. illus. 27 cm. [TT168.W5 1958] 58-8411
1. Manual training. I. Chamberlain, Duane Glen, 1902- joint author. II. Title. III. Title: Shop handbook.

Manual training—Methods and manuals.

BAYSINGER, Gerald Benjamin, 1904- 371.426
The student planning book industrial arts and vocational classes [by] Gerald B. Baysinger [and] G. Harold Silvius. 4th ed. Princeton, N. J., Van Nostrand [1960] 62p. illus. 28cm. First ed. published in 1941 under title: Student planning book for Industrial arts. [TT169.B37 1960] 60-13755
1. Manual training—Methods and manuals. I. Silvius, George Harold, 1906- joint author. II. Title.

BRYCE, Mayo. 372.5
Teacher's craft manual, by Mayo Bryce and Harry B. Green. San Francisco, Fearon Publishers [1956] 79 p. illus. 28 cm. [TT168.B7] 56-7133
1. Manual training—Methods and manuals. I. Green, Harry B., joint author. II. Title.

KIDD, Donald M 371.426
Methods of teaching shop and related subjects [by]Donald M.Kidd [and] Gerald B. Leigh body Albany, Delmar Publishers [1955] 201p. illus. 27cm. [TT168.K46] 55-57057
1. Manual training—Methods and manuals. I. Leighbody, Gerald B., joint author. II. Title.

LEIGHBODY, Gerald B. 607
Methods of teaching shop and technical subjects [by] Gerald B. Leighbody, Donald M. Kidd. [New York, Delmar Pubs., 1966] vi, 201p. illus. 27cm. Bibl. [TT168.L4] 66-26821 4.76
*1. Manual training—Methods and manuals. 2. Industrial arts—Study and teaching. I. Kidd, Donald M., joint author. II. Title.*BIP

PAUTLER, Albert J. 607'.1
Teaching shop and laboratory subjects [by] Albert J. Pautler. Columbus, Ohio, Merrill [1971] x, 185 p. 24 cm. (Merrill series in career programs) Includes bibliographical references. [TT168.P38] 75-150076 ISBN 0-675-09213-2
1. Manual training—Methods and manuals. I. Title.

SEXTON, Irwin, 1921- 371.426
Industrial techniques in the school shop. Milwaukee, Bruce Pub. Co. [1955] 74p. illus. 22cm. [TT168.S48] 55-1747
1. Manual training—Methods and manuals. I. Title.

Manufacturers—Connecticut—Biography.

BARNARD, Henry, 1811-1900, ed. 683'.43'0924 B
Armsmear : the home, the arm, and the armory of Samuel Colt : a memorial. [s.l. : s.n.], c1976. xviii, 399 p., [13] leaves of plates : ill. ; 27 cm. Reprint of the 1866 ed. privately printed by Alvord, New York. [TS533.3.C8C642 1976] 76-20422
1. Colt, Samuel, 1814-1862. 2. Manufacturers—Connecticut—Biography. I. Title.

Manufactures—Catalogs.

SEARS, Roebuck and Company. 745.1'0973
The best of Sears collectibles, 1905-1910 / edited by Leslie Parr, Andrea Hicks, Marie Stareck. New York : Arno Press, 1976. p. cm. Selected pages from the Sears, Roebuck catalogues of 1905-1910. [TS199.S435 1976] 75-43475 ISBN 0-405-06688-0 : 6.95
1. Manufactures—Catalogs. I. Parr, Leslie. II. Hicks, Andrea. III. Stareck, Marie. IV. Title. BIP

Manuscript—England—Oxford—Catalogs.

OXFORD. University. 016.091
Catalogue of the manuscripts in the Oxford colleges, by H. O. Coxe. Introd. by K. W. Humphreys. Wakefield, E. P. Publishing, 1972- v. 24 cm. Reprint of the 1852 ed. published under title: Catalogus codicum mss. qui in collegiis aulisque oxoniensibus hodie adservantur. [Z6621.O98 1972] 73-160785 40.00
1. Oxford. University. 2. Manuscript—England—Oxford—Catalogs. I. Coxe, Henry Octavius, 1811-1881. II. Title.
Distributed by Rowman & Littlefield, Inc.

Manuscripts.

MADAN, Falconer, 1851-1935. 091
Books in manuscript; a short introduction to their study and use. 2d ed., rev. New York, Haskell House Publishers, 1968. xv, 208 p. illus. 23 cm. "Facsimile of the 1927 revised edition." Bibliography: p. 195-203. [Z105.M17 1927a] 68-25315
1. Manuscripts. I. Title. BIP

Manuscripts, American—Catalogs.

UNITED States. Naval Academy, Annapolis. Museum. 016.091
Catalogue of manuscripts. Annapolis, 1957. unpaged. illus. 22 cm. [Z6621.U596] 58-60619
1. Manuscripts, American—Catalogs. 2. Manuscripts--Maryland—Annapolis.

Manuscripts, Anglo-Saxon—Catalogs.

CAMBRIDGE. University. Corpus Christi College. Library. 016.324'3
Anglo-Saxon and other manuscripts: catalogue of an exhibition in the library of Corpus Christi College, Cambridge. Cambridge, Corpus Christi College (Library) 1966. 16 p. 21 1/2 cm. 1/6 (B 66-10714) Bibliography: p. 16. [Z6621.C174C36] 66-76401
1. Manuscripts, Anglo-Saxon—Catalogs. I. Title.

Manuscripts, Arabic—Catalogs.

ARBERRY, Arthur John, 1905- 017'.6
The Chester Beatty Library. A handlist of the Arabic manuscripts, by Arthur J. Arberry. Dublin, E. Walker (Ireland), 1955- v. plates. 26 cm. Contents.Contents.—v. 1. MSS. 3001 to 3250.—v. 8. Indexes, by U. Lyons. [Z6623.B37A7] 71-12749
1. Manuscripts, Arabic—Catalogs. I. Lyons, Ursula. II. Chester Beatty Library. III. Title: A handlist of the Arabic manuscripts.

YALE University. Library. 595.78
Arabic manuscripts in the Yale University Library, compiled by Leon Nemoy. New Haven, 1956. 273 p. facsims. 24 cm. (Transactions of the Connecticut Academy of Arts and Sciences, v. 40, p. 1-273) [Q11.C9 vol. 40] A 57
1. Manuscripts, Arabic — Catalogs. I. Nemoy, Leon, 1901- comp. II. Title. III. Series: Connecticut Academy of Arts and Sciences, New Haven. Transactions, v. 40, p. 1-273 BIP

Manuscripts, Arabic—New Jersey—Princeton—Catalogs.

PRINCETON University. Library. 016.091
Catalogue of Arabic manuscripts (Yahuda section) in the Garrett Collection, Princeton University Library / by Rudolf Mach ; index by Robert D. McChesney. Princeton, N.J. : Princeton University Press, c1975. p. cm. (Princeton studies on the Near East) Includes index. [Z6621.P9453A76] 75-2999 ISBN 0-691-03908-9 : 100.00
1. Princeton University. Library. 2. Manuscripts, Arabic—New Jersey—Princeton—Catalogs. I. Mach, Rudolf, 1922- II. Title. III. Series. BIP

Manuscripts. Austria— Vienna—Catalogs.

KRAFT, Walter C 016.324'3
Codices Vindobonenses Hispanici; a catalog of the Spanish. Portuguese, and Catalan manuscripts in the Austrian National Library in Vienna. Corvallis, Oregon State College, 1957. 64p. facsims. 23cm. (Oregon. State College, Corvallis. Bibliographic series, no. 4) Bibliography: p. 57-58. [Z6621.V62V5] 57-63459
1. Manuscripts. Austria—Vienna—Catalogs. 2. Manuscripts, Spanish—Catalogs. 3. Manuscripts, Portguese—Catalogs. 4. Manuscripts, Catalan—Catalogs. I. Vienna. Nationalbibliothek. II. Title. III. Series. BIP

Manuscripts—Bibliography—Catalogs.

BIBLIOTHECA Corviniana: 745.6'7
the library of King Matthias Corvinus of Hungary. [Compiled by Csaba Csapodi, Klara Csapodi-Gardonyi, and Tibor Szanto. Translated by Zsuzsanna Horn; translation rev. by Alick West] New York, Praeger [1969] 398 p. 144 col. plates (incl. facsims., port.) 33 cm. Companion vol. to I. Berkovits' Illuminated manuscripts from the library of Matthias Corvinus, published in 1964. Includes bibliographical references. [Z725.M44B513 1969b] 69-11963 55.00
1. Matthias I, King of Hungary, 1440?-1490—Library. 2. Manuscripts—Bibliography—Catalogs. 3. Illumination of books and manuscripts—Specimens, reproductions, etc. I. Csapodi, Csaba. II. Csapodine Gardonyi, Klara. III. Szanto, Tibor.

Manuscripts—California—Berkeley—Catalogs.

CALIFORNIA. University. Bancroft Library. 091'.0973
A guide to the manuscript collections, edited by Dale L. Morgan and George P. Hammond. Berkeley, Published for the Bancroft Library by the University of California Press, 1963- v. 27 cm. (Bancroft Library publications. Bibliographical series) Vol. 2- edited by G. P. Hammond. Contents.Contents.—v. 1. Pacific and Western manuscripts (except California)—v. 2. Manuscripts relating chiefly to Mexico and Central America. [Z6621.C159] 63-16986 ISBN 0-520-01991-1 (v. 2) 20.00 (v. 2)
1. California. University. Bancroft Library. 2. Manuscripts—California—Berkeley—Catalogs. 3. America—History—Sources—Bibliography—Catalogs. I. Morgan, Dale Lowell, 1914- ed. II. Hammond, George Peter, 1896- ed. III. Title. IV. Series: California. University. Bancroft Library. Bancroft Library publications. Bibliographical series

Manuscripts. California—Catalogs.

CALIFORNIA. University. 016.091
Bancroft Library.
Guides to the manuscript collections. 1- [Berkeley, 1953- v. 28cm. [Z6621.C16B3] 53-3520
1. Manuscripts. California—Catalogs. 2. California—Hist.— Sources—Bibl. I. Title.

Manuscripts—California—Stanford—Catalogs.

STANFORD University. 026.091
Libraries. Division of Special Collections. Manuscripts Dept.
Cataloged manuscripts. [Stanford, Calif.] 1970. 13 l. 28 cm. [Z6621.S8615] 72-197290
1. Manuscripts—California—Stanford—Catalogs. I. Title.

Manuscripts—Catalogs.

ALEXANDER, Jonathan 016.091'0945
James Graham.
The Italian manuscripts in the library of Major J. R. Abbey, by J. J. G. Alexander and A. C. De la Mare. New York, Praeger [1969] xliv, 187 p. facsims., 86 plates (incl. facsims.; 6 col.) 32 cm. A catalogue of 63 MSS. dating from the early 12th to the late 16th century. Includes bibliographies. [Z6623.A39 1969b] 69-15589 40.00
1. Abbey, John Roland, 1896- —Library. 2. Manuscripts—Catalogs. I. De la Mare, Albinia Catherine, joint author. II. Title.

AMERICAN Philosophical 018'.2
Society, Philadelphia.
Guide to the archives and manuscript collections of the American Philosophical Society, compiled by Whitfield J. Bell, Jr. and Murphy D. Smith. Philadelphia, 1966. vii, 182 p. 26 cm. (Memoirs of the American Philosophical Society, v. 66) [Z6621.A513] 66-30208
1. Manuscripts—Catalogs. I. Bell, Whitfield Jenks, comp. II. Smith, Murphy D., comp. III. Title. IV. Series: American Philosophical Society, Philadelphia. Memoirs, v. 66 BIP

CAMBRIDGE. University. 016.324'3
Library.
Summary guide to accessions of Western manuscripts (other than medieval) since 1867, by A. E. B. Owen. Cambridge, University Library, 1966. 48 p. 22 cm. 7/6 [Z6621.C173] 66-70542
1. Manuscripts—Catalogs. I. Owen, Arthur Ernest Bion. II. Title.

CLARK, Kenneth Willis, 016.091
1898-
Checklist of manuscripts in St. Catherine's monastery, Mount Sinai, microfilmed for the Library of Congress, 1950. Washington, Library of Congress, Library of Congress Photoduplication Service, 1952. ix, 53 p. 27 cm. [Z6621.S45G72] 52-60038
1. Manuscripts—Catalogs. 2. Manuscripts. Sinaitic Peninsula—Catalogs. 3. Manuscripts, Greek—Catalogs. 4. Manuscripts, Oricntal.—Catalogs. I. Sinai. Saint Catharine (Basillan monastery). II. U. S. Library of Congress. III. Title.

[MASSACHUSETTS Historical 016.973
Society, Boston. Library]
Catalog of manuscripts of the Massachusetts Historical Society. Boston, G. K. Hall, 1969. 7 v. 37 cm. [Z6621.M3985] 73-16664
1. Manuscripts—Catalogs. 2. Manuscripts—Massachusetts—Boston—Catalogs. 3. U.S.—History—Sources—Bibliography. I. Title.

NORTH Carolina. 016.9175'03
University. Library. Southern Historical Collection.
The Southern Historical Collection; a guide to manuscripts, by Susan Sokol Blosser and Clyde Norman Wilson, Jr. Chapel Hill [1970] [251], 48, [17] p. 28 cm. [Z6621.N8S65] 70-630963
1. Manuscripts—Catalogs. 2. Southern States—History—Sources—Bibliography. I. Blosser, Susan Sokol. II. Wilson, Clyde Norman. III. Title.

PIERPONT Morgan Library, 016.9298
New York.
Autograph letters & manuscripts; major acquisitions of the Pierpont Morgan Library, 1924-1974. New York [1974] xv, 103 p. facsims., music. 30 cm. Erratum slip inserted. [Z6621.P6512] [Z602] 73-92927 ISBN 0-87598-043-0 8.00 (pbk.)
1. Pierpont Morgan Library, New York. 2. Manuscripts—Catalogs. 3. Autographs—Catalogs. I. Title.

Manuscripts — Collection and restoration.

BORDIN, Ruth Birgitta 026.091
Anderson, 1917-
The modern manuscript library, by Ruth B. Bordin and Robert M. Warner. New York, Scarecrow Press, 1966. 151 p. forms. 22 cm. Includes bibliographies. [Z110.C7B6] 66-13734
1. Manuscripts — Collection and restoration. I. Warner, Robert Mark, 1927- joint author. II. Title.

Manuscripts — Conservation and restoration.

BARROW, William J. 091
The Barrow method of restoring deteriorated documents. Richmond, Va., Author, State Lib. Bldg., [1965] 19p. 23cm. Bibl. [Z110.C7B27] 65-29519 price unreported pap.,
1. Manuscripts—Conservation and restoration. I. Title.

BARROW, William J. 025.3'4'102854
Manuscripts and documents: their deterioration and restoration. [2d ed.] Charlottesville, University Press of Virginia [1972] xxvii, 84 p. illus. 25 cm. Bibliography: p. [75]-84. [Z110.C7B3 1972] 72-89855 ISBN 0-8139-0408-0 7.95
1. Manuscripts—Conservation and restoration. I. Title.

KANE, Lucile M 025.171
A guide to the care and administration of manuscripts [by] Lucile M. Kane. [2d ed. Nashville] American Association for State and Local History [1966] 74 p. illus. 23 cm. Bibliography: p. [65]-74. [Z110.C7K3] 66-4914
1. Manuscripts — Conservation and restoration. I. American Association for State and Local History. II. Title. BIP

KATHPALIA, Yash Pal. 025.8'4
Conservation and restoration of archive materials. Paris, Unesco, 1973. 231 p. 21 cm. (Documentation, libraries and archives: studies and research, 3) Bibliography: p. 222-231. [Z110.C7K35] 74-181345 ISBN 9-231-01073-5
1. Manuscripts—Conservation and restoration. 2. Archives. I. Title. II. Series. Distributed by Unipub, 6.60 (pbk.).

Manuscripts, Coptic (Papyri)

WINLOCK, Herbert Eustis, 913.32
1884-1950.
The monastery of Epiphanius at Thebes. New York, 1926. [New York] Arno Press, 1973. 2 v. illus. 32 cm. Reprint of the ed. which was issued as v. 3-4 of the Publications of the Metropolitan Museum of Art Egyptian Expedition. At head of title: The Metropolitan Museum of Art Egyptian Expedition. Contents.Contents.—pt. 1. Winlock, H. E. The archaeological material. Crum, W. E. The literary material.—pt. 2. Crum, W. E. Coptic ostraca and papyri; edited with translations and commentaries. Evelyn-White, H. G. Greek ostraca and papyri; edited with translations and commentaries. [DT73.T3W48 1973] 72-168413 ISBN 0-405-02249-2 40.00
1. Epiphanius, Monastery of. 2. Manuscripts, Coptic (Papyri) 3. Manuscripts, Greek (Papri) 4. Ostraka. I. Crum, Walter Ewing, 1865-1944. II. Evelyn-White, Hugh Gerard, d. 1924, ed. III. Title. IV. Series: New York (City). Metropolitan Museum of Art. Egyptian Expedition. Publications, v. 3-4. BIP

Manuscripts—England—Catalogs.

LAMBETH Palace. Library. 016.091
A catalogue of manuscripts in Lambeth Palace Library, MSS. 1907-2340 / E. G. W. Bill. London : Oxford, 1976. xi, 379 p. ; 23 cm. Includes index. [Z6621.L8194] [Z792.L25] 77-358094 ISBN 0-19-920079-3 : 55.00
1. Lambeth Palace. Library. 2. Manuscripts—England—Catalogs. 3. Great Britain—Church history—19th century—Sources—Bibliography—Catalogs. 4. Great Britain—Church history—20th century—Sources—Bibliography—Catalogs. 5. Great Britain—History—Sources—Bibliography—Catalogs. I. Bill, Edward Geoffrey Watson. II. Title.
Distributed by Oxford University Press, N.Y. BIP

Manuscripts—England—London—Catalogs.

BRITISH Museum. Dept. of 016.091
Manuscripts.
Catalogue of the Stowe manuscripts in the British Museum. Reprograf. Nachdr. d. Ausg., London, 1895-96. Hildesheim, New York, Olms, 1973. 2 v. 20 cm. Contents.Contents.—v. 1. Text.—v. 2. Index. [Z6621.B85S83 1973] [DA26] 74-185865 ISBN 3-487-04783-7 DM198.00
1. British Museum. Dept. of Manuscripts. 2. Manuscripts—England—London—Catalogs. 3. Great Britain—History—Sources—Bibliography—Catalogs. I. British Museum. Mss. (Stowe). 1973. II. Title.

Manuscripts—England—Oxford—Catalogs.

DE LA MARE, 016.091'09425'7
Albinia Catherine.
Catalogue of the collection of medieval manuscripts bequeathed to the Bodleian Library, Oxford by James P. R. Lyell, compiled by Albinia de la Mare. Oxford, Clarendon P., 1971. xxxiii, 466 p. illus., plates, facsims. 24 cm. [Z6621.O972D45] 78-887676 ISBN 0-19-951326-0 £12.00
1. Manuscripts—England—Oxford—Catalogs. I. Lyell, James Patrick Ronaldson, 1871- II. Oxford. University. Bodleian Library.

Manuscripts, English—Catalogs.

HOUGHTON, Arthur Amory, 016.091
1906-
A checklist of manuscripts in the library of Arthur A. Houghton, Jr. Compiled by Robert F. Metzdorf. New York, 1969. 52 p. 23 cm. A revision and extension of the 1953 checklist which was based on a detailed catalog of Houghton's library prepared by William H. Bond. [Z6623.H68H68 1969] 74-172422
1. Houghton, Arthur Amory, 1906- —Library. 2. Manuscripts, English—Catalogs. I. Metzdorf, Robert Frederic, 1912- II. Title.

Manuscripts—Exhibitions.

HINDMAN, Sandra, 091'.074'015251
1944-
Pen to press : manuscripts and printed books in the first century of printing / by Sandra Hindman and James Douglas Farquhar. [College Park] : Art Dept., University of Maryland, 1977. p. cm. "An exhibition at the University of Maryland, Art Department Gallery, College Park, Maryland, September 15-October 23, 1977." Sponsored jointly by the Art Dept., University of Maryland and the Dept. of the History of Art, Johns Hopkins University. Includes index. Bibliography: p. [Z121.H6] 77-15026
1. College Park, Md.—Exhibitions. 2. Manuscripts—Exhibitions. 3. Bibliographical exhibitions. 4. Illumination of books and manuscripts—Exhibitions. I. Farquhar, James Douglas, 1941- joint author. II. Maryland. University. Dept. of Art. III. Johns Hopkins University. Dept. of the History of Art. IV. Maryland. University. Art Gallery. V. Title.

HIRSH, John C. 091
Western manuscripts of the twelfth through the sixteenth centuries in Lehigh University Libraries, a guide to the exhibition, by John C. Hirsh. Bethlehem, Pa., Rare Book Room, Linderman Library, Lehigh University, 1970. 32 p. illus. 23 cm. [Z6621.L496] 72-197768
1. Manuscripts—Exhibitions. I. Lehigh University, Bethlehem, Pa. Libraries. II. Title.

MICHIGAN. 018'.1'0977435
University. Library.
Manuscripts & papyri; an exhibition arranged for the XXVII International Congress of Orientalists, Ann Arbor, Michigan, August 13-19, 1967. [Ann Arbor? 1967] [v], 21 p. front. 23 cm. Catalog of the exhibition held at the University of Michigan Library, Aug. 7-Sept. 17, 1967. Bibliography: p. [v] [Z6621.M613O7] 68-64094
1. Manuscripts—Exhibitions. I. Title.

Manuscripts—Facsimiles.

JENKINSON, Hilary, Sir. 745.6'1
The later court hands in England from the fifteenth to the seventeenth century, illustrated from the Common paper of the Scriveners' Company of London, the English writing masters, and the public records. New York, Ungar [1969] vii, 199 p. illus. and portfolio ([6] l., 44 plates) 39 cm. Reprint of the 1927 ed. Companion volume to English court hand A.D. 1066 to 1500, by C. Johnson and H. Jenkinson. Includes bibliographies. [Z115.E5J57 1969] 68-8117 75.00
1. Manuscripts—Facsimiles. 2. Paleography, English. I. Title. BIP

Manuscripts, French—Catalogs.

DELISLE, Leopold 016.324'3
Victor, 1826-1910.
Inventaire general methodique des manuscrits francais de la Bibliotheque Nationale / Leopold Victor Delisle. Nachdr. d. Ausg. Paris 1876-1878. Hildesheim ; New York : Olms, 1975. 2 v. ; 19 cm. Cover title: Manuscrits francais de la Bibliotheque nationale. [Z6621.P223D44] 75-520491 ISBN 3-487-05301-2 (v. 1) : DM99.60
1. Paris. Bibliotheque nationale. 2. Manuscripts, French—Catalogs. I. Title. II. Title: Manuscrits francais de la Bibliotheque nationale.

Manuscripts—Great Britain—Catalogs.

BRITISH Museum. MSS. 016.091
(Lansdowne)
A catalogue of the Lansdowne manuscripts in the British Museum. With indexes of persons, places, and matters. Hildesheim, New York, G. Olms, 1974. 1 v. (various pagings) 29 cm. Reprint of the ed. published in London in 1819. [Z6621.B85L3 1974] 74-177997 ISBN 3-487-05184-2
1. British Museum. Mss. (Lansdowne) 2. Manuscripts—Great Britain—Catalogs. 3. Great Britain—History—Sources—Bibliography. I. Title.

BRITISH Museum. Dept. of 016.091
Manuscripts.
A catalogue of the Harleian manuscripts in the British Museum. With indexes of persons, places, and matters. Hildesheim, New York, G. Olms, 1973. 4 v. 25 cm. Half title: Manuscripts in the Harleian collection. Reprint of the London ed., published 1808-12. Based on the catalog begun in 1708 by H. Wanley. [Z6621.B85H3 1973] 74-164692 ISBN 3-487-05037-4 (v. 1)
1. Manuscripts—Great Britain—Catalogs. 2. Great Britain—History—Sources—Bibliography. I. Oxford, Robert Harley, 1st Earl of, 1661-1724. II. Oxford, Edward Harley, 2d Earl of, 1689-1741. III. Wanley, Humphrey, 1672-1726. IV. British Museum. MSS. (Harleian) V. Title. VI. Title: Manuscripts in the Harleian collection.

BRITISH Museum. Dept. of 016.091
Manuscripts.
A catalogue of the manuscripts in the Cottonian Library deposited in the British Museum. Hildesheim, New York, G. Olms, 1974. xv, 618, [75] p. 26 cm. Reprint of the ed. published in London in 1802.

[Z6621.B85C8 1974] 74-177966 ISBN 3-487-05018-8
1. British Museum. Mss. (Cottonian) 2. Manuscripts—Great Britain—Catalogs. 3. Great Britain—History—Sources—Bibliography. I. British Museum. Mss. (Cottonian) II. Title.

INDIA Office Library. 016.091
Index of post-1937 European manuscript accessions Boston, G. K. Hall, 1964. 156 p. 37 cm. Continues the library's Catalogue of manuscripts in European languages. [Z6621.G78E92] 74-166559
1. Manuscripts—Great Britain—Catalogs. 2. India—History—20th century—Sources—Bibliography. I. Title.

OXFORD. University. 016.324'3
Bodleian Library.
A summary catalogue of Western manuscripts in the Bodleian Library at Oxford. Oxford. Clarendon Press, 1895-1953. 7v. in 8. 23cm. [Z6621.O96W4] 9-24750
1. Manuscripts. Gt. Brit.—Catalogs. I. Hunt. Richard William, 1908- II. Madan, Falconer. 1851-1935. III. Record, P. D. IV. Title.
Contents omitted.

Manuscripts—Gt. Brit.—London—Catalogs.

TODD, Henry John, 1763-1845 091
A catalogue of the archiepiscopal manuscripts in the library at Lambeth Palace. With an account of the archiepiscopal registers and other records there preserved. London, Printer by Law and Gilbert, 1812. xi, 270, [68] p. facsim. 42cm. Photoreproduction. London, Gregg Pr., 1965. [Z6621.L82T6 1812a] 67-3964 35.00
1. Manuscripts—Gt. Brit.—London—Catalogs. I. Lambeth Palace. Library. II. Title.
Available from Gregg Pr., Ridgewood, N.J.

Manuscripts—Gt. Brit.—Oxford—Catalogs.

OXFORD, University. 016.091
Balliol College.
Catalogue of the manuscripts of Balliol College, Oxford. Compiled by R. A. B. Mynors. Oxford, Clarendon Press, 1963. ivii, 401 p. 24 cm. Bibliographical footnotes. [Z6621.O92] 63-4953
1. Manuscripts — Gt. Brit. — Oxford — Catalogs. I. Mynors, Roger Aubrey Baskerville, ed. II. Title.

OXFORD, University. Bodleian 011
Library
Catalogi codicum manuscriptorum bibliothecae Bodleianae. Oxonii, E. Typographeo Academico, [1966- v. 31cm. Vol. 4, 2d impression with corrections. [Z6621.O942] 68-78043 33.60
1. Manuscripts—Gt. Brit.—Oxford—Catalogs. I. Hackman, Alfred, 1811-1874. II. Tanner, Thomas, Bp. of St. Asaph, 1674-1735. III. Title.
Contents Omitted. Available from Oxford Univ. Pr., New York.

Manuscripts, Hebrew—Cambridge, Mass.—Catalogs.

HARVARD University. 016.296
Library. Houghton Library.
Hebrew manuscripts in the Houghton Library of the Harvard College Library : a catalogue / prepared by Mordechai Glatzer ; edited by Charles Berlin and Rodney Gove Dennis. Cambridge, Mass. : Harvard University Library, 1975. 68 p. : ill. ; 23 cm. Includes indexes. [Z6621.H34H44] [BM495] 75-329641
1. Harvard University. Library. Houghton Library. 2. Manuscripts, Hebrew—Cambridge, Mass.—Catalogs. 3. Manuscripts, Hebrew—Facsimiles. I. Glatzer, Mordechai. II. Title.

Manuscripts, Hebrew—Chicago—Catalogs.

SPERTUS College of 016.091
Judaica.
Spertus College of Judaica Yemenite manuscripts; an illustrated catalogue by Norman Golb. Chicago, Spertus College of Judaica Press, 1972. xv, 116 p. facsims. 29 cm. Includes bibliographical references. [Z6621.S7673H47 1972] 72-89585 25.00
1. Manuscripts, Hebrew—Chicago—Catalogs. 2. Manuscripts, Hebrew—Facsimiles. 3. Manuscripts, Arabic (Judeo-Arabic)—Chicago—Catalogs. 4. Mauuscripts, Arabic (Judeo-Arabic)—Facsimiles. 5. Jews in Yemen—Intellectual life. I. Golb, Norman. II. Title.

Manuscripts, Hebrew—Copenhagen—Catalogs.

EDELMANN, Rafael, 1902- 090
Hebraica from Denmark; manuscripts and printed books in the collection of the Royal Library, Copenhagen. Catalogue and introd. [New York, Printing by Marstin Print. Corp., 1969] [16] p. 4 plates (1 col.) 31 cm. A catalog of the 32 items exhibited in America through the cooperation of the Jewish Museum, the National Council of Jewish Women, the Danish Information Office, and SAS. [Z6621.C77H44] 77-83097
1. Manuscripts, Hebrew—Copenhagen—Catalogs. 2. Hebrew imprints. I. Jewish Theological Seminary of America. Jewish Museum. II. National Council of Jewish Women. III. Copenhagen. Kongelige Bibliotek. IV. Title.

Manuscripts, Hebrew—Facsimiles.

BURROWS, Millar, 1889- ed. 091
The Dead Sea scrolls of St. Mark's Monastery Edited for the trustees by Millar Burrows, with the assistance of John C. Trever and William H. Brownlee. New Haven, American Schools of Oriental Research, 1950- v. plates, port. 32 cm. The plates are facsim, reproductions of the original manuscripts. and are accompanied by printed Hebrew text. Contents.v. 1. The Isaiah manuscript and the Habakkuk commentary. [Z115Z.B58 I 8] 50-14067
1. Manuscripts, Hebrew—Facsimiles. I. Bible. Manuscripts. Hebrew. O. T. Isaiah. II. Bible. Manuscripts, Hebrew. O. T. Habakkuk. III. Jerusalem. St. Mark (Monastery) IV. Title.

Manuscripts, Hebrew—San Francisco—Catalogs.

CALIFORNIA. State 016.091
Library, Sacramento. Sutro Branch, San Francisco.
Sutro Library Hebraica: a handlist, by William M. Brinner. [Sacramento] California State Library, 1966. xiii, 82 p. 28 cm. [Z6621.C154H4] 68-64982
1. Manuscripts, Hebrew—San Francisco—Catalogs. I. Brinner, William M. II. Title.

Manuscripts—Hist.

DEUEL, Leo 091.09
Testaments of time; the search for lost manuscripts and records. New York, Knopf [c.]1965. xxxii, 590, xxi p. illus., maps, ports. 25cm. Bibl. [Z105.D4] 63-11118 8.95
1. Manuscripts—Hist. 2. Manuscripts—Conservation and restoration. I. Title.

Manuscripts—History—Juvenile literature.

CURRIER, Richard L. 417'.7
Ancient scrolls, by Michael Avi-Yonah. Retold for young readers by Richard L. Currier. Minneapolis, Lerner Publications Co. [1974, c1973] 95 p. illus. (part col.) 21 cm. (Digging up the past) (The Lerner archaeology series) A history of manuscripts, including discussions of early writing materials, preparation of scrolls and manuscripts, examples of surviving ancient literature, and the story of the Dead Sea Scrolls. [Z107.C87 1974] 72-10792 ISBN 0-8225-0827-3 (lib. bdg.)
1. Dead Sea scrolls—Juvenile literature. 2. Manuscripts—History—Juvenile literature. 3. Paleography—Juvenile literature. I. Avi-Yonah, Michael, 1904- II. Title. BIP

Manuscripts—Iowa—Iowa City—Catalogs.

IOWA. University. 017'.5'09777655
Libraries. Special Collections Dept.
Alphabetical index to manuscript collections. 3d revision. [Iowa City] 1969. 19 l. 28 cm. [Z6621.I663 1969] 76-636572
1. Manuscripts—Iowa—Iowa City—Catalogs. I. Title.

Manuscripts, Irish—Catalogs.

DE BRUN, Padraig, 1889- 016.091
Catalogue of Irish manuscripts in the King's Inn Library, Dublin. Dublin, Dublin Institute for Advanced Studies, 1972. xviii, 105 p. 22 cm. Includes bibliographical references. [Z6621.K4753I73] 74-157738
1. King's Inns, Dublin. Library. 2. Manuscripts, Irish—Catalogs. I. Title.

Manuscripts, Latin — Catalogs.

SILVERSTEIN, Theodore. 016.5
Medieval Latin scientific writings in the Barberini collection; a provisional catalogue. [Chicago] University of Chicago Press [1957] vii, 147 p. 24 cm. [Z6621.R78L19] 58-5492
1. Manuscripts, Latin — Catalogs. 2. Manuscripts. Italy — Catalogs. 3. Science, Medieval — Bibl. — Catalogs. I. Vatican, Biblioteca vaticana. Biblioteca barberiniana. II. Title. BIP

Manuscripts, Latin—Chicago—Exhibitions.

CHICAGO. University. 016.091
Library.
The Latin manuscript book; an exhibition held on the occasion of the seminars in Latin palaeography sponsored by the Division of the Humanities of the University of Chicago and the Medieval Academy of America, summer MCMLXXIII, selected from the collections of the University of Chicago Library. The Joseph Regenstein Library, July through September, 1973. [Chicago, 1973] [55] p. illus. 26 cm. Catalog. [Z114.C53 1973] 73-173470 1.50 (pbk.)
1. Chicago. University. Library. 2. Manuscripts, Latin—Chicago—Exhibitions. 3. Paleography, Latin—Exhibitions. I. Joseph Regenstein Library. II. Title.

Manuscripts, Latin—Facsimiles.

CODICES latini 471.7
antiquiores; a palaeographical guide to Latin manuscripts prior to the ninth century. Part II: Great Britain and Ireland. Edited by E. A. Lowe [under the auspices of the Union academique internationale for the American Council of Learned Societies and the Carnegie Institution of Washington] 2nd ed. Oxford, Clarendon Press, 1972. xxii, 60, [42] p. facsims. 45 cm. Revision of pt. 2, first published in 1935, of the original 12 pt. work. Bibliography: p. 47-60. [Z114.C676] 73-161496 ISBN 0-19-818222-8
1. Manuscripts, Latin—Facsimiles. 2. Paleography, English. 3. Paleography, Irish. I. Lowe, Elias Avery, 1879-1969, ed. II. International Union of Academies. III. American Council of Learned Societies Devoted to Humanistic Studies. IV. Carnegie Institution of Washington.
Distributed by Oxford University Press N.Y., 38.50.

Manuscripts—Maryland—Baltimore—Catalogs.

MARYLAND Historical 016.9752
Society.
The manuscript collections of the Maryland Historical Society. Compiled by Avril J. M. Pedley. Baltimore, 1968. 390 p. 26 cm. [Z6621.M3914] 68-23074 15.00
1. Manuscripts—Maryland—Baltimore—Catalogs. 2. Maryland—History—Sources—Bibliography. I. Pedley, Avril J. M., ed. II. Title. BIP

Manuscripts, Maya.

RAU, Jack. 091
The codex as a book form; three Maya codices: Dresden, Tro-Cortesianus, Per[e]sianus. New York, Pre-Columbian Press [1970] [15] p. 4 facsims. 16 cm. The facsims. are pages from the Dresdensis Maya (R 310) codex in the Sachsische Landesbibliothek, Dresden; the Tro-Cortesianus in the Museo Arqueologico Nacional, Madrid; and the Peresianus in the Bibliotheque nationale, Paris. "500 copies." [F1435.R29] 74-21823
1. Manuscripts, Maya. I. Title.

Manuscripts—New York City—Catalogs.

NEW York (City). Public 019'.1
Library. Manuscript Division.
Dictionary catalog. Boston, G. K. Hall, 1967. 2 v. 37 cm. At head of title: The New York Public Library Research Libraries. [Z6621.N5518] 68-4776
1. Manuscripts—New York City—Catalogs.

Manuscripts on microfilm.

ST. John's University, 091
Collegeville, Minn. Monastic Manuscript Microfilm Library.
The Monastic Manuscript Microfilm Library: its purpose and progress. [Text by Julian G. Plante. Collegeville? Minn., 1970] [24] p. (incl. cover) illus. (part. col.) 22 x 28 cm. [Z110.R4S24 1970] 74-192167
1. St. John's University, Collegeville, Minn. Monastic Manuscript Microfilm Library. 2. Manuscripts on microfilm. I. Plante, Julian G. II. Title.

Manuscripts on microfilm—Catalogs.

BRITISH Library. Dept. 010.8 s
of Manuscripts.
Register of microfilms and other photocopies in the Department of Manuscripts, British Library. London : Swift, 1976. [2], 239 p. ; 33 cm. (Special series - List and Index Society ; v. 9) Includes index. [CD1042.A2L56 Vol. 9] [Z6621.B837] 011 77-354423 ISBN 0-902573-53-5 : £5.00
1. British Library. Dept. of Manuscripts. 2. Manuscripts on microfilm—Catalogs. 3. Manuscripts—Facsimiles—Catalogs. I. Title. II. Series: List and Index Society. Special series ; v. 9.

UNITED States. Library of 016.091
Congress. Manuscript Division.
Manuscripts on microfilm; a checklist of the holdings of the Manuscript Division, compiled by Richard Bickel. Washington, Library of Congress, 1975. p. cm. [Z6621.U572 1975] 74-19073 ISBN 0-8444-0141-2
1. Manuscripts on microfilm—Catalogs. I. Bickel, Richard. II. Title.

Manuscripts—Oregon—Eugene—Catalogs.

OREGON. 018.1'09795'31
University. Library.
Catalogue of manuscripts in the University of Oregon Library. Compiled by Martin Schmitt. Eugene, University of Oregon [1971] 355 p. 26 cm. [Z6621.O713] 72-30080
1. Manuscripts—Oregon—Eugene—Catalogs. I. Schmitt, Martin Ferdinand. II. Title. BIP

Manuscripts (Papyri)

TURNER, Eric Gardiner. 091
The typology of the early codex / Eric G. Turner. [Philadelphia] : University of Pennsylvania Press, 1977. xxiii, 188 p. : ill. ; 27 cm. (The Eighteenth publication in the Haney Foundation series, University of Pennsylvania) Includes index. Bibliography: p. [vii]-[viii] [Z112.T87] 75-10125 ISBN 0-8122-7696-5 : 25.00
1. Manuscripts (Papyri) 2. Parchment. I. Title. BIP

Manuscripts—Pennsylvania—Philadelphia—Catalogs.

PENNSYLVANIA. University. Library. 018'.1
Catalogue of manuscripts in the libraries of the University of Pennsylvania to 1800, compiled by Norman P. Zacour and Rudolf Hirsch. Assisted by John F. Benton and William E. Miller. Philadelphia, University of Pennsylvania Press [c1965] viii, 279 p. illus. 25 cm. Major part of the Catalogue appeared originally in the Library chronicle, v. xXVI 2-XXIX 1. [Z6621.P44] 64-24501
1. Manuscripts—Pennsylvania—Philadelphia—Catalogs. I. Zacour, Norman P. II. Hirsch, Rudolf, 1906- III. Title.

Manuscripts, Persian—Catalogs.

THE Chester Beatty Library. 759.955 A catalogue of the Persian manuscripts and miniatures. Dublin, Hodges, Figgis, 1959- v. plates (incl. facsims.; part col.) 37 cm. Contents.Contents.—v. 1. MSS. 101-150, by A. J. Arberry, M. Minovi, and E. Blochet. Edited by J. V. S. Wilkinson.—v. 2. MSS. 151-220, by M. Minovi and others. Edited by A. J. Arberry. [Z6623.B37C52] 60-29727
1. Manuscripts, Persian—Catalogs. 2. Miniature painting, Iranian—Catalogs. I. Arberry, Arthur John, 1905- II. Minuvi, Mujtaba. III. Chester Beatty Library. IV. Title: A catalogue of the Persian manuscripts and miniatures.

Manuscripts, Spanish American—Catalogs.

UNITED States. Library of Congress. Manuscript Division. 016.091
Hans P. Kraus Collection of Hispanic American manuscripts; a guide, by J. Benedict Warren. Washington, Library of Congress, 1974. x, 187 p. illus. 25 cm. Bibliography: p. 165-171. [Z6621.U58K7] 74-1097 ISBN 0-8444-0118-8
1. United States. Library of Congress. Manuscript Division. 2. Kraus, Hans Peter, 1907- —Library. 3. Manuscripts, Spanish American—Catalogs. 4. Manuscripts—United States—Catalogs. 5. Latin America—History—Sources. I. Warren, J. Benedict. II. Title.

Manuscripts, Spanish — Catalogs.

INTERNATIONAL Congress of Hispanists. 1st, Oxford 1962 016.324'3
A catalogue of Hispanic manuscripts and books before 1700 from the Bodleian Library and Oxford college libraries exhibited at the Taylor Institution 6-11 September, 1962 [on the occasion of the] Primer Congreso Internacional de Hispanistas [Oxford, 1962] viii, 56 p. 22 cm. Exhibition arranged and catalog compiled by P. E. Russell and D. M. Rogers. Cover title: Hispanic manuscripts and books before 1700. [Z6621.I64] 65-73595
1. Manuscripts, Spanish — Catalogs. 2. Manuscripts — Gt. Brit. — Catalogs. I. Russell, Peter Edward, 1913- II. Rogers, David Morrison. III. Oxford. University. Bodielan Library. IV. Title. V. Title: Hispanic manuscripts and books before 1700.

RODRIGUEZ-MONINO, Antonio R., 1910- ed. 016.861
Catalogo de los manuscritos poeticos castellanos existentes en la Biblioteca de The Hispanic Society of America (siglos xv, xvi y xvii) por Antonio Rodriguez-Monino, Maria Brey Marino. New York, Hispanic Soc., 1965-66. 3v. illus., facsims., ports. 29cm. [Z6621.N5257] 66-31429 set, 50.00; lib. ed., set, 60.00
1. Manuscripts, Spanish—Catalogs. I. Brey Marino, Maria, joint ed. II. Hispanic Society of America. Library. III. Title.

Manuscripts, Spanish—England—London—Catalogs.

BRITISH Library. 016.091'0942
Catalogue of the manuscripts in the Spanish language in the British Library / Don Pascual de Gayangos. London : British Museum Publications for the British Library, 1976. 4 v. ; 26 cm. Reprint of the 1875 ed. published by the British Museum, Department of Manuscripts, London. [Z6621.B86S7 1976] 77-356349 ISBN 0-7141-0491-4 : £60.00
1. British Library. 2. Manuscripts, Spanish—England—London—Catalogs. I. Gayangos y Arce, Pascual de, 1809-1897. II. British Museum. Dept. of Manuscripts. Catalogue of manuscripts in the Spanish language in the British Museum. III. Title.

Manuscripts, Tibetan—Catalogs.

SNELLGROVE, David L. 011
The Chester Beatty Library. A catalogue of the Tibetan collection, by David L. Snellgrove, and A catalogue of the Mongolian collection, by C. R. Bawden. Dublin, Hodges, Figgis, 1969. 109 p. illus. (part col.) 26 cm. Includes bibliographies. [Z6621.C483T57] 73-200683
1. Manuscripts, Tibetan—Catalogs. 2. Manuscripts, Mongolian—Catalogs. 3. Block-books—Bibliography—Catalogs. 4. Lamaism—Bibliography—Catalogs. I. Chester Beatty Library. II. Bawden, Charles R. A catalogue of the Mongolian collection. 1969. III. Title: A catalogue of the Tibetan collection.

Manuscripts, Turkish—Catalogs.

MINORSKII, Vladimir Fedorovich, 1877-1966. 016.091
The Chester Beatty Library. A catalogue of the Turkish manuscripts and miniatures, by V. Minorsky. With an introd. by J. V. S. Wilkinson. Dublin, Hodges, Figgis, 1958. xxxv, [1], 145 p. 43 plates (incl. facsims., map; part col.) 37 cm. Bibliography: p. [xxxvi] [Z6623.M55] 62-3351
1. Manuscripts, Turkish—Catalogs. 2. Illumination of books and manuscripts, Turkish—Catalogs. I. Chester Beatty Library. II. Title: A catalogue of the Turkish manuscripts and miniatures.

Manuscripts—U. S.—Catalogs.

MICHIGAN. University. William L. Clements Library. 016.091
Guide to the manuscript collections in the William L. Clements Library, Compiled by William S. Ewing, curator of manuscripts. 2d ed. Ann Arbor, 1953. Ann Arbor, 1959. ix, 548p. 24cm. folder ([6] p.) 23cm. [Z6621.M63A25 1953] 54-62637
1. Manuscripts—U. S.— Catalogs. 2. U. S.—Hist.—Sources. I. Ewing, William S. II. Title. III. Title: —Supplement.

PIERPONT Morgan Library, New York. 016.0961
Italian manuscripts in the Pierpont Morgan Library; descriptive survey of the principal illuminated manuscripts of the sixth to sixteenth centuries, with a selection of important letters and documents. Catalogue compiled by Meta Harrsen and George K. Boyce; with an introd. by Bernard Berenson. New York, 1953. xii, 79p. 78 plates (incl. map. facsims.; part col.) 31cm. Includes bibliographical references. [Z6621.N55I8] 53-12411
1. Manuscripts. U. S.—Catalogs. 2. Manuscripts, Italian—Catalogs. I. Harrsen, Meta Philippine, 1891- II. Boyce, George Kenneth, 1906- III. Title.

WISCONSIN State Historical Society. 016.091
Guide to the manuscripts of the Wisconsin Historical Society; Supplement no. 2. ed. by Josephine L. Harper. Madison, State Hist. Soc. of Wis. [c.] 1966. x, 275p. 24cm. [Z6621.W772] 45-1974 9.00
1. Manuscripts—U. S.—Catalogs. 2. Wisconsin—Hist.—Sources—Bibl. I. Title.

Manuscripts. Virginia —Catalogs.

COLONIAL Williamsburg, inc. 016.091
Guide to the manuscript collections of Colonial Williamsburg, compiled by Lynette Adcock. Williamsburg, Va., 1954. 58p. 24cm. [Z6621.C72] 55-947
1. Manuscripts. Virginia —Catalogs. 2. Virginia—Hist.—Sources—Bibl. I. Adcock, Lynette. II. Title. III. Title: Manuscript collections of Colonial Williamsburg.

Manuscripts—West Virginia.

WEST Virginia. University. Library. West Virginia Collection. 016.9754
Guide to manuscripts and archives in the West Virginia Collection, by Charles Shetler. Morgantown, 1958 [i.e. 1959] x, 160 p. (West Virginia university bulletin, ser. 59, no. 10-1) [Z6621.W4] A59
1. Manuscripts — West Virginia. 2. West Virginia — Hist. — Sources. I. Shetler, Charles. II. Title.

WEST Virginia. University. Library. West Virginia Collection. 016.091
Guide to manuscripts and archives in the West Virginia Collection [by] James W. Hess. Morgantown, West Virginia University Library, 1974. viii, 317 p. 23 cm. "Describes collections listed in the first two guides [i.e. 1959-65 ed.] and materials added through June 1972." [Z6621.W42W48 1974] 73-78072 ISBN 0-87012-144-8
1. West Virginia. University. Library. West Virginia Collection. 2. Manuscripts—West Virginia. I. Hess, James W. II. Title.

Manuzio, family of printers, Venice.

STANFORD University. Libraries. Dept. of Special Collections. 070.5'092'2
The Aldine Press, 1494-1598, the first century of scholarly printing. An exhibition of books from libraries in San Francisco Bay area designed to illustrate the contributions of the Aldine Press to Renaissance scholarship and learning [Stanford, Calif.] 1973. [8] p. 31 cm. [Z232.M3S8 1973] 73-161507
1. Manuzio, family of printers, Venice. 2. Scholarly publishing—Venice—History—Exhibitions. 3. San Francisco Bay region—Libraries. I. Title.

Manzu, Giacomo, 1908—

MANZU, Giacomo, 1908- 730'.924
Exhibition of recent work by Giacomo Manzu, March 18 to April 27, 1968. New York, P. Rosenberg [1968] 63 p. (chiefly illus.) 31 cm. ([Rosenberg (Paul) and Company, New York.] Catalogue no. 159) Catalog of an exhibit held in the gallery of Paul Rosenberg & Co., March 18-April 27, 1968. "Friends of Manzu Committee. Collection of sculpture and graphic works": folder inserted in pocket. [NB623.M24R6] 68-30258
I. Rosenberg (Paul) and Company, New York. II. Title.

MANZU, Giacomo, 1908- 730.92'4
Giacomo Manzu [by] John Rewald. Greenwich, Conn., New York Graphic Society [1967, c1966] 327 p. illus. (part col.), plates (part col.) 31 cm. Bibliography: p. 315-322. [NB623.M24R413 1967b] 67-19374
I. Rewald, John, 1912-

MANZU, Giacomo, 1908- 730'.92'4 B
Giacomo Manzu. Text by Mario De Micheli. New York, H. N. Abrams [1974] Translated from the Italian. Bibliography: p. [NB623.M24M513] 73-14796 ISBN 0-8109-0261-3 35.00
1. Manzu, Giacomo, 1908- I. Micheli, Mario de. BIP

Maoris—Portraits—Exhibitions.

DUNEDIN Public Art Gallery. 704.94'2'099310740993157
Face value, a study in Maori portraiture : [exhibition catalogue]. [Dunedin, N.Z. : Dunedin Public Art Gallery], [1975] [44] p. : ill. (some col.) ; 19 x 26 cm. Cover title. Includes bibliographical references. [DU422.8.D86 1975] 75-325735
1. Maoris—Portraits—Exhibitions. I. Title.

Map collections.

SPECIAL Libraries Association. Geography and Map Division. Directory Revision Committee. 026'.912'02573
Map collections in the United States and Canada; a directory. 2d ed. New York, Special Libraries Association, 1970. xiii, 159 p. map. 23 cm. "Compiled by the Directory Revision Committee, David K. Carrington, chairman." First ed., 1954, by the division's Map Resources Committee. [GA193.U5S68 1970] 72-101336
1. Map collections. I. Carrington, David K., 1938- II. Special Libraries Association. Geography and Map Division. Map Resources Committee. Map collections in the United States and Canada.

SPECIAL Libraries Association. Geography and Map Division. Map Resources Committee. 016.912
Map collections in the United States and Canada, a directory. Marie Cleckner Goodman, chairman. New York, Special Libraries Association, 1954. 170p. fold. map. 22cm. [GA193.U5S7] 54-1345
1. Map collections. I. Goodman, Marie Cleckner. II. Title. BIP

Map collections—Canada.

NATIONAL Map Collection. 912'.71
Catalogue of the National Map Collection, Public Archives of Canada, Ottawa, Ontario. Boston : G. K. Hall, 1976. 16 v. ; 36 cm. English and French. [Z6028.N35 1976] [GA471] 76-379551 ISBN 0-8161-1215-0 lib.bdg. : 1250.00
1. National Map Collection. 2. Map collections—Canada. I. Title.

Map collections—Directories.

WORLD directory of map collections / compiled by the Geography and Map Libraries Sub-Section ; edited by Walter W. Ristow. 912'.075 Munchen : Verlag Dokumentation, 1976. 326 p. ; 22 cm. (IFLA publications ; 8) Bibliography: p. 325-326. [GA192.W67] 76-381150 ISBN 3-7940-4428-2
1. Map collections—Directories. I. Ristow, Walter William, 1908- II. International Federation of Library Associations. Geography and Map Libraries Sub-Section. III. Series: International Federation of Library Association. IFLA publications ; 8.

Map collections—History.

SPECIAL Libraries Association. Washington, D.C. Chapter. Geography and Map Group. 912'.08
Federal government map collecting; a brief history. Edited by Richard W. Stephenson. Washington, 1969. vii, 60 p. illus., maps. 22 cm. (Special Libraries Association. Washington, D.C. Chapter. Publication no. 2) Includes bibliographical references. [GA193.U5S73] 72-14281 3.00
1. Map collections—History. I. Stephenson, Richard W., ed. II. Title. III. Series.

Map collections—North America—Directories.

WESTERN Association of Map Libraries. 015'.794 s
Directory of map collections in: Alaska, Arizona, California, Hawaii, Idaho, Nevada, Oregon, Washington, Alberta, British Columbia. Sacramento, California State Library, Govt. Publications Section, 1969. 36 l. 29 cm. (California State Library. Government Publications Section. GPS publication no. 4) Cover title. [Z1223.Z7C35 no. 4] [GA193.N6] 026'.912'02573 73-623206
1. Map collections—North America—Directories. 2. Map collections—Hawaii—Directories. I. Title. II. Series: California. State Library, Sacramento. Government Publications Section. GPS publication no. 4.

SUBJECT INDEX MARGINALIA.

Map collections—United States—Directories.

CARRINGTON, David K., 1938- 026'.912'02573
Map collections in the United States and Canada : a directory / compiled by David K. Carrington and Richard W. Stephenson. 3d ed. New York : Special Libraries Association, 1978. p. cm. "A project of the Geography and Map Division, Special Libraries Association." Second ed., by the Directory Revision Committee, Geography and Map Division, Special Libraries Association, published in 1970. Includes index. [GA193.U5S68 1977] 77-26685 ISBN 0-87111-233-7 : 19.75
1. Map collections—United States—Directories. 2. Map collections—Canada—Directories. I. Stephenson, Richard W., joint author. II. Special Libraries Association. Geography and Map Division. III. Special Libraries Association. Geography and Map Division. Directory Revision Committee. Map collections in the United States and Canada. IV. Title.

Mapledurham, Eng.

BOND, Brian. 914.25'7
Mapledurham House, the historic home of the Blount family: official guide; history and description of contents by Brian Bond. Derby, English Life Publications, 1968. 20 p. illus., coat of arms, geneal. table, map. 14 x 21 cm. Illus. on lining papers. [DA690.M4097B6] 78-453197 unpriced
1. Blount family. 2. Mapledurham, Eng. I. Title.

Maps—Bibliography—Catalogs.

SMITH, Thomas Russell, 1910- 061.912
Maps of the 16th to 19th centuries in the University of Kansas Libraries; an analytical carto-bibliography, by Thomas R. Smith and Bradford L. Thomas. Lawrence, University of Kansas Libraries, 1963. 137 p. 26 cm. (University of Kansas publications. Library series, no. 16) Bibliography: p. 131-132. [Z6028.S55] 62-63443
1. Maps — Bibl. — Catalogs. I. Thomas Bradford L., joint author. II. Kansas.University. Libraries. III. Title. IV. Series: Kansas. University. Libraries. Library series, no. 16

Maps—Bibliography—Catalogs.

BERKOWITZ, David Sandler, 1913- 016.912
From Ptolemy to the moon: progress in the art of exploration and navigation; an exhibition of maps, charts, manuscripts, books, globes, and instruments held at the Rapaporte Treasure Hall, Brandeis University Library, June 2 to July 2, 1965, selected and described by David Sandler Berkowitz. Waltham, Mass., 1965. ix. 109 1. 28 cm. Includes bibliographies. [Z6028.B47] 65-9554
1. Mape — Bibl. — Catalogs. I. Brandeis University, Waltham, Mass. Library. II. Title.

RISTOW, Walter William, 1908- 016.911
Facsimiles of rare historical maps; a list of reproductions for sale by various publishers and distributors. Compiled by Walter W. Ristow [Geography and Map Division] Rev. Washington, Geography and Map Division, Library of Congress, 1966. i, 12 p. 26 cm. Issued in 1960 by the Library's Map Division, under title: Facsimiles of rare historical maps available for sale. [Z6022.R5 1966] 66-62298
1. Maps—Bibliography—Catalogs. I. U.S. Library of Congress. Map Division. Facsimiles of rare historical maps available for sale. II. U.S. Library of Congress. Geography and Map Division. III. Title.

RISTOW, Walter William, 1908- 016.911
Facsimiles of rare historical maps; a list of reproductions for sale by various publishers and distributors. Compiled by Walter W. Ristow, assisted by Mary E. Graziani, Geography and Map Division. 3d ed., rev. and enl. Washington [Library of Congress] 1968. 20 p. 26 cm. Issued in 1960 by the Library's Map Division, under title: Facsimiles of rare historical maps available for sale. [Z6022.R5 1968] 70-602104
1. Maps—Bibliography—Catalogs. I. U.S. Library of Congress. Map Division. Facsimiles of rare historical maps available for sale. II. U.S. Library of Congress. Geography and Map Division. III. Graziani, Mary E. IV. Title.

Maps, Early—Bibliography—Catalogs.

GEORGIA. Surveyor General. 016.912
Pre-nineteenth century maps in the collection of the Georgia Surveyor General Department : a catalog / compiled by Janice Gayle Blake, Surveyor General Department, Office of the Secretary of State. Atlanta : State Print. Off., 1975. xx, 173 p. ; 28 cm. Includes index. Bibliography: p. 153-157. [Z6022.G46 1975] [GA201] 75-620098
1. Georgia. Surveyor General. 2. Maps, Early—Bibliography—Catalogs. 3. North America—Maps—To 1800—Bibliography—Catalogs. I. Blake, Janice Gayle. II. Title.

Maps, Early—Collectors and collecting.

SKELTON, Raleigh Ashlin. 912'.075
Maps: a historical survey of their study and collecting [by] R. A. Skelton. Chicago, University of Chicago Press [1972] xvii, 138 p. port. 21 cm. (The Kenneth Nebenzahl, Jr., lectures in the history of cartography at the Newberry Library) "Published for the Hermon Dunlap Smith Center for the History of Cartography; the Newberry Library." "Raleigh Ashlin Skelton (1906-1970): a bibliography of published works": p. 111-131. [GA197.3.S55] 72-650049 ISBN 0-226-76164-9
1. Maps, Early—Collectors and collecting. 2. Cartography—History. I. Hermon Dunlap Smith Center for the History of Cartography. II. Title. III. Series. BIP

SKELTON, Raleigh Ashlin. 912'.09
Maps : a historical survey of their study and collecting / R. A. Skelton. Illustrated ed. Chicago : Published for the Hermon Dunlap Smith Center for the History of Cartography, the Newberry Library [by] the University of Chicago Press, 1975. xv, 138 p., [4] leaves of plates : ill. ; 21 cm. (The Kenneth Nebenzahl, Jr., lectures in the history of cartography at the Newberry Library) "Raleigh Ashlin Skelton (1906-1970): a bibliography of published works": p. 111-131. [GA197.3.S55 1975] 74-21344 ISBN 0-226-76164-9. ISBN 0-226-76165-7 pbk.
1. Maps, Early—Collectors and collecting. 2. Cartography—History. I. Title. II. Series.

TOOLEY, Ronald Vere, 1898- 912'.09
Collecting antique maps / [by] R. V. Tooley. London : Gibbons, 1976. 31 p. : maps ; 20 cm. (Stanley Gibbons guides) Bibliography: p. 31. [GA197.3.T66] 77-357385 ISBN 0-85259-850-5 : £0.75
1. Maps, Early—Collectors and collecting. I. Title.

Maps, Pictorial—History.

BEANS, George Harry, 1894- 912.52
A list of Japanese maps of the Tokugawa era. Jenkintown [Pa.] Tall Tree Library, 1951. 51 p. maps. 31 cm. (Tall Tree Library publication no. 23) "One hundred and fifty copies." "References": p. [46] [Z6027.J24B4] 911.52 52-41881
I. Title.

GEORGE, Wilma B. 526.8
Animals and maps [by] Wilma George. Pref. by Helen Wallis. Berkeley, University of California Press [1969] 235 p. illus., maps. 25 cm. Bibliography: p. [211]-220. [GA203.G4] 68-28808 9.50
1. Maps, Pictorial—History. I. Title. BIP

Marble sculpture, American.

GERDTS, William H. 730'.973
American neo-classic sculpture; the marble resurrection [by] William H. Gerdts. New York, Viking Press [1973] 160 p. illus. 24 cm. (A Studio book) Bibliography: p. 149-160. [NB1210.M3G47 1973] 75-100972 ISBN 0-670-12002-2 15.95
1. Marble sculpture, American. 2. Neoclassicism (Art)—United States. I. Title.

Marble sculpture, Greek—Greece—Tegea.

STEWART, Andrew F. 730'.92'4
Skopas of Paros / by Andrew F. Stewart. Park Ridge, N.J. : Noyes Press, c1977. xvi, 183 p., [28] leaves of plates : ill. ; 29 cm. Includes index. Bibliography: p. 149. [NB104.S73] 77-149 ISBN 0-8155-5051-0 : 32.00
1. Scopas, fl. 4th cent. B.C. 2. Tegea, Greece. Temple of Athena Alea. 3. Marble sculpture, Greek—Greece—Tegea. 4. Tegea, Greece—History. BIP

Marblehead, Mass.—History.

LORD, Priscilla Sawyer. 974.4'5
Marblehead; the spirit of '76 lives here [by] Priscilla Sawyer Lord [and] Virginia Clegg Gamage. Illustrated with line drawings by Marion Martin Brown. [1st ed.] Philadelphia, Chilton Book Co. [1971, c1972] xii, 395 p. illus. 24 cm. Bibliography: p. [372]-379. [F74.M3L6 1972] 73-169586 ISBN 0-8019-5596-3
1. Marblehead, Mass.—History. 2. Marblehead, Mass.—Description. I. Gamage, Virginia Clegg, joint author. II. Title.

Marbling.

AKERS, Robert C. 745.7
Marbling / [Robert C. Akers] Leicester : Dryad Press, 1976. 16 p. : ill. (chiefly col.) ; 15 x 21 cm. (Dryad leaflet ; 505) Cover title. [TT385.A43] 77-364706 ISBN 0-85219-103-0 : £0.45
1. Marbling. I. Title.

Marc, Franz, 1880-1916.

LEVINE, Frederick S. 759.3 B
The apocalyptic vision : the art of Franz Marc as German expressionism / by Frederick S. Levine. New York : Harper & Row, c1979. p. cm. (Icon editions) Includes index. Bibliography: p. [ND588.M194L46 1979] 78-4736 ISBN 0-06-435275-7 : 17.50
1. Marc, Franz, 1888-1916. 2. Painters—Germany—Biography. 3. Expressionism (Art)—Germany. I. Title. BIP

MARC, Franz, 1880-1916. 759.3
Franz Marc: watercolors, drawings, writings. With text and notes by Klaus Lankheit. [Translated from the German by Norbert Guterman] New York, H. N. Abrams [1960] 55p. illus., 16 removable col. plates, port. 33cm. 'Two slip-in frames' (for temporary framing of removable plates) in pocket. 60-11599 17.50
I. Lankheit, Klaus. II. Title.

SCHMIDT, Georg 759.3
Franz Marc. Translated by John Turnbull. Milan, Uffici Press [dist. New York, Crown, 1960] 30p. 10 mounted col. illus. 35cm. (The Uffici series in full colour) 60-4721 1.95 pap.,
1. Marc, Franz, 1880-1916. I. Title.

Marca-Relli, Conrad, 1913-

MARCA-RELLI, Conrad, 1913- 759.13
Marca-Relli, by William C. Agee. New York, Published for the Whitney Museum of American Art by F. A. Praeger [1967] 80 p. illus. (part col.), port. 25 cm. Exhibition held at the Whitney Museum of American Art. Bibliography: p. 78-80. [ND237.M238A62] 67-30560
I. Agee, William C. II. Whitney Museum of American Art, New York.

MARCA-RELLI, Conrad, 1913- 709'.24
Marca-Relli. [Catalog] Marlborough-Gerson Gallery Inc., New York. Associated galleries: Marlborough Fine Art (London) Ltd. [and] Marlborough Galleria d'Arte, Rome. New York, Marlborough-Gerson Gallery, 1970. 38 p. illus. 31 cm. "Cat. no. 267." [N6537.M36M37] 73-170845
1. Marca-Relli, Conrad, 1913- I. Marlborough-Gerson Gallery. II. Marlborough Fine Art, ltd., London. III. Marlborough galleria d'arte.

March, Winifred Petchey.

MARSH, Winifred Petchey. 759.11
People of the willow : the Padlimiut tribe of the Caribou Eskimo / portrayed in watercolours by Winifred Petchey Marsh. Toronto : Oxford University Press, 1976[i.e.1977] 63 p. : chiefly col. ill., map ; 23 x 26 cm. [ND1942.M34A53] 77-353618 ISBN 0-19-540271-5 : 10.95
1. March, Winifred Petchey. 2. Eskimos—Canada—Pictorial works. I. Title.
Distributed by Oxford University Press, New York BIP

Marden, Brice, 1938—

MARDEN, Brice, 1938- 759.13
Brice Marden : [catalogue of an exhibition] , the Solomon R. Guggenheim Museum, New York. New York : Solomon R. Guggenheim Foundation, 1975. 68 p. : ill. ; 22 cm. Bibliography: p. 61-67. [ND237.M239S64] 75-689 pbk. : 4.75
1. Marden, Brice, 1938- I. Solomon R. Guggenheim Museum, New York.

Maremont, Adele H., 1902- —Art collections.

CLASSICS of contemporary art from the Maremont Collection. 709.04
Phoenix, 1968. [24] p. illus. 22 cm. Catalog, by H. T. Broadley, of an exhibition held at the Phoenix Art Museum, May-November, 1968. [N6490.C585] 68-7022
1. Maremont, Adele H., 1902- —Art collections. 2. Art, Modern—20th century—Exhibitions. I. Broadley, Hugh T. II. Phoenix, Ariz. Art Museum.

Margaret Woodbury Strong Museum.

MARGARET Woodbury Strong Museum. 708'.147'89
The Margaret Woodbury Strong Museum. Director: H. J. Swinney. Photography by Richard Margolis. Rochester, N.Y. [1973] 48 p. illus. 18 x 26 cm. On cover: First stages: a brief report on the founder and the collections. [N718.A85] 73-171108
1. Margaret Woodbury Strong Museum. I. Swinney, Holman J., 1919- II. Title: First stages.

Margate, Eng. Grotto.

HASLAM, Ruby Mary. 942.2'3
The shell temple / by Ruby M. Haslam ; with illustrations by Graeme Wilkins. London ; New York : Regency Press, 1974. 107 p., [8] p. of plates : ill. ; 20 cm. [DA690.M42H37] 75-309346 ISBN 0-7212-0354-X : £1.20
1. Margate, Eng. Grotto. I. Title.

Margate, N.J. Lucy, the Margate Elephant (Architectural folly)

BOUCHER, Jack E. 917.49'84
Lucy, the Margate Elephant, by Jack E. Boucher. [2d ed. Margate, N.J., Save Lucy Committee, c1970] 16 p. illus. 24 cm. Cover title. [NA8460.B68 1970] 73-82995
1. Margate, N.J. Lucy, the Margate Elephant (Architectural folly) I. Title.

Marginalia.

PALM, Swante, 1815-1899. 920.1
Notes of a Texas book-collector, 1850-1899; selections from the marginalia of Swante Palm. With an introd. by Harry Ransom. [Austin] Texas Book Club, 1950 [i. e. 1953] 63p. 24cm. [CT275.P317A3] 53-35939
1. Marginalia. I. Title.

Mariette, Pierre Jean, 1694-1774.

STEINITZ, Kate 760'.092'2
Trauman.
Pierre-Jean Mariette & le Comte de Caylus and their concept of Leonardo da Vinci in the eighteenth century / by Kate T. Steinitz. Los Angeles : Zeitlin & Ver Brugge, 1974. 39 p. : ill. ; 26 cm. Edition limited to 500 copies. Bibliography: p. 38-39. [N7483.M3S8] 74-79450
1. Mariette, Pierre Jean, 1694-1774. 2. Caylus, Anne Claude Philippe, comte de, 1692-1765. 3. Leonardo da Vinci, 1452-1519. 4. Leonardo da Vinci, 1452-1519—Adaptations. I. Title.

Marin, John, 1870-1953.

HELM, MacKinley, 1896- 759.13
John Marin. New York, Kennedy Graphics, 1970 [c1948] 239 p. illus., col. plates, port. 26 cm. (Library of American art) [ND237.M24H4 1970] 75-87484
1. Marin, John, 1870-1953.

MARIN, John, 1870-1953. 769'.924
The complete etchings of John Marin. Catalogue raisonne by Carl Zigrosser. Philadelphia, Philadelphia Museum of Art, 1969. 20 p., 182 illus. 31 cm. Catalog of part 1 of the exhibition John Marin: etchings and related works, held at the Philadelphia Museum of Art, Jan. 17-Mar. 17, 1969. Bibliography: p. [168] [NE2012.M3Z5] 73-29687
I. Zigrosser, Carl, 1891- II. Philadelphia Museum of Art. III. Title.

MARIN, John, 1870-1953. 916
Drawings and water colors. New York, Twin Editions [1950] 1 portfolio ([11] p., 32 plates (part col.)) 34 cm. "125 copies of edition-I have been printed with an additional etching by the artist, numbered I-CXXv. No. LXXIV." [NC1075.M345A43] 75-205139
I. Title.

MARIN, John, 1870-1953. 759.13
John Marin. Edited by Cleve Gray. [1st ed.] New York, Holt, Rinehart and Winston [1970] 176 p. illus. (part col.), facsims., ports. 29 cm. [ND237.M24G7] 77-102144 22.95

MARIN, John, 1870-1953. 759.13
John Marin, 1870-1953; a centennial exhibition organized by the Los Angeles County Museum of Art. Selection and catalog by Larry Curry. [Los Angeles, Los Angeles County Museum of Art, 1970] 100 p. illus., plates (part col.), ports. 27 cm. Exhibition held at the Los Angeles County Museum of Art July 7-Aug. 30, 1970, and at other museums. Bibliography: p. 97-98. [ND237.M24C8] 77-128147
I. Curry, Larry. II. Los Angeles Co., Calif. Museum of Art, Los Angeles.

MARIN, John, 1870-1953. 741.973
John Marin drawings, 1886-1951, by Sheldon Reich. [Salt Lake City] University of Utah Press [1969] 120 p. illus. (part col.) 23 x 26 cm. "A retrospective exhibition honoring John Marin's centennial, organized by the University of Utah Museum of Fine Arts." Includes bibliographical references. [NC139.M27R4] 79-83660
I. Reich, Sheldon. II. Utah Museum of Fine Arts. BIP

MARIN, John, 1870-1953. 769'.924
John Marin [etchings, 1905-1951. Catalogue of an exhibition] February/March, 1971. New York, Marlborough Graphics [1971] 15 p. illus., port. 30 cm. [NE2012.M3M3] 72-198267
I. Marlborough Graphics Inc.

MARIN, John, 1870-1953. 759.13
John Marin in retrospect; an exhibition of his oils and watercolors, the Corcoran Gallery of Art, Washington, D.C., March 2-April 15, 1962; the Currier Gallery of Art, Manchester, New Hampshire, May 9-June 24, 1962. [Washington, D.C., 1962] 37 p. illus. (part col.) 25 cm. [ND237.M24C67] 73-172265
1. Marin, John, 1870-1953. I. Corcoran Gallery of Art, Washington, D.C. II. Currier Gallery of Art, Manchester, N.H.

MARIN, John, 1870-1953. 759.13
John Marin: oils, watercolors, and drawings which relate to his etchings, by Sheldon Reich. Philadelphia, Philadelphia Museum of Art, 1969. 9 p., 52 illus. 31 cm. Catalog of part 2 of the exhibition John Marin: etchings and related works, held at the Philadelphia Museum of Art, 1969. Includes bibliographical references. [N6537.M37R4] 77-29688
I. Reich, Sheldon. II. Philadelphia Museum of Art. III. Title.

MARIN, John, 1870-1953. 759.13
Letters of John Marin. Edited, with an introd. by Herbert J. Seligmann. Westport, Conn., Greenwood Press [1970] 1 v. (unpaged) facsims. 23 cm. Reprint of the 1931 ed. [ND1839.M35A3 1970] 77-109780 ISBN 0-8371-4270-9 201
A0021785NEW York. Museum of Modern

NEW York. Museum of Modern 759.13
Art.
John Marin; watercolors, oil paintings, etchings. Reprint ed. [New York] Published for the Museum of Modern Art by Arno Press, 1966 [c1936] 100 p. illus., plates, ports. 27 cm. Bibliography: p. 99-100. [ND237.M24] 66-26650
1. Marin, John, 1870-1953.

REICH, Sheldon. 759.13
John Marin: a stylistic analysis and catalogue raisonne. Tucson, University of Arizona Press [1970] 2 v. illus. (part col.), ports. 28 cm. Bibliography: v. 1., p. 273-297. [ND237.M24R4] 73-88861 60.00 (the set)
1. Marin, John, 1870-1953. I. Title.

WIGHT, Frederick [759.13] 927.5
Stallknecht, 1902-
John Marin, Frontiersman in John Marin: tributes by William Carlos Williams [etc.] Berkeley, Univ. of California Press, 1956. [ND237.M24J6] 56-6988
I. Title.

WILLIAMS, William Carlos, 759.13
1883-
John Marin: tributes by William Carlos Williams, Duncan Phillips [and] Dorothy Norman. Conclusion to a biography, by Mackinley Helm. John Marin, frontiersman, by Frederick S. Wight. Berkeley, University of California Press, 1956. [78]p. illus. (part col.) 28cm. Bibliography: p. [77]-[78] [ND237.M24J6] 927.5 56-6988
1. Marin, John, 1870-1953. I. Wight, Frederick Stallknecht, 1902- II. Title.

WILLIAMS, William Carlos, 759.13
1883-
John Marin: tributed by William Carlos Williams, Duncan Phillips [and] Dorothy Norman. Conclusion to a biography, by Mackinley Helm. John Marin, frontiersman, by Frederick S. Wight. Berkeley, University of California Press, 1956. [78]p. illus. (part col.) 28cm. Bibliography: p. [77]-[78] [ND237.M24J6] 927.5 56-6988
1. Marin, John, 1870-1953. I. Wieght, Frederick Stallknecht 1902- II. Title.

Marine painting.

BALLINGER, Harry Russell, 758.2
1892-
Painting surf and sea. New York, Watson-Guptill Publications, 1957. 93 p. illus. 27 cm. [ND1370.B3] 57-9618
1. Marine painting. I. Title.

FITZGERALD, Edmond 751.4'22
James, 1912-
Marine painting in watercolor, by Edmond J. Fitzgerald. New York, Watson-Guptill Publications [1972] 175 p. illus. 29 cm. Bibliography: p. 173. [ND2270.F58] 70-177379 ISBN 0-8230-3008-3 14.95
1. Marine painting. 2. Water-color painting—Technique. I. Title. BIP

KENT, Norman, 1903- ed. 758.2
Seascapes & landscapes in watercolor. New York, Watson-Guptill Publications, 1956. 126p. illus. (part col.) ports. 27cm. Companion volume to the editor's Watercolor methods. [ND2270.K4] 56-13775
1. Marine painting. 2. Landscape painting. 3. Water-color painting—Technique. 4. Painters, American. I. Title.

KENT, Norman, 1903-1972. 758.2
ed.
Seascapes & landscapes in watercolor. New York, Watson-Guptill Publications, 1956. 126 p. illus. (part col.) ports. 27 cm. Companion volume to the editor's Watercolor methods. [ND2270.K4] 56-13775
1. Marine painting. 2. Landscape painting. 3. Water-color painting—Technique. 4. Painters, American. I. Title.

*PATAKY, Denes 7584
Ships in art [by] Denes Pataky [and] Imre Marjai Budapest, Corvina Press, [1973] 42 p. 48 col. plates 24 cm. Bibliography, p. 37. [ND1373]
1. Marine painting. 2. Ships in art. I. Marjai, Imre, joint author II. Title.
Distributed by International Publications Service, N.Y. for 12.50. BIP

Marine painting, American.

STEIN, Roger B. 758'.2'0973
Seascape and the American imagination / Roger B. Stein. 1st ed. New York : C. N. Potter : distributed by Crown Publishers, [1975] xii, 144 p. : ill. (some col.) ; 26 cm. Published in association with the Whitney Museum of American Art. Includes index. Bibliography: p. 138-139. [ND1372.S8 1975] 75-8979 ISBN 0-517-52171-7 : 15.00
1. Marine painting, American. I. Whitney Museum of American Art, New York. II. Title.

Marine painting, American—Exhibitions.

AMERICAN 758'.2'09730740155416
marine painting : a loan exhibition on display at Virginia Museum, September 27-October 31, 1976, and the Mariners Museum, November 8-December 12, 1976 / organized by Frederick Robert Brandt : consultant on the exhibition, John Wilmerding. Richmond : Virginia Museum, c1976. 151 p. : ill. (some col.) ; 21x28 cm. Includes bibliographical references and index. [ND1372.A43] 76-28711 ISBN 0-917046-01-3 pbk. : 8.95
1. Marine painting, American—Exhibitions. I. Brandt, Frederick R., 1936- II. Virginia Museum of Fine Arts, Richmond. III. Mariners' Museum, Newport News, Va.

CUMMER Gallery of 758'.2'0973
Art.
American paintings of ports and harbors, 1774-1968. Organized by Joseph Jeffers Dodge, director. Foreword by Henry Bryan Caldwell [Jacksonville? Fla., 1969] [33] p. illus. 20 x 25 cm. Catalogue of an exhibition held at Cummer Gallery of Art, Jacksonville, Fla., Feb. 4-Mar. 16, 1969, and at Norfolk Museum of Arts and Sciences, Apr. 5-May 11, 1969. [ND1372.5.C8] 74-281657
1. Marine painting, American—Exhibitions. 2. Harbors in art. I. Dodge, Joseph Jeffers. II. Norfolk, Va. Museum of Arts and Sciences. III. Title.

SEA, sails, and 758'.2'07401471
ports : an exhibition of important marine paintings, from September 15 to October 29. New York : Kennedy Galleries, c1977. 24 p. : chiefly ill. (some col.) ; 28 cm. Includes index. [ND1372.5.S43] 77-154418
1. Marine painting, American—Exhibitions. 2. Marine painting, British—Exhibitions. 3. Marine painting—19th century—United States—Exhibitions. 4. Marine painting—19th century—Great Britain—Exhibitions. 5. Marine painting—20th century—United States—Exhibitions. 6. Marine painting—20th century—Great Britain—Exhibitions. I. Kennedy Galleries, inc., New York.

Marine painting, American—History.

WILMERDING, John. 758'.2'0973
A history of American marine painting. [1st ed. Salem, Mass.] Peabody Museum of Salem [1968] xxiii, 279 p. illus., plates (16 col.), ports. 30 cm. Bibliography: p. 257-268. [ND205.W53 1968] 68-22210 25.00
1. Marine painting, American—History. I. Peabody Museum of Salem, Salem, Mass. II. Title.

BIP

Marine painting, British.

BROOK-HART, Denys. 758'.2'0941
British 19th century marine painting / by Denys Brook-Hart. [Woodbridge, Eng.] : Antique Collectors' Club, [1974] 368 p. : ill. (some col.) ; 29 cm. Title on spine: Marine painting. Includes indexes. Bibliography: p. 127-130. [ND1373.G75B76] 75-302912 ISBN 0-902028-32-4 : £9.50
1. Marine painting, British. I. Title. II. Title: Marine painting.

CORDINGLY, David. 758'.2'0942
Marine painting in England, 1700-1900. [1st American ed.] New York, C. N. Potter; distributed by Crown Publishers [1974, c1973] 200 p. illus. (part col.) 30 cm. Bibliography: p. 183-191. [ND1373.G74C67] 73-84670 ISBN 0-517-51229-7 17.95
1. Marine painting, British. 2. Ships in art. I. Title. BIP

Marine painting—Catalogs.

KENNEDY 758'.2'07401471
Galleries, inc., New York.
Important marine paintings. New York : Kennedy Galleries, 1976. 24 p. : chiefly ill. ; 24 cm. Cover title. [ND1370.K4 1976] 77-353308
1. Kennedy Galleries, inc., New York. 2. Marine painting—Catalogs. I. Title.

MARINE painting : 758'.2
84 illustrations / selected and introduced by Richard Calvocoressi. Oxford : Phaidon ; New York : E. P. Dutton, 1978. 72 p. : chiefly ill. (some col.) ; 42 cm. (Phaidon giant art paperbacks) [ND1370.M37] 78-50079 ISBN 0-7148-1774-0 : 9.95
1. Marine painting—Catalogs. I. Calvocoressi, Richard.

Marine painting—Exhibitions.

EVERSON Museum of Art 758'.2'0973
of Syracuse and Onondaga County.
American ship portraits & marine painting. [Edited by Ruth S. Wilkins. Syracuse, N.Y., 1970] 64 p. illus. (part col.) 22 x 28 cm. Exhibition held Jan. 9-Mar. 8, 1970. [ND1370.E9] 75-112273
1. Marine painting—Exhibitions. 2. Ships—Pictorial works. I. Wilkins, Ruth S., 1926- II. Title.

Marine painting—Technique.

BALLINGER, Harry Russell, 758.2
1892-
Painting boats and harbors. New York, Watson-Guptill Publications, 1959. 96 p. illus. 27 cm. [ND1370.B28] 59-8410
1. Marine painting—Technique. I. Title.

BALLINGER, Harry Russell, 758.2
1892-
Painting sea and shore; a complete guide to the technique of marine painting in oils [by] Harry R. Ballinger. [New ed., edited by Susan E. Meyer] New York, Watson-Guptill Publications [1966] 174 p. illus. (part col.) 27 cm. Combines author's two books, Painting surf and sea, and Painting boats and harbors. [ND1370.B29] 66-18664
1. Marine painting—Technique. I. Title.

BROOKS, Walter, 1921- ed. 758.2
The art of seascape painting: oils, watercolor, polymer. [Designed and edited by Walter Brooks.] [New York] [Odyssey] [1966] 46 p. illus. (part col.) 32 cm. (A Grumbacher library book) [ND1370.B76] 66-17076
1. Marine paintings—Technique. I. Title.

CURTIS, Roger William, 751.4
1910-
How to paint successful seascapes : techniques in oil / by Roger W. Curtis ; edited by Charles Movalli. New York : Watson-Guptill Publications, 1975. 174 p. : ill. ; 29 cm. Includes index. Bibliography:

p. 171. [ND1370.C8 1975] 75-14025 ISBN 0-8230-2467-9 : 15.95
1. Marine painting—Technique. I. Title. BIP

DONALDSON, Theodore W. 758.2
Marine painting. New York, Pitman, c.1963. 1v. (unpaged) illus. (pt. col.) port. 20x26cm. (Pitman 44) 63-15304 1.00 pap.,
1. Marine painting—Technique. I. Title. BIP

OLSON, Herbert Vincent, 1905- 758'.2
Painting the marine scene in watercolor, by Herb Olsen. New York, Reinhold Pub. Corp. [1967] 128 p. (chiefly illus. (part col.)) 32 cm. [ND2270.O55] 67-24853
1. Marine painting—Technique. I. Title.

OLSON, Herbert Vincent, 1905-1973. 751.4'22
Painting the marine scene in watercolor / by Herb Olsen. New York : Galahad Books, [1976] c1967. 128 p. : chiefly ill. (some col.) ; 32 cm. Originally published by Reinhold Pub. Corp., New York. [ND2270.O55 1976] 75-37434 ISBN 0-88365-335-4
1. Marine painting—Technique. 2. Watercolor painting—Technique. I. Title.

RAYNES, John, 1929- 751
Painting seascapes: a creative approach. New York, Watson-Guptill Publications [1972, c1971] 118 p. illus. (part col.) 22 x 29 cm. Bibliography: p. 115. [ND1370.R3] 76-190515 ISBN 0-8230-3855-6 10.95
1. Marine painting—Technique. I. Title.

ROBINSON, E. John, 1932- 751.4'5
Marine painting in oil, by E. John Robinson. [New York, Watson-Guptill Publications [1973] 175 p. illus. (part col.) 22 x 29 cm. Bibliography: p. 172. [ND1370.R62] 73-9504 ISBN 0-8230-3007-5 15.00
1. Marine painting—Technique. I. Title. BIP

ROBINSON, E. John, 1932- 751.4'5
The seascape painter's problem book / by E. John Robinson. New York : Watson-Guptill Publications, 1976. 167 p. : ill. (some col.) ; 29 cm. Includes index. Bibliography: p. 163. [ND1370.R63 1976] 76-17120 ISBN 0-8230-4737-7 : 16.95
1. Marine painting—Technique. I. Title. BIP

SHUMAKER, Philip G. 758.2
Painting the sea [by] Philip G. Shumaker. New York, Sterling Pub. Co. [1966] 48 p. illus., plates (part col.) 29 cm. Bibliography: p. 47. [ND1370.S45 1966] 66-25198
1. Marine painting—Technique. I. Title.

SMART, Borlase. 758'.2'028
Seascape painting step-by-step. Rev. and enl. ed. New York, Watson-Guptill Publications [1969, c1965] 143 p. illus. (part col.) 29 cm. 1934 ed. published under title: The technique of seascape painting. [ND1370.S5 1969] 70-82748 15.00
1. Marine painting—Technique. I. Title. BIP

WOODWARD, Stanley Wingate, 1890- 751.4
Marine painting in oil and water color [by] Stanley Woodward. 3d ed., rev. and enl. New York, Watson-Guptill Publications [1967] 112 p. illus. (part col.) 27 cm. First ed. published in 1947 under title: Adventure in marine painting. [ND1370.W6 1967] 67-10334
1. Marine painting—Technique. I. Title.

WOODWARD, Stanley Wingate, 1890- 751.4
Marine painting in oil and watercolor. New York, Watson-Guptill Publications [1961] 96 p. illus. 26 cm. "Revised and expanded from ... [the author's] Adventure in marine painting." [ND1370.W6 1961] 61-6337
1. Marine painting—Technique. I. Title.

Marine painting—Technique—Juvenile literature.

PELLEW, John C., 1903- 751.4
Painting maritime landscapes [by] John C. Pellew. [New York, Watson-Guptill Publications [1973] 160 p. illus. (part col.) 29 cm. Bibliography: p. 157. Basic techniques for capturing the primary elements of the sea in oil, acrylic, and watercolor. [ND1370.P44] 73-5688 ISBN 0-8230-3695-2 15.00
1. Marine painting—Technique—Juvenile literature. I. Title. BIP

Marini, Marino, 1901—

BUSIGNANI, Alberto. 730'.92'4
Marini. London, New York, Hamlyn; [distributed by Crown Publishers, 1971] 96 p. illus. (part col.) 32 cm. (Twentieth-century masters) Translation of Marino Marini. Bibliography: p. 93-96. [NB623.M32B813 1971b] 74-152353
1. Marini, Marino, 1901-

MARINI, Marino, 1901- 709.24
Complete works. Introd. by Herbert Read. General text by Patrick Waldberg. Catalogues and notes by G. di San Lazzaro. New York, Tudor Pub. Co. [1970] 506 p. illus., plates (part col.), ports. 36 cm. Bibliography: p. 493-[494] [N6923.M27W3] 72-20429
I. Waldberg, Patrick. II. San Lazzaro, Gualtieri di.

MARINI, Marino, 1901- 759.5
Graphic work and paintings. Introd. by P. M. Bardi. New York, H. N. Abrams [1960] xix, 75 p. plates (part col.) 33 cm. Bibliography: p. 73. [ND623.M38B3] 60-14302
I. Bardi, Pietro Maria, 1900-

MARINI, Marino, 1901- 709.24
Marino Marini: sculpture, painting, drawing. Text by A. M. Hammacher. New York, H. N. Abrams [1970] 327 p. (chiefly illus. (part col.), ports.) 31 cm. Bibliography: p. 325-327. [N6923.M27H3] 69-18202 ISBN 0-8109-0274-5
I. Hammacher, Abraham Marie, 1897- II. Title.

MARINI, Marino, 1901- 730.945
The sculpture of Marino Marini. Photos. by Helmut Lederer. Text by Eduard Trier. [Translated from the German by Michael Bullock] New York Praeger [1961] xxiii, 146 p. illus. (part mounted col.) plates, port. 30 cm. (Books that matter) Bibliography: p. 145-146. [NB623.M32L43] 61-11063
I. Lederer, Helmut. II. Trier, Eduard.

Marion County, Tenn.—Antiquities.

FAULKNER, Charles H. 917.68'79'03
Westmoreland-Barber Site (40Mi-11) Nickajack Reservoir, season II [by Charles H. Faulkner and J. B. Graham Knoxville, Dept. of Anthropology, University of Tennessee, 1966. vi l., 150 p. illus., map, 28 plates. 29 cm. "Submitted in accordance with National Park Service contract 14-10-0131-1494." Bibliography: p. 146-150. [E78.T3F32] 67-63151
1. Marion County, Tenn.—Antiquities. I. Graham, J. B., 1916- joint author. II. Title.

Marisol, 1930-

MARISOL, 1930- 730'.92'4
Marisol; [catalogue of an exhibition] September 23 through November 14, 1971, Worcester Art Museum. Worcester, Mass. [Davis Press, 1971] [48] p. illus. 23 cm. [NB439.M3W67] 74-173509
1. Marisol, 1930- I. Worcester, Mass. Art Museum.

Mark, Mary Ellen, 1940—

MARCUS, Adrianne. 770'.92'2
The photojournalist, Mary Ellen Mark & Annie Leibovitz / text by Adrianne Marcus, with the editors of Alskog, inc. [New York] : T. Y. Crowell, [1974] 96 p. : ill. (some col.) ; 29 cm. (Masters of contemporary photography) Title on spine: Mark & Leibovitz: the photojournalist. [TR139.M28] 74-8229 ISBN 0-690-00619-5 : 7.95. ISBN 0-690-00620-9 pbk. : 3.95
1. Mark, Mary Ellen, 1940- 2. Leibovitz, Annie, 1949- 3. Photography, Journalistic. I. Mark, Mary Ellen, 1940- II. Leibovitz, Annie, 1949- III. Alskog, inc. IV. Title. V. Title: Mark & Leibovitz, the photojournalist.

Marks, Saul, 1905-1974.

DREYFUS, John. 070.5'092'4
Saul Marks and his Plantin Press / [by John Dreyfus]. [Los Angeles] : J. Zeitlin, [1975] [11] p. ; 24 cm. "Printed in memory of Saul Marks for Jacob Zeitlin." With device of Ward Ritchie's Laguna Verde press. [Z232.P73D73] 75-325104
1. Marks, Saul, 1905-1974. 2. Plantin Press, Los Angeles. I. Title.

Marlin Firearms Company.

WEST, Bill. 683'.4'0097468
Marlin & Ballard firearms & history. [1st ed.] Azusa, Calif. [1968] 1 v. (various pagings) illus., ports. 24 cm. "1970 Marlin centennial number." [TS533.3.C8W47] 68-29494
1. Marlin Firearms Company. I. Title.

Marling, Jacob, 1774-1833.

NORTH Carolina. Museum of Art, Raleigh. 759.13
Jacob Marling; retrospective exhibition, March 1-April 5, 1964. Raleigh, 1964] 55 p. illus., plan, ports. 26 cm. [ND237.M245N65] 64-64583
1. Marling, Jacob, 1774-1833. I. Title.

Marquetry.

FORGIONE, Joseph. 745.51
Wood inlay; art and craft [by] Joseph Forgione [and] Sterling McIlhany. Demonstration photos. by Alfred Russo. New York, Van Nostrand Reinhold Co. [1973] 102 p. illus. 21 cm. (An Art horizons book) [NK9920.F67] 72-9723 ISBN 0-442-22423-0 8.95
1. Marquetry. I. McIlhany, Sterling, joint author. II. Title.

PENNY, Clifford. 745.51
The fascination of marquetry. New York, Van Nostrand [1955?] 93p. illus. 20cm. [NK9920] 55-14452
1. Marquetry. I. Title.

Marsh, Reginald, 1898-1954.

MARSH, Reginald, 1898-1954. 760'.0924
East side, west side, all around the town; a retrospective exhibition of paintings, watercolors, and drawings, by Reginald Marsh. Tucson, University of Arizona Museum of Art [1969] 175 p. illus., 124 plates (part col.), port. 23 x 29 cm. [NC139.M28A44] 74-625733
I. Arizona. University. Museum of Art. II. Title.

MARSH, Reginald, 1898-1954. 769'.92'4
The prints of Reginald Marsh : an essay and definitive catalog of his linoleum cuts, etchings, engravings, and lithographs / Norman Sasowksy. 1st ed. New York : C. N. Potter ; distributed by Crown Publishers, c1976. 287 p. : chiefly ill. ; 26 cm. Includes index. Bibliography: p. [282]-284. [NE539.M27S28 1976] 75-45374 ISBN 0-517-52493-7 : 15.00
1. Marsh, Reginald, 1898-1954. I. Sasowsky, Norman. II. Title. BIP

MARSH, Reginald, 1898-1954. 759.13
Reginald Marsh, by Lloyd Goodrich. New York, H. N. Abrams [1972] 307 p. illus. 33 x 37 cm. Bibliography: p. 299-304. [ND237.M246G63] 72-2198 ISBN 0-8109-0280-X 50.00
I. Goodrich, Lloyd, 1897-

MARSH, Reginald, 1898-1954. 769.2
Reginald Marsh: etchings, engravings, lithographs, by Norman Sasowsky. Pref. by A. Hyatt Mayor; introd. by Isabel Bishop. New York, Praeger [1956] x, 60 p. (p. 1-46 illus.) 25 cm. (Books that matter) Catalog of the artist's works from which impressions may be obtained at the Kennedy Galleries, inc., New York ([4] p.) laid in. [NE539.M27S3] 56-1609
I. Sasowsky, Norman.

MARSH, Reginald, 1898-1954. 741.9'73
The sketchbooks of Reginald Marsh. [Compiled by] Edward Laning. Greenwich, Conn., New York Graphic Society [1973] 168 p. illus. (part col.) 27 cm. [NC139.M28L36] 73-78793 ISBN 0-8212-0538-2 15.00
1. Marsh, Reginald, 1898-1954. 2. New York (City) in art. I. Laning, Edward, 1906- comp.

OGUNQUIT, Me. Museum of Art. 709'.73
Paintings and drawings by Reginald Marsh. Paintings and sculpture by Americans of our times. Ogunquit, Me. [1970] [36] p. illus. 24 cm. Catalogue of an exhibition held July 4-Sept. 7, 1970. [N6512.O36] 73-171377 0.25
1. Marsh, Reginald, 1898-1954. 2. Art, American—Exhibitions. 3. Art, Modern—20th century—United States. I. Marsh, Reginald, 1898-1954. II. Title. III. Title: Paintings and drawings by Americans of our times.

Marshall, John, 1755-1835—Portraits, caricatures, etc.—Catalogs.

OLIVER, Andrew, 1906- 704.94'23'0973
The portraits of John Marshall / Andrew Oliver. Charlottesville : Published for the Institute of Early American History and Culture, Williamsburg, Va., by the University Press of Virginia, 1977. xi, 209 p., [1] leaf of plates : ill. ; 24 cm. Includes bibliographical references and index. [E302.6.M4O44] 76-13648 ISBN 0-8139-0633-4 : 12.50
1. Marshall, John, 1755-1835—Portraits, caricatures, etc.—Catalogs. I. Institute of Early American History and Culture, Williamsburg, Va. II. Title. BIP

Marshall, John, 1936—

MARSHALL, John, 1936- 739.2'3'724
John Marshall. Seattle [1973] 1 portfolio ([6] l., [15] l. of illus.) 22 cm. [NK7198.M37A48] 74-184591
1. Marshall, John, 1936- 2. Silversmithing—United States.

Marston, William Moulton, 1893-1947.

†FLEISHER, Michael. 741.5'973
The Wonder Woman encyclopedia / by Michael L. Fleisher, assisted by Janet E. Lincoln. New York : Collier Books, 1976. p. cm. (His The encyclopedia of comic book heroes ; v. 2) [PN6725.F5 1976b vol. 2] [PN6728.W6] 76-958 ISBN 0-02-080080-0 ISBN 0-02-538710-3 : 14.95
1. Marston, William Moulton, 1893-1947. Wonder Woman. I. Lincoln, Janet E., joint author. II. Title.

Martha's Vineyard, Mass.

EISENSTAEDT, Alfred. 779'.9'974494
Martha's Vineyard / photos. by Alfred Eisenstaedt ; text by Henry Beetle Hough. New York : Penguin Books, [1979] p. cm. [F72.M5E22 1979] 78-27369 ISBN 0-14-005165-1 pbk. : 5.95
1. Martha's Vineyard, Mass. I. Hough, Henry Beetle, 1896- II. Title. BIP

Martha's Vineyard, Mass.—Antiquities.

RITCHIE, William Augustus, 1903- 917.44'94
The archaeology of Martha's Vineyard: a framework for the prehistory of southern New England; a study in coastal ecology and adaptation, by William A. Ritchie. [1st ed.] Garden City, N.Y., Published for the American Museum of Natural History [by] the Natural History Press, 1969. xvi, 253 p. illus. 27 cm. Bibliography: p. 235-240. [E78.M4R5] 69-10987 15.00
1. Martha's Vineyard, Mass.—Antiquities. 2. Indians of North America—Massachusetts—Antiquities. I. Title.

Martienssen, Rex Distin, 1905-1942.

HERBERT, Gilbert. 720'.92'4 B
Martienssen and the international style : the modern movement in South African architecture / Gilbert Herbert. Cape Town

: Balkema (A.A.), 1976 xi, 283 p. : ill. ; 29 cm. Includes index. Bibliography: p. 271-278. [NA1596.M37H47] 76-350259 ISBN 0-86961-038-4 : 36.00
1. Martienssen, Rex Distin, 1905-1942. 2. International style (Architecture)—South Africa. 3. Architecture, Modern—20th century—South Africa. I. Title.
Distributed by Wittenborn

Martime Province, Siberia—Antiq.

OKLADNIKOV, Aleksei Pavlovich 915.77033
The Soviet Far East in antiquity; an archaeological and historical study of the Maritime Region of the U. S. S. R. Ed. by Henry N. Michael [Toronto] Pub. for the Arctic Inst. of North Amer. by Univ. of Toronto Pr. [1966, c.1965] v, 280p. illus., maps. 26cm. (Anthrop. of the North: trs. from Russian sources, no.6) At head of title: Arctic Institute of North America. Includes tr. of the t. p. of the Russian ed. reading The remote past of the Maritime Region; notes on the ancient and medieval history of the Maritime Kray [by] A. P. Okladnikov. Vladivostok, Pub. House of the Maritime Region, 1959. Bibl. [GN4.A65] 66-1592 6.00 pap.,
1. Martime Province, Siberia—Antiq. 2. Maritime Province, Siberia—Hist. I. Michael, Henry N., ed. II. Arctic Institute of North America. III. Title. IV. Series. BIP

Martin, Agnes, 1912—

MARTIN, Agnes, 1912- 709'.2'4
Agnes Martin. [Philadelphia, Printed by Falcon Press, 1973] 48 p. illus. 23 cm. Catalog of an exhibition held at the Institute of Contemporary Art, University of Pennsylvania, Philadelphia, Jan. 22-Mar. 1, 1973. Bibliography: p. 47-48. [N6537.M38P46] 73-163966
1. Martin, Agnes, 1912- I. Pennsylvania. University. Institute of Contemporary Art.

Martin, Alastair Bradley—Art collections.

THE Guennol 707'.4'01471
Collection : [exhibition] / edited by Ida Ely Rubin. New York : Metropolitan Museum of Art, c1975- v. : ill. ; 31 cm. Held at the Metropolitan Museum of Art in 1969. Includes bibliographical references. [N5220.M39G83] 75-33291 ISBN 0-87099-144-2 : 18.50
1. Martin, Alastair Bradley—Art collections. 2. Martin, Edith—Art collections. 3. Art—Exhibitions. I. Rubin, Ida Ely. II. New York (City). Metropolitan Museum of Art. BIP

Martin, Fletcher, 1904—

EBERSOLE, Barbara Warren. 1915- 927.5
Fletcher Martin. Foreword [by] William Saroyan. Gainesville, University of Florida Press, 1954. xvii, 51p. illus., port. 29cm. [ND237.M247E2] 54-7231
1. Martin, Fletcher, 1904- I. Title. BIP

MARTIN, Fletcher, 1904- 759.13
Fletcher Martin / H. Lester Cooke, Jr. New York : Abrams, 1977. 232 p. : ill. (some col.) ; 28 x 30 cm. Chiefly ill. Includes index. Bibliography: p. 226-228. [ND237.M247C66] 75-2472 ISBN 0-8109-0319-9 : 37.50
1. Martin, Fletcher, 1904- I. Cooke, Hereward Lester. BIP

Martin, Fred, 1927—

MARTIN, Fred, 1927- 760'.092'4
Fred Martin; paintings, collages, drawings, prints. [San Francisco, San Francisco Museum of Art, c1973] [48] p. illus. 21 x 28 cm. Catalog of an exhibition held at the San Francisco Museum of Art, Nov. 2-Dec. 30, 1973, with text by Suzanne Foley. Bibliography: p. [47] [N6537.M39F64] 73-88452
1. Martin, Fred, 1927- I. Foley, Suzanne. II. San Francisco. Museum of Art.

Martin, John, 1789-1854.

FEAVER, William. 759.2 B
The art of John Martin / William Feaver. Oxford : Clarendon Press, 1975. xv, 256 p., [9] leaves of plates : ill. ; 26 cm. Includes index. Bibliography: p. 239. [ND497.M37F42] 75-332728 ISBN 0-19-817334-2 : £7.00
1. Martin, John, 1789-1854. I. Martin, John, 1789-1854. II. Title. BIP

Martin, Keith, 1911- —Exhibitions.

BALTIMORE. Museum of Art. 709'.2'4
Keith Martin, collages : an exhibition, September 13-October 30, 1977, Baltimore Museum of Art. [Baltimore] : The Museum, [1977] 16 p. : ill. ; 28 cm. [N6537.M393B34 1977] 77-153882
1. Martin, Keith, 1911- —Exhibitions. I. Title.

Martin, Paul, 1864-1944.

FLUKINGER, Roy, 1947- 770'.92'4 B
Paul Martin : Victorian photographer / by Roy Flukinger, Larry Schaaf, and Standish Meacham. Austin : University of Texas Press, c1977. p. cm. Includes index. Bibliography: p. [TR140.M35F59] 77-4764 ISBN 0-292-76436-7 : 24.95
1. Martin, Paul, 1864-1944. 2. Photographers—England—Biography. I. Schaaf, Larry, 1947- joint author. II. Meacham, Standish, joint author. BIP

Martin, Saint, Bp. of Tours, 4th century—Art.

FREEMAN, Margaret Beam, 1899- 746.4'4
The St. Martin embroideries; a fifteenth-century series illustrating the life and legend of St. Martin of Tours [by] Margaret B. Freeman. [New York] Metropolitan Museum of Art; distributed by New York Graphic Society, Greenwich, Conn. [1968] 131, [1] p. illus. (part col.) 29 cm. Bibliography: p. 130-[132] [NK9208.F7] 68-21564 6.95
1. Martin, Saint, Bp. of Tours, 4th century—Art. 2. Embroidery, Medieval. I. Title. BIP

Martinez, Maria Montoya.

PETERSON, Susan. 738.3'092'4 B
The living tradition of Maria Martinez / Susan Peterson. 1st ed. Tokyo : Kodansha International ; New York : distributed through Harper & Row, 1977. 300 p. : ill. (some col.) ; 31 cm. Includes index. Bibliography: p. 289-296. [E99.S213M377] 77-75373 ISBN 0-87011-319-4 : 35.00
1. Martinez, Maria Montoya. 2. San Ildefonso, N.M.—Biography. 3. Pottery—New Mexico—San Ildefonso. 4. Indians of North America—New Mexico—Pottery. I. Title. BIP

Martinez, Maria (Montoya)—Juvenile literature.

*HYDE, Hazel. 738.3'092'4 [B]
Maria making pottery. [Santa Fe, N.M.] [Sunstone Pr.] [1973] 27 p. illus., ports. 15 x 23 cm. [E99] ISBN 0-913270-20-2 1.50 (pbk)
1. Martinez, Maria (Montoya)—Juvenile literature. 2. Pottery—Pueblo Indian—Juvenile literature. 3. Pottery—American—Juvenile literature. I. Title.
Publisher's address, P.O. Box 2321, Santa Fe, NM 87501.

NELSON, Mary Carroll. 738.3'092'4 B
Maria Martinez. Minneapolis, Dillon Press [1972] 77 p. illus. 24 cm. (The Story of an American Indian) A biography of the Pueblo Indian woman who became renowned for her skill in pottery. [E99.S213N44] 92 78-172871 ISBN 0-87518-038-8
1. Martinez, Maria (Montoya)—Juvenile literature. I. Title. BIP

NELSON, Mary Carroll. 738.3'092'4 B
Maria Martinez. Minneapolis, Dillon Press [1974, c1972] 74 p. illus. 24 cm. (The Story of an American Indian) A biography of the Pueblo Indian woman who became renowned for her skill in pottery. [E99.S213N44 1974] 92 74-12323 ISBN 0-87518-098-1
1. Martinez, Maria Montoya—Juvenile literature. I. Title.

Martinez Montanes, Juan, 1568-1648.

PROSKE, Beatrice Irene (Gilman) 1899- 730'.924 B
Juan Martinez Montanes; Sevillian sculptor, by Beatrice Gilman Proske. New York, Hispanic Society of America, 1967. ix, 190 p. 212 plates. 26 cm. (Hispanic notes & monographs; essays, studies, and brief biographies. Peninsular series) [NB813.M36P7] 67-66244
1. Martinez Montanes, Juan, 1568-1648. I. Title. II. Series. BIP

Martinez, Xavier, 1869-1943.

NEUBERT, George W. 759.13
Xavier Martinez (1869-1943) by George W. Neubert. Exhibition at the Oakland Museum Art Special Gallery, February 12 through April 7, 1974 [Oakland, Calif., 1974] 71 p. illus. (part col.) 25 cm. "Catalog of the exhibition.": p. 63-69. Bibliography: p. 61-62. [ND237.M253N48] 74-75062
1. Martinez, Xavier, 1869-1943. I. Oakland Museum.

Martinique—Description and travel.

BRUNETTI, Cosimo, ca.1620-ca.1680. 917.298'2
Cosimo Brunetti: three relations of the West Indies in 1659-1660 [edited by Susan Heller Anderson Philadelphia, American Philosophical Society, 1969. 49 p. maps. 30 cm. (Transactions of the American Philosophical Society, new ser., v. 59, pt. 6) Text in French or Italian, with editor's introduction in English. An outgrowth of the editor's thesis, Brown University. Contents.Contents.—Introduction, by S. H. Anderson.—Relation des Isles de l'Amerique.—Information succinte de quelques establissmens aux pays de l'Amerique Meridionale.—Relazione dell'Isole de Amerike. Bibliography: p. 47. [Q11.P6 n.s., vol. 59, pt. 6] 72-93501 3.00
1. Martinique—Description and travel. 2. Caribbean area—Description and travel. I. Anderson, Susan Heller, ed. II. Title: Three relations of the West Indies in 1659-1660. III. Series: American Philosophical Society, Philadelphia. Transactions, new ser., v. 59, pt. 6

Marussig, Piero.

MARUSSIG, Piero. 741.9'45
Marussig : disegni / Vanni Scheiwiller. [Oggiono] : Edizioni della seggiola, 1976. 128 p. : ill. ; 29 cm. (Documenti del disegno ; 3) English, French and Italian. Bibliography: p. 125-[129]. [NC257.M37S33] 77-478232
1. Marussig, Piero. I. Scheiwiller, Vanni. II. Title. III. Series.

Marvel Comics Group.

LEE, Stan. 741.5'973
Origins of Marvel Comics. New York, Simon and Schuster [1974] 254 p. illus. 26 cm. [PN6725.L4] 74-11141 ISBN 0-671-21864-6
1. Marvel Comics Group. 2. Comic books, strips, etc.—United States. I. Title. BIP

LEE, Stan. 741.5'973
Son of Origins of Marvel Comics / Stan Lee. New York : Simon and Schuster, [1975] 249 p. : col. ill. ; 26 cm. [PN6725.L44] 75-20029 ISBN 0-671-22170-1 : 10.95 ISBN 0-671-22166-3 pbk. : 6.95
1. Marvel Comics Group. 2. Comic books, strips, etc.—United States. I. Title. BIP

LEE, Stan. 741.5'973
The superhero women / by Stan Lee. New York : Simon and Schuster, c1977. p. cm. [PN6725.L424] 77-9500 ISBN 0-671-22766-1 : 10.95 ISBN 0-671-22928-1 pbk. : 6.95
1. Marvel Comics Group. 2. Comic books, strips, etc.—United States. 3. Women—Caricatures and cartoons. I. Title. BIP

Marx, Karl, 1818-1883.

*BAXANDALL, Lee. comp. 335.438701
Marx & Engels on literature & art. St. Louis, Telos Press [1974, c1973] 175 p. 19 cm. Bibliography: p. 157-172. [HX521.S63] 73-93501 ISBN 0-914386-01-8 6.95
1. Marx, Karl, 1818-1883. 2. Engels, Friedrich, 1820-1895. 3. Communism and art. I. Morawski, Stefan. joint comp. II. Title.
Pbk. 2.95; ISBN 0-914386-02-6. BIP

Marx, Robert Burle, 1909-

BARDI, Pietro Maria, 1900- 712.0981
The tropical gardens of Burle Marx. Photos. by M. Gautherot. New York, Reinhold [c.1964] 155p. illus. (pt. col.) 30cm. English, German, and Italian. Bibl. 63-19224 15.00
1. Marx, Robert Burle, 1909- 2. Landscape architecture—Brazil. 3. Tropical plants—Pictorial works. I. Title.

Mary Magdalene, Saint—Art.

DE JONG, Ralph. 755'.6
The life of Mary Magdalene in the paintings of the great masters / Ralph De Jong. [Albuquerque, N.M.] : Gloucester Art Press, [1979]. 14 leaves, [14] leaves of plates : ports. ; 28 cm. Cover title. [ND1430.D43] 79-834 ISBN 0-918968-3 : 19.75
1. Mary Magdalene, Saint—Art. 2. Painting. BIP

EMMINGHAUS, Johannes H. 704.9486
Mary Magdalene [by] Joh. H. Emminghard Kuppers. [Tr. from German by Hans Hermann Rosenwald] Recklinghausen [Ger.] A. Bongers; dist. Taplinger [New York, c.1964] 74p. col. illus. 18cm. (Saints in legend & art, v. 5) [N8080.E4413] 67-4499 2.50 bds.,
1. Mary Magdalene, Saint—Art. I. Kuppers, Leonhard, 1903- II. Title.

MALVERN, Marjorie M. 704.948'6
Venus in sackcloth : the Magdalen's origins and metamorphoses / by Marjorie M. Malvern. Carbondale : Southern Illinois University Press, [1975] xiii, 219 p. : ill. ; 25 cm. Includes index. Bibliography: p. 207-212. [NX652.M27M34] 75-6197 ISBN 0-8093-0707-3 : 8.95
1. Mary Magdalene, Saint—Art. 2. Mary Magdalene, Saint. 3. Arts. I. Title.

Mary Stuart, Queen of the Scots, 1542-1587.

SWAIN, Margaret H. 746.4'4 B
The needlework of Mary, Queen of Scots [by] Margaret Swain. New York, Van Nostrand Reinhold [1973] 128 p. illus. (part col.) 29 cm. Bibliography: p. 127. [DA787.A3S9] 73-1636 ISBN 0-442-29962-1 12.50
1. Mary Stuart, Queen of the Scots, 1542-1587. 2. Needlework—Great Britain—History. I. Title.

Mary, Virgin — Art.

DENNY, Don. 704.948'4
The Annunciation from the right : from early Christian times to the sixteenth century / Don Denny. New York : Garland Pub., 1977. p. cm. (Outstanding dissertations in the fine arts) Originally presented as the author's thesis, New York University, 1965. Bibliography: p. [N8070.D46 1977] 76-23611 ISBN 0-8240-2683-7 lib.bdg. : 32.50
1. Mary, Virgin—Art. 2. Mary, Virgin—Annunciation—Pictorial works. 3. Christian art and symbolism. 4. Christian art and symbolism—Renaissance, 1450-1600. I. Title. II. Series. BIP

ELWESS, Brewster. 755'.55
The most beautiful Jewish woman in the

SUBJECT INDEX MASKS—JUVENILE LITERATURE.

history of mankind / Brewster Elwess. Albuquerque : Gloucester Art Press, [1978] p. cm. Bibliography; p. [ND1430.E48] 78-26103 ISBN 0-930582-17-9 : 12.75 ISBN 0-930582-07-1 : 47.75
1. Mary, Virgin—Art. 2. Painting. I. Title.

FORSYTH, Ilene H. 731'.88'550944
The Throne of Wisdom; wood sculptures of the madonna in Romanesque France [by] Ilene H. Forsyth. Princeton, N.J., Princeton University Press [1972] xviii, 226, [64] p. illus. 29 cm. A revision of the author's thesis, Columbia, 1960. Bibliography: p. 209-218. [NB1255.F8F67 1972] 72-166372 ISBN 0-691-03837-6 30.00
1. Mary, Virgin—Art. 2. Sculpture, Romanesque—France. 3. Sculpture, French. 4. Wood-carving, French. I. Title.

GERHARD, Heinz Paul 755.55
The icons of the Mother of God [by] H. P. Gerhard. Tr. by Hans Rosenwald. [n.p.] Catholic Art Bk. Guild, [New York, dist. Taplinger 1966, c1964] 74p. 16 col. plates. 18cm. (Pictorial lib. of Eatern Church art, v.1) On cover: Icons: the Mother of God. Tr. of Muttergottes. [N8070.G433 1966] 66-9083 2.50 bds.,
1. Mary, Virgin—Art. I. Title. II. Title: Icons: the Mother of God.

GHEON, Henri, 1875-1944. 755.5
Mary, Mother of God. Introd. by Henri Gheon, with critical notices by Renee Zeller. Translated by Yetta Arenstein and Ethel Duncan. Chicago, H. Regnery Co. [1955] 194p. illus. (part mounted col.) 30cm. [N8070.G452] 55-4878
1. Mary, Virgin—Art. I. Zeller, Benee C. T. II. Title.

GUITTON, Jean. 704.94855
The Madonna. Illus. selected by Chantal Renaudeau d'Arc. Book design by Roger Krause. New York, Tudor Pub. Co. [1963] 143 p. illus. (part mounted col.) 22 cm. "Errata" slip inserted. Full name: Jean Marie Pierre Guitton. [N8070.G85] 63-25088
1. Mary, Virgin — Art. I. Title.

HARTMAN, Charles 755.55
The life of Mary, mother of Jesus; 91 masterworks of art. Text selection, introd. by Charles Hertman. Pref. by Walter M. Abbott. New York, Guild [dist. Golden, c.1963] 191p. col. plates. 28cm. Text selections in poetry and prose. 63-25570 10.00
1. Mary, Virgin—Art. 2. Mary, Virgin—Poetry. I. Title.

HARTMAN, Charles. 200
The life of Mary, mother of Jesus; 91 masterworks of art. Text selection and introd. by Charles Hartman. Pref. by Walter M. Abbott. New York, Guild Press [c1963] 191 p. col. plates. 28 cm. Text selections in poetry and prose. [N8070.H33] 63-25570
1. Mary, Virgin — Art. 2. Mary, Virgin — Poetry. I. Title.

HURLL, Estelle May, 704.948'55
1863-1924.
The Madonna in art. Boston, L. C. Page, 1898. Detroit, Gale Research Co., 1974. p. cm. Original ed. issued in series: Art lovers' series. Bibliography: p. [N8070.H9 1974] 78-159857 ISBN 0-8103-4083-6
1. Mary, Virgin—Art. 2. Painting, Renaissance. I. Title. II. Series: Art lovers' series.

JAMESON, Anna Brownell 704.948'55
(Murphy) 1794-1860.
Legends of the Madonna as represented in the fine arts. Forming the third series of Sacred and legendary art. By Mrs. Jameson. Illustrated by etchings and woodcuts. New ed. London, New York, Longmans, Green, 1890. Detroit, Gale Research Co., 1972. lxxv, 344 p. illus. 22 cm. Includes bibliographical references. [N8070.J36 1972] 70-89273
1. Mary, Virgin—Art. 2. Mary, Virgin—Legends. I. Title. BIP

KUPPERS, Leonhard, 1903- 200
Mary. [Translated from the German by Hans Hermann Rosenwald] Recklinghausen [Ger.] A. Oongers; distributed by Taplinger Pub. Co. [New York, 1967, c1965] 64 p. col. illus. 18 cm. (The Saints in legend and art, v. 14) [N8070.K7913] 67-4425
1. Mary, Virgin — Art. I. Title.

LEVI D'ANCONA, Mirella. 704.9485
The iconography of the Immaculate Conception in the Middle Ages and early Renaissance. [New York] Published by the College Art Association of America in conjunction with the Art bulletin, 1957. 82p., [8]p. of illus. 31cm. (Monographs on archaeology and fine arts, 7) [N8070.D3] 58-2663
1. Mary, Virgin—Art. 2. Immaculate Conception. I. Title.

THE most beautiful woman in the world / Rudolph Reni-Pallavicini. 755'.55
[Albuquerque, N.M.] : American Classical College Press, [1975] p. cm. Includes index. Bibliography: p. [N8070.M69] 74-33845 ISBN 0-913314-52-8 : 10.00
1. Mary, Virgin—Art. I. Reni-Pallavicini, Rudolph.

PARIS, Jean, 1921- 750' 117
Painting and linguistics : two lectures given at the College of Fine Arts in Carnegie-Mellon University on March 12 and 19, 1974 / Jean Paris. Pittsburgh : College of Fine Arts, Carnegie-Mellon University, [1975] 72 p. : ill. ; 23 cm. (Praxis/poetics series ; no. 1) Includes bibliographical references. [ND1140.P313] 75-310050
1. Mary, Virgin—Art. 2. Painting—Psychological aspects. 3. Visual perception. I. Title. II. Series.

PETTIT, Rhea Ferne. 704.948'55
The Madonna story. Montezuma, Iowa, Sutherland Print. Co. [1970] 137 p. illus. (part col.), port. 26 cm. Bibliography: p. 135. [N8070.P47] 73-134945 7.95
1. Mary, Virgin—Art. 2. Flower arrangement. I. Title.

Mary, Virgin—Cultus.

BACIGALUPA, Andrea, 1923- 759.13
Santos and saints' days. [1st ed.] Santa Fe, N.M., Sunstone Press, 1972. 32 p. illus. 22 cm. [BX2333.B3] 73-154725 ISBN 0-913270-09-1 2.95
1. Mary, Virgin—Cultus. 2. Saints—Cultus. 3. Santos (Art) I. Title.

Masaccio, Tommaso Guidi, known as, 1401-1428?

BERTI, Luciano. 759'.5
Masaccio. University Park, Pennsylvania State University Press, 1967. xii, 183 p. illus. (part col.), facsim., plan. 32 cm. Bibliography: p. 167-174. [ND623.M43B43] 66-25464
1. Masaccio, Tommaso Guidi, known as, 1401-1428? BIP

MASACCIO, Tommaso 759.9493'2
Guidi, known as, 1401-1428;
All the paintings of Masaccio. Text by Ugo Procacci. Translated by Paul Colacicchi. New York, Hawthorn Books [1962] 50p. plates (part col.) 18cm. (The Complete library of world art, v. 6) 'Bibliographical note;: p. 50. [ND623.M43P763] 62-10520
I. Procacci. Ugo. II. Title. III. Series.

Masereel, Frans, 1889-1972.

MASEREEL, Frans, 760'.092'4 B
1889-1972.
Frans Masereel / Roger Avermaete ; bibliography and catalogue by Pierre Vorms and Hanns-Conon von der Gabelentz. [Antwerp] : Fonds Mercator ; New York : Rizzoli, [1977, c1976] 318 p. : ill. (some col.) ; 35 cm. [N6973.M32A88] 76-11242 ISBN 0-8478-0034-2 : 70.00
1. Masereel, Frans, 1889-1972. I. Avermaete, Roger, 1893- II. Vorms, Pierre. III. Gabelentz, Hanns Conon von der, 1892-

Masks.

ALKEMA, Chester Jay. 731.7'5
Masks. New York, Sterling Pub. Co. [1971] 48 p. illus. (part col.) 20 cm. (Little craft book series) Directions for making a variety of masks from paper, papier mache, and cardboard. [TT898.A44 1971] 75-151712 ISBN 0-8069-5166-4
1. Masks. 2. Handicraft. I. Title.

ALKEMA, Chester Jay. 646.5
Monster masks. Photos. by the author. New York, Sterling Pub. Co. [1973] 48 p. illus. 20 cm. (Little craft book series) Instructions for making ghoulish masks from materials such as egg cartons, fibreboard, plastic foam, and aluminum. [TT898.A45] 72-95208 ISBN 0-8069-5256-3 2.95
1. Masks. I. Title. BIP

BARANSKI, Matthew. 731.75
Mask making: creative methods and techniques; illustrated by the author. Worcester, Mass., Davis Press, c1954. 101 p. illus. 27 cm. [GT1747.B3] 54-12542
1. Masks. I. Title. BIP

BIHALJI-MERIN, Oto, 1904- 391
Great masks. [Translated from the German by Herma Plummer] New York, H. N. Abrams [1972, c1971] 231 p. illus. (part col.) 29 cm. Translation of Masken der Welt. Bibliography: p. 229-230. [GT1747.B513] 74-156278 ISBN 0-8109-0276-1 17.50
1. Masks. I. Title.

GRATER, Michael, 1923- 745.54
Paper faces. Illustrated by the author. Photos. by Geoffrey Goode. New York, Taplinger Pub. Co. [1968, c1967] 134 p. illus. 26 cm. [TT870.G69 1968] 68-14775 5.50
1. Masks. 2. Paper work. I. Title.

GRATER, Michael, 1923- 745.54
Paper faces. Illustrated by the author. Photos. by Geoffrey Goode. New York, Taplinger Pub. Co. [1968, c1967] 134 p. illus. 26 cm. Specific suggestions, directions, techniques, and patterns for designing and decorating all kinds of masks, simple and elaborate, for all occasions. [TT870.G69 1968] AC 68
1. Masks. 2. Paper work. I. Title. BIP

LOMMEL, Andreas. 731'.75
Masks; their meaning and function. Translated by Nadia Fowler. New York, McGraw-Hill [1972] 227 p. illus. (part col.) 29 cm. Translation of Masken. Bibliography: p. 223-226. [GT1747.L613 1972] 74-148992 ISBN 0-07-038652-8 17.95
1. Masks.

MEYEROWITZ, Rick, 1943- 391'.43
Nose masks I : silly nasal disguises / Rick Meyerowitz. New York : Workman Pub. Co., [1978] p. cm. [GT1747.M47] 78-13100 ISBN 0-89480-041-8 (v. 1) pbk. : 3.95
1. Masks. 2. Masks—Anecdotes, facetiae, satire, etc. I. Title.

MEYEROWITZ, Rick, 1943- 391'.43
Nose masks II : serious nasal disguises / Rick Meyerowitz. New York : Workman Pub. Co., [1978] p. cm. [GT1747.M48] 78-13101 ISBN 0-89480-042-6 (v. 2) pbk. : 3.95
1. Masks. 2. Masks—Anecdotes, facetiae, satire, etc. I. Title.

SHALLECK, Jamie. 391'.43
Masks. New York, Viking Press [1973] xi, 163 p. illus. 23 cm. "A Subsistence Press book." Includes bibliographical references. [GT1747.S48 1973] 72-78988 ISBN 0-670-45996-8 12.50
1. Masks. I. Title.

SNOOK, Barbara. 731'.75
Making masks for school plays. [1st American ed.] Boston, Plays, inc. [1972] 96 p. illus. 23 cm. Bibliography: p. [93]-94. [TT898.S58 1972] 76-180545 ISBN 0-8238-0131-4 5.95
1. Masks. 2. College and school drama. I. Title. BIP

Masks—Africa, Sub-Saharan—Catalogs.

BLEAKLEY, Robert. 732'.2'0967
African masks / Robert Bleakley. New York : St. Martin's Press, 1978. [88] p. : 40 col. ill. ; 28 cm. [NB1255.S88B56 1978] 77-95303 ISBN 0-312-00970-4 pbk. : 5.95
1. Masks—Africa, Sub-Saharan—Catalogs. 2. Sculpture, African—Africa, Sub-Saharan—Catalogs. 3. Sculpture, Primitive—Africa, Sub-Saharan—Catalogs. I. Title.

Masks, African.

SEGY, Ladislas. 731'.75'096
Masks of Black Africa / Ladislas Segy. New York : Dover Publications, 1976. 248 p., [1] leaf of plates : ill. ; 28 cm. Bibliography: p. 247. [GN645.S39 1976] 74-15005 ISBN 0-486-23181-X pbk. : 6.00
1. Masks, African. I. Title. BIP

Masks, African—Africa, West.

MONTI, Franco. 731.7'5'096
African masks; [translated from the Italian by Andrew Hale]. London, New York, Hamlyn, 1969. 3-157 p. 69 col. illus. 20 cm. (Cameo) Translation of Le maschere africane. [NB1097.W4M613] 73-437272 ISBN 6-00-012166- 15/-
1. Masks, African—Africa, West. 2. Sculpture, Primitive—Africa, West. I. Title.

Masks, African—Exhibitions.

HARVARD University. 732'.2'096
Peabody Museum of Archaeology and Ethnology.
Masterpieces of black African art; an exhibition. [Text by] Lee Parsons. Cambridge, Mass. [1969] [24] p. illus. 23 cm. Bibliographical footnotes. [NB1080.H37] 77-15128 1.25
1. Masks, African—Exhibitions. 2. Negro art. I. Parsons, Lee A., 1932- II. Title. BIP

Masks—Congo.

SIDOFF, Phillip G. 732'.2'096751
Art of the Congo / by Phillip G. Sidoff. [Milwaukee] : Milwaukee Public Museum, 1974. iv, 42 p. : ill. ; 23 cm. (Special publication in anthropology and history ; no. 1) Bibliography: p. 41-42. [NB1099.C6S52] 76-353957
1. Masks—Congo. 2. Sculpture, Congo. 3. Sculpture, Primitive—Congo. I. Title. II. Series.

Masks—Exhibitions.

CALIFORNIA. University. 391'.43
University at Los Angeles. Museum of Cultural History.
Image and identity; the role of the mask in various cultures. [Los Angeles, 1972] 36 p. illus. 24 cm. An exhibition organized by the UCLA Museum of Cultural History, April 11-June 3, 1972, and held at the Museum of Cultural History Galleries. [GT1747.C3] 72-182843
1. Masks—Exhibitions. I. Title.

Masks—Japan.

BETHE, Monica. 731'.75'0952
Bugaku masks / Kyotaro Nishikawa ; translated and adapted by Monica Bethe. 1st ed. Tokyo ; New York: Kodansha International Ltd. and Shibundo, 1978. 194 p. : ill. ; 27 cm. (Japanese arts library ; v. 5) Includes index. Bibliography: p. [187]-189. [GT1747.B4313] 77-75971 ISBN 0-87011-312-7 : 12.95
1. Masks—Japan. 2. Bugaku. I. Nishikawa, Kyotaro. II. Title. III. Series. BIP

Masks—Juvenile literature.

†COX, Marcia Lynn. 792'.027
Make-up monsters / by Marcia Lynn Cox. New York : Grosset & Dunlap, c1976. 94 p. : ill. ; 22 cm. (Tempo books) Complete make-up instructions for twelve monster masks including a werewolf, a vampire, and a mummy. [TT898.C68] 76-19461 ISBN 0-448-12396-7 pbk. : 0.95.
1. Masks—Juvenile literature. 2. Monsters—Juvenile literature. 3. Make-up, Theatrical—Juvenile literature. I. Title.

GARDNER, Richard M. 792
101 masks; false faces and make-up for all ages, all occasions. Written and illustrated by Richard Cummings. New York, D. McKay Co. [1968] xiv, 173 p. illus. 21 cm. [TT160.G3] 68-17510

1. Masks—Juvenile literature. I. Title.

HETZER, Linda. 745.5
Playtime crafts / by Linda Hetzer ; photos. by Steven Mays ; [illustrators, Lynn Matus, Sally Shimizu]. Milwaukee : Raintree, c1978. 48 p. : ill. (some col.) ; 27 cm. Introduces various techniques in making musical instruments and masks and doing magic tricks. Includes step-by-step instructions for a selection of projects involving each craft. [TT898.H47] 77-28790 ISBN 0-8172-1182-9 lib.bdg. : 7.93
1. Masks—Juvenile literature. 2. Musical instruments—Construction—Juvenile literature. 3. Conjuring—Juvenile literature. I. Mays, Steven. II. Shimizu, Sally. III. Matus, Lynn. IV. Title. BIP

LALIBERTE, Norman. 391'.43
Masks, face coverings, and headgear [by] Norman Laliberte and Alex Mogelon. Demonstration photos. by Fortune Monte. New York, Van Nostrand Reinhold Co. [1973] 105 p. chiefly illus., part col. 21 cm. (An Art horizons book) Traces the history of masks and headgear, discusses their various uses, and suggests projects for making a variety of head coverings. [GT1747.L3] 72-4131 ISBN 0-442-24606-4 8.95
1. Masks—Juvenile literature. I. Mogelon, Alex, joint author. II. Monte, Fortune, illus. III. Title.

MEYER, Carolyn. 731'.75
Mask magic / by Carolyn Meyer ; illustrated by Melanie Gaines Arwin. 1st ed. New York : Harcourt Brace Jovanovich, c1978. 90 p. : ill. ; 22 cm. Includes index. Information on how masks have been used by various peoples over the centuries and directions for making similar masks out of easily available materials. [TT898.M48] 77-14080 ISBN 0-15-253107-6 : 7.95
1. Masks—Juvenile literature. I. Arwin, Melanie Gaines. II. Title. BIP

PETERS, Joan. 731'.75
Creative masks for stage and school / Joan Peters and Anna Sutcliffe. 1st American ed. Boston : Plays, 1976, c1975. 95 p. : ill. ; 21 cm. Published in 1975 under title: Make a mask. Instructions for constructing masks for use on school stages using a variety of materials. [TT898.P47 1976] 75-9901 ISBN 0-8238-0186-1 : 8.95
1. Masks—Juvenile literature. I. Sutcliffe, Anna, joint author. II. Title. BIP

PRICE, Christine, 1928- 392
The mystery of masks / by Christine Price. New York : Scribner, c1978. 64 p. : ill. ; 34 cm. An illustrated overview of masks with emphasis on their meaning and importance in each of the cultures that produced them. [GN419.5.P74] 77-27558 ISBN 0-684-15653-9 lib.bdg. : 7.95
1. Masks—Juvenile literature. I. Title. BIP

ROSS, Laura. 792.3'026
Mask-making with pantomime and stories from American history / Laura Ross ; drawings by Frank Ross, Jr. ; constructed mask photos by George Haddad. New York : Lothrop, Lee & Shepard Co., [1975] 112 p. : ill. ; 25 cm. Includes index. Bibliography: p. 110. Instructions for making masks and using them with pantomime dramatizations of four popular stories from American history. [TT898.R67] 75-11960 ISBN 0-688-41721-3 : 5.95 ISBN 0-688-51721-8 lib.bdg. : 5.11
1. Masks—Juvenile literature. 2. United States—History—Drama. I. Ross, Frank Xavier, 1914- II. Title. BIP

Masks (Sculpture)

GREGOR, Joseph, 1888-1960. 731.7'5'0222
Masks of the world; an historical and pictorial survey of many types & times. New York, B. Blom [1968] 31 p., 255 illus. on 91 l. 34 cm. First published 1936-37. Translation of Die Masken der Erde. [NB1310.G73 1968] 68-18150
1. Masks (Sculpture) I. Title. BIP

HOLY, Ladislav. 730'.96
Masks and figures from Eastern and Southern Africa; text by Ladislav Holy; photographed by Dominique Darbois. London, Hamlyn, 1967. 69p. 121 plates, 155 illus. (incl. 25 col.) maps 28cm. (Art of Africa) Bibl. [NB1097.E3H6] 68-84926 9.95
1. Masks (Sculpture) 2. Sculpture—Africa, East. 3. Sculpture—Africa, South. I. Darbois, Dominique. illus. II. Title.

HUNT, Kari. 731.75
Masks and mask makers [by] Kari Hunt and Bernice Wells Carlson. New York, Abingdon Press [1961] 67 p. illus. 25 cm. Includes bibliography. [NB1310.H85] 61-5097
1. Masks (Sculpture) I. Carlson, Bernice Wells, joint author. BIP

NOMA, Seiroku. 731.75
Masks. English adaptation by Meredith Weatherby. [1st English ed.] Tokyo, Rutland, Vt., C. E. Tuttle Co. [1957] 1 v. (unpaged) illus., plates (part col.) 20 cm. (Arts & crafts of Japan, no. 1) [NB1310.N6] 57-8793
1. Masks (Sculpture) 2. Sculpture—Japan. I. Series.

RILEY, Olive Lasette. 731.75
Masks and magic. New York, Studio Publications [1955] v, 122 p. plates (part col.) 28 cm. Bibliography: p. 122. [NB1310.R5] 55-9220
1. Masks (Sculpture) 2. Magic. I. Title.

SLADE, Richard 731.75
Masks and how to make them. With line illus. by Clive Kidder. London, Faber & Faber [1964] 48p. illus. 26cm. [NB131O. S551] 65-7388 3.75
1. Masks (Sculpture) I. Title.
Available from Transatlantic, New York.

Masks (Sculpture)—Catalogs.

NEW York (City). Museum of Primitive Art. 730'.74'013
Masks and sculptures from the collection of Gustave and Franyo Schindler. Greenwich, Conn., Distributed by the New York Graphic Society, 1966. [40] p. (chiefly illus.) 28 cm. [NB1310.N4] 68-7960
1. Masks (Sculpture)—Catalogs. 2. Sculpture, Primitive—Catalogs. 3. Sculpture—Private collections. I. Schindler, Gustave. II. Schindler, Franyo. III. Title.

Maskwa River site, Man.

SAYLOR, Stanley. 971.27'4
The Maskwa River site / by Stanley Saylor. [Winnipeg] : Dept. of Tourism, Recreation & Cultural Affairs, Historic Resources Branch, 1976. 32 p. : ill. ; 26 cm. (Preliminary report - Historic Resources Branch ; 1) (Papers in Manitoba archaeology) Cover title. [E78.M25S39] 77-354174
1. Maskwa River site, Man. I. Title. II. Series. III. Series: Manitoba. Historic Resources Branch. Preliminary report — Historic Resources Branch ; 1.

Mason, Benjamin Franklin, 1804-1871.

FRANKENSTEIN, Alfred Victor, 1906- [759.13]
Two journeymen painters. Co-authors: Alfred Frankenstein [and] Arthur K. D. Healy. Middlebury, Vt., Sheldon Museum, 1950. 63 p. ports. 28 cm. Bibliography: p. 43. [ND237.M26F7] 927.5 50-13112
1. Mason, Benjamin Franklin, 1804-1871. 2. Tuthill, Abraham G. D., 1775 of 6-1843. I. Healy, Arthur K. D. joint author. II. Title.

Mason family (Miles Mason, 1752-1822)

GODDEN, Geoffrey A. 738.3'7
The illustrated guide to Mason's patent ironstone china and related wares; stone china, new stone, granite china, and their manufacturers [by] Geoffrey A. Godden. New York, Praeger [1971] xiv, 175 p. illus., 8 col. plates. 26 cm. (The Illustrated guides to pottery and porcelain) Includes bibliographical references. [NK4210.M3G6 1971] 72-135513 20.00
1. Mason family (Miles Mason, 1752-1822) 2. Potters—England—Directories. I. Title. II. Title: Mason's patent ironstone china.

Mason, John, 1927-

LOS Angeles Co., Calif. Museum of Art, Los Angeles. 730'.92'4
John Mason: sculpture. An exhibition organized by the Los Angeles County Museum of Art, November 16, 1966-February 1, 1967. [Los Angeles, 1966] 1 v. (unpaged) illus. 23 cm. "Sponsored by the Museum's Contemporary Art Council." Includes bibliography. [NB237.M35L6] 66-30476
1. Mason, John, 1927- I. Los Angeles Co., Calif. Museum of Art, Los Angeles. Contemporary Art Council. II. Title.

MASON, John, 1927- 730'.92'4
John Mason ceramic sculpture, Pasadena Museum of Modern Art, May 7-June 23, 1974. An exhibition organized by Barbara Haskell. [Pasadena, Pasadena Museum of Modern Art, 1974] 32 p. illus. 25 cm. Bibliography: p. 27-30. [NK4210.M29H37] 74-176122
1. Mason, John, 1927- 2. Ceramic sculpture—United States. I. Haskell, Barbara. II. Pasadena Museum of Modern Art. III. Title.

Mason, Miles, 1752-1822.

HAGGAR, Reginald George, 1905- 338.7'61'7380922
Mason porcelain and ironstone 1796-1853 : Miles Mason and the Mason manufactories / by Reginald Haggar and Elizabeth Adams. London : Faber, 1977. 2-135 p., A-H, [80] p. of plates : ill. (some col.), facsim., plan ; 26 cm. (Faber monographs on pottery and porcelain) Includes index. Bibliography: p. 125-126. [NK4210.M3H27] 77-372940 ISBN 0-571-10945-4 : 34.95
1. Mason, Miles, 1752-1822. 2. Mason, Charles James, 1791-1856. 3. Potters—England—Biography. 4. Porcelain, English. I. Adams, B. Elizabeth, joint author. II. Title.
Distributed by Faber and Faber, Salem, Mass.

Masonry.

*WATSON, Lewis 721.0441.
How to build a low-cost house of stone by Lewis and Sharon Watson 3rd edition. Sweet, Idaho, Stonehouse [1975] 60p. ill. 21 cm. Bibliography: p. 56-59. [TH1201.] 3.00 (pbk.)
1. Masonry. I. Watson, Sharon,joint author II. Title. BIP

Masques.

JONES, Inigo, 1573-1652 741.90924
Designs by Inigo Jones for masques & plays at court; a descriptive catalogue of drawings for scenery and costumes mainly in the collection of His Grace the Duke of Devonshire, K. G., with introd. and notes by Percy Simpson & C. F. Bell. New York, Russell & Russell, 1966. xii, 158p. illus. (1 mounted) 51 plates, port. 33cm. [NC1115.J57 1966] 66-13236 35.00
1. Masques. 2. Theaters—Stage-setting and scenery. 3. Costume. 4. Theater—England. I. Devonshire, Victor Christian William Cavendish, 9th duke of, 1868-1938. II. Bell, Charles Francis, 1871- III. Simpson, Percy 1865- IV. Title. BIP

Mass media—Collections.

DENITTO, Dennis, comp. 700'.9'24
Media for our time; an anthology. New York, Holt, Rinehart and Winston [1971] xiv, 496 p. illus. (part col.) 23 cm. Includes bibliographical references. [P87.D38] 77-138405 ISBN 0-03-084700-1
1. Mass media—Collections. 2. The arts, Modern—20th century—Collections. I. Title.

Massachusetts Institute of Technology. School of Architecture and Planning.

SHILLABER, Caroline, 1908- 720'.9773'11
Massachusetts Institute of Technology School of Architecture and Planning, 1861-1961; a hundred year chronicle. [Cambridge, Massachusetts Institute of Technology, 1963] 134 p. illus., diagrs., plans. 25 cm. "References": p. 127-134. [NA2300.M4S5] 63-3586
1. Massachusetts Institute of Technology. School of Architecture and Planning. I. Title.

The Masses.

FITZGERALD, Richard. 741.5'973
Art and politics; cartoonists of the Masses and Liberator. Westport, Conn., Greenwood Press [1973] xiv, 254 p. illus. 24 cm. (Contributions in American studies, no. 8) Contents.Contents.—The Masses and the Liberator.—Art Young.—Robert Minor.—John Sloan.—K. R. Chamberlain.—Maurice Becker.—Bibliography (p. 235-241) [NC1305.F57] 72-609 ISBN 0-8371-6006-5 14.50
1. The Masses. 2. The Liberator. 3. Cartoonists—United States. 4. American wit and humor, Pictorial. I. Title. BIP

Masson, Andre, 1896-

GALERIE Louise Leiris, Paris. 759.4
Andre Masson: peintures 1960-1961 [Dist. New York, Wittenborn, 1962] [7]p. 45 illus. (pt. col.) 17cm. (Its Catalogue. Ser. A, no. 15) 62-4363 2.00 pap.,
1. Masson, Andre, 1896- I. Title.

JUIN, Hubert 759.4
Andre Masson [in French] [,paris, G. Fall, dist New York, Efron, c.1963] 88p. illus. (pt. col.) 19cm. (Le Musee de poche) 63-5299 2.25 pap.,
1. Masson, Andre, 1896- I. Title.

†RUBIN, William Stanley. 759.4 B
Andre Masson / by William Rubin and Carolyn Lanchner. New York : Museum of Modern Art, c1976. 232 p. : ill. (some col.) ; 25 cm. "Bibliography, compiled by Inga Forslund": p. 225-232. [ND553.M36R82] 76-1492 ISBN 0-87070-465-6 : 20.00.
1. Masson, Andre, 1896- 2. Painters—France—Biography. I. Lanchner, Carolyn, joint author.
Contents omitted. BIP

Master E S, 15th cent.

SHESTACK, Alan. 769'9924
Master E S, five hundredth anniversary exhibition, September fifth through October third, Phildelphia Museum of Art. Catalogue by Alan Shestack. [Philadelphia, Philadelphia Museum of Art, 1967] 1 v. (unpaged) illus. 28 cm. [NE805.M3S5] 67-9531
1. Master E S, 15th cent. I. Philadelphia Museum of Art. II. Title.

Master of Claude of France.

STERLING, Charles, 1901- 091
The Master of Claude, Queen of France, a newly defined miniaturist / by Charles Sterling ; with 101 ill. New York : H. P. Kraus, 1975. 71 p. : ill. (some col.) ; 27 cm. (Rare books monograph[s] series ; v. 5) Includes bibliographical references. [ND3363.C58S8] 74-22065 18.00
1. Master of Claude of France. 2. Claude, Queen Consort of Francis I, King of France, 1499-1524. 3. Hours, Books of. 4. Prayer-books. 5. Illumination of books and manuscripts, Medieval. I. Title. II. Series.

Master of the Amsterdam Cabinet, 15th century.

HUTCHISON, Jane C. 769'.92'4
The Master of the Housebook [by] Jane C. Hutchison. New York, Collectors Editions [1972] ix, 190 p. illus. 30 cm. (Northern European engravers of the fifteenth century) Bibliography: p. 81-96. [NE468.A5H87] 74-110442 ISBN 0-87681-041-5
1. Master of the Amsterdam Cabinet, 15th century. I. Title. II. Series.
Available from Van Nostrand 60.00

1. Matisse, Henri, 1869-1954. I. Matisse, Henri, 1869-1954.

RUSSELL, John, 1919- 759.4
The world of Matisse, 1869-1954, by John Russell and the editors of Time-Life Books New York, Time-Life Books [1969] 190 p. illus. (part col.), facsims., ports. 32 cm. (Time-Life library of art) Bibliography: p. 185. [ND553.M37R8] 69-19503
1. Matisse, Henri, 1869-1954. I. Time-Life Books. II. Title. BIP

SELZ, Jean. 759.4
Matisse. [Translated from the French by A. P. H. Hamilton] New York, Crown Publishers [1964] 94 p. illus. (part mounted, part col.) ports. (part mounted, part col.) 29 cm. Bibliography: p. 94. [ND553.M37S383] 64-54749
1. Matisse, Henri, 1869-1954. BIP

Matta Echaurren, Roberto Sebastian, 1911—

CLURMAN, Irene. 759.9493
Surrealism and the painting of Matta and Magritte. Stanford, Calif. [Humanities Honors Program, Stanford University] 1970. viii, 45 p. illus. 23 cm. (Stanford honors essay in humanities, no. 14) Bibliography: p. 42-45. [NX600.S9C55] 70-134703
1. Matta Echaurren, Roberto Sebastian, 1911- 2. Magritte, Rene, 1898-1967. 3. Surrealism. I. Title. II. Series.

MATTA Echaurren, Roberto 730'.924
Sebastian, 1911-
Judgments; original etchings [by] Matta. Yorktown Heights, N.Y., Editions of the Blue Moon Gallery [1967?] 1 portfolio ([4] l., 7 plates (part col.)) 52 x 68 cm. 100 copies printed. no. 14. The etchings were printed at the presses of Georges Visat, Paris, between August and October, 1967. [NE2210.M4A45] 68-3970
I. Title.

MATTA Echaurren, Roberto 709'.2'4
Sebastian, 1911-
Matta : a totemic world : paintings, drawings, sculpture, January 11-February 15, 1975 / introd. by Nicolas Calas. New York : Andrew Crispo Gallery, c1974. [60] p. : chiefly ill. (some col.) ; 23 x 27 cm. Bibliography: p. [59]-[60]. [N6669.M38A72] 74-33223
1. Matta Echaurren, Roberto Sebastian, 1911- I. Andrew Crispo Gallery. BIP

Matthews, John, 1933—

MATTHEWS, John, 1933- 730'.92'4
John Matthews : sculpture. [s.l. : s.n., 1976] [26] p. : chiefly ill. ; 29 cm. Cover title. [NB249.M33A48] 77-355792
1. Matthews, John, 1933-

Matthias I, King of Hungary, 1440?-1490—Library.

BIBLIOTHECA Corviniana: 745.6'7
the library of King Matthias Corvinus of Hungary. [Compiled by Csaba Csapodi, Klara Csapodi-Gardonyi, and Tibor Szanto. Translated by Zsuzsanna Horn; translation rev. by Alick West] New York, Praeger [1969] 398 p. 144 col. plates (incl. facsims., port.) 33 cm. Companion vol. to I. Berkovits' Illuminated manuscripts from the library of Matthias Corvinus, published in 1964. Includes bibliographical references. [Z725.M44B513 1969b] 69-11963 55.00
1. Matthias I, King of Hungary, 1440?-1490—Library. 2. Manuscripts—Bibliography—Catalogs. 3. Illumination of books and manuscripts—Specimens, reproductions, etc. I. Csapodi, Csaba. II. Csapodine Gardonyi, Klara. III. Szanto, Tibor.

Maundy coins.

TROWBRIDGE, Richard J. 737.49'42
Maundy coins of Great Britain, by Richard J. Trowbridge. [1st ed. Long Beach, Calif., Coins of the British World, 1969] iv, 48 p. illus. 22 cm. [CJ2482.T7] 74-11068 2.00
1. Maundy coins. I. Title.

Maurer, Alfred Henry,

MCCAUSLAND, Elizabeth, 927.5
1899-
A. H. Maurer. New York, Published for the Walker Art Center by A. A. Wyn, 1951. 289 p. illus., ports. 24 cm. Bibliography: p. 279-282. [ND237.M35M3] 51-4396
1. Maurer, Alfred Henry, I. Title.

Maurice Spertus Museum of Judaica.

FAITH & 726'.3'09773074017311
form : an exhibition / organized by the Maurice Spertus Museum of Judaica ; introductory material, Arthur M. Feldman, Grace Cohen Grossman. Chicago : Spertus College Press, 1976. 101 p. : ill. ; 22 x 28 cm. Contents.Contents.—Gutstein, M. A. The roots and the branches.—Rader, L. W. Synagogue architecture in Illinois. Includes bibliographical references. [NA5230.I3F34] 77-356182
1. Maurice Spertus Museum of Judaica. 2. Synagogue architecture—Illinois—Exhibitions. 3. Jews in Chicago—History. I. Maurice Spertus Museum of Judaica. II. Gutstein, Morris Aaron, 1905- The roots and the branches. 1976. III. Rader, Lauren Weingarden. Synagogue architecture in Illinois. 1976.

Mauser pistol.

BELFORD, James N. 623.4'43
The Mauser self-loading pistol, by James N. Belford and Jack Dunlap. [1st ed.] Alhambra, Calif., Borden Pub. Co., 1969. 208 p. illus. 29 cm. [TS537.B4] 70-79646 12.50
1. Mauser pistol. I. Dunlap, Jack, joint author. II. Title. BIP

BREATHED, John W. 683'.43
System Mauser; a pictorial history of the model 1896 self-loading pistol, by John W. Breathed, Jr., and Joseph J. Schroeder, Jr. Chicago, Handgun Press [1967] xiv, 273 p. illus. 26 cm. Bibliography: p. 273. [TS537.B72] 67-30346
1. Mauser pistol. I. Schroeder, Joseph J., joint author. II. Title.

PENDER, Roy G. 683'.43
Mauser pocket pistols, 1910-1946, by Roy G. Pender, III. [1st ed.] Houston, Tex., Collectors Press, 1971. 307 p. illus. 27 cm. Bibliography: p. 307. [TS537.P4] 71-126635 14.50
1. Mauser pistol. I. Title. BIP

Mauser rifle.

OLSON, Ludwig Elmer, 683'.42
1916-
Mauser bolt rifles / Ludwig Olson. 3d ed. Montezuma, Iowa : F. Brownell, 1976. ix, 364 p. : ill. ; 29 cm. Includes index. Bibliography: p. 351-353. [TS536.6.B6O45 1976] 76-9459
1. Mauser rifle. I. Title.

Mauzey, Merritt, 1898—

MISSISSIPPI. University 769'.92'4
of Southern Mississippi, Hattiesburg. Library.
The catalog of Merritt Mauzey Collection in the Library of the University of Southern Mississippi. Prepared by Warren Tracy. Hattiesburg, University of Southern Mississippi Press, 1972. 56 p. illus. 24 cm. [NE2312.M38M57] 73-170755
1. Mauzey, Merritt, 1898- I. Tracy, Warren Francis, 1914- II. Title.

Maverick, Peter, 1780-1881.

STEPHENS, Stephen DeWitt. 927.6
The Mavericks, American engravers. New Brunswick, N.J., Rutgers University Press, 1950. xx, 219 p. illus., ports. 26 cm. "Maverick engravings and lithographs": p. [81]-180. Bibliography: p. 184-185. [NE539.M3S7] 50-9453
1. Maverick, Peter, 1780-1881. I. Title.

Maximilian I, Emperor of Germany.

BURGKMAIR, Hans, 1473- 769.943
1531
The triumph of Maximilian I; 137 woodcuts by Hans Burgkmair, others. Tr. [from German] of descriptive text., introd., notes by Stanely Applebaum. New York, Dover [c.1964] 1v. (various p.) illus. 24x29cm. Plates reproduced from the 1883-1884 Holzhausen ed. Basic text here tr. is that of a 1512 ms. preserved in Vienna. Bibl. [NE1205.B8A63] 63-19488 3.00 pap.,
1. Maximilian I, I. Emperor of Germany, 1459-1519. II. Title.

BURGKMAIR, Hans, 1473- 769.943
1531
The triumph of Maximilian I; 137 woodcuts by Hans Burgkmair and others. Tr. of descriptive text, introd., notes by Stanley Applebaum [Gloucester, mass., P. Smith, 1965, c.1964] 1v. (various p.) illus. 24x29cm. Plates reproduced from the 1883-84 Holzhausen ed. Basic text tr. from the 1512 ms. held in Vienna (Dover bk. rebound) Bibl. [NE1205.B8A63] 5.50
1. Maximilian I. Emperor of Germany, 1459-1519. II. Title.

Maximilian I, Emperor of Germany, 1459-1519.

BURGKMAIR, Hans, 1473- 769.943
1531.
The triumph of Maximiliam I; 137 woodcuts by Hans Burgkmair and others. With a translation of descriptive text, introd. and notes by Stanley Appelbaum. New York, Dover Publications [c1964] 1 v. (various pagings) illus. 24 x 29 cm. "Plates . . . reproduced from the 1883-1884 Hoizhausen edition . . . The basic text here translated is that of a 1512 manuscript preserved in Vienna." Bibliography: p 19-20. [NE1205.B8A63] 63-19488
1. Maximilian I, Emperor of Germany, 1459-1519. I. Title.

Maxwell, John, 1905-1962.

MCCLURE, David. 759.9411 B
John Maxwell / by David McClure. Edinburgh : Edinburgh University Press, c1976. 69 p. : ill. (some col.) ; 16 x 22 cm. (Modern Scottish painters ; no. 4) Bibliography: p. 66. [ND497.M48M33] 77-362553 ISBN 0-85224-300-6 : 5.00
1. Maxwell, John, 1905-1962. 2. Painters—Scotland—Biography.
Distributed by Edinburgh University Press, Totowa, N.J.

Maxwell Museum of Anthropology.

RODEE, Marian E. 746.1'4
Southwestern weaving / Marian E. Rodee. 1st ed. Albuquerque : University of New Mexico Press, c1977. x, 176 p. : ill. (some col.) ; 27 cm. A catalog of textiles from the collection of the Maxwell Museum of Anthropology, University of New Mexico. Bibliography: p. 175-176. [E78.S7R6] 76-21517 ISBN 0-8263-0425-7 : 15.00. ISBN 0-8263-0426-5 pbk. : 6.95
1. Maxwell Museum of Anthropology. 2. Indians of North America—Southwest, New—Textile industry and fabrics—Catalogs. 3. Navaho Indians—Textile industry and fabrics—Catalogs. I. Maxwell Museum of Anthropology. II. Title. BIP

May, Morton D., 1914- —Art collections.

THE Morton D. 759.3'074'017866
May collection of 20th century German masters. [St. Louis, City Art Museum, 1970] 159 p. illus. (part col.) 30 cm. Catalog of the exhibition organized by the Marlborough-Gerson Gallery, New York, and the City Art Museum of St. Louis in honor of Morton D. May. It was shown at the Marlborough-Gerson Gallery from Jan.-Feb., 1970, and at City Art Museum from July-Aug., 1970. Includes bibliographical references. [ND568.M6] 75-282779
1. May, Morton D., 1914- —Art collections. 2. Paintings, German—Exhibitions. 3. Painting, Modern—20th century—Germany. I. Marlborough-Gerson Gallery. II. St. Louis. City Art Museum.

PARSONS, Lee Allen, 730'.099
1932-
Ritual arts of the South Seas : the Morton D. May Collection : the St. Louis Art Museum, 22 August-19 October, 1975 / catalogue by Lee A. Parsons ; photos. by Jack Savage. [St. Louis : The Museum], c1975. 204, [3] p., [2] leaves of plates : 250 ill. (some col.), 3 maps ; 25 cm. Bibliography: p. [207] [N7410.P37] 75-24647
1. May, Morton D., 1914- —Art collections. 2. Art—Oceanica—Exhibitions. 3. Art, Primitive—Oceanica—Exhibitions. I. Savage, Jack. II. St. Louis Art Museum. III. Title.

May, Saidie Adler, 1879-1951—Art collections.

BALTIMORE. Museum of 708'.152'6
Art.
Saidie A. May Collection. [Catalogue of an exhibition. Baltimore, 1972] 87 p. illus. (part col.) 26 cm. "An issue of the Baltimore Museum of Art Record, v. 3, no. 1, 1972." Includes bibliographical references. [N5220.M54B34 1972] 74-171020
1. May, Saidie Adler, 1879-1951—Art collections. 2. Art—Exhibitions. I. Baltimore. Museum of Art. Record, v. 3, no. 1. II. Title.

Mayas.

MORLEY, Sylvanus Griswold, 917.2
1883-1948.
In search of Maya glyphs; from the archaeological journals of Sylvanus G. Morley. Edited with an introd. by Robert H. Lister and Florence C. Lister. [Santa Fe] Museum of New Mexico Press [1970] 170 p. illus., maps, port. 24 cm. Bibliography: p. 169-170. [F1435.M753] 77-128565
1. Mayas. 2. Yucatan—Description and travel. 3. Guatemala—Description and travel. I. Title. BIP

THOMPSON, John Eric 972.015
Sidney, 1898-.
Maya archaeologist. [1st American ed.] Norman, University of Oklahoma Press [1963] xvii, 284 p. illus., 16 plates (incl. ports.) maps. 24 cm. [F1435.T495] 63-8994
1. Mayas. 2. Central America — Antiq. 3. Mexico — Antiq. 4. Central America — Descr. & trav. 5. Mexico — Descr. & trav. I. Title. BIP

Mayas—Antiquities.

AGUIAR, Walter R. 972
Maya land in color / text and photos. by Walter R. Aguiar. New York : Hastings House, [1978] p. cm. (Profiles of America) [F1435.A56] 78-2537 ISBN 0-8038-4703-3 : 5.95
1. Mayas—Antiquities. 2. Mexico—Antiquities. 3. Central America—Antiquities. 4. Mexico—Description and travel—1951- —Guide-books. 5. Central America—Description and travel—1951- —Guide-books. I. Title. BIP

ARNOLD, James MacKeever. 301.2 s
A survey of Maya state, religious, and secular architecture, by James MacKeever Arnold and James Robert Moriarty III. [Greeley] University of Northern Colorado, Museum of Anthropology, 1971. 14 l. illus. 29 cm. (Museum of Anthropology miscellaneous series, no. 27) Bibliography: leaves 13-14. [GN4.U53 no. 27] [F1435.3.A6] 722.91 72-191318
1. Mayas—Antiquities. 2. Indians of Mexico—Architecture. 3. Indians of Central America—Architecture. 4. Mexico—Antiquities. 5. Central America—Antiquities. I. Moriarty, James Robert, joint author. II. Title. III. Series: University of Northern Colorado. Museum of Anthropology. Miscellaneous series, no. 27.

BRUNHOUSE, Robert 913'.031'0922
Levere, 1908-
In search of the Maya; the first archaeologists [by] Robert L. Brunhouse. Albuquerque, University of New Mexico Press [1973] vii, 243 p. illus. 22 cm.

Bibliography: p. 215-232. [F1435.B874] 73-75904 ISBN 0-8263-0276-9 7.95
1. Mayas—Antiquities. 2. Archaeologists—Biography. 3. Mexico—Antiquities. 4. Central America—Antiquities. I. Title. BIP

CORSON, Christopher. 732'.2
Maya anthropomorphic figurines from Jaina Island, Campeche / by Christopher Corson. Ramona, Calif. : Ballena Press, c1976. ii, 218 p. : ill. ; 28 cm. (Ballena Press studies in Mesoamerican art, archaeology, and ethnohistory ; no. 1) Based on the author's thesis, University of California, Berkeley, 1972. Bibliography: p. 211-218. [F1435.1.J3C67] 76-362758 pbk : 7.50
1. Mayas—Antiquities. 2. Jaina Island—Antiquities. 3. Mayas—Art. 4. Indians of Mexico—Campeche—Jaina Island—Art. 5. Mexico—Antiquities. I. Title.

FERGUSON, William M. 972
Maya ruins of Mexico in color : Palenque, Uxmal, Kabah, Sayil, Xlapak, Labna, Chichen Itza, Coba, Tulum / by William M. Ferguson, in collaboration with John Q. Royce. 1st ed. Norman : University of Oklahoma Press, c1977. p. cm. Includes index. Bibliography: p. [F1435.F4] 77-9110 ISBN 0-8061-1442-8 : 25.00
1. Mayas—Antiquities. 2. Mexico—Antiquities. I. Royce, John Q., joint author. II. Title. BIP

HUNTER, C. Bruce. 917.2'03
A guide to ancient Maya ruins, by C. Bruce Hunter. [1st ed.] Norman, University of Oklahoma Press [1974] p. cm. Bibliography: p. [F1435.H86] 74-9587 ISBN 0-8061-1214-X
1. Mayas—Antiquities. 2. Mexico—Antiquities. 3. Central America—Antiquities. I. Title.

MAUDSLAY, Alfred Percival, 1850-1931. 972
Archaeology. by A. P. Maudslay. Facsim. ed. prepared and introd. written / by Francis Robicsek. New York : Milpatron Pub. Corp. : distributed by Arte Primitivo Inc., [1974?] 6 v. in 4 : ill. ; 28-31 cm. (Biologia Centrali-Americana) Photoreprint of the 1889-1902 ed. published for the editors by R. H. Porter and Dulau, London. Contents.Contents.—v. 1-4. Plates.—v. 5. Text.—v. 6. Goodman, J. T. Appendix. Includes bibliographical references. [F1435.M44 1974] 74-30688 ISBN 0-89088-001-8
1. Mayas—Antiquities. 2. Central America—Antiquities. 3. Mexico—Antiquities. 4. Mayas—Writing. I. Goodman, J. T. II. Title. III. Series.

SPINDEN, Herbert Joseph, 1879- 972.015
Maya art and civilization. Rev. and enl. with added illus. [Indian Hills, Colo.] Falcon's Wing Press [1957] xliii, 432 p. illus. (part col.) maps. 27 cm. First published in 1913 under title: A study of Maya art. Bibliography: p. [399]-415. [F1435.3.A7S75 1957] 56-5124
1. Mayas—Antiquities. 2. Art, Maya. I. Title.

TOTTEN, George Oakley, 1866-1939. 722'.91
Maya architecture. New York, B. Franklin [1973] p. Reprint of the 1926 ed. Bibliography: p. [F1435.3.A6T7 1973] 71-122845 ISBN 0-8337-3560-8 48.50
1. Mayas—Antiquities. 2. Indians of Mexico—Architecture. 3. Indians of Central America—Architecture. 4. Mexico—Antiquities. 5. Central America—Antiquities. I. Title. BIP

Mayas—Antiquities—Addresses, essays, lectures.

ARCHAEOLOGICAL studies in Middle America 917.2'03'08 s [by] E. Wyllys Andrews IV [and others] New Orleans, Middle American Research Institute, Tulane University, 1970. 199 p. illus. 27 cm. ([Tulane University of Louisiana. Middle American Research Institute] Publication 26) Contents.Contents.—Andrews, E. W. A revision of some dates on the hieroglyphic stairway, Copan, Honduras.—Berlin, H. and Kelley, D. H. The 819-day count and color-direction symbolism among the classic Maya.—Haviland, W. A. Maya settlement patterns: a critical review.—Carmack, R. M. Toltec influence on the postclassic culture history of highland Guatemala.—Haviland, W. A. Ancient lowland Maya social organization.—De Borhegyi, S. F. Archaeological reconnaissance of Chinkultic, Chiapas, Mexico.—Berlin, H. The tablet of the 96 glyphs at Palenque, Chiapas, Mexico.—Morley, S. G. The stela platform at Uxmal, Yucatan, Mexico.—Folan, W. J. The open chapel of Dzibilchaltun, Yucatan. Includes bibliographies. [F1421.T95 no. 26] [F1435] 970.3 74-153732
1. Mayas—Antiquities—Addresses, essays, lectures. 2. Mexico—Antiquities—Addresses, essays, lectures. 3. Central America—Antiquities—Addresses, essays, lectures. I. Title. II. Series.

GRAHAM, John Allen, comp. 913'.031'08 s
Studies in the archaeology of Mexico and Guatemala. Edited by John A. Graham. Berkeley, University of California, Dept. of Anthropology, 1972. ii, 122 p. illus. 28 cm. (Contributions of the University of California Archaeological Research Facility, no. 16) Contents.Contents.—Adams, R. E. W. Maya highland prehistory.—Sedat, D. W. and Sharer, R. J. Archaeological investigations in the northern Maya highlands.—Graham, J. A. and Berger, R. Radiocarbon dates from Copan, Honduras.—Graham, J. A. and Fitch, S. R. The recording of Maya sculpture.—Kelly, D. H. The nine lords of the night.—Troike, R. C., Troike, N. P., and Graham, J. A. Preliminary report on excavations in the archaeological zone of Rioverde, San Luis Potosi, Mexico.—Robertson, M. G. Notes on the ruins of Ixtutz, southeastern Peten.—Hester, T. R., Jack, R. N., and Heizer, R. F. Trace element analysis of obsidian from the site of Cholula, Mexico.—Graham, J. A., Hester, T. R., and Jack, R. N. Sources for the obsidian aOStudies in the archaeology of Mexico and Guatemala. Edited by John A. Graham. Berkeley, University of California, Dept. of Anthropology, 1972. ii, 122 p. illus. 28 cm. (Contributions of the University of California Archaeological Research Fa
1. Mayas—Antiquities—Addresses, essays, lectures. 2. Indians of Mexico—Antiquities—Addresses, essays, lectures. 3. Mexico—Antiquities—Addresses, essays, lectures. 4. Guatemala—Antiquities—Addresses, essays, lectures. I. Title. II. Series: California. University. Archaeological Research Facility. Contributions, no. 16.

Mayas—Antiquities—Collections.

MONOGRAPHS and papers in Maya archaeology. 917.281'03 Edited by William R. Bullard, Jr. Cambridge, Mass., Peabody Museum, 1970. ix, 502 p. illus., maps. 27 cm. (Papers of the Peabody Museum of Archaeology and Ethnology, Harvard University, v. 61) Includes bibliographies. [E51.H337 vol. 61] 73-105721 13.50
1. Mayas—Antiquities—Collections. I. Bullard, William Rotch, 1926- ed. II. Series: Harvard University. Peabody Museum of Archaeology and Ethnology. Papers, v. 61 BIP

Mayas—Antiquities—Pictorial works.

CRAVEN, Roy C. 917.2'03'0222
Ceremonial centers of the Maya. Photography by Roy C. Craven, Jr. Introd. by William R. Bullard, Jr. Site descriptions by Michael E. Kampen. Gainesville, University Presses of Florida, 1974. 152 p. illus. 28 cm. "A University of Florida book." "The collapse of Maya civilization, by William R. Bullard, Jr.": p. 1-19. Bibliography: p. 152. [F1435.C79] 74-2016 ISBN 0-8130-0447-0 20.00
1. Mayas—Antiquities—Pictorial works. 2. Central America—Antiquities—Pictorial works. 3. Mexico—Antiquities—Pictorial works. I. Bullard, William Rotch, 1926-1972. II. Kampen, Michael Edwin. III. Title. BIP

Mayas—Architecture.

ANDREWS, George F., 1918- 301.36'3'09701
Maya cities: placemaking and urbanization [by] George F. Andrews. [1st ed.] Norman, University of Oklahoma Press [1975] xviii, 468 p. illus. 23 x 26 cm. (The Civilization of the American Indian series, v. 131) Bibliography: p. 457-462. [F1435.3.A6A52] 73-19390 ISBN 0-8061-1187-9
1. Mayas—Architecture. 2. Cities and towns, Ruined, extinct, etc.—Mexico. 3. Cities and towns, Ruined, extinct, etc.—Central America. 4. Mexico—Antiquities. 5. Central America—Antiquities. I. Title. II. Series.

POTTER, David F. 722'.91
Maya architecture of the Central Yucatan Peninsula, Mexico / David F. Potter. New Orleans : Middle American Research Institute, Tulane University, 1977. xi, 118 p., [1] fold. leaf of plates : ill. ; 27 cm. (Publication - Middle American Research Institute, Tulane University ; 44) At head of title: National Geographic Society—Tulane University Program of Research in Campeche. Bibliography: p. 116-118. [F1435.3.A6P67] 77-154450
1. Mayas—Architecture. 2. Mayas—Antiquities. 3. Indians of Mexico—Architecture. 4. Mexico—Antiquities. I. National Geographic Society—Tulane University Program of Research in Campeche. II. Title. III. Series: Tulane University of Louisiana. Middle American Research Institute. Publications ; 44.

Mayas— Art.

ANTON, Ferdinand. 709'.01'109701
Art of the Maya. [English translation by Mary Whittall. 1st American ed.] New York, Putnam [1970] 344 p. illus. (part col.) 33 cm. Translation of Kunst der Maya. Bibliography: p. 337-340. [F1435.3.A7A6513 1970b] 70-108741 20.00
1. Mayas—Art. 2. Indians of Central America—Art. 3. Indians of Mexico—Art. I. Title. BIP

COE, Michael D. 709.01
Three Maya relief panels at Dumbarton Oaks, by Michael D. Coe and Elizabeth P. Benson. Washington, Dumbarton Oaks Trustees for Harvard University, 1966. 36 p. illus. (2 fold.) 27 cm. (Studies in pre-Columbian art and archaeology no. 2) Bibliography: p. 36. [E51.S85 no. 2] 66-30016
1. Mayas—Art. 2. Mayas—Antiquities. 3. Mayas-Writing. I. Benson, Elizabeth P., joint author. II. Title. BIP

GREENE, Merle 709.01
Ancient Maya relief sculpture: rubbings by Merle Greene. Introd., notes by J. Erick S. Thompson. New York, Museum of Primitive Art: dist. by N. y. Graphic, Greenwich, Conn., 1967. 1 v. (unpaged) map, plates, 32cm. Issued in a case. Bibl. [F1435.3.A7G69] 67-27900 15.00 pap.,bxd.
1. Mayas— Art. 2. Indians of Mexico—Sculpture. 3. Indians of Central America—Sculpture. 4. Relief (Sculpture) I. Thompson, John Eric Sidney, 1898- II. New York. Museum of Primitive Art. III. Title.

KUBLER, George, 1912- 709.01'1
Studies in classic Maya iconography. New Haven, Conn., Published by the Academy; to be obtained from Archon Books, Hamden, Conn., 1969. vi, 111 p. illus. 30 cm. (Memoirs of the Connecticut Academy of Arts & Sciences, v. 18) Bibliography: p. [49]-53. [Q11.C85 vol. 18] 78-7139 18.00
1. Mayas—Art. I. Title. II. Series: Connecticut Academy of Arts and Sciences, New Haven. Memoirs, v. 18 BIP

SPINDEN, Herbert Joseph, 1879-1967. 709'.01'1
A study of Maya art, its subject matter and historical development / Herbert J. Spinden ; with a new introd. and bibliography by J. Eric S. Thompson. New York : Dover Publications, 1975. xxvi, 285 p., [15] leaves of plates : ill. ; 29 cm. Originally published in 1913 by the Peabody Museum of American Archaeology and Ethnology, Harvard University, Cambridge, Mass., as v. 6 of its Memoirs. Based on the author's thesis, Harvard, 1909. Includes index. Bibliography: p. [263]-276. [F1435.3.A7S75 1975] 74-20300 ISBN 0-486-21235-1 pbk. : 5.95
1. Mayas—Art. 2. Indians of Mexico—Art. 3. Indians of Central America—Art. I. Title. II. Series: Harvard University. Peabody Museum of Archaeology and Ethnology. Memoirs ; v. 6.

Mayas—Art—Exhibitions.

ART Museum of South Texas. 738
The Barbachano Ponce Mayan art collection : [exhibition], Art Museum of South Texas, Corpus Christi, January 23-February 29, 1976, University of Texas at Austin, March 15-May 2, 1976. Corpus Christi : Golden Banner Press, c1976. 32 p. : chiefly ill. (some col.) ; 22 cm. Cover title: Maya. [F1435.3.A7A69 1976] 76-372833
1. Mayas—Art—Exhibitions. 2. Barbachano Ponce, Manuel—Art collections. 3. Indians of Mexico—Art—Exhibitions. 4. Indians of Central America—Art—Exhibitions. I. Texas. University at Austin. II. Title. III. Title: Maya.

FLORIDA. University, Gainesville. University Gallery. 732'.2
The Maya; a special exhibition of photographs and artifacts marking the event of the 20th annual Latin American conference. Gainesville [1970] [20] p. illus. 24 cm. Label mounted on t.p.: Supplied by Worldwide Books, inc., Boston. "Catalogue": p. [14]-[15] [F1435.3.A7F56] 70-633965
1. Mayas—Art—Exhibitions. I. Title.

Mayas—Kings and rulers.

KUBLER, George, 1912- 970 s
Aspects of classic Maya rulership on two inscribed vessels / George Kubler. Washington : Dumbarton Oaks, Trustees for Harvard University, 1977. 60 p. : ill. ; 27 cm. (Studies in pre-Columbian art and archaeology ; no. 18) Bibliography: p. 57-60. [E51.S85 no. 18] [F1435.3.P7] 972 77-84830 pbk. : 3.00
1. Mayas—Kings and rulers. 2. Mayas—Writing. 3. Indians of Mexico—Writing. 4. Indians of Central America—Writing. I. Title. II. Series.

Mayas—Pottery.

DUMBARTON Oaks. 738.3'7
Classic Maya pottery at Dumbarton Oaks / Michael D. Coe. [Washington : Dumbarton Oaks, Trustees for Harvard University, 1975] 1 portfolio (30 p., [16] leaves of plates : ill. (some col.)) ; 45 cm. Bibliography: p. 29-30. [F1435.3.P8D84 1975] 75-1727
1. Dumbarton Oaks. 2. Mayas—Pottery. 3. Indians of Mexico—Pottery. 4. Indians of Central America—Pottery. I. Coe, Michael D. II. Title. BIP

GIFFORD, James C. 917.282'03
Ancient Maya pottery; a folio of Maya pottery from the site of Barton Ramie in British Honduras, by James C. Gifford. Pref. by Gordon R. Willey. Col. illus. by Muriel Kirkpatrick. [Philadelphia, Order from: M. Kirkpatrick, Laboratory of Anthropology, Temple University, 1973] 1 portfolio (ii, 20 p. (chiefly illus., part col.)) 30 cm. Title from portfolio. Bibliography: p. 20. [F1435.3.P8G53] 73-89611 6.00
1. Mayas—Pottery. 2. Barton Ramie site, British Honduras. I. Kirkpatrick, Muriel, illus. II. Title.

GIFFORD, James C. 972.82
Ancient Maya pottery-2 : a second folio of Maya pottery from the site of Barton Ramie in British Honduras (Belize) / by James C. Gifford and Muriel Kirkpatrick ; color ill. by Muriel Kirkpatrick. Philadelphia : Order from Kirkpatrick, Laboratory of Anthropology, Temple University, c1975. 1 portfolio (20 p. : ill.) ; 30 cm. Title from portfolio. Bibliography: p. 20. [F1435.3.P8G54] 75-26237 6.50
1. Mayas—Pottery. 2. Barton Ramie site, British Honduras. 3. Indians of Central America—British Honduras—Pottery. I. Kirkpatrick, Muriel, joint author. II. Title.

MILLER, Mary Ellen. 738.8
Jaina figurines : a study of Maya iconography : [catalogue of an exhibition held at the Art Museum, May 3-June 29, 1975] / Mary Ellen Miller ; with an appendix by David Joralemon. Princeton, N.J. : Art Museum, Princeton University, c1975. 71 p. : ill. ; 24 cm. Bibliography: p. 69-71. [F1435.1.J3M54] 75-4409
1. Mayas—Pottery. 2. Mayas—Antiquities. 3. Mexico—Antiquities. 4. Indians of Mexico—Pottery. 5. Figurines—Mexico. I. Princeton University. Art Museum. II. Title.

REINA, Ruben E. 738.3'097281
The traditional pottery of Guatemala / by Ruben E. Reina and Robert M. Hill II. Austin : University of Texas Press, c1978. xxii, 299 p. : ill. ; 29 cm. (Texas Pan American series) Includes index. Bibliography: [283]-286. [F1465.3.P68R44] 77-17455 ISBN 0-292-78024-9 : 30.00 pre-Jan., 1979 : 27.00
1. Mayas—Pottery. 2. Indians of Central America—Guatemala—Pottery. 3. Pottery—Guatemala. I. Hill, Robert M., 1952- BIP

Mayas—Pottery—Exhibitions.

COE, Michael D. 738.3'82
Lords of the underworld : masterpieces of classic Maya ceramics / Michael D. Coe ; photos. by Justin Kerr. Princeton, N.J. : Art Museum, Princeton University : distributed by Princeton University Press, c1978. 142 p. : ill. (some col.) ; 29 cm. Catalogue of an exhibition held at the Princeton University Art Museum, Mar. 4-June 18, 1978. Bibliography: p. 141-142. [F1435.3.P8C63] 77-72144 ISBN 0-691-03917-8 : 45.00
1. Mayas—Pottery—Exhibitions. 2. Mayas—Art—Exhibitions. 3. Indians of Mexico—Pottery—Exhibitions. 4. Indians of Central America—Pottery—Exhibitions. 5. Indians of Mexico—Art—Exhibitions. 6. Indians of Central America—Art—Exhibitions. I. Kerr, Justin. II. Princeton University. Art Museum. III. Title.

Mayas—Sculpture.

MAYER, Karl Herbert. 732'.2
Maya monuments : sculptures of unknown provenance in Europe / by Karl Herbert Mayer ; translated from the German by Sandra L. Brizee. Ramona, Calif. : Acoma Books, 1978. 44 p., [28] leaves of plates : ill. ; 28 cm. Bibliography: p. 40-44. [F1435.3.S34M39] 78-110775 ISBN 0-916552-11-X pbk. : 12.00
1. Indians of Central America—Sculpture. 2. Indians of Central America—Writing. 3. Mayas—Sculpture. 4. Mayas—Writing. I. Title. BIP

RANNEY, Edward. 917.2'03
Stonework of the Maya. [1st ed.] Albuquerque, University of New Mexico Press [1974] xiv, 119 p. illus. 26 cm. Bibliography: p. 115-117. [F1435.3.A7R36] 73-82769 ISBN 0-8263-0277-7 9.95 (pbk.).
1. Mayas—Sculpture. 2. Mayas—Architecture. 3. Indians of Mexico—Sculpture. 4. Indians of Central America—Sculpture. 5. Indians of Mexico—Architecture. 6. Indians of Central America—Architecture. I. Title. BIP

Mayas—Writing.

GATES, William Edmond, 1863-1940. 497'.4
An outline dictionary of Maya glyphs, with a concordance and analysis of their relationships : with the author's "Glyph studies" reprinted from the Maya Society quarterly / by William Gates. New York : Dover Publications, 1978. xii, 204 p. : ill. ; 22 cm. Reprint of the 1931 ed. published by Johns Hopkins Press, Baltimore. [F1435.3.P6G38 1978] 77-92481 ISBN 0-486-23618-8 pbk. : 3.50
1. Mayas—Writing. 2. Maya language. I. Title.

KELLEY, David H. 497'.4
Deciphering the Maya script / David Humiston Kelley. Austin : University of Texas Press, c1976. xvii, 334 p., [3] fold. leaves of plates ; ill. ; 32 cm. Includes indexes. Bibliography: p. [299]-316. [F1435.3.P6K44] 75-17989 ISBN 0-292-71504-8 : 27.50
1. Mayas—Writing. 2. Mayas—Antiquities. 3. Mexico—Antiquities. 4. Central America—Antiquities. I. Title. BIP

MORLEY, Sylvanus Griswold, 1883-1948. 497'.4
An introduction to the study of the Maya hieroglyphs / Sylvanus Griswold Morley ; with a new introd. and bibliography by J. Eric S. Thompson. New York : Dover Publications, 1975. xxviii, 284 p., 32 leaves of plates : ill. ; 22 cm. Reprint of the 1915 ed. published by the Govt. Print Off., Washington and issued as Bulletin 57 of the Bureau of American Ethnology, Smithsonian Institution. Includes bibliographies and index. [F1435.3.P6M67 1975] 74-82503 ISBN 0-486-23108-9 pbk. : 4.00
1. Mayas—Writing. 2. Calendar, Maya. 3. Maya language. I. Title. II. Series: United States. Bureau of American Ethnology. Bulletin ; 57. BIP

THOMPSON, John Eric Sidney, 1898- 970.3
Maya hieroglyphic writing; an introduction [by] J. Eric S. Thompson. [3d ed.] Norman, University of Oklahoma Press [1971] xxii, 347, [128] p. illus. 30 cm. (Civilization of the American Indian series, no. 56) Includes bibliographies. [F1435.3.P6T47 1971] 72-190588 ISBN 0-8061-0447-3 25.00
1. Mayas—Writing. 2. Calendar, Maya. I. Title. II. Series. BIP

Mayas—Writing—Exhibitions.

COE, Michael D. 917.2'03
The Maya scribe and his world [by] Michael D. Coe. New York, Grolier Club, 1973. 160 p. illus. 29 x 43 cm. Includes items from the Grolier Club exhibit held Apr. 20-June 5, 1971 in New York. Bibliography: p. 156-157. [F1435.3.P6C55] 73-17731 ISBN 0-8139-0568-0
1. Mayas—Writing—Exhibitions. 2. Mayas—Art—Exhibitions. I. Grolier Club, New York. II. Title. BIP

Maybeck, Bernard R.

CARDWELL, Kenneth H., 1920- 720'.92'4 B
Bernard Maybeck : artisan, architect, artist / Kenneth H. Cardwell. Santa Barbara : Peregrine Smith, 1977. p. cm. Includes index. Bibliography: p. [NA737.M435C37] 77-13773 ISBN 0-87905-022-5 : 24.95
1. Maybeck, Bernard R. 2. Architects—California—Biography. BIP

Mayger, Chris.

MAYGER, Chris. 759.2
The marine paintings of Chris Mayger / edited and introduced by David Larkin. London : Pan Books, 1976. [93] p. : chiefly ill. (chiefly col.) ; 29 cm. [ND497.M485A5 1976b] 77-359766 ISBN 0-330-24832-4 : £2.95
1. Mayger, Chris. 2. Ships in art. I. Title.

MAYGER, Chris. 759.2
The marine paintings of Chris Mayger / edited and introduced by David Larkin. 1st U.S. ed. New York : Bantam Books, 1976. [13] p., 40 leaves of plates : ill. (some col.) ; 29 cm. "A Peacock Press/Bantam book." [ND497.M485A5] 75-38077 6.95
1. Mayger, Chris. 2. Ships in art. I. Title. BIP

Mazepa, Ivan Stepanovych, Hetman of the Cossacks, 1644-1709, in fiction, drama, poetry, etc.

BABINSKI, Hubert F., 1936- 809'.933'51
The Mazeppa legend in European romanticism [by] Hubert F. Babinski. New York, Columbia University Press, 1974. 164 p. 23 cm. Bibliography: p. [155]-161. [NX652.M3B32] 74-6152 ISBN 0-231-03825-9 12.00
1. Mazepa, Ivan Stepanovych, Hetman of the Cossacks, 1644-1709, in fiction, drama, poetry, etc. 2. Mazepa, Ivan Stepanovych, Hetman of the Cossacks, 1644-1709—Portraits, caricatures, etc. 3. Mazepa, Ivan Stepanovych, Hetman of the Cossacks, 1644-1709—Songs and music—History and criticism. 4. Romanticism in art. I. Title. BIP

Mazzola-Bedoli, Girolamo, ca. 1500-1569.

MILSTEIN, Ann Rebecca. 759.5
The paintings of Girolamo Mazzola Bedoli / by Ann Rebecca Milstein. New York : Garland Pub., [1978] (Outstanding dissertations in the fine arts) Originally presented as the author's thesis, Harvard, 1977. Bibliography: p. [ND623.M528M54 1978] 77-94710 lib bdg : 47.50
1. Mazzola-Bedoli, Girolamo, ca. 1500-1569. I. Title. II. Series. BIP

Mazzoni, Guido, 1450 (ca.)-1518.

VERDON, Timothy. 730'.92'4 B
The art of Guido Mazzoni / Timothy Verdon. New York : Garland Pub., 1978. p. cm. (Outstanding dissertations in the fine arts) Originally presented as the author's thesis, Yale, 1975. Bibliography: p. [NB623.M459V47 1978] 77-94719 ISBN 0-8240-3253-5 : lib.bdg. : 35.00
1. Mazzoni, Guido, 1450 (ca.)-1518. 2. Sculpture, Renaissance—Italy. I. Title. II. Series. BIP

Mazzuoli, Francesco, called Il Parmigianino, 1503-1540.

FREEDBERG, Sydney Joseph. 759.5
Parmigianino: his works in painting [by] Sydney J. Freedberg. Westport, Conn., Greenwood Press [1971, c1950] xx, 265 p. 167 plates. 26 cm. Bibliography: p. 247-251. [ND623.M55F68 1971] 72-95120 ISBN 0-8371-3717-9
1. Mazzuoli, Francesco, called Il Parmigianino, 1503-1540.

FREEDBERG, Sydney Joseph. 759.5
Parmigianino: his works in painting. Cambridge, Harvard University Press, 1950. xx, 265 p. plates. 26 cm. "A first draft was submitted to Harvard University as a doctoral thesis in 1940." Bibliography: p. 247-251. [ND623.M55F68] 50-8064
1. Mazzuoll, Francesco, called H Parmigianino, 1506-1540. 2. Mannerism (Art) I. Title. BIP

MAZZUOLI, Francesco, called Il Parmigianino, 1503-1540. 741.9'45
Catalogue of the drawings of Parmigianino, by A. E. Popham. New Haven, Published for the Pierpont Morgan Library [by] Yale University Press, 1971. 3 v. illus. 35 cm. (The Franklin Jasper Walls lectures, 1969) Includes bibliographical references. [NC257.M4P6 1971] 76-104619 ISBN 0-300-01300-0
I. Popham, Arthur Ewart, 1889- II. Title. III. Series. BIP

Meadows Museum.

MEADOWS Museum. 708'.164'2812
The Meadows Museum : a visitor's guide to the collection / by William B. Jordan. Dallas : Southern Methodist University, 1974. 137 p., [2] leaves of plates : ill. (some col.) ; 26 cm. Errata slip inserted. Includes bibliographical references. [N557.A86] 75-305020
1. Meadows Museum. 2. Art—Dallas—Catalogs. I. Jordan, William B., 1940-

Meagher Co., Mont.—History—Pictorial works.

MEAGHER County Historical Society. 978.6'612'0222
Meagher County; an early-day pictorial history, 1867-1967. Material gathered by Centennial Pictorial History Committee. White Sulphur Springs, Mont., Meagher County news [1968] 76 p. illus., map (on lining papers), ports. 28 cm. [F737.M4M4] 68-7204
1. Meagher Co., Mont.—History—Pictorial works. I. Title.

Meaning (Psychology)

CARVER, George Alexander. 101
Aesthetics and the problem of meaning; the application to aesthetics of the logical positivists' verifiability criterion of cognitive meaning. New Haven, Yale University Press, 1952. ix, 90 p. 24 cm. (Yale University. Undergraduate prise essays, v. 9) Bibliography: p. 88-89. [BF455.C28] 701.17 52-5364
1. Meaning (Psychology) 2. Logical positivism. 3. Aesthetics. I. Title. II. Series.

Mears, Norman B., 1904—

COHN, Angelo. 686.2'092'4 B
Norman B. Mears, the man behind the shadow mask. Minneapolis, T. S. Denison [1972] 228 p. illus. 23 cm. (Men of achievement series of biographies) A biography of the Minnesota businessman who developed a small graphic arts company into a large business dealing in printing, photo-engraving, and electronics. [TR140.M38C63] 92 76-183713 ISBN 0-513-01231-1
1. Mears, Norman B., 1904- I. Title.

Mechanical drawing.

ALMON, Joseph J 741.422
Visualized basic mechanical drawing. Milwaukee, Bruce Pub. Co. [1961] 160p. (chiefly illus.) 26cm. [T353.A44] 61-13462
1. Mechanical drawing. I. Title.

ARNOLD, Joseph Norman. 744.43
Introductory graphics [by] J. Norman Arnold, with the assistance of Myrl H. Bolds [and others] New York, McGraw-Hill, 1958. 543p. 26cm. [T353.A77] 57-14684
1. Mechanical drawing. I. Title.

AUDEL (Theo.) and Company, New York. 744.422
Audels mechanical drawing guide, by Audel staff. New York [1960] 158, 10p. illus. 23cm. [T353.A85 1960] 60-50544
1. Mechanical drawing. 2. Machinery—Drawing. I. Title. II. Title: Mechanical drawing guide.

BERG, Edward. 744
Mechanical drawing: instruction units and problems. Books I and II. 3d ed., rev. Milwaukee, Bruce Pub. Co. [1954] 228 p. illus. 27 cm. [T351.5.B4] 54-14436
1. Mechanical drawing.

BERG, Edward. 744.422
Mechanical drawing; instruction units and problems. Books I and II. 6th ed., rev. Milwaukee, Bruce Pub. Co. [1966] x, 244 p. illus., plans. 27 cm. [T353.B449 1966] 67-994
1. Mechanical drawing.

BERG, Edward. 744.076
Mechanical drawing problems, by Edward Berg and Emil F. Kronquist. Peoria, Ill., C. A. Bennett Co. [1956] 188p. illus. 16x21cm. [T353.B45 1956] 56-2949
1. Mechanical drawing. I. Kronquist, Emil Fritjoff. 1882- joint author. II. Title.

BERG, Edward. 744.076
Mechanical drawing problems, by Edward Berg and Emil F. Kronquist. Peoria, Ill., C. A. Bennett Co. [1956] 188p. illus. 16x21cm. [T353.B45 1956] 56-2949
1. Mechanical drawing. I. Kronquist, Emil Fritjoff, 1882- joint author. II. Title.

BLACK, Erl D 744.4
Graphical communication; drafting, sketching, and blueprint reading. New York, McGraw-Hill, 1959. 328p. illus. 24cm. [T353.B57] 58-9848
1. Mechanical drawing. I. Title.

BROWN, Walter Charles, 1918- 744.422
Drafting. Chicago, Goodheart-Willcox Co. [1961] 112 p. illus. 27 cm. (Goodheart-Willcox's build-a-course series) [T353.B87] 61-5335
1. Mechanical drawing. I. Title.

CHICAGO. Public Schools. Dept. of Vocational Education. 744.42
Drafting. [Chicago, 1951] 4 v. illus. 29 cm. At head of title of v. 3: Introduction to machine drafting; v. 4: Introduction to

Serial 5739-4. [Ed. 5] Scranton, International Correspondence Schools [1968] 125 p. illus., port. 19 cm. (His Engineering drawing, pt. 3) [T353.H235 1968] 79-871
1. Mechanical drawing. I. International Correspondence Schools, Scranton, Pa.

HARRIS, Michael Godfrey. 744.4'22
Light engineering production draughting [by] Michael G. Harris. London, Foulis [1967] ix, 166p. illus., tables, diagrs. 26cm. [T353.H297] 67-112521 7.25 bds.,
1. Mechanical drawing. I. Title.
Distributed by Transatlantic, Levittown, N.Y. BIP

HAWKINS, Nehemiah, b. 1833 744.422
Rogers' drawing and design; a practical treatise relating to linear drawing, machine design, working drawings, power transmission, metal working machines, lathes, drawing instruments, free hand drawing, tables, etc. New York, Audel [1963] 388p. illus. 18x24cm. 63-24728 3.00
1. Mechanical drawing. 2. Machinery—Design. I. Title. II. Title: Drawing and design.

HAWKINS, Nehemiah, b. 1833. 744.4
Rogers' drawing and design; a practical treatise relating to: linear drawing, machine design, working drawings, power transmission, metal working machines, lathes, drawing instruments, freehand drawing, tables, etc. New York, T. Audel [1960] 410p. illus. 18cm. [T353.H38 1960] 60-1012
1. Mechanical drawing. 2. Machinery—Design. I. Title. II. Title: Drawing and design.

HAYNES, Clarence S 744.4
General drafting; drawing assignments. Courses I and II. Rev. and enl. Boston, Christopher Pub. House [c1955] 94p. illus. 25cm. [T353.H398 1955] 55-24321
1. Mechanical drawing. 2. Drawing instruments. 3. Projection. I. Title.

HEALY, William L 744.4
Simplified drafting practice, a modern approach to industrial drafting[by] W. L. Healy & A. H. Rau. [Student ed.] New York, Wiley [1953] 156p. illus. 29cm. (General Electric series) [T352.H4 1953] 52-14176
1. Mechanical drawing. 2. Drawing-room practice. I. Rau, Arthur H., joint author. II. Title.

HICKS, G. A. 744.4'22
Modern technical drawing [by] G. A. Hicks. [1st ed.] Oxford, New York, Pergamon Press [1967- v. illus. 29 cm. (Commonwealth and international library. C.S.E. division) [T353.H47 1967] 66-17785
1. Mechanical drawing. I. Title.

HIGGINS Ink Company, inc., Brooklyn. 744
Technical illustration [compiled by Bertram Cholet, sales promotion manager. Brooklyn, 1953] 62p. illus. 28cm. [T353.H48] 53-3309
1. Mechanical drawing. I. Title.

HOELSCHER, Randolph Philip, 1890- 744.422
Basic drawing for engineering technology [by] Randolph P. Hoelscher, Clifford H. Springer, Jerry Dobrovolny. New York, Wiley [c.1964] ix, 396p. illus., diagrs. 29cm. 63-20632 6.95
1. Mechanical drawing. I. Title.

HOELSCHER, Randolph Philip, 1890- 744
Engineering drawing and geometry [by] Randolph P. Hoelscher [and] Clifford H. Springer. New York, Wiley [1956] 1v. illus. 29cm. [T353.H625] 56-5067
1. Mechanical drawing. 2. Geometry, Descriptive. I. Springer, Clifford Harry, 1896- joint author. II. Title.

HOELSCHER, Randolph Philip, 1890- 744.422
Engineering drawing and geometry [by] Randolph P. Hoelscher, Clifford H. Springer. 2d ed. New York, Wiley [1961, c.1956, 1961] various p. illus. 26cm. 61-11176 8.95
1. Mechanical drawing. 2. Geometry, Descriptive. I. Springer, Clifford Harry, 1896- joint author. II. Title.

HOOD, George Jussen, 1877-1965. 744.4'22
Geometry of engineering drawing [by] George J. Hood, Albert S. Palmerlee [and] Charles J. Baer. 5th ed. New York, McGraw-Hill [1969] vi, 469 p. illus. 24 cm. Bibliography: p. 462-463. [T353.H772 1969] 69-17182
1. Mechanical drawing. 2. Geometry, Descriptive. I. Palmerlee, Albert Seward, 1908-1969, joint author. II. Baer, Charles J., joint author. III. Title. BIP

HORNUNG, William J 744
Mechanical drafting. Englewood Cliffs, N.J., Prentice-Hall [1957] 240p. illus. 29cm. (Prentice-Hall technical-industrial-vocational series) [T353.H774] 57-7561
1. Mechanical drawing. I. Title.

INTERNATIONAL Correspondence Schools, Scranton, Pa. 744.4'22
Engineering drawing, by I.C.S. staff. Serial 5598-6. [Ed. 5] Scranton [1967- v. illus. 19 cm. Contents.Contents.—pt. 1. Geometrical drawing. [T353.I452] 67-3290
1. Mechanical drawing.

JENSEN, Cecil Howard, 1925- 744.4'22
Drafting fundamentals [by] C. H. Jensen [and] F. H. S. Mason. 2d ed. Toronto, New York, McGraw-Hill Co. of Canada [1967] viii, 242 p. col. illus. 26 cm. [T353.J45 1967] 67-8280
1. Mechanical drawing. I. Mason, Frederick Harry Sextus, 1926- joint author. II. Title.

JENSEN, Cecil Howard, 1925- 744.4'22
Engineering drawing and design. Edited and compiled by C. H. Jensen. Toronto, New York, McGraw-Hill Co. of Canada [1968] xvi, 750 p. illus. 29 cm. [T353.J47] 68-20742
1. Mechanical drawing. 2. Engineering design. I. Title. BIP

JERVIS, William. 744
General mechanical drawing; a psychological approach to a practical subject. Ed. 1. Scranton, International Textbook Co., 1950. xiii, 291 p. illus. 24 cm. (The Arts and industries series) [T353.J53] 50-5850
1. Mechanical drawing. I. Title.

JOHNSON, Lewis Olof. 744.422
Engineering graphics problems; a modern approach, by Lewis O. Johnson, Irwin Wladaver. New York, Reinhold [1962, c.1961] 82 1. illus. 28cm. 62-9529 5.25 pap.,
1. Mechanical drawing. I. Wladaver, Irwin, 1905- joint author. II. Title.

KEPLER, Frank Roy, 1875- 744.422
Mechanical drafting handbook: standards, conventions, and procedures [by] Frank Roy Kepler, William Bettencourt. 1963 ed., rev., enl. Milwaukee, Bruce [c.1963] 191p. illus. 23cm. 62-21389 2.76 pap.,
1. Mechanical drawing. I. Bettencourt, William, 1902- joint author. II. Title.

KLEIN, John A. 744.45
Practical projection, by John A. Klein. Scranton, International Correspondence Schools [1965- pts. illus. 19 cm. Part 1: Serial 1949A-1 [Ed. 2] pt. 3: Serial 1949C-1. [Ed. 3] [T363.K55] 65-4779
1. Mechanical drawing. 2. Projection. I. International Correspondence Schools, Scranton, Pa. II. Title.

LEVENS, Alexander Sander, 1900- 744
Problems in mechanical drawing, first course [by] A. S. Levens and A. E. Edstrom. Keyed to Mechanical drawing, by French and Svensen. 2d ed. New York, McGraw-Hill [1957] unpaged. illus. 28cm. [T353.L633 1957] 57-9426
1. Mechanical drawing. I. Edstrom, Alfred E., joint author. II. French, Thomas Ewing, 1871-1944. Mechanical drawing for high schools. III. Title.

LEVENS, Alexander Sander, 1900- 744.422
Problems in mechanical drawing, first course [by] A. S. Levens, A. E. Edstrom [workbook] Keyed to Mechanical drawing, by French and Svensen. 2d ed. New York, McGraw [1962, c.1957] unpaged. illus. 28cm. 4.95 pap.,
1. Mechanical drawing. I. Edstrom, Alfred E., joint author. II. French, Thomas Ewing, 1871-1944. Mechanical drawing for high schools. III. Title. BIP

LINCOLN Electric Company. 744.5
How to read shop drawings, with special reference to welding and welding symbols. Welding symbols as standardized by the American Welding Society. [1st ed.] Cleveland [1961] 187 p. illus. 28 cm. [T357.L53] 61-13942
1. Mechanical drawing. 2. Welding. I. Title. II. Title: Shop drawing.

LOMBARDO, Josef Vincent. 744.4
Engineering drawing [by] Josef Vincent Lombardo, Lewis O. Johnson [and] W. Irwin Short. Albert J. Lombardo, editor. New York, Barnes & Noble [c1953] 432p. illus. 21cm. (College outline series, 86) [T353.L86] 53-7989
1. Mechanical drawing. 2. Drawing practice. I. Title.

LOMBARDO, Josef Vincent. 744.4
Engineering drawing [by] Josef Vincent Lombardo, Lewis O. Johnson [and] W. Irwin Short. Albert J. Lombardo, editor. New York, Barnes & Noble [c1956] 432p. illus. 21cm. (College outline series, 86) [T353.L86 1956] 56-10847
1. Mechanical drawing. 2. Drawing-room practice. I. Title.

LUZADDER, Warren Jacob 744.422
Fundamentals of engineering drawing for technical students and professional draftsmen. 5th ed. Englewood Cliffs, N.J., Prentice [c.1943-1965] 726p. illus., plans. 26cm. Bibl. [T353.L88] 65-10056 9.95
1. Mechanical drawing. I. Title.

LUZADDER, Warren Jacob. 744.422
Fundamentals of engineering drawing for technical students and professional draftsmen. 4th ed. Englewood Cliffs, N. J., Prentice-Hall, 1959. 720p. illus. 24cm. Includes bibliography. [T353.L88 1959] 59-6531
1. Mechanical drawing. I. Title.

LUZADDER, Warren Jacob. 744.422
Fundamentals of engineering drawing for technical students and professional draftsmen [by] Warren J. Luzadder. 5th ed. Englewood Cliffs, N.J., Prentice-Hall [1965] 726 p. illus., plans. 26 cm. Sixth ed. published under title: Fundamentals of engineering drawing for design, communication, and numerical control. "Bibliography of engineering drawing and allied subjects": p. 710-714. [T353.L88 1965] 65-10056
1. Mechanical drawing. I. Title.

LUZADDER, Warren Jacob. 744.42
Graphics for engineers. Englewood Cliffs, N. J., Prentice-Hall, 1957. 597p. illus. 24cm. [T353.L882] 57-7673
1. Mechanical drawing. 2. Graphic methods. I. Title.

LUZADDER, Warren Jacob. 744
Technical drafting essentials. Architectural drafting section by William J. Hornung. 2d ed. Englewood Cliffs, N. J., Prentice-Hall [1956] 343p. illus. 24cm. (Prentice-Hall technical-industrial-vocational series) First ed. published in 1950 under title: Technical drafting essentials for vocational and technical students. [T353.L887 1956] 56-7228
1. Mechanical drawing. I. Title.

MCCARTNEY, T. O. 744.422
Precision perspective drawing. New York, McGraw [c.1963] 239p. illus. 24cm. 63-11108 11.00
1. Mechanical drawing. 2. Perspective. I. Title.

MCGEE, Richard Allen, 1897- 744.422
General mechanical drawing [by] R. A. McGee, W. W. Sturtevant [and] Glen O. Fuglsby. Rev. ed. Milwaukee, Bruce Pub. Co. [1959] 200p. illus. 25cm. [T353.M16 1959] 59-13649
1. Mechanical drawing. I. Title.

MAGNAN, George. 744.429
Visual art for industry. [New York] Reinhold Pub. Corp. [1961] 176p. illus. 27cm. [T353.M2] 61-14820
1. Mechanical drawing. I. Title.

MARTIN, C. Leslie. 744.422
Design graphics. New York, Macmillan [1962?] 274 p. illus. 30 cm. [T353.M36] 62-7518
1. Mechanical drawing. I. Title. BIP

MARTIN, C. Leslie. 744.4
Design graphics [by] C. Leslie Martin. 2d ed. New York, Macmillan [c.1968] xii, 307p. illus. 29cm. [T353.M36 1968] 68-10247 8.95
1. Mechanical drawing. I. Title.

MEYER, Jerome Sydney, 1895- 744.422
The key to mechanical drawing, by Jerome S. Meyer. [Owings Mills, Md.] Ottenheimer Publishers [1964] 140 p. illus. 18 cm. (A New imperial book) "3520-3." [T353.M6135] 64-6535
1. Mechanical drawing. I. Title.

MEYER, Jerome Sydney, 1895- 744.422
The key to mechanical drawing [Owings Mills, Md.] Ottenheimer [c.1964] 140p. illus. 18cm. (New Imperial bk., 3520-3) 64-6535 .95 pap.,
1. Mechanical drawing. I. Title.

MOTT, Leslie Charles. 744.422
Engineering drawing and construction [by] L. C. Mott. London, New York, Oxford University Press, 1965- v. illus. 26 cm. [T353.M72] 66-710
1. Mechanical drawing. I. Title. BIP

MUSACCHIA, John B., 1916- 744.4
Drafting by the model method, by John B. Musacchia, Henri A. Fluchere [and] Melvin J. Grainger. [New York] Arco Pub. Co. [1953] 143p. illus. 22x29cm. [T357.M87] 53-1510
1. Mechanical drawing. 2. Models and modelmaking. I. Title.

NELSON, Howard C 744.4
A handbook of drafting rules and principles. [1st ed.] Bloomington, Ill., McKnight & McKnight Pub. Co. [1958] 96p. illus. 22cm. [T353.N42] 58-1926
1. Mechanical drawing. I. Title.

ORTH, Herbert Denny, 1885- 744.422
Theory and practice of engineering drawing [by] H. D. Orth, R. R. Worsencroft [and] H. B. Doke. [2d ed.] Dubuque, Iowa, W. C. Brown Co. [1959] 484p. illus. 24cm. Published in 1946 under title: Basic engineering drawing. [T353.O68 1959] 59-16861
1. Mechanical drawing. I. Title.

PARKINSON, Albert Charles. 744.4'22
Geometrical and mechanical drawing, by A. C. Parkinson and E. A. Ayres. London, Pitman. 1967-- Stamped on t. p. dist. by SportShelf, New Rochelle, N. Y. Contents.Bk. 2. pt. 2. Mechanical Solid geometry. pt. 3. Mechanical drawing. [T353.P265] 68-81647 5.50 bds.,
1. Mechanical drawing. 2. Geometrical drawing. I. Ayres, E. A. joint author. II. Title.

PYEATT, A D 744.429
Technical illustration. New ed. New York, Higgins Ink Co., 1960. 113p. illus. 28cm. Published in 1953 by the Higgins Ink Company, Brooklyn. [T353.P9 1960] 60-4503
1. Mechanical drawing. I. Title.

REYNOLDS, R Wallace. 744.42
Problems for modern engineering drawing. San Francisco, Fearon Publishers [c1956- v. illus. 28x45cm. [T353.R47] 56-11438
1. Mechanical drawing. I. Title.

ROTMANS, Elmer A. 744.4
Drafting simplified. Albany, Delmar Publishers [1950] vii, 397 p. diagrs. 27 cm. [T353.R797] 50-38012
1. Mechanical drawing.

ROTMANS, Elmer A. 744.4'22
Drafting technology [by] Elmer A. Rotmans [and] Homer L. Horton. Albany, N.Y., Delmar Publishers [1967] v, 387 p. illus. 27 cm. [T353.R798] 67-19033

Medals, Renaissance. 3. Coins, Roman. I. Title.

U. S. National Gallery of Art 737.4
Renaissance medals: from the Samuel H. Kress Collection at the National Gallery of Art; based on the catalogue of Renaissance medals in the Gustave Dreyfus Collection, by G. F. Hill, rev., enl. by Graham Pollard. London, Phaidon Pr., for the Samuel H. Kress Found. [1967] x, 307p. 1209 illus. 31cm. Bibl. [CJ5510.U55] 67-105399 18.50
1. Medals, Renaissance. I. Dreyfus, Gustave, 1837-1914. II. Hill, Sir George Francis, 1867-1948. III. Pollard, Graham. IV. Samuel H. Kress Foundation. V. Title. VI. Title: The Gustave Dreyfus collection.
American distributor: Praeger, New York.

Medals—Switzerland.

KRAUSE, Delbert Ray 737.2
Swiss shooting talers and medals, by Delbert Ray Krause with Lawrence Block. Racine, Wis., Whitman Pub. [c.1965] 160p. illus. 20cm. [CJ6323.K7] 66-1565 3.00 bds.,
1. Medals—Switzerland. 2. Shooting contests. I. Block, Lawrence, joint author. II. Title.

Medals—U.S.

BELDEN, Bauman Lowe, 1862-1931. 737.2
Indian peace medals issued in the United States. New Milford, Conn., N. Flayderman [1966] 46 p. illus., port. 29 cm. [CJ5807.B4 1966] 66-20865
1. Medals—U.S. 2. Indians of North America—Medals. I. Title. BIP

CULVER, Virginia. 737'.0973
Guidebook of Franklin Mint issues / edited by Virginia Culver and Chester L. Krause. [2d ed.] Iola, Wis. : Krause Publications, 1975. 222 p. : ill. ; 28 cm. Includes indexes. [CJ5813.F732C84 1975] 76-364213 ISBN 0-87341-005-X pbk. : 6.50
1. Franklin Mint. 2. Medals—United States. 3. Tokens—United States. I. Krause, Chester L., joint author. II. Title.

KERRIGAN, Evans E. 355.1'34
American war medals and decorations. New York, Viking Press [1964] xiv, 149 p. illus., 4 col. plates. 24 cm. (A Studio book) Bibliography: p. 141. [CJ5805.K4] 63-17073
1. Medals—United States. 2. Decorations of honor—United States. I. Title. II. Title: Current American war medals and decorations, 1963-1969.

KERRIGAN, Evans E. 355.1'34
American war medals and decorations, by Evans E. Kerrigan. Newly rev. and expanded. New York, Viking Press [1971] xiv, 173 p. illus., 4 col. plates. 24 cm. (A Studio book) Bibliography: p. 165. [CJ5805.K4 1971] 77-124322 ISBN 0-670-12101-0 8.50
1. Medals—U.S. 2. Decorations of honor—U.S. I. Title.

KIDD, J. Archie. 737'.2
Silver art bars : a guide book of 1-ounce, .999 fine / produced by J. Archie Kidd. 2d ed. [s.l. : Kidd, 1976. 143 p. : ill. ; 29 cm. [CJ5806.K52 1976] 76-375320
1. Medals—United States. I. Title.

KRAUSE, Chester L. 737'.0973
Guidebook of Franklin Mint issues / edited by Chester L. Krause. [3d ed.]. Iola, Wis. : Krause Publications, 1976. 222 p. : ill. ; 28 cm. First-2d ed. written by V. Culver and C. L. Krause. Includes indexes. [CJ5813.F732C84 1976] 76-7254 ISBN 0-87341-009-2 : 6.50
1. Franklin Mint. 2. Medals—United States. 3. Tokens—United States. I. Culver, Virginia. Guidebook of Franklin Mint issues. II. Title.

LOUBAT, Joseph Florimond, duc de, 1831-1927. 355.1'34
The medallic history of the United States of America, 1776-1876. With 170 etchings by Jules Jacquemart. New Milford, Conn., N. Flayderman [1967] lxix, 460 p. illus. 24 cm. Reprint of the 1878 ed. [CJ5805.L8 1967] 67-28353
1. Medals—United States. I. Title.

Medals—United States—Exhibitions.

NORTON (R. W.) Art Gallery. 737'.2
Medallic art of the United States, 1800-1972. [Exhibition] August 8 to September 17, 1972. [Shreveport, La., 1972] 40 p. illus. (part col.) 28 cm. Bibliography: p. 39. [CJ5802.2.S48N67] 72-187912 ISBN 0-9600182-9-8
1. Medals—United States—Exhibitions. 2. Medals—History. I. Title. BIP

Medici, House of—Art collections.

ADY, Cecilia Mary, 1881-1958. v. 12
Lorenzo dei Medici and Renaissance Italy. New York, Collier Books [1962] 158 p. 18 cm. (Men and history) "First Collier Books edition [AS 421V]" Bibliography, p. [152] [NUC63-70132]
I. Title.

DETROIT. Institute of Arts. 709'.45'51
The twilight of the Medici; late baroque art in Florence, 1670-1743. Detroit, the Detroit Institute of Arts, 27 March-2 June, 1974. Florence, Palazzo Pitti, 28 June-30 September, 1974. Exhibition sponsored by Founders Society, the Detroit Institute of Arts, and the City of Florence. [Florence] Centro Di; [distribution in U.S.: Wayne State University Press, Detroit, 1974] 507 p. illus. (part col.) 24 cm. (Centro Di catalog 43) Bibliography: p. 494-503. [N6921.F7D47 1974] 74-176274 15.00
1. Medici, House of—Art collections. 2. Art, Florentine—Exhibitions. 3. Art, Baroque—Florence. I. Founders Society. II. Florence. Palazzo Pitti. III. Title. BIP

MORASSI, Antonio, 1892- 708.5
Art treasures of the Medici. Greenwich, Conn., New York Graphic Society [1964, c1963] 38, [3] p. illus. (part mounted col.) 31 cm. ([The Great masters of the past series, 10]) Art treasures from the Musco degli argenti, Florence. Translation of Il tesoro del Medici. Bibliography: p. [39]-[41] [NK480.F58M63] 63-16434
1. Medici, House of—Art collections. 2. Art objects—Florence. I. Florence. Museo degli argenti. II. Title. III. Series: The great masters of the past, 10

Medicine and art.

DAUMIER, Honore Victorin, 1808-1879 769.944
Doctors & medicine in the works of Daumier [by] Henri Mondor. Notes and catalogue by Jean Adhemar. Pref. by Arthur W. Heintzelman. [Tr. from French by C. de Chabanne] Boston, Boston Book and Art Shop, 657 Boylston St. [c. 1960] 134p. illus. 33cm. 60-12468 12.50 buck.,
1. Medicine and art. I. Mondor, Henri, 1885- II. Title.

DUKE University, Durham, N.C. Medical Center. Library. 769
Reflections of medicine: the graphic art [catalogue of] a loan exhibition cosponsored by the Trent Collection, Duke University Medical Center Library and the Duke University Museum of Art, Durham, North Carolina. November 17, 1972-January 7, 1973. [Durham, N.C., 1972] [22] p. illus. 25 cm. [NE962.M4D84 1972] 74-157595
1. Medicine and art. 2. Prints—Exhibitions. I. Associates of the Trent Collection. II. Duke University, Durham, N.C. Art Museum. III. Title.

MACKINNEY, Loren Carey, 1891- 704.94961
Medical illustrations in medieval manuscripts. Berkeley, Univ. of Calif., Pr. [c.]1965. xvii, 262p. plates. (pt. col.) 26cm. Bibl. [N8223.M25] 65-21268 15.00
1. Medicine and art. 2. Illumination of books and manuscripts—Speciments, reproductions, etc. I. Title.

PHILADELPHIA Museum of Art. 704.94961
Ars medica; a collection of medical prints presented to the Philadelphia Museum of Art by Smith, Kline & French Laboratories. Catalogue compiled by Carl Zigrosser. [Philadelphia, c1959] 90 p. illus. 26 cm. [N8223.P5 1959] 68-42697
1. Medicine and art. 2. Prints—Exhibitions. I. Zigrosser, Carl, 1891- II. Title.

PHILADELPHIA Museum of Art. 769.4
Ars medica; a collection of medical prints by great artists of the past, presented to the Art Museum by Smith, Kyline French Laboratories. Catalogue compiled by Carl Zigrosser. [Philadelphia, 1955] [52] p. (incl. cover) illus. 26cm. Cover title. [N8223.P5] 56-29873
1. Medicine and art. 2. Engravings—Exhibitions. 3. Art—Exhibitions, Traveling. I. Zigrosser, Carl, 1891- II. Title.

PHILADELPHIA Museum of Art. 704.94961
Ars medica; a collection of medical prints presented to the Philadelphia Museum of Art by Smith, Kline & French Laboratories. Catalogue compiled by Carl Zigrosser. [Philadelphia, c1959] 90 p. illus. 26 cm. [N8223.P5 1959] 68-42697
1. Medicine and art. 2. Prints—Exhibitions. I. Zigrosser, Carl, 1891- II. Title.

ROUSSELOT, Jean, 1915- 704.94/9/61
Medicine in art; a cultural history. Jean Rousselot, general ed. New York, McGraw [1967] 333p. illus. (pt. col.) 32cm. [N8223.R6] 66-24885 22.00
1. Medicine and art. I. Title.

SCHOUTEN, Jan. 704.94'9'61
The rod and serpent of Asklepios, symbol of medicine, by J. Schouten. [Translated from the Dutch by M. E. Hollander] Amsterdam, New York, Elsevier Pub. Co., 1967. 260 p. illus. 25 cm. Bibliography: p. 239-246. [N8223.S313] 66-25766
1. Medicine and art. 2. Medicine and art. I. Title.

ZIGROSSER, Carl, 1891- comp. 769'.4'961
Medicine and the artist; 137 great prints, selected with commentary by Carl Zigrosser. 3d enl. ed. New York, Dover Publications [1970] xi, 177 p. illus., ports. 28 cm. "Enlarged and slightly altered republication of the second revised edition (1959) of the Ars medica catalogue originally published by the Philadelphia Museum of Art." [N8223.Z5 1970] 69-17472 ISBN 0-486-62133-2 3.75
1. Medicine and art. 2. Prints—Exhibitions. I. Philadelphia Museum of Art. Ars medica. II. Title. BIP

Medicine and art—Juvenile literature.

COEN, Rena Neumann. 704.94'9'61
Medicine in art. Designed by Patricia Koskey. Minneapolis, Lerner Publications Co., 1970. 64 p. illus. (part col.), ports. (part col.) 26 cm. (Fine art books for young people) Text and examples of drawings, paintings, and sculpture from many eras describe man's concept of illness and various medical practices throughout the centuries. [N8223.C6] 79-84408
1. Medicine and art—Juvenile literature. I. Title.

Medicine bottles—Catalogs.

WILSON, Bill, 1926- 615'.1
19th century medicine in glass, by Bill & Betty Wilson [Amador City, Calif., 19th Century Hobby & Pub. Co., 1971] 147, [2] p. illus. 29 cm. Bibliography: p. [149] [NK5440.B6W48] 78-155464
1. Medicine bottles—Catalogs. I. Wilson, Betty, 1932- joint author. II. Title.

Medicine-man.

LOMMEL, Andreas. 291.6'2
Shamanism; the beginnings of art. New York, McGraw [1966,c.1967] 175p. illus. (pt. col.) 27cm. Tr. of Die Welt der fruhen Jager, Medizinmanner, Schamanen, Kunstler. Bibl. [GN477.L613] 66-24886 12.00
1. Medicine-man. I. Title.

Medinet=Abu.

CHICAGO. University. Oriental Institute. Epigraphic Survey. 913.32
Medinet Habu. Field director, Harold Hayden Nelson. Chicago, University of Chicago Press [1930-64] 7 v. illus., plans, plates (part col.) 49-61 em. The University of Chicago Oriental Institute publications, v. 8-9, 23, 51, 83-84, 93) Chicago. University. Oriental Institute. Publications, v. 8-9 [etc.] Contents.v. 1. Earlier historical records of Ramses iii. -- v. 2. Later historical records of Ramses iii. -- v. 3. The Calendar, the "slaughterhouse," and minor records of Ramses iii. -- v. 4. Festival scenes of Ramses iii. -- v. 5. The Temple proper. pt. 1. The portico, the treasury, and chapels adjoining the first hypostyle hall with marginal material from the forecourts. -- v. 6. The Temple proper. [DT73.M3C42] 30-22847
1. 2. Ramses iii, King of Egypt. 2. Medinet=Abu. 3. Egyptian language — Inscriptions. I. Nelson, Harold Hayden, 1878-1954. II. Title. III. Series. BIP

Meegeren, Han van, 1889-1947.

KILBRACKEN, John Raymond Godley, baron, 1920- 927.5
The master forger; the story of Han van Meegeren. New York, W. Funk [1951?] 223p. illus. 20cm. [ND653.M58K53 1951a] 51-7661
1. Meegeren, Han van, 1889-1947. 2. Vermeer, Johannes, 1632-1675. 3. Hooch, Pieter de, 17th cent. 4. Forgery of works of art. 5. Paintings—Expertising. I. Title.

KILBRACKEN, John Raymond Godley, Baron, 1920- 759.9492
Van Meegeren, master forger [by] Lord Kilbracken. New York, Scribner [1968, c1967] 197 p. illus., ports. 22 cm. [ND653.M58K56] 68-17337
1. Meegeren, Han van, 1889-1947. I. Title.

KILBRACKEN, John Raymond Godley, Baron, 1920- 759.9492
Van Meegeren, master forger [by] Lord Kilbracken. New York, Scribner [1968, c1967] 197 p. illus., ports. 22 cm. [ND653.M58K56 1968] 68-17337
1. Meegeren, Han van, 1889-1947.

Mefferd, Boyd.

COE, Ralph T. 709'.73
Boyd Mefferd: light in motion [by Ralph T. Coe. Dallas? 1968?] [12] p. illus. 26 cm. Exhibition held Jan. 17 to Feb. 18, 1968, at the Dallas Museum of Fine Arts. [N6537.M4C6] 68-2356
1. Mefferd, Boyd. I. Dallas. Museum of Fine Arts. II. Title: Light in motion.

Megalithic monuments—Ireland.

IRELAND (Eire). Ordnance Survey. 726'.8'09415
Survey of the megalithic tombs of Ireland / Ruaidhri de Valera and Sean O Nuallain. Dublin : Stationery Office, 1961- v. : ill. ; 33 cm. Contents.Contents.—v. 1. County Clare.—v. 3. Counties: Galway, Roscommon, Leitrim, Longford, Westmeath, Laoighis, Offaly, Kildare, Cavan. Includes bibliographical references. [GN792.I7I73 1961] 75-316418
1. Megalithic monuments—Ireland. 2. Ireland—Antiquities. 3. Tombs—Ireland. I. De Valera, Ruaidhri. II. O Nuallain, Sean. III. Title.

Meier, Richard, 1934—

MEIER, Richard, 1934- 720'.92'4
Richard Meier, architect : buildings and projects, 1966-1976 / introd. by Kenneth Frampton ; postscript by John Hejduk. New York : Oxford University Press, 1976. 238 p. : ill. ; 26 cm. (A Galaxy book) [NA737.M44A55] 75-38096 15.00
1. Meier, Richard, 1934- I. Title. BIP

Meiss, Millard.

STUDIES in late medieval and Renaissance painting in honor of Millard Meiss / edited by Irving Lavin and John Plummer. New York : New York 759.03

University Press, 1977[i.e. 1976] p. cm. Contributions in English, French, or Italian. Includes bibliographical references. [ND140.S88] 75-27118 75.00
1. Meiss, Millard. 2. Painting, Medieval—Addresses, essays, lectures. 3. Painting, Renaissance—Addresses, essays, lectures. I. Meiss, Millard. II. Lavin, Irving, 1927- III. Plummer, John. BIP

Meissen porcelain.

DUCRET, Siegfried 738.37
Meissen porcelain [Eng. tr. by Marjorie Gibson Craig] Berne, Hallwag [New York, Taplinger, 1965, c1964] 9p., 19 col. plates. 19cm. (Orbis pictus, 13) [NK4380.D813] 65-6984 2.50 bds.,
1. Meissen porcelain. I. Title. BIP

MEISSEN. Staatliche 738.2'7
Porzellanmanufaktur.
Meissen china; an illustrated history. K. Berling, editor. New York, Dover Publications [1972] xvi, 191 p. illus. 29 cm. Translation of Festschrift zur 200 jahrigen Jubelfeier der altesten europaischen Porzellanmanufaktur. Reprint of the 1911 ed. published by Royal Saxon China Manufactory, Meissen, under title: Festive publication to commemorate the 200th jubilee of the oldest European china factory, Meissen. Contents.Contents.—The Meissen china manufactory from 1710 to 1910, by prof. Dr. Berling.—The development of the chemico-technical management from the beginning to the present time, by Counsellor Superior of Mines Dr. Heintze.—Organization, financial management and social statistics, by Privy Counsellor of Commerce Gesell.—The celebration of the 200th anniversary of the Royal China Manufactory on June 6th 1910, by Privy Counsellor of Commerce Gesell. Includes bibliographical references. [NK4380.M413 1972] 72-75580 ISBN 0-486-21958-5 6.00
1. Meissen. Staatliche porzellanmanufaktur. 2. Meissen porcelain. I. Berling, Karl, 1857-1940, ed. II. Title. BIP

MORLEY-FLETCHER, Hugho. 738.2
Antique porcelain in color: Meissen. [1st ed. in U.S.A.] Garden City, N.Y., Doubleday [1971] 119 p. col. illus. 31 cm. [NK4380.M65 1971] 74-134440 12.95
1. Meissen porcelain. I. Title.

SMITHSONIAN Institution. 738.27
National Collection of Fine Arts.
Meissen and other German porcelain in the Alfred Duane Pell collection, by Paul Vickers Gardner, curator of ceramics. Washington, Smithsonian Institution, 1956. vi, 66 p. illus. (part col.) 26 cm. (Smithsonian Institution Publication no. 4256) Bibliography: p. 66. [NK4380.S6] 56-61670
1. Meissen procelain. 2. Meissen. Staatliche Porzellanmanufaktur. 3. Porcelain, German. 4. Porcelain — Marks. 5. Porcelain — Washington, D.C. — Catalogs. I. Gardner, Paul Vicker, 1908- II. Pell, Alfred Duane. III. Title.

Meissen. Staatliche porzellanmanufaktur.

MEISSEN. Staatliche 738.2'7
Porzellanmanufaktur.
Meissen china; an illustrated history. K. Berling, editor. New York, Dover Publications [1972] xvi, 191 p. illus. 29 cm. Translation of Festschrift zur 200 jahrigen Jubelfeier der altesten europaischen Porzellanmanufaktur. Reprint of the 1911 ed. published by Royal Saxon China Manufactory, Meissen, under title: Festive publication to commemorate the 200th jubilee of the oldest European china factory, Meissen. Contents.Contents.—The Meissen china manufactory from 1710 to 1910, by prof. Dr. Berling.—The development of the chemico-technical management from the beginning to the present time, by Counsellor Superior of Mines Dr. Heintze.—Organization, financial management and social statistics, by Privy Counsellor of Commerce Gesell.—The celebration of the 200th anniversary of the Royal China Manufactory on June 6th 1910, by Privy Counsellor of Commerce Gesell. Includes bibliographical references. [NK4380.M413 1972] 72-75580 ISBN 0-486-21958-5 6.00
1. Meissen. Staatliche porzellanmanufaktur. 2. Meissen porcelain. I. Berling, Karl, 1857-1940, ed. II. Title. BIP

Meissner, Kurt, 1909—

FORSTER-HAHN, 741.9'074'094945
Franziska.
Old master drawings from the Collection of Kurt Meissner, Zurich. Catalogue by Francoise Forster-Hahn. [Stanford, Calif.] Dept. of Art, Stanford University [1969] 117 p. 88 illus. 24 cm. (Stanford art book 10) Catalogue of an exhibition held at Stanford Art Gallery, Nov. 2-Dec. 14, 1969; Detroit Institute of Arts, Jan. 27-Mar. 8, 1970; and Finch College Museum of Art, Apr. 1-June 15, 1970. Label mounted on t.p.: Supplied by Worldwide Books, inc., Boston. Includes bibliographical references. [NC33.S92M44] 70-21381 4.50
1. Meissner, Kurt, 1909- 2. Drawings—Exhibitions—Art collections. I. Stanford University. Thomas Welton Stanford Art Gallery. II. Detroit. Institute of Arts. III. Finch College, New York. Museum of Art. IV. Title. V. Series.

Meister, Peter Wilhelm.

FESTSCHRIFT fur Peter 069'.9'7
Wilhelm Meister zum 65. [i.e. funfundsechzigsten] Geburtstag am 16. Mai 1974 / [hrsg. von Annaliese Ohm u. Horst Reber]. Hamburg : Hauswedell, [1975] 331 p. : ill., maps ; 30 cm. Includes three contributions in English. Bibliography of works by P. W. Meister: p. 327. [N7442.M442] 75-504057 DM240.00
1. Meister, Peter Wilhelm. 2. Art—Addresses, essays, lectures. I. Meister, Peter Wilhelm. II. Ohm, Anneliese. III. Reber, Horst.

Mel'nikov, Konstantin Stepanovich, 1890—

STARR, S. Frederick. 720'.92'4 B
Melnikov : solo architect in a mass society / S. Frederick Starr. Princeton, N.J. : Princeton University Press, c1978. xvii, 276 p. : ill. ; 29 cm. Includes index. Bibliography: p. [263]-270. [NA1199.M37S7] 77-85566 ISBN 0-691-03931-3 : 25.00
1. Mel'nikov, Konstantin Stepanovich, 1890- 2. Architects—Russian Republic—Biography. I. Title. BIP

Melamed, Abraham, 1914- —Art collections.

ELVEHJEM Art 769'.944'074017584
Center.
Cubist prints from the Collection of Dr. & Mrs. Abraham Melamed. Madison, Wis. [1972] 43 p. illus. 21 x 23 cm. Catalog of an exhibition held 5 February-12 March 1972, prepared by Arthur R. Blumenthal. Bibliography: p. 7. [NE492.C8E4] 72-187232
1. Melamed, Abraham, 1914- —Art collections. 2. Prints—Exhibitions. 3. Cubism. I. Blumenthal, Arthur R. II. Title.

Melbourne. Botanic Garden.

PESCOTT, Richard Thomas 712'.5 B
Martin, 1905-
W. R. Guilfoyle, 1840-1912 : the master of landscaping / [by] R. T. M. Pescott. Melbourne ; New York : Oxford University Press, 1974. xvii, 153 p., 13 p. of plates : ill., facsims., front., map on lining papers ; 25 cm. Includes index. Bibliography: p. 143-145. [SB470.G84P47] 75-320160 ISBN 0-19-550454-2 : 9.75
1. Guilfoyle, William Robert, 1840-1912. 2. Melbourne. Botanic Garden. 3. Landscape gardening—Australia—Melbourne.

Melbourne—Description—Views.

LIARDET, Wilbraham 759.994
Frederick Evelyn, 1799-1878.
Liardet's water-colours of early Melbourne. Introduction and captions by Susan Adams, edited by Weston Bate. Carlton, Vic., Melbourne University Press on behalf of the Library Council of Victoria, [1972, i.e. 1973] xi, 101 p. illus., maps, col. plates. 24 x 31 cm. Bibliography: p. 99-101. [ND1942.L46A65] 73-165144 25.00
1. Liardet, Wilbraham Frederick Evelyn, 1799-1878. 2. Melbourne—Description—Views. I. Adams, Susan. II. Bate, Weston Arthur, ed. III. Library Council of Victoria. IV. Title.
Distributed by International Scholarly Book Service. BIP

Melchers, Gari, 1860-1932.

GARI Melchers (1860-1932) 759.13
: [catalogue] : selections from the Mary Washington College collection, Fredericksburg, Virginia, 1973. [Fredericksburg, Va. : Art Dept., Mary Washington College, 1973] 56 p. : ill. ; 29 cm. "Prepared by the students in the Connoissership Course of the ... College Art Department." Bibliography: p. 55-56. [ND237.M42M37] 75-304332
1. Melchers, Gari, 1860-1932. I. Mary Washington College, Fredericksburg, Va. Art Dept.

Mellon, Paul—Art collections

BASKETT, John. 741.9'42'07401471
English drawings and watercolors, 1550-1850, in the Collection of Mr. and Mrs. Paul Mellon [by John Baskett and Dudley Snelgrove] New York, Pierpont Morgan Library, 1972. xxi, 107 p. 150 plates (part col.) 29 cm. "Exhibition of the Mellon Collection, 13 April to 28 July 1972, the Pierpont Morgan Library." Bibliography: p. xvii-xx. [NC228.B3] 77-190656 ISBN 0-87598-035-X
1. Mellon, Paul—Art collections 2. Mellon, Rachel Lambert (Lloyd)—Art collections. 3. Drawings, English—Exhibitions. 4. Water-colors, English—Exhibitions. I. Snelgrove, Dudley, joint author. II. Pierpont Morgan Library, New York. III. Title.

CONSTABLE, John, 1776-1837. 759.2
John Constable; a selection of paintings from the Collection of Mr. and Mrs. Paul Mellon. Washington, National Gallery of Art, 1969. 61 p. illus. 26 cm. Exhibition held Apr. 30-Nov. 1, 1969. [ND497.C7A53] 79-84207
1. Mellon, Paul—Art collections. 2. Mellon, Rachel Lambert (Lloyd)—Art collections. I. U.S. National Gallery of Art. II. Title.

HOGARTH, William, 1697- 759.2
1764.
William Hogarth; a selection of paintings from the collection of Mr. and Mrs. Paul Mellon. Washington, National Gallery of Art [1971] 50 p. illus. 26 cm. Exhibition held Feb. 12 to May 30, 1971. [ND497.H7A44] 75-148159
1. Mellon, Paul—Art collections. 2. Mellon, Rachel Lambert (Lloyd)—Art collections. I. U.S. National Gallery of Art. BIP

U.S. National 759.4'074'0153
Gallery of Art.
French paintings from the Collections of Mr. and Mrs. Paul Mellon and Mrs. Mellon Bruce; twenty-fifth anniversary exhibition, 1941-1966. [2d ed.] Washington [1966] 256 p. (chiefly illus. (part col.)) 26 cm. Exhibition held March 17-May 1, 1966. [ND547.U58 1966b] 71-18036
1. Mellon, Paul—Art collections. 2. Mellon, Rachel Lambert (Lloyd)—Art collections. 3. Bruce, Ailsa (Mellon)—Art collections. 4. Paintings, French—Exhibitions. I. Title.

WHITE, 760'.0942'07401468
Christopher.
English landscape, 1630-1850 : drawings, prints & books from the Paul Mellon Collection : an exhibition, April 19-July 17, 1977 / by Christopher White. New Haven : Yale Center for British Art, c1977. xxv, 126 p., [91] leaves of plates : ill. (some col.) ; 29 cm. Catalogue of an exhibition held at Yale Center for British Art, New Haven. Includes bibliographical references. [N8214.5.G7W48] 77-71656
1. Mellon, Paul—Art collections. 2. England in art. 3. Art, English—Exhibitions. 4. Art, Modern—17th-18th centuries—England—Exhibitions. 5. Art, Modern—19th century—England—Exhibitions. I. Yale Center for British Art. II. Title.

YALE Center 760'.0942'07401468
for British Art.
The pursuit of happiness : a view of life in Georgian England : an exhibition selected from the Paul Mellon Collection, Yale Center for British Art, New Haven, April 19 to September 18, 1977 / J. H. Plumb ; catalogue entries by Edward J. Nygren and Nancy L. Pressly. [New Haven] : The Center, c1977. 139 p., [6] leaves of plates : ill. (some col.) ; 28 cm. Includes index. [N6766.Y34 1977] 77-71640
1. Mellon, Paul—Art collections. 2. Art, English—Exhibitions. 3. Art, Georgian—England—Exhibitions. I. Plumb, John Harold, 1911- II. Title.

YALE 741.9'42'07401468
University. Art Gallery.
English drawings and watercolors, from the collection of Mr. and Mrs. Paul Mellon, April 15 - June 20, 1965. [New Haven, c1965] [46] p. (chiefly illus.) 22 cm. [NC228.Y34] 73-168190
1. Mellon, Paul—Art collections. 2. Mellon, Rachel Lambert (Lloyd)—Art collections. 3. Drawings, English—Exhibitions. 4. Watercolors, English—Exhibitions. I. Title.

Mells, Eng.

SOMERSET, Eng. 711'.4'094238
Planning Dept.
Mells conservation area. Taunton, Somerset (County) Council, 1969. 8 p. illus., col. map. 30 cm. Cover title. [DA690.M555S6] 72-522425 4/-
1. Mells, Eng. I. Title.

Memling, Hans, 1430?-1494.

DUMONT, Georges Henri. 759.9493'1
Hans Memling. [Translator: Haydn Barnes. Editor: Anthony Bosman] New York, Barnes & Noble [1967, c1966] 88 p. plate (part col.) 18 cm. (Barnes & Noble art series) "No. 628." [ND673.M5D813] 67-1532
1. Memling, Hans, 1430?-1494. I. Bosman, Anthony, ed.

MCFARLANE, Kenneth 759.9493
Bruce.
Hans Memling, by K. B. McFarlane. Edited by Edgar Wind with the assistance of G. L. Harriss. Oxford [Eng.] Clarendon Press, 1971. xv, 74 p. 153 illus. 30 cm. Bibliography: p. [61] - 66. [ND673.M5M3] 72-200900 ISBN 0-19-817179-X 19.50 (U.S.)
1. Memling, Hans, 1430?-1494.

Memory.

WRIGHT, J M von. 701.16
Forgetting and interference, by J. M. von Wright. Helsingfors, 1959. 124 p. diagrs., tables. 23 cm. (Societas Scientiarum Fennica. Commentationes humanarum literrarum XXVI,1) Bibliography: p. [118]-124. [P9.F5t.26, no. 1] A64
1. Memory. 2. Recollection (Psychology) I. Title. II. Series: Finska vetenskaps-societeten, Helsingfors. Commentationes humanarum litterarum, XXVI, 1

Memphis. Egypt—Antiq.

ANTHES, Rudolf. 1896- 913.32
Mit Rahineh 1955. With contributions by Hasan S.K. Bakry[and others] Philadelphia. University Museum. University of Pennsylvania, 1959. v. 93p. illus., fold. col. map (in pocket) 28cm. (University Museum. University of Pennsylvania. Museum monographs) Report of the first season of excavations from Feb. to Apr. 1955. Bibliography: p.89-93. [DT73.M5A78] 59-1939
1. Memphis. Egypt—Antiq. I. Title. II. Series: Pennsylvania. University. University Museum. Museum monographs BIP

SUBJECT INDEX MERU, Y. Y.

Men in art.

SELZ, Peter Howard, 1919- 704.94'2
New images of man. With statements by the artists. [New York, Published for the Museum of Modern Art by Arno Press, 1969] 159 p. illus. 25 cm. Reprint of the 1959 ed. "Errata": p. [2] "Selected bibliography by Ilse Falk": p. 155-159. [N7570.S38 1969] 76-86447
1. Men in art. 2. Art, Modern—20th century. I. New York (City). Museum of Modern Art. II. Title. BIP

WALTERS, Margaret, 1938- 704.94'23
The nude male : a new perspective / Margaret Walters. New York : Paddington Press : distributed by Grosset & Dunlap, c1978. 352 p. : ill. ; 26 cm. Includes index. Bibliography: p. 339. [N7572.W34] 77-20967 ISBN 0-448-23168-9 : 12.95
1. Men in art. 2. Nude in art. I. Title. BIP

Men—Portraits.

WOMEN photograph men / edited by Dannielle B. Hayes ; introd. by Molly Haskell. New York : Morrow, c1977. ca. 150 p. : chiefly ill. ; 28 cm. [TR681.M4W64] 77-6905 ISBN 0-688-03214-1 : 15.95 779'.23'0922
1. Men—Portraits. 2. Women photographers. I. Hayes, Dannielle B. BIP

WOMEN see men / edited by Yvonne Kalmus, Rikki Ripp, Cheryl Wiesenfeld ; introd. and text by Ingrid Bengis ; designed by Geri Davis. New York : McGraw Hill, c1977. p. cm. [TR681.M4W65] 77-8860 ISBN 0-07-033248-7 : 12.95 ISBN 0-07-033249-5 pbk. : 7.95 779'.23'0922
1. Men—Portraits. 2. Women photographers. I. Kalmus, Yvonne. II. Ripp, Rikki. III. Wiesenfeld, Cheryl. IV. Bengis, Ingrid.

Mendelsohn, Erich, 1887-1953.

MENDELSOHN, Erich, 1887-1953. 720'.924
The drawings of Eric Mendelsohn, by Susan King. With the cooperation of the Graham Foundation for Advanced Studies in the Fine Arts. [San Francisco, Printed by California Print. Co., 1969] 119 p. illus., ports. 18 cm. Catalogue of an exhibition held at the University of California Art Museum, March, 1969. Bibliography: p. 117. [NC1145.M44K5] 73-625801
I. King, Susan. II. California. University. Art Museum. III. Graham Foundation for Advanced Studies in the Fine Arts.

VON ECKARDT, Wolf 720.943
Eric Mendelsohn. New York, G. Braziller, 1960. 128 p. illus., plates. 26 cm. (The Masters of world architecture series) "Selected bibliography of books and articles written by Eric Mendelsohn": p. 119. "Selected bibliography on Eric Mendelsohn": p. 121. [NA1088.M57V6] 60-14514
1. Mendelsohn, Erich, 1887-1953. I. Title. II. Series. BIP

WHITTICK, Arnold, 1898- 927.2
Eric Mendelsohn. [2d ed.] New York, F. W. Dodge Corp. [1956] 219 p. illus., ports., plans. 28 cm. Bibliography: p. 208-210. [NA1088.M57W5 1956a] 56-14374
1. Mendelsohn, Erich, 1887-1953. I. Title.

Men's clothing.

BACHARACH, Bert. 687.11
Book for men; illustrated by Jesse Washington. New York, A.S. Barnes [1953] 159p. illus. 20cm. [TT585.B3] 52-13822
1. Men's clothing. 2. Etiquette. I. Title.

BACHARACH, Bert. 687.11
Right dress; success through better grooming. Illustrated by Norman Garbo and Jesse Washington. New York, Barnes [1955] 125p. illus. 20cm. [TT618.B14] 55-10216
1. Men's clothing. I. Title.

BENNETT-ENGLAND, Rodney Charles. 687'.11
Dress optional; the revolution in menswear, by Rodney Bennett-England. [Chester Springs, Pa.] Dufour, 1968. 240 p. illus. 23 cm. [TT617.B4 1968] 68-29951 8.95
1. Men's clothing. 2. Fashion. I. Title.

ESQUIRE 391
Esquire fashions for men, by the eds. of Esquire magazine. Introd. by Oscar E. Schoeffler. Illus. by Lealand Gustavson, others. New York, Harper c.1957-1966 253p. illus. 22cm. [TT618.E82] 66-13857 5.95
1. Men's clothing. 2. Fashion. I. Title.

HIX, Charles. 646'.32
Dressing right / by Charles Hix, with Brian Burdine. New York : St. Martin's Press, [1978] p. cm. Includes index. [TT618.H58] 78-3972 ISBN 0-312-21968-7 : 17.50
1. Men's clothing. 2. Grooming for men. I. Burdine, Brian, joint author. II. Title. BIP

JUSTER, Harry 646
Clothes make the man; the do's and don'ts of looking your best at all times. Illus. by Sidney Buchalter [New York, Macfadden, 1965] 175p. illus. 19cm. [TT618.J87] 65-9388 .75 pap.,
1. Men's clothing. I. Title.

LYLE, Dorothy Siegert. 646'.32
Clothing for young men, written by Dorothy Siegert Lyle for the Home Economics Education Association. [Washington, Home Economics Education Association, 1970] 32 p. illus. (part col.) 28 cm. Bibliography: p. 31-32. [TT580.L94] 78-135579 2.50
1. Men's clothing. I. Home Economics Education Association. II. Title. BIP

MOLLOY, John T. 646'.32
Dress for success / by John T. Molloy. New York : P. H. Wyden, [1975] x, 245 p., [2] leaves of plates : ill. ; 22 cm. [TT618.M64] 75-7647 ISBN 0-88326-078-6 : 8.95
1. Men's clothing. 2. Grooming for men. I. Title. BIP

RHINEHART, Jane. 646.4'3'02
How to make men's clothes / by Jane Rhinehart ; ill. by B. J. Shewbart. 1st ed. Garden City, N.Y. : Doubleday, 1975. 206 p. : ill. ; 24 cm. Includes index. [TT575.R45] 74-12706 ISBN 0-385-01850-9 : 8.95
1. Men's clothing. 2. Tailoring. I. Title. BIP

SCHOEFFLER, O. E., 1899- 391'.07'10904
Esquire's encyclopedia of 20th century men's fashions [by] O. E. Schoeffler and William Gale. New York, McGraw-Hill [1973] x, 709 p. illus. 28 cm. [TT617.S36] 72-9811 ISBN 0-07-055480-3 35.00
1. Men's clothing. 2. Costume—History—20th century. I. Gale, William, 1925- joint author. II. Title. III. Title: Encyclopedia of 20th century men's fashions.

SEAR, Hazel M. 646.4'3'02
The sew-easy guide to menswear : or, How to keep him in stitches / Hazel M. Sear. New York : Hawthorn Books, c1975. xii, 145 p. : ill. ; 26 cm. Bibliography: p. 145. [TT580.S4 1975] 74-27904 ISBN 0-8015-6754-8 pbk. : 4.95
1. Men's clothing. 2. Tailoring. I. Title.

SPEER, Michael L. 646'.32
Put your best foot forward / Michael L. Speer. Nashville : Broadman Press, c1977. 167 p. : ill. ; 21 cm. [TT618.S67] 77-79787 ISBN 0-8054-5585-X : 4.95
1. Men's clothing. 2. Grooming for men. I. Title. BIP

Mental retardation facilities—U.S.

U.S. Dept. of Health, Education, and Welfare. Secretary's Committee on Mental Retardation. 725'.53'0973
Mental retardation construction program: research centers, university-affiliated facilities, community facilities. Washington, 1969. vi, 65 p. illus. 27 cm. [HV3006.A1A558] 76-602667
1. Mental retardation facilities—U.S. I. Title.

Mentally handicapped in art.

COBER, Alan E. 741.9'73
The forgotten society : 92 drawings / by Alan E. Cober. New York : Dover Publications, 1975. 95 p. : chiefly ill. ; 24 cm. [NC139.C58A45 1975] 74-76981 ISBN 0-486-21405-2 pbk. : 3.50
1. Cober, Alan E. 2. Mentally handicapped in art. 3. Aged in art. 4. Prisoners in art. I. Title.

Mercantile buildings.

FERNANDEZ, Jose Antonio, 1898- 725.213
The specialty shop, a guide. With a foreword by Leopold Arnaud. New York, Architectural Book Pub. Co. [1950] 304 p. illus., diagrs., plans. 28 cm. ["Designing for business" series] [NA6220.F4] 50-8897
1. Mercantile buildings. I. Title.

SNIBBE, Richard W 725.2
A photographic record of 100 selected designs for small commercial buildings, executed within the last 20 years, with a challenging introd., plans of each project, and critical text. New York, Reinhold [1956] 216 p. illus. 31 cm. (The Progressive architecture library) [NA6210.S6] 56-11750
1. Mercantile buildings. 2. Architecture — Designs and plans. I. Title. II. Title: Small commercial buildings.

SNIBBE, Richard W. 725.2
A photographic record of 100 selected designs for small commercial buildings, executed within the last 20 years, with a challenging introd., plans of each project, and critical text. New York, Reinhold [1956] 216 p. illus. 31 cm. (The Progressive architecture library) [NA6210.S6] 56-11750
1. Mercantile buildings. 2. Architecture—Designs and plans. I. Title: Small commercial buildings.

Mercantile buildings—United States.

BUILDINGS for commerce and industry / edited by Charles King Hoyt. New York : McGraw-Hill, c1978. ix, 228 p. : ill. (some col.) ; 31 cm. "An Architectural record book." Includes index. [NA6212.B84] 78-1421 ISBN 0-07-002329-8 : 22.50 725
1. Mercantile buildings—United States. 2. Office buildings—United States. I. Hoyt, Charles King. II. Architectural record.

Mercator, Gerardus, 1512-1594.

OSLEY, A. S. 745.6'1
Mercator: a monograph on the lettering of maps, etc., in the 16th century Netherlands, with a facsimile and translation of his treatise on the italic hand and a translation of Ghim's Vita Mercatoris. [By] A. S. Osley, with a foreword by R. A. Skelton. New York, Watson-Guptill [1969] 209 p. illus., facsims., maps, plates, ports. 29 cm. Bibliography: p. 195-202. [Z43.A3O8 1969b] 78-79762 35.00
1. Mercator, Gerardus, 1512-1594. 2. Penmanship. I. Mercator, Gerardus, 1512-1594. Literarum latinarum. II. Ghymmius, Gualterus, 1530-1611. Vita Mercatoris.

Mercer, Henry Chapman, 1856-1930.

MERCER, Henry Chapman, 1856-1930. 917.48'18
The tiled pavement in the Capitol of Pennsylvania / Henry C. Mercer ; rev. and edited by Ginger Duemler ; illustrated by Linda Brown. State College : Pennsylvania Guild of Craftsmen, [1975] xv, 83 p. : ill. ; 23 cm. Revision of the author's Guide book to the tiled pavement in the Capitol of Pennsylvania. Fold. sheet inserted: Chronological guide and numerical reference list to the tiled pavement. Includes index. [NA3860.M47D83 1975] 75-318013
1. Mercer, Henry Chapman, 1856-1930. 2. Harrisburg, Pa. State Capitol. 3. Pavements, Tile—Pennsylvania—Harrisburg. 4. Pavements, Mosaic—Pennsylvania—Harrisburg. 5. Pennsylvania in art. I. Duemler, Ginger. II. Title.

Meresankh III, Queen of Egypt.

DUNHAM, Dows, 1890- 913.32
The mastaba of Queen Mersyankh III, G7530-7540, by Dows Dunham and William Kelly Simpson. Boston, Dept. of Egyptian and Ancient Near Eastern Art, Museum of Fine Arts, Boston, 1974. v, 26 p., [49] p. of illus. (part fold.) 35 cm. (Giza mastabas, v. 1) "Based upon the excavations and recording of late George Andrew Reisner and William Stevenson Smith, Museum of Fine Arts—Harvard University Expedition." Includes bibliographical references. [DT73.G5D85] 73-88232
1. Meresankh III, Queen of Egypt. 2. Giza—Tombs. I. Simpson, William Kelly. II. Reisner, George Andrew, 1867-1942. III. Smith, William Stevenson. IV. Title. V. Series.

Mergenthaler, Ottmar, 1854-1899.

MENGEL, Willi. 926.55
Ottmar Mergenthaler and the printing revolution. With an introd. by Lin Yutang. Brooklyn, Mergenthaler Linotype Co., 1954. 63p. illus. 26cm. [Z232.M56M4] 54-34221
1. Mergenthaler, Ottmar, 1854-1899. 2. Linotype. I. Title.

Mergenthaler, Ottmar, 1854-1899 — Juvenile literature.

LEVINE, Israel E j92
Miracle man of printing; Ottmar Mergenthaler. New York, J. Messner [1963] 190 p. 22 cm. Bibliography: p. 185-186. [Z232.M56L4] 63-16784
1. Mergenthaler, Ottmar, 1854-1899 — Juvenile literature. I. Title.

Merriam, Clinton Hart, 1855-1942—Art collections.

JETT, Stephen C., 1938- 746.4'1
Interwoven heritage : a bicentennial exhibition of Southwestern Indian basketry and textile arts, featuring the C. Hart Merriam collection of baskets and the Stephen C. Jett collection of Navajo weaving, January 9-February 8, 1976 : [catalogue] / Stephen C. Jett. Davis : University of California, Davis, Memorial Union Art Gallery, c1976. 44 p., [2] leaves of plates : ill. ; 28 cm. Bibliography: p. 41-44. [E78.S7J47] 76-359672
1. Merriam, Clinton Hart, 1855-1942—Art collections. 2. Jett, Stephen C., 1938- — Art collections. 3. Indians of North America—Southwest, New—Basket making—Exhibitions. 4. Navaho Indians—Textile industry and fabrics—Exhibitions. 5. Indians of North America—Southwest, New—Textile industry and fabrics—Exhibitions. I. California. University, Davis. Art Gallery. II. Title.

Merrymount Press, Boston.

UPDIKE, Daniel Berkeley, 1860-1941. 070.5'09744'61
Notes on the Merrymount Press & its work, by Daniel Berkeley Updike; with a bibliographical list of books printed at the Press, 1893-1933, by Julian Pearce Smith. With views of the Press at various periods, specimens of types alluded to, &c. &c. &c. Boston, Milford House [1973] p. Reprint of the 1934 ed. published by the Harvard University Press, Cambridge, Mass. [Z232.M57U82 1973] 73-10387 ISBN 0-87821-066-0 25.00 (lib. bdg.)
1. Merrymount Press, Boston. I. Smith, Julian Pearce. II. Title. BIP

Meru, Y. Y.

MERU, Y. Y. 730'.92'4
Attunement [by Y. Y. Meru. Monterey, Calif., c1973] 33 p. (chiefly illus., part col.) 37 cm. "Book no. 6 of 73 copies. First issue." [NB237.M43A42] 73-83182
1. Meru, Y. Y. Attunement. I. Title.

Meryet-Amun, Queen, consort of Amenhctep II, King of Egypt.

WINLOCK, Herbert 913.32'03'1
Eustis, 1884-1950.
The tomb of Queen Meryet-Amun at Thebes. Photos. by Harry Burton. Plans by Walter Hauser and catalogue by Charlotte R. Clark. New York, 1932. [New York] Arno Press, 1973. xi, 96 p., 46 plates. illus. 32 cm. Reprint of the ed. published by the Museum, which was issued as v. 6 of the Publications of the Metropolitan Museum of Art Egyptian Expedition. At head of title: The Metropolitan Museum of Art Egyptian Expedition. Includes bibliographical references. [DT73.T3W5 1973] 70-168415 ISBN 0-405-02253-0
1. Meryet-Amun, Queen, consort of Amenhctep II, King of Egypt. 2. Thebes, Egypt—Tombs. I. Title. II. Series: New York (City). Metropolitan Museum of Art. Egyptian Expedition. Publications, v. 6.

Meryon, Charles, 1821-1868.

MERYON, Charles, 1821- 769'.92'4
1868.
Prints & drawings : [exhibition] Toledo Museum of Art, Toledo, Ohio, 29 September-27 October 1974 : Yale University Art Gallery, New Haven, Connecticut, 21 November 1974-19 January 1975 : St. Louis Art Museum, St. Louis, Missouri, 14 February-6 April 1975 / Charles Meryon ; catalogue by James D. Burke. [New Haven : Yale University Art Gallery, 1974] xii, 113, [108] p. : ill. ; 28 cm. Includes bibliographical references. [NE2049.5.M43B87] 74-82945
1. Meryon, Charles, 1821-1868. I. Burke, James Donald, 1939- II. Toledo. Museum of Art. III. Yale University. Art Gallery. IV. St. Louis Art Museum.

Meszaros, Andor, 1900-1972.

SEMMENS, Kelman. 730'.92'4
Andor Meszaros. Melbourne, Hawthorn Press, 1972. 32 p. illus. 25 cm. [NB522.5.M47S45] 73-163010 ISBN 0-7256-0091-8 8.50
1. Meszaros, Andor, 1900-1972. I. Meszaros, Andor, 1900-1972.

Metabolism in architecture (movement)

KUROKAWA, Noriaki, 720'.92'4
1934-
Metabolism in architecture / Kisho Kurakawa [i.e. N. Kurokawa]. Boulder, Colo. : Westview Press, 1977. 208 p. : ill. ; 26 cm. Includes index. Bibliography: p. 205-207. [NA1559.K83A5 1977] 77-1042 ISBN 0-89158-734-9 lib.bdg. : 22.50
1. Kurokawa, Noriaki, 1934- 2. Metabolism in architecture (movement) I. Title.

Metal bonding.

AMERICAN Welding Society. 671.5
Modern joining processes, edited by Arthur L. Phillips. New York [1966] 139 p. illus. 24 cm. "Companion book to Current welding processes." Includes bibliographies. [TT211.A483] 66-20599
1. Metal bonding. I. Phillips, Arthur L., ed. II. Title. BIP

Metal curtain walls.

NATIONAL Research Council. 721.2
Building Research Institute.
The design potential of metal curtain walls; proceedings of a program conducted as part of the 1959 fall conferences of the Building Research Institute, Division of Engineering and Industrial Research. Washington, D. C. National Academy of Sciences, National Research Council, 1960. viii, 84p. illus., diagrs. 28cm. (National Research Council. Publication 788) 60-60053 5.00 pap.,
1. Metal curtain walls. I. Title. II. Series.

NATIONAL Research Council. 721.2
Building Research Institute. Conferences. Washington, D.C., fall, 1959.
The design potential of metal curtain walls; proceedings of a program conducted as part of the 1959 Fall Conferences of the Building Research Institute, Division of Engineering and Industrial Research. Washington, National Academy of Sciences-National Research Council, 1960. viii, 84 p.illus. 28 cm. (National Research Council. Publication 788) [TH2231.N35] 60-60053
1. Metal curtan walls. I. Title. II. Series.

Metal sculpture.

HALE, Nathan Cabot. 731.4
Welded sculpture. New York, Watson-Guptill Publications [1968] 191 p. illus. 27 cm. Bibliography: p. 187. [NB1220.H3] 67-21789
1. Metal sculpture. 2. Welding. I. Title. BIP

LYNCH, John. 739
Metal sculpture; new forms, new techniques. New York, Studio-Crowell [1957] 145p. illus. 24cm. [NB1220.L9] 57-6177
1. Metal sculpture. I. Title.

LYNCH, John, 1904- 739
Metal sculpture new forms, new techniques New York, Studio-Crowell [1957] 145 p. illus. 24 cm. [NB1220.L9] 57-6177
1. Metal sculpture.

MEILACH, Dona Z. 731.4
Direct metal sculpture; creative techniques and appreciation, by Dona Meilach, Don Seiden. New York, Crown [c.1966] xii, 210p. illus. (pt. col.) 27cm. [NB1220.M4] 65-28419 6.95
1. Metal sculpture. 2. Sculpture—Hist.—20th cent. I. Seiden, Don, joint author. II. Title. BIP

MORRIS, John D. 731.4'2
Creative metal sculpture: a step-by-step approach, by John D. Morris. New York, Bruce Pub. Co. [1971] 154 p. illus. 27 cm. [NB1220.M67] 75-158066 8.95
1. Metal sculpture. I. Title.

Metal-spinning.

JOHNSON, Harold V 671.33
Metal spinning techniques and projects. Milwaukee, Bruce Pub. Co. [1960] 130p. illus. 25cm. [TT206.J58] 60-8233
1. Metal-spinning. I. Title.

Metal-work.

ADAMS, Jeannette T. 684'.09
Metalworking handbook : principles and procedures / Jeannette T. Adams. New York : Arco Pub. Co., [1976] p. cm. [TT205.A43] 75-23577 ISBN 0-668-03857-8 lib bdg. : 10.00
1. Metal-work. I. Title. BIP

AKESON, Harold O 371.426871
Wood and art metal. Milwaukee, Bruce Pub. Co. [c1953] 62p. illus. 24cm. [TT205.A54] 55-2754
1. Metal-work. 2. Woodwork. 3. Handicraft. I. Title.

BARICH, Dewey F. 745.56
Metal work for industrial arts shops [by] Dewey F. Barich [and] Leonard C. Smith. Chicago, American Technical Society, 1952. 96 p. illus. 28 cm. [TT205.B315] 52-8345
1. Metal-work. I. Title.

BEDFORD, John Robert 739.1
Metalwork projects. London, J. Murray [dist. Hollywood-by-the-Sea, Fla., Transatlantic, c.1963]c96p. illus. 26cm. 64-385 3.00
1. Metal-work. I. Title.

BOLLINGER, Joseph 371.426871
Walter, 1897-
Fun with metalwork. Milwaukee, Bruce Pub. Co. [1958] 184p. illus. 24cm. Includes bibliography. [TT205.B6] 58-14747
1. Metal-work. I. Title.

BOYD, T. Gardner. 684'.09
Metalworking / by T. Gardner Boyd ; Walter C. Brown, consulting editor. South Holland, Ill. : Goodheart-Willcox Co., [1975] 120 p. : ill. ; 27 cm. (Goodheart-Willcox's build-a-course series) Includes index. Bibliography: p. 115. [TT205.B68 1975] 74-23306 ISBN 0-87006-187-9 : 4.40
1. Metal-work. I. Title. BIP

BOYE, David. 621.9'3
Step-by-step knifemaking : you can do it / by David Boye ; drawings by Robert J. Caradonna ; photos. by Grant Heidrich, David Boye, Franklin Avery. Emmaus, Pa. : Rodale Press, c1977. p. cm. Includes index. [TT213.B69] 77-22383 ISBN 0-87857-180-9 : 10.95. ISBN 0-87857-181-7 pbk. : 6.95
1. Metal-work. 2. Knives. I. Title. BIP

DRAGOO, Alva William. 671
General shop metalwork [by] A. W. Dragoo and Howard O. Reed. 4th ed. Bloomington, Ill., McKnight & McKnight Pub. Co. [1964] 144 p. illus. 26 cm. Bibliography: p. 139-141. [TT205.D7 1964] 64-3628
1. Metal-work. I. Reed, Howard Odin, 1906- joint author. II. Title. BIP

FEIRER, John Louis. 671
General metals. New York, McGraw-Hill [1952] 257 p. illus. 25 cm. (McGraw-Hill publications in industrial arts) [TT205.F39] 51-12564
1. Metal-work. I. Title. BIP

FEIRER, John Louis. 671
General metals. 2d ed. New York, McGraw-Hill [1959] 372 p. illus. 25 cm. (McGraw-Hill publications in industrial arts) Includes bibliography. [TT205.F39 1959] 58-13866
1. Metal-work. I. Title.

FEIRER, John Louis. 671
General metals [by] John L. Feirer. 3d ed. New York, McGraw-Hill [1967] x, 470 p. illus. (part col.) 25 cm. (McGraw-Hill publications in industrial education) [TT205.F39] 67-2038
1. Metal-work I. Title.

FEIRER, John Louis. 671
I.A. metalwork [by] John L. Feirer [and] John R. Lindbeck. Peoria, Ill., C. A. Bennett Co. [1965] 240 p. illus. 25 cm. Beginning with 2d ed. (1970) published under title: Metalwork. [TT205.F395] 65-18200
1. Metal-work. I. Lindbeck, John Robert, joint author. II. Title.

FEIRER, John Louis. 671
Metalwork [by] John L. Feirer [and] John R. Lindbeck. [2d ed.] Peoria, Ill., C. A. Bennett Co. [1970] 248 p. illus. 24 cm. 1965 ed. published under title: I.A. metalwork. [TT205.F395 1970] 75-14823
1. Metal-work. I. Lindbeck, John Robert, joint author. II. Title. BIP

FISCH, Arline M. 746'.04'53
Textile techniques in metal for jewelers, sculptors, and textile artists / Airline M. Fisch. New York : Van Nostrand Reinhold, c1975. 168 p. : ill. (some col.) ; 29 cm. Includes index. Bibliography: p. 165-166. [TT205.F57] 74-15249 ISBN 0-442-22400-1 : 15.00
1. Metal-work. 2. Textile crafts. 3. Metal cloth. I. Title.

FRASER, Roland R 371.426871
General metal: principles, procedures, and projects [by] Roland R. Fraser [and] Earl L. Bedell. New York, Prentice-Hall, 1955. 244p. illus. 25cm. [TT205.F7] 55-7954
1. Metal-work. I. Bedell, Earl L, joint author. II. Title.

GIACHINO, Joseph William, 671
1906-
Basic general metals, by J. W. Giachino. Milwaukee, Bruce Pub. Co. [1969] vii, 208 p. illus. (part col.) 24 cm. [TT205.G48] 68-28442
1. Metal-work. I. Title. BIP

GLASS, Frederick James, 739'.533
1881-1930.
Pewter craft. London, University of London Press, 1927. [Kentfield, Calif., N. K. Gregg, 1971] vii, 65 p. illus. 19 cm. (Gregg series of reprints on crafts and hobbies) Original ed. issued in the author's series: The artistic, practical handicraft series. [TT205.G64 1971] 74-163526 ISBN 0-912318-08-2
1. Metal-work. 2. Pewter. I. Title. BIP

GRONEMAN, Chris Harold, 694.024
1906-
Exploring the industries, for the general shop and laboratory of industries. Text ed. Austin, Tex., Steck Co. [1962] 155p. illus. 29cm. (The Steck industrial arts series) [TT153.G7 1962] 62-51407
1. Metal-work. 2. Woodwork. 3. Electricity. 4. Mechanical drawing. I. Title.

HOWELL, Percy G 673.38
21 construction projects in brass / illustrated by William T. Woodward. Detroit, Royalle Pub. Co. [1961] 1v. illus. 22x28cm. [TT205.H63] 61-17170
1. Metal-work. 2. Brass. I. Title.

JOHNSON, Harold V. 671
Technical metals, by Harold V. Johnson. Peoria, Ill., C. A. Bennett Co. [1968] 462 p. illus. (part col.) 27 cm. Bibliography: p. 455. [TT205.J55] 67-12639
1. Metal-work. I. Title. BIP

JOHNSON, Harold V. 671
Technical metals, by Harold V. Johnson. [Rev.] Peoria, Ill., C. A. Bennett Co. [1973] 476 p. illus. 27 cm. Bibliography: p. 469. [TT205.J55 1973] 73-166290 ISBN 0-87002-139-7 11.44
1. Metal-work. I. Title. BIP

KAUFFMAN, Henry 745.56
Machine shop and foundry projects. Bloomington, Ill., McKnight & McKnight Pub. Co. [dist., New York, Taplinger] [c.1959] 85p. illus. 27cm. 59-4096 3.80
1. Metal-work. I. Title.

KAUFFMAN, Henry J 1908- 745.56
Machine shop and foundry projects. [1st ed.] Bloomington, Ill., McKnight & McKnight Pub. Co. [1959] 85p. illus. 27cm. [TT205.K3] 59-4096
1. Metal-work. I. Title.

LUX, Donald G. 745.56
Contemporary metal home furnishings [by] Donald G. Lux [and] Edward R. Towers. [1st ed.] Bloomington, Ill., McKnight & McKnight [1957] 185p. illus., diagrs. 27cm. [TT213.L9] 57-1296
1. Metal-work. 2. Furniture. I. Towers, Edward R., joint author. II. Title.

MALCOLM, W. F. 671.3
Metalwork notes [by] W. F. Malcolm. Oxford, New York, Pergamon [1966] vii, 79p. 20cm. (Commonwealth intl. lib. Applied arts crafts div.) [TT205.M28 1965] 65-22916 1.50 pap.,
1. Metal-work. I. Title.

MARSHALL, Cyril Leek, 745.56
1906-
Foilcraft / Cyril Marshall. Harrisburg, Pa. : Stackpole Books, c1977. 160 p. : ill. : 25 cm. Includes index. Bibliography: p. 154-156. [TT205.M32 1977] 77-7573 ISBN 0-8117-0647-8 : 12.95
1. Metal-work. 2. Metal foils. I. Title. BIP

MATTSON, Elmer B 745.56
Creative metalworking. Milwaukee, Bruce Pub. Co. [1960] 121p. illus. 25cm. [TT205.M34] 60-3825
1. Metal-work. I. Title.

PARKINSON, Kenneth. 671
Metalwork; theory and practice. [1st ed.] Oxford, New York, Pergamon Press [1967] 154 p. illus. 25 cm. (The Commonwealth and international library. Applied arts and crafts) [TT205.P3 1967] 67-24302
1. Metal-work. I. Title.

RULEY, Morris J 745.56
Projects in general metalwork. Bloomington, Ill., McKnight & McKnight Pub. Co., 1951. 78 p. illus. 24 cm. [TT205.R75] 51-10333
1. Metal-work. I. Title.

SMITH, Robert Ernest, 1879- 671
Bench metal work Rev. ed. Bloomington, Ill., McKnight & McKnight Pub. Co. [1952] 72 p. illus. 27 cm. First ed. published in 1939 under title: Units in bench metal work. [TT205.S63 1952] 52-43011
1. Metal-work. I. Title.

SMITH, Robert Ernest, 1879- 671
Etching, spinning, raising, tooling metal. [Rev. ed.] Bloomington, Ill., McKnight & McKnight Pub. Co. [1951] 88 p. illus. 27 cm. Published in 1939 under title: Units in

SUBJECT INDEX MEXICO (CITY). MUSEO

etching, spinning, raising, and tooling metal. [TT205.S64 1951] 51-6611
1. Metal-work. I. Title.

TUSTISON, Francis Elwood, 1886- 671.8
Metalwork essentials [by] F. E. Tustison, Ray F. Kranzusch [and] Dan C. Blide. Rev. ed. Milwaukee, Bruce Pub. Co. [1962] 236 p. illus. 25 cm. [TT205.T8 1962] 62-19086
1. Metal-work. BIP

WALKER, John R. 684'.09
Exploring metalworking basic fundamentals / by John R. Walker. South Holland, Ill. : Goodheart-Willcox Co., c1976. 256 p. : ill. ; 29 cm. Includes index. Bibliography: p. 250. [TT205.W33 1976] 75-31808 ISBN 0-87006-199-2 : 6.80
1. Metal-work. I. Title. BIP

WALKER, John R. 671
Metal projects. bk.1 by John R. Walker Homewood, Ill., Goodheart-Willcox, [1966] Homewood, Ill., Goodheart-Willcox, [1966] 111p. illus. 29cm. [TT213.W3] 66-31265 3.75
1. Metal-work. I. Title. BIP

WALKER, John R. 671
Metal projects / by John R. Walker. South Holland, Ill. : Goodheart-Willcox Co., c197 v. : ill. ; 28 cm. Includes index. Contents.Contents.— —book 3. English and metrics. [TT205.W335] 77-21602 ISBN 0-87006-238-7 : 4.00
1. Metal-work. I. Title.

WALKER, John R 621.75
Projects for metals. Chicago, Goodheart-Willcox Co. [1957] 80 p. (chiefly illus.) 28 cm. [TT205.W34] 57-12977
1. Metal-work. 2. Manual training. I. Title.

WAY, Robert Barnard, 1890- 680
Metal working in the home, by R. Barnard Way and Noel D. Green, illustrated by R. B. Way. Redhill, Surrey, Wells, Gardner, Darton [1952] 118p. illus. 19cm. [TT205.W38] 53-24502
1. Metal-work. I. Green, Noel Dutton, 1890- joint author. II. Title.

WEYGERS, Alexander G. 621.9'08
The recycling, use, and repair of tools / Alexander G. Weygers ; illustrated by the author. New York : Van Nostrand Reinhold Co., [1978] p. cm. [TT213.W48] 78-17188 ISBN 0-442-29357-7 : 11.00. ISBN 0-442-29358-5 pbk. : 7.00
1. Metal-work. 2. Woodwork. 3. Tools. I. Title. BIP

Metal-work—Amateurs' manuals.

DANIELE, Joseph William. 684.09
Early American metal projects. [1st ed.] Bloomington, Ill., McKnight & McKnight Pub. Co. [1971] viii, 145 p. illus. 27 cm. [TT205.D35] 75-130495 ISBN 0-87345-142-2 5.97
1. Metal-work—Amateurs' manuals. 2. Art metal-work, American. I. Title. BIP

GRANSTROM, K. E., 1924- 684.09
Creating with metal [by] K. E. Granstrom. [Edited in English by Clara Fried Zwiebel] New York, Reinhold Book Corp. [1968] 92 p. illus. 23 cm. (Reinhold Scandinavian craft series) Translation of Metalslojd och klensmide. [TT205.G693] 67-24694
1. Metal-work—Amateurs' manuals. I. Title.

HACK, John. 739
Metal; designs, material, technique. New York, Van Nostrand Reinhold [1972] 88 p. illus. 21 cm. Translation of Metallarbeiten. [TT205.H1313] 70-183493 ISBN 0-442-03005-3
1. Metal-work—Amateurs' manuals. I. Title.

RULEY, Morris J. 684.09
Projects in general metalwork [by] M. J. Ruley. [Rev. ed.] Bloomington, Ill., McKnight & McKnight Pub. Co. [1969, c1968] 80 p. illus. 24 cm. Bibliography: p. 80. [TT205.R75 1969] 76-8114
1. Metal-work—Amateurs' manuals. I. Title.

THOMAS, Richard, 1917- 745.56
Metalsmithing for the artist-craftsman. 1st ed. Philadelphia, Chilton Co., Book Division [1960] 173 p. illus. 27 cm. (Arts and crafts series) Includes bibliography. [TT205.T45] 60-14633
1. Metal-work—Amateurs' manuals. I. Title. BIP

Metal-work—History.

FISKE, J. W. 739'.511
J. W. Fiske, 1893: copper weather vanes, bannerets, lightning rods, stable fixtures; illustrated catalog and historical introduction. [1st ed.] Princeton, Pyne Press [1971] 140 p. illus. 23 cm. (The American historical catalog collection) Facsim. of the 1893 catalog. Original t.p. reads: Illustrated catalogue and price list of copper weather vanes, manufactured by J. W. Fiske, 39 and 41 Park Place, New York. [NK9585.F5 1893a] 70-146205 ISBN 0-87861-003-0 4.00
I. Title. II. Series.

KNAUTH, Percy, 1914- 671'.09
The metalsmiths, by Percy Knauth and the editors of Time-Life Books. New York, Time-Life Books [1974] 160 p. illus. (part col.) 27 cm. (The Emergence of man) Bibliography: p. 157. [TT205.K57] 73-89680 7.95
1. Metal-work—History. 2. Mines and mineral resources—History. I. Time-Life-Books. II. Title.

LISTER, Raymond. 739'.09
The craftsman in metal. [1st American ed.] South Brunswick [N.J.] A. S. Barnes [1968, c1966] 208 p. illus. 22 cm. Bibliography: p. 201-203. [TT205.L58 1968] 68-14405
1. Metal-work—History. I. Title.

Metal-work—Juvenile literature.

GRONEMAN, Chris Harold, 1906- 684'.09
Getting started in metalworking / Chris H. Groneman, John L. Feirer. New York : McGraw-Hill, c1979. iv, 108 p. : ill. ; 24 cm. Includes index. A textbook introducing the fundamentals of metalworking and careers in the field. [TT205.G78] 78-19090 ISBN 0-07-024996-2 pbk. : 4.40
1. Metal-work—Juvenile literature. I. Feirer, John Louis, joint author. II. Title. BIP

HETZER, Linda. 745.5
Workshop crafts / by Linda Hetzer ; photos. by Steven Mays ; [illustrators, Lynn Matus and Sally Shimizu]. Milwaukee : Raintree, c1978. 48 p. : ill. (some col.) ; 26 cm. Presents a variety of projects for working with metal, wood, and self-hardening clay. [TT205.H37] 77-28707 ISBN 0-8172-1184-5 lib.bdg. : 7.93
1. Metal-work—Juvenile literature. 2. Woodwork—Juvenile literature. 3. Modeling—Juvenile literature. I. Mays, Steven. II. Matus, Lynn. III. Shimizu, Sally. IV. Title. BIP

METALWORKING / 671
Wilbur R. Miller ... [et al.]. 1st ed. Bloomington, Ill. : McKnight Pub. Co., 1979 iv, 123 p. : ill. (some col.) ; 24 cm. (Basic industrial arts) Includes index. Introduces basic skills of metalworking including planning the project, cutting and shaping, forging and forming, machine tool operations, and metal finishing. [TT205.M44] 78-53387 ISBN 0-87345-784-6 pbk. : 2.64
1. Metal-work—Juvenile literature. I. Miller, Wilbur R. II. Title. III. Series. BIP

PFLUG, Betsy. 745.56
You can. New York, Van Nostrand Reinhold [1969] 39 p. col. illus. 27 cm. Illustrations and simple directions explain how to make many useful items out of tin cans, their lids, and pop tops. [PZ10.P4478Yo] 70-78649 3.50
1. Metal-work—Juvenile literature. 2. Tin cans—Juvenile literature. I. Title.

Metal-work — Outlines, syllabi, etc.

ALSIP, Ben. 371.62
Course of study for general metals. Fayetteville, University of Arkansas, College of Education, Dept of Vocational Teacher Education, 1963. 119 l. illus. 23 cm. (University of Arkansas. Dept of Vocational Teacher Education. Monograph 62) Includes bibliography. [TT205.A56] 63-63304
1. Metal-work — Outlines, syllabi, etc. I. Title.

Metal-work—Problems, exercises, etc.

ROCCO, Louis R. 671
Basic metal science; workbook and shop and laboratory projects. Prepared by Louis R. Rocco. New Brunswick, N.J., Vocational Division, Curriculum Laboratory, 1960 [i.e. 1962] iii, 288 p. illus. 28 cm. Bibliography: p. 287-288. [TT205.R6] 62-9546
1. Metal-work—Problems, exercises, etc. 2. Metallurgy. I. New Jersey. Division of Vocational Education. Curriculum Laboratory, New Brunswick. II. Title.

Metallurgical plants—Design and construction.

CLOUGH, Robert T 1923- 725.4
The lead smelting mills of the Yorkshire dales; their architectural character, construction, and place in the European tradition. Foreword by Norman Culley. [Leeds! Eng.] 1962 [imprint on lebel: W.S. Heinman, New York] xxiv, 188p. illus., plates, maps, facsims., plans. 29cm. Bibliography: p. 169-172. [NA6510.C5] 62-52486
1. Metallurgical plants—Design and construction. 2. Metallurgical plants—Yorkshire, Eng. 3. Smelting. I. Title.

Metals in stage setting.

TAYLOR, Douglas C. 684'.09'024792
Metalworking for the designer and technician / by Douglas C. Taylor. New York : Drama Book Specialists, c1978. p. cm. Bibliography: p. [PN2091.M48T3] 78-23346 ISBN 0-910482-86-1 : 15.00
1. Metals in stage setting. 2. Metal-work. I. Title. BIP

Metalwork.

PARKINSON, Kenneth. 671
Metalwork: theory and practice. [1st ed.) Oxford, New York, Pergamon Press [1967] 154 p. illus. 25 cm. (The Commonwealth and international library. Applied arts and crafts. [TT205.P3] 67-24302
1. Metalwork. I. Title.

Metsu, Gabriel, 1629-1667.

ROBINSON, Franklin Westcott. 759.9492
Gabriel Metsu (1629-1667); a study of his place in Dutch genre painting of the golden age, by Franklin W. Robinson. New York, A. Schram [1974] p. cm. First prepared as the author's dissertation, Harvard. Bibliography: p. [ND653.M595R62] 74-19143 ISBN 0-8390-0130-4 45.00
1. Metsu, Gabriel, 1629-1667. 2. Painting, Dutch—History. 3. Painting, Modern—17th-18th centuries—Netherlands. I. Title.

Meulen, Adam Franz van der, 1632-1690.

MORRIS, Inga, 1924- 759.4
Adam Franz van der Meulen (1632-1690) [Munster?] 1970 [cover 1973] viii, 147 p. 21 cm. Inaug.-Diss.—Munster. Bibliography: p. 81-87. [ND553.M52M67] 74-175820
1. Meulen, Adam Franz van der, 1632-1690.

Mexico—Antiquities

ALSBERG, John L. 730'.972'3
Ancient sculpture from western Mexico; the evolution of artistic form. Text: John L. Alsberg. Photography: Rodolfo Petschek. Berkeley, Calif., Nicole Gallery, 1968. 135 p. illus. 35 cm. Bibliography: p. 130-131. [F1219.3.A7A45] 68-15904
1. Mexico—Antiquities. 2. Indians of Mexico—Antiquities. 3. Indians of Mexico—Sculpture. I. Petschek, Rodolfo, illus. II. Nicole Gallery. III. Title.

ANTON, Ferdinand. 709.01'1
Ancient Mexican art. [Translated from the German by Betty and Peter Ross. 1st American ed.] New York, Putnam [1969] 309 p. illus. (part col.), maps (part col.) 32 cm. Translation of Alt-Mexiko und seine Kunst. Bibliography: p. 299-301. [F1219.3.A7A513 1969] 77-75212 17.50
1. Mexico—Antiquities. 2. Indians of Mexico—Antiquities. 3. Indians of Mexico—Art. I. Title.

ARCHAEOLOGICAL studies among the ancient cities of Mexico. 970.4
Chicago, 1895-97; New York, Kraus Reprint, 1968. 516p. 2v. in 1. illus., lvii pl. (part fold., incl. plans) 25cm. (Chicago, Natural history museum. Fieldiana. Anthropology.) (Orig. Field Columbian museum. [Pubn. 8, 16] Anthropological series. v. 1) Orig. pub. in 2 parts. ea. with special t. -p. Orig. Contents.pt. 1. Monuments of Yucatan--pt. 2. Monuments of Chiapas, Oaxaca and the valley of Mexico. [GN2.F4 v.1] [F1435.H76] 3-17580 20.00 pap.
1. Mexico—Antiq. 2. Yucatan—Antiq. I. Holmes, William Henry, 1846-1933

GLUBOK, Shirley. 970.42
The art of ancient Mexico. Designed by Gerard Nook. Special photography by Alfred H. Tamarin. New York, Harper & Row [1968] 41 p. illus. (part col.) 26 cm. [F1219.3.A7G55] 68-14921
1. Mexico—Antiquities. 2. Indians of Mexico—Art. I. Title. BIP

JOYCE, Thomas Athol, 1878-1942. 970.4'2
Mexican archaeology; an introduction to the archaeology of the Mexican and Mayan civilizations of pre-Spanish America. New York, Hacker Art Books, 1970. xvi, 384 p. illus., maps, plans, 30 plates. 23 cm. First published in 1914. [F1219.J89 1970] 72-94900
1. Mexico—Antiquities. 2. Mayas—Antiquities. I. Title. BIP

REED, Alma M. 917.203
The ancient past of Mexico. Foreword by Eusebio Davalos Hurtado. New York. Crown [c.1966] xi. 388p. illus., maps, ports. 25cm. Bibl. [F1219.R3] 64-17847 7.50
1. Mexico—Antiq. 2. Indians of Mexico—Antiq. 3. Indians of Mexico—Art. I. Title.

SOUSTELLE, Jacques, 1912- 709'.72
Arts of ancient Mexico. With 206 photos. by Claude Arthaud and F. Hebert-Stevens. [Translated from the French by Elizabeth Carmichael] New York, Viking Press [1967] 160 p. illus. (part col.) maps, plans. 29 cm. (A Studio book) Bibliography: p. 147-151. [F1219.3.A7S613 1967a] 67-4718
1. Mexico—Antiquities. 2. Indians of Mexico—Antiquities. 3. Indians of Mexico—Art. I. Arthaud, Claude, 1927- illus. II. Hebert-Stevens, Francois, 1922- illus. III. Title.

Mexico (City). Museo Nacional de Antropologia.

NATIONAL Museum of Anthropology, Mexico City. 917.2'03
[Texts by Carlo Ludovico Ragghianti and Licia Ragghianti Collobi] New York, Newsweek [1970] 171 p. col. illus., plan. 30 cm. (Great museums of the world) Bibliography: p. 168. [GN37.M4N3] 71-127833
1. Mexico (City). Museo Nacional de Antropologia. I. Ragghianti, Carlo Ludovico. II. Ragghianti Collobi, Licia. III. Series: Great museums of the world (New York, Newsweek)

RAMIREZ QUESADA, Jaime. 970.4'2
The National Museum of Anthropology; Mexico: art, architecture, archaeology, anthropology [by] Pedro Ramirez Vazquez [and others]. Introd. by Ignacio Bernal. Designed and edited by Beatrice Trueblood. [Translation from the Spanish text: Mary Jean Labadie, Aza Zatz] New York, Abrams [1968] 257 p. illus. (part col.), maps, plans, ports. 32 cm. Bibliography: p. 252-255. [GN37.M4R38] 68-19150

1. Mexico (City) Museo Nacional de Antropologia.

Mexico—Descr. & trav.—Views.

AUDUBON, John Woodhouse, 741.91 1812-1862.
The drawings of John Woodhouse Audubon, illustrating his adventures through Mexico and California, 1849-1850. With an introd. and notes on the drawings by Carl Schaefer Dentzel. San Francisco, Book Club of California, 1957. 1 v. (unpaged) 34 plates (part col) 35cm. 'Four hundred copies ... printed at the Grabhorn Press.' Includes bibliographical references. [NC1075.A8D4] 58-1588
1. Mexico—Descr. & trav.—Views. 2. California— Descr. & trav.—Views. I. Title.

Mexico—Description and travel— 1951-

YEAGER, Bunny. 770
Camera in Mexico. Greenwich, Conn., Whitestone Publications [1967] 112 p. illus. 24 cm. (A Whitestone book, no. 78) Text and photos. by the author. [TR700.Y4] 67-8581
1. Mexico—Description and travel—1951- 2. Photography of the nude. 3. Travel photography. I. Title.

Mexico—Description and travel— 1951- —Views.

PENAFIEL, 779'.9'9720820924
Manuel.
Mexico / Manuel Penafiel. 1. ed. [s.l. : s.n.], 1976. 284 p. : chiefly col. ill. ; 29 x 42 cm. English, French, and Spanish. [F1216.P47] 77-358452
1. Mexico—Description and travel—1951- —Views. I. Title.

Meyer family.

GREER, Georgeanna H. 738.3'7
The Meyer family: master potters of Texas [by] Georgeanna H. Greer [and] Harding Black. San Antonio, Published for the San Antonio Museum Association, by Trinity University Press [1971] 97 p. illus. (part col.) 24 cm. "Published in conjunction with an exhibit of Meyer pottery held at the Witte Memorial Museum, Brackenridge Park, San Antonio, Texas from October 10 to December 31, 1971." [NK4210.M45G7] 72-179912 ISBN 0-911536-43-4
1. Meyer family. I. Black, Harding, joint author. II. San Antonio Museum Association. III. Witte Memorial Museum, San Antonio. IV. Title.

Mi, Fu, 1051-1107—Influence.

LEDDERHOSE, Lothar. 745.6'199'51
Mi Fu and the classical tradition of Chinese calligraphy / Lothar Ledderose. Princeton, N.J. : Princeton University Press, c1978. p. cm. Portions of this work originally presented as the author's Habilitationsschrift, Cologne University. Includes index. Bibliography: p. [NK3634.A2L43] 78-51177 ISBN 0-691-03937-2 : 25.00
1. Mi, Fu, 1051-1107—Influence. 2. Calligraphy, Chinese. I. Title. BIP

Michael, Marjorie M., 1920—

MICHAEL, Marjorie M., 730'.92'4 1920-
A woman's journey. Sculpture by Marjorie Michael. Words by Virginia Olsen Baron. Photography by Carole Lowenstein. [1st ed.] New York, Knopf, [distributed by Random House] 1974. [62] p. col. illus. 24 cm. [NB237.M5B37] 73-19681 ISBN 0-394-70670-6 3.95 (pbk.)
1. Michael, Marjorie M., 1920- I. Baron, Virginia Olsen. II. Title.

Michalczyk, Casimer, 1914—

MICHALCZYK, Casimer, 731.4'8 1914-
Restoration of the Genius of Connecticut. [Hartford] C.S.C.P.R.C., 1973. iii, 70 l.

illus. 28 cm. Cover title. [NB1200.M52C66] 75-304012
1. Michalczyk, Casimer, 1914- 2. Rogers, Randolph, 1825-1892. Genius of Connecticut. 3. Sculpture—Hartford—Conservation and restoration. I. Connecticut State Capitol Preservation and Restoration Commission. II. Title.

Michals, Duane.

BAILEY, Ronald H. 770
Duane Michals : the photographic illusion / text by Ronald H. Bailey, with the editors of Alskog, Inc. New York : Crowell, [1975] p. cm. (Masters of contemporary photography) "An Alskog book." [TR654.B26] 75-12884 8.95 ISBN 0-690-00788-4 pbk. : 4.95
1. Michals, Duane. 2. Photography, Artistic. I. Alskog, inc.

Michelozzo di Bartolommeo, 1396- 1472.

CAPLOW, Harriet McNeal, 730'.92'4 1928-
Michelozzo / Harriet McNeal Caplow. New York : Garland Pub., 1977. 2 v. (719 p.) : ill. ; 21 cm. (Outstanding dissertations in the fine arts) Bibliography: p. 661-704. [NB623.M517C36] 76-23604 ISBN 0-8240-2678-0 lib.bdg. : 85.00
1. Michelozzo di Bartolommeo, 1396-1472. I. Title. II. Series. BIP

Michelson, Leo, 1887-

BOURET, Jean. 759.4
Leo Michelson. [Translation of the French text into English by Rainer Esslen, into German by Friedrich Menke] New York, Arts; inc. [1963] 110 p. illus. (part col.) 30 cm. [Contemporary artists series] "A Golden griffin book. Text in English, French, and German. [ND553.M58B613] 63-20002
1. Michelson, Leo, 1887- . I. Title. II. Series.

Michener, James Albert, 1907- —Art collections.

TEXAS. 759.13'074'016431
University at Austin. Art Museum.
Selected paintings from the Michener Collection; [exhibition] November 2, 1969-January 5, 1970. [Austin, 1970?] 1 v. (unpaged) illus. 26 cm. [ND212.T42] 72-198153
1. Michener, James Albert, 1907- —Art collections. 2. Paintings, American—Exhibitions. 3. Painting, Modern—20th century—U.S. I. Title.

Michigan—Authors.

BEAMAN, Rossie. v. 12
This life we share. Illustrated by Leland Beaman. [Jackson, Mich., Stone Village Pub. Co., c1958] 111 p. illus. [NUC68-84357]
1. Michigan—Authors. I. Title.

Michigan—Description and travel— 1951- —Views.

BEAUTIFUL 779'.9'91774044
Michigan / photography by Michigan photographers. Portland, Or. : Beautiful America Pub. Co., c1978. 72 p. : chiefly ill. (some col.) ; 28 cm. [F567.B42] 78-105527 ISBN 0-915796-10-4 : 12.95 ISBN 0-915796-09-0 pbk. : 6.95
1. Michigan—Description and travel— 1951- —Views. BIP

Michigan. Northern Peninsula—Antiq.

BINFORD, Lewis Roberts, v. 12 1930-
Indian sites and chipped stone materials in the northern Lake Michigan area [by] Lewis R. Binford and George I. Quimby. [Chicago] Chicago Natural History Museum, 1963. 277-307 p. illus., tables. 24 cm. ([Chicago. Natural History Museum. Publication] no. 972) (Series. Series: Chicago. Natural History Museum. Fieldiana: anthropology, v. 36, no. 12)

GN2.F4 vol. 36, no. 12 Fieldiana: anthropology, v. 36, no. 12. Caption title. Bibliography: p. 307. [E78.M6B5 E51.F45 vol. 36, no. 12] 63-21954
1. Michigan. Northern Peninsula—Antiq. 2. Indians of North America—Michigan, Northern Peninsula. I. Quimby, George Irving, 1913- joint author. II. Title. III. Series.

Michigan—Public buildings.

MICHIGAN. Governor's 711'.3'09774
Special Commission on Architecture.
The State building process; analysis and recommendations. [Lansing, 1972?] vi, 108, [74] p. illus. 28 cm. Cover title. [NA4225.M5M52 1972] 73-623169
1. Michigan—Public buildings. 2. Architecture—Michigan. I. Title.

Michigan. University. William L. Clements Library.

MICHIGAN. University. 016.912'73
William L. Clements Library.
Research catalog of maps of America to 1860 in the William L. Clements Library, University of Michigan, Ann Arbor, Michigan. Edited by Douglas W. Marshall. Boston, G. K. Hall, 1972. 4 v. 37 cm. Bibliography: v. 1, p. viii. [Z6027.A5M53] 73-157170 ISBN 0-8161-1003-4 240.00
1. Michigan. University. William L. Clements Library. 2. America—Maps—Bibliography—Catalogs. I. Marshall, Douglas W., ed. II. Title. BIP

Mickey Mouse (Cartoon character)

MICKEY Mouse : 741.5'973
fifty happy years / edited by David Bain and Bruce Harris. New York : Harmony Books ; distributed by Crown Publishers, c1977. p. cm. Filmography: p. [NC1766.U52D55 1977] 77-11076 ISBN 0-517-52962-9 : 10.00
1. Disney (Walt) Productions—History. 2. Mickey Mouse (Cartoon character) I. Bain, David, 1949- II. Harris, Bruce S. BIP

Mies van der Rohe, Ludwig, 1886- 1969.

BLASER, Werner, 720'.7'1177311 1924-
After Mies : Mies van der Rohe, teaching and principles / Werner Blaser. New York : Van Nostrand Reinhold, 1977. 291 p. : ill. ; 25 cm. Translation of Mies van der Rohe, Lehre und Schule. Bibliography: p. 283-287. [NA1088.M65B5813] 76-28545 ISBN 0-442-20820-0 : 19.95
1. Mies van der Rohe, Ludwig, 1886-1969. 2. Illinois Institute of Technology, Chicago. Dept. of Architecture. 3. Architecture, Modern—20th century—United States. I. Title.

BLASER, Werner, 1924- 720'.92'4
Mies van der Rohe. [Rev. ed.] New York, Praeger [1972, c1965] 203 p. illus. 21 cm. [NA1088.M65B573 1972] 72-166163 8.50
1. Mies van der Rohe, Ludwig, 1886-1969.

BLASER, Werner, 1924- 720.924
Mies van der Rohe; the art of structure [Eng. version by D. Q. Stephenson. New York] Praeger [1965] 226p. illus. (pt. col.) plans, port. 27cm. [NA1088M65B573] 65-25278 25.00
1. Mies van der Rohe, Ludwig, 1886- I. Title.

CARTER, Peter James. 720'.92'4
Mies van der Rohe at work. New York, Praeger [1974] 196 p. illus. 25 x 30 cm. Bibliography: p. 193. [NA1088.M65C37] 72-88260
1. Mies van der Rohe, Ludwig, 1886-1969. I. Title.

DREXLER, Arthur. 720.973
Ludwig Mies van der Rohe. New York, G. Braziller, 1960. 127 p. illus., plates, port., plans. 26 cm. (The Masters of world architecture series) "Bibliography of articles written by Mies van der Rohe": p. 117. "Selected bibliography in Mies van der Rohe": p. 119-121. [NA1088.M65D7] 60-6077
1. Mies van der Rohe, Ludwig, 1886- I. Title. II. Series. BIP

HILBERSEIMER, Ludwig. 720.81
Mies van der Rohe. Chicago, P. Theobald, 1956. 199p. 187 illus., plans. 29cm. [NA1088.M65H5] 56-3870
1. Mies van der Rohe, Ludwig, 1886- I. Title.

MIES VAN DER ROHE, 720'.924
Ludwig, 1886-1969.
Mies van der Rohe. Introd. and notes by Martin Pawley. With 60 photos. by Yukio Futagawa. New York Simon and Schuster [1970] 134 p. illus. (part col.), plans, port. 27 cm. (Library of contemporary architects) Translation of Misu fan deru Roe. "New texts have been provided for this English language edition." Bibliography: p. 131. [NA1088.M65A513 1970] 73-119717 ISBN 0-671-20691-5 7.50
I. Pawley, Martin. II. Futagawa, Yukio, 1932-

NEW YORK (City). Museum 749.2'3 of Modern Art.
Ludwig Mies van der Rohe : furniture and furniture drawings from the Design Collection and the Mies van der Rohe Archive, the Museum of Modern Art, New York / by Ludwig Glaeser. New York : The Museum, c1977. 88 p. : ill. ; 26 cm. Bibliography: p. 86. [NK2554.M5N48 1977] 76-24509 ISBN 0-87070-555-5 pbk. : 4.95
1. Mies van der Rohe, Ludwig, 1886-1969. 2. Furniture—Germany—Exhibitions. 3. Furniture—Drawings—Exhibitions. I. Mies van der Rohe, Ludwig, 1886-1969. II. Glaeser, Ludwig. III. Mies van der Rohe Archive.

NEW YORK. Museum of 720.943 Modern Art.
Mies van der Rohe, by Philip C. Johnson. [2d ed., rev.] New York [c1953] 215p. illus., port., diagrs., plans. 26cm. Bibliography: p. 208-212. [NA1088.M65N4 1953] [NA1088.M65N4 1953] 720.81 54-7774 54-7774
1. Mies van der Rohe, Ludwig, 1886- I. Johnson, Philip Cortel you. 1906- II. Title.

SPEYER, A. James. 720'.924
Mies van der Rohe, by A. James Speyer. Catalogue entries by Frederick Koeper. [Chicago] Art Institute of Chicago, 1968. 120 p. illus., plans, ports. 26 cm. "A retrospective exhibition, organized by the Art Institute of Chicago in collaboration with the Graham Foundation for Advanced Studies in the Fine Arts." Held at the Art Institute of Chicago, April 27-June 30, 1968, and others. Bibliography: p. 120. [NA1088.M65S6] 68-4506
1. Mies van der Rohe, Ludwig, 1886- I. Koeper, Frederick. II. Chicago. Art Institute. III. Title.

Mies van der Rohe, Ludwig, 1886- 1969—Bibliography.

SPAETH, David A. 016.72 s
Ludwig Mies van der Rohe : an annotated bibliography and chronology / David A. Spaeth ; with a foreword by George Edson Danforth. New York : Garland Pub., 1978. p. cm. (Garland reference library of the humanities ; v. 115) (Papers - American Association of Architectural Bibliographers ; 13) Includes bibliographical references and index. [Z5941.A5 vol. 13] [Z8574.18] [NA1088.M65] 016.72'092'4 77-83355 ISBN 0-8240-9830-7 : lib.bdg. : 25.00
1. Mies van der Rohe, Ludwig, 1886-1969—Bibliography. 2. Mies van der Rohe, Ludwig, 1886-1969—Chronology. I. Title. II. Series. III. Series: American Association of Architectural Bibliographers. Papers ; 13. BIP

Milan. Pinacoteca di Brera.

BRERA Milan. 759.5'074'0521
[Texts by Roberto P. Ciardi and others] New York, Newsweek [1970] 171 p. col. illus., plan. 30 cm. (Great museums of the world) Bibliography: p. [168] [N2670.B7] 74-118562
1. Milan. Pinacoteca di Brera. I. Ciardi, Roberto Paolo. II. Series: Great museums of the world (New York, Newsweek)

SUBJECT INDEX MILLER (HERMAN) FURNITURE

Miles, Sally.

MILES, Sally. 745.92'8
Natural collage : the making of pictures with seeds, leaves, and grasses / Sally Miles ; with line drawings by Anthony Loynes. New York : Scribner, c1973. 127 p. : ill. (some col.) ; 26 cm. Includes index. [NK1535.M47A52] 74-5964 ISBN 0-684-13895-6 : 9.95
1. Miles, Sally. 2. Design, Decorative—Plant forms. 3. Design, Decorative—Animal forms. 4. Collage. I. Title. BIP

Miley, Michael, 1841-1918.

FISHWICK, Marshall William. 927.7
General Lee's photographer; the life and work of Michael Miley. [Chapel Hill] Published for the Virginia Historical Society by the University of North Carolina Press, 1954. 94 p. illus., col. plates, ports. 29 cm. "The Robert E. Lee series of negatives ... owned by the Virginia Historical Society": p. 77-87. Bibliographical footnotes. [TR140.M5F5] 54-13385
1. Miley, Michael, 1841-1918. 2. Lee, Robert Edward, 1807-1870. I. Virginia Historical Society, Richmond. II. Title.

Military architecture—Africa, West.

LAWRENCE, Arnold Walter, 1900- 725.180966
Trade castles & forts of West Africa. Stanford, Calif., Stanford Univ. Pr., 1964[c.1963] 389p. illus., map, plates. 24cm. Bibl. 64-23408 10.00
1. Military architecture—Africa, West. 2. Africa, West—Hist. I. Title.

Military architecture—History.

HUGHES, James Quentin. 725'.18
Military architecture / Quentin Hughes. New York : St. Martin's Press, 1975, c1974. 256 p., [4] leaves of plates : ill. ; 25 cm. (Excursions into architecture) Includes index. Bibliography: p. 244-251. [UG460.H84 1975] 74-25217 20.00
1. Military architecture—History. 2. Fortification—History. I. Title.

Military architecture—History—Addresses, essays, lectures.

HALE, John Rigby, 1923- 725'.18
Renaissance fortification : art or engineering? / J. R. Hale. [London] : Thames and Hudson, 1978. 64 p. : ill. ; 22 cm. (Walter Neurath memorial lecture ; 9) [UG460.H38] 78-309705 ISBN 0-500-55009-3 : 9.95
1. Military architecture—History—Addresses, essays, lectures. 2. Architecture, Renaissance—Addresses, essays, lectures. 3. Fortification—History—Addresses, essays, lectures. I. Title. II. Series.
Distributed by W. W. Norton, New York

Military architecture—India.

TOY, Sidney 725.18
The fortified cities of India. London, Heinemann [dist. New York, Hillary, c.1965] xiv. 118p. illus., map. plans. ports. 23cm. [NA497.I4T58] 65-29561 8.50
1. Military architecture—India. 2. Fortification—India. I. Title.

TOY, Sidney 725.183
The strongholds of India. Melbourne, W. Heinemann [New York, Hillary House, 1965, c.1957] 136p. illus. 23cm. [NA497.I4T6] 58-1640 6.00
1. Military architecture—India. 2. Fortification—India. I. Title.

Military history, Modern—20th cent.—Pictorial works.

CAPA, Robert, 1913-1954 908.4
Images of war, by Robert Capa, with text from his own writings. New York, Grossman [1966] 175p. illus., ports. 28cm. (Paragraphic bks.) [TR140.C28A3] 64-4621 3.50 pap.,
1. Military history, Modern—20th cent.—Pictorial works. I. Title.

Military miniatures.

ARNOLD, Arnold. 268'.432
The Arnold Arnold book of toy soldiers. Text and pictures by Arnold Arnold. New York, Random House [c1963] 8, [47] p. col. illus. 33 cm. Includes toy soldiers to push out and stand up, together with battle games. [GV1218.T55A7] 63-8998
1. Military miniatures. 2. War games. I. Title.

BALDET, Marcel 739.54
Lead soldiers and figurines Foreword by Peter J. Blum. Tr. by E. Stanton Russell. New York, Crown [1963, c.1961] 126, [3] p. illus., plates (pt. col.) 28cm. Bibl. 62-20064 12.50
1. Military miniatures. I. Title.

BLUM, Peter 745.59
Military miniatures. Photos. by Phillip Stearns. New York, Odyssey [c.1964] 34p. col. illus., col. map., col. ports. 11x17cm. (Odyssey lib. 12) 64-12890 .95 bds.,
1. Military miniatures. I. Title.

BLUM, Peter Joseph, 1930- 745.59
Military miniatures, by Peter Blum. Photos, by Phillip Stearns. New York, Odyssey Press [1964] 34 p. col. illus., col. map, col. ports. 11 x 17 cm. (The Odyssey library. 12) [NK494.M5B55] 64-12890
1. Military miniatures. I. Title.

CASSIN-SCOTT, Jack. 745.59'282
Making model soldiers of the world / Jack Cassin-Scott. New York : Hippocrene Books, [1974] c1973. 156 p. : ill. (some col.) ; 25 cm. Includes bibliographical references and index. [NK8475.M5C38 1974] 74-194418 ISBN 0-88254-268-0 : 10.95
1. Military miniatures. I. Title. BIP

FEATHERSTONE, Donald F. 745.59'282
Military modelling [by] Donald Featherstone. [1st American ed.] New York, A. S. Barnes [1971, c1970] 159 p. illus. 22 cm. Includes bibliographies. [NK8475.MF43 1971] 78-137364 ISBN 0-498-07832-9 6.95
1. Military miniatures. I. Title.

GOODENOUGH, Simon. 745.59'282
Military miniatures / Simon Goodenough and 'Tradition'. Radnor, Pa. : Chilton Book Co., 1978, c1977. 127 p. : ill. (some col.) ; 30 cm. Bibliography: p. 126. [U311.G66 1978] 77-93021 ISBN 0-8019-6721-X : 15.00. ISBN 0-8019-6722-8 pbk. : 8.50
1. Military miniatures. I. Tradition (Firm) II. Title. BIP

HARRIS, Henry Edward David, 1913- 745.59
Model soldiers. New York, Putnam [1962] 128 p. illus. (part col.) 22 cm. (Pleasures and treasures) [NK494.M5H3] 62-13079
1. Military miniatures. I. Title.

LINDSAY, Merrill. 739.7
Miniature arms. Photos. by Bruce Pendleton. [New York, Winchester Press; distributed by McGraw-Hill, 1970] 110 p. illus. (part col.) 15 x 23 cm. [NK8475.M5L5] 78-99753
1. Military miniatures. I. Title. BIP

RISLEY, Clyde A. 745.59
The model soldier guide; a handbook for the collecting, painting, and displaying of military miniatures, by Clyde A. Risley, William F. Imrie. Plus a survey of military uniforms, their origin and influence. Richmond Hill, Queens, N. Y., Imrie/Risley Miniatures, 114-05 101st Ave. [c.1965] ii, 67p. illus. 23cm. Bibl [NK494.M5R5] 65-4253 4.95 bds.,
1. Military miniatures. 2. Models and modelmaking I. Imrie, William F., joint author. II. Title.

WINDROW, Martin C. 745.59'282
Model soldiers / [by] Martin Windrow and Gerry Embleton. Cambridge : Stephens [for] Airfix Products Ltd., 1976. 64 p. : ill. ; 23 cm. (Airfix magazine guide ; 19) [U311.W56] 77-357552 ISBN 0-85059-234-8 : £1.40
1. Military miniatures. I. Embleton, Gerry, joint author. II. Title. BIP

Military miniatures—Collectors and collecting.

CARMAN, W. Y. 745.59'282
Model soldiers [by] W. Y. Carman. [1st American ed.] New York, World Pub. Co. [1972] 80 p. col. illus. 22 cm. (Collectors world all-color guides) Bibliography: p. 80. [NK8475.M5C37 1972] 72-77863 ISBN 0-529-04684-9 5.95
1. Military miniatures—Collectors and collecting. I. Title.

*GARRATT, John G. 745.592'82'075
Collecting model soldiers [by] John G. Garratt. New York, Arco Pub. Co. [1975] 187 p. 23 cm. Includes bibliographical references and index. [TT154] 74-24665 ISBN 0-668-03749-0 8.95
1. Military miniatures—Collectors and collecting. I. Title. BIP

HARRIS, Henry Edward David, 1913- 745.59
Collecting model soldiers [by] Henry Harris. Foreword by Peter Young. And a chapter on wargames, by Donald F. Featherstone. London, New York, Abelard-Schuman [1971] 200 p. illus., ports. 23 cm. First published in 1969 under title: How to go collecting model soldiers. Bibliography: p. 186-187. [NK8475.M5H3 1971] 75-141671 ISBN 0-200-71779-0 6.95 (U.S.)
1. Military miniatures—Collectors and collecting. I. Title.

MCKENZIE, Ian. 745.59'282
Collecting old toy soldiers / Ian McKenzie ; photography by Michael Hallett. London : B. T. Batsford, 1976. 155 p., [6] leaves of plates : ill. (some col.) ; 26 cm. Includes index. Bibliography: p. 152. [NK8475.M5M3] 76-359325 ISBN 0-7134-3036-2 : 14.95
1. Military miniatures—Collectors and collecting. I. Title.
Distributed by Hippocrene BIP

NICOLLIER, Jean, 1894- 745.59'2
Collecting toy soldiers. Rutland, Vt., C. E. Tuttle Co. [1967] 283 p. illus. (part col.) 24 cm. Translation of Soldats de collection. Bibliography: p. 269-270. [NK494.M5N53] 67-28905
1. Military miniatures—Collectors and collecting. I. Title.

Military miniatures—History.

GARRATT, John Geoffrey. 745.59'282
Model soldiers; an illustrated history [by] John G. Garratt. Greenwich, Conn., New York Graphic Society [1972] 248 p. illus. 26 cm. Bibliography: p. 241. [NK8475.M5G37 1972] 72-80417 ISBN 0-8212-0487-4 15.00
1. Military miniatures—History. I. Title.

Military miniatures—Juvenile literature.

STEARNS, Philip Olcott. 745.59'282
How to make model soldiers / written and photographed by Philip O. Stearns. New York : Arco Pub. Co., [1974] 80 p. : ill. (some col.) ; 26 cm. Includes bibliographical references and index. A how-to book that includes a history, production, display, and care of miniature soldiers. [U311.S83] 73-92267 ISBN 0-668-03446-7 : 5.95
1. Military miniatures—Juvenile literature. 2. Models and modelmaking—Juvenile literature. I. Title. BIP

Milk bottles—Collectors and collecting.

ROTH, Evelyn. 637'.135
The milky way. Ocean View, N.J. : E. Roth, [1974] 40 p. : ill. ; 23 cm. "Vol. 1." [NK5440.B6R64 1974] 75-302446
1. Milk bottles—Collectors and collecting. I. Title.

TAYLOR, Gordon A. 637'.135
Milkbottle manual; a collector's pictorial primer & pricing guide, by Gordon A. Taylor. [Salem, Or., Old Time Bottle Pub. Co., 1971] 111 p. illus. 22 cm. (A Collectors guide book for the U.S.A.) "Price guide" ([4] p.) inserted. Bibliography: p. 106. [NK5440.B6T3] 70-162919 ISBN 0-911068-07-4 3.95
1. Milk bottles—Collectors and collecting. I. Title. BIP

Millais, John Everett, Sir, bart., 1829-1896.

MILLAIS, John Guille, 1865-1931. 759.2 B
The life and letters of Sir John Everett Millais, president of the Royal Academy. New York, F. A. Stokes, 1899. [New York, AMS Press, 1973] 2 v. illus. 24 cm. [ND497.M6M5 1973] 72-148280 ISBN 0-404-04326-7 95.00
1. Millais, John Everett, Sir, bart., 1829-1896. BIP

SPIELMANN, Marion Harry, 1858-1948. 759.2
Millais and his works, with special reference to the exhibition at the Royal Academy 1898. With a chapter "Thoughts on our art of to-day", by J. E. Millais. Edinburgh, W. Blackwood, 1898. [New York, AMS Press, 1971] 190 p. illus., ports. 18 cm. [ND497.M6S7 1971] 74-148306
1. Millais, John Everett, Sir, bart., 1829-1896. I. London. Royal Academy of Arts. II. Title.

Millares, Manolo, 1926-1972.

MILLARES, Manolo, 1926-1972. 759.6
Homage to Manolo Millares : his last paintings, 1969-1971 : May 21-June 7, 1974, Pierre Matisse Gallery, 41 East 57th Street, New York. New York : The Gallery, [1974] [28] p. : ill. (some col.) ; 26 cm. Includes bibliographical references. [ND813.M495P5] 76-353693
1. Millares, Manolo, 1926-1972. I. Pierre Matisse Gallery, New York. II. Title.

Miller, Alfred Jacob, 1810-1874.

MILLER, Alfred Jacob, 1810-1874. 759.13
Braves and buffalo; Plains Indian life in 1837. Water-colours of Alfred J. Miller, with descriptive notes by the artist. Introduced by Michael Bell. [Toronto] University of Toronto Press [1973] 176 p. illus. (part col.) 24 x 31 cm. (The Public Archives of Canada series, 3) [ND1839.M54A42] 73-85088 15.00
1. Miller, Alfred Jacob, 1810-1874. 2. Indians of North America—Pictorial works. I. Title. II. Series: Canada. Public Archives. The Public Archives of Canada series, 3. BIP

WARNER, Robert C. 759.13
The Fort Laramie of Alfred Jacob Miller : a catalogue of all the known illustrations of the first Fort Laramie / by Robert C. Warner. Laramie : University of Wyoming, 1973. v, 163 leaves : ill. ; 29 cm. Thesis (M.A.)—University of Wyoming. Bibliography: leaves [156]-163. [N6537.M54W37] 74-186939
1. Miller, Alfred Jacob, 1810-1874. 2. Fort Laramie, Wyo.—Pictorial works. 3. The West in art. I. Title.

Miller, David Mason.

MILLER, David Mason. 759.13
Windows [by] David Miller. [Santa Fe, N.M., J. Muir Publications; distributed by Book People, Berkeley, Calif., c1973] [21] l., [46] l. of illus. (part col.) 25 cm. [ND1839.M55A57] 73-83377 ISBN 0-912528-06-0 6.00
1. Miller, David Mason. I. Title.

Miller (Herman) Furniture Company, inc., Zeeland, Mich.

CAPLAN, Ralph. 338.7'61'749217415
The design of Herman Miller / by Ralph Caplan. New York : Whitney Library of Design, 1976. 119 p. : ill. ; 23 cm. [TS880.C36 1976] 76-6489 ISBN 0-8230-7141-3 : 13.50
1. Miller (Herman) Furniture Company, inc., Zeeland, Mich. 2. Furniture design. I. Title.
Available from Watson-Guptill.

Miller, Kenneth Hayes, 1876-1952.

ROTHSCHILD, Lincoln, 1902- 759.13 B
To keep art alive; the effort of Kenneth Hayes Miller, American painter (1876-1952). Philadelphia, Art Alliance Press [1974] 104 p., [100] p. of illus. (part col.) 29 cm. Bibliography: p. 101-102. [ND237.M48R67] 73-9301 ISBN 0-87982-012-8
1. Miller, Kenneth Hayes, 1876-1952. I. Miller, Kenneth Hayes, 1876-1952, illus. II. Title.

Miller, William McE.—Art collections.

COLORADO Springs. Fine Arts Center. Taylor Museum. 759.01'1'099429
The art of Arnhem Land, from the collection of William McE. Miller, Jr. [Colorado Springs] 1966. [24] p. illus. 15 x 22 cm. Catalog of an exhibition. [ND1101.C64 1966] 74-171018
1. Miller, William McE.—Art collections. 2. Paintings, Australian (Aboriginal)—Exhibitions. 3. Painting, Primitive—Arnhem Land, Australia. I. Title.

Millersburg Glass Company.

EDWARDS, Bill. 748.2'9171'64
Millersburg, the queen of carnival glass / by Bill Edwards. Paducah, Ky. : Collector Books, c1975. 134 p. : col. ill. ; 22 cm. [NK5198.M54E38] 76-350543 ISBN 0-89145-002-5 : 8.95
1. Millersburg Glass Company. 2. Carnival glass. 3. Glassware—United States. I. Title.

Milles, Carl, 1875-1955.

ROGERS, Meyric Reynold, 1893- 730'.92'4
Carl Milles; an interpretation of his work, by Meyric R. Rogers. Port Washington, N.Y., Kennikat Press [1973, c1940] viii, 73 p., 163 [i.e. 164] plates. 31 cm. Bibliography: p. [62] [NB793.M5R6 1973] 72-85304 ISBN 0-8046-1707-4 25.00
1. Milles, Carl, 1875-1955.

Millet, Jean Francois, 1814-1875.

ADY, Julia Mary Cartwright, d.1924. 759.4
Jean Francois Millet. New York, AMS Press [1971] vii, 396 p. illus., port. 23 cm. Reprint of the 1896 ed. [ND553.M6A3 1971] 73-155629 ISBN 0-404-00297-8
1. Millet, Jean Francois, 1814-1875.

ADY, Julia Mary Cartwright, d.1924. 759.4
Jean Francois Millet: his life and letters. London, S. Sonnenschein; New York, Macmillan, 1896. St. Clair Shores, Mich., Scholarly Press, 1972. vii, 396 p. illus. 22 cm. [ND553.M6A64 1972] 76-115227 ISBN 0-403-00469-1
1. Millet, Jean Francois, 1814-1875. BIP

HERBERT, Robert L., 1929- 759.4
Jean-Francois Millet : [exhibition], Hayward Gallery, 22 January-7 March 1976 / Arts Council of Great Britain. [London] : [The Council], 1976. 235 p. : ill. ; 25 cm. Catalog by Robert Herbert in consultation with Michel Laclotte and Roseline Bacou. "An exhibition organized by the Reunion des musees nationaux and first held in the Galeries nationales d'exposition du Grand Palais, Paris from 17 October 1975 to 5 January 1976." Bibliography: p. 231-233. [N6853.M52H46] 76-365275 ISBN 0-7287-0079-4 : £5.25. ISBN 0-7287-0078-6 pbk.
1. Millet, Jean Francois, 1814-1875. I. Laclotte, Michel, joint author. II. Bacou, Roseline, joint author. III. Millet, Jean Francois, 1814-1875. IV. Arts Council of Great Britain. V. Hayward Gallery. VI. Reunion des musees nationaux, Paris.

SMITH, Charles Sprague, 1853-1910. 759.4
Barbizon days; Millet, Corot, Rousseau, Barye. Freeport, N.Y., Books for Libraries Press [1969] 232 p. illus., ports. 23 cm. (Essay index reprint series) Reprint of the 1902 ed. [N6847.S7 1969] 79-86784
1. Millet, Jean Francois, 1814-1875. 2. Corot, Jean Baptiste Camille, 1796-1875. 3. Rousseau, Theodore, 1812-1867. 4. Barye, Antoine Louis, 1796-1875. I. Title. BIP

TOMSON, Arthur. 759.4
Jean-Francois Millet and the Barbizon school. Freeport, N.Y., Books for Libraries Press [1973] p. Reprint of the 1903 ed. published by G. Bell, New York. Bibliography: [ND547.5.B3T65] 73-6507 ISBN 0-518-19070-6
1. Millet, Jean Francois, 1814-1875. 2. Barbizon school. 3. Painting, Modern—19th century—France. I. Title.

Millinery.

BORRETT, Eve. 646.5/04
How to make hats. London, Pitman, 1967. Stamped on t.p.: Dist. by Sportshelf, New Rochelle, N.Y. 92p. illus., diagrs. 20cm. [TT655.B57] 67-100486 4.25 bds.,
1. Millinery. I. Title.

BOTTOMLEY, Julia, ed. 646.6
The milliner's guide; a complete handy reference book for the workroom, embraces the professional experience of ages. Edited by Julia Bottomley. Rev., classified, and compiled by Emma Maxwell Burke. St. Clair Shores, Mich., Scholarly Press, 1972 [i.e. 1973] p. Reprint of the 1917 ed. [TT657.B6 1973] 72-11561 ISBN 0-403-02353-X
1. Millinery. 2. Receipts. I. Burke, Emma Maxwell. II. Title.

CARNAHAN, Ruby Ironside, 1890- 646.54
How to make hats; easy step by step instructions: 30 patterns, over 500 illustrations. [Chicago? 1952] 153 p. illus. 28 cm. [TT655.C3] 52-3989
1. Millinery. I. Title.

COLLINS, Wanda Summers, 1896- 646.54
The complete book of home millinery. New York, Funk & Wagnalls [1951] 108 p. illus. 23 cm. Pages 104-108, blank for "Notes [etc.]" [TT655.C65] 51-11258
1. Millinery. I. Title.

DRAGER, Brett Ours, 1905- 646.54
Hat tactics, written and illustrated by Brett Ours Drager. [1st ed.] [Oklahoma City?] [1950] 179 p. illus. 27 cm. [TT655.D7] 50-29975
1. Millinery. I. Title.

LOWRIE, Drucella. 646.54
Restyle your hats. New York, Studio Publications in association with Crowell [1952] 119 p. illus. 24 cm. [TT657.L6] 52-7380
1. Millinery I. Title.

ZAYLOR, Marianne Townsend, 1913- 646.54
How to make fabric hats; professional secrets revealed in a step-by-step guide. Cleveland, Immerman [1953] 64p. illus. 28cm. [TT655.Z3] 53-7516
1. Millinery. I. Title.

Mills, Donald, 1896—

MILLS, Donald, 1896- 741.9'73
Southwest impressions, by Mills. Glorieta, N.M., Rio Grande Press [1973] 125 p. (chiefly illus., part col.) 29 cm. [NC139.M54A55] 73-17268 ISBN 0-87380-090-7 10.00
1. Mills, Donald, 1896- 2. Southwest, New, in art. I. Title.

Mills, Flora Rupe—Art collections.

HARTLEY, Julia Magee. 748.2'913'07401645315
Old American glass : the Mills Collection at Texas Christian University / by Julia Magee Hartley. Fort Worth : Texas Christian University Press, [1975] xii, 279 p., [8] leaves of plates : ill. (some col.) ; 24 cm. On spine: The Mills Collection. Bibliography: p. 273-279. [NK5112.H28] 75-10110 10.00
1. Mills, Flora Rupe—Art collections. 2. Texas Christian University, Forth Worth. 3. Glassware—United States—Catalogs. I. Title. BIP

Mills, Robert, 1781-1855.

BALTIMORE. Museum of Art. 728.3'0924
Robert Mills' Waterloo Row—Baltimore 1816. [Baltimore, 1971] 24 p. illus., plans. 26 cm. Written by William Voss Elder, III, curator of decorative arts. Includes bibliographical references. [NA735.B3B3] 72-27509
1. Mills, Robert, 1781-1855. 2. Baltimore. Museum of Art. 3. Baltimore—Buildings. I. Elder, William Voss. II. Title.

GALLAGHER, Helen Mar (Pierce) d.1942. 720'.92'4 B
Robert Mills, architect of the Washington Monument, 1781-1855. New York, AMS Press, 1966 [c1935] xxv, 233 p. illus. 24 cm. Bibliography: p. [217]-220. [NA737.M5G3 1966] 72-183878
1. Mills, Robert, 1781-1855.

MARSH, Blanche. 720'.92'4
Robert Mills; architect in South Carolina. [Columbia, S.C.] R. L. Bryan Co., 1970. xi, 178 p. illus. 28 cm. Bibliography: p. 177-178. [NA737.M5M37] 72-125882
1. Mills, Robert, 1781-1855. 2. Architecture—South Carolina.

Milne, Alan Alexander, 1882-1956.

SHEPARD, Ernest Howard, 1879-. 741.942
Pooh, his art gallery. New York, Dutton [1962?] These pictures, selected from A. A. Milne's The world of Pooh and The world of Christopher Robin, are suitable for framing. [NC1115.S48A5] 62-51031
1. Milne, alan Alexander, 1882-1956 —Illustrations. I. Title. BIP

Milne, David Browne, 1882-1953.

TOVELL, Rosemarie. 759.11
David Milne : painting place = David Milne : un coin pour peindre / by Rosemarie L. Tovell. Ottawa : National Gallery of Canada, National Museum of Canada, 1976. 35 p. : ill. (some col.) ; 26 cm. (Masterpieces in the National Gallery of Canada ; no. 8) English and French. Bibliography: p. 34-35. [ND249.M5T68] 77-374601 ISBN 0-88884-313-5
1. Milne, David Browne, 1882-1953. Painting place. I. Milne, David Browne, 1882-1953. II. National Gallery of Canada. III. Title. IV. Series.

Milton, John, 1608-1674.

UPTON, Richard. 763
Credo: a sketch from John Milton's Paradise lost, with lithographs by Richard Upton. [Northampton] Printed at the Gehenna Press, 1967. 1 portfolio ([4] l., 12 plates) 70 cm. 20 copies, no. 11/20, signed by the artist. The lithographs were printed at the Erebus Press in Saratoga Springs. [NE2415.U6A45] 68-6068
1. Milton, John, 1608-1674. Paradise lost—Illustrations. I. Title.

Milton, John, 1608-1674—Influence.

POINTON, Marcia R. 760'.0942
Milton & English art [by] Marcia R. Pointon. [Toronto] University of Toronto Press [1970] xlii, 276 p. illus. 24 cm. Bibliography: p. [264]-269. [PR3588.P6 1970] 70-508609 14.50
1. Milton, John, 1608-1674—Influence. 2. Milton, John, 1608-1674—Illustrations. 3. Art, English. I. Title. BIP

Milton, John—Portraits.

MARTIN, John Rupert. 757'.9'0973
The portrait of John Milton at Princeton, and its place in Milton iconography. Princeton, N. J., Princeton University Library, 1961. vi, 34p. ports. (1 col.) 33cm. Bibliographical references includes in Notes' P. 31-33) [N7628.M5M3] 61-14263
1. Milton, John—Portraits. I. Title.

Milton, Peter, 1930- —Exhibitions.

MILTON, Peter, 1930- 769'.92'4
Prints by Peter Milton : an exhibition of prints from the collection of the artist / introd. by Kneeland McNulty ; organized and circulated by the International Exhibitions Foundation, 1977-1979. [Washington] : The Foundation, c1977. 32 p. : ill. ; 28 cm. Bibliography: p. 32. [NE2012.M54157] 77-82125
1. Milton, Peter, 1930- —Exhibitions. I. Title.

Minature painting—England.

HASSALL, A. G. 759.2
The Douce Apocalypse. Introd. and notes by A. G. and W. O. Hassall. New York, Yoseloff [c.1961] 32p. mounted col. illus. facsims. 29cm. (Lib. of illuminated manuscripts) Bibl. 61-16186 4.95
1. Minature painting—England. 2. Bible. N. T. Revelation—Pictures, illustrations, etc. I. Hassall. William Owen, joint author. II. Douce, Francis, 1757-1834. III. Title. IV. Series.

Minature painting, Iranian.

LILLYS, William, ed. 759.95
Oriental miniatures; Persian, Indian, Turkish. Ed., introductions, notes, by William Lillys, Robert Reiff, Emel Esin. Rutland, Vt., Tuttle [c.1965] 102p. illus. (pt. mounted, pt. col.) 31cm. Bibl. [ND3237.L5] 65-18961 9.50
1. Minature painting, Iranian. 2. Miniatures painting, Indic. 3. Miniature painting, Turkish. I. Reiff, Robert, ed. II. Esin, Emel (Tek) ed. III. Title.
Contents omitted

Miner, Dorothy Eugenia.

GATHERINGS in honor of 700
Dorothy E. Miner. Edited by Ursula E. McCracken, Lilian M. C. Randall [and] Richard H. Randall, Jr. Baltimore, Walters Art Gallery [1974] xviii, 353 p. illus. 29 cm. [N7442.2.M563] 74-170951 36.00
1. Miner, Dorothy Eugenia. 2. Art—Addresses, essays, lectures. I. Miner, Dorothy Eugenia. II. McCracken, Ursula E., ed. III. Randall, Lilian M. C., ed. IV. Randall, Richard H., ed. V. Walters Art Gallery, Baltimore. BIP

Ming ch'i—Catalogs.

CAPON, Edmund. 732'.7
Chinese tomb figures / Edmund Capon. London : H. M. Stationery Off., 1976. [12] p. : col. ill. ; 16 cm. (Victoria & Albert Museum ssmall colour book ; 11) [NK4165.C33] 77-368596 ISBN 0-11-290233-2 : £0.35
1. Ming ch'i—Catalogs. 2. Pottery, Chinese—Catalogs. I. Title. II. Series: Victoria & Albert Museum, South Kensington. Small colour book ; 11.

Ming porcelain.

FRANK, Ann. 738.2'0951
Chinese blue and white. New York, Walker [1970, c1969] 99 p. illus. (part col.) 22 cm. (Collectors' blue books) Bibliography: p. 98-99. [NK4565.F68 1970] 74-86409 4.50
1. Ming porcelain. I. Title.

MACINTOSH, Duncan. 738.2'7
Chinese blue & white porcelain / Duncan Macintosh. Rutland, Vt. : C. E. Tuttle Co., c1977. 152 p. : ill. (some col.) ; 29 cm. Includes index. Bibliography: p. 146-147. [NK4565.5.M3 1977b] 77-70845 ISBN 0-8048-1208-X : 15.00
1. Ming porcelain. 2. China trade porcelain. I. Title. BIP

Ming porcelain—Exhibitions.

VALENSTEIN, Suzanne G. 738.2'7
Ming porcelains : a retrospective : catalogue of a loan exhibition from museum and private collections in the United States, October 29, 1970 through January 31, 1971 / by Suzanne G. Valenstein. New York : China House Gallery, China Institute in America, c1970. 104 p. : ill. ; 24 cm. [NK4565.5.V34] 79-137202

1. *Ming porcelain—Exhibitions. I. China House Gallery. II. Title.*

Miniature bottles.

SNYDER, Robert E. 666'.19
Bottles in miniature, by Robert E. Snyder. Art: Bud McCaulley; photography: Ralph Leone. Amarillo, Tex., 1969- v. illus. (part col.) 26 cm. Vol. 3 has title: Bob Snyder's Bottles in miniature. Photography: Ray Wagner. [NK8475.B6S6] 73-13122 4.00
1. *Miniature bottles. I. Title.*

Miniature cameras.

BENTLEY, Thomas Leslie James 771.31
Newnes complete guide to the miniature camera. Colour illus. by courtesy of Kodak A. G. Stuttgart; other pictorial illus. by courtesy of Kodak A. G., Stuttgart; other pictorial illus. by the author. London, Newnes [Hollywood-by-the-Sea, Fla., Transatlantic, 1965, c.1964] viii, 376p. illus. (pt. col.) 23cm. Based in pt. on The manual of the miniature camera (5th ed.) [TR262.B4] 65-3136 13.50
1. *Miniature cameras. 2. Photography—Handbooks, manulas, etc. I. Title. II. Title: Guide to the miniature camera.*

COOPER, Joseph David, 1917- 771.3148
Ultra-miniature photography. New York, Amphoto; distributed by Garden City Books [1958] 160 p. illus. 24 cm. [TR146.C75] 57-14450
1. *Miniature cameras. 2. Photography—Handbooks, manuals, etc. I. Title.*

COOPER. JOSEPH DAVID, 1917- 771.3
The new Ultra-miniature photography. [2d ed., rev.] New York. Universal Photo Bks. [dist. Amphoto, c. 1958, 1961] 160p. illus. 61-14253 3.95bds.,
1. *Miniature cameras. 2. Photography—Handbooks, manuals, etc. I. Title. II. Title: Ultra-miniature photography.*

GAUNT, Leonard. 771.3
How to choose and use your 35mm camera. [2d ed.] New York, Amphoto [1969] 76 p. illus. 18 cm. (Viewfinder book) [TR262.G38 1969] 77-95585 1.25
1. *Miniature cameras. I. Title.*

GREEN, Thomas Leslie. 770.28
Ultra miniature camera technique [by] T. L. Green, [1st ed.] London, New York, Focal Press [1965] 216 p. illus. 22 cm. [TR262.G7] 66-6486
1. *Miniature cameras. 2. Photography—Handbooks, manuals, etc. I. Title.*

KEPPLER, Herbert. 771.3148
Official 35 mm camera rating guide. [1st ed.] New York, Universal Photo Books [1957] 128p. illus. 21cm. (A Universal photo guide) [TR260.K4] 57-10342
1. *Miniature cameras. I. Title.*

LAHUE, Kalton C. 770'.28
110 format photography / by Kalton C. Lahue. Los Angeles : Petersen Pub. Co., c1976. 79 p. : ill. (some col.) ; 28 cm. (Petersen's how-to photographic library) [TR262.L358] 75-18056 ISBN 0-8227-0113-8 : 3.95 ($4.50 Can)
1. *Miniature cameras. 2. Photography—Handbooks, manuals, etc. I. Title.*

POLLOCK, Norman. 771.3148
5 mm reference guide New York, Greenberg, c1956. 96p. illus. 20cm. (The Modern camera guide series) [TR260.P6] 56-7913
1. *Miniature cameras. I. Title.*

POLLOCK, Norman. 771.3148
35 mm reference guide. New York, Greenberg, c1956. 96p. illus. 20cm. (The Modern camera guide series) [TR260.P6] 56-7913
1. *Miniature cameras. I. Title.*

Miniature cameras—United States.

LAHUE, Kalton C. 771.3 s
The American 35 mm. [by Kalton C. Lahue and Joseph A. Bailey. New York, Amphoto [1972] 159 p. illus. 23 cm. (His Collecting vintage cameras, v. 1) [TR250.L34 vol. 1] [TR262] 771.3 72-186998
1. *Miniature cameras—United States. I. Bailey, Joseph A., joint author. II. Title.*

Miniature cameras—United States—History.

LAHUE, Kalton C. 771.3
Glass, brass, & chrome; the American 35 mm miniature camera, by Kalton C. Lahue and Joseph A. Bailey. [1st ed.] Norman, University of Oklahoma Press [1972] xix, 347 p. illus. 21 cm. [TR262.L35] 74-160496 ISBN 0-8061-0968-8 7.95
1. *Miniature cameras—United States—History. I. Bailey, Joseph A., joint author. II. Title.*

Miniature cases, American.

RINHART, Floyd. 745.59
American miniature case art [by] Floyd and Marion Rinhart. South Brunswick, A. S. Barnes [1969] 205 p. illus. (part col.) 28 cm. Bibliographical references included in "Notes to the text" (p. 181-183) Bibliography: p. 202. [NK8475.C3R5] 68-27207 20.00
1. *Miniature cases, American. I. Rinhart, Marion, joint author. II. Title.*

Miniature craft.

DUDA, Margaret B. 745.59'28
Miniature shops : how to design and make them / Margaret B. Duda ; photography by Joe Vigliano and Jon Sheckler. South Brunswick, N.J. : A. S. Barnes, c1977. 172 p., [4] leaves of plates : ill. ; 25 cm. Includes index. Bibliography: p. 168. [TT178.D82 1977] 76-10884 ISBN 0-498-01783-4 : 12.00
1. *Miniature craft. 2. Shops, Retail—Models. I. Title.* BIP

GREENHOWE, Jean. 745.59'2
Making miniature toys and dolls / Jean Greenhowe. New York : Van Nostrand Reinhold Co., [1977] p. cm. [TT178.G73] 77-6420 ISBN 0-442-22837-6 : 9.95. ISBN 0-442-22838-4 pbk. : 4.95
1. *Miniature craft. 2. Toy making. 3. Dollmaking. I. Title.* BIP

KRUSZ, Dorie. 745.59'23
Building miniature houses and furniture / by Dorie Krusz. [New York] : Arco Pub. Co., [1977] p. cm. Includes index. [TT178.K78] 77-1525 ISBN 0-668-04184-6 : 25.00
1. *Miniature craft. 2. Doll-houses. 3. Miniature furniture. I. Title.* BIP

MERAS, Phyllis. 745.59'2
Miniatures : how to make them, use them, sell them / Phyllis Meras. Boston : Houghton Mifflin, 1976. 149 p. : ill. ; 24 cm. [TT178.M47] 76-16493 ISBN 0-395-24344-0 : 12.95 pbk. : 6.95
1. *Miniature craft. I. Title.* BIP

O'BRIEN, Marian Maeve. 745.59'28
Make and furnish your own miniature rooms / by Marian Maeve O'Brien ; photos. by Sam Taylor ; drawings by Nancy Ovedovitz. New York : Hawthorn Books, c1976. 225 p., [8] leaves of plates : ill. ; 29 cm. Includes index. [TT178.O27] 75-41791 ISBN 0-8015-4808-X : 15.95
1. *Miniature craft. 2. Miniature rooms. I. Title.* BIP

PUIBOUBE, Daniel. 745.59'28
The art of making miniature models / by Daniel Puiboube. New York : Arco Pub. Co., [1978] p. cm. [TT178.P84] 77-27999 ISBN 0-668-04564-7 : 15.00. ISBN 0-668-04570-1 pbk. : 8.95
1. *Miniature craft. 2. Models and modelmaking. I. Title.* BIP

ROTH, Charlene Davis, 1945- 745.59'23
Making dollhouse accessories : patterns and directions for rooms, furniture, animal companions, utensils, and vehicles for full-size dolls / by Charlene Davis Roth. New York : Crown Publishers, c1977. vii, 112 p., [2] leaves of plates : ill. ; 29 cm. Includes index. [TT178.R67 1977] 77-6742 ISBN 0-517-52878-9 : 8.95 ISBN 0-517-52879-7 pbk. : 4.95
1. *Miniature craft. I. Title.* BIP

RUBIN, Cynthia. 684.1'04'0974
Shaker miniature furniture / Cynthia and Jerome Rubin. New York : Van Nostrand Reinhold, [1979] p. cm. Includes index. Bibliography: p. [TT178.R8] 78-15500 ISBN 0-442-27150-6 pbk. : 7.95
1. *Miniature craft. 2. Miniature furniture. 3. Furniture, Shaker. I. Rubin, Jerome, joint author. II. Title.*

RUTHBERG, Helen. 749
The book of miniatures : furniture and accessories / Helen Ruthberg ; with foreword by Sybil Harp. 1st ed. Radnor, Pa. : Chilton Book Co., c1977. xvi, 240 p. [4] leaves of plates : ill. ; 27 cm. (Chilton's creative crafts series) Includes index. Bibliography: p. 232-233. [TT175.5.R87 1977] 76-451 ISBN 0-8019-6365-6 : 13.95 ISBN 0-8019-6366-4 pbk. : 7.95
1. *Miniature craft. 2. Miniature furniture. 3. Miniature rooms. I. Title.* BIP

RUTHBERG, Helen. 747'.022'8
Miniature room settings / Helen Ruthberg. Radnor, Pa. : Chilton Book Co., c1978. xiv, 172 p., [4] leaves of col. plates : ill. ; 27 cm. (Chilton's creative crafts series) Includes index. Bibliography: p. 166-167. [TT178.R88 1978] 77-14742 ISBN 0-8019-6678-7 : 12.50. ISBN 0-8019-6679-5 pbk. : 6.95
1. *Miniature craft. 2. Miniature furniture. 3. Miniature rooms. I. Title.* BIP

WOODRUFF, Marie. 745.59'23
Early America in miniatures : the 18th century / by Marie Woodruff ; photography by Charles E. Woodruff. New York : Sterling Pub. Co., c1976. 176 p., [4] leaves of plates : ill. (some col.) ; 27 cm. Includes index. [TT178.W66] 76-19797 ISBN 0-8069-5370-5 : 10.95. ISBN 0-8069-5371-3 lib. bdg. : 9.29
1. *Miniature craft. 2. Doll-houses. 3. Art industries and trade, Early American. I. Title.* BIP

WORRELL, Estelle Ansley, 1929- 745.59'23
Make your own miniature rooms / Estelle Ansley Worrell ; photos. by Henry D. Widick and Dean D. Dixon. Riverdale, Md. : Hobby House Press ; New York : distributed to the trade by Scribner, c1978. 100 p. : ill. ; 21 x 26 cm. Includes index. [TT178.W67] 78-111311 ISBN 0-87588-139-4 : 8.95
1. *Miniature craft. 2. Miniature rooms. I. Title.*

Miniature furniture.

PIPE, Ann Kimball. 749.2
Reproducing furniture in miniature / Ann Kimball Pipe. Chicago : H. Regnery, c1976. viii, 228 p. : ill. ; 24 cm. Includes index. [TT175.5.P56 1976] 75-32981 ISBN 0-8092-8294-1 : 15.00 ISBN 0-8092-8072-8 pbk. :
1. *Miniature furniture. I. Title.* BIP

Miniature furniture—United States—Catalogs.

SCHIFFER, Herbert F., 1917- 749.2
Miniature antique furniture, by Herbert F. and Peter B. Schiffer. Wynnewood, Pa., Livingston Pub. Co. [1972] 264 p. illus. (part col.) 29 cm. Bibliography: p. 259-260. [NK2750.S35] 72-12679 ISBN 0-87098-049-1 20.00
1. *Miniature furniture—United States—Catalogs. I. Schiffer, Peter Berwind, joint author. II. Title.* BIP

Miniature glassware—Collectors and collecting.

LECHLER, Doris. 748.8
A collector's guide to children's glass dishes / by Doris Lechler and Virginia O'Neill. Nashville : T. Nelson, c1976. 224 p., [4] leaves of plates : ill. (some col. ; 25 cm. On spine: Children's glass dishes. Bibliography: p. 210. [NK8475.G55L42] 75-45085 ISBN 0-8407-4324-6 : 11.95
1. *Miniature glassware—Collectors and collecting. 2. Children's paraphernalia—Collectors and collecting. I. O'Neill, Virginia, joint author. II. Title. III. Title: Children's glass dishes.* BIP

Miniature heraldic porcelain—Catalogs.

WARD, Roland. 738.2'7
The price guide to the models of W. H. Goss / by Roland Ward. Woodbridge [Eng.] : Antique Collectors' Club, c1975. 189 p., 4 leaves of plates : chiefly ill. (some col.) ; 28 cm. Includes index. [NK4210.G583W37] 76-358880 ISBN 0-902028-20-0 : £6.95
1. *Goss, William Henry. 2. Goss China Company Ltd. 3. Miniature heraldic porcelain—Catalogs. I. Title.*

Miniature lamps—Catalogs.

DELMORE, Edward J., Mrs. 749'.63
Victorian miniature oil lamps, by Mrs. Edward J. Delmore. [Color photography by Frank L. Forward. Manchester, Vt., Forward's Color Productions, 1968] 1 v. (chiefly illus., 14 col. plates) 23 cm. Cover title. "All items illustrated are from the collection of Mr. & Mrs. Edward J. Delmore." [NK8475.L3D4] 74-240
1. *Delmore, Edward J., Mrs.—Art collections. 2. Delmore, Edward J.—Art collections. 3. Miniature lamps—Catalogs. I. Forward, Frank L., illus. II. Title.*

SMITH, Frank R., 1907- 749'.63
Miniature lamps, by Frank R. & Ruth E. Smith. [New York] Nelson [1968] 285 p. illus. (part col.), facsims. 24 cm. Bibliography: p. 285. 68-57930 12.50
1. *Miniature lamps—Catalogs. I. Smith, Ruth E., joint author. II. Title.* BIP

Miniature objects.

BRAUN, Susan Rogers. 745.5
Miniature vignettes / Susan Rogers Braun. New York : Scribner, [1975] 128 p. : ill. ; 28 cm. Includes index. [NK8470.B72] 75-11962 ISBN 0-684-14378-X : 14.95
1. *Miniature objects. 2. Models and modelmaking. I. Title.* BIP

MCCLINTON, Katharine (Morrison) 745.1
Antiques in miniature. New York, Scribner [1970] x, 182 p. illus. 26 cm. [NK8470.M3] 75-123843 8.95
1. *Miniature objects. I. Title.*

Miniature objects—Collectors and collecting.

LATHAM, Jean. 745.1'075
Collecting miniature antiques. New York, Scribner [1973, c1972] 177 p. illus. (part col.) 24 cm. Bibliography: p. 177. [NK8470.L37 1973] 72-12163 ISBN 0-684-13343-1 12.50
1. *Miniature objects—Collectors and collecting. I. Title.*

Miniature objects—Collectors and collecting—United States—Directories.

[HASKELL, Jane] 745'.025'73
Guide to American miniaturists. Rev. ed. [Northford, Conn. : J. Haskell], c1976. [66] p. ; 22 cm. Includes indexes. [NK8470.H37 1976] 76-358071 4.50
1. *Miniature objects—Collectors and collecting—United States—Directories. I. Title.*

Miniature objects, Senufo.

DE KOLB, Eric. 739'.512
Soothsayer bronzes of the Senufo. New York, Gallery d'Hautbarr [1968] 65 p. (chiefly illus., map) 23 cm. [NK8475.S4D4] 76-270
1. *Miniature objects, Senufo. 2. Bronzes, Senufo. 3. Fetishism. I. Title.*

Miniature objects—United States.

WORRELL, Estelle (Ansley) 1929- 745'.092'4
Americana in miniature. Photos. by Henry Widick. New York, Van Nostrand Reinhold Co. [1973] 64 p. illus 21 x 26 cm. [NK8470.W67] 72-9710 6.95
1. *Miniature objects—United States. 2.*

United States—History—Pictorial works. I. Title.

Miniature painters, British—Biography—Dictionaries.

FOSKETT, Daphne. 759.2
A dictionary of British miniature painters. New York, Praeger Publishers [1972] 2 v. 1069 illus. (100 col.) 29 cm. Vol. 2 consists of the monochrome illus. Bibliography: v. 1, p. 592-596. [ND1337.G7F463 1972] 72-112634 135.00
1. Miniature painters, British—Biography—Dictionaries. 2. Miniature painting, British. I. Title. II. Title: British miniature painters.
BIP

FOSKETT, Daphne. 759.2
A dictionary of British miniature painters. London, Faber and Faber, 1972. 2 v. (3-596 p., 31 leaves; 3-108, [1], 400 p.) ports. (some col.) 29 cm. Bibliography: v. 1, p. 592-596. [ND1337.G7F463 1972b] 72-193605 ISBN 0-571-08295-5
1. Miniature painters, British—Biography—Dictionaries. 2. Miniature painting, British. I. Title. II. Title: British miniature painters.
Available from Praeger, 135.00.

Miniature painting.

O'BRIEN, Donough, 1879- 757.7
Miniatures in the XVIIIth and XIXth centuries; an historical and descriptive record. London, New York, Batsford [1951] 193 p. 137 plates, 28 cm. Errata slip inserted. [ND1330.O2] 52-2350
1. Miniature painting. I. Title.

Miniature painting—Armenia.

DOURNOVO, Lydia A. 759.9566
Armenian miniatures. Pref. by Sirarpie Der Nersessian. [Text tr. from French by Irene J. Underwood] New York, Abrams [1961] 181p. mounted illus. (pt. col.) map 31cm. 61-15292 25.00
1. Miniature painting—Armenia. 2. Illumination of books and manuscripts—Armenia. I. Title.

Miniature painting—Ethiopia.

UNITED Nations Educational, Scientific and Cultural Organization. 096
Ethiopia; illuminated manuscripts. Introd. [by] Jules LeRoy. Texts [by] Stephen Wright and Otto A. Jager. [Greenwich, Conn.] New York Graphic Society by arrangement with UNESCO [1961] 25, [7] p. illus., 32 col. plates. 48 cm. (UNESCO world art series [15]) Material assembled by experts from UNESCO and the New York Graphic Society. Bibliography: p. [26] [ND3286.E8U5] 61-2206
1. Miniature painting—Ethiopia. 2. Illumination of books and manuscripts—Ethiopia. I. Wright, Stephen. II. Jager, Otto A. III. New York Graphic Society. IV. Series.

Miniature painting—France.

PORCHER, Jean. 759.4
Medieval French miniatures. [Translated from the French by Julian Brown] New York, H. N. Abrams [1960?] 275 p. illus. (part col.) col. plates. 31 cm. "Bibliographical commentary": p. 85-[94] [ND3147.P643] 59-12874
1. Miniature painting—France. 2. Illumination of books and manuscripts—France. I. Title.

Miniature painting—Gt. Brit.

MAYNE, Arthur. 741.7'0942
British profile miniaturists. [1st American ed.] Boston, Boston Book and Art [1970] 131 p. illus., facsims., col. plates, ports. (part col.) 26 cm. (Collectors library) Bibliography: p. 121. [N7616.M37 1970b] 72-129447
1. Miniature painting—Gt. Brit. 2. Silhouettes. 3. Portrait painters, British. I. Title.
BIP

REYNOLDS, Graham 757.7
English portrait miniatures. London, A. & C. Black [dist. New York. Barnes & Noble, 1964] 212p. illus. 23cm. (Lib. of Eng. art) [ND1337.G7R46] 53-8261 4.50
1. Miniature painting—Gt. Brit. 2. Portrait-painters, British. I. Title.

Miniature painting—History.

BOEHN, Max von, 1860-1932. 757'.7
Miniatures and silhouettes. Translated by E. K. Walker. New York, B. Blom [1970] ix, 214 p. illus., ports. 24 cm. Translation of Miniaturen und Silhouetten. Reprint of the 1928 ed. [N7616.B6 1970] 70-145772
1. Miniature painting—History. 2. Silhouettes. I. Title.
BIP

Miniature painting, India.

ARCHER, William George, 1907- 759.954
Indian miniatures. Color plates in collaboration with Madanjeet Singh. Greenwich, Conn., New York Graphic Society [1960] 16 p. 100 illus. (part mounted col.) map. 39 cm. [ND3247.A7] 60-5023
1. Miniature painting—India. 2. Illumination of books and manuscripts—India. I. Title. II. Series: The great masters of the past, 9

BUSSAGLI, Mario. 751.7'7'0954
Indian miniatures; [translated from the Italian by Raymond Rudorif]. Feltham, New York, Hamlyn, 1969. 3-158 p. 73 col. illus. 20 cm. (Cameo) Originally published as 'La miniatura Indiana'. Milano, Fabbri, 1966. [ND3247.B813] 72-437383 15/-
1. Miniature painting, India. I. Title.

ETTINGHAUSEN, Richard 759.954
Paintings of the sultans and emperors of India in American collections. [New Delhi, Pub. by B. C. Sanyal, for] Lalit Kala Akademi [dist. New York, Heinman, 1963] [35]p. mounted illus. (pt. col.) 35cm. (Lalit Kala ser. of Indian art) 64-114 8.00 pap.,
1. Maniature painting. India. 2. India—Kings and rulers. 3. Paintings—U.S. I. Title. II. Series.

REIFF, Robert, ed. 759.954
Indian miniatures: the Rajput painters. [1st ed.] Tokyo, Rutland, Vt., C. E. Tuttle Co. [1959] 32 p. plates (part col.) 30 cm. (Art treasures of Asia) Bibliography: p. 32. [ND3247.R4] 59-7576
1. Miniature painting—India. 2. Miniature painting—Reproductions, facsimiles, etc. 3. Paintings, Indic. I. Title. II. Title: The Rajput painters. III. Series.

Miniature painting, Indic—Catalogs.

ELVEHJEM Art Center. 751.7'7'0954
Indian miniature painting; the Collection of Earnest C. and Jane Werner Watson. Madison, Elvehjem Art Center, University of Wisconsin; distributed by the University of Wisconsin Press [1971] xxviii, 153 p. illus. (part col.) 18 x 23 cm. Catalog prepared by Pramod Chandra. [ND1337.I5E4] 70-157396 ISBN 0-299-97005-1
1. Watson, Earnest Charles, 1892- —Art collections. 2. Watson, Jane (Werner) 1915- —Art collections. 3. Miniature painting, Indic—Catalogs. 4. Illumination of books and manuscripts, Indic—Catalogs. I. Chandra, Pramod. II. Title.

EROTIC art of India 745.6'7'0954
/ [compiled by] Philip Rawson. New York : Universe Books, 1977. [88] p. : col. ill. ; 28 cm. [ND1337.I5E75 1977] 76-54568 ISBN 0-87663-962-7 pbk. : 6.95
1. Miniature painting, Indic—Catalogs. 2. Erotic art—India—Catalogs. I. Rawson, Philip S.

MINIATURE paintings on 745.6'7
display in Lahore Museum : Mughal and Rajasthani schools. Lahore : Lahore Museum, 1976. 24 p., [6] leaves of plates : ill. ; 21 cm. (Publication — Lahore Museum ; series 13) [ND1337.I5M56] 77-930123 Rs2.50
1. Lahore. Central Museum. 2. Miniature painting, Indic—Catalogs. 3. Painting, Mogul—Catalogs. 4. Rajput painting—Catalogs. 5. Miniature painting—Pakistan—Lahore—Catalogs. I. Lahore. Central Museum. II. Series: Lahore. Central Museum. Silsilah-yi intisharat-i Lahur 'Aja'ib Ghar ; 13.

Miniature painting, Indic. — Exhibitions.

ASIA Society 751.770954
Gods, thrones, and peacocks; Northern Indian Painting from two traditions: fifteenth to nineteenth centuries [by] Stuart Cary Welch, Milo Cleveland Beach. Catalogue of an exhibition: Asia House Gallery, Sept. 23-Dec. 12, 1965; the Baltimore Mus. of Art, Jan. 18-Feb. 27, 1966; Muson-Williams-Proctor Inst., Utica, N. Y., Apr. 3-May 15, 1966. [New York] dist. Abrams [c.1965] 129p. illus. (pt. col.) map. 28cm. An Asia House Gallery pubn. The exhibition was shown in the Asia House Gallery as an activity of the Asia Soc. Bibl. [ND3247.A8] 65-25427 10.00 bds.,
1. Miniature painting, Indic—Exhibitions. 2. Miniature painting, Islamic—Exhibitions. I. Welch, Stuart Cary. II. Beach, Milo Cleveland. III. Asia House Gallery, New York. IV. Baltimore. Museum of Art. V. Munson-Williams-Proctor Institute, Utica, N. Y. VI. Title.

ASIA Society. 751.7'7'0954
Gods, thrones, and peacocks : northern Indian painting from two traditions, fifteenth to nineteenth centuries : [catalogue of an exhibition] Asia House Gallery, September 23-December 12, 1965, the Baltimore Museum of Art, January 18-February 27, 1966, Munson-Williams-Proctor Institute, Utica, New York, April 3-May 15, 1966 / Stuart Cary Welch, Milo Cleveland Beach. New York : Arno Press, 1975, c1965. p. cm. (The Asia Society reprint collection) Reprint of the ed. published by the Society, New York. "Bibliography: Rajput painting": p. [ND3247.A82 1975] 75-6680 ISBN 0-405-06570-1 : 30.00
1. Miniature painting, Indic—Exhibitions. 2. Miniature painting, Islamic—Exhibitions. I. Welch, Stuart Cary. II. Beach, Milo Cleveland. III. Asia House Gallery, New York. IV. Baltimore. Museum of Art. V. Munson-Williams-Proctor Institute, Utica, N.Y. VI. Title. VII. Series.

ASIA Society. 751.770954
Gods, thrones, and peacocks: Northern Indian Painting from two traditions: fifteenth to nineteenth centuries [by] Stuart Cary Welch [and] Milo Cleveland Beach. Catalogue of an exhibition: Asia House Gallery, Sept. 23-Dec. 12, 1965; the Baltimore Museum of Art, Jan. 18-Feb. 27, 1966; Munson-Williams-Proctor Institute, Utica, N.Y., Apr. 3-May 15, 1966. [New York] Distributed by H. N. Abrams [1965] 129 p. illus. (part col.) map. 28 cm. "An Asia House Gallery publication." The exhibition was shown in the Asia House Gallery as an activity of the Asia Society. "Bibliography: Rajput painting": p. 127-129. [ND3247.A8] 65-25427
1. Miniature painting. Indic — Exhibitions. 2. Miniature painting, Islamic — Exhibitions. I. Welch, Stuart Cary. II. Beach, Milo Cleveland. III. Asia House Gallery, New York. IV. Baltimore, Museum of Art. V. Munson-Williams-Proctor Institute, Utica, N.Y. VI. Title. BIP

BINNEY, Edwin. 759.954
Indian miniature painting from the Collection of Edwin Binney, 3rd. An exhibition at the Portland Art Museum, Dec. 2, 1973—Jan. 20, 1974. Catalogue and text by Edwin Binney, 3rd. Portland, Or., Portland Art Museum [1974- c1973 v. illus. 20 x 22 cm. Contents.Contents.—1. The Mughal and Deccani schools. Bibliography: v. 1, p. 198-202. [ND1337.I5B56] 74-170338
1. Binney, Edwin—Art collections. 2. Miniature painting, Indic—Exhibitions. 3. Illumination of books and manuscripts, Indic—Exhibitions. I. Portland, Or. Art Museum. II. Title.

FLORIDA. University, Gainesville. University Gallery. 709.54
Miniatures and small sculptures from India. University Gallery, April 10th thru May 29th. 1966. Gainesville, Coll. of Archit. & Fine Arts, Univ. of Fla. [1966] 1 v. (unpaged) illus., map (on cover) 23cm. Special loan exhibition of the historical art of India from museums & collections in the U.S. [ND3247.F55] A66 2.95
1. Miniature painting, Indic.—Exhibitions. 2. Sculpture, Indic—Exhibitions. I. Title.

NEW York (City). Metropolitan Museum of Art. Dept. of Far Eastern Art. 759.954'074'01471
Indian miniatures from the Jeffrey Paley Collection : August 6-September 30, 1974 / by Martin Lerner. New York : Dept. of Far Eastern Art, Metropolitan Museum of Art, [1974] [27] p. : ill. ; 23 cm. Catalog of an exhibition. Bibliography: p. [26]-[27] [ND1337.I5N48 1974] 74-194437
1. Paley, Jeffrey—Art collections. 2. Miniature painting, Indic—Exhibitions. I. Lerner, Martin. II. Title.

SMITHSONIAN Institution. 016.091
Indian miniatures from the collection of Mildred and W.G. Archer, London. Circulated by the Smithsonian Institution. 1963-1964. [Washington, Smithsonian Institution, Traveling Exhibition Service, 1963] 1 v. (unpaged) illus. 22 cm. (Smithsonian publication 4520) Includes bibliography. [ND3247.S45] 64-60433
1. Miniature painting, Indic. — Exhibitions. 2. Miniature painting — Private collections. I. Archer, Mildred. II. Archer, William George, 1907- III. Smithsonian Institution. Traveling Exhibition Service. IV. Title.

Miniature painting—Iran.

LILLYS, William, ed. 757.7
Persian miniatures; the story of Rustam. Edited, with introd. and notes, by William Lillys. [1st ed.] Tokyo, Rutland, Vt., C. E. Tuttle Co. [1958] 32 p. mounted illus. (part col.) 30 cm. (Art treasures of Asia) Bibliography: p. 32. [ND3241.L5] 58-13429
1. Miniature painting—Iran. 2. Ferdowsi Shahnameh. I. Title. II. Series.

ROBINSON, Basil William. 757.7
A descriptive catalogue of the Persian paintings in the Bodleian Library. Oxford, Clarendon Press, 1958. xxv, 219 p. 41 plates. 28 cm. Bibliography: p. [xv]-xix. [ND3241.R596] 58-3433
1. Miniature painting—Iran. 2. Miniature painting—Reproductions, facsimiles, etc. I. Oxford. University. Bodleian Library. II. Title: Persian paintings in the Bodleian Library.

Miniature painting, Iranian—Exhibitions.

ROBINSON, Basil William. 751.7/7/0955
Persian miniature painting from collections in the British Isles [by] B. W. Robinson. London, H.M.S.O., 1967. 120p. col. front., 52 plates (incl facsims.). 25cm. (Large picture bk., no. 33) At head of title: Victoria and Albert Museum. [N1150.A752no.33] 67-114165 5.00 pap.,
1. Miniature painting, Iranian—Exhibitions. I. Title. II. Series: Victoria and Albert Museum, South Kensington. Large picture book, no. 33
Available from British Info., New York.

Miniature painting—Jerusalem. Latin kingdom, 1099-1244

BUCHTHAL, Hugo, 1909- 757.7
Miniature painting in the Latin kingdom of Jerusalem. With liturgical and palaeographical chapters by Francis Wormald. Oxford, Clarendon Press, 1957. xxxiv, 163p. 155 plates. 33cm. Bibliographical footnotes. [ND3239.J4B8] 58-446
1. Miniature painting—Jerusalem. Latin kingdom, 1099-1244 2. Miniature painting— Reproductions, facsimiles, etc. I. Title.
BIP

Miniature painting—Mexico.

ROBERTSON, Donald, 1919- 759.972
Mexican manuscript painting of the early colonial period: the Metropolitan Schools. New Haven, Yale University Press, 1959. xix, 234 p. 88 plates. 28 cm. (Yale historical publications History of art, 12)

Bibliography: p. 203-222. [ND3044.R6] 59-12700
1. Miniature painting—Mexico. 2. Illumination of books and manuscripts—Mexico. 3. Manuscripts, Mexican. I. Title. II. Series.

Miniature painting, Mogul—Exhibitions.

PINDER-WILSON, Ralph H.   745.6'7'095407402142
Paintings from the Muslim courts of India : [catalogue of] an exhibition held in the Prints and Drawings Gallery, British Museum, 13 April to 11 July 1976 / [compiled by R. H. Pinder-Wilson with the assistance of Ellen Smart and Douglas Barrett]. [London]. : World of Islam Festival Publishing Co. Ltd, 1976. 99 p., [8] p. of plates : ill. (some col.), geneal. table, map, ports. (1 col.) ; 26 cm. Bibliography: p. 96-99. [ND1337.I5P55] 76-380381 ISBN 0-905035-09-7. ISBN 0-905035-10-0 pbk. : £1.50
1. Miniature painting, Mogul—Exhibitions. 2. Illumination of books and manuscripts, Mogul—Exhibitions. I. Smart, Ellen, joint author. II. Barrett, Douglas E., joint author. III. British Museum. IV. Title.

Miniature painting—Punjab—History.

ARCHER, William George, 1907-   759.954
Indian paintings from the Punjab Hills; a survey and history of Pahari miniature painting, by W. G. Archer. Foreword by Sherman E. Lee. London, New York, Sotheby Parke Bernet, 1973. 2 v. illus. (part col.) 31 cm. Contents.Contents.—v. 1. Text.—v. 2. Plates. Bibliography: v. 1, p. 427-431. [ND1337.I5A72] 74-157913 ISBN 0-85667-002-2 84.00 (2 Vols.)
1. Miniature painting—Punjab—History. I. Title.
Publisher's address: 980 Madison Ave; New York, N.Y. 10021   **BIP**

Miniature painting—Reproductions, facsimiles, etc.

HORNE, fl.1288.   759.4
The Parisian miniaturist Honore. With an introd. and notes by Eric G. Millar. New York, T. Yoseloff [1959] 30p. 8 col. plates. 29cm. (The Library of illuminated manuscripts) 60-445 4.95
1. Miniature painting—Reproductions, facsimiles, etc. I. Title.

Miniature painting—Turkey.

ESIN, Emel (Tek)   759.9561
Turkish miniature painting. Rutland, Vt., C. E. Tuttle Co. [1960] 32p. illus. (part mounted col.) 30cm. (Art treasures of Asia) Bibl.: p.32 60-11513 2.50 bds.,
1. Miniature painting—Turkey. 2. Miniature painting—Reproductions, fascimiles, etc. 3. Paintings, Turkish. I. Title. II. Series.

UNITED Nations   759.9561
Educational, Scientific and Cultural Organization.
Turkey: ancient miniatures: Pref. [by] Richard Ettinghausen. Introd. [by] M. S. Ipsiroglu, S. Eyuboglu. [Greenwich, Conn.] N.Y. Graphic Society [c.1961] 26,[6]p. illus., 32 col. plates. 49cm. (UNESCO world art ser., 16) Bibl. 61-19744 18.00 bds.,
1. Miniature painting—Turkey. 2. Illumination of books and manuscripts—Turkey. I. New York Graphic Society. II. Title. III. Series.

Miniature painting—U. S.

LONDON, Hannah Ruth, 1894-   757.7
Miniatures of early American Jews. Springfield, Mass., Pond-Ekberg Co., 1953. x, 154p. ports. 27cm. 'Edition ... limited to one hundred fifty copies.' Bibliography: p. [73]-76. [ND1337.U5L6] 53-34128
1. Miniature painting—U. S. 2. Portrait-painters, American. 3. Jews in the U. S. I. Title.

Miniature paintings, Indic—Catalogs.

DIMAND, Maurice Sven.   759.954
Indian miniature paintings. Text by Maurice S. Dimand. New York, Crown Publishers [1967] 28 p. 10 col. illus. 31 cm. (The Folio art books) Cover title: Indian miniatures. [ND3247.D55] 68-1610
1. Miniature paintings, Indic—Catalogs. I. Title.

Miniature paintings, Iranian—Catalogs.

DIMAND, Maurice Sven.   759.955
Persian miniature paintings. Text by Maurice S. Dimand. New York, Crown Publishers [1967] 28 p. 10 col. illus. 31 cm. (The Folio art books) Cover title: Persian miniatures. [ND3241.D55] 68-1611
1. Miniature paintings, Iranian—Catalogs. I. Title.

Miniature rooms.

DULIN Gallery of Art.   747.7
A description of the Thorne miniature rooms in the permanent collection of the Dulin Gallery of Art, by Betsey B. Creekmore. Knoxville, Tenn. [1972] [23] p. illus. 20 x 27 cm. [NK2135.T45D8] 72-168263
1. Miniature rooms. I. Creekmore, Betsey Beeler. II. Thorne, Narcissa (Niblack) III. Title: The Thorne miniature rooms.

Miniature tableware.

PUNCHARD, Lorraine May.   738
Playtime dishes / by Lorraine May Punchard ; [photography by Gary Sherman]. Des Moines, Iowa : Wallace-Homestead Book Co., c1978. 115 p., [4] leaves of plates : ill. (some col.) ; 28 cm. Bibliography: p. 114. [NK8475.T33P86] 76-58068 ISBN 0-87069-212-7 pbk. : 9.95
1. Miniature tableware. I. Sherman, Gary. II.   Title.
BIP

Minimal art—Addresses, essays, lectures.

BATTCOCK, Gregory, 1937-   709.04
comp.
Minimal art; a critical anthology. [1st ed.] New York, E. P. Dutton, 1968. 448 p. illus. 21 cm. Includes bibliographical references. [N6494.M5B3 1968] 68-5528
1. Minimal art—Addresses, essays, lectures. I. Title.   **BIP**

Minimal art—Exhibitions.

ALBRIGHT-KNOX   759.13'074'014797
Art Gallery.
Modular painting. Buffalo [1970] [24] p. col. illus. 22 x 32 cm. Catalog, by R. M. Murdock, of the exhibition held Apr. 21-May 24, 1970. Includes bibliographical references. [N6512.5.M5A4] 73-18441
1. Minimal art—Exhibitions. 2. Minimal art—U.S. I. Murdock, Robert M. II. Title.

CONTEMPORARY Arts Center, 709.73
Cincinnati.
Monumental art. [Cincinnati, 1970] [14] p. illus. 46 cm. Cover title. Catalog of an exhibition organized by W. A. Leonard and held Sept. 13-Nov. 1, 1970. [N6512.5.M5C6] 75-198005
1. Minimal art—Exhibitions. 2. Minimal art—U.S. I. Leonard, William Albers. II. Title.

SHULMAN, Leon.   759.13'074'01443
The direct image in contemporary American painting; exhibition and catalogue ... Worcester Art Museum, October 16 to November 30, 1969. Worcester [Mass., 1969] [48] p. illus. 23 cm. Bibliography: p. [47]-[48] [N6512.5.M5S5] 74-23801
1. Minimal art—Exhibitions. 2. Art, Modern—20th century—U.S. I. Worcester, Mass. Art Museum. II. Title.

WASHINGTON, D.C. Gallery   730'.922
of Modern Art.
A new aesthetic. [Exhibition] May 6 - June 25, 1967, Washington Gallery of Modern

Art. [Baltimore, Printed by Garamond-Pridemark Press, c1967] 63 p. illus. 26 cm. Text by Barbara Rose. Includes bibliographies. [N6512.W36] 67-22134
1. Minimal art—Exhibitions. 2. Minimal art. I. Rose, Barbara. II. Title.

Minimal sculpture—20th century—Exhibitions.

SOLOMON R. Guggenheim   735'.29
Museum, New York.
Guggenheim international exhibition, 1971. [New York, Solomon R. Guggenheim Foundation, 1971] 1 case (43 p., 21 fold. sheets) illus. (part col.), ports. 29 x 23 cm. Title from case. Includes bibliographies. [NB198.5.M5S6] 79-152560
1. Minimal sculpture—20th century—Exhibitions. I. Title.

Minimal sculpture—Exhibitions.

SAN Francisco.   730'.74'019461
Museum of Art.
Unitary forms: [minimal sculpture, by Carl Andre and others. Exhibition, San Francisco Museum of Art, Sept. 16-Nov. 1, 1970. San Francisco, 1970] [16] p. plan. 23 cm. Includes bibliographies. [NB212.5.M5S25] 77-26426
1. Minimal sculpture—Exhibitions. 2. Minimal sculpture—U.S. I. Andre, Carl, 1935- II. Title.

Miniture cameras.

KEPPLER, Herbert.   771.3
Official 35mm camera rating guide. 2d ed. New York, Universal Photo Books [1959] 128p. illus. 21cm. (The Universal photographic library) [TR260.K4 1959] 59-65393
1. Miniture cameras. I. Title.

Minkkinen, Arno Rafael, 1945-

MINKKINEN, Arno   779'.21'0924
Rafael, 1945-
Frostbite : photographs / by Arno Rafael Minkkinen ; introd. by Ziva Kwitney. Dobbs Ferry, N.Y. : Morgan & Morgan, c1978. [95] p. : chiefly ill. ; 27 cm. [TR675.M56] 78-60179 ISBN 0-87100-143-8 pbk. : 10.95
1. Minkkinen, Arno Rafael, 1945- 2. Photography of the nude. I. Title.   **BIP**

Minneapolis. Institute of Arts—Catalogs.

MINNEAPOLIS. Institute of Arts.
Chinese jades : archaic and modern from the Minneapolis Institute of Arts / foreword by Samuel Sachs II ; introd. by Na Chih-liang ; [Harold Peterson, editor, Nancy Akre, associate editor ; Vera Shu-Ning Sun-Bailey, translator and researcher ; Gary Mortensen, photographer]. 1st ed. Rutland, Vt. : C. E. Tuttle Co., 1977. 176 p. : ill. (some col.) ; 28 cm. Bibliography: p. 171-174. [NK5750.M54 1977b] 78-102346 25.00
1. Minneapolis. Institute of Arts—Catalogs. 2. Jade art objects—China—Catalogs. 3. Jade art objects—Minnesota—Minneapolis—Catalogs. I. Sachs, Samuel. II. Na, Chih-liang. III. Peterson, Harold, 1935- IV. Title.   **BIP**

MINNEAPOLIS.   708.176'579
Institute of Arts.
A guide to the galleries of the Minneapolis Institute of Arts. [Minneapolis, 1970] 207 p. illus. 23 cm. [N582.6.A6] 70-135526
I. Title.

Minnesota—Capital and capitol.

INTERPRO, inc.   711'.4'09776581
Comprehensive plan for the Minnesota State Capitol area. [Saint Paul, 1970] 20 p. illus. (part col.), plans (part col.) 41 cm. Cover title. At head of title: Capitol Area Architectural and Planning Commission. [JK1651.M6515] 75-634977
1. Minnesota—Capital and capitol. 2. Cities and towns—Planning—St. Paul. I. Minnesota. Capitol Area Architectural and Planning Commission. II. Title.

Minnich, Dwight Elmer, 1890-1965—Art collections.

MINNEAPOLIS.   769'.074'0176579
Institute of Arts.
The Minnich Collection: the Collection of Dwight and Helen Minnich. [Minneapolis, 1970] 1 v. (unpaged) illus. 24 cm. Catalog of the exhibition held Sept. 24-Nov. 8, 1970. Includes bibliography. [N5220.M9M5] 70-135309
1. Minnich, Dwight Elmer, 1890-1965—Art collections. 2. Minnich, Helen Benton—Art collections. 3. Art—Exhibitions. I. Title.

Minolta camera.

COOPER, Joseph David,   771.3'1
1917-
Minolta system handbook, SR-T 101, SR-T 100, SR-M [by] Joseph D. Cooper. New York, Amphoto [1971, c1972- 1 v. (loose leaf) illus. 28 cm. [TR263.M47C63] 73-171941 ISBN 0-8174-0476-7
1. Minolta camera. 2. Photography—Handbooks, manuals, etc. I. Title.

COOPER, Joseph David,   771.3'1
1917-1975.
Minolta system handbook / Joseph D. Cooper. 2d ed. / rev. and enl. by the Amphoto editorial board. Garden City, N.Y. : Amphoto, c1976- 2 v. : ill. ; 28 cm. Loose-leaf for updating. Includes index. [TR263.M47C63 1976] 76-381517 ISBN 0-8174-2415-6 : 35.00
1. Minolta camera. 2. Photography—Handbooks, manuals, etc. I. Amphoto, New York. II. Title.

LONDON, Barbara.   771.3'1
A short course in Minolta photography / Barbara London. New York : Van Nostrand Reinhold Co., [1979] p. cm. Includes index. Bibliography: p. [TR263.M47L66] 78-23912 ISBN 0-442-26607-3 pbk. : 9.00 ISBN 0-442-26613-8 : 14.95
1. Minolta camera. 2. Photography—Handbooks, manuals, etc. I. Title.

NEUBAUER, John, 1929-   771.3'1
Minolta SR-T manual [by] John Neubauer [and] Robert Moeser. New York, Amphoto [1971] 191 p. illus. 24 cm. [TR263.M47N48] 70-160803 ISBN 0-8174-0540-2 8.95
1. Minolta camera. 2. Photography—Handbooks, manuals, etc. I. Moeser, Robert D., joint author. II. Title.

NEUBAUER, John, 1929-   771.3'1
Minolta SR T manual / John Neubauer, Robert Moeser. 2d ed. Englewood Cliffs, N.J. : Prentice-Hall, [1974] 191 p. : ill. ; 24 cm. Includes index. [TR263.M47N48 1974] 74-83643 ISBN 0-13-584607-2 : 9.95
1. Minolta camera. 2. Photography—Handbooks, manuals, etc. I. Moeser, Robert D., joint author. II. Title.

ROSENBERG, Ted.   771.3'1
Minolta-16 guide. Garden City, N.Y., American Photographic Book Pub. Co. [1973] 128 p. illus. 21 cm. [TR263.M47R67] 72-85821 ISBN 0-8174-0464-3 3.95
1. Minolta camera. 2. Photography—Handbooks, manuals, etc. I. Title.

TYDINGS, Kenneth S   771.31
Minolta camera guide. Philadelphia, Chilton Co., c1959. 127 p. illus. 20 cm. [TR263.M47T9] 59-1778
1. Minolta camera. 2. Photography—Handbooks, manuals, etc. I. Title.

WOLF, John C.   771.3'1
Minolta : reflex photography / John C. Wolf. Garden City, N.Y. : Amphoto, c1977. 191 p. : ill. ; 24 cm. Includes index. [TR263.M47W63] 76-16460 ISBN 0-8174-2409-1 : 10.95
1. Minolta camera. 2. Photography—Handbooks, manuals, etc. I. Title.

WOLF, John C.   771.3'1
The Minolta guide / John Wolf. Garden City, N.Y. : Amphoto, 1979. p. cm. Includes bibliographical references and index. [TR263.M47W62] 78-21451 ISBN 0-8174-2453-9 : 10.95. ISBN 0-8174-2128-9 pbk. : 5.95

1. Minolta camera. 2. Photography—Handbooks, manuals, etc. I. Title.

WOLF, John C. 771.3'1
Minolta SR-T101/100 guide, by John C. Wolf. New York, Amphoto [1972] 127 p. illus. 20 cm. [TR263.M47W64] 70-171940 ISBN 0-8174-0169-5 pap. 2.50
1. Minolta camera. 2. Photography—Handbooks, manuals, etc. I. Title. BIP

WOLF, John C. 771.3'1
Minolta SR-T 102/101/100 guide, by John C. Wolf. Garden City, N.Y., Amphoto [1974] 127 p. illus. 21 cm. Published in 1972 under title: Minolta SR-T 101/100 guide. [TR263.M47W64 1974] 74-166233 ISBN 0-8174-0169-5 3.95 (pbk.)
1. Minolta camera. 2. Photography—Handbooks, manuals, etc. I. Title.

WOLF, John C. 771.3'1
Official Minolta SR-T guide, by John C. Wolf. Garden City, N.Y., Amphoto [1974] 127 p. illus. 21 cm. Also issued under title: Minolta SR-T 102/101/100 guide. Published in 1972 under title: Minolta SR-T 101/100 guide. [TR263.M47W64 1974b] 74-176296 ISBN 0-8174-0169-5 4.00
1. Minolta camera. 2. Photography—Handbooks, manuals, etc. I. Title.

Minox camera.

COOPER, Joseph David, 1917- 771.3'1
The Minox manual [by] Joseph D. Cooper. [3d rev. ed.] Philadelphia, Chilton Book Co. [1968] 191 p. illus. (part col.) 24 cm. [TR263.M5C6 1968] 68-8555 7.95
1. Minox camera. 2. Photography—Handbooks, manuals, etc. I. Title.

COOPER, Joseph David, 1917- 771.31
Minox pocket companion. [New York] Universal Photo Bks. [dist. Amphoto, c. 1962] 94p. illus. 15cm. (U-257) 62-14419 1.95, wire bdg.
1. Minox camera. 2. sPhotography—Handbooks, manuals, etc. I. Title.

TYDINGS, Kenneth S. 771.31
New Minox guide, including all ultra-miniature cameras. Philadelphia, Chilton, c.1963. 127p. illus. 20cm. (Modern camera guide ser.) 62-21963 1.95 pap.,
1. Minox camera. 2. Photography—Handbooks, manuals, etc. I. Title.

TYDINGS, Kenneth S 771.31
New Minox guide, including all ultra-miniature cameras. Philadelphia, Chilton Books, c1963. 127 p. illus. 20 cm. (Modern camera guide series) [TR263.M5T9] 62-21963
1. Minox camera. 2. Photography — Handbooks, manuals, etc. I. Title.

Mint Museum of Art.

MINT Museum of Art. 732.2
The Pre-Columbian Collection; [catalog] Research, text, and introd. by M. Keating Griffiss. [Charlotte, N.C., 1970] 20, [55] p. illus. 23 cm. [E59.A7M56 1970] 71-137507
1. Mint Museum of Art. 2. Indians—Art—Catalogs. I. Griffiss, M. Keating.

WILKINSON, Henrietta H. 708'.156'76
The Mint Museum of Art at Charlotte; a brief history [by] Henrietta H. Wilkinson. [1st ed.] Charlotte, Heritage Printers, 1973. 105 p. illus. 20 x 22 cm. [N529.C35W54] 73-89448 4.95
1. Mint Museum of Art. I. Title.

Mint—United States.

HERBERT, Alan. 737.4'9'73
The official guide to mint errors / Alan Herbert. New York : House of Collectibles, [1974] 176 p. : ill. ; 22 cm. Bibliography: p. 43-44. [HG457.H47] 74-79578 ISBN 0-87637-214-0 : 2.95
1. Mint—United States. 2. Coinage—United States. 3. Errors. I. Title. II. Title: Mint errors.

Minter, Marilyn, 1948—

MINTER, Marilyn, 1948- 759.13
Marilyn Minter. Syracuse, N.Y., Everson Museum of Art [1973] [4] p. illus. 21 x 24 cm. Cover title. Catalog of the exhibition held at the Everson Museum of Art, Syracuse, N.Y., Aug. 21-Sept. 24, 1973. [ND237.M53E93] 73-87449
1. Minter, Marilyn, 1948- I. Everson Museum of Art of Syracuse and Onondaga County.

Minton, John, 1917-1957.

READING, Eng. Museum and Art Gallery. 760'.092'4
John Minton, 1917-1957 : paintings, drawings, illustrations and stage designs : [catalogue of an exhibition held at] Reading Museum and Art Gallery, Nov. 2nd-30th, 1974, Graves Art Gallery, Surrey Street, Sheffield, Dec. 7th [1974]-Jan. 4th 1975. [Reading : The Museum, 1974] [19] p. : ill., port. ; 18 x 23 cm. Bibliography: p. [18]-[19] [N6797.M53R42 1974] 75-309550 ISBN 0-9501247-2-9 : £0.25
1. Minton, John, 1917-1957. I. Minton, John, 1917-1957. II. Graves Art Gallery, Sheffield, Eng.

Mintons Ltd.

ASLIN, Elizabeth. 738'.09424'63
Minton, 1798-1910 : [catalogue of an] exhibition, August-October 1976 / [organized by the] Victoria and Albert Museum [and] Thomas Goode & Company Limited ; [by] Elizabeth Aslin and Paul Atterbury. London : [The Museum], 1976. [1], 111, [1] p., 4 p. of plates : ill. (some col.) ; 20 x 21 cm. Held at the Museum. Includes index. Bibliography: p. 14-15. [NK4210.M55A84] 77-355059 ISBN 0-901486-96-5 : £3.00
1. Mintons Ltd. 2. Pottery, English—Exhibitions. 3. Porcelain, English—Exhibitions. I. Atterbury, Paul, joint author. II. Mintons Ltd. III. Victoria and Albert Museum, South Kensington. IV. Thomas Goode & Company. V. Title.

GODDEN, Geoffrey A. 738.2'7
Minton pottery & porcelain of the first period, 1793-1850 [by] Geoffrey A. Godden. New York, F. A. Praeger [1968] xvi, 168 p. illus., 12 col. plates, ports. 26 cm. [NK4210.M55G6 1968b] 68-31671 20.00
1. Mintons Ltd. I. Title. BIP

Mints—Nevada—Carson City.

HICKSON, Howard. 081 s
Mint mark: "CC"; the story of the United States mint at Carson City, Nevada. Edited by Guy Shipler. Carson City, Nevada State Museum [1972] 124 p. illus. 26 cm. (Nevada. State Museum, Carson City. Popular series, no. 4) Bibliography: p. 105-108. [AM101.N464 no. 4] [HG461.C3] 338.7'6'7183 70-626512
1. Mints—Nevada—Carson City. I. Title. II. Series.

Miranda camera.

AMPHOTO, New York. 771.31
Official Mirada manual, by the Amphoto Editorial Board. New York [1961] 123p. illus. 21cm. [TR263.M53A45] 60-15904
1. Miranda camera. 2. Photography—Handbooks, manuals, etc. I. Title.

AMPHOTO, New York. 771.31
official Miranda manual, by the Amphoto Editorial Board. New York [Author, c. 1961] 123p. illus. 60-15904 2.50 bds.,
1. Miranda camera. 2. Photography—Handbooks, manuals, etc. I. Title.

DANTZIC, Jerry. 771.3'1
The official Miranda manual. New York, American Photographic Book Pub. Co. [c1966] 128 p. illus. 24 cm. [TR263.M53D3] 65-17123
1. Miranda camera. 2. Photography — Handbooks, manuals, etc. I. Title.

TYDINGS, Kenneth S 771.31
New Miranda eye-level reflex guide. Philadelphia, Chilton Co., Book Division, c1962. 127 p. illus. 20 cm. (Modern camera guide series, 1061) [TR263.M53T9] 62-18422
1. Miranda camera. I. Title.

WOLF, John C. 771.3'1
Miranda Sensorex/Sensomat single-lens reflex guide, by John C. Wolf. New York, Amphoto [1971] 94 p. illus. 20 cm. (An Amphoto camera guide) [TR263.M53W65] 74-153477 ISBN 0-8174-0173-3 2.50
1. Miranda camera. 2. Photography—Handbooks, manuals, etc. I. Title.

Miro, Joan, 1893—

BONNEFOY, Yves. 709'.46
Miro. New York, Viking Press, 1967. 29 p., 64 plates (part col.) illus. 36 cm. (A Studio book) Bibliography: p. 28-29. [ND813] 67-31950
1. Miro, Joan, 1893-

DUPIN, Jacques. 759.6
Miro. [Translated from the French by Norbert Guterman] New York, H. N. Abrams [1961 or 2] 596 p. illus. (part mounted, part col.) ports. 31 cm. Bibliography: p. 577-591. [ND813.M5D83] 62-19132
1. Miro, Joan, 1893-

DUPIN, Jacques. 759.6
Miro. [Translated from the French by Norbert Guterman] Gerhard Nellhaus] and The marriage of Mr. Mississippi; a play [translated from the German by Michael Bullock] New York, Grove Press [1966? c1964] 596 p. illus. (part mounted, part col.) ports. 31 cm. (An Evergreen book, E-401) Bibliography: p. 577-591. [ND813.M5D83] 62-1913214
1. Miro, Joan, 1893- 2. Drama—History and criticism. I. Title: The marriage of Mr. Mississippi.

GASSER, Manuel 759.6
Joan Miro. [Tr.: Hydayden Barnes] New York, Barnes & Noble [c.1965] 90p. illus. (pt. col.) 18cm. (Barnes & Noble art ser., 621) [ND813.M5G333] 66-142 .75 pap.,
1. Miro, Joan, 1893- I. Title.

GREENBERG, Clement, 1909- 759.6
Joan Miro. [Rev. ed.] New York, Quadrangle Press, 1948 [i. e. 1950] 133 p. illus., col. plates, port. 29 cm. "Books illustrated by Miro": p. 128. "Bibliography, compiled by Hannah B. Muller": p. 123-127. [ND813.M5G7 1950] 50-56750
1. Miro, Joan, 1893- I. Title.

GREENBERG, Clement, 1909- 759.6
Joan Miro / Clement Greenberg. New York : Arno Press, 1969 [c1950] 133 p. : ill. ; 29 cm. (Arno series of contemporary art ; no. 25) Reprint of the ed. published by Quadrangle Press, New York. "Bibliography, compiled by Hannah B. Muller": p. 123-127. "Books illustrated by Miro": p. 128. [ND813.M5G7 1969] 77-91377
1. Miro, Joan, 1893- I. Miro, Joan, 1893- II. Title. III. Series.

MIRO, Joan, 1893- 759.6
Joan Miro. [Text: James Johnson Sweeney. Photography: Joaquim Gomis, Catala-Roca, and Reprocolor Llovet. Selection and sequence: Joan Prats Valles. New York, Tudor Pub. Co., 1971] 28 p., 247 p. of col. illus. 21 cm. (Fotoscop) [ND813.M5S88] 73-168804
1. Miro, Joan, 1893- I. Sweeney, James Johnson, 1900-

MIRO, Joan, 1893- 769'.92'4
Joan Miro. [Translated from the French by Peninah Neimark and E. J. W.] New York, Tudor Pub. Co. 1972- v. illus. (part col.) 33 cm. Translation of Miro. Vol. 1: Two essays by M. Leiris. Annotated catalog by F. Mourlot. Contents.Contents.—v. 1. Lithographs. [ND813.M5L4513] 73-184353 ISBN 0-8148-0494-2 75.00
1. Miro, Joan, 1893- I. Leiris, Michel, 1901- II. Mourlot, Fernand.
Deluxe 1500.00 ISBN 0-8148-0537-X.

MIRO, Joan, 1893- 760.946
Joan Miro, his graphic work. Introd. [by] Sam Hunter. New York, H. N. Abrams [1958] xxxv, 108 p. illus., plates (part col.) group port. 33 cm. "Books illustrated by Miro": p. 107-108. Half title. Bibliographical references included in "Footnotes" (p. xxxv) [NE702.M5H8] 58-13486
I. Hunter, Sam, 1923-

*MIRO, Joan, 1893- 959.6
Joan Miro: magnetic fields. New York, Solomon R. Guggenheim Foundation [1972] 159 p. illus. 26 cm. [ND813.M5] 72-89976 5.25
I. Solomon R. Guggenheim Museum. New York. II. Title.

MIRO, Joan, 1893- 759.6
Miro [by] Umbro Apollonio. [Translated from the Italian by Victor Corti. 1st American ed.] New York, Grosset & Dunlap [1971, c1969] 38 p. 80 col. plates. 18 cm. (The New Grosset art library, 29) Bibliography: p. 27. [ND813.M5A753 1971] 69-11558
I. Apollonio, Umbro, 1911-

MIRO, Joan, 1893- 730'.92'4
Miro sculptures; an exhibition organized by Walker Art Center. [Minneapolis, 1971] [48] p. illus. (part col.) 28 cm. Catalog of the exhibition held at the Walker Art Center, Minneapolis, Oct. 3-Nov. 28, 1971; the Cleveland Museum of Art, Feb. 2-March 12, 1972, and the Art Institute of Chicago, Apr. 15-May 28, 1972. [NB813.M56W3] 72-175538
I. Walker Art Center, Minneapolis. II. Cleveland Museum of Art. III. Chicago. Art Institute. IV. Title.

PENROSE, Roland, Sir. 759.6
Miro [by] Roland Penrose. New York, H. N. Abrams [1970?] 215 p. illus. (part col.) 22 cm. Bibliography: p. 205-206. [ND813.M5P4 1970b] 69-17033 ISBN 0-8109-0304-0
1. Miro, Joan, 1893-

PICON, Gaetan. 709'.2'4
Joan Miro : Catalan notebooks : unpublished drawings and writings / presented by Gaetan Picon ; [translated from the French by Dinah Harrison]. Geneva : Skira ; New York : Rizzoli, 1977. 157 p. : ill. (some col.) ; 31 cm. [NC287.M5P513] 76-62893 ISBN 0-8478-0093-8 : 25.00
1. Miro, Joan, 1893- I. Miro, Joan, 1893-

PIERRE Matisse Gallery, New York. 720'.924
Miro: sculpture in bronze and ceramic, 1967-1969; recent etchings and lithographs. New York [1970] 1 v. (unpaged) illus. (part col.) 26 cm. Catalog of the exhibition held May, 1970. [NB813.M56P5] 75-199987
1. Miro, Joan, 1893- I. Title.

RUBIN, William Stanley. 709'.2'4
Miro in the collection of the Museum of Modern Art, including remainder-interest and promised gifts [by] William Rubin. New York, Museum of Modern Art; distributed by New York Graphic Society, Greenwich, Conn. [1973] 139 p. illus. (part col.) 25 cm. Includes bibliographical references. [N7113.M54R82 1973] 72-95078 ISBN 0-87070-463-X 15.00
1. Miro, Joan, 1893- 2. New York (City). Museum of Modern Art. I. Miro, Joan, 1893- II. New York (City). Museum of Modern Art. III. Title.

SOBY, James Thrall, 1906- 759.6
Joan Miro. New York, Museum of Modern Art; distributed by Doubleday, Garden City, N.Y. [1959] 164 p. illus. (part col.), port. 25 cm. Bibliography: p. 153-161. [ND813.M5S6] 59-10311
1. Miro, Joan, 1893- BIP

SWEENEY, James Johnson, 1900- 759.6
Joan Miro. Reprint ed. New York, Published for the Museum of Modern Art by Arno Press, 1969 [c1941] 87 p. illus., ports. 27 cm. Bibliography: p. 85-87. [ND813.M5S9 1969] 78-86434
1. Miro, Joan, 1893- I. New York (City). Museum of Modern Art. BIP

TAILLANDIER, Yvon 759.4
Creation Miro 1961. Photoscop: Gomis-Prats. Photographie, Joaquin Gomis; selection et sequence, J. Prats Valles. [Barcelona] Editorial RM [dist. New York, Wittenborn, 1963] [14]p., 60 illus. (chiefly col., incl. port.) [40]p. 21cm. French, English, and German. 63-1810 9.00

SUBJECT INDEX MOCHICA INDIANS—ART.

1. Miro, Joan, 1893- I. Gomis, Joaquin. II. Prats Valles, Juan. III. Title.

Mirrors, Chinese.

TODD, Oliver Julian. 739'.512
Chinese bronze mirrors; a study based on the Todd collection of 1,000 bronze mirrors found in the five northern provinces of Suiyuan, Shensi, Shansi, Honan, and Hopei, China, by Milan Rupert and O. J. Todd. New York, Paragon Book Reprint Corp., 1966. iii, 259 p. illus. 25 cm. "Reprint of the work first published in ... 1935." Bibliography: p. [83] -84. [NK7983.T6 1966] 66-30335
1. Mirrors, Chinese. 2. Bronzes—Private collections. 3. Bronzes, Chinese. I. Rupert, Milan. II. Title.

Mirrors, English.

WILLS, Geoffrey. 748'.8
English looking-glasses; a study of the glass, frames, and makers (1670-1820). Foreword by John Howard. South Brunswick [N. J.] A. S. Barnes [1967, c1965] 160 p. plates. 29 cm. Includes bibliographical references. [NK8440.W5 1967] 66-24935
1. Mirrors, English. 2. Mirrors—Frames. I. Title.

Misericords—France.

KRAUS, Dorothy. 730'.944
The hidden world of misericords / by Dorothy and Henry Kraus. New York : G. Braziller, c1975. 191 p. : ill. ; 23 cm. Includes bibliographical references. [NK9749.A1K72 1975] 75-10869 ISBN 0-8076-0804-1 : 20.00
1. Misericords—France. 2. Civilization, Medieval, in art. 3. Wood-carving, Medieval—France. 4. Wood-carving—France. I. Kraus, Henry, 1905- joint author. II. Title. BIP

Mississippi River in art.

MCDERMOTT, John Francis, 1947- 759.13
Seth Eastman's Mississippi; a lost portfolio recovered. Urbana, University of Illinois Press [1973] xvii, 149 p. illus. 16 x 23 cm. Bibliography: p. 145-147. [ND1839.E23M32] 73-2457 ISBN 0-252-00192-3 10.00
1. Eastman, Seth, 1808-1875. 2. Mississippi River in art. I. Title. BIP

Mississippian culture.

HATHCOCK, Roy. 738.3
Ancient Indian pottery of the Mississippi River Valley / by Roy Hathcock. 1st ed. Camden, Ark. : Hurley Press, c1976. 232 p. : ill. (some col.) ; 32 cm. Bibliography: p. 228. [E99.M6815H37] 75-6102 30.00
1. Mississippian culture. 2. Indians of North America—Mississippi Valley—Pottery. I. Title.

Missouri — Antiq.

CHAPMAN, Carl Haley, 1915- 970.462
Indians and archaeology of Missouri, by Carl H. Chapman and Eleanor F. Chapman. Columbia, University of Missouri Press [for the College of Arts and Science, 1964] 161 p., illus., maps. 23 cm. (Missouri handbook no. 6) Includes bibliographies. [E78.M8C5] 64-64127
1. Missouri — Antiq. 2. Indians of North America — Missouri — Antiq. I. Chapman, Eleanor F., joint author. II. Title. III. Series. IV. Series: Missouri. University. Missouri handbook no. 6 BIP

Missouri—Description and travel—1951- —Views.

LYLE, Wes, 1934- 779'.9'977804
Missouri : faces and places / Wes Lyle, photographer ; John Hall, writer. Lawrence : Regents Press of Kansas, c1977. ca. 150 p. : ill. ; 24 cm. [F467.L93] 77-81508 ISBN 0-7006-0165-1 : 9.50
1. Missouri—Description and travel—1951- —Views. I. Hall, John, 1939- II. Title. BIP

Missouri in art.

BINGHAM, George Caleb, 1811-1879. 759.13
Bingham's Missouri. [Saint Louis : Bingham Sketches, inc., c1975] [56] p. : ill. (some col.) ; 23 x 27 cm. Cover title. Catalogue and text by George McCue. Catalogue of an exhibition held Sept. 26, 1975-Apr. 11, 1976, in Kansas City, Mo., at the Nelson Gallery—Atkins Museum and other museums. Bibliography: p. [56] [ND237.B587M32] 75-332334
1. Bingham, George Caleb, 1811-1879. 2. Missouri in art. I. McCue, George. II. William Rockhill Nelson Gallery and Mary Atkins Museum of Fine Arts, Kansas City, Mo. III. Title.

Mr. and Mrs. George Gard De Sylva Collection.

LOS Angeles Co., Calif. Museum, Los Angeles. 338.4'3745'10973
The Mr. and Mrs. George Gard De Sylva Collection of French impressionist and modern paintings and sculpture. [Catalogue, prepared by W. R. Valentiner. Los Angeles] 1950. 78 p. illus., ports. 27 cm. [N5220.L65] 67-5051
1. Mr. and Mrs. George Gard De Sylva Collection. I. Valentiner, Wilhelm Reinhold, 1880-1958. II. Title.

Mitchell, Joan, 1926—

MITCHELL, Joan, 1926- 759.13
Joan Mitchell, by Marcia Tucker. New York, Whitney Museum of American Art [1974] 47 p. illus. (part col.) 22 x 26 cm. "[Exhibition held at] Whitney Museum of American Art, New York, March 26-May 5, 1974." Bibliography: p. 45-47. [ND237.M58T82] 74-77025
1. Mitchell, Joan, 1926- I. Tucker, Marcia. II. Whitney Museum of American Art, New York.

MITCHELL, Joan, 1926- 759.13
"My five years in the country"; an exhibition of forty-nine paintings. Everson Museum of Art, Syracuse, New York, March 25 through April 21, 1972; Martha Jackson Gallery, New York, April 26 through June 3. [Syracuse, N.Y., 1972] 1 v. (chiefly illus.) and case (6 col. illus.) 32 cm. Includes bibliography. [ND237.M58E9] 72-77408
I. Everson Museum of Art of Syracuse and Onondaga County. II. Martha Jackson Gallery. III. Title.

Mitra, Rajendralala, Raja, 1824-1891.

FERGUSSON, James, 1808-1886. 726'.1'4
Archaeology in India, with especial reference to the works of Babu Rajendralala Mitra / James Fergusson. New Delhi : K. B. Publications, 1974. vii, 115 p. : ill. ; 23 cm. "Ist Indian reprint." First published in 1884. Includes bibliographical references. [NA6002.F44 1974] 74-904007 10.00
1. Mitra, Rajendralala, Raja, 1824-1891. 2. Temples—India. 3. Cave temples—India. I. Title.
Distributed by South Asia Books.

Mitsumura Suiko Shoin, Kyoto.

[TAKAKUMA, Gisel] 1894- 712.0952
A gateway to Japanese gardens. [Austin, Tex., Perkins Oriental, 1963] 106p. illus. (pt. col.) maps. 15x15cm. Japanese text. Introd. in English, French. Cover title. J64 2.50 pap.,
1. Mitsumura Suiko Shoin, Kyoto. I. Title.

Mixed media painting.

SANDERSON, Gretchen S. 751.4'22
Mixed media and watercolor, by Gretchen S. Sanderson & Alphonse J. Shelton. New York, Pitman Pub. Corp. [1973] 32 p. illus. (part col.) 20 x 27 cm. (Pitman art series, 73) [ND2422.S26] 74-120002 1.25 (pbk.)
1. Mixed media painting. 2. Water-color painting. I. Shelton, Alphonse J., joint author. II. Title. BIP

Mixtec Indians—Art.

CARMACK, Robert M., 1934- 301.2 s
Quichean art: a Mixteca-Puebla variant, by Robert M. Carmack and Lynn Larmer. Greeley, University of Northern Colorado, Museum of Anthropology, 1971. 24 l. illus. 29 cm. (Museum of Anthropology miscellaneous series, no. 23) Bibliography: leaves 8, 22-24. [GN37.G743 no. 23] [F1219] 709'.01'1 72-191331
1. Mixtec Indians—Art. 2. Indians of Mexico—Puebla (State)—Art. 3. Quiches—Art. 4. Mexico—Antiquities. 5. Guatemala—Antiquities. I. Larmer, Lynn, joint author. II. Title. III. Series: University of Northern Colorado. Museum of Anthropology. Miscellaneous series, no. 23.

Mobile, Ala.—Description—Views.

HILL, Jackson, 1949- 779'.9'976122
On Mobile streets : a rumor of the city : photographs / by Jackson Hill. Mobile, Ala. : Easter Pub. Co., c1978. 84 p. : all ill. ; 20 x 22 cm. [F334.M6H49] 78-8718 ISBN 0-930642-04-X pbk. : 6.95
1. Mobile, Ala.—Description—Views. 2. Mobile, Ala.—Social life and customs—Pictorial works. I. Title. BIP

Mobile home parks.

NEWCOMB, Robinson. 711'.557
Mobile home parks. Washington, Urban Land Institute [1971- v. illus. 28 cm. (Urban Land Institute. Technical bulletin 66-) Contents.Contents.—pt. 1. An analysis of characteristics. Bibliography: pt. 1, p. 76-80. [NA9000.U67 no. 66, etc.] [TX1105] 76-167878
1. Mobile home parks. I. Title. II. Series.

Mobiles.

ROMBERG, Jenean. 731'.55
Let's discover mobiles. New York, The Center for Applied Research in Education [1974] 64 p. illus. 28 cm. (Her Arts and crafts discovery units) [NB1272.R65] 74-14628 ISBN 0-87628-524-8
1. Mobiles. I. Title. BIP

Mobiles (Sculpture)

LYNCH, John, 1904- 735.291
How to make mobiles. New York, Studio Publications in association with Crowell [1953] 96 p. illus. 24 cm. [NB212.L9] 53-7528
1. Mobiles (Sculpture) I. Title. BIP

MOOREY, Anne. 731.55
Making mobiles, by Anne and Christopher Moorey. London, Studio Vista; New York, Watson-Guptill [1966] 95 p. illus., 8 plates (incl. 4 col.) diagrs. 19 cm. 10/6 (B 66-8511) [NB1272.M6 1966] 66-13007
1. Mobiles (Sculpture) I. Moorey, Christopher, joint author. II. Title.

SCHEGGER, Theresia Maria 731.55
Make your own mobiles [Tr. from German by Paul Kuttner] New York, Sterling [c.1965] 96 p. illus., port. 21 cm. [NB1315.S313] 64-24683 2.95; 2.99 lib. ed.,
1. Mobiles (Sculpture) I. Title.

WILLIAMS, Guy R. 731.5'5
Making mobiles [by] Guy R. Williams. New York, Emerson Books [1969, c1968] 94 p. illus. 22 cm. [NB1272.W5] 76-76580 ISBN 8-7523-1675-
1. Mobiles (Sculpture) I. Title. BIP

*ZACHY, Harry 747
Mobiles. Illus. by the author. Cleveland, World [1966] 47p. 19cm. (Little hobby bkshelf. ser.) 1.95; 2.60 lib. ed.,
I. Title.

ZARCHY, Harry. 731.55
Mobiles, written and illustrated by Harry Zarchy. Cleveland, World Pub. Co. [1966] 47 p. illus. (part col.) 19 cm. (The Little hobby bookshelf) A Holly book. [NB1272.Z3] 67-6
1. Mobiles (Sculpture) I. Title.

ZARCHY, Harry. 731.5
Mobiles, written and illustrated by Harry Zarchy. Cleveland, World Pub. Co. [1966] 47 p. illus. (part col.) 19 cm. (The Little hobby bookshelf) "A Holly book." Simple instructions for constructing mobiles from wood, metal, or paper. [NB1272.Z3] AC 66
1. Mobiles (Sculpture) I. Title.

Mobiles (Sculpture)—Juvenile literature.

CREATIVE Educational Society, Mankato, Minn. 731'.55
How to have fun making mobiles, by editors of Creative. Illustrated by Nancy Inderieden. [Mankato, Minn., Creative Education; distributed by Childrens Press, Chicago, 1973, c1974] 31 p. illus. (part col.) 25 cm. (Creative craft book) Gives instructions for creating simple mobiles using such materials as paper, cardboard, sticks, styrofoam, wood, clay, and wire. [TT910.C7 1973] 73-18210 ISBN 0-87191-293-7 4.95 (lib. bdg.)
1. Mobiles (Sculpture)—Juvenile literature. I. Inderieden, Nancy, illus. II. Title. BIP

HOLZ, Loretta. 731'.55
Mobiles you can make / by Loretta Holz ; illustrated with drawings by the author and photos. by George and Loretta Holz. New York : Lothrop, Lee & Shepard Co., [1975] 128 p. : ill. ; 25 cm. Includes index. Bibliography: p. 122-124. Instructions for making three basic kinds of mobiles—string, base, and wire—and other mobile projects from household materials. [TT899.H64] 75-8994 ISBN 0-688-41695-0 : 5.95 ISBN 0-688-51695-5 lib.bdg. : 5.11
1. Mobiles (Sculpture)—Juvenile literature. I. Holz, George. II. Title. BIP

POUNTNEY, Kate. 731'.55
Make a mobile. [1st U.S. ed.] New York, S. G. Phillips [1974] 48 p. illus. (part col.) 26 cm. Instructions for making progressively more difficult mobiles including moving toys, simple mobiles, and balanced mobiles. [TT910.P68 1974] 74-9824 ISBN 0-87599-206-4
1. Mobiles (Sculpture)—Juvenile literature. I. Title. BIP

Moccasins—Juvenile literature.

GRAINGER, Sylvia, 1942- 746.4
How to make your own moccasins / by Sylvia Grainger ; [diagrs. by Jean Krulis]. Philadelphia : Lippincott, c1977. p. cm. Bibliography: p. Directions for making soft leather footwear in styles adapted from original Indian designs. [TT678.5.G7] 77-4262 ISBN 0-397-31754-9 : 7.95 ISBN 0-397-31755-7 pbk. : 3.95
1. Moccasins—Juvenile literature. I. Krulis, Jean. II. Title. BIP

Mochica Indians—Art.

BENSON, Elizabeth P. 970 s
A man and a feline in Mochica art / Elizabeth P. Benson. Washington : Dumbarton Oaks, Trustees for Harvard University, 1974. 31 p. : ill. ; 27 cm. (Studies in pre-Columbian art and archaeology ; no. 14) Bibliography: p. 30-31. [E51.S85 no. 14] [F3430.1.M6] 730 74-18650
1. Mochica Indians—Art. 2. Indians of South America—Peru—Art. I. Title. II. Series. BIP

DONNAN, Christopher B. 709'.01'1
Moche art and iconography / Christopher B. Donnan. Los Angeles : UCLA Latin American Center, University of California, 1976. vii, 146 p., [6] leaves of plates : ill. (some col.) ; 24 cm. (UCLA Latin American studies ; v. 33) (A Book on lore) Includes index. Bibliography: p. 140-142. [F3430.1.M6D655] 75-620011 ISBN 0-87903-033-X : 12.50
1. Mochica Indians—Art. 2. Indians of South America—Peru—Art. I. Title. II. Series. III. Series: California. University. University at Los Angeles. Latin American Center. Latin American studies ; v. 33.

Mocsanyi, Paul.

VAN LOEN, Alfred 730.9492
Alfred Van Loen, by Paul Mocsanyi. Great Neck, N.Y., Channel Press [c.1960] [63]p. illus. 32cm. 60-16162 5.95 half cloth,
1. Mocsanyi, Paul. I. Title.

Model houses.

EICHEN, Carole, 1932- 747'.8'8
How to decorate model homes and apartments. Edited by June R. Vollman. Designer: Jan White. Illustrator: J. Dyck Fledderus. New York, House & Home Press [1974] 155 p. illus. (part col.) 28 cm. [NK2195.M6E35] 74-8713 ISBN 0-07-019107-7 24.95
1. Model houses. 2. Model apartments. 3. Interior decoration. I. Title.

Modeling.

AUERBACH, Arnold, 1898- 731.42
Modelled sculpture and plaster casting. New York, T. Yoseloff [1962, c1961] 116 p. illus. 26 cm. [NB1180.A8 1962] 62-13152
1. Modeling. 2. Plaster casts. 3. Sculpture—Technique. I. Title. BIP

BERENSOHN, Paulus. 738.1
Finding one's way with clay; pinched pottery and the color of clay. With photos. by True Kelly. New York, Simon and Schuster [1972] 159 p. illus. (part col.) 31 cm. Bibliography: p. 159. [NB1180.B47] 72-83911 ISBN 0-671-21324-5 9.95
1. Modeling. I. Title. BIP

DANCYGER, Irene. 731.4'2
Clay models and stone carving. New York, Drake Publishers [1974] 116 p. illus. 26 cm. (Pelham crafts series) [NB1180.D36] 73-17639 ISBN 0-87749-564-5 6.95
1. Modeling. 2. Stone carving. I. Title.

DIVALENTIN, Maria Messuri, 1911- 731.4
Sculpture for beginners with clay & wax / by Maria and Louis DiValentin. Combined ed., Sculpture for beginners, Sculpturing with wax. New York : Sterling Pub. Co., 1976. 208 p., [4] leaves of plates : ill. (some col.) ; 21 cm. Includes index. [NB1180.D553] 76-19805 ISBN 0-8069-5072-2 : 7.95 ISBN 0-8069-5377-2 lib.bdg. :
1. Modeling. 2. Models (Clay, plaster, etc.) 3. Wax-modeling. I. DiValentin, Louis, joint author. II. DiValentin, Maria Messuri, 1911- Sculpture for beginners. III. DiValentin, Maria Messuri, 1911- Sculpturing with wax. IV. Title.

HUXLEY-JONES, T. B. 731.74
Modelled portrait heads. [New York] Studio Publications [1955] 95p. illus. 26cm. (How to do it series, 60) [NB1180.H8] 56-2067
1. Modeling. 2. Sculpture—Technique. 3. Sculpture. I. Title.

HUXLEY-JONES, T. B. 731.42
Modelled portrait heads [Rev. ed.] London, Tiranti [Hollywood-by-the-Sea, Fla., Transatlantic. 1964] 110p. illus. 22cm. 64-55870 3.25 pap.,
1. Modeling. 2. Sculpture—Technique. 3. Sculpture. I. Title.

ISENSTEIN, Harald. 738.14
Creative claywork. [Translated by Barbara Evans Zimmer] New York, Sterling Pub. Co. [1960] 96 p. illus. 22 cm. Translation of Leg med ler. [NB1180.1753] 60-14326
1. Modeling. I. Title. BIP

KOWAL, Dennis. 731.4
Sculpture casting; mold techniques and materials, metals, plastics, concrete, by Dennis Kowal and Dona Z. Meilach. New York, Crown Publishers [1972] viii, 264 p. illus. 27 cm. (Crown's arts and crafts series) Bibliography: p. 257-258. [NB1180.K68 1972] 72-84319 ISBN 0-517-50059-0 8.95
1. Modeling. 2. Precision casting. I. Meilach, Dona Z., joint author. II. Title. BIP

LANTERI, Edouard, d. 1917 731.42
Modelling and sculpture; a guide for artists and students; 3v. New introd. by Nathan Cabot Hale [Gloucester, Mass., P. Smith, 1966, c.1965] 3v. (various p.) illus. 21cm. (Dover bks., T1418/20 rebound) Previously pub. by Chapman & Hall, London, 1902-1911 under the title Modelling; a guide for teachers and students [NB1180.L22] 12.75; 4.25 set, ea.,
1. Modeling. 2. Sculpture—Technique. I. Title.

LANTERI, Edward, d. 1917 731.42
Modelling and sculpture; a guide for artists and students. New introd. by Nathan Cabot Hale. New York, Dover [c.1965] 3v. (153; 159; 233p.) illus. 21cm. (T1418, T1419, T1420) Previously pub. under title: Modelling; a guide for teachers and students. [NB1180.L22] 65-25704 2.25 pap., ea.,
1. Modeling. 2. Sculpture—Technique. I. Title.

LUNS, Theo. 731.42
The beginner's book of clay modelling. Photos. by J. Schoen. Newton, Mass., C. T. Branford Co. [1959] 62 p. illus. 22 cm. "Translated by Jan Tholenaar from the Dutch publication 'Boetseren voor beginners.'" [NB1180.L813] 59-1881
1. Modeling. I. Title.

PAYNE, Gordon Clifford. 731.4
Adventures with clay, by G. C. Payne. New York, Warne [1969.c1967] 64p. illus. 26cm. [NB1180.P3 1969] 68-19483 2.95 lib. ed.
1. Modeling. I. Title.
First published in Britain by Kaye & Ward.

ROETTGER, Ernst. 731.42
Creative clay design. New York, Reinhold Pub. Corp. [1963, c1962] 95 p. illus. 21 cm. [[NB1180.R6]] 63-8676
1. Modeling. I. Title.

ROTTGER, Ernst. 731.42
Creative clay design. New York, Reinhold Pub. Corp. [1963, c1962] 95 p. illus. 21 cm. [NB1180.R6] 63-8676
1. Modeling. I. Title.

SLADE, Richard. 731.4
Modeling in clay, plaster, and papier-mache. [1st American ed.] New York, Lothrop, Lee & Shepard Co. [1968, c1967] 64 p. illus. 25 cm. Bibliography: p. [59]-60. Describes basic shapes in clay modeling and how to obtain and vary them, modeling in plaster, and fundamentals of papier-mache modeling. [NB1180.S53] AC 68
1. Modeling. I. Title. BIP

SLADE, Richard. 731.4'3
Your book of modelling. London, Faber, 1967. 56p. illus. 22cm. (Your bk. ser.) [NB1180.S54] 68-113309 3.25 bds.,
1. Modeling. I. Title.
Distributed by Transatlantic, New York. BIP

WEISS, Harvey. 731
Clay, wood, and wire; a how-to-do-it book of sculpture. New York, W. R. Scott, c1956. 48 p. illus. 29 cm. (Young Scott books) [NB1180.W4] 56-10693
1. Modeling. 2. Carving (Art industries) 3. Sculpture, American. I. Title.

YODER, Ray A., 1909- 745.5
Sculpture and modeling for the elementary school / R. A. Yoder. West Nyack, N.Y. : Parker Pub. Co., [1976] p. cm. Includes index. [TT916.Y6] 75-33386
1. Modeling. 2. Sculpture. I. Title. BIP

Modeling—Juvenile literature.

HAWKINSON, John, 1912- 731.4'2
A ball of clay. Chicago, A. Whitman [1974] 47 p. illus. (part col.) 23 cm. Introduces clay as an art medium with information on how to find it in nature, prepare it for handling, and use it to create a variety of non-permanent projects. [TT916.H38] 72-13350 ISBN 0-8075-0557-9 3.75
1. Modeling—Juvenile literature. I. Title. BIP

HELFMAN, Harry Carmozin, 1910- 731.4'2
Making your own sculpture [by] Harry Helfman. Illustrated with photos. by the author. New York, Morrow [1971] 48 p. illus. 24 cm. Instructions for making sculptures of dough, plastic cups, paper, papier-mache, straws, wire, etc. [NB1185.H4] 73-155992 3.75
1. Modeling—Juvenile literature. I. Title. BIP

LEWIS, Alan. 738.1
Let's model. New York, Van Nostrand Reinhold [1972] c1971. 31 p. illus. (part col.) 21 cm. (Starting points) Discusses making a variety of decorative clay objects such as pots, puppets, and mosaic pictures. [NB1180.L48 1972] 70-188484 1.45
1. Modeling—Juvenile literature. I. Title.

ROTTGER, Ernst. 731.4'2
Creative clay design. New York, Van Nostrand Reinhold [1972, c1962] 95 p. illus. (part col.) 20 x 21 cm. (Creative play series) Text and black and white photographs instruct in the creation of clay figures and objects. Includes a section of technical notes predominately on preparation and firing. [NB1180.R6 1972] 72-188375
1. Modeling—Juvenile literature. I. Title.

Models and model making.

COLBRIDGE, A. M. 745.59'28
Scale models in balsa [by] A. M. Colbridge. New York, Taplinger Pub. Co. [1972, c1971] 118 p. 21 cm. (Taplinger's teach-yourself-crafts series) [TT154.C58 1972] 72-2196 ISBN 0-8008-6999-0 5.95
1. Models and model making. 2. Balsa wood. I. Title. BIP

Models and modelmaking.

COLEMAN, H S 680
Modelmaking. New York, Crowell [1953?] 87p. illus. 23cm. [TT154] 53-9408
1. Models and modelmaking. I. Title.

DEAN, William Albert, 1923- 629.133'1
Bill Dean's book of balsa models, by Bill Dean. [1st U.S. ed., rev. and updated] New York, Arco Pub. Co. [1970] 62 p. illus. 28 cm. First published in 1957 under title: Eagle book of balsa models. [TT154.D4 1970] 72-105134 ISBN 0-668-02209-4 2.95
1. Models and modelmaking. 2. Aeroplanes—Models. 3. Balsa wood craft. I. Title. II. Title: Book of balsa models. BIP

ELLIS, Chris. 745.59'28
How to build plastic model kits. [Rev. and updated ed.] New York, Ballantine Books [1973] 188 p. illus. 21 cm. Published in 1968 under title: How to go plastic modelling. Tips for techniques, tools, and materials used in constructing, finishing, and displaying plastic models from kits. [TT154.E44 1973] 73-175207 2.95
1. Models and modelmaking. 2. Plastics craft. I. Title.

HOHAUSER, Sanford, 1933- 720'.2
Architectural and interior models, design and construction ... New York, Van Nostrand Reinhold [1970] 211 p. illus. 32 cm. [TT154.H58] 68-16029
1. Models and modelmaking. I. Title.

KNOBLAUGH, Ralph R. 745.2
Modelmaking for industrial design. New York, McGraw-Hill, 1958. 276 p. illus. 26 cm. Includes bibliography. [TT154.K6] 57-12585
1. Models and modelmaking. 2. Design, Industrial. I. Title.

LOZIER, Herbert. 745.59'28
Getting started in model-building. New York, Hawthorn Books [1971] x, 196 p. 24 cm. Instructions for making model planes, cars, and boats from cardboard, balsa, pine, plastic, and metal. [TT154.L68 1971] 79-75198 5.95
1. Models and modelmaking. I. Title.

LOZIER, Herbert. 688'.1
Model making. [1st ed.] Philadelphia, Chilton Book Co. [1967] vii, 165 p. illus. (part fold.) 26 cm. [TT154.L69] 67-28893
1. Models and modelmaking. I. Title.

LOZIER, Herbert 688'.1
Model Making Herbert Lozier. Radnor, Pa. : Chilton, 1976 c1967. vii, [194] p. ; ill., diagrams : 25 cm. [TT154.L69] ISBN 0-8019-5251-4 pbk. : 6.95
1. Models and Modelmaking. I. Title.
L.C. card no. for 1967 ed.: 67-28893.

MAGINLEY, C. J. 745.59'2
America in miniatures : how to make models of early American houses, furniture, and vehicles / C. J. Maginley ; illustrated by Elizabeth D. McKee and James MacDonald ; photos. by Joseph Moffet. 1st ed. New York : Harcourt Brace Jovanovich, c1976. 99 p. : ill. ; 24 x 27 cm. Compiled from the author's Models of America's past and Historic models of early America. [TT154.M24] 76-13002 ISBN 0-15-105587-4 pbk. : 2.45
1. Models and modelmaking. 2. Miniature objects—United States. 3. Miniature craft. I. Title. BIP

MAGINLEY, C. J. 745.51
Models of America's past and how to make them [by] C. J. Maginley. Illustrated by Elisabeth D. McKee. [1st ed.] New York, Harcourt, Brace & World [1969] 144 p. illus. 22 cm. [TT154.M25] 69-17116 3.75
1. Models and modelmaking. I. Title. BIP

PHILPOTT, Bryan. 745.59'28
Making and improving plastic models / Bryan Philpott. Newton Abbot ; North Pomfret, Vt. : David and Charles, 1975. 112 p. : ill. ; 22 cm. Includes index. [TT154.P49] 74-21510 ISBN 0-7153-6698-X : 9.95
1. Models and modelmaking. 2. Military miniatures. 3. Plastics craft. I. Title. BIP

SCHLEICHER, Robert H. 745.59'28
Building plastic models / by Robert Schleicher ; editor, Harold A. Edmonson. Milwaukee : Kalmbach Books, c1976. 64 p. : ill. (some col.) ; 29 cm. [TT154.S347] 76-10915 ISBN 0-89024-527-4 : 3.50
1. Models and modelmaking. 2. Plastics craft. I. Title. BIP

WILLIAMS, Guy R. 745.59
Instructions to young model-makers. London, Museum Press [1960 ; 124p. (bibls.) illus. 23cm. (Brompton library) 60-2210 3.75 bds.,
1. tamped: distributed by SportShelf, New Rochelle, N. Y.] 2. Models and modelmaking. I. Title.

WINTER, William John, 1912- 688.1
Handbook of model planes, cars, and boats [by Bill Winter. Greenwich, Conn., Fawcett Publications, 1965] 112 p. illus., ports. 24 cm. Cover title. [TT154.W517] 65-1799
1. Models and modelmaking. I. Title. BIP

Models and modelmaking—Juvenile literature.

BAKER, Frank W. 688.7
31 models from odds and ends. Illus. by Barry surie. Oxford, B. Blackwell [dist. New Rochelle, N.Y., Leisure Time, 1964, c.1958] 67p. illus. 26cm. [TT154.B23] 65-5917 3.00
1. Models and modelmaking—Juvenile literature. 2. Toys—Juvenile literature. 3. Handicraft—Juvenile literature. I. Title.

HILTON, Suzanne 688'.1
It's a model world. Philadelphia, Westminster Press [1972] 128 p. illus. 26 cm. Bibliography: p. 121-124. Describes a wide variety of scale models made by professionals and their use in such fields as architectural design and highway safety. [TT154.G68] 72-76435 ISBN 0-664-32515-7 5.95
1. Models and modelmaking—Juvenile literature. I. Title. BIP

HILTON, Suzanne. 688'.1
It's smart to use a dummy. Philadelphia, Westminster Press [1971] 116 p. illus. 26 cm. Bibiiography: p. 107-110. Describes the construction and function of many types of dummies used in museum displays, mechanical equipment tests, medical experiments, and other areas. [TT154.H54] 78-155902 ISBN 0-664-32500-9 5.50
1. Models and modelmaking—Juvenile literature. 2. Simulation methods—Juvenile literature. I. Title. BIP

SCARBOROUGH, Gerald. 745.59'28
Plastic modelling / [by] Gerald Scarborough. Cambridge (Bar Hill, Cambridge CB3 8EL) : Patrick Stephens

SUBJECT INDEX MODULAR COORDINATION (ARCHITECTURE)

Ltd. [for] Airfix Products Ltd., 1974. 64 p. : ill. ; 23 cm. (Airfix magazine guide ; 1) [TT154.S34] 75-308518 ISBN 0-85059-153-8 : £1.00
1. Models and modelmaking—Juvenile literature. 2. Plastics craft—Juvenile literature. I. Title. BIP

Models and modelmaking— Period.

AMERICAN modeler annual. 745.59
[New York, Street Smith Publications] v. in illus. 29cm. [TT154.A4] 62-42207
1. Models and modelmaking— Period. 2. Aeroplanes—Models—Period.

Models and modelmaking—Periodicals—Indexes.

CARDWELL, Paul. 016.745'28
Index of model periodicals, 1971 through 1975 / by Paul Cardwell, Jr. Metuchen, N.J. : Scarecrow Press, 1977. xxv, 764 p. ; 23 cm. [TT154.C34] 77-1737 ISBN 0-8108-1027-1 : 27.50
1. Models and modelmaking—Periodicals—Indexes. I. Title.

Models, Artists'.

SEGAL, Muriel. 751.3
Painted ladies; models of the great artists. New York, Stein and Day [1972] 184 p. illus. 24 cm. [N7574.S4 1972] 73-187312 ISBN 0-8128-1472-X 7.95
1. Models, Artists'. I. Title.

UPTON, Richard. 769'.924
Models; eight etchings. [Coventry, Conn.] Erebus Press, 1972. 1 portfolio ([12] l., 8 plates) 73 cm. "Edition of fifteen numbered copies ... Copy number X/XV." [NE2012.U65A5] 72-190926
1. Models, Artists'. I. Title.

Models, Artists'—Correspondence, reminiscences, etc.

LINDSAY, Rose. 760'.0924
Model wife; my life with Norman Lindsay. Sydney, London, Ure Smith [1967] 257p. illus., ports. 23cm. [N7405.L5L5] 67-16129 7.50 bds.,
1. Lindsay, Norman. 1879- 2. Models, Artists'—Correspondence, reminiscences, etc. I. Title.
American distributor: Taplinger, New York.

Models (Clay, plaster, etc.)

HAUSER, Christian. 731.4'5
Art foundry. [English version by Julian Snelling and Claude Namy] New York, Van Nostrand Reinhold Co. [1974, c1972] 127 p. illus. (part col.) 18 x 21 cm. (Craft and art) Translation of La fonte d'art. Bibliography: p. 123. [NB1180.H3613 1974] 73-8467 ISBN 0-442-29990-7 7.95
1. Models (Clay, plaster, etc.) 2. Foundry. I. Title.

Models, Fashion.

RENO, Terry. 659.15
The model. Photography by Dan McCoy. New York, McGraw-Hill [1967] 158 p. illus. 22 cm. (A Young pioneer book) (A Week with ... series.) A young model gives a description of her camera world, tells how she got there, and points out the fashion essentials for the beginner and the professional. "78018." [TT505.R4A3] AC 67
1. Models, Fashion. I. Title.

Models, Fashion—Juvenile literature.

RENO, Terry. 659.15'2
The model. Photography by Dan McCoy. New York, McGraw-Hill [1967] 158 p. illus. 22 cm. (A Young pioneer book) A Week with...series. "78018." [TT505.R4A3] 67-16936
1. Models, Fashion—Juvenile literature. I. Title.

Modernism (Aesthetics)—Addresses, essays, lectures.

CALINESCU, Matei. 111.8'5
Faces of modernity : avant-garde, decadence, kitsch / Matei Calinescu. Bloomington : Indiana University Press, c1977. p. cm. Includes index. Bibliography: p. [BH301.M54C34 1977] 77-72194 ISBN 0-253-32087-9 : 15.00
1. Modernism (Aesthetics)—Addresses, essays, lectures. 2. Avant-garde (Aesthetics)—Addresses, essays, lectures. 3. Kitsch (Aesthetics)—Addresses, essays, lectures. 4. Decadence in literature—Addresses, essays, lectures. I. Title. BIP

Modernism (Art)

DUTHUIT, Georges, 1891- 759.91
The Fauvist painters. [Translation by Ralph Manheim] New York, Wittenborn, Schultz [1950] xi, 126 p. plates (part col.) 26 cm. (Documents of modern art, 11) "Bibliography, by Bernard Karpel": p. 102-124. [ND1265.D] A 51
*1. Modernism (Art) 2. Painters. I. Title.*BIP

Modernism (Art)—History.

ROWLAND, Kurt F. 709'.04
A history of the modern movement: art architecture design. New York, Van Nostrand Reinhold [1973] 240 p. illus. 28 cm. [N6447.R68 1973] 73-7117 ISBN 0-442-27172-7 13.50
1. Modernism (Art)—History. I. Title.

Modigliani, Amedeo, 1884-1920.

AMEDEO Modigliani 759.5
(1884-1920) Text by Jacques Lipchitz. New York, H. N. Abrams in association with Pocket Books [1954] [74] p. 64 illus. (part col.) port. 18cm. (The Pocket library of great art, A16) An Abrams art book. Bibliography: p. [74] [ND623.M67L57] 927.5 54-4310
I. Modigliani, Amedeo, 1884-1920. II. Lipchitz, Jacques, 1891-

DIEHL, Gaston. 759.5 B
Modigliani. [Translated from the French by Eileen B. Hennessy] New York, Crown Publishers [1969] 92, [4] p. illus. (part col.) 29 cm. Bibliography: p. [94]-[95] [ND623.M67D513] 76-93407
1. Modigliani, Amadeo, 1884-1920. I. Title. BIP

FIFIELD, William, 1916- 759.5 B
Modigliani / by William Fifield. New York : Morrow, 1976. 317 p., [12] leaves of plates : ill. ; 24 cm. Includes index. [ND623.M67F53] 75-41362 ISBN 0-688-03039-4 : 9.95
1. Modigliani, Amedeo, 1884-1920.

HARVARD University. 741.945
William Hayes Fogg Art Museum.
Modigliani: drawings from the collection of Stefa Leon Brillouin. [Exhibition] 3 Nov.--12 Dec., 1959. Cambridge [1959] 36p. 32plates. 26cm. Bibliography: p. 35-36. [NC257.M6H3] 61-666
1. Modigliani, Amedeo, 1884-1920. I. Brillouin, Stefa. II. Title.

MIDIGLIANI, Amedeo, 1884- 759.5
1920
Modigliani. Introd. by Corrado Pavolini. New York. New Amer. Lib., by arrangement with UNESCO [1966] 24p. illus., port., 32 col. plates. 17cm. (Mentor-Unesco art bk.) MQ697. Bibl. [ND623. M67A49] 66-31707 .95 pap.,
I. Pavolini, Corrado. 1898- II. United Nations Educational, Scientific and Cultural Organization. III. Title.

MODIGLIANI, Amedeo, 1884- 759.5
1920.
Amedeo Modigliani. Text by Jacques Lipchitz. New York, H. N. Abrams [1970] 22 p. illus. (part col.) 33 cm. (The Library of great painters. Portfolio ed.) [ND623.M67L56 1970] 69-14754
I. Lipchitz, Jacques, 1891-

MODIGLIANI, Amedeo, 1884- 759.5
1920.
Amedeo Modigliani. Text by Jacques Lipchitz. Commentaries by Alfred Werner. New York, H. N. Abrams [1969] 40 p. illus. (part col.) 33 cm. (Great art of the ages) [ND623.M67L56 1969] 69-19711 ISBN 0-8109-5124-X
I. Lipchitz, Jacques, 1891- II. Werner, Alfred, 1911-

MODIGLIANI, Amedeo, 1884- 759.5
1920.
Amedeo Modigliani; loan exhibition, October 14-November 13, 1971, for the benefit of the Museum of Modern Art, New York. New York, Acquavella Galleries [1971] [76] p. 52 col. plates. 28 cm. Bibliography: p. [76] [ND623.M67N38] 73-168570
I. New York (City). Museum of Modern Art. II. Acquavella Galleries.

MODIGLIANI, Amedeo, 741.9'45
1884-1920.
The drawings of Modigliani. Introd. by Stephen Longstreet. [1st ed.] Alhambra, Calif., Borden Pub. Co. [1972] [48] p. illus. 31 cm. (Master draughtsman series) [NC257.M6L66] 70-188835
1. Modigliani, Amedeo, 1884-1920. I. Longstreet, Stephen, 1907- II. Title. BIP

MODIGLIANI, Amedeo, 1884- 759.5
1920.
Medigliani. New York, Skira [1955?] [4] p., 6 col. plates (in portfolio) 32cm. [ND623.M67A5] 55-3120
I. Title.

MODIGLIANI, Amedeo, 741.9'45
1884-1920.
Modigliani : disegni / Osvaldo Patani. [Oggiono] : Edizioni della seggiola, 1976. 138, [1] p. : ill. ; 29 cm. (Documenti del disegno ; 1) English, French, and Italian. Bibliography: p. 138-[139] [NC257.M6P37] 77-474520
1. Modigliani, Amedeo, 1884-1920. I. Patani, Osvaldo. II. Title. III. Series.

MODIGLIANI, Jeanne. 927.5
Modigliani: man and myth. Translated from the Italian by Esther Rowland Clifford. New York, Orion Press; distributed by Crown Publishers [1958] 116 p. illus. 25 cm. Includes bibliography. [ND623.M67M63] 759.5 58-13185
1. Modigliani, Amedeo, 1884-1920.

NEW York. Museum of Modern 759.5
Art.
Modigliani; paintings, drawings, sculpture, with an introd. by James Thrall Soby. The Museum of Modern Art, New York, in collaboration with the Cleveland Museum of Art. [New York, 1951] 55 p. illus. (part col.) port. 26 cm. "Catalogue of the exhibition": p. 51-53. Bibliography, by H. B. Muller: p. 54-55. [ND623.M67N4] 51-10620
1. Modigliani, Amedeo, 1884-1920. 2. Art, Italian — Exhibitions. I. Cleveland Museum of Art. II. Soby, James Thrall, 1906- III. Title.

NEW York. Museum of Modern 759.5
Art.
Modigliani; paintings, drawings, sculpture. With an introd. by James Thrall Soby. The Museum of Modern Art, New York in collaboration with the Cleveland Museum of Art. [New York] Published for the Museum of Modern Art by Arno Press, 1972 [c1951] 55 p. illus. 27 cm. Bibliography: p. 54-55. [ND623.M67N4 1972] 73-169318 ISBN 0-405-01576-3
1. Modigliani, Amedeo, 1884-1920. I. Cleveland Museum of Art. II. Soby, James Thrall, 1906-

PAINTINGS, drawings, 759.5
sculpture. With an introd. by James Thrall Soby. New York, Museum of Modern Art [1954] 59p. illus. (part col.) port. 26cm. First published in 1951 with the addition of a catalog for the Modigliani exhibition, held at the Museum of Modern Art, Apr. 10-June 10, 1951. 'Selected bibliography, compiled by Hannah B. Muller': p. 57-58. [ND623.M67N42] 927.5 55-1872
I. Modigliani, Amedeo, 1884-1920. II. Soby, James Thrall, 1906- III. New York. Museum of Modern Art.

ROY, Claude, 1915- 759.5
Modigliani. Translated by James Emmons and Stuart Gilbert. [New York?] Skira [1958] 133p. mounted col. illus. (part fold.) 19cm. (The Taste of our time, 23) Bibliography: p. 123-[124] [ND623.M67R63] 927.5 58-8336
1. Modigliani, Amedeo, 1884-1920. I. Title.

RUSSOLI, Franco. 759.5
Modigliani. Text by Franco Russoli. Pref. by Jean Cocteau. New York, H. N. Abrams [1959] 43, [1] p. illus. (part mounted col.) port. 37 cm. "Catalogues of exhibitions of Modigliani's works": p. 41. Bibliography: p. 42-[44] [ND623.M67R813] 59-14795
1. Modigliani, Amedeo, 1884-1920.

SALMON, Andre, 1881- 759.5
Modigliani, a memoir. [Tr. from French] by Dorothy and Randolph Weaver. New York, Putnam [1961, c.1957, 1961] 216p. illus. (part col.) 61-6898 5.00
1. Modigliani, Amedeo, 1884-1920. I. Title.

SICHEL, Pierre. 759.5
Modigliani; a biography of Amedeo Modigliani. [1st ed.] New York, Dutton, 1967. 597 p. illus., ports. 25 cm. Bibliography: p. 582-588 [ND623.M67S5] 67-11841
1. Modigliani, Amedeo, 1884-1920.

WERNER, Alfred, 1911- 759.4
Modigliani, Utrillo, Soutine, Text and notes by Alfred Werner. New York, Tudor Pub. Co. [1969] 40 p., [94] p. of col. illus. 18 cm. ([Great painters series]) Includes bibliographies. [ND36.W4] 68-30733 2.95
1. Modigliani, Amedeo, 1884-1920. 2. Utrillo, Maurice, 1883-1955. 3. Soutine, Haim, 1894-1943. I. Title.

Modotti, Tina, 1896-1942.

CONSTANTINE, Mildred. 770'.92'4 B
Tina Modotti : a fragile life : an illustrated biography / Mildred Constantine. New York : Paddington Press, [1975] 224 p. : ill. ; 29 cm. Includes index. Bibliography: p. 219. [TR140.M58C66] 73-20956 ISBN 0-8467-0027-1 : 14.95
1. Modotti, Tina, 1896-1942. BIP

Modular coordination (Architecture)

CROCKER, Alan E. 729'.2
Module and metric; the theory and practice of dimensional co-ordination in metric [by] Alan E. Crocker. New York, Praeger [1971] 135 p. illus. 31 cm. Bibliography: p. 133. [TH860.C76] 79-139223 12.50
1. Modular coordination (Architecture) 2. Metric system. I. Title.

DE CHIARA, Joseph, 1929- 729'.2
Time-saver standards for building types. Edited by Joseph DeChiara and John Hancock Callender. New York, McGraw-Hill [1973] xiii, 1065 p. illus. 29 cm. Outgrowth of the 4th ed. of Time saver standards; a handbook of architectural design, containing the material dealing with building types. The original material has been revised, reorganized, and greatly expanded into a completely new handbook. Includes bibliographical references. [NA2760.D42] 73-6663 27.50
1. Modular coordination (Architecture) 2. Building materials—Standards. I. Callender, John Hancock, joint author. II. Title. BIP

JEANNERET-GRIS, Charles 729.2
Edouard, 1887-
The modulor; a harmonious measure to the human scale universally applicable to architecture and mechanics by Le Corbusier [pseud. Translated by Peter de Francis and Anna Bostock. 2d ed.] Cambridge, Harvard University Press, 1958 [c1954] 243p. illus. 20cm. [NA2760.J413 1958] 59-536
1. Modular coordination (Architecture) I. Title.

JEANNERET-GRIS, Charles 729'.23
Edouard 1887-1965.
The modulor; a harmonious measure to the human scale, universally applicable to architecture and mechanics, by Le Corbusier. Translated by Peter de Francia and Anna Bostock. [2d ed.] Cambridge, Mass., M.I.T. Press [1968, c1954] 243 p. illus., facsims., plans. 19 cm. Bibliographical footnotes. [NA2760.J413 1968] 68-25376 3.45

1. Modular coordination (Architecture) I. Title.

JEANNERET-GRIS, Charles Edouard 1887-1965. 729'.23
Modulor 2, 1955 (let the user speak next) by Le Corbusier Translated by Peter de Francia and Anna Bostock. Cambridge, Mass., M.I.T. Press [1968, c1958] 336 p. illus., facsims., plans. 19 cm. [NA2760.J4213 1968] 68-6765 3.45
1. Modular coordination (Architecture) I. Title. **BIP**

MODULAR Building Standards Association. 729.2
Modular practice; the schoolhouse and the building industry. Editorial team: Robert P. Darlington, Chief editor, Melvin W. Isenberg, associate editor [and] David A. Pierce, associate editor. New York, Wiley [1962] 198p. illus. 29cm. [NA2760.M6] 62-109181
1. Modular coordination (Architecture) 2. Architecutre—Designs and plans. 3. Building. 4. School-houses. I. Darlington, Robert P., ed. II. Title.

ROYAL Institute of British Architects, London. 729.23
The coordination of dimensions for building London, Royal Institute of British Architects [1965] 87 p. diagrs. 30 1/2 cm. 35 - Bibliography: p. 72-83. [TH860.R6] 66-70258
1. Modular coordination (Architiecture) I. Title.

UNITED Nations. Dept. of Economic and Social Affairs. 729.23
Modular co-ordination in building: Asia, Europe and the Americas. New York, United Nations, 1966. v, 67 p. illus., map. 28 cm. ([United Nations. Document] ST/SOA/62/E/C.6/36/add.9/rev.1) "United Nations publication. Sales no.: 66.IV.4." "Prepared by ... Lennart Bergvall ... and by the Centre for Housing, Building and Planning." Glossary (in English, French and Spanish) of terms for modular co-ordination: p. 66-67. [JX1977.A2 ST/SOA/62/E/C.6/36/add.9/rev.1] 66-31586
1. Modular coordination (Architecture) I. Bergvall, Lennart. II. United Nations. Centre for Housing, Building and Planning. III. Title. IV. Series.

UNITED Nations. Working Group on Modular Co-ordination in Housing. 729*.2
Report. New York, United Nations, 1965. iv, 52 p. illus. 28 cm. (United Nations. [Document] ST/TAO/ser.C/59/rev.1; E/CN.12/CCE/SC.4/rev.2; E/C.6/36/add.8) At head of title: Department of Economic and Social Affairs. Report of a meeting of the working group sponsored by the Economic Commission for Latin America and others. [JX1977.A2 ST/T/TAO/ser.C/59/rev.1, etc,] 72-9362
1. Modular coordination (Architecture) I. United Nations. Dept. of Economic and Social Affairs. II. United Nations. Economic Commission for Latin America. III. Series: United Nations. Document ST/TAO/ser.C/59/rev.1. IV. Series: United Nations. Document E/CN.12/CCE/SC.4/rev.2. V. Series: United Nations. Document E/C.6/36/add.8

Modular coordination (Architecture)—Congresses.

SYMPOSIUM on Dimensional Coordination, Dublin, 1975. 721
Dimensional coordination in building : a review : proceedings of a symposium held in the Gresham Hotel, Dublin on August 26, 1975, under the auspices of An Foras Forbartha / [edited by Aodhagan Brioscu]. Dublin : Foras Forbartha, 1976. 84 p. : ill. ; 30 cm. Cover title: Comhordu toiseach. san bhfoirgniocht — Dimensional coordination in building. [NA2760.S94 1975] 77-364639 ISBN 0-900115-85-8 : £1.50
1. Modular coordination (Architecture)—Congresses. I. Brioscu, Aodhagan. II. Foras Forbartha. III. Title. IV. Title: Comhordu toiseach. san bhfoirgniocht.

Moffett, Ross.

MOFFETT, Ross. 760'.092'4
Ross Moffett 1888-1971 : Worcester Art Museum, May 30-July 6,1975, Provincetown Art association,August 29September 29,1975 [Worcester, Mass.] : Worcester Art Museum, 1975. [30] p. : ill. ; 18 x 23 cm. Cover title. Exhibition catalog by J. C. Del Deo. [N6537.M63D44] 75-327912
1. Moffett, Ross. I. Del Deo, Josephine Couch. II. Worcester, Mass. Art Museum. III. Provincetown Art Association.

Mogollon culture.

GIAMMATTEI, Victor Michael. 738.3'7
Art of a vanished race : the Mimbres classic black-on-white / by Victor Michael Giammattei and Nanci Greer Reichert ; drawings rendered by Darcy Paige. Woodland, CA : Dillon-Tyler, 1975. 15 p., 40 leaves of plates : chiefly ill. ; 30 cm. Bibliography: p. 15. [E99.M76G5] 75-28600 ISBN 0-916280-00-4 : 5.95
1. Mogollon culture. 2. Indians of North America—Southwest, New—Pottery. 3. Indians of North America—Southwest, New—Art. I. Reichert, Nanci Greer, joint author. II. Paige, Darcy. III. Title. **BIP**

SNODGRASS, Oliver Theodore, 1902- 738.3'83
Realistic art and times of the Mimbres Indians / by O. T. Snodgrass. El Paso, Tex. : Snodgrass, c1975. iv, 181 p. : ill. ; 28 cm. Bibliography: p. 179-181. [E78.N65S62] 75-328240
1. Mogollon culture. 2. Indians of North America—New Mexico—Pottery. 3. Indians of North America—New Mexico—Art. I. Title.

WESCHE, Alice. 743'.6
Wild brothers of the Indians : as pictured by the ancient Americans / Alice Wesche. Tucson, Ariz. : Treasure Chest Publications, c1977. 56 p. : ill. ; 28 cm. [E99.M76W46] 77-79064 ISBN 0-918080-21-5 : 4.95
1. Mogollon culture. 2. Indians—Art. 3. Drawing—Technique. 4. Animals in art. I. Title. **BIP**

Mohamed, Ethel Wright.

MOHAMED, Ethel Wright. 746.3'92'4
My life in pictures / Ethel Wright Mohamed ; edited by Charlotte Capers and Olivia P. Collins. Jackson : Mississippi Dept. of Archives and History, 1976. 40 p. : col. ill. ; 26 cm. [NK9298.M63A25] 77-356180
1. Mohamed, Ethel Wright. 2. Family in art. 3. Embroidery—Mississippi. I. Title.

Moholy-Nagy, Laszlo, 1895-1946.

KOSTELANETZ, Richard, comp. 709'.24
Moholy-Nagy. New York, Praeger [1970] xviii, 238 p. illus. (part col.), port. 23 cm. (Documentary monographs in modern art) Contributions chiefly by L. Moholy-Nagy. Bibliography: p. 223-233. [N7454.M6K6 1970] 70-121715 12.50
I. Moholy-Nagy, Laszlo, 1895-1946. **BIP**

MOHOLY-NAGY, Dorothea Maria Pauline Alice Sibylle Pietzsch, 927
Moholy-Nagy, experiment in totality. With an introd. by Walter Gropius. [1st ed.] New York, Harper [1950] ix, 253 p. illus. (part col.) ports. 25 cm. [N6838.M6M6] 50-8091
1. Moholy-Nagy, Laszlo, 1895-1946.

MOHOLY-NAGY, Dorothea Maria Pauline Alice Sibylle (Pietzsch) 759.39'1 B
Moholy-Nagy: experiment in totality [by] Sibyl Moholy-Nagy. With an introd. by Walter Gropius. [2d ed.] Cambridge, Mass., M.I.T. Press [1969] xvii, 259 p. illus. (part col.), ports. 25 cm. Bibliography: p. 253. Bibliographical footnotes. [N6838.M6M6 1969] 69-20265
1. Moholy-Nagy, Laszlo, 1895-1946.

MOHOLY-NAGY, Laszlo, 1895-1946. 779'.092'4
Photographs of Moholy-Nagy from the collection of William Larson / edited by Leland D. Rice and David W. Steadman. [Claremont, Calif.] : Galleries of the Claremont Colleges, 1975. 64 p. : chiefly ill. ; 28 cm. Catalogue of an exhibition held at the Galleries of the Claremont Colleges, Apr. 4-May 8, 1975; San Francisco Museum of Art, July 8-Aug. 24, 1975; University Art Museum, University of New Mexico, Sept. 28-Nov. 2, 1975. Bibliography: p. 61, 63. [TR647.M56A54] 75-4035 ISBN 0-915478-08-0
1. Moholy-Nagy, Laszlo, 1895-1946. 2. Photography, Artistic—Exhibitions. I. Claremont College, Claremont, Calif. Galleries. II. San Francisco. Museum of Art. III. New Mexico. University. Art Museum. IV. Title.

Mola, Pier Francesco, 1612-1666.

COCKE, Richard. 759.5
Pier Francesco Mola. Oxford, Clarendon Press, 1972. xiv, 93 p. 147 illus. 30 cm. (Oxford studies in the history of art and architecture) Bibliography: p. 77-84. [ND623.M674C6] 72-180533 ISBN 0-19-817175-7 £6.75
1. Mola, Pier Francesco, 1612-1666. I. Title. II. Series.

Molas.

PARKER, Ann. 746.9
Molas : folk art of the Cuna Indians / Ann Parker & Avon Neal ; photos. by Ann Parker. Barre, Mass. : Barre Pub. ; New York : distributed by Crown Publishers, 1977. 250 p. : ill. (some col.) ; 25 x 27 cm. Bibliography: p. 244-248. [F1565.2.C8P3 1977] 77-21739 ISBN 0-517-52911-4 : 25.00
1. Molas. I. Neal, Avon, joint author. II. Title. **BIP**

Molas—Exhibitions.

WASHINGTON, D.C. Textile Museum. 746.9
Molas: art of the Cuna Indians. [Edited and designed by Jeannette R. Mueller. Washington] Circulated by the international Exhibitions Foundation, 1973. 27 p. illus. 22 x 28 cm. At head of title: Under the patronage of the Ambassador of Panama and Mrs. Nicolas Gonzales-Revilla. Catalog of an exhibition held Apr. 3-Sept. 9, 1973, at the Textile Museum of Washington, D.C. Bibliography: p. 27. [F1565.2.C8W3] 73-161539
1. Molas—Exhibitions. 2. Cuna Indians—Art—Exhibitions. 3. Cuna Indians—Textile industry and fabrics—Exhibitions. 4. Indians of Central America—Panama—Art—Exhibitions. 5. Indians of Central America—Panama—Textile industry and fabrics—Exhibitions. I. Mueller, Jeanette R., ed. II. Title.

Molinari, Amanda—Medal collections.

BOWDOIN College. Museum of Art. 737.4'9'74191
Medals and plaquettes from the Molinari collection at Bowdoin College / by Andres S. Norris & Ingrid Weber ; with an introd. to the medals catalogue by Graham Pollard. Brunswick, Me. : [Bowdoin College Museum of Art], 1976. xi, 292 p. : ill. ; 29 cm. Published on the occasion of an exhibition of the collection held Apr. 21-May 23, 1976. Includes bibliographical references and indexes. [CJ5510.U62B783] 75-44691 ISBN 0-916606-00-7 : 40.00
1. Molinari, Amanda—Medal collections. 2. Medals—Europe. 3. Plaques, plaquettes—Europe. I. Norris, Andrea S. II. Weber, Ingrid. III. Title. **BIP**

Molinari, Guido, 1933—

THEBERGE, Pierre. 759.11 B
Guido Molinari : [exposition : catalogue] / par Pierre Theberge. Ottawa : Galerie nationale du Canada, 1976. vii, 160 p. : ill. (some col.) ; 26 cm. English and French. Bibliography: p. 153-159. [N6549.M6T48] 77-457773 ISBN 0-88884-307-0
1. Molinari, Guido, 1933- 2. Artists—Canada—Biography. I. Molinari, Guido, 1933- II. National Gallery of Canada.

Monachesi, Sante, 1910-

MONACHESI: 730.945
sculture, con testi e testimonianze di Alfredo Anitori [et al.] e con un primo catalogo delle opere. [Millano] B. Alfieri [1966] [60] p. illus., 77 plates (12 col.) port. 23x25cm. Stamped on t. p.: Amer. dist.: Wittenborn, New York. Italian, English and/or French. Bibl. [NB623.M63A6] 66-8513 10.00 bds.,
1. Monachesi, Sante, 1910- I. Anitori, Alfredo.

Monadnock, Mount, in art.

THE Grand 769'.4'99174272
Monadnock; [a literary, artistic & social history] An exhibition at the Louise E. Thorne Art Gallery, Keene State College, Keene, N.H. from June 23 to August 3, 1974, in cooperation with the Society for the Protection of New Hampshire Forests. [Concord, Society for the Protection of New Hampshire Forests, 1974] 48 p. illus. 26 cm. [NX653.M66G72] 74-178251
1. Monadnock, Mount, in art. 2. Arts, American—Exhibitions. 3. Artists—New England. 4. Monadnock, Mount. I. Louise E. Thorne Art Gallery. II. Society for the Protection of New Hampshire Forests.

Monasteries.

BRAUNFELS, Wolfgang. 726'.7'094
Monasteries of Western Europe; the architecture of the orders. [3d ed. Princeton, N.J.] Princeton University Press [1973, c1972] 263 p. illus. 30 cm. Includes "Selections from documentary sources" with parallel Latin text and English translation. Translation of Abendlandische Klosterbaukunst. Bibliography: p. 251-254. [NA4850.B713 1973] 73-2472 ISBN 0-691-03896-1 25.00
1. Monasteries. I. Title. **BIP**

Monasteries—Egypt—Natrun Valley.

EVELYN-WHITE, Hugh Gerard, d.1924. 913.32
The monasteries of the Wadi 'n Natrun. New York, Metropolitan Museum of Art, Egyptian Expedition, 1926-[33. New York] Arno Press, 1973. 3 v. illus. 32 cm. Original ed. issued as v. 2, 4, and 8 of Publications of the Metropolitan Museum of Art, Egyptian Expedition. Contents.Contents.—pt. 1. New Coptic texts from the Monastery of Saint Macarius, edited with an introd. on the Library at the Monastery of Saint Macarius; with an appendix on a Copto-Arabic ms. by G. P. G. Sobhy.—pt. 2. The history of the monasteries of Nitria and Scetis, edited by W. Hauser.—pt. 3. The architecture and archaeology, edited by W. Hauser. Includes bibliographies. [DT73.N28E92] 77-168409 ISBN 0-405-02242-5
1. Saint Macarius (Monastery) 2. Monasteries—Egypt—Natrun Valley. 3. Coptic language—Texts. I. Hauser, Walter, 1893- ed. II. Title. III. Series: New York (City). Metropolitan Museum of Art. Egyptian Expedition. Publications, v. 2 [etc.] **BIP**

PANAGOPOULOS, Beata Maria, 1925- 726'.7'09495
Cistercian and mendicant monasteries in medieval Greece / Beata Kitsiki Panagopoulos. Chicago : University of Chicago Press, 1979. p. cm. Includes index. Bibliography: p. [NA5593.P36] 78-10769 ISBN 0-226-64544-4 lib. bdg. : 24.00
1. Monasteries—Greece, Medieval. 2. Architecture, Cistercian—Greece, Medieval. 3. Achitecture, Gothic—Greece, Medieval. 4. Church architecture—Greece, Medieval. I. Title. **BIP**

Monasteries—Europe.

SITWELL, Sacheverell 726.7094
Monks, nuns, and monasteries. New York, Holt [c.1965] xiii, 205p. illus. (pt. col.) ports. 26cm. [NA4850.S5] 65-21951 12.50
1. Monasteries—Europe. 2. Convents and nunneries—Europe. 3. Architecture—Europe. I. Title.

SUBJECT INDEX MONEY.

SITWELL, Sacheverell, Sir, bart., 1897- 726.7094
Monks, nuns, and monasteries. [1st ed.] New York, Holt, Rinehart and Winston [1965] xiii, 205 p. illus. (part col.) ports. 26 cm. [NA4850.S5] 65-21951
1. Monasteries—Europe. 2. Convents and nunneries—Europe. 3. Architecture—Europe. I. Title.

Monasteries—France.

EVANS, Joan, 1893- 726.70944
Monastic architecture in France, from the Renaissance to the Revolution. [New York] Cambridge [c.]1964. xlii, 186p. 827 illus. (incl. plans) 29cm. Bibl. 64-2430 27.50
1. Monasteries—France. 2. Architecture—France—Hist. I. Title.

EVANS, Joan, 1893- 726.70944
Monastic architecture in France, from the Renaissance to the Revolution. Cambridge [Eng.] University Press, 1964. xiii, 186 p. 827 illus. (incl. plans) 29 cm. Bibliography: p. 153-158. [NA5544.E8] 64-2430
1. Monasteries — France. 2. Architecture — France — Hist. I. Title.

Monastic libraries—Italy.

O'GORMAN, James F. 726'.79
The architecture of the monastic library in Italy, 1300-1600; catalogue with introductory essay [by] James F. O'Gorman. New York, New York University Press for the College Art Association of America, 1972. xvi, 81 p., [31] p. of illus. 29 cm. (Monographs on archaeology and the fine arts, 25) Based on the author's thesis, Harvard, 1966. Bibliography: p. 76-81. [Z675.M7O37 1972] 72-75004 ISBN 0-8147-6152-6
1. Monastic libraries—Italy. 2. Library architecture—Italy—History. 3. Architecture, Renaissance—Italy. I. Title. II. Series. BIP

Mondriaan, Pieter Cornelis, 1872-1944.

BUSIGNANI, Alberto. 759.9492
Mondrian [the life and the work of the artist, illustrated with 80 full-color plates. Translated from the Italian by Caroline Beamish. 1st American ed.] New York, Grosset & Dunlap [1968] 39 p. illus., col. plates. 18 cm. (The New Grosset art library, 13) Bibliography: p. 29-32. [ND653.M76B83 1968b] 68-26687

ELGAR, Frank. 759.9492
Mondrian. [Translated from the French by Thomas Walton] New York, Praeger [1968] 255 p. 208 illus. (part col.) 22 cm. (A Praeger world of art profile) Bibliography: p. 231-233. [ND653.M76E43] 68-54499 7.50
1. Mondriaan, Pieter Cornelis, 1872-1944. I. Title.

JAFFE, Hans Ludwig C. 759.9492
Piet Mondrian. Text by Hans L. C. Jaffe. New York, H. N. Abrams [1970] 163 p. illus. (part col.) 34 cm. (The Library of great painters) Bibliography: p. 161-[164] [ND653.M76J3213 1970b] 70-95192 ISBN 0-8109-0325-3
1. Mondriaan, Pieter Cornelis, 1872-1944. I. Mondriaan, Pieter Cornelis, 1872-1944.

MONDRIAAN, Pieter Cornelis, 1872-1944. 759.9492
Mondrian. [Text by Sam Hunter] [New York] [H.N. Abrams] [1958] [38] p. illus. (part mounted col.) 37 cm. (An Abrams art book) In portfolio; title from cover. [ND653.M76H8] 58-9036
I. Hunter, Sam, 1923-

MONDRIAAN, Pieter Cornelis, 1872-1944. 759.9492
Mondrian [by] Italo Tomassoni. [Translated from the Italian] London, New York, Hamlyn, 1970. 96 p. illus. (some col.), port. 32 cm. (Twentieth-century masters) Distributed in U.S. by Crown Publishers. Translation of Piet Mondrian. Bibliography: p. 96. [ND653.M76T5713] 73-851789 ISBN 0-600-35925-5 £1.75
I. Tomassoni, Italo.

MONDRIAAN, Pieter Cornelis, 1872-1944. 759.9492
Mondrian. Introd. by Harry Holtzman. [New York, Pace Editions, 1970] 48 p. illus. (part col.), port. 23 cm. On cover: Mondrian: the process works. Exhibition held at the Pace Gallery, New York, Apr. 11-May 16, 1970 and Los Angeles County Museum, Los Angeles, Calif., July 14-Aug. 30, 1970. [ND653.M76A52] 79-130804
I. Pace Gallery. II. Los Angeles Co., Calif. Museum, Los Angeles. III. Title: Mondrian: the process works.

MONDRIAAN, Pieter Cornelis, 1872-1944. 741.9'492
Mondrian. Introd. by Harry Holtzman. [New York, Pace Editions, c1970] 64 p. illus. (part col.), ports. 23 cm. On cover: Mondrian: the process works. Exhibition held at the Pace Gallery, New York, April 11-May 16, 1970, and Los Angeles County Museum, Los Angeles, Calif., July 14-Aug. 30, 1970. [ND653.M76A52 1970b] 72-27438
I. Pace Gallery. II. Los Angeles Co., Calif. Museum, Los Angeles. III. Title: Mondrian: the process works.

WELSH, Robert P. 759.9492
Piet Mondrian's early career : the "naturalistic" periods / Robert P. Welsh. New York : Garland Pub., 1977. xvi, 232 p., [67] leaves of plates : ill. ; 21 cm. (Outstanding dissertations in the fine arts) Reprint of the ed. originally presented as the author's thesis, Princeton University, 1965. Bibliography: p. 228-232. [ND653.M76W4 1977] 76-23659 ISBN 0-8240-2738-8 lib.bdg. : 40.00
1. Mondriaan, Pieter Cornelis, 1872-1944. 2. Painters—Netherlands—Biography. I. Title. II. Series. BIP

Mondriaan, Pieter Cornelis, 1872-1944—Aesthetics.

CHANDLER, Arthur. 750'.117
The aesthetics of Piet Mondrian. New York, MSS Information Corp. [1972] 67 p. 23 cm. Includes bibliographical references. [ND653.M76C45] 72-7934 ISBN 0-8422-0266-8 3.75
1. Mondriaan, Pieter Cornelis, 1872-1944—Aesthetics. I. Title.

MONDRIAAN, Pieter Cornelis, 1872-1944. 759.9492
Piet Mondrian. Text by Sam Hunter. New York, H. N. Abrams [1971] 24 p. illus. (part col.) 33 cm. (The Library of great painters. Portfolio ed.) Originally published under title: Mondrian. [ND653.M76H8 1971] 78-130284 ISBN 0-8109-3047-1
I. Hunter, Sam, 1923- II. Title.

MONDRIAAN, Pieter Cornelis, 1872-1944. 759.9'492
Piet Mondrian, 1872-1944: centennial exhibition [held at] the Solomon R. Guggenheim Museum, New York. [New York, Solomon R. Guggenheim Foundation, 1971] 223 p. illus. (part col.) 28 cm. Bibliography: p. 218-219. [ND653.M76S6] 71-180663
I. Solomon R. Guggenheim Museum, New York. II. Title.

WIJSENBEEK, Louis Jacob Florus, 1912- 759.9492
Piet Mondrian, by L. J. F. Wijsenbeek. Translated from the Dutch by Irene R. Gibbons. Greenwich, Conn., New York Graphic Society [1968] 186 p. illus., plates (part col.) 26 cm. Bibliography: p. 167-176. [ND653.M76W513] 69-19514 13.50
I. Mondriaan, Pieter Cornelis, 1872-1944. II. Title.

Monet, Claude, 1840-1926.

COGNIAT, Raymond, 1896- 759.4
Claude Monet. Translated from the French by Anne Ross. New York, Crown Publishers [1969] 45 p. illus. (part col.) 19 cm. (Basic art library) [ND553.M7C5813] 77-87936 1.00
1. Monet, Claude, 1840-1926.

COGNIAT, Raymond, 1896- 759.4
Monet and his world. [Translated from the French by Wayne Dynes] New York, Viking Press [1966] 143 p. illus., col. plates, ports. 24 cm. (A Studio book) [ND553.M7C623 1966a] 66-11828
1. Monet, Claude, 1840-1926. I. Title.

ISAACSON, Joel. 759.4
Monet: le dejeuner sur l'herbe. [New York, Viking Press, 1972] 124 p. illus. 23 cm. (Art in context) Bibliography: p. [121]-122. [ND553.M7I8 1972] 78-165931 ISBN 0-670-48497-0 7.50
1. Monet, Claude, 1840-1926. Picnic. I. Title.

LEVINE, Steven Z. 759.4
Monet and his critics / Steven Z. Levine. New York : Garland Pub., 1976. 471 p., [1] leaf of plates : ill. ; 21 cm. (Outstanding dissertations in the fine arts) Originally presented as the author's thesis, Harvard, 1974. Includes indexes. Bibliography: p. [441]-461. [ND553.M7L48 1976] 75-23800 ISBN 0-8240-1995-4 lib.bdg. : 30.00
1. Monet, Claude, 1840-1926. I. Title. II. Series. BIP

MONET at Giverny / 759.4 B
text by Claire Joyes ; photographic and editorial research by Robert Gordon and Jean-Marie Toulgouat ; with a commentary on the paintings at Giverny, by Andrew Forge. New York : Two Continents Pub. Group, 1976, c1975. p. cm. Includes index. Bibliography: p. [ND553.M7M56 1976] 76-16720 ISBN 0-8467-0200-2 : 16.95
1. Monet, Claude, 1840-1926. 2. Monet, Claude, 1840-1926—Homes and haunts—France—Giverny. I. Joyes, Claire. II. Monet, Claude, 1840-1926. BIP

MONET, Claude, 1840-1926. 759.4
Claude Monet. New York, R. L. Feigen [1969] 70 p. illus. (part col.) 25 cm. Exhibition, October 15—November 15, 1969, for the benefit of the Metropolitan Museum of Art held by R. L. Feigen & Co. [ND553.M7A43] 74-104952
I. Richard L. Feigen & Co.

MONET, Claude, 1840-1926. 759.4
Claude Monet. Text by William C. Seitz. New York, H. N. Abrams [1971] 24 p. illus. (part col.) 33 cm. (The Library of great painters. Portfolio ed.) Originally published under title: Monet (1840-1926) [ND553.M7S43 1971] 72-130288 ISBN 0-8109-3048-X
I. Seitz, William Chapin. II. Title.

MONET, Claude, 1840-1926. 759.4
Claude Monet, 1840-1926. Text by Margaretta Salinger. New York, H. N. Abrams [1957] unpaged. illus. 17cm. (Pocket library of great art, A29) [ND553.M7S26] 927.5 58-4089
I. Salinger, Margaretta, 1907- II. Title.

MONET, Claude, 1840-1926 759.4
Monet, by Henri Dumont [pseud.] New York, Crown [1963] 36p. chiefly illus. (pt. col.) 18cm. (Little bks. on great artists) French, English and German. 63-3143 .69 bds.,
I. Immerman, Irene. II. Title.

MONET, Claude, 1840-1926. 759.4
Monet / John House. Oxford : [Eng.] : Phaidon ; New York : Dutton, 1977. 16 p., [24] leaves of plates : chiefly col. ill. ; 31 cm. Bibliography: p. 14. [ND553.M7H65] 77-78376 ISBN 0-7148-1809-7 : 7.95
1. Monet, Claude, 1840-1926. I. House, John.

MONET, Claude, 1840-1926. 759.4
Observation and reflection / Claude Monet ; [text by] Isaacson. Oxford : Phaidon ; New York : Dutton, 1978. 240 p. : ill. (some col.) ; 29 cm. Includes index. Bibliography: p. 234-253. [ND553.M7A4 1978b] 77-93079 ISBN 0-7148-1781-3 : 39.95
1. Monet, Claude, 1840-1926. I. Isaacson, Joel. II. Title. BIP

MONET, Claude, 1840-1926. 759.4
Paintings by Monet : [exhibition] March 15 through May 11, 1975, The Art Institute of Chicago / foreword by John Maxon ; edited by Susan Wise ; essays by Andre Masson, Grace Seiberling, J. Patrice Marandel. Chicago : Art Institute of Chicago, 1975. 179 p. : ill. ; 26 cm. "Catalogue" : p. 53-179. Bibliography: p. 40. [ND553.M7W57] 74-15412
1. Monet, Claude, 1840-1926. I. Wise, Susan. II. Chicago. Art Institute. III. Title.

MOUNT, Charles Merrill. 759.4
Monet, a biography. New York, Simon and Schuster [1967, c1966] 444 p. illus., ports. 25 cm. Bibliographical references included in "Notes" (p. 395-427) [ND553.M7M6] 66-24032
1. Monet, Claude, 1840-1926.

NEW York Museum of Modern Art. 759.4
Claude Monet: Reasons and moments by William C. seitz in collaboration with The Museum of Modern Art, New York. Garden City, N.Y. dist. Doubleday [1960] 64p. illus. (part col.) 24cm. 'Exhibition dates: the Museum of Modern art. . . March 9-May 15, 1960; Los Angeles County Museum, June 14-August 7, 1960.' 60-9682 3.50; 1.95 pap.,
1. Monet, Claude, 1840-1926. I. Seitz, William Chapin. II. Title.

NEW York. Museum of Modern Art. 759.4
Claude Monet: seasons and moments, by William C. Seitz. Reprint ed. [New York] Published for the Museum of Modern Art by Arno Press, 1969. 64 p. illus. 25 cm. Issued in connection with the exhibition held Mar. 9-May 15, 1960, in the Museum of Modern Art, New York, and June 14-Aug. 7, 1960, in the Los Angeles County Museum. [ND553.M7N4 1969] 72-86446
1. Monet, Claude, 1840-1926. I. Seitz, William Chapin. II. Los Angeles Co., Calif. Museum, Los Angeles.

ROUART, Denis. 759.4
Claude Monet. [Introd. and conclusion by Leon Degand. Historical and critical study by Denis Rouart. Translated by James Emmons. New York] Skira [1958] 129 p. mounted col. illus. 19 cm. (The Taste of our time, 25) Bibliography: p. 117-[118] [ND553.M7R65] 58-12920
1. Monet, Claude, 1840-1926. I. Degand, Leon.

SEITZ, William Chapin 759.4
Claude Monet. New York, H. N. Abrams 1960[ ] 158, 2p. illus.(part mounted col.) ports 33cm. (The Library of great painters) Bibl. 60-7800 .[160] 15.00 buck.,
1. Monet, Claude, 1840-1926. I. Title. BIP

TAILLANDIER, Yvon 759.4
Monet. [Tr. from French by A. P. H. Hamilton] New York, Crown [1963] 94p. col. illus. (pt. mounted) 29cm. Bibl. 63-24889 3.50 bds.,
1. Monet, Claude, 1840-1926. I. Title. BIP

WEEKES, C. P. 759.4
The invincible Monet. New York, Appleton-Century-Crofts [c.1960] viii, 244p. b(Bibl. p.242-244) 21cm. 60-13068 4.50 half cloth.,
1. Monet, Claude, 1840-1926. 2. Impressionism (Art) I. Title.

WILDENSTEIN, Daniel, 1917- 759.4
Monet; impressions. [Translated by Diana Imber] New York, French & European Publications [1967] 66 p. col. illus. 21 cm. (Rhythm and colour, no. 10) [ND553.M7W5313] 68-1830
1. Monet, Claude, 1840-1926. I. Title. II. Title: Impressions.

WILDENSTEIN, Daniel, 1917- 750.92
Monet; impressions. [Translated by Diana Imber] New York, French & European Publications [1967] 66 p. col. illus. 21 cm. (Rhythm and colour, no. 10) [ND553.M7W5313] 759.4 68-1830
1. Monet, Claude, 1840-1926. I. Title: Impressions.

Money.

EVANS, Eva (Knox) 1905- 737.4
The adventure book of money. Illus. [by] Raymond Burns; photography [by] Aldo Vinai. [New York] Capitol Pub. Co. [1956] 93 p. illus. 26 cm. Information for beginning coin collectors, covering starting a collection, the history of coins, foreign coins, cleaning and storing a collection, counterfeit money, tokens and medals, and aids for the collector. [HG221.5.E9] AC 68
1. Money. 2. Coins—Collectors and collecting. I. Burns, Raymond, illus. II. Title.

Money—Hawaiian Islands.

GOULD, Maurice M. 737.49969
1960 catalog of Hawaiian coins, tokens, and paper money; an illustrated history and price list of the coins, tokens, medals, patterns, paper money, and transportation tokens that were once issued for use in our 50th State—1836 to date, by Maurice M. Gould and Kenneth Bresset. Racine, Wis., Whitman Pub. Co. [1960] 45 p. illus. 19 cm. [CJ4634.G6] 60-1371
1. Money—Hawaiian Islands. I. Bressett, Kenneth. II. Title: Hawaiian coins, tokens, and paper money.

Money—Juvenile literature.

EVANS, Eva (Knox) 737.4
The question and answer book of coins. Illus. by Raymond Burns. Photogs. by Alfo Vinai. New York, Capitol [dist.] Golden [1963, c.1956] 96p. illus. 26cm. (Question & answer bks., 5103) Bibl. .50 pap.,
1. Money—Juvenile literature. I. Title.

WITTE, Eva (Knox) 1905- 737.4
The adventure book of money. Raymond Burns, illus.; Aldo Vinai, photography. [New York] Capitol Pub. Co. [1956] 93p. illus. 26cm. [HG221.5.W5] 56-11308
1. Money—Juvenile literature. I. Title.

Money, Primitive.

RIDGEWAY, William, Sir, 737.4'09
1853-1926.
The origin of metallic currency and weight standards. Detroit, Singing Tree Press, 1970. xii, 417 p. illus. 22 cm. Reprint of the 1892 ed. Includes bibliographical references. [HG235.R6 1970] 73-78221
1. Money, Primitive. 2. Weights and measures—History. I. Title.

Money—Puerto Rico.

GOULD, Maurice M. 737.4075
1962 catalog of the money of Puerto Rico, an illustrated history and price list of the coins, tokens and paper money which were once issued for use in the Commonwealth that may someday become our 51st State, by Maurice M. Gould Lincoln W. Higgie. Racine, Wis., Whitman [c.1962] 83p. illus. 20cm. 62-5580 1.00 flexible bds.,
1. Money—Puerto Rico. I. Higgie, Lincoln W., joint author. II. Title. III. Title: The money of Puerto Rico.

Money—Rome.

SUTHERLAND, Carol 737.49'37
Humphrey Vivian.
Coinage in Roman imperial policy, 31 B.C.-A.D. 68, by C. H. V. Sutherland. New York, Barnes & Noble [1971] xi, 220 p. illus. 23 cm. Reprint of the 1951 ed. Includes bibliographical references. [HG237.S8 1971] 75-24781 ISBN 0-389-04146-7
1. Money—Rome. 2. Coinage—Rome. I. Title.

Mongols in art.

MARTIN, Conny. 915'.03'2
The world of Genghis and Kubilai Khan. Lubbock, Tex., First National Bank, c1968. [29] p. (incl. cover) illus. (part col.) 25 cm. Bibliography: p. [29] [ND237.M2464M58] 76-19944
1. Mongols in art. I. Title.

Monk Bretton priory.

GREAT Britain. Ministry 914.28'25
of Public Building and Works.
Monk Bretton priory, Yorkshire / ... by the late Rose Graham ... [and] R. Gilyard-Beer. London : H.M.S.O., 1976. 23 p., fold. plate : ill., coat of arms, map ; 22 cm. (Department of the Environment official handbook) (Department of the Environment ancient monuments and historic buildings) Originally published in 1966. [NA5469.Y55G73 1976] 77-358291 ISBN 0-11-670025-4 : £0.25
1. Monk Bretton priory. I. Graham, Rose, 1875- II. Gilyard-Beer, R. III. Title. IV. Series: Great Britain. Dept. of the Environment. Official handbook — Great Britain, Dept. of the Environment. V. Series: Great Britain. Dept. of the Environment. Ancient monuments and historic buildings.

Monnier, Henri Bonaventure, 1799-1877.

MELCHER, Edith, 1901- 927.41
The life and times by Henry Monnier, 1799-1877. Cambridge, Harvard University Press, 1950. xiv, 253 p. illus., ports. 22 cm. Bibliography: p.[223]-235. [NC1499.M6M4] 50-7071
1. Monnier, Henri Bonaventure, 1799-1877. I. Title.

Monograms.

BERGLING, John Mauritz, 745.6
1866-1933
Art monograms and lettering; an encyclopedia of monograms for the use of engravers, designers, and all lovers of art. 20th ed., complete 1964 de luxe vol. Coral Gables 34, Fla., V. C. Bergling, Box 34-523 [c.1908-1964] 110p. illus. 28cm. 63-22577 10.00
1. Monograms. 2. Lettering. I. Title. BIP

CIRKER, Hayward, comp. 745.6'1
Monograms and alphabetic devices. Edited by Hayward and Blanche Cirker. New York, Dover Publications [1970] 227 p. illus. 28 cm. (Dover Pictorial archive series) [NK3640.C48 1970] 74-78827 4.00
1. Monograms. 2. Initials. I. Cirker, Blanche, joint comp. II. Title.

TURBAYNE, Albert Angus, 745.6'1
1866-1940.
Monograms & ciphers, designed and drawn by A. A. Turbayne and other members of the Carlton Studio. New York, Dover Publications [1968] xxi p. 136 plates. 24 cm. (Dover pictorial archives) "Unabridged and unaltered republication of the work originally published ... circa 1906." [NK3640.T8 1968] 68-55285 2.50
1. Monograms. I. Carlton Studio, London. BIP

Monotype (Engraving)

BROWN, Gwyneth King. 769'.924
Monoprints. [Meriden, Conn., Printed at the Meriden Gravure Co., 1968] [24] p. chiefly illus. 23 cm. [NE539.B77A5] 77-1010
I. Title.

LALIBERTE, Norman. 760'.28
The art of monoprint; history and modern techniques [by] Norman Laliberte [and] Alex Mogelon. New York, Van Nostrand Reinhold Co. [1974] 104 p. illus. (part col.) 21 cm. (An Art horizons book) [NE2242.L34] 73-1635 ISBN 0-442-24607-2 8.95
1. Monotype (Engraving) I. Mogelon, Alex, joint author. II. Title.

MARSH, Roger. 763
Monoprints for the artist. [1st American ed.] New York, Transatlantic Arts, 1969. 42, [60] p. illus., 6 col. plates. 22 cm. [NE2242.M3] 71-94644
1. Monotype (Engraving) I. Title. BIP

PALMER, Frederick, 1936- 760'.28
Introducing monoprints / Frederick Palmer. New York : Drake Publishers, 1975. 96 p. : chiefly ill. ; 21 cm. [NE2242.P34 1975] 75-315615 ISBN 0-87749-849-0 : 7.95
1. Monotype (Engraving) I. Title.

RASMUSEN, Henry N 766.7
Printmaking with monotype. [1st ed.] Philadelphia, Chilton Co., Book Division [1960] 182p. illus. 27cm. [NE850.R3] 60-14987
1. Monotype (Engraving) 2. Engraving—Technique. I. Title.

Monotype (Engraving)—Exhibitions.

HEYMAN, 769'.9794'074019466
Therese Thau.
Monotypes in California. Introd. by Therese Thau Heyman. [Oakland, 1972?] 16 p. 22 cm. Catalog of an exhibition held at the Oakland Museum, Oakes Gallery, Oct. 17-Dec. 17, 1972. Bibliography: p. 16. [NE2245.C3H48] 75-307960
1. Monotype (Engraving)—Exhibitions. 2. Monotype (Engraving)—California. I. Oakland Museum. II. Title.

Monotype (Engraving)—Technique.

SOLMAN, Joseph, 1909- 769'.92'4
The monotypes of Joseph Solman / introd. by Una E. Johnson ; with technical notes by the artist on the making of the prints. New York : Da Capo Press, 1977. [96] p. : chiefly col. ill. ; 22 x 29 cm. Bibliography: p. [96]. [NE2246.S64A5] 77-9923 ISBN 0-306-77425-9 lib.bdg. : 18.95
1. Solman, Joseph, 1909- 2. Monotype (Engraving)—Technique. I. Title. BIP

Monreale, Sicily.

KITZINGER, Ernst, 1912- 729.72
The mosaics of Monreale [v.1. Dist. New York, Wittenborn, 1962, c.1960] 132; xvp. illus. (pt. col., pt. fold.) 36 cm. Bibl. 62-5722 65.00 bxd.
1. Monreale, Sicily. 2. Mosaics—Monreale, Sicily. I. Title.

Monroe Co., N.Y.—Historic houses, etc.

MALO, Paul. 917.47'88'03
Landmarks of Rochester and Monroe County: a guide to neighborhoods and villages. Photos. by Hans Padelt and others. Landmark Society of Western New York, sponsor. [1st ed.] [Syracuse, N.Y.] Syracuse University Press, 1974. ix, 276 p. illus. 21 cm. Bibliography: p. 252-255. [NA730.N42M666 1974] 73-23095 15.00
1. Monroe Co., N.Y.—Historic houses, etc. 2. Rochester, N.Y.—Historic houses, etc. 3. Architecture—Monroe Co., N.Y. 4. Architecture—Monroe Co., N.Y.—Conservation and preservation. I. Landmark Society of Western New York. II. Title.
Pbk. 6.00; ISBN 0-8156-0104-2. BIP

Monsen, R. Joseph—Photograph collections.

AMERICAN 779'.0973'074019777
photography, past into present : prints from the Monsen Collection of American Photography / selected and with an introd. by Anita Ventura Mozley. Seattle : Seattle Art Museum : distributed by the University of Washington Press, c1976. 155 p. : ill. ; 29 cm. Exhibition held at the Seattle Art Museum. Bibliography: p. 155. [TR646.U6S433] 76-4145 ISBN 0-295-95508-2 : 20.00 ISBN 0-295-95509-0 pbk. :
1. Monsen, R. Joseph—Photograph collections. 2. Photography, Artistic—Exhibitions. 3. Photography—History—United States—Exhibitions. I. Mozley, Anita Ventura. II. Seattle. Art Museum.

Monsters in art.

EVANS, Larry, 743'.8'9001944
1939-
How to draw monsters / Larry Evans. San Francisco : Troubador Press, c1977. 64 p. : ill. ; 28 cm. [NC825.M6E88] 77-3731 ISBN 0-912300-75-2 pbk. : 2.95
1. Monsters in art. 2. Animals, Mythical, in art. 3. Drawing—Technique. I. Title. BIP

Montana—Description and travel—1951- —Views.

GRAETZ, Rick. 917.86'04'3
Beautiful Montana / photography by Ed Cooper ... [et al.] ; text by Rick Graetz. Portland, Or. : Beautiful West Pub. Co., c1977. 71 p. : col. ill. ; 29 cm. [F732.G72] 78-102354 ISBN 0-915796-25-2 : 12.95
1. Montana—Description and travel—1951- —Views. I. Cooper, Ed, 1937- II. Title.

MONTANA / 917.86'04'30222
photography by Rick Graetz and others ; introd. by A. B. Guthrie, Jr. Waukesha, Wis. : Country Beautiful, [1975] p. cm. [F732.M66] 75-34321 ISBN 0-87294-079-9 : 25.00
1. Montana—Description and travel—1951- —Views. I. Graetz, Rick. BIP

Montana—Description and travel—Views.

WOLSTAD, George, 917.86'04'30222
1913-
Those shining mountains of Montana. [Missoula, Mont., 1973] viii, 109 p. illus. 36 cm. [F732.W64] 74-152726
1. Montana—Description and travel—Views. I. Title.

Montana—Hist.—Pictorial works.

COLE, Philip G. 978.6
Montana in miniature; the pictorial history of Montana from early exploration to early statehood, by Philip G. Cole. Illus. by Olaf C. Seltzer. Ed. by Van Kirke Nelson, Cato K. Butler. [1st ed.] Kalispell, Mont., O'Neil Printers, 1966. vii, 216p. illus. (pt. col.) 28cm. [F732.C6] 66-29538 18.50
1. Montana—Hist.—Pictorial works. 2. Montana—Hist. I. Seltzer, Olaf C., illus. II. Title.

Montana in art.

KOERNER, William Henry 759.13
Dethlef.
W. H. D. Koerner and Montana; an exhibition arranged by the Montana Historical Society in association with Ruth Koerner Oliver, July-Sept., 1971. [Helena, Montana Historical Society, 1971] iii, 28 p. (chiefly illus. (part col.)) 28 cm. [ND237.K5953O4] 70-171028
1. Montana in art. I. Oliver, Ruth Koerner. II. Montana. Historical Society. III. Title.

Montana—Juvenile literature.

BAILEY, Bernadine 917.86
(Freeman), 1901-
Picture book of Montana. Rev. ed. Pictures by Kurt Wiese. Chicago, A Whitman, c.1961, 1965. 32p. illus. (pt. col.) 17x21cm. (U.S. bks.) [F731.3.B3] 61-9969 1.50
1. Montana—Juvenile literature. I. Title.

BAILEY, Bernadine j917.86
(Freeman) 1901-
Picture book of Montana, by Bernadine Bailey. Pictures by Kurt Wiese. Rev. ed. Chicago, A. Whitman,[1965] 32 p. illus. (part col.) map. 17 cm. (The United States books) [F731.3.B3] 65-8994
1. Montana—Juvenile literature. I. Title. BIP

Montclair, N.J. Art Museum.

MONTCLAIR, N.J. 759.13'074'014931
Art Museum.
The American painting collection of the Montclair Art Museum. Montclair, N.J. : The Museum, c1977. 268 p. : ill. (some col.) ; 29 cm. [ND205.M58 1977] 77-72003
1. Montclair, N.J. Art Museum. 2. Painting, American—Catalogs. 3. Painting—New Jersey—Montclair—Catalogs. I. Title.

Monterey, Calif.—Descr.—Views.

FRASCONI, Antonio 769.973
A Sunday in Monterey woodcuts [New York] Harcourt [1964] 1v. col. illus. 14x6cm. Folding bk.; woodcuts on continuous strip, 14x322cm., in case. 64-56865 3.00
1. Monterey, Calif.—Descr.—Views. I. Title.

Monticelli, Adolphe, 1824-1886.

MONTICELLI, Adolphe, 1824- 759.4
1886.
Loan exhibition of paintings by Adolphe Monticelli (1824-1886) November 15 to December 11, 1954. New York, P. Rosenberg [1954] 27 p. illus. 26 cm. (Paul Rosenberg & Co. Catalogue no. 91) Catalog. [ND553.M75A49] 73-171702
1. Monticelli, Adolphe, 1824-1886. I.

SUBJECT INDEX MOORE, HENRY SPENCER

Series: Rosenberg (Paul) and Company, New York. Catalogue no. 91.

Monuments—California.

REED, Merrill A 735.73
Historical statues & monuments in California. [San Francisco? 1956] 176p. illus. 24cm. [NA9350.C2R4] 56-8702
1. Monuments—California. 2. Statues. I. Title.

Monuments—Italy—Preservation.

UNITED Nations. Social Defence Research Institute. 364.1'62
The protection of the artistic and archaeological heritage : a view from Italy and India. Rome : United Nations Social Defence Research Institute, 1976. 259 p. ; 21 cm. (Its Publications ; no. 13) Includes bibliographical references. [N9003.U54 1976] 76-381171
1. Monuments—Italy—Preservation. 2. Art thefts—Italy. 3. Monuments—India—Preservation. 4. Art thefts—India. I. Title. II. Series.

Monuments—Ohio—Exhibitions.

†DOEZEMA, Marianne, 1950- 730'.973
The public monument and its audience / Marianne Doezema, June Hargrove. Cleveland : Cleveland Museum of Art ; Kent, Ohio : distributed by the Kent State University Press, c1977. 70 p. : ill. ; 22 cm. [NA9347.D63] 77-25428 ISBN 0-910386-38-2 : 4.00
1. Monuments—Ohio—Exhibitions. 2. Art and society—Ohio—Exhibitions. 3. Art, Municipal—Ohio—Exhibitions. 4. Community art projects—Ohio—Exhibitions. I. Hargrove, June Ellen, joint author. II. Cleveland Museum of Art. III. Title.

Monuments—Preservation.

CROSBY, Theo. 711'.4'01
The necessary monument; its future in the civilized city. Greenwich, Conn., New York Graphic Society [1970] 127 p. illus., facsims., port. 25 cm. Bibliography: p. 125-[126] [CC135.C74 1970b] 72-109176 8.50
1. Monuments—Preservation. I. Title.

UNITED Nations Educational, Scientific and Cultural Organization. 720'.28
Preserving and restoring monuments and historic buildings. Paris, Unesco, 1972. 267 p. illus. 22 cm. (Museums and monuments, 14) Includes bibliographical references. [N8850.U52] 73-189463
1. Monuments—Preservation. 2. Historic houses, etc.—Preservation. I. Title. II. Series.
Distributed by Unipub, N.Y; 14.00. BIP

Monuments—Preservation—Congresses.

NORTH American International Regional Conference, Williamsburg, Va. and Philadelphia, 1972. 069'.53
Preservation and conservation : principles and practices : proceedings of the North American International Regional Conference, Williamsburg, Virginia, and Philadelphia, Pennsylvania, September 10-16, 1972 : conducted under the auspices of the International Centre for Conservation, Rome, Italy and the International Centre Committee of the Advisory Council on Historic Preservation / edited by Sharon Timmons. Washington : Preservation Press, National Trust for Historic Preservation in the United States, 1976. xxi, 547 p. : ill. ; 25 cm. Includes bibliographies. [CC135.N67 1976] 75-13331 ISBN 0-89133-029-1 : 15.00
1. Monuments—Preservation—Congresses. 2. Architecture—Conservation and restoration—Congresses. I. Timmons, Sharon. II. International Centre for the Study of the Preservation and the Restoration of Cultural Property. III. United States. Advisory Council on Historic Preservation. International Centre Committee. IV. Title. BIP

Monuments—U.s.

BUTTERFIELD, Ben. 917.3
National monuments. [Prepared with the cooperation of the American Geographical Society] Garden City, N.Y., n. Doubleday [1963, c1958] 64 p. illus. 21 cm. (Know your America program) [E159.B95] 63-5697
1. Monuments—U.s. 2. Natural monuments—U.s. 3. U.S.—Historic houses, etc. I. Title.

Monuments — U.S. — Juvenile literature.

BURT, Olive (Woolley) 1894- 917.3
Old America comes alive; our restored villages, from colonial Williamsburg to Dodge City [by] Olive W. Burt. New York, J. Day Co. [1966] 160 p. illus., facsims., fold map., ports. 24 cm. [E159.B93] 65-10734
1. Monuments — U.S. — Juvenile literature. 2. U.S. — Historic houses, etc. — Juvenile literature. I. Title. BIP

DITZEL, Paul C. 973
How they built the national monuments / by Paul C. Ditzel. Indianapolis : Bobbs-Merrill, [1976] p. cm. Includes index. Stories behind the construction of ten famous United States landmarks including the White House, Liberty Bell, Washington Monument, Golden Gate Bridge, the Mt. Rushmore faces, Statute of Liberty, and Boulder Dam. [E159.D624] 76-11633 ISBN 0-672-52124-5 : 9.95
1. Monuments—United States—Juvenile literature. 2. Historic sites—United States—Juvenile literature. 3. Historic buildings—Washington, D.C.—Juvenile literature. 4. United States—Description and travel—1960- —Juvenile literature. I. Title.

LOBSENZ, Norman M., 1919- 917.3
The first book of national monuments. New York, F. Watts [1959] 90 p. illus. 23 cm. [E159.L6] 59-12205
1. Monuments—U.S.—Juvenile literature. 2. Natural monuments—U.S. 3. U.S.—Historic houses, etc.—Juvenile literature. I. Title.

Monuments—U.S.—Preservation.

BULLOCK, Orin M 721.072
The restoration manual; an illustrated guide to the preservation and restoration of old buildings, by Orin M. Bullock, Jr. Drawings by the author unless otherwise credited. Written for the Commitee on Historic Buildings of the American Institute of Architects. With a foreward by Morris Ketchum, Jr. [1st American ed.] Norwalk, Conn., Silvermine Publishers [1966] 181 p. illus., plans. 26 cm. Bibliography: p. 173-181. [NA702.B77] 66-15647
1. Monuments — U.S. — Preservation. 2. U.S. — Historic houses, etc. 3. Architecture — Conservation and restoration. I. American Institute of Architects. Committee on Historic Buildings. II. Title. BIP

HOSMER, Charles Bridgham, 1932- 720.973
Presence of the past; a history of the preservation movement in the United States before Williamsburg, by Charles B. Hosmer, Jr. New York, Putnam [1965] 386 p. illus., ports. 24 cm. Bibliography: p. 349-372. [E159.H77] 65-13292
1. Monuments—U.S.—Preservation. 2. U.S.—Historic buildings. 3. Architecture—Conservation and restoration. I. Title.

MINER, Ralph W. 711'.57
Conservation of historic and cultural resources, by Ralph W. Miner. [Chicago, Ill.] American Society of Planning Officials [1969] 56 p. illus. 28 cm. Bibliography: p. 49-56. [N8905.M5] 70-4672 5.00
1. Monuments—U.S.—Preservation. I. American Society of Planning Officials. II. Title.

Moon, Jeremy, 1943-1973.

LYNTON, Norbert. 759.2
Jeremy Moon : paintings and drawings, 1962-1973. [London] : Arts Council of Great Britain, 1976. 32 p. : ill. (some col.) ; 16 cm. Catalogue of an exhibition held in 1976 at Serpentine Gallery, London, April 3-25, City Art Gallery, Manchester, May 11-June 6, and Kettle's Yard Gallery, Cambridge, June 18-July 12. Includes index. Bibliography: p. 29 and 32. [N6797.M56L95] 77-350496 ISBN 0-7287-0091-3 : £0.75
1. Moon, Jeremy, 1943-1973. I. Moon, Jeremy, 1934-1973. II. Serpentine Gallery. III. Manchester, Eng. Art Gallery. IV. Kettle's Yard Gallery.

Moon, Michael, 1937—

MARLE, Judy. 759.2
Michael Moon / [by] Judy Marle. London : Tate Gallery Publications, 1976. 47 p. : ill. (some col.), port. ; 16 cm. Published for the exhibition of 18 June-25 July 1976. Distributed by Idea Books, Paris and Milan. Bibliography: p. 44. [ND497.M68M37] 76-384054 ISBN 0-905005-35-X
1. Moon, Michael, 1937- I. Tate Gallery, London. II. Title.

Moon, Milton, 1926-

PRYOR, Dennis. 738'.0924
Focus on Milton Moon. [St. Lucia. Brisbane] Univ. of Queensland Pr. [1967] 64p. illus., (pt. col.) 24cm. (Artists in Queensland) Aust. Title page on 2 pages. [NK4210.M6P7] 68-31943 8.95 bds.,
1. Moon, Milton, 1926- I. Title.
American distributor: Tri-Ocean, San Francisco. BIP

Moon—Photographs from space.

LOCKHEED Electronics Company. 778.3'53
Analysis of Luna 9 photography [Washington] National Aeronautics and Space Administration; for sale by the Clearinghouse for Federal Scientific and Technical Information, Springfield, Va. [1968] ix, 80 p. illus. (part fold.) 27 cm. (NASA contractor report, NASA CR-980) Prepared under contract no. NAS 9-5191 for Manned Spacecraft Center. [TL521.3.C6A3 no. 980] 68-61634
1. Moon—Photographs from space. 2. Lunar probes. I. U.S. Manned Spacecraft Center, Houston, Tex. II. Title. III. Series: U.S. National Aeronautics and Space Administration. NASA contractor report, NASA CR-980

Moore, Bruce, 1905—

WILCOX, Howard. 709'.2'4
Bruce Moore : notes toward a review of his life and art / by Howard Wilcox ; with research assistance by Dorothy Wilcox. Washington : Estate Book Sales, 1975. 150 p. : ill. ; 31 cm. Bibliography: p. 142-146. [N6537.M64W55] 75-308845 30.00
1. Moore, Bruce, 1905- I. Moore, Bruce, 1905- BIP

Moore, Charles Herbert, 1840-1960.

MATHER, Frank Jewett, 1868-1953. 759.13
Charles Herbert Moore, landscape painter. Princeton, Princeton University Press, 1957. xv, 85p. illus., ports. 22cm. [ND237.M65M3] [ND237.M65M3] 927.5 57-5450 57-5450
1. Moore, Charles Herbert, 1840-1960. I. Title.

Moore, Gary E., 1942—

MOORE, Gary E., 1942- 759.13
G. E. Moore : synthesis. [Denver : Denver Art Museum], c1976. 1 portfolio ([16] p. : ill.) ; 20 x 24 cm. Exhibition held at the Denver Art Museum, Sept. 4-Oct. 24, 1976. [ND237.M68D46] 77-351266
1. Moore, Gary E., 1942- I. Denver. Art Museum. II. Title: Synthesis.

Moore, Henry Spencer, 1898-

GROHMANN, Will 730.942
The art of Henry Moore. New York, H. N. Abrams [1960] 279p. Bibl.: p.275-276. illus., plates (part col.) ports. 28cm. 60-7798 15.00
1. Moore, Henry Spencer. I. Title.

MOORE, Henry Spencer, 1898- 730'.92'4
Henry Moore. Text by Giulio Carlo Argan. Translated by Daniel Dichter. New York, H. N. Abrams [1973, c1971] [46] p., [181] p. of illus. (part col.) 32 cm. Bibliography: p. [33]-[37] [NB497.M6A8213] 72-4443 ISBN 0-8109-0328-8 35.00
I. Argan, Giulio Carlo.

MOORE, Henry Spencer, 1898- 730'.924
Henry Moore [by] David Sylvester. New York, F. A. Praeger [1968] 167 p. illus. 21 x 27 cm. "Revised edition of a monograph originally published ... in association with the retrospective exhibition [1968] at the Tate Gallery." [NB497.M6S93 1968] 68-8254 10.00
I. Sylvester, David.

MOORE, Henry Spencer, 1898- 730.924
Henry Moore: sculpture and drawings. v.3. Ed. by Alan Bowness. Introd. by Herbert Read. New York, Wittenborn [1966] 32p. 177p. of plates (chiefly illus. (pt. col.)) 30cm. Contents.v.3. Sculpture 1955-64. Bibl. [NB497.M6B6] 65-28958 15.00
I. Read, Herbert Edward, Sir 1893- II. Bowness, Alan. ed. III. Title.

MOORE, Henry Spencer, 1898- 730.924
Henry Moore; Mother and child. Introd. by Herbert Read. New York, New Amer. Lib., by arrangement with UNESCO [1966] 24p. illus., port., 32 col. plates. 17cm. (Mentor-Unesco art bk.) MQ698. Bibl. [NB497.M6A46] 66-31706 .95 pap.,
I. Read, Herbert Edward, Sir 1893- II. United Nations Educational, Scientific and Cultural Organization. III. Title. IV. Series.

MOORE, Henry Spencer, 1898- 730'.924
Henry Moore: carvings ... bronzes 1961-1970; [joint exhibition] M. Knoedler [and] Marlborough Gallery [April-May 1970. New York, 1970] 108 p. illus., plates (part col.), ports. 31 x 30 cm. [NB497.M6A428] 76-199920
I. Knoedler (M.) and Company, inc. II. Marlborough Gallery. III. Title.

MOORE, Henry Spencer, 1898- 730
Henry Moore on sculpture; a collection of the sculptor's writings and spoken words edited, with an introd., by Philip James. New York, Viking Press [1967] 293 p. illus. (part col.), facsim. (on lining paper) 29 cm. (A Studio book) Bibliography: p. 281-293. [NB497.M6A35 1967] 66-20426
I. James, Philip Brutton, 1901- ed. II. Title.

MOORE, Henry Spencer, 1898- 730
Henry Moore on sculpture; collection of the sculptor's writings and spoken words edited with an introd. by Philip James. Rev. and expanded. New York, Viking Press [1971] 327 p. illus. 21 cm. (The Documents of 20th-century art) Bibliography: p. 313-321. [NB497.M6A35 1971] 76-150115 ISBN 0-670-01920-8 5.95
I. James, Philip Brutton, 1901- ed. II. Title. III. Series.

MOORE, Henry Spencer, 1898- 730'.924
Henry Moore; sculpture and drawings, 1921-1969. Text by Robert Melville. New York, H. N. Abrams [1970] 368 p. illus. (part col.), plates (part col.), col. port. 31 cm. Bibliography: p. 330. [NB497.M6M4 1970b] 68-28381 ISBN 0-8109-0332-6
I. Melville, Robert.

MOORE, Henry Spencer, 1898- 741.9'42
Henry Moore: unpublished drawings. Text by David Mitchinson. New York, H. N. Abrams [1972] xv p., 212 illus. 25 cm. [NC242.M7M5] 76-164711 ISBN 0-8109-0330-X 15.00
I. Mitchinson, David.

MOORE, Henry Spencer, 1898- 730'.924
Henry Spencer Moore. [Photographed and edited by John Hedgecoe. Words by Henry Moore. New York, Simon and Schuster, 1968] 524 p. illus. (part col.), facsims.,

ports. (part col.) 34 cm. [NB497.M6H4] 68-8313
1. Hedgecoe, John.

Moore, Henry Spencer, 1898.

ARIZONA. University. Art Gallery. 579.9
Henry Moore; a retrospective exhibition of sculpture and drawings, February 6 through March 14 [1965] Tuscon, Ariz. [1965] 106 p. illus., port. 80 cm. [NB497.M6A83] 65-63311 94
1. Moore, Henry Spencer, 1896- I. Title.

Moore, Henry Spencer, 1898—

ART Gallery of Ontario. 709'.2'4
Henry Moore : sculpture, drawings and prints / organized by the Curatorial Department and circulated by Extension Services, Art Gallery of Ontario. [Toronto] : The Gallery, 1976. 23 p. : ill. ; 21 cm. [N6797.M57A88 1976] 76-370546 ISBN 0-919876-14-5
1. Moore, Henry Spencer, 1898-

FEZZI, Elda. 730'.92'4
Henry Moore; [translated from the Italian] London, New York, Hamlyn, 1972. 97 p. illus. (some col.), ports. 32 cm. (Twentieth-century masters) Distributed in the United States by Crown Publishers inc. Bibliography: p. 96-[97] [NB497.M6F413] 73-162331 ISBN 0-600-35929-8 3.95
1. Moore, Henry Spencer, 1898-

HALL, Donald, 1928- 730.924
Henry Moore; the life and work of a great sculptor. [1st ed.] New York, Harper [1966] 181p. illus., ports. 24cm. [NB497.M6H3 1966] 66-15732 7.50
1. Moore, Henry Spencer, 1898- I. Title.

MOORE, Henry Spencer, 1898- 730'.924
As the eye moves ... a sculpture by Henry Moore. Photos. by David Finn. Words by Donald Hall. New York, H. N. Abrams [1970] 160 p. (chiefly illus., part col.) 26 x 37 cm. [NB497.M6F5] 73-82876 ISBN 0-8109-0331-8 25.00
I. Finn, David. II. Hall, Donald, 1928- III. Title.

MOORE, Henry Spencer, 1898- 730'.92'4
Energy in space [by] Henry Moore. Photos [by] John Hedgecoe. [Translation into German by Renate Zauscher. Translation into French by Emmanuela de Nora. Greenwich, Conn.] New York Graphic Society [1974, c1973] 88 p. illus. (part col.) 25 cm. Text in English, French, and German. [NB497.M6A42 1974] 73-89946 ISBN 0-8212-0589-7 15.00
1. Moore, Henry Spencer, 1898- I. Hedgecoe, John, illus. II. Title.

MOORE, Henry Spencer, 1898- 741.9'42
Henry Moore drawings / [selected, with accompanying text by] Kenneth Clark. 1st U.S. ed. New York : Harper & Row, [1974] 326 p. : ill. (some col.) ; 28 cm. [NC242.M7C55] 74-1800 ISBN 0-06-010787-1 : 40.00
1. Moore, Henry Spencer, 1898- I. Clark, Kenneth McKenzie, Baron Clark, 1903- ed. II. Title.

MOORE, Henry Spencer, 1898- 730'.92'4
A Henry Moore odyssey : his sculptures in their environments / text and photos. by David Finn ; foreword by Kenneth Clark ; commentaries by Henry Moore. New York : H. N. Abrams, [1976] p. cm. [NB497.M6F52] 76-12588 ISBN 0-8109-1313-5 : 37.50
1. Moore, Henry Spencer, 1898- I. Finn, David. II. Title.

MOORE, Henry Spencer, 1898- 769'.92'4
Henry Moore—prints, 1969-1974 : catalogue of an exhibition of prints from the collection of the artist / organized and circulated by the International Exhibitions Foundation; introd. by David Mitchinson Washington : The Foundation, c1975. 32 p. : ill. ; 29 cm. Bibliography: p. 31-32. [NE642.M6I57] 75-25136 3.50
1. Moore, Henry Spencer, 1898- I. International Exhibitions Foundation. II. Title.

NEUMANN, Erich. 730.942
The archetypal world of Henry Moore. Translated from the German by R. F. C. Hull. [New York] Pantheon Books [1959] 138 p. illus. 27 cm. (Bollingen series, 68) (Includes bibliography) [NB497.M6N43] 58-8988
1. Moore, Henry Spencer, 1898- I. Title.
BIP

NEUMANN, Erich. 730'.92'4
The archetypal world of Henry Moore / Erich Neumann ; translated from the German by R. F. C. Hull. New York : Harper & Row, 1965, c1959. xii, 200 p. : ill. ; 21 cm. (The Bollingen library) (Harper torchbooks ; TB 2020) "Translated from an unpublished manuscript: Henry Moore und der Archetyp des Weiblichen." German ed. published in 1961 under title: Die archetypische Welt Henry Moores. Reprint of the ed. published by Pantheon Books, New York, which was issued as no. 68 of the Bollingen series. Bibliography: p. 199-200. [NB497.M6N43 1965] 75-319899
1. Moore, Henry Spencer, 1898- I. Title. II. Series: Bollingen series ; 68.

READ, Herbert Edward, Sir, 1893- 730.924 B
Henry Moore; a study of his life and work [by] Herbert Read. New York, Praeger [1966, c1965] 284 p. illus. (part col.), ports. 22 cm. (A Praeger world of art profile) Bibliography: p. 265-266. [NB497.M6R39 1966] 66-12041
1. Moore, Henry Spencer, 1898-

RUSSELL, John, 1919- 730'.924
Henry Moore. New York, Putnam [1968] 231 p. illus., ports. (part col.) 29 cm. [NB497.M6R78 1968] 68-31740 12.50
1. Moore, Henry Spencer, 1898- BIP

RUSSELL, John, 1919- 730'.924
Henry Moore. [Harmondsworth, Eng.] Penguin [1973 c.1968] 274 p. photos. 20 cm. (A Pelican Book) [NK497.M6R78] ISBN 0-14-021622-7
1. Moore, Henry Spencer, 1898- I. Title.
Available from Penguin, Baltimore for 3.95 (pbk)

SELDIS, Henry J. 730'.92'4
Henry Moore in America, by Henry J. Seldis. [New York] Praeger [1973] 283 p. illus. (part col.) 28 cm. Bibliography: p. 276-277. [NB497.M6S44] 73-78377 ISBN 0-87587-054-6 16.95
1. Moore, Henry Spencer, 1898- I. Moore, Henry Spencer, 1898- II. Title.

Moorman, Theo.

MOORMAN, Theo. 746.3'92'4
Weaving as an art form : a personal statement / Theo Moorman ; black and white photography by Nicholas Large, color photography by John Walling. New York : Van Nostrand Reinhold Co., [1975] 104 p. : ill. ; 24 cm. Includes index. [TT848.M66] 74-18908 ISBN 0-442-25370-2 : 8.95
1. Moorman, Theo. 2. Hand weaving. I. Title. BIP

Moran, Mary Nimmo, 1842-1890.

MORAN, Thomas, 1837-1926. 759.13
Home-thoughts, from afar; letters of Thomas Moran to Mary Nimmo Moran. Edit. supervision by Amy O. Bassford. Introd., notes by Fritiof Fryxell. East Hampton, N.Y., East Hampton Free Lib., 1967. xv, 152p. illus. 24cm. Bibl. [NC139.M6A3] 67-24733 2.50
1. Moran, Mary Nimmo, 1842-1890. I. Bassford, Amy O., ed. II. Title.
Publisher's address: 159 Main St., East Hampton, N.Y. 11937.

Moran, Thomas, 1837-1926.

WILKINS, Thurman. 759.13 (B)
Thomas Moran, artist of the mountains, [1st ed.] Norman, University of Oklahoma Press [1966] xvi, 315 p. plates (Art col.) 24 cm. Bibliography: p. 261-293. [NC139.M6W5] 65-11235
1. Moran, Thomas, 1837-1926. I. Title.

Morandi, Giorgio, 1890-1964.

GIUFFRE, Guido. 759.5
Morandi; [translated from the Italian]. London, New York, Hamlyn, 1971. 94 p. illus. (some col.). 32 cm. (Twentieth-century masters) Distributed in the U.S.A. by Crown Publishers, Inc. Bibliography: p. 92-94. [ND623.M687G513 1971] 72-177787 ISBN 0-600-35930-1 £2.25
1. Morandi, Giorgio, 1890-1964.

Morassi, Antonio, 1892-

TIZIANO, Vecelli, 1477-1576 759.5
Titian. Text by Antonio Morassi. Greenwich, Conn., N.Y. Graphic [1965, c.1964] 69p. 32 illus. (1 mounted col.) 43 col. plates (1 fold.) 38cm. (Great masters of the past, 13) Bibl. [ND623.T7M67] 65-23598 27.50
1. Morassi, Antonio, 1892- I. Title. II. Series.

More, Thomas, Saint, Sir 1478-1535—Portraits, etc.

MORISON, Stanley, 1889- 759.9
The likeness of Thomas More; an iconographical survey of three centuries.Ed. and supplemented by Nicolas Barker. New York, Fordham [1964, c.1963] xii, 96p. illus., ports. (pt. col.) 30cm. Bibl. 64-4266 8.75
1. More, Thomas, Saint, Sir 1478-1535—Portraits, etc. I. Title. BIP

Moreau, Gustave, 1826-1898.

MOREAU, Gustave, 1826-1898. 759.4
Gustave Moreau [by] Julius Kaplan. [Los Angeles] Los Angeles County Museum of Art [1974] 149 p. illus. (part col.) 28 cm. Catalog. "Exhibition dates: Los Angeles County Museum of Art, July 23-September 1, 1974. California Palace of the Legion of Honor, September 14-November 3, 1974." Bibliography: p. 145-148. [ND553.M8K36] 74-76953 ISBN 0-87587-059-7 7.00 (pbk.).
1. Moreau, Gustave, 1826-1898. I. Kaplan, Julius. II. Los Angeles Co., Calif. Museum of Art, Los Angeles. III. California Palace of the Legion of Honor, San Francisco.

PALADILHE, Jean. 759.4
Gustave Moreau [by] Jean Paladilhe and Jose Pierre. Translated by Bettina Wadia. New York, Praeger Publishers [1972] 171, [5] p. illus. (part col.) 30 cm. Contents.Contents.—Gustave Moreau: his life and work, by J. Paladilhe.—Gustave Moreau through the eyes of succeeding generations, by J. Pierre. Bibliography: p. [174] [ND553.M8P313] 71-183385 30.00
1. Moreau, Gustave, 1826-1898. I. Pierre, Jose, 1927- Gustave Moreau au regard changeant des generations. English. 1972. II. Title: Gustave Moreau through the eyes of succeeding generations.

SELZ, Jean. 759.4 B
Gustave Moreau / by Jean Selz ; [translated from the French by Alice Sachs]. New York : Crown Publishers, [1979] p. cm. [ND553.M8S4413] 78-12107 ISBN 0-517-53449-5 : 5.95
1. Moreau, Gustave, 1826-1898. 2. Painters—France—Biography. BIP

Morgan, Julia, 1872-1957.

LONGSTRETH, Richard W. 720'.92'4
Julia Morgan, architect / Richard W. Longstreth. [Berkeley, Calif.] : Berkeley Architectural Heritage Association, 1977. 35 p. : ill. ; 19 x 22 cm. (Berkeley Architectural Heritage publication series ; no. 1) "Originally appeared in Perspecta 15: Yale papers on architecture under the title Julia Morgan: some introductory notes." [NA737.M68L66] 77-152920
1. Morgan, Julia, 1872-1957. 2. Architecture—California. I. Title. II. Series.

Morgan, Peter, 1951—

MORGAN, Peter, 1951- 769'.92'4
Peter Morgan. [Montreal : Federation des Cooperatives du Nouveau-Quebec], 1976. [20] p. : chiefly ill. ; 26 cm. An exhibition organized by the Canadian Eskimo Art Council. English and French. [NE543.M67C36] 77-465174
1. Morgan, Peter, 1951- 2. Eskimos—Canada—Pictorial works. I. Canadian Eskimo Art Council.

Morison, Stanley, 1889-1967.

BARKER, Nicolas. 686'.2'0942
The printer and the poet; an account of the printing of 'The Tapestry' based upon correspondence between Stanley Morison and Robert Bridges. Cambridge [Eng.] 1970. 43 p. 26 cm. "Of this book 500 copies were printed at the University Printing House, Cambridge for presentation by the University printer, Christmas 1970." Includes bibliographical references. [Z232.M85B37] 72-573145
1. Morison, Stanley, 1889-1967. 2. Bridges, Robert Seymour, 1844-1930. The tapestry. I. Bridges, Robert Seymour, 1844-1930. II. Morison, Stanley, 1889-1967. III. Title.

BARKER, Nicolas. 686.2'092'4
Stanley Morison. Cambridge, Mass., Harvard University Press, 1972. 566 p. illus. 25 cm. Includes bibliographical references. [Z250.A2B15] 76-189157 ISBN 0-674-83425-9
1. Morison, Stanley, 1889-1967. BIP

BARKER, Nicolas. 655.2'0924
Stanley Morison, 1889-1967: a radio portrait; compiled by Nicholas Barker & Douglas Cleverdon from recollections by T. F. Burns [and others]. Ipswich, Cowell, 1969. 5-39 p. plate. port. 22 cm. First broadcast in the B.B.C. third programme on Sunday, Feb. 2, 1969. [Z250.A2B16] 73-479161
1. Morison, Stanley, 1889-1967. I. Cleverdon, Douglas. II. Burns, Thomas F., 1873-

JONES, Herbert, 1905- 686.2'2'0924 B
Stanley Morison displayed an examination of his early typographic work / by Herbert Jones ; foreword by William Emrys Williams. London : F. Muller, 1976. 127 p. : ill. ; 26 cm. Includes bibliographical references and index. [Z250.A2M688 1976] 76-374574 ISBN 0-584-10352-2 : £8.50
1. Morison, Stanley, 1889-1967. 2. Type designers—England—Biography. 3. Printers—England—Biography. 4. Printing—Specimens. I. Morison, Stanley, 1889-1967. II. Title.

MORAN, James. 686.2'2'0924
Stanley Morison; his typographic achievement. [1st ed.] New York, Hastings House [1971] 184 p. illus. 31 cm. (Visual communication books) Bibliography: p. 171-177. [Z250.A2M69 1971b] 77-163559 ISBN 0-8038-6706-9 17.50
1. Morison, Stanley, 1889-1967.

Morison, Stanley, 1889-1967—Bibliography.

APPLETON, Tony. 016.6862'2
The writings of Stanley Morison : a handlist / compiled by Tony Appleton ; with a biographical & typographical supplement, and essays by Brooke Crutchley & John Dreyfus. Brighton : The author, 1976. xix, 119 p., plate : port. ; 24 cm. Includes indexes. [Z117.A67] 77-355712 ISBN 0-9502916-4-1 : £8.00
1. Morison, Stanley, 1889-1967—Bibliography. 2. Printing—Bibliography. 3. Type and type-founding—Bibliography. 4. Writing—Bibliography. I. Title.

Morisot, Berthe, 1841-1895.

HUISMAN, Philippe 759.4
Morisot. enchantment [Tr. by Diana Imber] New York, French & European Pubns. [1963] 65p. mounted col. illus. 21cm. (Rhythm & colour, 8) Bibl. 63-25750 3.95
1. Morisot, Berthe, 1841-1895. I. Title.

MORISOT, Berthe [Berthe Marie Pauline (Morisot) Manet] 1841-1895. 759.4
Drawings, pastels, watercolors, paintings. Introd. by Elizabeth Mongan. Pref. by Denis Rouart. Research and chronology by Elaine Johnson. Catalog Commentary by

SEWTER, A. C. 748.5'92
The stained glass of William Morris and his circle [by] A. Charles Sewter. New Haven, Published for the Paul Mellon Centre for Studies in British Art by Yale University Press, 1974. xii, 119 p., [324] p. of illus. (part col.) 32 cm. (Studies in British art) Bibliography: p. 103-107. [ND5343.S48] 72-91307 ISBN 0-300-01471-6 50.00
1. Morris, William, 1834-1896. 2. Glass painting and staining, Victorian—Great Britain. 3. Glass painters—Great Britain. I. Title. II. Series. BIP

THOMPSON, Susan Otis. 686.2'24
American book design and William Morris / by Susan Otis Thompson. New York : R. R. Bowker Co., 1977. p. cm. Includes index. Bibliography: p. [Z116.A3T47] 77-8783 ISBN 0-8352-0984-9 : 29.95
1. Morris, William, 1834-1896. 2. Book design. 3. Book industries and trade—United States—History. I. Title.

UPDIKE, Daniel Berkeley, 1860-1941. 655
Daniel Berkeley Updike to William Morris. San Marino, Calif. [Printed by members of the HEH Preparations Dept.] 1968. [8] p. 21 cm. A reproduction of Updike's ms. letter, dated Aug. 3. 1893, bought a Sotheby's in Dec. 1956 by the Henry E. Huntington Library. "Limited to 50 copies, of which the first 15 are numbered and signed by the printers." L.C. copy is neither numbered nor signed. [Z232.U784A4 1968] 79-3727
I. Morris, William, 1834-1896. II. Title.

VALLANCE, Aymer, 1862-1943. 709'.24
William Morris: his art, his writings, and his public life; a record. Kennebunkport, Me., Milford House, 1971. xiv, 462 p. illus., facsims., col. plate, port. 24 cm. Reprint of the 1897 ed. "Chronological list of the printed works of William Morris": p. [447]-452. [PR5083.V3 1971] 72-79486 ISBN 0-87821-015-6
1. Morris, William, 1834-1896.

VALLANCE, Aymer, 1862-1943. 709'.24
William Morris, his art, his writings, and his public life : a record / by Aymer Vallance. Boston : Longwood Press, 1977. p. cm. Reprint of the 1898 ed. published by G. Bell, London. Includes index. "Chronological list of the printed works of William Morris": p. [PR5083.V3 1977] 77-6968 ISBN 0-89341-208-2 lib.bdg. : 50.00
1. Morris, William, 1834-1896. 2. Authors, English—19th century—Biography. 3. Artists—England—Biography.

WARWICK, Frances Evelyn (Maynard) Greville, Countess of, 1861-1938. 709'.2'4
William Morris, his homes and haunts. With twelve drawings in crayon by A. Forestier and other illus. [Folcroft, Pa.] Folcroft Library Editions, 1974. xi, 68 p. illus. 24 cm. Reprint of the 1912 ed. published by T. C. & E. C. Jack, London, in series: The Pilgrim books. [PR5083.W3 1974] 73-13851 ISBN 0-8414-3462-X (lib. bdg.)
1. Morris, William, 1834-1896.

WATKINSON, Raymond. 709'.42
William Morris as designer. New York, Reinhold Pub. Co. [1967] 81 p. 92 illus. (incl. facsims., ports.; part col.) 26 cm. Bibliography: p. 80-[82]. [NK1498.M6W3 1967] 67-24704
1. Morris, William, 1834-1896. I. Title.

WEEKLEY, Montague. 709'.2'4 B
William Morris. London, Duckworth. [Folcroft, Pa.] Folcroft Library Editions, 1973. p. Reprint of the 1934 ed., which was issued as no. 33 of Great lives. Bibliography: p. [PR5083.W4 1973] 73-908 ISBN 0-8414-2800-X
1. Morris, William, 1834-1896. BIP

WILLIAM Morris Gallery and Brangwyn Gift, Walthamstow, Eng. 016.094
In fine print : William Morris as book designer : [catalogue of an exhibition held at the] William Morris Gallery & Brangwyn Gift, Lloyd Park, Forest Road, London E17 4PP ..., 18 December 1976-19 March 1977. London : London Borough of Waltham Forest, Libraries and Arts Department, 1976. [3], ii, 75 p. ; 30 cm. Fold. sheet of ill. inserted. Bibliography: p. 71-74. [Z232.M87W48 1976] 77-366307 ISBN 0-901974-05-6 : £1.00
1. Morris, William, 1834-1896. 2. Printing—England—History—Exhibitions. 3. Book design—Exhibitions. I. Morris, William, 1834-1896. II. Title.

WILLIAM Morris: 769'.92'4
Ornamentation and illustrations from the Kelmscott Chaucer. With an introd. by Fridolf Johnson. New York, Dover Publications [1973] xiv, 112 p. facsims. 31 cm. (Dover pictorial archives) Includes 100 p. reproduced from the Kelmscott ed. of The works of Geoffrey Chaucer, with illus. by Sir E. Burne-Jones, published in 1896. [NC242.M72W54 1973] 73-80560 ISBN 0-486-22970-X 3.50
1. Morris, William, 1834-1896. 2. Chaucer, Geoffrey, d. 1400—Illustrations. I. Morris, William, 1834-1896. II. Burne-Jones, Edward Coley, Sir, bart., 1833-1898, illus. III. Chaucer, Geoffrey, d. 1400. The works of Geoffrey Chaucer. IV. Title: Ornamentation and illustrations from the Kelmscott Chaucer.

Morris, William, 1834-1896—Addresses, essays, lectures.

DUNLAP, Joseph Riggs, 1913- 686.2'092'4 B
On the heritage of William Morris : some considerations, typographic & otherwise : an address delivered by the annual Typophiles Christmas luncheon, December 12, 1974. New York : The Typophiles, 1976. 26 p. ; 19 cm. (A Typophile monograph) [Z250.A2D86] 77-352486
1. Morris, William, 1834-1896—Addresses, essays, lectures. I. Title. II. Series: The Typophiles, New York. Typophile monographs.

NEEDHAM, Paul, 1943- 686.2'092'4 B
William Morris and the art of the book : with essays on William Morris, as book collector by Paul Needham, as calligrapher by Joseph Dunlap, and as typographer by John Dreyfus. New York : Pierpont Morgan Library, c1976. 140, cxiv p. : ill. (some col.) ; 30 cm. Includes bibliographical references. [Z232.M87N4] 76-29207 55.00 pbk. : 27.50
1. Morris, William, 1834-1896—Addresses, essays, lectures. 2. Bibliographical exhibitions. I. Dunlap, Joseph Riggs, 1913- joint author. II. Dreyfus, John, joint author. III. Pierpont Morgan Library, New York. IV. Title. BIP

Morris, William, 1834-1896—Criticism and interpretation.

DRINKWATER, John, 1882-1937. 709'.2'4
William Morris : a critical study / by John Drinkwater. Norwood, Pa. : Norwood Editions, 1975. 201 p. : port. ; 23 cm. Reprint of the 1912 ed. published by M. Secker, London. [PR5084.D7 1975] 75-42179 ISBN 0-88305-168-0 : 20.00
1. Morris, William, 1834-1896—Criticism and interpretation.

Morris, William, 1834-1896—Exhibitions.

†WILLIAM Morris Society. 700'.92'4 B
The work of William Morris : an exhibition arranged by the William Morris Society. Folcroft, Pa. : Folcroft Library Editions, 1976. 75 p. : ill. ; 26 cm. Exhibition held Oct. 25-Nov. 10, 1962, at the Times Bookshop, London. Reprint of the 1962 ed. published for the William Morris Society by the Times Bookshop, London. Bibliography: p. 6-7. [PR5083.W54 1976] 76-29610 ISBN 0-8414-6104-X lib. bdg. : 10.00
1. Morris, William, 1834-1896—Exhibitions. I. Times Bookshop, London. II. Title.

Morrison, George, 1919—

MORRISON, George, 1919- 741.9'73
George Morrison: drawings. [Minneapolis? 1973] [8] p. illus. 28 cm. Exhibition to be held at the Walker Art Center, Minneapolis, Apr. 15-May 27, 1973; at the Heard Museum, Phoenix, Ariz., June 23-Aug. 5, 1973; and at the Amon Carter Museum of Western Art, Fort Worth, Tex., Nov. 10-Jan. 5, 1974. [NC139.M67W34] 73-163779
1. Morrison, George, 1919- I. Walker Art Center, Minneapolis. II. Heard Museum of Anthropology and Primitive Art, Phoenix, Ariz. III. Amon Carter Museum of Western Art, Fort Worth, Tex.

Morrison, George, 1919- —Juvenile literature.

KOSTICH, Dragos D. 759.13 B
George Morrison / by Dragos D. Kostich. Minneapolis : Dillon Press, c1976. 66 p. : ill. ; 24 cm. (The Story of an American Indian) A biography of the Chippewa Indian whose many artistic achievements were crowned when in 1970 he began teaching at the University of Minnesota not only art, but American Indian studies. [E99.C6M864] 92 75-45210 ISBN 0-87518-110-4 : 4.95
1. Morrison, George, 1919- —Juvenile literature. 2. Chippewa Indians—Juvenile literature. I. Title. BIP

Morrow, Stanley J., 1843-1921.

HURT, Wesley Robert, 1917- 927.7
Frontier photographer; Stanley J. Morrow's Dakota years [by] Wesley R. Hurt and William E. Lass. [Vermillion] University of South Dakota [1956] 135 p. illus. 24 cm. Includes bibliography. [TR140.M6H87] 56-10996
1. Morrow, Stanley J., 1843-1921. 2. Northwestern States—History. 3. Dakota Indians. 4. Photography—History—U.S. I. Lass, William E., joint author. II. Title.

Morse, Earl—Art collections.

WHITFIELD, Roderick. 759.951
In pursuit of antiquity; Chinese paintings of the Ming and Ch'ing dynasties from the collection of Mr. and Mrs. Earl Morse. With an addendum by Wen Fong. [Princeton, N.J.] Art Museum, Princeton University [1969] 240 p. illus. (part col.), map. 26 cm. Catalogue of an exhibition held at the Art Museum, Princeton University, May 17-July 27, 1969. Bibliography: p. 239-240. [ND1043.5.W48] 70-86877
1. Morse, Earl—Art collections. 2. Paintings, Chinese—Exhibitions. I. Fong, Wen. II. Princeton University. Art Museum. III. Title.

Morse, Samuel Finley Breese, 1791-1872.

LARKIN, Oliver W. 927.5
Samuel F. B. Morse and American Democratic Art. [1st ed.] Boston, Little, Brown, 1954. viii, 215 p. illus., ports. 21 cm. (The Library of American biography) "A note on the sources": p. [201]-203. [ND237.M75L3] 926.2 54-8284
1. Morse, Samuel Finley Breese, 1791-1872. 2. Art—United States.—History. I. Title. II. Series.

LATHAM, Jean Lee. 621.382'0924 B
Samuel F. B. Morse, artist-inventor. Illustrated by Jo Polseno. Champaign, Ill., Garrard Press [1961] 80 p. illus. 23 cm. (A Discovery book) A brief biography of the inventor of the telegraph and Morse code, who planned from early childhood to be a painter of great historical pictures but first won recognition as a portrait painter. [ND237.M75L34] 92 AC 68
1. Morse, Samuel Finley Breese, 1791-1872. I. Polseno, Jo, illus. II. Title.

Morse, Samuel Finley Breese, 1791-1872—Juvenile literature.

LATHAM, Jean Lee. 92 (j)
Samuel F. B. Morse, artist-inventor. Illustrated by Jo Polseno. Champaign, Ill., Garrard Press [1961] 80 p. illus. 23 cm. (A Discovery book) [ND237.M75L34] 61-11144
1. Morse, Samuel Finley Breese, 1791-1872—Juvenile literature.

Morse, Sherry Zahira.

MORSE, Sherry Zahira. 741.9'73
Pictographia / Sherry Zahira Morse. Berkeley : Zia Press, 1976. [75] p., [32] leaves of plates : all ill. ; 23 x 27 cm. Eighty-eight copies printed. No. 6. [NC139.M672A48] 77-373224
1. Morse, Sherry Zahira. I. Title.

Mosaics.

ALLER, Doris, 1909- 729.7
Sunset mosaics, written and illustrated by Doris and Diane Lee Aller. [1st ed.] Menlo Park, Calif., Lane Pub. Co. [1959] 96 p. illus. 28 cm. (Sunset craft books) [NA3750.A54] 59-14313
1. Mosaics. I. Aller, Diane Lee, joint author. II. Title.

ALLER, Doris, 1909- 729.7
Sunset mosaics, written and illustrated by Doris & Diane Lee Aller. [1st ed.] Menlo Park, Calif., Lane Pub. Co. [1959] 96p. illus. 28cm. (Sunset craft books) [NA3750.A54] 59-14313
1. Mosaics. I. Aller, Diane Lee, joint author. II. Title.

ARGIRO, Larry. 729.7
Mosaic art today. Scranton, International Textbook Co. [1961] 242p. illus. 27cm. (International textbooks in art education) Includes bibliography. [NA3750.A7] 61-11878
1. Mosalcs. 2. Mosalcs—Technique. I. Title.

BOVINI, Giuseppe. 738.52
Ravenna mosaics; the so-called Mausoleum of Galla Placidia, the Baptistery of the Cathedral, the Archiepiscopal Chapel, the Baptistery of the Arians, the Basilica San Apollinare nuovo, the Church of San Vitale, the Basilica of San Apollinare in Classe. [Translated by Gustina Scaglia] Greenwich, Conn., New York Graphic Society [1956] 55, [2]p. illus., 46 plates (part col.) 39cm. (The Great masters of the past, 4] Bibliography: p. [56-57] [NA3780.B663] 57-1067
1. Mosaics. 2. Art—Ravenna. 3. Christian art and symbolism. I. Title. II. Series. BIP

BYZANTINE mosaic decoration; aspects of monumental art in Byzantium. Boston, Bostoh Book ; Art Shop [1955] xiii, 97p. 64 plates. 26cm. Bibliographical references included in 'Notes' (p. 87-94) [NA3780.D39 1955] [NA3780.D39 1955] 729.7 55-9572 55-9572 738.5
1. Mosaics. 2. Art, Byzantine. 3. Christian art and symbolism. I. Demus, Otto. BIP

FISCHER, Peter. 751.4'8
Mosaic, history and technique. New York, McGraw-Hill [1971] 152 p. illus. (part col.) 28 cm. "Rewritten and revised by the author from his book Das Mosaik." Bibliography: p. 149-150. [NA3750.F52 1971] 74-148984 ISBN 0-07-021078-0 12.95
1. Mosaics. I. Title.

HENDRICKSON, Edwin A. 745.59
Mosaic patterns. Contributing artists: Antonio Vazquez [and others] New York, Hill and Wang [1958] 95 p. illus. 29 cm. [NA3750.H398] 58-14158
1. Mosaics. I. Title.

HENDRICKSON, Edwin A 738.52
Mosaics: hobby and art. New York, Hill and Wang [1957] 111p. illus. 24cm. [NA3750.H4] 57-8589
1. Mosaics. I. Title.

HENDRICKSON, Edwin A. 745.59
Mosaics: hobby and art. New York, Cornerstone [1963, c.1957] 128p. illus. 21cm. (CN46) 1.00 pap.,
1. Mosaics. I. Title.

HENDRICKSON, Edwin A. 738.52
Mosaics: hobby and art. New York, Hill and Wang [1957] 111 p. illus. 24 cm. [NA3750.H4] 57-8589
1. Mosaics.

JENKINS, Louisa. 738.52
The art of making mosaics, by Louisa Jenkins and Barbara Mills. Princeton, N. J., Van Nostrand [1957] 132p. illus. 26cm.

Includes bibliography. [NA3750.J4] 57-11592
1. Mosaics. I. Mills, Barbara (Jenkins) joint author. II. Title.

ROSSI, Ferdinando, 729'.7
architect.
Mosaics, a survey of their history and techniques [by] Ferdinando Rossi. [Translated from the Italian by David Ross] New York, Praeger [1970] 200 p. illus. (part col.) 30 cm. Translation of Il mosaico. Bibliography: p. 194-195. [NA3750.R6713 1970] 72-89606 18.50
1. Mosaics. 2. Marquetry. 3. Carving (Art industries) I. Title.

UNITED nations 729.72
Educational, Scientific and Cultural Organization.
Greece: Byzantine mosiacs. Pref. [by] Andre Grabar Introd. [by] Monolis Chatzidakis. [Greenwich, Conn.] New York Graphic Society [1959 i.e. 1960] 21, [4] p. Bibliography p. [22] illus. 32 col. plates. 48 cm. (Unesco world art series, 13) 60-1214 18.00 bds.,
1. Mosaics. 2. Art Byzantine. 3. Art—Greece. I. Title.

YOUNG, Joseph L. 738.52
Course in making mosaics; an introduction to the art and craft. New York, Reinhold Pub. Corp., c1957. 60 p. illus. 27 cm. (Reinhold's series of art courses) [NA3750.Y7] 57-9557
1. Mosaics. I. Title.

Mosaics—Beverly Hills, Calif.—Catalogs.

SHERMAN, 759.94'074'019493
Anthony C.
The Gilbert Mosaic Collection, by Anthony C. Sherman. Edited by M. Barbara Scheibel. West Haven, Conn., Pendulum Press [1971] 61 p. (chiefly col. plates) 32 cm. [NA3755.B48G57] 71-172497
1. Gilbert, Arthur, 1913-—Art collections. 2. Mosaics—Beverly Hills, Calif.—Catalogs. I. Title.

Mosaics, Byzantine.

GARY, Dorothy Hales. 709.02
The splendors of Byzantium, by Dorothy Hales Gary. Text by Robert Payne. New York, Viking Press [1967] 120 p. illus. (part col.) 31 cm. (A Studio book) [NA3780.G3 1967] 67-25919
1. Mosaics, Byzantine. 2. Architecture, Byzantine. I. Payne, Pierre Stephen Robert, 1911- II. Title.

KITZINGER, Ernst, 1912- 759.95694
Israeli mosaics of the Byzantine period. Introd. by Ernst Kitzinger [New York] New Amer. Lib. by arrangement with UNESCO [c.1965] 24p., [3]p. (on fold. leaf) illus., 28 col. plates (pt. fold.) 17cm. (Mentor-Unesco art bk. MQ 640) Bibl. [NA3780] 65-29969 .95 pap.,
1. Mosaics, Byzantine. 2. Mosaics—Israel. I. United Nations Educational, Scientific and Cultural Organization. II. Title.

Mosaics, Byzantine—Cyprus—Lythrankomi.

†MEGAW, Arthur H. S. 738.5
The Church of the Panagia Kanakaria at Lythrankomi in Cyprus : its mosaics and frescoes / A. H. S. Megaw and E. J. W. Hawkins. Washington : Dumbarton Oaks Center for Byzantine Studies, Trustees for Harvard University ; Locust Valley, N.Y. : distributed by J. J. Augustin, 1977. xx, 173 p., [4]leaves of plates : ill. (some col.) ; 30 cm. (Dumbarton Oaks studies ; 14) Includes index. Bibliography: p. xvii-xx. [NA3780.M4] 77-99267 ISBN 0-88402-074-6 : 25.00
1. Panayia Kanakaria (Church) Lythrangomi, Cyprus. 2. Mosaics, Byzantine—Cyprus—Lythrankomi. 3. Mosaics—Cyprus—Lythrankomi. 4. Mural painting and decoration, Byzanthine—Cyprus—Lythrankomi. 5. Mural painting and decoration—Cyprus—Lythrankomi. 6. Lythrangomi, Cyprus—Antiquities. I. Hawkins, Ernest J. W., joint author. II. Title. III. Series. BIP

Mosaics—Exhibitions.

LOS Angeles 738.5'094'074019494
Co., Calif. Museum of Art, Los Angeles.
The art of mosaics : selections from the Gilbert Collection, Los Angeles County Museum of Art, 28 April-10 July, 1977 : [catalog] / Alvar Gonzalez-Palacios. Los Angeles : The Museum, c1977. 143 p. : ill. (some col.) ; 26 cm. Bibliography: p. [8] [NA3755.L67L674] 77-75331 ISBN 0-87587-080-5 pbk. : 6.50
1. Gilbert, Arthur, 1913- —Art collections—Exhibitions. 2. Mosaics—Exhibitions. I. Gonzalez-Palacios, Alvar. II. Title.

Mosaics, Greek.

GRABAR, Andre, 1896- 729.7
Greek mosaics of the Byzantine period. Introd. by Andre Grabar [New York] Pub. by the New Amer. Lib. of World Lit. by arrangement with UNESCO [c.1959, 1964] 24p.[3]p. (on fold. 1.) illus., 28 col. plates (pt. fold.) 17cm. (Mentor-Unesco art bk., MQ591) Bibl. [NA3780.G7] 65-268 .95 pap.,
1. Mosaics, Greek. 2. Mosaics, Byzantine. I. United Nations Educational, Scientific and Cultural Organization. II. Title.

Mosaics—Handbooks, manuals, etc.

HASWELL, J. Mellentin. 729'.7
Van Nostrand Reinhold Manual of Mosaic [by] J. Mellentin Haswell. New York, Van Nostrand Reinhold [1974, c1973] 240 p. illus. (part col.) 25 cm. (Van Nostrand Reinhold Manuals.) Bibliography: p. 231-232. [NA3750.H37 1974] 73-14117 ISBN 0-442-23197-0 12.00
1. Mosaics—Handbooks, manuals, etc. I. Title. II. Title: Manual of Mosaic.

Mosaics—History.

L'ORANGE, Hans Peter, 729.709
1903-
Mosaics [by] H. P. L'Orange, P. J. Nordhagen: tr. [from Norwegian] by Ann E. Keep. London, Methuen, 1966. x, 92p. col. front., 113 plates (incl. 3 col.) 26cm. (Methuen handbks. of archaeology) Bibl. [NA3750.L613] 66-69439 12.50
1. Mosaics—Hist. I. ,nordhagen, P. J. II. Title.

Mosaics—History.

ANTHONY, Edgar 729'.7'09
Waterman, 1890-1947.
A history of mosaics. New York, Hacker Art Books, 1968. 332 p., 80 p. of illus. 29 cm. Reprint of the 1935 ed. Bibliography: p. [299]-314. [NA3750.A55 1968] 68-9000 20.00
1. Mosaics—History. I. Title. BIP

Mosaics—Istanbul.

KAHLER, Heinz. 726'.5'094961
Hagia Sophia. With a chapter on the mosaics by Cyril Mango. Translated by Ellyn Childs. New York, Praeger [1967] 74 p. 103 illus. (part col.), fold. plans. 31 cm. Bibliography:p. 70-[72] [NA5870.A9K33] 67-29605
1. Istanbul. Ayasofya Muzesi. 2. Mosaics—Istanbul. I. Title.

MANGO, Cyril A. 729.72
Materials for the study of the mosaics of St. Sophia at Istanbul. Washington, Dumbarton Oaks Research Library and Collection, 1962. xvii, 145 p. illus. 30 cm. (Dumbarton Oaks studies, 8) Bibliographical footnotes. [NA5870.A9M3] 62-17509
1. Istanbul. Ayasofya Muzesi. 2. Mosaics—Istanbul. I. Title. II. Title: The mosaics of St. Sophia at Istanbul. III. Series. BIP

Mosaics—Juvenile literature.

CURRIER, Richard L. 729'.7'093
The art of mosaics. By Michael Avi-Yonah. Retold for young readers by Richard L. Currier. Minneapolis, Lerner Publications Co. [1975, c1974] 95 p. illus. 21 cm. (Digging up the past) (The Lerner archaeology series) Contents.Contents.— An introduction to mosaics, including the techniques of making mosaics and the history of wall and pavement mosaics in Greece, Egypt, Rome, Africa, the Holy Land, and the Byzantine world. [NA3750.C87 1975] 72-10793 ISBN 0-8225-0828-1 6.95 (lib. bdg.)
1. Mosaics—Juvenile literature. I. Avi-Yonah, Michael, 1904- Ancient mosaics. II. Title.

Mosaics, Medieval.

NEUMAYER, Heinrich, 1905- 759.02
Byzantine mosaics. Tr. [from German] by Margaret Shenfield. New York, Crown [1964, c.1963] 62p. 24 col. plates. 19cm. (Movements in world art) Bibl. 64-24748 .95 bds.,
1. Mosaics, Medieval. 2. Mosaics, Byzantine. I. Title.

Mosaics— Palestine.

UNITED Nations 729.7095694
Educational, Scientific and Cultural Organization.
Israel: ancient mosaics. Pref. [by] Meyer Schapiro. Introd. [by] Michael Avi-Yonah. [Greenwich. Conn.] New York Graphic Society [1960] 24, [7]p. Bibl. p.[26] illus., 32 col. plates. 48cm. (Unesco world art series [14]) 60-4113 18.00 half cloth,
1. Mosaics— Palestine. 2. Mosaics, Byzantine. I. New York Graphic Society. II. Title.

Mosaics, Roman—Africa, North.

DUNBABIN, Katherine 738.5'0939'7
M. D.
The mosaics of Roman North Africa : studies in iconography and patronage / Katherine M. D. Dunbabin. Oxford [Eng.] ; New York : Clarendon Press, 1978. p. cm. (Oxford monographs on classical archaeology) Includes index.. Bibliography: p. [NA3770.D83] 77-30358 ISBN 0-19-813217-4 : 94.00
1. Mosaics, Roman—Africa, North. 2. Mosaics—Africa, North. 3. Pavements, Mosaic—Africa, North. 4. Africa, North—Antiquities, Roman. I. Title. II. Series.
Distributed by Oxford University Press, NY BIP

Mosaics, Roman—Great Britain.

RAINEY, Anne. 729'.7'0942
Mosaics in Roman Britain; a gazetteer. Totowa, N.J., Rowman and Littlefield [1973] 205 p. illus. 22 cm. Bibliography: p. 193-195. [NA3770.R33 1973] 73-161232 ISBN 0-87471-158-4 7.50
1. Mosaics, Roman—Great Britain. 2. Mosaics—Great Britain. 3. Great Britain—Antiquities, Roman. I. Title.

Mosaics—Rome (City)

OAKESHOTT, Walter 729'.7'0945632
Fraser, 1903-
The mosaics of Rome, from the third to the fourteenth centuries [by] Walter Oakeshott. Greenwich, Conn., New York Graphic Society [1967] 388 p. illus. (part col.) 31 cm. Bibliography: p. 380-385. [NA3850.R6O15 1967b] 67-25494
1. Mosaics—Rome (City) 2. Mosaics, Early Christian—Rome (City) 3. Mosaics, Medieval—Rome (City) I. Title.

Mosaics—Technique.

ARGIRO, Larry. 729'.7
Mosaic art today. Rev. ed. Scranton, International Textbook Co. [1968] xiii, 258 p. illus. (part col.) 27 cm. (International textbooks in art education) Bibliography: p. 254-255. [NA3750.A7 1968] 68-31353
1. Mosaics—Technique. I. Title.

ARVOIS, Edmond. 751.48
Making mosaics. [Translated by Leonard F. Wise and adapted by Robert F. Scott from the original French edution] London, Oak Tree Press; New York, Sterling Pub. Co. [1964] 88 p. illus. (part col.) 22 cm. Translation of Savoir faire de la mosalque. [NA3750.A773] 64-15109
1. Mosaics — Tecunique. I. Title.

ARVOIS, Edmond. 751.4'8
Making mosaics. [Translated by Leonard F. Wise and adapted by Robert F. Scott from the original French edition] Totowa, N.J., Littlefield, Adams, 1974 [c1964] 88 p. illus. 21 cm. (A Littlefield, Adams quality paperback no. 288) Translation of Savoir faire de la mosaique. Reprint of the ed. published by Oak Tree Press, London and Sterling Pub. Co., New York. [NA3750.A773 1974] 74-11209 ISBN 0-8226-0288-1 2.95 (pbk.)
1. Mosaics—Technique. I. Title.

BERRY, John, 1927- 751.48
Making mosaics. London, Studio Vista; New York, Watson-Guptill [1966] 104p. illus. (pt. col.) 19cm. Bibl. [NA3750.B4] 67-10437 1.95 bds.,
1. Mosaics—Technique. I. Title.

BULL, Brian, 1933- 751.4'8
Mosaics : the secrets, tools, and techniques / Brian Bull ; foreword by John Piper. London : Triton Books, 1976. x, 115 p. : ill. ; 28 cm. Distributed by Macdonald & Jane's Publishers, London. Includes index. [NA3750.B84] 76-379946 ISBN 0-363-00037-2 : £3.95
1. Mosaics—Technique. I. Title.

GARNETT, Angelica. 729'.7
Mosaics. London, New York [etc.] Oxford U. P., 1967. 70 p. front., illus., diagrs. 20 1/2 cm. (Oxford paperbacks, handbooks for artists) Bibliography: p. 67-68. [NA3750.G3] 68-70680
1. Mosaics—Technique. I. Title.

HUTTON, Helen. 751.48
Mosaic making. London, Batsford; New York, Reinhold, 1966. 136 p. illus., 3 col. plates, plan, diagrs. 21 1/2 cm. 35/- Bibliography: p. 130. [NA3750.H8 1966] 66-22688
1. Mosaics — Technique. I. Title.

HUTTON, Helen. 738.5
Mosaic making techniques / Helen Hutton. New ed. New York : Scribner, 1977. 138 p., [2] leaves of plates : ill. (some col.) ; 25 cm. (Scribner library) (Emblem editions) Published in 1966 under title: Mosaic making. Includes index. Bibliography: p. 133. [NA3750.H8 1977b] 77-72063 ISBN 0-684-15136-7 : 12.00. ISBN 0-684-15356-4 pbk. : 6.95
1. Mosaics—Technique. I. Title. BIP

LAUPPI, Walter. 751.4'8
Mosaics with natural stones / by Walter Lauppi ; [translated by Manly Banister ; adapted by Burton Hobson]. New York : Sterling Pub. Co., [1974] 96 p., [4] leaves of plates : ill. (some col.) ; 29 cm. Translation of Stein an Stein. Includes index. Describes the stones and tools used in making a mosaic and instructs the beginner in stone splitting and planning, setting, displaying, and restoring mosaics. [NA3750.L2413] 73-83457 ISBN 0-8069-5266-0. ISBN 0-8069-5267-9 lib.bdg. : 6.89
1. Mosaics—Technique. I. Title.

LEWIS, Beatrice. 729'.7
Making mosaics [by] Beatrice Lewis and Leslie McGuire. New York, Drake Publishers [1973] 191 p. illus. (part col.) 28 cm. [NA3750.L48] 72-10519 ISBN 0-87749-420-7 7.95
1. Mosaics—Technique. I. McGuire, Leslie, joint author. II. Title.

THE Mosaics of Jeanne 729.7
Reynal. Text by Dore Ashton [and others] New York, G. Wittenborn [1964] 111 p. illus. (part col.) ports. 29 cm. "Writings about Jeanne Reynal": p. 110. Bibliography: p. 110-111. [NA3840.M68] 63-22336
1. Reynal, Jeanne, 1903- 2. Mosaics—Technique. I. Ashton, Dore.

SEIDELMAN, James E. 751.48
Creating mosaics, by James E. Seidelman and Grace Mintonye. Illustrated by Harriet Sherman. New York, Crowell-Collier Press [1967] 56 p. illus. (part col.) 29 cm. [NA3750.S4 1967] 67-5671
1. Mosaics—Techniques. I. Mintonye, Grace, joint author. II. Title. BIP

SEIDELMAN, James E. 751.4
Creating mosaics, by James E. Seidelman and Grace Mintonye. Illustrated by Harriet

Sherman. New York, Crowell-Collier Press [1967] 56 p. illus. (part col.) 29 cm. An introduction to the techniques of mosaic art, suggesting ways to use such soft materials as paper, boxes, or foodstuffs, and explaining the use of grout with pebbles, glass or tiles. Includes also directions for making a mosaic mural. [NA3750.S4 1967] AC 67
1. Mosaics—Technique. I. Mintonye, Grace, joint author. II. Sherman, Harriet, illus. III. Title.

SPENCER, Sylvia, 1921- 751.4'8
Stone Mosaics / Sylvia Spencer. [New York] : Pitman Pub., [1975] c1974. 54, [33] p. : ill. (some col.) ; 26 cm. [NA3750.S67 1975] 75-313665 ISBN 0-273-07088-6 : 8.95
1. Mosaics—Technique. I. Title.

STRIBLING, Mary Lou. 738.5
Mosaic techniques; new aspects in fragmented design. New York, Crown Publishers [1966] x, 244 p. illus., col. plates. 27 cm. Bibliography: p. 236-237. [NA3840.S7] 66-15121
1. Mosaics — Tecnique. I. Title. BIP

STRIBLING, Mary Lou. 738.5
Mosaic techniques; new aspects in fragmented design. New York, Crown Publishers [1966] x, 244 p. illus., col. plates. 27 cm. Bibliography: p. 236-237. [NA3840.S7] 66-15121
1. Mosaics—Technique. I. Title.

TANNER, June. 751.4'8
Let's make a mosaic. New York, F. Watts [1969, c1968] 54 p. illus. (part col.) 23 cm. Describes the techniques for creating various kinds of mosaics using paper, seeds, wood, tiles, and pebbles. [NA3750.T35 1969] 69-10885 3.95
1. Mosaics—Technique. I. Title.

TIMMONS, Virginia Gayheart. 751.48
Designing and making mosaics. Worcester, Mass., Davis Publications [1971] 112 p. illus. (part col.) 26 cm. [NA3750.T5] 77-163725 ISBN 0-87192-042-5 8.85
1. Mosaics—Technique. I. Title. BIP

TIMMONS, Virginia Gayheart. 751.4'8
Designing and making mosaics / Virginia Gayheart Timmons. Englewood Cliffs, N.J. : Prentice-Hall, c1977. xiv, 143 p., [4] leaves of plates : ill. (some col.) ; 24 cm. (The Creative handcrafts series) (A Spectrum book) [NA3750.T5 1977] 76-56194 ISBN 0-13-201954-X pbk. : 6.95
1. Mosaics—Technique. I. Title.

UNGER, Hans, 1915- 751.48
Practical mosaics. New York, Viking Press [1965] 96 p. illus. (part col.) 26 cm. (A Studio book) Bibliography: p. 95. [NA3750.U5] 65-14295
1. Mosaics—Technique. I. Title.

WILLIAMSON, Robert. 729.7
Mosaics: design, construction, and assembly. London, C. Lockwood; New York, Hearthside Press [1963] 103 p. illus., ports., diagrs. 20 x 26 cm. [NA3750.W5] 63-11740
1. Mosaics — Technique. I. Title.

YOUNG, Joseph L 738.5
Mosaics: Principles and practice. New York, Reinhold [1963] 128 p. illus. (part col.) ports. 27 cm. First published in 1957 under title: Course in making mosaics. Bibliography: p. 126-127. [NA3750.Y7] 63-14883
1. Mosaics — Technique. I. Title.

Mosaics—Tunisia.

UNITED Nations Educational, Scientific and Cultural Organization. 729.509611
Tunisia: Ancient mosaics. Pref. [by] Giacomo Caputo. Introd. [by] Abdelaziz Driss. [Greenwich, Conn.] New York Graphic Society [1962] 21, [7] p. illus., 32 col. plates. 48 cm. (UNESCO world art series, 18) Bibliography: p. [22] [NA3760.U5] 62-51220
1. Mosaics—Tunisia. 2. Mosaics, Ancient. I. Caputo, Giacomo. II. Series.

Moscow—Descr.—Views.

CHERNOV, Vladimir. 914.73/1/03
Splendors of Moscow and its surroundings. Text by Vladimir Chernov, Marcel Girard. Introd. by Marcel Girard. Tr. by James Hogarth. Photos. by Gerard Bertin. Cleveland, World [1967] [N6997.M7C45] 67-24482 29.95
1. Moscow—Descr.—Views. 2. Art—Moscow. I. Girard, Marcel. joint author. II. Title.

Moscow. Gosudarstvennaia Tret'iakovskaia gallereia.

MOSCOW. Gosudarstvennaia Tret'iakovskaia gallereia. 759.7'074'0731
Soviet painting in the Tretyakov Gallery / [compiled and annotated by N. Adaskina ... et al. ; introduced by E. Polishchuk ; translated by Glenys Kozlova]. Leningrad : Aurora Art Publishers, 1976. 135 p. : col. ill. ; 34 cm. Includes bibliographies in Russian. [ND688.M59 1976] 77-356226
1. Moscow. Gosudarstvennaia Tret'iakovskaia gallereia. 2. Painting, Russian—Catalogs. 3. Painting, Modern—20th century—Russia—Catalogs. 4. Socialist realism in art—Russia—Catalogs. 5. Painting—Russian Republic—Moscow—Catalogs. I. Adaskina, N. II. Title.

Moscow. Kremlin.

†BURIAN, Jiri. 708'.7'31
The Kremlin of Moscow / text by Jiri Burian and Oleg A. Shvidkovsky ; photographs by Karel Neubert. New York : St. Martin's Press, 1976, c1975. xxxvii, [1] p., [65] leaves of plates : ill. (some col.) ; 31 cm. Translation of Moskevsky Kreml. Bibliography: p. [xxxviii] [NA7771.M6B8713 1976] 74-21650 25.00
1. Moscow. Kremlin. I. Shvidkovskii, Oleg Aleksandrovich, joint author. II. Neubert, Karel. III. Title. BIP

DUNCAN, David Douglas. 709'.473'1
Great treasures of the Kremlin. [Rev. and enl. ed.] New York, H. N. Abrams [1968] 187 p. col. illus. 31 cm. 1960 ed. published under title: The Kremlin. Bibliography: p. 187. [N6997.M7D8 1968] 68-28379
1. Moscow. Kremlin. 2. Art—Moscow. 3. Russia—History. I. Title.

DUNCAN, David Douglas. 709.47
The Kremlin. Greenwich, Conn., New York Graphic Society [1960] 170 p. mounted col. illus. 31 cm. Bibliography: p. 170. [N6997.M7D8] 60-8919
1. Moscow. Kremlin. 2. Art—Moscow. 3. Russia—History.

VOYCE, Arthur. 708.7
The Moscow Kremlin: its history, architecture, and art treasures. Berkeley, University of California Press, 1954. xiii, 147p. illus. (part mounted col.) plans. 29cm. Bibliography: p. 130-142. [N6997.M7V6] 54-12167
1. Moscow. Kreml.' 2. Architecture—Moscow. 3. Art—Moscow. I. Title. BIP

VOYCE, Arthur. 708'.7
The Moscow Kremlin: its history, architecture, and art treasures. Westport, Conn., Greenwood Press [1971, c1954] xiii, 147 p. illus. 27 cm. Bibliography: p. 139-142. [N6997.M7V6 1971] 74-138135 ISBN 0-8371-5708-0 31.50
1. Moscow. Kremlin. 2. Architecture—Moscow. 3. Art—Moscow. I. Title.

Moses, 13th cent. B.C.—Tomb.

GABALLA, G. A. 932'.01
The Memphite tomb-chapel of Mose / G. A. Gaballa. Warminster, Eng. : Aris & Phillips ; Forest Grove, Or. : distributed in the USA and Canada by ISBS, c1977. v, 40 p., [32] leaves of plates : ill. ; 31 cm. Includes bibliographical references and indexes. [DT73.S3G32] 78-313344 ISBN 0-85668-088-5 : 36.00
1. Mose, 13th cent. B.C.—Tomb. 2. Sakkara—Tombs. 3. Egyptian language—Inscriptions. 4. Law—Egypt—Sources. 5. Egypt—Antiquities. I. Title. BIP

Moses, Anna Mary (Robertson) 1860-1961.

KALLIR, Otto, 1894- 759.13
Grandma Moses. New York, Abrams [1973] 357 p. illus. (part col.) 31 x 35 cm. Bibliography: p. 341-342. [ND237.M78K32] 73-6930 ISBN 0-8109-0166-8 32.50
1. Moses, Anna Mary (Robertson) 1860-1961. I. Moses, Anna Mary (Robertson) 1860-1961.

KALLIR, Otto, 1894- 759.13
Grandma Moses / Otto Kallir. New York : H. N. Abrams, [1975] p. cm. An abridgement of the 1973 ed. published by Abrams. [ND237.M78K322] 74-31269 ISBN 0-8109-2053-0
1. Moses, Anna Mary (Robertson) 1860-1961. I. Moses, Anna Mary Robertson, 1860-1961.

MOSES, Anna Mary (Robertson) 1860-1961. 759.13
Art and life of Grandma Moses. Edited by Otto Kallir. New York, Gallery of Modern Art, 1969. 168 p. illus., ports. 24 cm. Includes catalogues of exhibitions. [ND237.M78K3] 76-13522
I. Kallir, Otto, 1894- ed. II. Title.

Moses, Anna Mary (Robertson) 1860-1961—Juvenile literature.

ARMSTRONG, William Howard, 1914- 759.13
Barefoot in the grass; the story of Grandma Moses, by William H. Armstrong. [1st ed.] Garden City, N.Y., Doubleday [1970] 96 p. illus. (part col.) 24 cm. The life of the artist who began her prolific career at the age of seventy. [ND237.M78A8] 92 74-122338 4.95
1. Moses, Anna Mary (Robertson) 1860-1961—Juvenile literature. I. Title. BIP

GRAVES, Charles Parlin, 1911- 759.13 B
Grandma Moses: favorite painter, by Charles P. Graves. Illustrated by Victor Hays. Champaign, Ill., Garrard Pub. Co. [1969] 96 p. illus. (part col.), ports. 24 cm. (Americans all) A biography of the New England grandmother who began painting seriously at age seventy and kept it up until she was over a hundred years old. [ND237.M78G7] 92 69-14830 2.49
1. Moses, Anna Mary (Robertson) 1860-1961—Juvenile literature. I. Mays, Victor, 1927- illus. II. Title.

LAING, Martha. 759.13
Grandma Moses: the grand old lady of American art. Charlotteville, N.Y., SamHar Press, 1972. 30 p. 23 cm. (Outstanding personalities, no. 13) Bibliography: p. 29-30. A biography of the famous American painter who did not begin painting seriously until age seventy-eight when arthritis forced her to give up embroidery. [ND237.M78L34] 92 71-190231
1. Moses, Anna Mary (Robertson) 1860-1961—Juvenile literature. I. Title.

Moses, Robert, 1888—

CARO, Robert A. 974.7'04'0924 B
The power broker : Robert Moses and the fall of New York / Robert A. Caro. New York : Vintage Books, 1975, c1974. 1246, xxxiv p., [25] leaves of plates : ill. ; 24 cm. Includes index. Bibliography: p. [1173]-1177. [NA9085.M68C37 1975] 75-9557 ISBN 0-394-72024-5 pbk. : 7.95
1. Moses, Robert, 1888- I. Title. BIP

CARO, Robert A. 974.7'04'0924 B
The power broker: Robert Moses and the fall of New York, by Robert A. Caro. [1st ed.] New York, Knopf, 1974. ix, 1246, xxxiv p. illus. 25 cm. Bibliography: p. [1170]-1177. [NA9085.M68C37 1974] 73-20751 ISBN 0-394-48076-7 15.00
1. Moses, Robert, 1888- I. Title.

RODGERS, Cleveland, 1885- 927.1
Robert Moses, builder for democracy. Introd. by H. V. Kaltenborn. [1st ed.] New York, Holt [1952] 356 p. illus. 22 cm. [NA9085.M68R6] 52-10302
1. Moses, Robert, 1888- I. Title.

Moskowitz, Ira.

MOSKOWITZ, Ira. 760'.092'4
The Hasidim. Paintings, drawings, and etchings by Ira Moskowitz. Text by Isaac Bashevis Singer and the artist. New York, Crown Publishers [1973] 31, [122] p. illus. (part col.) 29 cm. [ND237.M79S56 1973] 72-84288 ISBN 0-517-50047-7 10.00
1. Moskowitz, Ira. 2. Hasidism—Pictorial works. I. Singer, Isaac Bashevis, 1904- II. Title.

MOSKOWITZ, Ira 759.13
Ira Moskowitz. Introd. by John Davis Hatch. Text by Raymond Charmet, Claude Roger Marx. New York, Shorewood [c.1966, i.e., 1967] 21p. 63 plates (pt. col.) illus. 34cm. [ND237.M79C45] 66-24163 12.50
I. Charmet, Raymond. II. Roger-Marx, Claude, 1888- III. Title.

Mosques—Turkey.

KURAN, Aptullah. 726'.2'09561
The mosque in early Ottoman architecture. Chicago, University of Chicago Press [1968] xvi, 233 p. illus., plans. 26 cm. (Publications of the Center for Middle Eastern studies, no. 2) Bibliographical references included in "Notes" (p. 218-222) [NA5863.K8] 68-16701
1. Mosques—Turkey. 2. Architecture—Turkey. I. Title. II. Series: Chicago. University. Center for Middle Eastern Studies. Publications, no. 2 BIP

Mother Lode (The phrase)

FABILLI, Mary. 741.9'73
Ray Boynton and the Mother Lode : the depression years : [exhibition], May 4 through August 15, 1976, the Oakland Museum, History Special Gallery / compiled by Mary Fabilli. [Oakland, Calif.] : History Dept., the Oakland Museum, c1976. 62 p. : ill. ; 21 x 31 cm. Bibliography: p. 18. [NC139.B69F3] 76-13276
1. Boynton, Ray, 1883-1951. 2. Mother Lode (The phrase) 3. California in art. 4. Gold mines and mining—California—Pictorial works. I. Boynton, Ray, 1883-1951. II. Oakland Museum. III. Title.

Mothers in art.

HOOTON, Bruce, ed. 704.9424
Mother and child in modern art, edited by Bruce Hooton and Nina N. Kaiden. Foreword by A. Hyatt Mayor. Commentary by Frances L. Ilg. [1st ed.] New York, Duell, Sloan and Pearce [1964] 17 p. 49 plates (part col.) 26 cm. Based on an exhibition sponsored by Clairol and presented on a two-year national tour by the American Federation of Art. [N7630.H75] 64-21992
1. Mothers in art. 2. Children in art. 3. Mothers. 4. Parent and child. I. Kaiden, Nina N., joint ed. II. American Federation of Arts. III. Title.

KING, Marian. 757.4
A gallery of mothers and their children, with text by Marian King. Philadelphia, Lippincott [1958] 62p. illus. 26cm. [N7630.K5] 58-10139
1. Mothers in art. 2. Hcildren in art. I. Title.

MOTHER and child : 757'.4
100 works of art with commentaries by more than 100 distinguished people / compiled by Mary Lawrence ; pref. by Helen Hayes. New York : Crowell, [1975] 223 p. : col. ill. ; 31 cm. (A Balance House book) Includes indexes. [N7632.M67] 75-11652 ISBN 0-690-00970-4 : 27.95
1. Mothers in art. I. Lawrence, Mary, 1918-

Mothers—Portraits.

LANGSTON, Shelley. 779'.24
The mother. Photos. by Shelley Langston. Compiled by Hubert Bermont. New York, Essandess Special Edition, 1968. 1 v. (chiefly illus.) 23 cm. [TR680.L34] 68-5135
1. Mothers—Portraits. 2. Children—

Portraits. I. Bermont, Hubert Ingram. II. Title. BIP

Motherwell, Robert.

ARNASON, H. Harvard. 759.13
Robert Motherwell [by] H. H. Arnason. New York, H. N. Abrams [1974] p. cm. Bibliography: p. [ND237.M852A89] 74-14763 ISBN 0-8109-0289-3
1. Motherwell, Robert. BIP

MOTHERWELL, Robert. 759.13
The collages of Robert Motherwell: a retrospective exhibition, Museum of Fine Arts, Houston, November 15, 1972-January 14, 1973. With an introductory note by Philippe de Montebello, and text and catalogue by E. A. Carmean, Jr. [Houston, Museum of Fine Arts, c1972] 93 p. illus. (part col.) 24 x 28 cm. Bibliography: p. 43-46. [N6537.M67C37] 72-87521
1. Motherwell, Robert. I. Carmean, E. A. II. Houston, Tex. Museum of Fine Arts. III. Title.

MOTHERWELL, Robert. 769'.92'4
Robert Motherwell, selected prints, 1961-1974 : exhibition, November 23-December 21, 1974, Brooke Alexander, inc. / foreword by Arthur A. Cohen. New York : [B. Alexander, 1974] 13, [1] p. : ill. ; 26 x 31 cm. Title from cover flap. Bibliography: p. [14] [NE539.M67B76] 74-21727
1. Motherwell, Robert. I. Brooke Alexander, inc.

NEW York, Museum of Modern 759.13 Art
Robert Motherwell: with selections from the artist's writings by Frank O'Hara. Garden City, N.Y. Doubleday [1966, c.1965] 96p. illus. (pt. col.) ports. 24x26cm. Catalog for a retrospective exhibition held at the Mus. of Mod. Art. New York, Sept.30-Nov. 28. 1965. and to circulate in Europe during 1966 [ND237.M852N4] 65-25728 6.95: 2.95 pap.,
1. Motherwell, Robert. I. O'Hara, Frank, ed. II. Title.

ROBERT Motherwell: recent 759.13 *work;* [catalogue of an exhibition, January 5-February 17, 1973] Art Museum, Princeton University, Princeton, N.J. [1973] 83 p. illus. 22 cm. "Organized by the graduate students of the Department of Art and Archaeology, Princeton University." [N6537.M67R62] 73-89943
1. Motherwell, Robert. I. Motherwell, Robert. II. Princeton University. Art Museum. III. Princeton University. Dept. of Art and Archaeology.

SMITH College. Museum of 759.13 Art.
An exhibition of the work of Robert Motherwell, January 10-28, 1963, to accompany the first Louise Lindner Eastman memorial lecture, January 14, 1963. Northampton, Mass., 1963. unpaged. illus. 25 cm. [ND237.M852S6] 63-4240
1. Motherwell, Robert. I. Title.

Motion-picture projection.

RHODE, Ellis Gray, 1888- 778.55
Audio-visual lab manual and projectionists handbook. Illus. by Dale Perkins. [San Francisco?] c1951. 56 l. illus. 28 cm. [TR890.R4] 52-18399
1. Motion-picture projection. 2. Sound — Recording and reproducing. 3. Lantern projection. I. Title.

Motion picture theaters—U.S.

HALL, Ben M. 791.430973
The best remaining seats; the story of the golden age of the movie palace. [1st ed.] New York, C. N. Potter [1961] 266 p. illus. (part col.) ports. 29 cm. [NA6845.H3] 61-11763
1. Motion picture theaters—U.S. 2. Amusements—U.S. I. Title.

Motor bus lines—U.S.

PEAT, Marwick, Livingston 711'.73 & Co.
Evaluation of a bus transit system in a *selected urban area;* [Final report. New York] 1969. xv, 142 p. illus. (part col.) maps (part col.) 28 cm. "Prepared for the Bureau of Public Roads, Federal Highway Administration." [HE5623.P35] 77-610059
1. Motor bus lines—U.S. 2. Motor bus lines—Baltimore metropolitan area. I. U.S. Bureau of Public Roads. II. Title.

Mottahedeh, Rafi—Art collections—Catalogs.

HOWARD, David 738.2'0951 Sanctuary.
China for the West : Chinese porcelain & other decorative arts for export illustrated from the Mottahedeh Collection / David Howard and John Ayers ; foreword by Nelson A. Rockefeller. London ; New York : Sotheby Parke Bernet, 1978. 2 v. (698 p.) : ill. (some col.) ; 34 cm. Includes index. Bibliography: p. 673-678. [NK4565.5.H67] 78-319971 ISBN 0-85667-035-9 : 170.00 (2 vols.)
1. Mottahedeh, Rafi—Art collections—Catalogs. 2. Mottahedeh, Mildred—Art collections—Catalogs. 3. China trade porcelain—Catalogs. 4. China trade art—Catalogs. I. Ayers, John, joint author. II. Title. BIP

Mottoes.

LANDAUER, Bella Clara, 655.1 1874- comp.
Printers mottoes; a collection of sentiments taken from title-pages and colophons of books issued by printers and publishers, booksellers, artists and patrons from the 15th century to the present, compiled and edited by Bella C. Landauer. New York, Priv. print., 1926. 4p. l., 122p., 1 l. front., plates. 32cm. 'Of this edition there have been printed by Douglas C. McMurtrie, New York, in August 1926, one hundred and seventy-five copies, of which one hundred and fifty copies are offered for sale.'This copy not numbered. [Z235.L25] 27-2645
1. Mottoes. 2. Printers marks. I. Title.

Mount Rushmore National Memorial.

BORGLUM, Lincoln. 731.76
My father's mountain: Mt. Rushmore National Memorial and how it was carved. [Rapid City, S. D., Fenwyn Press, 1966] 1 v. (unpaged) illus. (part col.) 35 cm. [NB237.B6B6] 66-20565
1. Mount Rushmore National Memorial. 2. Borgium, John Gutzon de la Mothe, 1867-1941. I. Title.

FITE, Gilbert Courtland, 978.3 1918-
Mount Rushmore. [1st ed.] Norman, University of Oklahoma Press [1952] xiv, 272 p. illus., ports., maps. 22 cm. Bibliography: p. 255-260. [NB237.B6F5] 52-7919
1. Borglum, John Gutzon de la Mothe, 1867-1941. 2. Mount Rushmore National Memorial. I. Title. BIP

Mount, William Sidney, 1807-1868.

FRANKENSTEIN, Alfred 759.13 Victor, 1906-
William Sidney Mount, by Alfred Frankenstein. New York, Abrams [1974] p. [ND237.M855F72] 74-4007 ISBN 0-8109-0315-6 25.00
1. Mount, William Sidney, 1807-1868. I. Mount, William Sidney, 1807-1868. BIP

MOUNT, William Sidney, 741.9'73 1807-1868.
Drawings and sketches by William Sidney Mount, 1807-1868, in the collections of the Suffolk Museum & Carriage House at Stony Brook, Long Island, N.Y. [Stony Brook, N.J., Suffolk Museum & Carriage House, 1974] 80 p. illus. 21 cm. Cover title: Sketches and drawings by William Sidney Mount. [NC139.M68S94] 74-178206
1. Mount, William Sidney, 1807-1868. 2. Suffolk Museum, Stony Brook, N.Y. I. Suffolk Museum, Stony Brook, N.Y. II. Title. III. Title: Sketches and drawings by William Sidney Mount.

MOUNT, William Sidney, 759.13 1807-1868.
Painter of rural America: William Sidney Mount, 1807-1868. By Alfred Frankenstein. Introd. by Jane des Grange. [Washington, Printed by H.K. Press, c1968] 70 p. illus. (part col.), ports. (part col.) 27 cm. Sponsored by the Suffolk Museum at Stony Brook, Long Island and circulated by the International Exhibitions Foundation. Held at the National Gallery of Art, Washington D.C., Nov. 23, 1968-Jan. 5, 1969, and at 3 other museums, Jan. 18-May 31, 1969. [ND237.M855F7] 68-57955
1. Frankenstein, Alfred Victor, 1906- II. Suffolk Museum, Stonybrook, N.Y. III. International Exhibitions Foundation. IV. U.S. National Gallery of Art. V. Title.

Mountain Artisans.

LEWIS, Alfred Allan. 746.4'6
The Mountain Artisans quilting book. New York, Macmillan [1973] ix, 179 p. illus. 28 cm. [TT835.L48] 72-91259 10.00
1. Mountain Artisans. 2. Quilting. I. Mountain Artisans. II. Title. BIP

Moustakas, Evangelos, 1930—

GARDNER, W. Stephen. 730'.924 B
Evangelos Moustakas: essays in form and line [by] W. Stephen Gardner. Durham, N.C. [1970] 35 p. illus. 23 cm. Catalog of an exhibition, 8 March-3 May, 1970, Duke University Art Museum. [NB603.M6G3] 70-29244 1.25
1. Moustakas, Evangelos, 1930- I. Duke University, Durham, N.C. Art Museum. II. Title.

Movement, Aesthetics of.

BEST, David. 701.1
Expression in movement the arts; a philosophical enquiry. London; Lepus Books, [1975 c1974] xvi, 203 p. ill. 23 cm. Bibliography: p. 201-203. [BH301.M6B47] 75-317340 ISBN 0-86019-003-X
1. Movement, Aesthetics of. I. Title. Distributed by Plays, Inc. for 8.95. BIP

HALAS, John. 791.43
Art in movement: new directions in animation, by John Halas, in collaboration with Roger Manvell. New York, Hastings House [1970] 192 p. illus. (part col.) 28 cm. (Visual communication books) [NC1765.H26 1970] 73-118937 ISBN 8-03-803443- 17.50
1. Movement, Aesthetics of. 2. Moving-picture cartoons. I. Manvell, Roger, 1909- II. Title.

Moving-picture actors and actresses—Caricatures and cartoons.

HARMAN, Bob, 1931- 741.59'73
Hollywood panorama. [1st ed.] New York, Dutton [1971] 95 p. (chiefly illus., part col.) 23 x 31 cm. [NC1429.H3325A47] 76-31807 ISBN 0-525-47323-8 3.95 ($4.75 Can)
1. Moving-picture actors and actresses—Caricatures and cartoons. I. Title.

Moving-picture actors and actresses—United States—Portraits.

HOLLYWOOD glamor 779'.9'2 *portraits :* 145 photos of stars, 1926-1949 / edited by John Kobal. New York : Dover Publications, 1976. xiv, 144 p. : chiefly ill. ; 29 cm. [PN1998.A2H614] 76-19671 ISBN 0-486-23352-9 pbk. : 5.00
1. Moving-picture actors and actresses—United States—Portraits. 2. Glamour photography. I. Kobal, John. BIP

MOVIE-STAR portraits of 779'.2 *the forties :* 163 glamor photos / edited by John Kobal. New York : Dover Publications, 1977. xii, 162 p. : chiefly ill. ; 29 cm. Includes indexes. [PN2285.M65] 77-80118 ISBN 0-486-23546-7 : 6.00 ($6.95 Can.)
1. Moving-picture actors and actresses—United States—Portraits. I. Kobal, John. BIP

Moving-picture cameras.

MATZKIN, Myron A 778.5349
8m and 16mm movie equipment rating guide New York, Universal Photo Books [1958] 127p. illus. 21cm. (Universal photo guides) [TR880.M36] 58-59838
1. Moving-picture cameras. I. Title.

TYDINGS, Kenneth S 778.5
The Keystone movie guide. New York, Greenberg, c1954. 128p. illus. 20cm. (The Modern camara guide series) [TR880.T9] 53-12837
1. Moving-picture cameras. 2. Cinematography. I. Title.

Moving-picture cartoons.

STEPHENSON, Ralph. 741.5'8
Animation in the cinema. London, A. Zwemmer; New York, A. S. Barnes, 1967. 176 p. plates (incl. ports.) 16 cm. (International film guide series) 12/6 Bibliography: p. 165. [NC1765.S7] 67-94362
1. Moving-picture cartoons. I. Title.

Moving-picture theaters.

SHARP, Dennis. 725'.822
The picture palace and other buildings for the movies. New York, F. A. Praeger [1969] 224 p. illus. (part col.) 25 cm. (Excursions into architecture) Bibliography: p. 220-222. [NA6845.S46 1969b] 68-31529 12.50
1. Moving-picture theaters. I. Title.

Moving-picture theaters—Australia.

THORNE, Ross. 725'.822'0994
Picture palace architecture in Australia / [by] Ross Thorne. South Melbourne, Vic. : Sun Books, 1976. 27 p., [27] leaves of plates : chiefly ill. (some col.) ; 29 cm. (Sun-academy series) Includes bibliographical references. [NA6846.A8T48] 77-351326 ISBN 0-7251-0226-8
1. Moving-picture theaters—Australia. I. Title.

Moving-picture theaters—U.S.

HALL, Ben M. 791.43
The best remaining seats; the story of the golden age of the movie palace. New York, Bramhall House [1961] 266 p. illus. [NA6845.H304]
1. Moving-picture theaters—U.S. 2. Amusements—U.S. I. Title.

Moving-pictures.

NIL'SEN, Vladimir S 778.5
The cinema as a graphic art (on a theory of representation in the cinema) With an appreciation by S. M. Eisenstein. Translated by Stephen Garry, with editorial advice from Ivor Montagu. New York, Hill and Wang [1959] 226p. illus. 25cm. [PN1995.N52 1959] 59-8663
1. Moving-pictures. 2. Cinematography. I. Title. BIP

Mower, Margaret—Art collections.

THE Elsa Durand Mower 741.9'4 *Collection of French and Italian drawings.* [Exhibition] the Art Museum, Princeton University, Feb. 13 through Mar. 17, 1968. [Princeton, 1968] [62] p. illus. 26 cm. [NC15.P7P74] 75-9458
1. Mower, Margaret—Art collections. 2. Drawings—Exhibitions. I. Princeton University. Art Museum.

Moyens, H. Marc—Art collections.

CORCORAN Gallery of 707'.4'0153 Art, Washington, D.C.
The H. Marc Moyens Collection; a selection of paintings, drawings, and sculpture. [Washington, D.C., c1969] 35 p. illus. (1 col.) 25 cm. Catalog of the exhibition held at the Corcoran Gallery of Art, Dec. 12, 1969-Jan. 18, 1970. [N6490.C657] 79-111198

1. Moyens, H. Marc—Art collections. 2. Art, Modern—20th century—Exhibitions.

Mucha, Alphonse Marie, 1860-1939.

MOUNT Royal Station 769'.92'4 Gallery.
Poster artist Mucha; exhibition: Oct. 9-31, the Mount Royal Station Gallery of the Maryland Institute, College of Art. [Catalogue. Baltimore? 1973] 20 p. 31 cm. Cover title. [NC1850.M8M68 1973] 73-178348
1. Mucha, Alphonse Marie, 1860-1939. I. Title.

MUCHA, Alphonse 741.6'092'4 Marie, 1860-1939.
Alphonse Mucha / Jiri Mucha, Marina Henderson, Aaron Scharf. Rev. enl. ed. New York : St. Martin's Press, 1974. 144 p. : ill. (some col.) ; 30 cm. Includes index. Bibliography: p. [6] [NC1850.M8M8 1974] 73-90408 22.50
1. Mucha, Alphonse Marie, 1860-1939. I. Mucha, Jiri, 1915- II. Henderson, Marina. III. Scharf, Aaron, 1922-

MUCHA, Alphonse Marie, 741.6'0924 1860-1939.
Alphonse Mucha: posters and photographs. [Text by] Jiri Mucha, Marina Henderson [and] Aaron Scharf. New York, St. Martin's Press [1971] 136 p. illus. (part col.) 30 cm. On spine: Mucha. Bibliography: p. 134. [NC1850.M8M8 1971b] 76-184422 15.00
1. Mucha, Alphonse Marie, 1860-1939. I. Mucha, Jiri, 1915- II. Henderson, Marina. III. Scharf, Aaron, 1922- IV. Title. V. Title: Posters and photographs.

MUCHA, Alphonse Marie, 741.9'44 1860-1939.
Drawings of Mucha : 70 works / by Alphonese Maria Mucha. New York : Dover Publications, 1978. x, 57 p., [4] leaves of plates : chiefly ill. (some col.) 31 cm. [NC312.C93M792 1978] 78-52613 ISBN 0-486-23672-2 pbk. : 4.00
1. Mucha, Alphonse Marie, 1860-1939—Catalogs. I. Title. BIP

MUCHA, Alphonse Marie, 769'.92'4 1860-1939.
Posters of Mucha. New York : Harmony Books, [1975] 47 p. : col. ill. ; 39 cm. [NC1850.A1M82 1975] 75-9558 ISBN 0-517-52006-0 : 15.00. ISBN 0-517-52043-5 pbk. : 5.95
1. Mucha, Alphonse Marie, 1860-1939. I. Title. BIP

MUCHA, Jiri, 1915- 709.437(B)
Alphonse Mucha: his life and art, by his son; research by M. K. London, Heinemann, 1966. viii, 391p. 24 plates (incl. ports.) 23cm. Bibl. [N6838.M8M79] 67-70081 10.00
1. Mucha, Alphonse Marie, 1860-1939. I. Title.
American distributor: Humanities, New York.

Mucha, Jiri, 1915—

MUCHA, Jiri, 1915- 741.9'44
Mucha. New York : Rizzoli, 1977. [8] p., [48] leaves of plates : chiefly col. ill. ; 24 cm. [NC1850.M8A49] 76-42187 ISBN 0-8478-0067-9 pbk. : 4.95
1. Mucha, Jiri, 1915- I. Title.

Mukarovsky, Jan—Addresses, essays, lectures.

MUKAROVSKY, Jan. 111.8'5
Structure, sign, and function : selected essays by Jan Mukarovsky ; translated by John Burbank and Peter Steiner. New Haven : Yale University Press, 1978, c1977. p. cm. (Yale Russian and East European studies ; 14) Includes index. "Selected bibliography of Jan Mukarovsky's writings": p. [BH39.M8175 1978] 77-76310 ISBN 0-300-02108-9 : 15.00
1. Mukarovsky, Jan—Addresses, essays, lectures. 2. Aesthetics—Addresses, essays, lectures. 3. Arts—Addresses, essays, lectures. I. Title. II. Series. BIP

Mulholland, Roger, 1740-1818.

BRETT, Charles Edward 720'.92'4 B Bainbridge, 1928-
Roger Mulholland : architect, of Belfast, 1740-1818 / by C. E. B. Brett. [Belfast] : Ulster Architectural Heritage Society, 1976. 20 p. : ill., map, plans, port. ; 26 cm. [NA997.M8B73] 77-363170 ISBN 0-900457-20-1 : £0.80
1. Mulholland, Roger, 1740-1818. 2. Architecture—Northern Ireland—Belfast.

Mulier, Pieter, 1637-1701.

ROTHLISBERGER, Marcel. 759.9492
Cavalier Pietro Tempesta and his time [by] Marcel Roethlisberger-Bianco. [Newark] University of Delaware Press, 1970. 143, [178] p. of illus. (part col.) 31 cm. Bibliography: p. 139-140 (1st group) [ND653.M9R63] 78-101052
1. Mulier, Pieter, 1637-1701. 2. Paintings, Modern—17th-18th centuries—Catalog. I. Mulier, Pieter, 1637-1701. II. Title. BIP

Muller, Jan. 1922-1958.

SOLOMON R. Guggenheim 707.4 Museum, New York.
Jan Muller, 1922-1958. [New York, Solomon R. Guggenheim Foundation, 1962] unpaged, illus. 28 cm. Catalog of the exhibition, Jan. 11-Feb. 25, 1962. Includes bibliography. [ND237.M864S6] 62-12622
1. Muller, Jan. 1922-1958. I. Title.

Muller, Jorg.

MULLER, Jorg. 741.9'494
The changing city / Jorg Muller. 1st American ed. New York : Atheneum Publishers, c1977. 8 fold. leaves in portfolio : all col. ill. ; 33 cm. Translation of Hier Fallt ein Haus, dort steht ein Kran und ewig droht der Baggerzahn oder Die Veranderung der Stadt. Cover title. "A Margaret K. McFlderry book." [NC293.M82A4313 1977] 76-46646 ISBN 0-689-10782-X : 9.95
1. Muller, Jorg. 2. Switzerland in art. 3. Landscape in art. I. Title. BIP

MULLER, Jorg. 741.9'494
The changing countryside / Jorg Muller. 1st American edition. New York : Atheneum Publishers, 1977. 7 fold. leaves in portfolio : all. col. ill. ; 33 cm. Translation of Alle Jahre wieder saust der Presslufthammer nieder oder Die Veranderung der Landschaft. "A Margaret K. McElderry book." [NC293.M82A4213 1977] 76-46647 ISBN 0-689-10783-8 : 9.95
1. Muller, Jorg. 2. Switzerland in art. 3. Landscape in art. I. Title. BIP

Mullins, Patricia, 1952—

MULLINS, Patricia, 1952- 759.994
Fabulous beasts / [by] Patricia Mullins. Sydney : Collins, 1976. [30] p. : col. ill. ; 30 cm. [ND1105.M84A45] 77-352653 ISBN 0-00-185019-9
1. Mullins, Patricia, 1952- 2. Animals, Mythical, in art—Juvenile literature. 3. Animals, Mythical—Juvenile literature. I. Title.

Multiple art—Exhibitions.

TANCOCK, John L. 708'.148'11
Multiples: the first decade; [catalogue] by John L. Tancock. [Philadelphia, Philadelphia Museum of Art; distributed by Boston Book and Art, Boston, 1971] [107] p. (on double leaves) illus. 23 cm. "[Exhibition held at] Philadelphia Museum of Art, March 5-April 4, 1971." [N6494.M8T3] 74-156314
1. Multiple art—Exhibitions. I. Philadelphia Museum of Art. II. Title.

Mummy portraits.

THOMPSON, David L. 708'.194'93 s
The artists of the mummy portraits / David L. Thompson. [Malibu, Calif.] : J. Paul Getty Museum, c1976. 20 p., [24] leaves of plates : 56 ill. ; 22 cm. (Publication - J. Paul Getty Museum ; no. 7) "Amplified text of a lecture at the J. Paul Getty Museum on March 22, 1974, presented earlier as the first William Stevenson Smith memorial lecture at the Museum of Fine Arts, Boston." Bibliography: p. 20. [N582.M25A6 no. 7] [ND1327.E3] 757'0932 76-8380 ISBN 0-89236-002-X pbk. : 3.95
1. Mummy portraits. 2. Portrait painters—Egypt. I. Title. II. Series: Getty (J. Paul) Museum. Publication ; no. 7.

Mummy portraits—Exhibitions.

MUMMY portraits from 704.94'2 *Roman Egypt.* [Detroit, 1967] 36 p. illus. 26 cm. "An exhibition organized by William H. Peck [and held at] the Detroit Institute of Arts, March 22-April 30, 1967." Includes bibliographies. [N7588.M8] 67-7541
1. Mummy portraits—Exhibitions. 2. Portraits, Roman—Egypt. I. Peck, William H. II. Detroit. Institute of Arts.

Munakata, Shiko, 1903-1975.

MOKUHAN : 769'.952'074011134 the woodcuts of Munakata & Matsubara / Joan Stanley-Baker. Victoria, B.C. : Art Gallery of Greater Victoria, 1976. 110 p. : ill. ; 31 cm. Exhibition held at the Art Gallery of Greater Victoria. Includes bibliographical references. [NE1184.5.M86M64] 77-365126
1. Munakata, Shiko, 1903-1975. 2. Matsubara, Naoko. I. Munakata, Shiko, 1903-1975. II. Matsubara, Naoko. III. Stanley-Baker, Joan. IV. Art Gallery of Greater Victoria.

Munch, Edvard, 1863-1944.

BENESCH, Otto, 1896- 759.81
Edvard Munch. [Tr. from German by Joan Spencer] [dist. Garden City New York, Doubleday, c.1960] 143p. illus. (col.) 27cm. [Alpha books] Bibl. 61-16003 3.95 bds.,
1. Munch, Edvard, 1863-1944. I. Title.

DEKNATEL, Frederick B. [927.5]
Edvard Munch. With an introd. by Johan H. Langaard. Boston, Institute of Contemporary Art [1950] 120 p. illus. (part col.) ports. 26 cm. Published also as Oslo kommunes Kunstsamlinger catalog no. 6. Bibliography: p. 116-120. [ND773.M8D4 1950a] 759.81 50-58176
1. Munch, Edvard, 1863-1944. I. Title. BIP

GUENTHER, Peter W. 709'.2'4
Edvard Munch : an exhibition presented by the Sarah Campbell Blaffer Gallery, the University of Houston, April 9-May 23, 1976, also to be exhibited at the New Orleans Museum of Art, June 11-July 18, 1976, the Witte Memorial Museum, San Antonio, July 28-September 12, 1976 / catalogue researched and written by Peter W. Guenther. [Houston, Tex.] : The Gallery, c1976. 255 p., [1] leaf of plates : ill. ; 26 cm. Errata slip inserted. Bibliography: p. 246-254. [N7053.M86G83] 76-150548
1. Munch, Edvard, 1863-1944. I. Sarah Campbell Blaffer Gallery. II. New Orleans Museum of Art. III. Witte Memorial Museum, San Antonio.

HELLER, Reinhold. 759.81
Edvard Munch: The Scream. [New York, Viking Press, 1973, c1972] 127 p. illus. 23 cm. (Art in context) Includes bibliographical references. [ND773.M8H4] 70-180829 ISBN 0-670-28955-8 7.50
1. Munch, Edvard, 1863-1944. Scream. I. Title.

HODIN, Josef Paul. 759.81
Edvard Munch [by] J. P. Hodin. New York, Praeger [1972] 216 p. illus. (part col.) 22 cm. Bibliography: p. 211. [N7073.M8H59] 76-99313 10.00
1. Munch, Edvard, 1863-1944. BIP

LANGAARD, Johan Henrik, 759.81 1899-
Edvard Munch: malerier og grafikk [av] Johan H. Langaard, Reidar Revold. English, French, and German summary. Oslo. Norsk kunstreroducsjon [dist. Chester Springs, Pa., Dufour, 1964, 0 64-554523
1. Munch, Edvard, 1863-1944. I. Revold, Reidar, 1918- joint author. II. Title.

LANGAARD. Johan Henrik, 759.81 1899-
Edvard Munch; masterpices from the artist's collection in the Munch Museum in Oslo [by] Johan H. Langaard. Reidar Revold. Tr. from German by Michael Bullock. New York, McGraw [c.1964] 62p. mounted illus. (pt. col.) 80cm. 64-20212 23.50
1. Munch, Edvard, 1863-1944. I. Revold, Reidar, 1918- joint author. II. Oslo. Munch-museet. III. Title.

LANGAARD, Johan Henrik, 759.81 1899-
Edvard Munch: the university murals, graphic art and paintings [by] Johan H. Langaard, Reidar Revold. Oslo, Forlaget Norsk kunstreproduksjon [dist. Chester Springs, Pa., Dufour, 1963] 99p. illus., col. plates. 33cm. Bibl. 62-6635 15.00
1. Munch, Edvard, 1863-1944. 2. Oslo. Universitet. 3. Mural painting and decoration—Oslo. I. Revold. Reider, 1918- joint author. II. Title.

MADSEN, Stephan Tschudi 759.81
An introduction to Edvard Munch's wall paintings in the slo University Aula. [Translated from the Norwegian by Christopher Norman] New York, Wttenborn [1959 i.e.1960] 27p. illus. 23cm. 60-1424 1.00 pap.,
1. Munch, Edvard, 1863-1944. 2. Oslo, Universittet. 3. Mural painting and decoration—Oslo. I. Title.

MOEN, Arve 704.9424
Edvard Munch: woman and Eros; graphic art and paintings. [Tr. by Christopher Norman] Oslo, Forlaget Norsk Kunstreproduksion [dist. Chester Springs, Pa., Dufour. 1963] 109, [3]p. illus. (pt. mounted col.) 33cm. Bibl. 15.00, bxd.
1. Munch, Edvard, 1863-1944. 2. Women in art. I. Title.

MOEN, Arve 709.481
Edvard Munch: nature and animals; graphic art and paintings. [Tr. by Christopher Norman] Oslo, Forlaget Norsk Kunstreproduksjon [dist. Chester Springs, Pa., Dufour, 1963] 109, [3]p. illus. (pt. mounted col.) 32cm. Bibl. A63 15.00
1. Munch, Edvard, 1863-1944. 2. Nature (Aesthetics) I. Title.

MUNCH, Edvard, 1863-1944. 759.81
Edvard Munch / Ian Dunlop. New York : St. Martin's Press, 1977. [8] p., 40 leaves of plates : chiefly col. ill. ; 29 cm. [N7073.M8D86 1977] 77-71078 ISBN 0-312-23822-3
1. Munch, Edvard, 1863-1944. I. Dunlop, Ian, 1940-

MUNCH, Edvard, 1863-1944. 759.81
Edvard Munch. Text by Thomas M. Messer. New York, H. N. Abrams [1971 or 2] 166 p. illus. (part col.) 34 cm. (The Library of great painters) Bibliography: p. 161-162. [ND773.M8M47] 70-142738
1. Munch, Edvard, 1863-1944. I. Messer, Thomas M.

MUNCH, Edvard, 1863-1944. 759.81
Edvard Munch; a selection of his prints from American collections [by] William S. Lieberman. New York, Museum of Modern Art. [New York] Published for the Museum of Modern Art by Arno Press, 1972. 39 p. illus. 27 cm. Reprint of the 1957 ed. [NE694.M8L5 1972] 79-169306 ISBN 0-405-01565-8 9.00
I. Lieberman, William Slattery, 1924- II. Title.

MUNCH, Edvard, 1863- 769'.92'4 1944.
Some examples from our collection of etchings, woodcuts and lithographs / by Edvard Munch. Oslo : Galleri KB, 1976. [80] p. : chiefly ill. ; 25 cm. [NE694.M8G253] 77-356109
1. Munch, Edvard, 1863-1944. I. Galleri K.B., Oslo. II. Title.

MUNCH, Edvard, 1863- 769'.924 1949.
Edvard Munch: lithographs, etchings, woodcuts. Introd. by William S. Lieberman. Notes by Ebria Feinblatt. [Exhibition] Los Angeles County Museum of Art, January 28-March 9, 1969. [Los

SUBJECT INDEX MURAL PAINTING AND

Angeles, 1969] xvi, 118 p. illus. (part col.), port. 27 cm. Bibliography: p. 117-118. [NE694.M8A43] 69-11718 4.50 (pbk.)
1. Lieberman, William Slattery, 1924- II. Los Angeles Co., Calif. Museum of Art, Los Angeles.

NEW York (City). Museum of Modern Art. 769'.92'4
The prints of Edvard Munch; [checklist of the exhibition, February 13-April 29, 1973. New York, 1973] 1 sheet. illus. 36 x 50 cm. fold. to 18 x 13 cm. [NE694.M8N48] 73-166317
1. Munch, Edvard, 1863-1944. I. Munch, Edvard, 1863-1944.

SELZ, Jean. 769'.92'4
E. Munch / by Jean Selz ; [translated from the French by Eileen B. Hennessy]. New York : Crown Publishers, [1974] 95 p. : ill. (some col.) ; 29 cm. Bibliography: p. 94. [N7073.M8S4413] 74-76242 ISBN 0-517-51571-7 : 3.95
1. Munch, Edvard, 1863-1944.

TIMM, Werner. 769.924
The graphic art of Edvard Munch. Translated from the German by Ruth Michaelis-Jena with the collaboration of Patrick Murray. [Greenwich, Conn.] New York Graphic Society [1969] 313 p. illus. (part col.) 29 cm. Translation of Edvard Munch Graphik. Bibliography: p. [117] [NE694.M8T4813] 78-81079 15.00
1. Munch, Edvard, 1863-1944. I. Title. BIP

Munch, Edvard, 1863-1944—Catalogs.

MUNCH, Edvard, 1863-1944. 760'.092'4
Munch / [text by] John Boulton Smith. Oxford : Phaidon, 1977. 16 p., 48 p. of plates : chiefly col. ill. ; 32 cm. Bibliography: p. 14. [N7073.M8A4 1977b] 77-80141 ISBN 0-7148-1799-6 pbk. : 7.95
1. Munch, Edvard, 1863-1944—Catalogs. I. Smith, John Boulton.
Distributed by Dutton, New York

Muncie, Ind. Beneficence (Statue)

MYERS, Robert Henry, 1894- 731'.76'0977265
Beneficence; the statue on the campus of Ball State University, Muncie, Indiana. Robert Henry Myers, editor. Muncie, Ind., Ball State University, 1972. 128 p. illus. 26 cm. Bibliography: p. 123-128. [NB237.F7M93] 72-619607
1. French, Daniel Chester, 1850-1931. 2. Indiana. Ball State University, Muncie. 3. Muncie, Ind. Beneficence (Statue) I. Title.

Munich—Description.

SASEK, Miroslav. 914.3
This is Munich. [New York] Macmillan [1961] 60 p. illus. 32 cm. A pictorial tour of the Bavarian capital, presenting drawings of the historic buildings and monuments, parks, transportation, and the celebration of Oktoberfest in this large city of southern Germany. [ND1946.S2A54] AC 68
1. Munich—Description. I. Title. BIP

Munich—Description—Views.

SASEK, Miroslav. 759.37
This is Munich. [New York] Macmillan [1961] 60 p. illus. 32 cm. [ND1946.S2A54] 61-2984
1. Munich—Description—Views. I. Title.

Munich. Pinakothek, Alte.

BUCHNER, Ernst, 1892- 759.0838
Art treasures of the Pinakothek. [Translated from the German by Peter Gorge] New York, H. N. Abrams [1957] 58 p. 42 mounted col. illus., 98 plates. 35 cm. Translation of Die Alte Pinakothek, Munchen; Meisterwerke der europaischen Malerei. [N2325.B8213] A 58
1. Munich. Pinakothek, Alte. 2. Paintings, European. 3. Paintings—Munich. I. Title.

DUBE, Wolf Dieter. 759.94'074'0336
The Pinakothek, Munich. [Translated from the German by J. Wood] New York, H. N. Abrams [1970] 304 p. illus. (part col.), ports. (part col.) 22 cm. Translation of Alte Pinakothek Munchen. [N2325.D813 1970b] 74-117932 ISBN 0-8109-0409-8
1. Munich. Pinakothek, Alte. I. Title.

PINAKOTHEK, Munich. 708.3'36
[Texts by Roberto Salvini and others] New York, Newsweek [1969] 171 p. col. illus. 30 cm. (Great museums of the world) Bibliography: p. [168] [N2325.P5] 69-19062
1. Munich. Pinakothek, Alte. I. Salvini, Roberto. II. Series: Great museums of the world (New York, Newsweek)

Municipal buildings—Northampton, Eng.

GLAZEBROOK, Christopher John. 914.25'5
The history of Northampton's town halls, by C. J. Glazebrook. Northampton, J. Glazebrook, 1970. 37 p., 5 plates. illus., plan. 23 cm. Published in 1967 under title: A short history of Northampton's town halls. [DA690.N8G58] 76-503290 12/6
1. Municipal buildings—Northampton, Eng. I. Title.

GLAZEBROOK, Christopher John. 914.25'5
A short history of Northampton's town halls. Information collected & edited by C. J. Glazebrook. Northampton, 1967. 40 p. illus. 21 cm. Cover title. Published in 1970 under title: The history of Northampton's town halls. Bibliography: p. 34. [DA690.N8G58 1967] 72-196592
1. Municipal buildings—Northampton, Eng. 2. Northampton, Eng.—Buildings. I. Title.

Municipal research—West Haven, Conn.

WEST Haven Redevelopment Agency. 711'.4'097468
Limited urban observatory: West Haven; final report, prepared by West Haven Redevelopment Agency; New Haven Census Use Study, U.S. Dept. of Commerce; [and] Municipal Information Technology Program, University of Connecticut. [Final reports prepared by William L. Clarke and Joseph L. Sweeney. Storrs? Conn., 1969] 39, 49 p. illus., maps. 28 cm. Cover title. [HT110.W46] 74-630853
1. Municipal research—West Haven, Conn. I. Clarke, William Leonard, 1937- II. Sweeney, Joseph L. III. U.S. New Haven Census Use Study. IV. Connecticut. University. Municipal Information Technology Program. V. Title.

Municipal universities and colleges.

DOBBINS, Charles G., ed. 711.57
The university, the city, and urban renewal. Washington, D.C., Amer. Council on Educ. [c.1964] x, 58p. 23cm. Report of a regional conf. sponsored by the Amer. Council on Educ. and the West Philadelphia Corp., Philadelphia, March 25, 1963. 64-18211 1.50 pap.,
1. Municipal universities and colleges. 2. Urban renewal. I. American Council on Education. II. West Philadelphia Corporation. III. Title.

Municipal universities and colleges — Buildings.

DESIGN FETE, Rice University, 1962. 371.62
10 designs ; community colleges / Bill N. Lacey, editor. Houston, Tex., Dept. of Architecture, Rice University 1962] 100 p. illus. (part col.) col. map. plans, ports. 27 cm. "Sponsored by ... Educational Facilities Laboratories, inc., of New York City." [NA6600.D4] 62-21721
1. Municipal universities and colleges — Buildings. I. Lacey, Bill Neal, ed. II. William Marsh Rice University, Houston, Tex. Dept. of Architecture. III. Educational Facilities Laboratories. IV. Title.

Munsell, Joel, 1808-1880.

EDELSTEIN, David Simeon, 1913- 686'.20924
Joel Munsell: printer and antiquarian, by David S. Edelstein. New York, AMS Press, 1967 [c1950] 420 p. 23 cm. (Studies in history, economics, and public law, no. 560) Originally presented as the author's thesis, Columbia University. Bibliography: p. 389-407. [Z232.M923E4 1967] 75-164751
1. Munsell, Joel, 1808-1880. 2. Munsell, firm, publishers. I. Series: Columbia studies in the social sciences, 560.

Munting, Abraham, 1626-1683.

MUNTING, Abraham, 1626-1683. 769'.92'4
Decorative floral engravings : 118 plates from the 1696 Accurate description of terrestrial plants / by Abraham Munting ; edited by Theodore Menten. New York : Dover Publications, [1975] vi, 120 p. : ill. ; 32 cm. (Dover pictorial archive series) Edition for 1696 published under title: Naauwkeurige beschryving der aardgewassen. Includes index. [QK98.M85213 1975] 74-83764 ISBN 0-486-23117-8 : 3.50
1. Munting, Abraham, 1626-1683. Naauwkeurige beschryving der aardgewassen—Illustrations. 2. Botany—Pictorial works. 3. Botany—Pre-Linnean works. I. Title.

Mural painting and decoration.

ANTHONY, Edgar Waterman, 1890-1947. 751.73
Romanesque frescoes. Princeton, Princeton University Press, 1951. x, 208 p. 500 illus. 31 cm. Bibliographical footnotes. [ND2580.A5] 51-3518
1. Mural painting and decoration. 2. Church decoration and ornament. 3. Art, Romanesque. 4. Christian art and symbolism. I. Title.

GABRIEL, Mabel McAfee, 1885- 751.73
Livia's garden room at Prima Ports. New York, New York University Press, 1955. vii, 55p. 43illus. (incl. plan) 32cm. Bibliographical footnotes. [ND2575.G3] 55-10111
1. Mural painting and decoration. 2. Decoration and ornament— Italy—Prima Ports. 3. Livia Drusilla, wife of the Emperor Augustus, 56 B. C. (ca.)-29A.D. I. Title.

GOMBRICH, Ernst Hans Josef, 1909- 751.7'3
Means and ends : reflections on the history of fresco painting / E. H. Gombrich. London : Thames and Hudson, 1977,c1976. 72 p. : ill. ; 22 cm. (Walter Neurath memorial lectures ; no. 8) Includes bibliographical references. [ND2550.G65] 77-359594 ISBN 0-500-55008-5 : 9.95
1. Mural painting and decoration. I. Title. II. Series.
Distributed by W.W. Norton

HALE, Gardner, 1894-1931 751.44
The technique of fresco painting. Additional chapters prepd. from Mr. Hale's notes by Shaemas O'Sheel. Pref. by Jose Clemente Orozco. New York, Dover [1966] 69p. plates. 22cm. First pub. in 1933 under title Fresco painting [ND2470.H3] 66-15937 3.25
1. Mural painting and decoration. I. O'Sheel, Shaemas. 1886-1954. II. Title. BIP

HALE, Gardner. 1894-1931 751.44
The technique of fresco painting. With additional chapters prepd. from Mr. Hale's notes by Shaemas O'Sheel. Pref. by Jose Clemente Orozco [Gloucester, Mass., P. Smith, 1966] 69p. plates 22cm. (Dover bk. T1550 rebound) First pub. in 1933 by William Edwin Rudge under the title Fresco painting [ND2470.H3 1966] 3.25
1. Mural painting and decoration. I. O'Sheel, Shaemas, 1886-1954. II. Title.

KIVA mural decorations at Awatovi and Kawaika-a, 970.1 with a survey of other wall paintings in the Pueblo Southwest. With 9 plates in serigraph by Louie Ewing. Cambridge, Mass., The Museum, 1952. xxi, 363p. illus. (part col.) maps. 28cm. (Reports of the Awatovi Expedition. Report no. 5) Papers of the Peabody Museum of American Archeology and ethnology, Harvard University, v. 37. Errata slip inserited. References;: p. 327-347. [E51.H337 vol. 37] [E51.H337 vol. 37] 970.57172 A53 A53
1. Mural painting and decoration. 2. Decoration and ornament— Arizona. 3. Pueblo Indians—Art. 4. Awatovi, Ariz. I. Smith, Watson, 1897- II. Series: Harvard University. Peabody Museum of American Archaeology and Ethnology. Awatovi Expedition. Reports, no. 5 III. Series: Harvard University. Peabody Museum of American Archaeology and Ethnology. Papers, v. 37)

LITTLE, Nina Fletcher, 1903- 751.73
American decorative wall painting, 1700--1850. Sturbridge, Mass., Old Sturbridge Village, in cooperation with Studio Publications, New York City, 1952. xvi 145 p. illus. (part col.) 29 cm. Bibliography: p. 138-140. [ND2606.L58] 52-10836
1. Mural painting and decoration. 2. Decoration and ornament—U.S. I. Title. BIP

LITTLE, Nina Fletcher, 1903- 751'.73
American decorative wall painting, 1700-1850. New enl. ed. New York, Dutton, 1972. xx, 169 p. illus. (pt. col.) 29 cm. (Dutton pbk., D335) Originally published in 1952 by Old Sturbridge Village in cooperation with Studio Pubns. Bibl.: p. 138-140. [ND2606.L58] ISBN 0-525-47335-1 pap., 7.50;
1. Mural painting and decoration. 2. Decoration and ornament—U.S. I. Title.

OAKLEY, Violet, 1874- 751.73
The holy experiment, our heritage from William Penn; series of mural paintings in the governor's reception room in the Senate chamber, and in the supreme courtroom of the State Capitol at Harrisburg, Pennsylvania, U.S.A. [Philadelphia, Cogsela Studio Publications, 1950] 158 p. illus., plates. 32 cm. Bibliography: p. 147-149. [ND237.O3A3 1950] 50-11573
1. Mural painting and decoration. 2. Pennsylvania—Capital and capitol. I. Title.

WALL-PAINTINGS by snake charmers in Tanganyika. 759.01 New York, Grove Press [1953] 99p. illus. (part mounted col.) 26cm. [ND2866.T3] [ND2866.T3] 750.901 53-9824 53-9824
1. Mural painting and decoration. 2. Painting—Tanganyika Territory. 3. Art, Primitive. I. Cory, Hans.

WARSHAW, Howard. 759.13
Warshaw: a decade of murals. [Brunswick, Me.] Bowdoin College Museum of Art, 1972. [86] p. illus. (part col.) 20 x 28 cm. Catalog of the exhibition held Sept. 22-Nov. 5, 1972 at Bowdoin College Museum of Art, Brunswick, Me. and Feb. 10-March 11, 1973, at Santa Barbara Museum of Art, Santa Barbara, Calif. [ND237.W3533B68] 72-90514
I. Bowdoin College. Museum of Art. II. Santa Barbara, Calif. Musuem of Art. III. Title.

Mural painting and decoration—20th century—United States.

COCKCROFT, Eva. 751.7'3'0973
Toward a people's art : the contemporary mural movement / Eva Cockcroft, John Weber, and Jim Cockcroft ; foreword by Jean Charlot. New York : Dutton, c1977. xxvii, 292 p., [8] leaves of plates : ill. (some col.) ; 22 cm. Includes index. Bibliography: p. 280-284. [ND2608.C63 1977] 76-10038 ISBN 0-525-22165-4 : 12.95. ISBN 0-525-47426-9 pbk. : 7.95
1. Mural painting and decoration—20th century—United States. 2. Mural painting and decoration, American. 3. Community art projects—United States. 4. Art and society—United States. I. Weber, John, joint author. II. Cockcroft, James D., joint author. III. Title. BIP

GRIMES, Les. 751.7'3'0979493
The great murals of Farmer John Brand, Clougherty Meat Packing Co. in Vernon,

California. Concept and realization by Susan Hopmans. Photographed by Peter Kenner. [New York] Colorcraft Lithographers [1971] 1 v. (chiefly illus.) 18 x 27 cm. Based on S. Hopman's thesis (M.F.A.) Hunter College. [ND237.G66H65] 72-182722
1. Hopmans, Susan. II. Clougherty Meat Packing Co. III. Title.

Mural painting and decoration—Ajanta.

SINGH, Madanjeet. 759.95484
Ajanta; Ajanta painting of the sacred and the secular. New York, Macmillan [1965] 189 p. illus., plans, 82 plates (part col.) 31 cm. Bibliography: p. 189. [ND2827.S48] 65-22616
1. Mural painting and decoration — Ajanta. 2. Art, Buddhist. 3. Cave temples. I. Title. II. Title: Ajanta painting of the sacred and the secular.

UNITED Nations Educational, Scientific and Cultural Organization. 751.73
The Ajanta caves; early Buddhist paintings from India. Introd. by Benjamin Rowland [New York] New Amer. Lib. [c.1954, 1963] 24, [5]p. illus., 28 col. plates. 17cm. (Mentor-Unesco art bk.; MQ510) Bibl. 63-25402 .95 pap.,
1. Mural painting and decoration—Ajanta. 2. Art, Buddhist. 3. Cave temples. I. Rowland, Benjamin, 1904- II. Title.

Mural painting and decoration—Albany.

NEW York (State). University. 759.13
Mural paintings in the rotunda of the State Education Buildings, Albany, [designed and painted in the years 1913-18 by Will H. Low. Text by Leonard Freedman and Beverly Burke] Albany, 1967. iii, 32 p. illus. 14 x 22 cm. [ND2638.A3N4 1967] 68-64266
1. Albany. New York State Education Building. 2. Mural painting and decoration—Albany. I. Low, Will Hicok, 1853-1932. II. Freedman, Leonard. III. Burke, Beverly. IV. Title.

Mural painting and decoration, American.

ALLEN, Edward B. 751.7'3'0974
Early American wall paintings, 1710-1850, by Edward B. Allen. New York, Kennedy Graphics, 1971 [c1926] xiv, 110 p. illus. 27 cm. (Library of American art) [ND2606.A5 1971] 77-77694 ISBN 0-306-71332-2
1. Mural painting and decoration, American. I. Title.

ALLEN, Edward B. 759.13
Early American wall paintings, 1710-1850 [by] Edward B. Allen. Watkins Glen, N.Y., Century House [1969] 110 p. illus. 23 cm. (Classics in the visual arts) First published in 1926. [ND2606.A5 1969] 70-96942
1. Mural painting and decoration, American. I. Title. BIP

Mural painting and decoration—Antwerp.

MARTIN, John Rupert. 759.9493
The ceiling paintings for the Jesuit Church in Antwerp. London, New York, Phaidon, 1968. xvii, 241 p. illus., plan. 27 cm. (Corpus Rubenianum Ludwig Burchard, pt. 1) Bibliography: p. 13-17. [ND673.R9C63 pt. 1] 68-21258 1500.00
1. Antwerp. St. Charles Borromeo (Church) 2. Mural painting and decoration—Antwerp. I. Title. II. Series.

Mural painting and decoration—Bohemia.

DVORAKOVA, Vlasta. 759.37
Gothic mural painting in Bohemia and Moravia, 1300-1378 [by] Vlasta Dvorakova [and others. Translation from the Czech by Roberta Finlayson-Samsour and Iriv Urwin] London, New York, Oxford University Press, 1964. 160 p. maps. plates (part col.) 30 cm. Bibliography: p. 153-160. [ND2744.C9G63] 64-57059
1. Mural painting and decoration — Bohemia. 2. Mural painting and decoration — Moravia. 3. Mural painting and decoration, Gothic. I. Title.

GOTHIC moral painting in 759.37
Bohemia and Moravia, 1300-1378 by Viasta Dvorakava others. Tr. from Czech by Roberta Finlayson-Samsour, Iris Urwin. New York, Oxford [c.]1964. 160p. maps, plates (pt. col.) 30cm. Bibl. 64-57059 8.80
1. Mural painting and decoration—Bohemia. 2. Mural painting and decoration—Moravia. 3. Mural painting and decoration, Gothic. I. Dvorakova, Vlasta.

Mural, painting and decoration, Bulgarian.

UNITED Nations Educational, Scientific and Cultural Organization. 751.73
Bulgaria, mediaeval wall paintings. Pref. [by] Andre Grabar. Introd. [by] Krsto Mijatev. [Greenwich, Conn.] N. Y. Graphic [1962, c.1961] 26, [5]p. illus. (pt. col.) 48cm. (UNESCO world art ser., 17) Bibl. 62-3577 18.00,bds., bxd.
1. Mural, painting and decoration, Bulgarian. 2. Mural painting and decoration, Medieval. I. Grabar, Andre, 1896- II. Title. III. Series.

Mural painting and decoration, Byzantine.

UNITED Nations Educational, Scientific and Cultural Organization 751.73
Byzantine frescoes from Yugoslav churches. Introd. by David Talbot Rice. [New York] New Amer. Lib. [c.1955, 1963] 24, [6]p. illus., 28 col. plates. 17cm. (MentorUnesco art bk.; MQ514) Bibl. 63-25401 .95 pap.,
1. Mural painting and decoration, Byzantine. 2. Mural painting and decoration, Serbian. 3. Mural painting and decoration, Macedonian. I. Rice, David Talbot, 1903- II. Title.

Mural painting and decoration, Byzantine—Turkey.

RESTLE, Marcell, 1932- 751.7'3'09561
Byzantine wall painting in Asia Minor. Greenwich, Conn., New York Graphic Society [1968, c1967] 3 v. illus. (part col.), maps, plans. 28 cm. Translation of Die bysantinische Wandmalerei in Kleinasien. Contents.Contents.—1. Text.—2-3. Plates. Bibliography: v. 1, p. 9-12. [ND2794.R413] 68-12371 75.00
1. Mural painting and decoration, Byzantine—Turkey. 2. Mural painting and decoration—Turkey. I. Title.

Mural painting and decoration, Chinese.

FAIRBANK, Wilma. 751.7'3'0951
Adventures in retrieval; Han murals and Shang bronze molds. Cambridge, Mass., Harvard University Press, 1972. 201 p. illus. 26 cm. (Harvard-Yenching Institute studies, 28) Includes bibliographical references. [ND2848.F34] 79-173410 ISBN 0-674-00575-9
1. Mural painting and decoration, Chinese. 2. Bronzes, Chinese—To 221 B.C. I. Title. II. Series. BIP

Mural painting and decoration—Dura, Syria—Addresses, essays, lectures.

THE Dura-Europes 755'.9'6
synagogue; a re-evaluation (1932-1972). Edited by Joseph Gutmann. [Chambersburg, Pa.] American Academy of Religion, 1973. 190 p. illus. 21 cm. (Religion and the arts 1) Bibliography: p. [157]-159. [ND2819.S93D872] 73-85879 ISBN 0-88414-024-5
1. Dura, Syria. Synagogue—Addresses, essays, lectures. 2. Mural painting and decoration—Dura, Syria—Addresses, essays, lectures. 3. Jewish art and symbolism—Addresses, essays, lectures. I. Gutmann, Joseph, ed. II. Title. III. Series.

Mural painting and decoration, Egyptian.

MEKHITARIAN, Arpag. 751.7'3'0932
Egyptian painting / text by Arpag Mekhitarian ; [translated from the French by Stuart Gilbert]. New York : Skira, 1978. 164 p. : col. ill. ; 28 cm. Includes index. Bibliography: p. 158. [ND2863.M4413 1978] 78-110973 ISBN 0-8478-0161-6 : 22.50 ISBN 0-8478-0159-4 pbk. : 13.95
1. Mural painting and decoration, Egyptian. I. Title.
Distributed by Rizzoli Int'l, NYC

Mural painting and decoration, English.

CAIGER-SMITH, A. 751.730942
English medieval mural paintings. Oxford, Clarendon Pr. [dist. New York. Oxford, c.1963] 190p. plates (1 col.) 25cm. Bibl. 63-5041 7.20
1. Mural painting and decoration, English. 2. Mural painting and decoration, Medieval. I. Title.

Mural painting and decoration, Etruscan.

MORETTI, Mario. 751.7'3'09375
New monuments of Etruscan painting. Foreword by Massimo Pallottino. English translation by Dawson Kiang. University Park, Pennsylvania State University Press, 1970. xxxvii, 359 p. illus. (part col.), maps (part col.), plans. 38 cm. (Series of monographs in archaeology. Etruscan painting, v. 1) Translation of Nuovi monumenti della pittura etrusca. Bibliography: p. 343-344. [ND2565.M613] 68-8548 ISBN 0-271-00079-1
1. Mural painting and decoration, Etruscan. I. Title. BIP

Mural painting and decoration, Euboea.

IOANNOU, Andreas Spyridonos 709.02
Byzantine frescoe of Euboea. Title transliterated: Byzantines toichographies tes Euboias. A' thirteenth and fourteenth centuries. [distributor: Wittenborn, New York, 1959, i.e. 1960] xiii, 100, xx p. (chiefly illus., part mounted col.) map. 26cm. Greek and English 60-1944 10.00 half cloth,
1. Mural painting and decoration, Euboea. 2. Mural painting and decoration, Byzantine. I. Title. II. Title: Byzantine frescoes of Euboea,

Mural painting and decoration—Exhibitions.

JEWISH Theological Seminary of America. Jewish Museum. 751.7'3'07401471
Using walls (indoors). [New York, 1970] [28] p. illus. 26 cm. Catalog of the exhibition held at the Jewish Museum, New York May 13-June 21, 1970. Includes bibliographical references. [ND2550.J4] 73-125483
1. Mural painting and decoration—Exhibitions. I. Title.

Mural painting and decoration, Greco-Roman—Pompeii.

LITTLE, Alan MacNaughton Gordon. 757'.6'094572
A Roman bridal drama at the Villa of the Mysteries [by Alan M. G. Little. Wheaton, Md., 1972] 47 p. illus. 28 cm. "Companion piece to Roman perspective painting and the ancient stage." Includes bibliographical references. [ND2575.L57] 73-151705 3.00
1. Mural painting and decoration, Greco-Roman—Pompeii. 2. Mural painting and decoration—Pompeii. 3. Marriage in art. 4. Dionysia. 5. Pompeii. Villa dei misteri dionisiaci. I. Title.

Mural painting and decoration—Himalaya region.

SINGH, Madanjeet. 709'.54
Himalayan art; wall-painting and sculpture in Ladakh, Lahaul, and Spiti, the Siwalik Ranges, Nepal, Sikkim, and Bhutan. Greenwich, Conn., New York Graphic Society [1968] 295 p. illus. (part col.), col. map. 34 cm. (Unesco art books) Bibliography: p. 294-295. [N7307.H5S56] 68-28652 35.00
1. Mural painting and decoration—Himalaya region. 2. Sculpture—Himalaya region. I. Title. II. Series: United Nations Educational, Scientific and Cultural Organization. Unesco art books

SINGH, Madanjeet. 709.54
Himalayan art; wall-painting and sculpture in Iadakh, Lahaul and Spiti, the Siwalik Ranges, Nepal, Sikkim, and Bhutan. [New York] Macmillan [1971, c1968] 287 p. illus. (part col.), map. 22 cm. (Unesco art books) "Published in agreement with Unesco." Bibliography: p. 281-282. [N7307.H5S56 1971] 77-24701
1. Mural painting and decoration—Himalaya region. 2. Sculpture—Himalaya region. I. Title. II. Series: United Nations Educational, Scientific and Cultural Organization. Unesco art books BIP

Mural painting and decoration, Indic.

BARRETT, Douglas E. 759.954
Indian painting / text by Douglas Barrett and Basil Gray. New York : Skira, 1978. 213 p. : col. ill. ; 29 cm. (Treasures of Asia) Published in 1963 under title: Painting of India. Includes indexes. Bibliography: p. 195-196. [ND2827.B37 1978] 78-110976 ISBN 0-8478-0160-8 : 25.00. ISBN 0-8478-0158-6 pbk. : 14.95
1. Mural painting and decoration, Indic. 2. Miniature painting, Indic. I. Gray, Basil, 1904- joint author. II. Title. III. Series.
Distributed by Rizzoli Intl., 715 Fifth Ave., New York, NY 10019

Mural painting and decoration, Italian—Exhibitions.

THE Great age of fresco: 759.5
Giotto to Pontormo; an exhibition of mural paintings and monumental drawings. [New York] Metropolitan Museum of Art, 1968. 233 p. illus. (part col.) 24 cm. "Organized in collaboration with the Soprintendenza of the Florentine Galleries." Held during 1968-69 at the Metropolitan Museum of Art, the Rijks museum in Amsterdam, and the Hayward Gallery in London. Includes bibliographies. [ND2755.G7] 73-3720
1. Mural painting and decoration, Italian—Exhibitions. I. Italy. Soprintendenza alle gallerie per le provincie di Firenze, Arezzo e Pistoria. II. New York (City) Metropolitan Museum of Art. III. Amsterdam. Rijks-Museum. IV. Hayward Gallery.

Mural painting and decoration, Jewish.

LEVEEN, Jacob, 1891- 096'.1
The Hebrew Bible in art / by Jacob Leveen. New York : Hermon Press, [1974] xx, 140 p., [21] leaves of plates : ill. ; 24 cm. Reprint, with a new pref. and addenda and corrigenda by the author, of the 1944 ed. published for the British Academy by H. Milford, Oxford University Press, London, in series: The Schweich lectures of the British Academy, 1939. Includes index. Bibliography: p. [129]-135. [N8023.L47 1974] 74-78239 ISBN 0-87203-045-8 : 12.50
1. Bible. O.T.—Pictures, illustrations, etc. 2. Mural painting and decoration, Jewish. 3. Illumination of books and manuscripts, Jewish. I. Title. II. Series: The Schweich lectures ; 1939. BIP

Mural painting and decoration, Medieval—Italy.

MEISS, Millard. 751.7'3'0945
The great age of fresco; discoveries, recoveries, and survivals. New York, G. Braziller in association with the Metropolitan Museum of Art, 1970. 251 p. illus. (part col.) 32 cm. Bibliography: p.

Murray, Dean L.—Art—Collections.

MURRAY, Dean L.   748.8
More cruets only. [Illustrated by Dean L. Murray. Phoenix, Ariz., Killgore Graphics, 1973] 78 p. col. illus. 23 cm. [NK5440.C75M87] 73-168224 7.95
1. Murray, Dean L.—Art—Collections. 2. Cruets—Catalogs. I. Title.
Publisher's Address: 1401 E. Washington Ave., Phoenix, Ariz. 85004.   **BIP**

Murray Hill, New York.

PINS, Anita.   974.7'1
An historic district in Murray Hill / by Anita Pins. New York : Murray Hill Committee, c1977. 86 p. : ill. ; 23 cm. Bibliography: p. 83-86. [F128.68.M87P56] 77-152158
1. Murray Hill, New York. 2. Historic buildings—New York (City)—Conservation and restoration. 3. New York (City)—Dwellings. I. Title.

Museo de Arte de Cataluna.

OLIVAR Daydi, Marcal.   708.6'72
The Art Museum of Catalonia, Barcelona. Text by Marcial Olivar. [Translated from the Italian by James Brockway] New York, Meredith Press [1968] 160 p. (chiefly illus. (part col.)) 28 cm. (Great galleries series) Translation of Museo d'arte di Catalogna, Barcellona. [N3410.5.O413] 71-4548 8.95
1. Museo de Arte de Cataluna. I. Title.

Museum architecture—Exhibitions.

NEW YORK (City). Museum of   727'.6
Modern Art.
Architecture of museums; [exhibition] September 24-November 11, 1968. [New York, 1968] [20] p. illus. 22 cm. [NA6700.N46] 68-17129
1. Museum architecture—Exhibitions. I. Title.

Museum directors—United States—Biography.

KRAKEL, Dean   069'.9'70924 B
Fenton, 1923-
Adventures in Western art / by Dean Krakel. Kansas City, Mo. : Lowell Press, [1977] p. cm. Bibliography: p. [N654.K7] 76-21136 ISBN 0-913504-35-1 : 11.95
1. Krakel, Dean Fenton, 1923- 2. National Cowboy Hall of Fame and Western Heritage Center. 3. Museum directors—United States—Biography. 4. The West in art. I. Title.   **BIP**

Museum finance—U.S.

MCGRATH, Kyran M.   338.43
1971 financial and salary survey, by Kyran M. McGrath. [Washington, D.C., American Association of Museums, 1971] 92 p. illus. 21 cm. [AM122.M3] 70-175923 5.00
1. Museum finance—U.S. I. American Association of Museums. II. Title.

MCGRATH, Kyran M.   338.4'3
1973 museum salary and financial survey, by Kyran M. McGrath. [Washington] American Association of Museums [1973] xii, 110 p. 21 cm. [AM122.M32] 73-11020 10.00
1. Museum finance—United States. I. American Association of Museums. II. Title.

Museum libraries.

ANDERSON, Linda M.   026'.069
Libraries for small museums [by] Linda M. Anderson. Columbia, Museum of Anthropology, University of Missouri, 1971. ii, 80 l. 28 cm. (Museum brief 7) Bibliography: leaf 80. [E151.M87 no. 7] [Z675.M94] 71-635476
1. Museum libraries. I. Title. II. Series: Museum briefs, 7

ANDERSON, Linda M.   026'.069
Libraries for small museums / by Linda Anderson, Marcia R. Collins. 2d ed. Columbia : Museum of Anthropology, University of Missouri-Columbia, 1975. iii,

48 p. ; 28 cm. (Miscellaneous publications in anthropology ; no. 4) Bibliography: p. 48. [Z675.M94A53 1975] 76-353333 ISBN 0-913134-96-1
1. Museum libraries. I. Collins, Marcia R., joint author. II. Title. III. Series.

COLLINS, Marcia R.   026'.069
Libraries for small museums / by Marcia Collins, Linda Anderson. [3d ed.]. Columbia : Museum of Anthropology, University of Missouri-Columbia, c1977. iii, 48 p. : ill. ; 28 cm. (Miscellaneous publications in anthropology ; # 4) Anderson's name appeared 1st on t.p. of 2d ed. Bibliography: p. 48. [Z675.M94A53 1977] 78-620740 ISBN 0-913134-90-2
1. Museum libraries. I. Anderson, Linda M., joint author. II. Title. III. Series.

Museum manikins.

COFER, Janet.   069'.53
Manikins for the small museum. Columbia, Museum of Anthropology, University of Missouri-Columbia, 1970. 20 l. illus. 28 cm. (Museum briefs, no. 2) Bibliography: leaves [19]-20. [E151.M87 no. 2] [AM151] 75-635477
1. Museum manikins. I. Title. II. Series.

Museum of Graphic Art.

CASSATT, Mary, 1845-   760'.0924
1926
The graphic art of Mary Cassatt. Introd. by Adelyn D. Breeskin. Foreword by Donald H. Karshan. [New York] Museum of Graphic Art [1967] 111 p. illus. 26cm. Exhibition organized by the Mus. of Graphic Art, New York. Participating museums: Cincinnati Art Mus. [and others] [NE539.C3B7 1967] 67-30432 8.50 4.50 pap.,
1. Museum of Graphic Art. I. Cincinnati. Art Museum. II. Title.

Museum registration methods.

CHENHALL, Robert   069'.52'02854
G., 1923-
Museum cataloging in the computer age [by] Robert G. Chenhall. Nashville, American Association for State and Local History, 1975. viii, 261 p. illus. 24 cm. Includes bibliographical references. [AM139.C48 1975] 74-16439 ISBN 0-910050-12-0 17.50
1. Museum registration methods. 2. Museums—Data processing. I. Title.   **BIP**

DUDLEY, Dorothy H.   069'.52
Museum registration methods [by] Dorothy H. Dudley, Irma Bezold Wilkinson, and others. Rev. Washington, American Association of Museums, 1968. viii, 294 p. illus., forms, plans. 26 cm. Includes bibliographies. [AM139.D8 1968] 68-20274
1. Museum registration methods. I. Wilkinson, Irma Bezold, joint author. II. American Association of Museums.

Museum techniques.

NEAL, Arminta.   069'.5
Exhibits for the small museum : a handbook / Arminta Neal ; with an introductory essay by H. J. Swinney. Nashville : American Association for State and Local History, c1976. ix, 169 p. : ill. ; 26 cm. [AM151.N37] 76-21812 ISBN 0-910050-48-1 pbk. 8.00
1. Museum techniques. I. Title.   **BIP**

NELSON, George, 1908- ed.   069.53
Display. [New York, Whitney Publications, 1953] 190p. (chiefly illus., part col.) 32cm. (Interiors library, 3) [AM151.N4] 53-13449
1. Museum techniques. I. Title.

WARREN, Jefferson T.   069'.53
Exhibit methods, by Jefferson T. Warren. New York, Sterling Pub. Co. [1972] 80 p. illus. (part col.) 29 cm. [AM151.W37] 72-81046 ISBN 0-8069-5230-X
1. Museum techniques. I. Title.

Museums.

BRAWNE, Michael   727.7
The new museum: architecture and display [Tr. into German by Wolfgang Pehnt] New York, Praeger [1966, c1965] 208p. illus. 29cm. English and German. Bibl. [NA6700.A1B7] 66-11013 20.00
1. Museums. 2. Architecture—Designs and plans. 3. Museum techniques. I. Title.

COLEMAN, Laurence Vail,   727.6
1893-
Museum buildings. Washington, American Association of Museums, 1950- v. illus. 29 cm. Contents.v. 1. A planning study. [NA6700.A1C6] 50-58201
1. Museums. 2. Art—Galleries and museums. I. Title.

NEVADA. State   069'.2'0979357
Museum, Carson City.
Nevada State Museum guide. 3d revision. [Carson City, 1968] [32] p. illus. 17 x 26 cm. (Information series) Cover title. [AM101.N465 1968] 79-625796
I. Title. II. Series.

Museums and schools.

ZETTERBERG, Hans Lennart,   069'.1
1927-
Museums and adult education [by] Hans L. Zetterberg. New York, A. M. Kelley for the International Council of Museums, 1969 [c1968] xi, 89 p. 2 plates. 25 cm. Sponsored by the Icom Committee for Education and Cultural Action with the help of Unesco. Bibliography: p. 76-89. [LB3291.Z4 1969] 70-95622
1. Museums and schools. 2. Adult education. I. International Council of Museums. Committee for Education and Cultural Action. II. United Nations Educational, Scientific, and Cultural Organization. III. Title.   **BIP**

Museums — Furniture, equipment, etc.

AMERICAN Association of   v. 12
Museums.
Museum suppliers registry. 1964- ed. Washington. v. 23 cm. annual Cover title, 1964- [AM127.A6A9] 64-4478
1. Museums — Furniture, equipment, etc. I. Title. II. Title: MSR; museum suppliers registry.

Museums—Handbooks, manuals, etc.

NEAL, Arminta.   069'.53
Help! for the small museum; a handbook of exhibit ideas and methods. Boulder, Colo., Pruett Press [1969] 200 p. illus. 28 cm. Bibliography: p. 195-199. [AM151.N38] 70-75438 7.50
1. Museums—Handbooks, manuals, etc. I. Title.   **BIP**

Museums—Illinois—Directories.

WHITTAKER, Mary Jo.   069'.025'773
Museums of Illinois. [1st ed.] Salem, Ill., Weekends [1974] 160 p. illus. 26 cm. [AM12.I3W46] 74-172693 3.00
1. Museums—Illinois—Directories. I. Title.

Museums—Kansas.

ARY, Noel.   917.81'7'03
Museums of Southwest Kansas. Dodge City, Kan., Cultural Heritage and Arts Center [1969] 63 p. illus., map. 22 cm. "Title III, ESEA project no. 68-5772." [AM12.K2A78] 79-17160
1. Museums—Kansas. I. Cultural Heritage and Arts Center. II. Title.

Museums—Management.

GUTHE, Carl Eugen,   658'.91'069
1893-
So you want a good museum; a guide to the management of small museums, by Carl E. Guthe. [Washington] American Association of Museums [1973] iii, 37 p. 25 cm. Reprint of the 1957 ed., which was issued as new ser., no. 17 of American Association of Museums publications. Bibliography: p. 35. [AM121.G87 1973] 73-4804

1. Museums—Management. I. Title. II. Series: American Association of Museums. Publications, new ser., no. 17.

ROYAL Ontario Museum.   658'.91'069
Communications Design Team.
Communicating with the museum visitor : guidelines for planning / prepared by the Communications Design Team of the Royal Ontario Museum. Toronto : Royal Ontario Museum, 1976. xx, 498 p. : ill. ; 28 cm. At head of title: ROM. Includes index. Bibliography: p. 477-491. [AM121.R69 1976] 77-361681 ISBN 0-88854-193-7
1. Museums—Management. 2. Museum attendance. I. Title.

Museums—Massachusetts.

BERKSHIRE Museum,   708.144'1
Pittsfield, Mass.
A guide to the collections. Pittsfield, Mass. [1968] 47 p. (chiefly illus.) 22 cm. [N711.A54] 68-4362
I. Title.

MASSACHUSETTS. Dept. of   917.44'03
Commerce and Development.
Guide to Massachusetts museums. [Boston, 1968] 120 p. 23 x 11 cm. Cover title. [AM12.M4A47] 79-628274 0.20
1. Museums—Massachusetts. I. Title.

Museums — Security measures.

KECK, Caroline (Kohn) ed.   069.54
A primer on museum security. by Caroline K. Keck. [others] Cooperstown, N. Y., N. Y. State Hist. Assn., 1966. vi, 85p. illus. 23cm. The substance of a course entitled "Museum security" presented during the seminars held by N. Y. State Hist. Assn. July 13-18, 1964, at Cooperstown. Ed. from the tape-recorded talks and discussions by Caroline Keck and the other authors. Bibl. [AM148.K4] 66-8629 1.95 pap.,
1. Museums — Security measures. I. New York State Historical Association. II. Title. III. Title: Museum security.
Available from the Farmers' Museum Shop, Cooperstown, N. Y. 13326.   **BIP**

Museums—Texas—Directories.

TEXAS. State   069'.025764
Historical Survey Committee.
Texas museums directory. Rev. Austin, Distributed by the Texas Highway Dept. and T.H.S.C., 1970. 61 p. 22 x 10 cm. [AM12.T45T48 1970] 73-170214
1. Museums—Texas—Directories. I. Title.

Museums—Trustees—Addresses, essays, lectures.

NAUMER, Helmuth J.   658.4'2
Of mutual respect and other things : an essay on museum trusteeship / Helmuth J. Naumer. Washington : American Association of Museums, c1977. 31 p. ; 23 cm. Bibliography: p. 29-31. [AM121.N38] 77-152889
1. Museums—Trustees—Addresses, essays, lectures. I. Title.

Museums—Washington (State)

WASHINGTON (State).   069'.09797
State Library, Olympia.
Museums of the State of Washington. [Olympia] 1971. 22 l. 28 cm. Cover title. [AM12.W2A5] 78-636701
1. Museums—Washington (State) I. Title.

Museums—Wyoming.

WYOMING. State Museum,   069'.09787
Cheyenne.
Guide to museums in Wyoming. [1st ed.] Cheyenne, 1969. 52 l. maps. 28 cm. [AM12.W9W9] 79-629500 0.50
1. Museums—Wyoming. I. Title.

Music—Bibliography—Manuscripts.

ALBRECHT, Otto Edwin,   781.973
1899-
A census of autograph music manuscripts

SUBJECT INDEX MUSICAL INSTRUMENTS IN

of European composers in American libraries. Philadelphia, University of Pennsylvania Press, 1953. xvii, 331p. 24cm. Cover title: Census of European music manuscripts. Includes lists of present and former owners of manuscripts (p. 317-328) Bibliography: p. 329-331. [ML135.A2A4] 53-1163
1. Music—Bibl.—Mamuscripts. 2. Music—Manuscripts—U. S. I. Title. II. Title: Census of European music manuscripts.

Music—Bibliography—Catalogs.

PIERPONT Morgan Library, 016.78
New York.
The Mary Flagler Cary Music Collection; printed books and music, manuscripts, autograph letters, documents, portraits. New York [1970] xii, 108 p. xlix plates (facsims.) 28 cm. Catalog. Bibliography: p. 107-108. [ML136.N52P5] 73-133290
1. Music—Bibliography—Catalogs. 2. Music—Bibliography—Manuscripts. I. Cary, Mary Flagler. II. Title. BIP

Music—Bibliography—Manuscripts.

GOMBOSI, Marilyn, 781'.973'2
comp.
Catalog of the Johannes Herbst Collection. Edited by Marilyn Gombosi. Chapel Hill, University of North Carolina Press [1970] xix, 255 p. facsims., music. 24 cm. Thematic catalog of Moravian Church music copied by Johannes Herbst. [ML97.H375G6] 72-97011
1. Music—Bibliography—Manuscripts. 2. Church music—Moravian Church—Bibliography. I. Herbst, Johannes, 1735-1812. II. Title.

WINDSOR Castle. St. 016.783'026
George's Chapel.
The musical manuscripts of St. George's Chapel, Windsor Castle: a descriptive catalogue, by Clifford Mould. Windsor, Oxley and Son (Windsor) Ltd for the Dean and Canons of St. George's Chapel in Windsor Castle, 1973. ix, 76 p. music. 28 cm. (Historical monographs relating to St. George's Chapel, Windsor Castle, v. 14.) [ML138.W45] 74-163307 ISBN 0-902187-16-3 £1.25
1. Music—Bibliography—Manuscripts. 2. Music—Bibliography—Catalogs. 3. Music—Manuscripts—England. I. Mould, Clifford. II. Title. III. Series.

Music—Denmark—History and criticism—Sources.

HAMMERICH, Angul, 1848- 781.7'489
Mediaeval musical relics of Denmark / by Angul Hammerlich ; translated from Danish by Margaret Williams Hamerik. New York : AMS Press, 1976. viii, 124 p. : ill. ; 26 cm. Reprint of the 1912 ed. published by Breitkopf & Hartel, Leipzig. "With subvention of the Carlsberg Fund." Bibliography: p. [114]-116. [ML93.H2313 1976] 74-24104 ISBN 0-404-12952-8 : 24.50
1. Music—Denmark—History and criticism—Sources. 2. Music—Manuscripts—Facsimiles. 3. Church music—Denmark—History and criticism. 4. Church music—Catholic church. 5. Music—Theory—Medieval, 400-1500. I. Hamerik, Margaret Williams, 1867-1942. II. Title. BIP

Music-halls—Juvenile literature.

LERNER, Sharon 725
Places of musical fame. Illus. by George Overlie. Prepared under supervision of Robert W. Surplus. Minneapolis, Lerner Pubns. [c.1962] 48p. col. illus. 24cm. (Musical bks. for young people) 62-20803 2.75 bds.,
1. Music-halls—Juvenile literature. I. Title. BIP

Music—History and criticism.

LANG, Paul Henry, 1901- 780.9
A pictorial history of music [by] Paul Henry Lang and Otto Bettmann. [1st ed.] New York, Norton [1960] vii, 242 p. illus., facsims., ports. 29 cm. "Text based on Music in Western civilization, by Paul Henry Lang, copyright 1941." [ML89.L15] 60-6822
1. Music—History and criticism. 2. Music in art. 3. Musicians—Portraits. 4. Musical instruments in art. I. Bettmann, Otto, joint author. II. Title. BIP

Music in art.

BECK, Sydney. 726'.5'094223
Music in prints [by] Sydney Beck and Elizabeth E. Roth. [New York] New York Public Library, 1965. 1 v. (unpaged) facsims. 26 cm. "The publication of Music in prints was inspired by ... an exhibition on the same subject recently prepared by the Prints Division of The New York Public Library." [ML85.B34] 65-13045
1. Music in art. 2. Musical instruments — Pictorial works. I. Roth, Elizabeth E., joint author II. Title. BIP

CELENDER, Donald D. 704.94978191
Musical instruments in art, by Donald Celender. Designed by Wendell Carroll. Minneapolis, Lerner Publications Co., [1966] 72 p. illus. (part col.) port. 27 cm. (Fine art books for young people) [ML85.C44] 65-29037
1. Music in art. I. Title. BIP

HESS, Albert Gunter. 758.878
Italian Renaissance paintings with musical subjects; a corpus of such works in American collections, with detailed descriptions of the musical features. [Limited ed.] New York, Libra Press, 1955- v. plates. 31cm. Cover title. Issued in parts. Bibliography: fasc. 11, p. [8] [ML85.H4] 55-7004
1. Music in art. 2. Paintings, Renaissance. 3. Paintings, Italian. 4. Paintings— U. S. I. Title.

LESURE, Francois. 780'.08
Music and art in society. Foreword by Denis Stevens. Preface by Pierre Francastel. [Translated by Denis and Sheila Stevens] University Park, Pennsylvania State University Press, 1968. xxvi, 59 p. 96 plates (part col.) 29 cm. Bibliography: p. 55-59. [ML85.L4813] 67-27113
1. Music in art. 2. Music and society. I. Title.

MCALEER, Ken. 741.9'73
A progressive rock portfolio. [Illustrated, designed by Ken McAleer. Limited 1st ed. Syracuse, N.Y., Central New Yorker, 1970] [96] l. of illus. 26 x 34 cm. [ML85.M22] 78-18244 8.95
1. Music in art. I. Title.

MEDEIROS, Walter Patrick. 769'.5
San Francisco rock concert posters: imagery and meaning. [n.p., 1972] vi, 126 l. illus. 28 cm. Thesis—University of California, Berkeley. Bibliography: leaves 123-126. [ML85.M42] 74-172934
1. Music in art. 2. Rock music—History and criticism. 3. Music and society. I. Title.

MUSIC. 704.94978
Greenwich, Conn., N. Y. Graphic [1965] 64p. illus., 20 col. plates. 32cm. (Man through his art, v.2) Bibl. [ML85.M97] 65-3602 7.95
1. Music in art.

Music—Manuscripts.

COUSSEMAKER, Edmond de, 016.78
1805-1876.
Notice sur les collections musicales de la Bibliotheque de Cambrai et des autres villes du department du Nord / Charles Edmond Henri de Coussemaker. Hildesheim ; New York : G. Olms, 1975. 180, 40 p. : ill., music ; 19 cm. Reprint of the 1843 ed. published by C. Techner, Paris. Includes bibliographical references and index. [ML136.C17C8 1975] 76-450668 ISBN 3-487-05857-X
1. Music—Manuscripts. 2. Music—France—Bibliography. 3. Manuscripts—France. I. Title: Notice sur les collections musicales de la Bibliotheque de Cambrai ...

Music—Philosophy and aesthetics.

MEYERBAER KATHI 1892-3 780'.1
meyerbaer kathi 1892
Music of the spheres and the dance of death; studies in musical iconology. Princeton, Princeton University Press, 1970. xxii, 376 p. illus., facsims. 25 cm. Includes bibliographical references. [ML3849.M58] 68-15768 13.50
1. Music—Philosophy and aesthetics. 2. Death in music. 3. Music in art. I. Title.

Music printing.

GAMBLE, William, 1864- 686'.284
1933.
Music engraving and printing; historical and technical treatise. New York, B. Blom, 1971. ix, 266 p. illus. 22 cm. Reprint of the 1923 ed. [ML112.G16 1971b] 72-173166
1. Music printing. I. Title. BIP

GAMBLE, William, 1864- 686'.284
1933.
Music engraving and printing; historical and technical treatise. New York, Da Capo Press, 1971. x, 266 p. illus., facsims., music. 24 cm. (Da Capo Press music reprint series) Reprint of the 1923 ed. [ML112.G16 1971] 70-155576 ISBN 0-306-70168-5
1. Music printing. I. Title.

KROHN, Ernst Christopher, 780'.65
1888-
Music publishing in the middle western states before the Civil War, by Ernst C. Krohn. Detroit, Information Coordinators, 1972. 44 p. 23 cm. (Detroit studies in music bibliography, 23) Includes bibliographical references. [ML112.K74] 70-175173 ISBN 0-911772-47-2 4.00
1. Music printing. 2. Publishers and publishing—Middle West. I. Title. II. Series. BIP

KRUMMEL, Donald William, 686.284
1929-
Graphic analysis, its application to early American engraved music, by Donald W. Krummel. [Washington, D.C., 1959] 213-[233] p. illus. 23 cm. L.C. copy imperfect: p. 233 wanting. Offprint from Music Library Association Notes, 2d ser., vol. 16, no. 2, March, 1959. [ML112.K76] 68-128470
1. Music printing. 2. Publishers and publishing—United States. I. Title.

ROSS, Ted. 686'.284
The art of music engraving and processing; a complete manual, reference and text book on preparing music for reproduction and print. Miami, Hansen Books [1970] x, 278 p. illus. 23 cm. Bibliography: p. 277. [ML112.R75] 78-125460 9.95
1. Music printing. I. Title.

Music title-pages.

FRAENKEL, Gottfried 781'.97
Samuel, 1901- comp.
Decorative music title pages; 201 examples from 1500 to 1800. Selected, introduced, annotated by Gottfried S. Fraenkel Magnolia, Mass., Peter Smith, 1968] xvi, 230p. illus. 201 plates (facsims.) 29cm. (Dover bk. rebound) [ML112.5.F73] 6.00
1. Music title-pages. 2. Music printing. I. Title.

FRAENKEL, Gottfried 781'.97
Samuel, 1901- comp.
Decorative music title pages; 201 examples from 1500 to 1800. Selected, introduced, and annotated by Gottfried S. Fraenkel. New York, Dover Publications [1968] xvi, 230 p. illus., 201 plates (facsims.) 29 cm. [ML112.5.F73] 67-27232
1. Music title-pages. 2. Music printing. I. Title. BIP

KLAMKIN, Marian. 769'.5
Old sheet music : a pictorial history / Marian Klamkin ; photos. by Charles Klamkin. New York : Hawthorn Books, c1975. 214 p., [4] leaves of plates : facsims. (some col.) ; 29 cm. Includes index. [ML112.5.K55] 74-18695 ISBN 0-8015-5500-0 : 19.95
1. Music title-pages. 2. Music, Popular (Songs, etc.)—United States—History and criticism. I. Title.

LEVY, Lester S. 769'.5
Picture the songs : lithographs from the sheet music of nineteenth-century America / Lester S. Levy. Baltimore : Johns Hopkins University Press, c1976. x, 213 p. : ill. ; 29 cm. Includes index. Bibliography: p. 206-211. [ML112.5.L43] 76-13518 ISBN 0-8018-1814-1 : 25.00
1. Music title-pages. 2. Lithographs, American. 3. United States—Popular culture. I. Title. BIP

SPELLMAN, Doreen. 769'.5
Victorian music covers, by Doreen and Sidney Spellman. With a foreword by Sacheverell Sitwell. [1st U.S. ed.] Park Ridge, N.J., Noyes Press [1972, c1969] 72 p. illus., facsims. 21 cm. Bibliography: p. 72. [ML112.5.S73 1972] 72-76733 ISBN 0-8155-5004-9 7.00
1. Music title-pages. I. Spellman, Sidney, joint author. II. Title.

TATHAM, David. 769'.5
The lure of the striped pig; the illustration of popular music in America, 1820-1870. Barre, Mass., Imprint Society, 1973. 157 p. illus., 60 facsims. (part col.) 38 cm. "Bibliographic note": p. 157. [ML112.5.T38] 72-93852 ISBN 0-87636-051-7 40.00
1. Music title-pages. 2. Illustrators, American. I. Title.

Music title pages—United States.

DAVISON, Nancy R. 081 s
American sheet music illustration: reflections of the nineteenth century; a guide to an exhibition in the Museum of Art, October 12-November 18, by Nancy R. Davison. [Ann Arbor] William L. Clements Library, University of Michigan, 1973. 24 p. facsims. 24 cm. (William L. Clements Library, University of Michigan. Bulletin 79) [E172.M53 no. 79] 769'.5 74-620850
1. Music title pages—United States. I. Title. II. Series: Michigan. University. William L. Clements Library. Bulletin 79.

Music—U.S.—Hist. & crit.

SMITH, Cecil Michener, 728.81
1906-
Musical comedy in America. New York, Theatre Arts [1962, c.1950] x, 374p. illus. 22cm. 2.60 pap.,
1. Music—U.S.—Hist. & crit. 2. Musical revue, comedy, etc. I. Title. BIP

Musical instruments—Bibliography—Catalogs.

VICTORIA and Albert 016.7819'1
Museum, South Kensington. National Art Library.
Musical instruments : a list of books and articles in the National Art Library / compiled by Michael I. Wilson. [Rev., enl. and updated ed.]. [London] : Victoria and Albert Museum, 1976. iv, 126 p. : ill. ; 30 cm. Earlier eds. published under title: A bibliography of books on musical instruments in the Library of the Victoria and Albert Museum. [ML136.L8V55 1976] 77-368392
1. Victoria and Albert Museum, South Kensington. National Art Library. 2. Musical instruments—Bibliography—Catalogs. I. Wilson, Michael I. II. Title.

Musical instruments in art.

ARMAN, 1928- 759.4
Arman : lyrical surfaces, December 3, 1975—January 5, 1976. New York : Andrew Crispo Gallery, 1975. [48] p. : ill. (some col.) ; 23 x 26 cm. Bibliography: p. [47] [ND1950.A74A84] 75-39556
1. Arman, 1928- 2. Musical instruments in art. I. Andrew Crispo Gallery.

SCHREIBER, Georges, 1904- 759.13
"Symphonic variations 1971-1973"; exhibition of oils, watercolors, and drawings, September 13-29, 1973. New York, Kennedy Galleries [1973] 1 v. (unpaged) illus. 28 cm. [ND1839.S36A55] 73-181602
1. Schreiber, Georges, 1904- 2. Musical instruments in art. I. Title.

WINTERNITZ, Emanuel. 704.94'9'78191
Musical instruments and their symbolism in Western art : studies in musical iconology / Emanuel Winternitz. [2d ed.]. New Haven : Yale University Press, 1979. p. cm. "Bibliography of relevant writings by Emanuel Winternitz since 1940.": p. [ML85.W58 1979] 78-65482 ISBN 0-300-02324-3 : 24.95
1. Musical instruments in art. I. Title. BIP

Musical instruments (Mechanical)

BOWERS, Q. David. 737'.3
A tune for a token : a catalogue of tokens and medals relating to automatic musical instruments, circa 1850-1930 / Q. David Bowers. 1st ed. Thiensville, Wis. : Token and Medal Society, 1975. 79 p. : ill. ; 28 cm. Cover title. Includes indexes. [ML1050.B64] 75-320709
1. Musical instruments (Mechanical) 2. Tokens—United States. I. Title.

Musical instruments—Pictorial works.

BONNER, Stephen. 781'.91
Angel musicians above the entrance porch of the parish church of Pulham St. Mary the Virgin, near Diss, Norfolk, England; text by Stephen Bonner. Cambridge, Stephen Bonner, 59 Moorfield Rd., Duxford, 1967. [21] p. illus., map. 22 cm. [ML85.B63] 68-117660
1. Pulham, St. Mary the Virgin. Parish Church. 2. Musical instruments—Pictorial works. 3. Music in art. I. Title.

BONNER, Stephen. 726'.5'094223
Early Norman secular musicians on the church of Barfreston in Kent; drawings by Roy Bishop. Cambridge, Bois de Boulogne, 1969. [14] p. 5 illus. (1 col.). 22 cm. "This first edition is limited to sixty copies only, of which this is no. 28." Bibliography: p. [14] [ML85.B635] 72-463152 20/-
1. Barfreston, Church. 2. Musical instruments—Pictorial works. 3. Music in art. I. Title.

RICHARDSON, Allen L., 1920- 778.1
Tooters, tweeters, strings and beaters; an instrument book for all young readers. Illus. by Art Seiden. New York, Grosset [c.1964] 45p. illus. (pt. col.) 28cm. (2950) 64-9779 2.50
1. Mivical instruments—Juvenile literature. I. Title.

Musical revue, comedy, etc.—London—Pictorial works.

MANDER, Raymond. 782.8'1'09421
Musical comedy; a story in pictures, by Raymond Mander & Joe Mitchenson. Foreword by Noel Coward. New York, Taplinger Pub. Co. [1970, c1969] 64 p. illus., ports. 26 cm. [ML89.M35 1970] 70-94125 10.00
1. Musical revue, comedy, etc.—London—Pictorial works. I. Mitchenson, Joe, joint author. II. Title. BIP

MANDER, Raymond. 782.8'1'09421
Revue; a story in pictures, by Raymond Mander & Joe Mitchenson. Foreword by Noel Coward. New York, Taplinger Pub. Co. [1971] viii, 55 p. 225 illus. 26 cm. [ML89.M353] 76-163477 ISBN 0-8008-6789-0 10.95
1. Musical revue, comedy, etc.—London—Pictorial works. I. Mitchenson, Joe, joint author. II. Title. BIP

Musicians.

ZAIDENBERG, Arthur, 1903- 743'.4
How to draw musicians and musical instruments. London, New York, Abelard-Schuman [1970, c1969] 64 p. illus. 26 cm. [NC825.M8L3] 79-95138 3.33
1. Musicians. 2. Musical instruments—Pictorial works. I. Title. BIP

Musicians—Portraits.

SIEGEL, Adrian. 779'.9'785062748110924
Concerto for camera; a photographic portrait of the Philadelphia Orchestra. [Philadelphia, Philadelphia Orchestra Association, 1972] 207 p. illus. 26 cm. [ML200.8.P52O747] 72-8993
1. Philadelphia Orchestra. 2. Musicians—Portraits. I. Title.

Mustache cups.

HAMMOND, Dorothy M. 738
Mustache cups: history and marks, by Dorothy Hammond. [Des Moines, Wallace-Homestead Book Co., c1972. vi, 157 p. illus. (part col.) 23 cm. Bibliography: p. 157. [NK4695.M8H35] 73-173500
1. Mustache cups.

Muybridge, Eadweard, 1830-1904.

HAAS, Robert Bartlett. 770'.92'4 B
Muybridge : man in motion / by Robert Bartlett Haas. Berkeley : University of California Press, c1976. x, 207 p. : ill. ; 24 cm. Includes bibliographical references and index. [TR849.M87H3] 73-78542 ISBN 0-520-02464-8 : 18.50
1. Muybridge, Eadweard, 1830-1904. BIP

STANFORD University. Dept. of Art. 779'.092'4
Eadweard Muybridge; the Stanford years, 1872-1882. [Stanford, Calif., 1972] 135 p. illus. 22 x 27 cm. (Stanford art book 14) Catalog of an exhibition held at the Stanford University Museum of Art, Oct. 7-Dec. 4, 1972; the E. B. Crocker Art Gallery, Sacramento, Dec. 16, 1972-Jan. 14, 1973; and the University Galleries, University of Southern California, Los Angeles, Feb. 8-Mar. 11, 1973. Errata sheet inserted. Bibliography: p. 134-135. [TR849.M87S7] 72-92567
1. Muybridge, Eadweard, 1830-1904. I. Muybridge, Eadweard, 1830-1904. II. Stanford University. Museum. III. Crocker Art Gallery, Sacramento, Calif. IV. Los Angeles. University of Southern California. Art Galleries. V. Title. VI. Series.

Muzeul de Arta al Republicii Socialiste Romania. Galeria de Arta Universala.

MUZEUL de Arta al Republicii Socialiste Romania. Galeria de Arta Universala. 750'.74'094982
World painting in the Art Museum of the Socialist Republic of Romania : [album / Benedict Cristian ... et al. ; translated into English by Florin Ionescu ; preface, Ion Frunzetti]. Bucharest : Meridiane, 1976. [1], viii, 68 p., [54] leaves of plates : ill. (some col.) ; 34 cm. Translation of Pictura universala in Muzeul de Arta al Republicii Socialiste Romania. Includes index. Bibliography: p. 61-[67] [N3690.R9B86 1976] 76-373693 lei120
1. Muzeul de Arta al Republicii Socialiste Romania. Galeria de Arta Universala. 2. Paintings—Bucharest—Catalogs. I. Benedict, Cristian. II. Title.

Muzzle-loading firearms.

GOODMAN, Hank. 683'.42
Muzzle-loader's manual / by Hank Goodman. Hawthorne, N.J. : Ultra-Hi Products Co., 1975. 144 p. : ill. ; 21 cm. [TS536.6.M8G66] 75-27368
1. Muzzle-loading firearms. I. Title.

NONTE, George C. 683'.42
Home guide to muzzle-loaders [by] George C. Nonte, Jr. [Harrisburg, Pa.] Stackpole Books [1974] 219 p. illus. 28 cm. [TS536.6.M8N66] 74-16168 ISBN 0-8117-2101-9 6.95 (pbk.)
1. Muzzle-loading firearms. I. Title.

WALKER, Ralph T., 1931- 683'.4
Black powder gunsmithing / by Ralph T. Walker. Northfield, Ill. : DBI Books, c1978. 288 p. : ill. ; 28 cm. [TS536.6.M8W34] 78-52907 ISBN 0-695-80943-1 : 7.95
1. Muzzle-loading firearms. 2. Gunsmithing. I. Title. BIP

Mycenae

CHADWICK, John, 1920- 595.78
The Mycenne tablets III. With contributions from Emmett L. Bennett, Jr. [and others] Philadelphia, American Philosophical Society, 1963. 76 p. illus., maps, facsims., plans. 30 cm. (Transactions of the American Philosophical Society, new serv., v. 52, pt. 7, 1962) Includes bibliographical references. [Q11.P6] 63-1749
1. Mycenae 2. Inscriptions, Linear B. I. Bennett, Emmett Leslie, 1918- II. Title. III. Series. IV. Series: American Philosophical Society, Philadelphia. Transactions, new ser., v. 52, pt. 7

Mycenae—Tombs—Addresses, essays, lectures.

VERMEULE, Emily. 709'.01'3
The art of the shaft graves of Mycenae : delivered April 30 and May 1, 1973, the University of Cincinnati / by Emily Townsend Vermeule. Norman : University of Oklahoma Press, 1975. 61 p., [6] leaves of plates : ill. ; 22 cm. (Lectures in memory of Louise Taft Semple : 3d series) Bibliography: p. [53]-57. [DF221.M9V47] 75-313739
1. Mycenae—Tombs—Addresses, essays, lectures. 2. Tombs—Greece, Modern—Mycenae—Addresses, essays, lectures. 3. Mycenae—Antiquities—Addresses, essays, lectures. I. Title. II. Series: Cincinnati. University. Lectures in memory of Louise Taft Semple.

Mysteries, Religious, in art.

BIANCHI, Ugo. 709'.38
The Greek mysteries / by Ugo Bianchi. Leiden : Brill, 1976. 46 p., [24] leaves of plates : ill. ; 26 cm. (Iconography of religions ; section 17, Greece and Rome, fasc. 3) Includes bibliographical references. [N7760.B5] 76-380838 ISBN 9-00-404486-8 : fl 38.00
1. Mysteries, Religious, in art. 2. Mythology, Greek, in art. 3. Art, Greek. I. Title. II. Series.

Mystic Seaport, Mystic, Conn.

STACKPOLE, Edouard A 1905- 736.4
Figureheads & ship carvings at Mystic Seaport, by Edouard A. Stackpole. Mystic, Conn., Marine Historical Association, 1964. xiv, 134 p. illus. 26 cm. ([Marine Historical Association, Mystic Conn. Publication] no. 43) [E182.M32 no. 43] 65-1489
1. Mystic Seaport, Mystic, Conn. 2. Figureheads of ships. I. Title. II. Series.

Mythology.

AGARD, Walter Raymond, 1894- 731.87
Classical myths in sculpture. [Madison] University of Wisconsin Press [1951] xvi, 203 p. illus. 26 cm. "Bibliography and catalog": p. [177]-183. [NB1920.A35] 51-62409
1. Mythology. 2. Sculpture. I. Title.

CAMPBELL, Joseph, 1904- 291'.13
The masks of God. New York, Viking, 1959-[68] 4v. illus. 22cm. Contents.[4] Creative mythology. Bibl. [GN470.C32] 59-8354 10.00
1. Mythology. I. Title. BIP

Mythology, Australian (Aboriginal)

ROBERTS, Ainslie. 759.994
The dawn of time; Australian aboriginal myths in paintings by Ainslie Roberts, with text by Charles P. Mountford. Line illus. by Ainslie Roberts. New York, Taplinger Pub. Co. [1972, c1969] 79 p. illus. (part col.) 25 cm. [BL2610.R58 1972] 77-175042 ISBN 0-8008-2121-1 6.95
1. Mythology, Australian (Aboriginal) 2. Art and mythology. I. Mountford, Charles Pearcy, 1890- II. Title.

ROBERTS, Ainslie. 759.994
The first sunrise; Australian aboriginal myths in paintings by Ainslie Roberts, with text by Charles P. Mountford. Line illus. by Ainslie Roberts. New York, Taplinger Pub. Co. [1972, c1971] 79 p. illus. (part col.) 25 cm. [BL2610.R593 1972] 70-175043 ISBN 0-8008-2745-7 6.95
1. Mythology, Australian (Aboriginal) 2. Art and mythology. I. Mountford, Charles Pearcy, 1890- II. Title.

Mythology, Classical, in art.

ALBRICUS, philosophus. 704.94'7
Allegoriae poeticae : Paris, 1520 / Albricus. Theologia mythologica : Antwerp, 1532 / Georgius Pictorius. Apotheoseos ... : Basel, 1558 / Georgius Pictorius. New York : Garland Pub., 1976. p. cm. (The Renaissance and the gods ; no. 4) Reprint of the 1520 ed. of Allegoriae poeticae, of the 1532 ed. of Theologia mythologica, and of the 1558 ed. of Apotheoseos. [N7760.A44 1976] 75-27845 ISBN 0-8240-2053-7 : 40.00
1. Mythology, Classical, in art. 2. Mythology, Classical. I. Pictorius, Georg, 1500 (ca.)-1569. Theologia mythologica, 1976. II. Pictorius, Georg, 1500 (ca.)-1569. Apotheoseos ... 1976. III. Title. IV. Series. BIP

ANDERSON, Eleanor Cleveland. 759.13
Muses first; an exhibition of paintings and eleven poems. Presented May 11th through June 30th, 1973 by the Monterey Peninsula Museum of Art. Monterey, Calif. [Monterey Peninsula Museum of Arts, 1973] [22] l. 30 cm. "Fifty copies ... copy no. 50." "Catalogue of paintings": leaves [16]-[21]. [NX512.A52M66] 73-173364
1. Anderson, Eleanor Cleveland. 2. Mythology, Classical, in art. I. Monterey Peninsula Museum of Art. II. Title.

MAROLLES, Michel de, 1600-1681. 704.94'7
Tableaux du temple des muses : Paris, 1655 / Michel de Marolles. Iconologia : or, Moral emblems : London, 1709 / Cesare Ripa. New York : Garland Pub., 1976. p. cm. (The Renaissance and the gods ; no. 31) Reprint of the 1655 ed. of the Tableaux du temple des muses, published by N. L'Anglois, Paris, and of the 1709 ed. of the Iconologia, published by P. Tempest, London. [NE1680.M32 1976] 75-27876 ISBN 0-8240-2080-4 : 40.00
1. Mythology, Classical, in art. 2. Engravings. I. Ripa, Cesare, fl. 1600. Iconologia. English. 1976. II. Title. III. Series. BIP

MAYERSON, Philip. 700
Classical mythology in literature, art, and music. Waltham, Mass., Xerox College Pub. [1971] xv, 509 p. illus., geneal. tables, map. 26 cm. Bibliography: p. 483-487. [NX650.M9M38] 77-138393
1. Mythology, Classical, in art. I. Title. BIP

Mythology, Classical, in art—Juvenile literature.

PRODDOW, Penelope. 704.94'7'0938
Art tells a story : Greek and Roman myths / Penelope Proddow ; with introd. by Elizabeth Slinn. 1st ed. Garden City, N.Y. : Doubleday, c1978. p. cm. [N7760.P74] 76-18363 ISBN 0-385-11111-8 : 6.95. ISBN 0-385-11112-6 lib. bdg. : 7.90
1. Mythology, Classical, in art—Juvenile literature. I. Title. BIP

Nabi.

CHASSE, Charles, 1883- 759.4
The Nabis & their period. Translated by Michael Bullock. New York, Praeger [1969] 136 p. illus. (part col.), ports. 27 cm. Translation of Les nabis et leur temps. "Bibliographies and exhibitions": p. [125]-130. [ND547.C3713] 69-19189 12.50
1. Nabi. 2. Painting, Modern—19th century—France. I. Title.

MAUNER, George L., 1931- 700'.944
The Nabis: their history and their art, 1888-1896, by George L. Mauner. [New York] 1967. xiv, 326 l. 29 cm. Thesis—Columbia University. The original work also comprises a second volume containing illustrations. The second volume is deposited with the original copy in the Library of Columbia University. Bibliography: leaves 316-326. [N6847.5.N3M38] 74-191933

1. Nantucket, Mass.—Description and travel—Views. 2. Historic buildings—Massachusetts—Nantucket—Pictorial works. I. Sherman, Howard R., 1899-1974. II. Title.

Nantucket, Mass.—History—Pictorial works.

MATSUBARA, Naoko. 769'.924
Nantucket woodcuts, by Naoko Matsubara. Text by Fritz Eichenberg. Barre, Mass., Barre Publishers [1967] [61] p. illus. (part col.), map. 24 x 29 cm. [NE1217.M36E35] 67-26097
1. Nantucket, Mass.—History—Pictorial works. I. Eichenberg, Fritz, 1901- II. Title.

Napata site, Sudan.

DUNHAM, Dows, 1890- 916.25
The Barkal temples. Excavated by George Andrew Reisner. Boston, Museum of Fine Arts, 1970. xix, 103, lxiii p. illus., plans (part col., in pocket) 35 cm. [DT73.N25D85] 71-123877 45.00
1. Napata site, Sudan. 2. Temples—Sudan—Napata site. I. Reisner, George Andrew, 1867-1942. II. Title. BIP

Napkin rings, Victorian—United States.

SCHNADIG, Victor K. 739.2'3'773
American-Victorian figural napkin rings, by Victor K. Schnadig. Des Moines, Wallace-Homestead Book Co. [1971] xvii, 153 p. illus. 30 cm. [NK7242.N3S3] 72-178325
1. Napkin rings, Victorian—United States. 2. Silver-plated ware, Victorian—United States. I. Title. II. Title: Figural napkin rings.

Naples. Arco trionfale di re Alfonso d'Aragona.

HERSEY, George L. 728.8'1'094573
The Aragonese arch at Naples, 1443-1475 [by] George L. Hersey. New Haven, Yale University Press, 1973. xiv, 119 p. 123 illus. 29 cm. (Yale publications in the history of art, 24) Bibliography: p. 101-111. [NA9380.N3H47] 72-91297 ISBN 0-300-01611-5 15.00
1. Naples. Arco trionfale di re Alfonso d'Aragona. I. Title. II. Series.

Naranjo, Michael—Juvenile literature.

NELSON, Mary Carroll. 730'.92'4 B
Michael Naranjo / by Mary Carroll Nelson. Minneapolis : Dillon Press, [1975] 66 p. : ill. ; 23 cm. A biography of the Pueblo Indian sculptor who was blinded in Vietnam in 1968. [E99.P9N276] 92 75-14366 ISBN 0-87518-111-2 : 4.95
1. Naranjo, Michael—Juvenile literature. 2. Naranjo, Michael. 3. Pueblo Indians—Juvenile literature. I. Title. BIP

Narrative painting.

LUCIE-SMITH, Edward. 754
Work and struggle : the painter as witness 1870-1914 / Edward Lucie-Smith, Celestine Dars. New York : Paddington Press ; [New York] : distributed by Grosset & Dunlap, c1977. 243 p. : ill. (some col.) ; 29 cm. Includes index. [ND1450.L83] 76-53622 ISBN 0-448-22616-2 : 16.95
1. Narrative painting. 2. Labor and laboring classes in art. 3. Realism in art. I. Dars, Celestine, joint author. II. Title.

SITWELL, Sacheverell, Sir, bart., 1897- 759.2
Narrative pictures; a survey of English genre and its painters. With notes on the illustrations, by Michael Sevier. New York, B. Blom, 1972. vi, 122 p. illus. 26 cm. Reprint of the 1937 ed. [ND1452.G73S5 1972] 72-180039
1. Narrative painting. 2. Painting, Victorian. I. Sevier, Michel, 1886- II. Title. BIP

Narrative painting—Exhibitions.

MOURE, Nancy Dustin Wall. 754'.0973
American narrative painting : [exhibition, October 1-November 17, 1974] / catalog notes by Nancy Wall Moure ; essay by Donelson F. Hoopes. [Los Angeles] : Los Angeles County Museum of Art, [1974] 192 p. : ill. (some col.) ; 26 cm. Includes index. Bibliography: p. 184-188. [ND1451.M68] 74-7858 ISBN 0-87587-060-0 pbk. : 5.95
1. Narrative painting—Exhibitions. 2. Narrative painting—United States. 3. Genre painting, American. I. Hoopes, Donelson F. II. Los Angeles Co., Calif. Museum of Art, Los Angeles. III. Title.

Nash, John, 1752-1835.

DAVIS, Terence, 1924- 720'.924
John Nash, the Prince Regent's architect. [1st American ed.] South Brunswick [N.J.] A. S. Barnes [1967, c1966] 115 p. illus., plans. 26 cm. Bibliographical footnotes. [NA997.N3D33 1967] 67-20198
1. Nash, John, 1752-1835.

DAVIS, Terence, 1924- 720'.92'4
John Nash: the Prince Regent's architect. [New] ed. with corrections. Newton Abbot, David and Charles, 1973. 118, [43] p. illus., map, plans, ports. 26 cm. Includes index. Bibliography: p. 111-112. [NA997.N3D33 1973] 73-173291 ISBN 0-7153-5959-2
1. Nash, John, 1752-1835.
Distributed by David and Charles, Vermont, 12.00.

Nash, Paul, 1889-1946.

*EATES, Margot 709.2'4
Paul Nash; the master of the image 1889-1946 New York, St. Martins, [1974 c1973] xvi., 156 p. illus. 30 cm. [ND497] 74-76711 ISBN 0-7195-2671-X 15.95
1. Nash, Paul, 1889-1946. I. Title.

Nashville. Parthenon.

CREIGHTON, Wilbur F., 1883-1968. 727'.7'0976855
The Parthenon in Nashville; from a personal viewpoint, by Wilbur F. Creighton. [Nashville?] 1968. 48 p. illus. 23 cm. [NA281.C7] 68-5821
1. Nashville. Parthenon. 2. Athens. Parthenon. I. Title.

Nason, Thomas Willoughby, 1889—

NASON, Thomas Willoughby, 1889- 769'.92'4
The work of Thomas W. Nason, N.A. / by Francis Adams Comstock and William Fletcher ; with a biographical essay by Walter Muir Whitehill ; foreword by Philip J. McNiff ; edited by Sinclair H. Hitchings ; with commentaries on prints by Paul Swenson ; Nason's own essay on the history and practice of wood engraving ; and a reprinting of John Taylor Arms' essay on Nason's prints. Boston : Boston Public Library, 1976. p. cm. Includes index. [NE539.N37C65] 76-10852 ISBN 0-89073-012-1 : 65.00
1. Nason, Thomas Willoughby, 1889- I. Comstock, Francis Adams. II. Fletcher, William. III. Whitehill, Walter Muir, 1905- IV. Title. BIP

Nast, Thomas, 1840-1902.

KELLER, Morton. 817'.4
The art and politics of Thomas Nast. New York, Oxford University Press, 1968. vii, 353 p. illus., port. 31 cm. Bibliography: p. 351-353. [NC1429.N3K4] 68-19762
1. Nast, Thomas, 1840-1902. I. Nast, Thomas, 1840-1902. II. Title. BIP

NAST, Thomas, 1840-1902. 759.13
Five paintings from Th. Nast's grand caricaturama. Introd. and commentary by Lloyd Goodrich. [New York, Swann Collection of Caricature and Cartoon, 1970] 14 p. illus. (5 fold. col.) 20 x 25 cm. Catalog of an exhibition held Mar. 24-May 10, 1970, at the Whitney Museum of American Art, New York, and July 1-Aug. 30, 1970, at the National Collection of Fine Arts, Washington, D.C. "An exhibition from the Swann Collection of Caricature and Cartoon, New York." [NC1429.N3G6] 76-118821
I. Goodrich, Lloyd, 1897- II. Whitney Museum of American Art, New York. III. Smithsonian Institution. National Collection of Fine Arts. IV. Swann Collection of Caricature and Cartoon. V. Title.

NAST, Thomas, 1840-1902. 741.5973
Thomas Nast, political cartoonist, by J. Chal Vinson. Athens, University of Georgia Press [1967] x, 46 p., 154 illus. 29 cm. Bibliography: p. 42. [NC1429.N3V5] 66-27605
I. Vinson, John Chalmers.

NAST, Thomas, 1840-1902. 741.9'73
Thomas Nast's Christmas drawings / by Thomas Nast ; with an introd. by Thomas Nast St. Hill. New York : Dover Publications, 1978. viii, 69 p. : chiefly ill. ; 29 cm. Reprint of the 1890 ed. published by Harper, New York, under title: Thomas Nast's Christmas drawings for the human race: with new introd. [NC139.N3A4 1978] 78-52251 ISBN 0-486-23660-9 pbk. : 3.50
1. Nast, Thomas, 1840-1902. 2. Christmas in art. I. Title. II. Title: Christmas drawings. BIP

PAINE, Albert Bigelow, 1861-1937. 320'.973
Th. Nast, his period and his pictures. New York, B. Blom, 1971. xxi, 583, xx p. illus. 26 cm. Reprint of the 1904 ed. [NC1429.N3P3 1971] 78-177504
1. Nast, Thomas, 1840-1902.

PAINE, Albert Bigelow, 1861-1937. 741.5'973
Th. Nast, his period and his pictures / by Albert Bigelow Paine. Princeton : Pyne Press, [1974] xxi, 583, xx p., [1] leaf of plates : ill. ; 24 cm. Reprint of the 1904 ed. published by Macmillan, New York. Includes indexes. [NC1429.N3P3 1974] 74-80488 ISBN 0-87861-079-0 : 12.50
1. Nast, Thomas, 1840-1902.

PAINE, Albert Bigleow, 1861-1937 741.5973
Th. Nast: his period and his pictures. Gloucester, Mass., Ep. Smith, 1967 [1904] xxi, 583p. illus., facsims., ports. 21cm. [NC1429.N3P3 1967] 67-3735 6.50
1. Nast, Thomas, 1840-1902. I. Title. BIP

Natchez, Miss. Longwood.

MCADAMS, Ina May (Ogletree) 1906- comp. 728.8'4'0976226
The building of "Longwood" ... Natchez, Mississippi. Transcribed from original sources, edited, arr. and published by Ina May Ogletree McAdams. Austin, Tex. [1972] vii, 131 p. illus. 20 cm. [NA7238.N33M32] 72-194086
1. Natchez, Miss. Longwood. I. Title.

WHITWELL, William L. 976.2'26
The heritage of Longwood / William L. Whitwell. Jackson : University Press of Mississippi, [1975] ix, 110 p. : ill. ; 26 cm. Includes index. Bibliography: p. 103. [NA7238.N33W45] 74-17510 ISBN 0-87805-064-7 pbk. : 4.95
1. Natchez, Miss. Longwood. I. Title. BIP

National bank notes.

SOCIETY of Paper Money Collectors. 769'.559'73
The national bank note issues of 1929-1935. Edited by M. Owen Warns. Authors: Peter Huntoon [and others] [Anderson, S.C., 1970] 212 p. illus. 29 cm. Bibliography: p. 212. [HG607.S6] 70-17805
1. National bank notes. I. Warns, M. Owen, ed. II. Huntoon, Peter. III. Title.

National Commemorative Society.

THE National Commemorative Society and its first fifty issues [by Joseph M. Segel and others. Philadelphia, National Historical Foundation, c1969] 166 p. illus., ports. 32 cm. [CJ1820.N35] 72-110053 737.4
1. National Commemorative Society. 2. Commemorative coins—U.S. I. Segel, Joseph M. II. National Historical Foundation.

National Endowment for the Arts.

NATIONAL Council on the Arts. 338.4'3
The first five years: fiscal 1966 through fiscal 1970 [Washington, 1970] 1 v. (various pagings) 27 cm. Cover title. [NX22.N254] 72-175973
I. Title.

NATIONAL Council on the Arts. 700'.79
Programs of the National Endowment for the Arts through August 30, 1968. Washington [1968] 1 v. (various pagings) 27 cm. [NX730.N3] 68-67274
1. National Endowment for the Arts. I. Title.

NETZER, Dick, 1928- 338.4'7'700973
The subsidized muse : public support for the arts in the United States / Dick Netzer. Cambridge ; New York : Cambridge University Press, 1978. ix, 289 p. ; 24 cm. "A Twentieth Century Fund study." Includes index. bibliography: p. 264-280. [NX730.N4] 77-25441 ISBN 0-521-21966-3 : 14.95
1. National Endowment for the Arts. 2. Federal aid to the arts—United States. 3. Arts—Scholarships, fellowships, etc.—United States. 4. Art commissions—United States. I. Title. BIP

National Exhibition Centre.

MILLS, Edward David. 725'.91'0942497
The National Exhibition Centre : a shop window for the world / [by] Edward D. Mills. London : Crosby Lockwood Staples, 1976. [8], 88 p. : ill., maps, plans, ports. ; 28 cm. Bibliography: p. 87. [NA6750.L6N375 1976] 76-377510 ISBN 0-258-97066-9 : £2.50
1. National Exhibition Centre. I. Title. BIP

National Gallery of Canada.

NATIONAL Gallery of Canada. 708'.113'84
Slide catalogue / The National Gallery of Canada. Ottawa : National Gallery of Canada, 1976. 71, 73 p. ; 22 x 10 cm. Added t.p.: Repertoire des diapositives. Text in English and French; French text on inverted pages. Bibliography: p. [2] of cover. [N910.O7A7] 77-369226 ISBN 0-88884-319-4 : 5.00
1. National Gallery of Canada. 2. Art—Slides—Catalogs. I. Title. II. Title: Repertoire des diapositives.

National League of American Pen Women.

NATIONAL League of American Pen Women. 706.273
Membership roster. Washington. v. 20 cm. [PN121.N355] 50-18477
I. Title.

NATIONAL League of American Pen Women. Utah State Organization. 700'.92'2 B
Utah State National League of American Pen Women in review. Provo, J. G. Stevenson, 1972. v, 152 p. illus. 25 cm. Page 152 blank for "Autographs." [NX24.U8N37] 73-170756
1. National League of American Pen Women. Utah State Organization. I. Title.

National Map Collection.

NATIONAL Map Collection. 912'.71
Catalogue of the National Map Collection, Public Archives of Canada, Ottawa, Ontario. Boston : G. K. Hall, 1976. 16 v. ; 36 cm. English and French. [Z6028.N35 1976] [GA471] 76-379551 ISBN 0-8161-1215-0 lib.bdg. : 1250.00
1. National Map Collection. 2. Map collections—Canada. I. Title.

SUBJECT INDEX NATURE CRAFT—JUVENILE LITERATURE.

National Portrait Gallery, Washington, D.C.

NATIONAL 704.94'23'09730740153 Portrait Gallery, Washington, D.C. *A gallery of presidents* : the Hall of Presidents in the National Portrait Gallery / Marc Pachter. Washington : Smithsonian Institution Press, 1979. p. cm. [N7593.N23 1977] 78-22471 ISBN 0-87474-743-0 pbk. : 3.95
1. National Portrait Gallery, Washington, D.C. 2. Presidents—United States—Portraits. 3. Portraits, American. I. Pachter, Marc. II. Title. BIP

National socialism and architecture.

TAYLOR, Robert Ratcliffe, 1939- 720'.943 *The word in stone;* the role of architecture in the National Socialist ideology [by] Robert R. Taylor. Berkeley, University of California Press [1974] xv, 298 p. illus. 24 cm. Bibliography: p. [281]-287. [NA1068.5.N37T39] 79-186110 ISBN 0-520-02193-2 15.00
1. National socialism and architecture. 2. Architecture, Modern—20th century—Germany. I. Title. BIP

National socialism and architecture—Bibliography.

WILLIS, Victoria Jane. 016.3092 *Architecture and politics* : building as a means to National Socialist identity / Victoria Jane Willis. Monticello, Ill. : Council of Planning Librarians, 1977. 17 p. ; 28 cm. (Exchange bibliography - Council of Planning Librarians ; 1348) Cover title. Abstract of thesis (M.A.)—Cornell. Bibliography: p. 3-6. [Z5942.C68 no. 1348] [Z5944.G4] [NA1068.5.N37] 016.72'0943 77-153487 pbk. : 1.50
1. National socialism and architecture—Bibliography. 2. Architecture, Modern—20th century—Germany—Bibliography. 3. Germany—History—1789-1900—Chronology. 4. Germany—History—20th century—Chronology. I. Title. II. Series: Council of Planning Librarians. Exchange bibliography ; 1348.

National Trust for Places of Historic Interest or Natural Beauty.

NATIONAL Trust for Places 708'.2 of Historic Interest or Natural Beauty. *Treasures of the National Trust* / edited by Robin Fedden ; associate editor, Rosemary Joekes. London : J. Cape, 1976. 208 p. : ill. (some col.) ; 26 cm. Includes index. Bibliography: p. [187]-188. [N6761.N37 1976] 76-376406 ISBN 0-224-01241-X : £5.95
1. National Trust for Places of Historic Interest or Natural Beauty. 2. Art, British. 3. Art—Great Britain. I. Fedden, Henry Romilly, 1908- II. Joekes, Rosemary. III. Title. BIP

Nationalsozialistische Deutsche Arbeiter-Partei—Portraits.

CARGILL, Morris. 778.9'2 *A gallery of Nazis* / edited by Morris Cargill. 1st ed. Secaucus, N.J. : L. Stuart, c1978. 224 p. : ill. ; 23 x 26 cm. Includes index. [DD243.C37] 77-18102 ISBN 0-8184-0256-3 : 12.00
1. Nationalsozialistische Deutsche Arbeiter-Partei—Portraits. 2. World War, 1939-1945—Atrocities—Pictorial works. I. Title. BIP

Natkin, Robert, 1930—

NATKIN, Robert, 1930- 759.13 *Robert Natkin* : recent paintings / essay by Peter Fuller. New York : Andre Emmerich Gallery, 1976. [32] p. : col. ill. ; 18 x 23 cm. Exhibition catalog. Bibliography: p. [11] [ND237.N3F84] 76-381940
1. Natkin, Robert, 1930- I. Fuller, Peter.

NATKIN, Robert, 1930- 759.13 *Robert Natkin; an exhibition organized by the San Francisco Museum of Art.* [San Francisco, 1969] [23] p. illus. (part col.) 24 cm. Held at the San Francisco Museum of Art, Sept. 25-Nov. 9, 1969, and the Laguna Beach Art Association Gallery, Feb. 1-Feb. 28, 1970. Bibliography: p. [23] [ND237.N3A54] 72-99434
I. San Francisco. Museum of Art. II. Laguna Beach Art Association. Gallery.

Natsuzakaya.

DOMOTO, Insho, 1901- 759.952 *New formative arts of Insho Domoto.* Tokyo, Moiji-Shobo Pubs.[dist. Austin, Tex., Perkins Oriental, 1964] 24p. illsus. (pt. mounted col.) port. 37cm. Text in Japanese. Added t.p. in English. 64-779 25.00
1. Natsuzakaya. I. Title. II. Title: (transliterated)Domoto Insho shin zokei sakuin.

Natural history—Outdoor books—Juvenile literature.

GRAHAM, Ada. 745.5 *Foxtails, ferns, and fish scales* : a handbook of art and nature / by Ada Graham ; ill. by Dorothea Stoke, photos by Jon Stoke. New York : Four Winds Press, c1976. p. cm. Bibliography: p. Suggestions for craft projects using materials such as algae, leaves, and seeds collected outdoors. [QH48.G74] 76-17131 ISBN 0-590-07378-8 : 8.95
1. Natural history—Outdoor books—Juvenile literature. 2. Handicraft—Juvenile literature. I. Stoke, Dorothea. II. Stoke, Jon. III. Title. BIP

Natural history—Pictorial works.

FEININGER, Andreas, 1906- 779'.3'0924 *Roots of art* : the sketchbook of a photographer / Andreas Feininger. New York : Viking Press, 1975. 176 p. : ill. (some col.) ; 29 cm. (A Studio book) [QH46.F43 1975] 74-6998 ISBN 0-670-60807-6 : 18.95
1. Natural history—Pictorial works. 2. Nature (Aesthetics) I. Title.

JAQUES, Florence (Page) 1890-1972. 759.13 B *Francis Lee Jaques: artist of the wilderness world* [by] Florence Page Jaques. Foreword by Roger Tory Peterson. A treasury of prose writings from the six Jaques books. Three new appraisals of the artist's work. Memorials to Francis Lee Jaques by Sigurd F. Olson and to Florence Page Jaques by Harriet Buchheister. With 64 paintings and dioramas in full color [and] 100 drawings in scratchboard, pen and ink, and pencil. [1st ed.] Garden City, N.Y., Doubleday, 1973. xxi, 370 p. illus. (part col.) 30 cm. [QH31.J36J36] 72-94561 ISBN 0-385-02239-5 25.00
1. Jaques, Francis Lee, 1887-1969. 2. Natural history—Pictorial works. I. Jaques, Francis Lee, 1887-1969.

KLUTE, Jeannette, 1918- 779.3 *Woodland portraits.* [1st ed.] Boston, Little, Brown [1954] [36] p. illus. (part col.) 50 col. plates. 44 cm. [QH46.K55] 54-5821
1. Natural history—Pictorial works. I. Title.

STRACHE, Wolf, 1910- 779'.3'0924 *Forms and patterns in nature.* New York, Pantheon Books [1973, c1956] 22 p. 88 plates. 31 cm. Reprint of the ed. published by Pantheon, New York, with one new illus. [QH46.S79 1973] 73-3468 ISBN 0-394-42541-3 3.95 (pbk.)
1. Natural history—Pictorial works. 2. Nature photography. I. Title.

Natural history—The West—Pictorial works.

LOWE, Don. 779'.36'0978 *Alpine country of the West* / by Don Lowe ; text by David Sumner. Portland, Ore. : C. H. Belding, c1977. 128 p. : chiefly col. ill. ; 36 cm. [QH104.5.W4L69] 77-72232 ISBN 0-912856-34-3 : 25.00
1. Natural history—The West—Pictorial works. 2. Alpine flora—The West—Pictorial works. 3. The West—Description and travel—Views. I. Sumner, David. II. Title. BIP

Natural history—United States—Pictorial works.

RUGOFF, Milton Allan, 1913- comp. 779'.3'0973 *The wild places;* a photographic celebration of unspoiled America. Pictures collected and edited by Milton Rugoff and Ann Guilfoyle. Commentary by Ann and Myron Sutton. Photos. by Tom Algire [and others. 1st ed.] New York, Harper & Row [1973] 1 v. (unpaged (chiefly col. illus.)) 32 cm. "A chanticleer Press edition." [QH104.R83] 73-1075 ISBN 0-06-014176-X 27.50
1. Natural history—United States—Pictorial works. 2. Wilderness areas—United States—Pictorial works. I. Guilfoyle, Ann, joint comp. II. Algire, Tom, illus. III. Title. BIP

Natural monuments—U. S.

COLBY, Carroll B. 719.352 *America's natural wonders;* strange forests, mysterious caverns, and amazing formations. New York, Coward-McCann [1956] 48 p. illus. 28 cm. [QH77.U6C6] 56-9948
1. Natural monuments—U. S. I. Title. BIP

Natural resources—United States.

ADAMS, Ansel Easton, 1902- 779.3 *This is the American earth* [by] Ansel Adams [and] Nancy Newhall. San Francisco, Sierra Club [1960] xviii, 89 p. illus., group port. 35 cm. ([Sierra Club exhibit format series, 1]) [HC103.7.A68] 60-1364
1. Natural resources—United States. 2. Photography—Exhibitions. 3. National parks and reserves—United States. I. Newhall, Nancy (Wynne), joint author. II. Sierra Club. III. Title.

Nature (Aesthetics)

*LACEY, Jeannette F. 707 *Young Art:* nature and seeing, a fundamental program for teachers [by] Jeannette F. Lacey. Photographs by Georgia Voisard. New York, Van Nostrand Reinhold [1973] 94, [1] p. illus. (part. col.) 28 cm. [N8217.E3] 76-184824 ISBN 0-442-24650-1 5.95
1. Nature (Aesthetics) I. Voisard, Georgia, illus. II. Title.

MOEN, Arve 709.481 *Edvard Munch:* nature and animals; graphic art and paintings. [Tr. by Christopher Norman] Oslo, Forlaget Norsk Kunstreproduksjon [dist. Chester Springs, Pa., Dufour, 1963] 109, [3]p. illus. (pt. mounted col.) 32cm. Bibl. A63 15.00
1. Munch, Edvard, 1863-1944. 2. Nature (Aesthetics) I. Title.

SCHWENK, Theodor. 701'.17 *Sensitive chaos* : the creation of flowing forms in water and air / Theodor Schwenk ; translated by Olive Whicher and Johanna Wrigley ; ill. in the text by Walther Roggenkamp. New York : Schocken Books, 1976, c1965. 144, 87 p. : ill. ; 25 cm. Translation of Das sensible Chaos. Reprint of the ed. published by Rudolf Steiner Press, London. Includes index. Bibliography: p. 140-144. [N7438.S4513 1976] 76-9134 ISBN 0-8052-3636-8 : 14.95
1. Nature (Aesthetics) 2. Proportion (Art) I. Title. BIP

SHAFER, Elwood L. 634.9'0974 s *It seems possible to quantify scenic beauty in photographs,* by Elwood L. Shafer, Jr. and James Mietz. Upper Darby, Pa., U.S. Northeastern Forest Experiment Station, 1970. 12 p. illus. 23 cm. (U.S.D.A. Forest Service research paper NE-162) Cover title. Bibliography: p. 12. [SD11.A455493 no. 162] [BH301.N3] 111.8'5 78-609978
1. Nature (Aesthetics) 2. Nature photography. I. Mietz, James, joint author. II. Title. III. Series: United States. Northeastern Forest Experiment Station, Upper Darby, Pa. U.S.D.A. Forest Service research paper NE -162.

SHEPARD, Paul, 1925- 111.8'5 *Man in the landscape;* a historic view of the esthetics of nature. [1st ed.] New York, Knopf; [distributed by Random House] 1967. xx, 290, v p. illus. 22 cm. Based on the author's thesis, Yale University. Bibliography: p. [275]-290. [BH301.N3S45] 66-19398
1. Nature (Aesthetics) 2. Landscape. I. Title.

*STEINKRAUS, Warren W. 701.17 *Philosphy of art,* by Warren W. Steinkraus. Beverly Hills, Calif., Benziger [1974]. xii, 210 p. 22 cm. [BH301.N3] 72-94674 4.95 (pbk.)
1. Nature (Aesthetics) 2. Art—Philosophy. I. Title.

THOREAU, Henry David, 1817-1862. 779'.3 *"In wildness is the preservation of the world," from Henry David Thoreau* / selections & photos. by Eliot Porter ; introd. by Joseph Wood Krutch. 2d rev. print. New York : Ballantine Books, 1974. 144 p. : col. ill. ; 30 cm. "A Sierra Club/Ballantine book." [PS3042.P64 1974] 75-309124 ISBN 0-345-24313-7 : 5.95
I. Porter, Eliot, 1901- II. Sierra Club. III. Title.

Nature craft.

ALKEMA, Chester Jay. 745.5 *Crafting with nature's materials.* Photos. by the author. New York, Sterling Pub. Co. [1972] 48 p. illus. (part col.) 20 cm. (Little craft book series) Instructions for using materials such as seeds, grass, leaves, and rocks to create mosaics, collages, and sculptures. [TT880.A63 1972] 72-81038 ISBN 0-8069-5214-8
1. Nature craft. I. Title. BIP

GEARY, Ida. 745.5 *Plant prints & collages* / Ida Geary. New York : Viking Press, 1978. 101 p. : ill. ; 24 cm. (A Studio book) Bibliography: p.95-97. [TT910.G43 1978] 77-26266 ISBN 0-670-55890-7 : 12.50
1. Nature craft. 2. Plant prints. 3. Collages. 4. Pressed flower pictures. I. Title.

MUSSELMAN, Virginia W. 745.5 *Learning about nature through crafts,* by Virginia W. Musselman. [Harrisburg, Pa.] Stackpole Books [1969] 128 p. illus. 22 cm. Bibliography: p. 128. A simple guide to nature study describing the characteristics of common trees, flowers, and animals. Also includes directions for making handicrafts out of easily available materials. [TT157.M82] 78-85646 ISBN 0-8117-0938-8 3.95
1. Nature craft. 2. Nature study. I. Title. BIP

PHILLIPS, Lois Brandt. 745.5 *Wildlife woodcraft* / Lois Brandt Phillips. Happy Camp, CA : Naturegraph, c1978. 64 p. : ill. ; 22 cm. Presents step-by-step instructions for nature craft projects including plaques, boxes, wooden items, and three-dimensional scenes set in logs. [TT157.P47] 78-5267 ISBN 0-87961-067-0 : 7.00. ISBN 0-87961-066-2 pbk. : 3.00
1. Nature craft. 2. Design, Decorative—Animal forms. 3. Nature craft. I. Title. BIP

Nature craft—Juvenile literature.

FIAROTTA, Phyllis. 745.5 *Snips & snails & walnut whales* : nature crafts for children / by Phyllis Fiarotta with Noel Fiarotta. New York : Workman Pub. Co., 1975. 280 p. : ill. ; 21 x 23 cm. Instructions for making a variety of useful and decorative objects using raw materials from nature. [TT160.F49] 75-9574 ISBN 0-911104-75-5 : 9.95. ISBN 0-911104-49-6 pbk. : 4.95
1. Nature craft—Juvenile literature. I. Fiarotta, Noel, joint author. II. Title. BIP

NASSIET, Claude. 745.5 *What to make with nuts & grains* / by Claude Nassiet ; photographs by Pierre Roche ; drawings by Jeannine Janvier ; [translated by Maxine Hobson]. New York : Sterling Pub. Co., c1976. 32 p. : col. ill. ; 22 cm. (Easy craft series) Translation of Coques et graines. Includes index. Directions for using grains and nuts to make a lamp, bank, dolls, and other craft items. [TT160.N3713] 76-19821 ISBN 0-

8069-5410-8 : 3.95 ISBN 0-8069-5411-6 lib. bdg. : 3.99
1. Nature craft—Juvenile literature. 2. Nuts—Juvenile literature. 3. Grain—Juvenile literature. I. Roche, Pierre. II. Janvier, Jeannine. III. Title. IV. Series. BIP

Nature in literature.

KROEBER, Karl, 1926- 759'.2
Romantic landscape vision: Constable and Wordsworth. [Madison] University of Wisconsin Press [1975] xi, 142 p. illus. 23 cm. Includes bibliographical references. [PR5892.N2K7] 74-5905 ISBN 0-299-06710-6 10.00
1. Wordsworth, William, 1770-1850—Criticism and interpretation. 2. Constable, John, 1776-1837. 3. Nature in literature. 4. Romanticism, English. 5. Landscape painting, English. 6. Romanticism in art—England. I. Title.

Nature photography.

ANGEL, Heather. 778.3
Nature photography; its art and techniques. London, Fountain Press, 1972, [i.e. 1973] [16], 222, [24] p. illus. (some col.) 26 cm. Includes bibliographies and index. [TR721.A53] 74-164991
1. Nature photography. I. Title.
Distributed by International Publications Service, 15.00.

BANNETT, Edna. 778.9'3
Nature photography. 3d ed. Philadelphia, Chilton Book Co. [1967] 126 p. illus. 21 cm. [QH245.B4 1967] 67-25843
1. Nature photography.

BENNETT, Edna. 778.93
Nature photography. New York, Universal Photo Books [1961] 125p. illus. 20cm. [QH245.B4] 61-14248
1. Nature photography. I. Title.

BENNETT, Edna. 778.93
Nature photography. 3d ed. Philadelphia, Chilton Book Co. [1967] 126 p. illus. 21 cm. [QII245.B4] 67-25843
1. Nature photography. I. Title.

BENNETT, Edna 778.93
Nature photography., 2d ed. New York, Universal Photo Books [1965] 125 p. illus. 21 cm. [QII245.B4 1965a] 65-28043
1. Nature photography. I. Title.

BENNETT, Edna. 778.93
Nature photography. 2. ed. Philadelphia, Chilton Books [1965] 125 p. illus. 21 cm. [QH245.B4 1965] 65-7783
1. Nature photography.

BENNETT, Edna 778.93
Nature photography. 2d ed. New York, Universal Photo. [dist. Amphoto. c.1961, 1965] 125p. illus. 21cm, [QH245.B4] 65-28043 1.95 pap.,
1. Nature photography. I. Title.

BENNETT, Edna. 778.9/3
Nature photography. 3d ed. New York, Amphoto [1967] 126p. illus. 20cm. (136) [QH245B4 1967] 67-25843 1.95 pap.,
1. Nature photography. I. Title.
The hardcover edition is available from Chilton.

BENNETT, Edna. 778.9'3
Nature photography simplified / by Edna Bennett. Garden City, N.Y. : Amphoto, [1975] 96 p., [2] leaves of plates : ill. (some col.) ; 26 cm. (A Modern photoguide) Includes index. [TR721.B46] 75-1967 ISBN 0-8174-0184-9 : 3.45
1. Nature photography. I. Title. BIP

BLAKER, Alfred A., 1928- 778
Field photography : beginning and advanced techniques / Alfred A. Blaker. San Francisco : W. H. Freeman, c1976. xxi, 451 p., [6] leaves of plates : ill. (some col.) ; 24 cm. & field manual. Includes index. Bibliography: p. [431]-440. [TR721.B55] 75-33382 ISBN 0-7167-0518-4 : 19.95
1. Nature photography. I. Title. BIP

CRUICKSHANK, Allan D., ed. 778.71
Hunting with the camera; a guide to techniques and adventure in the field [by] Allan D. Cruickshank, editor [and others] [1st ed.] New York, Harper [1957] 215 p. illus. 25 cm. [HQ245.C75] 57-8197
1. Nature photography. I. Title.

DEAN, Roy. 779'.23'0924
Before the hand of man. Words and photos. by Roy Dean. [1st ed.] Los Angeles, Rho-Delta Press [1972] 103 p. illus. 32 cm. [TR721.D4] 72-75166 15.00
1. Nature photography. 2. Photography of the nudes. I. Title. BIP

EISENSTAEDT, Alfred. 779'.3
Witness to nature. New York, Viking Press [1971] 126 p. (chiefly col. illus.) 30 cm. (A Studio book) [TR721.E36 1971] 71-155658 ISBN 0-670-77685-8 16.95
1. Nature photography. I. Title.

FEININGER, Andreas, 1906- 779.3
The anatomy of nature; how function shapes the form and design of animate and inanimate structures throughout the universe. New York, Crown Publishers [1956] ix, 168 p. (chiefly illus.) 32 cm. [QH345.F44] 56-11364
1. Nature photography. I. Title. BIP

FEININGER, Andreas, 1906- 779'.092'4
The mountains of the mind : a fantastic journey into reality / Andreas Feininger. New York : Viking Press, [1977] p. cm. (A Studio book) [TR721.F44] 76-51762 ISBN 0-670-49129-2 : 17.95
1. Nature photography. 2. Photography, Artistic. I. Title.

GUYLER, Vivian Varney. 779'.0924
Design in nature. Worcester, Mass., Art Resource Publications [1970] 122 p. illus. 29 cm. [TR721.G8] 76-93119 9.95
1. Nature photography. 2. Photography, Artistic. I. Title. BIP

HOSKING, Eric John. 778.9'32
Wildlife photography; a field guide [by] Eric Hosking and John Gooders. New York, Praeger [1974, c1973] 192 p. (p. 182-192 blank for "Notes and records") 21 cm. Bibliography: p. [171]-172. [TR721.H66 1974] 73-19680
1. Nature photography. I. Gooders, John, joint author. II. Title. BIP

JIRU, Vaclav 779.3
Nature in camera. [dist. New York. Tudor Publishing Co., 1961, c.1960] 162p. (mainly illus., part col.) 31cm. 61-1348 9.95
1. Nature photography. I. Title.

KINNE, Russ. 778.943
The complete book of nature photography. With an introd. by Roger Tory Peterson. New York, Barnes [1962] 191 p. illus. 26 cm. (A Ziff-Davis book) [QH245.K5 1962] 62-10991
1. Nature photography.

KINNE, Russ. 778.9'3
The complete book of nature photography. With an introd. by Roger Tory Peterson. Philadelphia, Chilton Book Co. [1971] xi, 192 p. illus. (part col.) 26 cm. [TR721.K55 1971] 70-20151 8.95
1. Nature photography. I. Title. BIP

KINNE, Russ. 778.9'3
The complete book of nature photography. With an introd. by Roger Tory Peterson. New York, Amphoto, [1971] 192 p. illus. (part col.) 26 cm. [TR721.K55 1971b] 79-134590 ISBN 0-8174-0387-6 8.95
1. Nature photography. I. Title.

KIRK, Ruth. 574.909'5'4
Desert life. With photos. by Ruth and Louis Kirk. [1st ed.] Garden City, N.Y., Published for the American Museum of Natural History [by] Natural History Press [1970] [64] p. col. illus. 20 x 24 cm. Describes the fauna, flora, climate, and the changing sands of the desert. [TR721.K57] 71-92859 4.50
1. Nature photography. I. Kirk, Louis, illus. II. American Museum of Natural History, New York. III. Title.

LINTON, David, 1923- 778.93
Photographing nature. Garden City, N.Y., Published for the American Museum of Natural History [by] the Natural History Press, 1964. xvi, 262 p. illus., diagrs. 19 cm. (American Museum science books) "B7." "An annotated bibliography": p [247]-251. [QH245.L56 1964] 64-10026
1. Nature photography. I. Title.

*MCCURDY, John Chang 770
Of all things most yielding; photographs. Selections from oriental literature by Marc Lappe. Edited, with a foreward by David R. Brower. New York, McGraw-Hill, [1974] 128 p. col. illus. 29 cm. [QH245] 14.95.
1. Nature photography. I. Brower, David R., comp. II. Title.

MARCHINGTON, John. 778.9'32
An introduction to bird and wildlife photography; in still and movie [by] John Marchington and Anthony Clay, with photographs by the authors. London, Faber and Faber [1974] 149 p. illus. 23 cm. [TR721.M34] 74-183305 ISBN 0-571-10171-2
1. Nature photography. 2. Wildlife cinematography. I. Clay, Anthony. II. Title.
Distributed by Transatlantic Arts, Inc., 10.50.

MARCHINGTON, John. 778.9'32
Your book of photographing wild life, with photographs by the author. London, Faber & Faber, 1971. 3-56 p. 20 plates. illus. 22 cm. (The Your book series) [TR721.M35] 76-596758 ISBN 0-571-09601-8
1. Nature photography. I. Title.
Distributed by Transatlantic Arts, Levittown, N.Y., for 4.50. BIP

MOON, G. J. H. 778.9'3
Photographing nature [by] G. J. H. Moon. Rutland, Vt., C. E. Tuttle Co. [1970] 144 p. illus. (part col.) 22 cm. [TR721.M66] 70-118605
1. Nature photography. I. Title. BIP

NATURAL history 778.9'3
photography / edited by D. M. Turner Ettlinger. London ; New York : Academic Press, 1974. xxvii, 395 p. : ill. ; 24 cm. Includes bibliographies and indexes. [TR721.N37] 73-19024 ISBN 0-12-703950-3 : 23.25
1. Nature photography. I. Turner Ettlinger, D. M. BIP

NORTON, Boyd. 778.9'3
Wilderness photography : text and photographs / by Boyd Norton. 1st ed. New York : Reader's Digest Press : distributed by Crowell, 1977[i.e.1976] p. cm. Includes index. [TR721.N67 1977] 76-48156 ISBN 0-88349-114-1 : 12.95. ISBN 0-88349-115-X pbk. : 6.95
1. Nature photography. I. Title. BIP

†NURIDSANY, Claude. 778.9'3
Photographing nature / text and photographs by Claude Nuridsany and Marie Perennou ; translated [from the French] by J. W. Steward. London : Kaye and Ward ; New York : Oxford University Press, 1976. 4-157 p. : ill. (chiefly col.) ; 29 cm. Translation of Photographier la nature. Includes index. Bibliography: p. 156-157. [TR721.N8713 1976] 76-9256 ISBN 0-19-519885-9 (Oxford U.P.) : 17.95
1. Nature photography. 2. Macrophotography. I. Perennou, Marie, joint author. II. Title.

*PEARSON, John, 1934- 778.9'3
The sun's birthday. [Foreword by Anais Nin] Garden City, N.Y., Doubleday, 1973. 110 p. chiefly illus. (some col.) 28 cm. [TR721] 70-185426 ISBN 0-385-07412-3 5.95 (pbk.)
1. Nature photography. 2. Photography, Artistic. I. Title. BIP

PFEIFFER, C. Boyd. 770'.28
Field guide to outdoor photography / C. Boyd Pfeiffer ; photos. by the author. Harrisburg, Pa. : Stackpole Books, c1977. 224 p. : ill. ; 16 cm. Includes index. [TR721.P45 1977] 76-55380 ISBN 0-8117-2261-9 pbk. : 2.95
1. Nature photography. 2. Photography of sports. I. Title. BIP

SHUMWAY, Herbert D 778.93
Nature photography guide. Photos. by the author. New York, Greenberg, c1956. 125p. illus. 20cm. (The Modern camera guide series) [QH245.S46] 56-6019
1. Nature photography. I. Title.

*STOCK, Dennis 779.3'0924
Brother sun a photographic appreciation with selections from the literature of the sun by Christopher Collins and an introduction by J. G. Mitchell San Francisco, Sierra Club [1974] 86 p. col. illus. 27 cm. [QH46] 74-76311 ISBN 0-87156-104-2 14.95
1. Nature photography. I. Title.

STRACHE, Wolf, 1910- 779.3
Forms and patterns in nature. [Descriptive list of plates by Horst Janus; translation by Felix Kaufmann] [New York] Pantheon [1956] 22 p., 88 plates, 32 cm. [QH245.S863] 56-10416
1. Nature photography. I. Title. BIP

THOREAU, Henry David, 1817-1862 779.93
In wildness is the preservation of the world, from Henry David Thoreau. Selections, photos. by Eliot Porter. Introd. by Joseph Wood Krutch. New York, Sierra Club-Ballantine [1967, c. 1962] 160p. col. illus. 24cm. (U9800) [TR660.T5] 62-20527 3.95 pap.,
1. Nature photography. I. Porter, Eliot, 1901- II. Title.
Order from Ballantine. BIP

THOREAU, Henry David, 1817-1862. 779.93
In wildness is the preservation of the world, from Henry David Thoreau. Selections & photos. by Eliot Porter. Introd. by Joseph Wood Krutch. San Francisco, Sierra Club [1962] 167 p. col. illus. 35 cm. ([Serra Club exhibit format series, 4]) [TR660.T5] 62-20527
1. Nature photography. I. Porter, Eliot, 1901- II. Serra Club. III. Title.

TIME-LIFE Books. 778.9'3
Photographing nature, by the editors of Time-Life Books. New York [1971] 234 p. illus. (part col.) 27 cm. (Life library of photography) Bibliography: p. 231. [TR721.T52] 74-173835
1. Nature photography. I. Title. BIP

VILLIARD, Paul. 778.9'3
Through the seasons with a camera. With sixty-eight photos. by the author. [1st ed.] Garden City, N.Y., Doubleday [1970] xv, 105 p. illus., ports. 25 cm. [TR721.V54] 69-12238 3.95
1. Nature photography. I. Title.

WILSON, Arnold. 778.9'3
Creative techniques in nature photography / Arnold Wilson. Philadelphia : Lippincott, c1979. p. cm. Includes index. Bibliography: p. [TR721.W54] 78-26226 ISBN 0-397-01354-X pbk. : 17.50
1. Nature photography. I. Title.

Nature photography—Handbooks, manuals, etc.

FEININGER, Andreos, 1906- 779'.092'4
The mountains of the mind : a fantastic journey into reality / Adreas Feininger. New York : Viking Press, 1977 p. ; cm. (A Studio book) [TR721F44] 76-51762 ISBN 0-670-49129-2 : 17.95
1. Naute photography. 2. Photography-Artistic. I. Title.

MAYE, Patricia. 778.9'3
Fieldbook of nature photography. With a foreword by Ansel Adams and drawings by Nicholas Fasciano. San Francisco, Sierra Club [1974] 209 p. illus. 16 cm. (A Sierra Club totebook) [TR721.M39] 73-86880 ISBN 0-87156-085-2 6.95 (pbk.).
1. Nature photography—Handbooks, manuals, etc. I. Title. BIP

WILSON, Arnold. 778.9'3
Creative techniques in nature photography / Arnold Wilson. Philadelphia : Lippincott, c1979. p. cm. Includes index. Bibliography: p. [TR721.W54] 78-26226 ISBN 0-397-01354-X pbk. : 17.50
1. Nature photography. I. Title.

Nature photography—Juvenile literature.

HOBAN, Tana. 779'.3
Look again! New York, Macmillan [1971] [22] p. (chiefly illus.) 24 cm. Look through the square cut in the page and see part of

SUBJECT INDEX NAVAJO INDIANS—TEXTILE INDUSTRY

the photograph. Turn the page and experience the full concept of the picture. [TR721.H62] 72-127469 4.95
1. Nature photography—Juvenile literature. I. Title. BIP

Nauman, Bruce, 1941—

NAUMAN, Bruce, 1941- 709'.2'4
Bruce Nauman: work from 1965 to 1972. [Essays by] Jane Livingston & Marcia Tucker. [Los Angeles] Los Angeles County Museum of Art and Praeger, New York [1973, c1972] 172 p. (p. 53-156 illus.) 25 cm. Published in connection with the exhibition held Dec. 19, 1972-Feb. 18, 1973 at the Los Angeles County Museum of Art, and at the Whitney Museum of American Art, Mar. 29-May 13, 1973. Bibliography: p. 167-171. [N6537.N38L58] 72-91440 ISBN 0-87587-051-1 17.50
1. Nauman, Bruce, 1941- I. Livingston, Jane. II. Tucker, Marcia. III. Los Angeles Co., Calif. Museum of Art, Los Angeles. IV. Whitney Museum of American Art, New York. V. Title.

Nauvoo, Ill. Temple.

HARRINGTON, Virginia S. 917.73'43
Rediscovery of the Nauvoo Temple; report on the archaeological excavations, by Virginia S. Harrington & J. C. Harrington. Salt Lake City, Nauvoo Restoration, 1971. 54 p. illus., col. plate. 29 cm. Bibliography: p. 51-52. [NA5235.N3H3] 76-31744
1. Nauvoo, Ill. Temple. I. Harrington, Jean Carl, 1901- joint author. II. Title.

Navaho Indians.

ANDERSON, Susanne. 779'.9'97900497
Song of the earth spirit / by Susanne Anderson ; edited, with a foreword by David R. Brower. San Francisco : Friends of the Earth, [1973] 126 p. : ill. (some col.) ; 29 cm. (Celebrating the earth) [E99.N3A52] 72-3938 14.95
1. Navaho Indians. I. Title. II. Series. BIP

MAXWELL, Gilbert S. 746.72
Navajo rugs: past, present & future. With Eugene L. Conrotto. Palm Desert, Calif., Desert-Southwest [c.1963] 72p. illus. (pt. col.) port., map. 22cm. Bibl. 64-3381 2.00 pap.,
1. Navaho Indians. 2. Indians of North America—Textile industry and fabrics. I. Title.

PERCEVAL, Don Louis. 743.99703
A Navajo sketch book. With a descriptive text by Clay Lockett. [1st ed.] Flagstaff, Ariz., Northland Press, 1962. 98 p. (chiefly illus., part col.) 29 cm. [NC1075.P46] 62-21125
1. Navaho Indians. 2. Indians of North America—Pictures, illustrations, etc. I. Title. BIP

REICHARD, Gladys Amanda, 1893-1955. 746.1'09701
Navajo shepherd and weaver. Glorieta, N.M., Rio Grande Press [1968] xviii, 222 p. illus., map (on lining papers). 24 cm. (A Rio Grande classic) Reprint of 1936 ed. Bibliography: p. 215. [E99.N3R39 1968] 68-25390
1. Navaho Indians. 2. Navaho Indians—Textile industry and fabrics. 3. Indians of North America—Southwest, New—Textile industry and fabrics. I. Title. BIP

REICHARD, Gladys Amanda, 1893-1955. 746.1'09701
Spider woman; a story of Navajo weavers and chanters. Glorieta, N.M., Rio Grande Press [1968] x, 287 p. illus., map (on lining papers), ports. 24 cm. (A Rio Grande classic) Reprint of 1934 ed. [E99.N3R4 1968] 68-25391
1. Navaho Indians. 2. Navaho Indians—Textile industry and fabrics. 3. Indians of North America—Southwest, New—Textile industry and fabrics. I. Title. BIP

Navaho Indians—Antiquities.

SCHAAFSMA, Polly. 736'.5
Early Navaho rock paintings and carvings. [Santa Fe, N.M., Museum of Navaho Ceremonial Art, c1966] 32 p. illus., col. map (on cover) 24 cm. Cover title. Bibliography: p. 31-32. [E99.N3S33] 67-3748
1. Navaho Indians—Antiquities. 2. Petroglyphs—Southwest, New. 3. Rock paintings—Southwest, New. 4. Southwest, New—Antiquities. I. Title.

Navaho Indians—Art.

HATCHER, Evelyn Payne. 709.01'1
Navaho art; a methodological study in visual communication. Minneapolis, Intermittent Press, 1967. vii, 308 l. illus. 28 cm. Thesis--University of Minnesota. Bibliography: leaves 301-308. [E99.N3H34] 67-9813
1. Navaho Indians—Art. I. Title.

HATCHER, Evelyn Payne. 709'.01'1
Visual metaphors : a formal analysis of Navajo art / Evelyn Payne Hatcher ; with an introd. by Anthony F. C. Wallace. St. Paul : West Pub. Co., [1974] xvi, 272 p. : ill. ; 24 cm. (Monograph - The American Ethnological Society ; 58) Includes indexes. Bibliography: p. 249-261. [E99.N3H35] 74-20691 ISBN 0-8299-0026-8
1. Navaho Indians—Art. 2. Indians of North America—Southwest, New—Art. I. Title. II. Series: American Ethnological Society. Monographs ; 58.

Navaho Indians—Costume and adornment.

FRANK, Lawrence Phillip. 739.27'0979
Indian silver jewelry of the Southwest, 1868-1930 / by Larry Frank, with the assistance of Millard J. Holbrook II ; photography by William J. Salman. 1st ed. Boston : New York Graphic Society, c1978. p. cm. Includes index. Bibliography: p. [E99.N3F82] 78-7071 ISBN 0-8212-0740-7 : 32.50
1. Navaho Indians—Costume and adornment. 2. Indians of North America—Southwest, New—Costume and adornment. 3. Jewelry—Southwest, New. I. Holbrook, Millard J., joint author. II. Title. BIP

Navaho Indians—Exhibitions.

KOENIG, Seymour H. 709'.01'1
Sky, sand, and spirits; Navajo and Pueblo Indian art and culture. [An exhibition organized for the Hudson River Museum by Seymour H. Koenig. Yonkers, N.Y., Hudson River Museum, 1972] [90] p. illus. 28 cm. Exhibition held Jan. 9-Mar. 5, 1972, at the Hudson River Museum. [E99.N3K64] 72-198437
1. Navaho Indians—Exhibitions. 2. Pueblo Indians—Exhibitions. I. Hudson River Museum. II. Title.

Navaho Indians—Industries.

BENNETT, Noel, 1939- 746.7'2
Working with the wool; how to weave a Navajo rug, by Noel Bennett and Tiana Bighorse. With drawings by Robert Jacobson. Flagstaff [Ariz.] Northland Press [1971] xiii, 105 p. illus. 25 cm. Bibliography: p. 105. [E99.N3B49] 73-174994 ISBN 0-87358-084-2
1. Navaho Indians—Industries. 2. Indians of North America—Textile industry and fabrics. 3. Hand weaving. I. Bighorse, Tiana, 1917- joint author. II. Title. BIP

Navaho Indians—Industries—Exhibitions.

KAHLENBERG, Mary Hunt. 746.9'2
The Navajo blanket [by] Mary Hunt Kahlenberg and Anthony Berlant. [New York] Praeger [1972] 112 p. illus. (part col.) 31 cm. Catalogue of an exhibition first held at Los Angeles County Museum of Art, June 27-Aug. 27, 1972, and subsequently at other museums. Bibliography: p. 111. [E99.N3K3] 79-189549 ISBN 0-87587-050-3
1. Navaho Indians—Industries—Exhibitions. 2. Indians of North America—Textile industry and fabrics—Exhibitions. I. Berlant, Anthony, joint author. II. Los Angeles Co., Calif. Museum of Art, Los Angeles. III. Title.

Navaho Indians—Portraits.

ABEITA, Jim. 759.13
The American Indians of Abeita : "his people" / introd. by Joseph Stacey ; special dedication and song by Johnny Cash. 1st U.S. ed. Scottsdale, Ariz. : Rick Tanner Publications, c1976. [72] p. : all col. ill. ; 30 cm. [ND237.A23A43 1976] 76-27119
1. Abeita, Jim. 2. Navaho Indians—Portraits. 3. The West in art. I. Title.

Navaho Indians—Silversmithing.

BEDINGER, Margery. 739.2'3'09701
Indian silver; Navajo and Pueblo jewelers. [1st ed.] Albuquerque, University of New Mexico Press [1973] xiv, 264 p. illus. 24 cm. Bibliography: p. 243-255. [E99.N3B39] 72-94659 ISBN 0-8263-0273-4 15.00
1. Navaho Indians—Silversmithing. 2. Pueblo Indians—Silversmithing. 3. Indians of North America—Silversmithing. I. Title.

Navaho Indians—Textile industry and fabrics.

AMSDEN, Charles Avery, 1899-1941. 746.1'4
Navaho weaving, its technic and history / by Charles Avery Amsden ; foreword by Frederick Webb Hodge. Salt Lake City : Peregrine Smith, 1975. xviii, 261 p., [66] leaves of plates : ill. ; 23 cm. Reprint of the 1934 ed. published by The Fine Arts Press, Santa Ana, Calif. Includes index. Bibliography: p. [241]-249. [E99.N3A46 1975] 75-26555 ISBN 0-87905-063-2 pbk. : 8.50
1. Navaho Indians—Textile Industry and fabrics. 2. Indians of North America—Southwest, New—Textile industry and fabrics. I. Title.

ARIZONA. University. Museum of Art. 746.9'7
Navajo blankets, from the collection of Anthony Berlant; [exhibition] Text by Joseph Ben Wheat. [Tucson, 1974] [15] p. 36 p. of illus. (part col.) 32 cm. Bibliography: p. [53]-[54] [E99.N3A79 1974] 74-76013
1. Berlant, Anthony—Art collections. 2. Navajo Indians—Textile industry and fabrics. 3. Indians of North America—Southwest, New—Textile industry and fabrics. I. Wheat, Joe Ben. II. Title.

BENNETT, Noel, 1939- 746.1'4'09701
The weaver's pathway; a clarification of the "spirit trail" in Navajo weaving. [1st ed.] Flagstaff [Ariz.] Northland Press [1974] xiii, 64 p. illus. 25 cm. Bibliography: p. 63-64. [E99.N3B489] 73-78002 ISBN 0-87358-108-3 8.95
1. Navaho Indians—Textile industry and fabrics. 2. Indians of North America—Southwest, New—Textile industry and fabrics. I. Title. BIP

BERLANT, Anthony. 746.1'4
Walk in beauty : the Navajo and their blankets / by Anthony Berlant & Mary Hunt Kahlenberg. Boston : New York Graphic Society, [1977] p. cm. Includes index. Bibliography: p. [E99.N3B5] 76-30363 ISBN 0-8212-0691-5 : 27.50
1. Navaho Indians—Textile industry and fabrics. 2. Navaho Indians—History. 3. Indians of North America—Southwest, New—Textile industry and fabrics. I. Kahlenberg, Mary Hunt, joint author. II. Title. BIP

CERNY, Charlene. 746.3'9791
Navajo pictorial weaving / by Charlene Cerny ; foreword by Joe Ben Wheat ; photography by David Stein. 1st ed. Santa Fe : Published by the Museum of New Mexico Foundation for the Museum of New Mexico, c1975. 32 p. : ill. (some col.) ; 24 cm. "This publication arises from an exhibition presented at the Museum of International Folk Art, Santa Fe, in 1975-1976." Bibliography: p. 31. [E99.N3C44] 76-351425
1. Navaho Indians—Textile industry and fabrics. 2. Indians of North America—Southwest, New—Textile industry and fabrics. I. Santa Fe, N.M. Museum of New Mexico. II. Title. BIP

DEDERA, Don. 746.7'2
Navajo rugs : how to find, evaluate, buy, and care for them / by Don Dedera ; with a foreword by Clay Lockett. 1st ed. [Flagstaff, Ariz.] : Northland Press, c1975. xii, 114 p., [1] leaf of plates : ill. (some col.) ; 24 cm. Includes index. Bibliography: p. 111. [E99.N3D34] 74-31617 ISBN 0-87358-138-5 pbk. : 7.50
1. Navaho Indians—Textile industry and fabrics. 2. Indians of North America—Southwest, New—Textile industry and fabrics. I. Title.

JAMES, George Wharton, 1858-1923. 746.9'7
Indian blankets and their makers. New York, Dover Publications [1974] xvi, 213 p. illus. 24 cm. Reprint of the 1920 ed. published by A. C. McClurg, Chicago. Includes bibliographical references. [E99.N3J3 1974] 73-90526 ISBN 0-486-23068-6 5.00 (pbk.)
1. Navaho Indians—Textile industry and fabrics. 2. Indians of North America—Southwest, New—Textile industry and fabrics. I. Title. BIP

JAMES, George Wharton, 1858-1923. 746.9
Indian blankets and their makers. Glorieta, N.M., Rio Grande Press [1970, c1914] xvi, 213 p. illus. (part col.), map (on lining papers) 29 cm. (A Rio Grande classic) Cover title: Indian blankets and their makers: the Navaho. Includes bibliographical references. [E99.N3J3 1970] 74-114965 ISBN 0-87380-015-X
1. Navaho Indians—Textile industry and fabrics. 2. Indians of North America—Southwest, New—Textile industry and fabrics. I. Title.

JAMES, Harold L., 1933- 746.7'2
Posts and rugs : the story of Navajo rugs and their homes / by H. L. James. Globe, Ariz. : Southwest Parks and Monuments Association, c1976. x, 126 p. : ill. (some col.) ; 31 cm. (Popular series - Southwest Parks and Monuments Association ; no. 15) Includes index. Bibliography: p. 119-120. [E99.N3J33] 75-10108 ISBN 0-911408-33-9 : 12.00
1. Navaho Indians—Textile industry and fabrics. 2. Indians of North America—Southwest, New—Textile industry and fabrics. 3. Navaho Indians—Trading posts. 4. Indians of North America—Southwest, New—Trading posts. I. Title. II. Series: Southwest Parks and Monuments Association. Popular series ; no. 15. BIP

MERA, Harry Percival, 1875-1951. 746.1'4'0979
Navajo textile arts / H. P. Mera. New ed. / additions by Roger and Jean Moss. Santa Barbara : Peregrine Smith, 1975. ix, 122 p. : ill. ; 24 cm. [E99.N3M518 1975] 75-16296 ISBN 0-87905-040-3 pbk. : 4.95
1. Navaho Indians—Textile industry and fabrics. 2. Indians of North America—Southwest, New—Textile industry and fabrics. I. Title. BIP

PENDLETON, Mary. 746.1'09701
Navajo and Hopi weaving techniques. New York, Macmillan [1974] 158 p. illus. 29 cm. Includes bibliographies. [E99.N3P46 1974] 73-18256 ISBN 0-02-595500-4
1. Navaho Indians—Textile industry and fabrics. 2. Hopi Indians—Textile industry and fabrics. 3. Weaving. I. Title. BIP

REICHARD, Gladys Amanda, 1893-1955. 746.9'7
Weaving a Navajo blanket / by Gladys A. Reichard. New York : Dover Publications, 1974. xviii, 222 p., [8] leaves of plates : ill., diagrs. ; 21 cm. Reprint of the 1936 ed. published by J. J. Augustin, New York, under title: Navajo shepherd and weaver. Includes index. Bibliography: p. 215. [E99.N3R39 1974] 73-86437 ISBN 0-486-22992-0 : 3.00
1. Navaho Indians—Textile industry and fabrics. 2. Indians of North America—Southwest, New—Textile industry and fabrics. I. Title. BIP

Naval architecture—Bibliography.

SOCIETY of Naval 623.8'01'6
Architects and Marine Engineers, New York.
Index to SNAME publications, 1961-1966. New York [1967] 71 p. 23 cm. Cover title. [Z6834.S5S6] 72-8105
1. Naval architecture—Bibliography. 2. Marine engineering—Bibliography. I. Title.

SOCIETY of Naval 623.8'01'6
Architects and Marine Engineers, New York.
Index to SNAME publications, 1961-1969. New York [1970] 59 p. 28 cm. [Z6834.S5S6 1970] 77-17149 2.00
1. Naval architecture—Bibliography. 2. Marine engineering—Bibliography. I. Title.

Naval architecture—Indexes.

SOCIETY of Naval 016.6238
Architects and Marine/Engineers, New York.
Index of SNAME publications, 1961-1973. New York : The Society, [1974] 86 p. ; 28 cm. [Z6834.S5S6 1974] 74-191731 ISBN pbk. : 3.00
1. Society of Naval Architects and Marine Engineers, New York—Bibliography. 2. Naval architecture—Indexes. 3. Marine engineering—Indexes. I. Title.

Naval battles in art.

CUST, Charles 769'.4'99047
Leopold, Sir, 3d, bart., 1864-
Naval battles from the collection of prints formed and owned by Commander Sir Charles Leopold Cust, bart. The chronological arrangement of the prints with descriptive and historical notes by Harry Parker, and an introd. by Charles Napier Robinson. New York, B. Franklin [1974] Reprint of the 1911 ed. published by T. H. Parker, London. [NE957.C8 1974] 74-9854 ISBN 0-8337-4668-5 19.50 (lib. bdg.)
1. Cust, Charles Leopold, Sir, 3d, bart., 1864- —Art collections. 2. Naval battles in art. 3. Naval prints—Catalogs. I. Parker, Harry, 1884- II. Title.

Naval pottery—Great Britain.

PUGH, Patterson David 738'.0942
Gordon.
Naval ceramics, by P. D. Gordon Pugh assisted by Margery Pugh. Newport, Ceramic Book Co., 1971. xxvi, 113, [133] p. illus. (some col.). 31 cm. Includes index. Bibliography: p. 105-107. [NK4085.P83] 73-174238 ISBN 0-900272-10-4 £12.60
1. Naval pottery—Great Britain. 2. Naval porcelain—Great Britain. I. Pugh, Margery. II. Title.

Naval prints, American—Exhibitions.

UNITED 769'.4'935940973074013
States. Naval Academy, Annapolis. Museum.
American naval prints : from the Beverly R. Robinson Collection, U.S. Naval Academy Museum, Annapolis, Maryland / introd. by Roger B. Stein ; circulated by the International Exhibitions Foundation, 1976-1977. [Washington] : The Foundation, c1976. 121 p. : ill. ; 22 x 26 cm. Participating museums: Mariners Museum, Newport News, Va., and five others. [NE957.2.U54 1976] 76-21904 pbk. : 7.00
1. Robinson, Beverley Randolph, 1876-1951—Art collections. 2. Naval prints, American—Exhibitions. 3. Naval battles in art—Exhibitions. I. International Exhibitions Foundation. II. Mariners Museum, Newport News, Va. III. Title.

Naval prints—Catalogs.

KENNEDY Galleries, inc., 769'.973
New York.
Three centuries of seafaring. [New York] 1964. 2 pts. illus. 23 cm. (The Kennedy quarterly, v. 4, no. 4) Contents.Contents.—pt. 1. Prints.—pt. 2. Paintings, watercolors & drawings. [N8640.K4 vol. 4, no. 4 pt. 1-2] 70-11537
1. Naval prints—Catalogs. I. Title. II. Series.

Naval prints—United States—Catalogs.

SMITH, Edgar Newbold. 769'.4'9359
American naval broadsides : a collection of early naval prints (1745-1815) / by Edgar Newbold Smith ; foreword by M. V. Brewington. 1st ed. [Philadelphia] : Philadelphia Maritime Museum, [1974] xix, 225 p. : 117 ill. (some col.) ; 29 cm. Bibliography: p. 223-225. [NE957.2.S58 1974] 74-83106 ISBN 0-517-51761-2 : 35.00
1. Naval prints—United States—Catalogs. 2. Naval battles in art. 3. Prints—Collectors and collecting. I. Title.

Nazarenes (German painters)

ANDREWS, Keith. 759.3
The Nazarenes; a brotherhood of German painters in Rome. Oxford, Clarendon Press, 1964. xvii, 148 p. 81 plates (part col.) 29 cm. "Select bibliography": p. [138]-141. [ND567.A5] 64-6050
1. Nazarenes (German painters) I. Title.

Near East—Antiquities—Pictorial works.

BREASTED, James Henry, 779'.9'939
1865-1935.
The 1919/20 Breasted expedition to the Near East : a photographic study / compiled by Ruth Marcanti. Chicago : University of Chicago Press, 1977. v, 29 p. : map ; 22 cm. & microfiche (2 sheets : all ill. ; 11 X 15 cm.) in pocket. (A University of Chicago Press text/fiche) At head of title: The Oriental Institute. Includes bibliographical references. [DS44.5.B73 1977] 77-2731 ISBN 0-226-69473-9 : 14.00
1. Near East—Antiquities—Pictorial works. I. Marcanti, Ruth. II. Chicago. University. Oriental Institute. III. Title.

Nebraska—Capital and capitol.

BROWN, Elinor L. 725.1
Architectural wonder of the world: Nebraska's State Capitol Building. Photog. by Richard Hufnagle. [Ceresco, Neb., Midwest Pub. Co., c.1965] 180p. illus. (pt. col.) ports. 29cm. [NA4412.N2B7] 65-5889 10.00; 7.50 lib. & Sch. ed.,
1. Nebraska—Capital and capitol. I. Hufnagle, Richard, illus. II. Title.

BROWN, Elinor L 725.1
Architectural wonder of the world: Nebraska's State Capitol Building [by] Elinor L. Brown. Photography by Richard Hufnagle. [Ceresco, Neb., Midwest Pub. Co., 1965] 180 p. illus. (part col.) ports. 29 cm. [NA4412.N2B7] 65-5889
1. Nebraska — Capital and capitol. I. Hufnagle, Richard, illus. II. Title.

CUNNINGHAM, Harry Francis, 725.11
1885--
The capitol, Lincoln, Nebraska; an architectural masterpiece. Lincoln, Neb., Johnsen Pub. Co., c1954. unpaged. illus. 23cm. [NA4412.N2C3 1954] 55-28732
1. Nebraska—Capital and capitol. I. Title.

Nebraska. State College, Wayne.

MIDWEST review. 769'.973
Wayne, Neb., Wayne State College. v. 24 cm. annual. Began publication in 1959. Cf. New serial titles, 1962. INDEXES: Vols. 1-5, 1959-63, in v. 5. [AP2.M5552] 64-35459
1. Nebraska. State College, Wayne.

Nebraska. University. Sheldon Memorial Art Galley.

NEBRASKA. University. 70s.1784111
A checklist of the art collections at the University of Nebraska. [Lincoln, 1963] 1 v. (unpaged) 23 x 11 cm. Cover title. Published on the occasion of the opening of the Sheldon Memorial Art Gallery, May, 1963. [N582.L5A52] 63-64437
1. Nebraska. University. Sheldon Memorial Art Galley. I. Title.

Neckties.

KIRSCHEN, Jerry. 646.4'8
How to make ties & tablecloths. New York, Grosset & Dunlap [1973] 95 p. illus. 21 cm. [TT616.K57] 73-157887 ISBN 0-448-01169-7 1.50
1. Neckties. 2. Table-cloths. I. Title.

Needlepoint.

HANLEY, Hope 746.44
New methods in needlepoint. New York, Scribners [1966] 96p. illus. (pt. col.) 24cm. Bibl. [TT771.H22] 66-20459 5.95
1. Needlepoint. I. Title. BIP

PICKEN, Mary (Brooks) 746.44
1886-
Needlepoint made easy: classic and modern, by Mary Brooks Picken and Doris White. Drawings and layout by Claire Valentine. New York, Harper [1955] 149p. illus. 22cm. [TT771.P5] 55-8059
1. Needlepoint. I. White, Doris Wilson, joint author. II. Title. BIP

PITTSBURGH, University. v. 12
Henry Clay Frick Fine Arts Dept.
A wonderland of steel; an exhibition of needlepoint tapestries by Mildred T. Johnstone. The Henry Clay Frick Fine Arts Dept., University of Pittsburgh, November 10-December 9, 1960. Pittsburgh [1960] unpaged (chiefly illus.) 30cm. [NK9198.J6P5] 61-34247
1. Needlepoint. 2. Tapestry— Exhibitions. I. Johnstone, Mildred T. II. Title.

Needlepoint lace.

NORDFORS, Jill Denny. 746.2'2
Needle lace & needleweaving: a new look at traditional stitches. Photos. by Beverly Rush. Line drawings by the author. New York, Van Nostrand Reinhold Co. [1974] 159 p. illus. 26 cm. Bibliography: p. 156. [TT800.N67] 73-10893 ISBN 0-442-26059-8 9.95
1. Needlepoint lace. 2. Drawn-work. I. Title. BIP

Needlework.

ALFORD, Marianne Margaret 746.4'4
Compton Cust, Vicountess, 1817-1888.
Needlework as art / M. M. Cust, Vicountess Alford. New York : Garland Pub., 1978. xxiii, 422 p., [64] leaves of plates : ill. ; 24 cm. (The Aesthetic movement & the arts and crafts movement) Reprint of the 1886 ed. published by Sampson Low, Marston, Searle, and Rivington, London. Includes bibliographical references and index. [NK9104.A43 1978] 76-17770 ISBN 0-8240-2474-5 : lib.bdg. : 35.00
1. Needlework. I. Title. II. Series. BIP

BAXTER, Nancy. 746.4
Needlecraft for home decoration. Great Neck, N.Y., Hearthside Press [1971] 255 p. illus. 29 cm. [TT750.B3 1971] 72-163563 7.95
1. Needlework. 2. Fancy work. I. Title.

BAXTER, Nancy. 746.4
Needlecraft for home decoration. New York, Hearthside Press [1966] 223 p. illus. 29 cm. ([Home and garden bookshelf]) [TT750.B3] 65-24615
1. Needlework. 2. Fancy work. I. Title.

BEITLER, Ethel Jane. 746.4
Creating from remnants : stitchery with imperfect fabrics / by Ethel Jane Beitler. New York : Sterling Pub. Co., [1974] 48 p. : ill. (some col.) ; 20 cm. (Little craft book series).) Includes index. Explores the potentials in combining imperfect fabric lengths with stichery to create both functional and decorative items. [TT715.B42 1974] 74-82325 ISBN 0-8069-5306-3 : 4.50 lib.bdg. : 3.69
1. Needlework. I. Title. BIP

BELFER, Nancy. 746.4'4
Designing in stitching and applique / Nancy Belfer. Rev. paperback ed. Englewood Cliffs, N.J. : Prentice-Hall, c1977. viii, 152 p., [4] leaves of plates : ill. ; 24 cm. (The Creative handcrafts series) (A Spectrum book ; S-CR-17) Bibliography: p. 149-152. [TT750.B45 1977] 76-57240 ISBN 0-13-202010-6 pbk. : 7.95
1. Needlework. 2. Applique. I. Title. BIP

BIG book of needlecraft 746.4
(The); a book of practical information and interest for the home needlewoman, the dressmaker, the embroideress, the knitter, and the craftswoman. London, Odhams Pr. [1956] 576p. illus. 22cm. On label mounted on t.p.: Metuchen, N.J., Textile Book Service. [TT705.B46] 66-31778 6.00
1. Needlework. 2. Sewing. 3. Dressmaking. 4. Embroidery.

BUTLER, Winifred. 746.4
The complete book of needlework and emboidery. [1st American ed.] New York, Putnam [1967, c1966] ix, 196 p. illus. 21 cm. First published in 1966 under title: Needlework and embroidery. [TT705.B796 1967] 67-29481
1. Needlework. 2. Embroidery. I. Title. II. Title: Needlework and embroidery.

BUTLER, Winifred. 746.4
The complete book of needlework and embroidery. [1st American ed.] New York, Putnam [1967, c1966] ix, 196 p. illus. 21 cm. First published in 1966 under title: Needlework and embroidery. [TT705.B796 1967] 67-29481
1. Needlework. 2. Embroidery. I. Title. II. Title: Needlework and embroidery.

BUTLER, Winifred. 746.4'4
Needlework / Winifred Butler ; photographs by John Warren ; drawings by Mary French. London : Pan Books, 1976. 88 p. : ill. (some col.) ; 25 cm. (Pan craft books) Includes index. [TT750.B88] 77-368591 ISBN 0-330-24794-8 : £1.50
1. Needlework. I. Title.

BUTLER, Winifred. 746.4
Teach your child needlework. London, Pearson [1964] 94 p. illus. 21 cm. On label mounted on t. p.: Sole distributor for the U.S.A.: Transatlantic Arts, New York. [TT705.B8] 66-4351
1. Needlework. I. Title.

CARTER, Jean, 1930- 746.4
Creative play with fabrics and threads. New York, Taplinger Pub. Co. [1969, c1968] 96 p. illus. (part col.) 22 cm. Bibliography: p. 95-96. [TT750.C34 1969] 69-12455 5.95
1. Needlework. I. Title.

CHRISTOPHER, Rosemary 746.4'4
Brinley, 1918-
Needlework, by Rosemary Brinley. New York, Drake Publishers [1972] 95 p. illus. 20 cm. [TT750.C48] 72-184089 ISBN 0-87749-202-6 3.95
1. Needlework.

DAY, Lewis Foreman, 1845- 746.4'4
1910.
Art in needlework; a book about embroidery, by Lewis F. Day & Mary Buckle. London, B. T. Batsford, 1900. Detroit, Singing Tree Press, 1971. xxi, 262 p. illus. 19 cm. Original ed. issued in series: Text-books of ornamental design. Rev. ed. published in 1974 under title: Art nouveau embroidery. [TT770.D27 1971] 74-159927
1. Needlework. 2. Embroidery. I. Buckle, Mary, joint author. II. Title. III. Series: Text-books of ornamental design. BIP

DAY, Lewis Foreman, 1845- 746.4'4
1910.
Art in needlework / Lewis F. Day with Mary Buckle. New York : Garland Pub., 1977. xxi, 262 p. : ill. ; 19 cm. (The Aesthetic movement & the arts and crafts movement) Reprint of the 1900 ed. published by B. T. Batsford, London, in series: Text-books of ornamental design. [TT770.D27 1977] 76-17769 ISBN 0-8240-2473-7 lib.bdg. : 35.00
1. Needlework. 2. Embroidery. I. Buckle, Mary, joint author. II. Title. III. Series. IV. Series: Text-books of ornamental design.

DAY, Lewis Foreman, 1845- 746.4'4
1910.
Art Nouveau embroidery. Art in needlework / by Lewis F. Day and Mary Buckle ; introd. by Erica Wilson. Rev. ed.

New York : Sterling Pub. Co., [1974] x, 262 p. : ill. ; 22 cm. "A Discovery House book." Includes index. [TT770.D27 1974] 74-82335 ISBN 0-8069-8000-1 : 6.95. ISBN 0-8069-8001-X lib. bdg. : 6.39
1. Needlework. 2. Embroidery. 3. Art nouveau. I. Buckle, Mary, joint author. II. Title.

DEAN, Beryl 746.44
Church needlework. [dist. Newton, Mass., Branford, 1962, c.1961] 136p. illus. 23cm. 4.95 bds.,
1. Needlework. 2. Embroidery. 3. Church vestments. I. Title.

ENCYCLOPEDIA of needlework; a complete guide to stitches, designs, materials, and colors, with full working instructions, detailed diagrams, 2000 illustrations, and a full index. [New, entirely rev. ed.] New York, Hearthside [c.]1963. xvi, 876p. illus. (pt. col.) 24cm. 63-9933 7.95 746.4
1. Needlework.

FAMILY circle Creative needlecrafts / by the editors of Family circle. New York : Columbia House ; Englewood Cliffs, N.J. : distributed to the trade by Prentice-Hall, c1978. 240 p. : ill. (some col.) ; 29 cm. [TT750.F22] 79-103460 ISBN 0-13-301853-9 : 14.95 746.4
1. Needlework. I. Family circle. II. Title: Creative needlecrafts. BIP

FANNING, Robbie. 746.4'4
Here and now stitchery from other times and places / Robbie and Tony Fanning ; [color photos. by Lars Speyer, ill. by Tony Fanning, black and white photos. by Robbie and Tony Fanning]. New York : Butterick Pub., c1978. 200 p. : ill. ; 26 cm. Includes bibliographies and index. [TT751.F33] 77-92586 ISBN 0-88421-047-2 : 9.95
1. Needlework. I. Fanning, Tony, joint author. II. Title. BIP

FELDMAN, Annette. 746.4
Annette Feldman's Needlework for the home / photography by Doug Long. Englewood Cliffs, N.J. : Prentice-Hall, 1978. p. cm. "A Rutledge book." [TT751.F44] 78-10690 ISBN 0-13-036897-0 : 14.95
1. Needlework. I. Title. II. Title: Needlework for the home. BIP

FELDMAN, Annette. 746.4
Beginner's needlecraft. [1st ed.] New York, Harper & Row [1974] p. [TT750.F43] 73-14259 ISBN 0-06-011232-8 7.95
1. Needlework. 2. Fancy work. I. Title.

FELDMAN, Annette. 746.4
The needlework boutique / by Annette Feldman ; color photography by Keith Sheridan ; ill. by Carol Hines. New York : Rutledge Books, 1977. p. cm. Includes index. [TT750.F44] 77-7061 ISBN 0-87469-012-9 : 12.95
1. Needlework. I. Title. BIP

GUILD, Vera P 746.4
Good housekeeping's complete book of needlecraft. New York, Good Housekeeping, Book Dept. [1959] 498p. illus. 27cm. [TT750.G86] 59-6356
1. Needlework. I. Title.

GUILD, Vera P. 746.4
Painting with stitches : a guide to embroidery, needlepoint, crochet, and macrame / Vera P. Guild. Worcester, Mass. : Davis Publications, c1976. 95 p. : ill. (some col.) ; 27 cm. [TT750.G87] 75-41543 ISBN 0-87192-080-8 : 9.95
1. Needlework. 2. Fancy work. 3. Macrame. I. Title. BIP

HUGHES, Therle. 746.44
English domestic needlework, 1660-1860. New York, Macmillan [1961] 255 p. illus. 23 cm. [TT750.H92] 61-19567
1. Needlework. I. Title.

JOHN, Edith. 746.4'4
Ideas for needlecraft. [Newton Center, Mass.] C. T. Branford Co. [1968] 96 p. illus. 26 cm. Bibliography: p. 96. [TT760.J63 1968] 68-14347
1. Needlework. I. Title.

JOHN, Edith. 746.4'4
New stitches for needlecraft. New York, Dover Publications [1973, c1968] 95 p. illus. 26 cm. First published under the title: Ideas for needlecraft. [TT760.J63 1973] 73-84801 ISBN 0-486-22971-8 2.00 (pbk.).
1. Needlework. I. Title. BIP

JOHNSON, Jann. 746.9'2
The jeans book. Cover and book design by Vincent J. Yannie. New York, Ballantine Books [1972] 64 p. illus. 28 cm. [TT751.J58] 73-168325 ISBN 0-345-02550-4 2.95
1. Needlework. 2. Design, Decorative. 3. Jeans (Clothing) I. Title.

KOHL, Marguerite. 746.4
Pick-up needlework, by Marguerite Kohl and Frederica Young. Illustrated by Cynthia Rockmore. New York, D. McKay Co. [1955] 285 p. illus. 22 cm. [TT705.K6] 55-4707
1. Needlework. I. Young, Frederica, joint author. II. Title.

KRoNCKE, Grete. 746.4'4
Mounting handicraft; ideas and instructions for assembling and finishing. [Drawings and diagrs. by Grete Petersen] New York, Van Nostrand Reinhold [1970, c1967] 96 p. illus. 23 cm. ([Reinhold Scandinavian craft series]) Translation of Montering af handarbejder. Step-by-step instructions for mounting paintings, collages and embroidered fabrics to make wall hangings, cushions, book covers, handbags, jewelry boxes, and other objects. [TT751.K7513] 72-123380 ISBN 0-442-04539-5
1. Needlework. I. Petersen, Grete, illus. II. Title.

LAURY, Jean Ray. 746.4
A treasury of needlecraft gifts for the new baby / Jean Ray Laury. 1st ed. New York : Taplinger Pub. Co., 1976. p. cm. [TT751.L38 1976] 76-12186 ISBN 0-8008-7858-2 : 12.95
1. Needlework. 2. Infants' supplies. I. Title. BIP

LEE Wards complete library of needlecraft. New York : Fuller & Dees, c1975. 3 v. (864 p.) : col. ill. ; 29 cm. Includes index. [TT705.C75] 74-32451 ISBN 0-87197-085-6 : 24.95 746
1. Needlework. 2. Fancy work. 3. Textile crafts.

LOCKWOOD, Mary Smith, 1831-1922. 746.4'4
Art embroidery / M. S. Lockwood and [E.] Glaister. New York : Garland Pub., 1978. 83 p., [12] leaves of plates (3 fold.) : ill. ; 29 cm. (The Aesthetic movement & the arts and crafts movement) Running title: Art needlework. Reprint of the 1878 ed. published by M. Ward, London. [TT750.L6 1978] 76-17758 ISBN 0-8240-2462-1 lib. bdg. : 35.00
1. Needlework. I. Glaister, Elizabeth, joint author. II. Title. III. Series. BIP

LOPO, Ana G. 746.4
The needlecraft, manual : crochet, knitting, needlepoint, crewel, quilting, sewing, rugmaking, macrame, other techniques / Ana G. Lopo, Bruce W. Murphy. New York : Drake Publishers, 1977. 192 p. : ill. ; 28 cm. Bibliography: p. 189-192. [TT750.L66] 77-80197 ISBN 0-8473-1573-8 : 9.95
1. Needlework. I. Murphy, Bruce W., joint author. II. Title.

MCCALL'S treasury of needlecraft. New York, Simon and Schuster, 1955. 368 p. illus. 29 cm. [TT750.M2] 54-8652 746
1. Needlework. I. Title: Treasury of needlecraft.

MAREIN, Shirley. 746.4'4
Stitchery, needlepoint, applique, and patchwork : a complete guide / Shirley Marein ; renderings by Eleanor Bello, photos. by Alan Sweetman. New York : Penguin Books, 1976, c1974. 207 p. : ill. ; 26 cm. (Penguin handbooks) Includes index. Bibliography: p. 202. [TT750.M28 1976] 75-41374 ISBN 0-670-67055-3 : 12.95 ISBN 0-14-046249-X pbk. :
1. Needlework. I. Title. BIP

MEILACH, Dona Z. 746
Creating art from fibers and fabrics [by] Dona Z. Meilach. Chicago, Regnery [1972] 163 p. illus. (part col.) 29 cm. [TT750.M39] 75-183816 8.95
1. Needlework. 2. Fancy work. 3. Hand weaving. I. Title.

MEILACH, Dona Z. 746.4'45
Creative stitchery [by] Dona Z. Meilach [and] Lee Erlin Snow. Chicago, Reilly & Lee [1970] vii, 118 p. illus. (part col.) 29 cm. [TT750.M4] 76-126158 6.95
1. Needlework. I. Snow, Lee Erlin, joint author. II. Title.

MEILACH, Dona Z. 746.3
Creative stitchery / Dona Z. Meilach, Lee Erlin Snow. New York : Galahad Books, [1974], c1969. vii, 118 p. : ill. ; 29 cm. Includes index. [TT750.M4 1974] 74-184813 ISBN 0-88365-040-1 : 7.95
1. Needlework. I. Snow, Lee Erlin, joint author. II. Title.

MEILACH, Dona Z. 746.4
Exotic needlework, with ethnic patterns, techniques, trends / by Dona Z. Meilach and Dee Menagh ; photography, Dona and Mel Meilach ; drawings, Dee Menagh. New York : Crown Publishers, c1978. p. cm. Includes index. Bibliography: p. [TT751.M35 1978] 78-932 ISBN 0-517-52953-X : 12.95. ISBN 0-517-52954-8 pbk. : 7.95
1. Needlework. 2. Embroidery. 3. Design, Decorative. I. Menagh, Dee, joint author. II. Title.

MERRILL, Virginia. 746.4
Needlework in miniature : techniques and inspiration for making miniature rugs, upholstery, pillows, bedspreads, bed trimmings, doll clothes, and many more / Virginia Merrill & Jean Jessop. New York : Crown Publishers, c1978. x, 198 p., [4] leaves of plates : ill. ; 27 cm. Includes index. Bibliography: p. 187-188. [TT751.M38 1978] 77-20102 ISBN 0-517-52824-X : 10.95 ISBN 0-517-52825-8 pbk. : 5.95
1. Needlework. 2. Miniature craft. I. Jessop, Jean, joint author. II. Title. BIP

MESSENT, Jan. 746.4'4
Designing for embroidery from ancient and primitive sources / by Jan Messent ; [photographs by Gene Sparks]. London : Studio Vista, 1976. 127, [1] p. : ill. (some col.) ; 28 cm. American ed. published under title: Designing for needlepoint and embroidery from ancient and primitive sources. Includes index. Bibliography: p. 126. [TT751.M4 1976b] 77-353754 ISBN 0-289-70600-9 : £4.95
1. Needlework. 2. Embroidery. I. Title.

MESSENT, Jan. 746.4'4
Designing for needlepoint and embroidery from ancient and primitive sources / Jan Messent. New York : Macmillan, 1976. p. cm. Includes index. Bibliography: p. [TT751.M4] 76-7589 ISBN 0-02-584431-8 : 14.95
1. Needlework. 2. Embroidery. I. Title. BIP

MORRIS, Mair. 746.4
Creative thread design. Newton Centre, Mass., C. T. Branford Co. [1974] p. [TT750.M68] 73-17334 ISBN 0-8231-7033-0 8.75
1. Needlework. 2. Hand weaving. I. Title. BIP

THE Needleworker's constant companion / Susannah Read, general editor. New York : Viking Press, [1978] p. cm. (A Studio book) [TT705.N43] 78-16709 ISBN 0-670-50576-5 : 29.95 746.4
1. Needlework. I. Read, Susannah.

ODHAMS encyclopaedia of needlecraft. Contributors: Dorothy M. Howlett [and others] London, Odhams Press [1954; label: New York, J. Elstein] 512p. illus. 23cm. [TT705.O3] 56-962 646
1. Needlework. I. Howlett, Dorothy M.

O'SHAUGHNESSY, Marjorie, 1907- 646.2
Needlecraft for the home [by] Eileen Franklin. Edited by Miriam B. Reichl. [New York] Homemaker's Encyclopedia [1952] 256 p. illus. 21 cm. (The Homemaker's encyclopedia) [TT705.O38] 52-2456
1. Needlework. I. Homemaker's Encyclopedia, Inc., New York. II. Title.

PALUDAN, Lis. 746.4'4
New ideas in embroidery / Lis Paludan. 1st American ed. New York : Macmillan, 1976. p. cm. Translation of Nieuwe borduur ideeen. Includes index. [TT750.P2413 1976] 76-12426 ISBN 0-02-594660-9 : 8.95
1. Needlework. 2. Fancy work. 3. Embroidery. I. Title.

PASSADORE, Wanda. 746.4'3
The needlework book. New York, Simon and Schuster [1971, c1969] 208 p. illus. 31 cm. [TT750.P2913] 77-139654 ISBN 0-671-20842-X
1. Needlework. I. Title. BIP

RAINEY, Sarita R. 746.3
Wall hangings: designing with fabric and thread [by] Sarita R. Rainey. Worcester, Mass., Davis Publications [1971] 156 p. illus. (part col.), ports. 24 x 25 cm. Bibliography: p. 155. [TT750.R33] 70-142423 ISBN 0-87192-035-2 8.95
1. Needlework. 2. Fabric pictures. I. Title. BIP

ROSENTHAL, Iris. 746.4
The not-so-nimble needlework book / by Iris Rosenthal. New York : Grosset & Dunlap, c1977. 160 p. : ill. ; 28 cm. Includes index. [TT751.R57] 76-560 ISBN 0-448-12449-1 pbk. : 5.95
1. Needlework. I. Title.

RUSH, Beverly. 746.4'4
Stitch with style / Beverly Rush. Seattle, Wash. : Madrona Publishers, c1979. p. cm. (Connecting threads) [TT715.R87] 79-14559 ISBN 0-914842-39-0 pbk. : 5.95
1. Needlework. 2. Embroidery. I. Title. II. Series. BIP

RUSH, Beverly. 746.4
The stitchery idea book. New York, Van Nostrand Reinhold Co. [1974] 176 p. 29 cm. [TT750.R87] 74-1999 ISBN 0-442-27161-1
1. Needlework. I. Title.

RYAN, Mildred (Graves) 1905- 746.4
Needlecraft handbook. New York, Arco Pub. Co. [1954] 144p. illus. 26cm. (Arco handi-books for better living) Originally published as Fawcett book no. 234. [TT751.R9 1954] 54-9245
1. Needlework. I. Title.

RYAN, Mildred (Graves) 1905- 746.4
Needlecraft handbook. Photos., unless otherwise credited, by Simon Nathan. Greenwich, Conn., Fawcett Publications, c1954. 144p. illus. 24cm. (A Fawcett book, no. 234) [TT750.R9] 55-25491
1. Needlework. I. Title.

SCHARF, Bella. 746.4
Butterick's fast & easy needlecrafts : over 50 fashion and decorating projects you can make in less than a day / Bella Scharf. New York : Butterick Pub., c1977. 200 p. : ill. ; 27 cm. Includes index. [TT750.S3] 76-56596 ISBN 0-88421-029-4 : 9.95
1. Needlework. I. Butterick Publishing. II. Title. III. Title: Fast & easy needlecrafts. BIP

SHAUGHNESSY, Margery. 646.2
Needlecraft for the home [by]Eileen Franklin [pseud.] Edited by Miriam B. Reichl. [New York] Homemaker's Encyclopedia [1952] 256 p. illus. 21 cm. (The Homemaker's encyclopedia) [TT705.S48] 52-2456
1. Needlework. I. Title.

SILVERSTEIN, Mira. 746.4'4
Mira Silverstein's Guide to looped and knotted stitches : exciting needlework projects, patterns, and designs anyone can make / artwork by Roberta Frauwirth ; photos. by Sandy L. Studios. New York : McKay, c1977. p. cm. [TT760.S5] 77-11643 ISBN 0-679-50821-X : 5.95. ISBN 0-679-50785-X pbk. : 3.95
1. Needlework. 2. Embroidery. I. Title. II. Title: Guide to looped and knotted stitches. BIP

SPENCE, Anne. 746.4'4
Creative embroidery : a complete guide / Anne Spence. New York : Viking Press, 1976, c1975. 152 p. : ill. (some col.) ; 25 cm. (A Studio book) Includes index. Bibliography: p. 145-146. [TT750.S65 1976] 74-32660 ISBN 0-670-24653-0 : 14.95

1. Needlework. 2. Fancy work. 3. Embroidery. I. Title.

UNTERMYER, Irwin 746.394
English and other needlework, tapestries and textiles in the Irwin Untermyer collection. Text by Yvonne Hackenbroch. Published for the Metropolitan Museum of Art. Cambridge, Harvard University Press, 1960[ ] 1xxxi, 80p. illus., 183 plates (part col.) 31cm. (The Irwin Untermyer collection [4]) Bibl.: p.[71]-77. A60 25.00 half cloth,
1. Needlework. 2. Tapestry—Private collections. 3. Tapestry, English. 4. Textile industry and fabrics—Private collections. 5. Textile industry and fabrics—Gt. Brit. I. Hackenbroch, Yvonne. II. Title. III. Series.

*WARREN, Mrs. 746.4'4
Treasures in needlework / by Mrs. Warren and Mrs. Pullman. New York : Berkley Pub. Co., 1976. 448p. : ill. ; 20 cm. (A Berkley Windhover book) Facsimile ed. of the work first published in 1870. [TT770] ISBN 0-425-03108-X pbk. : 3.95
1. Needlework. 2. Embroidery. I. Pullman, Mrs. joint author. II. Title.

*WATSTEIN, Esther. 746'.4'4
Design your own needlepoint. Illus. by Maryweld Luhrs. [New York, Bantam Books [1974] 89 p. illus. 14 cm. (A Bantam minibook) [TT750] 0.60 (pbk.)
1. Needlework. I. Title.

*WATSTEIN, Esther. 746.4'4
Needlepoint and Bargello needlepoint. [New York, Bantam Books, 1974] 90 p. illus. 14 cm. (A Bantam Minibook) [TT750] 0.60 (pbk.)
1. Needlework. I. Title.

WESTFALL, Fran. 746
New idea; handcrafts made easy. [Melbourne] Lansdowne [1969] 158 p. illus. (part col.) diagrs., tables. 29 cm. [TT750.W44] 75-79354 6.50
1. Needlework. I. Title. II. Title: Handcrafts made easy.

WHITE, Alice Violet 746.44
Needlecraft for juniors. [dist. Newton, Mass., Charles T. Branford Co. c.1960] 184p. illus. 23cm 61-1266 3.50 bds.,
1. Needlework. I. Title.

WILLCOX, Donald J., 1933- 746.4'4
New design in stitchery [by] Donald J. Willcox. New York, Van Nostrand Reinhold Co. [1970] 120 p. illus. (part col.) 22 cm. Bibliography: p. 119. [NK9104.W54] 74-126869
1. Needlework. 2. Design, Decorative. I. Title.

WILLCOX, Donald J. 1933- 746.4'4
New design in stitchery [by] Donald J. Willcox. New York, Van Nostrand Reinhold, [1975 c1970] 120 p. ill. (part col.) 22 cm. Bibliography: p. 119. [NK9104.N54] ISBN 0-442-29473-5 5.95 (pbk.)
1. Needlework. 2. Design, Decorative. I. Title.
L.C. card no. for original ed.: 74-126869.

WILLIAMS, Elsa S. 746.4'4
The joy of stitching / Elsa Williams. New York : Van Nostrand Reinhold Co., [1978] p. cm. A collection of articles previously published in the author's newspaper column. Includes index. [TT750.W54] 78-17189 ISBN 0-442-29465-4 : 8.95
1. Needlework. 2. Embroidery. I. Title. **BIP**

WOELDERS, Ann. 746.4'4
Stitchery; free expression: fabrics, stitches, designs. [Translated from Dutch by Danielle Adkinson] New York, Van Nostrand Reinhold Co. [1973] 104 p. illus. (part col.) 25 cm. [TT750.W613] 72-7848 ISBN 0-442-29973-7 7.95
1. Needlework. I. Title.

THE Workbasket. 746.4
Workbasket handbook. Greenwich, Conn., Fawcett Publications, c1953. 144p. illus. 24cm. (A Fawcett book, no. 194) 'Material...has been reprinted from the Workbasket.' [TT751.W6] 53-40203
1. Needlework. I. Title.

THE Workbasket. 746.4
Workbasket handbook. New York, Arco Pub. Co. [1955? c1953] 144p. illus. 24cm. (The Do-it-yourself series) An Arco how-to book. Originally published as Fawcett book no. 194 'Material...has been reprinted from the Workbasket.' [TT751.W6 1955] 55-10822
1. Needlework. I. Title.

Needlework boxes—History.

ANDERE, Mary. 746'.028
Old needlework boxes and tools, their story and how to collect them. New York, Drake [1971] 184 p. illus., col. plate. 23 cm. Bibliography: p. 175. [NK8551.A5 1971b] 75-173732 ISBN 0-87749-085-6 5.95
1. Needlework boxes—History. 2. Needlework boxes—Collectors and collecting. 3. Sewing—Equipment and supplies—History. 4. Sewing—Equipment and supplies—Collectors and collecting. I. Title.

Needlework—Dictionaries.

CAULFEILD, Sophia 746.4'03
Frances Anne, 1824-1911.
The dictionary of needlework, an encyclopaedia of artistic, plain, and fancy needlework, dealing fully with the details of all the stitches employed, the method of working, the materials used, the meaning of technical terms, and, where necessary, tracing the origin and history of the various works described. Illustrated with upwards of 800 wood engravings. Plain sewing, textiles, dressmaking, appliances, and terms, by S. F. A. Caulfeild. Church embroidery, lace, and ornamental needlework, by Blanche C. Saward. London, L. U. Gill, 1882. Detroit, Singing Tree Press, 1971. 528 p. illus. 29 cm. [TT750.C35 1971] 75-172439
1. Needlework—Dictionaries. I. Saward, Blanche C. II. Title.

CAULFEILD, Sophia 746.4'03
Frances Anne, 1824-1911
Encyclopedia of Victorian Needlework [Dictionary of needlework by] S. F. A. Caulfeild and Blanche C. Saward. Magnolia, Mass. Peter Smith [1973 c1972] 2 v. illus. 28 cm. (Dover bk rebound) "An unabridged republication of the 2nd ed. (1887) of the work originally published...in 1882 under the title The dictionary of needlework: an encyclopedia of artistic, plain and fancy needlework." [TT750.C35 1972] 79-182103 ISBN 0-8446-4523-0 16.00 set.
1. Needlework—Dictionaries. I. Saward, Blanche C., joint author II. Title. **BIP**

RAMELLI Dieci, Giuliana. 746.4
A treasury of needle arts: stitch for stitch, thread for thread. New York, Drake Publishers [1974] p. cm. Translation of Puntoperpunto, filoperfilo. [TT750.R3413] 74-6438 ISBN 0-87749-711-7 19.95
1. Needlework—Dictionaries. 2. Fancy work—Dictionaries. 3. Needlework—Patterns. I. Title.

Needlework—Great Britain.

WARREN, Geoffrey. 746.4'0941
A stitch in time : Victorian and Edwardian needlecraft / Geoffrey Warren. New York : Taplinger Pub. Co., 1976. 144 p. : ill. ; 24 cm. Includes index. Bibliography: p. 137-139. [TT751.W37 1976] 76-12187 ISBN 0-8008-7435-8 : 9.95
1. Needlework—Great Britain. 2. Needlework, Victorian. 3. Needlework, Edwardian. I. Title. **BIP**

WARREN, Geoffrey. 746.4'0941
A stitch in time : Victorian and Edwardian needlecraft / Geoffrey Warren. Newton Abbot : David and Charles, 1976. 144 p. : ill., port. ; 24 cm. Includes index. Bibliography: p. 137-139. [TT751.W37 1976b] 77-368490 ISBN 0-7153-7218-1 : £4.95
1. Needlework—Great Britain. 2. Needlework, Victorian. 3. Needlework, Edwardian. I. Title.

Needlework—Great Britain—History.

SWAIN, Margaret H. 746.4'4 B
The needlework of Mary, Queen of Scots [by] Margaret Swain. New York, Van Nostrand Reinhold [1973] 128 p. illus. (part col.) 29 cm. Bibliography: p. 127. [DA787.A3S9] 73-1636 ISBN 0-442-29962-1 12.50
1. Mary Stuart, Queen of the Scots, 1542-1587. 2. Needlework—Great Britain—History. I. Title.

Needlework—History.

BRIDGEMAN, Harriet. 746.4'09
Needlework : an illustrated history / by Harriet Bridgeman and Elizabeth Drury. New York : Paddington Press, [1978] p. cm. Includes index. Bibliography: p. [TT750.B84] 78-7238 ISBN 0-448-22066-0 : 24.95
1. Needlework—History. I. Drury, Elizabeth, joint author. II. Title.

Needlework—Implements and appliances—History.

WHITING, Gertrude. 746.4
Old-time tools and toys of needlework. New York, Dover Publications [1971] xiii, 357 p. illus. 24 cm. First published in 1928 under title: Tools and toys of stitchery. [TT845.W48 1971] 77-154866 ISBN 0-486-22517-8 5.00
1. Needlework—Implements and appliances—History. I. Title. **BIP**

Needlework, Jewish.

ROCKLAND, Mae Shafter. 746.4'4
The work of our hands; Jewish needlecraft for today. New York, Schocken Books [1973] xiii, 258 p. illus. 25 cm. [TT750.R6] 72-91608 10.00
1. Needlework, Jewish. 2. Decoration and ornament, Jewish. I. Title. **BIP**

ROCKLAND, Mae Shafter. 746.4'4
The work of our hands : Jewish needlecraft for today / Mae Shafter Rockland. New York : Schocken Books, [1975] c1973. p. cm. (Schocken paperback edition) [TT750.R6 1975] 75-21572 ISBN 0-8052-0488-1 pbk. : 5.95.
1. Needlework, Jewish. 2. Decoration and ornament, Jewish. I. Title.

Needlework—Juvenile literature.

ENTHOVEN, Jacqueline. 372.5'4
Stitchery for children; a manual for teachers, parents, and children. New York, Reinhold Book Corp. [1968] 172 p. illus. (part col.), ports. 27 cm. [TT712.E55 1968] 67-24702
1. Needlework—Juvenile literature. 2. Needlework—Study and teaching. I. Title.

MEYER, Carolyn. 746.4'4
Stitch by stitch; needlework for beginners. Written and illustrated by Carolyn Meyer. [1st ed.] New York, Harcourt, Brace, Jovanovich [1970] 93 p. illus. 23 cm. Step-by-step directions for using various stitches to decorate pillow cases, handbags, place mats, potholders, and other objects. [TT712.M48] 77-117618 4.53
1. Needlework—Juvenile literature. I. Title. **BIP**

NEEDLEWORK, macrame & 746.4
knitting. [Translated by Angela Bailie] New York, Watts [1972] 175 p. illus. 31 cm. (Color crafts) Translation of Lana, hilo y aguja. Describes the basic techniques of knitting, needlework, crochet, and macrame and gives instructions for using them to make household items, gifts, and clothing. [TT750.L3513] 72-3837 ISBN 0-531-02588-8
1. Needlework—Juvenile literature. 2. Macrame—Juvenile literature. 3. Knitting—Juvenile literature. 4. Crocheting—Juvenile literature. I. Title. II. Series.

RAGBAG treasures 746.4
[by] Francoise Douvaines [and others] Translated by Halina Tunikowska. London, Mills and Boon [1972] [34] p. col. illus. 23 cm. Label mounted on t.p.: Transatlantic Arts, Inc., New York, Sole distributor for the U.S.A. Translation of Tresors de fil en aiguille. Instructions for using scraps, buttons, and yarn to make such treasures as dolls, pictures, and puppets. [TT751.T8413] 73-166408 ISBN 0-263-05066-1 3.95
1. Needlework—Juvenile literature. I. Douvaines, Francoise.

Needlework—Miscellanea.

WILSON, Erica. 746.4'4
Ask Erica / by Erica Wilson. New York : Scribner, [1977] p. cm. Includes index. [TT751.W53] 77-11617 ISBN 0-684-15296-7 : 5.95. ISBN 0-684-15295-9 pbk. : 2.50
1. Needlework—Miscellanea. 2. Embroidery—Miscellanea. I. Title.

Needlework—Nova Scotia—Patterns.

A Nova Scotia work basket 746.4
: some needlework patterns traditionally used in the province / by Marlene Davis ... [et al.] ; photographs by Ronald E. Merrick. Halifax : Nova Scotia Museum, 1976. 113 p. : ill. ; 22 x 28 cm. Bibliography: p. 110-111. [TT753.N69] 77-358110 ISBN 0-919680-02-X
1. Needlework—Nova Scotia—Patterns. I. Davis, Marlene.

Needlework—Patterns.

AMIR, Ziva, 1930- 746.4'4
Arabesque : decorative needlework from the Holy Land / Ziva Amir. New York : Van Nostrand Reinhold, [1977] p. cm. [TT753.A46] 76-41849 ISBN 0-442-20290-3 : 12.95
1. Needlework—Patterns. 2. Needlework—Israel. 3. Embroidery—Patterns. 4. Embroidery—Israel. I. Title. **BIP**

GORHAM, Georgia L. 746.4'4
A treasury of charted designs for needleworkers : 141 motifs including birds, flowers, animals, toys, etc. / Georgia L. Gorham and Jeanne M. Warth. New York : Dover Publications, 1977. 41 p. : chiefly ill. ; 28 cm. (Dover needlework series) [TT753.G67 1977] 77-77050 ISBN 0-486-23558-0 pbk. : 1.50
1. Needlework—Patterns. I. Warth, Jeanne M., joint author. II. Title. **BIP**

GROW, Judith K. 746.4
Classic needlework : contemporary designs inspired by the American past / Judith K. Grow. New York : Van Nostrand Reinhold, [1976] p. cm. Includes index. [TT753.G75] 76-8681 ISBN 0-442-22881-3 : 15.00
1. Needlework—Patterns. 2. Embroidery—Patterns. I. Title. **BIP**

HANLEY, Hope. 746.4'4
Hope Hanley's Patterns for needlepoint / drawings by Trudy Nicholson, photos. by Bonnie Boyle. New York : Scribner, c1976. 110 p. : ill. (some col.) ; 28 cm. Bibliography: p. 109-110. [TT753.H36 1976] 75-25627 ISBN 0-684-14468-9 : 14.95
1. Needlework—Patterns. I. Title. II. Title: Patterns for needlepoint. **BIP**

HOUCK, Carter. 746.4'4
The boat buff's book of embroidery / by Carter Houck and Myron Miller. New York : Scribner, c1979. p. cm. [TT753.H68] 78-22049 ISBN 0-684-16051-X : 14.95 ISBN 0-684-16052-8 pbk. : 7.95
1. Needlework—Patterns. 2. Embroidery—Patterns. 3. Design, Decorative—Themes, motives. 4. Boats and boating. I. Miller, Myron, 1918- joint author. II. Title.

HOUCK, Carter. 746.4'4
The boat buff's book of embroidery / by Carter Houck and Myron Miller. New York : Scribner, c1979. p. cm. [TT753.H68] 78-22049 ISBN 0-684-16051-X : 14.95 ISBN 0-684-16052-8 pbk. : 7.95
1. Needlework—Patterns. 2. Embroidery—Patterns. 3. Design, Decorative—Themes, motives. 4. Boats and boating. I. Miller, Myron, 1918- joint author. II. Title. **BIP**

JOHNSON, Mary Elizabeth, 746.4'4
1944-
Needlecraft designs from our best quilts : 20 favorite quilt designs graphed for needlework / Mary Elizabeth Johnson and Zuelia Ann Hurt. Birmingham, Ala. : Oxmoor House, c1978. 80 p. : ill. ; 28 cm. [TT753.J63] 77-95151 ISBN 0-8487-0493-5 pbk. : 4.95

1. Needlework—Patterns. 2. Quilting—Patterns. I. Hurt, Zuelia Ann, joint author. II. Title. BIP

KERIMOV, Liatif Gusein ogly, 1906- 746.7'59'0222
Folk designs from the Caucasus for weaving and needlework / by Lyatif Kerimov. New York : Dover Publications, 1974. 120 p. : chiefly ill. ; 29 cm. "A selection of designs from volume 1 (1961) of the [author's] work Azerbaidzhanskii kovyor." [TT753.K472] 73-80558 ISBN 0-486-23014-7 pbk. : 3.50
1. Needlework—Patterns. 2. Needlework—Caucasus. 3. Weaving—Patterns. 4. Weaving—Caucasus. I. Title. BIP

KERIMOV, Liatif Gusein ogly, 1906- 746.4'4
Persian rug motifs for needlepoint : charted for easy use / by Lyatif Kerimov. New York : Dover Publications, 1975. 47 p. : all ill. ; 28 cm. (Dover needlework series) "A selection of designs from volume 1 (1961) of the [author's] work 'Azerbaidzhanskii kovyor'." [TT753.K482 1975] 75-3650 ISBN 0-486-23187-9 pbk. : 1.50
1. Needlework—Patterns. 2. Design, Decorative—Azerbaijan. I. Title. BIP

MAREIN, Shirley. 746.4'4
Oriental images : new designs for needlepoint and stitchery / Shirley Marein. New York : Viking Press, [1978] p. cm. (A Studio book) [TT753.M35] 78-2269 ISBN 0-670-52861-7 : 17.95
1. Needlework—Patterns. 2. Embroidery—Patterns. 3. Design, Decorative—Near East. 4. Design, Decorative—East Asia. I. Title. BIP

MILLER, Heather Swan. 745.4
A needleworker's botany : fifty examples of early botanical art from the Library of the Massachusetts Horitcultural Society adaptd for needlework / Heather S. Miller. Somersworth : New Hampshire Pub. Co., [1978?] 102 p. : ill. ; 24 cm. Bibliography: p. 101-102. [TT753.M54] 78-59803 ISBN 0-912274-81-6 : 12.50 ISBN 0-912274-99-9 pbk. : 6.95
1. Needlework—Patterns. 2. Design, Deocrative—Plant forms. I. Massachusetts Horticultural Society. Library. II. Title. BIP

NEEDLEWORK classics : nostalgic designs from the Butterick archives for decorating clothing and accessories / edited by Becky Stevens Cordello ; [fashion ill. by Susan Blackman ; fashion photography by Bob Jaffe ; still photography by Laurence Cox]. New York : Butterick Pub., c1976. 128 p. : ill. ; 34 cm. Includes index. [TT753.N4] 75-35417 ISBN 0-88421-023-5 : 13.95 746
1. Needlework—Patterns. 2. Design, Decorative. I. Cordello, Becky Stevens. II. Butterick Publishing Co. BIP

NEEDLEWORK nostalgia : a collection of authentic needlework designs from the Butterick archives / edited by Barbara Weiland. New York : Butterick Pub., [1975] viii, 96 p. : col. ill. ; 34 cm. [TT753.N43] 74-29072 ISBN 0-88421-021-9 : 12.95 746.4'4
1. Needlework—Patterns. I. Weiland, Barbara. II. Butterick Publishing Co. BIP

OLDE time needlework patterns and designs. Seabrook, N.H. : Tower Press, c1976. 6 v. : ill. ; 28 cm. (Big book library ; v. 1-6) Cover title. [TT753.O4] 76-361397 746.4
1. Needlework—Patterns. 2. Design, Decorative.

OLESON, Karen E. 746.4'4
Floral patterns for needlecraft and the decorative arts / Karen E. Oleson. New York : Van Nostrand Reinhold, 1978. 208 p. : ill. ; 28 cm. Includes index. Bibliography: p. 205. [TT753.O42] 77-19324 ISBN 0-442-26282-5 pbk. : 10.95
1. Needlework—Patterns. 2. Design, Decorative—Plant forms. I. Title. BIP

ROTH, An. 746.4'4
Mosaic masterpieces in needlework and handicraft, based on motifs from the Holy Land / Ann Roth. New York : Scribner, c1975. 63 p. : ill. (some col.) ; 33 cm. [TT753.R67] 74-7799 ISBN 0-684-14062-4 : 10.00
1. Needlework—Patterns. 2. Cross-stitch—Patterns. 3. Mosaics—Israel. I. Title.

ROTH, An. 746.4'4
Needlepoint designs from the mosaics of Ravenna / Ann Roth. New York : Scribner, c1975. 63 p. : chiefly ill. (some col.) ; 33 cm. [TT753.R68] 75-4401 ISBN 0-684-14469-7 : 10.00
1. Needlework—Patterns. 2. Mosaics—Ravenna. I. Title.

RUSSIAN peasant design motifs for needleworkers and craftsmen / V. Stasov. New York : Dover Publications, 1976. 32 p. : all ill. ; 28 cm. (Dover pictorial archive series) "A new selection of 30 plates from Russkii narodnyi ornament. Vypusk pervyi: Shit'ye, tkani, kruzheva ... (Russian folk ornament. Part one: Embroidery, weaving, lace ... with an explanatory text by V. Stasov)" [TT753.R87 1976] 75-32224 ISBN 0-486-23235-2 pbnk. : 1.50 746
1. Needlework—Patterns. 2. Decoration and ornament—Russia. I. Stasov, Vladimir Vasil'evich, 1824-1906. BIP

SIBMACHER, Johann, d.1611. 746.4'4
Baroque charted designs for needlework / engraved by Johan Sibmacher. New York : Dover Publications, 1975. 36 p. : chiefly ill. ; 28 cm. (Dover needlework series) "Republication of the 1880 edition of Newes Modelbuch .... Inn Druck verfertigt, a work originally published in Nuremberg in 1604. The 1880 edition was published by Ernst Wasmuth in Berlin in 1880 under the title Kreuzstich-Muster 36 Tafeln der Ausgabe v. 1604 ("Cross-stitch patterns, 36 plates of the 1604 edition") ... contains new translations of the original 1604 title page and dedication." [TT753.S4913 1975] 75-2820 ISBN 0-486-23186-0 pbk. : 1.50
1. Needlework—Patterns. 2. Decoration and ornament, Baroque. I. Title. BIP

SIEGLER, Susan. 746.4'4
Needlework Patterns from the Metropolitan Museum of Art / Susan Siegler. 1st ed. Boston : New York Graphic Society, c1976. 184 p. : ill. (some col.) ; 29 cm. Bibliography: p. 184. [TT753.S495 1976] 76-10097 ISBN 0-8212-0639-7 : 17.50
1. Needlework—Patterns. 2. Canvas embroidery—Patterns. I. New York (City). Metropolitan Museum of Art. II. Title. BIP

SILVERSTEIN, Mira. 746.4'4
International needlework designs / Mira Silverstein ; artwork by Roberta Frauwirth ; photography by Sandy L. Studios. New York : Scribner, c1978. x, 180 p. : ill. ; 28 cm. Bibliography: p. 180. [TT705.S493] 77-21189 ISBN 0-684-15169-3 : 16.95
1. Needlework—Patterns. I. Title. BIP

SJODIN, Kerstin. 746.4
Ideas in textiles and threads. New York, Van Nostrand Reinhold [1973, c1972] 88 p. illus. 21 cm. (A Reinhold craft paperback) Translation of Textila ideer. [TT753.S5413] 72-1856 ISBN 0-442-29960-5 2.95
1. Needlework—Patterns. I. Title.

SPRINGER, Jo. 746.4
Creative needlework. Solweig Hedin, designer. Edith Noonberg, editor. [Expanded ed.] New York, Westport Corp. [1974] 256 p. illus. (part col.) 29 cm. [TT753.S68 1974] 74-166279 9.95
1. Needlework—Patterns. I. Title.
Publisher's address: 174 Fifth Ave., N.Y. 10010

STORY, Dorothy P. 746.7'4
Full-color American Indian designs for needlepoint rugs, charted for easy use / by Dorothy P. Story. New York : Dover Publications, 1975. [32] p. : all col. ill. ; 28 cm. (Dover needlework series) Cover title. [TT753.S76] 75-9176 ISBN 0-486-23190-9 pbk. : 1.75
1. Needlework—Patterns. 2. Rugs. 3. Indians of North America—Textile industry and fabrics. I. Title: Full-color American Indian designs for needlepoint rugs ...

THEULET-LUZIE, Bernadette. 746'.04'31
Wool craft. New York, Drake Publishers [1973] p. Translation of Les brins de laine. [TT753.T4713] 73-3194 ISBN 0-87749-471-1
1. Needlework—Patterns. I. Title.

TILLETT, Leslie, 1915- 746.4'4
American needlework, 1776-1976 : needlepoint and crewel patterns adapted from historic American images / by Leslie Tillett; foreword by Rose Kennedy Boston : New York Graphic Society, 1975. p. cm. [TT753.T54] 75-9096 ISBN 0-8212-0664-8 : 13.50
1. Needlework—Patterns. 2. Needlework, American. 3. Crewelwork—Patterns. I. Title.

TILLETT, Leslie, 1915- 746.4'4
The zoophabet needlework book : an alphabet for needleworkers / compiled by Leslie Tillett. New York : Crowell, c1977. 5 p., [26] leaves of plates : ill. ; 31 cm. [TT753.T55 1977] 76-45763 ISBN 0-690-01211-X : 14.95
1. Needlework—Patterns. 2. Alphabets. 3. Design, Decorative—Animal forms. I. Title. BIP

WARREN, Eliza. 746.4
Treasures in needlework, by Mrs. Warren and Mrs. Pullan. New York, Lancer Books [1973] xv, 448 p. illus. 20 cm. (A Lancer Larchmont book) "First published in 1870." [TT753.W37 1973] 73-162084 1.95 (pbk)
1. Needlework—Patterns. I. Pullan, Matilda Marian (Chesney) joint author. II. Title. BIP

WEISS, Rita. 746.4'4
Needlepoint designs after illustrations by Beatrix Potter : charted for easy use / by Rita Weiss. New York : Dover Publications, 1976. viii, 24 p. : ill. ; 28 cm. (Dover needlework series) [TT753.W44 1976] 75-9177 ISBN 0-486-20218-6 : 1.50
1. Needlework—Patterns. I. Potter, Beatrix, 1866-1943. II. Title. BIP

WINTER, Adalee. 746.4
Needlecraft kingdom / by Adalee Winter. Birmingham, Ala. : Oxmoor House, 1976, c1975. 64 p. : ill. ; 28 cm. (Family guidebook series) [TT753.W57 1976] 75-32265 pbk. : 3.95
1. Needlework—Patterns. 2. Graphic methods. I. Title. BIP

WINTER, Adalee. 746.4'4
Religious designs for needlework / Adalee Winter ; [editor, Mary Elizabeth Johnson ; photography, David Matthews]. Birmingham, Ala. : Oxmoor House, c1977. 64 p. : ill. ; 28 cm. (Family guidebook series) [TT753.W58] 77-74196 ISBN 0-8487-0470-3 pbk. : 3.95
1. Needlework—Patterns. 2. Christian art and symbolism. 3. Jewish art and symbolism. I. Title.

ZIMILES, Martha. 746.4'4
A treasury of needlework designs : ready-to-use patterns for needlepoint and embroidery / Martha Rogers Zimiles. New York : Van Nostrand Reinhold Co., [1976] p. cm. Includes index. [TT753.Z55] 76-11452 ISBN 0-442-29584-7 pbk. : 8.95
1. Needlework—Patterns. 2. Embroidery—Patterns. I. Title. BIP

Needlework—Pennsylvania.

SCHIFFER, Margaret Berwind. 746.4'4
Historical needlework of Pennsylvania [by] Margaret B. Schiffer. New York, Scribner [1968] 160 p. illus. (part col.) 27 cm. Bibliographical references included in "Notes" (p. 157-158) [NK9110.S35] 68-17348 7.50
1. Needlework—Pennsylvania. I. Title. BIP

Needlework—Study and teaching.

ENTHOVEN, Jacqueline. 372.5
Stitchery for children; a manual for teachers, parents, and children. New York, Reinhold Book Corp. [1968] 172 p. illus. (part col.), ports. 27 cm. Suggestions and instructions for progressively harder stitchery projects for children from pre-school age through high school, and for children with special needs. [TT712.E55 1968] AC 68
1. Needlework—Study and teaching. I. Title. BIP

Needlework, Turkoman.

ANDREWS, Mugul. 746'.0955
Turkmen needlework : dressmaking and embroidery among the Turkmen of Iran / by Mugul and Peter Andrews. London : Central Asian Research Centre, 1976. 61 p. : ill. ; 21 cm. (Central Asian monographs ; no. 2) Includes bibliographical references. [TT715.A65] 77-355571 ISBN 0-903424-10-X : £3.50
1. Needlework, Turkoman. 2. Needlework—Iran. I. Andrews, Peter, joint author. II. Title. III. Series.

Needlework—United States.

MUSHENO, Elizabeth J. 746.4
Book of colonial needlework : a handbook of contemporary projects ... / Elizabeth J. Musheno. New York : Van Nostrand Reinhold Co., [1975] 136 p. : ill. ; 29 cm. Includes index. [TT750.M87] 75-12166 ISBN 0-442-25607-8 : 16.95
1. Needlework—United States. 2. United States—History—Colonial period, ca. 1600-1775. I. Title.

SWAN, Susan Burrows. 746.4'4
A Winterthur guide to American needlework / Susan Burrows Swan. New York : Crown Publishers, 1976. p. cm. (A Winterthur book/Rutledge books) Bibliography: p. [NK8812.S95 1976] 76-10602 ISBN 0-517-52785-5 : 6.95 ISBN 0-517-52177-6 pbk. : 3.95
1. Henry Francis du Pont Winterthur Museum. 2. Needlework—United States. I. Henry Francis du Pont Winterthur Museum. II. Title. BIP

Needlework—United States—History.

SWAN, Susan Burrows. 301.41'2
Plain and fancy : American women and their needlework, 1700-1850 / Susan Burrows Swan. 1st ed. New York : Holt, Rinehart and Winston, c1977. 240 p. : ill. ; 24 cm. "A Rutledge book." Includes index. Bibliography: p. 235-237. [TT715.S9] 77-1627 ISBN 0-03-015121-X : 14.95
1. Needlework—United States—History. I. Title. BIP

Needlework—Yearbooks.

MCCALL'S needlework & crafts annual. v.1-1950- [New York, McCall Corp. v. illus. 35cm. Title varies: v.1, McCall needlework annual. [TT740.M34] 52-43420 745
1. Needlework—Yearbooks. 2. Handicraft—Yearbooks.

Needlwork—Dictionaries.

CAULFEILD, Sophia Frances Anne, 1824-1911. 746.4'03
The dictionary of needlework; an encyclopaedia of artistic, plain, and fancy needlework [by] S. F. A. Caulfeild [and] Blanche C. Saward. New York, Arno Press; distributed by Crown Publishers, 1972. 528 p. illus. 29 cm. Reprint of the 1882 ed. [TT750.C35 1972] 72-2139 ISBN 0-405-00695-0 6.95
1. Needlwork—Dictionaries. I. Saward, Blanche C. II. Title. BIP

Nefer-hotep.

DAVIES, Norman de Garis, 1865-1941. 913.32'03'1
The tomb of Nefer-hotep at Thebes, by Norman de Garis Davies. With plates in color by Nina de Garis Davies. New York, 1933. [New York] Arno Press, 1973. 2 v. in 1. illus., 68 plates. 31 cm. At head of title: The Metropolitan Museum of Art Egyptian Expedition. Plates in reprint ed. are in black and white. Reprint of the ed. which was issued as v. 9 of the Publications of the Metropolitan Museum of Art Egyptian Expedition. Includes bibliographical references. [DT73.T3D316 1973] 71-168402 39.00
1. Nefer-hotep. 2. Thebes, Egypt—Tombs. I. Davies, Nina M. (Cummings) illus. II. New York (City). Metropolitan Museum of Art. Egyptian Expedition. III. Title. IV. Series: New York (City). Metropolitan

Museum of Art. Egyptian Expedition. Publications, v. 9. BIP

Negre, Charles, 1820-1880.

NEGRE, Charles, 1820-1880. 779'.092'4
Charles Negre 1820-1880 / James Borcoman. Ottawa : National Gallery of Canada, 1976. 261 p. : chiefly ill. ; 30 cm. English and French in parallel columns. Includes indexes. Bibliography: p. 257-258. [TR652.N43 1976] 76-378760 ISBN 0-88884-268-6
1. Negre, Charles, 1820-1880. 2. Photography, Artistic. 3. Photographers—France—Biography. I. Borcoman, James.

Negro art.

DOVER, Cedric. 709.73
American Negro art. [Greenwich, Conn.] New York Graphic Society [1960] 186 p. illus., col. plates, ports. 25 cm. "Bibliography by Maureen Dover": p. 57-60. [N6538.N5D6 1960] 60-51364
1. Negro art. 2. Art, American. I. Title. BIP

KOCHNITZKY, Leon, 1894- 709.675
Negro art in Belgian Congo. 3d, rev. ed. New York, Belgian Government Information Center, 1952. 83p. illus. 23cm. (Art. life and science of Belgium, no. 10) [N7397.C6K6 1952] 61-40767
1. Negro art. 2. Art—Congo, Belgian. 3. Art, Primitive. I. Title.

LEWIS, Samella S. 709'.22
Black artists on art, [edited by] Samella S. Lewis and Ruth G. Waddy. [Los Angeles, Contemporary Crafts Publishers, 1969- v. illus. (part col.), ports. (part col.) 27 cm. [N6538.N5L4] 76-97788 14.50
1. Negro art. 2. Negro artists—United States. I. Waddy, Ruth G., 1909- joint author. II. Title.

MEAUZE, Pierre. 732'.2
African art: sculpture. [1st ed.] Cleveland, World Pub. Co. [1968] 219 p. illus. (part col.), map. 33 cm. Translation of L'Art negre: sculpture. Bibliography: p. 217. [NB1097.W4M43] 67-24467
1. Negro art. 2. Sculpture—Africa, West. I. Title.

Negro art—Africa, South.

DEJAGEN, E. J. 709'.68
Contemporary African art in South Africa, by E. J. De Jager. Cape Town, C. Struik, 1973. 31 p. illus. (part col.), 128 plates. 29 cm. Includes bibliographical references. [N7392.D4] 74-156464 ISBN 0-86977-025-X
1. Negro art—Africa, South. 2. Art, Modern—20th century—Africa, South. 3. Negro artists—Africa, South. I. Title.
Distributed by Verry; 22.50. BIP

Negro art—Catalogs.

GUILLAUME, Paul, 1891- comp. 732'.2
Sculptures negres; 24 photographies precedees d'un avertissement de Guillaume Apollinaire et d'un expose de Paul Guillaume. Collection Andre Breton et Paul Eluard: Sculptures d'Afrique, d'Amerique, d'Oceanie; Me Alph. Bellier, commissaire-priseur ... New York, Hacker Art Books, 1972 [i.e. 1973] [12] p., 24 plates, 50 p., 24 plates. map. 34 cm. "Sculptures negres first published in Paris by Paul Guillaume, 1917. Sculptures d'Afrique, d'Amerique, d'Oceanie first published in Paris, 1931. Reprinted 1973." [NB1098.G84] 71-143336 ISBN 0-87817-056-1
1. Breton, Andre 1896-1966—Art collections. 2. Eluard, Paul, 1895-1952—Art collections. 3. Negro art—Catalogs. 4. Sculpture—Africa, West—Catalogs. 5. Sculpture, Primitive—Catalogs. I. Apollinaire, Guillaume, 1880-1918. II. Bellier, Alphonse. III. Sculptures d'Afrique, d'Amerique, d'Oceanie. 1973. IV. Title. V. Title: Collection Andre Breton et Paul Eluard. BIP

Negro art—Exhibitions.

AFRO-AMERICAN 759.13'074'014461
artists: New York and Boston; [exhibition] The Museum of the National Center of Afro-American Artists, the Museum of Fine Arts [and] the School of the Museum of Fine Arts, Boston, 19 May-23 June, 1970. [Boston? 1970] 1 v. (unpaged) illus. 26 cm. [N6538.N5A35] 77-19423
1. Negro art—Exhibitions. 2. Negro artists—New York (City) 3. Negro artists—Boston. I. National Center of Afro-American Artists. Museum. II. Boston. Museum of Fine Arts. III. Boston. Museum of Fine Arts. School of the Museum of Fine Arts.

CROCKER Art Gallery Association. 709'.2'2
West coast 74, Black image : 1974 invitational exhibition : [exhibition dates, E. B. Crocker Art Gallery, Sacramento, California, September 13-13 October, 1974, Los Angeles Municipal Art Gallery, Barnsdall Park, Los Angeles, California, January 22-16 February, 1975] / Crocker Art Gallery Association and E. B. Crocker Art Gallery. Sacramento, Calif. : Crocker Art Gallery, [1974] [69] p. : ill. ; 23 cm. Bibliography: p. [68] [N6538.N5C76 1974] 74-84704
1. Negro art—Exhibitions. 2. Negro art—California. 3. Art, Modern—20th century—California. I. Crocker Art Gallery, Sacramento, Calif. II. Los Angeles. Municipal Art Gallery. III. Title. IV. Title: Black image.

DIMENSIONS of 709.1'74'96
Black. [Exhibition] La Jolla Museum of Art, February 15-March 29, 1970. Jehanne Teilhet, editor. [San Diego? 1970] vi, 154 p. illus., map. 23 x 26 cm. The exhibition and this catalog result from a student project of the University of California, San Diego. Bibliography: p. 150-153. [N7428.5.D54] 72-630858
1. Art, European—Negro influences. 2. Negro art—Exhibitions. 3. Art—Africa, West. I. Teilhet, Jehanne, ed. II. La Jolla, Calif. Museum of Art. III. California. University, San Diego.

DOTY, Robert M. 709.73'074'01471
Contemporary Black artists in America, by Robert Doty. New York, Whitney Museum of American Art [1971] 64 p. illus. (part col.) 25 cm. Catalogue of an exhibition held at Whitney Museum of American Art, April 6-May 16, 1971. Bibliography: p. 60-64. [N6538.N5D58] 74-154608
1. Negro art—Exhibitions. I. Whitney Museum of American Art, New York. II. Title.

EXISTENCE/BLACK; an exhibition of African-American artists. [Exhibition coordinated by Phillip Hampton. Edwardsville, Ill., 1972] [40] p. illus. 21 cm. "Presented ... for the Ethnic and Special Studies Workshop, June 10-July 21, Southern Illinois University, Edwardsville, Illinois." [N6538.N5E99] 72-195409
1. Negro art—Exhibitions. 2. Negro artists—United States. I. Hampton, Phillip J. II. Ethnic and Special Studies Workshop, Southern Illinois University, 1972.

HARLEM Cultural Council. 709'.73'07401471
New black artists; an exhibition organized by the Harlem Cultural Council, in cooperation with the School of the Arts, and the Urban Center of Columbia University. Brooklyn Museum, Oct. 7 to Nov. 9, 1969; Columbia University, Nov. 20 to Dec. 12, 1969. Foreword by Edward K. Taylor. [New York, Printed by Clarke & Way, 1969] [54] p. (chiefly illus., ports.) 26 cm. [N6538.N5H28] 73-25306
1. Negro art—Exhibitions. I. Brooklyn Institute of Arts and Sciences. Museum. II. Columbia University. III. Title.

HARMON Foundation, inc. 709'.22
Negro artists; an illustrated review of their achievements, including exhibition of paintings by the late Malvin Gray Johnson and sculptures by Richmond Barthe and Sargent Johnson. Presented by the Harmon Foundation in cooperation with the Delphic Studios April 22-May 4, 1935, inclusive. Freeport, N.Y., Books for Libraries Press, 1971. 59 p. illus., ports. 23 cm. (The Black heritage library collection) Reprint of the 1935 ed. [N6538.N5H34 1971] 72-161262 ISBN 0-8369-8821-3
1. Negro art—Exhibitions. I. Title. II. Series. BIP

HERBERT F. Johnson Museum of Art. 709'.73
Directions in Afro-American art : [exhibition] September 18 through October 27, 1974, Herbert F. Johnson Museum of Art, Cornell University, cosponsored by the Africana Studies and Research Center, Cornell University. Ithaca, N.Y. : Office of University Publications, Cornell University, [1974] [81] p. : ill. ; 31 cm. Bibliography: p. [77]-[81] [N6538.N5H47 1974] 74-1624
1. Negro art—Exhibitions. 2. Negro art—United States. 3. Art, Modern—20th century—United States. I. Cornell University. Africana Studies and Research Center. II. Title.

MINNEAPOLIS. Institute of Arts. 709'.73
Contemporary Black artists. [New York, Ruder & Finn, c1969] [44] p. illus. 28 cm. Catalog of an exhibition originally entitled: 30 contemporary Black artists. [N6538.N5M49 1969] 79-106382
1. Negro art—Exhibitions. 2. Negro artists—United States. I. Ruder & Finn. II. Title.

MINNEAPOLIS. Institute of Arts. 709'.73
30 contemporary black artists; an exhibition organized by the Minneapolis. Institute of Arts with the assistance of Ruder & Finn, inc. New York. [Minneapolis, 1968] [20] p. illus. 22 cm. Held at the Minneapolis Institute of Arts, Minneapolis, Minnesota, October 17-November 24, 1968: and will also be shown at the High Museum of Art, Atlanta; Flint Institute of Arts, Flint, Mich.; Everson Museum of Art, Syracuse; and the San Francisco Museum of Art. Catalog published in 1969 under title: Contemporary Black artists. [N6538.N5M5] 68-58877
1. Negro art—Exhibitions. 2. Negro artists—United States. I. Ruder & Finn. II. Title.

NATIONAL Center of Afro-American Artists. Museum. 759.13
Five famous Black artists presented by the Museum of the National Center of Afro-American Artists: Romare Bearden, Jacob Lawrence, Horace Pippin, Charles White, Hale Woodruff. [Exhibition] Feb. 9-Mar. 10, 1970. [Boston, 1970] [45] p. illus. 26 cm. Label mounted on t.p.: Supplied by Worldwide Books, Boston. [N6538.N5N3] 70-21664
1. Negro art—Exhibitions. I. Title.

NEW York (City). City University of New York. 709'.73
The evolution of Afro-American artists, 1800-1950. New York, 1967. 70 p. illus. 27 cm. Catalog of an exhibition organized by the City University of New York in cooperation with the Harlem Cultural Council and the New York Urban League, and held at Great Hall, the City College. [N6538.N5N4] 68-7881
1. Negro art—Exhibitions. 2. Negro art—United States. 3. Negro artists—United States. I. Harlem Cultural Council. II. Urban League of Greater New York. III. Title.

NEW York. Museum of Modern Art. 709'.73
African Negro art, edited by James Johnson Sweeney. Reprint ed. New York, Published for the Museum of Modern Art by Arno Press, 1966 [c1935] 58 p. illus., maps (part fold.) plates. 27 cm. Bibliography: p. 25-29. [N7380] 66-26124
1. Negro art—Exhibitions. 2. Art, African—Exhibitions. I. Sweeney, James Johnson, 1900- ed. II. Title. III. Title: Negro art. BIP

NEWARK Museum Association, Newark, N.J. 759.13'074'014932
Black artists: two generations [exhibition held at] the Newark Museum, May 13-Sept. 6, 1971. [Newark, 1971] 1 v. (chiefly illus.) 26 cm. Cover title. [N6538.N5N45] 72-198389
1. Negro art—Exhibitions. 2. Art, Modern—20th century—U.S. I. Title.

PORTER, James Amos, 1905- 709'.73
Ten Afro-American artists of the Nineteenth century. Washington, Gallery of Art, Howard University [1967] 33 p. illus. 25 cm. Catalog, prepared by J. A. Porter, of an exhibition commemorating the centennial of Howard University held Feb. 3-Mar. 30, 1967, Gallery of Art, Howard University. Bibliography: p. 32-33. [N6538.N5P62] 67-19362
1. Negro art—Exhibitions. 2. Negro artists—United States. I. Howard University, Washington, D.C. Gallery of Art. II. Title.

SOME American history 709.73
[by] Larry Rivers [and others] Introduced by Charles Childs. [Houston, 1971] 20 p., 49 plates (part col.) 23 cm. "[Exhibition] organized and circulated by the Institute for the Arts, Rice University, February 1971." "Film circulated with the exhibition: Slavery: the Black man and the man, conceived by June Jordan and directed by John Chandler." [N6538.N5S6] 72-153088
1. Negro art—Exhibitions. 2. Negroes in art. I. Rivers, Larry, 1923- II. William Marsh Rice University, Houston, Tex. Institute for the Arts.

TOLEDO. Museum of Art. 709'.73
Black artists of Toledo; [catalog of] an exhibition co-sponsored by the Confederation of Black Artists and the Toledo Museum of Art, August 5 through September 3, 1973. [Toledo, 1973] [11] p. 21 cm. [N6538.N5T64 1973] 74-158371
1. Negro art—Exhibitions. 2. Negro art—Toledo. I. Confederation of Black Artists. II. Title.

Negro art—United States.

FINE, Elsa Honig. 709'.73
The Afro-American artist; a search for identity. New York, Holt, Rinehart and Winston [1973] x, 310 p. illus. 26 cm. Bibliography: p. 288-300. [N6538.N5F56] 73-1235 9.95
1. Negro art—United States. 2. Negro artists—United States. I. Title.

LOCKE, Alain LeRoy, 1886-1954. 709'.22
The Negro in art; a pictorial record of the Negro artist and of the Negro theme in art. Edited and annotated by Alain Locke. Chicago, Afro-Am Press, 1969. 224 p. illus. 28 cm. Reprint of the 1940 ed. [N6538.N5L6 1969] 79-99389 ISBN 0-8411-0060-8
1. Negro art—United States. 2. Negroes in art. I. Title. BIP

LOCKE, Alain LeRoy, 1886-1954. 709'.2'2
The Negro in art; a pictorial record of the Negro artist and of the Negro theme in art. Edited and annotated by Alain Locke. New York, Hacker Art Books, 1971. 224 p. illus. 32 cm. Reprint of the 1940 ed. Bibliography: p. 224. [N6538.N5L6 1971] 68-9006 ISBN 0-87817-013-8
1. Negro art—United States. 2. Negroes in art. I. Title.

PORTER, James Amos, 1905- 709.73
Modern Negro art [by] James A. Porter. New York, Arno Press, 1969. viii, 272 p. illus. 23 cm. (The American Negro, his history and literature) Reprint of the 1943 ed., with a new pref. by the author. Bibliography: p. 183-192. [N6538.N5P6 1969] 69-18593 10.00
1. Negro art—United States. 2. Negro artists—United States. I. Title. II. Series. BIP

Negro art—U.S.—History.

CHASE, Judith Wragg. 709'.73
Afro-American art and craft. New York, Van Nostrand Reinhold Co. [1971] 142 p. illus. 29 cm. Bibliography: p. 138-139. [N6538.N5C5] 76-163485
1. Negro art—U.S.—History. I. Title.

SUBJECT INDEX NEIZVESTNYI, ERNEST, 1926—

Negro artists.

UNITED States Committee 709.73 for the First World Festival of Negro Arts
Dix artistes negres des Etats-Unis: premier Festival mondial des arts negres, Dakar, Senegal. 1966. Ten Negro artists from the United States: first World Festival of Negro Arts, Dakar. Senegal. 1966. An exhibition produced. sponsored by the U. S. Comm. for the First World Festival of Negro Arts. inc. and the National Collection of Fine Arts. Smithsonian Instn. [Text tr. prepd. by Denise and Michel Berthier. New York, 1 v. (unpaged) illus., ports. 21cm. The exhibition will be circulated in the United States by the Amer. Federation of Arts. English and French. [N6538.N5U513] 66-20330 1.75 pap.,
1. Negro artists. 2. Art. American—Exhibitions. I. Smithsonian Institution, National Collection of Fine arts. II. World Festival of Negro Arts. 1st. Dakar, 1966. III. Title. IV. Title: Ten Negro artists from the United States.

Negro artists—Louisiana.

THOMAS, Morris Taft. 709'.2'2
Contributions of Negro artists in Louisiana. Photos. by John L. Cooper, except as noted. [Pineville, La., Printed by Fitzgerald's Print. Co., 1973] vi, 50 p. ports. 23 cm. [N6538.N5T45] 73-166282
1. Negro artists—Louisiana. 2. Negro art—Louisiana. I. Title.

Negro artists—U.S.

BEARDEN, Romare, 1914- 709'.2'2
Six Black masters of American art [by] Romare Bearden and Harry Henderson. [1st ed.] New York, Zenith Books, 1972. 119 p. illus. (part col.) 21 cm. "Z23." Contents.Contents.—Joshua Johnston.—Robert S. Duncanson.—Henry Ossawa Tanner.—Horace Pippin.—Augusta Savage.—Jacob Lawrence. [N6538.N5B4] 70-175358 1.95
1. Negro artists—U.S. I. Henderson, Harry Brinton, 1914- joint author. II. Title. BIP

FAX, Elton C. 709'.22
Seventeen black artists [by] Elton C. Fax. New York, Dodd, Mead [1971] xiv, 306 p. illus., ports. 22 cm. [N6538.N5F3] 72-165671 ISBN 0-396-06391-8 7.95
1. Negro artists—U.S. I. Title. BIP

Negro artists—United States—Indexes.

ST. Louis. Public Library. 709'.73
An index to Black American artists. [St. Louis, 1972?] 50 p. 28 cm. Cover title: Black American artists index. Bibliography: p. 47-50. [N6538.N5S24 1972] 74-152308
1. Negro artists—United States—Indexes. 2. Negro art—United States—Indexes. I. Title. II. Title: Black American artists index. BIP

Negro arts—Africa, West.

STOKES, Olivia Pearl, 1916- comp. 398.2'0966
The beauty of being Black; folktales, poems and art from Africa. Edited by Louise Crane. Illustrated by Karen Tureck. New York, Friendship Press [1971] 63 p. illus. 23 cm. A collection of folktales, poems, and short stories from Africa. Also includes photographs and discussions of Africa's art. [NX589.S8] 70-29279 ISBN 0-377-11611-4 2.50
1. Negro arts—Africa, West. I. Tureck, Karen, illus. II. Title. BIP

THE Traditional artist in African societies. 700'.966 Warren L. d'Azevedo, editor. Bloomington, Indiana University Press [1973] xxi, 454 p. illus. 25 cm. Erratum slip inserted. Bibliography: p. 435-454. [NX589.T72] 79-160126 ISBN 0-253-39901-7 16.00
1. Negro arts—Africa, West. I. D'Azevedo, Warren L., ed. BIP

Negro arts—Africa, West—Juvenile literature.

PRICE, Christine, 1928- 700'.966
Made in West Africa. Illustrated with photos. and drawings. [1st ed.] New York, Dutton [1975] vii, 150 p. illus. 25 cm. Bibliography: p. 147. Discusses the influences of African customs, history, and geography upon art in West Africa. Includes dress, textiles, jewelry, metal sculpture, carving, masks, and pottery. [NX589.P54 1975] 74-4202 ISBN 0-525-34400-4
1. Negro arts—Africa, West—Juvenile literature. I. Title. BIP

Negro arts—Exhibitions.

NEW York Cultural Center. 709'.73
Blacks: U.S.A.: 1973. [Exhibition held at] the New York Cultural Center, in association with Fairleigh Dickinson University, September 26 to November 15, 1973. [New York, 1973] [27] p. illus. 28 cm. [N6538.N5N42 1973] 73-88677
1. Negro arts—Exhibitions. 2. Negro artists—United States. I. Fairleigh Dickinson University. II. Title.

Negro arts—Harlem, New York (City)

HUGGINS, Nathan Irvin, 1927- 700'.97471
Harlem renaissance. New York, Oxford Univ. Pr. [1973, c.1971] 343 p. illus., ports. 21 cm. (Galaxy bk., GB384) Bibl. refs. [NX512.3.N5H8] 70-159646 ISBN 0-19-501665-3 pap., 2.95
1. Negro arts—Harlem, New York (City) 2. The arts, Modern—20th century—Harlem New York (City) I. Title. BIP

Negro arts—United States.

BRAWLEY, Benjamin Griffith, 1882-1939. 700'.973
The Negro in literature and art in the United States. New York, Duffield, 1930. St. Clair Shores, Mich., Scholarly Press, 1972. xii, 231 p. 22 cm. Bibliography: p. 213-228. [PS153.N5B65 1972] 72-131644 ISBN 0-403-00531-0
1. Negro arts—United States. 2. Negroes in art. I. Title. BIP

BUTCHER, Margaret (Just) 1913- 700'.973
The Negro in American culture, based on materials left by Alain Locke. 2d ed. New York, Knopf, 1972 [c1971] x, 313, xiv p. 23 cm. [NX512.3.N5B8 1972] 74-38321 ISBN 0-394-47943-2 7.95
1. Negro arts—United States. I. Title. BIP

GAYLE, Addison, 1932- comp. 709.73
The Black aesthetic. [1st ed.] Garden City, N.Y., Doubleday, 1971. xxiv, 432 p. 22 cm. [NX512.3.N5G38] 71-123692 8.95
1. Negro arts—U.S. I. Title. BIP

LOCKE, Alain LeRoy, 1886-1954, ed. 917.3'06'96073
The new Negro. With a new pref. by Robert Hayden. New York, Atheneum, 1970 [c1925] xxiv, 452 p. illus. 21 cm. (Atheneum paperbacks. Studies in American Negro life, NL 10) Bibliography: p. 415-452. [NX512.3.N5L6 1970] 68-55749
1. Negro arts—United States. I. Title. BIP

Negro arts—United States—Bibliography.

IRVINE, Betty Jo. 016.709'73
Fine arts and the Black American, compiled by Betty Jo Irvine, and Music and the Black American, compiled by Jane A. McCabe. [Bloomington] Indiana University Libraries, 1969. 33 p. 28 cm. (Focus: Black America bibliography series) [Z5961.U5I78] 73-620746
1. Negro arts—United States—Bibliography. 2. Negro artists—United States. I. Indiana. University. Libraries. II. McCabe, Jane A. Music and the Black American. 1969. III. Title. IV. Title: Music and the Black American. V. Series.

Negro arts—United States—Biography.

*CEDERHOLM, Theresa Dickason. 700'.973
Afro-American artists; a bio-bibliographical directory, comp. and edited by Theresa Dickason Cederholm. [Boston, Mass.] Trustees of the Boston Public Library, 1973. 348 p. 24 cm. Bibliography: p. 325-348. [PS153] 73-84951 10.00 (pbk.)
1. Negro arts—United States—Biography. 2. Negroes in art—United States—Biography. I. Title.
Order from Information Office, Boston Public Library, Box 286, Boston, MA 02117. BIP

Negro musicians—Exhibitions.

RAMSEY, Frederic, 1915- 779'.2'0924
Where the music started; a photographic essay. [New Brunswick, N.J.] Rutgers University Institute of Jazz Studies [1970] 34 p. ports. 22 cm. A descriptive guide for an exhibit of photographs taken in the Deep South, 1951-60. [ML141.R88R3] 73-172396
1. Negro musicians—Exhibitions. 2. Negro musicians—Portraits, etc.—Catalogs. I. Title.

Negroes—Civil rights—Pictorial works.

JACKSON, Billy Morrow. 741.973
Protest drawings: a graphic response to the civil rights drama. [Chicago, Galaxie Press, 1966] [3], 4 l. 28 cm. and portfolio (8 plates (part col.)) 76 cm. Caption title. [NC1075.J3A55] 67-7776
1. Negroes—Civil rights—Pictorial works. I. Title.

Negroes—Iconography.

MURRAY, Freeman Henry Morris. 731'.8'9326
Emancipation and the freed in American sculpture; a study in interpretation. Introd. by John Wesley Cromwell. Freeport, N.Y., Books for Libraries Press, 1972. xxviii, 239 p. illus. 23 cm. (The Black heritage library collection) Reprint of the 1916 ed., issued in series: Black folk in art series. "This monograph is chiefly the expansion of papers which were read as lectures ... at the Summer School and Chautauqua of the National Religious Training School at Durham, N.C., in 1913." Includes bibliographical references. [E185.89.I2M9 1972] 70-38016
1. Negroes—Iconography. 2. Sculpture, American. I. Title. II. Series. III. Series: Black folk in art series. BIP

Negroes in art.

BOWDOIN College. Museum of Fine Arts. 704.94'9'30145196
The portrayal of the Negro in American painting; [exhibition] the Bowdoin College Museum of Art. [Catalogue. Brunswick? Me.] 1964. 1 v. (unpaged) illus., ports. 26 cm. [N8232.B6] 64-4946
1. Negroes in art. 2. Paintings, American — Exhibitions. I. Title.

MARK, Peter, 1948- 759.02
Africans in European eyes : the portrayal of Black Africans in fourteenth and fifteenth century Europe / by Peter Mark. [Syracuse, N.Y.] : Maxwell School of Citizenship and Public Affairs, Syracuse University, 1974. iv, 98 p. ; 23 cm. (Foreign and comparative studies : Eastern Africa ; 16) A revision of the author's thesis (M.A.), Syracuse University, 1972. Includes bibliographical references. [N8232.M37 1974] 74-25878 4.50
1. Negroes in art. 2. Negroes in Africa. 3. Art, Renaissance. I. Title. II. Series.

Negroes in art—Juvenile literature.

COEN, Rena Neumann. 704.94'2
The Black man in art. Designed by Patricia Koskey. Minneapolis, Minn., Lerner Publications Co. [1970] 71 p. illus. (part col.) 27 cm. Discusses, with examples of paintings and sculpture, the appearance of the black man in the art of various eras and cultures. [N8232.C6 1970] 78-84405
1. Negroes in art—Juvenile literature. I. Title. BIP

Negroes—Pictorial works.

HIGGINS, Chester. 779'.9'91730696073
Drums of life; a photographic essay on the Black man in America. Photos. by Chester Higgins, Jr. Text by Orde Coombs. [1st ed.] Garden City, N.Y., Anchor Press, 1974. 131 p. illus. 28 cm. [E185.H53] 73-11728 ISBN 0-385-07134-5 5.95 (pbk.).
1. Negroes—Pictorial works. I. Coombs, Orde.

WARNER, James A. 778.9'9'91730696073
The darker brother. [Photos. by] James A. Warner. [Edited by] Styne M. Slade. [1st ed.] New York, Dutton, 1974. 164 p. illus. 29 cm. (A Dutton visual book) [E185.W29 1974] 74-3639 ISBN 0-525-49502-9 18.95
1. Negroes—Pictorial works. I. Slade, Styne M., comp. II. Title. BIP

Negroes—Social life and customs—Pictorial works.

LUCAS, Leroy. 779'.9'91730696073024 B
Growing up Black. Photos. by Leroy Lucas. [Introductory statement by Leroy Lucas. New York, New York State Council on the Arts, c1971] [4] p., 50 plates. 37 cm. Issued in a case. "An exhibit portfolio produced by the New York State Council on the Arts for the New York Museums Collaborative." [E185.86.L82] 72-171184
1. Negroes—Social life and customs—Pictorial works. I. New York (State). State Council on the Arts. II. Museums Collaborative. III. Title.

Neighborhood Garden Association.

BUSH-BROWN, Louise (Carter) 1897- 712'.6
Garden blocks for urban America [by] Louise Bush-Brown. New York, Scribner [1969] 126 p. illus. (part col.) 27 cm. [NA9052.B78] 69-17051 10.00
1. Neighborhood Garden Association. 2. Urban beautification—Philadelphia. I. Title.

Neillot, Louis, 1898—

NEILLOT, Louis, 1898- 759.4
L. Neillot: watercolors, 1930-1973; a homage to the artist on his seventy-fifth birthday. [Catalog] Chicago, R. S. Johnson-International Gallery, 1973. 15 p. illus. 25 cm. Includes bibliographical references. [ND1950.N44J64] 73-83090
1. Neillot, Louis, 1898- I. Johnson (R. S.)-International Gallery.

Neiman, LeRoy, 1927—

NEIMAN, LeRoy, 1927- 741.9'73
Art & lifestyle / LeRoy Neiman. New York : Felicie, [1974] 285 p. : chiefly ill. (some col.) ; 34 cm. [N6537.N39A42] 74-8355 ISBN 0-9600692-3-2 : 35.00
1. Neiman, LeRoy, 1927- I. Title.

Neizvestnyi, Ernest, 1926—

BERGER, John. 709'.47
Art and revolution; Ernst Neizvestny and the role of the artist in the U.S.S.R. [1st American ed.] New York, Pantheon Books [1969] 191 p. illus. 21 cm. [NB699.N4B4 1969] 68-26045 1.95
1. Neizvestnyi, Ernest, 1926- 2. Socialism and art. I. Title.

BERGER, John. 730'.924
Art and revolution: Ernst Neizvestny and the role of the artist in the U.S.S.R. Harmondsworth, Penguin, 1969. 191 p. 89 illus., facsim., 5 ports. 20 cm. (Pelican books, A 1078) Bibliographical footnotes. [NB699.N4B4 1969c] 74-525631 12/-
1. Neizvestnyi, Ernest, 1926- 2. Socialism and art. I. Title.

Nelson, Horatio Nelson, 1758-1805—Monuments, etc.

MACE, Rodney. 942.1'32
Trafalgar Square : emblem of empire / Rodney Mace. London : Lawrence and Wishart, 1976. 338 p., [20] leaves of plates : ill. ; 24 cm. Includes index. Bibliography: p. 323-338. [DA685.T84M32] 76-378564 ISBN 0-85315-368-X : £8.00. ISBN 0-85315-367-1 pbk.
1. Nelson, Horatio Nelson, 1758-1805—Monuments, etc. 2. London—Plazas—Trafalgar Square. I. Title. BIP

Nelson McCoy Pottery Company—Catalogs.

HUXFORD, Sharon. 738.3'7
The collectors encyclopedia of McCoy pottery / by Sharon and Bob Huxford. 1st ed. Paducah, Ky. : Collector Books, c1978. 239 p. : ill. (some col.) ; 29 cm. Includes index. Bibliography:p. 238. [NK4210.M23A4 1978] 78-107663 ISBN 0-89145-068-8 : 17.95
1. Nelson McCoy Pottery Company—Catalogs. 2. Brush-McCoy Pottery Company—Catalogs. 3. Pottery, American—Ohio—Catalogs. I. Huxford, Bob, joint author. II. Title. BIP

Neo-impressionism (Art)

STEADMAN, William E. 760'.094
Homage to Seurat; paintings, watercolors, and drawings by the followers of Seurat, collected by Mr. and Mrs. W. J. Holliday. [Catalog by William E. Steadman] Tucson, University of Arizona Art Gallery [1968] [14] p., 73 plates (part col.) 29 cm. On cover: The Holliday Collection. Text on versos of plates. Includes bibliographies. [N6465.P6S7] 67-65947
1. Seurat, Georges Pierre, 1859-1891—Influence. 2. Holliday, William J., Mrs.—Art collections. 3. Neo-impressionism (Art) 4. Holliday, William J.—Art collections. I. Arizona. University. Art Gallery. II. Title. III. Title: The Holliday Collection.

SUTTER, Jean. 759.4
The neo impressionists. Edited by Jean Sutter with contributions by Robert L. Herbert [and others. Translated from the French by Chantal Deliss] Greenwich, Conn., New York Graphic Society [1970] 232 p. illus. (part col.) 29 cm. Bibliography: p. 221-223. [N6465.N44S913 1970] 70-126029 ISBN 0-8212-0224-3
1. Neo-impressionism (Art) I. Herbert, Robert L., 1929- II. Title.

Neoclassicism (Architecture)—England—Cambridge—Exhibitions.

WATKIN, David, 1941- 720'.9426'5907402659
The triumph of the classical : Cambridge architecture, 1804-1834 : exhibition / catalogued with an introd. by David Watkin. Cambridge ; New York : Cambridge University Press for the Fitzwilliam Museum, 1977. 58 p., [13] leaves of platess : ill. ; 20 x 28 cm. At head of title: Fitzwilliam Museum, Cambridge. Errata slip inserted. [NA971.C3W37] 77-12164 ISBN 0-521-21854-3 : 10.95
1. Neoclassicism (Architecture)—England—Cambridge—Exhibitions. 2. Architecture, Modern—19th century—England—Cambridge—Exhibitions. 3. Cambridge—Buildings. I. Cambridge. University. Fitzwilliam Museum. II. Title. BIP

Neoclassicism (Architecture)—Great Britain.

BEARD, Geoffrey W. 720'.92'4
The work of Robert Adam / Geoffrey Beard. New York : Arco, [1978] p. cm. [NA997.A4B4] 78-641 ISBN 0-668-04535-3 : 16.95
1. Adam, Robert, 1728-1792. 2. Neoclassicism (Architecture)—Great Britain. I. Adam, Robert, 1728-1792. II. Title. BIP

Neoclassicism (Architecture)—Italy.

GUINNESS, Desmond. 724'.1
Palladio : a western progress / Desmond Guinness and Julius Trousdale Sadler, Jr. New York : Viking Press, 1976. 183 p. : ill. (some col.) ; 29 cm. (A Studio book) Includes index. Bibliography: p. 179-180. [NA1123.P2G78 1976] 75-38760 ISBN 0-670-53732-2 : 14.95
1. Palladio, Andrea, 1508-1580. 2. Neoclassicism (Architecture)—Italy. 3. Neoclassicism (Architecture)—England. 4. Neoclassicism (Architecture)—Ireland. 5. Neoclassicism (Architecture)—United States. 6. Neoclassicism (Architecture)—West Indies. I. Sadler, Julius Trousdale, joint author. II. Title.

Neoclassicism (Architecture)—Italy—Exhibitions.

WHITEHEAD, Walter Muir, 1905- 720'.92'4
Palladio· in America / [texts by Walter Muir Whitehill and Frederick Doveton Nichols]. Milan : Electa, c1976. 127 p. : ill. ; 25 cm. Catalog of the exhibition held in the United States in 1976. Bibliography: p. 126. [NA1123.P2W48] 77-351242
1. Palladio, Andrea, 1508-1580. 2. Palladio, Andrea, 1508-1580—Influence. 3. Neoclassicism (Architecture)—Italy—Exhibitions. 4. Neoclassicism (Architecture)—United States—Exhibitions. I. Nichols, Frederick Doveton, joint author. II. Palladio, Andrea, 1508-1580. III. Title. BIP

Neoclassicism (Architecture)—United States.

†CLASSICAL America IV 720'.973
/ William A. Coles, editor. 1st ed. [New York] : Norton, c1977. 232 p. : ill. ; 29 cm. (The Classical America series in art and architecture) [NA710.5.N4C55 1977] 78-103153 ISBN 0-393-04497-1 : 14.95
1. Neoclassicism (Architecture)—United States. 2. Architecture, Modern—19th century—United States. 3. Architecture, Modern—20th century—United States. I. Coles, William A. II. Series. BIP

Neoclassicism (Art)

EITNER, Lorenz Edwin Alfred, comp. 709'.033
Neoclassicism and romanticism, 1750-1850; sources and documents [compiled by] Lorenz Eitner. Englewood Cliffs, N.J., Prentice-Hall [1970] 2 v. illus. 23 cm. (Sources and documents in the history of art series) Contents.Contents.—v. 1. Enlightenment/Revolution.—v. 2. Restoration/Twilight of humanism. Bibliographical footnotes. [N6425.N4E35] 74-94425
1. Neoclassicism (Art) 2. Romanticism in art. I. Title. II. Series.

HONOUR, Hugh. 709'.033
Neo-classicism. [Baltimore] Penguin Books [1973, c1968] 221 p. illus. 20 cm. (Pelican books, A978) (Style and civilization) Bibliography: p. 209-211. [N6425.N4H6] 71-384062 3.40 (pbk.)
1. Neoclassicism (Art) I. Title. II. Series. BIP

ROSENBLUM, Robert. 760'.094
The international style of 1800 : a study in linear abstraction / Robert Rosenblum. New York : Garland Pub., 1976. vii, 282 p. : ill. ; 21 cm. (Outstanding dissertations in the fine arts) Reprint of the author's thesis, New York University, 1956. Bibliography: p. 230-255. [N6425.N4R67 1976] 75-23813 ISBN 0-8240-2006-5 lib.bdg. : 25.00
1. Neoclassicism (Art) 2. Art, Modern—17th-18th centuries. 3. Art, Modern—19th century. I. Title. II. Series.

Neoclassicism (Art)—Addresses, essays, lectures.

ROCOCO to Romanticism : 709 s
art and architecture, 1700-1850. New York : Garland Pub., 1976. p. cm. (The Garland library of the history of art ; v. 10) Includes bibliographical references. [N5300.G32 vol. 10] [N6425.N4] 709'.03'3 76-14072 ISBN 0-8240-2420-6 lib.bdg. : 35.00
1. Neoclassicism (Art)—Addresses, essays, lectures. 2. Art, Modern—17th-18th centuries—Addresses, essays, lectures. 3. Romanticism in art—Addresses, essays, lectures. 4. Art, Modern—19th century—Addresses, essays, lectures. I. Series.
Contents omitted

Neoclassicism (Art)—Exhibitions.

POMPEII as source 704.94'9'9377
and inspiration : reflections in eighteenth- and nineteenth-century art : an exhibition / organized by the 1976-77 graduate students in the museum practice program, April 7-May 15, 1977, the University of Michigan Museum of Art, Ann Arbor. Ann Arbor : The Museum, [1977] ix, 58 p. : ill. ; 28 cm. Errata slip inserted. Catalogue. Bibliography: p. 55-56. [N6425.N4P65] 77-622974
1. Neoclassicism (Art)—Exhibitions. 2. Art, Modern—17th-18th centuries—Exhibitions. 3. Art, Modern—19th century—Exhibitions. 4. Art, Greco-Roman—Italy—Pompeii—Influence. 5. Pompeii. I. Michigan. University. Museum of Art.

Neoclassicism (Art)—France.

ERIKSEN, Svend. 745.4'49'44
Early Neo-Classicism in France : the creation of the Louis Seize style in architectural decoration, furniture and ormolu, gold and silver, and sevres porcelain in the mid-eighteenth century / by Svend Eriksen ; translated from the Danish [MS.] and edited by Peter Thornton. London : Faber, 1974. 3-432 p., [8] leaves of plates, [285] p. of plates : ill. (some col.) geneal. table ; 29 cm. (Faber monographs on furniture) Includes chapters in French with English translations. Ill. on lining papers. Includes bibliographical references and index. [N6846.5.N4E7413] 74-186862 ISBN 0-571-08717-5 : 105.00
1. Neoclassicism (Art)—France. 2. Decoration and ornament—Louis XVI style. I. Title.
Distributed by Humanities. BIP

GONZALEZ-PALACIOS, Alvar. 709'.44
The age of Louis XVI; [translated from the Italian by M. H. L. Jones London, New York [etc.] Hamlyn, 1969. 3-158 p. 68 col. illus. 20 cm. (Cameo) Originally published as Il Luigi XVI. Milan, Fabbri, 1966. [N6846.G6313] 76-437593 15/-
1. Neoclassicism (Art)—France. 2. Decoration and ornament—Louis XVI style. I. Title.

HOWARD, Seymour, 1928- 741.9'44
A classical frieze by Jacques Louis David : Sacrifice of the hero : the Roman years / Seymour Howard. Sacramento, Calif. : E. B. Crocker Art Gallery, c1975. 132 p. : ill. ; 28 cm. (Monograph series - E. B. Crocker Art Gallery) Includes bibliographical references and index. [NC248.D35H68] 75-16779
1. David, Jacques Louis, 1748-1825. Burial of Patroclus. 2. Neoclassicism (Art)—France. I. David, Jacques Louis, 1748-1825. II. Title. III. Title: Sacrifice of the hero. IV. Series: Crocker Art Gallery, Sacramento, Calif. Monograph series — E. B. Crocker Art Gallery.

KELDER, Diane. 759.4
Aspects of "official" painting and philosophic art, 1789-1799 / Diane M. Kelder. New York : Garland Pub., 1976. 237 p. : ill. ; 21 cm. (Outstanding dissertations in the fine arts) Originally presented as the author's thesis, Bryn Mawr, 1966. Bibliography: p. 181-195. [ND546.5.N4K44 1976] 75-23797 ISBN 0-8240-1992-X lib.bdg. : 25.00
1. Neoclassicism (Art)—France. 2. Painting, Modern—17th-18th centuries—France. 3. France—History—Revolution, 1789-1799—Art. 4. History in art. 5. Art—Philosophy. I. Title. II. Series. BIP

LEVITINE, George. 759.4
Girodet-Trioson : an iconographical study / George Levitine. New York : Garland, [1978] p. cm. (Outstanding dissertations in the fine arts) Originally presented as the author's thesis, Harvard, 1952. [ND553.G6L48 1978] 77-94702 ISBN 0-8240-3235-7 : lib.bdg. : 42.50
1. Girodet-Trioson, Anne Louis Girodet de Roussy, known as, 1767-1824. 2. Neoclassicism (Art)—France. I. Title. II. Series. BIP

Neoclassicism (Art)—Italy.

WILTON-ELY, John. 769'.92'4
The mind and art of Giovanni Battista Piranesi / John Wilton-Ely. London : Thames and Hudson, c1978. 304 p. : ill. ; 32 cm. Includes index. Bibliography: p. 298-300. [N6923.P495W54] 77-92272 ISBN 0-500-09122-6 : 39.95
1. Piranesi, Giovanni Battista, 1720-1778. 2. Neoclassicism (Art)—Italy. I. Title.
Distributed by W. W. Norton, New York, NY 10036 BIP

Nervi, Pier Luigi.

HUXTABLE, Ada Louise. 720.945
Pier Luigi Nervi. New York, G. Braziller, 1960. 128 p. plates, port., plans. 26 cm. (The Masters of world architecture series) "Bibliography of books and articles written by Pier Luigi Nervi": p. 119-120. "Selected bibliography on Pier Luigi Nervi": p. 121-122. [NA1123.N4H8] 60-6076
1. Nervi, Pier Luigi. I. Title. II. Series. BIP

SAN Francisco. Museum of Art. 720.945
Pier Luigi Nervi: space and structural integrity. [Exhibition] 12 May-18 June, 1961. [n. p., Associated Arts Foundation, 1961] 52p. illus. 31cm. [NA1123.N4S3] 61-34918
1. Nervi, Pier Luigi. I. Title.

THE works of Pier Luigi 720.945
Nervi. Pref. by Pier Luigi Nervi; introd. by Ernesto N. Rogers; explanatory notes to illus. by Jurgen Joedicke; translation by Ernest Priefert. New York, F. A. Praeger [1957] 141p. (chiefly illus., port.) 23 x 29cm. (Books that matter) [NA1123.N4A56] 720.81 56-9676
I. Nervi, Pier Luigi.

Nesbitt, Lowell, 1933—

NESBITT, Lowell, 1933- 759.13
Athens in ruins; Rome in ruins; New York in ruins. [New York, Gimpel & Weitzenhoffer, 1971] 1 v. (chiefly illus.) 25 cm. Cover title. Catalog of an exhibition held March 9-27, 1971, by Gimpel & Weitzenhoffer, ltd., New York. [ND237.N445A42] 70-27527
I. Gimpel & Weitzenhoffer.

NESBITT, Lowell, 1933- 759.13
Lowell Nesbitt, an autobiography : January 23-February 21, 1976, Andrew Crispo Gallery. New York : The Gallery, c1976. [110] p. : ill. (some col.) ; 23 x 27 cm. Errata slip inserted. Bibliography: p. [6] [ND237.N445A83] 75-42999
1. Nesbitt, Lowell, 1933- I. Andrew Crispo Gallery. II. Title.

Nesch, Rolf, 1893—

DETROIT. Institute of Arts. 769'.924
The graphic art of Rolf Nesch. Detroit [1969] viii, 84 p. illus. (part col.) 31 cm. Catalog of an exhibition held at the Detroit Institute of Arts, Mar. 18-Apr. 27, 1969, and at other museums. Bibliography: p. 60-61. [NE654.N4D4] 74-80117
1. Nesch, Rolf, 1893- I. Title. BIP

Netherlands—Civilization.

BALET, Leo, 1878- 759.9492
Rembrandt and Spinoza. New York, Philosophical [c.1962] 222p. illus. 22cm. Bibl. 61-18686 4.50
1. Rembrandt Hermanszoon van Rijn, 1606-1669. 2. Spinoza, Benedictus de, 1632-1677. 3. Netherlands—Civilization. I. Title.

BALET, Leo, 1878- 759.9492
Rembrandt and Spinoza. New York, Philosophical Library [1962] 222p. illus.

SUBJECT INDEX NEVELSON, LOUISE, 1900—

22cm. Includes bibliography. [ND653.R4B2] 61-18686
1. Rembrandt Hermanszoon van Rijn, 1606-1669. 2. Spinoza, Benedictus de, 1632-1677. 3. Netherlands— Civilization. I. Title.

Netherlands—Description and travel—1945- —Views.

BLOEMENDAL, Frederik Arnold Herman. 779'.9'914920924
Holland in color / photos. by F. A. H. Bloemendal ; text by Margaret Hides. New York : Scribner, c1975. 110 p. : ill. ; 30 cm. [DJ24.B5] 74-29023 ISBN 0-684-14188-4 : 12.95
1. Netherlands—Description and travel—1945- —Views. I. Hides, Margaret. II. Title.

Netsukes.

BARBANSON, Adrienne 730.952
Fables in ivory: Japanese netsuke and their legends. Pref. by Felix Tikotin. Rutland, Vt., Tuttle [c.1961] 116p. illus. (part col.) 26x27cm. Bibl. 61-6220 7.50 bds.,
1. Netsukes. 2. Legends—Japan. I. Title.

BROCKHAUS, Albert, 1855-1921. 736'.6
Netsukes, by Albert Brockhous. Translated by M. F. Watty. Edited by E. G. Stillman. New York, Hacker Art Books, 1969. xvii, 175 p. illus. 24 cm. Reprint of the 1924 ed. Bibliography: p. 173-175. [NK6050.B83 1969] 71-78364 12.50
1. Netsukes. 2. Art—Japan. I. Stillman, Ernest Goodrich, 1884- ed. BIP

BUSHELL, Raymond. 736'.68
An introduction to netsuke. Rutland, Vt., C. E. Tuttle Co. [1971] 78 p. 30 illus. 19 cm. [NK6050.B87] 78-147176 ISBN 0-8048-0905-4 3.50
1. Netsukes. I. Title. BIP

JONAS, Frank Morris, 1878- 736.68
Netsuke Rutland, Vt., C. E. Tuttle Co. [1960] 185 p. illus. (part col.) 22 cm. [NK6050.J6 1960] 60-11840
1. Netsukes. I. Title. BIP

KINSEY, Miriam. 736'.68
Contemporary netsuke / Miriam Kinsey ; with a foreword by Hans Conried ; photographs by Tomo-o Ogita and Tsune Sugimura ; sketches by Adelheid Roth Roscher. Rutland, Vt. : C. E. Tuttle Co., c1977. 261 p. : ill. ; 27 cm. Includes index. Bibliography: p. 249-251. [NK6050.K56] 77-72596 ISBN 0-8048-1159-8 : 42.50
1. Netsukes. I. Ogita, Tomoo. II. Sugimura, Tsune, 1926- III. Title. BIP

RYERSON, Egerton. 736'.68
The netsuke of Japan; legends, history, folklore, and customs. London, T. Yoseloff; South Brunswick [N.J.] A. S. Barnes [1967, c.1958] 88p. illus. (pt. col.) 27cm. Bibl. [NK6050.R9 1967] 67-30527 12.50
1. Netsukes. 2. Art—Japan. I. Title.

TOLLNER, Madeline R 736.68
Netsuke; the life and legend of Japan in miniature. [San Francisco Fearon Publishers, 1960] 358 p. illus. (part col.) 29 cm. Bibliography: p. [347] [NK6050.T6 1960] 61-40065
1. Netsukes. I. Title.

UEDA, Reikichi. 736.68
The netsuke handbook, Adapted from the Japanese by Raymond Bushell. Tokyo, Rutland, Vt., C. E. Tuttle Co. [1961] 325 p. illus. (part col.) 24 cm. Bibliography: p. 313-314. [NK6050.U3] 61-8739
1. Netsukes. I. Title.

VOLKER, T 736.68
The animal in Far Eastern art and especially in the art of the Japanese netsuke with references to Chinese origins, traditions, legends and art. Leiden, E. J. Brill, 1950. 190 p. plates. 26 cm. (Mededelingren van bet Rijkamuseum voor Volkenkunde, Leiden, no. 6-7) "Errata": leaf inserted. Bibliography: p. [178] [NK6050.V64] 52-64320
1. Netsukes. 2. Animals in art. 3. Art — Japan. I. Title. II. Series: Leyden. Rijkamuseum voor Volkenkunde. Mededelingren, no. 6-7

Netsukes—Catalogs.

BARKER, Richard. 736'.68'07402142
Netsuke : the miniature sculpture of Japan / Richard Barker & Lawrence Smith. London : British Museum Publications for the Trustees of the British Museum, c1976. 184 p. : ill. (some col.) ; 26 cm. Includes index. Bibliography: p. 174. [NK6050.B34] 76-374796 ISBN 0-7141-1409-X : £8.50
1. Netsukes—Catalogs. I. Smith, Lawrence R. H., joint author. II. Title.

DAVEY, Neil K. 736'.68
Netsuke : a comprehensive study based on the M. T. Hindson Collection / Neil K. Davey ; pref. by W. W. Windworth. New York : Sotheby Parke Bernet, 1974. 564 p., [2] leaves of plates : ill. ; 31 cm. "Catalogue of the M. T. Hindson Collection": p. [13]-275; catalog of other netsuke: p. 276-439. Includes index. [NK6050.D38 1974] 74-187939 ISBN 0-85667-013-8 : 70.00
1. Hindson, Mark T.—Art collections. 2. Netsukes—Catalogs. I. Title.

Netsukes—Collectors and collecting.

ALTMAN, H. B. 736'.68'075
A guide to collecting and selling netsuke / by H. B. Altman and Michele Hibbs. New York : Pilot Books, c1977. 25 p. ; 22 cm. Bibliography: p. 25. [NK6050.A47] 77-7060 ISBN 0-87576-061-9 : 2.50
1. Netsukes—Collectors and collecting. I. Hibbs, Michele, joint author. II. Title. BIP

BUSHELL, Raymond. 736'.68'075
Netsuke, familiar and unfamiliar : new principles for collecting / by Raymond Bushell. 1st ed. New York : Weatherhill, 1975. 259 p. : ill. (some col.) ; 27 cm. Slip inserted: Size of illustrations. Includes index. Bibliography: p. 241-242. [NK6050.B874 1975] 75-22420 ISBN 0-8348-0115-9 : 75.00
1. Netsukes—Collectors and collecting. I. Title. BIP

HURTIG, Bernard, 1928- 736'.68
Masterpieces of netsuke art; one thousand favorites of leading collectors. [1st ed.] New York, Published for the International Netsuke Collectors Society [by] Weatherhill [1973] 245 p. col. illus. 31 cm. Bibliography: p. 233. [NK6050.H87] 73-3202 ISBN 0-8348-0085-3 90.00
1. Netsukes—Collectors and collecting. I. International Netsuke Collectors Society. II. Title. BIP

O'BRIEN, Mary Louise 736.68075
Netsuke: a guide for collectors. Photog. by Margaret Dhaemers. Rutland, Vt., Tuttle [c.1965] 245p. 145 illus. (pt. col.) 21x22cm. [NK6050.O2] 65-11837 10.00
1. Netsukes—Collectors and collecting. I. Title.

O'BRIEN, Mary Louise. 736.68075
Netsuke: a guide for collectors. Photography by Margaret Dhaemers. Rutland, Vt., C. E. Tuttle Co. [1965] 245 p. 145 illus. (part col.) 21 x 22 cm. [NK6050.O2] 65-11837
1. Netsukes — Collectors and collecting. I. Title.

Netsukes—Exhibitions.

SPINK and Son ltd., London. 736'.68'07402132
Netsuke : to be exhibited for sale / by Spink & Son Ltd. London : Spink & Son, c1976. 48 p. : chiefly ill. ; 23 cm. Catalog of netsuke exhibited June 21-July 2, 1976. Includes index. Bibliography: p. 46-47. [NK6050.S65 1976] 77-373020
1. Netsukes—Exhibitions. I. Title.

Netting.

HOLDGATE, Charles. 746.4
Net making. With drawings by the author and photos. by Alec Davis. New York, Emerson Books [1972] 136 p. illus. 21 cm. [TT840.H65] 72-84056 ISBN 0-87523-180-2
1. Netting. I. Title. BIP

Netting—Juvenile literature.

HARTZELL, Warren M. 746.4
Net-making & knotting / by Warren M. Hartzell & Lura LaBarge. New York : Sterling Pub. Co., [1974] 56 p. : ill. (some col.) ; 20 cm. (Little craft book series) Includes index. Describes the tools, materials, and techniques for net-making and offers suggestions for a variety of projects. [TT840.H32] 74-82328 ISBN 0-8069-5310-1 : 3.50 ISBN 0-8069-5311-X lib.bdg. : 3.69
1. Netting—Juvenile literature. 2. Knots and splices—Juvenile literature. 3. Macrame—Juvenile literature. I. LaBarge, Lura, joint author. II. Title. BIP

Neuberger Museum.

NEUBERGER Museum. 708'.147'277
The making of a museum: 1. Neuberger Museum, State University of New York, College at Purchase: May 1974. [Purchase, N.Y., 1974] [116] p. 77 illus. 16 x 23 cm. "Catalog for the inaugural installation and opening of the Neuberger Museum." [N714.P8N48 1974] 74-181593
1. Neuberger Museum. 2. Art—Purchase, N.Y.—Catalogs. I. Title.

Neuberger, Roy R.—Art collections.

THE Neuberger Collection: 708.13
an American collection; paintings, drawings, and sculpture. [Providence? 1968] 463 p. illus. (part col.) 28 cm. A combined catalog of 2 exhibitions of works selected from the collection of Roy R. Neuberger and held May 8-June 30, 1968, at the Museum of Art, Rhode Island School of Design, and Annmary Brown Memorial, Brown University. Most of the works were also shown at the National Collection of Fine Arts, Smithsonian Institution, Aug. 15-Sept. 25, 1968. [N6512.N34] 68-12325
1. Neuberger, Roy R.—Art collections. 2. Art, American—Exhibitions. I. Rhode Island School of Design, Providence. Museum of Art. II. Brown University. Annmary Brown Memorial. III. Smithsonian Institution. National Collection of Fine Arts. IV. Title: An American collection.

Neutra, Richard Joseph.

MCCOY, Esther 720.973
Richard Neutra [New York, George Braziller, c.1960] 128p. 'Selected bibl. of books and articles written by Richard Neutra': p.29. 'Selected bibl. on Richard Neutra': p.30. illus., plates, plans. 26cm. (The Masters of world architecture series) 60-51015 4.95 half cloth,
1. Neutra, Richard Joseph. I. Title. II. Series.

NEUTRA, Richard Joseph, 1892- 927.2
Life and shape. [1st ed.] New York, Appleton-Century-Crofts [1962] 374 p. illus. 22 cm. [NA737.N4A2] 62-8498
I. Title.

NEUTRA, Richard Joseph, 1892- 720.973
Richard Neutra: 1950-60. Buildings and projects. Bauten und Projekte. Realisations et projets. Edited by W. Boesiger New York, Praeger [1959] 240 p. illus. 24 x 29 cm. (Books that matter) [NA737.N4B6] 59-7395

Nevelson, Louise, 1900—

GLIMCHER, Arnold B. 730'.92'4
Louise Nevelson [by] Arnold B. Glimcher. New York, Praeger [1972] 172 p. illus. 29 cm. Includes bibliographical references. [NB237.N43G55] 70-145946 29.50
1. Nevelson, Louise, 1900- BIP

GLIMCHER, Arnold B. 730'.92'4 B
Louise Nevelson / Arnold B. Glimcher. 2d ed., rev. and enl. New York : Dutton, c1976. 197 p., [5] leaves of plates : ill. (some col.) ; 28 cm. [NB237.N43G55 1976] 76-150542 ISBN 0-525-47439-0 : 11.95
1. Nevelson, Louise, 1900- 2. Sculptors—United States—Biography.

GORDON, John, 1912- 730'.924
Louise Nevelson. New York, Published for the Whitney Museum of American Art, by Praeger [1967] 67 p. illus., port. 24 cm. Exhibition held at the Whitney Museum of American Art, March 8-April 30, 1967. Bibliography: p. 66-67. [NB237.N43G6] 67-19733
1. Nevelson, Louise, 1900- I. Whitney Museum of American Art, New York.

NEVELSON, Louise, 1900- 730'.92'4 B
Dawns and dusks : taped conversations with Diana Mackown / Louise Nevelson. New York : Scribner, [1976] p. cm. [NB237.N43A23] 76-20634 ISBN 0-684-14781-5 : 9.95
1. Nevelson, Louise, 1900- 2. Sculptors—United States—Correspondence, reminiscences, etc. I. Mackown, Diana. II. Title. BIP

NEVELSON, Louise, 1900- 730'.92'4
Louise Nevelson / [introductory text and selections by] Germano Celant. New York : H. N. Abrams, [1975] p. cm. Bibliography: [NB237.N43C4413] 75-2419 ISBN 0-8109-0339-3 : 37.50
1. Nevelson, Louise, 1900- I. Celant, Germano. BIP

NEVELSON, Louise, 1900- 760'.0924
Louise Nevelson; prints and drawings, 1953-1966. [Text by Una E. Johnson. Research by Jo Miller. Brooklyn, Brooklyn Museum; distributed by Shorewood Publishers, New York, c1967] 62 p. illus., port. 24 cm. (American graphic artists of the twentieth century. Monograph no. 5) Bibliography: p. 61-62. [NE539.N4J6] 67-13451
I. Johnson, Una E. II. Brooklyn Institute of Arts and Sciences. Museum. III. Title. IV. Series.

NEVELSON, Louise, 1900- 730'.924
Louise Nevelson [exhibition] The Museum of Fine Arts, Houston, Tex., Oct. 23 to Dec. 14, 1969 [and] University of Texas, College of Fine Arts, Jan. 15 to Feb. 15, 1970. [Houston? Tex., 1969] 44 p. illus., port. 28 cm. [NB237.N43A48] 77-103874
I. Houston, Tex. Museum of Fine Arts. II. Texas. University. College of Fine Arts. III. Title.

NEVELSON, Louise, 1900- 730'.92'4
Nevelson : sky gates and collages, May 4-8 June, 1974, The Pace Gallery ... New York. New York : Pace Gallery, [1974] [28] p. : chiefly ill. ; 28 cm. [NB237.N43P32] 74-79437
1. Nevelson, Louise, 1900- I. Pace Gallery. II. Title. III. Title: Sky gates and collages.

NEVELSON, Louise, 1900- 730'.92'4
Nevelson at Purchase : the metal sculptures : [exhibition], May 8-September 11, 1977, Neuberger Museum, State University of New York, College at Purchase, Purchase, New York. [Purchase, N.Y.] : The Museum, c1977. [31] p. : ill. ; 26 cm. Bibliography: p. [29] [NB237.N43N48] 77-152095
1. Nevelson, Louise, 1900- I. Neuberger Museum. II. Title.

NEVELSON, Louise, 1900- 730'.924
Nevelson; recent wood sculpture. New York, Pace Gallery [1969] [34] p. (chiefly illus.) 28 cm. Bibliography: p. [32]-[33] [NB237.N43A52] 79-83522
I. Title.

NEVELSON, Louise, 1900- 730'.92'4
Nevelson: wood sculptures; [catalog of] an exhibition organized by Walker Art Center, by Martin Friedman. [1st ed.] New York, E. P. Dutton, 1973. 80 p. illus. 22 x 26 cm. Exhibition held at the Walker Art Center, Minneapolis, Nov. 10-Dec. 30, 1973, San Francisco Museum of Art, Jan. 25-Mar. 10, 1974, Dallas Museum of Fine Arts, Apr. 17-May 19, 1974, The High Museum of Art, Atlanta, July 6-Aug. 18, 1974, William Rockhill Nelson Gallery of Art, Kansas City, Mo., Sept. 21-Nov. 3, 1974, and the Cleveland Museum of Art, Jan. 28-Mar. 9, 1975. Bibliography: p. 75-79. [NB237.N43F74] 73-89272 ISBN 0-525-47367-X 4.00
1. Nevelson, Louise, 1900- I. Friedman, Martin L. II. Walker Art Center, Minneapolis. III. Title.

New Brunswick Museum.

NEW Brunswick Museum. 749.2'115'074011532
Heritage furniture Le mobilier traditionnel : a catalogue featuring selected heritage furniture from the collection of the New Brunswick Museum catalogue de meubles anciens choisis parmi les collections du Musee du Nouveau-Brunswick / edited, with an introd. by A. Gregg Finley ; photography ... by Don Simpson. Saint John, N.B. : New Brunswick Museum, 1976. 63 p. : chiefly ill. (some col.) ; 26 cm. (NBM collection catalogue ; 2) English and French. Bibliography: p. 60-61. [NK2441.N48 1976] 77-559484
1. New Brunswick Museum. 2. Furniture—New Brunswick—Saint John—Catalogs. I. Finley, A. Gregg. II. Title. III. Title: Le mobilier traditionnel. IV. Series: New Brunswick Museum. NBM collection catalogue ; 2.

New England—Description and Travel—Views.

KAPPEL, Philip. 917.4'04'4
New England gallery. With an introd. by Walter Muir Whitehill. [1st ed.] Boston, Little, Brown [1966] xvi, 349 p. illus. 29 cm. [NE2210.K3A47] 66-14900
1. New England—Description and travel—Views. 2. New England—Historic houses, etc. I. Title.

LORING, Paule Stetson, 1899- 741.973
Marine sketchbook [by] Paule Loring. Edited by Nathan C. Fuller. [1st ed. Rockland, Me., Maine Profiles, 1964] 56 p. (chiefly illus.) 19 x 28 cm. [NC1075.L86F8] 64-55016
1. New England — Descr. & trav. — Views. I. Title.

THOREAU country : 818'.3'09 B
photographs and text selections from the works of H. D. Thoreau / by Herbert W. Gleason ; edited by Mark Silber ; introd. by Paul Brooks. San Francisco : Sierra Club Books, 1975. xv, 143 p. : ill. ; 36 cm. [TR653.T47] 75-8865 ISBN 0-87156-140-9 : 32.50. ISBN 0-87156-144-1 pbk. : 9.95
1. Gleason, Herbert Wendell, 1855-1937. 2. Thoreau, Henry David, 1817-1862—Illustrations. 3. New England—Description and travel—Views. 4. Nature photography. I. Thoreau, Henry David, 1817-1862. Selections. 1975. BIP

WENGENROTH, Stow, 1906- 769.924
Stow Wengenroth's New England, with notes and observations, by David McCord. Introd. by Sinclair Hitchings. Barre, Mass., Barre Publishers, 1969. 108 p. illus. 22 x 29 cm. On spine: New England. [NE2415.W38M3 1969] 69-12344 12.50
1. New England—Description and travel—Views. I. McCord, David Thompson Watson, 1897- II. Title: New England.

New England—Description and travel—1951- —Views.

SMITH, Clyde H. 779'.9'974
New England / photography by Clyde H. Smith ; text by Ann[e] Glickman. Portland, Or. : C. H. Belding, [1975] 192 p. : col. ill. ; 36 cm. [F5.S64] 74-33866 ISBN 0-912856-17-3 : 30.00
1. New England—Description and travel—1951- —Views. I. Glickman, Anne, 1941- II. Title. BIP

SMITH, Clyde H. 779'.9'974
New England coast / photography by Clyde H. Smith ; text by M. Cronan Minton. Portland, Or. : C. H. Belding, c1976. 128 p. : col. ill. ; 36 cm. [F5.S65] 75-41843 ISBN 0-912856-24-6 : 25.00
1. New England—Description and travel—1951- —Views. 2. Coasts—New England—Pictorial works. I. Minton, Michael Cronan. II. Title. BIP

New Haven—Description—Views.

NEW Haven Colony Historical Society, New Haven. 758'.1
The New Haven scene; an exhibition of paintings, watercolors and drawings, April 19 through June 14, 1970. New Haven, Conn. [1970] 1 v. (unpaged) illus., map. 19 x 26 cm. [N6505.N43] 75-20478
1. New Haven—Description—Views. 2. Art, American—Exhibitions. I. Title.

New Haven—Plazas—Wooster Square.

HOMMANN, Mary. 711'.59
Wooster Square design; a report on the background, experience, and design procedures in redevelopment and rehabilitation in an urban renewal project. New Haven, New Haven Redevelopment Agency, 1965. 191 p. illus., maps, plans. 26 cm. [NA9072.N48H6] 73-12472
1. New Haven—Plazas—Wooster Square. 2. Urban beautification—New Haven. I. New Haven Redevelopment Agency. II. Title.

New Mexico—Description and travel—Views.

MARIN, John, 1870-1953. 759.13
Marin in New Mexico, 1929 & 1930. [Albuquerque, University Art Museum, University of New Mexico, 1968] 32 p. illus. (part col.), map, port. 24 cm. Catalog of an exhibition organized by the University Art Museum, the University of New Mexico, and shown at the University Art Museum, Nov. 18-Dec. 29, 1968; Marion Koogler McNay Art Institute, San Antonio, Tex., Feb. 7-Mar. 7, 1969; Amon Carter Museum, Fort Worth, Tex., Mar. 21-May 12, 1969. Bibliographical references included in "Notes to the text" (p. 26) [ND1839.M35A52] 68-66880
1. New Mexico—Description and travel—Views. I. New Mexico. University. Art Museum. II. Marion Koogler McNay Art Institute, San Antonio. III. Amon Carter Museum of Western Art, Fort Worth, Texas. IV. Title.

New Orleans — Descr. — Views.

WOODWARD, William? 1859-1939. 759.13
Early views of the Vieux Carre; guide book to the French Quarter. Scenes painted by William Woodward, from the collection . . in the Isasc Delgado Museum of Art. [Text and notes prepared by James B. Byrnes. 3d ed.] New Orleans, Isaac Delgado Museum of Art [1965] [90] p. (chiefly illus. (part col.) plans, col. port) 14 x 19 cm. [ND237.W83B88 1965a] 67-4796
1. New Orleans — Descr. — Views. I. Byrnes, James B. II. Isaac Delgado Museum of Art, New Orleans. III. Title.

New Orleans—Dwellings.

BRUCE, Curt. 976.3'35
The great houses of New Orleans / written and photographed by Curt Bruce. 1st ed. New York : Knopf, 1977. xi, 207 p., [2] leaves of plates : ill. ; 25 cm. Includes indexes. [NA7238.N5B78 1977] 76-47932 ISBN 0-394-40716-4 : 15.00
1. New Orleans—Dwellings. 2. Architecture, Domestic—Louisiana—New Orleans. I. Title. BIP

New Orleans—Historic houses, etc.

HUBER, Leonard Victor, 1903- 728.3109763355
Baroness Pontalba's buildings, their site and the remarkable woman who built them, by Leonard V. Huber, Samuel Wilson, Jr. New Orleans, New Orleans Chapter of the Louisiana Landmarks Soc. [1964] iv, 62p. illus., ports. 24cm. Bibl. 63-22709 price unreported
1. Pontalba, Miraela Leonarda (Almonester) 1795-1874. 2. New Orleans—Historic houses, etc. I. Wilson, Samuel, 1911- joint author. II. Title. BIP

HUBER, Leonard Victor, 1903- 71019
Baroness Pontalba's buildings, their site and the remarkable woman who built them, by Leonard V. Huber and Samuel Wilson, Jr. [2d ed.] New Orleans, New Orleans Chapter of the Louisiana Landmarks Society and the Friends of the Cabildo [1966, c1964] iv, 63 p. illus., ports. 24 cm. Bibliography: p. 61. [68-96710]
1. Pontalba, Micaela Leonarda (Almonester) 1795-1874. 2. New Orleans—Historic houses, etc. I. Wilson, Samuel, 1911- joint author. II. Friends of the Cabildo, inc., New Orleans. III. Louisiana Landmarks Society. IV. Title.

New Orleans—Parks—Audubon Park—Pictorial works.

CALLATAY, Xavier de. 741.9'73
Xavier de Callatay in Audubon Park; a series of ink drawings, color sketches and historical notes published for the enjoyment of the artist and his viewers, New Orleans, Louisiana. [New Orleans, 1970] 23 l. (in portfolio) illus., 2 col. plates. 32 x 41 cm. "500 numbered copies ... Twenty-six copies from A to Z." Copy Z. [NC139.C28A58] 72-26118
1. New Orleans—Parks—Audubon Park—Pictorial works.

New Orleans. Vieux Carre.

BUREAU of Governmental Research, New Orleans. 711'.59'09763355
Plan and program for the preservation of the Vieux Carre; historic district demonstration study, conducted by Bureau of Governmental Research, New Orleans, for the City of New Orleans. [Prepared under the supervision of Marcou, O'Leary and Associates, Washington, D.C. New Orleans, 1968] xiii, 170 p. illus., maps (part col.), plans. 22 x 28 cm. Bibliography: p. 168-169. [NA735.N4B8] 68-59463
1. New Orleans. Vieux Carre. 2. Architecture—New Orleans—Conservation and restoration. I. Marcou, O'Leary and Associates. II. Title. III. Title: Vieux Carre.

LEMANN, Bernard, 1905- 720.9763'35
The Vieux Carre—a general statement. With a foreword by John W. Lawrence. New Orleans, School of Architecture, Tulane University [1966] 91 p. illus. 26 cm. [NA735.N4l4] 720.973 78-294654
1. New Orleans. Vieux Carre. 2. Architecture—New Orleans—Conservation and restoration. I. Title.

New York. Cathedral of St. John the Divine.

HALL, Edward Hagaman, 1858-1936. 726.6097471
A guide to the Cathedral Church of Saint John the Divine in the City of New York. 17th ed. New York, The Dean and Chapter of the Cathedral Church, 1965. 231 p. illus., ports. 23 cm [BX5980.N5J65] 66-813
1. New York. Cathedral of St. John the Divine. I. Title.

New York (City). Art Students' League.

NEW York (City). Art Students' League. 707'.1
Art Students League : centennial, 1875-1976. [New York : Art Students League of New York, 1976?] 96 p. : ill. ; 23 cm. Cover title. [N330.N52A772 1976] 76-369956
1. New York (City). Art Students' League.

NEW York (City). Art Students' League. 707'.10747'1
Art Students League, centennial decade, 1968-1969. [New York, 1969] 112 p. illus. 24 cm. Catalogue of the 93rd regular session, Sept. 16, 1968 to May 28, 1969. [N330.N52A772] 73-171378
1. New York (City). Art Students' League. I. Title.

New York (City)—Buildings.

GOLDSTONE, Harmon Hendricks, 1911- 917.47'1'044
History preserved; a guide to New York City landmarks and historic districts, by Harmon H. Goldstone and Martha Dalrymple. New York, Simon and Schuster [1974] 576 p. illus. 25 cm. Bibliography: p. [530]-532. [F128.7.G64] 73-19096 ISBN 0-671-21610-4 12.95
1. New York (City)—Buildings. 2. New York (City)—Dwellings. I. Dalrymple, Martha, joint author. II. Title. BIP

SILVER, Nathan. 917.471'03
Lost New York. [Boston] Houghton Mifflin, 1967. xiii, 242 p. illus. 29 cm. [F128.37.S55] 66-11220
1. New York (City)—Buildings. 2. New York (City)—Dwellings. 3. Architecture—New York (City) I. Title. BIP

New York (City)—Culture.

COMMISSION for Cultural Affairs of the City of New York. 700'.9747'1
New York City as a national cultural resource : a report to the American people. [New York] : Commission for Cultural Affairs of the City of New York, [1977?] 70 p. : ill. ; 23 cm. [NX511.N4C65 1977] 77-71265
1. New York (City)—Culture. 2. New York (City)—Museums. 3. New York (City)—Theaters. I. Title. BIP

New York (City)—Description.

GARELICK, May, 1910- 917.471
Manhattan Island. Woodcuts by John Ross and Clare Romano Ross. New York, Crowell [1957] 53p. illus. 26cm. [F128.52.G3] 56-9801
1. New York (City)— Descr. I. Title.

New York (City)—Description.

ATKINSON, Oriana Torrey. 917.471
Manhattan and me. Drawings by Hirschfeld. [1st ed.] Indianapolis, Bobbs-Merrill [1954] 267 p. illus. 23 cm. [F128.5.A88] 54-6501
1. New York (City)—Description. I. Title.

SASEK, Miroslav. 917.471
This is New York. New York, Macmillan [1960] 60 p. illus. 32 cm. A pictorial tour of Manhattan Island presenting drawings of its neighborhoods, transportation and traffic, buildings, and the city's activities, from the local shoeshine stall to Wall Street. [ND1946.S2A55] AC 68
1. New York (City)—Description. I. Title.

New York (City)—Description—1951-

HERMANN, Bernard, 1941- 917.47'104'40222
New York / photos. by Bernard Hermann ; text by Gilbert Millstein. New York : Abrams, [1977] p. cm. [F128.52.H43] 77-1860 0-8109 15.00
1. New York (City)—Description—1951- I. Millstein, Gilbert. II. Title.

WAGENVOORD, James. 974.7'1'04
City lives / written and photographed by James Wagenvoord. 1st ed. New York : Holt, Rinehart and Winston, c1976. 226 p. : ill. ; 26 cm. [F128.52.W38] 75-21492 ISBN 0-03-015131-7 : 12.95 pbk. : 7.95
1. Wagenvoord, James. 2. New York (City)—Description—1951- 3. New York (City)—Social conditions. I. Title. BIP

New York (City)—Description—1951- —Tours.

ROSEBROCK, Ellen Fletcher. 917.47'1
Walking around in South Street; discoveries in New York's old shipping district. New York, South Street Seaport Museum [1974] 62 p. illus. 20 cm. [F128.18.R67] 74-181592 ISBN 0-913344-17-6
1. New York (City)—Description—1951- —Tours. 2. New York (City)—Streets—South Street. I. Title.

New York (City)—Description—1951- —Views.

LEHNARTZ, Klaus. 779'.9'9747104
New York in the sixties / photos. by Klaus Lehnartz ; text by Allan R. Talbot. New

York : Dover Publications, 1978. 120 p. : chiefly ill. ; 28 cm. "Photographs are a selection ... originally published ... in New York. [F128.37.L5 1978] 78-53190 ISBN 0-486-23674-9 : 5.00
1. New York (City)—Description—1951- —Views. 2. New York (City)—Social life and customs—Pictorial works. I. Talbot, Allan R. II. Title. BIP

New York (City)—Description—Guide-books.

NEW York walk book. 917.47'04'4
Pen sketches by Robert L. Dickinson and Richard Edes Harrison. Introduction to the geology of the region by Christopher J. Schuberth. 4th ed. completely rev. under the sponsorship of the New York-New Jersey Trail Conference and the American Geographical Society. Garden City, N.Y., Doubleday/Natural History Pr. [1973, c.1971] xxiv, 326 p. illus., col. maps. 21 cm. First-3rd ed. Written by Raymond H. Torrey, Frank Place, Jr., & Robert L. Dickinson. Bibl. [F128.68.A1N44] 70-150876 ISBN 0-385-03256-0 pap., 5.95
1. New York (City)—Description—Guide-books. 2. New York (State)—Description and travel—Guide-books. 3. New Jersey—Description and travel—Guide-books. 4. Hiking. 5. New York-New Jersey Trail Conference. I. American Geographical Society of New York. II. Torrey, Raymond H. New York walk book. BIP

New York (City)—Description—Juvenile literature.

SASEK, Miroslav. 917.47'1'044
This is New York [by] M. Sasek. Abridged. New York, Collier Books, 1973. 48 p. illus. 23 cm. A pictorial tour of Manhattan's neighborhoods, transportation and traffic, buildings, and the city's activities, from the local shoeshine stall to Wall Street. [F128.33.S29] 72-90994 0.95 (pbk.)
1. New York (City)—Description—Juvenile literature. I. Title.

THOMAS, Katrina. 917.471
My skyscraper city; a child's view of New York. Photos, by Katrina Thomas. Verses by Penny Hamond. [1st ed.] Garden City, N.Y., Doubleday [1963] 60 p. illus. 32 cm. [F128.33.T5] 63-13854
1. New York (City) — Descr. — Juvenile literature. 2. New York (City) — Views. I. Hamond, Penny. II. Title.

New York (City)—Description—Pictorial works.

THE Way it was 769'.4'99747103
: New York, 1850-1890 / [compiled by] Clarence P. Hornung. New York : Schocken Books, 1977. xi, 212 p. : ill. ; 32 cm. Includes indexes. Bibliography: p. 205-207. [NE954.2.W39] 76-49975 ISBN 0-8052-3642-2 : 25.00
1. New York (City)—Description—Pictorial works. 2. New York (City) in art. 3. Wood-engraving, American. 4. Wood-engraving—19th century—United States. I. Hornung, Clarence Pearson. BIP

New York (City)—Description—Views.

ABBOTT, Berenice, 1898- 917.47'1'034
New York in the thirties (formerly titled: Changing New York), as photographed by Berenice Abbott. Text by Elizabeth McCausland. New York, Dover Publications [1973, c1939] ix p., 97 illus. 26 x 29 cm. First published by Dutton, New York. [F128.37.A23 1973] 73-77375 ISBN 0-486-22967-X 3.00 (pbk.).
1. New York (City)—Description—Views. I. McCausland, Elizabeth, 1899-1966. II. Title. BIP

BEARD, John, comp. 917.47'2
Blue water views of old New York including Long Island and the Jersey shore. Embellished with commentary of the time selected by John Beard from out-of-print sources. [Centerville, Mass.] Scrimshaw Press; distributed by Barre Publishers, Barre, Mass. [1970] 127 p. illus., maps, music. 28 cm. (Scrimshaw illustrated Americana) Half title: America as it once was. [F128.37.B48] 69-18952 3.95
1. New York (City)—Description—Views. 2. Long Island—Description and travel—Views. I. Title. II. Title: America as it once was.

BUSSE, Fritz. 917.471
New York, city on many waters. Sketches by Fritz Busse; text by Meyer Berger. New York, Arts [1956?] unpaged (chiefly illus.) 18x21 cm. (Golden griffin books) [NC1145.B87] 56-161
1. New York (City)—Descr.—Views. I. Berger, Meyer, 1898- II. Title.

FEININGER, Andreas, 1906- 917.471
The face of New York; the city as it was and as it is. Photos. by Andreas Feininger. Text by Susan E. Lyman. [Rev. ed.] New York, Crown Publishers [1964] 1 v. (unpaged) illus. (part fold.) 31 cm. [F128.3.F4] 64-17838
1. New York (City)—Descr.—Views. I. Lyman, Susan Elizabeth. II. Title.

FEININGER, Andreas, 1906- 974.7'1'03
New York [von] Andreas Feininger. Texte von Kate Simon. [1. Aufl.] Wien, Econ-Verlag [1964] 159 p. illus. (part col.) facsims., map. 31 cm. [F128.37.F455] 65-79853
1. New York (City)—Descr.—Views. I. Simon, Kate. II. Title.

FEININGER, Andreas, 1906- 917.471
New York. Photos. by Andreas Feininger. Text by Kate Simon. New York, Viking Press [1964] 150 p. illus. (part col.) facsims. (incl. map) 31 cm. (A Studio book) [F128.52.F4] 64-11203
1. New York(City)—Descr. —Views. I. Simon, Kate. II. Title.

FEININGER, Andreas, 1906- 974.7'1'040222
New York in the forties / Andreas Feininger ; with text by John von Hartz. New York : Dover Publications, 1978. 178 p. : ill. ; 28 cm. [F128.37.F457] 77-87344 ISBN 0-486-23585-8 : 6.00
1. New York (City)—Description—Views. 2. New York (City)—Social life and customs—Pictorial works. I. Von Hartz, John. II. Title. BIP

FELLIG, Arthur, 1900-1968. 779'.9'97471
Naked city / by Weegee [i.e. A. Fellig]. New York : Da Capo Press, 1975, c1945. 243 p. : ill. ; 23 cm. Reprint of the ed. published by Essential Books, New York. [F128.5.F387 1975] 75-4840 ISBN 0-306-70724-1 lib.bdg. : 12.95
1. New York (City)—Description—Views. 2. New York (City)—Social conditions—Pictorial works. 3. New York (City)—Social life and customs—Pictorial works. I. Title. BIP

FELLIG, Arthur, 1900-1968. 779'.9'97471
Weegee's people. New York : Da Capo Press, 1975, c1946. ca. 250 p. : ill. ; 23 cm. Reprint of the ed. published by Essential Books, New York. [F128.5.F388 1975] 75-4846 ISBN 0-306-70723-3 lib.bdg. : 12.95
1. New York (City)—Description—Views. 2. New York (City)—Social life and customs—Pictorial works. I. Title. BIP

FIFTY years the New York Daily news in pictures 974.7'1'04
/ Worth Gatewood, editor. 1st ed. Garden City, N.Y. : Doubleday, 1979. 224 p. : ill. ; 30 cm. [F128.37.F53] 78-24843 ISBN 0-385-15025-3 : 17.95. ISBN 0-385-15024-5 pbk. : 8.95.
1. New York (City)—Description—Views. 2. New York (City)—History—Pictorial works. I. Gatewood, Worth. II. Daily news, New York, 1919- III. Title: Fifty years in pictures. BIP

KING, Moses, 1853-1909. 917.47'1'0340222
King's views of New York & Brooklyn: 1896, 1908/09, 1915. New introd. by A. E. Santaniello. New York, B. Blom, 1974. p. cm. Reprint of the editions published in Boston. [F128.37.K52 1974] 73-76084 25.00 ea. (2 vols.)
1. New York (City)—Description—Views. 2. Brooklyn—Description—Views. I. Title.

KOUWENHOVEN, John Atlee, 1909- 917.47'1
The Columbia historical portrait of New York; an essay in graphic history, by John A. Kouwenhoven. New York, Harper & Row [1972, c1953] 550 p. illus. 27 cm. (Icon editions, IN-30) [F128.3.K6 1972] 72-169081 ISBN 0-06-430030-7 Pap. $6.95
1. New York (City)—Description—Views. 2. New York (City)—History—Pictorial works. I. Columbia University. II. Title. BIP

KOUWENHOVEN, John Atlee, 1909- 917.471
The Columbia historical portrait of New York; an essay in graphic history in honor of the tricentennial of New York City and the bicentennial of Columbia University. With a foreword by Grayson L. Kirk. [1st ed.] Garden City, N. Y., Doubleday, 1953. 550 p. (chiefly illus. (part col.) ports., maps) 28 cm. [F128.3.K6] 53-8181
1. New York (City)—Description—Views. 2. New York (City)—History—Pictorial works. I. Columbia University. II. Title.

KRUSE, Werner. 741.9'43
New York [by] Robinson. New York, Funk & Wagnalls [1967] 64p. (chiefly illus., map, ports.) 34cm. [NC1140.K713] 68-13266 3.95 bds.,
1. New York (City)—Deser.—Views. I. Title.

LAREDO, Victor. 917.47'1'00222
New York City; a photographic portrait. 170 prints by Victor Laredo. With captions by Thomas Reilly. New York, Dover Publications [1973] 137 p. (chiefly illus.) 29 cm. Most of the photographs were originally published in New York: people and places by P. Seitlin. [F128.52.L29 1973] 72-91058 ISBN 0-486-22852-5 3.50
1. New York (City)—Description—Views. 2. New York (City)—Social life and customs—Pictorial works. 3. Architecture—New York (City)—Pictorial works. I. Reilly, Thomas. II. Seitlin, Percy. New York: people and places. III. Title.

LYON, Danny. 917.471
The destruction of Lower Manhattan. [New York] Macmillan [1969] 75 plates (incl. ports.) 28 cm. [F128.37.L96] 69-17103
1. New York (City)—Description—Views. 2. Manhattan (Borough) I. Title.

MAYER, Grace M 917.471
Once upon a city; New York from 1890 to 1910 as photographed by Byron and described by Grace M. Mayer. With a foreword by Edward Steichen. New York, Macmillan, 1958. xii, 511p. illus., ports. 29cm. 'The photographs reproduced ... are from the Byron Collection, Museum of the City of New York.' [F128.37.M3] 57-10777
1. New York (City)—Descr.—Views. 2. New York (City)—Hist. 3. New York (City)— Soc. life & cust. I. Byron, Percy C. II. New York. Museum of the City of New York. Byron Collection. III. Title.

NEW York Historical Society. 917.47'1'00222
Old New York in early photographs, 1853-1901. Mary Black: curator of painting and sculpture. New York, Dover Publications [1973] xvi, 228 p. (chiefly illus.) 31 cm. [F128.37.N7 1973] 72-90527 ISBN 0-486-22907-6 6.00 (pbk.)
1. New York (City)—Description—Views. I. Black, Mary C. II. Title. BIP

NEW York Historical Society. 974.7'1'04
Old New York in early photographs, 1853-1901 : 196 prints from the collection of the New-York Historical Society / Mary Black. 2d. rev. ed. New York : Dover Publications, c1976. xvi, 228 p. : chiefly ill. ; 31 cm. Includes indexes. [F128.37.N7 1976] 76-371335 ISBN 0-486-22907-6 pbk. : 6.00
1. New York (City)—Description—Views. I. Black, Mary C. II. Title.

NEW York. Museum of Modern Art. 760
Manhattan observed; selections of drawings and prints. Edited by William S. Lieberman. Greenwich, Conn., Distributed by New York Graphic Society [1968] 43 p. (chiefly illus.) 17 x 19 cm. [NE215.U7N4] 68-54924
1. New York (City)—Description—Views. 2. Prints—Catalogs. I. Lieberman, William Slattery, 1924- ed. II. Title.

RIZZUTO, Angelo, 1906-1967. 917.47'1'0340222
Angelo Rizzuto's New York: "In little old New York, by Anthony Angel." Washington, Library of Congress, 1972. 55 p. (chiefly illus.) 22 x 26 cm. [F128.37.R5] 72-3243 ISBN 0-8444-0025-4
1. New York (City)—Description—Views. 2. New York (City)—Social life and customs—Pictorial works. I. United States. Library of Congress. II. Title. III. Title: "In little old New York, by Anthony Angel."

SASEK, Miroslav 759.37
New York. [dist. New York, Macmillan, c.1960, 1961] 60p. col. illus. (Encyclopedie Casterman) Translation of This is New York. 61-65641 2.50 bds.,
1. New York (City)—Descr.—Views. I. Title.

SASEK, Miroslav 759.37
This is New York. New York, Macmillan [1960] 60p. illus. (col.) 32cm. 60-16324 4.00
1. New York (City)—Descr.—Views. I. Title. BIP

SZASZ, Suzanne. 917.471
Young folks' New York, by Suzanne Szasz and Susan Lyman. New York, Crown Publishers [1960] 124 p. illus. 17 cm. [F128.33.S95] 60-15396
1. New York [City] — Descr. — Views. 2. New York [City] — Descr. — Juvenile literature. 3. Photography of children. I. Lyman, Susan E. II. Title.

SZASZ, Suzanne. 917.471
Young folks' New York, by Suzanne Szasz and Susan Lyman. Rev. ed. New York, Crown Publishers [1968] 144 p. illus. 29 cm. Photographs and brief text describe all the sights and activities in New York of special interest to children. Includes zoos, holiday celebrations, museums, theaters, parks, and international shops and exhibits—all the famous favorites and many more. [F128.33.S95 1968] AC 68
1. New York (City)—Description—Views. 2. New York (City)—Description. I. Lyman, Susan Elizabeth, joint author. II. Title.

TRESS, Arthur. 309.1'747'1040222
Open space in the inner city; ecology and the urban environment. Photos. by Arthur Tress. [Introductory statement by Arthur Tress. New York, New York State Council on the Arts, c1971] [4] p., 50 plates. 37 cm. Issued in a case. "An exhibit portfolio produced by the New York State Council on the Arts for the New York Museums Collaborative." [F128.52.T73] 72-171187
1. New York (City)—Description—Views. 2. Photography, Artistic. I. New York (State). State Council on the Arts. II. Museums Collaborative. III. Title.

WHITEHOUSE, Roger, 1939- comp. 917.47'1'034
New York, sunshine and shadow : a photographic record of the city and its people from 1850 to 1915 / [compiled by] Roger Whitehouse. 1st ed. New York : Harper & Row, [1974] xvi, ca. 200 p. : chiefly ill. ; 32 cm. Includes indexes. [F128.37.W47 1974] 73-14300 ISBN 0-06-014616-8 : 15.00
1. New York (City)—Description—Views. 2. New York (City)—Social life and customs—Pictorial works. I. Title.

YOORS, Jan 917.471034
Only one New York. Photos. by Jan Yoors. Text by Charles Samuels. New York, S. & S. [1965] 136p. (chiefly illus.) 31cm. [F128.37.Y6] 64-25192 7.95 bds.,
1. New York (City)—Descr.—Views. I. Samuels, Charles. II. Title. BIP

New York (City). Edgar Laing Stores (The building)

WAITE, John G., comp. 725'.21'097471
Iron architecture in New York City; two studies in industrial archeology: The Edgar Laing stores (1849), by John G. Waite [and] The Cooper Union (1853-59), compiled by William Rowe, III. Edited by John G. Waite. [Albany] New York State

Historic Trust, 1972. 83, [17] p. illus. 29 cm. Includes bibliographical references. [NA6220.W34] 73-621396
1. Cooper Union for the Advancement of Science and Art, New York (The building) 2. New York (City). Edgar Laing Stores (The building) 3. Building, Iron and steel. 4. Architecture—Details. I. Waite, John G. The Edgar Laing stores (1849). 1972. II. Rowe, William, 1941- The Cooper Union (1853-59) 1972. III. Title.

New York (City). Empire State Building.

JAMES, Theodore. 947'.1
The Empire State Building / Theodore James, Jr. 1st ed. New York : Harper & Row, [1975] 180 p. : ill. ; 24 cm. Includes index. Bibliography: p. 175. [F128.8.E46J35 1975] 74-1821 ISBN 0-06-012172-6 : 10.00
1. New York (City). Empire State Building. I. Title. BIP

New York (City)—Foreign population—Pictorial works.

THE Lower East 779.9'91747'106
Side; immigrant portal to America from 1875 to 1925. [Introductory statement by Allon Schoener. New York, c1971] [4] p., 50 plates. 37 cm. Issued in a case. "An exhibit portfolio produced by the New York State Council on the Arts for the New York Museums Collaborative." [F128.9.A1L68] 72-193754
1. New York (City)—Foreign population—Pictorial works. I. New York (State). State Council on the Arts. II. Museums Collaborative.

New York (City)—Harbor.

BRAYNARD, Frank Osborn, 741.973
1916-
A tugman's sketchbook; pen and ink impressions of New York Harbor and the ships that use it, big and small. [Tuckahoe, N.Y.] De Graff [c.1965] 143p. illus. 29cm. [NC1075.B68A56] 65-21840 8.00
1. New York (City)—Harbor. 2. Ships in art. I. Title.

New York (City)—Harbor—Pictorial works.

ROSEBROCK, Ellen 917.47'1'044
Fletcher.
South Street : a photographic guide to New York City's historic seaport / text by Ellen Fletcher Rosebrock ; photos. by Edmund V. Gillon, Jr. New York : Dover Publications, c1977. x, 108 p. : ill. ; 24 cm. Some of the material was originally published in the author's Walking around South Street. [F128.63.R67 1977] 76-62807 ISBN 0-486-23396-0 : 4.00
1. New York (City)—Harbor—Pictorial works. 2. New York (City)—Streets—South Street—Pictorial works. I. Gillon, Edmund Vincent. II. Title. BIP

New York (City)—History.

STOKES, Isaac Newton 974.71
Phelps, 1867-1944
The iconography of Manhattan Island, 1498-1909. [Comp. from orig. sources. Illus. by photo-intaglio reprodns. of important maps, plans, views, and documents in public and private collections. New York] Arno [1967] 6v. illus. (pt. col.), facsims., maps (pt. fold. (pt. col.)) 29cm. Reprint of 1915-28 ed. Bibl. by Victor H. Paltsits: v.6, p. [181]-281 [F128.3.S856] 67-13560 795.00 set,
1. New York (City)—Hist. 2. New York (City)—Descr.—Views. 3. New York (City&-Maps. 4. America—Maps, Early. I. Title.

New York (City)—Historic houses, etc.

THE Heritage of New 917.471
York; historic-landmark plaques of the New York Community Trust. Pref. by Whitney North Seymour. New York, Fordham University Press, 1970. xxi, 402 p. (chiefly illus., maps) 26 cm. "Walking-guide to The heritage of New York" (22 p.) inserted in pocket. [F128.7.H47] 69-13762
1. New York (City)—Historic houses, etc. 2. Historical markers—New York (City) I. New York Community Trust. BIP

ULMANN, Albert, 1861-1948. 974.71
A landmark history of New York; also the origin of street names and a bibliography. Port Washington, N.Y., I. J. Friedman [1969] xvi, 285 p. illus., maps, ports. 18 cm. (Empire State historical publications series, no. 70) Reprint of the 1901 ed. Bibliography: p. 267-279. [F128.37.U42 1969] 70-101023
1. New York (City)—Historic houses, etc. 2. New York (City)—Streets. 3. New York (City)—Bibliography. I. Title. II. Series: Empire State historical publication 70 BIP

New York (City)—History.

LONGSTREET, Stephen, 974.7'1
1907-
City on two rivers : profiles of New York—yesterday and today / Stephen Longstreet ; illustrated with the author's drawings and with old photos. New York : Hawthorn Books, c1975. xiv, 305 p. : ill. ; 25 cm. Includes index. Bibliography: p. 291-293. [F128.3.L87 1975] 74-15647 ISBN 0-8015-1310-3 : 12.95
1. New York (City)—History. 2. New York (City)—Biography. I. Title.

PATTERSON, Jerry E. 974.7'1
Unfinished city : a history of New York / by Jerry Patterson ; illustrated from the collections of the Museum of the City of New York. New York : H. N. Abrams, [1978] p. cm. Includes index. Bibliography: p. [F128.3.P27] 77-15631 ISBN 0-8109-1708-4 : 19.95
1. New York (City)—History. I. New York (City). Museum of the City of New York. II. Title.

New York (City)—History—1775-1865.

SMITH, Thomas Edward 917.47'1'033
Vermilye, 1857-1922.
The city of New York in the year of Washington's inauguration, 1789. Introd. by Joseph Veach Noble. Riverside, Conn., Chatham Press [1973] 244 p. illus. 23 cm. Facsim. reprint of the 1889 ed. printed for the author by Trow's Print. and Bookbinding Co., New York, with a new selection of period illustrations. [F128.44.S67 1889a] 72-92013 ISBN 0-85699-057-4 2.95 (pbk.)
1. Washington, George, Pres. U.S., 1732-1799—Inauguration. 2. New York (City)—History—1775-1865. 3. New York (City)—Description. I. Title.

New York (City)—History—Revolution, 1775-1783.

SHUMWAY, Floyd 974.7'1'03
Mallory.
Seaport city : New York in 1775 / by Floyd M. Shumway. New York : South Street Seaport Museum, c1975. 64 p. : ill. ; 22 cm. Bibliography: p. 63-64. [F128.44.S48] 75-3940 ISBN 0-913344-20-6 pbk. : 1.95
1. New York (City)—History—Revolution, 1775-1783. 2. New York (City)—History—Colonial period, ca. 1600-1775. I. Title. BIP

New York (City) in art.

KRUSE, Werner, fl.1959- 741.9'43
New York [by] Robinson. New York, Funk & Wagnalls [1967] [64] p. (chiefly illus., map, ports.) 34 cm. [NC251.K78A5313] 68-13266
1. Kruse, Werner, fl. 1959- 2. New York (City) in art. I. Title.

MARSH, Reginald, 1898- 741.9'73
1954.
The sketchbooks of Reginald Marsh. [Compiled by] Edward Laning. Greenwich, Conn., New York Graphic Society [1973] 168 p. illus. (part col.) 27 cm. [NC139.M28L36] 73-78793 ISBN 0-8212-0538-2 15.00
1. Marsh, Reginald, 1898-1954. 2. New York (City) in art. I. Laning, Edward, 1906- comp.

New York (City) in art—Catalogs.

LAX, David, 1910- 759.13
New York City in the fifties; [paintings] New York, Washington Irving Gallery [1971] 1 v. (chiefly col. plates) 26 cm. "Dutchess Community College ... has undertaken to assemble this group of paintings for its permanent collection." [ND237.L35W3] 71-174668
I. Washington Irving Gallery. II. Dutchess Community College. III. Title.

SLOAN, John, 1871-1951. 769'.92'4
New York etchings (1905-1949) / John Sloan ; edited by Helen Farr Sloan. New York : Dover Publications, c1978. xi p., [33] leaves of plates : chiefly ill. ; 29 cm. [NE2012.S56A4 1978] 77-94929 ISBN 0-486-23651-X : 4.00
1. Sloan, John, 1871-1951—Catalogs. 2. New York (City) in art—Catalogs. I. Sloan, Helen Farr, 1911- II. Title. BIP

New York (City). Metropolitan Museum of Art.

GRINNELL, Isabel 726'.1'208
Hoopes.
Greek temples. New York, 1943. [New York] Arno Press, 1974. xxi, 59 p. illus. 32 cm. At head of title: The Metropolitan Museum of Art. Includes bibliographies. [NA275.G7 1974] 79-168420 ISBN 0-405-02258-1 20.00
1. New York (City). Metropolitan Museum of Art. 2. Temples, Greek. I. New York (City). Metropolitan Museum of Art. BIP

HOWE, Winifred Eva, 708'.147'1
1876-
A history of the Metropolitan Museum of Art, with a chapter on the early institutions of art in New York, by Winifred E. Howe. New York, 1913. [New York] Arno Press, 1974. xvi, 361 p. illus. 23 cm. Reprint of v. 1 of the 2 v. work originally published, 1913-46, by the Metropolitan Museum of Art, New York. [N610.H76] 76-168422 ISBN 0-405-02260-3 27.00
1. New York (City). Metropolitan Museum of Art. 2. Art—New York (City)—Galleries and Museums. 3. New York (City)—Museums. I. Title. BIP

IVINS, William Mills, 1881- 769
1961.
Prints and books; informal papers. New York, Da Capo Press, 1969 [c1926] x, 375 p. illus., ports. 23 cm. (Da Capa Press series in graphic art, v. 11) The essays are chiefly about prints and books in the Metropolitan Museum of Art. [NE53.N618 1969] 76-75295 10.00
1. New York. Metropolitan Museum of Art. 2. Prints—New York (City) I. Title. BIP

LERMAN, Leo. 708.1'471
The museum: one hundred years and the Metropolitan Museum of Art. Introd. by Thomas P. F. Hoving. New York, Viking Press [1969] 400 p. illus. (part col.), map, plans, ports. 30 cm. (A Studio book) [N610.L4 1969] 70-87252 16.95
1. New York (City). Metropolitan Museum of Art. I. Title.

THE Metropolitan 708'.147'1
Museum of Art, New York / [texts by Licia Collobi Ragghianti and the curatorial staff of the Metropolitan Museum of Art]. New York : Newsweek, c1978. 171 p. : col. ill. ; 30 cm. (Great museums of the world) Includes indexes. Bibliography: p. 168. A brief history of the founding and development of the Metropolitan Museum of Art with a pictorial survey of selected works of art in the museum's collections. [N610.M47] 77-17667 ISBN 0-88225-241-0 : 13.95
1. New York (City). Metropolitan Museum of Art. I. Ragghianti Collobi, Licia. II. New York (City). Metropolitan Museum of Art. III. Title. IV. Series. BIP

NEW York 749.2'14'07401471
(City). Metropolitan Museum of Art.
American furniture of the colonial period / Marvin D. Schwartz. [New York] : Metropolitan Museum of Art, [1976] 93 p. : ill. (some col.) ; 24 cm. Bibliography: p. 93. [NK2406.N37 1976] 76-18763 ISBN 0-87099-149-3 : 6.95
1. New York (City). Metropolitan Museum of Art. 2. Furniture, Colonial—United States—Catalogs. 3. Furniture—United States—Catalogs. I. Schwartz, Marvin D. II. Title. BIP

NEW York (City). 738.3'82'093 s
Metropolitan Museum of Art.
Attic black-figured neck-amphorae / Mary B. Moore and Dietrich von Bothmer. New York : Metropolitan Museum of Art, c1976. 1 portfolio (76 p., 52 leaves of plates) : ill. ; 33 cm. (Corpus vasorum antiquorum : United States of America ; fasc. 16 : The Metropolitan Museum of Art, New York ; fasc. 4) At head of title: Union academique internationale. Includes bibliographical references and indexes. [NK4640.C6U5 fasc. 16] [NK4650.A6] 738.3'82 75-25613 ISBN 0-87099-134-5 30.00
1. New York (City). Metropolitan Museum of Art. 2. Amphoras—New York (City)—Catalogs. I. Moore, Mary B. II. Von Bothmer, Dietrich, 1918- III. Title. IV. Series: Corpus vasorum antiquorum : United States of America ; fasc. 16. BIP

NEW York (City). 708'.147'1
Metropolitan Museum of Art.
The chase, the capture : collecting at the Metropolitan / Thomas Hoving, director ; with essays by members of the staff, Dietrich von Bothmer ... [et al.]. New York : Metropolitan Museum of Art, [1975] 234 p. : ill. ; 23 cm. [N610.A82] 75-34076
1. New York (City). Metropolitan Museum of Art. 2. Art—Collectors and collecting. I. Hoving, Thomas Pearsall Field, 1931- II. Von Bothmer, Dietrich, 1918- III. Title. BIP

NEW York (City). 708'.1471
Metropolitan Museum of Art.
The Metropolitan Museum of Art : notable acquisitions, 1965-1975. New York : The Museum, c1975. 300 p. : ill. ; 23 cm. [N610.A6745] 75-31761 ISBN 0-87099-141-8
1. New York (City). Metropolitan Museum of Art. 2. Art—New York (City)—Catalogs. BIP

NEW York (City). 759.94'074'01471
Metropolitan Museum of Art.
The picture galleries / [by Theodore Rousseau]. [New York : Metropolitan Museum of Art, 1954?] 56 p. : chiefly ill. ; 26 cm. Cover title. [N610.A726] 75-320286
1. New York (City). Metropolitan Museum of Art. 2. Paintings—New York (City) I. Rousseau, Theodore, 1912- II. Title.

NEW York (City). 380.1'45'7
Metropolitan Museum of Art.
Report on art transactions, 1971-1973 / the Metropolitan Museum of Art. [New York] : The Museum, 1973. 24, 5, 11 p. ; 28 cm. Cover title. [N610.A425] 75-305896
1. New York (City). Metropolitan Museum of Art. I. Title.

NEW York (City). 737'.6
Metropolitan Museum of Art.
Sasanian stamp seals in the Metropolitan Museum of Art / Christoper J. Brunner. New York : The Museum, 1978. p. cm. Includes indexes. Bibliography: p. [CD6255.N48 1978] 78-2845 ISBN 0-87099-176-0 : 35.00
1. New York (City). Metropolitan Museum of Art. 2. Seals (Numismatics)—Iran. 3. Sassanids. I. Brunner, Christopher J. II. Title.

NEW York (City). 708.1471
Metropolitan Museum of Art.
The second century; the comprehensive architectural plan for the Metropolitan Museum of Art. [New York, 1971] 62 p. illus. (part col.), map, plans (part col.) 29 cm. [N610.A85] 75-24450
I. Title.

NEW York (City). 759.951
Metropolitan Museum of Art.
Sung and Yuan paintings [collected by] Wen Fong. With catalogue by Marilyn Fu. New York; distributed by New York Graphic Society [1973] 162 p. illus. (part col.) 22 x 28 cm. Bibliography: p. 153-156. [ND1043.4.N48 1973] 73-15763 12.50

(chiefly illus.) 16 x 23 cm. Black and white photographs and a poem in free verse show the natural aspects of a park in four seasons. [F128.65.C3L4] 68-28917 3.95
1. New York (City)—Parks—Central Park—Pictorial works. I. Buttfield, Helen, illus. II. Title. BIP

New York (City)—Pictorial works.

*KERTESZ, Andre. 779
Of New York. . . . / Andre Kertesz ; edited by Nicolas Ducrot. New York : Knopf, c1976. [192 p.] : chiefly ill. ; 29 cm. (A Borzoi book). [TR647] 76-13673 ISBN 0-394-40511-0 : 22.50
1. New York (City)—Pictorial works. I. Ducrot, Nicolas, comp. II. Title.

New York (City)—Plazas—Washington Square.

KERTESZ, Andre. 917.47'1
Washington Square / Andre Kertesz ; with an appreciation by Brendan Gill. New York : Grossman Publishers, 1975. p. cm. [F128.65.W3K47] 75-19032 ISBN 0-670-00601-7 pbk. : 4.95
1. New York (City)—Plazas—Washington Square. I. Title.

New York (City). Public Library. Berg Collection.

SZLADITS, Lola L. 016.098'3
Documents: famous & infamous; selected from the Henry W. and Albert A. Berg Collection of English and American Literature, by Lola L. Szladits. [New York] New York Public Library, 1972. 34 p. illus. 26 cm. [Z42.S95] 73-153602 ISBN 0-87104-240-1
1. New York (City). Public Library. Berg Collection. 2. Autographs—Collections. 3. Literary forgeries and mystifications—Bibliography—Catalogs. I. New York (City). Public Library. Berg Collection. II. Title. BIP

New York (City). Public Library. Prints Division.

NEW York (City). 019'.1'097471
Public Library. Prints Division.
Dictionary catalog of the Prints Division. Boston : G. K. Hall, 1975. 5 v. ; 36 cm. At head of title: The New York Public Library, Astor, Lenox & Tilden Foundations, the Research Libraries. [Z5950.N562 1975] [NE53] 75-332052 ISBN 0-8161-1148-0 lib.bdg. : 425.00
1. New York (City). Public Library. Prints Division. 2. Prints—New York (City)—Bibliography—Catalogs. I. Title. BIP

New York (City)—Social life and customs.

CRILLEY, Joseph J 917.471
New York; island of islands. photos. by Joseph J. Crilley; test by Arthur Carduner. Design by Clifford N. Hehr; editing by Charles J. O'Connor. [Limited ed.] Buffalo, W. J. Keller [1965] 124 p. illus. 24 x 32 cm. [F128.52C7] 65-3675
1. New York (City)—Soc. life & cust. 2. New York (City)—Descr.—Views. I. Carduner, Arthur R. II. Title.

CRILLEY, Joseph J. 917.471
New York: island of islands. Photos. by Joseph J. Crilley; text by Arthur Carduner. Design by Clifford N. Hehr; ed. by Charles J. O'Connor. W. J. Keller [dist. New Hope, Bucks Co., Pa, 19838 Vanity Fair, Box 121] c.1965. 124p. illus. 24x32cm. [F128.52.C7] 65-3675 10.00, lim. ed.
1. New York (City)—Soc. life & cust. 2. New York (City)—Descr.—Views. I. Carduner, Arthur R. II. Title.

SINGLETON, Esther, 917.471'03'2
d.1930.
Social New York under the Georges, 1714-1776: houses, streets, and country homes, with chapters on fashions, furniture, china, plate, and manners. New York, B. Blom [1968] xix, 407 p. illus. 24 cm. Reprint of the 1902 ed. [F128.4.S61 1968] 68-26018
1. New York (City)—Social life and customs. I. Title. BIP

SINGLETON, Esther, 917.471'03'2
d.1930-
Social New York under the Georges, 1714-1776; houses, streets, and country homes, with chapters on fashions, furniture, china, plate, and manners. Port Washington, N.Y., I. J. Friedman [1969] 2 v. in 1 (xix, 407 p.) illus., ports. 24 cm. (Empire State historical publications series, no. 60) Reprint of the 1902 ed. with a new introd. by Ralph Adams Brown. [F128.4.S61 1969] 68-58928
1. New York (City)—Social life and customs. I. Title. II. Series.

SLOAN, John, 1871-1951. 759.13
John Sloan's New York scene; from the diaries, notes, and correspondence, 1906-1913. Edited by Bruce St. John, with an introd. by Helen Farr Sloan. [1st ed.] New York, Harper & Row [1965] xxvi, 658 p. illus. (part col.) ports. 24 cm. [ND237.S57A2] 64-25122
1. New York (City) — Soc. life & cust. I. Title. II. Title: New York scene.

New York (City)—Statues.

LEDERER, Joseph. 917.47'1'044
All around the town : a walking guide to the outdoor statues of New York City / text by Joseph Lederer ; photos. by Arley Bondarin. New York : Scribner, [1975] p. cm. Includes index. [NB235.N5L4] 75-12863 ISBN 0-684-14256-2 : 12.50
1. New York (City)—Statues. 2. Sculpture—New York (City) 3. New York (City)—Description—1951- —Tours. I. Bondarin, Arley. II. Title. BIP

New York (City)—Streets.

BRIERLY, J Ernest. 974.71
The streets of old New York; a pictorial rebirth of a vanished city. New York, Hastings House [1953] 127p. illus. 22cm. [F128.67.A1B75] 53-6147
1. New York (City)—Streets. I. Title.

New York (City)—Streets—100th Street.

DAVIDSON, Bruce, 1933- 917.471
East 100th Street. Cambridge, Mass., Harvard University Press, 1970. [129] p. (chiefly illus.) 32 cm. [F128.67.O5D3] 76-120714 ISBN 0-674-22435-3
1. New York (City)—Streets—100th Street. 2. Harlem, New York (City)—Description—Views. I. Title.

New York. Grand Central Terminal.

MIDDLETON, 385'.314'097471
William D., 1928-
Grand Central, the world's greatest railway terminal / William D. Middleton. San Marino, Calif. : Golden West Books, c1977. 160 p. : ill. ; 29 cm. Includes index. Bibliography: p. 154-156. [TF302.N7M53] 77-24507 ISBN 0-87095-071-1 : 11.95
1. New York. Grand Central Terminal. I. Title. BIP

New York Historical Society.

NEW York Historical 757'.9'0973
Society.
Catalogue of American portraits in the New York Historical Society. New Haven : Published for the New York Historical Society by Yale University Press, 1974. 2 v. (ix, 964 p.) : ports. ; 29 cm. Includes index. Bibliography: p. 939-955. [N7593.N5 1974] 74-79974 ISBN 0-300-01477-5 : 50.00
1. New York Historical Society. 2. Portraits, American—Catalogs. 3. Portraits—New York (City)—Catalogs. 4. United States—Biography—Portraits. I. Title. BIP

NEW York Historical 748.8
Society.
Glass paperweights of the New-York Historical Society / by Paul Hollister ; photos. by H. Landshoff ; foreword by Mary Black. 1st ed. New York : C. N. Potter : distributed by Crown, [1974] xiii, 210 p. : ill. (120 col.) ; 32 cm. Includes index. [NK5440.P3N48 1974] 74-14333 ISBN 0-517-51667-5 : 25.00
1. New York Historical Society. 2. Paperweights—Catalogs. I. Hollister, Paul M., 1918- II. Landshoff, H., ill. III. Title. BIP

New York School.

ASHTON, Dore. 700'.9747'1
The New York school : a cultural reckoning / by Dore Ashton. New York : Penguin Books, 1979. p. cm. Published in 1972 under title: The life and times of the New York school. Includes bibliographical references and index. [NX504.A87 1979] 79-11429 ISBN 0-14-005263-1 pbk. : 5.95
1. New York School. 2. Arts, Modern—20th century—United States. I. Title. BIP

ASHTON, Dore. 700'.9747'1
The New York school; a cultural reckoning. New York, Viking Press [1973, c1972] x, 246 p. illus. 22 cm. Published in 1972 under title: The life and times of the New York school. Includes bibliographical references. [NX504.A87 1973] 72-80897 ISBN 0-670-50912-4 10.00
1. New York School. 2. Arts, Modern—20th century—United States. I. Title.
Pbk. 4.95; ISBN 0-670-00368-9.

SANDLER, Irving, 1925- 709'.747'1
The New York School : the painters and sculptors of the fifties / by Irving Sandler. 1st ed. New York : Harper & Row, c1978. xi, 366 p. : ill. ; 26 cm. (Icon editions) Includes index. Bibliography: p. [326]-344. [N6512.5.N4S26 1978] 77-82357 ISBN 0-06-438505-1 : 30.00
1. New York School. 2. Art, American. 3. Art, Modern—20th century—United States. I. Title. BIP

New York (State)—Aerial photographs—Catalogs.

NEW York (State). Map 016.912'747
Information Unit.
Inventory of aerial photography and other remotely sensed imagery of New York State, 1975. Albany : Map Information Unit, New York State Dept. of Transportation, 1975. 116 p. : ill. ; 28 cm. Chiefly tables. [Z6027.U5N48 1975] [GA441] 76-621164 5.00
1. New York (State)—Aerial photographs—Catalogs. I. Title: Inventory of aerial photography and other remotely sensed imagery ...

New York (State)—Description and travel—1951- —Views.

SMITH, Clyde H. 779'.9'91747044
New York / by Clyde H. Smith ; text by Lionel Atwill. Portland, Or. : Graphic Arts Center Pub. Co., c1977. 160 p. : chiefly col. ill. ; 36 cm. [F120.S64] 77-72228 ISBN 0-912856-33-5 : 27.50
1. New York (State)—Description and travel—1951- —Views. I. Atwill, Lionel. II. Title. BIP

New York (State) in art.

BARBER, John Warner, 769'.92'4
1798-1885.
Early woodcut views of New York and New Jersey : 304 illustrations from the "Historical collections" / by John W. Barber and Henry Howe. New York : Dover Publications, 1975. 118 p. : chiefly ill. ; 29 cm. (Dover pictorial archive series) Includes index. [NE1112.B37H68] 75-3823 ISBN 0-486-23196-8 : 3.50
1. Barber, John Warner, 1798-1885. 2. Howe, Henry, 1816-1893. 3. New York (State) in art. 4. New Jersey in art. I. Howe, Henry, 1816-1893, joint author. II. Barber, John Warner, 1798-1885. Historical collections of the State of New York. III. Barber, John Warner, 1798-1885. Historical collections of the State of New Jersey. IV. Title. BIP

New York State Museum, Albany.

MUSEUM guide leaflet. 069.09747
no.1- Albany, New York State Museum [1951- v. illus. 22 cm. [AM101.N54] A 52
1. New York State Museum, Albany.

New York. State Prison, Auburn.

EVERSON Museum of Art of 759.13
Syracuse and Onondaga County.
From within; selected works by the artists/inmates of New York State Correctional Facility at Auburn (maximum security). [Exhibition held at] the National Collection of Fine Arts, Smithsonian Institution, Washington, D.C., February 2-March 25, 1973. [Washington, 1973] [35] p. illus. 26 cm. [ND230.N4E93] 72-95537
1. New York. State Prison, Auburn. 2. Prisoners as artists. 3. Paintings, American—Exhibitions. 4. Painting, Modern—20th century—New York (State) I. Smithsonian Institution. National Collection of Fine Arts. II. Title.

New York (State). State University.

NEW York (State). 338.4'7'7009747
State University. Washington Office.
Support for the arts; a survey of possible sources for State University of New York. [Susan G. Sorrels, editor] Washington] 1973. 164 p. 24 cm. Bibliography: p. 161-164. [NX705.5.U62N77 1973] 73-176026 2.00
1. New York (State). State University. 2. Arts—Scholarships, fellowships, etc.—New York (State) 3. Federal aid to the arts—New York (State) I. Sorrels, Susan G., ed. II. Title.

New York. Turtle Bay Gardens.

DETMOLD, Mabel Alice 635.9097471
(Porter) 1888-1964.
The brownstones of Turtle Bay Gardens. New York, East 49th Street Association [1964] 77 p. front., map (on lining papers) 22 cm. [F128.68.T85D4] 64-8538
1. New York. Turtle Bay Gardens. I. Title.

New York University. Hall of American Artists.

PARIS, William Francklyn, 709'.22
1871-1954.
Personalities in American art. Freeport, N.Y., Books for Libraries Press [1970- v. ports. 23 cm. (Essay index reprint series) Vols. 2-10 have title: The Hall of American Artists. Reprint of the 1930-ed. [N6536.P32] 72-107731
1. New York University. Hall of American Artists. 2. Artists, American. I. Title. II. Title: The Hall of American Artists. BIP

New Zealand—Biography.

EASTGATE, Nigel. 769'.563'09931
Stamp out kiwis / Nigel Eastgate. Dunedin [N.Z.] : J. McIndoe, 1976. [24] p. : ill. ; 22 cm. [CT2888.E2A37] 77-354610 ISBN 0-908565-15-1
1. Eastgate, Nigel. 2. New Zealand—Biography. 3. Postage-stamps—New Zealand—Miscellanea. I. Title.

New Zealand in art.

HAMON, Rei Paul F. 741.9'931
Rei Hamon : artist of the New Zealand bush : second collection. Auckland : Collins, 1976. 93 p. : ill. ; 38 cm. [NC374.H3A55] 77-465035 ISBN 0-00-216912-6
1. Hamon, Rei Paul F. 2. New Zealand in art. I. Title: Artist of the New Zealand bush.

MCCORMICK, Eric Hall, 759.9931
1906-
Eric Lee-Johnson, with a biographical introduction / by E. H. McCormick ; edited by Janet Paul. Hamilton, N.Z. : Paul's Book Arcade, 1956. 52 p., [16] leaves of plates : ill. (some col.) ; 22 cm. [ND2092.Z8L435] 75-317978
1. Lee-Johnson, Eric, 1908- 2. New Zealand in art.

Niepce, Joseph Nicephore, 1765-1833.

FOUQUE, Victor, b.1802. 770'.92'4
The truth concerning the invention of photography: Nicephore Niepce, his life, letters, and works [Translated by Edward Epstean] New York, Arno Press, 1973. 163 p. 23 cm. (The Literature of Photography) Translation of Laverite surl'invention de la photographie. Reprint of the 1935 ed. Includes bibliographical references. [TR140.N5F72 1973] 72-9198 ISBN 0-405-04907-2 10.00.
1. Niepce, Joseph Nicephore, 1765-1833. 2. Photography—History. I. Title. II. Series. BIP

Nietzsche, Friedrich Wilhelm, 1844-1900—Aesthetics.

LUDOVICI, Anthony Mario, 1882- 701.17'0924
Neitzsche and art, by Anthony M. Ludovici. New York, Haskell House, 1971. xvi, 236 p. illus. 23 cm. Reprint of the 1911 ed. [B3318.A4L8 1971] 72-148824 ISBN 0-8383-1229-2
1. Nietzsche, Friedrich Wilhelm, 1844-1900—Aesthetics. I. Title.

Nikkormat camera.

REYNOLDS, Clyde. 771.3'1
The Nikkormat book for EL and FT2 users / Clyde Reynolds London ; New York : Focal Press, 1976. 136 p. : ill. (some col.) ; 22 cm. (Focal camera books) Includes index. [TR263.N48R49] 76-376246 ISBN 0-240-50908-0 : £2.25
1. Nikkormat camera. 2. Photography—Handbooks, manuals, etc. I. Title.

Nikon camera.

AMPHOTO, New York. 771.31
official Nikon F and Nikkorex F manual, by the Amphoto edit. bd New York, Author ,53c. 1962] 126p. illus. 21cm. 62-17655 2.50bds.,
1. Nikon camera. 2. Photography—Handbooks, manuals, etc. I. Title.

AMPHOTO, New York. 771.3'1
Official Nikon F and Nikkormat manual, by the Amphoto Editorial board. [4th ed.] New York [1967] 126 p. illus. 21 cm. 1962 ed. published under title: Official Nikon F and Nikkorex manual. [TR263.N5A47 1967] 67-29189
1. Nikon camera. 2. Photography—Handbooks, manuals, etc. I. Title.

AMPHOTO, New York. 771.3'1
Official Nikon F and Nikkormat manual, by the Amphoto editorial board. [5th ed.] New York [1969] 126 p. illus. 22 cm. First ed. (1962) published under title: Official Nikon F and Nikkorex F manual; 7th ed. (1975) under title: Official Nikon-Nikkormat manual. [TR263.N5A47 1969] 78-83538
1. Nikon camera. 2. Photography—Handbooks, manuals, etc. I. Title.

AMPHOTO, New York. 771.3'1
Official Nikon F and Nikkormat manual, by the Amphoto editorial board. [6th ed.] New York [1972] 126 p. illus. 22 cm. First ed. (1962) published under title: Official Nikon F and Nikkorex F manual; 7th ed. (1975) under title: Official Nikon-Nikkormat manual. [TR263.N5A47 1972] 79-186232 ISBN 0-8174-0477-5 3.50
1. Nikon camera. 2. Photography—Handbooks, manuals, etc. I. Title.

AMPHOTO, New York. 771.31
Official Nikon F reflex manual. New York, c1960. 126p. illus. 21cm. [TR263.N5A45] 60-15902
1. Nikon camera. 2. Photography—Handbooks, manuals, etc. I. Title.

AMPHOTO, New York. 771.3'1
Official Nikon-Nikkormat manual / by the Amphoto editorial board. 7th ed. Garden City, N.Y. : Amphoto, [1975] 160 p. : ill. ; 24 cm. First ed. (1962) published under title: Official Nikon F and Nikkorex F manual; 2-6th ed. (1964-72) under title: Official Nikon F and Nikkormat manual. Includes index. [TR263.N5A47 1975] 74-84031 ISBN 0-8174-0582-8 : 7.95
1. Nikon camera. 2. Photography—Handbooks, manuals, etc. I. Title. BIP

COOPER, Joseph David, 1917- 771.31
Nikon F, Nikkorex F, pocket companion. New York, Amphoto [1967, c. 1963] 126p. illus. 15cm. [TR263.N5C6] 63-20734 1.95 pap.,
1. Nikon camera 2. Photography—Handbook manuals, etc. I. Title.

COOPER, Joseph David, 1917- 771.3'1
Nikon F, Nikkormat handbook of photography [by] Joseph D. Cooper and Joseph C. Abbott. Philadelphia, Chilton Book Co. [1968] 1 v. (various pagings) illus. 27 cm. [TR263.N5C63] 67-18630
1. Nikon camera. 2. Photography—Handbooks, manuals, etc. I. Abbott, Joseph C., joint author. II. Title.

COOPER, Joseph David, 1917- 771.3'1
Nikon F. Nikkormat, pocket companion, by Joseph D. Cooper. New York, Amphoto [1967] 126 p. illus. 15 cm. [TR263.N5C6 1967] 67-9318
1. Nikon camera. 2. Photography—Handbooks, manuals, etc. I. Title.

COOPER, Joseph David, 1917- 771.3'1
Nikon-Nikkormat Handbook / Joseph D. Cooper. Garden City, N.Y. : Amphoto, [1974- 2 v. : ill. (come col.) ; 27 cm. Loose-leaf for updating. Includes index. [TR263.N5C633] 73-92419 ISBN 0-8174-0566-6 : 37.50(set)
1. Nikon camera. 2. Photography—Handbooks, manuals, etc. I. Title.

COOPER, Joseph David, 1917- 771.31
Nikron F, Nikkorex F, pocket companion [New York, Amphoto, c. 1963] 126p. illus. 15cm. (Universal photo bks..) 63-20734 1.95 wore bdg.
1. Nikon camera. 2. Photography—Handbooks, manuals, etc. I. Title.

CRAWLEY, Geoffrey. 771.3'1
The Nikon system; the Nikon F, Nikkormat, lenses and accessory equipment. Reviewed by Geoffrey Crawley. Compiled by Jeremy Haworth. [2d ed.] New York, Amphoto [1970, c1969] 121 p. illus. 23 cm. [TR263.N5C7 1970] 74-125364 3.95
1. Nikon camera. I. Title.

LAHUE, Kalton C. 771.3'1
Nikon system / by Kalton C. Lahue. Los Angeles : Petersen Pub. Co., c1975. 80 p. : ill. ; 28 cm. (Petersen's camera systems library) [TR263.N5L33] 75-21831 ISBN 0-8227-0119-7 pbk. : 3.95
1. Nikon camera. I. Title.

LONDON, Barbara, 1936- 771.3'1
A short course in Nikon photography / Barbara London. New York : Van Nostrand Reinhold Co., [1979] p. cm. Includes index. Bibliography: p. [TR263.N5L66] 78-23903 ISBN 0-442-26608-1 pbk. : 9.00 ISBN 0-442-26614-6 : 14.95
1. Nikon camera. 2. Photography—Handbooks, manuals, etc. I. Title.

SHIPMAN, Carl. 771.3'1
How to select use Nikon & Nikkormat SLR cameras / Carl Shipman. [Tucson, Ariz.] : H. P. Books, [c1978] 208 p. : ill. (some col.) ; 28 cm. Cover title. [TR263.N5S47] 78-52274 ISBN 0-912656-77-8 : 5.95
1. Nikon camera. 2. Nikkormat camera. 3. Photography—Handbooks, manuals, etc. I. Title. II. Title: Nikon & Nikkormat SLR cameras. BIP

TYDINGS, Kenneth S 771.31
Nikon F eye-level reflex guide including Nikon S series and Nikkorex-35. Philadelphia, Chilton Co., c1962. 127 p. illus. 20 cm. (Modern camera guide series, 285) [TR263.N5T88] 62-8216
1. Nikon camera. 2. Photography — Handbooks, manuals, etc. I. Title.

TYDINGS, Kenneth S. 771.3'1
Nikon F eye-level reflex guide [by] Kenneth S. Tydings. New York, American Photographic Book Pub. Co., 1966, c1963. 127 p. illus. 20 cm. (The Modern camera guide series 253) "Revised to include Nikon S series, Nikkorex-35, Nikkorex F, Nikkorex Zoom-35, Nikkorex Auto-35, Nikkorex lenses." [TR263.N5T88 1966] 63-20210
1. Nikon camera. 2. Photography—Handbooks, manuals, etc. I. Title. II. Series.

TYDINGS, Kenneth S 771.3148
The Nikon guide. New York, Greenberg, [1957] 1956. 128p. illus. 20cm. (The Modern camera guide series) [TR263.N5T9] 56-12019
1. Nikon camera. 2. Photography—Handbooks, manuals, etc. I. Title.

WOLF, John C. 771.3'1
The Nikon guide / John C. Wolf. Garden City, N.Y. : Amphoto, c1978. 120 p., [4] leaves of plates : ill. (some col.) ; 26 cm. (Modern camera guide series) Includes bibliographical references and index. [TR263.N5W64] 77-93561 ISBN 0-8174-2432-6 : 10.95 ISBN 0-8174-2110-6 pbk. : 6.95
1. Nikon camera. 2. Photography—Handbooks, manuals, etc. I. Title. II. Series.

WRIGHT, George Benjamin, 1913- 770.2
The Nikon manual; a complete handbook of 35mm technique. Technical assistance by Joseph C. Abbott [and] Cora Wright. [1st ed.] New York, Universal Photo Books [1957] 288 p. illus. 24 cm. [TR263.N5W7] 57-10344
1. Nikon camera. 2. Photography — Handbook, manuals, etc. I. Title.

Nikonos camera.

ROBERTS, Fred M. 771.3'1
Nikonos photography : the camera and system / by Fred M. Roberts. 2d ed. Dana Point, Calif. : F. M. Roberts Enterprises [1974] 127 p. : ill. ; 22 cm. (A photographic technology book) Includes index. Bibliography: p. 124. [TR263.N5R62 1974] 74-187864 ISBN 0-912746-00-9 : 3.95
1. Nikonos camera. 2. Photography, Submarine—Handbooks, manuals, etc. I. Title. BIP

ROBERTS, Fred M. 771.3'1
Nikonos photography : the camera and system / by Fred M. Roberts. 3d ed. Dana Point, Calif. : fmRoberts Enterprises, c1977. 161 p. : ill. (some col.) ; 22 cm. (A Photographic technology book) Includes index. [TR263.N5R62 1977] 77-80027 ISBN 0-912746-00-9 pbk. : 4.95
1. Nikouos camera. 2. Photography, Submarine—Handbooks, manuals, etc. I. Title.
Publisher's address : P.O. Box 608, Dana Pt., Calif.92629

TAYLOR, Herb, 1942- 778.73
Underwater with the Nikonos & Nikon systems / Herb Taylor. Garden City, N.Y. : AMPHOTO, c1977. 160 p., [6] leaves of plates : ill. ; 24 cm. Includes index. Bibliography: p. 158. [TR263.N5T39] 76-16462 ISBN 0-8174-2401-6 : 9.95
1. Nikonos camera. 2. Nikon camera. 3. Photography, Submarine—Handbooks, manuals, etc. I. Title. BIP

Nimschke, Louis Daniel, 1832-1904.

WILSON, Robert Lawrence, 1939- 739.15
L. D. Nimschke, firearms engraver, by R. L. Wilson. Pref. by John J. McKendry. Teaneck, N.J., J.J. Malloy [1965] xxxxviii,108 p. illus. 35 cm. [NK6998.N5W5] 65-29644
1. Nimschke, Louis Daniel, 1832-1904. I. Title.

Nippon Toki Kobushiki Kaisha.

MEYER, Florence E. 738.2'0952
The colorful world of Nippon, by Florence E. Meyer. Des Moines, Iowa, Wallace-Homestead Book Co. [1971] [51] p. (incl. cover) illus., 19 col. plates. 23 cm. [NK4567.M53] 72-177700
1. Nippon Toki Kobushiki Kaisha. 2. Porcelain, Japanese. 3. Porcelain—Marks. I. Title. BIP

Nishi, Hongwanji, Kyoto.

MIYAZAKI, Enjun, 1906- 708.952
Nishi-Hongwanji, by Enjun Miyazaki, Yuzuru Okada, Tomohiko Horie. Photo Taikichi Irie, Sose Kuzunishi, Harumi Konishi [Dist. New York, Perkins Oriental, 1962] 274p. chiefly illus. col. front. 22cm. Japanese text; added t.p. in English. J62 3.50 bds.,
1. Nishi, Hongwanji, Kyoto. 2. Art, Buddhist. I. Irie, Taikichi, 1905- II. Title.

Niven, Thornton MacNess, 1806-1895.

DOWNS, Arthur Channing, 1930- 720'.924
The architecture and life of the Hon. Thornton MacNess Niven (1806-1895), with accounts of architecture and building practices in Newburgh, Goshen, Monticello, and Riverhead, N.Y., and of newly discovered architecture by Andrew J. Downing, A. J. Davis, Russell Warren, and Calvin Pollard [by] Arthur Channing Downs, Jr. [1st ed. Goshen, N.Y., Orange County Community of Museums & Galleries, 1971] 60 p. illus. 28 cm. Cover title. Includes bibliographical references. [NA737.N5D6] 71-174676
1. Niven, Thornton MacNess, 1806-1895.

Nixon, Richard Milhous, 1913- — Cartoons, satire, etc.—Exhibitions.

WATERGATE, the 760'.074'016947 s
unmaking of a President : Lexington, January 12-February 9, 1975 / organized and edited for the University of Kentucky Art Gallery by Richard B. Freeman. [Lexington : University of Kentucky Art Gallery, 1975] 96 p. : chiefly ill. ; 28 cm. (Graphics ; 17, 1975) Catalog of the exhibition held at the University of Kentucky Art Gallery. [NE45.K4K45 no. 17, 1975] [E860] 364.1'32 75-312669
1. Nixon, Richard Milhous, 1913- — Cartoons, satire, etc.—Exhibitions. 2. Watergate Affair, 1972- —Caricatures and cartoons—Exhibitions. 3. American wit and humor, Pictorial—Exhibitions. I. Freeman, Richard B., 1908- II. Series: Kentucky. University. Art Gallery. Graphics ; 17, 1975.

Nizami Ganjavi, 1140 or 41-1202 or 3—Manuscripts—Addresses, essays, lectures.

CHELKOWSKI, Peter J. FIC
Mirror of the invisible world : tales from the Khamseh of Nizami / [adapted and translated by] Peter Chelkowski, with an essay by Priscilla P. Soucek. New York : Metropolitan Museum of Art, 1975. p. cm. "Published on the occasion of the opening of the new Islamic Galleries at the Metropolitan Museum of Art." [PZ4.C516Mi] [PS3553.H348] 813'.5'4 75-28305 ISBN 0-87099-142-6 : 17.50
1. Nizami Ganjavi, 1140 or 41-1202 or 3—Manuscripts—Addresses, essays, lectures. I. Nizami Ganjavi, 1140 or 41-1202 or 3. Khamsah. II. New York (City). Metropolitan Museum of Art. III. Title.
Contents omitted. BIP

Noguchi, Isamu, 1904—

HUNTER, Sam, 1923- 730'.92'4
Isamu Noguchi / by Sam Hunter. New York : Abbeville Press, c1978. p. cm. Includes index. [NB237.N6H86] 78-5288 65.00
1. Noguchi, Isamu, 1904- 2. Sculptors—United States—Biography. BIP

NOGUCHI, Isamu, 1904- 730'.92'4
Noguchi : steel sculptures : [exhibition] the Pace Gallery ... New York, May 10-June 20, 1975. [New York : Pace Editions, inc., 1975] [36] p. : chiefly ill. (some col.) ; 28 cm. Catalog. Bibliography: p. [35]-[36] [NB237.N6P32] 75-10742
1. Noguchi, Isamu, 1904- I. Pace Gallery.

NOGUCHI, Isamu, 1904- 730'.924
A sculptor's world. Foreword by R.

Buckminster Fuller. [1st U.S. ed.] New York, Harper & Row [1968] 259 p. 268 illus. (part col.) 27 cm. [NB237.N6F8 1968] 67-22505
I. Title.

Noguchi, Isamu, 1904- —Juvenile literature.

TOBIAS, Tobi. 730'.92'4 B
Isamu Noguchi; the life of a sculptor. New York, Crowell [1974] 42 p. illus. 23 cm. (A Biography for young people) A brief biography of the renowned Japanese-American sculptor. [NB237.N6T56 1974] 92 72-7560 ISBN 0-690-45014-1 5.95
1. Noguchi, Isamu, 1904- —Juvenile literature. I. Title. **BIP**

Nolan, Sidney, 1917-

LYNN, Elwyn. 759.994
Sidney Nolan: myth and imagery. London, Melbourne, Macmillan, 1967. 92 p. front. (port.), illus. (some col.) 30 1/2 cm. 75/-(B67-19180) [ND1105.N6L87] 67-106660
1. Nolan, Sidney, 1917- I. Title.

Noland, Kenneth, 1924—

FRIED, Michael. 759.2
Three American painters: Kenneth Noland, Jules Olitski, Frank Stella. [Cambridge, Mass., Fogg Art Museum, 1965] 59 p. plates. 22 cm. An exhibition sponsored and held at the Fogg Museum, 21 Apr.-30 May 1965, and also at the Pasadena Art Museum, 6 July-3 Aug. 1965. [ND236.F7] 65-11623
1. Noland, Kenneth, 1924- 2. Olitski, Jules, 1922- 3. Stella, Frank. I. Harvard University. William Hayes Fogg Art Museum. II. Pasadena, Calif. Art Museum. III. Title.

FRIED, Michael. 759.13'074'01444
Three American painters : Kenneth Noland, Jules Olitski, Frank Stella : Fogg Art Museum, 21 April-30 May 1965. New York : Garland Pub. Co., [1978] c1965. 59 p., [10] leaves of plates : ill. ; 22 cm. Exhibition held also at the Pasadena Art Museum, 6 July-3 Aug. 1965. Includes bibliographical references. [ND212.F67 1978] 77-2760 ISBN 0-8240-1957-1 : 15.00
1. Noland, Kenneth, 1924- 2. Olitski, Jules, 1922- 3. Stella, Frank. 4. Painting, Modern—20th century—United States—Exhibitions. I. Harvard University. William Hayes Fogg Art Museum. II. Pasadena, Calif. Art Museum. III. Title.

MOFFETT, Kenworth. 759.13
Kenneth Noland / by Kenworth Moffett. New York : H. N. Abrams, [1977] p. cm. Includes index. Bibliography: [ND237.N594M63] 76-50564 ISBN 0-8109-1351-8 : 37.50
1. Noland, Kenneth, 1924- I. Noland, Kenneth, 1924- **BIP**

NOLAND, Kenneth, 1924- 759.13
Kenneth Noland : a retrospective / the Solomon R. Guggenheim Museum, New York / by Diane Waldman. New York : Solomon R. Guggenheim Foundation, 1977. 160 p. : ill. (some col.) ; 22 x 29 cm. Bibliography: p. 157-159. [ND237.N594W34] 77-70424 ISBN 0-89207-009-9
1. Noland, Kenneth, 1924- I. Waldman, Diane. II. Solomon R. Guggenheim Museum, New York.

Nolde, Emil, 1867-1956.

NOLDE, Emil, 1867- 760'.092'4 1956.
Emil Nolde : paintings, watercolours, drawings and graphics. London : Fischer Fine Art Limited, [1976]. [24] p. (2 fold.) : chiefly ill. (some col.) ; 18 cm. English and German. Catalogue of an exhibition held at Fischer Fine Art Limited in 1976. [N6888.N6F57] 76-380806 ISBN 0-904867-08-0 : £1.12
1. Nolde, Emil, 1867-1956. I. Fischer Fine Art Limited.

NOLDE, Emil, 1867-1956. 759.3
Emil Nolde: landscapes; watercolors and drawings [by] Martin Urban. [Translated

from the German by Paul Stevenson] New York, Praeger [1970] 38 p. illus. (part col.), 21 col. plates. 33 cm. Translation of Emil Nolde, Landschaften. "Produced under the auspices of the Ada and Emil Nolde Foundation-Seebull." [ND1954.N6U7213 1970b] 73-99926 25.00
I. Urban, Martin. II. Stiftung Seebull Ada und Emil Nolde.

NOLDE, Emil, 1867-1956. 759.3
Emil Nolde: unpainted pictures. [Translated from the German by Inge Goodwin] Rev. ed. New York, Praeger [1972, c1965] 39, [160] p. 40 col. plates. 33 cm. At head of title: Werner Haftmann. "Words in margin," by E. Nolde: p. 34-39. Translation of Emil Nolde, Ungemalte Bilder. [ND588.N6H33 1972] 73-161222 35.00
I. Haftmann, Werner. II. Title. III. Title: Unpainted pictures.

NOLDE, Emil, 1867-1956 759.43
Flowers and animals; watercolors and drawings. [Comp. by] Martin Urban. Tr. by Barbara Berg. New York, Praeger [1966, c.1965] 42p. illus. (pt. col.) ports. 33cm. [ND1964.N6U713 1966] 66-21795 20.00 bds.,
I. Urban, Martin, ccmp. II. Title.

NOLDE, Emil, 1867-1956. 759.3
Nolde: watercolors and drawings, by Martin Gosebruch. Translated by E. M. Kustner and J. A. Underwood. New York, Praeger [1973, c1972] 75, [1] p. illus. (part col.) 27 cm. Translation of Nolde: Aquarelle und Zeichnungen. Bibliography: p. [76] [ND1954.N6G613] 72-80695 9.95
1. Nolde, Emil, 1867-1956. I. Gosebruch, Martin.

NOLDE, Emil, 1867-1956. 759.3
Unpainted pictures [Text by] Werner Haftmann. [Tr. from German by Inge Goodwin] New York, Praeger [c.1963, 1965] New York, Abrams [1965] 35, 40p., 40 col. plates. 33cm. 79p. plates (12 col.) ports. 34cm. [ND588.N6H33] [ND1950.S3H313] 759.3 65-19284 65-12093 25.00 17.50
I. Haftmann, Werner. n3 II. Schulze, Alfred Otto Wolfgang, 1913-1951 III. Haftmann, Werner, ed. IV. Title. V. Title: Wols:

SELZ, Peter. 707.4
Emil Nolde. New York, Museum of Modern Art, distributed by Doubleday, Garden, N.Y. [1963] 88 p. illus. 23 cm. "Exhibitions: the Museum of Modern Art, New York, March 4, 1963; San Francisco Museum of Art, May 28, 1963; the Pasadena Art Museum, July 27, 1963." Includes bibliography. [ND588.N6S4] 63-12115
I. New York (City) Museum of Modern Art.

Norman, Henry C., 1850-1913.

NORMAN, Henry C., 770'.092'4 1850-1913.
Norman's Natchez : an early photographer and his town / Joan W. Gandy and Thomas H. Gandy. Jackson : University Press of Mississippi, 1978. p. cm. Includes index. Bibliography: p. [TR652.N67 1978] 78-15570 ISBN 0-87805-078-7 : 25.00
1. Norman, Henry C., 1850-1913. 2. Photography, Artistic. 3. Natchez, Miss.—Description—Views. I. Gandy, Joan W. II. Gandy, Thomas H. III. Title. **BIP**

North America—Antiq.

HABERLAND, Wolfgang. 709.01'1
The art of North America. New York, Crown [1968,c.1964] 251p. illus. (pt. col.), maps. 24cm. (Art of the world; European cultures; the hist., sociol. & religious backgrounds) Tr. of Nordamerika, Indianer, Eskimo, Westindien. Bibl. [E98.A7H243] 68-15660 6.95
1. North America—Antiq. 2. Indians of North America—Art. I. Title. II. Series: Art of the world; the historical, sociological, and religious backgrounds

Northwest. Pacific—Antiq.

SEAMAN, Norma Gilm, 970.4'95 1873-
Indian relics of the Pacific Northwest [by] N. G. Seaman. [2d ed.] Portland, Or., Binfords & Mort [1967] 255 p. illus. 22 cm. [E78.N77S4 1967] 66-28021
1. Northwest. Pacific—Antiq. 2. Indians of North America—Northwest, Pacific—Antiq. I. Title. **BIP**

Northwest, Pacific—History—Pictorial works—Catalogs.

WASHINGTON State 709'.795 Historical Society.
Northwest history in art 1778-1963 Tacoma [1963] 1 v. (unpaged) illus. (part col.) 26 cm. (Pacific Northwest historical pamphlet, no. 3) Cover title. [N6528.W3] A 68
1. Northwest, Pacific—History—Pictorial works—Catalogs. 2. Artists, American—Northwest, Pacific. I. Title. II. Series.

Northwestern States—History.

HURT, Wesley Robert, 1917- 927.7
Frontier photographer; Stanley J. Morrow's Dakota years [by] Wesley R. Hurt and William E. Lass. [Vermillion] University of South Dakota [1956] 135 p. illus. 24 cm. Includes bibliography. [TR140.M6H87] 56-10996
1. Morrow, Stanley J., 1843-1921. 2. Northwestern States—History. 3. Dakota Indians. 4. Photography—History—U.S. I. Lass, William E., joint author. II. Title.

Norton family.

OSGOOD, Cornelius, 1905- 738.37
The jug and related stoneware of Bennington. [1st ed.] Rutland, Vt., C. E. Tuttle Co. [1971] 222 p. illus., geneal. table, maps, col. plates. 28 cm. Bibliography: p. 207-212. [NK4027.B4O8] 73-152111 ISBN 0-8048-0888-0 15.00
1. Norton family. 2. Bennington pottery. I. Title. **BIP**

Norwich Cathedral.

THURLOW, A G G *726.5 726.6
Norwich Cathedral. Photographed by S. J. Brown. Norwich, Jarrold [1951] unpaged. illus. 18 cm. [NA5471.N8T48] 52-43398
1. Norwich Cathedral. I. Title.

THURLOW, Gilbert. 726'.6'094261
Norwich Cathedral. Norwich, Jarrold [1966] [25] p. front. (col. plan) illus. (some col.) 25 cm. (A Jarrold "Sandringham" book) [NA5471.N8T49] 67-80840
1. Norwich Cathedral.

Norwich, Conn.—Historic houses, etc.

O'KEEFE, Marian K. 728'.09'7465
Norwich historic homes & families. Researched and written by Marian K. O'Keefe and Catherine Smith Doroshevich. Consultant editor: Philip A. Johnson. Photography by Marian K. O'Keefe. Published in cooperation with the Society of the Founders of Norwich. Stonington, Conn., Pequot Press [1967] viii, 112 p. illus., map (on lining papers) 24 cm. Bibliography: p. 109. [F104.N93O37] 66-30461
1. Norwich, Conn.—Historic houses, etc. 2. Norwich, Conn.—Biography. I. Doroshevich, Catherine Smith, joint author. II. Title.

Norwich, Eng.—Description—Views.

SHAW, Michael. 914.26'15
Norwich old and new / [compiled by] Michael Shaw ; [contemporary photographs by Cliff Middleton]. Wakefield : EP Publishing, 1974. [5], 99 p. : of ill. ; 18 x 24 cm. [DA690.N88S53] 75-310076 ISBN 0-7158-1059-6 : £1.95
1. Norwich, Eng.—Description—Views. I. Middleton, Cliff. II. Title.

Notre Dame, Ind. University—Photograph collections—Exhibitions.

GABRIEL, 745.6'7'094074017289 Astrik Ladislas, 1907-
The Ambrosiana Collection at the University of Notre Dame : the Frank M. Folsom Ambrosiana Microfilm and Photographic Collection, a project of the Samuel H. Kress Foundation : an exhibition of selected manuscript leaves and miniatures from the 9th to the 16th century, master drawings from the 15th to the 17th century, a photographic documentation : catalogue / by Astrik L. Gabriel. [Chicago] : Sears Bank and Trust Co., c1976. 64 p. : ill. (some col.) ; 26 cm. Exhibition of material from the Medieval Institute of the University of Notre Dame, held at the Sears Bank and Trust Co., Nov. 29, 1976-Jan. 28, 1977, and at the Art Gallery, University of Notre Dame, Apr. 17-June 12, 1977. [N4010.N67N673] 76-53846
1. Notre Dame, Ind. University—Photograph collections—Exhibitions. 2. Illumination of books and manuscripts—Exhibitions. 3. Miniature painting—Exhibitions. 4. Drawing, Renaissance—Exhibitions. 5. Drawing, Baroque—Exhibitions. I. Milan. Biblioteca ambrosiana. II. Sears Bank and Trust Company. III. Notre Dame, Ind. University. Mediaeval Institute. IV. Notre Dame, Ind. University. Art Gallery. V. Title.

Nottinghamshire — Historic houses, etc.

PEVSNER, Nikolaus, 1902- 720.942
Nottinghamshire. Harmondsworth, Middlesex, Penguin Books [1951] 248 p. illus., map. 19 cm. (The Buildings of England, BE 2) [NA969.N6P4] 51-12868
1. Nottinghamshire — Historic houses, etc. 2. Churches — England — Nottinghamshire. I. Title. II. Series.

Nowicki, Matthew, 1910-1950.

NOWICKI, Matthew, 1910- 720'.92'4 1950.
The writings and sketches of Matthew Nowicki. [Compiled by] Bruce Harold Schafer. Charlottesville, University Press of Virginia [1973] 58 p. illus. 23 cm. Bibliography: p. [57]-58. [NA737.N68S32] 73-88126 ISBN 0-8139-0533-8 12.50
1. Nowicki, Matthew, 1910-1950. I. Schafer, Bruce Harold, ed. II. Title.

Noyon, France. Notre-Dame (Cathedral)

SEYMOUR, Charles, 726'.6'094435 1912-
Notre-Dame of Noyon in the twelfth century; a study in the early development of gothic architecture New York, Norton [1968] xx, 202 p. illus., plans. 20 cm. (The Norton library, N464) Reprint of the 1939 ed. Includes bibliographical references. [NA5551.N6S4 1968] 77-683 2.95
1. Noyon, France. Notre-Dame (Cathedral) 2. Architecture, Gothic—Noyon, France. I. Title. **BIP**

Nude in art.

ARCHER, John F., 1946- 769'.973
Susohn : a personal journey / John F. Archer. San Diego, Calif. : Atavistic Press, 1976. 1 portfolio ([4] leaves of plates : 17 ill.) ; 23 cm. "Of an edition of 30, this is number 29." [NE2232.5.A72A57] 75-40290 ISBN 0-915718-01-4 : 150.00
1. Archer, John F., 1946- 2. Nude in art. 3. Women in art. I. Title. **BIP**

AYMAR, Brandt. 704.94'23
The young male figure: in paintings, sculptures, and drawings, from ancient Egypt to the present. New York, Crown Publishers [1970] vii, 247 p. illus. 29 cm. Bibliography: p. 238-244. [N7572.A9 1970] 78-127501 7.95
1. Nude in art. 2. Men in art. I. Title.

BROOKLYN 759.13'074'01471
Institute of Arts and Sciences. Museum. brooklyn 1961 unpaged. illus. 23cm. [ND205.B68] 61-66601
1. Nude in art. 2. Paintings, American—Exhibitions. I. Title.

CINOTTI, Mya. 731.84
The nude in sculpture. Translated by Helen Slonim. Novara, Uffici Press [195-] 64p. illus. 21cm. Translation of La donna nuda nella sculture. [NB1930.C553] 57-23169
1. Nude in art. 2. Sculpture. 3. Women in art. I. Title.

CLARK, Kenneth McKenzie, Sir 1903- 704.942
The nude; a study in ideal form. [New York] Pantheon Books [c1956] xxi, 458p. illus. 27cm. (Bollingen series, 35. The A. W. Mellon lectures in the fine arts, 2) Bibliography: p. 417-421. [N73.C55] 56-10423
1. Nude in art. I. Title. II. Series: Bollingen series, 35. Series: The A.W. Mellon lectures in the fine arts, 2

CLARK, Kenneth McKenzie, Baron Clark, 1903- 704.94'21
The nude; a study in ideal form [by] Kenneth Clark. [Princeton, N.J.] Princeton University Press [1972, c1956] xxi, 458 p. illus. 26 cm. (The A. W. Mellon lectures in the fine arts, 2) Bibliography: p. [415]-421. [N7570.C55 1972] 74-164124 ISBN 0-691-09792-5 6.95 (pbk.)
1. Nude in art. I. Title. II. Series. III. Bollingen series, 35

CLARK, Kenneth McKenzie, Baron Clark, 1903- 704.94'21
The nude; a study in ideal form, by Kenneth Clark. Garden City, N.Y., Doubleday Anchor Books, 1959 [c1956] 575 p. illus. 18 cm. (Bollingen series, no. 35. The A. W. Mellon lectures in the fine arts, 2) Bibliography: p. [524]-529. [N7572.C55] 74-175159
1. Nude in art. I. Title. II. Series: Bollingen series, no. 35. III. Series: The A. W. Mellon lectures in the fine arts, 2.

CORMACK, Malcolm. 760'.094
The nude in western art / selected & introduced by Malcolm Cormack. Oxford [Eng.] : Phaidon, 1976. 96 p. : chiefly ill. (some col.) ; 42 cm. Cover title: The nude. [N7572.C67] 76-366417 ISBN 0-7148-1668-X : pbk. : 7.95
1. Nude in art. I. Title. II. Title: The nude.
Distributed by Dutton.

D'AGUILAR, Paul, 1927- 743.4
Nudes. [1st Amer. ed. New York, Watson-Guptill 1966] 55p. illus. 18cm. (Watson-Guptill drawing bks.) Cover title: Drawing nudes. [NC765.D3 1966] 66-19737 1.00 pap.,
1. Nude in art. I. Title. II. Title: Drawing nudes.

DORF, Barbara. 751.4
Beginner's guide to painting the nude. [London] Pelham Books [1973] 170 p. illus. 23 cm. Label mounted on t.p.: Transatlantic Arts, Inc., Levittown, New York, sole distributor for the U.S.A. Includes bibliographies. [ND1290.5.D67 1973] 74-162979 ISBN 0-7207-0636-X 8.75 (U.S.)
1. Nude in art. 2. Painting—Technique. I. Title. BIP

GERDTS, William H. 704.94'21'0973
The great American nude; a history in art [by] William H. Gerdts. New York, Praeger [1974] 224 p. illus. (part col.) 29 cm. (American art & artists) Bibliography: p. 216-219. [N7574.4.G47] 72-88496 ISBN 0-275-43510-5 25.00
1. Nude in art. 2. Art, American—History. I. Title. II. Series.

GRAVES, Douglas R. 751.4'5
Figure painting in oil, by Douglas R. Graves. New York, Watson-Guptill Publications [1973] 158 p. illus. (part col.) 29 cm. Bibliography: p. 155. [ND1290.5.G72] 72-12676 ISBN 0-8230-1702-8 15.00
1. Nude in art. 2. Painting—Technique. I. Title.

HAMM, Glenn, 1936- 751.4
Painting the nude. New York, Van Nostrand Reinhold [1971] 144 p. illus. (part col.) 29 cm. (Art-in-practice series) [ND1290.7.H3] 70-163316
1. Nude in art. 2. Women in art. 3. Painting—Technique. I. Title.

KRUCKMAN, Herbert Lincoln, 1904- 743.4
The nude and modern art. New York, Citadel Press [1959] 186p. illus. 27cm. [N73.K7] 59-11135
1. Nude in art. 2. Art, Modern—20th cent. 3. Drawing—Instruction. I. Title.

MACHOTKA, Pavel. 704'.94'21
The nude / Pavel Machotka. London ; New York : Wiley, c1978. p. cm. "A Halsted Press book." [N7572.M28] 78-8515 ISBN 0-470-26426-8 : 17.50
1. Nude in art. 2. Art—Psychology. 3. Aesthetics—Physiological aspects. I. Title. BIP

PARRISH, Maxfield, 1870-1966. 741.9'73
"In the beginning" : twenty-five Maxfield Parrish drawings from the Men's Day Life Class at the Pennsylvania Academy of the Fine Arts, 1892-1894 / compiled by Virginia Hunt Reed. [s.l. : s.n., c1976] ([Hartford, Vt. : Imperial Printers]) ix, 25 p. : chiefly ill. ; 28 cm. Bibliography: p. ix. [NC139.P29R43] 77-355245 15.00
1. Parrish, Maxfield, 1870-1966. 2. Nude in art. I. Reed, Virginia Hunt. II. Pennsylvania Academy of the Fine Arts, Philadelphia. III. Title.

RAWLINGS, John. 779.2
100 studies of the figure. [New York, Studio Publications in association with Crowell, 1951] 96 p. illus. 32 cm. [N73.R3] 51-8544
1. Nude in art. 2. Anatomy, Artistic. I. Title.

RELOUGE, Josef Egon, ed. 757.2
Masterpieces of figure painting. Introd. by Bodo Cichy. [English translation by Mervyn Savill] New York, Viking Press [c1959] 262p. illus., col. plates. 29cm. (A Studio book) Translation of Gemalte Schonheit. [N7630.R413 1959a] 60-3798
1. Nude in art. 2. Women in art. 3. Paintings. I. Title.

SERRA, Francisco, 1912- 751.4
Painting the nude / [by] Francesc Serra, J. M. Parremon ; [translated from the Spanish]. Kings Langley : Fountain Press, 1976. 112 p. : chiefly ill. (some col.), ports. ; 26 cm. (Improve your painting and drawing ; no. 14) (Fountain art series) Translation of El desnudo al oleo. [ND1290.7.S4713] 77-361625 ISBN 0-85242-449-3 pbk. : 4.95
1. Nude in art. 2. Women in art. 3. Painting—Technique. I. Parramon, Jose Maria, joint author. II. Title.
Distributed by Camera Graphic, P.O. Box 1702, F.D.R. Sta., N.Y., N.Y. 10022

SHEPPARD, Joseph, 1930- 743'.43
Drawing the male figure / by Joseph Sheppard. New York : Watson-Guptill Publications, 1976. p. cm. Bibliography: p. [NC765.S44 1976] 76-22733 ISBN 0-8230-1405-3 : 14.95
1. Nude in art. 2. Men in art. 3. Drawing—Instruction. I. Title. BIP

ZAIDENBERG, Arthur, 1903- 741.4
Life class: studying the nude. New York, Bantam Books [1967] 1 v. (chiefly illus.) 18 cm. [NC760.Z33] 67-23526
1. Nude in art. I. Title.

Numbers in art.

BING, Ilse. 741.9'43
Numbers in images : illuminations of numerical meanings / by Ilse Bing. 1st ed. New York : Ilkon Press, 1976. [171] p. : ill. ; 24 x 32 cm. [NC251.B53A52] 76-5739 ISBN 0-916832-00-7 : 9.95
*1. Bing, Ilse. 2. Numbers in art. I. Title.*BIP

Numismatics.

AMERICAN Numismatic Society. 737.06273
The American Numismatic Society, 1858-1958, by Howard Adelson [staff member] New York, 1958. 390p. illus. 26cm. [C.J15.A63] 59-225
I. Adelson, Howard L. II. Title. BIP

BALE, Don, Jr. 737.4
Complete guide for profitable coin investing. Crescent Pub. Co. dist. Sioux Falls, S. Dak., Bale Bks., 2008 W. Madison c.1963 208p. illus., tables 22cm. Bibl. 64-49 3.95 pap., wire bdg.
1. Numismatics. I. Title. II. Title: Profitable coin investing. BIP

BALE, Don. 737.4
Complete guide for profitable coin investing and collecting. 2d ed. Sioux Falls, S.D., Bale Publications [1969] 210 p. illus. 22 cm. [CJ63.B3 1969] 70-7780 5.00
1. Numismatics. I. Title.

BOEHM, David Alfred, 1914- 737.4
Coin collecting, by Robert V. Masters, Fred Reinfeld. [Rev. ed.] New York, Sterling [1966,c.1964] 128p. illus. 21cm. (Worthwhile how-to paperbacks) First pub. in 1952 under title: Coinometry. [CJ89.B6 1964] 66-25208 1.95 bds.,
1. Numismatics. 2. Paper money. I. Reinfeld, Fred, 1910-1964, joint author. II. Title.

BOEHM, David Alfred, 1914- 737.4
Coin collecting, by Robert V. Masters [pseud.] and Fred Reinfeld. [Rev. ed.] New York, Sterling Pub. Co. [c.1958, 1960] 128p. illus. (Worthwhile how-to paperbacks, 401) First published in 1952 under title: Coinometry. 60-50988 1.00 pap.,
1. Numismatics. 2. Paper money. I. Reinfeld, Fred, 1910- joint author. II. Title.

BOEHM, David Alfred, 1914- 737.4
Coinometry; an instructive historical introduction to coins and currency for the young collector, by Robert V. Masters [pseud.] and Fred Reinfeld. Illustrated by Howard Simon. New York, Sterling Pub. Co., c1952. 93p. illus. 23x26cm. [CJ89.B6] 52-14418
1. Numismutics. 2. Paper money. I. Reinfeld, Fred, 1910- joint author. II. Title.

BOEHM, David Alfred, 1914- 737.4
Coinometry; an instructive historical introductions to coins and currency for the young collector, by Robert V. Masters and Fred Reinfeld. Illustrated by Howard Simon. [Rev. ed.] New York, Sterling Pub. Co.; distributed to the coin trade by President Coin Corp. [1965] 93 p. illus. 23 x 26 cm. [CJ89.B6 1965] 65-4703
1. Numismatics. 2. Paper money. I. Reinfeld, Fred, 1910-1964, joint author. II. Title.

BROWN, Laurence A 737.49
Coins through the ages. New York, Sterling Pub. Co. [1962, c1961] 185 p. illus. 20 cm. (Sterling collectors series) [CJ75.B7] 62-12591
1. Numismatics. I. Title.

CARSON, Robert Andrew Glindinning. 737.4
Coins of the world. New York, Harper [1962] xiii, 642 p. 64 plates. 24 cm. Bibliography: p. 571-586. [CJ75.C3] 62-15732
1. Numismatics. I. Title. BIP

GRIERSON, Philip. 737.4
Numismatics / Philip Grierson. London ; New York : Oxford University Press, 1975. viii, 211 p. : ill. ; 21 cm. (A Galaxy book ; GB 440) Includes index. Bibliography: p. [201]-203. [CJ75.G74] 75-323282 ISBN 0-19-885098-0 11.95 ISBN 0-19-888098-7 pbk. : 4.95
1. Numismatics. I. Title. BIP

GRYZEWSKI, Tadeusz. 769'.569438
The stamps and postal service of the first Polish Corps in Russia / by Tadeusz Gryzewski ; translation by Elizabeth Gobby. [Chicago : Polonus Philatelic Society, 1977] 37 p. : ill. ; 28 cm. (Polonus handbook) On cover: The occupation of Russia by the Polish I Corps. Includes bibliographical references and index. [UH85.P7G7813] 77-153542
1. Poland. Armia. 1. Korpus—Postal service. I. Polonus Philatelic Society. II. Title. III. Title: The occupation of Russia by the Polish I Corps. IV. Series.

HARTMAN, Dennis, 1894- 737.4
The coin story; [collectors handbook] Los Angeles, American Press [c1966] 216 p. 24 cm. Bibliography: p. 131-216. [CJ81.H3] 67-1349
1. Numismatics. I. Title.

KOPKIN, Stanley 737.4
Paths to wealth through coin investments, by Stanley Kopkin, Eric W. Roberts. Rev. ed. Lynbrook, N. Y., World-Wide Numismatic [1965] 153p. illus. 23cm. [CJ75.K6] 65-3597 price unreported
1. Numismatics. I. Roberts, Eric W., joint author. II. Title.

LANE-POOLE, Stanley, 1854-1931 ed. 737
Coins and medals; their place in history and art, by the authors of the British Museum official catalogues, Reginald Stuart Poole [others] Chicago, Argonaut, 1968. 156p. illus. 25cm. (Argonaut lib. of antiquities) Reissue, with new typesetting of the 1885 ed. [CJ75.L3 1968] 66-19182 10.00
1. Numismatics. 2. Medals. I. Poole, Reginald Stuart, 1832-1895. II. Title.
Contents Omitted.

LAZENBY, Ruth Williams, 1934- 737.4
Coins for profit, by R. W. West [pseud.] Charlotte, N. C., Imperial Pub. Co. [1962] 56p. 21cm. [CJ85.L3] 62-2849
1. Numismatics. I. Title.

MACDONALD, George, Sir, 1862-1940. 737.4
Coin types; their origin and development. [1st American ed.] Chicago, Argonaut, 1969. x, 275 p. illus. 24 cm. "Unchanged reprint of the edition: Glasgow, 1905." Contains lectures delivered on the invitation of the Council of the Society of Antiquaries of Scotland. Includes bibliographical references. [CJ129.M2 1969] 67-17581
1. Numismatics. I. Title. BIP

MACKAY, James Alexander. 737
Value in coins and medals [by] James A. Mackay. [1st American ed.] New York, Transatlantic Arts [1969, c1968] 224 p. 12 plates. 23 cm. [CJ89.M3 1969] 77-4449
1. Numismatics. I. Title. BIP

RAWLINGS, Gertrude Burford. 737
Ancient, medieval, modern coins and how to know them [by] G. B. Rawlings. [1st American ed.] Chicago, Ammon Press, 1966. xix, 360 p. plates. 22 cm. First published in 1908 under title: Coins and how to know them. Bibliography: p. [337]-338. [CJ81.R2 1966] 66-19186
1. Numismatics. I. Title.

*SLABAUGH, Arlie R. 737.4'9'73
United States commemorative coins; the drama of America as told by our coins, by Arlie R. Slabaugh. 2nd ed. Racine, Wis., Whitman Coin Products, 1975. 160 p. ill. 20 cm. [CJ1845] ISBN 0-307-09377-8 4.00.
1. Numismatics. 2. Coins, American. I. Title.

SUTHERLAND, Carol Humphrey Vivian. v. 12
Art in coinage; the aesthetics of money from Greece to the present day. New York, Philosophical Library [1956] 223p. illus., ports. 23cm. 'Some notes on books and public collections': p. 210-212. [CJ151.S] A 56
1. Numismatics. I. Title.

Numismatics—Addresses, essays, lectures.

AMERICAN Numismatic Society. 737.4082
Centennial publication. Edited by Harald Ingholt. New York, 1958. xii, 712p. 53 plates. 29cm. Errata slip inserted. [CU35.A5] 58-14826
1. Numismatics— Addresses, essays, lectures. I. Jugholt, Harald, 1896- ed. II. Title.

THE Numismatist. 737.4082
Selections from the Numismatist: modern foreign currency, by American Numismatic Association. Reprint Advisory Committee: James W. Curtis [and others] Racine, Wis., Whitman Pub. Co., c1961. 320p. illus. 24cm. (The Numismatist reprint series) [CJ1747.N8] 61-1813
1. Numismatics—Addresses, essays, lectures. I. American Numismatic

SUBJECT INDEX NUMISMATICS—COLLECTORS AND COLLECTING.

Association. II. Title. III. Title: Modern foreign currency.

NUMISMATIST, (The) 737.4082
Selections from the Numismatist: Modern foreign currency. by the American Numismatic Association. Reprint advisory committee. Racine, Wis., Whitman Pub. Co., c.1961. 320p. illus. (Numismatist reprint series) 61-1813 3.75
1. Numismatics—Addresses, essays, lectures. I. American Numismatic Association. II. Title.

Numismatics—Aenus, Greece.

MAY, John Maunsell 737.4
Frampton.
Ainos, its history and coinage, 474-341 B. C. London, Oxford University Press, 1950. xvi, 288 p. plates, maps. 23 cm. (Oxford classical & philosophical monographs) Bibliographical footnotes. [CJ559.A3M3] 50-9101
1. Numismatics—Aenus, Greece. 2. Coins, Greek. Aenus, Greece—Hist. I. Title.

Numismatics—Africa.

DAVENPORT, John Stewart, 737.4
1907-
The dollars of Africa, Asia, & Oceania [by] John S. Davenport. Galesburg, Ill., 1969. 208 p. illus. 24 cm. "Valuations, May 1969" ([2] p.) inserted. Bibliography: p. 208. [CJ1529.D3] 76-7369
1. Numismatics—Africa. 2. Numismatics—Asia. 3. Numismatics—Oceanica. 4. Counterstamp (Numismatics) I. Title.

Numismatics—Africa, North.

HAZARD, Harry W 737.4
The numismatic history of late medieval North Africa. New York, American Numismatic Society, 1952. 377p. 8 plates, fold. map. 28cm. (Numismatic studies, no. 8) 'An early version of this study, without corpus or indices, was accepted by Princeton University ... for the doctoral degree in oriental languages and literatures. The present volume has been drastically revised and completely rewritten.' 'Corrigenda and addenda': [4] p. inserted. Bibliography: p. [286]-306. [CJ3914.H3] 53-5759
1. Numismatics—Africa, North. I. Title. II. Series.

Numismatics, Ancient.

LAING, Lloyd Robert. 737.4'3
Coins and archaeology [by] Lloyd R. Laing. New York, Schocken Books [1970, c1969] xvi, 336 p. illus., maps. 23 cm. Bibliography: p. [300]-326. [CJ233.L3 1970] 75-97253 9.50
1. Numismatics, Ancient. I. Title.

THE Numismatist. 737.493
Selections from the Numismatist: ancient and medieval coins. By American Numismatic Association. Reprint Advisory Committee, Ancient and Medieval Coins: James W. Curtis [and others] Reprint Pub. Committee: P. K. Anderson [and others] Racine, Wis., Whitman Pub. Co., c1960. 318p. illus. 24cm. (The Numismatist reprint series) [CJ233.N8] 61-1163
1. Numismatics, Ancient. 2. Numismatics, Medieval. I. American Numismatic Association. II. Title. III. Title: Ancient and medieval coins.

NUMISMATIST, (The) 737.493
Selections from the Numismatist: Ancient and medieval coins. by the American Numismatic Association. Reprint advisory committee. Racine, Wis., Whitman Pub. Co., c.1960. 318p. illus. (Numismatist reprint series) 61-1163 3.75
1. Numismatics, Ancient. 2. Numismatics, Medieval. I. American Numismatic Association. II. Title.

REGLING, Kurt Ludwig, 737.49'37
1876-1935.
Ancient numismatics; the coinage of ancient Greece and Rome. Translation by Terry Merz. Chicago, Argonaut Inc., 1969. 79 p. 22 cm. (The Argonaut library of antiquities) Translation of Munzkunde from Einleitung in die Altertumswissenschaft, edited by Alfred Gercke and Eduard Norden (II. Band, 2. Heft), published in 1930. Includes bibliographical references. [CJ233.R43] 65-26122
1. Numismatics, Ancient. I. Title.

WEAR, Ted Graham, 1902- 737.4938
Ancient coins; how to collect for fun and profit [by] Ted G. Wear. [1st ed.] Garden City, N.Y., Doubleday, 1965. viii, 152 p. illus. 22 cm. [CJ237.W4] 65-11052
1. Numismatics, Ancient. I. Title.

Numismatics—Arabia.

HILL, George Francis, 737.49'39'4
Sir, 1867-1948.
The ancient coinage of southern Arabia. Chicago, Argonaut, 1969. 28 p. illus. 23 cm. "Reprint of the 1915 Edition (Proc. Brit. Acad. vol. vii, 1915)." Bibliographical footnotes. [CJ3474] 78-6470
1. Numismatics—Arabia. I. Title.

Numismatics, Arabic.

MILES, George Carpenter, 737.4
1904-
The coinage of the Umayyads of Spain Published in cooperation with the Hispanic Society of America. New York, American Numismatic Society, 1950. 2 v. (xi, 591 p.) plates 23 cm. (Hispanic numismatic series, monograph no. 1) [CJ3194.M5] 51-1466
1. Numismatics, Arabic. 2. Numismatics-Spain. 3. Omayyade in Spain. I. Title. II. Series.

Numismatics—Armenia.

BEDOUKIAN, Paul Z. 737.49566
Coinage of Cilician Armenia. New York, Amer. Numismatic, 1962. xxxi, 494p. illus., map. 23cm. (Numismatic notes and monographs, no. 147) Bibl. 62-52595 15.00 pap.,
1. Numismatics—Armenia. I. Title. II. Series.

Numismatics — Athens.

THE new style silver 737.49385
coinage of Athens. by Margaret Thompson. New York, American Numismatic Society, 1961. 2 v. plates. 28 cm. (Numismatic studies, no. 10) Contents.v. 1. Text. -- v. 2. Plates. [CJ359.T45] 62-3776
1. Numismatics — Athens. **BIP**

Numismatics—Australia.

HANLEY, Tom 737.4994
Collecting Australian coins [by] Tom Hanley. Bill James. Sydney, Murray [1966] 223p. illus., ports. 24cm. [CJ4406.H3] 66-75789 6.95 bds.,
1. Numismatics—Australia. I. James, Bill joint author. II. Title.
Available from Tri-Ocean, San Francisco.

Numismatics—Bibliography.

ATTINELLI, Emanuel J. 016.737
A bibliography of American numismatic auction catalogues, 1828-1875 / Emmanuel Joseph Attinelli Lawrence, Mass. : Quarterman Publications, [1976] vi, 149 p. ; 24 cm. Originally published under title: Numisgraphics. Reprint of the 1876 ed. published in New York, with new foreword and price guide. Includes index. [Z6866.A88 1976] [CJ47] 75-32394 ISBN 0-88000-072-4 : 20.00
1. Numismatics—Bibliography. 2. Coins—Bibliography. 3. Numismatics—United States—Bibliography. 4. Coins, American—Bibliography. I. Title. **BIP**

Numismatics—Bibliography—Catalogs.

†AMERICAN Numismatic 016.737
Association. Library.
Library catalogue of the American Numismatic Association / Geneva Karlson. 2d ed. Colorado Springs, Colo. : The Association, c1977. xlii, 768 p. ; 23 cm. Includes index. [Z6870.A48 1977] [CJ76] 77-93078 ISBN 0-89637-000-3 : 25.00
1. American Numismatic Association. Library. 2. Numismatics—Bibliography—Catalogs. I. Karlson, Geneva. II. Title. **BIP**

AMERICAN Numismatic 016.737
Society. Library.
Dictionary catalogue of the Library of the American Numismatic Society. Boston : G. K. Hall, 1962. 6 v. (5194 p.) ; 36 cm. [Z6870.A52 1962a] [CJ59] 76-356280
1. American Numismatic Society. Library. 2. Numismatics—Bibliography—Catalogs. I. Title.

Numismatics—Byzantine Empire.

BRITISH Museum. Dept. 737.094961
of Coins and Medals.
Imperial Byzantine coins in the British Museum, by Warwick Wroth, assistant-keeper of the coins and medals. [1st American ed.] Chicago, Argonaut Publishers, 1966. 2 v. in 1 (cxii, 683 p.) 79 plates. 25 cm. First published in 1908 under title: Catalogue of the Imperial Byzantine coins in the British Museum. [CJ1215.B72 1966] 66-19329
1. Numismatics — Byzantine Empire. I. Wroth, Warwick William, 1858-1911. II. Title.

HENDY, Michael F. 731.49'495
Coinage and money in the Byzantine Empire, 1081-1261, by Michael F. Hendy. Washington, Dumbarton Oaks Center for Byzantine Studies, trustees for Harvard University; [distributed by J. J. Augustin, Locust Valley, N.Y.] 1969. xviii, 453 p. 3 fold. illus., 2 fold. maps, 51 plates. 30 cm. (Dumbarton Oaks studies, 12) Bibliography: p. xiii-xvii. [CJ1229.H44] 72-16909 20.00
1. Numismatics—Byzantine Empire. 2. Coins, Byzantine. I. Title. II. Series.

WHITTING, Philip D. 737.4'9'495
Byzantine coins, by P. D. Whitting. New York, Putnam [1973] 311 p. illus. 25 cm. (The World of numismatics) Errata slip inserted. [CJ1229.W53 1973] 73-76714 ISBN 0-399-11028-3 25.00
1. Numismatics—Byzantine Empire. 2. Coins, Byzantine. I. Title. II. Series.

Numismatics—California.

BURNIE, Robert Harry, 737.42
1916-
Small California and territorial gold coins: quarter dollars, half dollars, dollars. [Pascagoula? Miss., 1955] 96p. 30cm. Based on California gold quarters-Halves-dollars. by E. M. Lee. [CJ1848.C3B8] 55-37497
1. Numismatics- California. I. Lee, Edward Melvin, 1871- California gold quarters-halves-Dollars. II. Title.

LEE, Kenneth W. 737.4
California gold dollars, half dollars, quarter dollars; a descriptive listing of the varieties of fractional issues in the personal collection of the author, plus a few additions noted and examined by the author, by Kenneth W. Lee. [Los Angeles, University Press, 1970] xii, 138 p. 23 cm. [CJ1848.C3L43] 79-249906
1. Numismatics—California. I. Title.

Numismatics - Canada - Collectors and collecting.

*DUSHNICK, Stephan E. 737.4'9'71
Silver and nickel dollars of Canada : 1911 to date / by Stephan E. Dushnick. First ed. Hicksville, NY : Brooks Pub. Co., 1978. 171p. : ill., photos ; 24 cm. Bibliography: p. 171. [CJ1869] 9.50
1. Numismatics — Canada — Collectors and collecting. 2. Coins, Canadian. I. Title.
Publishers address: P.O. Box 70 31 Maple Place, Hicksville, N.Y. 11802.

Numismatics—Caulonia, Italy.

NOE, Sydney Philip. 737.49377
The coinage of Caulonia. [Catalogue] New York, American Numismatic Society, 1958. 62p. 20 plates. 28cm. (Numismatic studies, no. 9) Bibliographical footnotes. [CJ526.C3N6] 59-16277
1. Numismatics—Caulonia, Italy. I. Title. II. Series.

Numismatics—Ceylon.

LAPA, Frank A. 737.49'5493
Kandy kings of Ceylon, 1055-1295 A.D. [by]Frank A Lapa [Beverly Hills, Calif., 1968] 44 p. illus. 22 cm. Bibliography: p. 43. [CJ3551.L3] 78-958
1. Numismatics—Ceylon. I. Title.

Numismatics—China—Bibliography.

COOLE, Arthur 016.7374'9'51 s
Braddan, 1900-
A bibliography on Far Eastern numismatology and a coin index, by Arthur Braddan Coole, assisted by Hitoshi Kozono [and] Howard F. Bowker. [1st ed. Denver, 1967] viii, 581 p. ports. 24 cm. (His An encyclopedia of Chinese coins, v. 1) [CJ3496.C62 vol. 1] [Z6869.C5] 016.7374'9'5 73-160585
1. Numismatics—China—Bibliography. 2. Numismatics—East (Far East)—Bibliography. 3. Coins, Chinese. 4. Coins, Oriental. I. Kozono, Hitoshi. II. Bowker, Howard Franklin. III. Title. IV. Series.

Numismatics—Collectors and collecting.

ABBOTT, John J. 332.678
Fell's guide to investing in United States and foreign coins. New York, Fell [c.1965] 161p. 20cm. Bibl. [CJ101.A33] 65-15498 3.95 bds.,
1. Numismatics—Collectors and collecting. I. Title. II. Title: Guide to investing in United States and foreign coins.

ANGUS, Ian. 737.4'09
Fell's guide to coins and money tokens of the world. New York, F. Fell Publishers [1974, c1973] 128 p. illus. 27 cm. First published in 1973 under title: Coins and money tokens. Bibliography: p. 125. [CJ89.A54 1974] 74-75383 ISBN 0-8119-0237-4 8.95
1. Numismatics—Collectors and collecting. 2. Tokens. I. Title. II. Title: Guide to coins and money tokens of the world. **BIP**

BAUSHER, Jess 737.4075
'Its only money!' A comedy of errors: an illustrated reference and price guide for major mint errors. token errors. Canadian errors. foreign errors, by Jess Bausher. Charles Dolan. [Birdsboro. Pa., Numismatic Enterprises. 1966] ix, 291p. illus. 24cm. [CJ101.B3] 66-7641 8.75
1. Numismatics—Collectors and collecting. I. Dolan, Charles V., joint author. II. Title.

BERSON, Fred. 737.49'73
Secrets of a professional coin dealer, by Fred Berson and Abner Berson. New York, F. Fell [1967] v, 153 p. illus. 22 cm. [CJ1832.B4 1967] 67-4457
1. Numismatics—Collectors and collecting. I. Berson, Abner, 1946- joint author. II. Title. **BIP**

BERSON, Fred. 737.4973
Secrets of a professional coin dealer, by Fred Berson and Abner Berson. New York, Pocket Books [1966] v, 153 p. illus. 21 cm. (A PB special) [CJ1832.B4] 66-23511
1. Numismatics—Collectors and collecting. I. Berson, Abner, 1946- joint author. II. Title.

BRESSETT, Kenneth E. 737.4075
Let's collect coins; an introduction to a fascinating hobby, with price guide of valuable coins. Racine, Wis., Whitman Pub., c.1966. 64p. illus. 20cm. [CJ89.B66] 66-4544 .50 pap.,
1. Numismatics—Collectors and collecting. I. Title.

BRESSETT, Kenneth E. 737.4'075
Let's collect coins; an introduction to a fascinating hobby, with price guide of valuable coins, by Ken Bressett. Racine, Wis., Whitman Pub. Co., 1967. 64 p. illus. 20 cm. [CJ89.B66 1967] 68-2006
1. Numismatics—Collectors and collecting. I. Title.

BRESSETT, Kenneth E. 737.4'075
Let's collect coins : an introduction to a fascinating hobby, with price guide of valuable coins / by Ken Bressett. Racine, Wis. : Western Pub. Co., c1976. 64 p. : ill.

; 20 cm. [CJ89.B66 1976] 76-6208 ISBN 0-307-09380-8 pbk. : 0.75
1. Numismatics—Collectors and collecting. I. Title.

COFFIN, Joseph, 1899- 737.4075
The complete book of coin collecting. New York, Coward-McCann [1959] 251 p. illus. 21 cm. Completely rev. and expanded ed. of the author's Coin collecting. [CJ81.C6 1959] 59-11009
1. Numismatics—Collectors and collecting. I. Title. II. Title: Coin collecting.

COFFIN, Joseph, 1899- 737.4'075
The complete book of coin collecting / Joseph Coffin. 6th rev. ed. New York : Coward, McCann & Geoghegan, 1979. p. cm. Bibliography: p. [CJ81.C6 1979] 78-10529 ISBN 0-698-10954-6 : 8.95
1. Numismatics—Collectors and collecting. I. Title.

COFFIN, Joseph, 1899- 737.4'075
The complete book of coin collecting. 2d rev. ed. New York, Coward-McCann [1967] 251 p. illus. 21 cm. First published in 1938 under title: Coin collecting. Includes bibliographies. [CJ81.C6] 67-21506
1. Numismatics—Collectors and collecting. I. Title. II. Title: Coin collecting.

COFFIN, Joseph, 1899- 737.4'075
The complete book of coin collecting / Joseph Coffin. 5th rev. ed. New York : Coward, McCann & Geoghegan, 1976. 251 p., [8] leaves of plates : ill. ; 21 cm. Includes bibliographies. [CJ81.C6 1976] 75-40409 ISBN 0-698-10738-1 : 7.95
1. Numismatics—Collectors and collecting. I. Title.

COIN collectors' guide 737.4075
(old coins for profit) the complete guide to old coin collecting, includes catalog and price list of United States coins. 1960-62 ed. Harriman, Tenn., Pioneer Press [c.1960] 76p. illus. 23cm. Vols. for (1958-59--1960-62) prepared by Deane Sears [pseud.] and Martin Rywell. 58-11077 1.50 pap.,
1. Numismatics—Collectors and collecting. I. Rywell, Martin.

FORRER, Leonard Steyning. 737.4
The art of collecting coins; a practical guide to numismatics. Foreword by C. H. V. Sutherland. New York, Citadel Press, 1955. 183p. 16 plates. 22cm. Bibliography: p. 157-183. [CJ75] 55-4247
1. Numismatics—Collectors and collecting. I. Title.

FORTUNE RESEARCH, New York. 737.4
Money-making report. [New York? 1964] 71 p. illus. 29 cm. Cover title: Report. [CJ1832.F65] 64-5603
1. Numismatics — Collectors and collecting. 2. Coins, American. I. Title.

FRANK, Charles. 737.4075
Coin preservation handbook. 1st ed. [Brooklyn] Coingard Industries, 1964. xx, 135 p. illus., maps. 21 cm. Bibliography: p. 134-135. [CJ101.F7] 64-20863
1. Numismatics—Collectors and collecting. I. Title.

GOULD, Maurice M. 737.4'075
Gould's gold and silver guide to coins [by] Maurice M. Gould. New York, Fleet Press Corp. [1969] 255 p. illus. 21 cm. [CJ36.G6] 70-76025 8.95
1. Numismatics—Collectors and collecting. I. Title. II. Title: Gold and silver guide to coins. BIP

*HENDIN, David. 737.4'075
Collecting coins / by David Hendin. New York : New American Library, 1978. 170p. : ill. ; 18 cm. Includes index. [CJ89] ISBN 0-451-08405-5 pbk. : 1.95
1. Numismatics — Collectors and collecting. I. Title.

HOBSON, Burton. 737.4'075
Coins you can collect. New and rev. ed. New York, Hawthorn Books [1970] 128 p. illus. 24 cm. [CJ89.H58 1970] 79-113192 4.95
1. Numismatics—Collectors and collecting. I. Title.

HOBSON, Burton. 737.4'075
Coins you can collect. [1st ed.] New York, Hawthorn Books [1967] 128 p. illus. 24 cm. (Action books for today's young people) [CJ89.H58] 66-15359
1. Numismatics—Collectors and collecting. I. Title.

HOBSON, Burton 737.4075
Getting started in coin collecting. New York, Sterling [c.1961] 124p. illus. 61-15852 2.50
1. Numismatics—Collectors and collecting. I. Title.

HOBSON, Burton 737.4075
Getting started in coin collecting. New York, Cornerstone Lib., dist. to the coin trade by President Coin Corp. [1962, c.1961] 124p. illus. 21cm. (CN36) 1.00 pap.,
1. Numismatics—Collectors and collecting. I. Title.

HOBSON, Burton. 737.4'075
Getting started in coin collecting. [Rev. ed.] New York, Sterling Pub. Co.; distributed to the coin trade by President Coin Corp. [1967] 124 p. illus. 21 cm. [CJ89.H6 1967] 67-3283
1. Numismatics—Collectors and collecting. I. Title.

HOBSON, Burton. 737.4'075
Getting started in coin collecting. [Rev. ed.] New York, Sterling Pub. Co.; distributed to the coin trade by President Coin Corp. [1969] 124 p. illus. 21 cm. [CJ89.H6 1969] 70-13629
1. Numismatics—Collectors and collecting. I. Title.

HOBSON, Burton. 737.4'075
Pictorial guide to coin conditions, by Burton Hobson and Fred Reinfeld. [Rev. and] enl. ed. Garden City, N.Y., Doubleday [1968] 160 p. illus. 21 cm. [CJ101.H6 1968] 68-5032
1. Numismatics—Collectors and collecting. I. Reinfeld, Fred, 1910-1964, joint author. II. Title. III. Title: Coin conditions.

HOBSON, Burton. 737.4075
Pictorial guide to coin conditions, by Burton Hobson and Fred Reinfeld. New York, Sterling Pub. Co.; distributed to the coin trade by President Coin Corp. [1962] 128 p. illus. 17 cm. [CJ101.H6] 62-12605
1. Numismatics—Collectors and collecting. I. Reinfeld, Fred, 1910- joint author. II. Title: Coin conditions.

HOLZER, Hans W., 1920- 737.4'075
Collectors' guidebook to coins, by Hans Holzer. New York, Maco Pub. Co., c1967. 128 p. illus., maps. 24 cm. [CJ63.H6 1967] 70-2942 0.95
1. Numismatics—Collectors and collecting. I. Title.

HOLZER, Hans W 1920- 737.4075
Collectors' guidebook to coins, by Hans Holzer. New York, Simon and Schuster, 1965. 128 p. illus., maps. 25 cm. "A Maco publications book." [CJ63.H6] 65-23601
1. Numismatics — Collectors and collecting. I. Title.

HOLZER, Hans W., 1920- 737.4075
Collectors' guidebook to coins; how and why to collect, stories behind famous, valuable coins of the world, all American denominations [New York, Maco Mag., 1965] 128p. illus. 24cm. Cover title [CJ63.H6] 65-2877 .75 pap.,
1. Numismatics—Collectors and collecting. I. Title.

HOOD, Clyde. 737.4075
Numistic authority. [Mattoon, ill., Numistic Authority Publ Co. [1965] 61 p. illus. 20 cm. [CJ1832.H6] 65-9796
1. Numismatics — Collectors and collecting. 2. Coins, American. I. Title.

HUMPHREYS, Henry Noel, 737.4
1810-1879.
The coin collector's manual, or, guide to the numismatic student in the formation of a cabinet of coins: comprising an historical and critical account of the origin and progress of coinage, from the earliest period to the fall of the Roman Empire; with some account of the coinages of modern Europe, more especially of Great Britain. Detroit, Gale Research Co., 1971. 2 v. illus. 23 cm. (Bohn's illustrated library) Reprint of the 1853 ed. [CJ81.H8 1971] 74-124584
1. Numismatics—Collectors and collecting. I. Title.

JACOBS, Saul. 737.4'075
Collecting coins. New York, Grosset & Dunlap [1968] 82 p. illus. 21 cm. [CJ89.J33] 68-12748
1. Numismatics—Collectors and collecting. I. Title.

JOACHIM, E. E. 737.4'075
Coins beautiful, by E. E. Joachim. Photography by Shirley Hecht. Atlanta, Capitol Press; distributed by International Import Co., Stone Mountain, Ga. [1968] 100 l. illus. 22 cm. Includes bibliographical references. [CJ101.J6] 68-57173
1. Numismatics—Collectors and collecting. I. Title.

LINECAR, Howard W. A. 737.4/075
Beginner's guide to coin collecting, [by] Howard Linecar. London, Pelham, 1966. 159p. 16 plates. 22cm. Bibl. [CJ89.L48] 67-86617 6.95 bds.,
1. Numismatics—Collectors and collecting. I. Title.
American distributor: Transatlantic, Levittown, N.Y. BIP

LINECAR, Howard W. A. 737.4'09
Coins and coin collecting [by] Howard Linecar. Feltham, New York, Hamlyn, 1971. 2-143 p. illus. (some col.), facsim., maps (some col.), ports. 29 cm. Bibliography: p. 136-137. [CJ89.L53 1971] 73-161840 ISBN 0-600-31605-X £1.75
1. Numismatics—Collectors and collecting. 2. Numismatics—History. I. Title.

MILNE, Joseph Grafton, 737.4
1867-
Coin collecting, by J. G. Milne, C. H. V. Sutherland and J. D. A. Thompson. [London] Oxford University Press [1950] xii, 152 p. 44 plates. 21 cm. Bibliography: p. 133-134. [CJ81.M6] 50-10599
1. Numismatics — Collectors and collecting. I. Title.

PAPPAS, James G 737.4075
Know about coin collecting, by James G. Pappas. [1st ed.] New Augusta, Ind., Editors and Engineers [1965] 96 p. illus. 18 cm. (Skillfact library, 630) [CJ89.P3] 65-27954
1. Numismatics — Collectors and collecting. I. Title.

REINFELD, Fred, 1910- 737.4075
How to build a coin collection [Rev. by Burton Hobson] New York, Sterling [c.1958-1966] 127p. illus. 21cm. [CJ81.R4] 58-12544 2.95; 2.99 lib. ed.,
1. Numismatics—Collectors and collecting. I. Title. BIP

REINFELD, Fred, 1910- 737.4'075
1964.
How to build a coin collection. Revised by Burton Hobson. [Rev. ed.] New York, Collier Books [1973] 157 p. illus. 20 cm. [CJ81.R4] 54-3453 1.95 (pbk.)
1. Numismatics—Collectors and collecting. I. Title.

REINFELD, Fred, 1910- 737.4075
1964.
How to build a coin collection. [Rev. ed.] New York, Sterling Pub. Co. [1966] 159 p. illus. 21 cm. "Revised by Burton Hobson." [CJ81.R4 1966] 66-4622
1. Numismatics—Collectors and collecting. I. Hobson, Burton. II. Title.

REINFELD, Fred, 1910- 737.4075
1964
How to build a coin collection. Rev. ed. New York, Barnes & Noble, 1965[c.1958-1965] 159p. illus. 21cm. (Everyday handbks.; educational paperbacks, no.208) [CJ81.R4] 65-8822 1.50 pap.,
1. Numismatics—Collectors and collecting. I. Title.

REINFELD, Fred, 1910- 737.4'075
1964.
How to build a coin collection, by Fred Reinfeld. Rev. by Burton Hobson. New York, Sterling Pub. Co. [1970] 159 p. illus. 21 cm. [CJ81.R4 1970] 70-19869 ISBN 0-8069-6006-X
1. Numismatics—Collectors and collecting. I. Hobson, Burton. II. Title.

REINFELD, Fred, 1910- 737.4'075
1964.
How to build a coin collection, by Fred Reinfeld. Rev. by Burton Hobson. [Rev. ed.] New York, Sterling Pub. Co. [1972] 159 p. illus. 20 cm. [CJ81.R4 1972] 72-188378 ISBN 0-8069-6006-X
1. Numismatics—Collectors and collecting. I. Hobson, Burton. II. Title.

REINFELD, Fred, 1910- 737.4'075
1964.
How to build a coin collection [by] Fred Reinfeld. Rev. by Burton Hobson. [Rev. ed.] New York, Collier Books [1973] 159 p. illus. 21 cm. [CJ81.R4 1973] 73-175440 1.50 (pbk.)
1. Numismatics—Collectors and collecting. I. Hobson, Burton. II. Title.

REINFELD, Fred, 1910- 737.4'075
1964.
How to build a coin collection / by Fred Reinfeld ; rev. by Burton Hobson. Rev. ed. New York : Sterling Pub. Co., c1977. 159 p. : ill. ; 21 cm. Includes index. [CJ81.R4 1977] 77-152197 ISBN 0-8069-6007-8 : 4.95
1. Numismatics—Collectors and collecting. I. Hobson, Burton. II. Title.

REINFELD, Fred, 1910- 737.4'075
1964.
How to build a coin collection, by Fred Reinfeld. Rev. by Burton Hobson. [Rev. ed.] New York, Sterling Pub. Co.; distributed to the coin trade by President Coin Corp. [1973] 159 p. illus. 21 cm. [CJ81.R4 1973] 74-162865 ISBN 0-8069-6006-X. 3.95
1. Numismatics—Collectors and collecting. I. Hobson, Burton. II. Title.
Library binding 3.99, ISBN 0-8069-6007-8.

REIT, Seymour. 737.4075
Coins and coin collecting. Illustrated by W. T. Mars. New York, Golden Press [1965] 105 p. illus. (part col.) 28 cm. [CJ85.R4] 65-22521
1. Numismatics — Collectors and collecting. I. Title.

THOMAS, E. P. 737.4973
The ABC's of coin investing. Gardena, Calif., Payne Pub. Co. 16408 South Bway [c.1965] 86p. illus., map. 22cm. [CJ63.T5] 65-5722 2.50 pap.,
1. Numismatics—Collectors and collecting. I. Title.

WEAR, Ted Graham, 1902- 737.4075
Coin collecting in a nutshell. [1st ed.] Garden City, N.Y., Doubleday, 1963. 144 p. illus. 22 cm. [CJ89.W4] 63-16630
1. Numismatics—Collectors and collecting. I. Title.

ZIMMERMAN, Walter J., 737.4'075
1910-
The coin collector's fact book, by Walter J. Zimmerman. New York, Arco [1974] 135 p. illus. 25 cm. Bibliography: p. 9-11. [CJ81.Z55] 73-77839 ISBN 0-668-02991-9 5.95
1. Numismatics—Collectors and collecting. I. Title. BIP

Numismatics—Collectors and collecting—Juvenile literature.

BRESSETT, Kenneth E. 081 s
Coin collecting / by Kenneth Bressett. Rev. ed. North Brunswick, N.J. : Boy Scouts of America, 1975. 32 p. : ill. ; 21 cm. (Merit badge series ; no. 3390) Bibliography: p. 32. A handbook for earning the Boy Scout merit badge in coin collecting. [HS3313.Z95C6 1975] [CJ89] 737.4'075 76-356777 ISBN 0-8395-3390-X
1. Numismatics—Collectors and collecting—Juvenile literature. I. Title. II. Series: Boy Scouts of America. Merit badge series ; no. 3390.

BURTON, Hobson. 737.4'075
Coin collecting as a hobby. Enl. & rev. ed. New York, Sterling Pub. Co. [1972] 175 p. illus. 20 cm. (Coin and stamp books) [CJ89.B56] 67-27759 ISBN 0-8069-6018-3 3.50;
1. Numismatics—Collectors and collecting—Juvenile literature. I. Title.
lib. ed., 3.99 ISBN 0-8069-6019-1

HOBSON, Burton. 737.4'075
Coin collecting as a hobby. New York,

Sterling Pub. Co. [1967] 128 p. illus. 21 cm. [CJ89.H56] 67-27759
1. Numismatics — Collectors and collecting — Juvenile literature. I. Title.

HOBSON, Burton. 737.4'075
Coin collecting as a hobby / by Burton Hobson. Enl. and rev. ed. New York : Sterling Pub. Co., c1977. 191 p. : ill. ; 22 cm. [CJ89.H56 1977] 77-153071 ISBN 0-8069-6018-3 : 4.95 ISBN 0-8069-6019-1 lib.bdg. : 4.99
1. Numismatics—Collectors and collecting—Juvenile literature. I. Title.

Numismatics—Commonwealth of Nations.

HARRIS, Robert P. 737.4
A guide book of modern British Commonwealth coins, by Robert P. Harris. Racine, Wis., Western Pub. Co. [1970] 128 p. (p. 126-128 blank for "Notes") illus. 20 cm. On spine: Modern British Commonwealth coins. Bibliography: p. 124-125. [CJ2480.H3] 75-16091
1. Numismatics—Commonwealth of Nations. I. Title. II. Title: Modern British Commonwealth coins.

Numismatics—Crete.

MACDONALD, George, 737.4'9'3918
Sir, 1862-1940.
The silver coinage of Crete : a metrological note / by George Macdonald. Chicago : Obol International, 1974. 29 p., [1] leaf of plates : ill. ; 22 cm. Originally published in 1920 for the British Academy by H. Milford, London. Includes bibliographical references. [CJ474.M3 1974] 74-187946
1. Numismatics—Crete. 2. Silver coins. I. Title. BIP

Numismatics — Dictionaries.

BEALS, Gary. 737.4
Numismatic terms of Spain and Spanish America. San Diego, Calif, [1966] ii. 88 p. illus. 22 cm. Bibliography: p. 84-85. [CJ69.B4] 66-7910
1. Numismatics — Dictionaries. I. Title.

CHAMBERLAIN, Christopher 737.4'03
Churchill.
The world of coins : a dictionary of numismatics / [by] C. C. Chamberlain. 3rd ed. / revised by Arthur Blair. London : Teach Yourself Books, 1976. 203 p., [8] p. of plates : ill. ; 18 cm. (Teach yourself books) Edition for 1960 published under title: The teach yourself guide to numismatics. Bibliography: p. [199]-203. [CJ67.C48 1976] 77-372356 ISBN 0-340-21022-2 : £1.50
1. Numismatics—Dictionaries. I. Title.

HOBSON, Burton. 737.4'03
Illustrated encyclopedia of world coins [by] Burton Hobson and Robert Obojski. Garden City, N.Y., Doubleday [1970] 512 p. illus. 25 cm. [CJ67.H6 1970] 76-81030 12.95
1. Numismatics—Dictionaries. I. Obojski, Robert, joint author. II. Title.

Numismatics — Direct.

NUMISMATIC directory, 737.058
1957- St. Louis. v. 22cm. Compilers: 1957- D. W. Johnson, W. H. Breen. [CJ63.N72] 57-8605
1. Numismatics — Direct. I. Johnson, D. Wayne, comp. II. Breen, Walter H., comp.

Numismatics—Europe.

HAZLITT, William Carew, 737.4'9'4
1834-1913.
The coinage of the European continent, Middle Ages-20th century : with an introduction and catalogues of mints, denominations, and rulers / by W. Carew Hazlitt. A new ed. with a pref. and reference bibliography by Al N. Okonomides. Chicago : Ares, 1974. xxviii, 554, vii, 193 p. : ill. ; 24 cm. "Supplement to the coinage of the European continent, by W. Carew Hazlitt": vii, 193 p. (3d and 4th groups) Includes index. Bibliography: p. vii-x. [CJ2456.H33 1974] 74-77880 ISBN 0-89005-037-6 : 30.00
1. Numismatics—Europe. I. Oikonomides, Al. N. II. Title.

Numismatics—Georgia (Transcaucasia)

LANG, David Marshall. 737.4
Studies in the numismatic history of Georgia in Transcaucasia, based on the collection of the American Numismatic Society. New York, American Numismatic Society, 1955. x, 138p. illus., maps (1 fold.) 23cm. (Numismatic notes and monographs, no. 130) Bibliography: p. 126-131. [CJ3789.G4L3] 55-14891
1. Numismatics—Georgia (Transcaucasia) I. Title. II. Series.

Numismatics—Germany.

CRAIG, William D 737.4
Germanic coinages (Charlemagne through Wilhelm II) [Mountain View? Calif., 1954] vii, 242p. illus. 26cm. [CJ2710.C7] 54-12763
1. Numismatics—Germany. I. Title.

Numismatics—Goths.

MILES, George Carpenter, 737.4
1904-
The coinage of the Visigoths of Spain, Leovigild to Achila II. Published in co-operation with the Hispanic Society of America. New York, American Numismatic Society, 1952. xv, 519p. illus., fold. map. 28cm. (Hispanic numismatic series, monograph no. 2) Bibliography: p. [1]-20. [CJ3194.M52] 52-14385
1. Numismatics—Goths. 2. Numismatics—Spain. 3. Coins, Gothic. 4. Visigoths in Spain. I. Title.

Numismatics—Gt. Brit.

KENYON, Robert Lloyd, 737.49'42
1848-1931.
Kenyon's gold coins of England. Including an addendum by Norris D. McWhirter. New York, A. M. Kelley, 1970. 217 p. illus. 23 cm. Reprint of the 1884 ed. published under title: The gold coins of England, with "Listing gold coins issued up to 1969," by N. D. McWhirter added. [CJ2484.K5 1970] 77-111204
1. Numismatics—Gt. Brit. 2. Gold coins. I. Title.

Numismatics—Greece, Modern.

GARDIAKOS, S. 737.49'495
The coinage of modern Greece, Crete, the Ionian Islands & Cyprus [by] S. Gardiakos. Chicago, Argonaut, 1969. 96 p. illus., maps, 16 plates. 22 cm. Includes bibliographical references. [CJ2887.G3] 67-21044
1. Numismatics—Greece, Modern. 2. Numismatics—Crete. 3. Numismatics—Cyprus. 4. Numismatics—Ionian Islands. 5. Coins, Greek. I. Title. BIP

Numismatics, Greek.

DE TABLEY, John Byrne 737.49'38
Leicester Warren, baron, 1835-1895.
Greek federal coinage, by J. Leicester Warren. Chicago, Argonaut, 1969. 73 p. maps. 24 cm. (The Argonaut library of antiquities) Reprint of the 1863 ed., which was published under title: An essay on Greek federal coinage. [CJ335.D5 1969] 67-29115
1. Numismatics, Greek. I. Title.

GARDNER, Percy, 1846- 737.4938
1937.
Archaeology and the types of Greek coins. With an introd. by Margaret Thompson. Chicago, Argonaut Publishers, 1965. xvi, 217 p. 16 plates. 29 cm. "First American edition of...The types of Greek coins, an archaelogical essay, 1883." [CJ373.G2 1965] 65-15461
1. Numismatics, Greek. I. Title.

GARDNER, Percy, 1846- 737.4'9'38
1937.
A history of ancient coinage, 700-300 B.C. / by Percy Gardner Chicago : Ares Publishers, [1974] xvi, 463 p., [6] leaves of plates : ill. ; 24 cm. Reprint of the 1918 ed. published by Clarendon Press, Oxford. Includes bibliographical references and indexes. [CJ335.G3 1974] 74-77879 ISBN 0-89005-007-4 : 15.00
1. Numismatics, Greek. 2. Coins, Ancient. 3. Coinage. I. Title.

HEAD, Barclay Vincent, 737.49'38
1844-1914.
Historia numorum; a manual of Greek numismatics, by Barclay V. Head, assisted by G. F. Hill, George Macdonald, and W. Wroth. New and enl. [1st American] ed. Chicago, Argonaut, 1967. Chicago, Argonaut, 1968. ixxxviii, 966 p. illus., port. 25 cm. 64 p. 40 plates. 25 cm. Reprint of the 1911 ed. Cover title: Historia numorum. Authors' names in reverse order on spine. "A new edition adapted from the Greek original as a companion to the reprint edition of Historia numorum, edited by Alyce Marie Cresap." CJ335.H45 1967 Atlas Bibliography: p. [xxi]-xxxi. [CJ335.H45 1967] 67-25818
1. Numismatics, Greek. I. Sboronos Ioannes N., 1863-1922. II. Cresap, Alyce Marie, ed. III. Title. IV. Title: The illustrations of the Historia numorum, an atlas of Greek numismatics V. Title: The illustrations of the Historia numorum. BIP

HILL, George Francis, 737.40938
Sir 1867-1948.
Ancient Greek and Roman coins; a handbook, by G. F. Hill. New and enl. ed. [1st American ed.] Chicago, Argonaut, 1964. xv, 302 p. illus., 16 plates. 22 cm. (Argonaut library of antiquities) First published in 1899 under title: A handbook of Greek and Roman coins. Bibliography: p. [297]-302. [CJ237.H6 1964] 64-23439
1. Numismatics, Greek. 2. Numismatics, Roman. I. Title.

HILL, George Francis, 737.4938
Sir 1867-1948.
Historical Greek coins. Chicago, Argonaut, 1966. xvii, 180 p. illus., plate. 22 cm. (Argonaut library of antiquities) Companion volume to the author's Historical Roman coins. Bibliographical footnotes. [CJ339.H6 1966] 66-19179
1. Numismatics, Greek. I. Title. BIP

JENKINS, G. Kenneth. 737.4'9'38
Ancient Greek coins, by G. K. Jenkins. New York, Putnam [1972] 310 p. illus. 25 cm. (The World of numismatics) Includes bibliographical references. [CJ335.J45 1972] 70-187894 25.00
1. Numismatics, Greek. 2. Coins, Greek. I. Title. II. Series.

KRAAY, Colin M. 737.4'9'38
Archaic and classical Greek coins / Colin M. Kraay. Berkeley : University of California Press, c1976. xxvi, 390 p., [32] leaves of plates : ill. ; 26 cm. (The Library of numismatics) Includes indexes. Bibliography: p. [335]-344. [CJ401.K72] 76-14303 ISBN 0-520-03254-3 : 60.00
1. Numismatics, Greek. I. Title. II. Series. BIP

SELTMAN, Charles 737.4'9'385
Theodore, 1886-1957.
Athens : its history and coinage before the Persian invasion / by C. T. Seltman. Chicago : Ares Publishers, 1974. xix, 228 p., [12] leaves of plates : ill. ; 29 cm. Reprint of the 1924 ed. published by The University Press, Cambridge, England. Includes index. Bibliography: p. [xiv]-xvi. [CJ401.S44 1974] 74-77518 ISBN 0-89005-002-3 : 25.00
1. Numismatics, Greek. 2. Athens—History. BIP

Numismatics—History.

HOYT, Edwin Palmer. 737.4'09
Coins, collectors, and counterfeiters / by Edwin P. Hoyt. 1st ed. Nashville : T. Nelson, c1977. 159 p. ; 21 cm. Includes index. Bibliography: p. 143-144. [CJ59.H69] 76-58015 ISBN 0-8407-6537-1 : 6.95
1. Numismatics—History. 2. Counterfeits and counterfeiting—History. I. Title.

PORTEOUS, John. 737.4'09
Coins in history. New York, Putnam [1969] 251 p. illus. (part col.), facsims., maps. 26 cm. Bibliography: p. [250]-251. [CJ59.P65 1969b] 71-77174 15.00
1. Numismatics—History. I. Title.

SCHWARZ, Theodore. 737.4'09
Coins as living history / Ted Schwarz. New York : Arco Pub. Co., c1976. 224 p. : ill. ; 25 cm. Includes index. Beginning with Greek coins of the seventh century B.C., explains how coins and currency have reflected and affected the course of history. [CJ59.S38] 75-2708 ISBN 0-668-03791-1 : 8.95
1. Numismatics—History. I. Title. BIP

Numismatics—India.

RAPSON, Edward James, 737.49'34
1861-1937.
The coinage of ancient and medieval India. [2d reprint ed.] San Diego, Calif., Malter-Westerfield Pub. Co. [1969] 56 p. illus. 26 cm. First published in 1897 under title Indian coins, as II Bd., 3 Hft., B of Grundriss der indo-arischen Philologie, edited by G. Buhler. Includes bibliographical references. [CJ1391.R34 1969] 75-1800
1. Numismatics—India. I. Title.

RAPSON, Edward James, 737.49'34
1861-1937.
The coinage of ancient and medieval India. San Diego, Calif. Malter-Westerfield Pub. Co. [1967?] 56 p. illus. 26 cm. Imprint covered by label: Chicago, Argonaut, 1967. First published in 1897 under title Indian coins, as ii bd., 3 lift., B of grundriss der indo-arischen Philologie, edited by G Bilhler. Ncludes bibliographical references. [CJ1391.R34] 67-29130
1. Numismatics—India. I. Title.

Numismatics, Islamic.

CODRINGTON, 737.4'0917'671
Oliver, d.1921.
A manual of Musalman numismatics. New York, B. Franklin [1973] p. Reprint of the 1904 ed., which was issued as v. 7 of the Asiatic Society monographs. Bibliography: p. [CJ3410.C7 1973] 72-10050 ISBN 0-8337-0613-6
1. Numismatics, Islamic. I. Title. II. Series: Asiatic Society monographs, v. 7.

Numismatics—Israel.

GOULD, Jean, 1911- 737'.095694
The story of Israel in coins [by] Jean & Maurice M. Gould. Hollywood, Calif., Wilshire Book Co. [1971] 137 p. illus. 21 cm. [CJ3867.G67] 71-153460 2.00
1. Numismatics—Israel. 2. Coins, Israeli. 3. Medals—Israel. I. Gould, Maurice M., joint author. II. Title. BIP

HAFFNER, Sylvia 737.49'5694
The history of modern Israel's money. 1917 to 1967, including state medals and Palestine mandate, 1st ed. [La Mesa? Calif., 1967] 196p. illus. 23cm. Bibl. [CJ3867.H3] 67-7636 5.25; 3.25 pap.,
1. Numismatics—Israel. I. Title.
Available from the author at: Box 2153, Stn. A., La Mesa, Calif. 92041.

HAFFNER, Sylvia. 737.49'5694
The history of modern Israel's money, 1917-1970, including state medals and Palestine mandate, Turkish and Egyptian currency used in Palestine. [2d ed. Tarzana, Calif.] P. J. Matthew [1970] 366 p. illus. 23 cm. Bibliography: p. 364-365. [CJ3867.H32] 69-17332
1. Numismatics—Israel. I. Title.

Numismatics — Jews

REINACH, Theodore, 737.4933
1860-1928.
Jewish coins. Translated by Mary Hill. With an appendix by G. F. Hill. [1st American ed.] Chicago, Argonaut, 1966. xv, 77 p. illus. 22 cm. Bibliographical footnotes. [CJ1375.R513] 66-29171
1. Numismatics—Jews. I. Hill, George Francis, Sir, 1867-1948. II. Title. BIP

WIRGIN, Wolf, 1902- 737.4
The history of coins and symbols in ancient Israel [by] Wolf Wirgin and Siegfried Mandel. [1st ed.] New York, Exposition Press [1958] 264 p. illus. 21 cm. (An Exposition-university book) Includes bibliography. [CJ1375.W5] 58-1382

1. Numismatics — Jews I. Mandel, Siegfried, joint author. II. Title.

Numismatics—Juvenile literature.

ROSENFELD, Sam. 737.4
The story of coins. Illustrated by James E. Barry. Irvington-on-Hudson, N. Y., Harvey House [1968] 126 p. illus. (part col.) 26 cm. (A Story of science series book) [CJ89.R6] 67-16903
1. Numismatics—Juvenile literature. I. Title. BIP

Numismatics—Latin America.

HARRIS, Robert P. 737.4'098
Pillars & portraits; an illustrated catalogue of the numismatic history of the Spanish American Empire ... by Robert P. Harris. 1st ed. San Jose, Calif., Bonanza Press [1968] 96 p. illus. 20 cm. Bibliography: p. 94-96. [CJ1819.H33] 68-5513
1. Numismatics—Latin America. I. Title.

RAMSAY, Robert M. 737.49'8
A tentative checklist of Spanish-American bust-type silver, by Robert M. Ramsay. Chicago, Hewitt Bros., c1969. 67 p. illus. 20 cm. (Hewitt's numismatic information series) [CJ1819.R25] 73-19859 2.50
1. Numismatics—Latin America. 2. Silver coins. I. Title.

Numismatics—Lithuania.

RACKUS, Alexander Michaels, 1893- 737'.0947'5
Cyclopedia of Lithuanian numismatics, by Alexander M. Rackus. Chicago, Balzekas Museum of Lithuanian Culture, 1965- v. illus. (part col.) 29 cm. Added to t.p.: Zinynas apie Lietuvos numizmatika. English and Lithuanian parallel text. Contents.Contents.—v. 1. Primitive money in prehistoric times. Pirmyksciai pinigai priesistorijos gadyneje. Bibliography: v. 1, p. 329-331. [CJ3028.L5R3] 74-173431
1. Numismatics—Lithuania. 2. Lithuania—Antiquities. I. Title. II. Title: Zinynas apie Lietuvos numizmatika.

Numismatics—Lydia.

HEAD, Barclay Vincent, 1844-1914 737.49'3
The coinage of Lydia and Persia. An Diego, Calif., Pegasus Pub. Co. [n. d.] viii, 55p. illus. 28cm. Imprint covered by label: Chicago, Argonaut 1967. Bib. footnotes. [CJ618.H4] 68-4150 3.50 pap.,
1. Numismatics—Lydia. 2. Numismatics—Iran. I. Title.

Numismatics—Macedonia.

RAYMOND, Doris. 737.4
Macedonian regal coinage to 413 B. C. New York, American Numismatic Society, 1953. xi, 170p. 15 plates. 23cm. (Numismatic notes and monographs, no. 126) Bibliographical footnotes. [CJ545.R3] 53-8602
1. Numismatics—Macedonia. I. Title. II. Series.

Numismatics—Maritime Provinces, Can.

BECKER, J. Richard. 737.4'9'715
The decimal coinage of Nova Scotia, New Brunswick, and Prince Edward Island / by J. Richard Becker. 1st ed. Acton Centre, Mass. : Becker, c1975. 72 p. : ill. ; 23 cm. "500 copies." Includes bibliographical references. [CJ1879.M37B4] 75-1589
1. Numismatics—Maritime Provinces, Can. 2. Maritime Provinces, Can.—History. I. Title: The decimal coinage of Nova Scotia ...

Numismatics—Mexico.

MESMITH, Robert I 737.4
The coinage of the Americas at Mexico City, 1536-1572. New York, American Numismatic Society, 1955. vii, 139p. illus., plates. 23cm. (Numismatic notes and monographs. no. 131) Bibliographical footnotes. [CJ1905.N4] 56-802
1. Numismatics—Mexico. I. Title. II. Series.

NESMITH, Robert I. 737.4'9'729
The coinage of the first mint of the Americas at Mexico City, 1536-1572 / Robert I. Nesmith. Lawrence, Mass. : Quarterman Publications, c1977. 169 p., [6] leaves of plates : ill. ; 24 cm. On spine: Coinage at Mexico City. Each of the plates accompanied by a transparent overlay. Reprint of the 1955 ed. published by the American Numismatic Society, New York, which was issued as no. 131 of Numismatic notes and monographs. Includes a new foreword, additions to the catalogue, and valuation guide. Includes bibliographical references. [CJ1905.N4 1977] 75-1789 ISBN 0-88000-064-3 pbk. : 30.00
1. Numismatics—Mexico. I. Title. II. Title: Coinage at Mexico City. III. Series: Numismatic notes and monographs (New York) ; no. 131. BIP

Numismatics—Miscellanea.

ALLENBAUGH, Carl. 737.4'075
Coins : questions and answers / by Carl Allenbaugh ; edited by Robert M. Poeschl. 2d ed. Iola, Wis. : Krause Publications, c1976. 128 p. : facsims. ; 21 cm. Rev. ed. of Coins; questions and answers: what, when, why, published in 1964. [CJ81.A45 1976] 76-1543 ISBN 0-87341-008-4 pbk. : 1.50
1. Numismatics—Miscellanea. I. Title.

EDGE, Brian. 737.4'076
Coins and all about them: a numismatic quiz; 600 questions and answers. London, Faber and Faber [1973] 143 p. 21 cm. Label mounted on t.p.: Transatlantic Arts, Inc., Levittown, N.Y.: sole distributor for the U.S.A. Includes bibliographical references. [CJ1529.E3] 73-175482 ISBN 0-571-09984-X 6.95
1. Numismatics—Miscellanea. I. Title. BIP

Numismatics—Monaco.

VOS, Raymond de. 737'.0944'949
History of the monies, medals, and tokens of Monaco, 1640-1977 / by Raymond de Vos. [s.l. : s.n.] ; New York : distributed by S. J. Durst, 1978. (Monaco : Testa Press) ca. 350 p. : ill. (some col.) ; 28 cm. Limited ed. of 500 copies. No. 22. Includes bibliography. [CJ2693.V67] 78-302484 80.00
1. Numismatics—Monaco. 2. Coins, Monacan. I. Title. BIP

Numismatics—New South Wales.

SPALDING, Philip. 737.4'9'944
The world of the holey dollar. [1st ed. Santa Barbara, Ca[lif.] Priv. print. [by] Channel Lithograph Co., 1973] xvii, 252, a xii p. illus. 28 cm. Bibliography: p. a xi-a xii. [CJ4435.S6] 73-77615
1. Numismatics—New South Wales. 2. Currency question—New South Wales. 3. Tokens—New South Wales. I. Title. II. Title: Holey dollar.

Numismatics—North America.

LIEBERS, Arthur, 1913- 737.497
The guide to North American coins. New York, Arco Pub. Co. [c.1961] 107p. illus. 25cm. 61-10021 3.00
1. Numismatics—North America. I. Title. II. Title: North American coins.

Numismatics—Norway.

SKAARE, Kolbjorn, 1931- 737.4'9'481
Coins and coinage in Viking-age Norway : the establishment of a national coinage in Norway in the XI century, with a survey of the preceding currency history / Kolbjorn Skaare. Oslo : Universitetsforlaget, [1976] 272 p. : ill. ; 26 cm. Includes indexes. Bibliography: p. 207-[215] [CJ3154.S58] 76-369330 ISBN 8-200-01542-4 : kr120.00
1. Numismatics—Norway. 2. Coins, Norwegian. 3. Coin hoards—Norway. 4. Norway—History. I. Title. BIP

Numismatics—Panama.

GRIGORE, Julius. 737.4'9'862
Coins and currency of Panama. [Iola, Wis., Krause Publications, 1972] 202 p. illus. 24 cm. Includes bibliographical references. [CJ2036.G74] 72-83631
1. Numismatics—Panama. 2. Numismatics—Canal Zone. I. Title.

STICKNEY, Brian R. 737.49'862
Numismatic history of Republic of Panama, by Brian R. Stickney. San Antonio, Almanzar's Coins of the World [1971] 64 p. illus. 22 cm. Bibliography: p. 63-64. [CJ2047.S77] 75-25466
1. Numismatics—Panama. 2. Coins, Panamanian. I. Title.

Numismatics—Parthia.

CALEY, Earle Radcliffe, 1900- 737.4
Chemical composition of Parthian coins. New York, American Numismatic Society, 1955. v, 104p. diagrs., tables. 23cm. (Numismatic notes and monographs, no. 129) Bibliographical footnotes. [CJ692.C3] 55-14881
1. Numismatics—Parthia. I. Title. II. Series.

GARDNER, Percy, 1846-1937. 737.49'35
The coinage of Parthia. Introd. and supplementary catalog of a recent hoard by Joel L. Malter. San Diego, Calif., Malter-Westerfield Pub. Co. [1968] iv, 68 p. illus. 29 cm. Running title: Numismata orientalia. Imprint covered by label: Argonaut, Chicago, 1967. 1877 ed. published under title: The Parthian coinage. Bibliographical footnotes. [CJ692.G3 1968] 68-5104
1. Numismatics—Parthia. 2. Parthia—History. I. Title. II. Title: Numismata orientalia.

Numismatics—Period.

AMERICAN journal of numismatics . . . v.1-53; May 1866-1919. 737.06
New York, American Numismatic and Archaeological Soe. [New York, Johnson Reprint, 1965] 53v. (various p.) illus., plates, photos., ports., maps, facsims., atbles. 28cm. Monthly, May 1866-Apr. 1870; quarterly, July 1870-Dec. 1912; annually, 1913-19. Title varies. [CJ1.A6] 12-6563 580.00 set,
1. Numismatics—Period. I. American Numismatic Society, New York. II. Boston Numismatic Society.

AMERICAN journal of numismatics . . . v. 1-53; May 1866-1919. 737'.05
New York, Amer. Numismatic & Archaeological Soc., 1866]-1924. New York, Johnson Reprint, 1968. 53v. illus., plates, photos., ports., maps, gacsims., tables. 27x28cm. Monthly. May 1866-Apr. 1870; quarterly, July 1870-Dec. 1912; annually, 1913-19. Title varies. [CJ1.A6] 12-6563 580.00 set, unbound
1. Numismatics—Period. I. Norton, Frank Henry, 1836-1921, ed. II. Anthon, Charles Edward, 1822-1883, ed. III. Appleton, William Sumner, 1840-1903, ed. IV. Green, Samuel Abbott, 1830-1918, ed. V. Colburn, Jeremiah, 1815-1891, ed. VI. Marvin, William Theophilus Rogers, 1832-1913, ed. VII. American numismatic society, New York. VIII. Boston numismatic society.

AMERICAN Numismatic Society, New York 737.06273
Museum notes. [no.] 13. New York, 1967. v. illus., plates. 23cm. [CJ1.A63] 47-5435 7.50 pap.,
1. Numismatics—Period. I. Title.

AMERICAN Numismatic Society, New York. 737.06273
Museum notes. no. 9. New York, Author, Broadway at 156 St., 1960[ ] iii, 243, xvi p. (bibl. footnotes) illus., plates 23cm. 5.00 pap.,
1. Numismatics—Period. I. Title.

Numismatics— Persepolis.

MILES, George Carpenter, 1901- 737.4935
Excavation coins from the Persepolis region. New York, American Numismatic Society, 1959. 124p. 21plates, map. 23cm. (Numismatic notes and monographs, no. 143) Bibliographical footnotes. [CJ3421.M5] 59-16303
1. Numismatics— Persepolis. 2. Colns, Oriental. I. Title. II. Series.

Numismatics, Roman.

ADELSON, Howard L. 737.4937
A bronze hoard of the period of Zeno I. by Howard L. Adelson, George L. Kustas. New York, Amer. Numismatic, 1962. ix, 89p. illus., 23cm. (Numismatic notes and monographs, no. 148) Bibl. 62-52656 3.50 pap.,
1. Numismatics, Roman. I. Kustas, George L., joint author. II. Title. III. Series.

BUTTERY, Theore V 737.4
The triumvisa portrait gold of the quattuorviri monetales of 42 B. C. New York, American Numismatic Society, 1956. x, 69p. 9plates. 23cm. (Numismatic notes and monographs, no. 137) Bibliographical footnotes. [CJ941.B8] 57-1487
1. Numismatics, Roman. I. Title. II. Series.

BUTTREY, Theodore V 737.4
The triumviral portrait gold of the quattuorviri monetales of 42B. C. New York, American Numismatic Society, 1956. x, 69p. 9plates. 23cm. (Numismatic notes and monographs, no. 137) Bibliographical footnotes. [CJ941.B8] 57-1487
1. Numismatics, Roman. I. Title. II. Series.

GRANT, Michael. 737.4
Aspects of the principate of Tiberius; historical comments on the colonial coinage issued outside Spain. New York, American Numismatic Society, 1950. xviii, 199 p. illus. 24 cm. (Numismatic notes and monographs, no. 116) Bibliography: p. 173-187. [CJ1001.G75] 50-13148
1. Numismatics, Roman. 2. Tiberius, Emperor of Rome, 42 B. C.- 37 A. D. I. Title. II. Series.

GRANT, Michael. 737
Roman anniversary issues; an exploratory study of the numismatic and medallic commemoration of anniversary years 49 B. C.-A. D. 375. Cambridge [Eng.] University Press, 1950. xxiv, 204 p. plates. 23 cm. Bibliography: p. [185]-186. [CJ843.G7] 51-5048
1. Numismatics, Roman. 2. Medals, Roman. 3. Rome—Centennial celebrations, etc. I. Title. BIP

HILL, George Francis, Sir 1867-1948. 737.4937
Historical Roman coins. Chicago, Argonaut, 1966. xvi, 191 p. plates. 22 cm. (Argonaut library of antiquities) Companion to the author's Historical Greek coins. Bibliographical footnotes. [CJ833.H6 1966] 66-19180
1. Numismatics, Roman. I. Title. BIP

SMITH, Henry Roy William, 1891- 737.4
Problems historical and numismatic in the reign of Augustus. Berkeley, University of California Press, 1951. viii, 133-230 p. illus. 26 cm. (University of California publications in classical archaeology, v. 2, no. 4) Bibliographical footnotes. [DE1.C3] A 51
1. Numismatics. Roman. 2. Cinna, Cnaeus Cornelius. 3. Rome—Hist.—Augustus, 30 A.c.-14 A.D. I. Title. II. Series: California. University. University of California publications in classical archaeology, v. 2, no. 4

Numismatics, Roman—Addresses, essays, lectures.

BOYCE, Aline Abaecherli 737.4937
Festal and dated coins of the Roman Empire: four papers. New York, Amer. Numismatic Soc. Bway, between 155 & 156 Sts., 1965. x, 102p. 16 plates. 23cm. (Numismatic notes and monographs, no. 153) Bibl. [CJ969.B6] 65-5565 4.00 pap.,

cm. Includes bibliographical references. [NA735.P5D52] 76-369125
1. Oak Lane, Philadelphia. 2. Architecture—Philadelphia—Catalogs. 3. Architecture—Philadelphia—Statistics. I. Girondi, Vincent A., joint author. II. Title.

Oakland, Calif.—Description—Views.

URBAN, Roger F.   779'.9'9179466
Oakland, a mediterranean city : a book of photographs / by Roger F. Urban. [s.l.] : Urban, c1976. 48 p. : chiefly col. ill. ; 24 x 32 cm. [F869.O2U72] 76-50300
1. Oakland, Calif.—Description—Views. I. Title.

Oakland Museum.

OAKLAND Museum.   069'.09794'66
The first five years / the Oakland Museum, [text by Jinx Morgan]. [Oakland, Calif.] : The Museum, c1974. 4 pamphlets in 1 v. : ill. ; 18 x 21 cm. Contents.Contents.—[1] Creation.—[2] Fulfillment.—[3] Milestones.—[4] Guide. [AM101.O29A47] 75-311674
1. Oakland Museum. I. Morgan, Jinx. II. Title.

Oakland Museum. Art Dept.

OAKLAND Museum.   759.13'074'019466
Art Dept.
The Kahn Collection of nineteenth-century paintings by artists in California / by Marjorie Arkelian. [Oakland] : Oakland Museum, Art Dept., 1975. 63 p. : ill. (some col.) ; 23 x 31 cm. Includes index. Bibliography: p. 56-62. [ND230.C3O15 1975] 75-77188
1. Oakland Museum. Art Dept. 2. Paintings, American—Catalogs. 3. Painting, Modern—19th century—California. 4. Paintings—Oakland, Calif.—Catalogs. I. Arkelian, Marjorie. II. Title.

Oaxaca, Mexico (State) — Antiq.

BOOS, Frank H. 1892-   732.2
The ceramic sculptures of ancient Oaxaca [by] Frank H. Boos. South Brunswick [N. J.] A. S. Barnes [1966] 488 p. (chiefly illus. (part col.)) 35 cm. Bibliographical footnotes. [F1219.1.O11B65] 65-20531
1. Oaxaca, Mexico (State) — Antiq. 2. Indians of Mexico — Oaxaca (State) — Art. 3. Indians of Mexico — Pottery. 4. Terra-cottas — Oaxaca, Mexico (State) I. Title.

Obelisks.

HABASHI, Labib, 1906-   932
The obelisks of Egypt / by Labib Habachi ; edited by Charles C. Van Siclen III. New York : Scribner, [1977] p. cm. Includes index. Bibliography: p. [DT62.O2H32] 76-54646 ISBN 0-684-14805-6 : 15.00
1. Obelisks. I. Title.   BIP

Oberlin College. Dudley Peter Allen Memorial Art Museum.

OBERLIN College.   741.9'771'23
Dudley Peter Allen Memorial Art Museum.
Catalogue of drawings and watercolors in the Allen Memorial Art Museum, Oberlin College / by Wolfgang Stechow. Oberlin, Ohio : Oberlin College, 1976. p. cm. Includes index. [NC25.O25O256] 76-23495 ISBN 0-521-20955-2 : 15.95
1. Oberlin College. Dudley Peter Allen Memorial Art Museum. 2. Drawings—Oberlin, Ohio—Catalogs. 3. Water-colors—Oberlin, Ohio—Catalogs. I. Stechow, Wolfgang, 1896-1974. II. Title.

Obrebski, Jozef

MASSACHUSETTS.   778.9'9'4765
University. Art Gallery.
Yesterday's people: peasants of Polesie; [catalogue of] an exhibition of photographs of rural eastern Poland of the 1930's by Joseph Obrebski, October 3 to October 14, 1973, University Art Gallery. Amherst, [1973?] [16] p. illus. 26 cm. Cover title.

Includes bibliographical references. [DK511.P62M37 1973] 75-303505
1. Obrebski, Jozef 2. Ethnology—Polesie—Exhibitions. I. Obrebski, Jozef. II. Title.

Obsidional coins.

LAPA, Frank A.   737.4
Check list of siege coins and necessary issues, 16th-20th century, compiled by Frank A. Lapa. San Diego, Calif., Pegasus Pub. Co. [1968] [28] p. 22 cm. Bibliography: p. [28] [CJ1539.L36] 68-1049
1. Obsidional coins. I. Title.

NELSON, Philip.   332.4942
The obsidional money of the Great Rebellion, 1642-1649. San Diego, Calif., Malter-Westerfield Pub. Co. [196-?] 71 p. illus., map. 23 cm. Reprint of the 1907 ed. [CJ2482.N4] 68-4757
1. Obsidional coins. 2. Numismatics—Gt. Brit. I. Title.

Occidentals in Oriental art.

BURLAND, Cottie Arthur,   709'.5
1905-
The exotic white man; an alien in Asian and African art [by] Cottie A. Burland. Photos. by Werner Forman. [1st American ed.] New York, McGraw-Hill [1969, c1968] 140 p. illus. (part col.) 28 cm. Bibliography: p. 140. [N7260.B78] 71-87834 10.95
1. Occidentals in Oriental art. I. Forman, Werner, illus. II. Title.

PHILADELPHIA   796'.952'074014811
Museum of Art.
Foreigners in Japan; Yokohama and related woodcuts in the Philadelphia Museum of Art. Philadelphia, 1972. 39, [l] p. illus. 26 cm. Bibliography: p. [40] [NE1317.P48P485] 72-76728
1. Occidentals in Oriental art. 2. Color-prints, Japanese—Catalogs. 3. Yokohama—Description—Views. I. Title.

Occupations in art.

LEHMANN-HAUPT,   769'.4'930155
Hellmut, 1903-
The book of trades in the iconography of social typology / by Hellmut Lehmann-Haupt. Boston : Trustees of the Public Library of the City of Boston, [1976] p. cm. (Maury A. Bromsen lecture in humanistic bibliography ; no. 1) [NE1150.5.A45L43] 76-8399 ISBN 0-89073-010-5
1. Amman, Jost, 1539-1591. 2. Sachs, Hans, 1494-1576. Das Standebuch—Illustrations. 3. Occupations in art. I. Title. II. Series.   BIP

PYNE, William Henry,   769'.924
1769-1843.
Microcosm; or, A picturesque delineation of the arts, agriculture, and manufactures of Great Britain in a series of above a thousand groups of small figures for the embellishment of landscape. Drawn and etched by William Henry Pyne. Aquatinted by J. Hill. Explanations of the plates by C. Gray. Introd. by A. E. Santaniello. New York, B. Blom, 1971. 284 p. illus. 26 cm. Reprint of the 1845 ed. published under title: Picturesque groups for the embellishment of landscape, with a new introd. [NC825.O3P9 1971] 68-56512
1. Occupations in art. I. Title. II. Title: A picturesque delineation of the arts, agriculture, and manufactures of Great Britain.

PYNE, William Henry,   769'.92'4
1769-1843.
Picturesque views of rural occupations in early nineteenth-century England : all 641 illustrations from Ackermann's edition of the "Microcosm" / by W. H. Pyne. New York : Dover Publications, c1977. 120 p. : chiefly ill. ; 31 cm. (Dover pictorial archive series) [NC242.P9A4 1977] 77-80117 ISBN 0-486-23547-5 : 4.50
1. Pyne, William Henry, 1769-1843. 2. Occupations in art. I. Pyne, William Henry, 1769-1843. Microcosm. II. Title.   BIP

ZAIDENBERG, Arthur, 1903-   743'.4
How to draw people at work. London,

New York, Abelard-Schuman [1970] 64 p. illus. 26 cm. Sketches and brief text demonstrate how to capture the physical characteristics, emotional expressions, and bearing of people doing many different kinds of work. [NC825.O3Z3] 76-105257 3.75
1. Occupations in art. 2. Drawing—Instruction—Juvenile literature. I. Title.

Oceanica—Descr. & trav.—Views.

DANIELSSON, Bengt   759.4
Gauguin in the South Seas [Tr. from Swedish by Reginald Spink. 1st Amer ed.] Garden City, N. Y., Doubleday, 1966 [c1964, 1965] 336p. illus. (pt. col.) ports. (pt. col.) 24cm. Bibl. [ND553.G27D33] 65-12363 7.95
1. Gauguin, Paul, 1848-1903. 2. Oceanica—Descr. and trav. Views. I. Title.

LEWIS, Jack, 1912-   759.13
Pacific Odyssey. [Bridgeville?Del., 1950] 1v. (unpaged) plates (part col.) 31cm. [ND1839.L45A45] 51-1261
1. Oceanica—Descr. & trav.—Views. I. Title.

Oceanica in art.

SMITH, Bernard William,   709'.4
European vision and the South Pacific, 1768-1850: a study in the history of art and ideas by Bernard Smith. London, New York, Oxford U.P., 1969. xix, 287 p., 114 plates. 21 cm. (Oxford paperbacks, 162) Bibliography: p. [258]-274. [N7428.5.S6 1969] 75-463300 28/-
1. Oceanica in art. 2. Philosophy of nature. I. Title.   BIP

Ochikubo, Tetsuo, 1923—

SCHMECKEBIER, Laurence   760'.092'4
Eli, 1906-
Tetsuo Ochikubo, paintings, drawings, lithographs; a review based on a retrospective exhibition of his work held in the galleries of the Joe and Emily Lowe Art Center, October 5-30, 1964, by Laurence Schmeckebier. Syracuse, N.Y., School of Art, Syracuse University [1964?] [34] p. illus. 23 cm. [N6537.O26S35] 75-308325
1. Ochikubo, Tetsuo, 1923- I. Ochikubo, Tetsuo, 1923- II. Syracuse University. Joe and Emily Lowe Art Center.

Odessa, Del. Corbit House.

SWEENEY, John A H   728.8309751
Grandeur on the Appoquinimink; the house of William Corbit at Odessa, Delaware. [Newark] University of Delaware Press, 1959. xiv, 146 p. plates, facsims., geneal. table, plans. 27 cm. (Winterthru series) [NA7238.O3S9] 59-7532
1. Odessa, Del. Corbit House. I. Title. II. Series.

O'Doherty, Brian.

O'DOHERTY, Brian.   730'.92'4
Rope drawings by Patrick Ireland : an exhibition / organized by the La Jolla Museum of Contemporary Art. [La Jolla, Calif.] : La Jolla Museum of Contemporary Art, [1977?] [32] p. : ill. (some col.) ; 23 cm. Exhibition held at the La Jolla Museum of Contemporary Art, Jan. 28-Mar. 20, 1977; Seattle Art Museum, Nov. 7-Dec. 18, 1977; Contemporary Arts Center, Cincinnati, May 5-June 18, 1978. Bibliography: p. [31] [NB237.O35L3] 77-357019
1. O'Doherty, Brian. 2. Rope in art. I. La Jolla Museum of Contemporary Art. II. Seattle. Art Museum. III. Contemporary Arts Museum, Cincinnati. IV. Title.

Odysseus—Art.

STANFORD, William   704.94'7
Bedell.
The quest for Ulysses [by] W. B. Stanford and J. V. Luce. New York, Praeger [1974] 256 p. illus. 26 cm. Bibliography: p. 236-242. [NX652.O3S72] 70-154604 8.95

1. Odysseus—Art. I. Luce, John Victor, 1920- joint author. II. Title.   BIP

Oenochoes—Catalogs.

THOMPSON, Dorothy (Burr)   738.3'83
1900-
Ptolemaic oinochoai and portraits in faience; aspects of the ruler-cult. Oxford, Clarendon Press, 1973. xxviii, 221 p. illus. 29 cm. (Oxford monographs on classical archaeology) Bibliography: p. [xxi]-xxv. [NK4659.T48] 73-178773 ISBN 0-19-813211-5 57.75
1. Oenochoes—Catalogs. 2. Ptolemies, Kings of Egypt—Art. 3. Cultus, Alexandrian. 4. Pottery, Hellenistic—Egypt. I. Title. II. Series.
Distributed by Oxford University Press, New York.   BIP

Ofek, Avraham, 1935—

OFEK, Avraham, 1935-   759.95694
Avraham Ofek. [New York, Jewish Museum, 1972] [23] p. illus. (part col.) 21 x 25 cm. Catalogue of an exhibition held at the Jewish Museum, Dec. 20, 1972-Mar. 18, 1973. Bibliography: p. [23] [ND979.O34J48] 72-96382
1. Ofek, Avraham, 1935- I. Jewish Theological Seminary of America. Jewish Museum.

Office buildings.

ANGILLY, Arthur O   725.23
Life insurance buildings. 1st ed. New York, Life Office Management Association [c1954] 130p. illus. 29cm. [NA6227.L5A5] 55-59506
1. Office buildings. I. Title.

ARCHITECTURAL record.   725.23
Office buildings. New York, F. W. Dodge Corp. [1961] viii, 248p. illus., diagrs. 30cm. [NA6230.A7] 61-14017
1. Office buildings. 2. Skyscrapers. 3. Building. I. Title.

BOY Scouts of America.   728.44
Design and planning of a council office building. New Brunswick, N.J., c1957. 73p. illus. 22x28cm. [HS3313.B74A573] 57-46410
1. Office buildings. I. Title.

HOHL, Reinhold.   725'.23
Office buildings; an international survey. [Translation into English: E. Rockwell] New York, Praeger [1968] 173 p. illus., plans. 29 cm. English and German. Translation of Burogebande, international. [NA6230.H5313] 68-31532 18.50
1. Office buildings.

JOEDICKE, Jurgen.   725.23
Office buildings. New York, Praeger [1962] 219p. illus., diagrs., plans. 29cm. (Books that matter) 'Translated by C. V. Amerongen from the German Burobauten.' Bibliography: p. 219. [NA6230.J63] 62-10829
1. Office buildings. 2. Architecture—Designs and plans. 3. Building. I. Title.

MANASSEH, Leonard.   725.23
Office buildings [by] Leonard Manasseh and Roger Cunliffe. New York, Reinhold Pub. Corp. [1962] viii, 208p. illus., diagrs., plans. 25cm. Bibliography: p. 203-204. [NA6230.M3 1962] 62-9729
1. Office buildings. 2. Architecture—Designs and plans. I. Cunliffe, Roger, joint author. II. Title.

NATIONAL Association of   725.23
Real Estate Boards. National Institute of Real Estate Brokers.
Office planning and design. Sponsor: William T. Beazley. Chicago, 1960. 63p. illus. 27cm. [NA6227.R4N3] 60-37830
1. Office buildings. I. Title.

RIPNEN, Kenneth H   725.23
Office building and office layout planning. New York, McGraw-Hill, 1960. ix, 182p. illus., plans. 26cm. [NA6230.R33] 59-8559
1. Office buildings. I. Title.

SUBJECT INDEX OLDENBURG, CLAES, 1929—

Office buildings—Design and construction.

OPEN-PLAN offices : 725'.23 new ideas, experience and improvements / Kraemer, Sieverts & Partners ; English translation by James L. Ritchie. London ; New York : McGraw-Hill, c1977. 135 p. : ill. ; 24 cm. This enquiry was carried out by Hans-Ludger John and Dieter Reichel & the project was undertaken by Kraemer, Sieverts & Partners in collaboration with the School of Building Design and Construction at the University of Brunswick. Bibliography: p. 133-135. [TH4311.G7613] 77-30261 ISBN 0-07-084497-6 : 11.00
1. Office buildings—Design and construction. 2. Office layout. I. John, Hans-Ludger. II. Reichel, Dieter. III. Kraemer, Sieverts und Partner. IV. Brunswick. Technische Universitat. Lehrstuhl A fur Gebaudelehre und Entwerfen von Hochbauten.

Office layout.

GREAT Britain. Dept. of the Environment. Directorate of Building Development. 725'.23
Office space : a primer for users and designers / Directorate of Building Development, Property Services Agency, Department of the Environment. London : H.M.S.O., 1976. 103 p. : ill. (some col.), plans ; 30 cm. [HF5547.G718 1976] 77-364047 ISBN 0-11-670593-0 : £10.00
1. Office layout. I. Title.

PILE, John F. 747'.8'523
Interiors 3rd book of offices / by John Pile New York : Whitney Library of Design, 1976. 208 p. : ill. ; 32 cm. Includes index. [HF5547.P52] 76-20812 ISBN 0-8230-7305-X : 24.95
1. Office layout. I. Title. BIP

Offices—Location.

MCKEEVER, James Ross, 1910- 711'.552
Business parks, office parks, plazas & centers; a study of development practices and procedures, by J. Ross McKeever. Washington, Urban Land Institute [1970] 125 p. illus., plans. 28 cm. (Urban Land Institute. Technical bulletin 65) Bibliography: p. 122. [NA9000.U67 no. 65] 72-127217 10.00
1. Offices—Location. 2. Office buildings. I. Title. II. Series. BIP

Offset printing.

HALPERN, Bernard R 655.32
Offset stripping, black-and-white. [1st ed.] New York Lithographic Technical Foundation [1958] 360p. illus. 22cm. 'A revision of the original volume [by Arthur Sharples, Jr.] published in 1945.' [TR940.H28] 57-14955
1. Offset printing. 2. Photolithography. 3. Photomechanical processes. I. Title.

KARCH, Robert Randolph, 1902- 655.3
Graphic arts procedures: the offset processes; includes strike-on and film composition [by] R. Randolph Karch [and] Edward J. Buber. Chicago, American Technical Society [1967] 570 p. illus., port. 22 cm. Running title: The offset processes. [Z252.5.O5K3] 66-12164
1. Offset printing. I. Buber, Edward J., joint author. II. Warrington, P. S. III. Title. IV. Title: The offset processes.

LATIMER, Henry C. 655.325
Advertising production planning and copy preparation for offset printing, by H. C. Latimer. Norwalk, Conn., Five Mile River Press [1965] v, 145 p. illus. 28 cm. [Z252.5.O5L35] 65-29528
1. Offset printing. 2. Advertising layout and typography. 3. Art, Commercial—Reproduction. I. Title.

LATIMER, Henry C. 686.2'315
Advertising production planning and copy preparation for offset printing / by H. C. Latimer. 3d ed. New York : Art Direction Book Co., c1974. 136 p. : ill. ; 29 cm. Includes index. [Z252.5.O5L35 1974] 74-14111 ISBN 0-910158-18-5
1. Offset printing. 2. Advertising layout and typography. I. Title.

LAWSON, L. E. 655.315
Offset lithography [by] L. E. Lawson. London, Vista Bks. [1963] 184p. illus., plates. 21cm. (Facts of print ser.) ffset printing. [Z252.5.O5L37] 66-83284 5.00 bds.,
I. Title.
American distributor: Dufour in Chester Springs, Pa.

REED, Robert Findley, 1890- 655.32
Offset platemaking: surface. [1st ed.] New York, Lithographic Technical Foundation [1957] 177p. illus. 22cm. (Lithographic Technical Foundation, inc. Foundation publications. Skilled craft texts, 502) On spine: Surface platemaking. 'A revision of the original text [by Joseph W. Mazzaferri] published in 1945 under the title Offset platemaking--Albumin process.'SPhotolithography. [TR940.R4 1957] 775 58-185
1. Offset printing. 2. Lithography—Metal plate processes. I. Title. II. Title: Surface platemaking.

Ogata, Korin, 1658-1716.

RANDALL, Doanda. 759.952
Korin. New York, Crown Publishers [1960] 26 p. illus., plates (part col.) geneal. table. 18 x 19 cm. (Art of the East library) Bibliography: p. 26. [ND1059.O35R3] 60-16038
1. Ogata, Korin, 1658-1716. I. Series.

Oglethorpe Co., Ga.—Historic houses, etc.

RODGERS, Ava D. 720.9758'.175
The housing of Oglethorpe County, Georgia, 1790-1860 [by] Ava D. Rodgers. Tallahassee, Florida State University Press, 1971. xi, 79 p. illus. 29 cm. Bibliography: p. 79. [F292.O4R6] 72-137857 12.00
1. Oglethorpe Co., Ga.—Historic houses, etc. I. Title. BIP

Okanagan Valley, B.C.—Description and travel—Views.

REDIVO, Hugo. 779'.9'97114204
The Okanagan / photos. by Hugo Redivo ; introd. by Eric Sismey. Toronto : Oxford University Press, 1978. [96] p. : chiefly col. ill. ; 23 x 28 cm. [F1089.O5R43] 78-320164 ISBN 0-19-540286-3 : 9.95
1. Okanagan Valley, B.C.—Description and travel—Views. I. Title.
Distributed by Oxford University Press, N.Y BIP

O'Keefe, Georgia, 1887—

AMON Carter Museum of Western Art, Fort Worth, Tex. 759.13
Georgia O'Keeffe; an exhibition of the work of the artist from 1915 to 1966. Edited by Mitchell A. Wilder. Fort Worth, 1966 30 p. illus., ports. 27 cm. " Held at the Amon Carter Museum of Western Art, March 17-May 8, 1966." [ND237.O5A7] 66-20333
1. O'Keeffe, George, 1887- I. Wilder, Mitchell A., ed. II. Title.

O'KEEFFE, Georgia, 1887- 741.9'73
Drawings. Introd. by Lloyd Goodrich. New York, Atlantis Editions [1968] 1 portfolio ([8] p., 10 plates (1 col.)) 70 cm. "Two hundred and fifty copies ... of which two hundred and thirty are numbered and signed by the artist ... Copy K [signed]" [NC139.O45A43] 70-24761

O'KEEFFE, Georgia, 1887- 759.13 B
Georgia O'Keeffe / Georgia O'Keeffe. New York : Viking Press, [1976] p. cm. (A Studio book) [ND237.O5A46] 76-23452 ISBN 0-670-33708-0 : 75.00. ISBN 0-670-33709-9 lim. ed. : 275.00
1. O'Keeffe, Georgia, 1887- BIP

O'KEEFFE, Georgia, 1887- 759.13
Georgia O'Keeffe, by Lloyd Goodrich and Doris Bry. New York, Published for the Whitney Museum of American Art by Praeger [1970] 195 p. illus., col. plates, port. 29 cm. "Published on the occasion of the retrospective exhibition of Georgia O'Keeffe's works organized by the Whitney Museum of American Art in 1970 and shown subsequently at the Art Institute of Chicago and the San Francisco Museum of Art." Bibliography: p. 191-195. [ND237.O5G6] 72-129108 18.50
I. Goodrich, Lloyd, 1897- II. Bry, Doris. III. Whitney Museum of American Art, New York. IV. Chicago. Art Institute. V. San Francisco. Museum of Art.

O'KEEFFE, Georgia, 1887- 741.9'73
Some memories of drawings / Georgia O'Keeffe. New York : Atlantis Editions, 1974. 1 case ([97] p., 21 leaves of plates : 21 ill. (some col.)) ; 23 cm. "One hundred and twenty copies ..." No. T. [NC139.O45A45] 74-14986
1. O'Keeffe, Georgia, 1887- 2. Artists—United States—Correspondence, reminiscences, etc. I. Title. BIP

Old age.

RICHARDSON, Bessie Ellen, 1901- 704.94'9'301435
Old age among the ancient Greeks; the Greek portrayal of old age in literature, art, and inscriptions, with a study of the duration of life among the ancient Greeks on the basis of inscriptional evidence. New York, AMS Press [1969] xv, 376 p. illus. 23 cm. Reprint of the 1933 ed. Bibliography: p. 363-372. [DF78.R4 1969b] 74-93775
1. Old age. 2. Greece—Social life and customs. 3. Greek literature—History and criticism. 4. Art, Greek. 5. Human figure in art. 6. Inscriptions, Greek. I. Title. BIP

RICHARDSON, Bessie Ellen, 1901- 704.94'9'301435
Old age among the ancient Greeks; the Greek portrayal of old age in literature, art, and inscriptions, with a study of the duration of life among the ancient Greeks on the basis of inscriptional evidence. New York, Greenwood Press [1969, c1933] xv, 376 p. illus. 23 cm. (The Johns Hopkins University studies in archaeology, no. 16) Bibliography: p. 363-372. [DF78.R4 1969] 69-14056
1. Old age. 2. Greece—Social life and customs. 3. Greek literature—History and criticism. 4. Art, Greek. 5. Human figure in art. 6. Inscriptions, Greek. I. Title. II. Series.

Old age—Pictorial works—Juvenile literature.

FORRAI, Maria S. 779'.9'301435
A look at old age / photos. by Maria S. Forrai ; text by Rebecca Anders. Minneapolis : Lerner Publications Co., c1976. p. cm. (Lerner awareness series) Text and photographs introduce the joys, problems, and contributions of the elderly. [HQ1061.F62 1976] 75-38467 ISBN 0-8225-1304-8 lib.bdg. : 4.95
1. Old age—Pictorial works—Juvenile literature. I. Anders, Rebecca. II. Title. III. Title: Old age.

Old Stone House, Washington, D.C.

STANLEY, Joan H. 917.53
The Old Stone House in Georgetown, D.C.: its eighteenth century occupants and furnishings, parts C & D for furnishing plan, by Joan H. Stanley. [Washington?] Division of History, U.S. Office of Archeology and Historic Preservation, 1968. vi, 74 l. illus. 27 cm. Bibliographical footnotes. [F204.O4S8] 77-601812
1. Old Stone House, Washington, D.C. I. U.S. Office of Archeology and Historic Preservation. Division of History. II. Title.

U. S. Office of National Capital Parks. 975.3
The Old Stone House, by Cornelius W. Heine, historian. [Washington] 1955. v. 106 l. illus., maps. 27cm. Bibliography: leaves 96-106. [F204.O4U5] 56-60097
1. Old Stone House, Washington, D. C. I. Heine, Cornelius W. II. Title.

Old Sturbridge Village, Sturbridge, Mass.

CHAMBERLAIN, Samuel. 917.44'3
A tour of Old Sturbridge Village. New York, Hastings House [1972] 72 p. illus. 21 cm. [F74.S93C46 1972] 72-8861 ISBN 0-8038-7128-7 1.25 (pbk.)
1. Old Sturbridge Village, Sturbridge, Mass. I. Title.

CHAMBERLAIN, Samuel, 1895- 917.443
A tour of Old Sturbridge Village. [Rev. ed.] New York, Hastings House [1965] 72 p. illus. 21 cm. [F74.S93C46 1965] 65-6126
1. Old Sturbridge Village, Sturbridge, Mass. I. Title.

CHAMBERLAIN, Samuel, 1895- 917.44'3
A tour of Old Sturbridge Village. [Rev. ed.] New York, Hastings House [1969] 72 p. illus. 21 cm. [F74.S93C46 1969] 79-15123
1. Old Sturbridge Village, Sturbridge, Mass. I. Title.

Oldenburg, Claes, 1929—

JOHNSON, Ellen H. 709'.24
Claes Oldenburg, by Ellen H. Johnson. [Baltimore, Penguin Books, 1971] 64 p. illus. (part col.) 23 cm. (Penguin new art 4) Includes bibliographical references. [N6537.O4J6] 70-139845 ISBN 0-14-070624-0 3.65
1. Oldenburg, Claes, 1929- BIP

OLDENBURG, Claes, 1929- 730'.92'4
Claes Oldenburg : May 1974 - August 1976. Stuttgart ; London ; Reykjavik : H. Mayer, 1976. 2 v. : ill. (some col.) ; 24 cm. Issued on the occasion of the artist's exhibition of his work at the Leo Castelli Gallery in New York, Nov. 6-27, 1976. Contents.Contents.—[1] Photo Log.—[2] Press Log. Includes bibliography. [NB237.O42L46] 77-363145 DM30.00
1. Oldenburg, Claes, 1929- I. Leo Castelli Gallery.

OLDENBURG, Claes, 1929- 760'.0924
Drawings and prints. Introd. and commentary by Gene Baro. London, New York, Chelsea House [1969] 274 p. illus., col. plates. 31 cm. (A Paul Bianchini book) [NC1075.O4B3] 68-8894
I. Baro, Gene.

OLDENBURG, Claes, 1929- 769'.92'4
Notes. [Los Angeles, Gemini G. E. L., 1968] [v] p., xiii l. 12 col. plates. 24 cm. In portfolio. This sample ed. is a pre-publication announcement of sale. Contains copies of the 12 lithographs and 13 text pages of the projected work. [NE2312.O52A55] 73-170127
1. Oldenburg, Claes, 1929-

OLDENBURG, Claes, 1929- 741.9'73
Notes in hand. New York, E. P. Dutton [1971] 1 v. (unpaged, on double leaves) col. illus. 16 cm. Includes bibliography. [NC139.O4A52 1971] 73-166166 ISBN 0-525-16905-9 6.95
I. Title. BIP

OLDENBURG, Claes, 1929- 709'.73
Oldenburg. [New York? c1967] [24] p. illus., port. 28 cm. On label on t.p.: Supplied by Worldwide Books, New York. "An exhibition of new work by Claes Oldenburg, April 26 to May 27, 1967 at Sidney Janis ... N.Y." [N6537.O4S5] 68-30096
I. Sidney Janis Gallery.

OLDENBURG, Claes, 1929- 709'.2'4
Oldenburg : six themes : [exhibition] / introd. by Martin Friedman and interviews with Claes Oldenburg. Minneapolis : Walker Art Center, [1975] 99 p. : ill. (some col.) ; 26 cm. "Checklist of the exhibition, 6 April-25 May 1975, Walker Art Center, Minneapolis" (9 p.) inserted at end. Bibliography: p. 99. [NB237.O42W34] 75-7702
1. Oldenburg, Claes, 1929- I. Walker Art Center, Minneapolis.

OLDENBURG, Claes, 1929- 709'.24
Proposals for monuments and buildings, 1965-69. Chicago, Big Table Pub. Co. [1969] 196 p. illus. (part col.) 25 cm. ([A

Big Table book]) Bibliography: p. [171]-175. [NC1075.O4A53] 69-13384 12.95
I. Title.

ROSE, Barbara. 730'.924
Claes Oldenburg. New York, Museum of Modern Art; distributed by New York Graphic Society, Greenwich, Conn. [1970] 221 p. illus. (part col.) 22 x 37 cm. "This book was undertaken at the invitation of the Museum of Modern Art in conjunction with its major retrospective exhibition of the work of Claes Oldenburg (September 25-November 23, 1969)." Bibliography: p. 206-214. [N6537.O4R6] 69-11450
1. Oldenburg, Claes, 1929- I. New York (City). Museum of Modern Art. BIP

O'Leary, Dennis, 1945—

O'LEARY, Dennis, 1945- 730'.92'4
Dennis O'Leary : an exhibition organized by the La Jolla Museum of Contemporary Art, 7 May-6 June, 1976. La Jolla, Calif. : La Jolla Museum of Contemporary Art, c1976. 32 p. : ill. ; 21 x 23 cm. Bibliography: p. 31. [NB237.O43L34] 76-12429
1. O'Leary, Dennis, 1945- I. La Jolla Museum of Contemporary Art. II. Title.

Olitski, Jules, 1922—

JULES Olitski: recent 759.13
paintings; an exhibition organized by the Institute of Contemporary Art, University of Pennsylvania, in collaboration with the Hayden Gallery, Massachusetts Institute of Technology. Exhibition dates: Institute of Contemporary Art, Philadelphia, February 21 to March 26, 1968; Massachusetts Institute of Technology, Cambridge, March 29 to April 23, 1968. [Philadelphia, Printed by Falcon Press, 1968?] [31] p. illus. (part col.) 22 cm. Essay by Rosalind E. Krauss. Bibliography: p. [30] [ND237.O52J8] 77-282940
1. Olitski, Jules, 1922- I. Krauss, Rosalind E. II. Pennsylvania. University. Institute of Contemporary Art. III. Hayden Gallery.

OLITSKI, Jules, 1922- 759.13
Jules Olitski. Boston, Museum of Fine Arts; distributed by New York Graphic Society, Greenwich, Conn. [1973] 71 p. illus. (part col.) 26 x 31 cm. Catalogue of an exhibition to be held at Museum of Fine Arts, Boston, Apr. 6-May 13, 1973; at Albright-Knox Art Gallery, Buffalo, May 31-July 29, 1973; at Whitney Museum of American Art, New York, Sept. 7-Nov. 4, 1973. Includes bibliographical references. [ND237.O52B66] 72-94431 ISBN 0-87846-070-5 17.50
1. Olitski, Jules, 1922- I. Boston. Museum of Fine Arts. II. Albright-Knox Art Gallery. III. Whitney Museum of American Art, New York.

Oliveira, Nathan, 1928-

CALIFORNIA. University. 759.13
University at Los Angeles. Art Galleries.
Nathan Oliveira. [Exhibition] organized by the UCLA Art Galleries. Presented at University of California, Los Angeles, San Francisco Museum of Art, Fort Worth Art Center, Colorado Springs Fine Arts Center, 1963-1964. [Los Angeles, 1964?] v. (unpaged) illus. 28 cm. [ND237.O53C3] 66-49543
1. Oliveira, Nathan, 1928- I. Title.

SAN Francisco. Museum 760'.0924
of Art.
Nathan Oliveira; works on paper, 1960-1969. [San Francisco, 1969] [16] p. illus. 24 cm. Catalog of a loan exhibition held July 31-Aug. 31, 1969. [NC139.O46S2] 73-12405
1. Oliveira, Nathan, 1928-

SAN Francisco. Museum 760'.0924
of Art.
Nathan Oliveira: works on paper, 1960-1969. [Exhibition] San Francisco Museum of Art, July 31-Aug. 31, 1969. [San Francisco, 1969] [16] p. illus. 24 cm. Catalogue essay by J. Humphrey. [N6537.O44S2] 70-283476
1. Oliveira, Nathan, 1928- I. Humphrey, John, 1909- II. Title.

Olivera, Fortino.

RUTGERS University, 746.3'9'22
New Brunswick, N.J. University Art Gallery.
Contemporary Mexican tapestries: Fortino Olivera and Isaac Gutierez. [Exhibition] March 7 through April 16, 1967. [New Brunswick? N.J., c1967] 12 p. illus. 24 cm. (Its Bulletin, v. 1, no. 2) [N722.A3 vol. 1, no. 2] 73-17724
1. Olivera, Fortino. 2. Gutierez, Isaac. I. Title. II. Series.

Olmecs.

GAY, Carlo T. E. 732'.2
Xochipala: the beginning of Olmec art [by] Carlo T. E. Gay. [Princeton, N.J., Distributed by Princeton University Press, 1972] 61, [2] p. illus. 27 cm. Published in connection with the exhibition held Jan. 11-Feb. 13, 1972, at the Art Museum of Princeton University. "The text is taken from a work in progress on preclassic ceramic figures from central and midwestern Mexico, by Carlo T. E. Gay and Frances Pratt." Bibliography: p. [63] [F1219.1.G93G32] 70-187566 ISBN 0-691-03877-5 8.00
1. Olmecs. 2. Xochipala Valley, Mexico—Antiquities. I. Princeton University. Art Museum. II. Title.

HOUSTON, Tex. Museum of 707.4
Fine Arts.
The Olmec tradition [exhibition] June 18 to August 25, 1963. Houston, Author [1963] [73]p. illus., map. 28cm. 63-21043 apply
1. Olmecs. 2. Indians of Mexico—Art. I. Title.
Contents omitted.

Olmecs—Art.

BENSON, Elizabeth P. 917 s
An Olmec figure at Dumbarton Oaks [by] Elizabeth P. Benson. Washington, Dumbarton Oaks, Trustees for Harvard University, 1971. 39 p. illus. 27 cm. (Studies in pre-Columbian art and archaeology, no. 8) Bibliography: p. 38-39. [E51.S85 no. 8] [F1219] 732'.2 70-184640 2.00
1. Olmecs—Art. I. Dumbarton Oaks. II. Title. III. Series. BIP

CALIFORNIA. 730'.972'6
University. Archaeological Research Facility.
Colossal heads of the Olmec culture. [By] C. William Clewlow [and others] Berkeley, 1967. xi, 170 p. illus., maps, plan. 28 cm. (Its Contributions, no. 4) Includes bibliographies. [E51.C2] 68-63596
1. Olmecs—Art. 2. Indians of Mexico—Sculpture. 3. Vera Cruz, Mexico (State)—Antiq. 4. La Venta site. I. Clewlow, C. William. II. Title. III. Series: California. University. Archaeological Research Facility. Contributions, no. 4

CALIFORNIA. 730'.972'6
University. Archeological Research Facility.
Colossal heads of the Olmec culture. [By] C. William Clewlow [and others] Berkeley, 1967. xi, 170 p. illus., maps, plan. 28 cm. (Its Contributions, no. 4) Includes bibliographies. [E51.C2 no. 4] 68-63596
1. Olmecs—Art. 2. Indians of Mexico—Sculpture. 3. Vera Cruz, Mexico (State)—Antiquities. 4. La Venta site. I. Clewlow, C. William. II. Title. III. Series: California. University. Archaeological Research Facility. Contributions, no. 4

GROVE, David C. 917 s
The Olmec paintings of Oxtotitlan Cave, Guerrero, Mexico [by] David C. Grove. With photos. and drawings by the author and renderings by Felipe Davalos. Washington, Dumbarton Oaks, 1970. 36 p. illus. 27 cm. (Studies in pre-Columbian art and archaeology, no. 6) Bibliography: p. 35-36. [E51.S85 no. 6] [F1219.3.A7] 732'.2 71-127458
1. Olmecs—Art. 2. Indians of Mexico—Art. 3. Oxtotitlan Cave, Mexico. I. Dumbarton Oaks. II. Title. III. Series. BIP

JORALEMON, Peter David. 917
A study of Olmec iconography. Washington, Dumbarton Oaks, 1971. 95 p. illus. 27 cm. (Studies in pre-Columbian art and archeology, no. 7) Bibliography: p. 92-95. [E51.S85 no. 7] [F1219.3.A7] 79-169917
1. Olmecs—Art. 2. Indians of Mexico—Art. I. Dumbarton Oaks. II. Title. III. Series.

WICKE, Charles R. 980.3
Olmec: an early art style of Precolumbian Mexico [by] Charles R. Wicke. Tucson, University of Arizona Press [1971] xvii, 188 p. illus., map. 27 cm. Bibliography: p. 169-180. [F1219.W53] 71-122581 ISBN 0-8165-0185-8 12.00
1. Olmecs—Art. I. Title.

Olmecs—Sculpture.

CLEWLOW, C. 913'.031'08 s
William.
A stylistic and chronological study of Olmec monumental sculpture [by] Carl William Clewlow, Jr. Berkeley, University of California, Dept. of Anthropology, 1974. vii, 229 p. illus. 28 cm. (Contributions of the University of California Archaeological Research Facility, no. 19) Revision of the auhtor's thesis, University of California, Berkeley, 1972. Bibliography: p. 216-229. [E51.C2 no. 19] [F1219] 732'.2'09701 74-621854
1. Olmecs—Sculpture. 2. Indians of Mexico—Sculpture. I. Title. II. Series: California. University. Archaeological Research Facility. Contributions, no. 19.

Olmsted, Frederick Law, 1822-1903.

BARLOW, 711'.558'097471
Elizabeth.
Frederick Law Olmsted's New York. Text by Elizabeth Barlow. Illustrative portfolio by William Alex. New York, Praeger, in association with the Whitney Museum of American Art [1972] 173 p. illus. 20 x 26 cm. First published on the occasion of an exhibition of the same title presented by the Whitney Museum of American Art in New York City, Oct. 19-Dec. 3, 1972, organized and directed by William Alex. Bibliography: p. [172]-173. [F128.65.C3B37 1972] 72-82771 12.50
1. Olmsted, Frederick Law, 1822-1903. 2. New York (City)—Parks—Central Park. 3. Brooklyn—Parks—Prospect Park. I. Alex, William. II. Whitney Museum of American Art, New York. III. Title.

FABOS, Julius Gy. 712'.0924 B
Frederick Law Olmsted, Sr.; founder of landscape architecture in America [by] Julius Gy. Fabos, Gordon T. Milde, & V. Michael Weinmayr. [Amherst] University of Massachusetts Press, 1968. 114 p. illus. (part fold.), maps, plans, ports. 26 cm. [SB470.O5F32] 68-19670 12.00
1. Olmsted, Frederick Law, 1822-1903. 2. Parks—United States. I. Milde, Gordon T., joint author. II. Weinmayr, V. Michael, joint author.

FEIN, Albert. 712'.092'4
Frederick Law Olmsted and the American environmental tradition. New York, G. Braziller [1972] xi, 180 p. illus. 26 cm. (Planning and cities) "Selected list of the writings of Frederick Law Olmsted": p. 171-176. [NA737.O4F4 1972] 72-75831 ISBN 0-8076-0650-2 10.00 3.95 (pbk)
1. Olmsted, Frederick Law, 1822-1903. 2. Architecture and society. 3. Urban beautification. I. Title.

OLMSTED, Frederick Law, 712'.08 s
1822-1903.
The formative years, 1822 to 1852 / Charles Capen McLaughlin, editor, Charles E. Beveridge, associate editor. Baltimore : Johns Hopkins University Press, c1977. xx, 423 p. : ill. ; 25 cm. (The Papers of Frederick Law Olmstead ; v. 1) Includes bibliographical references and indexes. [SB470.O5A2 1977 vol. 1] 712'.08 76-47378 ISBN 0-8018-1798-6 : 20.00
1. Olmsted, Frederick Law, 1822-1903. 2. Landscape architects—United States—Correspondence. 3. Landscape architects—United States—Biography. I. Title.

OLMSTED, Frederick 712'.5'0924
Law, 1822-1903.
Forty years of landscape architecture: Central Park [by] Frederick Law Olmsted, Sr. Edited by Frederick Law Olmsted, Jr. and Theodora Kimball. Cambridge, Mass., MIT Press [1973, c1928] xviii, 575 p. illus. 21 cm. Reprint of v. 2 of the author's Frederick Law Olmsted landscape architect, 1822-1903, published by Putnam, New York. Bibliography: p. 563-575. [F128.65.C3O52 1973] 73-14121 ISBN 0-262-15009-3 4.95 (pbk.)
1. Olmstead, Frederick Law, 1822-1903. 2. New York (City)—Parks—Central Park. I. Olmsted, Frederick Law, 1870-1957, ed. II. Hubbard, Theodora (Kimball), 1887-1935, ed. III. Title.

ROPER, Laura Wood. 712'.092'4 B
Flo: A biography of Frederick Law Olmsted. Baltimore, Johns Hopkins University Press [1973] xvii, 555 p. illus. 25 cm. Includes bibliographical references. [SB470.O5R66] 73-8125 ISBN 0-8018-1508-8 15.00
1. Olmsted, Frederick Law, 1822-1903. 2. Landscape architecture—United States. I. Title.

STEVENSON, 712'.092'4 B
Elizabeth, 1919-
Park maker : a life of Frederick Law Olmstead / by Elizabeth Stevenson. New York : Macmillan, c1977. xxv, 484 p., [8] leaves of plates : ill. ; 25 cm. Includes index. Bibliography: p. 453-469. [SB470.O5S73] 76-52942 ISBN 0-02-614440-9 : 17.95
1. Olmsted, Frederick Law, 1822-1903. 2. Landscape architects—United States—Biography. I. Title. BIP

Olmsted, Frederick Law, 1822-1903—Archives.

UNITED States. 016.712'092'4
Library of Congress. Manuscript Division.
Frederick Law Olmsted : a register of his papers in the Library of Congress. Rev. ed. Washington : Manuscript Division, Research Dept., Library of Congress, 1977. p. cm. (Registers of papers in the Manuscript Division of the Library of Congress ; no. 28A) [Z6616.O5U53 1977] [SB470.O5] 76-608382 ISBN 0-8444-0229-X
1. Olmsted, Frederick Law, 1822-1903—Archives. 2. United States. Library of Congress. Manuscript Division. 3. Landscape architecture—United States—History—Sources—Bibliography—Catalogs. I. Series: United States. Library of Congress. Manuscript Division. Registers of papers in the Manuscript Division of the Library of Congress ; no. 28A.

Olmsted, Frederick Law, 1822-1903—Collected works.

OLMSTED, Frederick Law, 712'.08
1822-1903.
The papers of Frederick Law Olmstead / Charles Capen McLaughlin, editor, Charles E. Beveridge, associate editor. Baltimore : Johns Hopkins University Press, c1977- v. : ill. ; 25 cm. Contents.Contents.—v. 1. The formative years, 1822 to 1852. Includes bibliographical references and index. [SB470.O5A2 1977] 77-741 ISBN 0-8018-1798-6 (v.1) : 20.00
1. Olmsted, Frederick Law, 1822-1903—Collected works. 2. Landscape architects—United States—Correspondence—collected works. 3. Landscape architects—United States—Biography—Collected works.

Olmsted, Frederick Law, 1822-1903—Juvenile literature.

JOHNSTON, Johanna. 712'.092'4 B
Frederick Law Olmsted : partner with Nature / Johanna Johnston. New York : Dodd, Mead, [1975] 125 p. ; 24 cm. Includes index. Bibliography: p. 121-122. A biography of the self-taught landscape architect who designed many large park systems, including the first large city park in America, Central Park in New York. [SB470.O5J63] 92 74-25519 ISBN 0-396-07079-5 : 4.95
1. Olmsted, Frederick Law, 1822-1903—Juvenile literature. 2. Parks—United States—Juvenile literature. 3. Landscape architecture—United States—Juvenile literature. I. Title. BIP

NOBLE, Iris. 712'.092'4 B
Frederick Law Olmsted, park designer.
New York, J. Messner [1974] 190 p. 21
cm. Bibliography: p. 185-186. A biography
of the nineteenth-century park and city
planner and conservationist who designed
New York's Central Park, among countless
others, and was instrumental in the
creation of the National Park Service.
[SB470.O5N62] 92 74-7585 ISBN 0-671-
32675-9 5.95
*1. Olmsted, Frederick Law, 1822-1903—
Juvenile literature. 2. Parks—United
States—History—Juvenile literature. 3.
Landscape architecture—United States—
History—Juvenile literature. I. Title.*
Library binding; 5.29, ISBN 0-671-3267-7.

Olovson, Gudmar, 1936—

OLOVSON, Gudmar, 1936- 730'.92'4
Gudmar Olovson : [first one-man
exhibition in the United States] : April 28-
May 12, 1976. N[ew] Y[ork] : Kennedy
Galleries, c1976. [8] p. : chiefly ill. ; 28
cm. [N7093.O46K46] 76-368576
*1. Olovson, Gudmar, 1936- I. Kennedy
Galleries, inc., New York.*

Olympic games (in numismatics)

DANAHER, Mary A., 1938- 737.4
*The commemorative coinage of modern
sports* / Mary A. Danaher. South
Brunswick [N.J.] : A. S. Barnes, c1978.
183 p. : ill. ; 25 cm. Includes index.
Bibliography: p. 177-178. [CJ161.S65D36
1978] 75-20610 ISBN 0-498-01787-7
9.95
*1. Olympic games (in numismatics) 2.
Sports (in numismatics) I. Title.* BIP

Olympus camera.

COOPER, Joseph David, 771.31
1917-
Olympus camera guide. New York, Univ.
Photo Bks. [dist. Amphoto, c. 1962] 128p.
illus. 61-14254 1.95pap.,
*1. Olympus camera. 2. Photography—
Handbooks, manuals, etc. I. Title.*

EMANUEL, Walter Daniel, 771.3'1
1908-
*Olympus compact 35mm guide; how to use
the Olympus trip, Olympus 35 SP,
Olympus compact 35 EC and ECR,
Olympus 35 RC, and Olympus compact 35
DC,* by W. D. Emanuel. London, New
York, Focal Press; distributed in the
U.S.A. by Amphoto. New York [1972] 63
p. illus. 16 cm. (Focal camera guides)
[TR263.O4E48] 72-89547 ISBN 0-8174-
0761-8 2.50 (U.S.)
*1. Olympus camera. 2. Photography—
Handbooks, manuals, etc. I. Title.*

HEIBERG, Milton. 771.3'1
The OLympus guide / Milton Heiberg.
Garden City, N.Y. : Amphoto, c1978. 118
p., [4] leaves of plates : ill. (some col.) ; 26
cm. (A Modern camera guide series)
Includes index. [TR263.O4H44] 77-28695
ISBN 0-8174-2449-0 : 9.95. ISBN 0-8174-
2104-1 pbk. : 5.95
*1. Olympus camera. 2. Photography—
Handbooks, manuals, etc. I. Title. II.
Series: The Modern camera guide series.*
BIP

JACOBS, Lou. 771.3'1
Olympus OM camera manual / Lou
Jacobs, Jr. Garden City, N.Y. : Amphoto,
c1977. 192 p. : ill. ; 24 cm. Includes index.
[TR263.O4J3] 76-16459 ISBN 0-8174-
2412-1 : 11.95
*1. Olympus camera. 2. Photography—
Handbooks, manuals, etc. I. Title.* BIP

LONDON, Barbara, 1936- 771.3'1
A short course in Olympus photography /
Barbara London. New York : Van
Nostrand Reinhold Co., [1979] 191 p.
Includes index. Bibliography: p.
[TR263.O4L66] 78-23904 ISBN 0-442-
26606-5 pbk. : 9.00 ISBN 0-442-26616-2 :
14.95
*1. Olympus camera. 2. Photography—
Handbooks, manuals, etc. I. Title.*

Oman, Charles Chichele, 1901-

VICTORIA and Albert 739.23742
Museum, South Kensington
English Silversmiths' work. civil and
domestic: an introduction-by Charles
Oman London, H.M.S.O. New York
British Info., 1966. c.1965 [5]. 16p. front.,
192 plates (incl. facsim.) 26cm. [NK
7143.V492] 66-2654 8.40
*1. Oman, Charles Chichele, 1901- 2.
Silversmiths'—Gt. Brit. I. Oman, Charles
Chichele, 1901- II. Title.*

Onderdonk family.

STEINFELDT, Cecilia. 759.13 B
The Onderdonks : a family of Texas
painters / Cecilia Steinfeldt. [San Antonio]
: Published for the San Antonio Museum
Association by Trinity University Press,
1975, c1976. 238 p. : ill. (some col.) ; 24 x
29 cm. "Published in conjunction with an
exhibition ... held at the Witte Memorial
Museum, Brackenridge Park, San Antonio,
Texas, January 16, 1975 to July 31, 1975."
Includes index. Bibliography: p. 232-233.
[ND237.O54S73] 74-29009 ISBN 0-
911536-57-4 : 25.00
*1. Onderdonk family. 2. Painters—Texas—
Biography. I. San Antonio Museum
Association. II. Witte Memorial Museum,
San Antonio. III. Title.* BIP

O'Neill, Rose Cecil, 1874-1944.

MCCANSE, Ralph Alan. 740'.924 B
*Titans and kewpies; the life and art of
Rose O'Neill.* [1st ed.] New York, Vantage
Press [1968] 220 p. illus., ports. 21 cm.
[NC139.O5M3] 68-1950
1. O'Neill, Rose Cecil, 1874-1944. I. Title.

RUGGLES, Rowena Fay 741.6
(Godding)
*The one Rose, mother of the immortal
Kewpies;* a biography of Rose O'Neill and
the story of her work, by Rowena Godding
Ruggles. [Oakland? Calif., 1964] xi, 80 p.
plates, ports. 25 cm. [NC139.O5R8] 64-
6933
1. O'Neill, Rose Cecil, 1874-1944. I. Title.

RUGGLES, Rowena Fay 741'.092'4 B
(Godding)
*The one Rose, mother of the immortal
Kewpies;* a biography of Rose O'Neill and
the story of her work, by Rowena Godding
Ruggles. 2d ed. with supplemental
material. [Albany, Calif., 1972] xiii, 96 p.
illus. 25 cm. [NC139.O5R8 1972] 72-
178759 15.00
1. O'Neill, Rose Cecil, 1874-1944. I. Title.

Opal glass.

HARTUNG, Marion T. 748.2'913
Opalescent pattern glass, by Marion T.
Hartung. [1st ed. Emporia, Kan., 1971]
112 p. illus. (part col.) 27 cm.
[NK5112.H36] 76-30617
1. Opal glass. I. Title. BIP

Opera—Pictorial works.

BROIDO, Lucy. 769'.5
French opera posters, 1868-1930 / Lucy
Broido. New York : Dover Publications,
1976. ix, 52, xv-xxv p. : chiefly ill. (some
col.) ; 31 cm. Bibliography: p. vii.
[ML89.B76] 75-32586 ISBN 0-486-23306-
5 : 5.00
*1. Opera—Pictorial works. 2. Theatrical
posters, French. I. Title.* BIP

Oppenheim, Moritz, d. 1882.

OPPENHEIM, Moritz, d.1882. 759.3
Pictures of traditional Jewish family life /
by Moritz Daniel Oppenheim ; with an
introd. by Alfred Werner. New York :
Ktav Pub. House, 1976. p. cm. (The
Library of Jewish art) Translation of Bilder
aus dem altjudischen Familienleben.
[ND588.O58A4313] 76-41250 ISBN 0-
87068-472-8 : 25.00
*1. Oppenheim, Moritz, d. 1882. 2. Jewish
way of life in art. I. Title.*

Oprescu, George, 1881-

GRIGORESCU, Nicolae, 759.9498
1838-1907
Grigorescu, 1838-1907 [by] G. Oprescu.
[dist. New York, Vanous, 1962] 180p.
illus. (pt. mounted col.) col. plates. 30cm.
62-2910 13.90
1. Oprescu, George, 1881- I. Title.

Optical art.

BARRETT, Cyril. 709'.04
Op art. New York, Viking Press [1970]
192 p. illus. (part col.) 26 cm. (A Studio
book) Bibliography: p. [188]
[N6494.O6B28 1970b] 70-109217 10.95
1. Optical art. I. Title.

GRAFTON, Carol Belanger. 701'.8
Optical designs in motion : with moire
overlays / Carol Belanger Grafton. New
York : Dover Publications, c1976. [32] p. :
chiefly ill. (1 in pocket) ; 31 cm.
[NC260.5.G7 1976] 75-40775 ISBN 0-486-
23284-0 pbk. : 3.00
1. Optical art. 2. Visual perception. I. Title.

LARCHER, Jean, 1947- 741.9'44
Optical and geometrical allover patterns :
70 original drawings / by Jean Larcher.
New York : Dover Publications, 1979. [76]
p. : all ill. ; 28 cm. (Dover pictorial archive
series) Pref. in English and French.
[NC248.L335A4 1979] 78-72985 ISBN 0-
486-23758-3 : 3.50
*1. Larcher, Jean, 1947- 2. Optical art. 3.
Visual perception. I. Title.* BIP

PAROLA, Rene. 709.04
Optical art; theory and practice. New
York, Reinhold Book Corp. [1969] 144 p.
illus. (part col.) 29 cm. Bibliography: p.
143. [N6494.O6P3] 68-16031
1. Optical art. I. Title.

Optical art—Exhibitions.

CALIFORNIA. University, 709'.73
Irvine. Art Gallery.
*New York: the second breakthrough, 1959-
1964.* [Exhibition] March 18 to April 27,
1969. [Irvine, 1969] 31 p. illus. (part col.)
25 cm. "Catalog of the exhibition": p. 30-
31. [N6512.C27] 76-626168
1. Optical art—Exhibitions. I. Title.

Optical illusions.

LANNERS, Edi, comp. 152.1'48
Illusions / edited by Edi Lanners ;
translated and adapted by Heinz Norden.
New York : Holt, Rinehart and Winston,
[1977] 159 p., [8] leaves of plates : ill. ; 28
cm. Bibliography: p. 157. [N7430.5.L2913]
77-71375 ISBN 0-03-020891-2 : 12.95.
ISBN 0-03-020886-6 pbk. : 6.95
*1. Optical illusions. 2. Visual perception. I.
Title.* BIP

Optima camera.

EMANUEL, ,walter Daniel, 771.31
1908-
*Optima guide: original Optima, Optima I,
II, IIS, IIIS, and Optima Reflex.* New
York, Focal Pr. [dist. Amphoto, c. 1962]
56p. illus. 17cm. (Focal camera guide) 62-
4568 1.90
*1. Optima camera. 2. Photography —
Handbooks, manuals, etc. I. Title.*

Orchids—Indexes.

HAMILTON, Robert 769'.4'958415016
M., 1912- comp.
Orchid flower index; a world list of
reproductions in color in books and
periodicals 1736 to 1966. Repertoire des
fleurs orchidees; catalogue mondial des
illustrations en couleurs figuerant [sic] dans
les livres et periodiques de 1736 a 1966.
Das Orchideenblumenverzeichnis eine
Weltlist der Farbreproduktionen in
Buchern und Zeitschriften 1736-1966.
Richmond, B.C., 1967. x, 204 p. col. illus.
26 cm. Title and note on "Sources" in
English, French and German.
[QK495.O64H24] 67-95157
1. Orchids—Indexes. I. Title.

Oregon—Description and travel—
1951- —Views.

ATKESON, Ray. 779'.9'97950924
Beautiful Oregon / featuring Ray Atkeson
photography ; text by Paul M. Lewis.
Eugene, Or. : Beautiful Oregon
Publications, 1974. 70 p. : chiefly ill. (some
col.) ; 28 cm. [F877.A77] 75-314222
*1. Oregon—Description and travel—1951-
—Views. I. Lewis, Paul M. II. Title.* BIP

LEWIS, Paul M. 779'.9'91795044
Oregon coast / text by Paul M. Lewis.
Portland, Or. : Beautiful West Pub. Co.,
1977. 72 p. : col. ill. ; 29 cm. Cover title:
Beautiful Oregon coast. [F877.L48] 78-
102344 ISBN 0-915796-21-X : 12.95.
*1. Oregon—Description and travel—1951-
—Views. 2. Coasts—Oregon—Pictorial
works. I. Title. II. Title: Beautiful Oregon
coast.*

Oriental antiquities.

CHILDE, Vere Gordon, 1892- 913.3
1957.
New light on the most ancient East. [4th
ed.] New York, F. A. Praeger [1953] xiii,
255 p. illus., maps. 23 cm. (Books that
matter) First published 1928 under title:
The most ancient East. Bibliography: p.
245-246. [DS11.C52 1953] 52-13107
*1. Oriental antiquities. 2. Man, Prehistoric.
3. Civlization, Ancient. I. Title.* BIP

Origami.

ARNSTEIN, Bennett. 736'.98
*Origami polyhedra; how to make
threedimensional geometric models. With
diagrams and photos.* [1st ed.] New York,
Exposition [1968] 112p. illus. 25cm.
(Exposition-banner bk.) Bibl. [TT870.A7]
67-26388 5.00
1. Origami. 2. Polyhedra—Models. I. Title.

*HAPPY origami; 736.9
the Japanese art of paper folding* [2v. by
Tatsuo Miyawaki. Rutland, Vt., Japan
Pubns., c.1964] unpaged illus. (pt. col.)
20x27cm. Contents.[1] Butterfly books.--[2]
Tortoise book. 2.50 bds., ea.,
1. Origami. I. Miyawaki, Tatsuo.

HARBIN, Robert, 1909- 736'.98
Origami : a step by step guide / Robert
Harbin. London ; New York : Hamlyn,
1974. 79 p. : ill. (some col.) ; 26 cm.
Includes index. Bibliography: p. [78]
[TT870.H317] 74-195806 ISBN 0-600-
38109-9 : £1.25
1. Origami.

HARBIN, Robert, 1909- 736'.98
Secrets of origami: the Japanese art of
paper folding; illustrated by the author;
photographs by Kingsley Mitchell and
Robert Harbin. London, New York,
Octopus Books Ltd, 1971. 248 p. illus.,
ports. 28 cm. Bibliography: p. 246-247.
[TT870.H32] 73-158594 ISBN 0-7064-
0005-4 £1.50
1. Origami. I. Title.

HONDA, Isao 736.9
Pocket guide to origami, Japanese paper
folding. Rutland, Vt., Japan Pubns. [1963,
c.1959] 31p. col. illus. (pt. fold.) 1.00 pap.,
1. Title.

HONDA, Isao, 1888- 736.9
All about origami. Tr. [from Japanese] by
H. G. Nielsen. [dist. New York,
International Publications Service, 1961,
c.1960] 196p. illus. (part col.) 28cm. 61-
1569 6.95, bxd.
1. Origami. I. Title.

HONDA, Isao, 1888- 736.9
All about origami. [Tr. by H. G. Nielsen]
Tokyo, Toto Bunka Co.; dist. [Rutland,
Vt.] Japan Pubns. Trading Co. 11-13
Center St. [1963, c.1960], 196p. illus. (pt.
col.) 28cm. 61-1569 7.50
1. Origami. I. Title.

HONDA, Isao, 1888- 736.9
Living origami; Bk. 1. Japanese paper
folding. [Dist.] Rutland, Vt., Tuttle
[c.1962] 25p. col. illus. (pt. fold in pocket)
27cm. 62-6628 2.95 bds.,
1. Origami. I. Title.

HONDA, Isao, 1888- 736.9
Noshi; classic origami in Japan [Tr. by Masatsugu Tsuzawa, Donald C. Mann [Rutland, Vt.] Japan Pubns. [c.1964] 64p. illus. (pt. col.) 22cm. 64-6531 1.50 pap.,
1. Origami. I. Title.

HONDA, Isao, 1888- 736.98
The world of origami. [Translated by Richard L. Gage.] 1st ed.] Tokyo, New York. Japan Publications Trading Co. [1965] 264 p. illus., col. plates. 31 cm. Bibliography: p. 261-262. [TT870.H653] 65-27101
1. Origami. I. Title. BIP

KENNEWAY, Eric. 736'.98
Folding faces : making portraits in paper / Eric Kenneway. New York : Paddington Press ; distributed by Grosset & Dunlap, c1978. 95, [1] p. : ill. ; 28 cm. Bibliography: p. 96. [TT870.K43] 77-20990 ISBN 0-448-22557-3 pbk. : 4.95
1. Origami. 2. Portraits. I. Title. BIP

LEWIS, Shari 736.98
Folding paper masks [by] Shari Lewis, Lillian Oppenheimer. Orig.masks created by Giuseppe Baggi. New York, Dutton [c.1965] 93p. illus. 27cm. Bibl. [TT870.L45] 65-24481 3.95 bds.,
1. Origami, 2. Masks. I. Oppenheimer, Lillian, joint author. II. Title.

LEWIS, Shari. 736.9
Folding paper toys, by Shari Lewis and Lillian Oppenheimer. New York, Stein and Day [1963] 93 p. illus. 27 cm. Bibliography: p. 93. [TT870.L46] 63-20060
1. Origami. 2. Toys. I. Oppenheimer, Lillian, joint author. II. Title. BIP

MIYAWAKI, Tatsuo 736.9
Happy origami the Japanese art of paper folding. Hiroshima, Japan, Biken-sha, dist. [Rutland, Vt.] Japan Pubns. Trading Co., 11-13 Center St. [1963] c.1960. cunpaged. illus. (pt. col.) 20x27cm. 2.50 bds.,
1. Origami. I. Title.

MIYAWAKI, Tatsuo. 736
Origami playtime. New York, Japan Publications Trading Co. [1967] 51 p. illus. (part col.) 27 cm. Colored paper for making origami designs in pocket. A picture book as well as a manual for origami enthusiasts. Includes illustrations that can be enhanced by the reader's own origami figures. [TT870.M5] AC 67
1. Origami. 2. Picture books. I. Title.

MIYAWAKI, Tatsuo 736.9
Pop-up origami. Hiroshima, Japan, Biken-sha; dist. [Rutland Vt.] Japan Pubns. Trading Co., 11-13 Center St. [1963] c.1962. unpaged (chiefly illus., pt. col.) 20cm. 2.50 bds.,
1. Origami. I. Title.

ORIGAMI zoo, 736.9
[2v.] Origami designs by Isao Honda, Explanations of birds by Tadamichi Koga. Tokyo Toto Shuppan Co., dist. Rutland Vt. Japan Pubns. Trading Co., 11-13 Center St,. 1963 c. 1961 [2v.] 28;28p. illus. (pt. col.) 27x38cm. Contents.[v.1] Animal book.--[v.2] Bird book. 3.95, pap., ea. bxd.
1. Origami. I. Honda, Isao. II. Koga, Tadamichi.

POCKET guide to origami 736.9
[Tokyo, Japan, Asahi Origami Club, dist. Rutland, Vt., Japan Pubns., 1963, c.1960] 28p. col. illus. 19cm. (Bunny bk.) 1.00 pap.,

RANDLETT, Samuel. 736.9
The art of origami; paper folding, traditional and modern. Illus. by Jean Randlett; pref. by Lillian Oppenheimer; introd. by Edward Kallop. [1st ed.] New York, Dutton [1961] 192 p. illus. 27 cm. [TT870.R3] 61-6021
1. Origami. I. Title.

RANDLETT, Samuel. 736.9
The best of origami; new models by contemporary folders. Line drawings and photos. by Jean Randlett. Pref. by Martin Gardner. [1st ed.] New York, Dutton [1963] 185 p. illus., diagrs. 26 cm. Bibliography: p. 183. [TT870.R32] 63-15776
1. Origami. I. Randlett, Jean, illus. II. Title.

SAKADE, Florence 736.9
Origami storybook; Japanese paper-folding play, Illustrated by Kazuhiko Sono. Rutland, Vt., C. E. Tuttle Co. [1960] 30p. illus. (part. mounted, part col.) 31cm. 60-10952 4.50 bds.,
1. Origami. 2. Children's stories. I. Title.

SAKODA, James Minoru, 736'.98
1916-
Modern origami. New York, Simon and Schuster [1969] 144 p. illus. 28 cm. Bibliography: p. 141. [TT870.S27] 77-84130 2.95
1. Origami. I. Title.

**SUNNY origami* 736.98
[Rutland, Vt., Japan Pubns., 1966] 1v. (unpaged) col. illus. 28x28cm. (Angel bk.) 2.50 pap.,
1. Origami.

TEMKO, Florence. 736
Paperfolding to begin with, by Florence Temko and Elaine Simon. Pictures by Joan Stoliar. [1st ed.] Indianapolis, Bobbs-Merrill [1968] 31 p. col. illus. 22 x 29 cm. Simple illustrated directions for making various toys—cats, boats, butterflies, whales, etc.—by Origami, the Japanese art of paperfolding. [LB1542.T4] AC 68
1. Origami. 2. Paper work. I. Simon, Elaine, joint author. II. Stoliar, Joan, illus. III. Title.

WILLIAMS, Ned. 736'.98
New adventures in origami; the art of paper-folding [by] Robert Harbin. New York, Funk & Wagnalls [1972, c1971] vi, 186 p. illus. 18 cm. (A Funk & Wagnalls paperbook, F81) First published in 1971 under title: More origami. [TT870.W47 1972] 76-190495 1.25
1. Origami. I. Title.

WILLIAMS, Ned. 736'.98
Origami; the art of paper folding [by] Robert Harbin. [1st American ed. New York] Funk & Wagnalls [1969] v, 186 p. illus. 18 cm. (A Funk & Wagnalls paperbook, F67) First published in 1968 under title: Teach yourself origami. Bibliography: p. 185-186. [TT870.W5 1969] 73-4168 1.25
1. Origami. I. Title.

Origami—Juvenile literature.

DAVIDSON, Georgie. 736'.98
Origami / Georgie Davidson. New York : Larousse, 1975. 96 p. : ill. ; 26 cm. (The Larousse craft series) Step-by-step instructions with diagrams for creating origami toys, wrappings, decorations, and other items. [TT870.D295] 75-4492 ISBN 0-88332-026-6 : 7.95. ISBN 0-88332-027-4 pbk. : 5.95
1. Origami—Juvenile literature. I. Title.

FUKUDA, Keinichi 736
Sunny origami. [Gumma, Japan, Jomo Hagaku Kogyosha; dist.: Japan Pubns., Tokyo, San Francisco, 1967] 1 v. (unpaged) illus. (pt. col.) 19x28cm. (Swan bk.) Cover title. [TT870.F8] 66-25568 2.50 pap.,
1. Origami—Juvenile literature. I. Title. II. Series: Swan books series

MIYAWAKI, Tatsuo. 736 (j)
Origami playtime. New York, Japan Publications Trading Co. [1967] 51 p. illus. (part col.) 27 cm. Colored paper for making origami designs in pocket. [TT870.M5] 67-20792
1. Origami—Juvenile literature. I. Title.

SAKADE, Florence 736.9
Fold-and-paste origami storybook, by Florence Sakade, Kazuhiko Sono. Rutland, Vt., Tuttle [1964] 31p. col. illus. (Tuttle handicraft bks.) Packet of paper. for folding, in pocket. 64-22899 price unreported
1. Origami— Juvenile literature. 2. Children's stories. I. Sono, Kazuhiko, j author. II. Title. BIP

SARASAS, Claude 736
The ABC's of origami; paper folding for children. Illus. by the author. Rutland, Vt., Tuttle [c.1964] 55p. col. illus. 27cm. 64-17160 2.95 bds.,
1. Origami—Juvenile literature. I. Title. II. Title: Paper folding for children. BIP

Origin and destination traffic surveys—Addresses, essays, lectures.

ORIGIN and destination 711'.73
technology; 9 reports. Washington, Highway Research Board, National Research Council, 1968. 96 p. illus., maps. 25 cm. (Highway research record no. 250) (National Research Council. Publication 1397.) Papers sponsored by Committee on Origin and Destination. Includes bibliographies. [TE7.H5 no. 250] 73-600534 3.40
1. Origin and destination traffic surveys—Addresses, essays, lectures. I. National Research Council. Highway Research Board. Committee on Origin and Destination. II. Title. III. Series.

Orkin, Ruth.

ORKIN, Ruth. 779'.9'97471040924
A world through my window / photos. by Ruth Orkin ; text compiled by Arno Karlen. 1st ed. New York : Harper & Row, c1978. p. cm. [TR654.O74] 78-2153 ISBN 0-06-013293-0 : 20.00
1. Orkin, Ruth. 2. Photography, Artistic. 3. New York (City)—Description—Views. I. Karlen, Arno. BIP

Ornamental horticulture—Study and teaching.

ORNAMENTAL 373.2'46'09773 s
horticulture; a guide for developing the instructional program. Springfield, State of Illinois, Vocational and Technical Education Div., 1966. 35, [1] l. illus. 28 cm. (Illinois. Board of Vocational Education and Rehabilitation. [Bulletin] Series B—Misc. no. 37A) At head of title: Floriculture, landscaping, turf management, nursery management. Cover title. Imperfect copy: lower half of leaf [36] not printed. Companion vol. to the division's Careers in ornamental horticulture. Bibliography: leaves 35-[36] [LC1046.I3A4 no. 37A] [SB403.5] 635.9'07'1 77-630965
1. Ornamental horticulture—Study and teaching. I. Illinois. Vocational and Technical Education Division. II. Series: Illinois. Board of Vocational Education and Rehabilitation. Bulletin, misc. no. 37A.

Ornamental horticulture—Study and teaching (Secondary)—Virginia.

BASS, Bruce 635.93'071'2755
Carter, 1908-
Competencies needed by teachers of high school ornamental horticulture courses, by B. C. Bass. Blacksburg, Virginia Polytechnic Institute and State University, 1970. 50 p. 28 cm. (Virginia Polytechnic Institute and State University. Research Division bulletin, 23) Errata slip inserted. Includes bibliographical references. [AS36.V512 no. 23] [SB403.5] 70-634634
1. Ornamental horticulture—Study and teaching (Secondary)—Virginia. I. Title. II. Series: Virginia Polytechnic Institute and State University. Research Division. Bulletin, 23

Ornamental horticulture—Vocational guidance.

MOORE, Stanley B. 635.9'023
Ornamental horticulture as a vocation [by] Stanley B. Moore. Fairborn, Ohio, Munkus Pub. Co. [1969] xiv, 364 p. illus. 24 cm. Bibliography: p. 363-364. [SB472.M65] 76-6818
1. Ornamental horticulture—Vocational guidance. I. Title. BIP

Ornamental trees.

ZION, Robert L. 715'2
Trees for architecture and the landscape [by] Robert L. Zion. Photos by Maude Dorr, Peter Lieberstein, and others. New York, Van Nostrand Reinhold [1975 c1968] 284 p. illus. (part col.), map. 32 cm. Bibliography: p. 277. [SB435.Z5] 66-14437 ISBN 0-442-11232-7 25.00
1. Ornamental trees. I. Title.
Pbk., 12.95; ISBN 0-442-29579-0 BIP

Ornithologists—South Africa—Biography.

KEMP, Alan C. 759.941
The biography of Claude Gibney Finch-Davies, 1875-1920 : observer, student and highly skilled illustrator of Southern African birds / text by A. C. Kemp. Pretoria : Transvaal Museum, c1976. 33 p., [30] leaves of plates : ill. (some col.), facsims. ; 36 cm. Includes bibliographical references. [QL31.F52K45] 77-368019 ISBN 0-620-02081-4
1. Finch-Davies, Claude Gibney, 1875-1920. 2. Ornithologists—South Africa—Biography. 3. Birds—Africa, Southern—Pictorial works. I. Title.

Ornithologists—United States—Biography.

CHANCELLOR, John. 598.2'092'4 B
Audubon : a biography / by John Chancellor. New York : Viking Press, 1978. 224 p. : ill. ; 26 cm. (A Studio book) Includes index. Bibliography: p. 219. [QL31.A9C43] 78-8465 ISBN 0-670-14053-8 : 16.95
1. Audubon, John James, 1785-1851. 2. Ornithologists—United States—Biography. BIP

Ornithologists—United States—Juvenile literature.

SANGER, Marjory 574'.092'4 B
(Bartlett)
Billy Bartram and his green world; an interpretative biography. [1st ed.] New York, Farrar, Straus & Giroux [1972] 207 p. plates. 24 cm. Bibliography: p. [197]-202. A biography of the eighteenth-century man who devoted his life to studying and drawing birds, animals, and plants in America's wilderness. [QL31.B33S35 1972] 92 78-175822 ISBN 0-374-30707-5 6.50
1. Bartram, William, 1739-1823—Juvenile literature. 2. Ornithologists—United States—Juvenile literature. I. Title. BIP

Orozco, Jose Clemente, 1883-1949.

HELM, MacKinley, 1896- 759.972 B
Man of fire: J. C. Orozco; an interpretative memoir. Westport, Conn., Greenwood Press [1971, c1953] ix, 245 p. illus. 27 cm. Bibliography: p. 111-117. [ND259.O7H43 1971] 79-106689 ISBN 0-8371-3361-0
1. Orozco, Jose Clemente, 1883-1949. I. Title.

HELM, MacKinley, 1896- 927.5
Man of fire: J. C. Orozco; an interpretative memoir. [1st ed.] New York, Harcourt, Brace [1953] ix, 245 p. illus., 67 plates (4 col.) port. 26 cm. Bibliography: p. 111-117. [ND259.O7H43] 759.972 52-13764
1. Orozco, Jose Clemente, 1883-1949. I. Title.

OROZCO, Jose Clemente, 759.972
1883-1949.
The artist in New York: letters to Jean Charlot and unpublished writings, 1925-1929. Foreword and notes by Jean Charlot. Letters and writings translated by Ruth L. C. Simms. Austin, University of Texas Press [1974] 99 p. illus. 22 cm. (The Texas pan American series) Includes bibliographical references. [ND259.O7C513] 74-5235 ISBN 0-292-70309-0
1. Orozco, Jose Clemente, 1883-1949. I. Charlot, Jean, 1898- II. Title.

OROZCO, Jose Clemente, 760'.0924
1883-1949.
Orozco; a catalogue of his graphic work [by] Jon H. Hopkins. Flagstaff, Northern Arizona University Publications, 1967. 136 p. illus. 29 cm. Bibliography: p. 129-136. [NE546.O7H6] 67-64938
I. Hopkins, Jon H. II. Title.

REED, Alma M. 927.5
Orozco. New York, Oxford University Press, 1956. 308 p. illus. 25 cm. [ND259.O7R4] 759.972 56-5428
1. Orozco, Jose Clemente, 1883-1949.

1. Owls in art. 2. Owls in literature. 3. Owls—Legends and stories. I. Title.

Oxford almanac—Illustrations.

PETTER, Helen Mary. 769'.942
The Oxford almanacks / Helen Mary Petter. Oxford : Clarendon Press, 1974. xi, 128 p., 4 leaves of plates : ill. ; 23 x 29 cm. Includes bibliographical references and index. [NE628.P47] 74-185495 ISBN 0-19-817329-6 : 32.00
1. Oxford almanac—Illustrations. 2. Engravings, British—Catalogs. I. Title.
Distributed by Oxford University Press, N.Y. BIP

Oxford—Hist.

GAUNT, William, 1900- 378.4257
Oxford. Photos. by Eric de Mare. New York, Hastings [1966,c.1965] 191p. illus., maps. 23cm. [DA690.O98G3] 66-31940 5.95
1. Oxford—Hist. 2. Oxford. University — Hist. 3. Architecture—Oxford. I. Title.

Oxford in art.

ATALAY, Bulent. 769'.92'4
Oxford and the English countryside; impressions in ink. Oxford [Eng.] Washington, Eton House [1974] iii, 8 p. 25 plates. 36 x 42 cm. Bibliography: p. 8. [NC296.A92A52] 74-77145
1. Atalay, Bulent. 2. Oxford in art. 3. England in art. I. Title.

Oxford. University.

OXFORD. University. 016.091
Catalogue of the manuscripts in the Oxford colleges, by H. O. Coxe. Introd. by K. W. Humphreys. Wakefield, E. P. Publishing, 1972- v. 24 cm. Reprint of the 1852 ed. published under title: Catalogus codicum mss. qui in collegiis aulisque oxoniensibus hodie adservantur. [Z6621.O98 1972] 73-160785 40.00
1. Oxford. University. 2. Manuscript—England—Oxford—Catalogs. I. Coxe, Henry Octavius, 1811-1881. II. Title.
Distributed by Rowman & Littlefield, Inc.

Oxford. University. Ashmolean Museum.

ITALIAN 741.9'45'07402574
drawings in Oxford : from the collections of the Ashmolean Museum and Christ Church / text and commentary by Terisio Pignatti ; [translated from the Italian by Barbara Luigia la Penta]. Oxford : Phaidon, 1977. 256 p. : ill. (chiefly col.), ports. (some col.) ; 32 cm. Translation of I grandi disegni Italiani nelle collezione di Oxford. Includes index. Bibliography: p. 83-86. [NC255.G6613] 78-305501 ISBN 0-7148-1764-3 : 49.95
1. Oxford University. Ashmolean Museum. 2. Oxford University. Christ Church. Picture Gallery. 3. Drawing, Italian—Catalogs. 4. Drawing—England—Oxford—Catalogs. I. Pignatti, Terisio, 1920- II. Oxford. University. Ashmolean Museum. III. Oxford. University. Christ Church. Picture Gallery.

OXFORD. University. 737.4'9'37
Ashmolean Museum.
Catalogue of coins of the Roman Empire in the Ashmolean Museum. Oxford [Eng.] : Clarendon Press, 1975- v. : ill. ; 39 cm. Includes indexes. Contents.Contents.—pt. 1. Sutherland, C. H. V. and Kraay, C. M. Augustus (c. 31 B.C.-A.D. 14) Bibliography: pt. 1, p. xi. [CJ969.O93 1975] 76-352677 ISBN 0-19-813189-5 : 56.00
1. Oxford. University. Ashmolean Museum. 2. Coins, Roman. I. Title.
Dist. by Oxford U. Press N.Y. N.Y. BIP

OXFORD. 736'.2'093807402574
University. Ashmolean Museum.
Catalogue of the engraved gems and finger rings / Ashmolean Museum, Oxford ; by John Boardman and marie-Louise Vollenweider. Oxford : Clarendon Press ; New York : Oxford University Press, 1978- v. : ill. ; 29 cm. Includes index. Contents.Contents.—1. Greek and Etruscan. [NK5565.O93 1978] 77-30290 ISBN 0-19-813195-X (v. 1) : 62.50 (vol. 1)
1. Oxford. University. Ashmolean Museum. 2. Gems, Classical—Catalogs. 3. Gems—England—Oxford—Catalogs. 4. Rings, Classical—Catalogs. 5. Rings—England—Oxford—Catalogs. I. Boardman, John, 1927- II. Vollenweider, Marie-Louise. III. Title.

OXFORD. 738.3'82'0938507402574
University. Ashmolean Museum.
Oxford, Ashmolean Museum / by John Boardman. London ; New York : Published for the British Academy by Oxford University Press, 1975- v. : ill. ; 31 cm. (Corpus vasorum antiquorum : Great Britain ; fas. 14 : Oxford ; fas. 3) At head of title: Union academique internationle. Issued in portfolio. Includes bibliographical references and indexes. [NK4623.5.G7O926 1975] 76-354773 ISBN 0-19-725953-7 (v. 1) : 47.00 (U.S.) (v. 1)
1. Oxford. University. Ashmolean Museum. 2. Vases—Greece—Catalogs. 3. Vases—England—Oxford—Catalogs. I. Boardman, John, 1927- II. Title. III. Series: Corpus vasorum antiquorum : Great Britain ; fas. 14.

OXFORD. University. 914.22'5
Ashmolean Museum.
Report of the visitors. Oxford. v. 22cm. annual. [AM101.O773] 57-50624
I. Title.

Oxford. University. Ashmolean Museum. Dept. of Western Art.

OXFORD. 741.9'42'07402574
University. Ashmolean Museum. Dept. of Western Art.
Seventeenth and eighteenth century English drawings in the Ashmolean Museum [Department of Western Art]. Oxford ([University of Oxford, Oxford OX1 2PH]) : Ashmolean Museum, 1974. [4], 31 p. : (chiefly ill.). ; 19 cm. Cover title. [NC228.O93 1974] 75-320478 ISBN 0-900090-15-4 : £0.30
1. Oxford. University. Ashmolean Museum. Dept. of Western Art. 2. Drawings, English. I. Title.

Oxford. University. Bodleian Library.

HASSALL, A. G. 745.6'7'07402574
Treasures from the Bodleian Library / A. G. and W. O. Hassall ; introd. by R. W. Hunt. New York : Columbia University Press, 1976. 160 p. : col. ill. ; 37 cm. Includes bibliographical references and index. [ND2897.O93H37 1976] 75-33231 ISBN 0-231-04060-1 : 60.00
1. Oxford. University. Bodleian Library. 2. Illumination of books and manuscripts—Oxford. I. Hassall, William Owen, joint author. II. Title. BIP

OXFORD. 016.7456'7'07402574
University. Bodleian Library.
Illuminated manuscripts : an index to selected Bodleian Library color reproductions / compiled and edited by Thomas H. Ohlgren. New York : Garland Pub., 1977. p. cm. (Garland reference library of humanities ; v. 89) [ND2920.O9 1977] 76-52689 ISBN 0-8240-9884-6 lib.bdg. : 75.00
1. Oxford. University. Bodleian Library. 2. Illumination of books and manuscripts, Medieval—Catalogs. 3. Illumination of books and manuscripts, Medieval—Indexes. 4. Illumination of books and manuscripts—Slides—Indexes. 5. Illumination of books and manuscripts—England—Oxford—Catalogs. 6. Illumination of books and manuscripts—England—Oxford—Indexes. I. Ohlgren, Thomas H., 1941- II. Title.

Oxford. University. Christ Church.

BYAM Shaw, 741.9'4'07402574
James, 1903-
Drawings by old masters at Christ Church, Oxford / by James Byam Shaw. Oxford : Clarendon Press, 1976. 2 v. : ill. ; 31 cm. Contents.Contents.—v. 1. Catalogue. —v. 2. Plates. Includes bibliographical references and indexes. [NC27.G7O932] 76-375903 ISBN 0-19-817323-7 : 115.00
1. Oxford. University. Christ Church. 2. Drawings—Oxford—Catalogs. I. Title.
Dist. by Oxford University Press New York N.Y. BIP

BYAM Shaw, James, 741.9'4'0740153
1903-
Old master drawings from Christ Church, Oxford; a loan exhibition. Introd. and catalogue by James Byam Shaw. [Washington, International Exhibitions Foundations, 1972] 70 p., [114] p. of illus. 26 cm. Circulated by the International Exhibitions Foundation, 1972-73. Participating museums: National Gallery of Art, Washington, D.C., and others. [NC15.W37N372] 72-83826
1. Oxford. University. Christ Church. 2. Drawings—Exhibitions. I. International Exhibitions Foundation. II. United States. National Gallery of Art. III. Title. BIP

Oxford University Press—History.

BARKER, Nicolas. 070.5'94'094257
The Oxford University Press and the spread of learning, 1478-1978 : an illustrated history / by Nicolas Barker ; with a preface by Charles Ryskamp. Oxford [Eng.] : Clarendon Press, 1978. xiii, 69 p., [103] leaves of plates : chiefly ill. ; 31 cm. Includes bibliographical references and index. [Z232.O98B37] 77-30541 ISBN 0-19-951086-5 : 25.00
1. Oxford University Press—History. 2. Printing—England—History—Exhibitions. 3. Publishers and publishing—England—Exhibitions. I. Title.
Distributed by Oxford Universitty Press, NY BIP

OXFORD University Press. 655.142
The first minute book of the delegates of the Oxford University Press, 1668-1756. Edited by Strickland Gibson and John Johnson. Oxford, Clarendon Press [1966) xxxii, 104 p. 26 cm. Reprint of a work first published in 1943. Bibliographical footnotes. [Z232.O98O87] 66-6804
I. Gibson, Strickland, 1877-1958. ed. II. Johnson, John de Monins, 1882-1956, ed. III. Title.

Oyster-culture — California.

BARRETT, Elinore M 639'.08 s
The California oyster industry. [Sacramento, Calif.] 1963. 103 p. illus., maps. 23 cm. (California. Dept. of Fish and Game. Fish bulletin, 123) "Originally ... submitted is partial fulfillment of the requirements for the degree of master of arts in geography at the University of California, Berkeley." Bibliography: p. 96-103. [SH11.C27] [SH365.C2A5] 779'.9'6394110975518 63-64317
1. Oyster-culture — California. I. Title. II. Series.

Ozenfant, Amedee, 1886-1966.

OZENFANT, Amedee, 1886- 759.4
1966.
Ozenfant / John Golding. New York : M. Knoedler, c1973. 46, [2] p. : ill. (some col.) ; 22 cm. "Catalogue of the exhibitions": p. [47]-[48] Bibliography: p. 46. [ND553.O9G64] 75-304298
1. Ozenfant, Amedee, 1886-1966. I. Golding, John. II. Knoedler (M.) and Company, inc.

Paccioli, Luca, d. ca. 1514.

MORISON, Stanley, 1889- 745.6'1
1967.
Fra Luca de Pacioli of Borgo S. Sepolcro. New York, Grolier Club, 1933. [New York, Kraus Reprint Co. 1969] vii, 105 p. illus., port. 32 cm. "Bibliographical notes on the works of Luca de Pacioli, by Philip Hofer": p. [91]-98. Bibliography: p. [99]-100. "Selected recent publication on Pacioli and on geometric alphabets, compiled by James Wells": p. [101]-102. [NK3615.P34 1969] 68-58494
1. Paccioli, Luca, d. ca. 1514. De divina proportione. 2. Alphabets. 3. Lettering. BIP

TORNIELLO, Franceso. 745.6'197
The alphabet of Francesco Torniello da Novara [1517] Followed by a comparison with the alphabet of Fra Luca Pacioli. Introduction by Giovanni Mardersteig. Verona [Officina Bodoni] 1971. xxviii, 104 p. illus. 28 cm. (Editiones Officinae Bodoni) Original Italian and English translation of Opera del modo de fare le littere maiuscole antique. Issued in a limited ed. of 160 copies of which this is no. 86. Bibliography: p. xxviii. [NK3631.T65A5 1971] 76-885850
1. Paccioli, Luca, d. ca 1514. I. Mardersteig, Hans, 1892- II. Title.

Pacher, Michael, 15th cents.

*RONEN, Avraham. 755
The Peter and Paul altarpiece and Friedrich Pacher. New York, Humanities Press [1975] vi, 106 p. col. ill. 27 cm. Bibliography: p. 104-106. [NK2190] ISBN 0-391-00356-9 19.50.
1. Pacher, Michael, 15th cents. 2. Altarpieces. I. Title. BIP

Pachner, William.

AMERICAN Federation of 759.13
Arts.
William Pachner [by] Kenneth Donahue. New York 28, Amer. Federation of Arts, 1083 Fifth Ave. [c.1959] 28p. Bibl.: p. [24]-25. illus. (part col.) port. 19cm. Catalog of retrospective exhibition circulated by the American Federation of Arts. 60-3573 2.00, .50 pap.,
1. Pachner, William. I. Donahue, Kenneth. II. Title.

Pacific coast in art.

STENZEL, Franz. 759.13
James Madison Alden : Yankee artist of the Pacific coast, 1854-1860 : [catalog] accompanying exhibition presented at Amon Carter Museum, Fort Worth ... [et al.] / by Franz Stenzel. Fort Worth [Tex.] : The Museum, [1975] xiii, 209 p. : ill. (some col.) ; 25 cm. Includes index. Bibliography: p. 200-202. [ND1839.A44S83] 74-18766 ISBN 0-88360-011-0 : 25.00
1. Alden, James Madison, 1834-1922. 2. Pacific coast in art. I. Alden, James Madison, 1834-1922. II. Amon Carter Museum of Western Art, Fort Worth, Tex. BIP

Packaging.

NEW York. Museum of Modern 745.2
Art.
The package. [Exhibition: Sept. 9-Nov. 1, 1959. New York, 1959] 39p. illus. 26cm. (Its Bulletin, v. 27, no. 1) 60-6270 1.25 pap.,
1. Packaging. I. Title.

**PACKAGING 3 :* 741.6
an international survey of package design / edited by Walter Herdeg. Zurich, Switzerland : Graphis Press, c1977. 251p. : ill.(part col.) ; 30 cm. In English, German and French. [TS195] ISBN 0-8038-2684-2 : 39.50
1. Packaging. 2. Containers. 3. Commercial art. I. Herdeg, Walton.
Distributed by Hastings House.

Padlocks—Catalogs.

ARNALL, Franklin M. 381'.45'68332
The padlock collector; illustrations and prices of 270 padlocks of the past 100 years, by Franklin M. Arnall, with the cooperation of Alan and Michael, collectors. 1st ed. [Mentone, Calif., The Collector] 1972. 54 p. illus. 22 cm. [NK8205.A68] 72-183082 3.00
1. Padlocks—Catalogs. 2. Padlocks—Collectors and collecting. I. Title. BIP

Page, William 1811-1885.

TAYLOR, Joshua Charles, [759.13
1917-
William Page, the American Titian. [Chicago] University of Chicago Press [1957] xxii, 292 p. illus., ports. 28 cm. "Catalogue of works":p. 246-280. Bibliography: p. 281-286. [ND237.P17T3] 927.5 57-6991
1. Page, William 1811-1885. I. Title.

Pageants—Italy—Exhibitions.

ELVEHJEM Art Center. 741.9'45
Italian Renaissance festival designs. Madison, Wis., 1973. 126 p. illus. 23 cm. Catalog prepared by Arthur R. Blumenthal. Exhibition held at the Elvehjem Art Center, March 15-May 6, 1973. Bibliography: p. 124-125. [PN3261.E5] 73-161628
1. Pageants—Italy—Exhibitions. 2. Theaters—Italy—Stage-setting and scenery—Exhibitions. I. Blumenthal, Arthur R. II. Title.

Pictures—Catalogs.

SPECIAL Libraries Association. Picture Division. 708.1
Picture sources. Celestine G. Frankenberg, editor. 2d ed. New York, Special Libraries Association [1964] viii, 216 p. 27 cm. [N4000.S7 1964] 64-15089
1. Pages 204-216 blank for "User's notes." 2. Pictures — Catalogs. I. Frankenberg, Celestine Gilligan, ed. II. Title.

Pahari mural painting and decoration.

SETH, Mira. 751.7'3'095452
Wall paintings of the western Himalayas / Mira Seth. New Delhi : Publications Division, Ministry of Information and Broadcasting, Govt. of India, 1976. 136 p., [28] leaves of plates : ill. (some col.), map ; 33 cm. Includes quotations in Hindi. Includes index. Bibliography: p. [125]-130. [ND2828.H55S47] 76-904150 Rs100.00 ($30.00 U.S.)
1. Pahari mural painting and decoration. 2. Mural painting and decoration—India—Himachal Pradesh. I. Title.

Pahari painting—Exhibitions.

ARCHER, William George, 1907- 751.7'7'0954074
Visions of courtly India : the Archer collection of Pahari miniatures / introd. and catalogue by W. G. Archer ; circulated by International Exhibitions Foundation, Washington, D.C., 1976-1978. Washington : Foundation, c1976. xiii, 156 p. : ill. (some col.) ; 26 cm. Bibliography: p. 155-156. [ND1337.I5A74] 76-18030 ISBN 0-85667-032-4
1. Archer, William George, 1907- —Art collections. 2. Archer, Mildred—Art collections. 3. Pahari painting—Exhibitions. 4. Miniature painting, Indic—Exhibitions. I. International Exhibitions Foundation. II. Title. BIP

Paine, Josephine Ruth, joint author.

HODGSON, Mary Anne. 746.4'4
Fast and easy needlepoint / Mary Anne Hodgson and Josephine Ruth Paine ; photos. by Michael Pitts and Richard Fowlkes. 1st ed. Garden City, N.Y. : Doubleday, c1977. p. cm. Includes index. Uses a series of learning designs to teach the basic needlepoint stiches, then guides the reader into original designs for a belt, pillow, guitar strap, and other objects. [TT778.C3H63] 76-56302 ISBN 0-385-12431-7 : 5.95.
1. Paine, Josephine Ruth, joint author. 2. Canvas embroidery—Juvenile literature. I. Pitts, Michael. II. Fowlkes, Richard. III. Title. BIP

Paint—Handbooks, manuals, etc.

ORGANIC finishing 667.6
handbook. Westwood, N. J., Finishing Publications. v. illus. 20cm. [TT305.O7] 55-28853
1. Paint—Handbooks, manuals, etc. 2. Finishes and finishing.

Painted enamel.

WINTER, Edward. 738.4
Enamel painting techniques. New York, Praeger [1970] xiii, 86 p., 118 p. of plates (part col.) 26 cm. Bibliography: p. 78-82. [NK5000.W55 1970] 78-107222 14.95
1. Painted enamel. I. Title.

Painted enamel, Chinese—Exhibitions.

HYDE, John Alden Lloyd. 738.4'0951
Chinese painted enamels from private and museum collections, by J. A. Lloyd Hyde. New York, China House Gallery, China Institute in America [1969] 48 p. illus. 23 cm. Catalogue of an exhibition, Oct. 23, 1969- Feb. 1, 1970 at the China House Gallery. [NK5024.H9] 70-31512
1. Painted enamel, Chinese—Exhibitions. I. China House Gallery. II. Title.

Painted enamel, Renaissance—Catalogs.

WALTERS Art Gallery, Baltimore. 738.4
Catalogue of the painted enamels of the Renaissance, by Philippe Verdier. Baltimore, The Trustees, Walters Art Gallery, 1967. xxviii, 423 p. illus. (part col.) 28 cm. On spine: Painted enamels of the Renaissance. Includes bibliographies. [NK5014.W3] 68-2513
1. Painted enamel, Renaissance—Catalogs. 2. Enamel and enameling—Baltimore—Catalogs. I. Verdier, Philippe. II. Title. III. Title: Painted enamels of the Renaissance.

Painters.

CHUBB, Edwin Watts, 1865-1959. 759.94
Sketches of great painters. Freeport, N.Y., Books for Libraries Press [1968] 263 p. illus. 22 cm. (Essay index reprint series) Reprint of the 1915 ed., from a copy in the collections of the New York Public Library, Astor, Lenox and Tilden Foundations. Contents.Contents.—Raphael.—Millet.—Leonardo da Vinci.—Rembrandt.—Whistler.—Turner.—Titian.—Rubens.—Corot.—Michelangelo.—Reynolds.—Murillo.—Velasquez.—Rosa Bonheur.—Van Dyck. [ND36.C5 1968] 68-55843
1. Painters. 2. Paintings. I. Title. BIP

GEORGES-MICHEL, Michel, 1883- 739.4
From Renoir to Picasso; artists in action. With 50 illus. by or of those artists. Translated by Dorothy and Randolph Weaver. [1st American ed.] Boston, Houghton Mifflin, 1957 [c1954] 282p. illus. 24cm. [ND36.G373 1957a] [ND36.G373 1957a] 927.5 57-9025 57-9025
1. Painters. I. Title.

HALE, Philip Leslie, 1865-1931, ed. 759.9'4
Great masters in art. Introd. by Edward Alden Jewell. Freeport, N.Y., Books for Libraries Press [1968] 352 p. illus., ports. 24 cm. (Essay index reprint series) Reprint of the 1935 ed. Contents.Contents.—Giotto.—Leonardo da Vinci.—Michelangelo.—Raphael.—Titian.—Rubens.—Rembrandt.—El Greco.—Velasquez.—Goya.—Locations of principal paintings. [ND36.H3 1968] 68-20306
1. Painters. I. Title. BIP

HOLLMANN, Clide Anne. 759.18
Five artists of the Old West: George Catlin, Karl Bodmer, Alfred Jacob Miller, Charles M. Russell [and] Frederic Remington, by Clide Hollmann. With reproductions of the artists' paintings. New York, Hastings House [1965] 128 p. illus. (part col.) 24 cm. Bibliography: p. 124. [ND225.H6] 64-8123
1. Painters. 2. Painting — The West — Hist. 3. The West — Descr. & trav. — Views. I. Title.

LANE, James Warren, 1898- 759
Masters in modern art [by] James W. Lane. Freeport, N.Y., Books for Libraries Press [1966] 118 p. illus. 19 cm. (Essay index reprint series) "First published 1936." Contents.Contents.—Paul Cezanne (1839-1906).—Vincent van Gogh (1853-1890).—Paul Gauguin (1848-1903).—Henri-Matisse (1869-).—John Marin (1870-).—Andre Derain (1880-).—Charles Demuth (1883-1935).—Georgia O'Keeffe (1887-).—Jean Charlot (1898-). [ND190.L3 1966] 67-22100
1. Painters. 2. Painting, Modern—19th century. 3. Painting, Modern—20th century. I. Title.

MCKINNEY, Roland Joseph, 1898- 927.5
Famous old masters of painting. New York, Dodd, Mead, 1951. 135 p. illus. 23 cm. [Famous biographies for young peoples] [ND150.M3] 51-11037
1. Painters. I. Title.

MATHER, Frank Jewett, 1868-1953. 750
Estimates in art. New York, AMS Press [1971] x, 315 p. illus. 19 cm. Reprint of the 1916 ed. Contents.Contents.—Claude Lorrain: teacher.—Sandro Botticelli.—El Greco.—Goya and his art.—Rembrandt after three centuries, 1906.—Vermeer of Delft.—The painting of Sorolla.—Eugene Carriere.—Watts and his art.—John La Farge, an appreciation.—Far Eastern painting. [ND1142.M3 1971] 79-137261 ISBN 0-404-04256-2
1. Painters. 2. Painting. I. Title. BIP

MYERS, Bernard Samuel, 1908- 759
Fifty great artists. New York, Bantam [1965, c.1953] xix, 266p. illus. (pt. col.) ports. (pt. col.) 18cm. (Matrix ed., KM1029) Bibl. [ND36.M9] 65-26641 1.25 pap.,
1. Painters. I. Title.

MYERS, Bernard Samuel, 1908- 927.5
50 great artists. 1st ed. New York, Bantam Books, 1953] xviii, 232, [6] p. illus. (part col.) 18cm. (A Bantam fifty, F 1171) Bibliography: p. [234]-[236] [ND36.M9] 54-16488
1. Painters. I. Title.

THE Reader's digest. 759
Reader's digest family treasury of great painters and great paintings. Pleasantville, N.Y., Reader's Digest Association; distributors: Little, Brown, Boston [1965] 192 p. col. illus., col. ports. 32 cm. [ND36.R4] 65-24672
1. Painters. 2. Paintings. I. Title. II. Title: Family treasury of great painters and great paintings.

READER'S digest (The) 759
Reader's digest family treasury of great painters and great paintings. Reader's Digest Assn.; dist. Boston, Little [c.1965] 192p. col. illus., col. ports. 32cm. [ND36.R4] 65-24672 14.95
1. Painters. 2. Paintings. I. Title: Family treasury of great painters and great paintings.

RODITI, Edouard. 704
Dialogues on art. New York, Horizon Press [1961, c1960] 198p. illus. 23cm. [ND36.R6 1961] 61-14760
1. Painters. 2. Sculptors. I. Title.

RODITI, Edouard. 704
Dialogues on art. London, Secker & Warburg; [covered by label: New York, Humanities Press] 1960. 198p. illus. 23cm. [ND36.R6] 60-4000
1. Painters. 2. Sculptors. I. Title.

RODITI, Edouard [D'Israeli] 704
Dialogues on art. London, Secker & Warburg; covered by label: New York, Humanities Press, 1960 198p. illus. 23cm. 60-4000 6.00 bds.,
1. Painters. 2. Sculptors. I. Title.

SCHERMAN, Bernardine (Kielty) 759
Masters of painting: their works, their lives, their times [by] Bernardine Kielty. [1st ed.] Garden City, N.Y., Doubleday [1964] 183 p. illus. (part col.) ports. 33 cm. [ND36.S34] 63-15118
1. Painters. 2. Paintings. I. Title.

SYMONS, Arthur, 1865-1945. 750'.8
Studies on modern painters. Freeport, N. Y., Books for Libraries Press [1967] 88 p. 24 cm. (Essay index reprint series) Reprint of the 1925 ed. [ND190.S7 1967] 67-30233
1. Painters. 2. Painting. I. Title.
-Contents omitted BIP

THOMAS, Henry, 1886- 927.5
Living biographies of great painters, by Henry Thomas and Dana Lee Thomas. Garden City, N.Y., Garden City Books [1959] 312 p. 22 cm. [ND36.T45 1959] 59-2614
1. Painters. I. Thomas, Dana Lee, 1918- joint author. II. Title.

TURNGREN, Annette. 927.5
Great artists; 26 master painters. New York, Abelard Press [1953] 286p. 22cm. [ND36.T79] 53-6814
1. Painters. I. Title.

WECHSLER, Herman Joel, 1904- ed. 759.03
The pocket book of old masters; containing 64 reproductions of paintings by Da Vinci [others] Text by W. Somerset Maugham [others] New York, Washington Sq. [1962, c.1949] 112p. 16cm. (W-731) .60 pap.,
1. Painters. 2. Paintings. I. Title.

Painters, American.

BAUR, John Ireland Howe, 1909- ed. 759.13
New art in America: fifty painters of the 20th century, by John I. H. Baur, editor [and others] Greenwich, Conn., New York Graphic Society in cooperation with Praeger, New York [1957] 280 p. illus. (part col.) 32 cm. [ND212.B38] 57-9100
1. Painters, American. 2. Paintings, American. I. Title.

BELKNAP, Waldron Phoenix, 1899-1949. 759.13
Research notes concerning early New York State records and early American painters and paintings. [Boston] c1955. 981. 28cm. Cover title. Facsimile reproduction of ms. copy. [ND230.N4B4] 56-29062
1. Painters, American. I. Title.

BIZARDEL, Yvon 759.13
American painters in Paris. Translated by Richard Howard. New York, Macmillan [c.]1960. 177p. illus. 24cm. 60-14765 5.95
1. Painters, American. 2. Painting—Paris. I. Title.

CHAMBERLAIN, Georgia Stamm, 1910-1961. 709.73
Studies on American painters and sculptors of the nineteenth century. [Annandale? Va., 1965] vii, 66 p. illus. 26 cm. Bibliographical footnotes. [N6510.C5] 66-391081
1. Painters, American. 2. Sculptors, American I. Title.

FLEXNER, James Thomas, 1908- 759.13
America's old masters. Rev. [i.e. 2d] ed. New York, Dover [1967] 365p. illus., ports. 22cm. [ND207.F55 1967] 67-16702 2.75 pap.,
1. West, Benjamin, 1738-1820. 2. Copley, John Singleton, 1737-1815. 3. Peale, Charles Willson, 1741-1827. 4. Stuart, Gilbert, 1755-1828. 5. Painters, American. I. Title.
Contents Omitted.

FRANKENSTEIN, Alfred Victor, 1906- 927.5
After the hunt; William Harnett and other American still life painters, 1870-1900. Berkeley, University of California Press, 1953. xiii, 189 p. plates (1 col.) 29 cm. Bibliographical footnotes. [ND237.H315F7] 759.13 53-11237
1. Harnett, William Michael, 1848-1892. 2. Painters, American. 3. Still-life painting. 4. Painting, American. I. Title. BIP

GLACKENS, Ira, 1907- 759.13
William Glackens and the Ashcan group; the emergence of realism in American art. New York, Crown Publishers [1957] 267 p. illus. (part col.) 24 cm. [ND237.G5G55] 927.5 57-8771
1. Glackens, William J., 1870-1938. 2. Painters, American. 3. Realism in art. I. Title.

JANIS, Sidney, 1897- 759.13
They taught themselves; American primitive painters of the 20th century [Reissue] Foreword by Alfred H. Barr, Jr. Port Washington, N. Y., Kennikat [1965, c.1942] 236p. illus., ports. 24cm. [ND212.J3] 64-25539 9.00
1. Painters, American. 2. Painting—U. S. I. Title.

MCKINNEY, Roland Joseph, 1898- 927.5
Famous American painters. Illustrated with reproductions of the artists' paintings. New York, Dodd, Mead, 1955. 125p. illus.

22cm. (Famous biographies for young people) [ND236.M26] 55-9420
1. Painters, American. I. Title.

NARODNY, Ivan. 759.13
American artists. Introd. by Nicholas Roerich. Freeport, N.Y., Books for Libraries Press [1969] viii, 110 p. illus. 22 cm. (Essay index reprint series) "First published 1930." Contents.Contents.—Robert W. Chanler.—John E. Costigan.—Leon Dabo.—Howard Everett Giles.—Eugene Higgins.—Charles W. Hawthorne.—Rockwell Kent.—Leon Kroll.—Gari Melchers.—Eugene Speicher. [ND212.N3 1969] 74-93365
1. Painters, American. 2. Painting, Modern—20th century—U.S. I. Title. BIP

RICHTER, Hans, 1888- 700'.924
Hans Richter. Edited by Cleve Gray. New York, Holt, Rinehart and Winston [1971] 191 p. illus. (part col.) 29 cm. [NX93.R5G7] 75-155510 ISBN 0-03-083475-9 27.50
I. Gray, Cleve, ed. II. Title.

WATSON, Ernest William, 1884- 759.13
Twenty painters and how they work. [1st ed.] New York, Watson-Guptill Publications [1950] 158 p. illus. (part col.) ports. 31 cm. [Creative arts library] Contents.Contents. -- Louis Bosa. -- Jessie Arms Botke. -- Louis Bouche. -- Roy Brown. -- James Chapin. -- John Costigan. -- Russell Cowles. -- Francis de Erdely. -- Grigory Gluckmann. -- Julian Levi. -- Donald Mattison. -- Henry Mattson. -- Henry Lee McFee. -- William Palmer. -- Hobson Pittman. -- Iver Rose. -- Andree Ruelian. -- Helen Sawyer. -- Frederick Taubes. -- Paul Trebilcock. [ND236.W3] 50-12462
1. Painters, American. I. Title.

WHITNEY Museum of American Art, New York. 759.13918
The new decade; 35 American painters and sculptors. [Edited by John I. H. Baur, curator. Research by Rosalind Irvine, associate curator. New York, Macmillan, 1955. 96p. illus. 27cm. 'The result of an exhibition held at the Whitney Museum of American Art in the spring of 1955.' 'Catalogue of the exhibition': p.92-96. [ND212.W45] 55-3046
1. Painters. American. 2. Sculptors, American. I. Baur, John Ireland Howe, 1909- ed. II. Title.

YOUNG, Mahonri Sharp, 1911- 759.13
The eight; the realist revolt in American painting. New York, Watson-Guptill [1973] 160 p. illus. (part col.) 29 cm. Bibliography: p. 157. [ND236.Y67] 73-6865 ISBN 0-8230-1607-2 25.00
1. Painters, American. 2. Painting, American—History. 3. Painting, Modern—19th century—United States—History. 4. Painting, Modern—20th century—United States—History. 5. Realism in art. I. Title.

Painters, American—Correspondence, reminiscences, etc.

HEALY, George Peter Alexander, 1813-1894. 759.13
Reminiscences of a portrait painter. New York, Kennedy Graphics, 1970. ix, 221 p. ports. 23 cm. (Library of American art) Reprint of the 1894 ed. [ND237.H4A3 1970] 78-96439
1. Painters, American—Correspondence, reminiscences, etc. I. Title. BIP

Painters, American—Dictionaries.

BEREA, T. B. 759.13
Handbook of 17th, 18th and 19th century American painters [by] T. B. Berea. [Chattanooga? 1968] 86 p. 21 cm. [ND236.B53] 68-5710
1. Painters, American—Dictionaries. I. Title.

Painters, American—Juvenile literature.

BRAIDER, Donald, 1923- 759.13 B
Five early American painters: Benjamin West, John Singleton Copley, Charles Willson Peale, Gilbert Stuart, John Trumbull. [1st ed.] New York, Meredith Press [1969] 188 p. ports. 24 cm. Brief biographies of five early American painters including Benjamin West, John Singleton Copley, Charles Willson Peale, Gilbert Stuart, and John Trumbull. [ND236.B67] 920 71-91007 5.95
1. Painters, American—Juvenile literature. I. Title.

LEIPOLD, L. Edmond, 1902- 759.13 B
Famous American artists, by L. Edmond Leipold. Minneapolis, Denison [1969] 83 p. 25 cm. (His Famous American heroes and leaders series) Brief portraits of ten outstanding American artists: James McNeill Whistler, Benjamin West, Gilbert Stuart, Arthur Davies, Grant Wood, Mary Cassatt, Charles Willson Peale, George Caleb Bingham, Winslow Homer, and John Singer Sargent. [ND236.L45] 920 75-91284
1. Painters, American—Juvenile literature. I. Title.

LEIPOLD, L. Edmond, 1902- 759.13
Great American artists, by L. Edmond Leipold. Minneapolis, T. S. Denison [1973] 62 p. illus. 25 cm. (Lives of great Americans) Brief biographies of five American painters: Benjamin West, Winslow Homer, James McNeil Whistler, Grant Wood, and Oscar Howe. [ND236.L46] 920 76-190688 ISBN 0-513-01240-0 3.99
1. Painters, American—Juvenile literature. I. Title. II. Series: Lives of great Americans (Minneapolis)

Painters, American—Knoxville, Tenn.

KNOXVILLE artists: 759.16885
Robert Birdwell, Richard Clarke, C. Kermit Ewing, Joanna Higgs, Walter H. Stevens [and] Carl Sublett. [Knoxville, Tenn., 1960] [55]p. illus., ports. 26cm. [ND235.K5K55] 60-64167
1. Painters, American—Knoxville, Tenn.

Painters, American—Southwest, New.

AINSWORTH, Edward Maddin, 1902- 759.19
Painters of the desert; glimpses at those who captured for themselves and for their fellowmen the beauty and message of the American desert. Palm Desert, Calif., Desert magazine, [c:]1960 111p. illus. (part col.) 35cm. 61-3322 11.00
1. Painters, American—Southwest, New. 2. Paintings, American. 3. Southwest, New—Descr. & trav.—Views. I. Title.

AINSWORTH, Edward Maddin, 1902- 759.19
Painters of the desert glimpses at those who captured for themselves and for their fellowmen the beauty and message of the American desert. Palm Desert, Calif., Desert magazine. 1960 [i.e. 1961] 111p. illus. (part col.) ports. 25cm. [ND225.A4] 61-16101
1. Painters. American Southwest, New. 2. Paintings, American. 3. Southwest, New Descr. & trav Views. I. Title.

Painters, American—The West.

KENNEDY Galleries, inc., New York. 760'.922
"The Wild riders and the vacant land"; a century of Western paintings: from Peter Rindisbacher to the Taos school. New York, 1966. 65-128 p. illus. 24 cm. (The Kennedy quarterly, v. 6, no. 2) [N8640.K4 vol. 6, no. 2] 68-5817
1. Painters, American—The West. 2. Paintings, American—Catalogs. I. Title. II. Title: A century of Western paintings. III. Series.

Painters. American — Washington, D. C.

WASHINGTON, D. C. Gallery of Modern Art. 759.153
The Washington color painters, Morris Louis, Kenneth Noland, Gene Davis, Thomas Downing, Howard Mehring [and] Paul Reed; an exhibition. [Washington, 1965] 50 p. col. illus., ports. 26 cm. Bibliography: p. 49. [ND235.W3W3] 66-8224
1. Painters. American — Washington, D. C. 2. Painting, American — Exhibitions. I. Title.

Painters—Anecdotes, facetiae, satire, etc.

BECKFORD, William, 1760-1844. 750'.2'07
Biographical memoirs of extraordinary painters. Edited with an introd. and notes by Robert J. Gemmett. Rutherford [N.J.] Fairleigh Dickinson University Press [1969] 111 p. illus., port. 22 cm. Bibliography: p. 109-111. [N7470.B4 1969] 69-19434 ISBN 0-8386-7367-8 6.00
1. Painters—Anecdotes, facetiae, satire, etc. I. Gemmett, Robert J., ed. II. Title.

BECKFORD, William, 1760-1844. 750'.2'07
Biographical memoirs of extraordinary painters, 1780 / [by] William Beckford. [1st ed. reprinted] ; with an introduction by Philip Ward. Cambridge : Oleander Press, 1977. [17], 158 p. : ports. ; 21 cm. Reprint of the 1780 ed. published by J. Robson, London. Includes bibliographical references. [ND1155.B42 1977] 77-366203 ISBN 0-900891-13-0 pbk. : 9.50
1. Painters—Anecdotes, facetiae, satire, etc. I. Ward, Philip. II. Title.
Available from Oleander Press, 210 Fifth Ave., New York 10010. BIP

Painters—Austria—Correspondence, reminiscences, etc.

KOKOSCHKA, Oskar, 1886- 759.2 B
My life / Oskar Kokoschka ; translated by David Britt. 1st American ed. New York : Macmillan, 1974. 240 p., [8] leaves of plates : ill. ; 24 cm. Translation of Mein Leben. Includes index. [ND511.5.K6A213 1974] 74-2645 10.00
1. Kokoschka, Oskar, 1886- 2. Painters—Austria—Correspondence, reminiscences, etc. I. Title.

Painters—Belgium—Biography.

BAUDOUIN, Frans. 759.9493 B
Pietro Pauolo Rubens / Frans Baudouin ; translated by Elsie Callander. New York : Abrams, 1977. 405 p. : ill. (some col.) ; 34 cm. Text in English. Includes bibliographical references and indexes. [ND673.R9B238 1977b] 77-82339 ISBN 0-8109-1586-3 : 60.00
1. Rubens, Peter Paul, Sir, 1577-1640. 2. Painters—Belgium—Biography.

ENSOR, James, Baron, 1860-1949. 759.9493
Ensor / David Farmer. New York : G. Braziller, 1976. 48, p., [40] leaves of plates : ill. (some col.) ; 28 cm. [ND673.E6F37] 76-16639 ISBN 0-8076-0836-X : 9.95
1. Ensor, James, Baron, 1860-1949. 2. Painters—Belgium—Biography. I. Farmer, John David. II. Title.

JANSSENS, Jacques. 759.9493 B
Ensor / by Jacques Janssens. New York : Crown Publishers, c1978. p. cm. Bibliography: p. [ND673.E6J3613] 78-9884 ISBN 0-517-53284-0 pbk. : 5.95
1. Ensor, James, baron, 1860-1949. 2. Painters—Belgium—Biography. BIP

LANGUI, Emile 759.9493
Erits van den Berghe, 1883-1939. Catalogue raisonne de son oeuvre peint Erits van den Berghe eighteen eighty-three-nineteen thirty-nine Bruxelles, Edite par Laconti pour le Ministere de l'education nationale et de la culture, 1966. 1 v. (unpaged) illus., facsims., plates (pt. col.) ports. 33cm. (Maitres de la peinture contemporaine en Belgique, v. 2) Captions in French and Dutch. Bibl. [ND673.B48L3] 67-4108 25.00
I. Berghe, Frits van den, 1883-1939. II. Title. III. Series.
Distributed by Wittenborn in New York City.

Painters—Biography.

CANADAY, John Edwin, 1907- 759 B
The lives of the painters [by] John Canaday. [1st ed.] New York, Norton [1969] 4 v. plates (part col.) 24 cm. Contents.Contents.—v. 1. Late Gothic to High Renaissance.—v. 2. Baroque.—v. 3. Neoclassic to post-impressionist.—v. 4. Plates and index. [ND35.C35] 67-17666
1. Painters—Biography. I. Title. BIP

†NORMAN, Geraldine. 759.05
Nineteenth-century painters and painting : a dictionary / Geraldine Norman. Berkeley : University of California Press, 1977. 240 p. : ill. (some col.) ; 28 cm. Bibliography: p. 223-229. [ND190.N57 1977b] 76-24594 ISBN 0-520-03328-0 : 35.00
1. Painters—Biography. 2. Painting, Modern—19th century. I. Title. BIP

Painters, British.

PROCTER, Ida. 759.2
Masters of British painting: an introduction to their lives and works. New York, Roy Publishers [1956?] 192p. illus. 21cm. [ND496.P73] 927.5 54-10463
1. Painters. British. I. Title.

RITCHIE, Andrew Carnduff. 759.2
English painters, Hogarth to Constable; lectures delivered April 9, 10, 11, 16, 17, 1940, at the Johns Hopkins University [by] Andrew C. Ritchie. Freeport, N.Y., Books for Libraries Press [1968, c1942] xii, 61 p. 36 plates. 22 cm. (Essay index reprint series) "Delivered as part of a community art program sponsored by the Carnegie Corporation of New York." Bibliographical footnotes. [ND496.R5 1968] 68-57337
1. Painters, British. I. Carnegie Corporation of New York. II. Title. BIP

*ROTHENSTEIN, John 759.2
Modern English painters Wood to Hockney. New York, St. Martin's, [1974] 262 p. illus. 23 cm. [N6768] 73-89998 11.95
1. Painters, British. I. Title. BIP

SHIPP, Horace, 1891- 759.2
The English masters. New York, Philosophical Library [1956] 128p. 41 plates (part col.) 25cm. [ND461] 56-13859
1. Painters, British. 2. Painting—Gt. Brit. I. Title.

Painters—Canada—Biography.

BORDUAS, Paul Emile. 759.11
Paul-Emile Borduas / Francois-Marc Gagnon. Toronto : National Gallery of Canada, 1976. 93 p. : ill. (some col.) ; 24 cm. (Canadian artists series ; no. 3) Bibliography: p. 93-95. [ND249.B6G33] 77-360042 ISBN 0-88884-271-6
1. Borduas, Paul Emile. 2. Painters—Canada—Biography. I. Gagnon, Francois. II. Title. III. Series.

GRAY, Margaret Blair. 759.11 B
A. J. Casson / Margaret Gray, Margaret Rand, Lois Steen. Agincourt, Ont. : Gage Pub., c1976. 58 p. : ill. (some col.) ; 24 cm. (Canadian art series ; 1) Bibliography: p. 58. [ND249.C33G7] 77-359767 ISBN 0-7715-9962-5 : 14.95
1. Casson, Alfred Joseph, 1898- 2. Painters—Canada—Biography. I. Rand, Margaret, 1918- joint author. II. Steen, Lois, joint author.

HARRIS, Lawren Stewart, 1885-1970. 759.11
Lawren Harris / edited by Bess Harris and R. G. P. Colgrove ; and with an introd. by Northrop Frye. Toronto : Macmillan of Canada, 1976, c1969. xii, 146 p. : ill. (some col.) ; 22 x 28 cm. [ND249.H28H3 1976] 77-368957 ISBN 0-7705-1453-7 : 14.95
1. Harris, Lawren Stewart, 1885-1970. 2. Painters—Canada—Biography. I. Harris, Bess, ed. II. Colgrove, R. G. P., ed.

REID, Dennis R. 759.11
Edwin Holgate / Dennis Reid. Ottawa : National Gallery of Canada, 1976. 87 p. : chiefly ill. (some col.) ; 24 cm. (Canadian artists series ; no 4) Bibliography: p. 85 [ND249.H7R44] 77-358365 ISBN 0-88884-314-3
1. Holgate, Edwin H. 2. Painters—Canada—Biography. I. Holgate, Edwin H. II. Title. III. Series.

Painters—Colombia—Biography.

BOTERO, Fernando, 1932- 759.9861
Botero / Klaus Gallwitz ; [translated from the German by John Gabriel]. New York : Rizzoli, 1976. 87, [1] p. : chiefly ill. (some col.) ; 21 x 23 cm. Bibliography: p. 86-[88] [ND379.B6G3413] 76-11502 ISBN 0-8478-0045-8 : 7.95
1. Botero, Fernando, 1932- 2. Painters—Colombia—Biography. I. Gallwitz, Klaus.

Painters—Cuba—Biography.

LAM, Wifredo. 759.97291 B
Wifredo Lam / Max-Pol Fouchet. New York : Rizzoli, 1976. 266 p. : chiefly ill. (some col.) ; 30 cm. Includes index. Bibliography: p. 261-266. [ND305.L3F6813] 76-11245 ISBN 0-8478-0032-6 : 50.00
1. Lam, Wifredo. 2. Painters—Cuba—Biography. I. Fouchet, Max Pol. BIP

Painters—Dictionaries.

BERCKELAERS, Ferdinand Louis, 1901- 759
Dictionary of abstract painting, with a history of abstract painting [by] Michel Seuphor [pseud. Translated from the French by Lionel Izod, John Montague and Francis Scarfe] New York, Tudor Pub. Co. [1957] 304, [1]p. illus. (part col.) 2icm: Bibliography: p.[295]-[305] [ND35.B] A58
1. Painters—Dictionaries. 2. Art, Abstract. 3. Painting—Hist. I. Title.

CHAMPLIN, John Denison, 1834-1915, ed. 759
Cyclopedia of painters and paintings. Edited by John Denison Champlin, Jr. Critical editor: Charles C. Perkins. Port Washington, N.Y., Kennikat Press [1969] 4 v. illus., ports. 25 cm. Reprint of the 1886-1887 ed. Bibliography: v. 1, p. xix-xxxvi. [ND30.C4 1969] 77-86249
1. Painters—Dictionaries. 2. Paintings. I. Perkins, Charles Callahan, 1823-1886. II. Title. BIP

JAKOVSKY, Anatole 759
Peintres naifs: a dictionary of primitive painters. New York, Universe Bks [1967] 398p. illus. (pt. col.), ports. 26cm. Text in English, French, and German. Bibl. [ND35.J28] 67-15570 29.50
1. Painters—Dictionaries. 2. Primitivism in art. I. Title. II. Title: A dictionary of primitive painters.

KEIRSTEAD, C. Fraser. 704.948'5
Art studies in the life of Christ, and lives of the artists, by C. Fraser Keirstead. Needham Heights, Mass., Whittemore Associates [1967] 64 p. illus., ports. 19 cm. [N8050.K38] 68-771
1. Jesus Christ—Art. 2. Painters—Dictionaries. I. Title.

Painters, Dutch.

SHIPP, Horace, 1891- 759.9492
The Dutch masters. New York, Philosophical Library [1953] 128 p. 41 plates (part col.) 25 cm. [ND652.S47] 53-7904
1. Painters, Dutch. 2. Paintings, Dutch. I. Title.

Painters, Dutch — Haarlem.

ALLENTOWN, Pa. Art Museum. 759.4923
Seventeenth century painters of Haarlem. [Exhibition] April 2-June 13, 1965. Allentown, Pa. [1965] 80 p. illus. 26 cm. [ND651.H25A65] 66-59141
1. Painters, Dutch — Haarlem. 2. Painting, Dutch — Hist. I. Title.

Painters—England—Biography.

LEHMANN, John, 1907- 760'.092'4 B
Edward Lear and his world / John Lehmann. New York : Scribner, c1977. 128 p. : ill. ; 25 cm. Includes index. Bibliography: p. 118. [ND497.L48L44 1977] 77-73133 ISBN 0-684-15173-1 : 9.95
1. Lear, Edward, 1812-1888. 2. Painters—England—Biography. 3. Authors, English—19th century—Biography. I. Title. BIP

LINDSAY, Jack, 1900- 760'.092'4 B
Hogarth : his art and his world / Jack Lindsay. New York : Taplinger Pub. Co., 1979, c1977. p. cm. Includes index. Bibliography: p. [ND497.H7L77 1979] 78-21289 ISBN 0-8008-3916-1 : 14.95
1. Hogarth, William, 1697-1764. 2. Painters—England—Biography. BIP

RABIN, Lucy Feiden. 759.2 B
Ford Madox Brown and the pre-Raphaelite history-picture / Lucy Rabin. New York : Garland Pub., 1979 p. cm. (Outstanding dissertations in the fine arts) Originally presented as the author's thesis, Bryn Mawr College, 1973. Bibliography: p. [ND497.B73R3 1978] 77-94725 ISBN 0-8240-3246-2 : 25.00
1. Brown, Ford Madox, 1821-1893. 2. Painters—England—Biography. 3. Preraphaelitism—Europe. I. Title. II. Series. BIP

ROTHENSTEIN, William, Sir, 1872-1945. 759.2 B
Men and memories : recollections, 1872-1938 / by William Rothenstein ; edited by Mary Lago. Columbia : University of Missouri Press, 1978. 263 p., [5] leaves of plates : ill. ; 23 cm. Includes index. Bibliography: p. [241]-246. [ND497.R85A2 1978] 77-1470 17.00
1. Rothenstein, William, Sir, 1872-1945. 2. Painters—England—Biography. I. Lago, Mary. II. Title. BIP

SHONE, Richard. 759.21'42
Bloomsbury portraits : Vanessa Bell, Duncan Grant, and their circle / Richard Shone. Oxford : Phaidon ; New York : E. P. Dutton, 1976. 272 p., [4] leaves of plates : ill. (some col.) ; 26 cm. Includes index. Bibliography: p. 266-269. [ND497.B44S56] 76-5354 ISBN 0-7148-1628-0 : 18.95
1. Bell, Vanessa Stephen, 1874-1961. 2. Grant, Duncan James Corrowr, 1885- 3. Painters—England—Biography. 4. Bloomsbury group. I. Title.

STEEGMAN, John, 1899-1966. 759.2 B
Sir Joshua Reynolds / by John Steegmann [i.e. Steegman]. Folcroft, Pa. : Folcroft Library Editions, 1977. 136 p. ; 23 cm. Reprint of the 1933 ed. published by Macmillan, New York, in series: Great lives, 5. Bibliography: p. 136. [ND497.R4S75 1977] 77-17594 ISBN 0-8414-7867-8 lib. bdg. : 12.50
1. Reynolds, Joshua, Sir, 1723-1792. 2. Painters—England—Biography. BIP

Painters—England—Correspondence.

ROSSETTI, Dante Gabriel, 1828-1882. 759.2 B
The Rossetti-Leyland letters : the correspondence of an artist and his patron / edited by Francis L. Fennell, Jr. Athens : Ohio University Press, c1978. xxxiv, 111 p. : ports. ; 24 cm. Includes bibliographical references and index. [ND497.R8A3 1978] 75-14552 ISBN 0-8214-0207-2 : 11.00
1. Rossetti, Dante Gabriel, 1828-1882. 2. Painters—England—Correspondence. I. Leyland, Frederick Richard, 1831-1892, joint author. II. Fennell, Francis L. III. Title. BIP

Painters, England—Correspondence, reminiscences, etc.

WARD, Leslie, Sir, 1851-1922. 759.2 B
Forty years of "Spy". Detroit, Singing Tree Press, 1969. xvi, 351 p. illus., facsims., ports. 22 cm. [ND497.W255A3 1969] 70-81512
1. Painters, England—Correspondence, reminiscences, etc. I. Title. BIP

Painters, English.

ROTHENSTEIN, John Knewstub Maurice, Sir 1901- 759.2
Modern English painters. New York, Macmillan, 19 v. illus. 23cm. [ND496.R652] 58-1601
1. Painters, English. I. Title. BIP

Painters, Flemish.

ELST, Joseph van der, Baron, 1896- 759.9493
The last flowering of the Middle Ages. Port Washington, N.Y., Kennikat Press [1969, c1944] 127, [1] p. illus., plates, ports. 28 cm. (Essay and general literature index reprint series) Bibliography: p. [128] [ND665.E4 1969] 68-8230
1. Painters, Flemish. 2. Flanders—Social life and customs. 3. Paintings, Flemish. I. Title. BIP

Painters—France.

MUEHSAM, Gerd, 1913- comp. 759.4
French painters and paintings from the fourteenth century to post-impressionism; compiled and edited, with an introd., by Gerd Muehsam. New York, Ungar [1970] xli, 646 p. illus. 25 cm. (A Library of art criticism) Bibliography: p. 573-619. [ND552.M8] 70-98344 ISBN 0-8044-3210-4 22.50
1. Painters—France. 2. Paintings, French. I. Title. BIP

SLOCOMBE, George Edward, 1894- 759.9'4
Rebels of art: Manet to Matisse, by George Slocombe. With a commentary by Murdock Pemberton. Port Washington, N.Y., Kennikat Press [1969] xxii, 304 p. illus., ports. 25 cm. (Essay and general literature index reprint series) Reprint of the 1939 ed. [ND552.S5 1969] 68-8229
1. Painters—France. 2. Painting, French. 3. Impressionism (Art)—France. I. Pemberton, Murdock, 1888- II. Title. BIP

Painters—France—Biography.

ADLER, Kathleen. 759.4 B
Camille Pissarro : a biography / Kathleen Adler. New York : St. Martin's Press, 1978, c1977. 208 p., [8] leaves of plates : ill. ; 25 cm. Includes bibliographical references and index. [ND553.P55A85 1977] 77-10307 ISBN 0-312-11459-1 : 12.95
1. Pissarro, Camille, 1830-1903. 2. Painters—France—Biography.

CALLEN, Anthea. 759.4 B
Renoir / Anthea Gallen. 1st U.S. ed. New York : Two Continents/Oresko, 1978. p. cm. (Oresko art book series) Includes index. Bibliography: p. [ND553.R45C32 1977] 77-10354 ISBN 0-8467-0377-7 : 15.95
1. Renoir, Auguste, 1841-1919. 2. Painters—France—Biography. I. Title. II. Series.

CAMFIELD, William A. 759.4 B
Francis Picabia : his art, life, and times / by William Camfield. Princeton, N.J. : Princeton University Press, c1978. p. cm. Includes index. Bibliography: p. [ND553.P47C36] 77-85533 ISBN 0-691-03932-1 : 35.00
1. Picabia, Francis, 1879-1953. 2. Painters—France—Biography. BIP

COGNIAT, Raymond, 1896- 759.4' B
Sisley / by Raymond Cogniat ; [translated by Jeanine Warnod]. New York : Crown Publishers, c1978. p. cm. Bibliography: p. [ND553.S62C6313] 77-26315 ISBN 0-517-53321-9 : 5.95
1. Sisley, Alfred, 1839-1899. 2. Painters—France—Biography. 3. Impressionism (Art)—France. BIP

GAUGUIN, Paul, 1848-1903. 759.4 B
The writings of a savage / Paul Gauguin ; edited by Daniel Guerin ; with an introduction by Wayne Andersen ; translated by Eleanor Levieux. New York : Viking Press, [1977] p. cm. Includes index. [ND553.G27A4813] 76-53574 ISBN 0-670-53309-2 : 15.00
1. Gauguin, Paul, 1848-1906. 2. Painters—France—Biography. I. Title. BIP

MCLEAVE, Hugh. 759.4 B
A man and his mountain : a biography of Paul Cezanne / by Hugh McLeave. New York : Macmillan, 1977. p. cm. [ND553.C33M33] 77-9511 ISBN 0-02-5836,0-6 : 9.95
1. Cezanne, Paul, 1839-1906. 2. Painters—France—Biography. I. Title. BIP

MATHIEU, Georges, 1921- 759.4
Mathieu / by Dominique Quignon-Fleuret. New York : Crown Publishers, 1977, c1973. p. cm. Bibliography: p. [ND553.M368Q5413 1977] 77-5886 ISBN 0-517-53086-4 pbk. : 4.95
1. Mathieu, Georges, 1921- 2. Painters—France—Biography. I. Quignon-Fleuret, Dominique, 1943- BIP

MOSBY, Dewey F., 1942- 759.4 B
Alexandre-Gabriel Decamps, 1803-1860 / Dewey F Mosby New York : Garland Pub., 1977. 2 v. (xli, 699 p., 232 leaves of plates) : ill. ; 21 cm. (Outstanding dissertations in the fine arts) Thesis—Harvard, 1973. Bibliography: v. 2, p. [665]-699. [ND553.D29M83 1977] 76-23651 ISBN 0-8240-2714-0 : 95.00
1. Decamps, Alexandre Gabriel, 1803-1860. 2. Painters—France—Biography. I. Title. II. Series. BIP

O'BRIAN, Patrick. 759.4 B
Pablo Ruiz Picasso : a biography / Patrick O'Brian. London : Collins, 1976. 511 p., [8] p. of plates : ill., geneal. tables, ports. ; 24 cm. American ed. published under title: Picasso. Includes index. [ND553.P5O27 1976b] 77-362548 ISBN 0-00-211685-5 : £6.95
1. Picasso, Pablo, 1881-1973. 2. Painters—France—Biography.

O'BRIAN, Patrick. 759.4 B
Picasso : Pablo Ruiz Picasso : a biography / by Patrick O'Brian. New York : Putnam, c1976. 511 p. ; 24 cm. Includes index. [ND553.P5O27 1976] 75-41334 12.95 12.95
1. Picasso, Pablo, 1881-1973. 2. Painters—France—Biography. I. Title.

ROGER-MARX, Claude, 1888- 759.4 B
Vuillard, his life and work / by Claude Roger Marx ; [translated from the French by E. B. D'Auvergne]. New York : AMS Press, [1976] p. cm. Translation of Vuillard et son temps. Reprint of the 1946 ed. published by P. Elek, London. Bibliography: p. [ND553.V9R62 1976] 75-41229 ISBN 0-404-14718-6 : 25.00
1. Vuillard, Edouard, 1868-1940. 2. Painters—France—Biography. BIP

†RUBIN, William Stanley. 759.4 B
Andre Masson / by William Rubin and Carolyn Lanchner. New York : Museum of Modern Art, c1976. 232 p. : ill. (some col.) ; 25 cm. "Bibliography, compiled by Inga Forslund": p. 225-232. [ND553.M36R82] 76-1492 ISBN 0-87070-465-6 : 20.00.
1. Masson, Andre, 1896- 2. Painters—France—Biography. I. Lanchner, Carolyn, joint author.
Contents omitted. BIP

SELZ, Jean. 759.4 B
Gustave Moreau / by Jean Selz ; [translated from the French by Alice Sachs]. New York : Crown Publishers, [1979] p. cm. [ND553.M8S4413] 78-12107 ISBN 0-517-53449-5 : 5.95
1. Moreau, Gustave, 1826-1898. 2. Painters—France—Biography. BIP

STAEL, Nicolas de, 1914-1955. 759.4 B
Nicolas de Stael / by Guy Dumur ; translated by Fintan O'Connell ; photography by Henry B. Beville ... [et al.]. New York : Crown Publishers, c1976. p. cm. [ND553.S8D8413] 76-27652 ISBN 0-517-52611-5 : 4.95
1. Stael, Nicolas de, 1914-1955. 2. Painters—France—Biography. I. Dumur, Guy, 1921- II. Title.

STANTON, Theodore, 1851-1925, ed. 759.4 B
Reminiscences of Rosa Bonheur / edited by Theodore Stanton. New York : Hacker Art Books, 1976. xvii, 413 p., [23] leaves of plates : ill. ; 25 cm. Reprint of the 1910 ed. published by D. Appleton, New York. Includes indexes. [ND553.B6S8 1976] 74-147039 ISBN 0-87817-096-0 : 30.00
1. Bonheur, Rosa, 1822-1899. 2. Painters—France—Biography. I. Title. BIP

THOMSON, Richard. 760'.092'4 B
Toulouse-Lautrec / Richard Thomson. 1st U.S. ed. New York : Two Continents, c1977. p. cm. (The Oresko art book series) Includes index. Bibliography: p.

[ND553.T7T47 1977] 77-21483 ISBN 0-8467-0372-6 : 15.95 9.95
1. Toulouse-Lautrec Monfa, Henri Marie Raymond de, 1864-1901. 2. Painters—France—Biography. I. Title. II. Series.

VAN DYKE, John Charles, 1856-1932, ed. 759.4 B
Modern French masters : a series of biographical and critical reviews by American artists / edited by John C. Van Dyke ; with thirty-seven wood-engravings and twenty-eignt half-tone ill. New York : Garland Pub., 1976, c1896. p. cm. (The Art experience in late nineteenth-century America) Reprint of the ed. published by Century Co., New York. [ND547.V3 1976] 75-28885 ISBN 0-8240-2243-2 lib.bdg. : 35.00
1. Painters—France—Biography. 2. Painting, French. 3. Painting, Modern—19th century—France. I. Title. II. Series.
Conntents omitted

VERRIER, Michelle. 759.4
Fantin-Latour / Michelle Verrier. New York : Harmony Books, 1978. p. cm. Bibliography: p. [ND553.F3V47 1978] 78-1374 ISBN 0-517-53413-4 pbk. : 6.95
1. Fantin-Latour, Ignace Henri Jean Theodore, 1836-1904. 2. Painters—France—Biography. I. Fantin-Latour, Ignace Henri Jean Theodore, 1836-1904. II. Title. BIP

WAKEFIELD, David. 759.4
Fragonard / David Wakefield. New York : Two Continents Pub. Group, c1976. p. cm. Includes index. Bibliography: p. [ND553.F7W34 1976] 77-70919 ISBN 0-8467-0246-0 : 13.95. ISBN 0-8467-0245-2 pbk. : 7.95
1. Fragonard, Jean Honore, 1732-1806. 2. Painters—France—Biography. BIP

WERNER, Alfred, 1911- 759.4
Chaim Soutine / text by Alfred Werner. New York : H. N. Abrams, 1977. 167 p. : ill. (some col.) ; 34 cm. (The Library of great painters) Includes index. Bibliography: p. 163. [ND553.S7W4] 77-1249 ISBN 0-8109-0468-3 : 25.00
1. Soutine, Haim, 1894-1943. 2. Painters—France—Biography. I. Soutine, Haim, 1894-1943.

ZIFF, Norman D. 759.4 B
Paul Delaroche : a study in nineteenth-century French history painting / Norman D. Ziff. New York : Garland Pub., 1977. xv, 410 p. : ill. ; 21 cm. (Outstanding dissertations in the fine arts) Originally presented as the author's thesis, New York University, 1974. Bibliography: p. 308-328. [ND553.D3553 1977] 76-23663 ISBN 0-8240-2741-8 lib.bdg. 40.00
1. Delaroche, Hippolyte, called Paul, 1797-1856. 2. Painters—France—Biography. 3. History in art. I. Delaroche, Hippolyte, called Paul, 1797-1856. II. Title. III. Series. BIP

Painters—France—Biography—Juvenile literature.

BAKER, Donna. 759.4 B
Picasso / by Donna Baker. Chicago : Childrens Press, [1977] p. cm. (Artists in our world) A brief biography of one of the major artists of the twentieth century. [ND553.P5B24] 92 77-4848 ISBN 0-516-03683-1 lib.bdg. : 6.60
1. Picasso, Pablo, 1881-1973—Juvenile literature. 2. Painters—France—Biography—Juvenile literature. I. Title. II. Series.

Painters—France—Correspondence.

CEZANNE, Paul, 1839-1906. 759.4 B
Paul Cezanne, letters / edited by John Rewald ; [translated from the French by Marguerite Kay]. 4th ed. rev. and enl. Oxford [Eng.] : B. Cassirer, 1976. 374 p. ; 22 cm. "The letters of Zola represent nearly one-third of the whole correspondence." Includes index. [ND553.C33A212 1976] 77-359768 ISBN 0-85181-061-6 : £6.50
1. Cezanne, Paul, 1839-1906. 2. Painters—France—Correspondence. I. Rewald, John, 1912- ed. II. Zola, Emile, 1840-1902. III. Kay, Marguerite, tr.

Painters—France—Correspondence, reminiscences, etc.

PISSARRO, Camille, 1830-1903. 759.4 B
Camille Pissarro: letters to his son Lucien, edited with the assistance of Lucien Pissarro by John Rewald. 3d ed., rev. and enl. Mamaroneck, N.Y., P. P. Appel, 1972. 399 p. illus. 26 cm. Includes the letters of Lucien to Camille Pissarro published for the first time in English translation. [ND553.P55P4813 1972] 77-162499 ISBN 0-911858-22-9 22.50
1. Pissarro, Camille, 1830-1903. 2. Painters—France—Correspondence, reminiscences, etc. I. Rewald, John, 1912- ed. II. Pissarro, Lucien, 1863-1944. III. Title.

VOROBEV, Marevna, 1892- 700'.944'361
Life with the painters of La Ruche [by] Marevna. [Translation from the original Russian by Natalia Heseltine. 1st American ed.] New York, Macmillan [1974] x, 213 p. illus. 22 cm. [ND553.V67A2413 1974] 73-10564 6.95
1. Vorobev, Marevna, 1892- 2. Painters—France—Correspondence, reminiscences, etc. I. Title. BIP

Painters. French.

WECHSLER, Herman Joel, 1904- 927.5
Lives of famous French painters, from Ingres to Picasso. New York, Pocket Books [1952] 208 p. illus. 16 cm. (A Cardinal ed., C-28) [ND552.W4] 52-28626
1. Painters. French. I. Title.

Painters, French—Correspondence, reminiscences, etc.

DELACROIX, Eugene, 1798-1863. 759.4
Selected letters, 1813-1863. Selected and translated by Jean stewart. With an introd. by John Russell. New York, St. Martin's Press [1971, c1970] xiv, 414 p. 49 plates. 25 cm. "Extracts translated ... [and] selected from Correspondance generale d'Eugene Delacroix ... [and] Lettres intimes; correspondance inedite [originally published 1935-8 and 1954, respectively]" Bibliography: p. 392-393. [ND553.D33A39213 1971b] 70-150246 15.00
1. Painters, French—Correspondence, reminiscences, etc.

Painters, French—Juvenile literature.

MCKINNEY, Roland Joseph 759.4
Famous French painters. Illustrated with reporductions of the artists' paintings. New York, Dodd, Mead, [c.]1960. 157p. illus. 22cm. (Famous biographies for young people) 60-9152 3.00
1. Painters, French—Juvenile literature. I. Title. BIP

Painters, German.

THE German expressionists; a generation in revolt. New York, Praeger [1957] 401p. illus. (part mounted, part col.) ports. 29cm. Bibliography:p. 369-389. [ND568.M9] [ND568.M9] 927.5 57-11147 57-11147 759.3
1. Painters, German. 2. Paintings, German. 3. Expressionism (Art) I. Myers, Bernard Samuel, 1908-

MYERS, Bernard Samuel, 1908- 759.3
The German expressionists, a generation in revolt [Concise ed.] New York, McGraw [1963] 348p. illus. (pt. col.) ports. 23cm. Bibl. 63-19912 8.95
1. Painters, German. 2. Paintings, German. 3. Expressionism (Art) I. Title.

MYERS, Bernard Samuel, 1908- 759.3
The German expressionists, a generation in revolt [concise ed.] New York, Praeger [1966] 348p. illus. (pt. col.) 22cm. (Praeger paperbacks, P209) Bibl. 4.95 pap.,
1. Painters, German. 2. Paintings. German. 3. Expressionism (Art) I. Title.

MYERS, Bernard Samuel, 1908- 759.3
The German expressionists; a generation in revolt [by] Bernard S. Myers. [Concise ed.] New York, Prueger [1966] 348 p. illus. (part col.) 22 cm. (Praeger paperbacks) Books that matter. Bibliography: p. 325-342. [ND568] 67-217
1. Painters, German. 2. Paintings, German. 3. Expressionism (Art) I. Title.

Painters, German—Colmar.

SCHMITT, Pierre 759.3
Mathias Grunewald and other old masters in Colmar. Introd. by Pierre Schmitt. [Tr. from German by Gladys Wheelhouse] With 28 color plates by E. Ohresser. New York, A. S. Barnes [1963, c.1961] 67p. mounted col. illus. 22cm. [Metropolis bks.] 63-6133 4.95
1. Grunewald, Mathias, 16th cent. 2. Painters, German—Colmar. I. Title.

Painters—Germany—Biography.

DOMSAITIS, Pranas, 1880-1965. 741.973
Pranas Domsaitis / [text] by Elsa Verloren van Themaat. Cape Town : Struik (C.), 1976. 64 p. : chiefly ill. (some col., 1 fold.) ; 25 x 28 cm. (South African art library ; 6) Includes index. Bibliography: p. 63. [ND588.D65V37] 77-558243 ISBN 0-86977-070-5 : R9.75
1. Domsaitis, Pranas, 1880-1965. 2. Painters—Germany—Biography. I. Verloren van Themaat, Elsa. II. Title. III. Series.

FRIEDRICH, Caspar David, 1774-1840. 759.3
Caspar David Friedrich / edited by Jorg Traeger. New York : Rizzoli, c1976. 97 p. : ill. (some col.) ; 25 cm. English, German and French. [ND588.F75T7] 76-151002 ISBN 0-8478-0033-4 : 16.50
1. Friedrich, Caspar David, 1774-1840. 2. Painters—Germany—Biography. I. Traeger, Jorg, 1942-

FRIEDRICH, Caspar David, 1774-1840. 759.3
Caspar David Friedrich / hrsg. von Jorg Traeger ; [transl. into Engl. by Gillian Turner ; trad. francaise par Denise Baumann]. Munchen : Bruckmann, 1976. 97 p. : chiefly ill. (some col.) ; 25 cm. English, French, and German. [ND588.F75T7 1976b] 77-484085 ISBN 3-7654-1649-5 : DM35.00
1. Friedrich, Caspar David, 1774-1840. 2. Painters—Germany—Biography. I. Traeger, Jorg, 1942-

LEVINE, Frederick S. 759.3 B
The apocalyptic vision : the art of Franz Marc as German expressionism / by Frederick S. Levine. New York : Harper & Row, c1979. p. cm. (Icon editions) Includes index. Bibliography: p. [ND588.M194L46 1979] 78-4736 ISBN 0-06-435275-7 : 17.50
1. Marc, Franz, 1888-1916. 2. Painters—Germany—Biography. 3. Expressionism (Art)—Germany. I. Title. BIP

Painters—Germany—Correspondence, reminiscences, etc.

SCHLEMMER, Oskar, 1888-1943. 700'.92'4 B
The letters and diaries of Oskar Schlemmer. Selected and edited by Tut Schlemmer. Translated from the German by Krishna Winston. [1st ed.] Middletown, Conn., Wesleyan University Press [1972] xiii, 425 p. illus. 24 cm. Translation of his Briefe und Tagebucher. [ND588.S2818A3413] 77-184362 ISBN 0-8195-4047-1 19.95
1. Schlemmer, Oskar, 1888-1943. 2. Painters—Germany—Correspondence, reminiscences, etc. BIP

Painters—Germany, West—Biography.

LACKNER, Stephan. 759.3
Max Beckmann / text by Stephan Lackner. New York : H. N. Abrams, 1977. 175 p. : ill. (some col.) ; 34 cm. (The Library of great painters) Includes index. Bibliography: p. 169-170. [ND588.B37L297] 74-22446 ISBN 0-8109-0269-9 : 25.50
1. Beckmann, Max, 1884-1950. 2. Painters—Germany, West—Biography.

Painters—Great Britain.

BATE, Percy H., 1868-1913. 759.2
The English pre-Raphaelite painters; their associates and sucessors. London, Bell. [New York, AMS Press, 1972] xvi, 126 p. illus. 24 cm. Reprint of the 1901 ed. [ND467.5.P7B3 1972] 79-129383 ISBN 0-404-00691-4 12.00
1. Painters—Great Britain. 2. Preraphaelitism—Great Britain. I. Title. BIP

BATE, Percy H., 1868-1913. 759.2
The English Pre-Raphaelite painters; their associates and successors. Freeport, N.Y., Books for Libraries Press [1970, c1901] xix, 124 p. illus. 23 cm. [ND467.5.P7B3 1970] 71-140350 ISBN 0-8369-5593-5
1. Painters—Great Britain. 2. Preraphaelitism. I. Title.

Painters—Great Britain—Biography.

CARLINE, Richard. 759.2 B
Stanley Spencer at war / Richard Carline. London ; Boston : Faber and Faber, 1978. 224 p. : ill. ; 23 cm. Includes bibliographical references and index. [ND497.S75C37] 79-300467 ISBN 0-571-11028-2 : 21.95
1. Spencer, Stanley, Sir, 1891-1959. 2. Painters—Great Britain—Biography. I. Title.
Dist. by merrimack, Salem, NH 03079 BIP

JARRETT, Derek. 760'.092'4 B
The ingenious Mr Hogarth / Derek Jarrett. London : M. Joseph, 1976. 223 p., [12] leaves of plates : ill. ; 24 cm. Includes index. Bibliography: p. [214]-217. [ND497.H7J37] 76-380637 ISBN 0-7181-1489-2 : £7.00
1. Hogarth, William, 1697-1764. 2. Painters—Great Britain—Biography. I. Title.

LENNIE, Campbell, 1926- 759.2 B
Landseer : the Victorian paragon / [by] Campbell Lennie. London : Hamilton, 1976. [10], 259 p., 16 p. of plates : ill., ports. ; 24 cm. Includes index. Bibliography: p. 250-252. [ND497.L2L46 1976] 76-375309 ISBN 0-241-89432-8 : £6.95
1. Landseer, Edwin Henry, Sir, 1802-1873. 2. Painters—Great Britain—Biography. BIP

MESSUM, David. 759.2 B
The life and work of Lucy Kemp-Welch / by David Messum ; edited by Laura Wortley. [Woodbridge] : Antique Collectors' Club, 1976. 111 p. : ill. (some col.), ports. ; 29 cm. Includes catalogue of the L. Kemp-Welch Studio Collection exhibited at the David Messum Gallery, Spring 1976. Ill. on lining papers. [ND497.K446M47] 77-360045 ISBN 0-902028-43-X : 30.00
1. Kemp-Welch, Lucy, 1869-1958. 2. Painters—Great Britain—Biography. 3. Animals in art. I. Kemp-Welch, Lucy, 1869-1958. II. David Messum Gallery. The Lucy Kemp-Welch studio collection. 1976. III. Title.
Distributed by Antique Collectors' Club 1515 Broadway, New York

NICOLL, John. 759.2 B
Dante Gabriel Rossetti / John Nicoll. 1st American ed. New York : Macmillan, 1976, c1975. 175 p. : ill. (some col.) ; 28 cm. Includes bibliographical references and index. [ND497.R8N52 1976] 75-23267 ISBN 0-02-589340-8 : 22.50
1. Rossetti, Dante Gabriel, 1828-1882. 2. Painters—Great Britain—Biography. I. Rossetti, Dante Gabriel, 1828-1882.

ROTHENSTEIN, John Knewstub Maurice, Sir, 1901- 759.2 B
Modern English painters / by John Rothenstein. Rev. ed. New York : St. Martin's Press, 1976- v. : ill. ; 23 cm. Contents.Contents.—v. 1. Sickert to Smith.—v. 2. Lewis to Moore. Includes bibliographical references and indexes. [ND496.R652 1976] 77-362026 11.95 per vol.

1. Painters—Great Britain—Biography. I. Title.

SARTIN, Stephen. 759.2 B
Thomas Sidney Cooper, C.V.O., R.A., 1803-1902 / [compiled] by Stephen Sartin. Leigh-on-Sea : F. Lewis, 1976. 79 p., [40] p. of plates : ill. (incl. 1 tipped in) ; 30 cm. Limited ed. of 500 copies. Bibliography: p. 79. [ND497.C73S27] 77-354191 ISBN 0-85317-037-1 : £15.50
1. Cooper, Thomas Sidney, 1803-1902. 2. Painters—Great Britain—Biography.

SUTTON, Denys. 759.2 B
Walter Sickert : a biography / [by] Denys Sutton. London : Joseph, 1976. 272 p., leaf of plate, [24] p. of plates : ill., ports. ; 24 cm. Includes index. Bibliography: p. 252-262. [ND497.S48S97 1976] 76-373164 ISBN 0-7181-1436-1 : £10.50
1. Sickert, Walter, 1860-1942. 2. Painters—Great Britain—Biography.

SWANSON, Vern G. 759.2 B
Alma-Tadema : the painter of the Victorian vision of the ancient world / by Vern G. Swanson. New York : Scribner, 1977. 144 p. : ill. (some col.) ; 31 cm. Includes index. Bibliography: p. 132-134. [ND497.A4S9] 77-77549 ISBN 0-684-15304-1 : 15.95
1. Alma-Tadema, Lawrence, Sir, 1836-1912. 2. Painters—Great Britain—Biography. 3. Egypt in art. 4. Greece in art. 5. Rome in art.

TOWNSEND, William, 1909- 759.2 B 1973.
The Townsend journals : an artist's record of his times, 1928-51 / edited by Andrew Forge. London : Tate Gallery Publications, 1976. 3-98 p. : ill., ports. ; 26 cm. Includes index. [ND497.T755A55 1976] 77-358156 ISBN 0-900874-97-X : £3.50
1. Townsend, William, 1909-1973. 2. Painters—Great Britain—Biography. 3. Great Britain—Social life and customs—20th century. I. Title.

WORMAN, Isabelle. 759.2 B
Thomas Gainsborough : a biography 1727-1788 / by Isabelle Worman. Lavenham [Eng.] : T. Dalton, 1976. 148 p. : ill. (some col.) ; 24 cm. Includes index. Bibliography: p. 145. [ND497.G2W65] 77-355134 ISBN 0-900963-69-7 : £4.80
1. Gainsborough, Thomas, 1727-1788. 2. Painters—Great Britain—Biography. I. Gainsborough, Thomas, 1727-1788. BIP

Painters—Great Britain—Biography—Dictionaries.

FISHER, Stanley W. 759.2
A dictionary of watercolour painters, 1750-1900, by Stanley W. Fisher. London, New York, Foulsham, 1972. 245, [16] p. illus. 26 cm. Bibliography: p. 241-245. [ND1928.F54] 72-169716 ISBN 0-572-00794-9 £4.90
1. Painters—Great Britain—Biography—Dictionaries. 2. Water-color painting—Great Britain. I. Title.

Painters—Great Britain—Correspondence, reminiscences, etc.

PALMER, Samuel, 1805- 759.2 B 1881.
The letters of Samuel Palmer / edited by Raymond Lister. Oxford : Clarendon Press, 1974, [i.e.1975] 2 v. ; 23 cm. Contents.Contents.—v. 1. 1814-1859.—v. 2. 1860-1881. Includes bibliographical references and index. [ND497.P3A24] 75-311327 ISBN 0-19-817309-1 : 80.00
1. Palmer, Samuel, 1805-1881. 2. Painters—Great Britain—Correspondence, reminiscences, etc.
Distributed by Oxford University Press New York. BIP

REYNOLDS, Joshua, Sir, 759.2 B 1723-1792.
Letters of Sir Joshua Reynolds / collected and edited by Frederick Whiley Hilles. New York : AMS Press, [1976] p. cm. Originally presented as the editor's thesis, Yale University, 1926. Reprint of the 1929 ed. published by the University Press, Cambridge, Eng. Includes index. Bibliography: p. [ND497.R4A35 1976] 75-4122 13.50
1. Reynolds, Joshua, Sir, 1723-1792. 2. Painters—Great Britain—Correspondence, reminiscences, etc. I. Title.

SHEPHERD, David, 1931- 759.2 B
The man who loves giants : an artist among elephants and engines : David Shepherd's autobiography. New York : Scribner, c1975. 164 p. : ill. (some col.) ; 24 cm. [ND497.S46A25 1975b] 75-21663 ISBN 0-684-14509-X : 12.50
1. Shepherd, David, 1931- 2. Painters—Great Britain—Correspondence, reminiscences, etc. I. Title.

Painters—Indiana.

PEAT, Wilbur David, 1898- 759.13
Pioneer painters of Indiana. [Indianapolis] Art Association of Indianapolis, Indiana, 1954. xix, 254p. illus., ports., maps. 25cm. Bibliographical references included in 'Notes' (p. 211-219) 'Bibliographical guide; books referred to in the roster of painters that follows': p. 221-223. [ND230.I5P4] [ND230.I5P4] 759.172 54-14826 54-14826
1. Painters—Indiana. I. Title.

Painters—Israel—Interviews.

BAK, Samuel. 759.95694
Bak : paintings of the last decade. Artistic development ; The metaphysical works / Paul T. Nagano. Conversation with the artist / A. Kaufman. 2d ed. New York : Aberbach Fine Art, 1976. 156, [5] p. : ill. (some col.) ; 29 cm. Bibliography: p. [157]-[158] [ND979.B27A23] 77-358850
1. Bak, Samuel. 2. Painters—Israel—Interviews.

Painters, Italian.

BERENSON, Bernhard, 1865- 759.5
The Italian painters of the Renaissance. New York, Meeridian Books, 1957. 340p. illus. 18cm. (Meridian books, M40) [ND615] 57-6673
1. Painters, Italian. 2. Art, Renaissance. I. Title. BIP

BERENSON, Bernhard, 1865- 759.5
The Italian painters of the Renaissance. New York, Phaidon Publishers; distributed by Garden City Books [1952] xiii, 488p. plates (part col.) 27cm. [ND615.B55 1952] 53-5930
1. Painters, Italian. 2. Art, Renaissance. I. Title.

BERENSON, Bernhard, 1865- 759.5
The Italian painters of the Renaissance. [Dist. New York, Oxford, 1962] xiii, 488p. illus. (pt. col.) 27cm. Companion vol. to the author's Italian pictures of the Renaissance. 6.25
1. Painters, Italian. 2. Art, Renaissance. I. Title. BIP

BERENSON, Bernhard, 1865- 759.5 1959
The Italian painters of the Renaissance, by Bernard Berenson. [Illus., ed. reprinted]. London, Phaidon [1967] xiii, 488p. col. front., 400 illus., 16 col. plates. 27cm. [ND615.B55 1967] 68-11755 price unreported
1. Painters, Italian. 2. Painting, Renaissance. I. Title.
Distributed by N.Y. Graphic 140 Greenwich Ave, Greenwich, Conn. 06830

BERENSON, Bernhard, 1865- 759.5 1959.
The Italian painters of the Renaissance, by Bernard Berenson. London, New York, Phaidon, 1968. 2 v. 416 illus. (16 col.), ports. 25 cm. (Phaidon paperback) Contents.Contents.—v. 1. The Venetian painters. The North Italian painters.—v. 2. The Florentine painters. The Central Italian painters. [ND615.B55 1968] 68-18913 ISBN 0-7148-1335-4 (v. 1)
1. Painters, Italian. 2. Painting, Renaissance—Italy. I. Title.

MOIR, Alfred. 759.5
The Italian followers of Caravaggio. Cambridge, Harvard University Press, 1967. 2 v. 403 illus. 27 cm. Bibliography: v. 1, p. 319-345. [ND623.C26M6] 66-10315
1. Caravaggio, Michelangelo Merisi da, 1573-1610—Influence. 2. Painters, Italian. 3. Painting, Italian—History. I. Title. BIP

VENTURI, Lionello, 1885- 759.5
La peinture italienne. Etudes critiques de Lionello Venturi. Commentaires historiques de Rosabianca Skira-Venturi. [2d ed. Geneve, New York] A. Skira [1952, c1950- v. mounted illus. (part col.) 35 cm. (Peinture, couleur, histoire, 4 Contents.[1] Les Createurs de la Renaissance. [ND622.V39] 58-50457
1. Painters, Italian. 2. Painting, Italian — Hist. 3. Paintings, Italian. I. Skira-Venturi, Rosablanca. II. Title.

VENTURI, Lionello, 1885- 759.5 1961.
Italian painters of today. [Translated by Dorothy Cater] [New York] Universe Books [1959] 174 p. illus. (part mounted col.) 29 cm. "Biographies and bibliographies of the individual painters": p. 163-172. [ND618.V44] 59-11871
1. Painters, Italian. 2. Paintings, Italian. I. Title.

VENTURI, Lionello, 1885- 759.5 1961.
Italian painting; the Renaissance. Critical studies by Lionello Venturi. Historical surveys by Rosabianca Skira-Venturi. Translated by Stuart Gilbert. Geneva, New York, A Skira [1951] 168 p. mounted illus. (part col.) 35 cm. (Painting, colour, history) [ND622.V373] 52-1918
1. Painters, Italian. 2. Painting, Italian—History. I. Skira-Venturi, Rosabianca.

Painters—Italy—Biography.

LEGOUIX, Susan. 759.5
Botticelli / Susan Legouix. 1st U.S. ed. New York : Two Continents/Oresko, c1977. p. cm. (Oresko art book series) Includes index. Bibliography: p. [ND623.B7L43 1977] 77-10355 ISBN 0-8467-0376-9 : 15.95 pbk. : 9.95
1. Botticelli, Sandro, 1447?-1510. 2. Painters—Italy—Biography. I. Botticelli, Sandro, 1447?-1510. II. Title. III. Series.

LIGHTBOWN, R. W. 759.5 B
Sandro Botticelli / Ronald Lightbown. Berkeley : University of California Press, c1978. 2 v. : ill. (some col.) ; 29 cm. On spine: Botticelli. Contents.Contents.—v. 1. Life and work.—v. 2. Complete catalogue. Includes bibliographies and indexes. [ND623.B7L53 1978b] 76-46237 ISBN 0-520-03372-8 : 120.00
1. Botticelli, Sandro, 1447?-1510. 2. Painters—Italy—Biography. I. Botticelli, Sandro, 1447?-1510. BIP

PAYNE, Pierre Stephen 759.5 B Robert, 1911-
Leonardo / Robert Payne. 1st ed. Garden City, N.Y. : Doubleday, 1978. xix, 344 p., [36] leaves of plates : ill. ; 24 cm. Includes index. Bibliography: p. [321]-326. [ND623.L5P37] 78-869 ISBN 0-385-04154-3 : 12.95
1. Leonardo da Vinci, 1452-1519. 2. Painters—Italy—Biography. I. Title.

Painters—Italy—Correspondence, reminiscences, etc.

CHIRICO, Giorgio de, 1888- 759.5
The memoirs of Giorgio de Chirico. Translated from the Italian and with an introd. by Margaret Crosland. Coral Gables, Fla., University of Miami Press [1971] 262 p. illus. 23 cm. Translation of Memorie della mia vita, di Giorgio de Chirico. Bibliography: p. 253-258. [ND623.C56A2713 1971b] 74-102694 ISBN 0-87024-125-7 12.50
1. Chirico, Giorgio de, 1888- 2. Painters—Italy—Correspondence, reminiscences, etc. I. Title. BIP

Painters—Italy—Juvenile literature.

JACOBS, David, 1939- 759.5
Master painters of the Renaissance. New York, Viking Press [1968] 143 p. illus. (part col.) 26 cm. Bibliography: p. 142-143. [ND615.J3 1968] 67-20957
1. Painters—Italy—Juvenile literature. 2. Paintings, Renaissance—Italy. I. Title.

WILLIAMS, Francis S. 795.5
Painting in Mantua, Padua, Siena and Urbino, by Francis Williams. [1st ed.] Oxford, New York, Pergamon Press [1970] ix, 60 p. 23 illus. (part col.), 5 col. plates. 18 x 25 cm. (The Commonwealth and international library. Painting, sculpture and fine arts division) Profiles of the lives and works of twenty-seven early Renaissance painters from north-central Italy. [ND622.W53 1970] 920 78-99997
1. Painters—Italy—Juvenile literature. 2. Painting—Mantua. 3. Painting—Padua. 4. Painting—Siena. 5. Painting—Urbino. I. Title.

Painters—Japan—Biography.

KANO, Eitoku, 1543-1590. 759.952
Kano Eitoku / Tsuneo Takeda ; translated and adapted by H. Mack Horton and Catherine Kaputa. 1st ed. Tokyo ; New York : Kodansha International, 1977. 178 p. : ill. (some col.) ; 27 cm. (Japanese arts library ; v. 3) Includes index. Bibliography: p. [169]-174. [ND1059.K17T3413] 76-44155 ISBN 0-87011-295-3 : 15.00
1. Kano, Eitoku, 1543-1590. 2. Painters—Japan—Biography. I. Takeda, Tsuneo, 1925- II. Title. III. Series. BIP

Painters, Japanese — Dictionaries.

TOYO BIJUTSU KOKUSAI 759.952 KENKYUKAI.
Index of Japanese painters. Compiled by the Society of Friends of Eastern Art. Tokyo, Rutland, Vt., C. E. Tuttle Co. [1958] 160 p. fold. table. 19 cm. "Offset reprint of the original edition [published in 1940]" [ND1058.T65] 58-9985
1. Painters, Japanese — Dictionaries. I. Title. BIP

Painters, Latin American—Biography.

GARCIA Cisneros, F., 1924- 759.98
Latin-American painters in New York. Pintores Latino-americanos en Nueva York; a monographic book, by F. Garcia Cisneros. [Miami, Fla., Printed by Rema Press, 1964] 273 p. illus. 22 cm. On spine: 40 pintores Latinoamericanos en New York. On cover: 40 Latin American painters in New York. English and Spanish. Includes bibliographical references. [ND238.L3G37] 73-158682
1. Painters, Latin American—Biography. 2. Painters, Latin American—New York (City) I. Title. II. Title: Pintores Latino-americanos en Neuva York. III. Title: Cuarenta pintores Latinoamericanos en New York. IV. Title: 40 Latin American painters in New York.

Painters—Louisiana—New Orleans—Biography.

CRUISE, Boyd. 759.13
Boyd Cruise. 1st ed. New Orleans : Kemper and Leila Williams Foundation, c1976. 72 p. : ill. (some col.) ; 29 cm. Published in conjunction with the artist's exhibition held at the Historic New Orleans Collection, December 1976-February 1977. "Biography of the artist [by] Mary Louise Christovich": p. 2-13. [ND237.C843C48] 76-24712 ISBN 0-917860-01-2
1. Cruise, Boyd. 2. Painters—Louisiana—New Orleans—Biography. I. Christovich, Mary Louise. II. Historic New Orleans Collection.

Painters—Netherlands.

BODE, Wilhelm von, 1845- 759.9492 1929.
Great masters of Dutch and Flemish painting. Translated by Margaret L. Clarke. Freeport, N.Y., Books for Libraries Press [1967] ix, 358 p. 39 plates. 22 cm. (Essay index reprint series) Reprint of the 1909 ed. "Translated from the second and revised edition of Dr. Bode's 'Rembrandt und seine Zeitgenossen.'" [ND631.B613 1967] 67-22057
1. Painters—Netherlands. 2. Painters, Flemish. I. Clarke, Margaret L., tr. II. Title. BIP

MANDER, Carel van, 1548-1606. 759.9492 B
Dutch and Flemish painters. [Translation from the Schilderboeck and introd. by Constant van de Wall] New York, Arno Press, 1969. lxix, 560 p. map. 24 cm. Reprint of the 1936 ed. Includes bibliographical references. [ND625.M24 1969] 71-88823
1. Painters—Netherlands. 2. Painters, Flemish. I. Title. BIP

Painters—Netherlands—Biography.

LEYMARIE, Jean. 759.9492 B
Van Gogh / [text by Jean Leymarie ; translated from the French by James Emmons]. New ed. New York : Rizzoli International Publications, 1977. 210 p. : ill. (some col.) ; 35 cm. (Discovering the nineteenth century) Translation of Qui etait van Gogh? Includes index. Bibliography: p. 199-[200] [ND653.G7L463 1977] 78-100029 ISBN 0-8478-0119-5 : 45.00
1. Gogh, Vincent van, 1853-1890. 2. Painters—Netherlands—Biography. I. Title. II. Series.

POLLOCK, Griselda. 759.9492 B
Vincent van Gogh, artist of his time / Griselda Pollock and Fred Orton. New York : Dutton, 1978. 80 p. : ill. (some col.) ; 29 cm. Bibliography: p. 6 [ND653.G7P64] 78-56652 ISBN 0-7148-1883-6 : 12.95. ISBN 0-7148-1906-9 pbk : 6.95
1. Gogh, Vincent van, 1853-1890. 2. Painters—Netherlands—Biography. I. Orton, Fred, joint author. II. Gogh, Vincent van, 1853-1890. III. Title.

WELSH, Robert P. 759.9492
Piet Mondrian's early career : the "naturalistic" periods / Robert P. Welsh. New York : Garland Pub., 1977. xvi, 232 p., [67] leaves of plates : ill. ; 21 cm. (Outstanding dissertations in the fine arts) Reprint of the ed. originally presented as the author's thesis, Princeton University, 1965. Bibliography: p. 228-232. [ND653.M76W4 1977] 76-23659 ISBN 0-8240-2738-8 lib.bdg. : 40.00
1. Mondriaan, Pieter Cornelis, 1872-1944. 2. Painters—Netherlands—Biography. I. Title. II. Series. BIP

WELSH-OVHAROV, Bogomila. 759.9492 B
Vincent van Gogh : his Paris period 1886-1888 / Bogomila Welsh-Ovcharov. Utrecht : Editions Victorine, 1976. xi, 302 p. : ill. ; 28 cm. Thesis—Toronto. Includes index. Bibliography: p. 255-261. [ND653.G7W43] 77-465148
1. Gogh, Vincent van, 1853-1890. 2. Painters—Netherlands—Biography. 3. Painters—France—Paris—Biography.

WILKIE, Kenneth, 1942- 759.9492 B
The van Gogh assignment / Kenneth Wilkie. New York : Paddington Press : distributed by Grosset & Dunlap, c1978. 207 p. : ill. ; 22 cm. [ND653.G7W54] 77-20966 ISBN 0-448-23167-0 : 7.95
1. Gogh, Vincent van, 1853-1890. 2. Painters—Netherlands—Biography. I. Title. BIP

Painters—Netherlands—Correspondence, reminiscences, etc.

GOGH, Vincent van, 1853-1890. 759.9492 B
My life & love are one : quotations from the letters of Vincent Van Gogh to his brother Theo / edited by Irving and Jean Stone ; selected and arranged by Susan Polis Schutz and Nancy Hoffman ; designed by Stephen Schutz. Boulder, Colo. : Blue Mountain Arts, 1976. 63 p. : ill. ; 22 cm. [ND653.G7A344] 75-37346 ISBN 0-88396-016-8 pbk. : 3.50
1. Gogh, Vincent van, 1853-1890. 2. Gogh, Theo van, 1857-1891. 3. Painters—Netherlands—Correspondence. I. Title.

Painters—Netherlands—Correspondence, reminiscences, etc.

GOGH, Vincent van, 1853-1890. 759.9492
Van Gogh's "diary"; the artist's life in his own words and art. Edited by Jan Hulsker. New York, Morrow, 1971 [c1970] 168 p. illus. (part col.) 27 cm. Translation of "Dagboek" van Van Gogh. [ND653.G7A2813] 70-158078 12.50
1. Painters—Netherlands—Correspondence, reminiscences, etc. I. Hulsker, Jan, ed. II. Title.

Painters—New Zealand—Biography.

CANADAY, Frank H., 1896-1976. 759.9931
Triumph in color : the life and art of Molly Morpeth Canaday / Frank H. Canaday ; with art commentary by Janet Paul. Canaan, N.H. : Phoenix Pub., c1977. vii, 152 p. : ill. (some col.) ; 29 cm. Includes index. [ND1108.C36C36] 76-30866 ISBN 0-914016-38-5 : 20.00
1. Canaday, Molly Morpeth, 1903-1971. 2. Canaday, Molly Morpeth, 1903-1971. 3. Painters—New Zealand—Biography. I. Title. BIP

Painters—Pennsylvanis.

PENNSYLVANIA. State University. 759.13
Pennsylvania painters; centennial exhibition, October 7- November 6, 1955, commemorating the 100th anniversary of the Pennsylvania State University. Mineral Industries Gallery, University Park, Pennsylvania. [Text by Harold B. Dickson. University Park, 1955] 1v. (unpaged) 50 illus. 26cm. Includes bibliography ([2]p.) [ND230.P4P4] [ND230.P4P4] 759.148 55-63069 55-63069
1. Painters—Pennsylvanis. 2. Paintings, American—Exhibitions. I. Dickson, Harold Edward, 1900- II. Title.

Painters—Russian Republic—Biography.

ALEXANDER, Sidney, 1912- 759.7 B
Marc Chagall : the artist with seven fingers / by Sidney Alexander. New York : Putnam, c1978. p. cm. Includes index. [ND699.C5A67 1978] 77-16526 15.00
1. Chagall, Marc, 1887- 2. Painters—Russian Republic—Biography.

Painters—Scotland—Biography.

BUCHANAN, William. 759.9411 B
Joan Eardley / by William Buchanan. Edinburgh : Edinburgh University Press, c1976. 91 p. : ill. (some col.) ; 16 x 22 cm. (Modern Scottish painters ; no. 5) Bibliography: p. 88. [ND497.E25B8] 77-360043 ISBN 0-85224-301-4 : 5.00
1. Eardley, Joan. 2. Painters—Scotland—Biography. I. Eardley, Joan.
Distributed by Edinburgh Univ. Press, c/o Biblio Distribution Center, 81 Adams Dr., Totowa, NJ07512

LINDSAY, John Maurice, 1918- 759.9411 B
Robin Philipson / by Maurice Lindsay. Edinburgh : Edinburgh University Press, c1976. 79 p. : ill. (some col.) ; 16 x 22 cm. (Modern Scottish painters ; no. 6) Bibliography: p. 75. [ND497.P48L56] 77-360047 ISBN 0-85224-302-2 : 5.00
1. Philipson, Robin. 2. Painters—Scotland—Biography. I. Philipson, Robin.
Distributed by Edinburgh Univ. Press, c/o Biblio Distribution Ctr., 81 Adams Dr., Totowa, NJ 07512

MCCLURE, David. 759.9411 B
John Maxwell / by David McClure. Edinburgh : Edinburgh University Press, c1976. 69 p. : ill. (some col.) ; 16 x 22 cm. (Modern Scottish painters ; no. 4) Bibliography: p. 66. [ND497.M48M33] 77-362553 ISBN 0-85224-300-6 : 5.00
1. Maxwell, John, 1905-1962. 2. Painters—Scotland—Biography.
Distributed by Edinburgh University Press, Totowa, N.J.

Painters—Spain—Biography.

KAHR, Madlyn Millner. 759.6 B
Velazquez : the art of painting / Madlyn Millner Kahr. 1st ed. New York : Harper & Row, c1976. xii, 233 p. : ill. ; 24 cm. (Icon editions) Includes index. Bibliography: p. [221]-225. [ND813.V4K24 1976] 75-39563 ISBN 0-06-433575-5 : 12.50
1. Velazquez, Diego Rodriguez de Silva y, 1599-1660. 2. Painters—Spain—Biography.

MULLER, Joseph Emile. 759.6 B
Velazquez / Joseph-Emile Muller ; [translated from the French by Jane Brenton]. London : Thames and Hudson, 1976. 264 p. : ill. (some col.) ; 22 cm. Translation of Velazquez. Label mounted on t.p.: Transatlantic Arts, Levittown, N.Y. sole distributor for the U.S.A. Includes index. Bibliography: p. 251. [ND813.V4M7413 1976] 76-378650 ISBN 0-500-18152-7 : 12.95 ISBN 0-500-20147-1 pbk. : 6.95
1. Velazquez, Diego Rodriguez de Silva y, 1599-1660. 2. Painters—Spain—Biography.

WEST, Nancy Glass, 1940- 759.6 B
Jose Vives-Atsara, his life and his art / by Nancy Glass West Austin, Tex. : Shoal Creek Publishers, c1976. p. cm. Includes index. Bibliography: p. [ND813.V58W47] 76-47664 ISBN 0-88319-027-3 : 50.00
1. Vives-Atsara, Jose, 1919- 2. Painters—Spain—Biography.

ZURBARAN, Francisco, 1598-1664. 759.6
Zurbaran, 1598-1664 / biography and critical analysis by Julian Gallego ; catalogue of the works by Jose Gudiol. New York : Rizzoli, 1977. 415 p. : ill. (some col.) ; 30 cm. Includes indexes. Bibliography: p. 411-415. [ND813.Z85A4 1977] 77-77657 ISBN 0-8478-0118-7 : 60.00
1. Zurbaran, Francisco, 1598-1664. 2. Painters—Spain—Biography. I. Gallego, Julian. II. Gudiol i Ricart, Josep. BIP

Painters—Spain—Castile—Biography.

VOLK, Mary Crawford. 759.6 B
Vicencio Carducho and seventeenth century Castilian painting / Mary Crawford Volk. New York : Garland Pub., 1977, i.e.1978 428 p., [76] leaves of plates : ill. ; 22 cm. (Outstanding dissertations in the fine arts) Reprint of the author's thesis, Yale, 1973. Bibliography: p. 415-428. [ND813.C287V64 1977] 76-23650 ISBN 0-8240-2734-5 lib.bdg. : 45.00
1. Carducci, Vincenzio, 1578-1638. 2. Painters—Spain—Castile—Biography. I. Title. II. Series.

Painters—Spain—Correspondence, reminiscences, etc.

DALI, Salvador, 1904- 759.6 B
The unspeakable confessions of Salvador Dali / as told to Andre Parinaud ; translated from the French by Harold J. Salemsom. New York : Morrow, 1976. 300 p., [9] leaves of plates : ill. ; 24 cm. Translation of Comment on devient Dali. [ND813.D3P3713] 75-25924 ISBN 0-688-02995-7 : 10.00
1. Dali, Salvador, 1904- 2. Painters—Spain—Correspondence, reminiscences, etc. I. Parinaud, Andre, 1924- II. Title.

Painters—Switzerland—Biography.

MANNERS, Victoria Alexandra Elizabeth Dorothy, Lady, 1876-1933. 759.9494 B
Angelica Kauffmann, R. A., her life and her works / by Lady Victoria Manners and G. C. Williamson. New York : Hacker Art Books, 1976. xiii, 268 p., [32] leaves of plates : ill. ; 28 cm. Reprint of the 1924 ed. published by Bodley Head, London. Includes index. Bibliography: p. 247. [ND853.K29M36 1976] 75-10527 ISBN 0-87817-183-5 lib.bdg. : 40.00
1. Kauffmann, Maria Anna Angelica Catharina, 1741-1807. 2. Painters—Switzerland—Biography. I. Williamson, George Charles, 1858-1942, joint author.

Painters—Texas—Biography.

STEINFELDT, Cecilia. 759.13 B
The Onderdonks : a family of Texas painters / Cecilia Steinfeldt. [San Antonio] : Published for the San Antonio Museum Association by Trinity University Press, 1975, c1976. 238 p. : ill. (some col.) ; 24 x 29 cm. "Published in conjunction with an exhibition ... held at the Witte Memorial Museum, Brackenridge Park, San Antonio, Texas, January 16, 1975 to July 31, 1975." Includes index. Bibliography: p. 232-233. [ND237.O54S73] 74-29009 ISBN 0-911536-57-4 : 25.00
1. Onderdonk family. 2. Painters—Texas—Biography. I. San Antonio Museum Association. II. Witte Memorial Museum, San Antonio. III. Title. BIP

Painters—United States.

CAFFIN, Charles Henry, 1854-1918. 759.13
American masters of painting, being brief appreciations of some American painters. Freeport, N.Y., Books for Libraries Press [1970] x, 195 p. illus. 23 cm. (Essay index reprint series) Reprint of the 1902 ed. [ND236.C3 1970] 73-128217 ISBN 0-8369-1868-1
1. Painters—United States. I. Title. BIP

FRANKENSTEIN, Alfred Victor, 1906- 759.13
After the hunt; William Harnett and other American still life painters, 1870-1900 [by] Alfred Frankenstein. Rev. ed. Berkeley, University of California Press, 1969. xix, 200 p. illus., col. front. 29 cm. (California studies in the history of art, 12) Bibliographical footnotes. [ND237.H315F7 1969] 68-31417 16.50
1. Harnett, William Michael, 1848-1892. 2. Painters—United States. 3. Still-life painting, American. I. Title. II. Series.

MATHER, Frank Jewett, 1868-1953. 759.13
Estimates in art. Series II. Sixteen essays on American painters of the nineteenth century. Freeport, N.Y., Books for Libraries Press [1970, c1931] xii, 337 p. illus., ports. 23 cm. (Essay index reprint series) Contents.Contents.—Face-painter and feminist [Gilbert Stuart].—The art of S. F. B. Morse.—George Inness.—Elihu Vedder.—Afterthoughts on Whistler.—George Fuller.—Homer D. Martin.—Albert Pinkham Ryder.—Winslow Homer.—Thomas Eakins.—The enigma of Sargent.—Edwin Austin Abbey.—Kenyon Cox.—Alden Weir.—William M. Chase.—Arthur B. Davies. [ND210.M3] 70-93356 ISBN 0-8369-1527-5
1. Painters—United States. 2. Painting, Modern—19th century—United States. I. Title.

O'DOHERTY, Brian. 759.13
American masters: the voice and the myth. Photographed by Hans Namuth. New York, Random House [1973] 288 p. illus. (part col.) 32 cm. "A Ridge Press book." [ND212.O36] 73-4867 ISBN 0-394-46423-0 25.00
1. Painters—United States. 2. Painting, Modern—20th century—United States. I. Title.
Contents omitted.

SHELDON, George William, 1843-1914. 759.13
American painters, with one hundred and four examples of their work engraved on wood. Enl. ed. New York, B. Blom, 1972. 228 p. illus. 27 cm. Reprint of the 1881 ed. [ND236.S5 1972] 70-173144
1. Painters—United States. 2. Painters, American. 3. Paintings, American. I. Title. BIP

Painters—United States—Biography.

ADAMS, Philip Rhys, 1908- 759.13
Walt Kuhn, painter : his life and work / by Philip Rhys Adams. Columbus : Ohio State University Press, [1978] p. cm. Includes index. [ND237.K8A84] 78-3502 ISBN 0-8142-0258-6 : 30.00
1. Kuhn, Walt, 1877-1949. 2. Painters—United States—Biography. I. Title. BIP

ALBERTS, Robert C. 759.13 B
Benjamin West : a biography / Robert C.

Painters—United States—Biography—Juvenile literature.

Painters—United States—Bishop Hill, Ill.—Biography.

Painters—United States—Correspondence, reminiscences, etc.

Painters—United States—Interviews.

Painters—United States—Juvenile literature.

HEIDERSTADT, Dorothy. 759.13
Painters of America. New York, D. McKay Co. [1970] x, 180 p. 15 illus. 21 cm. Contents.Contents.—Benjamin West.—John Trumbull.—George Catlin.—Thomas Cole.—Karl Bodmer.—Alfred Jacob Miller.—George Caleb Bingham.—Emanuel Leutze.—George Inness.—Alfred Bierstadt.—Winslow Homer.—Frederic Remington.—Charles Schreyvogel.—Charles Marion Russell.—Grant Wood.—Bibliography (p. 171-173) [ND236.H43] 920 75-125655 4.95
1. Painters—United States—Juvenile literature. I. Title.

Painters, Victorian—Biography—Dictionaries.

WOOD, Christopher. 759.2
Dictionary of Victorian painters; with guide to auction prices, ... and index to artists' monograms. [Woodbridge] Antique Collectors' Club, 1971. v-xvi, 435 p. illus. 28 cm. Bibliography: p. xiv-xv. [ND35.W6] 72-188506 ISBN 0-902028-10-3 £8.00
1. Painters, Victorian—Biography—Dictionaries. I. Title.

Painters—Yugoslavia—Biography.

GENERALIC, Ivan. 759.9497 B
The magic world of Ivan Generalic / [edited] by Nebojsa Tomasevic ; translated from the Italian by John Shepley. New York : Rizzoli, 1976, c1975. 223 p. : ill. (some col.) ; 31 cm. Translation of Il mondo magico di Ivan Generalic. [ND953.G4T6513 1976] 76-11251 ISBN 0-8478-0044-X : 27.50
1. Generalic, Ivan. 2. Painters—Yugoslavia—Biography. 3. Primitivism in art—Yugoslavia. I. Tomasevic, Nebojsa. II. Title.

Painting.

ART always changes; 759.06
how to understand modern painting. With illus. and diagrs. by the author. New York, Hastings House [1958] 96p. illus. 21cm. (Visual communication books) [ND1142.B4] [ND1142.B4] 759.91 58-9006 58-9006
1. Painting. I. Bethers, Ray, 1902-

BERGER, Rene 759
Discovery of painting. [Tr. from French by Richard James] New York, Viking [c.1959, 1963] 391p. 453 illus. (pt. mounted col.) 29cm. (Studio bk.) Bibl. 63-11815 25.00, 22.50 until Dec. 31,
1. Painting. 2. Paintings. I. Title.

BERGER, Rene. 759
Discovery of painting, [Translated from the French by Richard James] New York, Viking Press [1963] 391 p. 453 illus. (part mounted col.) 29 cm. (A Studio book) Bibliography: p. 389-390. [ND1135.B443] 63-11815
1. Painting. 2. Paintings. I. Title.

BLANSHARD, Frances 750'.18
Margaret (Bradshaw) 1895-1966.
Retreat from likeness in the theory of painting. 2d ed., rev. & enl. Freeport, N.Y., Books for Libraries Press [1972, c1949] x, 178 p. illus. 23 cm. Bibliography: p. [159]-164. [ND1140.B55 1972] 72-37913 ISBN 0-8369-6733-X
1. Painting. 2. Aesthetics. I. Title. BIP

BOAS, George, 1891- 750
What is a picture? [By] George Boas, Harold Holmes Wrenn. New York. Schocken [1966, c1964] 182p. illus. 21cm. [ND1142.B6 1966] 66-14867 6.00; 2.45 pap.,
1. Painting. I. Wrenn, Harold Holmes, joint author. II. Title.

BOAS, George, 1891- 750
What is a picture? [By] George Boas and Harold Holmes Wrenn. [Pittsburgh] University of Pittsburgh Press [1964] xv, 183 p. illus. 27 cm [ND1142.B6] 64-13229
1. Painting. I. Wrenn, Harold Holmes, joint author. II. Title. BIP

*BROOKS, Walter, comp. 751.4
Creative ways with flower painting edited by Walter Brooks. New York, Golden Press [1973] 32 p. illus. 29 cm. (Golden Press Art Instruction Ser.) [ND1400] 73-88432 1.25 (pbk.)
1. Painting. I. Title. BIP

CALIFORNIA. University. 759.06
Dept. of Art, Los Angeles.
Looking at modern painting. A study-discussion program prepared by the Dept. of Art in cooperation with University Extension, University of California, Los Angeles. [Los Angeles, c1957] 123p. illus., plates (part col.) 30cm. Includes bibliographies. [ND160.C24] [ND160.C24] 759.91 58-63001 58-63001
1. Painting. 2. Paintings. 3. Painters. I. Title.

CHURCHILL, Winston Leonard 751
Spencer Sir 1874-
Painting as a pastime. New York, Cornerstone Lib. [dist. Affiliated Pubs., 1961] 32p. col. plates, port. (CN9) 1.00 pap.,
1. Painting. I. Title.

ELWESS, Brewster. 755'.55
The most beautiful Jewish woman in the history of mankind / Brewster Elwess. Albuquerque : Gloucester Art Press, [1978] p. cm. Bibliography; p. [ND1430.E48] 78-26103 ISBN 0-930582-17-9 : 12.75 ISBN 0-930582-07-1 : 47.75
1. Mary, Virgin—Art. 2. Painting. I. Title.

FREEDMAN, Leonard, ed. 759.06
Looking at modern painting [by] Gibson A. Danes [others] New York, Norton [c.1957, 1961] 140p. illus. (pt. col.) 28cm. Bibl. 61-9154 4.50 pap.,
1. Painting. 2. Paintings. 3. Art, Modern—20th cent. I. Danes, Gibson A. II. Title. BIP

GIARDELLI, Arthur. 750
The delight of painting : the W. D. Thomas memorial lecture delivered at the University College of Swansea on November 18, 1975 / by Arthur Giardelli. Swansea : University College of Swansea, 1976. 22, [1] p., [6] leaves of plates : ill. ; 22 cm. Bibliography: p. [23] [ND1140.G52] 77-366197
1. Painting. I. Title.

GOODHEART-WILLCOX'S painting 698 *and decorating encylopedia;* a complete librry of professional know-how on painting, decorating, and wood finishing in one easy-to-use volume. Edited by Wm. Don Jarvis. Chicago, Goodheart-Willcox Co. [1957] 288p. illus. 28cm. [TT320.G6] 56-6205
1. Painting. I. Jarvis, William Don, ed.

GROSSER, Maurice Richard, 751
1903-
The painter's eye. New York, Rinehart [1951] xii, 244 p. illus. 21 cm. [ND1135.G7] 51-14320
1. Painting. I. Title.

GROSSER, Maurice Richard, 751
1903-
The painter's eye. [New York] New American Library [1956, c1955] 192p. illus. 18cm. (A Mentor book, M159) [ND1135.G7 1956] 56-278
1. Painting. I. Title.

HAFTMANN, Werner. 759.06
Painting in the twentieth century. [Translated by Ralph Manheim] New York, Praeger [1961, c1960] 2 v. illus. (part col.) ports. 26 cm. (Books that matter) [ND195.H323 1961] 60-16468
1. Painting. 2. Painters. 3. Paintings. I. Title.

HESS, Thomas B. 759.915
Abstract painting; background and American phase. New York, Viking Press, 1951. 164 p. illus. (part col.) 29 cm. "A Lee Ault edition." [ND195.H4] 51-14481
1. Painting. 2. Painting, American. 3. Art, Abstract. I. Title.

HILL, Adrian Keith Graham, 751.4
1895?-
The pleasures of painting with practical demonstrations. New York, Pitman Pub. Corp. [1953] 102p. illus. 26cm. [ND1142] 53-12236
1. Painting. I. Title.

HULTON, Nika. 750
First steps in art appreciation. New York, Pitman Pub. Cor. [1958] 54 p. illus. 26 cm. [ND1142.H8] 59-1527
1. Painting. I. Title.

HUNT, William Morris, 1824- 750
1879.
W. M. Hunt's Talks about art / with a letter from J. E. Millais. New York : AMS Press, 1975. viii, 124 p. ; 23 cm. Reprint of the 1878 ed. published by Macmillan, London. [ND1135.H9 1975] 76-148797 ISBN 0-404-03448-9 : 10.50
1. Painting. I. Title: Talks about art. BIP

HUNT, William Morris, 1824- 750
1879.
William Morris Hunt on painting and drawing / with a new introduction by Charles Movalli. New York : Dover Publications, 1976. xiv, 175 ; 22 cm. (Dover art instruction and reference books) "Unabridged republication of Talks on art, first series, and Talks on art, second series." [ND1135.H9 1976] 76-3236 ISBN 0-486-23398-7 pbk. : 2.75
1. Painting. 2. Drawing. I. Title.

JANSON, Horst Woldemar, 1913- 759
The story of painting, from cave painting to modern times / H. W. Janson and Dora Jane Janson. New York : H. N. Abrams, 1977. 173 p. : ill. (some col.) ; 30 cm. First ed. published in 1952 under title: The story of painting for young people. Companion volume: The story of American painting, by A. A. Davidson. Includes index. [ND50.J335 1977] 77-2238 ISBN 0-8109-2068-9 pbk. : 7.95
1. Painting. I. Janson, Dora Jane, 1916- joint author. II. Title.

JOHNSON, Charles, 1896- 750
The language of painting. New York, Greenwood Press [1969] xii, 276 p. illus. 24 cm. Reprint of the 1949 ed. [ND1135.J65 1969] 73-90151
1. Painting. I. Title. BIP

JUIN, Hubert. 759.4
Sixteen painters of the young school of Paris. Edited by J. C. Lambert. Photos. by Luc Joubert. Translated by Haakon Chevalier. [New York] Arts, inc. [c1958] 60p. illus. 19cm. (The Pocket museum) Golden griffin books. [ND548.J813] 58-13501
1. Painting. I. Title.

LEEPA, Allen. 701.16
The challenge of modern art; with a foreword by Herbert Read. [Rev. ed.] New York, T. Yoseloff [1957] 256p. illus. 25cm. [ND195.L4 1957] 57-13766
1. Painting. 2. Art, Modern—20th cent. 3. Modernism (Art) I. Title.

MERRIFELD, Mary 751.4'5'08
Philadelphia, 1804or5-1889, comp.
Original treatises on the arts of painting, by Mary P. Merrifield. With a new introd. and glossary by S. M. Alexander. New York, Dover Publications [1967] 2 v. (cccxii, 918 p.) 22 cm. "Unabridged and unaltered republication of the work orginally published ... in 1849 [under title: Original treatises, dating from the XIIth to XVIIIth centuries on the arts of painting ...]" Original treatises in English and Latin. Bibliographical footnotes. [ND25.M52] 64-18860
1. Painting. 2. Painting—Technique. I. Title.

MILNER, Marion (Blackett) 751.4
On not being able to paint. Illustrated by the author. With a foreword by Anna Freud. 2d ed. New York, International Universities Press [1957, i. e. 1958] 184p. illus. 23cm. [ND1140.M5 1957] 58-327
1. Painting. 2. Creation (Literary, artistic, etc.) I. Title. BIP

MILNER, Marion (Blackett) 153.3'5
On not being able to paint, by Marion Milner (Joanna Field); illustrated by the author, with a foreword by Anna Freud. 2nd ed. London, Heinemann Educational, 1971. xxii, 184 p. illus. 22 cm. (An H.E.B. paperback) Bibliography: p. 167-170. [ND1140.M5 1971] 77-885810 ISBN 0-435-80590-8
1. Painting. 2. Creation (Literary, artistic, etc.) I. Title.
Available from International Universities Press, 5.50.

MOORE, Lamont. 759
The first book of paintings; an introduction to the appreciation of pictures. New York, Watts [1960] 69 p. illus. 23 cm. [ND1142.M6] 60-5576
1. Painting. 2. Paintings. I. Title.

PHILLIPS, Lois Brandt. 745.7'2
Decorative painting using patterns from nature / by Lois Brandt Phillips. New York : Crown Publishers, c1978. 96 p., [4] leaves of plates : ill. (some col.) ; 29 cm. Includes index. Bibliography: p. 93. [TT385.P48 1978] 77-19190 ISBN 0-517-53395-2. ISBN 0-517-53396-0 pbk. : 7.95
1. Painting. 2. Design, Decorative—Animal forms. 3. Design, Decorative—Plant forms. I. Title. BIP

PROTTER, Eric, ed. 750.88
Painters on painting. [1st ed.] New York, Grosset and Dunlap [1963] xvi, 272 p. illus., ports. 21 cm. (Universal library, UL156) Bibliography: p. 261-266. 63-10197
1. Painting. 2. Artists—Correspondence, reminiscences, etc. I. Title.

PROTTER, Eric, ed. 750'.1
Painters on painting, selected and edited by Eric Protter. [Rev. ed.] New York, Grosset & Dunlap [1971] xvii, 294 p. illus., ports 21 cm. (The Universal library, UL 156) Bibliography: p. 279-287. [ND1140.P7 1971] 73-120428 ISBN 0-448-00156-X 2.95
1. Painting. 2. Painters—Correspondence, reminiscences, etc. I. Title.

RUHEMANN, Helmut. 750.74
The artist at work [by] H. Ruhemann and E. M. Kemp. Baltimore, Penguin Books [1951] 72 p. illus. (part col.) 19 x 24 cm. (Penguin books, E 37) [ND1140.R8] 52-2686
1. Painting. I. Kemp, Ellem M., joint author. II. Title.

SOLOMON R. Guggenheim 701.16
Museum, New York.
Elements of modern painting [by] Thomas M. Messer [director. New York, c1961] unpaged. illus. 26 x 12 cm. [ND195.S67] 62-746
1. Painting. 2. Art, Modern — 20th cent. I. Messer, Thomas M. II. II. Title. III. Title: Modern painting.

TURNER, Percy Moore. 750'.11
The appreciation of painting. Freeport, N.Y., Books for Libraries Press [1971] 244 p. illus. 23 cm. Reprint of the 1921 ed. [ND1143.T8 1971] 71-179542 ISBN 0-8369-6671-6
1. Painting. 2. Art appreciation. I. Title. BIP

WHELPTON, Barbara 759.94
(Crocker)
Getting to know pictures. New York, Philosophical Library [1960] 144p. illus. (part col.) 20cm. 60-4148 4.75 bds.,
1. Painting. I. Title.

ZAIDENBERG, Arthur, 1903- 750
The joy of painting. [1st ed.] Garden City, N. Y., Hanover House [1955] 190 p. illus. 27 cm. [ND1142.Z3] 55-9358
1. Painting. I. Title.

ZUCKER, Paul, 1889- 750
Styles in painting, a comparative study. New York, Viking Press, 1950. xiii, 338 p. 241 illus. 26 cm. [ND1135.Z8 1950] 50-9742
1. Painting. I. Title.

ZUCKER, Paul, 1889- 750
Styles in painting, a comparative study [Gloucester, Mass., P. Smith, c.1950, 1963] xiii, 338p. illus. 21cm. (Dover bk. rebound) 4.00
1. Painting. I. Title. BIP

ZUCKER, Paul, 1889- 759
Styles in painting, a comparative study [New York] Dover [1964] xiii, 338p. illus., ports. 21cm. (T760) unabridged, corrected repubn. of the work first pub. in 1950. 64-9083 2.00 pap.,
1. Painting. I. Title.

Painting, Abstract—Ecuador—Exhibitions.

BARNITZ, Jacqueline. 759.9866'074'01471
Abstract currents in Ecuadorian art : Araceli, Maldonado, Molinari, Rendon, Tabara, Villacis / Jacqueline Barnitz, guest curator. [New York] : Center for Inter-American Relations, c1977. 47 p. : ill. (some col.) ; 18 x 25 cm. [ND385.5.A26B37] 77-156050 6.00
1. Painting, Abstract—Ecuador—Exhibitions. 2. Paintings, Ecuadorian—Ecuador—Exhibitions. 3. Painting, Modern—20th century—Ecuador—Exhibitions. 4. Painters—Ecuador—Biography. I. Center for Inter-American Relations. II. Title.
Publisher's address: 680 Park Avenue, New York, NY 10021

Painting—Addresses, essays, lectures.

BERGER, John. 759
The moment of cubism, and other essays. [1st American ed.] New York, Pantheon Books [1969] 139 p. illus. 22 cm. Contents.Contents.—The moment of cubism.—The historical function of the museum.—The changing view of man in the portrait.—Art and property now.—Image of imperialism.—Nude in a fur coat: Rubens.—The painter in his studio: Vermeer.—Et in Arcadia ego: Poussin.—The Maja dressed and the Maja undressed: Goya.—Grunewald.—Lowry.—Toulouse-Lautrec.—Giacometti.—Bonnard.—Hals.—Rodin. Bibliographical footnotes. [ND1150.B42 1969b] 69-20197 5.95
1. Painting—Addresses, essays, lectures. 2. Art criticism—Addresses, essays, lectures. I. Title.

THE Book of art. 709
New York : Grolier, 1977, c1976 3 v. : col. ill. ; 26 cm. Includes index. Contents.Contents.—v. 1. How to look at art. Origins of Western art. Italian art to 1800.—v. 2. Flemish and Dutch art. German and Spanish art to 1900. French art from 1350 to 1850. British and North American art to 1900.—v. 3. Impressionists and post-impressionists. Modern art. Chinese and Japanese art. [ND1150.B66 1976] 76-23528 ISBN 0-7172-1301-3 : 90.00
1. Painting—Addresses, essays, lectures. 2. Visual perception—Addresses, essays, lectures.

COX, Kenyon, 1856-1919. 750'.8
The classic point of view; six lectures on painting. Freeport, N.Y., Books for Libraries Press [1968] xi, 232 p. illus. 22 cm. (Essay index reprint series) Reprint of the 1911 ed. Contents.Contents.—The classic spirit.—The subject in art.—Design.—Drawing.—Light and shade and color.—Technique. [ND1150.C6 1968] 68-22907
1. Painting—Addresses, essays, lectures. I. Title.

GROSSER, Maurice Richard, 1903- 750.81
Painting in our time. Bobbs [dist. New York, Macfadden, c.1948, 1964] xix, 233p. 21cm. (Charter bk. 151) First pub. in 1948 under title: Painting in public. 64-3317 1.85 pap.,
1. Painting—Addresses, essays, lectures. I. Title.

LA FARGE, John, 1835-1910. 759
Considerations on painting; lectures given in the year 1893 at the Metropolitan Museum of Art. New York, Kennedy Galleries, 1969 [c1895] vi, 270 p. 23 cm. (Library of American art) [ND1135.L15 1969] 70-96111
1. Painting—Addresses, essays, lectures. I. Title. BIP

ZAIDENBERG, Arthur, 1903- comp. 704.92
The art of the artist; theories and techniques of art by the artists themselves. New York, Crown Publishers [1951] 175 p. illus. (part col.) 29 cm. [ND1150.Z3] 51-12016
1. Painting—Addresses, essays, lectures. I. Title.

Painting—Alexandria, Egypt.

BROWN, Blanche R 759.932
Ptolemaic paintings and mosaics and the Alexandrian style. Cambridge, Mass, Archaeological Institute of America, 1957. xvii, 108p. illus., 45 plates. 31cm. (Monographs on archaeology and fine arts, 6) Bibliography: p.xv-xvii; Bibliographical footnotes. [ND1084.A4B7] 58-3466
1. Painting—Alexandria, Egypt. 2. Mosaics. 3. Alexandria, Egypt—Antiq. I. Title. II. Series.

Painting, American.

ANDRUS, Lisa Fellows. 759.13
Measure and design in American painting, 1760-1860 / Lisa Fellows Andrus. New York : Garland Pub., 1977. 433 p. : ill. ; 21 cm. (Outstanding dissertations in the fine arts) Originally presented as the author's thesis, Columbia, 1976. Bibliography: p. 327-358. [ND207.A68 1977] 76-23601 ISBN 0-8240-2675-6 lib.bdg. : 40.00
1. Painting, American. 2. Painting, Colonial—United States. 3. Painting, Modern—19th century—United States. 4. Composition (Art) 5. Visual perception. I. Title. II. Series. BIP

BAIGELL, Matthew. 759.13
The American scene: American painting of the 1930's. New York, Praeger [1974] 214 p. illus. (part col.) 27 x 29 cm. (American art & artists) Bibliography: p. 212. [ND212.B28] 72-89639 29.50
1. Painting, American. 2. Federal Art Project. 3. Social realism. I. Title. II. Series.

BAUR, John Ireland Howe, 1909- 759.135
American painting in the nineteenth century; main trends and movements. New York, Praeger [1953] 59p. illus. 26cm. (Books that matter) An outgrowth of a catalogue written by the author to accompany an exhibition of 100 nineteenth century American paintings shown in Germany in 1953, with illustrations drawn from the exhibit. [ND210.B32] 53-9521
1. Painting, American. I. Title.

BROWN, Milton Wolf, 1911- 759.13
American painting, from the Armory Show to the depression. Princeton, Princeton University Press, 1955. xii, 243 p. illus. 29 cm. Bibliography: p. 201-237. [ND212.B74] 53-10147
1. Painting, American. I. Title. BIP

DAVIDSON, Abraham A. 759.13
The eccentrics and other American visionary painters / Abraham A. Davidson. 1st ed. New York : Dutton, c1978. xxii, 202 p., [6] leaves of plates : ill. (some col.) ; 21 cm. Includes index. Bibliography: p. 189-196. [ND210.5.R6D34 1978] 78-55775 ISBN 0-525-47500-1 : 9.95 ($12.50 Can)
1. Painting, American. 2. Romanticism in art—United States. 3. Surrealism—United States. 4. Fantasy in art. 5. Painting, Modern—19th century—United States. I. Title.

GELDZAHLER, Henry 759.13
American painting in the twentieth century. Metropolitan Mus. of Art; dist. Greenwich, Conn., N.Y. Graphic [c.1965] 236p. illus. 25cm. Bibl. [ND212.G36] 65-16668 7.50
1. Painting, American. 2. Painters, American. 3. Painting. Modern—20th cent. I. New York. Metropolitan Museum of Art. II. Title.

HASSRICK, Royal B. 759.13
Western painting today : painters of the contemporary American West / Royal B. Hassrick. New York : Watson-Guptill, 1975. p. cm. Includes index. Bibliography: p. [ND212.H34] 75-12862 ISBN 0-8230-5710-0 : 27.50
1. Painting, American. 2. Painting, Modern—20th century—United States. 3. The West in art. I. Title.

HELLER, Nancy. 759.13
The regionalists / by Nancy Heller and Julia Williams. New York : Watson-Guptill Publications, 1976. p. cm. Includes index. Bibliography: p. [ND212.H43] 76-12424 ISBN 0-8230-4516-1 : 35.00
1. Painting, American. 2. Painting, Modern—20th century—United States. 3. Art, Regional—United States. 4. United States in art. I. Williams, Julia, joint author. II. Title.

HENKES, Robert. 755'.4
The crucifixion in American painting : 80 American painters and the crucifixion theme / by Robert Henkes. New York : Gordon Press, 1977. p. cm. Includes index. [ND205.H4] 77-12369 ISBN 0-8490-1370-4 lib.bdg. : 44.95
1. Jesus Christ—Crucifixion—Art. 2. Painting, American. 3. Painters—United States. I. Title. BIP

INGRAM, O'Neal, 1941- 759.13
O'Neal Ingram; paintings, 1966-1971. Portland Museum of Art, May 28-July 11, 1971. [Written and designed by Robert B. Rettig Portland, Me., Portland Museum of Art, 1971] 79 p. illus. (part col.) 16 x 24 cm. [ND237.I48A54] 74-164034
I. Portland Museum of Art.

MORGAN, Howard Wayne. 759.13
New muses : art in American culture, 1865-1920 / by H. Wayne Morgan. 1st ed. Norman : University of Oklahoma Press, c1978. xiv, 232 p. : ill. ; 21 cm. Includes index. Bibliography: p. 183-224. [ND210.M6] 78-3524 ISBN 0-8061-1479-7 : 14.95
1. Painting, American. 2. Painting, Modern—19th century—United States. 3. Painting, Modern—20th century—United States. 4. Art and society—United States. I. Title. BIP

PICKHARDT, Carl E. 759.13
Carl Pickhardt. Text by Parker Tyler. [New York] Horizon Press [1972] 142 p. (chiefly illus., part col.) 27 cm. [ND237.P48T9] 72-182573 17.50
I. Tyler, Parker.

PROWN, Jules David. 759.13
American painting : from the Colonial period to the present / introd. by John Walker ; text by Jules David Prown and Barbara Rose. New updated ed. New York : Rizzoli, 1977. 276 p. : col. ill. ; 35 cm. Earlier ed. (1969) published in 2 separate v.: American painting, from its beginnings to the Armory Show, by J. D. Prown, and American painting, the 20th century, by B. Rose. Includes index. Bibliography: p. 255-[264] [ND205.P74 1977] 77-154746 ISBN 0-8478-0049-0 : 45.00
1. Painting, American. 2. Painters—United States. I. Prown, Jules David. American painting, from its beginnings to the Armory Show. II. Rose, Barbara. American painting, the 20th century. III. Title.

SHELDON, George William, 1843-1914. 759.13
Recent ideals of American art / George William Sheldon. New York : Garland Pub., 1977, [c1888] 13, 158, iv p., [79] leaves of plates : ill. ; 37 cm. (The Art experience in late nineteenth century America ; 16) Includes index. Reprint of the ed. published by D. Appleton, New York. [ND210.S52 1977] 75-28882 ISBN 0-8240-2240-8 lib.bdg. : 60.00
1. Painting, American. 2. Painting, Modern—19th century—United States. 3. Idealism in art. 4. Painting—Private collections—United States. I. Title. II. Series. BIP

SOLMAN, Joseph, 1909- 759.13
Joseph Solman. Introd. by A. L. Chanin. New York, Crown [1966] 16 p. [127] p. of illus. (part col.) illus. 29 cm. [ND237.S6327A47] 66-15519
I. Title.

SPENCER, Niles, 1893-1952. 759.13
Niles Spencer, by Richard B. Freeman; With a tribute by Ralston Crawford. [Lexington] University of Kentucky [1965] 79 p. illus., port. 28 cm. "A centennial publication of the University of Kentucky." Exhibition held at University of Kentucky Art Gallery, Oct. 10-Nov; 6, 1965, and others. "Tentative catalogue of Spencer's paintings": p; 29-36. Bibliography: p. 43. [ND237.S644E7] 67-5643
I. Freeman, Richard B., 1908- II. Kentucky. University. Art Gallery. III. Title.

TRUMBLE, Alfred. 759.13
Representative works of contemporary American artists / [text by Alfred Trumble]. New York : Garland Pub., 1977 [c1887] p. cm. (The Art experience in late nineteenth century America) Reprint of the ed. published by Scribner, New York. [ND210.T7 1977] 75-28879 ISBN 0-8240-2237-8 lib.bdg. : 50.00
1. Painting, American. 2. Painting, Modern—19th century—United States. I. Title. II. Series. BIP

VARIAN, Elayne H. 759.13'074'01471
Art in process; the visual development of a painting. Prepared by Elayne H. Varian, with statements by the artists. Special photographic assistance: Jonathan Holstein. New York, Finch College Museum of Art, Contemporary Study Wing [1965] 1 v. (unpaged) illus. 22 x 28 cm. Issued in connection with an exhibition which opened Feb. 25, 1965. [ND212.V37] 73-155868
1. Painting, American. 2. Painting, Modern—20th century—United States. 3. Painting—Psychological aspects. I. Finch College, New York. Museum of Art. Contemporary Study Wing. II. Title.

VISIONS / 759.13
with an introd. by Walter Hopps. Corte Madera, Calif. : Pomegranate Publications, c1977- v. : chiefly col. ill. ; 28 cm. [ND212.V54] 76-24519 ISBN 0-917556-00-3 (v. 1) pbk. : 7.95
1. Painting, American. 2. Painting, Modern—20th century—United States. I. Hopps, Walter.

WASSERBERGER, Nathan. 759.13
Nathan Wasserberger [paintings. New York, Eminent Publications, 1967] 102 p. illus. (part col., 1 fold in pocket) 19 x 24 cm. [ND237.W3535A49] 67-31176
I. Title.

WATSON, Ernest William, 1884-1969. 759.13
Color and method in painting as seen in the work of 12 American painters. Freeport, N.Y., Books for Libraries Press [1970, c1942] 141 p. illus. (part col.), ports. 31 cm. (Essay index reprint series) Contents.Contents.—Charles Burchfield.—Eugene Speicher.—Gladys Rockmore Davis.—Eliot O'Hara.—Stanley Woodward.—Andrew Wyeth.—Ogden M. Pleissner.—Leon Kroll.—Robert Brackman.—Paul Sample.—John F. Carlson.—Peppino Mangravite. [ND212.W36 1970] 72-117858
1. Painting, American. 2. Painting, Modern—20th century—U.S. 3. Painters, American. 4. Painting—Technique. I. Title.

YOUNG, Mahonri Sharp, 1911- 759.13 B
American realists, Homer to Hopper / by Mahonri Sharp Young. New York : Watson-Guptill Publications, 1977. 208 p. : chiefly ill. (some col.) ; 30 cm. Includes index. Bibliography: p. 204-205. [ND210.5.R4Y68] 77-5416 ISBN 0-8230-0215-2 : 35.00
1. Painting, American. 2. Realism in art—United States. 3. Painting, Modern—19th century—United States. 4. Painting, Modern—20th century—United States. 5. Painters—United States—Biography. I. Title.

Painting, American—Addresses, essays, lectures.

A selection of American paintings in the collection / Honolulu Academy of Arts. 759.13
Honolulu, Hawaii : The Academy, 1974. 69 p. : ill. (some col.) ; 26 cm. (Journal - Honolulu Academy of Arts ; v. 1) Collection of articles by various authors on the paintings. Includes bibliographical references. [ND205.S4] 75-329850
1. Painting, American—Addresses, essays, lectures. 2. Paintings, American. I. Honlulu Academy of Arts.

Painting, American—Bibliography.

KEAVENEY, Sydney Starr. 016.75913
American painting; a guide to information sources. Detroit, Gale Research Co. [1974] xiii, 260 p. 22 cm. (Art and architecture, v. 1) (Gale information guide library)

[Z5949.A45K4] 73-17522 ISBN 0-8103-1200-X 18.00
1. Painting, American—Bibliography. I. Title.

Painting, American—Catalogs.

CHRYSLER 759.13'074'0155521
Museum at Norfolk.
48 masterpieces ; from the Collection of Edgar William & Bernice Chrysler Garbisch Norfolk, Va. : Chrysler Museum at Norfolk, [1975] 68 p. : ill. ; 22 x 28 cm. On cover: The gift of American naive paintings from the collection of Edgar William & Bernice Chrysler Garbisch. [ND207.5.P7C49 1975] 75-13524
1. Garbisch, Edgar William—Art collections. 2. Garbisch, Bernice Chrysler—Art collections. 3. Chrysler Museum at Norfolk. 4. Paintings, America—Catalogs. 5. Primitivism in art—United States—Catalogs. 6. Paintings, Colonial—United States—Catalogs. 7. Painting, Modern—19th century—United States—Catalogs. I. Title.

KELLY, Felix. 759.9931
Felix Kelly: a romantic realist. [Shreveport, La.] R. W. Norton Art Gallery [1972] 24 p. illus. (part col.) 28 cm. Catalog of the loan exhibition held Apr. 16-May 14, 1972, at the R. W. Norton Art Gallery, Shreveport, La. [ND497.K44N67] 72-78863 ISBN 0-9600182-7-1
I. Norton (R. W.) Art Gallery. II. Title. **BIP**

MONTCLAIR, N.J. 759.13'074'014931
Art Museum.
The American painting collection of the Montclair Art Museum. Montclair, N.J. : The Museum, c1977. 268 p. : ill. (some col.) ; 29 cm. [ND205.M58 1977] 77-72003
1. Montclair, N.J. Art Museum. 2. Painting, American—Catalogs. 3. Painting—New Jersey—Montclair—Catalogs. I. Title.

RUSSELL, Josephine Dorr. 759.13
Spied a blossom passing fair; paintings. [1st ed. Cleveland, Ohio, World Pub. Co., 1969] [55] p. col. illus. 26 cm. [ND1839.R78A55] 69-19616 5.95
I. Title.

Painting, American—Exhibitions.

ACQUISITION 759.13'074'01471
priorities : aspects of postwar painting in America, including Arshile Gorky, works 1944-1948 : [exhibition] the Solomon R. Guggenheim Museum, New York. New York : Solomon R. Guggenheim Foundation, 1976. 119 p. : ill. (some col.) ; 28 cm. "Exhibition 76/3." [ND212.5.A25A25] 76-29096 ISBN 0-89207-005-6
1. Gorky, Arshile, 1904-1948. 2. Painting, American—Exhibitions. 3. Painting, Abstract—United States—Exhibitions. 4. Painting, Modern—20th century—United States—Exhibitions. I. Solomon R. Guggenheim Museum, New York. II. Title: Aspects of postwar painting in America. III. Title: Arshile Gorky, works 1944-1948.

AGEE, William 759.13'074'01641411
C.
Modern American painting, 1910-1940 : toward a new perspective : the Museum of Fine Arts, Houston, July 1-September 25, 1977 / William C. Agee. Houston, Tex. : The Museum, c1977. 23 p. : ill. ; 28 cm. Includes bibliographical references. [ND212.A447] 77-81839
1. Painting, American—Exhibitions. 2. Painting, Modern—20th century—United States—Exhibitions. I. Houston, Tex. Museum of Fine Arts. II. Title.

FORT Worth Art Center- 759.13
Museum.
Milton Resnick: selected large paintings; an exhibition organized by the Fort Worth Art Center Museum for showing there and at the Milwaukee Art Center —1971. [Fort Worth? 1971] [30] p. illus. (part col.), col. port. 26 cm. [ND237.R38F6] 70-198237
I. Resnick, Milton, 1917- II. Milwaukee. Art Center.

KENSETT, John 760'.0924
Frederick, 1816-1872.
John Frederick Kensett. [Exhibition] selected by John K. Howat. Organized and circulated by the American Federation of Arts, New York. [New Haven, Printed by Eastern Press, 1968] 47, [1] p. illus. 21 x 26 cm. Bibliography: p. [48] [ND237.K46H6 1968] 68-57157
I. Howat, John K. II. American Federation of Arts.

LAFARGE, John, 1835-1910. 759.13
John LaFarge: oils and watercolors, January 24-February 14, 1968. New York, Kennedy Galleries [1968] [36] p. 24 illus. 28 cm. Bibliography: p. [36] [ND237.L2A48] 68-1641
I. Kennedy Galleries, inc., New York.

LEVINE, Jack, 1915- 759.13
Jack Levine. Text by Frank Getlein. New York, Abrams [1966] 26p., 169 plates (pt. col.) port. 28cm. [ND237.L615G4] 66-10297 25.00
I. Getlein, Frank. II. Title. **BIP**

LEVINE, Jack, 1915- 759.13
Jack Levine: recent paintings. New York, Kennedy Galleries, inc. [1972] 1 v. (unpaged) illus. (part. col.) 28 cm. Catalog of the exhibition held Apr. 12-May 6, 1972, in the Kennedy Galleries, inc. [ND237.L615K46] 72-195720
I. Kennedy Galleries, inc., New York. II. Title.

NEWARK Museum 759.13'074'014931
Association, Newark, N.J.
Aspects of a collection : 18th and 19th century American painting from the Newark Museum : April 6-30, 1977. [New York] : M. Knoedler, c1977. 44 p. : ill. (some col.) ; 22 cm. Catalogue of the exhibition. [ND207.N43 1977] 77-152719
1. Painting, American—Exhibitions. 2. Painting, Colonial—United States—Exhibitions. 3. Painting, Modern—19th century—United States—Exhibitions. I. Knoedler (M.) and Company, inc. II. Title.

PEINTURE americaine en 759.13
Suisse 1950-1965 : [exposition], Musee d'art et d'histoire, Geneve, 8 juillet-4 octobre 1976 : [catalogue]. Geneve : Le Musee, 1976. 36 p. : ill. (some col.) ; 27 cm. English and French. [N6512.P44] 77-483337
1. Painting, American—Exhibitions. 2. Painting, Modern—20th century—United States—Exhibitions. 3. Painting, American—Switzerland—Exhibitions. I. Geneva. Musee d'art et d'histoire.

QUICK, Michael. 759.13'074'013
American expatriate painters of the late nineteenth century / Michael Quick. Dayton, Ohio : Dayton Art Institute, 1976. 158 p. : ill. (some col.) ; 28 cm. Prepared for an exhibition held at the Dayton Art Institute Dec. 4, 1976-Jan. 16, 1977, at the Pennsylvania Academy of the Fine Arts Feb. 4-Mar. 20, 1977, and at the Los Angeles County Museum of Art Apr. 12-May 29, 1977. Bibliography: p. 145-158. [ND210.Q5] 76-48792
1. Painting, American—Exhibitions. 2. Painting, Modern—19th century—United States—Exhibitions. 3. Americans in foreign countries. I. Dayton Art Institute, Dayton, Ohio. II. Pennsylvania Academy of the Fine Arts, Philadelphia. III. Los Angeles Co., Calif. Museum of Art, Los Angeles. IV. Title.

SALT Lake Art Center, 759.192
Salt Lake City.
100 years of Utah painting; selected works from the 1840s to the 1940s. Narrative and documentation by James L. Haseltine. [Salt Lake City, c1965] 62 p. illus. (part col.) 23 x 27 cm. "[Exhibition] October 22nd to November 23rd, 1965, Salt Lake Art Center, Salt Lake City, Utah. Sponsored by the Salt Lake Tribune." Bibliography: p. 50-51. [ND230.U7S3] 66-1719
1. Painting. American—Exhibitions. 2. Painters, American—Utah. I. Haseltine, James L. II. Salt Lake tribune. III. Title.

WALTON, Henry, 760'.0924
fl.1836-1850.
Henry Walton, 19th century American artist. [New York] Ithaca College Museum of Art [1968] 75 p. (chiefly illus. (part col.), ports. (part col.)) 27 cm. Catalog of the exhibition held Dec. 9, 1968 to Jan. 4, 1969 at the Ithaca College Museum of Art. "Genealogical chart showing the descent and alliances from the Colonial Period of the issue of Cruger, son of Henry Walton": 1 leaf inserted. Bibliography: p. 74-75. [N6537.W25A47] 79-12582
I. Ithaca College, Ithaca, N.Y. Museum of Art. II. Title.

Painting, American—History.

DODD, Loring Holmes, 1879- 759.13
With an eye on the gallery; American painters in oil. Cambridge, Mass., Dresser [1966] 251p. illus. 21cm. [ND205.D6] 66-19598 5.95
1. Painting, American—Hist. 2. Painters, American. I. Title.

FLEXNER, James Carey 759.1309
Thomas, 1908-
That wilder image; the painting of America's native school from Thomas Cole to Winslow Homer. Boston, Little [c.1962] 407p. illus. 28cm. 62-16956 15.00
1. Painting, American—Hist. I. Title. **BIP**

FLEXNER, James Thomas, 759.132
1908-
First flowers of our wilderness. Boston, Houghton Mifflin, 1947. xxi, 367p. illus., col. plates. 25cm. (His American painting. 1) A Life-in-America prize book. Includes bibliographies. [ND207.F57] 47-12171
1. Painting, American—Hist. 2. Paintings, American. I. Title. II. Series: Life in America series

FLEXNER, James Thomas, 759.13
1908-
The light of distant skies, 1760-1835. [1st ed.] New York, Harcourt, Brace [1954] xiii, 306p. 102 illus. 25cm. (His American painting. 2) 'Catalogue of illustrations':p. 285-293. Bibliography: p. 253-283. [ND207.F58] 54-9727
1. Painting, American—Hist. I. Title. **BIP**

FLEXNER, James Thomas, 750.973
1908-
The pocket history of American painting. New York, Pocket Books [1950] ix, 118 p. 48 plates. 16 cm. (Pocket book, 708) "Published simultaneously by Houghton Mifflin Company under the title: A short history of American painting." Bibliography: p. 116. [ND205.F5 1950a] 50-58206
1. Painting, American—Hist. I. Title.

FLEXNER, James Thomas, 750.973
1908-
A short history of American painting. Boston, Houghton Mifflin, 1950. ix, 118 p. 52 plates (part col.) 17 cm. "Being published simultaneously by Pocket Books, inc. under the title: The pocket history of American painting." Bibliography: p. 116. [ND205.F5 1950] 50-10505
1. Painting, American—Hist. I. Title.

MCCOUBREY, John W. 709.73
American tradition in painting. New York, Braziller [c.]1963. 128p. plates. 24cm. Bibl. 63-11371 4.95 bds.,
1. Painting, American—Hist. I. Title. **BIP**

NEW York. Metropolitan 759.13
Museum of Art
American paintings; a catalogue of the collection of the Metropolitan Museum of Art, v.1 [By] Albert Ten Eyck Gardner, Stuart P. Feld. Greenwich. Conn., N. Y. Graphic [c.1965] ix, 292p. illus., ports. 25cm. Bibl. [ND205.N364] 65-16834
1. Painting, American—Hist. 2. Paintings, American—Catalogs. 3. Paintings—New York (City)—Catalogs. I. Gardner, Albert Ten Eyck. II. Feld, Stuart P. III. Title.
Contents omitted.

PERLMAN, Bennard B. 759.1309
The immortal eight; American painting from Eakins to the Armory show (1870-1913) Introd. by Mrs. John Sloan. New York, Exposition [c.1962] 226p. illus. 21cm. 62-21058 6.00
1. Painting, American—Hist. I. Title.

Painting, American—History.

BAIGELL, Matthew. 759.13
A history of American painting. New York, Praeger Publishers [1971] 288 p. illus. (part col.) 22 cm. (Praeger world of art series) Bibliography: p. 269-271. [ND205.B2] 70-125485 9.95
1. Painting, American—History. I. Title.

BARKER, Virgil, 1890- 759.13
From realism to reality, in recent American painting. Freeport, N.Y., Books for Libraries Press [1968, c1959] 93 p. illus. 22 cm. (Essay index reprint series) [ND212.B33 1968] 68-57301
1. Painting, American—History. 2. Realism in art—United States. I. Title.

BENNETT, Ian. 759.13
A history of American painting. London, New York, Hamlyn, 1973. 240 p. illus. (some col.), ports. (some col.). 31 cm. [ND205.B45] 74-165637 ISBN 0-600-34400-2 £4.25
1. Painting, American—History. I. Title.

BURROUGHS, Alan, 1897- 759.13
1965.
Limners and likenesses; three centuries of American painting. New York, Russell and Russell, 1965 [c1936] ix, 246 p. plates. 26 cm. (Harvard-Radcliffe fine arts series) Bibliography: p. 223-226. [ND205.B8 1965] 65-18793
1. Painting, American—History. I. Title. II. Series. **BIP**

CAFFIN, Charles Henry, 759.13
1854-1918.
The story of American painting; the evolution of painting in America from colonial times to the present. With a new introd. by Stuart Levine. New York, Johnson Reprint Corp., 1970. xxxv, xiii, 396 p. illus., ports. 23 cm. (Series in American studies) Reprint of the edition published in New York by F. A. Stokes in 1907, with Levine's introd. added. Bibliography: p. xxxiii-xxxv. [ND205.C2 1970] 79-107852
1. Painting, American—History. 2. Painters—United States. I. Title. **BIP**

DAVIDSON, Abraham A. 759.13
The story of American painting [by] Abraham A. Davidson. New York, H. N. Abrams [1974] 168 p. illus. (part col.) 30 cm. Companion volume: The story of painting, by H. W. and D. J. Janson. [ND205.D23] 74-5116 ISBN 0-8109-0498-5
1. Painting, American—History. I. Title. **BIP**

FLEXNER, James Thomas, 759.13
1908-
First flowers of our wilderness; American painting, the colonial period. New York, Dover Publications [1969, c1947] xxix, 369 p. illus. 22 cm. Includes bibliographical references. [ND207.F57 1969] 68-8811 3.50
1. Painting, American—History. 2. Paintings, American. I. Title.

FLEXNER, James Thomas, 759.13
1908-
The light of distant skies, 1760-1835. New York, Dover Publications [1969] xviii, 307 p. illus. 22 cm. (His American painting, 2) "An unabridged republication, with minor corrections, of the work originally published in 1954 ... contains a new preface by the author and a new publisher's note." Bibliography: p. 253-283. "Catalogue of illustrations": p. 285-293. [ND207.F58 1969] 68-54073 3.00
1. Painting, American—History. I. Title.

FLEXNER, James Thomas, 759.13
1908-
Nineteenth century American painting. [1st ed.] New York, Putnam [1970] 256 p. illus. (part col.), ports. (part col.) 31 cm. "A Chanticleer Press edition." [ND210.F55 1970] 78-112988
1. Painting, American—History. 2. Painting, Modern—19th century—U.S. I. Title.

FLEXNER, James Thomas, 759.13
1908-
That wilder image; the painting of America's native school from Thomas Cole to Winslow Homer. New York, Dover Publications [1970] xxii, 344 p. 110 illus. 22 cm. "An unabridged republication of the work orginally published in 1962." Bibliography: p. 311-315. [ND210.F6 1970] 76-125911 ISBN 0-486-22580-1 4.00
1. Painting, American—History. 2. Painting, Modern—19th century—U.S. I. Title.

FREEDGOOD, Lillian. 759.13
An enduring image; American painting from 1665. New York, Crowell [1970] xvii, 387 p. illus. 26 cm. Bibliography: p. 368-374. [ND205.F7] 71-101928 ISBN 0-690-26619-7 7.95
1. Painting, American—History. I. Title. BIP

NOVAK, Barbara. 759.13
American painting of the nineteenth century; realism, idealism, and the American experience. New York, Praeger [1969] 350 p. illus. (part col.) 26 cm. Includes bibliographical references. [ND210.N68 1969] 77-76792 13.95
1. Painting, American—History. 2. Painting, Modern—19th century—U.S. I. Title.

RICHARDSON, Edgar Preston, 1902- 759.13
Painting in America, from 1502 to the present [by] E. P. Richardson. New York, Crowell [1965] xiii, 456 p. illus. (part col.) ports. 26 cm. Bibliography: p. 425-435. [ND205.R53 1965] 65-23777
1. Painting, American—History. I. Title.

RICHARDSON, Edgar Preston, 1902- 759.1
A short history of painting in America; the story of 450 years. New York, Crowell [c.1956, 1963] 348p. illus. 22cm. Abridgment, with a new concluding chapter and other new matter, of Painting in America: the story of 450 years. Bibl. 63-9206 6.95
1. Painting, America—Hist. I. Title. BIP

WILMERDING, John. 759.13
The genius of American painting. Editor: John Wilmerding. Contributors: R. Peter Mooz [and others] New York, Morrow [1973] 352 p. illus. (part col.) 30 cm. Bibliography: p. 344-348. [ND205.W52] 74-150417 ISBN 0-688-00193-9 24.95
1. Painting, American—History. I. Mooz, R. Peter. II. Title. BIP

Painting, American—History—Juvenile literature.

ALDEN, Carella. 759.13
From early American paintbrushes; colony to new nation. New York, Parents' Magazine Press [1971] 64 p. illus. (part col.) 24 cm. (Art tells a story series) "Based on the production from Yankee paintbrushes, presented in the Art entertainments series for young people, at the Metropolitan Museum of Art." Discusses the sculpture, painting, signs, furniture, and other artistic works produced in America from 1620 to the early nineteenth century. [ND207.A67] 73-156949 ISBN 0-8193-0477-8
1. Painting, American—History—Juvenile literature. I. Title. BIP

Painting, American—Indexes.

SMITH, Lyn Wall. 759.13
Index to reproductions of American paintings appearing in over 400 books primarily published since 1960 / by Lyn Wall Smith, Nancy Dustin Wall Moure. Metuchen, N.J. : Scarecrow Press, 1977. p. cm. [ND205.S575] 77-14498 ISBN 0-8108-1084-0 : 45.00
1. Painting, American—Indexes. I. Moure, Nancy Dustin Wall, joint author. II. Title.

Painting, American—Michigan—Exhibitions.

OMOTO, Sadayoshi. 759.174'074'017427
Early Michigan paintings : Kresge Art Center, Michigan State University, East Lansing, November 21, 1976-January 2, 1977 / [catalogue was prepared by Sadayoshi Omoto] ; introductory essay by Sadayoshi Omoto. [East Lansing, Mich. : The University], c1976. 142 p. : ill. ; 23 cm. Includes bibliographical references. [ND230.M5O48] 77-355843
1. Painting, American—Michigan—Exhibitions. 2. Painting, Modern—19th century—Michigan—Exhibitions. 3. Painting, Modern—20th century—Michigan—Exhibitions. I. Kresge Art Gallery. II. Title.

Painting, Ancient.

BELLONE, Gianguido 759.01
Prehistoric to classical painting. [Tr. from Italian by Annabella Cloudsly] New York, Golden [c.1962] [56]p. 24 col. illus., map. 38cm. (Art of the Western World) 62-53398 5.00 bds.,
1. Painting, Ancient. I. Title. II. Series.

Painting, Ancient—History.

RICE, David Talbot, 1903- 709
A concise history of painting from prehistory to the thirteenth century. New York, F. A. Praeger [1968, c1967] 287 p. illus. (part col.), facsims. (part col.) 22 cm. (Praeger world of art series) Bibliography: p. 269. [ND60.R5 1968] 68-12645
1. Painting, Ancient—History. 2. Painting, Medieval—History. I. Title.

Painting, Argentine—Hist.

SAN MARTIN, Maria Laura 759.982
Pintura argentina contemporanea. [In Spanish. Dist. New York, Wittenborn, 1962,c.] 1961, 265p. illus. (pt. col.) 27cm. (Coleccion Panoramas del siglo xx) Bibl. 62-3789 9.00
1. Painting, Argentine—Hist. I. Title.

Painting — Asia, Central — Hist.

BUSSAGLI, Mario. 759.939
Painting of Central Asia. [Translated from the Italian by Lothian Small. Geneva] Skira; [distributed in U.S. by World Pub., 1963] 135 p. mounted illus. (part col.) map. 29 cm. (Treasures of Asia, v. 6) Bibliography: p. 127-128. [ND991.B813] 63-20242
1. Painting — Asia, Central — Hist. 2. Paintings, Asiatic. I. Title. II. Series.

Painting, Australian.

GLEESON, James. 759.994
Masterpieces of Australian painting. Melbourne, Lansdowne [1969] 222 p. 21 illus., 96 plates. 32 cm. (Australian art library) [ND1100.G6] 72-487319 17.50
1. Painting, Australian. 2. Paintings, Australian. I. Title.

Painting, Australian—History.

SMITH, Bernard William. 709.94
Australian painting, 1788-1960. Melbourne, New York, Oxford University Press, 1962 [i. e. 1963] 357 p. illus. 26 cm. Includes bibliography. [ND1100.S55 1963] 63-2263
1. Painting, Australian—History. I. Title.

SMITH, Bernard William. 759.994
Australian painting, 1788-1970 [by] Bernard Smith. [2nd ed.] Melbourne, New York, Oxford University Press [1971] 483 p. illus. (part col.) 26 cm. Bibliography: p. 459-461. [ND1100.S553 1971] 72-193474 ISBN 0-19-550372-4 17.50
1. Painting, Australian—History. I. Title.

Painting, Baroque.

TRAPIER, Elizabeth Du Gue, 1893- [759.6] 927.5
Valdes Leal, baroque concept of death and suffering in his paintings. New York, Hispanic Society of America, 1956. 49 p. illus. 23 cm. (Hispanic notes & monographs; essays, studies, and brief biographies) [ND813.V2T7] 56-14473
1. Valdes Leal, Juan de, 1622-1690. 2. Painting, Baroque. 3. Death — Art. I. Title.

Painting, Basoli.

SINHA, Rajeshwar Prasad Narain. 759.954
Geeta govind in Basohli school of Indian painting. Foreword by Rajendra Prasad. Introd. by R. P. N. Sinha. New Delhi, [India] Oxford Book & Stationery Co. [dist., S. Pasadena, Calif., Hutchins Oriental Books, 1958, i.e., 1960] 15p. 9 pages (part col. and part-mounted) 34cm. 60-51363 4.00 pap.,
1. Jawadeva, son of Bhojadeva. Gitagovinda. 2. Painting, Basoli. I. Title.

Painting—Belgium—Hist.

SALKIN, Alex. 759.9493
Modern painting in Belgium. 2d ed. New York, Belgian Govt. Information Center, 1948. 64p. illus. 23cm. (Art, life and science in Belguium, no. 8) [ND664.S3 1948] 53-16486
1. Painting—Belgium—Hist. I. Title.

Painting books.

STEINER, Charlotte. v. 12
A Kiki double-fan Doubleday giant coloring book. Based on scenes from the famous Kiki books. 1st ed. Garden City, N.Y., Doubleday, 1963. unpaged (chiefly illus.) 46 cm. (Doubleday book toy) [[ND2399]] 63-12877
1. Painting books. I. Title.

Painting, British.

THE Century of change : 759.941
British painting since 1900 / Richard Shone. Oxford : Phaidon, 1977. 240 p. : ill. (some col.) ; 29 cm. Includes index. Bibliography: p. [46] [ND468.C46 1977] 77-75312 ISBN 0-7148-1782-1 : 24.95
1. Painting, British. 2. Painting, Modern—20th century—Great Britain. I. Shone, Richard.
Distributed by Dutton, N.Y. BIP

FRY, Roger Eliot, 1866-1934. 759.2
Reflections on British painting. Freeport, N.Y., Books for Libraries Press [1969] 147 p. 40 plates (incl. ports.) 23 cm. (Essay index reprint series) Reprint of the 1934 ed. [ND461.F7 1969] 76-99695
1. Painting, British. I. Title. BIP

GAUNT, William, 1900- 759.941
The restless century : painting in Britain, 1800-1900 / William Gaunt. 2d ed . Oxford : Phaidon Press ; New York : distributed by E. P. Dutton, 1978. 255 p. : ill. (some col.) ; 25 cm. Includes index. Bibliography: p. [251]-252. [ND467.G32 1978] 78-51023 ISBN 0-7148-1835-6 pbk. : 17.50
1. Painting, British. 2. Painting, Modern—19th century—Great Britain. I. Title. BIP

GAUNT, William, 1900- 759.2
The restless century: painting in Britain, 1800-1900. London, Phaidon, 1972. 255 p. chiefly illus. (some col.) 29 cm. Distributed in the USA by Praeger, New York. Bibliography: p. [251]-252. [ND467.G32] 72-81919 ISBN 0-7148-1544-6 25.00
1. Painting, British. 2. Painting, Modern—19th century—Great Britain. I. Title.

MAAS, Jeremy. 759.2
Victorian painters. [1st American ed.] New York, Putnam [1969] 257, [4] p. illus. (part col.), ports. (on lining papers) 30 cm. Bibliography: p. [259]-[261] [ND467.M26 1969b] 69-12341 22.50
1. Painting, British. 2. Painting, Victorian. I. Title.

Painting, British—Catalogs.

MANCHESTER, Eng. Art Gallery. 759.941'074'02733
Concise catalogue of British paintings / Manchester City Art Gallery. Manchester : City of Manchester Cultural Services, 1976- v. : ill., ports. ; 21 cm. Errata slip inserted in v. 1. Includes indexes. Contents.Contents.—v. 1. British artists born before 1850. [ND461.M36 1976] 77-352258 ISBN 0-901673-07-2 : £2.50
1. Manchester, Eng. Art Gallery. 2. Painting, British—Catalogs. 3. Painting—England—Manchester—Catalogs. I. Title.

TATE Gallery, London 708.21
The collections of the Tate Gallery; British painting, modern painting, and sculpture. [London] Tate Gallery; exclusively dist. in USA & Canada by Arno Pr., New York, 1967. 210p. 22cm. [N1080.A6153 1967b] 68-9468 5.95
1. Painting, British—Catalogs. 2. Art, Modern—20th cent.—Catalogs. I. Title. BIP

Painting, British—Exhibitions—Catalogs.

BRADSHAW, Maurice. 759.941
Royal Society of British Artists, members exhibiting, 1931-1946 / [compiled] by Maurice Bradshaw. Leigh-on-Sea : F. Lewis, 1976. [8], 80 p. ; 29 cm. Cover title: R.B.A. exhibitors 1931-1946. [ND468.B722] 76-383755 ISBN 0-85317-044-4 : £14.50
1. Royal Society of British Artists, London. 2. Painting, British—Exhibitions—Catalogs. 3. Painting, Modern—20th century—Great Britain—Exhibitions—Catalogs. I. Royal Society of British Artists, London. II. Title. III. Title: R.B.A. exhibitors 1931-1946.

Painting, British—Great Britain.

WATERHOUSE, Ellis Kirkham, 1905- 759.2
Painting in Britain, 1530 to 1790 / Ellis Waterhouse 4th ed. New York : Penguin Books, [1978] p. cm. (The Pelican history of art) Includes index. Bibliography: p. [ND464.W37 1978] 77-19107 pbk. : 14.95
1. Painting, British—Great Britain. 2. Painting, Renaissance—Great Britain. 3. Painting, Modern—17th-18th centuries—Great Britain. I. Title. II. Series.

Painting— Bulgaria—Hist.

KRUSTEV, Kiril 759.94977
Stara bulgarska zhivopis. [title transliterated] 1960 [dist.: New York, 21, Arthur Vanous, 406 E. 70th St.] 210p. 90 plates (part col.) Summaries and notes in Russian, French, English and German. Title trans.: Old Bulgarian painting. 33cm. 60-50994 11.00 bxd.,
1. Painting— Bulgaria—Hist. 2. Christian art and symbolism. I. Zakhariev, Vasil, 1895- II. Title.

Painting, Byzantine.

BYRON, Robert, 1905-1941. 759.9'4
The birth of Western painting; a history of colour, form, and iconography, illustrated from the paintings of Mistra and Mount Athos, of Giotto and Duccio, and El Greco, by Robert Byron and David Talbot Rice. New York, Hacker Art Books, 1968. xvi, 236 p. 94 plates. 29 cm. Reprint of the 1930 ed. Bibliography: p. 220-226. [ND53.B9 1968] 68-9002
1. Theotocopuli, Dominico, called El Greco, d. 1614. 2. Painting, Byzantine. 3. Christian art and symbolism. 4. Mural painting and decoration, Byzantine. 5. Paintings—Athos, Mount. 6. Paintings—Mistra, Greece. I. Rice, David Talbot, 1903- joint author. II. Title.

CHATZEDAKES, Manoles 759.02
Byzantine and early Medieval painting [by] Manolis Chatzidakis, Andre Grabar. Tr. by Simon Watson Taylor. New York, Viking [1966, c.1965] 54p., 176p. of illus. (pt. col.) 20cm. (Compass bks. CA4. Compass hist. of art) [ND142C5] 66-10722 2.25 pap.,
1. Painting, Byzantine. 2. Painting, Medieval. I. Grabar, Andre, 1896- II. Title.

CUTLER, Anthony, 1934- 755'.2
Transfigurations : studies in the dynamics of Byzantine iconography / Anthony Cutler. University Park : Pennsylvania State University, [1975] p. cm. Includes bibliographical references and index. [ND142.C87] 75-1482 ISBN 0-271-01194-7
1. Painting, Byzantine. 2. Icon painting—Byzantine Empire. 3. Christian art and symbolism. I. Title. BIP

Painting, Byzantine—History.

RICE, David Talbot, 1903- 759.02
Byzantine painting: the last phase. New York, Dial Press, 1968. 223 p. illus. (part col.), maps. 26 cm. Bibliographical references included in "Notes" (p. 211-217) [ND142.R52 1968b] 68-28689 22.50
1. Painting, Byzantine—History. I. Title.

Painting, Canadian.

GODSELL, Patricia. 759.11 B
Enjoying Canadian painting / Patricia Godsell. Don Mills, Ont. : General Pub. Co., 1976. viii, 275 p. : ill. (some col.), col. map ; 29 cm. Includes index. Bibliography: p. 263-265. [ND240.G62] 77-361410 ISBN 0-7736-0053-1 : 19.95
1. Painting, Canadian. 2. Painters—Canada—Biography. I. Title. BIP

†HARPER, J. Russell. 759.11
Painting in Canada : a history / J. Russell Harper. 2d ed. Toronto ; Buffalo : University of Toronto Press, 1977, c1966. vii, 463 p. : ill., ports. ; 24 cm. (Canadian university paperbooks ; 198) Includes index. Bibliography: p. [439]-443. [ND240.H3 1977] 78-302907 ISBN 0-8020-2271-5 : 29.50. ISBN 0-8020-6307-1 pbk. : 12.50
1. Painting, Canadian. I. Title.

HARPER, J. Russell. 759.11
A people's art : primitive, naive, provincial, and folk painting in Canada / J. Russell Harper. Toronto ; Buffalo : University of Toronto Press, [1974] 176 p. : ill. (some col.) ; 32 cm. Includes bibliographical references and index. [ND240.5.P7H37] 74-77739 ISBN 0-8020-2153-0 : 22.50
1. Painting, Canadian. 2. Primitivism in art—Canada. I. Title. BIP

Painting, Canadian—History.

HARPER, J. Russell. 759.11
Painting in Canada; a history [by] J. Russell Harper. [Toronto] University of Toronto Press [1966] viii, 443 p. illus. (part col.) ports. (part col.) 29 cm. Bibliography: p. 431-432. [ND240.H3] 66-9832
*1. Painting, Canadian—History. I. Title.*BIP

REID, Dennis R. 759.11
A concise history of Canadian painting [by] Dennis Reid. Toronto, Oxford University Press, 1973. 319 p. illus. (part col.) 22 cm. [ND240.R44 1973] 74-157032 ISBN 0-19-540207-3 9.50
*1. Painting, Canadian—History. I. Title.*BIP

Painting—China—History.

BINYON, Laurence 1869-1943 759.95
Painting in the Far East: an introduction to the history of pictorial art in Asia, especially in China and Japan. 394 ed., rev throughtout. New York, Dover Publications, [1959] xx, 297p. Bibl. notes; p.279-290) illus. 24cm. (T520) 2.00 pap.,
1. Painting—China—History. 2. Painting—Japan—Hist. I. Title. BIP

KUO, Jo-hsu, fl.1074. 759.951
Experiences in painting (T'u-hua chien-wen chih) An eleventh century history of Chinese painting, together with the Chinese text in facsimile; translated and annotated by Alexander Coburn Soper. Washington, American Council of Learned Societies, 1951. xiii, 216 p., facsim.: [68] p. 26 cm. (American Council of Learned Societies. Studies in Chinese and related civilizations, no. 6) [ND1040.K783] 52-190
1. Painting—China—Hist. 2. Painters, Chinese. I. Soper, Alexander Coburn. tr II. Title. III. Series: American Council of Learned Societies Devoted to Humanistic Studies. Studies in Chinese and related civilizations, no. 6

SIREN, Osvald, 1879- 759.951
Chinese painting; leading masters and principles. New York, Ronald Press 1956- v. plates. 29 cm. "Annotated lists of paintings and reproductions of paintings by Chinese artists": 95 p. at end of v. 2. Contents.pt. 1. The first millennium. v. 1. Early Chinese painting. v. 2. The Sung period. v. 3. Plates. Bibliography: v. 1, p. 231-235. [ND1040.S49] A 57
1. Painting — China — Hist. 2. Paintings, Chinese. 3. Painters, Chinese. I. Title. BIP

Painting, Chinese.

BRIESSEN, Fritz van. 759.95
The way of the brush; painting techniques of China and Japan. Tokyo, Rutland, Vt., C. E. Tuttle Co. [1962] 329 p. illus. (part col.) 28 cm. Bibliography: p. 323-324. [ND1040.B69 1962] 62-14119
1. Painting, Chinese. 2. Painting, Japanese. 3. Painting—Technique. I. Title. BIP

BUSH, Susan. 759.951
The Chinese literati on painting; Su Shih (1037-1101) to Tung Ch'i-ch'ang (1555-1636). Cambridge, Harvard University Press, 1971. x, 227 p. illus. 25 cm. (Harvard-Yenching Institute studies, 27) Bibliography: p. [205]-213. [ND1043.B88] 78-152698 ISBN 0-674-12425-1 7.00
1. Painting, Chinese. I. Title. II. Series.

BUSSAGLI, Mario. 759.951
Chinese painting; [translated from the Italian by Henry Vidon]. Feltham, New York, Hamlyn, 1969. 3-157 p. 74 col. illus. 20 cm. (Cameo) Originally published as 'La pittura Cinese'. Milano, Fabbri, 1966. [ND1040.B813] 77-437379 15/-
1. Painting, Chinese. I. Title.

CHANG, Shu-ch'i. 751.42
Painting in the Chinese manner. English text by Helen F. Chang. New York, Viking Press [1960] 79 p. illus., (part mounted col.) 29 cm. (A Studio book) English and Chinese; added t. p. [ND1045.C423] 60-14089
1. Painting, Chinese. 2. Painting—Technique. I. Title.

CHIANG, I. 759.951
The Chinese eye; an interpretation of Chinese painting [by] Chiang Yee. With a pref. by S. I. Hsiung. New York, Norton [1960] xvi, 239p. illus. 20cm. 60-16220 3.95
1. Painting, Chinese. I. Title. BIP

CHIANG, I, 1903- 759.951
The Chinese eye; an interpretation of Chiese painting. Pref. by S. I. Hsiung. 239p. illus. 20cm. Bloomington, Ind. Univ. Pr. [1964] 239p. illus. 20cm. (Midland bk. MB62) 2.45 pap.,
1. Painting, Chinese. I. Title.

†CHOU, Ju-hsi. 759.951
The Hua-yu-lu and Tao-chi's theory of painting / by Ju-hsi Chou. Tempe : Center for Asian Studies, Arizona State University, 1977. 49 p. ; 23 cm. (Occasional paper - Center for Asian Studies, Arizona State University ; no. 9) Includes bibliographical references. [ND1049.T3C47] 77-623250 1.25
1. Tao-chi, 1630-1707. Hua yu lu. 2. Painting, Chinese. 3. Painting—Technique. I. Title. II. Series: Arizona. State University, Tempe. Center for Asian Studies. Occasional paper ; no. 9.

ECKE, Gustav. 759.951
Chinese painting in Hawaii in the Honolulu Academy of Arts and in Arts, 1965- v. (chiefly illus. (part col.) plates (part col.] 32 cm. Bibliography: v. 1. p. 317-322. [ND1040.E3] 63-22537
1. Painting, Chinese. 2. Paintings—Honolulu. 3. Brush drawing. I. Honolulu Academy of Arts. II. Title.

GOEPPER, Roger 759.951
Chinese painting; the later tradition. [English tr. by John L. McHale] Berne, Hallwag [1966] 9, [39] p. col. illus. 19cm. (Orbis pictus 18) [ND1043.G613] 66-31662 2.50 bds.,
1. Painting Chinese. I. Title.
American distributor: Taplinger, New York.

GOEPPER, Roger. 759.951
The essence of Chinese painting. [Translated by Michael Bullock. 1st American ed.] Boston, Boston Book and Art Shop [c1963] 244 p. illus. (part mounted col.) 30 cm. Corrigenda slip inserted. Bibliographical references included in "Notes" (p. 227-232) [ND1040.G613] 63-17534
1. Painting, Chinese. I. Title.

JENYNS, Roger Soame, 1904- 759.951
A background to Chinese painting. New York, Schocken [c.1966] xxii, 208p. illus., facsims. 22cm. Reprint of the work first pub. in 1935. with a new pref. by the author. Bibl. [ND1040.J4 1966] 66-14873 6.00; 2.45 pap.,
1. Painting, Chinese. I. Title. BIP

MARCH, Benjamin, 1899-1934. 759.9'51
Some technical terms of Chinese painting. New York, Paragon Book Reprint Corp., 1969. xiii, 55 p. illus. 27 cm. (American Council of Learned Societies. Studies in Chinese and related civilizations, no. 2) "Unabridged and unaltered reprint of the edition first printed ... in 1935." [ND1040.M3 1969] 76-88188
1. Painting, Chinese. 2. Art—Terminology. I. Title. II. Series: American Council of Learned Societies Devoted to Humanistic Studies. Studies in Chinese and related civilizations, no. 2 BIP

ROWLEY, George. 759.951
Principles of Chinese painting. [2d ed.] Princeton, N. J., Princeton University Press, 1959. 85p. 47 illus. 29cm. (Princeton monographs in art and archaeology, 24) [ND1040.R6 1959] 60-325
1. Painting, Chinese. I. Title. II. Series. BIP

SIREN, Osvald, 1879- 759.951
The Chinese on the art of painting: translations and comments. New York, Schocken Books [1963] 261 p. illus. 23 cm. (Schocken paperbacks, SB57) Bibliographical footnotes. [ND1040.S48 1963] 63-20262
1. Painting, Chinese. I. Title. BIP

SULLIVAN, Michael, 1916- 759.951
The three perfections : Chinese painting, poetry, and calligraphy / Michael Sullivan. London : Thames and Hudson, [1975] c1974. 64 p. : ill. ; 22 cm. (Walter Neurath memorial lectures ; 6) Label mounted on t.p.: Transatlantic Arts, inc., sole distributor for the U.S.A. Includes bibliographical references. [ND1040.S78] 75-315630 8.75
1. Painting, Chinese. 2. Calligraphy, Chinese—Inscriptions. I. Title. II. Series.

SZE, Mai-mai 759.951
The tao of painting; a study of the ritual disposition of Chinese painting. With a tr. of the Chieh tzu yuan chuan; or, Mustard Seed Garden manual of painting, 1679-1701. [2d ed., with corrections. New York] Pantheon [1964,c. 1956,1963] 2 v.in 1. illus., plates (pt. fold., pt. col.) 27cm. (Bollingen ser., 49) 64-2864 17.50 bxd.
1. Painting, Chinese. I. Wang, Kai, fl. 1677-1705, ed. Chieh tzu yuan hua chuan. II. Title. III. Title: Mustard Seed Garden manual of painting.

WALEY, Arthur. 759.951
An introduction to the study of Chinese painting. New York, Grove Press [1958] xii, 261 p. 49 plates (part col) 29 cm. Bibliography: p. 253-254. [[ND1040] 58-6228
1. Painting, Chinese. I. Title. BIP

WALEY, Arthur. 759.951
An introduction to the study of Chinese painting. New York, Scribner, 1923. [New York, AMS Press, 1974] xii, 261 p., 49 p. of illus. front. 24 cm. On spine: Study of Chinese painting. Bibliography: p. 253-254. [ND1040.W3 1974] 74-38092 ISBN 0-404-56967-6 28.50
1. Painting, Chinese. I. Title. II. Title: Study of Chinese painting.

WANG, Kai, fl. 1677. 759.951
The tao of paintings, a study of the ritual disposition of Chinese painting; with a translation of the Chieh tzu yuan hua chuan or, Mustard Seed Garden manual of painting, 1679-1701, by Mai-mai Sze. [New York] Pantheon Books [1956] 2v. illus., plates (part col.) 27cm. (Bollingen series, 49) Contents.v. 1. The tao of painting.--v. 2. The Chieh tzfl yilan hua. chuan. Bibliography: v. 1. p. [123]- 136. [ND1043.W333] 56-10424
1. Painting. Chinese. I. Sze, Mai-mai. II. Title. III. Series.

WANG, Kai 759.951
The way of Chinese painting, its ideas and technique; with selections from the seventeenth-century Mustard Seed Garden manual of painting, by Mai-mai Sze. New York, Random House [c. 1956,1959] xxi, 456p. illus. 19cm. (Modern library paperbacks, P-57) Includes bibliography. 60-754 1.45 pap.,
1. Painting, Chinese. I. Sze, Mai-mai. II. Title. BIP

WANG, Kai, fl.1677. 759.951
The tao of painting, a study of the ritual disposition of Chinese painting; with a translation of the Chieh tzu yuan hua chuan; or, Mustard Seed Garden manual of painting, 1679-1701, by Mai-mai Sze. [New York] Pantheon Books [1956] 2 v. illus., plates (part col.) 27 cm. (Bollingen series, 49) Contents.v. 1. The tao of painting. -- v. 2. The Chieh tzu yuan hua chuan. Bibliography: v. 1, p. [125]-136. [ND1043.W333] 56-10424
1. Painting, Chinese. I. Sze, Mai-mai. II. Title. III. Series.

Painting, Chinese—20th century.

LAI, T'ien-ch'ang. 759.951
Three contemporary Chinese painters : Chang Da-chien, Ting Yin-yung, Ch'eng Shih-fa / [T. C. Lai]. Seattle : University of Washington Press, c1975. 128 p. : ill. (some col.) ; 23 cm. Includes bibliographical references (Chinese and English). [ND1045.L34] 75-327590 10.00
1. Chang, Ta-ch'ien, 1899- 2. Ting, Yin Yung, 1902- 3. Ch'eng, Shih-fa. 4. Painting, Chinese—20th century. I. Title. BIP

Painting, Chinese—Addresses, essays, lectures.

ARTISTS and traditions 759.951
: uses of the past in Chinese culture / edited by Christian F. Murck. Princeton, N.J. : The Art Museum, Princeton University : distributed by Princeton University Press, 1977,1976. xxi, 230 p. : ill. ; 27 cm. Includes bibliographical references and index. [ND1040.A77] 74-77300 ISBN 0-691-03909-7 : 35.00
1. Painting, Chinese—Addresses, essays, lectures. 2. Art and society—China—Addresses, essays, lectures. I. Murck, Christian F.

Painting, Chinese—Catalogs.

CLASSICAL Chinese 759.951
painting : [monograph / translated into English by Leon Levitchi]. Bucharest : "Meridiane", 1976. 31 p., [31] leaves of plates : ill. (some col.) ; 32 cm. Translation of Pictura chineza clasica. lei40.00 Contents.Contents.—Frunzetti, I. The spirit of Chinese painting.—Stanculescu Zamfirescu, N. Brief historical survey and selection of illustrations. Bibliography: p. [27] [ND1042.P5213] 77-350152
1. Painting, Chinese—Catalogs. 2. Painting, Chinese—History. I. Stanculescu-Zamfirescu, Nina.

Painting, Chinese—China—Shensi—Hu-hsien—Exhibitions.

ARTS Council of Great Britain. 759.951'43
Peasant paintings from Hu county, Shensi province, China ; [catalogue] / Arts Council of Great Britain ; edited and designed by Hugh Shaw. London : The Council, 1976. 67 p. : ill. ; 21 cm. [ND1046.H8A77 1976] 77-359599 ISBN 0-7287-0103-0 : £1.50
1. Painting, Chinese—China—Shensi—Hu-hsien—Exhibitions. 2. Painting—20th century—China—Shensi—Hu-hsien—Exhibitions. 3. Socialist realism in art—China—Shensi—Hu-hsien—Exhibitions. I. Shaw, Hugh. II. Title.

Painting, Chinese—Congresses.

CHINESE painting and the 759.951
decorative style / edited by Margaret Medley. [London] : University of London School of Oriental and African Studies, Percival David Foundation of Chinese Art, [1976] [9], 165 p. : ill. ; 26 cm. (Colloquies on art and archaeology in Asia ; no. 5) "A colloquy held 23-25 June 1975". Includes bibliographical references. [ND1040.C576] 76-380379 ISBN 0-7286-0028-5 : £3.50
1. Painting, Chinese—Congresses. 2. Art, Decorative—China—Congresses. I. Medley, Margaret. II. London. University. Percival David Foundation of Chinese Art. III. Title. IV. Series.

Painting, Chinese—Exhibitions.

QUEENS 759.951'074'0147243 Museum.
Masters of the brush : Chinese painting & calligraphy from the 16th to the 19th century, January 8 to March 6, 1977, the Queens Museum. Flushing, N.Y. : The Museum, c1977. [36] p. : ill. ; 20 x 21 cm. Bibliography: p. [36] [ND1043.5.Q43 1977] 77-357003
1. Painting, Chinese—Exhibitions. 2. Painting, Chinese—Ming-Ch'ing dynasties, 1368-1912—Exhibitions. 3. Calligraphy, Chinese—Exhibitions. I. Title.

Painting, Chinese—History.

CAHILL, James Francis, 759.951 1926-
Chinese painting. [Geneva?] Skira; [distributed in the U.S. by World Pub. Co., Cleveland, 1960] 211 p. mounted col. illus. 29 cm. (Treasures of Asia) Bibliography: p. 199-[200] [ND1043.C28] 60-15594
1. Painting, Chinese—History. 2. Paintings, Chinese. I. Title. II. Series.

CAHILL, James Francis, 759.951 1926-
Fantastics and eccentrics in Chinese painting / James Cahill. New York : Arno Press, 1975, [c1967] p. cm. (The Asia Society reprint collection) Catalogue of an exhibition selected by J. Cahill, and held at the Asia House Gallery, New York, Mar. 23-May 28, 1967; Los Angeles County Museum of Art, June 20-Aug. 13, 1967; and M. H. De Young Memorial Museum, San Francisco, Sept. 15-Nov. 5, 1967. Reprint of the ed. published by the Asia Society, New York. Bibliography: p. [ND1040.C3 1975] 75-6570 ISBN 0-405-06561-2 : 30.00
1. Painting, Chinese—History. I. Asia House Gallery, New York. II. Los Angeles Co., Calif. Museum of Art, Los Angeles. III. De Young Memorial Museum, San Francisco. IV. Title. V. Series.

CAHILL, James Francis, 759.951 1926-
Fantastics and eccentrics in Chinese painting [by] James Cahill. [New York] Asia Society; distributed by Abrams [1967] 122 p. illus. (part col.) 28 cm. Includes the catalog, edited by Virginia Field, of the exhibition held at Asia House Gallery, New York City, March 23-May 28, 1967; Los Angeles County Museum ofArt, June 20-Aug. 13, 1967; and M. H. De Young Memorial Museum, San Francisco, Sept. 15-Nov. 5, 1967. Bibliography: p. 122. [ND1040.C3] 67-16859
1. Painting, Chinese—Hist. I. Field, Virginia. II. Asia House Gallery, New York. III. De Young Memorial Museum, San Francisco. IV. Los Angeles Co., Calif. Museum, Los Angeles. V. Title.

PRIEST, Alan, 1898- 59.951
Aspects of Chinese painting. New York, Macmillan, 1954. 134p. illus. (part col.) 27cm. [ND1040.P7] 54-13066
1. Painting, Chinese—Hist. I. Title.

SIREN, Osvald, 1879- 759.951
Chinese painting : leading masters and principles / Osvald Siren. New York : Hacker Art Books, 1973 [i.e. 1974] 7 v. : ill. ; 29 cm. Includes bibliographies and indexes. [ND1040.S492] 74-182842 195.00
1. Painting, Chinese—History. 2. Paintings, Chinese. 3. Painters—China. I. Title. Contents omitted.

Painting, Chinese—Ming-Ch'ing dynasties, 1368-1912.

CAHILL, James Francis, 759.951 1926-
Parting at the shore : Chinese painting of the early and middle Ming dynasty, 1368-1580 / James Cahill. 1st ed. New York : Weatherhill, 1978. xiv, 281 p. : ill. (some col.) ; 31 cm. (His A history of later Chinese painting, 1279-1950 ; v. 2) Includes index. Bibliography: p. 265-268. [ND1043.C33 vol. 2] [ND1043.5] 77-8682 ISBN 0-8348-0128-0 : 30.00
1. Painting, Chinese—Ming-Ch'ing dynasties, 1368-1912. I. Title. BIP

Painting, Chinese—Sung-Yuan dynasties, 960-1368.

CAHILL, James Francis, 759.951 1926-
Hills beyond a river : Chinese painting of the Yuan Dynasty, 1279-1368 / James Cahill. 1st ed. New York : Weatherhill, 1976. xv, 198 p. : ill. ; 31 cm. Includes index. Bibliography: p. 183-187. [ND1043.4.C33 1976] 75-44083 ISBN 0-8348-0120-5 : 25.00
1. Painting, Chinese—Sung-Yuan dynasties, 960-1368. I. Title. BIP

EIGHTEEN songs of a nomad flute: the story of Lady Wen-chi; 759.951 a fourteenth-century handscroll in the Metropolitan Museum of Art. Introd., commentary, and translation of poems by Robert A. Rorex and Wen Fong. [New York] Metropolitan Museum of Art; distributed by New York Graphic Society [Greenwich, Conn., 1974] 1 v. (unpaged) illus. (part col.) 25 x 28 cm. The text of the poems on the scroll reproduced here is by Liu Shang; the paintings are by an unknown artist. Includes bibliographical references. [ND3399.L55E37] 74-11140 ISBN 0-87099-095-0 18.50
1. Liu, Shang, 8th cent. Hu chia shih pa p'ai—Illustrations. 2. New York (City). Metropolitan Museum of Art. 3. Ts'ai, Yen, ca. 177-ca. 239—Art. 4. Painting, Chinese—Sung-Yuan dynasties, 960-1368. I. Rorex, Robert A., ed. II. Fong, Wen, ed. III. New York (City). Metropolitan Museum of Art. IV. Liu, Shang, 8th cent. Hu chia shih pa p'ai. English. 1974.

FONG, Wen. 758'.1'0951
Summer mountains : the timeless landscape / Wen Fong. [New York] : Metropolitan Museum of Art, 1975. [74] p. : ill. ; 35 cm. Includes bibliographical references. [ND1049.F66] 75-23008 ISBN 0-87099-135-3 : 25.00
1. Hsia-shan-t'u (Scroll) 2. Painting, Chinese—Sung-Yuan dynasties, 960-1368. 3. Painting, Chinese—Ming-Manchu (Ch'ing) dynasties, 1368-1912. 4. Landscape in art. 5. Mountains in art. 6. Paintings—Attribution. I. Title.

Painting, Chinese—Sung-Yuan dynasties, 960-1368—Catalogs.

CHINESE painting and 759.951'074 *calligraphy :* a pictorial survey : 69 fine examples from the John M. Crawford, Jr., Collection / [text and photography by] Wan-go Weng ; with a pref. by Thomas Lawton. New York : Dover Publications, 1978. xxxvi, 155 p. : chiefly ill. ; 30 cm. Includes bibliographical references. [ND1043.4.C44 1978] 78-57835 ISBN 0-486-23707-9 : 7.95
1. Painting, Chinese—Sung-Yuan dynasties, 960-1368—Catalogs. 2. Painting, Chinese—Ming Ch'ing dynasties, 1368-1912—Catalogs. 3. Calligraphy, Chinese—Catalogs. 4. Crawford, John M.—Art collections—Catalogs. I. Weng, Wango H. C. BIP

Painting, Colonial—Australia.

GLEESON, James. 759.99'4
Colonial painters 1788-1880. [Melbourne] Lansdowne [1971] 127 p. illus. (part col.) 26 cm. (Australian painting studio series) (Australian art library) Bibliography: p. 124. [ND1100.G58] 79-883629 ISBN 0-7018-0393-2 4.50
1. Painting, Colonial—Australia. 2. Painting, Australian. 3. Painters, Australian. I. Title.

Painting, Colonial—Latin America.

SHALKOP, 759.972'074'018856 Robert L.
Reflections of Spain II: a comparative view of Spanish colonial painting. [Colorado Springs] Taylor Museum of the Colorado Springs Fine Arts Center [1970] 68 p. illus. 23 cm. Catalog of a loan exhibition held at the Taylor Museum. Bibliography: p. 67-68. [ND202.S45] 70-15914
1. Painting, Colonial—Latin America. 2. Paintings, Latin American—Exhibitions. I. Colorado Springs. Fine Arts Center. Taylor Museum. II. Title.

Painting, Colonial—U.S.

WINTERTHUR Conference on 759.13 Museum Operation and Connoisseurship, 17th, 1971.
American painting to 1776: a reappraisal. Edited by Ian M. G. Quimby Charlottesville, Published for the Henry Francis du Pont Winterthur Museum [by] the University Press of Virginia [1971] x, 384 p. illus. 23 cm. (Winterthur Conference report, 1971) Includes bibliographical references. [ND207.W5 1971] 75-173917 ISBN 0-8139-0378-5
1. Painting, Colonial—U.S. 2. Painting, American. I. Quimby, Ian M. G., ed. II. Henry Francis du Pont Winterthur Museum. III. Title. IV. Series: Winterthur Conference on Museum Operation and Connoisseurship. Report, 1971.

Painting—Conservation and restoration.

KECK, Caroline Kohn. 751.6
How to take care of your paintings / by Caroline K. Keck ; ill. by Ruth Sheetz Eisendrath. New York : Scribner, c1978. 96 p. : ill. ; 24 cm. Published in 1954 under title: How to take care of your pictures. Includes index. [ND1640.K4 1978] 77-28085 ISBN 0-684-15551-6 : 10.95. ISBN 0-684-15552-4 pbk : 5.95
1. Painting—Conservation and restoration. I. Title. BIP

Painting, Cuban—Catalogs.

MUSEUM of Arts an 759.97291 Sciences.
Cuban paintings from the Collection of General Fulgencio Batista / with an introd. by Gary Russell Libby. Daytona Beach, Fla. : Museum of Arts and Sciences, c1977. 48 p. : chiefly ill. (some col.) ; 21 cm. [ND303.M87 1977] 77-152462
1. Batista y Zaldivar, Fulgencio, Pres. Cuba, 1901-1973—Art collections. 2. Museum of Arts and Sciences. 3. Painting, Cuban—Catalogs. I. Title.

Painting—Cuzco, Peru.

COSSIO DEL POMAR, Felipe, 759.985 1889-
Peruvian colonial art; the Cuzco school of painting. Tr. from Spanish by Genaro Arbaiza. New York, Wittenborn [1965] 197p. illus., plates (pt. col.) 28cm. Tr. in part from the author's earlier work pub. under title: Arte del Peru colonial. [ND417.C8C593] 65-2351 10.00
1. Painting—Cuzco, Peru. 2. Paintings, Peruvian. 3. Art, Peruvian—Hist. I. Cossio del Pomar, Felipe, 1889- Arte del Peru colonial. II. Title.

Painting—Dictionaries.

BARRON, John N. 750'.3
The language of painting; an informal dictionary. Written, illus. by John N. Barron. Cleveland, World [1967] 207p. illus. 21cm. Bibl. [ND30.B32] 67-21388 4.95
1. Painting—Dictionaries. I. Title.

A Dictionary of modern painting. 750.3 [Translated from the French by Alan Bird, and others] General editors: Carlton Lake and Robert Maillard. New York, Tudor Pub. Co. [1956?] 328p. illus. (part col.) 22cm. [ND30] 56-1915
1. Painting—Dictionaries. I. Lake, Carlton, ed. II. Maillard, Robert, ed.

DICTIONARY of modern painting. 759.05 General editors: Carlton Lake and Robert Maillard. [Translated from the French by Lawrence Samuelson and others] [3d ed., rev. and enl.] New York, Tudor Pub. Co. [1964] 416 p. illus. (part col.) 22 cm. [ND30.D515 1964] 65-1420
1. Painting—Dictionaries. I. Lake, Carlton, ed. II. Maillard, Robert, ed.

DICTIONARY of modern painting. 750.3 [Translated from the French by Alan Bird, and others] General editors: Carlton Lake and Robert Maillard. New York, Paris Book Center [1955] 328p. illus. (part col.) 22cm. Imprint covered by label: New York. Tudor Pub. Co. [ND30.D515] 55-13835
1. Painting—Dictionaries. I. Lake, Carlton, ed. II. Maillard, Robert, ed.

ENCYCLOPEDIA of painting; 750.3 painters and painting of the world from prehistoric times to the present day. Bernard S. Myers, editor. Contributing associates: Milton W. Brown [and others] New York, Crown Publishers, 1955. 511p. illus. (part col.) 29cm. [ND30.E5] 55-12456
1. Painting—Dictionaries. 2. Painters—Dictionaries. I. Myers, Bernard, 1908- ed.

LAKE, Carlton, ed. 750.3
A Dictionary of modern painting. Published under the direction of Fernand Hazan. General editors: Carlton Lake and Robert Maillard. New York, Tudor Pub. Co. [1956?] 328 p. illus. (part col.) 22 cm. Translated from the French by Alan Bird, and others. On spine: Paris Book Center, inc. [ND30.D515 1956a] 56-1915
1. Painting — Dictionaries. I. Mallard, Robert, ed. II. Title.

WOLF, Martin L 750.3
Dictionary of painting; With an introd. by Eric Partridge. New York, Philosophical Library [1958] viii, 335 p. 22 cm. [ND30.W6] 58-1338
1. Painting — Dictionaries. I. Title. BIP

Painting—Dresden—Catalogs.

DRESDEN, Gemaldegalerie 759.94 Neue Meister.
Dresden Gallery: modern masters [by] Horst Zimmermann. [Boston] Boston Book and Art Shop [1966, c1964] 88 p., 125 plates (part col.) 32 cm. Includes bibliographical references. [N2280.5.A46] 64-66311
1. Painting—Dresden—Catalogs. I. Zimmerman, Horst, 1930- II. Title.

Painting, Dutch.

DUTCH & Flemish painting 759.9492 *:* 110 illustrations / selected & introduced by Christopher Brown. Oxford : Phaidon ; New York : E. P. Dutton, 1977. 96 p. : chiefly ill. (some col.) ; 42 cm. (Giant art paperbacks) [ND636.D87] 76-62638 pbk. : 7.95
1. Painting, Dutch. 2. Painting, Flemish. 3. Painting, Modern—17th-18th centuries—Netherlands. 4. Painting, Modern—17th-18th centuries—Belgium—Flanders. I. Brown, Christopher, 1948- BIP

FUCHS, Rudolf Herman, 759.9492 1942-
Dutch painting / R. H. Fuchs. New York : Oxford University Press, 1978. p. cm. (The World of art) Includes index. Bibliography: p. [ND644.F8] 78-2631 ISBN 0-19-520060-8 : 12.95 ISBN 0-19-520061-6 pbk. : 7.95
1. Painting, Dutch. I. Title. II. Series.

KAHR, Madlyn Millner. 759.9492
Dutch painting in the seventeenth century / by Madlyn Millner Kahr. 1st ed. New York : Harper & Row, c1978. p. cm. (Icon editions) Includes index. Bibliography: p. [ND646.K26 1978] 78-337 ISBN 0-06-433576-3 : 29.95
1. Painting, Dutch. 2. Painting, Modern—17th-18th centuries—Netherlands. I. Title. BIP

MARIUS, G. Hermine. 759.9492
Dutch painters of the 19th century / Marius ; [translated from the Dutch by Alexander Teixeira de Mattos]; edited by Geraldine Norman. Woodbridge : Antique Collectors' Club, 1973. [5], viii, 307 p. : chiefly ill. (some col.) ; 28 cm. First ed. published in 1908 under title: Dutch painting in the nineteenth century. Includes index. [ND647.M4 1973] 74-195743 ISBN 0-902028-21-9 : £8.75
1. Painting, Dutch. 2. Painting, Modern—19th century—Netherlands. I. Title.

NASH, John Malcolm. 759.9492
The age of Rembrandt and Vermeer; Dutch painting in the seventeenth century [by] J. M. Nash. New York, Holt, Rinehart, and Winston [1972] 271 p. illus. (part col.) 29 cm. [ND646.N37 1972] 78-190474 ISBN 0-03-091870-7 25.00

1. Rembrandt Harmenszoon van Rijn, 1606-1669. 2. Vermeer, Johannes, 1632-1675. 3. Painting, Dutch. 4. Painting, Modern—17th-18th centuries—Netherlands. I. Title. BIP

ROSE, Barbara. 759.9492
The golden age of Dutch painting. New York, F. A. Praeger [1969, c1965] 192 p. illus., plates (part col.) 31 cm. [ND646.R58] 68-30942 6.95
1. Painting, Dutch. 2. Painting, Modern—17th-18th centuries—Netherlands. I. Title.

SCIENTIFIC examination of early Netherlandish painting : applications in art history / [editors, J. R. J. van Asperen de Boer, J. P. Filedt Kok]. Bussum : Fibula-van Dishoeck, 1976. x, 268 p. : ill. ; 27 cm. (Nederlands kunsthistorisch jaarboek ; deel 26) English, French, or German. Includes bibliographical references. [N5.N4 deel 26] [ND1635] 759.9492 77-555659 ISBN 9-02-284429-3 705 s
1. Painting, Dutch. 2. Painting, Flemish. 3. Painting—Radiography. 4. Painting—Expertising. I. Filedt Kok, J. P. II. Asperen de Boer, J. R. J. van III. Title. IV. Series.

WILENSKI, Reginald Howard, 1887- 759.9422
Dutch painting. [1st American ed.] New York, Beechhurst Press [1955] 211 p. plates (part col.) 26 cm. First published in London in 1929 under title: An introduction to Dutch art. [ND641.W5 1955] 55-13709
1. Painting, Dutch. 2. Painters, Dutch.

WRIGHT, Christopher, 1945- 759.9492
The Dutch painters : 100 seventeenth century masters / by Christopher Wright. 1st U.S. ed. Woodbury, N.Y. : Barron's, c1977. p. cm. Includes index. Bibliography: p. [ND646.W74 1977] 77-21988 ISBN 0-8120-5163-7 : 19.95
1. Painting, Dutch. 2. Painting, Modern—17th-18th centuries—Netherlands. 3. Painters—Netherlands. I. Title.

Painting, Dutch—Delft.

WHEELOCK, Arthur K. 759.9492'3
Perspective, optics, and Delft artists around 1650 / Arthur K. Wheelock, Jr. New York : Garland Pub., 1977. 11, xii, 345 p., [29] leaves of plates : ill. ; 21 cm. (Outstanding dissertations in the fine arts) Originally presented as the author's thesis, Harvard, 1973, under the title: The shifting relationship of perspective to optics and its manifestation in paintings by artists in Delft around 1650. Bibliography: p. [328]-345. [ND651.D4W46 1977] 76-23661 ISBN 0-8240-2740-X : 40.00
1. Painting, Dutch—Delft. 2. Painting, Modern—17th-18th centuries—Delft. 3. Perspective. 4. Visual perception. 5. Optics. I. Title. II. Series.

Painting, Dutch—History.

FRIEDLANDER, Max J., 1867-1958 759.92
Early Netherlandish painting. Pref. by Erwin Panofsky. Comments, notes by Nicole Veronee-Verhaegen. Tr. by Heinz Norden. New York, Praeger [1967- v. illus. 28cm. Tr. of Die Altniederlandische Malerei. Contents.v. 1. The Van Eycks-Petrus Christus. Bibl. [ND645.F723] 67-13538 18.50
1. Painting, Dutch—Hist. 2. Painting, Dutch. 3. Painters, Dutch. I. Veronee-Verhaegen, Nicole, ed. II. Title.

MARTIN, Wilhelm, 1876- 759.9492
Dutch painting of the great period, 1650-1697. Illustrated by 337 examples from Dutch museums.[Translated from the Dutch by D. Horning] London, New York, Batsford [1951] 401 p. plates (part col.) 28 cm. Translation of De schilderkunst in de tweede helft van de seventlende eeuw. Bibliography: p. 77-78. [ND646.M313] 52-1826
1. Painting. Dutch—Hist. I. Title.

ROBINSON, Franklin Westcott. 759.9492
Gabriel Metsu (1629-1667); a study of his place in Dutch genre painting of the golden age, by Franklin W. Robinson. New York, A. Schram [1974] p. cm. First prepared as the author's dissertation, Harvard. Bibliography: p. [ND653.M595R62] 74-19143 ISBN 0-8390-0130-4 45.00
1. Metsu, Gabriel, 1629-1667. 2. Painting, Dutch—History. 3. Painting, Modern—17th-18th centuries—Netherlands. I. Title.

ROSENBERG, Jakob, 1893- 759.9492
Dutch art and architecture, 1600-1800 [by] Jakob Rosenberg, Seymour Slive[and] E.H. ter Kuile. Harmondsworth (Middx.) Penguin, 1966. xxvi, 330 p. col. front., 208 plates, map, 7 plans. 26 1/2 cm. (The Pelican history of art, Z27) 5/5/- (B 66-17406) In slip case. Includes architecture & sculpture. Bibliography: p. 279-308. [ND636.R6 1966a] 66-77800
1. Painting, Dutch — Hist. 2. Architecture — Netherlands — Hist. I. Slive, Seymour, 1920- . II. Kulie, Engelbert Hendrik ter. III. Title. IV. Series. BIP

ROSENBERG, Jakob, 1893- 759.9492
Dutch art and architecture: 1600 to 1800 [by] Jakob Rosenberg, Seymour Slive and E. H. ter Kuile. [Rev. ed. Harmondsworth, Eng.] Penguin Books [1972] 500 p. illus. 21 cm. (The Pelican history of art, PZ27) Bibliography: p. [441]-468. [ND646.R59 1972] 79-128579 ISBN 0-14-056127-7 9.95 (U.S.)
1. Painting, Dutch—History. 2. Painting, Modern—17th-18th centuries—Netherlands. 3. Architecture—Netherlands—History. 4. Architecture, Modern—17th-18th centuries—Netherlands. I. Slive, Seymour, 1920- II. Kuile, Engelbert Hendrik ter. III. Title. IV. Series.

Painting—Early works to 1800.

ALBERTI, Leone Battista, 1404-1472. 750
On painting. Translated with introd. and notes by John R. Spencer. New Haven, Yale University Press, 1956. 141p. diagrs. 23cm. (Rare masterpieces of philosophy and science) 'Sources': p. 33-35. [N7420.A35] 56-58458
1. Painting—Early works to 1800. 2. Sculpture—Early works to 1800. I. Title.

ALBERTI, Leone Battista, 1404-1472. 750
On painting. Translated with introd. and notes by John R. Spencer. [Rev. ed.] New Haven, Yale University Press [1966] 141 p. illus. 21 cm. (A Yale paperbound, Y-175) Bibliographical references included in "Notes to text" (p. 99-136) [ND1130.A483 1966] 67-4305
1. Painting—Early works to 1800.

ALBERTI, Leone Battista, 1404-1472. 759
On painting [by] Leon Battista Alberti. Translated with introd. and notes by John R. Spencer. [Rev. ed.] New Haven, Yale University Press [1966] 141 p. 21 cm. Translation of De pictura. Bibliography: p. 33-35. [ND1130.A483 1966b] 759 76-279648
1. Painting—Early works to 1800. I. Spencer, John Richard, ed. II. Title.

ALBERTI, Leone Battista, 1404-1472. 750
On painting / Leon Battista Alberti ; translated with introd. and notes by John R. Spencer. Westport, Conn. : Greenwood Press, 1976. p. cm. Translation of De pictura. Reprint of the 1966 rev. ed. published by Yale University Press, New Haven. Includes index. Bibliography: p. [ND1130.A483 1976] 76-22485 ISBN 0-8371-8974-8 lib.bdg. : 11.25
1. Painting—Early works to 1800. I. Spencer, John Richard. II. Title.

ARMENINI, Giovanni Battista, 1533?-1609. 750
On the true precepts of the art of painting / Giovanni Battista Armenini, 1533?-1609 ; edited and translated from the Italian with an introductory study, critical and historical notes, and bibliography by Edward J. Olszewski. New York : B. Franklin, [1977] p. cm. Translation of De' veri precetti della pittura. Includes index. Bibliography: p. [ND1130.A713] 77-21772 ISBN 0-89102-100-0 pbk. : 9.95
1. Painting—Early works to 1800. I. Olszewski, Edward J., 1937- II. Title. BIP

CENNINI, Cennino 751.4
The craftsman's handbook; translated [from the Italian] by Daniel V. Thompson, Jr. New York, Dover Publications [1960, c.1933] xxvii, 142p. (Bibl. footnotes) illus. 21cm. 1.25 pap.,
1. Painting—Early works to 1800. 2. Painting—Technique. I. Thompson, Daniel Varney, tr. II. Title. BIP

CENNINI, Cennino, 15th cent. 751
The craftsman's handbook; translated by Daniel V. Thompson, Jr. New York, Dover Publications [1954, c1933] xxvii, 142p. illus. 25cm. 'An unabridged republication of the Thompson translation first published . . . in 1933 [as v. 2 of the author's Il libro dell'arte]' [ND1130.C3822] 54-3194
1. Painting—Early works to 1800. 2. Painting—Technique. I. Thompson, Daniel Varney, 1902- tr. II. Title.

COSTA, Felix da, 1639-1712 759
The antiquity of the art of painting. Introd., notes by George Kubler. Tr. by George Kubler [others] New Haven, Yale Univ. Pr., 1967. viii, 516p. illus. 28cm. Facsimile of the 1696 MS.:p. 55-354. Cover title: Antiguidade da arte da pintura. [ND1130.C67 1967] 66-21523 20.00
1. Painting — Early works to 1800. I. Kubler, George, 1912- ed. and tr. II. Title. III. Title: Antiquidade da arte da pintura. BIP

DU FRESNOY, Charles Alphonse, 1611-1665. 750
The art of painting (De arte graphica) [Translated into English verse by William Mason with annotations by Sir Joshua Reynolds] New York, Arno Press, 1969. xix, 213 p. 29 cm. Reprint of the 1783 ed. English and Latin. Translation of De arte graphica. [ND1130.D8 1969] 76-88819
1. Painting—Early works to 1800. 2. Painters. I. Mason, William, 1725-1797, tr. II. Title. BIP

LEONARDO da Vinci, 1452-1519. 759.5
The genius of Leonardo da Vinci; Leonardo da Vinci on art and the artist, the material assembled, edited and introduced by Andre Chastel. Translated from the French by Ellen Callmann. New York, Orion Press [1961] xxiv, 226 p. illus. (part mounted col.) ports., facsims. 20 x 25 cm. The French ed., Traite de la peinture, was translated from the original, Trattato della pittura. Bibliographical references included in Notes. [ND1130.L513] 61-9300
1. Painting—Early works to 1800. I. Chastel, Andre, 1912- ed. and tr. II. Title.

LEONARDO da Vinci, 1452-1519. 759
La peinture [par] Leonard de Vinci. Textes traduits reunis et annotes, par Andre Chastal avec la collaboration de Robert Klein Paris, Hermann [1964] 199, [1] p. illus. 21 cm. Translation of Trattato della pittura. Bibliography: p. 199-[200] [ND1130.L514] 65-49118
1. Painting — Early works to 1800. I. Chastel, Andre, 1912- ed and tr. II. Title.

LEONARDO da Vinci, 1452-1519. 751
Leonardo da Vinci on painting: a lost book (Libro A) reassembled from the Codex Vaticanus Urbinas 1270 and from the Codex Leicester by Carlo Pedritti. With a chronology of Leonardo's Treatise on painting. Foreword by Sir Kenneth Clark. Berkeley, Univ. of Calif. Pr. [c.]1964. xvi, 301p. illus.9 facsims. 28cm. (Calif. studies in the hist. of art, 3) Text in English and Italian; commentary in English. Bibl. [ND1130.L513] 64-17171 12.00
1. Painting—Early works to 1800. I. Title. II. Series.

LEONARDO da Vinci, 1452-1519. 751
Leonardo da Vinci on painting: a lost book (Libro A) reassembled from the Codex Vaticanus Urbinas 1270 and from the Codex Leicester by Carlo Pedritti. With a chronology of Leonardo's Treatise on painting. Foreword by Sir Kenneth Clark. Berkeley, University of California Press, 1964. xvi, 301 p. illus., facsims. 28 cm. (California studies in the history of art, 3) Text in English and Italian; commentary in English. Bibliography: p. [267]-273. [ND1130.L513 1964] 64-17171
1. Painting — Early works to 1800. I. Pedretti, Carlo. II. Title. III. Series. BIP

LEONARDO DA VINCI 1452-1519. 751
The art of painting. New York, Philosophical Library [1957] 224p. illus., diagrs. 20cm. Translation of Trattato della pittura. [ND1130.L515 1957] 57-1834
1. Painting— Early works to 1800. I. Title.

LEONARDO DA VINCI 1452-1519. 751
Treatise on painting Codex urbinas latinus 1270 Translated and annotated by A. Philip McMahon. With an introd. by Ludwig H. Heydenreich. Princeton, Princeton University Press, 1956. 2 v. illus. 25 cm. The facsimile, a reproduction of the Italian text which is a compilation by Francesco Meizl of notes from the original mss. of Leonardo, has caption title: Libro di pittvra di bi. Lionardo da Vinci . . . 'A selective bibliography, compiled from the notes of A. Philip McMahon and supplemented by Kate trauman Steinitz': v. 1, p. [359]-396. Contents.v. 1. Translation.--v. 2. Facsimile. [ND1130.L515] 52-13164
1. Painting—Early works to 1800. I. McMahon, Amos Phillip 1890-1947 tr. II. Vatican. Biblioteca vaticana. Mass. III. Title.

LEONARDO DA VINCI 1452-1519. 751
Treatise on painting (Codex urbinas latinus 1270) Translated and annotated by A. Philip McMahon. With an introd. by Ludwig H. Heydenreich. Princeton, Princeton University Press, 1956. 2 v. illus. 23cm. The facsimile, a reproduction of the Italian text which is a compilation by Francesco Meizi of notes from the original mss. of Leonardo, has caption title: Libro di pittvra di M. Lionardo da Vinci ... Contents.--v. 1. Translation.--v. 2. Facsimile. 'A selective bibliography, compiled from the notes of A. Philip McMahon and supplemented by Kate Traumau Steinitz': v. 1, p. [359]-396. [ND1130.L515] 52-13164
1. Painting—Early works to 1800. I. McMahon, Amos Philip. 1890-1947. tr. II. Vatican. Biblioteca vaticana. Mss. (Urb. lat. 1270) III. Title.

PHILOSTRATUS, Flavius. 704.94'7'0938
Les images / Philostratus; translated by Blaise de Vigenere New York : Garland Pub., 1976. p. cm. (The Renaissance and the gods ; no. 22) Translation of Imagines. Reprint of the 1614 ed. published by A. L'Angelier, Paris. [PA4272.A5F7 1976] 75-27866 ISBN 0-8240-2071-5 lib.bdg. : 40.00
1. Painting—Early works to 1800. 2. Mythology, Classical, in art. I. Title. II. Series.

ROSKILL, Mark W., 1933- 759
Dolce's Aretino and Venetian art theory of the Cinquecento, by Mark W. Roskill. [New York] Published for the College Art Association of America by New York University Press, 1968. 354 p. front. 22 cm. (Monographs on archaeology and fine arts, 15) Revision of the author's thesis, Princeton, 1961. Includes text and translation of Dolce's L'Aretino. Bibliographical footnotes. [ND1130.D573R6] 68-19901
1. Dolce, Lodovico, 1508-1568. L'Aretino. 2. Painting—Early works to 1800. I. Title. II. Series.

STRASSBURG, Stadtbibliothek. MSS. (A.v.1.19) 750.7
The Strasburg manuscript a medieval painters handbook. Tr. from the Old German by Viola & Rosamund Borradaile; eds.' text tr. into German by Johanna M. Franck. Foreword by John Harthan. [1st Amer. ed.] New York, Transatlantic, 1966. 116p. 22cm. German and English on opposite pages; added t.p. in German. German text from a transcript, in the National Gallery, London, made before the destruction of the original Strassburg manuscript in 1870. Portions of the manuscript contain instructions of Heinrich von Lubbegge and Andres von Colmar. [ND1130.S813 1966] 67-547 6.75 bds.,
1. Painting—Early works to 1800. 2. Painting—Handbooks, manuals, etc. I. Borradaile, Viola, ed. and tr. II. Borradaile, Rosamund, ed. and tr. III. Heinrich von Lubbegge. IV. Andres von Colmar. V.

Paintings, European. I. Traz, Georges de, 1881- joint author. II. Title.

GAY, Claire. 759.94
Eighteenth century painting. New York, Funk & Wagnalls [1972] 207 p. illus. (part col.) 28 cm. (History of painting, v. 6) Translation of Le 18e siecle. Bibliography: p. 204. [ND456.G3513 1972] 75-100538 7.95
1. Painting, European—History. 2. Painting, Modern—17th-18th centuries—Europe. I. Title.

Painting—Exhibitions.

CHRYSLER Museum at Norfolk. 750'.74'016855
Treasures from the Chrysler Museum at Norfolk and Walter P. Chrysler, Jr. : special selections exhibition, Tennessee Fine Arts Center at Cheekwood, Nashville, Tennessee, June 12-September 5, 1977 : catalogue / by Mario Amaya and Eric M. Zafran ; edited by Mario Amaya. [Norfolk, Va.] : The Museum, c1977. [60] p., 60 leaves of plates : ill. (some col.) ; 28 cm. Includes bibliographical references and index. [N5020.N36C473] 77-81411
1. Painting—Exhibitions. 2. Sculpture, Modern—20th century—Exhibitions. I. Chrysler, Walter Percy, 1909- II. Amaya, Mario. III. Zafran, Eric. IV. Tennessee Fine Arts Center. V. Title.

Painting, Finnish.

SMITH, John Boulton. 759.71
Modern Finnish painting and graphic art. New York, Praeger Publishers [1970] 62 p. illus., 64 plates (part col.) 20 cm. ([The Modern arts in Finland, 3]) [ND955.F5S6] 72-117393 4.50
1. Painting, Finnish. 2. Painting, Modern—20th century—Finland. I. Title.

Painting—Flanders—Hist.

SHIPP, Horace, 1891- 759.9493
The Flemish masters. New York, Philosophical Library [1954] 128p. 40 plates (part col.) 25cm. [ND665] 54-1965
1. Painting—Flanders—Hist. 2. Paintings, Flemish. I. Title.

Painting, Flemish.

FROMENTIN, Eugene, 1820-1876 759.9492
The old masters of Belgium & Holland. Introd. by Meyer Schapiro. [Tr. from French by Mary C. Robins] New York, Schocken [1964, c.1949, 1963] xliv, 342p. illus., ports. 21cm. (SB54) 63-18396 2.45 pap.,
1. Painting, Flemish. 2. Painting, Dutch. I. Title.

HELD, Julius Samuel, 1905- 759.9493'1
Flemish painting. Text by Julius S. Held. New York, H. N. Abrams [1971] 24 p. illus. (part col.) 33 cm. (The Library of great painters. Portfolio ed.) [ND669.F5H4 1971] 71-124298 ISBN 0-8109-3015-3
1. Painting, Flemish. 2. Paintings, Flemish.

LARSEN, Erik. 759.29
Flemish painting, seventeenth century. New York, McGraw-Hill [1967] 47 p. illus., 24 col. slides (in pockets) 25 cm. (Color slide program of the world's art) [ND666.L3] 66-22521
1. Painting, Flemish. 2. Paintings, Flemish. 3. Lantern slides. I. Title.

LES Primitifs flamands; corpus de la peinture des anciens Pays-Bas meridionaux au quinzieme siecle. Bruxelles, [Centre national de Recherches. "Primities-flamands" Stamped on t.p.: Wittenborn, New York, 1966. Bruxelles, [Centre national de Recherches. "Primities-flamands] Stamped on t.p.: Wittenborn, New York, 1966. v. illus. 30cm. Edite par le Centre national de recherches 'Primitifs flamands.' Bibl. [ND665.P66] 53-16100 22.50 759.9493
1. Painting, Flemish. I. Centre national de recherches 'Primitifs flamands.'
Contents omitted.

Painting, Flemish—Catalogs.

FLEMISH painting / 759.9493'1
[compiled by] Anthea Peppin and William Vaughan. Oxford, [Eng.] : Phaidon ; New York : Dutton, 1977. 16 p., [24] leaves of plates : chiefly col. ill. ; 31 cm. [ND669.F5F57] 77-73886 ISBN 0-7148-1747-3 : 6.95
1. Painting, Flemish—Catalogs. I. Peppin, Anthea. II. Vaughan, William.

Painting, Flemish—History.

759.9493
Flemish painters, 1430-1830. New York, Viking Press [1960] xiii,783p.; xvii, 896 plates, plates (part col.) 28cm. (A Reynal book) Vol. 1 includes 'A dictionary of Flemish painters' from 1430 to 1900. Vol. 2: Plates, 'Notes on the literature': v. 1, p. 725-759. [ilenski, Reginald Howard] 50-1574 37.50
1. Painting, Flemish—Hist. 2. Painters, Flemish—Dictionaries. 3. Paintings, Flemish—Dictionaries. 4. Paintings, Flemish. I. Title.

GENAILLE, Robert. 759.9493
Flemish painting from Van Eyck to Brueghel. Translated by Leslie Schenk. New York, Universe Books [1959, c1954] 145 p. mounted illus. (part col.) 24 cm. Bibliography: p. 144. [ND665.G413 1959] 59-13048
1. Painting, Flemish—History. 2. Paintings, Flemish. I. Title.

LASSAIGNE, Jacques, 1910- 759.9493
Flemish painting. Text by Jacques Lassaigne. [Translated by Stuart Gilbert. New York] A. Skira [1957- v. mounted col. illus. 35cm. (Painting, color, history) Vol. 2: Text by Jacques Lassaigne and Robert L. Delevoy. Contents.[1] The century of Van Eyck. --[2] From Bosch to Rubens. Includes bibliographies. [ND665.L33] 57-11640
1. Painting, Flemish—Hist. 2. Paintings, Flemish. I. Title.

PUYVELDE, Leo van, 1882- 759.9'493'2
Flemish painting, the age of Rubens and Van Dyck [by] Leo van Puyvelde and Thierry van Puyvelde. Translated by Alan Kendall. New York, McGraw-Hill [1971] 243 p. illus., 42 col. plates. 29 cm. Translation of La peinture flamande au siecle de Rubens. Bibliography: p. 236-237. [ND669.F5P8513] 70-150466 ISBN 0-07-067130-3 24.50
1. Painting, Flemish—History. 2. Painting, Baroque—Flanders. I. Puyvelde, Thierry van, joint author. II. Title.

WILENSKI, Reginald Howard, 1887- 759.9493
Flemish painters, 1430-1830 New York, Viking Press [1960] 2 v. plates (part col.) 28 cm. (A Reynal book) Vol. 1 includes "A dictionary of Flemish painters" from 1430 to 1900. Vol. 2: Plates. "Notes on the literature": v. 1. p. 725-759. [ND672.W5] 60-1574
1. Painting. Flemish — Hist. 2. Painters, Flemish — Dictionaries. 3. Paintings. Flemish. I. Title.

Painting—Florence—History.

MEISS, Millard. 750.945
Painting in Florence and Siena after the Black Death. Princeton, Princeton University Press, 1951. xiv, 194 p. 169 illus. 31 cm. Full names: Millard Lazare Meiss. Bibliographical footnotes. [ND621.F7M4] 51-14790
1. Painting — Florence — Hist. 2. Painting — Siena — Hist. 3. Paintings, Italian. 4. Painting, Renaissance. I. Title.

MEISS, Millard Lazare. 759.5
Painting in Florence and Siena after the Black Death; the arts, religion and society in the mid-fourteenth century, by Millard Meiss. by Millard Meiss. New York, Harper [1973] xii, 195 p. 169 illus. 21 cm. (Icon editions, IN (t)37) First published in 1951. Bibliographical footnotes. [ND621.F7M4] ISBN 0-06-430037-4 3.95 (pbk.)
1. Painting—Florence—History. 2. Painting—Siena—History. 3. Painting, Italian. 4. Painting, Renaissance. I. Title.
L.C. card no. for the hardbound edition: 51-14790.

Painting, Florentine.

BERENSON, Bernhard, 1865-1959 759.5
Italian pictures of the Renaissance; a list of the principal artists and their works, with an index of places [pt. 2, 2v. Rev. ed.] Phaidon Pub., dist. Greenwich, Conn., N.Y. Graphic [c.1963] 2v. (various p.) 1482 illus. (col. fronts) 27cm. Contents.[Pt. 2, v.1-2] The Florentine school. 63-4419 25.00 set,
1. Painting, Florentine. 2. Painters, Italian—Florence. 3. Paintings, Renaissance. I. Title. BIP

COLE, Bruce, 1938- 759.5
Giotto and Florentine painting, 1280-1375 / Bruce Cole. 1st ed. New York : Harper & Row, c1976. x, 209 p. : ill. ; 22 cm. (Icon editions) Includes index. Bibliography: p. [195]-197. [ND623.G6C57 1976] 75-7632 ISBN 0-06-430900-2 : 8.50
1. Giotto di Bondone, 1266?-1337. 2. Painting, Florentine. 3. Painting, Gothic—Florence. I. Title. BIP

Painting—France.

GORDON, Jan, 1882-1944. 759.4
Modern French painters. Freeport, N.Y., Books for Libraries Press [1970] xii, 188 p. illus. 24 cm. (Essay index reprint series) Reprint of the 1923 ed. [ND548.G6 1970] 73-99697 ISBN 0-8369-1573-9
1. Painting—France. 2. Painting, Modern—20th century—France. 3. Painters—France. I. Title.

Painting—France—Hist.

WILENSKI, Reginald Howard 759.4
Modern French painters. v. 1, 1863-1903 v.2, 1904-1938. New York, Vintage Books [c.]1960 llus. 19cm. v. 1, 398, xx p. (Bibl. p. [351] -398; v. 2, 271, xvii p. (bibl. p. [247] -263) (K-97A, K-97B 1.65 pap., ea.
1. Painting—France—Hist. 2. Painters, French. 3. Art—Hist.—20th cent. I. Title.

WILENSKI, Reginald Howard, 1887- 759.4
Modern French painters. New York, Vintage Books, 1960. 2 v. illus. 10 cm. [ND547.W5 1960] 60-2590
1. Painting — France — Hist. 2. Painters, French. I. Title.

Painting, French.

BROWN, Milton Wolf, 1911- 759.4
The painting of the French revolution, by Milton W. Brown. New York, Critics group [c1938] 96p. XII pl. (incl. ports.) on 6 l. 21cm. (On cover: Critics group series. 8) Bibliography: p. 94-96. [ND546.B7] 40-7790
1. Painting, French. 2. France—Hist.—Revolution—Art. I. Title. II. Series.

FRY, Roger Eliot, 1866-1934. 759.04
French, Flemish, and British art. New York, Coward-McCann [1951] 215 p. illus. 23 cm. Contains the author's characteristics of French art, Flemish art, and Reflections on British painting. [ND454.F7 1951a] 51-13714
1. Painting, French. 2. Painting, Flemish. 3. Painting, British. I. Title.

HAMERTON, Philip Gilbert, 1834-1894. 759.4
Contemporary French painters, an essay. With 16 photographic illus. Freeport, N.Y., Books for Libraries Press [1973] p. (Essay index reprint series) Reprint of the 1895 ed. [ND547.H25 1973] 72-10745 ISBN 0-8369-7222-8
1. Painting, French. 2. Painting, Modern—19th century—France. 3. Painters, French. I. Title.

HUNTER, Sam, 1923- 759.4
Modern French painting, 1855-1956. [New York, Dell Pub. Co., 1956] 256p. illus. 17cm. (A Dell first edition, FE98) [ND547.H8] 55-7514
1. Painting, French. I. Title.

LEMOISNE, Paul Andre, 1875-1964. 759.4
Gothic painting in France, fourteenth and fifteenth centuries. Translated from the French by Ronald Boothroyd. New York, Hacker Art Books, 1973. xi, 165 p. 88 plates. 32 cm. "First published in Florence, 1931." Bibliography: p. 121-136. [ND543.L43 1973] 76-143356 ISBN 0-87817-075-8 35.00
1. Painting, French. 2. Painting, Gothic—France. I. Title.

LEVITINE, George. 759.4
The dawn of Bohemianism : the Barbu rebellion and primitivism in neoclassical France / George Levitine. University Park : Pennsylvania State University Press, [1978] p. cm. Includes index. Bibliography: p. [N6847.5.P68L48] 77-13892 ISBN 0-271-00527-0 : 18.50
1. Painting, French. 2. Primitivism in art—France. 3. Painting, Modern—19th century—France. 4. Avant-garde (Aesthetics)—France. I. Title. BIP

LOVGREN, Sven. 759.4
The genesis of modernism: Seurat, Gaguin, Van Gogh, & French symbolism in the 1880's. Rev. ed. Bloomington, Indiana University Press [1971] xiii, 241 p. illus., ports. 25 cm. Bibliography: p. 197-204. [ND547.5.N3L6 1971] 76-135009 ISBN 0-253-32560-9 9.50
1. Painting, French. 2. Symbolism in art—France. 3. Symbolism in literature. I. Title.

THE new Cezanne; 759.4
from Monet to Mondriaan. In commemoration of the 50th anniversary of Paul Cezanne's death. Red Wing, Minn., Art History [1958] 111p. illus. 25cm. [ND553.C33B5] [ND553.C33B5] 927.5 58-10644 58-10644
1. Cezanne, Paul, 1839-1906. 2. Painting, French. I. Biederman, Charles Joseph, 1906- BIP

RAYNAL, Maurice. 759.4
Modern French painters. [Translated by Ralph Roeder] New York, Arno Press [1969] 275 p. plates. 27 cm. (Arno series of contemporary art, no. 32) Translation of Anthologie de la peinture en France de 1906 a nos jours. Originally published in 1928. Includes bibliographical references. [ND548.R413 1969] 76-91374
1. Painting, French. 2. Painting, Modern—20th century—France. I. Title.

SLOANE, Joseph C 759.4
French painting between the past and the present; artists, critics, and traditions, from 1848 to 1870. Princeton, Princeton University Press, 1951. xii, 241 p. plates. 31 cm. (Princeton monographs in art and archaeology, 27) Bibliography: p. 227-235. [ND547.S55] 51-13872
1. Painting, French. I. Title. II. Series. BIP

WRIGHT, Christopher, 1945- 759.4
French painting / by Christopher Wright. New York : Mayflower Books, [1979] p. cm. (In the history of art) [ND544.W74] 78-25567 ISBN 0-8317-3566-X : 12.95 ISBN 0-8317-3567-8 pbk. : 6.95
1. Painting, French. 2. Painting, Renaissance—France. 3. Painting, Modern—France. I. Title. II. Series.

WRIGHT, Christopher, 1945- 759.4
French painting / by Christopher Wright. New York : Mayflower Books, [1979] p. cm. (In the history of art) [ND544.W74] 78-25567 ISBN 0-8317-3566-X : 12.95 ISBN 0-8317-3567-8 pbk. : 6.95
1. Painting, French. 2. Painting, Renaissance—France. 3. Painting, Modern—France. I. Title. II. Series. BIP

Painting, French—Dutch influences.

BANKS, Oliver T. 759.4
Watteau and the north : studies in the Dutch and Flemish baroque influences on French rococo painting / Oliver T. Banks. New York : Garland Pub., 1977, i.e.1978 xiv, 302 p., [105] leaves of plates : ill. ; 21 cm. (Outstanding dissertations in the fine

SUBJECT INDEX PAINTING—GT. BRIT.

arts) Originally presented as the author's thesis, Princeton, 1975. Bibliography: p. 296-302. [ND546.B34 1977] 76-23602 ISBN 0-8240-2676-4 lib.bdg. : 45.00
1. Watteau, Jean Antoine, 1684-1721. 2. Painting, French—Dutch influences. 3. Painting, French—Flemish influences. 4. Painting, Baroque—Influence. 5. Painting, Rococo—France. I. Title. II. Series.

Painting, French—Exhibitions.

DETROIT. Institute of Arts. 759.4
French painting from David to Courbet. The Detroit Institute of Arts, Feb. 1st through Mar. 5, 1950. [Detroit, 1950] 60 p. illus., ports. 25 cm. Cover title: From David to Courbet. Includes bibliographies. [ND547.D45] 50-14005
1. Painting, French—Exhibitions. I. Title. II. Title: From David to Courbet.

UNITED States. 759.4'074'0153
National Gallery of Art.
Small French paintings from the bequest of Ailsa Mellon Bruce : [catalogue / written by David E. Rust]. Washington : National Gallery of Art, 1978. xvii, 121 p. : ill. (some col.) ; 27 cm. Includes bibliographies and index. [ND547.5.I4U6 1978a] 78-606019 7.00
1. Bruce, Ailsa Mellon—Art collections—Exhibitions. 2. Painting, French—Exhibitions. 3. Impressionism (Art)—France—Exhibitions. 4. Post-impressionism (Art)—France—Exhibitions. 5. Painting, Modern—19th century—France—Exhibitions. I. Rust, David E. II. Title.

Painting, French—History.

CHATELET, Albert. 759.4
French painting, from Fouquet to Poussin, [by]Albert Chatelet [and] Jacques Thuillier. [Translated from the French by Stuart Gilbert. Geneva] Skira [1963; distributed in the U.S. by World Pub. Co., Cleveland] 243 p. mounted col. illus. 35 cm. (Painting, color, history) Bibliography: p. 229-232. [ND544.C433] 63-18588
1. Painting, French — Hist. 2. Paintings, French. I. Thuillier, Jacques. joint author. II. Title.

FRIEDLAENDER, Walter F. 759.4
David to Delacroix; translated by Robert Goldwater. Cambridge, Harvard University Press, 1952. xii, 136 p. 83 illus. 25 cm. [ND547.F75] 52-5395
1. Painting, French—Hist. 2. Paintings, French. I. Title. BIP

GAUSS, Charles Edward, 759.4
1909-
The aesthetic theories of French artists, 1855 to the present. Geneva Skira; corot. Cleveland, World c.1966 x, 111p. 21cm. (JH-23) Bibl. [ND547.G25] 49-11002 1.45 pap.,
1. Painting, French—Hist. 2. Esthetics. I. Title. BIP

HUYGHE, Rene. 709'.44
La peinture francaise des XVII et XVIII siecles. [Paris] Flammarion [1962] 103 p. mounted col. illus. 30 cm. [ND546.H8] 65-30620
1. Painting, French — Hist. I. Title.

LEYMARIE, Jean. 759.4
French painting, the nineteenth century. Translated from the French by James Emmons. Yeneva Skira distributed in the U.S. by World Pub. Co., Cleveland, 1962 229 p. mounted col. illus. 35 cm. (Painting, color, history) Bibliography: p. 215-[218] [ND547.L533] 62-21023
1. Painting, French — Hist. 2. Paintings, French. I. Title.

TAYLOR, Basil. 759.4
French painting. 12 colour plates and 139 photogravure plates. Introductory note by Geoffrey Grigson. London, New York, Thames and Hudson [1951] 64 p. plates (part col.) 31 cm. [ND544.T3] 52-3890
1. Painting. French — Hist. 2. Paintings. French. I. Title.

TRAZ, Georges de 1881- 759.4
French painting: Nineteenth century painters, 1800-1870 [by] Francois Fosca [pseud.] Translated by Peter Simmons. New York, Universe Books [1960] 151 p. mounted col. illus. 25 cm. Bibliography: p. 151. [ND547.T73] 60-9597
1. Painting, French — Hist. 2. Paintings, French. Full name: Georges Albert Edouard de Traz. I. Title.

Painting, French—History.

DIMIER, Louis, 1865-1943. 759.4
French painting in the sixteenth century. New York, Arno Press, 1969. xvi, 330 p. illus. 23 cm. Reprint of the 1904 ed. "This book has been translated from Monsieur Dimier's French MS. by Mr. Harold Child." Includes bibliographical references. [ND545.D6 1969] 74-88821
1. Painting, French—History. 2. Painting, Renaissance—France. I. Title. BIP

FRIEDLAENDER, Walter F., 759.4
1873-1966.
David to Delacroix. Translated by Robert Goldwater. New York, Schocken Books [1968, c1952] xii, 136 p. 83 illus. 21 cm. Translation of Von David bis Delacroix. [ND547.F7613 1968] 68-9567 2.45
1. Painting, French—History. 2. Paintings, French. I. Title.

LEYMARIE, Jean. 759.4
French painting, the nineteenth century. [Translated from the French by James Emmons] [Geneva] Skira [distributed in the U.S. by World Pub. Co., Cleveland] [1962] 229 p. mounted col. illus. 35 cm. (Painting, color, history) Bibliography: p. 215-[218] [ND547.L533] 62-21023
1. Painting, French—History. 2. Paintings, French. I. Title.

LUCIE-SMITH, Edward. 759.4
A concise history of French painting. New York, Praeger [1971] 288 p. illus. (part col.) 22 cm. Bibliography: p. 280-281. [ND541.L8 1971b] 76-135514 8.50
1. Painting, French—History. I. Title. BIP

SALINGER, Margaretta M., 759.4
1907-
French painting: the seventeenth century. New York, McGraw-Hill [1966, c1965] 48 p. illus., 24 col. slides (in pockets) 25 cm. (Color slide program of the world's art) [ND546.S2] 65-19417
1. Painting, French—History. 2. Painters, French. 3. Lantern slides. I. Title. II. Series.

THUILLIER, Jacques. 759.4
French painting, from Le Nain to Fragonard [by] Jacques Thuillier [and] Albert Chatelet. [Translated from the French by James Emmons. Geneva] Skira; [distributed in the U.S. by World Pub. Co., Cleveland, 1964] 275 p. mounted col. illus. 35 cm. (Painting, color, history) Bibliography: p. 259-[262] [ND546.T5] 63-23077
1. Painting, Frency — Hist. 2. Paintings, French. I. Chatelet. Albert, joint author. II. Title.

TRAZ, Georges de, 1881- 759.4
French painting: nineteenth century painters, 1800-1870 [by] Francois Fosca (pseud.) Translated by Peter Simmons. New York, Universe Books [1960] 151 p. mounted col. illus. 25 cm. Bibliography: p. 151. [ND547.T73] 60-9597
1. Painting, French—History. 2. Paintings, French.

WILENSKI, Reginald Howard, 759.4
1887-
French painting, by R. H. Wilenski. 3d rev. ed. New York, Dover Publications [1973] xvii, 316 p. illus. 24 cm. [ND541.W5 1973] 72-92760 ISBN 0-486-22931-9 5.00
1. Painting, French—History. 2. Painters, French. I. Title. BIP

Painting from photographs.

COKE, Van Deren, 1921- 759'.06
The painter and the photograph; from Delacroix to Warhol. [Rev. and enl. ed.] Albuquerque, University of New Mexico Press [1972] 324 p. illus. 29 cm. Rev. and enl. from the 1964 exhibition catalog issued under the same title. Includes bibliographical references. [N72.P5C6 1972] 75-129804 32.00
1. Painting from photographs. 2. Paintings—Exhibitions. 3. Photography—Exhibitions. I. Title. BIP

COKE, Van Deren, 1921- 111.8
The painter and the photograph. [1st ed.] Albuquerque] University of New Mexico Press [1964] 79 p. illus. 26 cm. Catalog for an exhibition organized by the staff of the Art Gallery, University of New Mexico, and shown during 1964 and 1965 at Rose Art Museum, Brandeis University. and at other institutions. Includes bibliographical references. [N72.P5C58] 64-24357
1. Painting from photographs. 2. Paintings—Exhibitions. 3. Photography—Exhibitions. I. New Mexico. University. Art Museum. II. Brandeis University, Waltham, Mass. Rose Art Museum. III. Title.

DE REYNA, Rudy, 1914- 751.4
Creative painting from photographs / by Rudy de Reyna. New York : Watson-Guptill Publications, 1975. 156 p. : ill. (some col.) ; 29 cm. Includes index. [ND1505.D46 1975] 74-23815 ISBN 0-8230-1092-9 : 15.95
1. Painting from photographs. 2. Painting—Technique. I. Title. BIP

SCHARF, Aaron. 770.1'1
Art and photography. [Harmondsworth, Eng., Baltimore, Penguin, 1974] 397 p. illus. 23 cm. Includes bibliographical references. [N72.P5S3 1974] 74-170324 ISBN 0-14-021722-3 5.95 (pbk.).
1. Painting from photographs.

Painting, German.

DEUSCH, Werner Richard, 759.3
1903-
German painting of the sixteenth century; Durer and his contemporaries, by Werner R. Deusch. With a pref. by F. Winkler. New York, Hacker Art Books, 1973. 32 p., 104 p. of illus. 32 cm. Translation of Deutsche Malerei des sechzehnten Jahrhunderts. Bibliography: p. 23. [ND565.D413 1973] 73-79047 ISBN 0-87817-133-9 30.00
1. Painting, German. 2. Painting, Renaissance—Germany. I. Title. BIP

FINKE, Ulrich. 759.3
German painting from romanticism to expressionism / Ulrich Finke. Boulder, Colo. : Westview Press, [1975] p. cm. Includes index. Bibliography: p. [ND567.F56] 75-19426 ISBN 0-89158-503-6 : 29.50
1. Painting, German. 2. Painting, Modern—19th century—Germany. 3. Painting, Modern—20th century—Germany. I. Title. BIP

ROTHEL, Hans Konrad, 1909- 759.3
Modern German painting. Translated from the German by Desmond and Louise Clayton. New York, Reynal [1957] 103p. illus. (part col.) 33cm. 'Biographies and literature on the artists: p.85-98. Bibliography: p.99-103. [ND568.R613] 58-2667
1. Painting, German. 2. Art, Modern—20th cent. I. Title.

SCHRADE, Hubert, 1900- 759.3
German romantic painting / Hubert Schrade ; translated from the German by Maria Pelikan. New York : H. N. Abrams, 1977, c1967. 135 p. : ill. (some col.) ; 34 cm. Translation of Deutsche Maler der Romantik. Includes index. Bibliography: p. 131-132. [ND567.5.R6S3713 1977] 72-149856 ISBN 0-8109-0141-2 : 25.00
1. Painting, German. 2. Painting, Modern—19th century—Germany. 3. Romanticism in art—Germany. I. Title. BIP

Painting, German—History.

BENESCH, Otto, 1896-1964. 759.3
German painting, from Durer to Holbein. Text by Otto Benesch [translated from the German by H. S. B. Harrison. Geneva] Skira; [distributed in the U.S. by the World Pub. Co., Cleveland, 1966] 107 p. mounted col. illus. 35 cm. (Painting, color, history) "Select bibliography by Eva Benesch": p. 183-[188] [ND565.B413] 66-22489
1. Painting, German — Hist. 2. Painting, Renaissance. I. Title.

GERMAN expressionist 759.05
painting. Berkeley, University of California Press. 1957. xx, 379p. 37illus., 180plates (part col.) 29cm. Bibliographical references Included in 'Notes' (p.[327]-353) Bibliography:p. [354]- 370. [ND568.S4] 759.915 57-10501
1. Painting, German—Hist. 2. Paintings, German. 3. Expressionism (art) I. Selz, Peter. BIP

SELZ, Peter. 759.05
German expressionist painting. Berkeley, University of California Press [1974, c1957] xviii, 379 p. illus., plates (part. col.) 24 cm. Bibliographical references included in "Notes" (p. [327]-353) [ND568.S4] 759.915 ISBN 0-520-02515-6 10.95 (pbk.)
1. Painting, German—Hist. 2. Paintings, German. 3. Expressionism (Art) I. Title. L.C. card no. for original edition: 57-10501.

Painting, German—History.

BRION, Marcel, 1895- 759.943
German painting. Translated by W. J. Strachan. New York, Universe Books [1959] 177 p. mounted col. illus. 24 cm. [ND564.B713] 59-13044
1. Painting, German—History. I. Title.

LANDOLT, Hanspeter. 759.3
German painting; the late Middle Ages (1350-1500). Translated by Heinz Norden [Geneva] Skira [1968] 167 p. 89 illus. (72 col.) 35 cm. (Painting, color, history) "Distributed in the United States by the World Publishing Company ... Cleveland." Translation of Die deutsche Malerei: das Spatmittelalter (1350-1500) Bibliography: p. 155-[160] [ND563.L313] 68-54210 29.50
1. Painting, German—History. 2. Painting, Medieval—Germany. I. Title.

Painting, Gothic—Hist.

SOUCHAL, Genevieve. 759.02
Gothic painting [by] Genevieve Souchal, Enzo Carli [and] Jose Gudiol. Translated by Michael Aeburn and William Harris] New York, Viking Press [1965] 67 p. 176 plates (part col.) 20 cm. (Compass history of art, CA6) Compass books. Contents.--Gothic painting in France, by G. Souchal.--Gothic painting in Italy, by E. Carli. Gothic painting in northern and central Europe, by E. Carli.--Gothic painting in Spain, by J. Gudiol. [ND140.S613] 65-141066
1. Painting, Gothic—Hist. I. Carli, Enzo, 1910- II. Gudiol y Ricart, Josep. III. Title.

Painting, Gothic—Italy.

JAMESON, Anna Brownell 759.5
(Murphy) 1794-1860.
Memoirs of the early Italian painters. Freeport, N.Y., Books for Libraries Press [1973] p. (Essay index reprint series) Reprint of the 1889 ed. published by Houghton, Mifflin, Boston. [ND614.J35 1973] 73-4569 ISBN 0-518-10085-5
1. Painting, Gothic—Italy. 2. Painting, Renaissance—Italy. 3. Painters, Italian. I. Title.

Painting—Gt. Brit.

HUBBARD, Eric Hesketh, 750.942
1892-
A hundred years of British painting, 1851-1951. London, New York, Longmans, Green [1951] xii, 325 p. plates, ports. 23 cm. Errata slip inserted. Bibliography: p. 299-302. [ND467.H85] 51-14717
1. Painting—Gt. Brit. I. Title.

WATERHOUSE, Ellis 750.942
Kirkham, 1905-
Painting in Britain, 1530-1790. London, Baltimore, Penguin Books [1953] xiii, 270 p. 192 p. of illus. 27 cm. (The Pelican history of art, Z1) Bibliography: p. 247-252. [ND464.W37 1953] 53-2410
1. Painting—Gt. Brit. 2. Paintings—Gt. Brit. I. Series. BIP

WATERHOUSE, Ellis Kirkham, 1905- 759.2
Painting in Britain, 1530 to 1790 [by] Ellis Waterhouse. 3rd ed. Harmondsworth, Penguin, 1969. 275 p. 193 plates, illus. (incl. 1 col.). 27 cm. (The Pelican history of art Z1) Bibliography: p. 250-256. [ND464.W37 1969] 77-437912 5/10/-
1. Painting—Gt. Brit. 2. Paintings—Gt. Brit. I. Title. II. Series.

Painting—Great Britain—History.

SHORT, Ernest Henry, 1875- 750.942
A history of British painting. London, Eyre & Spottiswoode. 1953 304p. illus., ports. 23cm. List of principal British painters: p.291-304. [ND461.S46] 54-1230 5.00 bds.,
1. Painting—Gt. Brit.—Hist. I. Title.
Available from Hillary House, New York.

Painting, Great Britain—History.

*PIPER, David comp. 759.41
Genius of British painting. New York, Morrow, 1975, 1975 352 p. illus. (part col.) 30 cm. Bibliography: p. 337-341. [ND261] 74-19879 ISBN 0-688-00313-3 27.50.
1. Painting, Great Britain—History. I. Title. BIP

Painting, Greek.

PFUHL, Ernst, 1876-1940. 759.938
Masterpieces of Greek drawing and painting. Translated, with a foreword, by J. D. iNew York, Macmillan [1955] viii, 151p., 126p. of illus. (part col.) 29cm. 'The plates contain a selection from the eight hundred reproductions in my three-volume work Malerel und Zeichnung der Griechen (Munich, 1923, Bruchmann)'--Pref. The text of the 1926 edition is republished unaltered, but the bibliography has been brought up to date.--Cf. Foreword. Bibliography: p.144-145. [ND110.P] A56
1. Painting. Greek. 2. Vase-painting. Greek. 3. Pottery, Greek. I. Title.

SPETERES, Tones P. 759.938
Greek and Etruscan painting [by] Tony Spiteris. Translated by Janet Sondheimer. New York, Funk & Wagnalls [1969, c1965] 207 p. illus. (part col.) 28 cm. (History of painting, v. 3) Translation of La peinture grecqe et etrusque. "Dictionary": p. [145]-203. Bibliography: p. [204] [ND110.S613] 69-13026 7.95
1. Painting, Greek. 2. Painting, Etruscan. I. Title.

Painting, Greek—Hist.

DEVAMBEZ, Pierre, 1902- 759.938
Greek painting. [Tr. by Jean Steward] New York, Viking [1963, c.1962] 36p. illus. (pt. col.) map. 20cm. (Compass bks., CA1. Compass hist. art) 62-12142 2.25 pap.,
1. Painting, Greek—Hist. 2. Vase painting, Greek—Hist. I. Title.

Painting —Hist.

BAZIN, Germain. ed. 704
Histoire de la peinture moderne. Texte, recherches, biographies, bibliographies, par Gaston Diehl [et al.] New York, Edition Hyperion [1950] 391 p. illus. (part col.) 19 cm. Bibliography: p. 341-346. [ND190.B26] 51-4542
1. Painting—Hist. 2. Art—Hist.—19th cent. 3. Art—Hist.—20th cent. 4. Painters. I. Title.

BAZIN, Germain. ed. 750.903
History of modern painting. Published under the supervision of Germain Bazin. Translated from the French by Rosamund Frost. [Edited by Andre Gloeckner] Text, research, illus., biographies, bibliography by Gaston Diehl [and others] New York, Hyperion Press; distributed by Macmillan [1951] 391 p. illus. (part col.) 19 cm. Erratum slip inserted. Bibliography: p. 341-346. [ND190.B264] 51-5448
1. Painting—Hist. 2. Art—Hist.—19th cent. 3. Art—Hist.—20th cent. 4. Painters. I. Title.

COGNIAT, Raymond, 1896- 759.04
Seventeenth-century painting [Tr. by Frances Partridge] New York, Viking [c.1964] 37p. 176 plates (pt. col.) 20cm. (Compass bks., CA9. Compass hist. of art) 63-15219 2.25 pap.,
1. Painting—Hist. I. Title.

CRAVEN, Thomas, 1889- 927.5
Men of art. Garden City, N. Y., Halcyon House [1950, '1931] xviii, 524 p. 32 plates. 25 cm. "Bibliography and acknowledgments": p. 515-516. [ND50.Cm 1950] 50-3370
1. Painting—Hist. 2. Painters. I. Title.

DIEHL, Gaston 759.05
The moderns; a treasury of painting throughout the world. [Tr. from French by Edward Lucie Smith] New York, Crown [1961] 219p. illus. (pt. mounted col.) col. plates. 33cm. Bibl. 61-15792 12.50
1. Painting—Hist. 2. Paintings. 3. Art, Modern—20th cent. I. Title. BIP

DUPONT, Jacques. 750.903
The seventeenth century; the new developments in art from Caravaggio to Vermeer. Text by Jacques Dupont and Francois Mathey. Translated by S. J. C. Harrison. Geneva, New York, Skira [1951] 135 p. mounted col. illus. 29 cm. (The Great centuries of painting) Bibliography: p. 132. [ND180.D8 1951a] 52-43278
1. Painting—Hist. 2. Paintings. 3. Painters. I. Mathey, Francois. joint author. II. Title. III. Series.

JANSON, Horst Woldemar, 1913- 759
The picture history of painting, from cave painting to modern times; an abridged ed. [by] H. W. Janson, Dora Jane Janson, New York, Washington Square Press [dist. Pocket Books, 1961, c.1957, 1961] 224p. illus. (part col.) (W1036) .90 pap.,
1. Painting—Hist. 2. Paintings. I. Janson, Dora Jane, 1916- joint author. II. Title.

JANSON, Horst Woldemar, 1913- 750.9
The story of painting for young people, from cave painting to modern times, by H. W. Janson and Dora Jane Janson. [1st ed.] New York, H. N. Abrams [c1952] 164p. illus (part col.) 31cm. [An Abrams art book] [ND1146.J35] 52-14236
1. Painting—Hist. 2. Art—Juvenile literature. I. Janson, Dora Jane, 1916- joint author. II. Title.

JONG, Casper de 759
Paintings of the Western world. Tr. from Dutch by Hans Koningsberger. Concluding chapter written by John Sedgwick. [New York] Barnes & Noble [c. 1963] viii. 246p. illus. 21cm. (Everyday handbks., no. 281) 63-19460 4.95; 1.75 pap.,
1. Painting—Hist. I. Title.

LEVEY, Michael 759
A concise history of painting, from Giotto to Cezanne. New York, Praeger [1963, c.1962] 324p. 549 col. illus. 22cm. (ppraeger paperbacks, P132) 3.95 pap.,
1. Painting—Hist. I. Title. BIP

MULLER, Joseph Emile. 759.06
Modern painting from Manet to Mondrian. [Translated from the French by Betty Forster] New York, Castle Books [c1960] 159p. illus. (part mounted col.) 32cm. [ND195.M783 1960] 61-19940
1. Painting—Hist. 2. Art, Modern—20th cent. I. Title.

MUNSTERBERG, Hugo, 1916- 750.904
Twentieth century painting. New York, Philosophical Library [1951] 102 p. illus. 24 cm. [ND195.M8] 51-14569
1. Painting — Hist. 2. Modernism (Art) I. Title.

MYERS, Bernard Samuel, 1908- 759.05
Modern art in the making. 2d ed. New York, McGraw-Hill, 1959. 486p. illus. 26cm. Includes bibliography. [ND195.M9 1959] 59-8554
1. Painting—Hist. 2. Modernism (Art) I. Title.

NEWMEYER, Sarah. 759.91
Enjoying modern art. New York, Reinhold [1955] vi, 216p. illus. 24cm. [ND160.N4] 55-9946
1. Painting—Hist. I. Title.

PLATTE, Hans. 701.16
Malerei. Hamburg, Standard- Verlag [1957] 318p. illus. (part col.) 22cm. (Die Kunst des 20. Jahrhunderts) 'Biographische Notizen : p. 301-311. [ND195.P5] 58-26145
1. Painting —Hist. 2. Art —Hist.—20th cent. I. Title.

PONENTE, Nello. 759.06
Modern painting, contemporary trends. [Translated from the Italian by James Emmons. New York] Skira; [distributed by World Pub. Co., Cleveland, 1960] 214p. mounted col. illus. 35cm. (Painting, color, history) 'General biography: p. 179-[180] Bibliographical and bibliographical notices': p. 181-[207] [ND195.P63 1960] 60-15614
1. Painting—Hist. 2. Paintings. 3. Art, Modern—20th cent. I. Title.

PONENTE, Nello 759.06
Modern painting, contemporary trends. [Translated from the Italian by James Emmons. New York Skira; distribution by World Pub. Co., Cleveland, 1960 214p. mounted col. illus. 35cm. (Painting, color, history [series ed. by Albert Skira], Bibl.: p.179-[180] and Biographical bibls.: p.181-[207] 60-15614 27.50, buck., bxd.
1. Painting—Hist. 2. Paintings. 3. Art, Modern—20th cent. I. Title.

READ, Herbert Edward, Sir 1893 759.06
A concise history of modern painting. New York, Praeger [1962, c.1959] 376p. illus. (pt. col.) 22cm. (PPS-74) Bibl. 3.95 pap.,
1. Painting—Hist. 2. Art, Modern—20th cent. I. Title. BIP

ROBB, David Metheny, 1903- 750.9
The Harper history of painting: the occidental tradition. Introd. by Francis Henry Taylor. New York, Harper [1951] xv, 1006 p. illus., col. plates. 27 cm. Bibliography: p. 965-983. [ND50.R6] 51-7191
1. Painting — Hist. I. Title.

SAUVAGE, Tristan 759.5
Nuclear art. [Traduction francaise de Gualtiero Schoenenberger. English tr. by John A Stephens] New York, M. Maestro [dist. Wittenborn, c.1962] 242p. illus. (pt. col.) 31cm. Italian, French. and English. Bibl. 62-4639 17.50, bxd.
1. Painting—Hist. 2. Painters. Italian. I. Title.

SCHMIDT-DEGENER, Henri. 759
The teach yourself history of painting. Based on the original work of H. Schmidt Degener, and edited for English readers by William Gaunt. New York, Roy [1956?- v. illus. (part col.) map. 25cm. Translation of Inleiding tot de geschiedenis der schilderkunst. Contents.v. 1. The Italian school i.--v. 2. The Italian school Includes bibliographies. [ND50] 56-5078
1. Painting—Hist. I. Title.

Painting — Hist. — 19th cent.

GOWANS, Alan. 759.05
The restless art; a history of painters and painting, 1760-1960. [1st ed.] Philadelphia, Lippincott [1966] 414 p. illus. 24 cm. Includes bibliographical references. [ND190.G6] 66-10346
1. Painting — Hist. — 19th cent. 2. Painting — Hist. — 20th cent. I. Title.

PEILLEX, Georges 759.05
Nineteenth-century painting [Tr. by Angus Malcolm] New York, Viking [1965, c.1964] 51p. 176 plates (pt. col.) 20cm. (Compass bks., CA11; Compass hist. of art) [ND190.P363] 64-19703 2.25 pap.,
1. Painting—Hist.—19th cent. 2. Paintings. I. Title.

RITHENSTEIN, Sir John Knewstub Maurice, 1901- 759'.05
Nineteenth-century painting; a study in conflict, by John Rothenstein. Freeport, N. Y., Books for Libraries Press [1967] x, 191 p. illus., ports. 22 cm. (Essay index reprint series) Reprint of the 1932 ed. Contents.CONTENTS.--The historical background.--Ingres.--Constable.--Bonington.--Turner.--Rousseau.--Corot.--Delacroix.--Daumler.--Millet.--Courbet.--Impressionism.--Bibliography (p. 181-186). [ND190.R6] 67-28739
1. Painting—Hist.—19th cent. 2. Impressionism (Art) I. Title.

Painting—Hist.—20th cent.

JAFFE, Hans Ludwig C. 759.06
Twentieth-century painting [Tr. by Margaret Shenfield] New York, Viking [1964, c.1963] 1v. (various p.) 176 plates (pt. col.) 20cm. (Compass bks. CA 12. Compass hist. of art) 'Captions': folder ([7] p.) inserted. 63-12645 2.25 pap.,
1. Painting—Hist.—20th cent. I. Title.

ROBBINS, Daniel 759.06
Painting between the wars, 1918-1940. New York, McGraw [1966] 47p. illus., 24 col. slides (in pockets) 25cm. (Color slide program of the world's art) [ND195.R6] 65-26486 8.95 bds.,
1. Painting—Hist.—20th cent. 2. Painters. 3. Lantern slides. I. Title. II. Series. BIP

SCHWARZ, Arturo, 1924- 759.5
Nuclear art [by] Tristan Sauvage. [Traduction francaise de Gualtiero Schoenenberger. English translation by John A. Stephens] New York, M. Maestro [1962] 242 p. illus. (part col.), ports. 31 cm. Italian, French, and English. Bibliography: p. 233-234. [ND195.S3813] 62-4639
1. Painting—Hist.—20th cent. 2. Painters, Italian. I. Title.

Painting—Hist.—Juvenile literature.

CUNNINGHAM, Margrete 759
Picture book of painters of the past. New York, Sterling [c.1963] 64p. illus. 26cm. (Visual hist. ser.) 62-18643 1.00 pap.,
1. Painting—Hist.—Juvenile literature. I. Title. II. Title: Painters of the past. III. Series.

JANSON, Horst Woldemar, 1913- 759
The story of painting, from cave painting to modern times [by] H. W. Janson, Dora Jane Janson. New York, Abrams [1966 i.e. 1967] 164p. illus. (pt. col.) 32cm. First ed. pub. in 1952 under title: The story of painting for young people [ND1146.J35 1966] 66-18590 5.95
1. Painting—Hist.—Juvenile literature. I. Janson, Dora Jane, 1916- joint author. II. Title.

JANSON, Horst Woldemar, 1913- j759
The story of painting for young people, from cave painting to modern times, by H. W. and Dora Jane Janson. Textbook ed. New York, Abrams [1962] 259 p. illus. 22 cm. [ND1146.J35 1962] 60-13033
1. Painting—Hist.—Juvenile literature. I. Janson, Dora Jane, 1916- joint author. II. Title. BIP

JANSON, Horst Woldemar, 1913- 759
The story of painting for young people, from cave painting to modern times, by H. W. and Dora Jane Janson. Textbook ed. New York, Abrams [1962?] 259p. illus. 22cm. [ND1146.J35 1962] 60-13033
1. Painting—Hist.—Juvenile literature. I. Janson, Dora Jane, 1916- joint author. II. Title.

ROGERS, William Garland, 1896- 759.06
A picture is a picture: a look at modern painting. New York, Harcourt [c.1964] 194p. 6 plates. 21cm. Bibl. 64-11495 3.95
1. Painting—Hist.—Juvenile literature. I. Title.

Painting, Hungarian.

RADOCSAY, De'nes 759.391
Gothic panel painting in Hungary [Tr. by Gedeon Dienes. Budapest] Corvina Pr. [New York, Heinman, 1964, c.1963] 64p. 48 mounted col. illus., facsims. 33cm. [ND517.R313] 64-47961 20.00
1. Painting, Hungarian. 2. Painting, Gothic. I. Budapest. Szepmuveszeti Muzeum. II. Esztergom, Hungary. Kereszteny Muzeum. III. Title.

Painting—Illinois—Chicago—Catalogs.

CHICAGO. Art Institute. 750'.74'017311
The Art Institute of Chicago : 100 masterpieces / [editor and coordinator, Janice J. Feldstein, co-editor, Maureen Smith]. Chicago : The Institute : distributed by Rand McNally, c1978. 159 p. : ill. (some col.) ; 36 cm. Includes indexes. [N530.A534] 78-56322 35.00
1. Chicago. Art Institute—Catalogs. 2. Painting—Illinois—Chicago—Catalogs. I. Feldstein, Janice J. II. Smith, Maureen, 1945-

Painting—India.

ARCHER, Mildred. 759.954
Indian painting for the British, 1770-1880; an essay by Mildred and W. G. Archer [London] Oxford University Press, 1955. xiv, 145p. 25 plates, map. 26cm. Bibliography: p. [125]-136. [ND1003.A7] 56-13543
1. Painting—India. 2. Paintings, Indic. I. Archer, William George, 1907- joint author. II. Title.

Painting, India—Hist.

BARRETT, Douglas E 759.954
Painting of India, text by Douglas Barrett and Basil Gray. [Geneva?] Skira; [distributed in the U.S. by World Pub. Co., Cleveland [1963] 213 p. mounted col. illus., map. 29 cm. (Treasurers of Asia) Bibliography: p. 195-196. [ND1002.B3] 63-8982
1. Painting — India — Hist. I. Gray, Basil, 1904- joint author. II. Title. III. Series.

RAWSON, Philip S 759.954
Indian painting. Paris, P. Tisne; New York, Universe Books [1961] 169p. illus. (part mounted col.) map. 24cm. Bibliography: p. 161-[163] [ND1001.R3] 61-14468
1. Painting, India—Hist. I. Title.

Painting, Indian—North America.

HIGHWATER, Jamake. 759.13
Song from the earth : American Indian painting / Jamake Highwater. 1st ed. [Greenwich, Conn.] : New York Graphic Society, c1976. p. cm. Includes index. Bibliography: p. [ND238.A4H53] 75-37201 ISBN 0-8212-0698-2 : 19.95
1. Painting, Indian—North America. I. Title. BIP

Painting, Indic.

ARCHER, William George, 1907- 759.954
India and modern art. New York, Macmillan [1959] 143 p. illus. 26 cm. Includes bibliography. [ND1004.A8] 60-4311
1. Painting, Indic. 2. Paintings, Indic. 3. Modernism (Art) I. Title.

BHATTACHARYA, Asok K. 759.954
Technique of Indian painting : a study chiefly made on the basis of the silpa texts / Asok K. Bhattacharya ; with a foreword by S. K. Saraswati. 1st ed. Calcutta : Saraswat Library, 1976. vi, 174 p., [8] leaves of plates : ill. (some col.) ; 25 cm. "Glossary": p. 169 [i.e. 159]-164. Includes index. Bibliography: p. 165-169. [ND1001.B47] 76-901597 Rs50.00
1. Painting, Indic. 2. Painting—Technique. I. Title.

CHAITANYA, Krishna, 1918- 751.7'30954
A history of Indian painting / Krishna Chaitanya. New Delhi : Abhinav Publications, 1976- v. : ill. ; 23 x 29 cm. Contents.Contents.—[1] The mural tradition. Includes bibliographical references and index. [ND1001.C46] 76-900494 27.50(v.1)
1. Painting, Indic. I. Title.
Distributed by South Asia Books.

CHANDRA, Moti. 759.954
Studies in early Indian painting / Moti Chandra. New York : Asia Pub. House, c1974. viii, 160 p., [37] leaves of plates : ill. (some col.) ; 25 cm. (Rabindranath Tagore memorial lectures ; 1964) Includes index. [ND1002.C46] 75-309643 ISBN 0-210-22310-3 : 35.00
1. Painting, Indic. 2. Mural painting and decoration, Indic. I. Title. II. Series. BIP

Painting, Indic-British influences—Exhibitions.

WELCH, Stuart Cary. 759.954
Room for wonder : Indian painting during the British period, 1760-1880 / by Stuart Cary Welch. New York : American Federation of Arts, c1978. 191 p. : ill. (some col.) ; 25 cm. Catalog of AFA exhibition 78-1, circulated Apr. 1978-Feb. 1979. Bibliography: p. 188-191. [ND1002.W44] 78-50093 8.00
1. Painting, Indic-British influences—Exhibitions. I. American Federation of Arts. II. Title.
Publisher's address: 41 E. 65th St., New York, NY 10021 BIP

Painting, Indic—India—Mithila.

VEQUAUD, Yves. 755'.9'45095412
Women painters of Mithila / Yves Vequaud. London : Thames and Hudson, 1977. 112 p. : chiefly ill. (some col.) ; 28 cm. Translation of L'art du Mithila. [ND1007.M55V4613 1977b] 78-308556 ISBN 0-500-27093-7 : 8.95
1. Valmiki. Ramayana—Illustrations. 2. Mahabharata—Illustrations. 3. Painting, Indic—India—Mithila. 4. Painting—India—Mithila. 5. Painting, Hindu—India—Mithila. 6. Hindu symbolism. 7. Symbolism in art—India—Mithila. I. Title.
Distributed by W. W. Norton, New York, NY 10036 BIP

Painting, Industrial.

COBB, Hubbard H., 1917- 667'.6
How to paint anything; the complete guide to painting and refinishing [by] Hubbard H. Cobb. New York, Macmillan [1972] x, 206 p. illus. 21 cm. [TT305.C65] 75-165566 6.95
1. Painting, Industrial. I. Title. BIP

GROSS, William F. 667'.9
Applications manual for paint and protective coatings; a guide to types of coatings, methods of surface preparation, and hand application techniques [by] William F. Gross. New York, McGraw-Hill [1970] viii, 270 p. illus. 23 cm. Bibliography: p. 253-255. [TT305.G82] 71-107290 ISBN 0-07-024970-9
1. Painting, Industrial. 2. Protective coatings. I. Title. BIP

HIGHLAND, Harold Joseph. 698
Audels painting and decorating manual. New York, T. Audel [1961] 592 p. illus. 18 cm. [TT305.H55] 62-16017
1. Painting, industrial. I. Title. II. Title: Painting and decorating manual.

HIGHLAND, Harold Joseph. 698
Audels painting and decorating manual. New York, T. Audel [1963] 600 p. illus. 19 cm. [TT305.H55 1963] 63-24358
1. Painting, Industrial. I. Title. II. Title: Painting and decorating manual.

NICHOLSON, Durward E 667.6
Painting. by Durward E. Nicholson and David T. Jones. Serial 6227A-3[--B-2. Ed. 3] Scranton, International Correspondence Schools, c1961-62. 2v. illus. 19cm. [TT305.N5] 61-45422
1. Painting, Industrial. I. Jones, David Thomas, joint author. II. International Correspondence Schools, Scranton, Pa. III. Title.

O'NEIL, Isabel. 684.1'043
The art of the painted finish for furniture & decoration; antiquing, lacquering, gilding, & the great impersonators. New York, Morrow [1971] 382 p. illus. 26 cm. "A House & garden book." Bibliography: p. [381]-382. [TT305.O64] 70-151928 19.95
1. Painting, Industrial. 2. Furniture painting. I. Title. BIP

PARRY, John P. 698
Modern technique in painting & decorating. London, New York, Longmans, Green [1950] 228 p. illus. 23 cm. [TT305.P33] 51-9409
1. Painting. Industrial. 2. House decoration. I. Title.

U.S. Bureau of Reclamation. 698.1
Paint manual for the control of paints and painting; Reclamation manual specialist supplement. Rev. reprint. Denver, 1953 [i. e. 1954] xii, 203 p. illus. 19 cm. [TT305.U5 1954] 54-61980
1. Painting, Industrial. 2. Protective coatings. I. U.S. Bureau of Reclamation. Reclamation manual. II. Title.

WARNER Electric Company, inc. Chicago. 745.59
How to "ceramize" for pleasure and profit; how the art of "ceramizing" enables you to turn hundreds of ordinary things into objects of art that can be sold at high profits or used to beautify your home. Chicago [1951] 119 l. illus. 28 cm. [TT370.W3] 51-6619
1. Painting, Industrial. 2. Glazing. 3. Handicraft. I. Title.

ZAHN, E A 698.1
Industrial finishing and common sense. With an introd. by Paul N. Gardner. Dayton, Ohio Research Press, 1958. 335 p. 21 cm. [TT305.Z33] 58-6900
1. Painting, Industrial. I. Title.

Painting, Industrial—Examinations, questions, etc.

ARCO Publishing Company, New York. 698.1'076
Painter: Federal, State, municipal jobs: all grades and kinds, by the Arco Editorial Board. [1st ed.] New York [1969] 192 p. illus. 26 cm. (Arco civil service test tutor) At head of title: The complete study guide for scoring high. [TT305.A7] 68-23046 5.00
1. Painting, Industrial—Examinations, questions, etc. 2. Civil service—U.S.—Examinations. I. Title.

Painting, Islamic.

ARNOLD, Sir Thomas Walker, 1864-1930. 759.956
Painting in Islam; a study of the place of pictorial art in Muslim culture. With a new introd. by B. W. Robinson. New York, Dover Publications [1965] xviii, 159 p. illus. 24 cm. Unabridged republication of the work first published in 1928, with a new introd. Bibliographical footnotes. [ND198.A7] 65-12451
1. Painting, Islamic. 2. Illumination of books and manuscripts. 3. Civilization, Islamic. I. Title.

ARNOLD, Thomas Walker, Sir 1864-1930 759.956
Painting in Islam: a study of the place of pictorial art in Muslim culture. New introd. by B. W. Robinson [Gloucester, Mass., P. Smith, c.1965] xviii, 159p. illus. 24cm. (Dover bk. T1310 rebound) [ND198.A7] 5.00
1. Painting, Islamic. 2. Illumination of books and manuscripts. 3. Civilization, Islamic. I. Title. BIP

ARNOLD, Thomas Walker, Sir 1864-1930 759.956
Painting in Islam; a study of the place of pictorial art in Muslim culture. New introd. by B. W. Robinson. New York, Dover [c.1965] xviii, 159p. illus. 24cm. (T1310) Unabridged repubn. of the work first pub. in 1928, with a new introd. Bibl. [ND198.A7] 65-12451 2.50 pap.,
1. Painting, Islamic. 2. Illumination of books and manuscripts. 3. Civilization, Islamic. I. Title.

BLOCHET, Edgar, 1870- 759.917'671
Musulman painting, XIIth-XVIIth century / by E. Blochet ; translated from the French by Cicely M. Binyon ; with an introd. by Sir E. Denison Ross. New York : Hacker Art Books, 1975. x, 123 p., 200 leaves of plates : ill. ; 27 cm. Reprint of the 1929 ed. published by Methuen, London. Includes index. [ND146.B5613 1975] 74-78544 ISBN 0-87817-155-X lib.bdg. : 30.00
1. Painting, Islamic. I. Title.

Painting, Italian.

BALLO, Guido, 1914- 759.5
Modern Italian painting, from futurism to the present day. [Translated from the Italian by Barbara Wall] New York, Praeger [1958] 215 p. mounted col. illus. 34 cm. (Books that matter) [ND618.B313] 58-8186
1. Painting, Italian. 2. Painters, Italian. 3. Paintings, Italian. 4. Art, Modern—20th century. I. Title.

BALLO, Guido 1914- 750.5
Modern Italian painting, from futurism to the present day. [Translated from the Italian by Barbara Wall] New York, Praeger [1958] 215p. mounted col. illus. 34cm. (Books that matter) [ND618.B313] 58-8186
1. Painting, Italian. 2. Painters, Italian. 3. Paintings, Italian. 4. Art, Modern—20th cent. I. Title.

BARASH, Moshe. 759.5
Light and color in the Italian Renaissance theory of art / Moshe Barasch. New York : New York University Press, 1978. xix, 232 p. ; 24 cm. Includes index. bibliography: p. 213-225. [ND615.B29] 77-92324 ISBN 0-8147-0995-8 : 22.50
1. Painting, Italian. 2. Painting, Renaissance—Italy. 3. Light in art. 4. Color in art. I. Title. BIP

BOLOGNA, Ferdinando 759.5
Early Italian painting; romanesque and early medieval art [Tr. from Italian. Princeton, N.J.] Van Nostrand [1964, c.1963] 227p. col. illus. 35cm. (Italian painting) Bibl. [ND613.B613] 65-7059 20.00
1. Painting. Italian. 2. Painting, Romanesque. 3. Painting, Medieval. I. Title.

BRIGANTI, Giuliano. 759.5
Italian mannerism. [Translated from the Italian by Margaret Kunzle. Princeton, N.J., Van Nostrand [c1962] 166 p. 100 col. illus. 35 cm. (Italian painting) Bibliography: p. [163]-166. [ND615.B732] 64-2678
1. Painting, Italian. 2. Mannerism (Art) I. Title.

CLARK, Kenneth McKenzie, Sir 1903- 759.5
A failure of nerve: Italian painting 1520-1535, by Sir Kenneth Clark, Oxford, Clarendon P., 1967. iv, 28 p. 16 plates 21 1/2 cm. (B 67-18648) (H. R. Bickley memorial lecture) Bibliographical footnotes. [ND615.C5] 67-110273
1. Painting, Italian. 2. Painting, Renaissance—Italy. I. Title. II. Series.

DEWALD, Ernest Theodore, 1891-1968. 759.5
Italian painting, 1200-1600 / Ernest T. DeWald. New York : Hacker Art Books, 1978, c1961. x, 613 p. : ill. ; 27 cm. Reprint of the ed. published by Holt, Rinehart, and Winston, New York. Includes indexes. Bibliography: p. 571. [ND615.D44 1978] 77-76786 ISBN 0-87817-219-X lib bdg : 40.00
1. Painting, Italian. 2. Painting, Medieval—Italy. 3. Painting, Renaissance—Italy. 4. Mannerism (Art)—Italy. I. Title.

FREEDBERG, Sydney Joseph. 759.5
Painting in Italy, 1500-1600 / S. J. Freedberg. 1st (rev.) ed. Harmondsworth : Penguin Books, 1975. 759 p. : ill. ; 21 cm. (The Pelican history of art ; PZ35) Includes index. Bibliography: p. 713-725. [ND615.F66 1975] 75-15156 12.95
1. Painting, Italian. 2. Painting, Rennaissance—Italy. 3. Mannerism (Art)—Italy. I. Title. II. Series. BIP

FREEDBERG, Sydney Joseph. 759.5
Painting in Italy, 1500 to 1600 [by] S. J. Freedberg. [Harmondsworth, Middlesex, Baltimore] Penguin Books [1971, c1970] xix, 554 p. 300 illus., col. plate. 27 cm. (The Pelican history of art) Bibliography: p. 515-527. [ND615.F66 1971] 78-27513 ISBN 0-14-056035-1 29.50
1. Painting, Italian. 2. Painting, Renaissance—Italy. 3. Mannerism (Art)—Italy. I. Title. II. Series.

HALE, John Rigby, 1923- 759.5
Italian Renaissance painting from Masaccio to Titian / John Hale. Oxford : Phaidon ;

New York : Dutton, 1977. 271 p. : chiefly ill. (some col.) ; 29 cm. Includes index. Bibliography: p. [263] [ND615.H38] 76-5355 ISBN 0-7148-1599-3 : 24.95
1. Painting, Italian. 2. Painting, Renaissance—Italy. I. Title.

ITALIAN Renaissance 759.5
painting / [text by] Keith Roberts. Oxford : Phaidon ; New York : Dutton, 1976. 16 p., 48 p. of plates : col. ill. ; 31 cm. [ND615.I79 1976] 76-1345 ISBN 0-7148-1745-7 : 6.95
1. Painting, Italian. 2. Painting, Renaissance—Italy. 3. Paintings, Italian. 4. Paintings, Renaissance—Italy. I. Roberts, Keith, 1937-

SIREN, Osvald, 1879- 759.5
Giotto and some of his followers / by Osvald Siren ; English translation by Frederic Schenck. New York : Hacker Art Books, 1975. 2 v. (x, 285 p., [110] leaves of plates) in 1 : ill. ; 27 cm. Reprint of the 1917 ed. published in 2 v. by Harvard University Press, Cambridge, Mass. Includes bibliographical references. [ND615.S5 1975] 75-189860 ISBN 0-87817-112-6 : 75.00
1. Giotto di Bondone, 1266?-1337. 2. Painting, Italian. 3. Painting, Gothic—Italy. 4. Painters—Italy. I. Title. BIP

SMART, Alastair, 1922- 759.5
The dawn of Italian painting, 1250-1400 / Alastair Smart. Ithaca, N.Y. : Cornell University Press, 1978. viii, 152 p., [64] leaves of plates : ill. (some col.) ; 25 cm. (Cornell paperbacks) Includes index. Bibliography: p. [141]-146. [ND613.S] 77-78657 ISBN 0-8014-1124-6 : 29.50
1. Painting, Italian. 2. Painting, Gothic—Italy. I. Title.

WATERHOUSE, Ellis Kirkham, 759.5
1905-
Italian baroque painting; with 200 illus. Phaidon dist. by NewYork Graphic, Greenwich, Conn., [1963, c.1962] 237p. illus. (pt. col.) 26cm. Bibl. 63-770 7.50
1. Painting. Italian. 2. Painting, Baroque. I. Title.

Painting, Italian—Addresses, essays, lectures.

BERENSON, Bernhard, 1865- 759.5
1959.
The study and criticism of Italian art : first series / by Bernhard Berenson. New York : AMS Press, 1976. xiv, 152 p., [43] leaves of plates : ill. ; 23 cm. Reprint of the 1920 ed. published by G. Bell, London. Includes bibliographical references and index. [ND611.B39 1976] 75-41028 ISBN 0-404-14758-5 : 17.50
1. Painting, Italian—Addresses, essays, lectures. I. Title.

Painting, Italian—History.

COLUMBIA University. Dept. 659.5
of Art History and Archaeology.
A home study course in the history of Italian painting, prepared under the supervision of the Dept. of Fine Arts, Columbia University. New York, Columbia University Press, 1930. 161 p. 20 cm. Includes bibliographies. [ND611.C73] 31-3073
1. Painting, Italian — Hist. I. Title.

GODFREY, Frederick M. 759.5
History of Italian painting, 1250-1800 [Vs.] 1 & 2. 2d ed., rev, enl. New York, Taplinger [c.1965] 2v. (xii, 456p.) illus. (pt. col.) map. 22cm. Bibl. 2d rev., enl. ed. of A student's guide to early Italian painting, 1250-1500 and A student's guide to later Italian painting, 1500-1800. [ND615.G54]
1. Painting—Italian—Hist. 2. Painters, Italian. I. Title.
Contents omitted. BIP

Painting, Italian—History.

CROWE, Joseph Archer, Sir, 759.5
1825-1896.
A history of painting in Italy: Umbria, Florence, and Siena, from the second to the sixteenth century, by J. A. Crowe & G. B. Cavalcaselle. Edited by Langton Douglas, assisted by S. Arthur Strong. New York, Scribner, 1903-14. St. Clair Shores, Mich., Scholarly Press, 1972. 6 v. illus. 22 cm. Vol. 3 edited by L. Douglas; v. 4 edited by L. Douglas assisted by G. de Nicola; v. 5-6 edited by T. Borenius. Contents.Contents.—v. 1. Early Christian art.—v. 2. Giotto and the Giottesques.—v. 3. The Sienese, Umbrian & north Italian schools.—v. 4. Florentine masters of the fifteenth century.—v. 5. Umbrian and Sienese masters of the fifteenth century.—v. 6. Sienese and Florentine masters of the sixteenth century. Includes bibliographical references. [ND611.C8 1972] 72-107171 ISBN 0-403-00431-4
1. Painting, Italian—History. I. Cavalcaselle, Giovanni Battista, 1820-1897, joint author. II. Title. BIP

MCCOMB, Arthur Kilgore, 759.5
1895-
The baroque painters of Italy; an introductory historical survey, by Arthur McComb. New York, Russell & Russell [1968, c1934] xii, 145 p. illus. 25 cm. Bibliography: p. [131]-140. [ND616.M3 1968] 68-10931
1. Painting, Italian—History. 2. Painters, Italian. 3. Painting, Baroque—Italy. I. Title. BIP

MAHON, Denis. 759.5
Studies in seicento art and theory. Westport, Conn., Greenwood Press [1971] ix, 351 p. illus. 24 cm. Reprint of the 1947 ed. Includes bibliographical references. [ND616.M34 1971] 73-114544 ISBN 0-8371-4743-3
1. Painting, Italian—History. 2. Painting, Modern—17th-18th centuries—Italy. I. Title. BIP

MARLE, Raimond van, 1888- 759.5
1936.
The development of the Italian schools of painting. New York, Hacker Art Books, 1970. 19 v. illus. 25 cm. Reprint of the 1923-38 ed. Includes bibliographical references. [ND611.M272] 70-116366
1. Painting, Italian—History. I. Title. BIP

MATHER, Frank Jewett, 1868- 759.5
1953.
A history of Italian painting. New York, Greenwood Press [1969, c1951] vi, 497 p. illus. 23 cm. "Revised edition." Bibliography: p. 491-492. [ND611.M4 1969] 78-95127 ISBN 8-371-25340-
1. Painting, Italian—History. I. Title. BIP

*MEISS, Millard Lazare, 750.945
1904-
Painting in Florence and Siena after the black death. New York, Harper [1964, c.1951] xiv, 194p. illus. 21cm. (Acad. Lib.; Torchbk. TB-1148) 2.25 pap.,
I. Title. BIP

OERTEL, Robert. 759.5
Early Italian painting to 1400 New York, Praeger [1968, c1966] 376 p. 137 plates (part col.) 25 cm. Translation of Die Fruhzeit der italienischen Malerei. Bibliographical references included in "Notes on the text" (p. 337-371) [ND613.O3213] 68-13133 18.50
1. Painting, Italian—History. 2. Painters, Italian. I. Title. II. Title: Italian painting to 1400.

SCHMECKEBIER, Laurence Eli, 759.5
1906-
A handbook of Italian Renaissance painting / by Laurence Schmeckebier. New York : AMS Press, [1976] p. cm. Reprint of the 1938 ed. published by Putnam, New York. Includes indexes. Bibliography: p. [ND615.S38 1976] 75-41241 ISBN 0-404-14700-3 : 23.00
1. Painting, Italian—History. 2. Painting, Renaissance—Italy—History. I. Title. BIP

Painting, Italian—Italy—Naples.

RINALDIS, Aldo de, 1882- 759.5'73
1949.
Neapolitan painting of the Seicento / by Aldo de Rinaldis. New York : Hacker Art Books, 1976. viii, 63 p., [80] leaves of plates : ill. ; 29 cm. "First published, Florence, 1929." Includes index. Bibliography: p. 57-[61] [ND621.N2R5 1976] 75-11055 ISBN 0-87817-177-0 : 40.00
1. Painting, Italian—Italy—Naples. 2. Painting, Modern—17th-18th centuries—Italy—Naples. I. Title. BIP

Painting, Italian—Italy, Northern.

RICCI, Corrado, 1858-1934. 759.5
North Italian painting of the cinquecento : Piedmont, Liguria, Lombardy, Emilia / by Corrado Ricci. New York : Hacker Art Books, 1976. viii, 68 p., 84 leaves of plates : ill. ; 29 cm. Includes index. [ND619.N67R5 1976] 75-11064 ISBN 0-87817-171-1 : 40.00
1. Painting, Italian—Italy, Northern. 2. Painting, Renaissance—Italy. I. Title. BIP

UCCELLO, Paolo di Doni, 759.5
known as, 1396or7-1475.
Paolo Uccello, complete edition, [by] John Pope-Hennessy. [2d ed.] London, New York, Phaidon [1969] 188 p. illus., plates (part col.) 31 cm. First published in 1950 under title: The complete work of Paolo Uccello. [ND623.U4P56 1969] 69-19810 25.00
I. Pope-Hennessy, John Wyndham, 1913-

UCCELLO, Paolo di Dono, 759.5
known as, 1396or7-1475
Paolo Uccello. Text by Paolo d'Ancona. [Tr. by Elizabeth Andrews] 35 plates in black and white, 47 plates in colour. New York, McGraw [1961, c.1960] 23p. 39cm. (Silvana collection) Bibl. 61-14995 20.00, bxd.
I. Ancona, Paolo d'. 1878- II. Title.

Painting, Italian—Italy—Venice—Exhibitions.

LONDON. National 759.5'31
Gallery.
The National Gallery lends : pictures from eighteenth-century Venice. [London] : Arts Council, 1976. [26] p. : ill., 2 ports. ; 21 cm. Cover title. Catalog prepared by H. Potterton. "Places of showing: Bristol City Museum & Art Gallery, 23rd October-5th December 1976, Norwich, Castle Museum, 11th December-23rd January 1977, Wolverhampton, Central Art Gallery, 31st January-13th March 1977." [ND621.V5L58 1976] 77-366202 ISBN 0-7287-0111-1 : £0.75
1. Painting, Italian—Italy—Venice—Exhibitions. 2. Painting, Modern—17th-18th centuries—Italy—Venice—Exhibitions. I. Potterton, Homan. II. Bristol, Eng. City Art Gallery. III. Norwich Castle Museum, Norwich, Eng. IV. Wolverhampton Art Gallery. V. Title. VI. Title: Pictures from eighteenth-century Venice.

Painting—Italy— Hist.

MAIURI, Amedeo, 1886- 759.5
New York] Skira [1959] 199p. mounted col. illus. 35cm. (Painting, color, history) Includes bibliographies. [ND611.M2313] 59-12843
1. Painting—Italy— Hist. 2. Paintings, Italian. I. Venturi, Lionello, 1885- II. Title.

Painting—Italy, Northern.

CROWE, Joseph Archer, Sir, 759.5
1825-1896.
A history of painting in north Italy : Venice, Padua, Vicenza, Verona, Ferrara, Milan, Friuli, Brescia, from the fourteenth to the sixteenth century / by J. A. Crowe and G. B. Cavalcaselle ; edited by Tancred Borenius. New York : AMS Press, 1976. 3 v. : ill. ; 23 cm. Reprint of the 1912 ed. published by J. Murray, London. Includes indexes. Bibliography: v. 3, p. 461-489. [ND619.N67C76 1976] 76-22574 ISBN 0-404-09290-X : 32.50
1. Painting—Italy, Northern. 2. Painting, Gothic—Italy, Northern. 3. Painting, Renaissance—Italy, Northern. I. Cavalcaselle, Giovanni Battista, 1820-1897, joint author. II. Title. BIP

Painting—Japan—History.

TODA, Kenji. 759.952
Japanese scroll painting. New York, Greenwood Press [1969] ix, 167 p. illus., map. 27 cm. Reprint of the 1935 ed. "Important works of Japanese scroll painting": p. 144-149. [ND1053.T6 1969] 69-14119
1. Painting—Japan—History. 2. Illumination of books and manuscripts, Japanese. I. Title. BIP

Painting, Japanese.

BOWIE, Henry P 759.952
On the laws of Japanese painting; an introduction to the study of the art of Japan, with prefatory remarks Iwaya Sazanami and Hirai Kinza. [New York] Dover Publications [c1951] xv, 117p. 66 plates. 25cm. [ND1050.B6 1951] 52-9794
1. Painting, Japanese. I. Title.

BRONSTEIN, Leo. 759.952
Five variations on the theme of Japanese painting. Freeport, Me., Published for Brandeis University, by the Bond Wheelwright Co. [1969] xvi, 373 p. illus. (part col.) 28 cm. Bibliographical references included in "Notes" (p. 345-362) [ND1050.B7] 65-27614
1. Painting, Japanese. 2. Harmony (Aesthetics) 3. Art—Psychology. I. Brandeis University, Waltham, Mass. II. Title. BIP

DAWSON'S Book Shop, 759.952'021'6
Los Angeles
Japanese picture scrolls and paintings; a priced and indexed catalogue. Los Angeles, 1967. 191p. illus. 22cm. Combines the firm's Catalogues 343, 346, 349, 351, 357, 366, first issued separately 1964-1967. Bibl. [ND1050.D3] 67-8094 5.00
I. Paintings, Japanese. II. Title.

DE LA SALLE, Innocent. 759.952
The illustrated guidebook of Japanese painting : from primitive art to the 18th century / Innocent De La Salle. [Albuquerque, N.M.] : American Classical College Press, [1978] p. cm. (A Promotion of the arts library book) Bibliography: p. [ND1050.D4] 78-26398 ISBN 0-89266-138-0 : 9.75 ; de luxe $27.50
1. Painting, Japanese. I. Title. BIP

IENAGA, Saburo, 1913- 759.952
Painting in the Yamato style. Translated by John M. Shields. [1st English ed.] New York, Weatherhill [1973] 162 p. illus. (part col.) 24 cm. (The Heibonsha survey of Japanese art [10]) Translation of Yamatoe. [ND1054.5.I3413] 73-3489 ISBN 0-8348-1016-6 8.95
1. Painting, Japanese. 2. Japan in art. I. Title. II. Series. BIP

MCDOWELL, Jack. 751.425
The art of Japanese brush painting [by] Jack McDowell and Takahiko Mikami. New York, Crown Publishers [1961] 127 p. illus. 26 cm. [ND1050.M25] 61-10314
1. Painting, Japanese. 2. Sumie—Technique. 3. Painting—Technique. I. Mikami, Takahiko, joint author. II. Title. III. Title: Japanese brush painting.

OI, Motoi 751.425
Step by step in Sumi-painting; v.7. [dist. Rutland, Vt. Japan Pubns.] c.1963. 24p. illus. 30cm. (Instructions in Sumi-painting, v.7) Contents.v.7. Landscapes. 3.00 pap.,
1. Painting, Japanese. 2. Painting—Technique. I. Title.

OKUDAIRA, Hideo, 1905- 751.7
Emaki; Japanese picture scrolls. [1st American ed.] Rutland, Vt., C. E. Tuttle Co. [1962] iii, 241 p. illus., plates (part fold.; part col.) 28 cm. "List of emaki and their English title (alphabetical order)" p. 206-233. [ND1053.O36 1962] 62-20798
1. Painting, Japanese. 2. Paintings, Japanese. I. Title. BIP

SAITO, Ryukyu. 751.425
Japanese ink-painting; lessons in Suiboku technique. Rutland, Vt., C. E. Tuttle Co. [1959] 96p. illus. 21x22cm. [ND1050.S3] 59-6634
1. Painting, Japanese. 2. Painting—Technique. I. Title. II. Title: Suiboku technique. BIP

SAITO, Ryukyu. 751.425
Suiboku; studies in Japanese ink painting. Translated and adapted by Charles Pomeroy. [1st ed.] Tokyo, Kodansha International; [distributed by Japan Publications Trading Co., Rutland, Vt.]

SUBJECT INDEX PAINTING, MODERN—17TH-18TH CENTURIES—NETHERLANDS—CATALOGS.

[1965] 104 p. illus. (part col.) 25 cm. Translation of Suibokuga nyumon (romanized) [ND1050.S323] 65-19188
1. Painting, Japanese. 2. Brush drawing. I. Title. II. Title: Studies in Japanese ink painting.

SECKEL, Dietrich, 1910- 759.952
Emakimono: the art of the Japanese painted hand-scroll. Foreword and photos. by Akihisa Hase. Text by Dietrich Seckel. Translated from the German by J. Maxwell Brown-John. [New York] Pantheon Books [1959] 238p. illus., col. plates. 30cm. Bibliography: p. 233-237. [ND1053.S443] 59-4934
1. Painting, Japanese. 2. Paintings, Japanese. I. Hase, Aklhisa, 1918- II. Title.

SHIMUZI, Yutaka 759.952
Nara picture books. Translated [from the Japanese] by Richard Zumwinkle. Los Angeles, Dawsons Book Shop [160] ncludes bibliographical references. 46p. illus. Part mounted, part. col. 26cm. 60-16197 4.75 pap.,
1. Painting, Japanese. 2. Illustrations of books—Japan. I. Title. BIP

SUMIYOSHI, Akeji. 759.9'52
The mystery of things: evocations of the Japanese supernatural; seventeen calligraph-paintings by Akeji Sumiyoshi. Text by Patrik Le Nestour, with the collaboration of Audie Bock. [1st ed.] Tokyo, New York, J. Weatherhill [1972] 141 p. illus. 27 cm. "Japanese title: Mono no ke." [ND1457.J36S93] 70-169151 ISBN 0-8348-0066-7 8.95
I. Le Nestour, Patrik. II. Title. III. Title: Mono no ke.

THOMPSON, Kay Morrissey. 751.425
The art and technique of sumi-e; Japanese ink-painting as taught by Ukai Uchiyama. [1st ed.] Tokyo, Rutland, Vt., C. E. Tuttle Co. [1960] 71 p. illus. 30 x 31 cm. [ND1055.T45] 60-10951
1. Uchiyama, Ukai, 1907- 2. Painting, Japanese. 3. Painting — Technique. I. Title. BIP

Painting, Japanese—History.

AKIYAMA, Terukazu, 1918- 759.952
Japanese painting. [Geneva?] Skira; [distributed by World Pub. Co., Cleveland, 1961] 216p. mounted col. illus., maps, tables. 29cm. (Treasures of Asia) Original text in French. English translation by James Emmons. 'Selected bibliography of books and articles on Japanese painting in Western languages': p. [200] [ND1050.A413] 61-15270
1. Painting, Japanese—Hist. 2. Paintings, Japanese. I. Title. II. Series. BIP

TODA, Kenji 759.952
Japanese painting. a brief history. Rutland, Vt., Tuttle [c.1965] 102p. illus. 21cm. [ND1050.T58] 65-22634 2.50 pap.,
1. Painting, Japanese—Hist. I. Title.

Painting, Japanese—History.

KONDO, Ichitaro, 1910-1961. 759.952
Japanese genre painting: the lively art of Renaissance Japan. Translated by Roy Andrew Miller. Tokyo, Rutland, Vt., C. E. Tuttle Co. [1961] 148 p. illus. (part mounted col.) 36 cm. [ND1053.K6] 60-15605
1. Painting, Japanese—History. 2. Genre painting. I. Title.

MIZUO, Hiroshi, 1930- 759.952
Edo painting: Sotatsu and Korin. Translated by John M. Shields. [1st English ed.] New York, Weatherhill [1972] 162 p. illus. (part col.) 24 cm. (The Heibonsha survey of Japanese art [18]) Translation of Sotatsu to Korin. [ND1053.5.M5913] 72-79122 ISBN 0-8348-1011-5 7.95
1. Tawaraya, Sotatsu, d. 1643. 2. Ogata, Korin, 1658-1716. 3. Hon'ami, Koetsu, 1558-1637. 4. Ogata, Kenzan, 1663-1743. 5. Painting, Japanese—History. I. Title. II. Series. BIP

Painting, Japanese—Kamakura, Momoyama periods, 1185-1600.

DOI, Tsugiyoshi, 1906- 759.952
Momoyama decorative painting / by Tsugiyoshi Doi ; translated by Edna B. Crawford. 1st English ed. New York : Weatherhill, 1977. 166 p. : ill. (some col.) : 24 cm. (The Heibonsha survey of Japanese art ; v. 14) Translation of Momoyama no shohekiga. [ND1053.4.D6413 1977] 76-44338 ISBN 0-8348-1024-7 : 12.50
1. Painting, Japanese—Kamakura, Momoyama periods, 1185-1600. 2. Screen painting, Japanese. I. Title. II. Series. BIP

Painting, Japanese—Meiji period, 1862-1912.

HARADA, Minoru, 1925- 759.952
Meiji Western painting, by Minoru Harada. Translated by Akiko Murakata. Adapted with an introd. by Bonnie F. Abiko. [1st ed.] New York, Weatherhill [1974] 143 p. illus. (part col.) 24 cm. (Arts of Japan, 6) Translation of Meiji no Yoga. Bibliography: p. [139] [ND1054.5.H3713] 73-88475 ISBN 0-8348-2708-5 7.95
1. Painting, Japanese—Meiji period, 1862-1912. 2. Painting, Japanese—Occidental influences. 3. Painters, Japanese. I. Title. Pbk. 6.95, ISBN 0-8348-2709-3. BIP

Painting—Juvenile literature.

*DEACON, Eileen. 751.4
It's fun to make pictures. Illustrated by Belinda Lyon. New York, Grosset & Dunlap [1974 c1972] 61 p. illus. 32 cm. Originally published under title My fun to make pictures book. [ND1471] 93-10688 ISBN 0-448-11634-0 3.95
1. Painting—Juvenile literature. I. Title. Lib. bdg. 4.99, ISBN 0-448-13167-6

FISHER, Leonard Everett. 751.4'5
The art experience: oil painting, 15th-19th centuries. [New York] F. Watts, 1973. 58 p. illus. (part col.) 27 cm. Discusses, with reference to specific paintings, the technique of oil painting and its development over four centuries. [ND1146.F5] 72-5406 ISBN 0-531-02609-4 5.95
1. Painting—Juvenile literature. 2. Painting—Technique—Juvenile literature. I. Title. II. Title: Oil painting, 15th-19th centuries.

Painting—Kangra, Punjab (District)

RANDHAWA, Mohindar Singh, 1909- 759.954
Kangra paintings of the Gita Govinda. Introd. by W. G. Archer. New Delhi, Natl. Mus. [dist. Honolulu, Hawaii. East-West Center Pr., 1965, c.1963] 132p. 48 illus. (20 mounted col.) 38cm. Includes 'Texts on paintings' and the orig. Sanskrit poem. Bibl. [ND1007.K35R315] SA65 25.00
1. Painting—Kangra, Punjab (District) 2. Paintings, Indic. I. Javadeva, son of Bhojadeva, Gita Govinda. II. Title.

Painting, Korean.

JANATA, Alfred. 759.9519
Korean painting. Translated by Margaret Shenfield. New York, Crown Publishers [1964] 64 p. 24 col. plates (incl. ports) 19 cm. (Movements in world art) Bibliography: p. 64. [ND1060.J313] 64-24747
1. Painting, Korean. 2. Paintings, Korean. I. Title.

Painting, Latin American—History.

MESSER, Thomas M. 759.98
The emergent decade; Latin American painters and painting in the 1960's. Text by Thomas M. Messer. Artists' profiles in text and pictures by Cornell Capa. [Ithaca, N.Y., Cornell University Press, 1966] xv, 172 p. illus. (part col.) ports. (part col.) 33 cm. "Prepared under the auspices of the Cornell University Latin American Year, 1965-1966, and the Solomon R. Guggenheim Museum." Bibliography: p. 170-172. [ND202.M4] 66-15382
1. Painting, Latin American—History. 2. Painters, Latin American. I. Capa, Cornell. II. Cornell University. III. Solomon R. Guggenheim Museum, New York. IV. Title.

Painting, Medieval.

BERENSON, Bernhard, 1865-1959. 759.02
Studies in medieval painting. New York, Da Capo Press, 1971 [c1930] xxii, 148 p. illus. 27 cm. [ND140.B4 1971] 73-153884 ISBN 0-306-70292-4
1. Painting, Medieval. 2. Illumination of books and manuscripts, Medieval. I. Title. BIP

BERENSON, Bernhard, 1865-1959. 091
Studies in medieval painting / by Bernard Berenson. New York : Da Capo Press, 1975, c1930. xxii, 148 p., [67] leaves of plates : ill ; 26 cm. (A Da Capo paperback) Reprint of the ed. published by Yale University Press, New Haven. Includes indexes. [ND140.B4 1975] 74-22036 ISBN 0-306-80010-1 pbk. : 2.95
1. Painting, Medieval. 2. Illumination of books and manuscripts, Medieval. I. Title.

BROWN, Stephanie. 755'.4
Religious painting : Christ's passion and crucifixtion in the history of art / by Stephanie Brown. New York : Mayflower Books, [1979] p. cm. [ND1430.B76] 78-24454 ISBN 0-8317-7370-7 : 12.95 ISBN 0-8317-7371-5 pbk. : 6.95
1. Jesus Christ—Passion—Art. 2. Jesus Christ—Crucifixion—Art. 3. Painting, Medieval. 4. Painting, Renaissance. 5. Painting, Baroque. I. Title. BIP

DODWELL, Charles Reginald. 759.02
Painting in Europe, 800 to 1200 [by] C. R. Dodwell. [Harmondsworth, Eng.] Penguin Books [1971] xxviii, 261 p. illus., 4 maps, 240 plates. 27 cm. (The Pelican history of art) Bibliography: p. 237-241. [ND140.D63] 70-851354 ISBN 0-14-056034-3 27.50 (U.S.)
1. Painting, Medieval. I. Title. II. Series. BIP

GRABAR, Andre, 1896- 750.902
Early medieval painting from the fourth to the eleventh century: Mosaics and mural painting, by Andre Grabar. Book illumination, by Carl Nordenfalk. Translated by Stuart Gilbert. [New York] Skira [1957] 241 p. illus. (part mounted, part col.) map. 29 cm. (The Great centuries of painting) Bibliography: p. 223-225. [ND140.G7] 57-11641
1. Painting, Medieval. 2. Paintings, Medieval. I. Nordenfalk, Carl Adam Johan, 1907- II. Title. III. Series.

MARCUCCI, Luisa 759.02
Medieval painting; a history of European painting, text by Luisa Marcucci and Emma Micheletti. [Translated from the Italian by H. E. Scott] New York, Viking Press [1960] 207p. mounted col. illus. 34cm. (A Studio book) Bibl.: p.200-201. 60-52147 25.00
1. Painting, Medieval. 2. Paintings, Medieval. I. Micheletti, Emma. II. Title.

RICKERT, Margaret Josephine, 1888- 750.942
Painting in Britain: the Middle Ages. London, Baltimore, Penguin Books [1954] xxvi, 253p. illus., maps. 27cm. (The Pelican history of art, Z5) Bibliography: p. 233-238. [ND463.R5 1954] 55-1759
1. Painting, Medieval. 2. Painting—Gt. Brit. I. Title.

Painting, Medieval—Addresses, essays, lectures.

STUDIES in late medieval and Renaissance painting in honor of Millard Meiss / edited by Irving Lavin and John Plummer. New York : New York University Press, 1977[i.e. 1976] p. cm. Contributions in English, French, or Italian. Includes bibliographical references. [ND140.S88] 75-27118 75.00 759.03
1. Meiss, Millard. 2. Painting, Medieval—Addresses, essays, lectures. 3. Painting, Renaissance—Addresses, essays, lectures. I. Meiss, Millard. II. Lavin, Irving, 1927- III. Plummer, John. BIP

Painting, Medieval—England.

†BORENIUS, Tancred, 1885-1948. 759.2
English medieval painting / by Tancred Borenius, and E. W. Tristram. New York : Hacker Art Books, 1976. 66 p., 101 leaves of plates : ill. ; 29 cm. First published in 1927. Bibliography: p. 58-61. [ND463.B5 1976] 75-11051 ISBN 0-87817-167-3 : 40.00
1. Painting, Medieval—England. 2. Painting, English. I. Tristram, Ernest William, 1882-1952, joint author. II. Title. BIP

Painting, Medieval—History.

BAZIN, Germain. 759
The avant-garde in painting. Translated from the French by Simon Watson Taylor. New York, Simon and Schuster [1969] 323 p. 265 illus. (52 col.) 32 cm. Translation of Histoire de l'avante-garde en peinture de XIIIe au XXe siecle. [ND137.B3714] 73-92199 29.95
1. Painting, Medieval—History. 2. Painting, Modern—History. I. Title.

Painting, Mexican.

HELM, MacKinley, 1896- 759.972
Modern Mexican painters. Freeport, N.Y., Books for Libraries Press [1968, c1941] xxi, 205 p. illus. 26 cm. (Essay index reprint series) [ND255.H4 1968] 68-22917
1. Painting, Mexican. 2. Painters, Mexican. I. Title. BIP

HELM, MacKinley, 1896- 759.972
Modern Mexican painters. New York, Dover Publications [1974, c1941] xxi, 205 p. 82 plates. 24 cm. Reprint of the ed. published by Harper, New York. [ND255.H4 1974] 73-91489 ISBN 0-486-22889-4 5.00 (pbk.)
1. Painting, Mexican. 2. Painting, Modern—20th century—Mexico. 3. Painters—Mexico. I. Title.

MYERS, Bernard Samuel, 1908- 759.972
Mexican painting in our time. New York, Oxford University Press, 1956. xiv, 283 p. illus. 29 cm. Bibliography: p. 269-276. [ND255.M9] 56-5166
1. Painting, Mexican. I. Title.

Painting, Modern—17th-18th centuries—Italy—Rome (City)

DIFEDERICO, Frank R. 759.5
Francesco Trevisani, eighteenth-century painter in Rome : a catalogue raisonne / by Frank R. DiFederico. Washington : Decatur House Press, c1977. xvi, 124 p., [55] leaves of plates : ill. ; 26 cm. (Art history series ; 1) Includes index. Bibliography: p. 103-108. [ND623.T924D53] 76-30904 ISBN 0-916276-02-3 : 50.00
1. Trevisani, Francesco, 1656-1746. 2. Painting, Modern—17th-18th centuries—Italy—Rome (City) 3. Painting—Italy—Rome (City) I. Title.

Painting, Modern—17th-18th centuries—Netherlands—Catalogs.

HOFSTEDE de Groot, Cornelis, 1863-1930. 016.7599492
A catalogue raisonne of the works of the most eminent Dutch painters of the seventeenth century, based on the works of John Smith / by C. Hofstede de Groot. Teaneck, N.J. : Somerset House, 1976. 10 v. in 3 ; 23 cm. Translation of Beschreibendes und kritisches Verzeichnis der Werke der hervorragendsten hollandischen Maler des XVII. Jahrhunderts. "The English translation was originally published in eight volumes by Macmillan & Co. Ltd., London, 1908-27. This reduced facsimile reprint reproduces the eight-volume English translation in two-volumes and vols. 9 & 10 of the original German edition in one volume." On spine: Catalogue of works of Dutch painters. Includes indexes. [ND646.H613 1976] 75-32592 ISBN 0-914146-37-8(v.1) : 198.00

1. Painting, Modern—17th-18th centuries—Netherlands—Catalogs. 2. Painting, Dutch—Catalogs. I. Title: A catalogue raisonne of the works of the most eminent Dutch painters ... II. Title: Catalogue of the works of Dutch painters. III. Title: Beschreibendes und kritisches Verzeichnis der Werke der hervorragendsten hollandischen Maler ...

Painting, Modern—17th-18th century.

LEVEY, Michael. 759.04
Rococo to Revolution; major trends in eighteenth-century painting. New York, Praeger [1966] 252 p. illus. (part col.) ports. (part col.) 22 cm. (Praeger world of art series) "Based on a series of lectures given at Cambridge during ... [the author's] tenure there as Slade Professor of Art." Bibliography: p. 240-241. [ND180.L4] 66-21785
1. Painting, Modern—17th-18th century. I. Title. BIP

Painting, Modern—19th century.

BELL, Clive, 1881- 759.94
Landmarks in nineteenth-century painting. Freeport, N. Y., Books for Libraries Press [1967] xiii, 214 p. illus. 22 cm. (Essay index reprint series) Reprint of the 1927 ed. [ND190.B3 1967] 67-30197
1. Painting, Modern—19th cent.—Hist. I. Title. BIP

BRION, Marcel, 1895- 709.034
Art of the romantic era; romanticism, classicism, realism. New York, Praeger [1966] 286 p. illus. (part col.) 22 cm. (Praeger world of art series) Translation of L'art romantique. Bibliography: p. 267-268. [ND457.B713] 65-20070
1. Painting, Modern—19th century. 2. Romanticism in art. 3. Art and society. I. Title.

CICHY, Bodo, 1924- 759.06
Great modern paintings. [1st American ed.] New York, Putnam [1971] 242 p. illus. (part col.) 33 cm. Translation of Moderne Malerei von Renoir bis Buffet. [ND190.C4813] 70-116154 25.00
1. Painting, Modern—19th century. 2. Painting, Modern—20th century. I. Title.

COOK, Clarence Chatham, 759.05
1828-1900.
Art and artists of our time / Clarence Cook. New York : Garland Pub., 1977 [c1888] p. cm. (The Art experience in late nineteenth-century America) Reprint the ed. published by S. Hess, New York. [ND190.C6 1977] 75-28881 ISBN 0-8240-2239-4 lib.bdg. : 175.00
1. Painting, Modern—19th century. 2. Painting, American—European influences. 3. Painters. I. Title. II. Series. BIP

MULLER, Joseph Emile. 759.06
A century of modern painting [by] Joseph-Emile Muller [and] Frank Elgar. [Rev. and enl. ed.] New York, Tudor Pub. Co. [1972] 192 p. illus. (part col.) 32 cm. Translation of Un siecle de peinture moderne, which is a revision and enlargement of La peinture moderne de Manet a Mondrian, published in 1960. [ND190.M8613] 72-85392
1. Painting, Modern—19th century. 2. Painting, Modern—20th century. I. Elgar, Frank, joint author. II. Title. BIP

MULLER, Joseph Emile. 759.06
One hundred years of modern painting [by] Joseph-Emile Muller [and] Frank Elgar. New York, Tudor Pub. Co. [1966] 191 p. illus. (part col.) 32 cm. Translation of Peinture moderne, which was first published in 1960 under title: La peinture moderne de Manet a Modrian. "Abstract painting [by] Frank Elgar": p. 132-164. [ND190.M853 1966] 66-31998
1. Painting—Modern—19th century. 2. Painting—Modern—20th century. I. Elgar, Frank. II. Title.

PRIMITIVE painters, 759.06
1835-1975 [compiled by] Roger Cardinal. New York : St. Martin's Press, 1978. p. cm. [ND189.P74] 78-19944 ISBN 0-312-64527-9 pbk. : 5.95 5.95
1. Painting, Modern—19th century. 2. Painting, Modern—20th century. 3. Primitivism in art. I. Cardinal, Roger.

RAYNAL, Maurice. 750.903
The nineteenth century; new sources of emotion from Goya to Gauguin. Translated by James Emmons. Geneva, New York, Skira [1951] 147 p. mounted col. illus. (The Great centuries of painting) Bibliography: p. 144. [ND190.R39] 51-14572
1. Painting, Modern—19th century. 2. Paintings. 3. Painters. I. Title. II. Series.

ROTHENSTEIN, John 759'.05
Knewstub Maurice, Sir, 1901-
Nineteenth-century painting; a study in conflict, by John Rothenstein. Freeport, N.Y., Books for Libraries Press [1967] x, 191 p. illus., ports. 22 cm. (Essay index reprint series) Reprint of the 1932 ed. Contents.Contents.—The historical background.—Ingres.—Constable. —Bonington.—Turner.—Rousseau.—Corot.—Delacroix.—Daumier. —Millet.—Courbet.—Impressionism.—Bibliography (p. 181-186). [ND190.R6 1967] 67-28739
1. Painting, Modern—History—19th century. 2. Impressionism (Art) I. Title. BIP

SHELDON, George William, 759.05
1843-1914.
Hours with art and artists / G. W. Sheldon. New York : Garland Pub., 1978 [c1882] 13, vii, 184 p., [12] leaves of plates : ill. ; 32 cm. (The Art experience in late nineteenth-century America) Reprint of the ed. published by D. Appleton, New York. [ND190.S44 1978] 75-28873 ISBN 0-8240-2233-5 lib.bdg. : 40.00
1. Painting, Modern—19th century. 2. Painters. I. Title. II. Series. BIP

Painting, Modern—19th century—Addresses, essays, lectures.

PAINTING from 1850 to the 709 s
present. New York : Garland Pub., 1976. p. cm. (The Garland library of the history of art ; v. 12) Includes bibliographical references. [N5300.G32 vol. 12] [ND189] 759.06 76-14075 ISBN 0-8240-2422-2 lib.bdg. : 35.00
1. Painting, Modern—19th century—Addresses, essays, lectures. 2. Painting, Modern—20th century—Addresses, essays, lectures. I. Series.
Contents omitted

Painting, Modern—19th century—Europe.

VENTURI, Lionello, 1885- 759.4
1961.
Modern painters. New York, Cooper Square Publishers, 1973. 2 v. illus. 25 cm. Vol. 2 has title: Impressionists and symbolists. Translation of Pittori moderni. Reprint of the 1947-50 ed. published by Scribner, New York. Contents.Contents.—[v. 1] Goya, Constable, David, Ingres, Delacroix, Corot, Daumier, Courbet.—v. 2. Manet, Degas, Monet, Pissarro, Sisley, Renoir, Cezanne, Seurat, Gauguin, Van Gogh, Toulouse-Lautrec. Includes bibliographies. [ND457.V415 1973] 72-97507 12.50
1. Painting, Modern—19th century—Europe. 2. Painters—Europe. I. Title. II. Title: Impressionists and symbolists. BIP

Painting, Modern—19th century—Exhibitions.

SELECTIONS from 759.94'074'017796
the Collection of Mrs. Fred Bohen : [exhibition], November 13, 1977-January 1, 1978, Des Moines Art Center. [Des Moines] : The Center, c1977. [10] p., [10] leaves of plates : ill. (some col.) ; 23 cm. [ND189.S44] 77-92746
1. Bohen, Mildred M.—Art collections—Exhibitions. 2. Painting, Modern—19th century—Exhibitions. 3. Painting, Modern—20th century—Exhibitions. I. Des Moines Art Center.

Painting, Modern—19th century—France.

DURET, Theodore, 1838- 759.4
1927.
Manet and the French Impressionists: Pissaro—Claude Monet—Sisley—Renoir—Berthe Morisot—Cezanne—Guillaumin. Translated by J. E. Crawford Flitch. Freeport, N.Y., Books for Libraries Press [1971] 256 p. illus. 27 cm. "First published 1910." "Catalogue of the paintings and pastels of Edouard Manet": p. 221-254. [ND547.5.I4D813 1971] 74-37340 ISBN 0-8369-6687-2
1. Manet, Edouard, 1832-1883. 2. Painting, Modern—19th century—France. 3. Impressionism (Art)—France. I. Title.

Painting, Modern—19th century—History.

LEWISOHN, Sam Adolph, 759.05
1884-
Painters and personality; a collector's view of modern art, by Sam A. Lewisohn. Rev. ed. Freeport, N.Y., Books for Libraries Press [1971, c1948] xxiv, 323 p. illus. 24 cm. [ND190.L55 1971] 70-152188 ISBN 0-8369-2238-7
1. Painting, Modern—19th century—History. 2. Painting, Modern—20th century—History. 3. Painters. I. Title. BIP

PICON, Gaetan. 759.05
Modern painting, from 1800 to the present / by Gaeton [i.e. Gaetan] Picon ; [translated from the French by Henry A. La Farge]. New York : Newsweek Books, c1974. 192 p. : ill. (some col.) ; 27 cm. (World of culture) Includes index. Bibliography: p. 185. [ND189.P513] 74-83889 ISBN 0-88225-113-9. ISBN 0-88225-114-7 de luxe
1. Painting, Modern—19th century—History. 2. Painting, Modern—20th century—History. I. Title.

Painting, Modern—19th century—Scotland—Glasgow.

MARTIN, David, 759.9414'43 B
artist.
The Glasgow School of painting / David Martin. Edinburgh : P. Harris, 1976. [7], 72 p., [12] p. of plates : ill., ports. ; 16 cm. Reprint of the 1897 ed. published by G. Bell & Sons, London. [ND481.G5M4 1976] 77-375308 ISBN 0-904505-15-4 : £2.00
1. Glasgow school of painting. 2. Painting, Modern—19th century—Scotland—Glasgow. 3. Painters—Scotland—Biography. I. Title.

Painting, Modern—19th century—Spain.

LIPSCHUTZ, Ilse Hempel. 759.6
Spanish paintings and the French Romantics. Cambridge, Harvard University Press, 1972. xvii, 407 p. illus. 24 cm. (Harvard studies in Romance languages, v. 32) Bibliography: p. 327-358. [ND807.L56] 74-172322 ISBN 0-674-83110-1
1. Painting, Modern—19th century—Spain. 2. Painting, Spanish. 3. French literature—19th century—History and criticism. 4. Romanticism—France. I. Title. II. Series.

Painting, Modern—19th century—United States.

BRECKENRIDGE, Hugh Henry, 759.13
1870-1937.
The paintings of Hugh H. Breckenridge, 1870-1927. [Dallas, Valley House Gallery, c1967] 61 p. illus. (part col.), ports. 24 cm. Stamped on t.p.: Worldwide Books, inc., New York. Catalog of an exhibition held Nov., 1967, at the Valley House Gallery, Dallas. [ND237.B82A57] 68-1234
1. Valley House Gallery. II. Title.

EDMONDSON, Edward, 1830- 709 s
1884.
The paintings of Edward Edmondson (1830-1884). By Bruce H. Evans. [Dayton, Ohio, Dayton Art Institute, 1972] 36 p. illus. 23 cm. (Dayton Art Institute bulletin, v. 30, no. 2) "Special exhibition issue, January 1972." "Dayton Art Institute, January 8-February 13, 1972." Includes bibliographical references. [N559.D3A25 vol. 30, no. 2] [ND237.E395] 759.13 72-198136
I. Evans, Bruce H. II. Dayton Art Institute, Dayton, Ohio. III. Title. IV. Series: Dayton Art Institute, Dayton, Ohio. Bulletin, v. 30, no. 2

PRENDERGAST, Maurice 759.13
Brazil, 1859-1924.
Paintings and water colors; [catalogue] A loan exhibition, November 1 through 26, 1966. New York, Knoedler Galleries [1966] [13] p., [58] p. of illus. 28 cm. [ND237.P85K55] 75-992
I. Knoedler (M.) and Company, inc.

WILMERDING, John. 759.13
Painting in nineteenth-century America. New York, H. N. Abrams [1973] p. Bibliography: p. [ND210.W528] 72-4404 ISBN 0-8109-0348-2
1. Painting, Modern—19th century—United States. 2. Painting, American. I. Title.

Painting, Modern—20th century.

GALLOWAY, John Crozier. 709.041
Origins of modern art, 1905-1914, by John Galloway. New York, McGraw-Hill [1965] 47 p. illus., 24 col. slides (in pockets) 25 cm. (Color slide program of the world's art) [N6490.G27] 65-26478
1. Painting, Modern—20th century. 2. Paintings. I. Title. II. Series. BIP

HAFTMANN, Werner. 759.06
Painting in the twentieth century. [Newly designed and expanded ed.] New York, Praeger [1965] 2 v. illus. (part col.) 24 cm. Contents.Contents.—1. An analysis of the artists and their work. Translated by R. Manheim.—2. A pictorial survey. Translated by J. Seligman. [ND195.H323 1965] 65-25066
1. Painting, Modern—20th century. 2. Painters. I. Title.

KULTERMANN, Udo. 759.06
New painting / Udo Kultermann ; translated from the German Neue Formen des Bildes by Wesley V. Blomster. Boulder, Colo. : Westview Press, [1977] p. cm. Translated from the 2d German ed., 1975. Includes index. Bibliography: p. [ND195.K8413 1977] 76-26656 ISBN 0-89158-622-9 lib.bdg. : 38.75
1. Painting, Modern—20th century. I. Title. BIP

MUNSTERBERG, Hugo, 1916- 759.06
Twentieth century painting. Port Washington, N.Y., Kennikat Press [1970, c1951] xiii, 102 p. illus. 23 cm. [ND195.M8 1970] 70-93065
1. Painting, Modern—20th century. I. Title.

READ, Herbert Edward, 759.06
Sir, 1893-1968.
A concise history of modern painting. New York, Praeger [1959] 376 p. illus. (part col.) 22 cm. (Books that matter) "Text references": p. 338-345. Bibliography: p. 346-348. [ND195.R4] 59-8136
1. Painting, Modern—20th century.

READ, Herbert Edward, 701'.8
Sir, 1893-1968.
A concise history of modern painting. New York, Praeger [1966] 378 p. illus. (part col.) 22 cm. (Praeger world of art series) Bibliography: p. 347-349. [ND195.R4 1966] 68-9164 7.50
1. Painting, Modern—20th century. I. Title. II. Title: Modern painting.

READ, Herbert Edward, 759.06
Sir, 1893-1968.
A concise history of modern painting / Herbert Read. Enl. and updated 3d ed. / pref. by Benedict Read ; additional material by Caroline Tisdall and William Faver. New York : Praeger, 1975, c1974. 392 p. : ill. (some col.) ; 21 cm. (Praeger world of art paperbacks) Includes index. Bibliography: p. 374-392. [ND195.R4 1975] 74-15682 11.50. ISBN 0-275-71730-5 pbk. : 6.95
1. Painting, Modern—20th century. I. Title. II. Title: Modern painting.

SOBY, James Thrall, 1906- 759.06
Contemporary painters. Reprint ed. New York, Published for the Museum of Modern Art by Arno Press, 1966 [c1948] 151 p. illus. 27 cm. [ND195.S63 1966] 66-26119
1. Painting, Modern—20th century. I. New York (City) Museum of Modern Art. II. Title. BIP

SUBJECT INDEX PAINTING—NEW YORK (CITY)

WADDINGTON, Conrad Hal, 1905- 759.06
Behind appearance; a study of the relations between painting and the natural sciences in this century [by] C. H. Waddington. [1st ed.] Cambridge, Mass., MIT Press [1970, c1969] x, 256 p. illus., col. plates. 31 cm. Includes bibliographical references. [ND195.W27 1970] 77-97772 25.00
1. Painting, Modern—20th century. 2. Art and science. I. Title.

WOLFE, Tom. 759'.06
The painted word / Tom Wolfe. New York : Farrar, Straus and Giroux, 1975. 121 p. : ill. ; 21 cm. [ND195.W64 1975] 75-8978 ISBN 0-374-22878-7 : 9.95
1. Painting, Modern—20th century. 2. Painting—Psychological aspects. I. Title.
BIP

Painting, Modern—20th century—Australia.

GLEESON, James. 759.99'4
Modern painters 1931-1970. [Melbourne] Lansdowne [1971] 128 p. col. illus. 26 cm. (Australian painting studio series) (Australian art library) Bibliography: p. 128. [ND1100.G62] 71-883627 ISBN 0-7018-0174-3 4.50
1. Painting, Modern—20th century—Australia. 2. Painting, Australian. 3. Painters, Australian. I. Title.

Painting, Modern—20th century—Exhibitions.

IAN McGugan and Ed Perera 759.06
: paintings : [catalogue of an exhibition held] 9 October to 9 November 1976 [at] Woodlands Art Gallery. London : London Borough of Greenwich, [1976] [11] p. : ill. ; 21 cm. "Ed Perera": [1] leaf inserted. [ND195.I2] 77-369106 ISBN 0-9504033-5-0
1. McGugan, Ian, 1932- 2. Perera, Ed, 1936- 3. Painting, Modern—20th century—Exhibitions. I. McGugan, Ian, 1932- II. Perera, Ed, 1936- III. Woodlands Art Gallery.

OBREGON, Alejandro, 1920- 759.9861
Alejandro Obregon. A loan exhibition of paintings from 1952 to the present. April 30-June 14, 1970. New York, Center for Inter-American Relations, Art Gallery [1970] [20] p. illus. 22 cm. Bibliography: p. [17] [ND813.O2A42] 71-21947
I. Center for Inter-American Relations. Art Gallery.

Painting, Modern—20th century—Germany.

MUNICH. Stadtische Galerie. 759.3'074'0336
The Blue Rider, with a catalog of the works by Kandinsky, Klee, Macke, Marc, and other Blue Rider artists in the Municipal Gallery, Munich [by] Hans K. Roethel. New York, Praeger Publishers [1971] 174 p. illus. (part col.) 29 cm. Translation of Der blaue Reiter. Includes bibliographical references. [ND568.5.E9M813] 75-148140 17.50
1. Blauer Reiter. 2. Painting, Modern—20th century—Germany. 3. Paintings, Modern—20th century—Exhibitions. I. Roethal, Hans Konrad, 1909-

Painting, Modern—20th century—History.

WASSERMAN, Burton. 759.06
Modern painting: the movements, the artists, their work. Worcester, Mass., Davis Publications [1970] 128 p. illus. (part col.) 27 cm. [ND195.W29] 72-108885 ISBN 0-87192-033-6
1. Painting, Modern—20th century—History. I. Title.

Painting, Modern—20th century—United States.

TEXANA, 1918-. 759.13
People of the world. Painted by Texana. Peuple du monde. Peintures de Taxana. Los Angeles [1965] 2 portfolios. illus., 28 col. plates. 37 cm. [ND237.T4A54] 66-4788
I. Title.

YOUNG, Mahonri Sharp, 1911- 759.06
Early American moderns; painters of the Stieglitz Group. New York, Watson-Guptill Publications [1974] 159 p. illus. (part col.) 32 cm. Bibliography: p. 156-157. [ND212.5.S75Y67] 74-9909 ISBN 0-8230-1598-X 24.50
1. Stieglitz Group. 2. Stieglitz, Alfred, 1864-1946—Art patronage. 3. Painting, Modern—20th century—United States. I. Title.

Painting, Modern—20th century—United States—Exhibitions.

BLUME, Peter, 1906- 759.13
Peter Blume. [Hartford, Printed by Connecticut Printers, 1968] 1 v. (chiefly illus. (part col.)) 28 cm. Catalogue of an exhibition, Feb. 20-Mar. 9, 1968, Kennedy Galleries, inc., New York, with introductory text by Frank Getlein. [ND237.B67G4] 68-1734
I. Getlein, Frank. II. Kennedy Galleries, inc., New York.

BOWMAN, Richard, 1918- 759.13
Paintings and reflections, 1943-1961. Published on the occasion of an exhibition at the San Francisco Museum of Art, Nov. 3d through Dec. 3d, 1961. San Francisco [c1961] unpaged. illus. 26cm. [ND237.B737A53] 62-5706
I. San Francisco. Museum of Art. II. Title.

CADMUS, Paul, 1904- 709'.73
Paul Cadmus; prints and drawings, 1922-1967. [Text by Una E. Johnson. Research by Jo Miller. Brooklyn, Brooklyn Museum, 1968] 66 p. illus. 24 cm. (American graphic artists of the twentieth century. Monograph no. 6) Bibliography: p. 64-65. [NE539.C25A54] 68-17379
I. Johnson, Una E. II. Brooklyn Institute of Arts and Sciences. Museum. III. Title. IV. Series.

CARSMAN, Jon, 1944- 759.13
Jon Carsman, paintings & watercolors : February, 1979. New York : A. Crispo Gallery, c1979. [58] p. : ill. (some col.) ; 23 x 27 cm. [ND237.C286A4 1979] 79-63309 10.00
1. Carsman, Jon, 1944- —Exhibitions. I. Andrew Crispo Gallery. II. Title.
Publisher's address: 41 E. 57th ST. New York, NY 10022

DORAZIO, Piero, 1927- 759.5
Piero Dorazio: paintings 1965-1968. New York, Marlborough-Gerson Gallery, 1969. [28] p. illus. (part col.), port. 30 cm. Catalogue of an exhibition held at the Marlborough-Gerson Gallery in New York City in February, 1969. "Cat. no. 243." [ND623.D64M3] 70-297781
I. Marlborough-Gerson Gallery.

FRIED, Michael. 759.13'074'01444
Three American painters, Kenneth Noland, Jules Olitski, Frank Stella : Fogg Art Museum, 21 April-30 May 1965. New York : Garland Pub. Co., [1978] c1965. 59 p., [10] leaves of plates : ill. ; 22 cm. Exhibition held also at the Pasadena Art Museum, 6 July-3 Aug. 1965. Includes bibliographical references. [ND212.F67 1978] 77-2760 ISBN 0-8240-1957-1 : 15.00
1. Noland, Kenneth, 1924- 2. Olitski, Jules, 1922- 3. Stella, Frank. 4. Painting, Modern—20th century—United States—Exhibitions. I. Harvard University. William Hayes Fogg Art Museum. II. Pasadena, Calif. Art Museum. III. Title.

HANSEGGER, John Konstantin, 1908- 759.13
Paintings, 1949-1960. By Martica Sawin New York, Arts, inc. [1962] 118 p. illus. (part col.) port. 29 cm. [Contemporary artists series) A Golden Griffin book. [ND853.H3S3] 61-18346
I. Sawin, Martica. II. Title. III. Series.

SARKISIAN, Paul, 1928- 759.13
Paul Sarkisian; an exhibition of six paintings, October 23 through November 15, 1970, the Santa Barbara Museum of Art. [Santa Barbara, Calif., Santa Barbara Museum of Art] 1970. [13] p. (chiefly illus.) 23 x 28 cm. [ND237.S32A56] 71-145428
I. Santa Barbara, Calif. Museum of Art. II. Title.

SOLOMON R. Guggenheim Museum, New York. 759.38
Fangor. [New York, Solomon R. Guggenheim Foundation, 1970] 33 p. illus. (part col.), port. 26 cm. "Margit Rowell, ... in concert with the artist, selected the works, mounted the show, and prepared this catalogue." Catalog of Exhibition 70/7, of W. Fangor's works, held in 1970. Bibliography: p. 33. [ND955.P63S64] 70-142939
I. Fangor, Wojciech, 1922- II. Rowell, Margit.

Painting, Modern—Netherlands.

SLIVE, Seymour, 1920- 759.9492
Dutch painting. New York, Abrams [1970] 24 p. illus. (part col.) 33 cm. (The Library great painters. Portfolio ed.) [ND644.S55 1970] 69-14744
1. Painting, Modern—Netherlands. 2. Paintings, Dutch. I. Title.

Painting, Modern—United States.

NORELLI, Martina R. 759.06
American wildlife painting, 1720-1920 / Martina R. Norelli. New York : Watson-Guptill, 1975. p. cm. Includes index. Bibliography: p. [ND1382.N67] 75-15856 ISBN 0-8230-0217-9 : 27.50
1. Painting, Modern—United States. 2. Painting, American. 3. Painters, American. 4. Birds in art. 5. Animals in art. I. Title.

Painting, Mogul.

BROWN, Percy, 1872-1955. 759.954
Indian painting under the Mughals A.D. 1550 to A.D. 1750 / by Percy Brown. New York : Hacker Art Books, 1975. 204 p., [77] leaves of plates : ill. (some col.) ; 32 cm. Includes index. Bibliography: p. 200-201. [ND1002.B7 1975] 73-86328 ISBN 0-87817-147-9 lib.bdg. : 50.00
1. Painting, Mogul. I. Title.

Painting, Mohammedan.

ETTINGHAUSEN, Richard. 759.956
Arab painting. Skira [dist. Cleveland, World, c.1962] 208p. mounted illus. (pt. col.) map. 29cm. (Treasures of Asia) Bibl. 62-10990 22.50, bxd.
1. Painting, Mohammedan. 2. Illusmination of books and manuscripts, Mohammedan. I. Title. II. Series.
BIP

Painting, Mongolian.

IPSIROGLU, Mazhar Sevket 759.517
Painting and culture of the Mongols [by] M. S. Ipsiroglu. [Tr. from German by E. D. Phillips] New York, Abrams [1966] 112p. illus. (pt. col.), map. 27 cm. Tr. of Malerei der Mongolen. Bibl. [ND1046.M61613] 66-26608 12.50
1. Painting, Mongolian. 2. Illumination of books and manuscripts. Mongolian. I. Title.

Painting—Netherlands.

KONINGSBERGER, Hans. 759.9492
Modern Dutch painting, an introduction. New York, Netherlands Information Service [195-] 61p. illus. 26cm. [ND648.K65] 55-2584
1. Painting—Netherlands. 2. Painters, Dutch. I. Title.

KONINGSBERGER, Hans. 759.9492
Modern Dutch painting, an introduction. New York, Netherlands Information Service [195-] 61p. illus. 26cm. [ND648.K65] 55-2584
1. Painting—Netherlands. 2. Painters, Dutch. I. Title.

Painting—Netherlands—History.

LEYMARIE, Jean. 759.9492
Dutch painting. [Translated by Stuart Gilbert. Geneva, New York] Skira [1956] 213p. mounted col. illus. 34cm. (Painting, color, history) Bibliography: p.201-204. [ND644.L42] 56-9861
1. Painting—Netherlands—Hist. 2. Paintings, Dutch. I. Title.

PANOFSKY, Erwin, 1892-1968. 759.9492
Early Netherlandish painting, its origins and character. Cambridge, Harvard University Press, 1953. 2 v. plates. 32 cm. Contents.Contents.—v. 1. Text.—v. 2. Plates. Bibliography: v. 1, p. [513]-535. [ND635.P35] 52-5402
1. Painting—Netherlands—History. 2. Paintings, Dutch. I. Title.

Painting—New England.

LITTLE, Ning Fletcher 759.14
Country art in New England, 1790--1840 Sturbridge, Mass., Old Sturbridge Village [c.1960] 32p. illus. 22cm. (Old Strubridge Village booklet series, 11) 60-3831 .75 pap.,
1. Painting—New England. 2. Folk art—New England. I. Title.

Painting—New York (City)

LOS Angeles Co., Calif. Museum of Art, Los Angeles. 759.147'1'074019494
New York school, the first generation: paintings of the 1940s and 1950s. Foreword by Maurice Tuchman. Greenwich, Conn., New York Graphic Society [1971] 228 p. illus. (part col.) 22 cm. "A revised edition of the original Los Angeles County Museum catalog of an exhibition during July-August 1965." Bibliography: p. [159]-220. [ND235.N45L65 1971] 77-86265 ISBN 0-8212-0389-4 8.95
1. Painting—New York (City) 2. Paintings, American—Exhibitions. 3. New York School. I. Tuchman, Maurice. II. Title.

LOS Angeles Co., Calif. Museum of Art, Los Angeles. 759.1471074019494
New York school, the first generation: paintings of the 1940s and 1950s ... With statements by the artists and critics, and a bibliography. Edited by Maurice Tuchman. [Los Angeles, 1965?] 253 p. plates (part col.) 23 cm. "A catalogue of the exhibition ... July 16 to August 1, 1965, Lytton Gallery ... organized with the cooperation of the Contemporary Art Council of the Los Angeles County Museum of Art." Erratum slip inserted. Bibliography: p. 210-252. [ND235N45L65] 65-22605
1. Painting — New York (City) 2. Paintings, American — Exhibitions. 3. Painters, American. I. Tuchman, Maurice, ed. II. Title.

LOS Angeles County Museum, Los Angeles 759.1471074019494
New York school, the first generation: paintings of the 1940s and 1950s. With statements by the artists and critics. and a bibliography. Ed. by Maurice Tuchman. [Los Angeles, 1965?] 253p. plates (pt. col.) 23cm. 'A catalogue of the exhibition . . . July 16 to Aug. 1, 1965, Lytton Galley . . . org. with the cooperation of the Contemporary Art Council of the Los Angeles County Mus. of Art.' Erratum slip inserted. Bibl. [ND235.N45L65] 65-22605 10.00
1. Painting—New York (City) 2. Painting. American. 3. Painters. American. 4. Paintings—Exhibitions. I. Tuchman, Maurice. ed. II. Title.
Distributed in 1966 by New York Graphic of Greenwich, Conn.

NEW work: New York. 759.1471'074'01471
Selected by Richard Lanier. [New York, American Federation of Arts, 1970] 1 v. (unpaged) illus. 21 cm. Catalog of the exhibition circulated 1970-71 by the American Federation of Arts. "AFA exhibition number 70-10." [ND235.N45N4] 70-135037
1. Painting—New York (City) 2. Painting, American—Exhibitions. I. Lanier, Richard. II. American Federation of Arts.

Painting—New York (City)—Catalogs.

NEW York. Museum of Modern Art. 709'.04'07401471
Painting and sculpture in the Museum of Modern Art, 1929-1967 / [compiled by] Alfred H. Barr, Jr. New York : The Museum, c1977. xiv, 657 p. : chiefly ill. ; 29 cm. Includes indexes. Bibliography: p. 611-612. [N620.M9A62] 68-54923 ISBN 0-87070-540-7 : 40.00
1. Painting—New York (City)—Catalogs. 2. Sculpture—New York (City)—Catalogs. I. Barr, Alfred Hamilton, 1902- II. Title. BIP

Painting, New Zealand—History.

DOCKING, Gilbert Charles, 1919- 759.9931
Two hundred years of New Zealand painting [by] Gil Docking. [Melbourne] Lansdowne [1971] 212 p. illus., 145 plates (part col.) 32 cm. Includes bibliographical references. [ND1106.D63] 72-186259 ISBN 0-7018-0365-7 27.50
1. Painting, New Zealand—History. I. Title. BIP

Painting—Old Lyme, Conn.

CONNECTICUT College for Women, New London 759.1465
The art colony at Old Lyme, 1900-1935. Ed. by Jane Hayward William Ashby McCloy. Introd. by Robin Richman. An exhibition presented by the members of the mus. seminar of Connecticut Coll. in cooperation with the Lyman Allyn Mus., New London, Connecticut, Feb. 5th to March 13th, 1966. [New London, Conn., Lyman Allyn Mus., 1966] 67p. illus. 27cm. Bibl. [ND235.O4C6] 66-5587 1.50 pap.,
1. Painting—Old Lyme, Conn. 2. Paintings. American—Exhibitions. I. Hayward, Jane, ed. II. McCloy. William Ashby, ed. III. Lyman Allyn Museum, New London, Conn. IV. Title. V. Title: Old Lyme.

HEMING, Arthur Henry Howard, 1870-1940. 704'.361
Miss Florence and the artists of Old Lyme. Illustrated by James Stevenson. Foreword by Nelson C. White. Essex, Conn., Pequot Press [1971] 69 p. illus., facsims., col. port. 28 cm. [ND235.O4H4] 78-124471
1. Griswold, Florence, 1850-1937. 2. Painting—Old Lyme, Conn. I. Title. BIP

Painting, Oriental.

EMERSON, James Christopher, 1913- 755'.5
The life of Christ in the conception & expression of Chinese and oriental artists : the mystery of Christ as conceived by the oriental mind / James Christopher Emerson. Albuquerque, N.M. : Gloucester Art Press, [1978] p. cm. Bibliography: p. [N8050.E45] 78-16581 ISBN 0-930582-13-6 : 39.75
1. Jesus Christ—Art. 2. Painting, Oriental. I. Title.
Publisher's address : P.O. Box 4526, Albuquerque, NM 87106 BIP

WANG. CHI-YUAN, 1895- 751.4
Oriental brushwork, by Wang Chi-yuan with Ruth Martin. New York, Pitman [c.1966] 95p. illus., ports. 23cm. [ND1260.W24] 64-20399 3.95
1. Painting, Oriental. 2. Painting—Technique. I. Martin, Ruth. II. Title. BIP

WANG, Chi-yuan, 1895- 751.425
Oriental brushwork, by Wang Chi-yuan, with Ruth Martin. New York, Pitman Pub. Corp. [1966] 95 p. illus., ports. 23 cm. [ND1260.W24 1966] 66-5595
1. Painting, Oriental. 2. Painting—Technique. I. Martin, Ruth. II. Title.

WANG, Chi-yuan, 1895- 751.4'25
Oriental brushwork, by Wang Chi-yuan with Ruth Martin. New York, Pitman Pub. Corp. [1968] 95 p. illus., ports. 23 cm. [ND1260.W24 1968] 68-4770
1. Painting, Oriental. 2. Painting—Technique. I. Martin, Ruth. II. Title.

WANG, Chi-yuan, 1895- 701
Oriental brushwork, by Wang Chi-yuan with Ruth Martin. New York, Pitman Pub. Corp. [1964] 46 p. illus., ports. 20 x 26 cm. (Pitman $1.00 art books, 51) [ND1260.W24] 64-20399
1. Painting, Oriental. 2. Painting — Technique. I. Martin, Ruth. II. Title.

Painting—Outlines, syllabl, etc.

BALDWIN, Doris E 759
A list of famous paintings of the masters old and new, compiled by Doris E. Baldwin and Bernice De Somer. [Chicago] Chicago playing Card Collectors, c1958. 1v. 30cm. [ND55.B3] 58-30026
1. Painting—Outlines, syllabl, etc. I. De Somer, Bernice, joint author. II. Title. III. Title: Famous paintings of the masters old and new.

Painting—Paris.

DORIVAL, Bernard. 759.4
The School of Paris in the Musee d'art moderne. [translated from the French by Cornelia Brookfield and Ellen Hart] New York, Abrams [1962] 316 p. illus. (part col.) 22 cm. [ND550.D613] 62-14853
1. Painting—Paris. 2. Paintings. I. Paris. Musee national d'art moderne. II. Title.

HYSLOP, Francis Edwin, 1909- 759.9493
Henri Evenepoel : Belgian painter in Paris, 1892-1899 / Francis E. Hyslop. University Park : Pennsylvania State University Press, [1975] x, 145 p. : ill. ; 24 cm. Bibliography: p. 145. [ND673.E8H974] 75-2227 ISBN 0-271-01191-2 : 14.50
1. Evenepoel, Henri Jacques Edouard, 1872-1899. 2. Painting—Paris. I. Title. BIP

NACENTA, Raymond. 759.4
School of Paris; the painters and the artistic climate of Paris since 1910. Greenwich, Conn., New York Graphic Society [1960] 366p. illus. (part mounted col.) ports. 103 col. plates. 32cm. [ND550.N3 1960] 59-9329
1. Painting—Paris. 2. Art—Paris. 3. Paintings. 4. Painters. I. Title.

NEW York, Museum of Modern Art. 759.4
The School of Paris; paintings from the Florene May Schoenborn and Samuel A. Marx collection.Pref. by Alfred H. Barr, Jr. Introd. by James Thrall Solby. Notes by Lucy R. Lippard. New York, Museum of Modern Art; distributed by Doubleday, Garden City, N.Y. [1965] 55 p. illus. (part col.) 24 cm. Catalog of an exhibition arranged by the Museum of Modern Art and shown there and at four other museums, Nov. 1, 1965-Oct. 2, 1966. [ND550.N46] 65-25727
1. Painting — Paris. 2. Paintings — Private collections. 3. Paintings — Exhibitions. I. Schoenborn, Florene May. II. Marx, Samuel A. III. Lippard, Lucy R. IV. Title.

Painting—Psychological aspects.

PARIS, Jean, 1921- 750'.117
Painting and linguistics : two lectures given at the College of Fine Arts in Carnegie-Mellon University on March 12 and 19, 1974 / Jean Paris. Pittsburgh : College of Fine Arts, Carnegie-Mellon University, [1975] 72 p. : ill. ; 23 cm. (Praxis/poetics series ; no. 1) Includes bibliographical references. [ND1140.P313] 75-310050
1. Mary, Virgin—Art. 2. Painting—Psychological aspects. 3. Visual perception. I. Title. II. Series.

Painting, Renaissance.

BAXANDALL, Michael. 750'.1
Giotto and the orators: humanist observers of painting in Italy and the discovery of pictorial composition, 1350-1450. Oxford, Clarendon Press, 1971. xii, 185 p., 16 plates; illus., facsim. 25 cm. (Oxford-Warburg studies) Includes texts in Greek and Latin. Bibliography: p. [178]-180. [ND170.B37] 79-851462 ISBN 0-19-817178-1 £3.75
1. Giotto di Bondone, 1266?-1337. 2. Painting, Renaissance. 3. Composition (Art) I. Title. BIP

*EYCK, Jan van, c.1389-1441 759.03
The adoration of the Mystic Lamb. Text by Valentin Denis. Tr. by Michael Langley. Milano, Arti Grafiche Ricordi [dist. Palisade, N.J., Meldona, Inc., Box 794.01965] 95p. 25 col. plates (pt. mounted) 41 cm. 150.00 bxd.,
1. Painting, Renaissance. 2. Painting—Flemish. I. Denis, Valentin. II. Langley, Michael., tr. III. Title.

HURLL, Estelle May, 1863-1924. 704.948'55
The Madonna in art. Boston, L. C. Page, 1898. Detroit, Gale Research Co., 1974. p. cm. Original ed. issued in series: Art lovers' series. Bibliography: p. [N8070.H9 1974] 78-159857 ISBN 0-8103-4083-6
1. Mary, Virgin—Art. 2. Painting, Renaissance. I. Title. II. Series: Art lovers' series.

Painting, Renaissance—Addresses, essays, lectures.

MEISS, Millard. 759.03
The painter's choice : problems in the interpretation of Renaissance art / Millard Meiss. 1st ed. New York : Harper & Row, c1976. p. cm. (Icon editions) Includes index. [ND170.M4 1976] 75-12290 ISBN 0-06-435657-4 : 15.00. ISBN 0-06-430068-4 pbk. : 6.95
1. Painting, Renaissance—Addresses, essays, lectures. I. Title. BIP

Painting, Renaissance—Europe.

CUTTLER, Charles D. 759.9'4
Northern painting from Pucelle to Bruegel: fourteenth, fifteenth, and sixteenth centuries [by] Charles D. Cuttler. New York, Holt, Rinehart and Winston [1968] xii, 500 p. illus. (part col.) 29 cm. Bibliography: p. 486-491. [ND454.C8] 68-20103 17.95
1. Painting, Renaissance—Europe. 2. Painting—Europe. I. Title.

Painting, Renaissance—Germany.

ROSE, Patricia, 1929- 759.3
Wolf Huber studies : aspects of Renaissance thought and practice in Danube School painting / Patricia Rose. New York : Garland Pub., 1977. iii, 540 p. : ill. ; 21 cm. (Outstanding dissertations in the fine arts) Reprint of the author's thesis, Columbia University, 1973. Bibliography: p. 524-540. [ND588.H8R67 1977] 76-23711 ISBN 0-8240-2725-6 : 45.00
1. Huber, Wolfgang, 1485 (ca.)-1553. 2. Donauschule. 3. Painting, Renaissance—Germany. I. Title. II. Series. BIP

Painting, Renaissance—Hist.

RUSSOLI, Franco 759.03
Renaissance painting. [Tr. by Angus Malcom] New York, Viking [1963, c.1962] 40, 11p. illus. (pt. col.) 20cm. (Compass bks., CA8. Compass hist. of art) 62-12141 2.25 pap.,
1. Painting, Renaissance—Hist. I. Title.

Painting, Renaissance—Italy.

BAXANDALL, Michael. 759.5
Painting and experience in fifteenth century Italy; a primer in the social history of pictorial style. Oxford, Clarendon Press, [1973 c1972] viii, 165 p. illus. (part col.) 21 cm. Bibliography: p. 155-161. [ND615.B32] 73-156125 ISBN 0-19-817321-0 11.95
1. Painting, Renaissance—Italy. 2. Painting, Italian—History. 3. Painting—Psychological aspects. 4. Italy—History—15th century—Pictorial works. I. Title.
Distributed by Oxford University Press N.Y.

FAHY, Everett. 759.5
Some followers of Domenico Ghirlandajo / Everett Fahy. New York : Garland, 1976. 230 p., [22] leaves of plates : ill. ; 21 cm. (Outstanding dissertations in the fine arts) Originally presented as the author's thesis, Harvard, 1968. Includes bibliographies. [ND615.F34 1976] 75-23790 ISBN 0-8240-1986-5 lib.bdg. : 27.50
1. Ghirlandaio, Domenico Bigordi, known as, 1449-1494—Influence. 2. Painting, Renaissance—Italy. 3. Painting, Italian. 4. Painters—Italy. I. Title. II. Series. BIP

UCCELLO, Paolo di Dono, known as, 1396 or 7-1475. 759.5
The complete work of Paolo Uccello, by John Pope-Hennessey. [Complete ed.] New York Phaidon Publishers; distributed by Oxford University Press 1950] 173 p. illus., plates (part col.) 31 cm. "Catalogue": p. [139]-173. [ND623.U4P56] 50-11833
I. Pope-Hennessy, John, 1913- II. Title.

Painting, Renaissance—Rome (City)—History.

FREEDBERG, Sydney Joseph. 759.5
Painting of the high Renaissance in Rome and Florence [by] S. J. Freedberg. New York, Harper & Row [1972] 2 v. illus. 24 cm. (Icon editions, IN-13-14) Reprint of the 1961 ed. Contents.Contents.—v. 1. Text.—v. 2. Plates. Includes bibliographical references. [ND615.F67 1972] 72-186226 ISBN 0-06-430013-7 6.95 (v. 1) 7.95 (v. 2)
1. Painting, Renaissance—Rome (City)—History. 2. Painting, Renaissance—Florence—History. 3. Paintings, Italian. I. Title.

Painting, Romanesque.

GRABAR, Andre, 1896- 750.902
Romanesque painting from the eleventh to the thirteenth century: Muray painting, by Andre Grabar. Book illumination, by Carl Nordenfalk. [Translated by Stuart Gilbert] [New York] Skira [1958] 229 p. mounted illus. (part col.) map. 29 cm. (The Great centuries of painting) Translation of De la fin de l'eopque romaine au onzieme siecle. Bibliography: p. 211-214. [ND140.G683] 58-8335
1. Painting, Romanesque. I. Nordenfalk, Carl Adam Johan, 1907- II. Title. III. Series.

Painting. Romanesque—Hist.

AINAUD DE LASARTE, Juan. 759.02
Romanesque painting [by] Juan Ainaud [and] Andrea Held. [Translated by Jean Stewart] New York, Viking Press [1963] 1 v. (various pagings) 176 plates (part col.) maps. 20 cm. (Compass books, CA 5. Compass history of art.) Captions: folder (7 p.) inserted. Includes bibliography. [ND140.A353] 63-14099
1. Painting. Romanesque—Hist. I. Held, Andre, joint author. II. Title.

Painting—Rome (City)—Hist.

FREEDBERG, Sydney Joseph 759.5
Painting of the high Renaissance in Rome and Florence. [2.v.] Cambridge, Mass., Harvard [c.]1961 644; 514p. plates. 27cm. Bibl. 61-7390 30.00 set,
1. Painting—Rome (City)—Hist. 2. Painting, Florentine—Hist. 3. Paintings, Italian. I. Title.

Painting, Russian.

ZIMENKO, Vladislav Mstislavovich. 759.7
The humanism of art / Vladislav Zimenko. Moscow : Progress Publishers, 1976. 242 p. : ill. (some col.) ; 23 cm. Translation of Gumanizm iskusstva. Includes bibliographical references. [ND688.Z4713] 77-359598
1. Painting, Russian. 2. Humanism in art. 3. Socialist realism in art—Russia. I. Title.

Painting, Russian—Catalogs.

MOSCOW. Gosudarstvennaia Tret'iakovskaia gallereia. 759.7'074'0731
Soviet painting in the Tretyakov Gallery / [compiled and annotated by N. Adaskina ... et al. ; introduced by E. Polishchuk ; translated by Glenys Kozlova]. Leningrad : Aurora Art Publishers, 1976. 135 p. : col. ill. ; 34 cm. Includes bibliographies in Russian. [ND688.M59 1976] 77-356226
1. Moscow. Gosudarstvennaia Tret'iakovskaia gallereia. 2. Painting,

SUBJECT INDEX PAINTING—TECHNIQUE.

Russian—Catalogs. 3. Painting, Modern—20th century—Russia—Catalogs. 4. Socialist realism in art—Russia—Catalogs. 5. Painting—Russian Republic—Moscow—Catalogs. I. Adaskina, N. II. Title.

Painting, Scottish.

HARDIE, William R. 759.9411
Scottish painting, 1837-1939 / [by William Hardie] London : Studio Vista, 1976. 112 p., [96] p. of plates : ill. (some col.), ports. ; 29 cm. Ill. on lining papers. Includes index. Bibliography: p. 105-109. [ND478.H37] 77-363450 ISBN 0-289-70482-0 : £12.00
1. Painting, Scottish. 2. Painting, Modern—19th century—Scotland. 3. Painting, Modern—20th century—Scotland. I. Title. BIP

Painting, Scottish—History.

IRWIN, David G. 759.9411
Scottish painters at home and abroad, 1700-1900 / David Irwin and Francina Irwin London : Faber, 1975. 508 p., [58] leaves of plates : ill. (some col.) ; 26 cm. Includes index. Bibliography: p. 453-477. [ND477.I78] 75-326635 ISBN 0-571-08822-8 : 49.95
1. Painting, Scottish—History. 2. Painting, Modern—17th-18th centuries—Scotland. 3. Painting, Modern—19th century—Scotland. 4. Painters—Scotland—Biography. I. Irwin, Francina, joint author. II. Title.
Distributed by Faber and Faber, Salem, New Hampshire

Painting—Self-instruction.

HILL, Adrian Keith Graham, 1895- 751.45
The beginner's book of oil painting, written and illustrated by Adrian Hill. New York, Emerson Books [1959, c1958] 76 p. illus. 23 cm. [ND1142.H48] 59-7999
1. Painting—Self-instruction. I. Title.

Painting, Sienese.

WEIGELT, Curt H., 1883- 759.5'58
Sienese painting of the Trecento, by Curt H. Weigelt. New York, Hacker Art Books, 1974. xii, 107 p., 120 plates. 32 cm. Reprint of the 1930 ed. published by Pantheon casa editrice, Firenze, and Harcourt, Brace, New York, in series: The Pantheon series. Includes bibliographical references. [ND621.S6W4 1974] 70-143368 ISBN 0-87817-087-1 40.00
1. Painting, Sienese. 2. Painting, Gothic—Siena. I. Title. II. Series: The Pantheon series. BIP

Painting—South Asia—Bibliography.

HINGORANI, Ratan Pribhdas. 016.759954
Painting in South Asia : a bibliography / by R. P. Hingorani. 1st ed. Delhi : Bharatiya Pub. House, 1976. xxxi, 253 p. ; 22 cm. [Z5949.S6H55] [ND1000] 76-904592 Rs50.00
1. Painting—South Asia—Bibliography. I. Title.

Painting, Spanish.

BROWN, Jonathan. 759.6
Images and ideas in seventeenth-century Spanish painting / Jonathan Brown. Princeton, N.J. : Princeton University Press, c1978. p. cm. (Princeton essays on the arts ; 6) Based on the author's thesis, Princeton University, 1964. Includes index. Bibliography: p. [ND806.B76] 78-52485 ISBN 0-691-03941-0 : 20.00. ISBN 0-691-00315-7 pbk. : 6.95
1. Painting, Spanish. 2. Painting, Baroque—Spain. 3. Art and society—Spain. 4. Catholic Church in art. I. Title. BIP

CAFFIN, Charles Henry, 1854-1918. 759.6
The story of Spanish painting. New York, AMS Press [1969] xi, 203 p. plates. 23 cm. Reprint of the 1910 ed. [ND804.C2 1969] 72-100521 ISBN 0-404-01361-9
1. Painting, Spanish. 2. Painting, Modern—Spain. 3. Painters—Spain. I. Title. BIP

Painting, Spanish—Hist.

JEDLICKA, Gotthard, 1899- 759.6
Spanish painting [Tr. from German by J. Maxwell Brownjohn] New York, Viking [1964, c.1963] 204p. (p.[77]-[196] illus.) 9 mounted col. illus. 32cm. (Studio bk.) 64-11433 12.50
1. Painting, Spanish—Hist. 2. Paintings, Spanish. I. Title.

LASSAIGNE, Jacques, 1910- 759.6
Spanish painting. Translated by Stuart Gilbert. [Geneva, New York] Skira [1952] 2v. mounted col. illus., map. 35cm. (Painting, color, history. v.6, 8) 'Bibliographical and bibliographical notices by A. Busuioceanu : v. 1, p. [125]-[135]: v. 2, p. [135] -146. [ND801.L343] 52-10110
1. Painting, Spanish—Hist. 2. Paintings, Spanish. I. Title.
Contents omitted.

POST, Chandler Rathfon, 1881- 759.6
A history of Spanish painting, vs. 13-14. Cambridge Mass., Harvard [c.] 1966. 2 v. (455; 280p.) 24cm. Contents.v. 13, The schools of Aragon and Navarre in the early Renaissance.--v. 14, The later Renaissance in Castile. Ed. by Harold E. Wethey. Bibl. [ND801.P6] 30-7776 v. 13, 20.00; v. 14, 15.0
1. Painting, Spanish—Hist. I. Title.

Painting. Structural.

NICHOLSON, Durward E 667.6
Painting of steel structures, by Durward E. Nicholson and David T. Jones. Serial 6250-1. [Ed. 2] Scranton, International Correspondence Schools, c1961. 64p. illus. 19cm. [TT305.N52 1961] 62-29218
1. Painting. Structural. 2. Steel—Corrosion. I. Jones David Thomas, joint author. II. International Correspondence Schools, Scranton, Pa. III. Title.

Painting—Study and teaching.

BETHERS, Ray, 1902- 751
How paintings happen. With diagrs. by the author. [1st ed.] New York, Norton [1951] 150p. illus. 25cm. [ND1143.B46] 51-1933
1. Painting—Study and teaching. 2. Paintings. I. Title.

BETHERS, Ray, 1902- 759
The language of paintings; form and content. Adapted from Pictures, painters, and you. New York, Pitman Pub. Corp. [c1963] [ND1143.B47] 63-15303
1. Painting — Study and teaching. 2. Paintings. I. Title.

BROOKS, Leonard, 1911- 760
Painter's workshop; a basic course in contemporary painting and drawing. New York, Van Nostrand Reinhold Co. [1969] 159 p. illus. (part col.) 29 cm. "A schedule for Painter's workshop" [1] l. in pocket. Bibliography: p. 155-156. [ND1115.B76] 69-16382
1. Painting—Study and teaching. 2. Drawing—Instruction. I. Title.

COOKE, Hereward Lester. 751.4
Painting lessons from the great masters. New York, Watson-Guptill Publications [1967] 239 p. illus., plates (part col.) 34 cm. "Published in cooperation with the National Gallery of Art." Revised and enl. ed. published in 1972 under title: Painting techniques of the masters. Bibliography: p. 236. [ND1120.C6] 67-21788
1. Painting—Study and teaching. 2. Painting—Technique. I. United States National Gallery of Art. II. Title.

COOKE, Hereward Lester. 751.4
Painting techniques of the masters. [Rev., enl. ed.] New York, Watson-Guptill Publications [1972] 269 p. illus. (part col.) 29 cm. "Published in cooperation with the National Gallery of Art." "A revised and enlarged edition of Painting lessons from the great masters [published in 1967]" Bibliography: p. 266. [ND1120.C6 1972] 75-188323 ISBN 0-8230-3863-7
1. Painting—Study and teaching. 2. Painting—Technique. I. United States. National Gallery of Art. II. Title. BIP

KRIESBERG, Irving, 1919- 759
Looking at pictures, a guide to intelligent appreciation; a discussion guide for use with a selected group of reproductions of great paintings. [Chicago] Center for the Study of Liberal Education for Adults, 1955. 193p. illus. 24cm. [ND1143.K7] 56-793
1. Painting—Study and teaching. 2. Art criticism. I. Title.

RANDALL, Arne W 372.5
Painting in the classroom; a key to child growth, by Arne W. Randall [and] Ruth Elise Halvorsen. Worcester, Mass., Davis Publications [1962] 102p. illus. 28cm. [ND1115.R3] 62-14732
1. Painting—Study and teaching. 2. Painting—Technique. I. Halvorsen, Ruth Elise, joint author. II. Title.

TIMMONS, Virginia Gayheart. 750'.7
Painting in the school program. Worcester, Mass., Davis Publications [1968] 135 p. illus. (part col.) 26 cm. [ND1115.T5] 68-20663
1. Painting—Study and teaching. 2. Artist's materials. I. Title. BIP

Painting, Swiss—History.

DEUCHLER, Florens, 1931- 759.9494
Swiss painting : from the Middle Ages to the dawn of the twentieth century / Florens Deuchler, Marcel Roethlisberger, Hans Luthy ; [English translation by James Emmons]. Geneva : Skira ; New York : Rizzoli, c1976. 197 p. : ill. (some col.) ; 35 cm. Translation of Schweizer Malerei. Includes index. Bibliography: p. 183-[185] [ND844.D4813] 76-15491 ISBN 0-8478-0056-3 : 45.00
1. Painting, Swiss—History. 2. Painting, Medieval—Switzerland—History. 3. Painting, Renaissance—Switzerland—History. 4. Painting, Modern—Switzerland—History. I. Rothlisberger, Marcel, joint author. II. Luthy, Hans, joint author. III. Title. BIP

Painting—Technique.

ABELS, Alexander. 751
Painting : materials and methods / Alexander Abels & Allen Koss. New York : Pitman Pub. Corp., c1968. 48 p. : ill. ; 20 x 26 cm. (Pitman art books ; 28) [ND1500.A23 1968] 75-329162
1. Painting—Technique. 2. Artists' materials. I. Koss, Allen, joint author. II. Title.

ABELS, Alexander. 751
Painting: materials and methods. Book design and illus. by Allen Koss. New York, Pitman Pub. Corp. [1959] 47 p. illus. 20 x 26 cm. (Pitman art series, 28) [ND1262.A2] 59-11226
1. Painting—Technique. 2. Artists' materials.

ALGER, Joseph 751.45
Get in there and paint. Illustrated by Bob Ritter [2nd] Rev. ed. New York, Crowell [c.1946, 1960] 122p. illus. 21cm. 60-6242 2.95 bds.,
1. Painting—Technique. I. Title.

ALSTON, Rowland Wright. 751.4
Painter's idiom, a technical approach to painting. London, New York, Staples Press [1954] 165p. illus. 22cm. Bibliography: p.161-162. [ND1260.A44] 55-20214
1. Painting—Technique. I. Title.

ANGELOCH, Robert, 1922- 751.4'5
Basic oil painting techniques. New York, Pitman Pub. Corp. [1970] 32 p. illus. (part col.) 20 x 26 cm. (Pitman art books, no. 67) [ND1262.A53] 69-10527 1.00
1. Painting—Technique. I. Title. BIP

THE art of acrylic painting. 751.4'2
[Designed and edited by Walter Brooks. New York, Golden Press, 1969] 47 p. illus. (part. col.), col. port. 32 cm. (A Grumbacher library book) [ND1262.A74] 68-29901 1.00
1. Painting—Technique. 2. Polymer painting. I. Brooks, Walter, 1921- ed. II. Title: Acrylic painting.

THE Art of painting; 751.4
step-by-step instruction and demonstration in color mixing and painting techniques, selected from the Grumbacher library. [Designed and edited by Walter Brooks] New York, Golden Press [1968] 190 p. illus. (part col.) 33 cm. [ND1260.A68] 68-29675 9.95
1. Painting—Technique. I. Brooks, Walter, 1921- ed. II. Grumbacher (M.) inc., New York.

BARRIO, Raymond. 751
The big picture; how to experiment with modern techniques in art. [1st ed.] Sunnyvale, Calif., Ventura Press [1967] 60 p. illus., port. 21 x 26 cm. [ND1262.B34] 67-2205
1. Painting—Technique. 2. Artists' materials. I. Title.

BARRIO, Raymond. 751.4
Experiments in modern art [by] Ray Barrio. New York, Sterling Pub. Co. [1968] 88 p. illus., col. plates, port. 29 cm. [ND1260.B32] 68-18788
1. Painting—Technique. 2. Artists' materials. I. Title.

BATEMAN, James, 1893- 751.45
Oil painting. London, New York, The Studio Publications [1957] 96 p. illus., plates (part col.) 26 cm. (The How to do it series, no. 68) [ND1260.B33] 57-3416
1. Painting—Technique. I. Series: How to do it series (London, The Studio) no. 68

BAZZI, Maria. 741.4
The artist's methods and materials. Translated by Francesea Priult. New York, Pitman [1960] 228p. illus. 23cm. Translation of Abecedario pittorico. [ND1260.B353] 61-2380
1. Painting—Technique. 2. Artists materials. 3. Paintings—Conservation and restoration. I. Title.

BERKMAN, Aaron, 1900- 751.4
The functional line in painting. New York, T. Yoseloff [1957] 103p. illus. 26cm. [ND1260.B4] 57-6909
1. Painting—Technique. 2. Painting—Hist. 3. Line (Art) I. Title.

BETHERS, Ray, 1902- 751.4
How to find your own style in painting; what style is, and how the kind of a person you are will influence your style. With diagrs. by the author. New York, Hastings House [1957] 96 p. illus. 22 cm. (Visual communication books) [ND1262.B4] 57-8643
1. Painting—Technique. I. Title. II. Title: Style in painting.

BLAKE, Wendon. 751.4'26
Complete guide to acrylic painting. New York, Watson-Guptill Publications [1971] 207 p. illus. (part col.) 29 cm. "Edited by Heather Meredith-Owens." Bibliography: p. 203. [ND1535.B55] 70-154028 ISBN 0-8230-0790-1 15.00
1. Painting—Technique. 2. Polymer painting. I. Title. BIP

BLAKE, Wendon. 751.4'5
Creative color: a practical guide for oil painters. New York, Watson-Guptill Publications [1972] 175 p. col. illus. 32 cm. Bibliography: p. 171. [ND1490.B55 1972] 79-190521 ISBN 0-8230-1035-X
1. Painting—Technique. 2. Color in art. I. Title. BIP

BLANCH, Arnold, 1896- 751
It's fun to paint; painting for enjoyment, by Arnold Blanch and Doris Lee. New York, Tudor Pub. Co. [1961? c1947] 128p. illus. 28cm. First published in 1947 under title: Painting for enjoyment. [ND1262.B55 1961] 61-4050
1. Painting —Technique. I. Lee, Doris (Emrick) 1905- joint author. II. Title.

BONE, Stephen, 1904- 751.4
Oil painting. Princeton, N. J., Van Nostrand [c1956] 85p. illus. 25c7. [HD1260B52 1956] 751.4 58-9 58-9
1. Painting—Technique. I. Title.

BRACKETT, Ward. 751.4
When you paint; a complete guide for practicing artists. New York, McGraw-Hill [1974] 127 p. illus. (part col.) 34 cm. "A North Light book." Bibliography: p. 127. [ND1500.B66] 74-77082 ISBN 0-07-007029-6 17.95

1. Painting—Technique. I. Title.

BRADSHAW, Percy Venner. 751.4
Sketching & painting indoors [by] Percy V. Bradshaw and Rowland Hilder. London, New York, Studio Publications [1956] 96 p. illus. (part col.) 26 cm. (The How to do it series, no. 67) [ND1260.B63] 57-1200
1. Painting—Technique. 2. Drawing—Instruction. I. Hilder, Rowland, illus. II. Title. III. Series: How to do it series (London, The Studio) no. 67

BRANDT, Warren, 1918- 751.4'5
Painting with oils. New York, Van Nostrand Reinhold [1971] 143 p. illus. (part col.) 29 cm. (Art-in-practice series) [ND1500.B7] 71-149250
1. Painting—Technique. I. Title.

BROOKS, Leonard, 1911- 751.45
Oil painting, traditional and new. New York, Reinhold Pub. Corp. [1959] 160 p. illus. 27 cm. [ND1260.B65] 59-11376
1. Painting—Technique. I. Title.

BROOKS, Leonard, 1911- 751.4'5
Oil painting; basic and new techniques. New York, Van Nostrand Reinhold [1971] 96 p. illus. (part col.) 21 cm. Bibliography: p. 95. [ND1471.B7] 70-146182
1. Painting—Technique. I. Title.

BROOKS, Leonard, 1911- 751.4'5
Oil paintings ... traditional and new / Leonard Brooks. New York : Galahad Books, [1974] c1959. 160 p. : ill. (some col.) ; 27 cm. Bibliography: p. 160. [ND1500.B74 1974] 73-90503 ISBN 0-88365-128-9 : 12.50
1. Painting—Technique. I. Title.

BROOKS, Leonard, 1911- 751.4
Painting and understanding abstract art; an approach to contemporary methods. New York, Reinhold Pub. Corp. [1964] 144 p. illus. (part col.) 27 cm. Bibliography: p. 142. [ND1265.B733] 64-22421
1. Painting—Technique. 2. Art, Abstract. I. Title.

BROOKS, Walter, 1921- ed. 751.45
The art of oil painting; still lifes, flowers, landscapes, waterfronts, portraits. [Designed and edited by Walter Brooks. New York, Odyssey, 1965] 1 v. (unpaged) illus. (part col.) 32 cm. (A Grumbacher library book) [ND1260.B64] 65-15432
1. Painting—Technique. I. Title.

BROOKS, Walter, 1921- 751.4'5
Creative ways with oil painting. Designed and edited by Walter Brooks. New York, Golden Press [1974] 32 p. illus. (part col.) 29 cm. (The Golden Press art instruction series) [ND1500.B76] 73-88426 1.25 (pbk.)
1. Painting—Technique. I. Title. II. Title: Oil painting. BIP

BUCHANAN, Norman. 752
Painting and the joy of colour. London, New York, F. Warne, 1968. 48 p. illus. (some col.) 29 cm. [ND1262.B76] 68-16852 ISBN 0-7232-0919-7 15/-
1. Painting—Technique. 2. Color in art. I. Title.

BURTON, Laurence V. 751
Week-end painter. New York, McGraw [1963, c.1948] xi, 218p. illus (pt. col.) 21cm. (McGraw paperbacks 09291) Bibl. 2.45 pap.,
1. Painting—Technique. I. Title.

CAMERON, Alison Stilwell. 751.4
Chinese painting techniques. Rutland, Vt., C. E. Tuttle Co. [1968, c1967] 226 p. illus. (part col.). 26 x 27 cm. Bibliography: p. 221. [ND1260.C17] 67-15140
1. Painting—Technique. 2. Painting, Chinese. I. Title. BIP

CARVER, Michael 751.45
Painting in oil by the 5-color method. New York, McGraw [1962, c.1961] viii, 223p. illus. (pt. col.) 29cm. 61-15908 8.95
1. Painting—Technique. I. Title.

CHEREPOV, George, 1909- 751.4'5
Discovering oil painting. New York, Watson-Guptill Publications [1971] 159 p. illus. (part col.) 29 cm. [ND1500.C57 1971] 73-137423 ISBN 0-8230-1345-6 11.95
1. Painting—Technique. I. Title. BIP

CHIEFFO, Clifford T. 751.4'5
The contemporary oil painter's handbook : a complete guide to oil painting : materials, tools, techniques, and auxiliary services, for the beginning and professional artist / Clifford T. Chieffo. Englewood Cliffs, N.J. : Prentice-Hall, c1976. xiii, 130 p. : ill. ; 24 cm. Includes index. Bibliography: p. 117. [ND1500.C574] 75-40302 ISBN 0-13-170167-3 : 11.50
1. Painting—Technique. 2. Artists' materials. I. Title. BIP

COLQUHOUN, Norman. 751
Painting, a creative approach; a guide to modern methods and materials. 2d rev. ed. New York, Dover Publications [1969] viii, 183 p. 22 cm. "Revised and enlarged republication of the work originally published in 1953 ... under the title Paint your own pictures." [ND1262.C75 1969] 68-21280 1.75
1. Painting—Technique. I. Title.

CONSTABLE, William George, 1887- 751
The painter's workshop. Boston, Beacon [1963, c.1954] 148p. 24 plates 21cm. (BP163) Bibl. 1.95 pap.,
1. Painting—Technique. I. Title.

CONSTABLE, William George, 1887- 751
The painter's workshop. London, New York, Oxford University Press, 1954. xiii, 148p. 25plates. 25cm. Bibliography: p.[137]-139. [ND1260.C6] 54-1765
1. Painting—Technique. I. Title. BIP

DANIELS, Alfred 751.4
Painting and drawing. [New York] Arc Eds. [dist. Arco, 1962, c.1961] 159p. illus. 18cm. (860) 62-12116 .95 pap.,
1. Painting—Technique. 2. Drawing—Instruction. I. Title.

DANIELS, Leslie R. 751.45
Learning how to paint in oils; illustrated step by step on TV storyboard, by Les Daniels. [1st ed.] Garden City, N.Y., Doubleday [1964] 127 p. illus. 27 cm. ([A Doubleday artcraft book]) [ND1262.D3] 64-16560
1. Painting—Technique. I. Title. BIP

DAVIDSON, Morris, 1898- 751.4
Painting with purpose. Englewood Cliffs, N. J. Prentice [c.1964] x, 170p. illus., col. plaes. 24cm. 64-10057 7.95
1. Painting—Technique. I. Title.

DAWLEY, Joseph. 751.4'5
The painter's problem books; 20 problem subjects and how to paint them, by Joseph Dawley as told to Gloria Dawley. New York, Watson-Guptill Publications [1973] 149 p. illus. (part. col.) 22 x 29 cm. Bibliography: p. 145. [ND1473.D39] 72-12704 ISBN 0-8230-3515-8 15.00
1. Painting technique. 2. Artists' materials. I. Dawley, Gloria. II. Title.

DAWLEY, Joseph. 751.4'5
The second painter's problem book / by Joseph Dawley as told to GloriaDawley. New York : Watson-Guptill Publications, 1978. 143 p. : ill. (some col.) ; 32 cm. Continues The painter's problem book. Includes index. Bibliography: p. 141. [ND1500.D38 1977] 77-27427 ISBN 0-8230-4749-0 : 18.50
1. Painting—Technique. 2. Artists' materials. 3. Painting—Themes, motives. I. Dawley, Gloria, joint author. II. Title. BIP

DOUST, Len A. 751.45
Oil painting. London, New York, Warne [1960] 53p. illus. (part col.) (Doust sketch books) 60-14709 2.00 bds.,
1. Painting—Technique. I. Title.

DUNLOP, Ronald Ossory, 1894- 751.4
How to paint for pleasure, a handbook for beginners. New York, Pellegrini & Cudahy [1952] 143 p. illus. 22 cm. Published in London in 1951 under title: Painting for pleasure. [ND1262.D8 1952] 51-12759
1. Painting—Technique. I. Title.

DUNSTAN, Bernard, 1920- 750'.18
Composing your paintings. New York, Watson-Guptill Publications [1971] 104 p. illus. (part col.) 24 cm. Bibliography: p. 102. [ND1500.D85] 70-114195 ISBN 0-8230-0870-3 7.95
1. Painting—Technique. 2. Composition (Art) I. Title. BIP

DUNSTAN, Bernard, 1920- 751.4
A course in painting. New York, Pitman [c.1962] unpaged. illus. (pt. col.) 20x26cm. (Pitman art bks., 39) 62-17741 1.00 pap.,
1. Painting—Technique. I. Title. BIP

DUNSTAN, Bernard, 1920- 751.4
Learning to paint. New York, Watson-Guptill [1970] 173 p. illus. (part col.) 29 cm. [ND1471.D8] 77-125843 12.50
1. Painting—Technique. I. Title. BIP

DUNSTAN, Bernard, 1920- 751.4'5
Painting in progress / Bernard Dunstan. [New York] : Pitman, [1976] p. cm. [ND1500.D86] 75-44084 ISBN 0-8230-3874-2
1. Painting—Technique. I. Title.

EGBERT, Lyn. 751.4
Free brush designing, by Lyn Egbert and Ruth Baruet. Largely illustrated with original designs by Pupils of Lyn Egbert and students of the Abbott Art School, Washington, D. C. Photos. by F. Robert Barnet, Lettie Thomas, and others. New York, Lothrop, Lee & Shepard Co. [1955] 118p. illus. 29cm. [ND1262.E3] 53-6751
1. Painting—Technique. 2. Design. I. Barnet, Ruth, joint author. II. Title.

FABRI, Ralph, 1894- 751.4
Painting cityscapes. New York, Watson-Guptill Publications [1969] 192 p. illus. (part col.) 29 cm. [ND1410.F3] 73-82273 15.00
1. Painting—Technique. I. Title.

FABRI, Ralph, 1894- 751.4'5
Painting outdoors. New York, Watson-Guptill Publications [1969] 175 p. illus. (part col.) 29 cm. [ND1260.F25] 69-12493 12.50
1. Painting—Techinque. I. Title.

FABRY, Alois. 751.45
Oil painting is fun. New York, Studio Publications [1957] 95 p. illus. 21 cm. [ND1262.F24] 57-5635
1. Painting—Technique. I. Title.

FAMOUS Artists Painting Course, inc., Westport, Conn. 751
Famous artists painting course. Westport, c1953. 1v. illus. 35cm. 'Consists of a handbook and ten lessons.' [ND1262.F35] 53-36906
1. Painting—Technique. I. Title.

FARNSWORTH, Jerry, 1895- 751.45
Learning to paint in oil. New York, Watson-Guptill Publications, 1957. 125 p. illus. 27 cm. [ND1260.F28] 57-9780
1. Painting—Technique. I. Title.

FARNSWORTH, Jerry, 1895- 751.4
Portrait & figure painting. New York, Watson-Guptill [1964, c.1963] 143p. illus. (pt. col.) 27cm. Rev., enl. ed. of Learning to paint in oil. 63-18773 9.25 bds.,
1. Painting—Technique. 2. Portrait painting. 3. Figure painting. I. Title.

FIENE, Ernest, 1894- 751.45
Complete guide to oil painting. New York, Watson-Guptill Publications [1964] 207 p. illus. (part col.) ports. 27 cm. [ND1260.F535] 64-14764
1. Painting—Technique. I. Title.

FITZGERALD, Edmond James, 1912- 751
Painting and drawing in charcoal and oil. New York, Reinhold [1959] 128 p. illus. 27 cm. Includes bibliography. [ND1260.F55] 59-6280
1. Painting—Technique. 2. Drawing—Instruction. 3. Charcoal-drawing. I. Title.

FRANKLIN-WHITE, Edmund. 751.45
The beginners' book of oil painting. New York, Reinhold [1962, c1961] 71 p. illus. 19 x 20 cm. [ND1262.F7 1962] 61-17056
1. Painting—Technique. I. Title. BIP

FRIEND, David, 1899- 751.4
The creative way to paint. New York, Watson-Guptill Publications [1966] 214 p. illus. (part col.) 29 cm. [ND1260.F7] 66-13001
1. Painting—Technique. I. Title. BIP

GARBO, Norman. 751.4
Pull up an easel. [New York] Barnes [1955] 244 p. illus. 22 cm. [ND1262.G25] 55-6643
1. Painting—Technique. I. Title. BIP

GARBO, Norman. 751.4
Pull up an easel / Norman Garbo. Rev. ed. Cranbury, N.J. : A. S. Barnes, c1976. x, 261 p., [2] leaves of plates : ill. ; 22 cm. [ND1473.G37 1976] 75-9020 ISBN 0-498-01777-X : 9.95
1. Painting—Technique. I. Title.

GASSER, Henry M., 1909- 751.4
Casein painting; methods and demonstrations. Edited by Arthur L. Guptill. [1st ed.] New York, Watson-Guptill Publications, 1950. 67 p. illus. (part col.) 31 cm. [ND1260.G3] 50-12144
1. Painting—Technique. I. Title.

GASSER, Henry M. 1909- 751.4
Guide to painting; [the techniques of handling oil, water-color, and casein] Photos. by Frank Patterson. New York, Golden Press [1964] 160 p. illus. (part col.) 16 cm. (A Golden handbook) "24348." [ND1260.G32] 64-11590
1. Painting—Technique. I. Title.

GASSER, Henry M., 1909- 751.45
Oil painting: methods and demonstrations. New York, Reinhold [1953] 128 p. illus. (part col.) port. 30 cm. [ND1260.G33] 53-9172
1. Painting—Technique.

GASSER, Henry M., 1909- 751.4
Techniques of picture making. New York, Reinhold [1963, c.1962] 128p. illus. (pt. col.) 27cm. 62-19486 8.95
1. Painting—Technique. I. Title.

GAUNT, William, 1900- 759
A guide to the understanding of painting. New York, H. N. Abrams [1968] 288 p. illus. (part col.) 22 cm. Includes bibliographical references. [ND1143.G32] 68-12936
1. Painting—Technique. 2. Paintings. 3. Art appreciation. I. Title.

GONZALEZ, Xavier. 751.4
Notes about painting. [1st ed.] Cleveland, World Pub. Co. [c1955] unpaged, illus. 19 x 32 cm. [ND1262.G6] 55-5911
1. Painting—Technique. I. Title.

GORDON, Conni 751.45
You can paint a picture in full-color oils in minutes by the Conni Gordon method. New York, Pocket Books c.1960. 32p. illus. 35cm. (A Pocket book special) 60-1059 1.95 pap.,
1. Painting—Technique. I. Title.

GORE, Frederick. 751.4
Painting: some basic principles. London, Studio Vista; New York, Reinhold Pub. Corp., [1965] 95 p. illus. (part col.) 21 cm. [ND1260.G58 1965] 65-13371
1. Painting — Technique. I. Title.

GROSSER, Maurice Richard, 1903- 751.4
Painter's progress [by] Maurice Grosser. [1st ed.] New York, C. N. Potter [1971] 246 p. illus. (part col.) 27 cm. [ND1500.G7 1971] 70-169048 8.95
1. Painting—Technique. I. Title.

GRUPPE, Emil A., 1896- 751.4'5
Gruppe on painting : direct techniques in oil / by Emil A. Gruppe ; edited by Charles Movalli and John Lavin. New York : Watson-Guptill Publications, 1976. 167 p. : ill. (some col.) ; 29 cm. Includes index. Bibliography: p. 165. [ND1500.G73 1976] 75-40291 ISBN 0-8230-2157-2 : 16.95
1. Painting—Technique. I. Title. BIP

GRUSKIN, Alan D., 1904- 759.13
The painter and his techniques: William Thon, by Alan D. Gruskin. Notes by the artist. New York, Viking [c.1964] 151p. illus., col. plates, ports. 29cm. (Studio bk.) 64-13302 8.50
1. Thon, William. 2. Painting—Technique. I. Title.

GUPTILL, Arthur Leighton, 1891-1956. 751.45
Oil painting step-by-step. [Rev. ed.] New York, Watson-Guptill Publications [1958]

SUBJECT INDEX PAINTING—TECHNIQUE.

267 p. illus. 24 cm. [ND1260.G8 1958] 59-1816
1. Painting—Technique. I. Title. BIP

GUPTILL, Arthur Leighton, 1891-1956. 751.45
Oil painting, step-by-step. [3d ed.] New York, Watson-Guptill Publications [1965] 259 p. illus. (part col.) 27 cm. [ND1260.G8 1965] 65-15945
1. Painting—Technique. I. Title.

GUPTILL, Arthur Leighton, 1891-1956. 751.45
Oil painting step-by-step. [1st ed.] New York, Watson-Guptill Publications [1953] 272 p. illus. 24 cm. (Step-by-step series) [ND1260.G8] 53-10490
1. Painting—Technique. I. Title.

HAROLD, Margaret, comp. 751.4
How to paint a prize winner; paintings and water color the easy step-by-step way. [Fort Lauderdale, Fla., Allies Publications 1965- v. illus. (part col.) ports. 34 cm. Cover title. [ND1260.H33] 65-23507
1. Painting — Technique. I. Title.

HARTLEY, Paul. 751.4
How to paint better; for those who now paint pictures either for fun or livelihood, for art students, art lovers, and those who would view art through the eyes of the artist. [New York] Harper [1951] 150 p. illus. 24 cm. [ND1260.H342] 51-13951
1. Painting—Technique. I. Title.

HAWTHORNE, Charles Webster, 1872-1930. 751.4
Hawthorne on painting, from students' notes collected by Mrs. Charles W. Hawthorne. With an introd. by Edwin Dickinson, and an appreciation by Hans Hofmann. New York, Dover Publications [1960, c.1938, 1960] 91p. 21cm. (T653) 60-50099 1.00 pap.,
1. Painting— Technique. I. Title. BIP

HAYES, Colin 751.45
The technique of oil painting. New York. Reinhold [1966, c.1965] 163p. illus., plates (pt. col.) 26cm. [WND1260.H4] 65-26474 9.95
1. Painting—Technique. I. Title.

HERBERTS, Kurt. 751.4
The complete book of artists' techniques. New York, Praeger [1958] 351 p. illus., 80 col. plates. 21 cm. (Books that matter) Translation of Die Maltechniken. Bibliography: p. 344-346. [ND1260.H463 1958] 58-12424
1. Painting—Technique. 2. Art—Technique.

HERRING, Jan, 1923- 750'.1
The painter's composition handbook. [1st ed. Clint, Tex., Poor-Henry Pub. Co., 1971] 191 p. illus. (part col.) 29 cm. [ND1475.H46] 70-26364 12.95
1. Painting—Technique. 2. Composition (Art) I. Title.

HILER, Hilaire, 1898- 751
Notes on the technique of painting. With a pref. by Sir William Rothenstein. New York, Exposition Press [1955] 346 p. illus. 23 cm. (A Banner book) [ND1260.H6 1955] 55-2670
1. Painting—Technique.

HILER, Hilaire, 1898-1966. 751.4
Notes on the technique of painting. With a pref. by Sir William Rothenstein. New York, Watson-Guptill Publications [1969] xiv, 347 p. illus. 23 cm. Bibliography: [304] -334. [ND1500.H5 1969] 69-12965
1. Painting—Technique. I. Title. BIP

HILL, Adrian Keith Graham, 1895- 751.4
Painting as a hobby. [dist. New Rochelle, N. Y. SportShelf, 1961, c.1959] 127p. illus. 61-19592 3.75 bds.,
1. Painting—Technique. I. Title.

HILL, Adrian Keith Graham, 1895- 751.4
Sketching and painting indoors, written and illustrated by Adrian Hill. New York, Pitman Pub. Corp. [1961] 71p. illus. 23cm. [ND1260.H64] 61-13483
1. Painting— Technique. 2. Drawing—Instruction. 3. Still-life painting. I. Title.

HILL, Adrian Keith Graham, 1895- 751.4
Sketching and painting out of doors, written and illustrated by Adrian Hill. New York, Pitman Pub. Corp. [1961] 75p. illus. 23cm. [ND1260.H65] 61-13482
1. Painting—Technique. 2. Drawing—Instruction. 3. Landscape painting—Technique. I. Title.

HOURS, Madeleine, 1913- 751.6
Secrets of the great masters; a study in artistic techniques. [New York, Putnam, 1968, c1964] 216 p. illus. (part col.) 26 cm. Translation of Les secrets des chefs-d'ouvre. [ND1140.H613] 68-22259 12.95
1. Painting—Technique. 2. Paintings—Expertising. I. Title.

HOURS, Madeleine, 1913- 751
Secrets of the great masters: a study in artistic techniques; [translated from the French]. Feltham, Hamlyn [1968] 216 p. illus. (incl. 5 col.) 26 cm. Translation of Les secrets des chefs-d'ouvre. [ND1140.H613 1968b] 78-402923 90/-
1. Painting—Technique. 2. Paintings—Expertising. I. Title.

JAMESON, Kenneth. 751.4
Painting : a complete guide / Kenneth Jameson. New York : Viking Press, 1975. 152 p. : ill. (some col.) ; 25 cm. (A Studio book) Includes index. Bibliography: p. 147-149. [ND1500.J35] 74-21746 ISBN 0-670-53573-7 : 14.95
1. Painting—Technique. I. Title.

JOHNSTON, F. C. 751.4
Sketching & painting : a step by step introduction / F. C. Johnston. New York : St. Martin's Press, 1976. 157 p. : ill. (some col.) ; 26 cm. Includes index. [ND1500.J57 1976] 76-14586 7.95
1. Painting—Technique. 2. Drawing—Technique. I. Title. BIP

KAMPMANN, Lothar. 751.4'22
Creating with poster paints. New York, Reinhold Book Corp. [1968] 76 p. illus. (part col.) 22 cm. (Art media series) Translation of Deckende Farben. [ND1262.K2213] 68-26803
1. Painting—Technique. I. Title.

KAN, Diana, 1926- 751.4'25
The how and why of Chinese painting. Photos. by Sing-Si Schwartz. Text by Diana Kan, with Miriam Mermey. New York, Van Nostrand Reinhold Co. [1974] 175 p. illus. (part col.) 29 cm. (Art-in-practice series) [ND1505.K36] 73-16711 ISBN 0-442-24243-3 16.50
1. Painting—Technique. 2. Painting, Chinese. I. Mermey, Miriam. II. Title. BIP

KELLEY, Ramon, 1939- 751.4
Ramon Kelley paints portraits and figures / by Ramon Kelley and Mary Carroll Nelson. New York : Watson-Guptill, [1977] p. cm. Includes index. [ND237.K442N44] 77-9919 ISBN 0-8230-4505-6 : 17.50
1. Kelley, Ramon, 1939- 2. Painting—Technique. 3. Portrait painting—Technique. 4. Human figure in art. I. Nelson, Mary Carroll, joint author. II. Title. BIP

KERR, Alfred (Paddy) 751.45
Anyone can paint pictures; a book of simplified instruction in oils and water colors for the recreational painter. New York, Pitman Pub. Corp. [1960] 127p. illus. (part col.) 23cm. 60-1091 3.95 bds.,
1. Painting—Technique. I. Title.

KOMINSKY, Nancy Circelli. 751.4'5
Instant painting; a guide for the absolute beginner, the only book with color formulas in exact amounts. Indianapolis, Bobbs-Merrill [1970] vii, 65 p. illus. (part col.) 27 cm. [ND1262.K6] 75-106637 4.95
1. Painting—Technique. 2. Artists' materials—Formulae, tables, etc. I. Title.

*KOMINSKY, Nancy Circelli. 751.45
More Instant Painting; A guide for the absolute beginner. The only book with color formulas in exact amounts by Nancy Circelli Kominsky. New York, Bobbs-Merrill [1972] xi, 91 p. illus. 26 cm. [ND1500] 75-106637 5.95
1. Painting—Technique. I. Title.

KOMINSKY, Nancy Circelli. 751.4'5
Paint along with Nancy Kominsky. New York : Warner Books, c1979- v. : ill. (some col.) ; 27 cm. Contents.Contents.—Book 1. Landscapes. [ND1500.K67] 79-106699 ISBN 0-446-87791-3 pbk. : 5.95
1. Painting—Technique. I. Title. BIP

LAIDMAN, Hugh. 750.4
How to make abstract paintings. New York, Viking Press, 1961. 136 p. illus. 26 cm. (A Studio book) [ND1260.L2] 61-6794
1. Painting—Technique. 2. Art, Abstract. I. Title.

LAMADE, Erich, 1894- 751
The craft of the artist; a simple text for fine arts painting. New York [1952] 206 p. illus. 28 cm. [ND1260.L22] 52-40977
1. Painting—Technique. 2. Artists' materials. I. Title.

LAMB, Lynton 751
Preparation for painting; the purpose and materials of the artist. Baltimore, Penguin Books [1960] 175p. Bibl.: p.170-171 illus., diagrs. 18cm. (Penguin Handbook PH 58) .95 pap.,
1. Painting—Technique. I. Title.

LAMB, Lynton. 751
Preparation for painting; the purpose and materials of the artist. London, New York, Oxford University Press, 1954. xiii, 166 p. illus. 22 cm. Bibliography: p. 161-162. [ND1260.L222] 54-11993
1. Painting—Technique. I. Title.

LAURIE, Arthur Pillans, 1861-1949. 751
The painter's methods & materials. New York, Dover Publications [1967] 249 p. illus. 21 cm. (Dover art instruction and reference books) Reprint of the 1960 ed. first published in 1926. [ND1260.L27 1967] 67-30385
1. Painting—Technique. 2. Artists' materials. I. Title. BIP

LEONARDO da Vinci, 1452-1519. 751.4
Leonardo da Vinci's advice to artists. Edited by Emery Kelen. Drawings by Leonardo da Vinci. [1st ed.] Nashville, T. Nelson [1974] 140 p. illus. 21 cm. Compiled from Leonardo's notebooks and his Treatise on painting. Bibliography: p. 140. Some of Leonardo da Vinci's thoughts on anatomy, motions and emotions, historical compositions, draperies, color, and landscapes are presented from his notebooks. Da Vinci's illustrations accompany text. [ND1475.L46 1974] 74-5144 ISBN 0-8407-6377-8 6.95
1. Painting—Technique. 2. Composition (Art) I. Kelen, Emery, 1896- ed. II. Title. III. Title: Advice to artists. BIP

LEVY, Mervyn. 751.45
Painting with sunshine; an introduction to oils for young people. With a foreword by John Newsom. New York, Roy Publishers [1955?] 95 p. illus. 19 cm. [ND1260.L4] 55-9188
1. Painting—Technique. I. Title.

LOBLEY, Robert. 751.4
Your book of painting / Robert Lobley. London : Faber, 1977. 68 p. : ill. ; 16 x 22 cm. (The Your book series) Includes index. [ND1500.L6] 78-300953 ISBN 0-571-10776-1 : 5.95
1. Painting—Technique. I. Title.
Distributed by Faber and Faber, Salem, NH BIP

LOOMIS, Andrew, 1892- 751.45
The eye of the painter and the elements of beauty. New York, Viking Press [1961] 144p. illus. 31cm. [ND1260.L6] 61-7388
1. Painting—Technique. 2. Aesthetics. I. Title.

MARKS, Mickey Klar 751.4
Painting free: lines, colors, and shapes. Paintings by Edith Alberts. Photos. by David Rosenfeld. New York, Dial [c.]1965. 64p. illus. (pt. col.) 21cm. [ND1260.M327] 65-15326 3.95
1. Painting—Technique. I. Title.

MARTIN-BARBAZ, Jean Bernard, 1910- 751.4
The holiday painter. Translated from the French by J. Holman Mason. New York, Emerson Books [1961, c1960] 190p. illus. 20cm. Translation of Le peintre du dimanche. London ed. (S. Paul) has title: The weekeud painter. [ND1260.M3343 1961] 61-10958
1. Painting—Technique. I. Title.

MARTIN-BARBAZ, Jean Bernard, 1910- 751.4
The holiday painter. Tr. from French by J. Holman Mason. New York, Emerson Books [1961, c.1960] 190p. illus. Published in Gt. Britain under title: The weekend painter. 61-10958 2.95
1. Painting—Technique. I. Title. BIP

MAYER, Ralph, 1895- 751
The artist's handbook of materials and techniques. Rev. ed. New York, Viking Press, 1957. 721 p. illus. 22 cm. Includes bibliography. [ND1260.M35 1957] 56-9222
1. Painting—Technique. 2. Artists' materials. 3. Pigments. I. Title. BIP

MAYER, Ralph, 1895- 751.4
The artist's handbook of materials and techniques. 3d ed., rev. and expanded. New York, Viking Press [1970] xv, 750 p. illus. 25 cm. Bibliography: p. 685-717. [ND1500.M3 1970] 75-18183 12.50
1. Painting—Technique. 2. Artists' materials. I. Title.

MAYER, Ralph, 1895- 751
The painter's craft; an introduction to artists' methods and materials. Princeton, N. J., Van Nostrand [1966] ix, 226 p. illus. 24 cm. [ND1260.M357] 66-3363
1. Painting—Technique. 2. Artists' materials. 3. Pigments. I. Title.

MAYER, Ralph, 1895- 751
The painter's craft : an introduction to artists' methods and materials / Ralph Mayer. New York : Penguin Books, [1979, c1975] p. cm. Includes index. Bibliography: p. [ND1500.M32 1979] 78-27281 ISBN 0-14-046369-0 pbk. : 7.95
1. Painting—Technique. 2. Artists' materials. I. Title. BIP

MAYER, Ralph, 1895- 751
The painter's craft : an introduction to artists' methods and materials / Ralph Mayer. 3d ed. New York : Viking Press, 1975. 200 p. : ill. ; 25 cm. (A Studio book) Includes index. Bibliography: p. 194-195. [ND1500.M32 1975] 75-1578 ISBN 0-670-53569-9 : 12.95
1. Painting—Technique. 2. Artists' materials. I. Title.

MILLS, John, 1917- 751.45
Oil painting. New York, Pitman [1961] 116p. illus. 23cm. (A Step-by-step book) [ND1262.M53] 62-11192
1. Painting—Technique. I. Title.

MILLS, John, 1917- 350.p25
Painting made easy. New York, Sterling Pub. Co. [1961, c1960] 124p. illus. 21cm. First published in 1960 under title: Instructions to young artists. [ND1262.M5 1961] 61-15859
1. Painting—Technique. I. Title.

MILLS, John FitzMaurice, 1917- 751
Instructions to young artists. London, Museum Press [1960: stamped: distributed by Sportshelf, New Rochelle, N.Y.] 116 p. illus. 23 cm. (The Brompton library) [ND1262.M5] 60-4180
1. Painting — Technique. I. Title.

MILLS, John FitzMaurice, 1917- 751.45
Oil painting. New York, Pitman [1961] 116 p. illus. 23 cm. (A Step-by-step book) [ND1262.M53] 62-11192
1. Painting — Technique. I. Title.

MILLS, John FitzMaurice, 1917- 751.45
Oil painting. New York, Pitman [1962, c.1961] 116p. illus. (pt. col.) 23cm. (Step-by-step bk.) 62-11192 3.95 bds.,
1. Painting—Technique. I. Title.

MILLS, John FitzMaurice, 1917- 751.4
The young artist, by John Mills. [Rev. ed.] New York, Sterling Pub. Co. [1968] 132 p. illus. 21 cm. First ed., 1960, has 2d ed. title: Instructions to young artists. An introductory explanation of materials and techniques for painting with watercolors, oils, charcoal, pastels, etc. Includes

introductions on composition, perspective and shadow. [ND1262.M5 1968] AC 68
1. Painting—Technique. I. Title.

MORGAN, Henry 751.4
Painting for pleasure. London. W. & G. Foyle [dist. New Rochelle, N.Y., SportShelf. 1965, c.1963] 92p. illus., 4 plates. 19cm. (Foyles handbks.) [ND1262.M6] 65-2733 1.50 bds.,
1. Painting—Technique. I. Title.

MUGNAINI, Joseph A. 751.4
Oil painting; techniques and materials [by] Joseph Mugnaini. New York, Van Nostrand Reinhold Co. [1969] 160 p. illus. (part col.) 29 cm. [ND1260.M8] 69-17635 15.00
1. Painting—Technique. 2. Artists' materials. I. Title.

NORDMARK, Olle. 751.45
Course in beginning oil painting. New York, Reinhold [1960?] 4 v. illus., col. plates. 27 cm. [ND1262.N6] 60-11327
1. Painting—Technique. I. Title.

OWEN, Peter. 751.4
Painting. London, New York, Oxford University Press, 1970. xv, 300 p. illus. (part col.) 21 cm. (The Appreciation of the arts, 5) [ND1471.O9 1970] 73-18634 10.75 (U.S.)
1. Painting—Technique.

PETTERSON, Henry. 751
Exploring with paint [by] Henry Petterson and Ray Gerring. New York, Reinhold Pub. Corp. 1964 68 p. illus. (part col.) 21 x 22 cm. [ND1260.P45] 63-19228
1. Painting—Technique. I. Gerring, Ray, joint author. II. Title.

POGANY, Willy, 1882- 751.45
Oil-painting lessons. New York, D. McKay [1954] 63p. illus. 29cm. [ND1260.P65] 53-11378
1. Painting— Technique. I. Title.

POMERANTZ, Louis, 1919- 751
Is your contemporary painting more temporary than you think? Vital technical information for the present-day artist. Drawings by Paula Gerard. Chicago, Intl. Bk. Co. 62p. 19cm. (Chicago Chapter Artists Equity Pubn.) 62-15290 2.15 pap.,
1. Painting—Technique. 2. Artists' materials. 3. Paintings—Conservation and restoration. I. Title. BIP

RAYNES, John, 1929- 751.45
Starting to paint in oils. London. Studio Vista; New York, Watson-Guptill [c.1966] 96p. illus., 8 plates (incl. 4 col.) tables. 19cm. [ND1263.R3 1966] 66-13004 1.95 bds.,
1. Painting—Technique. I. Title.

RET, Etienne. 751.4
Advice to a young artist. New York, Dodd, Mead, 1951. 86 p. illus. 25 cm. [ND1260.R35] 51-12107
1. Painting—Technique. 2. Drawing—Instruction. I. Title.

RICHMOND, Leonard. 751.45
From the sketch to the finished picture, oil painting. New York, Pitman Pub. Corp. [1953] xi, 81p. illus. (part col.) 26cm. [ND1260] 53-13025
1. Painting—Technique. I. Title.

RICHMOND, Leonard. 751.4'5
Fundamentals of oil painting. New York, Watson-Guptill Publications [1970] 144 p. illus. (part col.) 29 cm. 1931 ed. published under title: The technique of oil painting. Bibliography: p. 141. [ND1260.R5 1970] 74-98152 15.00
1. Painting—Technique. I. Title. BIP

RICHMOND, Leonard. 751
Imaginative techniques in painting. New York, Reinhold Pub. Co. [1964] 120 p. illus. (part col.) 27 cm. [ND1262.R48] 64-13642
1. Painting — Technique. I. Title.

RICHMOND, Leonard. 751.45
Oil painting. New York, Pitman Pub. Corp., c1961. unpaged. illus. 20x26cm. (Pitman art series, 33) [ND1262.R5] 61-7711
1. Painting—Technique. I. Title. BIP

SALEMME, Lucia A. 751.4'5
Compositional exercises for the painter [by] Lucia A. Salemme. New York, Watson-Guptill [1973] 167 p. illus. (part col.) 29 cm. [ND1475.S24] 73-6888 ISBN 0-8230-0877-0 15.00
1. Painting—Technique. 2. Composition (Art) I. Title.

SCHMIDT, Maurice. 751.4
How to achieve mastery in painting and drawing; an illustrated guide to the fundamental principles and techniques of art. With paintings and drawings by the author. Photos. of paintings by Roy Hammond. [1st ed.] New York, Exposition Press [1974] 112 p. illus. 21 cm. (An Exposition-banner book) Bibliography: p. 111-112. [ND1500.S34] 73-82092 ISBN 0-682-47770-2 6.00
1. Painting—Technique. 2. Drawing—Instruction. I. Title. BIP

SEDDON, Richard Harding, 1915- 701
The academic technique of oil painting [by] Richard Seddon. London, New York, Artist Pub. Co. [1960] 72 p. illus. (part col.), ports. 22 cm. (The Artist's series) [ND1260.S44] 68-128592
1. Painting—Technique. I. Title.

SEDGWICK, John P. 759.06
Discovering modern art; the intelligent layman's guide to painting from impressionism to pop [by] John P. Sedgwick, Jr. New York, Random House [1966] xii, 208 p. illus., col. plates. 25 cm. [ND1265.S4] 66-21463
1. Painting—Technique. 2. Painting—Modern—20th century. I. Title.

SEIDELMAN, James E. 751.4
Creating with paint [by] James E. Seidelman and Grace Mintonye. Illustrated by Peter Landa. New York, Crowell-Collier Press [1967] 58 p. illus. (part col.) 28 cm. An introduction to painting, suggesting experiments with brushes, papers, colors, and materials like string, crayons, and your hands. Also gives many suggestions for subjects of paintings, from dreams to portraits. [ND1260.S45] AC 68
1. Painting—Technique. I. Mintonye, Grace, joint author. II. Landa, Peter, illus. III. Title. BIP

SHEAKS, Barclay. 751.4'5
Painting with oils : the complete process / Barclay Sheaks. Worcester, Mass. : Davis Publications, 1978, c1977. viii, 120 p., [8] leaves of plates : ill. (some col.) ; 26 cm. [ND1500.S47] 77-78827 11.95
1. Painting—Technique. I. Title. BIP

SHEPPARD, Joseph, 1930- 751.4'5
Learning from old the masters / by Joseph Sheppard. New York : Watson-Guptill Publications, [1979] p. cm. Includes index. Bibliography: p. [ND1500.S48 1979] 79-4407 ISBN 0-8230-2672-8 : 19.50
1. Painting—Technique. 2. Painting, Renaissance—Technique. 3. Painting, Modern—17th-18th centuries—Technique. I. Title. BIP

SINGER, Joe, 1923- 759.13
Charles Pfahl, artist at work / by Joe Singer. New York : Watson-Guptill Publications, 1977. p. cm. Includes index. Bibliography: p. [ND237.P45S56] 77-8693 ISBN 0-8230-0620-4 : 17.95
1. Pfahl, Charles Alton, 1946- 2. Painting—Technique. I. Title.

SLATER, Frank. 751.45
Oil painting for everyone. New York, Scribner [1958] 96 p. illus. 24 cm. [ND1260.S56] 58-10860
1. Painting — Technique. I. Title.

SLATER, Frank. 751.4'5
Oil painting for everyone; a practical introduction for the serious beginner to the fundamentals of painting. New York, Scribner [1973, c1958] 96 p. illus. 19 cm. (The Scribner library, SL445. Emblem editions) [ND1500.S55 1973] 72-12175 2.95 (pbk.)
1. Painting—Technique. I. Title.

SORGMAN, Mayo. 751.4
Brush and palette; painting techniques for young adults. New York, Reinhold Pub. Corp. [1965] 168 p. illus. (part col.) 21 cm. [ND1260.S62] 65-12975
1. Painting—Technique. I. Title.

SOYER, Moses, 1899- 751.4'5
Oil painting in progress [by] Moses Soyer and Peter Robinson. New York, Van Nostrand Reinhold Co. [1972] 63 p. illus. 21 cm. [ND1505.S68] 79-90324
1. Painting—Technique. I. Robinson, Peter, 1915- II. Title.

SPARKES, Roy. 751.4
Painting without a brush / Roy Sparkes. London : Batsford, 1978. 96 p. : ill. ; 26 cm. Includes index. Bibliography: p. 92-93. [ND1146.S7] 78-320234 ISBN 0-7134-0189-3 : 9.50
1. Painting—Technique—Juvenile literature. I. Title.
Distributed by Hippocrene Books, New York, NY BIP

SULLY, Thomas, 1783-1872 751
Hints to young painters; a historic treatise on the color, expression, and painting techniques of American artists of the Colonial and Federal periods. Reprinted in new format from the orig. ed. of 1873, with a special introd. by Faber Birren. New York, Reinhold [c.]1965. xxiii, 46p. illus., facsim. 21cm. [ND1262.S9] 65-15055 7.95, bds., lim. ed.
1. Painting—Technique. 2. Portrait painting. I. Birren, Faber, 1900- II. Title.

TAUBES, Frederic, 1900- 751.4'26
Acrylic painting for the beginner. New York, Watson-Guptill Publications [1971] 143 p. illus. (part col.) 26 cm. [ND1535.T38] 77-137424 ISBN 0-8230-0060-5 9.95
1. Painting—Technique. 2. Polymer painting. I. Title.

TAUBES, Frederic, 1900- 751.45
Guide to oil painting. New York, Reinhold [c.1965] 95p. illus. (pt. col.) 21cm. [ND1260.T263] 65-24060 6.95
1. Painting—Technique. I. Title.

TAUBES, Frederic, 1900- 751.4
A guide to traditional and modern painting methods. New York, Viking Press [1963] 135 p. illus. 24 cm. (A Studio book) [ND1260.T264] 63-10935
1. Painting—Technique. 2. Painting—History.

TAUBES, Frederic, 1900- 751.45
The mastery of oil painting. New York, Studio Publications in association with Crowell [1953] 256 p. illus. (part col.) 25 cm. [ND1260.T267] 53-7530
1. Painting—Technique. 2. Painting—History. 3. Color. I. Title.

TAUBES, Frederic, 1900- 751
New techniques in painting. New York, Dodd, Mead [1962] 128 p. illus. 24 cm. [ND1260.T3] 62-12580
1. Painting—Technique. I. Title.

TAUBES, Frederic, 1900- 751.45
Oil painting for the beginner. [3d ed., rev.] New York, Watson-Guptill Publications [1954, c1944] 148p. illus. 26cm. [ND1260] 54-3801
1. Painting—Technique. I. Title. BIP

TAUBES, Frederic, 1900- 751
The quickest way to paint well, a manual for the part-time painter. New York, Studio Publications in association with Crowell [1950] 99 p. illus. (part col.) port. 25 cm. [ND1260.T275] 50-12500
1. Painting—Technique. I. Title.

TAYLOR, Bertha Fanning. 751.4
Form and feeling in painting, [1st ed.] New York, Pageant Press [1959] 92 p. illus. 21 cm. [ND1260.T33] 59-14416
1. Painting — Technique. 2. Painting. I. Title.

THOMPSON, Daniel Varney, 1902- 751
The materials and techniques of medieval painting. With a foreword by Bernard Berenson. New York, Dover Publications [1956] 239 p. 21 cm. Unabridged and unaltered republication of the first ed. published in 1936 under title: The materials of medieval painting. [ND1500.T5 1956] 57-4711
1. Painting — Technique. 2. Pigments. 3. Painting, Medieval. I. Title. BIP

TIMMONS, Virginia Gayheart. 751.4
Painting, ideas, materials, processes / Virginia Gayheart Timmons. Worcester, Mass. : Davis Publications, c1978. 138 p. : ill. (some col.) ; 27 cm. Bibliography: p. 134. [ND1500.T55] 78-58904 ISBN 0-87192-102-2 : 13.50
1. Painting—Technique. 2. Composition (Art) 3. Artists' materials. I. Title.

TONEY, Anthony. 701.8
Creative painting and drawing. Illustrated with reproductions of the artist's work. With an introd. by Rudolf Arnheim. New York, Dover Publications [1966] 202 p. illus. (part col.) 29 cm. [ND1263.T6] 66-14557
1. Painting—Technique. 2. Drawing—Instruction. 3. Composition (Art) I. Title. BIP

TRACY, Lois Bartlett. 750.4
Painting principles & practices, by Bartlett Tracy. Asheville, N.C., Kir-Ban Enterprises [1965] Indianapolis, Boobs-Merrill [1965] 129 p. illus. 23 cm. x, 210 p. 22 cm. [ND1260.T7] [TX753.T7] 641.694 65-24976 64-15666
1. Painting — Technique. 2. Cookery (Shellfish) I. Tracy, Marian (Coward) II. Title. III. Title: The shellfish cookbook,

20 oil painters and how 751.4'5
they work : from the pages of American artist / edited by Susan E. Meyer New York : Watson-Guptill Publications, [1978] p. cm. Includes index. [ND1500.T86 1978] 78-9612 ISBN 0-8230-5491-8 : 19.95
1. Painting—Technique. 2. Painters—Psychology. I. Meyer, Susan E. II. American artist.

[WANG, Kai], fl.1677-1705. 751.4'25
The Mustard Seed Garden manual of painting = Chieh Tzu Yuan hua chuan, 1679-1701 : a facsimile of the 1887-1888 Shanghai edition with the text translated from the Chinese and edited by Mai-mai Sze. Princeton, N.J. : Princeton University Press, 1977, c1956. vii, 624 p. : ill. ; 22 x 23 cm. (Bollingen series) Includes original t.p. in Chinese. "The Mustard Seed Garden manual of painting was originally part of a larger work, The tao of painting." Includes index. [ND1505.W313 1977] 77-312 ISBN 0-691-09940-5 : 20.00 pbk. : 8.95
1. Painting—Technique. 2. Painting, Chinese. 3. Painters—China. I. Sze, Mai-mai. II. Title. III. Series. BIP

WATSON, Dori. 750.4
The techniques of painting. New York, Van Nostrand Reinhold [1970] 160 p. illus., ports. 29 cm. Bibliography: p. 158. [ND1260.W28] 78-90321
1. Painting—Technique. I. Title.

WHITAKER, Frederic 751.4
Guide to painting better pictures. New York, Reinhold [c.1965] 96p. illus. (pt. col.) 27cm. [ND1260.W46] 65-12978 7.50
1. Painting—Technique. I. Title.

WHITING, John Downes, 1884- 752.4
Light and color for the vacation painter. New York, Comet Press Books, 1958. 107 p. illus. 21 cm. (A Reflection book) [ND1262.W5] 58-2511
1. Painting — Technique. I. Title.

WILLIAMS, Guy R. 751.4
Paint now, learn later. New York, Emerson [c.1966] 128p. illus. plates. 22cm. [ND1260.W48] 66-19979 3.95
1. Painting—Technique. I. Title. BIP

WILLIAMS, Guy R 751.4
Paint now, learn later [by] Guy R. Williams. New York, Emerson Books [1966] 128 p. illus., plates. 22 cm. [ND1260.W48] 66-19979
1. Painting — Technique. I. Title.

WILLIAMS, Hiram. 751.4
Notes for a young painter. Englewood Cliffs, N.J., Prentice-Hall [1963] xii, 106, [1] p. illus. 21 cm. (A Spectrum book) Bibliography: p. [107] [ND1260.W5] 63-21223
1. Painting — Technique. 2. Painting. I. Title.

WYETH, Paul. 751.45
How to paint in oils. [By] Paul Wyeth and Tom Horbin. London, New York, Elek [1953] 86 p. illus. 26 cm. [ND1260.W9] 54-856
1. Painting—Technique. I. Horabin, Tom, joint author. II. Title.

century. [By] Cornelis Ch. Goslinga. Assen, Van Gorcum & Comp., 1967. xvi, 128p. with illus. 24cm. Bibl. [ND430.G6] 67-106416 6.75 pap.,
1. Painting, Venezuelan. 2. Romanticism in art. I. Title.
Distriubted by Wittenborn, New York.

Painting, Victorian.

LISTER, Raymond. 759.2
Victorian narrative paintings. New York, C. N. Potter [1966] 159 p. illus. (part col.) 26 cm. Bibliography: p. 159. [ND467.L54 1966a] 66-24779
1. Painting, Victorian. 2. Narrative painting. I. Title.

Painting, Victorian—Great Britain.

STRONG, Roy C. 759.941
And when did you last see your father? : the Victorian painter and British history / Roy Strong. London : Thames and Hudson, 1978. 176 p. : ill. (some col.), ports. ; 24 cm. Includes bibliographical references and index. [ND467.S73] 78-323777 ISBN 0-500-23281-4 : 16.95
1. Painting, Victorian—Great Britain. 2. Painting, Modern—19th century—Great Britain. 3. History in art. 4. Great Britain—History—Pictorial works. I. Title.
Available from W. W. Norton, NYC

Painting, Zen—Exhibitions.

FONTEIN, Jan. 759.952'074'014461
Zen painting & calligraphy; an exhibition of works of art lent by temples, private collectors, and public and private museums in Japan, organized in collaboration with the Agency for Cultural Affairs of the Japanese government [by] Jan Fontein & Money L. Hickman. Boston, Museum of Fine Arts; distributed by New York Graphic Society, Greenwich, Conn. [1971, c1970] liv, 173 p. illus. (part col.) 29 cm. Catalog of the exhibition held Nov. 5-Dec. 20, 1970, at the Boston Museum of Fine Arts. [ND197.F6 1971] 76-127853 ISBN 0-87846-000-4 18.50
1. Painting, Zen—Exhibitions. 2. Calligraphy, Zen—Exhibitions. I. Hickman, Money L., joint author. II. Japan. Bunkacho. III. Boston. Museum of Fine Arts. IV. Title.

Paintings.

BILZER, Bert, ed. 759.074
Paintings of the world's great galleries the histories and treasures of the 30 most famous galleries in the world. Ed. by Bert Bilzer, Hermann Boekhoff, Fritz Winzer. [Tr. from German by Peter Gorge] New York, Praeger [1961, c.1960] 584p. illus., col. plates. 30cm. 61-15288 14.95; 18.50 after Dec. 1.
1. Paintings. 2. Art—Galleries and museums. I. Title.

CAFFIN, Charles Henry, 1854-1918. 759
How to study pictures by means of a series of comparisons of the painters' motives and methods. With additions by Roberta M. Fansler. Edited by Alfred Busselle, Jr. Rev. ed. Freeport, N.Y., Books for Libraries Press [1968, c1941] xiv, 544 p. illus. 22 cm. (Essay index reprint series) Bibliography: p. 523-525. [ND1143.C4 1968] 68-58776
1. Paintings. 2. Painting—Study and teaching. I. Fansler, Roberta (Murray) 1903- II. Busselle, Alfred, 1905- ed. III. Title.

CHASE, Alice Elizabeth. 759.0838
Famous paintings; an introduction to art for young people. New York, Platt and Munk [1951] 102 p. illus. 27 cm. [ND1146.C52] 51-12875
1. Paintings. 2. Art—Juvenile literature. I. Title.

CLARK, Kenneth McKenzie, Baron Clark, 1903- 759.94
Looking at pictures. New York, Holt, Rinehart and Winston [1960] 199 p. illus. 25 cm. [ND1145.C5 1960] 60-10106
1. Paintings. I. Title.

CRAVEN, Thomas, 1889- ed. 759
A treasury of art masterpieces, from the Renaissance to the present day. Rev. and enl. New York, Simon and Schuster, 1952. xvi, 327 p. illus., 160 col. plates. 34 cm. [ND1170.C7 1952] 52-13980
1. Paintings. I. Title. **BIP**

CRAVEN, Thomas, 1889- ed. 759
A treasury of art masterpieces : from the Renaissance to the present day / Edited by Thomas Craven. New York : Simon and Schuster, 1977. xvi, 327p. : ill., 160 col. plates ; 28 cm. (A Fireside Book) [ND1170.C7] ISBN 0-671-22776-9 pbk. : 9.95
1. Pantings. I. Title.
L.C. card no. for 1952 Simon and Schuster ed.:52-13980.

GETLEIN, Frank. 759
1000 famous masterpieces from the world's great museums. New York, H. N. Abrams [1974] p. cm. [N4000.G47] 74-14626 ISBN 0-8109-0517-5
1. Paintings. 2. Art—Galleries and museums. I. Title.

HOLME, Bryan, 1913- 759
Pictures to live with. New York, Viking Press [1959] 152 p. illus. (part col.) 26 cm. (A Studio book) [ND1170.H6] 59-13417
1. Paintings. 2. Engravings. I. Title.

JOHNSON, Ivan E. 758.9
Instructor modern art series. [Paintings selected by Ivan E. Johnson. Notes on artists and paintings by Guy Hubbard. Dansville, N.Y., F.A.Owen Pub. Co., c1962] 24 folders. mounted col. illus. 41 cm. Contents.1. Edgar Degas: Rehearsal on the state. -- 2. Paul Cezanne: The great pine. -- 3. Henri Rousseau: Repast of the lion. -- 4. Paul Gauguin: We greet thee Mary. -- 5. Vincent van Gohg: The postman Roulin. -- 6. Georges Seurat: Sunday afternoon on La Grande Jatte. -- 7. Henri de Toulouse-Lautrec: Cirque Fernando. -- 8. Wassily Kandinsky: Composition iv. -- 9. Henri Matisse: The painter's family, -- 10. John Marin: Lower Manhattan. -- 11. Georges Rouault: The parade. -- 12. Piet Mondrian: Broadway boogie-woogie. -- 13. Maurice de Viaminck: Road of Mamers. -- 14. Raoul Dufy: Threshing. -- 15. Paul Klee: Clown 1929. -- 16. Andre Derain: The pool of London. -- 17. Hans Hofmann: Exuberance. -- 18. Fernand Leger: The builders. -- 19. Pablo Picasso: Seated woman (1947) -- 20. MauOInstructor modern art series. [Paintings selected by Ivan E. Johnson. Notes on artists and paintings by Guy Hubbard. Dansville, N.Y., F.A.Owen Pub. Co., c1962] 24 folders. mounted col. illus. 41 cm. Contents.1. Edgar Degas: Rehearsal
1. Paintings. I. Hubbard, Guy. II. Title.

LEWIS, Wilmarth Sheldon, 1895- 759
See for yourself. [1st ed.] New York, Harper & Row [1971] viii, 118 p. 10 col. plates. 27 cm. (A Cass Canfield book) [ND1145.L4] 78-156532 ISBN 0-06-012601-9 15.00
1. Paintings. I. Title.

LOOK. 758.9
The story behind the painting. Text by Leo Rosten. Art direction by Allen Hurlburt. New York, Cowles Magazines & Broadcasting; book trade distribution by Doubleday, Garden City, N.Y. [1962] 165 p. illus. (part col.) ports. 34 cm. Includes bibliographies. [ND1170.L64] 62-19710
1. Paintings. 2. Painters. I. Rosten, Leo Calvin, 1908- II. Title.

LORGUES-LAPOUGE, C. 759.94
The old masters: Byzantine, Gothic, Renaissance, Baroque. Tr. from French by Anthony Rhodes. New York, Crown [1963] 210p. illus. (pt. mounted col.) col. plates. 33cm. 63-21120 12.50
1. Paintings. 2. Drawings. I. Title.

MASTERPIECES in the history of painting Under the general editorship of Robert Maillard Contributors: Luc Benois [others] Tr. [from French, with the exception of the Eng. lang. contributions, by Margaret Shenfield, Ricahrd Waterhouse] New York, Holt [1963, c.1961] 343p. col. illus. 24cm. 5.95 759
1. Paintings. 2. Painting—Hist. I. Benois, Luc, 1893- II. Maillard, Robert, ed.

MATHEWS, Wendell. 750
The world of painting. Saint Louis, Concordia Pub. House [1968] 112 p. illus. 18 cm. (The Christian encounters) Bibliography: p. 109. [ND1142.M34] 68-8397 1.25
1. Paintings. I. Title. II. Series.

NEW York. Museum of Modern Art 707.4
Two decades of American painting [New York, 1967] 80p. illus. (pt. col.) 25cm. The exhibition org. by the Mus. and selected by Waldo Rasmussen, under the auspices of the Intl. Council of the Mus. for showings in Tokyo, Oct. 15-Nov. 27, 1966 and in Kyoto, Dec. 10. 1966-Jan. 22, 1967. Text in English (12p.) inserted at end. Text in Japanese. [ND212.N397] 67-20892 2.50 pap.,
1. Paintings. I. Rasmussen, Waldo. II. Kokuritsu Kindai Bijutsukan, Tokyo. III. International Council of the Museum of Modern Art, New York. IV. Title. V. Title: Two decades of American painting. Title romanized: Gendai Amerika kaiga ten.

100 masterpieces in colour; introduction by Christopher Wood. London, New York, Hamlyn, 1972. 2-124 p. chiefly illus. (chiefly col.) 32 cm. Illus. on lining papers. [ND1145.O49] 73-150211 ISBN 0-600-31277-1 6.98 759
1. Paintings. I. Wood, Christopher.

100 of the world's most beautiful paintings. [New York] R. T. V. Sales, 1966] 1 v. (unpaged) 100 col. plates. 38 cm. On spine: The book of the world's most beautiful paintings. [ND1145.O5] 67-5658 750'.1
1. Paintings. 2. The book of the world's most beautiful paintings.

SCHAEFFER Galleries, inc., New York. 706'.5
Twenty-fifth anniversary, 1936-1961. New York [1961] [75]p. (chiefly illus. (part col.)) 36cm. Includes bibliographies. [N8660.S37A3] 62-5549
1. Paintings. 2. Drawings. I. Title.

SCHWARTZ, Paul Waldo. 759
Great paintings of all time; 100 masterpieces from the early Renaissance to abstract expressionism. Introd. by Sir John Rothenstein. New York, Simon and Schuster [1965] 208 p. col. illus. 25 cm. [ND1210.S3] 65-27472
1. Paintings. I. Title. **BIP**

STRAIN, Pamela. 759
Pleasure from pictures; a book for young and old. London, New York, Studio Publications [1950] 128 p. illus. (part col.) 25 cm. "A collection of pictures ... with some notes about them and the artists who painted them." [ND1145.S78] 50-8379
1. Paintings. 2. Painters. I. Title.

TUDOR history of painting in 1000 color reproductions. Under the general editorshop of Robert Maillard. Contributors: Luc Benoist [others. Tr., with the exception of the English language contributions, by Margaret Shenfield, Richard Waterhouse] New York, Tudor [c.1961] 325, [8]p. col. illus. 61-17425 10.00 759
1. Paintings. 2. Painting—Hist. I. Benoist, Luc, 1893- II. Maillard, Robert, ed.

VENTURE, Lionello, 1885- 759
Painting and painters; how to look at a picture, from Giotto to Chagall. Cleveland, World [1963, c.1945] 250p. illus. 21cm. (Forum bks. F258) Bibl. 1.95 pap.,
1. Paintings. 2. Painters. I. Title.

WALKLING, Christine, 1946- 759.94
Let's look at pictures / by Christine Walkling. London : Medici Society, 1976. 24 p. : col. ill. ; 19 x 22 cm. (Medici art books) Includes index. [ND1145.W34] 76-380174 ISBN 0-85503-035-6 : £0.60
1. Paintings. 2. Art appreciation. I. Title.

Paintings—Aberdeen, Scot.—Catalogs.

ABERDEEN Art Gallery, Aberdeen, Scot. 759.2'074'0941235
A picture book of landscapes in the collections of the Aberdeen Art Gallery. [Aberdeen] 1952. unpaged. illus. 14x22cm. [N1185.A2A57] 55-35346
1. Paintings—Aberdeen, Scot.—Catalogs. 2. Landscape painting. I. Title.

Paintings—Ajanta.

DEY, Mukul Chandra, 1895- 751.73
My pilgrimages to Ajanta and Bagh. With an introd. by Laurence Binyon. [2d ed.] [Bombay, New York] Indian Branch, Oxford University Press [1950] 185 p. illus. 23 cm. [ND2827.D4 1950] 53-20293
1. Paintings—Ajanta. 2. Paintings—Bagh, India. 3. Mural painting and decoration. 4. Cave temples. 5. Temples—India. I. Title.

Paintings, American.

ANDERSON, Clarence William, 1891- 759.13
Before the bugle, by C. W. Anderson. New York, Macmillan, 1968. [4] p., 8 col. plates (in portfolio) 41 cm. [ND237.A64A42] 68-21301
I. Title.

ARIZONA. University. Art Gallery. 707.4
American art collection. Tucson [196] 1 v. (chiefly illus.) 28 x 31 cm. [ND235.T8A73] 64-64315
1. Paintings, American. 2. Paintings — Tucson, Ariz. — Catalogs. I. Title.

BOSTON. Museum of Fine Arts. 759.13
American paintings, 1815-1865; one hundred and thirty-six paintings from the M. and M. Karolik collection in the Museum of Fine Arts, Boston, together with fourteen paintings from the private collection of Maxim Karolik; circulated by the Museum of Fine Arts, Boston, 1957-1959. [Boston, 1956] 112p. illus. 23cm. [ND210.B727] 57-414
1. Paintings, American. 2. Painters, American. 3. Paintings—Boston—Catalogs. I. Karolik, Maxim. II. Karolik, Martha Catherine (Codman) III. Title.

BOSTON. Museum of Fine Arts. 759.13
American paintings, 1815-1865; one hundred and thirty-six paintings from the M. and M. Karolik collection in the Museum of Fine Arts, Boston, together with fourteen paintings from the private collection of Maxim Karolik; circulated by the Museum of Fine Arts, Boston, 1957-1959. [Boston] [1956] 112 p. illus. 23 cm. [ND210.B727] 57-414
1. Paintings, American. 2. Painters, American. 3. Paintings—Boston—Catalogs. I. Karolik, Maxim. II. Karolik, Martha Catherine Codman. III. Title.

BOUTON, Margaret. 759.13
American painting in the National Gallery of Art. Washington, [National Galley of Art] [1959] 43p. col. illus. 19cm. (U. S. National Gallery of Art. Booklet no. 1) 60-60573 pap., apply
1. Paintings, American. I. Title. II. Series.

CARLSON, Raymond, 1906- ed. 759.13
Gallery of Western paintings. [1st ed.] New York, McGraw-Hill [1951] 85 p. illus. 32 cm. [ND225.C3] 51-12661
1. Paintings, American. 2. Painters, American. 3. The West—Description and travel—Views

CHILCOTT, Nicholas. 704'.75 B
A champion of American art / by Nicholas Chilcott. 1st ed. Chicago : Adams Press, c1975. x, 101 p. : ill. ; 18 cm. [N5220.J73C47] 75-20784
1. Johnson, William J., 1860-1942—Art patronage. 2. Paintings, American. 3. Paintings, Modern—19th century—United States. 4. Paintings, Modern—20th century—United States. I. Title.

COUNTRY beautiful 759.13
The beauty of America in great American art; with selections from the writings of renowned American authors, by the eds. of Country beautiful. Pref. by Eric F. Goldman. Introd. by Tracy Atkinson. New York, Country Beautiful Found. in assn. with Morrow [c.1965] 162p. illus. (pt. col.) 31cm. [ND205.C6] 65-26257 20.00
1. Paintings. American. 2. American literature (Selections: extracts, etc.) 3. U.S.—Descr. & trav.—Views. I. Title. **BIP**

MONRO, Isabel Stevenson. 759.13
Index to reproductions of American paintings; a guide to pictures occurring in more than eight hundred books, by Isabel Stevenson Monroand Kate M. Monro. New York, H. W. Wilson Co., 1948. 731 p. 26 cm. v. 26 cm. Supplement. New York, H. W. Wilson Co., 1964- [ND205.M57] 48-9663
1. Paintings, American. 2. Painters, American. I. Monro, Kate M., joint author. II. Title. BIP

MONRO, Isabel Stevenson 759.13
Index to reproductions of American paintings: a guide to pictures occurring in more than eight hundred books; first supplement, by Isabel Stevenson Monro, Kate M. Monro. New York, Wilson [c.] 1964. 480p. 27cm. Contents.1st supp. A guide to pictures occurring in more than four hundred works. 48-9663 15.00
1. Paintings, American. 2. Painters, American. I. Monro, Kate M., joint author. II. Title.

NEW York. Metropolitan 759.13
Museum of Art.
100 American painters of the 20th century; works selected from the collections of the Metropolitan Museum of Art. New York, 1950. xxiii, 111 p. plates (part col.) 26 cm. [ND212.N39] 50-13015
1. Paintings, American. I. Hale, Robert Beverly, 1901- II. Title. III. Title: With an introd. by Robert Beverly Hale.

NORDNESS, Lee, ed. 759.13
Art: USA: now. Text by Allen S. Weller. New York, Viking Press [1963] 2 v. (475 p.) illus. (part col.) ports. 25 cm. (A Studio book) [ND212.N6] 62-19607
1. Paintings, American. 2. Painters, American. I. Weller, Allen Stuart, 1907- II. Title.

PEARCE, John Newton, 1935- 759.13
American painting, 1560-1913, by John Pearce. New York, McGraw-Hill [1964] 48 p. illus., 24 col. slides (in pockets) 25 cm. (Color slide program of the world's art) [ND205.P4] 64-21907
1. Paintings, American. 2. Painting, American. 3. Lantern slides. I. Title. II. Series.

POUSETTE-DART, Nathaniel, 759.13
1886- ed.
American painting today. New York, Hastings House [c1956] 127p. (chiefly illus. (part col.) 28cm. 'Suggested reading, compiled by Muriel Baldwin': p. 122-123. [ND212.P65] 56-10969
1. Paintings, American. I. Title.

PRICE, Vincent, 1911- 759.13
The Vincent Price treasury of American art. Waukesha, Wis., Country Beautiful Corp. [1972] 320 p. illus. (part col.) 34 cm. [ND205.P73] 72-86463 ISBN 0-87294-031-4 25.00
1. Paintings, American. I. Title. II. Title: Treasury of American art.

RUSCHA, Edward. 760'.092'4
Edward Ruscha (Ed-werd Rew-shay) young artist; a book accompanying the exhibition of prints, drawings, and books of Edward Ruscha at the Minneapolis Institute of Arts, April 18-May 28, 1972. [Minneapolis? 1972] 1 v. (chiefly illus.) 12 cm. [N6537.R87M56] 72-75834
I. Minneapolis. Institute of Arts.

SALINAS, Porfirio. 759.13
Bluebonnets and cactus; an album of southwestern paintings. With an introd. by Joe B. Frantz, a pref. by Dewey Bradford, and five short stories. Austin, Prepared for Fine Arts Corp. by Pemberton Press, 1967. 111 p. col. illus. 22 x 30 cm. [ND237.S25A42] 68-5780
I. Fine Arts Corp. II. Title.

Paintings, American—Catalogs.

BALTIMORE, Museum of Art. 759.13
The Edward Joseph Gallagher III memorial collection, the Baltimore Museum of Art. Baltimore [1964] 33 p. (chiefly illus., port.) 19 x 22 cm. Collection presented to the museum by Edward J. Gallagher, Jr. [ND212.B32] 64-7204
1. Paintings, American—Catalogs. I. Gallagher, Edward Joseph. II. Title.

BOWDOIN 759.13'074'014191
College. Museum of Art.
Nineteenth century American paintings at Bowdoin College : [catalog]. [Brunswick, Me.] : The Museum, 1974. [77] p. : chiefly ill. ; 24 cm. [ND210.B74 1974] 75-322572
1. Bowdoin College. Museum of Art. 2. Paintings, American—Catalogs. 3. Paintings, Modern—19th century—United States—Catalogs. 4. Paintings—Brunswick, Me.—Catalogs. I. Title.

COLUMBUS 759.13'074'017157
Gallery of Fine Arts, Columbus, Ohio.
American paintings in the Ferdinand Howald Collection. Catalogue prepared by Marcia Tucker, with research assistance and biographies by Kasha Linville. Introd. by Edgar P. Richardson. [Columbus, c1969] 119 p. illus., col. plates. 28 cm. Includes bibliographical references. [ND212.C65] 72-95250
1. Howald, Ferdinand—Art collections. 2. Paintings, American—Catalogs. 3. Painting, Modern—20th century—U.S. I. Tucker, Marcia. II. Title.

DELAWARE Art Museum. 708'.151'2
American painting and sculpture / Delaware Art Museum ; Elizabeth H. Hawkes, assistant curator. [Wilmington] : The Museum, c1975. 182 p. : ill. (some col.) ; 26 cm. Includes bibliographical references and indexes. [ND205.D28 1975] 75-19934
1. Paintings, American—Catalogs. 2. Sculpture, American—Catalogs. I. Hawkes, Elizabeth H. II. Title.

HASSAM, Childe, 1859-1935. 759.13
Childe Hassam, 1859-1935. Tucson, University of Arizona Museum of Art, 1972. 150 p. illus. (part col.) 27 cm. Catalog of an exhibition held at the University of Arizona Museum of Art, Feb. 5-Mar. 5, 1972, and at the Santa Barbara Museum of Art, Mar. 26-Apr. 30, 1972. Bibliography: p. 150. [ND237.H345A85] 76-188054
I. Arizona. University. Museum of Art. II. Santa Barbara, Calif. Museum of Art.

KENNEDY Galleries, inc., 759.13
New York.
America at home; American homes in American paintings of the eighteenth and nineteenth centuries. New York [1969] 204-276 p. illus. (part col.) 23 cm. (The Kennedy quarterly, v. 8, no. 4) "All paintings are for sale, except where noted." [N8640.K4 vol. 8, no.4] 70-13664 2.00
1. Paintings, American—Catalogs. 2. Painting, Modern—17th-18th centuries—U.S. 3. Painting, Modern—19th century—U.S. 4. Architecture, Domestic, in art. I. Title. II. Series.

KENNEDY Galleries, inc., 760'.922
New York.
An American survey; paintings from two centuries. New York, Kennedy Galleries [1967] 76 p. illus. 23 cm. (The Kennedy quarterly, v. 7, no. 1) [N8640.K4 vol. 7, no. 1] 68-5818
1. Paintings, American—Catalogs. I. Title.

KENNEDY Galleries, inc., 759.13
New York.
Past and present: two hundred years of American painting. New York, 1966. 2 pts. illus., ports. 23 cm. (The Kennedy quarterly, v. 6, no. 3-4) Contents.Contents.—pt. 1. Eighteenth and nineteenth centuries.—pt. 2. Nineteenth and twentieth centuries. [N8640.K4 vol. 6, no. 3-4 pt. 1-2] 75-11541
1. Paintings, American—Catalogs. I. Title. II. Series.

KENNEDY 759.13'074'01471
Galleries, inc., New York.
Recently acquired American masterpieces of the 19th and 20th centuries. [New York, 1974] [44] p. col. illus. 28 cm. [ND210.K46 1974] 74-177234 5.00 (pbk.)
1. Paintings, American—Catalogs. 2. Painting, Modern—19th century—United States. 3. Painting, Modern—20th century—United States. 4. Water-colors, American—Catalogs. I. Title.

LANSKOY, Andre, 1902- 759.4
Lanskoy: recent paintings, November 7-December 10, 1960 New York, Albert Loeb Gallery [1960] [3] l., 11 plates (part col.) 33 cm. [ND553.L227L6] 68-7206
I. Loeb (Albert) Gallery, New York.

NEW York (City). 759.13'074'01471
Metropolitan Museum of Art.
A concise catalogue of the American paintings in the Metropolitan Museum of Art. Compiled by Albert Ten Eyck Gardner, associate curator of American art. New York, 1957. 51 p. 25 cm. [ND205.N373] 73-155821
1. Paintings, American—Catalogs. 2. Paintings—New York (City)—Catalogs. I. Gardner, Albert Ten Eyck. II. Title.

OAKLAND Museum. 759.13'074'019466
Art Dept.
The Kahn Collection of nineteenth-century paintings by artists in California / by Marjorie Arkelian. [Oakland] : Oakland Museum, Art Dept., 1975. 63 p. : ill. (some col.) ; 23 x 31 cm. Includes index. Bibliography: p. 56-62. [ND230.C3O15 1975] 75-77188
1. Oakland Museum. Art Dept. 2. Paintings, American—Catalogs. 3. Painting, Modern—19th century—California. 4. Paintings—Oakland, Calif.—Catalogs. I. Arkelian, Marjorie. II. Title.

PARIS, Harold Persico, 730'.92'4
1925-
Harold Paris: the California years. Edited by Peter Selz. [Berkeley, Calif., University Art Museum, 1972] 66 p. illus. (part col.) 26 cm. Catalog of an exhibition held at the University Art Museum, Berkeley, Calif. Bibliography: p. 65. [N6537.P25S4] 76-189051
I. Selz, Peter Howard, 1919- ed. II. California. University. Art Museum. III. Title.

RANDOLPH-MACON Woman's 759.13
College, Lynchburg, Va.
Catalogue of the collection of American painting at Randolph-Macon Woman's College [by] Mary Frances Williams. Lynchburg, Va., 1965. xxiii, 128 p. illus. (part col.) 23 cm. Half-title: The collection of Randolph-Macon Woman's College. [ND212.R35] 65-24452
1. Paintings, American — Catalogs. 2. Paintings — Lynchburg, Va. — Catalogs. I. Williams, Mary Frances. II. Title.

RHODE Island Historical 759.13
Society.
American paintings in the Rhode Island Historical Society, by Frank H. Goodyear, Jr. Providence, 1974. x, 116 p. illus. (part col.) 29 cm. [ND207.R48 1974] 73-91890
1. Paintings, American—Catalogs. 2. Painting, Colonial—United States. 3. Painting, Modern—19th century—United States. 4. Paintings—Providence—Catalogs. I. Goodyear, Frank Henry, 1944- II. Title. BIP

SANCHEZ, Emilio. 759.9'7291
Emilio Sanchez; [exhibition] Center for Inter-American Relations, September 29-November 7, Coe Kerr Gallery, September 29-October 16, Associated American Artists, September 29-October 16. [New York, Center for Inter-American Relations, 1971] 1 v. (chiefly plates, part col.) 23 cm. Text in English and Spanish. [ND305.S2C4] 74-198447
I. Center for Inter-American Relations. II. Coe Kerr Gallery. III. Associated American Artists.

SHATTUCK, Aaron Draper, 759.13
1832-1928.
Aaron Draper Shattuck, N.A., 1832-1928; a retrospective exhibition. Organized and arr. by the New Britain Museum of American Art, March 17th-April 26, 1970 New Britain, Conn. [1970] [60] p. illus. 21 x 26 cm. Bibliography: p. [60] [ND237.S468A42] 79-24967
I. New Britain Museum of American Art.

U.S. National 759.13'074'0153
Gallery of Art.
American paintings and sculpture: an illustrated catalogue. Washington, 1970. 192 p. illus. 23 cm. [N6505.A27] 73-91593
1. Paintings, American—Catalogs. 2. Sculpture, American—Catalogs. I. Title. BIP

WILLIAM A. 759.13'074'014153
Farnsworth Library and Art Museum, Rockland, Me.
American paintings and drawings in the William A. Farnsworth Library and Art Museum, Rockland, Maine. Rockland : The Library and Art Museum, c1975. 169 p. : ill. (some col.) ; 28 cm. [ND205.W515 1975] 75-324272
1. William A. Farnsworth Library and Art Museum, Rockland, Me. 2. Paintings, American—Catalogs. 3. Paintings—Rockland, Me.—Catalogs. 4. Drawings, American—Catalogs. 5. Drawings—Rockland, Me.—Catalogs. I. Title: American paintings and drawings ...

Paintings, American—Catalogs—Indexes.

SMITHSONIAN 016.01675913
Institution. National Collection of Fine Arts.
Directory to the Bicentennial inventory of American paintings executed before 1914. 1st ed. New York : Published for the National Collection of Fine Arts, Smithsonian Institution by Arno Press, 1976. p. cm. [ND205.S6 1976] 76-12616 ISBN 0-405-09545-7
1. Paintings, American—Catalogs—Indexes. 2. Paintings, Modern—17th-18th centuries—United States—Catalogs—Indexes. 3. Paintings, Modern—19th century—United States—Catalogs—Indexes. 4. Paintings, Modern—20th century—United States—Catalogs—Indexes. I. Title.

Paintings, American — Exhibitions.

AMERICA the 759.13'074'016399
beautiful : a bicentennial exhibition, October 5-November 16, 1975, the R. W. Norton Art Gallery, Shreveport, La. : R. W. Norton Art Gallery, c1975. 38 p. : ill. (some col.) ; 28 cm. Cover title. Catalogue of an exhibition of 47 paintings by eight regional contemporary artists. [ND212.A448] 75-28257 ISBN 0-913060-07-0 pbk. : 3.00
1. Paintings, American—Exhibitions. 2. Paintings, Modern—20th century—United States—Exhibitions. 3. United States in art. I. Norton (R. W.) Art Gallery.

AMERICAN Federation of 759.13'074
Arts.
Americans: individualists at work, from the Sara Roby Foundation Collection. New York [1972] [16] p. illus. 20 x 23 cm. [ND212.A515] 72-87727
1. Sara Roby Foundation, New York—Art collections. 2. Paintings, American—Exhibitions. 3. Painting, Modern—20th century—United States. I. Title.

AMERICAN Federation of 759.13'074
Arts.
The realist revival. Guest director: Scott Burton. [New York, 1972] [24] p. illus. 21 x 23 cm. "AFA exhibition number 72-4. Circulated 1972-1973." [ND212.5.R4A43] 72-87725
1. Paintings, American—Exhibitions. 2. Painting, Modern—20th century—United States. 3. Realism in art. I. Burton, Scott. II. Title. BIP

AMERICAN naive painting of 759.13
the 18th and 19th centuries; 111 masterpieces from the collection of Edgar William and Bernice Chrysler Garbisch. Foreword by John Walker. Pref. by Lloyd Goodrich. Introd. by Albert Ten Eyck Gardner. [New York] American Federation of Arts [1969] 159 p. illus. (part col.) 25 cm. Catalog of an exhibition being circulated through the United States and Europe 1968-70 under the auspices of the American Federation of Arts. Translation of Peintures naives americaines, xviiie-xixe siecles. [ND207.P413] 72-85150
1. Paintings, American—Exhibitions. 2. Primitivism in art—United States. I. Garbisch, Edgar William. II. Garbisch, Bernice (Chrysler) III. American Federation of Arts.

AMERICAN painting: 759.13
the 1940's. Selected by Lamar Dodd and William D. Paul, Jr. Co-sponsored by the Cultural Affairs Committee of the University of Georgia and AFA. New York [American Federation of Arts, 1967] 40 p. illus. 21 x 22 cm. [ND212.A56] 67-9313
1. Paintings, American—Exhibitions. I. Dodd, Lamar. II. Paul, William D. III. Georgia. University. Cultural Affairs

Committee. IV. American Federation of Arts.

AMERICAN 759.13'074'015818 *painting:* the 1950's. Selected by Gordon B. Washburn. [New Haven, Conn., Printed by Eastern Press, c1968] [36] p. illus. 21 cm. Catalog of an exhibition, organized and circulated by the American Federation of Arts, and co-sponsored by the Georgia Museum of Art and the AFA. "Exhibition number 68-14/circulated 1968-1969." Includes essay "American painting in the nineteen-fifties," by G. B. Washburn. [ND212.A562] 68-59253
1. Paintings, American—Exhibitions. 2. Painting, Modern—20th century—United States. I. Washburn, Gordon Bailey, 1904- II. American Federation of Arts. III. Georgia Museum of Art.

AMERICAN 759.13'074'015818 *painting: the 1960's.* [New York? 1969?] [36] p. illus. 21 cm. Includes the catalog of the exhibition organized and circulated by the American Federation of Arts, co-sponsored by the Georgia Museum of Art, the University of Georgia, and the American Federation of Arts. "American painting in the nineteen-sixties," by S. A. Green: p. [7]-[22] [ND212.A563] 79-103155
1. Paintings, American—Exhibitions. 2. Painting, Modern—20th century—United States. I. Green, Samuel Adams. II. American Federation of Arts. III. Georgia Museum of Art.

AMERICAN 759.13'074'014967 *paintings* : a gathering from three centuries : an exhibition organized by the Historical Society of Princeton, New Jersey, October 1975 / catalogue essay by Ellwood Parry ; sponsored by Squibb Corporation, New York City, and E. R. Squibb & Sons, Inc., Princeton, New Jersey. [Princeton? N.J.] : The Society?, c1975. 12, [51] p. : ill. ; 22 cm. Includes bibliographical references. [ND205.A66] 75-328825
1. Paintings, American—Exhibitions. 2. Paintings, Modern—18th century—United States. 3. Paintings, Modern—19th century—United States. 4. Paintings, Modern—20th century—United States. I. Parry, Ellwood. II. Historical Society of Princeton.

AMERICAN 759.13'074'018186 *paintings from Newport, from the Redwood Library and other collections.* [Wichita? Kan., 1969?] 76 p. illus., ports. 23 cm. Page 76 blank for "Notes." "[Catalogue of an exhibition] organized by the Wichita Art Museum in collaboration with the Cincinnati Art Museum, the Delaware Art Center, and the M. H. De Young Memorial Museum. Exhibitiors: Delaware Art Center, Wilmington, Delaware, October 3-November 2, 1969 [and others]" Bibliography: p. 12. [ND205.A67] 76-199833
1. Paintings, American—Exhibitions. I. Wichita Art Museum. II. Redwood Library and Athenaeum, Newport, R.I. III. Delaware Art Center, Wilmington.

THE American 759.13'074'0166 *sense of reality.* [Tulsa? Philbrook Art Center?, 1969] 56 p. illus. 21 x 26 cm. Cover title. Catalog of the exhibition held Mar. 4-25, 1969, at the Philbrook Art Center, Tulsa, and Apr. 6-May 11, 1969, at the Museum of Art, University of Oklahoma, Norman, and the Oklahoma Art Center, Oklahoma City. [ND205.A68] 72-22561
1. Paintings, American—Exhibitions. 2. Realism in art—United States. I. Philbrook Art Center, Tulsa, Okla. II. Oklahoma. University. Museum of Art. III. Oklahoma Art Center.

THE American 759.13'074'01471 *vision;* paintings 1825-1875. [New York] Public Education Association, 1968. 1 v. (unpaged) plates (part col., incl. ports.) 28 cm. Catalog of the exhibition held Oct. 8-Nov. 2, 1968, by the Public Education Association in M. Knoedler and Co., Hirschl and Adler Galleries, and Paul Rosenberg and Co. [ND210.A73] 73-20212
1. Paintings, American—Exhibitions. 2. Painting, Modern—19th century—U.S. I. Public Education Association of the City of New York.

AMERICANS at 759.13'074'01641411 *home and abroad, 1870-1920;* a loan exhibition for the benefit of the American Association of Museums. Houston, M. Long [1971] 58 p. illus. (part col.) 28 cm. Catalog of the exhibition held Mar. 26-Apr. 9, 1971, at the Meredith Long Gallery, Houston. [ND210.A75] 71-155816
1. Paintings, American—Exhibitions. 2. Painting, Modern—19th century—U.S. 3. Painting, Modern—20th century—U.S. I. American Association of Museums. II. Meredith Long Gallery.

ARIZONA. 759.13'074'01471
University. Art Gallery.
American painting, 1765-1964. [Selections from the Lawrence A. and Barbara Fleischman collection of American art. Exhibition, February 1 through March 28, 1964. Catalog.] Tucson 1964] 119 p. illus. (part col.) ports. (part col.) 26 cm. Cover title. [ND205.A75] 64-63116
1. Paintings, American — Exhibitions. 2. Paintings — Private collections. I. Fleischman, Lawrence A. II. Fleischman, Barbara. III. Title.

ARIZONA. University. Art 759.13
Gallery.
The West: 80 contemporaries; an invitational exhibition of paintings Tucson [1967] 95 p. (chiefly illus. (part col.)) 30 cm. Exhibition sponsored by the University of Arizona Art Gallery, and held March 19-April 30, 1967. [ND225.A7] 67-65524
1. Paintings, American—Exhibitions. 2. Artists, American—The West. I. Title.

ARKANSAS Arts Center, 759.13
Little Rock.
The James A. Michener collection of twentieth century American paintings. [Catalogue of the exhibition, May 3 through June 3, 1962. Little Rock, 1962] unpaged. illus. 21cm. [ND212.A65] 62-15684
1. Paintings. American—Exhibitions. 2. Paintings—Private collections. I. Michener, James Albert, 1907- II. Title.

ART Association of v. 12
Indianapolis, Indiana. John Herron Art Institute.
The first hundred years of Indiana painting. Indiana sesquicentennial celebration. [Exhibition] Herron Museum of Art, Indianapolis, Oct. 4-Nov. 13, 1966. [Indianapolis 1966] 1 v. (unpaged) illus., ports. 26 cm. Preceding page contains descriptive text of illus. opposite. [NUC67-80204]
1. Paintings, American — Exhibitions. 2. Painting — Indiana. 3. Painters, American — Indiana. I. Title.

ART Museum of 759.13'074'0164113
South Texas.
18th and 19th century American paintings from the Boston Museum of Fine Arts : [exhibition, Art Museum of South Texas, March 12 through May 2, 1976, Corpus Christi, Texas.[Corpus Christi : Golden Banner Press, c1976. 32 p. : chiefly ill. ; 22 cm. [ND207.A69 1976] 76-371913
1. Paintings, American—Exhibitions. 2. Painting, Colonial—United States—Exhibitions. 3. Paintings, Modern—19th century—United States—Exhibitions. I. Title.

ASSOCIATION of College 759.13
Unions.
American painting, 1910 to 1960; a special exhibition celebrating the 50th anniversary of the Association of Collge Unions, April 19th until May 10th, 1964, Fine Arts Gallery, Indiana University. Bloomington, 1964. 1 v. (unpaged) 71 illus. (1 mounted col.) 28 cm. Cover title. Includes bibliography. [ND212.A75] 65-63079
1. Paintings, American — Exhibitions. I. Indiana. University. Museum of Art. II. Title.

BAUR, John Ireland Howe, 759.13
1909-
George Grosz. [Research by Rosalind Irvine] New York, Published for the Whitney Museum of American Art by Macmillan, 1954. 67p. illus. (part col.) port. 26cm. 'The result of a retrospective exhibition of the work of George Grosz held by the Whitney Museum of American Art in January and February 1954.'--p. 67. 'Catalogue of the exhibition': p. 60-63. Bibliography: p. 65-67. [ND237.G68B3] 54-802 927 54-802
1. Grosz, George, 1893- 2. Paintings. American—Exhibitions. I. Whitney Museum of American Art, New yYork. II. Title.

BAUR, John Ireland Howe, 927.5
1909-
Loren MacIver. I. Rice Pereira. New York, Published for the Whitney Museum of American Art by Macmillan, 1953. 71 p. illus. (part col.) ports. 27 cm. "This book is the result of a retrospective exhibition...held by the Whitney Museum of American Art in January and February 1953." Includes bibliographies. [ND237.M214B38] 53-6459
1. MacIver, Loren, 1909- 2. Pereira, Irene Rice, 1907- 3. Paintings, American—Exhibitions. I. Whitney Museum of American Art, New York.

BENGSTON, Billy Al. 759.13
Billy Al Bengston [by] James Monte. [Exhibition] Los Angeles County Museum of Art, Lytton Hall, November 26, 1968-January 12, 1969. [Los Angeles, Los Angeles County Museum of Art, 1968] [64] p. illus. (part col.) 23 cm. Cover title: Billy. "Sponsored by the Contemporary Art Council, Corcoran Gallery—Dupont Center, Washington, D.C. [and] Vancouver Art Gallery, Vancouver, B.C." [ND237.B457M6] 68-58689
I. Monte, James. II. Los Angeles Co., Calif. Museum of Art, Los Angeles. Contemporary Art Council. III. Corcoran Gallery—Dupont Center. IV. Vancouver, B.C. Art Gallery.

BLACK, Mary C. 759.13'07407471
What is American in American art. Introd. by Lloyd Goodrich. Catalogue by Mary Black. [1st ed.] New York, C. N. Potter [1971] 80 p. illus. (part col.) 23 cm. Catalog of an exhibition held at the new M. Knoedler & Company, Inc., gallery. [ND205.B53 1971] 70-153674 9.50
1. Paintings, American—Exhibitions. 2. National characteristics, American. I. Knoedler (M.) and Company, inc. II. Title.

BOSTON. Institute of 759.13
Contemporary Art.
American painting now. [Catalogue of the exhibition at] Horticultural Hall, Boston, December 15, 1967-January 10, 1968, sponsored by the Institute of Contemporary Art. Boston, [1967] [24] p. illus. (part col.), ports. 19 cm. "An exhibition organized by Alan Solomon for the United States Information Agency, shown originally in the United States Pavilion at Expo 67, Montreal." [ND212.B63] 67-31691
1. Paintings, American—Exhibitions. 2. Painting, Modern—20th century—United States. I. Solomon, Alan R. II. Expo 67. III. Title.

BOSTON. Institute of 759.13
Contemporary Art.
Contemporary painters of Japanese origin in America, by Thomas M. Messer and Anne L. Jenks. [Exhibition and catalogue. Boston] 1958. unpaged. illus. 20cm. [ND212.B65] 61-3209
1. Paintings, American—Exhibitions. 2. Painters, Japanese. I. Messer, Thomas M. II. Jenks, Anne L. III. Title.

BOSTON. Museum 759.13'074'0159121
of Fine Arts.
American paintings, 1815-1865; one hundred and fifty paintings from the M. and M. Karolik collection in the Museum of Fine Arts, Boston. Boston, 1956 [cover 1957] 109 p. illus. 23 cm. Catalog of an exhibition to be held in 12 museums during a two-year period. [ND210.B727 1957] 71-283373
1. Karolik, Maxim—Art collections. 2. Paintings, American—Exhibitions. 3. Painting, Modern—19th century—United States. I. Karolik, Maxim. II. Karolik, Martha Catherine (Codman) III. Title.

BRENSON, Theodore, 759.94743
1893-
Light into color, light into space; paintings by Theodore Brenson, exhibited at the Art Gallery of Douglass College, Rutgers, the State University, New Brunswick, N. J., April 8-29, 1959. [New York, Wittenborn] c1959. unpaged. illus. 24cm. Includes bibliography. [ND237.B84A5] 59-2333
1. Paintings, American—Exhibitions. I. Rutgers University, New Brunswick, N. J. Douglass College. II. Title.

BROOKLYN 759.13'074'0159121
Institute of Arts and Sciences. Museum.
American painting: selections from the collection of Daniel and Rita Fraad. A special exhibition [held at] the Brooklyn Museum, June 9 to September 20, 1964 [and] Addison Gallery of American Art, Phillips Academy, Andover, Massachusetts, October 10 to November 8, 1964. [Brooklyn] Brooklyn Museum [1964] 87 p. illus. (part col.) ports. 23 cm. Includes bibliographical references. [ND210.B75] 64-23067
1. Paintings, American — Exhibitions. 2. Paintings — Private collections. I. Phillips Academy, Andover, Mass. Addison Gallery of American Art. II. Fraad, Daniel. III. Fraad, Rita. IV. Title.

BUFFALO Fine Arts Academy. 759.13
Eugene Speicher; a retrospective exhibition of oils and drawings, 1908-1949. September 29-October 26, 1950. Buffalo, Buffalo Fine Arts Academy, Albright Art Gallery [1950] 26 p. 23 plates. 26 cm. "Eugene Speicher, by Charles E. Burchfield": p. 9-12. Catalogue: p. 15-23. Bibliography: p. 14. [ND237.S64B8] 51-823
1. Speicher, Eugene Edward, 1883- 2. Paintings, American—Exhibitions. 3. Drawings, American—Exhibitions. I. Title.

BUTLER Art Institute, 759.13
Youngstown, Chic.
Annual mid-year show. [Catalogue] [Youngstown] v. illus. 15x24 cm. [ND212.B84] 55-30425
1. Paintings, American—Exhibitions. I. Title.

CALIFORNIA. University. 759.13
Art Museum.
The reality of appearance; the trompe l'oil tradition in American painting, by Alfred Frankenstein. Published by New York Graphic Society Ltd. for an exhibition organized by University Art Museum, Berkeley, in conjunction with National Gallery of Art [and others. Greenwich, Conn., 1970] 156 p. illus. (part col.) 27 cm. Exhibition held March 21-October 31, 1970. [ND210.C3] 78-104385 10.00
1. Paintings, American—Exhibitions. 2. Trompe l'oil painting—U.S. I. Frankenstein, Alfred Victor, 1906- II. U.S. National Gallery of Art. III. Title.

CENTURY 759.13'074'01471
Association, New York.
Robert Henri & five of his pupils: George Bellows, Eugene Speicher, Guy Pene Du Bois, Rockwell Kent [and] Edward Hopper. Loan exhibition of paintings, April 5 to June 1, 1946. Freeport, N.Y., Books for Libraries Press [1971] [61] p. illus. 27 cm. (Biography index reprint series) Text signed: Helen Appleton Read. Reprint of the 1946 ed. [ND212.C4 1971] 74-160918 ISBN 0-8369-8081-6
1. Henri, Robert, 1865-1929. 2. Bellows, George Wesley, 1882-1925. 3. Speicher, Eugene Edward, 1883-1962. 4. Du Bois, Guy Pene, 1884-1958. 5. Kent, Rockwell, 1882- 6. Hopper, Edward, 1882-1967. 7. Paintings, American—Exhibitions. 8. Ashcan School. I. Read, Helen Appleton. II. Title. BIP

•CHICAGO. Art Institute 708.173
Annual American exhibition; directions in contemporary painting and sculpture. Chicago, Author [1964] unpaged. illus. 28cm. Title varies. 52-38452 2.00 pap.,
1. Paintings, American—Exhibitions. 2. Sculpture, American—Exhibitions. I. Title.

CHICAGO. Art Institute. 759.13
Sargent, Whistler, and Mary Cassatt, by Frederick A. Sweet. [A catalogue of the exhibition] The Art Institute of Chicago, January 14 through February 25, 1954 [and] theMetropolitan Museum of Art, March 25 through May 23, 1954. [Chicago, 1954] 101p. illus. (part col.) ports. 26cm. [ND210.C47] 54-811
1. Sargent, John Singer, 1856-1925. 2. Whistler, James Abbott McNelli, 1834-1903. 3. Cassatt, Mary, 1845-1926. 4. Paintings, American—Exhibitions. I. Sweet, Frederick Arnold, 1903- II. New York. Metropolitan Museum of Art. III. Title.

CINCINNATI. Art 759.13'074'017178 Museum.
American paintings on the market today. [Cincinnati, 1968] 15 p. illus., ports. 26 cm. Catalog of the exhibition held Apr. 9-May 12, 1968. [ND205.C44] 70-15090
1. Paintings, American—Exhibitions. 2. Paintings—Collectors and collecting. I. Title.

CORGAN (D. Leonard) 759.13 Library.
Catalogue of the Edward Welles, Jr. Collection of paintings by artists in Wyoming Valley in the D. Leonard Corgan Library, King's College. Compiled by Mary Barrett. Rev. ed. Wilkes-Barre, Pa., King's College Press, 1974. 89 p. port. 23 cm. (Wyoming Valley series, no. 2) (Publications of the D. Leonard Corgan Library) Includes Painting in Wyoming Valley, 1808-1957, by G. G. Raddin; a series of 17 articles originally published in the Sunday Independent, Wilkes-Barre, Pa., Mar. 31-July 21, 1957: p. 23-80. [ND230.P4W962 1974] 74-170439 4.00 (pbk.).
1. Welles, Edward, 1894-1970—Art collections. 2. Paintings, American—Exhibitions. 3. Painting—Wyoming Valley, Pa. I. Barrett, Mary, 1910- II. Raddin, George Gates, 1906- III. Title. IV. Series: Corgan (D. Leonard) Library. Publications. V. Series: Wyoming Valley series (Wilkes-Barre, Pa.) no. 2.

CRANBROOK Academy of Art, 759.13 Bloomfield Hills, Mich.
Biennial exhibition [of] American painting [and] Sculpture. 1st- 1953- Bloomfield Hills, Mich. v. illus. 26cm. Exhibition held at the Museum ofCranbrook Academy of Art. [ND212.C67] 55-25695
1. Paintings, American—Exhibitions. 2. Sculpture, American—Exhibitions. I. Title.

CUMMER Gallery 759.13'074'0159121 of Art.
American paintings from the Collection of Mr. and Mrs. Fred D. Bentley, Sr., and Mr. and Mrs. J. Alan Sellars : [catalog of an exhibition], the Cummer Gallery of Art, Jacksonville, Florida, March 12-April 27, 1975. [Jacksonville, Fla.] : The Gallery, 1975. 96 p. : ill. (some col.) ; 21 cm. On cover: Bentley-Sellars Collection. Errata slip inserted. Includes index. [ND210.C78 1975] 75-314877
1. Bentley, Fred D.—Art collections. 2. Sellars, J. Alan—Art collections. 3. Paintings, American—Exhibitions. 4. Painting, Modern—19th century—United States—Exhibitions. 5. Painting, Modern—20th century—Exhibitions. I. Title: American paintings ...

CURRY, Larry. 759.13
The American West; painters from Catlin to Russell. With a foreword by Archibald Hanna. [New York] Viking Press [1972] 198 p. illus. (part col.) 22 x 24 cm. Catalog of an exhibition held Mar. 21-May 28, 1972, at the Los Angeles County Museum of Art, June 9-Sept. 17, 1972, at the M. H. de Young Memorial Museum, San Francisco, and Nov. 2-Dec. 31, 1972, at the St. Louis Art Museum. Bibliography: p. 192-195. [ND210.C83 1972] 79-185984
1. Paintings, American—Exhibitions. 2. Painting, Modern—19th century—United States. 3. The West in art. I. Los Angeles Co., Calif. Museum of Art, Los Angeles. II. De Young Memorial Museum, San Francisco. III. St. Louis Art Museum. IV. Title.

DALLAS. Museum 759.13'074'0159121 of Fine Arts.
Famous paintings and famous painters; [exhibition] October 4 through November 2, 1958. [Dallas, 1958?] 1 v. (chiefly illus.) 26 cm. [ND210.D3] 66-45006
1. Paintings, American — Exhibitions. I. Title.

DALLAS. Museum 759.13'074'016428 of Fine Arts.
The romantic vision in America. [Dallas, 1971] 1 v. (unpaged) plates (1 col.) 26 cm. Catalog, prepared by C. Robbins, of the exhibition held Oct. 9-Nov. 28, 1971 at the Dallas Museum of Fine Arts. Includes bibliographical references. [ND210.5.R6D3] 72-31297
1. Paintings, American—Exhibitions. 2. Painting, Modern—19th century—United States. 3. Romanticism in art—United States. I. Robbins, Carol. II. Title.

D'ARCANGELO, Allan, 1930- 759.13
Allan D'Arcangelo; paintings, 1963-1970 [Philadelphia] Institute of Contemporary Art, University of Pennsylvania [1971] [28] p. illus. (part col.) 22 cm. "An exhibition organized by Institute of Contemporary Art, University of Pennsylvania,..., March 10 to April 16, 1971, in collaboration with Albright-Knox Art Gallery, Buffalo,..., May 16 to June 27, 1971." Bibliography: p. [24]-[27] [ND237.D24P4] 70-28807
I. Pennsylvania. University. Institute of Contemporary Art. II. Albright-Knox Art Gallery.

DE Young 759.13'074'019461 Memorial Museum, San Francisco.
Three centuries of American painting; from the collection of the M. H. de Young Memorial Museum and the California Palace of the Legion of Honor. [By] F. Lanier Graham. San Francisco, 1971. 111 p. illus. (part col.) 26 cm. Combined exhibition catalog and guide to the collection. "Catalogue ... of the paintings selected for exhibition at the California Palace of the Legion of Honor from December 19, 1970, to February 7, 1971": p. 100-111. [ND205.D46] 77-153049
1. Paintings, American—Exhibitions. I. Graham, F. Lanier. II. California Palace of the Legion of Honor, San Francisco. III. Title. BIP

DELAWARE Art Museum. 759.13
Contemporary American paintings from the Lewis Collection : [exhibition] Delaware Art Museum, September 13-October 27, 1974. Wilmington, Del. : The Museum, [1974] 45 p. : ill. (some col.) ; 21 cm. [ND212.D44 1974] 74-193211
1. Lewis, Sydney—Art collections. 2. Paintings, American—Exhibitions. 3. Painting, Modern—20th century—United States. I. Title.

DES Moines Art Center. 759.13
Twenty-five years of American painting, 1948-1973. [Exhibition held at] Des Moines Art Center, March 6-April 22, 1973. Introd. by Max Kozloff. [Des Moines, Iowa, 1973] 18, [54] p. illus. (part col.) 25 cm. Bibliography: p. [52]-[53] [ND212.D47] 73-75776
1. Paintings, American—Exhibitions. 2. Painting, Modern—20th century—United States. I. Kozloff, Max. II. Title.

DETROIT. Institute of 759.13 Arts.
Travelers in Arcadia; American artists in Italy, 1830-1875. The Detroit Institute of Arts [and] the Toledo Museum of Art. [Detroit] 1951. 68 p. illus. 23 cm. "Catalogue": p. [15]-66. [ND210.D46] 51-4709
1. Paintings, American—Exhibitions. I. Toledo Museum of Art. II. Title.

FIFTEEN under 759.147'074'014748 *forty;* paintings by young New York State Black artists, Emma Amos [and others] Ernest Crichlow, director of the exhibition. Romare Bearden, consultant. [Albany, N.Y., Division of the Humanities and the Arts, 1970] 1 v. (unpaged) illus. 25 cm. Label mounted on t.p.: Supplied by Worldwide Books, Boston. Exhibition held at Gallery Museum, Hall of Springs, Saratoga Performing Arts Center, July 1st through July 31, 1970; sponsored by the Division of the Humanities and the Arts, the State Education Dept. of New York. [ND238.N5F5] 72-633963
1. Paintings, American—Exhibitions. 2. Negro artists—New York (State) I. Amos, Emma, 1938- II. Crichlow, Ernest T., 1914- III. Saratoga Performing Arts Center. IV. New York (State). Division of the Humanities and the Arts.

THE Forum exhibition of 759.13 *modern American painters, 1916.* Reprint ed. New York, Arno Press [1968, c1916] 78 p. illus. 26 cm. (Arno series of contemporary art no. 19) The Forum exhibition of modern American painters, March 13 to March 25, 1916, on view at the Anderson Galleries, New York. Bibliography: p. 77-78. [ND212.F57 1968] 68-9240
1. Paintings, American—Exhibitions. 2. Painting, Modern,—20th century—U.S. I. Anderson Galleries, New York. BIP

GARBISCH, Edgar William 759.13
101 masterpieces of American primitive paintings, from the collection of Edgar William & Bernice Chrysler Garbisch. [Rev. ed.] Forword by James J. Rorimer. Pref. by John Walker. Introd. by Albert Ten Eyck Gardner. [New York] Amer. Federation of Arts [1962, c.1961] 157p. col. illus. 30cm. These paintings have been selected for an exhibition that is being shown in many of the major museums in the United States. 61-18662 12.50; 5.00 pap.,
1. Paintings, American—Exhibitions. 2. Paintings—Privates collections. 3. Primitivism in art. I. Garbisch, Bernice (Chrysler) II. Title.

GARBISCH, Edgar William. 759.13
101 masterpieces of American primitive painting, from the collection of Edgar William & Bernice Chrysler Garbisch. Foreword by James J. Rorimer. Pref. by John Walker. Introd. by Albert Ten Eyck Gardner. New ed. [New York] American Federation of Arts; distributed by Doubleday [1962] 159 p. col. illus. 31 cm. Exhibition of paintings shown in various museums in the United States from November 17, 1961-May 15, 1964. [ND207.G3 1962] 64-6629
1. Paintings, American — Exhibitions. 2. Paintings — Private collections. 3. Primitivism in art. I. Garbisch, Bernice (Chrysler) II. Title.

GINGOLD, Diane 759.13'074'016147 J.
American painting, 1900-1939 : selections from the Whitney Museum of American Art: exhibition June 29 through August 8, 1976, Montgomery Museum of Fine Arts, Montgomery Alabama [Montgomery] : Montgomery Museum of Fine Arts, 1976. 110 p. : ill. ; 25 cm. Catalog prepared by D. J. Gingold. Includes index. Bibliography: p. 105-107. [ND212.G5] 76-21911 ISBN 0-89280-003-8
1. Whitney Museum of American Art, New York. 2. Paintings, American—Exhibitions. 3. Paintings, Modern—20th century—United States—Exhibitions. I. Montgomery Museum of Fine Arts. II. Title.

GODFREY, Robert, 757'.9'0973 1941-
The figure in recent American painting / organized by Robert Godfrey. New Wilmington, Pa. : Art Dept., Westminster College, 1974. 44 p. : ill. ; 21 x 23 cm. Catalogue of exhibition to be held at Westminster College, New Wilmington, Pa., Oct. 1-Nov. 5, 1974; at 4 other institutions, Nov. 22, 1974-Apr. 4, 1975. Includes bibliographical references. [ND212.5.R4G62] 74-83533
1. Paintings, American—Exhibitions. 2. Realism in art—United States. 3. Human figure in art. 4. Painting, Modern—20th century—United States. I. Title.

GOLDSTONE, Herbert A 708.1471
The Herbert A. Goldstone collection of American art [Catalogue of] a special exhibition, June 15-September 12, 1965. Brooklyn, Brooklyn Museum [c1965] 128 p. illus. 22 x 23 cm. Collection owned by Hilda and Herbert Goldstone. [ND212.G6] 65-23183
1. Paintings, American — Exhibitions. 2. Sculpture — Exhibitors 3. Paintings — Private collections. 4. Sculpture — Private collections. I. Goldstone, Hilda. II. Brooklyn Institute of Arts and Sciences, Museum. III. Title.

GREENWICH Gallery, New 759.13 York.
Fifty contemporary American artists: opening exhibition. New York [1957] 1v. (unpaged) illus., ports. 27cm. [N6512.G7] 57-59420
1. Paintings, American—Exhibitions. 2. Sculpture, American—Exhibitions. 3. Artists, American. I. Title.

HALLMARK CARDS, inc. 759.0838
The Hallmark art award [sponsored by Hall Brothers] Wildenstein, Institute of Contemporary Art, Corcoran Gallery of Art, Los Angeles County Museum, William Rockhill Nelson Gallery of Art. Proceeds for the benefit of American Red Cross. [New York? 1949] 87 p. illus. 24 cm. "The list of United States museums where the Hallmark Traveling Exhibition will be shown was incomplete at the time of printing of this catalogue." [ND212.H3] 50-531
1. Paintings, American—Exhibitions. 2. Paintings, French—Exhibitions. I. Wildenstein and Company, inc., New York. II. Title.

HAROLD, Margaret. 759.13
Prize-winning oil paintings and why they won the prize. With comments by Gus Baker. Designed by Harold G. Oliphant. [Nashville] Allied Publications [c1960] 111p. illus. 31cm. [ND212.H36] 60-53333
1. Paintings, American—Exhibitions. I. Title.

HAWES, 758'.1'09730740172255 Louis.
The American scene 1820-1900; an exhibitions of landscape and outdoor genre held in honor of the sesquicentennial of Indiana University. [Bloomington, Indiana University Art Museum, 1970] 142 p. illus. (part col.) 26 cm. (Indiana University Art Museum publication no. 1970/1) Catalog of the exhibition, held Jan. 18-Feb. 28, 1970, at the Indiana University Art Museum. [ND210.H38] 72-630910
1. Paintings, American—Exhibitions. 2. Painting, Modern—19th century—United States. 3. Landscape in art. 4. Genre painting. I. Indiana. University. Museum of Art. II. Title. III. Series: Indiana. University. Museum of Art. Publication no. 1970/1

HECKSCHER Art 759.13'074'014725 Museum, Huntington, N.Y.
The image in twentieth century America. [Huntington, N.Y., 1968] 20 p. illus. 26 cm. Catalog of the exhibition held Sept. 14-Oct. 27, 1968. [ND212.H4] 70-283501
1. Paintings, American—Exhibitions. 2. Painting, Modern—20th century—U.S. I. Title.

THE Henry G. Keller [759.13] *memorial exhibition;* catalogue of an exhibition of works by Henry G. Keller, sponsored by the Cleveland Institute of Art and the Cleveland Museum of Art. Held at the Cleveland Museum of Art, February first through March nineteenth, 1950. [Cleveland] Cleveland Museum of Art, 1950. Cleveland [1952] 56 p. 48 plates (incl. port.) 23 cm. [ND237.K44C6] 927.5 50-13110
1. Keller, Henry George, 1869-1949. 2. Paintings, American—Exhibitions. 3. After-dinner speeches. I. Cleveland. Institute of Art. II. Cleveland Museum of Art. III. Title: Friendly speeches.

HILLS, Patricia. 759.13
The painters' America: rural and urban life, 1810-1910 [organized for the Whitney Museum of American Art by] Patricia Hills. New York, Praeger [1974] xxiii, 160 p. illus. (part col.) 25 cm. Exhibition held at the Whitney Museum of American Art, New York, Sept. 20-Nov. 10, 1974; at the Museum of Fine Arts, Houston, Dec. 5, 1974-Jan. 19, 1975; and at the Oakland Museum, Feb. 10-Mar. 30, 1975. Bibliography: p. 154-156. [ND210.H47] 74-1721 ISBN 0-275-43700-0 15.00
1. Paintings, American—Exhibitions. 2. Painting, Modern—19th century—United States. 3. Painting, Modern—20th century—United States. 4. United States in art. I. Whitney Museum of American Art, New York. II. Houston, Tex. Museum of Fine Arts. III. Oakland Museum. IV. Title.

HIRSCHL & Adler 708.749*33 Galleries.
The American painting collection of the Montclair Art Museum. The subjects illustrated in this catalogue comprise Montclair in Manhattan, a loan exhibition presented by the Hirschl & Adler Galleries, New York, N.Y., November 7-25, 1961. [New York, 1961] 68 p. illus. (part col.) 26 cm. On cover: The Hirschl & Adler Galleries present the exhibition Montclair in Manhattan; a selection of American paintings on loan from the Montclair Art Museum, New Jersey, November 7-25, 1961. [ND210.H5] 72-210432
1. Paintings, American—Exhibitions. 2. Painting, Modern—19th century—United States. 3. Painting, Modern—20th century—United States. I. Montclair, N.J. Art Museum. II. Title. III. Title: Montclair in Manhattan.

HIRSCHL & Adler Galleries. 759.13'07401471
Forty masterworks of American art. [Exhibition held] Oct. 28 through Nov. 14, 1970. New York [1970] 57 p. illus. (part col.), ports. (part col.) 26 cm. [ND205.H5] 78-22620
1. Paintings, American—Exhibitions. I. Title.

HOOD, Dorothy, 1919- 759.13
Dorothy Hood paintings. Everson Museum of Art, Syracuse, New York, July 6 through August 3, 1972. [Syracuse, N.Y., Everson Museum of Art, 1972] 24 p. illus. (part col.) 24 cm. Bibliography: p. 22. [ND237.H72E8] 72-85863
I. Everson Museum of Art of Syracuse and Onondaga County.

HUNTER Museum of Art. 759.13'074'016882
A Southern sampler : American paintings in Southern museums : Hunter Museum of Art, September 21 through October 31, 1975, inaugural exhibition. [Chattanooga] : The Museum, [1975] 28 p. : ill. ; 23 cm. [ND205.H85] 76-354086
1. Paintings, American—Exhibitions. 2. Paintings, American—Southern States. 3. Art—Southern States—Galleries and museums. I. Title.

HUNTINGTON Galleries. 759.13'074'015442
American art : from the Limners to the Eight : [exhibition], February 1 through May 2, 1976, Huntington Galleries, Huntington, West Virginia. [Ashland, Ky.] : Ashland Oil, 1976. 128 p. : ill. (some col.) ; 26 cm. Catalog. Bibliography: p. 125. [ND205.H86 1976] 76-462
1. Paintings, American—Exhibitions. 2. Paintings, Colonial—United States—Exhibitions. 3. Paintings, Modern—17th-18th centuries—United States—Exhibitions. 4. Paintings, Modern—19th century—United States—Exhibitions. 5. Paintings, Modern—20th century—United States—Exhibitions. 6. Paintings, American—Appalachian region. I. Title.

ILLINOIS. Arts Council. 759.13'074'0173
Six Illinois painters 67/69; exhibit 1-[4] [Chicago, 1970?] 4 v. illus. 26 cm. Cover title. Each vol. contains one exhibit of six different painters. [ND230.I3A5] 77-635657
1. Paintings, American—Exhibitions. 2. Painting, Modern—20th century—Illinois. 3. Painters—Illinois. I. Title.

ILLINOIS. University. College of Fine and Applied Arts. 759.13
Contemporary American painting and sculpture. [Catalog] Krannert Art Museum. February 26 through April 2, 1961. Urbana, Univ. of Illinois Press [c.1961] 223p. illus. 26cm. annual A48 3.50 pap.,
1. Paintings, American—Exhibitions. I. Title.

ILLINOIS. University. College of Fine and Applied Arts 759.13
Contemporary American painting and sculpture, 1965. Introd. by Allen S. Weller Urbana, Author [c.1965] 210p. illus. 26cm. Catalogue of the 12th exhibition, Mar. 7-Apr. 11,1965. Krannert Art Mus., Champaign. Title varies. [ND212.A1I4] A48 3.50 pap.,
1. Paintings, American—Exhibitions. I. Title.

INDIANA. University. Museum of Art. 759.13'074'0172255
The American scene, 1900-1970; an exhibition of twentieth century painting held in honor of the Sesquincentennial of Indiana University. Organized by Thomas T. Solley, with an introd. by Henry R. Hope. april 6-may 17, 1970, Indiana University Art Museum. [Bloomington, 1970] 119 p. illus. (part col.) 26 cm. (Its Publication no. 2/1970) [ND212.I5] 71-632904
1. Paintings, American—Exhibitions. 2. Painting, Modern—20th century—U.S. I. Title. II. Series.

IOWA. University. School of Fine Arts. 759.13
Annual fine arts festival. [Catalog of] paintings by American masters. [Iowa City] v. illus. 23x29cm. [ND212.A116] 55-34835
1. Paintings, American—Exhibitions. 2. Painters, American. I. Title.

JUNIOR League of Albuquerque 759.13
Impressionism in America; an exhibition presented by the Junior League of Albuquerque in collaboration with the Univ. of N. M. Art Gallery. Univ. of N. M. Art Gallery, Albuquerque, Feb. 9-March 14, 1965; M. H. De Young Memorial Mus., San Francisco, March 30-May 5, 1965 [Albuquerque, N. M., Author, c.1965] 72p. illus. (pt. col.) 25cm. Bibl. [ND205.J8] 65-63397 4.50; 2.50 pap.,
1. Paintings, American—Exhibitions. 2. Impressionism (Art) I. New Mexico. University. Art Gallery. II. Title.

KANSAS. University. Museum of Art. 759.1
Legacy of the land, a selection of American landscape paintings from the museum collection; an exhibition in honor of the Conference of the American Association of Land Grant Colleges and State Universities, November 12, 1961 through January 15, 1962. Lawrence [1961] unpaged. illus. 15x23cm. (Its Miscellaneous publications, no. 45) [ND1351.K3] 62-62629
1. Paintings, American— Exhibitions. 2. Landscape painting, American. I. Title.

KENNEDY Galleries, inc., New York. 759.13
American masters, 18th and 19th centuries: exhibition March 14 through April 7, 1973, at Kennedy Galleries New York [New York, 1973] 63 p. illus. (part col.) 26 cm. Catalog. [ND207.K46 1973] 74-157597
1. Paintings, American—Exhibitions. 2. Painting, Colonial—United States. 3. Painting, Modern—19th century—United States. I. Title.

KENNEDY Galleries, inc., New York. 759.13
Western words; an exhibition of important paintings of the American West. New York [1969] 75 p. illus. (part col.) 23 cm. (The Kennedy quarterly, v. 9, no. 1) "The Kennedy quarterly is written ... by Maria Naylor." [N8640.K4 vol. 9, no. 1] 79-13007 2.00
1. Paintings, American—Exhibitions. 2. The West in art. I. Naylor, Maria. II. Title. III. Series.

LANDGREN, Marchal E. 739.13'074'015251
American pupils of Thomas Couture; [an exhibition] Text and catalogue by Marchal E. Landgren. [College Park, University of Maryland Dept. of Art, 1970] 64 p. 44 illus., port. 22 x 26 cm. On spine: Couture: American pupils. "Museum training program, 1969-1970." Held at the University of Maryland Art Gallery, Mar. 19-Apr. 26, 1970. Includes bibliographical references. [ND210.L34] 71-120903
1. Paintings, American—Exhibitions. 2. Painting, Modern—19th century—U.S. I. Maryland. University. Art Gallery. II. Title.

LANGDALE, Cecily. 759.13'074'01471
The American scene; a survey of the life and landscape of the 19th century. New York, Hirschl & Adler Galleries [1969] 72 p. illus. (part col.) 26 cm. Label mounted on t.p.: Supplied by Worldwide Books, inc., Boston. Catalogue of an exhibition held at Hirschl & Adler Galleries, Oct. 29 through Nov. 22, 1969. [ND210.L36] 75-104395
1. Paintings, American—Exhibitions. 2. Painting, Modern—19th century—U.S. 3. America in art. I. Hirschl & Adler Galleries. II. Title.

LONG Beach, Calif. Museum of Art. 759.194
California painting: 40 painters, selected by Samuel Heavenrich [director of the exhibition] and Grace L. McCann Morley, with statements by the artists. The Municipal Art Center, Long Beach, in collaboration with the San Francisco Museum of Art. [Long, Beach, 1956?] unpaged. illus. 26cm. [ND230.C3L6] 59-3736
1. Paintings, American— Exhibitions. 2. Painters, American—California. I. Heavenrich, Samuel. II. Morley, Grace Louise (McCann) 1900- III. Title.

LOS Angeles Co., Calif. Museum, Los Angeles. 759.1
A catalogue of the Mr. and Mrs. William Preston Harrison galleries of American art, compiled and arranged by Preston Harrison. Los Angeles Museum (Exposition Park) Los Angeles, Saturday night Pub. Co., 1934. 74 p. illus., plates, ports. 24 cm. Includes the terms of the Harrison gifts, printed in full (p. 3-13; 55-61) "Books on American art"; p. 18. [N582.L7A63] 34-11633
1. Paintings, American — Exhibitions. 2. Water-colors, American — Exhibitions. I. Harrison, William Preston, 1870-1940, comp. II. Title.

LOS Angeles Co., Calif. Museum, Los Angeles. 708.147
First Pan-American exhibition of oil paintings, November 27, 1925 to February 28, 1926. Los Angeles, Calif., Los Angeles Museum [1925] 60 p. illus., 20 plates. 20 cm. English and Spanish. [ND201.L6] 42-43904
1. Paintings, American — Exhibitions. 2. Paintings, Latin American — Exhibitions. 3. Paintings, Canadian — Exhibitions. I. Title.

LOS Angeles County Museum, Los Angeles. 759.13
Four abstract classicists [Karl Benjamin, Lorser Feitelson, Frederick Hammersley, and John McLaughlin. Los Angeles, 1959] 70p. illus. (part col.) ports. 19x21cm. Catalogue of exhibition, Sept. 16-Oct. 18, 1959, presented with the cooperation of the San Francisco Museum of Art. [ND212.L67] 61-43041
1. Paintings, American—Exhibitions. I. Title.

LOUISIANA. State University and Agricultural and Mechanical College. Library. 759.0838
Louisiana paintings of the nineteenth century, lent by Mr. and Mrs. W. E. Groves, New Orleans; an exhibition in the Louisiana State University Library October and Novemner, 1959. [Catalog by Corinne McNeir] Baton Rouge [1959] unpaged. illus. 22cm. [ND230.L8L8] 60-62623
1. Paintings, American—Exhibitions. 2. Paintings— Louisiana. I. Groves, William E., 1906- II. Groves, Gladys (Rhodes) III. Title.

LOWE Art Museum. 759.13
French impressionists influence American artists. Coral Gables, Fla. [1971] 96 p. illus. (part col.) 26 cm. Catalog of the exhibition held Mar. 19-Apr. 25, 1971. [ND210.5.I4L6] 77-198331
1. Paintings, American—Exhibitions. 2. Impressionism (Art)—U.S. 3. Painting, American—French influences. 4. Paintings, French—Exhibitions. 5. Impressionism (Art)—France. I. Title.

MAXWELL Galleries. 759.194
One hundred years of California painting from 1849; [exhibition held] March 4 through 26, 1966. San Francisco [1966] [16] p. illus. 28 cm. Cover title. Catalog. [ND230.C3M38 1966] 75-303958
1. Paintings, American—Exhibitions. 2. Painting, Modern—19th century—California. 3. Painting, Modern—20th century—California. I. Title.

MAYTHAM, Thomas N. 759.13'074
Great American paintings from the Boston and Metropolitan Museums. [Exhibition] National Gallery of Art [Nov. 30, 1970-Jan. 10, 1971]; City Art Museum, St. Louis [Jan. 28-Mar. 7, 1971]; Seattle Art Museum [Mar. 25-May 9, 1971] By Thomas N. Maytham. [Seattle] Seattle Art Museum [1970] 163 p. illus. (part col.) 25 cm. Bibliography: p. 155-156. [ND205.M33] 77-137432
1. Paintings, American—Exhibitions. I. Boston. Museum of Fine Arts. II. New York (City). Metropolitan Museum of Art. III. U.S. National Gallery of Art. IV. St. Louis. City Art Museum. V. Seattle. Art Museum. VI. Title.

MAYTHAM, Thomas N. 759.13'074
Great American paintings from the Boston and Metropolitan Museums, by Thomas N. Maytham. New York, Viking Press [1971] 163 p. illus. (part col.) 26 cm. (A Studio book) Catalogue of an exhibition of 100 paintings organized by the Seattle Art Museum in celebration of the centennial (1970) of the Boston and Metropolitan Museums. The exhibition toured the Art Museum, Seattle, the National Gallery of Art, Washington, D.C., and the City Art Museum, St. Louis. [ND205.M33 1971] 77-144837 ISBN 0-670-34838-4 12.50
1. Paintings, American—Exhibitions. I. Boston. Museum of Fine Arts. II. New York (City). Metropolitan Museum of Art. III. Seattle. Art Museum. IV. U.S. National Gallery of Art. V. St. Louis. City Art Museum. VI. Title.

MILWAUKEE. Art Center. 759.13
American painting, 1760-1960; a selection of 125 paintings from the collection of Mr. and Mrs. Lawrence A. Fleischman, Detroit. [Exhibition] March 3d through April 3d, 1960. [By Edward H. Dwight, director. Milwaukee, 1960] 145p. illus. (1 col.) 24cm. [ND205.M49] 60-1845
1. Paintings, American— Exhibitions. 2. Paintings—Private collections. I. Fleischman, Lawrence A. II. Fleischman, Barbara. III. Dwight, Edward H. IV. Title.

MINNESOTA. University. University Gallery. 759.13
40 American painters, 1940-1950; [exhibit] June 4- August 30, 1951. [Minneapolis, 1951] 1 v. (unpaged) illus. 23 cm. Cover title. [ND212.M5] 51-9543
1. Paintings, American — Exhibitions. I. Title.

MODERN 759.13'074'0178411
American painting from the Commerce Trust Company Collection. [Lawrence, Kan., 1966] 1 v. (unpaged) illus. 16 x 23 cm. (Miscellaneous publications of the Museum of Art, no. 64) "Catalogue ... prepared by art history students at the University of Kansas in a seminar on museum techniques, directed by Mr. Bret Waller [for the exhibition held at the museum Dec. 4, 1966-Jan. 1, 1967]" [ND212.M6] 68-63544
1. Commerce Trust Co., Kansas City, Mo.—Art collections. 2. Paintings, American—Exhibitions. 3. Painting, Modern—20th century—U.S. I. Kansas. University. Museum of Art. II. Series: Kansas. University. Museum of Art. Miscellaneous publications, no. 64

MOURE, Nancy Dustin Wall. 759.13'074'019493
Los Angeles painters of the nineteen-twenties. Introd. by Arthur Miller. Claremont, Calif., Pomona College Gallery [1972] [39] p. illus. 23 cm. Catalogue of an exhibition held Apr. 5-May 3, 1972 at Pomona College Gallery. Includes bibliographical references. [ND235.L6M6] 72-192452
1. Paintings, American—Exhibitions. 2. Painting, Modern—20th century—Los Angeles. 3. Painters, American—Los Angeles. I. Pomona College, Claremont, Calif. Gallery. II. Title.

NEW directions in painting. 759.13
[Exhibiting artists: Elmer Bischoff, Richard Diebenkorn, and others. Exhibition schedule: Florida State University Gallery, Tallahassee, March, 1959. John and Mable Ringling Museum of Art, Sarasota, April, 1959. Norton Gallery and School of Art, West Palm Beach, May, 1959. Tallahassee, 1959] unpaged (chiefly illus.) 26cm. [ND212.N368] 59-2222
1. Paintings, American—Exhibitions. I. Florida State University, Tallahassee.

NEW Jersey. State Museum, Trenton. 759.13'0740149'66
Four views. [Exhibition] September 19-November 15, 1970. Trenton [1970] [24] p. illus. 22 cm. [ND212.N3685] 79-633962
1. Paintings, American—Exhibitions. 2. Painting, Modern—20th century—U.S. I. Title.

NEW York. Art Students' League. 759.13
American masters; Art Students League. New York, c1967. 126 p. 45 illus. 26 cm. "Exhibition number 67: 25." Catalog of an exhibition circulated by the American Federation of Arts to celebrate the start of the tenth decade of the Art Students League of New York. [ND212.N3695] 68-3659
1. Paintings, American—Exhibitions. 2. Painters—United States. I. American Federation of Arts. II. Title.

22 x 26 cm. [ND237.R56W4] 72-75006 ISBN 0-8271-7215-X
I. Weeks, Edward, 1898-

SANTA Barbara, Calif. v. 12
Museum of Art.
Pacific coast biennial exhibition of paintings and watercolors [catalog] [Santa Barbara?] v. illus. 24cm. Began publication in 1955. [ND228.S3] 58-43995
1. Paintings. American—Exhibitions. 2. Painters, American—Pacific States. I. Title.

SANTA Barbara, Calif. 759.13
Museum of Art.
Two hundred years of American painting; a handbook listing the museum's holdings, including the newly acquired Preston Morton collection. Commemorating the opening of the Preston Morton Wing and the museum's twentieth anniversary, 1941-1961. [Santa Barbara, 1961] unpaged. illus. 24cm. [N742.S15A56] 61-3832
1. Paintings, American—Exhibitions. I. Title.

SARGENT'S Boston, 759.13
with an essay a biographical summary & a complete check list of Sargent's portraits. Boston, Museum of Fine Arts, 1956. 132p. illus. (part col.) ports. 26cm. 'Catalogue of a centennial exhibition, Sargent's Boston, January 3 to February 7, 1956':p. 67-75. [ND237.S3M3] [ND237.S3M3] 927.5 56-1995 56-1995
1. Sargent, John Singer, 1856-1925. 2. Paintings, American—Exhibitions. I. McKibbin, David. II. Boston, Museum of Fine Arts.

SELZ, Peter 759.13'074'0155451
Howard, 1919-
American painting, 1970. Directed by Peter H. Selz. Exhibition at the Virginia Museum from May 4 through June 7 [Cincinnati, Printed by J. W. Ford Co., 1970] 1 v. (unpaged) illus. (part col.) 31 cm. [ND212.S44] 73-115777
1. Paintings, American—Exhibitions. 2. Painting, Modern—20th century—United States. I. Virginia Museum of Fine Arts, Richmond. II. Title.

SHALKOP, Robert 759.13'074'018856
L.
A show of color; 100 years of painting in the Pike's Peak region. An exhibition in honor of the centennial of Colorado Springs, 1871-1971. [Catalogue by] Robert L. Shalkop. [Colorado Springs] Colorado Springs Fine Arts Center [1971] 92 p. illus. 27 cm. [ND230.C52P56] 72-194172
1. Paintings, American—Exhibitions. 2. Painting—Pike's Peak region. I. Colorado Springs. Fine Arts Center. II. Title.

SKOWHEGAN, Me. School of 759.13
Painting and Sculpture.
Four centuries of American masterpieces; an exhibition arranged by the Skowhegan School of Painting and Sculpture. Introd. by Donelson F. Hoopes;foreword by August Heckscher. [New York? 1964] 1 v. (Chiefly illus. (part col.)) 27 cm. Catalogue of exhibition held at the Gallery at the Better Living Center, New York World's Fair, 1964-65, May 22, 1964 through Oct. 18, 1964. [ND205.S56] 65-3158
1. Paintings, American — Exhibitions. 2. Sculpture, American — Exhibitions. I. Hoopes, Donelson F. II. New York. World's Fair, 1964-1965. III. Title.

SMITHSONIAN Institution. 759.13
National Collection of Fine Arts.
American landscape: A changing frontier. [Exhibition presented April 28 to June 19, 1966] in commemoration of the fiftieth anniversary of the National Park Service. Washington, Smithsonian Institution, 1966. 8 p., 34 p. of illus. 21 x 25 cm. (Smithsonian publication 4671) "Catalogue of the exhibition": 10, 2 p. inserted. [ND205.S6] 66-61720
1. Paintings, American—Exhibitions. 2. United States—Description and travel—Views. I. United States National Park Service. II. Title.

SOLOMON, Alan R. 759.13
Painting in New York: 1944 to 1969, by Alan Solomon. Exhibition dates: November 24, 1969-January 11, 1970, Pasadena Art Museum. [Pasadena, 1969] 76 p. illus. (part col.) 25 cm. Bibliography: p. 72-75. [ND235.N45S6] 72-99958
1. Paintings, American—Exhibitions. 2. Painting, Modern—20th century—New York (City) 3. Painting—New York (City) I. Pasadena, Calif. Art Museum. II. Title.

SOLOMON R. Guggenheim 759.06
Museum, New York.
American abstract expressionists and imagists. New York [1961] 131 p. illus. (part col.) 28 cm. Catalogue of the exhibition to be held Oct.-Dec. 1961. Bibliography: p. 97-131. [ND212.S59] 61-18230
1. Paintings, American — Exhibitions. 2. Art, Abstract — Exhibitions. 3. Expressionism (Art) I. Title.

SOLOMON R. Guggenheim 759.13
Museum, New York.
Systemic painting. [New York, Solomon R. Guggenheim Foundation, 1966] 65 p. illus. (part col.) 26 cm. Exhibition assembled and introduction written by Lawrence Alloway, curator; held Sept.-Nov., 1966 at the Guggenheim Museum. Bibliography: p. 56-65. [ND212.S598] 66-28425
1. Paintings, American—Exhibitions. I. Title.

SOLOMON R. Guggenheim 759.13
Museum, New York.
Younger American painters, a selection. [Exhibition] May 12 to July 25, 1954. New York [1954] [96]p. illus. 26cm. [ND212.S6] 55-1140
1. Paintings, American— Exhibitions. I. Title.

TEXAS. 759.13'074'016431
University at Austin. Art Museum.
Selected paintings from the Michener Collection; [exhibition] November 2, 1969-January 5, 1970. [Austin, 1970?] 1 v. (unpaged) illus. 26 cm. [ND212.T42] 72-198153
1. Michener, James Albert, 1907- —Art collections. 2. Paintings, American—Exhibitions. 3. Painting, Modern—20th century—U.S. I. Title.

TEXAS. University at 759.13
Austin. Art Museum.
Visual r & d: a corporation collects; the Ciba-Geigy Collection of contemporary paintings, June 10-August 12, 1973 [catalogue. Austin] University Art Museum, University of Texas at Austin [1973] [24] p. col. illus. 26 cm. [ND212.T42 1973] 74-171008
1. Ciba-Geigy Corporation—Art collections. 2. Paintings, American—Exhibitions. 3. Painting, Modern—20th century—United States. I. Ciba-Geigy Corporation. II. Title.

TOLEDO. Museum 759.13'074'017113
of Art.
Image, color, and form : recent paintings by eleven Americans : [exhibition] January 12 through February 9, 1975 : organized by the Toledo Museum of Art and the Toledo Modern Art Group. [Toledo, Ohio] : Toledo Museum of Art, [1975] 31 p. : ill. ; 26 cm. Bibliography: p. 30-31. [ND212.T6 1975] 74-31742
1. Paintings, American—Exhibitions. 2. Painting, Modern—20th century—United States. I. Toledo Modern Art Group. II. Title.

TROPICAL; 759.13'074'0194
tropical scenes by the 19th century painters of California. [Oakland? Calif., 1971 or 2] 50 p. illus (part col.) 23 cm. Catalogue of an exhibition held at the Oakland Museum, Oct. 5-Nov. 14, 1971, the Santa Barbara Museum of Art, Dec. 7, 1971-Jan. 23, 1972, and the E. B. Crocker Art Gallery, Feb. 19-Mar. 19, 1972. [ND230.C3T76] 72-198392
1. Paintings, American—Exhibitions. 2. Painting, Modern—19th century—California. 3. Tropics in art. I. Oakland Museum. II. Santa Barbara, Calif. Museum of Art. III. Crocker Art Gallery, Sacramento, Calif.

U. S. National Gallery of 759.13
Art.
American primitive paintings from the collection of Edgar William and Bernice Chrysler Garbisch. Washington, 1954- v. illus. 24cm. Catalogue of a series of exhibitions of opening May 9, 1954. Contents.pt. 1. Oil paintings. [ND207.A52] 54-11098
1. Paintings, American—Exhibitions. I. Garbisch, Edgar William. II. Garbisch, Bernice Chrysler. III. Title.

U. S. National Gallery of 759.13
Art.
George Bellows; a retrospective exhibition, January 19 through February 24, 1957. Washington [1957] 126p. plates. 24cm. [ND237.B45U5] [ND237.B45U5] 927.5 57-61111 57-61111
1. Bellows, George Wesley, 1882-1925. 2. Paintings, American—Exhibitions. I. Title.

VIRGINIA Museum of Fine 759.1
Arts, Richmond.
American painting, 1954. [Exhibition] directed by Dwight Kirsch at the Virginia Museum, 26 Feb. through 21 March; at the Des Moines Art Center, 4 April through 2 May, 1954. [Richmond, 1954] unpaged. illus. 15 x 22cm. [ND212.V48] 55-94
1. Paintings, American—Exhibitions. I. Kirsch, Dwight, 1899- II. Title.

VIRGINIA Museum of Fine 759.13
Arts, Richmond.
Twelve American painters : an exhibition of paintings by twelve American artists, organized by William Gaines, on display at the Virginia Museum from September 30 to October 27, 1974. Richmond : The Museum, [1974] 84 p., [12] leaves of plates : ill. (some col.) ; 27 cm. [ND212.V52 1974] 74-12843 ISBN 0-8139-0609-1 : 5.50
1. Paintings, American—Exhibitions. 2. Painting, Modern—20th century—United States. I. Gaines, William Harris, 1918- II. Title.

WALKER Art Center, 759.13
Minneapolis.
60 American painters, 1960; abstract expressionist painting of the fifties.?An exhibition, April 3-May 8, 1960. Editor of the catalogue Nancy B. Miller. Minneapolis, 1961] 79 p. illus. (part col.) 28 cm. Bibliography: p. 54-78. [ND212.W33] 61-42786
1. Paintings, American — Exhibitions. 2. Art, Abstract. 3. Expressionism (Art) I. Miller, Nancy B., ed. II. Title.

WALKER Art Center, 759.13
Minneapolis.
The precisionist view in American art. An exhibition organized by the Walker Art Center, Minneapolis, in cooperation with the Whitney Museum of American Art [and others] November 13 through December 25, 1960. Minneapolis, c1960. 62 p. illus. (part fold., part col.) 28 cm. Bibliography: p. 60-62. [ND212.W28] 61-65404
1. Paintings, American — Exhibitions. I. Title.

WASHINGTON and 759.13'074'0155852
Lee University, Lexington, Va.
American painting at Washington and Lee University : some nineteenth-century examples : an exhibition presented by Washington and Lee University, Lexington, Virginia, January 5-22, 1976. [Lexington, Va.] : The University, c1976. [48] p. : ill. (some col.) ; 29 cm. Bibliography: p. [3] of cover. [ND201.W37 1976] 76-354772
1. Paintings, American—Exhibitions. 2. Paintings, Modern—19th century—United States—Exhibitions. I. Title.

WASHINGTON University, St. 759.13
Louis Gallery of Art.
The development of modernist painting: Jackson Pollock to the present. St. Louis [1969?] [34] p. 21 col. illus. 20 cm. Catalogue of an exhibition sponsored by Steinberg Art Gallery Associates, held at the Washington University Gallery of Art on Apr. 1-30, 1969. [ND212.W347] 73-171524
1. Paintings, American—Exhibitions. 2. Painting, Modern—20th century—United States. I. Steinberg Art Gallery Associates. II. Title.

WHERE liberty 759.13'074'014797
dwells : 19th-century art by the American people : works of art from the Collection of Mr. and Mrs. Peter Tillou / catalogue by Peter H. Tillou ; introd., Robert P. Buck, Jr. [Buffalo, N.Y. : Albright-Knox Art Gallery], c1976. 114 p. : ill. (some col.) ; 26 cm. "Exhibition schedule: January 17-February 22, 1976, Albright-Knox Art Gallery, Buffalo, New York; July 25-August 29, 1976, Milwaukee Art Center, Milwaukee, Wisconsin; January 14-February 20, 1977, Pennsylvania Academy of Fine Arts, Philadelphia, Pennsylvania; April 3-May 29, 1977, Munson-Williams-Proctor Institute, Utica, New York." Bibliography: p. 111-114. [ND210.5.P7W45] 76-362663
1. Tillou, Peter H.—Art collections. 2. Paintings, American—Exhibitions. 3. Primitivism in art—United States—Exhibitions. 4. Paintings, Modern—19th century—United States—Exhibitions. I. Albright-Knox Art Gallery.

WHITNEY Museum 759.13'074'01471
of American Art, New York.
Lyrical abstractions. [New York, 1971] 46 p. illus. 19 x 21 cm. Catalogue of an exhibition held May 25-July 6, 1971. [ND212.5.A25W48] 73-162569
1. Aldrich, Larry—Art collections. 2. Paintings, American—Exhibitions. 3. Abstract expressionism—U.S. I. Title.

WHITNEY Museum of 759.13'074'0147
American Art, New York.
The structure of color, by Marcia Tucker. New York [1971] 31 p. 28 cm. Catalog of an exhibition held at the Whitney Museum of American Art from February 25 to April 18, 1971. Bibliography: p. 25-31. [ND212.W46] 73-154613
1. Paintings, American—Exhibitions. 2. Painting, Modern—20th century—U.S. 3. Color in art. I. Tucker, Marcia. II. Title.

WHITNEY Museum of 708.147
American Art, New York.
Young America; thirty American painters and sculptors under thirty-five. [Exhibition catalog] 1957- New York. v. illus. 26 cm. [N6512.W53] 57-1835
1. Paintings, American — Exhibitions. 2. Sculpture, American — Exhibitions. 3. Artists, American. I. Title.

WHITNEY Museum of 708.1471
American Art, New York.
Young America, 1960; thirty American painters under thirty-six [by] Lloyd Goodrich and John I. H. Baur. New York, Praeger [c.1960] unpaged illus. 23cm. 3.50
1. Paintings, American—Exhibitions. 2. Sculpture, American—Exhibitions. 3. Artists, American. I. Title.

WHITNEY Museum of 708.147
American Art, New York
Young America, 1965; thirty American artists under thirty-five, by Lloyd Goodrich. New York, Pub. for the Whitney Mus. of Amer. Art by Praeger [c.1965] 1v. (unpaged) illus. 23cm. [N6512.W53] 57-1835 4.00
1. Paintings, American—Exhibitions. 2. Sculpture, American—Exhibitions. 3. Artists, American. I. Title.

WIESENDANGER, 759.13'074'016318
Martin.
19th century Louisiana painters and paintings from the Collection of W. E. Groves. [By Martin and Margaret Wiesendanger. Gretna [La.] Pelican Pub. Co., 1971. 118 p. illus. 24 cm. [ND230.L8W53] 73-156076 ISBN 0-911116-52-4
1. Groves, William E., 1906- —Art collections. 2. Paintings, American—Exhibitions. 3. Painting, Modern—19th century—Louisiana. 4. Painters—Louisiana. I. Wiesendanger, Margaret, joint author. II. Title.

THE William Sommer [927.5]
memorial exhibition; catalogue of an exhibition of works by William Sommer held November first through December tenth in the Cleveland Museum of Art, 1950. [Cleveland, 1950] 98 p. illus., port. 26 cm. [ND237.S633C6] 759.13 50-11266
1. Sommer. William, 1867-1949. 2. Paintings. American—Exhibitions. I. Cleveland Museum of Art.

WILLIAMS, Gluyas, 1888- 741.9'73
The best of Gluyas Williams. With a foreword by Charles Dana Gibson, and a pref. by Robert Benchley. New York, Dover Publications [1971] viii, 119 p. (chiefly illus.) 29 cm. [NC1429.W56A43] 73-177890 ISBN 0-486-22737-5 2.50
I. Title.

WILLIS, John Ralph. 759.13'074'014967
Fragments of American life : an exhibition of paintings, January 25-March 28, 1976, the Art Museum, Princeton University / catalogue by John Ralph Willis ; biographies and bibliographies compiled by Anne Jones Willis. Princeton, N.J. : Art Museum, Princeton University, c1976. 75 p. : ill. ; 21 x 25 cm. Bibliography: p. 75. [ND212.W52] 75-42839
1. Paintings, American—Exhibitions. 2. Paintings, Modern—20th century—United States—Exhibitions. I. Willis, Anne Jones. II. Princeton University. Art Museum. III. Title.

YALE University. Art Gallery. 709'.73
American art from alumni collections. [New Haven, 1968] 1 v. (unpaged) 144 illus. 27 cm. Catalog of an exhibition held April 25-June 16, 1968, Yale University Art Gallery. [ND205.Y3] 68-4152
1. Paintings, American—Exhibitions. 2. Paintings—Private collections. I. Title.

Paintings, American—History.

HAYES, Bartlett H., 1904- 759.13
Roots and promise; aspects of American art history, by Bartlett H. Hayes. Andover, Mass., Addison Gallery of American Art, Phillips Academy [1966] 1 v. (unpaged) illus. 16 x 23 cm. "Published in connection with an exhibition held at Winterfest, the Prudential Building, Boston, under the auspices of the Cultural Foundation of Boston, February 18th-27th, 1966." [ND205.H3] 67-866
1. Paintings, American—History. I. Phillips Academy, Andover, Mass. Addison Gallery of American Art. II. Title.

Paintings—Amsterdam—Catalogs.

RIJKSMUSEUM 750'.74'094923
Amsterdam; paintings. [Texts by Giorgio T. Faggin, Ugo Ruggeri, and Raffaele Monti. Translation and editing: editors of Art news] New York, Newsweek [1969] 171 p. col. illus., plans, col. ports. 30 cm. (Great museums of the world) [N2460.R5] 69-19063
1. Paintings—Amsterdam—Catalogs. I. Faggin, Giorgio T. II. Ruggeri, Ugo. III. Monti, Raffaele. IV. Amsterdam. Rijks-Museum. V. Series: Great museums of the world (New York, Newsweek)

Paintings, Australian.

GRAY, Jocelyn. 759.994
Early Australian paintings. Melbourne, New York [etc.] Oxford University Press [1967] 31 p. illus. 22 cm. (National Gallery booklets) Bibliography: p. 31. [ND1100.G7] 68-87282 0.70 Aust.
1. Paintings, Australian. 2. Painting, Australian—History. I. Title. II. Series: Victoria, Australia. National Gallery, Melbourne. Booklets

GREAT Australian 759.9'94
paintings. [Melbourne] Lansdowne Press [1971] 72 p. col. illus. 31 cm. Bibliography: p. 72. [ND1100.G73] 72-178934 ISBN 0-7018-0434-3
1. Paintings, Australian.

Paintings, Australian (Aboriginal)

MOUNTFORD, Charles Pearcy, 1890- 759.994
Aboriginal paintings from Australia. Introd. by Charles P. Mountford [New York] Pub. by the New Amer. Lib. of World Lit. by arrangement with UNESCO [c.1954, 1964] 24p. [3]p. (on fold. 1.) illus., 28 col. plates. 17cm. (Mentor-Unesco art bk., MQ582) Bibl. [ND1101.M6] 65-266 .95 pap.,
1. Paintings, Australian (Aboriginal) I. United Nations Educational, Scientific and Cultural Organization. II. Title.

Paintings, Australian (Aboriginal)—Exhibitions.

COLORADO Springs. Fine Arts Center. Taylor Museum. 759.01'1'099429
The art of Arnhem Land, from the collection of William McE. Miller, Jr. [Colorado Springs] 1966. [24] p. illus. 15 x 22 cm. Catalog of an exhibition. [ND1101.C64 1966] 74-171018
1. Miller, William McE.—Art collections. 2. Paintings, Australian (Aboriginal)—Exhibitions. 3. Painting, Primitive—Arnhem Land, Australia. I. Title.

MOUNTFORD, Charles Pearcy, 1890- 759.01'1'099429
Aboriginal art from Australia; [bark paintings and sculpture lent by the National Gallery of South Australia, Adelaide. Catalogue by Charles P. Mountford. Exhibition: Worcester Art Museum, February 17-April 3, 1966; Allentown Art Museum, April 14-May 12, 1966. Worcester, Mass., Printed by Commonwealth Press, 1966] 96 p. illus., maps. 23 cm. [ND1101.M59] 68-650
1. Paintings, Australian (Aboriginal)—Exhibitions. 2. Sculpture, Primitive—Exhibitions. I. South Australia. National Gallery, Adelaide. II. Worcester, Mass. Art Museum. III. Allentown, Pa. Art Museum. IV. Title.

Paintings, Australian—Catalogs.

BONYTHON, Kym. 759.994
Modern Australian painting, 1970/1975 / [selected by] Kym Bonython ; [introduction by] Elwyn Lynn. Adelaide : Rigby, 1976. 87 p. : chiefly col. ill. ; 29 cm. [ND1100.B66 1976] 76-372026 ISBN 0-7270-0087-X
1. Paintings, Australian—Catalogs. 2. Paintings, Modern—20th century—Australia—Catalogs. I. Title.

Paintings, Australian—Exhibitions.

SMITH, Robert, 1928- 759.994'074
Australian painting today: a survey of the past ten years [catalogue. Brisbane, Printed by Rowan Morcom, 1963] [27] p. illus. 24 cm. On label: Supplied by Worldwide Books, inc., Boston. "Exhibition ... arranged [by the Queensland Art Gallery] with the cooperation of the State art galleries and the Commonwealth Art Advisory Board for showing in Australia and Europe from 1963 to 1965." [ND1100.S57] 74-199716
1. Paintings, Australian—Exhibitions. 2. Painting, Modern—20th century—Australia. I. Queensland Art Gallery. II. Title.

Paintings, Austrian—Exhibitions.

SOLOMON R. Guggenheim Museum, New York. 759.36
Gustav Klimt and Egon Schiele [Exhibition 65/1, February-April 1965] New York, Author [1965] 119p. illus. (pt. col.) ports. 28cm. Bibl. [ND538.K57S6] 65-16678 5.50 pap.,
1. Klimt, Gustav, 1862-1918. 2. Schiele, Egon, 1890-1918. 3. Paintings, Austrian—Exhibitions. 4. Drawings, Austrian—Exhibitions. I. Title.

Paintings, Balinese.

COLORADO Springs. Fine Arts Center. Taylor Museum. 759.9923
Balinese painting Taylor Museum collection. [By] Leland W. Gralapp. [Colorado Springs] c.1961. 56p. illus. Bibl. 61-19742 1.25 pap.,
1. Paintings, Balinese. I. Gralapp, LLand W. II. Title. BIP

Paintings—Baltimore—Catalogs.

BALTIMORE. Museum of Art. 759.0838
Cone collection; a handbook with a catalogue of paintings and sculpture. Baltimore [c1955] 55 p. illus. (part col.) 26 cm. Cover title: Handbook of the Cone collection. [N515.A53] 56-2463
1. Paintings—Baltimore—Catalogs. 2. Sculpture—Baltimore—Catalogs. I. Cone, Claribel. II. Cone, Etta. III. Title.

Paintings, Baroque—Exhibitions.

CALIFORNIA State University, Northridge. Fine Arts Gallery. 759.04
Baroque masters from the J. Paul Getty Museum. [Catalogue of an exhibition] February 26-March 30, 1973. [Northridge, California State University, 1973] 30, [21] p. illus. 23 cm. Includes bibliographical references. [ND182.B3C33 1973] 73-75353
1. Paintings, Baroque—Exhibitions. I. Getty (J. Paul) Museum. II. Title.

CALIFORNIA. University. Art Museum. 750'.74'09465
A university collects: the University of California, Berkeley. Introd. by Peter Selz. New York [1968] 47 p. illus. (part col.) 23 cm. "Exhibition number 68-18. Circulated 1968-69." Catalogue of an exhibition of part of the collection of the Art Museum of the University of California, Berkeley, organized and circulated by the American Federation of Arts. Includes brief essays originally published in catalogues of the museum's collection. Bibliographical footnotes. [ND182.B3C3] 68-54166
1. Paintings, Baroque—Exhibitions. 2. Painting, Baroque—Italian influences. I. American Federation of Arts. II. Title.

DENVER. Art Museum. 759'.04
Baroque art: era of elegance; one of two inaugural exhibitions, October 3-November 15, 1971. [Assembled and edited by Cile M. Bach. Denver? 1971] 120 p. illus. 23 cm. [ND182.B3D46 1971] 74-159779
1. Paintings, Baroque—Exhibitions. I. Title.

OSTROW, Stephen E. 759.04
Baroque painting; Italy and her influence. Selection and catalogue by Stephen E. Ostrow. [Exhibition] organized and circulated by the American Federation of Arts. [New Haven, Printed by Eastern Press, 1968] [38] p. illus. 24 cm. "Exhibition number 68-10. Circulated 1968-1969." [ND182.B3O8] 68-57158
1. Paintings, Baroque—Exhibitions. 2. Painting, Baroque—Italian influences. I. American Federation of Arts. II. Title.

SPEAR, Richard E., 1940- 759.94
Caravaggio and his followers / by Richard E. Spear. Rev. ed. New York : Harper & Row, c1975. x, 244 p. : ill. ; 24 cm. (Icon editions ; IN-34) Bibliography: p. 231-242. [ND182.B3S65 1975] 75-328941 ISBN 0-06-430034-X : 5.95
1. Caravaggio, Michelangelo Merisi da, 1573-1610—Influence. 2. Paintings, Baroque—Exhibitions. I. Title.

SPEAR, Richard E., 1940- 759.94
Caravaggio and his followers, by Richard E. Spear. [Cleveland] Cleveland Museum of Art [1971] x, 214 p. illus. (part col.) 26 cm. Exhibition catalog. Bibliography: p. 203-211. [ND182.B3S65] 76-169620 ISBN 0-910386-17-X 15.00
1. Caravaggio, Michelangelo Merisi da, 1573-1610—Influence. 2. Paintings, Baroque—Exhibitions. I. Title. BIP

Paintings—Bennington, Vt.—Catalogs.

BENNINGTON, Vt. Historical Museum and Art Gallery. Colyer Collection. 708.143
A descriptive list of the Colyer Collection of paintings and sculptures in the Bennington Historical Museum and Art Gallery by John Spargo, director-curator Bennington, 1952. 112 p. illus. port. 26 cm. [N516.B8A4] 52-3310
1. Paintings—Bennington, Vt.—Catalogs. 2. Sculpture—Bennington. Vt.—Catalogs. I. Colyer, Joseph Henry, 1882 or 3-1948. II. Title.

Paintings—Berlin—Catalogs.

BERLIN. Gemaldegalerie (West Berlin) 759.94
The Berlin-Dahlem Gallery; great paintings from the former Kaiser Friedrich Museum. With an introd. and commentary by Edwin Redslob. Translated from the German by Sophie Wilkins. New York, Macmillan [1967] xiv, 242 p. illus. (part col.) 34 cm. Translation of Gemaldegalerie Berlin-Dahlem. [N2230.A6413] 67-19551
1. Paintings—Berlin—Catalogs. I. Redslob, Edwin, 1884- II. Berlin. Museum Dahlem.

Paintings—Boston—Catalogs.

BOSTON. Museum of Fine Arts. 759.135
M. and M. Karolik collection of American paintings, 1815 to 1865. Cambridge, Published for Museum of Fine Arts, Boston [by] Harvard University Press, 1949 [i. e. 1951] ix, 544 p. 233 illus. 32 cm. Errata leaf inserted. [ND210.B73] 51-8136
1. Paintings—Boston—Catalogs. 2. Paintings, American. 3. Painters, American. I. Karolik, Maxim. II. Karolik, Martha Catherine (Codman) III. Title.

ISABELLA Stewart Gardner Museum, Boston. 750'.074'014461
European and American paintings in the Isabella Stewart Gardner Museum, by Philip Hendy. Boston, Trustees of the Isabella Stewart Gardner Museum [1974] 316 p. illus. (part col.) 29 cm. Includes bibliographies. [N521.I7A52] 74-79188 ISBN 0-914660-00-4
1. Isabella Stewart Gardner Museum, Boston. 2. Paintings—Boston—Catalogs. I. Hendy, Philip, Sir, 1900- II. Title. BIP

Paintings, British.

BEDDINGTON, Jack, comp. 759.2
Young artists of promise. London, New York, Studio Publications [1957] 127 p. (chiefly illus. (part col.)) 30 cm. [ND468.B4] 58-518
1. Paintings, British. 2. Sculpture, British. 3. Artists, British. I. Title.

COOKE, Hereward Lester 759.2
British painting in the National Gallery of Art. Washington, D.C., National Gallery of Art [c.1960] 43p. col. illus. 19cm. () U.S.] (National Gallery of Art. Booklet no.8) 60-61608 .25 pap.,
1. Paintings, British. I. Title.

GORDON, Irene. 759.2
Masterpieces of British painting. New York, Abrams [1971] 24 p. illus. (part col.) 33 cm. (The Library of great painters. Portfolio ed.) [ND464.G64 1971] 79-130287 ISBN 0-8109-3003-X
1. Paintings, British. 2. Painting, Modern—Great Britain. I. Title. II. Title: British painting.

WARK, Robert R. 759.2
Ten British pictures, 1740-1840, by Robert R. Wark. San Marino, Huntington Library, 1971. xiv, 137 p. illus. (part col.) 27 cm. Includes bibliographical references. [ND466.W3] 74-169905 10.00
1. Paintings, British. 2. Painting, Modern—17th-18th centuries—Gt. Brit. 3. Painting, Modern—19th century—Gt. Brit. I. Title. BIP

WOODWARD, John O. 759.2
British painting; a picture history. London, Vista Bks. [dist. Chester Springs, Pa., Dufour, 1965, c.1962] 160p. of illus (pt. col.) 29cm. [ND464.W8] 65-4081 7.50
1. Paintings, British. I. Title.

Paintings, British—Catalogs.

CONTEMPORARY British 759.2
painting. Introd. by Alan Bowness. New York, Praeger [1968, c1967] 159 p. illus. (part col.) 25 cm. "This publication is derived from the catalogue which accompanied the first showing of the Peter Stuyvesant Foundation Collection at the Tate Gallery, London. The exhibition was entitled 'Recent British painting' and took place from 15 November to 22 December 1967." Includes bibliographies. [ND468.C6 1968] 68-19133
1. Paintings, British—Catalogs. 2. Painting, Modern—20th century—Great Britain. I. Bowness, Alan. II. Peter Stuyvesant Foundation. III. Tate Gallery, London. Recent British painting.

Paintings, British—Exhibitions.

COLUMBUS Gallery of Fine Arts, Columbus, Ohio. 759.2'0740171'57
British art, 1890-1928. [Columbus, Ohio, 1971] 13, [40] p., [64] p. of illus. (part col.) 25 cm. Catalog of an exhibition held at the Columbus Gallery of Fine Arts, February

5th - March 7th, 1971. [ND467.C65] 71-198299
1. Paintings, British—Exhibitions. 2. Painting, Modern—19th century—Gt. Brit. 3. Painting, Modern—20th century—Gt. Brit. I. Title.

NEW York. Museum of Modern Art. 759.2
Masters of British painting, 1800-1950, the Museum of Modern Art, New York, in collaboration with the City Art Museum of St. Louis and the California Palace of the Legion of Honor, San Francisco. Andrew Carnduff Ritchie [director of the exhibition.] New York, 1956] 160 p. illus. (part col.) 25 cm. "Catalog of the exhibition": p. 153-156. Bibliography: p. 157-160. [ND467.N4] 56-11778
1. Paintings, British—Exhibitions. 2. Painters, British. I. Ritchie, Andrew Carnduff. II. Title.

NORTH Carolina. Museum of Art, Raleigh. 759.2
Young British painters. [Exhibition, October 18-November 15, 1964, Sandra Blow, Alan Davie, Donald Hamilton Fraser, Terry Frost, Gwyther Irwin, Bryan Wynter. Raleigh [1965?] [27] p. illus., ports. 26 cm. [ND468.N67] 66-64892
1. Paintings, British—Exhibitions. 2. Painting, Modern—20th century—Gt. Brit. I. Title.

Paintings—Bucharest—Catalogs.

MUZEUL de Arta al Republicii Socialiste Romania. Galeria de Arta Universala. 750'.74'094982
World painting in the Art Museum of the Socialist Republic of Romania : [album / Benedict Cristian ... et al. ; translated into English by Florin Ionescu ; preface, Ion Frunzetti]. Bucharest : Meridiane, 1976. [1], viii, 68 p., [54] leaves of plates : ill. (some col.) ; 34 cm. Translation of Pictura universala in Muzeul de Arta al Republicii Socialiste Romania. Includes index. Bibliography: p. 61-[67] [N3690.R9B86 1976] 76-373693 lei120
1. Muzeul de Arta al Republicii Socialiste Romania. Galeria de Arta Universala. 2. Paintings—Bucharest—Catalogs. I. Benedict, Cristian. II. Title.

Paintings. Canadian—Catalogs.

TORONTO. University. Hart House. 759.11
Canadian paintings in Hart House. With a foreword by Vincent Massey. Selected and arr., with notes, by J. Russell Harper [formerly curator of the Lee collection. Toronto] Art Committee of Hart House, University of Toronto, 1955. xii, 90p. illus. (part col.) 29cm. 'Catalogue of the Hart House collection and index to the plates': p. 85-90. [ND240.T6] 56-2066
1. Paintings. Canadian—Catalogs. 2. Paintings—Toronto— Catalogs. I. Harper, J. Russell, ed. II. Title.

Paintings, Canadian—Exhibitions.

MOLINARI, Barbeau, 759.11
Tousignant, Goguen, Kiyooka, Hurtubise, Juneau. [Cambridge, Mass., M.I.T. Press, 1968] [27] p. illus. (part col.), ports. 22 cm. (M.I.T. visual arts series, v. 1, no. 1) On cover: Seven Montreal artists. Exhibition held Jan. 24-Feb. 18, 1968, at the Hayden Gallery, Massachusetts Institute of Technology, and Apr. 10-May 5, 1968, at the Washington Gallery of Modern Art. [ND248.M6] 68-26667
1. Paintings, Canadian—Exhibitions. 2. Painters, Canadian—Montreal. I. Hayden Gallery. II. Washington, D.C. Gallery of Modern Art. III. Title: Seven Montreal artists. IV. Series: Massachusetts Institute of Technology. M.I.T. visual arts series, v. 1, no. 1

Paintings — Caricatures and cartoons.

REIT, Seymour. 741.5973
Canvas confidential; a backward glance at the world of art, by Sy Reit and Frank Jacobs. Paintings by Kelly Freas. New York, Dial Press, 1963. unpaged (chiefly illus.) 23 cm. [ND1156.R4] 62-17685
1. Paintings — Caricatures and cartoons. I. Jacobs, Frank, joint author. II. Freas, Kelly, illus. III. Title.

Paintings, Catalan.

HERMANN, Fritz 759.946
Catalonian paintings of the Romanesque period. New York, Taplinger [c.1962] 9, [39]p. 20 co6. illus. 19cm. (Orbis pictus, 8) 62-51005 2.00 bds.,
1. Paintings, Catalan. 2. Paintings, Romanesque. I. Title.

Paintings—Catalogs.

ALINARI, Fratelli, Florence. 704.9485
Pitture di venti secoli; [catalogo] Peintures de vingt siecles. Paintings of twenty centuries. Firenze, Fratelli Alinari, Istituto di edizioni artistiche; U. S. distributors: International Art Pub. Co., Detroit [1964] 239 p. (chiefly illus.) 34 cm. "Le piccole illustrazioni monocrome ... presentano i primi mille e cinquecento dipinti che i'Istituto di edizioni artistiche Alinari ha riprodotto in fotografia diretta a colori." [ND1170.A45 1964] 68-44781
1. Paintings—Catalogs 2. Paintings of twenty centuries. I. Title. II. Title: Peintures de vingt siecles.

DEERFIELD Academy, Deerfield, Mass. 750'.74'014422
The Charles P. Russell Collection. Deerfield, American Studies Group, Deerfield Academy [1969] 76 p. illus., ports. 21 x 29 cm. Bibliography: p. 72-74. [N5220.R82D4] 70-23153
1. Russell, Charles P., 1840-1923—Art collections. 2. Paintings—Catalogs. I. Deerfield Academy, Deerfield, Mass. American Studies Group.

HADDAD'S Fine Arts. 381'.45'75
Reproductions; a selective illustrated collection of fine prints. 2d ed., rev. and enl. Buena Park, Calif., 1974 [c1973] xiv, 266 p. (chiefly illus., part col.) 30 cm. Errata slip inserted. [N4035.H3H32 1973] 73-86624 ISBN 0-88445-001-5 22.00
1. Paintings—Catalogs. I. Title.
Publisher's address: 7427 D Orangethrope, Buena Park, Ca. 96620. BIP

KAPLAN (Arthur A.) Company, inc., New York. 338.4'7'75029
Catalog: fine art reproductions. New York [1969] 72 l. (chiefly col. illus.) 32 cm. [N4035.K28A6] 79-17704
1. Paintings—Catalogs.

MASTERPIECES of Biblical art. 755'.4
St. Paul, Catholic Digest Edition, College of St. Thomas, 1973. xvi, 95 plates of col. illus. 29 cm. [ND1430.M33 1973] 74-176212 ISBN 0-8326-1802-0 14.95
1. Bible—Pictures, illustrations, etc. 2. Paintings—Catalogs.

101 great art masterpieces. 759
[Editorial director: Paul A. Harris, Text: Lawrence B. Thomas.] New York, Columbia House, c1973] 1 v. (various pagings) col. illus. 36 cm. [N4035.C64O53] 73-89549
1. Paintings—Catalogs. I. Harris, Paul A., ed. II. Thomas, Lawrence B.

SMITHSONIAN Institution. National Collection of Fine Arts. 759.13
Catalogue of the Alice Pike Barney memorial lending collection, by Delight Hall. Washington [1965] 195 p. illus. (part col.) 22 cm. (Smithsonian publication no. 4522) [ND237.B265S6] 67-60378
1. Paintings — Catalogs. I. Barney, Alice (Pike) 1857-1931. II. Hall, Delight. III. Title.

Paintings—Catalonia.

CIRLOT, Juan Eduardo. 709.02
Romanesque art, the Art Museum of Catalonia. Photos. in color: Otto Schwarz. Photos. in black and white: Archivo Mas. New York, Philosophical Library [c1955] 93p. illus. (part mounted col.) 29cm. [N7109.C3C5] 57-971
1. Paintings—Catalonia. 2. Sculpture—Catalonia. 3. Paintings, Romanesque. 4. Sculpture, Romaneeque. I. Barcelons. Museo de Bellas Artes. II. Title.

Paintings, Central America — Exhibitions.

KANSAS. University. Museum of Art. v. 12
Pintores centroamericanos; an exhibition of contemporary art from Central America, December 1962, January 1963. Lawrence [1962] 63 p. illus. 23 cm. (Its Miscellaneous publications, no. 48) Spanish and English. [ND260.K3] 63-63250
1. Paintings, Central America — Exhibitions. I. Title.

Paintings—Ceylon.

DHANAPALA, D. B. 759.5488
Buddhist paintings from shrines and temples in Ceylon. Introd. by D. B. Dhanapala. [New York] Pub. by the New Maer. Lib. of World Lit. by arrangement with UNESCO [c.1957, 1964] 24p. [4]p. (on fold 1.) illus., 28 col. plates. (pt. fold.) 17cm. (Mentor-Unesco art bk., MQ585) Bibl. [ND1005.D5] 65-269 .95 pap.,
1. Paintings—Ceylon. 2. Art, Buddhist. I. United Nations Educational, Scientific and Cultural Organization. II. Title.

Paintings—Chicago—Catalogs.

CHICAGO. Art Institute 759.0838
Paintings in the Art Institute of Chicago; a catalogue of the picture collection. [Chicago, Author, c.1961] 490p. illus. (part col.) Bibl. 61-6403 10.00
1. Paintings—Chicago—Catalogs. I. Title.

Paintings, Chinese.

CAHILL, James Francis, 1926- 759.951
Chinese paintings, XI-XIV centuries. New York, Crown Publishers [1960] 40 p. illus., 27 plates (part col.) 18 cm. (Art of the East library) Bibliography: p. 40. [ND1043.C3] 60-10061
1. Paintings, Chinese. I. Title.

WALMSLEY, Lewis Calvin, 1897- 700'.924
Wang Wei, the painter-poet, by Lewis Calvin & Dorothy Brush Walmsley. [1st ed.] Rutland, Vt., C. E. Tuttle Co. [1968] 182 p. illus., maps, ports. 22 cm. Bibliography: p. 153-160. [ND1049.W33W3] 68-21117 6.00
1. Wang, Wei, 699-759. 2. Paintings, Chinese. I. Walmsley, Dorothy Brush, 1894-1968, joint author. II. Title. BIP

Paintings, Chinese—Catalogs.

NEW York (City). Metropolitan Museum of Art. 759.951
Sung and Yuan paintings [collected by] Wen Fong. With catalogue by Marilyn Fu. New York; distributed by New York Graphic Society [1973] 162 p. illus. (part col.) 22 x 28 cm. Bibliography: p. 153-156. [ND1043.4.N48 1973] 73-15763 12.50
1. New York (City). Metropolitan Museum of Art. 2. Paintings, Chinese—Catalogs. 3. Painting, Chinese—Sung-Yuan dynasties, 960-1368. 4. Paintings—New York (City)—Catalogs. I. Fong, Wen. II. Fu, Marilyn. III. Title.

Paintings, Chinese—Catalogs—Bibliography.

LOVELL, Hin-cheung. 016.759951
An annotated bibliography of Chinese painting catalogues and related texts. Ann Arbor, Center for Chinese Studies, University of Michigan, 1973. vi, 141 p. 23 cm. (Michigan papers in Chinese studies, no. 16) A companion to J. C. Ferguson's Li tai chu lu hua mu. "a review of each of the 108 titles used by him in Li-tai chu-lu hua mu ... In addition to the reviews of the 108 titles used by Ferguson, there is a supplement of reviews of twenty-two other texts not used by him but which are pertinent to our purpose." [Z5949.C5L67] 74-164391 3.00 (pbk.)
1. Paintings, Chinese—Catalogs—Bibliography. I. Ferguson, John Calvin, 1866-1945. Li tai chu lu hua mu. II. Title. III. Series.

Paintings, Chinese—Exhibitions.

CLEVELAND Museum of Art. 759.951
The colors of ink : Chinese paintings and related ceramics from the Cleveland Museum of Art / Sherman E. Lee ; with catalogue contributions by James Robinson. New York : Arno Press, 1975, c1974. p. cm. (The Asia Society reprint collection) "Catalogue of an exhibition shown in the Asia House Gallery in the winter of 1974." Reprint of the ed. published by Asia Society, New York. Bibliography: p. [ND2068.C57 1975] 75-6587 ISBN 0-405-06564-7 : 30.00
1. Paintings, Chinese—Exhibitions. 2. Pottery, Chinese—Exhibitions. 3. Porcelain, Chinese—Exhibitions. I. Lee, Sherman E. II. Asia House Gallery, New York. III. Title. IV. Series. BIP

CLEVELAND Museum of Art. 759.951
The colors of ink: Chinese paintings and related ceramics from the Cleveland Museum of Art. [By] Sherman E. Lee, with catalogue contributions by James Robinson. [New York] Asia Society; distributed by New York Graphic Society [1974] 139 p. illus. 29 cm. "An Asia House Gallery publication." "Catalogue of an exhibition shown in the Asia House Gallery in the winter of 1974 as an activity of the Asia Society." Bibliography: p. 136-137. [ND2068.C57 1974] 73-90483 ISBN 0-87848-042-0 18.50
1. Paintings, Chinese—Exhibitions. 2. Pottery, Chinese—Exhibitions. 3. Porcelain, Chinese—Exhibitions. I. Lee, Sherman E. II. Asia Society. III. Asia House Gallery, New York. IV. Title.

CRAWFORD, John M 745.6'1'9951
Catalogue of the exhibition of Chinese calligraphy and painting in the collection of John M. Crawford, Jr. [Edited by Laurence Sickman] New York, 1962. 53 p. plates. 26 cm. Abbreviated version of the full catalogue published in October, 1962, by the three participating museums, Pierpont Morgan Library, New York, Fogg Art Museum, Harvard University, and William Rockhill Nelson Gallery of Art, Kansas City, Missouri, under title: Chinese calligraphy and painting in the collection of John M. Crawford, Jr. [ND1042.C72] 63-5
1. Paintings, Chinese—Exhibitions. 2. Paintings—Private collections. 3. Penmanship. I. Sickman, Laurence C. S., ed. II. Pierpont Morgan Library, New York. III. Title. BIP

CRAWFORD, John M. 759.951
Chinese calligraphy and painting in the collection of John M. Crawford, Jr. [Laurence Sickman, ed. New York [Pierpont Morgan Lib.; dist. Philip C. Duschnes] 1962. 302p. illus. (pt. fold., pt. col.) 32cm. Catalogue prepared for an exhibition held at Pierpont Morgan Lib., New York, Fogg Art Museum, Harvard Univ., and William Rckhill Nelson Gallery of Art, Kansas City, Missouri. Bibl. 62-53674 100.00
1. Paintings, Chinese—Exhibitions. 2. Paintings—Private collections. 3. Penmanship, Chinese. I. Sickman, Laurence C. S., ed. II. Pierpont Morgan Library, New York, III. Title.

CRAWFORD, John M., Jr. 759.951
Chinese calligraphy and painting in the collection of John M. Crawford, Jr. [Laurence Sickman, ed.; Pierpont Morgan Lib., Cambridge, Mass., Fogg Art Mus., Harvard, 1963, c.]1962. 302p. illus. (pt. fold., pt. col.) 32cm. Catalogue prepared for an exhibition held at Pierpont Morgan Lib., New York, Fogg Art Mus., Harvard Univ., and William Rockhill Nelson Gallery of Art, Kansas City, Mo. Bibl. 62-53674 3.25 pap.,
1. Paintings, Chinese—Exhibitions. 2. Paintings—Private collections. 3. Penmanship, Chinese. I. Sickman, Laurence C. S., ed. II. Pierpont Morgan Library, New York. III. Title.

PARKE-BERNET Galleries, inc., New York. 759.951'021'6
Chinese paintings from the Chiang Er-Shih Collections. Public auction. Friday March 5 at 2 p.m. New York, 1971. xvi, 88 p. illus. (part. col.) 28 cm. Errata slip inserted. "Sale number 3167." Includes bibliographical references. [ND1043.P37] 73-156727 7.00

1. Paintings, Chinese—Exhibitions. 2. Chiang, O-shih—Art collections. I. Title.

WHITFIELD, Roderick.   759.951
In pursuit of antiquity; Chinese paintings of the Ming and Ch'ing dynasties from the collection of Mr. and Mrs. Earl Morse. With an addendum by Wen Fong. [Princeton, N.J.] Art Museum, Princeton University [1969] 240 p. illus. (part col.), map. 26 cm. Catalogue of an exhibition held at the Art Museum, Princeton University, May 17-July 27, 1969. Bibliography: p. 239-240. [ND1043.5.W48] 70-86877
1. Morse, Earl—Art collections. 2. Paintings, Chinese—Exhibitions. I. Fong, Wen. II. Princeton University. Art Museum. III. Title.

WILSON, Marc F.   745.6'1'9951
Friends of Wen Cheng-ming : a view from the Crawford Collection : [catalogue of the exhibition] : October 24, 1974 through January 26, 1975 / by Marc F. Wilson and Kwan S. Wong. New York : China House Gallery, China Institute in America, [1974] 128 p. : ill. (some col.) ; 24 cm. "After January 26, 1975, this collection will be exhibited at ... the William Rockhill Nelson Gallery of Art and Atkins Museum of Fine Arts, Kansas City, Missouri [and] Seattle Art Museum, Seattle, Washington." Bibliography: p. 127-128. [ND1042.W54] 74-84780
1. Crawford, John M.—Art collections. 2. Paintings, Chinese—Exhibitions. 3. Calligraphy, Chinese—Exhibitions. I. Wong, Kwan S., joint author. II. China House Gallery. III. Title.

Paintings—Cincinnati—Catalogs.

ART Association of   750'.74'017252
Indianapolis, Indiana. John Herron Art Institute.
Complete list of European and American paintings in the permanent collection of the John Herron Art Museum, September 1958. [Indianapolis] : Art Association of Indianapolis, Indiana, [1958] [44] p. ; 23 cm. [N577.A55 1958] 75-318279
1. Art Association of Indianapolis, Indiana. John Herron Art Institute. 2. Paintings—Cincinnati—Catalogs. I. Title: Complete list of European and American paintings ...

Paintings—Cleveland—Catalogs.

CLEVELAND Museum of Art.   759.0838
Paintings in the Cleveland Museum of Art. [Cleveland] 1952. 63 p. (chiefly illus., part col.) 23 cm. (Its Picture book, no. 4) [N552.A86] 52-4780
1. Paintings—Cleveland—Catalogs. I. Title. II. Series.

Paintings— Columbia, S. C.— Catalogs.

COLUMBIA, S. C. Museum of   759.5
Art.
Art of the Italian Renaissance from the Samuel H. Krees collection. Columbia, Columbia Museum of Art, 1954. 63p. illus. 28cm. [ND615.C58] 56-23423
1. Paintings— Columbia, S. C.—Catalogs. 2. Paintings, Italian. 3. Paintings, Renaissance. I. Samuel H. Krees Foundation. II. Title.

Paintings — Conservation and preservation.

KECK, Caroline (Kohn)   751.6
A handbook on the care of paintings, for historical agencies and small museums, by Caroline K. Keck. [Nashville] American Association for State and Local History [c1965] xii, 132 p. illus., ports. 23 cm. Bibliography: p. 128-129. [ND1640.K38] 66-3920
1. Paintings — Conservation and preservation. I. American Association for State and Local History. II. Title.

Paintings— Conservation and restoration.

BRADLEY, Morton Clark,   751.6
1912-
The treatment of pictures. Cambridge,

Mass, Art Technology, 1950. 304p. illus. 23cm. [ND1640.B7] 51-2893
1. Paintings—Conservation and restoration. I. Title.

CLARKE, Carl Dame, 1904-   751.6
Pictures, their preservation and restoration. Butler, Md., Standard Arts Press [1959] 270p. illus. 26cm. Includes bibliography. [ND1640.C55] 59-48827
1. Paintings — Conservation and restoration. I. Title.

KECK, Caroline (Kohn)   751.6
A handbook on the care of paintings, by Caroline K. Keck. New York, Published for the American Association for State and Local History by Watson-Guptill Publications [1967, c1965] xii, 136 p. illus., ports. 24 cm. Bibliography: p. 128-129. [ND1640.K38 1967] 67-13743
1. Paintings—Conservation and restoration. I. American Association for State and Local History. II. Title.   **BIP**

KECK, Caroline (Kohn)   751.6
How to take care of your pictures; a primer of practical information. Illus. by Ruth Sheetz Eisendrath. [New York] Museum of Modern Art & the Brooklyn Museum [1954] 54p. illus. 26cm. [ND1640.K4] 54-2825
1. Paintings—Conservation and restoration. I. Title.

KELLY, Francis.   751.6
Art restoration; a guide to the care and preservation of works of art. [1st ed.] New York, McGraw-Hill [1972] 235 p. illus. 25 cm. Bibliography: p. [220]-229. [ND1650.K4] 72-177591 ISBN 0-07-033890-6 9.95
1. Paintings—Conservation and restoration. 2. Prints—Conservation and restoration. I. Title.

RUHEMANN, Helmut.   751.6
The cleaning of paintings; problems and potentialities. With bibliography and supplementary material by Joyce Plesters and foreword by Sir Philip Hendy. New York, Praeger [1968] 508 p. illus. (part col.) 26 cm. [ND1640.R8] 68-17958 25.00
1. Paintings—Conservation and restoration. I. Title.

STOUT, George Leslie.   751.6
The care of pictures / by George L. Stout. New York : Dover Publications, [1975], c1948. xiv, 122 p., [12] leaves of plates : ill. ; 24 cm. Reprint of the ed. published by Columbia University Press, New York; with new introd. and rev. bibliography. Bibliography: p. [114]-118. [ND1640.S86 1975] 74-25487 ISBN 0-486-23165-8 pbk. : 3.00
1. Paintings—Conservation and restoration. I. Title.   **BIP**

WRIGHT, Dorothy E   751.6
Picture restoration. New York, Pitman Pub. Corp. [1955] 54p. 19cm. (The Artist's handbooks, no.7) [ND1640.W7] 57-2948
1. Paintings—Conservation and restoration. I. Title.

Paintings—Conservation and restoration—Addresses, essays, lectures.

CONSERVATION and   751.6
restoration of pictorial art / edited by Norman Brommelle and Perry Smith. London ; Boston : Butterworths, 1976. p. cm. "Consist[s] substantially of papers presented at a congress in Lisbon of the International Institute for Conservation of Historic and Artistic Works in October 1972." [ND1640.C57] 75-32570 ISBN 0-408-70712-7 : 34.50
1. Paintings—Conservation and restoration—Addresses, essays, lectures. I. Brommelle, Norman. II. Smith, Perry. III. International Institute for Conservation of Historic and Artistic Works.   **BIP**

Paintings—Conservation and restoration—Handbooks, manuals, etc.

EMILE-MALE, Gilberte.   751.6
The restorer's handbook of easel painting / Gilberte Emile-Male. New York : Van Nostrand Reinhold, [1976] p. cm. Translation of La restauration des

---

peintures de chevalet. Includes index. Bibliography: p. [ND1650.E4713] 76-15802 ISBN 0-442-22301-3 : 20.00
1. Paintings—Conservation and restoration—Handbooks, manuals, etc. 2. Artists' materials. I. Title.   **BIP**

Paintings—Detroit—Catalogs.

DETROIT. Institute of   708.174
Arts.
Catalogue of the paintings and sculpture given by Edgar B. Whitcomb and Anna Scripps Whitcomb to the Detroit Institute of Arts. [Detroit] 1954. 134p. illus. (part col.) 29cm. Includes bibliographical references. [N560.A52] 54-2704
1. Paintings—Detroit—Catalogs. 2. Sculpture—Detroit—Catalogs. I. Whitcomb, Edgar B., 1866-1953. II. Whitcomb, Anna (Scripps) III. Title.

Paintings—Dresden.

MENZ, Henner.   708.3
The Dresden Gallery. [Translated from the German by Daphne Woodward] New York, Abrams [1962] 320p. illus. (part col.) 22cm. [N2280.M413] 62-18732
1. Dresden, Gemalde- Galerie. 2. Paintings—Dresden. I. Title.

Paintings—Dublin—Catalogs.

DUBLIN. National   750'.74'094183
Gallery of Ireland.
Catalogue of the paintings. [Michael Wynne, compiler. Dublin] 1971. 223 p. 25 cm. [N1250.A545] 72-170419
1. Paintings—Dublin—Catalogs. I. Wynne, Michael. II. Title.

DUBLIN. National Gallery   759.94
of Ireland.
Concise catalogue of the oil paintings. Dublin, Stationary Off. [1964] 147 p. 23 cm. [N1250.D64] 77-6041
1. Paintings—Dublin—Catalogs. I. Title.

Paintings, Dutch.

BAIRD, Thomas P.   759.9492
Dutch painting in the National Gallery of Art. Washinaton, D.C., National Gallery of Art [c.1960] 43p. col. illus. 19cm. ([U.S.] National Gallery of Art. Booklet no. 7) 60-61609 .25 pap.,
1. Paintings, Dutch. I. Title.

CORCORAN Gallery of Art,   759.9492
Washington, D. C. W. A. Clark Collection.
A handbook of Dutch and Flemish paintings in the William Andrews Clark Collection, by James D. Breckenridge. [Washington] Corcoran Gallery of Art, 1955. 52p. illus. 24cm. Includes bibliographical references. [ND363.C6] 56-4378
1. Paintings, Dutch. 2. Paintings, Flemish. 3. Paintings—Washington, D. C.—Catalogs. I. Breckenridge, James D. II. Clark, William Andrews, 1839-1925. III. Title.

MEIJER, Emil R.   709.495
Dutch painting, seventeenth century. New York, Mcgraw [1963, c.1962] 47 p. illus. 24 col. slides (in pockets) 25 cm. (Color slide bks. of the world's art) 62-18982 bds., 8.95
1. Paintings, Dutch. 2. Lantern slides. I. Title. II. Series.

WEIGERT, Hans   759.9492
Dutch painting, 17th century. Translated by Desmond and Camille Clayton. Milan, Uffici Press [dist. New York, Crown, 1960] 31p. 16 mounted col. illus. (incl. cover) 35cm. (The Uffici series in full colour) 60-4703 1.95 pap.,
1. Paintings, Dutch. I. Title.

Paintings. Dutch — Catalogs.

CZOBER, Agnes.   759.9492
Rembrandt and his circle. [Translated by Lili Halapy] New York, Taplinger Pub. Co. [1970, c1969] 25 p. 48 col. plates. 25 cm. Translation of Rembrandt es kore. Bibliography: p. 19. [ND646.C9313 1970] 74-107012 7.95

---

1. Rembrandt Harmenszoon van Rijn, 1606-1669—Influence. 2. Paintings, Dutch—Catalogs. I. Budapest. Szepmuveszety Muzeum. II. Esztergom, Hungary. Kereszteny Muzeum. III. Title.

JACOBS, Alan.   759.9492 B
17th century Dutch and Flemish painters : a collectors' guide / compiled by Alan Jacobs. London ; New York : McGraw-Hill, 1977,c1976 297 p. : ill. (some col.) ; 22 x 28 cm. "A revision of A classified synopsis of the principal painters of the Dutch and Flemish schools, their scholars, imitators, and analogists, by George Stanley, published in London by Henry G. Bohn, 1855." Includes bibliographical references and index. [ND646.J32] 76-26521 ISBN 0-07-084477-1: 7.95
1. Paintings, Dutch—Catalogs. 2. Paintings, Modern—17th-18th centuries—Netherlands—Catalogs. 3. Paintings, Flemish—Catalogs. 4. Paintings, Modern—17th-18th centuries—Flanders—Catalogs. 5. Painters—Netherlands—Biography. 6. Painters—Flanders—Biography. I. Stanley, George. A classified synopsis of the principal painters of the Dutch and Flemish schools .... II. Title.

MOJZER, Miklos.   759.9'492
Dutch genre paintings. [Translated by Eva Racz] New York, Taplinger Pub. Co. [1969, c1967] 30 p., 48 col. plates. 24 cm. At head of title: Museum of Fine Arts, Budapest. Istvan Dobo Museum, Eger. Bibliography: p. 27. [ND646.M613 1969] 69-15913 7.95
1. Paintings, Dutch—Catalogs. 2. Genre painting. I. Budapest. Szepmuveszeti Muzeum. II. Eger, Hungary. Dobo Istvan Varmuzeum. III. Title.   **BIP**

OXFORD. University.   758.4074
Ashmolean Museum.
Catalogue of the collection of Dutch and Flemish still-life pictures bequeathed by Daisy Linda Ward. Oxford, Printed at the University Press, 1950. ix, 211 p. plates (1 col.) 26 cm. Title on spine: Ward collection of still-life pictures. Bibliography: p. 205. [ND636.O9] 51-21531
1. Paintings. Dutch — Catalogs. 2. Paintings, Flemish — Catalogs. 3. Still-life paintings. I. Ward, Daisy Linda (Travers) 1883-1937. II. Title.

SELECTIONS from the   759.9492
Bader Collection. With an introd. by Wolfgang Stechow. Milwaukee, 1974. [71] p. illus. 29 cm. Includes bibliographies. [ND636.S38] 74-79521
1. Bader, Alfred, 1924- — Art collections. 2. Paintings, Dutch—Catalogs. 3. Painting, Modern—17th-18th centuries—Netherlands. 4. Paintings, Flemish—Catalogs. 5. Painting, Modern—17th-18th centuries—Flanders.

TOTH-UBBENS, Magdi.   759.9492
Mauritshuis, The Hague; Dutch painting [by] Magdi Toth-Ubbens; tr. from Dutch by J. J. Kliphuis. Munich, Ahrbeck, Knorr & Hirth [1967] Label mounted on t. p.: W. S. Heinman, New York. 79p. col. plates. 18cm. (Little art bk.) [ND646.T6713] 68-8612 4.50
1. Hague. Kabinet van Schilderijen. 2. Paintings, Dutch—Catalogs. I. Title.

URBACH, Zsuzsa.   759.9492'074'039
Early Netherlandish painting, by Susan Urbach. [Translated by Mari Kuttna] New York, Taplinger [1972, c1971] 26 p., 48 col. plates. 24 cm. Translation of Korai nemetalfoldi tablakepek. Reproductions of paintings from the collections of the Museum of Fine Arts, Budapest, and the Christian Museum, Esztergom, Hungary. [ND635.U713 1972] 79-164681 ISBN 0-8008-2353-2 7.95
1. Paintings, Dutch—Catalogs. 2. Paintings, Renaissance—Netherlands. 3. Paintings, Flemish—Catalogs. I. Budapest. Szepmuveszeti Muzeum. II. Esztergom, Hungary. Kereszteny Muzeum. III. Title.

Paintings, Dutch—Exhibitions.

ART Association of   759.9492
Indianapolis, Indians. John Herron Art Institute.
The young Rembrandt and his times, a loan dxhibition of Dutch painting of the first four decades of the seventeenth century. John Herron Art Museum,

Indianapolis, Indiana, February 14-March 23, 1958. The Fine Arts Gallery, San Diego, California, April 11-May 18, 1958. [Indianapolis, 1958] [112]p. illus. (part col.) map. 25cm. [ND646.A82] [ND646.A82] 927.5 58-2164 58-2164
1. Paintings, Dutch—Exhibitions. 2. Rembrandt Hermanszoon van Rijn, 1606-1669. I. San Diego, Calif. Fine Arts Gallery. II. Title.

BOSTON. Museum of Fine Arts. 759.9'492
The Age of Rembrandt; an exhibition of Dutch paintings of the seventeen century. [New York, Published by October House for the Museum of Fine Arts, Boston, 1967,1966] 155 p. 108 plates (part col.) 19 x 23 cm. Catalog of an exhibition shown in the California Palace of the Legion of Honor, San Francisco, Oct. 10-Nov. 13, 1966; the Toledo Museum of Art, Nov. 26, 1966-Jan 8, 1967; and the Museum of Fine Arts, Boston, Jan. 21-Mar. 5, 1967. [ND646.A67] 66-25449
1. Paintings, Dutch—Exhibitions. I. California Palace of the Legion of Honor, San Francisco. II. Toledo. Museum of Art. III. Title.

BRANDEIS University, Waltham, Mass. Poses Institute of Fine Arts. 759.9492
17th century painting from the Low Countries, by Creighton Gilbert. [Waltham, Mass., 1966] 59 p. illus. 26 cm. "An exhibition of the Poses Institute of Fine Arts at the Rose Art Museum ... February 27-March 27, 1966." Bibliographical footnotes. [ND636.B7] 66-65088
1. Paintings, Dutch—Exhibitions. 2. Paintings, Flemish—Exhibitions. I. Gilbert, Creighton. II. Title.

LONDON. Queen's Gallery, Buckingham Palace. 759.9492'074'021
Dutch pictures from the royal collection. [1st ed.] University Park, Pennsylvania State University Press [1971] 96 p. plates (part col.) 23 cm. Catalog of an exhibition held at the Queen's Gallery at Buckingham Palace in 1971. Introd. (p. 7-36) by O. Millar. Includes bibliographical references. [ND646.L64 1971b] 79-172996 ISBN 0-271-01109-2 6.50
1. Windsor, House of—Art collections. 2. Paintings, Dutch—Exhibitions. 3. Painting, Modern—17th-18th centuries—Netherlands. I. Millar, Oliver, 1923- II. Title. BIP

ROBINSON, Franklin Westcott. 759.9492'074'0158231
Dutch life in the golden century : an exhibition of seventeenth century Dutch painting of daily life, presented under the auspices of the Royal Netherlands Embassy, Washington, D.C. : [exhibition dates, Museum of Fine Arts, St. Petersburg, Florida, January 21-March 2, 1975, High Museum of Art, Atlanta, Georgia, April 4-May 4, 1975] : catalogue essay and notes / by Franklin W. Robinson. [St. Petersburg, Fla. : The Museum, 1975] 52 p., [20] leaves of plates : 38 ill. ; 23 cm. Includes bibliographical references and index. [ND646.R56] 74-31811
1. Paintings, Dutch—Exhibitions. 2. Painting, Modern—17th-18th centuries—Netherlands. 3. Netherlands—Social life and customs—Pictorial works. I. St. Petersburg, Fla. Museum of Fine Arts. II. High Museum of Art. III. Title.

Paintings, Early Christian.

VOLPE, Carlo. 709.01
Early Christian to medieval painting. [Translated from the Italian by Pearl Sanders] New York, Golden Press [1963] [56] p. 24 col. illus. 38 cm. (Art of the Western World) [ND140.V613] 63-4649
1. Paintings, Early Christian. 2. Paintings, Medieval. I. Title. II. Series.

Paintings, Egyptian.

UNITED Nations Educational, Scientific and Cultural Organization. 759.932
Egypt: paintings from tombs and temples. Introd. by Jacques Vandier. [Greenwich, Conn.] New York Graphic Society [1954] 10 p. illus., 32 col. plates. 48 cm. (UNESCO world art series, 2) Material assembled by experts from UNESCO and the New York Graphic Society. [ND75.U5] 54-13079
1. Paintings, Egyptian. I. Vandier, Jacques, 1904- II. New York Graphic Society. III. Title. IV. Series.

Paintings—England—Catalogs.

MILLAR, Oliver, 1923- 750'.74'02
The Queen's pictures / Oliver Millar. 1st American ed. New York : Macmillan, 1977. 240 p., [24] leaves of plates : ill. (some col.) ; 30 cm. Includes bibliographical references and index. [N5247.W56M54 1977] 76-30894 ISBN 0-02-584690-6 : 35.00
1. Windsor, House of—Art collections. 2. Paintings—England—Catalogs. I. Elizabeth II, Queen of Great Britain, 1926- II. Title. BIP

Paintings—England—London—Catalogs.

LONDON. National Gallery. 759.94'074'02132
A guide to the National Gallery / [by] Homan Potterton ; with a foreword by Michael Levey .... London : The Gallery, [1976] 168, [2] p. (2 fold.) : ill., geneal. table, plans, ports. ; 21 cm. Includes indexes. [N1070.A67] 76-382243 ISBN 0-901791-60-1 : £0.50
1. London. National Gallery. 2. Paintings—England—London—Catalogs. I. Potterton, Homan. II. Title.

LONDON. University. Courtauld Institute of Art. 759.94'074'02142
The painting collections of the Courtauld Institute of Art / Philip Troutman ; foreword by Peter Lasko. Chicago : University of Chicago Press, c1978. p. cm. (Chicago visual library) At head of title: The Courtauld Institute of Art. Includes index. Bibliography: p. [N1165.U45A66] 78-13168 ISBN 0-226-68904-2 : 60.00
1. London. University. Courtauld Institute of Art—Catalogs. 2. Painting—England—London—Catalogs. I. Troutman, Philip. II. Title. BIP

Paintings, English.

CHURCHILL, Winston Leonard Spencer, Sir, 1874-1965. 759.2
Churchill: his paintings; a catalog, compiled by David Coombs. Foreword by Lady Spencer-Churchill. Cleveland, World Pub. Co. [1967] 272 p. illus., col. plates. 29 cm. [ND497.C548C6] 67-24472
I. Coombs, David. II. Title.

FRIEDMAN, Winifred H. 759.2'074'0212
Boydell's Shakespeare gallery / Winifred H. Friedman. New York : Garland Pub., 1976. 266 p., [103] leaves of plates : ill. ; 21 cm. (Outstanding dissertations in the fine arts) Originally presented as the author's thesis, Harvard, 1974. Bibliography: p. 246-256. [PR2883.B553F7 1976] 75-23791 ISBN 0-8240-1987-3 lib.bdg. : 30.00
1. Boydell, John, 1719-1804. The gallery of illustrations for Shakespeare's dramatic works. 2. Shakespeare, William, 1564-1616—Illustrations. 3. Paintings, English. 4. Paintings, Modern—17th-18th centuries—England I. Title. II. Series. BIP

KITSON, Michael. 759.942
English painting [by] Michael Kitson and Alexandra Wedgwood. New York, Golden Press [1964] [52] p. col. illus. 37 cm. (Art of the Western world) [ND466] 73-4448
1. Paintings, English. I. Wedgwood, Alexandra (Gordon Clark) 1938- II. Title. III. Series.

Paintings, English — Exhibitions.

ALEXANDER Galleries. 759.2'074'02842
The paintings of Atkinson Grimshaw & his followers. Harrogate : Alexander Galleries, 1976. [43] p. : chiefly ill. ; 26 cm. Cover title. [ND497.G74A8] 76-380890 £2.25
1. Grimshaw, John Atkinson, 1836-1893. 2. Paintings, English—Exhibitions. 3. Influence (Literary, artistics, etc.) I. Grimshaw, John Atkinson, 1836-1893. II. Title.

FROST and Reed. 758'.3
A superb collection of English sporting paintings. New York, National Art Museum of Sport [1970?] 39 p. illus. (part col.) 25 x 31 cm. Exhibition presented by Frost and Reed gallery at the National Art Museum of Sport opening Nov. 4, 1970. [ND1388.G7F7] 70-198036
1. Paintings, English—Exhibitions. 2. Sports in art. I. National Art Museum of Sport. II. Title.

VIRGINIA Museum of Fine Arts, Richmond. 704.9432
Painting in England 1700-1850; collection of Mr. & Mrs. Paul Mellon. [Catalogue by Basil Taylor Richmond, 1963. 2 v. illus. (part col.) 21 x 23 cm. "Exhibited at the Virginia Museum of Fine Arts in 1963." Vol. [1] contains text and illustrations while v. [2] reproduces many of the paintings. "Errata" slip mounted on p. [232], v. [2] [ND466.V5] 62-63444
1. Paintings, English — Exhibitions. 2. Paintings — Private collections. I. Mellon, Paul. II. Taylor, Basil. III. Title.

Paintings—Europe—Mutiliation, defacement, etc.

UNITED Nations Educational, Scientific and Cultural Organization. 759.94
An illustrated inventory of famous dismembered works of art: European painting; with a section on dismembered tombs in France. Paris, 1974. 221 p. illus. 30 cm. Includes bibliographical references. [ND450.U47 1974] 74-194851 ISBN 9-231-01040-9
1. Paintings—Europe—Mutiliation, defacement, etc. 2. Sculpture—France—Mutilation, defacement, etc. I. Title.
Distributed by Unipub, 23.10.

Paintings, European.

HUBBARD, R H ed. 759.0838
European paintings in Canadian collections: earlier schools, edited with an essay on picture collecting in Canada. Toronto, Oxford University Press, 1956. xxv, 154p. illus. (part col.) 29cm. Includes bibliographies. [ND454.H8] 56-59212
1. sPaintings, European. 2. Paintings—Canada. I. Title.

HUBBARD, Robert H., ed. 759.0838
European paintings in Canadian collections: modern schools, v.2, ed., essays on the collecting of modern pictures in Canada by Robert H. Hubbard. [New York] Oxford [1963, c.1962] 164p. illus. (pt. col.) 29cm. 56-59212 8.75
1. Paintings, European. 2. Paintings—Canada. I. Title.

HUBBARD, Robert Hamilton, 1916- 759.0838
European paintings in Canadian collections; edited with an essay on picture collecting in Canada. Toronto, Oxford University Press, 1956-62. 2 v. illus. (part. col.) 29 cm. Vol. 2: Edited with an essay on the collecting of modern pictures in Canada. Contents.Contents.--[1] Earlier schools.--2. Modern schools. Includes bibliographies. [ND454.H8] 56-59212
1. Paintings, European. 2. Paintings—Canada. I. Title.

KELLER, Hiltgart Leu, 1893- 759.94
20 centuries of great European painting; a collection of masterpieces. By Keller and bodo Cichy. Introd. by Maxim Dasio. New York, Sterling Pub. Co. [c1957] 235p. illus., col. plates. 32cm. [ND1170.K39] 59-16002
1. Paintings, European. 2. Painters, European. I. Cichy, Bodo, 1924- joint author. II. Title.

MARTIN, Gregory. 759.94
European painting; the eighteenth century. New York, McGraw-Hill [1967, c1966] 47 p. illus., 24 col. slides (in portfolio) 25 cm. [ND454.M3] 65-26483
1. Paintings, European. 2. Painting, European—Hist. 3. Lantern slides. I. Title.

SELVIG, Forrest, ed. 759.94'074'01471
European paintings in the Minneapolis Institute of Arts. [Minneapolis] c1963. [85] p. plates, ports. 28 cm. "The first of a new series of picture books of objects in the Minneapolis Institute of Arts." [ND454.S4] 64-1382
1. Paintings. European. 2. Paintings—Minneapolis. I. Minneapolis. Institute of Arts. II. Title.

Paintings, European—Catalogs.

LENINGRAD, Ermitazh. 759.06'074'0745
Western European painting on the nineteenth and twentieth centuries / the Hermitage ; [introd. and notes by A. Kostenevich ; translated by N. Johnstone and H. Perham]. Leningrad : Aurora Art Publishers, 1976. 306 p. : col. ill. ; 29 cm. [ND457.L4613] 76-378101
1. Leningrad. Ermitazh. 2. Paintings, European—Catalogs. 3. Paintings, Modern—19th century—Europe—Catalogs. 4. Paintings, Modern—20th century—Europe—Catalogs. 5. Paintings—Leningrad—Catalogs. I. Kostenevich, Al'bert Grigor'evich. II. Title.

MILLER, Dwight Cameron, 1923- 759.94'074'017252
Catalogue of European paintings [by Dwight Miller. Indianapolis] Indianapolis Museum of Art, 1970. xi, 225 p. illus. (part col.), ports. 26 cm. [ND450.M5] 78-140928
1. Paintings, European—Catalogs. 2. Paintings—Indianapolis—Catalogs. I. Indianapolis Museum of Art. II. Title.

MINNEAPOLIS. Institute of Arts. 759.94'074'0176579
European paintings from the Minneapolis Institute of Arts. New York, Praeger Publishers [1971] 548 p. illus. (part col.) 29 cm. [ND454.M55] 72-23830 25.00
1. Paintings, European—Catalogs. 2. Painting, Modern—Europe. 3. Paintings—Minneapolis—Catalogs. I. Title.

TIMKEN Art Gallery. 759.94'074'019498
European paintings in the Timken Art Gallery. Compiled by Agnes and Elizabeth Mongan. Foreword by Walter Ames. Introd. by Agnes Mongan. San Diego, Calif., Putnam Foundation, 1969. 136 p. col. illus. 22 cm. Cover title: Timken Art Gallery. Includes bibliographies. [N737.5.A63] 68-58364
1. Paintings, European—Catalogs. 2. Paintings—San Diego, Calif.—Catalogs. I. Mongan, Agnes. II. Mongan, Elizabeth. III. Title.

WORCESTER, Mass. Art Museum. 759.94'074'01443
European paintings in the collection of the Worcester Art Museum. Worcester, Mass. : The Museum, 1974. 2 v. (vii, 666 p.) : ill. ; 25 cm. Includes index. Contents.Contents.—[1] Text.—[2] Plates. [ND450.W67 1974] 73-90538
1. Worcester, Mass. Art Museum. 2. Paintings, European—Catalogs. 3. Paintings—Worcester, Mass.—Catalogs. I. Title.

Paintings, European—Exhibitions.

ILLINOIS. University. Krannert Art Museum. 759.94
Seventeenth and eighteenth century paintings from the University of Notre Dame. Catalogue by Dwight C. Miller. [Exhibition] Feb. 3 through Feb. 25, 1962. [Urbana, 1962] [55]p. illus. 25cm. Errata slip inserted. [ND456.I 4] 62-63769
1. Paintings, European — Exahibitions. I. Miller, Dwight Cameron, 1923- II. Notre Dame, Ind. University. III. Title.

Paintings, European—Exhibitions.

DUKE University, Durham, N.C. 750'.74'05656
Older European paintings from the Collection of Harry L. Dalton. A loan exhibition, Duke University, Durham, N.C., February 28-April 4, 1965. [Durham, 1965?] 1 v. (unpaged) illus. 23 cm. [ND454.D8] 67-63858

M. B. McNamee. St. Louis. dist. by Pius XII Memorial Library, 3655 West Pine Blvd., St. Louis 8. Mo.]1960 1.v. (unpaged) 117 illus. 28cm. Erratum slip inserted. Includes 'German expressionism: selected bibliography.' 60-1450 3.00 pap.,
1. Paintings—Exhibitions. 2. Paintings—Private collections. 3. Paintings. German—Exhibitions. 4. Expressionism (Art) I. May, Morton D., II. May, Marge Wolcott. III. McNamee, Maurice B. IV. Title.

SOLOMON R. Guggenheim 750.74
Museum, New York
Guggenheim International Award 1964. New York, Solomon R. Guggenheim Foundation [1963] 122 p. illus. (part col.) 28 cm. Catalogue of "Exhibition 64/1, January, February, March 1964." Bibliography: p. [106]-122. [N5020.N64] 63-14482
1. Paintings—Exhibitions. I. Title.

SOLOMON R. Guggenheim 750.7401471
Museum, New York
Paintings from the collection of the Solomon R. Guggenheim Museum [New York, Author, 1965] 83p. illus. (pt. col.) 28cm. Catalog of exhibition 65/4 Apr.-Sept., 1965. [N620.S63A56] 65-21985 3.50
1. Paintings—Exhibitions. I. Title.

WALKER Art Center, 759.0838
Minneapolis.
Expressionism, 1900-1955; the Walker Art Center, Minneapolis; the Institute of Contemporary Art, Boston; the San Francisco Museum of Art; the Cincinnati Art Museum, and Contemporary Arts Center; the Baltimore Museum of Art; the Albright Art Gallery, Buffalo. Catalog: James H. Elliott, editor Minneapolis, 1956] [56] p. illus. 27 cm. "Sources for biographical notes": p. [3] of cover. [N5020.M69] 56-2499
1. Paintings — Exhibitions. 2. Sculpture — Exhibitions. 3. Expressionism (Art) I. Elliott, James Heyer, 1924- ed. II. Title.

WALKER Art Center, 759.4
Minneapolis.
School of Paris, 1959: the internationals; Karel Appel, Hans Hartung, Andre Lanskoy, Jean-Paul Riopelle, Gerard Schneider, Pierre Soulages, Maria Helena Vieira da Silva, Zao Wou-Ki. An exhibition organized by the Walker Art Center, April 5-May 17, 1959. [Minneapolis, 1959] 59 p. illus. 28 cm. Includes bibliography. [N5020.M72] 59-2732
1. Paintings — Exhibitions. 2. Painting — Paris. I. Title.

WORCESTER, Mass. Art 704.9489
Museum.
Annual exhibition of oil paintings. [Worcester] v. illus. 20 cm. [N5020.W856] 61-56175
1. Paintings — Exhibitions. I. Title.

YALE University. Art 759.0838
Gallery.
Pictures collected by Yale alumni; exhibition, May eight to June eighteen, 1956. New Haven [1956] 1 v. (unpaged) 250 illus. 26 cm. [N5020.N128] 57-3806
1. Paintings — Exhibitions. I. Title.

Paintings—Expertising.

BRANNER, Robert. 729'.8
The painted medallions in the Sainte-Chapelle in Paris. Philadelphia, American Philosophical Society, 1968. 42 p. illus. 30 cm. (Transactions of the American Philosophical Society, new ser., v. 58, pt. 2) Bibliographical footnotes. [Q11.P6 vol. 58, pt. 2] 68-19147
1. Paris. Sainte-Chapelle. 2. Paintings—Expertising. I. Title. II. Series: American Philosophical Society, Philadelphia. Transactions, new ser., v. 58, pt. 2 BIP

DEINHARD, Hanna. 701
Meaning and expression; toward a sociology of art. Boston, Beacon Press [1970] 120 p. illus. 21 cm. First published under the title: Bedeutung und Ausdruck: Zur Soziologie der Malerei. Contents.Contents.—Timeless and time-bound art.—Enguerrand Quarton: "The coronation of the Virgin.".—Giotto: "The massacre of the innocents".—Bruegel: "The massacre of the innocents".—Rubens: "The massacre of the innocents".—Results of the analyses.—The artist and the public. Includes bibliographical references. [ND1145.D413 1970] 75-119676 ISBN 0-8070-6664-8 8.50
1. Paintings—Expertising. 2. Art—Psychology. 3. Art and society. I. Title.

SPECK, Douglas. 759.5
The authenticity of a Titian painting / by Douglas Speck. Minneapolis : T. S. Denison, c1976. ix, 92 p. : ill. ; 24 cm. Includes bibliographical references and index. [ND623.T7S64] 75-32867
1. Tiziano Vecelli, 1477-1576. Madonna and Child with rabbit. 2. Paintings—Expertising. I. Title.

Paintings. Flemish.

BROADLEY, Hugh T. 759.9493
Flemish painting in the National Gallery of Art. Washington, D. C., [National Gallery of Art] [1960] 43p. col. illus. 19cm. (U. S. National Gallery of Art. Booklet no. 5) 60-60831 .25 pp.,
1. Paintings, Flemish. I. Title.

DELEVOY, Robert L. 759.9493
Early Flemish painting. New York, McGraw-Hill [1963] 47 p. illus., 24 col. slides (in pockets) 25 cm. (The Color slide books of the world's art) With slide-viewer. [ND665.D4] 62-18983
1. Paintings, Flemish. 2. Painting, Flemish. 3. Lantern slides. I. Title. II. Series.

LES Primitifs 759.9493
flamands; corpus de la peinture des anciens Pay-Bas meridionaux au quinzieme siecle in French Brussels, Centre National de Recherches Primitifs Flamands. [New York, Heinman, 1963] ix, 318p. illus. (pt. col.) 30cm. Contents.v.u. Musee National du Louvre by Helene Adhemar. 53-16100 20.00
1. Paintings, Flemish. I. Centre national de recherches 'Primitifs flamands.'

LES primitifs flamands; 759.9493
I. Corpus de la peinture des anciens Pays-Bas meridionaux auquinzieme siecle. [fasc. 8] [New York, Heinman, c.1965] 68p. 121 plates. 30cm. Edite par le Centre national de recherches 'Primitifs flamands. Contents.8. Le Musee de L'Ermitage, Leningrad [par] Vladimir Loewinson--Lessing, Nicolas Nicouline. [ND665.P66] 53-16100 22.50
1. Paintings, Flemish. I. Centre national de recherches 'Primitifs flamands.

PRIMITIFS flamands 759.9493
(Les); corpus de la peinture des anciens Pay-Bas meridionaux au quinzieme siecle [v.7] Brussels, Centre national de Recherches Promitifs flamands [dist. New York, Wittenborn] 1964. various p. illus. (pt. col.) 30cm.Kv.7. Le palais ducal d'Urbin, by Jacqueslavalleye. 20.00
1. Paintings, Flemish. I. Centre national de recherches 5Primitifs flamands.'

PRIMITIFS flammands(Les); 759
corpus de la peinture des anciens Pays-Bas meridionaux au quinzieme siecle [v.6] Brussels. Centre national de Recherches Primitifs flamands [dist. New York. Heinman, 1964, c.1963. 354p. illus. (pt. col.) 30cm. Contents.v.6. La Chapelle Rovale de Grenade by Roger Van Schoute. Bibl. 25.00
1. Paintings. Flemish. I. Centre national de recherches Primitifs flamands. II. Van Schoute, Roger.

Paintings, Flemish—Catalogs.

JOHN G. 759.9492'074'014811
Johnson Collection, Philadelphia.
Catalogue of Flemish and Dutch paintings. Philadelphia, 1972. vi, 330 p. illus. 28 cm. A revision of W. R. Valentiner's Flemish and Dutch paintings, originally published as v. 2 of Catalogue of a collection of paintings and some art objects, by J. G. Johnson, 1913-14. Includes bibliographical references. [ND634.J63] 72-89967
1. Paintings, Flemish—Catalogs. 2. Paintings, Dutch—Catalogs. 3. Paintings—Philadelphia—Catalogs.

Paintings—Florence.

ROSSI, Filippo 750.740551
Art treasures of the Uffizi and Pitti [Tr. from Italian] Text by Filippo Rossi. New York, Abrams [1966] 40p. 116 illus. (pt. mounted col.) 33cm. [N2571.R6] 65-20321 25.00
1. Paintings—Florence. I. Florence. Galleria degli Uffizi. II. Florence. Galleria palatina. III. Title.

Paintings—Florence—Catalogs.

FRANCINI Ciaranfi, Anna 708.5'51
Maria.
The Pitti Gallery (Galleria Palatina). Visitors' guide and catalogue of paintings ... With 78 plates. [Translated by Evelyn Sandberg Vavala] Florence, Arnaud, 1967. vii, 153 p. 37 plates. 17 cm. Translation of Pitti, Galleria palatina. [N2560.F713] 68-110726 L 750
1. Florence. Galleria palatina. 2. Paintings—Florence—Catalogs. I. Title.

Paintings, Florentine.

CARLI, Enzo, 1910- 709.4551
Florentine painting. [Translated from the Italian by Pearl Sanders] New York, Golden Press [1963] [56] p. 24 col. illus. 38 cm. (Art of the Western World) [ND621.F7C33] 63-4650
1. Paintings, Florentine. I. Title. II. Series.

UCCELLO, Paolo di Dono, 759.5
known as, 1396or7-1475.
All the paintings of Paolo Uccello. Text by Enzo Carli. Translated from the Italian by Mario Fitzallan. New York, Hawthorn Books [c1963] 78 p. illus. (part col.) 18 cm. (The Complete library of world art, v. 22) Bibliography: p. 77-78. [ND623.U4C33 1963] 63-20694
I. Carll, Enzo, 1910- II. Title. III. Series.

Paintings, Florentine—Catalogs.

NEW York (City). 759.55'1
Metropolitan Museum of Art.
Italian paintings: Florentine school; a catalogue of the collection of the Metropolitan Museum of Art [by] Federico Zeri, with the assistance of Elizabeth E. Gardner. [New York] Distributed by New York Graphic Society [Greenwich, Conn., 1971] viii, 234 p. illus., map. 26 cm. Includes bibliographical references. [ND621.F7N4] 71-127080 ISBN 0-87099-019-5 15.00
1. Paintings, Florentine—Catalogs. 2. Paintings—New York (City)—Catalogs. 3. Paintings, Renaissance—Florence. I. Zeri, Federico. II. Title.

Paintings—Frederiction, N. B.—Catalogs.

BEAVERBROOK Art 708'.113'32
Gallery, Fredericton, N. B.
Beaverbrook Art Gallery; [paintings. 1st ed.] Fredericton, 1959. 71p. 68 plates (part col.) 23cm. 'A preliminary catalogue listing all paintings acquired prior to July 1st, 1959.' [N910.F7B4] 61-40316
1. Paintings—Frederiction, N. B.—Catalogs. I. Title.

Paintings, French.

BESSON, George. 1882- 759.4
Masters of French painting, 1850-1950, with a selection of old masters. New York, E. S. Hermann [1958] 155 p. col. illus. 29 cm. [ND547.B38 1958a] 58-14995
1. Paintings, French. 2. Paintings. I. Title.

DALE, Chester, 1883- 759.4
French paintings from the Chester Dale collection. [6th ed.] Washington, National Gallery of Art, 1953. 93 p. (chiefly illus.) 25 cm. [ND547.D33 1953] 53-4058
1. Paintings, French. 2. Paintings—Private collections. I. U. S. National Gallery of Art. II. Title.

MAUGHAM, William Somerset, 758.9
1874-1965.
Purely for my pleasure. [1st ed. in the U. S. A.] Garden City, N. Y., Doubleday, 1963 [i. e. 1962] 92 p. mounted col. illus., col. port. 33 cm. [ND547.M48 1962a] 62-15861
1. Paintings, French. 2. Paintings—Private collections. I. Title.

SALINGER, Margaretta M., 759.4
1907-
Masterpieces of French painting. Text by Margaretta M. Salinger. New York, H. N. Abrams [1971] 24 p. illus. (part col.) 33 cm. (The Library of great painters. Portfolio ed.) [ND544.S3 1971] 76-130289 ISBN 0-8109-3020-X
1. Paintings, French. I. Title.

SALINGER, Margaretta M., 758.9
1907-
Masterpieces of French painting, fifteenth to mid-nineteenth centuries. Text by Margaretta Salinger. [London, Beaverbrook Newspapers, c1959] 6 p. illus., 16 col. plates (plate 1 on jacket) 36 cm. (An Express art book) Caption title. [ND544] 74-2576
1. Paintings, French. I. Title.

STERLING, Charles, 1901- 759.4
Great French Painting in the Hermitage [Translated by Christopher Ligota. 2d ed.] New York, Abrams [1958] 250 p. illus. (part mounted col.) 35 cm. Translation of Musee de l'Ermitage: la peinture francaise de Poussin a nos jours. "Both reproductions of, and references to, a number of important pictures belonging to the Pushkin Museum in Moscow will be found in this book." Bibliography: p. 229-230. [ND544.S753] 58-9031
1. Paintings, French. I. Leningrad, Ermitazh. II. Moscou. Gostdarstvenny? muzel izebrazitelnykh iskuss(v.) III. Title.

VERGNET-RUIZ, Jean 759.4
Great French paintings from the regional museums of France [by] Jean Vergnet-Ruiz, Michel Laclotte. [Tr. from French by Norbert Guterman] New York, Abrams [1965] viii, 256p. illus. (pt. mounted col.) 3ocm. [ND544.V3813] 65-19229 25.00
1. Paintings, French. 2. Paintings—French. I. Laclotte, Michel, joint author. II. Title.

WECHSLER, Herman Joel, 759.4
1904-
French impressionists. Text by Herman J. Wechsler. New York, H. N. Abrams [1969] 40 p. illus., col. plates. 33 cm. (Great art of the ages) [ND547.5.I4W4 1969] 69-19707 ISBN 0-8109-5112-6
1. Paintings, French. 2. Impressionism (Art)—France. I. Title.

WECHSLER, Herman Joel, 759.4
1904-
French impressionists and their circle. New York, H. N. Abrams in association with Pocket Books [1953] [74] p. 39 illus (part col.) 18cm. (The Pocket library of great art. A7) An Abrams art book. Bibliography: p. [74] [ND547.W35] 53-13417
1. Paintings. French. 2. Impressionism (Art) I. Title.

Paintings, French—Catalogs.

COOKE, Hereward Lester. 759.4
French painting of the 16th-18th centuries in the National Gallery of Art. Washington, D.C., National Gallery of Art [c.1959] 43p. col. illus. 19cm. (U.S. National Gallery of Art. Booklet no. 4) 60-60501 pap., apply
I. Title.

EVANS, Grose. 759.4
French painting of the 19th century in the National Gallery of Art. Washington, D.C., National Gallery of Art. [c.1959] 43p. col. illus. 19cm. (U.S. National Gallery of Art. Booklet no. 2) 60-60574 pap., apply
I. Title.

LENINGRAD. 759.4'074'0745
Ermitazh.
The Hermitage, Leningrad: French 20th century masters; introduction by A. N. Izergina and notes by A. G. Barskaya, A. N. Izergina and B. A. Zernov. Feltham, New York, Hamlyn, 1970. ix, [180] p. col. illus. 31 cm. Translation of Ermitazh, Leningrad: frantsuzskie mastera 20-go stoletiia (romanized form) [ND548.L4513] 75-594202 ISBN 0-600-01789-3 4.20
1. Paintings, French—Catalogs. 2. Painting, Modern—20th century—France. 3. Paintings—Leningrad—Catalogs. I. Title.

NEW York. Metropolitan Museum of Art 759.4
A catalogue of French paintings, by Charles Sterling [senior res. fellow] Cambridge, Pub. for the Mus. by Harvard, 1955-[67] 3 v. illus., maps. 25cm. Vols. 2-3 have title: French paintings; a catalogue of the collections of the Metropolitan Museum of Art, by Charles Sterling, Margaretta M. Salinger. Pub. by the Mus.; dist. by N. Y. Graphic, Greenwich, Conn. Contents.[1] xvxviii centuries. -- 2. xix century. -- 3. xixxx centuries. Bibl. [ND544.N48] 67-6366 Vs. 2 & 3 ea., 7.50
1. Paintings, French—Catalogs. 2. Paintings—New York (City)—Catalogs. I. Sterling, Charles, 1901- II. Salinger, Margaretta M., 1907- III. Title.

Paintings, French—Exhibitions.

BALTHUS, 1908- 741.9'44
Balthus [a benefit exhibition of Balthus paintings and drawings for the City School of Detroit (L'Ecole francaise) November 24th to December 20th, 1969. Detroit, Donald Morris Gallery, 1969 or 70] [50] p. plates. 22 cm. Cover title; Bibliography: p. [46]-[47] [N6853.B3A42] 78-18768
I. Donald Morris Gallery.

BOSTON. Institute of Contemporary Art. [759.084]
Jacques Villon, Lyonel Feininger, with Reflections on painting by Jacques Villon and critical essays by George Heard Hamilton, Thomas B. Hess, and Frederick S. Wight. New York, Published for the Institute of Contemporary Art, Boston, by Chanticleer Press [1949 or 50] 46 p. illus., ports. 25 cm. "Catalogue of the exhibition": p. 44-46. Bibliography: p. 13, 35 [ND553.V54B6] 927.5 50-12872
1. Villon. Jacques, 1875- 2. Feininger, Lyonel Charles Adrian, 1871- 3. Paintings, French—Exhibitions. 4. Paintings, American—Exhibitions. I. Title.

CHICAGO. Art Institute. 759.4
Cezanne: paintings, watereolors & drawings; a loan exhibition, the Art Institute of Chicago, the Metropolitan Museum of Art. [Chicago, 1952] 100 p. illus. 26 cm. [ND553.C33C47] 52-1163
1. Cezanne, Paul, 1839-1906. 2. Paintings, French—Exhibitions. 3. Drawings, French—Exhibitions. I. New York. Metropolitan Museum of Art. II. Title.

CUMMER Gallery of Art. 709'.44
Masterpieces of French painting through two and a half centuries. Inaugural loan exhibition, Cummer Gallery of Art, Jacksonville, Florida, November 10-December 31, 1961. Lent by Wildenstein & Co., inc., New York. [Jacksonville, Fla., 1961] 40 p. illus. 23 cm. [ND546.C84] 72-215255
1. Paintings, French—Exhibitions. 2. Painting, Modern—17th-18th centuries—France. 3. Painting, Modern—19th century—France. I. Wildenstein and Company, inc., New York. II. Title.

DETROIT. Institute of Arts. 759.4
The two sides of the medal; French painting from Gerome to Gauguin. [Exhibition. Catalogue designed by William A. Bostick. Detroit] 1954. 71p. illus. 25cm. [ND547.D46] 55-28733
1. Paintings, French—Exhibitions. I. Title.

FINCH College, New York. Museum of Art. 759.4
Vouet to Rigaud, French masters of the seventeenth century; a loan exhibition, April 20-June 18, 1967. [Catalogue] New York [1967] [52] p. 62 illus. (2 col. (1 on cover)) 23 cm. Introd. signed: Robert L. Manning. [ND546.F5] 77-268910
1. Paintings, French—Exhibitions. 2. Painting, Modern—17th-18th centuries—France. I. Manning, Robert L. II. Title.

FRENCH painting 1774-1830, the Age of Revolution : 759.4'074 Grand Palais, Paris, 16 November 1974-3 February 1975, the Detroit Institute of Arts, 5 March-4 May 1975, the Metropolitan Museum of Art, New York, 12 June-7 September 1975 : exhibition sponsored by Founders Society the Detroit Institute of Arts, the Metropolitan Museum of Art, and the Reunion des Musees Nationaux, Paris.... English language ed. Detroit : distributed by Wayne State University Press, [1975] 712 p. : ill. (some col.) ; 22 cm. French translation has title: De David a Delacroix : la peinture francaise de 1774 a 1830. Includes index. Bibliography: p. 689-706. [ND546.5.N4D43] 75-322567 pbk. : 14.95
1. Paintings, French—Exhibitions. 2. Neoclassicism (Art)—France—Exhibitions. 3. Romanticism in art—France—Exhibitions. I. Paris. Grand Palais. II. Detroit. Institute of Arts. III. New York (City). Metropolitan Museum of Art. IV. Founders Society. V. Reunion des musees nationaux, Paris.

FRENCH paintings from 759.44
French museums, xvii-xviii centuries. Fine Arts Gallery of San Diego, September 29-November 5, 1967, California Palace of the Legion of Honor, November 17, 1967-January 1, 1968. E. B. Crocker Art Gallery, January 19-February 25, 1968 (and) Santa Barbara Museum of Art, March 15-April 28, 1968. [San Diego, Calif., Printed by Studio Printers, 1967] [83] p. illus. (part col.) 27 cm. [ND546.F7] 68-512
1. Paintings, French—Exhibitions. I. San Diego, Calif. Fine Arts Gallery. II. California Palace of the Legion of Honor, San Francisco. III. Crocker Art Gallery, Sacramento, Calif. IV. Santa Barbara, Calif. Museum of Art.

HASTINGS, Baird. 759.4
Christian Berard, painter, decorator, designer. With an introd. by Louis Jouvet. [New York, Published by Chanticleer Press for] Institute of Contemporary Art, Boston [1950] 62 p. illus. 25 cm. [ND553.B519H3] 52-1071
1. Berard, Christian, 1902-1949. 2. Paintings, French—Exhibitions. I. Title.

HERBERT, Robert L., 1929- 759.94
Neo-impressionism [by] Robert L. Herbert. [New York, Solomon R. Guggenheim Foundation, 1968] 261 p. illus. (part col.) 28 cm. Catalog of an exhibition held Feb.-Apr. 1968 at the Solomon R. Guggenheim Museum. Bibliography: p. [250]-251. [ND547.H54] 68-16803
1. Paintings, French—Exhibitions. 2. Neo-impressionism (Art) I. Solomon R. Guggenheim Museum, New York. II. Title.

KNOEDLER (M.) & Company, inc. 758.4
Impressionist and post-impressionist paintings from the U.S.S.R., lent by the Hermitage Museum, Leningrad [and] the Pushkin Museum, Moscow. New York, 1973. 120 p. col. illus. 28 cm. Catalogue of an exhibition at the National Gallery of Art, Washington, and the Knoedler Gallery, New York. Errata slip inserted. Includes bibliographical references. [ND547.5.I4K57] 73-77732
1. Paintings, French—Exhibitions. 2. Impressionism (Art)—France. 3. Post-impressionism (Art)—France. 4. Paintings, French—Russia. I. Leningrad. Ermitazh. II. Moscow. Gosudarstvennyi muzei izobrazitel'nykh iskusstv. III. United States. National Gallery of Art. IV. Title.

LEGER. 759.4
[Catalogue of the exhibition organized by] the Art Institute of Chicago in collaboration with the Museum of Modern Art, New York [and] the San Francisco Museum of Art. By Katharine Kuh. [Chicago, 1953] 90p. illus. (part col.), port. 26cm. 'A selected bibliography, complied by Hannah B. Muller': p. 77-83. [ND553.L58C47] [ND553.L58C47] 927.5 53-1501 53-1501
1. Leger, Fernand, 1881- 2. Paintings, French—Exhibitions. 3. Drawings, French—Exhibitions. I. Chicago. Art Institute. II. Kuh, Katharine.

MARANDEL, J. Patrice. 759.4'074'01641411
French oil sketches from an English collection, seventeenth, eighteenth, and nineteenth centuries : [exhibition] 1973-1975, the Museum of Fine Arts, Houston / by J. Patrice Marandel. Houston : The Museum, c1975. 107 p. : ill. ; 22 x 27 cm. [ND546.M28] 75-10693
1. Paintings, French—Exhibitions. 2. Paintings, Modern—17th-18th centuries—France—Exhibitions. 3. Paintings, Modern—19th century—France—Exhibitions. 4. Artists' preparatory studies—France—Exhibitions. I. Houston, Tex. Museum of Fine Arts. II. Title: French oil sketches from an English collection ...

MINNEAPOLIS. Institute of Arts. 759.4
The past rediscovered: French painting, 1800-1900. [Minneapolis, 1969] 1 v. (unpaged) illus. (part col.) 22 cm. Catalog of a loan exhibition held at the Minneapolis Institute of Arts, July 3-Sept. 7, 1969. Includes bibliographical references. [ND547.M64] 77-89799
1. Paintings, French—Exhibitions. 2. Paintings, Modern—19th century—France. I. Title.

NEW York (City) Museum of Modern Art. 759.4
Soutine, by Monroe Wheeler. New York, Museum of Modern Art, in collaboration with the Cleveland Museum of Art [1950] 115 p. illus., col. plates, ports. 26 cm. "Catalog of the exhibition" p. 112-114. Bibliography, by H. B. Muller: p. 114-115. [ND553.S7N4] 927.5 50-11267
1. Soutine, Haim, 1894-1943. 2. Paintings, French—Exhibitions. I. Cleveland Museum of Art. II. Wheeler, Monroe, 1899-

NEW York (City) Museum of Modern Art. 759.4
Yves Tanguy; [exhibition and catalogue] by James Thrall Soby. New York, [1955] 71 p. illus., plates (part col.) ports. 25 cm. Bibliography: p. 69-70. [ND553.T26N4] 55-11796
1. Tanguy, Yves, 1900-1955. 2. Paintings, French—Exhibitions. I. Soby, James Thrall, 1906-

NEW York. Museum of Modern Art. 759.4
Edouard Vuillard, by Andrew Carnduff Ritchie. The Museum of Modern Art, New York, in collaboration with the Cleveland Museum of Art. [New York, 1954] 104p. illus. (part col.) ports. (part col.) 26cm. [ND553.V9N4] [ND553.V9N4] 927.5 54-6136 54-6136
1. Vullard, Edouard, 1868-1940. 2. Paintings, French—Exhibitions. I. Ritchie, Andrew Carnduff. II. Cleveland Museum of Art. III. Title.
Contents omitted.

ROSENBERG, Pierre. 759.4'074'01
The age of Louis XV : French painting 1710-1774 : [exhibition] 1975-1976, the Toledo Museum of Art, October 26-December 7, the Art Institute of Chicago, January 10-February 22, the National Gallery of Canada, March 21-May 2 / Pierre Rosenberg [Toledo, Ohio] : Toledo Museum of Art, [1975] xv, 94 p., [62] leaves of plates : ill. (some col.) ; 26 cm. Bibliography: p. 87-94. [ND546.R66] 75-21037
1. Paintings, French—Exhibitions. 2. Paintings, Modern—17th-18th centuries—France—Exhibitions. I. Toledo. Museum of Art. II. Art Institute of Chicago. III. National Gallery of Canada. IV. Title.

SAN Diego, Calif. Fine Arts Gallery. 759.44
French paintings from the French museums, seventeenth-eighteenth century Fine Arts Gallery of San Diego, September 29-November 5, 1967, California Palace of the Legion of Honor, November 17, 1967-January 1, 1968, E. B. Crocker Art Gallery, January 19-February 25, 1968 [and] Santa Barbara Museum of Art, March 15-April 28, 1968. [San Diego, Calif., Printed by Studio Printers, 1967] [83] p. illus. (part col.) 27 cm. [ND546.F7] 68-512
1. Paintings. French—Exhibitions. I. California Palace of the Legion of Honor, San Francisco. II. Crocker Art Gallery, Sacramento, Calif. III. Santa Barbara, Calif. Museum of Art. IV. Title.

SCHONEMAN Galleries. 759.4
To commemorate thirty years on Fifty-Seventh Street: from our collection, 30 masterpieces of French art. [Exhibition] November 20 to December 9, 1967. New York, [1967] 35 p. illus. 28 cm. [ND547.5.I4S34 1967] 74-152070
1. Paintings, French—Exhibitions. 2. Impressionism (Art)—France. 3. Post-impressionism (Art)—France. I. Title: 30 masterpieces of French art.

STERLING and Francine Clark Art Institute, Williamstown, Mass. 750'.74'01441
French paintings of the nineteenth century. May 8th, 1956. Williamstown, Mass. [1956?] [89] p. plates. 25 cm. (Its Exhibit 5) Cover title. Includes bibliographies. [N867.A27 no. 5] 68-46107
1. Paintings, French—Exhibitions. I. Title. II. Series.

U. S. National Gallery of Art 759.4
French Paintings from the collections of Mr. and Mrs. Paul Mellon and Mrs. Mellon Bruce twentyfifth anniversary exhibition, 1941- 1966. [2d ed.] Washington [1966] 1 v. (chiefly illus. (pt. col.)) 26cm. [ND547.U58] 66-61423 price unreported
1. Paintings, French—Exhibitions. 2. Painting—Private collections. I. Mellon, Paul. II. Mellon, Rachel Lambert (Lloyd) III. Bruce, Ailsa (Mellon) IV. Title. BIP

U.S. National Gallery of Art. 759.4'074'0153
French paintings from the Collections of Mr. and Mrs. Paul Mellon and Mrs. Mellon Bruce; twenty-fifth anniversary exhibition, 1941-1966. [2d ed.] Washington [1966] 256 p. (chiefly illus. (part col.)) 26 cm. Exhibition held March 17-May 1, 1966. [ND547.U58 1966b] 71-18036
1. Mellon, Paul—Art collections. 2. Mellon, Rachel Lambert (Lloyd)—Art collections. 3. Bruce, Ailsa (Mellon)—Art collections. 4. Paintings, French—Exhibitions. I. Title.

U.S. National Gallery of Art. 759.4
Masterpieces of impressionist and post -- impressionist paintings. [Exhibition] April 25 -- May 24, 1959. Washington [1959] 63 p. illus., 26 cm. [ND547.U6] 59-61075
1. Paintings, French — Exhibitions. 2. Impressionism (Art) 3. Post — impressionism (Art) I. Title.

WALTERS Art Gallery, Baltimore. 759.4
A selection of nineteenth-century paintings. Baltimore [1965] [35] p. 29 illus. 24 cm. (A Walters Art Gallery picture book) [ND547.W3] 36-58391
1. Paintings, French — Exhibitions. I. Title. II. Series.

WALTERS Art Gallery, Baltimore. 759.4
A selection of nineteeth-century paintings. Baltimore, Author [1966] [35] p. 29 illus. 24cm. (Walters Art Gallery picture bk) [ND547.W3] 66-58391 .85 pap.,
1. Paintings, French—Exhibitions. I. Title. II. Series.

WILDENSTEIN and Company, inc., New York. 759.4
Romantics and realists; [catalogue of] a loan exhibition for the benefit of the Citizens' Committee for Children of New York, inc., under the patronage of the consul general of France in New York and Madame Michel Legendre and the cultural counselor to the French Embassy and Madame Edouard Morot-Sir, April 7th to May 7th, Wildenstein ... New York. [New York, 1966] 1 v. (unpaged) illus. (part col.) 28 cm. Introduction signed by M. Roy Fisher. Half-title: Eight French painters; romantics and realists. On spine: Chasseriau, Corot, Courbet ... [ND547.W49] 67-1853
1. Paintings, French—Exhibitions. 2. Romanticism in art—France. I. Fisher, M. Roy. II. Citizens' Committee for Children of New York City. III. Title.

Paintings, French—Hist.

CARDIFF, Wales. National Museum of Wales. 759.4
The Davies collection of French art [by] John Ingamells. Cardiff, National Museum of Wales, 1967. xiv, 115 p. 58 plates (incl. 8 col.), tables, 25 1/2 cm. 60/- (B67-19170) Bibliography: p. [102]-105. [ND547.C28] 67-106924
1. Paintings, French—Hist. 2. Paintings—Private collections. I. Ingamells, John. II. Title.

Paintings, German.

BROADLEY, Hugh T. 759.3
German painting in the National Gallery of Art. Washington, D.C., National Gallery of Art [c.1960] 43p. col. illus. 19cm. (U.S. National Gallery of Art. Booklet no. 9) 60-62153 .25 pap.,
1. Paintings, German. I. Title.

MYERS, Bernard Samuel, 1908- 759.3
The German expressionists, a generation in revolt [Concise ed.] New York, McGraw [1963] 348p. illus. (pt. col.) ports. 23cm. Bibl. 63-19912 8.95
1. Painters, German. 2. Paintings, German. 3. Expressionism (Art) I. Title.

WERNER, Alfred, 1911- 759.3
German painting, the old masters. New York, McGraw-Hill [1964] 48 p. (p. 48 advertisement) illus., ports., 24 col. slides (in pockets) 25 cm. (The Color slide book[s] of the world's art) [ND565.W4] 64-22200
1. Paintings, German. 2. Painting, German. 3. Lantern slides. I. Title. II. Series. BIP

Paintings, German—Exhibitions.

CHAMPA, Kermit S. 759.3'074'013
German painting of the 19th century. Introd. and catalogue by Kermit S. Champa with Kate H. Champa. New Haven, Conn., Yale University Art Gallery [1970] 239 p. illus. (part col.) 26 cm. Exhibition: Yale University Art Gallery, Oct. 15-Nov. 22, 1970; The Cleveland Museum of Art, Dec. 9, 1970-Jan. 24, 1971; The Art Institute of Chicago, Feb. 27-Mar. 28, 1971. Bibliography: p. 237-239. [ND567.C45] 78-137506
1. Paintings, German—Exhibitions. 2. Painting, Modern—19th century—Germany. I. Champa, Kate H. II. Yale University. Art Gallery. III. Cleveland Museum of Art. IV. Chicago. Art Institute. V. Title.

THE Morton D. 759.3'074'017866
May collection of 20th century German masters. [St. Louis, City Art Museum, 1970] 159 p. illus. (part col.) 30 cm. Catalog of the exhibition organized by the Marlborough-Gerson Gallery, New York, and the City Art Museum of St. Louis in honor of Morton D. May. It was shown at the Marlborough-Gerson Gallery from Jan.-Feb., 1970, and at City Art Museum from July-Aug., 1970. Includes bibliographical references. [ND568.M6] 75-282779
1. May, Morton D., 1914- —Art collections. 2. Paintings, German—Exhibitions. 3. Painting, Modern—20th century—Germany. I. Marlborough-Gerson Gallery. II. St. Louis. City Art Museum.

Paintings—Germany (Democratic Republic, 1949-)

SCHEIDIG, Walther 759.94
Unfamiliar masterpieces of painting in East German collections. [Tr. from German by Anthony Rhodes] New York, October House [1966, c.1964] 159p. 159 plates (pt. col.) 28cm. Bibl. [ND450.S313] 65-14358 17.50
1. Paintings—Germany (Democratic Republic, 1949-) 2. Paintings, European. I. Title.

Paintings—Gt. Brit.

PIPER, David, ed. 759
Enjoying paintings. Baltimore, Md., Penguin [c.1964] 242p. illus., 12 col. plates. 20cm. (Pelican bk., A624) Bibl. 64-57195 1.95 pap.,
1. Paintings—Gt. Brit. 2. Paintings, European. 3. Painting, European. I. Title.

Paintings, Haitian—Exhibitions.

APRAXINE, Pierre. 759.97294
Haitian painting: the naive tradition; [catalog of] an exhibition selected by Pierre Apraxine, organized and circulated by the American Federation of Arts. New York, American Federation of Arts [1973] 64 p. illus. 23 cm. Bibliography: p. 58-63. [ND306.A67] 73-90272 3.75 (pbk.).
1. Paintings, Haitian—Exhibitions. 2. Primitivism in art—Haiti. I. American Federation of Arts. II. Title.

MILWAUKEE. Art Center. 759.97294
Haiti, the naive tradition: the Flagg Tanning Corporation Collection. Milwaukee [1974] 120 p. illus. (part col.) 26 cm. Catalogue of an exhibition which opened Dec. 6, 1973. [ND306.M54 1974] 74-78457
1. Flagg Tanning Corporation—Art collections. 2. Paintings, Haitian—Exhibitions. 3. Primitivism in art—Haiti. I. Title.

Paintings—Honolulu— Catalogs.

HONOLULU Academy of Arts. 759.0838
The Samuel H. Kress collection in the Honolulu Academy of Arts. [Honolulu] 1952. 63p. illus. 22cm. [ND615.H55] 53-30734
1. Paintings—Honolulu— Catalogs. 2. Paintings, Italian. 3. Paintings, Renaissance. I. Samuel H. Kress Foundation. II. Title.

Paintings—Indexes.

MONRO, Isabel Stevenson. 016.759
Index to reproductions of European paintings; a guide to pictures in more than three hundred books, by Isabel Stevenson Monro and Kate M. Monro. New York, Wilson, 1956. 668p. 27cm. [ND45.M6] 55-6803
1. Paintings—Indexes. I. Monro, Kate M., joint author. II. Title.

Paintings—Indianapolis.

ART Association of Indianapolis, Indiana. John Herron Art Institute. 759.0838
105 paintings in the John Herron Art Museum. [Indianapolis] Art Association of Indianapolis, Indiana [1951] unpaged. illus. 17 cm. [N577.A575] 52-1955
1. Paintings—Indianapolis. I. Title.

Paintings—Indianapolis—Catalogs.

INDIANAPOLIS Museum of Art. 708'.172'52 s
A catalogue of the Clowes Collection, by A. Ian Fraser. With a pref. by Carl J. Weinhardt. [Indianapolis, 1973] xlix, 195 p. illus. 26 cm. (Its Bulletin/catalogue, new ser., v. 2, no. 1-2) Cover title: Clowes Collection. [N577.A4 n.s. vol. 2, no. 1-2] [N5220.C68] 759.94'074'017252 72-93036
1. Clowes, George Henry Alexander, 1877-1958—Art collections. 2. Indianapolis Museum of Art. 3. Paintings—Indianapolis—Catalogs. I. Fraser, A. Ian. II. Title. III. Title: Clowes collection. IV. Series.

INDIANAPOLIS Museum of Art. 708'.172'52 s
40 master-works; a selection of paintings in the Indianapolis Museum of Art, honoring the inaugural year of the Museum, 1970-71 [Indianapolis, 1970] 41 p. (chiefly illus. (part col.)) 26 cm. (Its Bulletin/catalogue, v. 57, no. 1) [N577.A4 vol. 57, no. 1] [N577] 750'.74'01252 74-160767
1. Indianapolis Museum of Art. 2. Paintings—Indianapolis—Catalogs. I. Title. II. Series.

Paintings, Indic—Exhibitions.

WELCH, Stuart Cary. 751.7'7'095407401471
A flower from every meadow: Indian paintings from American collections. With contributions by Mark Zebrowski. [New York] Asia Society; distributed by New York Graphic Society [1973] 142 p. illus. (part col.) 26 cm. Catalog of the exhibition held at the Asia House Gallery, New York, in the spring of 1973 as an activity of the Asia Society. Bibliography: p. 140-142. [ND1001.W44] 72-93985 ISBN 0-87848-040-4 17.50
1. Paintings, Indic—Exhibitions. 2. Paintings, Indic—United States. I. Zebrowski, Mark. II. Asia House Gallery, New York. III. Asia Society. IV. Title.

Paintings, Italian.

BERENSON, Bernhard, 1865-1959. 759.5
Looking at pictures with Bernard Berenson / selected and with an introd. by Hanna Kiel ; with a personal reminiscence by J. Carter Brown. New York : Abrams, c1974 [i.e.1975] 360 p. : ill. (some col.) ; 31 cm. Includes index. Bibliography: p. 355-[357] [ND614.B38 1974] 72-125795 ISBN 0-8109-0042-4 : 35.00
1. Paintings, Italian. 2. Painting, Gothic—Italy. 3. Painting, Renaissance—Italy. 4. Art appreciation. I. Kiel, Hanna. II. Title.

BOREA, Evelina. 759.5
The high Renaissance Italian painting. New York, McGraw-Hill [1963] 47 p. illus., 24 col. slides (in pockets) 25 cm. (The Color slide books of the world's art) Includes a "slide viewer." [ND615.B658] 62-20525
1. Paintings, Italian. 2. Art, Italian. 3. Lantern slides. I. Title. II. Series.

DRUDI GAMBILLO, Maria 759.5
After Boccioni; futurist paintings and documents from 1915 to 1919. Pref. by Claudio Bruni. Biographical notes, criticisms by Maria Drudi Gambillo. The writings, documents and letters have been collected and arr. by Maria Drudi Gambillo, Claudio Bruni. [Tr. by Helen Graham Heath] Ed. Mediterranee. [dist. New York, Wittenborn, 1961] 80p. illus. (col.) English and Italian. 61-66788 6.00 pap.,
1. Paintings, Italian. 2. Futurism (Art) I. Title.

EINSTEIN, Lewis, 1877- 759.5
Looking at Italian pictures in the National Gallery of Art. Washington, National Gallery of Art, Smithsonian Institution [1951] 116 p. illus. 17 cm. [ND614.E4] 51-8876
1. Paintings, Italian. 2. Paintings—Washington, D. C. 3. U. S. National Gallery of Art. I. Title.

EMILIANI, Andrea 759.5
Italian painting: Perugino to Caravaggio. New York, Golden [1963] [56]p. col. illus., map. 38cm. (Art of the western world) 63-25678 5.00
1. Paintings, Italian. I. Title. II. Series.

FRIEDLAENDER, Walter F., 1873- 759.5
Mannerism and anti-mannerism in Italian painting. Introd. by Donald Posner. New York, Schocken [c.1957, 1965] xix, 89p. plates. 21cm. (SB94) [ND615.F7] 4.00; 1.75 pap.,
1. Paintings, Italian. 2. Painting—Italy—Hist. 3. Manerism (Art) I. Title. BIP

GOULD, Cecil Hilton Monk, 1918- 759.5
Early Renaissance: fifteenth century Italian painting, by C. H. M. Gould. New York, Mcgraw-Hill [1965] 47 p. illus., 24 col. slides (in pockets) 25 cm. (Color slide program of the world's art) [ND615.G68] 65-19418
1. Paintings, Italian. 2. Painting, Italian. 3. Paintings, Renaissance. 4. Lantern slides. I. Title. II. Series.

ISAAC Delgado Museum of Art, New Orleans. 759.5
The Samuel H. Kress collection in the Isaac Delgado Museum of Art. New Orleans, 1953. 67p. illus. 26cm. [ND615.I75] 55-15005
1. Paintings, Italian. 2. Paintings—New Orleans—Catalogs. I. Samuel H. Kress Foundation. II. Title.

LEVEY, Michael. 759.5
The later Italian pictures in the collection of Her Majesty the Queen. [London] Phaidon Publishers; distributed by New York Graphic Society, Greenwich, Conn. [1964] 282 p. illus. (part mounted col.) 31 cm. Half title: The pictures in the collection of Her Majesty the Queen; the later Italian pictures. Catalogue no;. 350-714. Includes bibliographical references. [ND616.L4] 64-54941
1. Paintings, Italian. 2. Paintings — Gt. Brit. 3. Gt. Brit. — Kings and rulers. The pictures in the collection of Her Majesty the Queen. I. Title.

PREVITALI, Giovanni, 1934- 759.5
Early Italian painting. New York, McGraw-Hill [1964] 48 p. illus., 24 col. slides (in pockets) 25 cm. (The Color slide book of the world's art) [ND615.P67] 64-14335
1. Paintings, Italian. 2. Painting, Italian. I. Title. II. Series. BIP

RUSSOLI, Franco, ed. 759.5
The Berenson collection. Pref. by Nicky Mariano. Introd., catalogue by Franco Russoli [Tr. from Italian, ed. by Frances and Sidney Alexander]. Milano, Art grafiche Ricordi [dist. New York 22, Kimberley-Dormann Corp., 59 E. 54 St.] c.1964. 32p. illus., facsim., plates (pt. col.) port. 37cm. (Edizioni Beatrice d'Este) Pub. under the auspices of the Italian commission for UNESCO and the natl. commission for UNESCO of the United States of America. Harvard College, present owners of the Berenson Collection at Villa 'I Tatti, Florence. Bibl. 64-56193 100.00 bxd,
1. Paintings, Italian. 2. Paintings—Private collections. I. Berenson Bernhard, 1865-1950. II. Mariano, Nicky. III. Harvard University. Villa IV. Tatti, Florence. V. Title.

SHAPLEY, Fern Rusk. 759.5
Early Italian painting in the National Gallery of Art. Washington [D.C., National Gallery of Art] [c.1959] 43p. col. illus. 19cm. (U. S. National Gallery of Art. Booklet no. 3) 60-60500 pap., apply
1. Paintings, Italian. I. Title. II. Series.

SHAPLEY, Fern Rusk 759.5
Later Italian painting in the National Gallery of Art. Washington, D.C. [National Gallery of Art] [c.1960] 43p. col. illus. 19cm. (U.S. National Gallery of Art. Booklet no. 6) 60-60830 .25 pap.,
1. Paintings, Italian. I. Title.

THOMPSON, James W., 1924- 759.5
Masterpieces of Italian painting. Text by James W. Thompson. New York, H. N. Abrams [1970] 24 p. illus., 10 col. plates. 33 cm. (The Library of great painters. Portfolio ed.) [ND615.T47 1970] 69-14750
1. Paintings, Italian. 2. Painting, Renaissance—Italy. I. Title.

VAN SCHAACK, Eric 759.5
Baroque art in Italy. New York, McGraw [1965, c.1964] 47p. illus., 24 col. slides (in pockets) 25cm. (Color slide prog. of the world's art) [ND616.V3] 64-21908 8.95 bds.,
1. Paintings, Italian. 2. Painting, Italian. 3. Art, Baroque. I. Title. II. Series. BIP

Paintings, Italian—Catalogs.

ISABELLA Stewart Gardner Museum, Boston. 759.4'074'014461
A selection of paintings, drawings, and watercolors / Isabella Stewart Gardner Museum. Chicago : University of Chicago Press, [1976] p. cm. [ND615.I77 1976] 76-21230 ISBN 0-226-69181-0 : 15.00
1. Isabella Stewart Gardner Museum, Boston. 2. Paintings, Italian—Catalogs. 3. Paintings, Renaissance—Italy—Catalogs. 4. Paintings—Boston—Catalogs. I. Title. BIP

†JOHN and Mable Ringling Museum of Art, Sarasota, Fla. 759.5'074'015961
Catalogue of the Italian paintings before 1800 / by Peter Tomory. [Sarasota, Fla.] : John & Mable Ringling Museum of Art, 1976. xiii, 198 p., [8] leaves of plates : ill. (some col.) ; 27 cm. Cover title: The Italian paintings before 1800. Includes bibliographical references and indexes. [ND615.J58 1976] 76-730 ISBN 0-916758-01-X : 27.50
1. John and Mable Ringling Museum of Art, Sarasota, Fla. 2. Paintings, Italian—Catalogs. 3. Paintings, Renaissance—Italy—Catalogs. 4. Paintings, Modern—17th-18th centuries—Italy—Catalogs. 5. Paintings—Sarasota, Fla.—Catalogs. I. Tomory, P. A., 1922- II. Title. III. Title: The Italian paintings before 1800.
Publisher's address 5401 Bayshore Rd., Sarasota, Fla. 33580

JOHN G. Johnson Collection, Philadelphia. 759.5
Catalogue of Italian paintings. Philadelphia, 1966. xv, 247 p. illus. (part col.), ports. 28 cm. "Note on the catalogue" signed:

SUBJECT INDEX PAINTINGS, JAPANESE—EXHIBITIONS.

Barbara Sweeny. "Foreword" signed: Henri Marceau. Bibliographical footnotes. [ND614.J6] 66-25541
1. Paintings, Italian—Catalogs. 2. Paintings—Private collections. I. Sweeny, Barbara. II. Marceau, Henri, 1896- III. Title.

WALTERS Art 759.5'074'01526
Gallery, Baltimore.
Italian paintings in the Walters Art Gallery / by Federico Zeri ; with condition notes by Elisabeth C. G. Packard ; edited by Ursula E. McCracken. Baltimore : Walters Art Gallery, 1976. 2 v. (xx, 647 p., [158] leaves of plates) : ill. (some col.) ; 28 cm. Includes bibliographical references and indexes. [ND611.W34 1976] 75-28513 75.00
1. Walters Art Gallery, Baltimore. 2. Paintings, Italian—Catalogs. 3. Paintings—Baltimore—Catalogs. I. Zeri, Federico. II. Title. BIP

YALE University. 759.5'074'01468
Art Gallery.
Early Italian paintings in the Yale University Art Gallery; a catalogue, by Charles Seymour, Jr. New Haven, Published for the Yale University Art Gallery by Yale University Press, 1970. xxvi, 312 p. illus. 27 cm. Includes bibliographical references. [ND615.Y3] 71-99841 10.00
1. Paintings, Italian—Catalogs. 2. Painting, Gothic—Italy. 3. Painting, Renaissance—Italy. I. Seymour, Charles, 1912- II. Title. BIP

Paintings, Italian—Exhibitions.

ALEXANDER, 759.5'074'017197
Sidney, 1912-
Selected paintings and drawings of the Italian Renaissance : [exhibition], Trisolini Gallery of Ohio University, Athens, Ohio, February, 1975 / organized by Sidney Alexander M. Barry Katz. Athens : Trisolini Gallery of Ohio University, 1975. [15] p. : ill. ; 28 cm. [ND615.A39] 75-617
1. Paintings, Italian—Exhibitions. 2. Paintings, Renaissance—Italy—Exhibitions. 3. Drawings, Italian—Exhibitions. 4. Drawings, Renaissance—Italy—Exhibitions. I. Katz, M. Barry, joint author. II. Trisolini Gallery. III. Title.

ART Association of 759.5
Indianapolis, Indiana. John Herron Art Institute.
Pontormo to Greco, the age of mannerism; a loan exhibition of paintings and drawings of the century 1520-1620. February 14-March 28, 1954. Indianapolis 1954] v, 71p. illus., map. 25cm. Errate slip inserted. [ND617.A75] 54-4733
1. Paintings, Italian—Exhibitions. 2. Drawings, Italian—Exhibitions. I. Title.

CHICAGO. Art Institute. 759.5
Painting in Italy in the eighteenth century; rococo to romanticism. An exhibition organized by the Art Institute of Chicago, the Minneapolis Institute of Arts, and the Toledo Museum of Art. Edited by John Maxon and Joseph J. Rishel. Chicago, 1970. 251 p. illus. (part col.), maps, ports. 26 cm. Exhibition to be shown at the Art Institute of Chicago, Sept. 19-Nov. 1, 1970, at the Minneapolis Institute of Arts, Nov. 24, 1970-Jan. 10, 1971, and at the Toledo Museum of Art, Feb. 7-Mar. 21, 1971. [ND616.C5] 70-132024
1. Paintings, Italian—Exhibitions. 2. Painting, Modern—17th-18th centuries—Italy. I. Maxon, John, 1916- ed. II. Rishel, Joseph J., ed. III. Minneapolis. Institute of Arts. IV. Toledo. Museum of Art.

COLNAGHI (P. & 759.5'074'02132
D.) & Company, ltd., London.
Italian paintings, 1550-1780 : [catalogue of an exhibition held at] P. & D. Colnaghi & C. Ltd..., 26th May to 2nd July 1976. London : P. & D. Colnaghi & Co. Ltd., 1976. [1], 35 p., [36] p. of plates : ill. (incl. 1 col.) ; 25 cm. Includes bibliographical references. [ND615.C575 1976] 76-380391 ISBN 0-904221-11-3 : £1.00
1. Paintings, Italian—Exhibitions. 2. Mannerism (Art)—Italy—Exhibitions. 3. Paintings, Modern—17th-18th centurire—Italy—Exhibitions. I. Title.

DUKE University, Durham, 759.5
N.C. Art Museum.
The Italian paintings from the Mary and Harry L. Dalton Collection : the Duke University Museum of Art, September 29-November 12, 1974 : [catalog] [Durham, N.C.] : The Museum, [1974] [71] p. : ill. (some col.) ; 22 cm. [ND614.D84 1974] 74-195180
1. Dalton, Mary—Art collections. 2. Dalton, Harry L.—Art collections. 3. Paintings, Italian—Exhibitions. 4. Painting, Modern—Italy. I. Title.

FINCH College, New York. 759.5
Museum of Art.
Baroque painters of Bologna and neighboring cities; a loan exhibition, February twenty-seventh--April eighth, 1962. [Catalogue prepared by Robert L. Manning] New York [1962] 1 v. (unpaged) illus. (part col.) 23 cm. Cover title: Bolognese baroque painters. [ND616.F5] 68-1881
1. Paintings, Italian—Exhibitions. 2. Painting, Baroque—Bologna. I. Manning, Robert L. II. Title. III. Title: Bolognese baroque painters.

MINNESOTA 759.5'074'0176581
Museum of Art.
The introspective Italian. L'Italiano introspettivo. The 3M collection of paintings organized and circulated by the Minnesota Museum of Art. St. Paul [1971] [40] p. illus. (1 col.) 24 cm. Catalog of the exhibition held Sept. 23-Oct. 31, 1971 at the Minnesota Museum of Art, St. Paul. English and Italian. Bibliography: p. [34]-[35] [ND618.M5] 70-181073
1. Paintings, Italian—Exhibitions. 2. Painting, Modern—20th century—U.S. I. Minnesota Mining and Manufacturing Company. II. Title. III. Title: L'Italiano introspettivo.

QUINSAC, Annie 759.5'074'013
Paule.
Ottocento painting. Organization of the exhibition and catalogue by Annie Paule Quinsac. [Columbia, S.C., Printed by The Vogue Press, 1972] 111, [56] p. illus. (part col.) 21 cm. Catalog of a loan exhibition at the Columbia Museum of Art, Columbia, S.C., and other institutions, Nov. 15, 1972, to June 15, 1973. Bibliography: p. 26-31. [ND617.Q56] 72-80056
1. Paintings, Italian—Exhibitions. 2. Painting, Modern—19th century—Italy. I. Columbia, S.C. Museum of Art. II. Title.

YALE 755'.4'094507401468
University. Art Gallery.
Italian primitives; the case history of a collection and its conservation. [Contributors for the catalogue: David Arnheim and others. New Haven, 1972] 56 p. illus. 28 cm. Cover title. "An exhibition celebrating the centenary of Yale University's acquisition of the Jarves Collection, April—September, 1972." [ND1651.U6N47] 73-172477
1. Jarves, James Jackson, 1818-1888—Art collections. 2. Paintings, Italian—Exhibitions. 3. Paintings—Conservation and restoration—New Haven. I. Arnheim, David. II. Title.

Paintings, Italian—History.

CAVALLINI, Pietro, 759.5
ca.1250-ca.1330
Pietro Cavallini. Text by Pietro Toesca. [Tr. by Elizabeth Andrews] 25 plates in colour, 18 plates in monochrome. New York, McGraw [1961, c.1960] 18, [6]p. illus. (pt. col.) 38cm. (Silvana Collection) Bibl. 61-14992 16.00, bxd.
I. Toesca, Pietro, 1877- II. Title.

*DEWALD, Ernest Theodore. 759.5
Italian painting, 1200-1600 / Ernest T. DeWald. New York : Hacker Art Books, 1978, c1961. 613p. : ill. ; 26 cm. Includes index. Includes bibliograpies. [ND615.D44] ISBN 0-87817-219-X : 40.00
1. Paintings, Italian — History. 2. Paintings, Italian. I. Title.
Book carries L.C. card no.: 77-76786.

DEWALD, Ernest Theodore, 759.5
1891-
Italian painting, 1200-1600. New York, Holt [c.1961] 613p. illus. 25cm. Bibl. 61-8585 9.50
1. Paintings, Italian—Hist. 2. Paintings, Italian. I. Title.

Paintings, Italian—United States—Indexes.

FREDERICKSEN, Burton B. 759.5'097
Census of pre-nineteenth-century Italian paintings in North American public collections, by Burton B. Fredericksen and Federico Zeri. Cambridge, Harvard University Press, 1972. xxii, 678 p. 26 cm. [ND611.F73] 73-182813 ISBN 0-674-10491-9 25.00
1. Paintings, Italian—United States—Indexes. 2. Paintings, Italian—Canada—Indexes. I. Zeri, Federico, joint author. II. Title. BIP

Paintings, Japanese.

COVELL, Jon Etta Hastings 749.3
(Carter) 1910-
Masterpieces of Japanese screen painting: the Momoyam period (late 16th century) New York, Crown [1963, c.1962] 25p. illus., 14 col. plates. 43cm. Bibl. 63-1626 10.00
1. Paintings, Japanese. 2. Painters, Japanese. 3. Screens. I. Title.

DAWSON'S BOOK SHOP, 759.952'021'6
Los Angeles.
Japanese picture scrolls and paintings; a priced and indexed catalogue. Los Angeles, 1967. 191 p. illus. 22 cm. Combines the firm's Catalogues 343, 346, 349, 351, 357, 366, first issued separately 1964-1967. Includes bibliographies. [ND1050.D3] 67-8094
1. Paintings, Japanese. I. Title.

GAFU, Kazan 759.952
The sketchbook of Watanabe, Kazan; 2v. Dist. Austin, Texas, Perkins Oriental, 1963] 2v. (un-paged) chiefly illus. (pt. col.) 26cm. 12.00 bds., set,
1. Paintings, Japanese. I. Title.

GRILLI, Elise. 759.952
Golden screen paintings of Japan. New York, Crown Publishers [1960] 34 p. illus., plates (part col.) 18 cm. (Art of the East library) [ND1053.G72] 60-10059
1. Paintings, Japanese. 2. Screens. I. Title. II. Series.

GRILLI, Elise. 759.952
Japanese picture scrolls. New York, Crown Publishers [1958?] 24 p. illus., 28 plates (part col.) 18 x 19 cm. (Art of the East library) [ND1053.G73] 58-4760
1. Paintings, Japanese. 2. Illumination of books and manuscripts—Japan. I. Title. II. Series.

[HYAKUDAI, Shuga 759.952
A hundred pictures in watercolor, 5v. Dist. Austin Texas, Perkins Oriental, 1963] 5v. (unpaged) illus. (pt. col.) 25cm. 19.00 bds.,set,
1. Paintings, Japanese. 2. Water color paintings, Japanese. I. Title.

KAEMMERER, Eric A. 759.952
Trades and crafts of old Japan; leaves from a contemporary album. Tokyo, Rutland, Vt., Tuttle [c.1961] 112p. 49 plates (part col.) 61-14030 4.95, bxd.
1. Paintings, Japanese. 2. Art industries and trade—Japan. 3. Industry in art. I. Title.

[MANGA, Hokusai 759.952
The sketchbook of Hokusai, 15v. Dist. Austin, Texas, Perkins Oriental, 1963] 15v. (unpaged) chiefly illus. (pt. col.) 26cm. Japanese and English. 95.00 bds., set,
1. Paintings, Japanese. I. Title.

MIYAGAWA, Torao, 1908- 759.952
Modern Japanese painting; an art in transition. Tr., adapted by Toshizo Imai. [1st ed.] Tokyo, Palo Alto, Calif., Kodansha Intl. [1967] 131p. 36 plates (35 col.) 30cm. [ND1055.M513] 67-16770 10.00
1. Paintings, Japanese. 2. Painting—Japan. I. Title.

TAKAHASHI, Seiichiro, 759.952
1884- ed.
Kaiqetsudo (circa 1700-1750) English text by Richard Lane. [1st English ed.] Tokyo, Rutland, Vt., C. E. Tuttle Co. [1959] 88 p. illus. (part col.) 18 cm. (Kodansha library of Japanese art, no. 13) [ND1053.T213] 59-6633
1. Paintings, Japanese. 2. Color prints, Japanese. 3. Painters, Japanese. I. Title. II. Series.

UNITED Nations 759.952
Educational, Scientific and Cultural Organization
Japanese paintings from Buddhist shrines and temples. Introd. by Philip S. Rawson. [New York] New Amer. Lib. [c.1959,1963] 24, [7]p. illus., 28 col. plates. 17cm. (Mentor-Unesco art bk.; MQ518) Bibl. 63-25495 .95 pap.,
1. Paintings, Japanese. 2. Art, Buddhist. I. Rawson, Philip S. II. Title.

Paintings, Japanese—Catalogs.

NAKAMURA, Tanio. 759.952
Contemporary Japanese-style painting. Translated and adapted by Mikio Ito. New York, Tudor Pub. Co. [1969] 78, [162] p. illus. (163 col.), ports. 25 cm. [ND1055.N3313] 78-94757 9.95
1. Paintings, Japanese—Catalogs. 2. Painting, Modern—20th century—Japan. 3. Painters, Japanese. I. Ito, Mikio, 1917- II. Title.

Paintings, Japanese—Exhibitions.

CAHILL, James 759.952'074'013
Francis, 1926-
Scholar painters of Japan: the Nanga school [by] James Cahill. [New York] Asia Society; distributed by New York Graphic Society [1972] 135 p. illus. 31 cm. Catalog of an exhibition held at the Asia House Gallery, New York City, Jan. 12-Feb. 27, 1972; and University Art Museum, University of California, Berkeley, Apr. 3-30, 1972. Bibliography: p. 134. [ND1053.5.C3] 72-182236 ISBN 0-87848-038-2
1. Paintings, Japanese—Exhibitions. 2. Painting, Japanese—History. 3. Japan—History—Tokugawa period, 1600-1868. I. Asia House Gallery, New York. II. California. University. Art Museum. III. Title. BIP

FRENCH, Calvin L. 759.952
The poet-painters, Buson and his followers : an exhibition, the University of Michigan Museum of Art, Ann Arbor, January 9-February 17, 1974 ; the Seattle Art Museum, Washington, March 28-May 12, 1974 ; the Asia House Gallery, New York, October 3-December 1, 1974 / organized by Calvin L. French, in collaboration with Stephen Addiss ... [et al.]. [Ann Arbor] : University of Michigan Museum of Art, 1974. xv, 179 p., [3] leaves of plates : ill. (some col.) ; 31 cm. Catalog. Bibliography: p. 178-179. [ND1053.5.F73] 74-623083
1. Taniguchi, Buson, 1716-1784. 2. Taniguchi, Buson, 1716-1784—Influence. 3. Paintings, Japanese—Exhibitions. 4. Painting, Japanese—Edo period, 1600-1868. I. Michigan. University. Museum of Art. II. Seattle. Art Museum. III. Asia House Gallery, New York. IV. Title.

JAPAN. Cultural 759.952
Properties Protection Commission.
Exhibition of Japanese painting and sculpture sponsored by the Government of Japan. National Gallery of Art, Washington; the Metropolitan Museum of Art, New York; Museum of Fine Arts, Boston; the Art Institute of Chicago; Seattle Art Museum, Seattle. [Washington?] 1953. 207p. illus. (part col.) 28cm. Errata slip inserted. [ND1050.J25] 53-61152
1. Paintings, Japanese—Exhibitions. 2. Sculpture, Japanese— Exhibitions. 3. Art—Exhibitions, Traveling. I. U. S. National Gallery of Art. II. Title.

SHIMIZU, Yoshiaki. 759.9'52
Japanese paintings; from the collection of Joe D. Price. [Exhibition] 27 October/30 November, 1967, Museum of Art, University of Kansas. [Lawrence, 1967?] 68 p. illus. (part col.) 21 cm. (Miscellaneous publications of the Museum of Art, no. 68) Bibliography: p. 66-67. [ND1053.S4525] 68-64669
1. Paintings, Japanese—Exhibitions. 2. Paintings—Private collections. I. Price, Joe D. II. Kansas. University. Museum of Art.

III. Series: Kansas. University. Museum of Art. Miscellaneous publication, no. 68

Paintings—Juvenile literature.

BELVES, Pierre, 1909- 750
Enjoying the world of art [by] Pierre Belves [and] Francois Mathey. [American ed. New York] Lion Press [1968, c1966] 108 p. illus. (part col.) 22 x 26 cm. Translation of Premier livre d'art. An introduction to art with works by famous artists grouped under such headings as "Animal friends," "Art and music," and "At work." [ND1146.B413 1968] 78-3507
1. Paintings—Juvenile literature. 2. Painting—Juvenile literature. I. Mathey, Francois, joint author. II. Title. BIP

CAMPBELL, Ann Raymond. 750'.1
Paintings: how to look at great art, by Ann Campbell. New York, F. Watts [1970?] 136 p. illus., plates (part col.) 25 cm. Explains, with photographs of well-known paintings, the meaning of design, pattern, composition, space, perspective, light and shade, movement, sfumato, and many other concepts. [ND1146.C35] 70-97836 8.95
1. Paintings—Juvenile literature. I. Title.

CHASE, Alice Elizabeth. 758.9
Famous paintings; an introduction to art. A Chanticleer Press ed. New York, Platt & Munk [1962] 120 p. illus. (part col.) 29 cm. [ND1146.C52 1962] 62-9589
1. Paintings—Juvenile literature. 2. Art—Juvenile literature. I. Title.

WILLARD, Charlctte 759
What is a masterpiece New York, Putnam [c.1964] 62p. 14 illus. (13 col.) 27cm. 64-18028 3.50; 3.29 lib. ed.,
1. Paintings—Juvenile literature. 2. Art—Juvenile literature. I. Title.

Paintings, Latin American—Exhibitions.

CONTEMPORARY 759.98'074'016686
Latin American painting; [an exhibit] Philbrook Art Center, Tulsa, October 7-28, 1969; Oklahoma Art Center, Oklahoma City, November 2-30, 1969; Museum of Art, University of Oklahoma, Norman, December 7-21, 1969. [Tulsa? 1969?] 50 p. illus., ports. 21 x 27 cm. [ND202.C6] 70-20143
1. Paintings, Latin American—Exhibitions. 2. Painting, Modern—20th century—Latin America. I. Philbrook Art Center, Tulsa, Okla. II. Oklahoma Art Center. III. Oklahoma. University. Museum of Art.

NEW Jersey 759.98'074'014966
State Council on the Arts.
Panorama of contemporary Latin American artists = Panorama de artistas latinoamericanos contemporaneos. [Trenton : New Jersey State Council on the Arts, 1975]. [60] p. : ill. (some col.) ; 23 cm. Catalogue of an exhibition held at the New Jersey State Museum, Sept. 5-Oct. 27, 1975, and four other institutions, Nov. 8, 1975-July 4, 1976. English and Spanish. Includes bibliographical references. [ND202.N48 1975] 75-35435
1. Paintings, Latin American—Exhibitions. 2. Paintings, Modern—20th century—Latin America—Exhibitions. I. New Jersey. State Museum, Trenton. II. Title. III. Title: Panorama de artistas latinoamericanos contemporaneos.

Paintings—Leningrad.

DESCARGUES, Pierre. 759.074
The Hermitage Museum, Leningrad. New York, H. N. Abrams [1961] 320 p. plates (part col.) 22 cm. [N3350.D4] 61-14628
1. Leningrad. Ermitazh. 2. Paintings—Leningrad.

Paintings—London.

HENDY, Philip, Sir 1900- 759.0838
London National Gallery. New York, H. N. Abrams [1957] 62p. illus. (part mounted col.) 39cm. (Great museums of the world) An Abrams art book. [N1070.H43] 58-395
1. Paintings—London. I. London. National Gallery. II. Title.

LONDON. National Gallery. 759.084
Art treasures of the National Gallery, London. Text by Philip Hendy [director. 1st ed.] New York, H. N. Abrams [1955] 195p. illus., col. plates. 34cm. (Library of great museums) [N1070.A765] 56-1207
1. Paintings—London. I. Hendy, Philip, 1900- II. Title.

LONDON. National 750.740212
Gallery.
Masterpieces of European painting in the National Gallery, London. New York, H. N. Abrams [1965] viii, 50 p., 50 col. plates. 28 cm. [N1070.A754] 65-26990
1. Paintings — London. I. Title.

LONDON. National 750.740212
Gallery
Masterpieces of European painting in the National Gallery, London. London, Natl. Gallery 1965. ix, 50p. 50 col. plates. 28cm. [N1070.A754 1965a] 66-74067 4.20
1. Paintings—London. I. Title.
Available from British Info. in New York.

LONDON. National Gallery. 750.74
The National Gallery, London, by Philip Hendy, director. New York, H. N. Abrams [1960] 318 p. illus., col. plates, plan. 22 cm. [N1070.A766] 60-8400
1. Paintings—London. I. Hendy, Philip, Sir, 1900-

LONDON. National 759.94'074'02132
Gallery.
The National Gallery, London [by] Philip Hendy, former director. [4th ed., revised.] London, Thames and Hudson, 1971. 320 p. illus. (some col.), plan, ports. 22 cm. [N1070.A766 1971] 72-190543 ISBN 0-500-18006-7
1. Paintings—London. I. Hendy, Philip, Sir, 1900-
Available from Abrams, 7.50, ISBN 0-8109-0338-5

VALSECCHI, Marco 750.74021
National Gallery. London: text by Marco Valsecchi. [Tr. from Italian by Anthony Firmin O'Sullivan] New York, Appleton-Century [dist. Meredith. 1965, c.1963] 158p. illus. (pt. col.) 28cm. (Great galleries ser.) [N1070.V333] 65-21680 8.95 bds.,
1. Paintings—London. I. London. National Gallery. II. Title.

Paintings—Los Angeles—Catalogs.

LOS Angeles Co., Calif. 759.4
Museum, Los Angeles.
Catalogue of paintings. [Los Angeles] Los Angeles County Museum [1954?- v. plates. 26 cm. Cover title. Contents.Contents.—1. A catalogue of Italian, French, and Spanish paintings, 14-18 century.—2. A catalogue of Flemish, German, Dutch, and English paintings, 15-18 century. [N582.L7A59] 74-154215
1. Los Angeles Co., Calif. Museum, Los Angeles. 2. Paintings—Los Angeles—Catalogs.

Paintings—Madrid.

MADRID. Museo Nacional de 759.94
Pintura y Escultura.
The Prado. [Translated from the French by James Cleugh] New York, H. N. Abrams [1959] 317 p. plates (part col.) plans. 22 cm. [N3450.M273] 59-11868
1. Paintings—Madrid. I. Sanchez Canton, Francisco Javier, 1891-

WEHLE, Harry Brandeis, 759.0838
1887-
Great paintings from the Prado Museum. Foreword by F. J. Sanchez Canton. New York, Abrams [1963] 211p. illus. (pt. mounted, pt. col.) 33cm. 63-19566 25.00
1. Paintings—Madrid. I. Madrid. Museo nacional de pintura y escultura. II. Title.

Paintings—Mantua.

VERHEYEN, Egon. 759.5'28
The paintings in the studiolo of Isabella d'Este at Mantua. New York, Published by New York University Press for the College Art Association of America, 1971. xiii, 105 p. illus. 29 cm. (Monographs on archaeology and the fine arts, 23) Bibliography: p. 105. [ND621.M3V4] 76-164021 ISBN 0-8147-8751-7
1. Isabella d'Este, consort of Francis II, Marquis of Mantua, 1474-1539. 2. Paintings—Mantua. 3. Mantua. Palazzo ducale. Studiolo. I. Title. II. Series. BIP

Paintings—Melbourne—Catalogs.

HOFF, Ursula. 759.94'074'09945
European paintings before eighteen hundred. [2nd ed. Melbourne] National Gallery of Victoria [1967] 223 p. illus. 25 cm. First ed., 1961, has title: Catalogue of European paintings before eighteen hundred. [N3948.H6] 78-545891
1. Paintings—Melbourne—Catalogs. I. Victoria, Australia. National Gallery, Melbourne. II. Title.

Paintings — Memphis, Tenn. — Catalogs.

BROOKS Memorial Art 70s.1784111
Gallery, Memphis, Tenn.
Paintings donated by Mr. and Mrs. Morrie A. Moss to the Brooks Memorial Art Gallery, 1954-1961. [Catalogue] Memphis, 1964. 30 p. illus. (1 col) 26 cm. Cover title: The Moss collection: paintings [N582.M4A64] 66-8189
1. Paintings — Memphis, Tenn. — Catalogs. I. Moss, Lillian. II. Moss, Morrie A. III. Title. IV. Title: The Moss collection: paintings.

Paintings, Mexican—Exhibitions.

BARNITZ, Jacqueline. 759.972
Young Mexicans: Corzas, Gironella, Lopez-Loza, Rojo [and] Toledo. New York, Art Gallery, Center for Inter-American Relations [1970] [44] p. illus. (part col.) 22 cm. Published in connection with the exhibition held Oct. 22, 1970-Jan. 3, 1971 at the Art Gallery, Center for Inter-American Relations, New York. Bibliography: p. [34]-[35] [ND255.B36] 79-199929
1. Paintings, Mexican—Exhibitions. 2. Painting, Modern—20th century—Mexico. I. Center for Inter-American Relations. Art Gallery. II. Title.

MEXICO, the new 759.9'72
generation. [Austin? Printed by the Print. Division of the University of Texas, 196-] [32] p. illus. 22 cm. Catalog of an exhibition held at the University Art Museum, University of Texas, and organized by the museum in conjunction with the Departamento de Artes Plasticas, Instituto Nacional de Bellas Artes, Mexico. Bibliography: p. [30] [ND255.M37] 68-6537
1. Paintings, Mexican—Exhibitions. 2. Paintings, Modern—20th century—Mexico. I. Texas. University. Art Museum. II. Mexico (City). Instituto Nacional de Bellas Artes. Departamento de Artes Plasticas.

Paintings, Modern.

GREAT masters of world 759.5
painting : Botticelli, Canaletto, Watteau, Cezanne, Titian / [edited by] Nathaniel Harris. London ; New York : Spring Books, 1974. [322] p. in various pagings : chiefly col. ill. ; 28 cm. [ND160.G73] 75-318023 ISBN 0-600-33976-9 : £2.95
1. Paintings, Modern. I. Harris, Nathaniel.

Paintings, Modern—17th-18th centuries—Catalog.

ROTHLISBERGER, Marcel. 759.9492
Cavalier Pietro Tempesta and his time [by] Marcel Roethlisberger-Bianco. [Newark] University of Delaware Press, 1970. 143, [178] p. of illus. (part col.) 31 cm. Bibliography: p. 139-140 (1st group) [ND653.M9R63] 78-101052
1. Mulier, Pieter, 1637-1701. 2. Paintings, Modern—17th-18th centuries—Catalog. I. Mulier, Pieter, 1637-1701. II. Title. BIP

Paintings, Modern—19th century—Catalogs.

UNITED Nations 016.759
Educational, Scientific and Cultural Organization.
Catalogue de reproductions de peintures 1860 a 1973 et quinze plans d'expositions = Catalogue of reproductions of paintings 1860 to 1973 with fifteen projects for exhibitions. 10. ed. mise a jour. Paris : Unesco, 1974 [i.e.,1975] 343 p. : ill. ; 23 cm. French, English, and Spanish. "SHC.73/XI. II 1/AFS." Includes indexes. [ND189.U54 1974] 75-508403 ISBN 92-3-001123-1 pbk. : 13.20
1. United Nations Educational, Scientific and Cultural Organization. 2. Paintings, Modern—19th century—Catalogs. 3. Paintings, Modern—20th century—Catalogs. 4. Paintings—Catalogs. I. Title. II. Title: Catalogue of reproductions of paintings 1860 to 1973 ...
Distributed by Unipub Distributed by Unipub.

Paintings, Modern—19th century—Exhibitions.

MODERN masters, Manet 759.06'074
to Matisse. the Museum of Modern Art, New York ; edited by William S. Lieberman. New York : MOMA, [1975?] 271 p. : ill. (some col.) ; 19 x 21 cm. "Schedule of the exhibition: Art Gallery of New South Wales, Sydney, April 10-May 1, 1975; National Gallery of Victoria, Melbourne, May 28-June 22, 1975; the Museum of Modern Art, New York, August 4-September 1, 1975." [ND189.M62] 76-355327
1. Paintings, Modern—19th century—Exhibitions. 2. Paintings, Modern—20th century—Exhibitions. I. Lieberman, William Slattery, 1924- II. Sydney. Art Gallery of New South Wales. III. Victoria, Australia. National Gallery, Melbourne. IV. New York (City). Museum of Modern Art.

MONTGOMERY 759.06'074'016147
Museum of Fine Arts.
Corporate collections in Montgomery : Montgomery Museum of Fine Arts, Montgomery, Alabama, May 15 through June 20, 1976. Montgomery : The Museum, c1976. 71 p. : ill. ; 25 cm. Exhibition catalog of selected works from the collections of 5 Montgomery, Ala. corporations. Includes index. [ND189.M66 1976] 76-15913 ISBN 0-89280-002-X pbk. : 2.00
1. Paintings, Modern—19th century—Exhibitions. 2. Paintings, Modern—20th century—Exhibitions. 3. Corporations—Art collections—Alabama—Montgomery. I. Title. BIP

SMITH College. 759.06'074'014423
Museum of Art.
19th & 20th century paintings from the Collection of the Smith College Museum of Art. Catalogue prepared by Mira Matherny Fabian, Michael Wentworth & Charles Chetham, [Northampton, Mass., Smith College Museum of Art, 1970] 41 p., 59 plates (1 col.) 26 illus. 23 cm. "A circulating exhibition sponsored by the American Federation of Arts." [N5015.A53S6] 73-118586
1. Paintings, Modern—19th century—Exhibitions. 2. Paintings, Modern—20th century—Exhibitions. I. Fabian, Mira Matherny. II. Wentworth, Michael. III. Chetham, Charles Scott. IV. American Federation of Arts. V. Title.

SPECTACLE of realism; 759.05
an exhibition of 19th century European and American paintings, October 20th-November 30th, 1968. San Diego, Calif., Orr's Gallery, 1968. [7] p., 51 p. of illus. (part col.) 24 cm. [ND192.R4S6] 79-16581
1. Paintings, Modern—19th century—Exhibitions. 2. Realism in art. I. Orr's Gallery.

Paintings, Modern—20th century.

INNOCENT art / 759.06
edited by David Larkin ; with an introd. and biographical notes by Martin Green ; picture research by Celestine Dars. New York : Ballantine Books, 1974. [96] p. : col. ill. ; 30 cm. [ND196.P7155] 75-311790 ISBN 0-345-24244-0 pbk. : 4.95
1. Paintings, Modern—20th century. 2. Primitivism in art. 3. Painters. I. Larkin, David.

KULTERMANN, Udo. 759.06
The new painting. [Translated from the

German by Gerald Onn] New York, Praeger [1969] 71, 207 p. illus. (part col.) 28 cm. Translation of Neue Formen des Bildes. Bibliography: p. 67-71 (1st group) [ND195.K8413] 75-89604 20.00
1. Paintings, Modern—20th century. I. Title.

Paintings, Modern—20th century—Catalogs.

NEW York (City). 759.06'074'01471
Museum of Modern Art.
An invitation to see; 125 paintings from the Museum of Modern Art. Introd. and comments by Helen M. Franc. New York, Museum of Modern Art; Distributed by New York Graphic Society, Greenwich, Conn. [1973] 159 p. col. illus. 27 cm. Bibliography: p. 149-151. [ND195.N48] 72-82887 ISBN 0-87070-231-9 9.95
1. Paintings, Modern—20th century—Catalogs. 2. Paintings—New York (City)—Catalogs. I. Franc, Helen Margaret, 1908- II. Title. BIP

Paintings, Modern—20th century—Exhibitions.

ALLENTOWN, Pa. Art Museum. 759.06
Modern art from Pittsburgh; a selection of contemporary paintings from the permanent collection of the Museum of Art, Carnegie Institute. [Catalog of an exhibition held] October 14 through December 2, 1973, Allentown Art Museum, Allentown, Pennsylvania. Allentown [1973] 35 p. illus. 28 cm. [ND195.A53 1973] 73-87162
1. Paintings, Modern—20th century—Exhibitions. I. Pittsburgh. Carnegie Institute. Museum of Art. II. Title.

BAZIOTES, William, 1912- 759.13
1963.
William Baziotes late work, 1946-1962 New York, Marlborough Gallery [1971] 28 p. illus. (part col.), port. 30 cm. Exhibition held at the Marlborough Gallery, New York, February-March 1971. [N6537.B35A57] 70-198076
I. Marlborough Gallery.

CALIFORNIA. University, 759.13
Santa Barbara. Art Galleries.
A selection of paintings from the 50's and 60's from the collection of Gifford and Joann Phillips. [Santa Barbara, Calif., Printed by Standard Printing, 1968] [36] p. illus. (part col.) 23 cm. Exhibition held Mar. 12-Apr. 7, 1968, at the Art Gallery, University of California, Santa Barbara, and sponsored by the Committee on Arts and Lectures. [N5220.P54] 68-63036
1. Phillips, Gifford—Art collections. 2. Phillips, Joann—Art collections. 3. Paintings, Modern—20th century—Exhibitions. I. California. University, Santa Barbara. Committee on Arts and Lectures. II. Title.

CALIFORNIA. 759'.074'09491
University, Santa Barbara. Art Galleries.
Trends in twentieth century art; a loan exhibition from the San Francisco Museum of Art, January 6 to February 1, 1970. Organized and selected by Ala Story. Santa Barbara [1970] 29 p. illus. (part col.) 23 cm. [ND195.C3] 71-628710
1. Paintings, Modern—20th century—Exhibitions. I. Story, Ala. II. San Francisco. Museum of Art. III. Title.

DUVENECK, Frank, 1848- 759.13 B
1919.
Frank Duveneck. New York, Chapellier Gallery [1972] [96] p. illus. (part col.) 26 cm. Catalog of an exhibition. Bibliography: p. [94]-[96] [ND237.D85C45] 72-198250
I. Chapellier Galleries.

LEICHMAN, Seymour. 759.13
Seymour Leichman: recent paintings; exhibition: September 12-30, 1972. [Introductory text by Dmitri Vasarion] New York, Kennedy Galleries Inc., [1972] [20] p. illus. (part col.) 28 cm. [ND237.L54V37] 72-171049
I. Vasarion, Dmitri. II. Kennedy Galleries, inc., New York.

NIERMAN, Leonardo, 1932- 759.9'52
Leonardo Nierman. [Texto de Carlos Pellicer, Mexico], Artes de Mexico. Stamped on t.p.: American dist.: Wittenborn, New York, [1967] [11], p., 44 col. plates (incl. part.) and phonodisc (2 s. 7 in. 33 rpm.) in pocket. 34cm. Text, captions and phonodisc in Spanish and English. [ND259.N5P4] 67-9738 20.00
I. Pellicer, Carlos, 1897- II. Title.

PIERRE Matisse Gallery, New 759.4
York.
Hantai; paintings, 1960-1970. [Exhibition] Oct.-Nov. 1970. [New York, 1970?] [12] p. 2 illus., port. 26 cm. English and French. Texts by Francois Mathey and by Andre Breton, both translated by William Richard Miller. [ND553.H22P5] 76-198241
I. Hantai, Simon.

SAN Francisco. 759.06'074'019461
Museum of Art.
A selection of American and European paintings from the Richard Brown Baker Collection : [exhibition], September 14-November 11, 1973, San Francisco Museum of Art, December 7, 1973-January 27, 1974, Institute of Contemporary Art, University of Pennysylvania, Philadelphia / organized by San Francisco Museum of Art. [San Francisco] : The Museum, c1973. [32] p. : ill. ; 26 cm. [ND195.S22 1973] 75-316853
1. Baker, Richard Brown—Art collections. 2. Paintings, Modern—20th century—Exhibitions. I. Pennsylvania. University. Institute of Contemporary Art. II. Title.

SELECTIONS from the 759.06
Ferdinand Howald Collection, the Columbus Gallery of Fine Arts, Columbus, Ohio. New York, American Federation of Arts [1970] 1 v. (unpaged) illus. 21 cm. Catalog of the exhibition circulated 1970-71 by the American Federation of Arts. "AFA exhibition number 70-1." [ND195.S39] 77-134911
1. Howald, Ferdinand—Art collections. 2. Paintings, Modern—20th century—Exhibitions. I. Columbus Gallery of Fine Arts, Columbus, Ohio. II. American Federation of Arts.

SOLOMON R. Guggenheim 759.13
Museum, New York.
William Baziotes; a memorial exhibition. New York [1965] 51 p. illus. (part col.) 26 cm. Catalog of "Exhibition 65/2 February-March, 1965." Bibliography: p. 44-51. [ND237.S6328A2] 65-16957
I. Baziotes, William, 1912-1963. II. Title.

WHITNEY, Stephen. 759.06
Twentieth century masterpieces from the Musee de Grenoble. Essay and catalogue by Stephen Whitney. Translations by Eda M. Levitine [College Park? Md., c1973] 111 p. illus. 22 x 27 cm. Exhibition held at the University of Maryland Art Gallery, Nov. 7-Dec. 21, 1973, J. B. Speed Art Museum, Jan. 7-Feb. 3, 1974, and University Art Museum, Austin, Tex., Feb. 17-Mar. 24, 1974. English and French. Includes bibliographical references. [ND195.W47] 73-620203
1. Paintings, Modern—20th century—Exhibitions. I. Grenoble. Musee de peinture et de sculpture. II. Maryland. University. Art Gallery. III. Speed Art Museum, Louisville, Ky. IV. Texas. University at Austin. Art Museum. V. Title.

Paintings, Modern—20th century—France—Exhibitions.

PICASSO, Braque, 759.4'074'013
Leger : masterpieces from Swiss collections. Minneapolis : The Minneapolis Institute of Arts, c1975. 83 p. : ill. (some col.) ; 31 cm. Catalog of an exhibition held at the Minneapolis Institute of Arts, Oct. 30, 1975-Jan. 4, 1976, the Sarah Campbell Blaffer Gallery, University of Houston, Tex., Jan. 17-Mar. 7, 1976, and the San Francisco Museum of Modern Art, Mar. 19-May 4, 1976. [ND553.P5P46] 75-34717
1. Picasso, Pablo, 1881-1973. 2. Braque, Georges, 1882-1963. 3. Leger, Fernand, 1881-1955. 4. Paintings, Modern—20th century—France—Exhibitions. 5. Paintings, French—Switzerland. I. Picasso, Pablo, 1881-1973. II. Braque, Georges, 1882-1963. III. Leger, Fernand, 1881-1955. IV. Minneapolis. Institute of Arts. V. Sarah Campbell Blaffer Gallery. VI. San Francisco Museum of Modern Art. BIP

Paintings, Modern—Exhibitions.

BROOKS Memorial 759.06'074'016819
Art Gallery, Memphis, Tenn.
Memphis collects paintings: a loan exhibition, September, 1964. [Memphis, Tenn., 1964] 24 p. illus. 23 cm. [ND160.B76 1964] 75-304007
1. Paintings, Modern—Exhibitions. 2. Paintings—Private collections—Memphis. I. Title.

PAINTINGS from 759.06'074'017
midwestern university collections, seventeenth—twentieth centuries. An exhibition organized by the Committee on Institutional Cooperation and the member universities. [Evanston? Ill., 1974?] 179 p. illus. (part col.) 25 cm. Catalogue of a traveling exhibition shown at Wildenstein & Co., New York, and other galleries and museums Oct. 1973-Apr. 1975. [ND160.P3] 72-13631
1. Paintings, Modern—Exhibitions. 2. Paintings, Modern—Middle West. I. Committee on Institutional Cooperation.

Paintings—Moscow.

MOSCOW. Gosudarstvennyi 750.74
muzei izobrazitel'nykh iskusstv.
Great paintings from the Pushkin Museum, Moscow. Text by K. M. Malitskaya, curator of Western European art. Introd. by I. Antonova, director. [Translated by Norbert Guterman] New York, H. N. Abrams [1965?] 15 p., 100 mounted col. illus. 33 cm. [N3321.A5] 64-15232
1. Paintings—Moscow. I. Malitskaia, Kseniia Mikhailovna, 1891- II. Title.

Paintings—New York (City)

NEW York (City) 708.1471
Metropolitan Museum of Art.
Great paintings from the Metropolitan Museum of Art; a selection from the European collections, presented by the curatorial staff. New York, H. N. Abrams [1959] 38 p. illus. (part mounted col.) 33 cm. "A revised excerpt from Art treasures of the Metropolitan, published in 1952." [N610.A6735] 59-8848
1. Paintings—New York (City) I. Title. BIP

NEW York (City). 759.94'074'01471
Metropolitan Museum of Art.
The picture galleries / [by Theodore Rousseau]. [New York : Metropolitan Museum of Art, 1954?] 56 p. : chiefly ill. ; 26 cm. Cover title. [N610.A726] 75-320286
1. New York (City). Metropolitan Museum of Art. 2. Paintings—New York (City) I. Rousseau, Theodore, 1912- II. Title.

ROUSSEAU, Theodore, 759.0838
1912-
The Metropoliti)0an, New York. New York, H. N. Abrams [1957] 60p. illus. (part mounted col.) 39cm. (Great paintings of the world) An Abrams art book. [N610.R6] 58-346
1. Paintings—New York (City) I. New York. Metropolitan Museum of Art. II. Title. III. Series.

Paintings—New York (City)—Catalogs.

THE Frick 750'.74'01471
Collection, New York.
Handbook of paintings. New York, 1971. 144 p. illus. 22 cm. [N620.F6A65] 79-118330 ISBN 0-912114-08-8
1. Paintings—New York (City)—Catalogs. I. Title.

NEW York. Gallery of 709.01'1
Modern Art Including the Huntington Hartford Collection.
Paintings from the Huntington Hartford collection in the Gallery of Modern Art. [New York, 1964] 1 v. (unpaged) illus., col. plates. 28 cm. [N620.G3A6] 64-19357
1. Paintings — New York (City) — Catalogs. 2. Paintings — Private collections. I. Title.

NEW York Historical 708.147
Society.
The Waldron Phoenix Belknap, Jr. collection of portraits and silver, with a note on the discoveries of Waldron Phoenix Belknap, Jr. concerning the influence of the English mezzotint on colonial painting. Edited by John Marshall Phillips, Barbara N. Parker [and] Kathryn C. Buhler, with a biographical note by Edward Weeks. Cambridge, Harvard University Press, 1955. vii, 177p. illus., ports. 26cm. Catalogue of the collection which was bequeathed to the New York Historical Society in 1949. 'Notes on New York City goldsmiths and silversmiths, by Waldron Phoenix Belknap. Jr.': p. 115-121. [N613.A65] 55-14415
1. Paintings—New York (City)—Catalogs. 2. Portraits, American—Catalogs. 3. Silversmithing—U.S. 4. Silversmithing—Catalogs. I. Belknap, Waldron Phoenix. II. Phillips, John Marshall, ed. III. Title.

NEW York. Metropolitan 708.471
Museum of Art.
The Adele and Arthur Lehman collection, by Claus Virch. New York, 1965. 114 p. illus. (part col.) 29 cm. Includes bibliographies. [N611.L4] 65-25643
1. Paintings — New York (City) — Catalogs. 2. Art — New York (City) — Catalogs. I. Lehman, Adele (Lewisohn) 1882-1965. II. Lehman, Arthur. III. Virch, Claus, 1927- IV. Title.

NEW York. Metropolitan 759.0838
Museum of Art.
A catalogue of the collection. New York [1967] v. illus. (incl. ports.) map. 25cm. At head of title: The Metropolitan museum of art. A brief biog. of each artist with an account of his artistic heritage is supplied and is followed by explanatory material about the pictures themselves.--Pref. V. 2 by Harry B. Wehle, Margaretta Salinger; v. 3 by Charles Sterling. V. 3 has imprint: Cambridge, Pub. for the Mus. by Harvard Univ. Pr. Contents.[v] 11. 19th century, by Charles Sterling, Margaretta M. Salinger [N610.A653] 41-7098 7.50; 2.95 pap.,
1. Paintings—New York (City)—Catalogs. 2. Painters. I. Wehle, Harry Brandeis, 1887- II. Salinger, Margaretta, 1907- III. Sterling, Charles, 1901- IV. Title.
Available from N.Y. Graphic in Greenwich, Conn.

NEW York. Metropolitan 759.0838
Museum of Art.
A concise catalogue of the European paintings in the Metropolitan Museum of Art, by Josephine L. Allen, associate curator, and Elizabeth E. Gardner, assistant curator, Dept. of Paintings. New York, 1954. 104p. 25cm. Cover title: European paintings in the Metropolitan Museum. [N610.A654] 54-3248
*1. Paintings—New York (City)—Catalogs.*Allen, Josephine L. I. Gardner, Elizabeth E. II. Title. III. Title: European paintings in the Metropolitan Museum.*

NEW York. Museum of 708.147
Modern Art.
The Museum of Modern Art, New York, painting and sculpture collection. [Edited by] Alfred H. Barr, Jr. Paris, Braun; agent pour U.S.A.: E. S. Hermann. New York [c1950] unpaged. illus. 17 cm. (Collection des maitres) English, French and German. [N620.M9A88] 52-4557
1. Paintings — New York (City) — Catalogs. 2. Sculpture — New York (City) — Catalogs. I. Barr, Alfred Hamilton, 1902- ed. II. Title.

NEW York. Museum of 708.1471
Modern Art.
Painting and sculptpure in the Museum of Modern Art: a catalog. New York, 1958. 71p. 25cm. Bibliography: p. 64-65. [N620.M9A43] 58-8007
1. Paintings—New York (City)—Catalogs. 2. Sculpture—New York (City)—Catalogs. I. Title.

Paintings—Omaha—Catalogs.

JOSLYN Art Museum. 750'.74'018225
Paintings in the Joslyn Art Museum; a check list of paintings acquired before July, 1970. Omaha [1970] 85 p. 28 cm. [N658.A6] 74-138833
1. Paintings—Omaha—Catalogs. I. Title.

Paintings. Oriental — Exhibitions.

SUGAHARA, Hisao, 1923- 760'.095
Japanese ink painting and calligraphy from the collection of the Tokiwayama Bunko,

Kamakura, Japan. With an introductory essay by Takaaki Matsushita. [Translated from the Japanese by Miyeko Murase and others. Brooklyn, 1967] v. 85 p. illus. 24 cm. "A special exhibition, March 28-June 25, 1967, the Brooklyn Museum." [ND1036.S8] 67-20722
1. Paintings. Oriental — Exhibitions. 2. Calligraphy, Japanese — Exhibitions. I. Tokiwayama Bunko. II. Brooklyn Institute of Arts and Sciences. Museum. III. Title.

Paintings—Oxford—Catalogs.

OXFORD. University. Christ Church 759.94
Paintings by old masters at Christ Church; catalogue by J. Byam Shaw. London, Phaidon; New York, Praeger, 1967. [5], 308p. 241 illus. (6 col.) 31cm. [N1450.A63] 67-29887 17.50
1. Paintings—Oxford—Catalogs. I. Byam Shaw, James, 1903- II. Title.

Paintings—Paris.

LEMOYNE de Forges, Marie Therese. 759.4
Impressionist painters at the Jeu de Paume Picture Gallery, from Cezanne to Toulouse-Lautrec. Text by Marie-Therese de Forges. (English translation by Marjorie Gibson Graig.) Berne, Hallwag, 1967. 1 v. (unpaged) col. plates. 19 cm. (Orois pictus, 20) [N2050.J4L383 1967] 67-24992 unpriced
1. Paris. Musee du jeu de paume. 2. Paintings—Paris. 3. Impressionism (Art) I. Title.

Paintings—Philadelphia—Catalogs.

PENNSYLVANIA. Historical Society. 757'.0973
Paintings and miniatures at the Historical Society of Pennsylvania. Rev. ed. compiled by Nicholas B. Wainwright. Philadelphia, 1974. xx, 334 p. illus. (part col.) 29 cm. Published in 1872 under title: Catalogue of the paintings and other objects of interest belonging to the Historical Society of Pennsylvania; and in 1942 under title: Catalogue, descriptive and critical, of the paintings and miniatures in the Historical Society of Pennsylvania. [N683.A5 1974] 73-91728 ISBN 0-910732-08-6 20.00
1. Paintings—Philadelphia—Catalogs. I. Wainwright, Nicholas B., ed. II. Title. BIP

Paintings—Pittsburgh—Catalogs.

PITTSBURGH. Carnegie Institute. Museum of Art. 750'.74'014886
Catalogue of painting collection. Pittsburgh [1973] iv, 196 p. 96 plates. 23 cm. On spine: Painting collection. [N710.A54] 73-180225
1. Pittsburgh. Carnegie Institute. Museum of Art. 2. Paintings—Pittsburgh—Catalogs. I. Title.

Paintings, Polish.

UNITED Nations Educational, Scientific and Cultural Organization. 759.38
Poland; painting of the fifteenth century. Pref.: Rene Huyghe. Introd: Michal Walicki. [New York] New York Graphic Society, [1964] 1 v. (various pagings) plates (part col.) 49 cm. (UNESCO world art series, 21) Includes bibliography. [ND691.U5] 64-7169
1. Paintings, Polish. 2. Paintings, Polish — Hist. 3. Christian art and symoblism. I. Title. II. Series.

Paintings, Polish—Exhibitions.

NEW York. Museum of Modern Art. 759.38
15 Polish painters / by Peter Selz. An exhibition. Garden City, N. Y., Distributed by Doubleday [1961] 64p. illus. 24cm. [ND691.N52] 61-16522
1. Paintings. Polish—Exhibitions. I. Selz, Peter. II. Title.

POLISH paintings; 759.38
a loan exhibition, August 1-August 21, 1957 [at] the Parrish Art Museum. Arranged by Boleslaw Mastai. [Southampton, Long Island, New York, c1957] 99 p. illus., ports. 23 cm. [ND691.P56] 78-5911
1. Paintings, Polish—Exhibitions. I. Mastai, Boleslaw. II. Parrish Art Museum.

Paintings—Prices.

GRAVES, Algernon. 338.4'7'75
Art sales from early in the eighteenth century to early in the twentieth century (mostly old master and early English pictures) New York, B. Franklin, 1970. 3 v. ports. 29 cm. (Art history and art reference, 30) (Burt Franklin bibliography and reference series, 340.) Reprint of the 1918-21 ed. Contents.Contents.—v. 1. A to G.—v. 2. H. to Reme.—v. 3. Reynolds to Z. [N8675.G72] 77-108428
1. Paintings—Prices. I. Title.

WORLD collectors 759.085
annuary; v.12, 1960. [Dist. New York, Heinman, 1962] 547p. illus. 27cm. Ed. 1960- F. A. van Braam. 52-494 55.00
1. Paintings—Prices. I. Braam. Frederik A. van ed. BIP

WORLD collectors 759.085
annuary; v. 14, Jan.-Dec. 1962. Ed. by Fred. A. van Braam [Amsterdam, Author; dist. New York, Heinman, 1964] v. illus. 27cm. 52-494 55.00
1. Paintings—Prices. I. Braam, Frederik A. van, ed.

WORLD collectors 759.085
annuary, vols ix,x art 1957-1958.Edited by Fred A. Van Braam. dist. New York W. S. Heinman, 1960 various paging. illus. (part col.) 28cm. 52-494 52.50 buck.,
1. Paintings—Prices. I. Braam, Frederik A. van, ed.

WORLD collectors 759.0851
annuary v. 13, January 1st-December 31st 1961. Ed. by Fred A. van Braam. [Amsterdam, Author, dist. New York, Heinman, 1962] various p. illus. 27cm. 52-494 55.00
1. Paintings—Prices. I. Braam, Frederik A. van, ed.

WORLD collectors 759.085
annuary. v. 11, 1959 Ed. by Fred A. Van Braam. New York, W. S. Heinman [1960] 459, 106p. illus. (part col.) 27cm. (122p.) With index to v. 1-11. 52-194 54.00
1. Paintings—Prices. I. Braam, Frederick A. van ed.

WORLD collectors 759'.085
annuary. Netherlands, Edition: World Collectors Annuary [1967] v. illus. Ed.: 1964- F.A. van Braam, A.B. Ter Haar Romeny. Contents.v. 17: January 1st - December 31st 1965 [ND47.W6] 52-494 60.00
1. Paintings — Prices. I. Braam, Frederik A. van, ed. II. Romeny, A.B. Ter Haar.

WORLD collectors 759.085
annuary. v. 16. Jan. 1st- Dec. 31st. 1964 Edition: World Collectors Annuary [New York, Heinman, 1966] 1v. (various p.) illus. 27cm. Editor: 1964- F. A. van Braam, A. B. Ter Haar Romeny [ND47.W6] 52-494 55.00
1. Paintings—Prices. I. Braam, Frederik A. van, ed. II. Romeny A. B. Ter Haar.

Paintings—Private collections.

BENNETT, Mrs. Edgar Assheton. 708.272
Catalogue of paintings and drawings from the Assheton Bennett collection. Manchester, City Art Galleries, 1965. 2-55 p. col. front., illus. 25 cm. N. T. Cover title: Paintings from the Assheton Bennett collection. Includes bibliographical references. [[B 66-2052)] [N5245.B39] 66-2353
1. Paintings — Private collections. Bennett, Edgar Assheton, 1873- if. Manchester, Eng. Art Gallery. III. Title. Manchester, Eng. Art Gallery. III. Title. I. Title.

BODKIN, Thomas, 1887- 927
Hugh Lane and his pictures. Dublin, Published by the Stationery Office for an Chomhairle Ealaion (the Arts Council) 1956. xv, 96p. 51 illus. 22cm. [N8386.L3B6 1956] 57-42308
1. Lane, Hugh Percy, Sir 1875-1915. 2. Paintings—Private collections. I. Title.

DALE, Chester, 1883- 759.4
Twentieth century French paintings from the Chester. Dale collection. [1st ed.] Washington, National Gallery of Art, Smithsonian Institution, 1952. 69 p. (chiefly illus. (part col.)) 26 cm. [ND548.D32] 53-326
1. Paintings—Private collections. 2. Paintings, French. I. U. S. National Gallery of Art. II. Title.

JOHN G. Johnson Art Collection, Philadelphia. 759.084
Johnson collection, two hundred and eighty-eight reproductions: Italian, Dutch, Flemish, German, Spanish, French, English & 19th century paintings. Philadelphia, 1953. vi, 272p. illus. (part col.) 27cm. [N5220.J67] 54-502
1. Paintings—Private collections. I. Title.

KNOEDLER (M.) and Company 759.0838
A loan exhibition of paintings and sculpture from the Niarchos collection; [catalogue] The Knoedler Gallery, New York, Dec. 3, 1957 to Jan. 18, 1958; the National Gallery of Canada, Ottawa, Feb. 5 to Mar. 2, 1958; the Museum of Fine Arts, Boston, Mar. 15 to Apr. 20, 1958. [2d and rev. ed. New York, 1958] 133p. plates (part col.) 28cm. Includes bibliographies. [N5270.N5 1958] 57-14505
1. Paintings—Private collections. 2. Paintings— Exhibitions. I. Niarchos, Stavros. II. Title.

LASKER, Albert Davis, 1876- 759.4
The Albert D. Lasker collection: Renoir to Matisse. Commentaries by Wallace Brockway. Introd. by Alfred Frankfurter. New York, Simon and Schuster [1957] xvii, 123. [2] p. 60 mounted col. illus. 37cm. 'Complete catalogue of the Albert D. Lasker collection': p. 122-[124] [N5220.L34] 58-1792
1. Paintings —Private collections. 2. Paintings, French. I. Brockway, Wallace, 1905- II. Title. III. Title: Renoir to Matisse.

MILLAR, Oliver Nicholas, 1923- 759.2
The Tudor, Stuart, and early Georgian pictures in the collection of Her Majesty the Queen 2v. London] Phaidon Pubs. dist. Greenwich, Conn., N. Y. Graphic [c.1963] 2v. (227;266p) plates, geneal. table. atlas (9p., plates, pt. col.) ports. (pt. col.) 30cm. 1st pt. of a catalogue raisonne of the royal collection of pictures. 63-25403 8.50; 12.50 text vol., plate vol.,
1. Paintings—Private collections. 2. Paintings, British. 3. Portraits, British. 4. Gt. Brit.—Biog. Portraits. I. Title.
Contents omitted.

PHILLIPS COLLECTION, Washington, D.C. 759.0838
The Phillips Collection, a museum of modern art and its sources. Catalogue. Washington, [1952] x, 148 p. plates (part col.) 26 cm. [N5220.P55] 52-4782
1. Paintings — Private collections. I. Title.

PORTLAND, Or. Art Museum. 338.4'3745'10973
Paintings from the collection of Walter P. Chrysler, Jr. An Exhibition organized 1956 by the Portland Art Museum, Portland, Oregon. [2d ed. Portland, Portland Art Association, 1956] 145p. illus. (part col.) 24 cm. A catalog of the exhibition which opened at the Portland Art Museum on Mar. 2, 1956 and ends its tour of the participating museums in Apr. 1957. [N5220.C5P6 1956a] 56-4427
1. Paintings—Private collections. 2. Paintings—Exhibitions. 3. Art—Exhibitions, Traveling. I. Chrysler, Walter Percy, 1909- II. Title.

Paintings—Private collections—U.S.

LEWISOHN, Adolph, 1849-1938. 709'.44
The Adolph Lewisohn Collection of modern French paintings and sculptures, by Stephan Bourgeois. Reprint ed. New York, Arno Press [1968] xiii, 254 p. illus. 32 cm. (Arno series of contemporary art, no. 20) Half title: Modern French paintings and sculptures. Reprint of the 1928 ed. [ND547.L5 1968] 68-9241
1. Paintings—Private collections—U.S. 2. Paintings, French—Catalogs. 3. Sculpture—Private collections—U.S. 4. Sculpture, French—Catalogs. I. Bourgeois, Stephan. BIP

RUKHIN, Evgenii, 1943- 759.7
Eugene Rukhin, a contemporary Russian artist : an exhibition of paintings from private collections in the United States and Canada, August 10 through September 14, 1975 / Moussa M. Domit, Ruth Mayfield, Doris E. Dunlavy. Raleigh : North Carolina Museum of Art, 1975. p. cm. Includes index. [ND699.R83D65] 75-25733 ISBN 0-88259-079-0
1. Rukhin, Evgenii, 1943- 2. Paintings—Private collections—United States. I. Domit, Moussa M. II. Mayfield, Ruth, 1940- III. Dunlavy, Doris E., 1914- IV. North Carolina. Museum of Art, Raleigh. V. Title.

Paintings—Radiography.

BURROUGHS, Alan, 1897-1965. 751.5'8
Art criticism from a laboratory. Westport, Conn., Greenwood Press [1971, c1938] xxiii, 277 p. illus. 24 cm. Includes bibliographical references. [ND1635.B87 1971] 70-110267 ISBN 0-8371-4493-0
1. Paintings—Radiography. 2. Forgery of paintings. I. Title. BIP

HOURS, Madeleine, 1913- 751.6
Conservation and scientific analysis of painting / Madeleine Hours. New York : Van Nostrand, [1976] p. cm. Translation of L'analyse scientifique et la conservation des peintures. Bibliography: p. [ND1635.H6813] 76-7343 ISBN 0-442-23549-6 : 20.00
1. Paintings—Radiography. 2. Paintings—Conservation and restoration. I. Title. BIP

Paintings—Raleigh, N.C.—Catalogs.

NORTH Carolina. Museum of Art, Raleigh. 750'.74'015655
Catalogue of paintings. [2d ed.] Raleigh, 1966- v. illus. (part col.) 26 cm. Contents.Contents.—v. 1. American paintings to 1900.—v. 2. British paintings to 1900. [ND235.R3N62] 77-26860
1. Paintings—Raleigh—Catalogs.

NORTH Carolina. Museum of Art, Raleigh. 759.0838
Catalogue of paintings, including three sets of tapestries, by W. R. Valentiner. Raleigh, 1956- v. plates, plans. 24cm. [ND235.R3N6] 56-63506
1. Paintings- Raleigh—Catalogs. I. Valentiner, Wilhelm Reinhold, 1880- II. Title.

NORTH Carolina. Museum of Art, Raleigh. 759'.074'015655
Masterpieces in the North Carolina Museum of Art, by Charles W. Stanford, Jr. Raleigh, 1966. 86 p. illus. (part col.) 19 cm. Bibliography: p. 84. [N715.R2A56] 67-64718
1. Paintings—Raleigh, N.C.—Catalogs. I. Stanford, Charles W. II. Title. BIP

NORTH Carolina. Museum of Art, Raleigh. 759.5
The Samuel H. Kress collection. Raleigh [1960] 146p. illus. (part col.) 26cm. Catalogue of the collection in the museum. Includes bibliographies. [N715.R2N6] 61-62607
1. Paintings—Raleigh, N. C.—Catalogs. 2. Paintings, Italian. I. Samuel H. Kress Foundation. II. Title.

NORTH Carolina. Museum of Art, Raleigh. 759
Selections from British and American painting and sculpture, North Carolina Museum of Art, by Charles W. Stanford, Jr. Raleigh, 1967. 86 p. illus. (part col.) 19 cm. "Companion textbook to Masterpieces in the North Carolina Museum of Art, published in 1966." Bibliography: p. 84. [N715.R2A63] 68-64746
1. Paintings—Raleigh, N.C.—Catalogs. 2. Paintings, British—Catalogs. 3. Paintings,

SUBJECT INDEX PAINTINGS, SPANISH —

American—Catalogs. I. Stanford, Charles W. II. Title.

Paintings—Reading. Pa.—Catalogs.

READING, Pa. Public 750.838
Museum and Art Gallery.
Catalogue of paintings. 4th ed. Reading, 1953. 113p. illus. 22cm. [N715.R4A5 1953] 59-19561
1. Paintings—Reading. Pa.—Catalogs. I. Title.

Paintings, Renaissance

PORTLAND, Or. 759.03'074'05632
Art Museum.
Paintings of the Renaissance; handbook of the Samuel H. Kress collection. Portland [1952?] 63 p. illus. 28 cm. "Addendum": [8] p. inserted. [ND170.P6] 64-54585
1. Paintings, Renaissance 2. Paintings—Portland, Or.—Catalogs. I. Samuel H. Kress Foundation. II. Title.

Paintings, Renaissance—Catalogs.

SPEAR, Richard 759.03'074'05632
E., 1940-
Renaissance and baroque paintings from the Sciarra and Fiano collections [by] Richard E. Spear. University Park, Pennsylvania State University Press [1972] 111 p. illus. (part col.) 27 cm. Includes bibliographical references. [ND170.S63] 72-1141 ISBN 0-271-01156-4
1. Almagia family—Art collections. 2. Paintings, Renaissance—Catalogs. 3. Paintings, Baroque—Catalogs. I. Title. BIP

Paintings, Renaissance—Exhibitions.

ART Association of 759.0838
Indianapolis, Indiana. John Herron. Art Institute.
Holbein and his contemporaries, a loan exhibition of painting in France, the Netherlands, Germany, and England, October 22-December 24, 1950. [Rev. ed. Indianapolis, 1950] unpaged. illus. 25cm. [N5020.I49 1950] 57-19946
1. Holbein, Hans, the younger. 1497-1543. 2. Paintings, Renaissance— Exhibitions. I. Title.

PHILBROOK Art 759.03'074'016686
Center, Tulsa, Okla.
Masterpieces of Renaissance and Baroque painting from the Collection of Colonel Frank W. Chesrow. [Tulsa, 1970?] 44 p. illus. (part col.) 28 cm. Exhibition held at the Philbrook Art Center, Oct. 5-28, 1970 and the Oklahoma Art Center, Nov. 8-Dec. 6, 1970. [ND170.P47] 73-172401
1. Chesrow, Frank W., 1903- —Art collections. 2. Paintings, Renaissance—Exhibitions. 3. Paintings, Baroque—Exhibitions. I. Oklahoma Art Center. II. Title.

Paintings, Renaissance—Italy.

BERENSON, Bernhard, 1865- 759.5
1959.
Homeless paintings of the Renaissance. Edited by Hanna Kiel. Introd. by Myron P. Gilmore. Bloomington, Indiana University Press [1970, c1969] 256 p. illus. 30 cm. Six essays, 3 of which were previously published in English in International studio, during 1929-1931; 2 in Italian in Dedalo, 1932; and 1 in Italian in Bolletino d'arte, 1932. [ND615.B52 1970] 68-29524 17.50
1. Paintings, Renaissance—Italy. 2. Paintings—Expertising. I. Kiel, Hanna, ed. II. Title.

Paintings—Rumania.

GREAT masters of painting 759.074
in the museums of Rumania. Pref. by G. Oprescu. 3rd rev. ed. Bucharest, Meridians [dist. New York, Vanous] 1963. [244]p. 115 col. illus. 30cm. Pub. in 1960 under title: Masters of world painting in Rumanian museums. 62-2636 9.75
1. Paintings—Rumania. I. Oprescu, George, 1881-

Paintings, Russian—Exhibitions.

NEW York. Gallery of Modern 759.7
Art Including the Huntington Hartford Collection.
A survey of Russian painting, fifteenth century to the present. [New York, 1967] 72 p. illus. (part col.) 24 cm. Catalog of an exhibition held June 14-Sept. 17, 1967. Bibliography: p. 72. [ND684.N4] 67-8112
1. Paintings, Russian—Exhibitions. 2. Art, Russian—Exhibitions. I. Title.

Paintings—Sacramento, Calif.—Conservation and restoration.

MUSKAVITCH, Charles. 751.6
The E. B. Crocker art collection; a study on its physical condition with recommendations for its future care. Davis, Calif., Laboratory for Research in the Fine Arts & Museology, University of California, 1965. 1 v. (various pagings) illus. 28 cm. [ND1643.C7M8] 67-64784
1. Paintings—Sacramento, Calif.—Conservation and restoration. I. Crocker Art Gallery, Sacramento, Calif. II. Title.

Paintings—Santa Barbara, Calif.

ARCHIVERO I; 759'.074'019491
research papers on works of art in the collection of the Santa Barbara Museum of Art, by Roger C. Burns [and others] Santa Barbara, Calif. [Santa Barbara Museum of Art] 1973. 189 p. illus. (part col.) 27 cm. Includes bibliographies. [N742.S15A95] 73-88840
1. Santa Barbara, Calif. Museum of Art. 2. Paintings—Santa Barbara, Calif. 3. Paintings—Expertising. I. Burns, Rogert C. II. Santa Barbara, Calif. Museum of Art.

Paintings—Santa Barbara, Calif.—Catalogs.

BAER, Kurt. 709.794
Painting and sculpture at Mission Santa Barbara. Washington, Academy of American Franciscan History, 1955. xx, 244p. 152 illus. 25cm. (Publications of the Academy of American Franciscan History. Monograph series, v.3) Catalogue: p. 59-[211] Bibliography: p. 235-238. [N7911.S3B3] 55-13610
1. Paintings—Santa Barbara, Calif.—Catalogs. 2. Sculpture—Santa Barbara, Calif.—Catalogs. 3. Art, Spanish—American. 4. Christian art and symbolism. 5. Church decoration and ornament—California—Santa Barbara. I. Santa Barbara Mission. II. Title. III. Series: Academy of American Franciscan History. Monograph series, v.3

Paintings, Scottish—Exhibitions.

ABERDEEN 759.9412'1'0740941235
Art Gallery, Aberdeen, Scot.
Artist and patron in the North East, 1700-1860 : [catalogue of] a loan exhibition supported by the Scottish Arts Council, Aberdeen Art Gallery, 10-31 May 1975. [Aberdeen] : The Gallery, [1975] 32 p. : ill., ports. ; 30 cm. Includes indexes. [ND495.G75A23 1975] 76-352403 ISBN 0-900017-08-2 : £0.50
1. Paintings, Scottish—Exhibitions. 2. Paintings, Modern—17th-18th centuries—Grampian region, Scot.—Exhibitions. 3. Paintings, Modern—19th century—Grampian region, Scot.—Exhibitions. 4. Art patrons—Grampian region, Scot.—Portraits—Exhibitions. I. Scottish Arts Council. II. Title.

OTTAWA. National Gallery 759'.941
of Canada.
Three centuries of Scottish painting. Trois siecles de peinture ecossaise. An exhibition arranged by the National Gallery of Canada. Ottawa, 1968. 68 p. illus. (part col.) 26 cm. Label mounted on t.p.: Supplied by Worldwide Books, New York. [ND475.O8] 68-30465 unpriced
1. Paintings, Scottish—Exhibitions. I. Title. II. Title: Trois siecles de peinture ecossaise.

Paintings, Serbian.

BIHALJI-MERIN, Oto, 759.9497
1904-
Byzantine frescoes and icons in Yugoslavia. Photos. by Toso Dabac, Dusan Stanimirovic, and others. With notes on the plates by Svetislav Mandic. New York, H. N. Abrams [1960, c1958] 15 p. 81 plates (part col.) map. 29 cm. Translation of Fresken und Ikonen. [ND943.B513] 60-9705
1. Paintings, Serbian. 2. Paintings, Macedonian. 3. Paintings, Byzantine. 4. Mural painting and decoration—Yugoslavia. 5. Icons. I. Dabac, Toso. II. Title.

Paintings — Sharon, Mass. — Catalogs.

KENDALL Whaling Museum, 708.1447
Sharon, Mass.
Paintings, [a catalog] by M. V. & Dorothy Brewington. Sharon, Mass., 1965. xiii, 137 p. (chiefly illus. (part col.)) 29 cm. Includes bibliographical references. [N748.A53] 65-28071
1. Paintings — Sharon, Mass. — Catalogs. 2. Marine painting. Whaling. I. Brewington, Marion Vernon, 1902- II. Brewington, Dorothy. III. Title.

Paintings, Sienese.

GIOTTO and his 759.5
contemporaries. Translated by Susan Bellamy. New York, Crown Publishers, 1958. 98p. (chiefly col. plates) 30cm. Bibliography: p. 98. [ND623.G6C273] [ND623.G6C273] 927.5 58-12886 58-12886
1. Giotto di Bondone. 1266?-1337. 2. Paintings, Sienese. 3. Paintings, Florentine. I. Carli, Enzo, 1910-

SIENESE painting. 759.5
Greenwich, Conn., New York Graphic Society [c1956] 77p. illus., plates (part col.) 36cm. [The Great masters of the past, 7] [ND621.S6C32] [ND621 S6C32] 927.5 57-13102 57-13102
1. Paintings, Sienese. 2. Painters, Italian — Siens. I. Carli, Enzo, 1910- II. Series.

Paintings—Slides.

BELZ, Carl. 759.4
Paul Cezanne. New York, McGraw-Hill [1974, i.e.1975] p. cm. (Color slide program of the great masters) [ND553.C33B38] 74-16088 ISBN 0-07-004417-1 10.95
1. Cezanne, Paul, 1839-1906. 2. Paintings—Slides. I. Title. II. Series.

Paintings, Spanish.

ABRAMS (Harry N.) inc. 759.6
Spanish painting (from El Greco to Goya). Text by the editorial staff. New York, [1971] 24 p. illus. (part col.) 33 cm. (The Library of great painters. Portfolio ed.) [ND804.A597 1971] 75-124300 ISBN 0-8109-3059-5
1. Paintings, Spanish. 2. Painting, Modern—Spain. I. Title.

BICCHI, Ugo 759.6
Spanish painting. New York, Golden [1963] [56]p. col. illus. 38cm. (Art of the Western world) 63-25679 5.00
1. Paintings, Spanish. I. Title. II. Series.

EL Greco and the Spanish 759'.6
golden age. Text and notes by Erik Larsen. New York, Tudor Pub. Co. [1969] 40 p. 91 col. plates. 18 cm. Bibliography: p. 18. [ND804.E4] 68-30736 2.95
1. Paintings, Spanish. 2. Painters—Spain. I. Larsen, Erik. II. Theotocopuli, Dominico, called El Greco, d. 1614.

EVANS, Grose 759.6
Spanish painting in the National Gallery of Art. Washington, D.C., National Gallery of Art [c.1960] 43p. col. illus. 19cm. (U.S. National Gallery of Art. Booklet no. 10) 60-62154 .25 pap.,
1. Paintings, Spanish. I. Title.

GOMEZ-MORENO, Carmen 759.6
Spanish painting: the golden century. New York, McGraw [c.1965] 48p. illus., 24 col. slides (in pockets) 25cm. (Color slide program of the world's art) [ND806.G6] 64-21909 8.95 bds.,
1. Paintings. Spanish. 2. Painting, Spanish. 3. Lantern Slides. I. Title. II. Series.

GOMEZ-MORENO, Carmen. 759.6
Spanish painting: the golden century. New York, McGraw-Hill [1965] 48 p. illus., 24 col. slides (in pockets) 25 cm. (Color slide program of the world's art) [ND806.G6] 64-21909
1. Paintings, Spanish. 2. Painting, Spanish. 3. Lantern slides. I. Title. II. Series.

Paintings, Spanish—Catalogs.

BUDAPEST. 759.6'074'0391
Szepmuveszeti Muzeum.
Spanish masters, by Marianne Haraszti-Takacs. [Translated by Eva Racz. 2d rev. ed.] New York, Taplinger Pub. Co. [1971? c1966] 29 p., 48 col. plates. 24 cm. Translation of Spanyol mesterek. Catalog of works selected from the Spanish collection in the Budapest Museum of Fine Arts. Bibliography: p. 27. [ND805.B8313 1971] 70-137414 ISBN 0-8008-7360-2
1. Paintings, Spanish—Catalogs. 2. Paintings—Budapest—Catalogs. I. Haraszti, Marianna (Takacs) II. Title.

Paintings, Spanish — Exhibitions.

ART Association of 759.6
Indianapolis, Indiana. John Herron Art Institute.
El Greco to Goya; a loan exhibition of Spanish painting of the seventeenth and eighteenth centuries, under the high patronage of His Excellency Senor Don Antonio Garrigues. John Herron Museum of Art, Indianapolis, Indiana, Feb. 10 through Mar. 24, 1963. Musuem of Art, Rhode Island School of Design, Providence, Rhode Island, April 19 through May 26, 1963. [Indianapolis 1963] 1 v. (unpaged) 88 plates, 26 cm. Includes bibliographies. [ND806.A7] 63-2196
1. Paintings, Spanish — Exhibitions. I. Rhode Island School of Design, Providence. Museum. II. Title.

LONDON. Royal 759.6'074'02132
Academy of Arts.
The golden age of Spanish painting : [catalogue of an exhibition held at the Royal Academy], 10 January-14 March [1976]. [London] : The Academy, 1976. 116 p. : ill. (some col.), ports. (chiefly col.) ; 30 cm. LC copy imperfect : p. 49-64 repeated. Text of the catalogue by A. E. Perez Sanchez and X. de Salas. Includes indexes. Bibliography: p. 19-23. [ND805.L66 1976] 76-362174 ISBN 0-900946-26-1 : £1.70
1. Paintings, Spanish—Exhibitions. 2. Paintings, Renaissance—Spain—Exhibitions. 3. Paintings, Modern—17th-18th centuries—Spain—Exhibitions. I. Perez Sanchez, Alfonso E. II. Salas, Xavier de. III. Title.

NEW York (City) Museum of 759.6
Modern Art.
New Spanish painting and sculpture: Rafael Canogar [and others] [by] Frank O'Hara. [Exhibition] Garden City, N. Y., Distributed by Doubleday [1960] 59 p. illus. 26 cm. Includes bibliography. [N7108.N45] 60-15021
1. Paintings, Spanish—Exhibitions. 2. Sculpture, Spanish—Exhibitions. I. O'Hara, Frank. II. Title.

SIMPSON, Shirley 759.6'074'0153
S.
Contemporary Spanish painters : Miro and after, a selection / organized and circulated by International Exhibitions Foundation, Washington, D.C., 1975-1976 ; introd. by James Johnson Sweeney. Washington : International Exhibitions Foundation, c1975. 55 p. : ill. ; 23 cm. "Participating museums: the New York Cultural Center, New York, New York, North Carolina Museum of Art, Raleigh, North Carolina, Meadows Museum and Sculpture Court, Dallas, Texas, Edwin A. Ulrich Museum of Art, Wichita, Kansas." [ND808.S48] 75-14854
1. Paintings, Spanish—Exhibitions. 2. Paintings, Modern—20th century—Spain—

Exhibitions. I. International Exhibitions Foundation. II. Title. **BIP**

Paintings, Tuscan.

OTTINO DELLA CHIESA, Angela 759.5
Botticelli and his contemporaries. New York, Crown Publishers [1960] 98 p. mounted col. illus. 30 cm. Bibliography: p. 98. [ND619.T9O8 1960] 60-50284
1. Paintings, Tuscan. 2. Painters, Italian—Tuscany. I. Title.

Paintings, Tuscan—Catalogs.

BOSKOVITS, Miklos. 759.5
Tuscan paintings of the early Renaissance. [Translated by Eva Racz] New York, Taplinger Pub. Co. [1970, c1968] 25 p., 48 col. plates. 24 cm. Paintings from the Budapest Museum of Fine Arts and Esztergom Christian Museum. Translation of Toszkan kora reneszansz tablakepek. Bibliography: p. 19-22. [ND619.T9B613] 71-87081
1. Paintings, Tuscan—Catalogs. 2. Painting, Renaissance—Tuscany. I. Budapest. Szepmuveszeti Muzeum. II. Esztergom, Hungary. Kereszteny Muzeum. III. Title.

Paintings—U.S.

MORSE, John D., 1906- 759.0838
Old masters in America; a comprehensive guide; more than two-thousand paintings in United States and Canada by forty famous artists. Chicago, Rand McNally [1955] 192 p. illus. 20 cm. [ND1242.M6] 55-9332
1. Paintings—U.S. 2. Paintings—Canada. 3. Painters. I. Title. **BIP**

Paintings—Vatican City.

THE Great 759.94'074'05634
masterpieces of the Vatican galleries / [compiled by] Mario Fellucci. Albuquerque, N.M. : American Classical College Press, [1975] p. cm. Includes index. Bibliography: p. [N2940.G73] 75-9969 ISBN 0-913314-54-4 : 25.00
1. Paintings—Vatican City. I. Fellucci, Mario.

Paintings, Venetian.

GIOSEFFI, Decio 759.5
Canaletto and his contemporaries. New York, Crown Publishers [1960] 98p. bBibl.: 60-50285 .98. mounted col. illus. 30cm. 7.95 bds.,
1. Paintings, Venetian. 2. Painters, Italian—Venice I. Title.

Paintings, Venetian—Catalogs.

BUDAPEST. 759.5'31
Szepmuveszeti Muzeum.
Eighteenth century Venetian paintings, by Klara Garas. New York, Taplinger Pub. Co. [1968] 29 p., 48 col. plates. 24 cm. Translation of A velencei settecento festeszete. Bibliography: p. 27. [ND621.V5B783 1968b] 68-9166 6.95
1. Paintings, Venetian—Catalogs. 2. Paintings—Budapest—Catalogs. I. Garas, Klara. II. Title.

NEW York (City). 759.5'31
Metropolitan Museum of Art.
Italian paintings: Venetian school; a catalogue of the collection of the Metropolitan Museum of Art [by] Federico Zeri, with the assistance of Elizabeth E. Gardner. [New York]; Distributed by New York Graphic Society, Greenwich, Conn., 1973. 114 p. 107 plates. 25 cm. Includes bibliographical references. [ND621.V5N49 1973] 73-9831 ISBN 0-87099-079-9 16.00
1. Paintings, Venetian—Catalogs. 2. Paintings—New York (City)—Catalogs. I.

Zeri, Federico. II. Gardner, Elizabeth E. III. Title.
Pbk 4.95; ISBN 0-87099-080-2.

Paintings, Venetian—Exhibitions.

THE Circle of Canaletto: 759.5
a special exhibition, sponsored by GAC Corporation and its Allentown units, GAC Finance Inc. and Stuyvesant Insurance Group, February 21-March 21, 1971, Allentown Art Museum. [Allentown? Pa., 1971] [52] p. illus. 15 x 26 cm. [ND621.V5C54] 72-198130
1. Canal, Antonio, called Canaletto, 1697-1768. 2. Paintings, Venetian—Exhibitions. 3. Venice in art. I. Allentown, Pa. Art Museum.

Paintings, Victorian—History.

BELL, Quentin. 759.2
Victorian artists. Cambridge, Mass., Harvard University Press, 1967. xiv, 111 p. 123 illus. 25 cm. Bibliography: p. 96-103. [ND467] 68-3531
1. Paintings, Victorian—History. 2. Painters—England. I. Title.

Paintings — Vienna

OBERHAMMER, 759.94'074'03613
Vinzenz.
Great paintings from the Kunsthistorisches Museum, Vienna. [The notes on the plates were written with the assistance of Gustav and Vita Maria Kunstler. Translated by Richard Waterhouse] New York, H. N. Abrams [1963] 211 p. mounted illus. (100 col.) 24 cm. Translation of Die Gemaldegalerie des Kunsthistorisches Museums in Wien. [N1680.O213] 63-19568
1. Paintings — Vienna 2. Vienna. Kunsthistorisches Museum. Gemalde-Galerie. I. Title.

Paintings—Washington, D.C.

U.S. National Gallery of 750.74
Art
A pageant of painting from the National Gallery of Art. Ed. by Huntington Cairns, John Walker [2v.] New York, Macmillan [c. 1966] 2v. (xviii, 518p.) col. plates. 37cm. [N856.A676] 66-11576 35.00 set,
1. Paintings—Washington, D.C. I. Cairns, Huntington, 1904- ed. II. Walker, John, Dec. 24, 1906- ed. III. Title.

U.S. National Gallery of 758.9
Art.
Treasures from the National Gallery of Art. Edited by Huntington Cairns and John Walker. New York, Macmillan, 1962. 183 p. col. illus. 39 cm. The reproductions of paintings are "accompanied by comments drawn from a variety of sources." [N856.A693] 62-7270
1. Paintings—Washington, D. C. I. Cairns, Huntington, 1904- ed. II. Walker, John, Dec. 24, 1906- ed. III. Title.

WALKER, John, 750.74
Dec.24,1906-
National Gallery of Art, Washington, D.C. New York, H. N. Abrams [1963] 347 p. illus., col. plates, diagrs. 21 cm. [N856.W33] 63-15446
1. United States. National Gallery of Art. 2. Paintings—Washington, D.C.

WALKER, John, 708'.153
Dec.24,1906-
National Gallery of Art, Washington, D.C. New York, H. N. Abrams [1975] p. cm. [N856.W33 1975] 74-10716 ISBN 0-8109-0336-9 25.00
1. United States. National Gallery of Art. 2. Paintings—Washington, D.C. I. Title.

Paintings — Washington, D.C. — Catalogs.

COOKE, Hereward 750'.74'0153
Lester.
Pictures within pictures in the National Gallery of Art. Book design by Sylvan Jacobson. [1st ed.] Richmond, Westover Pub. Co. [1970] [63] p. illus. 23 cm. [ND1471.C66] 73-133459
1. Paintings—Washington, D.C.—Catalogs.

2. Composition (Art) 3. Painting—Technique. I. U.S. National Gallery of Art. II. Title.

CORCORAN Gallery of Art, 759.13
Washington, D.C.
A catalogue of the collection of American paintings in the Corcoran Gallery of Art. Washington, D.C., Author [c.1966] 160p. illus. 27cm. Contents.v. 1. Painters born before 1850. [N850.A612] 66-4178 5.00 pap.,
1. Paintings—Washington, D.C.—Catalogs. 2. Paintings, American—Catalogs. I. Title.

UNITED States. 759.4'074'0153
National Gallery of Art.
European paintings : an illustrated summary catalogue. Washington, 1975. 417 p. illus. 24 cm. [N856.A6917] 74-16421
1. United States. National Gallery of Art. 2. Paintings—Washington, D.C.—Catalogs. I. Title.

U.S. National Gallery of 708.153
Art.
Paintings and sculpture from the Kress collection. [Washington] v, illus. 24 cm. [N856.A677] 56-2539
1. Paintings — Washington, D.C. — Catalogs. 2. Sculpture — Washington, D.C. — Catalogs. II. Title. III. Title: Title varies slightly.

Paintings—Williamstown, Mass.— Catalogs.

STERLING and 750'.74'01441
Francine Clark Art Institute, Williamstown, Mass.
List of paintings in the Sterling and Francine Clark Art Institute. [Williamstown, c1972] 144 p. illus. 25 cm. "A chronological list of the publications of the Sterling and Francine Clark Art Institute": p. 142-144. [N867.A6] 72-90682
1. Sterling and Francine Clark Art Institute, Williamstown, Mass. 2. Paintings—Williamstown, Mass.—Catalogs. I. Title.

Pairpoint Glass Works.

AVILA, George C. 748.2'9144'85
The Pairpoint glass story, by George C. Avila. [1st ed.] New Bedford, Mass. [Reynolds-De Walt Print.] 1968. xiv, 238p. illus. (pt. col.) facsims. 25cm. [NK5198.P3A9] 68-4866 15.00
1. Pairpoint Glass Works. I. Title.
Publisher's address: Industrial Park New Bedford, Mass. 02745

PADGETT, Leonard E. 748.2'91'4485
Pairpoint glass, by Leonard E. Padgett. Photography by Harry L. Cleveland. Edited by Marion A. James. [Washington] Printed by South Capitol Press [1968] 23 p. illus., facsims. 26 cm. [NK5112.P3] 68-3121
1. Pairpoint Glass Works. I. Title. **BIP**

Palaces.

BECK, Barbara L. 728.8
The first book of palaces. Pictures by Page Cary. New York, F. Watts [1964] 66 p. illus., plans. 23 cm. A survey of the homes of thirty kings, emperors, shahs, shoguns, pharoahs and other royalty during the history of civilization. Includes the palaces at Persepolis in Iran, the Alhambra in Spain, the Winter Palace in Russia, the Old Seraglio in Turkey, and the Angkor Thom in Cambodia. [NA7710.B4] AC 68
1. Palaces. I. Cary, Page, 1904- illus. II. Title.

Palaces—Crete.

GRAHAM, James Walter, 722.61
1906-
The palaces of Crete. Princeton, N.J., Princeton University Press, 1962. xii, 269 p. illus., maps, plans. 25 cm. Bibliography: p. 249-253. [NA279.C7G7] 62-7039
1. Palaces—Crete. 2. Architecture, Domestic—Crete. I. Title. **BIP**

GRAHAM, James 728.8'2'093918
Walter, 1906-
The palaces of Crete. Princeton, N.J.,

Princeton University Press [1969, c1962] xiv, 269 p. illus. 24 cm. (Princeton paperbacks) Bibliography: p. 249-251. [NA279.C7G7 1969] 77-8003 4.95
1. Palaces—Crete. 2. Architecture, Domestic—Crete. I. Title.

Palaces—England.

COLVIN, Howard Montagu. 728.8
Royal buildings [by] Howard Colvin. Feltham, Country Life Books, 1968. [1], 64 p. illus., plans. 23 cm. (RIBA drawings series) Bibliography: p. 64. [NA7745.C67] 76-391708 10/6
1. Palaces—England. 2. Castles—England. I. Title.

Palaces—Europe.

GREAT palaces of Europe. 725.17
Introd. by Sacheverell Sitwell. New York, Putnam [1964] 288 p. illus., plans, col. plates, ports. 33 cm. [NA7710.G7] 64-14747
1. Palaces—Europe. I. Sitwell, Sacheverell, Sir, bart., 1897-

SITWELL, Sacheverell, 728.8094
Sir, bart., 1897- ed.
Great houses of Europe. Photos. by Edwin Smith. New York, Putnam [1961] 318 p. illus. (part col.) 33 cm. [NA7710.S5] 61-9708
1. Palaces—Europe. 2. Architecture, Domestic—Europe. I. Smith, Edwin, 1912- photographer. II. Title.

SITWELL, Sacheverell, 728.8'2'094
Sir, bart., 1897-
Great houses of Europe, edited by Sacheverell Sitwell; photographs by Edwin Smith. London, New York, Spring Books, 1970. 320 p. illus. (some col.), facsims., plans, ports. 32 cm. [NA7710.S5 1970] 72-884895 ISBN 0-600-33843-6 £2.95
1. Palaces—Europe. 2. Architecture, Domestic—Europe. I. Smith, Edwin, 1912- II. Title.

Palaces—Italy.

HERSEY, George L. 728.8'2'0945
Pythagorean palaces : magic and architecture in the Italian Renaissance / G. L. Hersey. Ithaca : Cornell University Press, 1976. 216 p. : ill. ; 26 cm. Includes index. Bibliography: p. 199-212. [NA7755.H47] 76-13661 ISBN 0-8014-0998-5 : 22.50
1. Palaces—Italy. 2. Architecture, Renaissance—Italy. 3. Architecture—Composition, proportion, etc. 4. Pythagoras and Pythagorean school. I. Title. **BIP**

Palaces—Juvenile literature.

BECK, Barbara L. 725
The first book of palaces. Pictures by Page Cary. New York, Watts [1964] 66p. illus. (pt. col.) plans. 23cm. 64-12122 2.50
1. Palaces—Juvenile literature. I. Title.

Palatine, Ill. Clayson House.

HASBROUCK, Wilbert R. 728.3'7'028
Clayson house / [The office of Wilbert R. Hasbrouck, Historic Resources]. [Palatine, Ill.] : Palatine Historical Society, c1977. 36 p., [2] leaves of plates : ill. ; 28 cm. [NA7238.P23H37] 77-150934
1. Palatine, Ill. Clayson House. 2. Architecture, Domestic—Illinois—Palatine—Conservation and restoration. I. Historic Resources (Firm) II. Title.

Paleography. English.

BISHOP, Terence Alan 745.6'197
Martyn.
English Caroline minuscule, by T. A. M. Bishop. Oxford, Clarendon Press, 1971. xxx, 26 p., 24 plates. 28 facsims. 28 cm. (Oxford palaeographical handbooks) Bibliography: p. xxvii-xxviii. [Z115.E5B57] 72-179780 ISBN 0-19-818224-4 £3.50
1. Paleography, English. 2. Writing, Minuscule. I. Title. II. Series.

HECTOR, Leonard Charles. 421.7
The handwriting of English documents, by L. C. Hector. 2nd ed. London, Edward Arnold, 1966. 136 p. facsims., diagrs. 25 1/2 cm. (B66-15510) Bibliography: p. 132-133. [Z115.E5H4] 66-74454
1. Paleography. English. 2. Diplomatics. I. Title.

JENKINSON, Hilary, Sir. 745.6'1
The later court hands in England from the fifteenth to the seventeenth century, illustrated from the Common paper of the Scriveners' Company of London, the English writing masters, and the public records. New York, Ungar [1969] vii, 199 p. illus. and portfolio ([6] l., 44 plates) 39 cm. Reprint of the 1927 ed. Companion volume to English court hand A.D. 1066 to 1500, by C. Johnson and H. Jenkinson. Includes bibliographies. [Z115.E5J57 1969] 68-8117 75.00
1. Manuscripts—Facsimiles. 2. Paleography, English. I. Title. BIP

JOHNSON, Charles, 1870- 421'.7
English court hand A.D. 1066 to 1500, illustrated chiefly from the public records [by] Charles Johnson [and] Hilary Jenkinson. New York, F. Ungar Pub. Co. [1967] 2 v. illus., 45 plates. 24-51 cm. "Reprinted from the edition of 1915." Contents.Contents.—pt. 1. Text.—pt. 2. Plates. Bibliography: v. 1, p. [xl]-xliv. [Z115.E5J6 1967] 66-28836
1. Paleography, English. 2. Manuscripts—Facsimiles. I. Jenkinson, Hilary, Sir. II. Title. III. Title: Court hand.

KER, Neil Ripley. 421.7
English manuscripts in the century after the Norman Conquest. Oxford, Clarendon Press, 1960. viv, 67p., 29 plates. 38cm. (The Lyell lectures, 1952-3) Bibliographical footnotes. [Z115.E5K4] 60-2856
1. Paleography, English. I. Title. II. Series.

PARKES, Malcolm Beckwith. 745.6'1
English cursive book hands, 1250-1500, by M. B. Parkes. Oxford, Clarendon P., 1969. xxxii, 24 p., 24 plates. facsims. 28 cm. (Oxford palaeographical handbooks) Bibliography: p. xxvii. [Z115.E5P37] 74-452401 50/-
1. Paleography, English. I. Title. II. Series.

PETTI, Anthony G. 745.6'1
English literary hands from Chaucer to Dryden / Anthony G. Petti. Cambridge, Mass. : Harvard University Press, 1977. ix, 133 p. : facsims. ; 29 cm. Includes index. Bibliography: p. 126-128. [Z115.E5P47] 77-74782 ISBN 0-674-25666-2 : 22.50
1. Paleography, English. 2. Writing—England—History. 3. English literature—Early modern, 1500-1700—Manuscripts—Facsimiles. 4. English literature—Middle English, 1100-1500—Manuscripts—Facsimiles. I. Title. BIP

TANNENBAUM, Samuel Aaron, 421'.7 1874?-1948
The handwriting of the Renaissance, being the development and 0 New York, Ungar [1967, c.1930] xii, 210p. illus., 15 facsims. 23cm. Bibl. [Z113.T17 1967] 67-17875 6.00
1. Paleography, English I. shley H. Thorndike. II. Title.

Paleography, German.

PETZET, Erich, 1870-1928. 745.6'1
Deutsche Schrifttafeln de IX. bis XVI. Jahrhunderts aus Handschriften der Bayerischen Staatsbibliothek Munchen / [hrsg. von] Erich Petzet [und] Otto Glauning Hildesheim ; New York : G. Olms, 1975. 5 v. in 1 : facsims ; 29 cm. Reprint of the 1910-1930 editions published by C. Kuhn, Munich and K. W. Hiersemann, Leipzig. Includes bibliographical references. [Z115.G4P47 1975] 75-513156 ISBN 3-487-05685-2
1. Paleography, German. 2. Manuscripts, German—Facsimiles. I. Glauning, Otto, 1876-1941, joint author. II. Title: Deutsche Schrifttafeln des IX. bis XVI. Jahrhunderts...

Paleography, Greek.

THOMPSON, Sir Edward 481.7 Maunde, 1840-1929.
A handbook of Greek and Latin palaeography Chicago, Argonaut, 1966. 343 p. 3 fold. illus., facsims. 22 cm. (Argonaut library of antiquities) Reprint of a work first published in 1893. Includes bibliographies. [Z114.T473] 66-19175
1. Paleography, Greek. 2. Paleography, Latin. I. Title.

THOMPSON, Edward Maunde, 481.7 Sir, 1840-1929.
A handbook of Greek and Latin palaeography. Chicago, Argonaut, 1966. 343 p. 3 fold. illus., facsims. 22 cm. (Argonaut library of antiquities) Reprint of a work first published in 1893. Includes bibliographies. [Z114.T473] 66-19175
1. Paleography, Greek. 2. Paleography, Latin. I. Title. BIP

TURNER, Eric Gardiner. 091'.0938
Greek manuscripts of the ancient world, by E. G. Turner. Princeton, N.J., Princeton University Press, 1971. xi, 132 p. illus. 30 cm. An illustrative supplement to the author's Greek papyri: an introduction. Includes bibliographical references. [Z113.8.T86 1971b] 79-148945 ISBN 0-691-03541-5 12.50
1. Paleography, Greek. 2. Manuscripts, Greek—Facsimiles. I. Title.

Paleography—Handbooks, treatises, etc.

COPE, Emma Elizabeth 417'.7 (Thoyts) 1860-
How to read old documents, by E. E. Thoyts. With an introd. by C. Trice Martin. Christchurch [Eng.] Dolphin Press [1972, i.e. 1973] xii, 143 p. illus. 23 cm. Imprint covered by label: Distributed in the U.S.A. by Humanities Press, New York. Half title: How to decipher and study old documents. First ed. published in 1893 under title: The key to the family deed chest. [Z113.C75 1972] 73-162795 ISBN 0-85642-007-7 5.75
1. Paleography—Handbooks, treatises, etc. 2. Diplomatics. I. Title. II. Title: How to decipher and study old documents. BIP

Paleography, Italian.

DE LA MARE, Albinia 652.1'092'2 Catherine.
The handwriting of Italian humanists, by A. C. de la Mare. Oxford, Printed at the University Press for the Association internationale de bibliophilie, 1973- v. in plates. 28 cm. [Z115.I8D44] 73-177629
1. Paleography, Italian. 2. Writing, Humanistic. 3. Humanists—Italy. I. Association internationale de bibliophilie. II. Title.

Paleography, Latin.

CODICES latini 471.7
antiquiores; a palaeographical guide to Latin manuscripts prior to the ninth century, ed. by E. A. Lowe. Oxford, Clarendon Pr., 1966. v. facsims. 45cm. Ed. under the auspices of the Union academique internationale for the Amer. council of learned socs. and the Carnegie Inst. of Washington. A succinct description . . . of all known Latin literary manuscripts on papyrus, parchment, or vellum which may be regarded as older than the ninth century, accompanied by a specimen, unreduced, of the script, and supplemented by a selected bibliography. Contents.--pt.9. Hungary, Luxembourg, Poland, Russia, Spain, Sweden, U.S., and Yugoslavia [Z114.C677] 34-23797 26.00
1. Paleography, Latin. 2. Manuscripts, Latin—Facsimiles. 3. Manuscripts, Latin—Catalogs. 4. Abbreviation, Latin. I. Lowe, Elias Avery, 1879- ed. II. International union of academies. III. American council of learned societies devoted to humanistic studies. IV. Carnegie institution of Washington.
Available from Oxford Univ. R. in New York.

HAYES, James. 471.7
The roman letter; a study of notable graven and written forms from twenty centuries in which our Latin alphabet moved toward its high destiny as the basic medium of printed communication throughout the Western World. Prepared on the occasion of an exhibition dealing with this subject, held by R. R. Donnelley & Sons Company in its Lakeside Press Galleries, Chicago, Illinois, 1951-52. [Chicago, 1951] 54 p. illus. 26 cm. [Z114.H3] 52-2698
1. Paleography, Latin. I. Title.

THOMPSON, Edward Maunde, 481'.7 Sir, 1840-1929.
An introduction to Greek and Latin palaeography. New York, B. Franklin [1965] xvi, 600 p. facsims. 26 cm. (Burt Franklin bibliography and reference series, #71) Reprint of the 1912 ed. Bibliography: p. [571]-583. [Z114.T472 1965] 74-6461
1. Paleography, Latin. 2. Paleography, Greek. I. Title.

THOMSON, Samuel Harrison, 471'.7 1895-
Latin bookhands of the later Middle ages, 1100-1500 [by] S. Harrison Thomson. London, Cambridge U.P., 1969. xiv, [171] p. facsims. 36 cm. [Z114.T53] 69-12930 ISBN 5-210-66247- 15/-/- ($37.50)
1. Paleography, Latin. 2. Manuscripts, Latin—Facsimiles. I. Title.

Paleontology—Pictorial works.

CELEBONOVIC, Stevan. 779.3
The living rocks. Pref. by Andre Maurois; with a commentary by Geoffrey Grigson and photos. and magnifications by Stevan Celebonovic. Translations by Joyce Emerson and Stanley A. Pocock. New York, Philosophical Library [1957] 94 p. 64 plates. 29 cm. (Art and nature) [QE714.C4] 57-3123
1. Paleontology—Pictorial works. 2. Mineralogy—Pictorial works. I. Grigson, Geoffrey, 1905- II. Title.

Palermo. Cattedrale.

BELLAFIORE, 726'.6'0945823 Giuseppe.
The Cathedral of Palermo / Giuseppe Bellafiore. Palermo : S. F. Flaccovio, c1976. 418 p. : ill. (some col.) ; 33 cm. Includes indexes. Bibliography: p. 345-350. [NA5621.P3P44] 77-482111 L50000
1. Palermo. Cattedrale. I. Title.

Palestine—Description and travel—Views.

CONVERSE, Gordon N. 779'.9'2209
Come see the place : the Holy Land Jesus knew / photos. by Gordon N. Converse ; text by Robert J. Bull and B. Cobbey Crisler. Englewood Cliffs, N.J. : Prentice-Hall, c1978. [DS108.5.C65] 78-7054 ISBN 0-13-152538-7 : 12.95
1. Jesus Christ—Biography. 2. Palestine—Description and travel—Views. 3. Christian biography—Palestine. I. Bull, Robert J. II. Crisler, B. Cobbey, 1933- III. Title. BIP

Palestine—History.

AVI-YONAH, Michael, 709'.5694 1904-
The Holy Land. Special photography by Mario Carrieri. [1st ed.] New York, Holt, Rinehart and Winston [1973, c1972] 288 p. illus. 26 cm. (World cultural guides) [DS111.A88 1973] 72-83345 ISBN 0-03-003466-3 9.95
1. Palestine—History. 2. Palestine—Antiquities. 3. Art—Israel. I. Title. BIP

Palette knife painting.

GRUERIO, Anthony. 751.4
Painting with a palette knife [by] Anthony Gruerio. Text by Margaret Mettert. New York, Pitman Pub. Corp. [1974] 32 p. illus. (part col.) 20 x 27 cm. (The Pitman art series, 81) [ND1539.G78] 72-97546
1. Palette knife painting. I. Mettert, Margaret. II. Title. BIP

WAUGH, Coulton, 1896- 751.4
How to paint with a knife. New York, Watson-Guptill Publications [1971] 239 p. illus. (part col.) 29 cm. [ND1539.W3] 70-145666 ISBN 0-8230-3880-7 12.95
1. Palette knife painting. I. Title. BIP

Paley, Jeffrey—Art collections.

NEW York 759.954'074'01471 (City). Metropolitan Museum of Art. Dept. of Far Eastern Art.
Indian miniatures from the Jeffrey Paley Collection : August 6-September 30, 1974 / by Martin Lerner. New York : Dept. of Far Eastern Art, Metropolitan Museum of Art, [1974] [27] p. : ill. ; 23 cm. Catalog of an exhibition. Bibliography: p. [26]-[27] [ND1337.I5N48 1974] 74-194437
1. Paley, Jeffrey—Art collections. 2. Miniature painting, Indic—Exhibitions. I. Lerner, Martin. II. Title.

Palladio, Andrea, 1508-1580.

ACKERMAN, James S. 720.924
Palladio, by James S. Ackerman. Harmondsworth, Penguin, 1966. 195 p. illus., maps, plans. 20 cm. (The architect and society) Pelican books. "Bibliographical notes:" p. 187-191. [NA1123.P2A65] 66-69830
1. Palladio, Andrea, 1508-1580. BIP

ACKERMAN, James S. 728.8'4'0924
Palladio's villas, by James S. Ackerman. Locust Valley, N.Y., Published for the Institute of Fine Arts, New York University [by] J. J. Augustin [1967] xi, 79 p. illus., maps. plans. 24 cm. (Walter W. S. Cook alumni lecture) Bibliography: p. 31-33. [NA1123.P2A66] 67-5752
1. Palladio, Andrea, 1508-1580. I. Title. II. Series.

GUINNESS, Desmond. 724'.1
Palladio : a western progress / Desmond Guinness and Julius Trousdale Sadler, Jr. New York : Viking Press, 1976. 183 p. : ill. (some col.) ; 29 cm. (A Studio book) Includes index. Bibliography: p. 179-180. [NA1123.P2G78 1976] 75-38760 ISBN 0-670-53732-2 : 14.95
1. Palladio, Andrea, 1508-1580. 2. Neoclassicism (Architecture)—Italy. 3. Neoclassicism (Architecture)—England. 4. Neoclassicism (Architecture)—Ireland. 5. Neoclassicism (Architecture)—United States. 6. Neoclassicism (Architecture)—West Indies. I. Sadler, Julius Trousdale, joint author. II. Title.

PUPPI, Lionello. 720'.92'4
Andrea Palladio / Lionello Puppi ; [translated by Pearl Sanders]. Boston : New York Graphic Society, 1975, c1973. 465 p. : ill. ; 29 cm. [NA1123.P2P8213 1975b] 74-21496 ISBN 0-316-03970-5 : 47.50
1. Palladio, Andrea, 1508-1580. BIP

SEMENZATO, Camillo. 728.8'4'0924
The Rotonda of Andrea Palladio. Translated by Ann Percy. University Park, Pennsylvania State University Press [1968] 58 p. illus., plates (part col.) 35 cm. (Corpus Palladianum, v. 1) Bibliography: p. [53]-54. [NA1123.P2S413] 68-8186
1. Palladio, Andrea, 1508-1580. 2. Vicenza. Villa Rotonda. I. Title. II. Series. BIP

VENDITTI, Arnaldo. 720'.92'4
The Loggia del Capitaniato. With a note on the pictorial decoration by Franco Barbieri. University Park, Pennsylvania State University Press [1971] 84 p. illus. (part col.) 35 cm. (Corpus Palladianum, v. 4) Includes bibliographies. [NA7595.V47V413] 72-79837 ISBN 0-271-00089-9 16.50
1. Palladio, Andrea, 1508-1580. 2. Vicenza. Loggia del capitaniato. I. Barbieri, Franco. II. Title. III. Series. BIP

WHITEHEAD, Walter Muir, 720'.92'4 1905-
Palladio in America / [texts by Walter Muir Whitehill and Frederick Doveton Nichols]. Milan : Electa, c1976. 127 p. : ill. ; 25 cm. Catalog of the exhibition held in the United States in 1976. Bibliography: p. 126. [NA1123.P2W48] 77-351242
1. Palladio, Andrea, 1508-1580. 2. Palladio, Andrea, 1508-1580—Influence. 3. Neoclassicism (Architecture)—Italy—Exhibitions. 4. Neoclassicism (Architecture)—United States—Exhibitions. I. Nichols, Frederick Doveton, joint author. II. Palladio, Andrea, 1508-1580. III. Title. BIP

WITTKOWER, Rudolf. 720
Palladio and Palladianism. New York, G.

Braziller [1974] 224 p. illus. 26 cm. Includes bibliographical references. [NA1123.P2W57 1974] 73-90463 ISBN 0-8076-0735-5 22.50
1. Palladio, Andrea, 1508-1580. 2. Palladio, Andrea, 1508-1580—Influence. 3. Architecture—England. I. Title. BIP

Palliser Press.

TAYLOR, William Ferguson. 769'.9428'42
Engravings. [by] William F. Taylor. Harrogate : Palliser Press for the Publishing Group of the British Printing Society, 1976. [17] p. : of ill. ; 21 cm. Limited ed. of 110 numbered copies. No. 17. "A second book of blocks in use at the Palliser Press." [Z232.P15T38] 77-362613 ISBN 0-9504112-1-3 : £1.00
1. Palliser Press. 2. Color-prints. I. Title.

Palm frond weaving.

GOODLOE, William H., 1924- 746.4'1
Coconut palm frond weaving [by] William H. Goodloe. Illustrated by William & Ellen Goodloe. Rutland, Vt., C. E. Tuttle Co. [1972] 132 p. illus. 19 cm. (Tut books. H) [TT877.5.G66] 72-79018 ISBN 0-8048-1061-3 3.25 (pbk.)
1. Palm frond weaving. I. Goodloe, Ellen, illus. II. Title. BIP

Palmer, Frederick, 1944—

WOODLANDS Art Gallery. 760'.0942'07402162
Frederick Palmer and Max Middleton : paintings, drawings and prints : [catalogue of an exhibition held] 13 November to 14 December 1976 [at] Woodlands Art Gallery. London : London Borough of Greenwich, [1976] [11] p. : ill. ; 21 cm. [N6797.P23W66] 77-367509 ISBN 0-905950-00-3
1. Palmer, Frederick, 1944- 2. Middleton, Max J. I. Palmer, Frederick, 1944- II. Middleton, Max J. III. Title.

Palmer, Samuel, 1805-1881.

CECIL, David, Lord, 1902- 759.2 B
Visionary and dreamer; two poetic painters: Samuel Palmer and Edward Burne-Jones. [Princeton, N.J.] Princeton University Press [1970, c1969] xxii, 177 p. illus. (part col.) 27 cm. (Bollingen series, 35. The A. W. Mellon lectures in the fine arts, 15) Bibliography: p. 163-[166] [ND496.C4 1970] 68-57088
1. Palmer, Samuel, 1805-1881. 2. Burne-Jones, Edward Coley, Sir, bart., 1833-1898. I. Title. II. Series: Bollingen series, 35. III. Series: The A. W. Mellon lectures in the fine arts, 15 BIP

LISTER, Raymond. 769'.924
Samuel Palmer and his etchings. New York, Watson-Guptill Publications [1969] 131 p. illus., col. plate, ports. 26 cm. Bibliography: p. 125-126. [NE2195.P218L5 1969b] 78-75353 17.50
1. Palmer, Samuel, 1805-1881. I. Title.

MALINS, Edward Greenway. 760'.0924 B
Samuel Palmer's Italian honeymoon [by] Edward Malins. London, New York [etc.] Oxford U.P., 1968. xiv, 130 p. 20 plates, illus., facsims., map, ports. 23 cm. Bibliography: p. [123]-125. [ND497.P3M3] 79-356980 35/-
1. Palmer, Samuel, 1805-1881. 2. Linnell, John, 1792-1882. I. Title.

PALMER, Samuel, 1805-1881. 759.2 B
The letters of Samuel Palmer / edited by Raymond Lister. Oxford : Clarendon Press, 1974, [i.e.1975] 2 v. ; 23 cm. Contents.Contents.—v. 1. 1814-1859.—v. 2. 1860-1881. Includes bibliographical references and index. [ND497.P3A24] 75-311327 ISBN 0-19-817309-1 : 80.00
1. Palmer, Samuel, 1805-1881. 2. Painters—Great Britain—Correspondence, reminiscences, etc.
Distributed by Oxford University Press New York. BIP

PEACOCK, Carlos. 760'.0924 B
Samuel Palmer; Shoreham and after. Greenwich, Conn., New York Graphic Society [1968] 144 p. illus. (part col.) 30 cm. [ND497.P3P4 1968b] 69-12901
1. Palmer, Samuel, 1805-1881.

SELLARS, James. 760'.092'4 B
Samuel Palmer / James Sellars. New York : St. Martin's Press, 1974. 159 p. : ill. (some col.) ; 32 cm. Includes index. Bibliography: p. [155] [ND497.P3S44 1974] 74-81700 ISBN 0-85670-148-3 : 45.00
1. Palmer, Samuel, 1805-1881.

Panayia Kanakaria (Church) Lythrangomi, Cyprus.

†MEGAW, Arthur H. S. 738.5
The Church of the Panagia Kanakaria at Lythrankomi in Cyprus : its mosaics and frescoes / A. H. S. Megaw and E. J. W. Hawkins. Washington : Dumbarton Oaks Center for Byzantine Studies, Trustees for Harvard University ; Locust Valley, N.Y. : distributed by J. J. Augustin, 1977. xx, 173 p., [4]leaves of plates : ill. (some col.) ; 30 cm. (Dumbarton Oaks studies ; 14) Includes index. Bibliography: p. xvii-xx. [NA3780.M4] 77-99267 ISBN 0-88402-074-6 : 25.00
1. Panayia Kanakaria (Church) Lythrangomi, Cyprus. 2. Mosaics, Byzantine—Cyprus—Lythrankomi. 3. Mosaics—Cyprus—Lythrankomi. 4. Mural painting and decoration, Byzantine—Cyprus—Lythrankomi. 5. Mural painting and decoration—Cyprus—Lythrankomi. 6. Lythrangomi, Cyprus—Antiquities. I. Hawkins, Ernest J. W., joint author. II. Title. III. Series. BIP

Pandora—Art.

PANOFSKY, Dora 704.947
Pandora's box; the changing aspects of a mythical symbol [2d ed., rev.] by Dora and Erwin Panofsky. [New York] Pantheon [c.1956, 1962] xiv, 185p. illus. 26cm. (Bollingen ser., 52) Bibl. 5.00
1. Pandora—Art. I. Panofsky, Erwin, 1802- joint author. II. Title. III. Series. BIP

PANOFSKY, Dora. 704.947
Pandora's box; the changing aspects of a mythical symbol, by Dora and Erwin Panofsky. [New York] Pantheon Books [1956] xiv, 158p. illus. 27cm. (Bollingen series, 52) Bibliographical footnotes. [N7760.P29] 55-11598
1. Pandora—Art. I. Panofsky, Erwin, 1892- joint author. II. Title. III. Series.

Panel painting, Flemish.

WHINNEY, Margaret Dickens. 759.9'493
Early Flemish painting [by] Margaret Whinney. New York, Praeger [1968] 168, 96 p. illus. (part col.) 26 cm. Bibliography: p. 162-163. [ND666.W5 1968b] 68-25471 12.50
1. Panel painting, Flemish. I. Title.

Panel painting, Flemish—History.

PUYVELDE, Leo van, 1882- 759.9493
Flemish painting from the van Eycks to Metsys. Translated by Alan Kendall. New York, McGraw-Hill [1970] 263 p. illus. (part col.), maps. 29 cm. Translation of La peinture flamande des van Eyck a Metsys. Includes bibliographical references. [ND665.P8213 1970] 70-125111 ISBN 0-07-050980-8 24.50
1. Panel painting, Flemish—History. I. Title.

Panel painting, Italian—Catalogs.

†GARRISON, Edward B. 759.5'074
Italian Romanesque panel painting : an illustrated index / Edward B. Garrison. New York : Hacker Art Books, 1976. 266 p. : ill. ; 32 cm. Includes indexes. Bibliography: p. 247-253. [ND613.G3 1976] 75-11061 ISBN 0-87817-180-0 : 50.00
1. Panel painting, Italian—Catalogs. 2. Panel painting, Romanesque—Italy—Catalogs. I. Title. BIP

Panel painting, Italian—Exhibitions.

WADSWORTH Atheneum, Hartford. 755'.2'094507401463
An exhibition of Italian panels & manuscripts from the thirteenth & fourteenth centuries in honor of Richard Offner, April 9 to June 6, 1965. Hartford [1965] 60 p. illus. 21 cm. "Bibliography of Richard Offner": p. 59-60. [ND613.W32] 73-157735
1. Panel painting, Italian—Exhibitions. 2. Panel painting, Gothic—Italy. 3. Illumination of books and manuscripts, Italian—Exhibitions. 4. Illumination of books and manuscripts, Gothic—Italy. I. Offner, Richard, 1889-1965. II. Title.

Panel paintings, Renaissance—Catalogs.

VEGH, Janos. 751.2
Fifteenth century German and Bohemian panel paintings. [Translated by Zsuzsanna Horn] New York, Taplinger [1968, c1967] 25 p. 48 col. plates. 24 cm. Paintings from the Budapest Museum of Fine Arts and the Esztergom Christian Museum. Translation of XV. szazadi nemet es cseh tablakepek. Bibliography: p. 21. [ND565.V413 1968] 68-15854
1. Panel paintings, Renaissance—Catalogs. 2. Panel paintings, German—Catalogs. 3. Panel paintings, Bohemian—Catalogs. I. Budapest. Szepmuveszeti Muzeum. II. Esztergom, Hungary. Kereszteny Muzeum. III. Title.

Paolozzi, Eduardo, 1924—

KIRKPATRICK, Diane. 709.24
Eduardo Paolozzi. Greenwich, Conn., New York Graphic Society [1969?] 144 p. illus. (part col.) 26 cm. Bibliography: p. 139-141. [N6797.P25K5] 71-125993 14.50
1. Paolozzi, Eduardo, 1924-

PAOLOZZI, Eduardo, 1924- 709'.2'4
Eduardo Paolozzi : sculpture, drawings, collages, and graphics : an Arts Council exhibition, Newcastle, Laing Art Gallery, 17 April-16 May 1976 .... [London : Arts Council, 1976] 128 p. : chiefly ill. ; 20 cm. Includes bibliographical references. [N6797.P25A897] 77-357404 ISBN 0-7287-0090-5 : £1.65
1. Paolozzi, Eduardo, 1924- I. Arts Council of Great Britain. II. Laing Art Gallery, Newcastle-upon-Tyne.

PAOLOZZI, Eduardo, 1924- 769'.924
Eduardo Paolozzi; a print retrospective. [Berkeley, University Art Museum, University of California, 1968] [32] p. illus. (part col.) 30 cm. "Exhibition held at Worth Ryder Art Gallery, Department of Art, University of California, Berkeley, 15 May-9 June 1968." [NE1846.P3W6] 68-64287 3.50
I. Worth Ryder Art Gallery.

PAOLOZZI, Eduardo, 1924- 730'.92'4
Paolozzi [by] Uwe M. Schneede. [Translated from the German by W. Woodson Hand] New York, H. N. Abrams [1971, c1970] 75 p. illus. 21 x 23 cm. (Modern artists) Bibliography: p. 73-75. [NB497.P3S3213 1971b] 75-143483 ISBN 0-8109-4414-6
I. Schneede, Uwe M. BIP

Papago Indians—Industries.

KISSELL, Mary Lois. 746.4'1
Basketry of the Papago and Pima Indians. Glorieta, N.M., Rio Grande Press [1972] 117-264 p. illus. 29 cm. (A Rio Grande classic, 86) Reprint of the 1916 ed., which was issued as no. 17, pt. 4 of Anthropological papers of the American Museum of Natural History. [E99.P25K58 1972] 72-8827 ISBN 0-87380-095-8 8.00
1. Papago Indians—Industries. 2. Pima Indians—Industries. 3. Indians of North America—Basket making. I. Title. II. Series: American Museum of Natural History, New York. Anthropological papers, v. 17, pt. 4. BIP

Pape, Eva—Art collections.

SANTA Barbara, Calif. Museum of Art. 709'.438
Three Polish artists: Anna Guntner, Zbigniew Makowski [and] Josef Twirbutt. From the Collection of Eva Pape at the Santa Barbara Museum of Art, March 30-April 28, 1974; [catalogue. Santa Barbara, 1974] [16] p. illus. 20 x 26 cm. [N7255.P6S27 1974] 74-79200
1. Pape, Eva—Art collections. 2. Art, Polish—Exhibitions. 3. Art, Modern—20th century—Poland. I. Guntner, Anna, 1933- II. Makowski, Zbigniew, 1930- III. Twirbutt, Josef, 1930- IV. Title.

Paper.

OXFORD Paper Company. 025.7
Book publishers' guide; a manual on the selection of paper and the design and production of bound books. [2d ed.] New York [1960] 1v. illus. 30cm. [Z247.O9] 62-149
1. Paper. I. Title.

REED, Robert Findley, 1890- 676'.27
What the printer should know about paper, by Robert F. Reed. Pittsburgh, Graphic Arts Technical Foundation [1970] xiii, 209 p. illus. 23 cm. Complete revision of What the lithographer should know about paper, first published in 1949. [Z247.R36 1970] 79-114768 2.65 (to members)
1. Paper. I. Title.

YOUNG, Laurence Carvan. 686.2'028
Materials in printing processes, by L. C. Young. London, New York, Focal P., 1973. xiii, 293, 8 p. illus. 24 cm. (Library of printing technology) Bibliography: p. 246-251. [Z247.Y65 1973b] 73-158532 ISBN 0-240-50756-8
1. Paper. 2. Printing-ink. 3. Printing machinery and supplies. I. Title.
Distributed by Hastings House; 15.00. BIP

Paper airplanes.

GANTER, H. 745.59'2
Paper airplanes you can build and fly, by H. Ganter. New York, Drake Publishers [1974] p. [TL770.G28] 74-5970 ISBN 0-87749-689-7 3.95 (pbk.)
1. Paper airplanes. I. Title. BIP

KOELEWYN, Arie. 745.59'2
Paper airplanes : 1911 and 1973 / Arie Koelewyn. Philadelphia : Paper Airplane Press, 1977. 12 p. : ill. ; 22 cm. (Publication of the Paper Airplane Press ; no. 1) "25 copies have been made for private distribution (A-Y) and 25 copies for sale (1-25)" Unnumbered copy. [TL770.K59] 77-365985
1. Paper airplanes. I. Title.

*OLSON, Rik 745.54
The executive manual on the construction of paper aircraft, r How to build paper airplanes at the office. Written, illus. by Rik Olson [San Francisco, Pisani Pr., 1966] 64p. illus. 25cm. 1.00 pap.,
I. Title.

*SIMON, Seymour. 745.59'2
The paper airplane book. Illus. by Byron Barton. New York, Viking [1973, c.1971] 48 p. illus. 23 cm. (Seafarer Books) Summary: Step-by-step instructions for making paper airplanes with suggestions for experimenting with them. [TL770.S4 1971] 71-162669 ISBN 0-670-05078-4 0.75 (pbk.)
1. Paper airplanes. 2. Paper airplanes. I. Barton, Byron, illus. II. Title. BIP

STEIDL, Robert H. 745.59'2
Stick-paper airplanes [by] Robert H. Steidl. London, New York, Abelard-Schuman [1971] 253 p. illus. 28 cm. "Includes plans for 50 models by the author." [TL770.S73 1971] 73-141562 ISBN 0-200-71780-4 4.95 (U.S.)
1. Paper airplanes. I. Title.

Paper airplanes—Juvenile literature.

CREATIVE Educational Society, Mankato, Minn. 745.59'28
How to have fun making paper airplanes, by editors of Creative. Illustrated by Melva

Mickelson. [Mankato, Minn., Creative Education; distributed by Childrens Press, Chicago, 1973, c1974] 31 p. illus. (part col.) 25 cm. (Creative craft book) Simple instructions for making various types of airplanes from paper. [TL770.C76 1973] 73-19589 ISBN 0-87191-294-5 4.95
1. Paper airplanes—Juvenile literature. I. Mickelson, Melva, illus. II. Title. **BIP**

Paper-cutting, Japanese.

HONDA, Isao 736.9
Mon-kiri; Japanese paper cutting. [Rutland, Vt.] Japan Pubns. Trading Co. [1963, c.1959] 35p. col. illus. 18x26cm. 2.00 pap.,
1. Paper-cutting, Japanese. I. Title.

Paper doll making—Collected works.

STALL, Pat. 745.59'22
Paper doll design. [Baltimore] 1973- v. illus. 28 cm. [TT175.S7] 73-92176
1. Paper doll making—Collected works. I. Title.

Paper doll making—Juvenile literature.

ANTIQUE paper dolls, 745.59'22
1915-1920 / edited by Arnold Arnold New York : Dover Publications, 1975. [19] leaves : all col. ill. ; 32 cm. Paper dolls to cut out, with costumes representative of the period between 1915-1920. [TT175.A57 1975] 75-3822 ISBN 0-486-23176-3 pbk. : 2.00
1. Paper doll making—Juvenile literature. I. Arnold, Arnold.

HUFF, Vivian. 736'.98
Let's make paper dolls / by Vivian Huff. 1st ed. New York : Harper & Row, c1978. 28 p., [2] leaves of plates : ill. ; 18 x 22 cm. Presents instructions for making chains of paper dolls. [TT175.H83] 77-11842 ISBN 0-06-022643-9 pbk. : 1.95 ISBN 0-06-022644-7 lib. bdg. : 4.79
1. Paper doll making—Juvenile literature. I. Title. **BIP**

IMAGERIE Pellerin, 745.59'22
Epinal, France.
Antique paper dolls, the Edwardian era : 8 two-sided dolls & 32 complete costumes & accessories, all in full color, as produced by the Imagerie Pellerin at Epinal. New York : Dover Publications, c1975. [16] leaves : all col. ill. ; 32 cm. Cover title. Reproduction of 2 series of Poupees a habiller, genre superieur, originally published ca. 1908 and ca. 1914. Paper dolls to cut out, with costumes representative of the turn of the century to World War I. [TT175.I4 1975] 75-2935 pbk. : 2.00
1. Paper doll making—Juvenile literature. I. Title.

Paper dolls.

GRATER, Michael, 1923- 745.59'22
Paper people. Photos. by Geoffrey Goode. New York, Taplinger [1970, c1969] 192 p. illus. 25 cm. Gives instructions for making inexpensive toys, hand puppets, marionettes, jumping jacks, and other "paper people" from cut, folded, and molded paper of various kinds. [TT870.G693 1970] 77-99308 ISBN 0-8008-6255-4 6.95
1. Paper dolls. I. Title. **BIP**

WOODCOCK, Jean. 745.59'22
Paper dolls of famous faces; encyclopedia and price guide. [Binghamton, N.Y., Printed by Niles & Phipps, 1974] 284 p. illus. 29 cm. [NK8553.W66] 74-165258
1. Paper dolls. 2. Biography—Portraits. I. Title.

Paper—Exhibitions.

INDIANAPOLIS Museum of 760'.028
Art.
Works on Twinrocker handmade paper : an exhibition organized by the Indianapolis Museum of Art, 15 April-25 May, 1975. [Indianapolis] : The Museum, [1975] [15] p. : ill. ; 26 cm. Includes checklist of exhibition. [TS1083.U61535 1975] 75-7928
1. Twinrocker Handmade Paper Mill. 2. Paper—Exhibitions. I. Title.

ROBISON, Andrew. 760'.074'0153
Paper in prints / Andrew Robison. Washington : National Gallery of Art, 1977. 61 p. ; 26 cm. Exhibition held at the National Gallery of Art, May 1-July 4, 1977. Includes bibliographical references. [Z247.R6] 77-363767
1. Paper—Exhibitions. 2. Prints—Exhibitions. I. United States. National Gallery of Art. II. Title.

Paper flowers.

JANITCH, Valerie. 745.59'43
Paper flowers / Valerie Janitch. 1st ed. Radnor, Pa. : Chilton Book Co., 1977, c1976. 96 p. : ill. (some col.) ; 27 cm. (Chilton's creative crafts series) [TT892.J36 1977] 76-11006 ISBN 0-8019-6414-8 : 10.95 ISBN 0-8019-6415-6 pbk. : 6.95
1. Paper flowers. I. Title. **BIP**

KIRSCH, Dietrich. 745.59'43
Make your own paper flowers [by] Dietrich Kirsch [and] Jutta Kirsch-Korn. New York, Watson-Guptill Publications [1969, c1968] 54 p. illus. (part col.) 19 cm. Translation of Blumen aus Papier und Perlen. Instructions for making paper flowers and decorating them with beads. [TT892.K5713] 72-118114 ISBN 0-8230-2965-4 3.50
1. Paper flowers. 2. Beadwork. I. Kirsch-Korn, Jutta, joint author. II. Title.

LOBLEY, Priscilla. 745.92
Flower making for beginners. New York, Taplinger Pub. Co. [1971, c1970] 88 p. illus. 24 cm. Step-by-step instructions, illustrated with photographs, drawings, and diagrams, show the novice techniques for creating various types of paper flowers. [TT892.L63 1971] 71-127407 ISBN 0-8008-2805-4 5.95
1. Paper flowers. I. Title. **BIP**

STROSE, Susanne. 745.59
Making paper flowers, by Susanne Strose. [Translated by Josephine Krieger and Dale Cunningham. Photos. by Richard Sattelmair] New York, Sterling Pub. Co. [1970] 48 p. illus. (part col.) 20 cm. (Little craft book series) Translation of Papierblumen. Gives instructions for creating flowers from tissue and crepe paper and metallic foil and by folding paper. Includes suggestions for arranging and using paper flowers. [TT892.S813] 69-19490 ISBN 0-8069-5130-3
1. Paper flowers. I. Sattelmair, Richard, 1905- illus. II. Title. **BIP**

WILDER, Carolyn. 745.59
Making paper and fabric flowers. Drawings by Barbara Shapira. New York, Hearthside Press [1969] 128 p. illus. (part col.) 24 cm. [TT890.W55] 68-8520 4.95
1. Paper flowers. 2. Fabric flowers. I. Title. **BIP**

WOODS, Pamela. 745.59'43
Paper flower decorations. Illustrated by Michael Woods. New York, Taplinger Pub. Co. [1972] 88 p. illus. 25 cm. [TT892.W65] 79-182197 ISBN 0-8008-6253-8 8.95
1. Paper flowers. I. Title.

Paper making and trade—Bibliography.

HUNTER, Dard, 1883- 016.676'2
1966.
The literature of papermaking, 1390-1800. New York, B. Franklin [1971] 47 p. illus. 35 cm. (Burt Franklin bibliography and reference series, 411) Reprint of the 1925 ed. [Z7914.P2H93 1971] 68-56797 ISBN 0-8337-1769-3
1. Paper making and trade—Bibliography. I. Title. **BIP**

LOUDEN, Louise. 016.676'14
Pulping of bagasse and other papermaking materials / Louise Louden. Appleton, Wis. : Institute of Paper Chemistry, 1976. 123 p. ; 28 cm. (Bibliographic series ; no. 270) Supplements Pulping of bagasse and other papermaking fibers, issued by the Institute of Paper Chemistry. Includes indexes. [Z7914.P2L69] [TS1105] 76-29080
1. Paper making and trade—Bibliography. 2. Bagasse—Bibliography. I. Appleton, Wis. Institute of Paper Chemistry. Pulping of bagasse and other papermaking fibers. II. Title. III. Series: Appleton, Wis. Institute of Paper Chemistry. Bibliographic series ; no. 270.

POLLOCK, Vera. 676'.12
Pitch, problems and control / Vera Pollock and Jack Weiner. Appleton, Wis. : Institute of Paper Chemistry, 1976. 113 p. ; 28 cm. (Bibliographic series - The Institute of Paper Chemistry ; no. 268) Includes indexes. [Z7914.P2P55] [TS1109] 76-3081 pbk. : 17.00
1. Paper making and trade—Bibliography. 2. Pitch—Bibliography. I. Weiner, Jack, 1910- joint author. II. Title. III. Series: Appleton, Wis. Institute of Paper Chemistry. Bibliographic series ; no. 268.

WEINER, Jack, 1910- 016.676'12
Microorganism control / Jack Weiner. Appleton, Wis. : Institute of Paper Chemistry, 1977. 135 p. ; 28 cm. (Bibliographic series - The Institute of Paper Chemistry ; no. 276) "Expansion of Institute bibliography no. 170, 'Slime control and prevention.'" Includes indexes. [Z7914.P2W3445] [TS1109] 76-57836 pbk. : 23.00
1. Paper making and trade—Bibliography. 2. Micro-organisms—Control—Bibliography. I. Title. II. Series: Appleton, Wis. Institute of Paper Chemistry. Bibliographic series ; no. 276. **BIP**

WEINER, Jack, 1910- 016.676'23
Sheet forming on paper machines [by] Jack Weiner and Lillian Roth. Appleton, Wis., Institute of Paper Chemistry, 1969- v. 28 cm. (Institute of Paper Chemistry. Bibliographic series, no. 247) Contents.Contents.—v. 2. Fiber retention and sheet formation. [Z7914.P2W3476] 72-105903
1. Paper making and trade—Bibliography. I. Roth, Lillian, joint author. II. Title. III. Series.

Paper making and trade—History—Bibliography.

LEIF, Irving P., 016.676'209
1947-
An international sourcebook of paper history / by Irving P. Leif. Hamden, Conn. : Archon, 1978. viii, 160 p. ; 23 cm. Includes indexes. [Z7914.P2L4] [TS1090] 77-20485 ISBN 0-208-01691-0 : 19.50
1. Paper making and trade—History—Bibliography. I. Title. **BIP**

Paper money.

ANGUS, Ian. 769'.559
Paper money / Ian Angus. New York : St. Martin's Press, 1975, c1974. 128 p. : ill. ; 27 cm. Includes index. [HG348.A5 1975] 74-33903 6.95
1. Paper money. I. Title. **BIP**

BERESINER, Yasha. 769'.559
The story of paper money [by] Yasha Beresiner and Colin Narbeth. New York, Arco Pub. Co. [1973] 112 p. illus. 25 cm. [HG353.B47 1973b] 72-92286 ISBN 0-668-02905-6 6.95
1. Paper money. I. Narbeth, Colin, joint author. II. Title.

KELLER, Arnold, 332.53
numismatist.
Paper money of the world; translated from the German and edited by Jerome M. Eisenberg. New York, Royal Coin Co., c1956- v. illus. 22cm. Translation of Das Paplergeld des Zweiten Weltkriegs und der Nachkriegszeit. Contents.pt. 1. Modern issues of Europe. Includes bibliographies. [HG353.K413] 57-20712
1. Paper money. I. Title.

LAKE, Kenneth Robert. 769'.55
Investing in paper money, [by] Kenneth R. Lake. London, Pelham, 1972. 158, (16) p. facsims. 23 cm. Label mounted on t.p.: Transatlantic Arts, Inc., New York. Sole distributor for the U.S.A. Bibliography: p. 138-144. [HG353.L28] 73-150160 ISBN 0-7207-0546-0
1. Paper money. I. Title.
10.00

REINFELD, Fred, 1910- 332.53
The story of paper money; including Catalogue of values. [Rev. ed.] New York, Sterling Pub. Co., distributed by President Coin Corp. [c1960] 128p. illus. 26cm. [HG353.R4 1960a] 61-2032
1. Paper money. I. Title.

REINFELD, Fred, 1910-1964. 332.53
The story of paper money, including Catalogue of values. New York, Sterling Pub. Co. [1957] 128 p. illus. 26 cm. [HG353.R4] 57-11529
1. Paper money.

Paper money—Bolivia.

SEPPA, Dale Allan. 769'.55984
The paper money of Bolivia, by Dale A. Seppa and Al Almanzar. San Antonio, Tex., Almanzar's Coins of the World [1972] 50 p. illus. 22 cm. [HG827.S46] 72-94572 ISBN 0-88242-004-6 pap. 2.50
1. Paper money—Bolivia. 2. Paper money—Catalogs. I. Almanzar, Alcedo, joint author. II. Title.

Paper money—Brazil.

SEPPA, Dale Allan. 769'.55981
The paper money of Brasil / Dale A. Seppa. 2d ed. Chicago : Obol International, 1975. 102 p. : ill. ; 21 cm. Bibliography: p. 102. [HG837.S45 1975] 75-6032 pbk. : 4.00
1. Paper money—Brazil. 2. Paper money—Catalogs. I. Title. **BIP**

Paper money—Canada.

GINGRAS, Larry. 769'.559'71
Paper money of the Hudson's Bay Company. [Richmond, B.C., Author, P.O. Box 15] 1969. 22 p. illus. 23 cm. "Published under the auspices of the Canadian Numismatic Research Society." [HG657.G54] 71-512629 2.00
1. Hudson's Bay Company. 2. Paper money—Canada. I. Canadian Numismatic Research Society. II. Title.

Paper money— Catalogs.

LOEB, Walter M 769'.55
Catalog of paper money around the world. Edited by Lee Firester. Port Washington, N. Y., Universal Pub. Co. of Port Washington, c1961. 75p. illus. 28cm. [HG353.L6] 62-2723
1. Paper money— Catalogs. I. Title.

PICK, Albert. 769'.55'94
Catalogue of European paper money since 1900. New York, Sterling Pub. Co. [1971] 320 p. illus. 27 cm. Translation of Papiergeld Katalog Europa seit 1900. [HG353.P5213] 76-151707 ISBN 0-8069-6030-2
1. Paper money—Catalogs. 2. Paper money—Europe. I. Title.

PICK, Albert. 769'.5594
Catalogue of European paper money since 1900. 2d ed. New York, Sterling Pub. Co. [1974] 336 p. illus. 26 cm. Translation of Papiergeldkatalog. [HG353.P5213 1974] 74-178196 ISBN 0-8069-6030-2 16.95
1. Paper money—Catalogs. 2. Paper money—Europe. I. Title.
Library binding 13.98; ISBN 0-8069-6053-1.

STEN, George J 769.550216
Encyclopedia of world paper money; an illustrated guide-index, compiled as an aid in the identification and translation of all currency, 1661-1964, by George J. Sten. Port Washington, N.Y., Universal Pub. Co., 1965. 152 p. illus. 28 cm. Bibliography: p. 152. [HG353.S7] 65-6034
1. Paper money — Catalogs. I. Title.

Paper money—Collectors and collecting.

BERESINER, Yasha. 769'.55
A collector's guide to paper money / Yasha Beresiner. New York : Stein and Day, 1977. 255 p., [4] leaves of plates : ill. (some col.) ; 27 cm. Includes index. Bibliography: p. [244]-246. [HG353.B46 1977b] 77-80372 ISBN 0-8128-2351-6 : 15.95
1. Paper money—Collectors and collecting. 2. Paper money—Catalogs. I. Title. **BIP**

NARBETH, Colin. 769'.55'075
Collecting paper money; a beginner's guide. Chicago, H. Regnery Co. [1973, c1968] 134 p. facsims. 21 cm. Bibliography: p. 122-124. [HG353.N37 1973] 72-11185 5.95
1. Paper money—Collectors and collecting. I. Title.

SHAFER, Neil. 769'.55'075
Let's collect paper money! : An introduction to the exciting hobby of collecting paper money of the world / by Neil Shafer. Racine, Wis. : Western Pub. Co., c1976. 64 p. : ill. ; 20 cm. Bibliography: p. 64. [HG353.S48] 76-6209 ISBN 0-307-09381-6
1. Paper money—Collectors and collecting. I. Title. BIP

Paper money—Confederate States of America.

CRISWELL, Grover C. 737.3'0975
The official guide to Confederate money & Civil War tokens, tradesmen & patriotic, by Grover Criswell & Herb Romerstien [sic] Hal L. Cohen, design & editorial. [1st ed.] [New York] HC Publishers [1971] 144 p. illus. 15 cm. [HG526.C74] 79-181839 1.00
1. Paper money—Confederate States of America. 2. Tokens—United States. I. Romerstein, Herbert. II. Title.

Paper money—Confederate States of America—Catalogs.

CRISWELL, Grover C. 769'.55975
Confederate and Southern State currency : a descriptive listing, including rarity and prices / by Grover C. Criswell, Jr. 2d rev. ed. Citra, Fla. : Criswell's & Criswell's Publications, c1976. viii, 294 p. : ill. ; 24 cm. (Criswell's currency series ; v. 1) [HG526.C73 1976] 76-17386
1. Paper money—Confederate States of America—Catalogs. I. Title. II. Series.

Paper money—Estonia.

TIITUS, M. 769'.559'4741
Paper currencies of Estonia. Eesti paberrahad [by] M. Tiitus. [Menlo Park, Calif., 1971] 27 p. facsims., map. 29 cm. Cover title. English and Estonian. Bibliography: p. 26. [HG1080.2.Z8T55] 70-22803
1. Paper money—Estonia. 2. Paper money—Catalogs. I. Title.

Paper money—Florida.

FREEMAN, Harley L. 769'.559'759
Florida obsolete notes and scrip, by Harley L. Freeman. [1st ed. Glen Ridge? N.J.] Society of Paper Money Collectors [1967] 103 p. facsims. 29 cm. [HG627.F5F7] 67-8299
1. Paper money—Florida. I. Title.

Paper money—Indonesia.

FOLTZ, Donald L. 769'.559'91
Paper money of the Republic of Indonesia; an illustrated listing of the official paper money of the Republic of Indonesia, from the declaration of independence in 1945 to date, by Donald L. Foltz. 1st ed. Indianapolis, 1970. 19 p. illus. 22 cm. [HG1257.F65] 77-17086 2.00 (pbk)
1. Paper money—Indonesia. I. Title.

Paper money—Paraguay.

SEPPA, Dale Allan. 769'.559892
Paraguayan paper money, by Dale A. Seppa. [Chicago, Ill.] Obol International [1973, c1974] 50 p. illus. 21 cm. [HG887.S46] 73-90434 10.00; 3.00 (pbk.)
1. Paper money—Paraguay. 2. Paper money—Catalogs. I. Title.
Publisher's address: 8 South Michigan Avenue Chicago, Ill. 60603 BIP

Paper money—Philippine Islands.

SHAFER, Neil. 769'.559599
Philippine emergency and guerrilla currency of World War II, by Neil Shafer, with special support of Maurice M. Gould. Racine, Wis., Western Pub. Co. [1974] 464 p. illus. 24 cm. Bibliography: p. 455-456. [HG1267.S52] 73-83702 15.00
1. Paper money—Philippine Islands. 2. Money—Philippine Islands. 3. Paper money—Catalogs. I. Gould, Maurice M., joint author. II. Title.

Paper money—Ukraine.

KIKTA, Stepan. 769'.55947'71
Specialized catalog of paper money of Ukraine 1917-1920 = Spezialisierter katalog der Geldscheine des Ukrainischen Staates 1917-1920 = [Kataloh derzhavnykh hroshei Ukra"iny (romanized form)] / Stepan Kikta. Cleveland, Ohio : Ukrainian Museum-Archives, 1974. 20 p. : col. ill. ; 24 cm. English, German, and Ukrainian. Errata slip inserted. [HG1080.U38K54] 75-316393
1. Paper money—Ukraine. 2. Paper money—Catalogs. I. Title. II. Title: Spezialisierter Katalog der Geldscheine des Ukrainischen Staates, 1917-1920. III. Title: Kataloh derzhavnykh hroshei Ukrainy.

Paper money — U.S.

CRISWELL, Grover C. 769.55
North American currency; the standard paper money reference, by Grover C. Criswell, Jr. Iola, Wis., Krause Pubns. [1965] 910p. illus. 24cm. Bibl. [HG591.C7] 64-66240 15.00
1. Paper money—U.S. 2. Paper money—North America. I. Title.

DONLON catalog of 322.530973
United States small size paper money, by William P. Donlon. With additional material by Robert H. Lloyd and Lee F. Hewitt. Section on error notes by James Grebinger. 2d ed. Chicago, Hewitt Bros., 1966, c1965. 128 p. illus. 20 cm. (Hewitt's numismatic information series) Previous edition published under title: Price catalog of United States small size paper money. [HG591.D6 1966] 66-5537
1. Paper money — U.S.

DONLON, William P 332.5'3'0973
Donlon catalog of United States small size paper money, by William P. Donlon. With additional material by Robert H. Lloyd and Lee F. Hewitt. Section on error notes by James Grebinger. 3d ed. (Hewitt's numismatic information series) First ed. published in 1964 under title: Price catalog of United States small size paper money. [HG591.D6 1967] 67-2619
1. Paper money — U.S. I. Title.

DONLON, William P. 332.5'3'0973
Donlon catalog of United States small size paper money, by William P. Donlon. Section on error notes by James Grebinger. 5th ed., 1969. Chicago, Hewitt Bros., 1968. 136 p. illus. 20 cm. (Hewitt's numismatic information series) First ed. published in 1964 under title: Price catalog of United States small size paper money. [HG591.D6 1968b] 77-1498 1.50
1. Paper money—U.S. I. Title.

DONLON, William P. 769'.55973
Donlon catalog of United States small size paper money. Text by William P. Donlon [and others] 7th annual ed. Chicago, Hewitt Bros., 1971. 164 p. illus. 20 cm. (Hewitt's numismatic information series) First ed. published in 1964 under title: Price catalog of United States small size paper money. [HG591.D6 1971] 73-179215 1.50
1. Paper money—United States. I. Title. II. Title: Catalog of United States small size paper money.

DONLON, William P 332.5'3'0973
Donlon catalog of United States small size paper money, by William P. Donlon. With additional material by Robert H. Lloyd and Lee F. Hewitt. Section on error notes by James Grebinger. 3d ed. Chicago, Hewitt Bros., 1967, c1966. 128 p. illus. 20 cm. (Hewitt's numismatic information series) First ed. published in 1964 under title: Price catalog of United States small size paper money. [HG591.D6 1967] 67-2619
1. Paper money — U.S. I. Title.

DONLON, William P. 332.5'3'0973
Donlon catalog of United States small size paper money, by William P. Donlon. With additional material by Robert H. Lloyd and Lee F. Hewitt. Section on error notes by James Grebinger. 4th ed. Chicago, Hewitt Bros., 1968, c1967. 128 p. illus. 20 cm. (Hewitt's numismatic information series) First ed. published in 1964 under title: Price catalog of United States small size paper money. [HG591.D6 1968] 68-2272
1. Paper money—United States. I. Title.

DONLON, William P. 769'.55973
Hewitt-Donlon catalog of United States small size paper money / text by William P. Donlon ... [et al.]. 13th annual ed. Chicago : Hewitt Numismatic Publications, 1977, c1976. 192 p. : ill. ; 20 cm. (Hewitt's numismatic information series) [HG591.D6 1977] 77-363432 2.50
1. Paper money—United States. 2. Paper money—Catalogs. I. Title.

DONLON, William P. 769'.55973
Hewitt-Donlon catalog of United States small size paper money. Text by William P. Donlon [and others] 10th annual ed. Chicago, Hewitt Bros, 1974, c1973. 176 p. illus. 20 cm. (Hewitt's numismatic information series) Previous editions have been published under title: Price catalog of United States small size paper money. [HG591.D6 1974] 74-168263 1.75
1. Paper money—United States. 2. Paper money—Catalogs. I. Title.

DONLON, William P. 769'.55973
Hewitt-Donlon catalog of United States small size paper money / text by William P. Donlon ... [et al.]. 11th annual ed. Chicago : Hewitt Numismatic Publications, 1975, c1974. 176 p. : ill. ; 20 cm. (Hewitt's numismatic information series) First ed. published under title: Price catalog of United States small size paper money. [HG591.D6 1975] 75-304946 pbk. : 1.95
1. Paper money—United States. 2. Paper money—Catalogs. I. Title.

DONLON, William P. 332.530973
Price catalog of United States small size paper money Additional material by Robert H. Lloyd, Lee F. Hewitt. Chicago, Hewitt Bros., 7320 Milwaukee Ave., [1965]c.1964. 104p. illus. 20cm. (Hewitt58s numismatic infor. ser.) [HG591.D6] 65-1880 1.00 pap.,
1. Paper money—U.S. I. Title.

DONLON, William P. 769.'559'73
United States large size paper money, 1861 to 1923, by William P. Donlon. [Iola, Wis., Krause Publications, 1968] 176 p. illus., ports. 23 cm. [HG591.D64] 68-6323 3.00
1. Paper money—United States. I. Title.

DONLON, William P. 769'.559'73
United States large size paper money, 1861 to 1923, by William P. Donlon. 2d ed. Iola, Wis., Krause Publications, 1970. 176 p. illus., ports. 23 cm. [HG591.D64 1970] 74-17096 3.00
1. Paper money—U.S. I. Title.

DONLON, William P. 769'.55973
United States large size paper money, 1861 to 1923, by William P. Donlon. 3d ed., 1973-1974 Utica, N.Y. [1973] 183 p. illus. 23 cm. [HG591.D64 1973] 73-173334 3.50
1. Paper money—United States. I. Title.
Publisher's address: Hotel Utica Bldg., 102 Lafayette Utica, New York. 13503

FRIEDBERG, Robert, 769'.55973
1912-
Paper money of the United States; a complete illustrated guide with valuations, by Robert Friedberg. 7th ed., with additions and revisions by Jack Friedberg. New York, Coin and Currency Institute [1972] 327 p. illus. 29 cm. [HG591.F7 1972] 72-80202 ISBN 0-87184-507-5
1. Paper money—United States. I. Friedberg, Jack, ed. II. Title.

FRIEDBERG, Robert, 1912- 332.53
Paper money of the United States, a complete illustrated guide with valuations, large size notes, fractional currency, small size notes, enclosed postage stamps, from the first year of paper money, 1861, to the present, 2d ed. New York, Coin and Currency Pub. Institute [1955] 151p. illus. 29cm. Bibliography: p.8. [HG591.F7 1955] 55-4408
1. Paper money—U. S. I. Title. BIP

FRIEDBERG, Robert, 1912- 332.53
Paper money of the United States, a complete illustrated guide with valuations: large size notes, fractional currency, small size notes, encased postage stamps, from the first year of paper money, 1861, to the present. [1st ed.] New York, Coin and Currency Pub. Institute [1953] 128 p. illus. 29 cm. Bibliography: p. 8. [HG591.F7] 53-3202
1. Paper money—U.S. I. Title.

FRIEDBERG, Robert, 769'.55973
1912-
Paper money of the United States : a complete illustrated guide with valuations / by Robert Friedberg. 8th ed. / with additions and revisions by Jack Friedberg. New York : Coin and Currency Institute, [1975] 327 p. : ill. ; 29 cm. Includes bibliographical references. [HG591.F7 1975] 74-20035 ISBN 0-87184-508-3 : 17.50
1. Paper money—United States. I. Friedberg, Jack. II. Title.

FRIEDBERG, Robert, 332.530973
1912-
Paper money of the United States, a complete illustrated guide with valuations. Large size notes, fractional currency, small size notes, encased postage stamps from the first year of paper money, 1861, to the present. 5th ed., with additions and revisions by Jack Friedberg. New York, Coin and Currency Institute [1964] 305 p. illus. 29 cm. [HG591.F7 1964] 64-8150
1. Paper money—U.S. I. Friedberg, Jack, ed.

FRIEDBERG, Robert, 332.5'3'0973
1912-
Paper money of the United States; a complete illustrated guide with valuations. Large size notes, fractional currency, small size notes, encased postage stamps from the first year of paper money, 1861, to the present. 6th ed., with additions and revisions by Jack Friedberg. New York, Coin and Currency Institute [1968] 327 p. illus. 29 cm. [HG591.F7 1968] 67-30486
1. Paper money—United States. I. Friedberg, Jack, ed.

GOODMAN, Leon J. 769'.55973
Standard handbook of modern U.S. paper money, 1971-72, by Leon J. Goodman, Jr., John L. Schwartz [and] Chuck O'Donnell. Including: Special section on national bank notes, series of 1929, by Peter Huntoon. 3d ed. [Turnersville, N.J., Printed by Photo-Printers] 1971. 111 p. illus. 22 cm. [HG591.G6 1971] 74-168216 1.50
1. Paper money—United States. I. Schwartz, John L., joint author. II. O'Donnell, Chuck, joint author. III. Title.

HESSLER, Gene, 1928- 769'.55973
The comprehensive catalog of U.S. paper money. Chicago, H. Regnery Co. [1974] xiv, 456 p. illus. 24 cm. Bibliography: p. [455]-456. [HG591.H47] 73-6461 20.00
1. Paper money—United States. 2. Paper money—Catalogs. I. Title.

KEMM, Theodore. 769'.55973
The official guide of United States paper money. 6th ed. Hall Cohen, editor. New York, House of Collectibles, c1972. 192 p. illus. 14 cm. [HG591.K4 1972] 73-158138 1.00
1. Paper money—United States. I. Title. II. Title: United States paper money.

KEMM, Theodore. 332.5'3'0973
The official guide of United States paper money; listing and pricing of all U.S. paper money, 1861 to date. Hal L. Cohen, design & editorial. New York, H C Publishers [1967, c1968] 160 p. illus. 14 cm. [HG591.K4] 67-9625
1. Paper money—United States. I. Title. II. Title: United States paper money.

MUSCALUS, John 769'.55973
Anthony, 1909-
Lincoln portraits on State bank notes, college currency, and scrip, by John A. Muscalus. Bridgeport, Pa., Historical Paper Money Research Institute [1967] 11 p. (chiefly illus.) 23 cm. Cover title. [HG622.M816] 67-31869
1. Lincoln, Abraham, Pres. U.S., 1809-1865. 2. Paper money—United States. 3. Bank-notes—United States. I. Title.

O'DONNELL, Chuck. 769'.55973
The standard handbook of modern U.S. paper money / by Chuck O'Donnell ; including a special section on national bank notes by Peter Huntoon ; and a comprehensive listing of errors by Harry Jones. 4th ed. Williamstown, N.J. : O'Donnell, [1974] xxx, 257 p. : facsims. ; 27 cm. First-3d ed. by L. J. Goodman. Includes index. Bibliography: p. xxix. [HG591.O36 1974] 75-315845 7.50
1. Paper money—United States. 2. Bank-notes—United States. I. Goodman, Leon J. Standard handbook of modern U.S. paper money. II. Title.

O'DONNELL, Chuck. 769'.55973
The standard handbook of modern U.S. paper money / by Chuck O'Donnell ; including a special section on national bank notes by Peter Huntoon and a comprehensive listing of errors by Harry Jones. 5th ed. [s.l. : s.n., 1975] c1974 (Turnersville, N.J. : Center Print.) p. cm. First-3d ed. by L. J. Goodman. Includes index. Bibliography: p. A definitive description of all paper money printed by the U.S. government since 1928. [HG591.O36 1975] 74-30456 10.00
1. Paper money—United States. 2. Bank-notes—United States. I. Goodman, Leon J. Standard handbook of modern U.S. paper money. II. Title.

RAYMOND, Wayte, 1886- 332.53
The standard paper money catalogue. [5th ed.] New York, 1954- v. 23cm. Cover title. Contents.pt. 2. United States notes and fractional currency. [HG591.R3524] 54-27333
1. Paper money—U. S. I. Title.

RAYMOND, Wayte, 1886- 332.53
The standard paper money catalogue. New York [1950] 2 v. 23 cm. Cover title. Contents.-- pt. 1. Colonial and Continental currency. -- pt. 2. United States notes and fractional currency. [HG591.R352] 50-13180
1. Paper money — U.S. I. Title.

SHAFER, Neil 769.5
A guide book of modern United States currency. With special assistance from William P. Donlon. Racine, Wis., Whitman [c.1965] 160p. illus. 20cm. Bibl. [HG591.S5] 65-3573 1.75 bds.,
1. Paper money—U.S. 2. Money—U.S. I. Title.

SHAFER, Neil. 769'.559'73
A guide book of modern United States currency. 5th ed. Racine, Wis., Western Pub. Co. [1971] 160 p. illus. 20 cm. On spine: Modern U.S. currency. Bibliography: p. 160. [HG591.S5 1971] 70-28630
1. Paper money—U.S. 2. Money—U.S. I. Title. II. Title: Modern U.S. currency. BIP

SHAFER, Neil. 769'.55973
A guide book of modern United States currency. 6th ed. Racine, Wis., Western Pub. Co. [1973] 160 p. illus. 20 cm. Bibliography: p. 160. [HG591.S5 1973] 73-168836 2.50
1. Paper money—United States. 2. Money—United States. I. Title. II. Title: Modern U.S. currency.

SHAFER, Neil. 769'.559'73
A guide book of modern United States currency. With special assistance from William P. Donlon. 2d ed. Racine, Wis., Whitman Pub. Co., 1967. 160 p. illus., facsims. 20 cm. Bibliography: p. 157. [HG591.S5 1967] 67-8227
1. Paper money—United States. 2. Money—United States. I. Title.

SHAFER, Neil. 332.5'3'0973
A guide book of modern United States currency. With special assistance from William P. Donlon. 3d. ed. Racine, Wis., Western Pub. Co., Whitman Hobby Division, 1969 [c1968] 159 p. illus., facsims. 20 cm. Bibliography: p. 157. [HG591.S5 1968] 73-2829
1. Paper money—U.S. 2. Money—U.S. I. Title.

SHAFER, Neil. 332.5'3'0973
A guide book of modern United States currency. With special assistance from William P. Donlon. 4th ed. Racine, Wis., Western Pub. Co., 1970 [c1969] 160 p. illus., facsims. 20 cm. Title on spine: Modern U.S. currency. Bibliography: p. 160. [HG591.S5 1970] 75-14342
1. Paper money—U.S. 2. Money—U.S. I. Title. II. Title: Modern U.S. currency.

WERLICH, Robert, ed. 332.53084
Catalogue of United States, Canadian, and Confederate currency. [New ed.] Washington; Distributed by Quaker Currency Co. [1963] 114 p. facsims. 24 cm. Quaker Currency Co. deleted; replaced by stamp: Quaker Press. [HG591.W4] 63-2999
1. Paper money — U.S. 2. Paper money — Canada. I. Title.

WERLICH, Robert, ed. 769.5
Fully illustrated catalogue of United States, Canadian, and Confederate currency. Ed., pub. by Robert Werlich. Washington, D.C., dist. by Quaker [pr.] 3218 O St., N.W. [c.1965] 114p. facsims. 24cm. Cover title: United States, Canadian, and Confederate paper money [HG591.W4] 65-3534 5.00 pap.,
1. Paper money—U.S. 2. Paper money—Canada. I. Title. II. Title: Catalogue of United States, Canadian, and Confederate currency. tUnited States, Canadian, and Confederate paper money.

Paper money—United States—Catalogs.

HESSLER, Gene, 1928- 769'.55973
The comprehensive catalog of U.S. paper money / Gene Hessler. Completely rev. and updated. Chicago : H. Regnery, c1977. xviii, 503 p. : ill. ; 24 cm. Bibliography: p. 501-503. [HG591.H47 1977] 76-6269 ISBN 0-8092-7994-0 : 25.00
1. Paper money—United States—Catalogs. I. Title. BIP

SHAFER, Neil. 769'.55973
A guide book of modern United States currency : a comprehensive illustrated valuation catalog of all modern-size United States paper money from 1929 to the present, with historical data and official totals, also includes complete catalog listing of U.S. military payment certificates / by Neil Shafer. 7th ed. Racine, Wis. : Western Pub. Co., c1975. 160 p. : ill. ; 20 cm. (An Official Whitman guide) On spine: Modern U.S. currency. Bibliography: p. 160. [HG591.S5 1975] 76-352113 ISBN 0-307-09373-5
1. Paper money—United States—Catalogs. 2. Money—United States—Catalogs. I. Title. II. Title: Modern U.S. currency.

Paper money—United States—History.

NEWMAN, Eric P. 332.5'3'0973
The early paper money of America, by Eric P. Newman. [Racine, Wis.] [Whitman Pub. Co.] [1967] 360 p. facsims. 29 cm. Includes bibliographies. [HG591.N45] 67-16064
1. Paper money—U.S.—History. I. Title.

NEWMAN, Eric P. 332.4'044'0973
The early paper money of America : an illustrated, historical, and descriptive comilation of data relating to American paper currency from its inception in 1686 to the year 1800 ... / by Eric P. Newman ; supplemented by current values of generally available bills under the direction of Richard Picker. Bicentennial ed. [Racine, Wis. : Western Pub. Co.], c1976. 416 p. : ill. ; 29 cm. Includes bibliographies. [HG591.N45 1976] 76-8365 ISBN 0-307-09355-7 : 22.50
1. Paper money—United States—History. I. Title. II. Title: Bicentennial edition of The early paper money of America.

ROTHERT, Matt. 769.5
A guide book of United States fractional currency; an illustrated history and catalog listing with valuations for all issues of postage and fractional currency of the United States, 1862-1876. Racine, Wis., Whitman Pub. Co. [1963] 81 p. illus., port. 20 cm. Bibliography: p. 77. [HG613.R6] 63-236000
1. Paper money — U.S. — Hist. 2. Postage-stamps — U.S. — Hist. I. Title.

Paper money—Uruguay.

SEPPA, Dale Allan. 769'.55'9895
Uruguayan paper money / by Dale A. Seppa. Chicago : Obol International, 1974, c1975. 60 p. : ill. ; 22 cm. [HG907.S46] 74-18765
1. Paper money—Uruguay. 2. Paper money—Catalogs. I. Title. BIP

Paper money—Vermont.

COULTER, Mayre Burns. 769'.559743
Vermont obsolete notes and scrip. Iola, Wis., Published for the Society of Paper Money Collectors, by Krauss Publications [1972] xvii, 151 p. illus. 29 cm. [HG627.V4C67] 72-84130
1. Paper money—Vermont. I. Title. BIP

Paper money—Virginia.

AFFLECK, Charles J. 769'.559'755
The obsolete paper money of Virginia, by Charles J. Affleck. Designed by Frank R. Hannah. [Hampton] Virginia Numismatic Association, 1968-69. v. illus. 28 cm. Vol. 2: Obsolete bank notes, 1804-1865. [HG627.V5A6] 68-7590 12.50
1. Paper money—Virginia. I. Title.

Paper—Printing properties.

BIRD & Bull, number 13 686.2'3
[by] Henry Morris North Hills, Pa., Bird & Bull Press, 1972. 70 p. illus. 16 x 24 cm. [Z247.B53] 72-185284 25.00
1. Paper—Printing properties. 2. Printing, Practical—Presswork. 3. Printing—Miscellanea. I. Morris, Henry, 1927-

DANIELS, Chester J. 686.2'325
Quantification of paper material accumulation on offset printing blankets / by Chester J. Daniels. [Rochester, N.Y. : Graphic Arts Research Center, Rochester Institute of Technology, 1974] x, 138 leaves : ill. ; 28 cm. (Report - Graphic Arts Research Center, Rochester Institute of Technology ; no. 145) Includes bibliographical references. [Z247.D35] 75-302506
1. Paper—Printing properties. 2. Optical instruments. 3. Photography, High-speed. 4. Offset printing. I. Title. II. Series: Rochester Institute of Technology, Rochester, N.Y. Graphic Arts Research Center. Report ; no. 145.

Paper—Printing properties—Bibl.

WEINER, Jack, 1910- 016.67627
Runnability of printing papers [by] Jack Weiner, Lillian Roth. Appleton, Wis., Inst. of paper Chem., 1043 E.S. River St., 1965. 135p. 28cm. (Appleton, Wis. Inst. of Pap. Chem. Bibl. ser., no. 215) [Z7914.P2W349] 64-8232 7.50 pap.,
1. Paper—Printing properties—Bibl. I. Roth, Lillian, joint author. II. Title. III. Series.

Paper—Printing properties—Congresses.

INTERNATIONAL Conference of Printing Research Institutes, 8th Aulanko, 1965. 655.3
Paper in the printing processes proceedings. Ed. by W. H. Banks. Oxford, New York, Symp. Pubns. Div. Pergamon [1967] viii, 454p. illus. 23cm. (Advances in printing sci. & technol. v. 4) Conf. met. . . under its new organization, the Intl. Assn. of Res. Insts. for the Graphic Arts Indus. Bibl. [Z247.I52 1965] 67-13995 18.50
1. Paper—Printing Properties—Congresses. I. Banks, William H., ed. II. International Association of Research Institutes for the Graphic Arts Industry. III. Title. IV. Series.

INTERNATIONAL Conference of Printing Research Institutes, 9th, Rome, 1969. 655.2
Inks, plates and print quality; proceedings. Edited by W. H. Banks. Oxford, New York, Pergamon Press [1969] xii, 333 p. illus. 23 cm. (Advances in printing science and technology, v. 5) Held under the auspices of the International Association of Research Institutes for the Graphic Arts Industry. Includes bibliographies. [Z247.I54 1967] 69-16048
1. Paper—Printing properties—Congresses. 2. Printing plates—Congresses. I. Banks, William H., ed. II. International Association of Research Institutes for the Graphic Arts Industry. III. Title. IV. Series.

Paper quillwork.

CHRISTY, Betty. 745.54
Quilling: paper art for everyone [by] Betty Christy and Doris Tracy. Chicago, Regnery [1974] 205 p. illus. 23 cm. Bibliography: p. 201. [TT870.C52] 74-8481 ISBN 0-8092-8843-5 8.95 (pbk.).
1. Paper quillwork. I. Tracy, Doris, joint author. II. Title.

Paper quillwork—Juvenile literature.

†AMIDON, Eva V. 745.54
Easy quillery : projects with paper coils and scrolls / Eva V. Amidon ; illustrated by Charles H. Amidon, Jr. New York : Morrow, 1977. 95 p. : ill. ; 25 cm. Includes index. Twelve paper filigree projects with an introduction to techniques and suggestions for other projects. [TT870.A47] 77-6463 ISBN 0-688-22130-0 : 6.25
1. Paper quillwork—Juvenile literature. I. Amidon, Charles H. II. Title. BIP

Paper — Sample books.

TAYLOR, John W 1909- 676
The characteristics and functions of printing papers, by Jack W. Taylor. [Tulsa, Okla., 1950] 1 v. (unpaged) samples. 28 cm. Cover title. [Z247.T38] 50-23340
1. Paper — Sample books. I. Title.

Paper sculpture.

ALLPORT, Alan. 736'.98
Paper sculpture. New York, Drake Publishers [1971] 85 p. illus. 23 cm. Instructions for making dolls, models, miniature theaters, puppets, toys, and other objects from paper. [TT870.A43 1971b] 71-173723 ISBN 0-87749-134-8 5.95
1. Paper sculpture. 2. Models and modelmaking. I. Title.

ANGRAVE, Bruce. 731.258
Sculpture in paper. London, New York, Studio Publications [1957] 96p. illus. 26cm. (The How to do it series, no. 72) [NB1270.P3A55] 57-3418
1. Paper sculpture. I. Title.

*DUBIN, Sidney 745.59
Paper sculpture technique in craft foam [Great Neck. N.Y., Author, 4 Park Place, 1965, c.1964] 49p. illus. 28cm. 2.00 pap.,
I. Title.

FABRI, Ralph, 1894- 736'.98
Sculpture in paper. New York, Watson-Guptill Publications [1966] 165 p. illus. (part col.) 27 cm. [NB1270.P3F3] 66-19734
1. Paper sculpture. I. Title. BIP

GRATER, Michael, 1923- 736.9
One piece of paper, for children and for teachers. Illus. by the author. Photos. by Geoffrey Goode. London, Mills & Boon [dist. New York, Taplinger, c.1963] 117p. illus. 26cm. 63-6368 7.50
1. Paper sculpture. I. Title. BIP

JOHNSON, Pauline, 1905- 731.258
Creating with paper; basic forms and variations. Seattle, University of Washington Press, 1958. 207 p. illus. 28 cm. [NB1270.P3J58] 58-6007
1. Paper sculpture. I. Title. BIP

JOHNSTON, Mary Grace, 1899- 731.258
Paper sculpture. [Worcester, Mass., Davis Press, 1952] unpaged, illus. (in portfolio) 29 cm. [NB1270.P3J6] 52-13274
1. Paper sculpture. I. Title.

JOHNSTON, Mary Grace, 1899- 736.9
Paper sculpture. Rev. and enl. Worcester, Mass, Davis Publications [c1964] 82 p. illus. 29 cm. A revision of the author's Paper sculpture and Paper shapes and

sculpture for school use. [NB1270.P3J62 1964] 64-24721
1. Paper sculpture. I. Title.

JOHNSTON, Mary Grace, 1899- 372.53
Paper shapes and sculpture for school use. Worcester, Mass., Davis Publications, 1958. 69p. illus. 29cm. [NB1270.P3J62] 58-8125
1. Paper sculpture. I. Title.

MILLER, Josephine Virginia (Trapani) 1918- 731.258
Paper sculpture and construction. Models and drawings by the author. Photos. by Morton Bartlett and D. S. Hennesey. Peoria, Ill., C. A. Bennett Co., c1957. 56p. illus. 28cm. [NB1270.P3M5] 57-5431
1. Paper sculpture. I. Title.

PAULI, Anna E 372.53
Paper figures, by Anna E. Pauli and Margaret S. Mitzit. Peoria. Ill., C. A. Bennet Co. [1957] 102p. illus. 27cm. [NB1270.P3P3] 57-5432
1. Paper seculpture. I. Mitzit, Margaret S., joint author. II. Title.

PETHERBRIDGE, Elizabeth. 736'.98
Paper sculpture step by step. London, Bell, 1972. 122 p. illus. 25 cm. [NB1270.P3P47] 73-158885 ISBN 0-7135-1718-2
1. Paper sculpture. I. Title.
Available from Transatlantic Arts, Levittown, N.Y., for 8.95 BIP

SADLER, Arthur 736.98
An introduction to paper sculpture. London, Blandford Pr. [1965] 63p. illus., port. 23cm. [NB1270.P3S3] 66-7499 2.75 bds.,
1. Paper sculpture I. Title.
Available from Branford in Newton Centre, Mass. BIP

SADLER, Arthur. 731.258
Paper sculpture. New York, Pitman Pub. Corp. [1955?] 144 p. illus. 25 cm. [TT870.S2 1955] 55-14506
1. Paper sculpture. 2. Show-windows.

SADLER, Arthur 736.9
Paper sculpture, 5th rev ed., New York, Pitman [1965] 144 p. illus., port. 26 cm. [TT870.S2] 65-619 6.75
1. Paper sculpture. 2. Show-windows. I. Title.

Paper toy making—Juvenile literature.

GOGNIAT, Maurice, 1934- 745.59'2
Wild West toys you can make / by Maurice Gogniat ; photos. by Jean-Pierre Tesson ; [translated by Maxine Hobson]. New York : Sterling Pub. Co., c1976. 32 p. : col. ill. ; 22 cm. (Easy craft series) Translation of Jeux du Far-West. Includes index. Instructions for using paper and cartons and other easily available materials to make a variety of toys with an Old West theme. [TT174.5.P3G6313] 76-609 ISBN 0-8069-5414-0 : 3.95 lib.bdg. : 3.99
1. Paper toy making—Juvenile literature. I. Tesson, Jean-Pierre. II. Title. III. Series. BIP

Paper work.

ADACHI, Katsuyuki. 736.9
A Japanese paper-folding classic; excerpt from the "lost" Kan no mada. Interpreted and edited by Julia McLean Brossman and Martin W. Brossman. Translated by Thomas K. Takeshita and Katsuyo L. Takeshita. Washington, Pinecone Press [1961] 66 p. illus. 25 cm. Includes bibliography. [TT870.A313] 60-53639
1. Paper work. I. Brossman, Julia McLean, ed. II. Brossman, Martin W., ed. III. Title.

AIREY, Graham. 736'.98
New ideas in card and paper crafts [by] Graham Airey, Ben Bates [and] Ian Price. New York, Van Nostrand Reinhold [1974, c1973] 94 p. illus. (part col.) 23 x 26 cm. Photographs and brief text present progressively more difficult ideas for paper and cardboard creations, from flat modular figures to folded and three-dimensional constructions. [TT870.A35] 71-39887 ISBN 0-442-29951-6 5.95
1. Paper work. I. Bates, Ben, joint author. II. Price, Ian, joint author. III. Title. IV. Title: Card and paper crafts.

ALKEMA, Chester Jay. 745.54
Creative paper crafts in color. New York, Sterling Pub. Co. [1967] 179 p. illus. (part col.) 21 x 25 cm. (Sterling crafts books) [GV1218.P3A37] 67-27748
1. Paper work. I. Title.

ALKEMA, Chester Jay. 745.54
Tissue paper creations. Photos. by the author. New York, Sterling Pub. Co. [1973] 48 p. illus. (part col.) 20 cm. (Little craft book series) Offers instructions for creating a variety of decorative and useful objects with tissue paper. [TT870.A38] 73-83454 ISBN 0-8069-5288-1
1. Paper work. 2. Tissue paper. I. Title. BIP

ASPDEN, George. 745.5
Model making in paper, cardboard, and metal. Photos. by Derek Abbott. New York, Reinhold Pub. Corp. [1965, 1964] 88 p. illus. (part col.) 26 cm. [TT870.A8 1965] 64-25856
1. Paper work. 2. Models and modelmaking. I. Title.

ASPDEN, George. 736'.98
One piece of card. Photos. by Derek Abbott. New York, Taplinger [1973] 95 p. illus. 22 cm. Instructions for creating sixteen three-dimensional figures form one piece of stiff paper or light cardboard. [TT870.A82 1973b] 72-7792 ISBN 0-8008-5821-2 6.50
1. Paper work. 2. Models and modelmaking. I. Title.

BECKER, Edith C 736.9
Adventures with scissors and paper; a guide for teachers of children in the middle grades. Scranton, Pa., International Textbook Co., 1959. 116p. illus. 26cm. (International textbooks in art education) [TT870.B26] 59-145651
1. Paper work. I. Title.

BODGER, Lorraine. 745.54
Paper dreams / written & illustrated by Lorraine Bodger. New York : Universe Books, 1977. 126 p., [4] leaves of plates : ill. ; 27 cm. [TT870.B57] 76-21221 ISBN 0-87663-287-8. pbk. : 5.95
1. Paper work. I. Title. BIP

BORCHARD, George. 736'.98
Paper sculpture. New York, Taplinger Pub. Co. [1973] 93 p. illus. 21 cm. [TT870.B65 1973] 72-12432 ISBN 0-8008-6257-0 6.50
1. Paper work. I. Title.

CAMPBELL, Margaret W. 736.9
Paper toy making; foreword by R. R. Tomlinson. Newton, Mass., Charles T. Brandford, 1960. 78p. illus. (part col.) 3.50
I. Title. BIP

COLLIN, Lore 745.54
Stampcraft; picture play with postage stamps. Toyko, Rutland, Vt., C. E. Tuttle [1960] 32p. illus. (part col.) 26cm. 60-8078 1.00 pap.,
1. Paper work. 2. Postage—stamps. I. Title.

CONSTAS, Dorothy, 1923- 372.5'5
Treasury of arts and crafts paper projects for the elementary school / by Dorothy Constas. West Nyack, N.Y. : Parker Pub. Co., [1977] p. cm. Includes index. [TT870.C66] 77-8712 ISBN 0-13-930586-6 : 12.95
1. Paper work. 2. Creative activities and seat work. I. Title. BIP

DOCKREE, Yvonne. 745.54
A kaleidoscope of tissue paper crafts. [St. Albans] Y. Dockree, 1972. [1], 24 p. illus. 23 cm. Cover title. [TT870.D6] 72-172554 ISBN 0-9502488-0-0 £0.38
1. Paper work. 2. Tissue paper. I. Title.

DREHMAN, Vera L., 1929- 745.54
Holiday ornaments from paper scraps [by] Vera L. Drehman. New York, Hearthside Press [1970] 189 p. illus. 25 cm. [TT870.D7] 77-92496 4.95
1. Paper work. 2. Decoration and ornament. I. Title.

EISNER, Vivienne. 745.54
Crafting with newspapers / by Vivienne Eisner & William Shisler ; drawings by Guy Brison-Stack. New York : Sterling Pub. Co., c1976. 48 p. : ill. ; 20 cm. (Little craft book series) Describes the tools, materials, and techniques for creating a variety of objects with newspapers. [TT870.E59] 76-19771 ISBN 0-8069-5368-3 : 3.75 ISBN 0-8069-5369-1 lib.bdg. : 3.99
1. Paper work. I. Shisler, William, joint author. II. Brison-Stack, Guy. III. Title. BIP

EISNER, Vivienne. 745.54
The newspaper everything book : how to make 150 useful objects from old newspapers / Vivienne Eisner and Adelle Weiss. 1st ed. New York : Dutton, 1975. 128 p. : ill. ; 28 cm. "A Sunrise book." Includes index. [TT870.E36 1975] 75-19145 ISBN 0-87690-179-8 : 4.95
1. Paper work. 2. Newsprint. I. Weiss, Adelle, joint author. II. Title.

FAWCETT, Clara Evelyn (Hallard). 391.09
Paper dolls, a guide to costume; with illus. by the author. New York, H. L. Lindquist Publications, 1951. 225 p. illus. 26 cm. [TT870.F35] 51-14967
1. Paper work. 2. Dolls. 3. Costume. I. Title.

GERLINGS, Charlotte. 745.59'2
Noah's ark in paper and card [by] Charlotte Gerlings and Suzy Ives. New York, Taplinger Pub. Co. [1974] 112 p. illus. 23 cm. [TT870.G43 1974] 73-17673 ISBN 0-8008-5578-7 7.95
1. Paper work. 2. Noah's ark. I. Title. BIP

GLASS, Frederick James, 1881-1930. 745.54
Paper craft. London, University of London Press, 1927. [Kentfield, Calif., N. K. Gregg, 1971] viii, 76 p. illus. 19 cm. (Gregg crafts series) Original ed. issued in the author's series: The artistic, practical handicraft series. [TT870.G5 1971] 73-163531 ISBN 0-912318-03-1
1. Paper work. I. Title. BIP

GROL, Lini R. 745.54
Scissorscraft. New York, Sterling Pub. Co. [1970] 48 p. illus. (part col.) 20 cm. (Little craft book series) Instructions for cutting out a variety of simple and complex figures and shapes from paper. [TT870.G76] 70-126849 ISBN 0-8069-5160-5
1. Paper work. I. Title.

HARTUNG, Rolf 745.54
Creating with corrugated paper. New York, Reinhold [1966,c.1965] 96p. illus. 22cm. (Creative play ser., 7) [TT870.H35] 66-14648 5.50 bds.,
1. Paper work. 2. Paperboard. I. Title.

HAWKESWORTH, Eric. 736'.98
Paper cutting : making all kinds of paper shapes and figures / by Eric Hawkesworth ; illustrated by Margaret and Eric Hawkesworth. New York : S. G. Phillips, [1977] 95 p. : ill. ; 24 cm. [TT870.H378 1977] 76-30461 ISBN 0-87599-224-2 : 6.50
1. Paper work. I. Title. BIP

HAWKESWORTH, Eric. 736'.98
Pleated paper folding : methods and routines for the amateur performer / by Eric Hawkesworth ; with illustrations by Margaret and Eric Hawkesworth. London : Faber, 1975. 3-104 p. : ill. ; 21 cm. [TT870.H38] 76-364018 ISBN 0-571-10625-0 : 4.95 ISBN 0-571-10882-2 pbk. : 2.95
1. Paper work. I. Title.
Distributed by Faber and Faber, Salem, N.H. BIP

HOLLANDER, Annette. 745.7
Decorative papers & fabrics. New York, Van Nostrand Reinhold Co. [1971] 119 p. illus. (part col.) 22 cm. Bibliography: p. 115-117. [TT870.H56] 73-149256
1. Paper work. 2. Dyes and dyeing—Paper. 3. Textile printing. I. Title.

HONDA, Isao, 1888- 745.54
How to make origami; the Japanese art of paper folding. New York, McDowell, Obolensky [1959] 37 p. col. illus. (part fold. mounted) 26 cm. (An Astor book, #1) 16 sheets of col. paper in pocket. [TT870.H6] 59-16149
1. Paper work. I. Title. II. Title: The Japanese art of paper folding.

HONDA, Isao, 1888- 736/.98
Mon-kiri playtime; fold and cutout fun. [Tokyo] Japan Publications; [dist. by Japan Pubns. San Francisco, 1967] 63p. illus. (pt. col.) 27cm. [GV1218.P3H58] 67-28962 2.75 bds.,
1. Paper work. I. Title.

JABLONSKI, Ramona, 1939- 736'.98
Folk art designs to color or cut from Polish wycinanki and Swiss and German Scherenschnitte / Ramona Jablonski. Owings Mills, Md. : Stemmer House, 1978. p. cm. [TT870.J29] 78-13765 ISBN 0-916144-33-X : 2.95
1. Paper work. 2. Folk art—Germany. 3. Folk art—Poland. I. Title.

JABLONSKI, Romana, 1939- 736'.98
The paper cut-out design book : a sourcebook for creating and adapting the heritage of American folk art, Polish wycinanki, Chinese hua yang, Japanese kirigami, German Scherenschnitte, and others / by Romana Jablonski. 1st ed. Owings Mills, Md. : Stemmer House, 1976. ix, 102 p. : ill. ; 31 cm. Bibliography: p. 102. [TT870.J3] 76-2467 ISBN 0-916144-03-8 : 15.95. ISBN 0-916144-04-6 pbk. : 6.95
1. Paper work. I. Title. BIP

JENSEN, Thea Bank. 745.54
Play with paper. [Translated from the Danish by Virginia Allen Jensen] New York, Macmillan, 1962. 48 p. illus. 19 x 20 cm. Tells how to fold, tear, cut and crumple paper to create imaginative toys and mobiles. [TT870.J413] AC 68
1. Paper work. I. Title. BIP

KLEIN, Louis P. 736.9
Animals to fold; an illustrated cutout alphabet book based on origami. New York, Crown [1962] unpaged. illus. 24x26cm. 62-52823 1.95 pap.,
1. Paper work. I. Title.

KRINSKY, Norman 736.98
Paper construction for children [by] Norman Krinskv. Bill Berry. New York, Reinhold [c.1966] 85p. illus. (pt. col.) 21cm. [LB1542.K7] 66-11932 6.75 bds.,
1. Paper work. I. Berry, Bill, joint author. II. Title.

KUWABARA, Minoru, 1912- 736.9
Cut and paste, by Minoru Kuwabara, Kenzo Hayashi, Takanori Kumamoto. [Tr. from Japanese and abridged by Manabu Saito. New York, Ivan Obolensky [c.1961] 48p. col. illus. 27cm. (Astor book) 61-3354 3.95
1. Paper work. I. Title.

LEEMING, Joseph, 1897-1968. 745.54
Holiday craft and fun; party-craft for holidays, including invitations, favors, decorations and centerpieces, party hats, costumes and games, easily made at home. Illustrated by Jessie Robinson. [1st ed.] Philadelphia, Lippincott [1950] 93 p. illus. 26 cm. [TT870.L42] 50-14621
1. Paper work. 2. Handicraft. 3. Children's parties. I. Title. BIP

LEWIS, Shari. 736.9
Folding paper puppets, by Shari Lewis and Lillian Oppenheimer. New York, Stein and Day; distributed by Lippincott, Philadelphia, 1962. 77 p. illus. 27 cm. [GV1218.P3L48] 62-20094
1. Paper work. I. Oppenheimer, Lillian, joint author. II. Title. BIP

MAILE, Anne. 745.54
Tie-dyed paper / Anne Maile. New York : Taplinger Pub. Co., 1975. 135 p., [8] leaves of plates : ill. (some col.) ; 26 cm. Instructions for tie dyeing paper napkins and towels, tissue, wrapping, etc. and for making these into mobiles, flowers, collages, greeting cards, and other decorative objects. [TT870.M24 1975] 74-21644 ISBN 0-8008-7702-0 : 12.95
1. Paper work. 2. Tie-dyeing. I. Title. BIP

MASSOGLIA, Elinor Tripato. 793.9
Fun-time paper folding. Pictures by George Rhoads. [Chicago] Childrens Press [1959] 31 p. illus. 25 cm. [GV1218.P3M3] 59-16084
1. Paper work. I. Title.

MUNSON, Don. 745.54
The paper book; 187 things to make [by] Don Munson and Allianora Rosse. New York, Scribner [1970] xiii, 176 p. illus. 27 cm. Directions for making nearly 200 useful and decorative items from different

kinds of paper. [TT870.M84] 77-123830 8.95
1. Paper work. I. Rosse, Allianora, joint author. II. Title. BIP

NEWMAN, Thelma R. 745.54
Paper as art and craft; the complete book of the history and processes of the paper arts [by] Thelma R. Newman, Jay Hartley Newman [and] Lee Scott Newman. New York, Crown Publishers [1973] vii, 308 p. illus. 27 cm. Bibliography: p. 296-297. [NK1520.N45] 72-96648 ISBN 0-517-50378-6 9.95
1. Paper work. 2. Design, Decorative. I. Newman, Jay Hartley, joint author. II. Newman, Lee Scott, joint author. III. Title. BIP

ODY, Kenneth 736.98
Paper folding & paper sculpture. New York, Emerson [1965, c.1964] 174p. illus. 25cm. [TT870.O37] 65-20776 4.95
1. Paper work. I. Title. BIP

PALESTRANT, Simon S 730'.92'4 1908-
Practical papercraft; over 400 useful and decorative projects for fun and profit. New York, Homecrafts [1950] vii, 120 p. illus. 25 cm. [TT870.3] 745 50-10932
1. Paper work. I. Title.

PFLUG, Betsy. 736
Funny bags. Princeton, N.J., Van Nostrand [1968] 40 p. col. illus. 27 cm. How to make an ordinary brown paper bag into an animal or caricature mask, a puppet, a party favor, a hat, or a party decoration. [PZ10.P4478Fu] AC 68
1. Paper work. 2. Paper bags. I. Title. BIP

PORTCHMOUTH, John. 745.54
All kinds of papercrafts / John Portchmouth ; with ill. by the author. New York : Viking Press, 1973, c1972. 128 p. : ill. ; 26 cm. (A Studio book) Includes index. Bibliography: p. 126. [TT870.P74 1973] 72-80264 ISBN 0-670-11386-7 : 8.95
1. Paper work. I. Title.

RITCHIE, Carson I. A. 745.54'09
Art in paper / Carson I. A. Ritchie. South Brunswick : A. S. Barnes, [1975] p. cm. Includes index. Bibliography: p. [TT870.R55] 74-9296 ISBN 0-498-01489-4 : 9.95
1. Paper work. I. Title. BIP

ROMBERG, Jenean. 372.5'044
Let's discover tissue. New York, Center for Applied Research in Education [1973] 64 p. illus. 28 cm. (Her Arts and crafts discovery units) [NK70.R65] 73-15953 ISBN 0-87628-530-2 3.95
1. Paper work. 2. Tissue paper. 3. Activity programs in education. I. Title. BIP

ROTTGER, Ernst. 736.9
Creative paper design. New York, Reinhold Pub. Corp. [1961, c1959] 95 p. (chiefly illus.) 22 cm. (His Creative play series, 1) [TT870.R6 1961] 60-16591
1. Paper work. I. Title.

ROTTGER, Ernst. 736'.98
Creative paper design. New York, Van Nostrand Reinhold Co. [1972] 95 p. illus. (part col.) 20 x 21 cm. (Creative play series) Translation of Werkstoff Papier. Demonstrates various techniques for creating designs and crafts of paper. [TT870.R6 1972] 72-191111
1. Paper work. I. Title.

SAKADE, Florence. 745.54
Origami; Japanese paper folding. [1st ed.] Tokyo, Rutland, Vt., C. E. Tuttle Co. [1957-59] 3 v. illus. 26cm. [TT870.S25] 57-10685
1. Paper work. I. Title. II. Title: Japanese paper folding.

SATTLER, Helen Roney. 745.54
Kitchen carton crafts. With diagrs. by the author. New York, Lothrop, Lee & Shepard [1970] 94 p. illus. 25 cm. Instructions for more than forty-five toys, games, party and holiday favors, and gifts made from items easily available in the home. [TT870.S284] 77-101478 3.95
1. Paper work. I. Title. BIP

SEIDELMAN, James E. 745.54
Creating with paper [by] James E. Seidelman and Grace Mintonye. Illustrated by Marjorie Borgos Blumenkopf. New York, Crowell-Collier Press [1967] 56 p. col. illus. 29 cm. Tells how to make paper stick together; how to score, pleat, fold, and make three dimensional shapes. Gives instructions for making portraits, masks, puppets, animals, mobiles, pictures, and stained glass windows out of paper. [TT870.S4] AC 67
1. Paper work. I. Mintonye, Grace, joint author. II. Blumenkopf, Marjorie Borgos, illus. III. Title. BIP

SLADE, Richard. 745.54
Take an egg box; how to make some interesting models, written, illus. by Richard Slade. London, Faber & Faber [1965] 48p. illus. 26cm. [TT870] 65-29952 3.00
1. Paper work. I. Title.
American distributor: Transatlantic, Levittown, N.Y. BIP

SPERLING, Walter, 1897- 745.54
How to make things out of paper. New York, Sterling Pub. Co. [1961] 124 p. illus. 21 cm. First published in 1955 under title: Papier-Spiele. [GV1218.P3S73] 60-14331
1. Paper work. I. Title.

STEPHAN, Barbara B. 745.54
Creating with tissue paper; design, technique, decoration, by Barbara B. Stephan. New York, Crown Publishers [1973] 248 p. illus. 27 cm. Bibliography: p. 239. [TT870.S7] 73-82486 ISBN 0-517-50579-7 8.95
1. Paper work. 2. Tissue paper. I. Title. BIP

STODDART, Brigitte. 736'.98
Papercutting. New York, Taplinger Pub. Co. [1973] 96 p. illus. 21 cm. [TT870.S74 1973] 72-5302 ISBN 0-8008-6247-3 6.50
1. Paper work. I. Title. BIP

STONE, Anne. 745.54
Paper straw craft / by Anne Stone. New York : Sterling Pub. Co., [1974] 96 p. : ill. ; 22 cm. Includes index. [TT870.S75] 74-82334 ISBN 0-8069-5312-8 : 4.95 ISBN 0-8069-5313-6 lib.bdg. : 4.89
1. Paper work. I. Title. BIP

TAKEDA, Nobuo 736.9
Paper snips. Japanese art of paper crafts. Rutland, Vt., Japan Pubns. [1963, c.1960] 29cm. col. illus. (pt. fold.) 1.95 pap.,
I. Title.

TEMKO, Florence. 736'.98
Paper: folded, cut, sculpted. Illustrated by Virginia Davidson. New York, Collier Books [1974] 192 p. illus. 26 cm. Bibliography: p. 189-190. [TT870.T46 1974] 73-2125 ISBN 0-02-616910-X 10.95
1. Paper work. I. Title.
Pbk; 5.95.

TEMKO, Florence. 736'.98
Paperfolding to begin with, by Florence Temko and Elaine Simon. Pictures by Joan Stoliar. [1st ed.] Indianapolis, Bobbs-Merrill [1968] 31 p. col. illus. 22 x 29 cm. [LB1542.T4] 67-21397
1. Paper work. I. Simon, Elaine, joint author. II. Stoliar, Joan, illus. III. Title.

TISSUE paper activities. 745.54
Worcester, Mass., Davis Publications [1971] 34 p. illus. (part col.) 20 x 27 cm. (Basic concept series, no. 1) Instruction for making collages, three-dimensional constructions, papier-mache figures, and other objects with tissue paper. [TT870.T57] 76-166219 ISBN 0-87192-037-9
1. Paper work. BIP

VOORST, Dick van. 745.54
Corrugated carton crafting. [Translated by Eric Greweldinger] New York, Sterling Pub. Co. [1970] 48 p. illus. 20 cm. (Little craft book series) Translation of Nieuwe mogelijkheden met golfkarton. Introduces some techniques in dealing with corrugated cardboard and suggests both decorative and practical objects to make such as model planes and lampshades. [TT870.V6613 1970] 71-90803 ISBN 0-8069-5138-9
1. Paper work. 2. Corrugated paperboard. I. Title. BIP

WILLIAMS, Ned 736.9
Paper folding fun [by] Robert Harbin [pseud.] Illus. by Eve Chandler, Robert Harbin. Newton Centre, Mass., C. T. Branford Co. [1961, c.1960] 102p. 26cm. 61-1564 3.75
1. Paper work. I. Title.

WILLIAMS, Ned. 736.9
Paper magic; the art of paper folding, by Robert Harbin [pseud.] Illustrated by Rolf Harris. Newton Centre, Mass., C. T. Branford Co. [1961, c1957] 103 p. illus., diagrs. 26 cm. Bibliography: p. 99-101. [TT870] 63-22929
1. Paper work. I. Title.

WOOD, Louise. 745.54
Make it with paper [by] Louise and Orvelo Wood. New York, D. McKay Co. [1970] 247 p. illus. 21 cm. Directions for making simple and elaborate decorative paper objects by using such techniques as cutting, folding, curling, scoring, embossing, and sculpturing. [TT870.W65] 73-135583 5.95
1. Paper work. I. Wood, Orvelo, joint author. II. Title. BIP

YAMADA, Sadami, 1915- 745.54
New dimensions in paper craft, [by] Sadami Yamada [and] Kiyotada Ito. [Translated by Richard L. Gage. 1st ed.] Tokyo, Rutland, Vt., Japan Publications Trading Co. [1966] 263 p. (chiefly illus.) 31 cm. [TT870.Y2513] 66-21209
1. Paper work. I. Ito, Kiyotada, 1937- joint author. II. Title.

ZARCHY, Harry. 745.54 (j)
Papercraft, written and illustrated by Harry Zarchy. Cleveland, World Pub. Co. [1966] 48 p. illus. (part col.) 20 cm. (The Little hobby bookshelf) "A Holly book." [GV1218.P3Z3 1966] 67-4847
1. Paper work. I. Title.

Paper work—China.

CHINESE cut-paper designs 736'.98
/ selected by Theodore Menten. New York : Dover Publications, 1975. 92 p. : all ill. (some col.) ; 29 cm. (Dover pictorial archive series) [NK1483.A1C46] 75-22240 ISBN 0-486-23198-4 pbk. : 3.00
1. Paper work—China. 2. Design, Decorative—China. I. Menten, Theodore. BIP

Paper work—Juvenile literature.

ALTON, Walter George. 745.59'28
Making models from paper and card / Walter G. Alton. New York : Taplinger, 1974. 95 p. : ill. ; 21 cm. Instructions for folding paper and cardboard into animals, dwellings, and people. [TT870.A45 1974] 74-170 ISBN 0-8008-5054-8 : 7.95
1. Paper work—Juvenile literature. I. Title.

BEHRENS, June. 745.54
My brown bag book / by June Behrens ; photos. by Michele and Tom Grimm. [La Puerte, Calif.] : Jay Alden, [1974] 38 p., [1] leaf of plates : col. ill. ; 22 x 27 cm. Brief text and color photographs suggest ways to turn a paper bag into a house, game, mask, snowman, purse, puppet, and many other things. [TT870.B43] 74-193368 ISBN 0-914844-03-2 lib.bdg. : 4.97
1. Paper work—Juvenile literature. 2. Paper bags—Juvenile literature. I. Grimm, Michele, ill. II. Grimm, Tom, ill. III. Title.

*BENJAMIN, Ranana. 745.54
Origami for everyone; paper folding step by step in photographs plus O-Ronni-Gami games. Blauvelt, N.Y., Biograf Books, 1973. 128 p., illus., 28 cm. [TT870] 72-86343 ISBN 0-8334-4006-3 4.95 (pbk.)
1. Paper work—Juvenile literature. I. Title.

CARD and cardboard. 745.54
New York, F. Watts [1971, c1970] 173 p. illus. 31 cm. (Color crafts) First published in 1970 under title: Working with card and cardboard. Illustrated instructions of graded difficulty for making toys, hats, and other sculptured constructions from card and cardboard. [TT870.W66 1971] 71-158980 ISBN 0-531-02002-9 5.95
1. Paper work—Juvenile literature. 2. Paperboard—Juvenile literature. I. Title. II. Series.

CHENG, Hou-Tien. 736'.98
Scissor cutting for beginners / by Cheng Hou-tien. New York : Holt, Rinehart and Winston, c1978. p. cm. Introduces paper cutting, a traditional Chinese art form developed over 2,000 years ago. [TT870.C485] 77-26776 ISBN 0-03-039941-6 : 6.50
1. Paper work—Juvenile literature. I. Title. BIP

COMINS, Jeremy. 736'.98
Slotted sculpture from cardboard / Jeremy Comins. New York : Lothrop, Lee & Shepard, c1977. 96 p. : ill. ; 25 cm. Directions for constructing animals, people, and everyday objects by slotting together ordinary cardboard. [TT870.C618] 76-30473 ISBN 0-688-41793-0 : 5.95 ISBN 0-688-51793-5 lib.bdg. : 5.21
1. Paper work—Juvenile literature. 2. Paperboard—Juvenile literature. 3. Paper sculpture—Juvenile literature. I. Title. BIP

COMINS, Jeremy. 745.59'2
Totems, decoys, and covered wagons : cardboard constructions from early American life / Jeremy Comins. New York : Lothrop, Lee & Shepard Co., c1976. 127 p. : ill. ; 24 cm. Includes index. Bibliography: p. 121-122. Directions for making large-scale, cardboard replicas of objects representative of American Indian and colonial life, such as houses, furniture, toys, and other artifacts. [TT870.C62] 75-44182 ISBN 0-688-41739-6 : 5.95 ISBN 0-688-51739-0 lib.bdg. :
1. Paper work—Juvenilc literature. 2. Indian craft—Juvenile literature. 3. United States—History—Colonial period, ca. 1600-1775—Juvenile literature. I. Title. BIP

CURTIS, Annabelle. 745.54
The knowhow book of paper fun / [written and devised by Annabelle Curtis and Judy Hindley ; illustrated by Colin King]. New York : Corwin Books, c1976. 47 p. : chiefly col. ill. ; 29 cm. (The Knowhow books) Includes index. Provides instructions for paper projects ranging from newspaper trees to paper sculpture. [TT870.C87] 75-44853 ISBN 0-8069-8036-2 : 4.50
1. Paper work—Juvenile literature. I. Hindley, Judy, joint author. II. King, Colin. III. Title. BIP

DIETRICH, Wilson G. 745.54
Create with paper bags; a book of creative art experiences using paper bags, by Wilson G. Dietrich. Minneapolis, Denison [1972] 52 p. illus. (part col.) 29 cm. Simple directions for making puppets, animals, masks, and hats from paper bags. [TT870.D5] 78-174482 ISBN 0-513-01208-7
1. Paper work—Juvenile literature. 2. Paper bags—Juvenile literature. I. Title.

EISNER, Vivienne. 745.54
A boat, a bat, and a beanie : things to make from newspaper / Vivienne Eisner & Adelle Weiss ; illustrated with drawings by Adelle Weiss, and photographs by Daniel Dorn, Jr. New York : Lothrop, Lee & Shepard Co., c1977. 92 p. : ill. ; 24 cm. Instructions for creating a variety of items from old newspaper, including a puppet, tote bag, picture frame, and building bricks. [TT870.E358] 77-493 ISBN 0-688-41789-2 : 6.50 ISBN 0-688-51789-7 lib.bdg. : 6.91
1. Paper work—Juvenile literature. I. Weiss, Adelle, joint author. II. Dorn, Daniel. III. Title. BIP

JANITCH, Valerie. 745.54
All made from paper / Valerie Janitch. New York : Viking Press, 1974. 95 p. : ill. (some col.) ; 27 cm. (A Studio book) Gives instructions and patterns for creating a variety of useful, decorative, and amusing items from paper, including collage pictures, lampshades, mobiles, flowers, and greeting cards. [TT870.J35] 74-2747 ISBN 0-670-11394-8 : 9.95
1. Paper work—Juvenile literature. I. Title.

LIDSTONE, John. 745.54
Building with cardboard. Photography by Roger Kerkham. Princeton, N.J., Van Nostrand [1968] 95 p. illus. 23 x 26 cm. Instructions for using various techniques with cardboard to produce art works such as masks, posters, sculpture, and miniature buildings. [TT870.L48] 68-54839 4.95
1. Paper work—Juvenile literature. 2. Paperboard—Juvenile literature. I. Kerkham, Roger, illus. II. Title.

NESS, Evaline. 747'.8'83
American colonial paper house : to cut out and color / designed by Evaline Ness. New York : Scribner, c1975. [40] p. : ill. ; 26 cm. Book opens to form four rooms of an eighteenth-century American house. Includes patterns for and historical notes about the furnishings. [TT870.N45] 75-8342 ISBN 0-684-14461-1 : 6.95
1. Paper work—Juvenile literature. 2. Miniature rooms—Juvenile literature. I. Title. BIP

†NESS, Evaline. 745.59'23
This is a paper palace to cut out and color / designed by Evaline Ness. New York : Scribner, c1976. 27 leaves, [3] leaves of plates : chiefly ill. ; 26 x 27 cm. Book opens to form four palace rooms that can be decorated with furnishings constructed from accompanying patterns. [TT870.N46] 76-24958 ISBN 0-684-14708-4 : 6.95
1. Paper work—Juvenile literature. 2. Miniature rooms—Juvenile literature. I. Title.

PFLUG, Betsy. 745.54
Funny bags. Philadelphia, Lippincott, 1974 [c1968] 40 p. col. illus. 26 cm. Instructions for turning an ordinary brown paper bag into an animal or caricature mask, a puppet, a party favor, a hat, a party decoration, or whatever the imagination dictates. [TT870.P49 1974] 73-21723 ISBN 0-397-31549-X 4.95
1. Paper work—Juvenile literature. 2. Paper bags—Juvenile literature. I. Title.

SEVERN, William. 745.54
50 ways to have fun with old newspapers / Bill Severen ; illustrated by Elizabeth Green. New York : D. McKay Co., c1977. p. cm. Includes index. Simple instructions accompanied by detailed drawings on how to make games, puzzles, murals, mobiles, and other decorative objects with old newspapers. [TT870.S44] 77-2422 ISBN 0-679-20402-4 : 8.95
1. Paper work—Juvenile literature. 2. Games—Juvenile literature. 3. Newspapers—Juvenile literature. I. Green, Elizabeth Brown. II. Title.

SEVERN, William. 793.9
Magic with paper, by Bill Severn. Illustrated by Katharine Wood. New York, David McKay [1974, c1962] viii, 149 p. illus. 21 cm. [GV1218.P3S4] ISBN 0-679-20294-3 2.50 (pbk.)
1. Paper work—Juvenile literature. I. Title.
L.C. card no. for original ed.: 62-7764.

SLADE, Richard. 745.5
Carton craft. New York, S. G. Phillips [1973, c1972] 63 p. illus. 26 cm. Instructions for making a variety of games and toys from such household containers as plastic bottles and cardboard boxes. [TT870.S54] 73-1953 ISBN 0-87599-196-3 5.95
1. Paper work—Juvenile literature. 2. Plastics craft—Juvenile literature. I. Title.

TEMKO, Florence. 745.54
Paper cutting. Illustrated by Steve Madison. [1st ed.] Garden City, N.Y., Doubleday [1973] 64 p. col. illus. 22 cm. These twenty-five easy-to-cut paper designs include decorations, toys, puzzles, and party tricks. [TT870.T45] 72-90028 ISBN 0-385-09432-9 4.95
1. Paper work—Juvenile literature. I. Madison, Steve, illus. II. Title. BIP

TEMKO, Florence. 745.57
Self-stick craft. Illustrated by Linda Winchester. [1st ed.] Garden City, N.Y., Doubleday 1975. 64 p. col. illus. 22 cm. Describes and suggests uses of a self-adhesive plastic for decorating a number of useful objects and toys. [TT870.T47] 73-19487 ISBN 0-385-03841-0 5.95
1. Paper work—Juvenile literature. 2. Plastics craft—Juvenile literature. I. Winchester, Linda, illus. II. Title.

THOMSON, Ruth. 745.54
Exciting things to make with paper / by Ruth Thomson ; illustrated by Carol Lawson. Philadelphia : Lippincott, [1977] p. cm. (Look and make books) Things to make with paper by folding, cutting, twisting, and sticking. Includes paper flowers, window panels, jewelry, and masks. [TT870.T53] 76-39905 ISBN 0-397-31741-7 : 4.95
1. Paper work—Juvenile literature. I. Lawson, Carol. II. Title. BIP

WEISS, Harvey. 745.54
Working with cardboard and paper / Harvey Weiss. [Reading, Mass.] : Addison-Wesley, c1978. 72 p. : ill. (some col.) ; 29 cm. (The Beginning artist's library) "A Young Scott book." Instructions for projects made from cardboard and paper. Includes houses, castles, airplanes, boats, and mobiles. [TT870.W425] 77-21860 ISBN 0-201-09342-1 lib.bdg. : 1.95
1. Paper work—Juvenile literature. 2. Paperboard—Juvenile literature. I. Title. BIP

WEISS, Peter, 1945- 745.54
Cutting up with paper; a craft book, by Peter and Carol Weiss. Illustrated by Sally Gralla. New York, Lothrop, Lee & Shepard Co. [1973] 96 p. illus. 24 cm. Simple instructions for making toys, greeting cards, mobiles, costumes, and other objects from paper. [TT870.W43] 73-4955 ISBN 0-688-41561-X 4.50
1. Paper work—Juvenile literature. I. Weiss, Carol, joint author. II. Gralla, Sally, illus. III. Title.
Library binding 4.14, ISBN 0-688-51561-4. BIP

WORKING with paper. 745.54
New York, F. Watts [1971, c1970] 191 p. illus. 31 cm. (Color crafts) Illustrated instructions for making decorative paper items such as mobiles, animals, and jewelry, are color-coded to indicate degree of difficulty. [TT870.W67 1971] 73-158978 ISBN 0-531-02003-7 5.95
1. Paper work—Juvenile literature. I. Title. II. Series. BIP

YAMADA, Sadami, 1915- 736.98
Paper playtime. [Tr. by Richard L. Gage. 1st ed. Toyko] Japan Pubns. [1966] 1v. (unpaged) illus. (pt. col.) 27cm. [GV1218.P3Y313] 66-22391 2.50 bds.,
1. Paper work—Juvenile literature. I. Title.
Available from the publisher's Rutland, Vt. office.

ZUBROWSKI, Bernie. 793.4
Things to do with milk carton building blocks / by Bernie Zubrowski ; illustrated by Otto Coontz. 1st ed. Boston : Little, Brown, c1979. p. cm. (A Children's Museum book) Directions for making three sizes of building blocks from milk cartons and for building structures commonly found in houses and buildings, including towers, furniture, and arches. [TT870.Z8] 78-27215 3.95
1. Paperwork—Juvenile literature. 2. Cartons—Juvenile literature. 3. Milk—Containers—Juvenile literature. I. Coontz, Otto. II. Title. III. Title: Milk carton building blocks. IV. Series: Boston. Children's Museum. A Children's Museum book.

Paper work—Study and teaching (Elementary)

ROMBERG, Jenean. 745.54
Let's discover paper / Jenean Romberg. New York : Center for Applied Research in Education, [1975] 64 p. : ill. ; 28 cm. (Her Arts and crafts discovery units) [TT870.R65] 75-16356 ISBN 0-87628-525-6 : 3.95
1. Paper work—Study and teaching (Elementary) I. Title. BIP

Paperboard.

GRANIT, Inga. 745.5
Cardboard crafting; how to make things out of cardboard. [Translated by Elsa Bley, adapted by Robert F. Scott] New York, Sterling Pub. Co. [1964] 96 p. illus. 22 cm. [TT870.G68 1964] 64-15108
1. Paperboard. 2. Paper work. I. Title. II. Title: How to make things out of cardboard. BIP

Paperweights.

HOLLISTER, Paul M., 1918- 748'.8
The encyclopedia of glass paperweights, by Paul Hollister, Jr. [1st ed.] New York, C. N. Potter; distributed by Crown Publishers [1969] vi, 312 p. illus. (part col.) 26 cm. Bibliography: p. 290-298. [NK5440.P3H6] 68-14080
1. Paperweights. I. Title.

JOKELSON, Paul, 1905- 748.8
Antique French paperweights. With 360 black and white illus. and 8 color plates showing the different types of paperweights by Baccarat, Clichy, and Saint-Louis. [Scarsdale? N. Y., 1955] 254p. illus., col. plates, maps. 24cm. Bibliography: p. 253. [NK5440.P3J6] 56-15131
1. Paperweights. I. Title.

MACKAY, James Alexander. 748.8
Glass paperweights [by] James MacKay. New York, Viking Press [1973] 111 p. illus. 26 cm. (A Studio book) Bibliography: p. 110-111. [NK5440.P3M28] 72-13987 ISBN 0-670-34180-0 14.00
1. Paperweights. I. Title.

Paperweights, American.

MELVIN, Jean Sutherland. 748'.8
American glass paperweights and their makers; a story of glass-paperweight craftsmen of the United States, their processes, and their products. [New York] T. Nelson [1967] 192 p. illus., 12 col. plates, ports. 26 cm. Bibliography: p. 179-182. [NK5440.P3M4] 67-22425
1. Paperweights, American. I. Title. BIP

MELVIN, Jean Sutherland. 748'.8
American glass paperweights and their makers; a story of glass-paperweight craftsmen of the United States, their processes, and their products. Rev. and enl. ed. [Camden, N.J., T. Nelson [1970] 287 p. illus. 26 cm. Bibliography: p. 275-278. [NK5440.P3M4 1970] 76-145815 15.00
1. Paperweights, American. I. Title.

Paperweights—Catalogs.

HOLLISTER, Paul M., 1918- 748'.8
Glass paperweights at Old Sturbridge Village; the J. Cheney Wells Collection, by Paul Hollister, Jr. Sturbridge, Mass., Old Sturbridge Village [1969] 52 p. (chiefly illus.) 22 cm. (Old Sturbridge Village booklet series, 27) The collection is in the Village Glass Museum. [NK5440.P3H63] 70-21428
1. Wells, Joel Cheney, 1874-1960—Art collections. 2. Paperweights—Catalogs. I. Old Sturbridge Village, Sturbridge, Mass. II. Village Glass Museum. III. Title. IV. Series.

HOLLISTER, Paul M., 1918- 748.8
Paperweights : "flowers which clothe the meadows" / Paul Hollister, Dwight P. Lanmon ; [photography, Raymond F. Errett and Nicholas L. Williams]. Corning, N.Y. : Corning Museum of Glass, c1978. 167 p. : ill. (some col.) ; 28 cm. "A special exhibition [held at] the Corning Museum of Glass, Corning, New York, April 29-October 21, 1978." [NK5440.P3H65] 77-91357 ISBN 0-87290-065-7 : 20.00
1. Paperweights—Catalogs. I. Lanmon, Dwight P., joint author. II. Corning, N.Y. Museum of Glass. III. Title. BIP

NEW York Historical Society. 748.8
Glass paperweights of the New-York Historical Society / by Paul Hollister ; photos. by H. Landshoff ; foreword by Mary Black. 1st ed. New York : C. N. Potter : distributed by Crown, [1974] xiii, 210 p. : ill. (120 col.) ; 32 cm. Includes index. [NK5440.P3N48 1974] 74-14333 ISBN 0-517-51667-5 : 25.00
1. New York Historical Society. 2. Paperweights—Catalogs. I. Hollister, Paul M., 1918- II. Landshoff, H., ill. III. Title. BIP

Paperweights—Collectors and collecting.

SELMAN, Lawrence. 748.8
Paperweights for collectors : an illustrated history and identification guide for antique and modern paperweights / Lawrence H. Selman, Linda Pope-Selman. Santa Cruz, Calif. : Paperweight Press, c1975. 171 p. : ill. (some col.) ; 29 cm. Includes index. Bibliography: p. 171. [NK5440.P3S44] 75-37108 27.50
1. Paperweights—Collectors and collecting. I. Pope-Selman, Linda, joint author. II. Title. BIP

Paperweights, French.

MANHEIM, Frank J. 748'.8
A garland of weights; some notes on collecting antique French glass paperweights for those who don't [by Frank J. Manheim] New York, 1967. 188 p. 45 col. plates. 24 cm. Bibliographical footnotes. [NK5440.P3M3 1967] 67-31618
1. Paperweights, French. 2. Paperweights—Collectors and collecting. I. Title. BIP

Paperwork.

*IVES, Suzy. 745.54
Making paper flowers and decorations. New York, Taplinger Publishing Co., [1974, c1973] 96 p., illus., 20 cm. [TT870] 73-2325 ISBN 0-8008-5057-2 7.95
1. Paperworks. I. Title. BIP

Papier-mache.

ALKEMA, Chester Jay. 745.54
Starting with papier mache / by Chester Jay Alkema ; photos. by the author. New York : Sterling Pub. Co., [1974] 48 p. : ill. (some col.) ; 20 cm. (Little craft book series) Includes index. Introduces the materials and techniques for creating a variety of objects in papier mache. [TT871.A43 1974] 73-93596 ISBN 0-8069-5298-9 : 3.50 ISBN 0-8069-5299-7 lib.bdg. : 3.69
1. Papier-mache. I. Title. BIP

ANDERSON, Mildred. 745.54
Original creations with papier mache. New York, Sterling Pub. Co. [1968, c1967] 92 p. illus. (part col.) 22 cm. (Sterling crafts books) [TS1155.A48] 67-27751
1. Papier-mache. 2. Handicraft. I. Title.

ANDERSON, Mildred. 745.54
Original creations with papier mache. New York, Sterling Pub. Co. [1968, c1967] 92 p. illus. (part col.) 22 cm. (Sterling crafts books) Briefly explaines the technique of using papier mache and gives directions for making many useful and decorative objects, such as a bead curtain, lamp shades, dishes, and a puppet theater. [TS1155.A48] AC 68
1. Papier-mache. 2. Handicraft. I. Title.

ANDERSON, Mildred 745.54
Papier mache and how to use it. New York, Sterling [c.1965] 96p. illus. 22cm. [TS1155.A5] 64-24685 3.95; 3.69 lib. ed.,
1. Papier-mache. I. Title.

ANDERSON, Mildred. 745.54
Papier mache crafts / by Mildred Anderson. New York : Sterling Pub. Co., c1975. 128 p. : ill. ; 26 cm. (Little craft book series) Material selected and adapted from the author's Original creations with papier mache, and Papier mache and how to use it. Directions for making sunglasses, jewelry, dishes, a Nativity scene, chess set, and many more things from papier mache. [TT871.A5] 75-14520 ISBN 0-8069-5338-1 : 7.95 ISBN 0-8069-5339-X lib.bdg. :
1. Papier-mache. I. Title. BIP

BETTS, Victoria Bedford, 1913- 745.54
Exploring papier-mache. [Worcester, Mass.] [Davis Press] [1955] 132 p. illus. 28 cm. [TS1155.B45] 55-7962
1. Papier-mache. I. Title.

JOHNSON, Lillian Bass, 1916- 731.258
Papier-mache. New York, D. McKay [1958] 88 p. illus. 26 cm. [NK8555.J6] 58-9802
1. Papier-mache. BIP

KENNY, Carla. 745.54
The art of paper mache [by] Carla and John B. Kenny. With drawings and photos. by the authors. [1st ed.] Philadelphia, Chilton [1968] xiv, 143 p. illus. 27 cm. [TT871.K4] 68-26488
1. Papier-mache. I. Kenny, John B., joint author. II. Title.

KENNY, Carla. 745.54
Design in papier mache, by Carla and John B. Kenny. With drawings and photographs by the authors. [1st ed.] Philadelphia, Chilton Book Co. [1971] xiv, 190 p. illus.

world) Bibl. [N2030.L6] 68-19927 6.95; 8.95 deluxe ed.,
1. Paris. Musee National du Louvre. I. Dalli Regoli, Gigetta. II. Newsweek.

*MAGI, Giovonni 708.4
Masterpieces of the Louvre and the Jeu de Paume. Florence, Bonechi, [1974] [61 p.] col. illus. 26 cm. [N2030]
1. Paris. Musee national du Louvre. I. Title.
Distributed by International Publications, N.Y. for 7.50 (pbk.). BIP

SCHNEIDER, Pierre. 701*.18
Louvre dialogues. Translated from the French by Patricia Southgate. [1st ed.] New York, Atheneum, 1971. x, 243 p. illus. 25 cm. [N1476.S35 1971] 72-135572 10.00
1. Paris. Musee national du Louvre. 2. Art criticism—Addresses, essays, lectures. 3. Art—Psychology—Addresses, essays, lectures. I. Title. BIP

Paris. Notre-Dame (Cathedral)

BOTTINEAU, Yves. 726'.6'094436
Notre-Dame de Paris and the Sainte-Chapelle. Translated by by Lovett F. Edwards [Chicago] Rand McNally [1967, c1965] 91 p. 108 illus. (part col.), plans. 24 cm. Translation of Notre-Dame de Paris et la Sainte-Chapelle. [NA5550.N7B63 1967b] 67-11464 9.95
1. Paris. Notre Dame (Cathedral) 2. Paris. Sainte-Chapelle. I. Title.

TEMKO, Allan. 726.6 726.5*
Notre-Dame of Paris New York, Viking Press, 1955. viii, 341 p. illus., map, plans. 24 cm. Bibliography: p. [316]-319. [NA5550.N7T4] 55-9643
1. Paris. Notre-Dame (Cathedral) I. Title.

TEMKO, Allan. 726.6094436
Notre-Dame of Paris. Time reading program special ed. New York, Time Inc. [c1962] New York, Barnes & Noble [1966] 343 p. illus. 21 cm. xvi, 600 p. 24 cm. "First edition 1938." Bibliography: p. [xvii] [NA5550.N7T4] [Z2009.T28] 016.32742 63-1623 66-3780
1. Paris. Notre-Dame (Cathedral) 2. Gt. Brit. — Pol. & govt. — Bibl. 3. Gt. Brit. — For. rel. — Bibl. 4. Gt. Brit. — Government publications — Bibl. I. Temperley, Harold William Vazeille, 1879-1939, ed. II. Penson, Dame Lillian Margery, 1896-1963, joint ed. III. Title. IV. Title: A century of diplomatic blue books, 1814-1914;

Paris. Notre-Dame (Cathedral). Cloture du chour.

GILLERMAN, Dorothy 730'.944'361
W.
The cloture of Notre-Dame and its role in the fourteenth century choir program / Dorothy Gillerman. New York : Garland Pub., 1977. p. cm. (Outstanding dissertations in the fine arts) Originally prresented as the author's thesis, Harvard, 1973. Bibliography: p. [NK9749.P37G54 1977] 76-23623 ISBN 0-8240-2693-4 : 37.50
1. Paris. Notre-Dame (Cathedral). Cloture du chour. 2. Wood-carving, Gothic—France—Paris. 3. Wood-carving—France—Paris. I. Title. II. Series.

Paris—Palaces—Pictorial works.

PIQUE, Jean-Pierre. 728.8'2
Parisian palaces. Written and rendered by Jean-Pierre Pigue. With an appreciation by Allison Delarue. [New York, Priv. print.] American Review Press, 1969. [44] p. illus. 29 cm. [NK2135.P57A53] 73-151365
1. Paris—Palaces—Pictorial works. I. Title.

Paris porcelain.

PLINVAL de Guillebon, 738.2'7
Begine de.
Porcelain of Paris, 1770-1850. Translated by Robin R. Charleston. New York, Walker [1972] 361 p. illus. (part col.) 29 cm. Bibliography: p. 351-353. [NK4399.P33P55 1972] 72-80541 ISBN 0-8027-0395-X 35.00
1. Paris porcelain. I. Title. BIP

Paris. Saint-Sulpice (Church)

SPECTOR, Jack J. 759'.4
The murals of Eugene Delacroix at Saint-Sulpice [by] Jack J. Spector. New York, College Art Association of America, 1967. 171 p. illus. (part col.) 28 cm. (Monographs on archaeology and the fine arts, 16) Revision of the author's thesis, Columbia University. Includes bibliographical references. [ND553.D33S63 1967] 67-30384
1. Delacroix, Eugene, 1798-1863. 2. Paris. Saint-Sulpice (Church) I. Title. II. Series. BIP

Paris. Sainte-Chapelle.

BRANNER, Robert. 729'.8
The painted medallions in the Sainte-Chapelle in Paris. Philadelphia, American Philosophical Society, 1968. 42 p. illus. 30 cm. (Transactions of the American Philosophical Society, new ser., v. 58, pt. 2) Bibliographical footnotes. [Q11.P6 vol. 58, pt. 2] 68-19147
1. Paris. Sainte-Chapelle. 2. Paintings—Expertising. I. Title. II. Series: American Philosophical Society, Philadelphia. Transactions, new ser., v. 58, pt. 2 BIP

Paris. Salon.

THE Impressionists and 709'.44
the Salon (1874-1886) honoring the centennial of the first impressionist exhibition. California collections. An exhibition organized by the students in the Department of the History of Art, University of California, Riverside. [Riverside, Calif., 1974] 1 v. (unpaged) illus., col. plates. 26 cm. Catalog of a loan exhibition held at the Los Angeles County Museum of Art, Apr. 16-May 12, 1974, and at the Gallery, University of California, Riverside, May 20-June 20, 1974. Errata slip inserted. Includes bibliographies. [N6847.5.I4144] 74-176327
1. Paris. Salon. 2. Impressionism (Art)—Exhibitions. 3. Impressionism (Art)—France. 4. Art, Modern—19th century—France. I. California. University, Riverside. Dept. of the History of Art. II. Los Angeles Co., Calif. Museum, Los Angeles. III. California. University, Riverside. Art Gallery.

Paris—Theaters.

MOYNET, J. 792'.0944
French theatrical production in the nineteenth century = L'envers du theatre / by M. J. Moynet ; translated and augmented by Allan S. Jackson, with M. Glen Wilson ; edited by Marvin A. Carlson. [Binghamton, N.Y.] : Max Reinhardt Foundation with the Center for Modern Theatre Research, 1976. xiv, 239 p. : ill. ; 29 cm. (Rare books of the theatre series ; no. 10) Includes index. Bibliography: p. 235. [PN2087.F5M613] 76-8313
1. Paris—Theaters. 2. Theaters—Stage-setting and scenery. 3. Stage machinery. I. Jackson, Allan S. II. Wilson, Mardis Glen, 1923- III. Title. IV. Series: Books of the theatre series ; no. 10.

Park, David, 1911-1960.

CALIFORNIA. University. 759.13
Committee for Arts and Lectures.
David Park memorial exhibition; the university years, 1955-1960. Organized and presented by the Committee for Arts and Lectures, University of California. Circulated by the Intercampus Cultural Exchange Committee, University of California. [Berkeley, Printed by the University of California Print. Dept., 1964] 1 v. (unpaged) illus. (part col.) 26 cm. Catalog, prepared by Alice Erskine, of an exhibition held at University Art Gallery, University of California, Berkeley, October 6 through November 8, 1964: Dickson Art Center, University of California, Los Angeles, November 15 through December 20, 1964; Art Gallery, University of California, Santa Barbara, March 2 through March 28, 1965. [ND237.P24C3] 67-65160
1. Park, David, 1911-1960. I. Erskine, Alice. II. California. University. Art Museum. III. Dickson Art Center. IV. California. University, Santa Barbara. Art Gallery. V. Title.

PARK, David, 1911-1960. 759.13
David Park. [San Francisco] Maxwell Galleries [1970] 27 p. illus. (part col.) 28 cm. Label mounted on t.p.: Supplied by Worldwide Books, Boston. Catalogue of a retrospective exhibition, Aug. 14-Sept. 26, 1970. [ND237.P24A43] 78-21903
I. Maxwell Galleries.

Parker, Raymond, 1922—

WASHINGTON, D.C. Gallery 759.13
of Modern Art.
Ray Parker. [Exhibition. Washington, 1966] 23 p. illus. (part col.) 27 cm. "November 5 to December 31, 1966, Washington Gallery of Modern Art, Washington, D.C.; January 20 to March 5, 1967, San Francisco Museum of Art, San Francisco, California; April 23 to May 21, 1967, University Art Museum, University of New Mexico, Albuquerqoe." Text by Gerald Nordland. Bibliography: p. 18-19. [ND237.P252W3] 66-30159
1. Parker, Raymond, 1922- I. Nordland, Gerald. II. San Francisco. Museum of Art. III. New Mexico. University. Art Museum.

Parks.

FRENCH, Jere Stuart. 711'.558
Urban green; city parks of the Western World. Dubuque, Iowa, Kendall/Hunt Pub. Co. [1973] xi, 129 p. illus. 22 x 28 cm. At head of title: City parks of the Western World. Bibliography: p. 129. [SB481.F66] 73-83081 ISBN 0-8403-0755-1
1. Parks. 2. Cities and towns. 3. Landscape architecture. I. Title. II. Title: City parks of the Western World.

RUTLEDGE, Albert J. 712'.5
Anatomy of a park; the essentials of recreation area planning and design [by] Albert J. Rutledge. Illus. by Donald J. Molnar. New York, McGraw-Hill [1971] x, 180 p. illus., plans. 24 cm. Bibliography: p. 173-176. [SB481.R86] 78-141925 ISBN 0-07-054347-X
1. Parks. 2. Landscape architecture. I. Title.

Parks, Charles C., 1922—

BRANDYWINE River 730'.92'2
Museum.
Three sculptors of American realism: Charles Parks, Eric Parks, Christopher Parks. Essay: Michael Richman. Photography: A. Cypen Lubitsh. Chadds Ford, Pa. [1973] 63 p. illus. (part col.) 26 cm. Catalog of an exhibition. [NB237.P27B72] 73-84334
1. Parks, Charles C., 1922- 2. Parks, Eric. 3. Parks, Christopher. 4. Realism in art. I. Parks, Charles C., 1922- II. Parks, Eric. III. Parks, Christopher. IV. Richman, Michael. V. Title.

Parks—England—Hampshire.

TURNER, Barbara D. 712'.5'094227
M. Carpenter.
Open spaces open to the public in Hampshire; text by Barbara Carpenter Turner. 2d ed. Winchester, Hampshire County Council, 1966. [3], 45 p. illus., maps (some col.), diagrs. 27 x 21 cm. Bibliography: p. 2-3. [SB484.G7T85 1966] 68-113257 5/-
1. Parks—England—Hampshire. 2. Open spaces—Hampshire, Eng. I. Hampshire, Eng. County Council. II. Title.

Parks, Gordon, 1912- —Juvenile literature.

HARNAN, Terry. 770'.92'4 B
Gordon Parks: Black photographer and film maker. Illustrated by Russell Hoover. Champaign, Ill., Garrard Pub. Co. [1972] 96 p. illus. (part col.) 24 cm. (Americans all) A brief biography of the man who overcame many obstacles to become a renowned photographer and film maker. [TR140.P35H37] 92 76-182846 ISBN 0-8116-4572-X
1. Parks, Gordon, 1912- —Juvenile literature. I. Hoover, Russell, illus. II. Title.

TURK, Midge. 770'.924
Gordon Parks. Illus. by Herbert Danska. New York, T. Y. Crowell [1973, c.1971] 33 p. illus. (pt. col.) 23 cm. (Crowell crocodile) (Crowell biographies) An easy-to-read biography of the black man who became a well-known photographer and author. [TR140.P35T8 1971] [92] 75-113857 ISBN 0-690-33794-9 0.95 (pbk.)
1. Parks, Gordon, 1912- —Juvenile literature. I. Danska, Herbert, illus. II. Title.

Parks—History.

CHADWICK, George F. 712.509
The park and the town; public landscape in the 19th and 20th centuries [by] George F. Chadwick. New York, F. A. Praeger [1966] 388 p. illus., plans. 26 cm. Bibliography: p. [379]-383. [SB481.C5] 66-26019
1. Parks—History. 2. Landscape gardening. I. Title.

Parks—Juvenile literature.

RESSNER, Philip. 712'.5
The park in the city. Photos. by Bill Binzen. [1st ed.] New York, Dutton [1971] [32] p. illus. 27 cm. Describes those things that are particularly pleasant about a city park. [PZ10.R3354Par] 70-133111 ISBN 0-525-36620-2 3.95
1. Parks—Juvenile literature. I. Binzen, Bill, illus. II. Title.

Parks — Kentucky.

WELLS, Joseph 719.3209769
William, 1881-
Kentucky parks, by J. W. Wells. [Nashville, Tenn., 1966] 181, [2] p. illus., port. 19 cm. "Home in the Cumberlands" and "Home and mother" (both in close score) p. [181]-183] [F449.3.W4] 66-8404
1. Parks — Kentucky. I. Title.

Parks—Maine.

MAINE. State Park 719.352
Commission.
Report. [Augusta] v. 23 cm. [SB482.M2] 51-622110
1. Parks—Maine. I. Title.

Parks—Management.

DOELL, Charles Edward, 711.558
1894-
Elements of park and recreation administration. Minneapolis, Burgess Pub. Co. [1963] 340 p. illus. 23 cm. [SB481.D59] 63-13049
1. Parks—Management. I. Title: Park and recreation administration. BIP

Parks—Minnesota.

MINNESOTA. Division of state 719
parks.
The Minnesota state park and recreational area plan. [Minneapolis] 1939. x, 158p. incl. illus. (incl. maps, plan) tables, diagrs. fold. maps. 37cm. 'This report embodies the findings and recommendations of the Division of state parks of the Department of conservation.'--p. iv. [SB482.M6A5 1939] 39-28393
1. Parks—Minnesota. 2. Recreation areas—Minnesota. 3. Minnesota—Public lands. I. Title.

MINNESOTA. Division of 719.32
State Parks.
Minnesota State parks; memorials, recreational reserves, waysides and monuments. Designed and illustrated by Tom Kelly. St. Paul, 1948. 51p. illus. 19cm. On cover: State parks of Minnesota. [SB482.M6A5 1948] A48
1. Parks—Minnesota. I. Title.

Parks—Planning.

CHRISTIANSEN, Monty L., 1941- 711'.558
Park planning handbook : fundamentals of physical planning for parks and recreation areas / Monty L. Christiansen ; ill. by James R. DeTuerk. New York : Wiley, c1977. p. cm. Includes bibliographies and indexes. [SB481.C53] 76-51844 ISBN 0-471-15619-1 : 14.95
1. Parks—Planning. 2. Recreation areas—Planning. I. Title. BIP

ORR, James F. 016.3092'08 s
Neighborhood park planning / James F. Orr. Monticello, Ill. : Council of Planning Librarians, 1978. 27 p. ; 28 cm. (Exchange bibliography - Council of Planning Librarians ; 1553) Cover title. [Z5942.C68 no. 1553] [SB481] 712'.5 78-106282 pbk. : 2.50
1. Parks—Planning. 2. Parks—Planning—Bibliography. I. Title. II. Series: Council of Planning Librarians. Exchange bibliography ; 1553.

Parks—United States.

FABOS, Julius Gy. 712'.0924 B
Frederick Law Olmsted, Sr.; founder of landscape architecture in America [by] Julius Gy. Fabos, Gordon T. Milde, & V. Michael Weinmayr. [Amherst] University of Massachusetts Press, 1968. 114 p. illus. (part fold.), maps, plans, ports. 26 cm. [SB470.O5F32] 68-19670 12.00
1. Olmsted, Frederick Law, 1822-1903. 2. Parks—United States. I. Milde, Gordon T., joint author. II. Weinmayr, V. Michael, joint author.

Parks—United States—History—Juvenile literature.

NOBLE, Iris. 712'.092'4 B
Frederick Law Olmsted, park designer. New York, J. Messner [1974] 190 p. 21 cm. Bibliography: p. 185-186. A biography of the nineteenth-century park and city planner and conservationist who designed New York's Central Park, among countless others, and was instrumental in the creation of the National Park Service. [SB470.O5N62] 92 74-7585 ISBN 0-671-32675-9 5.95
1. Olmsted, Frederick Law, 1822-1903—Juvenile literature. 2. Parks—United States—History—Juvenile literature. 3. Landscape architecture—United States—History—Juvenile literature. I. Title.
Library binding; 5.29, ISBN 0-671-3267-7.

Parks—United States—Juvenile literature.

JOHNSTON, Johanna. 712'.092'4 B
Frederick Law Olmsted : partner with Nature / Johanna Johnston. New York : Dodd, Mead, [1975] 125 p. ; 24 cm. Includes index. Bibliography: p. 121-122. A biography of the self-taught landscape architect who designed many large park systems, including the first large city park in America, Central Park in New York. [SB470.O5J63] 92 74-25519 ISBN 0-396-07079-5 : 4.95
1. Olmsted, Frederick Law, 1822-1903—Juvenile literature. 2. Parks—United States—Juvenile literature. 3. Landscape architecture—United States—Juvenile literature. I. Title. BIP

Parma. San Giovanni Evangelista (Church)

GHIDIGLIA Quintavalle, Augusta. 759.5
Correggio; the frescoes in San Giovanni Evangelista in Parma. Pref. by Roberto Longhi. [Translated by Olga Ragusa] New York, H. N. Abrams [1964?] 61 p. illus. (1 mounted col.) facsim., 42 col. plates. 33 cm. Translation of Gil affreschi del Correggio in San Giovanni Evangelista a Parma. Bibliographical references included in "Notes" (p. 59-60) Bibliography: p. 61. [ND623.C7G513] 64-10758
1. Correggio, Antonio Allegri, known as, 1494-1534. 2. Parma. San Giovanni Evangelista (Church) I. Longhi, Roberto, 1390- . II. Title.

Parrish, Maxfield, 1870-1966.

BRANDYWINE River Museum. 759.13
Maxfield Parrish, master of make-believe : an exhibition, June 1 through September 2, 1974. Chadds Ford, Pa. : Brandywine River Museum, [1974] 47 p. : ill. ; 23 cm. [ND237.P25213B72 1974] 74-81079
1. Parrish, Maxfield, 1870-1966. I. Parrish, Maxfield, 1870-1966. II. Title.

KNOX, Harold. 016.741'092'4
Collector's guide to Maxfield Parrish / by Harold Knox. Limited ed. W. Lebanon, N.H. : Knox, c1972. 32 p. : ill. ; 28 cm. [NE539.P34K56] 75-319989
1. Parrish, Maxfield, 1870-1966. 2. Prints—Collectors and collecting. I. Title.

LUDWIG, Coy, 1939- 741'.092'4
Maxfield Parrish. [New York, Watson-Guptill Publications [1973] 223 p. illus. (part col.) 32 cm. Bibliography: p. [220] [NC975.5.P37L82] 73-5691 ISBN 0-8230-3897-1 25.00
1. Parrish, Maxfield, 1870-1966.

PARRISH, Maxfield, 1870-1966. 741.9'73
"In the beginning" : twenty-five Maxfield Parrish drawings from the Men's Day Life Class at the Pennsylvania Academy of the Fine Arts, 1892-1894 / compiled by Virginia Hunt Reed. [s.l. : s.n., c1976] ([Hartford, Vt. : Imperial Printers]) ix, 25 p. : chiefly ill. ; 28 cm. Bibliography: p. ix. [NC139.P29R43] 77-355245 15.00
1. Parrish, Maxfield, 1870-1966. 2. Nude in art. I. Reed, Virginia Hunt. II. Pennsylvania Academy of the Fine Arts, Philadelphia. III. Title.

PARRISH, Maxfield, 1870-1966. 741'.092'4
The Maxfield Parrish poster book. With an introd. by Maurice Sendak. New York, Harmony Books [1974] 47 p. col. illus. 41 cm. [NC1850.P37A53] 73-88217 ISBN 0-517-51402-8 5.95 (pbk.).
1. Parrish, Maxfield, 1870-1966. I. Title. BIP

SWEENEY, Marian S. 759.13
Maxfield Parrish prints : a collector's guide / by Marian S. Sweeney ; [introd. by William Morgan]. Dublin, N.H. : W. L. Bauhan, 1974. xx, 137 p., [8] leaves of plates : ill. ; 22 cm. Includes index. Bibliography: p. 114-120. [NE539.P34S93] 73-81165 ISBN 0-87233-029-X : 4.95
1. Parrish, Maxfield, 1870-1966. 2. Prints—Collectors and collecting. I. Title. BIP

Party decorations.

MCCANN, Karen Carlson. 745.59
Party and holiday decorations you can make, by Karen Carlson McCann with Sue T. Garmon. Drawings and photos. by Karen Carlson McCann. [1st ed.] Garden City, N.Y., Doubleday, 1970. xi, 94 p. illus. 24 cm. [TT900.P3M3] 70-111177 4.95
1. Party decorations. 2. Holiday decorations. I. Garmon, Sue T., joint author. II. Title.

Party decorations—Juvenile literature.

WILLIAMS, Barbara. 745.59'41
Cookie craft : no-bake designs for edible party favors and decorations / by Barbara Williams and Rosemary Williams. New York : Holt, Rinehart & Winston, [1977] p. cm. Directions for creating forty-five party favors and decorations from commercially prepared cookies. [TT900.P3W54] 77-3184 6.95
1. Party decorations—Juvenile literature. 2. Holiday decorations—Juvenile literature. 3. Cookies—Juvenile literature. I. Williams, Rosemary, joint author. II. Title. BIP

WILLIAMS, Barbara. 745.59'41
Cookie craft : no-bake designs for edible party favors and decorations / Barbara Williams and Rosemary Williams ; illustrated with photos. by Barbara Williams. New York : Holt, Rinehart, and Winston, [1979] c1977. p. cm. (Holt owlet) Includes index. Directions for creating 45 party favors and decorations from commercially prepared cookies. [TT900.P3W54 1979] 79-10356 ISBN 0-03-048971-7. : 3.50
1. Party decorations—Juvenile literatures. 2. Holiday decorations—Juvenile literature. 3. Cookies—Juvenile literature. I. Williams, Rosemary, joint author. II. Title.

Pasadena, Calif.—Buildings.

SILLO, Terry. 917.94'93
Around Pasadena : an architectural study / Terry Sillo & John Manion ; photography by Terry Sillo. Pasadena, Calif. : Gallery Productions, c1976. 69 p. : ill. ; 22 x 26 cm. Includes index. Bibliography: p. 67. [NA735.P39S54] 76-373086 8.50
1. Pasadena, Calif.—Buildings. 2. Architecture—Pasadena, Calif.—Guide-books. I. Manion, John, joint author. II. Title.

Pascin, Jules, 1885-1930.

DIEHL, Gaston. 760'.0924
Pascin. [Translated from the French by Rosalie Siegel] New York, Crown Publishers [1968] 94, [1] p. illus. (part col.), ports. (part col.) 29 cm. Bibliography: p. 94-[95] [ND893.P3D53] 68-9080 3.50
1. Pascin, Jules, 1885-1930.

FREUDENHEIM, Tom L. 759.4
Pascin, by Tom L. Freudenheim. Schedule of the exhibition, 1966/1967: November 15/December 18, University Art Museum, University of California, Berkeley [and others. Berkeley, c1966] 1 v. (unpaged) illus. (part col.) 22 cm. [ND893.P3F7] 66-64727
1. Pascin, Jules, 1835-1930. I. California. University. Art Museum. II. Title.

PASCIN, Jules, 1885-1930. 741.973
Pascin: 110 drawings. Selected, edited and introduced by Alfred Werner. [Magnolia, Mass.] [Peter Smith] [1973 c.1972] xviii p., 109 p. plates, 29 cm. (Dover paperback rebound) [NC302.P37A53 1972] 71-154346 ISBN 0-486-20299-2 5.00
I. Title.

PASCIN, Jules [Real name: Julius Pincas] 1885-1930 759.4
Pascin, by Alfred Warner. New York, Abrams [1962] 32, [89]p. illus., plates (pt. col.) 36cm. 59-6940 17.50
I. Werner, Alfred, 1911- II. Title. BIP

Paste jewelry.

LEWIS, Malcolm David Samuel. 739.27
Antique paste jewellery [by] M. D. S. Lewis. [1st American ed.] Boston, Boston Book and Art [1970] 80, 48 p. illus., facsim., plates (part col.), port. 26 cm. ([Faber collectors library]) Bibliography: p. 78. [NK7406.L4 1970b] 78-124159 10.95
1. Paste jewelry. I. Title.

Pastel drawing.

CSOKA, Stephen, 1897- 741.23
Pastel painting. New York, Reinhold Pub. Corp. [1962] 128 p. illus. (part col.) 26 cm. [NC880.C76] 62-8986
1. Pastel drawing.

GREENE, Daniel E. 741.2'35
Pastel, by Daniel E. Greene. Edited by Joe Singer. New York, Watson-Guptill Publications [1974] 159 p. illus. (part col.) 29 cm. Bibliography: p. 157. [NC880.G74] 74-13740 ISBN 0-8230-3899-8
1. Pastel drawing. I. Title. BIP

HENDERSON, Keith, 1883- 741.23
Pastels. London, New York, Studio Publications [1952] 96 p. illus. 26 cm. (The How to do it series, no. 43 [i. e. 44]) [NC880.H4] 52-7388
1. Pastel drawing.

LALIBERTE, Norman. 741.2
Pastel, charcoal, and chalk drawing; history, classical and contemporary techniques [by] Norman Laliberte, Alex Mogelon [and] Beatrice Thompson. New York, Van Nostrand Reinhold Co. [1973] 105 p. (chiefly illus., part col.) 21 cm. (An Art horizons book) [NC880.L34] 72-165927 ISBN 0-442-34603-4 8.95
1. Pastel drawing. 2. Charcoal-drawing. 3. Blackboard drawing. I. Mogelon, Alex, joint author. II. Thompson, Beatrice Terzian, joint author. III. Title.

MERRIOTT, Jack 741.23
Drawing and painting in pastel. Princeton, N.J., Van Nostrand [1964, c.1963] xii, 84p. illus., plates (pt. col.) 26cm. 64-2166 5.75
1. Pastel drawing. I. Title.

RICHMOND, Leonard. 741.2'35
Fundamentals of pastel painting, by Leonard Richmond and J. Littlejohns. New York, Watson-Guptill Publications [1970] 143 p. illus. (part col.) 29 cm. 1931 and 1963 editions published under title: The technique of pastel painting. Bibliography: p. 141. [NC880.R522 1970] 70-98151 15.00
1. Pastel drawing. 2. Pastels. I. Littlejohns, John, 1874- joint author. II. Title. BIP

RICHMOND, Leonard. 741.23
The technique of pastel painting, by Leonard Richmond and J. Littlejohns. [Abridged ed.] New York, Pitman Pub. Corp. [1963] 79 p. illus. 26 cm. [NC880.R522] 63-4418
1. Pastel drawing. 2. Pastels. I. Littlejohns, John, 1874- joint author. II. Title.

SAVAGE, Ernest. 741.2'35
Painting landscapes in pastel. New York, Watson-Guptill Publications [1971] 175 p. illus. (part col.) 29 cm. Bibliography: p. 173. [NC880.S34 1971] 76-154027 ISBN 0-8230-2610-8 12.50
1. Pastel drawing. 2. Landscape in art. I. Title.

SAVAGE, Ernest. 741.235
Pastels for beginners. London, Studio Vista; New York, Watson-Guptill [1966] 96 p. illus., 8 plates (incl. 4 col.) 19 cm. 10/6(B 66-8002) Bibliography: p. 95. [NC880.S35 1966] 66-13005
1. Pastel drawing. I. Title.

SEARS, Elinor Lathrop, 1902- 741.2'35
Pastel painting step by step. New York, Watson-Guptill Publications [1968] 175 p. illus. (part col.) 29 cm. Bibliography: p. 171. [NC880.S37 1968] 68-12402
1. Pastel drawing. I. Title.

SINGER, Joe, 1923- 743'.4
How to paint portraits in pastel. New York, Watson-Guptill Publications [1972] 175 p. illus. (part col.) 29 cm. [NC880.S5] 70-190519 ISBN 0-8230-2465-2 12.50
1. Pastel drawing. 2. Portrait drawing. I. Title. BIP

Pastel drawing—Juvenile literature.

HAWKINSON, John, 1912- 741.2 (j)
Pastels are great! Chicago, A. Whitman [1968] 48 p. illus. (part col.) 24 cm. [NC880.H36 1968] 68-22193
1. Pastel drawing—Juvenile literature. I. Title. BIP

Patchen, Kenneth, 1911-1972.

PATCHEN, Kenneth, 1911- 759.13
Kenneth Patchen: painter of poems. [Baltimore, Printed by Garamond/Pridemark Press, c1969] 48 p. illus. (part col.) 25 cm. Label mounted on t.p.: Supplied by Worldwide Books, Boston. Catalog of the exhibition held Dec. 12, 1969-Jan. 18, 1970 at the Corcoran Gallery of Art, Washington, D.C. [ND237.P254A47] 74-112061
I. Corcoran Gallery of Art, Washington, D.C. II. Title.

PATCHEN, Kenneth, 1911-1972. 709'.2'4
The argument of innocence : a selection from the picture works of Kenneth Patchen / [edited] by Peter Veres ; introd. by Miriam Patchen. San Francisco : Scrimshaw Press, [1975] p. cm. Bibliography: p. [N6537.P27V47] 75-9695 ISBN 0-912020-39-3 : 17.50
1. Patchen, Kenneth, 1911-1972. I. Veres, Peter, 1938- II. Title. BIP

Patchwork.

BOGEN, Constance. 746.4'6
A beginner's book of patchwork, applique,

and quilting. New York, Dodd, Mead [1974] 159 p. illus. 25 cm. [TT835.B55] 73-11989 ISBN 0-396-06863-4 4.95
1. Patchwork. 2. Quilting. 3. Applique. I. Title. BIP

CHATTERTON, Pauline. 746.4
Patchwork & applique / Pauline Chatterton. New York : Dial Press, 1977, c1976. xiii, 214 p., [4] leaves of plates : ill. ; 19 x 26 cm. [TT835.C44 1977] 76-47513 ISBN 0-8037-6854-0 : 14.95 pbk. : 7.95
1. Patchwork. 2. Applique. I. Title. BIP

*DITTRICK, Mark. 746.4'6
Patchwork, plain & fancy / Mark Dittrick & Susan Morrow. New York : Berkley Pub. Corp., 1976c1973. 171p. : ill. ; 20 cm. (A Berkley Windhover book) [TT835] ISBN 0-425-03194-2 pbk. : 2.95
1. Patchwork. 2. Quilted goods. 3. Quilting. I. Morrow, Susan, joint author. II. Title. BIP

DUDLEY, Taimi. 746.4'6
Seminole patchwork variations / by Taimi Dudley. New York : Drake Publishers, 1978. p. cm. Includes index. [TT835.D84] 78-56893 ISBN 0-8473-1777-3 pbk. : 6.95
1. Patchwork. 2. Seminole Indians—Costume and adornment. 3. Indians of North America—Florida—Costume and adornment. I. Title.

GAMMELL, Alice I. 746.4'6
Polly Prindle's book of American patchwork quilts, by Alice I. Gammell. New York, Grosset & Dunlap [1973] 238 p. illus. 26 cm. [TT835.G35] 72-92371 ISBN 0-448-01332-0 12.95
1. Patchwork. I. Title. II. Title: Book of American patchwork quilts.

GRAFTON, Carol Belanger. 746.9'7
Geometric patchwork patterns : full-size cut-outs and instructions for 12 quilts / Carol Belanger Grafton. New York : Dover Publications, 1975. 63 p. : ill. ; 28 cm. [TT835.G7 1975] 74-31894 ISBN 0-486-23183-6 pbk. : 2.00
1. Patchwork. 2. Quilting. I. Title. BIP

GREEN, Sylvia, 1915- 746.4'6
Patchwork for beginners. New York, Watson-Guptill [1972, c1971] 104 p. illus. (part col.) 24 cm. Bibliography: p. 102. [TT835.G74 1972] 72-190514 ISBN 0-8230-3925-0 7.95
1. Patchwork. I. Title. BIP

GREEN, Sylvia, 1915- 746.4'6
Patchwork for beginners. London, Studio Vista, 1971. 104 p. illus. (some col.) 19 cm. (A Pocket how to do it) Bibliography: p. 102. [TT835.G74 1971] 72-185237 ISBN 0-289-70091-4
1. Patchwork. I. Title.
7.95, ISBN 0-8230-3925-0. Available from Watson-Guptill.

HELLEGERS, Louisa Bumagin. 746.4'6
Pictures in patchwork / Marie-Janine Solvit ; photos. from Elle ; [translated by Walter A. Simson ; adapted by Louisa B. Hellegers]. English language ed. New York : Sterling Pub. Co., c1977. 112 p. : ill. (some col.) ; 24 cm. Adaptation of M.-J. Solvit's Le patchwork. Includes index. [TT835.H44] 76-51189 ISBN 0-8069-5380-2 : 8.95 ISBN 0-8069-5381-0 lib. bdg. : 8.59
1. Patchwork. 2. Fabric pictures. I. Solvit, Marie-Janine. Le patchwork. II. Title. BIP

IVES, Suzy. 746.4'6
Ideas for patchwork. Newton Centre, Mass., C. T. Branford Co. [1974] 112 p. illus. 23 cm. [TT835.I9] 74-597 ISBN 0-8231-5042-9 6.50
1. Patchwork. I. Title. BIP

JARNOW, Jill. 746.4'6
The patchwork point of view / Jill Jarnow. New York : Simon and Schuster, [1975] 157 p. : ill. ; 25 cm. Bibliography: p. 157. [TT835.J37] 74-26974 ISBN 0-671-21957-X : 8.95
1. Patchwork. 2. Applique. I. Title. BIP

LANE, Maggie. 746.9'2
Maggie Lane's Oriental patchwork. New York : Scribner, [1978] p. cm. Includes index. Bibliography: p. [TT835.L33] 78-7957 ISBN 0-684-15621-0 : 16.95
1. Patchwork. 2. Clothing and dress. I. Title. II. Title: Oriental patchwork. BIP

LOBLEY, Priscilla. 746.4'6
Your book of patchwork / by Priscilla Lobley ; photos. by Robert Lobley. New York : Taplinger Pub. Co., [1975] c1974. 74 p. : ill. ; 17 x 22 cm. (The Your book series) [TT835.L6 1975] 74-6048 ISBN 0-8008-8760-3 : 6.50
1. Patchwork. I. Title. BIP

MARSTON, Doris E. 746.4'6
Exploring patchwork [by] Doris E. Marston. [1st U.S. ed.] Newton Centre, Mass., C. T. Branford Co. [1972] 66 p. illus. 21 cm. Bibliography: p. [65]-66. [TT835.M37 1972] 72-83840 4.75
1. Patchwork. I. Title. BIP

NIELD, Dorothea. 746.4'6
Adventures in patchwork / Dorothea Nield. London : Mills & Boon, 1975. 84 p., [2] leaves of plates : ill. (some col.) ; 22 cm. Bibliography: p. 83. [TT835.N5 1975] 75-320811 ISBN 0-263-05591-4 : 5.50
1. Patchwork. I. Title.
Distributed by Transatlantic BIP

SVENNAS, Elsie. 746.4'6
Patchcraft; designs, material, technique. New York, Van Nostrand Reinhold [1972] 96 p. illus. (part col.) 22 cm. Translation of Led med lappar. Describes the necessary materials and techniques for making patchwork designs. [TT835.S8413] 73-183494 ISBN 0-442-08085-9
1. Patchwork. I. Title.

*TIMMINS, Alice. 746.4'6
Patchwork simplified. New York, Arco Publishing Co. [1973] 96 p. illus. (part col.) 22 x 21 cm. Bibliography: p. 95. [TT835] 73-79197 ISBN 0-668-03321-5 5.95
1. Patchwork. I. Title. BIP

Patchwork—Exhibitions.

RHODE Island School 746.4'6'09754 of Design, Providence. Museum of Art.
Mountain artisans; an exhibition of patchwork and quilting, Appalachia. Photos., films and collected music by John Cohen. [Providence, 1970] 1 v. (unpaged) illus. 18 x 22 cm. Catalog of the exhibition held Oct. 1-25, 1970. Includes a bibliography. [TT835.R46] 78-22316
1. Patchwork—Exhibitions. 2. Quilting—Exhibitions. 3. Needlework—Appalachian region—Exhibitions. I. Title.

Patchwork—Juvenile literature.

CHOATE, Judith. 746.4'6
Patchwork / by Judith Choate and Jane Green ; ill. by Carol Inouye. 1st ed. Garden City, N.Y. : Doubleday, [1975] p. cm. Describes the supplies and stiches used in making patchwork handicraft. Includes instructions for such projects as jean pocket, skirt, sneakers, pillows, and wall hangings. [TT835.C46] 74-33982 ISBN 0-385-09680-1 : 4.95. ISBN 0-385-09681-X lib.bdg. : 5.95
1. Patchwork—Juvenile literature. I. Green, Jane, joint author. II. Inouye, Carol. III. Title. BIP

RATNER, Marilyn. 746.4'6
Plenty of patches : an introduction to patchwork, quilting, and applique / Marilyn Ratner ; illustrated by Chris Conover. New York : Crowell, [1977] p. cm. Includes index. Instructions for creating various items using quilting, patchwork, and applique. [TT835.R35] 77-3401 7.95
1. Patchwork—Juvenile literature. 2. Quilting—Juvenile literature. 3. Applique—Juvenile literature. I. Conover, Chris. II. Title. BIP

SOMMER, Elyse. 746.4'6
A patchwork, applique, and quilting primer / Elyse Sommer, with Joellen Sommer ; illustrated by Giulio Maestro. New York : Lothrop, Lee & Shepard Co., [1975] 128 p. : ill. ; 25 cm. Includes index. Bibliography: p. 125. Basic instructions for developing skills in patchwork, applique, and quilting with a number of learn-by-doing projects for each technique. [TT835.S63] 74-34152 ISBN 0-688-41693-4 : 4.95 ISBN 0-688-51693-9 lib.bdg. : 4.59
1. Patchwork—Juvenile literature. 2. Quilting—Juvenile literature. 3. Applique—Juvenile literature. I. Sommer, Joellen, joint author. II. Maestro, Giulio, ill. III. Title. BIP

Patchwork—Patterns.

BEYER, Jinny. 745.4
Patchwork patterns : a revolutionary, simple way to create original and traditional patchwork patterns for all crafts that use geometric design, quilting, stained glass, mosaics, needlepoint, graphics, jewelry, weaving, and woodworking / Jinny Beyer. McLean, Va. : EPM Publications, c1979. p. cm. Includes index. [TT835.B43] 78-32055 ISBN 0-914440-26-8 : 24.95 ISBN 0-914440-27-6 pbk. : 15.95
1. Patchwork—Patterns. I. Title. BIP

GAMMELL, Alice I. 746.4'6
Polly Prindle's book of American patchwork quilts / by Alice I. Gammell ; revisions by Patricia Newkirk. New York : Grosset & Dunlap, c1976. v, 260 p. : ill. ; 26 cm. [TT835.G35 1976] 76-375110 ISBN 0-448-12181-6 : 6.95
1. Patchwork—Patterns. 2. Quilting—Patterns. I. Newkirk, Patricia. II. Title. III. Title: American patchwork quilts.

IVES, Suzy. 746.9'7
Patterns for patchwork quilts and cushions / Suzy Ives. Newton Centre, Mass. : C. T. Branford, 1977. 64 p. : ill. ; 25 cm. [TT835.I93] 77-153649 ISBN 0-8231-5050-X pbk. : 4.95
1. Patchwork—Patterns. 2. Coverlets. 3. Cushions. I. Title. BIP

Patenier, Joachim, 1485 (ca.)-1524.

KOCH, Robert A., 1919- 759.9'493
Joachim Patinir, by Robert A. Koch. Princeton, N.J., Princeton University Press, 1968. xvi, 98 p. col. illus., 92 plates. 31 cm. (Princeton monographs in art and archaeology, 38) Bibliography: p. 91-93. [ND673.P27K6] 68-10392
1. Patenier, Joachim, 1485 (ca.)-1524. I. Title. II. Series.

Patios.

STEWART, Shan. 728.991
Planning and building your patio. New York, Crown Publishers [1954] 123p. illus. 29cm. [NA8375.S78] 54-9889
1. Patios. I. Title.

SUNSET. 728.9
Patio book, by the editorial staffs of Sunset books & Sunset magazine. Rev. [i.e. 2d]ed. Menlo Park, Calif., Lane Book Co. [1961] 165 p. illus. 26 cm. [NA8375.S8 1961] 61-1647
1. Patios. I. Title.

Patri, Giacomo, 1898—

PATRI, Giacomo, 1898- 769'.92'4
White collar : a novel in linocuts / Giacomo Patri. Millbrae, Calif. : Celestial Arts, 1975. 127 p. : chiefly ill. ; 22 cm. [NE1336.P38A58] 75-9440 ISBN 0-89087-180-9 : 8.95. ISBN 0-89087-101-9 pbk. : 4.95
1. Patri, Giacomo, 1898- 2. United States—History—1933-1945—Pictorial works. 3. United States in art. I. Title.

Pattern coins.

JUDD, J. Hewitt, 1899- 737.4'9'73
United States pattern, experimental and trial pieces / by J. Hewitt Judd, with the collaboration of Walter H. Breen, Abe Kosoff. 5th ed. Racine, Wis. : Western Pub. Co., c1974. 260 p. : ill. ; 24 cm. Includes bibliographical references. [CJ1826.J8 1974] 75-304964 ISBN 0-307-09059-0
1. Pattern coins. 2. Proof coins. 3. Coins, American. I. Breen, Walter H., joint author. II. Kosoff, Abe, joint author. III. Title.

Pattern glass—United States.

HARTLEY, Julia Magee. 748.2'913
The States' series : Early American pattern glass / Julia Magee Hartley, Mary Magee Cobb, co-author. [Lubbock? Tex.] : Hartley, c1976. 88 p. : ill. ; 23 cm. Cover title: Early American pattern glass. Includes index. Bibliography: p. 79-83. [NK5439.P36H37] 76-27580
1. Pattern glass—United States. I. Cobb, Mary Magee, joint author. II. Title. III. Title: Early American pattern glass.

Pattern glass, Victorian.

HEACOCK, William. 748.2'913
Encyclopedia of Victorian colored pattern glass / by William Heacock ; color photography by Albert Perry & Wayne Rayburn. [Jonesville, Mich. : Antiques Publications], c1974- v. : ill. (some col.) ; 28 cm. Includes index. Contents.Contents.—book 1. Toothpick holders from A to Z. Bibliography: v. 1, p. 12. [NK5109.8.H42] 75-316434
1. Pattern glass, Victorian. 2. Glass, Colored. I. Perry, Albert. II. Rayburn, Wayne. III. Title.

Pattern glass, Victorian—Pennsylvania.

SHUMAN, Susan. 748.2'9148'11
"Lion" pattern glass / by Susan W. and John A. Shuman III. Boston : Branden Press, c1977. 29 p., [23] leaves of plates : ill. ; 22 cm. Bibliography: p. 29. [NK5198.G44A4 1977] 77-71739 ISBN 0-8283-1695-3 : 7.50
1. Gillinder and Sons. 2. Pattern glass, Victorian—Pennsylvania. 3. Lions in art. I. Shuman, John A., joint author. II. Title.

Paul, Saint, apostle—Art.

SCHULTZE, Jurgen 704.9486
Paul [by] Jurgen Schultze. Text of story and legend by Leonhard Kuppers. [Tr. from German by Hans Hermann Rosenwald] Reckl inghausen 153Ger.] A. Bongers dist. Taplinger [New York, c.1964] 60p. col. illus. 18cm. (Saints in legend and art, v.3) (Saints in legend and art, v.3) [N8080.S3813] 67-16586 2.50 bds.,
1. Paul, Saint, apostle—Art. I. Kuppers, Leonhard, 1903- II. Title.

Paulson, Ronald, comp.

HOGARTH, William 1697-1764. 769.942
Hogarth's graphic works. Compiled and with a commentary by Ronald Paulson. 1st complete ed. New Haven Yale University Press 1965. 2 v. 346 illus., col. map on lining papers, port. 26 x 32 cm. Contents.CONTENTS. -- v. 1. Introduction and catalogue. -- v. 2. Plates. Includes bibliographical references. [NE642.H6P3] 64-20930
1. Paulson, Ronald, comp. I. Title.

Pausanias. Descriptio Graeciae.

IMHOOF-BLUMER, Friedrich, 1838-1920. 737.4938
Ancient coins illustrating lost masterpieces of Greek art; a numismatic commentary on Pausanias, by F. W. Imhoof-Blumer [and] Percy Gardner. New enl. ed. with introd., commentary and notes by Al. N. Oikonomides. [1st American ed,] Chicago, Argonaut, 1964. lxxx, 176 p. illus., map, plates. 22 cm. (Argonaut library of antiquities) First published in Journal of Hellenic studies, v. 6, 1885, v. 7, 1886, and v. 8, 1887, under title: Numismatic commentary on Pausanias. Includes translations of the Greek quotations from Pausanias and "A new commentary on the statues represented on Athenian coins" by the editor. Bibliography: p. [175]-176. [CJ351.I5 1964] 64-23435
1. Coins, Greek. 2. Pausanias. Descriptio Graeciae. 3. Sculpture, Greek. I. Gardner, Percy 1846-1937, joint author. II. Oikonomides, Al. N., ed. III. Title.

Pavements, Tile—England.

WIGHT, Jane A. 729'.7'0942
Mediaeval floor tiles / Jane A. Wight. New York : St. Martin's Press, 1975. xi, 179 p., [2] leaves of plates : ill. (some col.) ; 24 cm. Includes index. Bibliography: p.

170-174. [NA3543.W54 1975] 75-18592 17.95
1. Pavements, Tile—England. 2. Tiles, Medieval—England. 3. Tiles—England. I. Title.   BIP

Pavements, Tile—Pennsylvania—Harrisburg.

MERCER, Henry Chapman,   917.48'18 1856-1930.
The tiled pavement in the Capitol of Pennsylvania / Henry C. Mercer ; rev. and edited by Ginger Duemler ; illustrated by Linda Brown. State College : Pennsylvania Guild of Craftsmen, [1975] xv, 83 p. : ill. ; 23 cm. Revision of the author's guide book to the tiled pavement in the Capitol of Pennsylvania. Fold. sheet inserted: Chronological guide and numerical reference list to the tiled pavement. Includes index. [NA3860.M47D83 1975] 75-318013
1. Mercer, Henry Chapman, 1856-1930. 2. Harrisburg, Pa. State Capitol. 3. Pavements, Tile—Pennsylvania—Harrisburg. 4. Pavements, Mosaic—Pennsylvania—Harrisburg. 5. Pennsylvania in art. I. Duemler, Ginger. II. Title.

Pavements, Tile—Wales.

LEWIS, John Masters.   738.6'09429
Welsh medieval paving tiles / written by J. M. Lewis ; [photographs by Eric Broadbent]. Cardiff : National Museum of Wales, 1976. 35 p. : chiefly ill. (some col.), map ; 16 x 23 cm. Bibliography: p. 35. [NA3547.A1L48] 76-371230 ISBN 0-7200-0057-2 : £0.60
1. Pavements, Tile—Wales. 2. Tiles, Medieval—Wales. 3. Tiles—Wales. I. Cardiff, Wales. National Museum of Wales. II. Title.

Pavia. Certosa. Facciata.

MORSCHECK, Charles R.   730'.945'29
Relief sculpture for the facade of the Certosa di Pavia, 1473-1499 / Charles R. Morscheck, Jr. New York : Garland Pub., 1978. p. cm. (Outstanding dissertations in the fine arts) Bibliography: p. [NB1291.P37M67] 77-94727 ISBN 0-8240-3243-8 : lib.bdg. : 47.50
1. Pavia. Certosa. Facciata. 2. Relief (Sculpture)—Italy—Pavia. 3. Relief (Sculpture), Renaissance—Italy—Pavia. I. Title. II. Series.   BIP

Pavia, Phillip.

WASHINGTON, D.C.   730'.92'4
Gallery of Modern Art.
Phillip Pavia. [Exhibition, November 5 to December 31, 1966, Washington Gallery of Modern Art. [Washington, 1966] 18 p. illus. 27 cm. Text by Gerald Nordland. Bibliography: p. 12. [NB237.P36W3] 66-30158
1. Pavia, Phillip. I. Nordland, Gerald.

Pavilions.

CONNOLLY, Cyril, 1903-   728.8
Les pavillons; French pavilions of the eighteenth century [by] Cyril Connolly, Jerome Zerbe. New York, Macmillan [c.] 1962. 205p. illus. (col. front.) 29cm. 62-8761 15.00
1. Pavilions. 2. Architecture, Domestic—France. I. Zerbe, Jerome, 1904- joint author. II. Title. III. Title: French pavilions of the eighteenth century.

Pavilions—China.

BLASER, Werner, 1924-   722'.1
Chinesische Pavillon Architektur : Qualitat, Gestalt, Gefuge am Beispiel China = Chinese pavilion architecture : quality, design, structure exemplified by China / Werner Blaser ; [English version, D. Q. Stephenson]. New York : Architectural Book Pub. Co., c1974. 192 p. : chiefly ill. ; 27 cm. Bibliography: p. 192. [NA8450.B48] 75-308765 45.00
1. Pavilions—China. I. Title. II. Title: Chinese pavilion architecture.

Paxson, E. S., 1852-1919.

STENZEL, Franz.   759.13
E. S. Paxson—Montana artist / by Franz R. Stenzel. Helena : Montana Historical Society, [1975?] 32 p. : ill. ; 27 cm. (Montana heritage series ; no. 14) Cover title. [ND237.P257S84] 75-328261 1.00
1. Paxson, E. S., 1852-1919. 2. The West in art. I. Title. II. Series.

Peabody Museum of Salem, Mass. East India Marine Hall.

SMITH, Philip   727'.7'097445
Chadwick Foster.
East India Marine Hall, 1824-1974 / by Philip Chadwick Foster Smith ; with a foreword by Walter Muir Whitehill ; and a biographical sketch of its architect, Thomas Waldron Sumner by Christopher P. Monkhouse. [Salem, Mass.] : Peabody Museum of Salem, 1974. [56] p. : ill. ; 14 x 22 cm. Includes bibliographical references. [NA6700.S24S64] 75-328462 ISBN 0-87577-050-9
1. Peabody Museum of Salem, Mass. East India Marine Hall. I. Title.   BIP

Peabody Museum of Salem, Salem, Mass.

PEABODY Museum of Salem,   739.7'2
Salem, Mass.
The Peabody Museum collection of Japanese sword guards : with selected pieces of sword furniture : [catalogue] / by John D. Hamilton ; photos. by Mark Sexton. Salem, Mass. : The Museum, 1975. xliii i.e. [86] p. : ill. (some col.) ; 29 cm. Cover title: The Japanese sword guards. Includes index. [NK6784.A1P4 1975] 74-7603 ISBN 0-87577-041-X
1. Peabody Museum of Salem, Salem, Mass. 2. Sword guards—Japan—Catalogs. I. Hamilton, John D., 1935- II. Title: Japanese sword guards.

Peake, Mervyn Laurence, 1911-1968—Biography.

WATNEY, John Basil,   741'.092'4 B
1915-
Mervyn Peake / John Watney. New York : St. Martin's Press, 1976. 255 p. : ill. ; 25 cm. Includes index. Bibliography: p. 246-249. [PR6031.E183Z95 1976] 76-17422 10.95
1. Peake, Mervyn Laurence, 1911-1968—Biography. 2. Authors, English—20th century—Biography. 3. Painters—England—Biography.   BIP

Peale, Charles Willson, 1741-1827.

BRIGGS, Berta N.   927.5
Charles Willson Peale, artist & patriot. New York, McGraw-Hill [1952] 262 p. illus. 21 cm. (They made America) [ND237.P27B7] 52-9763
1. Peale, Charles Willson, 1741-1827.

SELLERS, Charles   759.13 B
Coleman, 1903-
Charles Willson Peale. New York, Scribner [1969] xiv, 510 p. illus., facsims. (music), ports. 29 cm. Based on the author's Charles Willson Peale, published in 1947 as v. 23, pts. 1-2 of the Memoirs of the American Philosophical Society. Includes bibliographical references. [ND237.P27S44] 68-17345 20.00
1. Peale, Charles Willson, 1741-1827.

SELLERS, Charles Coleman,   757
1903-
Portraits and miniatures by Charles Willson Peale. Philadelphia, American Philosophical Society, 1952. 369 p. illus. (part col.) ports. (part col.) 30 cm. (Transactions of the American Philosophical Society, new ser., v. 42, pt. 1) Bibliography: p. 272-274. [Q11.P6] 52-11644
1. Peale, Charles Willson, 1741-1827. I. Title. II. Series: American Philosophical Society, Philadelphia. Transactions, new ser., v. 42, pt. 1

Peale, Charles Willson, 1741-1827—Juvenile literature.

KERR, Laura (Nowak)   759.13 B
1904-
Wonder of his world: Charles Willson Peale, by Laura Kerr. New York, Funk & Wagnalls [1968] 189 p. ports. 22 cm. [ND237.P27K4] 68-22146 3.95
1. Peale, Charles Willson, 1741-1827—Juvenile literature. I. Title.

PEARE, Catherine Owens.   92
Painter of patriots, Charles Wilson Peale. [1st ed.] New York, Holt, Rinehart and Winston [1964] 144 p. illus. 21 cm. [ND237.P27P38] 64-18255
1. Peale, Charles Willson, 1741-1827—Juvenile literature. I. Title.

Peale family.

DETROIT. Institute of Arts   759.13
The Peale family; three generations of American artists. [Exhibition] org. by Charles H. Elam. [Detroit] Detroit Inst. of Arts. 1967. 150p. illus. (pt. col.) geneal. table. 23cm. Sponsored by Founders Soc., Detroit Inst. of Arts & Munson-Williams-Proctor Inst., Utica, N.Y. Catalog by C. H. Elam; articles by C. C. Sellers. E. G. Paine & E. H. Dwight. Bibl. [ND236.D4] 67-16330 7.50; 4.95 pap.
1. Peale family. I. Elam, Charles H. II. Munson-Williams-Proctor Institute, Utica, N.Y. III. Title.

Peale, Sarah Miriam, 1800-1885.

BALTIMORE. Municipal   759.13
Museum.
Miss Sarah Miriam Peale, 1800-1885; portraits and still life, by Wilbur H. Hunter and John Mahey. Exhibition, February 5, 1967 through March 26, 1967, the Peale Museum, Baltimore, Maryland. [Baltimore, 1967] 36 p. illus. 26 cm. Cover title: Sarah M. Peale. [ND237.P32B3] 68-779
1. Peale, Sarah Miriam, 1800-1885. I. Hunter, Wilbur Harvey. II. Mahey, John. III. Title.

Peanut craft.

DONNA, Natalie.   745.5
Peanut craft, written and illustrated by Natalie Donna. New York, Lothrop, Lee & Shepard [1974] 128 p. 25 cm. Instructions for making toys, puppets, flowers, decorations, and three-dimensional pictures from whole peanuts, peanut shells, and sawdust. [TT880.D64] 73-18040 ISBN 0-688-41567-9 4.95
1. Peanut craft. I. Title.
Library ed. 4.59; ISBN 0-688-51567-3. BIP

Peanut craft—Juvenile literature.

SHOLINSKY, Jane.   745.59'2
Peanut parade / by Jane Sholinsky ; photos. by Dan S. Nelken. New York : J. Messner, c1979. p. cm. Directions for making animal figures from peanuts with several suggestions for peanut jewelry. [TT880.S55] 78-25852 ISBN 0-671-32944-8 : 7.29
1. Peanut craft—Juvenile literature. I. Nelken, Dan S. II. Title.   BIP

Pearce, Bryan.

JONES, Ruth.   759.2 B
The path of the son : a biography of Bryan Pearce / by Ruth Jones. Sheviock : Sheviock Gallery Publications, 1976. 104 p., [20] p. of plates : ill. (some col.), ports. ; 22 cm. [N6797.P34J65] 76-380640 ISBN 0-9504904-0-7 : £3.95
1. Pearce, Bryan. 2. Artists, Mentally handicapped—England—Cornwall—Biography. I. Title.

Pearl art glass.

LAFFERTY, James R.   748.2
Foval: pearl art glass, by James R. Lafferty, Sr. 1st ed. [Rochester? Pa.] [1967] 12 p. illus. (part col.) 23 cm. "Fry's art glass (Catalog no. 12), H. C. Fry Glass Company, Rochester, Penna." 18 p.

booklet mounted on back cover. [NK5112.L3] 67-9214
1. Pearl art glass. 2. Pearl art glass—Catalogs. I. Title.

Pearlman, Henry, 1895-   —Art collections.

BROOKLYN Institute of   709'.03'4
Arts and Sciences. Museum.
An exhibition of paintings, watercolors, sculpture, and drawings from the Collection of Mr. and Mrs. Henry Pearlman, and Henry and Rose Pearlman Foundation, [May 22-Sept. 29, 1974 : catalog]. [New York] : The Museum, 1974. [8] p., [68] leaves of plates : ill. (some col.) ; 36 cm. Includes bibliographies. [N6447.B76 1974] 74-77468
1. Pearlman, Henry, 1895-   —Art collections. 2. Art, Modern—19th century—Exhibitions. 3. Art, Modern—20th century—Exhibitions. I. Title.

Pearls.

DICKINSON, Joan   639'.412
(Younger) 1916-
The book of pearls: their history and romance from antiquity to modern times. New York, Crown Publishers [1968] vii, 248 p. illus., maps, ports. 24 cm. Bibliography: p. 228-232. [NK7680.D5] 68-20481
1. Pearls. I. Title.

Pearls—Juvenile literature.

YOUNG, Eleanor R.   639'.412
Pearls, by Eleanor R. Young. New York, Watts [1970] 85 p. illus., map, ports. 23 cm. (A First book) A history of the pearl as an ornament, as an industry, and as an object that inspires man to take great risks to possess it. [TS755.P3Y68] 72-104031
1. Pearls—Juvenile literature. I. Title.

Pearson, John, 1934—

PEARSON, John, 1934-   779'.092'4
Magic doors / by John Pearson. Reading, Mass. : Addison-Wesley Pub. Co., c1977. p. cm. Bibliography: p. [TR654.P39] 77-22382 ISBN 0-201-05668-2 : 10.95. ISBN 0-201-05669-0 pbk. : 6.95
1. Pearson, John, 1934- 2. Photography, Artistic. I. Title.   BIP

Pebbles—Collectors and collecting.

ROGERS, Cedric.   736'.2'028
Pebble polishing and pebble jewelry. London, New York, Hamlyn, 1973. 80 p. illus. (some col.) 26 cm. Includes index. Bibliography: p. 80. [QE432.R63] 74-168640 ISBN 0-600-37025-9 £1.25
1. Pebbles—Collectors and collecting. 2. Rock craft. I. Title.

Pebbles—Juvenile literature.

FLETCHER, Edward.   739.27
Pebble collecting & polishing. [Photos. by Michael Allman and Joe Rothstein. Drawings by John Wood. American ed.]. New York, Sterling Pub. Co. [1973] 96 p. illus. 22 cm. "Originally published in Great Britain under title: Pebble polishing. Bibliography: p. 94-95. Describes the techniques and necessary equipment for collecting, polishing, and making jewelry from pebbles. [QE432.2.F57 1973] 72-95210 3.95
1. Pebbles—Juvenile literature. 2. Jewelry making—Juvenile literature. I. Allman, Michael, illus. II. Rothstein, Joe, illus. III. Wood, John, 1922- illus. IV. Title.
Library binding, 3.99.

Peck, Sheldon, 1797-1868.

BALAZS, Marianne E.   759.13
Sheldon Peck / [by Marianne E. Balazs]. New York : Whitney Museum of American Art, [1975] p. 273-282 : ill. (some col.) ; 31 cm. Cover title. "Reprinted from the magazine Antiques, August 1975." [ND1329.P42B34] 76-351651 pbk. : 1.75
1. Peck, Sheldon, 1797-1868. 2.

Primitivism in art—United States. I. Peck, Sheldon, 1797-1868. II. Whitney Museum of American Art, New York.

Peck Village site, La.

FORD, James Alfred, 1911-1968. 976.3'74
Ceramic decoration sequence at an old Indian village site near Sicily Island, Louisiana / [by J. A. Ford]. Millwood, N.Y. : Kraus Reprint Co., 1975, c1935. p. cm. Reprint of the ed. published by the Dept. of Conservation, Louisiana Geological Survey, New Orleans, which was issued as no. 1 of its Anthropological study and also as no. 24 of Louisiana State University studies. Includes index. [E78.L8F673 1975] 75-9511 ISBN 0-527-03230-1 : 10.00
1. Peck Village site, La. 2. Indians of North America—Louisiana—Pottery. I. Louisiana. Geological Survey. II. Title. III. Series: Louisiana. Dept. of Conservation. Anthropological study ; no. 1. **BIP**

Pecos, N.M.

KIDDER, Alfred Vincent, 1885-1963. 738.3'7
The pottery of Pecos : the glaze-paint, culinary, and other wares / Alfred Vincent Kidder. New York : Garland Pub., 1979. p. cm. (Classics of anthropology ; #20) Reprint of v. 2 of The Pottery of Pecos, published for Phillips Academy by Yale University Press, New Haven, 1936, as no. 7 of Phillips Academy, Andover, Mass. Dept. of Archaeology. Papers of the Southwestern Expedition. "The technology of Pecos pottery, by Anna O. Shepard": p. Bibliography: p. [E99.P34K53] 78-13922 ISBN 0-8240-9628-2 : 87.00
1. Pecos, N.M. 2. Pueblo Indians—Pottery. 3. Indians of North America—New Mexico—Pottery. 4. Pottery—New Mexico—Pecos. I. Shepard, Anna Osler, 1903- II. Title. III. Series. IV. Series: Phillips Academy, Andover, Mass. Dept. of Archaeology. Papers of the Southwestern Expedition ; no. 7.

Peiffer-Watenphul, Max, 1896-1976.

PEIFFER-WATENPHUL, Max, 1896-1976. 741.973
Max Peiffer Watenphul / Friedrich Welz ; [transl. by Della Couling]. Salzburg : Verl. Galerie Welz, 1976. 22 p., [48] leaves of col. plates : ill. ; 18 cm. [N6888.P39W44] 77-561447 ISBN 3-85349-048-4 : S112.00
1. Peiffer-Watenphul, Max, 1896-1976. I. Welz, Friedrich, 1903-

Peking—Palaces.

SIREN, Osvald, 1879- 915.1'156
The imperial palaces of Peking : two hundred and seventy four plates in collotype after the photographs by the author : twelve architectural drawings and two maps with a short historical account / by Osvald Siren. New York : AMS Press, [1975] p. cm. Reprint of the 1926 ed. published by G. van Oest, Paris. [NA1547.P6S5 1975] 74-38084 ISBN 0-404-56950-1 : 195.00
1. Peking—Palaces. I. Title. **BIP**

Peladan, Josephin, 1859-1918.

PINCUS-WITTEN, Robert. 700'.944
Occult symbolism in France : Josephin Peladan and the Salons de la Rose-Croix / Robert Pincus-Witten. New York : Garland Pub., 1976. ix, 291 p. : ill. ; 21 cm. (Outstanding dissertations in fine arts) Originally presented as the author's thesis, University of Chicago, 1968, under the title: Josephin Peladan and the Salons de la Rose-Croix. Bibliography: p. 225-240. [NX549.A1P56 1976] 75-23809 ISBN 0-8240-2003-0 lib.bdg. : 27.50
1. Peladan, Josephin, 1859-1918. 2. Arts, French. 3. Symbolism in art—France. 4. Paris. Salons de la Rose-Croix. 5. Rosicrucians. I. Title. II. Series. **BIP**

Pelletreau, Elias, 1726-1810.

BROOKLYN Institute of Arts and Sciences. Museum. 739.2
Elias Pelletreau, Long Island silversmith, and his sources of design. [Exhibition. Brooklyn, 1959] unpaged. illus. 23cm. [NK7198.P38B7] 59-31924
1. Pelletreau, Elias, 1726-1810. 2. Silversmithing— Exhibitions. I. Title.

Pen drawing.

BORGMAN, Harry. 741.2'6
Drawing in ink / drawing for reproduction by Harry Borgman. New York : Watson-Guptill, 1977. 159 p. : ill. ; 29 cm. Includes index. Bibliography: p. 157. [NC905.B67] 76-48153 ISBN 0-8230-1385-5 : 14.95
1. Pen drawing. I. Title. **BIP**

COZENS, Alexander, 1717(ca.)-1786. 743'.8'36
A new method of landscape / by Alexander Cozens ; with a new introd. by Michael Marqusee. [New York] : Paddington : distributed by Grosset & Dunlap, c1977. xi, 33 p., [15] leaves of plates : ill. ; 28 cm. (Masterpieces of the illustrated book) Originally published in 1785 under title: A new method of assisting the invention in drawing original compositions of landscape. [NC795.C69 1977] 76-30518 ISBN 0-448-22120-9 pbk. : 4.95
*1. Pen drawing. 2. Landscape in art. 3. Drawing—Early works to 1800. I. Title.***BIP**

GILL, Robert W. 720'.28
Van Nostrand Reinhold manual of rendering with pen and ink [by] Robert W. Gill. New York, Van Nostrand Reinhold [1974, c1973] 368 p. illus. 25 cm. (Van Nostrand Reinhold manuals) Half title: Rendering with pen and ink. British ed. published in 1973 under title: The Thames and Hudson manual of rendering with pen and ink. Bibliography: p. 364-365. [NC905.G54 1974] 73-14116 ISBN 0-442-22689-6 12.50
1. Pen drawing. 2. Perspective. 3. Architectural rendering. I. Title. II. Title: Rendering with pen and ink.
Pbk. 6.95, ISBN 0-442-22694-2.

GUPTILL, Arthur Leighton, 1891-1956. 741.26
Drawing with pen and ink. Edited and rev. by Henry C. Pitz. New York, Reinhold Pub. Corp. [1961] 159 p. illus. 27 cm. Includes bibliography. [NC905.G8 1961] 61-10573
1. Pen drawing. 2. Architectural drawing. 3. Drawing—Instruction. I. Title.

GUPTILL, Arthur Leighton, 1891-1956. 720'.28
Rendering in pen and ink / by Arthur L. Guptill ; edited by Susan E. Meyer. [New ed.] New York : Watson-Guptill Publications, 1976. 255 p. : ill. ; 31 cm. Previous editions published under title: Drawing with pen and ink. Includes index. [NC905.G8 1976] 76-18759 ISBN 0-8230-4530-7 : 17.95
1. Pen drawing. 2. Architectural rendering. 3. Drawing—Instruction. I. Title. **BIP**

HOAR, Frank. 741.26
Pen and ink drawing, Acanthus--Frank Hoar. London, New York, Studio Publications [1955] 96p. illus. 26cm. (The How to do it series, no. 56) [NC905.H6] 55-14545
1. Pen drawing. I. Title.

HOGARTH, Paul, 1917- 741.2'6
Creative ink drawing. New York, Watson-Guptill Publications [1968] 159 p. illus. (part col.) 27 cm. [NC905.H67] 68-12403
1. Pen drawing. I. Title. **BIP**

JAQUES, Faith. 720'.28
Drawing in pen and ink. [1st American ed.] New York, Watson-Guptill Publications, 1964] 56 p. illus. 18 x 20 cm. (Watson-Guptill drawing books) [NC905.J3 1964] 65-19009
1. Pen drawing. I. Title.

KAMPMANN, Lothar. 741.2'6
Creating with colored ink. New York, Van Nostrand Reinhold [1969] 70 p. illus. (part col.) 21 cm. (Art media series) Translation of Tusche und Tinte. Illustrates various techniques of drawing and creating effects with pen and ink. [NC905.K313] 78-83388 5.95
1. Pen drawing. I. Title.

LALIBERTE, Norman. 741.2'6
Drawing with ink; history and modern techniques [by] Norman Liberte and Alex Mogelon. New York, Van Nostrand-Reinhold [1970] 104 p. illus. (part col.) 21 cm. (An Art horizons book) [NC905.L27] 71-90306
1. Pen drawing. I. Mogelon, Alex, joint author. II. Title.

MAXWELL, Donald, 1877- 741.26
Sketching in pen & ink. 2d ed. New York, Pitman Pub. Corp. [1950] 96 p. illus. 23 cm. [NC905.M3 1950] 51-5852
1. Penn drawing. I. Title.

PENNELL, Joseph, 1857-1926. 741.64
Pen drawing and pen draughtsmen : their work and their methods : a study of the art with technical suggestions / Joseph Pennell. New York : Hart Pub. Co., c1977. xxix, 318 p., [16] leaves of plates : ill. ; 32 cm. Includes index. [NC905.P45 1977b] 77-151920 ISBN 0-8055-1127-X : 15.00. ISBN 0-8055-0218-1 pbk. : 8.95
1. Pen drawing. 2. Illustration of books. 3. Illustrators. I. Title. **BIP**

PENNELL, Joseph, 1857-1926. 741.2'6
Pen drawing and pen draughtsmen, their work and their methods : a study of the art today with technical suggestions / by Joseph Pennell. New York : Da Capo Press, 1977, c1920. xxxvii, 432 p., [10] leaves of plates : ill. ; 28 cm. (A Da Capo paperback) Reprint of the ed. published by Macmillan, New York, which was issued as v. 3 of The Graphic arts series for artists, students, amateurs & collectors. [NC905.P45 1977] 76-30462 ISBN 0-306-80064-0 pbk. : 7.95
1. Pen drawing. I. Title. II. Series: The Graphic arts series for artists, students, amateurs & collectors.

PITZ, Henry Clarence, 1895- 741.26
Ink drawing techniques. New York, Watson-Guptill Publications, 1957. 144 p. illus. 27 cm. [NC905.P49] 56-12495
1. Pen drawing. I. Title. **BIP**

PITZ, Henry Clarence, 1895- 741.26
Sketching with the felt-tip pen; a new artist's tool. New York, Studio Publications [1959] 62 p. illus. 21 cm. [NC905.P53] 58-14269
1. Pen drawing. I. Title.

TAUBES, Frederic, 1900- 741.26
Pen and ink drawing. New York, Pitman [c.1962] unpaged. illus. 20x26cm. (Pitman art bks., 41) 62-17740 1.00 pap.,
1. Pen drawing. I. Title. **BIP**

TAUBES, Frederic, 1900- 741.26
Pen-and-ink drawing; art and technique. New York, Watson-Guptill Publications [1956] 53 p. illus. 24 cm. [NC905.T3] 56-13160
1. Pen drawing. I. Title.

WELLING, Richard, 1926- 741.2'6
Drawing with markers. New York, Watson-Guptill Publications [1974] 159 p. illus. 29 cm. Bibliography: p. 158. [NC905.W44] 73-20202 ISBN 0-8230-1462-2 14.95
1. Pen drawing. I. Title. **BIP**

ZAIDENBERG, Arthur, 1903- 741.26
How to draw with pen & brush; a book for beginners. New York, Vanguard [c.1965] 61p. illus. 28cm. [NC905.Z3] 65-17376 3.50 bds.,
1. Pen drawing. 2. Brush drawing. I. Title. **BIP**

Pen drawing—Technique.

LOHAN, Frank. 741.2'6
Pen and ink techniques / Frank Lohan. Chicago : Contemporary Books, c1978. xi, 93 p. : ill. ; 29 cm. Bibliography: p. 93. [NC905.L6 1978] 78-57478 ISBN 0-8092-7439-6 : 11.95 ISBN 0-8092-7438-8 pbk. : 5.95
1. Pen drawing—Technique. I. Title.

LOHAN, Frank J. 741.2'6
Pen and ink techniques / Frank J. Lohan. Chicago : Contemporary Books, [1978] p. cm. Includes index. [NC905.L6] 78-57478 ISBN 0-8092-7439-6 : 11.95 ISBN 0-8092-7438-8 pbk. : 5.95
1. Pen drawing—Technique. I. Title. **BIP**

Pencil drawing.

FABRY, Alois. 741.24
Sketching is fun with pencil and pen. New York, Studio Publications [1958] 94 p. illus. 21 cm. [NC890.F34] 58-5499
1. Pencil drawing. 2. Pen drawing. I. Title.

FREER, Howard. 741.24
You can paint with a pencil. [New York] Studio Publications in association with Crowell [1951] 96 p. illus. 21 cm. [NC890.F7] 51-2892
1. Pencil drawing. I. Title.

GUPTILL, Arthur Leighton, 1891-1956. 741.24
Pencil drawing step by step. 2d ed. New York, Reinhold Pub. Corp. [1959] 147 p. illus. 27 cm. [NC890.G78 1959] 59-13643
1. Pencil drawing.

GUPTILL, Arthur Leighton, 1891-1956. 741.2'4
Rendering in pencil / by Arthur L. Guptill ; edited by Susan E. Meyer. New York : Watson-Guptill, 1977. 271 p. : ill. ; 32 cm. Rev. ed. of the author's Sketching and rendering in pencil and Pencil drawing step-by-step. Includes index. [NC890.G8 1977] 76-50547 ISBN 0-8230-4531-5 : 17.95
1. Pencil drawing. 2. Architectural rendering. I. Meyer, Susan E. II. Title. **BIP**

HOGARTH, Paul, 1917- 741.24
Creative pencil drawing. New York, Watson-Guptill Publications [1964] 159 p. illus. 27 cm. [NC890.H64] 64-14762
1. Pencil drawing. I. Title. **BIP**

HUNTER, William Stanley. 743.72
Tree rhythm in pencil. London, New York, Studio Publications [1952] 64p. illus. 18cm. (The How to draw series) [NC890.H85] 52-14570
1. Pencil drawing. 2. Trees in art. I. Title.

KAUTZKY, Theodore, 1896-1953. 741.24
Pencil broadsides; a manual of broad stroke technique. [2d ed., enl.] New York, Reinhold [1960, c.1940, 1960] 63p. illus. 31cm. 60-15649 5.50
1. Pencil drawing. I. Title.

LALIBERTE, Norman. 741.2'4
Drawing with pencils; history and modern techniques [by] Norman Laliberte [and] Alex Mogelon. New York, Van Nostrand Reinhold [1969] 104 p. illus. (part col.) 22 cm. (An Art horizons book) [NC890.L3] 69-16375
1. Pencil drawing. I. Mogelon, Alex, joint author. II. Title.

MALLAN, Lloyd, ed. 743.4
Pencil drawing for fun. [Greenwich, Conn., Fawcett Publications, 1952] 144p. illus. 24cm. (A Fawcett book, no. 159) 'Based in part on ... Fun with a pencil ... by Andrew Loomis, and ... Figure drawing for all it's worth ... by the same author.' [NC890.M33] 53-38660
1. Pencil drawing. I. Title.

RINES, Frank M. 741.24
Landscape drawing with pencil, by Frank M. Rines. London, Oak Tree Press; New York, Sterling Pub. Co. [1964] 112 p. illus. 28 cm. (A Bridgman giant) [NC890.R53] 64-15120
1. Pencil drawing. 2. Landscape drawing. I. Title.

RUFFINO, Carlos. 741.2'4
A guide to pencil drawing. New York, Van Nostrand Reinhold Co. [1969] 64 p. illus. 32 cm. [NC890.R8] 68-22736
1. Pencil drawing. I. Title.

WANG, Thomas C. 741.2'4
Pencil sketching / Thomas C. Wang. New York : Van Nostrand Reinhold, c1977. 96 p. : ill. ; 22 x 28 cm. Includes index.

Bibliography: p. 94. [NC890.W25] 77-1095 pbk. : 5.95
1. Pencil drawing. I. Title. BIP

WATSON, Ernest William, 741.24
1884-
Course in pencil sketching. New York, Reinhold Pub. Corp., c1956- v. illus. 27 cm. [NC890.W29] 56-9613
1. Pencil drawing. I. Title.

WATSON, Ernest William, 741.24
1884-
Gallery of pencil techniques. New York, Reinhold Pub. Co. [1958] unpaged. illus. 27 cm. [NC890.W295] 58-7197
1. Pencil drawing. I. Title.

WATSON, Ernest William, 741.2'4
1884-1969.
The art of pencil drawing, by Ernest W. Watson. New York, Watson-Guptill Publications [1968] 158 p. illus. 29 cm. [NC890.W28] 68-27552 10.00
1. Pencil drawing. I. Title. BIP

WATSON, Ernest William, 741.24
1884-1969.
Course in pencil sketching. New York, Reinhold Pub. Corp., [1956-57] 3 v. illus. 27 cm. Contents.Contents.—book 1. Buildings and streets.—book 2. Trees and landscapes.—book 3. Boats and the harbors. [NC890.W29] 56-9613
1. Pencil drawing. I. Title.

Pencil drawing—Technique.

KAUTZKY, Theodore, 1896- 741.2'4
1953.
The Ted Kautzky pencil book. Combined ed. New York : Van Nostrand Reinhold Co., [1979] p. cm. Includes material originally published in the author's Pencil broadsides and Pencil pictures. [NC890.K34 1979] 78-32126 ISBN 0-442-21575-4 : 14.95 ISBN 0-442-21576-2 pbk. : 8.95
1. Pencil drawing—Technique. I. Title. BIP

WATSON, Ernest William, 741.2'4
1884-1969.
Ernest W. Watson's Course in pencil sketching : four books in one / Ernest W. Watson. New York : Van Nostrand Reinhold Co., 1978. 208 p. : ill. ; 26 cm. Contents.Contents.—Buildings and streets.—Trees and landscapes.—Boats and harbors.—Perspective for sketchers. [NC890.W29 1978] 78-19178 ISBN 0-442-29230-9 : 14.95 ISBN 0-442-29229-5 pbk. : 8.95
1. Pencil drawing—Technique. I. Watson, Ernest William, 1884-1969. Perspective for sketchers. 1978. II. Title. III. Title: Course in pencil sketching. BIP

Penelon, Henri, 1827?-1885.

DEWAR, John, 1911- 759.13
Adios, Mr. Penelon; Henri Penelon, 1827-1885, painter, photographer, El Pueblo de Los Angeles. Los Angeles, History Division, Los Angeles County Museum of Natural History, 1968. [22] p. illus., ports. 23 cm. Includes bibliographical references. [N6537.P38D48] 76-284027
1. Penelon, Henri, 1827?-1885. I. Los Angeles Co., Calif. Museum of Natural History, Los Angeles. History Division. II. Title.

Penland School of Handicrafts, Penland, N.C.

MORGAN, Lucy, 1889- 745.52071
Gift from the hills; Miss Lucy Morgan's story of her unique Penland School, with LeGette Blythe. [1st ed.] Indianapolis, Bobbs-Merrill [1958] 314 p. illus. 23 cm. [NK410.P4M6] 58-9153
1. Penland School of Handicrafts, Penland, N. C. I. Blythe, Le Gette, 1900- II. Title.

MORGAN, Lucy, 745.5'09756'865
1889-
Gift from the hills; Miss Lucy Morgan's story of her unique Penland School, with LeGette Blythe. Including an epilogue. [Enl. ed.] Chapel Hill, University of North Carolina Press [1971] 331 p. illus., ports. 23 cm. [NK410.P4P45 1971] 76-144337 ISBN 0-8078-1165-3 5.95
1. Penland School of Handicrafts, Penland, N.C. I. Blythe, LeGette, 1900- II. Title.

Penmanship.

BIGGS, John R. 744.43
The craft of the pen. London, Blandford Pr. [dist. New York. Pitman, 1962] 64p. illus. 23cm. [Craft ser., 20] 62-52915 2.95 bds.,
1. Penmanship. I. Title.

CRESCI, Giovanni 745.6'1'97
Francisco, 16thcent.
A Renaissance alphabet; Il perfetto scrittore, parte seconda [by] Giovan Francesco Cresci. With an introd. by Donald M. Anderson. Madison, University of Wisconsin Press [1971] xxii, [51] p. illus. 22 x 30 cm. Translation of the second part of Il perfetto scrittore. Bibliography: p. xxii. [Z43.A3C7513] 77-121765 ISBN 0-299-05761-5
1. Penmanship. 2. Alphabets. I. Title. BIP

DAY, Lewis Foreman, 745.6'197
1845-1910.
Penmanship of the XVI, XVII & XVIIIth centuries : a series of typical examples from English and foreign writing books / selected by Lewis F. Day. New York : Taplinger Pub. Co., 1979, c1978. ca. 150 p. : ill. ; 25 cm. "A Pentalic book." [Z43.D27 1979] 78-58919 ISBN 0-8008-6277-5 pbk. : 7.95
1. Penmanship. 2. Calligraphy. I. Title.

GOURDIE, Tom. 652'.1
A guide to better handwriting. New York, Viking Press [1967] 96 p. illus. 20 cm. (A Studio book) Bibliography: p. 96. [Z43.G67 1967] 67-31928
1. Penmanship. I. Title.

HANDWRITING Research 652.1
Institute, New York.
Handwriting made easy. New York, Noble and Boble [1957] 96p. illus. 28cm. [Z43.H22] 58-4161
1. Penmanship. I. Title.

OSLEY, A. S. 745.6'1
Mercator: a monograph on the lettering of maps, etc., in the 16th century Netherlands, with a facsimile and translation of his treatise on the italic hand and a translation of Ghim's Vita Mercatoris. [By] A. S. Osley, with a foreword by R. A. Skelton. New York, Watson-Guptill [1969] 209 p. illus., facsims., maps, plates, ports. 29 cm. Bibliography: p. 195-202. [Z43.A3O8 1969b] 78-79762 35.00
1. Mercator, Gerardus, 1512-1594. 2. Penmanship. I. Mercator, Gerardus, 1512-1594. Literarum latinarum. II. Ghymmius, Gualterus, 1530-1611. Vita Mercatoris.

SLOTE, Claire Trieb. 652.1
Improve your handwriting. [1st ed.] New York, McGraw-Hill [1958] 147 p. illus. 20 cm. [Z43.S6] 58-8861
1. Penmanship. I. Title.

*TARR, John Charles. 745.61
Calligraphy in the Chancery script [by] John C. Tarr. San Leandro, Calif. [Poggio Bracciolini Scriptors] 1973. 20 p. illus. 32 cm. (Studies in calligraphy) 4.00
1. Penmanship. I. Title.
Publisher's address: 360 Hollister Court, San Leandro, CA 94577.

THREE classics of Italian 652.1
calligraphy, an unabridged reissue of the writing books of Arrighi, Tagliente and Palatino. With an introd. by Oscar Ogg. [New York] Dover Publications [1953] x, 272 p. illus. 25 cm. Contains facsimile reproductions of the first combined ed. of La operina and Il modo de temperare dated 1523, the 1580 ed. of Lo prensente libro insegna, and the 1561 ed. of Libro nuovo. "A bibliography, compiled by A. F. Johnson": p. [249]-272. [Z43.A3T5] 53-3313
1. Penmanship. 2. Alphabets. I. Ogg, Oscar, ed. II. Ludovico degli Arrighi, Vincentino, fl. 1522. La operina. III. Ludovico degli Arrighi, Vincentino, fl. 1522. Il modo de temperare. IV. Tagliente, Giovanni Antonio. Lo presente libro insegna. V. Palatino, Giovanni Battista, 16th century. Libro nuovo. BIP

TOWNSEND, Rebecca Mae. 372.51
Teaching handwriting with the imaginary line handwriting series. Austin, Tex., Steck Co. [1956] 62 p. illus. 27 cm. [Z43.T75] 56-35801
1. Penmanship. I. Title.

THE Typophiles, New York. 652.1
Calligraphics: hands & forms, rendered by Twenty-five American scribes for the Typophiles. New York, 1955. xiv, 119p. 12x19cm. (Its Typophile chap books, 28) 'The essay-extracts are from Graphic forms ... published ... in 1949.' [Z43.T9] 55-4637
1. Penmanship. I. Title. II. Series.

WEST, Paul Vining, 1885- 652.1
Better handwriting. N[ew] Y[ork] Barnes & Noble [1958] 102 p. illus. 13 x 21 cm. (Everyday handbooks, 270) [Z43.W47] 58-6510
1. Penmanship. I. Title.

Penmanship—Addresses, essays, lectures.

OSLEY, A. S., ed. 741
Calligraphy and palaeography; essays presented to Alfred Fairbank on his 70th birthday, edited by A. S. Osley. New York, October House [1966] xxiii, 286 p. illus., facsims., port. 26 cm. Includes bibliographical references. [Z105.O8 1966] 66-15273
1. Penmanship—Addresses, essays, lectures. 2. Paleography—Addresses, essays, lectures. I. Fairbank, Alfred J. II. Title. BIP

Penmanship, American.

NASH, Ray, 1905- 745.6'1
American penmanship, 1800-1850; a history of writing and a bibliography of copybooks from Jenkins to Spencer Worcester, American Antiquarian Society, 1969. xii, 303 p. facsims. 25 cm. "Additions to John Jenkins bibliography": p. 261-264. [Z43.A2N26] 78-106556
1. Penmanship, American. 2. Penmanship—Copy-books—Bibliography. I. American Antiquarian Society, Worcester, Mass. II. Title. BIP

Penmanship—Copy-books.

LYON, Luther H 652.1
Applied penmanship. 2d ed. Cincinnati, South-western Pub. Co. [1960] 124p. illus. 28cm. [Z43.L96 1960] 60-5693
1. Penmanship—Copy-books. I. Title. BIP

LYON, Luther H. 652'.1
Applied penmanship / L. H. Lyon, Margaret Ann Ferguson. 3d ed. Cincinnati : South-Western Pub. Co., c1976. iv, 124 p. : ill. ; 28 cm. [Z43.L96 1976] 76-1756 ISBN 0-538-05790-4 wkbk. : 2.60
1. Penmanship—Copy-books. I. Ferguson, Margaret Ann, joint author. II. Title.

SMILANICH, Marie Eldred. 372.6'34
Print-script to handwriting. Minneapolis, Denison [1969] 32 p. 22 x 28 cm. [Z43.S64] 75-80475
1. Penmanship—Copy-books. I. Title.

WRITE italic; 411
A series of trace & copy books for ages 8 to 90. Caledonia, N.Y., Italimuse [1965] 3 v. illus. 18-22 cm. Contents.--v. 1. Italic shapes and joins with pencil.--v. 2. Introducting the broad pen and pen angle.--v. 3. Introducting the medium pen & single flourished capitals. [Z43.E12] 66-6277
1. Penmanship—Copy-books.

Penmanship— Copy-books—Bibl.

NASH, Ray, 1905- 016.6521
American writing masters and copybooks; history and bibliography through colonial times. Boston, Colonial Society of Massachusetts, 1959. xiii, 77p. xxxvi p. of facsims. 25cm. (Studies in the history of calligraphy, 3) [Z43.A2N28] 59-841
1. Penmanship— Copy-books—Bibl. I. Title. II. Series.

Penmanship—History.

DAWSON, Giles Edwin, 652.10942
1903-
Elizabethan handwriting, 1500-1650; a manual [by] Giles E. Dawson. Laetitia Kennedy-Skipton. New York, Norton [c.1966] ix, 130p. 54facsims. 27cm Bibl. [Z43.D264] 66-11642 6.95
1. Penmanship—Hist. I. Kennedy-Skipton, Laetitia. joint author. II. Title.

DAWSON, Giles Edwin, 652.10942
1903-
Elizabethan handwriting, 1500-1650; a manual [by] Giles E. Dawson [and] Laetitia Kennedy-Skipton. [1st ed.] New York, Norton [1966] ix, 130 p. 54 facsims. 27 cm. Bibliography: p. 129-230. [Z43.D264] 66-11642
1. Penmanship—History. I. Kennedy-Skipton, Laetitia, joint author. II. Title.

Pennsylvania—Description and travel—1951- —Views.

SMITH, Clyde H. 779'.9'974804
Pennsylvania / photography, Clyde Smith ; text, Cronan Minton. Portland, Or. : Graphic Arts Center Pub. Co., c1978. 192 p. (p. 192 blank) : chiefly col. ill. ; 35 cm. [F150.S64] 78-51218 ISBN 0-912856-40-8 : 27.50
1. Pennsylvania—Description and travel—1951- —Views. I. Minton, Cronan. II. Title. BIP

Pennsylvania Germans.

LERCH, Lila. 745.1'09748
Pennsylvania German antiques. Allentown, Pa., Schlechter's, 1970. viii, 157 p. illus. 24 cm. [NK1410.P4L4] 70-19215
1. Pennsylvania Germans. 2. Decoration and ornament—Pennsylvania. I. Title.

Pennsylvania in art.

RUGGIERI, Nick T. 759.13
Pennsylvania .... a commemorative portrait / by Nick T. Ruggieri ; text by John M. Baer ; [edited by Marion W. Milliron ; ill. cutlines by Thomas Coolidge]. Harrisburg, Pa. : Patriot-News Co., 1975. 140 p. : col. ill. ; 23 x 28 cm. "A Bicentennial collection of the Harrisburg Patriot-News Company." Includes indexes. [ND1839.R74B33] 75-21055
1. Ruggieri, Nick T. 2. Pennsylvania in art. I. Baer, John M. II. Title.

Pentagram Design Partnership.

LIVING by design / 745.4'49'41
the partners of Pentagram, Theo Crosby ... [et al.] ; editor, Peter Gorb. London : L. Humphries ; New York : Whitney Library of Design, 1978. 300 p. : ill. (some col.) ; 20 x 21 cm. [NK1535.P39L38] 77-95220 ISBN 0-8230-7355-6 (Whitney) : 15.00
1. Pentagram Design Partnership. 2. Design—Great Britain—History—20th century. I. Pentagram Design Partnership. II. Crosby, Theo. III. Gorb, Peter.

Pentax camera.

COOPER, Joseph David, 771.3'1
1917-
Honeywell Pentax manual / Joseph D. Cooper. Garden City, N.Y. : Amphoto, c1975. 1 v. : ill. (some col.) ; 27 cm. Loose-leaf for updating. Includes index. [TR263.P4C58] 75-1963 27.50
1. Pentax camera. 2. Photography—Handbooks, manuals, etc. I. Title. BIP

COOPER, Joseph David, 771.3'1
1917-
Pentax pocket companion. New York, Amphoto [1967, c.1962] 94p. illus. 15cm. [TR263.P4C6] 62-14420 1.95
1. Pentax camera. 2. Photography—Handbooks, manuals, etc. I. Title.

COOPER, Joseph David, 771.3'1
1917-
Pentax pocket companion, by Joseph D.

Cooper. New York, Amphoto [1970] 94 p. illus. 14 cm. [TR263.P4C6 1970] 76-20237
1. Pentax camera. 2. Photography—Handbooks, manuals, etc. I. Title.

COOPER, Joseph David, 1917- 771.31
Pentax pocket companion. [New York] Universal Photo Bks. [dist. Amphoto, c. 1962] 94p. illus. 15cm. (U-259) 62-14420 1.95, wire bdg.
1. Pentax camera. 2. Photography—Handbooks, manuals, etc. I. Title.

EMANUEL, Walter Daniel 771.31
Pentax guide; how to use the Pentax, Pentax S, Pentax K, and Pentax H2 cameras. London, New York, Focal Press [dist. by American Photographic Publishing Company] [1960] 80p. illus., diagrs. 17cm. (The Camera guide) 60-2209 1.95 flex. plastic.,
1. Pentax camera. 2. Photography—Handbooks,manuals, etc. I. Title.

EMANUEL, Walter Daniel, 1908- 771.31
Asahi Pentax guide: how to use the Asahi Pentax, Pentax S, Pentax K, Pentax S1 (H1), Pentax S1a, Pentax S2 (H2), Pentax Super S2, Pentax SV, Pentax S3 (H3) and Pentax Spotmatic cameras, by W. D. Emanuel. 8th ed. London, New York, Focal P., 1965. 16; 32; 17-71 p. illus., tables, diags, 16 1/2 dm. (The Camera guide) 10/6 (B 66-405) Earlier editions published under title: Pentax guide. [TR263.P4E4 1965] 66-70584
1. Pentax camera. 2. Photography — Handbooks, manuals, etc. I. Title. II. Series.

FITZIG, Irving. 771.3'1
Pentax single-lens reflex guide. New York, Amphoto [1968] 96p. illus. 19cm. (Amphoto camera guide) [TR263.P4F58] 67-18635 1.95 pap.,
1. Pentax camera. 2. Photography—Handbooks, manuals, etc. I. Title.

FUHRING, Robert 771.31
Pentax and single-lens reflex photography. New York, Amphoto [c. 1962] 123p. illus. 62-12301 2.50bds.,
1. Pentax camera. 2. Photography—Handbooks, manuals, etc. I. Title.

FUHRING, Robert. 771.3'1
Pentax and single-lens reflex photography. [4th ed., rev.] New York, Amphoto [c. 1967] 123p. illus. 21cm. [TR263.P4F8 1967] 68-1450 2.95 bds.,
1. Pentax camera. 2. Photography—Handbooks, manuals, etc. I. Title.

FUHRING, Robert. 771.3'1
Pentax and single-lens reflex photography. [5th ed.] New York, American Photographic Book Pub. Co. [1969] 124 p. illus. 21 cm. [TR263.P4F8 1969] 77-91405
1. Pentax camera. 2. Photography—Handbooks, manuals, etc. I. Title.

FUHRING, Robert. 771.3'1
Pentax and single-lens reflex photography. [6th ed., rev.] New York, American Photographic Book Pub. Co. [1972] 124 p. illus. 21 cm. [TR263.P4F8 1972] 72-76653 ISBN 0-8174-0480-5 3.50
1. Pentax camera. 2. Photography—Handbooks, manuals, etc. I. Title.

KEPPLER, Herbert. 771.3'1
The Asahi Pentax way: the Asahi Pentax photographer's companion [by] H. Keppler. 2nd ed. London, New York, Focal 1967. 352p. illus. (some col.), tables, diagrs. 22cm. [TR263.P4K387 1967] 68-115432 9.95
1. Pentax camera. 2. Photography—Handbooks, manuals, etc. I. Title. BIP

KEPPLER, Herbert. 771.3'1
The Honeywell Pentax way; the Pentax photographer's companion [by] H. Keppler. 1st ed. New York, Amphoto [1966] 352 p. illus. (part col.) 22 cm. [TR263.P4K4] 66-24249
1. Pentax camera. 2. Photography—Handbooks, manuals, etc. I. Title.

KEPPLER, Herbert. 771.3'1
The Honeywell Pentax way; the Pentax photographer's companion [by] H. Keppler. 2d ed. Philadelphia, Chilton Book Co. [1968] 352 p. illus. (part col.) 22 cm. [TR263.P4K4 1968] 68-29668 9.95
1. Pentax camera. 2. Photography—Handbooks, manuals, etc. I. Title.

KEPPLER, Herbert. 771.3'1
The Honeywell Pentax way : the Pentax photographer's companion / H. Keppler. 9th ed. Garden City, N.Y. : Amphoto, c1976. viii, 366 p. : ill. (some col.) ; 22 cm. Includes index. [TR263.P4K4 1976] 76-360659 ISBN 0-8174-0688-3 : 13.95
1. Pentax camera. 2. Photography—Handbooks, manuals, etc. I. Title.

MURPHY. BURT. 771.31
Heiland Pentax guide. New York, Verlan Books [1960] 128p. illus. 20cm. (A Universal photo book, U-228) [TR263.P4M8] 60-7948
1. Pentax camera. 2. Photography—Handbooks, manuals, etc. I. Title.

RESHOVSKY, Ernest. 771.3'1
Honeywell Pentax system / by Ernest Reshovsky. Los Angeles : Petersen Pub. Co., [1974] 80 p. : ill. ; 28 cm. (Petersen's camera systems library) Cover title. [TR263.P4R47] 73-92485 ISBN 0-8227-0056-5 pbk. : 2.00 2.00
1. Pentax camera. I. Title.

TYDINGS, Kenneth S 771.31
New Heiland Pentax SLR guide, Philadelphia, Chilton Co., Book Division,[c1961] 127 p. illus. 20 cm. (Modern camera guide series, 827) [TR263.P4T9] 61-12688
1. Pentax camera. 2. Photography — Handbooks, manuals, etc. I. Title.

Peploe. Samuel John, 1871-1935.

HONEYMAN, Tom John, 1891- 927.5
Three Scottish colourists: S. J. Peploe, F. C. B. Cadell, Leslie Hunter. London, New York, Nelson [1950] xi, 132 p. plates (part col.) ports. 24 cm. "As I remember them, by Ion R. Harrison": p. [117]-126. [ND496.H6 1950] 52-30535
1. Peploe. Samuel John, 1871-1935. 2. Cadell, Francis Campbell Bolleau, 1883-1937. 3. Hunter, Leslie, 1879-1931. I. Title.

Perates, John.

PERATES, John. 730'.92'4
Twentieth century American icons, John Perates : [exhibition] Cincinnati Art Museum, December 8, 1974-January 5, 1975. Cincinnati : The Museum, [1974] [12] p. : ill. (some col.) ; 23 cm. [N8189.5.P47C56] 75-308817
1. Perates, John. I. Cincinnati. Art Museum. II. Title.

Perception.

BEARDEN, Romare, 1914- 751.4
The painter's mind; a study of the relations of structure and space in painting, by Romare Bearden and Carl Holty. New York, Crown Publishers [1969] 224 p. illus., ports. 24 cm. [ND1263.B37 1969] 75-75067 6.95
1. Perception. 2. Painting—Technique. 3. Art—Psychology. 4. Composition (Art) I. Holty, Carl, 1900- joint author. II. Title.

EHRENZWEIG, Anton, 1908- 701.15
The psycho-analysis of artistic vision and hearing; an introduction to a theory of unconscious perception. [2d ed.] New York, G. Braziller [1965] xxxv, 272 p. illus. 22 cm. [BF315.E5 1965] 65-24651
1. Perception. 2. Psychoanalysis. 3. Art — Psychology. 4. Music — Psychology. I. Title. BIP

Perceptual learning.

WYMAN, Jenifer D. 701.15
Primer of perception [by] Jenifer D. Wyman [and] Stephen F. Gordon. Photos. by Harold Zipkowitz. New York, Reinhold [1967] 87 p. illus. (part. col.) 19 x 26 cm. [NC735.W9] 67-24693
1. Perceptual learning. 2. Form (Aesthetics) 3. Perspective. I. Gordon, Stephen F., joint author. II. Title.

Perceval, Don Louis.

DIXON, Maynard, 1875-1946. 741.9'73
Maynard Dixon sketch book. Introd. and descriptive text by Don Perceval. Foreword by Lawrence Clark Powell. Flagstaff, Ariz., Northland Press, 1967. 1 v. (unpaged) illus., port. 29 cm. "The text and most of the sketches ... were previously published in The Westerners brand book, book no. 8." [NC1075.D54P4] 68-1286
1. Perceval, Don Louis. I. The Westerners. Los Angeles Corral. The Westerners brand book. II. Title. BIP

Perceval, John, 1923—

PLANT, Margaret. 759.99'4
John Perceval. [Melbourne] Lansdowne [1971] 122 p. illus., 32 col. plates. 31 cm. (Australian art library) Bibliography: p. 109-110. [N7405.P4P55] 77-884951 ISBN 0-7018-0350-9 10.00
1. Perceval, John, 1923-

Perez, Luis, 1934—

LEWIS, Alfred Allan. 747
Decorating with fabric / by Alfred Allan Lewis ; photographed by Helen Buttfield. New York : Grosset & Dunlap, c1974. ix, 147 p., [8] leaves of plates : ill. (some col.) ; 29 cm. [NK2004.3.P47L48] 73-15128 ISBN 0-448-01303-7 : 15.00
1. Perez, Luis, 1934- 2. Textile fabrics in interior decoration. I. Title.

Performing arts.

DORIAN, Frederick, 1902- 706.992
Commitment to culture; art patronage in Europe, its significance for America [Pittsburgh, Pa.] Univ. of Pittburgh Pr. [c.1964] viii, 521p. 24cm. Bibl. 64-12488 10.00
1. Performing arts. 2. Art and state. 3. Art patronage. I. Title.

Performing arts—U. S.—Addresses, essays, lectures.

KOSTELANETZ, Richard. ed. 709.73
The new American arts. New York, Collier [1967,c.1965] 270p. 21cm. (05258) [PN1582.U6K6] 65-15368 1.95 pap.,
1. Performing arts—U. S.—Addresses, essays, lectures. 2. American literature—20th cent.—Addresses, essays, lectures. 3. Art, American—Addresses, essays, lectures. I. Title.
Contents Omitted. BIP

Performing arts—U.S.—Pictorial works.

CREATIVE America 709.73
[Text by John F. Kennedy, others. Photos. by Magnum. New York] Pub. for Natl. Cultural Center by Ridge Pr. [dist. Trident, 1964.c.1962] 127p. illus. (pt. col.) ports. (pt. col.) 29cm. 62-21401 5.95
1. Performing arts—U.S.—Pictorial works. 2. Art, American. 3. U.S.—Intellectual life. I. Kennedy, John Fitzgerald. Pres. U.S., 1917-1963. II. Magnum Photos, inc. III. U.S. John F. Kennedy Center for the Performing Arts.

Perret, Auguste, 1874-1954.

COLLINS, Peter. 693.54
Concrete: the vision of a new architecture; a study of Auguste Perret and his precursors. New York, Horizon Press [1959] 307 p. illus., plans. 26 cm. Bibliographical references: p. 288-300. [NA4125.C6] 59-1958
1. Perret, Auguste, 1874-1954. 2. Concrete construction. 3. Architecture. I. Title.

Perry, Dean and Stewart.

LEE, Kaiman. 720'.28
Computer-generated perspective drawings / by Kaiman Lee. Boston : Environmental Design & Research Center, [1974] 5, [32] leaves : chiefly ill. ; 29 cm. Cover title: Computer perspectives. [NA2728.L435] 75-305512 5.00
1. Perry, Dean and Stewart. 2. Electronic data processing—Architecture. 3. Computer drawing. I. Title. II. Title: Computer perspectives. BIP

Perseus—Art.

WOODWARD, Jocelyn M. 700'.38
Perseus : a study in Greek art and legend / by Jocelyn M. Woodward. New York : AMS Press, [1976] p. cm. Reprint of the 1937 ed. published at the University Press, Cambridge. Bibliography: p. [NX652.P43W66 1976] 75-41299 ISBN 0-404-14633-3 : 12.50
1. Perseus—Art. 2. Arts.

Perspective.

ASHLEY, Howard J. 742
Accurate perspective simplified [by] Howard J. Ashley. Illustrated by the author. Stamford, Conn., Abak Press [1974] 214 p. illus. 24 cm. "A small portion of this book originally appeared under the title: Perspective projection by the new method." [NC750.A82 1974] 73-89328 ISBN 0-914214-01-2 16.00
1. Perspective. I. Title. BIP

BALLINGER, Louise Bowen. 742
Perspective: space and design. New York, Van Nostrand Reinhold Co. [1969] 96 p. illus. (part col.) 21 cm. Bibliography: p. 96. [NC750.B24] 69-16378
1. Perspective. I. Title.

BATHO, Robert Lloyd. 744.4'29
A practical approach to technical illustration [by] Robert Batho. With drawings prepared for publication by Peter Dennison. [New York] Hart Pub. Co. [1968] 72 p. illus. 26 cm. [T369.B35 1968b] 68-3693
1. Perspective. 2. Mechanical drawing. 3. Technical illustration. I. Title.

BUNIM, Miriam (Schild) 1912- 751.4
Space in medieval painting and the forerunners of perspective. [1st AMS ed.] New York, AMS Press [1970, c1940] xviii, 261 p. illus. 24 cm. Bibliography: p. [205]-216. [ND141.B85 1970] 70-121231
1. Perspective. 2. Painting, Medieval. I. Title. BIP

BURNETT, Calvin, 1921- 742
Objective drawing techniques; new approaches to perspective and intuitive space. New York, Reinhold Pub. Corp. [1966] 224 p. illus. 29 cm. Bibliography: p. 223. [NC750.B97] 66-14431
1. Perspective. 2. Space-perception. I. Title.

CAPELLE, Friedrich W. 742
Professional perspective drawing for architects and engineers [by] Friedrich W. Capelle. New York, McGraw-Hill [1969] x, 164 p. illus. 29 cm. [T369.C37] 69-12407 13.50
1. Perspective. I. Title. BIP

CHEVINS, Hugh, 1931- 742
Perspective. [1st Amer. ed. New York, Watson-Guptill 1966] 55p. illus. 18cm. (Watson-Guptill drawing bks.) Cover title: Drawing perspective. [NC750.C44 1966] 66-19736 1.00 pap.,
1. Perspective. I. Title. II. Title: Drawing perspective.

COLE, Rex Vicat, 1870- 701'.8
Perspective for artists : the practice & theory of perspective as applied to pictures, with a section dealing with its application to architecture / by Rex Vicat Cole ; illustrated by 436 drawings & diagrams by the author & 36 pictures chiefly by old masters. New York : Dover Publications, 1976. 279 p. : ill. ; 22 cm. (Dover art instruction and reference books) Reprint of the 1921 ed. published by Seeley, Service, London under title: Perspective. Includes index. Bibliography: p. 271-273. [NC750.C65 1976] 77-157431 ISBN 0-486-22487-2 pbk. : 3.50
1. Perspective. I. Title.

DE POSTELS, Theodore August, 1873- 742
Fundamentals of perspective. Enl. 2d ed. [edited by Jeffrey H. Livingstone. New York] Reinhold [1951, '1950] 30 sheets.

illus. (part col.) 30 cm. In portfolio; title from cover. [T369.D4 1951] 51-9621
1. Perspective. I. Title.

DOBLIN, Jay, 1920- 742
Perspective; a new system for designers. [New York] [Whitney Publications] [1956] 66 p. illus. 32 cm. [NC750.D53] 56-12413
1. Perspective.

FULLER, Wilfred Henry. 742
How to draw perspectives to scale. [New York] Studio Publications [1952] 64 p. illus. 18 cm. (The How to draw series) [NC750.F95] 52-7390
1. Perspective. I. Title.

GRECO, Simon. 742
The art of perspective drawing. [New York, Odyssey, 1968] 48 p. illus. (part col.) 32 cm. (A Grumbacher library book) [NC750.G67] 68-6730 1.00
1. Perspective. 2. Drawing—Instruction. I. Title.

GRECO, Simon. 742
The art of perspective drawing. [New York, Western Pub. Co., c1968] 48 p. illus. 32 cm. (A Grumbacher library book) [NC750.G67 1968b] 68-20987 1.00
1. Perspective. 2. Drawing—Instruction. I. Title.

HOLLIS, Harold Francis. 742
Teach yourself perspective drawing. New York, Roy Publishers [1956] 198p. illus. 18cm. (The Teach yourself books) [NC750.H65] 56-9376
1. Perspective. I. Title. II. Title: Perspective drawing.

HOLMES, John M. 742
Applied perspective, for architects, painters, and art students, by John M. Holmes. London, I. Pitman [1967] Stamped on t.p.: Dist. by SportShelf, New Rochelle, N.Y. 55p. illus. 29cm. Reprint of the 2d ed. of 1938. [NC750.H67 1967] 68-3630 6.75 bds.,
1. Perspective. I. Title.

HULL, Joseph William, 1897- 742
Perspective drawing, freehand and mechanical. Berkeley, University of California Press, 1950. xviii, 137 p. illus. 22 x 28 cm. Bibliography: p. 137. [NC750.H94] 50-62854
1. Perspective. I. Title.

IVINS, William Mills, 1881-1961. 742
On the rationalization of sight, with an examination of three Renaissance texts on perspective [by] William M. Ivins, Jr. De artificiali perspectiva [by] Viator, reproducing both the 1st ed. (Toul, 1505) and the 2d ed. (Toul, 1509) New York, Da Capo Press, 1973. 44 p., [116] p. (chiefly illus.) 28 cm. (Da Capo Press series in graphic art, v. 13) Bibliography: p. 43-44. [NC749.I94 1973] 68-54843 ISBN 0-306-71189-3 15.00 (lib. bdg.)
1. Alberti, Leone Battista, 1401-1472. Della pittura libri tre. 2. Pelerin, Jean, d. 1524. De artificiali perspectiva. 3. Durer, Albrecht, 1471-1528. Underweysung der Messung. 4. Perspective. I. Pelerin, Jean, d. 1524. De artificiali perspectiva. 1973. II. Title. III. Title: De artificiali perspectiva.

JELLICO, John. 701.8
Artistic perspective, Serial 4800. [Ed. 1] Scranton, International Correspondence Schools [1966] 54 p. illus. 28 cm. [NC750.J36] 67-208
1. Perspective. I. International Correspondence Schools, Scranton, Pa. II. Title.

JONES, William T 742
Perspective drawing. Serial 900-2. [Ed. 2] Scranton, International Correspondence Xchools, c1961. 140p. illus. 19cm. [NC750.J6 1961] 61-40062
1. Perspecitce. I. International Correspondence Schools, Scranton, Pa. II. Title.

JONES, William T 372.52
Perspective drawing, by William T. Jones. Serial 900-3. [Ed. 3] Scranton, International Correspondence Schools [1966] 141 p. illus. 19 cm. "Figures 10, 23, 27, 36, 42, 67 and 72" (fold. sheet) inserted. [NC750.J6 1966] 66-6088
1. Perspective. I. International Correspondence Schools, Scranton, Pa. II. Title.

LALLI, Victor R. 742
Intermediate perspective; step-by-step lessons in perspective drawing. Illustrated by the author. [1st ed.] New York, Exposition Press [1959] 181p. illus. 21cm. (An Exposition-university book) [NC750.L3] 59-16382
1. Perspective. I. Title. **BIP**

LANING, Edward, 1906- 742
Perspective for artists. New York, Pitman Pub. Corp. [1967] 48 p. illus., port. 20 x 27 cm. [NC750.L36] 67-12128 1.00
1. Perspective. I. Title. **BIP**

MOREHEAD, James Caddall, 1877- 742
A handbook of perspective drawing, by James C. Morehead and James C. Morehead, Jr. 2d rev. ed. Houston, Elsevier Press, 1952. 168 p. illus. 32 cm. [NC750.M67] 52-5663
1. Perspective. 2. Drawing — Instruction. I. Title.

NORTON, Dora Miriam. 742
Freehand perspective. [Rev. ed.] New York, Sterling Pub. Co. [1957] 92p. illus. 26cm. Published in 1909 under title: Freehand perspective and sketching. [NC750.N74 1957] 57-11525
1. Perspective. I. Title.

NORTON, Dora Miriam 742
Freehand perspective [Rev. ed.] London, Oak Tree Pr.; New York, Sterling [c.1957, 1964] 91p. illus. 28cm. (Bridgman giant) First pub. in 1909 under title: Freehand perspective and sketching. 64-24679 1.95 pap.,
1. Perspective. I. Title.

PERARD, Victor Semon, 1870- 742
Perspective. New York, Pitman Pub. Corp. [c1957] unpaged. (chiefly illus.) 20x26cm. (Pitman drawing series) [NC750.P48 1957] 57-9132
1. Perspective. I. Title.

PERARD, Victor Semon, 1870-1957. 742
Perspective. New York, Pitman Pub. Corp. [1954] unpaged (chiefly illus.) 20 x 26 cm. (Pitman drawing series) [NC750.P48] 54-3990
1. Perspective.

PIRENNE, Maurice Henri Leonard. 760'.028
Optics, painting & photography [by] M. H. Pirenne. London, Cambridge U.P., 1970. xxiv, 199 p. illus., plans. 26 cm. Bibliography: p. 184-192. [NC750.P66] 71-108109 80/-
1. Perspective. 2. Visual perception. I. Title. **BIP**

SAVAGE, Lee. 742
Aldo's doghouse : drawings in perspective / by Lee Savage. New York : Coward, McCann & Geoghegan, c1978. [48] p. : ill. ; 23 cm. Eddie illustrates the principles of perspective to a skeptical Aldo. [NC750.S245 1978] 78-8580 ISBN 0-698-20458-1 : 5.95
1. Perspective. I. Title. **BIP**

SHAH, Motichand Gulabchand, 1927- 742
Principles of perspective drawing. by M. G. Shah, C. M. Kale. New York, Asia Pub. [dist. Taplinger. 1966.c.1965] 9, [29]p. illus. 45cm. Bibl. [T369.S45] 65-16040 5.50 pap.,
1. Perspective. 2. Mechanical drawing. 3. Architectural drawing. I. Kale, Chandrashekhar Mahadeo, 1934- joint author II. Title.

STOREY, George Adolphus, 1834-1919. 742
The theory and practice of perspective. New York, B. Blom, 1972. xii, 272 p. illus. 21 cm. Reprint of the 1910 ed. published by Clarendon Press, Oxford. [NC750.S8 1972] 74-174406 13.75
1. Perspective. I. Title. **BIP**

TOMIYASU, Kiyo. 742
The art of perspective drawing. [New York, Odyssey, 1968] 48 p. illus. (part col.) 32 cm. (A Grumbacher library book) [Z5838.L3T6] 68-21474 1.00
1. Perspective. 2. Drawing—Instruction. I. Title.

VRIES, Jan Vredeman de, b.1527. 742
Perspective. New introd. by Adolf K. Placzek. New York, Dover [1968] 49, 24p. (chiefly illus.) 21 x 29cm. (Dover pictorial archives ser.) T186. Unabridged, unaltered repub. of work orig. pub. in 1604. Latin text with trs: by Stanley Applebaum. [NC749.V67 1968] 67-16701 2.25
1. Perspective. I. Title. II. Series. **BIP**

WALKER, Theodore D. 720'.28
Perspective sketches, II / Theodore D Walker [2d ed.] West Lafayette, Ind. : PDA Publishers, [1975] 283 p. : chiefly ill. (some col.) ; 23 x 29 cm. [NC750.W24 1975] 75-551 ISBN 0-914886-03-7 : 20.00 ISBN 0-914886-02-9 pbk. : 14.00
1. Perspective. 2. Architectural rendering. 3. Drawings. I. Title.

WATSON, Ernest William, 1884- 742
How to use creative perspective [by] Ernest W. Watson. New York, Van Nostrand Reinhold [1974, c1955] 160 p. illus. 26 cm. [NC750.W37] ISBN 0-442-29228-7 9.95
1. Perspective. I. Title.
Pbk. 4.95, ISBN 0-442-29228-7 L.C. card no. for original ed.: 55-6280

WATSON, Ernest William, 1884-1969. 742
How to use creative perspective. New York, Reinhold Pub. Corp. [1955] 160 p. illus. 27 cm. [NC750.W37] 55-6280
1. Perspective. I. Title. **BIP**

WATSON, Ernest William, 1884-1969. 742
Perspective for sketchers. New York, Reinhold Pub. Corp. [1964] 48 p. illus. 27 cm. [NC750.W38] 64-13644
1. Perspective. I. Title.

WHITE, Gwen. 742
A book of pictorial perspective. New York, Morrow [1955?] 77p. illus. 22x27cm. [NC750] 55-4618
1. Perspective. I. Title. II. Title: Pictorial perspective.

WHITE, Gwen. 742
Perspective: a guide for artists, architects and designers. London, Batsford; New York Watson-Guptill, 1968. 80p. illus., plans. 23 x 29cm. [NC750.W46 1968] 68-20447 8.50
1. Perspective. I. Title.

WHITE, John, 1924- 759.5
The birth and rebirth of pictorial space. Boston, Boston Book and Art Shop [1970, c1967] 289 p. illus. 26 cm. Includes bibliographical references. [NC750.W48 1970] 73-12070 15.00
1. Perspective. 2. Painting, Italian. 3. Painting, Renaissance—Italy. I. Title.

WHITE, John, 1924- 759.5
The birth and rebirth of pictorial space [2d ed.] New York, Harper & Row [1972] 289 p. illus. 23 cm. (Icon editions, IN(t)-27) Includes bibliographical references. [NC750.W48 1972b] 73-172151 ISBN 0-06-430027-7 4.95
1. Perspective. 2. Painting, Italian. 3. Painting, Renaissance—Italy. I. Title.

WICKHAM, Geoffrey E. 742
Rapid perspective, by G. E. Wickham. [1st American ed.] New York, Transatlantic Arts, 1967. 79 p. illus. 22 cm. (SBN 85458-050) [NC750.W73 1967] 68-3103
1. Perspective. I. Title. **BIP**

Perspective—Early works to 1800.

IVINS, William Mills, 1881-1961. 742
On the rationalization of sight : with an examination of three Renaissance texts on perspective / William M. Ivins, Jr. De artificiali perspectiva : reproducing both the first edition (Toul, 1505) and the second edition (Toul, 1509) / Viator. New York : Da Capo Press, [1975] c1973. 43, [116] p., : ill. ; 26 cm. (A Da Capo paperback) Bibliography: p. 43-[44] [NC749.I94 1975] 74-22066 ISBN 0-394-71571-3 pbk. : 2.95
1. Alberti, Leone Battista, 1404-1472. Della pittura libri tre. 2. Pelerin, Jean, d. 1524. De Artificiali perspectiva. 3. Durer, Albrecht, 1471-1528. Underweysung der Messung. 4. Perspective—Early works to 1800. I. Pelerin, Jean, d. 1524. De artificiali perspectiva. 1975. II. Title. **BIP**

POZZO, Andrea, 1642-1709. 743.9'4
Rules and examples of perspective proper for painters and architects. New York, B. Blom, 1971. 1 v. (unpaged) illus. 34 cm. First t.p. of original ed. has title: Perspectiva pictorum et architectorum ... English and Latin. Reprint of the 1707 ed., "done into English from the original printed at Rome, 1693, in Lat. and Ital., by John James." [NC1479.P7 1971] 69-13250
1. Perspective—Early works to 1800. I. Title.

Perspective—History.

EDGERTON, Samuel Y., 1926- 742
The Renaissance rediscovery of linear perspective / Samuel Y. Edgerton, Jr. New York : Basic Books, [1975] xvii, 206 p. : ill. ; 24 cm. Includes bibliographical references and index. [NC748.E33] 73-91086 ISBN 0-465-06915-0 : 15.00
1. Perspective—History. 2. Visual perception—History. I. Title. **BIP**

PERSPECTIVE / 701'.8
introd. and commentary by Pierre Descargues ; translation by I. Mark Paris. New York : H. N. Abrams, 1977, c1976. 176 p. : ill. ; 30 cm. Translation of Traites de perspective. [NC748.T7213] 77-81949 ISBN 0-8109-1454-9. ISBN 0-8109-2075-1 pbk. : 6.95
1. Perspective—History. I. Descargues, Pierre.

Perth, Australia—Historic houses, etc.

OLDHAM, Ray 728.8
Western heritage; a study of the colonial architecture of Perth, Western Australia [by] Ray and John Oldham. Perth, Paterson Brokensha [New Rochelle, N.Y., Australian Bk. Ctr. 1965] 102p. illus. (pt. col.) plans, ports. 29cm. Bibl. [DU378.O4] 65-4285 8.50
1. Perth, Australia—Historic houses, etc. I. Oldham, John, joint author. II. Title.

Peru—Antiq.

SAWYER, Alan Reed, 1919- 738.0985
Ancient Peruvian ceramics: the Nathan Cummings colliection, by Alan R. Sawyer. Drawings by Milton F. Sonday, Jr. Photogs. by William F. Pons, William E. Lyall. [New York] Metropolitan Mus. of Art; dist. N.Y. Graphic, Greenwich, Conn. [1966] 144p. illus. (pt. mounted col.) maps. 29cm. Bibl. [F3429.3.P8529] 65-16883 8.50
1. Peru—Antiq. 2. Indians of South America—Peru—Antiq. 3. Indians of South America—Pottery. I. Cummings, Nathan. II. New York. Metropolitan Museum of Art. III. Title. **BIP**

Peru—Antiq.—Juvenile literature.

GLUBOK, Shirley 709.85
The art of ancient Peru. Designed by photography Nook, Special photography by Alfred H. Tamarin. New York, Harper [1966] 41p. illus. (pt. col.) 26cm. [F3429.3.A7G5] 66-18651 4.50; 4.11 lib. ed.,
1. Peru—Antiq.—Juvenile literature. 2. Indians of South America—Peru—Juvenile literature 3. Indians of South America—Art—Juvenile literature. I. Title.

Perugino, Pietro Vannucci, known as, 1446-1524.

ADAMS, Joseph D. 759.5
The hard-luck artist of the Renaissance [by] Joseph D. Adams. [Warrensburg, Central Missouri State College, 1971] [12] p. illus. 23 cm. (Faculty distinguished lecture series, no. 4) [ND623.P4A65] 74-637069
1. Perugino, Pietro Vannucci, known as, 1446-1524. I. Title. II. Series.

Pet supplies—Juvenile literature.

BARWELL, Eve. 745.59'3
Make your pet a present / by Eve Barwell ; illustrated by Giulio Maestro. New York : Lothrop, Lee & Shepard, c1977. 110 p. : ill. ; 25 cm. Instructions for making a variety of gifts for dogs, cats, birds, small caged animals, and their owners. [SF413.5.B37] 76-30663 ISBN 0-688-41788-4 : 6.50 ISBN 0-688-51788-9 lib.bdg. : 5.61
1. Pet supplies—Juvenile literature. 2. Handicraft—Juvenile literature. 3. Gifts—Juvenile literature. I. Maestro, Giulio. II. Title. BIP

Peter, Saint, Apostle— Art.

EMMINGHAUS, Johannes H. 704.9486
Peter [by] Joh. H. Emminghaus. Text of story and legend by Leonhard Kuppers. [Tr. from German by Hans Hermann Rosenwald] Recklinghausen [Ger.] A. Bongers; dist. Taplinger [New York, c.1964] 69p. col. illus. 18cm. (Saints in legend & art, v. 2) [N8080.E4513] 67-4500 2.50 bds.,
1. Peter, Saint, Apostle— Art. I. Kuppers, Leonhard, 1903- II. Title.

Peter, Saint, apostle — Tomb.

TOYNBEE, Jocelyn M C 726.82
The shrine of St. Peter and the Vatican excavations, by Jocelyn Toynbee and John Ward Perkins. London, New York, Longmans, Green [1956] xxii, 293 p. plates, plans. 26 cm. [NA5620.S9T6] 56-1914
1. Peter, Saint, apostle — Tomb. 2. Vatican City. San Pietro in Vaticano (Basilica) I. Ward-Perkins, John Bryan, 1912- joint author. II. Title.

TOYNBEE, Jocelyn M C 726.82
The shrine of St. Peter and the Vatican excavations, by Jocelyn Toynbee and John Ward Perkins. New York, Pantheon Books [1957] xxii, 293 p. plates, plans. 26 cm. Includes bibliographical references. [NA5620.S9T6] 56-13363
1. Peter, Saint, apostle — Tomb. 2. Vatican City. San Pietro in Vaticano (Basilica) I. Ward-Perkins, John Bryan, 1912- joint author. II. Title. BIP

Petersen, Christian, 1884 or 5-1961.

WILSON, Geraldine L. 730.973
Christian Petersen, sculptor. Photos by Louis Al Facto. Ames, Iowa State University Press [1962] 82 p. illus. 20 x 24 cm. [NB237.P4W5] 61-18448
1. Petersen, Christian, 1884 or 5-1961. I. Title.

Petri camera.

TYDINGS, Kenneth S. 771.31
Petri guide. Philadelphia, Chilton Co., c.1960. 127p. illus. 20cm. (Modern camera guide series, 568) 60-11252 1.95 pap.,
1. Petri camera. 2. Photography—Handbooks, manuals, etc. I. Title.

TYDINGS, Kenneth S 771.31
Petri guide. Rev. Philadelphia, Chilton Co., Book Division, 1961. 127 p. illus. 20 cm. (Modern camera guide series, 568) [TR263.P44T9 1961] 61-17954
1. Petri camera. 2. Photography — Handbooks, manuals, etc. I. Title.

Petri, Friedrich Richard.

NEWCOMB, William Wilmon, 759.13 1921-
German artist on the Texas frontier, Friedrich Richard Petri / by William W. Newcomb, Jr., with Mary S. Carnahan. Austin : University of Texas Press, c1978. p. cm. "Published in collaboration with the Texas Memorial Museum." Includes index. Bibliography: p. [ND588.P52N48] 77-28620 ISBN 0-292-72717-8 : 19.95
1. Petri, Friedrich Richard. 2. Indians of North America—Texas—Pictorial works. I. Petri, Friedrich Richard. II. Carnahan, Mary S., joint author. III. Texas. Memorial Museum, Austin. IV. Title.

Petrie Museum.

STEWART, H. M., B.A. 732'.8'07402142
Egyptian stelae, reliefs and paintings from the Petrie collection / H. M. Stewart. Warminster, Eng. : Aris & Phillips, c1976- v. : ill. ; 31 cm. Contents.Contents.—pt. 1. The New Kingdom. Includes bibliographical references and indexes. [DT59.L65S84] 76-372332 ISBN 0-85668-026-5(v.1) 27.50
1. Petrie Museum. 2. Egypt—Antiquities—Catalogs. 3. Stele (Archaeology)—Catalogs. 4. Bas-relief—Catalogs. 5. Sculpture, Egyptian—Catalogs. I. Petrie Museum. II. Title.
Distributed by International Scholarly Book Services.

Petroglyphs.

GRANT, Campbell, 1909- 709'.01'1
Canyon de Chelly, its people and rock art / Campbell Grant. Tucson : University of Arizona Press, c1978. xviii, 290 p. : ill. ; 27 cm. Includes index. Bibliography: p. 269-279. [E78.A7G72] 77-22352 ISBN 0-8165-0632-69 : 19.50 ISBN 0-8165-0523-3 pbk. : 9.95
1. Indians of North America—Arizona—Chelly Canyon. 2. Chelly Canyon. 3. Rock paintings—Arizona—Chelly Canyon. 4. Petroglyphs—Arizona—Chelly Canyon. I. Title.

NEW York (City). 732.2'074'01471 Museum of Modern Art.
Prehistoric rock pictures in Europe and Africa, from material in the archives of the Research Institute for the Morphology of Civilization, Frankfort-on-Main, by Leo Probenius and Douglas C. Fox. Reprint ed. [New York] Published for the Museum of Modern Art by Arno Press, 1972 [c1937] 79 p. illus. 27 cm. [GN799.P4N4 1972] 74-169302 ISBN 0-405-01561-5
1. Petroglyphs. 2. Rock paintings. I. Frobenius, Leo, 1873-1938. II. Fox, Douglas Claughton, 1906- III. Frankfurt am Main. Frobenius-Institut. IV. Title. BIP

Petroglyphs—California.

GRANT, Campbell, 1909- 732'.2
Rock drawings of the Coso Range, Inyo County, California; an ancient sheep-hunting cult pictured in desert rock carvings. With a foreword by Julian H. Steward. Special appendixes by James W. Baird and J. Kenneth Pringle. China Lake, Calif. [Maturango Press] 1968. xii, 145 p. illus., maps. 26 cm. (Maturango Museum. Publication 4) Bibliography: p. 139-142. [GN799.P4G67] 68-58316
1. Petroglyphs—California. 2. Indians of North America—California—Inyo Co.—Antiquities. 3. Inyo Co., Calif.—Antiquities. I. Title. II. Series.

Petroglyphs—Klamath Valley.

SWARTZ, B. K. 709'.01'1
Klamath Basin petroglyphs / by B. K. Swartz, Jr. Rev. and abridged. Socorrow, N.M. : Ballena Press, 1979,c1978. 54 p., [8] leaves of plates : ill. ; 28 cm. (Ballena Press anthropological papers ; no. 12) Bibliography: p. 39-44. [E78.C15S95 1978] 78-110040 ISBN 0-87919-078-7 pbk. : 5.95
1. Petroglyphs—Klamath Valley. 2. Indians of North America—Klamath Valley—Antiquities. 3. Klamath Valley—Antiquities. 4. California—Antiquities. I. Title. BIP

Petroglyphs—North Dakota.

MILLIGAN, Edward A. 732'.2
Petroglyphs, pictographs, and prehistoric art in the Upper Missouri River and the Red River of the North Valley areas, by Edward A. Milligan. Bottineau, N.D. [1968] [40] p. illus. 27 cm. [E98.P6M55] 70-5727
1. Petroglyphs—North Dakota. 2. Rock paintings—North Dakota. 3. Indians of North America—North Dakota—Antiquities. 4. North Dakota—Antiquities. I. Title.

Petroglyphs—Saudi Arabia.

FIELD, Henry, 1902- comp. 732'.2
Rock-drawings from Saudi Arabia. Miami, Field Research Projects, 1970. i l., 19 plates. 28 cm. (Field Research Projects. Occasional paper no. 11) Includes bibliographical references. [GN799.P4F53] 74-153583
1. Petroglyphs—Saudi Arabia. 2. Saudi Arabia—Antiquities. I. Title. II. Series.

Pewabic Pottery (Firm)

PEAR, Lillian Myers. 738'.09774'34
The Pewabic Pottery : a history of its products and its people / by Lillian Myers Pear. Bicentennial ed. Des Moines : Wallace-Homestead Book Co., c1976. 295 p. : ill. (some col.) ; 29 cm. Includes indexes. Bibliography: p. 263-265. [NK4210.P48P4] 75-23558 ISBN 0-87069-158-9 : 22.50
1. Pewabic Pottery (Firm) 2. Pottery, American—Detroit. I. Title. BIP

Pewter.

COTTERELL, Howard Herschel. 739'.533
National types of old pewter, by Howard Herschel Cotterell, Adolphe Riff, and Robert M. Vetter. With a new introd. by Charles V. Swain. Rev. and expanded ed. Princeton [N.J.] Pyne Press; [distributed by Scribner, New York, 1972] vii, 152 p. illus. 28 cm. [NK8404.C6 1972] 72-76871 ISBN 0-87861-027-8 4.95 (pbk)
1. Pewter. I. Riff, Adolphe, joint author. II. Vetter, Robert Maria, joint author. III. Title.

JACOBS, Carl. 739.53388
Guide to American pewter. Illustrated by Marion B. Wilson. New York, McBride, 1957. 216 p. illus. 25 cm. [NK8412.J3] 56-12017
1. Pewter. 2. Hall-marks. I. Title.

JACOBS, Celia. 739.533
Pocket book of American pewter; the makers and the marks. [Springfield? Mass.] c1960. vii, 85p. 14cm. [NK8412.J33] 61-1183
1. Pewter. 2. Hall-marks. I. Title. BIP

MOORE, Hannah (Hudson) 739'.5 1857-1927.
Old pewter, brass, copper, and Sheffield plate. Rutland, Vt., C. E. Tuttle Co. [1972] xvi, 229 p. illus. 20 cm. Reprint of the 1905 ed. [NK8404.M6 1972] 75-104206 ISBN 0-8048-0887-2 8.25
1. Pewter. 2. Brasses. 3. Copper articles. 4. Sheffield plate. i. Title.

WYLIE, Walker Gill, 1894- 739.533
Pewter, measure for measure. [Miami? Fla.] c1952. 68 p. illus. 24 cm. [NK8404.W8] 52-8937
1. Pewter. 2. Weights and measures. I. Title.

Pewter, American.

EBERT, Katherine. 739.5330973
Collecting American pewter. New York : Charles Scribner's Sons [1976c1973] vii, 163p. : ill. ; 27 cm. Includes index. Bibliography: p. 157-159. [NK8412.E23] ISBN 0-684-14548-0 pbk. : 5.95
1. Pewter, American. 2. Pewter-Collectors and collecting. I. Title.
L. C.card no. for original edition: 72-12147.

JACOBS, Celia. 739'.533'0973
Pocket book of American pewter; the makers and the marks. 2d ed., rev. and enl. Boston, Herman Pub. Service [1970] 93 p. illus. 18 cm. [NK8412.J33 1970] 70-111761 4.50
1. Pewter, American. 2. Hall-marks. I. Title.

KAUFFMAN, Henry J., 1908- 739'.533'0973
The American pewterer; his techniques & his products [by] Henry J. Kauffman. Drawings by Dorothy Briggs. [Camden, N.J.] T. Nelson [1970] 158 p. illus. 26 cm. Bibliography: p. 155. [NK8412.K3 1970] 77-113170
1. Pewter, American. I. Title.

Pewter, American — Catalogs.

BOSTON. 739'.533'0974074014461 Museum of Fine Arts. Dept. of American Decorative Arts and Sculpture.
American pewter in the Museum of Fine Arts, Boston, Department of American Decorative Arts and Sculpture. Photos. by Daniel Farber. Boston, Museum of Fine Arts; distributed by New York Graphic Society, Greenwich, Conn. [1974] xiii, 119 p. illus. 28 cm. Bibliography: p. 119. [NK8412.B67 1974] 74-78551 ISBN 0-87846-080-2 12.50
1. Boston. Museum of Fine Arts. 2. Pewter, American—Catalogs. 3. Pewter—Boston—Catalogs. 4. Hall-marks. I. Title. BIP

YALE University. Art Gallery. 739.5330973
American pewter; Garvan and other collections at Yale. With an introd. by Graham Hood. [New Haven?] 1965. 2, 50 p. illus. 26 cm. [NK8412.Y3] 66-31378
1. Pewter, American — Catalogs. I. Garvan, Francis Patrick, 1875-1937. II. Title.

Pewter, American—Exhibitions.

CURRIER Gallery of Art, Manchester, N.H. 739'.533'0973
Pewter in America, 1650-1900. Manchester, N.H. [1968] 75 p. illus. 26 cm. "An exhibition of the pewter of the Currier Gallery of Art supplemented by selected loans. October 6-November 3, 1968." [NK8412.C8] 68-7831
1. Pewter, American—Exhibitions. I. Title.

FLINT Institute of Arts. 739'.533'0973
American pewter (c. 1730 - c.1870) in the Collection of Dr. and Mrs. Melvyn D. Wolf. [Loan exhibition Dec. 14, 1973-Jan. 13, 1974 [Flint, Mich., 1973] 40 p. illus. 26 cm. Includes bibliographical references. [NK8412.F55 1973] 73-92367
1. Wolf, Melvyn D., 1932- —Art collections. 2. Pewter, American—Exhibitions. I. Title.

Pewter, British.

BEDFORD, John, 1907- 739.533
Pewter. New York, Walker [1966] 63 p. illus. 19 cm. (Collectors' pieces, 6) [NK8415.G7B4 1966] 66-22380
1. Pewter, British. 2. Pewter—Collectors and collecting. I. Title.

COTTERELL, Howard Herschel. 739.533
Old pewter, its makers and marks in England, Scotland, and Ireland; an account of the old pewterer & his craft. Rutland, Vt., C. E. Tuttle Co. [1963] xxii, 432 p. illus., 82 plates (incl. facsims.) 29 cm. Bibliography: p. 423. [NK8415.G7C6 1963] 63-4599
1. Pewter, British.

JACKSON, Radway. 739'.533'0278
English pewter touchmarks, including the marks of origin of some of the Scottish and Irish pewterers; edited and introduced by Ronald F. Michaelis. London, New York, Foulsham, 1970. 123 p.; illus. 18 cm. Bibliography: p. [121]-123. [NK7210.J3] 77-866555 ISBN 0-572-00743-4 £0.75
1. Pewter, British. 2. Hall-marks. I. Title.

MASSE, Henri Jean Louis Joseph, 1860- 739'.533
Chats on old pewter [by] H. J. L. J. Masse. Edited and rev. by Ronald F. Michaelis. With a new section, American pewter in the eighteenth and nineteenth centuries, by Henry J. Kauffmann. 3d rev. ed. New York, Dover Publications [1971] 276 p. illus. 22 cm. Includes bibliographies. [NK8415.G7M43 1971] 72-138803 ISBN 0-486-22129-6 3.00
1. Pewter, British. 2. Pewter, American. 3. Pewter—Collectors and collecting. I. Michaelis, Ronald F., ed. II. Title. BIP

MICHAELIS, Ronald F. 739'.533
Antique pewter of the British Isles; a brief survey of what has been made in pewter in England and the British Isles, from the

SUBJECT INDEX PHILADELPHIA—HISTORIC HOUSES, ETC.—CONSERVATION

time of Queen Elizabeth I to the reign of Queen Victoria [by] Ronald F. Michaelis. New York, Dover Publications [1971] xiv, 118 p. illus., 40 plates. 22 cm. Originally published in 1955. Bibliography: p. 114. [NK8415.G7M55 1971] 74-138387 ISBN 0-486-22706-5 2.50
1. Pewter, British. I. Title. BIP

ULLYETT, Kenneth. 739'.533'075
Pewter collecting for amateurs. London, Muller, 1967. xi, 147p. illus., 12 plates, diagrs. 19cm. [NK8415.G7U55] 67-87612 3.00 bds.,
1. Pewter, British. 2. Pewter—Collectors and collecting. I. Title.
Distributed by Barnes & Noble, New York.

Pewter, British—Exhibitions.

CURRIER Gallery of 739'.553'0942 Art, Manchester, N.H.
British pewter, 1600-1850. Manchester, N.H. [1974] 42 p. illus. 19 x 26 cm. Catalogue of an exhibition held at the Currier Gallery of Art, Apr. 1-28, 1974. Bibliography: p. 42. [NK8415.G7C84 1974] 74-80494
1. Pewter, British—Exhibitions. I. Title.

Pewter, British—History.

HATCHER, John. 739'.533'0942
A history of British pewter / John Hatcher and T. C. Barker. London : Longman, 1974. xii, 363 p., [16] leaves of plates : ill. ; 23 cm. Includes index. Bibliography: p. 323-340. [NK8415.G7H37] 73-93118 ISBN 0-582-50122-9 : 22.50
1. Pewter, British—History. I. Barker, Theodore Cardwell, joint author. II. Title.
Distributed by Longman New York.

Pewter—England.

PEAL, Christopher 739'.533'0278 A.
More pewter marks / [compiled by] Christopher A. Peal ; [for the Pewter Society]. Norwich : The compiler, 1976. 117 p. : ill. ; 22 x 31 cm. Distributed in the U.S. by Price-Glover, New York. [NK8415.G7P43] 77-364705 ISBN 0-9505288-0-3 : 25.00
1. Pewter—England. 2. Hall-marks. I. Pewter Society. II. Title.

Pewter—United States.

KERFOOT, John 739'.533'0973 Barrett, 1865-1927.
American pewter / by J. B. Kerfoot ; with ill. from photos. by the author, of specimens in his own collection. Detroit : Gale Research Co., 1975, c1924. p. cm. Reprint of the 1942 ed. published by Crown Publishers, New York. Includes index. [NK8412.K4 1975] 75-29215 ISBN 0-8103-4147-6 : 10.00
1. Pewter—United States. 2. Pewter—Collectors and collecting. I. Title.

LAUGHLIN, Ledlie 739'.533'0973 Irwin.
Pewter in America: its makers and their marks. Barre, Mass., Barre Publishers, 1969-71. 3 v. illus., facsims., ports. 29 cm. Vols. 1-2, reprint of the 1940 ed.; v. 3, corrects, supplements, and brings the material of v. 1-2 up to date. Bibliography: v. 2, p. 163-[192]; v. 3, p. 233-255. [NK8412.L33] 77-86912 ISBN 0-8271-6918-3 (v. 1-2) 27.50 per vol.
1. Pewter—United States. 2. Hall-marks. I. Title.

MONTGOMERY, Charles 739'.533'0973 F.
A history of American pewter / Charles F. Montgomery. Rev. and enl. ed. New York : Dutton, c1978. 307 p. : ill. ; 26 cm. (A Winterthur book) Includes index. Bibliography: p. 301-302. [NK8412.M66 1978] 77-77937 ISBN 0-525-47467-6 : 12.50
1. Pewter—United States. I. Title.

Pewter—United States—Exhibitions.

AMERICAN 739'.533'09730740155451
pewter : a loan exhibition, organized by Frederick R. Brandt, on display at the Virginia Museum from April 27 to June 6, 1976 : [catalog]. Richmond : Virginia Museum, c1976. p. cm. Bibliography: p. [NK8412.A43] 76-11723
1. Pewter—United States—Exhibitions. I. Brandt, Frederick R., 1936- II. Virginia Museum of Fine Arts, Richmond.

Pewter—United States—History.

AMERICAN and 739'.533'0973
British pewter : an historical survey / edited by John Carl Thomas. 1st ed. New York : Main Street/Universe Press, [1976] 156 p. : ill. ; 29 cm. (Antiques magazine library ; 6) Includes bibliographical references and index. [NK8412.A4] 76-5096 ISBN 0-87663-241-X : 11.95. ISBN 0-87663-949-X pbk. : 5.95
1. Pewter—United States—History. 2. Pewter—Great Britain—History. I. Thomas, John Carl.

MONTGOMERY, Charles 739'.533'0973 F.
A history of American pewter [by] Charles F. Montgomery. New York, Praeger [1973] 246 p. illus. 27 cm. (American decorative arts series) (A Winterthur book) Bibliography: p. 241-242. [NK8412.M66] 77-141362 17.50
1. Pewter—United States—History. I. Title. BIP

Pewtercraft.

CHARRON, Shirley. 739'.533
Modern pewter : design and techniques / Shirley Charron. New York : Van Nostrand Reinhold co., [1979] c1973 143p. : ill ; 26 cm. Includes index. Bibliography:p.135. [TT266.3C47] ISBN 0-442-21560-6 pbk. : 7.95
1. Pewtercraft. I. Title.
L.C. card no. for 1973 Van Nostrand Reinhold ed.:72-9704. BIP

CHARRON, Shirley. 739'.533
Modern pewter: design and techniques. New York, Van Nostrand Reinhold [1973] 143 p. illus. 27 cm. Bibliography: p. 135. [TT266.3.C47] 72-9704 ISBN 0-442-21548-7 9.95
1. Pewtercraft. I. Title.

Peyote.

TSA TO KE, Monroe, [299.7] 970.62 1904-1937.
The peyote ritual; visions and descriptions. San Francisco, Grabhorn Press [1957] xvii, 66 p. col. illus. 40 cm. "Three hundred and twenty-five copies printed at the Grabhorn Press." [E98.R3T8] 58-16338
1. Peyote. 2. Indians of North America — Rites and ceremonies. 3. Indians of North America — Art. 4. Klowa Indians. I. Title.

Pfahl, Charles Alton, 1946—

SINGER, Joe, 1923- 759.13
Charles Pfahl, artist at work / by Joe Singer. New York : Watson-Guptill Publications, 1977. p. cm. Includes index. Bibliography: p. [ND237.P45S56] 77-8693 ISBN 0-8230-0620-4 : 17.95
1. Pfahl, Charles Alton, 1946- 2. Painting—Technique. I. Title.

Pfeiffer, Gustavus Adolphus, 1872-1953—Art collections.

DENNIS, Jessie 731.8'9'79414 McNab.
Chess: east and west, past and present; a selection from the Gustavus A. Pfeiffer Collection. Catalogue by Jessie McNab Dennis and Charles K. Wilkinson. Introd. by Charles K. Wilkinson. New York, Metropolitan Museum of Art; distributed by New York Graphic Society, Greenwich, Conn. [1968] xxxvi p. 117 illus. (part col.) 21 cm. "An exhibition ... shown at the Brooklyn Museum from April to October, 1968, sponsored by that museum and the Metropolitan Museum of Art." [NK530.D4] 68-17256
1. Pfeiffer, Gustavus Adolphus, 1872-1953—Art collections. I. Wilkinson, Charles Kyrle, 1897- II. Brooklyn Institute of Arts and Sciences. Museum. III. New York. Metropolitan Museum of Art. IV. Title.

Pharmacy paraphenalia—Collectors and collecting.

MATTHEWS, Leslie G. 615'.4'028
Antiques of the pharmacy. London, Bell [1971, i.e. 1972] xiv, 120 p. 48 plates, illus., facsims. 24 cm. Bibliography: p. 105-109. [NK1125.M348] 71-851775
1. Pharmacy paraphenalia—Collectors and collecting. I. Title.
Available from Transatlantic Arts, Levittown, N.Y., for 12.50

Phenomenology—Congresses.

LEXINGTON Conference on 701.17 Pure and Applied Phenomenology, 4th, 1967.
Aisthesis and aesthetics. Edited by Erwin W. Straus and Richard M. Griffith. Pittsburgh, Pa., Duquesne University Press [1970] xv, 348 p. illus. 23 cm. Organized by the Veteran's Administration Hospital, Lexington, Ky. Includes bibliographies. [B829.5.L4 1967] 70-98553 ISBN 0-8207-0118-1 10.95
1. Phenomenology—Congresses. 2. Aisthesis (The word). 3. Creation (Literary, artistic, etc.) 4. Art and mental illness. 5. Music—Philosophy and aesthetics. I. Straus, Erwin Walter Maximilian, 1891- ed. II. Griffith, Richard Marion, 1921- ed. III. United States. Veterans Administration Hospital, Lexington, Ky. IV. Title.

Phidias, ca. 500-ca. 430 B.C.

WALSTON, Charles, Sir, 730'.92'4 1856-1927.
Essays on the art of Pheidias, by Charles Waldstein. Washington, McGrath Pub. Co., 1973 [c1885] xvii, 431 p. 24 cm. On spine: The art of Pheidias. Reprint of the ed. published by University Press, Cambridge, Eng. [NB100.W2 1973] 72-119284 ISBN 0-8434-0152-4 32.00
1. Phidias, ca. 500-ca. 430 B.C. I. Title: The art of Pheidias.

Phifer, Robert Fulenwider, 1849-1928—Art collections.

NORTH Carolina. Museum 704'.361 of Art, Raleigh.
Robert F. Phifer Collection; [exhibition] March 31-May 13, 1973. [Raleigh, 1973] 97 p. illus. 26 cm. [N5220.P48N67 1973] 73-622791 ISBN 0-88259-069-3 3.00 (pbk.)
1. Phifer, Robert Fulenwider, 1849-1928—Art collections. 2. Art—Exhibitions. BIP

Philadelphia. Art Alliance.

WHITE, Theophilus 706.274811 Ballou, 1902-
The philadelphia Art Alliance; fifty years: 1915-1965, by Theo B. White. Philadelphia, University of Pennsylvania Press [c1965] 144 p. illus., plates, ports. 29 cm. [NA6813.P5W5 1965] 65-24120
1. Philadelphia. Art Alliance. I. Title.

Philadelphia. Centennial Exhibition, 1876.

GORES, Stan. 745.1
1876 Centennial collectibles and price guide ; including a history of the Centennial exhibition, with comments on the famous Gillinder & Sons glassworks and a comprehensive report on centennial items of value to antique dealers and collectors. 1st ed. Fond du Lac, Wi[s.] Haber Print. Co. [1974] 163 p. illus. 23 cm. [NK1125.G643] 74-82544
1. Philadelphia. Centennial Exhibition, 1876. 2. United States—Centennial celebrations, etc.—Collectibles. I. Title.

Philadelphia. City Hall (Old)

NELSON, Lee H. 725'.1'0974811
Old City Hall, Independence National Historical Park, Pennsylvania, by Lee H. Nelson. Washington, Office of History and Historic Architecture, Eastern Service Center, 1970. 1 v. (various pagings) illus. 26 cm. "Historic structure report, architectural data section." Includes bibliographical references. [F158.8.C52N4] 79-614585
1. Philadelphia. City Hall (Old) 2. Independence National Historical Park, Philadelphia. I. Title.

Philadelphia. Free Library.

PHILADELPHIA. Free 974.8'004'31 s Library.
The Pennsylvania German Fraktur of the Free Library of Philadelphia : an illustrated catalogue / compiled by Frederick S. Weiser & Howell J. Heaney ; [photography by William B. Daub & Robert G. Hostetter ; translations by Larry M. Neff & Frederick S. Weiser]. Breinigsville : Pennsylvania German Society, 1976. 2 v. : ill. (some col.) ; 25 x 27 cm. (Publications of the Pennsylvania German Society ; v. 10-11) Includes bibliographical references and indexes. [GR110.P4A372 vol. 10-11] [ND3035.P4] 745.6'7'09748074014811 76-13357 ISBN 0-911122-32-X (v. 1). ISBN 0-911122-33-8 (v. 2)
1. Philadelphia. Free Library. 2. Illumination of books and manuscripts, Pennsylvania German—Catalogs. 3. Illumination of books and manuscripts—Pennsylvania—Philadelphia—Catalogs. I. Weiser, Frederick Sheely, 1935- II. Heaney, Howell J. III. Title. IV. Series: Pennsylvania-German Society. Publications ; v. 10-11. BIP

Philadelphia. Free Quaker Meeting House.

PETERSON, 726'.58'96074014811 Charles Emil, 1906-
Notes on the Free Quaker Meeting House, Fifth and Arch Streets, Philadelphia, built 1783-4. Compiled for Harbeson, Hough, Livingston and Larson, architects to the Commonwealth of Pennsylvania, from a study of the documents and of the fabric, by Charles E. Peterson. [Philadelphia] 1966. 1 v. (various pagings) illus., facsims., plans. 28 cm. Bibliographical references included in foreword. [F158.8.F7P4] 68-22779
1. Philadelphia. Free Quaker Meeting House. I. Harbeson, Hough, Livingston and Larson. II. Title.

PETERSON, 726'.58'96074014811 Charles Emil, 1906-
Notes on the Free Quaker Meeting House, Fifth and Arch Streets, Philadelphia, built 1783-4. Compiled for Harbeson, Hough, Livingston and Larson, architects to the Commonwealth of Pennsylvania, from a study of the documents and of the fabric, by Charles E. Peterson. [Philadelphia] 1966. 1 v. (various pagings) illus., facsims., plans. 28 cm. Bibliographical references included in foreword. [F158.8.F7P4] 68-22779
1. Philadelphia. Free Quaker Meeting House. I. Harbeson, Hough, Livingston and Larson. II. Title.

Philadelphia—Historic houses, etc.

MCCALL, Elizabeth B. 728.30974811
Old Philadelphia houses on Society Hill. 1750-1840 Photos. by Michael Maicher. New York, Architectural Bk. [c.1966] 192p. illus., map (on lining papers) 28cm. [NA7238.P5M3] 66-18357 12.50
1. Philadelphia—Historic houses, etc. 2. Architecture, Domestic—Philadelphia. I. Title. BIP

Philadelphia—Historic houses, etc.—Conservation and restoration.

MORRISON, Andrew 725'.24'0974811 Craig.
The interior of the Second Bank of the United States. Denver, Colo., Denver Service Center, National Park Service, 1973. xi, 160 p. illus. 27 cm. (Historic structure report) On cover: Independence National Historical Park, Pennsylvania. Issued as a supplement to The interior of the Second Bank of the United States, by N. Souder, published in 1970. [NA6243.P5B34] 73-602846

1. Bank of the United States (1816-1836)—Buildings. 2. Philadelphia—Historic houses, etc.—Conservation and restoration. I. Souder, Norman M. The interior of the Second Bank of the United States. II. Title. III. Title: Independence National Historical Park, Pennsylvania. IV. Series: Historic structures report.

Philadelphia in art.

SNYDER, Martin P. 760
City of independence : views of Philadelphia before 1800 / Martin P. Snyder. New York : Praeger Publishers, 1975. 304 p. : ill. (some col.) ; 29 cm. Includes bibliographical references and index. [N8214.5.U6S65] 74-29313 ISBN 0-275-22030-3 : 25.00
1. Philadelphia in art. 2. Art, Modern—17th-18th centuries. 3. Philadelphia—History. I. Title.

Philadelphia Museum of Art.

PHILADELPHIA Museum of Art. 708'.148'11
Treasures of the Philadelphia Museum of Art and the John G. Johnson Collection. [Editor: George H. Marcus] Philadelphia, 1973. 111 p. illus. (part col.) 29 cm. [N685.A67] 74-160937 4.95
1. Philadelphia Museum of Art. 2. John G. Johnson Collection, Philadelphia. 3. Art—Philadelphia—Catalogs. I. Marcus, George H., ed. II. Title.

ROBERTS, George, June26,1900- 927
Triumph on Fairmount. Fiske Kimball and the Philadelphia Museum of Art, by George and Mary Roberts. [1st ed.] Philadelphia, Lippincott [1959] 321p. illus. 22cm. [N8375.K5R6] 59-9327
1. Kimball, Ss094n5y 9sk5(0, 1888-1955. 2. Philadelphia Museum of Art. I. Roberts, Mary (Howland) joint author. II. Title.

Philadelphia Orchestra.

SIEGEL, Adrian. 779'.9'785062748110924
Concerto for camera; a photographic portrait of the Philadelphia Orchestra. [Philadelphia, Philadelphia Orchestra Association, 1972] 207 p. illus. 26 cm. [ML200.8.P52O747] 72-8993
1. Philadelphia Orchestra. 2. Musicians—Portraits. I. Title.

Philadelphia. Powel House.

TATUM, George B. 974.8'11
Philadelphia Georgian : the city house of Samuel Powel and some of its eighteenth-century neighbors / by George B. Tatum : with photos. of Philadelphia architecture by Cortlandt Van Dyke Hubbard. 1st ed. Middletown, Conn. : Wesleyan University Press, 1976. xvii, 187 p. : ill. ; 26 cm. Includes index. Bibliography: p. [171]-173. [NA707.T37] 75-39905 ISBN 0-8195-4095-1 : 17.50 ISBN 0-8195-4096-X (lim. ed.). pbk. : 4.95
1. Philadelphia. Powel House. 2. Architecture, Georgian—Philadelphia. 3. Architecture, Domestic—Philadelphia. I. Hubbard, Cortlandt Van Dyke. II. Title. BIP

Philadelphia. Vanna Venturi house.

VENTURI and Rauch. 728.3'7
Vanna Venturi house, Chestnut Hill, Philadelphia, Pennsylvania, 1962 : Peter Brant house, Greenwich, Connecticut, 1973 : Carll Tucker III house, Westchester County, New York, 1975 / Venturi and Rauch ; edited and photographed by Yukio Futagawa ; text by Paul Goldberger. Tokyo : A.D.A. Edita, 1976. 40 p. : ill. (some col.), plans : 37 cm. (Global architecture ; 39) Title also in Japanese. Text in English and Japanese. [NA737.V46F87] 76-377426
1. Venturi and Rauch. 2. Carll Tucker III house, New York (State) 3. Philadelphia. Vanna Venturi house. 4. Greenwich, Conn. Peter Brandt house. I. Futagawa, Yukio, 1932- II. Goldberger, Paul. III. Title.

Philipson, Robin.

LINDSAY, John Maurice, 1918- 759.9411 B
Robin Philipson / by Maurice Lindsay. Edinburgh : Edinburgh University Press, c1976. 79 p. : ill. (some col.) ; 16 x 22 cm. (Modern Scottish painters ; no. 6) Bibliography: p. 75. [ND497.P48L56] 77-360047 ISBN 0-85224-302-2 : 5.00
1. Philipson, Robin. 2. Painters—Scotland—Biography. I. Philipson, Robin.
Distributed by Edinburgh Univ. Press, c/o Biblio Distribution Ctr., 81 Adams Dr., Totowa, NJ 07512

Phillips, Coles, 1880-1927.

SCHAU, Michael, 1945- 741.9'73
All-American girl : the art of Coles Phillips / by Michael Schau. New York : Watson-Guptill, 1975. 176 p. : ill. (some col.) ; 32 cm. Includes index. [NC139.P43S32 1975] 75-12697 ISBN 0-8230-0173-3 : 22.50
1. Phillips, Coles, 1880-1927. I. Phillips, Coles, 1880-1927. II. Title.

Phillips Collection, Washington, D.C.

PHILLIPS Collection, Washington, D.C. 759.13'074'018795
American art from the Phillips Collection : a selection of paintings, 1900-1950 : [exhibition] University of Wyoming Art Museum, Laramie, Wyoming, September 28-November 2, 1975, Utah State University Galleries, Logan, Utah, November 14-December 19, 1975, Brigham Young University, Provo, Utah, December 29, 1975-February 2, 1976, Denver Art Museum, Denver, Colorado, February 18-March 28, 1976, University of New Mexico, Albuquerque, New Mexico, April 6-May 9, 1976, the Phillips Collection, Washington, D.C., May 29-September 5, 1976. Washington : The Collection, c1975. [40] p. : ill. ; 22 cm. Includes index. [ND212.P43 1975] 75-27021
1. Phillips Collection, Washington, D.C. 2. Paintings, American—Exhibitions. 3. Paintings, Modern—20th century—United States—Exhibitions. 4. Paintings—Washington, D.C.—Exhibitions. I. Wyoming. University. Art Museum. II. Title.

PHILLIPS Collection, Washington, D.C. 750'.74'0153
A collection in the making : works from the Phillips Collection / compiled by Kevin Grogan ; with a foreword by Milton W. Brown. Chicago : University of Chicago Press, c1976. ix, 60 p. ; 24 cm. & 5 sheets (11x15 cm.) in pocket. (A University of Chicago Press text/fiche) The sheets are microfiche. Includes 2 essays by D. Phillips: A collection in the making (1926) and A collection still in the making (1931) [N858.P4A53] 76-10817 ISBN 0-226-69538-7 : 27.50
1. Phillips Collection, Washington, D.C. 2. Art—Washington, D.C.—Catalogs. I. Grogan, Kevin. II. Phillips, Duncan, 1886-1966. A collection in the making. 1976. III. Title. BIP

Phillips, Duncan, 1886-1966.

HORMATS, Bess. 709'.24
Retrospective for a critic: Duncan Phillips. "The critical writing of Duncan Phillips" and catalogue. Pref. [by] George Levitine. Introd. [by] William H. Gerdts. Foreword [by] J. William Fulbright. [College Park, University of Maryland, 1969] viii, 61 p. illus., port. 26 cm. An exhibition of paintings, sculpture, and watercolors from the Phillips Collection relating to the critical writing of Duncan Phillips, Feb. 12 through Mar. 16, 1969, University of Maryland Art Dept. and Art Gallery, J. Millard Tawes Fine Arts Center, College Park, Md. Includes bibliographical references. "The published writing of Duncan Phillips": p. 27-31. Bibliography: p. 32. [N5020.C7364] 79-625394
1. Phillips, Duncan, 1886-1966. 2. Art—Exhibitions. I. Phillips Collection, Washington, D.C. II. Maryland. University. Dept. of Art. III. Maryland. University. Art Gallery. IV. Title.

PHILLIPS, Marjorie, 1895- 750'.74'0153
Duncan Phillips and his collection. With a foreword by Laughlin Phillips. [1st ed.] Boston, Little, Brown [1970] xvi, 347 p. illus. (part col.), ports. (part col.) 26 cm. "An Atlantic Monthly Press book." [N5220.P55P5] 78-128359 20.00
1. Phillips, Duncan, 1886-1966. 2. Phillips Collection, Washington, D.C. I. Title.

Phillips, Gifford—Art collections.

CALIFORNIA. University, Santa Barbara. Art Galleries. 759.13
A selection of paintings from the 50's and 60's from the collection of Gifford and Joann Phillips. [Santa Barbara, Calif., Printed by Standard Printing, 1968] [36] p. illus. (part col.) 23 cm. Exhibition held Mar. 12-Apr. 7, 1968, at the Art Gallery, University of California, Santa Barbara, and sponsored by the Committee on Arts and Lectures. [N5220.P54] 68-63036
1. Phillips, Gifford—Art collections. 2. Phillips, Joann—Art collections. 3. Paintings, Modern—20th century—Exhibitions. I. California. University, Santa Barbara. Committee on Arts and Lectures. II. Title.

Phillips, Harry, 1911—

TEMPLE Newsam House, Leeds, Eng. 730'.92'4
Harry Phillips, sculptor. [Leeds] : [Temple Newsam House], [1976] [14] p. : ill., ports. ; 30 x 11 cm. Catalogue of an exhibition held at Stable Court Exhibition Galleries, Temple Newsam House, 3 April-1 May 1976. [NB497.P43T45 1976] 76-378648 £0.25
1. Phillips, Harry, 1911- I. Phillips, Harry, 1911- II. Title.

Phillpotts, Beatrice.

PHILLPOTTS, Beatrice. 753'.7
The book of fairies / Beatrice Phillpotts. New York : Ballantine Books, 1979, c1978. p. cm. First published under title: Fairy paintings. Includes index. [ND237.P474A4 1979] 78-19680 ISBN 0-345-28091-1 : 15.00. ISBN 0-345-28092-X pbk. : 7.95
1. Phillpotts, Beatrice. 2. Fairies in art. I. Title. BIP

Philpot, Glyn Warren.

OXFORD. University. Ashmolean Museum. 759.2
Glyn Philpot, R.A., 1884-1937 : [catalogue of] a commemorative exhibition [held at the] Ashmolean Museum Oxford 15th September-28th November 1976. Oxford : The Museum, 1976. ix, 12 p. : ill., ports. ; 21 cm. [ND497.P54O93 1976] 77-366014 ISBN 0-900090-41-3 : £0.75
1. Philpot, Glyn Warren. I. Philpot, Glyn Warren.

Phonorecord jackets.

*HERDEG, Walter, comp. 769.5
Record covers. The evolution of graphics reflected in record packaging. Zurich, Graphis Press, [1974] 192 p. illus (part. col.) 25 cm. [NC1880] ISBN 0-8038-2669-9
1. Phonorecord jackets. I. Title.
Distributed by Hastings House, N.Y. for 21.50

PHONOGRAPHICS : 741.6
contemporary album cover art & design / [compiled] by Brad Benedict & Linda Barton. New York : Collier Books, 1977. 137 p. : col. ill. ; 31 cm. Includes index. [NC1882.P48] 77-82314 ISBN 0-02-000100-2 : 9.95
1. Phonorecord jackets. I. Benedict, Brad. II. Barton, Linda. BIP

Phonorecord jackets—United States.

†*PHONOGRAPHICS* : 741.6
contemporary album cover art & design / by Brad Benedict & Linda Barton. New York : Macmillan, c1977. 137 p. : chiefly col. ill. ; 31 cm. Includes index. [NC1883.U6P48 1977b] 78-104847 ISBN 0-02-507570-5 : 19.95
1. Phonorecord jackets—United States. I. Benedict, Brad. II. Barton, Linda.

Photo-engraving.

THE art of photoengraving. 655.32
[Chicago, 1952] 64 p. illus. 26 cm. [TR970.A58] 777 52-40424
1. Photo-engraving. 2. Photo-engraving—Dictionaries. I. American Photoengravers Association.

SOUBIRAN, Julien J *655.32 777
The art and technique of photo-engraving. [2d rev. ed.] [New York? 1952] 104 p. illus. 20 cm. [TR970.S68 1952] 52-9351
1. Photo-engraving. I. Title.

Photo-realism.

DAVIES, Ken, 1926- 759.13
Ken Davies, artist at work / by Ken Davies. New York : Watson-Guptill Publications, 1978. p. cm. Includes index. [ND237.D32A4 1978] 78-17520 ISBN 0-8230-2578-0 : 18.50.
1. Davies, Ken, 1926- 2. Photo-realism. 3. Painting—Technique.

Photochromic materials.

DORION, George Henry. 535.6
Photochromism: optical and photographic applications, by George H. Dorion, Alwyn F. Wiebe. London, New York, Focal P., 1970. 121 p. illus. 25 cm. (The Focal library) Includes bibliographies. [TR210.D68] 74-496800 5/5/-
1. Photochromic materials. I. Wiebe, Alwyn F., joint author. II. Title. BIP

Photocopying processes.

DENSTMAN, Harold. 778.1
Photographic reproduction; methods, techniques, and applications for engineering and the graphic arts [by] Harold Denstman [and] Morton J. Schultz. New York, McGraw-Hill [1963] 187 p. illus. 26 cm. Includes bibliography. [TR825.D4] 62-22198
1. Photocopying processes. 2. Photomechanical processes. I. Schultz, Morton J., joint author. II. Title. BIP

HAWKEN, William R. 778.12
Full-size photocopying. New Brunswick, N.J., Graduate School of Library Service, Rutgers, the State University, 1960. 397 p. illus. 23 cm. (The State of the library art, v. 5, pt. 3) Includes bibliography. [TR925.H3] 60-16770
1. Photocopying processes. I. Title. II. Series.

HAWKEN, William R 778.1
Photocopying from bound volumes; a study of machines, methods, and materials. Chicago, Library Technology Project, American Library Association [1962] Chicago, Library Technology Project, American Library Association, 1963. 208 p. illus. 24 cm. no. illus. 28 cm. (LTP publications, no. 4) [TR927.H3] 61-18876
1. Photocopying processes. I. American Library Association. Library Technology Project. II. Title. III. Title: Supplement. no. 1-

ROTT, Andre. 772'.1
Photographic silver halide diffusion processes [by] Andre Rott and Edith Weyde. London, New York, Focal Press, 1972. 302 p., 8 plates. illus. 25 cm. (The Focal library) Includes bibliographical references. [TR824.R68] 77-188893 ISBN 0-240-50726-6 £7.50
1. Photocopying processes. I. Weyde, Edith. II. Title. BIP

Photocopying processes—Congresses.

SYMPOSIUM on Non-silver Photographic Processes, Oxford, 1973. 686.4'4
Non-silver photographic processes : proceedings of the Symposium on Non-silver Photographic Processes held at New College, Oxford, September, 1973 / edited by R. J. Cox. London ; New York : Published for the Scientific and Technical

Group of the Royal Photographic Society by Academic Press, 1975. xii, 371 p. : ill. ; 24 cm. Organized by the Scientific and Technical Groups Committee of the Royal Photographic Society. Includes bibliographical references and index. [TR824.S95 1973] 74-5676 ISBN 0-12-194440-9 : 24.75
1. Photocopying processes—Congresses. 2. Photoresist—Congresses. I. Cox, R. J. II. Royal Photographic Society of Great Britain, London. III. Title.

Photocopying processes—Patents.

WEISS, Samuel, 1925- 636.4'02'72
Copy papers. Park Ridge, N.J., Noyes Data Corp., 1972. ix, 268 p. illus. 28 cm. [TR824.W44] 72-75226 ISBN 0-8155-0442-X 36.00
1. Photocopying processes—Patents. I. Title.

Photoengraving.

WALLIS, Frederick Gordon. 655.3'27
Letterpress platemaking, by F. G. Wallis and R. V. Cannon. [1st ed. Oxford, New York] Pergamon Press [1969] xi, 249 p. illus. 21 cm. (Library of industrial and commercial education and training. Printing division) Includes bibliographical references. [TR970.W34 1969] 70-77636
1. Photoengraving. I. Cannon, Rupert Vernon, joint author. II. Title.

Photoengraving — Halftone process.

INTERNATIONAL Conference of Printing Research Institutes. 7th, London, 1963. 655.327
Halftone printing; proceedings, Edited by W. H. Banks. Oxford, New York, Symposium Publications Division, Pergamon Press [1964] xii, 423 p. illus. 24 cm. (Advances in printing science and technology, v. 3) Includes bibliographies. [TR975.I5 1963] 64-24960
1. Photoengraving — Halftone process. I. Banks, William H., ed. II. Title. III. Series.

JAFFE, Erwin. 655.327
Halftone photography for offset lithography. [2d ed.] New York, Lithographic Technical Foundation [1960] 210p. illus. 22cm. Includes bibliography. [TR975.J3 1960] 60-15891
1. Photoengraving—Halftone process. I. Title.

NOEMER, Ewald Fred 655.327
The handbook of modern halftone photography, with complete concepts and practices. Demarest, N.J., 07627 [Box 62, Perfect Graphic Graphic Arts Supply Co. 1966, c.1965] 146p. illus. (pt. col.) 24cm. Bibl. [TR975.N6] 66-1217 11.80
1. Photoengraving—Halftone process. I. Title. II. Title: Halftone photography. BIP

NOEMER, Ewald Fred. 686.2'327
The handbook of modern halftone photography, with complete concepts & practices. [4th ed.] Demarest, N.J., Perfect-Graphic-Arts Supply Co. [1969, c1965] 158 p. illus. (part col.), ports. 24 cm. Bibliography: p. 158. [TR975.N6 1969] 72-107025 ISBN 0-911126-02-3
1. Photoengraving—Halftone process. I. Title. II. Title: Halftone photography.

NOEMER, Ewald Fred. 686.2'327
The handbook of modern halftone photography, with complete concepts & practices. [5th ed.] Demarest, N.J., Perfect Grafic-Arts [1972, i.e. 1973] 190 p. illus. 24 cm. Includes bibliographical references. [TR975.N6 1972] 72-78159 ISBN 0-911126-04-X 12.80
1. Photoengraving—Halftone process. I. Title.
Publisher's Address: Dept. 16, P.O. Box 62, Demarest, N.J. 07627.

SIPLEY, Louis Walton. *655.32 777.3
The photomechanical halftone. [Philadelphia] American Museum of Photography [1958] 62 p. illus. 24 cm. Includes bibliography. [TR975.S5] 58-9998
1. Photoengraving — Halftone process. I. Title.

Photoengraving—Halftone process—Handbooks, manuals, etc.

STERNBACH, Harvey. 655.3'27
Halftone reproduction guide, by Harvey Sternbach and Anthony J. Teano. [New York] Sterling-Roman Press [c1965] 100 l. illus. (part col.) 30 x 31 cm. [TR975.S72] 68-695
1. Photoengraving—Halftone process—Handbooks, manuals, etc. 2. Color-printing—Handbooks, manuals, etc. I. Teano, Anthony J., joint author. II. Title. BIP

Photoengraving—Outlines, syllabi, etc.

BENZE, Alexander. 686.2*327*07
An introduction to the art of photoengraving. New Brunswick, N.J., Vocational-Technical Curriculum Laboratory, 1969. iii, 151, 10 p. illus. 28 cm. [TR970.B45] 72-629185
1. Photoengraving—Outlines, syllabi, etc. I. Title.

Photoengraving—Patents.

GUTCHO, M. 686'.2327'0272
Plastic printing plates manufacture and technology [by] M. G. Halpern. Park Ridge, N.J., Noyes Data Corp., 1971. viii, 294 p. 28 cm. [TR970.G88] 79-164890 ISBN 0-8155-0390-3 36.00
1. Photoengraving—Patents. 2. Printing plates—Patents. 3. Plastics—Patents. I. Title.

Photogrammetry.

BAKER, Wilfred H 526.982
Elements of photogrammetry. New York, Ronald Press [1960] 199p. illus. 24cm. [TR693.B3] 60-14858
1. Photogrammetry. 2. Photography, Aerial. I. Title.

FAIRCHILD Camera and Instrument Corporation. 778.38
Calibration certificates used for type T-11, mapping camera. v.1- Syosset, Long Island, N. Y. [195-]- v. illus. 29cm. On spine, v. 1- : Calibration certificates. Camera serial nos. 51-001 to 51-100-- [TR693.F3] 53-34043
1. Photogrammetry. I. Title.

GHOSH, Sanjib Kumar, 1925- 526.9'82
Theory of stereophotogrammetry, by Sanjib K. Ghosh. Columbus, Ohio State University, Dept. of Geodetic Science [1968] xi, 219 p. illus. 23 cm. On spine: Stereophotogrammetry. Bibliography: p. 217-219. [TR693.G56] 68-5126
1. Photogrammetry. I. Title.

GHOSH, Sanjib Kumar, 1925- 526.9'82
Theory of stereophotogrammetry [by] Sanjib K. Ghosh. 2d ed. Columbus, Ohio State University, Dept. of Geodetic Science [1972] xviii, 206 p. illus. 24 cm. Title on spine: Stereophotogrammetry. Bibliography: p. 198-202. [TR693.G56 1972] 72-619604 12.50
1. Photogrammetry. I. Title.

LYON, Duane. 526.982
Basic metrical photogrammetry. St. Louis, Mo. [1959] 1v. illus. 22cm. 'Volume 1 in a proposed series of three textbooks on the subject of photogrammetry.' [TR693.L9] 59-44020
1. Photogrammetry. I. Title.

MCNEIL, Gomer T 770.28
Photographic measurements, problems and solutions. New York, Pitman Pub. Corp. [1954] unpaged. illus. 24cm. Includes bibliography. [TR693.M2] 54-13370
1. Photogrammetry. I. Title.

WILLIAMS, John C. C. 526.9'82
Simple photogrammetry: plan-making from small-camera photographs taken in the air, on the ground or underwater, by J. C. C. Williams. London, New York, Academic P., 1969. x, 211 p. illus., plans. 24 cm. Bibliography: p. 206. [TR693.W55] 70-92400 50/-
1. Photogrammetry. I. Title. BIP

WOLF, Paul R. 526.9'82
Elements of photogrammetry (with air photo interpretation and remote sensing) [by] Paul R. Wolf. New York, McGraw-Hill [1974] xiii, 562 p. illus. 24 cm. Includes bibliographies. [TR693.W64] 73-21856 ISBN 0-07-071337-5 16.50
1. Photogrammetry. 2. Aerial photogrammetry. 3. Photographic interpretation. I. Title.

Photogrammetry—Equipment and supplies—Catalogs.

CIMERMAN, Vjekoslav. 526.9'82
Atlas of photogrammetric instruments. [By] Vj. Cimerman and Z. Tomasegovic. Amsterdam, New York, Elsevier Pub. Co., 1970. viii, 216 p. with illus. 30 cm. Bibliography: p. [211] [TR696.C55] 67-12773 ISBN 0-444-40700-6 fl104.00
1. Photogrammetry—Equipment and supplies—Catalogs. I. Tomasegovic, Zdenko, joint author. II. Title. BIP

Photogrammetry—Tables, calculations, etc.

MERRITT, Everett L 778.38
Analytical photogrammetry. New York, Pitman Pub. Corp. [1958] 242p. illus. 24cm. [TR695.M4] 58-6204
1. Photogrammetry—Tables, calculations, etc. 2. Geometry, Analytic. I. Title.

Photograms.

BRUANDET, Pierre. 772'.1
Photograms. [Translated by Rodney J. Cox, and adapted by John M. Pickering] New York, Watson-Guptill Publications [1974, c1973] 95 p. illus. 21 cm. [TR656.B713 1974] 73-8855 ISBN 0-8230-4010-0 8.50
1. Photograms. BIP

HAFFER, Virna. 778.8
Making photograms; the creative process of painting with light. With an introd. by Jacob Deschin. New York, Hastings House [1969] 128 p. illus. 26 cm. (Visual communication books) [TR656.H34] 74-93093 10.00
1. Photograms. I. Title. BIP

MARINO, T. J. 770'.28
Pictures without a camera, by T. J. Marino. New York, Sterling Pub. Co. [1974] 48 p. illus. 20 cm. (Little craft book series) Instructions for using a variety of techniques to create photograms—photographic-type pictures made without a camera. [TR682.C37 1974] 73-93595 ISBN 0-8069-5296-2 3.50
1. Photograms. I. Title.
Lib. bdg. 3.69, ISBN 0-8069-5297-0.

SMITH, Henry Holmes. 779'.5'0924
Henry Holmes Smith. [Louisville, Ky.] Center for Photographic Studies [1973] 10 plates (in portfolio) 54 x 43 cm. (Center for Photographic Studies. Portfolio 2) Cover title. A limited ed. of 130 signed and numbered copies. L. C. copy no. 39. [TR656.S5] 73-170137 125.00
1. Photograms. 2. Photography, Artistic. I. Title. II. Series.

Photograms—Juvenile literature.

HOBAN, Tana. 779
Shapes and things. [New York] Macmillan [1970] 36 p. (chiefly illus.) 26 cm. Photographs, created without a camera, of familiar household objects. [TR682.H6] 70-102965 4.95
1. Photograms—Juvenile literature. I. Title. BIP

Photograph collections—Directories.

GREEN, Shirley L. 779'.074'0153
Pictorial resources in the Washington, D.C., area / compiled by Shirley L. Green, with the assistance of Diane Hamilton, for the Federal Library Committee. Washington : Library of Congress, 1976. xv, 297 p. : ill. ; 24 cm. Includes index. [TR12.G73] 75-619383 ISBN 0-8444-0202-8
1. Photograph collections—Directories. 2. Art—Collectors and collecting—Washington metropolitan area—Directories. I. Hamilton, Diane, 1943- joint author. II. United States. Federal Library Committee. III. United States. Library of Congress. IV. Title.

NATIONAL Photographic Record. 779'.0941'0740941
Directory of British photographic collections / compiled by the National Photographic Record, a department of the Royal Photographic Society of Great Britain ; editor, John Wall. London : Camera/Graphic Press, [1977]i.e.1978 p. cm. Includes indexes. Bibliography: p. [TR12.N37 1977] 77-74779 ISBN 0-918696-00-3 : 32.00
1. Photograph collections—Directories. I. Wall, John. II. Title.
Publisher's address: P. O Box 1702 F.DR Station, New York, NY 10022 BIP

Photographers.

GERNSHEIM, Helmut, 1913- ed. 770'.92'2
The man behind the camera / edited by Helmut Gernsheim ; foreword by Rathbone Holme. New York : Arno Press, 1979. p. cm. (The Sources of modern photography) Reprint of the 1948 ed. published by Fountain Press, London. [TR139.G4 1979] 76-24683 ISBN 0-405-09655-0 : 15.00
1. Photographers. 2. Photography, Artistic. I. Title. II. Series. BIP

RAYFIELD, Stanley. 927.7
Life photographers, their careers and favorite pictures. [Garden City, N. Y.] Doubleday [1957] 89p. illus. 37cm. [TR139.R3] 57-10628
1. Photographers. 2. Life (Chicago) I. Title.

WHO'S who in photography; the focal world register. [Compiled by Ruth Matthews] London, New York, Focal Press [1951] 340 p. 26 cm. [TR139.W49] 61-38402 770.58
1. Photographers.

Photographers, American—Addresses, essays, lectures.

OSTENDORF, Lloyd. 770'.92'2
Lincoln and his photographers; address at annual meeting, Lincoln Fellowship of Wisconsin, Madison, 1971. [Madison] 1972. 14 p. ports. 26 cm. ([Historical Fellowship of Wisconsin] Historical bulletin no. 27) Cover title. [TR681.F3O8] 73-151399
1. Lincoln, Abraham, Pres. U.S., 1809-1865—Portraits—Addresses, essays, lectures. 2. Photographers, American—Addresses, essays, lectures. I. Title. II. Series.

Photographers, British.

BOORD, W. Arthur. 770'.92'2
Sun Artists, edited by W. Arthur Boord. New York, Arno Press, 1973. 60 p. illus. 32 cm. (Literature of Photography) Originally published in 1891. [TR139.B6 1973] 72-9184 ISBN 0-405-04895-5. 30.00.
1. Photographers, British. 2. Photography, Artistic. I. Title. II. Series.

Photographers—Correspondence, reminiscences, etc.

BEATON, Cecil Walter Hardy, 1904- 927.7
The face of the world; an international scrapbook of people and places. New York, Day [1957] 240 p. illus., ports. 29 cm. [TR140.B4A27] 57-14526
1. Photographers—Correspondence, reminiscences, etc. I. Title.

BEATON, Cecil Walter Hardy, 1904- 927.7
Photobiography. [1st ed.] Garden City, N. Y., Doubleday, 1951. 255 p. illus., ports. 26 cm. [TR140.B4A3] 51-11655
1. Photographers—Correspondence, reminiscences, etc. I. Title.

DUNCAN, Charles. 927.7
A photographic pilgrim's progress; being the adventures of an itinerant photographer among cameras, cabbages, and kings. With

a pref. by Percy W. Harris. London, New York, Focal Press [1954] 160p. 19cm. [TR140.D8A3] 55-20528
1. Photographers —Correspondence, reminiscences, etc. I. Title.

GORE, Art, 1926- 779'.92'4
Images of yesterday / by Art Gore. Palo Alto, Calif. : American West Pub. Co., [1975] [103] p. : chiefly ill. ; 24 x 32 cm. [TR140.G65A32] 75-6322 ISBN 0-910118-67-1 : 12.95
1. Gore, Art, 1926- 2. Photographers—Correspondence, reminiscences, etc. 3. Country life—United States. I. Title. BIP

HILL, George Henry, 1900- 920.5
Yankee photographer; with photos. by the author. New York, Coward-McCann [1953] 184 p. illus. 21 cm. [TR140.H5A3] 53-8886
1. Photographers—Correspondence, reminiscences, etc. 2. Photography, Journalistic. I. Title.

IVENS, Joris, 1898- 791.43'023'0924 B
The camera and I. New York, International Publishers [1969] 279 p. illus., ports. 19 cm. [TR140.I77A3 1969] 75-10169 1.95
I. Title. BIP

KIRKLAND, Wallace. 920.5
Recollections of a Life photographer. Photos. by the author. Boston, Houghton Mifflin, 1954. 272p. illus. 22cm. [TR140.K5A3] 54-9121
1. Photographers —Correspondence, reminiscences, etc. 2. Life (Chicago) I. Title.

PARKS, Gordon. 770.924 [B]
A choice of weapons. New York, Harper & Row [1973 c.1966] 222 p. 18 cm. (Perennial Library) [PS3566.A73C5] ISBN 0-06-080305-3 1.25 (pbk.)
I. Title.
L.C. card no. for original ed.: 64-25119.

PARKS, Gordon, 1912- 770.924 B
A choice of weapons. [1st ed.] New York, Harper & Row [1966] x, 274 p. 22 cm. [PS3566.A73C5] 64-25119
I. Title.

PARKS, Gordon, 1912- 770.924
A choice of weapons. [New York] Berkley [1967, c.1966] 222p. 18cm. (Medallion bk., S1399) [PS3566.A73C5] .75 pap.,
I. Title. BIP

PENDRIGH, Ernest. 927.7
The magic box; exploits of a street-photographer. London, New York, J. Long [1954] 156p. illus. 22cm. [TR140.P4A3] 54-44344
1. Photographers—Correspondence, reminiscences, etc. I. Title.

RODGERS, H. J. 770'.92'4
Twenty three years under a sky-light; or, Life and experiences of a photographer, by H. J. Rodgers. New York, Arno Press, 1973 [c1872] 235 p. illus. 21 cm. (The Literature of Photography) [TR140.R63A35 1973] 72-9233 ISBN 0-405-04938-2 14.00.
I. Title. II. Series. BIP

STOBART, Tom. 778
I take pictures for adventure. [1st ed.] Garden City, N.Y., Doubleday, 1958. 288 p. illus. 22 cm. [TR440.S72A3] 58-10042
1. Photographers — Correspondence, reminiscences, etc. I. Title.

STOBART, Tom. 778
I take pictures for adventure. [1st ed.] Garden City, N.Y., Doubleday, 1958. 288 p. illus. 22 cm. [TR140.S72A3] 58-10042
1. Photographers—Correspondence, reminiscences, etc. I. Title.

Photographers—England—Biography.

ARNOLD, Harry John Philip, 1932- 770'.92'4 B
William Henry Fox Talbot : pioneer of photography and man of science / [by] H. J. P. Arnold. London : Hutchinson, 1977. 383 p., leaf of plate, [48] p. of plates : ill. (some col.), col. coat of arms, facsims., geneal. tables, ports. (some col.) ; 26 cm. Includes bibliographies and index. [TR140.T3A76] 78-320092 ISBN 0-09-129600-5 : 31.95
1. Talbot, William Henry Fox, 1800-1877. 2. Photographers—England—Biography.
Distributed by Merrimack Book Service BIP

BEATON, Cecil Walter Hardy, Sir, 1904- 770'.92'4 B
The restless years : diaries, 1955-63 / Cecil Beaton. London : Weidenfeld and Nicolson, c1976. 190 p., [6] leaves of plates : ill. ; 23 cm. [TR140.B4A32] 76-377856 ISBN 0-297-77155-8 : £4.95
1. Beaton, Cecil Walter Hardy, Sir, 1904- 2. Photographers—England—Biography. I. Title.

FLUKINGER, Roy, 1947- 770'.92'4 B
Paul Martin : Victorian photographer / by Roy Flukinger, Larry Schaaf, and Standish Meacham. Austin : University of Texas Press, c1977. p. cm. Includes index. Bibliography: p. [TR140.M35F59] 77-4764 ISBN 0-292-76436-7 : 24.95
1. Martin, Paul, 1864-1944. 2. Photographers—England—Biography. I. Schaaf, Larry, 1947- joint author. II. Meacham, Standish, joint author. BIP

HANNAVY, John. 770'.92'4 B
Fox Talbot : an illustrated life of William Henry Fox Talbot, "Father of modern photography," 1800-1877 / John Hannavy. Princes Risborough : Shire Publications, 1976. 48 p. : ill., facsims., ports. ; 21 cm. (Lifelines ; 38) Includes index. Bibliography: p. 46. [TR140.T3H36] 76-383859 ISBN 0-85263-319-X : £0.60
1. Talbot, William Henry Fox, 1800-1877. 2. Photographers—England—Biography.

Photographers—Interviews.

DANZIGER, James, 1953- 770'.92'2 B
Interviews with master photographers : Minor White, Imogen Cunningham, Cornell Capa, Elliott Erwitt, Yousuf Karsh, Arnold Newman, Lord Snowdon, Brett Weston / James Danziger, Barnaby Conrad III. New York : Paddington Press : distributed by Grosset & Dunlap, c1977. 175 p., [12] leaves of plates : ill. ; 24 cm. [TR139.D36] 76-53315 ISBN 0-448-22183-7 : 10.00
1. Photographers—Interviews. I. Conrad, Barnaby, 1953- joint author. II. Title. BIP

DUGAN, Thomas, 1938- 770'.92'2
Photography between covers : interviews with photo-bookmakers / Thomas Dugan. Rochester, N.Y. : Light Impressions, c1979. p. cm. Includes bibliographical references. [TR147.D83] 79-9260 ISBN 0-87992-012-2 : 15.00 ISBN 0-87992-011-4 (pbk.) : 8.95
1. Photographers—Interviews. 2. Publishers and publishing—Interviews. I. Title. BIP

LAPLANTE, Jerry C. 770'.92'2
Photographers on photography / by Jerry C. LaPlante. New York : Drake Publishers, [1978] p. cm. [TR147.L36] 78-7063 ISBN 0-8473-1764-1 pbk. 5.95
1. Photographers—Interviews. 2. Photography. I. Title. BIP

Photographers—Juvenile literature.

FORSEE, Aylesa. 770.922
Famous photographers; excellence in professional photography as seen through the lives and work of five masters: Edward Steichen, Ansel Adams, Cecil Beaton, Yousuf Karsh [and] David D. Duncan. Philadelphia, Macrae Smith [1968] 223 p. illus., ports. 24 cm. Bibliography: p. [213]-215. [TR139.F6] 68-18810
1. Photographers—Juvenile literature. I. Title.

Photographers—United States—Biography.

ATKINS, Ollie, 1916- 770'.92'4 B
The White House years : triumph and tragedy / Ollie Atkins. 1st ed. Chicago : Playboy Press, c1977. 244 p. : ill. ; 24 cm. [TR140.A82A38] 77-23545 ISBN 0-87223-494-0 : 12.50
1. Atkins, Ollie, 1916- 2. Nixon, Richard Milhous, 1913- 3. Photographers—United States—Biography. I. Title. BIP

†BOHN, Dave. 770'.92'2
Kinsey, photographer : a half century of negatives by Darius and Tabitha May Kinsey, with contributions by son and daughter, Darius, Jr., and Dorothea / produced by Dave Bohn and Rodolfo Petschek. San Francisco : Chronicle Books, 1977, c1975. p. cm. Contents.Contents.—v. 1. The family album & other early work.—v. 2. The magnificent years. Bibliography: p. [TR140.K45B64 1977] 78-1029 ISBN 0-87701-107-9 : 19.95
1. Kinsey, Darius, 1869-1945. 2. Kinsey, Tabitha May, 1875-1963. 3. Photographers—United States—Biography. 4. Lumbering—Washington (State)—Pictorial works. I. Petschek, Rodolfo, joint author. II. Title. BIP

BROWNING, Norma Lee. 770'.92'4 B
He saw a hummingbird / Norma Lee Browning and Russell Ogg. 1st ed. New York : Dutton, c1978. xi, 143 p., [4] leaves of plates : ill. ; 21 cm. [TR140.B785B76] 78-2559 8.95
1. Browning, Russell. 2. Photographers—United States—Biography. 3. Diabetic rutinopathy—Biography. I. Ogg, Russell, joint author. II. Title. BIP

GENTHE, Arnold, 1869-1942. 770'.92'4 B
As I remember / Arnold Genthe. New York : Arno Press, 1979, c1936. p. cm. (The Sources of modern photography) Reprint of the ed. published by Reynal & Hitchcock, New York. Includes index. [TR140.G4A3 1979] 76-24684 ISBN 0-405-09660-7 : 28.00
1. Genthe, Arnold, 1869-1942. 2. Photographers—United States—Biography. I. Title. II. Series. BIP

KUNHARDT, Dorothy Meserve, 1901- 770'.92'4 B
Mathew Brady and his world : produced by Time-Life Books from pictures in the Meserve collection / by Dorothy Meserve Kunhardt and Philip B. Kunhardt, Jr., and the editors of Time-Life Books. Alexandria, Va. : Time-Life Books ; Morristown, N.J. : school and library distribution by Silver Burdett Co., c1977. 303 p. : ill. ; 30 cm. [TR140.B7K8] 77-73043 ISBN 0-8094-1775-8 : 25.00
1. Brady, Mathew B., 1823 (ca.)-1896. 2. Meserve, Frederick Hill, 1865-1962—Photograph collections. 3. Photographers—United States—Biography. I. Kunhardt, Philip B., joint author. II. Time-Life Books. III. Title.

MELTZER, Milton, 1915- 770'.92'4 B
Dorothea Lange : a photographer's life / Milton Meltzer. New York : Farrar Straus Giroux, c1978. xii, 399 p. : ill. ; 24 cm. Includes index. Bibliography: p. 385-391. [TR140.L3M44 1978] 78-5509 ISBN 0-374-14323-4 : 15.00
1. Lange, Dorothea. 2. Photographers—United States—Biography.

NOVOTNY, Ann. 770'.92'4 B
Alice's world : the life and photography of an American original, Alice Austen, 1866-1952 / by Ann Novotny ; pref. by Oliver Jensen. Old Greenwich, Conn. : Chatham Press, c1976. 221 p. : ill. ; 31 cm. [TR140.A83N67] 76-18489 ISBN 0-85699-128-7 : 22.50
1. Austen, Alice, 1866-1952. 2. Photographers—United States—Biography. I. Austen, Alice, 1866-1952. II. Title. BIP

STEINER, Ralph, 1899- 770'.92'4 B
A point of view / Ralph Steiner. 1st ed. Middletown, Conn. : Wesleyan University Press, c1978. xii, 144 p. : ill. ; 27 cm. [TR140.S683A34] 77-20513 ISBN 0-8195-5019-1 : 20.00
1. Steiner, Ralph, 1899- 2. Photographers—United States—Biography. I. Title. BIP

WHITE, Minor. 770'.92'4 B
Minor White : rites & passages : his photographs accompanied by excerpts from his diaries and letters / biographical essays by James Baker Hall. Millerton, N.Y. : Aperture, 1978. 141 p., [1] leaf of plates : ill. ; 30 cm. Bibliography: p. 137-141. [TR650.W48] 77-80023 ISBN 0-89381-022-3 : 25.00
1. White, Minor. 2. Photography, Artistic. 3. Photographers—United States—Biography.

Photographers—United States—Biography—Juvenile literature.

BOESEN, Victor. 779'.9'970004970924 B
Edward S. Curtis, photographer of the North American Indian / Victor Boesen and Florence Curtis Graybill. New York : Dodd, Mead & Co., [1977] p. cm. Includes index. A biography of Edward Curtis who spent many years photographing, writing about, and recording the songs of the North American Indians. [TR140.C82B63] 92 76-53435 ISBN 0-396-07430-8 : 6.95
1. Curtis, Edward S., 1868-1952—Juvenile literature. 2. Photographers—United States—Biography—Juvenile literature. 3. Indians of North America—Juvenile literature. I. Graybill, Florence Curtis, joint author.

DUNHAM, Montrew. 770'.92'4 B
Margaret Bourke-White, young photographer / by Montrew Dunham ; illustrated by Robert Doremus. Indianapolis : Bobbs-Merrill, c1977. 192 p. : ill. ; 20 cm. (Childhood of famous Americans) A biography of the photographer and writer who was one of the original staff photographers for Life magazine and the first accredited woman war correspondent to be sent overseas during World War II. [TR140.B6D86] 92 75-34512 ISBN 0-672-52225-X : 3.95 ISBN 0-672-71413-2 lib.bdg. : 3.73
1. Bourke-White, Margaret, 1906-1971. 2. Photographers—United States—Biography—Juvenile literature. I. Doremus, Robert. II. Title.

HOOBLER, Dorothy. 770'.92'4 B
Photographing history : the career of Mathew Brady / by Dorothy and Thomas Hoobler. New York : Putnam, c1977. 143 p. : ill. ; 24 cm. Includes index. A biography of the photographer of famous men and women of his time who left his studio at the zenith of his career to travel with Union troops photographing the Civil War. [TR140.B7H59 1977] 92 77-3009 ISBN 0-399-20602-7 : 8.95.
1. Brady, Mathew B., 1823 (ca.)-1896—Juvenile literature. 2. Photographers—United States—Biography—Juvenile literature. I. Hoobler, Thomas, joint author. II. Title.

Photographic chemicals—Analysis.

RUSSELL, Gerald. 771.5
Chemical analysis in photography [by] G. Russell. London.New York. Focal P. [1966] 272 p. tables, diagrs. 25 cm. (The Focal library) 90/- Includes bibliographies. [TR212.R8] 66-71906
1. Photographic chemicals—Analysis. I. Title. BIP

Photographic chemistry.

CLERC, Louis Philippe, 1875- 771.5
Properties of photographic materials. Tr. from French by C. J. Duncan. London, Fountain Pr.[dist. New York, Morgan & Morgan, 1964, c.1950] 230p. illus. 23cm. Bibl. 51-28719 7.95
1. Photographic chemistry. 2. Photography—Apparatus and supplies. I. Title.

DYE sensitization: 771.5
symposium [held at] Bressanone; edited by W. F. Berg [and others] London, New York, Focal, 1970. 309 p. illus. 25 cm. (The Focal Library) "Organized by G. Semerano and U. Mazzucato." Includes bibliographies. [TR210.D9] 535.6 78-575485 £10.00
1. Photographic chemistry. 2. Dyes and dyeing. 3. Photographic emulsions. I. Berg, Wolfgang Friedrich. II. Semerano, Giovanni, 1907- III. Mazzucato, U. BIP

GLAFKIDES, Pierre, 1912- 771.5
Photographic chemistry; 2v. Tr. from French by Keith M. Hornsby. Foreword by L. P. Clerc London, Fountain Pr. [dist. New York, Morgan & Morgan, 1964] 2v. (xiii, 996p.) illus. 26cm. Bibl. 61-40118 21.00 set.
1. Photographic chemistry. I. Title.

HORNSBY, Keith M. 771.5
Basic photographic chemistry [London] Fountain Pr. [dist. New York, Morgan &Morgan, 1964, c.1956] 158p. illus. 20cm. (Fountain photobk.) 56-4566 3.95 bds.,
1. Photographic chemistry. I. Title.

HUNT, Robert, 1807-1887. 770'.1'54135
Researches on light New York, Arno Press, 1973. vii, 303 p. illus. 23 cm. (The Literature of Philosophy) Reprint of the 1844 ed. Includes bibliographical references. [TR210.H86 1973] 72-9213 ISBN 0-405-04921-8. 18.00.
1. Photographic chemistry. 2. Photochemistry. 3. Photography—Early works to 1850. I. Title. II. Series. **BIP**

JOHN, David Hugh Oakley. 771.5
Photographic chemistry [by] D. H. O. John and G. T. J. Field. New York, Reinhold Pub. Corp., 1963. ix, 330 p. illus. 23 cm. Includes bibliographies. [TR210.J6] 63-24072
1. Photographic chemistry. I. Field, G. T. J., joint author.

LIALIKOV, K. S. 771'.5
The chemistry of photographic mechanisms [by] K. S. Lyalikov; tr. from Russian in co-operation with the Department of Scientific and Industrial Research. by Grace E. Locke ed. by E. A. Southerns. London, New York, Focal Pr., 1967. 355p. 25cm. (Focal lib.) (romanized: Teoriia fotograficheskihn protsessov) Bibl. [TR210.L513] 67-101468 38.00
I. Photographic chemistry. II. Title. **BIP**

MASON, Leslie Frederick Alfred. 771.54
Photographic processing chemistry, by L. F. A. Mason. London, New York, Focal P. [1966] 321 p. 4 plates, tables, diagrs. 25 cm. (The Focal library) Includes bibliographies. [TR210.M38 1966] 67-70608
1. Photographic chemistry. 2. Photography—Developing and developers. I. Title. **BIP**

MASON, Leslie Frederick Alfred. 771'.54
Photographic processing chemistry / L. F. A. Mason. 2nd ed. London ; New York : Focal Press, 1975. 326 p., 4 p. of plates : ill. ; 25 cm. Includes bibliographical references and index. [TR210.M38 1975b] 75-326617 ISBN 0-240-50824-6 : 15.00
1. Photographic chemistry. 2. Photography—Developing and developers. I. Title.

Photographic chemistry—Congresses.

INTERNATIONAL Colloquium on Scientific Photography, Liege, 1959. 771.53
Scientific photography; proceedings. Sponsored by the patrimoine de l Universite de Liege. Edited by H. Sauvenier. Oxford New York, Symposium Publications Division, Pergamon Press, 1962. xx, 617p. illus. 25cm. Includes bibliographies. [TR5.I48 1959] 60-14185
1. Photographic chemistry— Congresses. 2. Photographic emulsions. I. Sauvenier, Henri, ed. II. Liege. Universite. III. Title.

INTERNATIONAL Congress of Photographic Science, Tokyo, 1967. 770
The photographic image: formation and structure: the invited papers presented at the International Congress of Photographic Science, Tokyo, 1967; edited by S. Kikuchi. London, New York, Focal, 1970. 210 p. illus. 25 cm. (The Focal library) By H. Ammann-Brass and others. Includes bibliographical references. [TR210.I58 1967] 72-193072 £6.00
1. Photographic chemistry—Congresses. 2. Photochemistry—Congresses. I. Kikuchi, Sadao, 1924- ed. II. Ammann-Brass, H. III. Title.

Photographic emulsions.

CARROLL, Burt Haring, 1896- 661'.808
The photographic emulsion, by B. H. Carroll, D. Hubbard and C. M. Kretschman. London, New York, Focal P. [1968] 276 p. 2 plates, illus. 25 cm. (The Focal library) Originally published as a series of papers in the U.S. Bureau of Standards Journal of research between 1928-1934. Includes bibliographies. [TR280.C36] 74-433694 5/5/-
1. Photographic emulsions. I. Hubbard, Donald, 1900- II. Kretchman, Charles Monroe, 1912- III. Title. **BIP**

ZELIKMAN, Vitalii L'vovich 770.281
Making and coating photographic emulsions [by] V. L. Zelikman, S. M. Levi [Tr. from Russian by Consultants Bur.,iNew York. New York, Focal [1965, c.1964] 312p. illus. 25cm. (Focal lib.) Bibl. [TR395.Z3713] 65-2520 23.00
1. Photographic emulsions. I. Levi, Sergei Maksimovich, joint author. II. Title.

Photographic emulsions—Patents.

JAMES, Ronald W. 772'.1
Photographic emulsions; recent developments [by] Ronald W. James. Park Ridge, N.J., Noyes Data Corp., 1973. x, 303 p. illus. 25 cm. (Chemical technology review no. 21) [TR280.J36] 73-85968 ISBN 0-8155-0512-4 36.00
1. Photographic emulsions—Patents. I. Title. II. Series.

Photographic gelatin.

CROOME, Ronald John. 661.808
Photographic gelatin, by R. J. Crooms and F. G. Clegg. London, New York, Focal Press [1965] 91 p. illus. 25 cm. (The Focal library) Includes bibliographies. [TR395.C75] 65-5915
1. Photographic gelatin. I. Clegg, F. G., joint author. II. Title.

Photographic gelatin—Congresses.

SYMPOSIUM on Photographic Gelatin, 3d, Cambridge, Eng., 1974. 661'.808
Photographic gelatin II : proceedings of the Symposium on Photographic Gelatin held at Gonville and Caius College and Little Hall, Cambridge, September, 1974 / edited by R. J. Cox. London ; New York : Published for the Scientific and Technical Group of the Royal Photographic Society by Academic Press, 1976. xiv, 390 p. : ill. ; 24 cm. Includes bibliographical references and index. [TR395.S97 1974] 76-372419 ISBN 0-12-194452-2 : 29.75
1. Photographic gelatin—Congresses. I. Cox, R. J. II. Title.

Photographic industry—Job descriptions.

NEW Jersey Occupational Research Center. 778'.023
Occupations in the film processing and finishing industry. [By Naomi R. Smith and Louis P. Clark. Trenton] New Jersey State Employment Service [1969] vii, 134 p. illus. 29 cm. Bibliography: p. 128-130. [TR154.N47] 79-631349
1. Photographic industry—Job descriptions. I. Smith, Naomi R. II. Clark, Louis P. III. Title.

Photographic interpretation.

AVERY, Thomas Eugene. 778.3'5
Interpretation of aerial photographs / Thomas Eugene Avery. 3d ed. Minneapolis : Burgess Pub. Co., c1977. xi, 392 p., [6] leaves of plates : ill. (some col.) ; 27 cm. Includes bibliographies and index. [TR810.A9 1977] 76-9253 ISBN 0-8087-0130-4 : 14.95
1. Photographic interpretation. 2. Photography, Aerial. I. Title.

RIB, Harold T. 625.7'08 s
Investigations into automatic interpretations of terrain features, by Harold T. Rib and Robert D. Miles. Lafayette, Ind., Purdue University, 1968. iii, 27 l. illus. 28 cm. (Purdue University. Joint Highway Research Project. Technical paper no. 10) "Joint Highway Research Project, project no. C-36-32U, file no. 1-4-21." "Prepared as part of an investigation conducted by Joint Highway Research Project, Purdue University." Bibliography: leaf 27. [TE1.P8 no. 10] [TR810] 778.3'5 73-160465
1. Photographic interpretation. I. Miles, Robert D., 1923- joint author. II. Purdue University, Lafayette, Ind. Engineering Experiment Station. Joint Highway Research Project. III. Title. IV. Series: Purdue University, Lafayette, Ind. Engineering Experiment Station. Joint Highway Research Project. Technical paper no. 10.

RICHASON, Benjamin F. 778.3'5
Atlas of cultural features; a study of man's imprint on the land, by Benjamin F. Richason. [Northbrook, Ill.] Hubbard Press [1972] 96 p. illus. 28 cm. [TR810.R47] 72-138629 ISBN 0-8331-1301-1
1. Photographic interpretation. 2. Topographical maps. I. Title.

STRANDBERG, Carl H. 778.3'52
Aerial discovery manual [by] Carl H. Strandberg. New York, Wiley [1967] xiv, 249 p. illus. (part col.), maps. 31 cm. (Wiley series on photographic science and technology and the graphic arts) [TR810.S8] 67-19945
1. Photographic interpretation. 2. Aerial photography in geology. 3. Aerial photography in hydrology. I. Title. **BIP**

Photographic interpretation—Addresses, essays, lectures.

SYMPOSIUM on Automatic Photointerpretation, Washington, D.C., 1967. 621.3819'5
Pictorial pattern recognition; proceedings. Edited by George C. Cheng [and others] Washington, Thompson Book Co., 1968. viii, 521 p. illus. 24 cm. "Sponsored by the Office of Naval Research, the University of Maryland, and the Pattern Recognition Society." Includes bibliographies. [TR705.S95 1967] 68-21811
1. Photographic interpretation—Addresses, essays, lectures. 2. Scanning systems—Addresses, essays, lectures. 3. Pattern perception—Congresses. I. Cheng, George Chiwo, 1929- ed. II. United States. Office of Naval Research.

Photographic optics.

BROCK, Gerald Clement, 1911- 778.3'5
Image evaluation for aerial photography: an appraisal of current techniques by G. C. Brock. London, New York, Focal P., 1970. 258 p., 3 plates. illus. 25 cm. (The Focal library) Includes bibliographical references. [TR220.B76] 74-549412 ISBN 0-240-50716-9 £5/5/-
1. Photographic optics. 2. Photographic interpretation. 3. Photography, Aerial. I. Title. **BIP**

CHAMBERLAIN, Katherine McFarlane, 1892- 770
An introduction to the science of photography. New York, Macmillan [1951] xiii, 292 p. illus. (part col.) 25 cm. Includes bibliographies. [TR220.C47] 51-530
1. Photographic optics. 2. Photography. I. Title.

COX, Arthur. 771.35
Optics; the technique of definition. 11th ed. London, New York, Focal Press [1956] 375p. illus. 19cm. (The Manual of photo-technique) [TR220.C72 1956] 56-47569
1. Photographic optics. 2. Lenses, Photographic. I. Title.

COX, Arthur. 771.35
Optics, the technique of definition. 10th ed. London, New York, Focal Press [1953] 376p. illus. 19cm. (The Manual of photo-technique) Includes bibliography. [TR220.C72 1953] 54-1094
1. Photographic optics. 2. Lenses, Photographic. I. Title.

COX, Arthur. 771.352
Photographic optics: a modern approach to the technique of definition. 13th ed. London, New York, Focal P., 1966. 490 p. illus., col. plate, tables, diagrs. 22 cm. (The Manual of photo-techniques) (The Manuals of phototechnique) Previous ed. published as Optics. "Distributed in U.S.A. by AMPHOTO ... New York." [TR220.C72 1966] 66-72220 50/-
1. Photographic optics. 2. Lenses, Photographic. I. Series.

COX, Arthur. 771.3'5
Photographic optics, a modern approach to the technique of definition. Expanded ed. London, New York, Focal Press, 1971. 502 p., plate. illus. (some col.) 22 cm. (The Manuals of photo-technique) "Distributed in the U.S.A. by Amphoto, New York, N.Y. First published in 1943 under title: Optics, the technique of definition. Bibliography p. 484-486. [TR220.C72 1971] 76-169525 ISBN 0-8174-0665-4 £3.00
1. Photographic optics. 2. Lenses, Photographic. I. Title.

FRANKE, Georg 771.352
Physical optics in photography tr. [from German] by R. S. Ankersmit New York Focal [dist Pitman c.1966] 218p. illus., col. plate. tables. diagrs. 25cm. (Focal lib.) Bibl. [TR220.F713] 66-71511 20.00
1. Photographic optics. I. Title. **BIP**

GREENLEAF, Allen R. 771.352
Photographic optics. New York, Macmillan, 1950. vii, 214 p. illus. 25 cm. Bibliography: p. 199-200. [TR220.G7] 50-14514
1. Photographic optics. I. Title.

THE wonders of light and 770'.28
shadow. New York, Arno Press, 1973. 106 p. illus. 22 cm. (The Literature of Photography) Reprint of the 1851 ed. [TR220.W6 1973] 72-9236 ISBN 0-405-04941-2 9.00.
1. Photographic optics. 2. Photography—Apparatus and supplies. 3. Photography—Special effects. I. Society for promoting Christian knowledge, London. General literature committee. II. Title. III. Series. **BIP**

Photographic reconnaissance systems.

JENSEN, Niels, 1932- 621.36
Optical and photographic reconnaissance svstems. New York, Wiley [1968] xi, 211p. illus. 23cm. (Wiley ser. on photographic sci. & technol. & the graphic arts) Bibl. [TR810.J4] 67-29936 13.95
1. Photographic reconnaissance svstems. 2. Electrooptical photography. I. Title.

Photographic sensitometry.

GOROKHOVSKII, I.U. N. 771.'534
Spectral studies of the photographic process [by] Yu. N. Gorokhovskii. London, New York, Focal Press [1965] 357 p. illus. 25 cm. (The Focal library) Translation of (romanized: Spektral'nye issledovaniia fotograficheskogo protsessa) Includes bibliographies. [TR280.G5713] 67-4085
1. Photographic sensitometry. 2. Color photography. 3. Spectrum analysis. I. Title. **BIP**

GOROKHOVSKII, IU. N. 771.534
General sensitometry [by] Yu. N. Gorokhovskii, T. M. Levenberg. [Tr. from Russian in co-operation with the Dept. of Sci. and Industrial Res., Natl. Lending Lib. for Sci. and Tech., Boston Spa (Yorks) by Grace E. Lockie] New York, Focal [dist. Pitman, 1966] 303p. illus. 25cm. (Focal lib.) Bibl. [TR196.G613] 66-1346 27.50
1. Photographic sensitometry. I. Levenberg, Tat'iana Mikhailovna, joint author. II. Title.

LOBEL, Leopold, 1881- 661'.808
Sensitometry; the technique of measuring photographic materials, by L. Lobel and M. Dubois. [1st ed.] London, New York, Focal Press [1955] 263p. illus. 19cm. (The Manual ofphoto-technique) 'Translated and adapted by E. F. Teal from the French edition Manuel de sensitometrie.' [TR196.L63] 56-2001
1. Photographic sensitometry. I. Dubois, M., chemical engineer. II. Title.

NEBLETTE, Carroll Bernard. 771.5345
Elementary photographic sensitometry [by] C. B. Neblette [and] H. N. Todd. Rochester, N. Y., Rochester Institute of Technology, 1950. 100 p. illus. 24 cm. Includes bibliographical references. [TR196.N4] 50-5614
1. Photographic sensitometry. I. Todd, Hollis N., joint author. II. Rochester Institute of Technology, Rochester, N.Y. III. Title.

TODD, Hollis N. 771'.534
Photographic sensitometry; the study of tone reproduction [by] Hollis N. Todd [and] Richard D. Zakia. [1st ed.] Hastings-on-Hudson, N.Y., Morgan & Morgan [1969] 312 p. illus. 22 cm. Bibliography: p. [303]-307. [TR196.T6] 75-82445 9.95
1. Photographic sensitometry. I. Zakia, Richard D., joint author. BIP

VIETH, Gerhard, 1921- 661'.808
Sensitometric testing methods = Messverfahren der Photographie / Gerhard Vieth. London ; New York : Focal Press, 1974. [17], 505 p. : ill. ; 25 cm. (The Focal library) Text in German; summaries in English. Includes index. Bibliography: p. 462-482. [TR280.V53] 75-328594 ISBN 0-240-50751-7 : £13.50
1. Photographic sensitometry. I. Title. II. Title: Messverfahren der Photographie. BIP

Photographic sensitometry—Congresses.

SYMPOSIUM on 661'.808
Sensitometry, Binghamton, N.Y., 1976. *Modern aspects & future trends* / Symposium on Sensitometry, September 15-17, 1976 ; edited by Robert Shannahan. Washington : Society of Photographic Scientists and Engineers, c1976. 78 p. (p. 77-78 blank) : ill. ; 23 cm. Includes bibliographical references and indexes. [TR280.S98 1976] 76-41605 ISBN 0-89208-087-6 : 12.00
1. Photographic sensitometry—Congresses. I. Shannahan, Robert. II. Society of Photographic Scientists and Engineers. III. Title.

Photographic sensitometry—Programmed instruction.

TODD, Hollis N. 770'.7'7
Photographic sensitometry : a self-teaching text / Hollis N. Todd. New York : Wiley-Interscience, c1976. p. cm. (Wiley series on photographic science and technology and the graphic arts) Includes bibliographical references and index. [TR280.T6] 76-22657 ISBN 0-471-87649-6 : 14.95
1. Photographic sensitometry—Programmed instruction. I. Title.

Photographic—Yearbooks.

GERMAN photographic 778.058
annual (The). 1963. Eds.: Wolf Strache, Otto Steinert [Tr. from German by Jane K. Bunjes, Werner E. Bunjes. Stuttgart, W. Strache. dist.] New York, Hastings [c.1962] 191p. illus. (pt. col.) 29cm. 56-4838 10.00, bxd.
1. Photographic—Yearbooks. 2. Photography, Artistic.

Photographs.

MASTERWORKS of photography 779
library. v.1- St. Paul, American Photographic Pub. Co. [1950- v. illus. 25 cm. [TR650.M4] 51-41035
1. Photographs. 2. Photography, Artistic.

PENN, Irving. 779
Moments preserved; eight essays in photographs and words. With an introd. by Alexander Liberman. Rosemary Blackman collaborated in the writing of the captions and text. New York, Simon and Schuster [1960] 183p. illus. (part col.) ports. (part col.) 34cm. [TR140.P43A3] 60-51925
1. Photographs. 2. Photography, Artistic. I. Title.

Photographs—Catalogs.

DONALD Art Company. 750'.2'9
Donald Art Company, inc. [Fine art reproductions of masters, old, modern and contemporary, American and foreign ... printed in offset lithography; catalogue. Port Chester, N.Y., 1967] 144 l. chiefly col. illus. 29 cm. [N4035.D6] 68-7830 10.00
1. Photographs—Catalogs.

PARRY, Pamela Jeffcott. 779'.01'6
Photography index : a guide to reproductions / compiled by Pamela Jeffcott Parry. Westport, Conn. : Greenwood Press, 1979. p. cm. [TR199.P37] 78-26897 ISBN 0-313-20700-3 lib. bdg. : 25.00
1. Photographs—Catalogs. I. Title. BIP

U. S. Library of 973.084
Congress. Prints and Photographs Division.
Pictorial Americana; a select list of photographic negatives in the Prints and Photographs Division of the Library of Congress. 2d ed. compiled by Milton Kaplan, Prints and Photographs Division, edited by Charles G. La Hood, Jr., Photoduplication Service. Washington, Library of Congress, 1955. 68p. 26cm. [N4010.A5 1955] 55-60012
1. Photographs— Catalogs. 2. U. S.—Descr. & trav.—Views—Catalogs. 3. U. S.—Hist.—Pictorial works—Catalogs. I. Kaplan, Milton, 1918- II. U. S. Library of Congress. Photoduplication Service. III. Title.

Photographs—Collectors and collecting.

DENNIS, Landt. 770'.75
Collecting photographs : a guide to the new art boom / Landt and Lisl Dennis. 1st ed. New York : Dutton, c1977. xii, 244 p. : ill. ; 24 cm. "A Sunrise book." Includes index. Bibliography: p. 208-211. [TR6.5.D46 1977] 76-51256 ISBN 0-87690-236-0 : 12.95 ISBN 0-87690-237-9 pbk. : 6.95
1. Photographs—Collectors and collecting. I. Dennis, Lisl, joint author. II. Title. BIP

HALLER, Margaret. 779'.075
Collecting old photographs / Margaret Haller. New York : Arco Pub. Co., c1977. p. cm. Includes index. Bibliography: p. [TR6.5.H34] 77-3328 ISBN 0-668-04244-3 lib. bdg. : 12.50
1. Photographs—Collectors and collecting. I. Title. BIP

Photographs — Coloring.

BAKER, Gla. 770.284
How to paint photographs for profit. New York, Carlton Press, 1962. 67p. 21cm. [TR485.B3] 62-1526
1. Photographs—Coloring. I. Title.

MARSHALL, Lucile 771.45
(Robertson)
Photo-oil coloring for fun or profit; a step by step course for the beginner, plus fine arts training for the professional colorist. New rev. enl. 7th ed. [Washington, Larum Pub. Co]; distributed by J. G. Marshall Mfg. Co., Brooklyn [1956, c1944] 148p. illus. 22cm. [TR485.M25 1956] 56-4535
1. Photographs—Coloring. 2. Painting—Technique. I. Title.

MARSHALL, Lucile 771.45
(Robertson)
Photo-oil coloring for fun or profit; a step by step course for the beginner, plus fine arts training for the professional colorist. New rev. enl. 8th ed. [Washington, Larum Pub. Co]; distributed by J. G. Marshall Mfg. Co.*Brooklyn [1958, c1944] Brooklyn *1958, c1944* 152p. illus. 21cm. Includes bibliography. [TR485.M25 1958] 58-14925
1. Photographs—Coloring. 2. Painting—Technique. I. Title.

WALL, Alfred H. 770'.284
A manual of artistic colouring, as applied to photographs [by] Alfred H. Wall. New York, Arno press, 1973. viii, 266 p. 22 cm. (The Literature of Photography) Reprint of the 1861 ed. [TR485.W28 1973] 72-9244 ISBN 0-405-04948-X 15.00.
1. Photographs coloring. 2. Photography portraits. I. Title. II. Series. BIP

WALLEY, Charles W. 770.284
Colouring, tinting and toning photographs [2d ed.] London, Fountain [dist. New York, Morgan & Morgan, 1964] 104p. illus. (pt. col.) 19cm. 47-6925 3.95bds.,
1. Photographs— Coloring. I. Title.

WEST, Kitty. 770.28
Hand coloring your photographs with oils and dyes. Philadelphia, Chilton Co., Book Division, c1961. 124 p. illus. 21 cm. (Modern camera guide series, 648) [TR485.W4] 61-12055
1. Photographs — Coloring. I. Title. BIP

WHITNEY, Edwina J. 770.284
Natural photo oil coloring, by Edwina J. Whitney. Philadelphia, Chilton Books [1965] 153 p. illus. (part col.) 24 cm. [TR485.W5] 65-17128
1. Photographs—Coloring. I. Title.

Photographs—Conservation and restoration.

DAVIES, Thomas L. 770'.28
Shoots : a guide to your family's photographic heritage / Thomas L. Davies. Danbury, N.H. : Addison House, c1977. 72 p. : ill. ; 21 cm. Includes index. Bibliography: p. 71. [TR465.D38] 77-154962 ISBN 0-89169-012-3 pbk. : 3.95
1. Photographs—Conservation and restoration. I. Title. BIP

SHAFRAN, Alexander. 778.1
Restoration and photographic copying; the techniques of copying and restoring old and damaged photographs. Philadelphia, Chilton Books [1967] 192 p. illus. 24 cm. [TR465.S5] 67-12530
1. Photographs—Conservation and restoration. 2. Photography—Copying. I. Title.

WEINSTEIN, Robert A. 770'.28
Collection, use, and care of historical photographs / Robert A. Weinstein and Larry Booth. Nashville : American Association for State and Local History, c1977. 222 p. : ill. ; 25 cm. Includes index. Bibliography: p. 211-215. [TR465.W44] 76-27755 ISBN 0-910050-21-X : 16.00
1. Photographs—Conservation and restoration. 2. Photographs—Collectors and collecting. I. Booth, Larry, joint author. II. Title. BIP

WILHELM, Henry Gilmer, 770'.28
1943-
Preservation of contemporary photographic materials / by Henry Gilmer Wilhelm. 1976-1977 ed. Grinnell, Iowa : East Street Gallery, [1976] p. cm. Bibliography: p. [TR465.W54] 75-9136 ISBN 0-916268-01-2 : 15.00. ISBN 0-916268-00-4 pbk. : 9.00
1. Photographs—Conservation and restoration. I. East Street Gallery. II. Title.

Photographs in interior decoration.

HOLLAND, John, 1943- 747'.9
Photo decor : a guide to the enjoyment of photographic art / written and designed by John Holland. 1st ed. [Rochester, N.Y.] : Eastman Kodak Co., c1978. 88 p. : ill. (chiefly col.) ; 28 cm. (Kodak publication ; no. 0-22) [NK2115.5.P47H64] 78-60317 ISBN 0-87985-220-8 : 8.95
1. Photographs in interior decoration. I. Title. BIP

Photographs—Marketing.

AHLERS, Arvel W., 1915- 658.89'77
Where & how to sell your photographs / by Arvel W. Ahlers. 8th rev. ed. Garden City, N.Y. : Amphoto, c1977. 253 p. : ill. ; 26 cm. [TR690.A35 1977] 77-151149 ISBN 0-8174-2416-4 pbk. : 5.95
1. Photographs—Marketing. I. Title.

Photography.

ABBOTT, Berenice, 1898- 770.2
New guide to better photography. Rev. ed. New York, Crown Publishers [1953] 180p. illus. 27cm. First published in 1941 under title: A guide to better photography. [TR145.A25 1953] 52-10765
1. Photography. I. Title.

ADAMS, Ansel Easton, 1902- 770
Basic photo [v.4] New York, Morgan & Morgan 1963, c.1952] 118p. 24cm. illus. Contents.4. Naturallight photography. 48-2069 3.95 bds.,
1. Photography. I. Title.

ADAMS, Ansel Easton, 1902- 770
Basic photo / Ansel Adams. Rev. ed. Boston : New York Graphic Society, c1976- v. : ill. ; 26 cm. Contents.Contents.—1 Camera and lens. [TR145.A42 1976] 76-27616 ISBN 0-8212-0716-4 : 14.95 (v. 1)
1. Photography. I. Title.

ADAMS, Ansel Easton, 1902- 770
Basic photo [by] Ansel Adams. [1st rev. ed.] Hastings-on-Hudson, N.Y., Morgan & Morgan [1970- v. illus., ports. 26 cm. Contents.Contents.—1. Camera and lens. Bibliography: v. 1, p. 299. [TR145.A42] 78-21737 ISBN 0-87100-056-3 12.00 (v. 1)
1. Photography. I. Title.

AMPHOTO, New York. 770
35mm photography simplified, by the Amphoto editiorial board. Englewood Cliffs, N.J., Prentice-Hall [1974] 99 p. illus. (part col.) 26 cm. (A Modern photoguide) (A Spectrum book S-PG-2) [TR146.A53 1974] 73-92423 ISBN 0-13-918888-6 7.95
1. Photography. I. Title.
Pbk. 2.95, ISBN 0-13-918888-6.

ANDERSON, Arthur James, 770'.28
1863-
The artistic side of photography, in theory and practice. New York, Arno Press, 1973. 359 p. illus. 23 cm. (Literature of Photography) Reprint of the 1910 ed. [TR145.A55 1973] 72-9179 ISBN 0-405-04890-4 20.00
1. Photography. I. Title. II. Series. BIP

ARIN, Michael Kenneth. 778
How to shoot weddings. Illus. by the author. New York, American Photographic Book Pub. Co. [1957] 127p. illus. 24cm. (An Amphoto book) [TR680.A68] 57-10938
1. Photography. 2. Marriage customs and rites. I. Title.

BAINES, Harry, 1901-1963. 770
The science of photography [by] H. Baines. Revised and edited by E. S. Bomback. [2d ed. New York] Wiley [1967] 318 p. illus. (part col.), ports. 23 cm. Bibliography: p. 317-318. [TR200.B3 1967a] 67-5041
1. Photography. I. Bomback, Edward S., ed. II. Title. BIP

BAUER, Erwin A. 778.7'1
Outdoor photography / by Erwin A. Bauer. 2d ed., rev. and updated. New York : Outdoor Life, [1975] c1974. ix, 143 p. : ill. ; 24 cm. Includes index. [TR146.B34 1974] 75-306729 ISBN 0-87690-161-5 : 6.95
1. Photography. 2. Nature photography. I. Title.

BERNER, Jeff. 770
The photographic experience / Jeff Berner. 1st ed. Garden City, N.Y. : Anchor Press, 1975. xii, 129 p., [2] leaves of plates : ill. (some col.) ; 21 cm. [TR183.B46] 74-12723 ISBN 0-385-01773-1 pbk. : 4.95
1. Photography. I. Title. BIP

BETHERS, Ray, 1902- 770
From eye to camera. New York, Pitman Pub. Corp. [1951] viii. 129p. illus. 23cm. [TR145.B45] 51-6216
1. Photography. I. Title.

BINGHAM, Robert J. 770'.28
Photogenic manipulation, by Robert J. Bingham. New York, Arno Press, 1973. 87, 60 p. illus. 22 cm. (The Literature of Photography) Reprint of the 1852 ed. (The 9th ed. of Part I and the 5th ed of Part II), which was issued as pts. 3 and 4 of manipulations in the scientific arts. [TR145.B48 1973] 72-9182 ISBN 0-405-04893-9. 10.00
1. Photography. I. Title. II. Series. III. Series: Manipulations in the scientific arts, pts. 3-4 BIP

BLACKMAN, Victor. 770'.28
My way with a camera; adventures and lessons of a career in photography. With a preface by R. H. Mason. London, New York, Focal Press [1973] x, 262 p. illus. 25 cm. [TR146.B633] 74-155852 ISBN 0-240-50817-3 £3.00
1. Photography. 2. Photography, Journalistic. I. Title. BIP

BOUCHER, Paul Edward, 1893- 770
Fundamentals of photography, with laboratory experiments. 4th ed. Princeton, N.J., Van Nostrand [1963] xiv, 535 p. illus., col. plates, diagrs., tables. 24 cm. Includes bibliographies. [TR145.B63 1963] 63-24071

with organizing tools, exposure, film developing, printing, flash photography, and finishing pictures. [TR146.G125] 77-6190 ISBN 0-8473-1568-1 : pbk. : 5.95
1. Photography. I. Title. BIP

GAUNT, Leonard. 770
Commonsense photography. Philadelphia, Chilton Book Co. [1969] 304 p. illus. 23 cm. [TR146.G27] 77-4816 ISBN 2-405-06790- 8.95
1. Photography. I. Title. BIP

GAUNT, Leonard. 770
Commonsense photography / [by] Leonard Gaunt. 2nd ed. revised. London ; New York : Focal Press, 1972. 304 p. : ill. (some col.) ; 22 cm. Includes index. [TR145.G28 1972] 74-186536 ISBN 0-240-50679-0 : £2.75
1. Photography. I. Title.

GAUNT, Leonard. 770
Commonsense photography / [by] Leonard Gaunt. 3rd ed., revised. London ; New York : Focal Press, 1975. 304 p. : ill. (some col.) ; 22 cm. Includes index. [TR145.G28 1975] 76-354219 ISBN 0-240-50924-2 : £4.00
1. Photography. I. Title.

GILLELAN, G., Howard. 770.24
The young sportsman's guide to photography. New York, Nelson [1964] 96 p. illus., ports. 22 cm. (The Young sportsman's library) [TR146.G5] 64-14120
1. Photography. I. Title.

GOOD photography. 770
Greenwich, Conn., Fawcett Publications, c1954. 144p. illus. 24cm. (AFawcett book, no. 235) [TR650.G58] 55-2226
1. Photography.

GOOD photography. 770
Greenwich, Conn., Fawcett Publications, c1956. 144p. illus. 24cm. (A Fawcett how-to book, 297) [TR650.G58 1956] 56-1653
1. Photography. I. Fawcett Publications, inc.

*GOTLOP, Philip. 770.232
Van Nostrand Reinhold Manual of professional photography. New York, Van Nostrand Reinhold [1974, c1973] 208 p. illus. (part col.) 25 cm. (Van Nostrand Reinhold Manuals.) [TR154] 73-14115 ISBN 0-442-22786-8 9.95
1. Photography. I. Title. II. Title: Manual of professional photography.

GOWER, H. D. 686.4
The camera as historian, by H. D. Gower, L. Stanley Jast and W. W. Topley. New York, Arno Press, 1973. xv, 259 p. illus. 23 cm. (The Literature of Photography) Reprint of the 1916 ed. [TR147.G68 1973] 72-9202 ISBN 0-405-04911-0. 18.00.
1. Photography. I. Jast, Louis Stanley, 1868-1944, joint author. II. Topley, William Whiteman, joint author. III. Title. IV. Series. BIP

*GRIMM, Tom. 770
The basic book of photography. Photographs by Tom and Michele Grimm. Drawings by Ezelda Garcia. New York, New American Library [1974] 288 p. illus. 21 cm. (A Plume Book) [TR145] 73-90907 4.95 (pbk)
1. Photography. I. Title. BIP

HALSMAN, Philippe 770.1
Halsman on the creation of photographic ideas. New York, Ziff-Davis [c.1961] 91p. illus. 61-14229 3.50
1. Photography. I. Title. II. Title: On the creation of photographic ideas.

HARRIS, Ross, 1938- 770'.28
Making photographs : a workbook of materials, tools, and processes / Ross Harris. New York : Van Nostrand Reinhold Co., [1977] p. cm. Includes index. Bibliography: p. [TR146.H29] 74-163317 16.95
1. Photography. 2. Photography—Processing. I. Title. BIP

HATTERSLEY, Ralph. 770'.28
Beginner's guide to photography. [1st ed.] Garden City, N.Y., Doubleday, 1974. ix, 149 p. illus. 26 cm. [TR146.H36 1974] 72-84964 ISBN 0-385-02083-X 3.95
1. Photography. I. Title.

HAWKEN, William R. 770
You and your camera [by] William R. Hawken. Garden City, N.Y., Amphoto [1973, c1974] 142 p. illus. 28 cm. [TR146.H38] 72-97052 ISBN 0-8174-0560-7 4.95
1. Photography. I. Title. BIP

HAZ, Nicholas. 770.282
Image arrangement, from the notes of Nicholas Haz. Compiled by Louise Haz. [Pittsburgh, Haz Book Co., 1956] 105p. illus. 23cm. 'Sequel to ... [the author's] 'Image management.' [TR147.H29] 56-58243
1. Photography. I. Haz., Louise, ed. II. Title.

HEDGECOE, John. 770'.28
The book of photography : how to see and take better pictures / John Hedgecoe. 1st American ed. New York : Knopf, 1976. 256 p. : ill. (some col.) ; 29 cm. Includes index. [TR145.H4 1976b] 75-36817 ISBN 0-394-49818-6 : 17.95
1. Photography. I. Title. BIP

HEDGECOE, John. 770
The book of photography : how to see and take better pictures / [photos. by] John Hedgecoe ; [text by John Hedgecoe and Adrian Bailey]. London : Edbury Press, 1976. 256 p. : ill. (some col.) ; 29 cm. Includes index. [TR145.H4 1976] 76-362287 ISBN 0-85223-086-9 : £8.95
1. Photography. I. Bailey, Adrian, 1928- II. Title.

HEDGECOE, John. 770'.28
Photography : materials and methods / John Hedgecoe and Michael Langford. London ; New York : Oxford University Press, 1974. 170 p. : ill. ; 21 cm. Includes index. Bibliography: p. 164-165. [TR146.H43 1974] 75-306745 ISBN 0-240-50895-5 : 12.95
1. Photography. I. Langford, Michael John, 1933- joint author.

HEDGECOE, John. 770'.28
Photography: materials and methods [by] John Hedgecoe and Michael Langford. London, New York, Oxford University Press, 1971. [6], 170 p. illus. (some col.) 21 cm. (Oxford paperbacks, handbooks for artists, 9) Bibliography: p. 164-165. [TR146.H43] 73-158791 ISBN 0-19-289909-0 £1.50
1. Photography. I. Langford, Michael John, 1933- joint author. II. Title.

HILLSON, Peter J. 770
Photography; a study in versatility [by] Peter J. Hillson. Garden City, N.Y., Doubleday, 1969. 191 p. illus. (part col.), port. 23 cm. (Doubleday science series) Bibliography: p. 186. [TR146.H647 1969] 76-77920 6.95
1. Photography. I. Title.

HORENSTEIN, Henry. 770'.28
Beyond basic photography : a technical manual / Henry Horenstein ; with photos. by the author and drawings by Henry Isaacs. 1st ed. Boston : Little, Brown, c1977. 242 p. : ill. ; 22 cm. Includes bibliographies and index. [TR145.N62] 77-4852 ISBN 0-316-37312-5 pbk.: 6.95
1. Photography. I. Title. BIP

HORENSTEIN, Henry. 770'.28
Black and white photography: a basic manual. Drawings by Claire Nivola. [1st ed.] Boston, Little, Brown [1974] 179 p. illus. 22 cm. (The Crafts series) Bibliography: p. 174-177. [TR146.H793] 73-20140 ISBN 0-316-37310-9 7.95
1. Photography. I. Title. BIP

HORRELL, C. William. 770
Introductory & publications photography / by C. Wm. Horrell and Robert A. Steffes. 3d ed., Rev. Eau Claire, Wis. : Kenilworth Press, c1976. 103 p. : ill. ; 28 cm. Cover title. Text on p. [3] of cover. Includes index. [TR145.H63 1976] 77-351479
1. Photography. I. Steffes, Robert A., joint author. II. Title. BIP

HUNT, Robert, 1807-1887. 770
A manual on photography. New York, Arno Press, 1973. x, 321 p. illus. 23 cm. (The Literature of Photography) Reprint of the 1853 ed. [TR145.H85 1973] 72-9212 ISBN 0-405-04918-8. 19.00.
1. Photography. I. Title. II. Series. BIP

JACOBS, Lou. 770
Photography today : principles, equipment, and techniques for personal expression / Lou Jacobs, Jr. Santa Monica, Calif. : Goodyear Pub. Co. ; [Northridge, Calif.] : trade distribution in the U.S. by Brooke House Publishers, c1976. p. cm. Includes index. Bibliography: p. [TR145.J3] 76-42205 ISBN 0-87620-669-0 : 14.95 ISBN 0-87620-668-2 pbk. : 11.95
1. Photography. I. Title. BIP

JACOBS, Mark.
Photography in focus : a basic text / Mark Jacobs, Ken Kokrda. Skokie, Ill. : National Textbook Co., c1975. 181 p. : ill. ; 24 cm. Bibliography: p. [174]-181. [TR146.J3] 75-20872
1. Photography. I. Kokrda, Ken, joint author. II. Title. BIP

JAMES, Thomas Howard, 1912- 770.28
Fundamentals of photographic theory, by T. H. James [and] George C. Higgins. [2d ed.] New York, Morgan & Morgan [1960] 345p. illus. 22cm. Includes bibliography. [TR200.J3 1960] 59-12575
1. Photography. I. Higgins, George Clinton, 1912- joint author. II. Title. III. Title: Photographic theory.

JOHNSON, Benjamin King, 1896- 770'.28
Practical photography. London, New York, Hutchinson's University Library [1954] 146p. illus. 19cm. (Hutchinson's university library: Mathematical and physical sciences) Includes bibliography. [TR146.J55] 54-4955
1. Photography. I. Title.

KATZ, Jerome. 770'.1
Photographic analysis; a textbook of photographic science, by Jerome Katz [and] Sidney J. Fogel. [1st ed.] Hastings-on-Hudson, N.Y., Morgan & Morgan [1971] xiv, 658 p. illus. 26 cm. Bibliography: p. 641-646. [TR200.K33] 75-122515 ISBN 0-87100-015-6 25.00
1. Photography. 2. Photographic chemistry. I. Fogel, Sidney J., joint author. II. Title. BIP

KEMP, Weston D., 1936- 770'.28
Photography for visual communicators [by] Weston D. Kemp. Designed by Tom Muir Wilson. Englewood Cliffs, N.J., Prentice-Hall [1973] 278 p. illus. (part col.) 24 cm. Bibliography: p. [273]-276. [TR145.K4] 73-4645 ISBN 0-13-665356-1 15.95
1. Photography. I. Title.

KIRILLOV, N. I. 770
Problems in photographic research and technology [by] N. I. Kirillov; translated from the Russian by Intercontinental Translators, London, edited by E. A. Sutherns. London, New York, Focal P. [1967] 205 p. illus., tables, diagrs. 25 cm. (The Focal library) F7/7/- (B 67-9191) Translation of 0romanized: Problemy fotografii) Includes bibliographies. [TR200.K513] 67-87118
1. Photography. I. Title.

KOWALISKI, Pawel, 1908- 770'.1'53
Applied photographic theory [by] Paul Kowaliski. London, New York, Wiley [1972] x, 533 p. illus. (part col.) 24 cm. (Wiley series on photographic science and technology and the graphic arts) Translation of Theorie photographique appliquee. Includes bibliographical references. [TR200.K6513] 72-613 ISBN 0-471-50600-1 32.50
1. Photography. I. Title. BIP

LACOUR, Marshall. 770
Photo technology [by] Marshall LaCour [and] Irvin T. Lathrop. Chicago, American Technical Society [1966] 263 p. illus. (part col.) 24 cm. [TR145.L315] 66-23580
1. Photography. I. Lathrop, Irvin T., joint author. II. Title. BIP

LACOUR, Marshall. 770
Photo technology [by] Marshall LaCour [and] Irvin T. Lathrop. [2d ed.] Chicago, American Technical Society [1972] 270 p. illus. (part col.) 24 cm. [TR145.L315 1972] 72-177237 ISBN 0-8269-2620-7
1. Photography. I. Lathrop, Irvin T., joint author. II. Title.

LAHUE, Kalton C. 770
Petersen's Big book of photography / by Kalton C. Lahue. Los Angeles : Petersen Pub. Co., c1977. 480 p. : ill. (some col.) ; 28 cm. [TR145.L317] 77-376766 ISBN 0-8227-4029-X pbk. : 11.95
1. Photography. I. Title. II. Title: Big book of photography. BIP

LANGFORD, Michael J. 770.28
Basic photography; a primer for professionals. New York, Focal [dist. Pitman, c.1965] 374p. illus., plates. 25cm. (Focal lib.) Bibl. [TR145.L32] 65-29975 10.75
1. Photography. I. Title.

LANGFORD, Michael John, 1933- 770
Advanced photography: a grammar of techniques [by] Michael J. Langford. London, New York, Focal, 1969. 435 p. illus. (some col.), facsims. 25 cm. (The Focal library) [TR145.L318] 71-396045 ISBN 0-240-50681-2 70/-
1. Photography. I. Title. BIP

LANGFORD, Michael John, 1933- 770
Advanced photography; a grammar of techniques [by] Michael J. Langford. 2d ed. London, New York, Focal Press [1972] 435 p. illus. 26 cm. (The Focal Library) Distributed in the U.S.A. by Amphoto, New York. Includes bibliographical references. [TR145.L318 1972] 70-188891 17.00 (U.S.)
1. Photography. I. Title.

LANGFORD, Michael John, 1933- 770
Basic photography; a primer for professionals [by] Michael J. Langford. 2d ed. New York, Amphoto [1971] 374 p. illus. 24 cm. (The Focal library) Bibliography: p. 357-359. [TR145.L32 1971] 71-153479 ISBN 0-8174-0640-9 7.95
1. Photography. I. Title.

LANGFORD, Michael John, 1933- 770
Basic photography : a primer for professionals / [by] Michael J. Langford. 4th ed. London ; New York : Focal Press, 1977, i.e.1978 [2], 397 p., [52] p. of plates : ill. ; 24 cm. Includes index. Bibliography: p. 371-373. [TR145.L32 1977] 78-304084 ISBN 0-240-50954-4 : 24.95 ISBN 0-240-50955-2 pbk. : 14.95
1. Photography. I. Title.

LANGFORD, Michael John, 1933- 770
The step-by-step guide to photography / by Michael Langford. New York : Knopf, 1978. p. cm. Includes index. Bibliography: p. [TR146.L295] 78-54894 ISBN 0-394-41604-X : 15.95
1. Photography. I. Title. BIP

LARMORE, Lewis. 770
Introduction to photographic principles. Englewood Cliffs, N. J., Prentice-Hall, 1958. 229p. illus. 24cm. (Prencitc Hall physics series) [TR145.L33] 58-11419
1. Photography. I. Title. II. Title: Photographic princoples.

LARMORE, Lewis. 770
Introduction to photographic principles. 2d ed. New York., Dover Publications [1965] ix, 229 p. illus. 22 cm. Includes bibliographies. [TR145.L33 1965] 65-20484
1. Photography. I. Title. II. Title: Photographic principles. BIP

MCCOMBS, Kenneth Monroe, 1911- 778
Commercial photography. Illus. by the author and his students of photography at the Los Angeles Trade-Technical Junior College. Chicago, American Technical Society, 1951. vii, 363 p. illus. 22 cm. [TR145.M24] 51-692
1. Photography 2. Photography. Commercial I. Title.

MALLAN, Lloyd, ed. 770
Good photography. Greenwich, Conn., Fawcett Publications, c1953. 144p. (chiefly illus.) 24cm. (A Fawcett book, no. 192) [TR145.M32] 53-34326
1. Photography. I. Title.

MEES, Charles Edward Kenneth, 1882- 770
The theory of the photographic process. Rev. ed. New York, Macmillan [1954] 1183p. illus. 24cm. Includes bibliography. [TR200.M4 1954] 54-11837
1. Photography. I. Title.

MEES, Charles Edward Kenneth, 1882-1960, ed. 771.5
The theory of the photographic process, edited by T. H. James with the technical assistance of Ardelle Kocher. Contributors: C. R. Berry [and others] 3d ed. New York, Macmillan [1966] xi, 591 p. illus. 29 cm. 1st and 2d editions edited by C. E. K. Mees. Includes bibliographical references. [TR200.M4 1966] 65-27328
1. Photography. I. James, Thomas Howard, 1912- ed. II. Title. III. Title: The photographic process.

*MILLER, Russell. 770.28
Click. New York, Arco, [1974] 120 p. illus. 30 cm. [TR15] 74-76267 6.95
1. Photography. I. Title.

MILLER, Thomas H. 1906- 770
This is photography, its means and ends, by Thomas H. Miller and Wyatt Brummitt. Rochester, N.Y., Published by Case-Hoyt Corp. for Garden City Books, Garden City, N.Y., c1959. 260 p. illus. 23 cm. [TR145.M54 1959] 59-3737
1. Photography. I. Brummitt, Wyatt, joint author. II. Title.

MILLER, Thomas H 1906- 770
This is photography, its means and ends, by Thomas H. Miller and Wyatt Brummitt. [Rochester, N. Y.] Published by the Case-Hoyt Corp. for Garden City Books, Garden City, N. Y., c1955. 260p. illus. 23cm. [TR145.M54 1955] 56-805
1. Photography. I. Brummitt, Wyatt, joint author. II. Title.

MUSE, Ken, 1925- 770'.23
Photo two : advanced photo text / by Ken Muse. Englewood Cliffs, N.J. : Prentice-Hall, c1977. xvii, 268 p. : ill. ; 28 cm. Includes index. [TR145.M78] 76-51428 ISBN 0-13-665307-3 pbk. : 7.95
1. Photography. 2. Photography, Commercial. I. Title. BIP

NEBLETTE, Carroll Bernard. 770
Fundamentals of photography [by] C. B. Neblette. New York, Van Nostrand Reinhold [1970] 351 p. illus. (part col.), ports. 22 cm. Includes bibliographies. [TR145.N38] 78-92168
1. Photography. I. Title.

NEBLETTE, Carroll Bernard. 770
Neblette's Handbook of photography and reprography : materials, processes, and systems. 7th ed. / John Sturge. New York : Van Nostrand Reinhold, [1976] p. cm. First published in 1927 under title: Photography, its principles and practice. Includes bibliographical references and index. [TR145N4 1976] 76-43356 ISBN 0-442-25948-4 : 47.50
1. Photography. 2. Copying processes. I. Sturge, John M. II. Title. III. Title: Handbook of photography and reprography. BIP

NEBLETTE, Carroll Bernard. 770
Photography, its materials and processes. 5th ed. New York, Van Nostrand [1952] 500 p. illus. 25 cm. Previous editions have title: Photography, its principles and practice. [TR145.N4 1952] 52-5744
1. Photography. I. Title.

NEBLETTE, Carroll Bernard. 770
Photography, its materials and processes. 6th ed. Princeton, N.J., Van Nostrand [1962] 508 p. illus. 25 cm. First published in 1927 under title: Photography, its principles and practices. [TR145.N4 1962] 62-53672
1. Photography. I. Title.

NORDHEIMER, Stuart. 770'.28
Beginner's photography simplified / by Stuart Nordheimer. Garden City, N.Y. : Amphoto, [1975] 96 p. : ill. (some col.) ; 26 cm. (A Modern photoguide) [TR146.N67] 74-79255 ISBN 0-8174-0182-2 pbk. : 3.45
1. Photography. I. Title. BIP

PAGE, Andre. 770'.28
Photographic interpretation. Illus. by the author. London, Pelham, 1973. 128, [12] p. illus. 21 cm. Label mounted on t.p.: Transatlantic Arts, Inc., Levittown, New York, sole distributor for the U.S.A. Includes index. [TR149.P33 1973] 73-174163 ISBN 0-7207-0633-5 7.50
1. Photography. I. Title. BIP

PATTERSON, Freeman, 1937- 770
Photography for the joy of it / Freeman Patterson. Toronto ; New York : Van Nostrand Reinhold, 1977. 168 p. : col. ill. ; 22 cm. Includes index. [TR145.P33] 77-89872 ISBN 0-442-29883-8 : 19.95 ISBN 0-442-29893-5 pbk. : 9.95
1. Photography. I. Title. BIP

PHOTOGRAPHING America : 770
know the land and the people ... through photography / edited by George Hornby and the editors of Eastman Kodak Company. New York : Crown Publishers, c1976. 256 p. : chiefly ill. ; 32 cm. Includes index. [TR146.P443] 76-13553 ISBN 0-517-52582-8 : 15.95
1. Photography. 2. United States—Description and travel—Views. I. Hornby, George. II. Eastman Kodak Company.

PRICE, Lake. 770'.28
A manual of photographic manipulation, by (William) Lake Price. New York, Arno Press, 1973. viii, 304 p. illus. 23 cm. (The Literature of Photography) Reprint of the 2d. ed., 1868. [TR145.P94 1973] 72-9223 ISBN 0-405-04930-7 18.00.
1. Photography. I. Title. II. Series.

PRITCHARD, Henry Baden, 1841-1884. 770
About photography and photographers. New York, Arno Press, 1973. iv, 220 p. illus. 22 cm. (The Literature of photography) Reprint of the 1883 ed., which was issued as no. 14 of Scovill photographic series. [TR145.P98 1973] 72-9225 ISBN 0-405-04931-5 14.00
1. Photography. I. Title. II. Series. BIP

REHM, Karl M. 770
Basic black and white photography / Karl M. Rehm. Garden City, N.Y. : Amphoto, c1976. 190 p. : ill. ; 28 cm. Includes bibliographical references and index. [TR146.R427] 75-42568 ISBN 0-8174-2403-2 : 6.95
1. Photography. I. Title. BIP

RHODE, Robert Bartlett, 1916- 770.2
Introduction to photography [by] Robert B. Rhode & Floyd H. McCall. New York, Macmillan [1965] 278 p. illus. 24 cm. Bibliography: p. 264-269. [TR145.R5] 65-15572
1. Photography. I. McCall, Floyd Haley, 1902- joint author. II. Title.

RHODE, Robert Bartlett, 1916- 770
Introduction to photography [by] Robert B. Rhode [and] Floyd H. McCall. 2d ed. New York, Macmillan [1971] viii, 264 p. illus. 26 cm. Bibliography: p. 253-258. [TR145.R5 1971] 72-130951
1. Photography. I. McCall, Floyd Haley, 1902- joint author. II. Title.

ROGERS, Houston. 770.24
Instructions to young photographers. London, Museum Press [1959; stamped: distributed by Sportshelf, New Rochelle, N. Y.] 120p. illus. 23cm. (Brompton library) [TR149.R6] 59-2077
1. Photography. I. Title.

ROOT, Marcus Aurelius, 1808-1888. 770.28
The camera and the pencil; or, The heliographic art. With an introd. by Beaumont Newhall. Pawlet [Vt.] Helios, 1971. 456 p. illus. 20 cm. Reprint of the 1864 ed. [TR145.R78 1971] 78-161557 ISBN 0-87931-400-1
1. Photography. I. Title. BIP

RYDER, James Fitzallan, 1826-1904. 770'.72'4
Voightlander and I in pursuit of shadow catching. New York, Arno Press, 1973 [c1901] 251 p. illus. 24 cm. (The Literature of Photography) [TR149.R9 1973] 72-9235 ISBN 0-405-04940-4 17.00.
1. Photography. I. Title. II. Series.

SHEPPARD, Julian. 770.28
Photo design methods. New York, Amphoto [1971] 221 p. illus. 26 cm. [TR145.S54 1971] 74-134589 9.95
1. Photography. I. Title.

SHEPPARD, Julian. 770'.24'74
Photography for designers. London, New York, Focal Press, 1971. [11], 221 p.; illus., facsims. 25 cm. American ed. (New York, Amphoto) has title: Photo design methods. [TR145.S54 1971b] 73-855118 ISBN 0-240-50708-8 £3.00
1. Photography. I. Title. BIP

SHIPMAN, Carl. 770
Understanding photography / Carl Shipman. Tucson, Az. : H. P. Books, 1974. 224 p. : ill. (some col.) ; 28 cm. (The New photo series ; 1) Caption title. Includes index. [TR146.S515] 74-82518 ISBN 0-912656-24-7 : 5.95
1. Photography. I. Title. BIP

SIMON, Michael. 770
First lessons in black-and-white photography / Michael Simon, Dennis Moore. New York : Holt, Rinehart and Winston, c1978. xi, 239 p. : ill. ; 27 cm. Includes bibliographical references and index. [TR146.S528] 77-10489 ISBN 0-03-042831-9 : 16.95
1. Photography. I. Moore, Dennis, joint author. II. Title. BIP

SKUDRZYK, Eugen J., 1913- 770
Photography for the serious amateur, by Eugen J. Skudrzyk. South Brunswick, A. S. Barnes [1971] 367 p. illus. (part col.) 27 cm. Includes bibliographical references. [TR145.S58] 68-27214 ISBN 0-498-06701-7 12.00
1. Photography. I. Title.

SNELLING, Henry Hunt, 1816-1897. 770*.9
The history and practice of the art of photography. With an introd. by Beaumont Newhall. Hastings-on-Hudson, N.Y., Morgan & Morgan [1970] vi, [v]-vii, 139, [v]-viii p. illus., facsim. 19 cm. Title on spine: Art of photography. Facsim. of the George Eastman House collection copy, published in 1849, with a new introd. [TR144.S67 1849a] 73-119993 ISBN 0-87100-014-8
1. Photography. 2. Daguerreotype. I. Title. II. Title: Art of photography.

SPARLING, Marcus. 770'.28
Theory and practice of the photographic art, by W. [ie. M.] Sparling. New York, Arno Press, 1973. 212 p. illus. 23 cm. (The Literature of Photography) Reprint of the 1856 ed. published by Houlston and Stoneman, London. [TR145.S652 1973] 72-9237 ISBN 0-405-04942-0 13.00.
1. Photography. I. Title. II. Series. BIP

SPOERL, Alexander, 1917- 770.2
Living with a camera [Tr., adapted from German by Otto Gregory. Rev. for Amer. ed. by Hubert p. Luckett] New York, Crowell [1964, c. 1957, 1963] 238p. illus. 21cm. 64-18892 3.95
1. Photography. I. Title.

SPRUNGMAN, Ormal I. 778.71
Photography afield. [1st ed.] Harrisburg, Pa., Stackpole Co. [1951] 449 p. illus. 27 cm. [TR615.S6] 51-13151
1. Photography. 2. Cinematography. I. Title.

STONE, George Eathl. 770.2
Progressive photography: a workbook and laboratory manual [for college students] rev. ed. Berkeley, California Book Co., 1950. 432, xiii p. 29 cm. Includes bibliographies. [TR145.S8] 50-12904
1. Photography. I. Title.

STRONG, William McCreery, 1898or9-1941. 770
Photography for fun; a simplified guide to better pictures [and] color photography with your camera [by] William E. [sic] Strong and Jack Garber. [Rev., with additions, Oct. 1952] New York, Sentinel Books Publishers [1953, c1938] 127p. illus. 20cm. (Sentinel book series on arts, crafts, hobbies, sports, games, education. 7) [TR146.S85 1953] 53-2488
1. Photography. I. Garber, Jack. II. Title.

SUMMER School on the Science of Photography, Liege, 1962 770.82
Photographic theory; Liege summer school, 1962. Org. by A. Hautot. New York Focal [1964,c. 1963] 272p. illus. 25cm. (Focal lib.) English, French, or German. Org. under the auspices of N. A. T. O. by the Univ. of Liege. Bibl. 64-6502 21.00
1. Photography. I. Hautot, A., ed. II. North Atlantic Treaty Organization. III. Liege. Universite. IV. Title.

THE Theory of the photographic process. 770
4th ed. / edited by T. H. James. New York : Macmillan, c1977. xvii, 714 p. : ill. ; 29 cm. First and 2d editions edited by by C. E. K. Mees. Includes bibliographical references and indexes. [TR200.M4 1977] 76-25432 ISBN 0-02-360190-6 : 45.00
1. Photography. I. James, Thomas Howard, 1912- II. Mees, Charles Edward Kenneth, 1882-1960. The theory of the photographic process.

TIME-LIFE Books. 770'.28
Frontiers of photography, by the editors of Time-Life Books. New York [1972] 202 p. illus. (part col.) 27 cm. (Life library of photography) Bibliography: p. 199. [TR147.T45] 72-77412
1. Photography. I. Title. BIP

TISSANDIER, Gaston, 1843-1899. 770'.9
A history and handbook of photography, translated from the French. Edited by J. Thomson. New York, Arno Press, 1973. xx, 400 p. illus. 23 cm. (The Literature of Photography) Reprint of the 1878 ed. Includes bibliographical references. [TR145.T5713 1973] 72-9238 ISBN 0-405-04943-9 23.00.
1. Photography. I. Title. II. Series. BIP

TOWLER, John, 1811-1889. 770
The silver sunbeam. With an introd. by Beaumont Newhall. [Facsim. ed.] Hastings-on-Hudson, N.Y., Morgan & Morgan [1969] 351 p. 20 cm. Original t.p. reads: The silver sunbeam: a practical and theoretical text-book on sun drawing and photographic printing: comprehending all the wet and dry processes at present known ... New York, J. H. Ladd, 1864. [TR145.T75 1864a] 78-88124
1. Photography. I. Title. BIP

U.S. Bureau of Naval Personnel. 770.2
Photographer's mate 2, prepared by [the Navy Training Publications Center] Washington, U.S. Govt. Print. Off., 1958 [i. e. 1959] 696 p. illus. 20 cm. (Its Navy training courses) [TR145.U62] 59-60900
1. Photography. I. Title.

U.S. Bureau of Naval Personnel. 770
Photographer's mate 3, prepared by [the U.S. Navy Training Publication Center, Memphis, Tenn., and the Training Division of the] Bureau of Naval Personnel. Washington, U.S. Govt. Print Off., 1958. 861 p. illus. 20 cm. (Its Navy training courses) [TR145.U63] 58-62166
1. Photography. 2. Photography, Military. I. Title.

U.S. Dept. of the Air Force. 770.2
Basic photograhy. [Washington] [1959] iv, 187 p. illus., diagrs. 28 cm. (Its AF manual 95-1) [UG633.A3763 no. 95-1 1959] 60-60188
1. Photography. I. Title. II. Series: U.S. Dept. of the Air Force Air Force Manual no. 95-1)

VESTAL, David. 770
The craft of photography. [1st ed.] New York, Harper & Row [1975] xix, 364 p. illus. 24 cm. [TR146.V49 1975] 74-1865 ISBN 0-06-014497-1 12.95
1. Photography. I. Title. BIP

VOGEL, Hermann Wilhelm, 1834-1898. 770'.1'54135
The chemistry of light and photography. New York, Arno Press, 1973. xi, 288 p. illus. 23 cm. (The Literature of Photography) Reprint of the 1875 ed., which was issued as v. 15 of the International Scientific Series. Translation of Die chemischen Wirkungen des Lichts und die Photographie. [TR145.V88 1973] 72-9242 ISBN 0-405-04946-3 17.00.
1. Photography. 2. Photochemistry. I. Title. II. Series. III. Series: The International Scientific Series (New York), v. 14. BIP

WAKEFIELD, George L. 770.28
An introduction to photography, by George L. Wakefield. Philadelphia, Chilton Book Co. [1969] 191 p. illus. 23 cm. [TR146.W163] 79-4862 8.95
1. Photography. I. Title. BIP

WALLS, Henry James. 770
Basic photo science : how photography works. 2nd revised and enlarged ed. / [by] H. J. Walls and G. G. Attridge. London ; New York : Focal Press, 1978. 418 p. : ill. ; 22 cm. (The Manual of photo-technique) First ed. published in 1959 under title: How photography works. Includes bibliographies and index. [TR145.W16 1977] 78-312176 ISBN 0-8038-0785-6 (Hastings House) 26.95
1. Photography. I. Attridge, G. G., joint author. II. Title.
Distributed by Hastings House Pubs, Inc, NYC **BIP**

WASLEY, John. 770'.28
Beginner's guide to photography. [London] Pelham [1973, i.e.1974] 202 p. illus. 22 cm. Label mounted on t.p.: Transatlantic Arts, Inc., Levittown, N.Y., Sole distributor for the U.S.A. [TR146.W28] 74-174487 ISBN 0-7207-0696-3 8.95
1. Photography. I. Title. **BIP**

WEISS, Harvey. 770'.28
Lens and shutter; an introduction to photography. [Reading, Mass.] Young Scott Books [1971] 120 p. illus. 28 cm. (The Beginning artist's library) An introduction to photography describing the parts of a camera, the use of light and composition to achieve various effects, and the developing of film. [TR149.W45] 79-155913 ISBN 0-201-09240-9
1. Photography. I. Title. **BIP**

WILSON, Edward Livingston, 1838-1903. 770'.28
Wilson's photographics. New York, Arno Press, 1973 [c1881] 366 p. illus. 24 cm. (The Literature of photography) [TR145.W72 1973] 72-9247 ISBN 0-405-04951-X 19.00
1. Photography. I. Title. II. Title: Photographics. III. Series. **BIP**

WINDISCH, Hans, 1891- 770.2
The manual of modern photography. [Rev. English text by Fred. Willy Frerk] 2d rev. ed. Vaduz [Liechtenstein] Heering Publications; Rayelle Publications, Philadelphia, sole U. S. agency, 1956. 291p. illus. 22cm. Translation of Die neue Foto-Schule, die Technik. [TR146.W55 1956] 56-2128
1. Photography. 2. Photographic optics. I. Title.

WITTKOWER, Rudolf. 709'.45
Idea and image : studies in the Italian Renaissance / Rudolf Wittkower. [New York] : Thames and Hudson, c1978. 255 p. : ill. ; 27 cm. (The Collected essays of Rudolf Wittkower) Includes bibliographical references and index. [N6915.W55] 78-62804 ISBN 0-500-85005-4 : 29.95
1. Art, Renaissance—Italy—Addresses, essays, lectures. 2. Art, Italian—Addresses, essays, lectures. I. Title.
Avail. from W. W. Norton, 500 Fifth Ave. NY, NY Contents omitted.

WOLBARST, John, 1915- ed. 779
Polaroid portfolio. Design and art direction by Ernest G. Scarfone. New York, American Photographic Book Pub. Co., c1959- v. (chiefly illus.) 31 cm. [TR263.P6W63] 59-15400
1. Photography. 2. Polaroid Land camera. I. Title.

WOOLLEY, Al E. 770'.28
Photography: a practical and creative introduction [by] A. E. Woolley. New York, McGraw-Hill [1973, c1974] x, 383 p. illus. 25 cm. Includes bibliographies. [TR145.W78 1974] 73-7867 ISBN 0-07-071860-1 9.95
1. Photography. I. Title.

WRIGHT, George Benjamin, 1913-1958, ed. 771.442
Available light and your camera. Contributors: Jacquelyn Balish [and others] 2d ed., rev. New York, American Photographic Book Pub. Co.; distributed to the book trade by Garden City Books, Garden City, N.Y. [1958] 182 p. illus. 25 cm. [TR147.W7 1958] 58-12007
1. Photography. I. Title.

YULSMAN, Jerry. 770'.28
The complete book of 35mm photography / by Jerry Yulsman, New York : Coward, McCann & Geoghegan, c1976. 216 p. : ill. ; 22 cm. [TR145.Y8 1976] 75-45425 ISBN 0-698-10734-9 : 8.95
1. Photography. I. Title. **BIP**

ZARCHY, Harry. 770
Photography, written and illustrated by Harry Zarchy. Cleveland, World Pub. Co. [1966] 48 p. illus. (part col.) 20 cm. (The Little hobby bookshelf) "A Holly book." Instructions for the beginning photographer on cameras, subject matter, and developing film. [TR149.Z3] AC 66
1. Photography.

Photography, Abstract.

COOKE, Robert W. 778.9'5
Designing with light on paper and film [by] Robert W. Cooke. Worcester, Mass., Davis Publications [1969] 88 p. illus. 26 cm. Bibliography: p. 87. [TR656.C6] 75-75730 7.50
1. Photography, Abstract. I. Title. **BIP**

CROY, Otto R., 1902- 778.3'11
Creative photo micrography [by] Croij. [English translation by Grace E. Lockie. English ed.] New York, Amphoto [1968] 151 p. illus. 26 cm. Translation of Mikro-Foto-Graphik. [TR650.C72413] 68-4460
1. Photography, Abstract. 2. Photography, Close-up. I. Title.

CROY, Otto R 1902- 778.3'11
Creative photo micrography [by] Croy; [translated from the German] London, New York, Focal P., 1968. 151 p. illus. 26 cm. 42/- (B 68-09379) SBN 240-50665-0 Translation of Mikro-Foto-Graphik. [TR650.C72413 1968b] 68-119222
1. Photography, Abstract. 2. Photography, Close-up. I. Title. **BIP**

CROY, Otto R., 1902- 779'.0924
Creative photography, by O. R. Croy. New York, Amphoto [1970] 127, [32] p. illus. 26 cm. Translation of Schopferishe Foto-Grafek. [TR656.C7613 1970] 77-101242 12.50
1. Photography, Abstract. I. Title.

HOWARD, David, 1948- 779'.092'4
Realities / David Howard. [San Francisco] : San Francisco Center for Visual Studies, c1976. [49] p. : chiefly ill. ; 28 cm. [TR656.H68] 76-47802 4.95
1. Howard, David, 1948- 2. Photography, Abstract. I. Title. **BIP**

WHITE, Minor. 779'.5
Sound of one hand. [Rochester? N.Y.] 1960. 1 portfolio ([1] l., 10 plates) 42 x 53 cm. [TR656.W48] 76-235360
1. Photography, Abstract. I. Title.

Photography—Addresses, essays, lectures.

LYONS, Nathan, ed. 770.8
Photographers on photography; a critical anthology. Englewood Cliffs, N.J., Prentice-Hall [1966] 190 p. 23 cm. (Prentice-Hall foundations of modern photography series) Bibliography: p. 177-190. [TR185.L9] 66-22343
1. Photography—Addresses, essays, lectures. I. Title. **BIP**

OUTDOOR photographer's digest / edited by Erwin and Peggy Bauer. Chicago : Follett Pub. Co., c1975. 288 p. : ill. ; 27 cm. [TR185.O88] 74-25250 ISBN 0-695-80526-6 : 7.95 770
1. Photography—Addresses, essays, lectures. 2. Nature photography—Addresses, essays, lectures. 3. Photography of sports—Addresses, essays, lectures. I. Bauer, Erwin A. II. Bauer, Peggy.

PERSPECTIVE world report 1966-69 of the photographic industries, technologies and science; edited by L. A. Mannheim. London, New York, Focal P., 1968. 440 p. 8 plates, illus. 26 cm. (The Focal library) On spine: Perspective photographic world report, 1966-1969. [TR185.P4] 74-381148 7/7/- 770'.9'046
1. Photography—Addresses, essays, lectures. I. Mannheim, Ladislaus Andrew, 1925- ed. II. Title: Perspective photographic world report, 1966-1969.

Photography, Advertising.

CROY, Otto R., 1902- 770'.28
Graphic effects by photography [by] Croy. Translated by F. Bradley. New York, Hastings House [1973] 200 p. illus. (part col.) 23 cm. (Visual communication books) Translation of Photos helfen zeichnen. [TR690.4.C7813] 73-6631 ISBN 0-8038-2661-3 12.95
1. Photography, Advertising. I. Title.

HAMMOND, Bill. 658'.91'6591323
How to make money in advertising photography / Bill Hammond. Garden City, N.Y. : Amphoto, c1976. 160 p., [8] leaves of plates : ill. (some col.) ; 29 cm. Includes index. [TR690.4.H35] 74-79950 ISBN 0-8174-0581-X : 14.95
1. Photography, Advertising. 2. Photography, Commercial. I. Title. **BIP**

KEPPLER, Victor. 770'.924 B
Man + camera; a photographic autobiography [by] Victor Keppler. Designed by Hal Rogers. New York, Amphoto [1970] 215 p. illus. (part col.) 33 cm. [TR690.4.K46] 75-97872
1. Photography, Advertising. I. Title.

NELSON, Norbert N. 770'.24'6591
Photographing your product for advertising & promotion; a handbook for designers & craftsmen [by] Norbert Nelson. New York, Van Nostrand Reinhold Co. [1970] 144 p. illus. (part col.) 24 cm. Bibliography: p. 139-140. [TR690.4.N4] 71-128613
1. Photography, Advertising. I. Title.

PINNEY, Roy. 659.13
Advertising photography; a visual communication book. New York, Hastings House [1962] 160p. illus. 28cm. [TR690.P5] 61-9376
1. Photography, Advertising. I. Title.

PROFESSIONAL photographic illustration techniques. 1st ed. Rochester, N.Y. : Eastman Kodak Co., c1978. 135 p., [6] leaves of plates : ill. ; 28 cm. (Kodak publication ; no. 0-16) [TR690.4.P76] 77-99272 ISBN 0-87985-190-2 : 7.50 659.13'23
1. Photography, Advertising. 2. Photography, Commercial. I. Eastman Kodak Company. **BIP**

Photography, Advertising—Yearbooks.

PHOTOGRAPHIS 1968 659.13
Zurich, Graphis Pr.; [dist. in the U.S. by Hastings, New York] v. illus. (pt. col.; 31cm. ([Visual communication bks.] pubn.] International annual of advertising photoraphy. English. French and German. Ed.: 1966- W. Herdeg. [TR690.A1P48] 66-4571 19.50
1. Photography, Advertising—Yearbooks. I. Herdeg, Walter, 1908- .... ed.

PHOTOGRAPHIS. '66 659.13
Zurich, Graphis Pr., [dist. New York, Hastings, 3c.1966] 277p. illus. (pt. col.) 31cm. (Visual communication bks. pub.) Intl. annual of adv. photography. English, French and German. Editor: 1966- W. Herdeg [TR690.A1P48] 66-4571 19.50
1. Photography, Advertising—Yearbooks. I. Herdeg, Walter, 1908- ed.

PHOTOGRAPHIS '67 659.13
International annual of advertising photography. Zurich, Switzerland, Walter Herdeg, the Graphis Pr. [1967] v. illus., col. plates. 31cm. (Visual communications bks.) Captions, introd. in English, German, French. Ed.: 1966- W. Herdeg [TR690.A1P48] 66-4571 19.50
1. Photography, Advertising—Yearbooks. I. Herdeg, Walter, 1908- ed.
American distributor: Hastings House. New York.

Photography, Aerial.

AMERICAN Geological Institute. Committee on Education. 778.35
Outstanding aerial photographs in North America, prepared by a sub-committee of the Committee on Education. Washington, American Geological Institute, 1951. 87p. illus. 27cm. (American Geological Institute. Report no. 5) Bibliography: p. 79-87. [QE1.A392 no.5] 52-61390
1. Photography, Aerial. 2. Physical geography—North America. 3. Geology—Study and teaching. I. Title. II. Series.

AVERY, Thomas Eugene. 778.3'52
Interpretation of aerial photographs [by] T. Eugene Avery. 2d ed. Minneapolis, Burgess Pub. Co. [1968] vii, 324 p. illus. (part col.), col. map (on lining paper) 27 cm. Includes bibliographies. [TR810.A9 1968] 68-20284
1. Photography, Aerial. 2. Photographic interpretation. I. Title. **BIP**

BROCK, Gerald Clement, 1911- 778.3'52
Physical aspects of aerial photography, by G. C. Brock. New York, Dover Publications [1967] viii, 267 p. illus. 24 cm. "An unabridged republication wtih [sic] minor corrections of the work first published in 1952 ... under the title Physical aspects of air photography." Includes bibliographies. [TR810.B7 1967] 67-18855
1. Photography, Aerial. 2. Photographic optics. I. Title.

BROCK, Gerald Clement, 1911- 778.35
Physical aspects of air photography. London, New York, Longmans, Green [1952] 267 p. illus. 26 cm. Includes bibliography. [TR810.B7] 52-11738
1. Photography, Aerial. 2. Photographic optics. I. Title.

DOWNIE, Don. 778.3'5
Taking pictures from the air; photography for pilots. With co-pilot and back-up photo assistance from Ruth and Dana Downie. New York [Sports Car Press, 1968] 127 p. illus. 21 cm. (Modern aircraft series) [TR810.D67] 68-58242 2.45
1. Photography, Aerial. I. Downie, Ruth, joint author. II. Downie, Dana, joint author. III. Title.

GODDARD, George W., 1889- 778.3'5
Overview; a life-long adventure in aerial photography [by] George W. Goddard, with DeWitt S. Copp. [1st ed.] Garden City, N.Y., Doubleday, 1969. xiii, 415 p. illus., ports. 22 cm. [TR140.G6A3] 75-78732 8.95
I. Copp, DeWitt S., joint author. II. Title.

HALL, H J ed. 778.352
Photographic considerations for aerospace. Authors: G. C. Brock [and others] Editors: H. J. Hall [and] H. K. Howell. [1st ed.] Lexington, Mass., Itek Corp. [1965] viii, 118 p. illus. 23 cm. Includes bibliographies. [TR810.H3] 66-93076
1. Photography, Aerial. I. Howell, Hutson Koger, 1924- joint ed. II. Brock, Gerald Clement, 1911- III. Itek Corporation, Lexington, Mass. IV. Title.

HALL, H J., ed. 526.9'82
Photographic considerations for aerospace. Authors: G. C. Brock [and others] Editors: H. J. Hall [and] H. K. Howell. [2d ed.] Lexington, Mass., Itek Corp. [1966] viii, 122 p. illus. 23 cm. Includes bibliographies. [TR810.H3] 66-6403
1. Photography, Aerial. I. Howell, Hutson Koger, 1924- joint ed. II. Brock, Gerald Clement, 1911- III. Itek Corporation, Lexington, Mass. IV. Title.

HEIMAN, Grover. 778.3'5
Aerial photography; the story of aerial mapping and reconnaissance. New York, Macmillan [1972] xi, 180 p. illus. 24 cm. (Air Force Academy series) Bibliography: p. 173-174. [TR810.H4] 72-83763 5.95
1. Photography, Aerial. **BIP**

ST. Joseph, John Kenneth Sinclair, ed. 778.352
The uses of air photography: nature and man in a new perspective. ed. by J. K. S. St. Joseph. Contributions by Lord Esher [others] New York, John Day [1966] 166p. illus., maps. 26 x 32 cm. Largely written by members of the Comm. for Aerial Photography of the Univ. of Cambridge [TR810.S28 1966a] 67-10110 15.00
1. Photography. Aerial. I. Cambridge. University. Committee for Arenal Photography. II. Title. **BIP**

SMITH, Frank Kingston. 778.3'5
How to take great photos from airplanes / Frank Kingston Smith. Blue Ridge Summit, Pa. : Tab Books, [1978] p. cm. Includes index. [TR810.S54] 78-13619 ISBN 0-

8306-9879-5 : 8.95. ISBN 0-8306-2251-9 pbk. : 5.95
1. Photography, Aerial. I. Title. **BIP**

Photography, Aerial—Congresses.

INTERNATIONAL Symposium on Photography and Navigation, Columbus, Ohio, 1970. 778.3'5
International Symposium on Photography and Navigation; [proceedings] Edited by Sanjib K. Ghosh. [Columbus, Dept. of Geodetic Science, Ohio State University] 1970. vii, 416 p. illus., charts. 24 cm. Introd. and abstracts of most of the papers in English, French, and German. Sponsored by the International Society of Photogrammetry, Commission I, the American Society of Photogrammetry, and the Dept. of Geodetic Science, Ohio State University. Pages 413-416, blank for "Notes." Includes bibliographies. [TR810.158 1970] 73-24727 5.00
1. Photography, Aerial—Congresses. 2. Aerial photogrammetry—Congresses. I. Ghosh, Sanjib Kumar, 1925- ed. II. International Society for Photogrammetry. Commission I. III. American Society of Photogrammetry. IV. Ohio. State University, Columbus. Dept. of Geodetic Science.

Photography, Aerial—Handbooks, manuals, etc.

AMERICAN Society of Photogrammetry. 778.3'5'0202
Manual of color aerial photography. Editor-in-chief: John T. Smith, Jr. Associate editor: Abraham Anson. 1st ed. [Falls Church, Va., 1968] xv, 550 p. illus. (part col.), col. maps. 28 cm. Part of illustrative matter in pocket. Includes bibliographies. [TR810.A5] 67-31748
1. Photography, Aerial—Handbooks, manuals, etc. 2. Color photography—Handbooks, manuals, etc. 3. Photographic interpretation—Handbooks, manuals, etc. I. Smith, John T., ed. II. Anson, Abraham, ed. III. Title. **BIP**

Photography, Aerial—History.

NEWHALL, Beaumont, 1908- 778.3'5'09
Airborne camera; the world from the air and outer space. New York, Hastings House [1969] 144 p. illus. (part col.) 27 cm. Bibliography: p. 139-140. [TR810.N48] 69-15057 10.00
1. Photography, Aerial—History. 2. Earth—Photographs from space. I. Title. **BIP**

Photography—Apparatus and supplies.

INSTRUMENTATION and high-speed photography. v. 1. ser. 2. New York, Society of Motion Picture and Television Engineers 55 W. 42 St. [c.1955-1960] 187p. illus. 29cm. 'Papers reprinted from the Journal of the SMPTE.' Bibl. 61-670 4.00 pap., 778.37082
1. Photography—Apparatus and supplies. 2. Photography, High-speed. I. Society of Motion Picture and Television Engineers.

LILLEY, Geoffrey I. 771
Make your own photo equipment. London, Fountain Press; New York, Macmillan [1961. c. 1959] 116p. illus. (Fountain Photobook) 61-4017 4.50
1. sPhotography—Apparatus and supplies. I. Title.

PHOTOGRAPHY directory & buying guide. 1967. [New York, ZiffDavis 1966. v. illus. 29cm. Formerly in the May issues of 1939-42, 1950-53, and in the Oct. issue of 1948 of Photography. Title varies: 1954-55, Directory and buying guide. Comp. by the eds. of Popular photography. [TR12.P53] 55-333 3.00 deluxe ed. 770.025
1. Photography—Apparatus andsupplies—Direct. 2. Popular photography (Chicago)
This deluxe ed. is distributed by SportShelf, New Rochelle, N.Y.

U.S. National Aeronautics and Space Administration. Technology Utilization Division. 771
Selected photographic techniques; a compilation. Washington; [For sale by the Clearinghouse for Federal Scientific and Technical Information, Springfield, Va.] 1968. iv, 7 p. illus. 27 cm. (NASA SP-5914 (01)) [TR196.U55] 68-62093 0.15
1. Photography—Apparatus and supplies. 2. Photography—Printing processes. I. Title. II. Series: U.S. National Aeronautics and Space Administration. NASA SP - 5914 (01)

UNITED States. National Aeronautics and Space Administration. Technology Utilization Division. 771
Selected photographic techniques; a compilation. [Washington; for sale by the National Technical Information Service, Springfield, Va., 1971?] iii, 28 p. illus. 27 cm. (NASA SP-5914 (02)) Cover title. [TR196.U55 1971] 74-156872 1.00
1. Photography—Apparatus and supplies. 2. Photography—Processing. I. Title. II. Series: United States. National Aeronautics and Space Administration. NASA SP - 5914 (02).

Photography—Apparatus and supplies—Catalogs.

FOTOSHOP almanac. 770.58
New York, Fotoshop, inc. v. illus. 27 cm. [TR198.F6] 51-39710
1. Photography—Apparatus and supplies—Catalogs. 2. Photography. I. Fotoshop, inc., New York.

PETERSEN'S photographic magazine equipment buyer's guide. [Los Angeles, Petersen Pub. Co., 1974] 192 p. illus. 28 cm. [TR197.P45] 74-75067 ISBN 0-8227-0052-2 2.95 (pbk.) 380.1'45'7710973
1. Photography—Apparatus and supplies—Catalogs. I. Petersen Publishing Company. II. Title: Photographic magazine equipment buyer's guide.

THE Photography catalog / edited by Norman Snyder, with Carole Kismaric and Don Myrus. 1st ed. New York : Harper & Row, c1976. p. cm. Includes index. Bibliography: [TR197.P52] 76-9202 ISBN 0-06-013979-X pbk. : 7.95 770'.28
1. Photography—Apparatus and supplies—Catalogs. 2. Photography—Catalogs. I. Snyder, Norman. II. Kismaric, Carole, 1942- III. Myrus, Donald, 1927-

Photography—Apparatus and supplies—Collectors and collecting.

KLAMKIN, Charles. 770'.75
Photographica : a guide to the value of historic cameras and images / Charles Klamkin, with Matthew Isenberg. New York : Funk & Wagnalls, [1977] p. cm. Includes index. Bibliography: p. [TR6.5.K58] 77-2849 ISBN 0-308-10298-3 : 12.95
1. Photography—Apparatus and supplies—Collectors and collecting. 2. Photographs—Collectors and collecting. I. Isenberg, Matthew, joint author. II. Title. **BIP**

Photography—Apparatus and supplies—Direct.

PHOTOGRAPHY directory & buying guide. 1954- [New York(etc., Ziff-Davis Pub. Co.] v. illus. 29cm. Formerly in the May issues of 1939-42, 1950-58, and in the Oct. issue of 1948 of Photography. Title varies: 1954-55, Directory and buying guide. 'Compiled by the editors of Popular photography.' [TR12.P53] 55-333 779'.074'0153
1. Photography—Apparatus and supplies—Direct. I. Popular photography (Chicago)

POPULAR photography (Chicago) 779'.074'0153
Directory and buying guide. 1954- [Chicago, Ziff-Davis Pub. Co.] v. illus. 29cm. Formerly in the May issues for 1939-42 and for 1950-53 and in the October issue for 1948 of Photography, the magazine of popular photography. [TR12.P53] 55-333
1. Photography—Apparatus and supplies—Direct. I. Title.

Photography—Apparatus and supplies—Handbooks, manuals, etc.

FAMOUS Photographers School, Westport, Conn. 771
Famous Photographers course, technical manual; a concise reference handbook of useful technical information for photographers. [Westport, 1964] 130 p. illus., tables. 30 cm. "Prepared exclusively for students of the Famous Photographers School, Westport Connecticut." [TR196.F34] 64-1866
1. Photography—Apparatus and supplies—Handbooks, manuals, etc. I. Title.

Photography—Apparatus and supplies—Testing.

KEPPLER, Herbert, ed. 771
124 ways you can test cameras, lenses, and equipment. New York, Amphoto [c. 1962] 117p. illus. 61-16854 2.50bds.,
1. Photography—Apparatus and supplies—Testing. I. Title.

Photography, Applied.

MICHEL, Kurt, 1909- 778.3'11
Die Mikrophotographie. Mit 550 teils farbigen Textabbildungen. 3. Aufl. Wien, New York, Springer-Verlag, 1967. xxxii, 736p. 26cm. (Die Wissenschaftliche und angewandte Photographie, 10. Bd.) Bibl. [TR145.W76 Bd.10 1967] 66-22393 45.75
I. Title.

TIME-LIFE Books. 770.282
Special problems, by the editors of Time-Life Books. New York [1971] 209 p. illus. (part col.) 27 cm. (Life library of photography) Bibliography: p. 205. [TR624.T55] 75-148526
1. Photography, Applied. I. Title. **BIP**

Photography, Architectural.

DE MARE, Eric Samuel, 1910- 778.94
Photography and architecture. New York, Praeger [c.1961] 208p. 130 illus. 29cm. 61-7817 13.50
1. Photography, Architectural. 2. Architecture—Pictorial works. I. Title.

GIEBELHAUSEN, Joachim. 778.94
Architectural photography. English-language ed. by E. F. Linssen. Munich, Verlag Grossbild-Technik; distributed in U.S.A. by Kling Photo Corp., New York, 1965] 256 p. illus. (part col.) 29 cm. [TR630.G513] 65-21739
1. Photography, Architectural. I. Title.

*MARE, Eric de 778.9'4
Architectural photography. London, B. T. Batsford, [1975] 96 p. ill. 22 cm. [TR659] ISBN 0-7134-2985-2
1. Photography, Architectural. I. Title.
Distributed by Hippocrene Books for 12.50.

MOLITOR, Joseph W. 778.9'4
Architectural photography / Joseph W. Molitor. New York : Wiley, [1976] p. cm. Includes index. [TR659.M64] 76-6537 ISBN 0-471-61312-6 : 22.50
1. Photography, Architectural. I. Title. **BIP**

SHULMAN, Julius. 778.94
Photographing architecture and interiors. Introd. by Richard J. Neutra. New York, Whitney Library of Design [1962] ix, 154 p. illus. (part col.) 31 cm. [TR630.S48] 62-18473
1. Photography, Architectural. I. Title.

SHULMAN, Julius. 778.9'9'7
The photography of architecture and design : photographing buildings, interiors, and the visual arts / by Julius Shulman. New York : Whitney Library of Design, 1977. p. cm. Includes index. [TR659.S58] 77-22243 ISBN 0-8230-7429-3 : 25.00
1. Photography, Architectural. 2. Photography of art. I. Title. **BIP**

VELTRI, John. 778.9'4
Architectural photography. Garden City, N.Y., American Photographic Book Publishers Co. [1974] 190, [2] p. illus. (part col.) 25 x 28 cm. Bibliography: p. [191] [TR659.V44] 72-91033 ISBN 0-8174-0556-9 17.50
1. Photography, Architectural. **BIP**

Photography, Architectural—Exhibitions.

NEWHALL, Beaumont, 1908- 779'.4'0924
Frederick H. Evans: photographer of the majesty, light, and space of the medieval cathedrals of England and France. [Millerton, N.Y., Aperture, 1973] 1 v. (unpaged) illus. 27 cm. "Published to accompany a major exhibition of British photographers prior to 1915 to be presented by the Alfred Stieglitz Center of the Philadelphia Museum of Art in 1975." Includes bibliographical references. [TR659.N48] 73-85260 ISBN 0-912334-48-7 7.50
1. Evans, Frederick H. 2. Photography, Architectural—Exhibitions. I. Alfred Stieglitz Center.

Photography, Artistic.

BOURKE-WHITE, Mararet, 1906-1971. 779'.092'4
The photographs of Margaret Bourke-White. Edited by Sean Callahan. Introd. by Theodore M. Brown. Foreword by Carl Mydans. [Greenwich, Conn.] New York Graphic Society, 1972. 208 p. illus. 32 cm. Bibliography: p. 203-208. [TR140.B6A29 1972] 72-80415 ISBN 0-8212-0462-9 15.00
1. Bourke-White, Margaret, 1906-1971. 2. Photography, Artistic. 3. Photography, Journalistic. I. Callahan, Sean. II. Title.

770
The invented eye : masterpieces of photography, 1839-1914 / Edward Lucie-Smith. New York : Paddington Press, [1975] 256 p. : ill. ; 29 cm. Includes index. Bibliography: p. 255-256. [TR652.L8] 74-15919 ISBN 0-8467-0040-9 : 16.95
1. Photography, Artistic. I. Title.

ADAL, 1948- 779'.092'4
The evidence of things not seen ... / Adal. New York : Published for Foto by Da Capo Press, 1975. p. cm. [TR654.A3] 74-31350 ISBN 0-306-70722-5. ISBN 0-306-80013-6 pbk. : 7.95
1. Photography, Artistic. I. Title.

ADAMS, Ansel Easton, 1902- 779'.092'4
Ansel Adams. Edited by Liliane De Cock. Foreword by Minor White. [Hastings-on-Hudson, N.Y.] Morgan & Morgan [1972] 1 v. (unpaged; chiefly illus.) 28 cm. Includes bibliography. [TR653.A3] 72-83114 ISBN 0-87100-030-X 12.00
1. Photography, Artistic. **BIP**

ADAMS, Ansel Easton, 1902- 779'.092'4
Ansel Adams—images, 1923-1974 / foreword by Wallace Stegner. Boston : New York Graphic Society, 1974. 127 p. : chiefly ill. ; 36 x 45 cm. Bibliography: p. 127. [TR654.A33 1974] 74-78740 ISBN 0-8212-0600-1 : 75.00
1. Photography, Artistic. I. Title.

ADAMS, Ansel Easton, 1902- 779'.092'4
The portfolios of Ansel Adams / introd. by John Szarkowski ; [edited by Tim Hill]. Boston : New York Graphic Society, c1977. xii, 124 p. : chiefly ill. ; 28 cm. [TR654.A34] 77-71628 ISBN 0-8212-0723-7 : 19.50
1. Adams, Ansel Easton, 1902- 2. Photography, Artistic. I. Title. **BIP**

ADAMS, Washington Irving Lincoln, 1865-1946, ed. 770'.28
Sunlight and shadow / edited by W. I. Lincoln Adams. New York : Arno Press, 1979 [c1897] p. cm. (The Sources of modern photography) Reprint of the ed. published by Baker & Taylor, New York. [TR642.A3 1979] 76-24669 ISBN 0-405-09646-1 : 15.00
1. Photography, Artistic. I. Title. II. Series.

ALCORN, Thomas John, 1956-1974. 779'.092'4
Photographs / Thomas Alcorn. New York : Rizzoli, 1976. [76] p. : chiefly ill. ; 28 cm. Title on cover: Thomas John Alcorn, New York, 28-4-1956—Firenze, 13-3-1974.

Introd. in English and Italian. [TR654.A46 1976] 76-377961 ISBN 0-8478-0057-1 pbk. : 8.95
1. Alcorn, Thomas John, 1956-1974. 2. Photography, Artistic. I. Title.

AMERICA & Alfred 779'.092'4
Stieglitz : a collective portrait / edited by Waldo Frank ... [et al.] ; with a new introd. by Dorothy Norman. New York : Octagon Books, 1975, c1934. xvi, 339 p., 32 leaves of plates : ill. ; 24 cm. Reprint of the 1st ed. published by Doubleday, Doran, Garden City, N.Y.; with a new introd. Includes index. Bibliography: p. 319-322. [TR140.S7A7 1975] 75-11881 ISBN 0-374-96117-4 : 17.00
1. Stieglitz, Alfred, 1864-1946. 2. Photography, Artistic. I. Frank, Waldo David, 1889-1967.

ANDERSON, Paul Lewis, 1880-1956. 770'.28
The fine art of photography. New York Arno Press, 1973 [c1919]. 314 p. illus. 21 cm. (Literature of Photography) [TR642.A53 1973] 72-9180 ISBN 0-405-04891-2 20.00
1. Photography, Artistic. I. Title. II. Series.

ANSCO. 770
Better photography made easy ... [Binghamton, 1946] 60p. illus. 19cm. [TR650.A56 1946] 47-21636
1. Photography, Artistic. 2. Photography—Exposure. I. Title.

ANSCO. 770
Better photography made easy. [Binghamton, N. Y., 1955] 58p. illus. 19cm. [TR650.A56 1955] 55-3718
1. Photography, Artistic 2. Photography—Exposure. I. Title.

ARMSTRONG, Duke. 779
100 famous paintings [San Francisco] Toltec Press [1970] 1 v. (unpaged) illus. 22 x 28 cm. 500 copies printed. [TR654.A74] 70-15394
1. Photography, Artistic. 2. Photography, Abstract. I. Title.

ATGET, Eugene, 1856-1927. 779
The world of Atget, by Berenice Abbott. New York, Horizon Press [1964] xxx p., 180 plates (incl. facsim., ports.) 34 cm. [TR140.A8A2] 64-24540
1. Photography, Artistic. I. Abbott, Berenice, 1898- II. Title. BIP

ATKESON, Mira. 779'.3'0924
The world of Mira Atkeson : photography / by Mira Atkeson ; literary vignettes by Luella O'Conner ; introd. by Ray Atkeson. Portland, Or. : C. H. Belding, c1977. 120 p. : col. ill. ; 27 cm. [TR654.A84] 77-77012 ISBN 0-912856-36-X : 19.50
1. Photography, Artistic. I. O'Conner, Luella. II. Title. BIP

AUSTRALIAN photography 779'.0994
1976 / edited by Laurence Le Guay. Sydney : Globe Pub. Co., [1976] 168 p. : chiefly ill. ; 26 x 27 cm. Includes index. [TR654.A95] 76-380551
1. Photography, Artistic. I. Le Guay, Laurence.

BAILEY, J. Edward, 1923- 779'.9'9177434034
The city within. Photos. by J. Edward Bailey, III. [Detroit] Detroit Institute of Arts, 1969. [36] p. (chiefly illus.) port. 26 cm. [TR654.B25] 74-25368
1. Photography, Artistic. 2. Detroit—Description—Views. I. Title. BIP

BAILEY, Ronald H. 770
Duane Michals : the photographic illusion / text by Ronald H. Bailey, with the editors of Alskog, Inc. New York : Crowell, [1975] p. cm. (Masters of contemporary photography) "An Alskog book." [TR654.B26] 75-12884 8.95 ISBN 0-690-00788-4 pbk. : 4.95
1. Michals, Duane. 2. Photography, Artistic. I. Alskog, inc.

BAKAL, Carl, 1918- 778.24
How to shoot for glamour. Illus. not otherwise credited are by the author. [1st ed.] San Francisco, Camera Craft Pub. Co. [1955] 128p. illus. 24cm. [TR675.B26] 55-11887
1. Photography, Artistic. 2. Photography of women. I. Title.

BALISH, Jacquelyn, ed. 779
Leica world. Designed by Ernest G. Scarfone. [New York] American Photographic Book Pub. Co., 1957. 172 p. illus. 29 cm. [TR650.B26] 57-11330
1. Photography, Artistic. 2. Leica camera. I. Title.

BALISH, Jacquelyn, ed. 779
Leica world. Designed by Ernest G. Scarfone. [New York, American Photographic Book Pub. Co., 1957. 172p. illus. 29cm. [TR650.B26] 57-11330
1. Photography, Aritic. 2. Lelca camera. I. Title.

BARREAUX, Adolphe, ed. 779
Beauty and the camera. Louisville, Ky., Whitestone Publications, c1957. 144p. illus. 24cm. (A Whitestone book, no. 21) [TR650.B275] 58-3645
1. Photography, Artistic. I. Title.

BASCH, Peter. 778.92
Form & figure. [New York, Amphoto, c1956] 109p. illus. 32cm. [TR675.B32] 56-12478
1. Photography, Artistic. I. Title.

BASCH, Peter. 778.921
Guide to figure photography, Text by Jack Rey. New York, Amphoto [1961 117p. illus. 26cm. [TR675.B34] 61-8770
1. Photography, Artistic. 2. Photography of the nude. I. Rey, Jack. II. Title. III. Title: Figure photography.

BASCH, Peter. 779.24
Peter Basch photographs beauty. [Adolphe Barreaux, editor. Louisville, Ky., Whitestone Publications, 1960] 144p. illus. 24cm. (A Whitestone book, no. 31) [TR675.B36] 61-2337
1. Photography, Artistic. I. Title.

BASCH, Peter. 779.25
Photo studies. Greenwich, Conn., Fawcett Publications, c1957. 144p. illus. 24cm. (A Fawcett how-to book, 350) [TR680.B32] 58-3686
1. Photography, Artistic. 2. Photography of the nude. I. Title.

BAUMGARTENER, Otto G 1893- 778
Beauty to behold. [1st ed.] New York, Pageant Press [1956] 149p. illus. 24cm. Includes photos. taken by the author and a selection of prose and poetry chosen from his wide reading. [TR650.B32] 56-10103
1. Photography, Artistic. I. Title.

BEARD, Michael. 779'.092'4
Duet / by Michael Beard, Jeff Shyshka. San Francisco : A. Wofsy Fine Arts, c1977. [47] p. : chiefly ill. ; 28 cm. [TR654.B4] 76-58640 ISBN 0-915346-25-7 pbk. : 6.95
1. Photography, Artistic. I. Shyshka, Jeff, joint author. II. Title. BIP

BEATON, Cecil Walter Hardy, 1904- 779'.0924
The best of Beaton, with notes on the photos. by Cecil Beaton. Introd. by Truman Capote. [1st American ed.] New York, Macmillan [1968] 248 p. illus. (part col.), ports. (part col.) 32 cm. [TR650.B38 1968] 68-22816 17.95
1. Photography, Artistic. 2. Photography—Portraits. I. Title.

BEATON, Cecil Walter Hardy, 1904- 779
Images. Pref., Dame Edith Sitwell. Introd. by Christopher Isherwood. New York, London House [1964, c.1963] 1v. (chiefly illus., ports.) 26cm. 64-11267 4.95
1. Photography, Artistic. I. Title.

BELLOCQ, E. J. 779'.24
Storyville portraits; photographs from the New Orleans red-light district, circa 1912 [by] E. J. Bellocq. Reproduced from prints made by Lee Friedlander. Pref. by Lee Friedlander. Edited by John Szarkowski. New York, Museum of Modern Art; distributed by New York Graphic Society, Greenwich, Conn. [1970] 17 p. illus., 33 plates. 29 cm. [TR653.B45] 70-86413 12.50
1. Photography, Artistic. 2. Prostitutes. 3. Photography of women. I. New York (City). Museum of Modern Art. II. Title.

BENNETT, Edna. 778.8
Tabletop and still life photography. New York, Universal Photo Books [c1961] 128p. illus. 21cm. [TR650.B46] 61-14249
1. Photography, Artistic. 2. Photography, Table-top. I. Title.

BENNETT, Edna. 778.8
Tabletop and still life photography. New York, Amphoto [1970] 128 p. illus. 20 cm. [TR683.5.B45 1970] 68-57667 2.50
1. Photography, Artistic. 2. Photography, Table-top. I. Title.

BENY, Roloff. 779.991338
A time of gods; a photographer in the wake of Odysseus. Quotations from Chapman's Homer. Notes edited by John Lindsay Opie. New York, Viking Press [1962] 272 p. mounted illus., plates, map. 32 cm. (A Studio book) [TR650.B468] 62-19609
1. Photography, Artistic. I. Homerus. Odyssea. II. Title.

BERNSTEIN, Gary. 779'.24'0924
Burning cold / photography by Gary Bernstein ; written by Bernie Taupin. New York : Harmony Books, c1978. [64] p. : col. ill. ; 33 cm. [TR654.B47 1978] 78-1579 ISBN 0-517-53357-X : 14.95
1. Photography, Artistic. 2. Photography of the nude. 3. Women—Portraits. I. Taupin, Bernie. II. Title. BIP

BETHERS, Ray, 1902- 778
Photo-vision. New York, St. Martin's Press [1957] 106 p. illus. 26 cm. [TR650.B49] 57-2727
1. Photography, Artistic. I. Title.

BISCHOF, Werner Adalbert, 1916-1954. 770'.92'4 B
Werner Bischof, 1916-1954 / [editors, Rosellina Bischof Burri, Rene Burri]. New York : Grossman Publishers, 1974. 93, [2] p. : ill. ; 23 cm. (ICP library of photographers ; v. 2) Bibliography: p. [95] [TR140.B5A33 1974] 73-14141 ISBN 0-670-75717-9 : 10.00. ISBN 0-670-75718-7 pbk : 5.95
1. Bischof, Werner Adalbert, 1916-1954. 2. Photography, Artistic. I. Series: International Fund for Concerned Photography. ICP library of photographers ; v. 2.

BLOTNICK, Elihu. 779'.092'4
Saltwater flats / Elihu Blotnick. [Berkeley, Calif.] : BBM Associates, [1975] c1974. [63] p. : chiefly ill. ; 28 cm. "A silent film." [TR654.B6 1975] 74-18166 ISBN 0-915090-00-7 : 6.95
1. Photography, Artistic. I. Title.

BONES, Jim. 779'.3
Texas earth surfaces; a photographic study. Foreword by Mort Baranoff. Austin, Encino Press, 1970. [68] p. (chiefly illus.) 27 cm. [TR654.B66] 72-185299 7.50
1. Photography, Artistic. 2. Nature photography. I. Title. BIP

BONES, Jim. 779'.9'97640924
Texas heartland : a hill country year / photos. by Jim Bones, Jr. ; text by John Graves. College Station : Texas A&M University Press, [1975] 40 p., [32] leaves of plates : col. ill. ; 31 cm. [TR654.B663] 75-16352 ISBN 0-89096-002-X : 21.50
1. Photography, Artistic. 2. Nature photography. 3. Texas—History. I. Graves, John, 1920- II. Title. BIP

BOSTON. Museum of Fine Arts. 779
Alfred Stieglitz: photographer, by Doris Bry. Boston; [Distributed by October House, New York, 1965] 28 p. 62 plates. 28 cm. Contents.Contents.—The Alfred Stieglitz collection in the Museum of Fine Arts.—Alfred Stieglitz: photographer, by D. Bray.—Chronology.—Bibliography (p. 25-26)—Catalogue. [TR140.S7B6] 65-24359
1. Stieglitz, Alfred, 1864-1946. 2. Photography, Artistic. I. Bry, Doris.

BOURKE-WHITE, Margaret, 1906-1971. 779
The photographs of Margaret Bourke-White, introduction by Theodore M. Brown, foreword by Carl Mydans. Boston, New York Graphic Society, 1975 c1972 208 p. ill. 30 cm. Bibliography: p. 203-208. [TR650] ISBN 0-8212-0656-7 7.50 (pbk.)
1. Bourke-White, Margaret, 1906-1971. 2. Photography, artistic. 3. Photography, journalistic. I. Callahan, Sean, comp. II. Title.
L.C. card number for original edition: 72-80415. BIP

BOWEN, Elisa. 779'.092'4
Celebration of life. Millbrae, Calif., Celestial Arts Pub. [1972] [77] p. illus. 17 cm. A collection of photographs accompanied by two stanzas of the Tao te ching by Lao-tzu, as adapted in English by Elisa Bowen. [TR654.B68] 77-185761 2.50
1. Photography, Artistic. I. Lao-tzu. Tao te ching. II. Title.

BRANDT, Bill 779
Shadow of light; a collection of photographs from 1931 to the present. Introd. by Cyril Connolly and notes by Marjorie Beckett. New York, Viking [1966] 128p. (chiefly illus. (pt. col.) ports.) 29cm. (Studio bk.) [TR650.B68] 66-25278 12.95
1. Photography, Artistic. I. Title.

BRANDT, Bill. 779
Shadow of light : photographs / by Bill Brandt ; with introductions by Cyril Connolly and Mark Haworth-Booth. 1st American ed. New York : Da Capo Press, 1977. p. cm. Bibliography: p. [TR654.B7 1977] 76-52463 ISBN 0-306-70858-2 lib.bdg. : 29.50
1. Photography, Artistic. I. Title. BIP

BRASSAI, Gyula Halasz, called, 1899- 770'.924
Brassai. With an introductory essay by Lawrence Durell. New York, Museum of Modern Art; distributed by New York Graphic Society, Greenwich, Conn. [1968] 79, [1] p. (chiefly illus., ports.) 23 cm. Bibliography: p. 78-[80] [TR650.B683] 68-54161 5.95
1. Photography, Artistic. 2. Paris—Description—Views. I. Durrell, Lawrence. II. New York (City). Museum of Modern Art.

BRASSAI, Gyula Halasz, called, 1899- 779'.2'0924
A portfolio of ten photographs by Brassai. New York, Witkin-Berley, 1973. 1 portfolio ([5] l., 10 plates) 2 ports. 53 cm. "A limited edition of fifty." No. 12. [TR653.B7] 73-217861
1. Photography, Artistic.

BRODATZ, Phil. 779
Textures; a photographic album for artists and designers. New York, Dover Publications [1966] xiv, 112 p. (chiefly illus.) 27 cm. [TR650.B69] 66-24124
1. Photography, Artistic. I. Title. BIP

BROOK, John, 1924- 779'.21
A long the riverrun. [San Francisco] Scrimshaw Press [1970] 1 v. (chiefly illus.) 22 x 27 cm. (The Scrimshaw Press publication no. 5) [TR647.B76A48] 73-18973 6.50
1. Photography, Artistic. I. Title. BIP

BROOME, L E 779.24
Posing patterns for creative photography. New York, Hastings House [1958] 200p. illus. 25cm. (Communication arts books) [TR675.B7] 58-4425
1. Photography, Artistic. 2. Photography of women. 3. Posture. I. Title.

BROWNE, Turner. 779'.9'9763
Louisiana Cajuns = Cajuns de la Louisiane / photos. by Turner Browne ; introd. by Peter Feibleman. Baton Rouge : Louisiana State University Press, c1977. p. cm. Captions and introd. in English and French. [TR654.B743] 77-24171 ISBN 0-8071-0363-2 : 14.95
1. Photography, Artistic. 2. Cajuns—Pictorial works. 3. Louisiana—Description and travel—Views. I. Feibleman, Peter S., 1930- II. Cajuns de la Louisiane. III. Title. BIP

BRUCE, David, 1939- comp. 779'.2'0922
Sun pictures; the Hill-Adamson calotypes. Greenwich, Conn., New York Graphic Society [1974, c1973] 247 p. illus. 30 cm. Bibliography: p. 243. [TR651.B78 1974] 73-87361 ISBN 0-8212-0588-9 17.50
1. Hill, David Octavius, 1802-1870. 2. Adamson, Robert, 1821-1848. 3. Photography, Artistic. 4. Calotype. I. Hill, David Octavius, 1802-1870. II. Adamson, Robert, 1821-1848. III. Title.

DOBELL, Byron, ed. 778
Creative pictures. New York, Maco Magazine Corp, c1956. 125p. illus. 24cm. (Maco, 48) [TR650.D59] 57-23185
1. Photography, Artistic. I. Title.

DONNELS, John, 1924- 779'.092'4
New Orleans/Vieux Carre, and other photographs by John Donnels. Words by Joe Schulte. [New Orleans] Starving Artist Press [1973] [71] p. (chiefly illus.) 28 cm. [TR654.D68] 73-87929
1. Photography, Artistic. 2. New Orleans—Description—Views. I. Schulte, Joe. II. Title.

DORR, Nell. 779'.94991727
The bare feet. [Greenwich, Conn., New York Graphic Society, 1962] [80] p. (chiefly illus.) 27 x 35 cm. [TR650.D67] 62-52119
1. Photography, Artistic. 2. Teotitlan del Valle, Mexico—Description—Views. I. Title.

DORR, Nell. 779'.0924
Of night and day. [Greenwich, Conn., New York Graphic Society, 1968] 95 p. illus. 24 x 29 cm. [TR650.D677] 68-12362
1. Photography, Artistic. I. Title. BIP

DUNCAN, David Douglas. 779'.092'4
Prismatics; exploring a new world. [1st ed.] New York, Harper & Row [1973] [11] p., 42 col. plates. 32 cm. [TR654.D87 1973] 72-9752 ISBN 0-06-011128-3 22.50
1. Photography, Artistic. 2. Photography—Special effects. I. Title.

EISENSTAEDT, Alfred. 770
The eye of Eisenstaedt, by Alfred Eisenstaedt as told to Arthur Goldsmith. New York, Viking Press [1969] 199 p. illus. (part col.), ports. 22 cm. (A Studio book) [TR647.E35A3] 69-17970 6.95
1. Photography, Artistic. 2. Photography, Journalistic. 3. Photography—Portraits. I. Goldsmith, Arthur A. II. Title.

ELAM, Jane. 770'.28
Photography, simple and creative : with and without a camera / Jane Elam. New York : Van Nostrand Reinhold, [1975] p. cm. Bibliography: p. [TR642.E4 1975] 75-12164 ISBN 0-442-22280-7 : 9.95 ISBN 0-442-22281-5 pbk. : 5.95 pbk.
1. Photography, Artistic. 2. Photography—Special effects. 3. Photograms. I. Title.

ENYEART, James. 770'.92'4 B
Bruguiere, his photographs and his life / by James Enyeart. New York : Knopf, [1977] p. cm. Bibliography: p. [TR140.B79E58] 77-75355 ISBN 0-394-40852-7 : 17.50 ISBN 0-394-73385-1 pbk. : 9.95
1. Bruguiere, Francis. 2. Photography, Artistic. 3. Photographers—United States—Biography. I. Title.

ERWITT, Elliott. 779'.092'4
Photographs and anti-photographs. Biographical essay by Sam Holmes. Introd. by John Szarkowski. Greenwich, Conn., New York Graphic Society [1972] 128 p. (chiefly illus.) 25 x 30 cm. [TR654.E78] 72-183972 ISBN 0-8212-0440-8 15.00
1. Photography, Artistic. I. Title.

ERWITT, Elliott. 770'.92'4
Recent developments / Elliott Erwitt ; introd. by Wilfred Sheed. New York : Simon and Schuster, c1978. p. cm. [TR654.E782] 78-17998 ISBN 0-671-24645-3 : 17.95 ISBN 0-671-24646-1 pbk. : 9.95
1. Erwitt, Elliott. 2. Photography, Artistic. I. Title. BIP

ESSA, Ahmed. 779'.0924
Images and eloquence; photographs for composition. Photographed, written, and designed by Ahmed Essa. New York, Holt, Rinehart and Winston [1971, c1972] 264 p. illus. 28 cm. [TR654.E88] 70-165030 ISBN 0-03-085289-7
1. Photography, Artistic. 2. English language—Composition and exercises. I. Title.

EVANS, Walker, 1903- 779.949747
Message from the interior. New York, Eakins Pr. [1966] [4] 1., 12 plates. 36cm. [TR650.E87] 66-23199 15.00; 7.95 pap.,
1. Photography, Artistic. I. Title.

EVANS, Walker, 1903- 779'.092'4 1975.
Walker Evans, first and last. 1st ed. New York : Harper & Row, c1978. 199 p. : all ill. ; 31 cm. [TR654.E915 1978] 77-11824 ISBN 0-06-011261-1 : 29.95
1. Evans, Walker, 1903-1975. 2. Photography, Artistic. I. Title.

FEINBERG, Sidney. 779
30 photographs by Sidney Feinberg New York, Amer. Bk.-Stratford Pr. [1967] 1 v. (unpaged) illus., port. 26cm. Exhibit at the Willoughby Camera Stores gallery. [TR650.F45] 67-66218 pap., price unreported
1. Photography, Artistic. I. Willoughby Camera Stores. II. Title.

FEININGER, Andreas, 779'.092'4 1906-
Andreas Feininger. Introd. and text by Ralph Hattersley. [Dobbs Ferry, N.Y., Morgan & Morgan, c1973] 160 p. (chiefly illus.) 28 cm. Bibliography: p. 156-157. [TR654.F44] 73-83131 ISBN 0-87100-042-3 12.00
1. Photography, Artistic. I. Hattersley, Ralph. BIP

FEININGER, Andreas, 1906- 770'.1
The perfect photograph. Garden City, N.Y., AMPHOTO [1974] 176 p. illus. 23 cm. [TR642.F44] 73-92420 ISBN 0-8174-0565-8 9.95
1. Photography, Artistic. I. Title. BIP

FEININGER, Andreas, 1906- 770'.28
Photographic seeing. Englewood Cliffs, N.J., Prentice-Hall [1973] 184 p. illus. (part col.) 23 cm. [TR642.F45] 73-7567 ISBN 0-13-665372-3 8.95
1. Photography, Artistic. I. Title. BIP

FEININGER, Andreas, 1906- 778.9
The world through my eyes; 30 years of photography. New York, Crown Publishers [1963] 52 p. 172 plates (part col.) 33 cm. "Bibliography [of] books written and photographed by Andreas Feininger": p. 6. [TR650.F42] 63-21114
1. Photography, Artistic. I. Title.

FELDMAN, Lou. 779'.092'4
Camera eye-deas of Lou Feldman. [Worcester? Mass.] : Feldman, 1978. 124 p. : chiefly ill. ; 28 cm. [TR654.F45] 78-109102 17.95
1. Feldman, Lou. 2. Photography, Artistic. I. Title.

FELDSTEIN, Mark, 779'.4'0924 1937-
Unseen New York / photos. by Mark Feldstein. New York : Dover Publications, [1975] 97 p. : chiefly ill. (some col.) ; 27 cm. [TR654.F46 1975] 75-2617 ISBN 0-486-20166-X pbk. : 4.00
1. Photography, Artistic. 2. Architecture—Details—Pictorial works. 3. New York (City)—Description—Views. I. Title. BIP

FINK, Peter. 779'.0924
Photographs. Introductory essay by Marjorie Morris. New York, Gallery of Modern Art, 1969. [48] p. (chiefly illus.) 28 cm. Selections from a retrospective exhibit of 160 photographs. [TR647.F5A2 1969] 75-11036
1. Photography, Artistic. I. New York (City). Gallery of Modern Art Including the Huntington Hartford Collection. II. Title.

FIRST portfolio: photographs 779 *from the Hamilton-Kirkland community.* [Assembled by Robert Ziegler and Robert Hesse. Clinton, N.Y., Wintersetl] 1972. [48] p. (chiefly illus.) 22 cm. [TR654.F55] 72-191810
1. Photography, Artistic. I. Ziegler, Robert, comp. II. Hesse, Robert, 1950- comp. III. Hamilton College, Clinton, N.Y. IV. Kirkland College.

FOX, Siv Cedering. 811'.5'4
Cup of cold water; poems and photographs, by Siv Cedering Fox. [New York] New Rivers Press; [distributed by Serendipity Books, Berkeley, Calif.] 1973. 92 p. illus. 27 cm. [PS3556.O955C8] 73-76236 ISBN 0-912284-47-1 7.50
I. Title. BIP

FRAGMENTS of a world 779'.09931 *:* a collection of photographs by New Zealand women photographers / [edited, compiled, and designed by Gillian Chaplin ... et al.]. Dunedin : J. McIndoe, 1976. 111 p. : chiefly ill. ; 25 cm. [TR654.F65] 77-364101 ISBN 0-908565-10-0
1. Photography, Artistic. 2. Women photographers. I. Chaplin, Gillian, 1948- BIP

FRANK, Larry. 779'.092'4
Larry Frank, photographer. Washington, Baker-Webster Print. Co. [1971] 30 p. (chiefly illus.) 25 cm. (Portfolio, 1) [TR654.F68] 73-174251
1. Photography, Artistic.

FRANK, Robert. 779'.092'4
The lines of my hand. [n.p., Lustrum Press; distributor: Light Impressions, Rochester, N.Y., 1972] 1 v. (chiefly illus.) 31 cm. [TR654.F7] 71-189074 ISBN 0-912810-04-1 7.95
1. Photography, Artistic. 2. Photography, Documentary. I. Title.

FRANK, Robert. 779'.092'4
Robert Frank. Millerton, N.Y. : Aperture, c1976. 95 p. : chiefly ill. ; 21 cm. (The Aperture history of photography series ; 2) [TR654.F724 1976] 76-22001 ISBN 0-89381-002-9 : 6.95
1. Photography, Artistic.

FREED, Arthur. 779'.0924
Eight photographs. [Garden City, N.Y.] Doubleday [1971] 1 portfolio ([1] l., 8 plates) 37 cm. (Doubleday/Projections) Title from portfolio. [TR654.F74] 70-23327
1. Photography, Artistic.

FREUND, Gisele. 770'.92'4
The world in my camera, trans. by June Guicharnaud. New York, Dial Press, 1974. 259 p. illus. (part. col.) 29 cm. Translation of Le Monde et ma camera. [TR140.F69A313] 72-1061 ISBN 0-8037-9732-X 15.00
I. Title. BIP

FROST, Miriam. 779'.092'4
Messiah : a photographic meditation on Handel's Messiah / by Miriam Frost and Keith McCormick. Minneapolis, MN : Winston Press, c1978. 60 p., [1] leaf of plates : ill. ; 20 x 22 cm. [TR654.F78] 78-59409 ISBN 0-03-045721-1 pbk. : 5.95
1. Handel, Georg Friedrich, 1685-1759. Messiah. 2. Photography, Artistic. I. McCormick, Keith, joint author. II. Handel, Georg Friedrich, 1685-1759. Messiah. III. Title. BIP

GALANTI, Pat. 779
The ad-maze; a photographic excursion into the dreams of an adman, created and photographed by Pat Galanti. South Brunswick [N.J.] A. S. Barnes [1968] 267 p. (chiefly illus.) 29 cm. Song by Pamela Edwards and John DeMaio: p. 266-267. [TR654.G3] 68-14409 7.50
1. Photography, Artistic. I. Title.

GEORGE Eastman House, 770'.1 Rochester, N.Y.
Photo-secession : Stieglitz and the fine-art movement in photography / Robert Doty ; with a foreword by Beaumont Newhall. New York : Dover Publications, 1978. 139 p. : ill. ; 28 cm. Reprint of the 1960 ed. published by George Eastman House, New York, which was issued as George Eastman House monograph no. 1. Bibliography: p. 135-136. [TD650.G36 1978] 77-20467 ISBN 0-486-23588-2 : 5.00
1. Stieglitz, Alfred, 1864-1946. 2. Photography, Artistic. I. Doty, Robert M. II. Title. III. Series: George Eastman House monograph ; no. 1. BIP

GEORGE Eastman House, 770.1'1 Rochester, N.Y.
Photography in the twentieth century, by Nathan Lyons. New York, Horizon Press in collaboration with the George Eastman House. Rochester, N.Y. [1967] xv, 143 p. (chiefly illus.) 26 x 28 cm. "Prepared by the George Eastman House of Photography on the occasion of the exhibition 'Photography in the twentieth century,' which opened at the National Gallery of Canada in February of 1967." [TR650.G37] 67-20818
1. Photography, Artistic. 2. Photography—Exhibitions. I. Lyons, Nathan. II. Ottawa. National Gallery of Canada. III. Title. IV. Title.

GERNSHEIM, Helmut, 1913- 779
Creative photography: aesthetic trends, 1839-1960. [1st American ed.] Boston, Boston Book & Art Shop [1962] 258 p. illus., ports. 29 cm. Bibliography: p. 251-254. [TR650.G385 1962] 62-20069
1. Photography, Artistic. 2. Photography — Hist. I. Title.

GERNSHEIM, Helmut, 779'.092'4 B 1913-
Julia Margaret Cameron : her life and photographic work / Helmut Gernsheim. [2d ed.]. Millerton, N.Y. : Aperture, [1975] 200 p. : ill. ; 28 cm. Includes index. Bibliography: p. 195-196. [TR140.C27G47 1975] 73-85258 ISBN 0-912334-50-9 : 20.00. ISBN 0-912334-51-7 pbk. : 12.50
1. Cameron, Julia Margaret Pattle, 1815-1879. 2. Photography, Artistic. 3. Photography—Portraits.

GIBSON, Henry Louis, 779'.0924 1906-
Light through the lens; a cross-section of approaches for coupling poetry and photography, by H. Lou Gibson. [N. Quincy, Mass., Christopher Pub. House, 1968] 123 p. illus. 27 cm. [TR650.G46] 68-31022 ISBN 0-8158-0003-7 4.95
1. Photography, Artistic. I. Title.

GIBSON, Ralph. 779'.092'4
Deja-vu. [New York, Lustrum Press, 1973] [52] p. (chiefly illus.) 31 cm. [TR654.G5] 72-96851 ISBN 0-912810-06-8 5.95
1. Photography, Artistic. I. Title.
Distributed by Light Impressions

GILLIES, John Wallace. 770'.28
Principles of pictorial photography. New York, Arno Press, 1973. [c1923] 253 p. illus. 24 cm. (The Literature of Photography) [TR642.G54 1973] 72-9201 ISBN 0-405-04910-2. 16.00.
1. Photography, Artistic. I. Title. II. Series.

GLYCK, Zvonko. 779
Photographic vision. Philadelphia, Chilton Books [1965] 1 v. (various pagings) illus. (part col.) 32 cm. [TR650.G56] 65-23147
1. Photography, Artistic. I. Title.

GOLDWATER, Barry Morris, 779 1909-
People and places; text and photos. by Barry Goldwater. New York, Random House [1967] 86 p. illus. 30 cm. [TR650.G59] 67-22640
1. Photography, Artistic. I. Title.

GORDON, Richard, 1945- 779'.092'4
New York. [Santa Cruz, Calif., Yowza Products, 1973] 1 v. (chiefly illus.) 16 x 24 cm. Edition of 100 copies. No. C1. Consists of photos. mounted on cardboard. [TR654.G67] 73-173333
1. Photography, Artistic. 2. New York (City)—Description—Views.

GORE, Art, 1926- 779'.092'4
Speak softly to the echoes / by Art Gore. 1st ed. Flagstaff, Ariz. : Northland Press, c1978. ix, 104 p., [1] leaf of plates : col. ill. ; 24 x 32 cm. [TR654.G673] 78-53971 ISBN 0-87358-176-8 : 25.00
1. Photography, Artistic. 2. Nostalgia. I. Title. BIP

GOWIN, Emmet, 1941- 779'.092'4
Emmet Gowin : photographs. 1st ed. New York : Knopf : distributed by Random House, c1976. p. cm. [TR654.G68] 76-13696 ISBN 0-394-40195-6 : 17.50. ISBN 0-394-73249-9 pbk. : 8.95
1. Photography, Artistic.

GOWLAND, Peter. 778.924
Figure photography. Greenwich, Conn., Fawcett Publications, c1954. 143p. illus. 24cm. (A Fawcett book no. 250) A Fawcett how-to book 250. [TR675.G63] 55-29774
1. Photography, Artistic. 2. Human figure in art. I. Title.

GREEN, Jonathan. 779
The snap-shot / edited with an introd. by Jonathan Green. Millerton, N.Y. : Aperture, [1974] 126 p. : ill. ; 28 cm. Corrected p. 65: 1 leaf inserted. [TR654.G73] 74-18754 ISBN 0-912334-67-3 : 12.00. ISBN 0-912334-68-1 pbk. : 7.50
1. Photography, Artistic. 2. Photography, Instantaneous. I. Title.

GRIFFIN, John Howard, 1920- comp. 770'.924
A hidden wholeness; the visual world of Thomas Merton. Photos. by Thomas Merton and John Howard Griffin. Text by John Howard Griffin. Boston, Houghton Mifflin, 1970. 146 p. illus., ports. 29 cm. [TR647.M4G7] 72-120827
1. Photography, Artistic. I. Merton, Thomas, 1915-1968. II. Title. **BIP**

GROEBLI, Rene, 1927- 778.6
Variation: Moglichkeiten der Farbfotograpfie, some suggested uses of colour photography; possibilites de la photographie eh couleurs. New York, Hastings [1966] 112p. illus. (pt. col.) 32cm. German. English, and French [TR650.G75] 66-2039 19.50 bds.,
1. Photography, Artistic. 2. Color photography. I. Title.

GROEBLI, Rene, 1927- 778.6
Variation 2: Kommunikative Moglichkeiten der Farbfotografie. Some suggested uses of communicative colour photography. Possibilities communicatives de la photographie en couleurs. New York, Hastings House [1971] 165 p. illus. (part col.) 32 cm. (Visual communication books) At head of title: Rene Groebli photo. German, English, and French. [TR650.G75 1971] 79-26263
1. Photography, Artistic. 2. Color photography. I. Title.

GROSSMAN, Sid, 1915-1955. 779
Journey to the Cape. Photos. by Sid Grossman; written by Millard Lampell. [New York, Distributed by Grove Press, 1960, c1959] unpaged. illus. 26cm. [TR140.G75A3] 60-285
1. Photography, Artistic. I. Lampell, Millard, 1919- II. Title.

GUEST, Anthony. 770'.1
Art and the camera. New York, Arno Press, 1973. viii, 159 p. illus. 23 cm. (The Literature of Photography) Reprint of the 1907 ed. [TR642.G8 1973] 72-9203 ISBN 0-405-04912-9. 11.00.
1. Photography, Artistic. I. Title. II. Series. **BIP**

HAJEK-HALKE, heinz. 779
Abstract pictures on film; the technical of making lightgraphics [by] Hajek-Halke. With an introd. by Franz Roh. [Translated by J. Maxwell Brownjohn] New York, Viking Press [1965] 1 v. (chiefly illus. (part col.] 31 cm. (A Studio book) Translation of Lichtgrafik. [TR650.H2393] 65-21147
1. Photography, Artistic. I. Title.

HALL, Norman, ed. 779
Photography today, for everyone who loves good pictures and especially for those who collect them. New York, St. Martin's Press [1958] 108p. (chiefly illus.) 26cm. [TR650.H245] 58-14948
1. Photography, Artistic. 2. Photographs. I. Title.

HANSON, Eugene Montgomery. 778.924
Glamour guide; how to photograph girls. All photographs by the author. [1st ed.] Minneapolis, American Photographic Pub. Co., 1950. xiii, 188 p. illus., port. 27 cm. [TR680.H27] 50-13213
1. Photography, Artistic. 2. Photography—Portraits. I. Title.

HARBUTT, Charles. 799'.092'4
Travelog. Cambridge, MIT Press [1973] 1 v. (chiefly illus.) 21 x 23 cm. [TR654.H37] 73-16041 ISBN 0-262-08064-8 12.50
1. Photography, Artistic. I. Title. **BIP**

HATTERSLEY, Ralph. 770.2'3
Discover your self through photography; a creative workbook for amateur and professional. New York, Association Press [1971] 320 p. illus. 29 cm. [TR650.H36] 72-132396 ISBN 0-8096-1784-6 14.95
1. Photography, Artistic. I. Title. **BIP**

HEATH, Dave, 1931- 779
A dialogue with solitude. [Culpeper, Va.] Community Press, 1965. 1 v. (chiefly illus.) 29 cm. [TR650.H38] 63-21721
1. Photography, Artistic. I. Title.

HENLE, Fritz, 1909- 779.24
Figure studies. Introd. by Jacquelyn Judge. New ed. New York, Viking [c.1954, 1962] 76p. illus. (pt. col.) 26cm. (Studio bk.) 62-11676 6.95 bds.,
1. Photography, Artistic. 2. Human figure in art. I. Title.

HENLE, Fritz, 1909- 799.24
Figure studies. Introd. by Jacquelyn Judge. New York, Studio Publications in association with Crowell [1954] 72p. (p. [18]-[64] illus.) 27cm. [TR675.H44] 54-6329
1. Photography, Artistic. 2. Human figure in art. I. Title.

HENLE, Fritz, 1909- 779
Fritz Henle's Rollei; photographs, with text by Vivienne Tallal Winterry. New York, Hastings House [1950] 124 p. (chiefly illus., port.) 26 cm. [TR650.H44] 51-609
1. Photography, Artistic. 2. Photographs. I. Winterry, Vivienne Tallal.

HERR, Dan, comp. 779'.092'4
Contrasts [compiled by] Dan Herr [and] Joel Wells. Photos. by Daniel Frasnay. Waco, Tex., Word Books [1972] [91] p. illus. 23 x 28 cm. [TR654.H47] 72-84162 3.95
1. Photography, Artistic. I. Wells, Joel, joint comp. II. Frasnay, Daniel, illus. III. Title.

HERRON, Gaylord Oscar. 770'.92'4 B
Vagabond / by Gaylord Oscar Herron. Tulsa, Okla. : Penumbra Projects, 1975. 132 p. : chiefly ill. ; 29 cm. [TR654.H48] 75-43695 pbk. : 12.95
1. Herron, Gaylord Oscar. 2. Photography, Artistic. I. Title. **BIP**

HIETT, Steve. 779'.092'4
Pleasure places / Steve Hiett. New York : Flash : distributed in the U.S.A. by Quick Fox, c1976. [60] p. : col. ill. ; 21 cm. [TR654.H52] 74-21210 ISBN 0-8256-3904-2 pbk. : 4.95
1. Photography, Artistic. I. Title. **BIP**

HILEY, Michael. 770'.92'4 B
Frank Sutcliffe, photographer of Whitby / Michael Hiley. Boston : D. R. Godine, c1974. 224 p. : ill. ; 30 cm. (Godine photographic monographs) Includes bibliographical references and index. [TR140.S74H55 1974b] 74-81519 ISBN 0-87923-105-X : 27.50
1. Sutcliffe, Frank, 1853-1941. 2. Photography, Artistic. I. Title.

HILL, David Octavius, 1802-1870. 779'.092'4
An early Victorian album : the photographic masterpieces (1843-1848) of David Octavius Hill and Robert Adamson / edited and with an introd. by Colin Ford ; and an essay by Roy Strong. 1st American ed. New York : Knopf, 1975, c1974. p. cm. London ed. (J. Cape) has subtitle: the Hill/Adamson collection. Includes bibliographical references and index. [TR651.H53 1974b] 74-21315 ISBN 0-394-49733-3 : 17.50
1. Hill, David Octavius, 1802-1870. 2. Adamson, Robert, 1821-1848. 3. Photography, Artistic. 4. Photography—Portraits. 5. Calotype. I. Adamson, Robert, 1821-1848. II. Ford, Colin John, 1934- III. Title. **BIP**

HINE, Lewis Wickes, 1874-1940. 779'.9'6
Men at work : photographic studies of modern men and machines / by Lewis W. Hine. [2d enl. ed.] / with a suppl. of 18 related photos. New York : Dover Publications, 1977. [61] p. : ill. ; 27 cm. "Reproduced from original prints in the collection of the International Museum of Photography at George Eastman House, Rochester." "An unabridged republication of the work originally published by the Macmillan Company, N.Y., in 1932." [TR653.H54 1977] 76-50337 ISBN 0-486-23475-4 pbk. : 3.00
1. Photography, Artistic. 2. Industry—Pictorial works. I. International Museum of Photography at George Eastman House. II. Title. **BIP**

HINE, Lewis Wickes, 1874-1940. 779'.2
[Reproductions from original Lewis W. Hine negatives in the George Eastman House archive. Rochester, N.Y., George Eastman House, 1970] 1 portfolio (4 p., 12 plates) 24 x 31 cm. Includes bibliographical references. [TR653.H55] 73-22442
1. Photography, Artistic. I. George Eastman House, Rochester, N.Y.

HOLME, Charles, 1848-1923, ed. 770'.9'041
Art in photography / edited by Charles Holme. New York : Arno Press, 1979. p. cm. (The Sources of modern photography) Reprint of the 1905 ed. which was published as a special number of the Studio, London, New York. [TR642.H64 1979] 76-24674 ISBN 0-405-09650-X : 25.00
1. Photography, Artistic. I. Studio international. II. Title. III. Series.

HOLMES, Wendy. 779'.092'4
Hudson City, the living river; an exhibit portfolio. [New York] Wave Hill Center for Environmental Studies [1972?] 1 portfolio ([16] p., 46 plates) 36 cm. Includes bibliography. [TR654.H64] 73-77294
1. Photography, Artistic. 2. Hudson River—Views. 3. New York (City)—Description—Views. I. Wave Hill Center for Environmental Studies. II. Title.

HOM, Jesper 779'.092'2
For kids only : [an adventure in reading without words] / introduction by Charles F. Reasoner. New York : Delacorte Press, c1977. ca. 500 p. : all. ill. ; 24 cm. By Jesper Hom and Sven Gronlykke. Original Danish ed. (c1975) published under title: Bornenes billedbog. Approximately 500 photographs of people, animals, and objects arranged to tell very brief stories without any words. [TR654.H6713] 76-28183 ISBN 0-440-02690-3 pbk. : 4.95 ISBN 0-440-02738-1 : 8.95
1. Photography, Artistic. 2. Picture-books for children. I. Gronlykke, Sven, joint author. II. Title.

HOUSTON, Robert. 779'.2
Legacy to an unborn son. [Boston] Beacon Press [1971] 1 v. (unpaged) illus. 24 cm. [TR654.H68 1971] 72-141874 ISBN 0-8070-6660-5 5.95
1. Photography, Artistic. '. Title.

HOW to enter & win photo contests / [by the editors of Photographic magazine]. Los Angeles : Petersen Pub. Co., c1977. 96 p. : ill. ; 28 cm. [TR650.H79] 77-152272 ISBN 0-8227-2020-5 pbk. : 1.95 770
1. Photography, Artistic. 2. Photography—Competitions. I. Petersen's photographic magazine.

HOWARD, David, 1948- 770'.9'04
Perspectives / David Howard. San Francisco : San Francisco Center for Visual Studies, c1978. [83] p. : chiefly ill. ; 28 cm. [TR654.H688] 77-90787 ISBN 0-930976-00-2 lib. bdg. : 6.95
1. Photography, Artistic. 2. Photographers—Interviews. I. Title. **BIP**

HUMAN face of Europe (The). New York, Hill & Wang [1962, c.1960] unpaged. illus. 24cm. (Terra magica bk.) 62-12003 3.50, bds., bxd 778.9
1. Photography, Artistic. I. Toth, Tas.

INTERNATIONAL Museum of Photography at George Eastman House. 779'.074'014789
The extended document. [Rochester, N.Y. : International Museum of Photography at George Eastman House, c1975] 32 p. : chiefly ill. ; 21 x 23 cm. Cover title. [TR654.I57 1975] 75-323939
1. Photography, Artistic. I. Title.

INTERNATIONAL photography : the critics' choice / commentary by Hugo Schottle. New York : Rizzoli, 1977, c1976. [127] p. : chiefly col. ill. ; 24 cm. Translation of Olympiade der Farbfotografie. Includes indexes. [TR654.O6713 1977] 76-27019 ISBN 0-8478-0065-2 pbk. : 8.95 770'.2
1. Photography, Artistic.

JACKSON, William Henry, 1843-1942. 779'.9'978800924
William Henry Jackson's Colorado / compiled by William C. Jones and Elizabeth B. Jones ; foreword by Marshall Sprague. Boulder, Colo. : Pruett Pub. Co., c1975. xx, 172 p. : chiefly ill. ; 30 cm. [TR652.J3 1975] 75-33046 ISBN 0-87108-092-3 : 27.95. ISBN 0-87108-093-1 de luxe : 76.00
1. Jackson, William Henry, 1843-1942. 2. Photography, Artistic. 3. Colorado—Description and travel—Views. I. Jones, William C., 1937- II. Jones, Elizabeth B., 1942- III. Title. **BIP**

JACOBS, Sylvester. 779'.2'0924
Portrait of a shelter. Text by Linette Martin. Foreword by Francis A. Schaeffer. Downers Grove, Ill., InterVarsity Press [1973] 128 p. illus. 32 cm. [TR654.J29] 72-97949 ISBN 0-87784-866-1 9.95
1. Photography, Artistic. I. Martin, Linette. II. Title. **BIP**

JACOBS, Sylvester. 779'.9'94208570924
Portrait of England / [by] Sylvester Jacobs ; foreword by Leila Berg. London : Joseph, 1976. 222 p. : of ill., ports. ; 31 cm. [TR654.J293 1976] 76-382230 ISBN 0-7181-1490-6 : £8.50
1. Photography, Artistic. 2. Photography—Portraits. 3. England—Description and travel—Views. I. Title.

*JAY, Bill 779'.O924
Robert Demachy 1859-1936: photographs and essays. New York, St. Martin's Press [1974] 50 p. illus. 30 cm. [TR647] 73-93435 ISBN 0-85670-185-8 16.50
1. Photography, Artistic. I. Title.

JONES, Dewitt. 779'.36'0924
What the road passes by / photos. by Dewitt Jones ; text by Eleanor Huggins. Portland, Or. : Graphic Arts Center Pub. Co., c1978. [90] p. : col. ill. ; 23 x 28 cm. [TR654.J65] 78-55309 ISBN 0-912856-43-2 : pbk. : 7.95
1. Photography, Artistic. 2. Photography—Landscapes. I. Huggins, Eleanor M. II. Title. **BIP**

JONES, Edgar Yoxall. 770'.92'4 B
Father of art photography, O. G. Rejlander, 1813-1875. Greenwich, Conn., New York Graphic Society [1973] 112 p. illus. 25 cm. Includes bibliographical references. [TR140.R43J66 1973b] 73-89945 ISBN 0-8212-0598-6
1. Rejlander, Oscar Gustav, 1813-1875. 2. Photography, Artistic. I. Rejlander, Oscar Gustav, 1813-1875. II. Title.

JOSEPH, Meryl. 779'.9'7455922
Who won second place at Omaha? : A journey / photographed by Meryl Joseph ; written by Diane Kagan. New York : Random House, [1975] p. cm. [TR654.J68] 75-6966 ISBN 0-394-49625-6 : 8.95. ISBN 0-394-73081-X pbk. : 4.95
1. Photography, Artistic. 2. Dolls. I. Kagan, Diane. II. Title.

KAHMEN, Volker, 1939- 770'.9
Art history of photography / Volker Kahmen ; translated by Brian Tubb. New York : Viking Press, 1974. 55 p., [116] leaves of plates : ill. ; 25 cm. (A Studio book) Translation of Fotografie als Kunst. Bibliography: p. 53-55. [TR653.K3313] 74-3703 ISBN 0-670-13437-6 : 15.95
1. Photography, Artistic. I. Title. **BIP**

KAUFMAN, Paul, 1920- 779'.092'4
Double exposure / by Paul Kaufman and Ruth Lisa Schechter. 1st ed. New York : Barlenmir House, c1978. [48] p. : ill. ; 29 cm. [TR654.K367] 78-58414 ISBN 0-87929-066-8 : 12.95
1. Kaufman, Paul, 1920- 2. Photography, Artistic. I. Schechter, Ruth Lisa, joint author. II. Title.

KERTESZ, Andre. 779
A. Kertesz, photographer. Introductory essay by John Szarkowski. New York, Museum of Modern Art [c1964] 63 p. illus. 23 cm. Based on an exhibition held at the Museum of Modern Art, New York. Bibliography: p. 61-62. [TR140.K4S9] 64-66100
1. Photography, Artistic. I. Szarkowski, John. II. New York. Museum of Modern Art. III. Title. IV. Title: A. Kertesz, photographer.

KERTESZ, Andre. 779
Andre Kertesz. Introd. by Anna Farova. Adapted for the American ed. by Robert Sagalyn. New York, Paragraphic Books [1967] 66 p. illus., ports. 18 cm. [TR140.K4F3 1967] 66-27188
1. Photography, Artistic.

KERTESZ, Andre. 779'.092'4
Andre Kertesz. Millerton, N.Y. : Aperture, c1977. 95 p. : chiefly ill. ; 21 cm. (The Aperture history of photography series ; 6) [TR653.K46 1977] 77-70070 ISBN 0-912334-96-7 : 6.95
1. Kertesz, Andre. 2. Photography, Artistic.

KERTESZ, Andre. 779'.092'4
Andre Kertesz : sixty years of photography / edited by Nicolas Ducrot. New York : Penguin Books, 1978. 224 p. : chiefly ill. ; 25 x 27 cm. Includes bibliographical references. [TR653.K47 1978] 77-19082 ISBN 0-14-004744-1 pbk. : 8.95
1. Kertesz, Andre. 2. Photography, Artistic. I. Ducrot, Nicolas.

KERTESZ, Andre. 779'.092'4
Andre Kertesz: sixty years of photography, 1912-1972. Edited by Nicolas Ducrot. New York, Grossman, 1972. 224 p. (chiefly illus.) 25 x 28 cm. Bibliography: p. 6. [TR653.K47 1972] 72-77700 ISBN 0-670-12385-4 19.95
1. Photography, Artistic.

KERTESZ, Andre. 779'.21'0924
Distortions / Andre Kertesz ; edited by Nicolas Ducrot ; with an introd. by Hilton Kramer. 1st ed. New York : Knopf : distributed by Random House, 1976. [91] leaves : chiefly ill. ; 29 cm. [TR653.K48] 76-13699 ISBN 0-394-40890-X : 22.50
1. Photography, Artistic. 2. Photography of the nude. 3. Photography—Special effects. I. Title. **BIP**

KERTESZ, Andre. 779'.9'028
On reading. New York, Grossman, 1971. 63 p. of illus. 22 cm. [TR654.K45 1971] 76-155564 ISBN 0-670-52459-X 5.95
1. Photography, Artistic. I. Title.

KEZYS, Algimantas. 779'.092'4
Form and content. Photos. by Algimantas Kezys. Chicago, Morkunas, 1972. xiii p., 64 plates. 29 cm. Bibliography: p. xiii. [TR654.K457] 72-82267
1. Photography, Artistic. I. Title.

KEZYS, Algimantas. 779
Photographs. Text, introducing 8 groups of photos., by Bruno Markaitis. Postscript by Hugh Edwards. Chicago, Loyola University Press [1966] 1 v. (unpaged) illus. 28 cm. [TR650.K45] 66-28777
1. Photography, Artistic. I. Markaitis, Bruno.

[KLINSKY, Emil Josef] 779
Laughing camera [by E. J. Klinsky] Hanns Reich. Text by Heinz Held. New York, Hill Wang [1967, c.1965] 71 p., illus., 24 cm. (Terra magica bk.) German ed. by E. J. Klinsky. [TR650.K4813] 67-14654 3.95 bds.,
1. Photography, Artistic. I. Reich, Hanns, joint author. II. Held, Jeinz. III. Title. **BIP**

KNOBLE, Jack. 779'.0924
Artist's photographic reference. Photography and printing by the author. [San Mateo? Calif., 1968] 1 v. (chiefly illus. (part col.)) 29 cm. [TR650.K5] 75-976
1. Photography, Artistic. I. Title.

KOMROFF, Manuel, 1890- 779
The third eye [by] Manuel Komroff, Nathan Resnick, Konrad Cramer. New York, Walker [c.]1962. 89p. illus. 23x28cm. 62-12748 7.50
1. Photography, Artistic. I. Resnick, Nathan. II. Cramer, Konrad. III. Title.

KRAUSE, George, 1937- 779'.092'4
George Krause-1. Introd. by Mark Power. 1st ed. Haverford, Pa., Toll & Armstrong, 1972. [73] p. chiefly illus. 24 cm. [TR654.K7] 72-77077 ISBN 0-912838-02-7 9.75
1. Photography, Artistic. I. Title.

KRAUTH, Harald. 770
Artistic photography : methods and techniques / Harald Krauth. Garden City, N.Y. : Amphoto, c1976. 128 p., [4] leaves of plates : ill. (some col.) ; 28 cm. [TR642.K7] 75-42771 ISBN 0-8174-2402-4 : 6.95
1. Photography, Artistic. I. Title. **BIP**

KRIMS, Leslie. 779'.0924
Eight photographs. [Introd. by A. D. Coleman. New York, Doubleday, 1970] 1 portfolio ([2] l., [8] plates) 37 x 29 cm. (Projections photography portfolios) [TR647.K7A45] 72-18938
1. Photography, Artistic. I. Title.

KRIZ, Vilem. 779'.092'4
Sirague City : photographs / by Kriz. Berkeley, Calif. : D. McPhail, 1975. [62] p. : chiefly ill. ; 26 cm. [TR654.K77] 75-14371 ISBN 0-915756-00-5 : 14.95 ISBN 0-915756-01-3 pbk. : 6.95
1. Photography, Artistic. I. Title. **BIP**

LANGE, Dorothea. 779'.092'2
To a cabin [by] Dorothea Lange [and] Margaretta K. Mitchell. New York, Grossman Publishers, 1973. 127 p. chiefly illus. 24 x 26 cm. [TR654.L26 1973] 73-6359 ISBN 0-670-71627-8 15.00
1. Photography, Artistic. 2. Photography of children. I. Mitchell, Margaretta. II. Title.

LANGER, Micha. 779'.092'4
Let everything that breathes. Photography by Micha Langer. Words by Robert Fulton. [Millbrae, Calif.] Celestial Arts Pub., 1972. 63 p. illus. 22 cm. [TR654.L3] 72-86577 2.95
1. Photography, Artistic. I. Fulton, Robert, 1923- II. Title.

LARMORE, Lewis 770
Introduction to Siskind, photographer. Ed., introd. by Nathan Lyons. Essays by Henry Holmes Smith, Thomas B. Hess. Statement by Aaron Siskind. George Eastman House; [dist. New York, Horizon, 1965] 74p. plates. 26x27cm. (George Eastman House monograph no.5) Bibl. [TR145.L33] 65-20484 7.50
1. Photography, Artistic. I. Lyons, Nathan, ed. II. Smith, Henry Holmes. III. Hess, Thomas B. (Series) IV. Title.

LARTIGUE, Jacques Henri, 1894- 779
Diary of a century. [Edited by Richard Avedon. Translation by Carla van Splunteren] New York, Viking Press [1970] 1 v. (unpaged) illus., ports. 34 cm. (A Studio book) [TR653.L37] 74-101776 27.50
1. Photography, Artistic. I. Title.

LARTIGUE, Jacques Henri, 1894- 779
Diary of a century / Jacques Henri Lartigue. New York : Penguin Books, [1978] p. cm. Reprint of the 1970 ed. published by Viking Press, New York, in series: A Studio book. [TR653.L37 1978] 78-17468 ISBN 0-14-004840-5 pbk. : 8.95
1. Photography, Artistic. I. Title. **BIP**

†LARTIGUE, Jacques Henri, 1894- 779'.092'4
Jacques-Henri Lartigue : [photographs]. Millerton, N.Y. : Aperture, c1976. 95 p. : chiefly ill. ; 21 cm. (The Aperture history of photography series ; 5) [TR654.L34 1976] 76-22000 ISBN 0-89381-001-0 : 6.95
1. Photography, Artistic. I. Title.

LAUGHLIN, Clarence John. 779'.092'4
Clarence John Laughlin: the personal eye. Introd. by Jonathan Williams. Stories by Lafcadio Hearn. Captions by the photographer. [Millerton, N.Y., Aperture, c1973] 132 p. illus. 28 cm. Catalogue of an exhibition held at the Philadelphia Museum of Art from Nov. 1973 to Jan. 1974. Bibliography: p. 130-131. [TR654.L36] 73-85263 ISBN 0-912334-53-3 12.50
1. Laughlin, Clarence John. 2. Photography, Artistic. I. Hearn, Lafcadio, 1850-1904. II. Philadelphia Museum of Art. **BIP**

LAUGHLIN, Clarence John. 779'.9'976335
Lost Louisiana : an essay in the poetry of remembrance / Clarence John Laughlin. 1st ed. New York : C. N. Potter : distributed by Crown Publishers, c1976. p. cm. [TR654.L37] 76-9038 ISBN 0-517-52496-1
1. Photography, Artistic. 2. New Orleans—Description—Views. I. Title.

LEEN, Nina, 1909- 779'.092'4
Images of sound / Nina Leen ; all photos. by the author. 1st ed. New York : Norton, c1977. [79] p. : chiefly ill. ; 24 cm. [TR654.L42 1977] 77-9438 ISBN 0-393-08795-6 : 6.95 ISBN 0-393-08800-6 pbk. : 3.95
1. Photography, Artistics. I. Title. **BIP**

LEEN, Nina, 1909- 779'.092'4
Love, sunrise, and elevated apes. All photos. by the author. [1st ed.] New York, Norton [1974] 1 v. (unpaged) photos. 21 cm. [TR654.L43] 74-171044 ISBN 0-393-08694-1 5.95
1. Photography, Artistic. 2. Quotations, English. I. Title.
Pbk. 2.50, ISBN 0-393-08699-2. **BIP**

LEEN, Nina, 1909- 779'.0924
Women, heroes, and a frog. Photos by the author. [1st ed.] New York, Norton [1970] 1 v. (unpaged) illus. 21 cm. [TR654.L44 1970] 71-116125 4.95
1. Photography, Artistic. 2. Quotations, English. I. Title. **BIP**

LEVERANT, Robert. 779'.092'2
On the transmission of photography. [San Francisco, Images Press, 1972] 56 p. illus. (part col.) 26 cm. Bibliography: p. 53-54. [TR654.L458] 79-189861 ISBN 0-9600374-2-X
1. Photography, Artistic. I. Title. **BIP**

LEVITT, Helen. 779.25
A way of seeing; photographs of New York. With an essay by James Agee. New York, Viking Press, [1965] 78 p. (chiefly illus.) 20 cm. [TR650.L45] 65-15718
1. Photography, Artistic. 2. Children — Portraits. 3. New York (City) — Descr. — Views. I. Agee, James, 1909-1955. II. Title. **BIP**

LIBHART, Myles, comp. 779
Photographs and poems by Sioux children from the Porcupine Day School, Pine Ridge Indian Reservation, South Dakota. Selected by Myles Libhart and Arthur Amiotte. With an essay by Arthur Amiotte. An exhibition organized by the Indian Arts and Crafts Board of the U.S. Department of the Interior. [Rapid City, S.D., Tipi Shop, 1971] 80 p. illus., ports. 25 cm. Bibliography: p. 80. [TR654.L46] 75-26672
1. Photography, Artistic. 2. American literature—Indian authors. 3. Children's writings. I. Amiotte, Arthur, joint comp. II. U.S. Indian Arts and Crafts Board. III. Title.

LIGHT7. 770'.1'53
Photos. from an exhibition on a theme, Hayden Gallery, Massachusetts Institute of Technology, Oct. 1968. Edited by Minor White. [Cambridge, MIT Press] 1968. 74 p. illus. 25 cm. (MIT visual arts series, v. 1, no. 2) "An Aperture book." Sponsored by the MIT Committee on the Visual Arts. [TR654.L5] 68-57982
1. Photography, Artistic. 2. Photography—Exhibitions. I. White, Minor, ed. II. Hayden Gallery. III. Massachusetts Institute of Technology. Committee on the Visual Arts. IV. Series: Massachusetts Institute of Technology. M.I.T. visual arts series, v. 1, no. 2

LOCAL light : 779'.9'976904
photographs made in Kentucky / collected by Guy Mendes. Lexington, Ky. : Gnomon Press, c1976. [61] p. : chiefly ill. ; 28 cm. [TR654.L59] 76-151233 ISBN 0-917788-02-8 pbk. : 5.00
1. Photography, Artistic. 2. Kentucky—Description and travel—Views. I. Mendes, Guy.

LOOTENS on photographic 778.13
enlarging and print quality. [6th ed.] Rev., enlarged. New York, Amphoto [1962, c.1958, 1961] 248p. illus. 23cm. Vols. for 1962; ed.: Betty Carol Brown 61-12971 4.95
1. Photography, Artistic. 2. Photography—Enlarging. I. Lootens, Joseph Ghislain.

LOOTENS on photographic 778.13
enlarging and print quality. Rev., enlarged by Lester Bogen. 7th rev. ed. Philadelphia, Chilton; New York Amphoto [1967] v. illus. 23cm. [TR650.L6] 61-12971 6.95
1. Photography, Artistic. 2. Photography—Enlarging. I. Lootens, Joseph Ghislain.

LOWENTHAL, Jeff 778.99792
Stage and theater photography. Philadelphia, Chilton [c.1965] 128p. illus., ports. 24cm. [TR680.L65] 65-17116 4.95
1. Photography, Artistic. 2. Musicians—Portraits. I. Title.

LYONS, Nathan. 779'.092'4
Notations in passing / visualized by Nathan Lyons. [Cambridge] : MIT Press, [1974] 121 p. : all ill. ; 21 x 23 cm. [TR654.L89] 74-18618 ISBN 0-262-12067-4. ISBN 0-262-62028-6 pbk. : 7.95
1. Photography, Artistic. I. Title. **BIP**

LYONS, Nathan. 770.1'1
The persistence of vision: Donald Blumberg, Charles Gill, Robert Heinecken, Ray K. Metzker, Jerry N. Uelsmann, John Wood; ed. by Nathan Lyons. New York, Horizon [1968, 1967] 66 p. illus., ports. 21 x 22 cm. On spine: Contemporary photographers. Prepd. on the occasion of the exhibition, The persistence of vision, which opened at the George Eastman House in June of 1967. [TR650.L88] 67-26913 5.95
1. Photography Artistic. 2. Photography Composite. I. George Eastman House, Rochester, N. Y. II. Title. III. Title: Contemporary photographers.

LYONS, Nathan 779
Under the sun the abstract art of camera vision, by Nathan Lyons. Syl Labrot [and] Walter Chappell. New York, G. Braziller [c.]1960. [22]p. 36 plates (part col.) 22x27cm. 60-12506 7.50
1. Photography, Artistic. I. Title.

LYONS, Nathan, comp. 779
Vision and expression. Edited by Nathan Lyons. New York, Horizon Press [1969] 175 p. (chiefly illus.) 21 x 22 cm. On spine: Contemporary photographers. "Prepared on the occasion of the exhibition, 'Vision and expression,' which opened at the George Eastman House in February of 1969." [TR654.L9] 76-78952 12.95
1. Photography, Artistic. I. George Eastman House, Rochester, N.Y. II. Title. III. Title: Contemporary photographers.

MACO Magazine Corporation, New York. 779
Creative pictures. New York, 1963. 125 p. (chiefly illus.) 24 cm. (Maco 109) [TR650.M34] 63-25046
1. Photography, Artistic. I. Title.

MACO Magazine Corporation, New York. 778
Creative pictures. Edited by Byron Dobell. New York, 1956. 125 p. illus. 24 cm. (Maco, 48) [TR650.M34] 57-23185
1. Photography, Artistic. I. Dobell, Byron, ed. II. Title.

MAINE, Tony. 779'.092'4
Two eggs any style : [45 photographs] / Tony Maine. Berkeley, Calif. : VIA Press, c1976. [47] p. : all ill. ; 22 x 28 cm. [TR654.M334] 75-43264 ISBN 0-9600946-1-X pbk. : 5.50
1. Photography, Artistic. I. Title.

MAKOS, Christopher, 1948- 779'.092'4
White trash / Christopher Makos. New York : Stonehill Pub. Co. : [distributed by Farrar Straus & Giroux], c1977. [97] p. chiefly ill. ; 31 cm. [TR654.M335] 77-81180 ISBN 0-88373-068-5 : 12.95
1. Photography, Artistics. I. Title. **BIP**

MALLAN, Lloyd, ed. 770.79
Prize winning photography. Greenwich, Conn., Fawcett Publications, c1953. 144p. illus. 24cm. (A Fawcett book, no. 187) [TR650.M3] 53-34039
1. Photography, Artistic. 2. Photography—Competitions. 3. Photographs—Catalogs. I. Title.

MANOS, Constantine. 914.95'04'7
A Greek portfolio. New York, Viking Press [1972] [12] p., 112 plates. 28 cm. (A Studio book) [TR654.M337 1972] 72-81677 ISBN 0-670-35315-9 12.95
1. Photography, Artistic. 2. Greece—Description and travel—Views. I. Title.

MARCHIORI, Giuseppe. 730'.924
Pierluca. Fotografie di Gianni Berengo Gardin. Venezia, Alfieri [1967] Stamped on t.p.: Amer. dist. : Wittenborn New York. 112p. (p. 37-[104] illus.) illus., port. 24x25cm. Text in Italian, French & English. Bibl. [NB623.P38M3] 68-72872 12.00 bds.,

SUBJECT INDEX PHOTOGRAPHY, ARTISTIC.

I. Pierluca, 1926- II. Title.

MARGARET, Karla. 779'.092'4
Spaces : poetry and photography / by Karla Margaret ; book design by Nancy Green. 1st ed. Mill Valley, Calif. : In Between Books Pub. Co., [1974] [95] p. : ill. ; 26 cm. [TR654.M339] 74-82631 5.00
1. Photography, Artistic. I. Title.

MEATYARD, Ralph Eugene, 1925-1972. 779'.092'4
Ralph Eugene Meatyard / edited with text by James Baker Hall ; reminiscence by Guy Davenport. Millerton, N.Y. : Aperture, inc., [1974] 136 p. : chiefly ill. ; 28 cm. Bibliography: p. 135-136. [TR654.M38 1974] 74-76879 ISBN 0-912334-62-2 : 12.50. ISBN 0-912334-61-4 pbk. : 8.50
1. Photography, Artistic. I. Hall, James B., ed. BIP

MELVIN, Betsy. 779'.9'974
Robert Frost country / Betsy and Tom Melvin ; foreword by William Meredith. Garden City, N.Y. : Doubleday, 1976. p. cm. [TR654.M455] 76-2806 ISBN 0-385-12180-6 : 14.95. ISBN 0-385-12127-X pbk. : 6.95
1. Frost, Robert, 1874-1963—Quotations. 2. Photography, Artistic. 3. New England—Description and travel—Views. I. Melvin, Tom, joint author. II. Frost, Robert, 1874-1963. III. Title. BIP

MERCER, John D. 779'.9'979461
Island of the Pelicans : a photographic essay of the Island of Alcatraz / by John D. Mercer ; introd. by Patricia Mercer. Sonoma, Ca. : Creative Eye Press, c1976. 45 p. : ill. ; 22 cm. [TR654.M463] 75-39153 ISBN 0-916480-01-1
1. United States. Penitentiary, Alcatraz Island, Calif. 2. Photography, Artistic. 3. Alcatraz Island, Calif.—Description—Views. I. Title. BIP

MEREDITH, Roy, 1908- 770'.92'4 B
Mr. Lincoln's camera man, Mathew B. Brady / Roy Meredith. 2d rev. ed New York : Dover Publications, [1974] xiii, 368 p. : ill. ; 29 cm. An unabridged and corrected republication of the work originally published in 1946 by Scribner, New York, with a new index of negative numbers. Bibliography: p. 365-368. [TR140.B7M4 1974] 73-92262 ISBN 0-486-23087-2 : 12.50 ISBN 0-486-23021-X : 6.95
1. Brady, Mathew B., 1823 (ca.)-1896. 2. Photography, Artistic. 3. United States—History—Civil war, 1861-1865—Pictorial works. I. Title.

MICHALS, Duane. 779'.0924
Sequences. [1st ed.] Garden City, N.Y., Doubleday [1970] 1 v. of illus. 21 cm. (A Doubleday projections book) [TR654.M52] 76-122577 4.95
1. Photography, Artistic. I. Title.

MILWAUKEE journal. 655.32
Production of r. o. p. color in the Milwaukee journal. [Milwaukee, 1950] vii (i.e. viii), 177 p. illus. (part col.) 29 cm. Bibliography: p. 177. [Z258.M6] 50-4513
1. Color-printing. I. Title.

MOHOLY-NAGY, Laszlo, 1895-1946 779
Painting, photography, film. With a note by Hans M. Wingler and a postscript by Otto Stelzer. Translated by Janet Seligman. Cambridge, Mass., MIT Press [1973, c.1969] 150 p. illus. 25 cm. Translation of Malerei, Fotografie, Film. [TR650.M6183] 69-20302 ISBN 0-262-63046-X 2.95 (pbk.)
1. Photography, Artistic. 2. Art and photography. 3. Form (Aesthetics) I. Title. BIP

MOHOLY-NAGY, Laszlo, 1895-1946 770'.1
Painting, photography, film. With a note by Hans M. Wingler and a postscript by Otto Stelzer. Translated by Janet Seligman. Cambridge, Mass., MIT Press [1973, c1969] 150 p. illus. 26 cm. Translation of Malerei, Fotografie, Film. [TR642.M6413 1973] 74-150414 ISBN 0-262-13058-0 2.95 (pbk.)
1. Photography, Artistic. 2. Art and photography. 3. Form (Aesthetics) I. Title.

MOREHOUSE, Marion. 778.9
Adventures in value, fifty photographs by Marion Morehouse. Text by E.E. Cummings. [1st ed.] New York, Harcourt, Brace & World [1962] 1v. (unpaged) illus., ports. 27cm. [TR650.M62] 62-19030
1. Photography, Artistic. I. Cummings, Edward Estlin, 1894- 1962. II. Title.

MORGAN, Barbara Brooks, 1900- 779'.092'4
Barbara Morgan. Edited-designed by Barbara Morgan. Introd. by Peter Bunnell. [Hastings-on-Hudson, N.Y.] Morgan & Morgan [1972] 159 p. (chiefly illus.) 27 cm. Includes bibliographical references. [TR653.M65] 72-92282 ISBN 0-87100-034-2 12.00
1. Photography, Artistic. 2. Photography, Composite. BIP

MORTENSEN, William. 770
The command to look. [Rev. ed.] Los Angeles, J. de Langre, 1967. 128 p. illus., port. 21 cm. On cover: The command to look; the pictorial imperative. [TR650.M638 1967] 67-29079
1. Photography, Artistic. I. Title.

MORTENSEN, William. 778.92
How to pose the mocel, by William Mortensen and George Dunham. All illus. by William Mortensen except where otherwise designated. [3d ed.] New York, Ziff-Davis Pub. Co. [1960, c1956] 160p. illus. 25cm. First ed. published in 1937 under title: The model, a book on the problems of posing. [TR675.M6 1960] 60-15563
1. Photography, Artistic. 2. Human figure in art. I. Dunham, George, joint author. II. Title.

MORTENSEN, William. 778.92
How to pose the model, by William Mortensen and George Dunham. All illus. by William Mortensen except where otherwise designated. [3d ed.] San Francisco, Camera Craft Pub. Co. [1956] u60p. illus. 25cm. [A Camera Craft plus value book] First ed. published in 1937 under title: The model, a book on the problems of posing. [TR675.M6 1956] 56-11559
1. Photography, Artistic. 2. Human figure in art. I. Dunham, George, joint author. II. Title.

MORTENSEN, William. 770'.11
monsters and madonnas. New York, Arno Press, 1973 [c1936] [59] p. illus. 32 cm. (The Literature of Photography) [TR653.M67 1973] 72-9220 ISBN 0-405-04927-7. 11.00.
1. Photography, Artistic. I. Title. II. Series.

MORTENSEN, William. 770.1'1
Monsters & madonnas. [Hollywood, Calif.] J. De Langre, 1967. [67] p. illus. (part col.) 35 cm. On cover: Monsters & madonnas: photographic methods. [TR650.M64 1967] 67-29078
1. Photography, Artistic. I. Title. BIP

MUCHA, Alphonse Marie, 1860-1939. 779'.092'4
Photographs / Alphonse Mucha ; [compiled by] Graham Ovenden. New York : St. Martin's Press, 1974. 95 p. : chiefly ill. ; 30 cm. On spine: Mucha photographs. [TR653.M82 1974] 73-89210 ISBN 0-85670-161-0 : 15.95
1. Photography, Artistic. I. Title: Mucha photographs.

THE Multiple image. 779'.074'014
[Kingston? University of Rhode Island Arts Council, 1972] [40] p. illus. 26 cm. Cover title. "An exhibition organized by Frank Martinelli ... at the Creative Photography Gallery, the Massachusetts Institute of Technology ... [and] at the University of Rhode Island, the Fine Arts Center." [TR654.M85] 73-151155
1. Photography, Artistic. 2. Photography, Trick. I. Martinelli, Frank. II. Massachusetts Institute of Technology. Creative Photography Gallery. III. Rhode Island. University. Fine Arts Center. IV. Rhode Island. University. Arts Council.

MUNKACSI, Martin. 779.24
Nudes. [Photographs] New York, Greenberg, c1951. 74 p. (chiefly illus) 31 cm. [TR675.M85] 51-11374
1. Photography, Artistic. 2. Nude in art. I. Title.

NEBRASKA. University. Sheldon Memorial Art Gallery. 779
American photography: the sixties; an invitational exhibition of recent trends, February 22 through March 20, 1966, Sheldon Memorial Art Gallery, University of Nebraska, Lincoln. [Lincoln, Neb., 1966] 47 p. (chiefly illus.) 22 x 28 cm. [TR650.N4] 66-64779
1. Photography, Artistic. 2. Photography—Exhibitions. I. Title.

NEGRE, Charles, 1820-1880. 779'.092'4
Charles Negre 1820-1880 / James Borcoman. Ottawa : National Gallery of Canada, 1976. 261 p. : chiefly ill. ; 30 cm. English and French in parallel columns. Includes indexes. Bibliography: p. 257-258. [TR652.N43 1976] 76-378760 ISBN 0-88884-268-6
1. Negre, Charles, 1820-1880. 2. Photography, Artistic. 3. Photographers—France—Biography. I. Borcoman, James.

NEW Jersey. State Museum, Trenton. 779'.0922
Two generations of photographs: Man Ray and Naomi Savage. [Exhibition] December 14, 1968-February 9, 1969. Trenton [1969] [12] p. illus. 22 cm. [TR650.N48] 78-625612
1. Ray, Man, 1890- 2. Savage, Naomi, 1927- 3. Photography, Artistic. I. Title.

NEW York (City). Museum of Modern Art. 779'.074'01471
Looking at photographs; 100 pictures from the collection of the Museum of Modern Art, by John Szarkowski. New York; distributed by New York Graphic Society, Greenwich, Conn. [1973] 215 p. illus. 29 cm. [TR650.N49] 72-82885 ISBN 0-87070-514-8 15.00
1. Photography, Artistic. I. Szarkowski, John. II. Title. BIP

NEW York. Museum of Modern Art 779
A. Kertesz, photographer. Introd. essay by John Szarkowski. [Dist. Garden City, N.Y., Doubleday, c.1964] 63p. illus. 23cm. Bibl. [TR140.K4N4] 64-66100 2.95 pap.,
1. Kertesz, Andre. 2. Photography, Artistic. I. Szarkowski, John. II. Title. III. Title: A. Kertesz, photographer.

NEW York. Museum of Modern Art. 779
Steichen the photographer. Texts by Carl Sandburg [and others] Biographical outline by Grace M. Mayer. Garden City, N. Y., Distributed by Doubleday [1961] 80p. plates, ports. 25cm. A selected bibliography by Bernard Karpel': p. 76-80. [TR140.S68N4] 61-12288
1. Steichen, Edward. 1879- 2. Photography, Artistic. 3. Photographs. I. Sandburg, Carl, 1878 II. Title.

NEWHALL, Beaumont, 1908- ed. 779
Masters of photography; edited and with an introd. by Beaumont and Nancy Newhall. New York, G. Braziller, 1958. 192 p. (chiefly illus., ports.) 30 cm. Includes bibliography. [TR650.N47] 58-11896
1. Photography, Artistic. 2. Photographers. I. Newhall, Nancy (Wynne) joint ed. II. Title.

NEWHALL, Beaumont 1908- ed. 779
Masters of photography edited and with an introduction by Beaumont and Nancy Newhall. New York, A & W Visual Library, 1975 c 1958 192 p. (chiefly illus., ports.) 31 cm. Bibliography: p. 189. [TR650.N47] 74-33783 ISBN 0-89104-010-2 6.95 (pbk.)
1. Photography, Artistic. 2. Photographers. I. Newhall, Nancy (Wynne), joint ed. II. Title.

NEWHALL, Beaumont, 1908- 779'.9'9178
William H. Jackson / by Beaumont Newhall & Diana E. Edkins ; with a critical essay by William L. Broecker. Dobbs Ferry, N.Y. : Morgan & Morgan, [1974] 158 p. : ill. ; 28 cm. [TR652.N48] 73-89076 ISBN 0-87100-045-8 : 14.00
1. Jackson, William Henry, 1843-1942. 2. Photography, Artistic. 3. The West—Description and travel—Views. I. Edkins, Diana E., 1947- joint author. BIP

NEWHALL, Nancy (Wynne) 927.7
Ansel Adams. San Francisco, Sierra Club [1964, c1963- v. illus. (part fold.), ports. 35 cm. (Sierra Club exhibit format series, 7) Contents.Contents.—v. 1. The eloquent light. [TR140.A55N4] 63-23019
1. Adams, Ansel Easton, 1902- 2. Photography, Artistic. I. Sierra Club. II. Title: The eloquent light.

NEWHALL, Nancy Wynne. 770'.92'4 B
P. H. Emerson : the fight for photography as a fine art / by Nancy Newhall. New York : Aperture, inc., c1975. 266 p. : ill. ; 24 x 27 cm. Also published as Aperture, v. 19, no. 3-4. Published to accompany an exhibition of British photographers prior to 1915 to be presented by the Alfred Stieglitz Center in 1978. Bibliography: p. 262-265. [TR140.E43N48] 74-76911 ISBN 0-912334-58-4 : 22.50. ISBN 0-912334-59-2 pbk. : 12.95
1. Emerson, Peter Henry, 1856-1936. 2. Photography, Artistic. BIP

NIECE, Robert Clemens 778
Photo-imagination. Philadelphia, Chilton [1966] 126p. illus. (pt. col.) 32cm. [TR650.N54] 66-23324 10.00
1. Photography, Artistic. I. Title.

NIECE, Robert Clemens 779
Photo- imagination. New York, Amphoto, [1966] 126p. (chiefly illus., pt. col.) 31cm. [TR650.N54 1966a] 67-603 10.00
1. Photography, Artistic. I. Title.

NORMAN, Henry C., 1850-1913. 770'.092'4
Norman's Natchez : an early photographer and his town / Joan W. Gandy and Thomas H. Gandy. Jackson : University Press of Mississippi, 1978. p. cm. Includes index. Bibliography: p. [TR652.N67 1978] 78-15570 ISBN 0-87805-078-7 : 25.00
1. Norman, Henry C., 1850-1913. 2. Photography, Artistic. 3. Natchez, Miss.—Description—Views. I. Gandy, Joan W. II. Gandy, Thomas H. III. Title. BIP

OLYMPICS of colour photography : outstanding entries / with commentaries and analyses by Hugo Schottle ; [transl. from the German by Ulla Dornberg and Dianne Reichart]. Frankfurt am Main : Umschau-Verlag, 1976. 98 p. : chiefly ill. (col.) ; 24 cm. Translation of Olympiade der farbfotografie. Includes index. [TR654.O6713 1976] 77-471618 ISBN 3-524-00698-1 779'.092'2
1. Photography, Artistic. 2. Color photography. I. Schottle, Hugo.

ORKIN, Ruth. 779'.9'97471040924
A world through my window / photos. by Ruth Orkin ; text compiled by Arno Karlen. 1st ed. New York : Harper & Row, c1978. p. cm. [TR654.O74] 78-2153 ISBN 0-06-013293-0 : 20.00
1. Orkin, Ruth. 2. Photography, Artistic. 3. New York (City)—Description—Views. I. Karlen, Arno. BIP

O'SULLIVAN, Timothy H. 779
T. H. O'Sullivan; photographer, by Beaumont and Nancy Newhart, with an appreciation by Ansel Adams. [Rochester, N.Y.] G. Eastman House [c1966] 1 v. (chiefly illus.) 21 x 22 cm. [TR140.O8N4] 66-25971
1. Photography. Artistic. 2. The west — Descr. & trav. — Views. 3. U.S. — Hist. — Civil War — Pictorial works. I. Newhall, Beaumont, 1908- II. Newhall, Nancy (Wynne) III. Title.

PARKS, Gordon, 1912- 779'.0924
Gordon Parks: whispers of intimate things. Introd.: Philip B. Kundhardt, Jr. New York, Viking Press [1971] [80] p. col. illus. 25 cm. (A Studio book) [TR654.P33 1971] 75-139273 ISBN 0-670-34667-5 8.95
1. Photography, Artistic. I. Title: Whispers of intimate things.

PARKS, Gordon, 1912- 779'.0924
In love. [1st ed.] Philadelphia, Lippincott [1971] 1 v. (unpaged) col. illus. 25 cm. Poems. [PS3566.A73I5] 70-154848 8.95
I. Title.

PARKS, Gordon, 1912- 779'.092'4
Moments without proper names / Gordon Parks. New York : Viking Press, 1975. 173 p. : chiefly ill. (some col.) ; 32 cm. (A Studio book) Poems. [TR654.P297 1975] 75-9547 ISBN 0-670-48472-5 : 19.95

1. Photography, Artistic. I. Title.

PARKS, Gordon, 1912- 779'.0924
A poet and his camera. Pref.: Stephen Spender. Introd.: Philip B. Kunhardt, Jr. New York, Viking Press [1968] [92] p. col. illus. 25 cm. (A Studio book) Poems. [TR654.P3] 68-23207 8.95
1. Photography, Artistic. I. Title.

PEARSON, John, 1934- 779'.092'4
Magic doors / by John Pearson. Reading, Mass. : Addison-Wesley Pub. Co., c1977. p. cm. Bibliography: p. [TR654.P39] 77-22382 ISBN 0-201-05668-2 : 10.95. ISBN 0-201-05669-0 pbk. : 6.95
1. Pearson, John, 1934- 2. Photography, Artistic. I. Title. BIP

PEARSON, John, 1935- 779'.0924
To be nobody else. [Palo Alto, Calif., Jomeri Publications; distributor: Book People, Berkeley, Calif., 1968] [63] p. (chiefly illus.) 28 cm. [TR654.P4] 79-2817 3.95
1. Photography, Artistic. I. Title.

PELADEAU, Marius B. 770'.92'4 B
Chansonetta : the life and photographs of Chansonetta Stanley Emmons, 1858-1937 / by Marius B. Peladeau ; introd. by Berenice Abbott. 1st ed. Waldoboro : Maine Antique Digest ; Dobbs Ferry, N.Y. : distributed by Morgan & Morgan, 1977. 96 p. : ill. ; 23 x 27 cm. Includes bibliographical references. [TR653.P44] 77-78057 ISBN 0-917312-01-5 pbk. : 8.95
1. Emmons, Chansonetta Stanley, 1858-1937. 2. Photography, Artistic. 3. Photographers—Maine—Biography. I. Emmons, Chansonetta Stanley, 1858-1937. II. Title. BIP

PETERSON, C A 778
Photographing unknown beauties. [Los Angeles, Trend Books, 1958] 128p. illus. 24cm. (Trend book 163) [TR675.P45] 58-27395
1. Photography, Artistic. 2. Photography of women. I. Title. II. Series.

PHOTOGRAPHERS' Gallery. 770'.1
Reading photographs : understanding the aesthetics of photography / The Photographers' Gallery ; by Jonathan Bayer, with essays by Ainslie Ellis, Ian Jeffrey, and Peter Turner. 1st American ed. New York : Pantheon Books, c1977. 87 p.: ill. ; 20 x 23 cm. Originally published under title: Concerning photography. Originally published as the catalogue of an exhibition held at the Photographers' Gallery, London, and Spectro Workshop, Newcastle upon Tyne, in 1977. [TR183.P47 1977] 77-88761 ISBN 0-394-50127-6 : 12.95. ISBN 0-394-73584-6 pbk. : 5.95
1. Photography, Artistic. 2. Photography, Artistic—Exhibitions. I. Bayer, Jonathan, 1936- II. Spectro Workshop. III. Title. BIP

PHOTOGRAPHING glamour, by 779.24
Peter Gowland [and others. Greenwich, Conn., Fawcett Publications, 1959] 144p. illus. 24cm. (A Fawcett book, no. 412) [TR650.P48] 59-4167
1. Photography, Artistic. 2. Photography of women. I. Gowland, Peter. II. Fawcett Publications, inc.

PHOTOGRAPHY, current 770
perspectives. Rochester, N.Y. : Light Impressions Corp., c1978. 264 p. : ill. ; 24 cm. Edited by J. Liebling. Originally published as a quarterly issue of the Massachusetts review. [TR642.P47] 79-103970 ISBN 0-87992-013-0 : 15.00
1. Photography, Artistic. I. Liebling, Jerome. II. The Massachusetts review.

PICKER, Fred. 779'.092'4
The fine print / Fred Picker. Garden City, N.Y. : Amphoto, [1975] 159 p. : ill. ; 24 x 28 cm. Includes index. [TR642.P5] 74-83645 ISBN 0-8174-0584-4 : 12.50
1. Photography, Artistic. I. Title. BIP

PLOWDEN, David. 779'.4'0973
Commonplace / David Plowden. 1st ed. [New York] : Sunrise Books, [1974] 117 p. : chiefly ill. ; 26 x 29 cm. "A Chatham book." [TR654.P56 1974] 74-81420 ISBN 0-87690-143-7 : 15.00
1. Photography, Artistic. 2. United States—Description and travel—Views. I. Title.

POGZEBA, Wolfgang, 1936- 779'.9'978
New vision : photographs of the American West / Wolfgang Pogzeba ; foreword by Peter H. Hassrick. 1st ed. Flagstaff, Ariz. : Northland Press, c1977. x, 109 p. : chiefly ill. ; 24 x 31 cm. [TR654.P63] 77-79012 ISBN 0-87358-165-2 : 17.50
1. Photography, Artistic. 2. The West—Description and travel—Views. I. Title.

POND-SMITH, David Adams. 779'.092'4
Manself. [Los Angeles, Printed by G. Rice; distributed by Light Impressions, Rochester, N.Y., c1973] [29] p. (chiefly illus.) 31 cm. [TR654.P66] 73-89234
1. Photography, Artistic. I. Title.

POTTEBAUM, Gerard A. 779'.092'4
Wonderings. Written by Gerard A. Pottebaum. Photos. by Jack Hamilton. Winona, Minn., St. Mary's College Press [1972] 69 p. illus. 15 cm. [PS3566.O694W6] 72-77719 2.00
I. Title. BIP

PRINET, Jean. 779'.0924
Nadar, par Jean Prinet et Antoinette Dilasser. Paris, A. Colin, 1966. 287 p. illus., facsims., port. 18 cm. ([Collection] Klosque, 15) 8.50 F. (F***) Bibliography: p. 265-[268] [TR140.T6P7] 67-78251
1. Tournachon, Felix, 1820-1910. II. Dilasser, Antoinette, joint author. III. Title.

PRIZE winning photography. 778
Greenwich, Conn., Fawcett, c.1963. 112p. illus. 24cm. (541) annual. 56-808 .75 pap.,
1. Photography, Artistic. 2. Photography—Competitions.

PRIZE winning photography. 778
[Greenwich, Conn., Fawcett Publications, 1954] 144p. illus. 24cm. (A Fawcett book, no. 227) [TR650.P7] 54-3106
1. Photography, Artistic. 2. Photography—Competitions. I. Fawcett Publications, inc.

RAMIREZ, Efren Convento, 1941- 779'.092'4
In pursuit of images / by Efren Convento Ramirez. San Francisco : Peace and Pieces Foundation, c1976. p. cm. [TR654.R33] 76-22548 ISBN 0-914024-24-8 pbk. : 7.50
1. Photography, Artistic. I. Title.

RAWLINGS, John. 779.24
Studies of the human form by two masters: John Rawlings and Edward Weston. New York, Maco Magazine Corp. [1957] 127p. illus. 25cm. (Great photography series, 1) [TR675.R3] 57-59062
1. Photography, Artistic. 2. Human figure in art. I. Weston, Edward, 1886- II. Title. III. Series.

RAY, Man, 1890- 779'.092'4
Man Ray : photographs, 1920-1934 ; introd. by A. D. Coleman. New York : East River Press, 1975. p. cm. [TR653.R39 1975] 75-23459 ISBN 0-89172-002-2 : 8.50
1. Photography, Artistic. 2. Photography—Portraits.

REICH, Hanns, comp. 779'.26
Lovers. New York, Hill and Wang [1968] [16] p., 64 p. of illus. 24 cm. (A Terra magica book) Poems and photos. Issued also in German with title: Liebespaare. [TR675.R4] 68-9301
1. Photography, Artistic. I. Title. BIP

REYNOLDS, Robert, 1925- 779'.092'4
Magic symbols : a photographic study on graffiti / by Robert Reynolds. Portland, Or. : Graphic Arts Center Pub. Co., [1975] [96] p. : chiefly col. ill. ; 27 cm. [TR654.R484] 75-1649 ISBN 0-912856-19-X : 18.50
1. Photography, Artistic. 2. Graffiti—Pictorial works. I. Title.

ROBINSON, Henry Peach, 1830-1901. 770'.1
The elements of a pictorial photograph. New York, Arno Press, 1973. 167 p. illus. 23 cm. (The Literature of Photography) Reprint of the 1896 ed. [TR642.R59 1973] 72-9228 ISBN 0-405-04934-X 11.00.
1. Photography, Artistic. I. Title. II. Series. BIP

ROBINSON, Henry Peach, 1830-1901. 770'.11
Pictorial effect in photography, being hints on composition and chiaroscuro for photographers. With a new introd. by Robert A. Sobieszek. Pawlet [Vt.] Helios, 1971. viii, 199 p. illus. 22 cm. Reprint of the 1869 ed., with a new introd. [TR642.R6 1971] 76-164013 ISBN 0-87931-002-2
1. Photography, Artistic. 2. Composition (Photography) I. Title.

ROBINSON, Henry Peach, 1830-1901. 770'.28
Picture-making, by photography. New York, Arno Press, 1973. vi, 134 p. illus. 23 cm. (The Literature of Photography) Reprint of the 5th ed., published in 1897. [TR642.R62 1973] 72-9230 ISBN 0-405-04936-6 9.00.
1. Photography, Artistic. I. Title. II. Series.

ROH, Franz, 1890-1965, comp. 779'.09'042
Photo-eye. 76 photos of the period. Edited byFranz Roh and Jan Tschichold. New York, Arno Press, 1973. [c1929] 18 p. illus. 29 cm. (The Literature of Photography) Text in German French and English. Reprint of the ed. published under title: Foto-Auge, 76 Fotos der Zeit. [TR653.R64 1973] 72-9234 ISBN 0-405-04939-0 11.00.
1. Photography, Artistic. I. Tschichold, Jan. 1902- joint comp. II. Title. III. Series.

ROTZLER, Willy. 779'.092'2
Photography as artistic experiment : from Fox Talbot to Moholy-Nagy / W. Rotzler ; [English translation, Maureen Oberli-Turner]. Garden City, N.Y. : AMPHOTO, c1976. 92 p. : ill. ; 27 cm. (Photography, men and movements) Translation of Photographie als kunstlerisches Experiment. Includes index. Bibliography: p. 91. [TR650.R6813] 75-34677 ISBN 0-8174-0317-5 : 5.95
1. Photography, Artistic. I. Title. BIP

RUBINSTEIN, Eva. 779'.092'4
Eva Rubinstein / preface by Sean Kernan. Dobbs Ferry, N.Y. : Morgan & Morgan, [1974] 67 p. : chiefly ill. ; 23 cm. [TR654.R82] 74-83235 ISBN 0-87100-084-9 pbk. : 6.95
1. Photography, Artistic. BIP

RUSCHA, Edward. 779'.34'0924
Colored people. [New York, American distributor: Wittenborn] 1972. [16] l. of col. illus. 18 cm. Imprint from label mounted on t.p. [TR654.R87] 73-156281
1. Photography, Artistic. 2. Cactus—Pictorial works. I. Title.

RUSSELL, Guy, 1945- 779'.092'4
Mojave / Guy Russell. Brookline, Mass. : Sigga Press, [1977] p. cm. [TR654.R875] 77-27298 ISBN 0-916348-17-2 pbk. : 4.95
1. Photography, Artistic. I. Title. BIP

RUSSELL, Guy, 1945- 779'.092'4
The space outside : photographs / by Guy Russell ; forward [sic] by David Pratt. Westport, Mass. : Sigga Press, [1975] p. cm. [TR654.R88] 75-35693 ISBN 0-916348-08-3. ISBN 0-916348-07-5
1. Photography, Artistic. I. Title. BIP

SAFFORD, Nancy. 917.44'94
Time's Island; portraits of the Vineyard. Cambridge, Mass., MIT Press [1973] 103 p. (chiefly illus.) 22 x 25 cm. [TR654.S22] 72-11648 ISBN 0-262-19110-5 12.50
1. Photography, Artistic. 2. Martha's Vineyard, Mass.—Description and travel—Views. I. Title.

*SAMSON, Hans. 770
In the beginning. [Secaucus, N.J.] Derbibooks 1974 1 vol. (unpaged chiefly illus.) 40 cm. [TR145] ISBN 0-89009-013-0 6.95 (pbk.)
1. Photography, Artistic. I. Rous, Laura. II. Title.

SAROYAN, Aram. 779'.0924
Words & photographs. Chicago, Big Table Pub. Co. [1970] 1 v. (unpaged) illus., ports. 17 cm. [TR654.S26 1970] 75-112482 4.95
1. Photography, Artistic. I. Title.

SCHAEFFER, Richard W., 1949- 778.9'4'0979313
Turquoise pleasures; featuring photographs of the fabulous hotel-casinos of Las Vegas, by Richard W. Schaeffer. [Rochester, N.Y.] Silver Screen Pub. Co.; [distributed by Light Impressions Corp., 1974] [65] p. (chiefly illus.) 24 x 31 cm. [TR654.S3] 74-12140 ISBN 0-914840-00-2
1. Photography, Artistic. 2. Photography, Architectural. 3. Las Vegas, Nev.—Description—Views. I. Title. BIP

SCHAEWEN, Deidi von, 1941- 779'.4'0924
Walls / Deidi von Schaewen. 1st American ed. New York : Pantheon Books, c1977. xvi, 142 p. : chiefly ill. ; 29 cm. Includes index. [TR654.S33 1977] 77-1982 ISBN 0-394-41039-4 : 15.00. ISBN 0-394-73390-8 pbk. : 8.95
1. Photography, Artistic. 2. Walls—Pictorial works. I. Title. BIP

SCHWEITZER, Martin. 779'.092'4
Stopping the world : photographs and text / by Martin Schweitzer. 1st ed. Garden City, N.Y. : Dolphin Books, 1977. p. cm. [TR654.S38] 76-23816 ISBN 0-385-11584-9 pbk. : 5.95
1. Photography, Artistic. I. Title. BIP

SHAHN, Ben, 1898-1969. 779'.9'9173039160924
Ben Shahn, photographer; an album from the thirties. Edited, with an introd., by Margaret R. Weiss. New York, Da Capo Press, 1973. [9] p., 82 plates. 22 x 27 cm. [TR653.S5 1973] 77-75271 ISBN 0-306-71312-8 10.00
1. United States. Farm Security Administration. 2. Photography, Artistic. 3. United States—Description and travel—Views. I. Weiss, Margaret R., ed. II. Title.

SHEPARD, Harriett Crim, 1915- 770.1
Posing for the camera; a professional guide, for the creative model, director, photographer, by Harriett Shepard and Lenore Meyer. New York, Hastings House [1960] 184p. illus., diagrs. 25cm. (Communication arts books) 60-9678 6.95 half cloth,
1. Photography, Artistic. 2. Models, Artists. I. Meyer, Lenore Florence, 1921- joint author. II. Title.

SHOOLERY, John. 779'.092'4
Tongue of the fish / created by John Shoolery and George Lawson ; words by Robin Williamson and Mike Heron. 1st ed. Garden City, N.Y. : Doubleday, 1976. p. cm. [TR654.S52] 73-10540 ISBN 0-385-08209-6 : 3.95
1. Photography, Artistic. I. Lawson, George, 1951- II. Williamson, Robin. III. Heron, Mike. IV. Title.

SISKIND, Aaron. 779'.092'4
Aaron Siskind : photographs. John Logan : poems. Rochester, N.Y. : Visual Studies Workshop, 1976. 34 p. : 16 ill. ; 26 cm. [TR654.S54] 76-382581
1. Photography, Artistic. I. Logan, John, 1923-

SISKIND, Aaron. 770
Aaron Siskind, photographer. Edited with an introd. by Nathan Lyons. Essays by Henry Holmes Smith and Thomas B. Hess. Statement by Aaron Siskind. Rochester, N. Y., George Eastman House; [distributed by Horizon Press, New York [1965] 74 p. plates. 26 x 27 cm. (George Eastman House monograph no. 5) Bibliography: p. 69-72. [TR140.S54A3] 65-20164
1. Photography, Artistic. I. Lyons, Nathan, ed. II. Smith, Henry Holmes. III. Hess, Thomas B. IV. Series.

SMITH, Del. 779'.9'9766050924
Bedrock : images from the wayside / photos. by Del Smith ; odes by Michael Cauthron ; foreword by Carl Albert ; introd. by Bill Moyers. 1st ed. Austin, Tex. : Madrona Press, c1975. xiii, 115 p. : ill. ; 29 cm. [TR654.S55] 75-16938 ISBN 0-89052-015-1 : 10.50
1. Photography, Artistic. 2. Photography, Documentary. I. Cauthron, Michael, joint author. II. Title. BIP

SMITH, W. Eugene, 1918- 779'.0924
W. Eugene Smith, his photographs and notes. Afterword by Lincoln Kirstein. New York [Aperture, inc.] 1969. 1 v. (chiefly illus.) 26 cm. Includes bibliography. [TR654.S57] 70-99254 8.50
1. Photography, Artistic.

SUBJECT INDEX PHOTOGRAPHY, ARTISTIC.

SNOWDON, Anthony 779'.2'0924
Armstrong-Jones 1stEarl of 1930-
Assignments [by] Snowdon. New York, Morrow, 1972. 1 v. (chiefly illus.) 19 x 31 cm. [TR654.S58] 72-169090 ISBN 0-688-00027-4 12.50
1. Photography, Artistic. I. Title. BIP

SONTAG, Susan, 1933- 770'.1
On photography / Susan Sontag. New York : Farrar, Straus an Giroux, 1977. p. cm. Bibliography: p. [TR183.S65 1977] 77-11916 ISBN 0-374-22626-1 : 7.95
1. Photography, Artistic. I. Title.
Contents omitted

SPLIT image, 779
[edited by John Julian and Ben Lewin. Melbourne] Melbourne University Union Council, 1969. 1 v. (unpaged) illus. 28 cm. [TR654.S6] 73-485727 2.95
1. Photography, Artistic. I. Julian, John, ed. II. Lewin, Ben, ed. III. Melbourne University Union. Council.

STAGE and theater photography. 778.99792
Philadelphia, Chilton Books [1965] 128 p. illus., ports. 24 cm. [TR680.L65] 65-17116
1. Photography, Artistic. 2. Musicians — Portraits.

STEICHEN, Edward, 1879- 779
A life in photography. Published in collaboration with the Museum of Modern Art. Garden City, N.Y., Doubleday, 1963. 1 v. (unpaged) 249 illus. (part col., incl. ports.) 30 cm. [TR140.S68A25] 63-11119
1. Photography, Artistic. I. Title. BIP

STEICHEN, Edward, 779'.092'4
1879-1973.
Edward Steichen. Millerton, N.Y. : Aperture, c1978. 95 p. : all ill. ; 21 cm. (The Aperture history of photography series ; 9) Bibliography: p. 95. [TR653.S73 1978] 77-70071 ISBN 0-89381-006-1 : 7.95
1. Photography, Artistic. BIP

STEICHEN, Edward, 779'.092'4
1879-1973.
Steichen : the master prints 1895-1914, the symbolist period / Dennis Longwell. New York : Museum of Modern Art ; Boston : distributed by New York Graphic Society, c1978. 180 p. : ill. (some col.) ; 29 cm. Includes index. Bibliography: p. 175-177. [TR654.S72 1978] 77-90995 ISBN 0-87070-581-4 : 35.00
1. Steichen, Edward, 1879-1973. 2. Photography, Artistic. I. Longwell, Dennis. II. New York (City). Museum of Modern Art. BIP

STETSER, Carol. 779'.092'4
Black and white / Carol Stetser. Oatman, Ariz. : Padma Press, c1977. [56] p. : chiefly ill. ; 28 cm. [TR654.S73] 76-46884 ISBN 0-917960-01-7 pbk. : 5.95
1. Photography, Artistic. I. Title. BIP

STETSER, Carol. 779'.092'4
Chopping wood, carrying water / Carol Stetser. Oatman, Ariz. : Padma Press, c1978. [55] p. : chiefly ill. ; 25 cm. [TR654.S763] 77-83081 ISBN 0-917960-02-5 pbk. : 6.95
1. Photography, Artistic. 2. Simplicity. I. Title. BIP

STETSER, Carol. 779'.092'4
Continuum : an autobiography at thirty / Carol Stetser. Oatman, Ariz. : Padma Press, c1979. [60] p. ; 27 cm. Photographs. [TR654.S764] 78-70872 ISBN 0-917960-03-3 : 9.95
1. Photography, Artistic. 2. Stetser, Carol. I. Title. BIP

STOLL, Jerry 778.9
I am a lover. With comment from various sources selected by Evan S. Connell, Jr. Sausalito, Calif., Angel Island Publications, Box 755 [c.1961] unpaged (chiefly illus.) 28cm. (Contact eds., CE3) 61-11002 2.95 pap.,
1. Photography, Artistic. 2. Quotations. I. Title. BIP

STOUMEN, Louis 791.43'092'4
Clyde.
Can't argue with sunrise : a paper movie / Lou Stoumen. Millbrae, Calif. : Celestial Arts, 1975. 185 p. : ill. ; 22 cm. "A Hand Press book." [TR654.S76] 75-262 ISBN 0-89087-052-7 : 14.95. pbk. : 9.45
1. Photography, Artistic. 2. Photography, Documentary. I. Title.

STRAND, Paul, 1890- 779'.092'4
1976.
Paul Strand : sixty years of photographs : excerpts from correspondence, interviews, and other documents / profile by Calvin Tomkins. Millerton, N.Y. : Aperture, c1976. 183 p. : ill. ; 30 cm. Bibliography: p. 178-181. [TR654.S77 1976] 76-42103 ISBN 0-912334-81-9 : 25.00. ISBN 0-900406-82-8 pbk.
1. Photography, Artistic.

STUART, Garry. 779'.9'942925
Hirael, a portrait : a selection from a photographic study = Hirael, portread : detholiad allan o astudiaeth ffotograffig / by Garry Stuart. [Caernarfon] : Gwynedd County Council, Archives Service, 1976. 16, [1] p. : chiefly ill. ; 18 x 24 cm. [TR654.S78] 77-476528 ISBN 0-901337-16-1
1. Photography, Artistic. 2. Bangor, Wales—Description—Views. I. Title. II. Title: Hirael, portread.

SUDEK, Josef, 1896- 770'.92'4 B
1976.
Sudek / Sonja Bullaty. 1st ed. New York : C. N. Potter : distributed by Crown Publishers, c1978. 189 p. : chiefly ill. ; 29 cm. Bibliography: p. 188-189. [TR140.S737A34 1978] 78-17573 ISBN 0-517-53865-2 : 45.00
1. Sudek, Josef, 1896-1976. 2. Photography, Artistic. 3. Photographers—Czechoslovakia—Prague—Biography. I. Bullaty, Sonja.

SUZUKAWA, George. 779.0924
Suzukawa, his search for truth in photography. Cleveland, World Pub. Co. [1966] 1 v. (unpaged) illus. (part col.) 26 cm. Cover title: Suzukawa. [TR650.S9] 66-28442
1. Photography, Artistic. I. Title.

SZARKOWSKI, John. 779
The photographer's eye. New York, Museum of Modern Art; distributed by Doubleday, Garden City, N.Y. [1966] 155 p. 24 cm. [TR650.S92] 65-25724
1. Photography, Artistic. I. Title.

TALBOT, William Henry 779'.092'4
Fox, 1800-1877.
William H. Fox Talbot, inventor of the negative-positive process [by] Andre Jammes. [English translation by Maureen Oberli-Turner] New York, Macmillan [1973] 96 p. plates. 28 cm. (Photography: men and movements, v. 2) Includes bibliographical references. [TR651.T3413] 73-10789 10.95
1. Talbot, William Henry Fox, 1800-1877. 2. Photography, Artistic. 3. Calotype. I. Jammes, Andre.

THOMPSON, Jay. 779'.0924
I am also a you; a book of thoughts with photographs. With an introd. by John Lennon. Design by Michael Lunstead. [1st ed.] New York, C. N. Potter [1971] [127] p. (chiefly illus.) 29 cm. [TR654.T46 1971] 71-150694 4.95
1. Photography, Artistic. I. Title. BIP

TICE, George A. 779'.092'4
Photographs, 1953-1973 [by George A. Tice.] New Brunswick, N.J., Rutgers University Press [1975] 120 p. of illus., [6] p. 28 cm. Bibliography: p. [125] [TR654.T523 1975] 74-14895 ISBN 0-8135-0792-8 20.00
1. Photography, Artistic. I. Title.
Pbk. 12.50, ISBN 0-8135-0793-6.

TIME-LIFE Books. 779
The art of photography, by the editors of Time-Life Books. New York [1971] 230 p. illus. (part col.) 27 cm. (Life library of photography) Bibliography: p. 227. [TR642.T55] 75-161201
1. Photography, Artistic. I. Title. BIP

TIME-LIFE Books. 779
Great photographers, by the editors of Time-Life Books. New York [1971] 246 p. illus. (part col.) 27 cm. (Life library of photography) Cover title: Great photographers: 1840-1960. Bibliography: p. 241-242. [TR650.T53] 73-166210
1. Photography, Artistic. 2. Photographers. I. Title. BIP

TRAGER, Philip, 1935- 779'.092'4
Echoes of silence. [Danbury, Conn.] Scroll Press, 1972. 12 plates. 36 x 39 cm. [TR654.T7] 72-84234
1. Photography, Artistic. I. Title. BIP

TRAUB, Charles, 1945- 779'.2'0924
Beach / Charles Traub. New York : Horizon Press, c1978. 60 p. : chiefly ill. ; 27 cm. [TR654.T715] 78-59734 ISBN 0-8180-1417-2 : 8.95
1. Traub, Charles, 1945- 2. Photography, Artistic. 3. Bathing beaches—Pictorial works. I. Title.

TRESS, Arthur. 779'.092'4
Theater of the mind / Arthur Tress. Dobbs Ferry, N.Y. : Morgan & Morgan, 1976. [93] p. : chiefly ill. ; 23 cm. [TR654.T73] 76-25392 ISBN 0-87100-106-3 : 7.95
1. Photography, Artistic. I. Title. BIP

TRIBBETT, Hershel Thoth. 770
Moonscapes : 50 self-discovery projects for photographers / Hershel Thoth Tribbett. San Rafael, Calif. : Tribbett, c1976. 79 p. : ill. ; 20 x 26 cm. [TR654.T74] 75-44913
1. Photography, Artistic. 2. Self-realization. 3. Moon—Photographs. I. Title,

TUCKER, Anne, comp. 779'.092'2
The woman's eye. Edited and with an introd. by Anne Tucker. [1st ed.] New York, Knopf; [distributed by Random House] 1973. 169, [1] p. illus. 26 cm. "Selections from the work of Gertrude Kasebier, Frances Benjamin Johnston, Margaret Bourke-White, Dorothea Lange, Berenice Abbott, Barbara Morgan, Diane Arbus, Alisa Wells, Judy Dater, Bea Nettles." Bibliography: p. [170] [TR650.T78 1973] 73-7283 ISBN 0-394-48678-1 4.95
1. Photography, Artistic. 2. Women photographers. I. Title. BIP

TULCHIN, Lewis. 778.92
The nude in photography; a treatise on the esthetics and techniques of nude photography. Illus. by the author. New York, Grayson Pub. Corp. [1950] ix, 86 p. illus. 29 cm. [TR675.T8] 50-1466
1. Photography, Artistic. 2. Nude in art. I. Title.

TURNER, Peter. 770'.92'4 B
P. H. Emerson : photographer of Norfolk / Peter Turner and Richard Wood. Boston : D. R. Godine, [1975] c1974. 108 p. : ill. ; 30 cm. (Godine photographic monographs ; 2) Includes bibliographical references. [TR140.E43T87 1975] 74-81518 ISBN 0-87923-106-8 : 19.95
1. Emerson, Peter Henry, 1856-1936. 2. Photography, Artistic. 3. Norfolk, Eng. (County)—Description and travel—Views. I. Wood, Richard, joint author.

UELSMANN, Jerry, 1934- 779'.0924
Eight photographs. [Introd. by William E. Parker. New York, Doubleday, 1970] 1 portfolio ([1] l., 8 plates) 37 x 39 cm. [TR647.U44A44] 76-18939 6.95
1. Photography, Artistic. I. Title.

UZZLE, Burk. 779'.092'4
Landscapes/photographs. [New York, Magnum Photos; distributed by Light Impressions Corp., Rochester, N.Y., c1973] [95] p. (chiefly illus.) 21 x 23 cm. Cover title. [TR654.U95] 73-86869 ISBN 0-914122-01-0 14.95
1. Photography, Artistic. I. Title.
Pbk. 6.95; ISBN 0-914122-00-2

VARNEY, Vivian. 770
The photographer as designer / Vivian Varney. Worcester, Mass. : Davis Publications, c1977. x, 196 p. : ill. ; 27 cm. [TR642.V37] 76-19943 ISBN 0-87192-078-6 : 13.95
1. Photography, Artistic. I. Title. BIP

WAX, Charles Chaim. 779'.092'4
Brooklyn songs. [New York, Chain Way Films and Photography, 1973- v. (chiefly illus.) 22 x 25 cm. [TR654.W35] 73-89052
1. Photography, Artistic. 2. Brooklyn—Description—Views. I. Title.

WAX, Marvin. 779'.4'09794
Mystique of the missions; photographic impressions by Marvin Wax. Descriptive passages by Charles Francis Saunders and J. Smeaton Chase, selected from The California padres and their missions, published in 1915. [1st ed.] Palo Alto, Calif., American West Pub. Co. [1974] 111 p. chiefly col. illus. 29 cm. (An Images of America series book) [TR654.W36] 74-77396 ISBN 0-910118-52-3. 12.50
1. Photography, Artistic. 2. Spanish missions of California—Pictorial works. I. Saunders, Charles Francis, 1859-1941. The California padres and their missions. Selections. 1974. II. Title.
Deluxe edition 15.00; ISBN 0-910118-53-1.

WEINER, Dan, 1919-1959. 770'.92'4
Dan Weiner, 1919-1959 / [editors, Cornell Capa, Sandra Weiner]. New York : Grossman Publishers, 1974. 96 p. : chiefly ill. ; 23 cm. (ICP library of photographers ; v. 5) Bibliography: p. 96. [TR140.W42A33 1974] 72-11008 ISBN 0-670-25645-5 : 10.00. ISBN 0-670-25646-3 pbk : 5.95
1. Weiner, Dan, 1919-1959. 2. Photography, Artistic. I. Series: International Fund for Concerned Photography. ICP library of photographers ; v. 5.

†WELSCH, Ulrike. 779'.092'4
The world I love to see / photos. by Ulrike Welsch. Boston : Boston Globe, 1977. 122 p. : ill. ; 26 cm. [TR654.W42] 76-49624 ISBN 0-395-25179-6 pbk. : 5.95
1. Photography, Artistic. I. Title.
Available from Houghton Miflin, Boston, MA BIP

WELTY, Eudora, 779'.9'91762036
1909-
One time, one place: Mississippi in the depression; a snapshot album. [1st ed.] New York, Random House [1971] xiv, 111 p. illus. (chiefly illus.) 21 cm. [TR653.W44] 73-162392 ISBN 0-394-47308-6 7.95
1. Photography, Artistic. 2. Mississippi—Description and travel—Views. I. Title. BIP

WESTON, Brett. 779
Brett Weston: photographs, by Merle Armitage. New York, E. Weyhe [c1956] 102 p. plates. 34 cm. Alternate pages blank. Erratum slip mounted on p. 15. [TR650.W38] 56-12210
1. Photography, Artistic. 2. Photographs. I. Armitage, Merle, 1896- II. Title.

WESTON, Brett. 779'.092'4
Europe. Carmel, Calif., 1973. 1 portfolio ([8] l., 12 plates) 48 cm. Edition limited to 100 copies signed by the author. [TR654.W44] 73-174809 500.00
1. Photography, Artistic. I. Title.

WESTON, Brett. 779'.092'4
Voyage of the eye / Brett Weston ; afterword by Beaumont Newhall. Millerton, N.Y. : Aperture, inc., c1975. 100, [3] p. : chiefly ill. ; 30 cm. Bibliography: p. [101] [TR654.W443 1975] 75-13610 ISBN 0-912334-83-5 : 17.50 pbk.: 9.50
1. Weston, Brett. 2. Photography, Artistic. I. Title.

WESTON, Edward, 1886- 770'.92'4 B
1958.
The daybooks of Edward Weston. Edited by Nancy Newhall. [Millerton, N.Y., Aperture, 1973] 2 v. illus. 27 cm. "An Aperture book." Contents.Contents.—v. 1. Mexico.—v. 2. California. Bibliography: v. 1, p. 207-208. [TR140.W45A32] 74-156819 30.00
I. Weston, Edward, 1886-1958. II. Title. BIP

WESTON, Edward, 1886- 779'.0924
1958.
Edward Weston; the flame of recognition: his photographs accompanied by excerpts from the daybooks & letters. Edited by Nancy Newhall. New York [Aperture] 1971. 104 p. illus. 26 cm. 1965 ed. published under title: Edward Weston, photographer. Bibliography: p. [101]-[103] [TR140.W45A33 1971] 78-149320 10.00
1. Photography, Artistic. I. Title: The flame of recognition. BIP

WESTON, Edward, 1886- 779'.092'4
1958.
Edward Weston: fifty years; the definitive volume of his photographic work. Illustrated biography by Ben Maddow. [1st ed. Millerton, N.Y., Aperture, Inc., 1973]

285 p. illus. 32 x 35 cm. Bibliography: p. 282-285. [TR653.W457 1973] 73-85262 ISBN 0-912334-38-X 40.00
1. Weston, Edward, 1886-1958. 2. Photography, Artistic. I. Maddow, Ben, 1909- II. Title.

WESTON, Edward, 1886-1958. 779
Edward Weston, photographer; the flame of recognition; his photographs accompanied by excerpts from the daybooks & letters. Edited by Nancy Newhall. New York, Grossman, 1965. 87, [1] p. illus. 24 cm. "An Aperture monograph." "Brief bibliography and guide to the work of E. Weston" (p. 86-[88]) [TR140.W45A33] 65-27407
1. Photography, Artistic. I. Title. II. Title: The flame of recognition.

WESTON, Edward, 1886-1958. 779'.092'4
Edward Weston portfolio. [Negatives by Edward Weston; prints by Cole Weston. New York, Witkin-Berley, 1971] 1 portfolio (4 l., 10 plates) in case. 47 cm. Title from case. Imprint from label on verso of each plate. 50 sets; no. 9. Each plate signed on verso by C. Weston. [TR653.W458 1971] 73-160732
1. Photography, Artistic. I. Weston, Cole.

WESTON, Edward, 1886-1958. 779'.0924
Eight photographs. [Garden City, N.Y.] Doubleday [1971] 1 portfolio ([1] l., 8 plates 37 cm. (Doubleday/Projections) Title from portfolio. [TR653.W46] 73-23328
1. Photography, Artistic.

WESTON, Edward Henry, 1886-1958 927.7
Daybooks [2] Ed. by Nancy Newhall. New York, Horizon Pr. in collaboration with the George Eastman House [1966] xi, 290p. plates. 26cm. v1. was George Eastman House monograph no. 2. Contents.v.2. California [TR140.W5A3] 61-18484 15.00
I. Title.

WHERE are we? 779
A book by the photography students of the College of DuPage. [Glen Ellyn, Ill., Photography Dept., College of DuPage] 1970. 1 v. (chiefly illus.) 27 cm. [TR654.W47] 75-130602
1. Photography, Artistic. I. DuPage Co., Ill. College.

THE White elephant book 779'.32
: a photographic essay. San Diego : Beta Books, c1977. p. cm. [TR654.W48] 77-6402 ISBN 0-89293-019-5 pbk. : 2.95
1. Photography, Artistic. 2. Elephants. BIP

WHITE, Minor. 779.0924
Mirrors, messages, manifestations. [New York] Aperture [1969] 242 p. (chiefly illus.) 32 cm. "An Aperture monograph." "Comments by Beaumont Newhall, Meyer Schapiro, Peter Bunnell, Jonathan Williams, Barbara Morgan, Ansel Adams": [11] p. in pocket. [TR647.W46A2 1969] 77-99253 35.00
1. Photography, Artistic. I. Title.

WILLIAMS, Harold A., 1916- 779
Bodine; a legend in his time, by Harold A. Williams. [1st ed.] Baltimore, Bodine, 1971. 82 p., [77] p. of illus. 27 cm. "The photography of A. Aubrey Bodine, 1924-1970": p. [1]-[75] (2d group) [TR140.B55W5] 70-169537 ISBN 0-910254-70-2 12.50
1. Bodine, A. Aubrey, 1907-1970. 2. Photography, Artistic. I. Bodine, A. Aubrey, 1907-1970. II. Title.

WILLIAMS, Mason Douglas, 1938- 779'.9'68161
Royal road test [by] Mason Williams, Edward Ruscha [and] Patrick Blackwell. [New York, G. Wittenborn, 1967] [53] p. (chiefly illus.) 25 cm. [TR654.W5] 74-2438
1. Photography, Artistic. I. Ruscha, Edward, joint author. II. Blackwell, Patrick, joint author. III. Title.

WILSON, Leslie Hamilton, 1883-1968. 779'.092'4
An Edwardian observer : the photographs of Leslie Hamilton Wilson / introd. by Edwin Newman ; text by Clark Worswick ; edited by Marilyn Penn. [New York] : Penwick Pub., c1978. 149 p. : ill. ; 24 x 29 cm. "A Pennwick/Crown book." [TR653.W54 1978] 78-69844 ISBN 0-517-53376-6 : 22.50
1. Wilson, Leslie Hamilton, 1883-1968. 2. Photography, Artistic. I. Worswick, Clark. II. Penn, Marilyn. III. Title. BIP

WOLBERG, Lewis Robert, 1905- 779'.0924
Micro-art; art images in a hidden world. Text and photos. by Lewis R. Wolberg. With a pref. by Brian O'Doherty. New York, H. N. Abrams [1970] xx, 292 p. illus. (part col.) 28 x 30 cm. Bibliography: p. 291-292. [TR682.W64] 78-119623 ISBN 0-8109-0302-4 25.00
1. Photography, Artistic. 2. Photomicrography. I. Title.

YEAGER, Bunny. 779
How to take figure photos. Louisville, Ky., Whitestone Publications, c1962. 112 p. illus. 24 cm. (A Whitestone book, no. 38) [TR650.Y4] 62-48057
1. Photography, Artistic. 2. Photography of the nude. I. Title.

Photography, Artistic—Directories.

*MCDARRAH, Fred W. 779.092'4
Photography market place, edited by Fred W. McDarrah. 1975-1976 ed. New York, Bowker [1975] viii, 436 p. 23 cm. [TR653] 75-833 ISBN 0-8352-0803-6 14.95 (pbk.)
1. Photography, Artistic—Directories. I. Title.

Photography, Artistic—Exhibitions.

ABBOTT, Berenice, 1898- 779'.092'4
Berenice Abbott : [exhibition], January 6-24, 1976, Marlborough Gallery ... New York ... April 3-May 10, 1976, Lunn Gallery/Graphics International Ltd. ... Washington, D.C. .... [New York? : Marlborough Gallery?, 1976] [27] p. : ill. ; 28 cm. Bibliography: p. [23] [TR647.A23 1976] 77-354899
1. Photography, Artistic—Exhibitions. I. Marlborough Gallery. II. Lunn Gallery. III. Title. BIP

ADAMS, Ansel Easton, 1902- 779'.092'4
Ansel Adams: recollected moments. [San Francisco, 1972] [28] p. illus. 26 cm. Catalog of an exhibition held Oct. 14, 1972-Jan. 14, 1973 at the San Francisco Museum of Art. Bibliography: p. [25]-[27] [TR647.A43A3] 72-90800
1. Photography, Artistic—Exhibitions. I. San Francisco. Museum of Art. II. Title.

ADAMS, Ansel Eaton, 1902- 779'.092'4
Singular images [by] Ansel Adams. Text by Edwin Land [and others. Dobbs Ferry, N.Y., Morgan & Morgan, 1974] 53 p. illus. 26 cm. [TR647.A43L36] 73-93872 ISBN 0-87100-046-6 7.95
1. Photography, Artistic—Exhibitions. I. Land, Edwin Herbert, 1909- II. Title. BIP

ALEXANDER, Nina, 1941- 779'.2'0922
Mothermilk : exhibition at the New Jersey State Museum / Nina Alexander and Herta Hilscher-Wittgenstein. [Trenton] : Focus 411, c1975. [47] p. : chiefly ill. ; 24 x 31 cm. [TR646.U6T732] 75-34660 ISBN 0-916388-00-X. ISBN 0-916388-01-8 pbk.
1. Photography, Artistic—Exhibitions. I. Hilscher-Wittgenstein, Herta, joint author. II. New Jersey. State Museum, Trenton. III. Title.

ALFRED Stieglitz Center. 770'.944
French primitive photography; [exhibition, Nov. 17th through Dec. 28th, 1969] Introd. by Minor White. Commentaries by Andre Jammes and Robert Sobieszek. New York [Aperture, inc.] 1970. [97] p. illus., ports. 26 cm. Also published in Aperture, v. 15, no. 1. Bibliography: p. [13] [TR646.A42] 79-107749 8.50
1. Photography, Artistic—Exhibitions. 2. Photography—History—France. I. Title. BIP

ALVAREZ Bravo, Manuel, 1902- 779'.0924
Manuel Alvarez Bravo. [Pasadena, Calif.] Pasadena Art Museum [1971] 48 p. (chiefly illus., port.) 26 cm. Catalog, prepared by Fred R. Parker, of the exhibition held at the Pasadena Art Museum, May 4-June 20, 1971, the Museum of Modern Art, July 7-Aug. 25, 1971, and George Eastman House, Sept. 6-Oct. 15, 1971. Bibliography: p. [54]-[55] [TR647.A48A45] 74-159750
1. Photography, Artistic—Exhibitions. I. Parker, Fred R. II. Pasadena, Calif. Art Museum. III. New York (City). Museum of Modern Art. IV. George Eastman House, Rochester, N.Y. BIP

AMERICAN photography, past into present 779'.0973'074019777
: prints from the Monsen Collection of American Photography / selected and with an introd. by Anita Ventura Mozley. Seattle : Seattle Art Museum : distributed by the University of Washington Press, c1976. 155 p. : ill. ; 29 cm. Exhibition held at the Seattle Art Museum. Bibliography: p. 155. [TR646.U6S433] 76-4145 ISBN 0-295-95508-2 : 20.00 ISBN 0-295-95509-0 pbk. :
1. Monsen, R. Joseph—Photograph collections. 2. Photography, Artistic—Exhibitions. 3. Photography—History—United States—Exhibitions. I. Mozley, Anita Ventura. II. Seattle. Art Museum.

ARBUS, Diane, 1923-1971. 779'.2'0924
Diane Arbus. Millerton, N.Y. [Aperture, 1972] 15 p., 80 plates. 29 cm. "Published in conjunction with a major exhibition of the photographs of Diane Arbus at the Museum of Modern Art. Edited and designed by Doon Arbus ... and Marvin Israel." [TR647.A7A69] 72-93191 ISBN 0-912334-40-1 15.00
1. Photography, Artistic—Exhibitions. I. Title. BIP

BALTZ, Lewis, 1945- 779'.9'9753
Lewis Baltz : The Corcoran Gallery of Art, Washington, D.C., June 19-September 12, 1976. Washington : The Gallery, 1976. [21] p. : chiefly ill. ; 21 cm. (The Nation's Capital in photographs, 1976) Bibliography: p. [21] [TR647.B34 1976] 76-19239
1. Photography, Artistic—Exhibitions. 2. Washington, D.C.—Description—Views. I. Corcoran Gallery of Art, Washington, D.C. II. Title. III. Series.

BECHER, Bernhard. 779'.9'6200922
Bernd and Hilla Becher; an exhibition organized by the La Jolla Museum of Contemporary Art, La Jolla, California, February 23-March 31, 1974. [La Jolla, Calif., La Jolla Museum of Contemporary Art, 1974] [40] p. (chiefly illus.) 25 cm. Catalog of the exhibition. Bibliography: p. [38] [TR646.U6L343] 74-76639
1. Photography, Artistic—Exhibitions. 2. Photography, Industrial—Exhibitions. I. Becher, Hilla, joint author. II. La Jolla Museum of Contemporary Art.

A Book of photographs from the collection of Sam Wagstaff. 779'.074'013
[New York] : Gray Press ; [Rochester, N.Y. : distributed by Light Impressions Corp.], 1978. 143 p. : all ill. ; 29 cm. "An exhibition organized by the Corcoran Gallery of Art, Washington, D.C., February 4-March 26, 1978." [TR646.U6W373] 77-92100 ISBN 0-930928-01-6. ISBN 0-930928-00-8 pbk. : 15.00
1. Photography, Artistic—Exhibitions. I. Corcoran Gallery of Art, Washington, D.C.
Publisher's address : P.O. Box 3012, Rochester, NY 14614

BOSTON. Museum of Fine Arts. 779'.092'2
Private realities: recent American photography [by] Emmet Gowin [and others] Boston [1974] [96] p. 40 illus. 31 cm. Catalog of an exhibition. [TR646.U6B672 1974] 73-90126 ISBN 0-87846-077-2
1. Photography, Artistic—Exhibitions. I. Gowin, Emmet, 1941- II. Title.
Publisher's address: 465 Huntington Ave., Boston, Mass. 02115

BRAKE, Brian. 779'.092'4
Brian Brake, 40 photographs : an exhibition / organized by the Dowse Gallery. Lower Hutt, N.Z. : Dowse Art Gallery, [1976] [48] p. : 40 col. ill. ; 22 cm. "Toured with assistance of the Queen Elizabeth II Arts Council of New Zealand." [TR647.B69 1976] 77-351597
1. Photography, Artistic—Exhibitions. I. Dowse Art Gallery. II. Queen Elizabeth the Second Arts Council of New Zealand. III. Title.

[BRETTELL, Richard] 779'.092'2
Four directions in modern photography: Paul Caponigro, John T. Hill, Jerry N. Uelsmann, Bruce Davidson; an exhibition at the Yale University Art Gallery, Dec. 14, 1972 through Feb. 25, 1973. [Meriden, Conn., Printed by Meriden Gravure Co., 1973] [22] p. illus. 23 cm. [TR646.U6N423] 74-157593
1. Photography, Artistic—Exhibitions. I. Yale University. Art Gallery. II. Title.

BULLOCK, Wynn. 779'.0924
Wynn Bullock: photographs. [San Francisco, 1969] 16 p. illus. 28 cm. Catalog of the exhibition held Nov. 25, 1969-Jan. 4, 1970 in the Museum of Art, San Francisco. [TR647.B8A2 1969] 70-11119
1. Photography, Artistic—Exhibitions. I. San Francisco. Museum of Art. II. Title.

CALIFORNIA photographers, 1970. 779'.074'0194
[Davis? Memorial Union Art Gallery, University of California? 1970] 78 p. (chiefly illus.) 21 x 22 cm. Catalog of the exhibition organized by Fred R. Parker and held at Memorial Union Art Gallery, University of California, Davis, Apr. 6-May 9; Oakland Museum, Oakland, Calif., May 26-June 28; and Pasadena Art Museum, Pasadena, Calif., July 14-Aug. 23, 1970. [TR646.C34] 76-633964
1. Photography, Artistic—Exhibitions. I. Parker, Fred R. II. California. University, Davis. Art Gallery. III. Oakland Museum. IV. Pasadena, Calif. Art Museum.

CELEBRATIONS : 779
an exhibition of original photographs, Hayden Gallery, Massachusetts Institute of Technology, Cambridge, Massachusetts, March 1 through March 30, 1974 / selection and text by Minor White and Jonathan Green ; pref. by Gyorgy Kepes ; photos. by Leonard Freed ...[et al.]. New York : Aperture, inc., 1974. 82 p., [1] leaf of plates : chiefly ill. ; 28 cm. "Sponsored by the MIT Committee on the Visual Arts." [TR646.U6C352] 75-301783 ISBN 0-912334-56-8 : 10.95
1. Photography, Artistic—Exhibitions. I. White, Minor. II. Green, Jonathan. III. Freed, Leonard. IV. Hayden Gallery. V. Massachusetts Institute of Technology. Committee on the Visual Arts.

CLATTENBURG, Ellen Fritz. 779'.2'0924
The photographic work of F. Holland Day : [exhibition] Wellesley College Museum, Wellesley, Massachusetts, February 21-March 24, 1975 : introduction and catalogue / by Ellen Fritz Clattenburg. Wellesley, Mass. : The Museum, [1975] 64 p. : ill. ; 26 cm. Includes bibliographical references. [TR647.D38C55] 74-33228
1. Day, Fred Holland, 1864-1933. 2. Photography, Artistic—Exhibitions. I. Day, Fred Holland, 1864-1933. II. Wellesley College. Jewett Arts Center.

COLNAGHI (P. & D.) & Company, ltd., London. 779'.074'02132
Photography : the first eighty years : [catalogue of an exhibition] 27 October to 1 December 1976 / [presented by P. & D. Colnaghi in association with Howard Ricketts and Harry Lunn, Jnr.]. London : P. & D. Colhaghi, c1976. 262 p. : ill. ; 25 cm. Includes index. Bibliography: p. 259-260. [TR646G72L6623 1976] 77-361666 £6.00
1. Photography, Artistic—Exhibitions. I. Ricketts, Howard. II. Lunn, Harry. III. Title.

COLUMBIA College, Chicago. Chicago Photographic Gallery. 779'.092'2
Contemporary trends : Bernhard, Crane, Dater, Gibson, Gowin, Heinecken, Hosoe, Metzker, Siskind, Walker, Welpott, White : [exhibition], the Chicago Photographic Gallery of Columbia College, Chicago, Illinois / [edited by Howard Kaplan]. Chicago : The Gallery, c1976. 62 p. : ill. (some col.) ; 22 x 23 cm. Includes bibliographical references. [TR646.U6C523] 76-12197

photographic exhibition. Edited by Charles Springman. [Raleigh, 1970?] [48] p. (chiefly illus.) 22 x 23 cm. [TR646.U6R346] 73-172029
1. Photography, Artistic—Exhibitions. 2. North Carolina—Description and travel—Views. I. Springman, Charles, ed. II. Title.

NORTH 779'.9'9730740156565 Carolina. University. William Hayes Ackland Memorial Art Center.
The American situation : the camera's century / the William Hayes Ackland Memorial Art Center. Chapel Hill : University of North Carolina, c1975. p. cm. Exhibition held Jan. 11 through Feb. 23, 1976. [TR646.U6C486 1975] 75-28225 ISBN 0-8078-1259-5 : 9.95
1. Photography, Artistic—Exhibitions. I. Title. BIP

PENN, Irving. 779'.092'4
Irving Penn, photographs in platinum metals : images—1947-1975 : [exhibition] September 9-October 11, 1977. New York : Marlborough Gallery, c1977. [32] p. : ill. ; 29 cm. [TR654.P45] 77-153303
1. Photography, Artistic—Exhibitions. 2. Photography—Printing processes—Platinotype—Exhibitions. I. Marlborough Gallery. II. Title.

PHILADELPHIA College of Art. 779'.0924
Frederick Sommer; an exhibition of photographs at Philadelphia College of Art, November 1 through November 30, 1968. [Philadelphia, 1968] 27 p. plates, ports. 32 cm. [TR647.S62P45] 76-286099
1. Sommer, Frederick, 1905- 2. Photography, Artistic—Exhibitions.

†*PHOTOGRAPHY and* 779'.0973 *language* / Lew Thomas, editor ; Donna-Lee Phillips, design. San Francisco : Camerawork Press ; [New York : distributed by Whirlwind Books, c1977] 86 p. : ill. ; 31 cm. "From the exhibition ... shown simultaneously at Camerawork Gallery and La Mamelle's Arts Center, San Francisco, 1976." Bibliography: p. 83. [TR646.U6S366] 76-43622 ISBN 0-917986-01-6 : 6.95
1. Photography, Artistic—Exhibitions. I. Thomas, Lew. II. Phillips, Donna-Lee. III. Camerawork Gallery. IV. La Mamelle's Arts Center.

RICE, Leland, 1940- 779'.092'4
The photography of Leland Rice : Hirshhorn Museum and Sculpture Garden, Smithsonian Institution. [Washington] : Smithsonian Institution Press, [1977] c1976. [12] p. : ill. ; 29 cm. Exhibition held June 16-Sept. 5, 1977. [TR647.R4 1977] 77-372239
1. Photography, Artistic—Exhibitions. I. Hirshhorn Museum and Sculpture Garden. II. Title.

RINKE, Klaus, 1939- 779'.092'4
Klaus Rinke : [catalogue of an exhibition held at the] Museum of Modern Art, Oxford, January 11th-February 15th 1976 / [translation from the German by Barbara Flynn]. [Oxford] : [The Museum], [1976] [176] p. : ill. ; 26 cm. [TR647.R46 1976] 77-363174
1. Photography, Artistic—Exhibitions. I. Museum of Modern Art, Oxford.

ROGOVIN, Milton, 1909- 779'.092'4
Milton Rogovin, lower West Side, Buffalo, New York / James N. Wood ; with an appreciation by Paul Strand. Buffalo : Albright-Knox Art Gallery, c1975. 64 p. : chiefly ill. ; 22 cm. "Appears in conjunction with the exhibition organized by the Albright-Knox Art Gallery, and shown from September 27 to November 9, 1975." [TR647.R62A52] 75-24770
1. Photography, Artistic—Exhibitions. I. Wood, James N. II. Albright-Knox Art Gallery. III. Title.

ROITZ, Charles J., 1935- 779'.092'4
Charles Roitz, photographs and photosculpture : [exhibition] Denver Art Museum, November 30, 1974-December 29, 1974. Denver : Denver Art Museum, [1974] [24] p. : ill. ; 31 cm. [TR647.R64A43] 74-25843 ISBN 0-914738-05-4
1. Photography, Artistic—Exhibitions. I. Denver. Art Museum. II. Title.

ROSENBLUM, Walter, 1919- 779'.092'4
Walter Rosenblum, photographer : [catalogue] : Fogg Art Museum, Harvard University, exhibition, March 7 through April 13, 1975. [Cambridge, Mass.] : The Museum, [1975] c1974. [28] p. : ill. ; 22 x 24 cm. Bibliography: p. [26] [TR647.R67A57 1975] 75-313235
1. Photography, Artistic—Exhibitions. I. Harvard University. William Hayes Fogg Art Museum.

ROSENBLUM, Walter, 1919- 779'.092'4
Walter Rosenblum retrospective. [Flushing, N.Y. : Queens Museum], c1976. [24] p. : ill. ; 21 cm. Cover title. Exhibition held Oct. 2-Nov. 14, 1976, at the Queens Museum, Flushing, N.Y. Bibliography: p. [22] [TR647.R67 1976] 76-381967
1. Photography, Artistic—Exhibitions. 2. Photography, Documentary—Exhibitions. I. Queens Museum. II. Title.

RUETHER, David. 779'.0924
Soft images. [Ithaca, N.Y.] Andrew Dickson White Museum of Art, Cornell University [1970] [6] p., [24] plates. 22 cm. "Complete catalog reproducing each print full scale by the offset process" of an exhibition held (1970?) at Andrew Dickson White Museum of Art, Cornell University. [TR647.R8A56] 78-140211
1. Photography, Artistic—Exhibitions. I. Cornell University. Andrew Dickson White Museum of Art. II. Title.

RUTGERS 779'.074'014942 University, New Brunswick, N.J. University Art Gallery.
New Jersey photography : [catalogue of] a juried exhibition of New Jersey photographers, University Art Gallery, Rutgers, the State University, New Brunswick, New Jersey, March 10-April 14. [s.l. : s.n., 1974] (Cranford, N.J. : Olsen Press) [35] p. : chiefly ill. ; 22 x 28 cm. [TR646.U6N417 1974] 74-620021
1. Photography, Artistic—Exhibitions. I. Title.

SAN Francisco. 779'.074'013 Museum of Art.
Women of photography : an historical survey : [exhibition] / organized by San Francisco Museum of Art, April 18-June 15, 1975 ; Museum of New Mexico, Santa Fe, Sept. 15-Oct. 26, 1975, Art History Galleries, University of Wisconsin, Milwaukee, Feb. 2-March 14, 1976, Wellesley College Museum, Wellesley, Mass., April 12-May 23, 1976. [San Francisco] : The Museum, c1975. ca. 150 p. : ill. ; 31 cm. Catalog. Includes a bibliography. [TR646.U6S368 1975] 75-5018
1. Photography, Artistic—Exhibitions. 2. Women photographers. I. Santa Fe, N.M. Museum of New Mexico. II. Wisconsin. University. Art History Galleries. III. Wellesley College. Jewett Arts Center. IV. Title.

SAN 779'.2'097946107401471 *Francisco renaissance* : photographs of the '50s and '60s : November 24 through December 20, 1975, Gotham Book Mart Gallery, New York / edited and with an introd. by Merril Greene ; exhibition organized by Robert E. Johnson. New York : Gotham Book Mart, c1975. [20] p. : ill. ; 28 cm. [TR646.U6N486] 75-39891 2.95
1. Photography, Artistic—Exhibitions. I. Greene, Merril. II. Johnson, Robert E. III. Gotham Book Mart and Gallery.

STRUSS, Karl, 1886- 779'.092'4
Karl Struss, man with a camera : the artist-photographer in New York and Hollywood ... Cranbrook Academy of Art/Museum ... [et al.] / [exhibition organized, and catalogue prepared, researched, written, and edited by Susan and John Harvith]. Bloomfield Hills, Mich. : The Museum, c1976. viii, 104 p. : ill. ; 26 cm. Bibliography: p. 103-104. [TR647.S88A44] 76-1404
1. Struss, Karl, 1886- 2. Photography, Artistic—Exhibitions. 3. Cinematographers—Correspondence, reminiscences, etc. I. Harvith, Susan. II. Harvith, John. III. Cranbrook Academy of Art, Bloomfield Hills, Mich. Museum. IV. Title.

SZARKOWSKI, John. 779'.092'2
New Japanese photography, edited by John Szarkowski and Shoji Yamagishi. New York, Museum of Modern Art; distributed by New York Graphic Society, Greenwich, Conn. [1974] 111 p. chiefly illus. 27 cm. Introd. in English and Japanese. Based on an exhibition held at Museum of Modern Art, New York. [TR646.U6N488] 73-91048 ISBN 0-87070-503-2 8.95
1. Photography, Artistic—Exhibitions. 2. Photographers—Japan. I. Yamagishi, Shoji, joint author. II. New York (City). Museum of Modern Art. III. Title. BIP

THE Target 779'.0973'07401641411 *collection of American photography* : [exhibition], February 25-May 1, 1977 / pref. by William C. Agee ; edited, and with an introd. by Anne Tucker. Houston : Museum of Fine Arts, c1976. 64 p. : chiefly ill. ; 21 cm. [TR646.U6H687] 76-152093
1. Photography, Artistic—Exhibitions. I. Tucker, Anne. II. Houston, Tex. Museum of Fine Arts.

TERRY Fox / 709'.2'4 Brenda Richardson. Berkeley, [Calif.] : University Art Museum, 1973. ca. 150 p. : ill. ; 21 x 26 cm. Includes filmography and bibliography. [TR647.F68A57] 73-620112
1. Fox, Terry, 1943- 2. Photography, Artistic—Exhibitions. I. Richardson, Brenda. II. California. University. Art Museum.

TURNER, Peter. 779'.074'02132
Other eyes : an exhibition of photographs taken in the British Isles ... / [catalog by Peter Turner]. [London] : Arts Council of Great Britain, 1976. [26] p. : ill. ; 21 cm. Photographs by Izis, Bruce Davidson, Burk Uzzle, Paul Caponigro, Gilles Peress, Charles Harbutt, Dennis Hearne, Mark Cohen, Thomas Joshua Cooper and Ralph Gibson. [TR646.G72L668] 77-366715 ISBN 0-7287-0102-2 : £0.45
1. Photography, Artistic—Exhibitions. I. Bidermanas, Izis. II. Arts Council of Great Britain. III. Title.

UNITED States. 779'.09485'0740153 Library of Congress.
Contemporary photographs from Sweden; an exhibition of the work of the TIO Photographers. Washington, 1971. [18] p. illus. 18 x 21 cm. Introd. signed by Alan Fern, Assistant Chief, Prints and Photographs Division. [TR646.U5] 70-37008 ISBN 0-8444-0011-4
1. Photography, Artistic—Exhibitions. I. Fern, Alan Maxwell, 1930- II. Tio fotografer. III. Title.

UNIVERSITY of 779'.0973'074015271 Maryland, Baltimore County. Library.
Extended realism : from an exhibition produced by the University of Maryland Baltimore County Library : photographs / by M. Richard Kirstel ... [et al.]. [Baltimore] : The Library, c1976. [88] p. : chiefly ill. ; 23 cm. [TR646.U6B348 1976] 75-37333
1. Photography, Artistic—Exhibitions. I. Kirstel, M. Richard, 1936- II. Title.

VANDERPANT, John. 779'.092'4
John Vanderpant photographs = John Vanderpant photographies / Charles C. Hill. Ottawa : National Gallery of Canada, 1976. 96 p. : chiefly ill. ; 24 cm. English and French. Bibliography: p. 93-96. [TR647.V35 1976] 77-364480 ISBN 0-88884-333-X
1. Photography, Artistic—Exhibitions. I. Hill, Charles C. II. Title.

VAN HAMERSVELD, John. 779'.092'4
So-Cal 76 / [John Van Hamersveld]. Long Beach, Calif. : Long Beach Museum of Art, c1976. 51 p. : chiefly ill. ; 31 cm. Catalog of an exhibition held June 27-July 25, 1976. "Bicentennial project no. 017205." [TR647.V36 1976] 76-18983
1. Photography, Artistic—Exhibitions. I. Long Beach, Calif. Museum of Art. II. Title.

WALKER Art Center, 779'.092'2 Minneapolis.
Photographers Midwest invitational. [Minneapolis, 1973] 1 v. (unpaged) illus. 28 cm. Catalog of an exhibition organized by the Center; shown there Sept. 9-Oct. 21, 1973, and later at four other museums. [TR646.U6M5688 1973] 73-87442
1. Photography, Artistic—Exhibitions. I. Title.

WALKER Art 779'.074'0176579 Center, Minneapolis.
Projected images : Peter Campus, Rockne Krebs, Paul Sharits, Michael Snow, Ted Victoria, Robert Whitman : Walker Art Center, 21 September-3 November 1974 : an exhibition / organized by Walker Art Center with the assistance of the Bush Foundation. [Minneapolis] : The Center, c1974. 46 p. : ill. (some col.) ; 28 cm. Includes bibliographies. [TR646.U6M5688 1974] 74-18860
1. Photography, Artistic—Exhibitions. I. Title.

WELLS, Lynton, 1940- 779
Lynton Wells. [Syracuse, N.Y., Printed by Estabrook Print., 1971] [10] p. (chiefly illus.) 19 x 28 cm. Cover title. Catalog of the exhibition held at the Everson Museum of Art, Syracuse, N.Y., Nov. 22-Dec. 17, 1971; and at the Cranbrook Academy of Art, Bloomfield Hills, Mich., Jan. 25-Feb. 27, 1972. Bibliography: p. [1] [TR647.W4A45] 72-185583
1. Photography, Artistic—Exhibitions. I. Everson Museum of Art of Syracuse and Onondaga County. II. Cranbrook Academy of Art, Bloomfield Hills, Mich.

WHITE, Minor. 770'.5 s
Octave of prayer; an exhibition on a theme. New York, Aperture, 1972. 91 p. (chiefly illus.) 25 cm. (Aperture, v. 17, no. 1) Issued in connection with the exhibition held Oct. 27-Nov. 26, 1972, in the Hayden Gallery and sponsored by the MIT Committee on the Visual Arts. [TR1.A62 vol. 17, no. 1] [TR646.U6] 779'.074'01444 72-87368
1. Photography, Artistic—Exhibitions. I. Hayden Gallery. II. Massachusetts Institute of Technology. Committee on the Visual Arts. III. Title. IV. Series. BIP

WHITECHAPEL Art 779'.092'4 Gallery, London.
Michael Druks, everybody's own yard, a photographic study : [catalogue of an exhibition held in the] Ideas Gallery [of Whitechapel Art Gallery], 26 February-4 April 1976. London : Whitechapel Art Gallery, [1976] 8 p. : ill., ports. ; 30 cm. Bibliography: p. 5. [TR647.D79W48 1976] 76-371762 ISBN 0-85488-029-1 : £0.32
1. Photography, Artistic—Exhibitions. I. Druks, Michael, 1940- II. Title.

WORTH, Don, 1924- 779'.092'4
Don Worth; photographs, 1956-1972. [San Francisco, 1973] [16] p. illus. 26 cm. Exhibition presented by the San Francisco Museum of Art, Jan. 16-Mar. 25, 1973. [TR647.W67A44] 73-159223
1. Photography, Artistic—Exhibitions. I. San Francisco. Museum of Art.

Photography, Artistic—Hist.

SCHARF, Aaron, 1922- 770.11
Creative photography. London, Studio Vista; New York, Reinhold Pub. Corp. 965] 95 p. illus. 21 cm. [TR650.S39] 65-13370
1. Photography, Artistic—Hist. I. Title.

Photography, Artistic—History and criticism.

COLEMAN, Allan D. 770'.8
Light readings : a photography critic's writings, 1968-1978 / A. D. Coleman. New York : Oxford University Press, 1979. p. cm. [TR642.C64] 78-11891 ISBN 0-19-502516-4 : 14.95
1. Photography, Artistic—History and criticism. I. Title. BIP

HARTMANN, Sadakichi, 1867-1944. 770
The vailant knights of Daguerre : selected critical essays on photography and profiles of photographic pioneers / by Sadakichi Hartmann ; edited by Harry W. Lawton and George Knox, with the collaboration of Wistaria Hartmann Linton ; foreword by Thomas F. Barrow ; bibliography compiled by Michael Elderman. Berkeley : University of California Press, c1978. xiii, 364 p. : ill. ; 28 cm. Includes index. Bibliography: p. 335-358. [TR642.H37

1978] 76-47987 ISBN 0-520-03356-6 : 25.00
1. Hartmann, Sadakichi, 1867-1944. 2. Photography, Artistic—History and criticism. I. Lawton, Harry W. II. Knox, George. III. Linton, Wistaria Hartmann. IV. Title.

Photography, Artistic—Juvenile literature.

GLUBOK, Shirley. 770
The art of photography / by Shirley Glubok ; designed by Gerard Nook. New York : Macmillan, c1977. 48 p. : ill. ; 26 cm. A survey of photography as a fine art from the 1830's to the present, focusing on outstanding photographers and their work. [TR642.G59] 77-4985 ISBN 0-02-736680-4 : 7.95
1. Photography, Artistic—Juvenile literature. I. Title.

Photography, Artistic—Study and teaching—United States.

LEWIS, Steven, 1947- 770
Photography: source & resource; a source book for creative photography, by Steven Lewis, James McQuaid & David Tait. [State College, Pa.] Turnip Press; [distributed exclusively by Light Impressions, Rochester, N.Y., 1973] viii, 214 p. 28 cm. Bibliography: p. 162-170. [TR161.L48] 73-88294 6.00 (pbk.).
1. Photography, Artistic—Study and teaching—United States. 2. Photography, Artistic—Directories. I. McQuaid, James, joint author. II. Tait, David, 1946- joint author. III. Title.

Photography as a profession.

ABEL, Charles, 1891- 770.692
Photography: careers & opportunities for you. Philadelphia, Chilton Co., c1961. 104p. (Modern camera guide series) 61-5894 2.95;1.95pap.,
1. Photography as a profession. I. Title.

BENNETT, Edna. 770.692
Careers in photography. New York, Universal Photo Books [1962] 128p. illus. 20cm. [TR154.B4] 61-14247
1. Photography as a profession. I. Title.

DESCHIN, Jacob 770.692
Photography in your future. New York, Macmillan [c.1965] viii, 181p. illus. 21cm. Bibl. [TR154.D4] 64-10967 3.95; 3.96 bds., lib. ed.,
1. Photography as a profession. I. Title.

GOLDSMITH, Arthur A. 770.2'32
The photography game; what it is and how to play it, by Arthur Goldsmith. New York, Viking Press [1971] 160 p. illus., ports. 24 cm. (A Studio book) [TR154.G64] 74-101784 ISBN 0-670-55280-1 8.95
1. Photography as a profession. 2. Photography, Commercial. I. Title.

HOOD, Robert E 770.692
Find a career in photography. New York, Putnam [1959] 159p. illus. 21cm. [TR190.H6] 59-11439
1. Photography as a profession. I. Title.

JOHNSON, Bervin M. 770.2'32
Opportunities in photography careers, by Bervin M. Johnson. New York, Educational Books Division of Universal Pub. and Distributing Corp. [1969] 144 p. 21 cm. (Vocational guidance manuals, V171) Bibliography: p. 132-133. [TR154.J64] 77-76323
1. Photography as a profession. I. Title. II. Title: Photography careers. BIP

KEPPLER, Victor 770.692
Your future in photography. New York, Rosen [c.1965] 159p. 20cm. (Careers in depth [54]) Bibl. [TR190.K4] 65-11626 2.95
1. Photography as a profession. I. Title. BIP

KEPPLER, Victor. 770'.232
Your future in photography. [Rev. ed.] New York, R. Rosen Press [1970] 159 p. illus. 23 cm. (Careers in depth, 66) Discusses the requirements, advantages, and drawbacks of many different kinds of photographic careers. [TR154.K45 1970] 78-88830 ISBN 0-8239-0180-7
1. Photography as a profession. I. Title.

KEPPLER, Victor. 770.2'32
Your future in photography. [Rev. ed.] New York, Arco [1971] 159 p. 21 cm. (Arco-Rosen career guidance series) Bibliography: p. 159. Discusses the skills and training needed for a career in photography and the opportunities in that field. [TR154.K45 1971] 71-114104 ISBN 0-668-02262-0 1.95
1. Photography as a profession. I. Title.

KEPPLER, Victor. 770'.232
Your future in photography / Victor Keppler. 2d ed. New York : Arco, 1974. 158 p. ; 21 cm. (Arco-Rosen career guidance series) Bibliography: p. 158. Discusses the skills and training needed for a career in photography and the opportunities in that field. [TR154.K45 1974] 74-80997 ISBN 0-668-01583-7 : 1.95
1. Photography as a profession. I. Title.

LIEBERS, Arthur, 1913- 770'.232
You can be a professional photographer. New York : Lothrop, Lee & Shepard Co., 1979. p. cm. (His Vocations in trades) Includes index. Bibliography: p. Discusses the education and preparation needed for a career in photography and how to get information about jobs in such areas as portrait, fashion, news, industrial, medical, and undersea photography. [TR154.L53] 79-12484 ISBN 0-688-41890-2. lib.bdg. : 6.25
1. Photography—Vocational guidance—Juvenile literature. I. Title. BIP

PINNEY, Roy. 770.692
Careers with a camera. [1st ed.] Philadelphia, Lippincott [1964] 128 p. illus., ports. 21 cm. [TR190.P5] 64-19045
1. Photography as a profession. I. Title.

Photography—Biography.

BEATON, Cecil Walter Hardy, Sir, 1904- 770'.92'2 B
The magic image : the genius of photography from 1839 to the present day / Cecil Beaton and Gail Buckland. 1st American ed. Boston : Little, Brown, c1975. 304 p. : ill. (some col.) ; 29 cm. [TR139.B4 1975] 74-7107 19.95
1. Photography—Biography. 2. Photography—History. I. Buckland, Gail, joint author. II. Title. BIP

SIPLEY, Louis Walton. 770.922
Photography's great inventors, selected by an international committee for the International Photography Hall of Fame. Philadelphia, American Museum of Photography [1965] xix, 170 p. illus., ports. 24 cm. "A selected chronology of photography" p. 137-150. Includes bibliographies. [TR139.S5] 65-28010
1. Photography — Biog. I. American Museum of Photography, Philadelphia. II. Title.

Photography—Business methods.

GUTENBERG, Arthur W. 658.9177
Profitable studio management, by Arthur W. Gutenberg, Val K. Alberecht. Philadelphia, Chilton [c.1965] 208p. illus. 24cm. [TR581.G8] 65-17119 6.95
1. Photography—Business methods. I. Albrecht, Val K., joint author. II. Title.

SCHWARZ, Theodore. 770.2'32
The business side of photography. New York, Amphoto [1969] 159 p. illus. 24 cm. [TR581.S34] 69-13153 7.95
1. Photography—Business methods. I. Title.

SCHWARZ, Theodore. 770.2'32
The business side of photography. Philadelphia, Chilton [1969] 159 p. illus. 24 cm. [TR581.S34 1969b] 71-6376 7.95
1. Photography—Business methods. I. Title. BIP

Photography, Close-up.

ADAMS, Charles Hubert. 770.282
Close range photography with standard or home-made equipment. London, New York, Focal Press [1956] 191p. illus. 19cm. [TR683.A3] 56-16897
1. Photography, Close-up. I. Title.

BOMBACK, Edward S. 778.324
Close-ups and copying in colour. London, Fountain [dist. New York, Morgan & Morgan, 1964, c.1962] 93p. illus. (pt. col.) diagrs. 17cm. (Fountain photobk. ser.) 64-3080 2.95 bds.,
1. Photography, Close-up. 2. Photography—Copying. 3. Color photography. I. Title.

†CLOSE-UP photography & photomacrography. 778.3'24 Rochester, N.Y. : [Professional and Finishing Markets Division], Eastman Kodak Co., c1977. 2 v. in 1 (160 p.) : ill. ; 28 cm. (Kodak publication ; no. N-12) Previous editions by H. L. Gibson. [TR683.G5 1977] 77-88930 ISBN 0-87985-206-2 : 8.00
1. Photography, Close-up. 2. Macrophotography. I. Gibson, Henry Louis, 1906- Close-up photography and photomacrography.

CROY, Otto R 1902- 778.324
Camera close up; same-size and larger than life photography. [English translation by L. A. Mannheim] London, New York, Focal Press [1961] 240 p. illus. 24 cm. Translation of Alles Uber Nahufnahmen. [TR683.C713] 61-66056
1. Photography, Close-up. I. Title.

GIBSON, Henry Louis, 1906- 778.3'24
Close-up photography and photomacrography, by H. Lou Gibson. [1st. combined ed.] Rochester, Eastman Kodak Co. [1970] 88, 95, 9 p. illus. (part col.) 29 cm. (Kodak technical publication, no. N-16) Includes bibliographies. [TR683.G5 1970] 78-20232
1. Photography, Close-up. I. Title. BIP

GIBSON, Henry Louis, 1906- 778.3'24
Close-up photography and photomacrography / by H. Lou Gibson. 2d combined ed. Rochester, N.Y. : Eastman Kodak Co., Professional and Finishing Markets Division, c1975. 88, 110 p. : ill. ; 29 cm. (Kodak technical publication ; N-16) Includes bibliographies. [TR683.G5 1975] 75-332340 ISBN 0-87985-160-0 : 13.95
1. Photography, Close-up. 2. Macrophotography. I. Title.

MARTIN, Harold. 778.324
Close-up photography with your camera. New York, Amphoto [1961] 122p. illus. 21cm. [TR683.M33] 61-6415
1. Photography, Close-up. I. Title.

OWENS, William J. 778.3'24
Close-up photography / by William J. Owens. Los Angeles : Petersen Pub. Co., [1975] 80 p. : ill. ; 28 cm. (Petersen's how-to photographic library) [TR683.O9] 74-31880 ISBN 0-8227-0094-8 pbk. : 2.95
1. Photography, Close-up. I. Title. BIP

RAY, Sidney F. 778.3'24
The Focalguide to close-ups / Sidney Ray. London : Focal Press ; New York : Focal/Hastings House, c1978. 188 p. : ill. (some col.) ; 19 cm. Includes index. [TR683.R39] 79-301182 ISBN 0-8038-2336-3 (Focal/Hastings House) : 6.95
1. Photography, Close-up. I. Title. BIP

Photography—Collected works.

EASTMAN Kodak Company. Research Laboratories. v. 12
Scientific publications from the Kodak Laboratories. Rochester, N. Y. 1966 v. illus., ports. 28 cm. Supersedes its Abridged scientific publications from the Kodak Research Laboratories. Issued by the laboratories' Dept. of Information Services. Issued in four sections: I. Organic, polymer and biological chemistry; II. Analytical and physical chemistry and chemical engineering; III. Physics, mathematics, and engineering; IV. Photographic science and technology. [TR7.E32] 68-3605
1. Photography—Collected works. 2. Science—Collected works. I. Eastman Kodak Company. Research Laboratories. Dept. of Information Services. II. Title.

PHOTO guide 1 v. 12
London, New York, Focal Press, 1941- no. illus., plates., diagrs. 16cm. Title varies: 1- The New photo guide.- A Focal photo guide (cover title) Editor: 1941- A. Kraszna-Krausz. [TR7.P5] 58-42424
1. Photography—Collected works. I. Kraszna-Krausz, Andor, 1904- ed.

Photography, Commercial.

ABEL, Charles, 1891- 770.69
Tested money-making ideas for photographers. New York, Greenberg [1952] 280 p. illus. 24 cm. [HF6201.P55A2] 52-5617
1. Photography, Commercial. 2. Photography—Portraits. I. Title.

AHLERS, Arvel W 1915- 658.8977
How & where to sell your pictures overseas, with over 560 foreign publication market listings [by] Arvel W. Ahlers & Paul Webb. Philadelphia, Chilton Books, 1963. 111 p. illus. Port. 21 cm. (Modern camera guide series) [TR690.A35] 63-23102
1. Photography, Commerical. I. -Webb, Paul V., joint author. II. Title. III. Series.

AHLERS, Arvel W., 1915- 658.89'77
Where & how to sell your photographs / by Arvel W. Ahlers. 7th rev. ed. Garden City, N.Y. : Amphoto, [1974] c1975. 253 p. : ill. ; 26 cm. First-6th ed. published under title: Where and how to sell your pictures. Includes index. [TR690.A35 1975] 74-83644 ISBN 0-8174-0583-6 : 7.95
1. Photography, Commercial. I. Title.

BENNETT, Edna. v. 12
How to sell your pictures at a profit; the photographer's market place, by E. Bennett and R. Maschke. Englewood, N. J. 158 p. illus. 19 cm. Includes bibliography. [NUC66-1855]
1. Photography, Commercial. I. Maschke, R., joint author. II. Title.

CORNFIELD, Jim. 770'.92'4
The photo illustration, Bert Stern / text by Jim Cornfield, with the editors of Alskog, inc. [New York] : T. Y. Crowell, [1974] 95 p. : ill. (some col.) ; 29 cm. (Masters of contemporary photography) [TR140.S687C67] 74-8228 ISBN 0-690-00617-9 : 7.95. ISBN 0-690-00618-7 pbk. : 3.95
1. Stern, Bert. 2. Photography, Commercial. I. Stern, Bert. II. Alskog, inc. III. Title.

EASTMAN Kodak Company. 770'.28
Photography with large format cameras. [1st ed.] Rochester, N.Y. [1973] 48 p. illus. 29 cm. (Kodak publication no. 0-18H) [TR690.E2] 72-96319 ISBN 0-87985-066-3 6.95
1. Photography, Commercial. I. Title. BIP

HANSON, Eugene Montgomery 770.692
How to make money in photography. New York, American Photographic Book Pub. Co. [1960,c. 1955] x, 302p. illus. 20cm. 54-12860 1.95 pap.,
1. Photography, Commercial. I. Title.

HARTER, Walter L 778.9907
How to shoot and sell money-making pictures. New York, Amphoto [1961] 121p. illus. 21cm. [TR690.H35] 61-8773
1. Photography, Commercial. I. Title.

HARTER, Walter L. 770'.23
How to shoot and sell money-making pictures, by Walter L. Harter. 2d ed. New York, Amphoto [1972] 123 p. illus. 22 cm. [TR690.2.H37 1972] 70-187819 ISBN 0-8174-0460-0 3.50
1. Photography, Commercial. I. Title.

HOLDEN, Stan. 658'.91'77
20 ways to make money in photography / Stan Holden. Garden City, N.Y. : Amphoto, c1977. 96 p., [2] leaves of plates : ill. ; 26 cm. Includes index. [TR690.H54] 77-74673 ISBN 0-8174-2106-8 pbk. : 5.95
1. Photography, Commercial. I. Title.

KELLEY, Victor E., 1935- 770'.232
How to get into the business of photography / by Victor E. Kelley. Palm Springs, Calif. : ETC Publications, c1979. p. cm. Includes index. [TR690.K34] 78-31195 ISBN 0-88280-067-1 : 8.95
1. Photography, Commercial. I. Title.

KOVARIK, Thomas J. 070.5'2
The photo marketplace, by Thomas J. Kovarik and John A. Hurst. [Rev.] Mundelein, Ill., Career Institute [1973, c1972] 112 p. 23 cm. [TR690.K68] 72-90502 ISBN 0-911744-52-5 3.95
1. Photography, Commercial. I. Hurst, John A., joint author. II. Title.

LANGFORD, Michael John, 1933- 770'.232
Professional photography: principles in practice / [by] Michael J. Langford. London ; New York : Focal Press, 1974. 312 p., [24] p. of plates. : ill. (some col.), forms ; 25 cm. Includes index. Bibliography: p. 301-304. [TR690.L26] 74-183325 ISBN 0-240-50843-2 : £4.75
1. Photography, Commercial. 2. Photography—Business. I. Title. BIP

MELNITSKY, Benjamin, 1919- 778
Industrial and business photography for amateurs. New York, Greenberg [1957] 124p. illus. 20cm. [TR690.M4] 57-12503
1. Photography, Commercial. I. Title.

MILLER, Gary. 658'.91'77
Free-lance photography / by Gary Miller. Los Angeles, Calif. : Petersen Pub. Co., [1975] 80 p. : ill. ; 28 cm. (Petersen's how-to photographic library) [TR690.2.M54] 74-29450 ISBN 0-8227-0090-5 pbk. : 2.95
1. Photography, Commercial. I. Title.

PERRY, Robin. 770'.92'4
Creative color photography of Robin Perry. Garden City, N.Y. : American Photographic Book Pub. Co., [1974] 128 p. : col. ill. ; 27 cm. [TR690.P43] 74-83491 ISBN 0-8174-0575-5 : 14.95
1. Photography, Commercial. 2. Color photography. I. Title. BIP

PERRY, Robin. 770
Photography for the professionals / by Robin Perry. Waterford, Conn. : Livingston Press, c1976. 325 p. ; 25 cm. [TR690.P44] 75-31045 ISBN 0-915772-02-7 : 12.95
1. Photography, Commercial. I. Title.

PHOTO market survey. 658.8'0977
Little Falls, N.J., Singer Communications, 1971. 1 v. (loose-leaf) illus. 30 cm. [TR690.P46] 71-183543
1. Photography, Commercial. 2. Glamour photography.

PINKARD, Bruce, 1932- 770'.28
Creative techniques in studio photography / Bruce Pinkard. Philadelphia : Lippincott, 1978. p. cm. Includes index. Bibliography p. [TR690.P49] 78-26109 ISBN 0-397-01353-1 : 17.50
1. Photography, Commercial. 2. Photography, Advertising. I. Title.

PINKARD, Bruce, 1932- 770'.28
Creative techniques in studio photography / Bruce Pinkard. Philadelphia : Lippincott, 1978. p. cm. Includes index. Bibliography p. [TR690.P49] 78-26109 ISBN 0-397-01353-1 : 17.50
1. Photography, Commercial. 2. Photography, Advertising. I. Title. BIP

SAGARA, Peter. 770.2'3
Written on film, by Peter Sagara, with R. E. Simon, Jr. [Chicago, Childrens Press, 1970] 64 p. illus., ports. 19 cm. (An Open door book) Autobiographical. A Japanese-American tells how he became an advertising photographer. Includes a section on the requirements for and opportunities in this profession. [TR140.S33A37] 92 69-14685
I. Simon, Richard Edward, 1945- joint author. II. Title.

SCHWARZ, Theodore. 658'.91'77
How to make money with your camera / Ted Schwarz. Tucson, Az. : H. P. Books, 1974. 192 p. : ill. ; 28 cm. (The New photo series ; 2) Caption title. [TR690.S36] 74-82517 ISBN 0-912656-30-1 : 5.95
1. Photography, Commercial. I. Title. BIP

SCHWARZ, Theodore. 658'.91'77
How to start a professional photography business / Ted Schwarz. Chicago : H. Regnery Co., c1976. viii, 276 p. ; 24 cm. Includes index. [TR581.S35 1976] 75-92989 ISBN 0-8092-8134-1 : 12.95 ISBN 0-8092-8070-1 pbk. :
1. Photography, Commercial. I. Title. BIP

TAYLOR, Alan Faulkner 770
Photography in commerce and industry. London, Fountain [dist. New York, Morgan & Morgan, 1964, c.1962] 416p. illus. (pt. col.) diagrs. 22cm. 64-3395 15.95
1. Photography, Commercial. 2. Photography, Industrial. I. Title.

Photography—Competitions.

PAGE, Andre. 770
Photographs for exhibitions and competitions; illustrations by the author. London, Pelham, 1973. 135 p. illus. 21 cm. Includes index. [TR147.P33] 74-160608 ISBN 0-7207-0623-8
1. Photography—Competitions. I. Title.
Distributed by Transatlantic Arts; 7.50. BIP

SIMMONS, Robert, 1931- 770.79
Fullname:RobertPrestonSimmons.
Guide to winning photo contests. New York, Greenberg, c1956. 143 p. illus. 20 cm. (The Modern camera guide series) [TR650.S48] 56-9280
1. Photography — Competitions. 2. Photography-Handbooks, manuals, etc. I. Title.

Photography, Composite.

ADES, Dawn. 778.8
Photomontage / Dawn Ades. London : Thames & Hudson, c1976. 112 p. : 171 ill. ; 28 cm. Chiefly ill. including an annotated list. [TR685.A26 1976b] 76-381256 ISBN 0-500-27080-5 : £2.50
1. Photography, Composite. 2. Propaganda. I. Title.

ADES, Dawn. 778.8
Photomontage / Dawn Ades. 1st American ed. New York : Pantheon Books, c1976. p. cm. [TR685.A26 1976] 76-9472 ISBN 0-394-40899-3. 10.95. ISBN 0-394-73255-3 pbk. : 5.95
1. Photography, Composite. 2. Propaganda. I. Title. BIP

BELDEN Beyda, Janet. 779'.092'4
Chers amis / photos. and text by Janet Belden Beyda, with the collaboration of Frank Beyda ; with an introd. by Nicholas Meyer. New York : Pomerica Press : distributed E. P. Dutton, 1978,c1977 [75] p. : col. ill. ; 30 cm. English translation of Chers amis. [TR685.B4413] 77-84875 ISBN 0-918732-01-8 : write for information
1. Photography, Composite. 2. Photography, Humorous. I. Beyda, Frank, joint author. II. Title.

BINZEN, Bill. 779'.092'4
Doubletake. New York, Grossman Publishers, 1972. 1 v. (chiefly illus.) 15 x 16 cm. [TR685.B56] 72-170610 ISBN 0-670-28054-2 8.95
1. Photography, Composite. I. Title.

CROY, Otto R., 1902- 778.8
Croy's camera trickery / by O. R. Croy ; [English translation by W. D. Emanuel]. New York : Hastings House, 1977. 136 p. : ill. ; 25 cm. (Visual communications books) Translation of Fotomontage und Verfremdung. [TR685.C713] 76-56678 ISBN 0-8038-1216-7 : 13.50
1. Photography, Composite. 2. Photography—Special effects. I. Title. II. Title: Camera trickery. BIP

HEARTFIELD, John, 1891-1968. 779'.9'320943085
Photomontages of the Nazi period / John Heartfield ; [essay by Wieland Herzfelde translated by Eva Bergoffen, all other translations from German by Nancy Reynolds]. New York : Universe Books, 1977. 143 p. : ill. ; 26 cm. Translation of Krieg im Frieden. Bibliography: p. 142. [TR685.H4213] 76-41663 ISBN 0-87663-281-9 : 10.00 ISBN 0-87663-954-6 pbk. : 5.95
1. Heartfield, John, 1891-1968. 2. Photography, Composite. 3. National socialism—Caricatures and cartoons. 4. German wit and humor, Pictorial. I. Herzfelde, Wieland. II. Title. BIP

HICKS, John, 1918- 770'.11
Conceptography. Design/photography [by] John and Regina Hicks. Carmel, Calif., Creative Books [1972] [52] p. illus. 22 x 27 cm. [TR685.H52] 71-189772
1. Photography, Composite. 2. Personality. I. Hicks, Regina, joint author. II. Title. BIP

SATTY, W. 769'.92'4
Time zone [by] Satty. [San Francisco] Straight Arrow Books; [distributed by Quick Fox, New York, 1973] 155 p. (chiefly illus.) 31 cm. [NE654.S24A57 1973] 73-79877 ISBN 0-87932-028-1 5.95 (pbk.)
1. Satty, W. 2. Photography, Composite. I. Title.

STEVENS, Harold. 778.8
Design in photo-college. New York, Reinhold [1967] 100 p. illus. (part col.) 22 cm. [TR685.S7] 67-14161
1. Photography, Composite. 2. Photography, Trick. I. Title.

UELSMANN, Jerry, 1934- 779'.092'4
Portfolio [by] Jerry N. Uelsmann. [Roslyn Heights, N.Y.] Witkin-Berley, 1972. 1 portfolio (4 l., 10 plates) 51 cm. "A limited edition of twenty-five, this portfolio being no. 15." [TR685.U35] 73-162069 390.00
1. Photography, Composite. 2. Photography, Artistic.

UELSMANN, Jerry, 1934- 779'.092'4
Silver meditations / Jerry N. Uelsmann ; introd. by Peter C. Bunnell. Dobbs Ferry, N.Y. : Morgan & Morgan, 1977, c1975. ca. 150 p. : chiefly ill. ; 27 cm. Includes bibliography. [TR685.U36 1977] 75-7850 ISBN 0-87100-087-3 : 10.95
1. Uelsmann, Jerry, 1934- 2. Photography, Composite. I. Title. BIP

Photography, Composite—Exhibitions.

UELSMANN, Jerry, 1934- 779'.0924
Jerry N. Uelsmann. Introd. by Peter C. Bunnell. Fables by Russell Edson. New York [Aperture, inc.] 1970. [93] p. illus. (part col.) 26 cm. Catalogue of an exhibition presented by the Alfred Stieglitz Center of the Philadelphia Museum of Art, Dec. 12, 1970-Feb. 7, 1971. Also published as Aperture, v. 15, no. 4. Bibliography: p. [89]-[91] [TR685.U34] 74-135448 8.50
1. Photography, Composite—Exhibitions. I. Edson, Russell. II. Alfred Stieglitz Center. BIP

Photography—Congresses.

ADVANCE printing of papers 778.3
: summaries, May 1-6, 1977 : 30th annual conference / edited by Lane Jacobsen. Washington : Society of Photographic Scientists and Engineers, c1977. 132 p. : ill. ; 23 cm. Includes bibliographical references and index. [TR5.A38] 77-73034 ISBN 0-89208-090-6 : 12.00
1. Photography—Congresses. I. Jacobsen, Lane. II. Society of Photographic Scientists and Engineers.

BERG, Wolfgang Friedrich, ed. 771.5
Photographic science; symposium; Torino 1963. Ed. by G. Semerano; U. Mazzucato. New York, Focal [dist. Pitman, 1966, c.1965] 248p. illus. 25cm. (Focal lib.) Contributions in English, French or German, with contents notes and index in all 3 languages. Bibl. [TR200.B4] 64-6530 30.00
1. Photography—Congresses. 2. Photographic chemistry—Congresses. I. Title.

BERG, Wolfgang Friedrich, ed. 771.5
Photographic science; symp., Zurich [Sept. 10-16]1961. New York, Fo cal Pr. [1964, c.1963] 456p. illus. 25cm. (Focal lib.) Contributions in English, French or German, with contents notes and index in all 3 languages. Bibl. 64-6530 28.00
1. Photography—Congresses. 2. Photographic chemistry—Congresses. I. Title.

COLLOQUIO internazionale sulla della fotografia, Turin, 1963 770.631
Photographic science; symposium, Torino, 1963. Ed. by G. Semerano, U. Mazzucato. New York, Focal [dist. Pitman, 1966, c.1965] 248p. illus. 25cm. (Focal lib.) Org. by the Univ. of Padua and Bologna with the sponsorship of the Italian Natl. Res. Council. Summaries in English: discussions and index in English, French, German or Italian [TR5.C57 1963] 66-3711 30.00
1. Photography—Congresses. 2. Photographic emulsions—Congresses. I. Semerano, Giovanni, 1907- ed. II. Mazzucato, U., ed. III. Padua. Universita. IV. Title.

CONFERENCE of Photographic Scientists and Engineers, 25th, San Francisco, 1972. 770
Preprints of paper summaries, 25th annual conference. [Washington, Society of Photographic Scientists and Engineers, 1972] xi, 131 p. illus. 22 cm. On cover: SPSE: image 72. Conference held May 9-12, 1972 and sponsored by Society of Photographic Scientists and Engineers and NASA Ames Research Center. Includes bibliographical references. [TR5.C58 1972] 72-172291
1. Photography—Congresses. I. Society of Photographic Scientists and Engineers. II. United States. Ames Research Center, Moffett Field, Calif. III. Title.

CONGRES international de science photographique. Paris, 1965. 771/.5/08
Photographic science: symposium, Paris 1965: ed. by J. Pouradier. London, New York. Focal [1967]. 613p. illus., tables, diagrs. 25cm. (Focal lib.) Contributions in English, French or German, with contents notes and index in all 3 languages. Sponsored by the Societe francaise de photographie and the Institut d'optique. Bibl. [TR200.C6 1965] 67-109875 44.00
1. Photography—Congresses. 2. Photographic chemistry—Congresses. I. Pouradier, J. ed. II. Societe francaise de photographie, Paris. III. Paris. Institut d'optique theorique et appliquee. IV. Title.

INTERNATIONAL Congress on High-Speed Photography. 778.37082
Proceedings. New York, Academic Press. v. illus. 26cm. Biennial. [TR593.I5] 57-9346
1. Photography—Congresses. 2. Photography, High speed. I. Title.

Photography—Copying.

CROY, Otto R., 1902- 778.1
Camera copying and reproduction [Tr. from German by L. A. Mannheim] London, Focal Pr.; New York, Amphoto [dist.] Hastings [c.1962, 1964] 256p. illus. (pt. col.) diagrs., facsims. (pt. col.) 24cm. 64-2230 8.95
1. Photography—Copying. I. Title. BIP

SIMMONS, Robert 1931- 778.324
Fullname:RobertPrestonSimmons.
Close-up photography and copying. Photos, by the author. Philadelphia, Chilton Co., Book Division, c1961. 128 p. illus. 20 cm. (Modern camera guide series, 842) Includes bibliography. [TR470.S54] 61-17152
1. Photography — Copying. 2. Photography, Close-up. I. Title.

WRIGHT, George Benjamin, 1913- 778.1
Copying technique. Minneapolis, American Photography Book Dept. [1951] 93 p. illus. 23 cm. [TR470.W7 1951] 52-10649
1. Photography — Copying. 2. Paintings — Expertising. I. Title.

Photography—Developing and developers.

FLOYD, Wayne 770.2
ABC's of developing, printing, and enlarging. New York, Amphoto; dist. Grosset [c.1964] 96p. illus. 22cm. (Better photo guides; 425) 63-20737 1.00 pap.,
1. Photography—Developing and developers. 2. Photography—Printing processes. 3. Photography—Enlarging. I. Title.

HAIST, Grant. 770.283
Monobath manual. [1st ed.]) Hastings-on-

Hudson [N.Y.] Morgan & Morgan [1966] 168 p. illus. 24 cm. Includes bibliographies. [TR295.H3] 66-20077
1. Photography — Developing and developers. 2. Photography — Printing processes. I. Title. BIP

HALL, Mildred Lillington, ed. 770.283
The photographic darkroom. London, Newnes [dist. Hollywood- by-the-Sea, Fla., Transatlantic, c. 1962] 110p. illus., diagrs. 23cm. A63 3.75
1. Photography—Developing and developers. 2. Photography—Printing processes. I. Title.

JONAS, Paul 770.283
Manual of darkroom procedures and techniques. [2d ed.] Philadelphia, Chilton [c.1962, 1965] 128p. illus. 21cm. (Universal Photo bks.) [TR290.J65] 65-7785 2.95; 1.95 pap.,
1. Photography—Developing and developers. 2. Photography—Printing processes. 3. Photography—Enlarging. I. Title. II. Title: Darkroom procedures and techniques.

MANNHEIM, Ladislaus Andrew, 1925- 772'.1
Do your own film processing [by] L. A. Mannheim. [2d ed.] New York, Amphoto [1969] 76 p. illus. 18 cm. (Viewfinder book) [TR287.M35 1969] 74-92577 1.25
1. Photography—Developing and developers. I. Title.

MANNHEIM, Ladislaus Andrew, 1925- 770.2835
Straightforward developing; how to get the best out of your own flims. 2d ed. London, New York, Focal Press [1952] 96p. illus. 22cm. [TR295.M3 1952] 52-65096
1. Photography—Developing and developers. I. Title.

NATHAN, Simon. 770.283
Good photography's darkroom guide. [Greenwich, Conn., Fawcett Publications, 1957] 144p. illus. 24cm. (A Fawcett book, 332) [TR147.N3] 57-1895
1. Photography—Developing and developers. 2. Photography—Enlarging. I. Title.

NATHAN, Simon. 770.283
Good photography's darkroom guide. New York, Arco Pub. Co., c1957. 139 p. illus. 25 cm. (The Do-it-yourself series) [TR147.N3 1957a] 58-4504
1. Photography—Developing and developers. 2. Photography—Enlarging. I. Title.

SHUMWAY, Herbert D 770.28
Guide to your photo darkroom. Philadelphia, Chilton Co., Book Division, c1959. 159 p. illus. 20 cm. (Modern camera guide series, 442) [TR146.S52] 59-11560
1. Photography — Developing and developers. 2. Photography — Printing processes. I. Title.

SHUMWAY, Herbert D 770.28
Guide to your photo darkroom. 2d print., rev. Philadelphia, Chilton Co., Book Division, 1960. 159 p. illus. 20 cm. (Modern camera guide series, 442) [TR146.S52 1960] 60-52249
1. Photography — Developing and developers. 2. Photography — Printinc processes. I. Title.

STENSVOLD, Mike. 770'.28
Increasing film speed / by Mike Stensvold. Los Angeles : Petersen Pub. Co., c1978. 80 p. : ill. ; 28 cm. (Petersen's how-to photographic library) [TR295.S75] 78-55566 ISBN 0-8227-4022-2 pbk. : 3.95
1. Photography—Developing and develops. I. Title. BIP

WIELLETTE, Joseph. 770'.283
Zone v film processing manual Watertown, Mass., Zone V, [1973] 30 p. illus. 22 cm. Cover title. [TR295.W48] 73-78717 1.95
1. Photography—Developing and developers. I. Title. II. Title: Film processing manual.

Photography—Dictionaries.

THE Encyclopedia of photography; the complete photographer: the comprehensive guide and reference for all photographers. New York, Greystone Press [1967- v. illus. (part col.), maps, ports. (part col.) 29 cm. Published in 1942-43 under title: The complete photographer, a complete guide to amateur and professional photography. Includes bibliographies. [TR145.C674] 67-7720 770'.3
1. Photography—Dictionaries. I. Title: The complete photographer, a complete guide to amateur and professional photography. BIP

THE Encyclopedia of photography : the complete photographer : the comprehensive guide and reference for all photographers / Willard D. Morgan, general editor. New York : Greystone Press, c1974. 20 v. (3840 p., [112] leaves of plates) : ill. (some col.) ; 29 cm. Published 1942-43 under title: The Complete photographer, a complete guide to amateur and professional photography. Includes index. Bibliography: p. 3745-3750. [TR9.E466 1974] 75-309489 770'.3
1. Photography—Dictionaries. I. Morgan, Willard Detering, 1900-1967.

THE Encyclopedia of photography: the complete photographer; the comprehensive guide and reference for all photographers. Willard D. Morgan, general editor. New York, Greystone Press [197 v. illus. (part col.) 29 cm. Published 1942-43 under title: The complete photographer, a complete guide to amateur and professional photography. Includes bibliographies. [TR145.C675] 70-26139 770'.3
1. Photography—Dictionaries. I. Morgan, Willard Detering, 1900- ed.

ENCYCLOPEDIA of photography the complete photographer: the comprehensive guide and reference for all photographers. Wilard D. Morgan, general ed. New York, Greystone [dist. Hawthorn, 1963] illus. (pt. col.) ports. (pt. col.) diagrs. 29cm. Pub. 1942-43 under title: The complete photographer, a complete guide to amateur and professionalphotography. Bibl. 63-5178 3.98 770.3
1. Photography—Dictionaries. I. Morgan, WillardDetering, 1900- ed.

FOCAL. 770.3
New York, Macmillan [1960] 1298p. illus., diagrs. ncyclopedia of photography, The ISSN Desk ed.t).Bibl.p 6.95, plastic cloth 60-51826
1. Photography—Dictionaries.

THE Focal encyclopedia of photography. Revised desk ed. London, New York, Focal P., 1969. xi, 1699 p. illus. 22 cm. [TR9.F6 1969] 77-381067 70/- 770'.3
1. Photography—Dictionaries.

THE Focal encyclopedia of photography. London, New York, Focal Press [1956?] xxxii, 1298p. illus. (part col.) ports. 25cm. Includes bibliographies. [TR9.F6 1956] 57-2631 770.3
1. Photography—Dictionaries. BIP

THE Focal encyclopedia of photography. [Rev.] desk ed. New York, McGraw-Hill [1969] xi, 1699 p. illus. 22 cm. Includes bibliographies. [TR9.F6 1969b] 69-11420 14.00 770'.3
1. Photography—Dictionaries.

FOCAL encyclopedia of photography (The); 2v. New York, Focal [dist. Pitman, 1966, c.1965] 2v. (xlviii, 1699p.) illus. (pt. col.) ports. 25cm. Bibl. [TR9.F6] 65-26661 39.00, set; bxd. 770.3
1. Photography—Dictionaries.

GAUNT, Leonard. 770'.3
The pictorial cyclopedia of photography; edited by Leonard Gaunt and Paul Petzold. London, New York, Focal P., 1968. 703 p. 96 plates, illus. (some col.). 23 cm. [TR9.G38] 68-123978
1. Photography—Dictionaries. I. Petzold, Paul. II. Title. BIP

HARWOOD, Mary, 1950- 770'.3
Running Press glossary of photography language / Mary Harwood. Philadelphia : Running Press, c1977. p. cm. A glossary of the language and terminology of photography for both layman and professional. [TR9.H28] 77-12760 ISBN 0-89471-024-9 pbk. : 1.95. ISBN 0-89471-025-7 lib. bdg. : 9.80
1. Photography—Dictionaries. I. Title.

HASELGROVE, Maurice L. 770.3
Photographers' dictionary. New York, Archer [c.1962, 1963] 202p. illus. 21cm. 63-14427 4.95bds.,
1. Photography—Dictionaries. I. Title.

JONES, Bernard Edward, 1879- ed. 770'.3
Cassell's cyclopaedia of photography / edited by Bernard E. Jones. New York : Arno Press, 1973. viii, 572 p., [23] leaves of plates : ill. ; 26 cm. (The literature of photography) Reprint of the 1911 ed. published by Cassell, London, New York. [TR9.J6 1973] 74-19443 ISBN 0-405-04922-6
1. Photography—Dictionaries. I. Title. II. Series. BIP

PHOTO dictionary; quick reference guide photographic terms, abbreviations, nomenclature for motion picture films and illumination, and a descriptive listing of chemicals used in photography. [1st ed.] New York, Morgan & Morgan [1957] 128p. 21cm. [TR9.P52] 57-11892 770.3
1. Photography—Dictionaries.

THE Pictorial cyclopedia of photography. [1st American ed.] South Brunswick, A. S. Barnes [1968] 703 p. illus. (part col.) 22 cm. Based on the Focal encyclopedia of photography. [TR9.F62 1968] 68-16746 770'.3
1. Photography—Dictionaries.

SNELLING, Henry Hunt, 1816-1897. 770'.3
A dictionary of photographic art / Henry Hunt Snelling and A comprehensive and systematic catalogue of photographic apparatus and material, manufactured, imported, and sold E. Anthony. New York : Arno Press, 1979. p. cm. (The Sources of modern photography) Reprint of the 1854 ed. published by H. H. Snelling, New York. [TR9.S67 1979] 76-23059 ISBN 0-405-09623-2 : 25.00
1. Anthony (E., Firm)—Catalogs. 2. Photography—Dictionaries. 3. Photography—Apparatus and supplies—Catalogs. I. Anthony (E., Firm). A comprehensive and systematic catalogye of photographic apparatus and material, manufactured, imported, and sold by E. Anthony. 1979. II. Title. III. Series.

SOWERBY, Arthur Lindsay McRae. 770.3
Dictionary of photography and reference book for amateur and professional photographers, edited and largely re-written by A. L. M. Sowerby. 18th ed. London, Iliffe: New York, Philosophical Library [1956] vi. 719 p. illus., diagrs., tables. 19 cm. Includes bibliographies. [TR9.S74 1956] 57-2875
1. Photography — Dictionaries. I. Title.

SPENCER, Douglas Arthur, 1901- 770'.3
The Focal dictionary of photographic technologies [by] D. A. Spencer. London, New York, Focal Press, 1973. xvi, 725 p. illus. 23 cm. Bibliography: p. 719-725. [TR9.S77 1973b] 73-168485 ISBN 0-240-50747-9 £8.50
1. Photography—Dictionaries. I. Title.

SPENCER, Douglas Arthur, 1901- 770'.3
The focal dictionary of photographic technologies, by Douglas A. Spencer. Englewood Cliffs, N.J., Prentice-Hall [1973] p. Bibliography: p. [TR9.S77] 72-97893 ISBN 0-13-322719-7 39.95
1. Photography—Dictionaries. I. Title. BIP

STROEBEL, Leslie. 770'.3
Dictionary of contemporary photography / by Leslie Stroebel & Hollis N. Todd. Dobbs Ferry, N.Y. : Morgan & Morgan, [1974] 217 p. : ill. ; 27 cm. [TR9.S88] 73-93536 ISBN 0-87100-065-2 : 20.00
1. Photography—Dictionaries. I. Todd, Hollis N., joint author. II. Title. BIP

TAYLOR, Herb, 1942- 770'.3
Encyclopedia of practical photography / Herb Taylor. Garden City, N.Y. : Amphoto, [1977- p. cm. Includes bibliographical references and index. [TR9.T34] 77-22562 11.95 (v. 1) lib.bdg. : 15.95
1. Photography—Dictionaries. I. Title.

Photography—Dictionaries—Polyglot.

EASTMAN Kodak Company. 770'.1'4
International glossary of photographic terms. [Rochester, N.Y.] 1973. 95 p. illus. 29 cm. Terms and definitions in 8 languages. [TR9.E27 1973] 73-79879 ISBN 0-87985-070-1 8.95
1. Photography—Dictionaries—Polyglot. 2. Dictionaries, Polyglot. I. Title.

ELSEVIER'S dictionary of photography in three languages: English, French, German. Comp., arr. on an English alphabetical base by A. S. H. Craeybeckx. New York, Amer. Elsevier. 1965. 660p. 23cm. [TR9.E46] 63-16076 30.00 770.3
1. Photography—Dictionaries—Polyglot. 2. Dictionaries, Polyglot. I. Craeybeckx, A. S. H., ed.

PHOTOWORDS in four languages. London, New York, Focal Press [1950?] 63 p. 14 cm. [TR9.P53] 51-20217 770.3
1. Photography — Dictionaries — Polyglot. 2. English language — Dictionaries — Polyglot.

Photography—Directories.

*MCDARRAH, Fred W., ed. 771'.025
Photography market place / edited by Fred W. McDarrah. Second ed. New York : R.R. Bowker, 1977. viii, 502p. ; 23 cm. Includes index. [TR12] 75-833 ISBN 0-8352-0922-9 pbk. : 15.50
1. Photography-Directories. I. Title. BIP

STOCK photo and assignment source book : where to find photographs instantly / edited by Fred W. McDarrah. New York : R. R. Bowker Co., 1977. ix, 481 p. ; 23 cm. Includes index. [TR12.S86] 77-80294 ISBN 0-8352-0879-6 : 19.95 770'.25
1. Photography—Directories. 2. Photographers—Directories. I. McDarrah, Fred W., 1926- BIP

Photography, Documentary.

BISCHOF, Werner Adalbert, 1916-1954. 779'.092'4
Werner Bischof : [photos. and drawings / text by] Niklaus Flueler ; [English translation, Maureen Oberli-Turner]. Garden City, N.Y. : AMPHOTO, c1976. 92 p. : ill. ; 27 cm. (Photography, men and movements) Includes bibliographical references and index. [TR820.5.B5713 1976] 75-34606 ISBN 0-8174-0318-3 : 5.95
1. Bischoff, Werner Adalbert, 1916-1954. 2. Photography, Documentary. I. Flueler, Niklaus, 1934- BIP

BOUBAT, Edouard, 1923- 779'.2'0924
Edouard Boubat [by] Bernard George. [English translation by Maureen Oberli-Turner] New York, Macmillan [1973] 18 p., 59 plates. 28 cm. (Photography: men and movements, v. 3) [TR820.5.B6813] 73-7351 10.95
1. Boubat, Edouard, 1923- 2. Photography, Documentary. I. George, Bernard.

DILLON, Richard H. 770'.92'4 B
Images of Chinatown : Louis J. Stellman's Chinatown photographs / Richard Dillon. San Francisco : Book Club of California, 1976. 68 p. : ill. ; 20 x 23 cm. (Publication ; Book Club of California ; no. 153) "Four hundred and fifty copies ... produced." [TR140.S686D54] 77-152440
1. Stellman, Louis John, 1877-1961. 2. Photography, Documentary. 3. Chinese in San Francisco. 4. Photographers—California—Biography. I. Stellman, Louis John, 1877-1961. II. Title. III. Series: Book Club of California, San Francisco. Publication ; no. 153.

EASTMAN Kodak Company. 770'.28
Help your community ... through photography. By the editors of Eastman Kodak Company. [Rochester, N.Y., Eastman Kodak Co., 1973] 160 p. illus. 28 cm. (Kodak publication, no. AC-7) [TR820.5.E18 1973] 73-174228 ISBN 0-87985-071-X 5.95

1. Photography, Documentary. I. Title.

HARE, Chauncey, 1934- 779'.9'30917309240924
Interior American / Chauncey Hare ; designed by Marvin Israel and Kate Morgan. Millerton, N.Y. : Aperture, inc., c1978. 174 p., [1] leaf of plates : chiefly ill. ; 24 x 30 cm. [TR820.5.H37] 78-66663 ISBN 0-89381-028-2 : 20.00
1. Hare, Chauncey, 1934- 2. Photography, Documentary. 3. United States—Social life and customs—Pictorial works. I. Title.

HINE, Lewis Wickes, 1874-1940. 779'.092'4
America & Lewis Hine : photographs 1904-1940 : [exhibition] / foreword by Walter Rosenblum ; biographical notes by Naomi Rosenblum ; essay by Alan Trachtenberg ; design by Marvin Israel. New York : Aperture, inc., c1977. 142 p. : ill. ; 25 x 30 cm. Published in conjunction with an exhibition organized by the Brooklyn Museum. [TR820.5.H56 1977] 77-70068 ISBN 0-89381-008-8 : 22.50.
1. Hine, Lewis Wickes, 1874-1940. 2. Photography, Documentary. 3. Photographers—United States—Biography. I. Trachtenberg, Alan. II. Brooklyn. Institute of Arts and Sciences. Museum. III. Title. BIP

HODGSON, Pat. 909
Early war photographs / compiled and written by Pat Hodgson. Boston : New York Graphic Society, [1974] 159 p. : ill. ; 26 cm. Includes index. Bibliography: p. 31-32. [TR820.5.H62 1974] 74-78767 ISBN 0-8212-0630-3 : 12.00
1. Photography, Documentary. 2. War photographers. I. Title.

HURLEY, Forrest Jack. 779'.9'917303916
Portrait of a decade; Roy Stryker and the development of documentary photography in the thirties [by] F. Jack Hurley. Photographic editing by Robert J. Doherty. Baton Rouge, Louisiana State University Press [1972] ix, 196 p. illus. 29 cm. Bibliography: p. 189-193. [TR820.5.H87] 72-79331 ISBN 0-8071-0235-0 12.95
1. Stryker, Roy Emerson, 1893- 2. United States. Farm Security Administration. 3. Photography, Documentary. I. Title. BIP

HURLEY, Forrest Jack. 779'.9'973916
Portrait of a decade : Roy Stryker and the development of documentary photography in the thirties / F. Jack Hurley ; photographic editing by Robert J. Doherty. New York : Da Capo Press, [1977] c1972. ix, 196 p. : ill. ; 28 cm. (A Da Capo paperback) Includes index. Bibliography: p. 189-193. [TR820.5.H87 1977] 76-51427 ISBN 0-306-80058-6 pbk. : 6.95
1. Stryker, Roy Emerson, 1893- 2. United States. Farm Security Administration. 3. Photography, Documentary. I. Title.

LANGE, Dorothea. 779'.9'9739170924
Living witness : selected F.S.A. photographs of Dorothea Lange / edited by A. J. Marks ; introd. by William Stott. New York : East River Press, 1976, i.e.1978 p. cm. [TR820.5.L36] 76-972 ISBN 0-89172-004-9 : 29.50
1. Lange, Dorothea. 2. United States. Farm Security Administration. 3. Photography, Documentary. I. United States. Farm Security Administration. II. Title.

LEE, Russel, 1903- 779'.92'4
Russell Lee, photographer / F. Jack Hurley ; introd. by Robert Coles. Dobbs Ferry, N.Y. : Morgan & Morgan, c1978. 206 p. : ill. ; 24 x 30 cm. Bibliography: p. 204-206. [TR820.5.L42] 78-61494 ISBN 0-87100-151-9 : 25.00
1. Lee, Russell, 1903- 2. Photography, Documentary. 3. Photographers—United States—Biography. I. Hurley, Forrest Jack. II. Title.

MORAN, Tom. 770'.92'2
The photo essay, Paul Fusco & Will McBride / text by Tom Moran, with the editors of Alskog, inc. [New York] : T. Y. Crowell, [1974] 94 p. : ill. (some col.) ; 29 cm. (Masters of contemporary photography) Title on spine: Fusco & Mcbride: the photo essay. [TR139.M58] 74-8231 ISBN 0-690-00621-7 : 7.95 ISBN 0-690-00622-5 pbk. : 4.95
1. Fusco, Paul. 2. McBride, Will, 1931- 3. Photography, Documentary. I. Fusco, Paul. II. McBride, Will, 1931- III. Alskog, inc. IV. Title. V. Title: Fusco & McBride, the photo essay.

SHAHN, Ben, 1898-1969. 779'.9'9739170924
The photographic eye of Ben Shahn / edited by Davis Pratt. Cambridge, Mass. : Harvard University Press, 1975. xiii, 147 p. : all ill. ; 25 x 27 cm. [TR820.5.S48 1975] 75-18543 15.00
1. United States. Farm Security Administration. 2. Photography, Documentary. I. Title. BIP

*SILBER, Mark. 779
The family album; photographs of the 1890s & 1900s, by Gilbert Wight Tilton & Fred W. Record. Assembled by Mark Silber. [Boston, Mass.] David R. Godine [1973] 93 p. illus. 26 cm. [TR820.5] 15.00
1. Photography—Documentary. 2. Maine—Photography. I. Tilton, Gilbert Wight, illus. II. Record, Fred W., illus. III. Title. BIP

STRYKER, Roy Emerson, 1893- 779'.9'973917
In this proud land : America, 1935-1943, as seen in the FSA photographs / Roy Emerson Stryker and Nancy Wood. New York : Galahad Books, c1973. 191 p. : chiefly ill. ; 32 cm. Bibliography: p. 189. [TR820.5.S87] 75-12259 ISBN 0-88365-313-3 : 20.00
1. United States. Farm Security Administration. 2. Photography, Documentary. I. Wood, Nancy C., joint author. II. Title. BIP

STRYKER, Roy Emerson, 1893- 779'.9'973917
In this proud land : America, 1935-1943, as seen in the FSA photographs / Roy Emerson Stryker and Nancy Wood. Boston : New York Graphic Society, 1975, c1973. 191 p. : ill. ; 31 cm. Bibliography: p. 189. [TR820.5.S87 1975] 73-78792 ISBN 0-8212-0673-7 pbk : 8.95
1. United States. Farm Security Administration. 2. Photography, Documentary. I. Wood, Nancy C., joint author. II. Title.

TIME-LIFE Books. 779
Documentary photography, by the editors of Time-Life Books. New York [1972] 241 p. illus. 27 cm. (Life library of photography) Bibliography: p. 239. [TR820.5.T55] 78-184661
1. Photography, Documentary. BIP

Photography, Documentary—Exhibitions.

THE Concerned photographer: 779
the photographs of Werner Bischoff, Robert Capa, David Seymour ("Chim"), Andre Kertesz, Leonard Freed, Dan Weiner. [Editor: Cornell Capa. Text: Robert Sagalyn, Judith Friedberg] New York, Grossman Publishers, 1968. 1 v. (unpaged) illus. 24 cm. Reflects an exhibit of 6 one-man shows created by the Fund for Concerned Photography and held in 1967 at the Riverside Museum of New York. [TR820.5.C66 1968] 68-31898
1. Photography, Documentary—Exhibitions. I. Bischoff, Werner Adalbert, 1916-1954. II. Fund for Concerned Photography. III. New York (City). Riverside Museum.

THE Concerned photographer 2; 779
the photographs of Marc Riboud, Foman Vishniac, Bruce Davidson, Gordon Parks, Ernst Haas, Hiroshi Hamaya, Donald McCullin, W. Eugene Smith. [text by Michael Edelson] Editor: Cornell Capa New York, Grossman Publishers, 1972. 1 v. (unpaged) illus. 25 cm. Based on an exhibit prepared by the International Fund for Concerned Photography to be shown at the Israel Museum, Jerusalem, Sept., 1973. Includes bibliographies. [TR820.5.C66 1972] 72-172303 ISBN 0-670-23556-3 14.95
1. Photography, Documentary—Exhibitions. I. Riboud, Marc. II. Edelson, Michael. III. Capa, Cornell, ed. IV. International Fund for Concerned Photography. V. Jerusalem. Israel Museum.

EVANS, Walker, 1903-1975. 779'.092'4
Walker Evans : photographs : [catalogue of] an exhibition circulated under the auspices of the International Council of the Museum of Modern Art, New York [held at the] Museum of Modern Art, Oxford, 18 September-31 October 1976. [London] : Arts Council of Great Britain, 1976. [16] p. : ill., 2 ports. ; 21 cm. [TR820.5.E9 1976] 77-364475 ISBN 0-7287-0110-3 : £0.65
1. United States. Farm Security Administration. 2. Evans, Walker, 1903-1975. 3. Photography, Documentary—Exhibitions. I. International Council of the Museum of Modern Art, New York. II. Museum of Modern Art, Oxford.

PHOTOGRAPHING the frontier : 779'.9'9780074
an exhibition / researched and organized by Eugene Ostroff ; developed and circulated by the Smithsonian Institution Traveling Exhibition Service, 1975-1978. Washington : Published for the Smithsonian Institution Traveling Exhibition Service by the Smithsonian Institution Press, 1976. 32 p. : ill. ; 22 cm. (Smithsonian Institution Press publication ; no. 6133) [TR820.5.P48] 75-619331
1. Photography, Documentary—Exhibitions. 2. The West—Description and travel—Views—Exhibitions. I. Ostroff, Eugene. II. Smithsonian Institution. Traveling Exhibition Service.

STARCK, Robert, 1945- 779'.9'978203
Nebraska photographic documentary project : [1975-1977] : Sheldon Memorial Art Gallery / Robert Starck and Lynn Dance. Lincoln : Distributed by University of Nebraska Press, c1977. ix, 109 p. : chiefly ill. ; 24 x 26 cm. "Book reproduces 110 prints exhibited at Sheldon Memorial Art Gallery in March 1977." [TR820.5.S7] 77-72782 ISBN 0-8032-5864-X : 12.95
1. Photography, Documentary—Exhibitions. 2. Nebraska—Description and travel—Views. I. Dance, Lynn, 1949- joint author. II. Sheldon Memorial Art Gallery. III. Title. BIP

Photography—Early works to 1850.

LEREBOURS, Noel Marie Paymal, 1807-1873. 772'.12
A treatise on photography. New York, Arno Press, 1973 xix, 216 p. illus. 22 cm. (The Literature of Photography) Translation of the 4th French ed.: Traite de Photographie. [TR144.L4613 1973] 72-9215 ISBN 0-405-04923-4 14.00.
1. Photography—Early works to 1850. 2. Daguerreotype. I. Title. II. Series.

TALBOT, William Henry Fox, 1800-1877. 772'.16
The pencil of nature. New York, Da Capo Press, 1969. [94] p. 24 plates. 32 cm. Reprint of the 1844-46 ed., with a new introd. by B. Newhall. [TR144.T2 1969] 68-25759 35.00
1. Photography—Early works to 1850. I. Title. BIP

Photography—Electronic equipment.

BROWN, Robert Michael, 1943- 681'.418
Electronics for shutterbugs, by Robert M. Brown & Mark Olsen. [1st ed.] Blue Ridge Summit, Pa., G/L Tab Books [1974] 204 p. illus. 23 cm. [TR196.B75] 74-75217 ISBN 0-8306-4679-5 8.95
1. Photography—Electronic equipment. I. Olsen, Mark, joint author. II. Title.
Pbk. 5.95; ISBN 0-8306-3679-X.

LINCOLN, Marshall. 771
Electronics for photographers. New York, Amphoto [1966] 159 p. illus. 24 cm. [TR196.L52 1966a] 67-1727
1. Photography—Electronic equipment. I. Title.

LINCOLN, Marshall. 771
Electronics for photographers. Philadelphia, Chilton Books [1966] 159 p. illus. 24 cm. [TR196.L52] 66-23322
1. Photography—Electronic equipment. I. Title.

WELS, Byron G. 771
Electronics in photography, by Byron G. Wels. [1st ed.] Indianapolis, H. W. Sams [1968] 128 p. illus. 22 cm. [TR196.W37] 68-58091 3.50 ($4.50 Can.)
1. Photography—Electonic equipment. I. Title.

Photography—Enlarging.

CARROLL, John, 1926- 771.318
Durst enlarger and copy camera guide, by Jack Carroll and Eddie Tarjan. New York, Greenberg [1957] 128p. illus. 20cm. (The Modern camera guide series) [TR475.C28] 57-10217
1. Photography—Enlarging. 2. Photography—Copying. I. Tarjan, Edward, joint author. II. Title.

COLES, Charles H 778.13
The Beseler enlarger guide. New York, Greenberg, c1955. 126p. illus. 20cm. (The Modern camera guide series) [TR475.C56] 55-11959
1. Photography—Enlarging. I. Title.

FOLDES, Joseph. 778.13
The practical way to perfect enlargements. All illus. by the author. [1st ed.] San Francisco, Camera Craft Pub. Co. [1954] 190p. illus. 25cm. (A Camera Craft plus value book) [TR475.F65] 54-12588
1. Photography—Enlarging. I. Title.

GIBSON, Henry Louis, 1906- 778.13
Perfecting your enlarging. Philadelphia, Chilton, c.1961. 128p. illus. (Modern camera guide ser., 830 61-14023 1.95 pap.,
1. Photography—Enlarging. I. Title.

HARRIS, Frank George, 1899- 778.13
Modern enlarging technique, by Frank Harris, George L. Wakefield. London, Fountain [dist. New York, Morgan & Morgan, 1964, c.1954] 196p. illus., diagrs. 19cm. (Fountain photobk.) 64-9859 3.50 bds.,
1. Photography—Enlarging. I. Wakefield, George L., joint author. II. Title.

JACOBSOHN, Kurt, 1906- 778.1'3
Enlarging [by] C. I. Jacobson [and] L. A. Mannheim. 20th rev. ed. New York, Amphoto [1969] 534 p. illus. 22 cm. (The manuals of photo-technique) [TR475.J3 1969b] 71-79081 12.50
1. Photography—Enlarging. I. Mannheim, Ladislaus Andrew, 1925- joint author. II. Title.

JACOBSOHN, Kurt, 1906- 778.1'3
Enlarging [by] C. I. Jacobson [and] L. A. Mannheim. 20th rev. ed. London, New York, Focal P., 1969. 534 p. illus. 22 cm. (Manual of photo-technique) [TR475.J3 1969] 77-421748 50/-
1. Photography—Enlarging. I. Mannheim, Ladislaus Andrew, 1925- joint author. II. Title.

JACOBSOHN, Kurt, 1906- 778.1'3
Enlarging. 19th rev. ed. [by] C. I. Jacobson [and] L. A. Mannheim. London, New York, Focal P., 1967. 533 p. illus., 32 plates, tables, diagrs. 22 cm. (The Manual of photo-techniques) [TR475.J3 1967] 67-91661
1. Photography—Enlarging. I. Mannheim, Ladislaus Andrew, 1925- joint author. II. Title.

MCINTYRE, Robert L 778.13
The Solar enlarger guide. New York, Greenberg, c1955. 128p. illus. 20cm. (The Modern camera guide series) [TR475.M3] 55-12087
1. Photography—Enlarging. I. Title.

NIBBELINK, Don D 778.13
Bigger and better, the book of enlarging. Drawings by Sherman E. Nelson. [Rochester, N.Y.] Published by John P. Smith Co. for Garden City Books, Garden City, N.Y. [1952] 253 p. illus. 22 cm. [TR475.N5] 52-3226
1. Photography — Enlarging. I. Title.

NIBBELINK, Don D. 770'.284
Bigger and better enlarging / by Don Nibbelink and Rex Anderson. Garden City, N.Y. : AMPHOTO, [1974] 288 p. :

ill. ; 24 cm. Includes index. [TR475.N49] 74-82158 ISBN 0-8174-0579-8 : 9.95
1. Photography—Enlarging. I. Anderson, Rex, 1915- joint author. II. Title. BIP

SPITZING, Gunter. 770'.28
The photoguide to enlarging. [Translated by Fred Bradley] Garden City, N.Y., Amphoto [1974] 184 p. illus. 19 cm. "Translation from Vergrossern, schwarzweiss & farbig." [TR475.S75613] 73-89736 ISBN 0-8174-0770-7 5.95
1. Photography—Enlarging. I. Title.

STEVENSON, Albert Charles 778.13
Build your own enlarger, by A. C. Stevenson. London, Fountain Pr. [dist. New York, Morgan Morgan, 1964] 50p. front., illus., diagrs. 25cm. 43-2842 3.50
1. Photography—Enlarging. I. Title.

TYDINGS, Kenneth S 778.13
The Omega enlarger guide 4th print. rev. Philadelphia, Chilton Co., Book Division, 1960, c1954. 120 p. illus. 20 cm. (Modern camera guide series, 338) [TR475.T9] 60-11253
1. Photography — Enlarging. 2. Photography — Apparatus and supplies. I. Title.

TYDINGS, Kenneth S 778.13
The Omega enuerger.) guide. [With special section on how to color photographs] New York, Greenberg, c1954. 128p. illus. 20cm. (The Modern camera guide series) [TR475.T9] 52-10867
1. Photography—Enlarging. 2. Photography—Apparatus and supplies. I. Title.

WAKEFIELD, George L. 770'.284
Exposure control in enlarging London, Fountain Press [1973, c.1972] viii, 194 p. illus. 23 cm. index [TR475.W34] 73-152625 ISBN 0-852-42005-6
1. Photography—Enlarging. 2. Photography—Exposure. I. Title.
Available from International Publications Service, New York, for 10.00. BIP

Photography, Erotic.

ARATOW, Paul, comp. 779'.28
100 years of erotica; a photographic portfolio of mainstream American subculture from 1845-1945 [San Francisco, Straight Arrow Books; distributed by Quick Fox, New York, 1973] 1 v. (unpaged, chiefly illus.) 22 x 29 cm. Issued in a case. [TR676.A7] 73-79838 ISBN 0-87932-064-8 10.00
1. Photography, Erotic. I. Title.

ECSTASY : 779'.28
exploring the erotic imagination. 1st ed. Chicago : Playboy Press, 1977,c1976 216 p., [4] leaves of plates : ill. ; 29 cm. [TR676.E25] 76-27200 ISBN 0-87223-480-0 : 19.95
1. Photography, Erotic.

EROTIC fantasies : 779'.28
14 pictorial love stories. Collector's ed. Los Angeles : Playgirl, c1976. [144] p. : chiefly ill. ; 29 cm. [TR676.E74] 77-373222 2.75
1. Photography, Erotic. I. Playgirl.

HAMILTON, David. 779'.24'0924
Dreams of a young girl, by David Hamilton and Alain Robbe-Grillet. New York, Morrow, 1971. 143 p. (chiefly illus.) 30 cm. Translation of Reves de jeunes filles. [TR676.H3513] 70-159733 14.95
1. Photography, Erotic. 2. Photography, Artistic. I. Robbe-Grillet, Alain, 1922- joint author. II. Title. BIP

HAMILTON, David. 779'.28'0924
Sisters. [Photos.] by David Hamilton. Text: Alain Robbe-Grillet. [English translation: Martha Egan] New York, Morrow, 1973. 135 p. illus. 30 cm. Translation of Les demoiselles. [TR676.H3613] 73-162094 ISBN 0-688-00166-1 15.95
1. Photography, Erotic. 2. Photography, Artistic. I. Robbe-Grillet, Alain, 1922- II. Title. BIP

JOLITZ, William R. 779'.28'0924
Deborah's dreams : a Victorian fantasy / photographed by William R. Jolitz. 1st ed. Chicago : Playboy Press, c1976. [110] p. : all ill. (some col.) ; 29 cm. [TR676.J57] 75-42586 2.75
1. Photography, Erotic. I. Title.

NEWTON, Helmut, 1920- 779'.28'0924
White women / Helmut Newton ; designed by Bea Feitler. New York : Stonehill, c1976. [98] p. : ill. (some col.) ; 32 cm. [TR676.N48] 77-357754 ISBN 0-88373-053-7 : 25.00
1. Photography, Erotic. I. Title. BIP

O'HARA, Sharon. 779'.28
Noelle and the twelve nights of Christmas / photographed by Francois Robert, Robert Keeling, Natacha Robert ; [Sharon O'Hara, text]. 1st ed. Chicago : Playboy Press, c1976. [112] p. : ill. (some col.) ; 28 cm. [TR676.O37] 76-40674 pbk. : 2.95
1. Photography, Erotic. I. Robert, Francois. II. Keeling, Robert. III. Robert, Natacha. IV. Title.

OVENDEN, Graham. 779'.24
Victorian erotic photography [by] Graham Ovenden & Peter Mendes. New York, St. Martin's Press [1973] 111 p. (chiefly illus.) 30 cm. [TR676.O95 1973] 73-87130 ISBN 0-85670-065-7 12.50
1. Photography, Erotic. 2. Photography of the nude. I. Mendes, Peter, joint author. II. Title. BIP

SANNES, Sanne. 779'.24'0924
The face of love. South Brunswick, A. S. Barnes [1972] 23 p., [182] p. of illus. 29 cm. [TR676.S27 1972] 70-107130 ISBN 0-498-06732-7 15.00
1. Photography, Erotic. I. Title.

SMITH, J. Frederick. 779'.28'0924
Sappho by the sea : an illustrated guide to the Hamptons / photography by J. Frederick Smith ; text by Mary Arrigan McCarthy ; designed by Susan Lusk. New York : Belvedere, 1976. p. cm. [TR676.S6] 76-21830 pbk. : 7.95
1. Photography, Erotic. 2. East Hampton, N.Y.—Description—Views. I. McCarthy, Mary Arrigan. II. Title.

STOCTAY, G. G. 779'.28
America's erotic past, 1868-1940; [an annotated collection of erotic photographs in America from the Civil War to today] by G. G. Stoctay. [San Diego, Calif., Greenleaf Classics, 1973] 1 v. (unpaged) illus. 27 cm. (A Greenleaf classic/GP645) Includes bibliography. [TR676.S78] 74-166456 3.95
1. Photography, Erotic. I. Title.

Photography—Examinations, questions, etc.

*RUDMAN, Jack. 770.232
Photographer; examination section, questions and answers. Brooklyn, N.Y., National Learning Corp., 1968. 1v. (various p.) 28 cm. (Passbk. ser., Passbks. for civil service exams., C582) 5.00, pap., plastic bdg.
1. Photography—Examinations, questions, etc. I. Title. BIP

Photography—Exhibitions.

GERNSHEIM, Helmut, 1913- 779
Operative photography, 1826 to the present an exhibition from the Gernsheim by Helmut and Alison Gernsheim. Detroit, Wayne State Univ. Pr. [c.]1963. 130p. 48 plates. 26cm. Bibl. 63-16564 2.95 pap.,
1. Photography—Exhibitions I. Gernsheim, Alison, joint author. II. Title.

HOUSTON, Tex. Museum of Fine Arts. 770'.75
Salon of photography. [Catalogue] [Houston] v. illus. 18 cm. annual. [TR6.H65] 52-18888
1. Photography—Exhibitions. I. Title.

INTO the 70's; 779
photographic images by sixteen artists/photographers. [Akron, Ohio, Akron Art Institute, 1970] 80 p. (chiefly illus. (part col.)) 21 x 24 cm. "Prepared on the occasion of the exhibit ... which opened at the Akron Art Institute in April, 1970." [TR646.I59] 70-29651
1. Photography—Exhibitions. I. Akron, Ohio. Art Institute.

LENT, Max. 779'.074'013
Photography galleries and selected museums : a survey and international directory / Max Lent & Tina Lent. Venice, Calif. : Garlic Press, 1978. ca. 200 p. ; 29 cm. Includes bibliography. [TR12.L46] 78-69605 ISBN 0-932798-01-2. : 17.95 ISBN 0-932798-00-4 pbk. : 8.95
1. Photography—Museums—Directories. I. Lent, Tina, joint author. II. Title. BIP

LYONS, Nathan, ed. 779
Contemporary photographers. 67 p. (chiefly illus., ports.) 21 x 22 cm. On spine: Contemporary photographers. A collection of work by the five contemporary photographers represented in the exhibition. "Toward a social landscape," held at the George Eastman House, December 1966. [TR6.L9] 66-30698
1. Photography — Exhibitions. 2. Photography, Artistic. I. Davidson, Bruce 1933- II. George Eastman House, Rochester, N.Y. III. Title.

LYONS, Nathan, ed. 779
Toward a social landscape [by] Bruce Davideson [and others] Edited by Nathan Lyons. New York, Horizon Press [1967, c1966] 67 p. (chiefly illus., ports.) 21 x 22 cm. On spine: Contemporary photographers. A collection of work by the five contemporary photographers represented in the exhibition. "Toward a social landscape," held at the George Eastman House, December 1966. [TR6.L9] 66-30698
1. Photography — Exhibitions. 2. Photography, Artistic. I. Davidson, Bruce 1933- II. George Eastman House, Rochester, N.Y. III. Title. IV. Title: Contemporary photographers.

NEBRASKA. University. Sheldon Memorial Art Gallery. 779'.074'078229
Five photographers; an international invitational exhibition shown at the Sheldon Memorial Art Gallery, University of Nebraska Art Galleries, May 7 through June 2, 1968. [Lincoln, 1968] [48] p. illus. 22 x 23 cm. Preparation of the exhibition and the catalogue by Michael McLoughlin, exhibition director. [TR6.N36] 70-81
1. Hosoe, Eiko, 1933- 2. Meatyard, Ralph Eugene, 1925- 3. Sudek, Josef, 1896- 4. Winogrand, Garry, 1928- 5. Wood, John, 1922- 6. Photography—Exhibitions. I. McLoughlin, Michael. II. Title.

PHOTO maxima; 779
the international small print photographic exhibition in book form. 1st- 1958- New York. v. illus. 27cm. annual. 'Sponsored by the Pictorial Division of the Photographic Society of America.' [TR6.N6] 58-22542
1. Photography—Exhibitions. I. Photographic Society of America. Pictorial Division.

STEICHEN, Edward, 1879- comp. 779.2
The family of man; the greatest photographic exhibition of all time—503 pictures from 68 countries— created by Edward Steichen for the Museum of Modern Art. New York, Published for the Museum of Modern Art by the Maco Magazine Corp., c1955. 192 p. (chiefly illus.) 28 cm. [TR6.N55 1955c] 55-11621
1. Photography—Exhibitions. I. New York (City). Museum of Modern Art. II. Title. BIP

WHITE House News Photographers Association. 779
News photo exhibit. Washington. v. illus. 23 cm. annual. [TR6.W5] 51-33254
1. Photography—Exhibitions. 2. Photography, Journalistic. I. Title.

WORLD exhibition of photography on the theme: what is man? 779
555 photos by 264 photographers from 30 countries. [Hamburg, Gruner & Jahr, 1967?] 1 v. (unpaged) illus. 26 cm. [TR6.W67] 70-355655 unpriced
1. Photography—Exhibitions. 2. Photography, Artistic.

YOUNG photographers. 779
[1st ed. Albuquerque? N.M., 1968] [36] p. illus. 24 cm. Exhibition held at the University Art Museum, University of New Mexico, Albuquerque, and other museums. [TR650.Y6] 68-21261
1. Photography—Exhibitions. 2. Photography, Artistic. I. New Mexico. University. Art Museum.

Photography—Experiments.

ZAKIA, Richard D. 770.28
101 experiments in photography [by] Richard D. Zakia [and] Hollis N. Todd. [1st ed.] Hastings-on-Hudson, N.Y., Morgan & Morgan [1969] 116 p. illus. 19 cm. Bibliography: p. 98-[99] [TR161.Z3 1969] 70-86657
1. Photography—Experiments. I. Todd, Hollis N., joint author. II. Title.

Photography—Exposure.

BERG, Wolfgang Friedrich. 770.282
Exposure, the fundamentals of camera technique. London, New York, Focal Press [1950] 432 p. (p. 428-132 advertisements) illus. 19 cm. (The Manual of photo-technique) [TR591.B46] 51-952
1. Photography—Exposure. I. Title. II. Series: The Manuals of phototechnique BIP

BERG, Wolfgang Friedrich. 770.282
Exposure: theory and practice [by] W. F. Berg. 4th rev. ed. New York, Amphoto [1971?] 457 p. illus. 22 cm. (A Focal manual of photo-technique) Includes bibliographical references. [TR591.B46 1971] 75-79082 ISBN 0-240-44781-6 15.00
1. Photography—Exposure. I. Title.

COLES, Charles H 770.282
Exposure meter guide. [Rev.] New York, Greenberg [1957] 103p. illus. 20cm. (The Modern camera guide series) [TR591.C7 1957] 57-59092
1. Photography—Exposure. I. Title.

FELTZ, Michael R. 778.3'7
Total photo computer manual, by Michael R. Feltz [and] James F. Jasek. [Waco, Tex., Total Photo Computer, 1973] 74 p. illus. 23 cm. "Total photo computer" (circular slide rule) in pocket. [TR591.F4] 73-76575
1. Photography—Exposure. 2. Slide-rule. I. Jasek, James F., joint author. II. Title.

MANNHEIM, Ladislaus Andrew, 1925- 770.282
How to use your exposure meter; hand-held, built-in, automatic [by] L. A. Mannheim. [2d ed.] New York, Amphoto [1969] 72 p. illus. (part col.) 19 cm. (Viewfinder book) [TR591.M27 1969] 79-95773 1.25
1. Photography—Exposure. I. Title.

MANNHEIM, Ladislaus Andrew, 1925- 770.282
The right exposure every time [by] L. A. Mannheim. [2d ed.] New York, Amphoto [1969] 72 p. illus. (part col.) 18 cm. (Viewfinder book) [TR591.M29 1969] 73-95584 1.25
1. Photography—Exposure. I. Title.

MANNHEIM, Ladislaus Andrew, 1925- 770.282
Successful exposure in photography. London, New York, Focal Press [1961] 164p. illus. 19cm. [TR591.M3] 61-4679
1. Photography—Exposure. I. Title.

SANDERS, Norman, 1927- 770'.28
Photographic tone control / Norman Sanders ; [ill., Benjamin Perez]. Dobbs Ferry, N.Y. : Morgan & Morgan, c1977. 113 p. : ill. ; 21 cm. Includes bibliographical references. [TR591.S33] 77-83265 ISBN 0-87100-117-9 : 8.95
1. Photography—Exposure. 2. Photography—Processing. I. Title. BIP

WRIGHT, George Benjamin, 1913- 770.282
Guide to perfect exposure, by George B. and Cora Wright, 3d ed., rev., by Cora Wright. New York, Universal Photo Books [1962] 128 p. illus. 21 cm. [TR591.W7 1962] 62-4783
1. Photography — Exposure. I. Wright, Cora, joint author. II. Title.

WRIGHT, George Benjamin, 1913- 770.282
Guide to perfect exposure, by George B. and Cora Wright. 4th ed., rev. by Cora Wright Kennedy. Philadelphia, Chilton [1967] 128p. illus. 21cm. [TR591.W7 1967] 67-17795 2.95
1. Photography—Exposure. I. Kennedy, Cora Wright, joint author. II. Title.

Photography—Failures.

ABEL, Charles, 1891- 770.23
What's wrong with this picture? New York, Greenberg [1950] viii, 184 p. illus. 24 cm. [TR147.A22] 50-6689
1. Photography—Failures.

FRITSHE, Kurt. 770'.28
Faults in photography: causes and correctives; translation [from the German] by L. A. Mannheim. London, New York, Focal P., 1968. 337 p. illus. 22 cm. Translation of Das Grosse Fotofehlerbuch. [TR147.F713] 68-114246 50/-
1. Photography—Failures. I. Title.

Photography — Films.

EASTMAN Kodak Company. 771'.5324
Kodak films : color & black-and-white. [Rochester, N.Y. : Eastman Kodak Co., c1978] 160 p. : ill. ; 22 cm. (Kodak publication ; no. Af-1) Cover title. [TR283.E392 1978] 78-102444 ISBN 0-87985-161-9 : pbk. : 3.95
1. Photography—Films. I. Title.

MANNHEIM, Ladislaus Andrew, 1925- 771'.5324
How to choose and use film and filter [by] L. A. Mannheim. [2d ed.] New York, Amphoto [1969] 70 p. illus. (part col.) 18 cm. (Viewfinder book) [TR283.M35 1969] 70-92601 1.25
1. Photography—Films. 2. Photography—Light filters. I. Title.

WOOLLEY, Al E 770.28
Photographic films and their uses. Philadelphia, Chilton Co., Book Division, c1960. 119 p. illus. 20 cm. (Modern camera guide series, 447) [TR283.W6] 60-7394
1. Photography — Films. I. Title.

Photography—Films—Congresses.

SYMPOSIUM on Photographic Sensitivity, Cambridge, 1972. 772'.1
Photographic sensitivity; proceedings of the Symposium on Photographic Sensitivity held at Gonville and Caius College and Little Hall, Cambridge, September, 1972, edited by R. J. Cox. London, New York, Published for the Scientific and Technical Group of the Royal Photographic Society by Academic Press, 1973. xv, 409 p. illus. 24 cm. Includes bibliographical references. [TR280.S97 1972] 73-7032 ISBN 0-12-194465-4 23.00
1. Photography—Films—Congresses. 2. Emulsions—Congresses. I. Cox, R. J., ed. II. Royal Photographic Society of Great Britain, London. III. Title. BIP

Photography — Films — Testing.

TYDINGS, Kenneth S 770.28
Instant film testing color response chart and book for color and black & white. Philadelphia, Chilton Books, 1963. col. plate. 50 x 40 cm. fold. to 20 x 13 cm. and 24 p. illus. 20 cm. (The Modern camera guide series) In portfolio; title from portfilio. [[TR283]] 63-14382
1. Photography — Films — Testing. I. Title. II. Title: Film testing color response chart. III. Series.

Photography, Flash-light.

ARNOLD, Rus. 771.447
Advanced flash photography. Rev. ed. Photos. by the author. New York, Crown Publishers [1953] 128p. illus. 18cm. (Little technical library, 42) [TR605.A68 1953] 53-7429
1. Photography, Flash-light. I. Title.

ARNOLD, Rus. 778.37
All-purpose flash photography -- electronic & bulb. New York, American Photographic Book Pub. Co.; distributed to the book trade by Grosset & Dunlap [1964] 96 p. illus. 22 cm. (Better photo guides) "427." [TR605.A69] 63-22231
1. Photography, Flash-light. I. Title.

ARNOLD, Rus. 771.447
Strobonar electronic flash guide: bottled lightning. New York, Greenberg [1957] 126p. illus. 20cm. (The Modern camera guide series) [TR605.A72] 57-6182
1. Photography, Flash-light. I. Title.

ARNOLD, Rus. 778.37
Strobonar electronic flash guide: bottled lightning. 2d ed. Philadelphia, Chilton Co., Book Division, c1959. 121 p. illus. 20 cm. (Chilton's modern camera guide series, 41) [TR605.A72 1959] 59-1699
1. Photography, Flash-light. I. Title.

ARNOLD, Rus. 778.37
Strobonar electronic flash guide: bottled lightning. 2d ed. Philadelphia. Chilton Co., Book Division, c1960. 121p. illus. 20cm. (Modern camera guide series, 244) [TR605.A72 1960] 60-52111
1. Photography, Flash-Light. I. Title.

ASPDEN, Ralph Leonard. 778.37
Electronic flash photography; a survey of principles and practical techniques in industry, research, and radiography. New York, Macmillan, 1960 [c1959] 192 p. illus. 23 cm. Includes bibliography. [TR605.T76] 60-1211
1. Photography, Flash-light. I. Title.

BARRIS, George. 771.447
Candid photography with hi-speed flash, by George Barris [and others] New York, Arco Pub. Co. [1954] 144p. illus. 24cm. (Arco handi-books for better living) Originally published as Fawcett book no. 165. [TR605] 54-11134
1. Photography, Flash-light. I. Title.

BARRIS, George. 771.447
Candid photography with hi-speed flash [by George Barris and others. Greenwich, Conn., Fawcett Publications, 1952] 144p. illus. 24cm. (A Fawcett book, no. 165) [TR605.B28] 52-68094
1. Photography, Flash-light. I. Title.

BOUIE, Bill. 778.37
Flash for better photography. [2d ed.] New York, Universal Photo Books [1958] 122p. illus. 21cm. (A Universal photo guide) [TR605.B6 1958] 59-9511
1. Photography, Flash-light. I. Title.

BOUIE, Bill. 771.447
Flash for better photography. [1st ed.] New York, Universal Photo Books [1956] 122 p. illus. 21 cm. (A Universal photo guide) [TR605.B6] 56-9381
1. Photography, Flash-light. I. Title.

EDGERTON, Harold Eugene, 1903- 778.3'7
Electronic flash, strobe [by] Harold E. Edgerton. New York, McGraw-Hill [1970] xiv, 362 p. illus. 23 cm. Includes bibliographical references. [TR605.E43] 69-18725
1. Photography, Flash-light. 2. Photography, High-speed. I. Title. BIP

GAUNT, Leonard. 778.3'7
Electronic flash guide. London, New York, Focal P., [1967]. [1], 85 p. illus., tables, diagrs. 16 1/2 cm. [TR605.G38] 74-356664 12/6
1. Photography, Flash-light. I. Title. BIP

GILBERT, Geoffrey, photographer. 771.447
Photo-flash in practice. 4th ed. London, New York, Eocal Press [1954] 304p. illus. 19cm. [TR605.G5 1954] 54-34307
1. Photography, Flash-light. I. Title.

GILBERT, Geoffrey. photographer. 771.447
Photo-flash in practice. 3d ed. London, New York, Focal Press [1950] 287 p. (p. 280-287 advertisements) illus. 20 cm. [TR605.G5 1950] 50-12682
1. Photography, Flash-light. I. Title.

GOWLAND, Peter. 778.3'7
Electronic flash simplified / by Peter Gowland. Garden City, N.Y. : Amphoto, c1975. 96 p., [2] leaves of plates : ill. (some col.) ; 26 cm. (A Modern photoguide) [TR605.G59] 75-1970 ISBN 0-8174-0185-7 : 3.45
1. Photography, Flash-light. 2. Photography, High-speed. I. Title. BIP

GOWLAND, Peter. 778.3'7
Guide to electronic flash. 3d ed. New York, Amphoto [1972] 128 p. illus. 20 cm. (An Amphoto book) [TR605.G6 1972] 76-186147 ISBN 0-8174-0451-1 2.50
1. Photography, Flash-light. I. Title.

GOWLAND, Peter. 771.447
Guide to electronic flash. 2d ed. New York, American Photographic Book Pub. Co. [1963] 128 p. illus., ports. 21 cm. (An Amphoto book) [TR605.G6 1963] 63-25289
1. Photography, Flash-light. I. Title. II. Title: Electronic flash.

HARRIS, Percy Wooton 778.37
Beginner's guide to flash photography. London, Newnes [Hollywood-by-the-Sea; Fla., Transatlantic, c.1964] 112p. illus. (pt. col.) 19cm. [TR605] 65-7012 3.00 bds.,
1. Photography, Flash-light. I. Title. II. Title: Flash photography.

JACOBS, Lou. 778.3'7
Electronic flash. All photos. by the author unless otherwise noted. 2d ed. New York, Amphoto [1971] 128 p. illus. 21 cm. [TR605.J23 1971b] 79-29099 3.50
1. Photography, Flash-light. I. Title. BIP

JACOBS, Lou. 778.3'7
Electronic flash. All photos. by the author unless otherwise noted. 2d ed. Philadelphia, Chilton Books [1971] 128 p. illus. 21 cm. [TR605.J23 1971] 79-28162 ISBN 0-8019-5654-4 3.50
1. Photography, Flash-light. I. Title.

JACOBS, Lou, Jr. 778.37
Electronic flash. Photos. by the author unless otherwise noted. New York, Amer. Photographic Bk. Pub. Co. [1964, c.1962] 127p. illus. 21cm. 62-17656 2.50 bds.,
1. Photography, Flash-light. I. Title.

KARSTEN, Kenneth Stephen, 1913- 778.3'7
Science of electronic flash photography, by Kenneth S. Karsten. Philadelphia, Chilton Book Co. [1968] 190 p. illus. 24 cm. [TR605.K3] 68-11994
1. Photography, Flash-light. I. Title. II. Title: Electronic flash photography.

LURAY, Howard Lee, 1919- 771.447
'Strobe,' the lively light. [2d ed. rev.] San Francisco, Camera Craft Pub. Co. [1954] 144p. illus. 24cm. [TR605.L87 1954] 54-8483
1. Photography, Flash-light. I. Title.

LURAY, Howard Lee, 1919- 778.37
Strobe—the lively light; how it works and how to use it. 3d rev. ed. New York, A. S. Barnes [1963] 170 p. illus. 22 cm. (A Ziff-Davis book) [TR605.L87 1963] 60-53228
1. Photography, Flash-light. I. Title.

LURAY, Howard Lee, 1919- 771.447
Your simple flash camera: how to use it. [1st ed.] San Francisco, Camera Craft Pub. Co. [1953] 96p. illus. 22cm. [TR605.L88] 53-11649
1. Photography, Flash-light. I. Title.

MANNHEIM, L. A. 778.37
Successful flash photography. New York, Amphoto Press [1959] 160p. illus. (part col.) 19cm. (Focal photobk.) 59-65056 1.95 flex. plastic
1. Photography, Flash-light. I. Title.

MANNHEIM, Ladislaus Andrew, 1925- 778.37
Successful flash photography. London, New York, Focal Press [1959] 160p. illus. 19cm. [TR605.M26] 59-65056
1. Photography, Flash-light. I. Title.

MORTENSEN, William. 771.448
Flash in modern photography. Supplementary notes by Don M. Paul. [3d ed.] San Francisco, Camera Craft Pub. Co. [1950] 224 p. illus. 24 cm. [A Camera Craft plus value book] [TR605.M65 1950] 50-13484
1. Photography, Flash-light. I. Paul, Don M. II. Title.

MOTT, Verl. 778.3'7
Electronic flash equipment. [1st ed.] Indianapolis, H. W. Sams [1974] 112 p. illus. 22 cm. [TR605.M67] 73-85141 ISBN 0-672-21020-7 4.50 (pbk.)
1. Photography, Flash-light. 2. Photography, High-speed. I. Title.

SNOW, Peter 778.37
Electronic flashlight photography. London, Fountain Pr. [dist. New York, Morgan & Morgan, 1964, c.1961] 174p. illus. (pt. col.) 23cm. 64-3084 7.95
1. Photography, Flash-light. I. Title.

SPITZING, Gunter. 778.3'7
The photoguide to flash. [Translated by E. F. Linssen] Garden City, N.Y., Amphoto [1974] 202 p. illus. 19 cm. Translation of Blitzbuch. [TR605.S66B] 73-89737 ISBN 0-8174-0771-5 5.95
1. Photography, Flash-light. I. Title.

TYDINGS, Kenneth S 778.37
Ultrablitz speedlight guide [by] Kenneth S. Tydings and Murray Duitz. Philadelphia, Chilton Co., Book Division, 1960. 100 p. illus. 20 cm. (Modern camera guide series, 498) [TR605.T9] 60-7641
1. Photography, Flash-light. I. Dultz, Murray, joint author. II. Title.

Photography Formulae, tables, etc.

AMPHOTO, New York. 770.282
Official depth of field tables for 35 mm cameras. Prepared by the Amphoto editorial board, under the supervision of Bennet Sherman, with the assistance of Herbert Keppler and Edward Meyers. New York [1962] unpaged. 29cm. [TR151.A45] 62-9222
1. Photography—Formulae, tables, etc. 2. Miniature cameras. I. Sherman, Bennet, ed. II. Title.

CARROLL, John S., ed. 770
Photo-lab index; the cumulative formulary of standard recommended photographic procedures [25th ed.] London, Fountain Pr.; Hastings-on-Hudson, N.Y., Morgan & Morgan [c.1966] 1v. (various p.) tables, diagrs. 22cm. Loose-leaf. Earlier eds. by Henry M. Lester. Kept up-to-date with quarterly supps. [TR151] 40-847 25.00, loose-leaf ring binder.
1. Photography Formulae, tables, etc. I. Title. BIP

WALL, Edward John, 1860-1928. 770'.28
Photographic facts and formulas / by E. J. Wall and Franklin I. Jordan. Rev. and extensively rewritten / by John S. Carroll. Englewood Cliffs, N.J. : Prentice-Hall, c1975. 480 p. : ill. ; 24 cm. Includes index. [TR151.W24 1975] 73-92418 ISBN 0-13-665364-2 : 19.95
1. Photography—Formulae, tables, etc. I. Jordan, Franklin Ingalls, 1876- joint author. II. Carroll, John S., 1911- III. Title. BIP

Photography—Great Britain—History.

COE, Brian, 1930- 770'.9'04
The snapshot photograph : the rise of popular photography, 1888-1939 / Brian Coe and Paul Gates. London : Ash & Grant, 1977. 144 p. : ill. ; 29 cm. On jacket: Available in the United States from Taplinger Pub. Co., New York. Includes index. Bibliography: p. 144. [TR57.C63] 78-307319 ISBN 0-904069-13-3 : 12.95
1. Photography—Great Britain—History. 2. Photography, Instantaneous—History. I. Gates, Paul, 1936- joint author. II. Title. BIP

HEYERT, Elizabeth M. 779'.2'0941
The glasshouse years : Victorian portrait photography, 1839-1870 / Elizabeth M. Heyert. Montclair, N.J. : Allanheld & Schram, [1798] p. cm. Includes index. Bibliography: p. [TR57.H49] 77-25432 ISBN 0-8390-0210-6 : 16.50
1. Photography—Great Britain—History. 2. Photography—Portraits. I. Title. BIP

Photography—Handbooks, manuals, etc.

AARONS, Jules. 778.7
Vacation and travel photography. New York, American Photographic Book Pub. Co; distributed to the book trade by Grosset & Dunlap [1964] 36 p. illus. 22 cm. (Better photo guides) "436." [TR700.A2] 63-22230
1. Photography — Handbooks, manuals, etc. 2. Travel. I. Title.

ABEL, Charles, 1891- 770.2
The Bolsey guide; a simple introduction to better pictures, by Charles Abel and

Kenneth S. Tydings. New York, Greenberg, '1951. 121 p. illus. (part col.) 20 cm. [TR146.A15] 51-10377
1. Photography—Handbooks, manuals, etc. 2. Bolsey camera. I. Tydings, Kenneth S. joint author. II. Title.

AHLERS, Arvel W. 1915- 770.2
The Ansco guide to picture fun made easy. Drawings by Robert O. Galligan. New York, Popular [c.1963] 215p. illus. (pt. col.) 18cm. (PC1021) 63-5103 .75 pap.,
1. Photography—Handbooks, manuals etc. I. Title.

ALLINSON, K L. 770.2
35 mm. photography with an Exakta. With special contributions by R. H. Rushton, Frank Sharman [and] C. D. Wharry. London, Fountain Press; New York, Exakta Publications [1952] 126 p. illus. 26 cm. [TR263.E9A4 1952] 52-43779
1. Photography—Handbooks, manuals, etc. 2. Exakta camers. I. Title.

ALLINSON, Kenneth Leslie. 770.2
35 mm photography with an Exakta / with special contributions by R. H. Rushton, Frank Sharman and C. D. Wharry. 3d rev. ed. London, Fountain Press; Bronxville, N. Y., Variety Books [1954, 1952] 126p. illus.26cm. (A Fountain photobook) [TR263.E] A56
1. Photography—Handbooks, manuals, etc. 2. Exakta camera. I. Title.

AMATEUR photographer and cinematographer (The) 770.2
Hints, tips, and gadgets for the amateur photographer selcted from the Amateur photographer. London, Fountain Pr. [dist. New York, Morgan & Morgan. 1964] 142p. illus. diagrs. 19cm. 44-14394 2.95 bds.,
1. Photography—Handbooks, manuals, etc. I. Title.

THE amateur photographer's handbook (The) 7th, rev. ed. 7th, rev. ed. New York, Crowell [c.1941-1965] 400p. illus. (pt. col.) diagrs. 24cm. Vol. for 1965 by A. Sussman. [TR146.A464] 61-18664 5.95 770.24
1. Photography—Handbooks, manuals, etc. I. Sussman, Aaron.

AMATEUR photographers handbook (The) by Aaron Sussman. 6th rev. ed. New York, Crowell [c. 1948-1962] 400p. illus. (col. front) 25cm. Annual. 61-18664 5.95 770.24
1. Photography—Handbooks, manuals, etc. I. Sussman, Aaron.

ANSCO. 771.53
Ansco graphic handbook. [Binghamton, N. Y., c1956] 56p. illus. 19cm. [TR146.A59 1956] 56-35569
1. Photography—Handbooks. manuals, etc. 2. Photography—Films. I. Title.

ANSCO. 771.53
Ansco graphic handbook. [Binghamton, N. Y., 1955] 56p. illus. 19cm. [TR146.A59 1955] 55-3830
1. Photography— Handbooks, manuals, etc. 2. Photography—Films. I. Title.

ARNOLD, Rus 770.2
Guide to 120/620 cameras. Philadelphia, Chilton 128p. illus. (Modern camera guide ser., 595) 1.95 pap.,
1. Photography—Handbooks, manuals, etc. I. Title.

ARNOLD, Rus. 770.2
Guide0to 120/620 cameras. Philadelphia, Chilton Co., Book Division, c1961. 128p. illus. 20cm. (Modern camera guide series, 595) [TR146.A85] 61-15090
1. Photography— Handbooks, manuals, etc. I. Title.

ASHER, Harry. 770.28
Photographic principles and practices. Philadelphia, Chilton Book Co. [1968] 288 p. illus. (part col.) 24 cm. [TR146.A87] 67-18631
1. Photography—Handbooks, manuals, etc. I. Title. BIP

ASHER, Harry. 770'.28
Photographic principles and practices / by Harry Asher. 2d ed. Garden City, N.Y. : Amphoto, [1975] 288 p., [4] leaves of plates : ill. (some col.) ; 24 cm. Includes index. [TR146.A87 1975] 75-501103 ISBN 0-8174-0507-0 : 11.95
1. Photography—Handbooks, manuals, etc. I. Title.

BARRY, Les. 770.2
Getting started in photography. 2d ed. Philadelphia, Chilton Book Co. [1967] 128 p. illus. 21 cm. [TR146.B32 1967] 67-25842
1. Photography—Handbooks, manuals, etc. 2. Cameras. I. Title. BIP

BARRY, Les. 770.2
Getting started in photography. [1st ed.] New York, Verlan Books [1960] 128p. illus. 21cm. (A Universal photo book, U-228) [TR146.B32] 60-10805
1. Photography— Handbooks, manuals, etc. 2. Cameras. I. Title.

BARRY, Les. 770'.28
Getting started in photography / by Les Barry. Garden City, N.Y. : Amphoto, c1975. 96 p., [2] leaves of plates : ill. (some col.) ; 26 cm. (A Modern photoguide) Includes index. [TR146.B32 1975] 75-1966 ISBN 0-8174-0187-3 pbk. : 3.45
1. Photography—Handbooks, manuals, etc. 2. Cameras. I. Title.

BAUER, Erwin A 778.71
Outdoor photography, by Erwin Bauer. New York, Outdoor life [1965] 142 p. illus., ports. 24 cm. (Outdoor life skill book) [TR146.B34] 65-14983
1. Photography — Handbooks, manuals, etc. 2. Nature photography. I. Title. BIP

BENEDICT, Joel Avery, 1909- 770'.2'02
Creative photography camera and darkroom manual / by Joel Avery Benedict, Ted W. Shenenberger. 2d ed. Tempe : Media Research & Development, Arizona State University, [1976] p. cm. Includes index. [TR146.B42 1976] 76-9044
1. Photography—Handbooks, manuals, etc. 2. Photography—Processing—Handbooks, manuals, etc. I. Shenenberger, Ted W., 1946- joint author. II. Title.

BETTER homes and gardens 770.2
Phoography for your family. De Monies, Iowa, Meredith [c.1964] 160p. illus. (pt. col.) 29cm. 64-4306 2.95 bds.,
1. Photography—Handbooks, manuals, tc. I. Title.

BETTER homes and gardens. 770'.28
Photography for your family. Des Moines, Meredith Press [1964] 160 p. illus. (part col.) 29 cm. [TR146.B48] 64-4306
1. Photography — Handbooks, manuals, etc. I. Title.

BOWLER, Stanley W 771.3
Beginner's guide to the miniature camera. New York, McBride Bks. [c. 1962] 143p. illus. (pt. col.) 19cm. 62-13553 2.95 bds.,
1. iniature cameras. 2. Photography—Handbooks, manuals, etc. I. Title.

BRUCE, Helen Finn. 770.2
Your guide to photography. [New York] Barnes & Noble [1965] vii, 311 p. illus. 21 cm. (Everyday handbooks, 285) [TR146.B8] 65-17008
1. Photography—Handbooks, manuals, etc. I. Title. BIP

BRUCE, Helen Finn. 770'.28
Your guide to photography / Helen Finn Bruce. 2d ed. New York : Barnes & Noble Books, 1974. vi, 323 p. : ill. ; 21 cm. (Everyday handbooks ; 342) Includes index. [TR146.B8 1974] 73-19475 ISBN 0-06-463342-X pbk. : 2.50
1. Photography—Handbooks, manuals, etc. I. Title.

BUNNELL, Walter. 770.2'4
The new photography. South Brunswick [N. J.] A. S. Barnes [1968] 422p. illus., ports. 26cm. [TR146.B945] 67-16457 8.50
1. Photography—Handbooks, manuals, etc. I. Title.

CARROLL, John S., 1911- 771'.5324
Amphoto black-and-white film data book [by] John S. Carroll. 1st ed. New York, Amphoto, 1972. 128 p. 18 cm. [TR150.C37] 74-187820 ISBN 0-8174-0548-8 4.95
1. Photography—Handbooks, manuals, etc. 2. Photography—Films. I. Title.

CARROLL, John S., 1911- 771'.5324
Amphoto black-and-white film data book / John S. Carroll. 2d ed. Garden City, N.Y. : Amphoto, 1975. 128 p. ; 17 cm. On spine: Black/white film data book. Includes index. [TR150.C37 1975] 75-330243 ISBN 0-8174-1548-3 pbk. : 3.95
1. Photography—Handbooks, manuals, etc. 2. Photography—Films. I. Title. II. Title: Black/white film data book.

CARROLL, John S., 1911- 770.2'02
Amphoto lab handbook [by] John S. Carroll. [1st ed.] New York, American Photographic Book Pub. Co. [1970- 1 v. (loose leaf) illus. 25 cm. [TR150.C372] 76-97875
1. Photography—Handbooks, manuals, etc. 2. Photography—Films. 3. Photography—Developing and developers. I. Title.

CARROLL, John S., 1911- 770.2
Photography with the Graflex '22.' [1st ed.] New York, Morgan & Lester [1954] 128p. illus. 23cm. [TR147.C3] 54-8479
1. Photography—Handbooks, manuals, etc. 2. Twin-lens cameras. I. Title.

CASH, James Allan. 770.2
The Arrow book of photography [by] J. Allan Cash. Arrow ed., completely revised. London, Arrow Books, 1966. 127 p. 16 plates, diagrs. 18 cm. (B 66-5226) Previous ed. published as Photography on a small income, London, Hutchison, 1953. [TR146.C33] 67-84921
1. Photography — Handbooks, manuals, etc. I. Title.

CATLING, Gordon 770.2
Miniature photography for the young cameraman [by] Gordon Cating, Richard Serijeant [pseud.] (who also did the sketches) London, N. Kaye [dist. New Rochelle, N.Y., SportShelf, 1963, c.1962] 128p. illus. 20cm. 63-967 3.75 bds.,
1. Photography—Handbooks, manuals, etc. 2. Miniture cameras. I. Van Essen, William, joint author. II. Title.

CAULFIELD, Patricia. 771.3
Beginner's guide to better pictures. New York, American Photographic Book Pub. Co.; distributed to the book trade by Grosset & Dunlap [1964] 95 p. illus. 22 cm. (Better photo guides) "428." [TR146.C38] 63-22233
1. Photography — Handbooks, manuals, etc. I. Title.

*CONSUMER guide. 770'.28
Complete buying guide to photographic equipment. [New York, New American Library ,1974] 386 p. illus. 18 cm. (A Signet book) Cover title. [TR146] 1.95 (pbk.)
1. Photography-handbooks, manuals, etc. I. Title.

COOPER, Joseph David, 1917- 778.322
Photography through monocular, binoculars, and telescopes. New York, Universal Photo Books [dist. Amphoto, c.1961] 128p. illus. (U-231) 61-8113 1.95 pap.,
1. Photography—Handbooks, manuals, etc. 2. Field-glasses. 3. Telescope. I. Title.

COOPER, Joseph David, 1917- 778.322
Photography through monoculars, binoculars and telescopes, by Joseph D. Cooper. 3d ed. Philadelphia, Chilton Books [1965] 128 p. illus. 21 cm. Bibliography: p. 121-122. [TR147.C6 1965] 65-7803
1. Photography—Handbooks, manuals, etc. 2. Field-glasses. 3. Telescope. I. Title.

COOPER, Joseph David, 1917- 778.322
Photography through monoculars, binoculars, and telescopes. 3d. rev. ed. New York, Universal Photo [1967] 128p. illus. 20cm. [TR147.C6] 61-8113 1.95 pap.,
1. Photography—Handbooks, manuals, etc. 2. Field-glasses. 3. Telescope. I. Title. Distributed by Amphoto. A clothbound edition is available from Chilton.

DAFFRON, Joe, ed. 770
Photography guide. 1964 ed. New York, Sci. &Mechanics [c.]1963. 148p. illus. 24cm. (Sci. & mechanics handbk., no. 663) 63-23675 .75 pap.,
1. Photography—Handbooks, manuals, etc. I. Title.

DANIELS, Dan. 770
Photography from A to Z. New York, Chilton Book Co. [1968] 142 p. illus. 24 cm. [TR146.D245] 68-12003
1. Photography—Handbooks, manuals, etc. I. Title.

DELAMOTTE, Philip Henry, 1821-1889. 770'.28
The practice of photography. New York, Arno Press, 1973. viii, 166 p. 23 cm. (The Literature of Photography) Reprint of the 1855 ed. [TR146.D352 1973] 72-9193 ISBN 0-405-04903-X 10.00.
1. Photography—Handbooks, manuals, etc. I. Title. II. Series. BIP

DESCHIN, Jacob. 770.2
35 mm photography : approaches and techniques with the miniature camera. 1st. ed. San Francisco, Camera Craft Pub. Co. [1953] 192p. illus. 25cm. [A Camera Craft plus value book] [TR147.D49] 53-11647
1. Photography— Handbooks, manuals, etc. 2. Miniature cameras. I. Title.

DESCHIN, Jacob. 770.2'02
The New York times guide to taking better pictures. New York, Golden Press [1969] 120 p. illus. (part col.) 18 cm. Bibliography: p. 118. [TR146.D413] 75-76273 1.25
1. Photography—Handbooks, manuals, etc. I. Title. II. Title: Guide to taking better pictures.

DESCHIN, Jacob. 770.2
Rollei photography; handbook of the Rolleiflex and Rolleicord cameras. [2d print., rev.] San Francisco, Camera Craft Pub. Co. [1953] 192p. illus. 25cm. [TR263.R6D47 1953] 53-36061
1. Photography—Handbooks, manuals, etc. 2. Rolleiflex camera. 3. Rolleicord camera. I. Title.

DESCHIN, Jacob. 771.3
35 mm photography; approaches and techniques with the miniature camera. [2nd ed.] San Francisco, Camera Craft Pub. Co. [1959] 102 p. illus. 25 cm. (A Camera Craft plus value book) [TR147.D49 1959] 59-7602
1. Photography—Handbooks, manuals, etc. 2. Miniature cameras. I. Title.

DEZETTEL, Louis M. 770.24
Amateur photography for the beginner. New Augusta, Ind., Editors & Engineers [c.1966] 96p. illus. 18cm. (Skillfact lib., 622) [TR146.D42] 65-27946 1.00 pap.,
1. Photography—Handbooks, manuals, etc. I. Title.

DOBBS, Wallace E 770
Beginner's book of photography. [Rev. ed.] New York, Crown Publishers [c1953] 136p. illus. 18cm. (Little technical library. 21) [TR146.D57 1953] 53-5681
1. Photography—Handbooks, manuals, etc. I. Title.

DOWNES, Bruce. 770.282
Photography with the Ciro-flex. New York, Photo Imex [1950] 132 p. illus. (part col.) 21 cm. [TR263.C5D6] 50-2607
1. Photography—Handbooks, manuals, etc. 2. Ciroflex cameras. I. Title.

EASTMAN Kodak Company. 770'.28
The here's how book of photography. [Rochester, N.Y., 1971] 394 p. illus. 23 cm. "A compilation of the first six Kodak here's how books." [TR147.E23] 73-184546 ISBN 0-87985-001-9 9.95
1. Photography—Handbooks, manuals, etc. I. Title. II. Title: Kodak here's how. BIP

EASTMAN Kodak Company. 770'.28
The 5th & 6th here's how. Combined ed. Rochester, N.Y. : Eastman Kodak Co., c1977. 136 p. : ill. (some col.) ; 22 cm. (Kodak photo book advanced ; AE-105) [TR147.E235 1977] 78-100121 ISBN 0-87985-196-1 : 4.25
1. Photography—Handbooks, manuals, etc. I. Title.

EASTMAN Kodak Company. 770'.28
The 3rd & 4th here's how. Combined ed. Rochester, N.Y. : Eastman Kodak Co., c1975. 128 p. : col. ill. ; 22 cm. (Kodak photo book advanced ; AE-104) [TR147.E23 1975] 75-7722 ISBN 0-87985-152-X : 3.50
1. Photography—Handbooks, manuals, etc. I. Title.

EMANUEL, Walter Daniel, 1908- 770.24
The all-in-one camera-book; the easy path to good photography, by W. D. Emanuel. 57th ed. London, New York, Focal P., 1965. 232 p. illus. (some col.) tables. 13 1/2 cm. 10/6 (B 66-403) [TR146.E5 1965] 66-70251
1. Photography — Handbooks, manuals, etc. I. Title. BIP

EMANUEL, Walter Daniel, 1908- 771.3'1
Exakta 35 mm. guide: how to use the Exakta i, ii, Exakta Varex v, xv, iia, also the Exakta i, ia, ii, iia iib and 500, by W.D. Emanuel. 7th ed. London, New York, Focal, 1967. 104p. illus., tables, diagrs. 17cm. (Camera guide) 1943 to 1956 eds. pub. under the title: Exakta guide. [TR263.E9E5 1967] 68-89896 1.95
1. Photography—Handbooks, manuals, etc. 2. Exakta camera. I. Title.
Distributed by Amphoto, New York.

EMANUEL, Walter Daniel, 1908- 771.3'1
Exakta 35 mm. guide; how to use the Exakta I, II, Exakta Varex V, VX, IIa, IIb, VX500, VX1000, RTL1000, also the Exa I, Ia, II, IIa, IIb and 500, by W. D. Emanuel. 9th ed. London, New York, Focal Press, 1972. 112 p. illus. 17 cm. (The Camera guide) 1943 to 1956 editions published under title: Exakta guide. Distributed in the USA by Amphoto, New York. [TR263.E9E5 1972] 73-188892 ISBN 0-8174-0629-8 £0.65 ($2.50 U.S.)
1. Photography—Handbooks, manuals, etc. 2. Exakta camera. I. Title.

EMANUEL, Walter Daniel, 1908- 771.3'1
Exakta 35mm. guide: how to use the Exakta I, II, Exakta Varex V, VX, IIa and IIb, also the Exakta I, Ia, II, IIa and IIb, by W. D. Emanuel. 8th ed. London, New York, Focal Press [1969] 104 p. illus. 17 cm. (Camera guides) 1943 to 1956 eds. published under title: Exakta guide. [TR263.E9E5 1969] 78-441628 10/6
1. Photography—Handbooks, manuals, etc. 2. Exakta camera. I. Title.

EMANUEL, Walter Daniel, 1908- 770.2
Exakta guide; how and why with the VP Exakta, Kine-Exakta I and II, Exakta Junior and the 11th ed. London, New York, Focal Press [1950] 112 p. (p. 111-112 advertisements) illus., port. 16 cm. (The Camera guide) [TR263.E9E5 1950] 51-25853
1. Photography—Handbooks, manuals, etc. 2. Exakta camera. I. Title.

EMANUEL, Walter Daniel, 1908- 770.2
Exakta guide; how and why with the VP Exakta, Kine-Exakta I, II, V, and VX, Exa, Exakta Junior, and the 3' X 3' Exakta. 6th rev. American ed. Hollywood-by-the-Sea, Fla., Transatlantic Arts, c1954. 112 p. illus. 17 cm. (The Camera guide) 'A Focal Press book.' [TR263.E9E5 1954] 54-771
1. Photography—Handbooks. manuals, etc. 2. Exakta camera. I. Title.

EMANUEL, Walter Daniel, 1908- 771.3148
Retina guide; how to get the best out of your Retina. 7th ed. London, New York, Focal Press [1950] 64 p. (p. 61-64 advertisements) illus. 16 cm. (The Camera guide) [TR263.R4E5 1950] 51-3381
1. Photography—Handbooks, manuals, etc. 2. Retina camera. I. Title.

EMANUEL, Walter Daniel, 1908- 771.3148
Retina guide; how to get the best out of your Retina. 1st American ed. Hollywood-by-the-Sea, Fla., Transatlantic Arts, '1952. 64 p. illus. 17 cm. (The Camera guide) "A Focal Press book." [TR263.R4E5 1952] 52-1751
1. Photography—Handbooks, manuals, etc. 2. Retina camera. I. Title.

EMANUEL, Walter Daniel, 1908- 771.3'1
Rolleicord guide: how to make full use of any Rolleicord camera, by W. D. Emanuel. 5th ed. London, New York, Focal P., 1968. [1], 102 p. illus. 17 cm. (The Camera guide) [TR263.R58E5 1968] 73-370395 12/6
1. Photography—Handbooks, manuals, etc. 2. Rolleicord camera. I. Title. II. Series.

EMANUEL, Walter Daniel, 1908- 770.2
Rolleiflex guide; how to use rolleiflexes and rolleicords. 19th ed. London, New York, Focal Press [1950] 112 p. (p. 108-112 advertisements) illus. 17 cm. (The Camera guide) Previous editions by F. W. Frerk. [TR263.R6E5 1950] 51-6047
1. Photography—Handbooks, manuals, etc. 2. Rolleiflex camera. I. Frerk, Friedrich Willy. Rolleiflex guide. II. Title. BIP

EMANUEL, Walter Daniel, 1908- 771.3'1
Rolleiflex guide: how to use all the twinlens 2 1/4 x 2 1/4. Rolleiflex. Rollei-Magic, and 1 5/8 x 1 5/8 Rolleiflex models, by W.D. Emanuel 36th ed. London, New York Focal, 1967. 72p. illus., tables, diagrs. 17cm. (Camera guide) [TR263.R6E5 1967] 68-89898 1.95
1. Photography—Handbooks, manuals, etc. 2. Rolleiflex camera. I. Title.
Distributed by Amphoto, New York.

EMANUEL, Walter Daniel, 1908- 770.2
Rolleiflex guide; how to use Rolleiflexes and Rolleicords. 7th rev. American ed. New York, Transatlantic Arts, 1951. 112 p. (p. 108-112 advertisements) illus. 17 cm. (The Camera guide) "A Focal Press book." Based on previous editions by F. W. Frerk. [TR263.R6E5 1951] 51-6049
1. Photography—Handbooks, manuals, etc. 2. Rolleiflex camera. I. Frerk, Friedrich Willy. Rolleifiex guide. II. Title.

EVERYBODY'S photography manual; how to get the most out of your camera and darkroom. New York, Popular Science Pub. Co. [1951] 255 p. illus. 25 cm. [TR146.E9] 51-5824 770.82
1. Photography—Handbooks, manuals, etc. I. Popular Science Publishing Company, inc., New York.

FEININGER, Andreas, 1906- 770
Successful photography. New York, Prentice-Hall [1954] 249 p. illus. 24 cm. [TR146.F43] 53-5731
1. Photography—Handbooks, manuals, etc. I. Title. BIP

FEININGER, Andreas, 1906- 770
Successful photography / by Andreas Feininger. Rev. ed. Englewood Cliffs, N.J. : Prentice-Hall, [1975] 320 p. : ill. ; 23 cm. Includes index. [TR146.F43 1975] 74-23537 ISBN 0-13-864603-1 : 9.95
1. Photography—Handbooks, manuals, etc. I. Title.

FENTEN, D. X. 770.24
Better photography for amateurs. New York, Universal Photo [1967, c.1965] 128p. illus. 20cm. (Universal photo bk.) [TR146.F45] 1.95 pap.,
1. Photography— Handbooks, manuals, etc. I. Title.

FENTEN, D. X. 770
Better photography for amateurs / by D. X. Fenten. Garden City, N.Y. : Amphoto, [1975] 96 p., [2] leaves of plates : ill. (some col.) ; 26 cm. (A modern photoguide) Includes index. [TR146.F45 1975] 75-1969 ISBN 0-8174-0183-0 pbk. : 3.45
1. Photography—Handbooks, manuals, etc. I. Title.

FENTON, D X 770'.28
Better photography for amateurs. [2d ed.] New York, Universal Photo Books [1963] 128 p. illus. 21 cm. [TR146.F45] 63-25348
1. Photography—Handbooks, manuals, etc. I. Title. BIP

FLOYD, Wayne 770.28
Floyd's photo tips [450 short cuts to better picture making] New York, Amphoto [c. 1960] unpaged. illus. 60-15899 2.50bds.,
1. Photography—Handbooks, manuals, etc.— I. Title. II. Title: Photo tips.

FLYNN, Jack O. 770.283
Develop, print, and enlarge your own pictures [by] Jack O. Flynn, Alan Kellock [and] Albert J. Rosenberg; with a foreword by Morris Germain. New York, McGraw-Hill [1952] 113 p. illus. 26 cm. On cover: How to develop, print, and enlarge your own pictures. [TR146.F55] 52-5346
1. Photography—Handbooks, manuals, etc. I. Title. II. Title: How to develop, print, and enlarge your own pictures.

FOCAL Press, ltd., London. 770.2
The camera touring guide to Europe. Compiled by the editors, overseas correspondents, and the Service Dept. of the Focal Press. New York, Ziff-Davis Pub. Co. [1960] 176p. illus. 19cm. 60-4107 2.95 flex plastic,
1. Photography— Handbooks, manuals, etc. 2. Europe—Descr. & trav.—Guide-books. 3. Photography—Apparatus and supplies—Direct. I. Title.

FORNEY, James. 770'.2'02
The Sylvania practical guide to good pictures. New York, Grosset & Dunlap [1967, c1966] 127 p. illus. (part col.) 21 cm. A Rutledge book. [TR146.F66] 66-13824
1. Photography—Handbooks, manuals, etc. I. Title.

FOX, Stuart. 770.28
Photography, using only available light. New York, Cornerstone Library; [distributed by Affiliated Publishers, 1966] 144 p. illus. (part col.) 20 cm. [TR146.F67] 65-22091
1. Photography—Handbooks, manuals, etc. I. Title.

FRANKEL, Godfrey 770.24
Photography. New York, Sterling [1961,c. 1954] c128p. illus. 'Originally published under the title of Short cut to photography.' (Worthwhile how-to paperbacks, 106) 61-65969 1.00pap.,
1. Photography—Handbooks, manuals, etc. I. Title.

FRANKEL, Godfrey. 770.2
Short cut to photography. New York, Sterling Pub. Co. [1954] 128 p. illus. 21 cm. [TR146.F74] 54-9948
1. Photography—Handbooks, manuals, etc. I. Title.

FREYTAG, Heinrich. 770.2
The Contax way; the Contax photographer's companion. [Translated and adapted by Gerald R. Sharp] London, New York, Focal Press [1953] 272p. illus. 22cm. [TR263.C6F73] 53-3151
1. Photography—Handbooks, manuals, etc. 2. Contax camera. 3. Photography—Enlarging. I. Title.

FREYTAG, Heinrich. 770.2
Reinhold's photo and movie book [by] H. Freytag. New York, Reinhold [1964] 416 p. illus. (part col.) 21 cm. Translation of Knaurs Foto-und Filmbuch. [TR146.F873] 64-22422
1. Photography—Handbooks, manuals, etc. I. Title.

GOLDSMITH, Arthur A 770.2
How to make better pictures. New York, Maco Magazine Corp., c1955. 144p. illus. 24cm. [TR146.G58] 55-1682
1. Photography-Handbooks, manuals, etc. I. Title.

GOLDSMITH, Arthur A 770.2
How to take better pictures. Indianapolis, Bobbs-Merrill, c1955. 144p. illus. 25cm. [TR146] 55-14604
1. Photography-Handbooks, manuals, etc. I. Title.

GOTLOP, Philip 770.24
Tackle photography this way. London, S. Paul [1959, i. e., 1960] [stamped: distributed by Sport-Shelf, New Rochelle, N. Y.] 125p. illus. 19cm. p3.25 60-1862
1. Photography—Handbooks, manuals, etc. I. Title.

HEDGECOE, John. 770'.28
John Hedgecoe's Pocket guide to practical photography. New York : Simon and Schuster, c1979. p. cm. (A Fireside book) Includes index. [TR146.H44] 79-805 ISBN 0-671-24929-0 : 4.95
1. Photography—Handbooks, manuals, etc. I. Title. II. Title: Pocket guide to practical photography.

HEDGECOE, John. 770'.28
John Hedgecoe's Pocket guide to practical photography. New York : Simon and Schuster, c1979. p. cm. (A Fireside book) Includes index. [TR146.H44] 79-805 ISBN 0-671-24929-0 : 4.95
1. Photography—Handbooks, manuals, etc. I. Title. II. Title: Pocket guide to practical photography. BIP

HEDGECOE, John. 770'.2'02
The photographers handbook / by John Hedgecoe. 1st ed. New York : Knopf, 1977. p. cm. [TR150.H36] 77-74981 ISBN 0-394-40754-7 : 16.95
1. Photography—Handbooks, manuals, etc. I. Title. BIP

HEERING, Walther, 1902- 770.2
The Rollei book; a textbook for the use of Rolleiflex and Rolleicord. 6th ed. [English translation: Fred Willy Freek] Vaduz [Liechtenstein] Heering Publications; sole U. S. agency: Rayelle Publications, Philadelphia, 1954 [i.e. 1956] 272, 20p. illus. 22cm. Supplement ... English adaptation by Norman Rothschild,' 1955: 20p. at end. [TR263.R6H413 1956] 56-13564
1. Photography—Handbooks, manuals, etc. 2. Rolleiflex camera. 3. Rolleicord camera. I. Title.

HENLE, Fritz, 1909- 770.28
Guide to Rollei photography. With the editorial assistance of George B. Wright. New York, Studio Publications [c1956] 208p. illus. 27cm. [TR263.R6H45] 56-10900
1. Photography—Handbooks, manuals, etc. 2. Rolleiflex camera. 3. Photography, Artistic. I. Title. II. Title: Rollei photography.

HENLE, Fritz, 1909- 770.24
Photography for everyone, by Fritz Henle with H. H. Kinzer. New York, Viking Press [1959] 144 p. illus. 21 cm. (A Studio book) [TR146.H52] 59-7766
1. Photography—Handbooks, manuals, etc. I. Title.

HERTZBERG, Robert Edward, 1905- 770.28
Photo darkroom guide. [2d ed.] New York, Universal Photo Books [1958] 122p. illus. 21cm. [TR146.H574 1958] 59-223
1. Photography—Handbooks, manuals, etc. I. Title. BIP

HERTZBERG, Robert Edward, 1905- 770.283
Photo darkroom guide. New York, Greenberg [1954] 122p. illus. 20cm. (The Modern camera guide series) [TR146.H574] 54-8125
1. Photography—Handbooks, manuals, etc. I. Title.

HIBBERT, L J 770
A manual of photographic technique. 4th ed. London, Pitman [1952] 142p. illus. 17cm. (Pitman's technical primer series) [TR146.H6 1952] 53-23697
1. Photography—Handbooks, manuals, etc. I. Title.

HIGHLAND, Harold Joseph. 770.2
Audels guide to creative photography. New York, T. Audel [1960] 400p. illus. 17cm. [TR146.H64] 60-51622
1. Photography—Handbooks, manuals, etc. 2. Photography, Artistic. I. Title. II. Title: Creative photography.

JOHNSON, Philip. 770.2
The complete photobook. London, Fountain Press U. S. representatives: Rayelle Publications, Philadelphia [1955] 255p. illus. 19cm. (A Fountain photobook) [TR146.J566] 56-20385
1. Photography—Handbooks, manulas, etc. I. Title.

JONAS, Paul. 771.3
Improved 35 mm techniques. 3d ed. New York, Universal Photo Books [c1965] 124 p. illus. 21 cm. [TR262.J6] 67-5618
1. Photography—Handbooks, manuals, etc. 2. Miniature cameras. I. Title.

JONAS, Paul. 770.28
Improved 35 mm techniques. 3d ed. Philadelphia, Chilton Books [1965] xii, 124 p. illus. 21 cm. [TR262.J6] 65-7784
1. Photography—Handbooks, manuals, etc. 2. Miniature cameras. I. Title.

JONAS, Paul. 771.3
Improved 35 mm techniques. [2d ed., rev.]

SUBJECT INDEX PHOTOGRAPHY—HANDBOOKS, MANUALS, ETC.

New York, Universal Photo Books [c1963] 124 p. illus. 21 cm. [TR262.J6] 63-25288
1. Photography—Handbooks, manuals, etc. 2. Miniature cameras. I. Title.

JONAS, Paul. 770.282
Improved 35 mm techniques. 4th ed. New York, American Photographic Book Pub. Co. [1967] 128 p. illus. 20 cm. [TR262.J6 1967b] 68-1451
1. Photography—Handbooks, manuals, etc. 2. Miniature cameras. I. Title.

JONAS, Paul. 771.3
Improved 35mm techniques [2d. ed.] New York, Universal Photo [dist. Amphoto, c. 1960,1963] 124p. illus. 21cm. 1.95pap.,
1. Photography—Handbooks, manuals, etc. 2. Miniature cameras. I. Title.

JONAS, Paul. 770.282
Improved 35mm techniques. 4th ed. Philadelphia, Chilton Book Co. [1967] 128 p. illus. 21 cm. [TR262.J6 1967] 67-25845
1. Photography—Handbooks, manuals, etc. 2. Miniature cameras. I. Title.

JONAS, Paul. 771.3
Improved 35mm techniques. [1st ed. New York, Verlan Books [1960] 124p. illus. 21cm. (A Universal photo book) [TR146.J62] 60-7946
1. Photography—Handbooks, manuals, etc. 2. Miniature cameras. I. Title.

JONAS, Paul. 770.283
Manual of darkroom procedures and techniques. New York, Universal Photo Books [1962] 128p. illus. 20cm. [TR146.J624] 62-12124
1. Photography—Handbooks, manuals, etc. 2. Photography—Studios and dark rooms. I. Title. II. Title: Darkroom procedures and techniques.

KANAMEISHI, Betty M 1926- ed. 770.2
How to take better photographs. [Chicago] Popular Mechanics Press [1954] 160p. illus. 24cm. [TR146.K33] 53-11869
1. Photography—Handbooks, manuals, etc. I. Title.

KEELEY, Joseph Charles, 1907- 770.2
Taking it easy with your camera. [1st ed.] New York, Duell, Sloan and Pearce [1957] 191 p. illus. 21 cm. [TR146.K38] 57-7576
1. Photography—Handbooks, manuals, etc. I. Title.

KEPPLER, Herbert. 770.24
How to make better pictures in your home. New York, Amphoto [1962] 127p. illus. 21cm. [TR146.K43] 62-12303
1. Photography—Handbooks, manuals, etc. I. Title.

KIDD, Maurice Kenneth, 1910- 770.2
Photography at school and college. London, New York, Focal Press [1951] 200 p. illus. 19 cm. [TR146.K5] 52-42687
1. Photography—Handbooks, manuals, etc. I. Title.

KINZER, Harless Mahlon. 770.2
Available light photography. [1st ed.] New York, Universal Photo Books [1955] 119p. illus. 21cm. (A Universal photo guide) [TR146.K54] 55-12262
1. Photography—Handbooks, manuals, etc. I. Title.

KINZER, Harless Mahlon 770.2
Available light photography. [3d ed. New York] Universal Photog Bks. [dist. Amphoto, c.1955-1961] 119p. illus. (Universal photo guide) 61-65794 1.95 pap.,
1. Photography—Handbooks, manuals, etc. I. Title.

KINZER, Harless Mahlon 770.2
Available light photography. 4th ed. New York, Universal Photo [dist. Amphoto, 1965,c.1955-1964] 119p. illus. 21cm. (Universal photo guide) [TR146.K54] 65-7780 1.95 pap.,
1. Photography—Handbooks, manuals, etc. I. Title.

KNOPF, Aaron A. 770.2
Secrets of taking good pictures. [1st ed.] Garden City, N.Y., Hanover House [1955] 144 p. illus. 22 cm. [TR146.K56] 55-6487
1. Photography—Handbooks, manuals, etc. I. Title.

KNOPF, Aaron A 770.2
Secrets of taking good pictures. New rev. [i. e. 2d] ed. Garden City, N. Y., Hanover House [1958] 144p. illus. 22cm. [TR146.K56 1958] 58-8095
1. Photography—Handbooks, manuals, etc. I. Title.

LANGER, M Donald. 770.2
.My hobby is photography. New York, Hart Book Co. [1956] 128p. illus. 25cm. Includes bibliography. [TR146.L29] 56-13872
1. Photography—Handbooks, manuals, etc. I. Title.

LANGER, M Donald. 770.24
Photography made simple. [1st ed.] Garden City, N.Y.,Doubleday [1964] viii, 184 p. illus. ports. 26 cm. (Made simple books, MS57) [TR146.L293] 63-18736
1. Photography — Hanbooks, manuals, etc. I. Title.

LATHAM, Sidney. 770.2
A guide to available light photography. New York, Greenberg, 1955. 126 p. illus. 20 cm. [TR145.L35] 55-11519
1. Photography—Handbooks, manuals, etc. I. Title.

LESSERE, Samuel E 770.2
What you must know when you travel with a camera. Greenlawn, N. Y., Harian Publications; trade distributor: Greenberg [New York] c1954. 96p. illus. 22cm. [TR146.L48] 54-3105
1. Photography—Handbooks, manuals, etc. I. Title.

LESSERE, Samuel E. 770.2
What you must know when you travel with a camera. Greenlawn, N. Y., Harian Publications; trade distributor; Greenberg [New York] c1956. 125p. illus. 22cm. [TR146.L48 1956] 56-2028
1. Photography—Handbooks, manuals, etc. I. Title.

LESSERE, Samuel E 770.2
What you must know when you travel with a camera. Greenlawn, N. Y., Harian Publications; trade distributor: Greenberg [New York] c1955. 125p. illus. 22cm. [TR146.L48 1955] 55-13961
1. Photography—Handbooks, manuals, etc. I. Title.

LESSERE, Samuel E 770.2
What you must know when you travel with a camera. 3d rev. and enl. ed. Greenlawn, N. Y., Harian Publications; trade distributor:Greenberg [New York] c1957. 125p. illus. 22cm. [TR146.L48 1957] 57-13813
1. Photography—Handbooks, manuals, etc. I. Title.

LESSERE, Samuel E 770.282
What you must know when you travel with a camera. 4th rev. and enl. ed. Greenlawn, N. Y., Harian Publications; trade distributor: Crown Publishers [New York] c1959. 125p. illus. 22cm. [TR146.L48 1959] 59-3554
1. Photography—Handbooks, manuals, etc. I. Title.

MCCOY, Robert A. 770.24
Practical photography. [2d ed.]*xiv, 291p. illus. (part col.), diagrs. 24cm. 60-287 4.00
1. Photography— Handbooks, manuals, etc. I. Title.

MCCOY, Robert A. 770
Practical photography. Bloomington,Ill., Mcknight & Mcknight [1950] xv, 221 p. illus. 24 cm. Bibliography: p. 187-188 [TR146.M25] 50-7631
1. Photography—Handbooks, manuals, etc. I. Title.

MCCOY, Robert A. 770'.28
Practical photography [by] Robert A. McCoy. [3d ed.] Bloomington, Ill., McKnight & McKnight [1972] xiii, 296 p. illus. 24 cm. Bibliography: p. 277-280. [TR146.M25 1972] 74-189178 ISBN 0-87345-431-6 9.00
1. Photography—Handbooks, manuals, etc. I. Title.

MCINTYRE, Robert L., ed. 770.76
1,000answers to questions about photography (1,000 photo questions answered by experts New York, Grosset [1962, c. 1959] 248p. illus. 21cm. (1934) First pub. in 1959 under title: 1000 photo questions answered by experts. cd62 1.95pap.,
1. Photography—Handbooks, manuals, etc. I. Title.

MCINTYRE, Robert L ed. 770.76
1,000 photo questions answered by experts. New York, Ziff-Davis Pub. Co. [c1959] 248p. illus. 24cm. [TR146.M28] 59-15253
1. Photography—Handbooks, manuals, etc. I. Title.

MANNHEIM, Ladislaus Andrew, 1925- 770.2
The Rollei way; the Rolleiflex and Rolleicord photographer's companion, with contributions by John Gay [and others] London, New York, Focal Press [1952?] 224p. illus. 22cm. [TR263.R6M35] 53-22987
1. Photography—Handbooks, manuals, etc. 2. Rolleiflex camera. I. Title. **BIP**

MARSHALL, Lucile Robertson. 770
Photography for teen-agers. [1st ed.] New York, Prentice-Hall [1951] ix, 165 p. illus. 21 cm. [TR146.M36] 51-11357
1. Photography—Handbooks, manuals, etc. I. Title.

MARSHALL, Lucile (Robertson) 770
Photography for teen-agers. 2d ed. Englewood Cliffs, N. J., Prentice-Hall [1957] 185p. illus. 21cm. [TR146.M36 1957] 57-10587
1. Photography—Handbooks, manuals, etc. I. Title.

MATHESON, Andrew. 771.3
Successful 35mm. photography. London, New York, Focal Press [c1959] 163p. illus. 19cm. [TR146.M365] 60-832
1. Photography—Handbooks, manuals, etc. 2. Miniature cameras. I. Title.

MILLER, Walter Homer, 1909- [917.55425] 798.94
Williamsburg pictures, how and where; photographs and text by Walter H. Miller. Richmond, Dietz Press [c1951] 118 p. illus. 26 cm. [TR146.M53] 51-14998
1. Photography — Handbook, manuals, etc. 2. Williamsburg, Va. — Descr. — Views. I. Title.

MORGAN and Morgan, inc. 770.2
Pocket photo data book. New York, Morgan & Morgan [1958] 136p. illus. 19cm. [TR150.M64] 58-9905
1. Photography—Handbooks, manuals, manuals, etc. I. Title. II. Title: Photo data book.

MORGAN and Morgan, inc. 770.28
Pocket photo data book. [4th ed.] Hastings-on-Hudson, N. Y. [1966] 112 p. illus. 19 cm. Photo data book. [TR150.M64 1966] 66-3387
1. Photography — Handbooks, manuals, etc. I. Title. II. Series.

MORGAN and Morgan, inc. 770.2
Pocket photo data book [3d ed.] New York, Author [c. 1964] 156p. illus. 19cm. 64-20636 3.95,plastic,ring binder hoto data book.
1. Photography-Handbooks, manuals, etc. I. Title.

MORGAN and Morgan, Inc. 770.2
Pocket photo data book [New 4th ed.] Hastings-on-Hudson, N.Y., Author [c.1966] 112p. tables. 19cm. [TR150.M64] 58-9905 3.95, in ring binder.
1. Photography—Handbooks, manuals, etc. I. Title. II. Title: Photo data book.

MORGAN, Willard Detering, 1900- 771.31
Leica manual and data book [by] Willard D. Morgan. Assoc. eds.: John S. Carroll, Dorothy S. Gelatt. Introd. by Manuel Kmroff. 14th rev. ed. New York, Morgan & Morgan [c. 1961] 456p. illus. 35-14997 6.95
1. Photography—Handbooks, manuals, etc. 2. Leica camera. I. Title.

MORGAN, Willard Detering, 1900-1967. 771.3'1
The Leica manual / by Willard D. Morgan, Henry M. Lester, and contributors ; with an introd. by Rolf Fricke. Facsim. ed. Dobbs Ferry, N.Y. : Morgan & Morgan, 1977 [c1935] 501 p. (p. 485-501 advertisements) : ill. ; 22 cm. Photoreprint ed. Includes index. [TR146.M772 1977] 77-378540 ISBN 0-87100-118-7 : 12.95
1. Photography—Handbooks, manuals, etc. 2. Leica camera. I. Lester, Henry M., joint author. II. Title.

MURPHY, Burt. 770.282
Creative camera techniques; advanced methods for rendering detail and applying diffusion. New York, Universal Photo Books [1961] 128p. illus. 20cm. [TR146.M84] 60-53553
1. Photography—Handbooks, manuals, etc. I. Title.

NATHAN, Simon. 771.3
Good photography Greenwich, Conn., Fawcett Publications, c1958. 144p. illus. 24cm. (A Fawcett how-to book, 392) [TR146.N25] 59-39
1. Photography—Handbooks, manuals, etc. 2. Miniature cameras. I. Title.

NATHAN, Simon. 771.3
Good photography's 35mm handbook Greenwich, Conn., Fawcett Publications, 1960. 144p. illus. 24cm. (A Fawcett how-to book, 456) [TR146.N25 1960] 60-50576
1. Photography—Handbooks, manuals, etc. 2. Miniature cameras. I. Title.

NETTIS, Joseph 770.24
Traveling with your camera; creative 35 mm photography. Philadelphia, Chilton [c.1965] 96p. illus. 21cm. [TR700.N4] 65-17115 2.95
1. Photography—Handbooks, manuals, etc 2. Travel. I. Title.

NEWCOMBE, Harry S 771.3148
Thirty-five mm. photo technique; miniature camera practice. 10th ed. London, New York, Focal Press [1955] 328p. illus. 20cm. [TR147.N46 1955] 56-13737
1. Photography—Handbooks, manuals, etc. 2. Miniature cameras. I. Title.

NEWCOMBE, Harry S 771.3148
35 mm. photo technique; miniature camera practice 6th ed. London, New York, Focal Press [1951] 327 p. illus. 20 cm. [TR147.N46] 52-42685
1. Photography — Handbooks, manuals, etc. 2. Miniature cameras. I. Title.

NEWCOMBE, Henry Sainsbury. 771.3
35mm. photo technique [by] H. S. Newcombe. 17th ed. London, New York, Focal Press, 1971. 325 p. illus. 22 cm. [TR147.N46 1971] 72-179572 ISBN 0-240-44880-4 £2.25
1. Photography—Handbooks, manuals, etc. 2. Miniature cameras. I. Title.

NIBBELINK, Don D 770.2
Photography for the traveler. Rev. by Mel Fauer. New York, Crown Publishers [1955] 109p. illus. 18cm. (Little technical library, 37) [TR147.N5 1955] 55-8884
1. Photography —Handbooks, manuals, etc. 2. Travel. I. Title.

ODHAM'S manual of photography: practical guide for amateurs. New York, Macmillan, 1961 [c. 1960] 352p. illus. (part col.) 26cm. 7.50 770.24
1. Photography—Handbooks, manuals, etc.

ODHAMS manual of photography: the practical guide for amateurs. London, Odhams Press label: Transatlantic Arts, inc., Hollywood, Fla [c1960;] 352p. illus. 26cm. [TR146.O27] 61-2616 770.24
1. Photography— Handbooks, manuals, etc.

OVINGTON, Ray, ed. 778.7
The compact book of outdoor photography. Contributors: Bob Zwirz [and others] New York, J. L. Pratt; [distributed by Kable News Co., 1964] 96 p. illus., ports. 18 cm. (The Compact outdoorsman's library) The American sports library, 112. Bibliography: p. 95. [TR146.O9] 64-10985
1. Photography — Handbooks, manuals, etc. 2. Nature photography. I. Title. II. Title: Outdoor photography.

PARKER, James E 770.2
An approach to photography. Ann Arbor, Mich., Lithoprinted [by] Edwards Bros. [1960] vi, 105p. illus., ports. 28cm.

Bibliography: p. 97-98. [TR146.P22] 60-1915
1. Photography—Handbooks, manuals, etc. I. Title.

PARTRIDGE, Edward C 770.2
Beginner's guide to photography. New York, McBride Books [1962] 144 p. illus. 19 cm [[TR146]] 62-13550
1. Photography—Handbooks, manuals, etc. I. Title.

PARTRIDGE,Edward C. 770.2
*Beginner's guide to photography*New York,* McBride Bks. [c. 1962] 144p. illus.cpt. col.) 19cm. 62-13550 2.95 bds.,
1. Photography-Handbooks, manuals,etc. I. Title.

PEARLMAN, Alec 771.31
Rollei handbook [3d ed.] London, Fountain Pr. [dist. New York, Morgan & Morgan, 1964, c. 1954] 169p. illus., diagrs. 12x15cm. (Fountain photobk.) 64-9862 2.95 bds.,
1. Photography—Handbooks, manuals, etc. 2. Rolleiflex camera. I. Title.

PEARLMAN, Alec 771.31
Rollei manual; the complete book of twin-lens photography [4th ed.] London, Fountain Pr. [dist. New York, Morgan & Morgan, 1964, c.1953-1960] 431p. illus. (pt. col.) 23cm. (Fountain photobk.) 9.95
1. Photography—Handbooks, manuals, etc. 2. Rolleiflex camera. 3. Rolleicord comera. I. Title.

THE Photo-amateur's 770.2
pocketbook; diary, directory, data-book. London, New York, Focal Press. v. illus. 15 cm. [TR146.P43] 51-36537
1. Photography — Handbooks, manuals, etc. 2. Photography — Societies.

PHOTOGRAPHERS' guide to 770
Britain. London, New York, Focal Press [1951] 200 p. illus. 17 cm. [TR150.P54] 52-16469
1. Photography — Handbooks, manuals, etc. 2. Gt. Brit. — Descr. & trav.

PHOTOGRAPHER'S 770'.2'02
handbook. [New York, Time Life Books, 1972] 64 p. illus. 21 cm. (Life library of photography) Cover title. [TR146.P436] 73-114406
1. Photography—Handbooks, manuals, etc. I. Time-Life Books.

†PHOTOGRAPHER'S 770'.2'02
handbook. [New York : Time Life Books], c1976. 64 p. : ill. ; 21 cm. (Life library of photography) Cover title. [TR146P436 1976] 76-368115 6.95
1. Photography—Handbooks, manuals, etc. I. Time-Life Books.

THE Photographer's 770.2
pocketbook, databook, directory. London, New York, Focal Press [1950?] 256 p. illus. 15 cm. [TR150.P56] 50-57202
1. Photography — Handbooks, manuals, etc.

PHOTOGRAPHY handbook. 770.2
[New York, Arco, 1955] 144p. illus. 26cm. [Arco handy books for better living] Fawcett book 269. [TR146.P445] 55-9429
1. Photography—Handbooks, manuals, etc.

POPULAR photography 770.2
(Chicago)
Popular photography's invitation to photography; a complete guide to picture-taking. [New York, Ziff-Davis Pub., c.1966] 112p. illus. (pt. col.) 29cm. Cover title. [TR146.P447] 66-6435 3.00 pap.,
1. Photography—Handbooks, manuals, etc. I. Title. II. Title: Invitation to photography.

PRESSMAN, Zev. 770
Handbook of better photography [by] Zev Pressman and Paul Lamle. [Rev. ed.] New York, Tudor Pub. Co. [1955] 127p. illus. 29cm. [TR145.P9 1955] 56-46567
1. Photography—Handbooks, manuals, etc. I. Lamle, Paul, joint author. II. Title.

REED, Alice S. 778.8
Simple photo tricks everyone can do. New York, Amphoto; dist. Grosset [c.1964] 96p. illu 63-22237
I. Title.

REID, Giorgina. 770.2
The delights of photography, a working manual. New York, Barnes [1963] 185 p. illus. 26 cm. [TR146.R43] 61-14235
1. Photography—Handbooks, Manuals, etc. I. Title.

RUSSELL, Henry George 771.3
A handbook of miniature photography, by Henry G. Russell ('Minicam') [4th (rev.) ed.] London, N. Kaye [1960]; stamped: distributed by SportShelf, New Rochelle, N. Y.] 280p. illus. 23cm. 60-50993 8.00bds.,
1. Photography—Handbooks, manuals, etc. 2. Miniature cameras. I. Title.

SATOW, Y Ernest. 771.3
35 mm negs. and prints and how to get the most from them New York, Amphoto [1962] 128p. illus. 21cm. [TR146.S36 1962] 62-12837
1. Photography—Handbooks, manuals, etc. 2. Miniature cameras. I. Title.

SATOW, Y Ernest. 778.719
Taking pictures after dark. New York, Amphoto [c1960] 119p. illus. 21cm. [TR147.S3] 60-15901
1. Photography— Handbooks, manuals, etc. I. Title.

SATOW, Y. Ernest 771.3
35mm negs & prints. Rev. ed. New York, Amphoto [c. 1960, 1962] 128p. illus. 21cm. 62-12837 2.50bds.,
1. Photography—Handbooks, manuals, etc. 2. Miniature cameras. I. Title.

SATOW, Y. Ernest. 770.28
35 mm negs & prints, and how to get the most from them [by] Y. Ernest Satow. 3d. ed. Philadelphia, Chilton Book Co. [1969] 160 p. illus., ports. 24 cm. [TR146.S36 1969b] 78-7908 5.95
1. Photography—Handbooks, manuals, etc. 2. Miniature cameras. I. Title.

SCAYLEA, Josef. 770'.28
Scaylea on photography : how he does it / by Josef Scaylea. Seattle : Superior Pub. Co., [1976] [64] p. : ill. ; 35 cm. "A Salisbury Press book." [TR146.S37] 76-2521 ISBN 0-87564-014-1 : 19.95
1. Photography—Handbooks, manuals, etc. I. Title. BIP

SPILLMAN, Ronald 770.24
Good basic photography. London, Arlington Bks. [New Rochelle, N.Y., SportShelf, 1966, c.1964] 70p. illus. 16cm. [TR146.S64] 66-1443 1.75 pap.,
1. Photography—Handbooks, manuals, etc. 2. Travel. 3. Travel. I. Title.

STETTNER, Louis, 1922- 770.2
U.S. Camera's 35mm photography New York, U.S. Camera Pub. Corp. [1956] 126 p. illus. 23 cm. [TR146.S815] 56-4696
1. Photography — Handbooks, manuals, etc. 2. Miniature cameras. I. Title.

STILLMAN, Peter R. 770'.28
Improving your camera handling, by Peter R. Stillman. Illustrated by the author. Charlotteville, N.Y., SamHar Press, 1973. 32 p. illus. 22 cm. (Hand crafts and hobbies) [TR146.S823] 73-76623
1. Photography—Handbooks, manuals, etc. 2. Cameras. I. Title. BIP

STROETHOFF, 778.9'9'7455928
Pieter.
Photography for the scalemodeller / by Pieter Stroethoff. New York : Drake Publishers, 1978, c1975. 79 p. : ill. ; 26 cm. [TR148.S77 1978] 78-55052 ISBN 0-8473-1800-1 pbk. : 5.95
1. Photography—Handbooks, manuals, etc. 2. Models and modelmaking. I. Title. BIP

SUSSMAN, Aaron. 770.2
The amateur photographer's handbook; rev. by the author, and with revisions by Bruce Downes. 4th ed. New York, Crowell [1952] 400 p. illus. 25 cm. [TR146.S9 1952] 52-7856
1. Photography — Handbooks, manuals, etc. I. Title. BIP

SUSSMAN, Aaron. 770
The amateur photographer's handbook. 8th rev. ed. New York, Crowell [1973, c1972] p. Previous editions are entered under title. [TR146.S887 1973] 72-8868 ISBN 0-690-05782-2
1. Photography—Handbooks, manuals, etc. I. Title.

SWEDLUND, Charles. 770.2'02
A guide to photography. [Buffalo, Partners' Press] 1967. 151 p. illus. 29 cm. Bibliography: p. 142-146. [TR146.S92] 67-30492
1. Photography—Handbooks, manuals, etc. I. Title.

SWEDLUND, Charles. 770
Photography: a handbook of history, materials, and processes. New York, Holt, Rinehart and Winston [1974] xvi, 368 p. illus. 26 cm. Bibliography: p. 352-358. [TR146.S93] 73-1236 ISBN 0-03-010751-2 12.95
1. Photography—Handbooks, manuals, etc. I. Title.

THOMAS, Woodlief, 1929- 770'.1'5
SPSE handbook of photographic science and engineering. Edited by Woodlief Thomas, Jr. New York, Wiley [1973] xii, 1416 p. illus. 24 cm. (Wiley series on photographic science and technology and the graphic arts) "A Wiley-Interscience publication." Includes bibliographical references. [TR150.T48] 72-10168 ISBN 0-471-81880-1 37.50
1. Photography—Handbooks, manuals, etc. I. Society of Photographic Scientists and Engineers. II. Title. BIP

TYDINGS, Kenneth S 770.2
Basic all-35mm camera shooting guide Philadelphia, Chilton Co., Book Division, c1960. 127 p. illus. 20 cm. (The Modern camera guide series. 584) [TR146.T9] 60-14473
1. Photography — Handbooks, manula, etc. 2. Miniature cameras. I. Title.

TYDINGS, Kenneth S. 770.2
Guide to Kodak miniature cameras. New York, Greenberg, c1952. 128 p. illus. 20 cm. [TR150.T9] 52-5624
1. Photography—Handbooks, manuals, etc. 2. Miniature cameras. I. Title: Kodak miniature cameras.

TYDINGS, Kenneth S 770.2
Guide to Kodak miniature cameras. Rev. New York, Greenberg, 1957. 128 p. illus. 20 cm. (The Modern camera guide series. 18) [TR150.T9] 57-14590
1. Photography — Handbooks, manuals, etc. 2. Miniature cameras. I. Title. II. Title: Kodak miniature cameras.

TYDINGS, Kenneth S 771.3
Handbook of 35mm camera practice. Philadelphia, Chilton Co., Book Division, c1961. 127 p. illus. 20 cm. (Modern camera guide series, 607) [TR146.R92] 60-15378
1. Photography — Handbooks, manuals, etc. 2. Miniature cameras. I. Title. II. Title: 35mm camera practice.

TYDINGS, Kenneth S 770.2
The modern Rolleiflex and Rolleicord guide. New York, Greenberg, c1952. 128 p. illus. 20 cm. (The Modern camera guide series) [TR263.R6T9] 52-8126
1. Photography — Handbooks, manuals, etc. 2. Rolleiflex camera. I. Title.

TYDINGS, Kenneth S 771.31
Praktica, Praktina, Pentacon, Edixaflex guide. Philadelphia, Chilton Co., Book Division, c1961. 127 p. illus. 20 cm. (Modern camera guide series, 421) [TR146.T93] 61-14026
1. Photography — Handbooks, manuals, etc. 2. Single-lens reflex cameras. I. Title.

TYDINGS, Kenneth S 770.2
Self-teaching all-camera photography. Long Beach [Calif.] Photolix, Book Division, 1963. 123 p. illus. 22 cm. (Visual self-teaching workbooks) "P1." [[TR146]] 63-6857
1. Photography — Handbooks, manuals, etc. I. Title.

WAGG, Alfred. 770.2
Know your camera. New York, W. Funk, 1956. 244 p. illus. 24 cm. [TR146.W15] 56-7748
1. Photography — Handbooks, manuals, etc. 2. Cameras. I. Title.

WAHL, Paul Francis, 1922- 770.2
The candid photographer. Philadelphia, Chilton Books, 1963. 96 p. illus. 20 cm. (Modern camera guide series) [TR146.W158] 63-16483
1. Photography—Handbooks, manuals, etc. 2. Miniature cameras. I. Title.

WAHL, Paul Francis, 1922- 771.31
Subminiature technique. Philadelphia, Chilton Co., Book Division [1960] 128 p. illus., diagrs., tables. 20 cm. (Modern camera guide series, 464) [TR146.W16] 60-10702
1. Photography—Handbooks, manuals, etc. 2. Miniature cameras. I. Title. II. Series.

WALLS, Henry James. 770
Camera techniques, fundamentals and equipment [by] H. J. Walls. 3d rev. ed. London, New York, Focal Press [1964] 408 p. illus. 22 cm. (The Manual of photo-technique) First ed. published in 1954 under title: Photo-technique, fundsmentals and equipment. [TR146.W25 1964] 65-9284
1. Photography—Handbooks, manuals, etc. I. Title. II. Series: The Manuals of photo technique

WALLS, Henry James. 770'.28
Photo technique, fundamentals and equipment. [1st ed.] London, New York, Focal Press [1954] 384p. illus. 19cm. (The Manual of photo -technique) [TR146.W25] 55-30849
1. Photography—Handbooks, manuals. etc. I. Title.

WEISBORD, Marvin. 770.24
Basic photography. Philadelphia, Chilton Co., Book Division, c1959. 141 p. illus. 21 cm. (Modern camera guide series, 458) [TR146.W33] 59-14576
1. Photography — Handbooks, manuals, etc. I. Title. BIP

WEISBORD, Marvin Ross. 770'.28
Basic photography [by] Marvin Weisbord. 3d ed. Garden City, N.Y., Amphoto [1973] 156 p. illus. 21 cm. [TR146.W33 1973] 72-93374 ISBN 0-8174-0423-6 3.95
1. Photography—Handbooks, manuals, etc. I. Title.

WHAL, Paul Francis, 1922- 770.2
*The candid photographer.*Philadelphia,* Chilton, c. 1963. 96p. illus. 20cm. (Mod. camera guide ser.) 63-16483 1.95
1. Photography—Handbooks. manuals, etc. 2. Miniature cameras. I. Title.

WHITE, Minor. 770.28
Zone system manual: previsualization, exposure, development, printing; the Ansel Adams zone system as a basis of intuitive photography. [1st ed.] New York, Morgan & Morgan [1961] 112 p. illus. 19 cm. [TR145.W5] 61-12640
1. Photography — Handbooks, manuals, etc. 2. Photography — Printing processes — Toning. 3. Photography — Exposure. I. Title. BIP

WOOLLEY, Al E 770.28
Creative 35 mm techniques. New York, A. S. Barnes [1963] 170 p. illus. 26 cm. [TR146.W7] 63-9362
1. Photography — Handbooks, manuals, etc. I. Title.

WOOLLEY, Al E. 771.3
Creative 35mm techniques [by] A. E. Woolley. [2d ed. New York, Amphoto [1970] 170 p. illus., ports. 26 cm. [TR146.W7 1970] 70-23417 ISBN 0-8174-0385-X 8.95
1. Photography—Handbooks, manuals, etc. I. Title.

WRIGHT, George Benjamin, 770.2
1913-1958.
How to take better pictures of your family [by] George and Cora Wright. New York, Studio Publications [1958] 98 p. illus. 21 cm. [TR146.W94] 58-12295
1. Photography—Handbooks, manuals, etc. I. Wright, Cora, joint author. II. Title.

ZIM, Herbert Spencer, 1909- 770.2
Photography; the amateur's guide to better pictures, by Herbert S. Zim and R. Will Burnett. Illus. and diagrs. by Herschel Wartik and Harry McNaught. New York, Simon and Schuster [1956] 100 p. illus. 16 cm. (A golden handbook) Includes bibliography. [TR146.Z5] 56-13956
1. Phogoraphy—Handbooks, manuals, etc. I. Burnett, Raymond Will. 1912- joint author. II. Title.

ZIM, Herbert Spencer, 1909- 770.24
Photography; the amateur's guide to better pictures, by Herbert S. Zim, R. Will Burnett [and] Wyatt B. Brummitt. Illus. and diagrs. by Herschel Wartik and Harry McNaught. Rev. ed. New York, Golden Press [1964] 169 p. illus. (part col.) 16 cm. (A Golden handbook) "406." [TR146.Z5 1964] 64-11591
1. Photography—Handbooks, manuals, etc. I. Burnett, Raymond Will, 1912- joint author. II. Title.

Photography, High-speed.

CORNFIELD, Jim. 778.3'7
Electronic flash photography / by Jim Cornfield. Los Angeles : Petersen Pub. Co., c1976. 80 p. : ill. (some col.) ; 28 cm. (Petersen's how-to photographic library) [TR593.C67] 76-1544 pbk. : 3.95
1. Photography, High-speed. 2. Photography, Flash-light. I. Title.

DUBOVIK, Aleksandr Semenovich. 778.3'7
Photographic recording of high-speed processes, by A. S. Dubovik. Tr. by W. E. Jones. Tr. ed. by George H. Lunn. [1st English ed.] Oxford, New York, Pergamon [1968] xxii, 496p. illus. (pt. col.) 23cm. (romanized: Fotograficheskaia registratsiia bystroprotekaiushchikh protsessov) Tr. of Bibl. [TR593.D813 1968] 67-16126 21.50
1. Photography, High-speed. I. Title. BIP

EDGERTON, Harold Eugene, 1903- 778.3'7
Moments of vision : the stroboscopic revolution in photography / Harold E. Edgerton and James R. Killian, Jr. Cambridge, Mass. : MIT Press, c1979. p. cm. Bibliography: p. [TR593.E33] 79-11647 ISBN 0-262-05022-6 : 20.00
1. Edgerton, Harold Eugene, 1903- 2. Photography, High-speed. 3. Stroboscope. I. Killian, James Rhyne, 1904- II. Title. BIP

HYZER, William G 778.3
Engineering and scientific high-speed photography. New York, Macmillan [1962] 536p. illus. 22cm. [TR593.H9] 61-5242
1. Photography, High-speed. 2. Photography— Scientific applications. I. Title.

SAXE, Raymond Frederick. 778.37
High-speed photography [by] R. F. Saxe. London, New York, Focal P. [1966] 137 p. illus., tables, diagrs. 25 cm. (The Focal library) 63/-(B 66-14076) Bibliography: p. 134. [TR593.S3] 66-73456
1. Photography, High-speed. I. Title. BIP

Photography, High-speed—Congresses.

HIGH speed optical techniques : [seminar], August 26-27, 1976, San Diego, California / Michel A. Duguay, Richard K. Petersen, editors ; presented by the Society of Photo-optical Instrumentation Engineers, in cooperation with American Academy of Microbiology ... [et al.]. Palos Verdes Estates, Calif. : SPIE, c1977. viii, 152 p. : ill. ; 28 cm. (Proceedings of the Society of Photo-optical Instrumentation Engineers ; v. 94) Proceedings of the seminar. Includes bibliographical references and indexes. [TR593.H53] 77-365438 ISBN 0-89252-121-X pbk. : 35.00 778.3'7
1. Photography, High-speed—Congresses. I. Duguay, M. A. II. Petersen, Richard K. III. Society of Photo-optical Instrumentation Engineers. IV. Series: Society of Photo-optical Instrumentation Engineers. Proceedings ; v.94.

Photography—History.

BRAIVE, Michel Francois. 770.9
The photograph; a social history [by] Michel F. Braive. [Translated from the French by David Britt] New York, McGraw-Hill [1966] 367 p. (chiefly illus., facsims.) 31 cm. Translation of L'age de la photographie; de Niepce & nos jours. Bibliography: p. 363-364. [TR15.B6613] 66-19461
1. Photography — Hist. I. Title.

NEWHALL, Beaumont, 1908- ed. 770.82
On photography; a source book of photo history in facsimile. Watkins Glen, N. Y., Century House [c1956] 192p. illus. col. plate, facsims. 28cm. [TR15.N48] 56-8933
1. Photography—Hist. 2. Photography—Addresses, essays, lectures. I. Title.

POLLACK, Peter. 770.9
The picture history of photography, from the earliest beginnings to the present day. [1st ed.] New York, H.N. Abrams [1958] 624p. illus. (part col.) ports. 29cm. Bibliography: p. 618-619. [TR15.P55] 58-11357
1. Photography—Hist. I. Title.

WENTZEL, Fritz. 770.9
Memoirs of a photochemist. Edited by Louis Walton Sipley. Philadelphia, American Museum of Photography [1960] 146 p. illus. 24 cm. [TR15.W44] 59-14970
1. Photography — Hist. 2. Photographic chemistry. I. Title.

Photography—History.

BUCKLAND, Gail. 770'.92'4 B
Fox Talbot and the invention of photography / Gail Buckland. New York : Camera/Graphic Press, [1978] p. cm. Includes bibliographical references and index. [TR140.T3B8] 78-4405 ISBN 0-918696-07-0 : 37.50
1. Talbot, William Henry Fox, 1800-1877. 2. Photography—History. 3. Photographers—England—Biography. I. Title. BIP

COE, Brian, 1930- 770'.9'034
The birth of photography : the story of the formative years, 1800-1900 / by Brian Coe. London : Ash & Grant, 1976. 144 p. : ill. ; 28 cm. Includes index. Bibliography: p. 140. [TR15.C59] 76-383967 ISBN 0-904069-06-0. ISBN 0-904069-07-9 pbk. : £2.95
1. Photography—History. I. Title. BIP

DANIELS, Patrick. 770'.9'034
Early photography / [by] Patrick Daniels. London : Academy Editions ; New York : St. Martin's Press, 1978. 87 p. : ill., ports. ; 20 cm. [TR15.D22 1978] 78-60790 ISBN 0-312-22465-6 pbk. : 4.95
1. Photography—History. I. Title. BIP

EDER, Josef Maria, 1855-1944. 770'.9
History of photography / by Josef Maria Eder ; translated by Edward Epstean. New York : Dover Publications, 1978, c1945. xx, 860 p. : port. ; 22 cm. Translation of Geschichte der photographie. "An unabridged and unaltered republication of the work originally published by Columbia University Press, N.Y." Includes bibliographical references and index. [TR15.E383 1978] 77-88114 ISBN 0-486-23586-6 : 10.00
1. Photography—History. I. Title. BIP

FOUQUE, Victor, b.1802. 770'.92'4
The truth concerning the invention of photography: Nicephore Niepce, his life, letters, and works [Translated by Edward Epstean] New York, Arno Press, 1973. 163 p. 23 cm. (The Literature of Photography) Translation of Laverite surl'invention de la photographie. Reprint of the 1935 ed. Includes bibliographical references. [TR140.N5F72 1973] 72-9198 ISBN 0-405-04907-2 10.00.
1. Niepce, Joseph Nicephore, 1765-1833. 2. Photography—History. I. Title. II. Series. BIP

GABRIEL, Michael R. 016.6864'0904
Micrographics, 1900-1977 : a bibliography / by Michael R. Gabriel. Mankato : Minnesota Scholarly Press, c1978. 266 p. ; 24 cm. Includes index. [Z265.A1G32] 79-101793 19.00
1. Microphotography—Bibliography. I. Title. BIP

GASSAN, Arnold. 770'.9
A chronology of photography; a critical survey of the history of photography as a medium of art. Athens, Ohio, Handbook Co.; [distributed by Light Impressions, Rochester, N.Y., 1972] 373 p. illus. 23 cm. [TR15.G33] 72-83426 ISBN 0-912808-01-2
1. Photography—History. I. Title.

GERNSHEIM, Helmut, 1913- 770.9
A concise history of photography [by] Helmut Gernsheim in collaboration with Alison Gernsheim. New York, Grosset & Dunlap [1965] 314 p. illus. (part col.), facsims., ports. (part col.) 22 cm. Bibliography: p. 291-294. [TR15.G36] 66-10281
1. Photography—History. I. Gernsheim, Alison, joint author. II. Title.

GERNSHEIM, Helmut, 1913- 770'.9
The history of photography from the camera obscura to the beginning of the modern era [by] Helmut Gernsheim, in collaboration with Alison Gernsheim. [2d ed.] New York, McGraw-Hill [1969] 599 p. illus., facsims., ports. 31 cm. First ed. published in 1955 under title: The history of photography from the earliest use of the camera obscura in the eleventh century up to 1914. Bibliography: p. [580]-581. [TR15.G37 1969] 69-18726 22.95
1. Photography—History. I. Gernsheim, Alison, joint author. II. Title.

GERNSHEIM, Helmut, 1913- 770.9
The history of photography from the earliest use of the camera obscura in the eleventh century up to 1914, by Helmut Gernsheim in collaboration with Alison Gernsheim. London, New York, Oxford University Press, 1955. xxviii, 395 p. illus. 28 cm. Second ed. published in 1969 under title: The history of photography from the camera obscura to the beginning of the modern era. Bibliography: p. [375]-376. Bibliographical footnotes. [TR15.G37] 55-13800
1. Photography—History. I. Gernsheim, Alison, joint author. II. Title.

GREAT Britain. Patent Office. 770'.2'72
Patents for inventions : abridgments of specifications, class 98, photography, periods 1839 through 1900 / Great Britain Patent Office. New York : Arno Press, 1979. p. cm. (The Sources of modern photography) Reprint of 8 v. published at the Patent Office, London, 1861-1903. [TR147.G73 1979] 76-23063 ISBN 0-405-09626-7 (2 vols.) : 90.00
1. Photography—Patents. 2. Patents—Great Britain. I. Title. II. Title: Abridgments of specifications, class 98, photography, periods 1839 through 1900. III. Series. BIP

GREENHILL, Ralph. 770.971
Early photography in Canada. Toronto, Oxford University Press, 1965. 173 p. illus., facsims., ports. 29 cm. Bibliography: p. 169. [TR26.G72] 65-4206
1. Photography — Hist. — Canada. 2. Canada — Descr. & trav. — Views. I. Title.

HARRISON, William Jerome, 1845-1909. 770'.9
A history of photography, written as a practical guide and an introduction to its latest developments. New York, Arno Press, 1973 [c1887] 136 p. port. 23 cm. (The Literature of photography) Original ed. issued in Scovill's photographic series. Includes bibliographical references. [TR15.H32 1973] 72-9204 ISBN 0-405-04913-7 9.00
1. Photography—History. I. Title. II. Series. BIP

JUSSIM, Estelle. 760
Visual communication and the graphic arts; photographic technologies in the nineteenth century. New York, R. R. Bowker Co., 1974. xv, 364 p. illus. 28 cm. Bibliography: p. 331-337. [TR15.J87] 74-12032 ISBN 0-8352-0760-9
1. Photography—History. 2. Photomechanical processes—History. 3. Graphic arts—History. I. Title.

LECUYER, Raymond. 770'.9
Histoire de la photographie / Raymond Lecuyer. New York : Arno Press, 1979. p. cm. (The Sources of modern photography) Reprint of the 1945 ed. published by S.N.E.P.-Illustration, Paris. [TR15.L4 1979] 79-566 ISBN 0-405-09609-7 : 40.00
1. Photography—History. I. Title. II. Series.

MARTIN, Paul. 770'.9
Victorian snapshots. New York, Arno Press, 1973. xv, 44 p. (72 p. illus.) 23 cm. (The Literature of Photography) Reprint of the 1939 ed. [TR15.M3 1973] 72-9219 ISBN 0-405-04926-9. 11.00.
1. Photography—History. 2. England—Social life and customs—Illustrations. 3. England—Social life and customs. I. Title. II. Series. BIP

MENTIENNE, Adrien, b.1841. 770'.9'034
La decouverte de la photographie en 1839 / Adrien Mentienne. New York : Arno Press, 1979. p. cm. (The Sources of modern photography) Reprint of the 1892 ed. published by Impr. P. Dupont, Paris. [TR15.M4 1979] 76-23037 ISBN 0-405-09600-3 : 15.00
1. Photography—History. 2. Photography—History—Sources. 3. Daguerreotype. I. Title. II. Series. BIP

NEWHALL, Beaumont, 1908- 770.9
The history of photography, from 1839 to the present day. Rev. and enl. ed. New York, Museum of Modern Art; distributed by Doubleday, Garden City, N.Y. [1964] 215 p. illus. 29 cm. Text first published in the exhibition catalog Photography, 1839-1937 by the Museum of Modern Art in 1937. In 1938 the text and ill. were reprinted with minor revisions as Photography: a short critical history. Bibliography: p. [205]-210. [TR15.N47 1964] 64-15285
1. Photography—History. I. Title.

NEWHALL, Beaumont, 1908- 770'.9'034
Latent image; the discovery of photography. [1st ed.] Garden City, N.Y., Doubleday, 1967. xii, 148 p. illus., ports. 22 cm. (Science study series) Bibliography: p. [139]-140. [TR15.N475] 67-22460
1. Photography—History. I. Title. II. Series.

POLLACK, Peter. 779
The picture history of photography, from the earliest beginnings to the present day. Rev. and enl. ed. New York, H. N. Abrams [1969] 708 p. illus. (part col.), ports. 29 cm. Bibliography: p. 698-701. [TR15.P55 1969] 76-76556
1. Photography—History. I. Title. BIP

POLLACK, Peter. 779
The picture history of photography from the earliest beginnings to the present day / Peter Pollack. New York : Abrams, 1977. 176 p. : ill. ; 30 cm. Includes index. [TR15.P55 1977] 76-51916 ISBN 0-8109-2056-5 pbk. : 8.95
1. Photography—History. I. Title.

POTONNIEE, Georges. 770'.9
The history of the discovery of photography. [Translated by Edward Epstean] New York, Arno Press, 1973. [c1936] x, 272 p. 24 cm. (The Literature of Photography) Translation of Histoire de la decouverte de la photographic Includes bibliographical references. [TR15.P6213 1973] 72-9222 ISBN 0-405-04929-3 16.00.
1. Photography—History. I. Title. II. Series. BIP

SCHARF, Aaron, 1922- 770'.9
Pioneers of photography : an album of pictures and words / written and compiled by Aaron Scharf ; by arrangement with the British Broadcasting Corporation. New York : H. N. Abrams, [1976] p. cm. Bibliography: p. [TR15.S34] 75-42216 ISBN 0-8109-0408-X : 18.50
1. Photography—History. 2. Photographers. I. British Broadcasting Corporation. II. Title. BIP

STENGER, Erich, 1878- 770'.9
The history of photography / Erich Stenger ; translation and footnotes by Edward Epstean. New York : Arno Press, 1979. p. cm. (The Sources of modern photography) Translation of Die Photographie in Kultur und Technik. Reprint of the 1939 ed. published by Mack Print. Co., Easton, Pa. Includes index. Bibliography: p. [TR15.S75213 1979] 76-23050 ISBN 0-405-09611-9 : 12.00
1. Photography—History. 2. Photography. 3. Photography—Apparatus and supplies. I. Title. II. Series. BIP

STORY, Alfred Thomas, 1842-1934. 770
The story of photography. Rochester,

N.Y., Visual Studies Workshop, 1974 [c1902] 169 p. illus. 19 cm. (A Visual studies reprint book) Reprint of the 1904 ed. published by McClure, Phillips, New York. Includes bibliographical references. [TR15.S88 1974] 73-22264 ISBN 0-87992-003-3 11.95
1. Photography—History. I. Title.
Pbk. 6.75, ISBN 0-87992-002-5. **BIP**

THOMAS, Alan.　　　　770'.9'034
Time in a frame / Alan Thomas. New York : Schocken Books, 1977. p. cm. Includes index. Bibliography: p. [TR15.T48] 77-75294 ISBN 0-8052-3674-0 : 17.95
1. Photography—History. 2. Nineteenth century. I. Title. **BIP**

WERGE, John.　　　　770'9
The evolution of photography. New York, Arno Press, 1973. viii, 312 p. illus. 22 cm. (The Literature of Photography) Reprint of the 1890 ed. [TR15.W48 1973] 72-9245 ISBN 0-405-04949-8 17.00
1. Photography History. I. Title. II. Series. **BIP**

WILLSBERGER, Johann, 1941-　770'.9
The history of photography : cameras, pictures, photographers / Johann Willsberger ; translated by Helga Halaki. Garden City, N.Y. : Doubleday, 1977. [182] p. : chiefly ill. ; 29 cm. Translation of Fotofaszination. [TR15.W4913] 77-374024 ISBN 0-385-12664-6 : 24.95
1. Photography—History. 2. Cameras—History. I. Title. **BIP**

Photography—History—Addresses, essays, lectures.

ONE hundred years of　　　770
photographic history : essays in honor of Beaumont Newhall / edited by Van Deren Coke. 1st ed. Albuquerque : University of New Mexico Press, c1975. x, 180 p. : ill. ; 29 cm. Includes bibliographical references and index. [TR15.O53] 74-83381 ISBN 0-8263-0344-7 : 17.50
1. Newhall, Beaumont, 1908- 2. Photography—History—Addresses, essays, lectures. I. Newhall, Beaumont, 1908- II. Coke, Van Deren, 1921-
Contents omitted

Photography—History—Great Britain.

HANNAVY, John.　　　　770'.941
Masters of Victorian photography / John Hannavy. New York : Holmes & Meier, 1976. 96 p. : ill. ; 26 cm. Includes index. Bibliography: p. 93. [TR57.H36 1976] 75-45255 ISBN 0-8419-0260-7 : 15.00
1. Photography—History—Great Britain. 2. Photographers—Great Britain. I. Title. **BIP**

HOWARTH-LOOMES, B. E. C. 770'.941
Victorian photography : an introduction for collectors and connoisseurs / B. E. C. Howarth-Loomes. New York : St. Martin's Press, 1974 [i.e. 1975] 99, [1] p., [2] leaves of plates : ill. ; 27 cm. Bibliography: p. [100] [TR57.H68 1975] 74-76282 8.95
1. Photography—History—Great Britain. I. Title.

INTERNATIONAL Museum of 770'.28
Photography at George Eastman House.
British masters of the albumen print : a selection of mid-nineteenth century Victorian photography on albumenized paper / International Museum of Photography at George Eastman House ; edited by Robert A. Sobieszek. Chicago : University of Chicago Press, [1976] p. cm. Bibliography: p. [TR57.I57 1976] 76-16546 ISBN 0-226-69171-3 : 17.50
1. Photography—History—Great Britain. 2. Photography, Artistic. 3. Albumen paper. I. Sobieszek, Robert A., 1943- II. Title. **BIP**

Photography—History—New Zealand.

KNIGHT, Hardwicke.　　　770'.993
Photography in New Zealand; a social and technical history. Dunedin, J. McIndoe [1971] 196 p. illus. 25 cm. Bibliography: p. 179. [TR122.5.K55] 72-192643
1. Photography—History—New Zealand. I. Title.

Photography—History—The West.

ANDREWS, Ralph Warren,　770.979
1897-
Picture gallery pioneers, 1850 to 1875, by Ralph W. Andrews. [1st ed. Seattle, Superior Pub. Co. [1964] 192 p. illus., facsims., ports. 28 cm. [TR23.6.A5] 64-21318
1. Photography—History—The West. 2. Photographers, American. I. Title.

Photography—History—United States.

ANDREWS, Ralph Warren,　770.979
1897-
Photographers of the frontier West; their lives and works, 1875 to 1915. Seattle, Wash., Superior [c.1965] 182p. illus., ports. 28cm. [TR23.6.A48] 65-23447 12.95
1. Photography—Hist.—The West. 2. Photographers, American. 3. The West—Descr. & trav.—Views. I. Title.

DOTY, Robert M.　　　　770'.973
Photography in America. Edited by Robert Doty. Introd. by Minor White. New York, Published for the Whitney Museum of American Art [by] Random House [1974] 255 p. illus. 32 cm. Prepared to accompany an exhibition of the same title shown at the Whitney Museum of American Art, New York, Nov. 20, 1974-Jan. 12, 1975. "A Ridge Press book." [TR23.D67] 74-4308 ISBN 0-394-49355-9
1. Photography—History—United States. 2. Photography, Artistic—Exhibitions. I. Whitney Museum of American Art, New York. II. Title.

HORAN, James David,　　770.924 B
1914-
Timothy O'Sullivan, America's forgotten photographer; the life and work of the brilliant photographer whose camera recorded the American scene from the battlefields of the Civil War to the frontiers of the West, by James D. Horan. [1st ed.] Garden City, N.Y., Doubleday, 1966. xiv, 334 p. illus. 29 cm. Bibliography: p. 324-326. [TR140.O8H6] 66-20922
1. O'Sullivan, Timothy H. 2. Photography—History—United States. 3. The West—Description and travel—Views. 4. United States—History—Civil War, 1861-1865—Pictorial works.

TAFT, Robert, 1894-1955　　770.973
Photography and the American scene; a social history, 1839-1889 [Gloucester, Mass., P. Smith, 1965, c.1938] x, 546p. illus., facsims., ports. 24cm. (Dover bk., T1201 rebound) First pub. by Macmillan in 1938. Bibl. [TR23.T3] 5.50
1. Photography—Hist.—U.S. 2. U.S.—Hist.—1783-1865. 3. U.S.—Hist.—1865-1898. I. Title.

TAFT, Robert, 1894-1955　　770.973
Photography and the American scene; a social history, 1839-1889. New York, Dover [1964, c.1938] x, 546p. illus., facsims., ports. 24cm. Unabridged, unaltered repubn. of the work first pub. by Macmillan in 1938. (T 1201) Bibl. [TR23.T3] 64-18373 3.00 pap.,
1. Photography—Hist.—U.S. 2. U.S.—Hist.—1783-1865. 3. U.S.—Hist.—1865-1898. I. Title. **BIP**

WALKER, Mary Frances (Lamson) 920
1865-
I remember -- I remember, 1865-1957. Photos. from the author's album. [Claremont, Calif.] Priv. print. by the Creative Press, c1960. 64 p. illus. 22 cm. [CT275.W2457A3] 60-7691
I. Title.

Photography—History—Utah.

WADSWORTH, Nelson B.,　779'.9'9792
1930-
Through camera eyes / Nelson B. Wadsworth. [Provo, Utah] : Brigham Young University Press, [1975] xi, 180 p. : ill. ; 29 cm. Includes index. Bibliography: p. 175-176. [TR24.U8W32] 75-8657 ISBN 0-8425-0435-4 : 10.95 10.95 pbk. : 6.95
1. Photography—History—Utah. 2. Utah—History. I. Title. **BIP**

Photography in archaeology.

CONLON, Vera M.　　778.9'9'913031
Camera techniques in archaeology [by] V. M. Conlon. New York, St. Martin's Press [1973] xiv, 109 p. illus. 23 cm. [TR775.C66 1973] 73-82631 11.95
1. Photography in archaeology. I. Title. **BIP**

PHOTOGRAPHY in　　　930'.1'028
archaeological research / edited by Elmer Harp, Jr. 1st ed. Albuquerque : University of New Mexico Press, c1975. xxiii, 380 p. : ill. ; 24 cm. (School of American Research advanced seminar series) "A School of American Research book." Includes index. Bibliography: p. 369-373. [TR775.P48] 75-2532 ISBN 0-8263-0376-5 : 20.00
1. Photography in archaeology. I. Harp, Elmer. II. Santa Fe, N.M. School of American Research. III. Series: Santa Fe, N.M. School of American Research. Advanced seminar series.

SIMMONS, Harold　778.9'9'913031
Champion.
Archaeological photography [by] Harold C. Simmons. New York, New York University Press, 1969. vi, 138 p. illus. 23 cm. Bibliography: p. 133-134. [TR775.S55] 68-24659
1. Photography in archaeology. I. Title. **BIP**

Photography in education.

CHILDREN are centers for　　372.5
understanding media. [Guest editors: Susan Rice and Rose Mukerji] Washington, Association for Childhood Education International [with the collaboration of the Center for Understanding Media, 1973] vii, 89 p. illus. 23 cm. Includes bibliographies. [TR816.C47] 72-92022 3.95
1. Photography in education. I. Rice, Susan, ed. II. Mukerji, Rose, ed. III. Association for Childhood Education International. IV. Center for Understanding Media. **BIP**

GRIFFITH, Jerry.　　　　770'.7
Classroom projects using photography : with tools and tips to help you / [prepared by Jerry Griffith, Lynn E. Miner, Twila E. Strandberg]. Rochester, N.Y. : Eastman Kodak Co., 1975. 2 v. : ill. (some col.) ; 28 cm. (Kodak publication ; no. ED 11-1, ED 12-1) Cover title. Contents.Contents.— v. 1. For the elementary school level.—v. 2. For the secondary school level. [LB1043.67.G74] 75-7866 ISBN 0-87985-102-3 (v. 1) : ISBN 0-87985-103-1(v.2) : 6.95per vol.
1. Photography in education. I. Miner, Lynn E., joint author. II. Strandberg, Twila E., joint author. III. Eastman Kodak Company. IV. Title.

Photography in nuclear physics.

BARKAS, Walter H　　　539.778
Nuclear research emulsions. New York, Academic Press, 1963- v. illus. 24 cm. (Pure and applied physics, v. 15) Contents.CONTENTS.— v. 1. Techniques and theory. Includes bibliography. [TR210.B27] 63-13639
1. Photography in nuclear physics. 2. Photographic emulsions. 3. Particles (Nuclear physics) I. Title. **BIP**

Photography, Indoor.

EASTMAN Kodak Company.　778.7'2
Indoor picture-taking / by the editors of Eastman Kodak Company. [Rochester, N.Y. : Consumer Markets Division, Kodak, 1974 [i.e.1975] 220 p. : ill. (some col.) ; 22 cm. (Kodak photo book ; AC-31) [TR600.E17] 74-186975 ISBN 0-87985-073-6 : 4.95
1. Photography—Artificial light. I. Title.
Distributed by Morgan, New York.

REED, Alice S　　　　778.72
How to take living indoor pictures, by A. S. Reed and Kathy Wersen. New York, American Photographic Book Pub. Co.; distributed to the book trade by Grosset & Dunlap [1964] 96 p. illus. 22 cm (Better photo guides) "433." [TR620.R4] 63-22238
1. Photography, Indoor. I. Wersen, Kathy, joint author. II. Title.

Photography, Industrial.

COLMER, Michael.　　　659.13'23
Industry in focus. London, Business Books, 1974. ix, 134 p. illus., form, ports. 26 cm. Includes index. [TR775.C64] 74-173862 ISBN 0-220-66242-8
1. Photography, Industrial. 2. Photography, Advertising. I. Title.
Distributed by Cahners; 27.50.

EASTMAN Kodak Company.　658.4
A way to do it better ...; a report on applications of photographic and related energy-sensitive processes by three leading industrial organizations. [Rochester, N.Y., 196-] vii, 122, 4 p. illus. 36 cm. Issued in a case. [TR706.E2] 72-197649
1. Photography, Industrial. I. Title.

SANSOM, Leslie, comp.　　620'.0065
Camera in the works; a miscellany of pictures from the Vickers archives. New York, American Elsevier Pub. Co., 1970. 146 p. of illus. (part col.), ports. 29 cm. [TR706.S25 1970b] 71-108779
1. Photography, Industrial. I. Vickers Limited. Photographic Dept. II. Title.

Photography, Industrial — Period.

WOLFMAN, Augustus, ed.　016.77
PMI; photo methods for industry. v. 1- Jan. 1958- [New York, Gellert-Wolfman, etc.] v. in illus. (part col.) diagrs. 29 cm. monthly. Running title, 1958- Photo methods for industry. Editors: 1958- A. Wolfman and others. Vols. for 1960- include an additional October issue called Directory (varies slightly) [TR1.P2] 62-53475
1. Photography, Industrial — Period. I. Title.

Photography, Infra-red.

EASTMAN Kodak Company.　778.3*4
Applied infrared photography. [Rochester, N.Y., 1968] 96 p. illus. (part col.) 28 cm. (A Kodak technical publication M-28) Cover title. [TR755.E28] 72-23857 2.00
1. Photography, Infra-red. I. Title. **BIP**

EASTMAN Kodak Company.　621.36'72
Infrared & ultraviolet photography. [1st combined ed.] Rochester [N.Y., 1972] 32, 88 p. illus. (part col.) 29 cm. (Kodak technical publication no. M-27/28-H) Contains two Kodak publications: no. M-27, Ultraviolet and fluorescence photography; no. M-28, Applied infrared photography. Includes bibliographies. [TR755.E32 1972] 72-75585 ISBN 0-87985-005-1 9.95
1. Photography, Infra-red. 2. Photography, Ultra-violet. I. Eastman Kodak Company. Ultraviolet and fluorescence photography. 1972. II. Eastman Kodak Company. Applied infrared photography. 1972. III. Title.

GIBSON, Henry Lou, 1906-　778.3'4
Photography by infrared : its principles and applications / H. Lou Gibson. A 3d ed. of Photography by infrared by Walter Clark. New York : Wiley, c1978. xxiv, 545 p., [1] leaf of plates : ill. ; 24 cm. (Wiley series on photographic science and technology and the graphic arts) "A Wiley-Interscience publication." Includes bibliographies and index. [TR755.C55 1978] 77-26919 ISBN 0-471-15895-X : 26.50
1. Photography, Infra-red. I. Clark, Walter, 1899- Photography by infrared. II. Title. **BIP**

MASSOPUST, Leo Carl,　　778.9961
1893-
Infrared photography in medicine. Springfield, Ill., Thomas [1952] 53 p. illus. 22 cm. (American lecture series, publication no. 152, American lectures in medical photography) Includes bibliography. [TR755.M3 1952] 52-12801
1. Photography, Infra-red. 2. Photography, Medical. I. Title.

NURNBERG, Albert.　　　621.36'72
Infrarot-Photographie. Halle (Saale) W. Knapp, 1957. 135p. illus. 22cm. Includes bibliographies. [TR755.N8] 57-28351
1. Photography, Infra-red. I. Title.

Photography, Instantaneous.

AMERICAN snapshots / 779'.092'2 selected by Ken Graves & Mitchell Payne ; introd. by Jean Shepherd. Oakland, Calif. : Scrimshaw Press, 1977. 117 p. : chiefly ill. ; 21 x 24 cm. [TR592.A43] 77-21861 ISBN 0-912020-64-4 : 13.50
1. Photography, Instantaneous. 2. Photography—United States. I. Graves, Ken, 1942- II. Payne, Mitchell, 1944-

DUCKWORTH, Paul 778.37
Family fun, games, and sports photography. New York, Universal [dist. Amphoto, c.1962] 127p. illus. 20cm. 62-12123 1.95 pap.,
1. Photography, Instantaneous. I. Title.

EDGERTON, Harold Eugene, 1903- 778.37
Flash! Seeing the unseen by ultra high-speed photography, by Harold E. Edgerton and James R. Killian, Jr. [2d ed.] Boston, C. T. Branford Co. [1954] 215p. illus. (part col.) ports. (part col.) 29cm. Bibliography: p. 211-213. [TR592.E3 1954] 54-7120
1. Photography, Instantaneous. 2. Stroboscope. 3. Photography—Scientific applications. I. Killian, James Rhyne, 1904- joint author. II. Title.

SELF, Charles. 770'.28
How to take action photographs / by Charles Self. 1st ed. Garden City, N.Y. : Doubleday, 1975. p. cm. [TR592.S4] 75-2285 ISBN 0-385-01285-3 : 2.95
1. Photography, Instantaneous. I. Title.

Photography—Interiors.

BRETT, James, 1927- 779'.4'0924
Looking into houses / by James Brett. New York : Watson-Guptill Publications, [1976] p. cm. Includes index. [TR620.B7] 76-25123 ISBN 0-8230-7358-0 : 25.00
1. Photography—Interiors. 2. Architecture, Domestic—Designs and plans. I. Title.

BYRON, Joseph. 779'.9'74721471
New York interiors at the turn of the century : in 131 photographs by Joseph Byron from the Byron Collection of the Museum of the City of New York / text by Clay Lancaster. New York : Dover Publications, 1976. xviii, 154 p. : ill. ; 28 cm. [TR620.B97 1976] 76-8308 ISBN 0-486-23359-6 pbk. : 5.00
1. Photography—Interiors. 2. New York (City)—Description—Views. I. Lancaster, Clay. II. New York (City). Museum of the City of New York. III. Title. BIP

CLEVELAND, Robert C 778.94
Architectural photography of house; how to take good pictures of exteriors and interiors. New York, F. W. Dodge Corp. [1953] 170p. illus. 30cm. [TR620.C59] 53-7214
1. Photography—Interiors. 2. Photography, Architectural. I. Title.

Photography, Journalistic.

AHLERS, Arvel W., 1915- 770.69
Where and how to sell your pictures. Photographic advisor: J. Walter Thompson Co. Market listings rev. by Joan Goodstein. 1th ed. rev. New York, American Photographic Book Pub. Co.; book trade: Garden City Books, Garden City., N. Y. [1959] 112p. illus. 20cm. [TR850.A35 1959] 59-1237
1. Photography, Journalistec. 2. American periodicals—Direct. 3. American newspapers—Direct. I. Title.

AHLERS, Arvel W., 1915- 770.69
Where & how to sell your pictures. Market listings compiled by Alice Melligon. New York, Photography Pub. Corp. [1952] 63p. 23cm. [TR820.A35] 53-808
1. Photography, Journalistic. 2. American periodicals—Direct. 3. American newspapers—Direct. I. Title.

AHLERS, Arvel W., 1915- 770.69
Where & how to sell your pictures. Market listings rev. by Susan L. Sill. 3d ed., rev. New York, American Photographic Book Pub. Co. [1956] 122p. 23cm. [TR820.A35 1956] 56-9096
1. Photography,Journalistic. 2. American periodicals—Direct. 3. American newspapers—Direct. I. Title.

AHLERS, Arvel W., 1915- 770.69
Where & how to sell your pictures. Market listings rev. by Florence A. Golden. [Rev. ed. New York] American Photographic Book Pub. Co. [1954] 120p. 23cm. [TR820.A35 1954] 54-2379
1. Photography, Journalistic. 2. American periodicals—Direct. 3. American newspapers—Direct. I. Title.

AHLERS, Arvel W., 1915- 770.69
Where and how to sell your pictures. U. S. market listings rev. by E. S. Woods. Foreign market data by P. Webb. 5th ed. rev. New York, Amphoto [1962] 164p. illus. 20cm. [TR820.A35 1962] 62-15603
1. Photography, Journalistic. 2. American periodicals Direct. 3. American newspapers Direct. I. Title.

AIGNER, Lucien. 770'.92'4
Lucien Aigner / [editor, John P. Aigner]. New York : International Center for [i.e. of] Photography, 1979. 127 p. : ill. ; 22 cm. (ICP library of photographers ; v. 7) Bibliography: p. 126-127. [TR820.A37] 78-66049 ISBN 0-933642-00-8 : 8.95
1. Aigner, Lucien. 2. Photography, Journalistic. I. Aigner, John P. II. Series: International Center of Photography. ICP library of photographers ; v. 7.

ARNOLD, Edmund C 778.9907
Feature photos that sell: 365 daily picture ideas. Photos. by Leslie A. Dodds. [1st ed.] New York, Morgan & Morgan [1960] 96p. illus. 19cm. [TR820.A7] 60-11975
1. Photography, Journalistic. I. Title.

ASSOCIATED Press. 779
The instant it happened / the Associated Press. New York : H. N. Abrams, [1976] c1972. 230 p., [1] leaf of plates : ill. ; 37 cm. [TR820.A78 1976] 75-42279 ISBN 0-8109-0376-8 : 22.50
1. Photography, Journalistic. I. Title. BIP

ATKINS, Ollie, 1916- 778
Camera on assignment, by Ollie Atkins and Charles Baptie. [Fairfax, Va., Fairfax Pub. Society, 1957] 64p. (chiefly illus.) 32cm. [TR820.A8] 58-16223
1. Photography, Journalistic. I. Baptie, Charles. II. Title.

BERGIN, David P. 778
Photo journalism manual [by] David P. Bergin. [1st ed.] Hastings-on-Hudson, N.Y., Morgan & Morgan [1967] 283 p. illus. 24 cm. Bibliography: p. 269-270. [TR820.B47] 67-20398
1. Photography, Journalistic. I. Title.

BOWDEN, Robert. 778.9'9'07
Get that picture / Robert Bowden. Garden City, N.Y. : Amphoto, [1977] p. cm. Includes index. [TR820.B68] 77-22064 ISBN 0-8174-2430-X : 13.95. ISBN 0-8174-2111-4 : 8.95
1. Photography, Journalistic. I. Title. BIP

BYRNE, Howard. 770
Without assignment; how to free lance in photography. New York, Pellegrini & Cudahy [1952] 198 p. illus. 21 cm. [TR820.B9] 51-12762
1. Photography, Journalistic. I. Title.

BYRNE, Howard. 770
Without assignment; a personal guide to free lance photo journalism, its business technique & practice. London, New York, Focal Press [1951] 199 p. illus. 20 cm. [TR820.B9 1951] 52-43009
1. Photography, Journalistic. I. Title.

CAPA, Robert, 1913-1954. 770'.92'4
Robert Capa, 1913-1954 / [editors, Cornell Capa, Bhupendra Karia]. New York : Grossman Publishers, 1974. 127 p. : ill. ; 23 cm. (ICP library of photographers ; v. 1) [TR140.C28A32 1974] 72-11005 ISBN 0-670-60095-4 : 12.50. ISBN 0-670-60096-2 pbk. : 6.95
1. Capa, Robert, 1913-1954. 2. Photography, Journalistic. I. Series: International Fund for Concerned Photography. ICP library of photographers ; v. 1.

DECKOFF, Harold B 778
The free lance photographer's hand-book. New York, Falk Pub. Co. [1956] 249p. illus. 23cm. [TR820.D38] 56-11528
1. Photography, Journalistic. 2. American periodicals—Direct. 3. American newspapers—Direct. I. Title.

EDOM, Clifton Cedric. 070.4'9
Photojournalism : principles and practices / Clifton C. Edom. Dubuque, Iowa : W. C. Brown Co., c1976. xvi, 306 p. : ill. (some col.) ; 29 cm. Includes indexes. Bibliography: p. 297-299. [TR820.E36] 75-3809 ISBN 0-697-04303-7
1. Photography, Journalistic. I. Title.

FABER, John 779
Great moments in news photography, from the historical files of the National Press Photographers Association. New York, T. Nelson [c.1960] 126p. illus. 29cm. 60-14863 4.95 half cloth,)
I. Title.

FABER, John. 770'.92'2
Great news photos and the stories behind them / by John Faber. 2d, rev. ed. New York : Dover Publications, 1978. 159 p. : ill. ; 29 cm. First ed. published in 1960 under title: Great moments in news photography. Bibliography: p. 157-159. [TR820.F3 1978] 77-27723 ISBN 0-486-23667-6 : 5.00
1. Photography, Journalistic. I. Title. BIP

FEINBERG, Milton. 770.28
Techniques of photojournalism. New York, Wiley-Interscience [1970] ix, 279 p. illus. 28 cm. (Wiley series on human communication) [TR820.F44] 73-96959
1. Photography, Journalistic. I. Title. BIP

FELLIG, Arthur, 1900-1968. 779'.092'4
Weegee. Millerton, N.Y. : Aperture, c1978. 95 p. : chiefly ill. ; 21 cm. (The Aperture history photography series ; 8) Bibliography: p. 95. [TR820.F46] 77-80020 ISBN 0-89381-021-5 : 7.95
1. Fellig, Arthur, 1900-1968. 2. Photography, Journalistic.

FELLIG, Arthur, 1900-1968. 779'.92'4
Weegee / [compiled and edited] by Louis Stettner. New York : Knopf, 1977. p. cm. Bibliography: p. [TR820.F45 1977] 77-75356 ISBN 0-394-40770-9 : 15.00 ISBN 0-394-73322-3 pbk. : 8.95
1. Fellig, Arthur, 1900-1968. 2. Photography, Journalistic. I. Stettner, Louis, 1922-

FORMAN, Harrison, 1904- 778
How to make money with your camera. Foreword by Ivan Dmitri. New York, McGraw-Hill [1952] 235 p. illus. 21 cm. [TR820.F6] 51-13605
1. Photography, Journalistic. I. Title.

FOX, Rodney. 778.9907
Creative news photography [by] Rodney Fox [and] Robert Kerns. Ames, Iowa State University Press [1961] 192 p. illus. 28 cm. Includes bibliography. [TR820.F66] 61-10551
1. Photography, Journalistic. I. Kerns, Robert, joint author. II. Title. BIP

FOX, Rodney, 778.9'9'07
Creative news photography / Rodney Fox, Robert Kerns. Ann Arbor, Mich. : Reprinted for Iowa State University Press by University Microfilms International, [1978, c1961] p. cm. Reprint of the ed. published by Iowa State University Press, Ames. Includes index. Bibliography: p. [TR820.F66 1978] 78-10451 ISBN 0-8357-0329-0 : 14.00
1. Photography, journalistic. I. Kerns, Robert, joint author. II. Title.

GARDNER, Gerald C. 741.5973
Who's in charge here? Photos by UPI and Wide World. New York, Pocket Bks., c.1962. unpaged. chiefly illus. 16x21cm. 62-52141 1.00 pap.,
I. Title.

GERMAR, Herb. 778
The student journalist and photojournalism. [1st ed.] New York, Richards Rosen Press [1967] 189 p. illus. 22 cm. (The Student journalist guide series) Bibliography: p. 189. [TR820.G4] 67-15471
1. Photography, Journalistic. 2. School photography. I. Title. BIP

GIDAL, Nachum. 779
Modern photojournalism: origin and evolution, 1910-1933 [by] Tim N. Gidal. [English translation by Maureen Oberli-Turner] New York, Macmillan [1973] 96 p. illus. 28 cm. (Photography: men and movements, v. 1) Includes bibliographical references. [TR820.G5313] 73-10788 10.95
1. Photography, Journalistic. I. Title.

GOULD, Lewis L. 770'.92'4 B
Photojournalist : the career of Jimmy Hare / by Lewis L. Gould & Richard Greffe. Austin : University of Texas Press, c1977. 157 p. : ill. ; 26 cm. Includes bibliographical references and index. [TR140.H37G68] 76-52920 ISBN 0-292-74004-2 : 12.95
1. Hare, James H., 1856-1946. 2. Photography, Journalistic. 3. Photographers—United States—Biography. I. Greffe, Richard, 1947- joint author. II. Title. BIP

JACOBS, Lou. 778
Free-lance magazine photography; a guide to the working photojournalist. Philadelphia, Chilton Books [1965] 160 p. illus. 24 cm. [TR820.J3] 65-23148
1. Photography, Journalistic. I. Title.

JACOBS, Lou. 070.4'9
Free-lance magazine photography; a guide to the working photojournalist. Photos. by the author. New York, Amphoto [1970] 160 p. illus., ports. 24 cm. [TR820.J3 1970] 779'.092'4 76-76434 7.95
1. Photography, Journalistic. I. Title.

KALISH, Stanley E. 070.4
Picture editing, by Stanley E. Kalish and Clifton C. Edom. New York, Rinehart [1951] 207 p. illus. 27 cm. [TR820.K3] 51-13237
1. Photography. Journalistic. I. Title.

LIFE (Chicago) 779
Memorable Life photographs. Foreword and comment by Edward Steichen. New York, Museum of Modern Art [c1951] 1 v. (chiefly illus.) 36cm. [TR820.L5] 52-10476
1. Photography, Journalistic. 2. Photographs. I. Steichen, Edward, 1879- II. Title.

LOGAN, Richard H. 778.5'38'07
Elements of photo reporting [by] Richard H. Logan, III. New York, Amphoto [1971] 323 p. illus., ports. 24 cm. Bibliography: p. 315-318. [TR820.L57] 73-97877 ISBN 0-8174-0523-2 12.50
1. Photography, Journalistic. I. Title.

LOOK. 778
School photojournalism, telling your school story in pictures by the editors of Look. Produced by Edward A. Hamilton. Washington, National School Public Relations Association [1958] 72p. illus. 28cm. [TR820.L6] 58-1322
1. Photography, Journalistic. 2. School publicity. I. Hamilton, Edward A. II. Title.

LOOSLEY, A. E. 778.9'9'07
The business of photojournalism [by] A. E. Loosley. New York, Amphoto [1971, c1970] 283 p. illus., ports. 23 cm. [TR820.L63 1971] 78-127414 12.95
1. Photography, Journalistic. I. Title.

LOOSLEY, A. E. 070.4'9
The business of photojournalism [by] A. E. Loosley. London, New York, Focal P., 1970. 283 p. illus. 23 cm. [TR820.L63] 779'.092'4 74-579747 ISBN 0-240-50730-4 60/-
1. Photography, Journalistic. I. Title.

MCCULLIN, Donald, 1935- 779'.092'4
The destruction business. [Melbourne] Sun Books [1971] 94 p. (chiefly illus.) 24 cm. [TR820.M2 1971b] 73-158974 ISBN 0-7251-0125-3 2.95
1. Photography, Journalistic. I. Title.

MCCULLIN, Donald, 1935- 779'.092'4
Is anyone taking any notice? A book of photographs and comments. With phrases drawn from the 1970 Nobel lecture by Alexander Solzhenitsyn. Cambridge, Mass., MIT Press [1973] 1 v. (unpaged) illus. 29 x 31 cm. First published in 1971 under title: The destruction business. [TR654.M33 1973] 72-7475 ISBN 0-262-13084-X 14.95
1. Photography, Journalistic. I.

Solzhenitsyn, Aleksandr Isaevich, 1918- Nobelevskaia lektsiia. English. Selections. 1973. II. Title.

MCINTOSH, Ian C. 770.692
Successful freelance photo- journalism. London, Fountain Pr. [dist. New York, Morgan & Morgan, 1964,c. 1963] 128p. illus., ports. 22cm. 64-3396 7.95bds.,
1. Photography, Journalistic. I. Title.

MARCUS, Adrianne. 770'.92'2
The photojournalist, Mary Ellen Mark & Annie Leibovitz / text by Adrianne Marcus, with the editors of Alskog, inc. [New York] : T. Y. Crowell, [1974] 96 p. : ill. (some col.) ; 29 cm. (Masters of contemporary photography) Title on spine: Mark & Leibovitz: the photojournalist. [TR139.M28] 74-8229 ISBN 0-690-00619-5 : 7.95. ISBN 0-690-00620-9 pbk. : 3.95
1. Mark, Mary Ellen, 1940- 2. Leibovitz, Annie, 1949- 3. Photography, Journalistic. I. Mark, Mary Ellen, 1940- II. Leibovitz, Annie, 1949- III. Alskog, inc. IV. Title. V. Title: Mark & Leibovitz, the photojournalist.

NATIONAL Press Photographers Association. 778
Complete book of press photography. [Joseph Costs, editor] New York, c1950. 206 p. illus. ports. 31 cm. "An annotated bibliography for the photo-journalist, by Clifton C. Edom": p. 127-137. [TR820.N3] 50-10702
1. Photography. Journalistic. I. Title.

NATIONAL Press Photographers Association. 779'.092'4
Humor in news photography from the historical files of the National Press Photographers Association. Selected by John Faber. New York, T. Nelson [1961] 128p. (chiefly illus.) 28cm. [TR820.percent9.907] 61-17520
1. Photography. Journalistic. 2. Wit and humor, Pictorial. I. Faber, John, ed. II. Title.

OHIO. State University, Kent. School of Journalism. 778
Digest, press photography short course. Kent. v. illus., ports. 27 cm. annual. Title varies: 19 News photography short course digest (cover title, 19 Digest, short course in news photography) [TR820.O45] 51-62405
1. Photography, Journalistic. I. Title. II. Title: Press photography short course.

PAYNE, Lee. 778.5'38'07
Getting started in photojournalism. Philadelphia, Chilton Book Co. [1967] 128 p. illus. 24 cm. [TR820.P3] 67-21699
1. Photography, Journalistic. I. Title.

PAYNE, Lee. 778.9
Getting started in photojournalism. Philadelphia, Chilton Book Co. [1967] 128 p. illus. 24 cm. A newspaper photographer discusses equipment, the professional news photographer, working under specific editors or in certain fields, composition, and selling to magazines. [TR820.P3] AC 67
1. Photography, Journalistic. I. Title.

PETERSON, C A 778
Photography for profit; a complete guide on how to shoot and sell your photos. [Los Angeles, Trend Books, 1956] 128p. illus. 24cm. (Trend book 139) [TR820.P45] 56-12638
1. Photography, Journalistic. 2. American periodicals—Direct. I. Title.

THE Photographer's market place. 779'.092'4 Englewood, N. J., R. Maschke. v. 20cm. [TR820.P5] 56-18043
1. Photography, Journalistic. 2. American periodicals— Direct.

PIGOZZI, Jean C. 779'.2'0924
Pigozzi's Journal of the seventies / by Jean C. Pigozzi ; wih an introd. by Jann Wenner. 1st ed. Garden City, N.Y. : Doubleday, 1979. ca. 200 p. : chiefly ill. ; 28 cm. (A Dolphin book) [TR820.P557] 78-66065 ISBN 0-385-15104-7 pbk. : 8.95
1. Pigozzi, Jean C. 2. Photography, Journalistic. 3. Photography—Portraits. I. Title. II. Title: Journal of the seventies. BIP

POUNCEY, Truman. 770
Photographic journalism, a guide for learning with the graphic. Dubuque, Iowa, W. C. Brown Co. [1952] 161p. illus. 29cm. [TR820.P68] 53-1334
1. Photography, Journalistic. I. Title.

QUICK, Watson, the camera : 779'.092'2 seventy-five years of news photography / edited by Delmar Watson ; text by Helen R. Weiner. Hollywood, CA : D Watson, 1975. 120 p. : chiefly ill. ; 29 cm. Includes index. [TR820.Q52] 75-15119 12.95
1. Photography, Journalistic. I. Watson, Delmar. II. Weiner, Helen R.

RHODE, Robert Bartlett, 1916- 778.9907
Press photography; reporting with a camera [by] Robert B. Rhode [and] Floyd H. McCall. New York, Macmillan [1961] 244p. illus. 22cm. [TR820.R45] 61-5158
1. Photography, Journalistic. I. McCall, Floyd Haley, 1902- joint author. II. Title.

RUBIN, Len S., 1916- 779'.0924
Editor with a camera; picture window on a small town, by Len S. Rubin. South Brunswick, A. S. Barnes [1969, c1968] 111 p. illus. 29 cm. [TR820.R8] 68-27224 8.00
1. Photography, Journalistic. 2. Maywood, N.J.—Description—Views. I. Title.

SALOMON, Erich. 779'.092'4
Erich Salomon. Millerton, N.Y. : Aperture, c1978. 95 p. : chiefly ill. ; 22 cm. (The Aperture history of photography series ; no. 10) Bibliography: p. 95. [TR820.S239] 77-80021 ISBN 0-89381-023-1 : 7.95
1. Salomon, Erich. 2. Photography, Journalistic. BIP

SELLMEYER, Ralph. 770.2'4
The professional approach to journalistic photography [by] Ralph Sellmeyer [and] Cal Wayne Moore. [Dallas] Taylor Pub. Co. [c1967] 119 p. illus. (part col.) 29 cm. [TR820.S38] 67-30143
1. Photography, Journalistic. I. Moore, Cal Wayne, joint author. II. Title.

SEYMOUR, David. 779
David Seymour-"Chim". Introd. by Judith Friedberg. New York, Paragraphic Books [1966] 23, [70] p. illus., ports. 18 cm. [TR140.S46A3] 66-26547
1. Photography, Journalistic. I. Friedberg, Judith. II. Title: Chim.

SEYMOUR, David. 770'.92'4
David Seymour—"Chim", 1911-1956 / [editors, Cornell Capa, Bhupendra Karia]. New York : Grossman Publishers, 1974. 95 p. : chiefly ill. ; 23 cm. (ICP library of photographers ; v. 3) Bibliography: p. 94-95. [TR140.S46A32 1974] 73-14140 ISBN 0-670-25831-8 : 10.00. ISBN 0-670-25832-6 pbk : 5.95
1. Seymour, David. 2. Photography, Journalistic. I. Series: International Fund for Concerned Photography. ICP library of photographers ; v. 3.

SHOTS; photographs from the underground press. 777 Edited by/David Fenton. Designed by Neil Shakery. [1st ed.] New York, Douglas Book Corp.; distributed by the World Pub. Co. [1971] 111 p. (chiefly illus.) 28 cm. "A Liberation News Service book." [TR820.S458] 77-146614 2.95
1. Photography, Journalistic. I. Fenton, David, ed.

SIDEY, Hugh. 778
1,000 ideas for better news pictures [by] Hugh Sidey [and] Rodney Fox. Ames, Iowa State College Press [1956] 192 p. illus. 28 cm. [PN4784.P5S5] 56-11773
1. Photography, Journalistic. I. Fox, Rodney, joint author. II. Title.

SIMMONS, Robert, 1931- 778
Fullname:RobertPrestonSimmons.
How and where to market your pictures. Photos, by the author unless otherwise credited. New York, Greenberg [1957] 128 p. illus. 20 cm. (The Modern camera guide series) [TR820.S46] 57-10216
1. Photography, Journalistic. 2. American periodicals — Direct. I. Title.

SOLOMON, Leo M., 1895- 778
There's money in pictures. New York, Published for Newsweek [by] Funk & Wagnalls [1951] 198 p. illus. 22 cm. (A Newsweek book) [TR820.S6] 51-14402
1. Photography, Journalistic. I. Title.

SPINA, Tony. 778.5'38'07
Press photographer. Text and photos. by Tony Spina. South Brunswick, [N.J.] A. S. Barnes [1968] 185 p. (chiefly illus., ports) 29 cm. [TR820.S68] 67-10743
1. Photography, Journalistic. I. Title.

STEIN, Barney 778
Spot news photography. New York, Verlan Books [1960] 126 p. illus. 21 cm. (A Universal photo book) [TR820.S77] 60-7951
1. Photography, Journalistic. I. Title.

SWEET, Ozzie. 778
My camera pays off. New York, American Photographic Book Pub. Co.; distributed by Garden City Books, Garden City, N.Y., [1959, c1958] 175 p. illus. 25 cm. [TR820.S85] 58-12011
1. Photography, Journalistic. I. Title.

TIME-LIFE Books. 070.4'9
Photojournalism, by the editors of Time-Life books. New York [1971] 227 p. illus. (part col.) 27 cm. (Life library of photography) Bibliography: p. 223. [TR820.T55] 74-144122
1. Photography, Journalistic. I. Title. BIP

WAR; 779'.9'9098
text by Albert R. Leventhal, picture research by Del Byrne. London, New York, Hamlyn, 1973. 252 p. chiefly illus., ports. 29 cm. [TR820.W37 1973b] 74-169000 ISBN 0-600-39304-6 £4.95
1. Photography, Journalistic. 2. War. I. Leventhal, Albert R. II. Byrne, Del.

WAR. 779'.9'9098
Text by Albert R. Leventhal. Picture research by Del Byrne. [1st ed. Chicago] Playboy Press [1973] 242 p. (chiefly illus.) 29 cm. "A Ridge Press book." [TR820.W37] 73-84340 16.95
1. Photography, Journalistic. 2. War. I. Leventhal, Albert R. II. Byrne, Del.

WAR / 779'.9'9098
text by Albert R. Leventhal ; picture research by Del Byrne. [New York] : Ridge Press, c1973. 242 p. : chiefly ill. ; 28 cm. "A Ridge Press Book/A & W Visual Library." [TR820.W37 1973c] 75-7827 ISBN 0-89104-014-5 : 7.95 ($8.95 Can)
1. Photography, Journalistic. 2. War. I. Leventhal, Albert R. II. Byrne, Del.

WARD, William G. 770'.28
The student journalist and creative photography : text and photos. / by Bill Ward. 1st ed. New York : R. Rosen Press, 1976. 95 p. : ill. ; 29 cm. (Student journalist guide series) A study of creative photojournalism and its use in school publications. [TR820.W39] 75-30781 ISBN 0-8239-0335-4 lib.bdg. : 12.50
1. Photography, Journalistic. 2. School photography. I. Title. BIP

WOOLLEY, Al E 070.4
Camera journalism; reporting with photographs, by A. E. Woolley. South Brunswick [N.J.] A. S. Barnes [1966] 192 p. illus. (part col.) ports. 26 cm. [TR820.W6] 66-13059
1. Photography Journalistic. I. Title.

WOOLLEY, Al E. 070.4
Camera journalism; reporting with photographs, by A. E. Woolley. South Brunswick [N.J.] A. S. Barnes [1966] 192 p. illus. (part col.) ports. 26 cm. [TR820.W6] 66-13059
1. Photography, Journalistic. I. Title.

Photography, Journalistic—Addresses, essays, lectures.

PHOTOGRAPHIC communication; 778.9'9'07 principles, problems and challenges of photojournalism. Edited, with commentaries and notes, by R. Smith Schuneman. [1st ed.] New York, Hastings House [1972] 379 p. illus. 25 cm. (Visual communication books) "Based on contributions from the Wilson Hicks international conference[s] on photocommunication arts, University of Miami, Florida [1957-1970]" [TR820.P53] 72-38937 ISBN 0-8038-5780-2 9.50
1. Photography, Journalistic—Addresses, essays, lectures. I. Schuneman, R. Smith, ed. II. Hicks, Wilson. III. Miami, University of, Coral Gables, Fla.

Photography, Journalistic—Awards.

LEEKLEY, Sheryle. 779'.0973
Moments : the Pulitzer Prize photographs / Sheryle and John Leekley. New York : Crown Publishers, c1978. 128 p. : ill. ; 24 x 31 cm. [TR820.L43 1978] 77-17277 12.95
1. Photography, Journalistic—Awards. 2. Pulitzer prizes. I. Leekley, John, joint author. II. Title. BIP

Photography, Journalistic—Exhibitions.

BROWN, Theodore M. 779'.092'4
Margaret Bourke-White, photojournalist [by] Theodore M. Brown. [Ithaca, N.Y.] Andrew Dickson White Museum of Art, Cornell University, 1972. 136 p. illus. 29 cm. "Catalog of the exhibition, Andrew Dickson White Museum of Art, Cornell University, March 15-April 23, 1972:" (p. [127]-131) Bibliography: p. [109]-119. [TR140.B6B76] 76-188882
1. Bourke-White, Margaret, 1905-1971. 2. Photography, Journalistic—Exhibitions. I. Cornell University. Andrew Dickson White Museum of Art. II. Title.

NEW York (City). Museum of Modern Art. 779'.2'07401471
From the picture press. Edited by John Szarkowski. New York, [1973] 95 p. (chiefly illus.) 26 cm. Catalog of an exhibition. [TR820.N4] 72-82886 ISBN 0-87070-334-X
1. Photography, Journalistic—Exhibitions. I. Szarkowski, John, ed. II. Title. BIP

SCOOP, scandal, and strife; 070.4'9 a study of photography in newspapers [by] Ken Baynes [and others] With contributions by Len Franklin [and others] Newspapers reproduced from the John Frost collection. Edited by Ken Baynes. [New York] Hastings House [1971] 144 p. illus. 30 cm. "Record of a Welsh Arts Council travelling exhibition which had its first showing at the National Museum of Wales, Cardiff, in August 1971." [TR820.S36] 75-174705 ISBN 0-8038-6707-7 15.00
1. Photography, Journalistic—Exhibitions. I. Baynes, Ken. II. Welsh Arts Council.

Photography, Journalistic—Yearbooks.

JUST one more. 778.058
[Los Angeles] Los Angeles Press Photographers' Association. v. illus. 31cm. annual. [TR820.J8] 57-39739
1. Photography, Journalistic—Yearbooks. I. Los Angeles Press Photographers Association.

Photography—Juvenile literature.

CATLING, Gordon. 770'.28
Better photography. [2d ed.] London, Kaye & Ward [1973, c1968] 94 p. illus. 23 cm. Stamped on t.p.: Distributed by Sportshelf, New Rochelle, N.Y. Advice for choosing and operating a camera and its equipment, taking pictures, developing film, and earning cash from your camera. [TR149.C37 1973] 74-161960 ISBN 0-7182-0489-1 6.50 (U.S.)
1. Photography—Juvenile literature. I. Title. BIP

FORBES, Robin. 770'.282
Click, a first camera book / by Robin Forbes. New York : Macmillan, c1979. p. cm. Simple instructions for those learning to handle a camera for the first time. [TR149.F67] 78-31756 ISBN 0-02-735640-X : 6.95 ISBN 0-02-043210-0 pbk. : 2.95
1. Photography—Juvenile literature. I. Title.

GERACE, Philip G., 1939- 770'.28
Communication—photography / Philip G. Gerace, Stephen S. Mangione ; consulting editor, Rex Miller. Englewood Cliffs, N.J. : Prentice-Hall, c1976. 119 p. : ill. ; 24 cm. (Modular exploration of technology series) Includes index. Describes the proper use of the camera and related photographic tools and discusses the techniques of developing, enlarging, and finishing photographic prints. [TR149.G47] 75-40429 ISBN 0-13-153247-2 : 5.95 ISBN 0-13-153239-1 pbk. : 2.60
1. Photography—Juvenile literature. I.

Mangione, Stephen S., 1943- joint author. II. Title.

HERDA, D. J., 1948- 770'.28
Photography : close-up / words and photos. by D. J. Herda ; ill. by Don Robison. Milwaukee : Raintree Editions ; Chicago : distributed by Childrens Press, c1977. 48 p. : ill. (some col.) ; 25 cm. Discusses adjustable cameras and lenses, the choosing of film for specific situations, different picture-taking angles and attitudes, and the effects of light on camera subjects. [TR149.H47] 76-45947 ISBN 0-8172-0020-7 : 4.95. ISBN 0-8172-0019-3 lib. bdg. : 4.95
1. Photography—Juvenile literature. I. Robison, Don. II. Title.

HERDA, D. J., 1948- 770
Photography, through the lens / words and photos. by D. J. Herda ; ill. by Andrea Eberbach. Milwaukee : Raintree Editions ; Chicago : distributed by Childrens Press, c1977. 48 p. : ill. (some col.) ; 25 cm. Discusses more advanced cameras, lighting techniques, filters, and meters and explores additional inexpensive equipment for the young photographer. [TR149.H48] 76-45778 ISBN 0-8172-0004-5 : 4.95.
1. Photography—Juvenile literature. I. Eberbach, Andrea. II. Title.

HOKE, John L. 770.28
The first book of photography. Illus. by Peter P. Plasencia. New York, Watts [c.1964, 1965] 81p. illus., ports. 23cm. [TR149.H6] 65-22600 2.65; 1.98 bds., lib. ed.,
1. Photography—Juvenile literature. I. Title.

HOKE, John L 1924- 770
The first book of photography. With photos. from many sources and drawings by Russel Hamilton. New York, F. Watts, c1954. 69p. illus. 23cm. ([First book series] 50) Includes bibliography. [TR149.H6] 54-5990
1. Photography—Juvenile literature. I. Title.

HOLLAND, Viki. 770
How to photograph your world. Photos by the author. New York, Scribner [1974] 63 p. illus. 21 x 26 cm. Briefly discusses the best kind of camera for a beginner and how it works and gives suggestions for choosing a subject and composing a picture. [TR149.H63] 73-19561 ISBN 0-684-13709-7 5.95
1. Photography—Juvenile literature. I. Title. BIP

JACOBS, Lou. 770
You and your camera. Illustrated with photos. New York, Lothrop, Lee & Shepard Co. [1971] 159 p. illus. 24 cm. Bibliography: p. 154-156. An introduction to photography which includes instructions on basic photographic techniques for beginners, discussions of various cameras and how they work, and advice on composition, lighting, picture ideas, darkroom techniques, and movie making. [TR149.J28] 70-133627 4.95
1. Photography—Juvenile literature. I. Title. BIP

JOHNSON, James Ralph. 770
Photography for young people. New York, McKay [1971] xi, 128 p. illus. 21 cm. Bibliography: p. 123-126. Discusses purchase, care, and use of photographic equipment. [TR149.J64] 74-144019 5.50
1. Photography—Juvenile literature. I. Title.

KIDD, Maurice Kenneth, 771.3 1910-
Cameras work like this. 45 illus. by W. J. Readhead. London, Phoenix House New York, Roy [c.1963] 56p. illus. (col. front.) 26cm. (Sci. works like this ser.) Bibl. 63-14985 2.95bds.,
1. Photography— Juvenile literature. 2. Cameras—Juvenile literature. I. Title.

KOHN, Eugene. j770.2
Photography; a manual for shutterbugs. Illustrated by Peter P. Plasencia. Englewood Cliffs, N.J., Prentice-Hall [1965] 64 p. illus. (part col.) 22 cm. [TR149.K595] 65-11772
1. Photography—Juvenile literature. I. Title. BIP

KOHN, Eugene 770.2
Photography: a manual for shutterbugs. Illus. by Peter P. Plasencia. Englewood Cliffs, N.J., Prentice-Hall [1975, c1965] 64 p. 21 cm. (A Treehouse paperback) [TK147.K595] 65-11772 ISBN 0-13-665018-X 1.25 (pbk.)
1. Photography—Juvenile literature. I. Title.

LANGFORD, Michael John, 1933- 770
Starting photography / Michael Langford ; [diagrs. by John Quinn]. New York : Hastings House, 1976. 128 p. : ill. ; 24 cm. Includes index. Discusses technical and artistic aspects of photography such as camera operation, darkroom procedures, and picture composition. [TR149.L35 1976] 76-13517 ISBN 0-8038-6736-0 : 7.95
1. Photography—Juvenile literature. I. Title. BIP

LAVERRIERE, Sophie. 770'.2'40544
Fun with photography / Sophie Laverriere ; photos. by the author, drawings by Nicole Claveloux. New York : Watts, 1975. 95 p. : ill. (some col.) ; 18 cm. (A Panda paperback) Explains photographic techniques and some unusual and humorous uses to which these techniques can be put. [TR149.L38] 75-318981 lib.bdg. : 1.95
1. Photography—Juvenile literature. I. Claveloux, Nicole. II. Title.

LEEN, Nina, 1909- 770'.28
Taking pictures / by Nina Leen. New York : Holt, Rinehart and Winston, c1977. 48 p. : ill. ; 24 cm. A guide for the young child in operating a camera, with suggestions for photographing animals and for making backgrounds for indoor shots. [TR149.L43] 76-41156 ISBN 0-03-018701-X : 5.95
1. Photography—Juvenile literature. I. Title. BIP

MERGENDAHL, T. E. Jr. 770.69
What does a photographer do? [By] T. E. Mergendahl, Jr., Sheldon Ramsdell. New York, Dodd, [c.1965] 64p. illus., ports. 22cm. [TR149.M4] 65-152744 2.75; 2.69 lib.ed.,
1. Photography—Juvenile literature. I. Ramsdell, Sheldon, joint author. II. Title.

NOREN, Catherine. 770'.28
Photography: how to improve your technique. Photos. by the author. New York, F. Watts, 1973. 63 p. illus. 24 cm. (A Concise guide) Bibliography: p. 59-60. Directions on choosing equipment and film, using light, developing film, and numerous other techniques that can improve photo-taking skills. [TR149.N67] 73-5687 ISBN 0-531-02640-X 3.95
1. Photography—Juvenile literature. I. Title.

PALDER, Edward L. 770
Magic with photography; simplified explanations and scientific demonstrations of basic photography, by Edward L. Palder. Illustrated by Ric Estrada. New York, Grosset & Dunlap [1969] v, 103 p. illus. 28 cm. Briefly traces the history of photography, explains, with suggestions for experiments, the scientific principles involved, and gives tips on taking photographs with any camera. [TR149.P35 1969] 70-88895 3.95
1. Photography—Juvenile literature. I. Estrada, Ric, illus. II. Title.

PHOTOGRAPHY / 770
Wilbur R. Miller ... [et al.]. 1st ed. Bloomington, Ill. : McKnight Pub. Co., 1979,c1978. iv, 92 p. : ill. ; 24 cm. (Basic industrial arts) Includes index. Introduces fundamentals of photography including operating a camera, developing films, composing a picture, and printing an enlargement. [TR149.P47] 78-53393 ISBN 0-87345-797-8 : 3.96 ISBN 0-87345-789-7 pbk. : 2.64
1. Photography—Juvenile literature. I. Miller, Wilbur R., 1944- II. Title. III. Series.

SPITZING, Gunter. 770
Peter and his camera; my first book about photography. Told by Gunter Spitzing and Karl Steinorth. Translated by Rolf Fricke. Illustrated by Hannelore Radetzky. Dobbs Ferry, N.Y., Morgan & Morgan [1973] 85 p. illus. (part col.) 18 cm. While learning to use the camera he receives as a gift, Peter learns how a camera works, its many uses, and the history of photography. [TR149.S6513] 72-83110 ISBN 0-87100-032-6 2.95 (pbk.)
1. Photography—Juvenile literature. I. Steinorth, Karl, joint author. II. Radetzky, Hannelore, illus. III. Title. BIP

STEINBERG, Phillip Orso. 770'.28
Photography / by Phil Steinberg ; pictures by George Overlie. Minneapolis : Lerner Publications Co., [1975] 32 p. : ill. ; 20 cm. (An Early craft book) Traces the history of photography, describes the various kinds of cameras, and explains how to take, develop, enlarge, and display photographs. [TR149.S69 1975] 74-11892 ISBN 0-8225-0869-9 lib.bdg. : 3.95
1. Photography—Juvenile literature. I. Overlie, George, illus. II. Title.

SULLIVAN, George, 1927- 770
Understanding photography. New York, F. Warne [1972] 128 p. illus. 24 cm. Bibliography: p. 121-122. Includes directions for choosing and caring for a camera, composing a picture, developing film, and making prints. [TR149.S83] 72-83127 4.50
1. Photography—Juvenile literature. I. Title. BIP

Photography —Landscapes.

ADAMS, Ansel Easton, 779.943 1902-
These we inherit; the parklands of America. San Francisco, Sierra Club [1962] 103 p. 42 plates. 35 cm. "Derived in large part from My camera in the national parks ... travel and photographic data have been omitted ... and the text has been rewritten." Includes bibliographical references. [TR660.A3] 62-18739
1. Photography—Landscapes. 2. National parks and reserves—U.S. I. Title.

BRODATZ, Phil. 779'.36
Land, sea, and sky : a photographic album for artists and designers / Phil Brodatz. New York : Dover Publications, 1976. xi, 99 p. : chiefly ill. ; 27 cm. Includes index. [TR660.5.B76 1976] 75-30178 ISBN 0-486-23249-2 pbk. : 4.50
1. Photography—Landscapes. I. Title. BIP

CAPONIGRO, Paul, 1932- 779'.092'4
The landscape : photographs / by Paul Caponigro. New York : McGraw-Hill, c1975. p. cm. (McGraw-Hill paperbacks) [TR660.C36] 75-24797 ISBN 0-07-009780-1 pbk. : 7.95
1. Photography—Landscapes. I. Title. BIP

GAYTON, Leonard. 770.24
Landscape photography [by] Leonard & Marjorie Gayton. London, New York, Focal Press [1953?] 216p. illus. 24cm. [TR660.G3] 54-39217
1. Photography—Landscapes. I. Gayton, Marjorie, joint author. II. Title.

MUENCH, David. 779'.9'97800924
Rendezvous country / photos. by David Muench ; text by Donald G. Pike. 1st ed. Palo Alto, Calif. : American West Pub. Co., [1975] 159 p. : ill. (some col.), map (on lining papers) ; 29 cm. (Images of America series) Includes index. [TR660.5.M83] 75-6323 ISBN 0-910118-65-5 : 18.50. ISBN 0-910118-66-3 de luxe : 22.00
1. Photography—Landscapes. 2. The West—Description and travel—Views. 3. Fur trade—The West. I. Pike, Donald G. II. Title.

ROBINSON, Henry Peach, 778.9'36 1830-1901.
Letters on Landscape photography. New York, Arno Press, 1973. 94 p. illus. 23 cm. (The Literature of Photography) Reprint of the 1888 ed., which was issued as no. 7 of Scovill photographic series [TR660.R66 1973] 72-9229 ISBN 0-405-04935-8. 9.00.
1. Photography landscape. 2. Photography, Artistic. I. Title. II. Series. BIP

WALL, Alfred H. 778.9'36
Artistic landscape photography, by A. H. Wall. New York, Arno Press, 1973. 171 p. illus. 23 cm. (The Literature of Photography) Reprint of the 1896 ed. [TR660.W34 1973] 722 ISBN 0-405.04947-1 11.00.
1. Photography—Landscapes. I. Title. II. Series. BIP

WOOLEY, Al E. 778.71
Outdoor four-seasons photography, in black-and-white and color. Philadelphia, Chilton, c.1962. 127p. illus. 20cm. (Modern camera guide ser., 884) 62-11594 1.95 pap.,
1. sPhotography—Landscapes. 2. Photography—Marines. I. Title.

WOOLLEY, Al E. 778.71
Outdoor four-seasons photography, in black-and-white and color. Philadelphia, Chilton Co. Book Division, c1962. 127 p. illus. 20 cm. (Modern camera guide series, 884) [TR660.W6] 62-11594
1. Photography — Landscapes. 2. Photography — Marines. I. Title.

WRIGHT, Cedric, 1889-1959. 779.3
Words of the earth. Ed. by Nancy Newhall. Foreword by Ansel Admas. San Francisco, Sierra Club [dist. New York, Knopf, c.1960] 93p. (chiefly illus.) 35cm. 60-53176 12.50
1. Photography—Landscapes. 2. Photography, Artistic. I. Title. BIP

Photography—Landscapes— Exhibitions.

BROWN, Dean, 1936- 779'.36'0973 1973.
Photographs of the American wilderness : [exhibition] / Dean Brown ; introduction by Carol Brown. Garden City, N.Y. : Amphoto, c1976. [133] p. : col. ill. ; 24 cm. Held at the Akron Art Institute from May 2 through June 13, 1976, and others. [TR660.5.B77] 76-17423 ISBN 0-8174-2413-X : 13.95
1. Photography—Landscapes—Exhibitions. 2. Wilderness areas—United States—Pictorial works. I. Akron, Ohio. Art Institute. II. Title.

GEORGE Eastman 779'.074014789
House, Rochester, N.Y.
Figure in landscape. [Catalogue of an exhibition. Rochester] 1971. 1 portfolio ([4] p., 5 plates) 38 cm. Introd. signed: Harold H. Jones III. Bibliography: p. [4] [TR660.5.G46] 72-181048
1. Photography—Landscapes—Exhibitions. I. Jones, Harold H. II. Title.

THE Land : 779'.36'0740941
twentieth century landscape photographs / selected by Bill Brandt. 1st American ed. New York : Da Capo Press, 1976. p. cm. "Based on an exhibition of the same title, The Land, held at the Victoria and Albert Museum in the winter of 1975-76 and afterwards circulated to the National Gallery of Modern Art, Edinburgh, the Ulster Museum, Belfast, and the National Museum of Wales, Cardiff." [TR660.5.L37 1976] 75-30640 ISBN 0-306-70753-5 : 15.00 ISBN 0-306-80026-8 pbk. :
1. Photography—Landscapes—Exhibitions. I. Brandt, Bill. II. Victoria and Albert Museum, South Kensington.

Photography— Law and legislation— U. S.

CHERNOFF, George. 770.2673
Photography and the law, by George Chernoff and Hershel Sarbin. Philadelphia, Chilton Books [1965] 128 p. illus. 24 cm. [[KF3067]] 65-7779
1. Photography—Law and legislation—U.S. I. Sarbin, Hershel, joint author. II. Title. BIP

CHERNOFF, George. 770
Photography and the law, by George Chernoff and Hershell Sarbin. New York, American Photographic Book Pub. Co.; distributed by Garden City Books, Garden City, N. Y. [1958] 127p. illus. 20cm. (An Amphoto book) 57-14986
1. Photography—Law and legislation—U. S. I. Sarbin, Hersbel, joint author. II. Title.

SHERWIN, Robert Veit. 770
Legal problems in photography. New York, Greenberg [1958, c1957] 126 p. illus. 20

cm. (The Modern camera guide series 19) 57-12728
1. Photography — Law and legislation — U.S. I. Title.

Photography, Legal.

MALLARE, Frank L. 347.07'5
Photographs "...worth a thousand words" as evidence [by] Frank L. Mallare & William D. Gehl. [Madison, Wis., Institute of Continuing Legal Education for Wisconsin, c1971] xiv, 113 p. 23 cm. On spine: Photographs as evidence. Includes bibliographical references. [TR822.M33] 79-185759
1. Photography, Legal. I. Gehl, William D., joint author. II. Title. III. Title: Photographs as evidence.

POUNTNEY, Harold. 770'.24'3632
Police photography. Amsterdam, London, New York, Elsevier, 1971. x, 197 p. 48 plates; illus. (some col.), facsims., plan. 26 cm. Bibliography: p. 178-179. [TR822.P68] 74-134290 ISBN 0-444-20104-1 £6.00
1. Photography, Legal. I. Title. BIP

SANSONE, Sam J. 364.12'8
Modern photography for police Sam J. Sansone. Cincinnati : Anderson Pub. Co., c1977. xv, 203, 12 p. : ill. ; 27 cm. (Law enforcement fieldbooks) Published in 1971 under title: Modern photography for police and firemen. Includes index. Bibliography: p. 191-194. [TR822.S26] 77-81216 ISBN 0-87084-772-4 : 11.95
1. Photography, Legal. I. Title. II. Series.

SANSONE, Sam J. 770'.24'363
Modern photography for police and firemen, by Sam J. Sansone. Cincinnati, W. H. Anderson Co. [1971] xii, 478 p. illus. (part col.) 27 cm. (Science in law enforcement series) Bibliography: p. 443-446. [TR822.S25] 78-150851
1. Photography, Legal. I. Title.

SILJANDER, Raymond P. 770'.2'4363
Applied police and fire photography / Raymond P. Siljander ; with forewords by John D. Douthit and Mel Hardy. Springfield, Ill. : Thomas, c1976. p. cm. Includes index. [TR822.S53] 76-7017 ISBN 0-398-03566-0
1. Photography, Legal. 2. Criminal investigation. 3. Fire investigation. I. Title. BIP

SILJANDER, Raymond P. 778.9'9'364128
Applied surveillance photography / by Raymond P. Siljander. Springfield, Ill. : Thomas, [1975] xi, 102 p. : ill. ; 24 cm. Includes index. [TR822.S54] 74-23471 ISBN 0-398-03376-5 : 10.50
1. Photography, Legal. I. Title. BIP

Photography—Library applications.

SHAW, Ralph Robert, 1907- 025.129
The use of photography for clerical routines, a report to the American Council of Learned Societies. Washington, American Council of Learned Societies, 1953. 85p. 22cm. [Z681.S4] 53-2373
1. Photography—Library applications. I. American Council of Learned Societies Devoted to Humanistic Studies. II. Title.

Photography—Light filters.

BAKAL, Carl, 1918- 771.356
Filter manual, including The filter dictionary. [1st ed.] San Francisco, Camera Craft Pub. Co. [1953] 136p. illus. 25cm. [TR453.B17] 53-11646
1. Photography—Light filters. I. Title. II. Title: The filer dictionary.

BATES, G. Gordon 771.356
How to use filters in colour and black-and-white photography. London, Fountain [dist. New York, Morgan & Morgan, 1964, c.1960] 94p. illus., diagrs., tables. 17cm. (Fountain photobk. ser.) 64-3074 2.95 bds.,
1. Photography—Light filters. I. Title.

LATHAM, Sidney. 771.356
Filter guide. Philadelphia, Chilton Books, 1962. 96p. illus. 20cm. (Modern camera guide series, 995) [TR590.5.L3] 62-20133
1. Photography—Light filters. I. Title. BIP

MANNHEIM, Ladislaus Andrew, 1925- 771.3'56
Filter practice [by] Hans Clauss [and] Heinz Meusel. [English translation and adaptation by L. A. Mannheim] Philadelphia, Chilton Book Co. [1969] 176 p. illus. (part col.) 22 cm. [TR590.5.M35] 69-16644 6.95
1. Photography—Light filters. I. Clauss, Hans. Filterpraxis. II. Title.

REYNOLDS, Clyde. 771.3'56
The photoguide to filters / Clyde Reynolds. London ; New York : Focal Press, 1976. 235 p. : ill. (some col.) ; 19 cm. (The Focal photoguides) Includes index. [TR590.5.R49] 77-360353 ISBN 0-240-50923-4 : pbk. : 6.95
1. Photography—Light filters. I. Title.

ROTHSCHILD, Norman 771.356
Filter guide: for color and black & white, by Norman Rothschild, Cora Wright. Rev. ed. New York, Amphoto [c.1959, 1962] 126p. illus. 21cm. 62-12836 2.50 bds.,
1. Photography—Light filters. I. Wright, Cora, joint author. II. Title.

ROTHSCHILD, Norman. 771.356
Filter guide, by Norman Rothschild and Cora Wright. New York, American Photographic Book Pub. Co. [1959] 128p. illus. 20cm. (An Amphoto book) [TR453.R6] 58-12010
1. Photography—Light filters. I. Wright, Cora, joint author. II. Title.

ROTHSCHILD, Norman. 771.3'56
Filter guide: for color and black & white, by Norman Rothschild and Cora Wright Kennedy. 3d ed. New York, Amphoto [1971] 126 p. illus. 21 cm. [TR590.5.R67 1971] 75-26593 3.50
1. Photography—Light filters. I. Kennedy, Cora Wright, joint author. II. Title.

ROTHSCHILD, Norman. 771.3'56
Filter guide for color and black & white, by Norman Rothschild and Cora Wright Kennedy. 3d ed. Philadelphia, Chilton Book Co. [1971] 126 p. illus. 21 cm. [TR590.5.R67 1971b] 70-131961 ISBN 0-8019-5611-0 3.50
1. Photography—Light filters. I. Kennedy, Cora Wright, joint author. II. Title.

SHANK, Bradford, 1908- 771.356
Filters and their uses. Rev. ed. New York, Crown Publishers [1954] 112p. illus. 18cm. (Little technical library, 3) [TR453.S45 1954] 54-6643
1. Photography—Light filters. I. Title.

SMITH, Robb. 771.3'56
Amphoto guide to filters / George Catlin [i.e. R. Smith]. Garden City, N.Y. : Amphoto, [1979] p. cm. Includes index. [TR590.5.S56] 78-21937 ISBN 0-8174-2458-X : 9.95 ISBN 0-8174-2132-7 pbk. : 5.95
1. Photography—Light filters. I. Title. BIP

SMITH, Robb. 771.3'56
The Tiffen practical filter manual / Robb Smith. Garden City, N.Y. : Amphoto, c1975. 96 p., [4] leaves of plates : ill. (some col.) ; 26 cm. Includes index. [TR590.5.S57] 75-21574 ISBN 0-8174-0180-6 pbk. : 4.95
1. Photography—Light filters. I. Title. BIP

STENSVOLD, Mike. 771.3'56
Photo filters / by Mike Stensvold. Los Angeles : Petersen Pub. Co., c1976. 80 p. : ill. ; 28 cm. (Petersen's how-to photographic library) [TR590.5.S73] 76-5980 ISBN 0-8227-4002-8 pbk. : 3.95
1. Photography—Light filters. I. Title. BIP

Photography—Lighting.

BUCKNER, Ken. 778.7
Available light / by Ken Buckner. Los Angeles : Petersen Pub. Co., c1976. 80 p. : ill. ; 28 cm. (Petersen's how-to photographic library) [TR595.B82] 76-15435 ISBN 0-8227-4003-6 pbk. : 3.95
1. Photography—Lighting. 2. Photography, Commercial. I. Title. BIP

CRICKS, R Howard. 770.282
Illumination; the technique of light. London & New York, Focal Press [1951] 320 p. illus. 19 cm. (The Manual of photo-technique) [TR590.C7] 51-32629
1. Photography—Lighting. 2. Lighting. I. Title.

DESCHIN, Jacob. 770.282
New lighting techniques in photography. New York, Crown Publishers [1953] 124p. illus. 18cm. (Little technical library, 44) [TR590.D47] 52-10770
1. Photography—Lighting. I. Title.

FEININGER, Andreas, 1906- 770'.28
Light and lighting in photography / by Andreas Feininger. Garden City, N.Y. : Amphoto, c1976. 296 p. : ill. ; 23 cm. Includes index. [TR590.F44] 76-16449 ISBN 0-8174-0585-2 : 11.95
1. Photography—Lighting. I. Title. BIP

GOWLAND, Peter 778.37
Guide to electronic flash. New York, American Photographic Book Pub. Co. [c.1960] 128p. illus. 20cm. (An Amphoto book) 59-10308 1.95 pap. sPhotography, Flash-light.
I. Title. II. Title: Electronic flash.

HALFORD, Russ. 770.282
Bounce lighting [with flood, flash, 'strobe,' or daylight] All illus. by the author except where otherwise designated 96p. illus. 22cm. [TR590.H3] 58-11858
1. Photography—Lighting. I. Title.

HATTERSLEY, Ralph. 778.7
Photographic lighting / Ralph Hattersley. Englewood Cliffs, N.J. : Prentice-Hall, c1979. p. cm. (A Spectrum book) Includes index. Bibliography: p. [TR590.H34] 79-1310 ISBN 0-13-665323-5 : 15.95 ISBN 0-13-665315-4 pbk. : 6.95
1. Photography—Lighting. 2. Visual perception. I. Title.

JACOBS, Lou. 770.15
ABC's of lighting. New York, Amphoto [1962] 117p. illus. 21cm. [TR590.J2] 62-12302
1. Photography—Lighting. I. Title.

JACOBS, Lou. 778.7
Amphoto guide to lighting / Lou Jacobs, Jr. Garden City, N.Y. : Amphoto, [1979] p. cm. Includes index. [TR590.J23] 78-21626 ISBN 0-8174-2467-9 : 9.95 pbk. : 5.95
1. Photography—Lighting. I. Title. II. Title: Guide to lighting. BIP

MURPHY, Burt. 770.15
Complete lighting guide. New York, Universal Photo Books [1962] 128p. illus. 20cm. [TR590.M8] 61-8117
1. Photography—Lighting. I. Title.

NIBBELINK, Don D 771.44
The complete book of lighting for color and black-and-white photography. Forest Park, Ill., Midland Publishers [1951, c1950] 256p. illus. 21cm. [TR590.N5] A51
1. Photography— Lighting. I. Title.

NURNBERG, Walter, 1907- 770.1'53
Lighting for photography; means and methods. 16th rev. ed. Philadelphia, Chilton Book Co. [1968] 209 p. illus. (part col.) 25 cm. [TR590.N8 1968] 79-130 9.95
1. Photography—Lighting. I. Title. BIP

PETZOLD, Paul. 778.7'1
Light on people. New York, Amphoto [1971] 152 p. illus. (part col.) 19 x 23 cm. (Visual communication books) [TR590.P48 1971] 70-134588 ISBN 0-240-50707-X 9.95
1. Photography—Lighting. I. Title.

SIMMONS, Robert, 1931- 770.15
Fullname:RobertPrestonSimmons.
Lighting in photography. Photos. by the author unless otherwise credited. Philadelphia, Chilton Co., c1959. 117 p. illus. 20 cm. (Modern camera guide series, 483) [TR590.S5] 59-14140
1. Photography — Lighting. I. Title.

TIME-LIFE Books. 770
Light and film, by the editors of Time-Life Books. New York [1970] 227 p. illus. (part col.) 27 cm. (Life library of photography) Buyer's guide to camera accessories (6 p.) inserted at end. Bibliography: p. 223. [TR590.T55] 77-116582
1. Photography—Lighting. 2. Photography—Exposure. 3. Photography—Films. I. Title. BIP

WRIGHT, George Benjamin, 1913- ed. 771.442
Available light and your camera. Contributors: Jacquelyn Judge [and others] New York, American Photographic Book Pub. Co. [1956, c1955] 181 p. illus. 24 cm. Photography. [TR147.W7] 55-12278
I. Title.

Photography—Marines.

ANTHONY, Gene. 779'.37'0924
The illustrated eternal sea : photographs / by Gene Anthony ; edited by Howard Chapnick. New York : Grosset & Dunlap, c1976. 192 p. : chiefly ill. ; 28 cm. (A Black star book) [TR670.A57 1976] 76-570 ISBN 0-448-12253-7 : 14.95
1. Photography—Marines. I. Title.

ATWOOD, Ann. 779'.37
New Moon Cove. Text and photographs by Ann Atwood. New York, Scribner [1969] [32] p. col. illus. 27 cm. Color photographs and brief text capture the inconstant patterns of a sea cove which change with every tide and season. [TR670.A8] 69-14347 3.95
1. Photography—Marines. I. Title.

CHURCH, Albert Cook. 779'.37
Albert Cook Church; photographs. And a biographical sketch [by Philip F. Purrington] New Bedford, 1969. 1 v. (chiefly illus., ports.) 19 x 26 cm. (Old Dartmouth historical sketches, no. 76) [F74.D25O4 no. 76] 75-9545
1. Photography—Marines. I. Purrington, Philip F. II. Title. III. Series.

FRITH, Francis. 779'.37'094107402162
A Victorian maritime album : 100 photographs from the Francis Frith Collection at the National Maritime Museum / chosen, introduced and explained by Basil Greenhill, director of the National Maritime Museum. Cambridge : Stephens, 1974. 144 p. : ill. ; 29 cm. [TR670.F74] 75-311002 ISBN 0-85059-170-8 : 19.95
1. Photography—Marines. 2. Great Britain—Description and travel—Views. I. Greenhill, Basil. II. Greenwich, Eng. National Maritime Museum. III. Title. Distributed by Haessner Publishing, Newfoundland, N.J. BIP

PARKHURST, Violet. 759.13
Parkhurst on seascapes; a beautiful presentation of our magnificent coastline. [1st ed. Santa Barbara, Calif., Art Made Famous Ltd., 1972] 120 p. illus. (part col.) 34 cm. [TR670.P37] 73-168196 25.00
1. Photography—Marines. 2. Marine painting. I. Title.

Photography, Medical.

BIOMEDICAL photography : 616.07'54 a Kodak seminar in print. 1st ed. Rochester, N.Y. : Eastman Kodak Co., 1976. 128 p. : ill. ; 28 cm. (Kodak publication ; no. N-19) [TR708.B56] 76-27101 ISBN 0-87985-183-X : 10.00
1. Photography, Medical. I. Eastman Kodak Company.

BROWN, Eileen M 778.9'49'61
Medical photography of patients, by Eileen M. Brown. London, H. K. Lewis, 1968. xii, 111 p. 155 illus. 22 cm. 35/- (B 68-01997) [[TR708]] 68-69689
1. Photography, Medical. 2. NLM: Photography. TR 705 B878m 1968] I. Title.

EASTMAN Kodak Company. 616.07'54 Professional, Commercial, and Industrial Markets Division.
Clinical photography; a Kodak medical publication for professional use only. [Rochester, N.Y., 1972] 118 p. illus. 28 cm. (Kodak publication no. N-3) "A Kodak data book." Bibliography: p. 117-118. [TR708.E18] 72-87504 ISBN 0-87985-035-3 2.95
1. Photography, Medical. I. Title. BIP

GIBSON, Henry Louis, 1906- 616.07'54
Medical photography; clinical-ultraviolet-infrared, by H. L. Gibson. Rochester, N.Y., Eastman Kodak Co., Professional and Finishing Markets Division [1973] 208 p.

illus. 29 cm. (Kodak medical publication no. N-18) Bibliography: p. 205-208. [TR708.G49] 73-83431 ISBN 0-87985-076-0 14.95
1. Photography, Medical. **BIP**

GIBSON, Henry Louis, 1906- 778.9961
The photography of patients, including discussions of basic photographic and optical principles. Springfield, Ill., Thomas [1952] 118 p. illus. 23 cm. (American lecture series, publication no. 95. American lectures in medical photography) [TR705.G5] 51-14668
1. Photography, Medical. I. Title.

HANSELL, Peter. 778.9961
A system of ophthalmic illustration. Springfield, Ill., C. C. Thomas [1957] xi, 114p. illus. (part col.) 26cm. (American lecture series, publication no. 289. A monograph in American lectures in medical photography) Includes bibliographies. [TR705.H25] 56-6392
1. Photography, Medical. 2. Ophthalmology. I. Title. II. Series: American lecture series, publication no. 289

LONGMORE, Thomas A. 778.9'9'61
Longmore's medical photography. Rev. and edited by Peter Hansell and Robert Ollerenshaw. 8th rev. ed. Philadelphia, Chilton Book Co. [1969] 538 p. illus., port. 23 cm. [TR708.L65 1969] 70-4971 ISBN 0-240-44862-6 15.00
1. Photography, Medical. 2. Radiography, Medical. I. Hansell, Peter, ed. II. Ollerenshaw, Robert, ed. III. Title. IV. Title: Medical photography.

LONGMORE, Thomas a 778.9961
Medical photography. Rev. and edited by Peter Hansell and Robert Ollerenshaw. 7th rev. ed. Philadelphia, Lippincott [c1962] 544 p. illus. 23 cm. [[TR705]] 62-212721
1. Photography, Medical. 2. Radiography. I. Title.

LONGMORE, Thomas A 778.9961
Medical photography, Radiographic and clinical. With a foreword by D. B. McGrigor. 5th ed. London, New York, Focal Press [1955] 990p. illus. 19cm. [TR705.L6 1955] 56-58855
1. Photography, Medical. 2. Radiography. I. Title.

MCCOMB, Stanley J, 1905- 778.9961
The preparation of photographic prints for medical publication. [1st ed.] Springfield, Ill., Thomas [1950] v. 69 p. illus. 23 cm. (American lecture series, no. 90. American lectures in medical photography) Bibliography: p. 67, 69. [TR705.M3 1950] 50-11025
1. Photography. Medical. I. Title. II. Series: American lecture series, no. 90. Series: American lectures in medical photography

SMIALOWSKI, Arthur 778
Photography in medicine, by Arthur Smialowski and Donald J. Currie. Springfield, Ill. Charles C Thomas [c.1960] xviii, 330p. Bibl.: p.314-316. illus. (part col.), diagrs. 27cm. 59-14210 14.50
1. Photography, Medical. I. Currie, Donald J., joint author. II. Title.

SMIALOWSKI, Arthur. 778
Photography in medicine, by Arthur Smialowski and Donald J. Currie. Springfield, Ill., Thomas [1960] 330 p. illus. 27 cm. Includes bibliography. [TR708.S6 1960] 59-11210
1. Photography. Medical. I. Currie, Donald J. joint author. II. Title. **BIP**

Photography, Medical—Congresses.

PHOTOGRAPHIC science and 610'.28
engineering in medicine—equipment and techniques. Proceedings, tutorial seminar, July 20-21, 1972, Marriott Motor Hotel, Newton, Mass. [Washington, Society of Photographic Scientists and Engineers, 1972] viii, 88 p. illus. 22 cm. Pages 84-88 blank for "Notes." Bibliography: p. 72-81. [TR708.P46] 72-195226
1. Photography, Medical—Congresses. I. Society of Photographic Scientists and Engineers.

Photography, Military—Handbooks, manuals, etc.

UNITED States. Dept. 355'.008 s
of the Army.
Army pictorial techniques, equipments and systems, still photography. [Washington] 1969. 1 v. (various pagings) illus. (part col.), maps. 27 cm. (Its Technical manual TM11-401-2) Cover title. "Supersedes so much of TM11-401, 10 December 1953, including C1, 28 June 1961, as pertains to still photography." [U408.3.A13 TM11-401-2] [UG476] 770'.28 78-605727
1. United States. Army—Photographers. 2. Photography, Military—Handbooks, manuals, etc. I. Title. II. Series: United States. Dept. of the Army. Training publication TM11-401-2.

Photography—Negatives.

JACOBSOHN, Kurt, 1906- 770.283
Developing: the negative technique, by C. I. Jacobsen. 16th ed. London, New York, Focal P., 1966. 370 p. illus., tables, diagrs. 22 cm. (The Manual of photo-technique) 50/- [TR290.J3] 66-70362
1. Photography—Negatives. 2. Photography—Developing and developers. I. Title. II. Series. III. Series: The Manual of photo technique **BIP**

JACOBSOHN, Kurt, 1906- 770.283
Developing, the negative-technique by C. I. Jacobson [pseud.] [11 ed.] London, New York, Focal Press [1951] 319p. illus. 19cm. (The Manual of photo-technique) [TR290.J3 1951] 53-22986
1. Photography—Negatives. 2. Photography—Developing and developers. I. Title.

JACOBSOHN, Kurt, 1906- 770.283
Developing: the negative technique [by] C. I. Jacobson and R. E. Jacobson. 17th ed. London, New York, Focal P., 1970. 391 p. illus., plans. 22 cm. (The Manual of photo-technique) [TR290.J3 1970] 71-540478 ISBN 0-240-44770-0 50/-
1. Photography—Negatives. 2. Photography—Developing and developers. I. Jacobson, R. E., joint author. II. Title.

Photography—New Mexico—History.

COKE, Van Deren, 1921- 770'.9789
Photography in New Mexico / Van Deren Coke ; foreword by Beaumont Newhall. 1st ed. Albuquerque : University of New Mexico Press, c1979. p. cm. Includes index. Bibliography: p. [TR24.N6C64] 78-21370 ISBN 0-8263-0495-8 : 24.95
1. Photography—New Mexico—History. 2. New Mexico—History. I. Title. **BIP**

Photography, Night.

AMPHOTO, New York. 778.7'19
Night photography simplified, by the Amphoto editorial board. Englewood Cliffs, N.J., Prentice-Hall [1974] 96 p. illus. (part col.) 26 cm. (A Modern photoguide) (A Spectrum book, S-PG-1) [TR610.A45 1974] 73-92425 ISBN 0-13-622373-7 7.95
1. Photography, Night. I. Title.
Pbk. 2.95, ISBN 0-13-622356-6. **BIP**

SOULE, Harold V. 778.7'19
Electro-optical photography at low illumination levels [by] Harold V. Soule, New York, Wiley [1967, c1968] xvi, 392 p. illus. 24 cm. (Wiley series on photographic science and technology and the graphic arts) Bibliography: p. 367-388. [TR610.S6] 67-23330
1. Photography, Night. 2. Electrooptical photography. I. Title.

WERSEN, Kathy. 778.719
Picture-taking at night, by Kathy Wersen and A. S. Reed. New York, American Photographic Book Pub. Co.; distributed to the book trade by Grosset & Dunlap [1964] 96 p. illus. 22 cm. (Better photo guides) "434." [TR610.W4] 63-22239
1. Photography, Night. I. Reed, Alice S., joint author. II. Title.

WOOLLEY, Al E. 771.4491
A guide to night photography. New York, Greenberg, c1956. 126 p. illus. 20 cm. (The Modern camera guide series) [TR610.W6] 56-6104
1. Photography, Night. 2. Photography, Artistic. I. Title.

Photography of animals.

BAUER, Erwin A. 778.9'32
Hunting with a camera : a world guide to wildlife photography / Erwin A. Bauer. New York : Winchester Press, [1974] viii, 324 p., [8] leaves of plates : ill. (some col.) ; 26 cm. Includes index. Bibliography: p. 314-316. [TR727.B26] 74-78698 ISBN 0-87691-143-2 : 12.95
1. Photography of animals. I. Title.

BAUFLE, Jean Marie. 778.9'32
Photographing wildlife [by] Jean-Marie Baufle [and] Jean-Philippe Varin. Translated from the French by Carel v. Amerongen. New York, Oxford University Press, 1972. 157 p. illus. 29 cm. Translation of La chasse photographique. Bibliography: p. 157. [TR727.B2813] 72-82675 ISBN 0-19-519714-3 15.00
1. Photography of animals. I. Varin, Jean Philippe, joint author. II. Title. **BIP**

CHANDOHA, Walter. 778.9'32
How to photograph cats, dogs, and other animals. New York, Crown Publishers [1973] 154 p. illus. 27 cm. [TR727.C47 1973] 72-96653 ISBN 0-517-50349-2 7.50
1. Photography of animals. I. Title. **BIP**

COTT, Hugh Bamford 778.932
Zoological photography in practice; a contribution to the techniqueand art of wild animal portraiture. Pref. by Julian S. Hunkey. London, Fountain Pr. [New York, Morgan & Morgan, 1964] 370p. illus., 68 plates. 23cm. (Photo practice ser.) Bibl. 57-440 12.50
1. Photography of animals. 2. Photography—Handbooks, manuals. etc. I. Title.

COTT, Hugh Bamford. 778.932
Zoological photography in practice; a contribution to the technique and art of wild animal portriture With a pref. by Julian S. Huxley. London, Fountain Press Philadelphia, Rayelle Publications [1956] 370p. illus., 68plates. 23cm. (Photo practice series) A Fountain photobook. Bibliography: p. 357-358. [QH245.C6] 57-440
1. Photography of animals. 2. Photography—Handbooks, manuals. I. Title.

DAMROTH, William G. 778.9'32
Passport to nature [by] William G. Damroth. Introd. by Arthur Godfrey. New York, Viking Press [1972] 94 p. illus. 24 x 28 cm. (A Studio book) [TR727.D35 1972] 77-178821 ISBN 0-670-54195-8 10.00
1. Photography of animals. 2. Animal pictures. I. Title.

DUNTON, Sam C 778.932
Guide to photographing animals. New York, Greenberg, c1956. 128p. illus. 20cm. (The Modern camera guide series) [QH245.D89] 56-7914
1. Photography of animals. I. Title. II. Title: Photographing animals.

FEIN, Nat. 779.32
Nat Fein's animals, photographed by Nat Fein, with text as told to Ferdi Backer & Ruth Biemiller. Foreword by Walt Kelly. New York, Gilbert Press; distributed by J. Messner [1955] unpaged. illus. 28 cm. [TR673.F4] 55-9853
1. Photography of animals. 2. Animal pictures. I. Backer, Ferdi. II. Biemiller, Ruth.

GARRISON, Ronald. 778.9'32
Secrets of zoo photography [by] Ronald Garrison, with Robert Gray. [1st ed.] Garden City, N.Y., Doubleday, 1972. 127 p. illus. 21 cm. Bibliography: p. [126]-127. [TR727.G37] 74-180121 2.50
1. Photography of animals. I. Gray, Robert, 1922- II. Title. III. Title: Zoo photography.

MACKENZIE, Compton, Sir 778.932
1883-
Catmint. With photos. specially taken for this book by Richard Herzenberg. [1st American ed.] New York, Taplinger Pub. Co., 1962 [c1961] 103p. illus. 25cm. [TR673.M3 1962] 62-10395
1. Photography of animals. 2. Cats—Pictures, illustrations, etc. I. Title.

RAITHBY, J. A. 778.9'32
How to photograph Australian wildlife [by] J. A. Raithby and H. Beste. [Melbourne] Periwinkle Books [1971] 112 p. illus. (part col.) diagrs. 19 cm. (Periwinkle colour guides) Bibliography: p. 109. [TR727.R35] 72-175237 ISBN 0-7018-0094-1 1.50
1. Photography of animals. I. Beste, H., joint author. II. Title.

SELL, Francis E., 1902- 778.932
Hunting with camera and binocular. Philadelphia, Chilton Co., Book Division, c1961. 128 p. illus. 21 cm. (Modern camera guide series, 547) [QH245.S43] 61-5908
1. Photography of animals. I. Title.

SHERMAN, John Burrowes. 778.932
Camera on safari; shooting big game through your lens. London, New York, Focal Press [1960] 128 p. illus. 24 cm. [TR673.S5] 61-19812
1. Photography of animals. I. Title.

SIMMONS, Albert Dixon. 778.932
Photography for sportsmen; profusely illustrated by the author. New York, D. Van Nostrand Co. [1951] 172 p. illus. 24 cm. [TR682.S5] 51-12775
1. Photography of animals. 2. Photography, Artistic. I. Title.

STAGG, Mildred. 778.932
Animal and pet photography. New York, Universal Photo Books [1961] 127 p. illus. 20 cm. [TR673.S8] 61-14260
1. Photography of animals. I. Title.

STAGG, Mildred. 778.9'32
Animal and pet photography. [2d ed., rev.] Philadelphia, Chilton Book Co. [1969] 127 p. illus. 21 cm. [TR727.S7 1969] 70-4183 3.50
1. Photography of animals. I. Title.

STAGG, Mildred. 778.9'32
Animal and pet photography. [2d ed., rev.] New York, American Photographic Book Pub. Co. [1969] 127 p. illus. 20 cm. (Amphoto photo books, 102) [TR727.S7 1969b] 69-13154
1. Photography of animals. I. Title.

STAGG, Mildred. 778.9'32
Animal & pet photography simplified / by Mildred Stagg. Garden City, N.Y. : Amphoto, [1975] 96 p., [2] leaves of plates : ill. (some col.) ; 26 cm. (A Modern photoguide) Includes index. [TR727.S72] 75-1972 ISBN 0-8174-0181-4 pbk. : 3.45
1. Photography of animals. I. Title. **BIP**

Photography of animals—History.

GUGGISBERG, Charles 770'.92'2 B
Albert Walter.
Early wildlife photographers / by C. A. W. Guggisberg ; foreword by Eric Hosking. New York : Taplinger Pub. Co., 1977. 128 p. : ill. ; 24 cm. Includes index. Bibliography: p. 120-127. [TR727.G83 1977b] 76-54404 ISBN 0-8008-2352-4 : 9.95
1. Photography of animals—History. 2. Wildlife cinematography—History. 3. Photographers. I. Title. **BIP**

Photography of animals—Juvenile literature.

REICH, Hanns, comp. 779
Laughing camera for children. Photos. by Backhaus [and others] New York, Hill and Wang [1971] c1970. 40 p. (chiefly illus.) 24 cm. First published in Munich in 1970 under title: Die lachende Kamera fur Kinder. A collection of humorous black and white photographs, the humor often being derived from the juxtaposition of photographs of animals and humans engaged in similar activities. [TR727.R4313 1971] 70-148231 ISBN 0-8090-2122-6
1. Photography of animals—Juvenile literature. I. Title. **BIP**

Photography of art.

DUNCAN, David Douglas. 779'.9'70924
Magic worlds of fantasy / by David Douglas Duncan. New York : Harcourt Brace Jovanovich, [1978] p. cm. "A Helen and Kurt Wolff book" Includes index. [TR657.D86] 78-1470 14.95
1. Photography of art. I. Title. BIP

LEWIS, John Noel Claude, 1912- 778.9'9'7
Reproducing art; the photography, graphic reproduction and printing of works of art [by] John Lewis and Edwin Smith. New York, Praeger [1969] 143 p. illus. (part col.) 26 cm. [TR657.L48] 75-78294 14.95
1. Photography of art. 2. Photography—Reproduction of plans, drawings, etc. I. Smith, Edwin, 1912- joint author. II. Title.

MACLEAN, Hector, R. P. S. 778.9'9'7
Photography for Artists. New York, Arno Press, 1973. 152 p. illus. 24 cm. (The Literature of Photography) Reprint of the 1896 ed. [TR657.M3 1973] 72-9218 ISBN 0-405-04925-0. 10.00.
1. Photography of Art. 2. Photography. I. Title. II. Series. BIP

MATES, Robert E. 778.9
Photographing art. by Robert E. Mates. Philadelphia, Chilton [1966] 128p. illus. (pt. col.) 26cm. Bibl. [TR625.M3] 66-23323 6.95
1. Photography of art. I. Title.

MATTHEWS, Sydney Kent. 778.9'9'913031
Photography in archaeology and art [by] S. K. Matthews. [New York] Humanities Press [1968] xii, 161 p. illus. (part col.) 26 cm. Bibliography: p. 155-156. [TR657.M37 1968b] 67-30790 15.00
1. Photography of art. 2. Photography in archaeology. I. Title.

SCHMID, Claus Peter. 778.9'9'7
Photography for artists and craftsmen / Claus-Peter Schmid. New York : Van Nostrand Reinhold Co., [1975] 103 p. : ill. ; 24 cm. [TR657.S35] 74-17545 ISBN 0-442-27393-2 : 9.95
1. Photography of art. I. Title. BIP

Photography of bark.

FOREL, Oscar Louis, 1891- 779'.34'0924
Hidden art in nature; synchromies [by] Oscar Forel. [1st U.S. ed.] New York, Harper & Row [1972] 125 p. (chiefly col. plates) 34 cm. Pages 18-125 consist of plates with captions on opposite pages. Translation of Synchromies. [TR726.B3F6713 1972] 72-79665 ISBN 0-06-011317-0 30.00
1. Photography of bark. I. Title.

Photography of birds.

AUSTING, G. Ronald. 778.932
I went to the woods: the autobiography of a bird photographer [by] Ronald Austing. [1st American ed.] New York, Coward-McCann [1964, c1963] 143 p. illus. (part col.) ports. 22 cm. [TR673.A8 1964] 64-13059
1. Photography of birds. I. Title.

HOSKING, Eric John. 778.932
Bird photography as a hobby [by] Eric Hosking and Cyril Newberry. New York, McBride Books [1962, c1961] 95p. illus. 20cm. [TR673.H6] 62-13554
1. Photography of birds. I. Newberry, Cyril William, joint author. II. Title.

HOSKING, Eric John. 770'.92'4 B
An eye for a bird; the autobiography of a bird photographer [by] Eric Hosking, with Frank W. Lane. Foreword by Prince Philip, Duke of Edinburgh. [1st American ed.] New York, P. S. Eriksson [1973, c1970] xviii, 302 p. illus. 24 cm. [TR140.H67A3 1973] 72-93312 ISBN 0-8397-0290-6 10.00
1. Hosking, Eric John. 2. Photography of birds. I. Lane, Frank Walter. II. Title.

SLOCUM, Perry D. 778.9'32
Birds of North America and how to photograph them; 100 species, by Perry D. Slocum. [Winter Haven, Fla., Published by Perry D. Slocum in cooperation with the Florida Audubon Society, 1971- v. col. illus. 28 cm. Cover title. [TR729.B5S56] 72-200969 12.95
1. Photography of birds. 2. Birds—North America. I. Florida Audubon Society. II. Title.

TUPHOLME, Cuthbert Hartland Seymour, 1896- 778.93
Photographing garden birds, with a 35-mm camera. London, Faber & Faber [dist. Hollywood-by-the-Sea, Fla., Transatlantic, c.1962] 127p. illus. (pt. col.) 21cm. Bibl. 63-282 4.50
1. Photography of birds. I. Title.

WARHAM, John. 778.9'32
The technique of bird photography. [3d rev. ed.] London, New York, Focal Press [1973] 218 p. illus. 23 cm. First published in 1956 under title: The technique of photographing birds. [TR729.B5W37 1973] 73-177794 ISBN 0-240-50882-3 £3.00
1. Photography of birds. I. Title. BIP

WARHAM, John. 778.9'32
The technique of bird photography. [3d ed. rev.] Garden City, N.Y., Amphoto [1973] 218 p. illus. 23 cm. First published in 1956 under title: The technique of photographing birds. [TR729.B5W37 1973b] 73-84538 ISBN 0-8174-0684-0 12.95
1. Photography of birds. I. Title. II. Title: Bird photography.

WARHAM, John. 778.93
The technique of photographing birds. London, New York, Focal Press [1956] 199 p. illus. 22 cm. [TR673.W3] 56-58883
1. Photography of birds. I. Title.

Photography of children.

ANKERSMIT, K S 770.2
Beginner's guide to photographing children and pets, by K. S. Ankersmit. London, Newnes, [1964] 128 p. illus. (part col.) 19 cm. Label mounted on t. p.: Transatlantic Arts, Hollywood-by-the-Sea, Fla. [[TR575]] 64-57298
1. Photography of children. 2. Photography of animals. I. Title. II. Title: Photographing children and pets.

BENNETT, Edna 778.925
Child photography simplified. New York, Amphoto; dist. Grosset *c.1964] 96p. illus. 22cm. (Better photo guides 430) 63-22229 1.00 pap.,
1. p)0Photography of children. I. Title.

BENNETT, Edna. 778.925
Child photography simplified. New York, American Photographic Book Pub. Co.; distributed to the book trade by Grosset & Dunlap [1964] 96 p. illus. 22 cm. [Better photo guides] "430." [TR680.B417] 63-22229
1. Photography of children. I. Title.

DONOVAN, Donald J. 778.925
Donovan on child portraiture. London, Fountain Pr. [dist. New York, Morgan & Morgan, 1964, c.1950] 128p. illus. 24cm. 51-4678 5.50
1. Photography of children. I. Title.

DORR, Nell. 779.25
Mother and child. [New York, Harper, 1954] [89]p. (chiefly illus.) 22cm. [TR675.D63] 54-12794
1. Photography of children. 2. Photography, Artistic. I. Title. BIP

DORR, Nell. 779'.25'0924
Mother and child. [2d ed. San Francisco, Scrimshaw Press, 1972] [104] p. (chiefly illus.) 26 cm. [TR681.C5D67 1972] 72-76271 ISBN 0-912020-23-7 8.95
1. Photography of children. 2. Photography, Artistic. I. Title.

DORR, Nell. 779'.25'0924
Mother and child. [2d ed. San Francisco, Scrimshaw Press, 1972] [104] p. (chiefly illus.) 26 cm. [TR681.C5D67 1972] 72-76271 ISBN 0-912020-23-7 8.95
1. Photography of children. 2. Photography, Artistic. I. Title.

FEARNLEY, Bernard. 778.9'25
Child photography. London, New York, Focal Press [1972] 132 p. illus. 25 cm. [TR681.C5F4] 76-186991 ISBN 0-240-50720-7 12.95 U.S.
1. Photography of children. I. Title.

HEYMAN, Ken. 778.925
Willie. Photos. by Ken Heyman. Words by Michael Mason. [New York] Ridge Press; [distributed by] Atheneum [1963] [88] p. (chiefly illus.) 27 cm. [TR680.H48] 63-11063
1. Photography of children. 2. Photography, Artistic. I. Mason, Michael. II. Title.

HOBAN, Tana. 778.925
How to photograph your child. Foreword by Jaquelyn Judge. New York, Crown Publishers [1955] 128p. illus. 18cm. (Little technical library, 46) [TR680.H6] 55-8885
1. Photography of children. I. Title.

KUHNER, Russ. 778.925
Family photography [by] Russ and Betty Kuhner. Philadelphia, Chilton Books, 1963. 96 p. illus. 24 cm. (Modern camera guide series) [TR680.K8] 63-17050
1. Photography of children. I. Kuhner, Betty, joint author. II. Title.

LAHUE, Kalton C. 778.9'25
Petersen's photographic magazine guide to photographing children [by Kalton C. Lahue, Hank Harris, and Sandra C. Wallace. Los Angeles, Petersen Pub. Co., 1974] 80 p. illus. 28 cm. Cover title. [TR681.C5L33] 74-78333 ISBN 0-8227-0063-8 2.00 (pbk.).
1. Photography of children. I. Harris, Hank, joint author. II. Wallace, Sandra C., joint author. III. Title. IV. Title: Photographing children.

MILLER, Wayne, 1918- 779.25
The world is young. New York, Distributed by Simon and Schuster [1958] 188p. (chiefly illus.) 29cm. [TR575.M5] 58-13035
1. Phtography of children. I. Title.

MOERKERK, J M 779.25
Camera in kinderland. Haarlem, Focus [1957] 186p. illus. 24cm. [TR680.M] A59
1. Photography of children. 2. Photography, Artistic. I. Title.

MURPHY, Burt. 770.2
Baby and child photography. [2d ed.] New York, Universal Photo Books [c1965] 128 p. illus. 21 cm. [TR575.M85] 67-66222
1. Photography of children. I. Title.

MURPHY, Burt. 778.925
Baby and child photography. [2d ed.] Philadelphia, Chilton Books [1965] 128 p. illus. 21 cm. [TR575.M85 1965] 65-7782
1. Photography of children. I. Title.

MURPHY, Burt. 778.925
Boy and child photography. New York, Verlan Books [1960] 128p. illus. 21cm. (A Universal photo book, U-223) [TR575.M85] 60-7947
1. Photography of children. I. Title.

PARSON, Jan. 779'.25'0924
Children of the Earth / by Jan Parson and Linda Jones-Cowing. Millbrae, Calif. : Celestial Arts, 1975. p. cm. Photos. and poems. [TR681.C5P37 1975] 74-25839 ISBN 0-89087-012-8 : 3.95
1. Photography of children. 2. Photography, Artistic. I. Jones-Cowing, Linda, joint author. II. Title.

PARSON, Jan. 779'.25'0924
Children of the Earth, by Jan Parson and Linda Jones-Cowing. Vol. 1. [Balboa Island, CA, Parson-Cowing Co., 1973] [104] p. illus. 26 cm. Photos. and poems. No more published. [TR681.C5P37 1973] 73-80916
1. Photography of children. 2. Photography, Artistic. I. Jones-Cowing, Linda, joint author. II. Title.

PARSON, Jan. 779'.25'0924
A world of children / by Jan Parson and D. Modin. Las Vegas, Nev. : Astro Press, c1975. [110] p. : ill. ; 26 cm. [TR681.C5P36] 75-15477 ISBN 0-89031-022-X : 7.95 ISBN 0-89031-023-8 pbk. : 4.50
1. Photography of children. 2. Children. I. Modin, D., joint author. II. Title.
Available from Phoenix House. BIP

PHOTOGRAPHING baby and child / edited by George Hornby and the editors of Eastman Kodak Company. New York : Crown Publishers, [1977] p. cm. Includes index. [TR575.P63] 77-6476 ISBN 0-517-53016-3 : 9.95 778.9'25
1. Photography of children. I. Hornby, George. II. Eastman Kodak Company.

REICH, Hanns. 779.25
Children of many lands. New York, Hill and Wang [1958, i.e., 1960] 119 p. (chiefly illus.) 29 cm. (A Terra magica book) 60-10510 5.95 bds.,
1. Photography of children. 2. Photography, Artistic. I. Title. BIP

SCHNEIDER, Josef Aaron, 1912- 778.925
Child photography made easy. New York, American Photographic Book Pub. Co. [1957] 134p. illus. 24cm. [TR575.S34] 57-10939
1. Photography of children. I. Title.

SCHNEIDER, Josef Aaron, 1912- 778.925
Child photography the modern way. Illus. by the author, sketches by Dorothy Tolmach. New York [American Photographic Book Pub. Co., 1955] 208p. illus. 24cm. (An Amphoto book) [TR575.S35 1955] 55-4385
1. Photography of children. I. Title.

SCHNEIDER, Josef Aaron, 1912- 778.925
Josef Schneider teaches child photography; a personalized home study course for hobbyist or professional. [New York] Academy of Practical Photography [1955- v. illus. (part col.) 38cm. [TR575.S36] 55-4866
1. Photography of children. I. Title.

STEWART, Jo Moore. 778.925
The camera's choice: children. Text and photos. by Jo Moore Stewart. South Brunswick [N.J.] A. S. Barnes [1966] 208 p. illus. 26 cm. [TR575.S77] 66-21604
1. Photography of children. I. Title.

SZASZ, Suzanne. 778.9'25
Child photography simplified / by Suzanne Szasz. Garden City, N.Y. : Amphoto, c1976. 96 p., [2] leaves of plates : ill. (some col.) ; 26 cm. (A Modern photoguide) [TR681.C5S88] 75-27833 ISBN 0-8174-0190-3 : 3.45 ($3.95 Can)
1. Photography of children. I. Title. BIP

SZASZ, Suzanne. 778.925
Guide to photographing children. New York, Greenberg [1957] 128 p. illus. 20 cm. [The Modern camera guide series] [TR680.S98] 57-12015
1. Photography of children. I. Title.

SZASZ, Suzanne 778.925
Guide to photographing children. dist. Philadelphia, Amphoto Chilton c.1966 Chilton c.1966 128p. illus. 20cm. (Mod. camera gd. set.) [TR680.S98] 2.95
1. Photography of children. I. Title.

SZASZ, Suzanne. 778.9'25
How I photograph children. New York, Amphoto [1972] 128 p. illus. 22 cm. [TR681.C5S9 1972] 72-182716 ISBN 0-8174-0453-8 3.50
1. Photography of children. I. Title.

WEINER, Leigh. 779.25
Here comes me. New York, Odyssey [1966] [91] p. (chiefly illus.) 30 cm. [TR680.W44] 66-20063
1. Photography of children. 2. Children—Portraits. I. Title.

Photography of fires.

LYONS, Paul R. 778.9'9'628925
Techniques of fire photography / by Paul Robert Lyons. 1st ed. Boston : National Fire Protection Association, c1978. xiv, 224 p., [1] leaf of plates : ill. ; 29 cm. Includes bibliographical references and index. [TR820.L94] 76-55155 ISBN 0-87765-090-X : 16.50
1. Photography of fires. I. Title. BIP

SUBJECT INDEX PHOTOGRAPHY OF THE

Photography of mountains.

HARMON, Byron, 779'.9'97110924 1876-1934.
Great days in the rockies : the photographs of Byron Harmon, 1906-1934 / edited by Carole Harmon and the Peter Whyte Foundation ; with a biography by Bart Robinson ; and an appreciation by Jon Whyte. Toronto ; New York : Oxford University Press, 1978. 86p. : ill. ; 23 x 28 cm. [TR787.H37 1978] 78-325354 ISBN 0-19-540288-X : 15.95
1. Harmon, Byron, 1876-1934. 2. Photography of mountains. 3. Photographers — Northwest Territories, Can. — Biography. 4. Rocky Mountains, Can. — Description and travel — Views. I. Harmon, Carole, 1947- II. Peter Whyte Foundation. III. Title. BIP

SCAYLEA, Josef. 779.'9'9179778
Moods of the mountain. [1st ed.] Seattle, Superior Pub. Co. [1967] [6] p., 48 plates. 35 cm. [TR787.S25] 67-20240
1. Photography of mountains. 2. Rainier, Mount—Description and travel—Views. I. Title. BIP

Photography of plants.

FENTEN, D. X. 778.934
Flower and garden photography. Amphoto [dist.] Philadelphia, Chilton [c.1966] 128p. illus. (pt. col.) 24cm. [TR674.F4] 66-16211 4.95
1. Photography of plants. I. Title. II. Title: Garden photography.

ROCHE, John Patrick, 778.934 1909-
Photographing your flowers; a practical guide for indoor and outdoor use, by John P. and Mary Alice Roche. New York, Greenberg [1954] 137 p. illus. 24 cm. [TR674.R6 1954] 54-8753
1. Photography of plants. 2. Photography, Artistic. I. Roche, Mary Alice, 1917- joint author. II. Title.

ROCHE, John Patrick, 778.934 1909-
Photographing your flowers; a practical guide for indoor and outdoor use, by John P. and Mary Alice Roche. New York, Greenberg [1954] 120p. illus. 20cm. (The Modern camera guide series) [TR674.R6 1954a] 54-7115
1. Photography of plants. 2. Photography, Artistic. I. Roche, Mary Alice, 1917- joint author. II. Title.

VOLZ, McLeod. 779.3
The woods, by McLeod Volz and Mary Mosteller. [Sausalito, Calif., Graphic Arts of Marin, 1963, c1962] 1 v. (unpaged, chiefly illus.) 28 cm. Cover title. [TR674.V6] 63-25383
1. Photography of plants. 2. Muir Woods National Monument. 3. Nature photography. I. Mosteller, Mary. II. Title.

Photography of rocks—Juvenile literature.

MUNARI, Bruno. 741.2'6
From afar it is an island. [Translated and adapted by Pierrette Fleutiaux] New York, World Pub. [1972, c1971] [38] p. illus. 22 cm. Translation of Da lontano era un'isola. Text and photographs introduce a variety of stones and suggest pictures to paint on them. 71-155071 ISBN 0-529-01284-7 3.95
1. Photography of rocks—Juvenile literature. 2. Rocks—Juvenile literature. I. Title.
PLB $3.95, ISBN 0-529-01285-5

Photography of sailing ships.

BEESTON, Diane. 779'.37'0924
Of wind, fog and sail; sailing on San Francisco Bay. San Francisco, Chronicle Books [1972] 160 p. (chiefly illus.) 25 x 35 cm. [TR670.5.B44] 72-85167 12.95
1. Photography of sailing ships. I. Title. BIP

WEINSTEIN, Robert 779'.37'0916432 A.
Tall ships on Puget Sound : the marine photographs of Wilhelm Hester / Robert A. Weinstein. Seattle : University of Washington Press, [1978] p. cm. [TR690.W43] 78-4372 ISBN 0-295-95619-4 : 14.95
1. Photography of sailing ships. 2. Puget Sound—Description and travel—Views. I. Hester, Wilhelm. II. Title. BIP

Photography of ships.

BARLOW, Peter. 779'.9'79710924
The marine photography of Peter Barlow. New York, Motor Boating & Sailing Books [1973] 173 p. illus. 26 cm. [TR670.5.B36] 72-89439 ISBN 0-910990-14-X 12.50
1. Photography of ships. 2. Photography of sailing ships. I. Title.

BUNTING, William 779'.37'0924 Henry, 1945-
Steamers, schooners, cutters, and sloops; the marine photographs of N. L. Stebbins taken from 1884 to 1907. Selected and annotated by W. H. Bunting. [Boston] Published for Society for the Preservation of New England Antiquities, by Houghton Mifflin Co., 1974. 126 p. illus. 23 x 29 cm. Includes bibliographical references. [TR670.5.B86] 74-12034 ISBN 0-395-19895-X 12.50
1. Stebbins, Nathaniel Livermore, 1847- 2. Photography of ships. 3. Steamboats. 4. Sailing ships. I. Stebbins, Nathaniel Livermore, 1847- illus. II. Title.

ROSENFELD, Morris, 1884- 779.93
Under full sail. [Golden anniversary collection] Photos. by Morris Rosenfeld; commentary by Everett B. Morris. Englewood Cliffs, N. J., Prentice- Hill [1957] 212p. illus. 29cm. [TR670.R63] 57-11973
1. Photography of ships. 2. Yachts and yachting. I. Morris, Everett B. II. Title.

SMYTH, Pete. 778.9'9'3872
A guide to marine photography. [1st ed. [New York, Norton, 1974] 144 p. illus. 29 cm. [TR670.5.S58 1974] 74-13741 ISBN 0-393-03182-9
1. Photography of ships. 2. Photography—Marines. I. Title. BIP

Photography of sports.

CALLAHAN, Sean. 770'.92'2
Photographing sports, John Zimmerman, Mark Kauffman and Neil Leifer / text by Sean Callahan and Gerald Astor, with the editors of Alskog, inc. Los Angeles : Alskog, inc., c1975. 96 p. : ill. (some col.) ; 29 cm. (Masters of contemporary photography) Title on spine: Zimmerman & Kauffman: photographing sports. [TR821.C34] 75-12965 ISBN 0-690-00785-X : 8.95.
1. Zimmerman, John, 1927- 2. Kauffman, Mark. 3. Leifer, Neil. 4. Photography of sports. I. Astor, Gerald, 1926- joint author. II. Alskog, inc. III. Title. IV. Title: Zimmerman & Kauffman : photographing sports.

CZAJA, Bruce. 778.9'9'796
How to take great sports action photos / Bruce Czaja. Blue Ridge Summit, Pa. : Tab Books, 1979. p. cm. Includes index. [TR821.C9] 78-11088 ISBN 0-8306-9855-8 : 8.95. ISBN 0-8306-1098-7 pbk. : 5.95
1. Photography of sports. I. Title. BIP

KAUFFMAN, Mark. 778.99796
Guide to photographing sports. New York, Greenberg [c1956] 123p. illus. 20cm. (The Modern camera guide series) [TR682.K3] 56-12486
1. Photography of sports. I. Title.

NEWCOMBE, Harry S. 778.996238
Camera a guide for those who go sailing with cameras. London, Focal Press [dist.] Amphoto. New York 23, 33 W. 60th St. [1960] 160p. illus. 25cm. 60-4468 5.95
1. Photography of sports. 2. Photography—Handbooks, manuals, etc. 3. Sailing. I. Title.

Photography of sports—Exhibitions.

BALTIMORE. 778.9'9'4979607407526 Museum of Art.
Man in sport; an international exhibition of photography, directed by Robert Riger. Baltimore [1967] 70 p. (chiefly illus., part col.) 22 x 28 cm. Exhibition held Dec. 12, 1967-Feb. 11, 1968. [TR821.B34] 778.9'9'796332640973 76-277371
1. Photography of sports—Exhibitions. I. Riger, Robert. II. Title. BIP

Photography of sports—Juvenile literature.

OLNEY, Ross Robert, 778.9'9'796 1929-
Photographing action sports / by Ross R. Olney and Chan Bush. New York : F. Watts, 1976. 116 p. : ill. ; 25 cm. Includes index. Advice for the amateur on photographing action sports, the equipment to use, and getting the photographs published. [TR821.O46] 75-34250 ISBN 0-531-01139-9 lib.bdg. : 5.90
1. Photography of sports—Juvenile literature. I. Bush, Chan, joint author. II. Title. BIP

Photography of the grotesque.

COLEMAN, Allan D. 779
The grotesque in photography / by A. D. Coleman. New York : Summit Books, c1977. p. cm. "A Ridge Press book." [TR686.C64] 77-22678 20.00. pbk. : 10.00
1. Photography of the grotesque. I. Title. BIP

Photography of the nude.

ABBOTT, Ashley. 778.921
Creative figure photography [by] Ashley Abbott and Allen Cobert. Jacket illus. by Allen Cobert. Philadelphia, Chilton Co., Book Division, c1960. 111p. illus. 21cm. (Modern camera guide series, 459) [TR675.A24] 60-9223
1. Photography of the nude. I. Cobert, Allen, joint author. II. Title.

ALLEN, Casey. 778.921
New concepts in nude photography. South Brunswick [N.J.] A. S. Barnes [1966] 133 p. illus. (part col.) 29 cm. [TR675.A4] 66-23188
1. Photography of the nude. I. Title.

ALLEN, Casey. 779'.21
The nude Aesop; camera fables for the modern man. South Brunswick, [N.J.] A. S. Barnes [1967] 152 p. illus. (part col.) 29 cm. [TR675.A43] 67-25167
1. Photography of the nude. I. Title.

BARR, Bill 779.9421
Barely speaking, by Bill Barr, Allen Camelli. With a revealing commentary by Henry Morgan. New York, Crown [c.1965] 1 v. (chiefly illus.) 25cm. [TR675.B267] 65-24319 1.95 pap.,
1. Photography of the nude. I. Camelli, Allen, joint author. II. Title.

BEAUTY which inspires 779.21
[v.2] Preface by Werner Zimmermann. Boston, Bruce Humphries [1962] unpaged. chiefly illus. 30cm. 62-2106 7.50
1. Photography of the nude.

BEREKMERI, Steve, 1924- 779'.24
Nudes in my camera. South Brunswick, A. S. Barnes [1971] 181 p. (chiefly illus.) 29 cm. [TR675.B48] 68-14416 ISBN 0-498-06733-5
1. Photography of the nude. I. Title.

BLAKEY, Roy. 779'.23'0924
He, photographed and designed by Roy Blakey. [New York, Distributed by Blaze Interprises, c1972] 1 v. (chiefly illus.) 36 cm. [TR675.B53] 73-159391
1. Photography of the nude. I. Title.

CLERGUE, Lucien 779.21
Naissance d'Aphrodite Birth of Aphrodite. [Photos de Lucien Clergue. Realise par Jean Petit. Textes de Federico Garcia Lorca. Tr. by Grace Davis. New York, Brussel & Bussel, 1966] [45] p. (chiefly illus.) 28cm. (Panoramas forces vives) [TR675.C53] 66-9782 10.00
1. Photography of the nude. I. Garcia Lorca, Federico, 1898-1936. II. Petit, Jean, poet, ed. III. Title. IV. Title: Birth of Aphrodite

COZZI, Angelo, 1934- 779'.24'0924
Innocence in the mirror / photos. by Angelo Cozzi ; introduced by Laurie Lee ; [translated from the Italian by Simon Pleasance]. New York : Morrow, 1978, c1977. ca. 150 p. : ill. (some col.) ; 27 cm. [TR681.G5C67 1978] 78-52475 ISBN 0-688-03376-8 : 12.95
1. Cozzi, Angelo, 1934- 2. Girls—Portraits. 3. Photography of the nude. I. Title. BIP

CURRIN, Tony, 1936- 779'.24'0924
Black woman : photographs / by Tony Currin. New York : Camera/Graphic Press, c1978. [128] p. : chiefly ill. ; 28 cm. [TR675.C87] 77-18649 ISBN 0-918696-05-4 : 9.95
1. Photography of the nude. 2. Afro-American women—Portraits. I. Title. BIP

DEAN, Roy. 779'.21
A time in Eden. [1st ed.] Los Angeles, Rho-Delta Press [1969] 1 v. (chiefly illus. (part col.)) 29 cm. [TR675.D36] 70-87784 15.00
1. Photography of the nude. 2. Eden. I. Title. BIP

DE DIENES, Andre, 770'.92'4 1913-
Nude variations / Andre De Dienes. Garden City, N.Y. : American Photographic Book Pub. Co., c1977. 91 p., [4] leaves of plates : ill. (some col.) ; 27 cm. [TR675.D413 1977] 78-178248 ISBN 0-8174-2417-2 : 9.95
1. Photography of the nude. 2. Photography—Special effects. I. Title.

DE DIENES, Andre, 779'.24'0924 1913-
Nudes, my camera and I. London, Focal Press, 1973. 160 p. chiefly illus., ports. 25 cm. [TR675.D428] 74-155151 ISBN 0-240-50782-7
1. Photography of the nude. I. Title.
Distributed by Amphoto, 13.95. BIP

DE DIENES, Andre, 1913- 779.21
Sun-warmed nudes. Elysium [dist. New York, Stuart. c.1965] unpaged (chiefly illus. (pt. col.)) 29cm. [TR675.D42] 65-6296 10.00 bds.,
1. Photography of the nude. I. Title. BIP

DE DIESNES, Andre, 1913- 779'.21
Natural nudes. New York, Amphoto [c1966] 160 p. illus. 31 cm. [TR675.D398] 66-16210
1. Photography of the nude. I. Title.

DE'LISLE, Gordon. 779'.21
Of woman, love and beauty. [Melbourne, Joey Books, 1970] [92] p. illus. 31 cm. [TR675.D436] 72-850415 ISBN 0-9599825-0-7 9.50
1. Photography of the nude. I. Title.

FARBER, Robert. 779'.24'0924
Images of woman / Robert Farber ; [text by Gail Lightipe]. Garden City, N.Y. : American Photographic Book Pub. Co., c1976. [95] p. : ill. (some col.) ; 29 cm. [TR675.F37] 75-39833 ISBN 0-8174-2404-0 : 16.95
1. Photography of the nude. I. Lightipe, Gail. II. Title. BIP

FRENCH, Jim. 779'.23'0924
Another man; photography. [Village Station, N.Y., State of Man, 1974] [64] p. (chiefly illus.) 37 cm. [TR675.F72] 74-162966
1. Photography of the nude. I. Title.

FRENCH, Jim. 779'.23'0924
Man; photography. [New York, c1972] [64] p. (chiefly illus.) 37 cm. [TR675.F73] 73-174051
1. Photography of the nude. I. Title.

FRENCH, Jim. 779'.23'0924
Quorum : [photography / by Jim French]. [Village Station, N.Y. : State of Man], c1976. [73] p. : all ill. (some col.) ; 32 cm. [TR675.F74] 76-44031
1. Photography of the nude. I. Title.

*GARDNER, Gerald. 779'.21
The streaking book. New York, Bantam Books [1974] 1 v. (chiefly(illus) 18 cm. (A Bantam extra) [TR675] 1.50 (pbk.)
1. Photography of the nude. I. Title.

GLOEDEN, Wilhelm, Baron 779'.23 von, 1856-1931.
Photographs of the classic male nude / photographs by Baron Wilhelm von Gloeden ; with a pref. by Jean-Claude Lemagny. New York : Camera/Graphic Press, [1977] c1975. p. cm. Translation of

Taormina, debut de siecle. [TR675.G4613] 77-9125 ISBN 0-918696-03-8 : 19.95
1. Photography of the nude. I. Title. BIP

GRAHAM, William M 778.921
What is a woman? by William M. Graham. Los Angeles, Elysium [1966] 95 p. illus. 32 cm. [TR675.G73] 66-7575
1. Photography of the nude. I. Title. BIP

HASKINS, Samuel. 779.24
Cowboy Kate, & other stories, by Sam Haskins. New York, Crown Publishers [1965] 1 v. (chiefly illus.) 36 cm. [TR675.H37] 65-18400
1. Photography of the nude. I. Title.

HASKINS, Samuel. 779'.28'0924
Haskinsposters; a book of miniposters, designed and photographed by Sam Haskins. [New York, Crowell, c1972] [2] p. [31] l. (chiefly illus., part col.) 48 cm. [TR675.H384 1972] 73-164449 ISBN 0-690-71832-2 16.95
1. Photography of the nude. 2. Photography, Composite. I. Title.

HASKINS, Samuel. 779'.24'0924
November girl [by] Haskins. New York, Madison Square Press [1967] 1 v. (chiefly illus.) 26 cm. [TR675.H39 1967b] 67-25791
1. Photography of the nude. I. Title.

HEDGECOE, John. 779'.24'0924
Possessions / John Hedgecoe ; [editor, Iain Parsons]. New York : A & W Publishers, 1978. ca. 150 p. : chiefly ill. ; 30 cm. [TR675.H396 1978] 78-54124 ISBN 0-89479-023-4 : 25.00
1. Photography of the nude. I. Parsons, Iain. II. Title. BIP

HENDIN, Arnie. 778.921
Nude landscapes, by Arnie Hendin & Martin S. Moskof. New Hyde Park, N. Y., University Books [1968] 1 v. (chiefly illus., 32 cm. $10.00 [TR675.H42] 67-31698
1. Photography of the nude. I. Moskof, Martin S., joint author. II. Title. BIP

HESTER, George M. 779'.21'0924
The classic nude, by George M. Hester. Garden City, N.Y., Amphoto [1973] 1 v. (unpaged) illus. 37 cm. [TR675.H47] 72-93373 ISBN 0-8174-0554-2 19.95
1. Photography of the nude. I. Title. BIP

HESTER, George M. 779'.21'0924
The classic nude / by George M. Hester ; design by George M. Hester. [New York] : A & W Visual Library, [1975], c1973. ca. 150 p. : chiefly ill. (some col.) ; 28 cm. [TR675.H47 1975b] 75-328239 ISBN 0-89104-015-3 pbk. : 7.95
1. Photography of the nude. I. Title.

HESTER, George M. 779'.23
Man / George M. Hester. Garden City, N.Y. : Amphoto, c1975. ca. 100 p. : chiefly ill. (some col.) ; 32 cm. [TR675.H48] 75-27835 ISBN 0-8174-0590-9
1. Photography of the nude. I. Title.

HESTER, George M. 779'.24
Woman / George M. Hester. Garden City, N.Y. : Amphoto, c1975. ca. 100 p. : chiefly ill. (some col.) ; 32 cm. [TR675.H486] 75-27834 ISBN 0-8174-0591-7 : 24.95
1. Photography of the nude. I. Title.

HOSOE, Eiko, 1933- 778.921
Man and woman [photogs.] by Eikoh Hosoe. Poems by Taro Yamamoto. Tokyo, Camerart [dist. New York, Perkins Oriental, 1962] unpaged. chiefly illus. 25cm. J62 5.00 bds.,
1. Photography of the nude. I. Yamamoto, Taro, 1925- II. Title.

JAY, Bill. 778.9'21
Views on nudes. New York, Amproto [1971] 151 p. illus. 19 x 23 cm. [TR674.J38] 79-153497 ISBN 0-8174-0797-9 9.95
1. Photography of the nude. I. Title. BIP

JAY, Bill. 778.9'21
Views on nudes. London, New York, Focal Press, 1971. 156 p. illus. 19 x 23 cm. [TR674.J38 1971b] 77-888149 ISBN 0-240-50731-2 £1.75
1. Photography of the nude. I. Title.

JENNINGS, Thomas, 1914- 779'.21
The female figure in movement. New York, Watson-Guptill Publications [1971] 175 p. chiefly illus. 32 cm. [TR675.J45] 75-133978 ISBN 0-8230-1650-1
1. Photography of the nude. I. Title.

KALEYA, Tana. 779'.23
Les hommes / by Tana Kaleya New York : Harmony Books, [1975] c1974. ca. 100 p. : chiefly ill. (some col.) ; 30 cm. English. Includes quotations from Michelangelo's sonnets translated by E. Jennings. [TR675.K34] 75-15048 ISBN 0-517-52437-6 : 19.95
1. Photography of the nude. I. Title. BIP

LANGE, June. 778.921
The wonderful Webbers, a dedication. Los Angeles, Elysium [1967] 91 p. illus. (part col.) 29 cm. [TR675.L26] 67-30895
1. Photography of the nude. 2. Nudism I. Title. BIP

MALIN, Karin. 778.9'21
Nude photography. South Brunswick, A. S. Barnes [1972] 111 p. (chiefly illus.) 29 cm. [TR674.M29] 78-124211 ISBN 0-498-06893-5 12.00
1. Photography of the nude. I. Title.

MEISNITZER, Fritz. 779'.21
Dreaming of Eve. South Brunswick, A. S. Barnes [1970] 144 p. illus. 29 cm. [TR675.M37] 71-115049
1. Photography of the nude. I. Title.

MINKKINEN, Arno Rafael, 1945- 779'.21'0924
Frostbite : photographs / by Arno Rafael Minkkinen ; introd. by Ziva Kwitney. Dobbs Ferry, N.Y. : Morgan & Morgan, c1978. [95] p. : chiefly ill. ; 27 cm. [TR675.M56] 78-60179 ISBN 0-87100-143-8 pbk. : 10.95
1. Minkkinen, Arno Rafael, 1945- 2. Photography of the nude. I. Title. BIP

MURPHY, Burt. 778.924
Nude. Figure and glamour photography. Photos. by Jack Anderson. New York, Universal Photo Books [1961] 128p. illus. 20cm. (Universal photo books, U-233) [TR675.M87] 61-8118
1. Photography of the nude. 2. Photography of Women. I. Title.

NIKOLAIDIS, George 778.921
Japanese nudes and the amateur photographer. Rutland, Vt., Tuttle [c.1965] 110p. illus. 18cm. [TR675.N5] 65-22635 2.95 pap.,
1. Photography of the nude. 2. Models, Artists. I. Title.

PARRELLA, Lew, ed. 799.21
Creative camera; three portfolios of beauty [by] Ferenc Berko, Peter Basch [and] Wynn Bullock. [New York, Maco Magazine Corp., 1960] 126p. (chiefly illus.) 24cm. (Maco, 87) [TR675.P36] 61-2396
1. Photography of the nude. I. Title.

RAWLINGS, John 778.921
The photographer and his model. New York, Viking [c.1966] 111p. (chiefly illus. (pt. col.)) 30cm. (Studio bk.) [TR675.R29] 66-12923 10.95 bds.,
1. Photography of the nude. I. Title.

RIDGE Press, inc., New York. 778.921
The model; a portrait of beauty by ten master photographers. [Prepared and produced by the Ridge Press. New York, Distributed by Pocket Books, 1959, c1958] 112p. illus. 28cm. [TR675.R5] 58-14477
1. Biehn, Betty. 2. Photography of the nude. I. Title.

ROTHMAN, Stewart. 77b.9'21
Nudes of 16 lands. New York, American Photographic Book Pub. Co. [1970] 160 p. illus. (part col.) 32 cm. [TR675.R63] 67-18637 15.00
1. Photography of the nude. I. Title.

RUBY, Erik A. 743'.4
The human figure : a photographic reference for artists / E. A. Ruby. New York : Van Nostrand Reinhold Co., [1974] 338 p. : all ill. ; 30 x 22 cm. [TR675.R8] 74-5948 ISBN 0-442-27160-3
1. Photography of the nude. 2. Human figure in art. I. Title.

SIMON, Peter, 1947- 779'.2'0924
Decent exposures / written and photographed by Peter Simon ; with an introd. by Asa Elliot. Berkeley, Calif. : Wingbow Press : distributed by Book People, [1974] 121 p. : ill. ; 26 cm. [TR675.S54] 74-80864 ISBN 0-914728-01-6 : 6.00
1. Photography of the nude. 2. Photography, Erotic. I. Title. BIP

SKREBNESKI, Victor. 779'.21
Skrebneski. New York, Ridge Press; [distributed by Grosset & Dunlap, 1969] [60] p. of illus. 36 cm. [TR675.S56] 71-94557
1. Photography of the nude.

STAGG, Mildred. 778.921
The nude in 101 moods. Photos. by Paul Duckworth. New York, Universal Photo Books [1961] 128 p. illus. 20 cm. [TR675.S674] 61-14259
1. Photography of the nude. I. Title.

TULCHIN, Lewis. 779'.0924
Creative figure photography. Text and photos. by Lewis Tulchin. South Brunswick [N.J.] A. S. Barnes [1967] 143 p. (chiefly illus., part col.) 29 cm. [TR675.T78] 67-13081
1. Photography of the nude. I. Title.

TULCHIN, Lewis. 778.921
Photographing the nude. With photos by the author. New York, Barnes [1962] 152 p. illus. 29 cm. [TR675.T82] 62-109927
1. Photography of the nude. I. Title.

TULCHIN, Lewis. 778.921
The photography of women; the nude as art. With photos. by the author. New York, A. S. Barnes [1964] 154 p. illus. (part col.) 29 cm. [TR675.T83] 64-15385
1. Photography of the nude. 2. Photography of women. I. Title.

VANCE, David. 779'.21'0924
Visions. [Coral Gables? Fla., 1973] [72] p. (chiefly illus.) 36 cm. On cover: A collection of photographic nudes. [TR675.V34] 73-174056
1. Photography of the nude. I. Title.

VERONESE, Marcel. 779'.21
Mademoiselle 1+1, by Marcel Veronese and Jean-Claude Peretz. Text and design by Alain Wienc. New York, Crown [1968] 1 v. (unpaged) illus. 36 cm. [TR675.V413] 68-29830
1. Photography of the nude. I. Peretz, Jean Claude, joint author. II. Wienc, Alain. III. Title.

VERONESE, Marcel. 779'.21
Youpi & the girls. New York, Crown Publishers [1969] 1 v. (chiefly illus.) 36 cm. [TR675.V42] 71-75066
1. Photography of the nude. I. Title.

WALTERS, Thomas. 779'.24
Nudes of the '20s and '30s / Thomas Walters London : Academy Editions ; New York : St. Martin's Press, 1976. 87 p. : ill. (some col.) ; 20 cm. [TR675.W34 1976] 76-44583 ISBN 0-85670-239-0 : 3.95 (U.S.)
1. Photography of the nude. I. Title. BIP

WESTON, Edward, 1886-1958. 779'.24'0924
Edward Weston nudes : his photographs accompanied by excerpts from the Daybooks & letters / remembrance by Charis Wilson. New York : Aperture, 1977. 116 p. : ill. ; 30 cm. [TR675.W48 1977] 77-80022 ISBN 0-89381-020-7 : 20.00.
1. Photography of the nude. I. Weston, Charis Wilson. II. Title.

WOLMAN, Baron. 779'.24'0924
Profiles. [Mill Valley, Calif.] Squarebooks [1974] 44 plates. 21 cm. [TR675.W58] 74-81290
1. Photography of the nude. 2. Breast—Pictorial works. I. Title. BIP

WOOLLEY, Al E 779'.21
35mm. nudes / by A. E. Woolley. by A. E Woolley New York, Amphoto [c1966] 160 p. illus. 82 cm. [TR675.W63] 66-16208
1. Photography of the nude. I. Title.

YEAGER, Bunny. 778.921
How I photograph nudes. New York, A. S. Barnes [1963] 144 p. illus. 29 cm. [TR675.Y39 1963] 63-18261
1. Photography of the nude. 2. Photography, Artistic. I. Title.

Photography of the nude—Exhibitions.

BE-ING without clothes. 778.9'21'074014461 New York, Aperture, 1970. 96 p. illus. 26 cm. Catalogue of an exhibition presented by the Massachusetts Institute of Technology, Nov. 3-29, 1970, with commentary by M. White. Also published as Aperture, v. 15, no. 3. [TR675.B46] 73-141030 8.50
1. Photography of the nude—Exhibitions. 2. Photography, Artistic—Exhibitions. I. White, Minor. II. Massachusetts Institute of Technology.

Photography of the nude — Hist.

LACEY, Peter. 778.921
The history of the nude in photography; Designed by Anthony LaRotonda. New York, Bantam Books [1964] 215 p. illus. 18 cm. (A Bantam gallery edition, RG9) [TR675.L23] 63-14181
1. Photography of the nude — Hist. I. Title.

STETTNER, Louis. 778.921
History of the nude in American photography. Greenwich, Conn., Whitestone Publications, 1966. 111 p. illus. 24 cm. (A Whitestone book no. 68) [TR675.S712] 66-31387
1. Photography of the nude — Hist. I. Title.

Photography of women.

ARNOLD, Eve. 779'.24'0924
The unretouched woman / Eve Arnold. 1st ed. New York : Knopf : distributed by Random House, 1976. 191 p. : ill. (some col.) ; 29 cm. [TR681.W6A76] 76-381518 ISBN 0-394-40194-8 : 20.00 ISBN 0-394-73260-X pbk. : 9.95
1. Photography of women. 2. Women—Portraits. I. Title. BIP

BARREAUX, Adolphe. 778.9'24
Glamor and the camera. Greenwich, Conn., Whitestone Publications [1968] 112 p. illus. 24 cm. (A Whitestone book, no. 87) [TR675.B275] 68-7333 0.95
1. Photography of women. 2. Photography of the nude. I. Title.

BARREAUX, Adolphe, ed. 778.924
The technique of figure photography. Louisville, Ky., Whitestone Publications, c1959. 144p. illus. 24cm. (A Whitestone book, no. 27) [TR675.B28] 59-65283
1. Photography of women. 2. Photography of the nude. I. Title. II. Title: Figure photography.

BASCH, Peter. 778.924
Glamour photography. Greenwich, Conn., Fawcett Publications, c1956. 143p. illus. 24cm. (A Fawcett how-to book, 313) [TR675.B33] 56-4940
1. Photography of women. 2. Photography of the nude. 3. Photography, Artistic. I. Title.

BASCH, Peter. 778.924
Peter Basch photographs: 100 famous beauties. Adolphe Barreaux, editor. Louisville, Ky., Whitestone Publications, 1965. 112 p. ports. 24 cm. (A Whitestone book, 59) [TR675.B345] 65-5874
1. Photography of women. I. Barreaux, Adolphe, ed. II. Title. III. Title: 100 famous beauties.

BASCH, Peter. 778.924
Peter Basch photographs glamorous women. [Greenwich, Conn., Fawcett Publications, 1959] 144p. illus. 24cm. (A Fawcett how-to book, 425) [TR675.B37] 59-65284
1. Photography of women. 2. Photography, Artistic. I. Title.

BASCH, Peter. 779'.0924
Peter Basch photographs the world of glamor. Greenwich, Conn., Whitestone Publications, c1967. 112 p. (chiefly illus., ports.) 24 cm. (A Whitestone book, no. 83) [TR675.B373] 68-2585
1. Photography of women. I. Title.

1. Photography—Period. 2. Photography,Artistic. *

INFINITY. 778
[New York] American Society of Magazine Photographers. no. in v. illus., ports. 29cm. irregular. Title varies: -July 1950, ASMP news.--Aug. 1950-Jan. 1952, American Society of Magazine Photographers news. [TR1.A58324] 58-30484
1. Photography—Period. 2. Photography, Journalistic. I. American Society of Magazine Photographers.

PHOTOGRAPHIC engineering 770.5
v. 1-7 Jan. 1950- Oct. 1957 [Washington] Society of Photographic Engineers. 7v. in Illus., ports., diagrs. 23cm. quarterly. Superseded by Photographic science and engineering. [TR1.P776] 58-23659
1. Photography—Period. I. Society of Photographic Engineers.

Photography, Pinhole.

SHULL, Jim. 770'.28
The hole thing; a manual of pinhole fotografy. [Dobbs Ferry, N.Y., Morgan & Morgan, 1974] [64] p. illus. (part col.) 21 cm. [TR268.S48] 73-93873 ISBN 0-87100-047-4 2.95 (pbk.)
1. Photography, Pinhole. I. Title. BIP

Photography, Police.

MURPHY. BURT. 778.993641
Police and crime photography. New York, Ver lan Books [1960] 127p. illus. 20cm. (A Universal photo book, U-225) [TR830.M8] 60-7949
1. Photography, Police. I. Title.

Photography—Popular works.

JACOBS, Lou. 770
Expressive photography / text by Lou Jacobs, Jr. Santa Monica, Calif. : Goodyear Pub. Co., c1978. p. cm. Includes index. Bibliography: p. [TR149.J27] 78-15600 ISBN 0-87620-283-0 : 15.95
1. Photography—Popular works. I. Title. BIP

Photography—Portraits

ARCHER, Fred Robert, 1889- 778.92
Fred Archer on portraiture. All illus. by the author except where otherwise designated. [2d ed.] San Francisco, Camera Craft Pub. Co. [1954] 224p. illus. 25cm.]A Camera Craft plus value book] [TR680.A65 1954] 54-1259
1. Photography—Portraits. 2. Photography, Artistic. I. Title.

ASTON, Kevin L 1930- 778.92
Candid photographic portraiture, by Kevin L. Aston. Philadelphia, Chilton Books [1965] 144 p. illus., ports. 26 cm. [TR575.A8] 65-17127
1. Photography — Portraits. I. Title.

ATTIE, David. 779'.2'0947
Russian self-portraits / David Attie. 1st ed. New York : Harper & Row, c1977. [96] p. : chiefly ill. ; 27 cm. "An Irwin Glusker book." [TR680.A87] 77-6881 ISBN 0-06-010171-7 pbk. : 6.95
1. Photography—Portraits. 2. Self-portraits—Russia. I. Title. BIP

AVEDON, Richard 301.2
Nothing personal. Photos by Richard Avedon. Text by James Baldwin. [New York] Dell [1965, c.1964] iv. (chiefly illus.) 24cm. [TR680.A89] 64-23632 1.50 pap.,
1. Photography—Portraits., I. Baldwin, James, 1924- II. Title.

AVEDON, Richard. 779.2
Observations. Photographs by Richard Avedon. Comments by Truman Capote. [New York, Simon and Schuster, 1959] 151p. illus., ports. 37cm. Cover title. [TR680.A9] 59-4425
1. Photography—Portraits. 2. Photography, Artistic. I. Capote, Truman, 1924- II. Title.

AVEDON, Richard. 779'.2'0924
Portraits / Richard Avedon ; [essay, Harold Rosenberg]. 1st ed. New York : Farrar, Straus, and Giroux, 1976. [141] p. : ports. ; 31 cm. [TR681.F3A93] 76-26752 ISBN 0-374-23638-0 : 25.00
1. Photography—Portraits. I. Rosenberg, Harold. II. Title.

BAILEY, David, 779'.2
photographer.
Goodbye baby & amen; a saraband for the Sixties [by] David Bailey & Peter Evans. [1st American ed.] New York, Coward-McCann [1969] 237 p. illus., ports. 37 cm. [TR681.F3B3 1969] 72-92772 15.00
1. Photography—Portraits. I. Evans, Peter, joint author. II. Title.

BECK, Otto Walter, 1864- 778.9'2
1954.
Art principles in portrait photography; composition, treatment of backgrounds, and the processes involved in manipulating the plate. New York, Arno Press, 1973 [c1907] p. (The Literature of photography) [TR575.B4 1973] 72-9181 ISBN 0-405-04892-0
1. Photography—Portraits. I. Title. II. Series. BIP

BENNETT, Edna. 779.25
Portrait guide 2d. ed., rev New York, American Photographic Book Pub. Co. [1963] 128 p. illus., ports. 21 cm. "An Amphoto edition bound book." [TR680.B42] 63-25290
1. Photography — Portraits. I. Title.

BENNETT, Edna. 778.92
Portrait guide. New York, American Photographic Book Pub. Co.; book trade: Garden City Books, Garden City, N. Y. [1958] 128p. illus. 20cm. (An Amphoto book) [TR680.B42] 58-12009
1. Photography—Portraits. I. Title.

BERGER, Charles, 779'.2'0924
1943-
Image Tibet. [Mill Valley, Calif.] Artisan Press; [distributed by Scrimshaw Press, San Francisco] 1973. [11] p., 30 col. plates, [6] p. 30 cm. [TR680.B45] 73-80938 ISBN 0-912020-32-6 25.00
1. Photography—Portraits. 2. Tibetans—Pictorial works. 3. Serigraphs (Prints) I. Title. BIP

BOMBACK, Edward S. 778.9'2
Portrait manual, by Edward S. Bomback and Arnold J. Coppel. [2d. ed.] South Brunswick, N.J., A. S. Barnes [1967, i.e. 1968] 238 p. illus., ports. 22 cm. The authors' names appear in reverse order in the first edition. [TR575.B58 1968] 68-14397
1. Photography—Portraits. I. Coppel, Arnold J. Portrait Manual. II. Title.

BOMBACK, Edward S. 778.92
Portraits in colour. London, Fountain [dist. New York, Morgan & Morgan, 1964, c.1962] 94p. illus. (part col.) 17cm. (Fountain photobk. ser.) 64-3010 2.95 bds.,
1. Photography—Portriats. 2. Color photography. I. Title.

BRADY, Mathew B., 779'.2'0973
1823(ca.)-1896.
Mathew Brady's Great Americans : prints from the original glass negatives in the Meserve collection / produced in collaboration with Time-Life Books. [Alexandria, Va.] : Time-Life Books, [1977,c1976] 1 case : ports. ; 30 cm. Title from case. Contains text (6 p.), by P. B. Kunhardt, Jr., 1 photoprint (9 x 11 in.), and 10 contact prints (3 x 4 in.), each mounted on a folder with accompanying descriptive text. [TR681.F3B7 1976] 77-150942 19.95
1. Brady, Mathew B., 1823 (ca.)-1896. 2. Photography—Portraits. 3. United States—Biography—Portraits. I. Time-Life Books. II. Title: Great Americans.

BROOKS, David, 1933- 778.9'24
Small camera portraiture / by David Brooks. Los Angeles : Petersen Pub. Co., c1977. 80 p. : ill. (some col.) ; 28 cm. (Petersen's how-to photographic library) [TR575.B76] 77-74099 ISBN 0-8227-4018-4 pbk. : 3.95
1. Photography—Portraits. 2. Photography of women. I. Title. BIP

BULL, Clarence Sinclair. 779'.2
The faces of Hollywood, by Clarence Sinclair Bull, with Raymond Lee. South Brunswick [N.J.] A. S. Barnes [1969, c1968] 256 p. illus. ports. 29 cm. [TR680.B8] 68-27205 10.00
1. Photography—Portraits. I. Lee, Raymond, joint author. II. Title. BIP

*CAMERON, Julia 779'2'0924
Margaret.
Victorian photographs of famous men & fair women. With introductions by Virginia Woolf & Roger Fry. Expanded and revised edition edited by Tristam Powell. New York, A & W Visual Library [1975 c1973] 32 p. 44 plates, 30 cm. [TR681] 75-12275 ISBN 0-88365-332-X 6.95 (pbk.)
1. Photography—Portraits. I. Title. BIP

CAMERON, Julia 779'.2'0924
Margaret Pattle, 1815-1879.
The Cameron collection / Julia Margaret Cameron ; with an introd. by Colin Ford. New York : Van Nostrand Reinhold, 1975. p. cm. Includes bibliographical references. [TR681.F3C35 1975] 75-26000 ISBN 0-442-20312-8 : 30.00
1. Cameron, Julia Margaret Pattle, 1815-1879. 2. Photography—Portraits. 3. Great Britain—Biography—Portraits. I. Title.

CAMERON, Julia 779'.2'0924
Margaret Pattle, 1815-1879.
Julia Margaret Cameron : an album. Washington : Lunn Gallery/Graphics International, c1975. 57 p. : all ill. ; 24 cm. [TR680.C28] 75-34962
1. Cameron, Julia Margaret Pattle, 1815-1879. 2. Photography—Portraits. I. Lunn Gallery.

CAMERON, Julia 779'.2'0924
Margaret Pattle, 1815-1879.
Victorian photographs of famous men & fair women / by Julia Margaret Cameron ; with introds. by Virginia Woolf & Roger Fry. Expanded and rev. ed. / edited by Tristram Powell. Boston : D. R. Godine, 1973. 32 p., 44 leaves of plates : ill. ; 33 cm. [TR681.F3C36 1973b] 73-81062 ISBN 0-87923-076-2
1. Photography—Portraits. 2. Great Britain—Biography—Portraits. I. Title.

CASTLE, Paul. 658'.91'77892
Promotional portrait photography; everything you always wanted to know about studio operation, but didn't know whom to ask ... With editorial assistance from Janet Marshall Victor. Upper Darby, Pa. [1974] vi, 182 p. illus. 29 cm. [TR581.C37] 74-163515
1. Photography—Portraits. 2. Photography—Business methods. I. Title. BIP

CATEWOOD, Charles. 778.9'2
People in focus / Charles Catewood. Garden City, N.Y. : Amphoto, [1977] p. cm. Includes index. Bibliography: p. [TR680.C39] 77-21897 ISBN 0-8174-2429-6 : 14.95. ISBN 0-8174-2107-6 pbk. : 8.95
1. Photography—Portraits. I. Title. BIP

CITY families : 778.9'2
Chicago and London / by Roslyn Banish. 1st ed. New York : Pantheon Books, c1976. p. cm. Consists of interviews and accompanying photos. of 80 families. [TR681.F28C57] 76-9981 ISBN 0-394-49906-9 : 15.00. ISBN 0-394-73236-7 pbk. : 7.95
1. Photography—Portraits. 2. Family—London. 3. Family—Chicago. I. Banish, Roslyn, 1942- BIP

CONSILVIO, Thomas. 779'.2'0924
Snapshooters. [Boston] A Mouse Press; [distributed by Light Impressions, Rochester, N.Y.] 1973. 1 v. (chiefly illus.) 18 x 25 cm. [TR681.S6C66] 73-81972 ISBN 0-913968-00-5 4.95
1. Photography—Portraits. I. Title. BIP

CROY, Otto R., 1902- 778.9'2
The photographic portrait, by O. R. Croy. [Translated by F. L. Dash] Philadelphia, Chilton Book Co. [1968] 245 p. illus. (part col.) 24 cm. [TR575.C713] 68-23444
1. Photography—Portraits. I. Title. BIP

†DISFARMER, Mike, 779'.2'09767285
1884-1959.
Disfarmer : the Heber Springs portraits, 1939-1946 : Disfarmer photographs from Peter Miller, The Group, inc. / text by Julia Scully. Danbury, N.H. : Addison House ; [Rochester, N.Y. : distributed by Light Impressions Corp.], c1976. 135 p. : ill. ; 29 cm. [TR680.D57 1976] 76-15886 ISBN 0-89169-003-4 : 22.50
1. Photography—Portraits. I. Scully, Julia. BIP

DIXON, John 778.24
Professional methods for amateur photographers. London, Fountain [dist. New York, Morgan & Morgan. 1964, c.1954] 140p. illus., diagrs. 24cm. 5.95
1. Photography—Portraits. 2. Photography of women. 3. Photography—Studies and dark rooms. I. Title.

EASTMAN Kodak Company. 778.9'2
Professional portrait techniques. [1st ed.] Rochester, N.Y. [1973] 68 p. col. illus. 29 cm. (Kodak publication, no. 0-4H) [TR575.E23] 72-95689 ISBN 0-87985-060-4 7.95
1. Photography—Portraits. I. Title.

EINSTEIN, Bob. 779
This is my first magic book so I'm a little nervous. Los Angeles, Price/Stern/Sloan Publishers [1970] 96 p. (chiefly illus.) 22 cm. [TR681.F3E5] 73-137336
1. Photography—Portraits. 2. Comedians—United States. 3. Wit and humor, Pictorial. I. Title.

EISENSTAEDT, Alfred. 779'.2'0924
Eisenstaedt's album : fifty years of friends and acquaintances / Alfred Eisenstaedt. New York : Viking Press, [1976] p. cm. (A Studio book) [TR680.E32] 76-26144 ISBN 0-670-29078-5 : 16.95
1. Photography—Portraits. I. Title. BIP

EISENSTAEDT, Alfred. 779'.2'0924
People. New York, Viking Press [1973] 259 p. illus. 34 cm. (A Studio book) [TR680.E33 1973] 73-5332 ISBN 0-670-54701-8 17.95
1. Eisenstaedt, Alfred. 2. Photography—Portraits. I. Title.

EISENSTAEDT, Alfred. 779'.2'0924
People / Alfred Eisenstaedt. New York : Penguin Books, [1979] p. cm. [TR680.E33 1979] 78-10683 ISBN 0-14-005073-6 pbk. : 11.95
1. Eisenstaedt, Alfred. 2. Photography—Portraits. I. Title.

EISENSTAEDT, Alfred. 778.9
Witness to our time. Foreword by Henry R. Luce. New York, Viking Press [1966] 343 p. (chiefly illus., ports.) 33 cm. (A Studio book) Part of illustrative matter col. [TR680.E34] 66-23565
1. Photography—Portraits. 2. Twentieth century—Pictorial works. I. Title.

EVANS, Walker, 1903- 779.2
Many are called. With an introd. by James Agee. Boston, Houghton Mifflin, 1966. 178 p. (chiefly ports.) 23 cm. [TR680.E9] 66-27491
1. Photography—Portraits. I. Title.

FALK, Edwin A. 778.9'2
Practical portrait photography for home and studio, by Edwin A. Falk, Sr., and Charles Abel. [2d ed.] Philadelphia, Chilton Books [1967] 223 p. illus., ports. 28 cm. [TR575.F3 1967] 67-17794
1. Photography—Portraits. I. Abel, Charles, 1891- joint author. II. Title. BIP

GALELLA, Ron. 779'.2'0924
Offguard : a paparazzo look at the beautiful people / by Ron Galella ; with an introd. by Bruce Jay Friedman. New York : McGraw-Hill, c1976. 192 p. : ill. ; 28 cm. Includes index. [TR681.F3G34] 75-46628 ISBN 0-07-022729-2 : 12.95. ISBN 0-07-022733-0 pbk. : 6.95
1. Photography—Portraits. 2. Photography, Journalistic. I. Title. BIP

GOWLAND, Peter. 778.924
How to take glamour photos. Greenwich, Conn., Fawcett Publications, c1955. 144p. illus. 24cm. (A Fawcett how-to book, 285) [TR680.G69] 56-806
1. Photography—Portraits. 2. Photography, Artistic. I. Title.

GRIFFIN, John Howard, 779'.2'0924
1920-
Twelve photographic portraits. Greensboro, N.C., Unicorn Press, 1973. 1 v. (unpaged) ports. 24 cm. (Unicorn keepsake series) [TR680.G698] 74-134755 ISBN 0-87775-036-X 4.00
1. Photography—Portraits. I. Title. BIP

SUBJECT INDEX PHOTOGRAPHY—PORTRAITS.

GRUBER, L. Fritz, ed. 779.2
Famous portraits. New York 16, Ziff-Davis Pub Co. [1 Park Ave.] [1960] 159p. mostly ports. 31cm. 60-50540 10.00
1. Photography—Portraits. 2. Biography. 3. Photographers. I. Title.

HALSMAN, Philippe. 779'.2'0924
Halsman sight and insight. Words and photos. by Philippe Halsman. Designed by Herb Lubalin. [1st ed.] Garden City, N.Y., Doubleday, 1972. 186 p. illus. 30 cm. [TR681.F3H35] 70-164720 25.00
1. Photography—Portraits. I. Title.

HATTERSLEY, Ralph. 778.9'2
Beginner's guide to photographing people / Ralph Hattersley. 1st ed. Garden City, N.Y. : Dolphin Books, 1978. 222 p. : ill. ; 26 cm. [TR575.H28] 77-12860 ISBN 0-385-12689-1 : 4.95
1. Photography—Portraits. I. Title. BIP

HILLIER, Bevis, 1940- 779'.2
Victorian studio photographs from the collections of Studio Bassaro and Elliott & Fry, London. by Bevis Hillier ; with contributions by Brian Coe, Russell Ash and Helen Varley. London : Ash and Grant, 1976. 144 p. : ports. ; 26 cm. Includes index. [TR681.F3H54] 77-355572 ISBN 0-904069-03-6 : £6.95
1. Photography—Portraits. 2. Great Britain—Biography—Portraits. I. Studio Bassano. II. Elliott and Fry (Firm). III. Title.

HOMOLKA, Florence 779.2
Focus on art; photography and notes by Florence Homolka. New York, Obolensky [1963, c.1962] xi, 116p. illus. (pt. col.) 29cm. 62-18786 12.50
1. Photography—Portraits. I. Title. BIP

HORST, Horst P., 1906- 910.03'09043
Salute to the thirties [by] Horst. Foreword by Janet Flanner. Photos. by Horst and George Hoyningen-Huene. Notes on the plates by Valentine Lawford. New York, Viking Press [1971] 192 p. (chiefly illus.) 29 cm. (A Studio book) [TR681.F3H66] 79-117061 ISBN 0-670-61638-9 16.95
1. Photography—Portraits. I. Hoyningen-Huene, George, 1900-1968. II. Lawford, Valentine. III. Title.

HUJAR, Peter, 1934- 779'.092'4
Portraits in life and death / by Peter Hujar ; introd. by Susan Sontag. New York : Da Capo Press, 1976. [91] p. : chiefly ill. ; 28 cm. [TR680.H77] 75-46627 ISBN 0-306-70755-1 : 17.95 pbk. : 8.95
1. Photography—Portraits. 2. Dead. I. Title. BIP

JOHNSTON, Frances Benjamin, 1864-1952. 779'.092'4 B
A talent for detail: the photographs of Miss Frances Benjamin Johnston, 1889-1910 / by Pete Daniel and Raymond Smock. New York : Harmony Books, [1974] 182 p. : chiefly ill. ; 22 x 28 cm. "All photographs ... from the Prints and Photographs Division of the Library of Congress." Includes index. [TR140.J64A34 1974] 74-79780 ISBN 0-517-51642-X : 15.00
1. Johnston, Frances Benjamin, 1864-1952. 2. Photography—Portraits. 3. Photography, Documentary. I. Daniel, Pete. II. Smock, Raymond. III. United States. Library of Congress. Prints and Photographs Division. IV. Title.

KALETT, Jim. 779'.2'0924
People and crowds, a photographic album for artists and designers / by Jim Kalett. New York : Dover Publications, 1978. 91 p. : chiefly ill. ; 27 cm. (Dover pictorial archive series) [TR680.K24 1978] 77-87844 ISBN 0-486-23696-X : 5.00
1. Photography—Portraits. 2. Crowds—Pictorial works. I. Title.

KARSH, Yousuf, 1908- 779'.2
Faces of our time. Toronto, Buffalo, University of Toronto Press [1971] 202 p. ports. 31 cm. [TR681.F3K37] 79-155956 ISBN 0-8020-1771-1 15.00
1. Photography—Portraits. I. Title.

KARSH, Yousuf, 1908- 779'.2'0924
Karsh Canadians / Yousuf Karsh. Toronto ; Buffalo : University of Toronto Press, c1978. 203 p. : ports. ; 31 cm. [TR681.T3K375] 79-302029 ISBN 0-8020-2317-7 :
1. Karsh, Yousuf, 1908- 2. Photography—Portraits. 3. Canada—Biography—Portraits. I. Title.

KARSH, Yousuf, 1908- 779'.2
Karsh portfolio. [London] Nelson [1967] 202p. illus. 31cm. [TR680.K28] 67-106656 10.00
1. Photography—Portraits. 2. Photography, Artistic. I. Title.

KARSH, Yousuf, 1908- 779'.2
Portraits by Karsh. [Meriden, Conn., Printed by the Meriden Gravure Co., 1968] [34] p. ports. 29 cm. Selections from an exhibition held at the Museum of Fine Arts, Boston, April 19-June 4, 1968. [TR680.K287] 68-26015
1. Photography—Portraits. I. Boston. Museum of Fine Arts. II. Title.

LAPOW, Harry. 779'.2'0924
Coney Island beach people / photos. by Harry Lapow ; with an introd. by David Toor. New York : Dover Publications, c1978. 136 p., [1] leaf of plates : chiefly ill. ; 28 cm. [TR680.L35 1978] 77-91232 ISBN 0-486-23614-5 pbk. : 5.00
1. Photography—Portraits. 2. Coney Island, N.Y.—Description—Views. I. Title. BIP

LARRAIN, Gilles. 779'.2'0924
Idols. Edited by Ralph Gibson. New York, Links [1973] [61] p. (chiefly col. ports.) 31 cm. [TR680.L36 1973] 73-81030 ISBN 0-8256-3020-7 9.95
1. Photography—Portraits. I. Title.
Pbk. 5.95, ISBN 0-8256-3019-3.

LEFEBVRE, Henry. 778.92
Candid wedding photography. [2d ed. New York, American Photographic Book Pub. Co., 1955] 106p. illus. 24cm. (An Amphoto book) [TR575.L4 1955] 55-11628
1. Photography—Portraits. 2. Photography—Business methods. I. Photography—Handbooks, manuals. etc. II. Title.

MAN, Felix H., 1893- 779'.2'0924
Felix H. Man : reportage portraits, 1929-76 : [catalogue of an exhibition held at the] National Portrait Gallery [1 October 1976 to 2 January 1977]. London : The Gallery, 1976. [19] p. : chiefly ports. ; 24 cm. Bibliography: p. [8] [TR681.F3M36] 77-364176 ISBN 0-904017-10-9 : £0.30
1. Man, Felix H., 1893- 2. Photography—Portraits. I. London. National Portrait Gallery.

MANNING, Jack. 778.9'2
The fine 35mm portrait / Jack Manning. Garden City, N.Y. : Amphoto, c1978. 200 p. : ill. (some col.) ; 29 cm. Includes index. [TR575.M35] 78-8558 ISBN 0-8174-2438-5 : 25.00
1. Photography—Portraits. I. Title. BIP

MISRACH, Richard, 1949- 779'.2
Telegraph 3 A.M. : the street people of Telegraph Avenue, Berkeley, California : photographs / by Richard Misrach. Berkeley, Calif. : Cornucopia Press, 1974. [80] p. : all ill. ; 27 cm. (Publication - Cornucopia Press ; no. 1) [TR680.M49] 74-16786 17.00
1. Photography—Portraits. 2. Berkeley, Calif.—Description—Views. I. Title.

MORTENSEN, William. 778.92
Outdoor portraiture. All illus. by the author except where otherwise designated. [2d ed.] San Francisco, Camera Craft Pub. Co. [1951] 208 p. illus. 25 cm. [TR575.M6 1951] 51-10916
1. Photography — Portraits. 2. Photography — Handbooks, manuals. I. Title.

MURAY, Nicholas, 1892-1965. 779'.2'0924
Muray's celebrity portraits of the twenties and thirties : 135 photographs / by Nickolas Muray ; introd. by Marianne Fulton Margolis. New York : Dover Publications, 1978. [140] p. : chiefly ill. ; 29 cm. [TR681.F3M87 1978] 77-87448 ISBN 0-486-23578-5 : 5.00 ($5.75 Can.)
1. Photography—Portraits. I. Title. BIP

MURAY, Nickolas, 1892-1965. 779'.0924
The revealing eye; personalities of the 1920's, in photographs by Nikolas Muray and words by Paul Gallico. [1st ed.] New York, Atheneum, 1967. xviii, 307 p. ports. 33 cm. [TR680.M87] 67-25487
1. Photography—Portraits. I. Gallico, Paul, 1897- II. Title.

NEWMAN, Arnold, 1918- 779'.2
One mind's eye : the portraits and other photographs of Arnold Newman / foreword by Beaumont Newhall ; introd. by Robert Sobieszek. Boston : D. R. Godine, c1974. xix, 192, [12] p. : chiefly ill. ; 24 x 29 cm. Includes index. Bibliography: p. [198]-[201] [TR680.N48] 74-81520 ISBN 0-87923-094-0 : 27.50
1. Newman, Arnold, 1918- 2. Photography—Portraits. 3. Photography, Artistic. I. Title.

NIBBELINK, Don D. 778.9'2
Picturing people / Don Nibbelink ; edited by and published for Eastman Kodak Company. Garden City, N.Y. : Amphoto, c1976. 255 p. : col. ill. ; 27 cm. Includes index. [TR575.N5] 75-27065 ISBN 0-8174-0576-3 : 12.95
1. Photography—Portraits. I. Eastman Kodak Company. II. Title. BIP

NOREN, Catherine. 929'.2
The camera of my family / Catherine Hanf Noren. 1st ed. New York : Knopf : distributed by Random House, 1976. 240 p. : chiefly ill. ; 24 x 29 cm. [TR680.N68 1976] 75-36805 ISBN 0-394-48838-5 : 20.00
1. Wallach family—Portraits. 2. Photography—Portraits. I. Title. BIP

PENN, Irving. 779'.2'0924
Worlds in a small room / by Irving Penn as an ambulant studio photographer. New York : Grossman, 1974. 95 p. : ill. ; 28 cm. [TR680.P46 1974] 74-6653 ISBN 0-670-79025-7 : 16.50
1. Photography—Portraits. I. Title. BIP

THE Photographer's image : self-portrayal / edited by James Alinder ; 101 contemporary self-portraits with essays by Peter Hunt Thompson, Dana Asbury, R. Duncan Wallace. Carmel, Calif. : Friends of Photography, c1978. [116] p. : chiefly ill. ; 26 cm. On cover: Self-portrayal. Contents.Contents.—Thompson, P. H. Self-portrayal.—Asbury, D. Photographing the interior.—Wallace, R. D. On self-portrayal. [TR680.P48] 78-71591 ISBN 0-933286-00-7 : 9.95 779'.0973
1. Photography—Portraits. 2. Self-portraits. I. Alinder, Jim. II. Thompson, Peter Hunt. III. Asbury, Dana. IV. Wallace, R. Duncan, 1938- V. Friends of Photography. VI. Title: Self-portrayal.

PYKE, Martha. 778.92
The portrait in photography. [Houston? Tex., c1952] 159p. illus. 28cm. [TR575.P9] 58-22481
1. Photography- —Portraits. I. Title.

SANDER, August. 779'.2'0924
August Sander. Millerton, N.Y. : Aperture, c1977. 94 p. : all ill. ; 22 cm. (The Aperture history of photography series ; 7) Bibliography: p. 93-94. [TR680.S22 1977] 77-70069 ISBN 0-89381-007-X : 7.95
1. Photography—Portraits. BIP

SANDER, August. 779'.2'0924
Men without masks; faces of Germany, 1910-1938. With an introd. by Gunther Sander and foreword by Golo Mann. [Translated from the German by Maureen Oberli-Turner] Greenwich, Conn., New York Graphic Society [1973] 313 p. illus. 31 cm. Translation of Menschen ohne Maske. London ed. published under title: August Sander: photographer extraordinary. [TR680.S2313 1973b] 73-77664 ISBN 0-8212-0533-1 27.50
1. Sander, August. 2. Photography—Portraits. I. Sander, Gunther, 1907- II. Title.

SANDERS, Norman, 1927- 779'.2'0924
At home : photographs / by Norman Sanders. Dobbs Ferry, N.Y. : Morgan & Morgan, 1977. 95 p. : chiefly ill. ; 29 cm. [TR680.S25] 77-83835 ISBN 0-87100-137-3 pbk. : 8.95
1. Photography—Portraits. I. Title. BIP

SEEFF, Norman. 779'.2'0924
Hot shots : photographs / by Norman Seeff. New York : Flash Books, [1974] 90 p. : all ill. ; 21 cm. [TR680.S38] 74-80024 ISBN 0-8256-3903-4 : 3.95
1. Photography—Portraits. I. Title.

SIPPRELL, Clara E. 779.2
Moment of light; photographs by Clara Sipprell. Introd. by Elizabeth Gray Vining. New York, John Day [1966] 1 v. (chiefly illus., ports.) 28cm. [TR680.S5] 66-21128 12.95
1. Photography—Portraits. I. Title.

SKREBNESKI, Victor. 779'.2'0924
Skrebneski portraits : a matter of record. 1st ed. Garden City, N.Y. : Doubleday, 1978. ca. 150 p. : chiefly ill. ; 31 cm. [TR681.F3S57] 78-18566 ISBN 0-385-14623-X : 27.50
1. Photography—Portraits. I. Title. BIP

SLOAN, James, 1926- 779.2
Faces in the crowd. [Redlands? Calif., 1964] 85 p. ports. 29 cm. [TR680.S55] 64-56394
1. Photography — Portraits. I. Title.

SLOAN, James, 1926- 778.9'2
More faces & places. [Redlands, Calif., 1970] 170 p. (chiefly illus. (part col.), ports.) 29 cm. [TR681.F3S58] 74-23418
1. Photography—Portraits. I. Title.

SLOAN, James, 1926- 779'.2
More faces in the crowd. [Redlands, Calif., Printed by Citrograph Print. Co., 1967] 81 p. (chiefly ports.) 29 cm. [TR680.S56] 68-80
1. Photography—Portraits. I. Title.

SPITZING, Gunter. 778.9'2
The photoguide to portraits. [Translated by Frank Dash] Garden City, N.Y., Amphoto [1974] 179 p. illus. (part col.) 19 cm. Translation of Portratfotos—gewusst wie. [TR575.S6613] 73-89745 ISBN 0-8174-0772-3 5.95
1. Photography—Portraits. I. Title.

STAGG, Mildred. 778.924
Hal Reiff's glamour manual. New York, Amphoto [1960] 121 p. illus. 21 cm. [TR675.S67] 61-8772
1. Photography — Portraits. 2. Photography of women. I. Reiff. Hal. II. Title.

STRELOW, Liselotte, 1908- 778.92
Photogenic portrait management tr., adapted[from German] by L. A. Mannheim. London, New York, Focal [1966] 176p. plates (ports.) 23cm. Orig. pub. as Das manipulierte Menschenbilonis. Dusseldorf, Econ- Verlag, 1961. [TR575.S873] 66-66275 6.95
1. Photography-Portraits. I. Title.
American distributor: Hastings, New York.

THEISEN, Earl. 778.92
Photographic approach to people. New York, Amphoto [1966] 160 p. illus. 26 cm. [TR575.T5 1966a] 66-31636
1. Photography—Portraits. I. Title.

THEISEN, Earl. 778.92
Photographic approach to people. Philadelphia, Chilton Books [1966] 160 p. illus., ports. 26 cm. [TR575.T5] 66-23326
1. Photography—Portraits. I. Title.

TOURNACHON, Felix, 1820-1910. 779'.2'0924
Nadar / Nigel Gosling. London : Secker & Warburg, 1976. 298 p. : ill. ; 31 cm. Includes index. [TR681.F3T68 1976] 77-355116 ISBN 0-436-18610-1 : £9.75
1. Tournachon, Felix, 1820-1910. 2. Photography—Portraits. 3. France—Biography—Portraits. I. Gosling, Nigel.

TOURNACHON, Felix, 1820-1910. 779'.2'0924
Nadar / Nigel Gosling. 1st American ed. New York : Knopf : distributed by Random House, 1976. 298 p. : ill. ; 31 cm. Includes index. [TR681.F3T68 1976b] 76-27546 ISBN 0-394-41106-4 : 25.00
1. Tournachon, Felix, 1820-1910. 2. Photography—Portraits. 3. France—Biography—Portraits. 4. Photographers—France—Biography. I. Gosling, Nigel. II. Title.

TYDINGS, Kenneth S 778.92
Portrait photography. Featuring the

portrait studies of Editta Sherman. Philadelphia, Chilton Co., c1960. 128 p. illus., ports. 20 cm. (The Modern camera guide series) [TR575.T93] 60-13941
1. Photography — Portraits. I. Title. II. Series. BIP

TYDINGS, Kenneth S. 778.92
Portriat photography. Featuring the portrait studies of Editta Sherman. Philadelphia, Chilton Co., c.1960. 128p. illus., ports, diagrs., charts. 20cm. (The Modern camera guide series) (585) 60-13941 1.95 pap.,
1. Photography—Portraits. (Sereis) I. Title.

VAN DERZEE, James 779'.2'0924
James Van DerZee / edited by Liliane De Cock and Reginald McGhee ; introd. by Regina A. Perry. Dobbs Ferry, N.Y. : Morgan & Morgan, [1974] c1973. 159 p. : chiefly ill., ports. ; 28 cm. [TR680.V27 1974] 73-83130 ISBN 0-87100-039-3 : 12.00
1. Photography—Portraits. 2. Negroes—Pictorial works.

VAN DERZEE, James. 779*.9*96073
The world of James Van DerZee: a visual record of Black Americans. Compiled and with an introd. by Reginald McGhee. New York, Grove Press [1969] [23] p., 165 p. of illus., ports. 29 cm. [TR680.V28] 71-97157 15.00
1. Photography—Portraits. 2. Negroes—History—Pictorial works. I. McGhee, Reginald, comp. II. Title.

VAN VECHTEN, Carl, 779'.092'4
1880-1964.
Portraits, the photography of Carl Van Vechten / compiled by Saul Mauriber. Indianapolis : Bobbs-Merrill, [1978] p. cm. [TR680.V29 1978] 78-55643 ISBN 0-672-52427-9 : 29.95
1. Van Vechten, Carl, 1880-1964. 2. Photography—Portraits. I. Mauriber, Saul. II. Title.

A Victorian album : 779'.2'0942
Julia Margaret Cameron and her circle / edited by Graham Ovenden ; introductory essay by David Cecil. 1st American ed. New York : Da Capo Press, 1975. vii, 252 p. : chiefly ill. ; 34 cm. Includes index. [TR681.F3V52 1975b] 75-18728 ISBN 0-306-70749-7 : 60.00
1. Cameron, Julia Margaret Pattle, 1815-1879. 2. Photography—Portraits. 3. Great Britain—Biography—Portraits. I. Ovenden, Graham. BIP

WEISSBERGER, L. Arnold. 779'.2
Close-up; a collection of photographs by L. Arnold Weissberger. New York, Arno Press, 1967. [64] p. (chiefly ports.) 28 cm. Exhibition of the Museum of the City of New York held Oct. 3, 1967. [TR680.W47] 67-30714
1. Photography—Portraits. I. New York. Museum of the City of New York. II. Title.

WEISSBERGER, L. 779'.2'0924
Arnold.
Famous faces; a photograph album of personal reminiscences, by L. Arnold Weissberger. New York, H. N. Abrams [1973] 443 p. ports. 28 x 30 cm. [TR681.F3W44] 72-706 ISBN 0-8109-0115-3 35.00
1. Photography—Portraits. 2. Performing arts—Biography—Portraits. I. Title.

WILLIAMS, Herbert 778.92
Camera portraiture; professional and amateur. London. New York, Focal Press [dist. American Photographic Book Pub. Co.] [1960] 168p. illus. 24cm. 60-1213 5.95
1. Photography—Portraits. I. Title.

WOLFF, Bernard 779'.2'0924
Pierre, 1930-
Friends and friends of friends / Bernard Pierre Wolff ; with an introd. by John Leonard. 1st ed. New York : E. P. Dutton, c1978. xviii, 121 p. : chiefly ill. ; 23 x 26 cm. [TR680.W64 1978] 78-55050 ISBN 0-525-47519-2 : 8.95
1. Wolff, Bernard Pierre, 1930- 2. Photography—Portraits. 3. Friendship—Pictorial works. I. Title. BIP

Photography—Portraits—Exhibitions.

AVEDON, Richard. 779'.2
Avedon. [Minneapolis, Minneapolis Institute of Arts, 1970] 1 portfolio. 24 cm. Consists of a pamphlet ([11] p. illus., ports.), 10 ports., and a sheet (240 illus. (chiefly ports.) 69 x 92 cm. fold. to 23 x 23 cm.) Catalogue of an exhibition held at the Minneapolis Institute of Arts, July 2-Aug. 30, 1970. Bibliography: p. [9] [TR681.F3A9] 78-118354
1. Photography—Portraits—Exhibitions. I. Minneapolis. Institute of Arts.

NOREN, Catherine. 779'.2'07401471
The camera of my family. [Catalogue of exhibition] April 11, 1973-September 3, 1973, Jewish Museum, New York. [New York, Jewish Museum, 1973] [12] p. illus. 24 cm. [TR680.N67] 73-78651
1. Wallach family—Portraits. 2. Photography—Portraits—Exhibitions. I. Jewish Theological Seminary of America. Jewish Museum. II. Title.

Photography—Portraits—History.

†MADDOW, Ben, 1909- 778.9'2'09
Faces : a narrative history of the portrait in photography / by Ben Maddow ; photos. compiled and edited by Constance Sullivan ; designed and coordinated by Massimo Vignelli and Gudrun Buettner. 1st ed. Boston : New York Graphic Society, 1977. 540 p. : ill. ; 32 cm. "A Chanticleer Press edition." Includes index. Bibliography: p. 532-535. [TR575.M32] 76-41139 ISBN 0-8212-0703-2 : 35.00
1. Photography—Portraits—History. I. Sullivan, Constance. II. Title. BIP

Photography—Portraits—Lighting and posing.

HARTMANN, Sadakichi, 778.9'2
1867-1944.
Composition in portraiture, by Sidney Allan (Sadakichi Hartmann) New York, Arno Press, 1973. [c1909] 116 p. illus. 23 cm. (The Literature of Photography) [TR573.H3 1973] 72-9205 ISBN 0-405-04914-5. 10.00.
1. Photography portraits lighting and posing. 2. Portraits. 3. Composition. (Photography) I. Title. II. Series. BIP

NURNBERG, Walter, 1907- 778.9'2
Lighting for portraiture; technique and application. [7th ed.] Philadelphia, Chilton Book Co. [1969] 186 p. illus. (part col.) 25 cm. [TR573.N8 1969] 79-5007 9.95
1. Photography—Portraits—Lighting and posing. I. Title.

NURNBERG, Walter, 1907- 778.92
Lighting for portraiture, technique and application. [3d ed.] London, New York, Focal Press [1957] 188p. illus. 25cm. [TR573.N8 1957] 57-4357
1. Photography—Portraits— Lighting and posting. I. Title. BIP

PETZOLD, Paul. 778.7'1
Light on people. London, New York, Focal Pr., 1971. 152 p. illus. (some col.) 19 x 22 cm. [TR575.P48] 79-585301 ISBN 0-240-50707-X £1.75
1. Photography—Portraits—Lighting and posing. I. Title. BIP

WOOLLEY, Al E. 778.7
Photographic lighting. New York, A. S. Barnes [c.1963] 154p. illus., ports. 26cm. 63-18253 7.50
1. Photography—Portraits—Lighting and posing. I. Title. BIP

WOOLLEY, Al E. 778.7'2
Photographic lighting [by] A. E. Woolley. New York, American Photographic Book Pub. Co. [1971] 136 p. illus., ports. 26 cm. [TR590.W6 1971] 72-21233 ISBN 0-8174-0356-6 8.95
1. Photography—Portraits—Lighting and posing. I. Title.

Photography—Printing papers.

ANSCO. 770.284
Ansco photographic papers, their properties and applications. [Binghamton, N.Y., 1954] 80p. illus. 20 cm. [TR285.A55] 54-26618
1. Photography—Printing papers. 2. Photography—Printing processes. I. Title.

MARX, M Richard. 770.284
Printing with variable contrast papers. 4th ed. San Francisco, Camera Craft Pub. Co. [1959] 96p. illus. 22cm. Previous editions published under title: Printing with Varigam. [TR285.M3 1959] 58-14231
1. Photography—Printing papers. I. Title.

MARX, M Richard. 770.284
Printing with variable contrast papers. All illus. by the author except where otherwise designated. [5th ed.] New York, Ziff-Davis Pub. Co. [1961] 96p. illus. 22cm. First ed. published in 1954 under title: Printing with Varigam. [TR285.M3 1961] 61-12009
1. Photography—Printing papers. I. Title.

MARX, M Richard. 770.284
Printing with 'Varigam.' [1st ed.] San Francisco, Camera Craft Pub. Co. [1954] 80p. illus. 22cm. [TR285.M3] 53-11648
1. Photography—Printing papers. I. Title.

MARX, M Richard. 770.284
Printing with Varigam. All illus. by the author except where otherwise designated. [3d ed.] San Francisco, Camera Craft Pub. Co. [1957] 96p. illus. 22cm. [TR285.M3 1957] 57-7819
1. Photography—Printing papers. I. Title.

MARX, M Richard. 770.284
Printing with Varigam. All illus. by the author except where otherwise designated. [2d ed.] San Francisco, Camera Craft Pub. Co. [1955] 84p. illus. 22cm. [TR285.M3 1955] 55-9872
1. Photography—Printing papers. I. Title.

Photography—Printing processes.

BUNNELL, Peter C., comp. 770'.28
Nonsilver printing processes: four selections, 1886-1927. Edited by Peter C. Bunnel. New York, Arno Press, 1973. 4 v. in 1 illus. 23 cm. (The Literature of photography) Reprint of Elements of photogravure, by C. N. Bennett, first published 1927; of the 2d ed., 1898, of Photo-aquatint, or The gum-bichromate processes, by A. Maskell and R. Demachy; of The oil and bromoil processes, by F. J. Mortimer and S. L. Coulthurst, first published 1909; and of Platinotype, by G. Pizzighelli and Baron A. Hubl, published 1886. [TR350.B83 1973] 72-9221 ISBN 0-405-04928-5 16.00
1. Photography—Printing processes. 2. Photogravure. I. Title. II. Series.
Pbk. 4.50.

BURBANK, William Henry. 770'.28
Photographic printing methods [by] W. H. Burbank. New York, Arno Press, 1973 [c1887] 225 p. illus. 23 cm. (The Literature of photography) Reprint of the 1891 ed., which was issued as no. 22 of Scovill's photographic series. Bibliography: p. [7]-8. [TR330.B94 1973] 72-9185 ISBN 0-405-04896-3 13.00
1. Photography—Printing processes. I. Title. II. Series. BIP

CROY, Otto. 770.284
The complete art of printing and enlarging. London, New York, Focal Press [1950] 255 p. (p. 255 advertisement) illus. 25 cm. [TR330.C7] 51-2621
1. Photography—Printing processes. 2. Photography—Enlarging. I. Title. BIP

CROY, Otto R., 1902- 770.284
The complete art of printing and enlarging, by O. R. Croy. 11th ed. New York, Amphoto [1970] 251 p. illus. 24 cm. [TR330.C7 1970] 74-18661 9.95
1. Photography—Printing processes. 2. Photography—Enlarging. I. Title.

CROY, Otto R., 1902- 770.284
The complete art of printing and enlarging, by O. R. Croy. 10th print., fully rev. Philadelphia, Chilton Book Co. [1969] 251 p. illus. 24 cm. [TR330.C7 1969] 77-4970 9.95
1. Photography—Printing processes. 2. Photography—Enlarging. I. Title.

CROY, Otto R., 1902- 770.284
The complete art of printing and enlarging, by Dr. O. R. Croy. 1st ed., 9th impression. London, New York, Focal P., 1967. 251 p. illus., tables, diagrs, 24 cm. 351 -- [TR330.C7 1967] 67-105429
1. Photography — Printing processes. 2. Photography — Enlarging. I. Title.

FRAZIER, William J. 770.284
Printing by flash, by William J. Frazier. Philadelphia, Chilton Book Co. [1967] 142 p. illus. 26 cm. [TR333.F7] 67-29521
1. Photography—Printing processes. I. Title.

FRAZIER, William J. 770.284
Printing by flash, by William J. Frazier. New York, American Photographic Book Pub. Co. [1967] 142 p. illus. 26 cm. [TR333.F7 1967b] 68-319
1. Photography—Printing processes. I. Title.

GASSAN, Arnold. 770'.28
Handbook for contemporary photography / by Arnold Gassan. 4th ed. Rochester, N.Y. : Light Impressions Corp., 1977. p. cm. [TR330.G38 1977] 77-14576 ISBN 0-87992-009-2 : 15.00 ISBN 0-87992-008-4 pbk. : 8.95
1. Photography—Printing processes. I. Title. BIP

HATTERSLEY, Ralph. 770'.28
Photographic printing / Ralph Hattersley. Englewood Cliffs, N.J. : Prentice-Hall, c1977. xxi, 265 p. : ill. ; 24 cm. (A Spectrum book) Includes index. [TR330.H37] 77-2835 ISBN 0-13-665299-9 : 15.95 ISBN 0-13-665281-6 pbk. : 6.95
1. Photography—Printing processes. I. Title. BIP

HAWKEN, William R. 770'.284
You and your prints / William R. Hawken. Garden City, N.Y. : Amphoto, c1978. 144 p. : ill. ; 29 cm. Includes index. [TR330.H378] 78-9459 ISBN 0-8174-2452-0 : 9.95. ISBN 0-8174-2114-9 pbk. : 5.95
1. Photography—Printing processes. I. Title. BIP

JACOBS, Lou. 770.284
How to use variable contrast papers. Photos. by the author. New York, Amphoto [c1960] 120p. illus. 21cm. [TR330.J3] 61-6413
1. Photography—Printing processes. 2. Photography— Printing papers. I. Title.

JACOBS, Lou. 770.284
How to use variable contrast papers [by] Lou Jacobs, Jr. 3d ed. New York, Amphoto [1970] 160 p. 24 cm. [TR330.J3 1970] 79-97873 6.95
1. Photography—Printing processes. 2. Photography—Printing papers. I. Title.

KOSAR, Jaromir. 771.5
Light-sensitive systems; chemistry and application of nonsilver halide photographic processes. New York, Wiley [1965] xv, 473 p.illus. 24 cm. (Wiley series on photographic science and technology and the graphic arts) Includes bibliographies. [TR350.K65] 65-22427
1. Photography — Printing processes. 2. Photographic chemistry. I. Title. II. Title: Nonsilver halide photographic processes.

STONE, Jim. 770'.28
Darkroom dynamics : an introduction to creative printing techniques / Jim Stone. New York : Van Nostrand Reinhold Co., [1979] p. cm. Includes index. [TR330.S84] 78-23902 ISBN 0-442-27925-6 : 17.95
1. Photography—Printing processes. I. Title. BIP

TIME-LIFE Books. 770'.28
The print, by the editors of Time-Life Books. New York [1970] 235 p. illus. (part col.), ports. 27 cm. (Life library of photography) "Buyer's guide to darkroom equipment" (6 p.) inserted at end. Bibliography: p. 231. [TR320.T55] 70-124382
1. Photography—Printing processes. I. Title.

SUBJECT INDEX PHOTOGRAPHY—RESEARCH.

WOODHEAD, Harold Charles. 770'.284
Creative photographic printing methods / Harold C. Woodhead. London ; New York : Focal Press, 1975. 180 p. : ill. ; 24 cm. Includes index. [TR330.W65] 76-351889 ISBN 0-240-50880-7 : £4.00
1. Photography—Printing processes. I. Title. BIP

WOOLLEY, Al E 770.284
Photographic print quality; procedure and papers. All photos. by the author. Philadelphia, Chilton Co., Book Division, c1961. 128 p. illus. 20 cm. (Modern camera guide series, 589) [TR320.W6] 61-7185
1. Photography — Printing processes. 2. Photography — Printing paper. I. Title.

Photography—Printing processes—Carbon.

WILSON, Edward Livingston, 1838-1903. 773'.1
The American Carbon Manual. New York, Arno Press, 1973 [c1868] 100 p. illus. 22 cm. (The Literature of Photography) [TR440.W55 1973] 72-9246 ISBN 0-405-04950-1 9.00
1. Photography—Printing processes—Carbon. I. Title. II. Series.

Photography—Printing processes—Gum-bichromate.

SCOPICK, David, 1944- 773'.5
The gum bichromate book : contemporary methods for photographic printmaking / David Scopick ; [illustrated by Michael Cote]. Rochester, N.Y. : Light Impressons, c1978. 88 p. : ill. ; 23 cm. Bibliography: p. 84-88. [TR445.S36] 78-8122 ISBN 0-87992-010-6 pbk. : 7.95
1. Photography—Printing processes—Gum-bichromate. I. Title. BIP

Photography—Printing processes—Silver.

ROBINSON, Henry Peach, 1830-1901. 772'.1
The art and practice of silver printing, by H. P. Robinson and Capt. Abney. New York, Arno Press, 1973. 128 p. illus. 22 cm. (The Literature of Photography) Reprint of the 1881 ed., which was issued as no. 4 of photographic handy-books. [TR385.R62 1973] 72-9227 ISBN 0-405-04933-1 10.00.
1. Photography—Printing processes—Silver. I. Abbey, William de Wiveleslie, Sir, 1844-1920, joint author. II. Title. III. Series. IV. Series: Photographic handy-books, no. 4. BIP

Photography—Processing.

AMPHOTO, New York. 770'.28
Developing, printing & enlarging simplified, by the Amphoto editorial board. Englewood Cliffs, N.J., Prentice-Hall [1974] 95 p. illus. 26 cm. (A Modern photoguide) (A Spectrum book, S-PG-3) [TR287.A46 1974] 73-92422 ISBN 0-13-205138-9 7.95
1. Photography—Processing. I. Title.
Pbk. 2.95, ISBN 0-13-205120-6.

CARROLL, John S., 1911- 770'.28
Amphoto home darkroom course : advanced black and white / John S. Carroll. Garden City, N.Y. : Amphoto, c1977. 1 case (160 p. : ill.) ; 26 cm. Title on case: Advanced B & W home darkroom course. Includes index. Bibliography: p. 158-159. [TR287.C374] 76-16683 ISBN 0-8174-0595-X : 9.95
1. Photography—Processing. I. Title. II. Title: Home darkroom course. III. Title: Advanced B & W home darkroom course.

EATON, George T. 338.476672
Photographic chemistry in black-and-white and color photography, by George T. Eaton. [2d ed.] Hastings-on-Hudson, N.Y., Morgan & Morgan [1965, 1957] 124 p. illus., ports. 23 cm. First ed. published in 1957 under title: Photo chemistry in black-and-white [TR210.E32 1965] 65-27034
I. Title.

EPSTEIN, Samuel, 1909- 770.28
How to develop, print, and enlarge pictures, by Samuel Epstein and David W. De Armand. New York, Grosset & Dunlap [1970] 96 p. illus. 28 cm. [TR287.E67 1970] 71-26202 1.95 ($2.50 Can)
1. Photography—Processing. I. De Armand, David W., joint author. II. Title.

FEININGER, Andreas, 1906- 770'.28
Darkroom techniques. Garden City, N.Y., Amphoto [1974] 2 v. illus. 23 cm. Contents.Contents.—v. 1. The darkroom, film development, basic photo-chemistry.—v. 2. Equipment materials, contact printing, enlarging. [TR287.F44] 73-82108 ISBN 0-8174-0562-3 15.00
1. Photography—Processing. I. Title. BIP

FINEMAN, Mark B. 770'.28
The home darkroom, by Mark B. Fineman. Garden City, N.Y., Amphoto [1973] 92 p. illus. 28 cm. [TR287.F56] 72-79608 ISBN 0-8174-0555-0 2.95
1. Photography—Processing. 2. Photography—Studios and dark rooms. I. Title. BIP

GAUNT, Leonard. 770'.28
The focalguide to the darkroom / Leonard Gaunt. London : Focal Press ; New York : Focal/Hastings, 1978. 176 p. : ill. (some col.) ; 19 cm. Includes index. [TR560.G38] 78-326451 ISBN 0-8038-2365-7 pbk. : 6.95
1. Photography—Studios and dark rooms. 2. Photography—Processing I. Title. BIP

HAIST, Grant Milford, 1922- 770'.28
Modern photographic processing / Grant Haist. New York : Wiley, [1978] p. cm. (Wiley series on photographic science and technology and the graphic arts) "A Wiley-Interscience publication." Includes indexes. Bibliography: p. [TR287.H28] 78-17559 ISBN 0-471-04286-2 : 40.00
1. Photography—Processing. I. Title. BIP

HATTERSLEY, Ralph. 770'.28
Beginner's guide to darkroom techniques / Ralph Hattersley. 1st ed. New York : Doubleday, c1976. p. cm. [TR287.H33] 76-1063 ISBN 0-385-11073-1 : 4.95
1. Photography—Processing. I. Title. BIP

HERTZBERG, Robert Edward, 1905- 770'.28
Elementary developing and printing, by Robert Hertzberg. Garden City, N.Y., Amphoto [1973] 128 p. illus. (part col.) 26 cm. [TR287.H39] 72-91032 ISBN 0-8174-0558-5 8.95
1. Photography—Processing. I. Title. BIP

HERTZBERG, Robert Edward, 1905- 770'.28
Photo darkroom guide / by Robert Hertzberg. 5th ed. Garden City, N.Y. : Amphoto, c1975. 128 p. : ill. ; 20 cm. Originally published in 1967 by Chilton Book Co., Philadelphia. Includes index. [TR287.H4 1975] 75-332956 ISBN 0-8174-1148-8 : 2.75
1. Photography—Processing. I. Title.

JACOBSON, R. E. 770'.28
The focalguide to home processing : colour and monochrome materials / R. E. Jacobson. 2d ed. London : Focal Press ; New York : Focal/Hastings House, 1978. 197 p. : ill. ; 19 cm. [TR287.J29 1978] 79-304532 ISBN 0-8038-2345-2 (Focal/Hastings House) : 6.95
1. Photography—Processing. I. Title. BIP

JONAS, Paul. 770.2
Manual of darkroom procedures and techniques. [2d ed.] New York, Universal Photo Books [c1965] 128 p. illus. 20 cm. [TR287.J65] 67-6041
1. Photography—Processing. I. Title. BIP

JONAS, Paul. 770.28
Manual of darkroom procedures and techniques. 3d ed. Philadelphia, Chilton Book Co. [1967] 128 p. illus. 21 cm. [TR287.J65 1967] 67-25846
1. Photography—Processing. I. Title. II. Title: Dark room procedures and techniques.

JONAS, Paul. 770.28
Manual of darkroom procedures and techniques. New York, Amphoto [1971] 160 p. illus. 24 cm. [TR287.J65 1971] 74-164637 ISBN 0-8174-0541-0 7.95
1. Photography—Processing. I. Title. II. Title: Darkroom procedures and techniques.

KIRKPATRICK, Kirk. 770'.28
Basic darkroom / by Kirk Kirkpatrick. Los Angeles : Petersen Pub. Co., c1975. 80 p. : ill. ; 28 cm. (Petersen's how-to photographic library) [TR287.K57] 75-27124 ISBN 0-8227-0121-9 pbk. : 2.95
1. Photography—Processing. I. Title. BIP

MANELLA, Douglas. 770'.28
Amphoto guide to black-and-white processing and printing / Douglas Manella. Garden City, N.Y. : Amphoto, [1978] p. cm. Includes index. [TR287.M33] 78-21632 ISBN 0-8174-2461-X : 9.95 ISBN 0-8174-2135-1 pbk. : 5.95
1. Photography—Processing. 2. Photography—Printing processes. I. Title. BIP

PICKER, Fred. 770'.28
Zone VI workshop; the fine print in black & white photography Garden City, N.Y., Amphoto [1974] 110 p. illus. 25 cm. [TR287.P5] 73-93529 ISBN 0-8174-0574-7 5.95
1. Photography—Processing. 2. Photography—Exposure. I. Title. BIP

Photography—Processing—Congresses.

SOCIETY of Photographic Scientists and Engineers. 770
Symposium on Photographic Processing; 1973 SPSE Technical Conference, May 6-11, 1973, Rochester, New York. Richmond C. Beach, editor. Washington, 1973. xv, 103 p. 23 cm. At head of title: SPSE. On cover: 26th annual conference, Society of Photographic Scientists and Engineers. Includes bibliographical references. [TR287.S64 1973] 73-166219
1. Photography—Processing—Congresses. I. Beach, Richmond C., ed. II. SPSE Symposium on Photographic Processing, Rochester, N.Y., 1973. III. SPSE Technical Conference, Rochester, N.Y., 1973. IV. Title.
Contents omitted.

SYMPOSIUM on Photographic Processing, University of Sussex, 1971. 772'.1
Photographic processing: proceedings of the Symposium on Photographic Processing held at the University of Sussex, Falmer, Sussex, September, 1971. Edited by R. J. Cox. London, New York, Published for the Scientific and Technical Group of the Royal Photographic Society by Academic Press, 1973. xii, 340 p. illus. 24 cm. Includes bibliographies. [TR287.S95 1971] 72-7710 ISBN 0-12-194460-3 16.50
1. Photography—Processing—Congresses. I. Cox, R. J., ed. II. Royal Photographic Society of Great Britain, London. III. Title. BIP

Photography—Processing—Handbooks, manuals, etc.

CARROLL, John S., 1911- 770'.28
Amphoto black-and-white processing data book [by] John S. Carroll. [1st ed.] New York, Amphoto [1972] 224 p. 18 cm. [TR287.C37] 78-187821 ISBN 0-8174-0549-6 6.95
1. Photography—Processing—Handbooks, manuals, etc. I. Title. II. Title: Black-and-white processing data book.

CARROLL, John S., 1911- 770'.28
Amphoto black-and-white processing data book / John S. Carroll. 2d rev. ed. Garden City, N.Y. : Amphoto, 1975. 240 p. ; 17 cm. On spine: Black/white processing data book. [TR287.C37 1975] 75-331107 4.95
1. Photography—Processing—Handbooks, manuals, etc. I. Title. II. Title: Black/white processing data book.

CARROLL, John S., 1911- 770'.28
Photographic lab handbook / John S. Carroll. Garden City, N.Y. : Amphoto, [1974] 636 p. in various pagings : graphs ; 24 cm. Includes index. [TR287.C38] 74-84030 ISBN 0-8174-0422-8 : 19.95
1. Photography—Processing—Handbooks, manuals, etc. I. Title.

CARROLL, John S., 1911- 770'.28
Photographic lab handbook / John S. Carroll. Rev. ed. Englewood Cliffs, N.J. : Prentice-Hall, c1976. 720 p. ; 23 cm. Includes index. Bibliography: p. 15-16. [TR287.C38 1976] 76-360809 ISBN 0-13-665448-7 : 9.95
1. Photography—Processing—Handbooks, manuals, etc. I. Title.

CARROLL, John S., 1911- 770'.28
Photographic lab handbook / John S. Carroll. 4th ed. Garden City, N.Y. : Amphoto, 1977. 720 p. ; 23 cm. Includes index. Bibliography: p. 15-16. [TR287.C38 1977] 77-365093 ISBN 0-8174-2427-X. ISBN 0-8174-2109-2 pbk. : 10.95
1. Photography—Processing—Handbooks, manuals, etc. I. Title.

CARROLL, John S., 1911- 770'.28
Photographic lab handbook / John S. Carroll. 5th ed. Englewood Cliffs, N.J. : Prentice-Hall, 1979. 656 p. ; 23 cm. Page 656 reserved for future expansion. Includes index. Bibliography: p. 15-16. [TR287.C38 1979] 79-107809 ISBN 0-13-665422-3 : 24.95
1. Photography—Processing—Handbooks, manuals, etc. I. Title. BIP

HERTZBERG, Robert E. 770.283
Photo darkroom guide, by Robert E. Hertzberg. 5th ed. New York, Amphoto [1967] 128p. illus. 20cm. (148) [TR287.H4 1967] 67-25844 1.95 pap.,
1. Photography—Processing—Handbooks, Manuals, etc. I. Title.
The hardcover edition is available from Chilton.

HERTZBERG, Robert Edward, 1905- 770.28
Photo darkroom guide, by Robert E. Hertzberg. 5th ed. Philadelphia, Chilton Book Co. [1967] 128 p. illus. 21 cm. [TR287.H4 1967] 67-25844
1. Photography—Processing—Handbooks, manuals, etc. I. Title.

MORGAN and Morgan, inc. 770.28
Pocket dark room data book. Hastings-on-Hudson, N.Y., Author [c.1966] 97p. 1v. (loose-leaf) forms. 18cm. [TR530.M62] 66-20078 3.95, loose-leaf ringbinder
I. Title. II. Title: Dark room data book.

Photography—Programmed instruction.

ROSEN, Marvin J. 770'.7'7
Introduction to photography : a self-directing approach / Marvin J. Rosen. Boston : Houghton Mifflin, c1976. xii, 322 p., [2] leaves of plates : ill. (some col.) ; 28 cm. Includes bibliographies and index. [TR146.R85] 75-31013 ISBN 0-395-20471-2 pbk. : 9.95
1. Photography—Programmed instruction. I. Title.

Photography—Reproduction of plans, drawings, etc.

INTERNATIONAL Association of Blue Print and Allied Industries. 778.1
Facilities survey of the blueprint, photocopy, and allied industries. [Chicago? 1951] 65 p. 28 cm. [TR900.I 5] 51-37827
1. Photography—Reproduction of plans, drawings, etc. 2. Blueprinting. I. Title.

LIETZE, Ernst. 686.4'2
Modern heliographic processes. Rochester, N.Y., Visual Studies Workshop, 1974 [c1888] viii, 143 p. illus. 26 cm. (The Visual Studies Workshop reprint series) Reprint of the ed. published by Van Nostrand, New York. [TR920.L53 1974] 73-22265 ISBN 0-87992-001-7 12.50
1. Photography—Reproduction of plans, drawings, etc. 2. Photography—Printing processes. I. Title.
Pbk., 7.95, ISBN 0-87992-000-9. BIP

Photography—Research.

MEES, Charles Edward Kenneth, 1882-1960. 770.72
From dry plates to ektachrome film; a story of photographic research. New York, Ziff-Davis Pub. Co., 1961. 312p. illus. 24cm. [TR15.M37] 61-2570
1. Photography—Research. I. Title.

Photography—Retouching.

ANTHONY, Anne J. 770.2838
Negative and print retouching for amateur and professional. Illus. by the author. New York, Greenberg [1950] 138 p. illus. 28 cm. [TR310.A36] 50-9677
1. Photography—Retouching.

CROY, Otto R., 1902- 770.283
Retouching: corrective techniques in photography [by] O. R. Croy. 5th impression. London, New York, Focal, 1967. 188p. illus. 22cm. (Manual of phototechnique) [TR310.C69 1967] 68-93605 9.95
1. Photography—Retouching. I. Title. II. Series: The Manuals of photo-technique
Distributed by Amphoto, New York. BIP

DRAPER, Ernest E 770.2838
Negative retouching and print finishing by Ernest E. Draper and Norris Harkness. Photographic illus. by Stephen Deutch. Rev. ed. New York, Crown Publishers [1954] 111p. illus. 18cm. (Little technical library, 29) [TR310.D7 1954] 54-6545
1. Photography—Retouching. I. Harkness, Norris, joint author. II. Title.

KING, Walter S. 770.2843
The airbrush technique of photographic retouching [by] Walter S. King and Alfred L. Slade. New York, Macmillan [1954] 115 p. illus. 29 cm. [TR310.K5] 54-1265
1. Photography—Retouching. I. Slade, Alfred L., joint author. II. Title.

LAHUE, Kalton C. 770'.28
Photo retouching and restoration / by Kalton C. Lahue. Los Angeles : Petersen Pub. Co., c1979. 80 p. : ill. ; 28 cm. (Petersen's how-to-photographic library) [TR310.L33] 78-78395 ISBN 0-8227-4034-6 pbk. : 5.50
1. Photography—Retouching. I. Title. BIP

OURDAN, J. P. 770'.284
The Art of Retouching, by Burrows and Colton [rev. by] J. P. Ourdan. New York, Arno Press, 1973. 108 p. illus. 23 cm. (Literature of Photography) Reprint of the 1880 ed. Originally published under title: Concise instructions in the art of retouching. [TR310.093 1973] 72-9187 ISBN 0-405-04898-X. 9.00
1. Photography—Retouching. I. Burrows and Colton, London. II. Title. III. Series.

SHAFRAN, Alexander. 770.284
Airbrush photo retouching manual; the techniques of airbrush retouching positive prints and negatives. New York, American Photographic Book Pub. Co. [1968] 174 p. illus. (part col.) 24 cm. [TR310.S47] 68-12001
1. Photography—Retouching. 2. Airbrush art. I. Title.

WEST, Kitty. 770.2838
Guide to retouching negatives and prints. New York, Greenberg [1955] 121p. illus. 20cm. (The Modern camera guide series) [TR310.W44] 55-9431
1. Photography—Retouching. I. Title. II. Title: Retouching negatives and prints. BIP

WEST, Kitty. 770'.283
Guide to retouching negatives and prints. 3d ed. New York, AMPHOTO [1972] 121 p. illus. 20 cm. (Amphoto guide books, 271) [TR310.W44 1972] 70-189391 ISBN 0-8174-0271-3 Pap. 2.50
1. Photography—Retouching. I. Title. II. Title: Retouching negatives and prints.

WEST, Kitty. 770.284
Modern retouching manual. Philadelphia, Chilton Book Co. [1967] 191 p. illus. (part col.) 24 cm. [TR310.W45] 67-21700
1. Photography—Retouching. I. Title.

WEST, Kitty. 770'.284
Modern retouching manual. 2d ed. Garden City, N.Y., Amphoto [1973] 191 p. illus. 24 cm. [TR310.W45 1973] 72-75556 ISBN 0-8174-0508-9 8.95
1. Photography—Retouching. I. Title.

WEST, Kitty. 770.284
Modern retouching manual. New York, Amer. Photographic Book. Co. [1967] 191p. illus. (pt. col.) 24cm. [TR310.W45 1967b] 68-256 7.95
1. Photography—Retouching. I. Title.
Available from Chilton, Philadelphia. BIP

Photography—Scientific applications.

ARNOLD, Christopher R. 778.3
Applied photography [by] C. R. Arnold, P. J. Rolls [and] J. C. J. Stewart; edited by D. A. Spencer. London, New York, Focal Press, 1971. 510, [24] p. illus. 25 cm. (The Focal Library) Includes bibliographies. [TR692.A75] 72-193450 ISBN 0-240-50723-1 £8.50
1. Photography—Scientific applications. I. Rolls, Peter J., joint author. II. Stewart, James C. J., joint author. III. Title. BIP

Photography—Societies, etc.

PHOTOGRAPHERS' Association 016.77 of America.
Directory of professional photography. [Milwaukee] v. 28cm. [TR1.P714] 54-34485
1. Photography—Societies, etc. I. Title.

Photography—Special effects.

AMPHOTO, New York. 770'.28
Photographic tricks simplified; a modern photoguide, by the Amphoto editorial board. Englewood Cliffs, N.J., Prentice-Hall [1974] 96 p. illus. (part col.) 26 cm. (A Spectrum book, S-PG-4) [TR148.A56 1974] 73-92424 ISBN 0-13-665562-9 7.95
1. Photography—Special effects. 2. Photography, Trick. I. Title.
Pbk. 2.95, ISBN 0-13-665554-8. BIP

BIGGS, Ken. 770'.28
Special effects / Ken Biggs. Los Angeles : Petersen Pub. Co., [1974] 80 p. : ill. (some col.) ; 28 cm. (Petersen's how-to photographic library) [TR148.B57] 74-14433 ISBN 0-8227-0084-0 pbk. : 2.95
1. Photography—Special effects. I. Title. BIP

BOYD, Harry. 770'.28
A creative approach to controlling photography / by Harry Boyd, Jr. Austin, Tex. : Heidelberg Publishers, 1974. xiv, 289 p. : ill. (some col.) ; 24 cm. Includes index. [TR148.B65] 73-92364 ISBN 0-913206-02-4 : 12.95
1. Photography—Special effects. I. Title. BIP

CROY, Otto R., 1902- 778.8
Graphic effects by photography [by] Croy; translated [from the German] by F. Bradley. London, New York, Focal Press, 1973. 199 p. illus. (some col.) 22 cm. Translation of Photos helfen zeichnen. Includes index. [TR148.C7613 1973b] 73-178566 ISBN 0-240-50832-7
1. Photography—Special effects. 2. Photography, Advertising. I. Title.
Distributed by Hastings House, 11.95. BIP

EASTMAN Kodak Company. 770'.28
Creative darkroom techniques. [1st ed. Rochester, N.Y., Consumer Markets Division, 1973] 292 p. illus. (part col.) 23 cm. (Kodak publication no. AG-18) [TR148.E18 1973] 73-87110 ISBN 0-87985-075-2 6.95; 2.95 (pbk.)
1. Photography—Special effects. 2. Photography—Processing. I. Title.

FEININGER, Andreas, 1906- 778.8
Andreas Feininger : experimental work / Andreas Feininger. Garden City, N.Y. : Amphoto, c1978. 144 p. : chiefly ill. ; 29 cm. [TR148.F38] 78-5167 ISBN 0-8174-2441-5 : 14.95. ISBN 0-8174-2116-5 pbk. : 9.95
1. Photography—Special effects. I. Title: Experimental work.

†FROBISCH, Dieter. 770'.28
Graphic photo design / Dieter Frobisch, Hartmut Lamprecht. Garden City, N.Y. : American Photographic Book Pub. Co., c1977 v. : ill. (some col.) ; 21 cm. Translation of Photo-Design. Contents.Contents.—[1] Lab techniques in color and black & white. [TR148.F7613] 77-81319 ISBN 0-8174-2434-2 : 14.95
1. Photography—Special effects. 2. Photography—Processing. I. Lamprecht, Hartmut, joint author. II. Title. BIP

LITZEL, Otto. 770'.28
Darkroom magic / by Otto Litzel. Rev. ed. Garden City, N.Y. : Amphoto, [1975] 160 p. : ill. ; 26 cm. [TR148.L5 1975] 75-303113 ISBN 0-8174-0509-7 : 9.95
1. Photography—Special effects. 2. Photography—Processing. I. Title.

LUNDQVIST, Par, 1937- 770'.28
Photographics; line and contrast methods. [Translated by Eric de Mare] New York, Van Nostrand Reinhold Co. [1972] 127 p. illus. 20 x 24 cm. Translation of Fotografik. [TR148.L813] 79-165926 9.95
1. Photography—Special effects. I. Title.

ROUTH, Robert D. 770
Photographics / by Robert D. Routh. Los Angeles : Petersen Pub. Co., c1976. 80 p. : ill. ; (some col.) ; 28 cm. (Petersen's how-to photographic library) [TR148.R68] 76-15436 ISBN 0-8227-4001-X pbk. : 3.95 3.95 ($4.50 Can)
1. Photography—Special effects. I. Title. BIP

RUGGLES, Joanne. 770'.28
Darkroom graphics : creative techniques for photographers and artists / Joanne & Philip Ruggles. Garden City, N.Y. : Amphoto, c1975. 160 p., [8] leaves of plates : ill. (some col.) ; 27 cm. Includes index. [TR148.R83] 76-350099 ISBN 0-8174-0573-9 : 13.95
1. Photography—Special effects. 2. Photography—Processing. I. Ruggles, Philip, joint author. II. Title. BIP

SICILIA, Dominic. 778.8
Instant photo/instant art : the new simple technique that turns SX-70 Polaroid photos into beautiful frameable paintings / by Dominic Sicilia. Los Angeles : Price/Stern/Sloan Publishers, c1977. 95 p. : ill. (some col.) ; 22 cm. [TR148.S53] 77-7120 ISBN 0-8431-0423-6 pbk. : 5.95
1. Photography—Special effects. 2. Polaroid Land camera. I. Title. BIP

STEVENS, Gloria. 778.8
The metaphorical eye : special effects in photography / Gloria Stevens. Garden City, N.Y. : AMPHOTO, c1976. 160 p., [8] leaves of plates : ill. ; 29 cm. [TR148.S73] 75-39834 ISBN 0-8174-0599-2 : 15.95
1. Photography—Special effects. I. Title. BIP

WALKER, Sandy. 770'.28
Solarization [by] Sandy Walker [and] Clarence Rainwater. Garden City, N.Y., Amphoto [1974] 160 p. illus. (part col.) 26 cm. Bibliography: p. 157-160. [TR148.W34] 73-91379 ISBN 0-8174-0561-5 14.95
1. Photography—Special effects. I. Rainwater, Clarence, 1920- joint author. II. Title. BIP

ZUCKERMAN, Jim. 778.8
Image magic / by Jim Zuckerman. Los Angeles : Petersen Pub. Co., c1978. 80 p. : ill. (some col.) ; 28 cm. (Petersen's how-to photographic library) [TR148.Z8] 78-50984 ISBN 0-8227-4016-8 pbk. : 3.95
1. Photography—Special effects. I. Title. BIP

Photography, Stereoscopic.

CHANDLER, Arthur. 778.4
Stereo views / by Arthur Chandler and Wayne Pope. San Francisco : Troubador Press, 1978. p. cm. Discusses the development and uses of stereoscopy, commonly known as three-dimensional photography. Includes 34 examples of these photographs and a pair of viewing glasses. [TR780.C47] 78-11761 ISBN 0-912300-96-5 : 5.95
1. Photography, Stereoscopic. I. Pope, Wayne, 1932- joint author. II. Title.

DARRAH, William Culp, 778.4'09 1909-
The world of stereographs / William C. Darrah. Gettysburg, Pa : Darrah, 1977. 246 p. : ill. (some col.) ; 29 cm. Includes index. Bibliography: p. 238-242. [TR780.D35] 77-92123 ISBN 0-913116-04-1 : 22.50
1. Photography, Stereoscopic. I. Title. BIP

GOWLAND, Peter. 778.4
The art and technique of stereo photography. De luxe ed. General editor: Aaron Sussman. New York, Crown Publishers [1954] 128p. illus. 26cm. [TR780.G6] 54-11184
1. Photography, Stereoscopic. I. Title.

GOWLAND, Peter. 778.4
Stereo photography. New York, Crown Publishers [1954] 186p. illus. 18cm. (Little technical library, 45) [TR780.G63] 54-6642
1. Photography, Stereoscopic. I. Title.

JONES, John, 1926- 779'.9'7784
Wonders of the stereoscope / [by] John Jones. London : Cape, 1976. 126 p. : ill. (some col.) ; 27 cm. & stereoscope with cards (48 cards : some col.) in case. Bibliography: p. 125. [TR780.J66 1976b] 77-357951 ISBN 0-224-01344-0 : £12.50
1. Photography, Stereoscopic. I. Title. BIP

JONES, John, 1926- 778.4
Wonders of the stereoscope / John Jones. 1st American ed. New York : Knopf ; distributed by Random House, 1976. 126 p. : ill. (come col.) ; 26 cm. & stereoscope cards (48 cards : col. ; 9 x 18 cm.) with viewer in container (26 cm.) Bibliography: p. 125. [TR780.J66 1976] 76-19125 ISBN 0-394-40882-9 : 25.00
1. Photography, Stereoscopic. 2. Stereoscope. I. Title.

KAISER, Julius B. 778.4
Make your own stereo pictures. New York, Macmillan [1955] 344 p. illus. 22 cm. [TR780.K3] 55-1603
1. Photography, Stereoscopic. I. Title.

MCKAY, Herbert Couchman, 778.4 1895-
Three-dimensional photography; principles of stereoscopy. Minneapolis, American Photography, Book Dept. [1951] 334 p. illus. 24 cm. First published in 1948 under title: Principles of stereoscopy. [TR780.M3 1951] 52-8521
1. Photography, Stereoscopic. I. Title.

MCKAY, Herbert Couchman, 778.4 1895-
Three dimensional photography; principles of stereoscopy. New York, American Photography, Book Dept. [1953] 333 p. illus. 24 cm. First published in 1948 under title: Principles of stereoscopy. [TR780.M3 1953] 53-23904
1. Photography, Stereoscopic. I. Title.

MORGAN, Willard Detering, 778.4 1900-
Stereo realist manual [by] Willard D. Morgan [and] Henry M. Lester, and 14 contributors. [1st ed.] New York, Morgan & Lester [1954] 400p. illus. 23cm. Includes bibliography. [TR780.M6] 54-11905
1. Photography, Stereoscopic. I. Lester, Henry M. II. Title. BIP

MOSS, George H. 778.4
Double exposure; early stereographic views of historic Monmouth County, New Jersey, and their relationship to pioneer photography, by George H. Moss Jr. With a foreword by Carlin Gasteyer. Sea Bright, N.J., Ploughshare Press [1971] xv, 176 p. illus., facsims. 32 cm. Stereoscope in pocket. Bibliography: p. 176. [TR780.M64] 70-154560 ISBN 0-912396-00-8 12.95
1. Photography, Stereoscopic. I. Title.

OKOSHI, Takanori, 1932- 774
Three-dimensional imaging techniques / Takanori Okoshi. New York : Academic Press, 1976. p. cm. Includes bibliographies. [TR780.O38] 75-13106 ISBN 0-12-525250-1 : 15.00
1. Photography, Stereoscopic. 2. Moving-pictures, Three-dimensional. 3. Holography. I. Title.

TYDINGS, Kenneth S 778.4
The Revere 33 Stereo Camera guide. New York, Greenberg, c1953. 124p. illus. 20cm. (The Modern camera guide series) [TR780.T89] 53-12220
1. Photography, Stereoscopic. I. Title.

TYDINGS, Kenneth S 778.4
The Stereo-Realist guide; stereo made easy for everyone. New York, Greenberg, c1951. 127 p. illus. 20 cm. [TR780.T9] 52-892
1. Photography, Stereoscopic. 2. Color photography. 3. Cameras. I. Title.

Photography—Studios and darkrooms.

PRITCHARD, H. Baden, 770'.28 1841-1884.
The photographic studios of Europe, by H.

SUBJECT INDEX PHOTOGRAPHY, TRICK.

Baden Pritchard. New York, Arno Press, 1973. 279 p. illus. 22 cm. (The Literature of Photography) Reprint of the 1882 ed. [TR550.P74 1973] 72-9226 ISBN 0-405-04932-3. 15.00.
1. Photography—Studios and dark rooms. I. Title. II. Series. BIP

ROBINSON, Henry Peach, 1830-1901. 770'.28
The studio: and what to do with it. New York, Arno Press, 1973. viii, 143 p. illus. 23 cm. (The Literature of Photography) Reprint of the 1891 ed. [TR550.R6 1973] 72-9231 ISBN 0-405-04937-4 10.00.
1. Photography studios and dark rooms. 2. Photography portraits. I. Title. II. Series.

TIME-LIFE Books. 770.28
The studio, by the editors of Time-Life Books. New York [1971] 236 p. illus. (part col.) 27 x 27 cm (Life library of photography) Bibliography: p. 233. [TR550.T55] 70-154544
1. Photography—Studios and dark rooms. 2. Fashion photography. 3. Photography—Portraits. 4. Photography, Table-top. I. Title.

Photography—Studios and darkrooms.

CURTIN, Dennis. 771'.1
The darkroom handbook : a complete guide to the best design, construction, and equipment / Dennis Curtin, Joe DeMaio. New York : Van Nostrand Reinhold Co., [1979] p. cm. Includes index. [TR560.C87] 78-23911 ISBN 0-442-21808-7 : 16.95
1. Photography—Studios and darkrooms. I. DeMaio, Joe, joint author. II. Title. BIP

Photography — Study and teaching.

KAY, Alan. 770'.7
Creative art through photography. Newton Centre, Mass., C. T. Branford Co. [1973] 96 p. illus. 26 cm. Bibliography: p. 95. [TR161.K38] 72-8378 7.50
1. Photography—Study and teaching. I. Title. BIP

SWENSON, Theodore H 770
Industrial arts: photography, teachers guide. Prepared by Theodore H. Swenson. New Brunswick, N.J. Vocational Division, Curriculum Laboratory, 1961 [i.e. 1962] 89 p. illus. 28 cm. "Audio visual aids": p. 79-83. Bibliography: p. 84-87. [TR161.S9 1962] A63
1. Photography — Study and teaching. I. New Jersey. Division of Vocational Education. Curriculum Laboratory, New Brunswick. II. Title.

Photography—Study and teaching (Elementary)

CYR, Don. 770'.28
Teaching your children photography : a step-by-step guide / Don Cyr. Garden City, N.Y. : Amphoto, c1977. 128 p. : ill. ; 29 cm. [TR161.C95] 77-72291 ISBN 0-8174-0597-6 : 9.95. ISBN 0-8174-2416-4 pbk. : 5.95 pbk.
1. Photography—Study and teaching (Elementary) I. Title. BIP

Photography, Submarine.

CLARKE, Arthur Charles, 1917- 778.73
The reefs of Taprobane; underwater adventures around Ceylon. With color and black-and-white photos. by Mike Wilson. [1st ed.] New York, Harper [1957] 205p. illus. 25cm. [TR800.C55] 57-6136
1. Photography, Submarine. 2. Diving, Submarine. 3. Ceylon—Descr. & trav. I. Title.

CROSS, Ellis Royal, 1913- 778.73
Underwater photography and television; a handbook of equipment and techniques. With a foreword by Roger Revelle and a chapter on deep-sea photography by Robert S. Dietz. [1st ed.] New York, Exposition Press [c1954] 258 p. illus. 21 cm. Includes bibliography. [TR800.C7] 54-10335
1. Photography, Submarine. 2. Television. I. Title.

DOBBS, Horace. 778.73
Camera underwater ; a practical guide to underwater photography / Horace Dobbs. 2nd. New York : Focal Press, 1972. 187 p. : ill. 24 cm. 79-188316 ISBN 0-8174-0636-0
1. Photography, Submarine. I. Title.

DOBBS, Horace E 778.73
Camera underwater; a practical guide to underwater photography. London, New York, Focal Press [1962] 187 p. illus. 24 cm. [TR800.D6] 63-4871
1. Photography, Submarine. I. Title. BIP

FREY, Hank. 778.7'3
Camera below; the complete guide to the art and science of underwater photography, by Hank Frey and Paul Tzimoulis. With a foreword by Edward C. Stephan and drawings by Kathleen M. Frey. New York, Association Press [1968] 224 p. illus. 26 cm. Bibliography: p. 215-216. [TR800.F7] 68-17774 12.00
1. Photography, Submarine. I. Tzimoulis, Paul, joint author. II. Title.

HERSEY, John Brackett, 1913- 778.7'3
Deep-sea photography, edited by John Brackett Hersey. Baltimore, Johns Hopkins Press, 1967. 310 p. illus. (part col.), maps. 29 cm. (The Johns Hopkins oceanographic studies, no. 3) [GC60.H4] 66-16038
1. Photography, Submarine. 2. Photography in oceanography. I. Title. II. Series. BIP

KENDALL, Bob. 778.7'3
Photographs underwater / Bob Kendall. 1st ed. Laguna Beach, Calif. : ICER Press, 1976. 104 p. : ill. (some col.) ; 29 cm. Includes bibliographical references. [TR800.K44] 76-15705 ISBN 0-914704-02-8 : 24.50
1. Photography, Submarine. I. Title. BIP

MCNEIL, Gomer T. 778.7'3
Optical fundamentals of underwater photography [by] Gomer T. McNeil. Rockville, Md., Photogrammetry, 1968. v, 115 p. illus. 28 cm. Bibliography: p. 112-113. [TR800.M24] 72-2905
1. Photography, Submarine. I. Title.

MERTENS, Lawrence Edwin. 778.7'3
In-water photography; theory and practice [by] Lawrence E. Mertens. New York, Wiley-Interscience [1970] xiii, 391 p. illus. 26 cm. (Wiley series on photographic science and technology and the graphic arts) Includes bibliographies. [TR800.M47] 75-111355
1. Photography, Submarine. I. Title. BIP

REBIKOFF, Dimitri, 1921- 778.73
A guide to underwater photography, by Dimitri Rebikoff and Paul Cherney. [2d ed.] New York, Greenberg [c1955] 113p. illus. 20cm. (The Modern camera guide series) [TR800.R4 1955] 56-13068
1. Photography, Submarine. I. Cherney, Paul, joint author. II. Title. III. Title: Underwater photography.

REBIKOFF, Dimitri, 1921- 778.73
Underwater photography [by] Dimitri Rebikoff and Paul Cherney. Philadelphia, Chilton Books [1965] 126 p. illus., ports. 23 cm. [TR800.R45] 65-17114
1. Photography, Submarine. I. Cherney, Paul, joint author.

REBIKOFF, Dimitri, 1921- 778.73
Underwater photography [by] Dimitri Rebikoff and Paul Cherney. New York, American Photographic Book Pub. Co. [1965] 126 p. illus. 23 cm. [TR800.R45] 65-4932
1. Photography. Submarine. I. Cherney, Paul, joint author. II. Title.

REBIKOFF, Dimitri, 1921- 778.7'3
Underwater photography / by Dimitri Rebikoff and Paul Cherney. 2d ed. Garden City, N.Y. : Amphoto, [1975] 143 p., [4] leaves of plates : ill. (some col.) ; 24 cm. Includes index. [TR800.R45 1975] 74-83492 ISBN 0-8174-0490-2 : 8.95
1. Photography, Submarine. I. Cherney, Paul, joint author. II. Title.

SCHENCK, Hilbert Van Nydeck, 1926- 778.73
Underwater photography, by Hilbert Schenck, Jr., and Henry Kendall. Cambridge, Md., Cornell Maritime Press, 1954. 110p. illus. 22cm. Includes bibliography. [TP800.S3] 53-9688
1. Photography, Submarine. I. Kendall, Henry Way, 1926- joint author. II. Title.

SCHENCK, Hilbert Van Nydeck, 1926- 778.73
Underwater photography, by Hilbert Schenck, Jr. and Henry W. Kendall. Illus. by John E. Johnson. Cambridge, Md., Cornell Maritime Press, 1957. 126p. illus. 23cm. [TR800.S3 1957] 57-11358
1. Photography, Submarine. I. Kendall, Henry Way, 1926- joint author. II. Title.

SCHULKE, Flip. 778.7'3
Underwater photography for everyone / Filp Schulke. Englewood Cliffs, N.J. : Prentice-Hall, c1978. xv, 220 p., [16] leaves of plates : ill. ; 24 cm. Includes index. Bibliography: p. 216. [TR800.S34] 78-9820 ISBN 0-13-936450-1 : 14.95
1. Photography, Submarine. I. Title. BIP

STARCK, Walter A. 778.73
The art of underwater photography, by Walter A. Starck II and Paul Brundza. New York, Amphoto [1966] 160 p. illus. (part col.) 24 cm. Bibliography: p. 159-160. [TR800.S7 1966a] 67-95
1. Photography, Submarine. I. Brundza, Paul, joint author. II. Title. BIP

STARCK, Walter A. 778.73
The art of underwater photography, by Walter A. Starck II and Paul Brundza. Philadelphia, Chilton Books [1966] 160 p. illus. (part col.) 24 cm. Bibliography: p. 159-160. [TR800.S7] 66-23325
1. Photography, Submarine. I. Brundza, Paul, joint author. II. Title.

STRYKOWSKI, Joe. 778.7'3
Divers and cameras : a complete textbook for students, instructors, and advanced underwater photographers / by Joe Strykowski ; ill. by Ernie Duerksen. Northfield, Ill. : Dacor Corp., [1974] iv, 212 p. : ill. ; 24 cm. Includes index. Bibliography: p. 206. [TR800.S77] 73-93201
1. Photography, Submarine. I. Title.

TOWNSEND, Derek 778.73
Underwater photography: movies and still. London, S. Paul [dist. New Rochelle, N.Y., SportShelf, 1965, c.1964] 160p. illus. 21cm. [TR800.T6] 65-2937 5.75 bds.,
1. Photography, Submarine. I. Title.

WALLIN, Doug. 778.7'3
Basics of underwater photography / Doug Wallin. Garden City, N.Y. : Amphoto, c1975. 128 p., [4] leaves of plates : ill. (some col.) ; 26 cm. Includes index. [TR800.W34] 74-79949 ISBN 0-8174-0578-X : 5.95
1. Photography, Submarine. I. Title. BIP

Photography, Submarine—Congresses.

UNDERWATER photo-optical instrumentation applications. 778.7'3 [Redondo Beach, Calif., Society of Photo-optical Instrumentation Engineers, 1968] ix, 194 p. illus., ports. 28 cm. (S.P.I.E. seminar proceedings, v. 12) Seminar-in-depth, San Diego, Calif., Feb. 5-6, 1968; co-sponsored by S.P.I.E. and Dept. of the Navy, Naval Undersea Warfare Center. Includes bibliographies. [TR800.U52] 76-8086
1. Photography, Submarine—Congresses. 2. Underwater exploration—Congresses. I. Society of Photo-optical Instrumentation Engineers. II. Naval Undersea Warfare Center, Pasadena, Calif. III. Series: Society of Photo-optical Instrumentation Engineers. S.P.I.E. seminar proceedings, v. 12 BIP

Photography, Submarine—Handbooks, manuals, etc.

GLOVER, T. 778.7'3
A manual of underwater photography / T. Glover, G. E. Harwood, J. N. Lythgoe. London ; New York : Academic Press, 1977. xiii, 219 p. : ill. ; 24 cm. Includes index. Bibliography: p. 202-203. [TR800.G56] 76-16967 ISBN 0-12-286750-5 : 18.75
1. Photography, Submarine—Handbooks, manuals, etc. I. Harwood, G. E., joint author. II. Lythgoe, J. N., joint author. III. Title.

Photography, Submarine—Juvenile literature.

ROBERTS, Howard R. 778.7'3
The beginner's guide to underwater photography / Howard R. Roberts. New York : D. McKay Co., c1978. 150 p. : ill. ; 24 cm. Includes index. Bibliography: p. 141. An introduction to underwater photographic equipment and techniques with a discussion of past, present, and future developments in the field. [TR800.R58] 77-14917 ISBN 0-679-20450-4 : 7.95
1. Photography, Submarine—Juvenile literature. I. Title. BIP

Photography, Submarine — Societies, etc.

UNDERWATER Photographic Society. 778.73
Journal. [Los Angeles] v. illus. (part col.) 28 cm. annual. [TR800.U5] 67-42331
1. Photography, Submarine — Societies, etc. I. Title.

Photography, Table-top.

BOMBACK, Edward S. 778.8
Table-tops and titles in colour. London, Fountain Pr. [dist. New York, Morgan & Morgan, 1964, c.1962] 94p. illus. (pt. col.) diagrs. 17cm. (Fountai ISSN photobk. ser.)) 64-3079 2.95 bds.,
1. Photography, Table-top. 2. Moving-pictures—Tilling. 3. Color photography. I. Title.

HEIMANN, Ernest. 778.8
Creative table-top photography. Foreword by Percy W. Harris. [2d ed.] London, Fountain Press; Philadelphia, Rayelle Publications [1957] 143p. illus. 23cm. [A Fountain photobook] [TR650.H433 1957] 58-34958
1. Photography, Table-top. I. Title.

WENDELL, Lehman 778.8
Camera phantasies. [Cranbury, N.J.] A. S. Barnes [c.1966] 115p. illus. 26cm. [TR650.W36] 66-13344 5.95
1. Photography, Table-top. I. Title.

Photography—Technique.

ROSENBLUM, Barbara. 770'.1
Photographers at work : a sociology of photographic styles / by Barbara Rosenblum. New York : Holmes & Meier, 1978. p. cm. Includes index. Bibliography: p. [TR183.R67] 78-8986 ISBN 0-8419-0402-2 : 25.00
1. Photography—Technique. 2. Photography, Journalistic. 3. Photography, Advertising. 4. Photography, Artistic. I. Title. BIP

Photography—The West—History.

CURRENT, Karen. 779'.9'978
Photographers of the Old West / text by Karen Current ; photos. selected and printed by William R. Current. New York : H. N. Abrams, [1978] p. cm. Bibliography: p. [TR23.6.C87] 77-27857 ISBN 0-8109-1412-3 : 19.95
1. Photography—The West—History. 2. Photographers—The West—Biography. I. Current, William. II. Title.

Photography, Time-lapse.

OTT, John Nash, 1909- 778.5
My ivory cellar; [the story of time-lapse photography] Chicago, Twentieth Century Press [1958] 157 p. illus. 24 cm. [TR857.O8] 58-59587
1. Photography, Time-lapse. I. Title. BIP

Photography, Trick.

DUCKWORTH, Paul. 778.8
Creative photographic effects simplified / by Paul Duckworth. Garden City, N.Y. : Amphoto, 1975. 95 p., [2] leaves of plates : chiefly ill. (some col.) ; 26 cm. (A modern photoguide) [TR148.D78] 75-1968 ISBN 0-8174-0188-1 pbk. : 3.45
1. Photography, Trick. 2. Photography—Special effects. I. Title. BIP

DUCKWORTH, Paul 778.8161-u425o
Experimental and trick photography. New York, Universal Photo Bks. [dist. Amphoto, c.1961] 127p. illus. 1.95 pap.,
1. Photography, Trick. I. Title.

DUCKWORTH, Paul. 778.8
Experimental and trick photography. [2d ed.] New York, American Photographic Book Pub. Co. [1967] 127 p. illus. 20 cm. [TR148.D8 1967] 67-9247
1. Photography, Trick. I. Title.

FELLIG, Arthur, 1900- 778.8
Weegee's creative camera, by Weegee [pseud.] with Roy Ald. Garden City, N.Y., Hanover House, 1959. 128 p. illus. 27 cm. [TR148.F4] 59-6262
1. Photography, Trick. I. Title.

LITZEL, Otto. 770.283
Darkroom magic. Philadelphia, Chilton Books [1967] 143 p. illus. 25 cm. [TR148.L5] 67-12529
1. Photography, Trick. I. Title. BIP

MOSER, Lida. 778.8
Fun in photography; special effects and tricks. Garden City, N.Y., Amphoto [1974] 160 p. illus. 24 cm. [TR148.M67] 73-82107 ISBN 0-8174-0564-X 8.95
1. Photography, Trick. 2. Photography—Special effects. I. Title. BIP

PETZOLD, Paul. 778.8
Effects and experiments in photography. London, New York, Focal Press, 1973. 160 p. illus. (some col.). 19 x 23 cm. Includes index. [TR148.P47] 73-167855 ISBN 0-240-50763-0 £2.50
1. Photography, Trick. 2. Photography—Special effects. I. Title. BIP

RICKARDS, Maurice 778.8
Off-beat photography. New York, Amphoto [Amer. Photographic Bk. Pub. Co., 1960] 35p. illuw. 21cm. 60-50219 2.50 bds.,
1. Photography, Trick. I. Title.

SPITZING, Gunter. 778.8
The photoguide to effects and tricks. [Translated by Fred Bradley] Garden City, N.Y., Amphoto [1974] 174 p. illus. (part col.) 19 cm. Translation of Das verruckte Fotobuch. [TR148.S6513] 73-89735 ISBN 0-8174-0769-3 5.95
1. Photography, Trick. 2. Photography—Special effects. I. Title.

WOODBURY, Walter E. 778.8
Photographic amusements, including tricks and unusual or novel effects obtainable with the camera, by Frank R. Fraprie and Walter E. Woodbury. New York, Arno Press, 1973. viii, 271 p. illus. 24 cm. (The Literature of Photography) Reprint of the 10th ed., rev. and enl., published in 1931. Editions of 1896-1922, by W. E. Woodbury. [TR148.W6 1973] 72-9199 ISBN 0-405-04908-0. 18.00.
1. Photography, Trick. I. Fraprie, Frank Roy, 1874- II. Title. III. Series. BIP

Photography, Trick—Juvenile literature.

WEBSTER, David, 1930- 778.8
Photo fun: an idea book for shutterbugs. Illustrated with photos. and diagrs. by David Webster. New York, Watts, 1973. 88 p. illus. 26 cm. Explains the use of special techniques and effects in producing unusual photographs. [TR148.W4] 72-8112 ISBN 0-531-02620-5 4.95
1. Photography, Trick—Juvenile literature. I. Title.

Photography—United States—Finance.

MOSER, Lida. 338.4'7'770973
Grants in photography : how to get them / Lida Moser. Garden City, N.Y. : Amphoto, c1978. p. cm. Includes index. [TR147.M67] 78-13364 ISBN 0-8174-2445-8 : 12.50
1. Photography—United States—Finance. 2. Photography—Research grants—United States. I. Title. BIP

Photography—United States—History.

WELLING, William B. 770'.973
Photography in America : the formative years, 1839-1900 / William Welling. New York : Crowell, [1977] p. cm. Includes index. Bibliography: p. [TR23.W44] 77-1983 ISBN 0-690-01451-1 : 29.95
1. Photography—United States—History. I. Title. BIP

Photography—United States—History—Juvenile literature.

SANDLER, Martin W. 770'.973
The story of American photography : an illustrated history for young people / by Martin W. Sandler. 1st ed. Boston : Little, Brown, c1978. p. cm. Includes index. Bibliography: p. Traces the development of photography in the United States. Illustrated with over 200 photographs. [TR23.S34] 78-24025 ISBN 0-316-77021-3 : 15.00
1. Photography—United States—History—Juvenile literature. I. Title. BIP

Photography—Yearbooks.

AMERICAN Society of Magazine Photographers. 779.058
ASMP picture annual. [New York] Simon and Schuster. 1957- v. illus., ports. 29 cm. Cover title, 1957- : Picture. [TR1.A6] 57-12784
1. Photography—Yearbooks. 2. Photography, Artistic. I. Title.

BEST photography. 779.21
[Los Angeles, Trend Books] v. illus. 24cm. annual. (Trend book) [TR1.B47] 59-47581
1. Photography— Yearbooks. 2. Photography of the nude. 3. Photography, Artistic. I. Trend Books, inc., Los Angeles.

GERMAN photographic annual (The). 778'.058
Das deutsches Lichtbild. 1968. New York, Hastings. v. illus. (pt. col.) 29 cm. Tr. from the German by Wolf Strache [TR1.G4] 56-4838 11.50
1. Photography—Yearbooks. 2. Photography, Artistic—Yearbooks.

GERMAN Photographic annual (The) 1962. 778.058
Eds.: Wolf Strache, Otto Steinert [Tr. from German by Jane K. Bunjes, Werner E. Bunjes] New York, Hastings, [1962, c.1961] 204p. illus. (pt. col.) 29cm. 56-4838 10.00
1. Photography—Yearbooks. 2. Photography, Artistic.

GERMAN photographic annual (The) 1966. 778.058
Das deutsche Lichtbild. Eds.: Wolf Strache, Otto Steinert. New York, Hastings [1966, c.1965] 215p. (chiefly plates, pt. col.) 29cm. [TR1.G4] 56-4838 11.50
1. Photography—Yearbooks. 2. Photography, Artistic. I. Strache, Wolf, ed. II. Steinert, Otto, joint ed.

INTERNATIONAL photography year book 1962. 779.058
ed. by Norman Hall. New York. St. Martin's [c.]1961[ ] 204p. illus. 28cm. Title varies. 36-13575 6.95
1. Photography—Yearbooks.

INTERNATIONAL photography year book, 1963. 779.058
ed. by Norman Hall. New York, St. Martin's [c.]1962. unpaged. chiefly illus. 28cm. Title varies. 36-13575 7.95
1. Photography—Yearbooks.

INTERNATIONAL photography year book. 1935- 779.058
New York [etc.] St. Martin's Press [etc.] v. illus. 28-31cm. Title varies: 1935-55, Photography year book. [TR1.P882] 36-13575
1. Photography—Yearbooks.

INTERNATIONAL photography year book 1961. 779.058
Edited by Norman Hall. New York, St. Martin's Press, 1960[ ] 216p. (mostly plates; part col., 1 fold-out) 28cm. Began publication with 1935/36 issue. Title varies: 1935-1955, Photography year book. 36-13575 6.95
1. Photography—Yearbooks.

INTERNATIONAL photography year book. 1968. 779.058
New York, A. S. Barnes [1968] v. illus. 28cm. London ed. has title: Photography year book. [TR1.P882] 36-13575 9.95
1. Photography—Yearbooks.
Earlier editions were published by St. Martin's Pr.

MALONEY, Thomas James, 1904- ed. 770.58
U.S. camera international pictures. (New York] 1964 [TR1.U53] 64-4075
1. Photography — Yearbooks. I. Title.

NATIONAL Fire Protection Association. 779.961484
Photo contest fire photographs. 1951- [Boston] v. illus. 24 cm. [TR1.N275] 52-43421
1. Photography — Yearbooks. 2. Photography — Competitions. 3. Fires. I. Title.

PHOTOGRAPHY annual, 770.58
1961: a selection of the world's finest photographs compiled by the Editors of Popular Photography. New York, Ziff-Davis Pub. Co. [c. 1960] (1961 edition) 224p. (mostly plates, part col.) 30cm. (Vol. 1, 1951-) 51-7159 2.95bds.,
1. Photography—Yearbooks. 2. Photographs. 3. Photography, Artistic. I. Popular photography (Chicago)

PHOTOGRAPHY year. 770'.15
Alexandria, Va. : Time-Life Books.
The 1977 ed. by the editors of Time-Life Books is available for 11.95. L.C. card no.:76-57807.

**PHOTOGRAPHY year,* 770.1'5
by the editors of Time-Life Books. 1974 ed. New York, Time-Life Books [1974] 236 p. illus. 26 cm. [TR9] 72-91518 11.95
1. Photography—Yearbooks. I. Time-Life Books.

POPULAR Photography (Chicago) 770.58
Photography annual; a selection of the world's greatest photographs. 1951- [Chicago, Ziff-Davis] v. illus. (part col.) 29 cm. Compiled by the editors of Popular photography. [TR1.P8813] 51-7159
1. Photography — Yearbooks. 2. Photographs. 3. Photography, Artistic. I. Title.

ROLLEI Jahrbuch der Rollei-Photographie. 770.58
Annual of Rolleiphotography. 1.-1951- Wien, New York, R. H. Hammer. v. illus. 26cm. [TR1.R64] 53-29757
1. Photography—Yearbooks. 2. Photography, Artistic. 3. Bolletflex camera. I. Title.

35 mm photography. 770.58
1959- [New York, Ziff-Davis Pub. Co.] v. illus (part col.) 29 cm. (Popular photography workshop annual) [TR1.T48] 59-3623
1. Photography — Yearbooks. 2. Miniature cameras — Yearbooks.

TIME-LIFE Books. 770'.5
Photography year / by the editors of Time-life Books. 1978 ed. Alexandria, Va. : Time-Life Books, [1978] p. cm. Includes index. Bibliography: p. [TR1.T55 1978] 78-2298 ISBN 0-8094-1667-0 : 12.95
1. Photography—Yearbooks. I. Title. BIP

U. S. Camera 1961. 770.58
The picture universe; 25th anniversary [ed.] Edited by Tom Maloney. Associate editors: Mary P. R. Thomas [and] Jack L. Terracciano. [dist. New York, Holt, Rinehart and Winston c. 1960] 306p. illus. (part col.), ports. 29 cm. annual, Title varies. Editor: 1935- T. J. Maloney. 35-24291 10.00bds.,
1. Photography—Yearbooks. I. Maloney, Thomas James, ed. II. Title.

U. S. camera 62 770.58
Ed. by Tom Maloney. Associate Eds.: Mary P. R. Thomas. Jack L. Terracciano. [New York] Duell [c. 1961] 215p. 29m. illus. annual. Title varies. (U.S. camera bk.) 35-24291 10.00 bds.,
1. Photography—Yearbooks. I. Maloney, Thomas James, 1904- ed.

U. S. camera international annual. 1964. 770.58
Ed. by Tom Maloney. Assoc. eds., Mary P. R. Thomas, Jack L. Terracciano [New York] Duell [dist.] Meredith [c. 1963] 231p. illus. (pt. col.) 29cm. Title varies. 1964 ed.: U. S. camera annual. 35-24291 10.00
1. Photography—Yearbooks. I. Maloney, Thomas James, 1904- ed.

U. S. camera international annual, 1963. 770.58
Ed. by Tom Maloney. Assoc. eds., Mary P. R. Thomas, Jack L. Terracciano [New York] Duell [dist.] Meredith [c. 1962] 207p. illus. (pt. col.) 29cm. Title varies. 35-24291 4.95 bds.,
1. Photography—Yearbooks. I. Maloney, Thomas James, 1904- ed.

Photogravure.

CARTWRIGHT, Mills. 777.1
Rotogravure; a survey of European and American methods, by H. M. Cartwright and Robert MacKay. Lyndon, Ky., MacKay Pub. Co. [1956] 303p. illus. 29cm. [TR980.C32] [TR980.C32] 57- 57-13537
1. Photogravure. 2. Rotogravures. I. MacKay, Robert, joint author. II. Title.

DENISON, Herbert. 686.2'327
A treatise on photogravure. Rochester, N.Y. Visual Studies Workshop, 1974. 140 p. illus. 21 cm. (The Visual Studies Workshop reprint series) Reprint of the 1895 ed. published by Iliffe, London. [TR980.D4 1974] 73-22263 ISBN 0-87992-005-X 11.95
1. Photogravure. I. Title.
Pbk. 6.50; ISBN 0-87992-004-1 BIP

Photolithography.

COGOLI, John E. 686.2'325
Everything to know about photo offset, by John E. Cogoli. [Philadelphia, North American Pub. Co., 1973] xiii, 442 p. illus. 27 cm. Bibliography: p. 433-434. [TR940.C63] 73-15253 ISBN 0-912920-21-1
1. Photolithography. I. Title.

JORGENSEN, George W 655.32
The sensitivity of bichromated coatings used in lithography, by George W. Jorgensen and Michael H. Bruno. [1st ed.] New York, Lithographic Technical Foundation [1954] 199p. illus. 22cm. (([Lithographic Technical Foundation, inc.] Research bulletin no. 218) [NE2250.L75 no.218] 775.1 55-24455
1. Photolitography. 2. Photographic sensitometry. I. Title.

LATHAM, Charles W 655.32
Photo composing. [1st ed.] New York, Lithographic Technical Foundation [1953] 82p. illus. 22cm. ([Lithographic Technical Foundation, inc.] Foundation publications, no. 515) [TR940.L32] 775 54-26622
1. Photolithography. I. Title.

LATHAM, Charles W 655.325
Photo composing; with an introduction to punch & pin register systems, by Charles W. Latham. [1st ed.] Rev. and expanded by Jack W. White. Pittsburgh, Graphic Arts Technical Foundation [1964] vii, 236 p. illus. 22 cm. [TR940.L32 1964] 63-23276
1. Photolithography. I. White, Jack W., ed. II. Title.

LATIMER, Henry C 655.32
Survey of lithography. [1st ed.] New York, Lithographic Technical Foundation [1955, c1954] 99p. illus. 22cm. ([Lithographic Technical Foundation, inc.] Foundation publications, 407) 'A revision of the original text [by David J. MacDonald and George Hart] published in 1945.' Includes bibliography. [TR940.L3] 775 55-24324
1. Photolithography. I. MacDonald, David James, 1875- Survey of lithography. II. Title.

†PRUST, Z. A., 1924- 686.2'325
Photo-offset lithography / by Z. A. Prust. South Holland, Ill. : Goodheart-Willcox Co., c1977. 160 p. : ill. ; 27 cm. Includes index. [TR940.P77] 77-21607 ISBN 0-87006-240-9 : 7.68
1. Photolithography. I. Title. BIP

REED, Robert Findley, 1890- 655.325
Offset platemaking, deep-etch. [2d ed.] New York, Lithographic Technical Foundation [1959] 224p. illus. 22cm. [TR920.R4 1959] 59-15902
1. Photolithography. 2. Offset printing. 3. Lithography—Metal plate processes. I. Title.

REED, Robert Findley, 1890- 655.32
Offset platemaking, deep-etch. [1st ed.] New York, Lithographic Technical Foundation [1955] 223p. illus. 22cm. ([Lithographic Technical Foundation, inc.] Foundation publications. Skilled craft texts, 504) On spine: Deep-etch platemaking. 'A revision of the original text [Offset platemaking, deep-etch (gum) process, by Joseph W. Mazzaferri] published in 1945.' [TR920.R4] [TR920.R4] 775 56-19076 56-19076
1. Photolithography. 2. Offset printing. 3. Lithography—Metal plate processes. I. Mazzaferri, Joseph W. Offset platemaking, deep-etch (gum) process. II. Title. III. Title: Deep-etch platemaking.

SAYRE, Irene Harvey, 1905- 655.325
Photography and platemaking for photo-lithography. Rev. and enl. Chicago, Lithographic Textbook Pub. Co. [1959] 454p. illus. 24cm. [TR940.S3 1959] 59-33750
1. Photolithography. 2. Lithography—Metal plate processes. 3. Photography. I. Title.

SHAPIRO, Charles, 1907- comp. 686.2'315
The lithographers manual. 4th ed. Pittsburgh, Graphic Arts Technical Foundation [1970, c1968] 1 v. (various pagings) illus. (part col.) 29 cm. Bibliography: p. 18:1-18:6. [TR940.S47 1970] 68-57213
1. Photolithography. 2. Lithography. I. Title.

SHAPIRO, Charles, 1907- comp. 655.3'25
The lithographers manual. Pittsburgh, Graphic Arts Technical Foundation [1966] 1 v. (various pagings) illus. (part col.) 29 cm. "Walter Soderstrom commemorative edition." The 20th anniversary ed., 1958, was edited by Victor Strauss. Bibliography: p. 18: 1-18: 5. [TR940.S47] 64-15377
1. Photolithography. 2. Lithography. I. Soderstrom, Walter E., 1895- comp. The photo-lithographer's manual. II. Strauss, Victor, ed. The lithographers manual. III. Title.

STUART, Duncan R. 655.3'25
The mass production of unique items, by Duncan R. Stuart and Fred Eichenberger. [Raleigh, Design Research Laboratory of the School of Design, North Carolina State University, 1968] 52 p. illus. (part col.) 25 x 27 cm. Cover title. [TR940.S84] 68-65660
1. Photolithography. 2. Combinations. I. Eichenberger, Fred, joint author. II. Title.

TORY, Bruce E 655.32
Photolithography. Sydney, Associated General Publications; Chicago, Graphic Arts Monthly [1953] 243p. illus. 28cm. [TR940.T6] 775 54-1185
1. Pholtolithography I. Title.

WHITE, Jack W. 763.23
How to make and run better aluminum surface plates. Compiled from the research of Robert F. Reed [and others. 1st ed.] New York, Lithographic Technical Foundation [1957] 187 p. illus. 22 cm. "Based on LTF's Research bulletin no. 6, The albumin process of photolithography, by Robert F. Reed and Paul W. Dorst." [TR940.W4] 57-13100
1. Photolithography. 2. Lithography — Metal plate processes. 3. Albumin. I. Title.

WHITE, Jack W 655.32
How to make and run better zinc surface plates; compiled from the research of Robert F. Reed [and others. 1st ed.] New York, Lithographic Technical Foundation [1953] 184p. illus. 22cm. ([Lithographic Technical Foundation, inc.] Foundation publications, 805) [TR955.W5] 776.1 54-26621
1. Photoiithography, Hithography—Metal plate process I. Title.

Photolithography— Abstracts.

LITHOGRAPHIC Technical Foundation, inc, 655.31
Lithographic abstracts. New York. v. 22cm. [TR940.L46] 54-31385
1. Photolithography— Abstracts. I. Title.

Photolithography—Patents.

DE RENZO, D. J. 686.2315
Polymers in lithography, 1971 [by] D. J. De Renzo. Park Ridge, N.J., Noyes Data Corp. [1971] vii, 216 p. illus. 28 cm. [TR940.D47] 74-161879 ISBN 0-8155-0388-1 36.00
1. Photolithography—Patents. 2. Polymers and polymerization—Patents. I. Title.

Photomechanical processes

BEATTIE, Kenneth Wilfred. 655.3'2
How to publish and print photomechanically, by K. W. Beattie and Dorsey Biggs. Philadelphia, North American Pub. Co., 1967. 256 p. illus. (part col.), plans. 29 cm. Advertising matter interspersed. [TR925.B33] 67-26589
1. Photomechanical processes. I. Biggs, Dorsey, joint author. II. Title.

BIGGS, John R. 655.3
Illustration and reproduction. New York, Pellegrini & Cudahy, 1952. 240p. illus. (part col.) 25cm. [TR925.B] A53
1. Photomechanical processes. I. Title.

BURDEN, James Walter, 1940- 778
Graphic reproduction photography. New York, Hastings House, [1973] 448 p., illus., 24 cm. (Visual communication books) [TR925.B87 1973b] 72-1158 ISBN 0-8038-2651-6 19.50
1. Photomechanical processes. I. Title. BIP

CANNON, Rupert Vernon. 655.3
Graphic reproduction; copy preparation and processes [by] R. V. Cannon and F. G. Wallis. London, Vista Books [1963] 123 p. illus. (part col.) 21 cm. (Facts of print series) Includes bibliographies. [TR925.C3] 64-55739
1. Photomechanical processes 2. Illustration of books. I. Wallis, Frederick Gordon, joint author. II. Title.

CANNON, Rupert Vernon 655.32
Graphic reproduction; copy preparation and processes [by] R. V. Cannon, F. G. Wallis. London, Vista Books. [Chester Springs, Pa., Dufour,] 1966, c.1963] 123p. illus. (pt. col.) 21cm. (Facts of print ser.) Bibl. [TR925.C3] 64-55739 5.00 bds.,
1. Photomechanical processes. 2. Illustration of books. I. Wallis, Frederick Gordon, joint author. II. Title.

FOSSETT, R. O. 686.2'32
Screen printing photographic techniques, by R. O. Fossett. 2d ed. Cincinnati, Signs of the Times Pub. Co. [1973] viii, 165 p. illus. 22 cm. [TR925.F64 1973] 73-163813 ISBN 0-911380-30-2 8.50
1. Photomechanical processes. 2. Screen process printing. I. Title. BIP

LEVENSON, Harvey R. 686.2'2544
Art & copy preparation [by] Harvey R. Levenson. An introduction to phototypesetting [by] Frank S. Benevento, Daniel J. Makuta [and] Raymond H. Stachowiak. Pittsburgh, Typographic Council of Graphic Arts Technical Foundation [1974] 76 p. illus. 28 cm. [TR925.L48] 74-81523 ISBN 0-88362-006-5
1. Photomechanical processes. 2. Graphic arts. 3. Phototypesetting. I. Benevento, Frank S. An introduction to phototypesetting. 1974. II. Title.

MAYFIELD, Jeanne (Bourges) 655.32
New techniques in practical art for reproduction [featuring the Bourges process] New York, Repro Art Press [1951] 140 p. illus. 34 cm. [TR977.M35] 774.7 51-13121
1. Photomechanical processes. 2. Color photography. 3. Color-printing. I. Title.

MERTLE, Joseph Stephen, 1899- 655.32
Photomechanics and printing; practical information on platemaking and presswork by recognized procedures [by] J. S. Mertle [and] Gordon L. Monsen. Chicago, Mertle Pub. Co., 1957. 423p. illus. 19cm. [TR925.M4] 58-14600
1. Photomechanical processes. I. Monsen, Gordon L., joint author. II. Title.

Photomechanical processes—Congresses.

NEW photo-technology trends in the graphic arts; 686.2'32 1972 annual symposium, SPSE, October 25-27, 1972, Marriott Twin-Bridges Hotel, Washington, D.C. Washington, Society of Photographic Scientists & Engineers, [1972] 180 p. illus. 25 cm. Includes bibliographical references. [TR925.N48] 73-153873
1. Photomechanical processes—Congresses. 2. Phototypesetting—Congresses. I. Society of Photographic Scientists and Engineers.

Photomechanical processes—Yearbooks.

PENROSE annual (The) 655.32058
v.60. 1967. New York, Hastings, 1967. v. illus. (pt. col.) 30cm. annual (Visual communications bks.) Ed.: 1965- H. Spencer [TR925.P4] 47-34609 16.50
1. Photomechanical processes—Yearbooks. I. Spencer, Herbert, ed.

PENROSE annual (The); 655.32058
v.59, 1966 [Ed. by Herbert Spencer. New York, Hastings, c.1966] 1v. (various p.) illus. (pt. col.) diagrs. 30cm. Part of the illus. matter is col., pt. fold., & pt. mount. (Visual communications bks.) [TR925.P4] 47-34609 14.50
1. Photomechanical processes—Year-books. I. Spencer, Herbert, ed.

PENROSE annual (The); 655.32058
v.58, 1965 [Ed. by Herbert Spencer. New York, Hastings, c.1965] 1v. (various p.) illus. (pt. col.) plates (pt. col.) diagrs. 30cm. Part of the illus. matter is col., pt. fold., & pt. mount. (Visual communications bks.) [TR925.P4] 47-34609 14.00
1. Photomechanical processes.—Yearbooks. I. Spencer, Herbert, ed.

Photomicrography.

ALLEN, Roy Morris, 1882- 778.31
Photomicrography. 2d ed. Princeton, N. J., Van Nostrand [1958] 441 p. illus. 24 cm. [QH251.A4 1958] 58-14411
1. Photomicrography. 2. Microphotography.

DRABKIN, David Lion, 1899- 778.3'1
Fundamental structure : nature's architecture / by David L. Drabkin. Philadelphia : University of Pennsylvania Press, [1975] 30 p., [26] leaves of plates : ill. (some col.) ; 29 cm. Includes reproductions of photos. and color transparencies by the author comprising an exhibition held at the Philadelphia Art Alliance, Apr. 3-27, 1958. Includes bibliographical references. [QH251.D7] 74-19577 ISBN 0-8122-7685-X : 25.00
1. Photomicrography. 2. Crystallization. 3. Hemoglobin—Pictorial works. I. Title. BIP

LAWSON, Douglas F. 778.3'1
Photomicrography [by] Douglas Lawson. London, New York, Academic Press, [1973, c1972] xiii, 494 p. illus. 24 cm. [QH251.L32] 71-185209 ISBN 0-12-439750-6 21.50
1. Photomicrography. BIP

LAWSON, Douglas F. 778.315
The technique of photomicrography. New York, Macmillan [c.]1960, [i.e. 1961] 256p. illus. (part col.) Bibl. 60-11652 12.75
1. Photomicrography. I. Title.

LOVELAND, Roger Platt. 778.3'11
Photomicrography; a comprehensive treatise [by] Roger P. Loveland. New York, Wiley [1970] 2 v. (x, 1039, I-xii p.) illus. 23 cm. (Wiley series on photographic science and technology and the graphic arts) Includes bibliographies. [QH251.L68] 70-88315 ISBN 0-471-54830-8
1. Photomicrography. BIP

THE Microscope as a camera. 778.3'1 Edited by H. A. Traber. New York, Amphoto [1971] 199 p. illus. (part col.) 23 cm. [QH251.M525] 73-117057 13.95
1. Photomicrography. I. Traber, Hans Arnold, 1921- ed.

WALKER, Michael Ivan. 778.3'1
Amateur photomicrography [by] M. I. Walker. London, New York, Focal Press, 1971. 189 p. illus. 23 cm. "Distributed in the U.S.A. by Chilton Book Company, Philadelphia." Bibliography: p. [177]-178. [QH251.W2] 71-178249 ISBN 0-8019-5699-4 13.95 (U.S.)
1. Photomicrography. I. Title. BIP

Photomicrography—Atlases.

WOLBERG, Lewis Robert, 1905- 779'.3'0924
Art forms from photomicrography / Lewis R. Wolberg. New York : Dover Publications, 1974. viii, 94 p. : chiefly ill. (some col.) ; 27 cm. (Dover pictorial archive series) [QH251.W586] 74-76837 ISBN 0-486-20298-4 pbk. : 4.00
1. Photomicrography—Atlases. 2. Art from photography. I. Title. BIP

Phototypesetting.

AUERBACH Publishers. 686.2'2544
Auerbach on automatic photocomposition. Princeton [1972] 128 p. illus. 26 cm. (Its Auerbach on series) "An expansion of material from Auerbach graphic processing reports." [TR1010.A8 1972] 76-171091 ISBN 0-87769-107-X
1. Phototypesetting. I. Title. II. Title: Automatic photocomposition.

BRUYNINCKX, Jozef. 655.3'2
Phototypography and graphic arts dimension control photography. [Los Angeles, Ad Compositors, c1969] 155 p. illus. 23 cm. [TR1010.B78] 74-115394
1. Phototypesetting. I. Title. BIP

CRAIG, James, 1930- 686.2'25
Phototypesetting : a design manual / by James Craig ; edited by Margit Malmstrom. New York : Watson-Guptill Publications, [1978] p. cm. Includes index. Bibliography: p. [TR1010.C73] 78-12276 ISBN 0-8230-4011-9 : 22.50
1. Phototypesetting. I. Malmstrom, Margit. II. Title. BIP

ROMANO, Frank J. 686.2'2544
Photocomposition and you, by Frank J. Romano. Salem, N.H., GAMA Communications [1974] 149 p. illus. 24 cm. [TR1010.R65] 74-172780
1. Phototypesetting. I. Title.

Phototypesetting—Equipment and supplies—Costs.

HUGHES, Thomas, 1922- 658.1'553
Handbook of operating costs and specifications for phototypesetting equipment / Thomas Hughes. Philadelphia : North American Pub. Co., [1975] 280 p. : ill. ; 29 cm. Includes index. [TR1010.H83] 74-25457 ISBN 0-912920-38-6 : 34.50
1. Phototypesetting—Equipment and supplies—Costs. I. Title: Handbook of operating costs ...

Phyfe, Duncan, 1768-1854.

CORNELIUS, Charles Over, 1890-1937. 749.213
Furniture masterpieces of Duncan Phyfe. Measured detail drawings by Stanley J. Rowland. New York, Dover Publications [1970] x, 86 p. illus. 24 cm. Reprint of the 1922 ed. [NK2439.P5C6 1970] 70-113861 2.50
1. Phyfe, Duncan, 1768-1854. I. Title. BIP

Physical laboratories.

AMERICAN Association of Physics Teachers. 727.553
Modern physics buildings: design and function. A project of the American Association of Physics Teachers and the American Institute of Physics supported by a grant from the Educational Facilities Laboratories, inc. [By] R. Ronald Palmer. project director [and] William Maxwell Rice, project archietect. New York, Progressive Architecture Library. Reinhold Pub. Corp. [1961] 324p. illus. 27cm. [NA6751.A5] 61-8456
1. Physical laboratories. 2. Architecture—Designs and plans. I. Palmer. Ralph Ronald, 1905 II. Rice, William Maxwell.

III. American Institute of Physics. IV. Title.

INSTITUTE of physics, 727.553
London. London and Home Counties Branch.
The design of physics research laboratories; a symposium held at the Royal Institution on 27 November, 1957. London, Chapman and Hall; New York, Reinhold, 1959. 108p. illus., plans. 25cm. Bibliography: p. 105. Bibliographical footnotes. [NA6751.I55 1957] 61-2894
1. Physical laboratories. 2. Architecture—Designs and plans. I. Title.

Piano music — Interpretation (Phrasing, dynamics, etc.)

VENABLE, Mary, 1866- 746.4'1'0924
The interpretation of piano music. Boston, O. Ditson [1913] viii, 252 p. 21 cm. (The music student's library) "From time to time, since July, 1902, much of the matter of this volume has appeared in the Musician, Boston, The Etude, Philadelphia, and the Courier, Cincinnati." -- Pref. [MT235.V46] 13-7501
1. Piano music — Interpretation (Phrasing, dynamics, etc.) I. Title.

Picabia, Francis, 1879-1953.

CAMFIELD, William A. 759.4 B
Francis Picabia : his art, life, and times / by William Camfield. Princeton, N.J. : Princeton University Press, c1978. p. cm. Includes index. Bibliography: p. [ND553.P47C36] 77-85533 ISBN 0-691-03932-1 : 35.00
1. Picabia, Francis, 1879-1953. 2. Painters—France—Biography. **BIP**

CAMFIELD, William A. 759.4
Francis Picabia, by William A. Camfield. New York, Solomon R. Guggenheim Museum [1970] 161 p. illus. (part col.), facsims., ports. 28 cm. Catalog of an exhibition organized by the Solomon R. Guggenheim Museum; participating institutions: Cincinnati Art Museum, Art Gallery of Ontario, Toronto, and the Detroit Institute of Arts. Bibliography: p. 149-156. [N6853.P48C3] 75-138304
1. Picabia, Francis, 1879-1953. I. Solomon R. Guggenheim Museum, New York.

Picasso, Pablo, 1881-1973.

ALLEY, Ronald. 759.6
Picasso: The three dancers. Newcastle upon Tyne, University of Newcastle upon Tyne, 1967. 20 p. illus. 24 cm. (Charlton lectures on art, 48, 1967) Bibliographical references included in "Notes" (p. 20) [ND553.P5A67] 70-368355 5/-
1. Picasso, Pablo, 1881- Three dancers. I. Title. II. Series: Charlton lecture, 48, 1967

ARNHEIM, Rudolf. 759.6
The genesis of a painting: Picasso's Guernica. Berkeley, University of California Press [1973, c.1972] 139 p. illus. 28 cm. First published in 1962 under title: Picasso's Guernica: The genesis of a painting. A few minor corrections have been added. Bibliographical references included in "Notes": p. [137]-139. [ND553.P5A75] 62-20637 ISBN 0-520-02353-6 5.95 (pbk)
1. Picasso, Pablo, 1881-1973. I. Title. II. Title: Picasso's Guernica.

ARNHEIM, Rudolf. 759.6
Picasso's Guernica; the genesis of a painting. Berkley, University of California Press, 1962. 139 p. illus. (1 fold., 1 col.) 29 cm. Bibliographical references included in "Notes" (p.[137]-139) [ND553.P5A75] 62-20637
1. Picasso, Pablo, 1881- I. Title.

†BALTIMORE. Museum of 741.9'44
Art.
Picasso : drawings and watercolors, 1899-1907 / by Victor I. Carlson. Baltimore : Baltimore Museum of Art, c1976. xxiv, 111 p. : ill. (some col.) ; 26 cm. Half title: Picasso, drawings and watercolors, 1899-1907, in the collection of the Baltimore Museum of Art. Bibliography: p. 109-111. [NC248.P5B27 1976] 76-41022 15.00
1. Picasso, Pablo, 1881-1973. I. Carlson, Victor I.

BERGER, John 759.6
The success and failure of Picasso [Magnolia, Mass., P. Smith, 1967, c.1965] 210p. illus. (inc. ports.) 20cm. (Penguin bk., 2383 rebound) [ND553.P5B45] 4.25
1. Picasso, Pablo, 1881- I. Title.

BERGER, John 759.6
The success and failure of Picasso. [Harmondsworth, Eng., Baltimore] Penguin [1966, c.1965] 210p. 120 illus. (incl. ports.) 20cm. (2383) [ND553.P5B45] 66-757 2.25 pap.,
1. Picasso, Pablo, 1881- I. Title.

BLUNT, Anthony, Sir, 1907- 759.6
Picasso's 'Guernica'. London, New York [etc.] Oxford U.P., 1969. [4], 60 p. plate, illus. 21 cm. (The Whidden lectures 1966) Bibliographical references included in "Notes" (p. 59-60) [ND553.P5B62] 73-83061 25/-
1. Picasso, Pablo, 1881- Guernica. I. Title. II. Series.

BLUNT, Anthony Frederick, 759.6
Sir 1907-
Picasso, the formative years; a study of his sources [by] Anthony Blunt, Phoebe Pool. [Greenwich, Conn.] N. Y. Graphic [c.1962] 32p. 173 illus. 31cm. 62-52668 8.50
1. Picasso, Pablo, 1881- I. Pool, Phoebe, joint author. II. Title.

BOECK, Wilhelm. 759.6
Picasso [by] Wilhelm Boeck [and] Jaime Sabartes. New York, H. N. Abrams [1955] 524 p. illus., plates (some col.), ports. 31 cm. Bibliography: p. 516-522. [ND553.P5B64] 56-1124
1. Picasso, Pablo, 1881- I. Sabartes, Jaime, 1881- joint author.

BRASSAI, Gyula Halasz, 759.6
called, 1899-
Picasso and company [by] Brassai. Translated from the French by Francis Price. Pref. by Henry Miller. Introd. by Roland Penrose. With photos. by the author. [1st ed.] Garden City, N.Y., Doubleday, 1966. xx, 289 p. illus., ports. 24 cm. Translation of Conversations avec Picasso. [ND553.P5B653] 66-24331
1. Picasso, Pablo, 1881- I. Title.

BUCHHEIM, Lothar Gunther. 759.6
Picasso, a pictorial biography. [translated by Michael Heron] New York, Viking Press [1959] 143 p. illus. (part col.) ports. 24 cm. (A Studio book) [ND553.P5B663] 59-16515
1. Picasso, Pablo, 1881-1973.

CASSOU, Jean, 1897- 759.6
Picasso. [Translated from the French by Edward Fitzgerald] New York, H. N. Abrams [1959] 88p. col. illus. 19cm. [ND553.P5C333] 59-11867
1. Picasso, Pablo, 1881- I. Title.

CHEVALIER, Denys. 759.6
Picasso: the blue and rose periods. [Translated from the French by Stephanie Winston] New York, Crown Publishers [1969] 96 p. illus. (part col.) 29 cm. Translation of Picasso, epoques bleue et rose. Bibliography: p. 94-95. [ND553.P5C4853] 70-82118 3.50
1. Picasso, Pablo, 1881- I. Title.

CIRLOT, Juan Eduardo. 741.944
Picasso, birth of a genius. Foreword by Juan Ainaud de Lasarte. New York, Praeger [1972] 288 p. illus. (part col.) 30 cm. Translation of El nacimiento de un genio. Bibliography: p. 176-182. [ND553.P5C5313] 72-186477 37.50
1. Picasso, Pablo, 1881- I. Title.

COGNIAT, Raymond, 1896- 759.6
Picasso; figures. [Translated by Diana Imber] New York, French & European Publications [1963] 60,[4] p. mounted col. illus. 21 cm. (Rhythm and colour, 5) Bibliography: p. 60-[61] [ND553.P5C663] 63-3612
1. Picasso, Pablo, 1881- I. Title.

COOPER, Douglas, 1911- 760'.0924
Picasso theatre. New York, H. N. Abrams [1968] 360 p. illus. (part col.), facsims. 30 cm. Includes facsims. of MS. letters, etc. of Picasso, E. Satie, and J. Cocteau. Bibliography: p. 359-360. [ND2885.C6413] 68-18127
1. Picasso, Pablo, 1881- 2. Theaters—Stage-setting and scenery—Illustrations. I. Title.

CRESPELLE, Jean Paul. 759.6
Picasso and his women. Translated from the French by Robert Baldick. [1st American ed.] New York, Coward-McCann [1969] 223 p. illus., ports. 25 cm. Translation of Picasso, les femmes, les amis, l'ouvre. Bibliography: p. [215]-217. [ND553.P5C713 1969] 68-14312 7.95
1. Picasso, Pablo, 1881- I. Title.

DAIX, Pierre. 759.6
Picasso. New York, F. A. Praeger [1965, c1964] 271 p. illus. (part col.) port. 22 cm. (Praeger world of art profiles) [ND553.P5D253] 65-20072
1. Picasso, Pablo, 1881-1973. I. Title.

DAIX, Pierre. 759.6
Picasso: the blue and rose periods; a catalogue raisonne of the paintings, 1900-1906 [by] Pierre Daix and Georges Boudaille. Catalogue compiled with the collaboration of Joan Rosselet. [Translated from the French by Phoebe Pool] Greenwich, Conn., New York Graphic Society [1967, c1966] 348 p. illus., col. plates, ports. 33 cm. "Bibliography and list of exhibitions": p. 345-347. [ND553.P5D2553] 66-19492
1. Picasso, Pablo, 1881- I. Boudaille, Georges, joint author. II. Title.

DIEHL, Gaston 759.6
Picasso. [Translated by Helen C. Slonim] New York, Crown Publishers, 1960[ ] 88, [8]p. bBibl.: p.[91]-[94]. illus. (part mounted, part col.) 29cm. 60-16348 2.95 bds.,
1. Picasso, Pablo, 1881- I. Title.

DOR DE LA SOUCHERE, 709.46
Romuald.
Picasso in Antibes. Text by Dor de la Sourchere. Photos. by Marianne Greenwood. [Translated from the French by W. J. Strachan. 1st American ed.] New York, Pantheon Books [1960] 57 p. illus., plates (part col.) port. 25 x 32 cm. [[N6853.P5]] 60-14805
1. Picasso, Pablo, 1881- I. Title.

DUNCAN, David Douglas. 759.4
Goodbye Picasso / David Douglas Duncan. 1st ed. New York : Grosset & Dunlap, [1974] 299 p. : ill. (some col.) ; 33 cm. [ND553.P5D77] 74-4059 ISBN 0-448-11619-7 : 35.00
1. Picasso, Pablo, 1881-1973. I. Title.

DUNCAN, David Douglas. 759.4
The silent studio / David Douglas Duncan. London : Collins, 1976. 109 p. : chiefly ill. ; 29 cm. [ND553.P5D83 1976b] 76-382816 ISBN 0-00-216768-9 : £5.50
1. Picasso, Pablo, 1881-1973. 2. Picasso, Jacqueline—Portraits, etc. 3. Mougins, France. Notre-Dame de Vie—Pictorial works. I. Title. **BIP**

DUNCAN, David Douglas. 759.4
The silent studio / David Douglas Duncan. 1st American ed. New York : Norton, c1976. 109 p. : chiefly ill. ; 29 cm. [ND553.P5D83 1976] 76-5571 ISBN 0-393-04442-4 : 12.50
1. Picasso, Pablo, 1881-1973. 2. Picasso, Jacqueline—Portraits, etc. 3. Mougins, France. Notre-Dame de Vie—Pictorial works. I. Title.

ELGAR, Frank 759.6
Picasso. A study of his work by Frank Elgar. A biographical study by Robert Maillard. Translated from the French by Francis Scarfe. New York, Praeger [1960, c.1956] 268p. bBibl.: p.[259-260] illus. (part col.) plates 21cm. 2.95
1. Picasso, Pablo. I. Maillard, Robert. II. Title.

ELGAR, Frank. 759.4
Picasso. A study of his work by Frank Elgar. A biographical study by Robert Maillard. Translated from the French by Francis Scrafe. New York, Praeger [1956] 314p. illus. (part col.) plates. 22cm. Bibliography: p. [259]-260. [ND553.P5E] A57
1. Picasso, Pabio, I. Maillard, Robert. II. Title.

ELGAR, Frank. 709'.2'4
Picasso. Study of his work by Frank Elgar. Biographical study by Robert Maillard. [Translated from the French by Francis Scarfe] Rev. and enl. ed. New York, Tudor Pub. Co. [1972] 247, [7] p. illus. (part col.) 28 cm. Bibliography: p. [249]-[254] [ND553.P5E43 1972] 72-85393 ISBN 0-8148-0512-4 15.00
1. Picasso, Pablo, 1881- I. Maillard, Robert.

GALERIE Louise Leiris, 741.944
Paris.
Picasso dessins 1959-1960; Galerie Louise Leiris, 30 novembre-31 decembre 1960. [dist. New York, Wittenborn, 1961] 89p. illus. (part col.) e(Its Catalogue. Serie A. no 12) 61-1305 1.50 pap.,
1. Picasso, Pablo, 1881- I. Title.

GALERIE Louise Leiris, 759.6
Paris.
Picasso: peinture 1962-1963; Galerie Louise Leiris, 15 janvier-15 fevrier 1964 [New York, Wittenborn] 1964. 62p. chiefly illus. (pt. col.) 17cm. (Its Catalogue. Ser. A. no. 18) 64-2380 3.00 pap.,
1. Picasso, Pablo, 1881- I. Title.

GALERIE Louise Leiris, 759.6
Paris.
Picasso; peintures (Vauvenargues, 1959-1961); Galerie Louise Leiris, 26 janvier-24 fevrier 1962. [New York, Wittenborn, 1962] [11] p., 31 illus. (pt. col.) (Its Catalogue. Serie A, no. 14) 62-2441 2.00 pap.,
1. Picasso, Pablo, 1881- I. Title.

GALLOWAY, John Crozier. 709'.24
Picasso [by] John Galloway. New York, McGraw-Hill [1969] 48 p. illus., 20 col. slides ((2 x 2 in.) in pockets) 29 cm. (Color slide program of the great masters) Bibliography: p. 48. [ND553.P5G279] 67-29889
1. Picasso, Pablo, 1881- I. Title. II. Series.

GALLWITZ, Klaus. 759.4
Picasso at 90; the late work. [1st American ed. New York, Putnam [1971] 221 p. illus. (part col.) 35 cm. Translation of Picasso laureatus. Bibliography: p. 216-217. [ND553.P5G2813 1971b] 76-157061 35.00
1. Picasso, Pablo, 1881- I. Picasso, Pablo, 1881- II. Title.

GILOT, Francoise, 1921- 927.5
Life with Picasso [by] Francoise Gulot and Charleto Lake New York New Amer. Lib. [1965, c.1964] 349p. 18cm. (Signet bk., Q2772) [ND553.P5G55] .95 pap.,
1. Picasso, Pablo, 1881- I. Lake, Carlton. II. Title.

GILOT, Francoise, 1921- 927.5
.
Life with Picasso [by] Francoise Gilot and Carlton Lake. [1st ed.] New York, McGraw-Hill [1964] 373 p. illus., plates (incl. ports.) 23 cm. [ND553.P5G55] 64-23276
1. Picasso, Pablo, 1881- I. Lake, Carlton. II. Title.

GILOT, Francoise, 1921- 759.4
Life with Picasso, [by] Francoise Gilot and [as told to] Carlton Lake. Harmondsworth (Mddx.), Penguin, 1966. 367 p. 16 plates (incl. ports.). 18 1/2 cm. [ND553.P5G55 1966] 759.4 79-359146 7/6
1. Picasso, Pablo, 1881- I. Lake, Carlton. II. Title.

GREENFELD, Howard. 759.4
Pablo Picasso; an introduction. Chicago, Follett [1971] 192 p. illus. (part col.) 25 cm. [ND553.P5G7] 70-118928 ISBN 0-695-80139-2 5.95
1. Picasso, Pablo, 1881-

HILTON, Timothy, 1941- 759.4
Picasso / Timothy Hilton. New York : Praeger, 1975. p. cm. (World of art) Includes index. Bibliography: p. [ND553.P5H54] 75-48 ISBN 0-275-49780-1 : 12.50. ISBN 0-275-71750-X pbk. : 6.95
1. Picasso, Pablo, 1881-1973. 2. Cubism.

HORODISCH, Abraham. 709.46
Picasso as a book artist. [Translation by I. Grafe. 1st ed.] Cleveland, World Pub. Co. [1962] 136p. illus., plates (part col.) facsims. 26cm. Bibliography: p. 112-131. [NC248.P5H63 1962] 62-9048
1. Picasso, Pablo, 1881- I. Title.

JAFFE, Hans Ludwig C. 759.6
Pablo Picasso [Tr. by Norbert Guterman] New York, Abrams [1964] 158, [2]p. illus.,

SUBJECT INDEX PICASSO, PABLO, 1881-1973.

col. plates, ports. 34cm. (Lib. of great painters) Bibl. [ND553.P5J253] 64-107624 15.00
1. Picasso, Pablo, 1881- I. Title.

JAFFE, Hans Ludwig C. 759.4
Picasso [by] Hans Jaffe [translated from the Italian] London, New York, Hamlyn, 1970. 96 p. illus. (some col.), ports. 32 cm. (Twentieth century masters) "Distributed in the U.S.A. by Crown Publishers. Bibliography: p. 96. [ND553.P5J2613] 78-599424 ISBN 0-600-36910-2 £1.75
1. Picasso, Pablo, 1881-

JOHNSON, Ron, 1937- 730'.92'4
The early sculpture of Picasso, 1901-1914 / Ron Johnson. New York : Garland Pub., 1976. p. cm. (Outstanding dissertations in the fine arts) Originally presented as the author's thesis, University of California, 1971. Bibliography: p. [NB553.P45J63 1976] 75-38622 lib.bdg. : 27.50
1. Picasso, Pablo, 1881-1973. I. Title. II. Series. BIP

JOHNSON, Ron, 1937- 730'.92'4
The early sculpture of Picasso, 1901-1914 / Ron Johnson. New York : Garland Pub., 1976. iv, 245 p. : ill. ; 22 cm. (Outstanding dissertations in the fine arts) Originally presented as the author's thesis, University of California, 1971. Bibliography: p. 181-187. [NB553.P45J63 1976] 75-23795 ISBN 0-8240-1990-3 lib.bdg. : 27.50
1. Picasso, Pablo, 1881-1973. I. Title. II. Series.

JUDKINS, Winthrop. 759.06
Fluctuant representation in synthetic cubism : Picasso, Braque, Gris, 1910-1920 / Winthrop Judkins. New York : Garland, 1976. viii, 526 p. : ill. ; 22 cm. (Outstanding dissertations in the fine arts) Originally presented as the author's thesis, Harvard, 1954, under title: The nature and techniques of fluctuant representation in synthetic cubism: Picasso, Braque, Gris. Bibliography: p. 329-330. [ND196.C8J82 1976] 75-23796 ISBN 0-8240-1991-1 lib.bdg. : 35.00
1. Picasso, Pablo, 1881-1973. 2. Braque, Georges, 1882-1963. 3. Gris, Juan, 1887-1927. 4. Cubism. 5. Painting, Modern—20th century. I. Title. II. Series. BIP

KAY, Helen, pseud. 709.46
Picasso's world of children. Introd. by Daniel-Henry Kahnweiler. Garden City, N. Y., Doubleday [1965] 241p. illus. (pt. col.) 33cm. Chanticleer pr. ed. [ND553.P5K3] 65-15754 25.00; 22.50 pre-Christmas,
1. Picasso, Pablo, 1881- 2. Children in art. I. Title.

LEYMARIE, Jean. 709'.2'4
Picasso : the artist of the century / text by Jean Leymarie ; with appreciations by poets and friends of the artist ; designed and edited by Albert Skira ; [translated from the French by James Emmons]. Geneva : Skira ; New York : Rizzoli, c1976. x, 309 p. : ill (some col.) ; 35 cm. Translation of Picasso, metamorphoses et unite. Includes index. Bibliography: p. 287-289. [ND553.P5L4413 1976] 76-62894 ISBN 0-8478-0090-3 (Rizzoli) : 50.00
1. Picasso, Pablo, 1881-1973. I. Picasso, Pablo, 1881-1973.

LEYMARIE, Jean. 741.946
Picasso drawings. Text by Jean Leymarie. Translated from the French by Stuart Gilbert. [Geneva] Skira; [distributed in the United States by the World Pub. Co., Cleveland, 1967] 107 p. illus., plates (part col.) 19 cm. (The Taste of our time) [NC1135.P5L42] 67-25116
1. Picasso, Pablo, 1881- I. Title.

LIPTON, Eunice. 759.4
Picasso criticism, 1901-1939 : the making of an artist-hero Eunice Lipton. New York : Garland Pub., 1976. 385 p. : ill. ; 21 cm. (Outstanding dissertations in the fine arts) Originally presented as the author's thesis, New York University, 1975. Bibliography: p. 349-367. [N6853.P5L56 1976] 75-23801 ISBN 0-8240-1996-2
1. Picasso, Pablo, 1881-1973. I. Title. II. Series.

LOS Angeles Co., Calif. 769.92
Museum of Art, Los Angeles.
Picasso: sixty years of graphic works; aquatints, dry points, engravings, etchings, linoleum cuts, lithographs, woodcuts. [Los Angeles, 1966] 167 [1] p. illus., col. plates. 21 cm. Exhibition organized with the cooperation of the Graphic Arts Council of the Los Angeles County Museum of Art. Bibliography: p. 167-[168] [NE650.P62L6] 66-29096
1. Picasso, Pablo, 1881- I. Los Angeles Co., Calif. Museum of Art, Los Angeles. Graphic Arts Council. II. Title.

MALRAUX, Andre, 1901- 759.4
Picasso's mask / by Andre Malraux ; translated and annotated by June Guicharnaud, with Jacques Guicharnaud. New York : Holt, Rinehart and Winston, 1976. p. cm. Translation of Le tete d'obsidienne. [ND553.P5M3313] 75-5469 ISBN 0-03-013751-9 : 10.00
1. Picasso, Pablo, 1881-1973. I. Title. BIP

MARRERO SUAREZ, Vicente, 759.6
1922-
Picasso and the bull. Translated by Anthony Kerrigan. Chicago, H. Regnery Co., 1956. 132p. illus. 22cm. [ND553.P5M372] [ND553.P5M372] 927.5 56-11852 56-11852
1. Picasso, Pablo, 1881- 2. Bulls in art. 3. Bull (in religion. folk-lore, etc.) I. Title.

MICHELI, Mario de. 759.6
Picasso. [Translated from the Italian by Pearl Sanders. 1st American ed.] New York, Grosset & Dunlap [1967] 39, [80] p. illus. (part col.) 18 cm. (The New Grosset art library, 4) On cover: Picasso; the life and work of the artist. Bibliography: p. 28-31. [ND553.P5M52 1967b] 67-24231
1. Picasso, Pablo, 1881-

NEW York (City). 760'.092'4
Museum of Modern Art.
Picasso in the collection of the Museum of Modern Art, including remainder-interest and promised gifts [by] William Rubin. With additional texts by Elaine L. Johnson and Riva Castleman. New York, Museum of Modern Art; distributed by New York Graphic Society, Greenwich, Conn. [1972] 246 p. illus. (part col.) 25 cm. Issued in honor of Picasso's 90th birthday. [N6853.P5N4] 70-164877 ISBN 0-87070-537-7 15.00
1. Picasso, Pablo, 1881- I. Rubin, William Stanley. II. Title.

NEW York. Museum of Modern 759.6
Art.
Picasso: 75th anniversary exhibition. ed. by Alfred H. Barr, Jr. New York [1957] 115p. illus. (part col.) 25cm. Errata leaf inserted. [ND553.P5N44] 927.5 57-3495
1. Picasso, Pablo. 1881- I. Barr, Alfred Hamilton, 1902- ed. II. Chicago. Art Institute. III. Title.

NEW York. Museum of Modern 759.6
Art.
The Picasso: 75th anniversary exhibition. The Museum of Modern Art, New York, May 22-Sept. 8, 1957; the Art Institute of Chicago, Oct. 29-Dec. 8, 1957. [Catalogue] edited by Alfred H. Barr, Jr. New York [1957] 115p. illus. (part col.) 25cm. Errata leaf inserted. [ND553.P5N44] [ND553.P5N44] 927.5 57-3495 57-3495
1. Picasso, Pabio, 1881- I. Barr, Alfred Hamilton, 1902- ed. II. Chicago, Art Institute. III. Title.

NEW York. Museum of 759.40924
Modern Art.
Picasso, fifty years of his art, by Alfred H. Barr, Jr. Reprint ed. New York, Published for the Museum of Modern Art by Arno Press, 1966 [c1946] 314 p. illus., plates, ports. 27 cm. Bibliography: 286-308. [ND553] 66-26126
1. Picasso, Pablo, 1881- I. Barr, Alfred Hamilton, 1902- ed. BIP

O'BRIAN, Patrick. 759.4 B
Pablo Ruiz Picasso : a biography / Patrick O'Brian. London : Collins, 1976. 511 p., [8] p. of plates : ill., geneal. tables, ports. ; 24 cm. American ed. published under title: Picasso. Includes index. [ND553.P5O27 1976b] 77-362548 ISBN 0-00-211685-5 : £6.95
1. Picasso, Pablo, 1881-1973. 2. Painters—France—Biography.

O'BRIAN, Patrick. 759.4 B
Picasso : Pablo Ruiz Picasso : a biography / by Patrick O'Brian. New York : Putnam, c1976. 511 p. ; 24 cm. Includes index. [ND553.P5O27 1976] 75-41334 12.95 12.95
1. Picasso, Pablo, 1881-1973. 2. Painters—France—Biography. I. Title.

OLIVIER, Fernande 759.6
Picasso and his friends. Tr. [from French] by Jane Miller [1st Amer. ed.] New York, Appleton-Century [dist. Meredith, 1965, c.1933-1964] 186p. illus., ports. 21cm. [ND553.P5O413] 65-25447 3.95
1. Picasso, Pablo, 1881- 2. Artists—Correspondence, reminiscences, etc. I. Title.

OTERO, Roberto. 759.4
Forever Picasso: an intimate look at his last years. Translated by Elaine Kerrigan. New York, Abrams [1974] 196 p. illus. (part col.) 29 cm. [ND553.P5O7413] 74-2304 ISBN 0-8109-0369-5
1. Picasso, Pablo, 1881-1973. I. Title.

PARMELIN, Helene. 759.6
Picasso: At Notre Dame de Vie. Text by Helene Parmelin. New York, H. N. Abrams [1966] 180 p. illus. (part col.) 31 cm. (Her Intimate secrets of a student. 3) [ND553.P5P323] 66-26611
I. Picasso, Pablo, 1881- II. Title. III. Title: At Notre Dame de Vie.

PARMELIN, Helene 759.6
Picasso: At Notre Dame de Vie. Text by Helene Parmelin. New York, Abrams [c.1966] 189p. illus. (pt. col.) 31cm. (Her Intimate secrets of a studio, 3) [ND553.P5P323] 66-26611 35.00
I. Picasso, Pablo, 1881- II. Title. III. Title: At Notre Dame de Vie.

PARMELIN, Helene. 927.5
Picasso plain; an intimate portrait. Translated from the French by Humphrey Hare. New York, St. Martin's Press [1963] 250 p. illus. 22 cm. Translation of Picasso sur la place. [ND553.P5P333] 63-15854
1. Picasso, Pablo, 1881-1973.

PARMELIN, Helene. 759.6
Picasso says ... Translated by Christine Trollope. [1st American ed.] South Brunswick [N.J.] A. S. Barnes [1969] 123 p. 22 cm. Translation of Picasso dit. [ND553.P5P313 1969b] 73-83368 5.00
1. Picasso, Pablo, 1881- I. Title.

PARMELIN, Helene 759.6
Picasso; the artist and his model, and other recent works [Tr. from French] New York, Abrams [1966] 183p. mounted illus. (pt. col.) 31cm. [ND553.P5P343] 65-23173 30.00
I. Picasso, Pablo, 1881- II. Title.

PENROSE, Roland 759.6
Picasso: his life and work. 2d ed. New York, Schocken. 1962[c.1958, 1962] 410p. illus. 21cm. (SB31) Bibl. 62-20157 2.45 pap.,
1. Picasso, Pablo, 1881- I. Title.

PENROSE, Roland, Sir. 759.4
Picasso : his life and work / Roland Penrose. [Revised ed.]. Harmondsworth : Penguin, 1971. xv, 518 p., [16] leaves of plates : ill. ; 20 cm. (Pelican biographies) Includes index. Bibliography: p. [492]-498. [ND553.P5P42 1971] 75-309868 ISBN 0-14-021408-9
1. Picasso, Pablo, 1881-1973. I. Title.

PENROSE, Roland, Sir. 759.6
Picasso: his life and work. New York, Harper [1959, c1958] 392 p. illus. 22 cm. Includes bibliography. [ND553.P5P42 1959] 58-8863
1. Picasso, Pablo, 1881-1973.

PENROSE, Roland, Sir. 759.6
Picasso: his life and work. [1st U.S. ed.] New York, Harper & Row [1973] xv, 518 p. illus. 22 cm. (Icon editions, IN-16) [ND553.P5P42 1973] 72-180702 15.00
1. Picasso, Pablo, 1881-1973. I. Title.
Pbk. 5.95; ISBN 0-06-430016-1

PENROSE, Roland, Sir. 759.4
Picasso, in retrospect. Advisory editors: Sir Roland Penrose [and] John Golding. [Authors] Daniel-Henry Kahnweiler [and others] New York, Praeger [1973] 283 p. illus. (part col.) 30 cm. Bibliography: p. 272-273. [ND553.P5P424] 71-163098 29.95
1. Picasso, Pablo, 1881-1973. I. Golding, John, joint author. II. Title.

PENROSE, Roland. 759.6
Portrait of Picasso. New York, Museum of Modern Art; distributed by Simon and Schuster [1957] 96p. illus., ports., map. 25cm. [ND553.P5P43] 927.5 57-7372
1. Picasso, Pablo, 1881- I. Title.

PENROSE, Roland, Sir. 759.4
Portrait of Picasso. [2d rev. and enl. ed.] New York, Museum of Modern Art; distributed by New York Graphic Society, Greenwich, Conn. [1971] 128 p. illus., ports. (part col.) 26 cm. [ND553.P5P43 1971] 71-162311 ISBN 0-87070-536-9 8.95
1. Picasso, Pablo, 1881- I. Title.

PENROSE, Roland, Sir. 730'.924
The sculpture of Picasso. Chronology by Alicia Legg. New York, Museum of Modern Art [1967] 231 p. illus., port. 31 cm. Issued in conjunction with the exhibition at the Museum of Modern Art, Oct. 11, 1967 to Jan. 1, 1968. "Bibliography on the sculpture and ceramics of Picasso, compiled by Inga Forslund" (p. 215-221) [NB553.P45P42] 67-29395
1. Picasso, Pablo, 1881- I. New York (City). Museum of Modern Art. II. Title.

PERLS, Frank. 769'.924
Picasso: 45 selected graphics from 1904 to 1968. Beverly Hills, Calif., 1971. 31 p. illus. (part col.) 28 cm. Cover title. Catalog of the exhibition held Oct. 25-Nov. 26, 1971, at the Beverly Hills gallery of F. Perls on occasion of P. Picasso's birthday. "Introduction by Frank Perls: 'Encounters with Picasso'": p. 7-18. [NE650.P62P4] 75-30649
1. Picasso, Pablo, 1881- I. Title.

PICASSO; 759.6
a loan exhibition of his paintings, drawings, sculpture, ceramics, prints, and illustrated books, January 8-February 23, 1958. [Pref. by Henry Clifford. Philadelphia, 1958] 129p. illus., col. plates ports. 26cm. [N6853.P5P5] 927.5 58-2453
1. Picasso, Pablo, 1881- I. Philadelphia Museum of Art. II. Clifford, Henry, 1904-

PICASSO, Braque, 759.4'074'013
Leger : masterpieces from Swiss collections. Minneapolis : The Minneapolis Institute of Arts, c1975. 83 p. : ill. (some col.) ; 31 cm. Catalog of an exhibition held at the Minneapolis Institute of Arts, Oct. 30, 1975-Jan. 4, 1976, the Sarah Campbell Blaffer Gallery, University of Houston, Tex., Jan. 17-Mar. 7, 1976, and the San Francisco Museum of Modern Art, Mar. 19-May 4, 1976. [ND553.P5P46] 75-34717
1. Picasso, Pablo, 1881-1973. 2. Braque, Georges, 1882-1963. 3. Leger, Fernand, 1881-1955. 4. Paintings, Modern—20th century—France—Exhibitions. 5. Paintings, French—Switzerland. I. Picasso, Pablo, 1881-1973. II. Braque, Georges, 1882-1963. III. Leger, Fernand, 1881-1955. IV. Minneapolis. Institute of Arts. V. Sarah Campbell Blaffer Gallery. VI. San Francisco Museum of Modern Art. BIP

PICASSO Coloring book 759.6
(The); paintings rendered in line by Joseph Solman. Ed. by Joseph K. Foster. NewYork, Crown [c.1966] 1 v. (unpaged) illus. (pt. col.) 32cm. (Edward Ernest bk.) 2.95 pap.,
I. Solmah, Joseph II. Forster, Joseph K., ed. III. Solmah, Joseph IV. Forster, Joseph K., ed.

PICASSO, Pablo 759.6
Picasso: the early years [by] Jiri Padrta. With a pref. by Jean Cocteau. [Translated by Iris Urwin] New York, Tudor Pub. Co. [1960] 16p. illus. 29 col. plates 28cm. 60-50595 7.95
I. Padrta, Jiri. II. Title.

PICASSO, Pablo, 1881- 759.6
The complete paintings of Picasso, blue and rose periods. Introd. by Denys Sutton. Notes and catalogue by Paolo Lecaldano. New York, Abrams [1972] 119 p. illus., col. plates, 32 cm. (Classics of the world's great art) Translation of L'opera completa di Picasso blu e rosa. Bibliography: p. 82. [ND553.P5L34513 1970] 70-92261 ISBN 0-8109-5514-8 5.95
1. Picasso, Pablo, 1881- I. Lecaldano, Paolo, ed. II. Title.

PICASSO, Pablo, 1881- 741.946
Drawings. Introd. [by] Maurice Jardot. New York, H. N. Abrams [1959] xiv, 159p. (chiefly illus. (part col.)) 34cm. [NC1135.P5J3] 59-11863
I. Jardot, Maurice. II. Title.

PICASSO, Pablo, 1881- 759.4
Homage to Picasso for his 90th birthday. Exhibition for the benefit of the American Cancer Society, Oct. 1971. Joint exhibition of paintings and works on paper: years 1901-1924, Saidenberg; years 1924-1971, Marlborough. [New York, 1971] 118 p. illus. (part col.) 30 cm. [ND553.P5M362] 78-198480
I. Marlborough Gallery. II. Saidenberg Gallery. III. Title.

PICASSO, Pablo, 1881- 709.46
Les dejeuners. Text by Douglas Cooper. [New York] Abrams [1963] 36p. illus., plates (pt. col.) 38cm. 62-21485 35.00 bxd.
I. Cooper, Douglas, 1911- II. Title.

PICASSO, Pablo, 1881- 759.6
Pablo Picasso: blue and rose periods. Text by William S. Lieberman. New York, H. N. Abrams in association with Pocket Books [1954] [74] p. 46 illus. (part col.) port. 18cm. (The Pocket library of great art, A20) An Abrams art book. Bibliography: p. [74] [ND553.P5L535] [ND553.P5L535] 927.5 54-14620 54-14620
I. Lieberman, William Slattery, 1924- II. Title.

PICASSO, Pablo, 1881- 759.4
Pablo Picasso: blue and rose periods. Text by William S. Lieberman. New York, H. N. Abrams [1971] 40 p. illus., col. plates. 33 cm. (Great art of the ages) [ND553.P5L53 1971] 69-19712 ISBN 0-8109-5127-4
I. Lieberman, William Slattery, 1924-

PICASSO, Pablo, 1881- 759.4
Pablo Picasso: blue and rose periods. Text by William S. Lieberman. New York, H. N. Abrams [1971] 24 p. illus. (part col.) 33 cm. (The Library of great painters. Portfolio ed.) [ND553.P5L53 1971b] 69-14755
I. Lieberman, William Slattery, 1924-

PICASSO, Pablo, 1881- 759.6
Picasso. Text by Robert Fisher. Edited by Theodore Reff. New York, Tudor Pub. Co. [1966] 36 p. 89 col. plates. 18 cm. [ND553.P5R4] 66-10560
I. Fisher, Robert, 1931- II. Reff, Theodore, ed.

PICASSO, Pablo, 1881- 759.44
Picasso. Text by Umbro Apollonio. Tr. from Italian by Cesare Foligno. New York, Crown [1965] 26p. illus. (10 mounted col.) 30cm. (Folio art bks.) Bibl. [ND553.P5A713] 65-5031 1.45 pap.,
I. Apollonio, Umbro, 1911- II. Title.

PICASSO, Pablo, 1881- 730.946
Picasso [by] Roland Penrose. New York, Universe Books [c.1961] [16]p. 32 plates, port. (Universe sculpture series) Captions in French, English, German, Dutch, and Spanish. Bibl. 60-14500 1.95 bds.,
I. Penrose, Roland. II. Title.

PICASSO, Pablo, 1881- 769'92'4
Picasso: recent etchings, lithographs and linoleum cuts. [Introd. by Kurt Leonhard. Biography and documentation by Hans Bolliger. Translation by Norbert Guterman.] New York, Abrams [1967, 1966] xxxiv, 144 p. (chiefly illus. (part col.)) 29 cm. Translation of L'oeuvre grav e. Bibliography of Picasso's graphic work:" p. 133-139. "Books illustrated by Picasso": p. 140-144. [NE650.P62L43] 67-12685
I. Leonhard, Kurt, 1910- II. Bollinger, Hans. III. Title.

PICASSO, Pablo, 1881- 709.46
Picasso at Vallauris. New York, Reynal [1959] [196]p. illus. (part. col.) 36cm. Includes three essays in French by D. H. Kahnweller, O. Elytis, and G. Ramie: with translations into English by Serge Hughes. 'Originally published in France [1951] as a double number of Verve., 25 and 26.' [N6853.P5A5] 59-5995
I. Title.

PICASSO, Pablo, 1881- 759.4
Picasso: cubism and after. Text by Sam Hunter. New York, H. N. Abrams [1971] 24 p. illus. (part col.) 33 cm. (The Library of great painters. Portfolio ed.) Published in 1957 with subtitle: cubism to the present. [ND553.P5H798] 72-191931 ISBN 0-8109-3075-7
I. Hunter, Sam, 1923- II. Title.

PICASSO, Pablo, 1881- 741.946
Picasso, dessins 1966-1967. Galerie Louise Leiris, 28 fevrier--23 mars 1968. [Paris Galerie L. Leiris,] 1968. Stamp on t.p.: American dist., Wittenborn, New York. 74p. illus. (pt. col.) 17cm. (Galerie Louise Leiris. Catalogue no 21, ser. A) Cover illus. in color. [NC248.P5A53] 68-102823 4.50 pap.,
I. Galerie Louise Leiris, Paris. II. Title.

PICASSO, Pablo, 1881- 769.2
Picasso: fifty-five years of his graphic work. [Introd. and selection by Bernhard Geiser. Biography and documentation by Hans Bolliger. Translation by Lisbeth Gombrich] New York, H. N. Abrams [1955?] xxvii, 177 p. (chiefly illus.) 29 cm. Translation of Picasso: das graphische Werk. "Bibliography of Picasso's graphic work": p. 174-175. "Books illustrated by Picasso": p. 176-177. [NE650.P62G35] 56-1080 [An Abrams art book]
I. Geiser, Bernhard.

PICASSO, Pablo, 1881- 769'.924
Picasso graphic art. Cambridge, Mass., Fogg Art Museum [1957] 28 p. (chiefly illus.) 20 cm. (Fogg Museum picture book no. 7) Prepared by the Dept. of Prints, Fogg Art Museum and the Dept. of Printing and Graphic Arts, Harvard Library for the Fogg Art Museum, Harvard University and the Art Institute of Chicago. [N527.A55 no. 7] 73-10364
I. Harvard University. William Hayes Fogg Art Museum. Dept. of Prints. II. Harvard University. Library. Dept. of Printing and Graphic Arts. III. Harvard University. William Hayes Fogg Art Museum. IV. Chicago. Art Institute. V. Title. VI. Series: Fogg picture book no. 7

PICASSO, Pablo, 1881- 709'.46
Picasso in Chicago: paintings, drawings, and prints from Chicago collections. [Exhibition at] the Art Institute of Chicago, February 3-March 31, 1968. [Chicago, Art Institute of Chicago, 1968] 120 p. illus. 26 cm. [ND553.P5C486] 68-21275
I. Chicago. Art Institute. II. Title.

PICASSO, Pablo, 1881- 760'.0924
Picasso in Milwaukee. [Exhibition] Milwaukee Art Center, Oct. 25-Nov. 28, 1971. [Milwaukee, 1971] [32] p. illus. 23 cm. [N6853.P5M5] 70-182184
I. Milwaukee. Art Center. II. Title.

PICASSO, Pablo, 1881- 769'.924
Picasso linocuts, 1958-1963, by Donald H. Karshan. New York, Tudor Pub. Co. [1968] xiv, 103 p. (chiefly illus. (part col.)) 23 x 38 cm. Prepared for an exhibition of the linocuts comprising the Computer Applications Incorporated collection, arranged by Trois Anges, ltd., New York, and held at the Nelson Gallery-Atkins Museum, Kansas City, Mo., and at other museums. Bibliography: p. xiv. [NE1334.P5K3] 68-56152 7.95
I. Karshan, Donald H. II. Computer Applications Incorporated. III. William Rockhill Nelson Gallery of Art and Mary Atkins Museum of Fine Arts, Kansas City, Mo. IV. Title.

PICASSO, Pablo, 1881- 769.946
Picasso linoleum cuts: bacchanals, women, bulls & bullfighters. Introd. by Wilhelm Boeck. New York, Abrams [1963.,c. 1962] xiii, 45 col. plates. 33x39cm. 63-8146 35.00 bxd.
I. Boeck, Wilhelm. II. Title.

PICASSO, Pablo, 1881- 769'.924
Picasso lithographs. [Translated from the French by Jean Didry. Boston] Boston Book and Art Publisher [1970] 299 p. illus. (part col.) 28 cm. Notes by Fernand Mourlot. [NE2349.5.P5M613] 70-129449
I. Mourlot, Fernand. II. Title.

PICASSO, Pablo, 1881- 769'.924
Picasso: master of graphic art; a retrospective exhibition of graphic works: 1904-1968, spring, 1971. Chicago, R. S. Johnson-International Gallery [1971] 78 p. illus., port. 25 cm. Bibliography: p. 68. [NE650.P62A516] 72-158147
I. Johnson (R. S.)-International Gallery.

PICASSO, Pablo, 1881- 769'.92'4
Picasso. recent Teachings. Lithographs, and linoleum cuts. [Introd. by Kurt Leonhard. Biography and documentation by Hans Bolliger. Tr. by Norbert Guterman.] New York, Abrams [1967, 1966] xxxiv, 144p. (chiefly illus. (pt. col.)) 29cm. Tr. of L'oeuvre grave. Bibl. of Picasso's graphic work: p. 133-139. Bks. illustrated by Picasso: p. 140-144. [NE650.P62L43] 67-12685 15.00
I. Leonhard, Kurt, 1910- II. bolliger, Hans. III. Title.

PICASSO, Pablo, 1881- 769'.924
Picasso 347. [1st ed.] New York, Random House [1970] 2 v. (22 p., 347 plates) 30 x 43 cm. "347 engravings that Picasso executed at Mougins from March 16th to October 5th, 1968." Includes the major part, in English, of Georges Bloch's introd. to Picasso's "Pablo Picasso. Catalogue de l'oeuvre grave et lithographie, 1904-1967," published in 1968. Issued in a case. [NE650.P62A52] 71-127545

PICASSO, Pablo, 1881- 741.9'44
Picasso; 20 drawings, 1967-1971. Exhibit in honor of Picasso's 90th birthday at the R.S. Johnson International Gallery. Chicago, fall 1971. [Chicago, 1971] 30 p. illus. (part col.) 25 cm. [NC248.P5J6] 79-178981
I. Johnson (R. S.)-International Gallery.

PICASSO, Pablo, 1881- 759.6
Picasso's Picassos, by David Douglas Duncan. New York, Harper [1961] 270 p. illus. (part col., part mounted) col. ports. 31 cm. [ND553.P5D78] 61-10205
I. Duncan, David Douglas.

PICASSO, Pablo, 1881- 730'.924
Picasso's third dimension. Photos. and text by Gjon Mili. [New York] Triton Press; [distributed by Tudor Pub. Co., c1970] 183 p. illus. (part col.), ports. (part col.) 28 cm. [NB553.P45M5] 74-138431 27.50
I. Mili, Gjon, 1904- II. Title.

PICASSO, Pablo, 1881- 759.4
A year of Picasso paintings: 1969. Text by rafael alberti. translated by Anthony kerrigan New York, H. N. Abrams [1972, c1971] 221 p. (chiefly illus., part col.) 33 cm. French translation has title: Picasso en Avignon. [ND553.P5A6513] 70-161634 ISBN 0-8109-0382-2 35.00
I. Alberti, Rafael, 1902- II. Title.

PICASSO, Pablo, 1881- 760'.092'4
1973.
Carnet Picasso : Madrid, 1898 / con una introduccion de Xavier de Salas. Barcelona : G. Gili, [1976?] 96 p. ; 11 x 18 cm. & sketchbook (30 leaves of plates : all ill.) In case. Title from case: Carnet Madrid, 17-22, III, 1898. Text in English, French, and Spanish. [NC248.P5A412] 77-463308
1. Picasso, Pablo, 1881-1973. I. Title. II. Title: Carnet Madrid.

PICASSO, Pablo, 1881- 709'.2'4
1973.
Child and caveman : elements of Picasso's creativity / [compiled by] Josep Palau i Fabre. New York : Rizzoli, [1978, c1977] 20, 69 p. : chiefly ill. (some col.) ; 21 cm. Bibliography: p. 20 (1st group) [N6853.P5A4 1978] 77-95343 ISBN 0-8478-0165-9 : 9.95
1. Picasso, Pablo, 1881-1973. 2. Creation (Literary, arrtistic, etc.)—Psychological aspects. I. Palau y Fabre, Jose. II. Title. **BIP**

PICASSO, Pablo, 1881-1973. 759.4
Designs for The three-cornered hat (Le tricorne) / Pablo Picasso ; edited by Parmenia Migel. New York : Dover Publications, 1978. xvi, 31 p. : chiefly ill. (some col.) ; 31 cm. "Includes the entire contents ... of the portfolio Le tricorne: ballet d'apres les dessins en couleurs de Picasso, originally published ... by Editions Paul Rosenberg, Paris, 1920." Bibliography: p. xv. [ND2888.P52A4 1978] 78-59924 ISBN 0-486-23709-5 : 5.00
1. Picasso, Pablo, 1881-1973. 2. Falla, Manuel de, 1876-1946. El sombrero de tres picos—Illustrations. I. Migel, Parmenia. II. Title.

PICASSO, Pablo, 1881- 741.9'44
1973.
Homage to Picasso, 1881-1973; fifty-two drawings, watercolors, and pastels, 1900-1972. [Catalog of an exhibition at the] R. S. Johnson-International Gallery. Chicago, 1973. 63 p. illus. 25 cm. [NC248.P5J58] 73-84352
1. Picasso, Pablo, 1881-1973. I. Johnson (R. S.)-International Gallery. II. Title.

PICASSO, Pablo, 1881-1973. 759.4
Picasso : a loan exhibition for the benefit of Cancer Care, inc., the National Cancer Foundation, April 15-May 17. New York : Acquavella Galleries, 1975. [64] p. : chiefly ill. (some col.) ; 28 cm. [ND553.P5A63] 75-3979
1. Picasso, Pablo, 1881-1973. I. Acquavella Galleries.

PICASSO, Pablo, 1881-1973. 709.46
Picasso at Vallauris. New York, Reynal [1959] [96] p. illus. (part col.) 36 cm. Includes three essays in French by D. H. Kahnweiler, O. Elytis, and G. Ramie; with translations into English by Serge Hughes. "Originally published in France [1951] as a double number of Verve, 25 and 26." [N6853.P5A5] 59-5995
I. Title.

PICASSO, Pablo, 1881- 741.9'44
1973.
Picasso: drawings, 1961-1968. [Exhibition] fall 1968 Chicago, International Galleries [1968] 39 p. (chiefly illus., part col.) 25 cm. Text by R. S. Johnson. Bibliography: p. 7. [NC248.P5I57] 74-187163
1. Picasso, Pablo, 1881-1973. I. International Galleries.

PICASSO, Pablo, 1881- 741.9'44
1973.
Picasso's posters. Compiled by Christopher Czwiklitzer. [1st American ed.] New York, Random House [1971] 1 v. (various pagings) illus. (part col.) 35 cm. Translation of Les affiches de Pablo Picasso. [NC1850.P5C913] 75-163490 ISBN 0-394-47222-5 60.00
I. Czwiklitzer, Christopher, comp. II. Title.

PICASSO, Pablo, 1881- 769'.92'4
1973.
Picasso's Vollard Suite / introd. by Hans Bolliger ; [translated by Norbert Guterman]. New York : H. N. Abrams, 1977. xviii, 100 p. : chiefly ill. ; 28 cm. Translation of Suite Vollard. Includes bibliographical references. [N] [NE2049.5P5APA5813 1977] 77-373226 ISBN 0-8109-2076-X 6.95
1. Picasso, Pablo, 1881-1973. 2. Vollard, Ambroise, 1867-1939. I. Title. **BIP**

PICASSO, Pablo Pablo 741.9346
Ruiz y Picasso 1881-
Toros: 15 wash drawings by Pablo Picasso. Poem by Pablo Neruda. Tr. from Spanish into French by Jean Marceau. [dist. Greenwich, Conn., New York Graphic Society, c.] 1960 [ ] unpaged text. 15 numbered prints. t.p. in French. 55x42cm. lim. numbered ed. silk-bound portflio, 225.00
I. Neruda, Pablo. II. Marceau, Jean, tr. III. Title.

QUINN, Edward. 759.6
Picasso at work; an intimate photographic study by Edward Quinn. Introd. and text by Roland Penrose. Garden City, N. Y., Doubleday [1964] 16 [259] p. illus. (part col.) ports. (part col.) 34 cm. [ND553.P5Q5] 64-24372
1. Picasso, Pablo, 1881- I. Penrose, Roland. II. Title.

RABOFF, Ernest Lloyd. 709
Pablo Picasso, by Ernest Raboff. Garden City, N.Y., Doubleday, 1968. [31] p. illus. (part col.), port. 29 cm. (Art for children) A Gemini-Smith book. A simplified discussion of the art of Pablo Picasso with examples showing the various techniques used in his works. [ND553.P5R24] AC 68
1. Picasso, Pablo, 1881- I. Title. **BIP**

RAMIE, Georges. 738'.092'4
Picasso's ceramics / Georges Ramie ; translated from the French by Kenneth Lyons. New York : Viking Press, 1976. 292 p. : ill. (some col.) ; 28 cm. (A Studio book) Translation of Ceramique de Picasso. Includes index. [NK4210.P5R2813

ed.] New York, Tudor Pub. Co. [1962] 154 p. illus. 25 cm. [N8550.L3 1962] 62-21160
1. Picture frames and framing.

NEWMAN, Thelma R., 1925- 749'.7
The frame book; contemporary design with traditional and modern methods and materials [by] Thelma R. Newman, Jay Hartley Newman [and] Lee Scott Newman. New York, Crown Publishers [1974] 144 p. illus. 29 cm. Bibliography: p. 132. [N8550.N48] 73-85858 5.95
1. Picture frames and framing. I. Newman, Jay Hartley, joint author. II. Newman, Lee Scott, joint author. III. Title. BIP

ROGERS, Harold. 745.51
How to make your own picture frames; step-by-step pictures of over 50 basic frame styles and how to finish them, for artists, students, photographers, decorators, home craftsmen [by] Hal Rogers [and] Ed Reinhardt. (Rev. ed.] New York, Watson-Guptill Publications [1964, c1958] 127 p. illus. 31 cm. [N8550.R63] 64-23733
1. Picture frames and framing. I. Reinhardt, Edwin, joint author. II. Title.

ROGERS, Harold. 745.51
How to make your own picture frames; step-by-step pictures of over 50 basic frame styles, and how to finish them; for artists, students, photographers, decorators, home craftsmen [by] Hal Rogers [and] Ed Reinhardt. [1st ed.] New York, Watson-Guptill Publications [1958] 125 p. illus. 23 x 31 cm. [N8550.R63] 58-13523
1. Picture frames and framing. I. Reinhardt, Edwin, joint author. II. Title. BIP

TAUBES, Frederic, 1900- 749.72
Better frames for your pictures. New York, Studio Publications, in association with Crowell [1952] 144 p. illus. 24 cm. [N8550.T3] 52-7382
1. Picture frames and framing. I. Title.

TAUBES, Frederic, 1900- 749.7
Better frames for your pictures. [New ed.] New York, Viking Press [1960] 144 p. illus. 24 cm. (A Studio book) [N8550.T3 1960] 60-8513
1. Picture frames and framing. I. Title.

TAUBES, Frederic, 1900- 749'.7
Better frames for your pictures. [3d rev. ed.] New York, Viking Press [1968] 144 p. illus. 24 cm. (A Studio book) [N8550.T3 1968] 68-22318
1. Picture frames and framing. I. Title.

TOSCANO, Eamon. 749'.7
Step-by-step framing; a complete introduction to the craft of framing. Conceived and edited by William and Shirley Sayles. New York, Golden Press [1971] 80 p. illus. 28 cm. (Golden Press step-by-step craft series) Bibliography: p. 80. [N8550.T6] 72-149095 2.50
1. Picture frames and framing. I. Title. II. Title: Framing.

WOLF, Jack, 1922- 749'.7
Professional picture framing for the amateur, by Jack & Barbara Wolf. [1st ed.] Blue Ridge Summit, Pa., G/L Tab Books [1974] 167 p. illus. 23 cm. [N8550.W55] 73-86764 ISBN 0-8306-3674-9 5.95
1. Picture frames and framing. I. Wolf, Barbara, joint author. II. Title.
Pbk. 3.95; ISBN 0-8306-2674-3. BIP

YOUNT, John T. 749'.7
Picture framing handbook, by John T. Yount. San Angelo, Tex., Educator Books, c1971. 151 p. illus. 22 cm. Bibliography: p. 149. [N8550.Y6] 73-180259 ISBN 0-912092-42-4 6.95
1. Picture frames and framing. I. Title. BIP

Picture frames and framing—History.

MARYANSKI, Richard A. 749'.7
Antique picture frame guide, by Richard A. Maryanski. Edited by Anne Lunde. Niles, Ill., Cedar Forest Co. [1973] 80 p. illus. (part col.) 29 cm. [N8550.M36] 73-180221 12.50
1. Picture frames and framing—History. 2. Mirrors—Frames—History. I. Title. BIP

Picture-writing, Indian.

HEIZER, Robert 571.709793
Fleming, 1915-
Prehistoric rock art of Nevada and eastern California [by] Robert F. Heizer and Martin A. Baumhoff. Berkeley, University of California Press, 1962. xvi, 412 p. illus., maps, diagrs. 27 cm. Includes bibliographies. [N5310.H33] 62-13074
1. Picture-writing, Indian. 2. Indians of North America—Nevada—Antiquities. 3. Indians of North America—California—Antiquities. 4. Nevada—Antiquities. 5. California—Antiquities. I. Baumhoff, Martin A., joint author. II. Title.

MALLERY, Garrick, 1831-1894. 497
Picture-writing of the American Indians. Foreword by J. W. Powell. New York, Dover Publications [1972] 2 v. (x, 822 p.) illus. 24 cm. Reprint of the 1893 ed. [E59.W9M3 1972] 76-188815 ISBN 0-486-22842-8 5.00 per vol.
1. Picture-writing, Indian. I. Title. BIP

Picture-writing, Indian—Exhibitions.

PREHISTORIC petroglyphs 732'.2
and pictographs in Utah. Edited by Roland Siegrist. [Salt Lake City] Utah State Historical Society [1972] 70 p. (chiefly illus. (part col.)) 20 x 23 cm. Catalogue of an exhibition held at the Utah Museum of Fine Arts. Includes bibliographical references. [E78.U55P7] 72-619505
1. Picture-writing, Indian—Exhibitions. 2. Indians of North America—Utah—Art—Exhibitions. 3. Utah—Antiquities—Exhibitions. I. Siegrist, Roland, ed. II. Utah State Historical Society. III. Utah Museum of Fine Arts.

Pictures.

JUDSON, Sylvia (Shaw) ed. 759.084
The quiet eye; a way of looking at pictures. Selections and introd. by Sylvia Shaw Judson. Chicago, H. Regnery Co., 1954. 4, [65] p. illus. (part col.) 28cm. [N370.J8] 55-443
1. Pictures. I. Title.

JUDSON, Sylvia (Shaw) ed. 028.5
The quiet eye; a way of looking at pictures. Selections and introd. by Sylvia Shaw Judson. [3rd ed.] Chicago, Regnery, 1954 [i.e. 1963] 4, [64] p. illus. (part col.) 28 cm. [N370.J8] 67-8761
1. Pictures. I. Title.

Pictures—Catalogs.

AARON Ashley, inc. 381'.45'769
Catalogue of fine color reproductions. Yonkers, N.Y. : A. Ashley, 1977. 133 p. : all col. ill. ; 29 cm. "A Collograph print." Includes index. [N4035.A17A45 1977] 76-42152
1. Pictures—Catalogs. 2. Color prints—Catalogs. I. Title.

DONALD Art Company. 338.4'7'75029
Fine art reproductions of masters, old, modern, and contemporary, American and foreign— many under exclusive contract with our company—printed in offset lithography. [Port Chester, N.Y., 1970] 246 p. (chiefly illus., part col.) 29 cm. [N4035.D6A5 1970] 76-279664
1. Pictures—Catalogs. I. Title.

SPECIAL Libraries 704.97
Association. Picture Division.
Picture sources; an introductory list. Helen Faye, editor. New York, Special Libraries Association [1959] 115 p. 26 cm. [N4000.S7] 59-10237
1. Pictures—Catalogs. I. Faye, Helen, ed. II. Title.

SPECIAL Libraries 025.2'1
Association. Picture Division.
Picture sources : collections of prints and photographs in the U.S. and Canada : a project of Picture Division, SLA, and American Society of Picture Professionals / Ann Novotny, editor, Rosemary Eakins, assistant editor. 3. New York : Special Libraries Association, 1975. xx, 387 p. : ill. ; 26 cm. Includes indexes. [N4000.S7 1975] 75-6582 ISBN 0-87111-206-X : 17.00
1. Pictures—Catalogs. I. Novotny, Ann. II. Eakins, Rosemary. III. American Society of Picture Professionals. IV. Title.

Pictures—Copying.

CHETHAM, Charles Scott. 759.9492
The role of Vincent van Gogh's copies in the development of his art / Charles Chetham. New York : Garland Pub., 1976. 288 p., [8] leaves of plates : ill. ; 21 cm. (Outstanding dissertations in the fine arts) Originally presented as the author's thesis, Harvard University, 1960. Bibliography: p. 284-288. [ND653.G7C4 1976] 75-23788 ISBN 0-8240-1984-9 lib.bdg. : 27.50
1. Gogh, Vincent van, 1853-1890. 2. Pictures—Copying. I. Title. II. Series. BIP

Pictures—Directories.

EVANS, Hilary, 1929- 001.4'3
The picture researcher's handbook : an international guide to picture sources, and how to use them / Hilary and Mary Evans and Andra Nelki. New York : Scribner, [1975] c1974. 365 p., [4] leaves of plates : ill. ; 25 cm. Includes indexes. [N4000.E8 1975b] 74-19684 ISBN 0-684-14133-7 : 15.00
1. Pictures—Directories. I. Evans, Mary, 1890- joint author. II. Nelki, Andra, joint author. III. Title. BIP

Pictures—Indexes.

GREER, Roger C., 1928- 011
Illustration index, by Roger C. Greer. 3d ed. Metuchen, N.J., Scarecrow Press, 1973. 164 p. 22 cm. Previous editions by L. E. Vance and E. M. Tracey. [N7525.G72 1973] 72-10918 ISBN 0-8108-0568-5 12.00
1. Pictures—Indexes. I. Vance, Lucile E. Illustration index. II. Title.

HEWLETT-WOODMERE Public 709
Library.
Index to art reproductions in books. Compiled by the professional staff of the Hewlett-Woodmere Public Library under the direction of Elizabeth W. Thomson. Metuchen, N.J., Scarecrow Press, 1974. xii, 372 p. 22 cm. Includes bibliographical references. [N7525.H48 1974] 74-1286 ISBN 0-8108-0711-4
1. Pictures—Indexes. I. Thomson, Elizabeth W. II. Title. BIP

MARSHALL, Stephen. 016.7
The picture index. New York, Research Book Co. [c1952- v. 28cm. Contents.v.1. An index of every pictured object in the New Funk & Wagnalls encyclopedia.--v.2. An index of every pictured object in Merriam-Webster's New International dictionary, second edition.--v.3. An index of every pictured object in Funk & Wagnalls new Standard dictionary. [N7525.M35] 54-28476
1. Pictures—Indexes. I. Title.

VANCE, Lucile E. 016.7
Illustration index. New York, Scarecrow Press, 1957. 192 p. 23 cm. "Books and periodicals indexed": p. 5. [N7525.V3] 57-6624
1. Pictures—Indexes. I. Title.

VANCE, Lucile E. 011
Illustration index by Lucile E. Vance, Esther M. Tracey. 2d ed. New York, Scarecrow [c.]1966. 527p. 22cm. Bibl. [N7525.V3] 65-13558 12.00
1. Pictures—Indexes. I. Tracey, Esther M., joint author. II. Title.

VANCE, Lucile E. 016.7
Illustration index. New York, Scarecrow Press, 1957. 192 p. 23 cm. "Books and periodicals indexed": p. 5. -- Supplement. 1st -- July 1956-1959 -- New York, Scarecrow Press. no. 22 cm. [N7525.V3] 57-6624
1. Pictures — Indexes. I. Title.

Pictures—Printing.

CHERRY, David. 686.2'8
Preparing artwork for reproduction / David Cherry. New York : Crown Publishers, 1976. 96 p. : ill. ; 26 cm. [Z257.C47] 76-4802 ISBN 0-517-52618-2 : 6.95
1. Pictures—Printing. 2. Commercial art—Printing. 3. Printing, Practical—Layout. I. Title.

STONE, Bernard 655
Preparing art for printing [by] Bernard Stone, Arthur Eckstein. New York, Reinhold [c.1965] 199p. illus. (pt. col.) 22 x 27 cm. [Z257.S75] 64-22426 15.00
1. Pictures—Printing. 2. Commercial art—Printing. I. Eckstein, Arthur, joint author. II. Title. BIP

WAKEMAN, Geoffrey. 769'.942
Victorian book illustration; the technical revolution. Detroit, Gale Research Co. [1973] 182 p. illus. 23 cm. Bibliography: p. 165-169. [Z257.W34 1973] 72-14042 12.50
1. Pictures—Printing. 2. Illustrated books—19th century. I. Title. BIP

Piening, Peter F.

PIENING, Peter F. 741.9'43
Peter F. Piening : Olbilder, Zeichnungen, 1973-1975 : [Ausstellung, Galerie Brockstedt, Hamburg, Dezember 1975-Januar 1976 : Katalog]. Hamburg : Galerie Brockstedt, [1975] [6] p., [24] leaves of plates : chiefly ill. ; 17 x 21 cm. Text by Stefanie Poley. [NC251.P53P64] 76-458552
1. Piening, Peter F. I. Poley, Stefanie. II. Galerie Brockstedt.

Pierpont Morgan Library, New York.

PIERPONT Morgan 730'.0935
Library, New York.
Ancient Mesopotamian art and selected texts : The Pierpont Morgan Library. New York : The Library, c1976. 42 p. : ill. ; 26 cm. Includes bibliographical references. [N5370.P53 1976] 76-45976 ISBN 0-87598-062-7
1. Pierpont Morgan Library, New York. 2. Art, Assyro-Babylonian. 3. Assyro-Babylonian language—Texts. 4. Iraq—Antiquities. I. Title. BIP

PIERPONT Morgan 686.2'2'07401471
Library, New York.
Art of the printed book, 1455-1955; masterpieces of typography through five centuries from the collections of the Pierpont Morgan Library. With an essay by Joseph Blumenthal. New York, 1973. xiv, 192 p. 125 plates. 31 cm. Catalog of an exhibition held at the Pierpont Morgan Library, Sept. 11-Dec. 2, 1973. Bibliography: p. 181-183. [Z121.P58 1973] 73-82830 ISBN 0-87598-041-4
1. Pierpont Morgan Library, New York. 2. Bibliographical exhibitions. I. Blumenthal, Joseph, 1897- II. Title.

PIERPONT Morgan Library, 016.9298
New York.
Autograph letters & manuscripts; major acquisitions of the Pierpont Morgan Library, 1924-1974. New York [1974] xv, 103 p. facsims., music. 30 cm. Erratum slip inserted. [Z6621.P6512] [Z602] 73-92927 ISBN 0-87598-043-0 8.00 (pbk.)
1. Pierpont Morgan Library, New York. 2. Manuscripts—Catalogs. 3. Autographs—Catalogs. I. Title.

PIERPONT Morgan Library, 741.9'4
New York.
Drawings. New York [1974] xxx, 103 p. 50 plates. 30 cm. (Its Major acquisitions, 1924-1974) [NC25.N4P536 1974] 73-92928 ISBN 0-87598-044-9 8.00 (pbk.)
1. Pierpont Morgan Library, New York. 2. Drawings—New York (City)—Catalogs. I. Title.

PIERPONT Morgan Library, New 093
York.
Early printed books. New York [1974] xvi, [105] p. facsims. 30 cm. (Its Major acquisitions, 1924-1974) Errata slip inserted. [Z240.P62 1974] 73-92930 8.00
1. Pierpont Morgan Library, New York. 2. Incunabula—Bibliography—Catalogs. I. Title.

PIERPONT Morgan 745.6'7'094
Library, New York.
Mediaeval & Renaissance manuscripts. New York [1974] xvi, 106 p. facsims. 30 cm. (Its Major acquisitions, 1924-1974) Errata slip inserted. Bibliography: p. 105-

Piranesi, Giovanni Battista, 1720-1778—Catalogs.

PIRANESI, Giovanni 741.9'45
Battista, 1720-1778.
Giovanni Battista Piranesi : drawings in the Pierpont Morgan Library / Felice Stampfle ; with a foreword by Charles Ryskamp. New York : Dover Publications, c1978. xxxiv, 121 p. : ill. ; 31 cm. Includes bibliographical references and index. [NC257.P49A4 1978] 78-54866 ISBN 0-486-23714-1 : 7.50
1. Piranesi, Giovanni Battista, 1720-1778—Catalogs. 2. Pierpont Morgan Library, New York—Catalogs. I. Stampfle, Felice. II. Pierpont Morgan Library, New York. BIP

Pisa. Battistero.

SMITH, Christine. 726'.4
The Baptistery of Pisa / Christine Smith. New York : Garland Pub., 1978. p. cm. (Outstanding dissertations in the fine arts) Originally presented as the author's thesis, New York University, 1975. Bibliography: p. [NA1121.P6S44 1978] 77-94715 ISBN 0-8240-3249-7 : lib.bdg. : 36.00
1. Pisa. Battistero. I. Title. II. Series. BIP

Pisa—Description.

LOOKING at Pisa / 913.4575
G. Barsali ... [et al.]. Firenze : Bonechi, 1976, c1974. 92 p. : chiefly col. ill., map (1 fold. col. in pocket) ; 28 cm. (Italia artistica : New ser. ; n. 4) Includes index. [DG975.P6L66] 77-459528 L3000
1. Pisa—Description. 2. Art—Italy—Pisa. I. Barsali, G.

Pisa—Hist.

HERLIHY, David. 945.5
Pisa in the early Renaissance; a study of urban growth. New Haven, Yale University Press, 1958. xx, 229p. map. 23cm. (Yale historical publications, Miscellany, 68) 'This book grew of a dissertation written at Yale University.' 'Notes on the sources': p. 215-221. Bibliographical footnotes. [DG975.P615H4] 58-6933
1. Pisa—Hist. I. Title. II. Series.

Pisanello, Antonio Pisano, known as, ca. 1395-ca. 1455.

PACCAGNINI, Giovanni, 1910- 759.5
Pisanello [translated from the Italian by Jane Carroll] London, Phaidon Press, 1973. 298 p. illus. (some col.) 29 cm. Distributed in the U.S.A. by Praeger Publishers, New York. Translation of Pisanello e il ciclo cavalleresco di Mantova. Includes index. Bibliography: p. 285-290. [ND623.P68P3213 1973] 72-86573 ISBN 0-7148-1556-X 45.00
1. Pisanello, Antonio Pisano, known as, ca. 1395-ca. 1455. I. Title.

PISANELLO, Antonio 741.945
Pisano, Known as, ca.1395-ca.1455
Drawing by Pisanello. A selection; with introd., notes. by George F. Hill. New York, Dover [1965] 60p. 65 plates. 29cm. (,t1484) Unabridged repubn. of the work first pub. in 1929 [NX1155.P55H55] 65-26653 2.00 pap.,
I. Hill. George Francis, Sir 1867-1948, ed. II. Title.

PISANELLO, Antonio 741.945
Pisano, Known as, ca.1395-ca.1455
Drawings by Pisanello. A selection, with introd., notes, by George F. Hill. [Gloucester. Mass., P. Smith. 1966] 60p. 65 plates. 29cm. (Dover bk., T1484 rebound) First pub. in Paris and Brussels in 1929 [NC1155.P55H55] 4.50
I. Hill, George Francis, Sir 1867-1948, ed. II. Title.

SINDONA, Enio. 759.5
Pisanello. [Translated from the Italian by John Ross] New York, H. N. Abrams [c1961] 148 p. illus., plates (part col.) 32 cm. Bibliography: p. 139. [ND623.P68S53] 63-12780
1. Pisanello, Antonio Pisano, known as, ca. 1395-ca. 1455. I. Title.

SNIDONA, Enio 759.5
Pisanello. [Tr. from Italian by John Ross] New York, Abrams [1964, c.1961] 148p. illus., plates. (pt. col.) 32cm. Bibl. 63-12780 25.00
1. Pisanello, Antonio Pisano, known as, ca. 1395-ca. 1455. I. Title.

Pisano, Giovanni, 1240?-1320?

AYRTON, Michael, 1921- 730.924
Giovanni Pisano, sculptor [by] Michael Ayrton. Introd. by Henry Moore. Photos. specially taken by Ilario Bessi in collaboration with Henry Moore. New York, Weybright & Talley [1969] 248 p. illus., 370 plates. 28 cm. Bibliography: p. 244-246. [NB623.P4A9] 75-87066 20.00
1. Pisano, Giovanni, 1240?-1320? I. Title.

Pissarro, Camille, 1830-1903.

ADLER, Kathleen. 759.4 B
Camille Pissarro : a biography / Kathleen Adler. New York : St. Martin's Press, 1978, c1977. 208 p., [8] leaves of plates : ill. ; 25 cm. Includes bibliographical references and index. [ND553.P55A85 1977] 77-10307 ISBN 0-312-11459-1 : 12.95
1. Pissarro, Camille, 1830-1903. 2. Painters—France—Biography.

BOULTON, Alfredo. 760'.0924
Pissarro in Venezuela. Introd. by Alfredo Boulton, translated and edited by Stanton L. Catlin and Phyllis Freeman. [New York, Printed by J. B. Watkins Co., 1968] 32 p. illus. 18 x 25 cm. "A loan exhibition presented in collaboration with the Banco Central de Venezuela in association with the Museo de Bellas Artes, Caracas, and the Drawing Society ... [held] February 1-March 6, 1968, Art Gallery, Center for Inter-American Relations, 680 Park Avenue, New York." The introd. (p. 5-18) is a translation of the Spanish portion of Camille Pissarro en Venezuela. [ND553.P55B613] 68-21908
1. Pissarro, Camille, 1830-1903. 2. Melbye, Fritz, 1826-1896. I. Center for Inter-American Relations. Art Gallery. II. Title. BIP

KUNSTLER, Charles, 1887- 759.4
Pissarro; cities and landscapes. New York, French & European Publications [1967] 64 p. col. illus. 21 cm. (Rythm [i.e. Rhythm] and colour, no. 11) Translation of Pissarro; villes et campagnes. Bibliography: p. 63-64. [ND553.P55K813] 68-1829
1. Pissarro, Camille, 1830-1903. I. Title. II. Title: Cities and landscapes.

PISSARRO, Camille, 1830- 759.4
1903-
Camille Pissarro. Text by John Rewald. New York, Abrams [1963] 158, [2]p. illus., col. plates, ports. 34cm. (Lib. of great painters) Bibl. 63-14212 15.00
I. Rewald, John, 1912- II. Title.

PISSARRO, Camille, 1830- 759.4
1903.
Camille Pissarro (1830-1903) Text by John Rewald. New York, H. N. Abrams in association with Pocket Books [1954] [74] p. 42 illus. (part col.) port. 18cm. (The Pocket library of great art, A18) An Abrams art book. Bibliography: p. [74] [ND553.P55R42] [ND553.P55R42] 927.5 54-14621 54-14621
I. Rewald, John, 1912- II. Title.

PISSARRO, Camille, 1830- 759.4 B
1903.
Camille Pissarro: letters to his son Lucien, edited with the assistance of Lucien Pissarro by John Rewald. 3d ed., rev. and enl. Mamaroneck, N.Y., P. P. Appel, 1972. 399 p. illus. 26 cm. Includes the letters of Lucien to Camille Pissarro published for the first time in English translation. [ND553.P55P4813 1972] 77-162499 ISBN 0-911858-22-9 22.50
1. Pissarro, Camille, 1830-1903. 2. Painters—France—Correspondence, reminiscences, etc. I. Rewald, John, 1912- ed. II. Pissarro, Lucien, 1863-1944. III. Title.

PISSARRO, Camille, 1830- 759.4
1903.
Pissarro / by Raymond Cogniat ; [translated from the French by Alice Sachs]. New York : Crown Publishers, c1975. 95 p. : ill. (some col.) ; 29 cm. Bibliography: p. 93-94. [ND553.P55C6313] 75-20697 ISBN 0-517-52477-5 : 4.95
1. Pissarro, Camille, 1830-1903. I. Cogniat, Raymond, 1896-

SHAPIRO, Barbara S. 769'.92'4
Camille Pissarro; the impressionist printmaker, by Barbara S. Shapiro. Boston, Museum of Fine Arts [1973] [56] p. illus. (1 col.) 28 cm. Exhibition catalog. Bibliography: p. [16] [NE650.P68S52] 73-79207 ISBN 0-87846-075-6 3.25
1. Pissarro, Camille, 1830-1903. I. Boston. Museum of Fine Arts. BIP

Pissarro, Lucien, 1863-1944.

MEADMORE, William Sutton. 927.5
Lucien Pissarro; un coeur simple. New York, Knopf, 1963 [1962] 251 p. illus. 22 cm. In English. [ND553.P56M4 1963] 63-14617
1. Pissarro, Lucien, 1863-1944. 2. Pissarro family.

Pistols.

DATIG, Fred A 1925- 623.4433
The Luger pistol (Pistole Parabellum): its history and development from 1893-1945. (Bevery Hills, Calif., Fadco Pub. Co., 1955 208p. illus. 24cm. [TS537.D3] 55-4634
1. Pistols. I. Title. BIP

DUNLAP, H J 683.4
American, British & Continental pepperbox firearms [by] Jack Dunlap. [Los Altos, Calif., 1964] 279 p. illus. 29 cm. "A portion of this book is published under the 1952 copyrights of Pepperbox firearms [by Lewis Winant]" [TS537.D75] 64-24121
1. Pistols. I. Winant, Lewis. Pepperbox firearms. II. Title. III. Title: Pepperbox firearms. BIP

DUNLAP, H. J. 683.4
American, British & Continental pepperbox firearms [by] Jack Dunlap. Palo Alto, Calif., Pacific Bks. [1967,c.1964] 279p. illus. 29cm. A portion of this bk. is pub. under the 1952 copyrights of Pepperbox firearms [by Lewis Winant.] [TS537.D75] 15.00
1. Pistols. I. Winant, Lewis. Pepperbox firearms. II. Title. III. Title: Pepperbox firearms.

NEAL, Robert J., 1933- 623.443
Smith and Wesson, 1857-1945 [by] Robert J. Neal and Roy G. Jinks. South Brunswick [N.J.] A. S. Barnes [1966] 360 p. illus., facsims., ports. 26 cm. Bibliography: p. 354-355. [TS537.N35 1966] 66-12902
1. Smith and Wesson, inc., Springfield, Mass. 2. Pistols. 3. Revolvers. I. Jinks, Roy G., 1936- joint author. BIP

SMITH, Walter Harold 623.443
Black, 1901-1959.
The book of pistols & revolvers, an encyclopedic reference work, by Walter H. B. Smith, and Supplement: post-war developments, by Kent Bellah. [4th ed.] Harrisburg, Pa., Military Service Division, Stackpole Co. [1960] xvi, 718 p. illus. 24 cm. Revised and enl. ed. of the author's The N. R. A. book of small arms, v. 1, Pistols and revolvers, published in 1946. [TS537.S54 1960] 60-6300
1. Pistols. 2. Revolvers. I. Title.

SMITH, Walter Harold 623.4'43
Black, 1901-1959.
Book of pistols and revolvers. Completely up-dated by Joseph E. Smith. [7th ed.] Harrisburg, Pa., Stackpole Books [1968] xvi, 816 p. illus. 24 cm. At head of title: The W. H. B. Smith classic. Revised and enl. ed. of the author's The N.R.A. book of small arms, v. 1, Pistols and revolvers, published in 1946. [TS537.S54 1968] 68-18959
1. Pistols. 2. Revolvers. I. Smith, Joseph Edward, 1921- ed. II. Title.

WILKINSON, Frederick 739.7'4'43
John, 1922-
Flintlock pistols; an illustrated reference guide to flintlock pistols from the 17th to the 19th century, by F. Wilkinson. [Harrisburg, Pa.] Stackpole Books [1968] 75 p. illus., port. 23 cm. (Stackpole arms and armour) Bibliography: p. 71-73. [TS537.W47] 68-31205 4.95
1. Pistols. I. Title. BIP

Pistols, American.

DURHAM, Charles. 683'.43
Firearms of the American Revolution : a bicentennial commemoration, 1776-1976 / [written and illustrated by Charles Durham]. [s.l.] : Durham, c1974. 1 portfolio ([17] p. (incl. cover), [5] leaves of plates) : ill. ; 34 cm. Title from portfolio. [TS537.D76] 75-312005
1. Pistols, American. 2. United States—History—Revolution, 1775-1783—Supplies. I. Title.

KIRKLAND, Turner. 683'.43
Southern derringers of the Mississippi Valley, by Tu[r]ner Kirkland. 2d ed. [Union City, Tenn., Pioneer Press] 1972. 102 p. illus. 22 cm. [TS537.K53 1972] 75-185226
1. Pistols, American. 2. Firearms industry and trade—Mississippi Valley. I. Title. BIP

Pistols, British.

DIXON, Norman. 739.7'4'43
Georgian pistols: the art and craft of the flintlock pistol, 1715-1840. York, Pa., G. Shumway [1972, c1971] 184 p. illus. 26 cm. Includes bibliographical references. [TS537.D58 1972] 72-166147 ISBN 0-87387-046-8 14.00
1. Pistols, British. I. Title. BIP

GLENDENNING, Ian. 623.4'4
British pistols and guns, 1640-1840. [New ed.] New York, Arco Pub. Co. [1967] viii, 195 p. illus., facsims. 19 x 26 cm. [TS535.G5 1967b] 67-18416
1. Pistols, British. 2. Firearms, British. I. Title.

Pistols—Collectors and collecting.

ALEXANDER, S. G. B. 739.7
Antique pistols. Illus. by Ronald Paton, with a commentary by S. G. B. Alexander. New York, Arco [1964, c.1963. 55]p. col. illus., diagr. 26x44cm. (Arco gun lib.,1176) Bibl. 64-11520 15.00
1. Pistols—Collectors and collecting. I. Paton, Ronald, illus. II. Title.

REESE, Michael, 1942- 355.8'2
Collector's guide to Luger values, by Michael Reese, II. 1972-73 ed. Gretna, La., Pelican Pub. Co., 1972. [23] p. illus. 14 cm. [TS532.4.R44] 72-86563 1.00
1. Pistols—Collectors and collecting. 2. Luger pistol. I. Title. BIP

THE William M. 683'.43'074017178
Locke Collection; [catalogue. By Frank M. Sellers and others. 1st ed.] East Point, Ga., Antique Armory Inc. [1973] 541 p. chiefly illus. (part col.) 29 cm. Bibliography: p. 538. [TS532.4.W56] 73-91748
1. Locke, William M., 1894-1972. 2. Pistols—Collectors and collecting. I. Locke, William M., 1894-1972. II. Sellers, Frank M. III. The Antique Armory Inc.

Pistols—Exhibitions.

NORTON (R. W.) 683'.43'074016399
Art Gallery.
Artistry in arms; the art of gunsmithing and gun engraving. [1st ed.] Shreveport, La. [1971] 42 p. illus. 28 cm. Catalog of the exhibition held May 16-June 27, 1971. Bibliography: p. 38-40. [TS532.2.U6S56] 75-164699 ISBN 0-9600182-4-7
1. Pistols—Exhibitions. I. Title. BIP

Pistols, German.

HOGG, Ian V., 1926- 683'.43
German pistols and revolvers, 1871-1945 [by] Ian V. Hogg. [Harrisburg, Pa.] Stackpole Books [1971] 160 p. illus. 30 cm. [TS537.H63] 70-162454 ISBN 0-8117-0700-8 12.95
1. Pistols, German. 2. Revolvers, German. I. Title.

HOGG, Ian V., 1926- 683'.43'0943
German pistols and revolvers, 1871-1945 / Ian V. Hogg. New York : Galahad Books,

[1975] c1971. 160 p. : ill. ; 29 cm.
Originally published by Stackpole Books,
Harrisburg, Pa. [TS537.H63 1975] 74-
29815 ISBN 0-88365-299-4 : 12.95
1. Pistols, German. 2. Revolvers, German.
I. Title.

Pistols—History.

BOOTHROYD, Geoffrey.   683'.43'09
The handgun. New York, Crown
Publishers [1970] 564 p. illus., ports. 29
cm. Includes bibliographical references.
[TS537.B65 1970] 70-108067 19.95
1. Pistols—History. I. Title.

FRITH, James   739.7
Antique pistol collecting (1400-1860) by
James Frith and Ronald Andrews. New
York, Arco Pub. Co. [c.1960, i.e., 1961]
122p. illus., 25 plates 28cm. 60-52068 7.50
1. Pistols—Hist. 2. Pistols—Collectors and
collecting. I. Andrews, Ronald, joint
author.   II.   Title.

HOGG, Ian V., 1926-   683'.43'0904
Pistols of the world : a comprehensive
illustrated encyclopedia of the world's
pistols and revolvers from 1870 to the
present day / by Ian V. Hogg and John
Weeks. London : Arms and Armour Press
; San Rafael, Calif. : Presidio Press, 1978.
306 p. : ill. ; 30 cm. Includes index.
[TS533.H65 1978] 78-318505 ISBN 0-
89141-068-6 (Presidio) : 24.95
1. Pistols—History. I. Weeks, John, joint
author. II. Title.

Pistols, Japanese.

LEITHE, Frederick   623.4'43'0952
E.
Japanese hand guns, by Frederick E.
Leithe. [1st ed.] Alhambra, Calif., Borden
Pub. Co. [1968] 1 v. (chiefly illus.) 23 x 29
cm. [TS537.L4] 67-29814
1. Pistols, Japanese. 2. Revolvers. I. Title.
    BIP

Pistols, Russian—History.

TARASSUK, Leonid.   623.4'43'0947
Russian pistols in the seventeenth century.
York, Pa., G. Shumway [1968] 34, [1] p.
39 illus. 23 cm. First published in the
Burlington magazine, v. 109, Nov. and
Dec. 1967. Bibliography: p. 34-[35]
[TS533.4.R9T3] 72-2546
1. Pistols, Russian—History. I. Title.

Pistols—United States—Collectors and collecting.

DYKE, Samuel E.   683'.43
Thoughts on the American flintlock pistol,
by S. E. Dyke. York, Pa., G. Shumway
[1974] 61 p. illus. 28 cm. (Longrifle series)
[TS532.4.D93] 74-174994 ISBN 0-87387-
070-0
1. Pistols—United States—Collectors and
collecting. I. Title.   BIP

Pitchers.

KAMM, Minnie Elizabeth   748.8
(Watson), 1886-
A fifth pitcher book. Drawings by the
author. [2d ed. Grosse Pointe Farms?
Mich., 1952] 209 p. illus. 22 cm.
[NK5112.K27 1952] 52-35548
1. Pitchers. 2. Glassware—U. S. 3.
Glassware—Collectors and collecting. I.
Title.

KAMM, Minnie Elizabeth   748.8
(Watson), 1886-
A second two hundred pattern glass
pitchers; drawings. by the author. [3d ed.
Grosse Pointe Farms, Mich., 1950] 141 p.
illus. 22 cm. [NK5112.K32 1950] 50-36723
1. Pitchers. 2. Glassware—U. S. 3.
Glassware—Collectors and collecting. I.
Title.

KAMM, Minnie Elizabeth   748.8
(Watson) 1886-
A seventh pitcher book. Drawings by the
author. [1st ed. Grosse Pointe, Mich.,

1953] 212p. illus. 22cm. [NK5112.K287]
53-2173
1. Pitchers. 2. Glassware—U. S. 3.
Glassware—Collectors and collecting. I.
Title.

KAMM, Minnie Elizabeth   748.8
(Watson) 1886-
A third Two hundred pattern glass
pitchers. Drawings by the author. [3d ed.]
Detroit, Printed by Motschall Co. [1953]
iv, 151p. illus. 22cm. [NK5112.K33 1953]
53-30731
1. Pitchers. 2. Glassware—U. S. 3.
Glassware—Collectors and collecting. I.
Title.

KAMM, Minnie Elizabeth   748.8
(Watson) 1886-
Two hundred pattern glass pitchers.
Drawings by the author. [5th ed.] Detroit,
Motschall Co. [1952] 138p. illus. 22cm.
[NK5112.K3 1952] 52-67703
1. Pitchers. 2. Glassware—U. S. 3.
Glassware—Collectors and collecting. I.
Title.

KAMM, Minnie Elizabeth   748.8
(Watson) 1886-1954.
A third two hundred glass patterns. [3d
ed.] Drawings by the author. [Detroit,
Kamm Publications, 1960] iv, 151 p. illus.
22 cm. Previous editions published under
title: A third two hundred pattern glass
pitchers. [NK5112.K33] 64-1383
1. Pitchers. 2. Glassware, American. 3.
Glassware — Collectors and collecting. I.
Title.

Pitchers—Collectors and collecting.

PATON, James.   745.1
Jugs : a collector's guide / by James Paton.
London : Souvenir Press, 1976. 144 p. : ill.
; 22 cm. Includes index. Bibliography: p.
140. [NK8592.P37 1976] 76-376247 ISBN
0-285-62214-5 : £4.50
1. Pitchers—Collectors and collecting. I.
Title.   BIP

Pitt, Ronald—Art collections.

SQUIRE, Gwen.   391'.45
Livery buttons : the Pitt Collection / [by]
Gwen Squire. Pulborough : Leghorn Co.,
1976. lxix p., 100 leaves of plates : chiefly
ill., port. ; 28 cm. Leaves printed on both
sides. Includes indexes. Bibliography: p.
lxix. [NK3670.S67 1976] 77-373031 ISBN
0-9504748-0-0 : £10.00
1. Pitt, Ronald—Art collections. 2. Livery
buttons—Catalogs. I. Title.

Pittsburgh. Carnegie Institute.

VAN TRUMP, James   917.48'86'034
Denholm, 1908-
An American palace of culture; the
Carnegie Institute and Carnegie Library of
Pittsburgh, by James D. Van Trump. With
foreword by James M. Walton, and introd.
by Charles Covert Arensburg. [1st ed.]
Pittsburgh, Carnegie Institute [1970] x, 56
p. illus. 24 cm. [AS36.P79V35] 71-100955
3.95
1. Pittsburgh. Carnegie Institute. 2.
Pittsburgh. Carnegie Library. I. Title.

Pittsburgh. Carnegie Institute. Museum of Art.

PITTSBURGH.   750'.74'014886
Carnegie Institute. Museum of Art.
Catalogue of painting collection. Pittsburgh
[1973] iv, 196 p. 96 plates. 23 cm. On
spine: Painting collection. [N710.A54] 73-
180225
1. Pittsburgh. Carnegie Institute. Museum
of Art. 2. Paintings—Pittsburgh—Catalogs.
I. Title.

Pittsburgh—Description—Views.

LEE, Edward Brown.   917.48'86'03
A pencil in Penn; sketches of Pittsburgh
and surrounding areas. Drawings by
Edward Brown Lee with text by Edward
Brown Lee, Jr. Pittsburgh, 1970. 122 p.
illus. (part col.) 22 cm. [NC139.L44A55]
73-125538 10.00
1. Pittsburgh—Description—Views. I. Lee,
Edward Brown, 1876-1956, illus. II. Title.

Pittsburgh. University—Descr.—Views.

KOERNER, Henry.   916
University of Pittsburgh in drawings.
[Pittsburgh c1962] unpaged. illus. 36cm.
[NC1075.K58A57] 62-18480
1. Pittsburgh. University—Descr.—Views.
I. Title.

Plamondon, Antoine, ca. 1802-1895.

OTTAWA. National Gallery   759.11
of Canada.
Antoine Plamondon / 1802-1895,
Theophile Hamel / 1817-1870; two
painters of Quebec/deux peintres de
Quebec. Catalogue and essay by R. H.
Hubbard, with a foreword by Jean
Sutherland Boggs. [Ottawa, 1970] 176 p.
plates (part col.) 26 cm. At head of title:
An exhibition organized by the National
Gallery of Canada. English and French.
Exhibition held at Musee du Quebec,
Quebec, 5-28 November, 1970; Art
Gallery of Ontario, Toronto, 11 December
1970 - 10 January, 1971; National Gallery
of Canada, Ottawa 22 January-21
February, 1971. [ND248.O8] 70-22917
1. Plamondon, Antoine, ca. 1802-1895. 2.
Hamel, Theophile, 1817-1870. I. Hubbard,
Robert Hamilton, 1916- II. Quebec (City).
Musee de la province de Quebec. III.
Ontario. Art Gallery.

Plant containers.

FRAMER, Jack, 1927-   745.59'3
Planters : make your own containers for
indoor and outdoor plants / by Jack
Kramer. 1st ed. New York : Ballantine
Books, 1977. 128 p. : ill. ; 28 cm.
[SB418.4.K7] 76-56426 ISBN 0-345-
25534-8 pbk. : 3.95
1. Plant containers. 2. Handicraft. I. Title.
    BIP

VERMEER, Jackie.   745.59'3
Making decorative planters from
practically anything / by Jackie Vermeer
and Marian Lariviere Frew ; photography
by Duane D. Davis. New York : Taplinger
Pub. Co., 1978. p. cm. [SB418.4.V83] 77-
92755 ISBN 0-8008-5065-3 : 9.95. ISBN
0-8008-5066-1 pbk. : 4.95
1. Plant containers. 2. Handicraft. I. Frew,
Marian Lariviere, joint author. II. Title.

Plant hangers.

MEILACH, Dona Z.   745.59'3
Plant hangers : ideas and techniques,
macrame, weaving, twining, coiling,
leather, antiques, and more / Dona Z.
Meilach ; photos. by Dona and Mel
Meilach. New York : Crown Publishers,
c1977. 96 p., [4] leaves of plates : ill. ; 28
cm. Includes index. Bibliography: p. 94.
[SB418.4.M44 1977] 76-58406 ISBN 0-
517-52924-6 : 7.95 ISBN 0-517-52925-4
pbk. : 4.95
1. Plant hangers. 2. Macrame. 3. Hand
weaving. I. Title.

Planters Peanuts (Firm)—Collectibles—Catalogs.

REDDOCK, Richard D.   664'.8
Planters Peanuts advertising and
collectibles, with current prices / by
Richard D. and Barbara Reddock. Des
Moines : Wallace-Homestead Book Co.,
c1978. 164 p. : ill. ; 28 cm. [NK808.R4]
76-45717 ISBN 0-87069-191-0 pbk. : 7.95
1. Planters Peanuts (Firm)—Collectibles—
Catalogs. I. Reddock, Barbara, joint author.
II.   Title.

Plantin, Christophe, ca. 1520-1589.

PLANTIN,   686.2'09493'2
Christophe, ca.1520-1589.
Ornamental initials : the woodcut initials
of Christopher Plantin : a complete
catalogue / by Stephen Harvard. New
York : American Friends of the Plantin-
Moretus Museum, 1974. xiii, 26, [169] p. :
chiefly ill. ; 32 cm. Includes bibliographical
references. [NK3631.P52H37] 74-75791
1. Plantin, Christophe, ca. 1520-1589. 2.
Initials. I. Harvard, Stephen. II. Antwerp.
Musee Plantin-Moretus. III. Title.

Plants.

VON BORSIG, Arnold, 1899-   779.34
Designs in nature [by] Tet Borsig. Introd.
by Adolf Portmann. [Translated from the
original German by Cynthia Harris] New
York, Viking Press [1961] 14 p. 80 plates.
25 cm. (A Studio book) Translation of
Verborgene Kunstformen. [QK50.V613]
62-7454
1. Plants. 2. Photography, Artistic. 3.
Botany—Pictorial works. I. Title.

Plants—Collection and preservation.

WACH, Natalie.   745.92
The elegant art of pressing and preserving
seeds, leaves, and flowers / by Natalie
Wach ; ill. by Natalie Wach and Carl
Moreus. Norwalk, Conn. : C. R. Gibson
Co., [1975] 48 p. : ill. ; 22 cm. Title on
spine: Seeds, leaves and flowers.
[SB447.W3] 74-76217 ISBN 0-8378-3007-
9 : 2.00
1. Plants—Collection and preservation. 2.
Pressed flower pictures. 3. Dried flower
arrangement. I. Title. II. Title: Seeds,
leaves, and flowers.

Plants, Decorative.

JAMES, Suzanne.   635.9663
Gifts from the garden. Drawings by Elsa.
New York, Hearthside Press [1961] 130 p.
illus. 25 cm. [SB449.J3] 61-16550
1. Plants, Decorative. 2. Handicraft. 3.
Flower arrangement. I. Title.

Plants—Drying.

KAREL, Leonard, 1912-   745.92
Dried grasses, grains, gourds, pods, and
cones / by Leonard Karel. Metuchen, N.J.
: Scarecrow Press, 1975. vii, 201 p. ; ill. ;
22 cm. Includes indexes. Bibliography: p.
31-34. [SB447.K293] 74-31178 ISBN 0-
8108-0792-0 : 8.00
1. Plants—Drying. 2. Dried flower
arrangement—Equipment and supplies. I.
Title.

Plants in art.

HUNT Botanical Library.   751.4'5
Catalogue of an exhibition of
contemporary botanical art and illustration,
6 April to 1 September 1964. Pittsburgh
[1964] 80 p. ports. 23 cm. [NE953.H8] 71-
248008
1. Plants in art. 2. Prints—Exhibitions. I.
Title. II. Title: Contemporary botanical art
and illustration.

Plants, Ornamental—Australia.

BROOKS, A. E.   635.96'76'0994
Australian native plants for home gardens,
by A. E. Brooks. [3rd ed.] Melbourne,
Lothian [1967] xvi, 149 p. illus. (part col.)
23 cm. Bibliography: p. 139-140.
[SB466.A7] 68-124501 4.50 Aust.
1. Plants, Ornamental—Australia. 2.
Botany—Australia. I. Title.

Plants, Useful—Dictionaries.

HARRIS, Ben Charles.   581.6'1
Make use of your garden plants / by Ben
Charles Harris ; drawings by Lauren
Jarrett. 1st ed. New York : C. N. Potter :
distributed by Crown Publishers, c1978. p.
cm. Includes index. Bibliography: p.
[QK98.4.A1H37 1978] 77-17894 ISBN 0-
517-53198-4 : 8.95
1. Plants, Useful—Dictionaries. 2. Plants,
Ornamental—Dictionaries. 3. Nature
craft—Dictionaries. I. Title.   BIP

Plaquettes—Denmark—Catalogs.

NEWMAN, Earl Nelson.   738.2'7
The Danish Royal Copenhagen plaquettes,
2010 series. [1st ed. Edmond? Okla., 1973]
xiii, 123 p. illus. 23 cm.
[NK4210.K58N48] 73-154713
1. Kongelige Porcelainsfabrik &
Fajancefabriken Aluminia a/s,
Copenhagen. 2. Plaquettes—Denmark—
Catalogs. I. Title.

Plaster casts.

BELL, Roy. 731.4'52
Taking casts in sand and other materials. [1st ed. Oxford, New York] Pergamon Press [1970] vii, 53 p. illus. 22 cm. (The Pergamon English library) [NB1190.B38 1970] 70-94937
1. Plaster casts. I. Title. II. Series.

CHANEY, Charles. 731.4'3
Plaster mold and model making [by] Charles Chaney and Stanley Skee. New York, Van Nostrand Reinhold [1973] 144 p. illus. 25 cm. Bibliography: p. 8. [NB1190.C45] 76-39805 ISBN 0-442-21511-8 9.95
1. Plaster casts. 2. Sculpture—Technique. I. Skee, Stanley, joint author. II. Title. BIP

MEILACH, Dona Z. 731.452
Creating with plaster, by Dona Z. Meilach. Chicago, Reilly & Lee Co. [1966] 73 p. illus. 29 cm. [NB1190.M4] 66-15160
1. Plaster casts. 2. Sculpture—Technique. I. Title.

MEILACH, Dona Z. 731.4'52
Creating with plaster / by Dona Z. Meilach. New York : Galahad Books, [1974] c1966. 73 p. : chiefly ill. ; 29 cm. [NB1190.M4 1974] 73-92080 ISBN 0-88365-075-4 : 6.95
1. Plaster casts. 2. Sculpture—Technique. I. Title.

TRAVERS, Ralph, 1913- *668.41
How to make professional moulds & castings, from plater to plastics. 2d ed., rev. Boston, Plastic Service Associates, 1952. 346 p. illus. 26 cm. [TT297.T7] 52-2201
1. Plaster casts. 2. Plastics — Molding. I. Title. II. Title: Professional moulds & castings

Plaster casts—Juvenile literature.

BATHO, Margot. 731.4'52
Sandcasting. Pictures by George Overlie. Minneapolis, Lerner Publications Co. [1973] 32 p. illus. 21 cm. (An Early craft book) Introduces the techniques and necessary tools for creating a variety of plaster and wax objects by making impressions in sand. [TT295.B37] 72-13345 ISBN 0-8225-0860-5 3.95
1. Plaster casts—Juvenile literature. 2. Candles—Juvenile literature. I. Overlie, George, illus. II. Title. BIP

Plaster craft.

FARNWORTH, Warren. 731.4
Creative work with plaster / Warren Farnworth. New York : Drake Publishers, 1975. 95 p. : ill. ; 21 cm. Bibliography: p. 95. [TT295.F37] 74-22578 ISBN 0-87749-784-2 : 6.95
1. Plaster craft. I. Title.

FRASER, B. Kay. 738.1'5
Decorative plastercraft : a complete guide to making plaster whiteware, casting, carving, sculpturing, painting, and antiquing / B. Kay Fraser. New York : Crown Publishers, [1974] 96 p., [4] leaves of plates : ill. ; 28 cm. Includes index. [TT295.F7 1974] 74-80316 5.95
1. Plaster craft. I. Title.

Plastic foams.

YATES, Brock 745.57
Plastic foam for arts and crafts. Drawings by Stan Fraydas. New York, Sterling [c.1965] 128p. illus. 21cm. [TT297.Y3] 64-24686 2.95; 2.99 lib. ed.,
1. Plastic foams. 2. Handicraft. I. Title.

Plastic sculpture.

BUNCH, Clarence. 730'.92'2
Acrylic for sculpture and design. New York, Van Nostrand Reinhold [1972] 144 p. illus. 29 cm. [NB1270.P5B85] 75-149251
1. Plastic sculpture. 2. Plastics industry and trade. I. Title.

DAWSON, Robert, 1921- 731.4
Practical sculpture; creating with plastic media. New York, Viking Press [1970] 111 p. illus., plates. 26 cm. ([A Studio handbook]) Bibliography: p. 108. [NB1170.D38 1970] 71-110357 ISBN 0-670-57127-X 6.95
1. Plastic sculpture. I. Title.

NEWMAN, Thelma R. 731.4
Plastics as sculpture [by] Thelma R. Newman. [1st ed.] Radnor, Pa., Chilton Book Co. [1974] 223 p. illus. 26 cm. Bibliography: p. [217] [NB1270.P5N48] 74-691 ISBN 0-8019-5767-2 14.95
1. Plastic sculpture. I. Title. BIP

PANTING, John. 731.2
Sculpture in fiberglass: the use of polyester resin and fiberglass in sculpture. New York, Watson-Guptill Publications [1972] 120 p. illus. 23 cm. [NB1270.P5P3] 72-2884 ISBN 0-8230-4672-9
1. Plastic sculpture. I. Title. BIP

ROUKES, Nicholas. 731.4
Sculpture in plastics. New York, Watson-Guptill Publications [1968] 175 p. illus. (part col.) 27 cm. Bibliography: p. 172. [NB1270.P5R6] 68-12401
1. Plastic sculpture. I. Title. BIP

ROUKES, Nicholas. 731.4
Sculpture in plastics / by Nicholas Roukes. New rev. and enl. ed. New York : Watson-Guptill Publications, 1978. 192 p. : ill. (some col.) ; 29 cm. Includes index. Bibliography: p. 189. [NB1270.P5R6 1978] 77-17479 ISBN 0-8230-4701-6 : 22.50
1. Plastic sculpture. I. Title.

SCHWARTZ, Therese, 1925- 731
Plastic sculpture and collage: designs, materials, methods. New York, Hearthside Press [1969] 128 p. illus. 25 cm. [NB1270.P5S3] 79-77779 5.95
1. Plastic sculpture. 2. Collage. I. Title.

Plastics.

BICK, Alexander Frederick, 1890- 745.59
Plastics for fun; a course of study for schools, hospitals, camps, and home workshops. Milwaukee, Bruce Pub. Co. [1954] 96p. illus. 27cm. [TT157.B47] 54-8220
1. Plastics. 2. Handicraft. I. Title.

BICK, Alexander Frederick, 1890- 745.57
Plastics: projects and procedures with polyesters. Milwaukee, Bruce Pub. Co. [1962] 108 p. illus. 27 cm. [TT297.B5] 62-10340
1. Plastics. 2. Laminated plastics.

COPE, Dwight W. 745.57
Plastics, by Dwight W. Cope, John O. Conaway. Walter C. Brown, consulting ed. Homewood, Ill., Goodheart-Willcox [c.1966] 96p. illus. 27cm. (Goodheart-Willcox's build-a-course ser.) [TT297.C6] 66-18989 3.50
1. Plastics. 2. Handicraft. I. Conaway, John O., joint author. II. Title.

COPE, Dwight W 745.57
Plastics book, edited by Floyd Dickey. Chicago, Goodheart-Willcox Co. [1960] 272 p. illus. 29 cm. [TP986.A2C65] 60-8667
1. Plastics. I. Title.

COPE, Dwight W 745.59
Plastics book; edited by Floyd Dickey. Chicago, Goodheart-Willcox Co. [1957] 272 p. illus. 29 cm. [TP986.A2C65] 57-11946
1. Plastics. I. Title.

Plastics as art material.

NEWMAN, Thelma R. 702'.8
Plastics as an art form [by] Thelma R. Newman. Rev. ed. Philadelphia, Chilton Book Co. [1969] xxi, 403 p. illus. 27 cm. Bibliography: p. 385-387. [N8530.N4 1969] 76-91122
1. Plastics as art material. I. Title.

NEWMAN, Thelma R. 702.8
Plastics as an art form [by] Thelma R. Newman. [1st ed.] Philadelphia, Chilton Books [1964] xii, 338 p. illus., ports. 26 cm. Bibliography: p. 319-321. [N8530.N4] 64-18240
1. Plastics as art material. I. Title. BIP

Plastics craft.

BARNSLEY, Alan. 745.57
Crafts in plastic foam. New York, Watson-Guptill [1973] 96 p. illus. (part col.) 21 cm. Bibliography: p. 93. Instructions for creating a variety of decorative objects from polystyrene materials. [TT297.B37 1973] 72-11573 ISBN 0-8230-0999-8 7.95
1. Plastics craft. 2. Polystyrene. I. Title.

BORGLUND, Erland, 1894- 736
Working in plastic, bone, amber, and horn [by] Erland Borglund and Jacob Flauensgaard. [Edited in English by Clara Fried Zwiebel] New York, Reinhold Book Corp. [1968] 96 p. illus. 23 cm. ([Reinhold Scandinavian craft series]) Translation of Gor det sjalv av plast, ben och horn. [TT297.B643] 67-24691
1. Plastics craft. 2. Bone carving. 3. Amber. 4. Horn carving. I. Flauensgaard, Jacob, joint author. II. Title.

BROUWER, Ab de. 745.57
Creating with flexible foam. [Translated by Manly Banister] New York, Sterling Pub. Co. [1971] 48 p. illus. 20 cm. (Little craft book series) Translation of Werken met schuimplastic. Instructions for sculpturing or constructing animals, human figures, and other decorative objects from a flexible foam plastic called polyurethane. [TT297.B7613 1971] 71-167657 ISBN 0-8069-5182-6
1. Plastics craft. I. Title. BIP

CHERRY, Raymond. 668'.41
General plastics; projects and procedures. [4th ed., enl. and completely rev.] Bloomington, Ill., McKnight & McKnight [1967] 318 p. illus. 27 cm. Bibliography: p. 309. [TT297.C5 1967] 65-19552
1. Plastics craft. I. Title.

COPE, Dwight W. 668.4
Plastics / by Dwight W. Cope, Lee E. Schaude. South Holland, Ill. : Goodheart-Willcox Co., c1977. 112 p. : ill. ; 27 cm. (Goodheart-Willcox's build-a-course series) Includes index. [TT297.C6 1977] 77-21618 ISBN 0-87006-239-5 : 4.40
1. Plastics craft. I. Schaude, Lee E., joint author. II. Title. BIP

EDWARDS, H. Wayne. 745.57
Karton kuties, written and illustrated by H. Wayne Edwards. San Antonio, Tex., Naylor Co. [1971] 44 p. illus. 22 cm. Simple instructions demonstrate that common household items can be used to create many entertaining things. [TT297.E28] 70-139592 ISBN 0-8111-0390-0 2.95
1. Plastics craft. I. Title.

EDWARDS, Lauton. 745.57
Industrial arts plastics. Peoria, Ill., C. A. Bennett Co. [1964] 280 p. illus. 24 cm. [TP986.5.A2E3] 64-14340
1. Plastics craft. I. Title. BIP

EDWARDS, Lauton. 745.57
Industrial arts plastics. 2d ed. Peoria, Ill., C. A. Bennett Co. [1973, c1974] 288 p. illus. 24 cm. A textbook describing the properties of different types of plastics with instructions for making a variety of items from these materials. [TT297.E26] 73-81458 ISBN 0-87002-146-X
1. Plastics craft. I. Title.

HARRIS, Tom. 745.57
Creating with styrofoam, and related materials. Text by Elsie Harley. Chicago, J. G. Ferguson Pub. Co.; distributed to the book trade by Doubleday [Garden City, N.Y., 1970] 32 p. illus. (part col.) 27 cm. (Art unlimited) Instructions for creating decorative and useful objects from styrofoam and related materials. [TT297.H37] 70-139497
1. Plastics craft. I. Harley, Elsie. II. Title.

HELLER, Beatrice. 745.57
Cooking crystal craft / Beatrice Heller. 1st ed. Radnor, Pa. : Chilton Book Co., [1975] xiii, 175 p., [4] leaves of plates : ill. (some col.) ; 27 cm. Includes index. [TT297.H44 1975] 75-4248 ISBN 0-8019-6181-5 : 12.50 ISBN 0-8019-6182-3 pbk. : 6.95
1. Plastics craft. I. Title. BIP

KONIJNENBERG-DE Groot, Jo. 745.57
Cellophane creations, with chicken wire, iron wire, glass, metal. [Photos. by Louis Van Beurden. Translated by Manly Banister] New York, Sterling Pub. Co. [1972] 48 p. illus. 20 cm. (Little craft book series) Translation of Cellofaan. Directions for making a variety of decorative objects, including Chinese lanterns, flowers, and mobiles, from this colorful, inexpensive material. [TT297.K6513 1972] 72-180457
1. Plastics craft. 2. Cellophane. I. Beurden, Louis van, illus. II. Title.

LANG, Nancy M. 745.57
Getting started in plastics [by] Nancy M. Lang. New York, Collier Books [1972] 95 p. illus. (part col.) 28 cm. (Getting started series) Bibliography: p. 91. Introduces the materials, tools, and techniques for creating a variety of decorative and useful items from plastics. [TT297.L28] 72-183408 2.95
1. Plastics craft. I. Title. BIP

LAPLANTE, Jerry C. 684.1'06
Plastic furniture for the home craftsman / Jerry C. LaPlante. New York : Drake Publishers, 1978. 154 p. : ill. ; 23 cm. Includes index. [TT297.L29] 77-87474 ISBN 0-8473-1664-5 : 5.95
1. Plastics craft. 2. Plastic furniture. I. Title. BIP

LAPPIN, Alvin R. 745.57
Plastics projects and techniques [by] Alvin R. Lappin. [1st ed.] Bloomington, Ill., McKnight & McKnight Pub. Co. [1965] 136 p. illus. 26 cm. Bibliography: p. 133-135. [TT297.L3] 64-22304
1. Plastics craft. 2. Handicraft. I. Title. BIP

LAWRENCE, L. L. 745.57
Polystyrene foam craft [by] L. L. Lawrence. Radnor, Pa., Chilton Book Co. [1974] x, 86 p. illus. 26 cm. (Chilton's creative crafts series) [TT297.L33] 73-22390 ISBN 0-8019-6117-3 9.95
1. Plastics craft. 2. Polystyrene. I. Title.

LEINWOLL, Stanley. 684.1'06
Plasticrafts. New York, Simon and Schuster [1973] 127 p. illus. 25 cm. [TT297.L37] 72-93514 ISBN 0-671-21496-9 6.95
1. Plastics crafts. I. Title. BIP

MOORE, Bob. 745.57
Introducing thermoplastics / Bob Moore. Sydney ; New York : J. Wiley, c1976. 44 p. : ill. ; 25 cm. Includes index. [TT297.M66] 77-353284 ISBN 0-471-02354-X
1. Plastics craft. 2. Thermoplastics. I. Title.

NEWMAN, Jay Hartley. 745.57
Plastics for the craftsman, by Jay Hartley Newman and Lee Scott Newman. New York, Crown [1972] ix, 214 p. illus. 27 cm. Bibliography: p. 200. [TT297.N47 1972] 75-185084 7.95
1. Plastics craft. I. Newman, Lee Scott, joint author. II. Title. BIP

NEWMAN, Thelma R. 745.57
Crafting with plastics / Thelma R. Newman. 1st ed. Radnor, Pa. : Chilton Book Co., [1975] xiii, 202 p., [4] leaves of plates : ill. ; 27 cm. (Chilton's basic crafts series) Includes index. Bilbiography: p. 200. [TT297.N49 1975] 75-22127 ISBN 0-8019-5936-5 pbk. : 13.95
1. Plastics craft. I. Title. BIP

O'MEARA-HUMPHREY, Deirdre. 745.57
Plastic crafts / Deirdre O'Meara-Humphrey. New York : Grosset & Dunlap, c1977. 143 p. : ill. ; 28 cm. Includes index. [TT297.O43] 76-50867 ISBN 0-448-13428-4 lib. bdg. ISBN 0-448-12950-7 pbk. : 4.95
1. Plastics craft. I. Title.

REES, David. 745.57
Creative plastics. New York, Viking Press [1974, c1973] 112 p. illus. 25 cm. (A Studio book) Bibliography: p. 110. [TT297.R43 1974] 73-8084 ISBN 0-670-24682-4 8.95
1. Plastics craft. I. Title.

ROUKES, Nicholas. 745.57
Crafts in plastics. New York, Watson-Guptill Publications [1970] 176 p. illus. (part col.) 29 cm. Bibliography: p. 6. [TT297.R68] 70-117075 ISBN 8-320-10007- 10.95
1. Plastics craft. I. Title.

SCARFE, Herbert. 745.57
Crafts in polyester resin. New York,

Watson-Guptill Publications [1973] 96 p. illus. (part col.) 21 cm. Bibliography: p. 94. [TT297.S28 1973] 72-11557 ISBN 0-8230-1004-X 7.95
1. Plastics craft. 2. Polyesters. I. Title. BIP

SCHMIDT, Lloyd H. 745.57
Basic plastics [by] Lloyd H. Schmidt. [1st ed.] Indianapolis. H. W. Sams [1969] 112 p. illus. 22 cm. [TT297.S3] 70-94807
1. Plastics craft. I. Title.

SMALE, Claude. 745.57
Creative plastics techniques. [New York, Van Nostrand Reinhold Co., 1973] 124 p. illus. 22 cm. Explains the properties of different plastics and describes some techniques for fabricating plastic items. [TT297.S54] 75-39888 ISBN 0-442-29952-4 6.95
1. Plastics craft. I. Title.

SMITH, Lura 745.57
Resin and glass aricraft for flower arrangers and craftsmen. Photos. by Doug Morris. New York, Barrows; dist. by Morrow, 1966. 115p. illus. (pt. col.) 21cm. [TT297.S58] 66-27950 4.95
1. Plastics craft. 2. Decoration and ornament. 3. Glass. Ornamental. I. Title.

TIRANTI, John. 668.4'94
Glass fibre for schools; hand lay-up with polyester resin. [1st American ed.] New York, Transatlantic Arts, 1972. viii, 104 p. illus. 23 cm. Bibliography: p. 103. [TT297.T57 1972b] 72-166293
1. Plastics craft. 2. Glass reinforced plastics. I. Title. BIP

WEIR, Donna J. 745.57
Treasures in resin; a complete guide to casting with liquid plastic, by Donna J. Weir [and] Stephen J. Schilt. Santa Ana, Calif., Saddleback Publications [1969] 59 p. illus. (part col.) 28 cm. Bibliography: p. 59. [TT297.W44] 74-9116
1. Plastics craft. I. Schilt, Stephen J., joint author. II. Title.

ZAHN, Millicent. 745.57
Millicent Zahn book of plastics craft. Edited by Sterling McIlhany. New York, Van Nostrand Reinhold Co. [1973] 96 p. illus. 28 cm. [TT297.Z33] 72-9711 ISBN 0-442-29583-9 8.95
1. Plastics craft. I. Title.
Pbk. 4.95; ISBN 0-442-29582-0.

ZECHLIN, Katharina. 745.57
Setting in clear plastic. New York, Taplinger Pub. Co. [1971] 72 p. illus. 22 cm. [TT297.Z43] 75-164672 ISBN 0-8008-7070-0
1. Plastics craft. 2. Biological specimens—Plastic embedment. I. Title. BIP

Plastics craft—Juvenile literature.

LEFEVRE, Gregg. 745.57
Creating with sheet plastic / by Gregg LeFevre ; photos. by the author. New York : Sterling Pub. Co., c1974. 48 p. : ill. ; 20 cm. (Little craft book series) Includes index. Introduces the tools, materials, and techniques for working with sheet plastic and suggests a variety of projects. [TT297.L35] 74-82326 ISBN 0-8069-5314-4 : 3.50 ISBN 0-8069-5315-2 lib.bdg. : 3.69
1. Plastics craft—Juvenile literature. I. Title. BIP

Plastics — Handbooks, manuals, etc.

COPE, Dwight W. 745.57
Cope's plastics book, by Dwight Cope. Edited by Floyd Dickey. South Holland, Ill., Goodheart-Willcox Co. [1973] 272 p. illus. 29 cm. Published in 1957 and 1960 under title: Plastics book. [TP1130.C64 1973] 74-151214 ISBN 0-87006-150-X
1. Plastics—Handbooks, manuals, etc. I. Title. II. Title: Plastics book.

DEWICK, Ernest S 745.57
Industrial arts; using plastics in the school shop. Prepared by Ernest De Wick. New Brunswick, N.J., Vocational Division, Curriculum Laboratory, 1960. 84 p. illus. 28 cm. Cover title: Industrial arts: plastics. [TT267.D4] A 60
1. Plastics — Handbooks, manuals, etc. I. New Jersey. Division of Vocational Education. Curriculum Laboratory, New Brunswick. II. Title. III. Title: Industrial arts: plastics.

Plate, English.

HAYWARD, John 739.2'3'722
Forrest, 1916-
The Courtauld silver : an introduction to the work of the Courtauld Family of Goldsmiths / J. F. Hayward. London ; New York : Sotheby Parke Bernet, [1975] 62 p. : ill. ; 26 cm. [NK7198.C63H38] 75-316374 ISBN 0-85667-018-9 : 15.00
1. Courtauld family. 2. Plate, English. I. Title. BIP

Plate, French.

CRIPPS, Wilfred 739.2'0944
Joseph, 1841-1903.
Old French silver. [Boston] Newbury Books [1973] vii, 101 p. illus., plates. 23 cm. Published in 1880 and 1893 under title: Old French plate. [NK7149.C8 1973] 73-78444 ISBN 0-912728-01-9 7.75
1. Plate, French. 2. Hall-marks. I. Title.

Plate—Gt. Brit.—History.

JACKSON, Charles James, 739.22742
Sir, 1849-1923.
English goldsmiths and their marks; a history of the goldsmiths and plate workers of England, Scotland, and Ireland. With over thirteen thousand marks reproduced in facsimile from authentic examples of plate, and tables of date-letters and other hall-marks used in the assay offices of the United Kingdom. 2d ed., rev. and enl. New York, Dover Publications [1964, c1921] xvi, 747 p. illus. 28 cm. "Unabridged and unaltered republication of the work first published ... in 1921." [NK7143.J15 1964] 64-18852
1. Plate—Gt. Brit.—History. 2. Goldsmiths, British. 3. Silversmiths, British. 4. Hall-marks. I. Title. BIP

Plate, Greek.

STRONG, Donald Emrys. 739.2
Greek and Roman gold and silver plate, [by] D. E. Strong. Ithaca, N.Y., Cornell University Press [1966] xxviii, 235 p. illus. 25 cm. Includes bibliographical references. [NK7107.S7] [RC150] 616.203 65-28837 65-8030
1. Plate, Greek. 2. Plate, Roman. I. Title.

Plate numbers (Postage-stamps)—Catalogs.

CATALOGUE of used 769.56973075
plate number singles. Gardena, Calif. v. illus. 23cm. Began publication in 1952? Editor: 19 A. Hebert. [HE6185.U6C28] 54-25789
1. Plate numbers (Postage-stamps)—Catalogs. I. Hebert, Antonio, 1897- ed.

Plateau d'Assy, France. Notre-Dame-de-Toute-Grace (Church).

RUBIN, William Stanley 709.04
Modern sacred art and the church of Assy. New York, Columbia, 1961[c.1960] xi, 185p. plates (part col.) plan. 25cm. Bibl. 61-15469 8.75
1. Plateau d'Assy, France. Notre-Dame-de-Toute-Grace (Church). 2. Christian art and symoblism. 3. Art, Modern—20th cent. 4. Catholic Church in France. I. Title.

Plates (Tableware)

WITT, Louise Schaub. 738.2'8
Wonderful world of plates: annual, Christmas [and] commemorative; with collector's price guide. [North Kansas City, Mo., Trojan Press, 1970- 1 v. (loose-leaf) illus., ports. 24 cm. [NK4695.P55W58] 72-26134
1. Plates (Tableware) I. Title.

Plates (Tableware)—Collectors and collecting.

BRADFORD Exchange. 738
The Bradford book of collector's plates : the official guide to all editions traded on the world's largest exchange / edited under the direction of Nadja K. Bartels, John G. McKinven. New York : McGraw-Hill, 1976. p. cm. Includes indexes. [NK8596.B72 1976] 76-16129 ISBN 0-07-007057-1 : 9.95
1. Plates (Tableware)—Collectors and collecting. 2. Plates (Tableware)—Catalogs. I. Bartels, Nadja K. II. McKinven, John G. III. Title.

CLARK, Eleanor. 730
Plate collecting / by Eleanor Clark. Secaucus, N.J. : Citadel Press, [1976] p. cm. Includes index. [NK8596.C55] 76-26098 ISBN 0-8065-0478-1 : 17.95
1. Plates (Tableware)—Collectors and collecting. I. Title. BIP

COHEN, Hal L. 738
Grosset's complete guide to collectible plates / Hal L. Cohen. 1st ed. New York : Grossett & Dunlap, c1974. 244 p. : ill. (some col.) ; 21 cm. Bibliography: p. 244-[245] [NK8596.C63] 73-16688 ISBN 0-448-11597-2 lib.bdg. : 7.95 pbk. : 6.95
1. Plates (Tableware)—Collectors and collecting. I. Title.

KOVEL, Ralph M. 738'.075
The Kovels' price guide for collector plates, figurines, paperweights, and other limited editions / Ralph & Terry Kovel. New York : Crown Publishers, c1978. xxiv, 200 p. : ill. ; 29 cm. [NK4695.P55K68 1978] 79-102149 ISBN 0-517-53533-5 : 12.95
1. Plates (Tableware)—Prices. 2. Figurines—Prices. 3. Paperweights—Prices. 4. Plaques, plaquettes—Prices. I. Kovel, Terry H., joint author. II. Title. III. Title: Price guide for collector plates, figurines, paperweights, and other limited editions.

Plates (Tableware)—United States—Catalogs.

WOOD, Richard H., 1908- 738.3'8
A catalogue of American historical china cup plates [by] Richard H. and Virginia A. Wood. Baltimore [1969] [26] p. (chiefly illus.) 31 cm. Cover title: Historical china cup plates. [NK4695.P55W65] 72-194267
1. Plates (Tableware)—United States—Catalogs. I. Wood, Virginia A., 1906- joint author. II. Title. III. Title: Historical china cup plates.

Platner, Warren, 1919—

TEN by Warren Platner 720'.92'4
/ with a foreword by Ezra Stoller. New York : McGraw-Hill, [1975] 193 p. : chiefly ill. (some col.) ; 32 cm. Photos by E. Stoller, A. Georges, and S. McCartney. [NA737.P47S76] 75-19214 ISBN 0-07-050285-4 : 19.95
1. Platner, Warren, 1919- I. Georges, Alexandre, joint author. II. McCartney, Susan, joint author. BIP

Playgrounds.

ALLEN, Marjory (Gill) 711'.558
Allen, Baroness, 1897-
Planning for play [by] Lady Allen of Hurtwood. Cambridge, Mass., M.I.T. Press [1969, c1968] 140, [4] p. illus., plans. 24 cm. Bibliographical references included in "Footnotes" (p. [141]-[143]) [GV423.A44 1969] 69-16908
1. Playgrounds. I. Title. BIP

BENGTSSON, Arvid. 711'.558
Environmental planning for children's play. New York, Praeger [1970] 224 p. illus., plans. 31 cm. [GV423.B43 1970b] 79-112771 17.50
1. Playgrounds. I. Title.

DATTNER, Richard. 711'.558
Design for play. New York, Van Nostrand Reinhold Co. [1969] 144 p. illus. 23 x 29 cm. Bibliography: p. 140. [GV423.D3] 69-16380 12.50
1. Playgrounds. I. Title.

DATTNER, Richard. 711'.558
Design for play. Cambridge, Mass., MIT Press [1974, c1969] 144 p. illus. 22 x 29 cm. Bibliography: p. 140. [GV423.D3 1974] 73-1884 ISBN 0-262-54023-1 4.95 (pbk.)
1. Playgrounds. I. Title.

GENDUSA, Sam, 1939- 731.4
Building playground sculpture & homes / by Sam Gendusa. Dayton, Or. : Master Press, 1974. 146 p : ill. ; 24 cm. Includes bibliographical references. [GV424.G46] 74-23019 7.95
1. Playgrounds. 2. Playgrounds—Apparatus and equipment. 3. Sculpture. 4. Environment (Art) I. Title. BIP

The Plaza, New York.

NICHOLS, Mary Eudora, 974.71'04
1901-
The Plaza; its life and times, by Eve Brown. [1st ed.] New York, Meredith Press [1967] xii, 244 p. illus., ports. 24 cm. (A Duell, Sloan and Pearce book) [F128.625.P55N5] 67-12634
1. The Plaza, New York.

Plochmann, Carolyn Gassan.

PLOCHMANN, Carolyn Gassan. 759.13
Carolyn Plochmann, recent paintings: exhibition, January 17-February 3, 1973. New York, Kennedy Galleries [1973] [22] p. illus. 28 cm. [ND237.P72K46] 73-158294
1. Plochmann, Carolyn Gassan. I. Kennedy Galleries, inc., New York.

Plunket, Jean Reasoner.

PLUNKET, Jean 741'.092'4
Reasoner.
Faces that won't sit still : celebrated subjects by a prominent portrait artist and how they were captured / by Jean Reasoner Plunket, with Barbara Brandt Ward. Washington : Acropolis Books, c1978. 201 p. : ill. ; 29 cm. [NC139.P57A2 1978] 78-14259 ISBN 0-87491-261-X : 18.00. pbk. : 9.95. ISBN 0-87491-260-1 lim. deluxe ed. : 35.00
1. Plunket, Jean Reasoner. 2. Portrait painters—United States—Biography. 3. Children—Portraits. 4. Portrait drawing—Technique. I. Ward, Barbara Brandt, joint author. II. Title.

Plymouth, Eng. Civic Centre.

PLYMOUTH, Eng. 725.13094235
Council.
The civic centre, Plymouth. Plymouth, City of Plymouth Entertainment and Publicity Manager [1966] [25] p. illus. (some col.) 29 1/2 cm. [DA690.P7P49] 67-71792
1. Plymouth, Eng. Civic Centre. I. Title.

Plywood.

DOUGLAS Fir Plywood 684
Association.
52 fir plywood home storage plans. Tacoma, Wash. [1955] 95 p. illus. 28 cm. [TT197.D67] 55-29584
1. Plywood. 2. Handicraft. I. Title.

HERTZBERG, Robert Edward, 674.83
1905-
Handy man's indoor and outdoor plywood projects. Greenwich, Conn., Fawcett Publications, c1954. 144p. illus. 24cm. (A Fawcett how-to book, 245) [TT200.H38] 55-19281
1. Plywood. 2. Handicraft. I. Title.

SCHARFF, Robert. 684.8
More plywood projects for the home craftsman. [1st ed.] New York, McGraw-Hill [1959] 184 p. illus. 26 cm. [TT200.S35] 58-8857
1. Plywood. 2. Handicraft. I. Title.

SHEA, John Gerald. 684
Plywood working for everybody. Princeton, N. J., Van Nostrand [1963] x, 212 p. illus., diagrs. 29 cm. [TT200.S42] 63-24099
1. Plywood. 2. Woodwork. I. Title.

SIBLEY, Hi [Hiram Walter 745.51
Sibley] ed.
95 plywood projects. Chicago, Goodheart-Willcox Co. [c.1960] 80p (chiefly illus. diagrs. 28cm. 60-9701 1.50 pap.,
1. Plywood. I. Title.

Pocket watches—United States—Catalogs.

CRISS, David. 681'.114
Collector's price guide to American pocket watches / by David Criss. [2d ed.]. [Imlay City, Mich.] : Criss, 1976. 102 p. : ill. ; 23 cm. Cover title. Includes index. [NK7492.C75 1976] 76-378916 4.75
1. Pocket watches—United States—Catalogs. 2. Pocket watches—United States—Collectors and collecting. I. Title.

CRISS, David. 681'.114
Collector's price guide to American pocket watches / by David Criss. 1st ed. Imlay City, Mich. : Criss, 1975. 95 p. in various pagings : ill. ; 22 cm. Cover title. Includes index. [NK7492.C75] 75-324336 3.50
1. Pocket watches—United States—Catalogs. 2. Pocket watches—United States—Collectors and collecting. I. Title.

Poetics.

ZIGROSSER, Carl, 1891- 769
Multum in parvo; an essay in poetic imagination. New York, Braziller [c.1965] 54p. 15plates 23cm. [PN1042.Z47] 65-19325 5.00
1. Poetics. 2. Creation (Literary, artistic, etc.) 3. Imagination. I. Title. BIP

Poetry.

MARITAIN, Jacques, 1882- 700'.1
Art and poetry. Translated by E. de P. Matthews. Port Washington, N.Y., Kennikat Press [1968, c1943] 104 p. 22 cm. (Essay and general literature index reprint series) Translation of 3 essays which were first published in 1935 in the author's Frontieres de la poesie et autres essais. Contents.Contents.—Three painters: Marc Chagall, Georges Rouault, Gino Severini.—Dialogues.—The freedom of song. [PQ2625.A78738F72 1968] 68-26243
1. Poetry. 2. Art—Philosophy. 3. Creation (Literary, artistic, etc.) I. Title.

Poets, English—19th century—Biography.

†BYROM, Thomas. 760'.092'4 B
Nonsense and wonder : the poems and cartoons of Edward Lear / by Thomas Byrom. 1st ed. New York : Dutton, c1977. 244 p. : ill. ; 24 cm. "A Brandywine Press book." Includes index. Bibliography: p. 239-242. [PR4879.L2Z59] 77-14560 ISBN 0-525-16835-4 : 12.95
1. Lear, Edward, 1812-1888. 2. Poets, English—19th century—Biography. 3. Artists—England—Biography. I. Lear, Edward, 1812-1888. Nonsense and wonder. 1977. II. Title. BIP

DAVIS, Michael. 760'.092'4 B
William Blake : a new kind of man / Michael Davis. Berkeley : University of California Press, 1977. 181 p., [20] leaves of plates : ill. (some col.) ; 25 cm. Includes index. Bibliography: p. 165-170. [PR4146.D34 1977] 77-71059 ISBN 0-520-03443-0 : 12.95
1. Blake, William, 1757-1827—Biography. 2. Poets, English—19th century—Biography. 3. Artists—England—Biography.

PRESTON, Kerrison. 700'.92'2
Blake and Rosetti / by Kerrison Preston. Folcroft, Pa. : Folcroft Library Editions, 1976. p. cm. Reprint of the 1944 ed. published by A. Moring, London. [PR4146.P7 1976] 76-29028 ISBN 0-8414-6782-X lib. bdg. : 17.50
1. Blake, William, 1757-1827. 2. Rossetti, Dante Gabriel, 1828-1882. 3. Poets, English—19th century—Biography. 4. Painters—England—Biography. I. Title.

Point Lobos Reserve.

WESTON, Edward, 1886- 779.3
My camera on Point Lobos; 30 photographs and excerpts, from E.W.'s daybook. Yosemite National Park, V. Adams; Boston, Houghton Mifflin, 1950. 79 [2] p. 30 plates. 27 cm. Bibliography: p. [81] [F868.M7W4] 50-4370
1. Point Lobos Reserve. 2. Photography, Artistic. I. Title.

WESTON, Edward, 1886-1958. 779'.3
My camera on Point Lobos. New York, Da Capo Press, 1968 [c1950] 79, [2] p. 30 illus. 36 cm. Bibliography: p. [81] [F868.M7W4 1968] 68-27727 27.50
1. Point Lobos Reserve. 2. Photography, Artistic. I. Title.

Poiret, Paul.

WHITE, Palmer. 746.9'2 B
Poiret. [1st American ed.] New York, C. N. Potter [1973] 192 p. illus. (part col.) 30 cm. Bibliography: p. 183-185. [TT505.P6W47] 73-78881 ISBN 0-517-50537-1 20.00
1. Poiret, Paul. I. Title.

Poison bottles—Collectors and collecting.

STIER, Wallis W. 666'.19
Poison bottles; a collectors' guide, by Wallis W. Stier. Photos. by author. [Boise, Idaho, 1969] 30, [1] p. illus. 28 cm. Bibliography: p. [31] [NK5440.B6S73] 73-20527 3.00
1. Poison bottles—Collectors and collecting. I. Title.

Polakovits, Mathias—Art collections.

RUBIN, James Henry. 741.9'44'074014967
Eighteenth-century French life-drawing : selections from the Collection of Mathias Polakovits / James Henry Rubin, in collaboration with David Levine ; foreword by Pierre Rosenberg. Princeton, N.J. : Art Museum, Princeton University : distributed by Princeton University Press, c1977. 103 p. : ill. ; 29 cm. Catalog of the exhibition held at the Princeton University Art Museum, April 2-May 8, 1977. Foreword also in French. Includes bibliographical references. [NC246.R82] 76-56719 ISBN 0-691-03926-7 : 24.50
1. Polakovits, Mathias—Art collections. 2. Drawing, French—Exhibitions. 3. Drawing—18th century—France—Exhibitions. 4. Nude in art. 5. Men in art. I. Levine, David, 1951- joint author. II. Princeton University. Art Museum. III. Title.

Polaroid Land camera.

ADAMS, Ansel Easton, 1902- 771.3'1
Polaroid Land photography / by Ansel Adams, with the assistance of Robert Baker. 1st rev. ed. Boston : New York Graphic Society, c1978. p. cm. First published in 1963 under title: Polaroid Land photography manual. Includes index. [TR263.P6A3 1978] 78-7069 ISBN 0-8212-0729-6 : 17.50
1. Polaroid Land camera. 2. Photography—Handbooks, manuals, etc. I. Baker, Robert. II. Title.

ADAMS, Ansel Easton, 1902- 771.31
Polaroid Land photography manual; a technical handbook. New York, Morgan & Morgan [1963] 192 p. illus. 24 cm. [TR263.P6A3] 63-10804
1. Polaroid Land camera. 2. Photography—Handbooks, manuals, etc. I. Title.

COLES, Charles H 771.3133
Polaroid Land guide. New York, Greenberg [1956] 118p. illus. 20cm. (The Modern camera guide series) [TR263.P6C6] 56-10100
1. Polarold Land camera. I. Title.

COOPER, Joseph David, 1917- 771.3'1
Polaroid land photography, pocket compahion, by Joseph D. Cooper with Byron S. Cooper. New York, Amphoto [1967] 128p. illus., ports. 15cm. [TR263.P6C63] 67-18633 1.95, wire bds.,
1. Polaroid Land camera. 2. Photography—Handbooks manuals, etc. I. Cooper, Byron S. II. Title.

COOPER, Joseph David, 1917- 771.3'1
Polaroid land photography, pocket companion, by Joseph D. Cooper with the assistance of Byron S. Cooper. New York, Amphoto [1967] 128 p. illus.,ports. 15 cm. [TR263.P6C63] 67-18633
1. Polaroid Land camera. 2. Photography—Handbooks, manuals, etc. I. Cooper, Byron S. II. Title.

KEMP, Wes. 771.3
Better Polaroid pictures in color and black & white. New York, American Photographic Book Pub. Co.; distributed to the book trade by Grosset & Dunlap [1964] 104 p. illus. (part col.) port. 22 cm. (Beter photo guides) "429." [TR263.P6K4] 63-22232
1. Polaroid Land camera. 2. Photography — Handbooks, manuals, etc. I. Title.

KEMP, Weston D., 1936- 771.3'1
How to take better Polaroid pictures / Weston Kemp. Englewood Cliffs, N.J. : Prentice-Hall, [1975] x, 86 p., [2] leaves of plates : ill. (some col.) ; 23 cm. (Modern photo guide) (A Spectrum book) [TR263.P6K43] 75-17776 ISBN 0-13-434969-5 : 10.95 ISBN 0-13-434944-X pbk. : 3.95
1. Polaroid Land camera. 2. Photography—Handbooks, manuals, etc. I. Title.

LAHUE, Kalton C. 771.3'1
Polaroid photography / [by Kalton C. Lahue] [Los Angeles] : Petersen Pub. Co., [1974] 80 p. : ill. (some col.) ; 28 cm. (Petersen's how-to photographic library) Cover title. [TR263.P6L33] 74-81318 ISBN 0-8227-0049-2 pbk. 2.00
1. Polaroid land camera. 2. Photography—Handbooks, manuals, etc. I. Title.

POPULAR photography (Chicago) 770.31
Polaroid Land photography, comp. by the eds. of Popular photography. [New York, A. S. Barnes, 1963] 112p. illus. 29cm. 63-5544 2.95
1. Polaroid Land camera. 2. Photography—Handbooks, manuals, etc. I. Title.

TYDINGS, Kenneth S 771.3
Dr. Tydings' Polaroid Land camera guide. Philadelphia, Chilton Co., Book Division, c1959. 152 p. illus. 20 cm. (Modern camera guide series) [TR263.P6T9] 59-13448
1. Polaroid Land camera. 2. Photography — Handbooks, manuals, etc. I. Title.

TYDINGS, Kenneth S 771.3
Tydings' Polaroid Land camera guide. Rev. Philadelphia, Chilton Co., Book Division, 1961. 127 p. illus. 20 cm. (Modern camera guide sereies) First published in 1950 under title: Dr. Tydings' Polaroid Land camera guide. [TR263.P6T9] 61-947
1. Polaroid Land camera. 2. Photography — Handbooks, manuals, etc. I. Title.

WOLBARST, John, 1912- 770.2
Pictures in a minute; how to get the most out of your Polaroid Land camera. [New York, American Photographic Book Pub. Co., 1956] 158 p. illus. 23 cm. [TR263] [P6W6] 771 56-7056
1. Polaroid Land camera. 2. Photography — Handbooks, manuals, etc. I. Title.

WOLBARST, John, 1915- 771.31
How to make better polaroid pictures with your J66 or J33 Polaroid Land camera. New York, Gellert-Wolfman Pub. Corp., c1962. 1 v. illus. 23 cm. [TR263.P6W59] 62-14848
1. Polaroid Land camera. 2. Photography — Handbooks, manuals, etc. I. Title.

WOLBARST, John, 1915- 771.3193
Pictures in a minute. 2d ed. [New York] [American Photographic Book Pub. Co.] [1958] 176 p. illus. 33 cm. [TR263.P6W6 1958] 58-9993
1. Polaroid Land camera. 2. Photography—Handbooks, manuals, etc. I. Title.

Polaroid Land camera—Juvenile literature.

JACOBS, Lou. 770'.28
Instant photography / Lou Jacobs, Jr. New York : Lothrop, Lee & Shepard Co., c1976. p. cm. Bibliography: p. [TR263.P6J3] 75-42438 ISBN 0-688-41741-8 : 5.95 ISBN 0-688-51741-2 lib.bdg. :
1. Polaroid Land camera—Juvenile literature. 2. Photography—Juvenile literature. I. Title. BIP

Polasek, Albin, 1879-1965.

POLASEK, Emily. 730'.92'4
Albin Polasek: man carving his own destiny. [Winter Park? Fla., c1970] 107 p. illus. 21 x 23 cm. [NB237.P6P64] 78-112350
1. Polasek, Albin, 1879-1965. I. Polasek, Albin, 1879-1965.

SHERWOOD, Ruth, 1890- 927.3
Carving his own destiny; the story of Albin Polasek. Chicago, R. F. Seymour [1954] 466p. illus. 25cm. [NB237.P6S45] 55-18870
I. Polasek, Albin, 1879- II. Title.

Police—Caricatures and cartoons.

PULLING, Christopher 363.2
Mr. Punch and the police [Washington, D.C.] Butterworths [1965, c.]1964. viii, 281p. illus. 26cm. [NC1478.P78] 65-6982 6.00; 9.00 deluxe ed.,
1. Police—Caricatures and cartoons. 2. Police—Anecdotes, facetiae, satire, etc. 3. Punch (London) I. Title.

Political cartoons, American.

*COBB, Ron. 741.5973
"Mah fellow Americans"; editorial cartoons from the Underground Press Syndicate [Los Angeles, Calif., Sawyer Pr., 1968] 1v. (unpaged) chiefly illus. 28cm. 1.95 pap.,
1. Political cartoons, American. I. Underground Press Syndicate. II. Title.
Publisher's address: Box 46-653, Los Angeles, Calif. 90046.

Political posters, Cuban.

STERMER, Dugald, 1936- comp. 769'.4'99729106
The art of revolution. Introductory essay by Susan Sontag. [1st ed.] New York, McGraw-Hill [1970] xxxvi p., 96 p. of illus. (part col.) 45 cm. [F1788.S7] 70-125887 ISBN 0-07-061195-5 7.95
1. Political posters, Cuban. 2. Posters, Cuban. I. Sontag, Susan, 1933- II. Title.

Political posters, Mexican.

MEXICAN student posters; posters from the uprising 1968. Studies in the Third World Inc. [Indianapolis, Bobbs-Merrill, 1971] 1 portfolio (16 plates (part col.)) 45 cm. Title from portfolio. A folder ([8] p. 23 x 10 cm.) in Spanish, English, and French, inserted. [F1235.M4] 78-142484 3.95 769'.4'9972082
1. Political posters, Mexican. 2. Students—Mexico—Political activity. I. Studies in the Third World Inc.

Politics in art.

ART and architecture in the service of politics / edited by Henry A. Millon and Linda Nochlin. Cambridge, Mass. : MIT Press, c1977. p. cm. Includes bibliographical references and index. [N8236.P5A77] 78-1311 ISBN 0-262-13137-4 : 45.00 701
1. Politics in art. 2. Art and revolution. I. Millon, Henry A. II. Nochlin, Linda.

THE Artists' response to political and social issues. [Show organized by Ben Goldstein. New York, National Emergency Civil Liberties Committee, 1971] [20] p. (incl. cover) 19 x 23 cm. Cover title. [N6512.A77] 73-170470 760'.0973
1. Politics in art. 2. Humanism in art. 3. Art, American—Exhibitions. 4. Art, Modern—20th century—United States. I. Goldstein, Ben. II. National Emergency Civil Liberties Committee.

HESS, Hans, art curator. 741.5'943
George Grosz. [1st American ed.] New York, Macmillan [1974] 272 p. illus. (part col.) 29 cm. Bibliography: p. 266-270. [NC1509.G78H47 1974] 74-7414 ISBN 0-02-551270-6 22.50
1. Grosz, George, 1893-1959. 2. Politics in art. 3. German wit and humor, Pictorial.

Politics in art—Juvenile literature.

MONDALE, Jean 704.94'9'320973
Adams.
Politics in art. Designed by Vicki Hall. Minneapolis, Lerner Publications Co. [1972] 71 p. illus. 27 cm. (Fine art books for young people) Discusses political commentary reflected in various works of art. [N6505.M58] 72-266 ISBN 0-8225-0170-8
1. Politics in art—Juvenile literature. 2. Art, American—History—Juvenile literature. I. Title.

Pollaiuolo, Antonio del, d. 1498.

EHRLICH, Evelyn. 769.92'4
The Gott impression of Pollaiuolo's Battle of the nudes [by] Evelyn Ehrlich [and] John H. Neff. Washington, National Gallery of Art, 1973. 28 p. illus. 26 cm. Includes bibliographical references. [NE662.P65E35] 73-88213
1. Pollaiulo, Antonio del, d. 1498. Battle of the nudes. I. Neff, John H., joint author. II. Pollaiuolo, Antonio del, d. 1498. Battle of the nudes. 1973. III. Title.

ETTLINGER, Leopold 709'.2'2
David, 1913-
Antonio and Piero Pollaiuolo : complete edition with a critical catalogue / Leopold D. Ettlinger. Oxford : Phaidon ; New York : Dutton, 1978. 183 p. : ill. (some col.) ; 29 cm. Includes indexes. Bibliography: p. 174-176. [N6923.P6E88 1978] 78-55008 ISBN 0-7148-1768-6 : 75.00
1. Pollaiuolo, Antonio del, d. 1498. 2. Pollaiuolo, Pietro del, d. 1496. I. Title. **BIP**

Pollak, Max.

TRITON Museum of Art. 769'.92'4
Max Pollak: in retrospect, 1886-1970. [Exhibition] May 13 to June 15, 1973. Santa Clara, Calif. [1973] [24] p. illus. 28 cm. Catalog. Bibliography: p. [8] [NE2012.P64T74 1973] 74-185072
1. Pollak, Max.

Polland, Don, 1932—

POLLAND, Don, 1932- 730'.92'4
The Old West in miniature : sculpture / by Don Polland. Shreveport, La. : R. W. Norton Art Gallery, [1974] 23 p. : ill. (some col.) ; 28 cm. Cover title. Catalog of an exhibition held at the R. W. Norton Art Gallery, Shreveport, La., Oct. 13-Nov. 24, 1974. [NB237.P65N67] 74-24491
*1. Polland, Don, 1932- 2. The West in art. I. Norton (R. W.) Art Gallery. II. Title.***BIP**

Pollock, Jackson, 1912-1956.

BUSIGNANI, Alberto. 759.13
Pollock [translated from the Italian] London, New York, Hamlyn, 1971. 96 p. (chiefly illus. (chiefly col.), ports.) 32 cm. (Twentieth-century masters) Distributed in the United States by Crown Publishers. Bibliography: p. 96. [ND237.P73B813] 72-182352 ISBN 0-600-36914-5 £2.25
1. Pollock, Jackson, 1912-1956.

FIELD, Richard S. 769'.92'4
Jasper Johns : prints 1970-1977 / by Richard S. Field. Middletown, Conn. : Wesleyan University, 1978. 127 p. : ill. (some col.) ; 28 x 26 cm. Catalog of a traveling exhibition to be held at the Center for the Arts, Wesleyan University and other institutions, Mar. 27, 1978-Nov. 18, 1979. Bibliography: p. 125-127. [NE539.J57A4 1978] 77-93988 ISBN 0-931266-00-9 pbk. : 10.00
1. Johns, Jasper, 1930- —Exhibitions. I. Wesleyan University, Middletown, Conn. Center for the Arts.

FRIEDMAN, Bernard 759.13 B
Harper, 1926-
Jackson Pollock; energy made visible, by B. H. Friedman. [1st ed.] New York, McGraw-Hill [1972] xx, 293 p. illus. 23 cm. Bibliography: p. [263]-278. [ND237.P73F7] 76-39411 ISBN 0-07-022421-8
1. Pollock, Jackson, 1912-1956.

JACKSON Pollock : 709'.2'4
new-found works : Yale University Art Gallery, New Haven, Connecticut, 5 October-26 November 1978, National Collection of Fine Arts, Washington, D.C., 22 December-11 February 1979, the David and Alfred Smart Gallery, the University of Chicago, Chicago, Illinois, 12 March-6 May 1979. New Haven : Yale University Art Gallery, c1978. [32] p. : ill. ; 27 cm. Bibliography: p. [32] [ND237.P73A4 1978] 78-9867 ISBN 0-89467-007-7 : 250.00
1. Pollock, Jackson, 1912-1956. I. Yale University. Art Gallery. II. Smithsonian Institution. National Collection of Fine Arts. III. David and Alfred Smart Gallery.

KLIGMAN, Ruth. 759.13
Love affair; a memoir of Jackson Pollack [i.e. Pollock] New York, Morrow, 1974. 220 p. group port. 21 cm. [ND237.P73K55] 73-14553 ISBN 0-688-00232-3 6.95
1. Pollock, Jackson, 1912-1956. 2. Kligman, Ruth. I. Title.

O'CONNOR, Francis V. 759.13
Jackson Pollock, by Francis V. O'Connor. New York, Museum of Modern Art [1967] 148 p. illus. (1 fold. col.), ports. 23 x 25 cm. Bibliography: p. 137-143. [ND237.P73O2] 67-26814
1. Pollock, Jackson, 1912-1956.

O'HARA, Frank. 759.13
Jackson Pollock. New York, G. Braziller, 1959. 125 p. illus. (part col.), port. 26 cm. (The Great American artists series) Bibliography: p. 119-120. [ND237.P73O4] 59-12228
1. Pollock, Jackson, 1912-1956.

POLLOCK, Jackson, 1912- 709'.2'4
1956.
Jackson Pollock : a catalogue raisonne of paintings, drawings, and other works / edited by Francis Valentine O'Connor and Eugene Victor Thaw. New Haven : Yale University Press, 1978. p. cm. Includes indexes. Contents.Contents.—v. 1. Paintings, 1930-1947.—v. 2. Paintings, 1948-1955.—v. 3. Drawings, 1930-1956.—v. 4. Other works, 1930-1956. Bibliography: p. [N6537.P57O24 1978] 77-16390 ISBN 0-300-02109-7 : 250.00 (set)
1. Pollock, Jackson, 1912-1956. I. O'Connor, Francis V. II. Thaw, Eugene V.

POLLOCK, Jackson, 1912- 741'.0924
1956.
Jackson Pollock; psychoanalytic drawings. Text by C. L. Wysuph. New York, Horizon Press [1970] 123 p. illus. (part col.) 25 cm. Bibliography: p. 119-121. [NC139.P6W95] 72-132329 5.95 (pbk.)
I. Wysuph, C. L., 1939-

POLLOCK, Jackson, 1912- 760'.0924
1956.
Jackson Pollock: works on paper. [Text by] Bernice Rose. New York, Museum of Modern Art, in association with the Drawing Society; distributed by New York Graphic Society, Greenwich, Conn. [1969] 106 p. illus. (part col.) 28 x 29 cm. [NC139.P6R6] 68-17128 15.00
I. Rose, Bernice. II. Drawing Society. III. Title.

POLLOCK, Jackson, 1912- 759.13
1956.
Pollock; [the life and work of the artist, illustrated with 80 full-color plates, by] Italo Tomassoni. [Translated from Italian by Caroline Beamish. 1st American ed.] New York, Grosset & Dunlap [1969, c1968] 39 p. illus., plates (part col.) 18 cm. (The New Grosset art library, 24) Bibliography: p. 27-29. [ND237.P73T63 1969] 69-11563 ISBN 0-448-00473-9 1.50
I. Tomassoni, Italo. **BIP**

PUTZ, Ekkehard. 759.13
Jackson Pollock, Theorie und Bild / Ekkehard Putz. Hildesheim ; New York : G. Olms, 1975. 340 p. : ill. ; 21 cm. (Studien zur Kunstgeschichte ; Bd. 4) Originally presented as the author's thesis, Ruhr-Universitat Bochum, 1973. Includes index. Bibliography: p. 307-325. [ND237.P92P64 1975] 76-451921 ISBN 3-487-05743-3
1. Pollock, Jackson, 1912-1956. I. Title. II. Series.

ROBERTSON, Bryan, 1912- 759.13
1956
Jackson Pollock. New York, H. N. Abrams [1960] 215p. plates (part col.) ports. 28cm. Bibl.: p.195-196. 60-8401 18.50
1. Pollock, Jackson, 1912-1956. I. Title.

Pollution—Caricatures and cartoons.

GERARD, Dave. 741.5'973
Citizen Smith fights pollution. Valley Forge, Judson Press [1972] 1 v. (chiefly illus.) 12 x 16 cm. [NC1429.G38A43] 74-181023 ISBN 0-8170-0550-1 1.00
1. Pollution—Caricatures and cartoons. I. Title.

Polychromy.

GATZ, Konrad. 724.9
Color in architecture; a guide to exterior design [by] Konard Gatz, Wilhelm O. Wallenfang. Collaboration: Werner Piepenburg. New York, Reinhold [1961, c.1960] 192p. chiefly illus. (part col.) 30cm. Captions in German, English, and French. 61-8451 16.95
1. Polychromy. 2. Architecture, Modern—20th cent. I. Wallenfang, Wilhelm Otto. II. Title. **BIP**

Polymer painting.

BROOKS, Walter, 1921- 751.4'26
Creative ways with acrylic painting. Designed and edited by Walter Brooks. New York, Golden Press [1974] 32 p. illus. (part col.) 29 cm. (The Golden Press art instruction series) [ND1535.B76] 73-88428 1.25 (pbk.)
1. Polymer painting. I. Title. II. Title: Acrylic painting. **BIP**

COVINO, Frank. 751.4'26
Discover acrylics with Frank Covino, an academic approach. Westport, Conn., North Light Publishers; distributed by Watson-Guptill Publications, New York [1974] 129 p. illus. (part col.) 24 x 31 cm. [ND1535.C68] 73-93004 ISBN 0-8230-1340-5 16.95
1. Polymer painting. I. Title. **BIP**

DANIELS, Alfred. 751.4'26
Enjoying acrylics / [by] Alfred Daniels ; line illustrations by Margot Hamilton Hill. London : Luscombe, 1976. 128 p., 8 p. of plates : ill. (some col.) ; 23 cm. Label mounted on t.p.: Transatlantic Arts, Inc., Levittown, N.Y., sole distributor for the U.S.A. Includes index. Bibliography: p. 126. [ND1535.D36] 76-377600 ISBN 0-86002-142-4 : 7.50
1. Polymer painting. I. Title.

FABRI, Ralph, 1894- 751
The art of polymer painting. New York, Reinhold Pub. Corp. [1966] 88 p. illus. (part col.) 27 cm. Cover title: Guide to polymer painting. [ND1260.F24] 66-22685
1. Polymer painting. I. Title. II. Title: Guide to polymer painting.

GUTIERREZ, Jose L. 751.4
Painting with acrylics, by Jose Gutierrez & Nicholas Roukes. Pref. by David Alfaro Siqueiros. New York, Watson-Guptil Publications [1965] 191 p. illus. (part col.) 27 cm. Bibliography: p. 189. [ND1260.G85] 65-25309
1. Polymer painting. 2. Artists' materials. I. Roukes, Nicholas, joint author. II. Title.

KORTLANDER, William 751.4'26
Clark, 1925-
Painting with acrylics [by] William Kortlander. Project director: Edward A. Hamilton. New York, Van Nostrand Reinhold [1973] 144 p. illus. (part col.) 29 cm. (Art-in-practice series) [ND1535.K67] 72-2664 ISBN 0-442-24514-9 12.50
1. Polymer painting. I. Title.

SHEAKS, Barclay. 751.4'26
Painting with acrylics, from start to finish. Worcester, Mass., Davis Publications [1972] xii, 114 p. illus. 26 cm. [ND1535.S5] 71-186596 ISBN 0-87192-048-4
1. Polymer painting. I. Title.

TORCHE, Judith. 751.2
Acrylic and other water-base paints for the artist. New York, Sterling Pub. Co., [1967] 80 p. illus. (part col.) 29 cm. Bibliography: p. 77-78. [ND1540.T6 1967] 66-25197
1. Polymer painting. I. Title.

WOODY, Russell O. 751
Painting with synthetic media [by] Russell O. Woody, Jr. Technical appendix by Henry W. Levison. New York, Reinhold Pub. Corp. [1965] 160 p. illus. (part col.) 29 cm. [ND1260.W66] 64-22420
1. Polymer painting. I. Title.

WOODY, Russell O. 751.4'2
Polymer painting and related techniques, with course outline and works of prominent artists [by] Russell O. Woody, Jr. New York, Van Nostrand Reinhold Co. [1969] 108 p. illus. (part col.) 20 cm. (A Van Nostrand Reinhold art paperback) [ND1260.W67 1969] 74-90304
1. Polymer painting. I. Title.

Polymer painting—Technique.

BLAKE, Wendon. 751.4'26
The acrylic painting book / by Wendon Blake ; paintings by Rudy de Reyna. New York : Watson-Guptill, 1979. p. cm. [ND1505.B55 1978] 78-4263 ISBN 0-8230-0067-2 : 22.50
1. Polymer painting—Technique. I. De Reyna, Rudy, 1914- II. Title. **BIP**

Pompeii.

GABRIEL, Mabel McAfee, 751.73
1885-
Masters of Campanian painting. New York, H. Bittner, 1952. vii, 66p. illus., 35 plates. 32cm. Bibliography: p. 63-64. [N5770.G3] 53-303
1. Pompeii. 2. Herculaneum. 3. Mural painting and decoration. I. Title.

Ponies.

THELWELL, Norman, 1923- 743.69725
Ponies. [1st Amer. ed. New York, Watson-Guptill, 1966] 56p. illus. 18cm. (Watson-Guptill drawing bks.) Cover title: Drawing ponies. [NC780.T48 1966] 66-19735 1.00 pap.,
1. Ponies. 2. Animals in art. I. Title. II. Title: Drawing ponies.

Pontalba, Micaela Leonarda (Almonester) 1795-1874.

HUBER, Leonard 728.3109763355
Victor, 1903-
Baroness Pontalba's buildings, their site and the remarkable woman who built them, by Leonard V. Huber, Samuel Wilson, Jr. New Orleans, New Orleans Chapter of the Louisiana Landmarks Soc. [1964] iv, 62p. illus., ports. 24cm. Bibl. 63-22709 price unreported
1. Pontalba, Miraela Leonarda (Almonester) 1795-1874. 2. New Orleans—Historic houses, etc. I. Wilson, Samuel, 1911- joint author. II. Title. **BIP**

HUBER, Leonard Victor, 71019
1903-
Baroness Pontalba's buildings, their site and the remarkable woman who built them, by Leonard V. Huber and Samuel Wilson, Jr. [2d ed.] New Orleans, New Orleans Chapter of the Louisiana Landmarks Society and the Friends of the Cabildo [1966, c1964] iv, 63 p. illus., ports. 24 cm. Bibliography: p. 61. [68-96710]
1. Pontalba, Micaela Leonarda (Almonester) 1795-1874. 2. New Orleans—Historic houses, etc. I. Wilson, Samuel, 1911- joint author. II. Friends of the Cabildo, inc., New Orleans. III. Louisiana Landmarks Society. IV. Title.

Ponting, Herbert George.

ARNOLD, Harry John 770'.92'4 B
Philip, 1932-
Photographer of the world; the biography of Herbert Ponting [by] H. J. P. Arnold. [1st American ed.] Rutherford [N.J.] Fairleigh Dickinson University Press [1972, c1969] 175 p. illus. 26 cm. Includes bibliographical references. [TR140.P6A7 1972] 75-156270 ISBN 0-8386-7959-5 8.50
1. Ponting, Herbert George. I. Title. **BIP**

Pontormo, Jacopo Carucci, known as, 1494-ca. 1556.

REARICK, Janet Cox 741.945
The drawings of Pontormo [v.1&2] Cambridge, Mass., Harvard [c.]1964. 2v. (452+various p. illus. 26cm. Contents.v.1. Text. Catalogue raisonne.--v.2. Illustrations. Bibl. 64-13427 35.00 set,
1. Pontormo, Jacopo Carrucci, known as Jacopo da, b. 1494. I. Title.

SHEARMAN, John K. G. 759.5
Pontormo's altarpiece in S. Felicita, by John Shearman. [Newcastle upon Tyne, Eng.] University of Newcastle upon Tyne, 1971. 30 p. illus. 24 cm. (Charlton lecture, 51) Includes bibliographical references. [ND623.P8S53] 73-160894
1. Pontormo, Jacopo Carucci, known as, 1494-ca. 1556. Entombment. 2. Chiesa di Santa Felicita. I. Title. II. Series.

Poor—Pictorial works.

SALZMANN, Laurence. 779'.2'0924
Neighbors on the block: life in single room occupancy hotels. Photos. by Laurence Salzmann. [Introductory statement by Laurence Salzmann. New York, New York State Council on the Arts, c1971] [4] p., 50 plates. 37 cm. Issued in a case. "An exhibit portfolio produced by the New York State Council on the Arts for the New York Museums Collaborative." [TR681.P6S24] 72-171181
1. Poor—Pictorial works. I. New York (State). State Council on the Arts. II. Museums Collaborative. III. Title.

Poor—United States.

RIIS, Jacob August, 1849-1914. 779'.9'9747104
Jacob A. Riis : photographer & citizen / by Alexander Alland, Sr. ; with pref. by Ansel Adams. Millerton, N.Y. : Aperture, [1974] 220 p. : ill. ; 24 x 28 cm. Includes index. Bibliography: p. 215. [HV4045.R5 1974] 74-21617 ISBN 0-912334-66-5 : 17.50
1. Riis, Jacob August, 1849-1914. 2. Poor—United States. I. Alland, Alexander.

Poor—United States—Pictorial works.

DOHERTY, Robert J., 1924- 779'.9'9173
Social-documentary photography in the USA / R. J. Doherty. Garden City, N.Y. : AMPHOTO, c1976. 92 p. : ill. ; 27 cm. (Photography, men and movements) Includes index. Bibliography: p. 91. [HV4044.D6] 75-34604 ISBN 0-8174-0316-7 : 5.95
1. Poor—United States—Pictorial works. 2. United States—Social conditions—1933-1945—Pictorial works. I. Title.

Pop art.

AMAYA, Mario. 709.04
Pop art ... and after. New York, Viking Press [1966, c1965] 148 p. plates (part col.) 26 cm. (A Studio book) Published in Great Britain in 1965 under title: Pop as art. Bibliography: p. 143-145. [N6490.A62 1966] 66-10679
1. Pop art. I. Title.

COMPTON, Michael. 709.04'6
Pop art. Feltham, New York, Hamlyn, 1970. 5-139 p. illus. (some col.), ports. (some col.). 22 cm. (Movements of modern art) Illus. (incl. 1 col.) on lining papers. [N6494.P6C6] 74-21988 ISBN 0-600-02637-X 35/-
1. Pop art.

KULTERMANN, Udo. 759.13
New realism. Greenwich, Conn., New York Graphic Society [1972] 1 v. (various pagings) illus. (part col.) 25 cm. Translation of Radikaler Realismus. Includes bibliography. [N6494.P6K813] 76-181341 ISBN 0-8212-0432-7 14.95
1. Pop art. 2. Art, Modern—20th century. I. Title.

LIPPARD, Lucy R 709.04
Pop art [by] Lucy R. Lippard. With contributions by Lawrence Alloway, Ancy Marmer [and] Nicolas Calas. New York, Praeger [c1966] 216 p. illus. (part col.) 22 cm. (Praeger world of art series) Bibliography: p. 206-208. [N6490.L53] 66-21787
1. Pop art. I. Title.

MERZ, Florian. 707'.1'2
Pop art in the school; an investigation of pop art and its application in educational theory and classroom practice. Foreword by Reinhard Pfennig. New York, Van Nostrand Reinhold Co. [1970] 103 p. illus. (part col.) 22 cm. Translation of Pop-Art in der Schule. On spine: Pop art: projects for young people. [N352.M4513] 79-90340
1. Pop art. 2. Children as artists. I. Title.

SCHOLZ-WANCKEL, Katharina. 709.04
Pop Import. Eine selektive Abhandlung uber Pop Artisten. Hamburg, Matari Verlag [1965]. 107 p. with illus. 25 cm. Bibliographical footnotes. [N6490.S32] 68-73733 DM19.80
1. Pop art. I. Title.

YAHN, Erle 709.04
You can be a pop-op artist! [dist. New York, Taplinger, c.1966] dist. New York, Taplinger, c.1966 79p illus. 25cm. [N6490.Y3] 66-15645 5.95; 2.95 pap.,
1. Pop art. I. Title. II. Title: Introd. by Andy Warhol. Photos. by Bram and Debbie Lucom

Pop art—England—Exhibitions.

POP Art in England 709'.42'074094
: Anfange einer neuen Figuration 1947-63 = beginnings of a new Figuration 1947-63 : [Ausstellung] Kunstverein in Hamburg 7. Februar bis 21. Marz 1976, Stadt. Galerie im Lenbachhaus Munchen 3. April bis 16. Mai 1976, York City Art Gallery 29 May-11 July 1976 / hrsg. vom Kunstverein in Hamburg ; Katalogredaktion und Texte, Uwe M. Schneede. Hamburg : Kunstverein, [1976] 134 p. : ill. (some col.) ; 23 cm. English and German. Includes bibliographies. [N6768.5.P65P66] 77-480356
1. Pop art—England—Exhibitions. 2. Art, Modern—20th century—England—Exhibitions. I. Schneede, Uwe M. II. Kunstverein in Hamburg. III. Munich. Stadtische Galerie im Lenbachhaus. IV. York, Eng. Art Gallery.

Pop art — Exhibitions.

KANSAS. University. Museum of Art. 704.9'2 s
Gene Swenson: retrospective for a critic. [Lawrence, Kan., 1971] 104 p. illus. (part col.) 26 cm. (Its Register, v. 4, nos. 6-7) Catalog of an exhibition held Oct. 24-Dec. 5, 1971. Bibliography: p. 83. [N582.L25A35 vol. 4, no. 6-7] [N6512.5.P6] 709'.2'4 76-198477
1. Swenson, Gene, 1934-1969—Art collections. 2. Pop art—Exhibitions. 3. Art, Modern—20th century—U.S. I. Title. II. Series.

KANSAS. University. Museum of Art. 701.16
Optics, illusion and art. [Exhibition] May 14-June 7, 1965, Museum of Art, The University of Kansas. [Lawerence, 1965] 1 v. (unpaged) illus. 19 cm. (Its miscellaneous publications, no. 59) [N6490.K3] 66-63693
1. Pop art — Exhibitions. I. Title. II. Series.

NEW York. Museum of Modern Art. 709.04
The object transformed. With an introd. by Mildred Constantine and Arthur Drexler. [New York, 1966] 35 p. illus. 25 cm. "Exhibition ... shown at the Museum of Modern Art from June 28 through August 21, 1966." [N6490.N43] 66-28128
1. Pop art—Exhibitions. I. Constantine, Mildred. II. Drexler, Arthur. III. Title.

OAKLAND, Calif. Art Museum. 709'.73'074019466
Pop art USA : an exhibition presented by the Oakland Art Museum and the California College of Arts & Crafts, organized by John Coplans, shown September 7 to 29, 1963, at the Oakland Art Museum. [Oakland, Calif.] : The Museum, [1963] 63 p. : ill. (some col.) ; 23 cm. [ND212.5.P6O14 1963] 75-320595
1. Pop art—Exhibitions. 2. Pop art—United States. 3. Painting, Modern—20th century—United States. I. Coplans, John. II. California College of Arts and Crafts, Oakland. III. Title.

RHODE Island School of Design, Providence. Museum of Art. 709.04
Recent still life. [Exhibition] February 23-April 4, 1966. Providence [1966] 1 v. (unpaged) illus. 22 cm. [N6490.R53455] 68-1616
1. Pop art—Exhibitions. 2. Art, Modern—20th century—Exhibitions. I. Title.

RUSSELL, John, 1919- comp. 709.04'6
Pop art redefined [by] John Russell [and] Suzi Gablik. New York, Praeger [1969] 240 p. illus. (part col.) 25 cm. Includes the catalog of an exhibition of Anglo-American pop art, sponsored by the Arts Council of Great Britain, and held in July and August 1969 at the Hayward Gallery in London. [N6494.P6R82] 74-85330 8.95
1. Pop art—Exhibitions. I. Gablik, Suzi, joint comp. II. Arts Council of Great Britain. III. Hayward Gallery. IV. Title.

Pop art—Gt. Brit.

MELLY, George, 1926- 700'.942
Revolt into style: the pop arts. Garden City, N.Y., Anchor Books, 1971 [1970] 270 p. 18 cm. [NX600.P66M4] 71-157644 1.95
1. Pop art—Gt. Brit. 2. Gt. Brit.—Popular culture. I. Title.

Pop art—U.S.

ALLEN, Don, 1941- 709.04
The electric humanities; patterns for teaching mass media & popular culture. Photography & graphics by Brent Warren. Dayton, Ohio, G. A. Pflaum [1971] 276 p. illus. 24 cm. [NX600.P66A4] 77-160514
1. Pop art—U.S. 2. The arts, Modern—20th century—U.S. 3. U.S—Popular culture. I. Title.

ALLOWAY, Lawrence, 1926- 709'.73
American pop art. New York, Collier Books [1974] xii, 144 p. illus. (part col.) 25 cm. "An exhibition organized for and shown at the Whitney Museum of American Art, April 6-June 16, 1974." Bibliography: p. 133-140. [N6512.5.P6A55 1974] 73-22532 ISBN 0-02-627700-X 9.95
1. Pop art—United States. 2. Art, Modern—20th century—United States. I. Whitney Museum of American Art, New York. II. Title.
Pbk. 4.95. BIP

LOWE Art Museum. 709'.73
Phases of new realism, January 20-February 20, 1972 [exhibition catalog] Coral Gables, Fla., Lowe Art Museum, University of Miami [1972] 44 p. illus. 26 cm. [N6512.5.P6L68] 74-157583
1. Pop art—United States. 2. Pop art—Exhibitions. 3. Art, Modern—20th century—United States. I. Title.

Pope, Alexander, 1688-1744 — Portraits, etc.

WIMSATT, William Kurtz, 1907- 704.9423
The portraits of Alexander Pope. New Haven, Yale University Press, 1965. xxxiii, 391 p. illus. (part col.) ports. 29 cm. Bibliographical footnotes. [PR3633.W5] 65-12549
1. Pope, Alexander, 1688-1744 — Portraits, etc. I. Title.

Pope, Arthur, 1880—

CARPENTER, James Morton, 1914- 752
Color in art; a tribute to Arthur Pope. With an introd. to color by Howard T. Fisher. Catalogue and text by James M. Carpenter. [Cambridge, Mass.] Fogg Art Museum, Harvard University [1974] 134 p. illus. (part col.) 27 cm. Exhibition held Apr. 24-June 16, 1974, at the Fogg Art Museum. Bibliography: p. 130. [ND1493.P66C37] 74-78661
1. Pope, Arthur, 1880- 2. Color in art. I. Pope, Arthur, 1880- II. Harvard University. William Hayes Fogg Art Museum.

Porcelain.

CAMPBELL Museum. 738'.074'014988
The Campbell Museum collection. Camden, N.J., 1969. [96] p. illus. (part col.) 26 cm. Bibliography: p. [93] [NK460.C3A53] 77-101017 3.00
I. Title.

CAMPBELL Museum. 738'.074'014988
The Campbell Museum collection. 2d ed., rev. and enl. Camden, N.J., 1972. 1 v. (unpaged) illus. (part col.) 26 cm. Includes bibliography. [NK460.C3A53 1972] 73-190079 4.00
I. Title.

*CUSHION, John P. 738.28
Pottery & porcelain tablewares / John P. Cushion. New York : William Morrow, c1976. 240p. : ill. (some col.) ; 27 cm. Includes index. Bibliography:p.140. [NK4373] 75-45518 ISBN 0-688-03055-6 : 22.50
1. Porcelain. 2. Tableware. 3. Pottery. I. Title. BIP

CUSHION, John Patrick. 738.2
Porcelain [by] John Cushion. New York, World Pub. [1973] p. (Connoisseur's library) Bibliography: p. [NK4370.C87] 72-10448 ISBN 0-529-05014-5
1. Porcelain. I. Title. II. Series: Connoisseur's library (New York)

*HARRIS, Nathaniel. 666.58
Porcelain figurines. [New York] Golden Press [1974] [80] p. illus. (part. col.) 30 cm. (Golden highlights library.) [TP822] 73-87967 2.95
1. Porcelain. I. Title.

TAIT, Hugh. 738.2'094
Porcelain. Revised ed. London, New York, Hamlyn, 1972. 96 p. illus. (some col.), map. 30 cm. Bibliography: p. 93. [NK4370.T3 1972] 73-152226 ISBN 0-600-37003-8 £1.50
1. Porcelain.

TRIMBLE, Alberta C. 738.2
Modern porcelain: today's treasures, tomorrow's traditions. [1st ed.] New York, Harper [1962] 224 p. illus. 24 cm. [NK1370.T7] 62-8618
1. Porcelain. I. Title.

Porcelain, American.

†PALLEY, Reese. 738.2'092'4
The porcelain art of Edward Marshall Boehm / by Reese Palley. New York : H. N. Abrams, [1976] p. cm. Includes index. [NK4210.B6P34] 76-20690 ISBN 0-8109-0701-1 : 35.00
1. Boehm, Edward Marshall, 1913-1969. 2. Porcelain, American. I. Title.

ROBERT Hudson/Richard 739.2'092'4
Shaw, work in porcelain. [Catalogue of an exhibition] May 11-July 1, 1973, San Francisco Museum of Art. [San Francisco, 1973] 35 p. illus. 26 cm. Bibliography: p. 34. [NK4210.H82R62] 73-164556
1. Hudson, Robert, 1938- 2. Shaw, Richard, 1941- 3. Porcelain, American. I. Hudson, Robert, 1938- II. Shaw, Richard, 1941- III. San Francisco. Museum of Art.

Porcelain, American—Exhibitions.

NORTON (R. W.) Art Gallery. 738.2'0973'074014966
The American porcelain tradition: 18th, 19th, and 20th centuries. A loan exhibition from the New Jersey State Museum, May 28 to June 25, 1972. [Shreveport, La., Printed by C. Young, 1972] 32 p. illus. (part col.) 28 cm. Bibliography: p. 29-30. [NK4405.N6] 72-82888 ISBN 0-9600182-8-X
1. Porcelain, American—Exhibitions. I. New Jersey. State Museum, Trenton. II. Title.

Porcelain, American—History.

SCHWARTZ, Marvin D. 738.2'0973
A history of American art porcelain, by Marvin D. Schwartz and Richard Wolfe.

[1st ed.] New York, Renaissance Editions [1967] 93 p. illus. (part col.) 28 cm. Bibliography: p. 93. [NK4405.S3] 66-30197
1. Porcelain, American—History. I. Wolfe, Richard, 1938- joint author. II. Title.

Porcelain, British.

GODDEN, Geoffrey A. 738.2'0942
British porcelain; an illustrated guide [by] Geoffrey A. Godden. [1st American ed.] New York, Clarkson N. Potter; distributed by Crown Publishers [1974] 451 p. illus. 26 cm. Bibliography: p. 446-448. [NK4485.G59 1974] 73-88984 ISBN 0-517-51305-6 15.00
1. Porcelain, British. BIP

Porcelain, British—Catalogs.

BATTIE, David. 738.2'0942
The price guide to 19th and 20th century British porcelain / by David Battie and Michael Turner. Woodbridge [Eng.] : Antique Collectors' Club, c1975. 507 p. : chiefly ill. ; 22 cm. Includes index. Bibliography: p. 503. [NK4485.B28] 75-330653 £5.95
1. Porcelain, British—Catalogs. 2. Porcelain—Collectors and collecting. I. Turner, Michael L., joint author. II. Title.

Porcelain, Chinese.

BEURDELEY, Michel. 738.20951
Chinese trade porcelain. [Translated by Diana Imber] Rutland, Vt., C. E. Tuttle Co. [1962] xii, 219p. illus. (part mounted col.) 'Orginally published in French under the title of 'Porcelaine de la companie des Indes.' Bibliography: p. 212-213. [NK4565.B453] 62-14115
1. Porcelain, Chinese. I. Title.

DONNELLY, P. J. 738.2'7
Blanc de Chine, the porcelain of Tehua in Fukien, by P. J. Donnelly. New York, Praeger [1969] xiv, 407, 160 p. illus. (part col.) 26 cm. (Monographs on pottery and porcelain) Includes bibliographical references. [NK4565.D6 1969b] 69-20262 30.00
1. Porcelain, Chinese. 2. Porcelain—Fukien, China (Province) I. Title.

HYDE, John Alden Lloyd. 738.2'0951'07401511
Oriental Lowestoft, Chinese export porcelain, Porcelaine de la Cie des Indes; with special reference to the trade with China and the porcelain decorated for the American market, by J. A. Lloyd Hyde. [3d ed.] Newport Monmouthshire, Ceramic Book Co. [1964] viii, 168 p. 37 plates (part col.) 31 cm. [NK4565.H9] 65-66468
1. Porcelain, Chinese. 2. Art industries and trade, Chinese. 3. Lowestoft porcelain. I. Title.

JU ware of the Sung dynasty. 738.20951
Comp. by the joint Board of Directors of the National Palace Museum and the National Central Museum, Taichung, Taiwan, Republic of China. Kowloon, Hong Kong, Cafa Co. [dist. New York 22, Paragon Bk. Gallery, 140 E. 49th St., 1963] 55p. col. illus. 39cm. Japanese and English. 30.00
1. Porcelain, Chinese.

KOYAMA, Fujio, 1900- comp. 738.2/0951
A selection of outstanding Kinrande porcelains in Japanese collections. [Kyoto, Unsodo Pub. Co., 1967] [6]. 55 col. plates (in portfolio) 43cm. [NK4565.K6] 68-275 80.00
1. Porcelain, Chinese. 2. Porcelain—Japan. I. Title.
Distributed by Perkins Oriental Bks., Pasadena, Calif.

MUDGE, Jean McClure 738.27
Chinese export porcelain for American trade, 1785-1835 Univ. of Delaware Pr. [dist. University Pubns., New York, 1963, c.]1962. 284p. iulls. (pt. col.) 26cm. (Winterthur ser. bk.) Bibl. 61-16518 15.00
1. Porcelain, Chinese. I. Title. BIP

OSGOOD, Cornelius, 1905- 738.2
Blue-and-white Chinese porcelain; a study of form. New York, Ronald Press Co. [1956] xvii, 166p. illus., 64plates. 27cm. Bibliography: p. 147-155. [NK4565.O78] 56-10176
1. Porcelain, Chinese. I. Title.

PHILLIPS, John Goldsmith. 738.2
China-trade porcelain; an account of its historical background, manufacture, and decoration, and a study of the Helena Woolworth McCann collection. Cambridge, Published for the Winfield Foundation and the Metropolitan Museum of Art [by] Harvard University Press, 1956. xxi, 234p. illus. (part col.) maps. 28cm. Bibliography: p.222-224. [NK4565.P55] 56-11749
1. Porcelain, Chinese. 2. Porcelain—Private collections. I. McCann, Helena Woolworth. II. Title. BIP

POPE, John Alexander, 1906- 738.2
Fourteenth-century blue-and-white; a group of Chinese porcelains in the Topkapu Sarayi Muzesi, Istanbul. Washington, 1952. iii, 85 p. 44 plates. 21 cm. (Freer Gallery of Art occasional papers, v. 2, no. 1) Smithsonian Institution. Publication 4089. Bibliography: p. 74-78. [NK4565.P6] 52-61397
1. Porcelain. Chinese. 2. Porcelain — Istanbul. I. Istanbul. Topkapu Sarayl Muzesi. II. Title. III. Series: Freer Gallery of Art, Washington, D.C. Occasional papers, v. 2, no. 1

SCHUSTER, Felicia. 738.2'095
Vases of the sea; Far Eastern porcelain and other treasures [by] Felicia Schuster and Cecilia Wolseley. New York, Scribner [1974] 157 p. col. illus. 25 cm. Bibliography: p. 153. [NK4565.S32] 73-7215 ISBN 0-684-13556-6 12.50
1. Porcelain, Chinese. 2. Porcelain, Japanese. 3. Art objects, Chinese. 4. Art objects, Japanese. I. Wolseley, Cecilia, joint author. II. Title.

WILLIAMSON, George Charles, 1858-1942. 738.2'0951
The book of famille rose. Rutland, Vt., Tuttle [1970] xxiv, 231 p. illus., 62 plates (19 col.) 27 cm. Bibliography: p. xxi-xxiv. [NK4565.W5 1970] 72-104208 ISBN 0-8048-0880-5 25.00
1. Porcelain, Chinese. I. Title. II. Title: Famille rose.

Porcelain, Chinese—Exhibitions.

AN Exhibition of China trade procelain designed to illustrate the wares imported to the port of New Haven. 738.2'0951
New Haven Colony Historical Society, March 3 through April 28, 1968. [New Haven, 1968] 99 p. illus. 22 cm. Catalogue compiled by John Devereux Kernan. Historical introd. by Mary Means Huber. Includes bibliographies. [NK4565.E96] 68-4007
1. Porcelain, Chinese—Exhibitions. I. Kernan, John Devereux, 1911- II. New Haven Colony Historical Society, New Haven.

Porcelain, Chinese—History.

LAUFER, Berthold, 1874-1934. 738.2'0951
The beginnings of porcelain in China. With a technical report by H.W. Nichols. [New York, Kraus Reprint Corp., 1967] 79-183 p. illus., 12 plates. 23 cm. (Field Museum of Natural History. Anthropological series, v. 15, no. 2) [Field Museum of Natural History] Publication 192. Title page includes original imprint: Chicago, 1917. "The Mrs. T.B. Blackstone Expedition." [GN2.F4 vol.15, no.2] 68-4205
1. Porcelain, Chinese—Hist. I. Nichols, Henry Windsor, 1868- II. Title. III. Series: Fieldiana: anthropology, v. 15, no. 2. Series: Field Museum of Natural History. Publication 192 BIP

Porcelain, Chinese—History.

DU BOULAY, Anthony. 738.20951
Chinese porcelain. New York, Putnam [1963] 128 p. illus. (part col.) 22 cm. (Pleasures and treasures) [NK4565.D78] 63-15525
1. Porcelain, Chinese—History. I. Title.

Porcelain, Chinese—Ming-Ch'ing dynasties, 1368-1912.

CHOU, Calvin. 738.2'0951
The hollow line in dating Chinese porcelains / Calvin Chou ; [macrophotography by Marvin Becker]. 1st ed. San Francisco : Chinese Art Appraisers Association, 1978. 120 p. (p. 107-120 advertisements) : ill. ; 26 cm. (Occasional publications - Chinese Art Appraisers Association) Bibliography: p. 98-101. [NK4565.5.C47] 77-87445 ISBN 0-930940-03-2 : 20.00. ISBN 0-930940-00-8 pbk. : 12.00
1. Porcelain, Chinese—Ming-Ch'ing dynasties, 1368-1912. 2. Porcelain—Dating. 3. Porcelain—Technique. I. Title. II. Series: Chinese Art Appraisers Association. Occasional publications — Chinese Art Appraisers Association. BIP

Porcelain—Collectors and collecting.

BERGES, Ruth. 738'.075
The collector's cabinet / Ruth Berges. South Brunswick [N.J.] : A. S. Barnes, c1979. p. cm. Includes index. Bibliography: p. [NK42130.B38] 77-84560 ISBN 0-498-02117-3 : 30.00
1. Porcelain—Collectors and collecting. 2. Faience—Collectors and collecting. 3. Majolica—Collectors and collecting. I. Title. BIP

BERGES, Ruth. 738'.075
Collector's choice of porcelain and faience. South Brunswick [N.J.] A. S. Barnes [1968, c1967] 264 p. illus. (part col.) 29 cm. Bibliography: p. 258-259. [NK4230.B4] 67-16884
1. Porcelain—Collectors and collecting. 2. Pottery—Collectors and collecting. I. Title.

RUST, Gordon. 738.2'075
Collector's guide to antique porcelain [by] Gordon A. Rust. New York, Viking Press [1973] 144 p. illus. 24 cm. (A Studio book) Bibliography: p. 136-141. [NK4230.R87 1973] 72-12062 ISBN 0-670-22917-2 9.95
1. Porcelain—Collectors and collecting. I. Title. II. Title: Antique porcelain.

THEUS, Will H. 738'.075
How to detect and collect antique porcelain and pottery [by] Will H. Theus. [1st ed.] New York, Knopf; [distributed by Random House] 1974. xii, 249, xix p. illus. 22 cm. Bibliography: p. [245]-249. [NK4230.T48 1974] 74-7747 ISBN 0-394-49130-0
1. Porcelain—Collectors and collecting. 2. Pottery—Collectors and collecting. I. Title. BIP

Porcelain, Czech.

BRISTOWE, William Syer. 738.28
Victorian china fairings [by] W. S. Bristowe. [1st American ed.] New York, Taplinger Pub. Co. [1965] 106 p. illus. 26 cm. [[NK4660.B7 1965]] 65-14390
1. Porcelain, Czech. 2. Porcelain, German. 3. Porcelain, English. I. Title. II. Title: China fairings. III. Title: Fairings.

Porcelain, English.

CHARLESTON, R. J., ed. 738.20942
English porcelain, 1745-1850. London E. Benn [Toronto] Univ. of Toronto Pr. [c.1965] 183p. illus., col. plates. 29cm. Bibl. [NK4485.C45] 65-8705 17.50
1. Porcelain, English. I. Title. BIP

EXLEY, Clifford Landseer. 338.4'7'6665
A history of the Torksey and Mansfield china factories, by C. L. Exley. Lincoln, G. R. G. Exley, 1970. 82 p. illus. (1 col.), geneal. table, map, plan. 22 cm. Bibliography: p. 80-82. [NK4210.T64E94] 74-163281 ISBN 0-9501465-0-1 25/-
1. Torksey China Factory. 2. Mansfield China Factory. 3. Porcelain, English. I. Title. BIP

GALPIN, John. 738.2'7
A handbook of Goss china. Portsmouth, J. Galpin (18 Lodge Ave., East Cosham), 1972. [2], 82 p. illus. 19 cm. Cover title: Goss china. [NK4210.G58G36] 73-168256 ISBN 0-9502548-0-0 £1.10
1. Goss China Company Ltd. 2. Porcelain, English. I. Title. II. Title: Goss china. BIP

GODDEN, Geoffrey A. 738.20942
Victorian porcelain. Foreword by Hugh Wakefield. New York, Nelson [1962, c.1961] 222p. illus. 25cm. (Victorian collector ser.) Bibl. 62-8329 8.50
1. Porcelain, English. I. Title.

HONEY, William Bowyer, 1889- 738.2'0942
Old English porcelain : a handbook for collectors / by W. B. Honey. 3d ed., rev., expanded and reset / rev. by Franklin A. Barrett. London : Faber and Faber, 1977. xxxiv, 440 p., [2] leaves of plates : ill. ; 23 cm. Includes index. Bibliography: p. 414-423. [NK4485.H7 1977] 78-300704 ISBN 0-571-04902-8 : 29.95
1. Porcelain, English. 2. Porcelain—Collectors and collecting. I. Barrett, Franklin Allen, 1906- II. Title.
Distributed by Faber and Faber, Salem, NH BIP

HUGHES, George Bernard, 1896- 738.2'0942
English porcelain and bone china, 1743-1850 [by] Bernard and Therle Hughes. New York, Praeger [1968] 256 p. illus. 23 cm. Bibliography: p. 244-248. [NK4485.H8 1968] 68-21583
1. Porcelain, English. I. Hughes, Therle, joint author. II. Title.

LANE, Arthur, [Edward Arthur Lane] 1909- 738.28
English porcelain figures of the eighteenth century. New York, Yoseloff [1961, c.1962] xi, 148p. 100 plates (pt. col.) 26cm. Bibl. 62-10188 8.95
1. Porcelain, English. I. Title.

REYNOLDS, Ernest Randolph, 1910- 738.2'0942
Collecting Victorian porcelain [by] Ernest Reynolds. New York, F. A. Praeger [1968, c1966] 128 p. illus. 23 cm. [NK4485.R4 1968] 68-16721
1. Porcelain, English. 2. Porcelain—Collectors and collecting. I. Title.

Porcelain, English—Catalogs.

SPERO, Simon, 1943- 738.2'0942
The price guide to eighteenth century English porcelain. Woodbridge (Suffolk), Antique Collectors' Club, 1970. [15], 448 p. illus. (1 col.) 22 cm. Bibliography: p. 444. [NK4485.S76] 78-597288 ISBN 0-902028-06-5 £3.15
1. Porcelain, English—Catalogs. 2. Porcelain—Prices. I. Title.

Porcelain, English—History.

BURTON, William, 1863- 738.2'0942
A history and description of English porcelain. [1st ed. reprinted] with a new introduction. Wakefield, EP Publishing Ltd, 1972. vii, xii, 196 p., 123 leaves. illus. 25 cm. Reprint of 1st ed., London, Cassell, 1902. Bibliography: p. [192] [NK4485.B9 1972] 73-161036 ISBN 0-85409-902-6 £3.50
1. Porcelain, English—History. 2. Porcelain—Marks. I. Title. BIP

EAGLESTONE, Archibald Arthur, 1892- 738.3'0942
The Rockingham pottery, by Arthur A. Eaglestone and Terrence A. Lockett. Clifton Park, Rotherham, Municipal Museum and Art Gallery, 1964. 152 p. illus. 23 cm. [NK4085.E2] 66-3118
1. Porcelain, English—Hist. I. Lockett, Terence A., joint author. II. Title. BIP

NIGHTINGALE, James Edward, d.1892. 338.4'3738'20942
Contributions towards the history of early English porcelain from contemporary sources; to which are added reprints from Messrs. Christie's sale catalogues of the Chelsea, Derby, Worcester and Bristol manufactories from 1769 to 1785, by J. E. Nightingale. Wakefield, EP Publishing, 1973. [1], xcv, 112 p. illus. 24 cm. Reprint of 1st ed., Salisbury, privatley printed, 1881. [NK4485.N53 1973] 74-163745 ISBN 0-85409-839-9 £2.50
1. Porcelain, English—History. I. Title. BIP

WATNEY, Bernard. 738.20942
English blue and white porcelain of the eighteenth century. [1st American ed.] New York, T. Yoseloff [1964, c1963] xiii, 137 p. illus. (part col.) 26 cm. (The Faber monographs on pottery and porcelain) Bibliography: p. 130-132. [NK4485.W3 1964] 64-57403
1. Porcelain, English — Hist. I. Title. BIP

Porcelain—Europe.

PENKALA, Maria. 738.2'094
European porcelain; a handbook for the collector. [2d ed.] Rutland, Vt., C. E. Tuttle Co. [1968] 256 p. illus. 25 cm. Bibliography: p. 246-250. [NK4230.P4 1968] 69-19604 12.50
1. Porcelain—Europe. 2. Porcelain—Collectors and collecting. I. Title.

Porcelain, European.

BACCI, Mina. 738.2'094
European porcelain; [translated from the Italian by Adeline Hartcup] Feltham, New York, Hamlyn, 1969. 3-157 p. 69 col. illus. 20 cm. (Cameo) Originally published as 'Le porcellane Europee'. Milano, Fabbri, 1966. [NK4083.B313] 70-437377 15/-
1. Porcelain, European. I. Title.

RHODE Island School of Design, Providence. Museum 738.2094
The Lucy Truman Aldrich collection of European porcelain figures of the eighteenth century, by Elizabeth Temple Casey. Mus. of Art of the R.I. Sch. of Design [dist. New York, Abrams, 1966, c.1965] 157p. plates (pt. col.) 26cm. Bibl. [NK4483.R5] 65-28229 9.00
1. Porcelain, European. 2. Porcelain—Providence—Catalogs. I. Aldrich, Lucy Truman, 1869-1955. II. Casey, Elizabeth Temple. III. Title.

WYNTER, Harriet. 738.2'094
An introduction to European porcelain. New York, Crowell [1972, c1971] xx, 255 p. illus. 25 cm. Bibliography: p. [244]-247. [NK4083.W9 1972] 72-167763 ISBN 0-690-44851-1 11.00
1. Porcelain, European. I. Title.

Porcelain, Far Eastern.

GOMPERTZ, Godfrey St. George Montague. 738.2'7
Celadon wares [by] G. St. G. M. Gompertz. New York, Praeger [1969, c1968] 104 [36] p. plates (part col.), maps. 23 cm. Bibliography: p. 98-99. [NK4563.G6 1969] 68-19135 7.95
1. Porcelain, Far Eastern. I. Title.

Porcelain, French.

LANDAIS, Hubert. 738.27
French porcelain. Translated from the French by Isabel and Florence McHugh. Photos. by E. Boudot-Lamotte. New York, Putnam [1961] 128 p. illus. 22 cm. (Pleasures and treasures) [NK4497.L313] 61-12201
1. Porcelain, French. I. Title.

Porcelain, French—Hist.

SAVAGE, George. 1909- 738.20944
Seventeenth and eighteenth century French porcelain. New York, Macmillan [1961, c.1960] 243p. Bibl. illus. (part col.) 61-1565 14.00
1. Porcelain, French—Hist. I. Title.

Porcelain, German.

DUCRET, Siegfried 738.20943
German porcelain and faience. Tr. [from German] by Diana Imber. New York, Universe [c.1962] 466p. illus. (pt. col.) 34cm. (Universe lib. of antique art) Bibl. 62-13886 37.50, bxd.
1. Porcelain, German. 2. Pottery, German. I. Title.

RAINES, Joan. 738.2'7
A guide to Royal Bayreuth figurals, by Joan and Marvin Raines. [New City, N.Y.] 1973. [45] p. (chiefly col. illus.) 23 cm. [NK4210.P58R34] 73-160546
1. Porzellanfabrik Tettau. 2. Porcelain, German. I. Raines, Marvin, joint author. II. Title.

WARE, George Whitaker, 1902- 738.20943
German and Austrian porcelain. New York, Crown Publishers [1964, c1963] 244 p. illus. (part mounted, part col.) col. maps. 26 cm. Bibliography: p. 227-228. [NK4499.W37 1964] 64-1631
1. Porcelain, German. 2. Porcelain, Austrian. 3. Porcelain—Marks. I. Title. BIP

Porcelain—History.

BACKLIN-LANDMAN, Hedy 738.209
The story of porcelain, by Hedy Backlin-Landman. Edna Shapiro. Illus. by Harry McNaught. New York, Odyssey, c.1965. 41p. illus. (pt. col.) 11x17cm. (Odvssey lib., 23) [NK4370.B15] 65-23289 .95 bds.,
1. Porcelain—Hist. I. Shapiro, Edna, joint author. II. McNaught, Harry, illus. III. Title.

SAVAGE, George, 1909- 738.209
Porcelain through the ages. [2d ed.] Baltimore, Penguin Books [1963] 347 p. illus. 18 cm. (Pelican books, A298) [NK4370.S3 1963] 63-5562
1. Porcelain—Hist. I. Title.

SAVAGE, George, 1909- 738.209
Porcelain through the ages. [Harmondsworth, Middlesex] Penguin Books [1954] 352p. illus. 18cm. (Pelican books A 298) Bibliography: p. 329-335. [NK4370.S3] 55-4560
1. Porcelain—Hist. I. Title.

SAVAGE, George, 1909- 738.209
Porcelain through the ages. London, Cassell [New York, Barnes & Noble, 1964, c.1954, 1961] xxiii, 333p. illus., 64 plates. 21cm. (Belle sauvage lib.) Bibl. 64-9556 5.00
1. Porcelain—Hist. I. Title.

SCOTT, Cleo M 738.209
Antique porcelain digest, by Cleo M. Scott and G. Ryland Scott, Jr. Newport, Mon., Ceramic Book Co. [1961] xvi, 200p. 180 plates (part col.) 29cm. Bibliography: p. 141. [NK4373.S35] 61-40313
1. Porcelain—Hist. 2. Porcelain—Collectors and collecting. I. Scott, George Ryland, joint author. II. Title.

SUTTENFIELD, Elise 738.209
The parade of porcelain; a history. New York, Exposition [1964, c.1963] 56p. illus. (pt. col.) 21cm. (EP41115) 64-908 4.00
1. Porcelain—Hist. I. Title.

Porcelain—History.

BERGES, Ruth. 738.209
From gold to porcelain; the art of porcelain and faience New York, T. Yoseloff [1964, c1963] 239 p. illus., col. plates. 29 cm. Bibliography: p. 226-227. [NK4370.B4] 63-18243
1. Porcelain—History. 2. Pottery—History. I. Title.

WEISS, Gustav, 1922- 738.2
The book of porcelain. Translated by Janet Seligman. New York, Praeger [1971] 335 p. illus., facsims., maps, plates (part col.) 24 cm. Translation of Ullstein Porzellanbuch. Bibliography: p. 318-320. [NK4370.W413] 74-107150 15.00
1. Porcelain—History. 2. Porcelain—Marks. I. Title.

Porcelain, Irish—Catalogs.

AN Illustrated guide to Irish Belleek Parian china. 738.2'7 Los Angeles, Calif., E. J. Lease [1969] viii, 85 p. illus. (part col.) 15 x 22 cm. Includes a reproduction of the 1937 Belleek catalog. [NK4210.B415] 74-12597 8.95
1. Porcelain, Irish—Catalogs. I. Lease (E. Jay) & Associates. II. Belleek Pottery, ltd. New illustrated catalogue of Parian china. 1969. III. Title: Irish Belleek Parian china.

Porcelain, Italian.

STAZZI, Francesco. 738.2'0945
Italian porcelain. New York, Putnam [1967] 127 p. 135 illus. (part col.) 22 cm. (Pleasures and treasures) [NK4503.S813] 67-11278
1. Porcelain, Italian. I. Title.

Porcelain, Japanese.

MEYER, Florence E. 738.2'0952
The colorful world of Nippon, by Florence E. Meyer. Des Moines, Iowa, Wallace-Homestead Book Co. [1971] [51] p. (incl. cover) illus., 19 col. plates. 23 cm. [NK4567.M53] 72-177700
1. Nippon Toki Kobushiki Kaisha. 2. Porcelain, Japanese. 3. Porcelain—Marks. I. Title. BIP

Porcelain, Japanese—Hist.

JENYNS, Roger Soame, 1904- 738.20952
Japanese porcelain, by Soame Jenyns. New York, Praeger [c.1965] xiii, 351, 120p. fold. map, plates (pt. col.) 26cm. Bibl. [NK4567.J4] 65-13447 20.00
1. Porcelain, Japanese—Hist. I. Title. BIP

Porcelain—Juvenile literature.

ALDRIDGE, Eileen. 738.2
Porcelain. Illustrated by Peter Morter and Design Bureau. New York, Grosset & Dunlap [1970] 159 p. col. illus. 22 cm. (A Grosset all-color guide, 7) Bibliography: p. 156. An introduction to porcelain from its earliest manufacture in China to the discovery of its secrets in eighteenth century Europe and its eventual manufacture in the United States. [NK4240.A4 1970] 70-120435 3.95
1. Porcelain—Juvenile literature. I. Morter, Peter, illus. II. Design Bureau. III. Title.

Porcelain—Marks.

POCHE, Emanuel. 738.2'02'78
Porcelain marks of the world / Emanuel Poche ; [translated from the Czech by Joy Moss-Kohoutova]. London ; New York : Hamlyn, [1975] 255 p. : chiefly ill., facsims. ; 20 cm. Includes index. Bibliography: p. 239. [NK4215.P6213] 76-352745 ISBN 0-600-39290-2 : £1.50
1. Porcelain—Marks. I. Title. BIP

SCHLEGELMILCH, Clifford J. 738.2'7
Handbook of Erdmann and Reinhold Schlegelmilch, Prussia-Germany, and Oscar Schlegemilch, Germany, porcelain marks, my ancestor's [sic] china, by Clifford J. Schlegelmilch. [3d ed. Flint, Mich., 1973] 44 p. illus. (part col.) 26 cm. On cover: R. S. Prussia Schlegelmilch. Previous editions published under title: Handbook of RS Prussia, RS Germany and Oscar Schlegelmilch porcelain marks. [NK4215.S34 1973] 73-171135
1. Schlegelmilch, Erdmann. 2. Schlegelmilch, Reinhold. 3. Schlegelmilch, Oscar. 4. Porcelain—Marks. I. Title.
Publisher's address: 3560 Rue Forest, Flint, Mich. 48504.

SCHLEGELMILCH, Clifford J. 738.2'7
Handbook of R S Prussia, R S Germany and Oscar Schlegelmilch porcelain marks [by Clifford J. Schlegelmilch, in collaboration with Louise J. Schlegelmilch. 2d ed. Flint, Mich., 1971] 32 p. illus., map. 21 cm. [NK4215.S34 1971] 71-25185
1. Schlegelmilch, Erdmann. 2. Schlegelmilch, Reinhold. 3. Schlegelmilch, Oscar. 4. Porcelain—Marks. I. Schlegelmilch, Louise J. II. Title.

SCHLEGELMILCH, Clifford J. 738.2'7
Handbook of R.S. Prussia, R.S. Germany and Oscar Schlegelmilch porcelain marks [by Clifford J. Schlegelmilch] 1st ed. Flint, Mich., Printed by Schultz Print. Co., c1970. 31 p. illus., map. 20 cm. Third ed. published in 1973 under title: Handbook of Erdmann and Reinhold Schlegelmilch, Prussia-Germany, and Oscar Schlegelmilch, Germany, porcelain marks. [NK4215.S34] 72-22490 3.00
1. Schlegelmilch, Erdmann. 2. Schlegelmilch, Reinhold. 3. Schlegelmilch, Oscar. 4. Porcelain—Marks. I. Title.

Porcelain—Private collections.

POST, Marjorie Merriweather. 738.2'0947
Russian porcelains; the Gardner, Iusupov, Batenin ... factories, by Marvin C. Ross. Foreword by Marjorie Merriweather Post. Norman, Univ. of Okla. Pr. [1968] xxviii, 427p. illus., plates (pt. col.) 26cm. (Her The Collections of Marjorie Merriweather Post) Bibl. [KN4511.P6] 67-15592 15.00
1. Porcleain—Private collections. 2. Porcelain, Russian—Catalogs. I. Ross, Marvin Chauncey, 1904- II. Title.

Porcelain, Spanish.

FROTHINGHAM, Alice Wilson. 738.2
Capodimonte and Buen Retiro porcelains, period of Charles III. Printed by order of the trustees. New York, Hispanic Society of America, 1955. viii, 55p. 55 illus. 23cm. (Hispanic notes & monographs; essays, studies, and brief biographies) Bibliographical references included in 'Notes' (p.50-52) [NK4523.F7] 55-13562
1. Porcelain, Spanish. 2. Procelain, Italian. I. Title. II. Series.

Porcelain—Washington, D.C.

KLAPTHOR, Margaret Brown. 738'.074'0153
Official White House china; 1789 to the present. [1st ed.] Washington, Smithsonian Institution Press ; [distributed by G. Braziller, New York] 1975. 283 p. illus. (part col.) 29 cm. (Smithsonian Institution Press publication no. 4826) Includes bibliographical references. [NK4427.W3K55] 74-6171 ISBN ISBN 0-87474-135-1 15.95
1. Porcelain—Washington, D.C. 2. Washington, D.C. White House. I. Title.
Distributed by Braziller.

Porches.

BROSTROM, Ethel. 728.991
How to plan your porch and patio. New York, Greenberg, c1956. 96 p. illus. 21 cm. (Room-by-room decorating series) [NA8375.B7] 56-10846
1. Porches. 2. Patios. I. Title.

SCHUSTER, Franz, 1892- 721.8
Balkone; Balkone, Laubengange und Terrassen aus aller Welt. Die Ubersetzung der Texte besorgte das Ubersetzungsburo Hans-Heinz Kaufmann [Dist. New York, Efron, c.1962] 148p. (chiefly illus., plans) 30cm. (Die Bauelement, Bd. 4) English, French, and German. 62-4004 14.00
1. Porches. 2. Porticoes. 3. Patios. I. Title. II. Series.

Portait painting.

CARR, Henry Marvell, 1894- 757
Portrait painting. London, New York, Studio Publiations [1952] 80p. illus. (part col.) 25cm. (The How to do it series, no. 45) 'Some book on method': p. 80. [ND1300.C37] 53-445
1. Portait painting. I. Title. II. Series: How to do it series (London, The Studio) n3. 45

Portait painting—Juvenile literature.

KAINZ, Luise C., 1902- 704.94'2
Portraits and personalities; an introduction to the world's great art [by] Luise C. Kainz, Olive L. Riley. New York, Abrams [1967 or 8] 127p. illus. (pt. col.) ports, (pt. col.) 26cm. [ND1302.K3] 68-15901 7.50
1. Portait painting—Juvenile literature. I. Riley, Olive Lasette. joint author. II. Title.

Porter, Arthur Kingsley, 1883-1933.

MEDIEVAL studies in memory of A. Kingsley Porter. 709.02 Edited by Wilhelm R. W. Koehler. Freeport, N.Y., Books for Libraries Press [1969, c1939] 2 v. (xxiv, 728 p.) illus., plans, port. 29 cm. (Essay index reprint series) "Bibliography of the

writings of A. Kingsley Porter": v. 1, p. [xvii]-xxiv. [N5975.M5 1969] 77-80391
1. Porter, Arthur Kingsley, 1883-1933. 2. Art, Medieval. 3. Archaeology, Medieval. I. Koehler, Wilhelm Reinhold Walter, 1884-1959, ed. BIP

Porter, Bernard H.

SCHEVILL, James Erwin, 1920- 701.1
The roaring market and the silent tomb. [Oakland, Calif., Abbey Press, 1957] 88p. illus. 23cm. [N6537.P6S3] 57-28736
1. Porter, Bernard H. I. Title.

Porter, Katherine, 1941—

ANDERSEN, Wayne V. 759.13
Katherine Porter [exhibition] Hayden Gallery, Massachusetts Institute of Technology, November 22 to December 21, 1974, sponsored by the MIT Committee on the Visual Arts : essay / by Wayne Andersen. [Cambridge? Mass. : s.n., 1974] [15] p. : ill. (some col.) ; 28 cm. Bibliography: p. [13] [ND237.P8134A63] 74-24799
1. Porter, Katherine, 1941- I. Porter, Katherine, 1941- II. Hayden Gallery.

Porter, Rufus, 1792-1884.

LIPMAN, Jean (Herzberg) 1909- 759.13 B
Rufus Porter, Yankee pioneer [by] Jean Lipman. Foreword by Gerard Piel. Pref. by John I. H. Baur. [1st ed.] New York, C. N. Potter; distributed by Crown [1968] ix, 202 p. illus. (part col.), coat of arms, facsims., ports. 29 cm. Bibliography: p. 189-192. [ND237.P8135L48] 68-26881 12.50
1. Porter, Rufus, 1792-1884.

Portland, Or.—Historic houses, etc.

VAUGHAN, Thomas. 720'.9795'49
A century of Portland architecture [by] Thomas Vaughan [and] George A. McMath. Portland, Oregon Historical Society, 1967. 226 p. illus., maps. 23 cm. Includes bibliographical references. [NA735.P55V3] 67-64659
1. Portland, Or.—Historic houses, etc. 2. Architecture—Portland, Or.—History. 3. Decoration and ornament, Architectural. I. McMath, George A., joint author. II. Title. BIP

Portland, Or. Skidmore Fountain.

SNYDER, Eugene E. 917.95'49
Skidmore's Portland: his fountain and its sculptor; from buckboards to bustles, by Eugene E. Snyder. [1st ed.] Portland, Or., Binfords & Mort [1973] 152 p. illus. 24 cm. Includes bibliographical references. [NA9410.P67S58] 73-85142 ISBN 0-8323-0228-7 6.95
1. Portland, Or. Skidmore Fountain. 2. Warner, Olin Levi, 1844-1896. 3. Skidmore, Stephen Griggs, 1838-1883. I. Title.

Portman, John Calvin.

PORTMAN, John Calvin. 728.5
The architect as developer / by John Portman and Jonathan Barnett. New York : McGraw-Hill, c1976. p. cm. [NA737.P63B37] 76-19062 ISBN 0-07-050536-5 : 22.95
1. Portman, John Calvin. 2. Atlanta. Hyatt Regency Atlanta. 3. San Francisco. Hyatt Regency San Francisco. I. Barnett, Jonathan, joint author. II. Title. BIP

STARBUCK, James C. 016.3092'08 s
John Portman : an introduction and bibliography / James C. Starbuck. Monticello, Ill. : Council of Planning Librarians, 1974. 8 p. ; 28 cm. (Exchange bibliography - Council of Planning Librarians ; 680) Cover title. [Z5942.C68 no. 680] [Z8706.8] [NA737.P63] 016.720'92'4 75-313593 1.50
1. Portman, John Calvin. I. Series: Council of Planning Librarians. Exchange bibliography ; 680.

Portrait drawing.

CARR, Henry Marvell, 1894- 743'.4
Portraits [by] Henry Carr. [1st American ed. New York, Watson-Guptill Publications, 1966, c1961] 54 p. illus. 18 x 20 cm. (Watson-Guptill drawing books) Cover title: Drawing portraits. [NC773.C3 1966] 65-19012
1. Portrait drawing. 2. Drawing—Instruction. I. Title: Drawing portraits.

GRAVES, Douglas R. 743'.4
Drawing portraits, by Douglas R. Graves. New York, Watson-Guptill Publications [1974] 159 p. illus. 29 cm. Bibliography: p. 157. [NC773.G72 1974] 74-9718 ISBN 0-8230-1430-4 13.50
1. Portrait drawing. I. Title. BIP

PORTRAIT of Robin 828'.9'1407
Crozier / [edited by Robin Crozier]. Sunderland : Ceolfrith Press, 1975. [70] p. : chiefly ill. ; 19 cm. Cover title. [NC773.P67] 75-316327 £0.75
1. Crozier, Robin. 2. Portrait drawing. I. Crozier, Robin.

Portrait drawing—Exhibitions.

STAMPFLE, Felice. 743.9'2'07401471
Artists and writers; nineteenth and twentieth century portrait drawings from the collection of Benjamin Sonnenberg. Catalogue by Felice Stampfle and Cara Dufour. With an introd. by Brendan Gill. [Exhibition held at] the Pierpont Morgan Library, New York, May 13 to July 30, 1971. [New York, 1971] 52 p., 64 plates. 28 cm. Includes bibliographies. [NC31.S6S8] 73-161537 ISBN 0-87598-004-X
1. Sonnenberg, Benjamin, 1901- —Art collections. 2. Portrait drawing—Exhibitions. 3. Artists—Portraits. I. Dufour, Cara, joint author. II. Pierpont Morgan Library, New York. III. Title.

Portrait miniatures—Great Britain—Catalogs.

WILLIAM Rockhill Nelson Gallery of Art and Mary Atkins Museum of Fine Arts, Kansas City, Mo. 757'.7'09420740178411
The Starr Collection of miniatures in the William Rockhill Nelson Gallery. With introd. by Graham Reynolds. Kansas City, 1971. 84 p. illus. (part col.) 25 cm. "The basic structure of this catalogue is patterned after ... [Reynold's] book English portrait miniatures." [ND1337.G7W47] 72-177685
1. Starr, John W., 1925- —Art collections. 2. Portrait miniatures—Great Britain—Catalogs. 3. Miniature painting—Kansas City, Mo.—Catalogs. I. Reynolds, Graham. II. Title.

Portrait miniatures—United States.

WEHLE, Harry Brandeis, 1887-1969. 757'.7'0973
American miniatures, 1730-1850; one hundred and seventy-three portraits selected with a descriptive account by Harry B. Wehle, & a biographical dictionary of the artists by Theodore Bolton. New York, Kennedy Galleries, 1970 [c1927] xxv, 127 p. 48 plates (ports., part col.) 27 cm. (Library of American art) Bibliography: p. [115]-118. [ND1337.U5W4 1970] 71-87684 ISBN 0-306-71708-5
1. Portrait miniatures—United States. 2. Portrait-painters, American. I. Bolton, Theodore, 1889- II. Title. BIP

Portrait miniatures—United States—Exhibitions.

NORTON (R. W.) Art Gallery. 757'.7'0974074016399
Portrait miniatures in early American history, 1750-1840 : a Bicentennial exhibition, April 18-June 13, 1976, the R. W. Norton Art Gallery. Shreveport, La. : The Gallery, c1976. 41 p. : ill. (some col.) ; 28 cm. Cover title. Includes bibliographical references and index. [ND1337.U5N67 1976] 77-356142 ISBN 0-913060-09-7
1. Portrait miniatures—United States—Exhibitions. 2. United States—History—Biography—Portraits—Exhibitions. 3. Miniature painters—United States—Biography. I. Title. BIP

Portrait painters.

*GORDON, Willard F. 757
The spirit of '76 . . . an American portrait : America's best known painting, least known artist Willard F. Gordon. Fallbrook, Ca. ; Aero Publishers : Distributed by Quail Hill Associates, c1976. 95 p. ; ill. : 28 cm. [N7593.2] 76-12646 7.95
1. Portrait painters. I. Title.
Distributor's address: Box 1776 92028.

KAINZ, Luise C., 1902- 709
Portraits and personalities; an introduction to the world's great art [by] Luise C. Kainz [and] Olive L. Riley. New York, H. N. Abrams [1967 or 8] 127 p. illus. (part col.), ports. (part col.) 26 cm. An introduction to the history and forms of portraiture, from ancient Egypt to Marisol, organized by period with brief historical background for each period and critical comments on the artists and reproductions included. [ND1302.K3] AC 68
1. Portrait painters. 2. Portraits. I. Riley, Olive Lasette, joint author. II. Title.

Portrait-painters, American.

MORGAN, John Hill, 1870-1945. 759.13
Gilbert Stuart and his pupils. Together with the complete notes on painting, by Matthew Harris Jouett, from conversations with Gilbert Stuart in 1816. New York, Kennedy Galleries, 1969 [c1939] 102 p. illus., ports. 24 cm. (Library of American art) Includes bibliographical references. [ND237.S8M6 1969] 72-96440
1. Stuart, Gilbert, 1755-1828. 2. Portrait painters, American. 3. Portraits, American. I. Jouett, Matthew Harris, 1788-1827. II. Title. BIP

SHERMAN, Frederic Fairchild, 1874-1940. 757
Early American portraiture. New York, B. Blom, 1972. 65 p. ports. 26 cm. Reprint of the 1930 ed. [ND1311.S5 1972] 72-84107
1. Portrait-painters, American. 2. Portraits, American. I. Title. BIP

Portrait painters—Ireland—Biography.

MURPHY, William Michael, 1916- 759.9415 B
Prodigal father : the life of John Butler Yeats, 1839-122 / William M. Murphy. Ithaca : Cornell University Press, 1978. 680 p. : ill. ; 25 cm. Includes index. Bibliography: p. [543]-547. [ND1329.Y43M86] 77-3122 ISBN 0-8014-1047-9 : 27.50
1. Yeats, John Butler, 1839-1922. 2. Portrait painters—Ireland—Biography. I. Title. BIP

Portrait painters—United States—Biography.

PLUNKET, Jean Reasoner. 741'.092'4
Faces that won't sit still : celebrated subjects by a prominent portrait artist and how they were captured / by Jean Reasoner Plunket, with Barbara Brandt Ward. Washington : Acropolis Books, c1978. 201 p. : ill. ; 29 cm. [NC139.P57A2 1978] 78-14259 ISBN 0-87491-261-X : 18.00. pbk. : 9.95. ISBN 0-87491-260-1 lim. deluxe ed. : 35.00
1. Plunket, Jean Reasoner. 2. Portrait painters—United States—Biography. 3. Children—Portraits. 4. Portrait drawing—Technique. I. Ward, Barbara Brandt, joint author. II. Title.

Portrait-painters—United States—Correspondence, reminiscences, etc.

DUNLAP, William, 1766-1839. 700'.924
Diary of William Dunlap, 1766-1839; the memoirs of a dramatist, theatrical manager, painter, critic, novelist, and historian. New York, B. Blom [1969] 3 v. in 1 (xxxv, 964 p.) illus., ports. 22 cm. (Collections of the New York Historical Society for the year 1929-31. The John Watts DePeyster publication fund series, 62-64) Reprint of the 1930 ed. "The Diary has been transcribed, edited and indexed by Dorothy C. Barck." Includes many of the portraits painted by Dunlap. [PS1561.A3 1969] 78-84204 28.50
I. Barck, Dorothy C., ed. II. Series: New York Historical Society. Collections. The John Watts De Peyster publication fund series, 62-64 BIP

STOCK, Joseph Whiting, 1815-1855. 759.13 B
The paintings and the journal of Joseph Whiting Stock / edited by Juliette Tomlinson ; with a checklist of his works compiled by Kate Steinway. Middletown, Conn. : Wesleyan University Press, [1976] p. cm. Includes index. Bibliography: p. [ND1329.S69A25] 76-7189 ISBN 0-8195-4098-6 : 30.00
1. Stock, Joseph Whiting, 1815-1855. 2. Portrait-painters—United States—Correspondence, reminiscences, etc. 3. Primitivism in art—United States. I. Tomlinson, Juliette, 1921- II. Title. BIP

Portrait painting.

ANSBACHER, Jessie. 743.4
Portraits. New York, Pitman Pub. Corp. [1959] unpaged. illus. 20 x 26 cm. (Pitman art series, 23) [ND1302.A5] 59-6584
1. Portrait painting. 2. Drawing—Instruction. I. Title.

AYMAR, Gordon Christian. 757
The art of portrait painting; portraits through the centuries as seen through the eyes of a practicing portrait painter [by] Gordon C. Aymar. [1st ed.] Philadelphia, Chilton Book Co. [1967] xiv, 337 p. illus. (part col.), ports. 28 cm. [ND1300.A9] 67-26026
1. Portrait painting. I. Title.

COVINO, Frank. 751.4'5
The fine art of portraiture: an academic approach. Westport, Conn., Fletcher Art Services; distributed by Van Nostrand Reinhold, New York [1970] 168, [7] p. 107 illus. (34 col.) 32 cm. [ND1302.C68] 78-128612
1. Portrait painting. I. Title.

DARGIE, William. 757
On painting a portrait. [1st ed.] New York, Pitman Pub. Corp. [1957] 72p. illus. 22cm. (The Artist's series) [ND1300.D3] 57-12737
1. Portrait painting. I. Title.

DAWLEY, Joseph. 741.4'5
Character studies in oil, by Joseph Dawley as told to Gloria Dawley. New York, Watson-Guptill Publications [1972] 141 p. illus. (part col.) 22 x 29 cm. [ND1300.D35 1972] 79-181488 ISBN 0-8230-0608-5 12.50
1. Portrait painting. I. Dawley, Gloria. II. Title.

DE RUTH, Jan1922- 731.8'9
Portrait painting. New York, Pitman Pub. Corp. [1964] 32 p. illus. (part col.) ports. (part col.) 20 x 26 cm. (Pitman $1.00 art books, 48) [ND1302.D4] 63-20130
1. Portrait painting. I. Title.

DUNSTAN, Bernard, 1920- 757
Starting to paint portraits. London, Studio Vista; New York, Watson-Guptill [1966] 96 p. illus., 8 plates (incl. 4 col.) diagrs. 19 cm. 10 6 [ND1300.D8] 66-13006
1. Portrait painting. I. Title. BIP

FINCK, Furman J., 1900- 757
Complete guide to portrait painting, by Furman J. Finck. New York, Watson-Guptill Publications [1970] 207 p. illus. (part col.) 29 cm. [ND1302.F5] 73-117073 15.00
1. Portrait painting. I. Title. II. Title: Portrait painting. BIP

HALS, Frans, 1584-1666. 757.3
The Civic Guard portrait groups. With a foreword by H. P. Baard. Amsterdam, Elsevier; New York, Macmillan, 1950. 31 p. illus., 54 plates (part col.) 35 cm. "C. H. Peacock ... prepared the English version of

Dr. Baard's introduction and notes." Translation of Schuttersstukken. "Bibliography on restoration": p. 28. [ND653.H2B32] 50-2192
I. Baard, H. P. II. Title.

HAMMOND, Peggy 743.4
Children's portraits in Conte; a lighthearted approach. New York, Watson-Guptill [c.]1961. 63p. illus. (part col.) 26cm. 60-13374 4.95
1. Portrait painting. 2. Drawing—Instruction. 3. Children—Portraits. I. Title.

HARRISON, Claude. 757
The portrait painters' handbook. London, Studio Vista; New York, Watson-Guptill, 1968. 96p. illus. (pt. col.) 26cm. Bibl. [ND1302.H3 1968] 68-13480 8.50 bds.,
1. Portrait painting. I. Title.

JACOBS, Michel, 1877- 757
Color in portrait painting. Chicago, D. M. Campana Art Co. [1957] 115p. illus. 28cm. [ND1300.J26] 57-48492
1. Portrait painting. I. Title.

KINSTLER, Everett Raymond. 751
Painting portraits. Edited by Susan E. Meyer. New York, Watson-Guptill Publications [1971] 175 p. illus. (part col.) 29 cm. [ND1302.K5] 76-159563 ISBN 0-8230-3820-3 12.50
1. Portrait painting. I. Meyer, Susan E., ed. II. Title.

OLSEN, Helen. 751.4
Painting portraits; how to capture likeness and personality. Photos. by George Olsen. London, Oak Tree Press; New York, Sterling Pub. Co. [1964, c1963] 112 p. illus., ports. (part col.) 22 cm. [ND1300.O4] 63-11583
1. Portrait painting. I. Title.

PRATTEN, John W. 757
Portrait painting for beginners. [1st ed.] New York, Watson-Guptill Publications [1955] 112 p. illus. 24 cm. (Step-by-step series) [ND1302.P7] 55-14650
1. Portrait painting. I. Title.

SLATER, Frank. 757.1
Getting a likeness. New York, Scribner [1954] 63p. illus. 25cm. [ND1300.S57] 54-7912
1. Portrait painting. I. Title.

SLATER, Frank. 757
Practical portrait painting. New York, Scribner [1950, c1949] 183 p. illus., 49 plates (1 fold. col.) 26 cm. Full name: Frank Edward Slater. [ND1300.S6] 50-9478
1. Portrait painting. I. Title.

SLATER, Frank Edward 751.4
Portrait painting: step by step. New York, Scribners [c.1961] 88p. illus. (pt. col.) 61-15772 4.50
1. Portrait painting. I. Title.

TAUBES, Frederic, 1900- 757
The art and technique of portrait painting. New York, Dodd, Mead, 1957. 113 p. illus. 26 cm. [ND1300.T3] 57-7449
1. Portrait painting. I. Title.

TAUBES, Frederic, 1900- 757
The technique of portrait painting. New York, Watson-Guptill Publications [1967] 159 p. illus. (part col.) 29 cm. [ND1300.T33] 67-21791
1. Portrait painting. I. Title. BIP

VAN WYK, Helen. 751.4'2
Acrylic portrait painting. [Edited by Susan E. Meyer] New York, Watson-Guptill [1970] 174 p. 156 illus. (16 col.) 29 cm. [ND1302.V35] 70-125844 ISBN 0-8230-0075-3 12.50
1. Portrait painting. 2. Polymer painting. I. Title. BIP

Portrait-painting, American—History.

BLACK, Mary C. 759.13
American folk painting, by Mary Black and Jean Lipman. [1st ed.] New York, C. N. Potter [1966] xxiv, 244 p. illus. (part col.) 32 cm. Bibliography: p. 233-244. [ND1311.B55] 66-22405
1. Portrait-painting, American—History. 2. Portrait-painters, American. I. Lipman, Jean (Herzberg) 1909- joint author. II. Title.

Portrait painting, American—Juvenile literature.

FISHER, Leonard Everett. 759.13
The limners; America's earliest portrait painters, written & illustrated by Leonard Everett Fisher. New York, F. Watts [1969] 47 p. illus., ports. 22 cm. (Colonial Americans) Discusses the motivation, materials, and techniques of the first "artists" in colonial America—the sign painters—and how their works contribute to a better understanding of early American history and society. [ND1311.F5] 79-83644
1. Portrait painting, American—Juvenile literature. I. Title.

Portrait painting, British—History.

JUDSON, Alexander Corbin, 1883- 001.3 s
Sidney's appearance; a study in Elizabethan portraiture, by Alexander C. Judson. Freeport, N.Y., Books for Libraries Press [1971, c1958] xii, 98 p. ports. 23 cm. (Indiana University publications. Humanities series, no. 41) (Biography index reprint series) Bibliography: p. 91-94. [AS36.I385 no. 41 1971] [ND1314.2] 757'.3'0942 73-179730 ISBN 0-8369-8098-0
1. Sidney, Philip, Sir, 1554-1586—Portraits, etc. 2. Portrait painting, British—History. I. Title. II. Series: Indiana. University. Indiana University humanities series, no. 41. BIP

Portrait painting — China.

LANCMAN, Eli. 759.951
Chinese portraiture. Rutland, Vt., C.E. Tuttle Co. [1966] 188 p. illus. (part col) ports. (part col.) 27 cm. Bibliography: p. 181-182. [ND1326.L3] 66-15265
1. Portrait painting — China. I. Title.

Portrait painting, English—Addresses, essays, lectures.

STEWART, J. Douglas. 757'.0942
English portraits of the seventeenth and eighteenth centuries; papers read at a Clark Library seminar, April 14, 1973, by J. Douglas Stewart [and] Herman W. Liebert. Los Angeles, William Andrews Clark Memorial Library, University of California, 1974. v, 95 p. illus. 23 cm. (William Andrews Clark Memorial Library seminar papers) Contents.Contents.—Stewart, J. D. Pin-ups or virtues? The concept of the "beauties" in late Stuart portraiture.—Liebert, H. W. Portraits of the author: Lifetime likenesses of Samuel Johnson. Includes bibliographical references. [ND1314.3.S73] 74-181610
1. Portrait painting, English—Addresses, essays, lectures. I. Liebert, Herman W. II. California. University. University at Los Angeles. William Andrews Clark Memorial Library. III. Title. IV. Series.

Portrait painting, Florentine—History.

ALAZARD, Jean, 1887-1960. 757'.09455'1
The Florentine portrait. New York, Schocken Books [1968] 235 p. ports. 22 cm. Reprint of the 1948 ed. Translation of Le portrait florentin de Botticelli a Bronzino. Bibliography: p. 229-235. [ND1318.A515 1968] 68-26731 7.50
1. Portrait painting, Florentine—History. I. Title. BIP

Portrait painting, Renaissance.

POPE-HENNESSY, John Wyndham, 1913- 757'.9
The portrait in the Renaissance [by] John Pope-Hennessy. [New York, Bollingen Foundation; distributed by] Pantheon Books [1966] xxxii, 348 p. illus. 27 cm. (Bollingen series, 35. The A. W. Mellon lectures in the fine arts, 12) Bibliographical references included in "Notes" (p. 303-327) [ND1308.P6] 66-16236
1. Portrait painting, Renaissance. Portraits, Renaissance. I. Title. II. Series. III. Series: Bollingen series, 35. Series: The A. W. Mellon lectures in the fine arts, 12 BIP

POPE-HENNESSY, John Wyndham, 1913- 757'.9
The portrait in the Renaissance [by] John Pope-Hennessy. London, Phaidon; New York, Bollingen Foundation [1966]. xxxii, 348 p. 330 illus. 26 1 2 cm. (Bollingen series, 35. The A. W. Mellon lectures in the fine arts, 12) 75/- Distributed by Pantheon Books, New York. Bibliographical references included in "Notes" (p. 303-327) [ND1308.P6] 67-93388
1. Portrait painting, Renaissance. 2. Portraits, Renaissance. I. Title. II. Series. III. Series: Bollingen series, 35. Series: The A. W. Mellon lectures in the fine arts, 12

Portrait painting—Technique.

BURNS, Paul Callan. 751.4'5
The portrait painter's problem book / by Paul C. Burns and Joe Singer. New York : Watson-Guptill Publications, 1979. p. cm. Includes index. Bibliography: p. [ND1302.B87 1979] 78-32012 ISBN 0-8230-4186-7 : 19.50
1. Portrait painting—Technique. I. Singer, Joe, 1923- joint author. II. Title.

BURNS, Paul Callan. 751.4'5
The portrait painter's problem book / by Paul C. Burns and Joe Singer. New York : Watson-Guptill Publications, 1979. p. cm. Includes index. Bibliography: p. [ND1302.B87 1979] 78-32012 ISBN 0-8230-4186-7 : 19.50
1. Portrait painting—Technique. I. Singer, Joe, 1923- joint author. II. Title. BIP

SANDEN, John Howard. 751.4'5
Painting the head in oil / by John Howard Sanden ; edited by Joe Singer. New York : Watson-Guptill Publications, 1976. 151 p. : ill. (some col.) ; 29 cm. Includes index. Bibliography: p. 149. [ND1302.S26 1976] 75-40175 ISBN 0-8230-3640-5 : 16.95
1. Portrait painting—Technique. 2. Head in art. I. Title. BIP

SILVERMAN, Burt, 1928- 751.4
Painting people / by Burt Silverman. New York : Watson-Guptill Publications, 1977. p. cm. Includes index. [ND1302.S57 1977] 77-8642 ISBN 0-8230-3815-7 : 17.95
1. Portrait painting—Technique. 2. Portrait drawing—Technique. 3. Pastel drawing—Technique. 4. Water-color painting—Technique. I. Title. BIP

SINGER, Joe, 1923- 751.4'5
Painting women's portraits / Joe Singer. New York : Watson-Guptill Publications, 1977. 151 p. : ill. (some col.) ; 29 cm. Includes index. Bibliography: p. 149. [ND1329.3.W6S56 1977] 76-57765 ISBN 0-8230-3882-3 : 16.95
1. Portrait painting—Technique. 2. Women—Portraits. I. Title. BIP

Portrait painting—U. S.—Hist.

BELKNAP, Waldron Phoenix, 1899-1949. 759.13
American colonial painting: materials for a history. Cambridge, Mass., Belknap Press of Harvard University Press, 1959. xi, 377p. ports., coats of arms. facsims. 28cm. 'Catalogue of prints and paintings': p. 270-322. Bibliographical footnotes. [ND1311.B39] 59-10313
1. Portrait painting—U. S.—Hist. 2. Portrait painters, American. 3. New York (State)—Geneal. I. Title. BIP

Portrait prints—Edinburgh.

EVANS, Hilary, 1929- 769'.92'4
John Kay of Edinburgh: barber, miniaturist and social commentator, 1742-1826 [by] Hilary and Mary Evans. Aberdeen, Impulse Publications Ltd, 1973. 53, [97] p. illus., ports. (1 col.) 27 cm. Illus. on lining papers. "Bibliography and iconography": p. 51-53 (1st group). [NE642.K39E92 1973] 74-152868 ISBN 0-901311-28-6 £6.00
1. Kay, John, 1742-1826. 2. Portrait prints—Edinburgh. I. Evans, Mary, 1890- joint author. II. Title.

Portrait prints—Stanford, Calif.—Catalogs.

STANFORD 769'.4'2094074019473
University. Libraries. Division of Special Collections.
Portraits: a catalog of the engravings, etchings, mezzotints, and lithographs presented to the Stanford University Library by Dr. and Mrs. Leon Kolb. Compiled by Susan V. Lenkey. [Stanford, Calif.] Stanford University, 1972. 373 p. port. 28 cm. On cover: Collection of Dr. and Mrs. Leon Kolb. [NE240.K64S72] 73-150724
1. Kolb, Leon, 1890-—Art collections. 2. Stanford University. Libraries. 3. Portrait prints—Stanford, Calif.—Catalogs. I. Lenkey, Susan V., comp. II. Title.

Portrait sculpture.

MARRITS, Louis E. 731.8'2
Modeled portrait sculpture, by Louis E. Marrits. South Brunswick, A. S. Barnes [1970] 374 p. illus., ports. 27 cm. [NB1293.M3 1970] 75-81673 8.50
1. Portrait sculpture. I. Title.

Portrait sculpture, English—Catalogs.

WHINNEY, Margaret Dickens. 731'.82
English sculpture 1720-1830, by Margaret Whinney. London, H.M. Stationery Off., 1971. 160 p. illus. 25 cm. (Victoria and Albert Museum. Museum monograph, no. 17) Includes bibliographical references. [NB1305.G7W45] 72-193412 ISBN 0-11-290083-6
1. Portrait sculpture, English—Catalogs. 2. Portrait sculpture—London—Catalogs. I. Title. II. Series: Victoria and Albert Museum, South Kensington. Museum monograph, no. 17.
Available from Pendragon. 8.50. BIP

Portrait sculpture, Japanese.

MORI, Hisashi, 1916- 732'.7
Japanese portrait sculpture / Hisashi Mori ; translator, Widayati Roesijadi. New York : Kodansha International, [1977] p. cm. (Japanese arts library ; v. 2) Translation of Shozo chokoku. Includes index. Bibliography: p. [NB1305.J3M6713 1977] 76-9353 ISBN 0-87011-286-4 : 12.95
1. Portrait sculpture, Japanese. 2. Sculpture, Buddhist—Japan. I. Title. II. Series. BIP

MORI, Hisashi, 1916- 732'.7
Portrait sculpture / by Hisashi Mori ; translated with an introd. by Widayati Roesijadi. 1st ed. New York : Weatherhill, 1975. p. cm. (Arts of Japan ; 9) Translation of Shozo chokoku. Includes index. Bibliography: p. [NB1305.J3M6713] 74-22097 ISBN 0-8348-2716-6. ISBN 0-8348-2717-4 pbk.
1. Portrait sculpture, Japanese. 2. Sculpture, Buddhist—Japan. 3. Sculpture, Japanese—Heian period, 794-1185. 4. Sculpture, Japanese—Kamakura-Momoyama periods, 1185-1600. I. Title.

Portrait sculpture, Roman.

BONANNO, Anthony. 733'.5
Portraits and other heads on Roman historical relief up to the age of Septimius Severus / [by] Anthony Bonanno. Oxford : British Archaeological Reports, 1976. [21], 227 p., [76] p. of plates : ill. ; 30 cm. (BAR supplementary series ; 6) ISSN 0306-1205) Cover title: Roman relief portraiture to Septimius Severus. Bibliography: p. 215-227. [NB1296.3.B66] 77-358366 ISBN 0-904531-38-4 : £5.90 ($13.00 U.S.)
1. Portrait sculpture, Roman. 2. Relief (Sculpture)—Rome. I. Title. II. Title: Roman relief portraiture to Septimius Severus. III. Series.

TOYNBEE, Jocelyn M. C. 730'.0937
Roman historical portraits / J. M. C. Toynbee. Ithaca, N.Y. : Cornell University Press, 1978. 208 p. : ill. ; 26 cm. (Aspects of Greek and Roman life) Includes bibliographical references and index. [NB1296.3.T69 1978b] 75-38428 ISBN 0-8014-1011-8 : 35.00

SUBJECT INDEX PORTRAITS, AMERICAN —

1. Portrait sculpture, Roman. 2. Rome—Biography—Portraits. 3. History, Ancient—Portraits. I. Title. II. Series. BIP

Portraits.

GASSER, Manuel. 704.942
Self-portraits: from the fifteenth century to the present day. Translated by Angus Malcolm. [1st ed.] New York, Appleton-Century [1963] 302 p. illus., col. plates. 23 cm. [N7592.G313] 63-18195
1. Portraits. 2. Painters. I. Title.

GRUBER, L Fritz, ed. v. 12
Fame; famous portraits of famous people by famous photographers. London, New York, Focal Press [1960] 159p. ports. 31cm. [TR680G74] 61-906
1. Portraits. 2. Photography, Artistic. I. Title.

THE Human face. 704.94'2
[1st ed.] Greenwich, Conn., New York Graphic Society [1969] 64 p. illus. (part col.) 31 cm. (Man through his art, v. 6) "Endorsed by the World Confederation of Organizations of the Teaching Profession." Includes bibliographies. [N7575.H77] 68-19202 8.95
1. Portraits. I. World Confederation of Organizations of the Teaching Profession. II. Title. III. Series.

KARSH, Yousuf, 1908- 779.2
Portraits of greatness. [London, New York] T. Nelson [1959] 207 p. ports. 32 cm. [TR680.K3] 59-65108
1. Portraits. 2. Photography, Artistic. I. Title.

LAX, David, 1910- 757
Portraits. New York, Associated American Artists [195-?] unpaged. illus. 28 cm. [ND237.L35A45] 52-30533
I. Title.

PAINTINGS by the masters; 750.8
a treasury of famous paintings: portraits, landscapes, still lifes. Text by Gus Baker, Paul H. Reno. Comp. by Margaret Harold. Fort Lauderdale. Fla., Allied Pubns. [1966] 1v. (various pagings) illus. (pt. col.) ports. (pt. col.) 35cm. First pub. as 3 separate titles: Portraits by the masters, with commentaries by Gus Baker (1963), Landscapes by the masters. with commentaries by Gus Baker (1965), Still life by the masters, with commentaries by Paul H. Reno (1965) [N7592.P23] 63-21285 7.50 bds.,
1. Portraits. 2. Landscape painting. 3. Stillipe paintings. I. Baker, Gus. II. Reno, Paul H. III. Harold Margaret, comp. IV. Title: Portraits by the masters. V. Title: Landscapes by the masters. VI. Title: Still life by the masters.

PORTRAITS by the masters 759.9
[Comp. by Margaret Haorld. Commentaries by Gus Baker. Fort Lauderdale, Fla., Allied Pubns., 1964, c.1963] 39p. illus. (pt. col.) ports. (pt. col.) 35cm. Cover title. 63-21286 1.95 pap.,
1. Portraits. 2. Paintings. I. Harold, Margaret, comp. II. Baker, Gus.

REID, Charles, 1937- 751.4'22
Portrait painting in watercolor. New York, Watson-Guptill Publications [1973] 156 p. illus. (part col.) 22 x 29 cm. Bibliography: p. 153. [ND2200.R44] 72-13569 ISBN 0-8230-4192-1 15.00
1. Portraits. 2. Water-color painting—Technique. I. Title. BIP

Portraits, American.

BOLTON, Theodore, 1889- 741.973
Early American portrait draughtsmen in crayons. New York, Kennedy Graphics, 1970 [c1923] xii, 111 p. ports. 24 cm. (Library of American art) [NC860.B64 1970] 74-77724
1. Portraits, American. 2. Portrait-painters, American. 3. Crayon drawings. I. Title. BIP

BOWDOIN College. Museum of Fine Arts. 757'.9
Colonial and Federal portraits at Bowdoin College [by] Marvin S. Sadik [director. Brunswick, Me.] 1966. 222 p. ports. (part col.) 25 cm. Bibliography: p. 10-13. [N7634.B6] 68-1270
1. Portraits, American 2. U. S.—Biog.—Portraits. I. Sadik, Marvin S. II. Title.

CIRKER, Hayward. 704.9'42'0973
Dictionary of American portraits. 4045 pictures of important Americans from earliest times to the beginning of the twentieth century. Edited by Hayward and Blanche Cirker and the staff of Dover Publications. New York, Dover Publications [1967] xiv, 756 p. (chiefly ports.) 34 cm. (Dover pictorial archive series) Bibliography: p. 713-715. [N7593.C53] 66-30514
1. Portraits, American. 2. United States—Biography—Portraits. I. Cirker, Blanche, joint ed. II. Dover Publications, inc., New York. III. Title. IV. Title: American portraits. V. Series.

FLAGG, James Montgomery, 1877- 741.91
Celebrities: a half-century of caricature and portraiture, with comments by the artist. Watkins Glen, N. Y., Century House, 1951. 104 p. illus. 27 cm. [NC1429.F53] 51-13183
I. Title.

KNOX, Katharine (McCook) 741'.092'2 B
The Sharples: their portraits of George Washington and his contemporaries; a diary and an account of the life and work of James Sharples and his family in England and America. New York, Kennedy Graphics, 1972 [c1930] xvi, 133 p. illus. 28 cm. (Library of American Art) [ND497.S445K6 1972] 70-87456 ISBN 0-306-71529-5
1. Sharples, James, 1750?-1811. 2. Sharpless family. 3. Washington, George, Pres. U.S., 1732-1799—Portraits. 4. Portraits, American. I. Title.

NATIONAL Society of the Colonial Dames of America. Delaware. 704.942
Portraits in Delaware, 1700-1850; a check list. Wilmington, 1951. 176 p. illus. 25 cm. Bibliography: p. [169] [N7593.N25] 51-7662
1. Portraits, American. 2. U.S. — Biog. — Portraits. I. Title.

NATIONAL Society of the Colonial Dames of America. North Carolina. 704.942
The North Carolina portrait index, 1700-1860. Compiled by Laura MacMillan, chairman of historic activities for the National Society of the Colonial Dames of America in the State of North Carolina. Chapel Hill, University of North Carolina Press [1963] viii, 272 p. ports. 29 cm. [N7593.N27] 63-4278
1. Portraits, American. 2. U.S. — Biog. — Portraits. 3. North Carolina — Biog. — Portraits. I. MacMillan, Laura, comp. II. Title.

PEAT, Wilbur David, 1898- 757'.3'09772074017252
Portraits and painters of the governors of Indiana, 1800-1978 / by Wilbur D. Peat ; biographies of the governors by Lana Ruegamer ; [photography, Robert Wallace]. Rev., edited, and with new entries / by Diane Gail Lazarus. Indianapolis : Indiana Historical Society, 1978. 104 p. : ill. ; 26 cm. Includes indexes. [ND1311.8.I6P42 1978] 79-107666
1. Indiana—Governors—Portraits. 2. Indiana—Governors—Biography. 3. Portraits, American. I. Lazarus, Diane Gail. II. Wallace, Robert, 1921- III. Title.

SEARS, Clara Endicott, 1863- 757'.9'0973
Some American primitives; a study of New England faces and folk portraits. Port Washington, N.Y., Kennikat Press [1968, c1941] xviii, 291, [1] p. ports. 22 cm. Bibliography: p. [292]. [ND1311.S4 1968] 67-27645
1. Portraits, American. 2. New England—Boigraphy—Portraits. 3. Portrait painting, American. United States. I. Title. II. Title: American primitives.

THOMPSON, Cephas, 1775-1856. 759.13
Cephas Thompson's memorandum of portraits. Northampton, Mass. [c1965] [78] p. 21 cm. Facsim, of the original Ms., which lists some of the sitters whose portraits the artist painted during the first quarter of the 19th century. [ND237.T552A35] 65-28618
I. Title.

WHITLEY, Edna Talbott, 1891- 757.9
Kentucky ante-bellum portraiture; illustrated by photos. from the collection of the National Society of the Colonial Dames of America in the Commonwealth of Kentucky. [Paris? Ky., 1956] xii, 848 p. ports. 25 cm. Bibliography: p. 787-806. [N7593.W45] 55-12502
1. Portraits. American. 2. Kentucky — Biog. 3. Kentucky — Biog. — Portraits. 4. Portrait-painters, American. I. National Society of the Colonial Dames of America. Kentucky. II. Title.

Portraits, American — Catalogs.

AMERICAN Philosophical Society, Philadelphia. 709.73
A catalogue of portraits and other works of art in the possession of the American Philosophical Society. Philadelphia, American Philosophical Society, 1961. viii, 173p. illus., ports. (1 col.) 24cm. (Memoirs of the American Philosophical Society, v. 54) [N7621.A7] 61-14631
1. Portraits. American—Catalogs. 2. Art—Philadelphia—Catalogs. I. Title. II. Series: American Philosophical Society, Philadelphia, Memoirs, v. 54

BEAL, Rebecca J. 759.13
Jacob Eichholtz, 1776-1842; portrait painter of Pennsylvania, by Rebecca J. Beal. Philadelphia, Historical Society of Pennsylvania, 1969. xxxiii, 401 [1] p. illus., ports. (part col.) 29 cm. Bibliography: p. [391]-[402] [ND237.E44B4] 78-93461 15.00
1. Eichholtz, Jacob, 1776-1842. 2. Portraits, American—Catalogs.

FEIGENBAUM, Rita. 757'.9'0973
American portraits, 1800-1850; a catalogue of early portraits in the collections of Union College Schenectady, N.Y., Union College Press, 1972. xxv, 155 p. ports. (1 col.) 24 cm. Originally presented as the author's thesis (M.A.) Union College, 1966-67. Bibliography: p. 143-150. [ND1311.2.F4 1972] 71-173916 ISBN 0-912756-01-2 10.95
1. Union College, Schenectady. 2. Portraits, American—Catalogs. 3. Portraits—Schenectady—Catalogs. I. Union College, Schenectady. II. Title. BIP

KENNEDY Galleries, inc., New York. 708'.147'1 s
Two hundred years of American portraits; a selection of portraits from the early eighteenth to the early twentieth century. New York [1970] 232-292 p. ports. (part. col.) 23 cm. (The Kennedy quarterly, v. 9, no. 4) [N8640.K4 vol. 9, no. 4] [ND1311] 757'.9'0973 72-196233 2.00
1. Portraits, American—Catalogs. 2. Portrait painting, American. I. Title. II. Series.

NATIONAL Portrait Gallery, Washington, D.C. 704.94'2'09730740153
Checklist of the permanent collection. Washington, Smithsonian Institution Press, 1973. 54 p. 27 cm. "Includes all portraits acquired by the gallery through 30 June 1972." [N857.8.A55] 72-674 1.25
1. Portraits, American—Catalogs. 2. Portraits—Washington, D.C.—Catalogs.

NATIONAL Portrait Gallery, Washington, D.C. 704.94'2'0973
This new man: a discourse in portraits. Edited by J. Benjamin Townsend and introd. by Charles Nagel. With an essay by Oscar Handlin. Washington, Published for the National Portrait Gallery by the Smithsonian Institution Press; [distributed by Random House, New York] 1968. 217 p. ports. (part col.) 27 cm. (Smithsonian publication 4752) [N7593.N23] 68-8535 6.95
1. Portraits, American—Catalogs. 2. United States—Biography—Portraits. I. Townsend, James Benjamin, 1918- II. Handlin, Oscar, 1915- III. Title.

NATIONAL Society of the Colonial Dames of America. Tennessee. Portrait Committee. 016.757
Portraits in Tennessee painted before 1866; preliminary checklist, compiled by Eleanor Fleming Morrisey, chairman. [Nashville?] National Society of the Colonial Dames of America in Tennessee, 1964. v. 147 p. ports. 23 cm. [N7593.N29] 65-824
1. Portraits, American — Catalogs. 2. Paintings — Tennessee — Catalogs. 3. U.S. — Biog. — Portraits — Catalogs. I. Morrissey, Eleanor Fleming. II. Title.

NEW York Historical Society. 757'.9'0973
Catalogue of American portraits in the New York Historical Society. New Haven : Published for the New York Historical Society by Yale University Press, 1974. 2 v. (ix, 964 p.) : ports. ; 29 cm. Includes index. Bibliography: p. 939-955. [N7593.N5 1974] 74-79974 ISBN 0-300-01477-5 : 50.00
1. New York Historical Society. 2. Portraits, American—Catalogs. 3. Portraits—New York (City)—Catalogs. 4. United States—Biography—Portraits. I. Title. BIP

PERKINS, Helen D. 759.13
An illustrated catalogue of known portraits by Jared B. Flagg, 1820-1899. Compiled by Helen D. Perkins. Hartford, Conn. [Stowe-Day Foundation, 1972] 64 p. illus. 26 cm. On cover: A catalogue of a Connecticut artist. Published for an exhibit of selected Flagg portraits, sponsored by the Stowe-Day Foundation, Mar. 1-June 30, 1972, held at Nook Farm Visitors' Center, Hartford, Conn. [ND1329.F55P46] 72-75449
1. Flagg, Jared Bradley, 1820-1899. 2. Portraits, American—Catalogs. I. Nook Farm Visitors' Center. II. Stowe-Day Foundation. III. Title. BIP

Portraits, American — Exhibitions.

ALEXANDRIA Association. 757.0838
Our town: 1749-1865 likenesses of this place & its people taken from life, by artists known and unknown. [Exhibition] sponsored by the Alexandria Association at Gadsby's Tavern, April 12-May 12, 1956. [1st ed. Alexandria, 1956] iv, 114p. ports. 23cm. [N7593.A27] 56-9988
1. Portraits, American—Exhibitions. 2. Alexandria, Va.—Biog.—Portraits—Catalogs. 3. Painters, American. I. Title.

BISHOP, Robert Charles. 759.13
The Borden Limner and his contemporaries : an exhibition, The University of Michigan Museum of Art, November 14, 1976-January 16, 1977 / organized by Robert C. H. Bishop. [Detroit : Michigan Council for the Arts], [1977] c1975. x, 90 p. : ill. (some col.) ; 21 x 26 cm. Includes bibliographical references. [ND1329.B64B57] 77-621415
1. The Borden Limner. 2. Portraits, American—Exhibitions. 3. Portrait painting, American—New England—Exhibitions. 4. Portrait painting—19th century—New England—Exhibitions. 5. Primitivism in art—New England—Exhibitions. I. Michigan. University. Museum of Art. II. Title.

BOWDOIN College. Museum of Art. 757'.9'074014461
The Winslows : pilgrims, patrons, and portraits : a joint exhibition at Bowdoin College Museum of Art and the Museum of Fine Arts, Boston / organized by Bowdoin College Museum of Art. [Brunswick, Me. : Bowdoin College, 1974] 40 p. : 20 ports. ; 23 cm. Includes bibliographical references. [ND1311.1.B68 1974] 75-327367
1. Winslow family—Portraits, etc.—Exhibitions. 2. Portraits, American—Exhibitions. I. Boston. Museum of Fine Arts. II. Title.

BROOKLYN Institute of Arts and Sciences. Museum. 757.9
Face of America, the history of portraiture in the United States; an exhibition at the Brooklyn Museum, November 14, 1957 - January 26, 1958. [Brooklyn, 1957] unpaged. illus. 24cm. [N7593.B74] 58-236
1. Portraits, American—Exhibitions. I. Title.

HENNESSEY, William James, 1901- 757'.0973'07401443
The American portrait: from the death of Stuart to the rise of Sargent, April 26 1973 - June 3 1973; [exhibition] Catalogue by

William J. Hennessey. Worcester, Mass., Worcester Art Museum [1973] 63 p. illus. 23 cm. [ND1311.2.H46] 75-304144
1. Portraits, American—Exhibitions. 2. Portrait painters—United States. I. Worcester, Mass. Art Museum. II. Title.

NATIONAL Portrait Gallery, Washington, D.C. 757.9'074'0153
Nucleus for a national collection, National Portrait Gallery, Smithsonian Institution. Entries compiled by Robert G. Stewart. Washington, Smithsonian Insitution, 1966. 1 v. (unpaged) ports. 23 cm. (Smithsonian publication 4653) "The exhibition described in this catalogue was on display September 15 through November 14, 1965 in the Arts and Industries Building." [N7593.N213] 67-60364
1. Portraits, American—Exhibitions. 2. United States—Biography—Portraits. I. Stewart, Robert G. II. Title.

NATIONAL Portrait Gallery, Washington, D.C. 757'.9'0740153
Recent acquisitions. Entries compiled by Robert G. Stewart. Washington, Smithsonian Institution, 1966. 1 v. (unpaged) illus. 24 cm. (Smithsonian publication 4685) [N7593.N22] 68-62941
1. Portraits, American—Exhibitions. I. Stewart, Robert G., comp. II. Title.

NEW York. New School for Social Research. New School Art Center. 704.942
Portraits from the American art world. [Exhibition] February 2-27, 1965 [New York, 1965] [64] p. illus. 18 cm. [N7593.N47] 66-59150
1. Portraits, American — Exhibitions. I. Title.

Portraits, Ancient.

BRECKENRIDGE, James Douglas, 1926- 731.7'4
Likeness; a conceptual history of ancient portraiture, by James D. Breckenridge. Evanston [Ill.] Northwestern University Press, 1968 [c1969] xvi, 293 p. illus. 26 cm. Includes bibliographical references. [N7580.B7] 68-29325
1. Portraits, Ancient. I. Title.

Portraits, British.

LONDON. National Portrait Gallery. 757.9
British historical portraits; a selection from the National Portrait Gallery, with biographical notes. Cambridge, Published for the National Portrait Gallery at the University Press, 1957. 265p. ports. 22cm. [N1090.A575] 57-4773
1. Portraits, British. 2. Gt. Brit.—Biog.—Portraits. I. Title.

TARKINGTON, Booth, 1869-1946. 757'.9'0942
Some old portraits; a book about art and human beings. Freeport, N.Y., Books for Libraries Press [1969, c1939] xx, 249 p. ports. 27 cm. (Essay index reprint series) Bibliography: p. 239-249. [N7598.T3 1969] 78-93382
1. Portraits, British. 2. Gt. Brit.—Biography—Portraits. I. Title. BIP

Portraits, British—Catalogs.

FINK, Frances Sharf 704.942
Heads across the sea; an album of eighteenth-century English literary portraits in America. Charlottesville, Bibliographical Society of the University of Virginia: distributed by the University of Virginia Press, [c.] 1959. 251p. Bibliography: p. [231]-235. 46 ports. 24cm. 60-16018 10.00
1. Portraits, British—Catalogs. 2. Gt. Brit.—Biog.—Portraits—Catalogs. 3. Art—U.S.—Catalogs. I. Title.

LONDON. National Portrait Gallery. 757.9
Catalogue of seventeenth-century portraits in the National Portrait Gallery, 1625-1714. Compiled by David Piper. Cambridge, Published for the Trustees of the National Portrait Gallery, at the University Press, 1963. xxviii, 409 p. ports. 26 cm. Includes bibliographical references. [N1090.A598] 63-2037
1. Portraits, British — Catalogs. 2. Gt. Brit. — Biog. — Portraits — Catalogs. I. Piper, David. II. Title.

Portraits—Catalogs.

A.L.A. portrait index; 016.757
index to portraits contained in printed books and periodicals. Edited by William Coolidge Lane and Nina E. Browne. New York, B. Franklin [196-?] 3 v. (1601 p.) 27 cm. (Burt Franklin bibliography and reference series, #68) Reprint of the 1906 ed. [N7620.A2 1960z] 77-6494
1. Portraits—Catalogs. I. Lane, William Coolidge, 1859-1931, ed. II. Browne, Nina Eliza, ed. III. American Library Association. BIP

MASON, George Champlin, 1820-1894. 759.13 B
The life and works of Gilbert Stuart. With selections from Stuart's portraits reproduced on steel and by photogravure. New York, B. Franklin Reprints [1974] x, 286 p. ports. 26 cm. (Burt Franklin research & source works series. Art history & reference series, 48) Reprint of the 1879 ed. published by Scribner, New York. [ND1329.S7M37 1974] 72-82298 ISBN 0-8337-5236-7
1. Stuart, Gilbert, 1755-1828. 2. Portraits—Catalogs. I. Title. BIP

SINGER, Hans Wolfgang, 1867- 016.757
Allgemeiner bildniskatalog, von Hans Wolfgang Singer. Leipzig, K. W. Hiersemann, 1930-1936. Nendeln, Liechtenstein, Kraus-Thomson Org., 1968 14v. 28cm. [N7575.S55] 31-15244 378.00 set,
1. Portraits—Catalogs. I. Title.
Order from Kraus-Thomson, 9491 Nendeln, Liechtenstein.

Portraits — Exhibitions.

BOWDOIN College. Museum of Art. 743'.4
The French visage; a century and a half of portraiture and caricature from the Artine Artinian Collection. [Brunswick, Me.] 1969. [20] p. illus., ports. 23 cm. Catalogue of an exhibition held at Bowdoin College Museum of art. [ND1301.6.A78B68] 72-194226
1. Artinian, Artine, 1907-—Art collections. 2. Portraits—Exhibitions. 3. Caricatures and cartoons—Exhibitions. I. Title.

KANSAS. University. Museum of Art. 704.94'2
Images: 23 interpretations; an exhibition of portrait and figure painting. Prepared by students in the Dept. of History of Art, the University of Kansas Museum of Art, Lawrence, Kansas, April 26 to June 3, 1964. [Lawrence, 1964] 56 p. illus. 23 cm. (University of Kansas. Miscellaneous publications of the Museum of Art, no. 54) [N7592.K3] 64-64363
1. Portraits — Exhibitions. I. Title. II. Series. III. Series: Kansas. University. Museum of Art. Miscellaneous publications, no. 54

MILWAUKEE. Art Center. 704.94'2
The inner circle; [exhibition] September 15 through October 23, 1966. [Milwaukee, Printed by Arrow Press, 1966] 1 v. (unpaged) illus. 23 cm. [N5020.M53] 67-68057
1. Portraits—Exhibitions. I. Title.

MILWAUKEE. Art Center. 757
Portraits from Milwaukee collections. [Milwaukee, 1971] 1 v. (unpaged) 65 ports. 23 cm. "[Catalogue] of an exhibition presented by the Milwaukee Art Center in co-sponsorship with The National Society of the Colonial Dames of America in the State of Wisconsin, September 3rd through October 10th, 1971." [ND1301.M5M52] 72-200916
1. Portraits—Exhibitions. 2. Portraits—Milwaukee. I. National Society of the Colonial Dames of America. Wisconsin. II. Title.

SAISSELIN, Remy Gilbert, 1925- 707.8
Style, truth, and the portrait. [Cleveland] Cleveland Museum of Art; distributed by H. N. Abrams [New York] [1963] 215 p. 91 ports. (part col.) 27 cm. Serves as a catalogue of the exhibition, Style, truth, and the portrait, held at Cleveland from Oct. 1 to Nov. 10, 1963, and as a study of the golden ages of portraiture. [ND1301.S24] 63-19063
1. Portraits—Exhibitions. 2. Portrait painting—History. I. Cleveland Museum of Art. II. Title.

TIME, inc. 704.942
Famous likeness; an exhibition co-originated by Time incorporated, New York and the Institue of Contemporary Art, Boston, in participation with the Columbus Gallery of Fine Arts, Columbus, Ohio and the Milwaukee Art Center, Milwaukee, Wisconsin, March-August, 1961. [Text: Francis Brennan. New York, 1961] unpaged. illus. 20 cm. [ND1301.T5] 61-19023
1. Portraits—Exhibitions. I. Boston. Institute of Contemporary Art. II. Title.

VIRGINIA Museum of Fine Arts, Richmond. 757.9
A souvenir of the exhibition entitled Healy's sitters; or, A portrait panorama of the Victorian Age, being a comprehensive collection of the likenesses of some of the most important personages of Europe & America, as portrayed by George Peter Alexander Healy between the years 1837 and 1899, supplemented with documents relating to the artist's life and furnishings of the period, on view at the Virginia Museum of Fine Arts ... 24 January-5 March 1950. [Richmond] 1950 94 p. illus., map. 26 cm [ND237.H4V5] 50-58174
1. Healy, George Peter Alexander, 1813-1894. 2. Portraits — Exhibitions. I. Title.

Portraits—Georgia.

NATIONAL Society of the Colonial Dames of America. Georgia. Historical Activities Committee. 757'.09758
Early Georgia portraits, 1715-1870 / compiled by the Historical Activities Committee, Marion Converse Bright, state chairman, for the National Society of the Colonial Dames of America in the State of Georgia. Athens : University of Georgia Press, c1975. xiii, 338 p. : ports. ; 29 cm. Includes index. [ND1311.8.N37 1975] 74-18581 ISBN 0-8203-0370-4 : 25.00
1. Portraits—Georgia. 2. Portrait painting—Georgia. 3. Georgia—Biography—Portraits. I. Bright, Marion Converse. II. Title. BIP

Portraits, Greek—Catalogs.

BOSTON. Museum of Fine Arts. 733
Greek & Roman portraits, 470 BC - AD 500. Boston, 1972. [82] p. illus. 22 cm. Includes bibliographical references. [N7585.B66 1972] 72-77975
1. Boston. Museum of Fine Arts. 2. Portraits, Greek—Catalogs. 3. Portraits, Roman—Catalogs. 4. Portraits—Boston—Catalogs. I. Title.

Portraits, Group—Rome.

KLEINER, Diana E. E. 733'.5
Roman group portraiture : the funerary reliefs of the late Republic and early Empire / Diana E. E. Kleiner. New York : Garland Pub., 1977. 270 p., [76] leaves of plates : ill. ; 21 cm. (Outstanding dissertations in the fine arts) Originally presented as the author's thesis, Columbia, 1975. Bibliography: p. 252-257. [NB1296.4.K55 1977] 76-23634 ISBN 0-8240-2703-5 : 45.00
1. Portraits, Group—Rome. 2. Relief (Sculpture)—Rome. 3. Sepulchral monuments—Rome. I. Title. II. Series.

Portraits—Louisiana—Catalogs.

BRUNS, Thomas Nelson Carter, Mrs. 757'.9'09763
Louisiana portraits / compiled by Mrs. Thomas Nelson Carter Bruns for the Historical Activities Committee. Bicentennial ed. New Orleans : National Society of the Colonial Dames of America in the State of Louisiana, 1975. 317 p. : ports. ; 28 cm. Includes index. [ND1311.8.L8B78] 75-29641
1. Portraits—Louisiana—Catalogs. 2. Louisiana—Biography—Portraits—Catalogs. I. National Society of the Colonial Dames of America. Louisiana. Historical Activities Committee. II. Title.

Portraits, Roman—Catalogs.

INAN, Jale 731.8207409561
Roman and early Byzantine portrait sculpture in Asia Minor, by Jale Inan, Elisabeth Rosenbaum. London, Pub. for the Brit. Acad. by Oxford 1966. xxv, 245p. 187 plates (incl. map) 29cm. Bibl. [N7588.I5] 66-72474 31.40
1. Portraits, Roman—Catalogs. 2. Portraits, Byzantine—Catalogs. 3. Sculpture—Asia Minor—Catalogs. I. Rosenbaum, Elisabeth, joint author. II. Title.
Available from publisher's New York office.

Portraits—U.S.—Indexes.

LEE, Cuthbert. 757'.016
Portrait register. [Asheville, N.C.] Biltmore Press [1968- v. ports. 24 cm. [N7620.L4] 73-3014
1. Portraits—U.S.—Indexes.

Portraits—Virginia—Catalogs.

HOOD, Graham, 1936- 759.155
Charles Bridges and William Dering : two Virginia painters, 1735-1750 / by Graham Hood. Williamsburg, Va. : Colonial Williamsburg Foundation ; Charlottesville : distributed by University Press of Virginia, c1978. xvi, 125 p., [5] leaves of plates : chiefly ill. ; 27 cm. Includes bibliographical references and index. [ND1329.B75H66] 77-13772 ISBN 0-87935-047-4 : 15.00
1. Bridges, Charles, 1670-1747. 2. Dering, William. 3. Portraits—Virginia—Catalogs. I. Title.

Porzellanfabrik Tettau.

RAINES, Joan. 738.2'7
A guide to Royal Bayreuth figurals, by Joan and Marvin Raines. [New City, N.Y.] 1973. [45] p. (chiefly col. illus.) 23 cm. [NK4210.P58R34] 73-160546
1. Porzellanfabrik Tettau. 2. Porcelain, German. I. Raines, Marvin, joint author. II. Title.

SALLEY, Virginia Sutton. 738.2'7
Royal Bayreuth china [by] Virginia Sutton Salley and George H. Salley. [Portland? Me.] 1969. [32] p. col. illus. 23 cm. [NK4210.S325A57] 74-13657
1. Porzellanfabrik Tettan. I. Salley, George H., joint author. II. Title.

Posada, Jose Guadalupe, 1852-1913.

POSADA, Jose Guadalupe, 1852-1913. 769'.92'4
Posada's popular Mexican prints; 273 cuts, by Jose Guadalupe Posada. Selected and edited, with an introd. and commentary, by Roberto Berdecio and Stanley Appelbaum. New York, Dover Publications [1972] xxi, 156 p. illus. 29 cm. Bibliography: p. [155]-156. [NE546.P6B47 1972] 77-178994 ISBN 0-486-22854-1 3.50
1. Posada, Jose Guadalupe, 1852-1913. I. Berdecio, Roberto, ed. II. Appelbaum, Stanley, ed. III. Title.

POSADA, Jose Guadalupe, 1852-1913. 769'.92'4
The works of Jose Guadalupe Posada = Das Werk von Jose Guadalupe Posada / edited and with an introd. by Hannes Jahn. Frankfurt am Main : Zweitausendeins, 1976. 753 p. : chiefly ill. ; 28 cm. English and German. Includes index. Bibliography: p. 741-744. [NE546.P6A58] 77-476165
1. Posada, Jose Guadalupe, 1852-1913.

Post, Frans, 1612 (ca.)-1680.

SOUSA Leao, Joaquim de, 1897- 759.9492
Frans Post, 1612-1680. Amsterdam, A. L. van Gendt, 1973. 176 p. illus. (part. col.) 34 cm. (Painters of the past) Distributed in the USA by Abner Schram (Schram Enterprises Ltd) New York. Bibliography: p. 169-170. [ND653.P6S5813] 72-92539 49.00

SUBJECT INDEX POSTAGE-STAMPS—ALBUMS.

1. Post, Frans, 1612 (ca.)-1680. I. Post, Frans, 1612 (ca.)-1680.

Post-impressionism (Art).

HANSON, Lawrence. 927.5
The sockers: Gaugin, Van Gogh, Cezanne [by] Lawrence and Elisabeth Hanson. New York, Random House [c1963] xv, 334 p. illus., ports. 25 cm. Bibliography: p. [325]-328. [ND553.G27H34] 63-11619
1. Gaugin, Paul, 1848-1903. 2. Gogh, Vincent van, 1853-1890. 3. Cezanne, Paul, 1839-1906. 4. Post-impressionism (Art) I. Hanson, Elisabeth M., joint author. II. Title.

REWALD, John, 1912- 759.915
Post-impressionism: From Van Gogh to Gauguin. New York, Museum of Modern Art [1956] 614 p. illus., col. plates, ports. 26 cm. Bibliography: 551-594. [ND1265.R43] 759.06* 56-14105
1. Post-impressionism (Art) 2. Painters.

REWALD, John, 1912- 391'.07'20903
Post-impressionism: from Van Gogh to Gauguin. [2d ed.] New York, Museum of Modern Art; distributed by Doubleday, Garden City, N.Y. [1962] 619 p. illus. (part col.) map (on lining papers) 26 cm. Includes bibliographies. [ND1265.R43] 62-13979
1. Post-impressionism (Art). 2. Painters. I. Title.

Post-impressionism (Art)—France.

HIND, Charles Lewis, 1862- 759.4
1927.
The post impressionists. Freeport, N.Y., Books for Libraries Press [1969] vii, 93 p. illus., ports. 24 cm. (Select bibliographies reprint series) Reprint of the 1911 ed. [ND547.H56 1969] 75-102244 ISBN 0-8369-5129-8
1. Cezanne, Paul, 1839-1906. 2. Gauguin, Paul, 1848-1903. 3. Gogh, Vincent van, 1853-1890. 4. Post-impressionism (Art)—France. I. Title. BIP

WERNER, Alfred, 1911- 759.4
Painting by the post-impressionists. New York, McGraw-Hill [1964, c1963] 48 p. illus., 24 col. slides (in pockets) 25 cm. (The Color slide book[s] of the world's art) [ND547.W39] 63-22386
1. Post-impressionism (Art)—France. 2. Paintings, French. I. Title. II. Series.

Post-impressionism (Art)—France—Catalogs.

THE Post-impressionists / 759.4
[text by] Frank Elgar. Oxford : Phaidon, 1978 16 p., 48 p. of plates : chiefly col. ill., col. ports. ; 31 cm. [ND547.5.P6P67] 77-79686 ISBN 0-7148-1810-0 pbk. : 7.95
1. Post-impressionism (Art)—France—Catalogs. 2. Painting, French—Catalogs. 3. Painting, Modern—19th century—France—Catalogs. I. Elgar, Frank. BIP

Postage-stamp design.

MORRIS, Thomas 769'.924 B
Francis, 1890-
The life and work of Thomas F. Morris, 1852-1898, by Thomas F. Morris, II. Edited by Barbara R. Mueller. [Larchmont? N.Y., 1968] 159 p. illus., ports. 26 cm. [HE6185.U5M65] 70-1130
1. Morris, Thomas Francis, 1852-1898. 2. Postage-stamp design. 3. Paper money design. I. Title.

Postage-stamps.

BOEHM, David Alfred, 1914- 383.22
Stampography; an instructive travel album for the young stamp collector, by Robert V. Masters [pseud.] Illustrated with full-color lithographs by Howard Simon. [Rev.] New York, Sterling Pub. Co. [1951] 80 p. illus. 23 x 26 cm. [HE6182.B6 1951] 51-14703
1. Postage-stamps. I. Simon, Howard, 1906- illus. II. Title.

*CHASE, Carroll. 769.569'73'69.
The 3 stamp of the United States 1851-1857 issue revised. Lawrence, Mass., Quarterman [1975] xx, 375p. ill. 23 cm. Includes index. Bibliography:p.354-361. [HE6185.] 75-18277 ISBN 0-88000-070-8. 30.00.
1. Postage-stamps. I. Title.

HERTSCH, Max. 769'.56
Famous stamps of the world. Berne, Hallwag [1968] 8 p. 19 col. plates. 19 cm. (Orbis pictus, 23) Translation of Die beruhmtesten Briefmarken. [HE6182.H413] 68-116672
1. Postage-stamps. I. Title. BIP

KELEN, Emery, 1896- 769
Stamps tell the story of the United Nations. [1st ed.] New York, Meredith Press [1968] 95 p. illus. 24 cm. Presents the stamps issued by the United Nations, the only international body which issues its own stamps, explaining the aspects of the U.N. and its missions that each stamp honors. Arranged in sections by the subjects of the stamps, for example, the main organs of the U.N., peace-keeping operations, or technical assistance. [JX1977.8.P8K4] AC 68
1. United Nations—Postal service. 2. Postage stamps. I. Title.

LIDMAN, David. 769'.56
Treasury of stamps : 1,000 rare and beautiful stamps in color / by David Lidman ; photos. by Herman Landshoff. [New York : H. N. Abrams, 1975] p. cm. Includes index. Bibliography: p. [HE6182.L52] 74-32120 ISBN 0-8109-0469-1
1. Postage-stamps. 2. Postage-stamps—Collectors and collecting. I. Title. BIP

STORER, Doug. 769.5609
Amazing but true stories behind the stamp Doug Storer. New York : Pocket Books ,1976. 208 p. : ill. ; 18 cm. [HE6182] ISBN 0-671-80781-1 pbk. : 1.50
1. Postage-stamps. I. Title.

SUTTON, Richard John. 383.22
Stamp curiosities. New York, Philosophical Library [1958, c1957] 285 p. illus. 22 cm. [HE6182.S84 1958] 58-59958
1. Postage-stamps. I. Title.

WAY, W Dennis. 383.22
Zoology in postage stamps, by W. Dennis Way and O. D. Standen. [New York] Philosophical Library, 1952. 113 p. illus. 25 cm. [HE6183.W38] 52-8824
1. Postage-stamps. 2. Zoology. I. Title.

Postage-stamps—Albania—Catalogs.

GREECE, Albania, 383.229495
Turkey stamp catalog. New York, Minkus Publications. v. illus. 23cm. Editor: 19 G.A. Tlamsa. [HE6224.G8] 60-28462
1. Postage-stamps—Albania—Catalogs. 2. Postage-stamps—Greece—Catalogs. 3. Postage-stamps—Turkey—Catalogs. I. Tlamsa, George Adolph Maria, 1915- ed. II. Minkus Publications, inc., New York.

Postage-stamps—Albums.

BLUMENTHAL, Ben, ed. 383.22
The all American stamp album, from 1847 to date; a fully illustrated album for the postage stamps of the United States. New York, Minkus Publications; distributed by Grosset & Dunlap [c1953] 1281. illus. 30cm. [HE6185.U5B5 1953] 53-2650
1. Postage-stamps—Albums. 2. Postage-stamps—U. S. I. Title.

BLUMENTHAL, Ben. ed. 383.22
The all American stamp album, from 1847 to date; a fully illustrated album for the postage stamps of the United States. New York, Minkus Publications; distributed by Grosset & Dunlap, '1952. 128 l. illus. 30 cm. [HE6185.U5B5] 52-4894
1. Postage-stamps—Albums. 2. Postage-stamps—U. S. I. Title.

GROSSMAN Stamp Co., inc., 383.22
New York.
The premier world stamp album. Capacity for approximately 12,000 postage stamps. More than 7,500 clear full size illustrations. Every important country represented with interesting facts of each. Guide for stamp collectors. Latest world maps. New York, c1955. 224p. illus. 31cm. [HE6221.G72] 55-24584
1. Postage-stamps—Albums. I. Title.

GROSSMAN Stamp Company, 383.22
inc., New York.
The aristocrat world stamp album. New York, c1956. 672p. illus. 31cm. [HE6221.G67] 56-20046
1. Postage-stamps—Albums. I. Title.

GROSSMAN Stamp Company, 383.22
inc., New York.
The paramount stamp album, for stamps of the world; also includes special section for U.S. blocks of four. Capacity for over 30,000 postage stamps with more than 15,000 full size illustrations. Most all the countries of the globe are represented. Also interesting facts and statistics of the major stamp issuing countries. Includes instructions in collecting stamps and directory of countries. New York, c1952. 608p. illus. 31cm. [HE6221.G7 1952] 52-65987
1. Postage-stamps—Albums. I. Title.

GROSSMAN Stamp Company, 383.22
inc., New York.
The paramount stamp album, for stamps of the world; also includes special section for U. S. blocks of four. Capacity for over 30,000 postage stamps with more than 15,000 full size illustrations. Most all the countries of the globe are represented. Also interesting facts and statistics of the major stamp issuing countries. Includes instructions in collecting stamps and directory of countries. New York, '1950. 608 p. illus., map (on lining paper) 31 cm. [HE6221.G7] 50-5465
1. Postage-stamps—Albums. I. Title.

GROSSMAN Stamp Company, 383.22
inc., New York.
The regent world stamp album. Capacity for approximately 50,000 postage stamps. More than 35,000 clear full size illustrations. Most every stamp issuing country represented with interesting facts of each country. Guide for stamp collectors. Latest world maps. New York, c1956. 928p. illus. 31cm. [HE6221.G73] 56-29860
1. Postage-stamps—Albums. I. Title.

HARRIS (H. E.) and 383.22
Company, Boston.
The new diplomat album for postage stamps of the world. Personally compiled and edited by H. E. Harris. Boston, c1960. 416p. illus. 31cm. [HE6221.H336] 61-23716
1. Postage-stamps—Albums. I. Harris, Henry Ellis, 1902- II. Title. III. Title: Diplomat album for postage stamps of the world.

HARRIS, Henry Ellis, 1902- 383.22
ed.
The pocket stamp album. New York, Pocket Books [1952] 288 p. illus. 17 cm. (Pocket book, 892) [HE6221.H36] 52-24127
1. Postage-stamps—Albums. I. Title.

MINKUS Publications, inc., 383.22
New York.
World stamp album; the ideal book for the beginning collector. New York, Distributed by Grosset & Dunlap, c1962. 94 p. illus. 28 cm. (A Minkus stamp album) [HE6221.M6165] 62-52263
1. Postage-stamps—Albums. I. Title.

THE New world wide postage 383.22
stamp album. 1955- New York, Minkus Publications. v. illus. 30cm. Issue for 1957 is loose-leaf. Editor: 1955- G. A. Tlamsa. [HE6221.T54] 57-59043
1. Postage-stamps— Albums. I. Tlamsa, George Adolph Maria, 1915- ed.

SCOTT Publications, inc., 383.22
New York;
The modern postage stamp album ... New York [1950] 1 v. (unpaged) illus. 28 cm. [HE6221.S54 1950] 51-352
1. Postage-stamps — Albums. I. Title.

SCOTT Publications, inc., 383.22
New York.
Scott's grand award album for postage stamps of the world. Spaces for more than a century of world postage stamps through the 1963 Standard postage stamp catalogue. New York, 1962- 1 v. (loose-leaf) illus. 30 cm. [HE6221.S414] 63-203
1. Postage-stamps—Albums. I. Title.

SCOTT Publications, inc., 383.22
New York.
Scott's imperial stamp album; spaces for over 12, 000 lower-priced, readily obtainable postage stamps of the world, with over 4,600 illus. New York, c1953. 1v. (unpaged) illus. 29cm. Published in 1940 under title: The imperial postage stamp album. [HE6221.S48 1953] 383
1. Postage-stamps—Albums. I. Title. II. Title: Imperial stamp album.

SCOTT Publications, inc., 383.22
New York.
United States commemorative postage stamps; contains spaces for singles and blocks of four commemorative stamps of the United States listed in the 1950 edition of the Standard postage stamp catalogue under the following classification, "Special stamps issued to commemorate some event of local, national, or historical importance." New York, c1950. 1 v. (unpaged) illus. 31 cm. (Its Specialty series) Added t.p., with imprint date c1949. [HE6221.S6536 1950] 52-663
1. Postage-stamps — Albums. I. Title. II. Title: Commemorative postage stamps.

TLAMSA, George Adolf 383.22
Maria, 1915- ed.
The comprehensive world wide stamp album; an up-to-date stamp album created to give the stamp collector the basis of obtaining the two great fundamentals from this hobby: fun & knowledge. [9th ed.] New York, Minkus Publications [1957] 704p. illus. 30cm. [HE6221.T52 1957] 57-29537
1. Postage-stamps—Albums. I. Title.

TLAMSA, George Adolph 383.22
Maria, 1915- ed.
The comprehensive world wide stamp album ... Spaces for over 31,000 stamps. Catalog numbers from the New American stamp catalog ... New York, Minkus Publications [1955] 704p. illus. 30cm. [HE6221.T52 1955] 55-56541
1. Postage-stamps—Albums. I. Title.

TLAMSA, George Adolph 383.22
Maria, 1915- ed.
The comprehensive world wide stamp album; an up-to-date stamp album created to give the stamp collector the basis of obtaining the two great fundamentals from this hobby: fun & knowledge. New York, Minkus Publications [1955, c1956] 704p. illus. 30cm. [HE6221.T52 1956] 56-19646
1. Postage—stamps—Albums. I. Title.

TLAMSA, George Adolph 383.22
Maria, 1915- ed.
The master global stamp album ... New York, Minkus Publications [1952- 1 v. (loose-leaf) illus. 31 cm. Kept up to date by annual supplements. [HE6221.T53] 52-7571
1. Postage stamps — Albums. I. Title.

TLAMSA, George Adolph 383.22
Maria, 1915- ed.
My first stamp album; the ideal book for the beginning collector, featuring stamps the beginning collector can easily obtain, spaces for over 4,300 stamps, over 2,500 illustrations ... historical and geographic descriptions of each country, requirements for Boy Scouts merit badge, guide to the beginning collector [and] stamp identifier. New York, Minkus Publications; distributed by Grosset & Dunlap, c1958. 94 p. illus., col. maps (on lining papers) 29 cm. [HE6221.T533] 59-21534
1. Postage-stamps — Albums. I. Title.

TLAMSA, George Adolph 383.22
Maria, 1915- ed.
The new world wide postage stamp album, an up-to-date stamp album ... Spaces for over 15,700 stamps... The catalog numbers in this album are from the New American stamp catalog. New York, Minkus Publications [1956] 348p. illus. 29cm. [HE6221.T54 1956] 56-41377
1. Postage-stamps—Albums. I. Title.

TLAMSA, George Adolph 383.22
Maria, 1915- ed.
The new world wide postage stamp album, an up-to-date stamp album providing spaces for over 15,000 stamps ... The catalog numbers in this album are from the New American stamp catalog ... New York, Minkus Publications [1955] 348p. illus. 29cm. [HE6221.T54] 55-56542

1. Postage-stamps—Albums. I. Title.

TLAMSA, George Adolph 383.22
Maria, 1915- ed.
The supreme global stamp album ... New York, Minkus Publications [1957- 2 v. (loose leaf) illus. 31 cm. [HE6221.T55] 57-39442
1. Postage-stamps — Albums. I. Title.

Postage-stamps—Arab countries.

WOLINETZ, Harvey D. 769'.564
Arab philatelic propaganda against the State of Israel / by Harvey D. Wolinetz. Ann Arbor, Mich. : Wolinetz, 1975. iii, 74 p. : ill. ; 25 cm. Revised and extended version of the author's thesis (M.A.), Yeshiva University, 1973. Includes bibliographical references. [HE6185.A59W64 1975] 75-332193
1. Postage-stamps—Arab countries. 2. Propaganda, Anti-Israeli—Arab countries. I. Title.

Postage-stamps—Asia—Catalogs.

MINKUS Publications, 383.2295
inc., New York.
Free Asia and Africa stamp catalog. George A. Tlamsa, editor in chief. 1960 ed. New York [1959] 894-1166p. illus. 23cm. [HE6224.M553] 60-17816
1. Postage-stamps—Asia—Catalogs. 2. Postage-stamps—Africa—Catalogs. I. Tlamsa, George Adolph Maria, 1915- ed. II. Title.

PATTERSON, Frank E. 383.229581
Afghanistan, its twentieth century postal issues, Introd. by R. Pazhwak. [New York] Pub. under the auspices of the Theodore E. Steinway Memorial Pubn. Fund [Collectors Club, 22 E. 35th St., 1965, c.1964] 208p. illus., map. 25cm. (Collectors Club handbk., no. 18) Bibl. [HE6185.A32P3] 65-3867 7.50
1. Postage-stamp—Afghanistan—Catalogs. I. Title.

Postage-stamps—Australia.

AUSTRALIA. Postmaster- 769'.56994
General's Dept.
The definitive stamps of the reign of King George VI / [by the] Australian Post Office. [Melbourne] : Postmaster-General's Dept., [1972?]. 39 p. : ill. ; 22 cm. (Australian postage stamps) [HE6185.A82A87 1972] 74-186199 0.50
1. Postage-stamps—Australia. I. Title. II. Series.

ROSENBLUM, Alec A. 769.56
The stamps of the Commonwealth of Australia a handbook for philatelists, by Alec A. Rosenblum. Prepd. with the collaboration of the Comm. and members of the Australian Commonwealth Specialists Soc. (Great Britain) and of numerous individuals. [6th ed., rev., brought completely up-to-date. Melbourne, Acacia Pr. [1966] 591p. illus. 24cm. [HE6185.A8R6 1966.] 67-404 13.45
1. Postage-stamps—Australia. I. Title.
American distributor: Tri-Ocean, San Francisco.

ROSENBLUM, Alec A. 769'.569'94
The stamps of the Commonwealth of Australia; a handbook for philatelists, by Alec A. Rosenblum. 6th [i.e. 7th] ed. Melbourne, Acacia Press [1968] 636 p. illus. 25 cm. Prepared with the collaboration of the committee and members of the Australian Commonwealth Specialists' Society (Great Britain) and of numerous individuals. [HE6185.A8R6 1968] 71-553588
1. Postage-stamps—Australia. I. Australian Commonwealth Specialists' Society (Great Britain) II. Title.

Postage-stamps—Australia—Catalogs.

COLLAS, Phil. 769.56994
Australian postage stamps [by] P. Collas. [Brisbane] Jacaranda Press; San Francisco, Tri-Ocean Books [1965] 110 p. illus., facsims., port. 29 cm. [HE6185.A82C6] 65-4800
1. Postage-stamps—Australia—Catalogs. I. Title.

THE Colour catalogue 769'.56994
of Australian stamps. Southsea : David Mortimer, 1976. [1], 30 p. : chiefly col. ill. ; 23 cm. [HE6185.A82C63] 77-376032 ISBN 0-905556-00-3 : £1.25
1. Postage-stamps—Australia—Catalogs.

Postage-stamps—Australia—History.

AUSTRALIA. Postmaster- 769'.56994
General's Dept.
The 1913-14 recess-printed series and the King George V sideface and pictorial definitive stamps [by Australian Post Office.] [Melbourne, Postmaster-General's Dept., 1971?] 32 p. illus. 23 cm. (Australian postage stamps) [HE6185.A8A5] 72-171874 ISBN 0-642-95563-8 0.50
1. Postage-stamps—Australia—History. I. Title. II. Series.

Postage stamps — Austria — Albums.

TLAMSA, George Adolph 383.229436
Maria, 1915- ed.
Austria: a complete album for the postage stamps of Austria and Bosnia & Herzegovina; spaces for every major number variety, with numbers from the New world-wide postage stamp catalog. New York, Minkus Publications [1958- 1 v. (loose-leaf) illus. 30 cm. [HE6185.A92T5] 59-24507
1. Postage stamps — Austria — Albums. I. Title.

Postage-stamps—Austria—Catalogs.

MINKUS Publications, 383.229436
inc., New York.
Austria, Switzerland, Liechtenstein stamp catalog. George A. Tlamsa, editor in chief. 1960 ed. New York [1959] 72p. illus. 23cm. [HE6185.A92M5] 60-17818
1. Postage-stamps—Austria—Catalogs. 2. Postage-stamps—Liechtenstein— Catalogs. 3. Postage-stamps—Switzerland—Catalogs. I. Tlamsa, George Adolph Maria, 1915- ed. II. Title.

POSTAGE stamp catalog 383.229436
of Austria, Switzerland, Bosnia & Herzegovina. New York, Minkus Publications. v. illus. 23cm. Editor: G. A. Tlamsa. [HE6185.A92P6] 59-44098
1. Postage-stamps—Austria— Catalogs. 2. Postage-stamps—Bosnia and Herzegovina—Catalogs. 3. Postage-stamps—Switzerland—Catalogs. I. Tlamsa, George Adolph Maria, 1915- ed.

Postage-stamps—Belgium—Catalogs.

MINKUS Publications, 383.229492
inc., New York.
Belgium, Netherlands, Luxembourg, colonies stamp catalog. George A. Tlamsa, editor in chief. 1960 ed. New York [1959] 101p. illus. 23cm. [HE6185.B42M5] 60-17819
1. Postage-stamps—Belgium—Catalogs. 2. Postage-stamps— Netherlands—Catalogs. 3. Postage-stamps—Luxemburg—Catalogs. I. Tlamsa, George Adolph Maria, 1915- ed. II. Title.

Postage — stamps — Booklets.

WORK, H. R. ed. 383.22
British Empire postage stamp booklets; study and evaluation. [n. p., 1957. unpaged. 30 cm. [HE6185.G6W6] 57-31973
1. Postage — stamps — Booklets. 2. Postage — stamps — Commonwealth of Nations. 3. Postage — stamps — Gt. Brit. — Colonies. I. Title.

WORK, H. R. ed. 383.22942
British Empire postage stamp booklets; study and evaluation. 2d ed. [New York?] c1958. unpaged. 29 cm. -- Supplement. 1st- [New York?] 1959- v. 28 cm. [HE6185.G6W6 1958] 58-19725
1. Postage — stamps — Booklets. 2. Postage — stamps — Commonwealth of Nations. 3. Postage — stamps — Gt. Brit. — Colonies. I. Title.

Postage-stamps —British America— Catalogs.

SCOTT Publications, inc., 383.22
New York.
Scott's dollar British America stamp catalogue, 1954; Canada and the British colonies and territories of the Western Hemisphere, from Scott's 1954 standard postage stamp catalogue. Edited by Gordon R. Harmer. New York [1953] 71p. illus. 24cm. [HE6185.B75S3 1954] 54-436
1. Postage-stamps —British America— Catalogs. I. Harmer, Gordon R., 1906- ed. II. Title.

Postage-stamps—Bulgaria—Catalogs.

MINKUS Publications, 383.229497
inc., New York.
Bulgaria. Hungary, Romania, Yugoslavia stamp catalog. George A. Tlamsa.a editor in chief. 1960 ed. New York [1959] 161p. illus. 23cm. [HE6224.M55] 60-17824
1. Postage-stamps—Bulgaria—Catalogs. 2. Postage-stamps—Hungary—Catalogs. 3. Postage-stamsp—Rumania—Catalogs. 4. Postage-stamps—Yugoslavia— Catalogs. I. Tlamsa, George Adolph Maria, 1915- ed. II. Title.

Postage-stamps—Canada.

BOGGS, Winthrop 769'.56971
Smillie, 1902-
The postage stamps and postal history of Canada / Winthrop S. Boggs. Lawrence, Mass. : Quarterman Publications, [1974] xxxvi, 870 p. : ill., facsims. ; 24 cm. Contains v. 1 and excerpts from v. 2 of the 1945 ed.; with a foreword and a section comprising the author's revisions added. Includes index. Bibliography: p. 750-751. [HE6185.C2B6 1974] 74-79893 ISBN 0-88000-042-2 : 40.00
1. Postage-stamps—Canada. 2. Postal service—Canada—History. I. Title. BIP

CALDER, James 769.56973075
Alexander, 1868-1956.
Some phases of the Canada '59 issue. [Plymouth, Eng., 19--] 53p. illus. 28cm. 'Reprinted from the London philatelist.' [HE6185.C2C2] 59-28868
1. Postage-stamps—Canada. I. Title.

HEYN, K. D. 769'.56971
Checklist of Canada's definitives, 1954-76 / by K. D. Heyn. Mill Valley, CA : Heyn, c1977. vi p., 29 leaves : ill. ; 22 cm. Cover title. [HE6185.C22H48 1977] 77-359026 2.50
1. Postage-stamps—Canada. I. Title.

HOWES, Clifton 769'.56971
Armstrong, 1872-
Canadian postage stamps and stationery / Clifton A. Howes. Lawrence, Mass. : Quarterman Publications, [1974] c1911. 287 p., [7] leaves of plates : ill. ; 27 cm. Reprint of the ed. published by the New England Stamp Co., Boston under title: Canada, its postage stamps and postal stationery. Includes bibliographical references. [HE6185.C2H6 1974] 73-86774 ISBN 0-88000-019-8 : 30.00
1. Postage-stamps—Canada. I. Title.

JARRETT, Fred. 769'.56971
Stamps of British North America / Fred Jarrett. Lawrence, Mass. : Quarterman Publications, c1975. xv, 595 p. : ill. ; 24 cm. Reprint of the 1929 ed. published in Toronto. [HE6185.C2J37 1975] 74-82308 ISBN 0-88000-052-X : 35.00
1. Postage-stamps—Canada. 2. Postage-stamps—Great Britain—Colonies. I. Title. BIP

Postage-stamps—Canada—Catalogs.

MINUSE, Kenneth. 769'.569'71
The essays and proofs of British North America. Compiled by Kenneth Minuse and Robert H. Pratt. 1st ed. [Federalsburg? Md., Sissons Publications] 1970. 198 p. illus. 27 cm. Caption title: The Essay-Proof Society catalog of the essays and proofs of British North America. [HE6185.C22M5] 74-24789
1. Postage-stamps—Canada—Catalogs. I. Pratt, Robert H., joint author. II. Essay Proof Society. III. Title. IV. Title: The Essay-Proof Society catalog of the essays and proofs of British North America.

Postage-stamps — Cape of Good Hope.

STEVENSON, David Alan. 383.2
The triangular stamps of Cape of Good Hope. London, New York, H. R. Harmer, 1950. xv, 142 p. illus. (part col.) 28 cm. Bibliography: p. 141-142. [HE6185.S6S8] 50-56383
1. Postage-stamps — Cape of Good Hope. I. Title.

Postage-stamps—Catalogs.

CONWAY, Herbert E. 769'.56
25 years of philatelic highlights / United Nations Postal Administration. 1st ed. New York : UN, 1976. 59 p. : ill. ; 23 cm. [HE6224.C75] 76-366546 2.50
1. United Nations—Postal service. 2. Postage-stamps—Catalogs. I. United Nations. Postal Administration. II. Title.

FERRIS, Carleton G., comp. 383.22
United States stamp auction review. 1912-13. Philadelphia, E. Klein. 192 p. 20 cm. Compiled by C. G. Ferris. No more published? [HE6226.U5] 58-52751
1. Postage-stamps — Catalogs. I. Title.

GIBBONS-WHITMAN 769'.56'0216
postage stamp catalogue. 1st- ed.: 1968- Racine, Wis., Whitman Pub. [1967] v. illus. 24cm. Amer. ed. Issued in 3 parts. pt. 1, United States of America and possessions, Great Britain and British Commonwealth, United Nations. [HE6224.G53] 67-27918 7.00 bds.,
1. Postage-stamps—Catalogs. I. Gibbons (Stanley) ltd., London.

HARRIS (H. E.) and 383.22
Company, Boston.
The stamp collectors' guide. Boston. v. illus. 18cm. [HE6226.H28] 056
1. Postage-stamps— Catalogs. I. Title.

HAUSDORFF, Henry. 383.22
Cash for your stamps. New York, Sterling Pub. Co. [1957] 128p. illus. 17cm. [HE6226.H39] 57-13281
1. Postage-stamps—Catalogs. I. Title.

INTERNATIONAL Philatelic v. 12
Exhibition, 6th, Washington, D.C., 1966.
Official catalogue. [Washington, National Philatelic Exhibitions of Washington, D.C., 1966] 196 p. illus. 26 cm. Catalogue of an exhibition (known also by its acronym, SIPEX) held May 21-30, 1966. Sponsored by the National Philatelic Exhibitions of Washington, D.C. [HE6191.I53 1966] 74-151691
1. Postage-stamps—Catalogs. I. National Philatelic Exhibitions of Washington, D.C., inc.

LUFF, Moe, 1911- 383.22
United States postal slogan cancel catalog. Rev., enl. & ed. Spring Valley, N. Y., 1968. 127p. illus. 22cm. First pub. in 1950 under title: United States postal slogan cancels. [HE6183.L8 1963] 63-25179 4.25 pap., spiral bdg.
I. Title.
Order from author: 12 Greene Road, Spring Valley, New York 10977. BIP

MINKUS New American stamp 383.22
catalog. 1966 ed. Ben Blumenthal, ed. in chief. Assoc. eds.: H. L. Lindquist [others] New York, Minkus [c.1965] x, 286p. illus., facsims. 24cm. [HE6185.U5N4] 55-13741 3.00
1. Postage-stamps—Catalogs. I. Tlamsa, George Ben, ed. II. Lindquist, H. L., joint ed.

MINKUS New world-wide 383.22
postage stamp catalog. 2v. 1966 George A. Tlamsa, ed. in chief New York, Minkus [c.1965] 2v. (vi. 1461: vi, 1482p.) illus. 24cm. Contents.v.1. The United States. its territories and possessions; the United Nations; the British Commonwealth of Nations; Ireland; Central and South America; Free states of Africa and Asia.-- v.2. Europe and colonies [HE6224.N4] 56-597 7.95 ea.,
1. Postage-stamps—Catalogs. I. Tlamsa, George Adolph Maria. 1915- ed.

handbook series) Spine title: Black Jacks. Bibliography: p. 147-148. [HE6207.A37L36] 75-322350
1. Allen, Harry Frederick, 1878-1965. 2. Postage-stamps—Collectors and collecting. 3. Postage-stamps—United States—History. I. Perry, Elliott. II. Title. III. Title: Black Jacks. IV. Series: American Philatelic Society. A.P.S. handbook series.

MARTIN, M. W. 769'.564'075
Topical stamp collecting / M. W. Martin. New York : Arco Pub. Co., c1975. xii, 159 p. : ill. ; 26 cm. Includes bibliographical references. [HE6215.M36] 74-19793 ISBN 0-668-03754-7 lib.bdg. : 8.95 ISBN 0-668-03662-1 pbk. : 5.95
1. Postage-stamps—Collectors and collecting. I. Title. BIP

MELVILLE, Frederick John, 1882-1940. 383.22
Stamp collecting for fun and profit. Rev. by Charles Skilton. New York, Arc Books [1963, c1961] vi, 190 p. illus. 18 cm. First published in 1940 under title: Modern stamp collecting. [HE6213.M53 1963] 63-19413
1. Postage-stamps—Collectors and collecting. I. Skilton, Charles, ed. II. Title.

MOURNING, Jim. 383.22
Guidebook to stamp collecting. [Los Angeles, Trend Books, c1958] 128p. illus. 25cm. (Trend book 179) [HE6215.M7] 59-38123
1. Postage-stamps—Collectors and collecting. I. Title.

MUELLER, Barbara R 383.22
Common sense philately. Princeton, N. J., Van Nostrand [1956] 173p. 24cm. [HE6213.M8] 56-8215
1. Postage-stamps—Collectors and collecting. I. Title.

NEW, Anthony S. B. 769'.56
The observer's book of postage stamps, by Anthony S. B. New. London, New York, F. Warne [1967] 240 p. illus. (part col.) 14 1/2 cm. (The Observer's pocket series, 42) Bibliography: p. 10. [HE6215.N4] 68-10043
1. Postage-stamps—Collectors and collecting. I. Title. II. Series. BIP

PATRICK, Douglas. 383.22
The international guide to stamps and stamp collecting. Includes the answers to 1200 questions most often asked about stamps. By Douglas and Mary Patrick. New York, Dodd, Mead [1962] 428 p. illus. 22 cm. [HE6215.P3] 62-17920
1. Postage-stamps—Collectors and collecting. I. Patrick, Mary, joint author. II. Title.

REINFELD, Fred, 1910- 383.22
A beginner's guide to stamp collecting, by Edward Young [pseud.] Baltimore, Ottenheimer Publishers [c1960] 52p. 19cm. [HE6215.R4] 61-3473
1. Postage-stamps— Collectors and collecting. I. Title.

REINFELD, Fred, 1910- 383.22
Fun with stamp collecting. Illustrated by W. T. Mars. Garden City, N.Y., Garden City Books [1957] 88 p. illus. 32 cm. [HE6213.R36] 57-11319
1. Postage-stamps—Collectors and collecting. I. Title.

REINFELD, Fred, 1910-1964. 769'.569'73
Stamp collectors' handbook, by Fred Reinfeld. Adapted by Burton Hobson. Garden City, N.Y., Doubleday [1970] 152 p. illus. 21 cm. [HE6215.R43] 77-111945 3.95
1. Postage-stamps—Collectors and collecting. I. Hobson, Burton. II. Title. BIP

REINFELD, Fred, 1910-1964. 769'.56973
Stamp collectors' handbook / by Fred Reinfeld ; adapted by Burton Hobson. Rev. ed. / by Beatrice Reinfeld. Garden City, N.Y. : Doubleday, c1976. 160 p. : ill. ; 21 cm. Includes index. [HE6215.R43 1976] 76-356786 ISBN 0-385-11682-9 : 5.95
1. Postage-stamps—Collectors and collecting. I. Hobson, Burton. II. Reinfeld, Beatrice. III. Title.

SCOTT'S new handbook for philatelists. 769'.56 New York, Simon and Schuster [1967] 192 p. illus. 25 cm. Bibliography: p. 116-143. [HE6215.S33] 67-19818
1. Postage-stamps—Collectors and collecting. I. Title: Handbook for philatelists.

SMITH, Eric 769.56075
Collecting stamps. London, Batsford, 1966. 72p. illus, facsims 22cm. [HE 6215.S6] 66-71852 5.00
1. Postage-stamps—Collectors and collecting. I. Title.
Available from Leisure Time Bks. in New Rochelle, New York.

SUTTON, Richard John. 383.22
Practical philately. London, New York, Hutchinson's Scientific and Technical Publications [1953] 216p. illus. 22cm. [HE6215.S85] 54-319
1. Postage-stamps—Collectors and collecting. I. Title.

THORP, Prescott Holden. 383.22
The complete guide to stamp collecting. New York, Minkus Publications [1961] 216 p. illus. 23 cm. [HE6213.T48 1961] 61-2962
1. Postage-stamps—Collectors and collecting. I. Title.

THORP, Prescott Holden. 769.56
The complete guide to stamp collecting. New York, Minkus Publications. [1965] xiii, 198 p. illus. 22 cm. [HE6213.T48] 66-7043
1. Postage-stamps — Collectors and collecting. I. Title.

THORP, Prescott Holden. 383.22
The complete guide to stamp collecting. New York, Minkus Publications; distributed by Grosset & Dunlap [1953] 175 p. illus. 23 cm. [HE6213.T48] 53-8501
1. Postage stamps—Collectors and collecting. I. Title.

THORP, Prescott Holden. 769'.56'075
The complete guide to stamp collecting. New York, Minkus Publications [1967] xiii, 198 p. illus., facsims., port. 23 cm. Bibliography: p. 191-192. [HE6213.T48 1967] 68-820
1. Postage-stamps—Collectors and collecting. I. Title. II. Title: Stamp collecting.

THORP, Prescott Holden. 769'.56'075
The complete guide to stamp collecting. New York, Minkus Publications [1971] xiii, 198 p. illus., facsims., port. 23 cm. Bibliography: p. 191-192. [HE6213.T48 1971] 74-25794 3.95
1. Postage-stamps—Collectors and collecting. I. Title. II. Title: Stamp collecting.

THORP, Prescott Holden. 383.22
A guide to stamp collecting; America's favorite family hobby. New York, Minkus Publications; distributed by Grosset & Dunlap [1962] 96 p. illus. 28 cm. (A Minkus stamp book) [HE6215.T48] 62-52285
1. Postage-stamps—Collectors and collecting. I. Title.

THORSEN, Harry D., 1913- 081 s
Stamp collecting / by Harry D. Thorsen, Jr. Rev. ed. North Brunswick, N.J. : Boy Scouts of America, 1974. 48 p. : ill. ; 21 cm. (Merit badge series ; 3359) [HS3313.Z95S78 1974] [HE6215] 769'.56'075 74-193205 ISBN 0-8395-3359-4 pbk. : 0.55
1. Postage-stamps—Collectors and collecting. 2. Postage-stamps—United States—History. I. Title. II. Series: Boy Scouts of America. Merit badge series ; 3359.

VILLIARD, Paul. 769'.56'075
Collecting stamps. With 77 photos. by the author. [1st ed.] Garden City, N.Y., Doubleday, 1974. xiv, 191 p. illus. 25 cm. [HE6215.V54] 73-10950 ISBN 0-385-01774-X 5.95
1. Postage-stamps—Collectors and collecting. I. Title. BIP

WILLIAMS, Leon Norman, 1914- 769'.56
Fundamentals of philately / by L. N. and M. Williams. Unabridged ed. State College, Pa. : American Philatelic Society, c1971. 629, xxx p. : ill. ; 26 cm. (A.P.S. handbook series) Includes bibliographical references and index. [HE6213.W5473 1971] 75-322349
1. Postage-stamps—Collectors and collecting. I. Williams, Maurice, 1905- joint author. II. Title. III. Series: American Philatelic Society. A.P.S. handbook series.

WILLIAMS, Leon Norman, 1914- 383.22
The postage stamp: its history and recognition [by] L. N. & M. Williams. [Harmondsworth, Middlesex, Baltimore] Penguin Books [1956] 272 p. illus. 18 cm. (A Pelican book, A374) [HE6213.W553] 57-3654
1. Postage-stamps — Collectors and collecting. I. Williams, Maurice, 1905- joint author. II. Title.

WISE, Ernest Harold, 1926- 769'.56'075
Forming a specialised stamp collection / [by] Ernest H. Wise. London : Gibbons, 1976. 30 p. : ill., facsims. ; 20 cm. (Stanley Gibbons guides) Includes bibliographical references. [HE6215.W57] 77-362230 ISBN 0-85259-840-8 : £0.75
1. Postage-stamps—Collectors and collecting. I. Title.

ZARCHY, Harry. 383.22
Stamp collector's guide, written and illustrated by Harry Zarchy. [1st ed.] New York, Knopf [1956] 178 p. illus. 22 cm. [HE6215.Z36] 56-5297
1. Postage-stamps—Collectors and collecting. I. Title. BIP

Postage-stamps—Collectors and collecting—Australia.

FINLAY, Ian F. 769'.569'94
Australian stamp collecting, [by] Ian F. Finlay. [Melbourne] Lansdowne [1971] 112 p. illus. (part col.) 24 cm. Bibliography: p. 111-112. [HE6185.A8F55] 72-178231 ISBN 0-7018-0304-5 3.95
1. Postage-stamps—Collectors and collecting—Australia. 2. Postage-stamps—Australia. I. Title.

Postage-stamps—Collectors and collecting—Directories.

MATHIAS, Virgil J. 769'.56'025
The philatelic index. Virgil J. Mathias, editor. [Columbus, Ohio] 1969- v. 28 cm. [HE6209.M34] 78-9606 5.00 (v. 1)
1. Postage-stamps—Collectors and collecting—Directories. I. Title.

Postage-stamps—Collectors and collecting—Europe—Handbooks, manuals, etc.

ALLEN, Jon L. 769'.56'075
Stamp collector's guide to Europe [by] Jon L. Allen and Paul H. Silverstone. New York, Arco [1974] ix, 309 p. illus. 25 cm. Includes bibliographical references. [HE6215.A45] 73-78494 3.95 (pbk.)
1. Postage-stamps—Collectors and collecting—Europe—Handbooks, manuals, etc. 2. Postal service—Europe—Handbooks, manuals, etc. I. Silverstone, Paul H., joint author. II. Title.
Hardbound 5.95; ISBN: 0-668-03343-6. BIP

Postage-stamps—Collectors and collecting—Juvenile literature.

CETIN, Frank. 383.2
Stamp collecting. New York, Putnam [1962] 127p. illus. 24cm. (Here is your hobby) [HE6215.C4] 62-14384
1. Postage-stamps—Collectors and collecting—Juvenile literature. I. Title.

FELIX, Ervin J., 1918- 769'.56'075
Let's collect stamps / by Ervin J. Felix. 2d ed. Racine, Wis. : Western Pub. Co., c1976. 64 p. : ill. ; 20 cm. Page 64 blank for "Notes." Introduces aspects of stamp collecting such as types of collections, stamp characteristics to look for, and collector's terminology. [HE6215.F43 1976] 76-6210 ISBN 0-307-06720-3
1. Postage-stamps—Collectors and collecting—Juvenile literature. I. Title. BIP

KEHR, Ernest Anthony, 1911- 383.22
My hobby is collecting stamps. Chicago, Childrens Press [1960, c1955] 127 p. illus. 25 cm. [[HE6215]] 62-5490
1. Postage-stamps — Collectors and collecting — Juvenile literature. I. Title.

LINDENBAUM, Arieh. 769'.56
Stamps tell the story of stamps. New York, Sabra Books [1970] 63 p. illus. (part col.) 22 cm. Traces the history of postage stamps discussing their use and value for collectors. [HE6182.L54] 71-124117 4.50
1. Postage-stamps—Collectors and collecting—Juvenile literature. I. Title.

OLCHESKI, Bill. 769'.56'075
Beginning stamp collecting / by Bill Olcheski. New York : H. Z. Walck, c1976. 135 p. : ill. ; 26 cm. Includes index. An introduction to stamp collecting with chapters on how to get stamps, picking an album, first-day covers, and stamp clubs and shows. [HE6215.O47] 74-25978 ISBN 0-8098-2429-9 : 7.95
1. Postage-stamps—Collectors and collecting—Juvenile literature. I. Title. BIP

STEINER, Barbara A. 769'.56'075
Your hobby: stamp collecting, by Barbara A. Steiner. [Minneapolis, Schmitt, Hall & McCreary Co., c1972] 53 p. illus. 20 x 25 cm. Bibliography: p. 49-50. Briefly describes the significance of stamps and gives suggestions for starting a collection and a stamp club. [HE6215.S68] 72-10318
1. Postage-stamps—Collectors and collecting—Juvenile literature. I. Title.

THE United States; 769'.563'0973 illustrated stories of important people, places, and events—with a catalogue of all postage stamps of the U.S. and the United Nations. Editor: Elena Marzulla. [De luxe limited ed.] Omaha, Scott Pub. Co. [1971] 216 p. illus. 19 cm. (Scott exploration series, v. 1) Highlights of United States history are incorporated in this catalogue of United States and United Nations stamps. [HE6217.U5] 72-176949
1. Postage-stamps—Collectors and collecting—Juvenile literature. 2. Postage-stamps—U.S.—Catalogs. I. Marzulla, Elena, ed.

Postage-stamps—Collectors and collecting—Period.

INTERNATIONAL Society for Japanese Philately. 383.2205
Japanese philately. [Philadelphia, etc., International Society for Japanese Philately] v. in illus. 29 cm. Frequency varies. [HE6187.J3] 66-93458
1. Postage-stamps—Collectors and collecting—Period. 2. Postage-stamps—Japan. I. Title.

PHILLIPS, Charles James, 1863-1940. 383.2205
Philatelic classics. v. 1-2 (no. 1-14); Mar. 1927-June 1931. New York. 2v. in 1. 19cm. irregular. L. C. set incomplete: no. 12 wanting. [HE6187.P646] 58-25900
1. Postage -stamps—Collectors and collecting—Period. I. Title.

Postage- stamps—Commonwealth of Nations—Catalogs.

MINKUS Publications, inc., New York. 383.22942
British Commonwealth stamp catalog. George A. Talasa. editor in chief. 1960 ed. New York [1959] 68-466p. illus. 23cm. [HE6185.G62M5] 60-17825
1. Postage- stamps—Commonwealth of Nations—Catalogs. 2. Postage-stamps—Gt. Brit.— Colonies—Catalogs. I. Tlamsa, George Adolph Maria, 1915- ed. II. Title.

MINKUS Publications, inc., New York. 383.22942
Minkus British Commonwealth stamp catalog. New York. v. illus. 24 cm. [HE6185.G62M5] 60-17825
1. Postage-stamps — Commonwealth of Nations — Catalogs. 2. Postage-stamps — Gt. Brit. — Colonies — Catalogs. I. Title.

SUBJECT INDEX POSTAGE-STAMPS—JUVENILE LITERATURE.

Postage-stamps—Dealers.

HERST, Herman. 383.22069
Nassau Street; a quarter century of stamp dealing. [1st ed.] New York, Duell, Sloan and Pearce [1960] 305 p. 21 cm. Autobiography. [HE6204.U5H4] 60-12829
1. Postage-stamps—Dealers. I. Title.

Postage stamps—Dictionaries.

MACKAY, James Alexander. 769'.56'03
The dictionary of stamps in color [by] James A. Mackay. New York, Macmillan [1973] 296 p. illus. 32 cm. [HE6196.M33] 72-11282 19.95
1. Postage-stamps—Dictionaries. I. Title. BIP

MACKAY, James Alexander. 769'.56904
Encyclopaedia of world stamps, 1945-1975 / [by] James A. Mackay. London : Lionel Leventhal Ltd, 1976. 3-160 p., 112 p. of plates : col. ill. ; 32 cm. American ed. published simultaneously under title: Encyclopedia of world stamps, 1945-1975. [HE6196.M34 1976b] 77-356534 ISBN 0-85368-231-3 : £10.95
1. Postage-stamps—Dictionaries. I. Title.

MACKAY, James Alexander. 769'.56'03
Encyclopedia of world stamps, 1945-1975 / by James A. Mackay New York : McGraw-Hill, 1976. p. cm. [HE6196.M34 1976] 76-17283 ISBN 0-07-044595-8 : 24.95
*1. Postage-stamp—Dictionaries. I. Title.*BIP

SPENCER, Charles Edward, 1890- 383.2203
The stamp collector's assistant; an alphabetical list designed to help collectors to quickly find names and former names of issuing countries, place of use of overprints and surcharges, with bits of information which will make the hobby of stamp collecting more interesting and entertaining. Los Angeles, Stamp Collector, inc.] e1959. 56 p. 22 cm. [HE6196.S65] 59-47358
1. Postage-stamps — Dictionaries. I. Title.

SUTTON, Richard John, comp. 383.22
The stamp collector's encyclopaedia. [4th ed.] New York, Philosophical Library [1955] 350p. illus. 22cm. [HE6196.S85 1955] 55-13767
1. Postage-stamps— Dictionaries. I. Title.

SUTTON, Richard John. 383.22
A stamp collector's encyclopaedia. [2d ed., rev.] New York, Philosophical Library [1952] 263 p. illus. 22 cm. [HE6196.S85 1952] 51-14234
1. Postage stamps—Dictionaries. I. Title.

SUTTON, Richard John. 383.22
The stamp collector's encyclopaedia. [4th ed., rev. and enl.] London, New York, Hutchinson's Scientific and Technical Publications [1955] 850p. illus. 22cm. [HE6196.S85 1955] 56-21108
1. Postage-stamps—Dictionaries. I. Title.

SUTTON, Richard John. 769.5603
The stamp collector's encyclopaedia. 6th ed., rev. by K. W. Anthony. [New York] Philosophical Library [1966] 370 p. illus. 22 cm. [HE6196.S85 1966] 66-5091
1. Postage-stamps—Dictionaries. I. Anthony, Kenneth W., ed. II. Title.

SUTTON, Richard John. 769'.56'03
The stamp collector's encyclopedia. Compiled by R. J. Sutton. 6th ed. rev. by K. W. Anthony. New York, Arco Pub. Co. [1973, c1966] 365 p. illus. 18 cm. (An ARC book) [HE6196.S85 1973] 72-3134 ISBN 0-668-02647-2 1.95
1. Postage-stamps—Dictionaries. I. Anthony, Kenneth W. II. Title. BIP

Postage-stamps—Dictionaries—German.

GERMANY Philatelic Society. Chapter No. 7, Fort Lauderdale, Fla. 769'.56'03
German-English philatelic dictionary. Compiled by Chapter No. 7 of the Germany Philatelic Society, Fort Lauderdale, Florida. [Valparaiso, Ind.] Germany Philatelic Society [1969] 101 p. ports. 24 cm. (GPS library booklet series, no. 4) [HE6196.G47] 73-100697 3.00
1. Postage-stamps—Dictionaries—German. 2. German language—Dictionaries—English. I. Title. II. Series: Germany Philatelic Society. GPS library booklet series, no. 4

Postage-stamps—Exhibitions.

FOSTER, C. E. 769'.56'074
How to prepare stamp exhibits, by C. E. Foster. [n.p.] New Mexico Philatelic Association [1973] iv, 212 p. illus. 29 cm. Originally serialized in the New Mexico philatelist, Aug. 1970-June 1973. [HE6215.F6] 73-181297
*1. Postage-stamps—Exhibitions. I. Title.*BIP

Postage-stamps—Forgeries.

FOURNIER, Francois, d.1914. 769'.562
The Fournier album of philatelic forgeries; a photographic composite for reference purposes. Edited by Lowell Ragatz. Worthington, Ohio, J. van den Berg [1970] a-z, aa-ai, 175 p. illus. 28 cm. Contains the author's 1914 price-list of philatelic forgeries, and Album de fac-similes, first published about 1928. [HE6184.F6F68 1970] 73-170677
1. Postage-stamps—Forgeries. 2. Postage-stamps—Catalogs. I. Fournier, Francois, d. 1914. Album de fac-similes. 1970. II. Title.

RAGATZ, Lowell Joseph, 1897- ed. 383.22
The early philatelic forgeries of all countries; a stamp collector's omnibus. Washington, Educational Research Bureau, 1953. 1v. 18cm. [HE6183.R25] 54-21590
1. Postage-stamps—Foregeries. I. Title. Contents omitted.

TYLER, Varro E. 769'.562'0922 B
Philatelic forgers, their lives and works / by Varro E. Tyler. London : Lowe, 1976. iv, 60 p. : facsims., ports. ; 25 cm. Includes bibliographical references and index. [HE6184.F6T94] 77-362339 £4.00
1. Postage-stamps—Forgeries. I. Title.

Postage-stamps—Forgeries—Catalogs.

THE Yucatan affair : 769'.562
the work of Raoul Ch. de Thuin, philatelic counterfeiter / James M. Chemi, editor-in-chief, James H. Beal and James T. De Voss, associate editors ; detailed and compiled through the assistance of an outstanding specialist editorial staff. Unabridged ed. State College, Pa. : American Philatelic Society, c1974. 523 p. : ill. ; 27 cm. (A.P.S. handbook series) [HE6184.F6Y8] 75-328159
1. Thuin, Raoul Charles de. 2. Postage-stamps—Forgeries—Catalogs. I. Chemi, James M. II. Beal, James H., 1922- III. DeVoss, James T. IV. Series: American Philatelic Society. A.P.S. handbook series.

Postage-stamps—France.

LESGOR, Raoul. 383.22
France: 19th century specialized; a special study of the issues of France, 1849-1900, varieties, shades, etc. Holmes, N. Y. [1956] 50p. illus., facsims. 23cm. [HE6185.F8L417] 57-15174
1. Postage-stamps—France. I. Title.

LESGOR, Raoul. 383.22
France, 20th century specialized; a special study of the issues of France, 1900-1930, with the price at which they can be obtained from Raoul Lesgor. Holmes, N. Y. [1955] 100p. illus. 23cm. [HE6185.F8L42] 55-59139
1. Postage-stamps—France. I. Title.

Postage-stamps—France—Catalogs.

MINKUS Publications, inc., New York. 383.22944
France. French community stamp catalog. George A. Tlamsa, editor in chief. 1960 ed. New York [1959] 247p. illus. 23cm. [HE6185.F82M5] 60-17817
1. Postage-stamps—France—Catalogs. 2. Postage-stamps—French community—Catalogs. I. Tlamsa, George Adolph Maria, 1915- ed. II. Title.

Postage-stamps—Gt. Brit.—Catalogs.

POSTAGE stamp catalog 383.22942
of British Europe & America. New York, Minkus Publications. v. illus. 23cm. Editor: G. T. Tlamsa. [HE6185.G62P6] 59-44099
1. Postage-stamps—Gt. Brit.—Catalogs. I. Tlamsa, George Adolph Maria, 1915- ed.

Postage-stamps—Gt. Brit.—Colonies.

HAYEK, Margit. 383.22
Adventure with stamps. With photographic illus. of 129 different stamps. New York, Roy Publishers [1956?] 144p. illus. 20cm. [HE6185] 56-8728
1. Postage-stamps—Gt. Brit.—Colonies. 2. Gt. Brit.—Colonies—Hist. I. Title.

SAMUEL, Marcus. 769.569171'241
Specimen stamps of the Crown Colonies, 1857-1948 / [by] Marcus Samuel. London : Royal Philatelic Society, 1976. 255 p. : facsims. ; 23 cm. Bibliography: p. [254]-255. [HE6185.G62S35] 76-382946 ISBN 0-900631-08-2 : £9.50
1. Postage-stamps—Great Britain—Colonies. 2. Cancellations (Philately)—Great Britain—Colonies. I. Title.

Postage stamps — Gt. Brit. — Colonies — America.

TLAMSA, George Adolph Maria, 1915- ed. 383.2297
British America: a complete album for the postage stamps of the British Commonwealth of Nations in America; spaces for every major number variety with numbers from the New world-wide postage stamp catalog. New York, Minkus Publications [c1958- 1 v. (loose-leaf) illus. 30 cm. [HE6185.G63B7] 59-28237
1. Postage stamps — Gt. Brit. — Colonies — America. I. Title.

Postage-stamps—Hawaii.

WESTERBERG, J. F. 769'.569'969
Plating the Hawaiian numerals [by] J. F. Westerberg. [Honolulu, Mission Press, 1968] x, 86 p. illus., facsims. 23 cm. Bibliography: p. 76-77. [HE6185.U53H3] 68-2066
1. Postage-stamps—Hawaii. I. Title.

Postage-stamps—History.

MACKAY, James Alexander. 769'.56'09034
The world of classic stamps; 1840-1870 [by James A. Mackay] New York, Putnam [1972] 334 p. illus. (part col.) 25 cm. Bibliography: p. 323. [HE6182.M23] 72-75945 25.00
1. Postage stamps—History. I. Title.

WILLIAMS, Leon Norman, 1914- 769'.56
Rare stamps [by] L. N. and M. Williams. New York, Putnam [1967] 120 p. illus. (part col.) 22 cm. (Pleasures and treasures) Bibliography: p. [4] [HE6184.R3W5 1967] 67-21988
1. Postage-stamps—History. I. Williams, Maurice, 1905- joint author. II. Title.

Postage-stamps—Ireland—Catalogs.

FELDMAN, David, 1947- 769'.569'415
Handbook of Irish philately. [1st ed. Dublin] D. Feldman, ltd. [1968] 176 p. (p. 174-176 advertisements) illus., facsims. 23 cm. On label inside front cover: Published in the United States by Dufour Editions, Chester Springs, Pa. [HE6185.I62F4] 77-281
1. Postage-stamps—Ireland—Catalogs. I. Title.

Postage-stamps —Israel.

FORSHER, Bruno J. 769'.569'5694
The interim period postage stamps of Israel, March to July 1948; a handbook, by Bruno J. Forsher. Photography by L. I. Erdos. [New York] Society of Israel Philatelists, 1969. iv, 124 p. illus. 26 cm. Cover title. Bibliography: p. 121-124. [HE6185.P14F65] 70-15867
1. Postage-stamps—Israel. I. Society of Israel Philatelists. II. Title.

LEVISON, Milton E. 769'.5694
The plate blocks and tabs of the Doar Ivri issue / Milton E. Levison. [Cleveland : Society of Israel Philatelists, Educational Fund], c1976. 31 p. : ill. ; 26 cm. [HE6185.I65L48] 77-359202
1. Postage-stamps—Israel. I. Society of Israel Philatelists. Educational Fund. II. Title.

RIBALOW, Harold Uriel, 1919- 383.22
The history of Israel's postage stamps. New York, Twayne Publishers [1956] 121p. illus. 23cm. [HE6185.P14R5] 56-4387
1. Postage-stamps —Israel. I. Title.

Postage-stamps — Israel — Catalogs.

WENGER, Kenneth R. 769.56973075
The Wenger Israel postage stamp catalog. 1st ed.: 1956- Belleville, N.J., K.R. Wenger. v. illus. 22 cm. [HE6185.P14W4] 56-45464
1. Postage-stamps — Israel — Catalogs. I. Title.

Postage-stamps—Japan.

WOODWARD, Alphonse Marie Tracey. 769'.56952
The postage stamps of Japan and dependencies / A. M. Tracey Woodward. Lawrence, Mass. : Quarterman Publications, c1976. xliv, 548 p., [123] leaves of plates : ill. ; 27 cm. Includes index. Bibliography: p. 525-528. [HE6185.J32W6 1976] 73-86773 ISBN 0-88000-020-1 : 50.00
1. Postage-stamps—Japan. I. Title. BIP

Postage-stamps—Japan—Albums.

SCOTT Publications, inc., New York. 769.56973075
Specialty album for postage stamps of Japan. Contains spaces for every major variety of postage stamp issued by Japan as listed in Scott's Standard postage stamp catalogue. New York, c1962. 1 v. (loose-leaf) illus. 31 cm. (Its Specialty series) [HE6185.J3S35] 62-45349
1. Postage-stamps—Japan—Albums. I. Title.

Postage-stamps—Juvenile Literature.

DEPREE, Mildred. 769'.56
A child's world of stamps; stories, poems, fun, and facts from many lands. New York, Parents' Magazine Press [1973] 126 p. col. illus. 24 cm. "In cooperation with the U.S. Committee for UNICEF." Postage stamps from around the world help introduce the geogrpahy, way of life, folklore, and poetry of many countries. [HE6217.D45] 72-10178 ISBN 0-8193-0661-4 4.95
1. Postage-stamps—Juvenile literature. I. United States Committee for UNICEF. II. Title.
Library binding 4.59; ISBN 0-8193-0662-2. BIP

GEMMING, Elizabeth. 769'.56
Learning through stamps, by Elizabeth and Klaus Gemming. Barre, Mass., Barre Pub. 1968-69. 3 v. illus., (part col.), map. 25 cm. Contents.Contents.—v. 1. The world of art.—v. 2. Around the world.—v. 3. Portraits of greatness. [HE6217.G38] 68-17069
1. Postage-stamps—Juvenile Literature. I. Gemming, Klaus, joint author. II. Title.

Postage-stamps—Korea.

KOREA Stamp Society. 769'.569'519
Philatelic handbook for Korea, 1884-1905. [Editorial committee: Warren Hahn [and others] Helen K. Zirkle, chairman and editor. New York, Collectors Club [1970] 128 p. illus., map. 23 cm. (Collectors Club handbook no. 23) On spine: Korea. Bibliography: p. 123-128. [HE6185.K7K6] 73-13516
1. Postage-stamps—Korea. I. Zirkle, Helen Kingsbury, ed. II. Title. BIP

Postage-stamps—Liechtenstein—Catalogs.

ZINSMEISTER, Marian Carne. 769'.569436'48
Liechtenstein stamps and their background, 1912-1973 / by Marian Carne Zinsmeister. 1st ed. [Lemont, Pa.] : Society of Philatelic Americans, 1975. 88 p. : ill. ; 23 cm. [HE6185.L52Z56] 75-329629 4.00
1. Postage-stamps—Liechtenstein—Catalogs. I. Title.

Postage-stamps, Local—Catalogs.

ROWCROFT, William. 383.220838
Catalog of local post issues. So. Ozone Pk., N. Y. [1960] 144p. illus. 22cm. [HE6230.R65] 60-24192
1. Postage-stamps, Local—Catalogs. I. Title.

Postage stamps — Manchuria.

ZIRKLE, Helen Kingsbury. 383.229518
The postage stamps and commemorative cancellations of Manchoukuo/Manshukoku, Manchou Tikuo, Manchukuo, by Helen K. Zirkle. [New York, Collectors Club, 1964] 131 p. illus. 23 cm. (Collectors Club handbook no. 16) Bibliography: p. 127-131. [HE6185.M3Z5] 64-5477
1. Postage stamps — Manchuria. 2. Cancellations (Philately) — Manchuria. I. Title.

Postage-stamps—Mexico—History.

CHAPMAN, Samuel, 1859-1943. 769'.56972
The postage stamps of Mexico, 1856-1868 / Samuel Chapman Lawrence, Mass. : Quarterman Publications, c1976. xxi, 376 p. ; 24 cm. "Contains two previously separate works: The postage stamps of Mexico from the commencement in 1856, to the end of the provisional period in 1868, by S. Chapman, originally published under the auspices of the Collectors' Club, New York City, as Handbook number four in 1926 ... and "Additions to 'The postage stamps of Mexico,' a book by S. Chapman," by Roberto Garcia-Larranaga, originally published in the Collectors Club Philatelist, vol. XXXII, no. 2, no. 4, no. 5, no. 6, and vol. XXXIII, no. 1." [HE6185.M5C53 1976] 75-40501 ISBN 0-88000-079-1 : 30.00
1. Postage-stamps—Mexico—History. I. Garcia-Larrananga, Roberto. Additions to The postage stamps of Mexico. 1976. II. Title. BIP

Postage-stamps—Netherlands.

DEKKER, Jan. 769'.56
The postal booklets of Netherlands, Dutch East Indies, Curacao. Written and compiled by Jan Dekker. Chicago, Netherlands Philatelic Society [1969] 33 p. illus. 28 cm. [HE6185.N42D43] 77-10495
1. Postage-stamps—Netherlands. 2. Postage-stamps—Indonesia. 3. Postage-stamps—Curacao. I. Netherlands Philatelic Society. II. Title.

Postage-stamps—New Brunswick.

ARGENTI, Nicholas. 769'.569715
The postage stamps of New Brunswick and Nova Scotia / Nicholas Argenti. Lawrence, Mass. : Quarterman Publications, c1976. 223 p., [17] leaves of plates : ill. ; 29 cm. Includes index. [HE6185.C23N45 1976] 76-19723 ISBN 0-88000-088-0 : 35.00
1. Postage-stamps—New Brunswick. 2. Postage-stamps—Nova Scotia. I. Title. BIP

Postage-stamps—New Hebrides.

HALS, Nathan. 769'.569'934
The New Hebrides; their postal history and postage stamps [by] Nathan Hals [and] Phil Collas. [New York? c1967] viii, 176 p. illus., facsims. 22 cm. (Collectors Club handbook 20) Bibliography: p. 175-176. [HE6185.G63N3] 68-2635
1. Postage-stamps—New Hebrides. 2. Postal service—New Hebrides—History. I. Collas, Phil, joint author. II. Title.

Postage-stamps—Newfoundland.

BOGGS, Winthrop Smillie, 1902- 769'.569718
The postage stamps and postal history of Newfoundland / Winthrop S. Boggs, with Postage stamps of Newfoundland / Bertram W. H. Poole, Harry E. Huber. Lawrence, Mass. : Quarterman Publications, c1975. 186, 65 p. : ill. ; 24 cm. Reprint of 2 works, the 1st originally published in 1942 by Chambers Pub. Co., Kalamazoo, Mich., in series: Chambers handbook series; and the 2d originally published in 1922 by Severn-Wylie-Jewett Co., Portland, Me.; with new foreword. Includes index. Bibliography: p. 179-180. [HE6185.C23N473] 75-1791 ISBN 0-88000-066-X : 20.00
1. Postage-stamps—Newfoundland. 2. Postal service—Newfoundland. I. Huber, Harry E. II. Poole, Bertram W. H. Postage stamps of Newfoundland. 1975. III. Title. IV. Title: Postage stamps of Newfoundland. BIP

Postage-stamps—Palestine.

LEWIS, Nahum H. 769'.569'5694
Specimen issues of mandate Palestine, 1918-1948, by Nahum H. Lewis and Fabius Schmerler. Loudonville? N.Y. [1967] 31, [23] p. illus. 28 cm. Bibliographical footnotes. [HE6185.P13L48] 68-945
1. Postage-stamps—Palestine. I. Schmerler, Fabius, joint author. II. Title.

Postage-stamps—Poland—History.

POLISH Philatelic Society of Australia. 769'.563'09438
Millennium Poloniae commemorative album. Album pamiatkowy, 966-1966. [Melbourne, 1966] [54] p. illus., facsims. 23 cm. Articles in English or Polish. Edition limited to 320 copies. [HE6185.P62P63] 74-384718 unpriced
1. Postage-stamps—Poland—History. 2. Water-marks. I. Title.

Postage-stamps—Portugal—Catalogs.

PORTUGAL, Spain, 383.22946
colonies stamp catalog. New York, Minkus Publications. v. illus. 23cm. Editor: 19 G. A. Tlamsa. [HE6185.P7P6] 60-29634
1. Postage-stamps—Portugal—Catalogs. 2. Postage- stamps— Spain—Catalogs. I. Tlamsa, George Adolph Maria, 1915- ed. II. Minkus Publications, inc., New York.

Postage-stamps—Scotland.

HILL, Cuthbert William. 383'.49'41
Scotland in stamps: a guide to the postal history, postage stamps and postmarks of Scotland [by] C. W. Hill. Aberdeen, Impulse Books, 1972. ix, 147, [10] p. illus., facsims. 23 cm. [HE6185.G63S354] 72-192892 ISBN 0-901311-14-6 £2.25
1. Postage-stamps—Scotland. 2. Postal service—Scotland. I. Title.

Postage stamps—Spanish-America—Catalogs.

LATIN America stamp 383.2298
catalog. 1960- ed. New York, Minkus Publications. v. facsims. 23cm. Editor: 1960- GA. Tlamsa. [HE6224.L3] 60-378
1. Postage stamps—Spanish-America—Catalogs. I. Tlamsa, George Adolph Maria, 1915- ed.

Postage-stamps—Switzerland—History.

MIRABAUD, Paul. 769'.569494
The postage stamps of Switzerland, 1843-1862 / Paul Mirabaud and Alex de Reuterskiold. Lawrence, Mass. : Quarterman Publications, c1975. xi, 266 p., [8] leaves of plates : ill. ; 27 cm. Translation of Les timbres-poste suisses, 1843-1862. Reprint of the 1899 ed. published by Librairies-imprimeries reunies, Paris. Includes index. Bibliography: p. [241]-259. [HE6185.S9M613 1975] 74-81948 ISBN 0-88000-050-3 : 35.00
1. Postage-stamps—Switzerland—History. I. Reuterskiold, A. de, joint author. II. Title. BIP

Postage-stamps—Tibet.

HAVERBECK, H D S 383.22
The postage stamps and postal history of Tibet. New York, Collectors Club, c1952. 52p. illus., maps. 26cm. Cover title. Reprinted from the Collectors Club philatelist, v. 31, no. 2-4, Mar.--July 1952. [HE6185.T5H3] 53-16413
1. Postage-stamps—Tibet. 2. Postal service—Tibet. I. Title.

HAVERBECK, Harrison Donald Seaman. 383.229515
The postage stamps and postal history of Tibet. [New enl. and completely rev. ed.] New York, Collectors Club, c1958. 80 p. illus. 26 cm. [HE6185.T5H3 1958] 59-22968
1. Postage-stamps — Tibet. 2. Postal service — Tibet. I. Title.

HAVERBECK, Harrison Donald Seaman. 383.22
The postage stamps and postal history of Tibet. New York Collectors Club, c1952. 52 p. illus., maps. 26 cm. Cover title. Reprinted from the Collectors Club philatelist, v. 31, no. 2-4, Mar.-July 1952. [HE6185.T5H3] 53-16413
1. Postage-stamps — Tibet. 2. Postal service — Tibet. I. Title.

Postage-stamps—Topics—Apollo 11 (Spacecraft)

KITCHEN, R. F., 1930- 769'.563
First men on the moon : handbook of stamps / R. F. Kitchen. 1st ed. New York : Vantage Press, c1976. 139 p. : ill. ; 21 cm. Includes bibliographical references. [HE6183.A64K57] 76-374880 ISBN 0-533-01957-5 : 5.95
1. Postage-stamps—Topics—Apollo 11 (Spacecraft) I. Title.

Postage-stamps—Topics—Art.

FARNESE, Drew. 769'.56
Art and paintings on stamps. [1968 ed. Orlando, Fla., United Philatelic International, c1967] 144 p. illus. (part col.) 22 cm. [HE6230.F3] 68-4790
1. Postage-stamps—Topics—Art. I. Title.

ZIEGLER, Kay, ed. 383.22
Checklist of artists. [Muskogee, Okla.] Fine arts philatelist [1957- v. illus. 28 cm. (v. 2: 23 cm.) [HE6230.Z47] 58-17028
1. Postage-stamps—Topics—Art. I. Fine arts philatelist. II. Title.

Postage-stamps—Topics—Astronautics.

KELEN, Emery, 1896- 769'.564
Stamps tell the story of space travel. [1st ed.] Nashville, T. Nelson [1972] 143 p. illus. 24 cm. [HE6183.A8K44] 74-181677 ISBN 0-8407-6212-7
1. Postage-stamps—Topics—Astronautics. I. Title.

Postage-stamps—Topics—Atomic energy.

ANGELO, Joseph A. 769'.564
Stamps tell the story of nuclear energy / by Joseph A. Angelo, Jr. [Washington : U.S. Energy Research and Development Administration, Office of Public Affairs, 1975] 100 p. : ill. ; 22 cm. Cover title. Bibliography: p. 75-77. [HE6183.A85A5] 73-600332
1. Postage-stamps—Topics—Atomic energy. I. Title.

Postage-stamps—Topics—Bible.

MATEK, Ord. 769'.564
The Bible through stamps. New York, Ktav Pub. House [1974] 230 p. illus. 24 cm. Bibliography: p. 220-222. [HE6183.B5M37] 73-23126 ISBN 0-87068-397-7
1. Postage-stamps—Topics—Bible. I. Title. BIP

Postage-stamps—Topics—Birds.

STANLEY, Willard Francis, 1901- 769.56'08 s
Birds of the world on stamps, by Willard F. Stanley, Beverly S. Ridgely [and] Gustavs E. Eglajs. [Milwaukee] American Topical Association [1974] 101 p. illus. 23 cm. (American Topical Association. Handbook no. 82) Cover title. Revision of the 1954 ed. by Sidney R. Esten. [HE6187.A635 no. 82] [HE6183.B53] 769'.564 74-165206 6.00
1. Postage-stamps—Topics—Birds. I. Ridgely, Beverly S., joint author. II. Eglajs, Gustavs E., joint author. III. Esten, Sidney, R. Birds of the world on stamps. IV. Title. V. Series: American Topical Association. Topical handbook no. 82.

Postage-stamps—Topics—Boy Scouts.

THORSEN, Harry D., 1913- 769'.563
Scouts on stamps of the world [by] Harry D. Thorsen, Jr. [and] W. Arthur McKinney. [Hicksville, N.Y.] Scouts on Stamps Society International [1968] 60 p. illus. 24 cm. Cover title. [HE6183.T5 1968] 68-5394 2.00
1. Postage-stamps—Topics—Boy Scouts. I. McKinney, W. Arthur, joint author. II. Title.

Postage-stamps—Topics—Catholica.

WEBER, Francis J. 769'.564
Catholica on American stamps / Francis J. Weber. Tilton, N.H. : Hillside Press, 1976, c1975. [103] p. ; 61 mm. "Spaces have been provided for affixing the appropriate stamps." Copernicus stamp affixed as frontispiece and on p. [101] of L.C. copy. "250 numbered copies." No. 16. [HE6183.C34W4 1976] 75-10167
1. Postage-stamps—Topics—Catholica. 2. Postage-stamps—United States. I. Title.

Postage-stamps — Topics — Christianity.

MUELLER, Barbara R 383.224
Postage stamps and Christianity. Saint Louis, Concordia Pub. House [1964] ix, 83 p. 15 plates. 24 cm. Bibliography: p. 82-83. [HE6183.M8] 64-16982
1. Postage-stamps — Topics — Christianity. 2. Postage-stamps — Collectors and collecting. I. Title.

Postage-stamps—Topics—Crowns.

PERNES, Rufino R. 769'.569171'2469
Crown stamps of the Portuguese colonies / by Rufino R. Pernes. Crete, Neb. : J-B Pub. Co., 1976. 35 p. : ill. ; 23 cm. Bibliography: p. 35. [HE6183.C68P47] 75-36294 ISBN 0-916170-01-2 pbk. : 6.00
1. Postage-stamps—Topics—Crowns. 2. Postage-stamps—Portugal—Colonies. I. Title.

Postage-stamps—Topics—Fishes.

LOWER vertebrates : 769'.564
fishes, amphibia and reptiles on stamps of the world / by George A. Bearse ... [et al.] . [Milwaukee] : American Topical Association, c1977. 119 p. : ill. ; 23 cm. (Handbook - American Topical Association ; no. 91) Cover title. Page 119 is p. [3] of

cover. Includes indexes. [HE6187.A635 no. 91] [HE6183.F54] 77-150421 8.00
1. Postage-stamps—Topics—Fishes. 2. Postage-stamps—Topics—Amphibians. 3. Postage-stamps—Topics—Reptiles. 1. Bearse, George A. II. Title: Fishes, amphibia and reptiles on stamps of the world. III. Series: American Topical Association. Handbook ; no. 91.

Postage-stamps — Topics — Freemasons.

DOMINGUE, Robert A comp. 769.564
Freemasonry in philately, compiled by Robert A. Domingue. [Andover Mass., 1966] 138.1 illus. 28 cm. Bibliography: leaf 138. [HE6183.D59] 66-5907
1. Postage-stamps — Topics — Freemasons. 2. Freemasons — Biog. I. Title.

LUCY, Gregory Ramsey, 383.224
1912-
An album for stamps that honor Freemasons of many nations, by Gregory R. Lucy. St. Louis, S. Wilson, 1964. 173 p. illus. 28 cm. [HE6183.L75] 64-6192
1. Postage-stamps — Topics — Freemasons. 2. Freemasons — Biog. I. Title.

Postage-stamps—Topics—History.

SONSKY, Aaron. 769.563
History of the United States : illustrated by postage stamps / Aaron Sonsky. Bicentennial ed. New York : Benchmark Products, c1975. [95] p. : ill. ; 27 cm. [HE6185.U5S65] 76-355189
1. Postage-stamps—Topics—History. 2. Postage-stamps—United States. 3. United States—History. I. Title.

WILLIAMSON, Omega. 769.563
American history through United States stamps : a philatelic education program / by Omega Williamson. [Tucson, Ariz.] : Western Postal History Museum, c1975. 179 p. in various pagings : ill. ; 28 cm. Includes index. [HE6185.U5W54] 75-326532
1. Postage-stamps—Topics—History. 2. United States—History. I. Western Postal History Museum. II. Title.

Postage-stamps—Topics—Jews.

ABER, Ita H. 769.563
International Judaica philatelic handbook. Edited by Ita Aber. Associate editor: Marvin Siegel. Riverdale, N.Y., S.A.R. Academy, Harry Aber Memorial Library Fund [1973] 1 v. (unpaged) 22 cm. [HE6183.J4A2] 73-83988
1. Postage-stamps—Topics—Jews. I. Siegel, Marvin, joint author. II. Title.

LINDENBAUM, Arieh. 769.563
Great Jews in stamps. New York, Sabra Books [1970] 67 p. illus. (part col.) 22 cm. [HE6183.J4L45] 79-124119 4.50
1. Postage-stamps—Topics—Jews. I. Title.

RICHTER, John Henry, 769.563
1919-
Judaica on postage stamps; an annotated checklist of stamps issued through December 31, 1972. Compiled with the generous advice and assistance of Irvin Girer and Ellen Shoshany Kaim. Ann Arbor, Mich. [May be ordered from I. Girer, Southfield, Mich.] 1974. 181 p. illus. 27 cm. (Judaica Historical Philatelic Society. Monograph, no. 2) [HE6183.J4R5] 74-182342 10.00
1. Postage-stamps—Topics—Jews. I. Title. II. Series: Judaica Historical Philatelic Society. Monograph — Judaica Historical Philatelic Society, no. 2.

Postage-stamps — Topics — Kennedy, John Fitzgerald, Pres., U.S., 1917-1963.

AYAL Publications, New 383.22
York.
Postage stamps honoring John Fitzgerald Kennedy, 35th President of the United States of America, and related issues. New York [1964- 1 v. (loose-leaf) illus. 30 cm. [HE6221.A83] 65-6337
1. Postage-stamps — Topics — Kennedy,

John Fitzgerald, Pres., U.S., 1917-1963. I. Title.

KELEN, Emery, 1896- 769
Stamps tell the story of John F. Kennedy. New York, Meredith Press [1968] 122 p. illus., ports. 24 cm. Bibliography: p. 120. The life of the thirty-fifth President of the United States, as commemorated in stamps issued in countries around the world. Includes description of the stamps. [HE6183.K44] AC 68
1. Kennedy, John Fitzgerald, Pres. U.S., 1917-1963. 2. Postage stamps—Topics—Kennedy, John Fitzgerald, Pres. U.S. 1917-1963. I. Title.

WENGER, Kenneth R. 769.563
John F. Kennedy memorial stamp issues of the world, edited by Kenneth R. Wenger. [Fort Lee, N.J., 1970] 189 p. illus. 21 cm. "A visual reference catalog with current market prices." [HE6183.K4W45] 79-15856 3.95
1. Postage-stamps—Topics—Kennedy, John Fitzgerald, Pres. U.S., 1917-1963. I. Title.

Postage-stamps—Topics—Lincoln, Abraham, Pres. U.S., 1809-1865.

FRAENKEL, Alexander, 1908- 383.22
ed.
Postage stamps commemorating the sesquicentennial of the birth of Abraham Lincoln and other commemorative issues of the world honoring the great President. New York, Ayal Publications, c1960. unpaged. illus. 29 cm. [HE6183.F684] 63-33356
1. Postage-stamps — Topics — Lincoln, Abraham, Pres. U.S., 1809-1885. I. Title.

THE Lincoln heritage 973.7'0924
trail. [Chicago, Keepsake Press, 1967?] [39] album l. 28 cm. Caption title. Leaf [1] with text; leaves [2]-[19] each with 2 mounted post cards, postage stamps affixed, some commemorative, cancelled on Lincoln's birthday, Feb. 12, 1967. One card was cancelled in each of 36 places associated with him in Kentucky, Indiana, and Illinois. The post cards have illustrative text and an outline drawing of the particular state. Leaves [20]-[39] blank for additions. [E457.6.L74] 71-223605 27.50
1. Lincoln, Abraham, Pres. U.S., 1809-1865—Monuments, etc. 2. Postage-stamps—Topics—Lincoln, Abraham, Pres. U.S., 1809-1865. 3. Postal cards—United States.

Postage-stamps—Topics—Lindbergh, Charles Augustus, 1902-

CARDINAL Spellman 769.563
Philatelic Museum, Weston, Mass.
Catalog of the Charles A. Lindbergh Collection. Compiled and edited by Sister M. Fidelma, executive director and curator, and Walter Curley, librarian. Weston, Mass., 1968. iv, 36, [39] l. illus., ports. 29 cm. [HE6183.L57C3] 72-196627
1. Postage-stamps—Topics—Lindbergh, Charles Augustus, 1902- I. Fielma, Sister, ed. II. Curley, Walter, ed. III. Title.

Postage-stamps—Topics—Maps.

KLINEFELTER, Walter, 769.564
1899-
A fourth display of old maps and plans : studies in postal cartography / by Walter Klinefelter. La Crosse [Wis.] : Sumac Press, 1978. 65 p. : ill. ; 24 cm. Includes bibliographical references. [HE6183.M3K49] 77-94176 ISBN 0-911462-11-2 : 6.00
1. Postage-stamps—Topics—Maps. I. Title.
BIP

KLINEFELTER, Walter, 769.564
1899-
A further display of old maps & plans. La Crosse, Wis., Sumac Press, 1969. [70] p. 23 cm. "300 copies printed." Includes

bibliographical references. [HE6183.M3K5] 78-20756
1. Postage-stamps—Topics—Maps. I. Title.

KLINEFELTER, Walter, 1899- 383.22
A small display of old maps and plans. Iowa City] Prairie Press [c 1962] 80 p.illus.17 cm. [HE6183.K55] 62-20625
1. Postage-stamps—Topics—Maps. I. Title.

KLINEFELTER, Walter, 769.564
1899-
A third display of old maps and plans; studies in postal cartography. La Crosse [Wis.] Sumac Press, 1973. 77 p. illus. 23 cm. "300 copies." Includes bibliographical references. [HE6183.M3K53] 73-86565 ISBN 0-911462-10-4 5.00
1. Postage-stamps—Topics—Maps. I. Title.
BIP

Postage stamps — Topics — Medical botany.

COCHRAN, Emory Ellsworth. 383.224
Philatelic therapy, by Emory E. Cochran. 1st ed. Federalsburg, Md., Printed by J. W. Stowell Print Co. [1964] 102 p. illus. 26 cm. Bibliography: p. 96-97. [HE6183.C54] 65-1225
1. Postage-stamps — Topics — Medical botany. I. Title.

GRIFFENHAGEN, George B. 769.564
Drugs and pharmacy on stamps, by George Griffenhagen. Milwaukee, American Topical Association [1967] 95 p. illus. 24 cm. (ATA medical handbook series, v. 2) (ATA topical handbook 55.) Cover title. Bibliography: p. 86-93. [HE6183.G73] 78-2664 5.00
1. Postage-stamps—Topics—Medical botany. I. Title. II. Series: American Topical Association. ATA medical handbook series, v. 2. III. Series: American Topical Association. Topical handbook 55

Postage-stamps—Topics—Medicine.

KYLE, Robert A., 1928- 769.564
comp.
Medicine and stamps. Edited by R. A. Kyle and M. A. Shampo. [Chicago, American Medical Association, 1970] xi, 216 p. illus. (part col.) 23 cm. "This edition is a compilation with revisions and additions of articles on stamps and medicine appearing in the Journal of the American Medical Association during 1961 to 1969, plus new articles specially prepared for this volume." [HE6183.M42K9] 70-112916 1.00
1. Postage-stamps—Topics—Medicine. I. Shampo, Marc A., joint comp. II. Title.

NEWERLA, Gerhard J., 769.564
1906-
Medical history in philately and numismatics, by Gerhard J. Newerla. [2d ed. Waltham, Mass., 1971] v, 473 p. 22 cm. Bibliography: p. 462-473. [HE6183.M42N4 1971] 79-169791
1. Postage-stamps—Topics—Medicine. 2. Numismatics—Collectors and collecting. I. Title.

Postage-stamps—Topics—Medicine—History.

NEWERLA, Gerhard J., 769.564
1906-
Medical history in philately [by] Gerhard J. Newerla. Milwaukee, American Topical Association [1964] 143 p. illus. 24 cm. (ATA topical handbook 39) Cover title. Bibliography: p. 137-141. 64-15875
1. Postage-stamps—Topics—Medicine—History. I. Title. II. Series. III. Series: American Topical Association. Topical handbook 39.

Postage stamps — Topics — Music.

WATSON, James, 1916- 383.224
Stamps and music. London, Faber and Faber [c1962] 160 p. illus., ports. 21 cm. Label mounted on t.p.: Transatlantic Arts, Hollywood-by-the-Sea, Fla. [HE6183.W344] 63-187
1. Postage stamps — Topics — Music. I. Title.

Postage-stamps—Topics—Physicians.

GOTTFRIED, Oscar, 1894- 383.22
Doctors philatelic. [1st ed.] New York, American Physician [1st ed. Illus. 22cm. Bibliography: p. 96. [HE6183.G58] 55-24937
1. Postage-stamps—Topics—Physicians. I. Title.

Postage-stamps — Topics — Portraits.

STILES, Kent B 383.22
Postal saints and sinners; who's who on stamps, by Kent B. Stiles. Brooklyn, T. Gaus' Sons, 1964. ix, 295 p. 23 cm. [HE6215.S7] 64-7712
1. Postage-stamps — Topics — Portraits. 2. Postage-stamps — Collectors and collecting. I. Title.

Postage-stamps—Topics—Rockets (Aeronautics)

ELLINGTON, Jesse T 769.564
Rocket mail catalog, 1904-1967. International unabridged. Co-editors: Jesse T. Ellington [and] Perry F. Zwisler. [New York? 1967] 245 p. illus. 24 cm. [HE6230.E53] 68-2887
1. Postage-stamps—Topics—Rockets (Aeronautics) I. Zwisler, Perry F., joint author. II. Title.

Postage-stamps — Topics — Roosevelt, Eleanor (Roosevelt) 1884-1962.

AYAL Publications, New 383.22
York.
Postage stamps: a tribute to Eleanor Roosevelt. The official album authorized by the Eleanor Roosevelt Memorial Foundation. New York [1964- 1 v. (loose-leaf) illus. 30 cm. [HE6221.A8] 65-4528
1. Postage-stamps — Topics — Roosevelt, Eleanor (Roosevelt) 1884-1962. I. Title.

Postage-stamps—Topics—Science.

TRUMAN, Roger W. 769.564'08 s
Science stamps / by R. W. Truman. Milwaukee, Wis. : American Topical Association, 1975. 118 p. : ill. ; 23 cm. (Handbook - American Topical Association ; no. 87) Cover title. Includes index. Bibliography: p. 118. [HE6187.A635 no. 87] [HE6183.S36] 769'.564 76-353347 7.00
1. Postage-stamps—Topics—Science. I. Title. II. Series: American Topical Association. Handbook — American Topical Association ; no. 87.

Postage-stamps—Topics—Ships.

AMERICAN Topical 769.56'08 s
Association. Ships on Stamps Unit.
Watercraft on stamps [by the] Ships on Stamps Unit. Kathy Herd, editor. Milwaukee, American Topical Association [1973] 82 p. illus. 24 cm. (ATA handbook no. 80) Cover title. [HE6187.A635 no. 80] [HE6183.S5] 769'.564 73-174244 5.00
1. Postage-stamps—Topics—Ships. I. Herd, Kathy, ed. II. Title. III. Series: American Topical Association. Topical handbook no. 80.
Publisher's address: 3306 North 50th Street, Milwaukee, Wis. 53216.

Postage-stamps—Topics—Sports.

BRUCE, Robert M. 769'.564'075 s
Checklist of sports & recreation, by Robert M. Bruce. [Rev. ed. Milwaukee, American Topical Association, 1973] 45 p. illus. 23 cm. (American Topical Association. Handbook no. 83) Cover title. "ATA LM no. 300." [HE6187.A635 no. 83] [HE6183.S6] 769'.564 75-332794 4.00
1. Postage-stamps—Topics—Sports. I. Title. II. Series.

ENHAGEN, Carl Olof. 383.224
Sports stamps. New York, Arco Pub. Co. [1961] 275 p. illus. 22 cm. (Arco hobby library) [HE6183.E58] 62-13446
1. Postage-stamps — Topics — Sports. I. Title.

Postage-stamps —Topics—Telecommunication—Catalogs.

ROSEN, Herbert. 383.2
Radio-philatelia. New York, Audio Master Corp. [c1956] unpaged. illus. 23cm. [HE6230.R6] 56-7689
1. Postage-stamps —Topics—Telecommunication—Catalogs. I. Title.

Postage-stamps—U. S.

AMERICAN Philatelic Society. 383.22
The perforation centennial, 1957-1957. the first perforated United States-stamp, 1c, 3c, 5c, 10c, 12c, 24 30c, 90c. 1937-1860. Sponsored by the 3c 1851-1857 Unit of the American Philatelic Society. July 4-6. 1957. National Philatelic Museum. Philadelphia. Philadelphia? c1957. 232p. illus. 23cm. [HE6185.U3A62] 57-4447
1. Postage-stamps—U. S. 2. Philadelphia, National Philatelic Museum. I. Title.

BLOOMGARDEN, Henry S. 769'.563'0973
American history through commemorative stamps [by] Henry S. Bloomgarden. New York, Arco Pub. Co. [1969] 141 p. facsims. 29 cm. [HE6185.U6B55] 69-17544 5.95
1. Postage-stamps—U.S. 2. U.S.—History. I. Title.

BRAZER, Clarence Wilson, 1880-1956. 769'.56973
Essays for U.S. adhesive postage stamps / Clarence W. Brazer Lawrence, Mass. : Quarterman Publications, [1977] xvi, 295 p. : ill. ; 24 cm. Reprint of the 1941 ed. published by the Handbook Committee, American Philatelic Society, Chicago, to which have been added selected addenda and a primer on essays and proofs written by C. Brazer for the first American Philatelic Congress book. Includes indexes. [HE6185.U5B69 1977] 75-40503 ISBN 0-88000-081-3 : 25.00
1. Postage-stamps—United States. I. Title.
BIP

BROOKMAN, Lester George. 769.56973
The United States postage stamps of the 19th century, by Lester G. Brookman. New York, H. L. Lindquist Publications, 1966- v. illus., facsims. 26 cm. [HE6185.U5B752] 67-747
1. Postage stamps—United States. I. Title.

COLE, Maurice F. 383.22
The Black Jacks of 1863-1867 Black Jacks of eighteen sixty-three--eighteen sixty-seven Kalamazoo, Chambers Pub. Co., 1950. 121 p. illus., port. 23 cm. (Chambers handbook series) [HE6185.U5C6] 50-23584
1. Postage-stamps—U. S. I. Title.

GLASS, Sol, 1893- 383.22
United States postage stamps, 1945-1952. West Somerville, Mass., Bureau Issues Association [1954] vii, 280p. illus., ports. 25cm. 'Series of articles ... first published in 'The Bureau specialist' ... from 1945 to 1952.' [HE6185.U6G6] 54-21974
1. Postage stamps—U. S. I. Title. II. Title: Foreword by R. A. Bryant.

HESSEN, Beatrice. 769'.563
The American Revolution stamp album. New York, Minkus Publications [1972- 1 v. (loose-leaf) illus. 30 cm. [HE6185.U6H45] 72-90931
1. Postage-stamps—United States. 2. United States—History—Revolution, 1775-1783. I. Title.

JOHL, Max G. 769'.56973
United States postage stamps, 1902-1935 : regular issues, parcel post, airmails / Max G. Johl Lawrence, Mass. : Quarterman Publications, c1976. xxii, 566 p. : ill. ; 24 cm. Contains chapters originally published in v. 1 (rev.) and v. 3 of The United States postage stamps of the twentieth century, by B. S. King and M. G. Johl. Includes indexes. [HE6185.U5J63] 75-18276 ISBN 0-88000-069-4 : 35.00
1. Postage-stamps—United States. I. King, Beverly S., d. 1935. The United States postage stamps of the twentieth century. II. Title.
BIP

NEINKEN, Mortimer L 1896- 383.22973
United States: the 1851-57 twelve cent stamp, by Mortimer L. Neinken, Foreword by Henry M. Goodkind. New York, Collectors Club, 1964. iv, 74 p. illus. 25 cm. (Collectors Club handbook, 17) [HE6185.U5N38] 64-55813
1. Postage-stamps — U.S. I. Title.

NEINKEN, Mortimer L 1896- 383.22973
The United States in cent stamps of 1855-1859; the plate reconstruction,some postal history,and postal makings of the stamps. [New York, Collectors Club, 1960] 252p. illus. 27cm. 'With special chapters reprinted from The United States ten cent stamp of 1855-1857 and The United States one cent stamp of 1851-1857 by Stanley B. Ashbrook.' [HE6185.U5N37] 60-51893
1. Postage-stamps—U. S. I. Title.

NEINKEN, Mortimer L., 1896- 769'.56973
The United States one cent stamp of 1851 to 1861 [by] Mortimer L. Neinken. [New York] U.S. Philatelic Classics Society [1972] xix, 552 p. illus. 27 cm. "Revision of volume 1 of Stanley B. Ashbrook's 'The United States one cent stamp of 1851-1857' with comments on the 1875 reprint plate and on demonetization." [HE6185.U6N4] 72-192871
1. Postage-stamps—United States. I. Ashbrook, Stanley B. The United States one cent stamp of 1851-1857. II. Title.

THORP, Prescott Holden. 769'.569'73
Catalogue of the 20th century stamped envelopes and wrappers of the United States, including an appendix listing price revisions of all 19th century entries as listed in Thorp-Bartels, Century edition. Compiled, completely rev. and edited by Prescott Holden Thorp. Editorial board: Richard C. Dahlem [and others]. 1st ed. Netcong, N.J. [1968] 205 p. illus., ports. 24 cm. [HE6185.U6T46] 68-2697
1. Postage-stamps—United States. 2. Stamped envelopes. I. Bartels, John Murray, 1871-1944. Thorp-Bartels Catalogue of the stamped envelopes and wrappers of the United States. II. Title.

UNITED States. Congress. House. Committee on the Judiciary. Subcommittee No. 1. 769'.56
Reproduction of color stamps. Hearing, Ninetieth Congress, second session, on H.R. 2622 ... March 13, 1968. Washington, U.S. Govt. Print. Off., 1968. iii, 15 p. 24 cm. "Serial no. 13." [KF27.J8666 1968j] 68-60944
1. Postage-stamps—United States. I. Title.

WILLARD, Edward L. 769'.569'0973
The United States two cent red brown of 1883-1887, by Edward L. Willard. New York, H. L. Lindquist Publications, 1970. 2 v. illus. 27 cm. [HE6185.U6W54] 70-15840
1. Postage-stamps—U.S. 2. Cancellations (Philately)—U.S. I. Title.

Postage-stamps—U. S.—Albums.

THE All American stamp album; 383.22973 a fully illustrated album for the postage stamps of the United States and the United Nations. New York, Minkus publications. v. illus. 30cm. annual. Began publication with the 1951 edition. Subtitle varies slightly. Editor: B. Blumenthal. [HE6185.U5A58] 57-19958
1. Postage-stamps—U. S.—Albums. I. Blumenthal, Ben, ed.

BLUMENTHAL, Ben, ed. 383.22
United States stamp album; a fully illustrated album for the postage stamps of the United States with stories of the men, women and places that have made America's history. The catalog numbers in this album are from the New American stamp catalog. New York, Minkus Publications; distributed by Grosset & Dunlap [1962- 96p. illus. 28cm. (A A Minkus stamp album) Kept up to date by yearly supplements. [HE6185.U5B55] 62-52262
1. Postage-stamps—U. S.—Albums. I. Minkus Publications, inc, New York. II. Title.

LUCY, Gregory Ramsey, 1912- 769.56973075
Freemasonry in the making of a nation; an historical stamp album. St. Louis, S. Wilson, 1963. 66 l. illus. 28 cm. [HE6185.U6L8] 63-46727
1. Postage-stamps — U.S. — Albums. 2. Postage-stamps — Topics — Freemasons. 3. Postage-stamps — Topics — Portraits. 4. Postage-stamps — Topics — History. 5. U.S. — Hist. I. Title.

Postage-stamps—U. S.—Catalogs.

DATZ, Stephen R. 769'.56973
Datz philatelic index of United States postage stamps / by Stephen R. Datz. 1976 ed. [Denver] : Matchless Pub. Co., 1976, c1975. 75 leaves ; 29 cm. [HE6185.U6D37 1976] 76-358503 ISBN 0-88219-011-3 : 17.50
1. Postage-stamps—United States—Catalogs. I. Title. II. Title: Philatelic index of United States postage stamps.

DATZ, Stephen R. 769'.56973
Datz philatelic index of United States postage stamps, by Stephen R. Datz. 1973 ed. Denver, Colo., Matchless Pub. Co. [1973] 75 l. 29 cm. [HE6185.U6D37 1973] 73-175532 ISBN 0-88219-009-1 12.50
1. Postage-stamps—United States—Catalogs. I. Title. II. Title: Philatelic index of United States postage stamps.

FREED, Lilly B. 769'.56
Scott's know your United States stamps; a guide to the identification of major and minor varieties of U.S. postage stamps as listed in Scott's Standard postage stamp catalogues, compiled and edited by Lilly B. Freed. [New York, Scott Publications, 1969] 94 p. illus. 26 cm. Includes bibliographies. [HE6185.U6F68] 77-78301 2.50
1. Postage-stamps—U.S.—Catalogs. I. Scott Publications, inc., New York. II. Title. III. Title: Know your United States stamps.

HARRIS (H. E.) and Company, Boston. 769'.569'7
Stamps of the United States, United Nations and British North America; plus: Confederate States, U.S. possessions, Americana; albums and accessories. Comprehensive U.S. stamp identifier. Boston, 1971. 192 p. (p. 168-192 advertisements) illus. 21 cm. First published in 1943 under title: United States stamps, U.S. possessions, and British North America. [HE6185.U5H35 1971] 70-23607 1.00
1. United Nations—Postal service. 2. Postage-stamps—U.S.—Catalogs. 3. Postage-stamps—Canada—Catalogs. I. Title.

HARRIS (H. E.) and Company, Boston. 769'.56973
Stamps of the United States, United Nations, and Canada and provinces ... Boston, 1974. 216 p. illus. 21 cm. [HE6185.U5H35 1974] 74-165246 1.00
1. United Nations—Postal service. 2. Postage-stamps—United States—Catalogs. 3. Postage-stamps—Canada—Catalogs. I. Title.

HARRIS (H. E.) and Company, Boston 769'.569'7
Stamps of the United States, U.S. possessions, United Nations, and British North America. New ed. Boston [1967] 192p. (p. [159]-192 advertisements) illus. 21cm. First pub. in 1943 under title: United States stamps, U.S. possessions, and British North America. [HE6185.U5H35 1967] 67-5713 1.00 pap.,
1. Postage-stamps—U.S.—Catalogs. 2. Postage-stamps—Canada—Catalogs. I. Title.

THE New American stamp catalog. 383.22 [1st]-ed.; 1954- New York, Minkus Publications. v. illus., facsims. 24cm. Editors: 1954, L. G. Brookman.--1956- G. A. Tiamsa. [HE6185.U5N4] 55-13741
1. Postage-stamps—U. S.—Catalogs. I. Brookman, Lester George, ed. II. Tlamsa, George Adolph Maria, 1915- ed.

SCOTT Publications, inc., New York. 383.22
Scott's dollar United States stamp catalogue, 1954; containing the United States section of Scott's 1954 standard postage stamp catalogue, and including Canal Zone, Guam, Hawaii, United Nations, and the U. S. and Spanish administration issues of Cuba, Philippines, and Porto Rico. Edited by Gordon R. Harmer. New York [1953] 123p. illus. 24cm. [HE6185.U5S32 1954] 54-438
1. Postage-stamps—U. S.—Catalogs. I. Harmer, Gordon R., 1906- ed. II. Title.

Postage-stamps—United States—Catalogs—Juvenile literature.

SCOTT Publishing Co. 769'.564'0973
United States stamps & stories. Editor: Elena Marzulla. Stamp quotations from the 1974 Scott catalog. [New York] Published for the United States Postal Service by Scott Pub. Co. [1973] 233 p. col. illus. 18 cm. Describes briefly events in United States history and the stamps that commemorate them. [HE6185.U6S29 1973] 73-85832 2.00
1. Postage-stamps—United States—Catalogs—Juvenile literature. I. Marzulla, Elena, ed. II. United States Postal Service. III. Title.

SCOTT Publishing Co. 769'.564'0973
United States stamps & stories. Illustrated stories of important people, places, and events. With a catalogue of all postage stamps of the U.S. and the United Nations. Editor: Elena Marzulla. [1st ed.] Edited and published for the United States Postal Service by Scott Pub. Co. New York [1972] 224 p. col. illus. 18 cm. Describes briefly events in United States history and the stamps that commemorate them. [HE6185.U6S29 1972] 72-80188
1. Postage-stamps—United States—Catalogs—Juvenile literature. I. Marzulla, Elena, ed. II. United States Postal Service. III. Title.

Postage-stamps—United States—History.

COLLECTORS Institute. 769'.56973
Pictorial treasury of U.S. stamps / edited and published by Collectors Institute, ltd. ; editor, Elena Marzulla ; art director, Max E. Watson, art production, Larry D. Cahill, Joseph N. Schiro ; consultants, Norman S. Hubbard, Wm. W. Wylie. Omaha : The Institute, [1974] viii, 223 p. : col. ill. ; 29 cm. (Collectors Institute reference library) Includes index. $19.95. Bibliography: p. 218-219. [HE6185.U5C64 1974] 74-15228
1. Postage-stamps—United States—History. 2. Postage-stamps—Collectors and collecting—United States. I. Marzulla, Elena, ed. II. Title. III. Series: Collectors Institute. Collectors Institute reference library.

SCHUEREN, Fred P. 769'.56973
The United States 1869 issue : an essay-proof history / by Fred P. schueren. Chicago : Collectors Club of Chicago, [1974] xiii, 127 p. : ill. ; 26 cm. Bibliography: p. 125-126. [HE6185.U5S26] 74-82406
1. Postage-stamps—United States—History. 2. Postage-stamp design. I. Collectors Club of Chicago. II. Title.

Postage-stamps—Vatican City.

KELEN, Emery, 1896- 769'.569'45634
Stamps tell the story of the Vatican. [1st ed.] New York, Meredith Press [1969] x, 132 p. illus. 24 cm. Bibliography: p. 132. Descriptions and explanations of postage stamps issued by the Vatican trace the religious and architectural history of the "Holy See." [HE6185.V3K43] 76-80285 4.95
1. Postage-stamps—Vatican City. 2. Vatican City—History. I. Title.

Postage-stamps — Venezuela.

WICKERSHAM, Cornelius Wendell, 1884- 383.22987
The early stamps of Venezuela. With an introd. by Henry M. Goodkind. New York, Collectors Club [1958] 156 p. illus. 28 cm. (A Collectors Club handbook)

SUBJECT INDEX POSTAL SERVICE.

Includes bibliography. [HE6185.V5W5] 59-31034
1. Postage-stamps — Venezuela. I. Title.

Postage-stamps—Victoria, Australia.

PURVES, James Richard William. 769'.569'945
Victoria, 1901-12 issue; the 3d., 4d., and 5d. values, with an addenda giving new information on the 1d., 2d., and 2 1/2d. values, by J. R. W. Purves. Melbourne, Hawthorn Press [1964] 41 p. illus., diagrs. 24 cm. (Series of monographs concerning the stamps of Australia and the Pacific Islands, no. 14) "The edition is limited to 300 copies." [HE6185.A83V535] 77-393965 unpriced
1. Postage-stamps—Victoria, Australia. I. Title.

Postage-stams—U. S.— Catalogs.

HARRIS (H. E.) and Company, Boston. 383.22
Stamps of the United States, U.S. possessions, and British North America 2d ed., 1960 Boston, c1960. 160p. illus. 21cm. First published in 1943 under title: United States stamsps, U. S. possessions, and British North America. [HE6185.U5H35 1960] 60-4362
1. Postage-stams—U. S.— Catalogs. 2. Postage-stamps—Canada—Catalogs. I. Title.

Postal cards.

BURDICK, Jefferson R 741.67
Pioneer post cards; the story of mailing cards to 1898, with an illustrated checklist of publishers and titles. [Syracuse? N. Y., c1957. 144p. illus. 27cm. [NC1872.B83] 741.68 57-24446
1. Postal cards. I. Title.

BURDICK, Jefferson R., ed. 741.68
Pioneer post cards: the story of mailing cards in 1898, with an illustrated checklist of publishers and titles. Franklin Square, N. Y., Nostalgia Pr., Box 283 [1964] 200p. illus. 26cm. Reprint of 1957 ed with brief notes by Clark H. Stevens. 64-55184 4.25 pap.,
1. Postal cards. I. Title.

CALEY, George L. 769'.5
Post cards of yesteryear: 1893-1926; Delaware and elsewhere, by George L. Caley. Smyrna, Del., Printed by Shane Quality Press [1973] 92 p. illus. 27 cm. [NC1875.U6C34] 73-85391
1. Caley, George L.—Art collections. 2. Postal cards. I. Title.

CARLINE, Richard. 769'.5
Pictures in the post; the story of the picture postcard and its place in the history of popular art. [1st U.S. ed.] Philadelphia, Deltiologists of America, 1972 [c1971] 127 p. illus. (part col.) 30 cm. Bibliography: p. 125-126. [NC1872.C3 1972] 70-190038 7.50
1. Postal cards. I. Title.

FANTASY postcards / 769'.5
[compiled by] William Ouellette ; with an introd. by Barbara Jones. 1st ed. in the U.S.A. Garden City, N.Y. : Doubleday, [1975] 87, [9] p. : chiefly ill. (some col.) ; 24 x 30 cm. Includes index. [ND1872.F36] 75-7893 ISBN 0-385-11175-4 14.95 ISBN 0-385-11230-0 pbk. : 7.95
1. Postal cards. 2. Fantasy in art. I. Ouellette, William.

FRENCH postcards. 741.5
New York, Avon Publications [1954] 125p. illus. 17cm. (Avon, 609) [NC1872.F7] 55-15010
1. Postal cards.

LAUTERBACH, Carl, comp. 741.6
Postcard album; also a cultural history. Lovingly collected and written by C. Lauterbach and A. Jakovsky. [Translated from French and German by Judith Bogianckino-Matthias and Elizabeth Earl. 1st American ed.] New York, Universe Books [1961] [64] p. (chiefly illus., ports.) 26x36cm. Bibliography: p.[63]-[64] [NC1872.L313 1961] 61-14472
1. Postal cards. I. Jakovsky, Anatole, joint comp. II. Title.

NoRGAARD, Erik. 769'.5
With love to you; a history of the erotic postcard. [1st American ed.] New York, C. N. Porter; distributed by Crown Publishers [1969] 120 p. illus. (part col.) 20 x 21 cm. Translation of Med karlig hilsen. [NC1878.E7N613 1969] 77-91448 5.00
1. Postal cards. 2. Erotic art. I. Title.

STAFF, Frank. 769.5
The picture postcard & its origins. New York, F. A. Praeger [1966] 95 p. illus. (part col.) 29 cm. [NC1872.S7 1966a] 66-18374
1. Postal cards. I. Title.

WEILL, Alain. 741.68
Art nouveau postcards : the posterists' postcards / by Alain Weill ; [translated from the French by Bernard Jacobson]. New York : Images Graphiques, 1977. 16 p., [32] leaves of plates : col. ill. ; 26 cm. Bibliography: p. 6. [NC1878.5.A75W4413] 77-94470 ISBN 0-89545-014-3 : 11.95 ISBN 0-89545-015-1 pbk. : 6.95
1. Postal cards. 2. Decoration and ornament—Art nouveau. I. Title. **BIP**

Postal cards—Bibliography.

LOWE, James L. 016.769'5
Bibliography of postcard literature; a list of references pertaining to the publishing and collecting of picture post cards, by James L. Lowe. [Folsom, Pa.] 1969. x p. illus. 27 cm. [Z5956.P6L67] 73-7510
1. Postal cards—Bibliography. I. Title.

Postal cards—Catalogs.

KADUCK, John M. 769'.5
Rare and expensive postcards : [a price guide] / by John M. Kaduck ; [photography by Otto Schutte]. 1st ed. Cleveland : Kaduck, 1974. 88 p. : chiefly ill. ; 28 cm. Includes index. [NC1877.K32] 74-186357 5.95
1. Postal cards—Catalogs. 2. Postal cards—Collectors and collecting. I. Title. **BIP**

LOWE, James L. 769'.4'997370924
Lincoln postcard catalog; a check list of Lincoln postcards, old and new [by] James L. Lowe. 1st ed. Folsom, Pa., Better Postcard Collectors' Club [1967] 65 p. illus. 28 cm. [E457.6.L83] 68-1365
1. Lincoln, Abraham, Pres. U.S., 1809-1865—Iconography. 2. Postal cards—Catalogs. I. Title.

LOWE, James L. 016.769'4'997370924
Lincoln postcard catalog; a check list of Lincoln postcards, old and new [by] James L. Lowe. Revised by Dean and Mrs. Charles W. Brennan. 1st revision. Folsom, Pa., Deltiologists of America [1973] 144 p. illus. 29 cm. [E457.6.L83 1973] 73-83549 ISBN 0-913782-05-X
1. Lincoln, Abraham, Pres. U.S., 1809-1865—Iconography. 2. Postal cards—Catalogs. I. Brennan, Charles W. II. Brennan, Charles W., Mrs. III. Title.
Publisher's address: 318 Roosevelt Ave., Folsom, PA. 19033.

Postal cards—Collectors and collecting.

BOOK Club of California, San Francisco. 769'.5
West coast expositions and galas. [San Francisco, 1970] 10 folders. illus. 26 cm. (Its Series of keepsakes, 1970) Contents.Contents.—no. 1. "Don't forget to send a card."—no. 2. California Midwinter International Exposition.—no. 3. Lewis and Clark Exposition.—no. 4. Alaska-Yukon-Pacific Exposition.—no. 5. The Portola celebration.—no. 6. Panama-Pacific International Exposition.—no. 7. Panama-California Exposition.—no. 8. The Tournament of Roses.—no. 9. Peace voyage of the U.S. white fleet.—no. 10. The Mid-Pacific Carnival. [NC1875.B6] 72-192313
1. Postal cards—Collectors and collecting. I. Title. II. Series: Book Club of California, San Francisco. Keepsake series, 1970.

BURDICK, Jefferson R 741.67
The handbook of Detroit Publishing Co. post cards; a guide for collectors with a detailed checklist of the later contract issues and all unnumbered cards. [Syracuse? N. Y.] 1954. unpaged. illus. 22cm. [NC1872.B8] 741.68 56-35720
1. Postal cards—Collectors and collecting. 2. Detroit Publishing Company. I. Title.

KLAMKIN, Marian. 769'.5
Picture postcards. Illustrated with photos. by Charles Klamkin. New York, Dodd, Mead [1974] 192 p. illus. 31 cm. Bibliography: p. 190. [NC1872.K55 1974b] 73-15063 ISBN 0-396-06889-8 15.00
1. Postal cards—Collectors and collecting. I. Title. **BIP**

LOWE, James L. 769'.5
Detroit Publishing Company collectors' guide / James L. Lowe and Ben Papell. 1st ed. Newton Square, Pa. : Deltiologists of America, c1975. 288 p. : ill. ; 28 cm. Includes index. [NC1872.L59] 75-4127 ISBN 0-913782-07-6
1. Detroit Publishing Company. 2. Postal cards—Collectors and collecting. I. Papell, Ben, joint author. II. Title.

Postal cards—England.

GREEN, Benny, 1927- 769'.5
I've lost my little Willie! : a celebration of comic postcards / [text] by Benny Green. London : Elm Tree Books, 1976. 160 p. : ill. (some col.), chiefly facsims. (some col.), ports. ; 28 cm. [NC1878.W58G73 1976] 77-373033 ISBN 0-241-89407-7 : £4.95
1. Postal cards—England. 2. English wit and humor, Pictorial. I. Title.

Postal cards—France.

HAMMOND, Paul. 741.68
French undressing : naughty postcards from 1900 to 1920 / by Paul Hammond. London : Jupiter Books, 1976. 136 p. : ill. (some col.) ; 31 cm. Bibliography: p. 136. [NC1878.E7H35] 76-368351 ISBN 0-904041-40-9 : £4.25
1. Postal cards—France. 2. Erotic art—France. I. Title. **BIP**

Postal cards—Germany—Catalogs.

WALLACE, Charles L. 769'.5
The catalogue of poly-chrome post cards made in Germany, 1905—1906—1907 / [Charles L. Wallace]. [Morongo Valley, Calif. : Wallace, 1974] 93 p. : ill., facsims. ; 28 cm. Includes index. [NC1877.W34] 75-312208
1. Postal cards—Germany—Catalogs. 2. Color photography. I. Title. II. Title: Poly-chrome post cards.

Postal cards—History.

WELSCH, Roger L. 769'.5
Tall-tale postcards : a pictorial history / Roger L. Welsch. South Brunswick : A. S. Barnes, c1976. 244 p., [1] leaf of plates : ill. ; 29 cm. Includes index. Bibliography: p. 240-241. [NC1872.W44 1976] 74-9303 ISBN 0-498-01606-4 : 17.50
1. Postal cards—History. I. Title. **BIP**

Postal cards—Ryukyu Islands—Catalogs.

SCHOBERLIN, Melvin, 1912- 769'.56952'81
Specialized catalogue of postal stationery of the Ryukyu Islands, issued under United States administration. Photography by J. C. Templeton, Jr. [Cincinnati] Society of Philatelic Americans [1968- v. 23 cm. Vol. 3 (called Part 3) has title: Handbook & specialized catalogue of postal issues of the Ryukyu (Liu Ch'iu) Islands (Issued under United States Administrations) Contents.Contents.—v. 1. The provisional issues, 1945-1953. —v. 3. The Nansei Shoto provisional postage stamps, 1945-1948. [HE6185.J32S35] 68-7732 3.00
1. Postal cards—Ryukyu Islands—Catalogs. 2. Postage-stamps—Ryukyu Islands—Catalogs. I. Title. II. Title: Handbook & specialized catalogue of postal issues of the Ryuku (Liu Ch'iu) Islands.

Postal cards—United States.

FRICKE, Charles A. 383'.122 s
Plating of the first United States postal card (an original research project) by Charles A. Fricke. [Belleair, Fla., United Postal Stationery Society, 1973] 70 p. illus. 24 cm. (Centennial handbook of the first issue United States postal card, v. 1) Cover title. [HE6187.C38 vol. 1] [HE6375] 769'.5 73-77501 5.00
1. Postal cards—United States. I. Title. II. Series: Centennial handbook of the first issue postal card, v. 1.

MILLER, George. 769'.5
Picture postcards in the United States, 1893-1918 / George and Dorothy Miller. 1st ed. New York : Crown Publishers, c1975. p. cm. Includes index. Bibliography: p. [NC1872.M54 1975] 75-29392 ISBN 0-517-52400-7 : 15.00
1. Postal cards—United States. 2. United States in art. I. Miller, Dorothy, joint author. II. Title. **BIP**

Postal cards—United States—Catalogs.

FRICKE, Charles A. 769'.56
The United States international single postal cards of 1879-1897-1898 / by Charles A. Fricke. Bloomington, Ill. : United Postal Stationery Society, [1974- v. : chiefly ill. ; 23 cm. Contents.Contents.—v. 1. Plating: a research project. Includes bibliographical references. [HE6185.U6F69] 74-21563
1. Postal cards—United States—Catalogs. I. Title.

KADUCK, John M. 769'.5
Patriotic postcards, by John M. Kaduck. [1st ed.] Des Moines, Iowa, Printed by Wallace-Homestead Co. [1974] 67 p. illus. 28 cm. [NC1878.P3K32] 74-177233 4.95
1. Postal cards—United States—Catalogs. 2. Patriotism in art. I. Title.

UNITED Postal Stationery Society. 769'.56973
United States postal card catalog; with a special appendix on exposition postal cards. Clark H. Stevens, editor, Frank B. Stratton, associate editor. 25th anniversary ed. Albany, Or., Printed [by] Van Dahl Publications, 1970. xvii, 136 p. illus. 23 cm. [HE6185.U6U56 1970] 73-138317 5.00
1. Postal cards—United States—Catalogs. I. Stevens, Clark H., ed. II. Stratton, Frank B., ed. III. Title.

UNITED Postal Stationery Society. 769'.56973
United States postal card catalog : with special appendix features—exposition postal cards, exposition cancels, machine cancels / United Postal Stationery Society ; editorial board, Clark H. Stevens, editor, Frank B. Stratton, editor, associate editors, Charles A. Fricke ... [et al.]. 30th anniversary ed. Bloomington, IL : The Society, 1975. xviii, 177 p. : ill. ; 23 cm. [HE6185.U6U56 1975] 75-3513
1. Postal cards—United States—Catalogs. I. Stevens, Clark H. II. Stratton, Frank B. III. Title.

Postal cards—United States—History.

FRICKE, Charles A. 383'.122 s
A contemporary account of the first United States postal card, 1870-1875, edited by Charles A. Fricke. [Philadelphia, 1973] v, 146 p. illus. 24 cm. (Centennial handbook of the first issue postal card, v. 2) Cover title. [HE6187.C38 vol. 2] [HE6375] 769'.5 73-76977
1. Postal cards—United States—History. I. Title. II. Series.

Postal service.

MEYER, Karl Friedrich, 1884- 383

Disinfected mail; [Historical review and tentative listing of catchets, handstamp markings, wax seals, wafer seals and manuscript certifications alphabetically arranged according to countries. In collaboration with C. Ravasini and others. Holton, Kan., Gossip Printery, 1962] 341 p. 29 cm. [HE6183.M48] 62-15592
1. Postal service. 2. Postmarks. I. Title.

Postal service—History.

ANGUS, Ian. 383'.09
Stamps, posts, and postmarks / Ian Angus. New York : St. Martin's Press, 1975, c1973. 128 p. : ill. ; 26 cm. Includes index. [HE6203.A72 1975] 74-33902 6.95
1. Postal service—History. 2. Postage-stamps—History. I. Title.

Posters.

ALLNER, Walter H, 1909- ed. 741.67
Posters; fifty artists and designers analyze their approach, their methods, and their solutions to poster design and poster advertising. New York, Reinhold [1952] 112 p. illus. (part col.) ports. 25 x 31 cm. [NC1810.A63] 52-10620
1. Posters. I. Title.

ART nouveau : 769'.94
posters & graphics / [compiled by] Roger Sainton. New York : Rizzoli, 1977. 95 p. : chiefly ill. (some col.) ; 30 cm. Introd. in English; captions in English, French, or German. [NC1845.A7A77] 76-51472 ISBN 0-8478-0073-3 : 13.95. pbk. : 7.95
1. Posters. 2. Illustration of books. 3. Decoration and ornament—Art nouveau. I. Sainton, Roger.

BIEGELEISEN, Jacob Israel, 1910- 741.67
Design and print your own posters / J. I. Biegeleisen. New York : Watson-Guptill Publications, 1976. 167 p. : ill. ; 26 cm. Includes index. Bibliography: p. 162-163. [NC1810.B48] 75-40176 ISBN 0-8230-1309-X : 11.95
1. Posters. 2. Lettering. 3. Screen process printing. I. Title. BIP

BOUGHNER, Howard. 704.94'32
Posters. New York, Pitman Pub. Corp. [1962] unpag ed. illus. 20x26cm. (Pitman art series, 38) [NC1810.B66] 62-9138
1. Posters. I. Title. BIP

CIRKER, Hayward, comp. 741.67
The golden age of the poster. Selected and edited by Hayward and Blanche Cirker. New York, Dover Publications [1971] 70 p. (chiefly col. illus.) 32 cm. [NC1845.A7C5] 79-164736 ISBN 0-486-22753-7 3.95
1. Posters. 2. Decoration and ornament—Art nouveau. I. Cirker, Blanche, joint comp. II. Title. BIP

COPLAN, Kate. 741.67
Poster ideas and bulletin board techniques for libraries and schools. Original art by Constance Rosenthal. Lettering art by Charles Cipolloni. Dobbs Ferry, N.Y., Oceana Publications [1962] 183 p. illus. 29 cm. [NC1810.C63] 62-11949
1. Posters. 2. Bulletin boards. 3. Handicraft. I. Title.

DC super heroes poster book / introd. by Isaac Asimov. New York : Harmony Books, c1978. 47 p. : chiefly col. ill. ; 39 cm. [PN6725.D2] 78-3414 ISBN 0-517-53329-4. : 5.95 769'.5
1. DC Comics, inc. 2. Posters, American. I. Title: Super heroes poster book. BIP

ECKERSLEY, Tom. 741.67
Poster design. London & New York, Studio Publications [1954] 96p. illus. (part col.) 26cm. (The How to do it series, no. 50) [NC1810.E25] 54-2833
1. Posters. I. Title. II. Series: How to do it series (London, The Studio)

EZELL, Mancil. 741.67
Making nonprojected visuals and displays / Mancil Ezell. Nashville : Broadman Press, [1975] 57 p. : ill. ; 23 cm. [NC1810.E93] 74-21565 ISBN 0-8054-3419-4 pbk. : 1.95
1. Posters. 2. Display boards. I. Title. BIP

GOINES, David Lance, 1945- 769'.92'4
The David Lance Goines poster book. New York : Harmony Books, 1979, c1978 47 p. : chiefly col. ill. ; 39 cm. [NC1850.G58A4 1978] 78-6543 ISBN 0-517-53488-6. : 6.95
1. Goines, David Lance, 1945- I. Title.

**GRAPHIS posters :* 769.5
the international annual of poster art / edited by Walter Herdeg. Zurich, Switzerland : Graphis Press, c1977. v. : ill. ; 30 cm. [NC1810] 35.00
1. Posters. 2. Commercial art. I. Herdeg, Walter, ed.
Distributed by Hastings House.

HILLIER, Bevis, 1940- comp. 769'.5
100 years of posters 1st u. s. ed. New York, Harper & Row [1972] xvi, 96 p. (chiefly illus. (part col.)) 42 cm. [NC1810.H52 1972] 72-79672 ISBN 0-06-011899-7
1. Posters. I. Title.

HILLIER, Bevis, 1940- 769'.5
Posters. New York, Stein and Day [1969] 296 p. illus. (part col.), ports. 26 cm. Bibliography: p. 289-290. [NC1810.H53] 74-86914 17.50
1. Posters.

HORN, George F. 741.67
Contemporary posters : design and techniques / George F. Horn. Worcester, Mass. : Davis Publications, c1976. 112 p. : ill. (some col.) ; 26 cm. [NC1810.H58] 75-41544 ISBN 0-87192-079-4
1. Posters. I. Title. BIP

HORN, George F. 741.67
Posters: designing, making, reproducing. Worcester, Mass., Davis Publications [1964] 96 p. illus. (part col.) 26 cm. [NC1810.H6] 64-12774
1. Posters. I. Title.

HUTCHISON, Harold Frederick. 769'.5
The poster; an illustrated history from 1860 [by] Harold F. Hutchison. New York, Viking Press [1968] 216 p. illus. (part col.) 30 cm. (A Studio book) Bibliography: p. 213-214. [NC1810.H8 1968] 69-10592 14.00
1. Posters. I. Title.

INTERNATIONAL poster annual. 13th 1967/68- New York, Hastings. v. illus. 30cm. Ed.: 13th A. Niggli. English, French, and German. [NC1800.157] 49-10559 16.00 741.67
1. Posters. I. Niggli, Arthur, ed.

INTERNATIONAL poster annual. Panorama international de part de l'affiche. Interna tales Plakatiahrbuch. 1962 Ed.; Arthur Niggli. New York, Hastings [c.1962] 132p. illus. (pt. col. 30cm. 49-10559 12.95 741.67
1. Posters. I. Niggli, Arthur. ed.

INTERNATIONAL poster annual; v.11. Ed. [by] Arthut Niggli. New York, Hastings [c.1963] 136p. chiefly illus. (pt. col.) 30cm. (Visual communication bks) English, French and German annual. 49-10559 12.95 741.67
1. Posters. I. Niggli, Arthur, ed.

INTERNATIONAL Poster Annual, 1960. Editor: Arthur Niggli. New York, Hastings House [1960] 132p. illus (part col.) 30cm. (Visual communication books) English, French and German 49-10559 12.00 nds., 741.67
1. Posters. I. Niggli, Arthur, ed.

LALIBERTE, Norman. 769'.5
The book of posters [by] Norman Laliberte [and] Alex Mogelon. Blauvelt, N.Y., Art Education [1970] 78 p. illus. (part col.) 41 cm. [NC1810.L34] 77-131936
1. Posters. I. Mogelon, Alex, joint author. II. Title. BIP

METZL, Ervine, 1899- 741.67
The poster: its history and its art. [New York] Watson-Guptill Publications [1963] 183 p. illus. 29 cm. [NC1810.M45] 62-21808
1. Posters.

MILLS, Vernon. 741.6'7
Making posters. London, Studio Vista; New York, Watson-Guptil [1967] 104 p. front., illus. (some col.), diagrs. 19 cm 10/6 (B67-6433) Bibliography: p. 102-103. [NC1810.M55] 67-13738
1. Posters. 2. Graphic arts — Technique. I. Title.

MOURLOT, Fernand. 741.67
Art in posters; the complete original posters of Braque, Chagall, Dufy, Leger, Matisse, Miro [and] Picasso. Monte Carlo, A. Sauret; New York, G. Braziller [1959] 247p. 102 plates (part col.) 33cm. [NC1810.M77] 59-13125
1. Posters. I. Title.

POSTERS by painters : 769'.5
29 posters by famous artists / Evelyn and Leo Farland. New York : H. N. Abrams, c1978. 62 p. : col. ill. ; 41 cm. [NC1810.P723] 77-14387 ISBN 0-8109-2085-9 pbk. : 8.95
1. Posters. I. Farland, Evelyn. II. Farland, Leo.

RICKARDS, Maurice, 1919- 741.6'7'09034
Posters at the turn of the century. New York, Walker [1968] 70 p. illus. (part col.) 21 cm. ([Collectors' blue books]) [NC1845.A7R5 1968] 68-22132 3.50
1. Posters. 2. Decoration and ornament—Art nouveau. I. Title.

RICKARDS, Maurice, 1919- 769'.5
Posters of the nineteen-twenties. New York, Walker [1968] 70 p. illus. (part col.) 21 cm. [NC1810.R54 1968] 68-22131 3.50
1. Posters. I. Title.

RICKARDS, Maurice, 1919- 769'.5
The rise and fall of the poster. New York, McGraw-Hill [1971] 111 p. illus. (part col.) 25 cm. [NC1810.R55 1971b] 71-155883 ISBN 0-07-052619-2 6.95
1. Posters. I. Title.

ROSSI, Attilio. 769'.5
Posters [translated from the Italian by Raymond Rudorff] London, New York, Hamlyn, 1969. 159 p.; col. illus. 20 cm. (Cameo) Translation of I manifesti. [NC1810.R6613] 71-883923 ISBN 0-600-01261-1 £0.90
1. Posters. I. Title.

THE Space art poster book / [compiled by] Ron Miller. Harrisburg, Pa. : Stackpole Books, c1979. p. cm. [NC1849.S63S66 1979] 79-12483 ISBN 0-8117-2077-2 pbk. : 8.95 769'.4'980883876
1. Outer space—Posters. I. Miller, Ron, 1947- BIP

Posters, American.

AMERICAN poster renaissance / by Victor Margolin. New York : Watson-Guptill Publications, 1975. 223 p. : ill. (some col.) ; 32 cm. Includes index. Bibliography: p. 220-221. [NC1807.U5A43 1975] 75-4813 ISBN 0-8230-0214-4 : 25.00 769'.5
1. Posters, American. 2. Decoration and ornament—Art nouveau. I. Margolin, Victor, 1941-

DISNEY (Walt) Productions. 769'.5
The Disney poster book / introd. by Maurice Sendak. New York : Harmony Books, c1977. 47 p. : chiefly col. ill. ; 39 cm. [NC1850.D5744 1977] 76-56735 ISBN 0-517-52936-X pbk. : 5.95
1. Disney (Walt) Productions. 2. Posters, American. I. Title. BIP

FREEMAN, Graydon La Verne, 1904- 769'.5
Victorian posters. Compiled by Larry Freeman for the Library of Victorian culture and sponsored by the American Life Foundation. Watkins Glen, N.Y. [Distributed by Century House, 1969] 304 p. illus. 28 cm. Bibliography: p. 278. [NC1807.U5F7] 68-55037
1. Posters, American. 2. Decoration and ornament—Victorian style. I. American Life Foundation, Watkins Glen, N.Y. II. Title. BIP

THE Golden age of the American poster : a concise edition of the American poster renaissance / Victor Margolin. New York : Ballantine Books, 1976. 31 p., 48 leaves of plates : ill. (some col.) ; 30 cm. Includes index. [NC1807.U5A432] 76-151349 ISBN 0-345-25129-6 pbk. : 6.95 769'.5
1. Posters, American. 2. Decoration and ornament—Art nouveau. I. Margolin, Victor, 1941- II. American poster renaissance. 1976. BIP

MAX, Peter, 1939- 709'.24
Peter Max superposter book. New York, Crown Publishers [1971] [38] p. illus. (part col.) 41 cm. [NC1429.M429A55 1971] 73-119918 3.95
I. Title. II. Title: Superposter book.

UNITED States Printing Company. Poster Dept. 741.67
A few good posters; being sundry half-tone reproductions of some posters we have made, together with a little friendly discourse on the subject of posters. Cincinnati [1960?] 32 p. illus. 28 cm. [NC1807.U5U5] 68-4200
1. Posters, American. I. Title.

Posters, American—Catalogs.

WALKER, Cummings G., comp. 741.6'7
The great poster trip: art eureka. Editor: Cummings G. Walker. Designer: Richard D. Teater. [Palo Alto, Calif.] Coyne & Blanchard [1968] 79 p. (chiefly illus., port col.) 28 cm. [NC1807.U5W3] 68-1614
1. Posters, American—Catalogs. I. Title. BIP

Posters, American—Exhibitions.

IMAGES of an era : 769'.5
the American poster, 1945-75 : [exhibition] . Washington : National Collection of Fine Arts, Smithsonian Institution, 1975. 20, [11] p., [132] leaves of plates : ill. (some col.) ; 25 cm. Catalog of the exhibition held Nov. 21-Jan. 4, at the Corcoran Gallery of Art, Washington, D.C., and elsewhere. Bibliography: p. [4]-[9] (2d group) [NC1807.U5I45] 75-34602
1. Posters, American—Exhibitions. I. Smithsonian Institution. National Collection of Fine Arts. II. Corcoran Gallery of Art, Washington, D.C.

Posters, American—Private collections.

AMERICAN advertising posters of the nineteenth century : from the Bella C. Landauer Collection of the New-York Historical Society / Mary Black. New York : Dover Publications, 1976. vii, 119 p. : chiefly ill. ; 37 cm. Includes indexes. [HF5843.A68] 76-20834 ISBN 0-486-23356-1 : 6.95 769.5
1. Landauer, Bella Clara, 1874-1960—Art collections. 2. New York Historical Society. 3. Posters, American—Private collections. I. Black, Mary C.

Posters, Belgian—Exhibitions.

OOSTENS-WITTAMER, Yolande. 760'.09493
La Belle Epoque; Belgian posters, watercolors and drawings from the collection of L. Wittamer-De Camps. Introd. and catalogue by Yolande Oostens-Wittamer. Pref. by Emile Langui. Circulated by International Exhibitions Foundation, 1970-1971. [New York] Grossman [1970] 93 p. illus. (part col.) 23 x 28 cm. "Participating institutions: Library of Congress [and others]" [NC1807.B4O55] 71-134209
1. Wittamer-De Camps, L.—Art collections. 2. Posters, Belgian—Exhibitions. 3. Decoration and ornament—Art nouveau. I. International Exhibitions Foundation. II. Title.

Posters—Catalogs.

MASTERS of the poster, 1896-1900 : reproduces the complete text and all the plates in the series "Les maitres de l'affiche" / preface by Roger Marx ; introd. by Alain Weill ; notes by Jack Rennert ; [translated by Bernard Jacobson]. New York : Images Graphiques, 1977. 32 p., [32] leaves of plates : col. ill. ; 28 cm. Includes index. [NC1845.A7M35] 77-94468 ISBN 0-89545-012-7 : 11.95 ISBN 0-89545-013-5 pbk. : 6.95 769'.5
1. Posters—Catalogs. 2. Decoration and ornament—Art nouveau. I. Les Maitres de l'affiche. BIP

Posters—Censorship.

RICKARDS, Maurice, 1919- 769'.5
Banned posters, presented and reviewed by Maurice Rickards. [1st U.S. ed.] Park

U.S. Philatelic Classics Society, 1968. xiv, 379 p. illus., ports. 26 cm. Continuation of United States railroad postmarks, 1837 to 1861, by C. W. Remule. Bibliography: p. 354-355. [HE6185.U6T82] 78-1904
1. Postmarks—U.S. I. Meyer, Henry Albert, 1894-1968, joint author. II. Remele, C. W. United States railroad postmarks, 1837 to 1861. III. Title.

Postmarks—United States—History.

CYCLOPEDIA of United 769'.56973
States postmarks and postal history / edited by Delf Norona. Lawrence, Mass. : Quarterman Publications, [1975]. vi, 405 p. : ill. ; 24 cm. Reprint, with new foreword, of the 1933-35 ed. published by D. Norona, Moundsville, W. Va. Includes bibliographies. [HE6185.U5C93 1975] 75-1788 ISBN 0-88000-063-5 : 30.00
1. Postmarks—United States—History. 2. Postal service—United States—History. I. Norona, Delf, 1895- BIP

Postmarks—Vermont.

SLAWSON, George 383'.09743
Clarke, 1905-
The postal history of Vermont, by George C. Slawson, Arthur W. Bingham [and] Sprague W. Drenan. New York, Collectors Club, 1969. xi, 308 p. illus., maps. 23 cm. (Collectors Club handbook, no. 21) Bibliographical footnotes. [HE6185.U7V47] 73-3546
1. Postmarks—Vermont. 2. Postage-stamps—Vermont. 3. Postal service—Vermont. I. Bingham, Arthur W., joint author. II. Drenen, Sprague W., joint author. III. Title.

Pot-lids—Great Britain.

BALL, Abraham, 1908- 738.3'83
The price guide to pot-lids and other underglaze colour prints on pottery, by A. Ball. Woodbridge, Antique Collectors' Club, 1970. [37], 496 p. (chiefly illus. (some col.)). 22 cm. [NK4695.L5B34] 73-158851 ISBN 0-902028-03-0 £4.20
1. Pot-lids—Great Britain. I. Title.

Potamkin, Meyer P., 1909- —Art collections.

DALLAS. 759.13'074'01642812
Museum of Fine Arts.
The M. P. Potamkin Collection. [Dallas, 1970] [12] p. 24 plates. 26 cm. Catalogue of a loan exhibition, Jan. 28-Mar. 8, 1970. [N5220.P72D3] 70-25288
1. Potamkin, Meyer P., 1909- —Art collections. 2. Art—Exhibitions. I. Title.

Potichomania.

POTICHOMANIA; decoupage 745.54
under glass, by Cynthia Alderdice [and others] Photos. by Roy H. Hoopes. [Bethesda, Md., American Art Associates Publications, 1972] 32 p. illus. (part col.) 28 cm. Cover title. [TT870.P75] 72-86469 2.98
1. Potichomania. 2. Electric lamps—Amateurs' manuals. I. Alderdice, Cynthia.

Potomac River—Description and travel.

LEWIS, Jack, 1912- 759.13
Potomac. [Limited ed. Dover, Del., Woodwend Studios, 1970] x, 224 p. illus. (part col.), ports. (part col.) 29 cm. "A portfolio of watercolors depicting the varied and scenic Potomac River from its source to its end ... " [F187.P8L48] 72-21371
1. Potomac River—Description and travel. I. Title.

Potter, Beatrix, 1866-1943.

HUTCHINGS, Margaret. 745.59'24
Toys from the tales of Beatrix Potter. With sections on the baskets by Eve Legg, and the furniture and accessories by Richard Hutchings. Photography by Eve Legg. New York, F. Warne [1974, c1973] 314 p. illus. 26 cm. [TT174.H87 1974] 73-75922 ISBN 0-7232-6098-2 15.00
1. Potter, Beatrix, 1866-1943. 2. Toy making—Amateurs' manuals. I. Legg, Evelyn. II. Hutchings, Richard. III. Title. BIP

POTTER, Beatrix, 1866-1943 828
The art of Beatrix Potter With an appreciation by Anne Carroll Moore [3d ed.] New York, Warne [1964] 336p. (chiefly illus. (pt. col.) facsims.) 24cm. [NC242.P6A43] 65-5380 18.50
I. Moore, Anne Carroll, 1871- II. Title.

POTTER, Beatrix, 1866- 741.642
1943.
The art of Beatrix Potter. With an appreciation by Anne Carroll Moore. London, New York, F. Warne [1955] 336p. (chiefly illus. (part col.) facsims.) 24cm. 'The Beatrix Potter books': p. 334-336. [NC233.P6A43] 55-13632
I. Moore, Anne Carroll, 1871 II. Title. BIP

POTTER, Beatrix, 1866- 741.642
1943.
The art of Beatrix Potter. With an appreciation by Anne Carroll Moore. [2d ed.] London, New York, F. Warne [1956] 336 p. (chiefly illus. (part col.) facsims.) 24 cm. "The Beatrix Potter books": p. 334-336. [NC233.P6A43 1956] 57-2629
I. Moore, Anne Carroll, 1871-

POTTER, Beatrix, 1866- 741.9'42
1943.
The art of Beatrix Potter / with an appreciation by Anne Carroll Moore and notes to each section by Enid and Leslie Linder. [5th ed.]. London ; New York : F. Warne, 1972. xxvi, 406 p. : chiefly ill. (some col.), facsims., port. ; 24 cm. Bibliography: p. 400-406. [NC242.P6L56 1972] 76-358049 ISBN 0-7232-1457-3 : £6.95
1. Potter, Beatrix, 1866-1943. I. Linder, Enid. II. Linder, Leslie. III. Title.

POTTER, Beatrix, 1866- 741.9'42
1943.
The art of Beatrix Potter: direct reproductions of Beatrix Potter's preliminary studies and finished drawings, also examples of her original manuscript; selected and arranged by L. Linder and W. A. Herring, with an appreciation by Anne Carroll Moore. 4th ed. London, New York, F. Warne, 1966. 336 p. illus. (some col.), facsims. plate. 24 cm. 84/- (B 68-00403) "The Beatrix Potter books": p. 334-336. [NC242.P6A43] 68-98286
I. Moore, Anne Carroll, 1871- II. Title.

POTTER, Beatrix, 1866- 730'.92'4
1943.
Letters to children. [Cambridge, Mass.] Harvard College Library, Dept. of Printing and Graphic Arts; New York, Walker, 1966 [i. e. 1967] 48 p. illus. 20 cm. Facsimiles and transcriptions of 9 holograph letters, 1896-1902, owned by Phillip Hofer. [PR6031.O72Z54] 67-13247
I. Title. BIP

Potter, Beatrix, 1866-1943—Biography.

LANE, Margaret, 1907- 741'.0924 B
The tale of Beatrix Potter: a biography. Revised ed. London, New York, F. Warne, 1968. 173 p. 47 plates, illus. (some col.), ports. 22 cm. "The Beatrice Potter books": p. 167-168. [PR6031.O72Z6 1968] 68-22444 ISBN 0-7232-0138-2 30/-
1. Potter, Beatrix, 1866-1934—Biography. I. Title. BIP

Potters.

MILLS, Flora Rupe. 738
Potters and glassblowers. San Antonio, Tex., Naylor Co. [1963] xiv, 112 p. illus. 22 cm. [NK4200.M5] 63-17569
1. Potters. 2. Glass-workers. 3. Pottery—Collectors and collecting. 4. Glassware — Collectors and collecting. I. Title.

Potters—England—Biography.

HAGGAR, Reginald 338.7'61'7380922
George, 1905-
Mason porcelain and ironstone 1796-1853 : Miles Mason and the Mason manufactories / by Reginald Haggar and Elizabeth Adams. London : Faber, 1977. 2-135 p., A-H, [80] p. of plates : ill. (some col.), facsim., plan ; 26 cm. (Faber monographs on pottery and porcelain) Includes index. Bibliography: p. 125-126. [NK4210.M3H27] 77-372940 ISBN 0-571-10945-4 : 34.95
1. Mason, Miles, 1752-1822. 2. Mason, Charles James, 1791-1856. 3. Potters—England—Biography. 4. Porcelain, English. I. Adams, B. Elizabeth, joint author. II. Title.
Distributed by Faber and Faber, Salem, Mass.

LEACH, Bernard 738'.092'4 B
Howell, 1887-
Beyond East and West : memoirs, portraits, and essays / Bernard Leach. London ; Boston : Faber, 1978. 320 p., [12] leaves of plates : ill. ; 26 cm. Includes index. [NK4210.L35A2 1978] 78-315916 ISBN 0-571-11138-6 : 15.95
1. Leach, Bernard Howell, 1887- 2. Potters—England—Biography. I. Title.
Distributed by Watson Publishing Co., 6608 Hesperia Ave. Reseda, CA 91335 BIP

Potters—England—Directories.

GODDEN, Geoffrey A. 738.3'7
The illustrated guide to Mason's patent ironstone china and related wares; stone china, new stone, granite china, and their manufacturers [by] Geoffrey A. Godden. New York, Praeger [1971] xiv, 175 p. illus., 8 col. plates. 26 cm. (The Illustrated guides to pottery and porcelain) Includes bibliographical references. [NK4210.M3G6 1971] 72-135513 20.00
1. Mason family (Miles Mason, 1752-1822) 2. Potters—England—Directories. I. Title. II. Title: Mason's patent ironstone china.

Potters—Great Britain—Biography.

CLARK, Garth. 738.3'092'4 B
Michael Cardew : a portrait / by Garth Clark. 1st ed. Tokyo ; New York : Kodansha International ; New York : distributed by Harper & Row, 1976. 228 p. : ill. (some col.) ; 26 cm. Includes index. Bibliography: p. 225-226. [NK4210.C29C55] 76-9358 ISBN 0-87011-277-5 : 25.00
1. Cardew, Michael, 1901- 2. Potters—Great Britain—Biography. BIP

Potters—Great Britain—Biography—Addresses, essays, lectures.

MICHAEL Cardew : 738.3'092'4 B
a collection of essays / with an introd. by Bernard Leach ; and contributions by Michael Cardew ... [et al.]. London : Crafts Advisory Council ; New York : distributed in the United States of America and Canada by Watson-Guptill, c1976. 80 p. : ill. ; 21 x 22 cm. Includes index. Contents.Contents.—Leach, B. Introduction.—Houston, J. The early years.—Finch, R. Working at Winchcombe in 1936.—Bouverie, K. P. A personal account.—Houston, J. Africa and Cornwall.—Cardew, M. Slipware and stoneware.—Chronology.—Pottery marks. Bibliography: p. 77-79. [NK4210.C29M5] 76-381211 ISBN 0-903798-07-7 : 9.95.
1. Cardew, Michael, 1901- —Addresses, essays, lectures. 2. Potters—Great Britain—Biography—Addresses, essays, lectures. I. Cardew, Michael, 1901-

Potters—Great Britain—Interviews.

POTTERS on pottery / 738'.092'2
[edited by] Elisabeth Cameron and Philippa Lewis. London : Evans, 1976. 168 p. : ill. (some col.) ; 26 cm. [NK4085.P59 1976b] 77-359493 ISBN 0-237-44855-6 : £6.50
1. Potters—Great Britain—Interviews. 2. Pottery, British. I. Cameron, Elisabeth. II. Lewis, Philippa.

Potters—Japan—Biography.

LEACH, Bernard 738.3'092'4 B
Howell, 1887-
Hamada, potter / Bernard Leach. London : Thames and Hudson, 1976. 306 p. : ill. (some col.), ports. ; 31 cm. Text in form of dialogue between the author and Hamada. Includes index. [NK4210.H32L4 1976] 76-377126 ISBN 0-500-23222-9 : £20.00
1. Hamada, Shoji, 1894- 2. Potters—Japan—Biography. I. Hamada, Shoji, 1894- II. Title. BIP

Potters—Tyne Valley.

BELL, Robert Charles, 738.3'7
1917-
The potteries of Tyneside [by] R. C. Bell and M. A. V. Gill. Newcastle upon Tyne, Graham, 1973. 40 p. illus., facsim. 22 cm. Bibliography: p. 39. [NK4087.T9B39] 73-164285 ISBN 0-902833-77-4 £0.60
1. Potters—Tyne Valley. 2. Pottery—Marks. I. Gill, Margaret Anne Violet, joint author. II. Title.

Potters—United States.

NANCE, John, 1935- 738'.092'4 B
The mud-pie dilemma : a master potter's struggle to make art and ends meet / John Nance. Forest Grove, Or. : Timber Press, c1978. vi, 116 p., [24] leaves of plates : ill. (some col.) ; 29 cm. (Timber Press series in arts and crafts) [NK4210.C63N37] 78-13888 ISBN 0-917304-18-7 : 14.95
1. Coleman, Thomas, 1945- 2. Potters—United States—Biography. I. Title. II. Series. BIP

WILDENHAIN, 738'.092'4 B
Marguerite.
The invisible core; a potter's life and thoughts. Photos. by Fran Ortiz. Palo Alto, Calif., Pacific Books [1973] 207 p. illus. 29 cm. [NK4210.W47A25] 72-80746 ISBN 0-87015-201-7 12.50
1. Wildenhain, Marguerite. 2. Potters—United States. I. Title. BIP

Pottery.

BALL, Frederick Carlton. 738.1'4
Decorating pottery with clay, slip, and glaze, by F. Carlton Ball. Columbus, Ohio, Professional Publications [1967] 63 p. illus., port. 28 cm. (A CM handbook) [NK4600.B3] 67-19833
1. Pottery. 2. Decoration and ornament. I. Title.

BALL, Frederick Carlton. 738.1'4
Decorating pottery with clay, slip, and glaze, by F. Carlton Ball. Columbus, Ohio, Professional Publications [1967] 63 p. illus., port. 28 cm. (A CM handbook) [NK4600.B3] 67-19833
1. Pottery. 2. Decoration and ornament. I. Title.

BARFORD, George. 666'.023
Clay in the classroom; a means to creative expressions. Worcester, Mass., Davis Publications [c1963] 118 p. illus. 28 cm. Bibliography: p. 114-117. [TP808.B34] 63-19347
1. Pottery. 2. Clay. I. Title.

BILLINGTON, Dora M. 738.1
The technique of pottery. New York, Hearthside Press [1962] ix, 222 p. illus., diagrs. 23 cm. Bibliography: p. 216. [TP807.B57 1962a] 63-11741
1. Pottery. I. Title.

BINNS, Charles Fergus, 666'.4
1857-1934.
The potter's craft. 4th ed., rev. by John F. McMahon. Princeton, N.J., Van Nostrand [1967] xiii, 144 p. illus. 21 cm. Bibliography: p. 124-125. [TP808.B6 1967] 67-18063
1. Pottery. I. McMahon, John Francis, 1900 ed. II. Title.

BOHROD, Aaron. 738.15
A pottery sketchbook. Madison, University of Wisconsin Press, 1959. 196 p. (chiefly illus.) 28 cm. [NK4250.B6] 59-14647
1. Pottery. 2. Design, Decorative. I. Title. BIP

BRENNAN, Thomas J. 738.1
Ceramics. Consulting editor: Walter C. Brown. Homewood, Ill., Goodheart-Willcox [1964] 96 p. illus. 27 cm. (Goodheart-Willcox's build-a-course series) Bibliography: p. 93. [TP808.B7] 64-12361
1. Pottery.

TAYLOR, Sally, 1914- 738
Ceramics for the table. New York, Fairchild Publications [1950] 160 p. illus. 22 cm. [NK4235.T3] 50-13495
1. Pottery. 2. Glassware. I. Title.

TETRAULT, Genevieve, 1879- 666.3
First steps in pottery; a manual of simple and practical instructions and suggestions in the art of fashioning pottery, prepared especially for beginners. Photography by Joan De Munbrun. Los Angeles, American Book Institute [1951] 78p. illus. 22cm. [TP808.T4] 52-1694
1. Pottery. I. Title.

THORP, Harold E. 738
Basic pottery for the student [by] Harold E. Thorp. [1st American ed.] New York, Transatlantic Arts, 1969. 99 p. illus., 45 plates. 22 cm. [TP808.T57 1969] 73-88660
1. Pottery. I. Title. BIP

TREVOR, Henry. 738.14
Pottery step-by-step. New York, Watson-Guptill Publications [1966] 127 p. illus. 27 cm. Bibliography: p. 121-122. [NK4225.T7] 66-13000
1. Pottery. I. Title.

TYLER, Keith. 738
Pottery without a wheel. Leicester, Dryad P., 1966. 2-77 p. front., illus., diagrs. 21 1/2 cm. (B 66-23946) Bibliography: p. 77. [NK4225.T95 1966] 67-72954
1. Pottery. I. Title.

VILLIARD, Paul. 666'.3
A first book of ceramics. New York, Funk & Wagnalls [1969] viii, 175 p. illus. 21 cm. [TP808.V54] 68-56463 5.95
1. Pottery. I. Title.

WALLIS, Ross Hamilton, 1902- 738.3
Hobby pottery, how its done! Los Angeles, Leisurecrafts, c1950. 54 p. illus. 28 cm. (A Leisurecrafts hobby book) [TP808.W27] 51-38473
1. Pottery. I. Title.

WILDENHAIN, Marguerite. 738.14
Pottery; form and expression. [New York] American Craftsmen's Council, 1959. 149 p. illus. 28 cm. [NK4225.W5] 59-4980
1. Pottery. I. Title. BIP

•WILDENHAIN, Marguerite. 738.1
Pottery: form and expression. Photo story by Otto Hagel. Palo Alto, Calif., American Crafts Council [&] Pacific Books Pubs. [1973] 157 p. illus. 29 cm. A reissue of the new & enl. ed. published by Reinhold Book Co. in 1962. [TP808] 62-16374 ISBN 0-87015-202-5 9.95
1. Pottery. I. Hagel, Otto, illus. II. Title.
Available from Pacific Books.

WILDENHAIN, Marguerite. 372.53
Pottery: form and expression. [Enl. ed.] New York [Published for] American Craftsmen's Council [by] Reinhold [1962] 157 p. illus. 29 cm. [NK4225.W5 1962] 62-16374
1. Pottery. I. Title.

WINKLEY, David. 738.3
Pottery. New York, Drake Publishers [1975] p. cm. [NK4225.W53 1975] 74-4058 ISBN 0-87749-661-7
1. Pottery. I. Title. BIP

WINTERBURN, Mollie. 738
The technique of handbuilt pottery. [American ed. adapted by Susan E. Meyer] New York, Watson-Guptill Publications [1969, c1966] 175 p. illus. 27 cm. English ed. published in 1966 under title: Hand-built pottery: a book for schools and students. [TP808.W63 1969] 69-12494 10.00
1. Pottery. I. Title. BIP

YOUNG, Helen. 738.14
Here is your hobby: ceramics. New York, Putnam [1962] 128 p. illus. 24 cm. Includes bibliography. [TP808.Y6] 62-14386
1. Pottery. I. Title.

Pottery—19th century—Addresses, essays, lectures.

CERAMIC art : 738'.09'04
comment and review, 1882-1977 : an anthology of writings on modern ceramic art / edited by Garth Clark. 1st ed. New York : E. P. Dutton, c1978. xxv, 197 p., [8] leaves of plates : ill. (some col.) ; 25 cm. Bibliography: p. 193-197. [NK3920.C47 1978] 78-53107 ISBN 0-525-47497-8 (DP). ISBN 0-525-07850-9 : 18.95
1. Pottery—19th century—Addresses, essays, lectures. 2. Pottery—20th century—Addresses, essays, lectures. 3. Form (Aesthetics)—Addresses, essays, lectures. I. Clark, Garth. BIP

Pottery—Addresses, essays, lectures.

MATSON, Frederick Rognald, 1912- ed. 738.30901
Ceramics and man. Ed. by Frederick R. Matson. Chicago, Aldine [c.1965] xii, 301p. illus. 28cm. (Viking Fund pubns. in anthro., no.41) Papers and discussion transcriptions of a symp. org. by the Wenner-Gren Found. for Anthrop. Res. and held at Burg Wartenstein, Austria, Sept. 2-12, 1961. Bibl. [NK4245.M3] 65-22492 7.50
1. Pottery—Addresses, essays, lectures. I. Wenner-Gren Foundation for Anthropological Research, New York. II. Title. III. Series.

Pottery, American.

BERKOW, Nancy Pratt. 738.3'7
Fiesta ware / by Nancy Berkow. Des Moines : Wallace-Homestead Book Co., c1978. i, 124 p. (p. 124 blank) : ill. (some col.) ; 21 cm. [NK4210.H65B47] 76-23908 ISBN 0-87069-200-3 pbk. : 8.95
1. Homer Laughlin China Company. 2. Pottery, American. I. Title. BIP

CHRISTENSEN, Erwin Ottomar, 1890- 738.15
Early American designs: ceramics. New York, Pitman Pub. Corp. [1962] 48 p. (chiefly illus.) 28 cm. [NK4005.C45] 52-2932
1. Pottery, American. 2. Decoration and ornament, American. I. Title.

DONHAUSER, Paul S. 738'.0973
History of American ceramics : the studio potter / Paul S. Donhauser. Dubuque, Iowa : Kendall/Hunt Pub. Co., c1978. xvi, 260 p., [5] leaves of plates : ill. (some col.) ; 29 cm. Includes index. Bibliography: p. 237-240. [NK4005.D66] 78-52547 ISBN 0-8403-1864-2 : 15.95
1. Pottery, American. I. Title. BIP

EVANS, Paul, 1937- 738.3'0973
Art pottery of the United States : an encyclopedia of producers and their marks / by Paul Evans. New York : Scribner, [1974] 353 p., [4] leaves of plates : ill. (some col.) ; 26 cm. Includes index. Bibliography: p. 345. [NK4007.E92] 74-19578 ISBN 0-684-14029-2 : 14.95
1. Pottery, American. 2. Pottery—Marks. I. Title. BIP

FELKER, Sharon Loraine. 738.3'7
Lovely Hull pottery / by Sharon L. Felker. [Des Moines, Iowa : Wallace-Homestead Book Co., 1974] [50] p. : ill. (some col.) ; 23 cm. Cover title. [NK4210.H84F44] 74-75949 5.95
1. Hull Pottery Company. 2. Pottery, American. I. Title.

GUILLAND, Harold F. 738.3'0973
Early American folk pottery [by] Harold F. Guilland. [1st ed.] Philadelphia, Chilton Book Co. [1971] xii, 321 p. illus. (part col.) 26 cm. Bibliography: p. 293-309. [NK4006.G8 1971] 70-159513 ISBN 0-8019-5436-3
1. Pottery, American. 2. Folk art—U.S. I. Title. BIP

HENZKE, Lucile. 738'.0973
American art pottery. Camden, T. Nelson [1970] 336 p. illus. (part col.) 28 cm. [NK4005.H45] 70-113171 17.50
1. Pottery, American. 2. Pottery—Marks. I. Title. BIP

HUXFORD, Sharon. 738.3'7
The collectors encyclopedia of Fiesta, with Harlequin and Riviera / by Sharon & Bob Huxford. Rev. 2d ed. Paducah, Ky. : Collector Books, c1976. 142 p. : col. ill. ; 22 cm. First ed. published in 1974 under title: The story of Fiesta. [NK4210.H65H89 1976] 77-361290 ISBN 0-89145-010-6 : 7.95
1. Homer Laughlin China Company. 2. Pottery, American. I. Huxford, Bob, joint author. II. Title.

HUXFORD, Sharon. 738.3'7
The collectors encyclopedia of Roseville pottery / by Sharon and Bob Huxford. 1st ed. Paducah, Ky. : Collector Books, c1976. 184 p. : ill. (some col.) ; 29 cm. Includes index. Bibliography: p. 179-182. [NK4210.R58H88] 76-358474 ISBN 0-89145-015-7 : 17.95
1. Roseville Pottery Company. 2. Roseville Pottery, inc. 3. Pottery, American. I. Huxford, Bob, joint author. II. Title. III. Title: Roseville pottery. BIP

JOHNSON, Deb. 738.3'0973
Beginner's book of American pottery; introduction to a field of collecting still relatively uncrowded, easy on the pocketbook, and full of delightful adventures, by Deb and Gini Johnson. Des Moines, Wallace-Homestead Book Co. [1974] 119 p. illus. (part col.) 23 cm. [NK4005.J64] 74-181611 ISBN 0-87069-079-5 5.95
1. Pottery, American. 2. Pottery—Collectors and collecting. I. Johnson, Gini, joint author. II. Title. III. Title: American pottery. BIP

KETCHUM, William C., 1931- 738'.0973
The pottery and porcelain collector's handbook; a guide to early American ceramics from Maine to California, by William C. Ketchum, Jr. New York, Funk & Wagnalls [1971] xx, 204 p. illus. 22 cm. [NK4005.K47] 71-137487 8.95
1. Pottery, American. 2. Porcelain, American. I. Title.

KOVEL, Ralph M. 738.3'0973
The Kovels' collector's guide to American art pottery / Ralph & Terry Kovel. New York : Crown Publishers, [1974] vi, 368 p., [8] leaves of plates : ill. (some col.) ; 26 cm. Includes bibliographies and index. [NK4005.K68 1974] 74-80295 ISBN 0-517-51676-4 : 12.95
1. Pottery, American. 2. Pottery—Collectors and collecting. 3. Pottery—Marks. I. Kovel, Terry H., joint author. II. Title. BIP

†RAMSAY, John, 1899- 738'.0973
American potters & pottery / by John Ramsay. Ann Arbor, Mich. : Ars Ceramica, 1976. xx, 304 p., [16] leaves of plates : ill. ; 27 cm. Reprint of the 1939 ed. published by Hale, Cushman & Flint, Boston; with new introd. Includes index. Bibliography: p. 244-251. [NK4005.R3 1976] 76-22944 ISBN 0-89344-006-X : 24.50
1. Pottery, American. 2. Potters—United States—Directories. I. Title. BIP

SCHWARTZ, Marvin D. 738'.0973
Collectors' guide to antique American ceramics, by Marvin D. Schwartz. [1st ed.] Garden City, N.Y., Doubleday, 1969. x, 134 p. illus. 22 cm. [NK4005.S3] 69-10989 4.95
1. Pottery, American. 2. Porcelain, American. 3. Pottery—Collectors and collecting—U.S. 4. Porcelain—Collectors and collecting—U.S. I. Title.

SMITH, Elmer Lewis. 738.3'0973
Pottery; a utilitarian folk craft. Compiled by Elmer L. Smith. Photographed by Bradford L. Rauschenberg. Lebanon, Pa., Applied Arts Publishers [1972] 32 p. illus. 29 cm. [NK4005.A1S75] 72-190943 1.25
1. Pottery, American. 2. Folk art—United States. I. Title.

SPARGO, John, 1876-1966. 738'.0973
Early American pottery and china / by John Spargo. Rutland, Vt. : C. E. Tuttle Co., 1974. xix, 393 p., 64 leaves of plates : ill. ; 20 cm. Reprint of the 1926 ed. published by Century Co., New York, issued in series: Century library of American antiques; with a new introd. [NK4006.S7 1974] 74-78148 ISBN 0-8048-1135-0 : 12.50
1. Pottery, American. I. Title. II. Series: Century library of American antiques. BIP

STEWART, Regina. 738.3'0973
Stoneware / Regina Stewart, Geraldine Cosentino. New York : Golden Press, c1977. 128 p. : ill. (some col.) ; 21 cm. (A Golden handbook of collectibles) Includes index. Bibliography: p. 127. [NK4007.S76] 76-55048 ISBN 0-307-43177-0 : 3.95
1. Pottery, American. 2. Pottery—19th century—United States. 3. Pottery—20th century—United States. I. Cosentino, Geraldine, joint author. II. Title. BIP

WEBSTER, Donald Blake. 738.3'83'097
Decorated stoneware pottery of North America. Rutland, Vt., C. E. Tuttle Co. [1971] 232 p. illus. 29 cm. Bibliography: p. 229-230. [NK4003.W4] 71-134032 ISBN 0-8048-0007-3 15.00
1. Pottery, American. 2. Pottery, Canadian. I. Title. BIP

Pottery, American—Catalogs.

HARBIN, Edith. 738.3'7
Blue & white stoneware, pottery & crockery / by Edith Harbin. Paducah, Ky. : Collector Books, c1977. 63 p. : col. ill. ; 22 cm. [NK4005.H36] 77-369197 pbk. : 7.95
1. Pottery, American—Catalogs. 2. Folk art—United States—Catalogs. I. Title. BIP

PETTERSON, Richard B., comp. 738'.0973
Ceramic art in America; a portfolio. Edited by Richard B. Petterson. [Columbus, Ohio, Professional Publications, 1969] [4] p., 32 plates (in portfolio) 36 cm. [NK4008.P4] 79-90375
1. Pottery, American—Catalogs. I. Title.

Pottery, American—Detroit.

PEAR, Lillian Myers. 738'.09774'34
The Pewabic Pottery : a history of its products and its people / by Lillian Myers Pear. Bicentennial ed. Des Moines : Wallace-Homestead Book Co., c1976. 295 p. : ill. (some col.) ; 29 cm. Includes indexes. Bibliography: p. 263-265. [NK4210.P48P4] 75-23558 ISBN 0-87069-158-9 : 22.50
1. Pewabic Pottery (Firm) 2. Pottery, American—Detroit. I. Title. BIP

Pottery, American — Exhibitions.

BARONS, Richard I. 738.3'0973'074014734
An exhibition of 18th and 19th century American folk pottery [by Richard I. Barons. New Paltz, N.Y., 1969] 35 p. illus. 18 x 26 cm. Held at College Art Gallery, State University College at New Paltz, N.Y., Feb. 25-Mar. 8, 1969. "Sponsored by the Student Art Guild." [NK4006.A1B3] 73-630459
1. Pottery, American—Exhibitions. 2. Folk art—U.S. I. New York (State). State University College, New Paltz. Art Gallery. II. New York (State). State University College, New Paltz. Student Art Guild. III. Title: 18th and 19th century American folk pottery.

CALIFORNIA. University, Irvine. Art Gallery. 738.30973
Abstract expressionist ceramics; [exhibition] Art Gallery, University of California, Irvine, October 28th to November 27th, 1966. [Irvine, 1966] 54 p. illus. (part col.) 24 cm. Bibliography: p. 49. [NK4008.C3] 66-65165
1. Pottery, American—Exhibitions. 2. Art, Abstract—Exhibitions. I. Title.

EVERSON Museum of Art of Syracuse and Onondaga County. 738'.0973
Ceramic national exhibition. [Syracuse, N.Y.] v. illus. 24-26 cm. Annual, 19 biennial, 1954- First exhibition held in 1932. Title varies: 19 National ceramic exhibition. -- 19 Ceramic national. Exhibitions for 19 organized by the Syracuse Museum of Fine Arts (with Onondaga Pottery Company, 19 [NK4008.E9] 67-1524
1. Pottery, American — Exhibitions. I. Syracuse, N.Y. Museum of Fine Arts. National ceramic exhibition. II. Onondaga Pottery Company, Syracuse, N.Y. III. Title.

NATZLER, Gertrud. 738'.0924
The ceramic work of Gertrud and Otto Natzler. [San Francisco, M. H. de Young Memorial Museum, 1971] 74 p. illus. (part col.), ports. 22 cm. Catalog of a retrospective exhibition held July 24 - September 6, 1971, at M. H. de Young Memorial Museum, San Francisco. Bibliography: p. 64-72. [NK4210.N3N3] 71-169966
I. Natzler, Otto. II. De Young Memorial Museum, San Francisco. III. Title.

NATZLER, Gertrud. 738'.0922
The ceramic work of Gertrud and Otto Natzler; a retrospective exhibition, 15th June-14th August, 1966, Los Angeles County Museum of Art, Lytton Gallery. [Los Angeles, Lithographed by Koltun Bros. for the Los Angeles County Museum of Art, 1966] 1 v. (unpaged) plates (part col.) 21 x 22 cm. [NK4200.N3] 68-6805
I. Natzler, Otto. II. Los Angeles Co., Calif. Museum of Art, Los Angeles. III. Title.

ROCHESTER Museum and Science Center. 738.3'09747'88
Clay in the hands of the potter; an exhibition of pottery manufactured in the Rochester and Genesee Valley Region, c. 1793-1900. Rochester,N.Y. [1974] 56 p. illus. 18 x 26 cm. Catalog of an exhibition held March 29-August 19, 1974. Bibliography: p. 56. [NK4025.N72R627 1974] 74-170873
1. Pottery, American—Exhibitions. 2. Pottery—Rochester region, N.Y. 3. Pottery—Genesee region, N.Y. I. Title.

WILLIAMS, Gerald. 738.3'0924
Gerry Williams: ceramics [exhibition] February 14 to March 15, 1970, the Currier Gallery of Art, Manchester, New Hampshire. [Manchester, N.H., Currier Gallery of Art, 1970] 31 p. illus., ports. 23 cm. Catalog of the exhibition. [NK4210.W5A45] 79-13634
I. Currier Gallery of Art, Manchester, N.H.

YOUNG 738'.0973'07401471
Americans : clay/glass : May 6-June 11, 1978, the Tucson Museum of Art, Tucson, Arizona, July 21-September 30, 1978, the Museum of Contemporary Crafts of the American Crafts Council / sponsored by the American Crafts Council ; exhibition organized by the Museum of Contemporary Crafts ; [photography by Joe Schopplein]. [New York] : The Council, c1978. [32] p. : ill. (some col.) ; 22 cm. [NK4008.Y68] 78-57040 ISBN 0-88321-025-8 pbk. : 4.85
1. Pottery, American—Exhibitions. 2. Pottery—20th century—United States—Exhibitions. 3. Glassware—United States—History—20th century—Exhibitions. I. Tucson Museum of Art. II. American Crafts Council. Museum of Contemporary Crafts.

Pottery, American—History.

BARBER, Edwin Atlee, 1851-1916. 738'.0973
Pottery and porcelain of the United States; an historical review of American ceramic art. With a new introduction and bibliography. Watkins Glen, N.Y., Century House Americana, 1971. 450 p. illus. 24 cm. Bibliography: p. 407-435. [NK4005.B23 1971] 79-96939
1. Pottery, American—History. 2. Pottery—Marks. I. Title.

Pottery, American—Minnesota—Red Wing.

VIEL, Lyndon C. 738.3'7
The clay giants : the stoneware of Red Wing, Goodhue County, Minnesota / by Lyndon C. Viel. Des Moines, Iowa : Wallace-Homestead Book Co., c1977. 128 p. : ill. (some col.) ; 28 cm. [NK4210.R4V53] 76-24235 ISBN 0-87069-175-9 : 9.95
1. Red Wing Potteries. 2. Pottery, American—Minnesota—Red Wing. I. Title. BIP

Pottery, American—New York (State)

KETCHUM, William C., 1931- 738.3'09'747
Early potters and potteries of New York State [by] William C. Ketchum, Jr. New York, Funk & Wagnalls [1970] x, 278 p. illus., map. 22 cm. Bibliography: p. 254-269. [NK4025.N7K4] 71-100537 10.00
1. Pottery, American—New York (State) 2. Pottery—New York (State) 3. Potters—New York (State) I. Title.

Pottery, American—Ohio—Catalogs.

HUXFORD, Sharon. 738.3'7
The collectors encyclopedia of Brush McCoy pottery / by Sharon and Bob Huxford. 1st ed. Paducah, Ky. : Collector Books, c1978. 190 p. : ill. ; 29 cm. Includes index. Bibliography: p. 188-189. [NK4210.B73H88] 78-113434 ISBN 0-89145-078-5 : 17.95
1. Brush—McCoy Pottery Company. 2. Pottery—Ohio—Collectors and collecting. I. Huxford, Bob, joint author. II. Title. BIP

HUXFORD, Sharon. 738.3'7
The collectors encyclopedia of McCoy pottery / by Sharon and Bob Huxford. 1st ed. Paducah, Ky. : Collector Books, c1978. 239 p. : ill. (some col.) ; 29 cm. Includes index. Bibliography:p. 238. [NK4210.M23A4 1978] 78-107663 ISBN 0-89145-068-8 : 17.95
1. Nelson McCoy Pottery Company—Catalogs. 2. Brush-McCoy Pottery Company—Catalogs. 3. Pottery, American—Ohio—Catalogs. I. Huxford, Bob, joint author. II. Title. BIP

Pottery, American—Ohio—Directories.

LEHNER, Lois. 738'.02'78
Ohio pottery and glass : marks and manufacturers / by Lois Lehner. Des Moines : Wallace-Homestead book Co., c1978. 113 p. : ill. ; 28 cm. Includes index. Bibliography: p. 109-113. [NK4025.O5L43] 76-15492 ISBN 0-87069-168-6 : 9.95
1. Pottery, American—Ohio—Directories. 2. Pottery—Marks. 3. Glassware—Ohio—Directories. 4. Glass—Trade-marks. I. Title.

Pottery, American—Ohio—Zanesville.

SIMON, Dolores H. 738.3'7
Shawnee pottery in color : [an illustrated value guide] / by Dolores H. Simon. Paducah, Ky. : Collector Books, c1977. 64 p. : ill. ; 22 cm. [NK4210.S52S55] 77-150235 ISBN 0-89145-030-0 : 7.95
1. Shawnee Pottery Company. 2. Pottery, American—Ohio—Zanesville. I. Title.

Pottery, American—Texas—Exhibitions.

HUMPHREYS, Sherry B. 738'.09764'0740164245
Texas pottery : Caddo Indian to contemporary / Sherry B. Humphreys, Johnell L. Schmidt. Washington, Tex. : Star of the Republic Museum, c1976. 45 p. : ill. (some col.) ; 21 x 22 cm. Catalog of an exhibition at the Star of the Republic Museum. Bibliography: p. 45. [NK4027.T4H85] 76-371313
1. Pottery, American—Texas—Exhibitions. 2. Pottery—Texas—Exhibitions. I. Schmidt, Johnell L., joint author. II. Star of the Republic Museum. III. Title.

Pottery, Ancient.

CURRIER, Richard L. 738.3'09'01
Pottery in ancient times / by Rivka Gonen ; retold for young readers by Richard L. Currier ; edited by Michael Avi-Yonah. Minneapolis : Lerner Publications Co., 1974, c1973. 94 p. : ill. (some col.) ; 21 cm. (The Lerner archaeology series) (Digging up the past) Includes index. [NK3800.C87 1974] 72-10796 ISBN 0-8225-0829-X
1. Pottery, Ancient. I. Gonen, Rivka. Ancient pottery. II. Title. BIP

NICHOLSON, Felicity 738.109
Greek, Etruscan, and Roman pottery and small terracottas; a brief guide for the small collector, with a note on Greek dress [London] Corv. Adams & Mackay [New York, Taplinger c.1965] 66 [1]p. illus. map (on lining paps.) 26cm. Bibl. [NK3835.N5] 66-67 5.50
1. Pottery, Ancient. 2. Terra-cottas. I. Title.

Pottery, Ancient—Bulgaria.

SULTOV, Bogdan. 738.3'0939'8
Ancient pottery centres in Moesia inferior / Bogdan Soultov ; artist, Dimiter Kartalev ; photogr., Toros Horisyan ; transl., Petroushka Tomova. Sofia : Sofia-Press, 1976. 111 p. : ill. (some col.) ; 26 cm. Bibliography: p. 111. [NK3855.B9S8413] 77-469914
1. Pottery, Ancient—Bulgaria. 2. Pottery—Bulgaria. 3. Pottery—Moesia Inferior. 4. Bulgaria—Antiquities. I. Title.

Pottery, Anglo-Saxon.

MYRES, John Nowell Linton. 738.3'0942
A corpus of Anglo-Saxon pottery of the pagan period / J. N. L. Myres. Cambridge [Eng.] ; New York : Cambridge University Press, 1977. 2 v. : ill. ; 31 cm. (Gulbenkian archaeological series) Includes indexes. Bibliography: p. v. 1, p. xxvi-xxxvi. [NK4085.M92] 76-11088 ISBN 0-521-21285-5 : 115.00 (2 vols.)
1. Pottery, Anglo-Saxon. 2. England—Antiquities. I. Title. BIP

Pottery, Arretine—Catalogs.

OXFORD. University. Ashmolean Museum. Dept. of Antiquities. 738.3'7
Catalogue of Italian terra-sigillata in the Ashmolean Museum, by A. C. Brown. Oxford, Clarendon Pr., 1968. xix, 39p. 26 plates, illus. 29cm. [NK3850.O9] 68-92654 10.10
1. Pottery, Arretine—Catalogs. 2. Pottery—Oxford—Catalogs. 3. Pottery—Marks. I. Brown, Ann Cynthia. II. Title.
Available from Oxford Univ. Pr., New York. BIP

Pottery as an investment.

MORLEY-FLETCHER, Hugo. 738
Investing in pottery & porcelain. New York, C. N. Potter [1968] 155 p. illus., col. plates. 31 cm. ([The New currency series]) [NK4230.M6 1968b] 68-26883 7.95
1. Pottery as an investment. 2. Porcelain as an investment. I. Title.

Pottery—Bennington, Vt.

BARRET, Richard Carter. 738
Bennington pottery and porcelain; a guide to identification. Halftone photos. by Lloyd Oppenheimer. New York, Crown Publishers, 1958. 342 p. illus. (part col.) 28 cm. [NK4027.B4B3] 58-8312
1. Pottery—Bennington, Vt. I. Title.

BARRET, Richard Carter. 738.3097438
How to identify Bennington pottery. Brattleboro, Vt., S. Greene Press, 1964. 71 p. illus. 22 cm. [NK4027.B4B32] 64-17558
1. Pottery — Bennington, Vt. I. Title. BIP

Pottery—Bibliography.

CAMPBELL, James Edward. 016.738
Pottery and ceramics : a guide to information sources / edited by James Edward Campbell. Detroit : Gale Research Co., [1977] p. cm. (Art and architecture information guide series ; v. 7) [Z7179.C35] [NK4225] 74-11545 ISBN 0-8103-1274-3 : 18.00
1. Pottery—Bibliography. I. Title. BIP

WEINRICH, Peter H. 016.738
A bibliographic guide to books on ceramics = Guide bibliographique des ouvrages sur la ceramique / Peter H. Weinrich. Ottawa : Canadian Crafts Council, 1976. xiii, 272 p. ; 24 cm. Limited ed. of 500 copies. Includes index. [Z7179.W44] [NK4225] 77-373015 ISBN 0-88980-000-6
1. Pottery—Bibliography. 2. Porcelain—Bibliography. I. Title. II. Title: Guide bibliographique des ouvrages sur la ceramique.

Pottery, British.

CASSON, Michael, 1925- 738.3
Pottery in Britain today. Melbourne, Flesch, 1967. 1 v. (chiefly plates) 29 cm. [NK4085.C3 1967c] 70-363386 8.50
1. Pottery, British. 2. Potters—Gt. Brit. I. Title.

CASSON, Michael, 1925- 738.3'0942
Pottery in Britain today. [1st American ed.] New York, Transatlantic Arts, 1967. 1 v. (unpaged) 244 illus. (1 col.) 30 cm. [NK4085.C3 1967b] 68-442
1. Pottery, British 2. Pottery—Great Britain. I. Title.

COYSH, Arthur Wilfred. 738'.0941
British art pottery, 1870-1940 / A. W. Coysh. Rutland, Vt. : C. E. Tuttle Co., c1976. 96 p. : ill. ; 24 cm. Includes index. Bibliography: p. 93. [NK4085.C65] 76-6748 ISBN 0-8048-1202-0 : 10.00
1. Pottery, British. 2. Decoration and ornament—Great Britain. I. Title. BIP

CUSHION, John Patrick. 738'.02'78
Pocket book of British ceramic marks, including index to registered designs, 1842-83 / compiled by J. P. Cushion. 3d enl. ed., rev. and reset. London; Salem, NH Faber & Faber 1976 431 p. : ill. ; 17 cm. First-2d ed. published under title: Pocket book of English ceramic marks and those of Wales, Scotland, and Ireland. Includes index. [NK4085.C8 1976] 76-353781 ISBN 0-571-04869-2 : 9.95
1. Pottery, British. 2. Pottery—Marks. I. Title: Pocket book of British ceramic marks ...

GODDEN, Geoffrey A. 738.3'0942
British pottery : an illustrated guide / Geoffrey A. Godden. 1st American ed. New York : C. N. Potter : distributed by Crown Publishers, 1975. 452 p., [10] leaves of plates : ill. (some col.) ; 26 cm. Includes index. Bibliography: p. 445-447. [NK4085.G599 1975] 74-14332 15.00
1. Pottery, British. I. Title.

GODDEN, Geoffrey A. 738.2
An illustrated encyclopedia of British pottery and porcelain [by] Geoffrey A. Godden. New York, Crown [1966] xxvi, 390 p. illus. (part col.) 26 cm. Bibliography: p. 385. [NK4085.G64 1966a] 66-23065
1. Pottery, British. 2. Porcelain, British. I. Title.

HUGHES, George Bernard, 1896- 738.37
Victorian pottery and porcelain. New York, Macmillan [1960, c1959] 184 p. illus. 26 cm. Includes bibliography. [NK40H5.H84 1960] 60-930
1. Pottery, British. 2. Porcelain, British. I. Title.

Pottery, British—Dictionaries.

GODDEN, Geoffrey A. 738.880942
Encyclopaedia of British pottery and porcelain marks, by Geoffrey A. Godden. New York, Crown [1964] 765 p. illus., map. 26 cm. Bibliography: p. [741]-744. [NK4085.G63] 64-22014
1. Pottery, British—Dictionaries. 2. Porcelain, British—Dictionaries. 3. Pottery—Marks. 4. Porcelain—Marks. I. Title.

Pottery, British—Handbooks, manuals, etc.

GODDEN, Geoffrey A. 738'.0278
The handbook of British pottery and porcelain marks. New York, Praeger [1968] 197 p. illus. 20 cm. Bibliography: p. 190-191. [NK4085.G635 1968b] 68-19134
1. Pottery, British—Handbooks, manuals, etc. 2. Porcelain, British—Handbooks, manuals, etc. 3. Pottery—Marks. 4. Porcelain—Marks. I. Title.

Pottery, British—History.

GODDEN, Geoffrey A. 738.30942
British pottery and porcelain, 1780-1850, by Geoffrey A. Godden [New York] A. S. Barnes [1964, c1963] 144 p. illus., map, col. plates. 28 cm. Bibliography: p. 138-140. [NK4085.G6 1964a] 64-57297
1. Pottery, British—History. 2. Porcelain, British—History. I. Title.

JEWITT, Llewellynn 738'.0942
Frederick William, 1816-1886.
Jewitt's Ceramic art of Great Britain, 1800-1900, by Geoffrey A. Godden. Being a rev. and expanded ed. of those parts of The ceramic art of Great Britain by Llewellynn Jewitt dealing with the nineteenth century. New York, Arco Pub. Co. [1972, c1971] xxviii, 282 p. illus. 26 cm. Bibliography: p. 263-266. [NK4085.J52 1792b] 76-184414 ISBN 0-668-02595-6 25.00
1. Pottery, British—History. I. Godden, Geoffrey A. II. Title. III. Title: Ceramic art of Great Britain, 1800-1900.

*LOCKETT, T. A. 738.3'7
Davenport pottery and porcelain 1794-1887. Rutland, Vt., C. E. Tuttle [1973, c1972] [112 p.] illus. 25 cm. [NK4087] ISBN 0-8048-1079-6. 10.00.
1. Pottery, British—History. I. Title. BIP

Pottery, Canadian.

WEBSTER, Donald Blake. 738.3'0971
Early Canadian pottery [by] Donald Webster. Greenwich, Conn., New York Graphic Society [1971] 256 p. illus. (part col.) 26 cm. Bibliography: p. 249-250. [NK4029.W38 1971] 75-162722 ISBN 0-8212-0409-2 12.50
1. Pottery, Canadian. I. Title.

Pottery—Catalogs.

CATALOG of Rookwood art 666'.3'74
pottery shapes. [Kingston, N.Y., P-B Enterprises, 1971- v. illus. 28 cm. Cover title. "This is no. 21 of a limited printing of 300 copies." [TP818.C37] 79-28292
1. Pottery—Catalogs.

Pottery, Chinese.

BARLOW, James Alan Noel, 730.951
bart., Sir 1881-
Chinese ceramics, bronzes and jades in the collection of Sir Alan and Lady Barlow, by Michael Sullivan. London, Faber & Faber [dist. New York, Paragon, c.1963] 173p. plates (pt. col.) maps. 29cm. Bibl. 63-24839 32.50
1. Pottery, Chinese. 2. Bronzes, Chinese. 3. Jade. 4. Art objects—Private collections. I. Sullivan, Michael, 1916- II. Title.

CHU, Yen. 738'.0951
Description of Chinese pottery and porcelain; being a translation of the T'ao shuo, with introd., notes, and bibliography, by Stephen W. Bushell. Oxford, Clarendon Press, 1910. [New York, AMS Press, 1973] xxxi, 222 p. 23 cm. "Appendix: Lettre[s] du pere d'Entrecolles Missionnaire de la Compagnie de Jesus: au pere Orry de la mesme Compagnie": p. [181]-222. Bibliography: p. [173]-179. [NK4165.C513 1973] 77-38058 ISBN 0-404-56914-5 12.50
1. Pottery, Chinese. 2. Porcelain, Chinese. I. Bushell, Stephen Wootton, 1844-1908, tr. II. Entrecolles, Francois Xavier d', 1663-1741. III. Title. BIP

HAYASHIYA, Seizo 738.0951
Chinese ceramics. by Seizo Hayashiva. Gakuji Hasebe. Tr. by Charles A. Pomerov. Rutland, Vt., Tuttle [c.1966] 95p., 114 plates (pt. col.) illus., map. 29cm. [NK4165.H313] 66-12057 15.00
I. Title.

HOBSON, Robert 738'.0951
Lockhart, 1872-1941.
Chinese pottery and porcelain : an account of the potter's art in China from primitive times to the present day / R. L. Hobson. New York : Dover Publications, 1976. xxx, 227, xvi, 326 p., [76] leaves of plates : ill. (some col.) ; 21 cm. Reprint of the 1915 ed. originally published in 2 v. by Funk and Wagnalls Co., New York. Includes index. Contents.Contents.—Pottery and early wares.—Ming and Ch'ing porcelain. Bibliography: p. xxvii-xxx. [NK4165.H7 1975] 76-372136 ISBN 0-486-23253-0 pbk. : 10.00
1. Pottery, Chinese. 2. Porcelain, Chinese. I. Title. BIP

HOBSON, Robert 738.20951
Lockhart, 1872-1941.
The wares of the Ming dynasty. Rutland, Vt., C. E. Tuttle Co. [1962] xvi, 208 p. 60 plates (part col.) 28 cm. Bibliography: p. 199-200. [NK4165.H8 1962] 62-18358
1. Pottery, Chinese. I. Title. BIP

JENYNS, Roger Soame, 1904- v. 12
Ming pottery and porcelain. New York, Pitman [1954] xi, 160 p. 124 plates (part col.) 26 cm. (The Faber monographs on pottery and porcelain) "Sequel to the author's Later Chinese porcelain." Bibliography: p. 156-157. [[NK165.J]] A56
1. Pottery, Chinese. 2. Porcelain, Chinese. I. Title.

KU kung po wu yuan, 738.0951
T'aichung, Formosa.
Kuan of the Sung dynasty, Comp. by the Joint Board of Directors of the National Palace Museum and the National Central Museum, Taichung, Taiwan, Republic of China. Kowloon, Hong Kong. Cafa Co. [dist. New York, Paragon Bk., 1963] 61p. col. plates (on double leaves) 40cm. (Porcelain of the Natl. Palace Mus.) Chinese and English; added colophon title in Chinese. 63-6524 35.00
1. Pottery, Chinese. I. Title. II. Title: Ku kung ts'ang tz'u—kuan yao. III. Series.

LAUFER, Berthold, 1874- 738.30951
1934.
Chinese poetry of the Han dynasty. [2d ed.] Rutland. Vt., C. E. Tuttle Co. [1962] 339p. illus. 21cm. [NK4165.L3 1962] 62-14935
1. Pottery, Chinese. I. Title.

NEAVE-HILL, W. B. R 738'.0951
Chinese ceramics / W. B. R. Neave-Hill ; foreword by Sir Harry Garner. New York : St. Martin's Press, 1976, c1975. 176 p. : ill. (some col.) ; 31 cm. Includes index. Bibliography: p. 171-172. [NK4165.N38 1976] 75-18991 20.00
1. Pottery, Chinese. 2. Porcelain, Chinese. I. Title.

PRODAN, Mario. 738.30951
The art of the Tang potter. New York, Viking Press [1961, c1960] 186p. mounted col. illus., plates. 32cm. (A Studio book) Bibliography: p. 179. [NK4165.P7] 61-8064
1. Pottery. Chinese. I. Title.

Pottery, Chinese—Catalogs.

GULBENKIAN Museum of 738'.0951
Oriental Art and Archaeology.
A descriptive and illustrated catalogue of the Malcolm Macdonald collection of Chinese ceramics in the Gulbenkian Museum of Oriental Art and Archaeology, School of Oriental Studies, University of Durham, by Ireneus Laszlo Lageza; with a foreword by Malcolm Macdonald. London, Oxford University Press, 1972. lxxxiii, 112, cxlvi p. illus. (some col.), map. 29 cm. Bibliography: p. 101-112. [NK4165.G8] 72-193708 ISBN 0-19-713135-2 £15.00
1. Macdonald, Malcolm, 1901- —Art collections. 2. Pottery, Chinese—Catalogs. 3. Porcelain, Chinese—Catalogs. I. Lageza, Ireneus Laszlo. II. Title.

Pottery, Chinese—Exhibitions.

CHINESE ceramics 738'.0951'074013
from Japanese collections : T'ang through Ming Dynasties / Seizo Hayashiya, and Henry Trubner ; in collaboration with Gakuji Hasebe ...[et al.]. [New York] : Asia Society, c1977. 135 p. : ill. (some col.) ; 26 cm. "An exhibition of Chinese ceramics from public and private collections in Japan organized under the joint sponsorship of the Agency for Cultural affairs of the Japanese Government and the participating institutions in the United States." Held at the Asia House Gallery, New York, and at three other museums. Bibliography : p. 133-135. [NK4165.C4796] 77-1654 ISBN 0-87848-049-8 : 19.95
1. Pottery, Chinese—Exhibitions. 2. Pottery—Collectors and collecting—Japan—Exhibitions. 3. Porcelain, Chinese—Exhibitions. 4. Porcelain—Collectors and collecting—Japan—Exhibitions. I. Hayashiya, Seizo. II. Japan. Bunkacho. III. Asia House Gallery, New York. BIP

KUWAYAMA, George. 738'.0951
Chinese ceramics: the Heeramaneck Collection, a gift from Nasli M. Heeramaneck. [Los Angeles, Los Angeles County Museum of Art, c1973] 48 p. illus. 26 cm. Catalog of an exhibition held at the Los Angeles County Museum of Art, Dec. 18, 1973-Mar. 3, 1974. Bibliography: p. 47-48. [NK4165.K9] 73-89351 ISBN 0-87587-057-0
1. Heeramaneck, Nasli M.—Art collections. 2. Pottery, Chinese—Exhibitions. 3. Porcelain, Chinese—Exhibitions. I. Los Angeles Co., Calif. Museum of Art, Los Angeles. II. Title. BIP

LOS Angeles County Museum, 738
Los Angeles.
Chinese ceramics, from the prehistoric period through Ch'ien Lung; a loan exhibition from collections in America and Japan. Mar. 14 to Apr. 27, 1952. [Los Angeles, 1952] 119p. illus., map. 27cm. Bibliography: p. 118-119. [NK4165.L65] 52-9160
1. Pottery, Chinese—Exhibition. I. Title.

SCHLOSS, Ezekiel. 738.2'0951
Foreigners in ancient Chinese art; from private and museum collections. [Exhibition] Mar. 27 through May 25, 1969, China House Gallery. New York, China Institute in America [1969] [48] p. illus., map. 23 cm. [NK4165.S29] 72-14545
1. Pottery, Chinese—Exhibitions. I. China Institute in America. II. Title.

Pottery, Chinese—Fou-liang, China (Kiangsi Province)

BRANKSTON, Archibald 738.2'0951
Dooley.
Early Ming wares of Chingtechen. Hong Kong, Vetch and Lee. New York, Paragon Book Reprint Corp. [1970, c1938] A-J, xvi, 102 p. illus., maps. 25 cm. "Reissued with a biographical and bibliographical notice of the author, and a note on 'The A. D. Brankston collection of Chinese porcelain in the British Museum', by Soame Jenyns (1954)" Bibliography: p. [89]-90. [NK4166.F6B7 1970b] 73-24987 ISBN 0-85331-275-3 60.00 (Hong Kong)
1. Pottery, Chinese—Fou-liang, China (Kiangsi Province) I. Title.

Pottery, Chinese—History.

MEDLEY, Margaret. 738'.0951
The Chinese potter : a practical history of Chinese ceramics / Margaret Medley. New York : Scribner, c1976. 288 p., [4] leaves of plates : ill. ; 26 cm. Includes index. Bibliography: p. 282-284. [NK4165.M39 1976b] 76-6023 ISBN 0-684-14684-3 : 20.00
1. Pottery, Chinese—History. 2. Porcelain, Chinese—History. I. Title.

VALENSTEIN, Suzanne G. 739'.0951
A handbook of Chinese ceramics / Suzanne G. Valenstein. New York : Metropolitan Museum of Art : distributed by New York Graphic Society, [1975] p. cm. Bibliography: p. [NK4165.V34] 75-22208 ISBN 0-87099-131-0 : 15.00. ISBN 0-87099-132-9 pbk. : 9.95
1. Pottery, Chinese—History. 2. Porcelain, Chinese—History. I. New York (City). Metropolitan Museum of Art. II. Title.

Pottery, Chinese—Ming-Ch'ing dynasties, 1368-1912.

HOBSON, Robert 738'.0951
Lockhart, 1872-1941.
The wares of the Ming dynasty / by R. L. Hobson. New York : Dover Publications, 1978. xiii, 238 p., [4] leaves of plates : ill. (some col.) ; 24 cm. Reprint of the 1923 ed. published by Benn Bros., London. Includes index. Bibliography: p. 231-232. [NK4165.5.H6 1978] 78-50103 ISBN 0-486-23652-8 : 6.00
1. Pottery, Chinese—Ming-Ch'ing dynasties, 1368-1912. 2. Ming porcelain. I. Title.

Pottery, Chinese—Sung dynasty, 960-1279.

MINO, Yutaka. 738'.0951
Ceramics in the Liao dynasty, north and south of the Great Wall. [New York, China Institute in America, 1973] 86 p. illus. 24 cm. Catalog of an exhibition at the China House Gallery, New York, Mar. 15 through May 28, 1973. Bibliography: p. 20-26. [NK4165.4.M56] 73-75676 3.00 (pbk.)
1. Pottery, Chinese—Sung dynasty, 960-1279. 2. Pottery, Chinese—Exhibitions. I. China House Gallery. II. Title.
Publisher's Address: 125 E. 65th St. N.Y. 10021.

Pottery—Collectors and collecting.

CURTIS, Tony. 738'.075
China / compiled and edited by Tony Curtis. Galashiels : Lyle Publications, 1976. 3-126 p. : ill. ; 16 cm. (Antiques and their values) Includes index. [NK4230.C78] 76-382223 ISBN 0-902921-43-6 : £1.50
1. Pottery—Collectors and collecting. 2. Pottery—Prices. 3. Porcelain—Collectors and collecting. 4. Porcelain—Prices. I. Title.

CUSHION, John Patrick. 738
Pottery & porcelain/ John P. Cushion; drawings by C. R. Evans. New York: Hearst Books: distributed by [Avon Books] 1976 c1972. 231, [8] p.: ill. (part col.); 22 cm. (The Connoisseur illustrated guides) Includes index. Bibliography: p. 221-222. [NK4230.C82] ISBN 0-87851-301-9 pbk.: 5.95
1. Pottery—Collectors and collecting. 2. Porcelain—Collectors and collecting. I. Title.
L.C. card no. for original ed.: 73-151693.

JACKSON, Mary L 738.3
If dishes could talk. Boston, Meador Pub. Co. [1959] 240p. illus. 21cm. Includes bibliography. [NK4230.J3] 59-14789
1. Pottery—Collectors and collecting. 2. Pottery—Hist. I. Title. BIP

KAMM, Minnie Elizabeth 738
(Watson), 1886-
Old China. Photos. by E. J. Santee; drawings by the author. [1st ed. Grosse Pointe Farms, Mich., 1951] 251 p. illus. 22 cm. [NK4230.K3] 52-389
1. Pottery—Collectors and collecting. 2. Pottery—Hist. 3. Pottery—Marks. I. Title.

WOLSELEY, Cecilia. 738.2'075
These minor monuments; fresh lights on china appreciation [by] Cecilia Wolseley and Felicia Schuster. New York, Arco [1971, c1970] xi, 115 p. illus. 23 cm. Bibliography: p. 115. [NK4230.W64] 70-134273 4.95
1. Pottery—Collectors and collecting. 2. Porcelain—Collectors and collecting. I. Schuster, Felicia, joint author. II. Title.

Pottery—Collectors and collecting—United States.

EARLE, Alice (Morse) 738'.075
1851-1911.
China collecting in America. Detroit, Singing Tree Press, 1970. xi, 429 p. illus. 22 cm. Reprint of the 1892 ed. [NK4230.E3 1970] 77-99044
1. Pottery—Collectors and collecting—United States. 2. Porcelain—Collectors and collecting—United States. I. Title. BIP

EARLE, Alice (Morse) 738'.075
1851-1911.
China collecting in America. Rutland, Vt., C. E. Tuttle Co. [1973] xiii, 429 p. illus. 19 cm. (Tut books, C.) Reprint of the 1892 ed. [NK4230.E3 1973] 78-142764 ISBN 0-8048-0958-5 3.25
1. Pottery—Collectors and collecting—United States. 2. Porcelain—Collectors and collecting—United States. I. Title.

Pottery craft.

BAGG, Graham W. 738.1
Pottery techniques on and off the wheel, by Graham W. Bagg. New York, Van Nostrand Reinhold Co. [1974] p. cm. [TT920.B33] 73-16698 ISBN 0-442-30023-9 7.95
1. Pottery craft. I. Title.

BALL, Frederick Carlton. 738.14
Making pottery without a wheel; texture and form in clay [by] F. Carlton Ball and Janice Lovoos. New York, Reinhold [1965] 159 p. illus. 29 cm. Bibliography: p. 158. [NK4225.B27] 65-12977
1. Pottery craft. I. Lovoos, Janice, joint author. II. Title. BIP

BILLINGTON, Dora M. 738
Pottery for everyone [by] Dora Billington. Rev. by John Colbeck. New York, Watson-Guptill [1974] 175 p. illus. 26 cm. Bibliography: p. 168-169. [TT920.B54 1974] 73-21808 ISBN 0-8230-5180-3 10.00
1. Pottery craft. I. Title.

BIRKS, Tony. 738.1
The potter's companion / Tony Birks. 1st [i.e. American] ed. New York : Dutton, 1977, c1974. 208 p. : ill. (some col.) ; 23 cm. "A Sunrise book." Includes index. [TT920.B57 1977] 76-39662 ISBN 0-87690-245-X : 9.95. ISBN 0-87690-246-8 pbk. : 4.95
1. Pottery craft. I. Title. BIP

BJoRN, Arne. 666'.4'3
Exploring fire and clay: man, fire, and clay through the ages. New York, Van Nostrand Reinhold [1969] 87 p. illus. 23 cm. ([Reinhold Scandinavian craft series]) Translation of Ild og ler. Bibliography: p. 85. [TP808.B6513] 72-118559 ISBN 0-442-07850-1
1. Pottery craft. 2. Kilns. I. Title.

BROADWATER, Elaine. 738.1
Clay craft at home / Elaine Broadwater. Radnor, Pa. : Chilton Book Co., c1978. vi, 152 p., [8] leaves of plates : ill, ; 26 cm. (Chilton's creative crafts series) Includes bibliographical references and index. [TT920.B76 1978] 78-7141 ISBN 0-8019-6487-3 : 12.50. ISBN 0-8019-6488-1 pbk. : 6.95
1. Pottery craft. I. Title.

BRODY, Harvey. 738
The book of low-fire ceramics / by Harvey Brody ; photos. by David Powers. 1st ed. New York : Holt, Rinehart, and Winston, c1979. p. cm. Includes index. Bibliography: p. [TT920.B78 1979] 79-944 ISBN 0-03-042116-0. : 14.95 ISBN 0-03-042111-X pbk. : 8.95
1. Pottery craft. I. Powers, David. II. Title. III. Title: Low-fire ceramics.

BROOKSHAW, Doreen. 738.1
Pottery craft. London, New York, F. Warne, 1967. x, 110 p. illus., 16 plates, diagrs. 22 1/2 cm. [TP808.B76] 68-10153 21/-
1. Pottery craft. I. Title.

CAMPBELL, Donald, 1928(Jan.7)- 738.1'42
Using the potter's wheel / Donald Campbell ; photos. by Adrienne Campbell. New York : Van Nostrand Reinhold Co., 1978. 96 p. : ill. ; 28 cm. Includes index. [TT920.C35] 77-28398 ISBN 0-442-21461-8 pbk. : 12.95
1. Pottery craft. I. Title. BIP

CARDEW, Michael, 1901- 738
Pioneer pottery. New York, St. Martin's Press [1971, c1969] xv, 327 p. illus. 26 cm. Bibliography: p. 310-311. [TP808.C37 1971] 74-141313 15.00
1. Pottery craft. I. Title. BIP

CASSON, Michael, 1925- 738.1'4
The craft of the potter / by Michael Casson ; edited by Anna Jackson ; [photography by Ed Buziak, drawings by Ray and Corrine Burrows]. Woodbury, N.Y. : Barron's, [1978, c1977] p. cm. "Published to accompany a series of programmes prepared in consultation with the BBC Further Education Advisory Council." Bibliography: p. [TT920.C38 1978] 78-15013 ISBN 0-8120-2028-6 : 5.95
1. Pottery craft. I. Jackson, Anna. II. British Broadcasting Corporation. Further Education Advisory Council. III. Title. BIP

CERAMIC projects; 738
a selection of projects for classroom, home and studio. Originally pub. in form of articles in Ceramics Monthly magazine. Prepared by the staff of Ceramics Monthly magazine, Thomas Sellers, Ed. Columbus, Ohio, Professional Pubns., 4175 N. High St. [c.1963] 64p. illus. 28cm. (CMhandbk.) 2.00 pap.,

CHRISTY, Judith. 738
Making pottery [by] Judith and Roy Christy. Baltimore, Penguin Books [1969] 138 p. illus. 19 cm. (Penguin handbooks, PH 145) Bibliography: p. [134] [TP808.C53] 73-8542 1.95
1. Pottery craft. I. Christy, Roy, 1920- joint author. II. Title.

CHROMAN, Eleanor. 738.1
The potter's primer. New York, Hawthorn Books [1974] xiii, 238 p. illus. 24 cm. [TT920.C49 1974] 73-11741 8.95
1. Pottery craft. I. Title. BIP

CONRAD, John W. 738.1'4
Contemporary ceramic techniques / John W. Conrad. Englewood Cliffs, N.J. : Prentice-Hall, [1979] p. cm. Includes index. Bibliography: p. [TT920.C64] 77-25456 ISBN 0-13-169540-1 : 12.95
1. Pottery craft. I. Title. BIP

COOPER, Emmanuel. 738.1'44
Glazes for the potter / by Emmanuel Cooper and Derek Royle. New York : Scribner, 1979. p. cm. British ed. published under title: Glazes for the studio potter. Includes index. Bibliography: p. [TT922.C66 1978] 78-16586 ISBN 0-684-16021-8 : 13.95
1. Pottery craft. 2. Glazes. I. Royle, Derek, joint author. II. Title. BIP

COTTIER-ANGELI, Fiorella. 738
Ceramics. [English version by Julian Snelling and Claude Namy] New York, Van Nostrand Reinhold [1974, c1972] 143 p. illus. (part col.) 18 x 21 cm. (Craft and art) Bibliography: p. 138. [TT920.C6713 1974] 73-13438 ISBN 0-442-30005-0 7.95
1. Pottery craft. I. Title.

COUNTS, Charles. 666'.3'75
Common clay. Photos. by Bill Haddox. [1st ed.] Atlanta, Ga., Droke House/Hallux [1971] 144 p. illus. (part col.) 29 cm. [TP808.C578] 77-172016 ISBN 0-8375-6760-2
1. Pottery craft. I. Title. BIP

COUNTS, Charles. 738.1
Pottery workshop; a study in the making of pottery from idea to finished form. Photos. by Bill Haddox. New York, Macmillan [1973] viii, 198 p. illus. 24 cm. Bibliography: p. 195-196. [TT920.C68] 72-86029 9.95
1. Pottery craft. I. Title. BIP

COWLEY, David. 738.1'42
Moulded and slip cast pottery and ceramics / David Cowley. New York : Scribner, c1978. 120 p., [2] leaves of plates : ill. ; 26 cm. Includes bibliographical references. [TT920.C69 1978] 78-126 ISBN 0-684-15752-7 : 10.95
1. Pottery craft. I. Title.

COYNE, John. 738
The Penland School of Crafts book of pottery / edited by John Coyne ; with photography by Evon Streetman. Indianapolis : Bobbs-Merrill, [1975] 192 p. : ill. (some col.) ; 24 cm. "A Rutledge book." [TT920.C7] 74-34008 ISBN 0-672-51968-2 : 12.95
1. Pottery craft. I. Penland School of Handicrafts, Penland, N.C. II. Title. BIP

CREATIVE crafts : 738
ceramics, mosaics, and stained glass / edited by Saul Lapidus. New York : D. McKay Co., c1977. p. cm. "A Courier book." [TT920.C74] 77-8008 ISBN 0-679-50762-0 pbk. : 6.95
1. Pottery craft. 2. Mosaics. 3. Glass craft. I. Lapidus, Saul.

DICKERSON, John. 738.1'4
Pottery in easy steps / John Dickerson ; [photos. by Alain Le Garsmeur]. London : Studio Vista, 1976. 64 p. : ill. ; 28 cm. [TT920.D48] 77-368573 ISBN 0-289-70721-8 : £1.95
1. Pottery craft. I. Title.

DICKERSON, John. 738.1
Pottery making : a complete guide / John Dickerson. New York : Viking Press, 1974. 152 p. : ill. (some col.) ; 25 cm. (A Studio book) Includes index. Bibliography: p. 147. [TT920.D5] 73-21059 ISBN 0-670-56864-3 : 14.00
1. Pottery craft. I. Title.

DUNCAN Ceramic Products. 738.1'5
30 exciting bisq-stain techniques Fresno, Calif. [1974] 41 p. illus. 28 cm. (Duncan library of ceramic decorating) Cover title. [TT922.D86 1974] 74-181636 2.50
1. Pottery craft. 2. Glazes. 3. Stains and staining. I. Title.

HAMILTON, David, 1940(Feb.24)- 738.1
Van Nostrand Reinhold manual of pottery and ceramics. New York, Van Nostrand Reinhold Co. [1974] 188 p. illus. (part col.) 25 cm. (Van Nostrand Reinhold manuals) Bibliography: p. 183. [TT920.H35 1974] 73-19428 ISBN 0-442-23086-9 10.95
1. Pottery craft. 2. Ceramics. I. Title.

HARVEY, David, fl.1976- 738.1
Imaginative pottery / David Harvey. London : Pitman, 1976. vi, 122 p., [4] p. of plates : ill. (some col.), plans ; 26 cm. Includes index. Bibliography: p. 118. [TT920.H37] 77-364687 ISBN 0-273-00748-3 : £3.95
1. Pottery craft. 2. Kilns. I. Title.

HOWELL, Frank, 1940- 738
The craft of pottery : a problem-solving approach to the fundamentals of pottery making / Frank Howell, Carol Woodward, Robert H. Woodward. 1st ed. New York : Harper & Row, [1975] x, 157 p. : ill. ; 26 cm. Includes index. Bibliography: p. 147-149. [TT920.H69 1975] 74-15859 ISBN 0-06-011966-7 : 9.95. ISBN 0-06-011959-4 pbk. : 4.95
1. Pottery craft. I. Woodward, Carol, 1927- joint author. II. Woodward, Robert Hanson, 1925- joint author. III. Title. BIP

KENNY, John B. 738
The complete book of pottery making / John B. Kenny ; photos. by the author ; drawings by Carla H. Kenny. Rev. ed. Radnor, Pa. : Chilton Book Co., c1976. p. cm. (Chilton's creative crafts series) Includes index. [TT920.K46 1976] 76-302 ISBN 0-8019-5932-2. ISBN 0-8019-5933-0 pbk.
1. Pottery craft. I. Title. BIP

KRIWANEK, Franz F. 738
Keramos [by] Franz F. Kriwanek. Dubuque, Iowa, Kendall/Hunt Pub. Co. [1970] xi, 131 p. illus., map, plans, ports. 22 x 28 cm. [TP808.K7] 74-129915 ISBN 0-8403-0279-7
1. Pottery craft. I. Title. BIP

KRIWANEK, Franz F. 738
Keramos : the teaching of pottery / Franz F. Kriwanek. Rev. ed. Dubuque, Iowa : Kendall/Hunt Pub. Co., 1976,c1975 xiii, 135 p. : ill. ; 22 x 28 cm. [TT920.K74 1975] 77-351961 ISBN 0-8403-0279-7 4.95
1. Pottery craft. I. Title.

LAKOFSKY, Charles. 738
Pottery. Dubuque, Iowa, W. C. Brown Co. [1968] xiii, 113 p. illus. 23 cm. (Art horizons series) Bibliography: p. 105. [TP808.L26] 68-14578
1. Pottery craft.

LARDEN, Ida Claire. 738.1
The off-wheel pottery book [by] Ida Claire Larden and Raymond Hull. New York, Scribner [1975] 154 p. illus. 24 cm. Bibliography: p. [TT920.L37] 74-18321 ISBN 0-684-14110-8 10.95
1. Pottery craft. I. Hull, Raymond, 1919- joint author. II. Title. BIP

LAUDER, Ian. 738.1'3
The home potter. New York, Universe Books [1971, c1970] 143 p. illus. 24 cm. [TP808.L27 1971] 71-130802 ISBN 0-87663-136-7 5.95
1. Pottery craft. I. Title.

LEACH, Bernard Howell, 1887- 738
The potter's challenge / Bernard Leach ; edited by David Outerbridge. 1st ed. New York : Dutton, [1975] 156 p. : ill. ; 21 cm. "A Sunrise book." Bibliography: p. 153-156. [TT920.L4 1975] 75-15520 10.95
1. Pottery craft. 2. Pottery. I. Title. BIP

LISSAMAN, Elizabeth. 738.1'4
Starting with ceramics / by Elizabeth Lissaman. New York : Sterling Pub. Co., [1975] 96 p. : ill. (some col.) ; 24 cm. Originally published in 1969 under title: Pottery for pleasure in Australia and New Zealand. Includes index. Procedures for making pottery, the essential tools and products, and the art of throwing are detailed through text, photographs, and a glossary. [TT920.L57 1975] 74-31709 ISBN 0-8069-5324-1 : 5.95 ISBN 0-8069-5325-X lib.bdg. : 5.69
1. Pottery craft. I. Title.

LYNGGAARD, Finn. 738.1
Pottery: raku technique; designs, material, technique. [Translated from the Danish by Joan Bulman] New York, Van Nostrand Reinhold Co. [1973] 79 p. illus. 22 cm. Translation of Raku. Bibliography: p. 78. [TT920.L9613] 72-12550 ISBN 0-442-29969-9 2.95 (pbk.)
1. Pottery craft. 2. Raku pottery. I. Title.

MEMMOTT, Harry Attridge. 738
The art of making pottery; from clay to kiln, by Harry Memmott. [1st American ed.] New York, C. N. Potter; distributed by Crown Publishers [1971] 250 p. illus. (part col.) 29 cm. [TP808.M38 1971] 77-143190 7.95
1. Pottery craft. I. Title.

MEMMOTT, Harry Attridge. 738.1
Discovering pottery [by] Harry Memmott. Sydney, New York, Hamlyn, 1972. 136 p. ill. 23 cm. "Abridged edition from The Australian pottery book." Index. [TT920.M452] 74-167379 ISBN 0-600-07119-7 1.95
1. Pottery craft. I. Title.

NAGUMO, Ryu, 1931- 738.1
Creative ceramics / by Ryu Nagumo. Tokyo : Japan Publications, 1974. 215 p. : ill. ; 27 cm. Distributed by Japan Publications Trading Co., San Francisco. Includes index. [TT920.N33] 74-76115 ISBN 0-87040-251-X : 14.95
1. Pottery craft. 2. Pottery, Japanese. I. Title. BIP

NIGROSH, Leon I. 738.1
Claywork : form and idea in ceramic design / Leon I. Nigrosh. Worcester, Mass. : Davis Publications, [1975] 222 p., [4] leaves of plates : ill. (some col.) ; 27 cm. Includes index. Bibliography: p. 194-195. [TT920.N53] 74-31687 ISBN 0-87192-069-7 : 12.95
1. Pottery craft. 2. Design. I. Title. BIP

PETTERSON, Henry. 738.1
Creating form in clay. New York, Reinhold Book Corp. [1968] 112 p. illus. 21 cm. An introduction to clay modeling which describes various methods of forming shapes, surface design and decoration, firing procedures, and safety precautions. [TP808.P47] 68-22735
1. Potterycraft. 2. Modeling. I. Title.

PLOWMAN, Thomas. 738.1
Craft pottery / [by] Thomas Plowman. Aylesbury : Shire Publications, 1976. 33 p. : ill. ; 21 cm. (Shire album ; 18) Bibliography: p. [33] [TT920.P56] 77-360710 ISBN 0-85263-347-5 : £0.45
1. Pottery craft. I. Title. BIP

POTTERY step-by-step. 738.1
1st American ed. New York : Collier Books, 1976. 64 p. : col ill. ; 29 cm. "A Studio Vista book." Bibliography: p. 64. [TT920.P63 1976b] 76-8826 ISBN 0-02-011810-4 pbk. : 4.95
1. Pottery craft.

POWELL, Harold. 738.1
The beginner's book of pottery. Buchanan, N.Y., Emerson Books, 1974. 120 p. illus. 23 cm. [TT920.P65 1974] 73-90300 ISBN 0-87523-182-9 6.95
1. Pottery craft. I. Title.

POWELL, Harold. 738.1'4
Pottery for beginners / Harold Powell. Poole : Blandford Press, 1979. 118 p. : ill. ; 22 cm. [TT920.P66] 79-303448 ISBN 0-7137-0910-3 : 8.95

1. Pottery craft. I. Title.
Distributed by Sterling Publishing, 2 Park Ave., New York, NY 10016 BIP

POWNALL, Glen. 738
Pottery. New York, Drake Publishers [1973] 75 p. illus. (part col.) 26 cm. (His Creative leisure series) [TT920.P68 1973] 72-10528 ISBN 0-87749-325-1 3.95
1. Pottery craft. I. Title.

PRIOLO, Joan B. 738.1'4
Ceramics by coil / Joan & Anthony Priolo. New York : Sterling Pub. Co., c1976. 48 p. : ill. (some col.) ; 19 cm. (Little craft book series) Includes index. [TT920.P73] 76-1178 ISBN 0-8069-5344-6 : 3.75 ISBN 0-8069-5345-4 lib.bdg. :
1. Pottery craft. I. Priolo, Anthony, joint author. II. Title. BIP

PRIOLO, Joan B. 738
Ceramics by slab, by Joan & Anthony Priolo. New York, Sterling Pub. Co. [1973] 48 p. illus. 19 cm. (Little craft book series) Introduces the techniques and necessary tools for creating a variety of ceramic objects by the slab method. [TT920.P74 1973] 72-95195 ISBN 0-8069-5240-7 2.95
1. Pottery craft. I. Priolo, Anthony, joint author. II. Title. BIP

PUCCI, Cora. 738.1
Pottery: a basic manual. Photos. by Peter Hunsberger. [1st ed.] Boston, Little, Brown [1974] 171 p. illus. 23 cm. (Little, Brown crafts series) Bibliography: p. 171. [TT920.P8] 74-1068 ISBN 0-316-72110-7 7.95
1. Pottery craft. I. Title.
Pbk. 3.95; ISBN 0-316-721115.

RHODES, Daniel, 1911- 738.1
Pottery form / Daniel Rhodes ; photos. by Thomas Liden. 1st ed. Radnor, Pa. : Chilton Book Co., c1976. xi, 243 p. : ill. ; 27 cm. (Chilton's creative crafts series) Includes index. [TT920.R49 1976] 76-301 ISBN 0-8019-5935-7 : 12.50
1. Pottery craft. I. Title. BIP

RIEGGER, Hal, 1921- 738.1
Electric kiln ceramics / Hal Riegger. New York : Van Nostrand Reinhold Co., 1978. p. cm. Includes index. Bibliography: p. [TT920.R53] 77-20509 ISBN 0-442-26961-7 : 15.00. ISBN 0-442-26958-7 pbk. : 8.95
1. Pottery craft. 2. Electric kilns. I. Title.

RIEGGER, Hal, 1921- 738.1'4
Primitive pottery. New York, Van Nostrand Reinhold [1972] 120 p. illus. 29 cm. Bibliography: p. 119. [TP808.R52] 75-184821
1. Pottery craft. I. Title. BIP

SANDERS, Herbert H. 738.1
How to make pottery, by Herbert H. Sanders. New York, Watson-Guptill Publications [1974] 143 p. illus. 28 cm. First ed. published in 1953 under title: Sunset ceramics book; 2d ed. published in 1964 under title: How to make pottery and ceramic sculpture. Bibliography: p. 140. [TT920.S26 1974] 73-20020 ISBN 0-8230-2420-2 10.00
1. Pottery craft. I. Title. BIP

SAPIRO, Maurice. 738.1'42
Clay, the potter's wheel / Maurice Sapiro ; photographs by Erwin Sapiro and the author. Worcester, Mass. : Davis Publications, c1977. 87 p. : ill. ; 26 cm. [TT920.S27] 77-84480 ISBN 0-87192-095-6 : 8.95
1. Pottery craft. I. Sapiro, Erwin. II. Title.

SHAFER, Thomas, 1937- 738.1'4
Pottery decoration / by Thomas Shafer. New York : Watson-Guptill Publications, 1976. 160 p. : ill. ; 29 cm. Includes index. Bibliography: p. 156-157. [TT920.S5 1976] 75-45355 ISBN 0-8230-4206-5 : 15.95
1. Pottery craft. 2. Decoration and ornament. 3. Glazes. I. Title. BIP

THOMAS, Gwilym. 738.1
Step by step guide to pottery. Feltham, New York, Hamlyn, 1973. 80 p. illus. (some col.) 26 cm. Includes index. Bibliography: p. 79. [TT920.T47] 74-166692 ISBN 0-600-38031-9 £0.95
1. Pottery craft. I. Title.

TONG, Gary. 738.1'4
Modeling with self-hardening clay / Gary Tong. New York : Larousse, 1976. 96 p. : ill. ; 26 cm. (Larousse craft series) [TT920.T66 1976] 76-15924 ISBN 0-88332-047-9 : 8.95. ISBN 0-88332-048-7 pbk. : 5.95
1. Pottery craft. 2. Clay. 3. Modeling. I. Title. BIP

WETTLAUFER, George. 738.1
Getting into pots : a beginning pottery manual / George & Nancy Wettlaufer. Englewood Cliffs, N.J. : Prentice-Hall, [1976] p. cm. Includes index. Bibliography: p. [TT920.W45] 76-20643 ISBN 0-13-354712-4 : 9.95 ISBN 0-13-354704-3 pbk. :
1. Pottery craft. I. Wettlaufer, Nancy, joint author. II. Title. BIP

WHITE, John Kennardh. 738.1
Pottery techniques of native North America : an introduction to traditional technology / John Kennardh White ; photos. by Stewart J. MacLeod. Chicago : University of Chicago Press, c1976. vii, 52 p. : ill. ; 21 cm. & 4 sheets (11x15 cm.) in pocket. The sheets are microfiche. Bibliography: p. 51-52. [TT920.W47] 76-10710 ISBN 0-226-69815-7 : 25.00
1. Pottery craft. 2. Indian craft. 3. Indians of North America—Pottery. 4. Cherokee Indians—Pottery. I. Title. BIP

WILDENHAIN, Marguerite. 738
Pottery: form and expression. Photo story by Otto Hagel. [Enl. ed.] Palo Alto, Calif., Pacific Books [1973, c1962] 157 p. illus. 29 cm. [TT920.W54 1973] 73-162763 ISBN 0-87015-202-5 9.95
1. Pottery craft. I. Title.

WOODY, Elsbeth S. 738.1'4
Handbuilding ceramic forms / Elsbeth S. Woody. New York : Farrar, Straus, Giroux, c1978. xiii, 225 p. : ill. ; 26 cm. Includes bibliographical references. [TT920.W65 1978] 78-9017 ISBN 0-374-16773-7 : 20.00
1. Pottery craft. I. Title. BIP

WOODY, Elsbeth S. 738.1'42
Pottery on the wheel / Elsbeth S. Woody ; photos. by Steven Smolker. New York : Farrar, Straus and Giroux, [1975] 205 p. : ill. ; 27 cm. Bibliography: p. 205. [TT920.W66 1975] 75-14223 ISBN 0-374-23656-9 : 15.00. ISBN 0-374-51234-5 6.95
1. Pottery craft. I. Smolker, Steven. II. Title. BIP

ZORZA, Rosemary. 738.1
Pottery; creating with clay [by] Rosemary Zorza. [1st ed. in the U.S.A.] Garden City, N.Y., Doubleday, 1974 [c1973] 160 p. illus. 26 cm. (Crafts and hobbies) Bibliography: p. 160. [TT920.Z66 1974] 72-92410 ISBN 0-385-00120-7 3.95 (pbk.)
1. Pottery craft. I. Title.

Pottery craft—Dictionaries.

FOURNIER, Robert L., 1915- 738'.03
Illustrated dictionary of practical pottery [by] Robert Fournier. Photos. by John Anderson. Diagrs. by Sheila Fournier. New York, Van Nostrand Reinhold Co. [1973] 256 p. illus. 26 cm. Bibliography: p. 254. [TT919.5.F68] 78-39886 ISBN 0-442-29950-8 12.50
1. Pottery craft—Dictionaries. I. Title. BIP

FOURNIER, Robert L., 1915- 738'.03
Illustrated dictionary of practical pottery / Robert Fournier ; photos. by John Anderson ; diagrs. by Sheila Fournier. Rev. ed. New York : Van Nostrand Reinhold Co., c1977. 256 p. : ill. (some col.) ; 26 cm. Bibliography: p. 254. [TT919.5.F68 1977] 76-41466 ISBN 0-442-22447-8 : 14.95
1. Pottery craft—Dictionaries. I. Title.

HAMER, Frank. 738.1'03
The potter's dictionary of materials and techniques. New York, Watson-Guptill Publications [1974] p. cm. Bibliography: p. [TT919.5.H35 1974] 74-703 ISBN 0-8230-4210-3 12.50
1. Pottery craft—Dictionaries. 2. Ceramic materials—Dictionaries. I. Title. BIP

Pottery craft—Equipment and supplies.

CHAPPELL, James, 1942- 738.1
The potter's complete book of clay and glazes / by James Chappell ; photography by Arleen Olson. New York : Watson-Guptill Publications, 1977. p. cm. Includes index. Bibliography: p. [TT921.5.C48] 76-42212 ISBN 0-8230-4202-2 : 24.95
1. Pottery craft—Equipment and supplies. 2. Clay. 3. Glazes. I. Title.

HARVEY, Roger, 1943- 681'.7666
Building pottery equipment, by Roger Harvey and Sylvia and John Kolb. New York, Watson-Guptill [1975] 208 p. illus. 29 cm. [TT921.5.H37 1975] 74-16375 ISBN 0-8230-0540-2 16.50
1. Pottery craft—Equipment and supplies. I. Kolb, Sylvia, 1912- joint author. II. Kolb, John, 1915- joint author. III. Title. BIP

Pottery craft—Juvenile literature.

BROCKWAY, Maureen. 738
Clay projects. Pictures by G. Overlie. Minneapolis, Lerner Publications Co. [1973] 32 p. illus. 21 cm. (An Early craft book) Traces briefly the use of clay throughout history and gives directions for making flower plaques, a bird feeder, a coil pot, and other objects from clay. [TT921.B76] 72-13337 ISBN 0-8225-0853-2 3.95
1. Pottery craft—Juvenile literature. I. Overlie, George, illus. II. Title. BIP

ELBERT, Virginie. 738.1
Potterymaking. Text and photography by Virginie Fowler Elbert. [1st ed.] Garden City, N.Y., Doubleday [1974] 64 p. illus. 22 cm. (Crafts for children) Introduces the materials, tools, and techniques needed for creating objects from clay such as pots, tiles, figures, and bowls. [TT920.E42] 73-9023 ISBN 0-385-08342-4 5.95
1. Pottery craft—Juvenile literature. I. Title. BIP

FISHER, Leonard Everett. 666'.3'973
The potters, written & illustrated by Leonard Everett Fisher. New York, F. Watts [1969] 47 p. illus., map. 22 cm. (His Colonial Americans) Traces the early history of pottery in Colonial America with descriptions of the clay used, techniques of making and decorating pots, and a listing of some of the famous potters of the time. [TP808.F5] 69-14499
1. Potterycraft—Juvenile literature. I. Title. BIP

GILBREATH, Alice Thompson. 738.1'4
Slab, coil, and pinch : a beginner's pottery book / by Alice Gilbreath ; illustrated by Barbara Fiore. New York : Morrow, 1977. 64 p. : ill. ; 24 cm. Thirteen different projects with complete directions introduce the three basic types of hand-built pottery. [TT921.G54] 76-48742 ISBN 0-688-22105-X : 5.50 ISBN 0-688-32105-4 lib.bdg. : 4.84
1. Pottery craft—Juvenile literature. I. Fiore, Barbara. II. Title. BIP

Pottery craft—Study and teaching (Primary)

FARNWORTH, Warren. 738.1
Beginning pottery. New York, Van Nostrand Reinhold [1974, c1973] 128 p. illus. 21 cm. Bibliography: p. 127. [TT290.F37 1974] 73-10654 ISBN 0-442-22374-9 5.95
1. Pottery craft—Study and teaching (Primary) I. Title. BIP

Pottery, Cypriote—Classification.

ADELMAN, Charles Martin. 738.3'09393'7
Cypro-geometric pottery, refinements in classification / by Charles Martin Adelman. Goteborg : [P. Astrom], 1976. xviii, 143, [34] p. : ill. ; 31 cm. (Studies in Mediterranean archaeology ; v. 47) Thesis—Gothenburg. Includes index. Bibliography: p. [123]-135. [NK4146.C9A33] 76-379412 ISBN 9-18-505869-6 : kr75.00
1. Pottery, Cypriote—Classification. I. Title. II. Series.

Pottery—Denmark.

HIORT, Esbjorn. 738.3
Modern Danish ceramics. Moderne dansk keremik. New York, Museum Books, 1955. 129p. plates (part col.) 31cm. English, French, German, and Danish. [NK4115.H5] 55-12562
1. Pottery—Denmark. I. Title.

Pottery—Dictionaries.

BARBER, Edwin Atlee, 1851-1916. 738'.03
The ceramic collectors' glossary. New York, Da Capo Press, 1967. 119 p. illus. 24 cm. (Da Capo Press series in architecture and decorative art, v. 7) (A Da Capo Press reprint edition.) Reprint of the 1914 ed. [NK3770.B3 1967] 67-27448
1. Pottery—Dictionaries. I. Title.

BOGER, Louise Ade. 738'.03
The dictionary of world pottery and porcelain. New York, Scribner [1971] 533 p. illus. (part col.) 28 cm. Bibliography: p. 525-533. [NK3770.B64] 72-123829 ISBN 0-684-10031-2 22.50
1. Pottery—Dictionaries. 2. Porcelain—Dictionaries. I. Title. BIP

THE Ceramic, furniture, and silver collectors' glossary / by Edwin Atlee Barber, Luke Vincent Lockwood, and Hollis French. New York : Da Capo Press, 1976. 119, 55, 164 p. : ill. ; 23 cm. (A Da Capo paperback) Reprint of 3 works originally published by the Walpole Society, New York: The ceramic collectors' glossary, by E. A. Barber, first published in 1914; The furniture collectors' glossary, by L. V. Lockwood, first published in 1913; and A silver collectors' glossary and a list of early American silversmiths and their marks, first published in 1917. [NK3770.C46] 76-8172 ISBN 0-306-80049-7 pbk. : 6.95 745.1
1. Pottery—Dictionaries. 2. Furniture—Dictionaries. 3. Silverware—Dictionaries. 4. Silversmiths—United States. 5. Hallmarks. 6. Antiques. I. Barber, Edwin Atlee, 1851-1916. The ceramic collectors' glossary. 1976. II. Lockwood, Luke Vincent, 1872-1951. The furniture collectors' glossary. 1976. III. French, Hollis, 1868-1940. A silver collectors' glossary and a list of early American silversmiths and their marks. 1976. BIP

CHARLES, Bernard H. 738'.03
Pottery and porcelain : a dictionary of terms / Bernard H. Charles. New York : Hippocrene Books, [1974] 320 p. : ill. ; 23 cm. Bibliography: p. 290-292. [NK3770.C48 1974b] 74-81392 ISBN 0-88254-278-8 : 14.95
1. Pottery—Dictionaries. 2. Porcelain—Dictionaries. I. Title.

PAYTON, Mary. 738'.03
The observer's book of pottery and porcelain [by] Mary and Geoffrey Payton. London, New York, F. Warne, 1973. 192, [8] p. illus. (some col.) 15 cm. (The Observer's pocket series, 51) Includes index. Bibliography: p. 179-181. [NK3770.P39] 73-80247 ISBN 0-7232-1518-9 £0.60 ($2.50 U.S.)
1. Pottery—Dictionaries. 2. Porcelain—Dictionaries. I. Payton, Geoffrey, joint author. II. Title. III. Series. BIP

RAY, Marcia. 738'.03
Collectible ceramics; an encyclopedia of pottery and porcelain for the American collector. New York, Crown Publishers [1974] 256 p. illus. (part col.) 26 cm. [NK3770.R38] 73-92104 9.95
1. Pottery—Dictionaries. 2. Porcelain—Dictionaries. 3. Pottery—Collectors and collecting—United States. 4. Porcelain—Collectors and collecting—United States. I. Title.

SAVAGE, George, 1909- 738'.03
An illustrated dictionary of ceramics; defining 3,054 terms relating to wares, materials, processes, styles, patterns, and shapes from antiquity to the present day [by] George Savage [and] Harold Newman. With an introductory list of the principal European factories and their marks,

SUBJECT INDEX POTTERY, ENGLISH—CATALOGS.

compiled by John Cushion. New York, Van Nostrand Reinhold Co. [1974] 319 p. illus. (part col.) 26 cm. [NK3770.S38 1974b] 73-17999 ISBN 0-442-27364-9 18.95
1. Pottery—Dictionaries. 2. Porcelain—Dictionaries. I. Newman, Harold, joint author. II. Cushion, John Patrick. III. Title. BIP

Pottery—Diyala, Mesopotamia.

DELOUGAZ, Pinhas. 738.3
Pottery from the Diyala region. Chicago, University of Chicago Press [1952] xxii, 182 p. illus., 205 plates (incl. maps) 31 cm. (University of Chicago. Oriental Institute publications, v. 63) Part of the illustrative matter is fold., part col. "This publication is one of a group planned to present as a whole the work of the Oriental Institute's Iraq Expedition in the Diyala region." Bibliographical footnotes. [NK3855.D5D4] 52-6876
1. Pottery—Diyala, Mesopotamia. 2. Excavations (Archaeology)—Mesopotamia. I. Title. II. Series: Chicago. University. Oriental Institute. Publications, v. 63

Pottery, Dutch—Exhibitions.

ACHTERBERGH, J. W. N. van. 738.2'0924
Omtrent bakbeesten en vuurlanders : overzichtstentoonstelling ceramiek van Hans de Jong, Museum Boymans-Van Beuningen, Rotterdam 10.10-21.11.76 / [tekst, J. W. N. van Achterbergh ; foto's, Dick Wolters]. [Rotterdam : Museum Boymans-Van Beuningen], 1976. 42 p. : ill. ; 25 cm. Bibliography: p. 24. [NK4210.J615A25] 77-461946
1. Jong, Hans de, 1932- 2. Pottery, Dutch—Exhibitions. I. Jong, Hans de, 1932- II. Rotterdam. Museum Boymans-Van Beuningen.

BALTIMORE. Museum of Art. 738'.092'4
Lea Halpern : dates of the exhibition, January 27-March 21, 1976. [Baltimore] : Baltimore Museum of Art, [1976?] [24] p., [8] leaves of plates : ill. (8 col. in pocket) ; 26 cm. "Catalogue of the exhibition": p. [11]-[24] [NK4210.H3B34 1976] 76-359580
1. Halpern, Lea Henny, 1901- 2. Pottery, Dutch—Exhibitions. I. Halpern, Lea Henny, 1901-

Pottery—Egypt.

KELLEY, Allyn L. 738.3'0932
The pottery of ancient Egypt : dynasty 1 to Roman times / Allyn L. Kelley. Toronto : Royal Ontario Museum, 1976. 55 p. ; 28 cm. & portfolio (ca. 875 leaves : ill. ; 30 cm.) Cover title. Includes index. Bibliography: p. 43-51. [DT62.P72K44] 77-360554
1. Pottery—Egypt. 2. Egypt—Antiquities. I. Title.

Pottery—England—Hist.

HAGGAR, Reginald George, 1905- 738.3'0942
A new guide to old pottery; English country pottery. New York, M. M. McBride [1950?] 160p. illus. 23cm. London ed. (Phoenix House) has title: English country pottery. Bibliography: p. 145-153. [NK4085.H] A52
1. Pottery—England— Hist. I. Title.

Pottery—England—Lambeth—Bibliography.

SCOTT, Patricia. 016.7383'09421'65
Pottery in Lambeth : a select bibliography / [compiled by Patricia Scott]. [London] : [Lambeth Amenity Services], [1976] 21 p. : ill. ; 21 cm. Issued in conjuction with an exhibition organized by the Lambeth Amenity Services. Includes index. [Z7179.S36] [NK4087.L27] 77-355552 ISBN 0-905208-01-3
1. Pottery—England—Lambeth—Bibliography. I. Title.

Pottery—England—London—Catalogs.

WALLACE Collection, London. 738'.074'02132
Catalogue of ceramics / Wallace Collection. London : Trustees of the Wallace Collection, 1976- v. : ill. (some col.) ; 24 cm. Includes indexes. Contents.Contents.—v. 1 Norman, A. V. B. Pottery, maiolica, faience, stoneware. Bibliography: v. 1, p. 386-406. [NK3745.G7W348 1976] 77-361360 ISBN 0-900785-06-3 : (v. 1) : £4.00
1. Wallace Collection, London. 2. Pottery—England—London—Catalogs. I. Norman, A. Vesey B. II. Title.

Pottery, English.

BIRKS, Tony. 738'.092'2
Art of the modern potter / Tony Birks. New York : Van Nostrand Reinhold, 1977, c1976. 206 p. : ill. (come col.) ; 29 cm. [NK4085.B38 1977] 76-26017 ISBN 0-442-20766-2 : 20.00
1. Pottery, English. 2. Potters—England. I. Title. BIP

BIRKS, Tony. 738'.092'2
Art of the modern potter / [by] Tony Birks ; [photographs by Michael Holford ... and others]. Revised and enlarged ed. London : Country Life Books, 1976. 208 p. : ill. (some col.), ports. ; 29 cm. [NK4085.B38 1976b] 77-358571 ISBN 0-600-37126-3 : £5.00
1. Pottery, English. 2. Potters—England. I. Title.

BREARS, Peter C. D. 738.3'0942
The English country pottery: its history and techniques [by] Peter C. D. Brears. Rutland, Vt., C. E. Tuttle Co. [1971] 266 p. illus., col. port. 23 cm. Bibliography: p. 251-253. [NK4085.B75 1971b] 78-152115 ISBN 0-8048-0986-0 8.50
1. Pottery, English. 2. Folk art—England. I. Title.

CUSHION, John Patrick. 738'.0942
English china collecting for amateurs [by] J. P. Cushion. London, Muller, 1967. viii, 168p. illus., 12 plates, tables, diagrs. 19cm. Bibl. [NK4085.C78] 67-110832 3.50 bds.,
1. Pottery, English. 2. Porcelain, English. I. Title.
Distributed by Barnes & Noble, New York.

ENGLISH art pottery, 1865-1915 / [compiled] by Malcolm Haslam. [Woodbridge, Eng.] : Antique Collectors' Club, c1975. 214 p. : ill. (some col.) ; 29 cm. [NK4085.E46] 76-352718 ISBN 0-902028-26-X : £9.50 738'.0942
1. Pottery, English. I. Haslam, Malcolm.

FALKNER, Frank. 738.3'7
The Wood family of Burslem. [1st ed. reprinted] with a note on the author by Michael Robert Parkinson. Wakefield, E. P. Publishing, 1972. vi, v-xx, 118 p. 59 leaves (1 fold.) illus., coats of arms, geneal. table, map, ports. 29 cm. Reprint of 1st ed., published in 1912 by Chapman and Hall, London. Includes index. [NK4210.W6F3 1972] 74-162337 ISBN 0-85409-911-5 £4.00
1. Wood family. 2. Pottery, English. 3. Staffordshire pottery. I. Title.

FISHER, Stanley W. 738'.0942
English ceramics; earthenware, Delft, stoneware, cream-ware, porcelain, including a section on Welsh factories, by Stanley W. Fisher. [1st American ed.] New York, Hawthorn Books [1967, c1965] 256 p. illus. (part col.) port. 20 cm. Bibliography: p. 47-50. [NK4085.F52 1967] 66-17842
1. Pottery, English. I. Title.

FISHER, Stanley W. 738'.0942
A start to collecting English pottery & porcelain, by S. W. Fisher. London, New York, Foulsham, 1971. [6], 90 p. illus. 23 cm. Bibliography: p. 85-88. [NK4085.F53] 72-192638 ISBN 0-572-00795-7 £1.70
1. Pottery, English. 2. Pottery—Collectors and collecting. 3. Porcelain, English. 4. Porcelain—Collectors and collecting. I. Title.

GODDEN, Geoffrey A. 738'.075
Antique glass and china; a guide for the beginning collector, by Geoffrey A. Godden. South Brunswick [N. J.] A. S. Barnes [1967, c1966] 94 p. illus. (part col.) 28 cm. Bibliography: p. 92. [NK4085.G594 1967] 66-25037
1. Pottery, English. 2. Glassware, English. 3. Pottery—Collectors and collecting. 4. Glassware—Collectors and collecting. I. Title.

HUGHES, George Bernard, 1896- 738.0942
The collector's pocket book of china [by] G. Bernard Hughes. Illus. by Therie Hughes. [1st Amer. ed.] New York, Hawthorn [1967, c.1965] 376p. illus. 16cm. First pub. in 1965 under title: The Country Life pocket book of china. [NK4085.H832 1967] 66-20615 4.50 bds.,
1. Pottery, English. 2. Porcelain, English. 3. Potters' marks. I. Title.

HUGHES, George Bernard, 1896- 738.30942
English and Scottish earthenware, 1660-1860. New York, Macmillan [1961, c.1960] 238p. illus. (part col.) 61-1648 8.50
1. Pottery, English. 2. Pottery, Scottish. I. Title.

HUGHES, George Bernard, 1896- 738.8
English pottery and porcelain figures [by] G. Bernard Hughes. New York, F. A. Praeger [1968, c1964] 224 p. illus. (part col.) 23 cm. Bibliography: p. 210-211. [NK4085.H837 1968] 68-14676
1. Pottery, English. 2. Porcelain, English. I. Title.

LEWIS, Griselda. 738.3'0942
English pottery. New York, Pellegrini & Cudahy, 1950. 95 p. (chiefly illus.) 22 cm. On spine: An introduction to English pottery. London ed. (Art and Technics) has title: An introduction to English pottery. [NK4085.L] A52
1. Pottery, English. I. Title.

MANKOWITZ, Wolf. 738
The concise encyclopedia of English pottery and porcelain, by Wolf Mankowitz & Reginald G. Haggar. New York, Hawthorn Books [1957] xv, 312p. illus. (part col.) 26cm. Includes bibliographical references. [NK4085.M34] 57-6366
1. Pottery, English. 2. Porcelain, English. 3. Pottery—Dictionaries. 4. Porcelain—Dictionaries. I. Haggar, Reginald George, 1905- joint author. II. Title.

MILLER, J. Jefferson. 738.3'7
English yellow-glazed earthenware / J. Jefferson Miller, II. Washington : Smithsonian Institution Press, 1974. xvii, 125 p. : ill. (some col.) ; 27 cm. Distributed by G. Braziller, New York. Includes index. Bibliography: p. 115-117. [NK4085.M54] 73-21328 20.00
1. Pottery, English. 2. Glazing (Ceramics) 3. Yellow in art. I. Title. BIP

MOORE, Hannah Hudson, 1857-1927. 738.2'0942
The old china book : including staffordshire, wedgwood, lustre, and other English pottery and porcelain / by N. Hudson Moore. Rutland, Vt. : C. E. Tuttle Co., 1974. xvi, 300 p., [38] leaves of plates : ill. ; 19 cm. (Tut books : C) Reprint of the 1903 ed. published by F. A. Stokes Co., New York. Includes bibliographical references and index. [NK4085.M66 1974] 73-90233 ISBN 0-8048-1126-1 pbk. : 3.95
1. Pottery, English. 2. Porcelain, English. I. Title. BIP

ORMSBEE, Thomas Hamilton, 1890- 738.3
English China and its marks. Drawings by W. Robert Suda. Great Neck, N.Y., Deerfield Editions [1959] 200 p. illus. 24 cm. [NK4085.O7] 59-4701
1. Pottery, English. 2. Porcelain, English. 3. Pottery—Marks. 4. Porcelain—Marks. I. Title.

ORMSBEE, Thomas Hamilton, 1890- 738.0278
English china and its marks, by Thomas H. Ormsbee. Drawings by W. Robert Suda. [Great Neck, N. Y.] Deerfield Bks.: dist. Hearthside New York [1967, c.1959] 200p. illus. 25cm. [NK4085] 67-17835 8.50 bds.,
1. Pottery, English. 2. Porcelain, English. 3. Pottery—Marks. 4. Porcelain— Marks. I. Title.

RACKHAM, Bernard, 1876- 738.3'0942
English pottery, by Bernard Rackham and Herbert Read. With an appendix on the Wrotham potters by J. W. L. Glaisher, and with a new pref. and introd. by Peter Walton. Totowa, N.J., Rowman and Littlefield [1972] xii, xxiv, 142 p. 115 plates (part col.) 29 cm. Reprint of the 1924 ed. Includes bibliographies. [NK4085.R3 1972] 73-150451 ISBN 0-87471-118-5 35.00
1. Pottery, English. I. Read, Herbert Edward, Sir, 1893-1968, joint author. II. Glaisher, James Whitbread Lee, 1848-1928. III. Title. BIP

REES, Diana. 738.2'7
A pictorial encyclopaedia of Goss china, by Diana Rees and Marjorie G. Cawley. Newport, Ceramic Book Company, 1970. viii, 29 p., 65 plates. illus. (1 col.), coat of arms, facsim., port. 30 cm. [NK4210.G58R42] 74-164439 ISBN 0-900272-01-5 £4.00
1. Goss China Company Ltd. 2. Pottery, English. 3. Porcelain, English. I. Cawley, Marjorie G., joint author. II. Title.

TILLEY, Frank. 738.38
Teapots and tea. With 10 colour plates, and over 200 monochrome illus. Newport, Mon., Eng., Ceramic Book Co. [1957] xv, 135 p. 77 plates (10 col.) 32 cm. [NK4085.T52] 58-44185
1. Pottery, English. 2. Porcelain, English. 3. Tea. I. Title.

WAKEFIELD, Hugh, 1915- 738.30942
Victorian pottery. New York, Nelson [1963, c1962] 208 p. illus. 25 cm. (The Victorian collector series) Includes bibliography. [NK4085.W3] 62-17803
1. Pottery, English. I. Title.

WILLIAM Rockhill Nelson Gallery of Art and Mary Atkins Museum of Fine Arts, Kansas City, Mo. 738'.0942
The Frank P. and Harriet C. Burnap Collection of English pottery in the William Rockhill Nelson Gallery. Rev. and enl. ed. by Ross E. Taggart. Kansas City, Mo., Nelson Gallery-Atkins Museum, 1967. 219 p. illus. (part col.) 29 cm. Bibliography: p. 212-215. [NK4085.W53 1967] 67-21666
1. Pottery, English. 2. Pottery—Kansas City, Mo.—Catalogs. I. Taggart, Ross E. II. Burnap, Frank P. III. Burnap, Harriet Call.

WILLIAM ROCKHILL NELSON GALLERY OF ART AND MARY ATKINS MUSEUM OF FINE ARTS, Kansas City, Mo. 738.37
The Frank P. and Harriet C. Burnap collection of English pottery in the William Rockhill Nelson Gallery of Art. Kansas City, Mo., Nelson-Atkins Gallery of Art, 1953. 128 p. illus. (part col.) 28 cm; Bibliography: p. 127. [NK4085.W53] 54-21992
1. Pottery, English. 2. Pottery — Kansas City, Mo. — Catalogs. I. Burnap, Frank P. II. Burnap, Harriet Call. III. Title.

WILLS, Geoffrey 738.2
The book of English china. [Cranbury, N.J.] A.S. Barnes [1966, c.1964] 96p. illus. (pt. col.) 26cm. [NK4085.W538] 65-24846 5.00
1. Pottery, English. 2. Porcelain, English. I. Title.

Pottery, English—Catalogs.

HOOD, Kenneth. 738.3'0942
English pottery from the fifteenth century to the nineteenth century. Melbourne, London, Oxford U.P., 1966. 27 p. illus. 22 cm. (National Gallery booklets) Bibliography: p. 27. [NK4085.H74] 71-400248 7 English shillings
1. Pottery, English—Catalogs. 2. Pottery—Victoria, Australia—Catalogs. I. Title. II. Series: Victoria, Australia. National Gallery, Melbourne. Booklets

MOUNT, Sally. 738.3'0942
The price guide to 18th century English pottery, by Sally Mount. Woodbridge, Antique Collectors Club, 1972. [11], 425 p. illus. 21 cm. Bibliography: p. 7. [NK4085.M68] 74-155000 £3.75
1. Pottery, English—Catalogs. 2. Pottery—

Collectors and collecting. 3. Pottery—Prices. I. Title.

TEMPLE Newsam House, Leeds, Eng. 738.3'0942'07402819
Creamware and other English Pottery at Temple Newsam House, Leeds : a catalogue of the Leeds Collection / by Peter Walton. Bradford [Eng.] : Manningham Press, c1976. xi, 293 p. : ill. (some col.) ; 30 cm. Includes index. Bibliography: p. 281-284. [NK4085.T4 1976] 77-356357 ISBN 0-905564-00-6 : £28.00
1. Temple Newsam House, Leeds, Eng. 2. Pottery, English—Catalogs. 3. Pottery—England—Leeds—Catalogs. I. Walton, Peter. II. Title.

Pottery, English—Dictionaries.

HUGHES, George Bernard, 1896- 738
The collector's encyclopaedia of English ceramics [by] Bernard and Therle Hughes. New York, Macmillan [1957] 172p. illus., plates. 26cm. Bibliography: p. 167-172. [NK4085] 57-13708
1. Pottery, English—Dictionaries. 2. Pottery—Marks. I. Hughes, Therle, joint author. II. Title. III. Title: Encyclopaedia of English ceramics.

MANKOWITZ, Wolf. 738
The concise encyclopedia of English pottery and porcelain, by Wolf Mankowitz & Reginald G. Haggar. New York, Praeger [1968, c1957] xv, 312 p. illus., plates (part col.) 26 cm. Includes bibliographies. [NK4085.M34 1968] 68-28655 18.50
1. Pottery, English—Dictionaries. 2. Porcelain, English—Dictionaries. I. Haggar, Reginald George, 1905- joint author. II. Title. III. Title: English pottery and porcelain.

Pottery, English—Exhibitions.

ASLIN, Elizabeth. 738'.09424'63
Minton, 1798-1910 : [catalogue of an] exhibition, August-October 1976 / [organized by the] Victoria and Albert Museum [and] Thomas Goode & Company Limited ; [by] Elizabeth Aslin and Paul Atterbury. London : [The Museum], 1976. [1], 111, [1] p., 4 p. of plates : ill. (some col.) ; 20 x 21 cm. Held at the Museum. Includes index. Bibliography: p. 14-15. [NK4210.M55A84] 77-355059 ISBN 0-901486-96-5 : £3.00
1. Mintons Ltd. 2. Pottery, English—Exhibitions. 3. Porcelain, English—Exhibitions. I. Atterbury, Paul, joint author. II. Mintons Ltd. III. Victoria and Albert Museum, South Kensington. IV. Thomas Goode & Company. V. Title.

DETROIT. Institute of Arts. 738.2
English pottery and porcelain, 1300-1850. [Exhibition] the Detroit Institute of Arts, January 19 to February 28, 19544 [Detroit, 1954] 111p. illus. 25cm. Catalogue compiled by Paul L Grigaut. Bibliography: p.109-110. [NK4085.D48] 54-27311
1. Pottery. English—Exhibitions. I. Grigaut, Paul L. II. Title.

TOLEDO. Museum of Art. 738'.074'017113
English and American ceramics of the 18th and 19th centuries; a selection from the collection of Mr. and Mrs. Harold G. Duckworth. [Exhibition] December 1, 1968-January 12, 1969. [Toledo, 1968] 53 p. illus. 23 cm. Bibliography: p. 52-53. [NK4085.T58] 68-59384
1. Pottery, English—Exhibitions. 2. Pottery, American—Exhibitions. I. Duckworth, Harold G. II. Title.

Pottery, English—History.

CONNOISSEUR (The) 738.30942
The Connoisseur new guide to antique English pottery, porcelain, and glass. Ed. by L. G. G. Ramsey. Introd. by G. Bernard Hughes. New York, Dutton [c.1961] 192p. illus. (col. front) 25cm. Bibl. 61-66004 4.95 bds.,
1. Pottery, English—Hist. 2. Porcelain, English—Hist. 3. Glassware, English—Hist. I. Ramsey, L. G. G., ed. II. Title. III. Title: Antique English pottery, porcelain, and glass.

HONEY, William Bowyer, 1889- 738.20942
English pottery and porcelain, 5th ed. rev. by R. J. Charleston. 72 illus. from photos., 12 from drawings, and 30 marks. London, A. & C. Black [dist. New York, Barnes & Noble. 1964, c.1962] xvi, 284p. illus., plates. 23cm. (Lib. of Eng. art) Reprinted, with minor rev. Bibl. [NK4085.H73] 65-672 6.00
1. Pottery, English—Hist. 2. Porcelain, English—Hist. I. Title. II. Series.

SAVAGE, George, 1909- 738.30942
English pottery and porcelain. [1st American ed.] New York, University Books [1961] 431p. illus. (part mounted col.) 34cm. (The Universe library of antique art) Bibliography: p.[428] [NK1085.S35] 61-11039
1. Pottery, English— Hist. 2. Porcelain, English—Hist. I. Title.

Pottery, English—History.

HODGKIN, John Eliot. 738.3'0942
Examples of early English pottery named, dated, and inscribed / by John Eliot Hodgkin and Edith Hodgkin. Wakefield : EP Publishing, 1973. [1], xix, 187 p. plate : ill. ; 26 cm. Reprint of the 1891 ed. published by Cassell, London. [NK4085.H7 1973] 75-320112 ISBN 0-85409-900-X : £5.00
1. Pottery, English—History. 2. Pottery—Marks. 3. Pottery—Collectors and collecting. I. Hodgkin, Edith, joint author. BIP

LEWIS, Griselda. 738.3'0942
A collector's history of English pottery. New York, Viking Press [1969] 221 p. illus. (part col.), ports. 26 cm. (A Studio book) [NK4085.L38 1969] 78-80264 12.00
1. Pottery, English—History. I. Title.

Pottery, English—Yorkshire.

GRABHAM, Oxley. 738.3'094274
Yorkshire potteries, pots and potters. [1st ed. reprinted]; with a new introduction by Peter Walton. Wakefield, S.R. Publishers, 1971. vii, 2-116 p.; illus. 25 cm. Reprint of 1st ed., York, Yorkshire Philosophical Society, 1916. Bibliography: p. [116] [NK4087.Y5G7 1971] 79-866830 ISBN 0-85409-659-0 £1.50
1. Pottery, English—Yorkshire. 2. Pottery—Yorkshire, Eng. I. Title. BIP

Pottery—Equipment and supplies.

HAMER, Frank. 738.1'2
Clays / Frank and Janet Hamer. New York : Watson-Guptill Publications, 1977. 90 p. : ill. ; 21 cm. (Ceramic skillbooks) Includes index. Bibliography: p. 80-81. [TT921.5.H35 1977] 77-199 ISBN 0-8230-0589-5 : 7.95
1. Pottery—Equipment and supplies. 2. Clay. I. Hamer, Janet. II. Title. III. Series. BIP

Pottery—Europe—History—Addresses, essays, lectures.

MEDIEVAL pottery from excavations : studies presented to Gerald Clough Dunning : with a bibliography of his works / edited by Vera I. Evison, H. Hodges, and J. G. Hurst. New York : St. Martin's Press, 1974. 262 p., [9] leaves of plates : ill. ; 24 cm. Includes bibliographies and index. [TP793.M4 1974] 74-82134 14.95 738.3'094
1. Dunning, Gerald Clough. 2. Pottery—Europe—History—Addresses, essays, lectures. I. Dunning, Gerald Clough. II. Evison, Vera I. III. Hodges, Henry, 1920- IV. Hurst, John G., 1927-
Contents omitted. BIP

Pottery, European.

SCHWARTZMAN, Paulette. 738'.075
A collector's guide to European and American art pottery / by Paulette Schwartzman ; photographed by Milton Parker. Paducah, Ky. : Collector Books, c1978. 104 p. : ill. (some col.) ; 22 cm. Includes index. Bibliography: p. 103. [NK4083.S34] 78-107594 ISBN 0-89145-072-6 : 9.95
1. Pottery, European. 2. Pottery, American. 3. Decoration and ornament—Art nouveau. 4. Art deco. 5. Pottery—Collectors and collecting. I. Parker, Milton. II. Title. III. Title: Art pottery. BIP

Pottery, European—Dictionaries.

HAGGAR, Reginald George, 1905- 738.37
The concise encyclopedia of continental pottery and porcelain. New York, Hawthorn Books [1960] 533p. Bibl.: p.523-533. illus., plates (part col.) 26cm. 60-10340 20.00
1. Pottery, European—Dictionaries. 2. Porcelain, European—Dictionaries. I. Title. II. Title: Continental pottery and porcelain.

HAGGAR, Reginald George, 1905- 738
The concise encyclopedia of continental pottery and porcelain, by Reginald G. Haggar. New York, Praeger [1968, c1960] 533 p. illus., plates (part col.) 26 cm. Bibliography: p. 523-533. [NK4083.H3 1968] 68-28656 18.50
1. Pottery, European—Dictionaries. 2. Porcelain, European—Dictionaries. I. Title. II. Title: Continental pottery and porcelain.

Pottery—Exhibitions.

EVERSON Museum of Art of Syracuse and Onondaga County. 738'.0973
Ceramics 70 plus woven forms; a national invitational exhibition organized by Everson Museum. Consultant to the exhibition: Toshiko Takqezu. [Syracuse, 1970] [34] p. col. illus. 21 cm. Exhibited at Everson Museum of Art, Syracuse, N.Y., Nov. 14, 1970-Jan. 3, 1971 and Albany Institute of History and Art, Albany, N.Y., Feb. 8-Mar. 31, 1971. [NK3712.S93E83 1970] 73-146786
1. Pottery—Exhibitions. 2. Wall hangings—Exhibitions. I. Albany Institute of History and Art. II. Title.

Pottery, Far Eastern—Exhibitions.

AGA-OGLU, Kamer, 1903- 738'.095'074017435
The Williams collection of Far Eastern ceramics. Chinese, Siamese, and Annamese ceramic wares selected from the collection of Justice and Mrs. G. Mennen Williams in the University of Michigan Museum of Anthropology. Catalogue of an exhibition held in the West Gallery of the Horace H. Rackham School of Graduate Studies, Mar. 1-30, 1972. Ann Arbor, University of Michigan, Museum of Anthropology [1972] v, 73 p. illus. 27 cm. Bibliography: p. 73. [NK4163.A34] 72-197785
1. Williams, G. Mennen, 1911- —Art collections. 2. Pottery, Far Eastern—Exhibitions. 3. Porcelain, Far Eastern—Exhibitions. I. Michigan. University. Museum of Anthropology. II. Title. BIP

Pottery, French.

GIACOMOTTI, Jeanne 738.37
French faience [Tr. from French by Diana Imber] New York, Universe [c.1963] 266p. illus., 52 col. plates. 30cm. (Univ. lib. of antique art) Bibl. 63-18339 27.50
1. Pottery, French. I. Title.

RAMIE, Georges. 738'.092'4
Picasso's ceramics / Georges Ramie ; translated from the French by Kenneth Lyons. New York : Viking Press, 1976. 292 p. : ill. (some col.) ; 28 cm. (A Studio book) Translation of Ceramique de Picasso. Includes index. [NK4210.P5R2813 1976] 76-2690 ISBN 0-670-55323-9 : 45.00
1. Picasso, Pablo, 1881-1973. 2. Pottery, French. 3. Ceramic sculpture—France. I. Title.

Pottery, French—History.

LANE, Arthur, 1909- 738.3'7
French faience. [2d ed.] New York, Praeger [1970] xi, 49 p., [96] p. of illus. 8 col. plates. 26 cm. Bibliography: p. 45. [NK4305.L3 1970b] 75-133087 17.50
1. Pottery, French—History. I. Title. BIP

Pottery—Galena, Ill.

HORNEY, Wayne B. 738.3
Pottery of the Galena area. [Valparaiso, Ind., Author, RR4. Box 349 1965] 48p. illus (pt. col.) 22cm. Cover title. [TP800.G3H6] 65-9243 3.50 pap.,
1. Pottery—Galena, Ill. I. Title.

Pottery, Gallo-Roman.

STANFIELD, Joseph Aloysius. 738.3
Central Gaulish potters, by J. A. Stanfield & Grace Simpson; with a pref. by Eric Birley. With drawings completed by Wilfred Dodds. London, New York, Oxford University Press. 1958. iiii, 300 p. illus., plates, map. 29 cm. (University of Durham publications) "A complete list of the published works of J. A. Stanfield": p. [xxi]-xxii. Bibliography: p. [xxv]-xxviii. [NK3850.S75] 58-800
1. Pottery, Gallo-Roman. 2. Gaul — Antiq. I. Simpson, Grace, joint author. II. Title. III. Series: Durham, Eng. University. Publications

Pottery, Great Britain.

*CAMERON, Elisabeth, comp. 738.'0942
Potters on pottery / Elizabeth Cameron, Philippa Lewis. New York : St. Martin's, c1976. 168p. : ill. ; 26 cm. [NK4085] 76-11329 11.95
1. Pottery, Great Britain. 2. Potters-Great Britain. I. Lewis, Phillips, joint comp. II. Title.
Contents omitted. BIP

WEBSTER, Graham. 738.3'09362
Romano-British coarse pottery : a student's guide / edited by Graham Webster. 3rd ed. London : Council for British Archaeology, 1976. 37 p. : ill. ; 21 cm. (CBA research report ; no. 6) Bibliography: p. 21-30. [NK3850.W4 1976] 77-363446 ISBN 0-900312-38-6 : £1.25
1. Pottery—Great Britain. 2. Pottery, Roman—Great Britain. 3. Pottery—Dictionaries. I. Title. II. Series: Council for British Archaeology. C.B.A. research reports ; no. 6.

Pottery, Greek.

COOK, R. M. 738.382
Greek painted pottery. Chicago, Quadrangle Books, 119 West Lake Street [1960] xxiii, 391p. (Bibliography: p.334-358.) illus., plates. 25cm. (Methuen's) handbooks of archaeology) 59-15809 12.50
1. Pottery, Greek. 2. Vases, Greek. 3. Vase-painting, Greek. I. Title.

COOK, Robert Manuel 738.0938
Greek painted pottery [by] R. M. Cook. London, Methuen Label mounted on t.p.: New York Barnes Noble. [1966,c.1960] xxiii, 395p. illus. plates. 25cm. (Methuen's handbks. of archeaology) Reprinted with corrections. [NK4645.C6 1966] 66-8479 13.50
1. Pottery, Greek. 2. Vases, Greek. 3. Vase-painting, Greek. I. Title.

COOK, Robert Manuel. 738.3'0938
Greek painted pottery [by] R. M. Cook. 2nd ed. [London] Methuen [1972] xxiv, 390 p. illus. 24 cm. ([Methuen's handbooks of archaeology series]) Distributed in the USA by Harper & Row; Barnes & Noble Import Division. Bibliography: p. 331-359. [NK4645.C6 1972] 72-193710 ISBN 0-416-76170-4
1. Pottery, Greek. 2. Vases, Greek. 3. Vase-painting, Greek. I. Title.
Available from Barnes and Noble, 35.00, 0-416-76170-4.

MINGAZZINI, Paolino. 738'.0945
Greek pottery painting; translated by F. B. Sear from the Italian. London, New York, Hamlyn, 1969. 3-157 p. col. illus. 20 cm. (Cameo) Translation of Ceramica greca. [NK4645.M7153] 70-454866 15/-
1. Pottery, Greek. 2. Vase-painting, Greek. I. Title.

SUBJECT INDEX POTTERY, JAPANESE—1868

WALTERS, Henry Beauchamp, 1867-1944. 738.3'82'0938
History of ancient pottery: Greek, Etruscan, and Roman. Based on the work of Samuel Birch. With 300 illus. Washington, McGrath Pub. Co., 1973. 2 v. illus. 24 cm. Reprint of the 1905 ed. published by J. Murray, London. Bibliography: v. 1, p. xix-xxxvi. [NK3835.W3 1973] 76-119285 ISBN 0-8434-0153-2 110.00
1. Pottery, Greek. 2. Pottery, Etruscan. 3. Pottery, Roman. 4. Mythology, Classical, in art. I. Birch, Samuel, 1813-1885. History of ancient pottery. II. Title.

Pottery, Greek—Greece—Corinth.

HERBERT, Sharon, 1944- 938'.7 s
The red-figure pottery / by Sharon Herbert. Princeton, N.J. : American School of Classical Studies at Athens, 1977. x, 88 p., [18] leaves of plates : ill. ; 32 cm. (Corinth ; v. 7 ; pt. 4) Erratum slip tipped in. Includes bibliographical references and index. [DF261.C65A6 vol. 7, pt. 4] [NK3840] 738.3'0938'7 77-3070 ISBN 0-87661-074-2 : 25.00
1. Pottery, Greek—Greece—Corinth. 2. Pottery—Greece—Corinth. 3. Corinth, Greece—Antiquities. I. Title. II. Series: American School of Classical Studies at Athens. Corinth ; v. 7, pt. 4.

Pottery, Greek—Handbooks, Manuals, etc.

FOLSOM, Robert Slade. 738.3'0938
Handbook of Greek pottery; a guide for amateurs [by] Robert S. Folsom. Greenwich, Conn., New York Graphic Society [1967] 213 p. illus., 16 plates. 26 cm. $14.00 Bibliography: p. 205-206. [NK3840.F64 1967b] 68-25740
1. Pottery, Greek—Handbooks, Manuals, etc. I. Title.

Pottery, Hellenistic—Corinth, Greece.

EDWARDS, G. Roger, 1914- 738.3'0938'7
Corinthian Hellenistic pottery, by G. Roger Edwards. Princeton, N.J., American School of Classical Studies at Athens [1975] p. cm. (Corinth; results of excavations conducted by the American School of Classical Studies at Athens, v. 7, pt. 3) Bibliography: p. [DF261.C65A6 vol. 7, pt. 3] [NK3840] 74-10623 ISBN 0-87661-073-4 : 35.00
1. Pottery, Hellenistic—Corinth, Greece. 2. Pottery—Corinth, Greece. I. Title. II. Series: American School of Classical Studies at Athens. Corinth, v. 7, pt. 3. **BIP**

Pottery—History.

CHAFFERS, William, 1811-1892 738.0278
Marks & monograms on European and oriental pottery and porcelain. 2v. The British section ed. by Geoffrey A. Godden. The European and oriental sections ed. by Frederick Litchfield. R. L. Hobson. 15th rev. ed. London, W. Reeves [New York. Dover. 1966,c.1965] 2v. (636,443p.) illus. 26cm. Bibl. [NK4215.C46] 66-38182 12.5
1. Pottery—Hist. 2. Pottery, Oriental. 3. Porcelain—Hist. 4. Porcelain, Oriental. 5. Pottery—Marks. I. Godden, Geoffrey A., ed. II. Litchfield, Frederick, 1850- ed. III. Hobson, Robert Lockhart, 1872-1941, ed. IV. Title. **BIP**

CHARLESTON, Robert J., 1916- 738'.09
World ceramics; an illustrated history edited by Robert J. Charleston. [Authors]: John Ayers [and others] New York, McGraw-Hill [1968] 352 p. illus. (part col.), maps. 35 cm. Bibliography: p. 8. [NK3780.C48] 68-24604 25.00
1. Pottery—History. 2. Porcelain—History. I. Ayers, John. II. Title.

COOPER, Emmanuel. 738'.09
A history of pottery / Emmanuel Cooper. New York : St. Martin's Press, 1972. 276 p., [4] leaves of plates : ill. (some col.) ; 26 cm. Includes index. Bibliography: p. 265-270. [NK3780.C66 1972] 72-85262
1. Pottery—History. I. Title.

HAGGAR, Reginald George, 1905- 738.309
Pottery through the ages. Illustrated by the author. New York, Roy Publishers [1959] 74p. illus. 22cm. [NK3780.H24] 59-10060
1. Pottery—Hist. I. Title.

HILLIER, Bevis, 1940- 738'.09
Pottery and porcelain, 1700-1914; England, Europe, and North America New York, Meredith Press [1968] 386 p. illus. (part col.), facsims., ports. 24 cm. (The Social history of the decorative arts) Bibliography: p. 361-368. [NK3900.H5 1968b] 68-27001 12.95
1. Pottery—History. 2. Porcelain—History. I. Title.

LITCHFIELD, Frederick, 1850- 738
Pottery and porcelain, a guide to collectors. 5th ed., enlarged and completed rev. by Frank Tilley New York, M. Barrows [1951] xii, 356 p. illus. (part col.) 26 cm. Containing the marks and monograms of the important factories. Bibliography: p. 331-334. [NK4230.L7 1951] 51-14172
1. Pottery—Hist. 2. Porcelain—Hist. 3. Pottery—Collectors and collecting. 4. Porcelain—Collectors and collecting. 5. Pottery—Marks. I. Title.

SAVAGE, George, 1909- 738.309
Pottery through the ages. [Harmondsworth, Middlesex] Penguin Books 1959] 247p. illus. 18cm. (Pelican books, A439) [NK3780.S3] 59-2187
1. Pottery—Hist. I. Title.

SAVAGE, George, 1909- 738.309
Pottery through the ages. London, Cassell [dist. New York, Barnes & Noble, 1964, c.1959] 246p. illus. 22cm. (Belle sauvage lib.) Bibl. 64-6041 6.00
1. Pottery—Hist. I. Title.

WYCKES-JOYCE, Max. 738.09
700 years of pottery and procelain. New York, Philosophical Library [1958] 276 p. illus. 23 cm. Includes bibliography. [NK3780.W9] 58-59648
1. Pottery — Hist. 2. Porcelain — Hist. I. Title.

Pottery, Hungarian.

PATAKY, Ilona (Brestyanszky) 738.3094391
Modern Hungarian ceramics. [Tr. by Lili Halapy] Budapest, Corvina [dist. New York, Vanous, 1963] 46p. 48 plates (pt. col.) 19cm. Bibl. 63-4886 2.90
1. Pottery, Hungarian. I. Title.

Pottery, Iranian.

YOSHIDA, Mitsukuni, 1921- 738.3'0955
In search of Persian pottery. Translated by John M. Shields. [1st English ed.] New York, Weatherhill [1972] 161 p. illus., col. plates. 22 cm. On spine: Persian pottery. Translation of Perushia no yakimono. [NK4147.Y613 1972] 72-76402 ISBN 0-8348-1510-9 6.95
1. Pottery, Iranian. I. Title. II. Title: Persian pottery.

Pottery, Iranian—Exhibitions.

IOWA. University. Museum of Art. 738.3'7
Calligraphic ceramics from eastern Iran : early Islamic pottery from the Collection of Ulfert Wilke : [exhibition] the University of Iowa Museum of Art, Iowa City, November 7 through December 15, 1974 / [Wendy Waldron]. [Iowa City] : The Museum, [1974?] 32 p. : ill. ; 28 cm. [NK4147.I58 1974] 75-624382
1. Wilke, Ulfert, 1907- —Art collections. 2. Pottery, Iranian—Exhibitions. 3. Pottery, Islamic—Iran—Exhibitions. 4. Paleography, Arabic (Cufic) in art. I. Wilke, Ulfert, 1907- II. Waldron, Wendy. III. Title.

Pottery, Islamic—Catalogs.

GRUBE, Ernst J. 738.3'0917'67107402176
Islamic pottery of the eighth to the fifteenth century in the Keir Collection / Ernst J. Grube. London : Faber and Faber, 1976, i.e. 1977 378 p., [14] col. leaves of plates : ill. (some col.) ; 29 cm. (The Keir Collection) Includes index. General bibliography: p. 308-332. [NK3880.G78] 76-383703 ISBN 0-571-09953-X : 75.00
1. De Unger, Edmund—Art collections. 2. Pottery, Islamic—Catalogs. I. Title. II. Series.
Distributed by Faber and Faber, Salem, New Hampshire

Pottery, Islamic—Exhibitions.

FREER Gallery of Art, Washington, D.C. 709'.5'0740153 s
Ceramics from the world of Islam, by Esin Atil. Washington, Smithsonian Institution, 1973. viii, 225 p. illus. (part col.) 31 cm. (Its Fiftieth anniversary exhibition, 3) Catalog of an exhibition. Includes bibliographical references. [N5020.W52F733 1973 vol. 3] [NK3880] 738.3'0917'671 74-168248
1. Pottery, Islamic—Exhibitions. I. Atil, Esin. II. Title. **BIP**

Pottery, Islamic—Neyshabur, Iran.

WILKINSON, Charles Kyrle, 1897- 738.3'0955'92
Nishapur: pottery of the early Islamic period [by] Charles K. Wilkinson. [New York] Metropolitan Museum of Art; distributed by New York Graphic Society, Greenwich, Conn. [1973] xlii, 374 p. illus. (part col.) 32 cm. Bibliography: p. 371-374. [NK4148.N49W56] 73-9795 ISBN 0-87099-076-4 45.00
1. Pottery, Islamic—Neyshabur, Iran. 2. Pottery—Neyshabur, Iran. I. Title.

Pottery, Israeli—Exhibitions.

KOCHAVI, Nora, 1934- 730'.92'4
Nora & Naomi: impressions from Sinai. [Catalogue of exhibition] Jewish Museum, New York, April 11, 1973-September 3, 1973. [New York, Jewish Museum, 1973] [12] p. illus. 24 cm. [NK4210.K55B57] 73-78652
1. Kochavi, Nora, 1934- 2. Bitter, Naomi, 1936- 3. Pottery, Israeli—Exhibitions. I. Bitter, Naomi, 1936- II. Jewish Theological Seminary of America. Jewish Museum. III. Title. IV. Title: Impressions from Sinai.

Pottery, Japanese.

BOWES, James Lord, 1834-1899. 730'.02'78
Japanese marks and seals / by James Lord Bowes. Ann Arbor, Mich. : Ars Ceramica, 1976. xxiii, 379 p. : ill. ; 24 cm. Reprint of the 1882 ed. published by H. Sotheran, London; with a new introd. Includes index. [NK4167.B75 1976] 76-15315 ISBN 0-89344-002-7 : 25.00
1. Pottery, Japanese. 2. Pottery—Marks. 3. Illumination of books and manuscripts, Japanese. 4. Book industries and trade—Japan. 5. Art industries and trade—Japan. 6. Artists' marks. 7. Seals (Numismatics)—Japan. I. Title. **BIP**

FIGGESS, John. 738'.0952
The heritage of Japanese ceramics, by Fujio Koyama. Translated and adapted by John Figgess with an introd. by John Alexander Pope. [1st ed.] New York, Weatherhill [1973] 252 p. illus. (part col.) 38 cm. Adapted from Nihon toji no dento, by F. Koyama. Bibliography: p. 248. [NK4167.K6142 1973] 73-4762 ISBN 0-8348-1513-3 40.00
1. Pottery, Japanese. I. Koyama, Fujio, 1900- Nihon toji no dento. II. Title.

GORHAM, Hazel H. 738.2'0952
Japanese and Oriental ceramics, by Hazel H. Gorham. Rutland, Vt., C. E. Tuttle Co. [1970, c1971] xiii, 256 p. illus., map. 22 cm. Bibliography: p. 237-241. [NK4167.G58 1971] 70-130416 7.50
1. Pottery, Japanese. I. Title. **BIP**

JENYNS, Roger Soame, 1904- 738.3'0952
Japanese pottery, by Soame Jenyns. New York, Praeger Publishers [1971] xiv, 380 p. illus., 4 col. plates. 26 cm. (Monographs on pottery and porcelain) Bibliography: p. 348-350. [NK4167.J4 1971b] 69-19121 32.50
1. Pottery, Japanese. I. Title. **BIP**

LEACH, Bernard Howell 738.3
A potter in Japan, 1952-1954. [Hollywood-by-the-Sea, Fla., Transatlantic Arts 1960] 246p. illus. 22cm. 60-2214 8.50
1. Pottery, Japanese. 2. Folk art—Japan. 3. Japan—Descr. & &trav.—1945- I. Title.

LEACH, Bernard Howell, 1887- 738.3
A potter in Japan, 1952-1954, by Bernard Leach. [1st American ed.] New York, Transatlantic Arts [1967] 246 p. illus., map, ports. 22 cm. [NK4167.L4 1967] 67-4140
1. Pottery, Japanese. 2. Folk art—Japan. 3. Japan—Description and travel—1945- I. Title.

MIKAMI, Tsugio, 1907- 738.2'0952
The art of Japanese ceramics. Translated by Ann Herring. [1st English ed.] New York, Weatherhill [1972] 185 p. illus. (part col.) 24 cm. (The Heibonsha survey of Japanese art, 29) Translation of Toki. [NK4167.M4613] 77-162681 ISBN 0-8348-1000-X 7.95
1. Pottery, Japanese. 2. Porcelain, Japanese. I. Title. II. Series. **BIP**

MILLER, Roy Andrew. 738.30952
Japanese ceramics. New York, Crown Publishers [1962] 19 p. illus., 29 plates (part col.) 18 x 19 cm. (Art of the East library) [NK4167.M48] 62-1506
1. Pottery, Japanese. I. Title. II. Series.

MUNSTERBERG, Hugo, 1916- 738.0952
The ceramic art of Japan; a handbook for collectors. Rutland, Vt., C. E. Tuttle Co. [1964] 272 p. illus. (part col.) col. map. 21 x 22 cm. Errata slip mounted on p. [150] Bibliography: p. 265-266. [NK4167.M85 1964] 63-20586
1. Pottery, Japanese. 2. Pottery—Collectors and collecting. I. Title.

NAGUMO, Ryu, 1931- 738.1
Japanese pottery as a hobby. Tokyo, Toto Shuppan Co.; [distributed solely by] Japan Publications Trading Co., Rutland, Vt. [c1963] 128 p. illus. (part col.) 31 cm. [TP808.N3] 63-22185
1. Pottery, Japanese I. Title.

SANDERS, Herbert H. 738'.0952
The world of Japanese ceramics, by Herbert H. Sanders, with the collaboration of Kenkichi Tomimoto. [1st ed.] Tokyo, Palo Alto, Calif., Kodansha International [1967] 267 p. illus. (part col.), map. 27 cm. [TP804.J3S3 1967] 67-16771
1. Pottery, Japanese. I. Tomimoto, Kenkichi, 1886-1963. II. Title. **BIP**

[SUGIMOTO, Katsuo] 738.0952
[The outline of Tamba pottery.] Kyoto, Japan, Heiando Shoten [dist. New York, Perkins, 1963] 157, 10p. illus. (pt. col.) 23cm. Text in Japanese with English summary. and caption title. J63 8.00
1. Pottery, Japanese. I. Title. II. Title: (Japanese) Romanized: Tamba no yakimono.

TANAKA, Kana, ed. 738.37
Ishizara and aburazara. Introd.notes by Soetsu Yanagi [others] Summary in English by Hidesaburo Suzuli. [dist. Los Angeles, Perkins Oriental Books, c.] 1960[ ] 33, 12p., illus. (part col.) Text and captions in Japanese. Title pages in English and Japanese. 26cm. J61 12.50, bds., bxd.
1. Pottery, Japanese. 2. Ishizara—Japanese pottery. 3. Aburazara—Japanese pottery. I. Title.

Pottery, Japanese—1868-

STITT, Irene. 738'.0952
Japanese ceramics of the last 100 years / by Irene Stitt. New York : Crown Publishers, [1974] ix, 214 p., [4] leaves of plates : ill. (some col.) ; 26 cm. Includes index. Bibliography: p. 207-208. [NK4167.6.S8 1974] 74-80304 ISBN 0-517-51664-0 : 9.95

1. Pottery, Japanese—1868- 2. Porcelain, Japanese—1868- I. Title.

Pottery, Japanese—Congresses.

INTERNATIONAL Symposium 738'.0952 on Japanese Ceramics, Seattle Art Museum, 1972.
International Symposium on Japanese Ceramics; [transcript. Seattle, Seattle Art Museum, 1973] 196 p. illus. 26 cm. Errata slip inserted. Includes bibliographical references. [NK4167.I57 1972] 73-179307 8.50 (pbk.)
1. Pottery, Japanese—Congresses. 2. Porcelain, Japanese—Congresses. I. Seattle. Art Museum.

Pottery, Japanese—Exhibitions.

BROOKLYN Institute of 730'.02'78 Arts and Sciences. Museum.
Japanese ceramics from the collection of Captain and Mrs. Roger Gerry. New York, c1961. unpaged. illus. 23cm. Includes biography. [NK4167.B85] 61-65403
1. Pottery, Japanese—Exhibitions. 2. Pottery—Private collections. I. Gerry, Roger, 1916- II. Gerry, Peggy, 1919- III. Title.

KOYAMA, Fujio, 1900- 738'.0952
Japanese ceramics from ancient to modern times; selected from collections in Japan and America. Edited by Fujio Koyama. A commemorative catalogue of an exhibition held at the Oakland Art Museum, Oakland, California, U.S.A., 1961. [Oakland, Calif., Oakland Art Museum, 1961] 70 p., 84 p. of illus. 8 col. plates. 31 cm. Bibliography: p. 69-70. [NK4167.K58] 79-244670
1. Pottery, Japanese—Exhibitions. I. Oakland, Calif. Art Museum. II. Title.

SEATTLE. Art 738'.0952'074019777 Museum.
Ceramic art of Japan; one hundred masterpieces from Japanese collections. Seattle [1972] 172 p. illus. (part col.) 27 cm. An exhibition initiated by the Seattle Art Museum and arranged under the joint sponsorship of the Agency for Cultural Affairs of the Japanese Government and participating museums in the United States. Held at the Seattle Art Museum, Sept. 7, 1972-Oct. 22, 1972, and at three other museums. Bibliography: p. 169-172. [NK4167.S42] 74-189738
1. Pottery, Japanese—Exhibitions. 2. Porcelain, Japanese—Exhibitions. I. Japan. Bunkacho. II. Title.

Pottery, Japanese—Hist.

OKUDA, Seiichi, ed 738.37
Japanese ceramics, by Roy Andrew Miller, after the Japanese text by Seiichi Okuda and others. With photos. by Manshichi Sakomoto, Tazaburo Yoneda, and Yoshihiko Maejima. Tokyo, Toto Shuppan Co.; distributed by C. E. Tuttle Co., Rutland, Vt. [1960] 240p. illus., 105 plates (19col.) map. 28cm. 60-16172 12.50, bxd.
1. Pottery, Japanese—Hist. I. Miller, Roy Andrew. II. Title.

Pottery, Jomon.

EGAMI, Namio, 1906- 738.3'0952
The beginnings of Japanese art. With supplementary chapters by Teruya Esaka and Ken Amakasu. Translated by John Bester. [1st English ed.] New York, Weatherhill [1973] 178 p. illus. (part col.) 24 cm. (The Heibonsha survey of Japanese art) Translation of Nihon bijutsu no tanjo. [NK4167.E3213] 72-78599 ISBN 0-8348-1006-9 8.95
1. Pottery, Jomon. 2. Pottery, Yayoi. 3. Terra-cottas, Japanese. I. Title. II. Series. BIP

KIDDER, Jonathan Edward. 738.3'7
Prehistoric Japanese arts; Jomon pottery, by J. Edward Kidder. With contributions by Teruya Esaka. [1st ed.] Tokyo, Palo Alto, Calif., Kodansha International [1968] 308 p. illus. 37 cm. Bibliography: p. 296-300. [NK3855.J6K5] 68-17458
1. Pottery, Jomon. I. Esaka, Teruya, 1919- joint author. II. Title.

Pottery—Juvenile literature.

VAL BAKER, Denys, 1917- 738
The young potter; a how-it-is-done book of pottery. New York, Warne [c.1963] 57p. illus. 29cm. Bibl. 63-7185 3.95
1. Pottery—Juvenile literature. I. Title. BIP

WEISS, Harvey. 738.1
Ceramics: from clay to kiln. New York, Young Scott Books [1964] 63 p. col. illus. 28 cm. [NK4240.W4] 64-13583
1. Pottery—Juvenile literature. I. Title. BIP

Pottery—Kansas City. Mo.—Catalogs.

WILLIAM Rockhill Nelson 738.3 Gallery of Art, Kansas City, Mo.
The Frank P. and Harriet C. Burnap collection of English pottery in the William Rockhill Nelson Gallery of Art. Kansas City, Mo., Nelson-Atkins Gallery of Art. 1953. 128p. illus. (part col.) 28cm. Bibliography: p.127. [NK3730.K3W5] 54-21992
1. Pottery—Kansas City. Mo.—Catalogs. 2. Pottery, English. I. Burnap, Frank P. II. Burnap, Harriet Call. III. Title.

Pottery, Korean.

GOMPERTZ, Godfrey St. George 738 Montague.
Korean pottery and porcelain of the Yi period, by G. St. G. M. Gompertz. New York, Praeger [1968] xx, 106 p., 128 plates (part col.) illus., maps. 26 cm. Includes bibliographies. [NK4168.5.G63 1968b] 68-22780
1. Pottery, Korean. 2. Porcelain, Korean. I. Title. BIP

KIM, Chae-won, 1909- 738.309519 ed.
The ceramic art of Korea, edited by Chewon Kim and G. St. G. M. Gompertz. New York, T. Yoseloff [1961] 222 p. 100 plates (part col.) 31 cm. [NK4168.5.K5] 61-19038
1. Pottery, Korean. I. Gompertz, Godfrey St. George Montague, joint ed. II. Title.

Pottery, Korean—Exhibitions.

GRIFFING, Robert P. 738'.09519
The art of the Korean potter; Silla, Koryo, Yi. [New York] Asia Soc.; dist. by N. Y. Graphic [Greenwich, Conn., 1968] 131p. illus. (pt. col.), map. 27cm. Asia House Gallery pubn. Catalogue of an exhibition selected by Robert P. Grining, Jr. & snown in spring 1968 as an activity of the Asia Society. Bibl. [NK4168.5.G7] 68-21015 12.00
1. Pottery, Korean—Exhibitions. I. Asia Society. II. Asia House Gallery, New York. III. Title.

HENDERSON, 738'.09519'074017157 Gregory.
Korean ceramics; an art's variety. Collection of Mr. and Mrs. Gregory Henderson. [Columbus] Divisions of Art Gallery, Ohio State University [1969] 60 p. illus. (part col.) 28 cm. Catalog of an exhibition held Feb. 9-Mar. 9, 1969 at Ohio State University. Bibliography: p. 18. [NK4168.6.A1H46] 73-171231
1. Pottery, Korean—Exhibitions. 2. Porcelain, Korean—Exhibitions. 3. Henderson, Gregory—Art collections. I. Ohio. State University, Columbus. II. Title.

Pottery, Korean—Yi dynasty, 1392-1910.

AKABOSHI, Goro, 1897- 738'.09519
Five centuries of Korean ceramics : pottery and porcelain of the Yi Dynasty / by Goro Akaboshi and Heiichiro Nakamaru ; translated by June Silla. 1st English ed. New York : Weatherhill, 1975. 159 p. : ill. (some col.) ; 22 cm. Translation of Chosen no yakimono. [NK4168.6.A1A6213] 74-23784 ISBN 0-8348-1514-1 : 12.50
1. Pottery, Korean—Yi dynasty, 1392-1910. I. Nakamaru, Heiichiro, 1908-1974, joint author. II. Title. BIP

Pottery—Kyoto—History.

SATO, Masahiko, 738'.0952'191 1925-
Kyoto ceramics. Translated and adapted by Anne Ono Towle and Usher P. Coolidge. [1st ed.] New York, Weatherhill [1973] 133 p. illus. (part col.) 23 cm. (Arts of Japan, 2) Translation of Kyoyaki, v. 28 (1968) in the series, Nihon no bijutsu. [NK4168.K86S2713 1973] 72-92256 ISBN 0-8348-2701-8 4.95
1. Pottery—Kyoto—History. I. Title. BIP

Pottery—Lancashire, Eng.

LOMAX, Abraham. 1738.34
Royal Lancastrian pottery, 1900-1938; its achievements and its makers. Bolton, 1957. 153p. illus. 24cm. [NK4087.L3L61] 57-45819
1. Pottery—Lancashire, Eng. 2. Lusterware. I. Title.

Pottery, Latin American.

LITTO, Gertrude, 1929- 738.3'098
South American folk pottery :/ by Gertrude Litto ; studio photography by Robert Emerson Willis ; ill. by Frank Litto. New York : Watson-Guptill Publications, 1976. 223 p. : ill. (some col.) ; 29 cm. Includes index. Bibliography: p. 221. [NK4002.L57] 76-3644 ISBN 0-8230-4873-X : 24.95
*1. Pottery, Latin American. 2. Folk art—Latin America. I. Litto, Frank. II. Title.*BIP

Pottery — Leed, Eng.

TOWNER, Donald C 738.37
The Leeds pottery [by] Donald Towner. [1st American Ed.] New York, Taplinger Pub. Co. [1965] x, 180 p. illus., facsims, map, plan, plates (part col.) 25 cm. Bibliogray: p. 175. [NK4088.L4T6] 65-14387
1. Pottery — Leed, Eng. I. Title.

Pottery—Marks.

BARBER, Edwin Atlee, 738'.027'8 1851-1916.
Marks of American potters. Southampton, N.Y., Cracker Barrel Press [1971?] 174 p. illus., facsims., ports. 21 cm. Reprint of the 1904 ed. [NK4215.B3 1971] 70-21077 3.00
1. Pottery—Marks. 2. Potters—United States. I. Title. BIP

BARBER, Edwin Atlee, 738'.02'78 1851-1916.
Marks of American potters / by Edwin Atlee Barber. Ann Arbor : Ars Ceramica, 1976. 174 p. : ill. ; 24 cm. Reprint of the 1904 ed. published by Patterson & White Co., Philadelphia. [NK4215.B3 1976] 76-15310 ISBN 0-89344-001-9 : 11.50
1. Pottery—Marks. 2. Potters—United States. I. Title.

[BURTON, William] 738.2'02'78 1863-
Collector's guide to pottery and porcelain marks. Edited by John Edwards. Stratford, Conn., J. Edwards, 1971 [c1928] x, [2], 213 p. illus. 24 cm. A reprint of Handbook of marks on pottery & porcelain, by W. Burton and R. L. Hobson. Bibliography: p. [xii] [NK4215.B8 1971] 72-180870 8.00
1. Pottery—Marks. 2. Porcelain—Marks. I. Hobson, Robert Lockhart, 1872-1941, joint author. II. Edwards, John, 1943- ed. III. Title.

[BURTON, William] 738.2'02'78 1863-
Collector's handbook to marks on porcelain and pottery. Edited by E. Paul and A. Petersen. Greens Farms, Conn., Modern Books and Crafts [1974] [10], 213 p. illus. 24 cm. Reprint of the 1928 ed. of Handbook of marks on pottery & porcelain by W. Burton and R. L. Hobson, published by Macmillan, London. Bibliography: 10th prelim. page. [NK4215.B8 1974] 74-180368 10.00
1. Pottery—Marks. 2. Porcelain—Marks. I. Hobson, Robert Lockhart, 1872-1941, joint author. II. Paul, Ethel, ed. III. Petterson, Ann, ed. IV. Title.

CUSHION, John 738.3'02'78 Patrick.
Dictionary of marks on earthenware and stoneware / John P. Cushion. New York : Van Nostrand Reinhold Co., [1976] p. cm. Includes index. Bibliography: p. [NK4215.C78] 76-23943 ISBN 0-442-21794-3 : 22.50
1. Pottery—Marks. I. Title.

FISHER, Stanley W. 738'.0942
English pottery and porcelain marks, by Stanley W. Fisher. Slough, New York, Foulsham, 1970. 3-98 p. illus., facsims. 18 cm. [NK4215.F5] 78-597296 ISBN 0-572-00711-6 £0.60
1. Pottery—Marks. 2. Porcelain—Marks. 3. Pottery, English. 4. Porcelain, English. I. Title. BIP

KOVEL, Ralph M. 738.88
Dictionary of marks: pottery and porcelain, by Ralph M. and Terry H. Kovel. New York, Crown Publishers [1953] x, 278 p. 22 cm. Bibliography: p. x. [NK4215.K68] 53-5247
1. Pottery—Marks. I. Kovel, Terry H., joint author. II. Title. BIP

PENKALA, Maria. 738'.027'8
European pottery; a handbook for the collector, 5780 marks on maiolica, faience, and stoneware. [2d ed.] Rutland, Vt., C. E. Tuttle Co. [1969, c1968] 472 p. illus. 25 cm. Bibliography: p. 459-462. [NK4215.P4 1969] 69-19602 15.00
1. Pottery—Marks. 2. Pottery—Europe—History. I. Title.

Pottery, Maya.

BRAINERD, George 970.657155 Walton, 1909-1956.
The archaeological ceramics of Yucatan. [Berkeley, University of California Press, 1958] iii, 378p. illus., maps, plans, tables. 28cm. (Anthropological records, v. 19) Bibliography: p. 101-106. [E51.A58 vol.19] A 58
1. Pottery, Maya. 2. Indians of Mexico—Pottery. 3. Yucatan—Antiq. I. Title. II. Series.

Pottery, Mexican.

WHITAKER, Irwin. 738'.0972
A potter's Mexico / Irwin & Emily Whitaker. 1st ed. Albuquerque : University of New Mexico Press, c1978. xvi, 136 p., [8] leaves of plates : ill. (some col.) ; 27 cm. Includes index. Bibliography: p. 130-133. [NK4031.W47] 77-29047 ISBN 0-8263-0472-9 : 17.50
*1. Pottery, Mexican. 2. Pottery—20th century—Mexico. 3. Potters—Mexico—Biography. I. Whitaker, Emily. II. Title.*BIP

Pottery, Moravian—North Carolina.

BIVINS, John, 1940- 738.3'09756
The Moravian potters in North Carolina, by John Bivins, Jr. Photography by Bradford L. Rauschenberg. Winston-Salem, Published for Old Salem, inc. by the University of North Carolina Press, Chapel Hill [1972] xiii, 300 p. illus. 27 cm. (The Old Salem series) Bibliography: p. 289-290. [NK4025.N8B5] 70-172396 ISBN 0-8078-1191-2
1. Pottery, Moravian—North Carolina. I. Old Salem, inc., Winston-Salem, N.C. II. Title. BIP

Pottery Mound site, N.M.

HIBBEN, Frank Cummings, 751.7'3 1910-
Kiva art of the Anasazi at Pottery Mound / by Frank C. Hibben. 1st ed. Las Vegas, Nev. : KC Publications, 1975. xiii, 145 p. : col. ill. ; 24 x 30 cm. Includes indexes. Bibliography: p. 139-140. [E99.P9H46] 75-19742 ISBN 0-916122-16-6 : 35.00
1. Pottery Mound site, N.M. 2. Pueblo Indians—Art. 3. Indians of North America—Southwest, New—Art. 4. Mural painting and decoration—New Mexico. I. Title.

1. Pottery—Shenandoah Valley. 2. Folk art—Shenandoah Valley. I. Title.

Pottery, South African.

CLARK, Garth. 738'.0968 B
Potters of Southern Africa / G. Clark, L. Wagner. 1st ed. Cape Town : C. Struik, 1974. 200 p. : ill. (some col.) ; 29 cm. Includes index. [NK4178.6.S6C52] 74-82877 ISBN 0-86977-046-2 : 27.50
1. Pottery, South African. 2. Potters—Africa, South. I. Wagner, Lynne, joint author. II. Title.
Distributed by Verry BIP

Pottery, Southeast Asian.

BROWN, Roxanna M. 738.3'0959
The ceramics of South-East Asia : their dating and identification / Roxanna M. Brown. Kuala Lumpur ; New York : Oxford University Press, 1977. xiv, 82 p., [42] leaves of plates : ill. (some col.) ; 29 cm. (Oxford in Asia studies in ceramics) Includes index. Bibliography: p. [71]-76. [NK4154.B77] 77-376446 ISBN 0-19-580315-9 : 39.50
1. Pottery, Southeast Asian. I. Title. BIP

Pottery, Southeast Asian—Exhibitions.

FRASCHE, Dean F. 738.3'0959'07401471
Southeast Asian ceramics : ninth through seventeenth centuries / Dean F. Frasche. [New York] : Asia Society, 1976. 144 p. : ill. (some col.) ; 26 cm. "An Asia House Gallery publication." "Catalogue of an exhibition shown in Asia House Gallery in the fall of 1976." Bibliography: p. 142-143. [NK4154.F7] 76-20204 ISBN 0-87848-047-1 : 25.00
1. Pottery, Southeast Asian—Exhibitions. I. Asia House Gallery, New York. II. Title. BIP

Pottery, Spanish.

LLORENS Artigas, Jose. 738.3'0946
Spanish folk ceramics of today. [By] J. Llorens Artigas [and] J. Corredor-Matheos. Photographer F. Catala Roca. [2d ed.] New York, Watson-Guptill Publications [1974, c1970] 235 p. illus. (part col.) 28 cm. First ed. published in Spanish and English under title: Ceramica popular espanola actual. Spanish folk ceramics of today. Bibliography: p. 235. [NK4123.L47 1974] 74-3296 ISBN 0-8230-4880-2
1. Pottery, Spanish. 2. Folk art—Spain. I. Corredor Matheos, Jose, 1929- joint author. II. Title.

Pottery—Stoddard, N.H.

FIELD, Anne E. 748.2'9142'9
On the trail of Stoddard glass / by Anne E. Field. Dublin, N.H. : W. L. Bauhan, [1975] 110 p. : ill. ; 22 cm. Includes index. Bibliography: p. 101-102. [NK4027.S86F54] 73-153379 ISBN 0-87233-021-4 : 4.95
1. Weeks and Gilson. 2. Pottery—Stoddard, N.H. I. Title. BIP

Pottery — Summit Co., Ohio.

BLAIR, C. Dean. 738.39077136
The potters and potteries of Summit County, 1828-1915, by C. Dean Blair. Akron, Ohio, Summit County Historical Society, 1965 [c1966] vi, 59 p. illus. facsims. 23 cm. Bibliography: p. 35-36. [NK4025.O5B5] 66-5976
1. Pottery — Summit Co., Ohio. 2. Potters — Summit Co., Ohio. I. Title.

Pottery—United States—Congresses.

WINTERTHUR Conference, 18th, 1972. 738'.09
Ceramics in America. Edited by Ian M. G. Quimby. Charlottesville, University Press of Virginia [1973] ix, 374 p. illus. 23 cm. (Winterthur Conference report, 1972) "Published for the Henry Francis du Pont Winterthur Museum." Includes bibliographical references. [NK4005.W5 1972] 72-96715 ISBN 0-8139-0476-5 4.50 (pbk.)
1. Pottery—United States—Congresses. I. Quimby, Ian M. G., ed. II. Henry Francis du Pont Winterthur Museum. III. Title. IV. Series: Winterthur Conference. Report, 1972.

Pottery—Washington, D.C.

KLAMKIN, Marian. 738'.074'0153
White House china. New York, Scribner [1972] xvi, 184 p. illus. 27 cm. Bibliography: p. 165-169. [NK3730.W37W484] 72-179553 ISBN 0-684-12758-X 12.50
1. Pottery—Washington, D.C. 2. Porcelain—Washington, D.C. 3. Washington, D.C. White House. I. Title.

Pottery — Yucatan.

THOMPSON, Raymond H 301.2'4
Modern Yucatecan Maya pottery making. Salt Lake City, Society for American Archaeology, 1958. 157 p. illus. 16 cm. (Memoirs of the Society for American Archaeology, no. 15) American antiquity, v. 23, no. 4, pt. 2, Apr. 1958. Bibliography: p. 151-157. [[E51.S7 no.15]] A59
1. Pottery — Yucatan. 2. Pottery, Maya. 3. Indians of Mexico — Pottery. I. Title. II. Series: Society for American Archaeology. Memoirs, no. 15

Pottery—Zanesville, Ohio—Catalogs.

PURVIANCE, Louise. 738'.09771'91
Zanesville art poetry in color, by Louise and Evan Purviance and Norris F. Schneider. Leon, Iowa, Mid-America Book Co. [1968] [50] p. col. illus. 23 cm. Items from the Louise and Evan Purviance collection displayed at White Pillars Antiques, Norwich, Ohio. [NK4027.Z3P8] 79-1241 4.95
1. Pottery—Zanesville, Ohio—Catalogs. I. Purviance, Evan, joint author. II. Schneider, Norris Franz, 1898- III. Title.

Pousette-Dart, Richard, 1916—

GORDON, John, 1912- 759.13
Richard Pousette-Dart. Foreword by Lloyd Goodrich. New York, Pub. for Whitney Mus. of Amer. Art by Praeger [c.1963] 55p. illus. (pt. col.) port. 24cm. Bibl. 63-14678 .50
1. poussette-Dart, Richard, 1916- I. Whitney Museum of American Art, New York. II. Title.

POUSETTE-DART, Richard, 1916- 759.13
Richard Pousette-Dart : [catalogue of the exhibition, November 7, 1974-January 5, 1975] / by James K. Monte. New York : Whitney Museum of American Art, [1974] 79 p. : col. ill. ; 23 cm. Bibliography: p. 71-78. [ND237.P817M66] 74-22531
1. Pousette-Dart, Richard, 1916- I. Monte, James K. II. Whitney Museum of American Art, New York.

Poussin, Nicolas, 1594?-1665.

BLUNT, sir Anthony, 1907- 759.4
Nicolas Poussin. London, Phaidon; New York, Bollingen Foundation, 1967 [i. e. 1968]. 2v. 265 plates, illus. 32 cm. (Bollingen series [35]. The A. W. Mellon lectures in the fine arts, 12) 9 ISSN -each vol. (B68-04555-B 68-04556))IContents.CONTENTS.-Text-Plates. Bibliography: v. 1, p. [381]-392 [DE553.P8B64 1968] 68-103532
1. Poussin, Nicolas, 1594?-1665. I. Title. II. Series: Bollingen series, 35 III. Series: The A. W. Mellon lectures in the fine arts, 12)

BLUNT, Anthony, Sir 1907- 759.4
Nicolas Poussin. [New York, Bollingen Foundation [dist. Princeton, N. J., Princeton, 1967] 2 v. illus., 265 plates. 32-24 x 31 cm. (Bollingen ser., 35. The A. W. Mellon lects. in the fine arts, 70) Contents.[1] Text.-- [2] Plates. [ND553.P8B64] 66-162373 25.00 set, ed.
1. Poussin, Nicolas, 1594-1665. I. Title. II. Series: Bollingen series, 35 III. Series: The A. W. Mellon lectures in the fine arts, 7)
Bollingen books are now distributed by Princeton.

BLUNT, Anthony, Sir 1907- 759.4
The paintings of Nicolas Poussin. Critical catalogue. London, Phaidon [1966] [7]. 271p. 38 plates. 32cm. Bibl. [ND553.P66B5] 67-31911 25.00
1. Poussin, Nicolas, 1594?-1665. I. Title.
American distributor: N. Y. Graphic in Greenwich, Conn.

FRIEDLAENDER, Walter F., 1873- 759.4
Nicolas Poussin; a new approach. New York, Abrams [1966] 203, [1] p. 130. illus., 49 col. plates. 33cm. (Lib. of great painters) Bibl. [ND553.P8F7] 64-10763 20.00
1. Poussin, Nicolas, 1594?-1665. I. Title.

FRIEDLAENDER, Walter F 1873- 759.4
Nicolas Poussin; a new approach [by] Walter Friedlaender. New York, H. N. Abrams, [1966?] 203, [1] p. 130 illus., 49 col. plates. 33 cm. (The Library of great painters) "Bibliographical note": p. [204] [ND553,P8F7] 64-10763
1. Poussin, Nicolas, 1594?-1665. I. Title.

MACGREEVY, Thomas 759.4
Nicolas Poussin. [dist. Chester Springs, Pa., Dufour Eds., c.1960] 47p. illus. 26cm. 61-3099 4.50, pap., limited ed.
1. Poussin, Nicolas, 1594?-1665. I. Title.

POUSSIN, Nicolas, 1594?-1665. 759.4
Poussin, 1594-1665. [Texte par] Pierre Marois. Paris, Braun; agent pour U.S.A.: E. S. Herrmann. New York [1950] [63] p. (p. [15]-[62] illus.) 17 cm. (Collection des maltres) French, English, and German. Bibliography:p. [63] [ND553.P8M36] 51-4653
I. Marois, Pierre, 1901- ed. II. Title. III. Series: Collection "Les Maltres"

REY, Robert, 1888- 759.4
Poussin paintings [tr. from French by Diana Imber] New York, French & European Pubns. [1964] 62p. mounted col. illus. 21cm. (Rhythm & colour, 10) Bibl. 64-5425 3.95
1. Poussin, Nicolas, 1594?-1665. I. Title.

Powder flasks.

NEW York. Metropolitan Museum of Art. 736.6
American engraved powder horns; a study based on the J. H. Grenville Gilbert collection, by Stephen V. Grancsay, curator emeritus, Dept. of Arms and Armor. New printing. Philadelphia. R. Riling Arms Books Co., 1965 [c1946] viii, 96 p. illus., map, 47 plates, port. 30 cm. Cover title: American powder horns. "Annotated bibliography": p. 89-96 [NK6020.N4 1965] 65-25087
1. Gilbert, J. H. Grenville. 2. Powder flasks. 3. Bone carving. I. Grancsay, Stephen Vincent, 1897- II. Title. III. Title: American powder horns. BIP

RYWELL, Martin, 1905-1972. 739.7
The powder flask; the complete guide for the collector of the principal accessory to the firearm. [Harriman, Tenn.] [Pioneer Press] [1959] 81 p. illus. 23 cm. [NK9990.P6R9] 59-3900
1. Powder flasks.

Powder flasks—United States—Catalogs.

SWAYZE, Nathan L. 736'.6
Engraved powder horns of the French and Indian War and Revolutionary War era / by Nathan L. Swayze ; [drawings by Don Troiana]. Yazoo City, Ms. : Gun Hill Pub. Co., c1978. 235 p. : ill. ; 23 x 29 cm. Bibliography: p. 235. [NK6020.S87] 78-53343 ISBN 0-87833-304-5 : 25.00
1. Powder flasks—United States—Catalogs. 2. Bone carving—United States—Catalogs. 3. United States—History—French and Indian War, 1755-1763. 4. United States—History—Revolution, 1775-1783. I. Title. BIP

Powell, Nowland Van.

POWELL, Nowland Van. 759.13
The American navies of the Revolutionary War : paintings / by Nowland Van Powell ; with descriptive notes by the artist ; introd. by Richard B. Morris. New York : Putnam, [1974] 126, [2] p. : col. ill. ; 28 x 34 cm. Bibliography: p. [128] [ND237.P819A43 1974] 73-78625 ISBN 0-399-11183-2 : 20.00
1. Powell, Nowland Van. 2. United States. Navy—History—Revolution, 1775-1783—Pictorial works. 3. United States—History—Revolution, 1775-1783—Naval operations—Pictorial works. I. Title. BIP

Powers, Asahel, 1759-1841.

LITTLE, Nina Fletcher, 1903- 759.13
Asahel Powers; painter of Vermont faces. [Catalog of an exhibition] Abby Aldrich Rockefeller Folk Art Collection, Williamsburg, Virginia, October 14-December 2, 1973. [Williamsburg, Va., Colonial Williamsburg Foundation, 1973] 49 p. illus. 21 x 26 cm. Includes bibliographical references. [ND1329.P68L57] 73-86269 ISBN 0-87935-015-6 4.00 (pbk.)
1. Powers, Asahel, 1759-1841. 2. Vermont—Biography—Portraits. I. Abby Aldrich Rockefeller Folk Art Collection, Williamsburg, Va.

Powers, Hiram, 1805-1873.

REYNOLDS, Donald M. 730'.92'4
Hiram Powers and his ideal sculpture / Donald Martin Reynolds. New York : Garland Pub., 1977. xxvii, 377, 1051-1118 p. : ill. ; 21 cm. (Outstanding dissertations in the fine arts) Originally presented as the author's thesis, Columbia, 1975. "The letters from Appendix A (Unpublished correspondence of Hiram Powers, pp. 378 through 1050) have been withheld at the request of the author. They are qvailable to the reader in the Hiram Powers archives at the National Collection of Fine Arts; Smithsonian Institution, Washington, D.C." Bibliography: p. 1109-1110. [NB237.P7R49 1977] 76-23685 ISBN 0-8240-2720-5 lib.bdg. : 45.00
1. Powers, Hiram, 1805-1873. 2. Sculptors—United States—Biography. I. Title. II. Series. BIP

WUNDER, Richard P. 730'.92'4 B
Hiram Powers: Vermont sculptor, by Richard P. Wunder. Published in cooperation with the Woodstock Historical Society. Taftsville, Vt., Countryman Press [1974] i, 39 p. illus. 23 cm. Includes bibliographical references. [NB237.P7W86] 74-18074 3.75
1. Powers, Hiram, 1805-1873. I. Powers, Hiram, 1805-1873.

Powers, Kimiko—Art collections.

ROSENFIELD, John M. 709.52
Traditions of Japanese art; selections from the Kimiko and John Powers Collection [by] John M. Rosenfield [and] Shujiro Shimada. [Cambridge, Mass.] Fogg Art Museum, Harvard University, 1970. 393 p. illus. (part col.), facsims., maps. 29 cm. Exhibition catalog. Includes bibliographical references. [N7352.R67] 76-133788 ISBN 0-674-90125-8 25.00
1. Powers, Kimiko—Art collections. 2. Powers, John—Art collections. 3. Art, Japanese—Exhibitions. I. Shimada, Shujiro, 1907- joint author. II. Harvard University. William Hayes Fogg Art Museum. III. Title. BIP

Pozzatti, Rudy, 1925—

GESKE, Norman A. 769'.924
Rudy Pozzatti: American printmaker [by] Norman A. Geske. Lawrence, University Press of Kansas [1971] viii, 63 p. 50 illus. 28 cm. Bibliography: p. 30. [NE539.P6G4] 75-121648 ISBN 0-7006-0065-5
1. Pozzatti, Rudy, 1925- I. Title.

Pozzo, Cassiano del, d. 1657.

VERMEULE, Cornelius 740.0740229
Clarkson, 1925-
The Dal Pozzo-Albani drawings of classical antiquities in the Royal Library at Windsor Castle [by] Cornelius C. Vermeule, III. Philadelphia, American Philosophical Society, 1966. 170 p. illus. 30 cm. (Transactions of the American Philosophical Society. New ser., v. 56, pt. 2, 1966) Bibliography: p. 7. [Q11.P6 n.s., vol. 56, pt. 2] 66-18701
1. Pozzo, Cassiano del, d. 1657. Museum chartaceum. 2. Albani, Alessandro, Cardinal, 1692-1779. 3. Drawings, Italian — Catalogs. 4. Classical antiquities — Catalogs. I. Windsor Castle. Royal Library. II. Title. III. Series: American Philosophical Society, Philadelphia. Transactions, new ser., v. 56, pt. 2 BIP

Pozzo, Cassiano del, d. 1657. Museum chartaceum.

VERMEULE, Cornelius 741.945
Clarkson, 1925-
The Dal Pozzo-Albani drawings of classical antiquities in the British Museum. Philadelphia, American Philosophical Society, 1960. 78 p. illus. 30 cm. (Transactions of the American Philosophical Society, new ser., v. 50, pt. 5) Bibliography: p. 8. [Q11.P6] 60-11139
1. Pozzo, Cassiano del, d. 1657. Museum chartaceum. 2. Albani, Alexxandro, cardinal, 1692-1779. 3. Drawings, Italian. 4. Classical antiquities. 5. Sculpture, Ancient. 6. British Museum. Dept. of Greek and Roman Antiquities. I. Title. II. Title: Pozzo-Albani drawings of classical antiquities in the British Museum. III. Series: American Philosophical Society, Philadelphia. Transactions, new ser., v. 50 pt. 5

VERMEULE, Cornelius 741.945
Clarkson, III
The Dal Pozzo-Albani drawings of classical antiquities in the British Museum. Philadelphia, American Philosophical Society [c.]1960. 78p. Bibl.: p.8. illus. 30cm. (Transactions of the American Philosophical Society, new ser., v.50, pt. 5) 60-11139 2.00 pap.,
1. Pozzo, Cassiano del, d. 1657. Museum chartaceum. 2. Albani. Alessandro, cardinal, 1692-1779. 3. Drawings, Italian. 4. Classical antiquities. 5. Sculpture, Ancient. I. British Museum. Dept. of Greek and Roman Antiquities. II. Title. III. Title: Pozzo-Albani drawings of classical antiquities in the British Museum. IV. Series: American Philosophical Society, Philadelphia. Transactions, new ser., v. 50, pt. 5

Prague. Hrad.

BURIAN, Jiri. 943.7'12
Prague Castle / [by] Jiri Burian and Antonin Hartmann ; [translated from the Czech by Jan Eisler] ; photographs by Karel Neubert. London ; New York : Hamlyn, 1975. 203 p. : ill. (chiefly col.), facsims., col. ports. ; 33 cm. [NA7721.P73B8713] 76-357364 ISBN 0-600-37062-3 : £5.95
1. Prague. Hrad. I. Hartmann, Antonin, joint author. II. Title.

Prairie School (Architecture)

BROOKS, Harold Allen, 720'.977
1925-
The prairie school : Frank Lloyd Wright and his midwest contemporaries / H. Allen Brooks. New York : Norton, [1976], c1972. p. cm. (The Norton library) Includes index. Bibliography: p. [NA722.B7 1976] 76-16576 ISBN 0-393-00811-8 pbk. : 7.95
1. Wright, Frank Lloyd, 1867-1959. 2. Prairie School (Architecture) 3. Architecture, Modern—20th century—Middle West. I. Title. BIP

BROOKS, Harold Allen, 1925- 724.9
The prairie school; Frank Lloyd Wright and his midwest contemporaries [by] H. Allen Brooks. [Toronto, University of Toronto Press, 1972] xxiii, 373 p. illus. 23 cm. Bibliography: p. [349]-352. [NA722.B7 1972] 72-151363 ISBN 0-8020-5251-7 25.00
1. Wright, Frank Lloyd, 1867-1959. 2. Prairie School (Architecture) 3. Architecture—Middle West. 4. Architecture, Modern—20th century—Middle West. I. Title.

MILWAUKEE. Art Center. 720'.977
Prairie Archives.
The Prairie school tradition / the Prairie Archives of the Milwaukee Art Center ; edited by Brian A. Spencer. New York : Whitney Library of Design, 1979. p. cm. Includes index. Bibliography: p. [NA722.M54 1979] 79-321 ISBN 0-8230-7432-3 : 30.00
1. Prairie school (Architecture) 2. Architecture, Modern—20th century—Middle West. I. Spencer, Brian A., 1942- II. Title.

WILSON, Richard Guy, 720'.9777
1940-
The Prairie School in Iowa / Richard Guy Wilson, Sidney K. Robinson. 1st ed. Ames : Iowa State University Press, 1977. p. cm. Includes bibliographical references. [NA730.I8W54] 77-2788 ISBN 0-8138-0915-0 pbk. : 6.50
1. Wright, Frank Lloyd, 1867-1959. 2. Sullivan, Louis Henri, 1856-1924. 3. Prairie School (Architecture) 4. Architecture—Iowa. 5. Architecture, Modern—20th century—Iowa. I. Robinson, Sidney K., 1943- joint author. II. Title. BIP

Praktica camera.

GAUNT, Leonard. 771.3'1
The Praktica way: the Praktica photographer's companion. 2nd ed. London, New York, Focal Press, 1972. 286 p. illus. 22 cm. [TR263.P7G38 1972] 73-154916 ISBN 0-240-50743-6 £2.75
1. Praktica camera. 2. Photography—Handbooks, manuals, etc. I. Title. BIP

ROSSING, Roger. 771.3'1
The Praktica book. [English translation from the German by K. S. Ankersmit]. 5th revised ed. London, New York, Focal P., 1969. 256 p. illus. (some col.). 22 cm. Translation of Fotografie mit der Praktica. [TR263.P7R613] 72-463302 35/-
1. Praktica camera. 2. Photography—Handbooks, manuals, etc. I. Title. BIP

Prang, Louis, 1824-1909.

FREEMAN, Graydon La 769'.92'4
Verne, 1904-
Louis Prang; color lithographer; giant of a man [by] Larry Freeman. Watkins Glen, N.Y., Century House [1971] 190 p. illus. (part col.) 29 cm. (Library of Victorian culture) [NE2312.P7F7] 70-145867
1. Prang, Louis, 1824-1909.

MCCLINTON, Katharine 769'.92'4
(Morrison)
The chromolithographs of Louis Prang. [1st ed.] New York, C. N. Potter; distributed by Crown Publishers [1973] 246 p. illus. (part col.) 32 cm. [NE2312.P7M32 1973] 72-87339 ISBN 0-517-50411-1 15.00
1. Prang, Louis, 1824-1909. 2. Prang (L) & Company, Boston. I. Title.

Prassinos, Mario, 1916-

FERRIER, Jean Louis 759.4
Prassinos. [Paris, G. Fall, dist. New York, Efron] c.1962. 74p. col. illus. 19cm. (Le Musee de poche) 62-52236 1.50 pap.,
1. Prassinos, Mario, 1916- I. Title.

Precancels—Georgia—Catalogs.

OGDEN, William C 769.56973075
1907- ed.
Official precancel catalog for Georgia. George C. Mynchenberg, managing editor. W. C. Ogden, State editor. Winter Park, Fla., G. W. Noble, c1958. 78p. illus. 22cm. [HE6185.U7G46] 59-31035
1. Precancels—Georgia—Catalogs. I. Mynchenberg George C., 1897- ed. II. Title.

Precancels—Iowa—Catalogs.

KIRKPATRICK, 769.56973075
Williard Hann, 1909- ed.
Official precancel catalog for Iowa, George C. Mynchenberg, managing editor. W. H. Kirkpatrick, State editor. Winter, Park, Fla., G. W. Noble, c1961. 168p. 23cm. [HE6185.U7I84] 62-735
1. Precancels—Iowa—Catalogs. I. Mynchenberg, George C., 1897- ed. II. Title.

Precancels—U. S.

CODA, Richard J 769.56973075
The G-C town list of post offices which do or did issue precancels. Newark, N. J., c1957. 54p. 22cm. [HE6185.U5C58] 58-17936
1. Precancels—U. S. I. Title.

Precancels—United States—Catalogs.

BESOM, Dale B ed. 769.56973075
The official integral precancel type list & handbook, all types illustrated. G. C. Mynchenberg, managing editor. Dale B. Besom, listing & pricing editor. 1st ed. Winter Park, Fla., G. W. Noble, c1962. 76p. illus. 23cm. [HE6185.U6B47] 62-32337
1. Precancels—U. S.—Catalogs. I. Mynchenberg, George C., 1897- ed. II. Title. BIP

BESOM, Dale B. ed. 769.56973
The official printed dated control precancel catalog; all types illustrated, all stamps priced. G. C. Mynchenberg, managing editor. Dale B. Besom, listing & pricing editor, assisted by Charles Metz & Tom Beddoes. 4th ed. Winter Park, Fla., G. W. Noble, 1966. 156 p. 23 cm. [HE6185.U6B48] 66-6729
1. Precanceis — U.S. — Catalogs. I. Mynchenberg, George C. 1897- ed. II. Title. BIP

METZ, Charles, ed. 769.56973075
Official precancel catalog for printed dated controls, printed dated integrals and early dated classics. Editor: Charles Metz; assoc. editor: Alvin F. Simon. 3d ed. Detroit, A. F. Simon, c1961. 80p. illus. 22cm. [HE6185.U6M4 1961] 61-47552
1. Precancels—U. S.—Catalogs. I. Title.

MYNCHENBERG, George 769.56973075
C 1897- ed.
The official precancel town & type list. 1st ed. Winter Park, Fla., G. W. Noble, 1960. 273p. 23cm. [HE6185.U6M9] 60-51752
1. Precancels—U. S.—Catalogs. I. Title. BIP

PRECANCELLED envolopes 769'.56973 *of the United States* / Ben Hedding, editor, John Randall, editor. 1st ed. Bloomington, IL : United Postal Stationery Society, 1976. 112 p. : ill. ; 28 cm. [HE6185.U6P73] 76-29537
1. Precancels—United States—Catalogs. I. Hedding, Ben. II. Randall, John M. III. United Postal Stationery Society.

Precious metals.

WELTER, Gerhard. 737.4'028
Cleaning and preservation of coins and medals / by Gerhard Welter ; including Paper money restoration and preservation by James J. Curto. New York : S. J. Durst, c1976. ix, 117 p. : ill. ; 24 cm. Translation of Die Reinigung und Erhaltung von Munzen und Medaillen. Includes index. Bibliography: p. 115. [TS729.W413] 76-3964 ISBN 0-915262-03-7 : 10.50
1. Precious metals. 2. Coins—Cleaning. 3. Coins—Preservation. I. Title. BIP

Precious stones.

ANDERSON, Basil William, 549
1901-
Gem testing [2d American ed.] New York, Emerson Books, 1959. 324p. illus. 23cm. First published in 1942 under title: Gem testing for jewellers. Includes bibliography. [TS752.A58 1959] 59-59
1. Precious stones. I. Title. BIP

DRAGSTED, Ove. 736'.2
Gems and jewelry in color / Ove Dragsted ; illustrated by Otto Frello. 1st American ed. New York : Macmillan, 1975. 232 p. : ill. (some col.) ; 19 cm. Includes index. Bibliography: p. 224-225. [TS752.D7 1975] 75-2391 ISBN 0-02-533500-6 : 7.95
1. Precious stones. 2. Jewelry. I. Frello, Otto. II. Title. BIP

GUBELIN, Eduard Josef, 736.2
1913-
Precious stones. Berne, Hallwag [dist. New York, Taplinger, c.1963] 10p. 18 col. plates. 19cm. (Orbis pictus, 9) 63-6242 2.00 bds.,
1. Precious stones. I. Title.

PADDOCK, Orlando S. 736'.2
Gemformation; a primer in gemology [by] Orlando S. Paddock. 1st ed. Dallas, Eskew Pub. Co. [1974] 107 p. illus. 23 cm. [TS752.P32] 74-174425
1. Precious stones. I. Title.

THE Rockhound buyers guide. 736.2 *1st- ed.;1953-* Palm Desert, Calif., Lapidary Journal. v. 25cm. Editor: 1953- L. Quick. Includes bibliography. [TN980.R6] 53-38776
1. Precious stones. I. Quick, Lelande, ed.

WEBSTER, Robert. 736'.2
Gem identification / by Robert Webster. New York : Sterling Pub. Co., c1977. 130 p., [3] leaves of plates : ill. (some col.) ; 26 cm. Published in 1975 under title: Gems in jewellery. Includes index. [TS752.W38 1977] 76-19800 ISBN 0-8069-3078-0 : 11.95 ISBN 0-8069-3079-9 lib. bdg. : 10.89
1. Precious stones. I. Title.

WEBSTER, Robert. 553'.8
Gems: their sources, descriptions, and identifications. [2d ed. Hamden, Conn.] Archon Books [1970] xvi, 836 p. illus. (part col.) 28 cm. Bibliography: p. 780-783. [TS752.W39 1970] 71-17205 45.00
1. Precious stones.

WEBSTER, Robert. 549
Practical gemmology : a study of the identification of gem-stones, pearls, and ornamental minerals / by Robert Webster. 6th ed. New York : Arco Pub. Co., 1978. 209 p. : ill. ; 20 cm. Includes index. [TS752.W4 1978] 78-2263 ISBN 0-668-04609-0 : 7.95
1. Precious stones. I. Title. BIP

Precision casting.

JACKSON, Harry, 1924- 731.4'56
Lost wax bronze casting; a photographic essay on this antique and venerable art. Foreword by John Walker. Flagstaff [Ariz.] Northland Press [1972] x, 127 p. illus. 30 cm. Bibliography: p. 123-215. [TS570.J33] 72-188289 ISBN 0-87358-093-1 20.00
1. Precision casting. 2. Bronze founding. 3. Sculpture—Technique. I. Title.

JACKSON, Harry, 1924- 731.4'56
Lost wax bronze casting : a photographic essay on this antique and venerable art / by Harry Jackson ; foreword by John Walker. New York : Van Nostrand Reinhold, 1979. p. cm. Reprint of the 1972 ed. published by Northland Press, Flagstaff, Ariz. Bibliography: p. [TS570.J33 1979] 78-26574 ISBN 0-442-26099-7 : 15.00
1. Precision casting. 2. Bronze founding. 3. Sculpture—Technique. I. Title. BIP

Prefabricated apartment houses—Design and construction.

DESIGN considerations 693.5'42 *for a precast prestressed apartment building.* Chicago : Prestressed Concrete Institute, c1975. 224 p. : ill. ; 23 cm. Cover title. "First presented at a special design seminar in conjunction with the 1972 PCI annual convention in Atlanta, Georgia, October 10, 1972," and subsequently published in serial form in the PCI Journal. Includes bibliographical references and index. [TH4820.D4] 75-27394
1. Prefabricated apartment houses—Design and construction. 2. Precast concrete construction. 3. Prestressed concrete construction. 4. High-rise apartment buildings—Design and construction. I. Prestressed Concrete Institute. BIP

Prefabricated houses.

ROWLAND, Norman. 728.2
Reston low income housing demonstration program [written by Norman Rowland, with the special assistance of Margaret Drury. Reston? Va.] 1969. 1 v. (various pagings) illus., plans. 28 cm. Half title: A report on factory produced multi-family housing utilizing light-gage steel frame modules. Based on research conducted by Gulf Reston, inc., and Divco-Wayne Industries, under grant no. VA-LIHD-1 from the U.S. Dept. of Housing and Urban Development to the Reston Virginia Foundation for Community Programs. Bibliography: p. 193-196. [TH4819.P7R68] 79-603847
1. Prefabricated houses. 2. Modular coordination (Architecture) 3. Housing—Reston, Va. I. Drury, Margaret J., joint author. II. Gulf Reston, inc. III. Divco-Wayne Industries. IV. Reston Virginia Foundation for Community Programs. V. Title. VI. Title: A report on factory produced multi-family housing utilizing light-gage steel frame modules.

Pregnancy—Pictorial works.

PHILLIPS, Royal, 1940- 779'.2
Life itself : a parenting experience / by Royal Phillips. Santa Barbara, Calif. : Royalt Pub. Co., 1976. 63 p. : ill. ; 27 cm. [RG525.P46] 76-51578
1. Pregnancy—Pictorial works. 2. Natural childbirth—Pictorial works. 3. Parent and child—Pictorial works. I. Title.

Preraphaelitism.

ANGELI, Helen (Rossetti) 704'.09
Pre-Raphaelite twilight; the story of Charles Augustus Howell. London, Richards Press, 1954. St. Clair Shores, Mich., Scholarly Press, 1971. xiii, 256 p. illus., ports. 22 cm. [PR466.A8 1971] 72-158494 ISBN 0-403-01312-7
1. Howell, Charles Augustus, d. 1890. 2. Preraphaelitism. I. Title. BIP

CARY, Elisabeth Luther, 1867-1936. 759.2
The Rossettis: Dante Gabriel and Christina. [Folcroft, Pa.] Folcroft Library Editions, 1973 [c1900] p. Reprint of the ed. published by Putnam, New York. "Christian Rossetti's poems": p. "List of the more important writings of Dante Gabriel Rossetti": p. [ND497.R8C3 1973] 73-12547 35.00
1. Rossetti, Dante Gabriel, 1828-1882. 2. Rossetti, Christina Georgina, 1830-1894. 3. Preraphaelitism. I. Title.

DICKASON, David Howard. 709.73
The daring young men; the story of the American Pre-Raphaelites. Bloomington, Indiana University Press, 1953. x, 304p. illus., ports. 25cm. Bibliographical references included in 'Notes' (p. 268-287) [N6510.D45] 53-10023
1. Preraphaelitism. 2. Art—U. S.—Hist. 3. American literature—19th cent.—Hist. & crit. I. Title.

DUNN, Henry Treffry, 1838-1899. 759.2
Recollections of Dante Gabriel Rossetti and his circle (Cheyne Walk life). Edited and annotated by the late Gale Pedrick. With a prefatory note by William Michael Rossetti. London, E. Mathews, 1904. [New York, AMS Press, 1971] 96 p. illus., port. 19 cm. Includes bibliographical references. [ND497.R8D8 1971] 73-129379 ISBN 0-404-02222-7
1. Rossetti, Dante Gabriel, 1828-1882. 2. Preraphaelitism. I. Title. BIP

GAUNT, William, 1900- 759.2
The pre-Raphaelite dream. New York, Schocken [c.1966] 294p. illus. 21cm. First pub. by Jonathan Cape, London, under title: The pre-Raphaelite tragedy [ND 467.G3 1966] 66-14869 6.00; 2.45 pap.,
1. Preraphaelitism. 2. Painters, British. 3. English poetry—19th cent.—Hist. & crit. I. Title. BIP

HILTON, Timothy, 1941- 759.2
The pre-Raphaelites. New York, H. N. Abrams [1971, c1970] 216 p. illus. (part col.) 22 cm. Includes bibliographical references. [ND467.5.P7H5 1971] 76-132634 ISBN 0-8109-0424-1 7.50
1. Preraphaelitism. I. Title. BIP

LAYARD, George Somes, 1857-1925. 760'.92'2
Tennyson and his pre-Raphaelite illustrators : a book about a book / by George Somes Layard. Folcroft, Pa. : Folcroft Library Editions, 1978. p. cm. Reprint of the 1894 ed. published by E. Stock, London. Contents.Contents.—Introductory.—As to the origin of 'P.R.P.'—Millais.—Holman Hunt.—Rossetti. [PR5577.L3 1978] 78-12687 ISBN 0-8414-5755-7 lib. bdg. : 12.50
1. Tennyson, Alfred Tennyson, Baron, 1809-1892—Illustrations. 2. Preraphaelitism. I. Title. BIP

ROSSETTI, William Michael, 1829-1919, ed. 759.2
Ruskin: Rossetti: Preraphaelitism; papers 1854 to 1862. New York, AMS Press [1971] xxi, 327 p. illus. 19 cm. Reprint of the 1899 ed. [ND467.5.P7R6 1971] 73-127453 ISBN 0-404-05437-4
1. Preraphaelitism. 2. Painters—England—Correspondence, reminiscences, etc. I. Ruskin, John, 1819-1900. II. Rossetti, Dante Gabriel, 1828-1882. III. Title.

WATKINSON, Raymond. 709'.42
Pre-Raphaelite art and design. Greenwich, Conn., New York Graphic Society [1970] 208 p. illus. (part col.) 26 cm. Bibliography: p. 197-201. [N6767.5.P7W3 1970b] 79-120101 13.50
1. Preraphaelitism. I. Title.

Preraphaelitism — Bibl.

FREDEMAN, William Evan, 1928- 016.70942
Pre-Raphaelitism; a bibliocritical study [by] William E. Fredeman. Cambridge, Harvard University Press, 1965. xix, 327 p. illus., facsims., ports. 25 cm. Based on thesis, University of Oklahoma, 1956. [Z5948.P9F7] 64-21242
1. Preraphaelitism — Bibl. 2. Painting, English — Hist. — Bibl. 3. English literature — 19th cent. — Hist. & crit. — Bibl. I. Title.

Preraphaelitism—England.

ALDEN, J. E. 759.2
The Pre-Raphaelites and Oxford; a descriptive handbook, by J. E. Alden. [Folcroft, Pa.] Folcroft Library Editions, 1974. 40 p. illus. 24 cm. Reprint of the 1948 ed. published by Alden, Oxford. [N6767.5.P7A43 1974] 74-1477 ISBN 0-8414-2964-2 (lib. bdg.)
1. Preraphaelitism—England. 2. Art, Modern—19th century—England. 3. Preraphaelitism—Oxford. 4. Art, Modern—19th century—Oxford. I. Title. BIP

CARY, Elisabeth Luther, 1867-1936. 760'.092'4
The Rossettis : Dante Gabriel and Christina / by Elisabeth Luther Cary. New York : Haskell House, 1974. iv, 310 p. : port. ; 22 cm. Reprint of the 1900 ed. published by Putnam, New York. Includes index. "List of the more important writings of Dante Gabriel Rossetti": p. 277-281. [NX547.6.R67C37 1974] 74-30190 ISBN 0-8383-1943-2 : 17.95
1. Rossetti, Dante Gabriel, 1828-1882. 2. Rossetti, Christina Georgina, 1830-1894. 3. Preraphaelitism—England. I. Title. BIP

GRIEVE, Alastair Ian. 759.2
The art of Dante Gabriel Rossetti: the Pre-Raphaelite period, 1848-50 [by] A. I. Grieve. Hingham, Real World Publications [1973] [4], 31 p. illus., ports. 30 cm. Includes bibliographical references. [ND497.R8G73] 73-164125 ISBN 0-903822-00-8 £1.10
1. Rossetti, Dante Gabriel, 1828-1882. 2. Preraphaelitism—England. I. Title.

HAMILTON, Walter, 1844-1899. 700'.942
The Aesthetic movement in England. 3d ed. [Folcroft, Pa.] Folcroft Library Editions, 1973. viii, 143 p. 24 cm. Reprint of the 1882 ed. published by Reeves & Turner, London. Contents.Contents.—The pre-Raphaelites.—The germ.—John Ruskin.—The Grosvenor Gallery.—Aesthetic culture.—Poets of the asthetic school.—Jonas Fisher: a poem in brown and white, and Mr. Robert Buchanan.—Punch's attacks on the asthetes.—Mr. Oscar Wilde.—A home for the asthetes. [NX543.H3 1973] 73-3203 ISBN 0-8414-2068-8 17.50
1. Preraphaelitism—England. I. Title.
Contents Omitted.

†HARDING, James. 759.2
The Pre-raphaelites / James Harding New York : Rizzdli 1977.c 96p. : ill.(some col.) ; 30 cm. Includes index. [ND467.5.PH33] 77-74338 ISBN 0-8478-0109-8 : 13.95 ISBN 0-8478-0108-X pbk. : 7.95
1. Preraphaelitism England. 2. Painting, English. 3. Painting, Modern 19th century England. I. Title. BIP

ROSSETTI, William Michael, 1829-1919. 700'.92'4 B
The P.R.B. journal : William Michael Rossetti's diary of the Pre-Raphaelite brotherhood, 1849-1853, together with other Pre-Raphaelite documents / edited from the original manuscript with an introd. and notes by William E. Fredeman. Oxford [Eng.] : Clarendon Press, 1975. xxvii, 282 p. : ill. ; 22 cm. Includes indexes. Bibliography: p. [251]-255. [ND467.5.P7R58 1975] 75-316365 ISBN 0-19-812505-4 : 32.00
1. Rossetti, William Michael, 1829-1919. 2. Preraphaelitism—England. I. Fredeman, William Evan, 1928- II. Title.
Distributed by Oxford University Press, New York. BIP

ROSSETTI, William Michael, 1829-1919, ed. 759.2
Preraphaelite diaries and letters, edited by William Michael Rossetti. London, Hurst and Blackett, 1900. [New York, AMS Press, 1974] 328 p. illus. 23 cm. Contents.Contents.—Some early correspondence of Dante Gabriel Rossetti, 1835-54.—Madox Brown's diary, etc., 1844-56.—The P.R.B. journal kept by W. M. Rossetti, 1849-53. Includes bibliographical references. [ND467.5.P7R59 1974] 70-148293 ISBN 0-404-08898-8
1. Rossetti, Dante Gabriel, 1828-1882. 2. Brown, Ford Madox. 3. Preraphaelitism—England. I. Title.

WOOD, Esther. 700'.942
Dante Rossetti and the Pre-Raphaelite movement. New York, Cooper Square Publishers, 1973. xii, 323 p. illus. 21 cm. Reprint of the 1894 ed. published by S. Low, Marston, London. Includes bibliographical references. [NX543.W66 1973] 72-91205 ISBN 0-8154-0445-X 9.50
1. Rossetti, Dante Gabriel, 1828-1882. 2. Preraphaelitism—England. I. Title.

Preraphaelitism—England—Catalogs.

THE Pre-Raphaelites / 759.2
[compiled by] Andrea Rose. Oxford : Phaidon, 1977. 16 p., 48 p. of plates : col. ill. ; 31 cm. [ND467.5.P7P74] 78-302479 ISBN 0-7148-1791-0 : 7.95
1. Preraphaelitism—England—Catalogs. 2. Painting, English—Catalogs. 3. Painting, Modern—19th century—England—Catalogs. I. Rose, Andrea.
Distributed by Dutton, New York

THE Pre-Raphaelites / 759.2
[compiled by] Andrea Rose. Oxford : Phaidon, 1977. 16 p., 48 p. of plates : col. ill. ; 31 cm. [ND467.5.P7P74] 78-302479 ISBN 0-7148-1791-0 : 7.95
1. Preraphaelitism—England—Catalogs. 2. Painting, English—Catalogs. 3. Painting, Modern—19th century—England—Catalogs. I. Rose, Andrea.
Distributed by Dutton, New York

Preraphaelitism—Exhibitions.

ART Association of Indianapolis, Indiana. John Herron Art Institute. 759.2
The Pre-Raphaelites; a loan exhibition of paints and drawings by members of the Pre-Raphaelite Brotherhood and their associates. Herron Museumof Art, Indianapolis, February 16 through March 27, 1964; Gallery of Modern Art Including the Huntington Hartford Collection, New York, April 27 through May 31, 1964. [Indianapolis, Printed by Allied Print. Service, 1964] [103] p. 84 illus. 26 cm. Introd. by Curtis G. Coley. Includes bibliographical references. [N6767.5.P7A7] 79-629089
1. Preraphaelitism—Exhibitions. I. Coley, Curtis G. II. New York (City). Gallery of Modern Art Including the Huntington Hartford Collection. III. Title.

CUMMER Gallery of Art. 759.2
Artists of Victoria's England. [Catalogue of exhibition] February 2-March 14, 1965. Jacksonville, Fla. [1965?] [21] p. illus. 22 x 29 cm. Cover title. [N6767.5.P7C85 1965] 74-184379
1. Preraphaelitism—Exhibitions. 2. Preraphaelitism—Great Britain. 3. Art, Modern—19th century—Great Britain. I. Title.

ELZEA, Rowland. 709'.03'4
The Pre-Raphaelite era, 1848-1914 : an exhibition in celebration of the Nation's Bicentennial, April 12-June 6, 1976, Delaware Art Museum, Wilmington, Delaware / Rowland and Betty Elzea; photos. of catalog entries by Will Brown...et al. [Wilmington] : Wilmington Society of the Fine Arts, c1976. 233 p. : ill. ; 29 cm. Errata slips inserted. Bibliography: p. 230-233. [N6465.P7E48] 76-9873
1. Preraphaelitism—Exhibitions. 2. Art, Modern—19th century—Exhibitions. 3. Art, Modern—20th century—Exhibitions. I. Elzea, Betty, joint author. II. Delaware Art Museum. III. Title.

LOWE Art Museum. 759.2
The revolt of the Pre-Raphaelites. Coral Gables, Fla. [1972?] 54 p. illus. 26 cm. Catalog of a loan exhibition held Mar. 5 through Apr. 9, 1972. Bibliography: p. 54. [ND467.5.P7L68] 73-172073
1. Preraphaelitism—Exhibitions. 2. Preraphaelitism—England. 3. Painting, Modern—19th century—England. I. Title.

Preraphaelitism—Great Britain.

MARILLIER, Henry Currie, 1865-1951. 759.2
Rossetti. [Folcroft, Pa.] Folcroft Library Editions, 1973. 112 p. illus. 23 cm. Reprint of the 1906 ed. published by G. Bell, London, in series: Bell's miniature series of painters. [ND497.R8M34 1973] 73-15949 ISBN 0-8414-6066-3 (lib. bdg.)
1. Rossetti, Dante Gabriel, 1828-1882. 2. Preraphaelitism—Great Britain. I. Series: Bell's miniature series of painters.

Preraphaelitism—Great Britain—Addresses, essays, lectures.

THE Germ; 700'.1
thoughts towards nature in poetry, literature, and art; being a facsimile reprint of the literary organ of the Pre-Raphaelite Brotherhood, published in 1850, with an introd. by William Michael Rossetti. [Folcroft, Pa.] Folcroft Library Editions, 1973. 30 p. 24 cm. Reprint of the 1901 ed. published by E. Stock, London. [NX543.G4 1973] 73-505 ISBN 0-8414-1561-7 6.50
1. Preraphaelitism—Great Britain—Addresses, essays, lectures. I. Rossetti, William Michael, 1829-1919. BIP

THE Germ: thoughts towards nature in poetry, literature, and art. 759.41
With an introd. by William Michael Rossetti. New York, AMS Press [1965] 192 p. illus. 24 cm. A reprint of the literary organ of the Pre-Raphaelite Brotherhood originally issued in four numbers from Jan. to May 1850; no. 1-2 under title: The Germ: thoughts towards nature in poetry, literature, and art; no. 3-4 under title: Art and poetry: being thoughts towards nature. [NX543.G4 1965] 700'.942 78-88238
1. Preraphaelitism—Great Britain—Addresses, essays, lectures. I. Rossetti, William Michael, 1829-1919. II. Pre-Raphaelite Brotherhood. III. Title: Art and poetry: being thoughts toward nature.

PRE-RAPHAELITISM : 700'.942
a collection of critical essays / edited and with an introd. by James Sambrook. Chicago : University of Chicago Press, 1974. 277 p. ; 24 cm. (Patterns of literary

SUBJECT INDEX

PRIMITIVISM IN ART—UNITED

criticism ; [12]) Includes index. Bibliography: p. [265]-270. [NX543.P73] 73-89790 ISBN 0-226-73452-8 : 13.50
1. Preraphaelitism—Great Britain—Addresses, essays, lectures. 2. Arts, English—Addresses, essays, lectures. I. Sambrook, James.

Preraphaelitism—Influence.

SPALDING, Frances. 759.2
Magnificent dreams : Burne-Jones and the late Victorians / Frances Spalding. New York : Dutton, 1978. 80 p. : ill. (some col.) ; 29 cm. Bibliography: p. 6. [ND497.B8S83 1978] 78-55004 ISBN 0-7148-1827-5 : 12.95. ISBN 0-7148-1909-3 pbk. : 6.95
1. Burne-Jones, Edward Coley, Sir, bart., 1833-1898. 2. Preraphaelitism—Influence. 3. Symbolism (Art movement)—England. 4. Painting, Victorian—England. I. Title. BIP

Preraphaelitism—U.S.

DICKASON, David Howard. 709.73
The daring young men; the story of the American Pre-Raphaelites. [New York] B. Blom [1970, c1953] x, 304 p. illus., ports. 24 cm. Includes bibliographical references. [N6510.D45 1970] 69-13235
1. Preraphaelitism—U.S. I. Title. BIP

Presidents—U.S.—Medals.

DUSTERBERG, Richard B. 737'.2
The official inaugural medals of the presidents of the United States / by Richard B. Dusterberg. 2d ed. Cincinnati, Ohio : Medallion Press, c1976. iv, 140 p. : ill. ; 24 cm. [CJ5813.D87 1976] 77-351423 17.95
1. Presidents—United States—Medals. 2. Presidents—United States—States—Inauguration. I. Title.

DUSTERBERG, Richard B. 737'.2
The official inaugural medals of the presidents of the United States; medals authorized by the Inaugural Committee to Commemorate the Inauguration of America's Presidents, by Richard B. Dusterberg. [1st ed.] Cincinnati, Ohio, Medallion Press [1971] viii, 107 p. illus. (1 col.), port. 24 cm. [CJ5813.D87] 72-24531
1. Presidents—U.S.—Medals. 2. Presidents—U.S.—Inauguration. I. Title.

Presidents—United States—Medals—Exhibitions.

MACNEIL, Neil, 1927- 745
The President's medal, 1789-1977 / by Neil MacNeil 1st ed. New York : Published in association with the National Portrait Gallery, Smithsonian Institution, by C. N. Potter : distributed by Crown Publishers, c1977. 160 p., [2] leaves of plates : ill. ; 31 cm. Include index. [CJ5802.2.W37M3 1977] 76-49563 ISBN 0-517-52917-3 : 12.95. ISBN 0-517-52918-1 pbk. : 7.95
1. Presidents—United States—Medals—Exhibitions. 2. Presidents—United States—Inauguration—Exhibitions. I. National Portrait Gallery, Washington D.C. II. Title. BIP

Presidents—United States—Portraits.

BERGER, Oscar, 1901- comp. 741.5973
The Presidents, from George Washington to the present. Edited and drawn in one line by Oscar Berger. New York, Crown Publishers [1968] 96 p. illus. 32 cm. "Sources of Presidential quotations": p. 88-94. [E176.1.B46] 68-9068 3.95
1. Presidents—United States—Portraits. 2. Quotations, American. I. Title.

LINCOLN, Abraham, Pres. U.S., 1809-1865. 973.7'092'4 B
An album of Lincoln photographs and words. [New York] : Eakins Press Foundation, c1976. [16] p. (on double leaves) : ill. ; 16 cm. (Eakins pocket album ; 3) Cover title. Folding book. [E457.92 1976] 77-152770 1.95
1. Lincoln, Abraham, Pres. U.S., 1809-1865—Quotations. 2. Lincoln, Abraham, Pres. U.S., 1809-1865—Portraits. 3. Presidents—United States—Portraits. I. Title.

NATIONAL Portrait Gallery, Washington, D.C. 704.94'23'09730740153
A gallery of presidents : the Hall of Presidents in the National Portrait Gallery / Marc Pachter. Washington : Smithsonian Institution Press, 1979. p. cm. [N7593.N23 1977] 78-22471 ISBN 0-87474-743-0 pbk. : 3.95
1. National Portrait Gallery, Washington, D.C. 2. Presidents—United States—Portraits. 3. Portraits, American. I. Pachter, Marc. II. Title. BIP

PURDY, Virginia C. 704.94'2
Presidential portraits, compiled and written by Virginia C. Purdy and Daniel J. Reed. Edited by J. Benjamin Townsend. Washington, Published for the National Portrait Gallery by the Smithsonian Institution Press, 1968. 73 p. ports. 26 cm. (Smithsonian publication 4748) [N7593.P84] 68-55302
1. Presidents—United States—Portraits. I. Reed, Daniel J., 1922- joint author. II. National Portrait Gallery, Washington, D.C. III. Title.

PURDY, Virginia C. 757.9
Presidential portraits, compiled and written by Virginia C. Purdy and Daniel J. Reed. Edited by J. Benjamin Townsend. Washington, Published for the National Portrait Gallery by the Smithsonian Institution Press, 1968 [i.e. 1969] 75 p. ports. 26 cm. (Smithsonian publication 4748) "Pages 73-75 of this catalogue were added in 1969." [N7593.P84 1969] 70-29697
1. Presidents—U.S.—Portraits. I. Reed, Daniel J., 1922- joint author. II. National Portrait Gallery, Washington, D.C. III. Title.

Pressed flower pictures.

FLESHER, Irene. 745.92'8
The pressed flower picture book : the art of collecting, pressing, arranging, and framing garden and wild flowers for your home / by Irene Flesher ; illustrated by Glory Brightfield. New York : Butterick Publishing, c1978. 192 p. : ill. (some col.) ; 26 cm. Includes bibliographical references. [SB449.3.P7F58] 77-92605 ISBN 0-88421-056-1 : 7.95
1. Pressed flower pictures. I. Title. BIP

GRUMANN, Velma K. 745.92'8
Painting with nature, by Velma K. Grumann. [1st ed. Dayton, Ohio, E. L. Kendall, c1972] v, 86 p. illus. (part col.) 21 cm. Cover title: Nature art. [SB449.3.P7G78] 72-93866
1. Pressed flower pictures. I. Title. II. Title: Nature art.

LASSNER, Jane. 745.92'8
Flower pressing, by Peter & Susanne Bauzen. [Translated by Paul Kuttner. Adapted by Jane Lassner] New York, Sterling Pub. Co. [1972] 48 p. illus. 20 cm. (Little craft book series) Adapted translation of Gepresste Blumen. [SB449.3.P7B3813 1972] 77-167661
1. Pressed flower pictures. I. Bauzen, Peter. Gepresste Blumen. II. Bauzen, Susanne. III. Title. BIP

MCDOWALL, Pamela. 745.92'8
Pressed flower pictures; a Victorian art revived. New York, Scribner [1970, c1969] 78, [49] p. illus. (part col.) 27 cm. [SB449.3.P7M3 1970] 70-106538 10.95
1. Pressed flower pictures.

Pressed flower pictures—Juvenile literature.

EATON, Marge. 745.92'8
Flower pressing. Pictures by George Overlie. Minneapolis, Lerner Publications Co. [1973] 32 p. illus. 19 cm. (An Early craft book) A how-to-do-it book explaining the technique of pressing and preserving plants, flowers, and leaves, including projects for independent learning. [SB449.3.P7E2] 72-13340 ISBN 0-8225-0855-9 3.95 (Lib. bdg.)
1. Pressed flower pictures—Juvenile literature. 2. Flowers—Collection and preservation—Juvenile literature. I. Overlie, George, illus. II. Title.

WAGNER, Lee. 745.92'8
How to have fun pressing flowers. Illustrated by Nancy Inderieden. [Mankato, Minn., Creative Education; distributed by Childrens Press, Chicago, 1974] p. cm. (Creative education craft series) A simple introduction to the art of pressing flowers and the uses of this craft. [SB449.3.P7W33] 74-8926 ISBN 0-87191-365-8 4.45 (lib. bdg.).
1. Pressed flower pictures—Juvenile literature. I. Inderieden, Nancy, illus. II. Title. BIP

Pressed glass.

HARTUNG, Marion T. 748.8'0973
Patterns and pinafores; pressed glass toy dishes, by Marion T. Hartung and Ione E. Hinshaw. [1st ed. Des Moines, Printed by Wallace-Homestead Co., c1971] 102 p. illus. 24 cm. [NK5112.H37] 72-181090 8.95
1. Pressed glass. 2. Miniature objects. I. Hinshaw, Ione E., joint author. II. Title.

REVI, Albert Christian. 748.2973
American pressed glass and figure bottles. New York, Nelson [1964] xi, 446 p. illus., diagrs. 29 cm. Bibliography: p. 413. [NK5112.R4] 64-14510
1. Pressed glass. 2. Glassware, American. 3. Bottles. I. Title. BIP

Pressed glass—United States.

BATTY, Bob H. 748.2'913
A complete guide to pressed glass / by Bob H. Batty ; drawings by John T. Hendricks. Gretna [La.] : Pelican Pub. Co., 1978. p. cm. Bibliography: p. [NK5203.B37] 77-19211 ISBN 0-88289-057-3 : 19.95
1. Batty, Bob H.—Art collections. 2. Pressed glass—United States. 3. Pattern glass—United States. 4. Glassware—United States—History—19th century. I. Title. BIP

Primitivism in art.

A.C.A. Galleries. 759.13'0740147'1
Four American primitives: Edward Hicks, John Kane, Anna Mary Robertson Moses, Horace Pippin. New York, [1972] [65] p. (incl. cover) illus. 28 cm. "February 22-March 11, 1972." [ND236.A14] 72-180613
1. Hicks, Edward, 1780-1849. 2. Kane, John, 1860-1934. 3. Moses, Anna Mary (Robertson) 1860-1961. 4. Pippin, Horace, 1888-1946. 5. Primitivism in art.

BIHALJI-MERIN. OTO 1904- 709
Masters of naive art: a history and worldwide survey. Translated by Russell M. Stockman. New York, McGraw-Hill [1971] 304 p. illus. (part col.) 33 cm. Translated from the author's unpublished ms. Bibliography: p. 301. [N7432.5.P7B513] 70-155880 ISBN 0-07-005257-3 25.00
1. Primitivism in art. I. Title.

BIHALJI-MERIN, Oto, 1904- 759
Modern primitives: masters of naive painting. [Translated from the German by Norbert Guterman] New York, H. N. Abrams [1961, c1959] 290 p. illus. (part mounted col.) plates (part col.) ports. 21 x 25 cm. Translation of Das naive Bild der Welt. Bibliography: p. 153-155. [ND1267.B513] 61-5784
1. Primitivism in art. 2. Painting. 3. Paintings. I. Title.

BIHALJI-MERIN, Oto, 1904- 709.497
Primitive artist of Yugoslavia. New York, McGraw-Hill, 1964. 200 p. illus. (part mounted col.) ports. 32 cm. [N7248.B49] 64-22730
1. Primitivism in art. 2. Art, Yugoslavian. I. Title.

GOLDWATER, Robert John, 1907- 709
Primitivism in modern art [by] Robert Goldwater. Rev. ed. New York, Vintage Books [1967] xxv, 289 p. illus. 19 cm. First ed. published in 1938 under title: Primitivism in modern painting. Includes bibliographical references. [ND1265.G63 1967] 67-12138
1. Primitivism in art. 2. Painting, Modern—20th century. I. Title.

KENNEDY Galleries, inc., New York. 708.147'1 s
American primitives; primitive, folk, and naive art from the 18th, 19th and 20th centuries. [New York, 1972] [129]-192 p. illus. 23 cm. (The Kennedy quarterly, v. 11, no. 3) [N8640.K4 vol. 11, no. 3] [N6507] 759.13'074'01471 72-186100 2.00
1. Primitivism in art. 2. Art, American—Catalogs. I. Title. II. Series.

LIPMAN, Jean (Herzberg) 1909- 759.13
American primitive painting [by] Jean Lipman. New York, Dover Publications [1972, c1942] 158 p. illus. (part col.) 29 cm. Bibliography: p. 139-142. [ND210.5.P7L56 1972] 79-184124 ISBN 0-486-22815-0 4.00 (pbk.)
1. Primitivism in art. 2. Painting, American. 3. Painting, Modern—19th century—United States. I. Title. BIP

UHDE, Wilhelm, 1874-1947. 759.4
Five primitive masters. [Translated by Ralph Thompson] New York, Arno Press [1969, c1949] 98 p. illus., port. 27 cm. (Arno series of contemporary art no. 35) [ND552.U3513 1969] 75-91371
1. Rousseau, Henri Julien Felix, 1844-1910. 2. Vivin, Louis, 1861-1936. 3. Bombois, Camille, 1883- 4. Bauchant, Andre, 1873-1958. 5. Louis, Seraphine, 1864-1942. 6. Primitivism in art. I. Title. BIP

Primitivism in art—Australia.

LEHMANN, Geoffrey, 1940- 759.994 B
Australian primitive painters / [by] Geoffrey Lehmann. St. Lucia, Q. : University of Queensland Press, 1977. 99 p. : ill. (some col.) ; 29 cm. Distributed in the United Kingdom by Prentice-Hall International, Hemel Hempstead, Eng. [ND1100.5.P7L43] 78-320865 ISBN 0-7022-1039-0 : 24.25
1. Primitivism in art—Australia. 2. Painting, Australian. 3. Painting, Modern—20th century—Australia. 4. Painters—Australia—Biography. I. Title.
Distributed by Technical Impex, 5 South Union St., Lawrence, MA 01843 BIP

Primitivism in art—Exhibitions.

CURTIS, Melinda. 709'.03'4074015251
Search for innocence : primitive and primitivistic art of the 19th century : Department of Art, University of Maryland Art Gallery ... 29 October-10 December 1975 / with an essay by George Levitine ; and text and catalogue by Melinda Curtis. [College Park] : University of Maryland Art Gallery, c1975. 130 p. : ill. (some col.) ; 27 cm. "University of Maryland Department of Art, Museum Training Program, 1974-1975." Includes bibliographical references. [N6465.P74C87] 75-21724 8.00
1. Primitivism in art—Exhibitions. 2. Art, Modern—19th century—Exhibitions. I. Levitine, George. II. Maryland. University. Art Gallery. III. Maryland. University. Dept. of Art. IV. Title.

WALKER Art Center, Minneapolis. 707'.4'0176579
Naives and visionaries : [catalogue of] an exhibition / organized by Walker Art Center, Minneapolis. 1st ed. New York : Dutton, [1974] 95 p. : ill. (some col.) ; 26 cm. Bibliography: p. 95. [N6512.5.P7W34 1974] 74-23454 ISBN 0-525-47393-9 : 8.95
1. Primitivism in art—Exhibitions. 2. Primitivism in art—United States. 3. Art, Modern—20th century—United States. I. Title.

Primitivism in art—United States.

ANDREW Crispo Gallery. 759.13
Edward Hicks, a gentle spirit : [catalog of an exhibition, May 16 thru June 28, 1975]. New York : A. Crispo Gallery, c1975. [67] p. : ill. (some col.) ; 23 x 26 cm. Includes bibliographical references. [ND237.H58A52 1975] 75-15072 pbk. : 10.00
1. Hicks, Edward, 1780-1849. 2. Primitivism in art—United States. I. Title.

Publisher's address: 41 E. 57th St., N.Y., N.Y. 10022.

BALAZS, Marianne E. 759.13
Sheldon Peck / [by Marianne E. Balazs]. New York : Whitney Museum of American Art, [1975] p. 273-282 : ill. (some col.) ; 31 cm. Cover title. "Reprinted from the magazine Antiques, August 1975." [ND1329.P42B34] 76-351651 pbk. : 1.75
1. Peck, Sheldon, 1797-1868. 2. Primitivism in art—United States. I. Peck, Sheldon, 1797-1868. II. Whitney Museum of American Art, New York.

GULICK, Henry Thomas, 759.13
1872-1964.
Henry Thomas Gulick, 1872-1964. [Exhibition] Montclair Art Museum, Montclair, New Jersey, April 21-June 23, 1974. [Montclair, N.J., Montclair Art Museum, 1974] [36] p. illus. (part col.) 18 x 26 cm. [ND237.G77M66] 74-171049
1. Gulick, Henry Thomas, 1872-1964. 2. Primitivism in art—United States. I. Montclair, N.J. Art Museum.

HIRSCHL & Adler 759.13'074'01471
Galleries.
Plain and fancy, a survey of American folk art. [New York, 1970] 72 p. illus. (part col.) 26 cm. Label mounted on t.p.: Supplied by Worldwide Books, inc., Boston. Catalogue of an exhibition held at Hirschl & Adler Galleries, Apr. 30 through May 23, 1970. "Introduction" signed by Stuart P. Feld. [N6507.H57] 73-18930
1. Primitivism in art—United States. 2. Art, American—Exhibitions. I. Feld, Stuart P. II. Title.

HOUSTON, Tex. Museum of 745.1
Fine Arts.
American primitive art; [exhibition] the Museum of Fine Arts of Houston, January 6-29, 1956. [Houston, 1956] 1 v. (unpaged) illus. 22 x 26 cm. [NK806.H6] 70-200293
1. Primitivism in art—United States. 2. Folk art—United States. 3. Folk art—Exhibitions. I. Title.

LIPMAN, Jean (Herzberg) 759.13
1909- comp.
Primitive painters in America, 1750-1950; an anthology by Jean Lipman and Alice Winchester. Freeport, N.Y., Books for Libraries Press [1971, c1950] 182 p. illus. 24 cm. (Biography index reprint series) Contents.Contents.—Why American primitives? By A. Winchester.—Primitive painters of the eighteenth century, by N. F. Little.—Eunice Pinney, by J. Lipman.—Ruth Henshaw Bascom, by A. M. Dods.—Edward Hicks, by A. E. Bye.—Mary Ann Willson, by J. Lipman.—Rufus Porter, by J. Lipman.—James Sanford Ellsworth, by F. F. Sherman.—Erastus Salisbury Field, by F. B. Robinson.—William Matthew Prior, by N. F. Little.—Deborah Goldsmith, by J. Lipman.—Joseph H. Davis, by F. O. Spinney.—Thomas Chambers, by N. F. Little.—Joseph Whiting Stock, by J. L. Clarke, Jr.—James and John Bard, by H. S. Sniffen.—Joseph H. Hidley, by J. Lipman.—Olaf Krans, by M. E. Jacobsen.—Paul Seifert, by J. Lipman.—Twentieth-century primitives, by S. Janis.—Record of primitive painters, by J. Lipman. [ND207.L47 1971] 7OPrimitive painters in America
1. Primitivism in art—United States. 2. Painters—United States. I. Winchester, Alice, joint comp. II. Title.

MITCHELL, Lucy B 1901- 759.13
The paintings of James Sanford Ellsworth, itinerant folk artist, 1802-1873.: catalog of an exhibition, by Lucy B. Mitchell. Williamsburg, Va., [The Colonial Williamsburg Foundation 1974 vii, 103 p. illus. 21 cm. Catalog of an exhibition presented by the Abby Aldrich Rockefeller Folk Art Collection, Williamsburg, Virginia, October 13-December 1, 1974. Bibliography: p. 101-103. [ND1337.U6E495] 74-14365 ISBN 0-87935-025-3 7.00 (pbk.)
1. Ellsworth, James Sanford, 1802-1873 or 4. 2. Primitivism in art—United States. I. Ellsworth, James Sanford, 1802-1873 or 4. II. Abby Aldrich Rockefeller Folk Art Collection, Williamsburg, Va. III. Title.

SHARON, Mary Bruce, 1878- 759.13
1961.
Mary Bruce Sharon, an American primitive. [Washington, Traveling Exhibition Service, Smithsonian Institute, 1973] [25] p. illus. 22 cm. "This exhibition has been organized by Mrs. Sharon's daughter. Henrietta Sharon Aument, and her cousin, John Harvey, and is being circulated by the Traveling Exhibition Service of the Smithsonian Institute, 1974-76." [ND237.S467A95] 73-178353
1. Sharon, Mary Bruce, 1878-1961. 2. Primitivism in art—United States. I. Aument, Henrietta Sharon. II. Harvey, John, 1947- III. Smithsonian Institution. Traveling Exhibition Service. IV. Title.

Primitivism in art—United States—Exhibitions.

VASSAR College. 709'.73'074014733
Art Gallery.
Primitive presence in the '70's : [exhibition], Vassar College Art Gallery, May 5-May 31, 1975. [Poughkeepsie, N.Y.] : The Gallery, 1975. 23 p. : ill. ; 22 x 28 cm. Bibliography: p. 22-23. [N6512.5.P7V37 1975] 76-358222
1. Primitivism in art—United States—Exhibitions. 2. Art, American—Exhibitions. 3. Art, Modern—20th century—United States—Exhibitions. I. Title. BIP

Primitivism in art—United States—History.

EBERT, Katherine. 759.13
American folk painting / by Katherine Ebert New York : Scribner, [1975] p. cm. Includes index. Bibliography: p. [ND205.E23] 75-11914 14.95
1. Primitivism in art—United States—History. 2. Painting, American—History. I. Title.

Prince Edward Island—Description and travel—Views.

BARRETT, Wayne. 779'.9'91717044
Prince Edward Island / photos. by Wayne Barrett and Edith Robinson. Toronto : Oxford University Press, 1977. [96] p. : chiefly col. ill. ; 23 x 28 cm. [F1047.8.B37] 77-379173 ISBN 0-19-540276-6 : 12.95
1. Prince Edward Island—Description and travel—Views. I. Robinson, Edith, joint author. II. Title.
Distributed by Oxford University Press, N.Y. BIP

Princeton University. Art Museum.

GIBBONS, 741.9'45'074014967
Felton Lewis, 1929-
Catalogue of Italian drawings in the Art Museum, Princeton University / by Felton Gibbons. Princeton, N.J. : Princeton University Press, c1977. 2 v. : ill. ; 29 cm. "Published for the Department of Art and Archaeology, Princeton University." Includes index. Contents.Contents.—1. Text.—2. Plates. [NC255.G45] 76-3252 ISBN 0-691-03888-0 : 50.00
1. Princeton University. Art Museum. 2. Drawings, Italian—Catalogs. 3. Drawings—Princeton, N.J.—Catalogs. I. Princeton University. Art Museum. II. Princeton University. Dept. of Art and Archaeology. III. Title. BIP

Princeton University. Chapel.

STILLWELL, Richard, 917.49'67'034
1899-
The Chapel of Princeton University. Princeton, N.J., Princeton University Press, 1971. xiv, 137 p. illus. (part col.) 29 cm. [NA5235.P75S8] 76-90961 ISBN 0-691-03864-3 15.00
1. Princeton University. Chapel. I. Title. BIP

Princeton University. Library.

PRINCETON University. 016.091
Library.
Catalogue of Arabic manuscripts (Yahuda section) in the Garrett Collection, Princeton University Library / by Rudolf Mach ; index by Robert D. McChesney. Princeton, N.J. : Princeton University Press, c1975. p. cm. (Princeton studies on the Near East) Includes index. [Z6621.P9453A76] 75-2999 ISBN 0-691-03908-9 : 100.00
1. Princeton University. Library. 2. Manuscripts, Arabic—New Jersey—Princeton—Catalogs. I. Mach, Rudolf, 1922- II. Title. III. Series. BIP

Print rental service.

INTERNATIONAL Graphic 016.779
Arts Society.
Print rental service; a study. [New York, 1964?] 46 p. 21 cm. "Report on the research and experimentation program establishing print rental collections in institutions of higher learning." [NE53.N5I55] 68-4713
1. Print rental service.

Printed ephemera.

LEWIS, John Noel Claude, 655.2
1912-
Printed ephemera; the changing uses of type and letter-forms in English and American printing [by] John Lewis. New York, Distributed in the U.S.A. by Dover Publications for W. S. Cowell, Ipswich, Eng. [1962] 288 p. facsims. (part col.) 32 cm. [Z116.A3L45] 66-21261
1. Printed ephemers. I. Title.

Printed ephemera—Collectors and collecting.

HECHTLINGER, Adelaide. 769'.5'075
The complete book of paper antiques [by] Adelaide Hechtlinger and Wilbur Cross. New York, Coward, McCann & Geoghegan [1972] 220 p. illus. 22 cm. Bibliography: p. 204-206. [NC1280.H36 1972] 72-79513 ISBN 0-698-10468-4 6.95
1. Printed ephemera—Collectors and collecting. I. Cross, Wilbur, joint author. II. Title. III. Title: Paper antiques.

LEWIS, John, 1912- 769'.5'075
Collecting printed ephemera : a background to social habits and social history, to eating and drinking, to travel and heritage, and just for fun / by John Lewis. London : Studio Vista, 1976. 160 p., [16] p. of plates : ill. (some col.), facsims. (some col.), forms, ports. (some col.) ; 31 cm. Bibliography: p. 158. [NC1280.L45] 77-354691 ISBN 0-289-70393-X : £8.50
1. Printed ephemera—Collectors and collecting. I. Title.

RICKARDS, Maurice, 769'.5'075
1919-
This is ephemera : collecting printed throwaways / Maurice Rickards. Brattleboro, Vt. : Gossamer Press : distributed by S. Greene Press, c1977. 64 p., [1] leaf of plates : ill. ; 21 cm. Includes index. [NC1280.R53] 77-81642 ISBN 0-8289-0322-0 : 7.00 ISBN 0-8289-0323-9 pbk. : 3.95
1. Printed ephemera—Collectors and collecting. I. Title. BIP

Printers—Direct.

LEAHART, John Mary, 1873- 655.058
Introduction to check-lists of names of places where typography was applied, of master printers, printers, workmen, publishers, promoters, etc. St. Louis, Central Bureau, Catholic Central Union (Verein) [1959] 130p. 28cm. [Z231.L4] 59-65162
1. Printers—Direct. I. Title.

Printers—England—Biography.

BLAKE, Norman 070.5'092'4 B
Francis.
Caxton : England's first publisher / N. F. Blake. New York : Barnes & Noble Books, 1976, c1975. 220 p. : ill. ; 25 cm. "Caxton's editions": p. [192]-196. Includes index. Bibliography: p. [211]-212. [Z232.C38B635 1976] 76-2874 ISBN 0-06-490450-4 : 22.50
1. Caxton, William, 1422(ca.)-1491. 2. Printers—England—Biography. BIP

BLAKE, Norman 070.5'092'4
Francis.
Caxton : England's first publisher / [by] N. F. Blake. London : Osprey Publishing, 1976. xi, 220 p. : ill., facsims., ports. ; 25 cm. Includes index. "Caxton's editions": p. [192]-196. [Z232.C38B635 1976b] 77-355083 ISBN 0-85045-106-X : £7.00
1. Caxton, William, 1422(ca.)-1491. 2. Printers—England—Biography. 3. Publishers and publishing—England—Biography.

CHILDS, Edmund 686.2'092'4
Lunness.
William Caxton : a portrait in a background / Edmund Childs. New York : St. Martin's Press, 1979. p. cm. Includes index. Bibliography: p. [Z232.C38C5 1978] 77-25770 ISBN 0-312-88031-6 : 10.00
1. Caxton, William, 1422 (ca)-1491. 2. Printers—England—Biography. BIP

CHILDS, Edmund 686.2'092'4 B
Lunness.
William Caxton : a portrait in a background / [by] Edmund Childs. London : Northwood Publications Ltd, 1976. 190 p., [4] p. of plates (2 fold.) : ill., facsims., map, ports. ; 21 cm. Includes index. Bibliography: p. 181-183. [Z232.C38C5] 76-380633 ISBN 0-7198-2579-2 : £3.50. ISBN 0-7198-2569-5 pbk.
1. Caxton, William, 1422 (ca.)-1491. 2. Printers—England—Biography.

PAINTER, George 686.2'092'4 B
Duncan, 1914-
William Caxton : a biography / by George D. Painter. 1st American ed. New York : Putnam, 1977, c1976. xi, 227 p., [4] leaves of plates : ill. ; 25 cm. Includes index. Bibliography: p. 196-202. [Z232.C38P33 1976] 76-41134 ISBN 0-399-11888-8 : 14.95
1. Caxton, William, 1422 (ca.)-1491. 2. Printers—England—Biography. 3. Printing—History—England.

PEARMAN, Naomi. 686.2'092'4 B
The Lincoln Caxton / [by] Naomi Pearman. [Lincoln] : [Lincoln Cathedral Library], 1976. 28 p. : ill. ; 22 cm. (Lincoln Cathedral Library publications ; no. 1) [Z232.C38P43] 77-369858 ISBN 0-9505083-0-6 : £0.60
1. Caxton, William, 1422 (ca.)-1491. 2. Jacobus de Varagine. Legenda aurea. 3. Lincoln Cathedral. Library. 4. Printers—England—Biography. I. Lincoln Cathedral. Library. II. Title. III. Series: Lincoln Cathedral. Library. Lincoln Cathedral Library publications ; no. 1.

SALE, William 686.2'092'4 B
Merritt, 1899-
Samuel Richardson : master printer / William M. Sale, Jr. Westport, Conn. : Greenwood Press, [1977?] c1950. vi, 389 p. : ill. ; 23 cm. Reprint of the ed. published by Cornell University Press, Ithaca, N.Y., which was issued as v. 37 of Cornel studies in English. Includes bibliographical references and index. [Z232.R595S3 1977] 77-22446 ISBN 0-8371-9732-5 lib.bdg. : 21.75
1. Richardson, Samuel, 1689-1761. 2. Printers—England—Biography. 3. Printing—England—History. I. Series: Cornell University. Cornell studies in English ; v. 37.

Printers—France—Biography.

RITCHIE, Ward, 686.2'092'4 B
1905-
Francois-Louis Schmied, artist, engraver, printer : some memories and a bibliography / by Ward Ritchie. Tucson : Graduate Library School, University of Arizona, c1976. vi, 41 p. : ill. ; 22 cm. (Bibliographic papers ; no. 1) Bibliography: p. [29]-41. [Z232.S253R58] 76-374430
1. Schmied, Francois Louis, 1873- 2. Printers—France—Biography. 3. Illustrators—France—Biography. 4. Engravers—France—Biography. I. Title.

WATTS, George Byron, 655.1'44
1890-
Philippe-Denis Pierres: first printer ordinary of Louis XVI [by] George B. Watts. [Charlotte, N. C., Printed by Heritage Printers, 1966] 56 p. 23 cm. Cover title. Pierres, Phillippe Denis. 1741-

1808. Bibliography: p. 52-56. [Z232.P59W3] 66-23874
I. Title.

Printers' marks.

IRWIN, Frank. 686.2
Printer's marks and colophons / by Frank Irwin. Tilton, N.H. : Hillside Press, 1976. 51, [4] p. : ill. ; 60 mm. "Limited to 250 numbered copies." No. 14. Bibliography: p. [53]-[55] [Z235.I77] 76-377482
1. Printers' marks. 2. Colophons. I. Title.

RYDER, John, 1917- 655.1
A suite of fleurons, or a preliminary enquiry into the history & combinable natures of certain printers' flowers. Boston, C. T. Branford [1957] 54 [1] p. typog., specimens, 19cm. Bibliography: p. [55] [Z235.R95] 56-12706
1. Printers' marks. I. Title.

RYDER, John, 1917- 655.1
A suite of fleurons, or a preliminary enquiry into the history & combinable natures of certain printers' flowers. Boston, C. T. Branford [1957] 54 [1] p. typog, specimens. 19cm. Bibliography: p. [55] [Z235.R95] 56-12706
1. Printers' marks. I. Title.

SULLIVAN, Eugene T. 686'.2
Marks of craftsmanship. [Text and design by Eugene T. and Marilynn Sullivan. Chicago, Book Binding Materials Division, Joanna Western Mills Company, 1969] 16 p. illus. (part col.) 23 x 29 cm. Cover title. [Z235.S9] 70-27302
1. Printers' marks. I. Sullivan, Marilynn, joint author. II. Title.

Printers' marks—Europe.

WINGER, Howard W. 769'.5
Printers' marks and devices / Howard W. Winger. Chicago : Caxton Club, 1976. 107 p. : ill. ; 25 cm. Bibliography: p. 103-107. [Z235.W54] 77-354957
1. Printers' marks—Europe. I. Title.

Printers—U. S.

FISHER, Paul Leslie, 655.069
1918-
An uncommon gentry. Columbia, Linotype School, School of Journalism, University of Missouri, 1952. xxiv, 54 p. 24 cm. [Z231.F5] 52-62413
1. Printers—U. S. 2. Printing—Hist.—U. S. I. Title.

Printers—United States—Directories.

CHECK Collectors Round 686.2
Table.
Security printers. 1st ed. Cincinnati [1974] 21 p. 28 cm. [HG350.C45 1974] 74-177139
1. Printers—United States—Directories. 2. Money—United States. 3. Negotiable instruments—United States. 4. Securities—United States. I. Title.

CHECK Collectors Round 686'.2
Table.
Security printers. 2d ed. Cincinnati : Check Collectors Round Table, c1976. 38 p. ; 29 cm. [HG350.C45 1976] 76-362044
1. Printers—United States—Directories. 2. Money—United States. 3. Negotiable instruments—United States. 4. Securities—United States. I. Title.

Printing.

GREENLAW, Dana S. 655.2
Amateur printing and cut making, by Dana S. Greenlaw. St. Petersburg, Fla. [1970] 114 p. illus. (part col.) 29 cm. [Z116.A3G7] 77-17820
1. Printing. 2. Engravings—Technique. I. Title.

MCLUHAN, Herbert Marshall. 655.1
The Gutenberg galaxy; the making of typographic man. [Toronto] University of Toronto Press [1962] 293 p. 25 cm. [Z116.M15] 62-4860
1. Printing. I. Title. BIP

POTTINGER, David Thomas, 686'.2
1884-1958.
Printers and printing. Freeport, N.Y., Books for Libraries Press [1971, c1941] viii, 143 p. illus. 23 cm. Bibliography: p. [131]-134. [Z116.P655 1971] 70-175709 ISBN 0-8369-6624-4
1. Printing. I. Title. BIP

*RUEGG, Ruedi. 686.22
Basic typography; handbook of technique and design, [by] Ruedi Ruegg [and] Godi Frohlich. Zurich, ABC Edition [1972] 220 p. illus. 26 cm. In German, French, and English. [Z250] ISBN 3-85504-028-1
1. Printing. I. Frohlich, Godi., joint author. II. Title.
Dist. by Hastings House. 37.50. BIP

Printing—Addresses, essays, lectures.

BENNETT, Paul A 1897- 655
Some notes on the engaging by-paths and enduring pleasures of fine book-making. This keepsake commemorates the dedication of the Morgan A. and Aline D. Gunst Memorial Library. The book, its art and history; an exhibition in the Albert M. Bender Room, Stanford University Libraries, Oct. 18, 1963. [Stanford Calif., 1963] 53 p. 23 cm. [Z116.AB4] 63-25525
1. Printing — Addresses, essays, lectures. I. Stanford University. Libraries. Gunst Memorial Library. II. Title. III. Title: The engaging by-paths and enduring pleasures of the fine book-making

JACKSON, Holbrook, 1874- 686'.2
1948.
The printing of books. Freeport, N.Y., Books for Libraries Press [1970] xiii, 285 p. illus. 23 cm. (Essay index reprint series) Reprint of the 1939 ed. Includes bibliographical references. [Z116.A3J33 1970] 70-134100 ISBN 0-8369-1931-9
1. Printing—Addresses, essays, lectures. 2. Book design. I. Title. BIP

MORISON, Stanley, 1889- 655.1
The typographic arts; two lectures. Cambridge, Harvard University Press, 1950. 106 p. illus. 24 cm. "References"6 p. 87-98. Contents.Contents. -- The typographic arts. -- The art of printing. [Z116.A3M65] 50-5263
1. Printing — Addresses, essays, lectures. 2. Printing — Hist. I. Title.

THE Printing press; 099
a little publication issued occasionally to lovers of good printing. San Francisco, E. & R. Grabhorn. no. 22cm. [Z116.A4P7] 57-50619
1. Printing—Addresses, essays, lectures. I. Grabhorn Press, San Francisco.

ROGERS, Bruce, 1870-1957. 686'.08
Pi; a hodge-podge of the letters, papers, and addresses written during the last sixty years. Freeport, N.Y., Books for Libraries Press [1972, c1953] ix, 185 p. illus. 23 cm. (Essay index reprint series) [Z232.R67A33 1972] 79-167407 ISBN 0-8369-2669-2
1. Printing—Addresses, essays, lectures. I. Title. BIP

STANDARD, Paul, 1900- 099
Chapters on writing and printing. Lexington [Ky.] Anvil Press, 1963. 70 p. illus., typog, specimens, 26 cm. (Publication of the Anvil Press 7) 134 copies printed. No. 38. Contents.CONTENTS. -- Calligraphy for the printer, by P. Standard. -- Digressions on the Roman letter, by V. Hammer. -- Printing from the blocks of Thomas Bewick, by R. H. Middleton. -- Notes on the Stamperia del Santuccio, by C. R. Hammer. [Z116.C44] 63-24614
1. Printing — Addresses, essays, lectures. I. Title.

WARDE, Beatrice Lamberton 665.04
(Becker) 1900-
The crystal goblet; sixteen essays on typography. Selected and edited by Henry Jacob. Cleveland, World Pub. Co., 1956. 221 p. 22 cm. [Z116.W24] 56-13673
1. Printing — Addresses, essays, lectures. I. Title.

WARDE, Beatrice Lamberton 686.2
Becker, 1900-1969.
The trump card of the small printer : from a speech by the late Beatrice Warde. [London] : British Printing Society, 1976. [12] p. ; 22 cm. [Z231.5.L5W37 1976] 77-365829 ISBN 0-9501973-6-X : £0.30
1. Printing—Addresses, essays, lectures. 2. Little presses—Addresses, essays, lectures. I. Title.

Printing—Bibliography.

ANDERSON, Frank J. 016.6862
Private presswork : a bibliographic approach to printing as an avocation / Frank J. Anderson. South Brunswick [N.J.] : A. S. Barnes, c1977. p. cm. Includes index. [Z117.A53] 75-38442 ISBN 0-498-01876-8 : 12.50
1. Printing—Bibliography. 2. Private presses—Bibliography. 3. Books—Bibliography. I. Title. BIP

APPLETON, Tony. 016.6862'2
The writings of Stanley Morison : a handlist / compiled by Tony Appleton ; with a biographical & typographical supplement, and essays by Brooke Crutchley & John Dreyfus. Brighton : The author, 1976. xix, 119 p., plate : port. ; 24 cm. Includes indexes. [Z117.A67] 77-355712 ISBN 0-9502916-4-1 : £8.00
1. Morison, Stanley, 1889-1967—Bibliography. 2. Printing—Bibliography. 3. Type and type-founding—Bibliography. 4. Writing—Bibliography. I. Title.

LEHMANN-HAUPT, Hellmut, 016.6862
1903-
One hundred books about bookmaking : a guide to the study and appreciation of printing / by Hellmut Lehmann-Haupt. Westport, Conn. : Greenwood Press, 1975, c1949. [83] p. ; 23 cm. Reprint of the ed. published by Columbia University Press, New York. Includes index. [Z117.L43 1975] 75-34148 ISBN 0-8371-8546-7 : 8.25
1. Printing—Bibliography. 2. Books—Bibliography. 3. Book industries and trade—Bibliography. I. Title. BIP

MILLS, George Jackson, 016.655
1920-
Guide to films, periodicals, and books, in printing, paper, publishing, printed advertising, and their closely related industries. Pittsburgh, School of Printing Management, Carnegie Institute of Technology, 1956. 64p. 27cm. [Z117.M48] 56-9733
1. Printing—Bibl. 2. Printing—Audio-visual aids. I. Title.

MILLS, George Jackson, 016.655
1920-
Sources of information in the American graphic arts. Pittsburgh, Carnegie Press, 1951. vii, 70 p. 24 cm. ([Carnegie Institute of Technology, Pittsburgh] Occasional papers, no. 2) [Z117.M5] 51-4375
1. Printing — Bibl. 2. Engraving — Bibl. I. Title. II. Series: Pittsburgh. Carnegie Institute of Technology. Occasional papers, no. 2

Printing—Chronology.

TIMPERLEY, Charles Henry. 686.2
Encyclopaedia of literary and typographical anecdote / C. H. Timperley ; with a new introd. by Terry Belanger. New York : Garland Pub., 1977. p. cm. (Garland reference library of the humanities ; v. 81) "The printer's manual": p. Reprint of the 1842 ed. published by H. G. Bohn, London, which was originally published in 1839 under title: A dictionary of printers and printing. Includes indexes. [Z116.T59 1977] 76-52671 ISBN 0-8240-9892-7 lib.bdg. : 60.00
1. Printing—Chronology. 2. Books—Chronology. 3. Publishers and publishing—Chronology. 4. Book industries and trade—Chronology. I. Timperley, Charles Henry. The printers' manual. 1977. II. Title.

Printing—Dictionaries.

AMERICAN dictionary of 686'.03
printing and bookmaking; containing a history of these arts in Europe and America, with definitions of technical terms and illustrated. New York, B. Franklin [1970] iv, 592 p. illus., ports. 26 cm. (Burt Franklin bibliography & reference series 382. American classics in history & social science, 158) Reprint of the 1894 ed. [Z118.A6 1970] 70-135172 ISBN 0-8337-0059-6 27.50
1. Printing—Dictionaries. 2. English language—Dictionaries—Polyglot.

AMERICAN dictionary of 655'.003
printing and bookmaking; containing a history of these arts in Europe and America, with definitions of technical terms and biographical sketches. Edited by W. W. Pasko. New introd. by Robert E. Runser. Detroit, Gale Research Co., 1967. 592 p. illus., facsims., ports. 26 cm. Title page includes original imprint: New York, H. Lockwood, 1894. [Z118.A6 1967] 66-27215
1. Printing—Dictionaries. 2. Book industries and trade—Dictionaries. 3. Printing—History—United States. I. Pasko, Wesley Washington, 1840-1897.

BAARLAER, Joseph L 655.03
Graphic arts encyclopedia; a compendium of literary and miscellaneous information based on material selected from many sources, with the addition of new information, containing numerous rules and regulations on varied subjects and diverse practices, compiled and edited by J. L. Baarlaer, Sr. [Cincinnati] Cincinnati Typesetting Co. [1966] 141 p. illus. 28 x 40 cm. [Z118.B2] 66-23076
1. Printing—Dictionaries. I. Title.

DICTIONARY of printing 655.03
terms ... 5th ed., rev. and enl. Salt Lake City, Porte Pub. Co. [1950] 173 p. 21 cm. "Copyright ... by Rhoda A. Porte." [Z118.D5 1950] 50-58087
1. Printing—Dictionaries. I. Porte, Rhoda A.

DICTIONARY of printing 686.2'03
terms : a comprehensive guide to the terms most commonly used in printing, paper, typesetting, origination, finishing, point of sale, premiums and promotions etc. / edited by Ian Foster. Rev. ed. London : Print Buyer Magazine, 1976. 112 p. : ill. ; 19 cm. On cover: DOT. [Z118.D48 1976] 77-363602 ISBN 0-905768-00-0 : £0.60
1. Printing—Dictionaries. I. Foster, Ian.

JACOBI, Charles Thomas, 655'.03
1853-1933.
The printers' vocabulary; a collection of some 2500 technical terms, phrases, abbreviations, and other expressions mostly relating to letterpress printing, many of which have been in use since the time of Caxton. London, Chiswick Press, 1888. Detroit, Gale Research Co., 1969. vi, 158 p. 22 cm. [Z118.J18 1969] 68-30613
1. Printing—Dictionaries. I. Title. BIP

MELCHER, Daniel. 655.03
Printing and promotion handbook; how to plan, produce, and use printing, advertising, and direct mail [by] Daniel Melcher [and] Nancy Larrick. 3d ed. New York, McGraw-Hill [1966] xi, 451 p. illus. 23 cm. (McGraw-Hill handbooks) [Z118.M4 1966] 66-14535
1. Printing—Dictionaries. I. Larrick, Nancy, joint author. II. Title.

MELCHER, Daniel. 655.03
Printing and promotion handbook; how to plan, produce, and use printing, advertising, and direct mail [by] Daniel Melcher [and] Nancy Larrick. 2d ed. New York, McGraw-Hill, 1956. xi, 438 p. illus. 24 cm. Bibliography: p. 397-411. "Graphic arts films": p. 412-417. [Z118.M4 1956] 56-6966
1. Printing—Dictionaries. I. Larrick, Nancy, joint author. II. Title. BIP

NATIONAL Association of 760'o.03
Printing Ink Manufacturers. Glossary Subcommittee.
Glossary of graphic arts terms (as applied in the printing ink industry), compiled by Glossary Sub-committee of the Technical Committee, National Association of Printing Ink Makers. Final ed. (June, 1964) [New York, 1964] 59 l. 28 cm. [Z118.N37 1964b] 71-14175
1. Printing—Dictionaries. I. Title. II. Title: Graphic arts terms.

SAVAGE, William, 1770- 1843. 655'.03
A dictionary of the art of printing. New York, B. Franklin [1965] viii, 815 p. illus. 24 cm. (Burt Franklin bibliography and references series, 82) Reprint of the 1841 London ed. [Z118.S26 1965] 75-6350
1. Printing—Dictionaries. I. Title. BIP

STEVENSON, George A. 655'.003
Graphic arts encyclopedia [by] George A. Stevenson. New York, McGraw-Hill [1968] xv, 492 p. illus. 24 cm. Bibliography: p. 421-422. [Z118.S82] 67-24445
1. Printing—Dictionaries. 2. Graphic arts—Dictionaries. I. Title. BIP

STEVENSON, George A. 686.2'03
Graphic arts encyclopedia / George A. Stevenson. 2d ed. New York : McGraw-Hill, c1979. p. cm. Includes indexes. Bibliography: p. [Z118.S82 1979] 78-7298 ISBN 0-07-061288-9 : 24.95
1. Printing—Dictionaries. 2. Graphic arts—Dictionaries. I. Title.

Printing — Dictionaries — Polyglot.

HOSTETTLER, Rudolf. 655.302
Technical terms of the printing industry. [3d rev. ed.] New York, Wittenborn [1959] 135 p. illus. 16 cm. English, French, German, Italian, and Dutch. First ed. published in 1949 under title: The printer's terms. [Z118] 65-7273
1. Printing — Dictionaries — Polyglot. I. Title.

Printing—Dictionaries—Spanish.

RODRIGUEZ, Cesar. 655.03
Bilingual dictionary of the graphic arts; English-Spanish, Spanish-English, by Cesar Rodriguez. New and complete ed., rev. and enl. by George A. Humphrey. Farmingdale, N.Y., G. A. Humphrey [1966] 448 p. 28 cm. Section covering A-L first published in 1956 under title: Diccionario bilingue de las artes graficas, ingles-espanol. Added title page in Spanish. [Z118.R6] 66-17570
1. Printing—Dictionaries—Spanish. 2. English language—Dictionaries—Spanish. I. Title.

Printing—England—History—Bibliography.

ST. Bride Printing Library. 686.2'092'4
Caxtoniana : or, The progress of Caxton studies from the earliest times to 1976 : [catalogue of] an exhibition at the St Bride Printing Library ... 20 September-29 October 1976 .... London : The Library, 1976. 16 p. : ill. ; 25 cm. Selected and with an introd. by Robin Myers. [Z232.C38S24 1976] 77-361465 ISBN 0-9504161-2-6 : £0.75
1. Caxton, William, 1422 (ca.)-1491—Bibliography. 2. Printing—England—History—Bibliography. 3. Bibliographical exhibitions. I. Myers, Robin, fl. 1967- II. Title. III. Title: The progress of Caxton studies from the earliest times to 1976.

Printing—England—History—Exhibitions.

BARKER, Nicolas. 070.5'94'094257
The Oxford University Press and the spread of learning, 1478-1978 : an illustrated history / by Nicolas Barker ; with a preface by Charles Ryskamp. Oxford [Eng.] : Clarendon Press, 1978. xiii, 69 p., [103] leaves of plates : chiefly ill. ; 31 cm. Includes bibliographical references and index. [Z232.O98B37] 77-30541 ISBN 0-19-951086-5 : 25.00
1. Oxford University Press—History. 2. Printing—England—History—Exhibitions. 3. Publishers and publishing—England—Exhibitions. I. Title.
Distributed by Oxford Universitty Press, NY BIP

BIRMINGHAM, Eng. Public Libraries. Reference Library. Language and Literature Dept. 015'.42
500 years of British printing, Caxton 1476-1976 : an exhibition in the Reference Library, Language and Literature Department Birmingham Public Libraries, 30 September-30 October 1976. [Birmingham] : [Birmingham Public Libraries], [1976] [1], 17 [i.e. 21] p. : facsims. ; 30 cm. Cover title. [Z121.B6B573] 77-359372 ISBN 0-901011-14-2 : £0.30
1. Printing—England—History—Exhibitions. I. Caxton, William, 1422 (ca.)-1491. II. Title.

WILLIAM Morris Gallery and Brangwyn Gift, Walthamstow, Eng. 016.094
In fine print : William Morris as book designer : [catalogue of an exhibition held at the] William Morris Gallery & Brangwyn Gift, Lloyd Park, Forest Road, London E17 4PP ..., 18 December 1976-19 March 1977. London : London Borough of Waltham Forest, Libraries and Arts Department, 1976. [3], ii, 75 p. ; 30 cm. Fold. sheet of ill. inserted. Bibliography: p. 71-74. [Z232.M87W48 1976] 77-366307 ISBN 0-901974-05-6 : £1.00
1. Morris, William, 1834-1896. 2. Printing—England—History—Exhibitions. 3. Book design—Exhibitions. I. Morris, William, 1834-1896. II. Title.

Printing—England—London—History.

MORAN, James. 686.2'092'4 B
Wynkyn de Worde, father of Fleet Street / James Moran. 2d ed. London : Wynkyn de Worde Society, 1976. 52, [8] p., [1] fold. leaf of plates : ill. ; 20 cm. Originally published in 1960. Includes index. Bibliography: p. [53] [Z232.W87M6 1976] 77-357537 ISBN 0-85331-388-1 : £2.95
1. Worde, Wynkyn de, d. 1534? 2. Printing—England—London—History. I. Wynkyn de Worde Society. II. Title.

Printing—England—Reading—History—Exhibitions.

READING, Eng. Museum and Art Gallery. 686.2'09422'93
Printing : past, present and future : Reading celebrates Caxton's quincentenary / [Reading Museum and Art Gallery]. [Reading] : Reading Museum and Art Gallery and Reading Libraries, 1976. 23 p., [8] p. of plates : ill., facsims., ports. ; 21 x 30 cm. Bibliography: p. [22] [Z121.R42 1976] 77-360628 ISBN 0-9501247-6-1 : £0.39
1. Printing—England—Reading—History—Exhibitions. 2. Reading, Eng.—Exhibitions. I. Title.

Printing—Exhibitions.

AMERICAN Institute of Graphic Arts. 655.53074
1964 paperbacks U.S.A.; an exhibition of covers and 30 complete books. New York, Amer. Inst. of Graphic Arts. 1059 Third Avenue [1965] 1v. (unpaged) 131 illus. 23cm. [Z121.A47] 65-1723 5.00 pap.,
1. Printing—Exhibitions. 2. Bibliography—Paperback editions. 3. Book covers. I. Title.

CAMBRIDGE. University. Library. 015'.47
Russian printing to 1917 : [a catalogue of an exhibition in the University Library, Cambridge 22 April to 29 June 1974] [Cambridge] : [The Library], 1974. [27] p. ; 21 cm. Cover title. [Z121.C18 1974] 76-356825 £0.05
1. Printing—Exhibitions. 2. Printing—History—Russia. I. Title.

LEHRER, Ruth Fine. 011
The Janus Press, 1955-75 : an exhibition at the Robert Hull Fleming Museum at the University of Vermont in Burlington, 1975 / catalogue raisonne / by Ruth Fine Lehrer. [Burlington] : Robert Hull Fleming Museum, University of Vermont, c1975. 43 p. : ill. ; 22 cm. "Essay and entries were originally prepared for the Private library." [Z121.L216] 76-356713
1. Janus Press. 2. Printing—Exhibitions. I. Vermont. University. Robert Hull Fleming Museum. II. Title.

LOWMAN, Al. 011
Printer at the pass : the work of Carl Hertzog : [catalog of an exhibition at the Institute of Texan Cultures from November 20, 1970, to January 31, 1971] / compiled by Al Lowman ; with an essay by William R. Holman. [San Antonio] : Institute of Texan Cultures, University of Texas at San Antonio, 1972. xix, 123 p. : ill. ; 24 cm. Includes index. Bibliography: p. 109-112. [Z232.H54L68] 75-320668
1. Hertzog, Carl. 2. Printing—Exhibitions. 3. El Paso, Texas—Imprints—Exhibitions. I. Institute of Texan Cultures. II. Title.

NEWBERRY Library, Chicago. 655.1
The scholar printers; two exhibitions at the Newberry Library in honor of the Association of American University Presses on the occasion of their visit to Chicago on May 31, 1964. Printers, Publishers, and scholars: books mainly from the John M. Wing Foundation, on the history of printing. The learned presses. Chicago, University of Chicago Press [1964] 59 p. illus., facsims. 22 cm. Prepared by James M. Wells. [Z121.N57] 64-5058
1. Printing — Exhibitions. I. Wells, James M. II. Association of American University Presses. III. Title.

ROCHESTER, N.Y. University. Memorial art gallery. 016.09
Catalogue of an exhibition of the history of the art of printing 1450-1920, during months of September & October in the year nineteen hundred and twenty. The Memorial art gallery, Rochester, N.Y. [Rochester, 1920] 76 p. 21 cm. Compiled by John Rothwell Slater. "Bibliography and history of printing: books of reference available to Rochester students of typography": p. 73-76. [Z121.R67] 25-6416
1. Printing—Exhibitions. 2. Title-page. I. Slater, John Rothwell, 1872- II. Title.

Printing—History—New Orleans.

KORN, Bertram Wallace. 655.1763355
Benjamin Levy: New Orleans printer and publisher, with a bibliography of Benjamin Levy imprints, 1817-1841. Portland, Me., Anthoensen Press, 1961. 78p. port., facsims. 24cm. 'Reprinted, in an edition of three hundred numbered copies, from The papers of the Bibliographical Society of America (copyright 1960)...Number 40.' Bibliographical footnotes. [Z232.L66K6] 61-11265
1. Levy, Benjamin, 1786-1860. 2. Printing—Hist.—New Orleans. I. Title.

Printing—History.

DOYLE, Anthony Ian, 1925- 686.2
Manuscript to print : tradition and innovation in the Renaissance book / by A. I. Doyle, Elizabeth Rainey, & D. B. Wilson. Durham : University of Durham, Library, 1975. [2], 33 p. : facsims. ; 32 cm. (Library guides : Special series ; 1) Cover title. Includes index. Bibliography: p. [33] [Z126.D74] 76-351690 ISBN 0-900009-02-0 : £1.00
1. Printing—History. 2. Books—History—1400-1600. 3. Bibliography—Early printed books—Exhibitions. I. Rainey, Elizabeth, joint author. II. Wilson, Dudley Butler, joint author. III. Title. IV. Series.

GASKELL, Philip. 686.2'09
A new introduction to bibliography / Philip Gaskell. [1st ed.] reprinted with corrections. Oxford : Clarendon Press, 1974. xxv, 438 p. : ill., facsims. ; 24 cm. Includes index. Bibliography: p. [392]-413. [Z116.A2G27 1974] 75-330050 ISBN 0-19-818150-7 : 9.95
1. Printing—History. 2. Book industries and trade—History. 3. Bibliography—Theory, methods, etc. 4. Books—Bibliography. I. Title.
Distributed by Oxford University Press, N.Y.,N.Y. BIP

HUNTER, John Marvin, 1880- 926.55
Peregrinations of a pioneer printer; an autobiography. Grand Prairie, Tex., Printed by Frontier Times Pub. House, c1954. 244p. illus. 23cm. [Z232.H85A3] 54-39743
1. Printing—Hist.—Texas. I. Title.

PLANTIN, Christophe, 1514-1589 655.14932
Correspondance de Christophe Plantin . . . Antwerpen, J. E. Buschmann, 1883-1918. Nendeln, Liechtenstein, Kraus-Thomson Org., 1968. 9v. in 8 24cm. (Half-title: Maatschappij der Antwerpsche bibliophilen. Ultgave n' 12, 15, 26, 29-33/34) . . . [Z232.P71P7] 3-24462 125.00 set,
1. Printing—Hist.—Antwerp. I. Rooses, Max, 1839-1914. II. Denuce, Jean, 1878- III. Antwerp. Musee Plantin-Moretus. IV. Title.

SPENCER, Herbert, 1924- 655.2'09'04
Pioneers of modern typography. [1st American ed.] New York, Hastings House [1970, c1969] 159 p. illus. (part col.), ports. 31 cm. (Visual communication books) Bibliography: p. 157-158. [Z116.A3S6 1970] 76-99155 ISBN 0-8038-5755-1 14.50
1. Printing—History. 2. Art, Modern—20th century—History. I. Title.

Printing—History—Addresses, essays, lectures.

CRUTCHLEY, Brooke. 686.2'094
Siberch celebrations, 1521-1971; edited by Brooke Crutchley. Cambridge, University Printing House, 1971. xi, 133 p. illus., facsims., music. 25 cm. Bibliography: p. 44. [Z232.S56C7] 72-190735 ISBN 0-903349-00-0 £0.75
1. Siberch, John, 1475 or 6-1554? 2. Printing—History—Addresses, essays, lectures. I. Title.

Printing—History—Alnwick, Eng.

ISAAC, Peter C. G. 655.1'428'2
William Davison of Alnwick: pharmacist and printer 1781-1858 [by] Peter C. G. Isaac. Oxford, Clarendon P., 1968. ix, 40 p. 2 plates, illus., facsims. 22 cm. Bibliography: p. 40. [Z232.D25I8] 68-114665 45/-
1. Davison, William, 1781-1858. 2. Printing—History—Alnwick, Eng.

Printing—History—Bibliography.

MCMURTRIE, Douglas Crawford, 1888-1944, ed. 016.6862'09
The invention of printing: a bibliography. Edited by Douglas C. McMurtrie, with the assistance of John Adamson. New York, B. Franklin [1970] xxiv, 413 p. 27 cm. (Burt Franklin bibliography and reference series, 40) "Originally published, 1936 [i.e. 1942]" [Z117.M18 1970] 71-153487 ISBN 0-8337-2342-1
1. Printing—History—Bibliography. I. Title. BIP

NEWBERRY Library, Chicago. John M. Wing Foundation. 016.011
Dictionary catalogue of the history of printing from the John M. Wing Foundation in the Newberry Library. Boston, G. K. Hall, 1961. 6 v. (6073 p.) 37 cm. Reproductions of "author, title, and subject entries, interfiled alphabetically ... a chronology file and a place-name file for place of printing or publishing of all incunabula and ZP's (books chosen as samples of printing)" Cf. Introd. Contents.Contents.—v. 5. Places, A-Z.—v. 6. Chronology, 1280-1960. [Z117.N54] A 64
1. Printing—History—Bibliography. 2. Printing—Bibliography. I. Wing, John Mansir, 1845-1917. II. Title.

Printing—History—England—Addresses, essasy, lectures.

CAXTON : 686.2'092'4 B
an American contribution to the quincentenary celebration / edited by Susan Otis Thompson. New York : The Typophiles, 1976. xvi, 54 p., [3] leaves of plates : ill. ; 19 cm. (Typophile chap book ; 52) Contents.Contents.—Blumenthal, J. Introduction.—Dunlap, J. R. From Westminster to Hammersmith vis Chiswick.—Lawton, J. Caxton's autograph?—Griffith, R. R. The early years of William Caxton. Includes bibliographical references. [Z232.C38C37] 76-29112
1. Caxton, William, 1422 (ca.)-1491—Addresses, essays, lectures. 2. Printing—History—England—Addresses, essay, lectures. I. Thompson, Susan Otis. II. The Typophiles, New York. III. Series: The

Typophiles, New York. Typophile chap books ; 52.

Printing—History—England—Exhibitions.

ENGLANDES earliest 016.093
printers : [catalogue of] an exhibition held in the monks dormitory, Durham Cathedral, to commemorate five hundred years of printing in England 1976 / [by Jan Rhodes]. Durham : The University Library, 1976. [2], 30 p. : ill. ; 21 cm. Cover title. Author statement provided by the British National Bibliography. "Drawn from three Durham libraries: the Cathedral, the University and Ushaw College." Includes bibliographical references. [Z121.E46] 77-350723 ISBN 0-900009-04-7 : £0.30
1. Printing—History—England—Exhibitions. I. Rhodes, Jan. II. Durham Cathedral, Library. III. Durham, Eng. University. Library. IV. Ushaw College, Durham, Eng. Library.

Printing—History—Exhibitions.

INDIANA. University. Lilly Library. 081 s
Exotic printing and the expansion of Europe, 1492-1840: an exhibit. [Bloomington] 1972. 81 p. illus. 28 cm. (Its Publication no. 14) Bibliography: p. 76-78. [Z881.I42P8 no. 14] [Z121] 686.2'09 72-611482
1. Printing—History—Exhibitions. I. Title. II. Series.

INDIANA. University. Lilly Library. 081 s
Printing and the mind of man. Bloomington, 1973. 81 p. 28 cm. (Lilly Library publication no. 19) Catalog of the exhibition held principally in the Lilly Library in 1973. The condensed descriptions of books in this catalog were taken from the 1963 catalog of the Eleventh International Printing Machinery and Allied Trades Exhibition. [Z881.I42P8 no. 19] [Z121] 686.2'09 74-620786 5.00
1. Printing—History—Exhibitions. 2. Civilization, Modern—History—Exhibitions. I. London. 1963. Printing and the mind of man. II. Title. III. Series: Indiana. University. Lilly Library. Publication no. 19.

Printing—History—Great Britain.

NICHOLS, John, 1745-1826. 686.2'092'2
Biographical and literary anecdotes of William Bowyer. With two memoirs of John Nichols. New York, Garland Pub., 1974. p. cm. (The English book trade, 1660-1853.) Reprint of Biographical and literary anecdotes of William Bowyer, printer, F.S.A., and of many of his learned friends, by J. Nichols, printed in 1782 by and for the author, London; of Brief memoirs of John Nichols, printed in 1804 by Nichols and Son, London; and of Memoir of John Nichols, Esq., F.S.A., by A. Chalmers, from the Gentleman's magazine for December 1826. [Z232.B79N498 1974] 74-16185 ISBN 0-8240-0971-1 22.00
1. Bowyer, William, 1699-1777. 2. Nichols, John, 1745-1826. 3. Printing—History—Great Britain. I. Brief memoirs of John Nichols. 1974. II. Title. III. Series.

Printing—History—New York (City)

GAINE, Hugh, 1726or7-1807. 070.5'0924
The journals of Hugh Gaine, printer. Paul Leicester Ford, editor. [New York] Arno [1970, c1902] xi, 239, 234 p. illus., facsims., port. 24 cm. (The American journalists) [Z232.G2F5 1970] 70-125694 ISBN 0-405-01671-9
1. Printing—History—New York (City) 2. United States—History—Revolution, 1775-1783—Personal narratives. I. Title. BIP

Printing—History—Northwest, Pacific.

SCHOENBERG, Wilfred P. 015.795
Jesuit mission presses in the Pacific Northwest; a history and bibliography of imprints, 1876-1899. [Portland, Or.] Champoeg Press, 1957. 76 p. illus., port., facsims. 26 cm. Includes bibliographical references. [Z231.5.C3S37] 58-17846
1. Printing—History—Northwest, Pacific. 2. Jesuits in the Northwest, Pacific. I. Title.

Printing—History—Origin and antecedents.

DE VINNE, Theodore Low, 1828-1914. 655.1'02'4
The invention of printing; a collection of facts and opinions descriptive of early prints and playing cards, the block-books of the fifteenth century, the legend of Lourens Janszoon Coster of Haarlem, and the work of John Gutenberg and his associates. Illustrated with facsims. of early types and woodcuts. New York, F. Hart, 1876. Detroit, Gale Research Co., 1969. 556 p. illus., facsims., maps, ports. 23 cm. Bibliography: p. [543]-545. [Z126.D49 1969] 68-17971
1. Printing—History—Origin and antecedents. I. Title.

DUFF, Edward Gordon, 1863-1924. 655.1
Early printed books. New York, Haskell House, 1968. 219 p. illus. 23 cm. Reprint of the 1893 ed. Bibliographical footnotes. [Z240.D85 1968] 68-25309
1. Printing—History—Origin and antecedents. 2. Incunabula—Bibliography. I. Title.

GOFF, Frederick Richmond, 1916- 686'.1'0924
Johann Gutenberg and the Scheide Library at Princeton / by Frederick R. Goff. [Princeton, N.J.] : Princeton University Press, 1976. p. 72-84, [2] leaves of plates : ill. ; 26 cm. Caption title. Extracted from v. 37, no. 2, winter 1976 issue of the Princeton University Library chronicle. Bibliography: p. 83-84. [Z126.Z7G59] 76-377522
1. Gutenberg, Johann, 1397?-1468. 2. Scheide Library. 3. Printing—History—Origin and antecedents. I. Title.

MCMURTRIE, Douglas Crawford, 1888-1944. 686'.1'0924 B
Wings for words; the story of Johann Gutenberg and his invention of printing. With the collaboration of Don Farran. Illustrated by Edward A. Wilson. New York, Rand McNally, 1940. Detroit, Tower Books, 1971. 175 p. illus. 24 cm. A biography of the man who developed the process of printing from moveable type in the fifteenth century. [Z126.Z7M32 1971] 92 78-167061
1. Gutenberg, Johann, 1397?-1468. 2. Printing—History—Origin and antecedents. I. Wilson, Edward Arthur, 1886- illus. II. Title. BIP

Printing—History—Tennessee.

DOBSON, John, 1924- 070.5'092'4
The lost Roulstone imprints : with a checklist of issues from George Roulstone's Tennessee press, 1793-1804 / by John Dobson. Knoxville : University of Tennessee Library, 1975. xiii, 70 p. : facsims. ; 24 cm. (Occasional publication - University of Tennessee Library ; no. 2) Bibliography: p. 69-70. [Z232.R753D6] 74-16840
1. Roulstone, George, 1767-1804. 2. Printing—History—Tennessee. 3. Legislslative journals—Tennessee—Bibliography. 4. Tennessee—History—Sources—Bibliography. I. Title. II. Series: Tennessee. University. Libraries. Occasional publication ; no. 2.

Printing—History—Utica, N.Y.

WILLIAMS, John Camp, 1859?-1929. 686.2'092'4
An Oneida County printer, William Williams, printer, publisher, editor, with a bibliography of the press at Utica, Oneida County, New York, from 1803-1838. New York, Scribner, 1906. Harrison, N.Y., Harbor Hill Books, 1974. xxvi, 211 p. illus. 22 cm. Bibliography: p. 18. [Z232.W7W7 1974] 74-14766 12.50
1. Williams, William, 1787-1850. 2. Printing—History—Utica, N.Y. 3. Utica, N.Y.—Imprints. I. Title.

Printing-ink.

HALPERN, George Martin, 1919- 655.32
Pressman's ink manual; with foreword by Fred J. Hartman. New York, Bullinger's Guides [1952] 182 p. illus. 22 cm. [Z247.H3] 52-1419
1. Printing-ink. I. Title.

†NATIONAL Association of Printing Ink Manufacturers. Product and Technical Publications Committee. 667'.5
Printing ink handbook / compiled by Product and Technical Publications Committee, National Association of Printing Ink Manufacturers, Inc. 3d ed. Harrison, N.Y. : The Association, c1976. 95 p. : ill. ; 28 cm. Previous editions entered under the earlier name of the subordinate body: Technical Committee. Bibliography: p. 82. [Z247.N35 1976] 75-37363 pbk. : 2.50
1. Printing-ink. I. National Association of Printing Ink Manufacturers. Technical Committee. Printing ink handbook. II. Title.

NATIONAL Association of Printing Ink Manufacturers. Technical Committee. 667.5
Printing ink handbook. Prepared by the Technical and Educational Committees of the National Association of Printing Ink Makers, assisted by the National Printing Ink Research Institute at Lehigh University. New York, National Association of Printing Ink Makers [1958] 59 p. illus. 28 cm. [Z247.N35 1958] 676 68-566
1. Printing-ink. I. National Association of Printing Ink Manufacturers. Education Committee. II. Title.

NATIONAL Association of Printing Ink Manufacturers. Technical Committee. 667'.5
Printing ink handbook. Compiled by Technical and Education Committees, National Association of Printing Ink Manufacturers, and the National Printing Ink Research Institute. 2d ed. [New York, 1967] 94 p. illus. (part col.) 28 cm. Bibliography: p. 71. [Z247.N35 1967] 67-30364
1. Printing-ink. I. National Association of Printing Ink Manufacturers. Education Committee. II. Lehigh University, Bethlehem, Pa. National Printing Ink Research Institute. III. Title.

U.S. Government Printing Office. 667'.5
GPO standard ink book. [Washington, 1969] 1 v. (unpaged) illus. 27 cm. Cover title. [Z247.U53] 75-606044
1. Printing-ink. I. Title.

WOLFE, Herbert Jay, 1904- 655.32
Pressmen's ink handbook. New York, Dorland Books, 1952. 267p. illus. 20cm. [Z247.W8] 53-175
1. Printing-ink. I. Title.

Printing—Invention—Juvenile literature.

HARRIS, Brayton. 686.1'092'4 B
Johann Gutenberg and the invention of printing. New York, Watts, 1972. xv, 144 p. illus. 22 cm. (A Franklin Watts biography) Bibliography: p. 141-142. A biography of the man who developed printing from moveable type in the fifteenth century. [Z126.Z7H37] 92 73-150377 ISBN 0-531-00967-X
1. Gutenberg, Johann, 1397?-1468—Juvenile literature. 2. Printing—Invention—Juvenile literature. I. Title.

Printing machinery and supplies—History.

THE Ernest A. Lindner 681'.62'09
Collection of antique printing machinery. Pasadena [Calif.] V. Gerry, 1971. 44, [6] p. illus. 20 x 23 cm. Bibliography: p. [46] [Z249.E735] 72-31995
1. Lindner, Ernest A. 2. Printing machinery and supplies—History.

HUSS, Richard E. 681'.62'0924 B
Dr. Church's "hoax" : an assessment of Dr. William Church's typographical inventions in which is enunciated Church's law / by Richard E. Huss. Lancaster, Pa. : Graphic Crafts, 1976. xiv, 78 p. : ill. ; 24 cm. Includes index. Bibliography: p. 77-78. [Z249.H88] 75-44946 12.00
1. Church, William, 1779-1863. 2. Printing machinery and supplies—History. I. Title. BIP

Printing plates.

BRITISH Printing Industries Federation. Sheet-fed Offset Study Group. 686.2'325
Selecting the right litho plate / [prepared by the Sheet-fed Offset Study Group of the British Printing Industries Federation]. London : The Federation, 1976. 39 p. : ill. ; 21 cm. Cover title. [Z249.B72 1976] 77-364614 ISBN 0-85168-100-X : £1.50
1. Printing plates. 2. Offset printing. I. Title.

REED, Robert Findley, 1890- 655.3'15
Offset lithographic platemaking, by Robert F. Reed. Pittsburgh, Graphic Arts Technical Foundation [1967] xi, 203 p. illus. 22 cm. [Z249.R38] 67-27780
1. Printing plates. I. Title.

Printing, Practical.

AMES, Richard D 655.2
Exercises in printing. Washington, Printed at Bell Vocational High School, c1955. 136p. illus. 20cm. [Z244.3.A735] 55-58429
1. Printing, Practical. I. Title.

AMMONDS, Charles Cyril. 655'.01'5
Printing: basic science, by Charles C. Ammonds. [1st ed. Oxford, New York] Pergamon Press [1970] viii, 364 p. illus. (1 col.) 22 cm. (Library of industrial and commercial education and training. Printing) [Z244.A6 1970] 71-89611
1. Printing, Practical. 2. Science. I. Title.

ARNOLD, Edmund C. 655.2
Ink on paper; a handbook of the graphic arts. [1st ed.] New York, Harper & Row [1963] 323 p. illus. 25 cm. [Z244.A83] 63-8009
1. Printing, Practical. I. Title.

ARNOLD, Edmund C. 686.2
Ink on paper 2; a handbook of the graphic arts [by] Edmund C. Arnold. New York, Harper & Row [1972] 374 p. illus. 25 cm. Includes bibliographies. [Z244.A83 1972] 70-156503 ISBN 0-06-010131-8 10.95
1. Printing, Practical. I. Title.

ARNOLD, Edmund C. 655.3
Processes of printing and engraving, by Edmund C. Arnold. Serial 6767. [Ed. 1] Scranton, International Correspondence Schools [1966] 72, 3 p. illus. (part col.) 23 cm. "Figures 37, 38, 39, 40, 41, and 42" (fold. sheet inserted) [Z244.3.A74] 68-74
1. Printing, Practical. 2. Photoengraving. I. International Correspondence Schools, Scranton, Pa. II. Title.

AUBLE, John Woodard, 1899- 655.3076
Arithmetic for printers. [2d ed.] Peoris, Ill., C. A. Benett Co. [1954] 188p. illus. 22cm. [Z245.A88 1954] 54-1677
1. Printing, Practical. 2. Arithmetic—Problems. exercises. etc. I. Title.

BALLINGER, Raymond A., 1907- 686.2'24
Art and reproduction : graphic-reproduction techniques / Raymond A. Ballinger. New York : Van Nostrand Reinhold, [1976] p. cm. Includes index. Bibliography: p. [Z244.B2] 76-5070 ISBN 0-442-20550-3 : 7.95 pbk. : 7.95
1. Printing, Practical. I. Title. BIP

BASTIEN, Alfred. 655.8
Practical typography, explained for apprentices and students. 2d rev. ed. West Drayton, Middesex, 1955. 118p. illus. 19cm. [Z244.B3 1955] 56-19026
1. Printing, practical. I. Title.

BIGGS, John R. 655
Basic typography [by] John R. Biggs. New York, Watson-Guptill Publications [1968]

176 p. illus. (part col.) 20 cm. Bibliography: p. 176. [Z244.3.B5] 68-12032 8.50
1. Printing, Practical. I. Title.

BROEKHUIZEN, Richard J. 686.2
Graphic communications [by] Richard J. Broekhuizen. [1st ed. Bloomington, Ill., McKnight, 1973] xiv, 380 p. illus. 24 cm. (A McKnight career publication) [Z244.B76] 73-80805 ISBN 0-87345-245-3 9.32
1. Printing, Practical. 2. Graphic arts. I. Title. BIP

CARLSEN, Darvet E. 760
Graphic arts. Peoria, Ill., C. A. Bennett [1964,c.1958] 158p. illus., diagrs. 26cm. Bibl. 64-820 4.00
1. Printing, Practical. 2. Graphic arts. I. Title. BIP

CARLSEN, Darvey E. 655
Graphic arts [by] Darvey E. Carlsen. 4th ed. Peoria, Ill., C. A. Bennett Co. [1970] 208 p. illus. (part col.) 25 cm. Bibliography: p. 201-202. [Z244.3.C3 1970] 74-16797 ISBN 0-87002-016-1
1. Printing, Practical. 2. Graphic arts.

CARLSEN, Darvey E. 686.2'24
Graphic arts / Darvey E. Carlsen. 5th ed. Peoria, Ill. : C. A. Bennett Co., c1977. 208 p. : ill. (some col.) ; 25 cm. Includes index. Bibliography: p. 201. [Z244.3.C3 1977] 75-37453 ISBN 0-87002-177-X : 7.20
1. Printing, Practical. 2. Graphic arts. I. Title.

CLEETON, Glen Uriel, 1895- 655.3
General printing [by] Glen U. Cleeton [and] Charles W. Pitkin. Bloomington, Ill., McKnight & McKnight, 1953. 195 p. illus. 27 cm. [Z122.C63 1953] 53-3674
1. Printing, Practical. I. Pitkin, Charles W., joint author. II. Title.

CLEETON, Glen Uriel, 1895- 655.3
General printing [by] Glen U. Cleeton [and] Charles W. Pitkin. Rev. by Raymond L. Cornwell. [3d ed.] Bloomington, Ill., McKnight & McKnight Pub. Co. [1963] xviii, 203 p. illus. 27 cm. Bibliography: p. 191-195. [Z122.C63 1963] 63-24644
1. Printing, Practical. I. Pitkin, Charles W., joint author. II. Title.

CLOWES, William Beaufoy. 686.2
A guide to printing; an introduction for print buyers [by] William Clowes. Westport, Conn., Greenwood Press [1973, c1963] x, 134 p. illus. 22 cm. Reprint of the ed. published by Heinemann, London. Bibliography: p. [126]-130. [Z244.C5 1973] 73-717 ISBN 0-8371-6786-8
1. Printing, Practical. I. Title.

COFFIN, Narry Bigelow, 1906- 655.3
Idea file; 100 illustrated ideas for printers, lithographers, agencies, designers, advertisers, publishers for announcements, booklets, broadsides, catalogs, reply cards, selfmailers, etc. New York, Moore Pub. Co., c1952. unpaged. illus. 22cm. 'An American printer book.' 'Reprinted from American printer, August 1949-November 1951.' [Z244.3.C635] 53-637
1. Printing, Practical. I. Title.

CRAIG, James, 1930- 686.2
Production for the graphic designer. Edited by Margit Malmstrom. New York, Watson-Guptill Publications [1974] 207 p. illus. 29 cm. Bibliography: p. 203. [Z244.C78 1974] 74-836 ISBN 0-8230-4415-7 18.50
1. Printing, Practical. 2. Book design. I. Title. BIP

DAVIS, Alec. 760
Graphics : design into production / by Alec Davis. New York : Pitman Pub. Corp., [1974] c1973. 154 p. : ill. (some col.) ; 26 cm. Includes bibliographies and index. [Z244.D27 1974] 74-80152 ISBN 0-273-07073-8 : 14.25
1. Printing, Practical. 2. Graphic arts. I. Title.

DENNIS, Ervin A. 686.2
Comprehensive graphic arts [by] Ervin A. Dennis [and] John D. Jenkins. [1st ed.] Indianapolis, H. W. Sams [1974] xi, 548 p. illus. 27 cm. [Z244.D36] 72-92620 ISBN 0-672-20886-5 15.95
1. Printing, Practical. 2. Graphic arts. I. Jenkins, John D., joint author. II. Title. III. Title: Graphic arts. BIP

DONDIS, Donis A. 686.2'2
Print media for public communication : a workbook / by Donis Dondis. Boston : Eikon Books, [1975] p. cm. [Z246.D65] 75-25856
1. Printing, Practical. I. Title.

EASTERN Press, inc., Brooklyn. 655.2
Typographical handbook. [Brooklyn, 1950] 64 p. illus. 23 cm. [Z246.E13 1950] 50-28062
1. Printing, Practical. I. Title.

GATES, David, 1927- 686.2'24
Graphic design studio techniques / by David Gates. New York : Watson-Guptill, 1978. p. cm. Includes index. Bibliography: p. [Z244.G3] 78-6520 ISBN 0-8230-2147-5 : 22.50
1. Printing, Practical. 2. Graphic arts—Technique. I. Title.

GROESBECK, Harry Appleton, 1879-1950. 655.2
A primer of engraving and printing, including composition, electrotyping, paper, presses, and ink. New York, Colton Press ['1950] 174 p. 19 cm. "Portions of this book were reprinted from the ninth Graphic arts production yearbook." [Z244.G9] 51-6698
1. Printing, Practical. 2. Engraving—Technique. 3. Lithography—Technique. I. Title.

HAGUE, Clifford Wilson, 1893- 655.2
Printing and allied graphic arts. Milwaukee, Bruce Pub. Co. [1957] 244 p. illus. 23 cm. [Z244.H13] 57-4247
1. Printing, Practical.

HALE, Frank David, 1878- 655.3
Printing methods for beginners. Jersey City [1950] 160 p. illus. 20 cm. [Z244.3.H27] 51-536
1. Printing, Practical. I. Title.

HYMES, David G, 1908- 655.2
Production in advertising; a guide book for students of advertising, magazine and newspaper journalism, publishing, printing and the graphic arts. New York, Colton Press [1950] 392 p. illus. 21 cm. [Z246.H9] 50-2269
1. Printing, Practical. 2. Advertising. I. Title.

INTERNATIONAL Typographical Union of North America. 655.2
I. T. U. lessons in printing. By I. T. U. Bureau of Education. Indianapolis, c19 v. illus. 23cm. Contents.[newspaper] unit 4. Newspaper advertising. [Z122.I6514] 57-32481
1. Printing, Practical. I. Title. II. Title: Lessons in printing.

INTERNATIONAL Typographical Union of North America. 655.2
I. T. U. lessons in printing. By I. T. U. Bureau of Education. Indianapolis, c1956- v. illus. 23cm. Contents.unit 1. Elements of composition.--unit 2. Display composition.--job unit 4. Design for printers.--unit 5. English for printers.--unit 6. Trade unionism. [Z122.I666] 57-32484
1. Printing, Practical. I. Title. II. Title: Lessons in printing.

INTERNATIONAL Typographical Union of North America. 655.2
I. T. U. lessons in printing. By I. T. U. Bureau of Education. Indianapolis, c1955- v. illus. 23cm. Contents.unit 1. Elements of compostion.--unit 2. Display composition.--[newspaper] unit 3. Newspaper practice.--unit 5. English for printers.--unit 6. Trade unionism.--unit 10. Photocomposition, ruling and pasteup. [Z122.I664] 57-32483
1. Printing, Practical. I. Title. II. Title: Lessons in printing.

INTERNATIONAL 686.2'2
Typographical Union of North America. *ITU lessons in printing.* [Colorado Springs] Bureau of Education International Typographical Union, c1973- v. illus. (part col.) 27 cm. [Z122.I675 1973] 74-161799
1. Printing, Practical. I. Title. II. Title: Lessons in printing.

INTERNATIONAL 686.2'2
Typographical Union of North America. *ITU lessons in printing.* [Colorado Springs, Colo.] Bureau of Education, International Typographical Union [1970-72] 2 v. illus. (part col.) 27 cm. [Z122.I675] 70-129221
1. Printing, Practical. I. Title. II. Title: Lessons in printing.

JACKSON, Hartley Everett. 655.2
Printing; a practical introduction to the graphic arts. Prepared for publication by M. Ardelle Cleverdon. New York, McGraw-Hill [1957] 286p. illus. 25cm. (McGraw-Hill publications in industrial arts) [Z244.J14] 56-13394
1. Printing, Practical. I. Title.

KARCH, Robert Randolph, 1902- 655
Graphic arts procedures. [2d ed., rev.] Chicago, American Technical Society [1957] 383 p. illus. 22 cm. [Z244.K3 1957] 57-7328
1. Printing, Practical. I. Title.

KARCH, Robert Randolph, 1902- 655
Graphic arts procedures; basic [by] R. Randolph Karch. 4th ed. Chicago, American Technical Society [1970] 409 p. illus., facsims. 22 cm. [Z244.K3 1970] 77-114265
1. Printing, Practical. I. Title.

KARCH, Robert Randolph, 1902- 655
Graphic arts procedures, by R. Randolph Karch. [3d ed. rev.] Chicago, American Technical Society [1965] xi, 388 p. illus. 22 cm. Includes bibliographical references. [Z244.K3 1965] 65-14747
1. Printing, Practical. I. Title.

KARCH, Robert Randolph, 1902- 655
How to plan and buy printing. New York, Prentice-Hall, 1950. viii, 169 p. illus. 29 cm. "Some of the material ... has been adapted from [the auther's] raphic arts procedures." [Z244.K33] 50-11596
1. Printing, Practical. I. Title.

KARCH, Robert Randolph, 1902- 655.2
Printing and the allied trades. 4th ed. New York, Pitman [1958] 318p. illus. 21cm. [Z244.3.K19 1958] 58-1611
1. Printing, Practical. 2. Type-setting. I. Title.

KARCH, Robert Randolph, 1902- 655.2
Printing and the allied trades. 3d ed. New York, Pitman [1954] 318p. illus. 22cm. [Z244.3.K19 1954] 54-10396
1. Printing, Practical. 2. Type-setting. I. Title.

KAY, Frederick George, 1911- 655
Printing, by E. George Kay. London, J. Baker; New York, Roy, 1968. 55p. 24 plates. [Z244.3K25] 68-119607 3.25
1. Printing, Practical. I. Title.

KOLLECKER, Eugen, 1884- ed. 001.55'2
Der moderne Druck; Handbuch der grafischen Techniken. Hrsg. von Eugen Kollecker und Walter Matuschke Hamburg, Hammerich & Lesser [1956] 672p. illus. (part fold.) plates (part col., part mounted) diagrs., plans. 25cm. (Bucher fur Betrieb und Wirtschaft) Bibliography: p. 671-672. [Z244.K74] 58-16810
1. Printing, Practical. I. Matuschke, Walter, 1903- joint ed. II. Title.

LEE, Marshall, 1921- ed. 655.074
Books for our time; edited and designed by Marshall Lee, with contributions by Herbert Bayer [and others] and a pref. by George Nelson. New York, Oxford University Press, 1951. 128 p. illus., facsims. 29 cm. "Conceived originally as the catalogue of the Books for Our Time Exhibition, opened in New York at the New Art Circle gallery under the auspices of the Trade Book Clinic of the American Institute ofGraphic Arts." [Z246.L5] 51-10911
1. Printing, Practical. 2. Printing—Exhibitions. I. Bayer, Herbert, 1900- II. American Institute of Graphic Arts. Trade Book Clinic. III. Title.

LIEBERMAN, J Ben. 655.069
Printing as a hobby. New York, Sterling Pub. Co. [1963] 128 p. illus. 22 cm. [Z244.L57] 63-11589
1. Printing, Practical. I. Title. BIP

LIEBERMAN, J Ben. 655.023
Printing as a hobby. [Rev. ed.] New York, Sterling Pub. Co. [1965] 128 p. illus. 22 cm. Bibliography: p. 124. [Z244.L57 1965] 65-8069
1. Printing. Practical. I. Title.

LOOP, James W 655.2
Printing for the beginning pupil. [Rev. and reprinted] Charleston, W. Va., 1956. 226p. illus. 24cm. [Z122.L86 1956] 57-3777
1. Printing, Practical. I. Title.

MARINACCIO, Anthony. 655
Exploring the graphic arts. 2d ed. Princeton, N. J., Van Nostrand [1959] 297p. illus. 24cm. [Z244.M36 1959] 59-14618
1. Printing. Practical. 2. Writing—Hist. 3. Engravings—Printing. I. Title.

MOXON, Joseph, 1627-1700. 655.3
Mechanick exercises on the whole art of printing, 1683-4. Edited by Herbert Davis & Harry Carter. London, Oxford, University Press, 1958. lxiii, 480 p., illus., plates, ports., maps, diagrs., facsims., typog. specimens. 26 cm. "Reprinted from a copy of Mechanick exercises, vol. II, 1683, in the Bodleian Library (Gibson 200)" "Later books on printing and their reliance on Moxon": p. 442-444. [Z244.A2M93 1958] 59-244
1. Printing, Practical. I. Title. BIP

MOXON, Joseph, 1627-1700. 686.2'24
Mechanick exercises on the whole art of printing (1683-4) / by Joseph Moxon ; edited by Herbert Davis & Harry Carter. 2d ed. New York : Dover Publications, 1978, c1962. lviii, 487 p. : ill. ; 24 cm. Folded leaf attached to p. 3 of cover. Originally reprinted in 1958 by Oxford University Press, London, from a copy of Mechanick exercises, vol. II, 1683, in the Bodleian Library (Gibson 200). This ed. represents a reprint of the Oxford University Press second ed. Includes index. Bibliography: p. 409-444. [Z244.A2M93 1978] 77-20468 ISBN 0-486-23617-X : 7.95
1. Printing, Practical. I. Davis, Herbert John, 1893-1967. II. Carter, Harry Graham. III. Title.

POLK, Ralph Weiss, 1890- 655
The practice of printing. Rev. and enl. Peoria, Ill., C. A. Bennett Co. [1952] 324 p. illus. 23 cm. [Z244.P76 1952] 52-13857
1. Printing, Practical. I. Title. BIP

POLK, Ralph Weiss, 1890- 001.55'2
The practice of printing; letterpress and offset, by Ralph W. Polk and Edwin W. Polk, Rev. Peoria, Ill., Bennett [1964] xii, 328 p. illus. (part col.) ports., facsims. 23 cm. Bibliography: p. 319-322. [Z244.P76] 64-1051
1. Printing, Practical. I. Polk, Edwin W., joint author II. Title.

POLK, Ralph Weiss, 1890- 686'.2312
The practice of printing: letterpress and offset, by Ralph W. Polk and Edwin W. Polk. 7th ed. Peoria, Ill., C. A. Bennett Co. [1971] xii, 328 p. illus. (part col.), facsims. 23 cm. Bibliography: p. 321-322. [Z244.P76 1971] 76-26064 ISBN 0-87002-101-X
1. Printing, Practical. I. Polk, Edwin W., joint author. II. Title.

PRACTICAL printing and binding; Odhams complete guide to the printer's craft. Fully rev. by specialist authors. London, Odhams Bks. [dist. Levittown, N.Y., Transatlantic, c.1965] 448p. illus. (pt. col.) 23cm. Third ed. of Practical printing and binding, orig. ed. by Harry Whetton [Z244.P85] 65-6481 9.75 655.3
1. Printing, Practical. 2. Bookbinding. I. Whetton, Harry, ed. Practical printing and binding.

RYDER, John, 1917- 686.2
Printing for pleasure / John Ryder. Rev. ed. Chicago : H. Regnery Co., 1977, c1976. 129 p. : ill. ; 19 cm. [Z244.3.R9 1977] 77-372224 ISBN 0-8092-7810-3 : 5.95
1. Printing, Practical. I. Title. BIP

SIMON, Oliver, 1895- 655.25
Introduction to typography. [Rev. ed. Harmondsworth, Middlesex] Penguin Books [1954] 117p. illus. 19cm. (Pelican books. A288) [Z244.3.S6 1954] 55-27354
1. Printing. Practical. I. Title.

STOWER, Charles, 1779?-1816 655.24
The printer's grammar. [By] Caleb Stower. London, Gregg Pr., [1966] xviii, 530p. illus. 21cm. (English bibl. sources. ser. 3: Printers' manuals [no.] 4) Reprint of the 1808 ed. [Z244.A2S8 1965] 67-3117 21.00
1. Printing, Practical. 2. Printing—Specimens. I. Title. II. Series: English bibliographical sources, ser. 3, no. 4

SWANN, Cal. 655.2
Techniques of typography. New York, Watson-Guptill Publications [1969] 96 p. of illus. 21 x 22 cm. [Z244.3.S97 1969b] 69-17669 7.50
1. Printing, Practical. I. Title.

THOMPSON, Samuel Winfield, 1906- 001.5'52
Basic layout design; a pattern for understanding the basic motifs in design and how to apply them to graphic art problems [by] Tommy Thompson. New York, Studio Publications in association with Crowell [c1950] 79 p. illus. (part col.) 24 cm. [Z246.T54] 655 51-534
1. Printing, Practical. 2. Design. I. Title.

TURNBULL, Arthur T. 655.2
The graphics of communication: typography, layout, design [by] Arthur T. Turnbull [and] Russell N. Baird. 2d ed. New York, Holt, Rinehart and Winston [1968] xiv, 395 p. illus., facsims. 24 cm. Bibliography: p. 353-355. [Z244.T86 1968] 68-13616
1. Printing, Practical. I. Baird, Russell N., joint author. II. Title.

TURNBULL, Arthur T. 655.3
The graphics of communication: typography, layout, design [by] Arthur T. Turnbull and Russell N. Baird. New York, Holt, Rinehart and Winston [1964] x, 342 p. illus., ports., diagrs., facsims. 24 cm. Bibliography: p. 309-310. [Z244.T86] 64-11979
1. Printing, Practical. I. Baird, Russell N., joint author. II. Title. BIP

TURNBULL, Arthur T. 686.2'2
The graphics of communication : typography, layout, design / Arthur T. Turnbull, Russell N. Baird. 3d. ed. New York : Holt, Rinehart and Winston, [1975] xiii, 462 p. : ill. ; 25 cm. Includes index. Bibliography: p. 432-437. [Z244.T86 1975] 74-26949 ISBN 0-03-089580-4 : 10.95
1. Printing, Practical. I. Baird, Russell N., joint author. II. Title.

WARFORD, H. S. 686'.22
Design for print production; the interaction between design, planning and production of print, by H. S. Warford. New York, Hastings House [1972, c1971] viii, 176 p. illus. 24 cm. (The Library of printing technology) (Visual communication books) Bibliography: p. 171-172. [Z244.W28] 77-178848 ISBN 0-8038-1543-3
1. Printing, Practical. I. Title.

Printing, Practical—Bibliography.

GERBER, Jack. 016.76
A selected bibliography of the graphic arts. Pittsburgh, Graphic Arts Technical Foundation [1967] 84 p. 22 cm. [Z117.G4] 67-27779
1. Printing, Practical—Bibliography. 2. Graphic arts—Bibliography. I. Title.

Printing, Practical—Dictionaries.

POCKET encyclopedia of paper & graphic arts terms. 655.303 [Kaukauna, Wis., Thomas Print. & Pub. Co., 1960] 94p. 16cm. [Z118.P6] 60-4619
1. Printing, Practical—Dictionaries. 2. Paper making and trade—Dictionaries. 3. Graphic arts—Dictionaries.

Printing, Practical —Handbooks, manuals, etc.

BURKE, Clifford. 686.2
Printing it; a guide to graphic techniques for the impecunious. With illus. by Chuck Miller. New York, Ballantine Books [1972] 127 p. illus. 21 cm. Bibliography: p. 126-127. [Z244.3.B95] 72-194117 ISBN 0-345-02694-2 2.95
1. Printing, Practical—Handbooks, manuals, etc. I. Title. BIP

INTERNATIONAL Paper Company. 655.302
The pocket pal [for printers, estimators and advertising production managers] 5th ed. New York, 1957. 114p. illus. 19cm. [Z244.3I58 1957] 57-58388
1. Printing, Practical —Handbooks, manuals, etc. I. Title.

INTERNATIONAL Paper Company. 686.2'2
Pocket pal : a graphic arts production handbook. 11th ed. New York : International Paper Co., 1974. 191 p. : ill. ; 19 cm. [Z244.3.I58 1974] 75-316438 1.50
1. Printing, Practical—Handbooks, manuals, etc. I. Title.

LEM, Dean Phillip, 1924- 686.2'02'02
Graphics master : a workbook of planning aids, reference guides and graphic tools for the design, estimating, preparation and production of printing and print advertising / Dean Phillip Lem. Los Angeles, Calif. : Dean Lem Associates, c1974. 25 [i.e. 74] p. : ill. (some col.) ; 30 cm. Includes index. [Z244.3.L42] 73-88192 ISBN 0-914218-01-8
1. Printing, Practical—Handbooks, manuals, etc. I. Title. BIP

LEM, Dean Phillip, 1924- 686.2'24
Graphics master 2 : [a workbook of planning aids, reference guides, and graphic tools for the design, estimating, preparation, and production of printing and print advertising] / Dean Phillip Lem. 2d ed. Los Angeles : Dean Lem Associates, c1977. 36 [i.e. 92] p. : ill. (some col.) ; 30 cm. Includes index. [Z244.3.L42 1977] 76-41508 ISBN 0-914218-02-6 : 37.50
1. Printing, Practical—Handbooks, manuals, etc. I. Title.

Printing, Practical—Imposition, etc.

WARNER, H. Wayne. 686.2'256
Planning for better imposition, by H. Wayne Warner. [2d ed. Washington, Printed by Judd & Detweiler, 1972] 42, 91 p. illus. 32 cm. [Z255.W36 1972] 76-102070
1. Printing, Practical—Imposition, etc. I. Title.

Printing, Practical — Juvenile literature.

BERGER, Melvin. 686.2
Printing plant / by Melvin Berger. New York : Watts, 1978. 66 p. : ill. ; 22 cm. (Industry at work) Includes index. Bibliography: p. 62-63. Describes various steps in the preparation and printing of materials including books, magazines, and newspapers and introduces various jobs of people involved in this work. [Z244.B563] 78-2529 ISBN 0-531-02207-2 lib. bdg. : 4.90
1. Printing, Practical—Juvenile literature. 2. Printing industry—Juvenile literature. I. Title. II. Series: Industry at work series. BIP

CARLSEN, Darvey E. 686.2'2
Communication—graphic arts / Darvey E. Carlsen, Vernon A. Tryon ; consulting editor, Rex Miller. Englewood Cliffs, N.J. : Prentice-Hall, c1976. 119 p. : ill. ; 24 cm. (Modular exploration of technology series) Includes index. Bibliography: p. 113. Includes such information as major printing processes, measurement, graphic arts materials and techniques, planning for reproduction and production, and finishing operations. [Z244.C267] 75-12635 ISBN 0-13-153197-2 : 5.95 ISBN 0-13-153189-1 pbk. : 2.60
1. Printing, Practical—Juvenile literature. I. Tryon, Vernon A., 1936- joint author. II. Title.

COOKE, David Coxe, 1917- 655.3
How books are made. New York, Dodd, Mead [1963] 63 p. illus. 19 x 24 cm. [Z244.C76] 63-15472
1. Printing, Practical—Juvenile literature. 2. Books—Juvenile literature. I. Title.

SPELLMAN, John A 655.2
Printing works like this [by] John A. Spellman. With 55 illus. by H. A. Johns. London, Phoenix House; New York, Roy Publishers [1964] viii, 56 p. illus. (part col.) 26 cm. (The 'Science works like this series) [Z244.S77] 64-10588
1. Printing, Practical — Juvenile literature. I. Title. BIP

Printing, Practical—Layout.

HURLBURT, Allen, 1910- 686.2'24
The grid : a modular system for the design and production of newspapers, magazines, and books / Allen Hurlburt. New York : Van Nostrand Reinhold Co., [1978] p. cm. Includes index. Bibliography: p. [Z246.H82] 78-3734 ISBN 0-442-23598-4 : 16.95
1. Printing, Practical—Layout. I. Title.

HURLBURT, Allen, 1910- 686.2'25
Layout : the design of the printed page / Allen Hurlburt. New York : Watson-Guptill Publications, 1977. 159 p. : ill. ; 28 cm. Includes index. Bibliography: p. 151-153. [Z246.H83] 77-701 ISBN 0-8230-2655-8 : 17.95
1. Printing, Practical—Layout. 2. Graphic arts. 3. Design. I. Title. BIP

JONES, Gerre L., 1926- 808'.025
How to prepare professional design brochures / Gerre Jones. New York : McGraw-Hill, c1976. viii, 277 p. : ill. ; 25 cm. Includes index. Bibliography: p. 271-272. [Z246.J66] 75-40383 ISBN 0-07-032801-3 : 16.50
1. Printing, Practical—Layout. 2. Architectural services marketing. 3. Engineering services marketing. I. Title. BIP

NELSON, Roy Paul. 070.5'3
Publication design / Roy Paul Nelson. 2d ed. Dubuque, Iowa : W. C. Brown Co., c1978. 295 p. : ill. ; 24 cm. Includes bibliographies and index. [Z246.N44 1978] 78-50177 ISBN 0-697-04324-X : 10.95
1. Printing, Practical—Layout. I. Title. BIP

Printing, Practical—Make-up.

BAIN, Eric K. 686'.22
Display typography [by] Eric K. Bain. London, New York, Focal, 1970. 182 p. illus. (some col.), facsims. 25 cm. Bibliography: p. 177-182. [Z253.5.B256] 79-594585 ISBN 0-240-50700-2 60/-
1. Printing, Practical—Make-up. I. Title.

BAIN, Eric K. 655.2
The theory and practice of typographic design [by] Eric K. Bain. New York, Hastings House [1970] 182 p. illus., facsims. 25 cm. (Visual communication books) On spine: Display typography. Bibliography: p. 177-182. [Z253.5.B26] 78-12571 12.50
1. Printing, Practical—Make-up. I. Title. II. Title: Display typography.

BALLINGER, Raymond A., 1907- 655.25
Layout. New York, Reinhold [1956] 244 p. illus. (part col.) 31 cm. Bibliography: p. 241. [Z253.5.B28] 56-9614
1. Printing, Practical—Make-up. I. Title.

BANTA (George) Company, inc. 655.2
Banta book of typographical tips. Menasha, Wis. [1969] v, 103 p. illus. 26 cm. "Reprinted from Banta book of types & typographical tips, 1961." [Z253.5.B29 1969] 70-231889
1. Printing, Practical—Make-up. 2. Proof-reading. I. Title.

BUTLER, Kenneth B. 016.051
A practical handbook on borders, ornamentation, and boxes in publication layout, by Kenneth B. Butler and George C. Likeness. Mendota, Ill., Butler Typo-Design Research Center [1960] 103 p. illus. 28 cm. (His A series of handbooks, no. 8) [Z253.5.B78] 66-94080
1. Printing. Practical—Make-up. I. Likeness, George C., joint author. II. Title.

BUTLER, Kenneth B 016.051
Practical handbook on double-spreads in publication layout, by Kenneth B. Butler, George C. Likeness and Stanley A. Kordek. Mendota, Ill., Butler Typo-Design Research Center [1956] 89p. illus. 28cm. 'No. 4 in a series of handbooks.' [Z253.5.B8] 56-2905
1. Printing, Practical—Make-up. I. Title. II. Title: Double-spreads in publication layout.

CONNECTICUT. Curriculum Committee for Printing Trades. 655.25
Printing layout and design. Albany, Delmar Publishers [1955] 201p. illus. 27cm. [Z253.5.C6] 55-11457
1. Printing, Practical—Make-up. I. Title. BIP

DARNELL, Tony. 655.5'3
Yearbook ideas on layout and photography [by] Tony Darnell [and] Aloysius J. Redd. San Angelo, Tex., Newsfoto Pub. Co. [1967] 281 p. (chiefly illus.) 32 cm. [Z253.5.D3] 67-6568
1. Printing. Practical — Make-up. 2. School yearbooks. I. Redd, Aloysius J., joint author. II. Title.

HARUM, Albert Edward. 655.25
Typography and newspaper makeup. Layout and illus. by C. M. Dugger, Jr.; photos, not otherwise credited, by W. G. Moeser. Dubuque, W. C. Brown Co. [1951] 82 p. illus. 28 cm. [Z253.5.H3] 52-2116
1. Printing, Practical—Make-up. 2. Type and type-founding. I. Title.

HEATH, Harry Eugene, 1919- 070.32
A guide to newspaper page makeup. [Ames] Iowa State College Press [1950] 15, [1] p. illus. 23 cm. Cover title. "Prepared for use with the Makeup editor's kit." Bibliography: p. [16] [Z253.H4] 50-3097
1. Printing, Practical—Make-up. I. Title.

LEE, Marshall, 1921- 655
Bookmaking: the illustrated guide to design & production. New York, Bowker [1965] 399 p. illus. 26 cm. (A Balance House book) Bibliography: p. [373]-380. [Z253.5.L4] 65-22380
1. Printing, Practical—Make-up. I. Title. BIP

NELSON, Roy Paul. 070.5'3
Publication design. Dubuque, Iowa, W. C. Brown Co. [1972] 232 p. illus. 24 cm. (Journalism series) Includes bibliographies. [Z253.5.N44] 78-176306 ISBN 0-697-04323-1
1. Printing, Practical—Make-up. I. Title.

NICYPER, Raymond, 1919- 686.2'2
Graphics underlay guides with reference data for media layout / by Raymond Nicyper. Westport, Conn. : Graphicraft, [1975] 136 p. : ill. ; 29 x 37 cm. (Graphics underlay guides) Includes index. [Z253.5.N56] 74-84417
1. Printing, Practical—Make-up. I. Title. II. Title: Media layout. III. Series.

REHE, Rolf F., 1935- 682.2'2
Typography : how to make it most legible / Rolf F. Rehe. Rev. ed. Indianapolis : Design Research Publications, 1974. 79 p. : ill. ; 21 cm. Originally presented as the author's thesis (M.A.), Indiana University, 1972. Bibliography: p. 65-78. [Z253.R36 1974] 74-18916
1. Printing, Practical—Make-up. I. Title.

SILVER, Gerald A 655.258
Modern graphic arts paste-up [by] Gerald A. Silver. Chicago, American Technical Society [1966] 141 p. illus. 26 cm. (Graphic arts series) Bibliography: p. 135. [Z253.5.S5] 66-12165
1. Printing, Practical—Make-up. I. Title.

SILVER, Gerald A. 686.2'25
Modern graphic arts paste-up [by] Gerald A. Silver. [2d ed.] Chicago, American Technical Society [1973] 160 p. illus. 26 cm. (Graphic arts series) Bibliography: p. 154. [Z253.5.S5 1973] 72-84254 ISBN 0-8269-2722-X pap. 4.90
1. Printing, Practical—Make-up. I. American Technical Society, Chicago. II. Title.

WARFORD, H. S. 686.2
Design for print production: the interaction between design, planning and production of print, by H. S. Warford. London, New York, Focal Press, 1971. viii, 176, [32] p. illus., facsims. 24 cm. (The library of printing technology) Bibliography: p. 171-172. [Z253.5.W37] 72-192652 ISBN 0-240-50741-X £3.25
1. Printing, Practical—Make-up. 2. Graphic arts. I. Title. BIP

Printing. Practical—Miscellanea.

BORKLUND, Carl Ernest, 1904- 655.3
Manual for editorial, production, typographic technicians. Mount Morris, Ill., Kable Print. Co. [1951] 56 p. illus. 23 cm. [Z244.3.B67] 51-4426
1. Printing. Practical—Miscellanea. I. Title.

Printing, Practical—Paste-up techniques.

GRAHAM, Walter B. 686.2'25
Complete guide to pasteup / Walter B. Graham. Philadelphia : North American Pub. Co., c1975. 247 p. : ill. ; 29 cm. Includes bibliographical references and index. [Z253.G7414] 75-8161 ISBN 0-912920-40-8 : 24.95
1. Printing, Practical—Paste-up techniques. I. Title. BIP

VAN UCHELEN, Rod 686.2'25
Paste-up : production techniques and new applications / Rod van Uchelen. New York : Van Nostrand Reinhold Co., [1976] p. cm. Includes index. [Z246.V29] 75-44584 ISBN 0-442-29022-5 : 12.95 pbk. : 7.95
1. Printing, Practical—Paste-up techniques. I. Title. BIP

Printing, Practical—Presswork.

HOCK, Fred William, 1891- 655.31
Handbook for pressmen, by Fred W. Hoch. [Rev. ed.] New York, F. W. Hoch Associates, 1966. xiii, 142 p. illus. 24 cm. [Z256.H68 1966] 66-6891
1. Printing, Practical—Presswork. I. Title.

Printing, Practical—Psychological aspects.

BURT, Cyril Lodowic, Sir 1883- 655.2
A psychological study of typography. With an introd. by Stanley Morison. Cambridge [Eng.] University Press, 1959. xix, 67p. illus. 26cm. Bibliography: p.56-[57] Bibliographical footnotes. [Z244.4.B8] 59-16185
1. Printing, Practical—Psychological aspects. I. Title.

Printing, Practical—Study and teaching—Addresses, essays, lectures.

THE Seventies; 338.4'7'6862
education and change. Pittsburgh, Graphic Arts Technical Foundation [1970] 70 p. ports. 16 x 23 cm. Addresses given at the 1970 GATF general education meeting. [Z122.S38] 77-128628
1. Printing, Practical—Study and teaching—Addresses, essays, lectures. 2. Printing industry—Management—Addresses, essays, lectures. I. Graphic Arts Technical Foundation.

Printing, Practical—Style manuals.

COUNCIL of Biology Editors. Committee on Form and Style. 686.2'252
CBE style manual. 3d ed. Washington, Published for the Council of Biology Editors by the American Institute of Biological Sciences [1972] xii, 297 p. illus. 24 cm. Previous editions issued by the Committee on Form and Style of the Conference of Biological Editors under title: Style manual for biological journals. Bibliography: p. 249-277. [Z250.6.B5C64 1972] 73-152333
1. Printing, Practical—Style manauls. 2. Technical writing. 3. Biological literature. I. Conference of Biological Editors. Committee on Form and Style. Style manual for biological journals. II. Title. BIP

Printing, Practical—Style manuals.

CABIBI, John F. J. 686.2'2
Copy preparation for printing [by] John F. J. Cabibi. New York, McGraw-Hill [1973] viii, 152 p. illus. 24 cm. Bibliography: p. 147-148. [Z246.C13] 72-10486 ISBN 0-07-009524-8 pap. 3.95 (text ed.)
1. Printing, Practical—Style manuals. 2. Printing, Practical—Make-up. I. Title. BIP

HARPER & Row author's manual. 655.5
Author's manual. New York [1966] vii, 141 p. illus. (part col.) 25 cm. [Z253.H32] 66-13190
1. Printing, Practical — Style manuals. I. Title.

KARCH, Robert Randolph, 1902- 355.25
Basic lessons in printing layout. Milwaukee, Bruce Pub. Co. [1952] 140p. illus. 23cm. [Z253.K25] 52-13218
1. Printing, Practical—Style manuals. I. Title.

Printing-press.

KAINEN, Jacob. 926.55
George Clymer and the Columbian press. San Francisco, Book Club of California, 1950. viii, 60 p. illus. 19 cm. 350 coples printed. "References": p. [51]-58. [Z249.K23] 50-13586
1. Clymer, George E., 1754-1834. 2. Printing-press. I. Title.

Printing-press—Catalogs.

STERNE, Harold E., 1929- 681'.62
Catalogue of nineteenth century printing presses / Harold E. Sterne. Cincinnati : Ye Olde Printery, c1978. 382 p. : ill. ; 16 x 24 cm. Includes index. [Z249.S827] 78-63314 ISBN 0-932606-00-8 : 19.50
1. Printing-press—Catalogs. I. Title. II. Title: Nineteenth century printing presses.

Printing-press—History.

MORAN, James. 681'.62
Printing presses; history and development from the fifteenth century to modern times. Berkeley, University of California Press [1973] 263 p. illus. 29 cm. Bibliography: p. [253]-254. [Z249.M748 1973] 72-75519 ISBN 0-520-02245-9 25.00
1. Printing-press—History. I. Title.

Printing—Private presses.

RANSOM, Will, 1878- ed. 655.4
Kelmscott, Doves, and Ashendene; the private press credos. [San Fransisco] Book Club of California 1952 vi, 197p. illus. 19cm. '300 copies printed.' Bibliography: p.[189]-196. [Z231.R35] [Z231.R35] 655.142 53-308 53-308
1. Printing—Private pressessAshendene Press. 2. Doves Press. 3. Kelmscott Press. I. Title.

RANSOM, Will, 1878- ed. 070.5'93
Kelmscott, Doves and Ashendene; the private press credos. [Los Angeles] The Typophiles, 1952. vi, 197p. illus. 18cm. (Typophile chap books. 27) 'Designed by Ward Ritchle and printed in Los Angeles by Anderson & Ritchie ... This edition comprises 400 copies for Typophile subscribers and contributors. An edition of 300 copies with the imprint of the Book Club of Caifornia has also been printed.' Bibliography: p.[189]-198. [Z231.R] A54
1. Printing—Private presses. 2. Kelmacott Press. 3. Doves Press. 4. Ashendene Press. I. Title. II. Series: The Typophiles, New York. Typophile chap books, 27

Printing—Private presses—Societies.

THE Fantasy collector. 686
Philadelphia, Fantasy Amateur Press Association, 19 no. 29 cm. [Z118.A3F3] 52-27791
1. Printing—Private presses—Societies. I. Fantasy Amateur Press Association.

Printing—Specimens.

BERRY, William Turner. 655.2403
The encyclopaedia of type faces [by] W. Turner Berry, A. F. Johnson [and] W. P. Jaspert. [3d ed., further rev. & enl.] New York, Pitman Pub. Corp. [1962] 420 p. typog. specimens. 26 cm. Bibliography: p. 407-408. [Z250.B5 1962] 62-21098
1. Printing—Specimens. I. Title. II. Title: Type faces.

BIEGELEISEN, Jacob Israel, 1910- 686'.224
Art directors' book of type faces; for artists, typographers, letterers, teachers & students [by] J. I. Biegeleisen. Introd. by Robert L. Leslie. [2d ed. New York, Arco Pub. Co., 1970] 231 p. illus. 31 cm. Bibliography: p. 229. [Z250.B56 1970] 72-125464 ISBN 0-668-01050-9
1. Printing—Specimens. 2. Type and type-founding. I. Title. BIP

BIEGELEISEN, Jacob Israel, 1910- 655.24
Art directors' work book of type faces, for artists, typographers, letterers, teachers & students. Introd. by Robert L. Leslie. New York, Arco Pub. Co. [1963] 212 p. illus. 32 cm. [Z250.B56] 63-10182
1. Printing—Specimens. 2. Type and type-founding. I. Title.

BIEGELEISEN, Jacob Israel, 1910- 686.2'24
Art directors' workbook of type faces : for artists, typographers, letterers, teachers & students / J. I. Biegeleisen ; introd. by Robert L. Leslie. 3d ed. New York : Arco Pub. Co., 1976. p. cm. First ed. published under title: Art directors' work book of type faces; 2d ed., under title: Art directors' book of type faces. Includes index. [Z250.B56 1976] 76-17128 ISBN 0-668-04041-6 : 12.95
1. Printing—Specimens. 2. Type and type-founding. I. Title. II. Title: Workbook of type faces.

BIEGELEISEN, Jacob Israel, 1910- 655.24
The book of 100 type face alphabets; a guide to better lettering. [Cincinnati, Signs of the Times Pub. Co., 1965] 215p. 24x32cm. [Z250.B562] 65-15691 10.00
1. Printing—Specimens. 2. Alphabets. I. Title.

BRUSHSTROKE and free-style alphabets : 686.2'24
100 complete fonts / selected and arr. by Dan X. Solo from the Solotype Typographers catalog. New York : Dover Publications, 1977. 100 p. ; 28 cm. (Dover pictorial archive series) [Z250.B888] 77-70048 ISBN 0-486-23488-6 pbk. : 3.00
1. Printing—Specimens. 2. Alphabets. I. Solo, Dan X. II. Solotype Typographers. BIP

BURNS, Aaron. 655.24
Typography. New York, Reinhold Pub. Corp., c1961. 111 p. illus. 37 cm. [Z250.B96] 61-14822
1. Printing—Specimens.

CARTER, Will, 1912- 686.2'24
Portfolio 2 : projects, backward glances, and jeux d'esprit / put together by Will and Sebastion Carter. Cambridge [Eng.] : Rampant Lions Press, 1974. 1 portfolio : ill. ; 28 cm. "This portfolio was concocted, designed and printed ... in an edition of about five hundred copies." [Z232.R17C37] 75-332423
1. Rampant Lions Press. 2. Printing—Specimens. I. Carter, Sebastian, joint author. II. Title.

COWELL (W. S.) ltd., Ipswich, Eng. 655.24
A book of typefaces, with some illustrated examples of text and display setting. Ipswich [1952] 74p. 26cm. [Z253.C84] 53-16952
1. Printing—Specimens. I. Title.

FRANKLIN Photolettering. 686.2'24
Modern display alphabets : 100 complete fonts / selected and arr. by Paul E. Kennedy, from the Franklin Photolettering catalogue. New York : Dover Publications, 1974. 100 p. ; 29 cm. [Z250.K4F7 1974] 74-79330 ISBN 0-486-23097-X pbk. : 2.50
1. Franklin Photolettering. 2. Printing—Specimens. I. Kennedy, Paul E. II. Title. BIP

GATES, David. 686.2'24
Type. New York, Watson-Guptill Publications [1973] 207 p. 31 cm. [Z250.G24] 72-10272 ISBN 0-8230-5522-1 8.95
1. Printing—Specimens. 2. Type and type-founding—History. I. Title. BIP

GRAPHIC Arts Typographers, inc., New York 655.24
Graphic arts typebook; v.1-2. New York, Reinhold [c.1965] 2v. (287;255p.) 30cm. Contents.v.1. Machine composition; serif faces.--v.2. Machine composition; sans serif, square serifs, miscellany. sorts [Z250.G74] 65-14035 5.95 ea.,
1. Printing—Specimens. I. Title.

HART, James David, 1911- 655.5'93
The private press ventures of Samuel Lloyd Osbourne and R. L. S., with facsimiles of their publications, by James D. Hart. [San Francisco] Book Club of California, 1966. 49 p. illus., facsims., port. 27 cm. (Book Club of California. Publication no. 123) "500 copies." "The Surprise, issues of March 6, March 20, June 1880; Davos news, issues of Dec. 17, Dec. 20, Dec. 22, 1880; Black Canyon; Not I, and other poems; To M. I. Stevenson; Moral emblems; Moral emblems, a second collection; The graver & the pen; Robin and Ben" (11 pamphlets) in pocket. [Z232.O7H35] 71-6498
1. Osbourne, Lloyd, 1868-1947. 2. Stevenson, Robert Louis, 1850-1894. 3. Printing—Specimens. I. Title. II. Series: Book Club of California, San Francisco. Publication no. 123

HUTCHINGS, Reginald Salis, 1915- ed. 655.24
A manual of decorated typefaces; a definitive guide to series in current use, including inline, outline, shaded, three-dimensional, stencil, cameo, halftone, with two-colour and embellished designs selected and arr. with an introd., commentaries and appendices, by R. S. Hutchings. New York, Hastings House [1965] 96 p. 26 cm. "Bibliographical note": p. 95. [Z250.H948 1965] 65-14976
1. Printing — Specimens. 2. Type and type-founding — Display type. I. Title.

HUTCHINGS, Reginald Salis, 1915- 655.24
The Western heritage of type design; a treasury of currently available typefaces demonstrating the historical development and diversification of form of printed letters. Selected and arr. with an introd., commentaries, and reference appendices [London] Cory, Adams & MacKay [New York, Hastings, 1965, c.1963] 127p. 26cm. Bibl. [Z250.H95] 65-7402 7.95
1. Printing—Specimens. I. Title.

ILLINOIS. Southern Illinois University, Carbondale. Printing Service. 655.24
Type faces. [Carbondale, 1958?] 1v. (unpaged) typog. specimens. 22cm. Cover title. [Z250.I4] A 58
1. Printing—Specimens. 2. Paper—Sample books. I. Title.

INTERTYPE Corporation, Brooklyn. 686.2'24
Intertype faces for photocomposition. [Brooklyn, N.Y., 1970?] [34] p. 27 cm. [Z250.I653] 72-196560
1. Printing—Specimens. I. Title.

JASPERT, W. Pincus. 686'.224
The encyclopaedia of type faces [by] W. Pincus Jaspert, W. Turner Berry [and] A. F. Johnson. [4th ed., entirely restyled and greatly enl.] New York, Barnes & Noble [1970] xiii, 420 p. 31 cm. In previous editions, W. T. Berry's name appeared first on t.p. [Z250.J36 1970] 70-22018 ISBN 0-389-04043-6
1. Printing—Specimens. I. Berry, William Turner, joint author. II. Johnson, Alfred Forbes, joint author. III. Title. IV. Title: Type faces.

LAMBERT, Frederick. 655.24
Letter forms, Formes de caracteres. Forme typografiche. Formas tipograficas. Buchstabenformen. New York, Hastings House [1964] 189 p. illus. 28 cm. (Visual communication books) [Z250.L237] 64-54842

1. Printing — Specimens. I. Title. BIP

LAMBERT, Frederick W. 686.2'24
Letter forms; 110 complete alphabets [by] Frederick Lambert. Edited by Theodore Menten. New York, Dover Publications [1972] 110 p. illus. 28 cm. [Z250.L237 1972] 70-182097 ISBN 0-486-22872-X 2.50
1. Printing—Specimens. I. Title.

LAMESLE, Claude. 655.2'4
The type-specimens. A facsimile of the first ed. printed at Paris in 1742. Introd. by A. F. Johnson. Amsterdam, Menno Hertzberger, 1965 [1966] 194p. 21cm. Tr. of Epreuves generales des caracteres qui setrouvent chez Claude Lemesle. [Z250.L2374 1742a] 68-81394 15.50 bds.,
1. Printing—Specimens. I. Title.
Distributed by Schram, New York.

LONGYEAR, William. 655.24
Type and lettering for typographers, letterers, designers; 350 selected styles. New York, Watson-Guptill, 1950. 128 p. illus. 31 cm. [Z250.L8518] 50-10402
1. Printing—Specimens. I. Title.

LONGYEAR, William Levwyn, 1899- 655.24
A dictionary of modern type faces and lettering, by William Longyear... 3d ed. rev.... Pelham, N.Y., Bridgman publishers, inc., 1936. 130 l. 23 cm. Text runs parrel with back of cover. [Z250.L85 1936] 37-838
1. Printing — Specimens. 2. Type and type-founding. I. Title.

LONGYEAR, William Levwyn, 1899- 655.24
Type & lettering [by] William Longyear. 4th ed., rev. and enl. New York, Watson-Guptill Publications [1966] 175 p. illus. 32 cm. [Z250.L8518 1966] 66-19739
1. Printing—Specimens. I. Title.

LONGYEAR, William Levwyn, 1899- 655.24
Type and lettering, for typographers, letterers, designers, 350 selected styles. New York, Watson-Guptill, 1950. 128 p. illus. 23 x 31 cm. [Z250.L8518 1950] 50-10402
1. Printing — Specimens. I. Title. BIP

LONGYEAR, William Levwyn, 1899- 655.21
Type and lettering, 350 selected styles: for students. typographers. letters, designers. Rev. ed. New York. Watson-Guptill Publications [1956] 124p. illus. 23 x 31cm. [Z250.L8518 1956] 56-2157
1. Printing—Specimens. I. Title.

LONGYEAR, William Levwyn, 1899- 655.24
Type & lettering for students, designers, letterers, typographers [Rev. ed.] New York, Watson-Guptill Publications [1961] 139p. illus. 23 x 31cm. [Z250.L8518 1961] 61-15098
1. Printing—Specimens. I. Title.

LONGYEAR, William Levwyn, 1899- 655.24
Type specimens for layout, printing, lettering, by William Longyear... New York, N.Y., Watson-Guptill publications, inc., c1940. ix, 116 p. illus. 23 x 30 cm. Text runs parallel with back of cover. Bibliography: p. 15. [Z250.L852] 41-6289
1. Printing — Specimens. I. Title.

MAURICE Jacobs, inc. 682.2'24
Maurice Jacobs, inc.; [type specimen book ... 20th anniversary of the founding of Maurice Jacobs, inc.] Philadelphia, 1970. 254 p. illus. 23 cm. [Z250.M38 1970] 73-168091
1. Printing—Specimens.

MERGENTHALER Linotype Company. 655.24
One-line specimens of linotype faces. Brooklyn [1950] xiv, 229 p. illus. 27 cm. [Z250.M4852] 51-659
1. Printing — Specimens. 2. Linotype. I. Title.

MERRIMAN, Frank. 411
A. T. A. type comparison book. [New York, Advertising Typographers Association of America, 1965] xv, 133 p. illus., facsims. 27 cm. [Z250.M57] 65-4289
1. Printing — Specimens. I. Advertising Typographers Association of America. II. Title.

THE Milwaukee journal. 655.24
Type faces and production techniques for creating effective advertisements. 3d ed. [Milwaukee, 1958] 174p. illus. 29cm. [Z250.M66 1958] 58-3399
1. Printing—Specimens. I. Title.

THE Milwaukee journal. 655.24
Type faces and production techniques for creating effective advertisements. [Milwaukee, 1950] 148 p. illus. 29 cm. "The Milwaukee journal type selector" (fold. leaf) laid in. [Z250.M66] 51-4148
1. Printing — Specimens. I. Title.

MONSEN Typographers, inc. 411
Monsen type library. Chicago, c1961. 2v. 32cm. [Z250.M78 1961] 62-5002
1. Printing—Specimens. I. Title.

MORGAN Press. 655.24
Morgan Press types; specimen lines from original foundry types in the Morgan Press collection from 1786 to 1960. Scarsdale, N. Y. [1960] 88 p. 24 cm. Imprint covered by label: Hastings-on-Hudson, N. Y., Morgan Press. [Z250.M854] 60-13692
1. Printing — Specimens. I. Title.

THE News, New York,1919- 655.24
The News type book. Produced in the mechanical departments of the New York News. Limited ed. [New York] News Syndicate Co., c1950. vii, 109 p. illus. 31 cm. "Reproduced ... are all the type faces and sizes tht are available in the composing room of the New York News." [Z250.N55] 51-1048
1. Printing — Specimens. I. Daily news, New York, 1919- II. Title.

NORTH Central Publishing Company. 655.2'4
North Central printing types. Saint Paul, 1967. 2 v. 24 cm. Contents.Contents.—v. 1. Monotype, foundry type, and Ludlow faces.—v. 2. Linotype and monotype text faces. [Z250.N635] 68-1438
1. Printing—Specimens. I. Title.

PAUL A. Bennett private press keepsake. 655
Gathered together by friends and typophiles. New York, The Typophiles [1969] 62 pieces (in case) 19 cm. Includes general t.p. with foreword by Charles Antin, 60 separately printed tributes, and list of contributors. 200 copies, distributed solely to the contributors. [Z239.A1P38] 73-5638
1. Bennett, Paul A., 1897-1966. 2. The Typophiles, New York. 3. Printing—Specimens. 4. Private presses. I. Bennett, Paul A., 1897-1966.

ROSEN, Ben. 686.2'24
Type and typography : the designer's type book / by Ben Rosen. Rev. ed. New York : Van Nostrand Reinhold Co., 1976. 406 p. : ill. ; 30 cm. Includes bibliographical references and index. [Z250.R79 1976] 75-43153 ISBN 0-442-27020-8 : 9.95
1. Printing—Specimens. I. Title.

SHIELDS, John Warnock, 1888- 655.24
Shields type manual. Bridgeport, Conn., c1951. 163 p. illus. 30 cm. [Z250.S56] 51-7678
1. Printing—Specimens. I. Title.

SUTTON, James, 1929- 655.2'4
An atlas of typeforms [by] James Sutton and Alan Bartram. [1st American ed.] New York, Hastings House [1968] 116 p. illus., facsims. 41 cm. (Visual communication books) [Z250.S935 1968] 68-24227
1. Printing—Specimens. I. Bartram, Alan, joint author. II. Title.

TILLOTSONS (Bolton) Ltd. 655.24
Type specimen book, incorporating the house style of typesetting and standard printers' and authors' proof corrections. [New ed.] Bolton [Eng., 1952] 133p. 26cm. [Z250.T5 1952] 53-39088
1. Printing—Specimens. I. Title.

V & M Typographical, inc. 686.2'24
The type specimen book; 544 different typefaces with over 3000 sizes shown in complete alphabets. New York, Van Nostrand Reinhold [1974] xxiv, 622 p. 29 cm. [Z250.V115 1974] 74-5951 ISBN 0-442-27916-7
1. Printing—Specimens. I. Title.

VICTORIAN display alphabets : 686.2'24
100 complete fonts / selected and arranged by Dan X. Solo from the Solotype Typographers catalog. New York : Dover Publications, 1976. 100 p. : all ill. ; 28 cm. (Dover pictorial archive series) [Z250.V53] 75-44586 ISBN 0-486-23302-2 pbk. : 3.00
1. Printing—Specimens. I. Solo, Dan X. II. Solotype Typographers. BIP

VISUAL Graphics Corporation. 686.2'24
The world-famous photo typositor alphabet library. New ed. [North Miami, Fla.] c1973. xi, 270 p. illus. 28 cm. [Z250.V67 1973] 74-75693
1. Printing—Specimens. 2. Type and type-founding—Display type. 3. Phototypesetting. I. Title. II. Title: Phototypositor alphabet library.

WALKLIN, Carol. 686.2'24
Designing with letters. New York, Drake Publishers [1974] p. cm. [Z250.W236] 74-5969 ISBN 0-87749-702-8 7.95
1. Printing—Specimens. 2. Signs and symbols. 3. Lettering. I. Title.

WEBB-LINN Printing Company, Chicago. 655.24
The Webb-Linn type book . . . [Designed and written by L. J. Weber and A. J. Falick] Chicago [1951] 243 p. illus. 24 cm. [Z250.W4] 51-6702
1. Printing — Specimens. I. Title.

WESTERN Typesetting Company. 686.2'24
The Western book of alphabets / Western Typesetting Company. 1st ed. Chicago : The Company, c1976- 1 v. ; 30 cm. On cover: Western type—book of alphabets. Loose-leaf for updating. "A complement to the Western book of keyboard composition faces." [Z250.W47 1976] 76-46825
1. Printing—Specimens. 2. Type and typefounding. I. Title.

WOOD type alphabets : 686.2'24
100 fonts / edited by Rob Roy Kelly. New York : Dover Publications, 1977. 100 p. : all ill. ; 28 cm. (Dover pictorial archive series) [Z250.W86 1977] 77-78607 ISBN 0-486-23533-5 : 3.50
1. Printing—Specimens. I. Kelly, Rob Roy. BIP

ZAPF, Hermann. 686.2'24
Manuale typographicum: 100 typographical arrangements with considerations about types, typography and the art of printing selected from past and present, printed in eighteen languages. Frankfurt, New York, Z-Presse, 1968. 119 l. 31 cm. Copy no. 174, signed by the author. [Z250.Z332] 655.24 79-411580 unpriced
1. Printing—Specimens. 2. Type and type-founding. 3. Books—Quotations, maxims, etc. I. Title.

ZAPF, Hermann. 655.2
Manuale typographicum. Cambridge, Mass., M.I.T. Press [1970] 123 l. 17 x 25 cm. On cover: 100 typographic pages with quotations from the past and present on types and printing in 16 different languages. On spine: MIT 147. Prefatory matter, annotations, and translations of texts from the typographic pages are in English. Includes bibliographical references. [Z250.Z325] 76-110239 5.95
1. Printing—Specimens. 2. Type and type-founding. 3. Books—Quotations, maxims, etc. I. Title. BIP

Printing — Specimens — Fine books — Bibl.

HENRY E. Huntington Library and Art Gallery. 094.074019493
Great books in great editions. Selected and described by Roland Baughman and Robert O. Schad. [Rev. ed.] San Marino, 1965. 65 p. illus., facsims. 25 cm. "Original edition ... was a catalogue of an exhibition held in 1940 at the Huntington Library." [Z121.H55] 65-5679
1. Printing — Specimens — Fine books — Bibl. 2. Bibliography — Rare books. I. Baughman, Roland Orvil, 1902- II. Schad, Robert Oliver, 1900- III. Title. BIP

Printmakers—Addresses, essays, lectures.

PRINT collector's quarterly : 769
an anthology of essays on eminent printmakers of the world / edited by Lauris Mason and Joan Ludman. Millwood, N.Y. : KTO Press, 1977. 10 v. (cxlvi, 6598 p.) : ill. ; 19 cm. Consists partly of selections from the Print collector's quarterly. Includes index. [NE400.P74] 77-161 ISBN 0-527-62205-2 lib.bdg. : 475.00 (set)
1. Printmakers—Addresses, essays, lectures. 2. Prints—Addresses, essays, lectures. I. Mason, Lauris. II. Ludman, Joan.

Printmakers—Belgium—Biography.

RIGGS, Timothy A., 1942- 769'.92'4 B
Hieronymus Cock, printmaker and publisher / Timothy A. Riggs. New York : Garland Pub., 1977, i.e.1978 xxxii, 416 p., [68] leaves of plates : ill. ; 21 cm. (Outstanding dissertations in the fine arts) Originally presented as the author's thesis, Yale, 1971. Bibliography: p. 395-416. [NE674.C6R43 1977] 76-23706 ISBN 0-8240-2724-8 lib.bdg. : 52.50
1. Cock, Hieronymus, 1510 (ca.)-1570. 2. Printmakers—Belgium—Biography. I. Title. II. Series.

Printmakers—England—Biography.

MITZMAN, Max E. 769'.92'4 B
George Baxter and the Baxter prints / Max E. Mitzman. Newton Abbot [Eng.] ; North Pomfret, Vt. : David and Charles, c1978. 176 p. : ill. (Chiefly col.) ; 24 cm. Includes indexes. Bibliography: p. [169] [NE1860.B2M57] 78-52165 ISBN 0-7153-7629-2 : 17.95
1. Baxter, George, 1804-1867. 2. Printmakers—England—Biography. 3. Color prints, English. I. Baxter, George, 1804-1867. II. Title. BIP

Printmakers—Japan—Biography.

BLAKEMORE, Frances. 769'.92'2 B
Who's who in modern Japanese prints / by Frances Blakemore. 1st ed. New York : Weatherhill, 1975. 263 p. : ill. ; 22 cm. [NE771.B55] 74-28174 ISBN 0-8348-0101-9 : 12.50
1. Printmakers—Japan—Biography. I. Title. BIP

STRANGE, Edward Fairbrother, 1862-1929. 760'.092'4 B
Hokusai, the old man mad with painting / by Edward F. Strange. Folcroft, Pa. : Folcroft Library Editions, 1977. 71 p., [9] leaves of plates : ill. ; 22 cm. Reprint of the 1906 ed. published by Siegel, Hill, London, which was issued as v. 17 of the Langham series. [NE1325.K3S77 1977] 77-357 ISBN 0-8414-7753-1 lib. bdg. : 10.00
1. Katsushika, Hokusai, 1760-1849. 2. Printmakers—Japan—Biography. I. Title. II. Series: The Langham series ; v. 17. BIP

Printmakers—United States—Biography.

ZIGROSSER, Carl, 1891- 769'.92'2 B
The artist in America : contemporary printmakers / by Carl Zigrosser. New York : Hacker Art Books, 1978, c1942. xxi, 207, v p., [46] leaves of plates : ill. ; 25 cm. Reprint of the 1st ed. published by Knopf, New York. Includes index. [NE508.Z45 1978] 77-73724 ISBN 0-87817-215-7 lib bdg : 30.00
1. Printmakers—United States—Biography. 2. Prints—20th century—United States. I. Title. BIP

Prints.

BEST engravings / 769
Skip Whitson, editor. Albuquerque, N.M. : Sun Pub. Co., 1975- v. ; ill. ; 28 cm. [NE486.B47] 76-357091 ISBN 0-914172-02-6. pbk. : 15.00
1. Prints. I. Whitson, Skip. BIP

CASTLEMAN, Riva. 769'.92'2
Contemporary prints. New York, Viking Press [1973] 172 p. illus. (part col.) 32 cm. (A Studio book) [NE490.C37 1973] 73-2338 ISBN 0-670-23986-0 38.50
1. Prints. 2. Printmakers. I. Title.

CASTLEMAN, Riva. 769'.904
Prints of the twentieth century / [by] Riva Castleman. London : Thames and Hudson, 1976. 216 p. : ill. (some col.) ; 22 cm. Includes index. Bibliography: p. 210-214. [NE490.C39] 76-373505 ISBN 0-500-18155-1 : £4.50
1. Prints. I. Title. **BIP**

HEGEDUS, Laszlo, 1920- 769'.994
Prints by Laszlo Hegedus. Introduction by Andor Meszaros. Melbourne [The Author, Flat 16, 20 Cardigan Street, East St. Kilda, Vic. 3183] 1969. 12 l. illus. 37 x 52 cm. Limited ed. of 75 numbered copies containing signed original prints; no. 48. Prints appearing in book form have been numbered from 76-150; print no. 123. Bibliography: leaf 2. [NE1171.H8H45] 79-870649 ISBN 0-9599996-0-4 75.00

IVINS, William Mills, 1881-1961. v. 12
How prints look: photographs with a commentary. Boston, Beacon Press [1958] 164 p. illus. 21 cm. (Beacon paperback, BP57) "Photographic reproduction of ... the first edition ... published by the Metropolitan Museum of Art ... in 1943." [NE863.I] A 60
1. Prints. I. New York. Metropolitan Museum of Art. II. Title.

LONGSTREET, Stephen, 1907- 769
A treasury of the world's great prints; a collection of the best-known woodcuts, etchings, engravings, and lithographs by twenty-three great artists, selected and presented by Stephen Longstreet. New York, Simon and Schuster [1961] 333 p. illus. (part col.) 31 cm. [NE900.L6] 61-12867
1. Prints. 2. Printmakers. I. Title.

PRINT Club, Cleveland. 769
The Print Club of Cleveland, 1919-1969. Cleveland [1969] 171 p. illus. 24 cm. [NE1.P6625] 78-104902
I. Title.

SACHS, Paul Joseph, 1878-1965. 769
Modern prints & drawings; a guide to a better understanding of modern draughtsmanship. Selected and with an explanatory text by Paul J. Sachs. New York, Knopf [1954] 261 p. illus. 27 cm. [NE940.S3] 54-6137
1. Prints. 2. Drawings. I. Title.

SIBLIK, Jiri. 769'.904
Twentieth-century prints [translated from the Czech by Till Gottheiner] London, New York, Hamlyn, 1970. 155 p. illus. (some col.), ports. 32 cm. [NE490.S49] 72-180439 ISBN 0-600-01659-5 £3.50
1. Prints. I. Title.

WECHSLER, Herman Joel, 1904- 769'.922
Great prints & printmakers [by] Herman J. Wechsler. New York, Abrams [1967] 244 p. illus., 100 plates (part col.) 33 cm. Bibliography: p. 244. [NE900.W35] 67-12686
1. Prints. 2. Printmakers. I. Title. **BIP**

ZIGROSSER, Carl, 1891- 769
The appeal of prints. [Philadelphia, Leary's Book Co., 1970] 151 p. illus. 23 cm. [NE400.Z54] 72-140388 12.50
1. Prints. I. Title.

ZIGROSSER, Carl, 1891- 769
Prints and their creators : a world history : an anthology of printed pictures and introduction to the study of graphic art in the West and the East / by Carl Zigrosser. 2d rev. ed. New York : Crown Publishers, [1974] vii, 136 p., [159] leaves of plates : 738 ill. ; 29 cm. Published in 1937 under title: Six centuries of fine prints; in 1948 and 1956 under title: The book of fine prints. Includes indexes. Bibliography: p. [115]-116. [NE430.Z5 1974] 74-80293 ISBN 0-517-51592-X : 14.95
1. Prints. I. Title.

Prints—15th century—Exhibitions.

GINGOLD, Diane J. 769'.94
Master prints from the fifteenth through eighteenth centuries : from the collection of Mr. and Mrs. Adolph Weil, Jr. : [exhibition] September 11 through November 6, 1977, Montgomery Museum of Fine Arts, Montgomery, Alabama, July 2 through August 14, 1978, Museum of Fine Arts, St. Petersburg, Florida. Montgomery, Ala. : Montgomery Museum of Fine Arts, 1977. 120 p. : ill. ; 28 cm. Catalog by D. J. Gingold. Includes index. [NE57.W44G56] 77-84545 ISBN 0-89280-007-0 pbk. : 9.00
1. Weil, Adolph—Art collections—Exhibitions. 2. Prints—15th century—Exhibitions. 3. Prints—16th century—Exhibitions. 4. Prints—17th century—Exhibitions. 5. Prints—18th century—Exhibitions. I. Montgomery Museum of Fine Arts. II. St. Petersburg, Fla. Museum of Fine Arts. III. Title. **BIP**

Prints—20th century.

†CASTLEMAN, Riva. 769'.904
Prints of the twentieth century : a history : with ill. from the collection of The Museum of Modern Art / Riva Castleman. New York : The Museum : distributed by Oxford University Press, 1976. 216 p. : ill. (some col.) ; 22 cm. Includes index. Bibliography: p. 210-214. [NE490.C39 1976b] 75-34694 ISBN 0-87070-520-2 : 12.50. pbk. : 7.95
1. Prints—20th century. I. New York (City). Museum of Modern Art. II. Title.

Prints, American.

AMERICAN prints, 1870-1950 / edited by Robert Flynn Johnson 769'.973
Chicago : University of Chicago Press, c1976. vi, 34 p. ; 21 cm. & microfiche (1 sheet : all ill. (some col.) ; 11 x 15 cm.) in pocket. At head of title: The Baltimore Museum of Art. "Based on an exhibition held at the Baltimore Museum of Art in 1974." Bibliography: p. 29-34. [NE507.A44] 76-13195 ISBN 0-226-68824-0 : 9.95
1. Prints, American. I. Johnson, Robert Flynn. II. Baltimore. Museum of Art.

CLIFT, John R. 769'.924
The alienation box [by] John R. Clift. Boston, Beacon Press [1971] 1 v. (chiefly illus.) 27 cm. [NE2237.5.C54A43 1971] 73-159845 ISBN 0-8070-6656-7 12.50
I. Title.

DUNN, Eugenia V 759.13
Portfolio, by Eugenia V. Dunn. [Little Rock? Ark.] 1964- no. plates, 36 cm. "Limited [to] 200 copies." [NE539.D77A54] 66-58074
I. Title.

EBERT, John. 769'.973
Old American prints for collectors [by John & Katherine Ebert. New York, Scribner [1974] ix, 277 p. illus. (part col.) 26 cm. Bibliography: p. 269-272. [NE505.E23] 73-19685 ISBN 0-684-13635-X 9.95
1. Prints, American. 2. Prints—Collectors and collecting. I. Ebert, Katherine, joint author. II. Title.

GREGORY, Albert. 769'.924
Leaves. Cambridge, Mass., 1968. [4] l., 32 col. plates, [1] l. 36 cm. Plates on folds numbered 1-16. Issued in portfolio (38 cm.) "100 copies." This copy designated "artist's proof A.6." [NE539.G7A45] 70-3616
I. Title.

HINDMAN, W C 769.973
Prairie coal and buffalo grass, gathered by 'Hiney' [pseud.] Hollywood, c1960. 1v. (chiefly illus.) 29x41cm. [NE2210.H5A5] 61-24041
I. Title.

KENT, Corita, 1918- 769'.924
Damn every thing but the circus; a lot of things put together. [1st ed.] New York, Holt, Rinehart and Winston [1970] 1 v. (unpaged) illus. (part col.) 28 cm. [NE2237.5.K4A44] 72-117263 ISBN 0-03-084884-9 12.50
I. Title.

NEW York (State). State University College, Buffalo. 769'.973
Centennial 1971, State University College at Buffalo. [Buffalo, 1971] 1 portfolio ([4] l., 12 plates) 50 cm. [NE508.N43] 73-160669
1. Prints, American. I. Title.

ROELOF-LANNER, V., ed. 769.973
Prints by American Negro artists. Los Angeles, Cultural Exchange Ctr. [c.1965] [11]p., [51] illus. (pt. col.) 31cm. [NE508.R6] 65-24998 price unreported
1. Prints, American. 2. Negro art. I. Title.

RUTHERFORD, Meg. 769'.924
The beautiful island. [1st ed.] Garden City, N.Y., Doubleday [1969] [71] p. (chiefly illus.) 20 x 24 cm. [NE789.R8] 72-78663 4.00 (special gift ed.)
I. Title.

WEITENKAMPF, Frank, 1866-1962. 769'.973
American graphic art. New York, H. Holt, 1912. Detroit, Gale Research Co., 1974 i.e.1975 x, 372 p. illus. 22 cm. [NE505.W4 1974] 74-6198 ISBN 0-8103-4020-8 15.00
1. Prints, American. I. Title. **BIP**

Prints, American—Catalogs.

MUSEUM of Graphic Art. 769'.973
American printmaking, the first 150 years. Pref. by A. Hyatt Mayor. Foreword by Donald H. Karshan. Introd. by J. William Middendorf II. Text by Wendy J. Shadwell. [New York, 1969] 180 p. illus. (part col.), ports. 26 cm. Bibliography: p. 175-178. [NE505.M8] 71-75748
1. Prints, American—Catalogs. I. Title.

TYLER, Valton, 1944- 769'.92'4
The first fifty prints, Valton Tyler. Text by Rebecca Reynolds. Dallas, Published for Valley House Gallery by Southern Methodist University Press [1972] 154 p. illus. 23 x 27 cm. [NE2012.T9R4] 75-189304 ISBN 0-87074-001-6 15.00
I. Reynolds, Rebecca. II. Title.
Pap. $12.50, ISBN 0-87074-002-4

U.S. Library of Congress. Prints and Photographs Division. 769'.973
American prints in the Library of Congress; a catalog of the collection. Compiled by Karen F. Beall and the staff of the Prints and Photographs Division of the Library of Congress. With an introd. by Alan Fern and a foreword by Carl Zigrosser. Baltimore, Published for the Library of Congress by the Johns Hopkins Press [1970] xxi, 568 p. illus. 27 cm. Bibliography: p. 541-547. [NE505.A47] 73-106134
1. Prints, American—Catalogs. 2. Prints—Washington, D.C.—Catalogs. I. Beall, Karen F., 1938- II. Title. **BIP**

Prints, American—Exhibitions.

[AMERICAN Artists' Congress] 769'.973'07413
Graphic works of the American thirties : a book of 100 prints. 1st paperback ed. New York : Da Capo Press, 1977. 14 p., 100 leaves of plates : chiefly ill. ; 28 cm. (A Da Capo paperback) Reprint of the 1936 ed. published by Equinox Cooperative Press, New York under title: America today; a book of 100 prints chosen and exhibited by the American Artists' Congress. [NE508.A55 1977] 77-371424 ISBN 0-306-80078-0 : 7.95
1. Prints, American—Exhibitions. 2. Prints—20th century—United States—Exhibitions. I. Title.

AVATI, Mario, 1921- 769'.924
Avati; prints from 1957 to 1967. [Los Angeles, 1967] [14] p. illus., port., 8 plates. 32 cm. Catalogue of an exhibition presented by the Grunwald Graphic Arts Foundation at the Dickson Art Center, University of California, Los Angeles, Feb. 27-Apr. 2, 1967. [NE650.A9A43] 73-215189
I. Grunwald Graphic Art Foundation. II. Dickson Art Center.

BARO, Gene. 769'.973'074014723
30 years of American printmaking, including the 20th National print exhibition / by Gene Baro Brooklyn : Brooklyn Museum ; New York : available to the trade only through Universe Books, [1976] 160 p. : ill. (some col.) ; 22 x 27 cm. Catalog of an exhibition held Nov. 20, 1976-Jan. 30, 1977. Includes indexes. [NE508.B27] 76-17486 ISBN 0-87663-249-5 : 15.00 ISBN 0-87273-058-1 pbk. : 8.95
1. Prints, American—Exhibitions. 2. Printmakers—United States. I. Brooklyn Institute of Arts and Sciences. Museum. II. Title: 30 years of American printmaking ...

BARO, Gene. 769'.973'074014723
Twenty-first national print exhibition / by Gene Baro. Brooklyn, N.Y. : Brooklyn Museum, c1978. 204 p. : ill. ; 24 cm. Catalog of the exhibition held Dec. 9, 1978-Feb. 11, 1979 at the Brooklyn Museum, Brooklyn, N.Y. Includes indexes. [NE508.B28] 78-26421 ISBN 0-87273-072-7 : 8.95
1. Prints, American—Exhibitions. 2. Prints—20th century—United States—Exhibitions. I. Brooklyn Institute of Arts and Sciences. Museum. II. Title. **BIP**

CASTELMAN, Riva. 769'.973'074094933
American prints, 1913-1963 : catalogue / by Riva Castelman Bruxelles : Bibliotheque royale Albert Ier, 1976. 152, [9] p. : 112 ill. ; 26 cm. "An exhibition circulated under the auspices of the International Council of the [Museum of] Modern Art, New York. Brussels 27.3-8.5.1976." "D/1976/0020/3." [NE508.C37] 76-364052
1. Prints, American—Exhibitions. I. Bibliotheque royale Albert Ier. II. International Council of the Museum of Modern Art, New York. III. Title.

CINCINNATI. Art Museum. 769'.973
San Francisco area printmakers. [Exhibition held at] the Cincinnati Art Museum, January 12 to March 18, 1973. [Cincinnati, 1973] [23] p. illus. 26 cm. Catalog: p. [8]-[18] [NE535.S26C56] 73-170353
1. Prints, American—Exhibitions. 2. Printmakers—San Francisco Bay region. I. Title.

DALLAS. Museum of Fine Arts. 760'.09764'07401642812
20th century united States fancy cancelations / exhibition dates, October 8-November 23, 1975. by Foster W. Loso and Heyliger de Windt. c6 [Dallas] : Dallas Museum of Fine Arts, 1975. [8] p. : ill. ; 28 cm. [NE524.6.D34 1975] 76-351665 1.50
1. Prints, American—Exhibitions. 2. Prints—Southwest, New—Exhibitions. 3. Drawings, American—Exhibitions. 4. Drawings—Southwest, New—Exhibitions. I. Title.

HONOLULU Academy of Arts. 769'.973'0740996931
1st Hawaii National Print Exhibition; [catalogue] Honolulu, Printed by the Star-Bulletin Print. Co.] 1971. [27] p. illus. 26 cm. Organized by and held at the Honolulu Academy of Arts, Feb. 4-Mar. 7, 1971. [NE508.H58] 72-192530
1. Prints, American—Exhibitions. I. Title.

HONOLULU Academy of Arts. 769'.973'0740996931
2d Hawaii National Print Exhibition, April 27-May 27, 1973; [catalogue] Honolulu, Printed by Edward Enterprises, 1973] [27] p. illus. 26 cm. [NE508.H58 1973] 74-160764
1. Prints, American—Exhibitions. I. Title.

HOOVER, Francis Louis, 1913- comp. 769'.973'07401471
Young printmakers. Edited by F. Louis Hoover. Normal, Ill., Art Resource Publications [1964-69] 2 v. (chiefly plates) 31 cm. Issued in portfolios. The prints in v. 1 were selected for the national high school print show on display at the Metropolitan Museum of Art in 1964. Vol. 2 has title: Young printmakers II; outstanding prints by high school students. Vol. 2 has imprint: Worcester, Mass., Art Resource Publications. [NE508.H6] 64-21686
1. Prints, American—Exhibitions. 2. Youth as artists. I. New York (City). Metropolitan Museum of Art. II. Title. III. Title: Young printmakers II.

IOWA. State University 769'.973
of Science and Technology, Ames. Design Center.
American prints: 72. Exhibition dates: April 1 to April 30, 1972, Memorial Union Gallery, Ames, Iowa. May 22 to June 22, 1972, Davenport Municipal Art Gallery, Davenport, Iowa Ames [1972] [36] p. illus. 26 cm. [NE508.I58] 73-172177
1. Prints, American—Exhibitions. I. Memorial Union Gallery. II. Davenport Municipal Art Gallery, Davenport, Iowa. III. Title.

LOS Angeles Co., Calif. 769'.973
Otis Art Institute, Los Angeles.
Biennial national invitational print exhibition. 1st-1962- Los Angeles. v. illus. 22 cm. Title varies: 1962. National annual print invitational exhibition. -- 1963. National invitational print exhibition. [NE508.L6] 67-6707
1. Prints, American — Exhibitions. I. Los Angeles Co., Calif. Otis Art Institute, Los Angeles. National annual print invitational exhibition. II. Title.

NEW York 769'.973'074014743
(State). State University, Albany. Art Gallery.
Big prints. [Albany, 1968] [52] p. (chiefly illus.) 25 cm. Cover title. Catalog of an invitational exhibition held Feb. 16-Mar. 24, 1968 at the Art Gallery, State University of New York at Albany. [NE508.N42] 70-635004
1. Prints, American—Exhibitions. I. Title.

PHILADELPHIA. Library 769'.973
Company.
Made in America: printmaking, 1760-1860; an exhibition of original prints from the collections of the Library Company of Philadelphia and the Historical Society of Pennsylvania, April-June, 1973. Philadelphia, 1973. iv, 59, [3] p. 48 plates. 23 cm. Bibliography: p. [60]-[62] [NE506.P48] 73-161317
1. Prints, American—Exhibitions. I. Pennsylvania. Historical Society. II. Title.

PRINTS 769'.9794'074019466
California : profile of an exhibition / co-sponsored by the California Society of Printmakers, the San Francisco Foundation, Administrators of the Phelan Awards ; Therese Thau Heyman, editor and compiler. [Oakland, Calif.] : Oakland Museum, 1975. [44] p. : ill. ; 23 cm. Catalog of the exhibition held Apr. 29-July 6, 1975 at the Oakland Museum, and Aug. 1-Sept. 2, 1975 at the Contemporary Graphics Center of the Santa Barbara Museum of Art. [NE535.C2P74] 75-13934
1. Prints, American—Exhibitions. 2. Prints—California—Exhibitions. 3. Printmakers—California. I. Heyman, Therese Thau. II. Oakland Museum. III. Santa Barbara, Calif. Museum of Art. Contemporary Graphics Center.

SOLOMON, Elke. 769.973'074'01471
Oversize prints. New York, Whitney Museum of American Art [1971] 32 p. illus. 28 cm. Catalogue of an exhibition held Nov. 2-Dec. 12, 1971. [NE508.S65] 74-182378
1. Prints, American—Exhibitions. I. Whitney Museum of American Art, New York. II. Title.

WALKER Art Center, 769'.973
Minneapolis.
Johns, Kelly, Lichtenstein, Motherwell, Nauman, Rauschenberg, Serra, Stella : prints from Gemini G.E.L. : an exhibition organized by Walker Art Center. [Minneapolis : The Center, 1974] 40 p. : ill. ; 28 cm. Held at Walker Art Center, Minneapolis, Aug. 17-Sept. 29, 1974, and at various other institutions through Aug. 1975. [NE508.W34 1974] 74-13773
1. Gemini G. E. L. (Firm) 2. Prints, American—Exhibitions. I. Gemini G. E. L. (Firm) II. Title. III. Title: Prints from Gemini G. E. L.

WALKER Art Center, 769'.973
Minneapolis.
Printmakers Midwest invitational. [Minneapolis, 1973] 1 v. (unpaged) illus. 28 cm. Catalog of an exhibition organized by the Center; shown there Sept. 9-Oct. 21, 1973, and later at four other museums. [NE518.W34 1973] 73-87443
1. Prints, American—Exhibitions. 2. Printmakers—Middle West. I. Title.

Prints, American—History.

GURDUS, Melissa. 760
Electronic variations. [Madison, Wis., 1966] 1 v. illus. 25 cm. Folding book; illus. on continuous strip, 24 x 704 cm. "Thirty copies ... printed from the original plates at the University of Wisconsin ... Number 11." Signed: M. C. Gurdus. [NE539.G8A44] 77-8752
I. Title.

MAYOR, Alpheus Hyatt, 769'.973
1901-
Popular prints of the Americas, by A. Hyatt Mayor. New York, Crown Publishers [1973] 183 p. (chiefly illus. (part col.)) 35 cm. Bibliography: p. 177. [NE501.M38 1973] 73-82943 ISBN 0-517-50601-7 15.95
1. Prints—America—History. I. Title. BIP

WINTERTHUR Conference on 769'.973
Museum Operation and Connoisseurship, 16th, 1970.
Prints in and of America to 1850. Edited by John D. Morse. Charlottesville, University Press of Virginia [1970] xx, 355 p. illus., facsims., ports. 23 cm. (Winterthur conference report, 1970) "Published for the Henry Francis du Pont Winterthur Museum." Includes bibliographical references. [NE505.W55 1970] 76-135506 ISBN 0-8139-0323-8
1. Prints, American—History. 2. Graphic arts, American—History. I. Morse, John D., 1906- ed. II. Henry Francis du Pont Winterthur Museum. III. Title. IV. Series: Winterthur Conference on Museum Operation and Connoisseurship. Report, 1970 BIP

Prints, Australian.

KEMPF, Franz, 1926- 769'.92'2 B
Contemporary Australian printmakers / Franz Kempf. Melbourne : Landsdowne, 1976. 100, 32 p. : ill. ; 31 cm. Includes Directory of Australian printmakers, 1976. Bibliography: p. 100. [NE789.4.K45] 77-365474 ISBN 0-7018-0469-6
1. Prints, Australian. 2. Prints—20th century—Australia. 3. Printmakers—Australia—Biography. 4. Printmakers—Australia—Directories. I. Directory of Australian printmakers. 1976. II. Title.

Prints, Austrian—Catalogs.

BINNEY, Edwin. 793.3'08 s
A century of Austro-German dance prints, 1790-1890. [New York, Dance Perspectives Foundation, 1971, c1970] 76 p. illus. 23 cm. (Dance perspectives, 47) Bibliography: p. 55-56. [GV1580.D27 no. 47] [NE643.3] 769'.4'97933 77-172958 2.95
1. Prints, Austrian—Catalogs. 2. Prints, German—Catalogs. 3. Dancing in art. I. Title. II. Series.

Prints, Austrian—Exhibitions.

SOTRIFFER, Kristian, 1932- 760
Contemporary graphic art from Austria. [Vienna, Schroll-Presse, 1969?] 47, [5] p. illus. 29 cm. Exhibition under the auspices of the Austrian Federal Ministry of Education and the Wiener Secession. Bibliography: p. [51] [NE643.4.S6] 72-197947
1. Prints, Austrian—Exhibitions. I. Austria. Bundesministerium fur Unterricht. II. Vereinigung Bildender Kunstler "Wiener Secession." III. Title.

Prints—Bibliography.

MASON, Lauris. 016.769'92'2
Print reference sources : a select bibliography, 18th-20th centuries / compiled by Lauris Mason ; assisted by Joan Ludman. Millwood, N.Y. : Kraus-Thomson Organization, 1975. ix, 246 p. ; 26 cm. [Z5947.A3M37] [NE850] 74-79901 ISBN 0-527-00372-7
1. Prints—Bibliography. 2. Printmakers—Bibliography. I. Ludman, Joan. II. Title. BIP

Prints—Boston—Congresses.

BOSTON prints and 015'.744'61 s
printmakers, 1670-1775; a conference held by the Colonial Society of Massachusetts, 1 and 2 April 1971. Boston, Colonial Society of Massachusetts; distributed by the University Press of Virginia [Charlottesville, 1973] xxv, 294 p. illus. 25 cm. (Publications of the Colonial Society of Massachusetts, v. 46) Includes bibliographical references. [F61.C71 vol. 46] [NE538] 769'.9744'61 72-96131 15.00
1. Prints—Boston—Congresses. 2. Printmakers—Boston—Congresses. I. Colonial Society of Massachusetts, Boston. II. Series: Colonial Society of Massachusetts, Boston. Publications, v. 46. BIP

Prints, British.

HUGHES, Therle. 769'.942
Prints for the collector; British prints from 1500 to 1900. New York, Praeger [1971] 216 p. illus., col. plates, ports. 26 cm. [NE628.H83 1971] 74-79071 15.00
1. Prints, British. 2. Prints—Collectors and collecting. I. Title.

Prints—Collectors and collecting.

BUCHSBAUM, Ann. 760'.75
Practical guide to print collecting / Ann Buchsbaum. New York : Van Nostrand Reinhold, 1975. 160 p. : ill. ; 24 cm. Includes index. Bibliography: p. 144-153. [NE885.B77] 75-2819 ISBN 0-442-21138-4 : 9.95
1. Prints—Collectors and collecting. I. Title. BIP

KNOX, Harold. 016.741'092'4
Collector's guide to Maxfield Parrish / by Harold Knox. Limited ed. W. Lebanon, N.H. : Knox, c1972. 32 p. : ill. ; 28 cm. [NE539.P34K56] 75-319989
1. Parrish, Maxfield, 1870-1966. 2. Prints—Collectors and collecting. I. Title.

LUCKEY, Carl F. 769'.075
Official guide to collector prints / by Carl F. Luckey. Florence, Ala. : House of Collectibles, c1976. v, 574 p., [16] leaves of plates : ill. (some col.) ; 18 cm. Includes index. [NE885.L82] 77-357306 ISBN 0-87637-335-X pbk. : 5.95
1. Prints—Collectors and collecting. I. Title. BIP

ROSEN, Randy. 760'.75
Prints, the facts and fun of collecting / by Randy Rosen. 1st ed. New York : Dutton, c1978. 218 p., [8] leaves of plates : ill. (some col.) ; 24 x 27 cm. Includes index. Bibliography: p. 215-216. [NE885.R58 1978] 77-79800 ISBN 0-525-18453-8 : 19.95
1. Prints—Collectors and collecting.

SHAPIRO, Cecile. 769'.075
Fine prints : collecting, buying, and selling / by Cecile Shapiro and lauris Mason ; with glossaries of French and German terms by Joan Ludman. 1st ed. New York : Harper & Row, c1976. p. cm. Includes bibliographical references and index. [NE885.S42 1976] 76-9200 ISBN 0-06-013853-X : 10.95
1. Prints—Collectors and collecting. I. Mason, Lauris, joint author. II. Title. BIP

SHAPIRO, Cecile. 769'.075
Fine prints : collecting, buying, and selling / Cecile Shapiro and Lauris Mason ; with glossaries of French and German terms by Joan Ludman. New York : Cornerstone Library, 1978, c1976. viii, 256p. : ill. ; 21 cm. Includes bibliographical references and index. [NE885.S42 1976] ISBN 0-346-12342-9 pbk. : 3.95
1. Prints — Collectors and collecting. 2. Prints — Marketing. I. Mason, Lauris, joint author. II. Title.
L.C. card no. for 1976 Harper & Row ed.: 76-9200.

SWEENEY, Marian S. 759.13
Maxfield Parrish prints : a collector's guide / by Marian S. Sweeney ; [introd. by William Morgan]. Dublin, N.H. : W. L. Bauhan, 1974. xx, 137 p., [8] leaves of plates : ill. ; 22 cm. Includes index. Bibliography: p. 114-120. [NE539.P34S93] 73-81165 ISBN 0-87233-029-X : 4.95
1. Parrish, Maxfield, 1870-1966. 2. Prints—Collectors and collecting. I. Title. BIP

VERSHBOW, Arthur. 769'.075
Print collecting today; a symposium held in the Wiggin Gallery, Boston Public Library, on May 3, 1968. The speakers: Arthur Vershbow, Sinclair Hitchings [and] R. E. Lewis. Boston [Printed for the Boston Public Library by the Stinehour Press, Lunenburg, Vt.; supplied by Worldwide Books, inc., Boston] 1969. 41 p. 23 cm. [NE885.V47] 70-93293
1. Prints—Collectors and collecting. I. Hitchings, Sinclair H. II. Lewis, Raymond Edwin, 1923- III. Boston. Public Library. IV. Title. BIP

WHITMAN, Alfred, 1860- 769'.075
1910.
The print-collector's handbook. London, G. Bell, 1901. Detroit, Tower Books, 1971. xi, 152 p. illus. 23 cm. [NE885.W6 1971] 72-177279
1. Prints—Collectors and collecting. I. Title. BIP

WHITMAN, Alfred, 1860- 769'.075
1910.
The print-collector's handbook, by Alfred Whitman. [3rd ed. reprint]; with a new introduction by H. F. B. Tregaskis. Wakefield, E. P. Publishing, 1973. ix, v-xi, 164 p., 77 leaves. illus. 23 cm. Facsimile reprint of 1907 reprint of 3rd ed., London, Bell, 1903. Includes index. Bibliography: p. 147-154. [NE885.W6 1973] 74-156023 ISBN 0-85409-800-3 £3.50
1. Prints—Collectors and collecting. I. Title.

WILLSHIRE, William Hughes, 769'.1
1816-1899.
An introduction to the study & collection of ancient prints. 2d ed., rev. and enl. Ann Arbor, Gryphon Books, 1971. 2 v. front. 22 cm. "A facsimile reprint of the 1877 edition." Bibliography: v. 2, p. [279]-293. [NE885.W74 1877a] 75-146923
1. Prints—Collectors and collecting. I. Title.

ZIGROSSER, Carl, 1891- 769'.1
A guide to the collecting and care of original prints, by Carl Zigrosser and Christa M. Gaehde. Sponsored by the Print Council of America. New York, Crown Publishers [1967, c1965] vi, 120 p. illus. 21 cm. "Based on What is an original print? Published by the Print Council in 1961." Bibliography: p. 11-12. [NE885.Z5 1967] 68-115
1. Prints—Collectors and collecting. I. Gaehde, Christa M., joint author. II. Print Council of America. What is an original print? III. Title. BIP

ZINGROSSER, Carl, 1891- 769.1
A guide to the collecting and care of original prints by Carl Zigrosser, and Christa M. Gaehde. Sponsored by the Print Council of America. New York, Crown [c.1965] vi, 120p. illus. 21cm. Bibl. [NE885.Z5] 65-24325 3.00
1. Prints—Collectors and collecting. I. Gaehde, Christa M., joint author. II. Print Council of America. III. Title.

Prints, Dutch—Exhibitions.

CONNECTICUT. 769'.9492
University. Museum of Art.
Hendrik Goltzius & the printmakers of Haarlem. [Storrs, 1972] 100 p. illus. 22 cm. Catalog, prepared by F. den Broeder, of the exhibition held Apr. 22-May 21, 1972. Includes bibliographical references. [NE670.G65C6] 72-184258
1. Goltzius, Hendrik, 1558-1617. 2. Prints, Dutch—Exhibitions. I. Goltzius, Hendrik, 1558-1617. II. den Broeder, Frederick. III. Title.

Prints, English.

CATCHPENNY prints; 769'.942
163 popular engravings from the eighteenth century originally published by Bowles and Carver. New York, Dover Publications [1970] vii p., 163 p. of illus. 28 cm. (Dover pictorial archive series) [NE628.2.C36] 79-103068 ISBN 0-486-22569-0 3.00

1. Prints, English. I. Bowles and Carver (Firm) BIP

JARROLD, 1770- 769'.065'4261
1970: a book of East Anglian prints and documents. Norwich, Jarrold & Sons [1970] [5] p., 30 plates (2 fold.). illus., facsims. 38 cm. Cover title. Plate size varies. [NE642.J3J3] 73-596287
1. Jarrold & Sons Limited. 2. Prints, English.

A Prospect of 769'.4'4094229
Berkshire : eight prints from the eighteenth century, selected from the local history collection at Reading Libraries. [Reading] : Reading Libraries, 1976. [10] leaves : of ill. ; 24 cm. One leaf printed on both sides. [NE954.3.G7P7] 77-364712
1. Prints, English. 2. Prints—18th century—England. 3. Berkshire, Eng., in art. I. Reading, Eng. Public Libraries.

Prints, English—Exhibitions.

GLEESON, Larry. 769'.942
Followers of Blake : The Santa Barbara Museum of Art, March 2-April 4, 1976 / Larry Gleeson, editor. [Santa Barbara, Calif.] : Santa Barbara Museum of Art, c1976. 40 p. : ill. ; 26 cm. Bibliography: p. 37-38. [NE628.G56] 76-4928
1. Shoreham Circle (Group of artists) 2. Blake, William, 1757-1827—Influence. 3. Prints, English—Exhibitions. I. Santa Barbara, Calif. Museum of Art. II. Title.

Prints—Europe, Eastern.

EASTERN European 769'.947
prints. Compiled and edited by Andrew Stasik. New York, Pratt Graphics Center [1970] 1 portfolio ([4] l., 10 plates (part col.)) 59 cm. "A folio of 10 prints issued in a limited edition of 100 sets signed and numbered by the artists. [No. 18]" Contents.Contents.—Czechoslovakia: Jiri John. Jaroslav Serych.—Hungary: Arnold Gross. Bela Kondor.—Poland: Danuta Lesczynska-Kluza. Ryszard K. Otreba.—Romania: Ion Bitzan. Marcel Chirnoaga.—Yugoslavia: Janez Bernik. Marjan Pogacnik. [NE625.E3] 73-267502 415.00
1. Prints—Europe, Eastern. I. Stasik, Andrew, ed.

Prints, European—Catalogs.

JOHNSON (R. S.)- 769'.94
International Gallery.
Master graphics, 1880-1970; some aspects of 90 years in the history of European printmaking. Chicago, 1972. 63 p. illus. 25 cm. Bibliography: p. 51-52. [NE625.3.J64] 74-190280
1. Prints, European—Catalogs. I. Title.

Prints, European—Exhibitions.

COOPER-HEWITT 769'.94'07401471
Museum of Decorative Arts and Design.
Master printmakers from Cooper Hewitt Museum of Decorative Arts and Design, Smithsonian Institution. Selected by Elaine Evans Dee, curator of prints and drawings. New York, American Federation of Arts [1970] [16] p. illus. 18 cm. "[Catalog of] AFA exhibition number 70-15, circulated 1970-1972." [NE625.C66] 79-132632
1. Prints, European—Exhibitions. I. Dee, Elaine Evans. II. American Federation of Arts. III. Title.

MILLER, Dwight Cameron, 769'.4'2
1923-
Street criers and itinerant tradesmen in European prints; catalogue by Dwight Miller. [Exhibition] Stanford Art Gallery, Stanford University, 10 March to 3 May 1970. Achenbach Foundation for Graphic Arts, California Palace of the Legion of Honor, 9 May to 5 July 1970. [Stanford] Dept. of Art, Stanford University [1970] 32 p. illus. 22 x 28 cm. (Stanford art book 11) Label on t.p.: Supplied by Worldwide Books, Boston. Bibliography: p. 31-32. [NE962.P4M55] 75-29134
1. Prints, European—Exhibitions. 2. Peddlers and peddling in art. I. Stanford University. Thomas Welton Stanford Art Gallery. II. Achenbach Foundation for Graphic Arts, San Francisco. III. Title. IV. Series.

Prints—Exhibitions.

BOWDOIN College. Museum 769'.074
of Art.
Language of the print; a selection from the Donald H. Karshan Collection. Pref. by A. Hyatt Mayor. Foreword and essay by Richard V. West. Catalogue commentary by Donald H. Karshan. [Brunswick, Me., 1968] 112 p. illus. 26 cm. Exhibition organized by Bowdoin College Museum of Art. "Participating museums: Addison Gallery of American Art, Andover, Massachusetts [and other museums] ... 1968-1969." Bibliography: p. 111-112. [NE57.B75] 68-25178
1. Karshan, Donald H.—Art collections. 2. Prints—Exhibitions. I. West, Richard V. II. Phillips Academy, Andover, Mass. Addison Gallery of American Art. III. Title.

BROOKLYN 769'.074'014723
Institute of Arts and Sciences. Museum.
Van Gogh's sources of inspiration; 100 prints from his personal collection. [Brooklyn, 1971] [39] p. illus. 23 cm. "The Brooklyn Museum, a special exhibition/February 1-April 4, 1971." Bibliography: p. [39] [NE59.S7G63] 70-151803
1. Gogh, Vincent van, 1853-1890—Art collections. 2. Prints—Exhibitions. I. Title.

BROWN University. Dept. 769'.924
of Art.
Jacques Callot, 1592-1635. [Exhibition held] at the Museum of Art, Rhode Island School of Design, Providence, Rhode Island, Mar. 5 through Apr. 11, 1970. [Providence, 1970] 1 v. (unpaged) illus. 21 x 22 cm. Includes bibliographical references. [NE650.C3B75] 76-566770
1. Callot, Jacques, 1592-1635. 2. Prints—Exhibitions. I. Rhode Island School of Design, Providence. Museum of Art.

CALIFORNIA. University, Santa 769
Barbara. Art Gallery.
The Ala Story Print Collection of the Art Gallery, University of California at Santa Barbara. [Exhibition] March 9 through March 26, 1967. [Santa Barbara, 1967] 11 p. 5 illus. 26 cm. Catalogue. Bibliography: p. 11. [NE42.S3C32] 67-63593
1. Story, Ala—Art collections. 2. Prints—Exhibitions. I. Title.

CASTLEMAN, Riva. 769'.904'074
Modern art in prints. New York, Museum of Modern Art [1973] 75 p. illus. (part col.) 23 cm. Issued in connection with an exhibition which was formed for circulation in Asia, New Zealand, and Australia, and was organized under the auspices of the International Council of the Museum of Modern Art. Bibliography: p. 73. [NE491.C37] 72-95073 ISBN 0-87070-461-3 3.95 (pbk.)
1. Prints—Exhibitions. I. International Council of the Museum of Modern Art, New York. II. Title.

CLISBY, Roger D. 760'.09'04
19th & 20th century prints & drawings from the Baltimore Museum of Art; catalogue [of an exhibition held at the E. B. Crocker Art Gallery, Nov. 3-Dec. 2, 1973, Honolulu Academy of Arts, Jan. 18-Feb. 17, 1974, and William Hayes Ackland Memorial Art Center, Apr. 2-Apr. 21, 1974] Introd. by Victor I. Carlson. Catalogue by Roger D. Clisby [Sacramento, Calif.] E. B. Crocker Art Gallery, 1973. [25] p. illus. 28 cm. [NE486.C54] 73-88934
1. Prints—Exhibitions. 2. Drawings—Exhibitions. I. Baltimore. Museum of Art. II. Crocker Art Gallery, Sacramento, Calif. III. Honolulu Academy of Arts. IV. North Carolina. University. William Hayes Ackland Memorial Art Center. V. Title.

COLNAGHI (P. & 769'.94'07402132
D.) & Company, ltd., London.
Five hundred years of fine prints : an exhibition, 10 February-10 March 1976. London : P & D Colnaghi, 1976. [150] p. : ill. ; 22 cm. "Price list": 1 leaf inserted. Includes index. [NE45.G7L663 1976] 76-377128
1. Prints—Exhibitions. I. Title.

DETROIT. Institute of 016.709'04
Arts.
Documenting a collection ; About the designer/"illem Sandberg ; Twentieth-century graphics : chekc lists for three exhibitions selected from the Winston-Malbin Collection shown in conjunction with Cobra and Contrasts at the Detroit Institute of ARts, September 25-November 17, 1974. Detroit : Founders Society, Detroit Institute of Arts, 1974. 40 p. ; 26 cm. Includes bibliographies. [Z5935.5.D44 1974] [N6487] 75-317139
1. Winston, Lydia, 1897- —Art collections—Bibliography—Exhibitions. 2. Winston, Harry Lewis—Art collections—Bibliography—Exhibitions. 3. Sandberg, Willem Jacob Henri Berend, 1897- 4. Prints—Exhibitions. I. Title.

DURER through 769'.94'07401441
other eyes : his graphic work mirrored in copies and forgeries of three centuries : an exhibition prepared by students in the Williams College-Clark Art Institute graduate program in art history, March 14 to June 15, 1975. Williamstown, Mass. : Sterling and Francine Clark Art Institute, c1975. 99 p. : ill. ; 27 cm. Errata sheet inserted. Includes index. Bibliography: p. 68-73. [NE42.W54S834] 76-354407
1. Durer, Albrecht, 1471-1528—Adaptations. 2. Durer, Albrecht, 1471-1528—Forgeries. 3. Prints—Exhibitions. I. Williams College. II. Sterling and Francine Clark Art Institute, Williamstown, Mass.

ELVEHJEM Art 769'.944'074017584
Center.
Cubist prints from the Collection of Dr. & Mrs. Abraham Melamed. Madison, Wis. [1972] 43 p. illus. 21 x 23 cm. Catalog of an exhibition held 5 February-12 March 1972, prepared by Arthur R. Blumenthal. Bibliography: p. 7. [NE492.C8E4] 72-187232
1. Melamed, Abraham, 1914- —Art collections. 2. Prints—Exhibitions. 3. Cubism. I. Blumenthal, Arthur R. II. Title.

FENTON, Jean. 769'.4'36094
Impressions of landscape; landscape in prints from 1450 to 1870. [Santa Barbara] University of California [1969] 40 p., [35] p. of illus. 26 cm. Catalog of an exhibition held at the Art Galleries, University of California Santa Barbara, Apr. 1-May 11, 1969. Bibliography: p. 27. [NE42.S3C34] 79-625753
1. Prints—Exhibitions. 2. Landscape in art. I. California. University. Santa Barbara. Art Gallery. II. Title.

FIFTEENTH and 769'.94'0740155365
sixteenth century prints from the Rosenwald Collection, National Gallery of Art, Washington, D.C. Fredericksburg, Va. [1971] [75] p. illus. 28 cm. Cover title. Prepared by the Connoisseurship Class for an exhibition at the Mary Washington College of the University of Virginia, Fredericksburg, Va., Feb. 8-Mar. 15, 1971. Bibliography: p. [73]-[75] [NE441.F5] 75-635469
1. Rosenwald, Lessing Julius, 1891- —Art collections. 2. United States. National Gallery of Art. 3. Prints—Exhibitions. I. Mary Washington College, Fredericksburg, Va.

GRUNWALD Center 760'.074'019493
for the Graphic Arts.
Twenty years of acquisition : evolution of a university study collection / the Grunwald Center for the Graphic Arts. Los Angeles : Frederick S. Wight Art Gallery, University of California, Los Angeles, 1974. 91 p. : ill. (some col.) ; 28 cm. Includes catalogue of the exhibition held Spring 1974 (p. 61-68) Bibliography: p. 89-91. [NE42.L6G784 1974] 74-623602
1. Prints—Exhibitions. I. Title.

HAIR; 769'.973
a pictorial tribute. A loan exhibition from the Library of Congress, Division of Prints and Photographs. Circulated by the International Exhibitions Foundation, 1972-1974. [Washington, 1972] folder (8 p.) 15 x 18 cm. [NE962.H3H3] 72-79900
1. Prints—Exhibitions. 2. Hair in art. I. United States. Library of Congress. Prints and Photographs Division. II. International Exhibitions Foundation.

HAMILTON, Richard. 769'.92'4
Prints, multiples, and drawings. [Catalog of an exhibition at] Whitworth Art Gallery, University of Manchester, Whitwork Park, Manchester, 22 January-19 February 1972. Manchester, Whitworth Art Gallery, 1972. 47 p. illus. 20 x 21 cm. [NE642.H32W5] 72-189323
I. Whitworth Art Gallery, Manchester, Eng.

HARBISON, Craig S. 769'.4'6094
Symbols in transformation; iconographic themes at the time of the Reformation. [Princeton, N.J., 1969] 110 p. illus. 26 cm. "An exhibition of prints in memory of Erwin Panofsky, The Art Museum, Princeton University, March 15-April 13, 1969." Introduction and catalogue entries by Craig Harbison. Bibliography: p. 35-[37] [NE42.P7P75] 72-19900
1. Prints—Exhibitions. 2. Symbolism in art. I. Panofsky, Erwin, 1892-1968. II. Princeton University. Art Museum. III. Title.

HARVARD University. 769.074
William Hayes Fogg Art Museum
Master prints of the 20th century; a tribute to Jakob Rosenberg, curator of prints at the Fogg Art Museum from 1939 to 1964. Master prints of the twentieth century Cambridge, Mass., Harvard [c.1965] [88]p. illus. 22cm. Catalog of the exhibition held Feb. 4-Mar. 31, 1965 at the Fogg Art Mus. Bibl. [NE40.H3] 65-1748 2.50 pap.,
1. Prints—Exhibitions. I. Rosenberg, Jakob, 1893- II. Title.

HENRY Art 769'.074'019777
Gallery.
Prints/multiples; an exhibition of original prints and multiples presented by the Henry Gallery and the Junior League of Seattle. [Seattle, 1969] 56 p. illus. 22 cm. Contains catalog of an exhibition held at Henry Gallery, University of Washington, Seattle, Nov. 16-Dec. 23, 1969, together with 8 essays. [NE491.H45] 70-25359
1. Prints—Exhibitions. I. Junior League of Seattle. II. Title.

JOHN and Mable 096'.1'074015961
Ringling Museum of Art, Sarasota, Fla.
Twentieth century illustrated books; a selection of important contemporary illustrated books from a Sarasota private collection. [Exhibition] Ringling Museum of Art, October 2-22, 1967. [Sarasota, 1967] 24 p. illus. 18 x 26 cm. Bibliography: p. 24. [NE491.J6] 73-275281
1. Prints—Exhibitions. 2. Prints—Private collections—Sarasota, Fla. 3. Illustrated books—20th century. I. Title.

JOHNSON (R. S.)- 769'.94'074017311
International Gallery.
Old master prints, 1470-1800 : an exhibit of fine and rare engravings, etchings and woodcuts from four centuries, fall 1974 / R. S. Johnson-International Gallery. Chicago, ; The Gallery, [1974] 87 p. : ill. ; 25 cm. Includes bibliographical references and index. [NE42.C5J64 1974] 74-82177
1. Prints—Exhibitions. I. Title.

JOHNSON (R. S.)- 769'.94
International Gallery.
A selection of nineteenth and twentieth century master graphics R. S. Johnson-International Gallery. Chicago : The Gallery, 1974. 31 p. : chiefly ill. ; 25 cm. Cover title: 19th & 20th century master graphics. Includes index. [NE485.J63 1974] 74-17871
1. Prints—Exhibitions. I. Title. II. Title: 19th & 20th century master graphics.

KANSAS. 760'.074'08165
University. Museum of Art.
The August W. Lauterbach Collection of prints and drawings; an exhibition from the collection of the late Senator August W. Lauterbach, given to the University of Kansas in honor of Dr. Franklin D. Murphy, 1960. Lawrence, Kan. [1966?] 16 p. illus. 23 cm. (Miscellaneous publication of the Museum of Art, no. 50) [NE42.L3K3] 66-65085
1. Lauterbach, August W.—Art collections. 2. Prints—Exhibitions. 3. Drawings—Exhibitions. I. Title. II. Series: Kansas. University. Museum of Art. Miscellaneous publications, no. 50

KARLSTROM, Paul J. 914.5'31'00222
An exhibition of views of Venice in the graphic arts from the late 15th through 18th century. [By Paul J. Karlstrom] The Grunwald Graphic Arts Foundation, Dickson Art Center, University of California, February 24 to March 30, 1969. [Los Angeles? 1969?] [39] p. illus. 22 x 28

cm. Half title: Venice panorama. Bibliography: p. [35] [NE42.L6K3] 78-235768
1. Prints—Exhibitions. 2. Venice in art. I. Grunwald Graphic Arts Foundation. II. Dickson Art Center. III. Title. IV. Title: Venice panorama.

KENNEDY Galleries, inc., New York. 769'.074'01471
Catalogue of an exhibition held October 28 through November 15, 1969 at the Kennedy Galleries, Print Department. New York [1969] 32 p. illus. 20 cm. (Art in prints, no. 4) Cover title: New acquisitions in the Kennedy Galleries Print Department. [NE70.A76 no. 4] 74-285246 2.00
1. Prints—Exhibitions. I. Title. II. Title: New acquisitions in the Kennedy Galleries Print Department. III. Series.

KENNEDY Galleries, inc., New York. 769'.074'01471
Master prints three: exhibition, October 7-30, 1976. N[ew] Y[ork] : Kennedy Galleries, c1976. 79 p., [1] leaf of plates : ill. ; 28 cm. Includes index. [NE42.N7K464] 77-363949
1. Prints—Exhibitions. I. Title.

KRANNERT Art Museum. 769
Extensions of the artist; prints from the Collection of Lydia and Harry Lewis Winston (Mrs. Barnett Malbin) Champaign [1969] 52 p. illus., port. 28 cm. Exhibition held Oct. 12-Nov. 16, 1969. Contents.Contents.—Introduction, by M. B. Christison.—Reflections on art collecting as a creative process, by L. K. Winston.—Catalogue of the exhibition. [NE42.C45K72 1969] 72-629118
1. Winston, Lydia, 1897- —Art collections. 2. Winston, Harry Lewis—Art collections. 3. Prints—Exhibitions. I. Title.

NIELSEN Gallery. 769'.074'014461
Twentieth century prints : [exhibition] fall 1975. Boston : Nielsen Gallery, 1975. [24] p. : ill. ; 20 cm. [NE491.N53 1975] 75-24203 2.00
1. Prints—Exhibitions. I. Title.

RHODE Island School of Design, Providence. Museum of Art. 769'.904'607401452
Selection III: Contemporary graphics from the museum's collection. [Providence, 1973] 1 v. (unpaged) illus. 27 cm. Catalog of the exhibition held Apr. 5-May 6, 1973. [NE42.P73R45 1973] 73-76521
1. Prints—Exhibitions.

ST. Louis. City Art Museum. 769'.074'017866
Graphic art from the Sidney and Sadie Cohen Foundation in the collection of City Art Museum of Saint Louis; [exhibition] December 18, 1970 through January 17, 1971. [St. Louis, 1970] 23, [1] p. illus. 24 cm. Bibliography: p. [24] [NE42.S25C54] 72-200037
1. Prints—Exhibitions. I. Title.

SHARP, Ellen. 769'.074'017434
Detroit collects prints and drawings. Detroit, Wayne State University Press [1972] 52 p. illus. 22 cm. "Catalogue of an exhibition of prints and drawings from six Detroit collections ... the Detroit Institute of Arts, 13 April through 21 May, 1972." Contents.Contents.—Charles E. Feinberg.—Gertrude Kasle.—Paul G. Lutzeier.—Lydia Winston Malbin.—Kurt Michel.—Albert H. Ratcliffe. [NE42.D47D47 1972] 72-79325 ISBN 0-8143-1486-4 5.00
1. Prints—Exhibitions. 2. Prints—Private collections—Detroit. 3. Drawings—Exhibitions. 4. Drawings—Private collections—Detroit. I. Detroit. Institute of Arts. II. Title.

TROCHE, Ernst Gunter. 769'.074'019461
Five centuries of prints, from the collection of the Achenbach Foundation for Graphic Arts, California Palace of the Legion of Honor, San Francisco, California. [Santa Barbara, 1967] 66 p. illus. 21 cm. Catalogue, by E. Gunter Troche, of an exhibition held at the Art Gallery, University of California, Santa Barbara, Jan. 5-29, 1967. [NE45.S24T7] 67-65507
1. Prints—Exhibitions. I. Achenbach Foundation for Graphic Arts, San Francisco. II. California. University, Santa Barbara. Art Galleries. III. Title.

VANCOUVER, B.C. Art Gallery. 769'.074'011133
Vancouver print international; exposition internationale de gravures. [Vancouver, 1967] 149 p. illus. 28 cm. Label mounted on t.p.: Supplied by Worldwide Books, Inc., New York. "Organized at a Centennial project by the Women's Auxiliary to the Vancouver Art Gallery." [NE40.V3] 68-30060
1. Prints—Exhibitions. I. Vancouver, B.C. Art Gallery. Women's Auxiliary. II. Title. III. Title: Exposition internationale de gravures.

Prints, Finnish—Exhibitions.

GRAPHIC art of Finland : 769'.9471'074 travelling exhibition 1976 : India, Indonesia, Singapore, Japan, Australia, New Zealand / catalogue ed[itor], Ritva-Liisa Elomaa ; organizers, Ministry for Foreign Affairs, and the Society of Finnish Graphic Artists, Helsinki. [s.l. : s.n.], 1976. [19] p. : ill. ; 21 x 22 cm. [NE735.F5G7] 77-469818
1. Prints, Finnish—Exhibitions. 2. Prints—20th century—Finland—Exhibitions. I. Elomaa, Ritva-Liisa. II. Finland. Ulkoasiainministerio. III. Suomen taidegraafikot ry.

Prints, French.

FURSTENBERG, Jean, 1890- 769'.944'074013
La gravure originale dans l'illustration du livre francais au dixhuitieme [sic] siecle = Die Original-Graphik in der franzosischen Buch-Illustration des achtzehnten Jahrhunderts / Jean Furstenburg ; [traduction allemande par Bernd von Arnim] Hamburg : E. Hauswedell, 1975. 438 p. : ill. ; 30 cm. French and German. Includes indexes. Bibliography: p. 432-434. [NE647.2.F87] 76-451492 ISBN 3-7762-0135-5
1. Prints, French. 2. Illustration of books—France. 3. Illustrated books—18th century. I. Title. II. Title: Die Original-Graphik in der franzosischen Buch-Illustration des achtzehnten Jahrhunderts.

IVES, Colta Feller. 769'.944
The great wave: the influence of Japanese woodcuts on French prints. [New York] Metropolitan Museum of Art; distributed by New York Graphic Society [1974] 112 p. illus. (part col.) 26 cm. Bibliography: p. 111-112. [NE647.6.I4I93] 74-16187 ISBN 0-87099-098-5
1. Prints, French. 2. Prints, French—Japanese influences. 3. Impressionism (Art)—France. 4. Ukiyoe. I. New York (City). Metropolitan Museum of Art. II. Title.

PASSERON, Roger. 769.944
French prints of the 20th century. [Translated from the French, by Robert Allen. New York, Praeger Publishers [1970] 181 p. illus. (part col.), ports. 30 cm. Translation of La Gravure francaise au XXe siecle. [NE647.P4713] 74-108245 20.00
1. Prints, French. I. Title.

PASSERON, Roger. 769'.944
Impressionist prints. New York, Dutton, 1974. 222 p. illus. (part col.) 37 cm. (A Dutton visual book) Translation of La gravure impressionniste. [NE647.6.I4P3713 1974] 74-3640 ISBN 0-525-49503-7 40.00
1. Prints, French. 2. Impressionism (Art)—France. I. Title.

A Portfolio of twenty-four reproductions of masterpieces of graphic art ... ; 769'.944 text of "An introduction to prints & printmaking" / by Herman J. Wechsler with an additional foreword for the portfolio. New York : Triton Press, [1974] 1 portfolio (6 p., 24 leaves of plates : ill. (some col.)) ; 44 cm. Consists of a print of each of the following artists: Manet, Degas, Cezanne, Gauguin, Renoir, Lautrec, Bonnard, Vuillard, Morisot, Cassatt, Redon, Matisse, Braque, Maillol, Rouault, Utrillo, Segonzac, Picasso, Chagall, Miro. Includes bibliographical references. [NE647.3.P67] 74-193293
1. Prints, French. 2. Prints. I. Wechsler, Herman Joel, 1904-

Prints, French—Catalogs.

THE Graphic works of the impressionists; 769'.944 Manet, Pissarro, Renoir, Cezanne, Sisley. [Text by] Jean Leymarie. Catalogue by Michel Melot. New York, H. N. Abrams [1972] 353 p. (chiefly illus. (part col.)) 33 cm. Translation of Les Gravures des impressionistes. [NE647.6.I4G713 1972b] 72-160222 ISBN 0-8109-0154-4 25.00
1. Prints, French—Catalogs. 2. Impressionism (Art)—France. I. Leymarie, Jean. II. Melot, Michel, conservateur.

Prints, French—Exhibitions.

AMERICANS in Paris, 1600-1900; 769'.944'07401471 one hundred and fifty/works from the Print Collection of the National Library in Paris. [New York? 1972] 48 p. illus. 23 cm. Catalogue of an exhibition held in the Art Center of the New School for Social Research, February 26 through April 22, 1972. [NE647.A68] 72-198172
1. Prints, French—Exhibitions. 2. United States—History—Pictorial works. 3. Portraits, American—Exhibitions. 4. Prints, American—Exhibitions. I. Paris. Bibliotheque nationale. Departement des estampes. II. New York (City). New School for Social Research. New School Art Center.

JOHNSON, Una E. 769'.944'074013
Ambroise Vollard, editeur : prints, books, bronzes / Una E. Johnson. New York : Museum of Modern Art ; Boston : distributed by New York Graphic Society, c1977. 176 p. : ill. (come col.) ; 24 cm. Published in 1944 under title: Ambroise Vollard, editeur, 1867-1939. Catalogue of an exhibition held at the Museum of Modern Art, New York, June 9-Sept. 6, 1977 and at the Art Gallery of Ontario, Toronto, the Krannert Art Museum, University of Illinois at Champaign, and the Toledo Museum of Art. "Catalogue raisonne": p. 125-171. Bibliography: p. 172-176. [NE647.3.J63 1977] 77-70042 ISBN 0-87070-062-6 : 17.50.
1. Vollard, Ambroise, 1867-1939. 2. Prints, Frech—Exhibitions. 3. Prints—19th century—France—Exhibitions. 4. Prints—20th century—France—Exhibitions. 5. Illustration of books—France—Exhibitions. 6. Bronzes—France—Exhibitions. I. New York (City). Museum of Modern Art. II. Title.

WEISBERG, Gabriel P. 769'.944
Social concern and the worker; French prints from 1838-1910, by Gabriel P. Weisberg. [Salt Lake City, Utah Museum of Fine Arts, c1973] 138 p. illus. 22 x 27 cm. Catalog of the exhibition held Jan. 13-Feb. 17, 1974 at the Utah Museum of Fine Arts, Salt Lake City, Mar. 12-May 12, 1974 at the Cleveland Museum of Art, Cleveland, and June 11-July 28, 1974 at the Indianapolis Museum of Art, Indianapolis. Bibliography: p. 133-138. [NE647.3.W44] 73-90715
1. Prints, French—Exhibitions. 2. Labor and laboring classes in art. 3. Peasants in art. I. Utah Museum of Fine Arts. II. Cleveland Museum of Art. III. Indianapolis Museum of Art. IV. Title.

Prints, German—Exhibitions.

PRINTS and drawings of the Danube School; 760'.0943 an exhibition of South German and Austrian graphic art of 1500 to 1560; [catalogue] Prepared by a graduate seminar in the history of art under the direction of Charles Talbot and Alan Shestack. [New Haven, Printed by the Carl Purington Rollins Printing-Office of the Yale University Press, 1969?] 109 p. 61 plates. 26 cm. Cover title: The Danube School. Held at: Yale University Art Gallery, Oct. 9-Nov. 16, 1969, City Art Museum of St. Louis, Dec. 11, 1969-Jan. 25, 1970, and Philadelphia Museum of Art, Feb. 10-March 24, 1970. Includes bibliographical references. [NE652.S6P7] 76-21443
1. Prints, German—Exhibitions. 2. Prints—Germany, Southern. 3. Prints, Austrian—Exhibitions. 4. Drawings, German—Exhibitions. 5. Drawings—Germany, Southern. 6. Drawings, Austrian—Exhibitions. I. Talbot, Charles W. II. Shestack, Alan. III. Yale University. Art Gallery. IV. St. Louis. City Art Museum. V. Philadelphia Museum of Art. VI. Title: The Danube School.

TEXAS. University at Austin. Art Museum. 769'.943
German graphics of the sixties. [Catalogue of an exhibition] February 17 - March 24, 1974, Archer M. Huntington Galleries, upper level, University Art Museum, University of Texas at Austin. [Austin, 1974] 1 v. (unpaged) illus. 18 cm. [NE651.4.T48 1974] 74-620013
1. Prints, German—Exhibitions. 2. Printmakers—Germany (Federal Republic, 1949-) I. Title.

Prints, German—U.S.

STECHOW, Wolfgang, 1896- 769'.924
Durer and America. Washington, National Gallery of Art, 1971. xv p. illus., ports. 28 cm. "This essay is adapted from a lecture delivered at the National Gallery of Art, April 25, 1971." Includes bibliographical references. [NE654.D9S7] 78-612415
1. Durer, Albrecht, 1471-1528. 2. Prints, German—U.S. I. Title.

Prints—Great Britain.

GODFREY, Richard T. 769'.941
Printmaking in Britain : a general history from its beginnings to the present day / by Richard T. Godfrey. New York : New York University Press, 1978. 244 p. : ill. (some col.) ; 26 cm. Includes index. Bibliography: p [240]-241. [NE628.G63] 78-53802 ISBN 0-8147-2973-8 : 24.50
1. Prints—Great Britain. 2. Printmakers—Great Britain. I. Title. **BIP**

Prints—History.

BELLA, Stefano della, 1610-1664. 769'.924
Presenting Stefano della Bella, seventeenth-century printmaker, by Phyllis Dearborn Massar. [New York] Metropolitan Museum of Art; distributed by New York Graphic Society [1971] 141 p. illus. 29 cm. [NE662.B38M3] 70-162340 ISBN 0-87099-109-4 12.95
I. Massar, Phyllis Dearborn. II. Title.

EICHENBERG, Fritz, 1901- 769'.9
The print: art, history and technics. New York, H. N. Abrams [1975] p. cm. [NE400.E32] 74-18024 ISBN 0-8109-0103-X
1. Prints—History. 2. Prints—Technique. I. Title.

IVINS, William Mills, 1881-1961. 769'.9
Prints and visual communication. New York, Da Capo Press, 1969. xxv, 190 p. illus. 24 cm. (Da Capo Press series in graphic art, v. 10) (A Da Capo Press reprint edition.) Reprint of the 1953 ed. [NE430.I85 1969] 68-31583 10.00
1. Prints—History. 2. Photomechanical processes. I. Title. **BIP**

LINDEMANN, Gottfried. 760'.09
Prints & drawings; a pictorial history. Translated by Gerald Onn. New York, Praeger Publishers [1970] 475 p. illus. (part col.) 31 cm. [NE430.L5513 1970] 71-111074 18.50
1. Prints—History. 2. Drawings—History. I. Title. **BIP**

LINDEMANN, Gottfried. 760'.09
Prints & drawings : a pictorial history / Gottfried Lindemann ; translated [from the German] by Gerald Onn. Oxford : Phaidon, 1976. 475 p. : ill. (some col.), ports. (some col.) ; 31 cm. Includes indexes. [NE430.L5513 1976] 77-350226 ISBN 0-7148-1760-0 : 16.95
1. Prints—History. 2. Drawing—History. I. Title.
Distributed by E.P. Dutton, N.Y.

MAYOR, Alpheus Hyatt, 1901- 769'.9
Prints & people; a social history of printed pictures [by] A. Hyatt Mayor. [New York]

Metropolitan Museum of Art; distributed by New York Graphic Society [1971] 1 v. (unpaged) 752 illus. 27 cm. [NE400.M3] 73-162341 ISBN 0-87099-108-6 20.00
1. Prints—History. 2. Art and society. I. New York (City). Metropolitan Museum of Art. II. Title. BIP

MUELLER, Earl George, 1914- 769'.9
The art of the print [by] Earl G. Mueller. Dubuque, Iowa, W. C. Brown Co. [1969] viii, 130 p. illus. 23 cm. (Studies in art series) Bibliography: p. 123-124. [NE430.M84] 69-12932
1. Prints—History. 2. Prints—Technique. I. Title.

NEW York (City). Metropolitan Museum of Art. 769'.94
Notes on prints, by William M. Ivins, Jr. Cambridge, Mass., M.I.T. Press [1969] 194 p. illus. 26 cm. Texts of the descriptive labels which accompanied a 1929 exhibition of prints from the Museum's collection. "Unabridged republication of the first edition published by the Metropolitan Museum of Art in 1930." [NE400.N4 1969] 70-6007 3.45
1. Prints—History. 2. Prints—Exhibitions. 3. Illustration of books—Exhibitions. I. Ivins, William Mills, 1881-1961. II. Title. BIP

NEW York. Metropolitan Museum of Art. 769
Notes on prints, by William M. Ivins, Jr. New York, Da Capo Press, 1967. 194 p. illus., ports. 26 cm. (Da Capo Press series in graphic art, v. 5) (A Da Capo reprint edition.) Reprint of the 1930 ed. Consists of the descriptive labels which accompanied an exhibition of prints held by the Metropolitan Museum of Art in 1929. [NE400.N4 1967] 67-25444
1. Prints—History. 2. Prints—Exhibitions. 3. Illustration of books—Exhibitions. I. Ivins, William Mills, 1881-1961. II. Title.

Prints, Italian.

BINNEY, Edwin. 769'.4'2
Sixty years of Italian dance prints, 1815-1875. [New York, Dance Perspectives Foundation, 1973] 60 p. illus. 23 cm. (Dance perspectives, 53) Bibliography: p. 41-42. [GV1580.D27 no. 53] [NE659.3] 73-76644 2.95 (pbk.)
1. Prints, Italian. 2. Dancing in art. I. Title. II. Series.

LAZZARI, Pietro, 1898- 759.13
I carbonizzati. Washington, [Printed by Yazge] 1967. v l., 41 plates (in portfolio) 52 cm. [ND237.L38A44] 67-31723
I. Title.

Prints, Japanese.

PETIT, Gaston, 1930- 769'.952
44 modern Japanese print artists / Gaston Petit; foreword by Kudo Sadajino ; preface by Stanley William Hayter Tokyo ; New York : Kodansha International, 1973. 2 v. : chiefly col. ill. ; 31 cm. & descriptive list of plates. [NE771.4.P47] 73-79759 ISBN 0-87011-202-3 : 100.00
1. Prints, Japanese. 2. Printmakers—Japan—Biography. I. Title.

WILKE, Ulfert, 1907- 741.973
One, two and more. Kyoto, Printed by Kuroyama Collotype Print Co., dist. New York, Wittenborn 1960. [2] 1., 23 plates (in portfolio) 51cm. 60-52334 20.00, bxd.
I. Title.

Prints, Japanese—Catalogs.

YOSEIDO Garo. 769'.952
Modern Japanese prints; a contemporary selection. Edited by Yuji Abe. [1st ed.] Rutland, Vt., C. E. Tuttle Co. [1971] 1 v. (chiefly illus. (part col.)) 19 cm. (A Tut books) [NE771.Y67] 70-120391 ISBN 0-8048-0926-7 2.25
1. Prints, Japanese—Catalogs. I. Abe, Yuji, ed. II. Title.

Prints, Japanese—Collections.

MICHENER, James A. 769.952
The modern Japanese print: an appreciation, with ten original, hand-printed, prize-winning works by ten of Janan's most outstanding print artists: Hiratsuka Un ichi [others] Rutland, Vt., Tuttle [1963] 56p. 57cm.10 col. illus. 150.00 lim. ed.
1. Prints, Japanese—Collections. I. Title.

Prints, Japanese—Exhibitions.

KUWAYAMA, George. 769'.952'074019494
Contemporary Japanese prints. [Los Angeles, Los Angeles County Museum of Art, 1972] 125 p. illus. (part col.) 21 cm. Catalog of an exhibition held at the Los Angeles County Museum of Art, Aug. 29-Oct. 22, 1972. Bibliography: p. 123. [NE771.4.K88] 72-87780 ISBN 0-87587-051-1
1. Prints, Japanese—Exhibitions. I. Los Angeles Co., Calif. Museum of Art, Los Angeles. II. Title. BIP

Prints, Japanese—Japan.

CHIBBETT, David G. 769'.952
The history of Japanese printing and book illustration / David Chibbett. 1st ed. Tokyo ; New York : Kodansha International ; New York : distributed by Harper & Row, 1977. 264 p. : ill. (some col.) ; 29 cm. Includes indexes. Bibliography: p. 237-238. [NE771.C48] 76-9362 ISBN 0-87011-288-0 : 50.00
1. Prints, Japanese—Japan. 2. Illustration of books—Japan. 3. Printing—History—Japan. I. Title. BIP

Prints, Latin American—Exhibitions.

NEW York (City). Museum of Modern Art. 769'.98
Latin American prints from the Museum of Modern Art. [New York] Center for Inter-American Relations [1974] [60] p. illus. (part col.) 21 cm. Catalog of an exhibition, Jan. 3-Mar. 24, 1974, held at the Center for Inter-American Relations, and later to be circulated in Latin America under the sponsorship of the International Council of the Museum of Modern Art. English and Spanish; added t.p.: Grabados latinoamericanos del Museo de Arte Moderno, Nueva York. [NE502.N48 1974] 74-175967 3.00 (pbk.)
1. Prints, Latin American—Exhibitions. I. Center for Inter-American Relations. II. International Council of the Museum of Modern Art, New York. III. Title. IV. Title: Grabados latinoamericanos del Museo de Arte Moderno, Nueva York. BIP

Prints—Marketing.

DONSON, Theodore B. 769'.1
Prints and the print market : a guide for buyers, collectors, and connoisseurs / Theodore B. Donson. New York : Crowell, [1976] [NE62.D66] 76-14487 ISBN 0-690-01160-1 : 12.95
1. Prints—Marketing. I. Title.

Prints, Mexican—Catalogs.

IMAGE of Mexico; 760'0972
the General Motors of Mexico Collection of Mexican graphic art. Editor: Harry H. Ransom; special editor; Thomas Mabry Cranfill; photographic editor: Hans Beacham [and others] Austin, University of Texas at Austin, 1969. 2 v. illus., ports. 26 cm. (The Texas quarterly, v. 12, no. 3-4) At head of title: A special issue. Articles, captions, and biographical sketches in English and Spanish. [AP2.T269 vol. 12, no. 3-4] [NE44.4] 77-30163 1.50 ea.
1. General Motors de Mexico—Art collections. 2. Prints, Mexican—Catalogs. 3. Drawings, Mexican—Catalogs. I. Cranfill, Thomas Mabry, ed. II. Beacham, Hans, ed. III. Title. IV. Series.

Prints, Mexican—Exhibitions.

GRABADOS mexicanos : 769'.972'074014423
an historical exhibition of Mexican graphics, 1839-1974 / organized and written by Art History Seminar 372 of Mexican graphics, Alicia Andraca '77 ... [et al.]. South Hadley, Mass. : Mount Holyoke College, c1974. 67 p. : ill. ; 24 cm. Bibliography: p. 66-67. [NE544.G68] 75-7990
1. Prints, Mexican—Exhibitions. I. Andraca, Alicia. II. Mount Holyoke College.

Prints—New York (City)

IVINS, William Mills, 1881-1961. 769
Prints and books; informal papers. New York, Da Capo Press, 1969 [c1926] x, 375 p. illus., ports. 23 cm. (Da Capa Press series in graphic art, v. 11) The essays are chiefly about prints and books in the Metropolitan Museum of Art. [NE53.N6I8 1969] 76-75295 10.00
1. New York. Metropolitan Museum of Art. 2. Prints—New York (City) I. Title. BIP

Prints—New York (City)—Bibliography—Catalogs.

NEW York (City). Public Library. Prints Division. 019'.1'097471
Dictionary catalog of the Prints Division. Boston : G. K. Hall, 1975. 5 v. ; 36 cm. At head of title: The New York Public Library, Astor, Lenox & Tilden Foundations, the Research Libraries. [Z5950.N562 1975] [NE53] 75-332052 ISBN 0-8161-1148-0 lib.bdg. : 425.00
1. New York (City). Public Library. Prints Division. 2. Prints—New York (City)—Bibliography—Catalogs. I. Title. BIP

Prints—New York (City)—Catalogs.

KENNEDY Galleries, inc., New York. 769'.074'01471
The Kennedy Galleries collection of fine graphics; [catalogue] New York [1974] 47 p. illus. 28 cm. [NE53.N7K464 1974] 74-178222
1. Kennedy Galleries, inc., New York. 2. Prints—New York (City)—Catalogs. I. Title.

NEW York (City). Public Library. 769.973
American historical prints: early views of American cities, etc. from the Phelps Stokes and other collections, by I. N. Phelps Stokes and Daniel C. Haskell. New York, New York Public Library, 1933. Detroit, Gale Research Co., 1972. xxxiii, 235 p. illus. 23 cm. [NE954.2.N39 1972] 77-180284 ISBN 0-8103-3950-1
1. Stokes, Isaac Newton Phelps, 1867-1944—Art collections. 2. Prints—New York (City)—Catalogs. 3. Drawings—New York (City)—Catalogs. 4. America—Description and travel—Views. 5. America—Description and travel—Maps, Early. 6. America—History—Pictorial works. I. Stokes, Isaac Newton Phelps, 1867-1944. II. Haskell, Daniel Carl, 1883- III. Title.

Prints—Oakland, Calif.—Catalogs.

MILLS College, Calif. Art Gallery. 769'.94'074019466
Selections from the print collection. [Catalogue and commentary by Harvey Jones] Oakland, Calif., 1971. 140 p. illus. 28 cm. Bibliography: p. 136-138. [NE53.O25M5] 72-194227
1. Prints—Oakland, Calif.—Catalogs. I. Jones, Harvey. II. Title.

Prints—Period.

ARTIST'S proof: 769.05
the annual of contemporary prints. v.7 [New York] Pratt Ctr. for Contemp. Printmaking in coop. with Barre Pubs. [1967] v. illus. 29cm. annual. (orig. semiannual) Subtitle orig.: A magazine of printmaking [NE1.A75] 67-26101 12.50
1. Prints—Period. I. Pratt Graphic Art Center, New York.

Prints, Spanish—Exhibitions.

COLNAGHI (P. & D.) & Company, ltd., London. 769'.946
Prints from Spain, Portugal and Latin America. London, P. & D. Colnaghi [1973] [68] p. illus. 22 cm. Stamped on t.p.: Supplied by World Wide books, Inc., Boston. "31st July-24th August 1973." Bibliography: p. [7] [NE699.C64 1973] 73-198366
1. Prints, Spanish—Exhibitions. 2. Print, Portuguese—Exhibitions. 3. Prints, Latin American—Exhibitions. I. Title.

Prints, Swiss—Exhibitions.

[DAVIS, Marian B] 769'.9494'074016431
Swiss concrete art in graphics : [exhibition] , February 23 - March 30, 1975, Archer M. Huntington Galleries, lower level, University Art Museum, University of Texas at Austin. [Austin] : The Museum, c1975. [87] p. : ill. (some col.) ; 18 cm. [NE707.6.C635D38] 75-328721
1. Prints, Swiss—Exhibitions. 2. Prints—Texas—Exhibitions. 3. Concrete art—Exhibitions. 4. Artists—Switzerland. I. Texas. University at Austin. Art Museum. II. Title.

Prints—Technique.

AMERY, Heather. 760'.028
The knowhow book of print and paint / [written and devised by Heather Amery and Anne Civardi ; assisted by Jim Corless ; illustrated by Malcolm English]. New York : Corwin Books, c1976. 47 p. : col. ill. ; 29 cm. (The Knowhow books) [NE860.A46 1976] 75-44858 ISBN 0-8069-8046-X : 4.50 ISBN 0-8069-8047-8 lib.bdg. :
1. Prints—Technique. 2. Painting—Technique. I. Civardi, Anne, joint author. II. Corless, Jim, joint author. III. English, Malcolm. IV. Title. BIP

ANDREWS, Michael F. 760
Creative printmaking, for school and camp programs. Englewood Cliffs, N.J., Prentice-Hall [1964] xi, 159 p. illus. 25 cm. Bibliography: p. 145-148. [NE850.A5] 64-10501
1. Prints—Technique. I. Title.

BANISTER, Manly Miles, 1914- comp. 761
Prints from linoblocks and woodcuts [by] Manly Banister. New York, Sterling Pub. Co. [1967] 76 p. illus. (part col.) 29 cm. [NE860.B3] 67-27749
1. Prints—Technique. I. Title.

BICKFORD, John H., 1926- 760'.2'8
New media in printmaking / by John Bickford. New York : Watson-Guptill Publications, 1976. p. cm. Includes index. Bibliography: p. [NE850.B52] 76-22481 ISBN 0-8230-3165-9 : 14.95
1. Prints—Technique. I. Title. BIP

CAPON, Robin. 760'.2'8
Introducing abstract printmaking. New York, Watson-Guptill [1973] 95 p. illus. (part col.) 21 cm. Bibliography: p. 94 [NE860.C28] 72-13405 ISBN 0-8230-6098-5 7.95
1. Prints, Technique. 2. Art, Abstract. I. Title.

A Complete guide to printmaking 760'.28
/ edited by Stephen Russ. New York : Viking Press, 1975. 152 p. : ill. (some col.) ; 25 cm. (A Studio book) Includes index. Bibliography: p. 144-145. [NE855.C65] 74-7692 ISBN 0-670-23422-2 : 14.95
1. Prints—Technique. I. Russ, Stephen.

DANIELS, Harvey, 1936- 760
Printmaking. New York, Viking Press [1971] 224 p. col. illus. 28 cm. (A Studio book) Includes bibliographical references. [NE850.D3 1971] 77-146054 ISBN 0-670-57757-X 14.95
1. Prints—Technique. I. Title.

EPPINK, Norman R. 761
101 prints; the history and techniques of printmaking, by Norman R. Eppink. [New ed.] Norman, University of Oklahoma Press [1972, c1971] xiii, 273 p. illus. (part col.) 28 cm. First ed. published in 1967 under title: 101 prints; each an original example of a printmaking process. Bibliography: p. 257-259. [NE850.E6 1972] 78-108806 ISBN 0-8061-0915-7 25.00
1. Prints—Technique. I. Title.

March 25, 1973. [Washington, 1973] [35] p. illus. 26 cm. [ND230.N4E93] 72-95537
1. New York. State Prison, Auburn. 2. Prisoners as artists. 3. Paintings, American—Exhibitions. 4. Painting, Modern—20th century—New York (State) I. Smithsonian Institution. National Collection of Fine Arts. II. Title.

Prisoners of war as artists.

GREEN, Gerald. 760'.09174'924
The artists of Terezin. [1st ed.] New York, Hawthorn Books [1969] ix, 191, [2] p. illus. (part col.) 27 cm. "A note on sources": p. [193] [N6886.T4G7] 69-16020 10.00
1. Prisoners of war as artists. 2. Children as artists. 3. Terezin (Concentration camp) I. Title.

GREEN, Gerald. 741.9'437'1
The artists of Terezin / Gerald Green. New York : Schocken Books, 1979. p. cm. Bibliography: p. [N6833.T47G73 1978] 78-59813 ISBN 0-8052-0609-4 pbk. : 7.95
1. Prisoners of war as artists. 2. Children as artists. 3. Terezin (Concentration camp) I. Title. BIP

GREEN, Gerald. 741.9'437'1
The artists of Terezin / by Gerald Green. New York : Hawthorn Books, c1978. ix, 191 p., [2] leaves of plates : ill. (some col.) ; 26 cm. Bibliography: p. [193] [N6833.T47G73 1978b] 78-108798 ISBN 0-8015-0420-1 : 12.50
1. Prisoners of war as artists. 2. Children as artists. 3. Terezin (Concentration camp) I. Title.

Prisons—Construction.

PRISON architecture : 725'.6
an international survey of representative closed institutions and analysis of current trends in prison design / prepared by Giuseppe Di Gennaro ... [et al.]. 1976 239 p. : ill. ; 31 x 43 cm. At head of title: United Nations Social Defence Research Institute. Summaries in English, French, and Spanish. Bibliography: p. 227-239. [HV8805.P74 1975] 76-365725 ISBN 0-85139-547-3 : 70.00
1. Prisons—Construction. I. Di Gennaro, Giuseppe. II. United Nations. Social Defence Research Institute.
Distributed by Nichols Pub. BIP

Prisons—Construction—Addresses, essays, lectures.

MOYER, Frederic D., comp. 725'.6
Correctional environments; a summary of recent endeavors to develop an effective correctional system comprised of programs and environments which support and encourage the development of full citizenship, edited by Frederic D. Moyer [and] Edith E. Flynn. [Urbana, Ill., National Clearinghouse for Correctional Programming and Architecture, c1971] 57 p. illus. 30 cm. Includes bibliographical references. [HV8805.M69] 74-155347
1. Prisons—Construction—Addresses, essays, lectures. 2. Corrections—Addresses, essays, lectures. I. Flynn, Edith E., joint comp. II. National Clearinghouse for Correctional Programming and Architecture. III. Title.

Prisons—Construction—History.

JOHNSTON, Norman Bruce, 725'.6'09
1921-
The human cage: a brief history of prison architecture [by] Norman Johnston. New York, Published for the American Foundation, Institute of Corrections by Walker [1973] 68 p. illus. 31 cm. Includes bibliographical references. [HV8805.J67] 72-95189 ISBN 0-8027-0424-7 5.95
1. Prisons—Construction—History. I. Title. BIP

Prisons—Construction—Standards—United States.

STANDARDS relating to 725'.6
architecture of facilities / recommended by the IJA-ABA Joint Commission on Juvenile Justice Standards, Irving R. Kaufman, chairman ; Allen F. Breed, chairman of drafting committee III, Allan M. Greenberg, reporter. Cambridge, Mass. : Ballinger Pub. Co., c1977. xi, 92 p. ; 23 cm. At head of title: Institute of Judicial Administration, American Bar Association, Juvenile Justice Standards Project. Bibliography: p. 87-92. [HV8827.S7] 77-14495 ISBN 0-88410-249-1
1. Prisons—Construction—Standards—United States. 2. Juvenile corrections—Standards—United States. 3. Juvenile detention homes—Design and construction—Standards—United States. I. Greenberg, Allan. II. IJA-ABA Joint Commission on Juvenile Justice Standards. III. Juvenile Justice Standards Project. BIP

Prisons—Illinois.

ILLINOIS. Bureau of 725'.6
Detention Facilities and Jail Standards.
Jail planning and construction standards. [Springfield] 1971. 39 p. illus. 28 cm. Cover title. Bibliography: p. 39. [HV8828.I3A5] 72-610366
1. Prisons—Illinois. 2. Prisons—Construction. I. Title.

Private presses—Addresses, essays, lectures.

MODERN fine printing; 655.1'794
papers read at a Clark Library seminar, March 11, 1967, by H. Richard Archer and Ward Ritchie. Los Angeles, William Andrews Clark Memorial Library, University of California, 1968. 44 p. 23 cm. (William Andrews Clark Memorial Library seminar papers) Contents.Contents.—The private press: its essence and recrudescence, by H. R. Archer.—Tradition and the printers of southern California, by W. Ritchie. Includes bibliographical references. [Z231.5.P7M6] 73-633434
1. Private presses—Addresses, essays, lectures. 2. Printing—History—California—Addresses, essays, lectures. I. Archer, Horace Richard. II. Ritchie, Ward, 1905- III. California. University. University at Los Angeles. William Andrews Clark Memorial Library. IV. Title. V. Title: Fine printing. VI. Series.

Privies.

LAMBTON, Lucinda. 747'.78
Temples of convenience / Lucinda Lambton. New York : St. Martin's Press, 1979, c1978. 12 p., [24] leaves of plates : ill. ; 25 cm. Bibliography: p. [4] [TD775.L35 1979] 78-60787 ISBN 0-312-79085-6 : 5.95
1. Privies. I. Title. BIP

Privies in art.

DEYOUNG, Harry Anthony, 741.9'73
1893-1956.
Texas out back / sketches by Harry Anthony DeYoung ; text by Leon Hale. 1st ed. Austin, Tex. : Madrona Press, c1973. 65 p. : ill. ; 24 cm. [NC139.D48H34] 75-314512
1. De Young, Harry Anthony, 1893-1956. 2. Privies in art. 3. Texas in art. I. Hale, Leon. II. Title. BIP

Project Apollo in art.

EYEWITNESS to 760'.074'0153
space; paintings and drawings related to the Apollo mission to the moon, selected, with a few exceptions, from the art program of the National Aeronautics and Space Administration (1963 to 1969) Written by Hereward Lester Cooke, with the collaboration of James D. Dean. Foreword by J. Carter Brown. Pref. by Thomas O. Paine. New York, H. N. Abrams [1971] 227 p. illus. (part col.) 32 x 43 cm. [N6512.E9] 76-141761 ISBN 0-8109-0112-9 35.00
1. Project Apollo in art. 2. Art, American—Catalogs. 3. Art, Modern—20th century—U.S. I. Cooke, Hereward Lester. II. Dean, James D. III. U.S. National Aeronautics and Space Administration.

Projectile points.

VAN BUREN, G. E. 739.7'3
Arrowheads and projectile points : with a classification guide for lithic artifacts / by G. E. Van Buren. 1st ed. Garden Grove, Calif. : Arrowhead Pub. Co., 1974- v. : ill. ; 29 cm. Includes indexes. Bibliography: p. 226-229. [GN799.W3V36] 75-306448 17.50
1. Projectile points. 2. Indians—Arms and armor. I. Title.

Projectile points—Prices—United States.

MOORE, Robert K. 739.7'3
Projectile point types of the American Indian; price guide, by Robert K. Moore. 2d ed. [Athens, Ala., Distributed by American Indian Books, 1973] 24 p. illus. 23 cm. Cover title. [E98.I4M68 1973] 73-158154 1.00
1. Projectile points—Prices—United States. 2. Indians of North America—Antiquities. 3. United States—Antiquities. I. Title.

Projection.

TURNER, William Wirt. 744.45
Projection drawing for architects. New York, Ronald Press Co. [1950] vi, 107 p. illus. 24 cm. [T363.T8] 50-7714
1. Projection. 2. Architectural drawing. I. Title.

Proof coins.

HOSCH, Charles R. 737.4
World proof and specimen issues since 1950, by Charles R. Hosch [Atlanta? c1971] 264 p. 23 cm. Stamped on t.p.: Distributed by HC Publishers, New York. [CJ1755.H67] 73-159318
1. Proof coins. 2. Coins. I. Title.

Proportion.

COLMAN, Samuel, 1832-1920. 701.8
Nature's harmonic unity; a treatise on its relation to proportional form. Edited by C. Arthur Coan. With 302 illus. by the author. The mathematical analysis by the editor. New York, B. Blom, 1971. viii, 327 p. illus. 28 cm. Reprint of the 1912 ed. [N7431.C65 1971] 78-177520
1. Proportion. I. Coan, Clarence Arthur, 1867-1934, ed. II. Title. BIP

GHYKA, Matila Costiescu, 701'.17
1881-1965.
The geometry of art and life / Matila Ghyka. New York : Dover Publications, 1977. xvii, 174 p. : ill. ; 22 cm. Reprint of the 1946 ed. published by Sheed and Ward, New York. [N7430.G47 1977] 77-78586 ISBN 0-486-23542-4 : 2.75
1. Proportion. 2. Proportion (Art) 3. Aesthetics. I. Title. BIP

Proportion (Art)

MUNARI, Bruno. 741.4
Discovery of the square. [English translation by Desmond O'Grady] New York, G. Wittenborn [1963] 84 p. illus. 16 cm. [N76.M8] 60-15446
1. Proportion (Art) 2. Square. I. Title.

MUNARI, Bruno 701.17
Discovery of the square. [Tr. by Desmond O'Grady] New York, Wittenborn [1966,c.1965] [87]p. illus. 16cm. Bibl. [N76.M8] 65-28615 4.50 pap.,
1. Proportion (Art) 2. Square. I. Title.

THOMAS, Brian, 1912- 110
Geometry in pictorial composition. Newcastle upon Tyne, Oriel Press, 1971. 152 p. illus. 23 cm. [NC745.T55 1971] 68-55977 ISBN 0-85362-052-0 £3.00
1. Proportion (Art) 2. Perspective. I. Title. BIP

WEYL, Hermann, 1885-1955. 701.17
Symmetry. Princeton, Princeton University Press, 1952. 168 p. illus. 23 cm. "Preface and bibliographical remarks": 5th and 6th prelim. pages. [N76.W4] 52-5830
1. Proportion (Art) 2. Aesthetics. BIP

Proportion (Art)—Addresses, essays, lectures.

PATTERNS of symmetry / 700'.1
edited by Marjorie Senechal and George Fleck. Amherst : University of Massachusetts Press, 1977. vii, 152 p. : ill. ; 24 cm. Includes the Proceedings of the Symmetry Festival, held at Smith College, February 1973. Bibliography: p. [147]-150. [NX650.P65P37] 76-56775 ISBN 0-87023-232-0 lib.bdg. : 12.00
1. Proportion (Art)—Addresses, essays, lectures. 2. Arts—Addresses, essays, lectures. 3. Symmetry—Addresses, essays, lectures. I. Senechal, Marjorie. II. Fleck, George M. III. Symmetry Festival, Smith College, 1973.

Propylon, Samothrace.

LEHMANN, Phyllis Lourene 733'.3
Williams, 1912-
Skopas in Samothrace [by] Phyllis Williams Lehmann. Northampton, Mass., Smith College, 1973. 85 p. illus. 23 cm. (The Katharine Asher Engel lectures, 1972) Includes bibliographical references. [NB104.L43] 73-88453 5.00
1. Scopas, fl. 4th century B.C. 2. Propylon, Samothrace. I. Title. II. Series.

Protestant Episcopal Church in the U.S.A.—Connecticut.

COIT, Richard M. 779'.4'0924
Churches in Episcopal Connecticut : photographs / by Richard M. Coit ; edited by Kenneth Walter Cameron. Hartford : Transcendental Books, [1974] 186 leaves : chiefly ill. ; 29 cm. [BX5917.C8C64] 74-193173
1. Protestant Episcopal Church in the U.S.A.—Connecticut. 2. Churches—Connecticut—Pictorial works. I. Title.

Providence—Recreation facilities.

PROVIDENCE. City 711'.558'097452
Plan Commission.
Master plan for public recreation and conservation. [Providence, 1966] 54 p. illus., plan. 29 cm. "Supplants the Master plan for playgrounds and playfields completed in 1951 and published thirteen years ago." [GV54.R5P6] 66-28612
1. Providence—Recreation facilities. I. Title.

Provincetown Art Association.

MOFFETT, Ross 706.27449
Art in narrow streets; the first thirty-three years of the Provinceton Art Association. Falmouth, Mass., Kendall Print. Co., 1964. 110p. illus., ports. 23cm. 64-55283 price unreported
1. Provincetown Art Association. I. Title.

Provincetown, Mass—Descr.—Views.

WAINWRIGHT, Wainwright 917.449
Johnson, 1917-
Cape Cod in picture and story Cotuit, Mass., Picture Book Press [1954] 64p. illus. 22cm. [F74.P96W3] 53-32934
1. Provincetown, Mass—Descr.—Views. I. Title.

WAINWRIGHT, Wainwright 917.449
Johnson 1917-
Provincetown, in picture and story. Cotuit, Mass., Picture Book Co. [1953] 95p. illus. 22cm. [F74.P96W3] 53-32934
1. Provincetown, Mass.—Descr.— Views. I. Title.

Provincetown, Mass.—Hist.

HATCH, Mellen C M. 974.49
The log of Provincetown and Truro on Cape Cod. Provincetown, Mass., 1939 [i. e. 1951] 86 p. illus. 21 cm. Includes bibliography. [F74.P96H3 1951] 51-7029
1. Provincetown, Mass.—Hist. 2. Truro, Mass.—Hist. I. Title.

SUBJECT INDEX

PUEBLO INDIANS—POTTERY.

Prudhomme, Edward C.

PRUDHOMME, Edward C. 739.7'4
E. C. Prudhomme, master gun engraver; a retrospective exhibition: 1946-1973. April 1 to May 13, 1973, the R. W. Norton Art Gallery. [Shreveport, La., R. W. Norton Art Gallery, 1973] 32 p. illus. 29 cm. Catalogue. [TS532.2.U6S563] 73-78704 ISBN 0-913060-01-1
1. Prudhomme, Edward C. 2. Firearms—Exhibitions. I. Norton (R. W.) Art Gallery. II. Title.

Prytaneums.

MILLER, Stephen G. 725'.1
The prytaneion : its function and architectural form / Stephen G. Miller. Berkeley : University of California Press, c1978. xiv, 258 p., [8] leaves of plates : ill. ; 25 cm. Includes indexes. Bibliography: p. 240-245. [NA278.P78M54] 76-24590 ISBN 0-520-03316-7 : 14.50
1. Prytaneums. I. Title. BIP

Psychiatric hospitals — Design and construction — Congresses.

GOOD, Lawrence R ed. 725.52
Therapy by design; implications of architecture for human behavior, compiled and edited by Lawrence R. Good, Saul M. Siegel [and] Alfred Paul Bay. Springfield, Ill., Thomas [1965] x. 193 p. illus. 27 cm. Report of a project entitled "Architectural mofification to meet functional change," undertaken at Topeka State Hospital in August, 1962, and made possible in part by the financial support of the National Institute of Mental Health, project grant OM-986. Includes proceedings of a conference held March 11-13, 1963, in Topeka, Kansas, to discuss the project. [RC439.G65] 65-11307
1. Psychiatric hospitals — Design and construction — Congresses. I. Siegel, Saul M., joint ed. II. Bay, Alfred Paul, joint ed. III. Kansas, State Hospital, Topeka. IV. Title.

Psychiatrists—Caricatures and cartoons.

SZEKELY-KOVACS, Olga illus. 741.5
Caricatures of 88 pioneers in psychoanalysis, drawn from life at the Eighth International Psychoanalytic Congress [by] Olga Szekely- Kovacs and Robert Bereny. New York, Basic Books [1954] [96]p. (chiefly illus.) 23cm. [NC1763.S9A43] 54-8202
1. Psychiatrists—Caricatures and cartoons. I. Bereny, Robert, joint illus. II. Title.

Psychiatry in art.

PICKFORD, Ralph William, 701.15
1903-
Studies in psychiatric art; its psychodynamics, therapeutic value, and relationship to modern art, by R. W. Pickford. Springfield, Ill., C. C. Thomas [1967] xix, 340 p. illus. 24 cm. Includes bibliographies. [N8237.5.P5] 67-12038
1. Psychiatry in art. 2. Art and mental illness. I. Title.

Psychical research.

ROBERTS, Jane, 1929- 759.4
The world view of Paul Cezanne : a psychic interpretation / by Jane Roberts ; introd. by Seth. Englewood Cliffs, N.J. : Prentice-Hall, c1977. xviii, 246 p. ; 22 cm. Includes index. [ND553.C33R587] 77-8079 ISBN 0-13-968859-5 : 7.95
1. Cezanne, Paul, 1839-1906. 2. Psychical research. I. Title. BIP

Psychoanalysis—Caricatures and cartoons.

FREEMAN, Paul K. 1929- 741.5973
An introduction to Sigmund Freud, M.D., and psychoanalysis, including the first public printing of Dr. Freud's paper, 'Der Mutti.' Written, illus. by Paul Freeman. Englewood Cliffs, N.J., Prentice [c.1965] 1v. (unpaged) col. illus. 21cm. [NC1429.F669] 65-15125 1.50 pap.,
1. Psychoanalysis—Caricatures and cartoons. I. Title.

Public buildings.

GUIDELINES 720'.28 s
Publications.
Commercial, institutional, and other heavy frame construction. Orinda, Calif. : Guidelines Publications, 1975, c1974. 52 p. ; 29 cm. (Its Architectural working drawing check list ; 1) [NA2700.G83 1974 vol. 1] [NA4170] 720'.28 75-326321 pbk. : 6.00
1. Public buildings. 2. Architecture—Details. I. Title.

PEVSNER, Nikolaus, Sir, 725'.09
1902-
A history of building types / Nikolaus Pevsner. Princeton, N.J. : Princeton University Press, c1976. 352 p. : ill. ; 30 cm. (A. W. Mellon lectures in the fine arts ; 19) Includes index. Bibliography: p. 295. [NA4170.P48] 75-4459 ISBN 0-691-09904-9 : 37.50
1. Public buildings. I. Title. II. Series. III. Bollingen series ; 35

Public housing—Richmond, Calif.—Case studies.

COOPER, Clare C. 711'.13
Easter Hill Village : some social implications of design / Clare C. Cooper. New York : Free Press, [1975] xxiv, 337 p. : ill. ; 24 cm. Includes index. Bibliography: p. 325-333. [HD7304.R47C66] 74-10311 ISBN 0-02-906670-0 : 15.95
1. Public housing—Richmond, Calif.—Case studies. 2. Public housing—Social aspects. 3. Row houses—Richmond, Calif.—Case studies. 4. Architecture, Domestic—Designs and plans. I. Title. BIP

Publishers and publishing—Handbooks, manuals, etc.

GIBSON, Joe A. 770.2'32
How to sell every photograph you take, by Joe A. Gibson. [San Angelo, Tex.] Educator Books [1970] 93 p. illus., port. 22 cm. [Z476.G5] 71-129077 4.95
1. Publishers and publishing—Handbooks, manuals, etc. 2. Photography as a profession. I. Title.

Puccinelli, Raimondo, 1904—

PUCCINELLI, Raimondo, 730'.92'4
1904-
An exhibition of the sculpture and drawings of Raimondo Puccinelli of Florence, Italy, September 29-November 12, 1974, the Duke University Museum of Art, Durham, North Carolina. [Durham, N.C. : Duke University Museum of Art, 1974] [47] p. : ill. ; 22 cm. "Catalog" : p. [16] [NB623.PD84] 74-193199
1. Puccinelli, Raimondo, 1904- I. Duke University, Durham, N.C. Art Museum. II. Title.

Pucelle, Jean, fl. 1320.

MORAND, Kathleen 745.67
Jean Pucelle. Oxford, Clarendon Pr. [dist. New York, Oxford, 1963, c.1962] xiv, 49p. 33 plates. 29cm. Based on thesis, University of London. Bibl. 63-1388 7.20
1. Pucelle, Jean, fl. 1320. 2. Illumination of books and manuscripts—France. I. Title.

Pueblo Bonito, N.M. Indians of North America — Architecture.

JUDD, Neil Merton, 1887- 722.91
The architecture of Pueblo Bonito, by Neil M. Judd. Washington, Smithsonian Institution, 1964. vii, 349 p. map, plans, 81 plates. 24 cm. (Smithsonian miscellaneous collections, v. 147, no. 1) Smithsonian Institution. Publication 4524. Bibliography: p. 235-240. [Q11.S7 vol. 147, no. 1] 64-62271 E78
1. Pueblo Bonito, N.M. Indians of North America — Architecture. I. Title. II. Series. III. Series: Smithsonian Institution. Smithsonian miscellaneous collections, v. 147, no. 1

Pueblo Indians.

HARLOW, Francis 738'.0917497
Harvey, 1928-
Historic Pueblo Indian pottery; painted jars and bowls of the period, 1600-1900. Text and drawings by Francis H. Harlow. Los Alamos, N.M., Printed by the Monitor Press: [distribution by the Museum of New Mexico, 1967] 49 p. illus. 23 cm. [E99.P9H27] 67-2610
1. Pueblo Indians. 2. Indians of North America — Pottery. I. Title. BIP

Pueblo Indians—Antiquities.

PACKARD, Gar. 732'.2
Suns and serpents; the symbolism of Indian rock art, by Gar and Maggy Packard. Drawings by Ow-u-Te-Wa. [1st ed. Santa Fe., N.M., Packard Publications, 1974] 64 p. illus. 28 cm. Bibliography: p. 63. [E99.P9P25] 73-93621 4.95
1. Pueblo Indians—Antiquities. 2. Petroglyphs—Southwest, New. 3. Southwest, New—Antiquities. I. Packard, Maggy, joint author. II. Title.

Pueblo Indians—Art.

BUNZEL, Ruth Leah, 1898- 738
The Pueblo potter; a study of creative imagination in primitive art, by Ruth L. Bunzel. New York, Dover Publications [1972] 134 p. illus. 26 cm. Originally presented as the author's thesis, Columbia. Reprint of the 1929 ed. published by Columbia University Press, New York. Bibliography: p. 129-130. [E99.P9B88 1972] 72-79159 ISBN 0-486-22875-4 3.00
1. Pueblo Indians—Art. 2. Indians of North America—Arizona—Pottery. 3. Indians of North America—New Mexico—Pottery. Title. BIP

BUNZEL, Ruth Leah, 1898- 738
The Pueblo potter; a study of creative imagination in primitive art, by Ruth L. Bunzel. New York, AMS Press [1969] 134 p. illus. 29 cm. "An investigation .. under the auspices of the Southwest Society and the Department of Anthropology of Columbia University." Issued also as thesis, Columbia University. Reprint of the 1929 ed. Bibliography: p. 129-130. [E99.P9B88 1969] 73-82257
1. Pueblo Indians—Art. 2. Indians of North America—Arizona—Pottery. 3. Indians of North America—New Mexico—Pottery. I. Archaeological Institute of America. Southwest Society, Los Angeles. II. Columbia University. Dept. of Anthropology. III. Title.

MERA, Harry Percival, 738.3'09701
1875-1951.
Pueblo designs; 176 illustrations of the "rain bird." Drawings by Tom Lea. New York, Dover Publications [1970, c1938] 113 p. illus. (part col.) 26 cm. Original ed., which has title The "rain bird": a study in Pueblo design, was issued as v. 2 of Memoirs of the Laboratory of Anthropology. Bibliography: p. [15] [E99.P9M4 1970] 73-127847 ISBN 0-486-22073-7 2.50
1. Pueblo Indians—Art. 2. Indians of North America—Art. I. Title. II. Series: Santa Fe, N.M. Laboratory of Anthropology. Memoirs, v. 2. BIP

UNDERHILL, Ruth Murray, 1884- 745
Pueblo crafts / by Ruth Underhill. New York : AMS Press, 1979. p. cm. Reprint of the 1945 ed. published by the Education Division, U.S. Indian Service, Washington, which was issued as 7 of Indian handcrafts. Bibliography: p. [E99.P9U315 1979] 76-43880 ISBN 0-404-15737-8 : 32.50
1. Pueblo Indians Art. 2. Indians of North America—Southwest, New—Art. 3. Pueblo Indians—Industries. 4. Indians of North America—Southwest, New—Industries. I. Title. II. Series: United States. Bureau of Indian Affairs. Indian handcrafts ; 7. BIP

Pueblo Indians—Embroidery.

MERA, Harry Percival, 746.4'4
1875-1951.
Pueblo Indian embroidery / by H. P. Mera ; drawings by the author. Santa Fe, N.M. : William Gannon, 1975. 73 p. : ill. (some col.) ; 26 cm. Reprint of the 1943 ed. published by University of New Mexico Press which was issued as v. 4 of the Memoirs of the Laboratory of Anthropology. Includes bibliographical references. [E99.P9M39 1975] 74-31607 ISBN 0-88307-512-1 : 15.00 ISBN 0-88307-513-X pbk. : 7.50
1. Pueblo Indians—Embroidery. 2. Indians of North America—Embroidery. I. Title. II. Series: Santa Fe, N.M. Laboratory of Anthropology. Memoirs ; v. 4. BIP

Pueblo Indians—Juvenile literature.

NELSON, Mary Carroll. 730'.92'4 B
Michael Naranjo / by Mary Carroll Nelson. Minneapolis : Dillon Press, [1975] 66 p. : ill. ; 23 cm. A biography of the Pueblo Indian sculptor who was blinded in Vietnam in 1968. [E99.P9N276] 92 75-14366 ISBN 0-87518-111-2 : 4.95
1. Naranjo, Michael—Juvenile literature. 2. Naranjo, Michael. 3. Pueblo Indians—Juvenile literature. I. Title. BIP

Pueblo Indians—Pottery.

BRETERNITZ, David A. 738'.09791 s
Prehistoric ceramics of the Mesa Verde region / compiled by David A. Breternitz, Arthur H. Rohn, Jr., and Elizabeth A. Morris.; general editor, Watson Smith, assistant editor, Kathleen Gratz. Flagstaff : Northern Arizona Society of Science and Art, 1974. ix, 70 p., 1 fold. leaf of plates : ill. ; 28 cm. (Museum of Northern Arizona ceramic series ; no. 5) Includes index. Bibliography: p. 65-67. [E78.S7F56a no. 5] [E99.P9] 738.3'09791 74-193295
1. Pueblo Indians—Pottery. 2. Indians of North America—Southwest, New—Pottery. 3. Pueblo Indians—Antiquities. 4. Southwest, New—Antiquities. I. Rohn, Arthur H., 1929- joint author. II. Morris, Elizabeth Ann, 1932- joint author. III. Title. IV. Series: Flagstaff, Ariz. Museum of Northern Arizona. Ceramic series ; no. 5. BIP

CHAPMAN, Kenneth Milton, 738.3'7
1875-1968.
The pottery of Santo Domingo pueblo, a detailed study of its decoration / Kenneth M. Chapman. Albuquerque : Published for the School of American Research [by the] University of New Mexico Press, 1977. xiv, 192 p. : ill. ; 32 cm. A reissue of the 1953 ed. Bibliography: p. 192. [E99.P9C47 1977] 77-81985 ISBN 0-8263-0460-5 : 22.50
1. Pueblo Indians—Pottery. 2. Santo Domingo, N.M. (Indian pueblo) 3. Indians of North America—New Mexico—Pottery. 4. Pueblo Indians—Art. 5. Indians of North America—New Mexico—Art. I. Santa Fe, N.M. School of American Research. II. Title.

FRANK, Lawrence Phillip. 738.3'83
Historic pottery of the Pueblo Indians, 1600-1880 / by Larry Frank and Francis H. Harlow ; photos. by Bernard Lopez. Boston : New York Graphic Society, 1974 [i.e.1975] xvi, 160 p., [16] leaves of plates : ill. (some col.) ; 28 cm. Bibliography: p. 158-160. [E99.P9F69] 73-89957 ISBN 0-8212-0586-2 : 25.00
1. Pueblo Indians—Pottery. 2. Indians of North America—Southwest, New—Pottery. I. Harlow, Francis Harvey, 1928- joint author. II. Title. BIP

GIFFORD, James C. 738.3'7
Gray corrugated pottery from Awatovi and other Jeddito sites in Northeastern Arizona / James C. Gifford and Watson Smith, with the assistance of Carol A. Gifford, Muriel Kirkpatrick, and Robert O'Haire ; compiled by Carol A. Gifford. Cambridge, Mass. : Peabody Museum of Archaeology and Ethnology, Harvard University, 1978. xi, 155 p. : ill. ; 27 cm. (Papers of the Peabody Museum of Archaeology and Ethnology, Harvard University ; v. 69) (Reports of the Awatovi Expedition ; no. 10) Bibliography: p. 153-155. [E51.H337 vol. 69] [E99.P9] 78-50909 ISBN 0-87365-194-4 pbk. : 15.00
1. Pueblo Indians—Pottery. 2. Indians of North America—Arizona—Pottery. 3. Awatovi, Ariz. 4. Jeddito Valley, Ariz.—Antiquities. 5. Arizona—Antiquities. I. Smith, Watson, 1897- joint author. II.

Gifford, Carol A. III. Title. IV. Series: Harvard University. Peabody Museum of Archaeology and Ethnology. Papers ; v. 69. V. Series: Harvard University. Peabody Museum of Archaeology and Ethnology. Awatovi Expedition. Reports ; no. 10.

HARLOW, Francis Harvey, 1928- 738.3'7
Modern Pueblo pottery, 1880-1960 / by Francis H. Harlow. 1st ed. Flagstaff : Northland Press, c1977. viii, 110 p. : ill. (some col.) ; 28 cm. Includes index. Bibliography: p. 107. [E99.P9H28] 76-52540 ISBN 0-87358-159-8 : 25.00
1. Pueblo Indians—Pottery. 2. Indians of North America—Southwest, New—Pottery. I. Title. BIP

MAXWELL Museum of Anthropology. 738.3'7
Seven families in Pueblo pottery / Maxwell Museum of Anthropology. Albuquerque : University of New Mexico Press, 1975, c1974. 112 p. : ill. (some col.) ; 18 cm. Originally published as the catalog of an exhibition held in 1974 at the Maxwell Museum of Anthropology. [E99.P9M36 1975] 75-17376 ISBN 0-8263-0388-9 pbk. : 4.95
1. Pueblo Indians—Pottery. 2. Indians of North America—Southwest, New—Pottery. I. Title. BIP

WASHBURN, Dorothy Koster. 738.3'7
A symmetry analysis of Upper Gila area ceramic design / Dorothy Koster Washburn ; ill. by Sarah Whitney Powell and Barbara Westman. Cambridge, Mass. : Peabody Museum of Archaeology and Ethnology, Harvard University, 1977. xiii, 193 p. : ill. ; 27 cm. (Papers of the Peabody Museum of Archaeology and Ethnology, Harvard University ; v. 68) Bibliography: p. 190-193. [E99.P9W37] 76-53125 ISBN 0-87365-193-6 lib.bdg. : 25.00
1. Pueblo Indians—Pottery. 2. Indians of North America—New Mexico—Catron Co.—Pottery. 3. Pueblo Indians—Antiquities. 4. New Mexico—Antiquities. 5. Catron Co., N.M.—Antiquities. I. Title. II. Series: Harvard University. Peabody Museum of Archaeology and Ethnology. Papers ; v. 68. BIP

Pueblo Indians—Pottery—Catalogs.

LISTER, Robert Hill, 1915- 738.3
Anasazi pottery : ten centuries of prehistoric ceramic art in the Four Corners country of the Southwestern United States, as illustrated by the Earl H. Morris memorial pottery collection in the University of Colorado Museum / by Robert H. Lister and Florence C. Lister. [Albuquerque] : Published for the Maxwell Museum of Anthropology, University of New Mexico, by the University of New Mexico Press, c1978. ix, 94 p. : ill. ; 28 cm. Edition of 1969 published under title: The Earl H. Morris memorial pottery collection. Bibliography: p. 94. [E99.P9L53 1978] 78-6825 ISBN 0-8263-0473-7 : 5.95
1. Morris, Earl Halstead, 1889-1956—Art collections. 2. Pueblo Indians—Pottery—Catalogs. 3. Indians of North America—Southwest, New—Pottery—Catalogs. I. Lister, Florence Cline, joint author. II. Title. BIP

Pugh, Clifton Ernest, 1924—

PUGH, Clifton Ernest, 1924- 759.994
Clifton Pugh (b. 1924, Richmond, Australia), recent paintings : [catalogue of an exhibition held] 4th-29th May 1976 [at the] Crane Kalman Gallery. London : The Gallery, [1976] [8] p. : chiefly ill. 17 x 26 cm. [ND1105.P8C7] 76-378649 ISBN 0-9503599-4-7 : £0.30
1. Pugh, Clifton Ernest, 1924- I. Crane Kalman Gallery.

Pugin, Augustus Welby Northmore, 1812-1852.

FERREY, Benjamin, 1810-1880. 720'.92'4 B
Recollections of A. N. Welby Pugin, and his father, Augustus Pugin; with notices of their works. With an appendix by E. Sheridan Purcell. New York, B. Blom, 1972. xv, 473 p. illus. 21 cm. "An appendix, in which the writings and character of Augustus Welby Northmore Pugin are considered in their Catholic aspect, by Edmund Sheridan Purcell": p. 307-465. Reprint of the 1861 ed. [NA997.P9F4 1972] 77-173143
1. Pugin, Augustus Welby Northmore, 1812-1852. 2. Pugin, Augustus Charles, 1762-1832. I. Purcell, Edmund Sheridan, 1824?-1899. II. Title.

STANTON, Phoebe B. 720.9'24
Pugin [by] Phoebe Stanton. Pref. by Nikolaus Pevsner. New York, Viking Press [1972, c1971] 216 p. illus. 22 cm. (A Studio book) Bibliography: p. 210-212. [NA997.P9S7 1972] 78-172898 ISBN 0-670-58216-6 7.95
1. Pugin, Augustus Welby Northmore, 1812-1852.

Pulham, St. Mary the Virgin. Parish Church.

BONNER, Stephen. 781'.91
Angel musicians above the entrance porch of the parish church of Pulham St. Mary the Virgin, near Diss, Norfolk, England; text by Stephen Bonner. Cambridge, Stephen Bonner, 59 Moorfield Rd., Duxford, 1967. [21] p. illus., map. 22 cm. [ML85.B63] 68-117660
1. Pulham, St. Mary the Virgin. Parish Church. 2. Musical instruments—Pictorial works. 3. Music in art. I. Title.

Punched work.

ILLES, Robert E. 746.4'4
Men in stitches / Robert E. Illes. New York : Van Nostrand Reinhold Co., [1975] 136 p. : ill. ; 25 cm. Includes index. [TT840.I42] 74-22512 ISBN 0-442-23630-1 : 13.95
1. Punched work. 2. Embroidery. 3. Needlework. I. Title. BIP

Puppet craft.

BRODY, Vera. 745.59'22
Fun with puppets / Vera Brody, Marie-Francoise Heron ; ill. by Christiane Neuville , photos. by Marie Dolar. New York : Watts, 1975. 95 p. : ill. (some col.) ; 18 cm. (A Panda paperback) [TT174.7.B76] 74-22509 ISBN 0-531-02802-X pbk. : 1.95
1. Puppet craft. I. Heron, Marie-Francoise, joint author. II. Neuville, Christiane. III. Dolar, Marie. IV. Title. BIP

Puppet making.

BINYON, Helen. 745.5922
Puppetry today; designing and making marionettes, hand puppets, rod puppets, and shadow puppets. New York, Watson-Guptil Publications [1966] 112 p. illus. 26 cm. Bibliography: p. 110-111. [PN1977.B5 1966] 66-12999
1. Puppet making. I. Title.

DEAN, Audrey Vincente. 745.59'22
Wooden spoon puppets / by Audrey Vincente Dean ; illustrated by the author. 1st American ed. Boston : Plays, inc., 1976. 92 p. : ill. (some col.) ; 26 cm. [TT174.7.D43 1976] 75-28202 ISBN 0-8238-0204-3 : 9.95
1. Puppet making. 2. Spoons. I. Title. BIP

FETTIG, Hansjurgen. 745.59'22
Hand and rod puppets; a handbook of technique. English version by John Wright and Susanne Forster. Boston, Plays, inc. [1974, c1973] 119 p. illus. 22 x 29 cm. Translation of Hand- und Stabpuppen. [TT174.7.F4713 1974] 72-3692 ISBN 0-8238-0140-3 9.95
1. Puppet making. I. Title.

KAMPMANN, Lothar. 745.59'22
Creating with puppets. New York, Van Nostrand Reinhold Co. [1972] 75 p. illus. (part col.) 21 cm. (Art media series) Discusses the making and staging of a wide variety of puppets. Illustrated with photographs. [TT174.7.K35] 71-142217
1. Puppet making. I. Title.

LEWIS, Shari. 745.5922
Making easy puppets. Illustrated by Larry Lurin. [1st ed.] New York, Dutton [1967] 86 p. illus. 26 cm. Bibliography: p. 86. [PN1972.L45] 67-20128
1. Puppet making. I. Title.

MCLAREN, Esme. 745.59'22
Making glove puppets. [1st American ed.] Boston, Plays, inc. [1973] 218 p. illus. 25 cm. [TT174.7.M3 1973] 73-1573 ISBN 0-8238-0144-6 12.95
1. Puppet making. I. Title. BIP

MORTON, Brenda. 745.59'22
Sleeve puppets / Brenda Morton ; with drawings by Juliet Renny. New York : Taplinger Pub. Co., 1978. 118 p. : ill. ; 22 cm. Contains patterns and directions for sewing puppets that are held on the puppeteer's arm. [TT174.7.M68 1978] 77-92754 ISBN 0-8008-7237-1 : 8.50
1. Puppet making—Juvenile literature. I. Renny, Juliet. II. Title. BIP

ROMBERG, Jenean. 745.59'22
Let's discover puppets / Jenean Romberg. West Nyack, N.Y. : Center for Applied Research in Education, c1976. p. cm. (Her Arts and crafts discovery units) [TT174.7.R65] 76-5786 ISBN 0-87628-528-0
1. Puppet making. I. Title. BIP

ROTH, Charlene Davis, 1945- 745.59'22
The art of making puppets and marionettes / Charlene Davis Roth. 1st ed. Radnor. Pa. : Chilton Book Co., [1975] p. cm. (Chilton's creative crafts series) [TT174.7.R67 1965] 75-19016 ISBN 0-8019-6185-8 : 12.50 ISBN 0-8019-6186-6 pbk. : 6.95
1. Puppet making. I. Title. BIP

SLADE, Richard. 745.5922
You can make a string puppet; a practical guide to puppetry. Photos. by John Watts. [1st American ed.] Boston, Plays, inc. [1966] 46 p. illus. 25 cm. [PN1972.S5 1966] 66-31567
1. Puppet making. I. Title. BIP

Puppet making—Juvenile literature.

ALKEMA, Chester Jay. 745.59'22
Puppet-making. New York, Sterling Pub. Co. [1971] 48 p. illus. (part col.) 20 cm. (Little craft book series) An introduction to creating twenty-nine puppets from paper, papier mache, cloth, and various items found around the house. [TT174.7.A4 1971] 72-167668 ISBN 0-8069-5174-5
1. Puppet making—Juvenile literature. I. Title. BIP

CREATIVE Educational Society, Mankato, Minn. 745.59'22
How to have fun making puppets, by the editors of Creative [Educational Society] Illustrated by Nan Brooks. [Mankato, Minn., Creative Education; distributed by Childrens Press, Chicago, 1974] 31 p. illus. (part col.) 25 cm. (Creative craft books) On spine: Puppets. Directions for making stick, paper sack, box, hand, finger, and arm puppets. [TT174.7.C73 1974] 73-18225
1. Puppet making—Juvenile literature. I. Brooks, Nan, illus. II. Title. BIP

†GATES, Frieda. 745.59'22
Easy to make puppets / written and illustrated by Frieda Gates. New York : Harvey House, c1976. 47 p. : ill. ; 24 cm. Introduces five types of hand and string puppets to make from easy patterns. Includes a puppet play with staging suggestions. [TT174.7.G37] 75-27481 ISBN 0-8178-5432-0 Lib. bdg. : 4.69
1. Puppet making—Juvenile literature. I. Title. BIP

GATES, Frieda. 745.59'22
Glove, mitten, and sock puppets / by Frieda Gates. New York : Walker, 1978. 47 p. : ill. ; 20 x 24 cm. Illustrated instructions for creating a variety of puppets with discarded or mis-matched mittens, gloves, socks, and other simple materials. [TT174.7.G38 1978] 78-3068 ISBN 0-8027-6326-X : 5.95. ISBN 0-8027-6327-8 lib. bdg. : 5.85
1. Puppet making—Juvenile literature. I. Title. BIP

LUCKIN, Joyce. 745.59'22
Easy-to-make puppets. Photos. by Livia Rolandini. [1st American ed.] Boston, Plays, inc. [1975] 48 p. illus. 26 cm. Instructions, patterns, and photographs reveal how to create twenty-one puppets—hand, glove, and marionette. [TT174.7.L8 1975] 74-17063 ISBN 0-8238-0178-0 7.95
1. Puppet making—Juvenile literature. I. Rolandini, Livia, illus. II. Title.

MOLONEY, Joan. 745.59'22
Making puppets and puppet theatres. [1st American ed.] Boston, Plays, inc. [1974, c1973] p. cm. Instructions for making glove, sock, shadow, and other puppets and for constructing simple theaters they can perform in. [TT174.7.M64 1974] 74-2415 ISBN 0-8238-0169-1 6.95
1. Puppet making—Juvenile literature. 2. Puppet theaters—Juvenile literature. I. Title. BIP

MORTON, Brenda. 745.59'22
Needlework puppets. [Rev. ed.] Boston, Plays, inc. [1975] p. cm. Offers detailed instructions for making a variety of puppets. [TT174.7.M67 1975] 74-18484 ISBN 0-8238-0179-9 4.95
1. Puppet making—Juvenile literature. I. Title. BIP

PHILPOTT, Alexis Robert. 745.59'22
Let's make puppets [by] A. R. Philpott. New York, Van Nostrand Reinhold [1972] 32 p. illus. (part col.) 21 cm. (Starting points) Instructions for making many kinds of puppets such as rod, string, hand, and shadow from a variety of materials. [TT174.7.P47] 75-188508 ISBN 0442-26554-9 1.45
1. Puppet making—Juvenile literature. I. Title.

PHILPOTT, Violet. 745.59'22
The Knowhow book of puppets / [written and devised by Violet Philpott and Mary Jean McNeil ; illustrated by Malcolm English ; photos. by Brian Marshall]. New York : Corwin Books, c1976. 47 p. : col. ill. ; 29 cm. (The Knowhow books) Includes index. Describes the construction and operation of simple puppets. Includes suggestions for three open-ended plays. [TT174.7.P48 1976] 75-44854 ISBN 0-8069-8036-2 : 4.50 ISBN 0-8069-8039-7 lib.bdg. :
1. Puppet making—Juvenile literature. I. McNeil, Mary Jean, joint author. II. English, Malcolm. III. Title. BIP

ROSS, Laura. 745.59'22
Scrap puppets : how to make and move them / Laura Ross ; illustrated by Frank Ross, Jr. New York : Holt, Rinehart, and Winston, c1978. p. cm. Presents instructions for making marionettes and hand, rod, and shadow puppets from scrap materials found in the home and at school. Includes directions for manipulating the puppets. [TT174.7.R66] 78-4282 ISBN 0-03-018511-4 : 6.95
1. Puppet making—Juvenile literature. I. Ross, Frank Xavier, 1914- II. Title. BIP

Puppets and puppet-plays.

BODOR, John J. 745.59'22
Creating and presenting hand puppets. New York, Reinhold [1967] 144 p. illus. 24 cm. Bibliography: p. 143-144. [PN1972.B6] 66-22683
1. Puppets and puppet-plays. 2. Puppet making. I. Title.

CREEGAN, George. 745.59'22
Sir George's book of hand puppetry. Cover illus. by Don Meighan. Chicago, Follett Pub. Co. [1966] 95 p. illus., ports. 21 cm. Includes the author's production script for the puppet adaptation of "The night it rained toys," by Dorothy Stephenson. [PN1972.C7] 67-5679
1. Puppets and puppet-plays. I. Stephenson, Dorothy. The night it rained toys. II. Title.

ENGLER, Larry. 745.59'22
Making puppets come alive; a method of learning and teaching hand puppetry [by] Larry Engler and Carol Fijan. Photography by David Attie. Demonstration puppets designed by Paul Vincent Davis. [1st ed.] New York, Taplinger [1973] 192 p. illus.

SUBJECT INDEX

PYRAMIDS—JUVENILE LITERATURE.

25 cm. [PN1972.E54] 72-6623 ISBN 0-8008-5074-2 9.95
1. Puppets and puppet-plays. I. Fijan, Carol, joint author. II. Title. **BIP**

FRASER, Peter, 1932- 745.59'22
Puppet circus. With illus. by the author. [1st American ed.] Boston, Plays inc. [1971] 152 p. illus. 23 cm. Includes bibliographical references. [PN1972.F7214 1971] 77-129014 ISBN 0-8238-0119-5 4.95
1. Puppets and puppet-plays. I. Title. **BIP**

MALKIN, Michael R., 1943- 745.59'22
Traditional and folk puppets of the world / Michael R. Malkin ; with photos. by David L Young, additional photos. by Alan G. Cook. South Brunswick [N.J.] : A. S. Barnes, c1977. 194 p., [4] leaves of plates : ill. ; 25 cm. Includes index. Bibliography: p. 187-191. [PN1972.M32] 76-26381 ISBN 0-498-01871-7 : 12.00
1. Puppets and puppet-plays. I. Title.

ROBINSON, Stuart. 745.59'22
Exploring puppetry [by] Stuart and Patricia Robinson. With drawings by the authors and title pictures by Sheila Robinson. New York, Taplinger [1967, c1966] 134 p. illus. (part col.) 26 cm. Bibliography: p. 128-129. [PN1972.R54 1967] 67-16600
1. Puppets and puppet-plays. I. Robinson, Patricia, joint author. II. Title.

SNOOK, Barbara 745.5922
Puppets. Newton Center, Mass Branford 1966, c.1965 94p. illus. 23cm. [PN1972.S55] 66-12304 3.95 bds.,
1. Puppets and puppet-plays. I. Title. **BIP**

STILL, William Frank. 745.59'22
Charming children with puppets, for 35 years, by Wm. Frank Still. Jacksonville, Fla., Paramount Press [1967] ix, 77 p. illus., facsim., ports. 26 cm. Autobiographical. [PN1972.S72] 68-558
1. Puppets and puppet-plays. I. Title.

WILLIAMS, DeAtna M. 745.59'22
Paper-bag puppets [by] DeAtna M. Williams. Palo Alto, Calif., Fearon Publishers [1966] 59 p. illus. 28 cm. [PN1972.W575] 66-25058
1. Puppets and puppet-plays. I. Title. **BIP**

Purcell & Elmslie.

PURCELL, William Gray, 1880-1965. 720'.924
The Work of Purcell and Elmslie, architects. With a new introd. by David Gebhard. [Park Forest, Ill., Prairie School Press, c1965] 96 p. illus., plans, ports. 33 cm. Reproduced three issues of The Western architect: Jan. 1913, Jan. 1915, July 1915. Cover title: The architecture of Purcell and Elmaslie. [NA737.P8G4] 67-6747
1. Purcell & Elmslie. 2. Elmslie, George Grant, 1871-1952. 3. Architecture — U.S. I. The Western architect. II. Title. III. Title: The architecture of Purcell and Elmslie.

Purcell, Roy, 1936—

PURCELL, Roy, 1936- 769'.92'4
The wayfarer : poetry and etchings / by Roy Purcell. Millbrae, Calif. : Celestial Arts, 1975. [96] p. : ill. ; 22 cm. [NE2012.P87A58] 74-25836 ISBN 0-89087-007-1 : 4.95
1. Purcell, Roy, 1936- 2. Southwest, New, in art. 3. Self-realization in art. I. Title.

Pure Land Buddhism in art.

FUKUYAMA, Toshio, 1905- 726'.1'43920952
Heian temples : Byodo-in and Chuson-ji / by Toshio Fukuyama ; translated by Ronald K. Jones. 1st English ed. New York : Weatherhill, 1976. 168 p., [2] fold. leaves of plates : ill. (some col.) ; 24 cm. (The Heibonsha survey of Japanese art ; v. 9) Translation of Byodoin to Chusonji. [N8193.3.P8F8413] 75-41337 ISBN 0-8348-1023-9 : 12.50
1. Pure Land Buddhism in art. 2. Art, Japanese—Heian period, 794-1185. I. Title. II. Series. **BIP**

OKAZAKI, Joji, 1925- 759.952
Pure land Buddhist painting / Joji Okazaki ; translator, Elizabeth ten Grotenhuis. New York : Kodansha International, [1977] p. cm. (Japanese arts library ; v. 4) Translation of Jodokyo ga. Includes index. Bibliography: p. [ND1053.4.O3413] 76-9354 ISBN 0-87011-287-2 : 12.95
1. Pure Land Buddhism in art. 2. Painting, Japanese—Kamakura-Momoyama periods, 1185-1600. 3. Painting, Buddhist—Japan. I. Title. II. Series. **BIP**

Push Pin Studios.

THE Push Pin style. 760'.0973
Palo Alto, Calif., Communication Arts Magazine [1970] 1 v. (unpaged (chiefly illus. (part col.), group port.)) 24 cm. Catalog of the exhibition of works by members of the Push Pin Studios held Mar. 18-May 18, 1970, at the Musee des arts decoratifs, Paris. Editorial matter in English and French. [NC999.4.P86P8] 77-14861
1. Push Pin Studios. I. Paris. Musee des arts decoratifs.

Pushkin, Aleksandr Sergeevich, 1799-1837.

REUTLINGER, Mathias von, 1897- 741.973
Pen and ink drawings, by Mathias Von Reutlinger. "The queen of spades" [and] "The captain's daughter," by A. S. Pushkin, "War and peace," by L. N. Tolstoy. Limited ed. [Philadelphia, c1970] 73 l. illus. 27 cm. Cover title. English and Russian. [NC975.5.P8R48] 77-16953
1. Pushkin, Aleksandr Sergeevich, 1799-1837. Pikovaia dama—Illustrations. 2. Pushkin, Aleksandr Sergeevich, 1799-1837. Kapitanskaia dochka—Illustrations. 3. Tolstoi Lev Nikolaevich, graf, 1828-1910. Voina i mir—Illustrations.

Puy, Jean, 1876-1960.

BESSON, George, 1882- 759.4
Jean Puy [Exposition] Musee de Lyon. [Lyon] 1963. 1 v. (unpaged) illus. (part col.) port. 25 cm. Text by G. Besson. [ND553.P94L9] 66-55763
1. Puy, Jean, 1876-1960. I. Title.

LYONS. Musee des beaux-arts. 759.4
Jean Puy [Exposition] Musee de Lyon. [Lyon] 1963. 1 v. (unpaged) illus. (part col.) port. 25 cm. Text by G. Besson. [ND553.P94L9] 66-55763
1. Puy, Jean, 1876-1960. I. Besson, George, 1882- II. Title.

Puzinas, Paul, 1907-1967.

PUZINAS, Paul, 1907-1967. 759.743
Puzinas / by Frederic Whitaker ; introd. by A. Puzinas. New York : Austra Publications, 1975. [72] p. : chiefly col. ill. ; 33 cm. Includes bibliographical references. [ND699.P89W45] 74-79812
1. Puzinas, Paul, 1907-1967. I. Whitaker, Frederic.

Pyle, Howard, 1853-1911.

THE Brandywine heritage: 759.13
Howard Pyle, N. C. Wyeth, Andrew Wyeth, James Wyeth. Chadds Ford, Pa., Brandywine River Museum; distributed by New York Graphic Society, Greenwich Conn. [1971] 121 p. illus. (part col.) 27 cm. Catalog of an exhibition held at the Brandywine River Museum, Chadds Ford, Pa. [ND236.B68] 78-164689 ISBN 0-912416-01-7 14.50
1. Pyle, Howard, 1853-1911. 2. Wyeth family. I. Brandywine River Museum.

DELAWARE Art Museum. 760'.0924
Howard Pyle; works in the collection of the Delaware Art Museum. [Wilmington] 1971. 56 p. illus. (part col.), port. 26 cm. Catalogue prepared by Rowland Elzea. [NC975.5.P9D4] 70-27589
1. Pyle, Howard, 1853-1911. I. Elzea, Rowland.

DELAWARE Art Museum. 759.13
Howard Pyle: diversity in depth. [Exhibition] March 5-April 15, 1973. [Wilmington, 1973] 81 p. illus. 22 x 28 cm. [ND237.P94D44] 72-97684
1. Pyle, Howard, 1853-1911. I. Title.

MORSE, Willard Samuel, 1856-1935, comp. 016.741973
Howard Pyle; a record of his illustrations and writings, compiled by Willard S. Morse and Gertrude Brinckle. Wilmington, Wilmington Society of the Fine Arts, 1921. Detroit, Singing Tree Press, 1969. x, 242 p. illus., port. 23 cm. [NC139.P8M6 1969] 68-31099
1. Pyle, Howard, 1853-1911. 2. Pyle, Howard, 1853-1911—Bibliography. I. Brinckle, Gertrude, joint comp.

NESBITT, Elizabeth. 741.0924
Howard Pyle. [1st American ed.] New York, H. Z. Walck [1966] 71, [1] p. port. 19 cm. Bibliography: p. 68-[72] [PS2671.N4 1966a] 66-31456
1. Pyle, Howard, 1853-1911.

PITZ, Henry Clarence, 1895- 760'.092'4
Howard Pyle—writer, illustrator, founder of the Brandywine school / by Henry C. Pitz. 1st ed. New York : C. N. Potter : distributed by Crown Publishers, [1975] viii, 248 p., [16] leaves of plates : ill. (some col.) ; 32 cm. Includes index. Bibliography: p. 231-244. [ND237.P94P57 1975] 74-77563 ISBN 0-517-51665-9(Crown) : 25.00.
1. Pyle, Howard, 1853-1911. I. Title.

PYLE, Howard, 1853-1911. 759.13
Howard Pyle / introd. by Rowland Elzea. 1st U.S. ed. New York : Scribner, 1975. [5] p., 43 leaves of plates : chiefly col. ill. ; 30 cm. "An original Peacock Press/Bantam Book." [ND237.P94A44 1975] 75-5196 ISBN 0-684-14415-8 : 10.00
1. Pyle, Howard, 1853-1911.

Pyle, Howard, 1853-1911—Influence.

BRANDYWINE 760'.0973'07401512
tradition artists; featuring the works of Howard Pyle, Frank E. Schoonover, the Wyeth family, Charles Colombo, David Hanna. With introductory essay by Rowland Elzea. [Exhibition held] October 1971-October 1972. Exhibitors: International Art Gallery, Pittsburgh, Pennsylvania [and others. New York, Great American Editions, 1971] 54 p. illus. 22 x 29 cm. Cover title: An album of Brandywine tradition artists. [N6512.B72] 72-180989 3.50
1. Pyle, Howard, 1853-1911—Influence. 2. Art, American—Exhibitions. 3. Art, Modern—20th century—U.S. I. International Art Gallery. II. Title: An album of Brandywine tradition artists.

PITZ, Henry Clarence, 1895- 760'.09748'13
The Brandywine tradition [by] Henry C. Pitz. Illustrated with 16 color and 32 black and white plates. Boston, Houghton Mifflin, 1969 [c1968] xv, 252 p. illus. (part col.), map, ports. 27 cm. Bibliography: p. [243]-246. [N6517.P5] 68-28457 12.95
1. Pyle, Howard, 1853-1911—Influence. 2. Artists, American—Brandywine Valley. I. Title.

Pyne, William Henry, 1769-1843.

PYNE, William Henry, 1769-1843. 769'.92'4
Picturesque views of rural occupations in early nineteenth-century England : all 641 illustrations from Ackermann's edition of the "Microcosm" / by W. H. Pyne. New York : Dover Publications, c1977. 120 p. : chiefly ill. ; 31 cm. (Dover pictorial archive series) [NC242.P9A4 1977] 77-80117 ISBN 0-486-23547-5 : 4.50
1. Pyne, William Henry, 1769-1843. 2. Occupations in art. I. Pyne, William Henry, 1769-1843. Microcosm. II. Title. **BIP**

Pyramid Lake, Calif.—Recreational use.

CALIFORNIA. Dept. of Water Resources. 711'.558
Pyramid Lake recreation development plan; initial facilities. [Sacramento] 1972. 12 p. illus. 28 cm. (Its Bulletin, no. 117-13) [GV54.C22P973 1972] 73-620985
1. Pyramid Lake, Calif.—Recreational use. I. Title. II. Series.

Pyramids.

EDWARDS, Iorwerth Eiddon Stephen. 913.32
The pyramids of Egypt [by] I. E. S. Edwards. New York, Viking Press [1972] 240 p. illus. 25 cm. (A Studio book) Bibliography: p. [227]-234. [DT63.E3 1972] 73-186741 ISBN 0-670-58361-8
1. Pyramids. I. Title.

EDWARDS, Iorwerth Eiddon Stephen. 913.32
The pyramids of Egypt [by] I. O. S. Edwards. Illus. by J. C. Rose. [Harmondsworth, Eng.] Penguin Books [1975, c1972] 319 p. illus. 18 cm. (A Pelican original) Bibliography: p. 299-311. [DT63.E3] ISBN 0-14-020168-8
1. Pyramids. I. Title.
Distributed by Penguin, Baltimore for 3.50 (pbk.) L.C. card number for original ed.: 51-2916. **BIP**

FAKHRY, Ahmed. 913.32
The pyramids. [Chicago] University of Chicago Press [1961] 260 p. illus., maps, plans. 24 cm. [DT63.F3] 61-8645
1. Pyramids. **BIP**

GHUNAIM, Muhammad Zakariya. 913.32
The buried pyramid. London, New York, Longmans, Green [1956] 155p. illus. 23cm. American ed. (New York, Rinehart) has title: The lost pyramid. [DT73.S3G5 1956a] 56-14553
1. Sekhem-khet, King of Egypt. 2. Pyramids. I. Title.

JEFFERY, Edmond C 913.32
The Pyramids and the patriarchs; a study of the exploration of the Great Pyramids of Egypt, their origin and their meaning for our time. New York, Exposition Press [1952] 176p. illus. 22cm. [DT63.5.J4] 52-5691
1. Pyramids. I. Title.

Pyramids—Construction.

MENDELSSOHN, Kurt. 913.32
The riddle of the pyramids. New York, Praeger [1974] 224 p. illus. 25 cm. Bibliography: p. 213-215. [DT63.M43] 73-18485 12.95
1. Pyramids—Construction. 2. Indians of Mexico—Pyramids. I. Title.

Pyramids—Construction—Juvenile literature.

MACAULAY, David. 690'.6'8
Pyramid / David Macaulay ; illustrated by the author. Boston : Houghton Mifflin, 1975. 80 p. : ill. ; 32 cm. Text and black-and-white illustrations follow the intricate step-by-step process of the building of an ancient Egyptian pyramid. [DT63.M25] 75-9964 ISBN 0-395-21407-6 : 7.95
1. Pyramids—Construction—Juvenile literature. I. Title. **BIP**

Pyramids—History.

COTTRELL, Leonard. 913.32
The mountains of Pharaoh. New York, Rinehart [1956] 285 p. illus. 22 cm. [DT63.C6] 56-5721
1. Pyramids—History. I. Title.

Pyramids—Juvenile literature.

WEEKS, John. 913.32
The pyramids. London, Cambridge University Press, 1971. 48 p. illus., maps. 21 cm. (Cambridge introduction to the history of mankind, topic books) [DT63.5.W4] 74-111135 ISBN 0-521-07240-9 £0.52
1. Pyramids—Juvenile literature. I. Title.

WEEKS, John. 932'.01
The pyramids / John Weeks. Minneapolis : Lerner Publications Co., 1977, c1971. p. cm. (A Cambridge topic book) Includes

1. Quilting. I. Title.

TAYLOR, Sibby, 1943- 746.9'7
New and easy quilting / Sibby Taylor ; photos. by Bob Mehesy. South Brunswick, [N.J.] : A. S. Barnes, c1977. 112 p., [4] leaves of plates : ill. ; 29 cm. Includes index. Bibliography: p. 110. [TT835.T34 1977] 76-27492 ISBN 0-498-02001-0 : 12.95
1. Quilting. I. Title. BIP

WEEKS, Linda S. 746.4'6
Patchwork & other quilting, by Linda S. Weeks. New York, Sterling Pub. Co. [1973] 48 p. illus. (part col.) 20 cm. (Little craft book series) [TT835.W43 1973] 73-83452 ISBN 0-8069-5290-3 3.50
1. Quilting. 2. Patchwork. I. Title.
Library binding; 3.29, ISBN 0-8069-5291-1.

WOOSTER, Ann-Sargent, 1946- 746.9'7
Quiltmaking; the modern approach to a traditional craft. New York, Drake Publishers [1972] x, 160 p. illus. (part col.) 26 cm. Bibliography: p. 159-160. [TT835.W66] 72-10733 ISBN 0-87749-288-3 8.95
1. Quilting. 2. Patchwork. 3. Applique. I. Title.

WOOSTER, Ann-Sargent, 1946- 746.9'7
Quiltmaking : the modern approach to a traditional craft / by Ann-Sargent Wooster. New York : Galahad Books, [1975] c1972. x, 160 p., [4] leaves of plates : ill. (some col.) ; 26 cm. Includes index. Bibliography: p. 159-160. [TT835.W66 1975] 74-15433 ISBN 0-88365-154-8 : 10.00
1. Quilting. 2. Patchwork. 3. Applique. I. Title.

Quilting—Canada—History.

CONROY, Mary, 1935- 746.9'7
300 years of Canada's quilts / mary Conroy Toronto : Griffin House, 1976. ix, 133 p. : ill. ; 18 x 26 cm. Bibliography: p. 130-133. [TT835.C65] 76-380946
1. Quilting—Canada—History. 2. Coverlets—Canada. I. Title.

Quilting—Kentucky.

CLARKE, Mary Washington. 746.9'7
Kentucky quilts and their makers / Mary Washington Clarke ; photo graphs by Ira Kohn. Lexington : University Press of Kentucky, c1976. viii, 119 p., [4] leaves of plates : ill. (some col.) ; 21 cm. (The Kentucky Bicentennial bookshelf) Includes indexes. Bibliography: p. 112-[113] [TT835.C57] 76-4435 ISBN 0-8131-0228-6 : 3.95
1. Quilting—Kentucky. 2. Quiltmakers—Kentucky. I. Title. II. Series.

Quilting—Patterns.

ECHOLS, Margit. 746.9'7
The new American quilt : an innovation in contemporary quilt design / by Margit Echols. 1st ed. Garden City, N.Y. : Doubleday, 1976. p. cm. [TT835.E36] 76-2839 ISBN 0-385-09924-X pbk. : 3.95
1. Quilting—Patterns. I. Title.

GRAFTON, Carol Belanger. 746.4'6
Traditional patchwork patterns : full-size cut-outs & instructions for 12 quilts / Carol Belanger Grafton. New York : Dover Publications, 1974. vi, 57 p. : ill. ; 28 cm. [TT835.G72] 74-82207 pbk. : 2.00
1. Quilting—Patterns. I. Title. BIP

HINSON, Dolores A. 746.4'6
A quilter's companion, by Dolores A. Hinson. New York, Arco [1973] 279 p. illus. 29 cm. [TT835.H48] 72-3333 ISBN 0-668-02666-9 8.95
1. Quilting—Patterns. I. Title. BIP

LARSEN, Judith LaBelle. 746.4'6
The patchwork quilt design & coloring book / by Judith LaBelle Larsen and Carol Waugh Gull ; [color ill. by Judy Larsen, Carol Gull, and Marilyn Gong, ill. by Phoebe Gaughan]. New York : Butterick Pub., c1977. 224 p. : ill. (some col.) ; 26 cm. [TT835.L34] 76-57296 ISBN 0-88421-028-6 : 7.95
1. Quilting—Patterns. 2. Patchwork—Patterns. I. Gull, Carol Waugh, joint author. II. Title. BIP

MCKAIN, Sharon. 746.4'6
The Great Noank Quilt Factory; how to make quilts & quilted things. Photography by Howard Park. Illus. by Richard M. Brown. New York, Random House [1974] 136 p. illus. 29 cm. Bibliography: p. 134-136. [TT835.M28] 73-20568 ISBN 0-394-49064-9 8.95
1. Quilting—Patterns. I. Title.

Quilting—Texas.

COOPER, Patricia. 976.4'06'0922 B
The quilters : women of the Southwest and their domestic art / by Patricia Cooper & Norma Bradley Buferd. 1st ed. New York : Doubleday, c1976. p. cm. Includes index. [TT835.C66] 76-2765 ISBN 0-385-11685-3 : 12.95
1. Quilting—Texas. 2. Quilting—New Mexico. I. Buferd, Norma Bradley, joint author. II. Title. BIP

Quilting—United States.

HECHTLINGER, Adelaide. 746.9'7
American quilts, quilting, and patchwork. [Harrisburg, Pa.] Stackpole Books [1974] 358 p. illus. 29 cm. (An Early American Society book) [TT835.H38] 74-13398 ISBN 0-8117-0092-5
1. Quilting—United States. 2. Patchwork—United States. I. Title.

Quilting—United States—Patterns.

DUBOIS, Jean, 1926- 746.9'7
The colonial history quilt / by Jean Dubois. Wheatridge, Colo. : Leman Publications, c1976. 56 p. : ill. ; 28 cm. [TT835.D78] 76-49695
1. Quilting—United States—Patterns. 2. United States—History—Colonial period, ca. 1600-1775. I. Title.

JOHNSON, Mary Elizabeth, 1944- 746.9'7
Country quilt patterns / Mary Elizabeth Johnson. Birmingham, Ala. : Oxmoor House, 1977. 80 p. : ill. (some col.) ; 28 cm. (Family guidebook series) [TT835.J588] 77-75689 ISBN 0-8487-0478-9 pbk. : 3.95
1. Quilting—United States—Patterns. 2. Coverlets, American. I. Title. BIP

JOHNSON, Mary Elizabeth, 1944- 746.9'7
Prize country quilts : designs, patterns, projects / Mary Elizabeth Johnson. 1st ed. Birmingham, Ala. : Oxmoor House, c1977. viii, 230 p. : ill. ; 29 cm. Includes index. Bibliography: p. 228. [TT835.J59] 76-40858 ISBN 0-8487-0444-4 : 12.95
1. Quilting—United States—Patterns. 2. Coverlets—United States. I. Title. BIP

MALONE, Maggie, 1942- 746.4'6
Classic American patchwork quilt patterns / Maggie Malone. New York : Drake Publishers, 1977. 192 p. : ill. ; 28 cm. Includes index. Bibliography: p. 189. [TT835.M35] 77-80195 ISBN 0-8473-1611-4 : 14.95. ISBN 0-8473-1572-X pbk. : 6.95
1. Quilting—United States—Patterns. 2. Patchwork—United States—Patterns. I. Title. BIP

STATE capitals quilt blocks : 50 patchwork patterns from "Hearth & home" magazine / collected and edited by Barbara Bannister and Edna Paris Ford. New York : Dover Publications, c1977. 71 p. : ill. ; 28 cm. "From Hearth and home magazine, 1912-1916." [TT835.S69 1977] 77-77049 ISBN 0-486-23557-2 pbk. : 2.25 ($2.60 Can) 746.4'6
1. Quilting—United States—Patterns. I. Bannister, Barbara. II. Ford, Edna Paris. III. Hearth and home (Agusta, Me.) BIP

Quinn, John, 1870-1924.

REID, Benjamin Lawrence. 704'.34'0924 B
The man from New York; John Quinn and his friends [by] B. L. Reid. New York, Oxford University Press, 1968. xviii, 708 p. illus., ports. 24 cm. Bibliography: p. 687-691. [CT275.Q55R4] 68-29724 12.50
1. Quinn, John, 1870-1924. I. Title.

ZILCZER, Judith. 709'.44'0740153
"The noble buyer" : John Quinn, patron of the avant-garde / Judith Zilczer. Washington : Published for the Hirshhorn Museum and Sculpture Garden, Smithsonian Institution, by the Smithsonian Institution Press, 1978. 198 p. : ill. (some col.) ; 31 cm. Includes index. Bibliography: p. 195-198. [N6487.W3H579] 78-2041 20.00
1. Quinn, John, 1870-1924—Art collections—Exhibitions. 2. Art, Modern—20th century—Exhibitions. 3. Avant-garde (Aesthetics)—Exhibitions. 4. Art, French—Exhibitions. 5. Art, Modern—20th century—France—Exhibitions. I. Hirshhorn Museum and Sculpture Garden. II. Title.

Quinn, Wayne, 1941—

QUINN, Wayne, 1941- 759.13
The art of Wayne Quinn. San Francisco : New Glide Publications, c1977. 93 p. : col. ill. ; 22 x 27 cm. (The Working artist) "A David Charlsen/New Glide book." [N6537.Q56A4 1977] 77-13667 ISBN 0-912078-57-X : 25.00
1. Quinn, Wayne, 1941- I. Title. II. Series. BIP

Quirt, Walter.

ÁMERICAN Federation of Arts. 759.13
Walter Quirt, by Robert M. Coates. New York Author [1083 Fifth Ave.] [c.1960] 28p. (Bibl.: p.20-23) illus., plates (part col.) port. 18cm. 2.00 .50 pap.,
1. Quirt, Walter. I. Title.

Rackham, Arthur, 1867-1939.

COLUMBIA University. Libraries. 741.942
The centenary of Arthur Rackham's birth, September 19, 1867: an appreciation of his genius and a catalogue of his original sketches, drawings, and paintings in the Berol Collection, by Roland Baughman. New York, Columbia University Libraries, 1967. 48 p. illus. (part col.) 31 cm. [NC242.R3C57] 68-1079
I. Rackham, Arthur, 1867-1939. II. Baughman, Roland Orvil, 1902- III. Berol, Alfred C., 1892- IV. Title.

GETTINGS, Fred. 741.9'42
Arthur Rackham / Fred Gettings. 1st American ed. New York : Macmillan, 1976, c1975. 192 p. : ill. (some col.) ; 29 cm. Includes index. Bibliography: p. 191. [NC242.R3G47 1976] 75-21767 ISBN 0-02-543080-7 : 20.00
1. Rackham, Arthur, 1867-1939. I. Rackham, Arthur, 1867-1939. II. Title.

HUDSON, Derek. 741.64
Arthur Rackham: his life and work. New York, Scribner [1960] 181 p. illus. (part mounted, part col.) ports. 29 cm. Bibliography: p. 159-160. "The printed work of Arthur Rackham, a check-list compiled by Bertram Rota": p. 164-181. [NC242.R3H8] 60-12994
1. Rackham, Arthur, 1867-1939.

*RACKHAM, Arthur 1867-1939 741.642
Arthur Rackham edited by David Larkin, Introduction by Leo John De Freitas New York, Peacock Press/Bantam Book [1975] [90 p.] Chiefly ill., plates), 30 cm. [NC965] 75-11188 5.95 (pbk.)
1. Rackham, Arthur 1867-1939 I. Larkin, David comp. II. Title.

Radcliffe College—Alumnae.

THE Discerning eye : 708'.144'4
[catalogue] : Radcliffe collectors' exhibition, Fogg Art Museum [Oct. 9-Nov. 24, 1974]. [Cambridge, Mass.] : Fogg Art Museum, [1974] [124] p. : chiefly ill. ; 25 cm. Addendum slip inserted. [N5020.C24F632] 74-17603
1. Radcliffe College—Alumnae. 2. Art—Exhibitions. 3. Art—Private collections—United States. I. Harvard University. William Hayes Fogg Art Museum.

Radford, Albert, 1862-1904.

RADFORD, Fred W. 738'.092'4 B
A. Radford; pottery, his life & works, by Fred W. Radford. [Columbia? S.C., 1973] 50 p. illus. 23 cm. [NK4210.R28R32] 73-161384
1. Radford, Albert, 1862-1904.

Radiography.

CHESNEY, D. Noreen 778.33
Radiographic photography [by] D. Noreen Chesney, Muriel O. Chesney. Oxford, Blackwell Scientific Pubns. [Philadelphia, F. A. Davis, c.1965] xiii, 453p. illus. 23cm. Bibl. [TR750.C55] 65-29515 10.00
1. Radiography. I. Chesney, Muriel O., joint author. II. Title. BIP

Radiography — Outlines, syllabl, etc.

MORGAN, James A 778.33
The art and science of medical radiography, by James A. Morgan. [Rev.] Saint Louis, Catholic Hospital Association [1963] xiii, 122 p. illus. 28 cm. Bibliography:p. 122. [[RC78]] 65-7954
1. Radiography — Outlines, syllabl, etc. I. Title. BIP

Raffaele Sanzio, 1483-1520.

BERTI, Luciano. 759.5
Raphael. Translated from the Italian by Sylvia Sprigge. New York, Norton [1961] 121 p. mounted illus., 44 col. plates. 21 cm. (Masters and movements) [ND623.R2B463] 61-15340
1. Raffaele Sanzio, 1483-1520. BIP

ERNEST, Brother, 1897- 927.5
Our Lady's portrait painter, a story of Raphael. Illus. reproductions from the works of Raphael. Notre Dame, Ind., Dujarie Press [1952] 94 p. illus. 24 cm. [ND623.R2E7] 52-3888
1. Raffaele Sanzio, 1483-1520. 2. Art—Juvenile literature. I. Title.

GILLETTE, Henry S. 92
Raphael; painter of the Renaissance, by Henry S. Gillette. New York, Watts [1967] 160 p. illus. 25 cm. (Immortals of art) Bibliography: p. 148-150. A biography of the sixteenth century Italian painter known for such works as the Sistine Madonna, La Belle Jardiniere, The School of Athens, and Triumph of Galatea. [ND623.R5G5] AC 67
1. Raffaele, Sanzio, 1483-1520. I. Title.

OPPE, Adolf Paul, 1878-1957. 759.5
Raphael [by] A. P. Oppe. Edited with an introd. by Charles Mitchell. [Rev. ed.] New York, Praeger [1970] xxiii, 130 p., 273 illus. 14 col. plates (2 fold.) 29 cm. First published 1909. Bibliography: p. 123-125. [ND623.R2O5 1970] 78-108987 35.00
1. Raffaele Sanzio, 1483-1520. I. Mitchell, Charles, 1912- ed.

RAPHAEL, 1483-1520. 759.5
The complete paintings of Raphael. Introd. by Richard Cocke. Notes and catalogue by Pierluigi de Vecchi. New York, H. N. Abrams [1969, c1966] 128 p. illus. (part col.) 32 cm. (Classics of the world's great art) Translation of L'opera completa di Raffaello. Bibliography: p. 82. [ND623.R2D413 1969b] 69-16897
I. De Vecchi, Pierluigi. II. Title.

VICTORIA and Albert Museum, South Kensington. 741.90924
The Raphael cartoons; introduction by John Pope-Hennessy. London, H.M.S.O.; Obtainable in the U.S. of Amer. from British Info. 1966. 40p. illus. (some col.) 19x25cm. (Its Colour book no 1). [NK3052.R7V5] 66-67579 1.30 pap.,
1. Raffaele Sanzio, 1483-1520. I. Title.

Raffaele Sanzio, 1483-1520—Juvenile literature.

RABOFF, Ernest Lloyd. 759.5
Raphael Sanzio, by Ernest Raboff. Garden City, N.Y., Doubleday [1971] [31] p. illus. (part col.), ports. 29 cm. (Art for children) (A Gemini Smith book) A brief biography of Raphael accompanies color reproductions and critical interpretations of many of his works. [ND623.R2R25] 75-139056 3.95
1. Raffaele Sanzio, 1483-1520—Juvenile literature. I. Title.

Raffia work.

JESSEN, Bibbi, 1910- 745.58
How to work with raffia. Milwaukee, Bruce Pub. Co. [1955] 57p. illus. 25cm. Translation of Smarte ting av bast. [TT875.J413] 55-954
1. Raffia work. I. Title.

KRoNCKE, Grete. 746.4'1
New ways with raffia: braid, weave, sew, knit, embroidy, crochet. New York, Van Nostrand Reinhold [1970, c1968] 95 p. illus. 23 cm. Translation of Nyt i bast. [TT875.K713] 78-123379 4.50
1. Raffia work. I. Title.

LAMMER, Jutta. 746.41
Make things with straw and raffia. New York, Watson-Guptill Publications [1965] 54 p. illus. (part col.) 20 cm. Translation of Bast, Stroh and Peddigrohr. [TT875.L2513] 65-24234
1. Raffia work. 2. Straw work. I. Title.

Ragamala painting—Exhibitions.

PAL, Pratapaditya. 759.9'54
Ragamala paintings in the Museum of Fine Arts, Boston. [Boston, 1967] 84 p. illus. 27 cm. "Exhibition held at the museum, December 1, 1967-January 14, 1968." Includes catalogue information from Ananda Coomaraswamy's Catalogue of Rajput paintings, 1925. "Abbreviations & selected bibliography": p. 6. [ND3247.P25] 68-3795
1. Ragamala painting—Exhibitions. 2. Music in art. I. Boston. Museum of Fine Arts. II. Title.

RAI—Radiotelevisione Italiana—Buildings.

MAZZARIOL, Giuseppe. 725/.23
Un edificio per la RAI, Roma, viale Mazzini. Con testi di Giuseppe Mazzariol, Francesco Berarducci e Marziano Bernardi. [Venezia] Alfieri [1967] Stamped on t.p.: Amer. dist.: Wittenborn, New York. [86]p. illus. (pt. col.) plans. 24x25cm. (Monografie diarchittetura, 3) Text in Italian and English. [NA1123.B38M3] 67-9834 9.00
1. RAI—Radiotelevisione Italiana—Buildings. I. Berarducci, Francesco. II. Bernardi, Marziano. III. Title.

Railroads—England—Stations.

COCKMAN, Frederick George. 725'.3
Railway architecture / [by] F. G. Cockman. Aylesbury : Shire Publications, 1976. 33 p. : ill. ; 21 cm. (Shire album ; 14) Bibliography: p. [33] [NA6315.G7C6] 77-350472 ISBN 0-85263-335-1 : £0.45
1. Railroads—England—Stations. I. Title.

SYMES, Rodney, 725'.31'09422
1934-
Railway architecture of the southeast [by] Rodney Symes & David Cole. Reading, Osprey, 1972. 128 p. chiefly illus. 22 cm. (Railway architecture series) [TF300.S93] 72-191748 ISBN 0-85045-070-5 £1.95
1. Railroads—England—Stations. I. Cole, David. II. Title.

Railroads—Great Britain.

ADAMS, John, 1912- 385'.36'10941
British Rail scrapbook, 1955 / [compiled by] John Adams & Patrick Whitehouse. London : Allan, 1976. 64 p. : chiefly ill. ; 25 cm. [TT57.A718] 77-354795 ISBN 0-7110-0694-6 : £1.60

1. Railroads—Great Britain. I. Whitehouse, Patrick Bruce, joint author. II. Title.

Railroads—Great Britain—Stations.

BIDDLE, Gordon. 385'.314'0941
The British railway station / G. Biddle and Jeoffry Spence ; drawings by Peter Fells. Newton Abbot [Eng.] ; North Pomfret, Vt. : David & Charles, 1977. 96 p. : chiefly ill. ; 26 cm. At head of title: Railway history in pictures. [TF302.G7B5] 78-304103 ISBN 0-7153-7467-2 : 9.95
1. Railroads—Great Britain—Stations. I. Spence, Jeoffry, joint author. II. Title. III. Title: Railway history in pictures. BIP

Railroads—Great Britain—Stations—History.

BIDDLE, Gordon. 725'.31'0942
Victorian stations; railway stations in England & Wales, 1830-1923; drawings by Peter Fells. Newton Abbot [Eng.] David & Charles [1973] 256 p. illus. 22 cm. Bibliography: p. 227-230. [NA6315.G7B52] 74-154891 ISBN 0-7153-5949-5 13.50
1. Railroads—Great Britain—Stations—History. 2. Architecture, Victorian—Great Britain. I. Title.
Distributed by David and Charles, Vermont. BIP

Railroads in art.

BEAUMONT, Anthony. v. 12
Traction engine prints; fifty rare items with descriptions. [Lingfield, Surrey] Oakwood Press,[1967] 53 p. (chiefly illus.) (Oakwood Library of Railway History, v. 61) (Series) [NUC68-30068]
I. Title. II. Series.

GREAT *railroad paintings /* 758
edited and with an introd. by Robert Goldsborough. 1st U.S. ed. New York : Peacock Press/Bantam Book, 1976. [96] p. : chiefly col. ill. ; 23 x 29 cm. [ND1460.R3G73] 76-15474 pbk. : 6.95
1. Railroads in art. 2. Railroads—United States—Pictorial works. 3. Paintings, American. I. Goldsborough, Robert. BIP

Railroads—London metropolitan area—Stations.

SYMES, Rodney, 725'.31'09421
1934-
Railway architecture of Greater London [by] Rodney Symes and David Cole. Reading, Osprey Publishing, 1973. 128 p., chiefly illus. 22 cm. (Railway architecture series) [NA6315.G72L67] 73-174689 ISBN 0-85045-123-X £1.95
1. Railroads—London metropolitan area—Stations. I. Cole, David, joint author. II. Title.

Railroads—London—Stations.

BETJEMAN, John, 385'.314'09421
Sir, 1906-
London's historic railway stations [by] John Betjeman, photographed by John Gay. [London] Murray [1972] 126 p. illus. 25 cm. [TF300.B48] 72-190187 ISBN 0-7195-2573-X
1. Railroads—London—Stations. I. Gay, John, illus. II. Title.
Distributed by Transatlantic 15.00 BIP

Railroads, Narrow-gage—Caricatures and cartoons.

FALLBERG, Carl 741.5973
Fiddletown & Copperopolis; the life and times of an uncommon carrier. Foreword by Lucius Beebe. Reseda, Calif., Hungerford Press. [6951 Reseda Blvd.] [c.] 1960 unpaged (chiefly illus.) 17 x 25cm. 60-9259 7.95
1. Railroads, Narrow-gage—Caricatures and cartoons. I. Title.

FALLBERG, Carl, 1915- 385'.5'0207
Fiddletown & Copperopolis; the life and times of an uncommon carrier. Foreword by Lucius Beebe. Reseda, Calif., Hungerford Press [1968] 1 v. (chiefly illus.)

16 x 25 cm. [NC1429.F275A45 1968] 68-58240 6.95
1. Railroads, Narrow-gage—Caricatures and cartoons. I. Title.

Railroads—Nebraska—Stations.

RAPP, William F. 725'.31'09782
Nebraska C.B.& Q. depots, by William F. Rapp. Crete, Neb., J-B Pub. Co. [1970] 46 p. illus., plans. 28 cm. [TF300.R37] 78-253249
1. Chicago, Burlington, and Quincy Railroad Company. 2. Railroads—Nebraska—Stations. I. Title.

Railroads—Ontario—Stations.

WILLMOT, Elizabeth 385'.314'09713
A., 1918-
Meet me at the station / Elizabeth A. Willmot. [Agincourt, Ont.] : Gage, 1976. 114 p. : ill. ; 24 x 26 cm. Includes index. [TF302.O6W54] 77-357818 ISBN 0-7715-9976-5
1. Railroads—Ontario—Stations. I. Title.

Railroads—Stations.

CARTER, Ernest Frank, 1899- 385.3
Famous railway stations of the world and their traffic; illustrated by Kenneth E. Carter. London, F. Muller stamped: distributed by Sportshelf, New Rochelle, N. Y. [c1958] 143p. illus. 20cm. (Globe books) [TF300.C3] 59-3279
1. Railroads—Stations. 2. Railroads—Hist. I. Title.

DROEGE, John Albert, 725'.31
1861-1961.
Passenger terminals and trains. With a special introd. by George W. Hilton. 1st ed. New York, McGraw-Hill, 1916. Milwaukee, Kalmbach Pub. Co., 1969. vii, 410 p. illus., maps, plans (part fold.) 24 cm. [TF305.D83 1969] 68-58723 7.50
1. Railroads—Stations. 2. Railroads—Passenger traffic. I. Title.

FAMOUS *railroad stations of* 385.1
the world, by Adele Gutman Nathan with W. C. Baker. Illustrated by Graham Bernbach. New York, Random House c100p. illus. 26cm. (Gateway books) [TF300.N3] 385.3 53-6276
1. Railroads—Station. I. Nathan, Adele (Gutman)

MEEKS, Carroll Louis 725.31
Vanderslice, 1907-
The railroad station; an architectural history. New Haven, Yale University Press, 1956. xxvi, 203 p. illus., plans. 28 cm. (Yale historical publications History of art, 11) "Bibliographical essay": p. 175-186. [NA6310.M4] 56-10872
1. Railroads—Stations. I. Title. II. Series. BIP

Railroads—Tucson, Ariz.—Airspace utilization.

ALBANESE, Charles A. 711'.75
Air rights - a study [by] Charles A. Albanese. Participating students: Dwayne L. Burton [and others. Tucson] College of Architecture, University of Arizona [1974] 39 p. illus. 22 x 28 cm. Bibliography: p. 39. [HE2781.T8A37] 74-176300
1. Railroads—Tucson, Ariz.—Airspace utilization. I. Burton, Dwayne L. II. Title.

Railroads—United States—Buildings and structures.

GROW, Lawrence. 725'.31'0973
Waiting for the 5:05 : terminal, station, and depot in America / compiled by Lawrence Grow; introd. by Clay Lancaster. New York : Main Street/Universe Books, 1977. 128 p. : ill. ; 26 cm. Based on an exhibition prepared by the Historic American Buildings Survey and the Historic American Engineering Record. Includes index. [NA6311.G76] 76-56632 ISBN 0-87663-283-5 : 12.50. ISBN 0-87663-957-0 pbk. : 6.95
1. Railroads—United States—Buildings and structures. II. Historic American Buildings Survey. II. Historic American Engineering Record. III. Title. BIP

Railroads—United States—Stations.

CAVALIER, Julian, 1931- 385'.314
North American railroad stations / Julian Cavalier. South Brunswick : A. S. Barnes, c1978. p. cm. Includes index. [TF302.U54C38] 77-84564 ISBN 0-498-02121-1 : 17.50
1. Railroads—United States—Stations. 2. Railroads—Canada—Stations. I. Title.

EDUCATIONAL Facilities 720
Laboratories.
Reusing railroad stations : a report from Educational Facilities Laboratories and the National Endowment for the Arts. New York : The Laboratories, 1975- v. : ill. ; 22 x 28 cm. [TF302.U54E38] 76-360818 4.00 (v. 2)
1. Railroads—United States—Stations. I. National Endowment for the Arts. II. Title.

HARDY Holzman Pfeiffer 385'.314
Associates.
Reusing railroad stations; a report from Educational Facilities Laboratories [research and writing by Hardy Holzman Pfeiffer Associates. New York, 1974] 78 p. illus. 22 x 28 cm. [NA6311.H37 1974] 74-77372 4.00
1. Railroads—United States—Stations. I. Educational Facilities Laboratories. II. Title.

SLOAN, Anthony R. 711'.75
Reestablishing the link; a study of the commuter rail station [by] Anthony R. Sloan [and] John W. Blatteau. [Philadelphia] Southeastern Pennsylvania Transportation Authority, 1970. 66 p. illus. 22 x 29 cm. "A report of the Planning-Marketing Projects Division." [TF300.S58] 74-629180
1. Railroads—U.S.—Stations. 2. Railroads—U.S.—Commuting traffic. I. Blatteau, John W., joint author. II. Southeastern Pennsylvania Transportation Authority. Planning-Marketing Projects Division. III. Title.

Railroads—United States—Stations—Bibliography.

SETO, Jack W. 016.3092'08 s
Railroad stations in the United States / Jack W. Seto. Monticello, Ill. : Council of Planning Librarians, 1978. 37 p. ; 28 cm. (Exchange bibliography - Council of Planning Librarians ; 1450) Cover title. [Z5942.C68 no. 1450] [Z7234.S74] [HE1613.A15] 016.385'314 78-308668 pbk. : 3.50
1. Railroads—United States—Stations—Bibliography. I. Title. II. Series: Council of Planning Librarians. Exchange bibliography ; 1450.

Railroads—United States—Stations—Designs and plans.

RAILROAD station 725'.31'0973
planbook / [edited by Harold A. Edmonson and Richard V. Francaviglia]. [Milwaukee : Kalmbach Pub. Co., c1977] 96 p. : ill. ; 21 x 29 cm. Cover title. Includes index. [NA6311.R34] 76-52194 ISBN 0-89024-531-2 : 4.00
1. Railroads—United States—Stations—Designs and plans. 2. United States—Public buildings—Designs and plans. I. Edmonson, Harold A. II. Francaviglia, Richard V. BIP

Railroads—U.S.—Stations—Pictorial works.

ALEXANDER, Edwin P. 625.1'8'0973
Down at the depot; American railroad stations from 1831 to 1920 [by] Edwin P. Alexander. [1st ed.] New York, C. N. Potter; distributed by Crown Publishers [1970] 320 p. illus., plans. 32 cm. [TF300.A4 1970] 76-86510 15.00
1. Railroads—U.S.—Stations—Pictorial works. I. Title.

BYE, Ranulph, 1916- 759.13
The vanishing depot. Wynnewood, Pa., Livingston Pub. Co. [1973] xiii, 113 p. illus. (part col.) 29 cm. [ND1839.B93A57] 73-16229 ISBN 0-87098-058-0 20.00
1. Bye, Ranulph, 1916- 2. Railroads—

United States—Stations—Pictorial works. I. Title.

Railway mail service—Great Britain.

POTTER, David, 1932- 769'.564
Great Britain railway letter stamps, 1957-1976 : a handbook and catalogue / compiled by David Potter. [New ed.] / edited by Peter Johnson. Leicester : Railway Philatelic Group, 1976. 36 p. : ill. ; 21 cm. [HE6939.R2P67 1976] 77-353884 ISBN 0-901667-08-0 : £1.60
1. Railway mail service—Great Britain. 2. Postage-stamps—Great Britain. I. Title.

Raku pottery.

DICKERSON, John. 738.1
Raku handbook; a practical approach to the ceramic art. New York, Van Nostrand Reinhold Co. [1972] 112 p. illus. 25 cm. Bibliography: p. 108. [TP808.D5 1972] 72-1442 ISBN 0-442-22092-8 7.95
1. Raku pottery. I. Title.

PIEPENBURG, Robert. 738.1
Raku pottery / Robert Piepenburg. 1st Collier Books ed. New York : Collier Books, 1976, c1972. 159 p., [4] leaves of plates : ill. (some col.) ; 28 cm. Includes index. Bibliography: p. 155. [NK4340.R3P53 1976] 77-358665 6.95
1. Raku pottery. I. Title.

PIEPENBURG, Robert E. 738.1
Raku pottery / Robert Piepenburg. New York : Collier Books [1976c1972] 159p. : ill. ; 28 cm. Includes index. Bibliography: p. 155. [NK4340.R3P53] 75-188768 pbk. : 6.95
1. Raku pottery. I. Title. BIP

RIEGGER, Hal, 1921- 738.1'4
Raku, art & technique. New York, Van Nostrand Reinhold [1970] 134 p. illus. (part col.) 29 cm. Bibliography: p. 134. [TP808.R53 1970] 77-102195
1. Raku pottery. I. Title. BIP

TYLER, Christopher, 1944- 738.1
Raku / by Christopher Tyler and Richard Hirsch. New York : Watson-Guptill Publications, 1975. 176 p. : ill. ; 30 cm. Includes index. Bibliography: p. 172-173. [TT920.T93 1975] 75-11934 ISBN 0-8230-4503-X : 14.95
1. Raku pottery. I. Hirsch, Richard, 1944- joint author. II. Title. BIP

Ramirez, Eduardo, 1923—

CENTER for Inter-American Relations. Art Gallery. 730'.924
Eduardo Ramirez, sculptor. New York, c1968] 12 p. illus. 22 cm. Prepared for an exhibition held in the Art Gallery of the Center for Inter-American Relations, New York, Nov. 7-Dec. 1, 1968. [NB379.R3C4] 76-4525
1. Ramirez, Eduardo, 1923-

Ramos, Mel, 1935—

RAMOS, Mel, 1935- 759.13
The girls of Mel Ramos / with a text by Elizabeth Claridge. 1st ed. Chicago : Playboy Press, c1975. 158 p. : ill. (some col.) ; 31 cm. Includes index. Bibliography: p. 152-153. [ND237.R125C5] 75-4182 ISBN 0-87223-434-7 : 17.95
1. Ramos, Mel, 1935- I. Claridge, Elizabeth. II. Title.

Rampant Lions Press.

CARTER, Will, 1912- 686.2'24
Portfolio 2 : projects, backward glances, and jeux d'esprit / put together by Will and Sebastion Carter. Cambridge [Eng.] : Rampant Lions Press, 1974. 1 portfolio : ill. ; 28 cm. "This portfolio was concocted, designed and printed ... in an edition of about five hundred copies." [Z232.R17C37] 75-332423
1. Rampant Lions Press. 2. Printing—Specimens. I. Carter, Sebastian, joint author. II. Title.

Ranch houses—Arizona—History.

STEWART, Janet Ann, 1925- 728.6'4
Arizona ranch houses; southern territorial styles, 1867-1900. Edited by John Bret Harte. With photos. by Louis S. Bencze. [Tucson] Arizona Historical Society [1974] 121 p. illus. 23 cm. (Historical monograph no. 2) Bibliography: p. 118-121. [NA7235.A6S83] 74-16374
1. Ranch houses—Arizona—History. I. Title. II. Series.

Ranches in art.

†ROGERS, Mondel, 1946- 759.13
Old ranches of the Texas plains : paintings / by Mondel Rogers ; foreword by Mitchell A. Wilder. 1st ed. College Station : Texas A & M University, c1976. 124 p., [1] leaf of plates : ill. (some col.) ; 24 x 32 cm. (The Joe and Betty Moore Texas art series ; no. 1) [ND1839.R63A56] 76-17980 ISBN 0-89096-019-4 : 27.50
1. Rogers, Mondel, 1946- 2. Ranches in art. 3. Ranches—Texas—Pictorial works. I. Title. II. Series. BIP

Randolph family.

KRUSEN, Jessie Ball Thompson. 975.5'455
Tuckahoe Plantation / by Jessie Ball Thompson Krusen ; drawings by Howard L. Rich ; photos. by Richard Cheek. Richmond : Krusen, 1975. 117 p. : ill. ; 31 cm. Includes index. Bibliography: p. 71-73. [NA7235.V52T824] 74-27255 25.00
1. Randolph family. 2. Tuckahoe Plantation, Va. 3. Architecture, Colonial—Virginia. I. Title.

Randolph-Macon Woman's College, Lynchburg, Va.

WILLIAMS, Mary Frances. 760'.0973'0740155671
Catalogue of the collection of American art at Randolph-Macon Woman's College : a selection of paintings, drawings, and prints / Mary Frances Williams. 2d ed. Charlottesville : University Press of Virginia, 1977. p. cm. First ed. (1965) issued by Randolph-Macon Woman's College under title: Catalogue of the collection of American painting at Randolph-Macon Woman's College. Bibliography: p. [N6505.W53 1977] 76-51281 ISBN 0-8139-0591-5 : 15.00
1. Randolph-Macon Woman's College, Lynchburg, Va. 2. Art, American—Catalogs. 3. Art—Virginia—Lynchburg—Catalogs. I. Randolph-Macon Woman's College, Lynchburg, Va. II. Randolph-Macon Woman's College, Lynchburg, Va. Catalogue of the collection of American painting at Randolph-Macon Woman's College. III. Title. BIP

Ranney, William, 1813-1857.

GRUBAR, Francis S. 759.13
William Ranney, Painter of the early West. Foreword by Hermann Warner Williams, Jr. New York, C. N. Potter [dist. Crown, 1963] iv, 65p. plates (2 col.) 26cm. Biog., catalogue prepared to accompany an exhibition organized by the Corcoran Gallery of Art. Bibl. 62-19291 7.50
1. Ranney, William, 1813-1857. I. Corcoran Gallery of Art, Washington, D.C. II. Title.

Raphael, 1483-1520.

BORTOLON, Liana. 759.5 B
The life and times of Raphael; text by Liana Bortolon, translator [from the Italian] Barbara Paterson. London, New York[etc.] Hamlyn, 1968. [1], 77 p. illus. (chiefly col.), ports. (some col.) 30 cm. (Portraits of greatness) [ND623.R2B64] 73-415496 ISBN 0-600-03134-9 17/6
1. Raphael, 1483-1520. I. Title.

THE Complete work of 759.5
Raphael. New York, Reynal [1969] 649 p. illus., col. plates. 38 cm. Contents.Contents.—Introduction, by M. Salmi.—Raphael and painting, by L. Becherucci.—Raphael's collaborators, by A. Marabottini.—The drawings, by A. Forlani Tempesti.—The architect, by G. Marchini.—Raphael and antiquity, by G. Becatti.—Raphael and ancient Rome, by F. Castagnoli.—Life, by V. Golzio.—The sonnets, by V. Golzio.—Raphael and his critics, by V. Golzio. Includes bibliographies. [ND623.R2C62] 77-7885 45.00
1. Raphael, 1483-1520. BIP

CROWE, Joseph Archer, Sir, 1825-1896. 759.5
Raphael: his life and works. With particular reference to recently discovered records, and an exhaustive study of extant drawings and pictures, by J. A. Crowe and G. B. Cavalcaselle. Freeport, N.Y., Books for Libraries Press [1972] 2 v. 22 cm. Reprint of the 1882-85 ed. [ND623.R2C8 1972] 72-2584 ISBN 0-8369-6852-2
1. Raphael, 1483-1520. I. Cavalcaselle, Giovanni Battista, 1820-1897, joint author. BIP

DUSSLER, Luitpold, 1895- 759.5
Raphael: a critical catalogue of his pictures, wall-paintings and tapestries [translated from the German by Sebastian Cruft] London, New York, Phaidon, 1971. xxiii, 220 p. illus. 28 cm. Translation of Raffael. Kritisches Verzeichnis der Gemalde, Wandbilder und Bildteppiche. Bibliography: p. ix-xxi. [ND623.R2D813] 76-139836 ISBN 0-7148-1469-5 £8.00
1. Raphael, 1483-1520.

GILLETTE, Henry S. 759.5
Raphael; painter of the Renaissance by Henry S. Gillette New York, Watts [1967] 160 p. illus. 25 cm. (Immortals of art) Bibliography: p. 148-150. [ND623.R5G5] 67-14177
1. Raphael, 1483-1520. I. Title.

MONTI, Raffaele. 759.5
Raphael. [1st Amer., ed. Tr. from Italian by Caroline Beamish] New York, Grosset [1967] 39, [80] p. illus. (pt. col.) 18cm. (New Grosset art lib., 8) On cover: Raphael; the life and work of the artist. [ND623.R2M753 1967] 67-24228 1.25 pap.,
I. Raffaele Sanzio, 1483-1520. II. Title.

MUNTZ, Eugene, 1845-1902. 759.5 B
Raphael, his life, works, and times / by Eugene Muntz. Rev. from the 2d French ed. / by Walter Armstrong. Boston : Longwood Press, 1977. p. cm. Reprint of the 1888 ed. published by Chapman and Hall, London. [ND623.R2M9 1977] 77-9327 ISBN 0-89341-202-3 lib.bdg. : 60.00
1. Raphael, 1483-1520. I. Armstrong, Walter, Sir, 1850-1918. II. Title.

PONENTE, Nello. 759.5
Who was Raphael? Text by Nello Ponente; translated from the Italian by James Emmons. Geneva, Skira, 1967. 149 p. illus. (part col.), ports. (part col.) 24 cm. (Who was?) Distributed in the United States by The World Publishing Company, Cleveland. Bibliography: p. [134] [ND623.R2P673] 67-25119
1. Raphael, 1483-1520. I. Title.

RAFFAELE SANZIO, 1483-1520. 759.5
All the frescos of Raphael. Edited by Ettore Camesasca. Translated by Paul Colacicchi. New York, Hawthorn Books [1963] 2 v. (94 p.) illus., plates (part col.) 19 cm. (The Complete library of world art, v. 12-13) "Bibliographical note": v. 2, p. 94. [ND623.R2C283] 63-8011
I. Camesasca, Ettore, 1922- ed. II. Title. III. Series.

RAFFAELE SANZIO, 1483-1520. 759.5
All the paintings of Raphael. Edited by Ettore Camesasca. Translated by Luigi Grosso. New York, Hawthorn Books [1963] 2 v. illus. 19 cm. (The Complete library of world art, v. 8-9) Includes bibliography. [ND623.R2C33] 62-16130
I. Camesasca, Ettore, 1922- ed.

RAFFAELE SANZIO, 1483-1520. 759.5
Raphael, 1483-1520. Text by Marco Valsecchi. New York, H. N. Abrams [1960] 79p. illus. (part col.) 18cm. (The Pocket library of great art, A38) Bibliography: p. 79. [ND623.R2V27] 60-14973
I. Valsecchi, Marco. II. Title.

RAFFAELE SANZIO, 1483-1520. 759.5
Raphael: panel paintings. Text by Mary Pittaluga. New York, H. N. Abrams [1955, c1954] 24 p. illus., 36 plates (part col.) 33 cm. (The Library of great painters) [An Abrams art book] [ND623.R2P5] 56-1123
I. Pittaluga, Mary.

RAPHAEL, 1483-1520. 759.5
Raphael. Text by Patricia Egan. New York, H. N. Abrams [1971] 24 p. illus. (part col.) 33 cm. (The Library of great painters. Portfolio ed.) [ND623.R2E35 1971] 75-130294 ISBN 0-8109-3050-1
I. Egan, Patricia.

RAPHAEL, 1483-1520. 759.5
Raphael. Text by James H. Beck. New York, H. N. Abrams [1974] p. (The Library of great painters) Bibliography: p. [ND623.R2B36] 73-12198 ISBN 0-8109-0432-2 1.95 (pbk.)
1. Raphael, 1483-1520. I. Beck, James H.

RIPLEY, Elizabeth, 1906- 759.5
Raphael; a biography. Philadelphia, Lippincott [1961] 68 p. illus. 26 cm. [ND623.R2R64] 61-6065
1. Raphael (Raffaelle Sansio da Urbino) 1483-1520.]

SHEARMAN, John K. G. 759.5
Raphael's cartoons in the collection of Her Majesty the Queen, and the tapestries for the Sistine Chapel, by John Shearman. London, Phaidon, 1972. viii, 258 p., [3] leaves. illus. (some col.), plans. 31 cm. "Distributors in the United States: Praeger publishers, Inc." Includes bibliographical references. [ND623.R2S45] 72-79553 ISBN 0-7148-1450-4 38.50
1. Raphael, 1483-1520. 2. Vatican. Cappella sistina. 3. Windsor, House of—Art collections. I. Title.

Rashid al-Din Tabib, 1247?-1318.

RICE, David Talbot, 1903-1972. 745.6'7'09553
The illustrations to the World history of Rashid al-Din / David Talbot Rice ; edited by Basil Gray. Edinburgh : Edinburgh University Press, c1976. viii, 192 p., [2] leaves of plates : facsims. ; 29 cm. & microfiche (2 sheets : col. ; 11 x 15 cm) in pocket. The illustrations are from Rashid al-Din Tabib's Collection of chronicles, reproduced from Edinburgh University Library's Ms. Arab 20. Includes bibliographical references and index. [ND3399.R33R5] 77-354203 ISBN 0-85224-271-9 : 30.00
1. Rashid al-Din Tabib, 1247?-1318. Jami 'al-tavarikh—Illustrations. I. Rashid al-Din Tabib, 1247?-1318. Jami 'al-tavarikh. II. Gray, Basil, 1904- III. Title.
Distributed by Edinburgh University Press, Totowa, New Jersey

Rashid al-Din Tabib, 1247?-1318. Jami 'al-tawarikh.

MAREK, Jiri 757.7
The Jenghiz Khan miniatures from the court of Akbar the Great. Photos. by Werner Forman. Text by J. Marek and H. Knizkova. Tr. by Olga Kuthanova. [London] Spring Bks. [dist. New York, Tudor, 1964, c.1963] 42p., 34 [i.e. 56] col. plates, geneal. table. 27cm. The miniatures are illus. of Rashid al-Din Tabib's History of the Mongols, reproduced from a MS. called Kitab-i Changeznama, property of the Imperial Lib. at Teheran. Bibl. 64-1971 5.95
1. Rashid al-Din Tabib, 1247?-1318. Jami 'al-tawarikh. 2. Akbar, Emperor of Hindustan, 1542-1605. 3. Jenghis Khan, 1162-1227— Iconography. 4. Miniature painting, Mogul. I. Knizkova, Hana, joint author. II. Forman, Werner. III. Title.

Rathbone, Perry Townsend, 1911—

BOSTON. Museum of Fine Arts. 708'.144'61
The Rathbone years; masterpieces acquired for the Museum of Fine Arts, Boston, 1955-1972, and for the St. Louis Art Museum, 1940-1955. Boston, 1972. 203 p. illus. (part col.) 25 cm. [N520.A718] 72-81916 ISBN 0-87846-067-5
1. Rathbone, Perry Townsend, 1911- 2. Art—Boston—Catalogs. 3. Art—St.

Louis—Catalogs. I. St. Louis Art Museum. II. Title. BIP

Rationing, Consumer—United States.

SOCIETY of Ration Token Collectors. 737'.3'0973
U.S. ration currency & tokens, 1942-1945. [Editor: Joseph A. Lowande. North Plainfield? N.J., 1971?- 1 v. (loose-leaf) illus. 29 cm. "Catalog." Illustrated with mounted samples of ration stamps and tokens. Includes O.P.A. forms of record. [HF5415.1.S6] 73-153544
1. Rationing, Consumer—United States. I. Lowande, Joseph A., ed. II. United States. Office of Price Administration. III. Title.

Rattle—Collectors and collecting—Gt. Brit.

ROTHERA, Diana. 745.59'2
Antique rattles: some examples from the collection, 1748-1920 [drawings by the author] Cambridge, Printed privately by Bois de Boulogne, 1970. [73] p. illus. 18 cm. [NK8610.R6] 76-587087 ISBN 0-9501460-0-5
1. Rattle—Collectors and collecting—Gt. Brit. I. Title.

Rattner, Abraham.

AMERICAN Federation of Arts. 759.13
Abraham Rattner, by Frank Getlein. New York, Author, 1083 Fifth Ave., c.1960. 28p. Bibl. 60-2679 .13-14, 17-23. illus. (part col.) port. 18cm. 2.00; .50 pap.,
1. Rattner, Abraham. I. Getlein, Frank. II. Title.

RATTNER, Abraham. 759.13
Abraham Rattner. New York, Kennedy Galleries, 1969. 47 p. illus. (part col.) 28 cm. Catalogue of an exhibition, Apr. 2-28, 1969, with introductory text by Frank Getlein. [ND237.R174A43] 79-13512
I. Getlein, Frank. II. Kennedy Galleries, inc., New York. BIP

RATTNER, Abraham. 759.13
Abraham Rattner; recent paintings. Exhibition, October 19-November 4, 1972. New York, Kennedy Galleries, 1972. [24] p. chiefly illus. 28 cm. [ND1839.R3K46] 72-196907
I. Kennedy Galleries, inc., New York.

RATTNER, Abraham. 759.13
The gallows of Baghdad. [Exhibition] New School Art Center, February 26-March 26, 1970. New York, 1970. 23 p. illus., port. 23 cm. (Art and society) [ND1839.R3A45] 77-199836
I. New York (City). New School for Social Research. New School Art Center. II. Title. III. Series.

Rauschenberg, Robert, 1925-

FORGE, Andrew. 709.24
Rauschenberg. New York, Abrams [1969] 230, [1] p. (incl. cover) illus. (part col.) 28 x 30 cm. Title page is p. [221] "Autobiography [of Rauschenberg]": p. 225-229. Bibliography: p. 230-[231] [N6537.R27F6] 69-12480
1. Rauschenberg, Robert, 1925- BIP

FORGE, Andrew. 759.13
Rauschenberg. New York, Abrams [1972] 87 p. (incl. 51 plates (part col.)) 21 x 23 cm. (Modern artists) "Autobiography [of Rauschenberg]": p. [79]-[83] Bibliography: p. 85-87. [N6537.R27F6 1972] 78-175944 ISBN 0-8109-4425-1 6.75
1. Rauschenberg, Robert, 1925- I. Rauschenberg, Robert, 1925-

JEWISH Theological Seminary of America. Jewish Museum. 707.4
Robert Rauschenberg, by Alan R. Solomon. [New York, Jewish Museum Fifth Ave. at 92 St.] 1963. [65]p. illus., port. 25cm. Catalog of the exhibition to be held Mar. 31 to May 12, 1963. Bibl. 63-15824 apply
1. Rauschenberg, Robert, 1925- I. Solomon, Alan R. II. Title.

RAUSCHENBERG graphic art. 769'.973
An exhibition organized by Institute of Contemporary Art, University of Pennsylvania, Philadelphia, Apr. 1 to May 10, 1970 ... Philadelphia, Institute of Contemporary Art, University of Pennsylvania [1970] 36 p. illus. 19 x 28 cm. Label on t.p.: Supplied by Worldwide Books, Boston, Mass. Includes bibliographical references. [N6537.R27R38] 79-18606
1. Rauschenberg, Robert, 1925- I. Pennsylvania. University. Institute of Contemporary Art.

RAUSCHENBERG, Robert, 1925- 769'.924
Robert Rauschenberg in black and white: paintings 1962-1963, lithographs 1962-1967; exhibition. [Balboa, Calif., Newport Harbor Art Museum, c1969] 1 v. (unpaged) illus. 28 cm. "Organized by the Newport Harbor Art Museum, Balboa, California, December 10, 1969-January 18, 1970; Phoenix Art Museum, Phoenix, Arizona, February 3-March 15, 1970; Seattle Art Museum, Seattle, Washington, May 22-June 21, 1970." Includes bibliographical references. [NE2415.R33A56] 70-19826
I. Newport Harbor Art Museum. II. Phoenix, Ariz. Art Museum. III. Seattle. Art Museum. IV. Title.

RAUSCHENBERG, Robert, 1925- 769'.924
Robert Rauschenberg: prints 1948/1970; [exhibition] Minneapolis Institute of Arts, August 6 through September 27, 1970. [Minneapolis? 1970] [100] p. (chiefly illus., port.) 26 cm. Includes bibliographical references. [NE539.R38A54] 73-140313
I. Minneapolis. Institute of Arts.

Ravenna. San Giovanni in Fonte (Baptistery)

KOSTOF, Spiro K 726.69
The Orthodox Baptistery of Ravenna [by] Spiro K. Kostof. New Haven, Yale University Press, 1965. xviii, 171 p. illus. (part col.) plans. 29 cm. (Yale publications in the history of art, 18) Revision of thesis, Yale University. "Bibliographical note": p. 157-165. [NA5621.R3K6] 65-22328
1. Ravenna. San Giovanni in Fonte (Baptistery) I. Title.

Ravens in art.

DEARMOND, Dale. 769'.92'4
Raven : a collection of woodcuts / by Dale Burlison DeArmond. Anchorage : Alaska Northwest Pub. Co., [1975] [128] p. : col. ill. ; 32 cm. Stories adapted from John Swanton's Tlingit myths and texts published in 1909 by the Bureau of American Ethnology in Bulletin 39. [NE1112.D42A56] 75-23002 ISBN 0-88240-040-1 : 100.00
1. DeArmond, Dale. 2. Ravens in art. I. Swanton, John Reed, 1873-1958. Tlingit myths and texts. II. Title. BIP

Raverat, Gwendolen Mary Darwin, 1885-1957.

RAVERAT, Gwendolen Mary Darwin, 1885-1957. 769'.92'4 B
Period piece / Gwen Raverat. New York : Norton, 1976, c1952. p. cm. (The Norton library) [NE1147.6.R28A2 1976] 76-18933 ISBN 0-393-00822-3 pbk. : 3.95
1. Raverat, Gwendolen Mary Darwin, 1885-1957. 2. Wood-engravers—Great Britain—Correspondence, reminiscences, etc. 3. Cambridge, Eng.—Social life and customs. I. Title. BIP

Ray, Man, 1890-1976.

LOS Angeles Co., Calif. Museum of Art, Los Angeles. 709.73
Man Ray; an exhibition organized by the Los Angeles County Museum of Art in cooperation with the museum's Contemporary Art Council and under the direction of Jules Langsner. [Los Angeles] Los Angeles County Museum of Art, Lytton Gallery, 1966. 148 p. illus. (part col.) ports. 22 x 23 cm. Errata slip inserted. Bibliography: p. 144-148. [N6537.R3L65] 66-29095
1. Ray, Man, 1890- I. Langsner, Jules. II. Los Angeles Co., Calif. Museum of Art, Los Angeles. Contemporary Art Council.

NEW Jersey. State Museum, Trenton. 779'.0922
Two generations of photographs: Man Ray and Naomi Savage. [Exhibition] December 14, 1968-February 9, 1969. Trenton [1969] [12] p. illus. 22 cm. [TR650.N48] 78-625612
1. Ray, Man, 1890- 2. Savage, Naomi, 1927- 3. Photography, Artistic. I. Title.

PENROSE, Roland, Sir. 709'.2'4
Man Ray / Roland Penrose. Boston : New York Graphic Society, c1975. 208 p. : ill. (some col.) ; 25 cm. Includes bibliographical references and index. [N6537.R3P45 1975b] 74-27250 ISBN 0-316-54489-2 : 14.95. ISBN 0-316-54487-6 pbk.
1. Ray, Man, 1890- I. Ray, Man, 1890-

RAY, Man, 1890- 709'.2'4
Man Ray. Conceived by Jean Saucet. Text by Sarane Alexandrian. Translated from the French by Eleanor Levieux. Chicago, J. P. O'Hara, c1973. 72 p. illus. (part col.) 31 cm. "A Howard Greenfeld book." Bibliography: p. 71-72. [N6537.R3A7913] 73-4747 ISBN 0-87955-603-X 15.00
1. Ray, Man, 1890- I. Alexandrian, Sarane.

RAY, Man, 1890- 927.5
Self portrait. [1st ed.] Boston, Little, Brown [1963] 402 p. illus. 24 cm. [ND237.R178A2] 63-8319
I. Title. BIP

SCHWARZ, Arturo, 1924- 709'.2'4
Man Ray : the rigour of imagination / Arturo Schwarz. New York : Rizzoli, 1977. 384 p. : ill. (some col.) ; 23 cm. Includes index. Bibliography: p. 338-358. [N6537.R3S38] 77-77759 ISBN 0-8478-0124-1 : 35.00
1. Ray, Man, 1890-1976. I. Ray, Man, 1890-1976. BIP

Raymond, Antonin, 1888—

RAYMOND, Antonin, 1888- 720'.92'4 B
Antonin Raymond; an autobiography. Rutland, Vt., C. E. Tuttle [1973] 328 p. illus. (part col.) 32 cm. [NA737.R33A22] 72-91552 ISBN 0-8048-1044-3 27.50
1. Raymond, Antonin, 1888- BIP

Reading, Eng., in art.

MARY Mitford's 769'.4'9942293
Reading : a selection of views of Reading, 1798-1845, with quotations from the works of Mary Russell Mitford. [Reading] : Reading Libraries, 1975. [7] leaves, [6] leaves of plates : ill. ; 34 cm. [NE954.3.E5M37 fol] 75-328645 ISBN 0-9501338-4-1 : £1.50
1. Reading, Eng., in art. 2. Prints, English. I. Mitford, Mary Russell, 1787-1855.

Reading, Eng. University. Dept. of Fine Art.

READING, Eng. Museum and Art Gallery. 709'.422'9307402293
Art and the University from 1860 : [catalogue of an exhibition held at Reading Museum and Art Gallery]. [Reading] : The Museum, [1976] [13] p., [4] p. of plates : ill., facsim., port. ; 30 x 11 cm. Cover title. "This exhibition using paintings, prints, drawings, sculpture, and documentary material offers a survey of the growth of the present Fine Art Department from its earliest beginnings. [N346.5.G72R47 1976] 77-355085 ISBN 0-9501247-5-3 : £0.30
1. Reading, Eng. University. Dept. of Fine Art. 2. Art, English—Exhibitions. 3. Art, Modern—19th century—England—Exhibitions. 4. Art, Modern—20th century—England—Exhibitions. I. Title.

Real estate office buildings.

NATIONAL Association of Real Estate Boards. National Institute of Real Estate Brokers. 725'.23
The modern real estate office. Sponsor: George E. Mayer. Chicago, 1967. 64 p. illus., plans. 27 cm. [NA6280.N3] 67-66270
1. Real estate office buildings. 2. Architecture—Designs and plans. I. Title.

Realism in art.

AESTHETIC realism: we have been there; 701.1
six artists on the Siegel theory of opposites [by] Ted Van Griethuysen [and others] New York, Definition Press [1969] 119 p. illus. 20 cm. "Material ... originally presented at the Terrain Gallery in New York City on November 18, 1967." [BH221.U54S5] 69-17523 4.95
1. Siegel, Eli, 1902- 2. Realism in art. 3. Aesthetics. I. Van Griethuysen, Ted, 1934- II. Terrain Gallery.

BRANDYWINE River Museum. 730'.92'2
Three sculptors of American realism: Charles Parks, Eric Parks, Christopher Parks. Essay: Michael Richman. Photography: A. Cypen Lubitsh. Chadds Ford, Pa. [1973] 63 p. illus. (part col.) 26 cm. Catalog of an exhibition. [NB237.P27B72] 73-84334
1. Parks, Charles C., 1922- 2. Parks, Eric. 3. Parks, Christopher. 4. Realism in art. I. Parks, Charles C., 1922- II. Parks, Eric. III. Parks, Christopher. IV. Richman, Michael. V. Title.

BROOKLYN Institute of Arts and Sciences. Museum. 759
Triumph of realism; an exhibition of European and American realist paintings, 1850-1910. [Brooklyn, Brooklyn Museum, 1967] 187 p. illus. (part col.) 23 cm. Catalog of an exhibition shown at the Brooklyn Museum Oct. 3-Nov. 19, 1967, the Virginia Museum of Fine Arts Dec. 11, 1967-Jan. 14, 1968, and the California Palace of the Legion of Honor Feb. 17-Mar. 31, 1968. [ND457.T7] 67-28914
1. Realism in art. 2. Paintings, European—Exhibitions. 3. Paintings, American—Exhibitions. I. Virginia Museum of Fine Arts, Richmond. II. California Palace of the Legion of Honor, San Francisco. III. Title.

CHIARI, Joseph 701
Realism and imagination. [dist. New York, Macmillan, 1961, c.1960] 216p. 61-804 6.00
1. Realism in art. 2. Imagination. 3. Art—Philosophy. I. Title. BIP

CHIARI, Joseph. 701.15
Realism and imagination. New York, Gordian Press, 1970 [c1960] 216 p. 23 cm. "Reprinted with a new preface." [N66.C47 1970] 74-131248 ISBN 0-87752-019-4
1. Realism in art. 2. Imagination. 3. Art—Philosophy. I. Title.

COST, James Peter, 1923- 759.13
Realism in retrospect: an exhibition of paintings & water colors by James Peter Cost, October 24-December 5, the R. W. Norton Art Gallery, Shreveport, Louisiana. [1st ed. Shreveport, La., 1971] 24 p. illus. (part col.) 28 cm. [ND237.C76N6] 75-164700 ISBN 0-9600182-3-9
I. Norton (R. W.) Art Gallery. II. Title. BIP

NOCHLIN, Linda. 709'.03'4
Realism. Harmondsworth, Penguin, 1971. 283 p. illus. 20 cm. (Style and civilization) Bibliography: p. 271-274. [N6465.R4N6] 71-149557 ISBN 0-14-021305-8 £1.10
1. Realism in art. 2. Art, Modern—19th century. I. Title. BIP

NOCHLIN, Linda. 709.034
Realism and tradition in art, 1848-1900; sources and documents. Englewood Cliffs, N.J., Prentice-Hall [1966] x, 189 p. facsim. 23 cm. (Sources and documents in the history of art series) Bibliographical footnotes. [N6450.N57] 66-23609
1. Realism in art. 2. Naturalism in art. 3. Art, Modern—19th century—Sources. I. Title. II. Series.

TRIUMPH of realism; 759
an exhibition of European and American realist paintings, 1850-1910. [Brooklyn] [Brooklyn Museum] [1967] 187 p. illus. (part col.) 23 cm. Catalog of an exhibition shown at the Brooklyn Museum Oct. 3-Nov. 19, 1967, the Virginia Museum of Fine Arts Dec. 11, 1967-Jan. 14, 1968, and the California Palace of the Legion of Honor Feb. 17-Mar. 31, 1968. [ND457.T7] 67-28914

SUBJECT INDEX REDOUTE, PIERRE JOSEPH

1. Realism in art. 2. Paintings, European—Exhibitions. 3. Paintings, American—Exhibitions. I. Brooklyn Institute of Arts and Sciences. Museum. II. Virginia Museum of Fine Arts, Richmond. III. California Palace of the Legion of Honor, San Francisco.

YOUNG, Mahonri Sharp, 1911- 759.13
The paintings of George Bellows. New York, Watson-Guptill Publications [1973] 151 p. illus. (part col.) 29 cm. Bibliography: p. 9. [ND237.B45Y67] 73-5695 ISBN 0-8230-3885-8 25.00
1. Bellows, George Wesley, 1882-1925. 2. Realism in art. I. Bellows, George Wesley, 1882-1925. II. Title.

Realism in art—Addresses, essays, lectures.

SUPER realism : 709'.04
a critical anthology / edited by Gregory Battcock. New York : Dutton, 1975. xxx, 322 p., 8 leaves of plates : ill. (some col.) ; 23 cm. Includes bibliographical references and index. [N6494.R4S94 1975] 75-324335 ISBN 0-525-47377-7 : 6.95
1. Realism in art—Addresses, essays, lectures. 2. Art, Modern—20th century—Addresses, essays, lectures. 3. Painting from photographs—Addresses, essays, lectures. I. Battcock, Gregory, 1937- Contents omitted. BIP

Realism in art—Canada—Exhibitions.

AGNES Etherington Art Centre. 709'.71'074011372
Realism : emulsion and omission / Agnes Etherington Art Centre, the Art Gallery of the University of Guelph. Kingston, Ont. : Agnes Etherington Art Centre, 1972. [40] p. : ill., ports. ; 21 x 22 cm. Catalogue of an exhibition held at the Agnes Etherington Art Centre, Sept. 19-Oct. 22, 1972 and at the Art Gallery of the University of Guelph, Nov. 8-Dec. 4, 1972. Includes bibliographies. [N6545.5.R4A35 1972] 75-319042 2.00
1. Realism in art—Canada—Exhibitions. 2. Art, Canadian—Exhibitions. 3. Art, Modern—20th century—Canada—Exhibitions. I. Guelph, Ont. University. Art Gallery. II. Title.

Realism in art—Exhibitions.

ROTHMANS of Pall Mall Canada Limited. 709'.04
Aspects of realism = Aspects du realisme : [13th international art exhibition / organized by Rothmans of Pall Mall Canada Limited]. [s.l.] : Rothmans of Pall Mall Canada Limited, [1976] 92 p. : col. ill. ; 31 cm. [N6494.R4R67 1976] 77-483635
1. Realism in art—Exhibitions. 2. Art, Modern—20th century—Exhibitions. I. Title. II. Title: Aspects du realisme.

Realism in art—France.

NOCHLIN, Linda. 759.4
Gustave Courbet : a study of style and society / Linda Nochlin. New York : Garland Pub., 1976. xvii, 240 p., [33] leaves of plates : ill. ; 21 cm. (Outstanding dissertations in the fine arts) Originally presented as the author's thesis, New York University, 1963, under the title: The development and nature of realism in the work of Gustave Courbet. Bibliography: p. 233-240. [ND553.C9N62 1976] 75-23803 ISBN 0-8240-1998-9 lib.bdg. : 27.50
1. Courbet, Gustave, 1819-1877. 2. Realism in art—France. I. Title. II. Series.

Realism in art—Russia.

VALKENIER, Elizabeth Kridl. 759.7
Russian realist art : the state and society : the Peredvizhniki and their tradition / by Elizabeth Valkenier. Ann Arbor : Ardis, c1977. xv, 251 p. : ill. ; 24 cm. (Studies of the Russian Institute, Columbia University) Includes index. Bibliography: p. 231-242. [ND687.5.R4V34] 77-151042 ISBN 0-88233-264-3 : 16.95
1. Realism in art—Russia. 2. Peredvizhniki. 3. Painting, Modern—19th century—Russia. 4. Socialist realism in art—Russia. 5. Art and state—Russia. I. Title. II. Series: Columbia University. Russian Institute. Studies.

Realism in art—United States.

MATHEY, Francois. 759.13
American realism : a pictorial survey from the early eighteenth century to the 1970's / by Francois Mathey. New York : Rizzoli, c1978. 191 p. : ill. (some col.) ; 35 cm. Includes index. [N6505.5.R42M37] 77-77764 ISBN 0-8478-0125-X : 50.00
1. Realism in art—United States. 2. Art, American. I. Title. BIP

MILWAUKEE. Art Center. 759.13
Aspects of a new realism. [Exhibition] Milwaukee Art Center, June 21 through August 10, 1969; Contemporary Arts Museum, Houston, September 17 through October 19, 1969; Akron Art Institute, November 9 through December 14, 1969. [Milwaukee, 1969] 75, [1] p. illus. (part col.), ports. 26 cm. (Directions 2) "[Exhibitions] organized by the Milwaukee Art Center and sponsored by the Jos. Schlitz Brewing Company in conjunction with the Friends of Art of the Milwaukee Art for The Lakefront Festival of the Arts." Bibliography: p. [76] [ND212.M48] 71-6447
1. Realism in art—United States. 2. Paintings, American—Exhibitions. 3. Painting, Modern—20th century—United States. I. Contemporary Arts Museum. II. Akron, Ohio. Art Institute. III. Title. IV. Series.

Realism in art—United States—Exhibitions.

SEVEN realists 759.13'074'01468
: [exhibition] Yale University Art Gallery, New Haven, Connecticut, March 28-June 2, 1974. [New Haven? : The Gallery?, 1975?] 47 p. : ill. ; 22 cm. "The brief essays about the seven artists in our show were written by students in the museum training course ... Eve Blau [and others]." [ND212.5.R4S48] 75-327548
1. Realism in art—United States—Exhibitions. 2. Paintings, American—Exhibitions. 3. Paintings, Modern—20th century—United States—Exhibitions. I. Blau, Eve. II. Yale University. Art Gallery.

Reaugh, Frank, 1860-1945.

HALEY, James Evetts 1901- 759.13
F. Reaugh: man and artist. El Paso, Tex., C. Hertzog, 1960. unpaged. illus. 24cm. [ND237.R25H3] 61-1411
1. Reaugh, Frank, 1860-1945. I. Title.

STROUD, Alice Bab. 927.5
F. Reaugh; Texas longhorn painter by Alice Bab Stroud and Modena Stroud Dailey. Dallas, Royal Pub. Co. [1962] 143 p. illus., ports. 21 cm. "Prose sketches to accompany the series of paintings by Frank Reaugh entitled, Twenty-four hours with the herd; the text based partly on an earlier sketch by 'Hondo' and written jointly by the painter and by Clyde Walton Hill . . . An exact reproduction of an old booklet": p. [113]-[132] [ND237.R25S7] 62-52452
1. Reaugh, Frank, 1860-1945. I. Dailey, Modena (Stroud) joint author. II. Title.

Recreation—California—San Diego metropolitan area.

SAN Diego, Calif. City Planning Dept. General Planning Section. 711'.558'0979498
Park and recreation planning study. San Diego, 1972. ix, 108 p. illus. 28 cm. [GV54.C22S267 1972] 75-310892
1. Recreation—California—San Diego metropolitan area. 2. Outdoor recreation—California—San Diego metropolitan area. 3. Parks—California—San Diego metropolitan area. I. Title.

Recreation—Congresses.

NATIONAL Facilities Conference, 3d, Indiana University, 1965. 711.558
Planning areas and facilities for health, physical education, and recreation. Rev. Chicago, Athletic Institute, 1965. viii, 272 p. illus., plans. 28 cm. First published as a guide for planning facilities for athletics, recreation, physical & health education, the report of the first conference held in 1946. Includes bibliographies. [GV401.N33 1965c] 65-27616
1. Recreation—Congresses. 2. Physical education facilities. I. National Facilities Conference, 1st, Jackson's Mill, W. Va., 1946. A guide for planning facilities for athletics, recreation, physical & health education. II. Title.

Recreation rooms.

ABRAMS, Jane. 747'.791
Family rooms and dens. Garden City, N.Y., Doubleday [1970] 80 p. illus. (part col.) 24 cm. (The Doubleday home decorating program) [NK2117.A26] 73-22643
1. Recreation rooms. I. Title.

Red.

COLMEY, Mary Jane. 752
Red, yellow, and blue. Minneapolis, Denison [c1967] 24p. col. illus. 29cm. [ND1283.C67] 67-28674 2.88 lib. ed.,
1. Red. 2. Yellow. 3. Blue. 4. Color—Study and teaching. I. Title. BIP

Red in art.

WOLFF, Robert Jay, 1905- 701.8 j
Seeing red. New York, Scribner [1968] 1 v. (unpaged) col. illus. 21 cm. [ND1283.W6] 67-24052
1. Red in art. 2. Color—Juvenile literature. I. Title. BIP

Red Wing Potteries.

VIEL, Lyndon C. 738.3'7
The clay giants : the stoneware of Red Wing, Goodhue County, Minnesota / by Lyndon C. Viel. Des Moines, Iowa : Wallace-Homestead Book Co., c1977. 128 p. : ill. (some col.) ; 28 cm. [NK4210.R4V53] 76-24235 ISBN 0-87069-175-9 : 9.95
1. Red Wing Potteries. 2. Pottery, American—Minnesota—Red Wing. I. Title. BIP

Reder, Bernard, 1897-

BAUR, John Ireland Howe, 1909- 730.9436
Bernard Reder. New York, Pub. for the Whitney Mus. of Amer. Art by Praeger [1962, c.1961] 120p. illus. 31cm. 62-16052 7.50
1. Reder, Bernard, 1897- I. Whitney Museum of American Art, New York. II. Title.

WHITNEY Museum of American Art, New York. 730.9436
Bernard Reder, by John I. H. Baur. Exhibition and catalogue by the Whitney Museum of American Art. [New York, Praeger, 1961] 120 p. illus., ports. 31 cm. (Books that matter) Exhibition to be held Sept. 27 -- Nov. 7, 1961. Bibliography: p. 118. [N6838.R4W45] 61-17285
1. Reder, Bernard, 1897- I. Baur, John Ireland Howe, 1900- II. Title.

Redon, Odilon, 1840-1916.

BERGER, Klaus, 1901- 759.4
Odilon Redon: fantasy and colour. Tr. by Michael Bullock. New York, McGraw [1965] 244p. illus. (pt. mounted col.) plates, ports. 31cm. Bibl. [ND553.R35B43] 65-18176 19.95
1. Redon, Odilon, 1840-1916. I. Title.

BRESDIN, Rodolphe, 1822-1885. 769'.92'4 B
Bresdin to Redon; six letters 1870 to 1881. Edited by Roseline Bacou. Translated by Seymour S. Weiner. [Northampton, Mass.] Gehenna Press, 1969. [21] p. port. 27 cm. Translation of chapter 3 of Lettres de Gauguin, Gide, Huysmans, Jammes, Mallarme, Verhaeren ... a Odilon Redon, 1960. "Four hundred copies have been printed ... A double portrait of Bresdin and Redon, etched by Leonard Baskin, is printed from the plate. The first hundred copies, specially bound, have an additional impression of the etching signed by the artist." No. 33. [NE2049.5.B7A33] 73-83577
I. Redon, Odilon, 1840-1916. II. Baskin, Leonard, 1922- III. Bacou, Roceline. Letters ... a Odilon Redon. IV. Title.

MELLERIO, Andre, 1862- 760'.0924
Odilon Redon. New York, Da Capo, 1968. 166p. 206 illus., port. 29cm. (Da Capo ser. in graphic art, v. 4) Unabridged repubn. of the first ed. pub. in Paris in 1913. Also includes the supplementary catalogue that appeared in Mellerio's Odilon Redon: peintre, dessinateur et graveur, pub. in Paris in 1923. Bibl. [NE650.R4M4 1968] 67-27461 45.00
1. Redon, Odilon, 1840-1916. I. Title.

NEW York. Museum of Modern Art. 759.4
Odilon Redon, Gustave Moreau [and] Rodolphe Bresdin. The Museum of Modern Art, New York, in collaboration with the Art Institute of Chicago. Garden City, N.Y., Distributed by Doubleday [1961] 184 p. illus. (part col.) 24 cm. "Exhibition dates: the Museum of Modern Art ... December 4, 1961-February 4, 1962; the Art Institute of Chicago, March 2, 1962-April 15, 1962." Bibliographies: p. 168-171. [ND553.R35N4] 61-17804
1. Redon, Odilon, 1840-1916. 2. Moreau, Gustave, 1826-1898. 3. Bresdin, Rodolphe, 1825-1885.

REDON, Odilon, 1840-1916. 769'.924
The graphic works of Odilon Redon. With an introd. by Alfred Werner. New York, Dover Publications [1969] xxvii p. 209 plates, ports. 31 cm. Includes 192 illus. which previously appeared in his Oeuvre graphique complet, published in 1913. [NE650.R4W4] 68-14351 4.00
I. Werner, Alfred, 1911- BIP

REDON, Odilon, 1840-1916. 759.4
Odilon Redon, by Jean Selz. [Translated from the French by Eileen B. Hennessy] New York, Crown Publishers [1971] 95 p. illus. (part col.) 29 cm. Bibliography: p. 92-93. [ND553.R35A5713] 73-147349
I. Selz, Jean.

REDON, Odilon, 1840-1916. 760'.092'4
Odilon Redon / edited by Carolyn Keay ; introd. by Thomas Walters. New York : Rizzoli, 1977. 80 p. : ill. (some col.) ; 31 cm. [N6853.R38K42] 76-62547 ISBN 0-8478-0070-9 : 13.95. ISBN 0-8478-0088-1 pbk.
1. Redon, Odilon, 1840-1916. I. Keay, Carolyn.

REDON, Odilon, 1840-1916. 759.4
Odilon Redon: loan exhibition, October 22-November 21, 1970, for the benefit of the Lenox Hill Hospital, New York. New York, Acquavella Galleries [1970] [20] p. 50 plates (part col.) 28 cm. [ND553.R35A56] 76-198008
I. Lenox Hill Hospital, New York. II. Acquavella Galleries.

WILSON, Michael. 760'.092'4
Nature and imagination : the work of Odilon Redon / Michael Wilson. New York : Dutton, 1978. 78 p. : ill. (some col.) ; 29 cm. Bibliography: p. 6. [N6853.R38W54 1978] 78-55002 ISBN 0-7148-1849-6 : 12.95. ISBN 0-7148-1905-0 pbk. : 6.95
1. Redon, Odilon, 1840-1916. I. Redon, Odilon, 1840-1916. II. Title. BIP

Redoute, Pierre Joseph, 1759-1840.

HUNT Botanical Library. 759.4
A catalogue of Redouteana exhibited at the Hunt Botanical Library 21 April to 1 August 1963. Pittsburgh, 1963. vii, 117 p. plates (part col.) 26 cm. Catalogue of 203 items in the Hunt Botanical Library.

Includes bibliographies. [QK31.R4H8] 70-229937
1. Redoute, Pierre Joseph, 1759-1840. 2. Botanical illustration. I. Title.

Rees, Lloyd Frederic, 1895—

FREE, Renee. 759.994
Lloyd Rees [by] Renee Free. General editor John Henshaw. Melbourne, Lansdowne, 1972. 107 p. illus., col. plates. 32 cm. (Australian art library) Bibliography: p. 106-107. [ND1105.R4F69] 73-164917 ISBN 0-7018-0133-6 12.95
1. Rees, Lloyd Frederic, 1895- 2. Landscape in art. I. Rees, Lloyd Frederic, 1895-

Reeves, Euchlin D.—Art collections.

EFIRD, Callie Huger. 738.2'0951
Chinese export porcelain from the Reeves Collection at Washington and Lee University, Lexington, Virginia. [Exhibition and catalogue prepared by Callie Huger Efird and Katharine Gross Farnham. Lexington, Va., Washington and Lee University, 1973] 56 p. illus. 28 cm. "These Chinese export pieces from the Reeves Collection were first exhibited to the public at the High Museum of Art, Atlanta, Georgia, February 23rd to April 8th, 1973." Bibliography: p. 56. [NK4565.5.E33] 73-76576
1. Reeves, Euchlin D.—Art collections. 2. Reeves, Louise C. Herreshoff—Art collections. 3. China trade porcelain—Exhibitions. I. Farnham, Katharine Gross, joint author. II. Washington and Lee University, Lexington, Va. III. High Museum of Art. IV. Title. BIP

Reeves, Louise C. Herreshoff.

REEVES, Louise C. 759.13
Herreshoff.
Louise Herreshoff : an American artist discovered : an exhibition, October 9-November 21, 1976 / sponsored by Washington and Lee University and the Corcoran Gallery of Art. Lexington, Va. : The University, 1976. 80 p. : ill. (some col.) ; 28 cm. Catalog of the exhibition held at the Corcoran Gallery of Art, Washington, D.C. Bibliography: p. 31. [ND237.R258W37] 76-150460
1. Reeves, Louise C. Herreshoff. I. Washington and Lee University, Lexington, Va. II. Corcoran Gallery of Art, Washington, D.C.

Reformation and art.

MOXEY, Keith P. F., 759.9493'2
1943-
Pieter Aertsen, Joachim Beuckelaer, and the rise of secular painting in the context of the Reformation / Keith P. F. Moxey. New York : Garland Pub., 1977. xii, 284 p., [37] leaves of plates : ill. ; 21 cm. (Outstanding dissertations in the fine arts) Thesis—Chicago, 1974. Bibliography: p. 269-284. [ND623.A32M68] 76-23656 ISBN 0-8240-2715-9 : 35.00
1. Aertsen, Pieter, 1508-1575. 2. Beuckelaer, Joachim, ca. 1533-ca. 1575. 3. Reformation and art. I. Title. II. Series. BIP

Regenstein, Helen—Art collections.

CHICAGO. Art 741.9'4'074017311
Institute.
The Helen Regenstein Collection of European drawings : catalogue / by Harold Joachim. [Chicago] : Art Institute of Chicago, 1974. 167 p. : ill. (some col.) ; 26 cm. [NC225.C53 1974] 74-79440
1. Regenstein, Helen—Art collections. 2. Chicago. Art Institute. 3. Drawings, European—Catalogs. 4. Drawings—Chicago—Catalogs. I. Joachim, Harold. II. Title.

Reid, Neel, 1885-1926.

REID, Neel, 1885-1926. 720'.92'4
Architecture of Neel Reid in Georgia [by] James Grady. Photography by Kenneth Kay. Special photography by Josephine von Miklos. Color photography by Carey Sutlive. [Athens] University of Georgia Press [1973] xxii, 204 p. illus. (part col.) 29 cm. "Commissioned by Peachtree-Cherokee Trust." Bibliography: p. 200-201. [NA737.R44G72] 73-85027 ISBN 0-8203-0323-2 29.75
1. Reid, Neel, 1885-1926. 2. Architecture—Georgia. I. Grady, James H. II. Peachtree-Cherokee Trust. III. Title.

Reinforced concrete construction.

MORANDI, Riccardo 720.924
The concrete architecture of Riccardo Morandi [by] Giorgio Boaga, Benito Boni. Introd. by Riccardo Morandi [New enl. ed.] New York, Praeger [1966, c.1965] 234p. (chiefly illus., plans, port.) 30cm. Bibl. [TA683.M7813] 66-11378 20.00 bds.,
1. Reinforced concrete construction. I. Boaga, Giorgio. II. Boni, Benito. III. Title.

NERVI, Pier Luigi. 721
Aesthetics and technology in building. Translated from the Italian by Robert Einaudi. Cambridge, Mass., Harvard University Press, 1965. 198 p. illus. 20 x 25 cm. (The Charles Eliot Norton lectures, 1961-1962) [NA4125.N413] 65-16686
1. Reinforced concrete construction. 2. Architecture — Addresses, essays, lectures. I. Title. II. Series. BIP

RAAFAT, Aly Ahmed. 721.975
Reinforced concrete in architecture. New York, Reinhold [1958] 240p. illus. 27cm. Includes bibliography. [NA4125.R2] 58-7196
1. Reinforced concrete construction. 2. Architecture, Modern—20th cent. I. Title.

Reinhardt, Adolph Frederick.

JEWISH Theological 759.13
Seminary of America. Jewish Museum.
Ad Reinhardt: paintings. [Essay] by Lucy R. Lippard. Pref. by Sam Hunter. With a chronology by the artist. New York, Jewish Museum [1966] 76 p. illus. (part col., part mounted) 25 cm. Catalogue of an exhibition held at the Jewish Museum, Nov. 23, 1966-Jan. 15, 1967. Includes bibliographies. [ND237.R316J4] 66-29794
1. Reinhardt, Adolph Frederick. I. Lippard, Lucy R. II. Title.

LIPPARD, Lucy R. 759.13
Ad Reinhardt / Lucy R. Lippard. New York : H. N. Abrams, [1980] p. cm. Bibliography: p. [ND237.R316L48] 79-101623 ISBN 0-8109-1554-5 : 55.00
1. Reinhardt, Adolph Frederick.

REINHARDT, Adolph 759.13
Frederick.
Ad reinhardt: black paintings, 1951-1967. New York, Marlborough Gallery, 1970. 27 p. illus., port. 30 cm. Catalog of the exhibition held March 1970 at the Marlborough Gallery. [ND237.R316A4] 71-18446
I. Marlborough Gallery. II. Title.

Reiss, Winold, 1886-1953.

REISS, Winold, 1886-1953. 759.3
Winold Reiss: Plains portraits. Exhibition October 4 through October 28, 1972, Kennedy Galleries, Inc. New York, [Kennedy Galleries, c1972] 32 p. illus. (part col.) 27 cm. [ND1329.R34K46] 73-170565
1. Reiss, Winold, 1886-1953. 2. Indians of North America—Portraits. I. Kennedy Galleries, inc., New York. II. Title.

Rejlander, Oscar Gustav, 1813-1875.

JONES, Edgar Yoxall. 770'.92'4 B
Father of art photography, O. G. Rejlander, 1813-1875. Greenwich, Conn., New York Graphic Society [1973] 112 p. illus. 25 cm. Includes bibliographical references. [TR140.R43J66 1973b] 73-89945 ISBN 0-8212-0598-6
1. Rejlander, Oscar Gustav, 1813-1875. 2. Photography, Artistic. I. Rejlander, Oscar Gustav, 1813-1875. II. Title.

THE Photography of O. 770'.92'4
G. Rejlander : two selections / edited by Peter C. Bunnell. New York : Arno Press, 1979. p. cm. (The Sources of modern photography) Reprint of two works, the 1st from the Journal of the Photographic Society of London, April 21, 1858; the 2d from The photographic news, July 1886-Feb. 1887. Contents.Contents.—Rejlander, O. G. On Photographic composition.—Wall, A. H. Rejlander's photographic art studies. [TR651.P46] 76-24658 ISBN 0-405-09637-2 : 10.00
1. Rejlander, Oscar Gustav, 1813-1875. 2. Photography, Artistic. I. Bunnell, Peter C. II. Rejlander, Oscar Gustav, 1813-1875. On photographic composition. 1979. III. Wall, Alfred H. Rejlander's photographic art studies. 1979. IV. Series.

Rekhmara, Vizir of Upper Egypt, ca. B.C. 1471-1448.

DAVIES, Norman de Garis, 913.32
1865-1941.
The tomb of Rekh-mi-Re' at Thebes. New York, 1943. [New York] Arno Press, 1973 [c1944] 2 v. in 1. (ix, 118 p. 122 plates) 32 cm. Reprint of the ed. published as vol. 11 of Publications of the Metropolitan Museum of Art, Egyptian Expedition. At head of title: The Metropolitan Museum of Art, Egyptian Expedition. Bibliography: p. 107-109. [DT73.T3D32 1973] 75-168403 ISBN 0-405-02267-0
1. Rekhmara, Vizir of Upper Egypt, ca. B.C. 1471-1448. 2. Thebes, Egypt—Tombs. 3. Mural painting and decoration, Egyptian—Thebes. I. Title. II. Series: New York (City). Metropolitan Museum of Art. Egyptian Expedition. Publications, v. 11. BIP

Relief printing.

BROMMER, Gerald F. 761
Relief printmaking [by] Gerald F. Brommer. Worcester, Mass., Davis Publications [1970] 148 p. illus. 26 cm. [NE1350.B7] 77-113860 ISBN 0-87192-034-4
1. Relief printing. I. Title. BIP

ROSS, John, 1921- 761'.028
The complete relief print; the art and technique of the relief print, children's prints, care of prints, collecting prints, dealer and the edition, sources, and charts [by] John Ross [and] Clare Romano. New York, Free Press [1974] xiv, 115 p. illus. (part col.) 31 cm. Bibliography: p. 109-111. [NE850.R594] 74-2694 6.95 (pbk.)
1. Relief printing. I. Romano, Clare, joint author. II. Title. BIP

ROTHENSTEIN, Michael, 1908- 761
Relief printing. With contributions by Trevor Allen [and others] Photos. by John Hunnex. Diagrs. by Duncan Mill. New York, Watson-Guptill Publications [1970] 224 p. illus. (part col.) 29 cm. [NE850.R6] 73-98988 15.00
1. Relief printing. I. Allen, Trevor. BIP

Relief (Sculpture)

ROGERS, Leonard Robert, 731'.8
1924-
Relief sculpture / L. R. Rogers. London ; New York : Oxford University Press, 1974. 229 p. : ill. ; 26 cm. (The Appreciation of the arts ; 8) Includes bibliographical references and index. [NB1280.R63] 74-184847 ISBN 0-19-211920-6 : 19.50
1. Relief (Sculpture) I. Title. BIP

RYBERG, Inez (Scott) 731.5'4
Panel reliefs of Marcus Aurelius. New York, Archaeological Institute of America, 1967. xii, 102 p., 63 plates. 31 cm. (Monographs on archaeology and the fine arts 14) On label: Stechert-Hafner Service Agency, New York. Bibliographical footnotes. [NB165.A85R9] 67-8802
1. Aurelius Antoninus, Marcus, Emperor of Rome, 121-180. 2. Relief (Sculpture) I. Title. II. Series.

Relief (Sculpture)—Italy—Pavia.

MORSCHECK, Charles R. 730'.945'29
Relief sculpture for the facade of the Certosa di Pavia, 1473-1499 / Charles R. Morscheck, Jr. New York : Garland Pub., 1978. p. cm. (Outstanding dissertations in the fine arts) Bibliography: p. [NB1291.P37M67] 77-94727 ISBN 0-8240-3243-8 : lib.bdg. : 47.50
1. Pavia. Certosa. Facciata. 2. Relief (Sculpture)—Italy—Pavia. 3. Relief (Sculpture), Renaissance—Italy—Pavia. I. Title. II. Series. BIP

Relief (Sculpture)—Turkey—Lycia.

CHILDS, William A. 732'.9'3928
P., 1942-
The city-reliefs of Lycia / William A. P. Childs. Princeton, N.J. : Princeton University Press, c1978. p. cm. (Princeton monographs in art and archaeology ; 42) Includes bibliographical references and index. [NB130.L9C48] 78-51159 27.50
1. Relief (Sculpture)—Turkey—Lycia. 2. Cities and towns in art. 3. Sepulchral monuments—Turkey—Lycia. 4. Lycia. I. Title. II. Series. BIP

Religion—Exhibitions and museums.

JEWISH Theological Seminary 732
of America. Jewish Museum.
Thou shalt have no other gods before me [Exhibition] New York, Author [c.]1964 [55]p. illus. 25cm. 64-20950 2.50 pap.,
1. Religion—Exhibitions and museums. I. Farkas, Ann. II. Title.
Contents omitted.

Religion in art.

BEIER, Ulli. 730'.92'4
The return of the gods : the sacred art of Susanne Wenger / Ulli Beier. Cambridge [Eng.] ; New York : Cambridge University Press, 1975. 120 p. : ill. ; 23 x 25 cm. Includes index. [NB511.5.W44B44] 74-12969 ISBN 0-521-20717-7 : 14.95
1. Wenger, Susanne, 1915- 2. Religion in art. 3. Yorubas—Religion. I. Wenger, Susanne, 1915- II. Title. BIP

Religion in poetry.

GARDNER, Charles, 760'.092'4
1874-
Vision & vesture; a study of William Blake in modern thought. [Folcroft, Pa.] Folcroft Library Editions, 1973. xi, 226 p. 23 cm. Reprint of the 1929 rev. ed. published by E. P. Dutton, New York. [PR4147.G32 1973] 73-15646 ISBN 0-8414-4470-6 (lib. bdg.)
1. Blake, William, 1757-1827. 2. Religion in poetry. 3. Literature, Modern—19th century—History and criticism. I. Title. BIP

Religions—Pictures, illustrations, etc.

MOORE, Albert C. 704.94'8
Iconography of religions : an introduction / Albert C. Moore. 1st American ed. Philadelphia : Fortress Press, 1977. vi, 337 p. : ill. ; 26 cm. Includes index. Bibliography: p. [323]-325. [N7790.M65 1977] 76-62598 ISBN 0-8006-0488-1 : 25.00
1. Religions—Pictures, illustrations, etc. I. Title. BIP

Rembrandt Harmenszoon van Rijn, 1606-1669.

ABELES, Elivn, 1909- 759.9492
The magic painter; the story of Rembrandt, told by Kerwin Bowles [pseud.] Illustrated by Mitchell Foster. New York, Stravon Publishers [1951] 31 p. illus. 22 x 28 cm. (A Child's book of great artists) Stravon great artist series, 3. [ND653.R4A65] 927.5 51-8432
1. Rembrandt Hermanszoon van Rijn, 1606-1669. 2. Art—Juvenile literature. I. Title.

BALET, Leo, 1878- 759.9492
Rembrandt and Spinoza. New York, Philosophical [c.1962] 222p. illus. 22cm. Bibl. 61-18686 4.50
1. Rembrandt Hermanszoon van Rijn, 1606-1669. 2. Spinoza, Benedictus de, 1632-1677. 3. Netherlands—Civilization. I. Title.

BALET, Leo, 1878- 759.9492
Rembrandt and Spinoza. New York, Philosophical Library [1962] 222p. illus. 22cm. Includes bibliography. [ND653.R4B2] 61-18686

Pennsylvania State University Press [1969] 2 v. illus., ports. 31 cm. Contents.—[1] Text.—[2] Plates. Bibliographical footnotes. [NE2165.R5W45 1969] 69-17493 29.50
1. Rembrandt Hermanzoon van Rijn, 1606-1669. I. Title.

Rembrandt Harmenszoon van Rijn, 1606-1669.

BAILEY, Anthony. 759.9492 B
Rembrandt's house / Anthony Bailey. Boston : Houghton Mifflin, 1978. 246 p. : ill. ; 24 cm. Includes index. Bibliography: p. 237-240. [N6953.R4B25] 77-26987 ISBN 0-395-25706-9 : 15.00
1. Rembrandt Harmenszoon van Rijn, 1606-1669. 2. Artists—Netherlands—Biography. 3. Rembrandthuis. 4. Amsterdam—Social life and customs. I. Title. BIP

BENESCH, Otto, 1896-1964. 759.9492
Rembrandt. Edited by Eva Benesch. [New York] Phaidon [1970] xx, 456 p. illus., ports. 26 cm. (His Collected writings, v. 1) "Essays originally printed in German have been translated by Gillian Mullins." Includes bibliographies. [N7483.B43A15 vol. 1] 69-12787 ISBN 0-7148-1365-6 15.00
1. Rembrandt Harmenszoon van Rijn, 1606-1669.

BIORKLUND, George. 769'.924
Rembrandt's etchings, true and false; a summary catalogue in a distinctive chronological order and completely illustrated, by George Biorklund with the assistance of Osbart H. Barnard. 2nd ed. Rev. and enl. Stockholm, New York [etc.] 1968. 199 p. illus., ports. 30 cm. Distributors in the U.S.A.: Museum Books, New York. "Printed in 600 numbered copies" No. 181. [NE2165.R5B5 1968] 68-55427 unpriced
1. Rembrandt Harmenszoon van Rijn, 1606-1669. I. Title.

BONNIER, Henry. 741.9'492
Rembrandt. [Translated by Victoria Benedict] New York, G. Braziller [1970, c1968] 117 p. illus. 25 cm. (The Great draughtsmen) Translation of L'Univers de Rembrandt. [NC263.R4B613 1970] 73-107229 7.95
1. Rembrandt Harmenszoon van Rijn, 1606-1669.

CAMBRIDGE. University. Fitzwilliam Museum. 741.9492
Rembrandt and his circle: [catalogue of] an exhibition of drawings from the collection of the Fitzwilliam Museum, Cambridge, February-June 1966. Cambridge, Fitzwilliam Museum [1966] [72] p. 22 1/2 cm. Bibliography: p. [8]-[11] [NC1055.R4C3] 67-76820
1. Rembrandt Harmenszoon van Rijn, 1606-1669. I. Title.

CLARK, Kenneth McKenzie, Baron Clark, 1903- 759.9492 B
An introduction to Rembrandt / Kenneth Clark. 1st U.S. ed. New York : Harper & Row, c1978. 153 p. : ill. ; 25 cm. (Icon editions) "Based on a series of television programmes ... made for the Ashwood Trust." Includes index. [N6953.R4C55 1978] 77-3745 ISBN 0-06-430860-X : 12.95
1. Rembrandt Harmenszoon van Rijn, 1606-1669. 2. Artists—Netherlands—Biography. I. Title.

FUCHS, Rudolf Herman, 1942- 759.9492
Rembrandt in Amsterdam [by] R. H. Fuchs. [Translated from the Dutch by Patricia Wardle and Alan Griffiths. 1st English language ed.] Greenwich, Conn., New York Graphic Society [1969, c1968] 80 p. illus. 26 cm. Includes bibliographical references. [ND653.R4F813 1969] 71-78380 9.50
1. Rembrandt Harmenszoon van Rijn, 1606-1669. I. Title.

HAAK, B. 759.9492 B
Rembrandt; his life, his work, his time [by] Bob Haak. [Translated from the Dutch by Elizabeth Willems-Treeman] New York, H. N. Abrams [1969] 348 p. illus., facsims., maps, ports. 36 cm. Translation of Rembrandt, zijn leven, zijn werk, zijn tijd. Part of the illustrative matter is colored. Bibliography: p. 337-340. [ND653.R4H153 1969b] 69-12481
1. Rembrandt Harmenszoon van Rijn, 1606-1669. I. Title.

HELD, Julius Samuel, 1905- 759.9492
Rembrandt's Aristotle, and other Rembrandt studies, by Julius S. Held. Princeton, N.J., Princeton University Press, 1969. xvi, 155, [82] p. illus. (part col.) 28 cm. Bibliographical footnotes. [ND653.R4H377] 69-18075 10.00
1. Rembrandt Harmenszoon van Rijn, 1606-1669. I. Title.

LEPORE, Mario, 1912- 759.9492
The life and times of Rembrandt; text by Mario Lepore, translator [from the Italian] Julia Shaw. London, New York [etc.] Hamlyn, 1968. 75 p. col. illus., facsim., ports. (some col.) 30 cm. (Portraits of greatness) Illus. on lining papers. [ND653.R4L413] 78-397565 ISBN 6-00-031543- 17/6
1. Rembrandt, Harmenszoon van Rijn, 1606-1669. I. Title.

MULLER, Joseph Emile. 759.9492
Rembrandt. [Translated from the French by Brian Hooley] New York, H. N. Abrams [1969] 271 p. 134 illus. (part col.) 22 cm. Bibliography: p. 271. [ND653.R4M7863 1969] 69-12441
1. Rembrandt Harmenszoon van Rijn, 1606-1669.

NASH, John Malcolm. 759.9492
The age of Rembrandt and Vermeer; Dutch painting in the seventeenth century [by] J. M. Nash. New York, Holt, Rinehart, and Winston [1972] 271 p. illus. (part col.) 29 cm. [ND646.N37 1972] 78-190474 ISBN 0-03-091870-7 25.00
1. Rembrandt Harmenszoon van Rijn, 1606-1669. 2. Vermeer, Johannes, 1632-1675. 3. Painting, Dutch. 4. Painting, Modern—17th-18th centuries—Netherlands. I. Title. BIP

REMBRANDT after three hundred years; an exhibition of Rembrandt and his followers. [Chicago] Art Institute of Chicago, 1969. 280 p. illus. (part col.) 26 cm. Held at the Art Institute of Chicago, the Minneapolis Institute of Arts, and the Detroit Institute of Arts. Contents.Contents.—Foreword, by C. C. Cunningham.—Introduction, by E. Haverkamp-Begemann.—Catalogue of paintings, by J. R. Judson.—Paintings, illustrations.—Catalogue of drawings, by E. Haverkamp-Begemann [and] A. M. Logan.—Drawings, illustrations. Includes bibliographical references. [N6946.R45] 76-96721 759.9492
1. Rembrandt Harmenszoon van Rijn, 1606-1669. 2. Art, Dutch—Exhibitions. 3. Art, Modern—17th-18th centuries—Netherlands. I. Judson, Jay Richard. II. Haverkamp Begemann, Egbert. III. Chicago. Art Institute. IV. Minneapolis. Institute of Arts. V. Detroit. Institute of Arts.

REMBRANDT Harmenszoon van Rijn, 1606-1669. 741.9'45
Drawings. Introd. by Stephen Longstreet. [1st ed.] Los Angeles, Borden Pub. Co. [1963] 1 v. (chiefly illus.) 31 cm. (Master draughtsman series) [NC1055.R4L8] 64-1291
I. Longstreet, Stephen, 1907- ed. II. Title.

REMBRANDT Harmenszoon van Rijn, 1606-1669. 741.9'492
More drawings of Rembrandt / introd. by Stephen Longstreet. 1st ed. Alhambra, Calif. : Borden Pub. Co., [1974] [48] p. : chiefly ill. ; 31 cm. (Master draughtsman series) [NC263.R4L66] 74-79306
1. Rembrandt Harmenszoon van Rijn, 1606-1669. I. Longstreet, Stephen, 1907-

REMBRANDT Harmenszoon van Rijn, 1606-1669. 741.9'492
Rembrandt drawings / Bob Haak ; [translated by Elizabeth Willems-Treeman]. London : Thames and Hudson, 1976. 223 p., [2] leaves of plates : ill. (some col.) ; 22 cm. Translation of Rembrandt. Bibliography: p. 222-223. [NC263.R4H3213] 76-382224 ISBN 0-500-18157-8 : £4.50
1. Rembrandt Harmenszoon van Rijn, 1606-1669. I. Haak, B. II. Title.

REMBRANDT, Harmenszoon van Rijn, 1606-1669. 769'.924
Rembrandt: experimental etcher. [Catalogue was prepared jointly by Felice Stampfle and others] Boston, Museum of Fine Arts; distributed by New York Graphic Society, Greenwich, Conn. [1969] 184 p. illus. 26 cm. Exhibition held at the Museum of Fine Arts, Boston, Oct. 1-Nov. 9, 1969, and at the Pierpont Morgan Library, New York, Nov. 26, 1969-Jan. 10, 1970. [NE2054.5.R4S7] 77-93138 20.00
1. Rembrandt Harmenszoon van Rijn, 1606-1669. I. Stampfle, Felice. II. Boston. Museum of Fine Arts. III. Pierpont Morgan Library, New York.

REMBRANDT Harmenszoon van Rijn, 1606-1669. 769'.92'4
Rembrandt, sessanta acqueforti = Rembrandt, sixty etchings / scelte e annotate da Antony De Witt. Firenze : La nuova Italia, 1976. 23, [22] p., 60 leaves of plates : ill. ; 20 cm. (Strumenti ; 36) English and Italian. Bibliography: p. [41] [NE2054.5.R4A85 1976] 77-468078 L1500
1. Rembrandt Harmenszoon van Rijn, 1606-1669. I. Antony de Witt, Antonio, 1876-1967. II. Title. III. Title: Rembrandt, sixty etchings.

REMBRANDT HARMENSZOON VAN RIJN, 1606-1669. 759.9492
Rembrandt. Text by Wilhelm Koehler. New York, H. N. Abrams [196-?] 24 p. illus., col. plates. 33 cm. (Library of great painters. Portfolio ed.) [ND653.R4K655 1960z] 69-14756
1. Rembrandt Harmenszoon van Rijn, 1606-1669. I. Koehler, Wilhelm Reinhold Walter, 1884-1959.

RIPLEY, Elizabeth, 1906- 927.5
Rembrandt, a biography. With drawings, etchings and paintings by Rembrandt. New York, Oxford University Press, 1955. 68 p. illus. 26 cm. (Oxford books for boys and girls) [ND653.R4R55] 55-8693
1. Rembrandt Harmenszoon van Rijn, 1606-1669.

ROSENBERG, Jakob, 1893- 760'.0924
Rembrandt: life & work. [3d ed.] London, New York, Phaidon [1968] xi, 386 p. illus., ports. 25 cm. (Paidon paperback, PH54) Includes bibliographical references. [ND653.R4R82 1968] 68-18911 ISBN 0-7148-1338-9 4.95
1. Rembrandt, Harmenszoon van Rijn, 1606-1669.

STEARNS, Monroe. 759.9'492 B
Rembrandt and his world. New York, F. Watts [1967] viii, 216 p. illus., ports. 25 cm. (Immortals of art) Bibliography: p. 206-209. [ND653.R4S7] 67-1733
1. Rembrandt Harmenszoon van Rijn, 1606-1669. I. Title.

U.S. National Gallery of Art. 760'.0924
Rembrandt in the National Gallery of Art, Washington, D.C. [Washington, 1969] 71 p. illus. 26 cm. Catalog of an exhibition commemorating the tercentenary of the artist's death held Mar. 16-May 11, 1969 at the National Gallery of Art. Bibliography: p. 9. [ND653.R4U5] 78-600475
1. Rembrandt Harmenszoon van Rijn, 1606-1669. I. Title.

WALLACE, Robert, 1919- 760'.0924
The world of Rembrandt, 1606-1669, by Robert Wallace and the editors of Time-Life Books New York, Time-Life Books [1968] 188 p. illus. (part col.) 31 cm. (Time-Life library of art) Issued in a case. Bibliography: p. 183. [ND653.R4W27 1968] 68-22321
1. Rembrandt Harmenszoon van Rijn, 1606-1669. I. Time-Life Books. II. Title. BIP

WHITE, Christopher. 927.5
Rembrandt and his world. New York, Viking Press [1964] 144 p. illus., facsims., map, col. plates, ports. 24 cm. (A Studio book) [ND653.R4W44] 64-18148
1. Rembrandt Harmenszoon van Rijn, 1606-1669. I. Title.

WRIGHT, Christopher, 1945- 759.9492
Rembrandt and his art / [by] Christopher Wright. London ; New York : Hamlyn, 1975. 128 p. : ill. (some col.), ports. (some col.) ; 34 cm. Includes index. Bibliography: p. 128. [ND653.R4W74] 76-356074 ISBN 0-600-36177-2 : £3.95
1. Rembrandt Harmenszoon van Rijn, 1606-1669. I. Title.

Rembrandt Harmenszoon van Rijn, 1606-1669—Influence.

CZOBER, Agnes. 759.9492
Rembrandt and his circle. [Translated by Lili Halapy] New York, Taplinger Pub. Co. [1970, c1969] 25 p. 48 col. plates. 25 cm. Translation of Rembrandt es kore. Bibliography: p. 19. [ND646.C9313 1970] 74-107012 7.95
1. Rembrandt Harmenszoon van Rijn, 1606-1669—Influence. 2. Paintings, Dutch—Catalogs. I. Budapest. Szepmuveszety Muzeum. II. Esztergom, Hungary. Kereszteny Muzeum. III. Title.

Rembrandt Harmenszoon van Rijn, 1606-1669.

WHITE, Christopher. 741.9493
The drawings of Rembrandt. London, Trustees of the British Museum; [stamped on cover: Agents in America. British Information Services, New York] 1962. 52 p. illus. 22 cm. Includes bibliography. [NC263.R4W5] 62-5907
1. Rembrandt Hermanazoon van Rijn, 1606-1669. I. Title.

Rembrandt, Harmenszoon van Rijn, 1606-1669.

ROGER-MARX, Claude, 1888- 759.9492
Rembrandt. Translated [from the French] by W. J. Strachan and peter Simmons. New York, Universe Books [1960] 365p. illus., col. plates. 29cm. notes: p.353-356. Bibl. 60-12417 20.00
1. Rembrandt Hermanszoon van Riin, 1606-1669. I. Title.

Remington Arms Co., inc.

PETERSON, Harold Leslie, 1922- 623.44
The Remington historical treasury of American guns, by Harold L. Peterson. Edinburgh, New York, T. Nelson [1966] 154 p. illus. (part col) 22 cm. "A Ridge press book." [TS535.P44] 66-13822
1. Remington Arms Co., inc. 2. Firearms. I. Title.

PETERSON HAROLD LESLIE, 1922- 623.44
The Remington treasury of American guns. New York, Grosset [1966] 154p. illus. 21cm. (Ridge Pr. bk., 1255) [TS535.P44] 1.00 pap.,
1. Remington Arms Co., inc. 2. Firearms. I. Title.

Remington Arms Company, inc.

WEST, Bill. 683'.4'00973
Remington arms & history. [1st ed.] Azusa, Calif. [1970] 1 v. (various pagings) illus., ports. 24 cm. [TS533.2.W46] 71-121899
1. Remington Arms Company, inc. 2. Firearms, American. I. Title.

Remington, Frederic, 1861-1909.

BAIGELL, Matthew. 709.2'4
The western art of Frederic Remington / by Matthew Baigell. 1st ed. New York : Ballantine Books, 1976. p. cm. [N6537.R4B24] 76-9744 ISBN 0-345-25128-8 pbk. : 5.95
1. Remington, Frederic, 1861-1909. 2. The West in art. I. Title. BIP

HASSRICK, Peter H. 759.13
Frederic Remington; an essay and catalogue to accompany a retrospective exhibition of the work of Frederic Remington, by Peter H. Hassrick. Fort Worth [Tex.] Amon Carter Museum [1973] 48 p. illus. 22 cm. Includes bibliographical references. [N6537.R4H37] 72-96833 3.00
1. Remington, Frederic, 1861-1909. 2. The

Publishers, 1958. 95p. illus. (part mounted, part col.) 29cm. Bibliography: p. 93-94. [ND553.R45S33] 58-13257
1. Renoir, Auguste, 1841-1919. I. Title.

SLATKIN (CHARLES E.) 707.4 GALLERIES, New York.
Renoir, Degas; a loan exhibition of drawings, pastels, sculptures, November 7 through December 6, 1958. New York [1958] unpaged (chiefly illus.) 29 cm. Includes bibliography. [ND553.R45S5] 59-23070
1. Renoir, Auguste, 1841-1919. 2. Degas, Hilaire Germain Edgar, 1834-1917. I. Title.

STERLING and 750'.74'01443 Francine Clark Art Institute, Williamstown, Mass.
Impressionist paintings; 32 Renoir, 2 Monet. September 18th, 1956. Williamstown, Mass. [1956?] [50] p. plates 25 cm. (Its Exhibit 6) Cover title. Includes bibliographies. [N867.A27 no. 6] 67-35668
1. Renoir, Auguste, 1840-1926. 2. Monet, Claude, 1841-1919. 3. Impressionism (Art) — Exhibitions. I. Title. II. Series.

[TRAZ, George Albert 759.4 Edouard de] 1881-
Renoir, his life and work [by] Francois Fosca [pseud. Tr. from French by Mary I. Martin] Englewood Cliffs, N. J., Prentice [1962, c1961] 271p. illus. (pt. col.) 22cm. 62-52349 6.95
I. Renoir, Auguste, 1841-1919. II. Title.

TRAZ, Georges de, 1881- 759.4 B
Renoir [by] Francois Fosca. [Translated from the French by Mary I. Martin] New York, H. N. Abrams [1969] 288 p. illus. (part col.), ports. (part col.) 22 cm. Translation of Renoir, l'homme et son ouvre. [ND553.R45T683 1969] 73-90892
1. Renoir, Auguste, 1841-1919.

TRAZ, Georges de, 1881- 759.4 B
*Renoir : his life and work / Francois Fosca [i.e. G. de Traz] ; [translated from the French by Mary I. Martin]. New York : Praeger, 1975. 288 p. : ill. (some col.) ; 21 cm. (Praeger world of art paperbacks) (A Praeger world of art profile) Translation of Renoir, l'homme et son ouvre. Includes index. [ND553.R45T683 1975] 74-8442 ISBN 0-275-71670-8 : 5.95
1. Renoir, Auguste, 1841-1919.*

WILDENSTEIN and Company, 759.4 inc., New york.
A loan exhibition of Renoir for the benefit of the New York Infirmary, March 23-April 29, 1950 at Wildenstein. [New York, 1950] 62 p. illus., ports. 26 cm. "The exhibition has been organized by Vladimir Visson and Daniel Wildenstein, with the collaboration of Ima N. Ebin." "Renoir, by Daniel Wildenstein": p.9-37. [ND553.R45W48] 50-2672
1. Renoir, Auguste, 1841-1919. 2. Paintings, French—Exhibitions. I. Wildenstein, Daniel, 1917- II. Title.

Renoir, Auguste, 1841-1919— Addresses, essays, lectures.

IMPRESSIONISM in 759.4 perspective / edited by Barbara Ehrlich White. Englewood Cliffs, N.J. : Prentice Hall, c1978. xiv, 165 p., [6] leaves of plates : ill. ; 23 cm. (The artists in perspective series) (A Spectrum book) Bibliography: p. 161-163. [ND547.5.I4I448] 77-21780 ISBN 0-13-452037-8 : 18.95 ISBN 0-13-452029-7 pbk. : 5.95
1. Renoir, Auguste, 1841-1919—Addresses, essays, lectures. 2. Pissarro, Camille, 1830-1903—Addresses, essays, lectures. 3. Monet, Claude, 1840-1926—Addresses, essays, lectures. 4. Impressionism (Art)—France—Addresses, essays, lectures. 5. Painting, Modern—19th century—France—Addresses, essays, lectures. I. White, Barbara Ehrlich.

Renoir, Auguste, 1841-1919. Full name: Georges Albert Edouard de Traz.

TRAZ, Georges de, 1881- 759.4
Renoir, his life and work [by] Francois Fosca [pseud. Translated from the French by Mary I. Martin. 1st American ed.]

Englewood Cliffs, N.J., Prentice-Hall [1962, c1961] 271 p. illus. 22 cm. [ND553.R45T683] 62-52349
1. Renoir, Auguste, 1841-1919. Full name: Georges Albert Edouard de Traz. I. Title.

Renoir, Auguste, 1848-1919—Juvenile literature.

RABOFF, Ernest Lloyd. 759.4
Pierre-Auguste Renoir, by Ernest Raboff. Garden City, N.Y., Doubleday [1970] [31] p. illus. (part col.), ports. (part col.) 29 cm. (Art for children) (A Gemini-Smith book.) A brief biography of the artist accompanies color reproductions and analyses of fifteen of his works. [ND553.R45R3] 72-93205 3.95
1. Renoir, Auguste, 1848-1919—Juvenile literature. I. Title.

Rensselaer Polytechnic Institute, Troy, N.Y.

DOXIADIS 727'.3'0974741 Associates, inc.
Campus planning in an urban area; a master plan for Rensselaer Polytechnic Institute. New York, Praeger Publishers [1971] xiii, 99 p. maps (part col.) 29 cm. (Praeger special studies in U.S. economic and social development) [T171.R49D68] 79-153391
1. Rensselaer Polytechnic Institute, Troy, N.Y. I. Title.

Repairing—Amateurs' manuals.

WAUGH, Andrew. 643'.7
Handyman's encyclopedia / Andrew Waugh ; U.S. editor, Bruce Scully. 1st U.S. ed. New York : Drake Publishers, 1976. 431 p. : ill. ; 29 cm. Includes index. [TT151.W38 1976] 76-16423 ISBN 0-8473-1079-5 : 14.95
1. Repairing—Amateurs' manuals. I. Title.

Report year ends June 30.

PHILLIPS Academy, 708.144 Andover, Mass. Addison Gallery of American Art.
Report. Andover. v. 28 cm. annual. [N512.A6P334] 51-38282
1. Report year ends June 30. I. Title.

Repousse work.

MERIEL Bussy, Yves. 739'.14
Repoussage: the embossing of metal. [Translated by Rhea Rollin. Adapted by Anne E. Kallem] New York, Sterling Pub. Co. [1970] 48 p. illus. 20 cm. (Little craft book series) Translation of Le Repoussage du metal. [NK6530.M413] 70-115445 ISBN 0-8069-5148-6
1. Repousse work. I. Title.

Research—United States

SMITHSONIAN 507.2'073 Institution. Office of Education and Training.
Smithsonian research opportunities: fine arts, history, science, 1967-1968. Washington, 1966. vi, 153 p. illus. 23 cm. (Smithsonian publication 4691) [Q11.S8A5] 67-60377
1. Smithsonian Institution. 2. Research—United States I. Title.

Restaurants, lunch rooms, etc.

ATKIN, William Wilson. 747.8571
Interiors book of restaurants, by William Wilson Atkin & Joan Adler. New York, Whitney Library of Design [1960] xl, 215 p. illus., diagrs., plans. 32 cm. Includes bibliography. [NA7855.A8] 60-16477
1. Restaurants, lunch rooms, etc. I. Adler, Joan, joint author. II. Title.

BACKUS, Harry. 747'.8'571
Designing restaurant interiors : a guide for food service operators / Harry Backus. New York : Lebhar-Friedman Books, c1977. iv, 92 p. : ill. ; 24 cm. Includes index. [NK2195.R4B3] 76-56638 ISBN 0-912016-58-2 : 11.00

1. Restaurants, lunch rooms, etc. 2. Interior decoration. I. Title. BIP

FENGLER, Max. 725'.71
Restaurant architecture and design; an international survey of eating places. New York, Universe Books [1972, c1971] xxiv, 176 p. illus. 31 cm. Translation of Restaurants, Cafes, Kantinen, Mensen. [NA7855.F413] 70-101444 ISBN 0-87663-112-X 18.50
1. Restaurants, lunch rooms, etc. I. Title.

LAWSON, Fred R 725'.71
Restaurant planning and design, by Fred Lawson. [New York] Van Nostrand Reinhold [1974, c1973] 180 p. illus., plans. 31 cm. Bibliography: p. 177. [NA7855.L38 1974] 73-11754 ISBN 0-999-84690-6 24.95
1. Restaurants, lunch rooms, etc. I. Title.

Restaurants, lunch rooms, etc.—Design and construction.

LAWSON, Fred R. 725'.71
Designing commercial food service facilities [by] Fred Lawson. New York, Whitney Library of Design [1974, c1973] p. Includes bibliographical references. [TX945.L34 1974] 73-21504 ISBN 0-8230-7146-4 24.95
1. Restaurants, lunch rooms, etc.—Design and construction. I. Title. BIP

Reswick, Katherine White—Art collections.

FAGG, William Buller. 730'.967
African tribal images; the Katherine White Reswick Collection [by] William Fagg. [Cleveland] Cleveland Museum of Art [1968] 1 v. (unpaged) illus., maps. 24 cm. Includes bibliography. [NB1080.F312] 68-31762 9.50
1. Reswick, Katherine White—Art collections. 2. Sculpture, African—Catalogs. I. Cleveland Museum of Art. II. Title.

Retina camera.

BOMBACK, Edward S 770.28
Retina handbook. London, Fountain Press; Philadelphia, Rayelle Publications [1957] 159p. illus. 12x15cm. (A Fountain photobook) [TR263.R4B57] 57-59471
1. Retina camera. 2. Photography—Handbooks, manuals, etc. I. Title.

COOPER, Joseph David, 771.31 1917-
Retina Reflex pocket companion. [New York]. Universal Photo Bks. [dist. Amphoto, c. 1962]c94p. illus. 15cm. (U-261) 62-14415 1.95, wire bdg.
1. Retina camera. 2. Photography—Handbooks, manuals, etc. I. Title.

CROY, Otto R 1902- 770.2
The Retina way; the Retina photographer's companion. London, New York, Focal Press [1952?] 239 p. illus. 22 cm. [TR263.R4C7] 52-43361
1. Retina camera. I. Title.

MANNHEIM, L. A. 771.31
The Retina Reflex way; the Retina Reflex photographer's companion. New York, [dist. Amphoto, c. 1960] 360p. illus. (part col.) 61-1088 7.50
1. Retina camera. 2. Photography—Handbooks, manuals, etc. I. Title.

MANNHEIM, Ladislaus 771.31 Andrew, 1925-
The Retina Reflex way; the Retina Reflex photographer's companion. New York, Focal Press [1960] 360p. illus. 22cm. [TR263.R4M3] 61-1088
1. Retina camera. 2. Photography—Handbooks, manuals, etc. I. Title.

TYDINGS, Kenneth S. 771.31
New Retina eye-level reflex guide, applicable to Retina rangefinder, Kodak 35, Pony, and Signet cameras. Philadelphia, Chilton, c.1963. 95p. illus. 20 cm. (Mod. camera gd. ser.) 63-10579 price unreported
1. Retina camera. 2. Photography—Handbooks, manuals, etc. I. Title. II. Series.

TYDINGS, Kenneth S 771.31
New Retina eye-level reflex guide, applicable to Retina rangefinder, Kodak 35, Pony, and Signet cameras. Philadelphia, Chilton Books, c1963. 95 p. illus. 20 cm. (The Modern camera guide series) [TR263.R4T92] 63-10579
1. Retina camera. 2. Photography — Handbooks, manuals, etc. I. Title. II. Series.

Revenue-stamps—Catalog.

GRIFFENHAGEN, George B. 769'.5
Medicine tax stamps: worldwide, by George Griffenhagen. Milwaukee, American Topical Association in cooperation with the American Institute of the History of Pharmacy [1971] 126 p. facsims. 23 cm. (ATA handbook no. 76) (ATA medical handbook series, v. 5) Cover title. Includes bibliographies. [HE6187.A635 no. 76] [HJ5315] 75-28799 6.00
1. Revenue-stamps—Catalog. 2. Drugs—Taxation. I. Title. II. Series: American Topical Association. Topical handbook, no. 76. III. Series: American Topical Association. ATA medical handbook series, v. 5.

Revenue-stamps—Great Britain— Catalogs.

FRANK, Samuel B. 769'.5
The stamp duty of Great Britain and Ireland; a catalogue of the embossing dies and of the impressed stamps used for fiscal purposes from 1694 onward, by Samuel B. Frank and Josef Schonfeld. With the indispensable contributions of William A. Barber and Marcus Samuel. Mamaroneck, N.Y., 1970-74. 3 v. illus. 28 cm. [HJ5404.Z7F7] 73-18650
1. Revenue-stamps—Great Britain—Catalogs. I. Schonfeld, Josef, joint author. II. Title.

Revenue-stamps—Mexico.

STEVENS, Richard B. 769'.569'72
The revenue stamps of Mexico, by Richard B. Stevens. Elmhurst, Ill., Elmhurst Philatelic Society [1968] xii, 238 p. illus., facsims. 29 cm. [HJ5377.Z7S7] 68-56299
1. Revenue-stamps—Mexico. I. Title.

Revenue-stamps—United States.

TURNER, George T. 769'.5
Essays and proofs of United States Internal Revenue stamps : a compilation with relative prices / by George T. Turner. Arlington, Mass. : Bureau Issues Association, 1974. xi, 446 p. : ill. ; 27 cm. Includes bibliographical references and index. [HJ5321.Z7T87] 74-20069
1. Revenue-stamps—United States. 2. Revenue-stamps—Collectors and collecting. I. Title. BIP

Revenue-stamps—U.S.—Catalogs.

GILMORE, Jene C. 769'.5
Art for conservation: the Federal duck stamps, by Jene C. Gilmore. Introd. by Robert Hines. Barre, Mass., Barre Publishers, 1971. 99 p. illus. 29 cm. [HJ5321.Z7G55] 78-163882 ISBN 0-8271-7122-6 14.95
1. Revenue-stamps—U.S.—Catalogs. 2. Game and game-birds—U.S. I. Title.

Revere moving-picture cameras.

MANKUS, Ed. 778.5
Revere movie guide. New York, Greenberg, c1955. 128p. illus. 20cm. (The Modern camera guide series) [TR880.M3] 55-11960
1. Revere moving-picture cameras. I. Title.

Revere, Paul, 1735-1818.

AMERICAN Antiquarian 769.2 Society, Worcester, Mass.
Paul Revere's engravings, by Clarence S. Brigham. Worcester, 1954. xvl, 181p. 77 plates (part fold., part col.) 32cm. [NE539.R5A57] 55-634

SUBJECT INDEX RICCI, SEBASTIANO, 1659-1734.

1. Revere, Paul, 1735-1818. I. Brigham, Clarence Saunders, 1877- II. Title.

AMERICAN Antiquarian 769.924
Society, Worcester, Mass.
Paul Revere's engravings [by] Clarence S. Brigham. [Rev. ed.] New York, Atheneum, 1969. xx, 262 p., illus. (part fold., part col.), facsims., ports. 29 cm. [NE539.R5A57 1969] 73-86552 27.50
1. Revere, Paul, 1735-1818. I. Brigham, Clarence Saunders, 1877-1963. II. Title.

THE Bloody Massacre; 769'.924
perpetrated in King-Street, Boston, on March 5th, 1770, by a party of the 29th Regiment. Together with a print of the event taken from the plate engraved by Paul Revere, the report from the Boston gazette, and a note by Richard Hale. Barre, Mass., Imprint Society, 1970. [16] p. plate (laid in) 29 x 31 cm. [NE539.R5B55] 79-126637 ISBN 0-87636-010-X
1. Revere, Paul, 1735-1818. Boston Massacre. I. Hale, Richard Walden, 1909- II. Imprint Society, Barre, Mass. III. Revere, Paul, 1735-1818. Boston Massacre. 1970.

BOSTON. Museum 709'.73'074014461
of Fine Arts. Dept. of American Decorative Arts and Sculpture.
Paul Revere's Boston, 1735-1818 : [exhibition, April 18-October 12, 1975] / contributors to the catalogue, introd. by Walter Muir Whitehill : Jonathan C. Fairbanks ...[etal.]. Boston : Dept. of American Decorative Arts and Sculpture, Museum of Fine Arts : distributed by New York Graphic Society, 1975. 234 p. : ill. (some col.) ; 28 cm. Bibliography: p. 216-218. [N6535.B7B77 1975] 74-21766 ISBN 0-87846-088-8
1. Revere, Paul, 1735-1818. 2. Art, American—Exhibitions. 3. Art, Colonial—Boston—Exhibitions. I. Fairbanks, Jonathan L. II. Title. BIP

REVERE, Paul, 1735-1818. 769'.924
The Boston Massacre, 1770, engraved by Paul Revere. [Washington] Library of Congress [1970] col. plate (in portfolio) 41 cm. (Library of Congress facsimile no. 4) Text on p. [2]-[3] of portfolio. [NE539.R5A43] 78-606227
1. Revere, Paul, 1735-1818. Boston Massacre. I. Series: U.S. Library of Congress. Facsimile no. 4

Revolvers.

ALBAUGH, William A 1908 623.4434
The original Confederate Colt; the story of the Leach & Rigdon and Rigdon-Ansley revolvers, by William A. Albaugh, III, and Richard D. Steuart. New York, Greenberg [1953] 62p. illus., map. 27cm. [TS537.A4] 53-5532
1. Colt, Samuel, 1814-1862. 2. Revolvers. 3. Confederate States of America. Army—Firearms. I. Steuart. Richard Dennis, 1882- joint author. II. Title.

COLBY, Carroll B. 623.443
Six-shooter: pistols, revolvers, and automatics, past and present. New York, Coward-McCann, c1956. 48 p. illus. 28 cm. [TS537.C6] 56-9951
1. Revolvers. 2. Pistols. I. Title.

PARSONS, John E. 623.4434
Smith & Wesson revolvers; the pioneer single action models. New York, Morrow, 1957. 242 p. illus., ports., facsims., tables. 25 cm. "Correspondence with Colonel Schofield": p. 177-214. Bibliographical references included in "Notes" (p. 217-227) Bibliography: p. 231-234. [TS537.P32] 57-8596
1. Smith and Wesson, Inc., Springfield, Mass. 2. Revolvers.

WEBSTER, Donald B. 623.4434
Suicide specials. Harrisburg, Pa., Stackpole Co., [1958] 192 p. illus. 23 cm. Includes bibliography. [NK5912.W4] 58-12382
1. Revolvers. 2. Firearms — Collectors and collecting. I. Title.

Revolvers, American.

FORS, W. Barlow. 683'.43
The collector's handbook of U.S. cartridge revolvers, 1856 to 1899, including brand names, patent listings, maker history, by W. Barlow Fors. [Northbrook, Ill., Barlow Book Co., 1973] 92 p. 22 cm. Bibliography: p. 89-90. [TS537.F67] 73-164596 6.00
1. Revolvers, American. I. Title.

Revolvers—History.

TAYLERSON, A. W. F. 623.443
The revolver, 1865-1888, by A. W. F. Taylerson. New York, Crown Publishers [1966] 292 p. illus. 24 cm. Bibliography: p. [275]-278. [TS537.T38] 66-18455
1. Revolvers—History. 2. Firearms industry and trade. I. Title.

TAYLERSON, A. W. F. 683'.43
Revolving arms [by] A. W. F. Taylerson. New York, Walker [1967] xvi, 123 p. illus. 24 cm. (Arms and armour series) [TS537.T39 1967] 67-13232
1. Revolvers—History. I. Title. II. Series.

Reweaving.

REDDEN, G O 646.2
Textile repairing. Milwaukee, Bruce Pub. Co. [c1959] 95p. illus. 22cm. [TT720.R4] 59-15806
1. Reweaving. I. Title.

SAUNDERS, Virginia. 646.24
Reweave it yourself. Princeton, N. J., Van Nostrand [1958] 126 p. illus. 27 cm. [TT720.S3] 58-13832
1. Reweaving. I. Title.

Reynal, Jeanne, 1903—

THE Mosaics of Jeanne 729.7
Reynal. Text by Dore Ashton [and others] New York, G. Wittenborn [1964] 111 p. illus. (part col.) ports. 29 cm. "Writings about Jeanne Reynal": p. 110. Bibliography: p. 110-111. [NA3840.M68] 63-22336
1. Reynal, Jeanne, 1903- 2. Mosaics—Technique. I. Ashton, Dore.

Reynard, Grant T., 1887-1968.

KNAUTZ, Harlan E. 759.13 B
Grant Reynard, N.A. : an American painter / by Harlan E. Knautz. Berea, Ohio : Baldwin-Wallace College, 1974. 172 p. : ill. (some col.) ; 29 cm. Includes index. Bibliography: p. 167-170. [ND237.R4K55] 74-15652
1. Reynard, Grant T., 1887-1968. I. Reynard, Grant T., 1887-1968.

Reynolds, Joshua, Sir, 1723-1792.

HILLES, Frederick Whiley, 828.608
1900-
The literary career of Sir Joshua Reynolds. [Hamden, Conn.] Archon Books, 1967. xx, 318 p. 2 facsims. 22 cm. Reprint of the 1936 edition. "A bibliography of Sir Joshua's writings": p. [277]-300. Bibliography: p. xi-xii. [ND497.R4H5 1967] 67-12978
1. Reynolds, Joshua, Sir, 1723-1792. I. Title. BIP

MORGAN, Eileen. 759.2
Sir Joshua Reynolds, 1723-1792; first president of the Royal Academy. [Plymouth, Plymouth Corporation and the Sir Joshua Reynolds Celebrations Committee, 1973] 44 p. illus. 21 cm. [ND497.R4M85] 74-162425 £0.40
1. Reynolds, Joshua, Sir, 1723-1792.

POTTERTON, Homan. 759.2'074'02132
Reynolds and Gainsborough / by Homan Potterton. London : National Gallery, [1976] 52 p. : ill., ports. ; 21 cm. (Themes and painters in the National Gallery : Series 2 ; no. 3) [ND497.R4P67] 76-380382 ISBN 0-901791-61-X : £0.75
1. Reynolds, Joshua, Sir, 1723-1792. 2. Gainsborough, Thomas, 1727-1788. I. London. National Gallery. II. Title. III. Series. BIP

REYNOLDS, Joshua, Sir, 759.2 B
1723-1792.
Letters of Sir Joshua Reynolds / collected and edited by Frederick Whiley Hilles. New York : AMS Press, [1976] p. cm. Originally presented as the editor's thesis, Yale University, 1926. Reprint of the 1929 ed. published by the University Press, Cambridge, Eng. Includes index. Bibliography: p. [ND497.R4A35 1976] 75-4122 13.50
1. Reynolds, Joshua, Sir, 1723-1792. 2. Painters—Great Britain—Correspondence, reminiscences, etc. I. Title.

REYNOLDS, Joshua, Sir, 759.2
1723-1792.
Reynolds [by] Ellis Waterhouse. [New York] Phaidon; [distributed by Praeger, 1973] 192 p. 127 plates (part col.) 29 cm. Includes bibliographical references. [ND497.R4W3 1973] 78-158100 ISBN 0-7148-1519-5 25.00
1. Reynolds, Joshua, Sir, 1723-1792. I. Waterhouse, Ellis Kirkham, 1905- BIP

STEEGMAN, John, 1899- 759.2 B
1966.
Sir Joshua Reynolds / by John Steeggmann [i.e. Steegman]. Folcroft, Pa. : Folcroft Library Editions, 1977. 136 p. ; 23 cm. Reprint of the 1933 ed. published by Macmillan, New York, in series: Great lives, 5. Bibliography: p. 136. [ND497.R4S75 1977] 77-17594 ISBN 0-8414-7867-8 lib. bdg. : 12.50
1. Reynolds, Joshua, Sir, 1723-1792. 2. Painters—England—Biography. BIP

Reynolds, Mary Louise—Art collections.

CHICAGO. Art 016.700'9'04
Institute.
Surrealism & its affinities: the Mary Reynolds collection; a bibliography compiled by Hugh Edwards. Chicago [1973] 147 p. illus. 26 cm. [Z5936.S8C45 1973] 73-132025
1. Reynolds, Mary Louise—Art collections. 2. Surrealism—Bibliography—Catalogs. I. Edwards, Hugh L. II. Title.

Rhino Horn (Group of painters)

RHINO Horn. 759.13
[Hackensack, N.J., Custombook, inc., 1971?] 23 p. col. illus., col. group port. 27 cm. Page 23: Rhino Horn, New School for Social Research, 66 West 12th St., N.Y.C. [N6512.5.R48R4] 71-199986
1. Rhino Horn (Group of painters) I. New York (City). New School for Social Research.

Rhode Island School of Design, Providence. Museum of Art.

RHODE Island School of 707'.11
Design, Providence.
Alumni directory, April 1956. Providence, c1956. 133p. 22cm. [N330.P77] 56-35083
I. Title.

RHODE Island School of 779'.2
Design, Providence.
Portfolio 1970. Providence [1970?] 302 p. (chiefly illus.) 26 cm. [N330.P72R486] 73-151303
I. Title.

RHODE Island 739.27'0938'07401452
School of Design. Providence. Museum of Art.
Classical jewelry / Tony Hackens. Providence : Museum of Art, Rhode Island School of Design, c1976. 159 p. : ill. ; 28 cm. (Its Catalogue of the classical collection) Also published under title: Selection VI: ancient jewelry from the museum's collection, as a volume in the Bulletin of Rhode Island School of Design, Museum notes, v. 62, no. 5, June 1976. Bibliography: p. 14-17. [NK7307.3.R49 1976] 76-16947
1. Rhode Island School of Design, Providence. Museum of Art. 2. Jewelry, Classical—Catalogs. 3. Jewelry—Rhode Island—Providence—Catalogs. I. Hackens, Tony, 1939- II. Title.

RHODE Island 733'.074'01452
School of Design, Providence. Museum of Art.
Classical sculpture, by Brunilde Sismondo Ridgway. [Providence, 1972] 244 p. illus. 28 cm. (Catalogue of the classical collection) Includes bibliographical references. [NB87.P76R457] 72-79496
1. Rhode Island School of Design, Providence. Museum of Art. 2. Sculpture, Greek—Catalogs. 3. Sculpture, Roman—Catalogs. 4. Sculpture—Providence—Catalogs. 5. Classicism in art. I. Ridgway, Brunilde Sismondo, 1929- II. Title.

Rhodes (City)—Sepulchral monuments.

FRASER, Peter Marshall. 732'.9'16
Rhodian funerary monuments / by P. M. Fraser. Oxford ; New York : Clarendon Press, 1977. 205 p., 1 fold. leaf, [76] leaves of plates : ill. ; 24 cm. Includes bibliographical references and indexes. [NB1800.F7] 78-314251 ISBN 0-19-813192-5 : 62.50
1. Rhodes (City)—Sepulchral monuments. 2. Sculpture, Greek—Greece, Modern—Rhodes (City) 3. Sculpture, Hellenistic—Greece, Modern—Rhodes (City) 4. Rhodes (City)—Antiquities, Greek. I. Title. BIP

Rhodes, Mary.

WOODLANDS Art 746.3'942'07402162
Gallery.
Mary Rhodes, her embroiderers and tapestry-weavers : [catalogue of an exhibition held] 6 May to 1 June 1976 [at the] Woodlands Art Gallery. London : London Borough of Greenwich, [1976] [12] p. : ill. ; 21 cm. [NK9243.W66 1976] 77-368379 ISBN 0-9504033-8-5
1. Rhodes, Mary. 2. Embroidery—England—Exhibitions. 3. Tapestry—England—Exhibitions. I. Rhodes, Mary. II. Title.

Ribbon work.

EVANS, Hilary. 746.2'7
Ribbonwork / by Hilary Evans. Indianapolis : Bobbs-Merrill, [1976] p. cm. Includes index. [TT880.E89] 75-33533 ISBN 0-672-52170-9 : 10.00
1. Ribbon work. I. Title. BIP

EVANS, Hilary. 746.2'7
Ribbonwork / Hilary Evans ; [drawings by the author ; photographs by Gordon Roberton]. London : Elm Tree Books, 1976. 111 p. : ill. (some col.) ; 26 cm. [TT880.E89 1976b] 77-367990 ISBN 0-241-89353-4 : £3.50
1. Ribbon work. I. Title.

Ribera, Jusepe de, called Lo Spagnoletto, 1588?-1652.

BROWN, Jonathan. 760'.092'4
Jusepe de Ribera: prints and drawings; [catalogue of an exhibition] The Art Museum, Princeton University, October-November 1973. Fogg Art Museum, Harvard University, December 1973-January 1974. [Princeton, N.J., Princeton University, 1973] 223 p. illus. 26 cm. Bibliography: p. 217-221. [NE2062.5.R52B76] 73-77440 5.95
1. Ribera, Jusepe de, called Lo Spagnoletto, 1588?-1652. I. Princeton University. Art Museum. II. Harvard University. William Hayes Fogg Art Museum.

Ricci, Sebastiano, 1659-1734.

DANIELS, Jeffery. 759.5
Sebastiano Ricci. [by] Jeffery Daniels. Hove : Wayland, 1976. xix, 172 p., leaf of plate, [136] p. of plates : ill. (some col.), facsim., plan, ports. ; 32 cm. Includes index. Bibliography: p. 158-164. [ND623.R644D35] 76-479298 ISBN 0-85340-057-1 : £45.00
1. Ricci, Sebastiano, 1659-1734. BIP

MILKOVICH, Michael. 759.5
Sebastiano and Marco Ricci in America. A loan exhibition. [Lexington] University of Kentucky [1965, c1966] 54 p. illus. 28 cm. Catalogue of the exhibition held at Brooks Memorial Art Gallery, Dec. 19, 1965-Jan. 23, 1966; University of Kentucky Art Gallery, Feb. 13-Mar. 6, 1966. Bibliography: p. 20-21. [ND622.M55] 68-63169
1. Ricci, Sebastiano, 1659-1734. 2. Ricci, Marco, 1676-1729. I. Brooks Memorial Art Gallery, Memphis, Tenn. II. Kentucky. University. Art Gallery. III. Title.

Rice, David Talbot, 1903-1972.

STUDIES in memory of David 709
Talbot Rice / editors, Giles Robertson, George Henderson. Edinburgh : Edinburgh University Press, [1975] 334 p., [48] leaves of plates : ill., maps ; 24 cm. Bibliography: p 317-325. [N7442.2.R527] 75-329001 ISBN 0-85224-253-0 : 30.00
1. Rice, David Talbot, 1903-1972. 2. Art—Addresses, essays, lectures. I. Rice, David Talbot, 1903-1972. II. Robertson, Giles. III. Henderson, George David Smith, 1931-
Distributed by Biblio distribution N.J.

Richards, Ceri, 1903-1971.

LIVERPOOL. Public 726'.595
Libraries, Museums, and Art Gallery. Walker Art Gallery.
Ceri Richards and the Metropolitan Cathedral of Christ the King : [catalogue of an exhibition held at the] Walker Art Gallery, Liverpool, 1975-6. [Liverpool] : [Walker Art Gallery], [1976] 15 p. : ill. ; 25 cm. [NC242.R52L58 1976] 77-355315 ISBN 0-901534-34-X : £0.50
1. Richards, Ceri, 1903-1971. 2. Liverpool. Metropolitan Cathedral of Christ the King. 3. Artists' preparatory studies—England—Exhibitions. I. Richards, Ceri, 1903-1971. II. Title.

Richards, William Trost, 1833-1905.

FERBER, Linda S. 759.13
William Trost Richards: American landscape & marine painter, 1833-1905. Catalogue compiled & written by Linda S. Ferber. The Brooklyn Museum, June 20-July 29, 1973. Pennsylvania Academy of the Fine Arts, Sept. 13-Oct. 21, 1973. [Brooklyn, N.Y.] Brooklyn Museum [1973] 105 p. illus. 22 x 26 cm. Bibliography: p. 104-105. [ND237.R5F47] 73-83703 6.50
1. Richards, William Trost, 1833-1905. I. Richards, William Trost, 1833-1905. II. Brooklyn Institute of Arts and Sciences. Museum. III. Pennsylvania Academy of the Fine Arts, Philadelphia.

Richardson family.

FALES, Martha 338.4'7'73923722 B
Gandy.
Joseph Richardson and family, Philadelphia silversmiths. [1st ed.] Middletown, Conn., Published for the Historical Society of Pennsylvania by Wesleyan University Press [1974] xviii, 340 p. illus. 28 cm. Bibliography: p. [312]-320. [TS730.F34] 74-5911 ISBN 0-8195-4076-5 17.50
1. Richardson family. 2. Silversmiths—Philadelphia. I. Pennsylvania. Historical Society. II. Title.

Richardson, Henry Hobson, 1838-1886.

EATON, Leonard K. 720'.973
American architecture comes of age; European reaction to H. H. Richardson and Louis Sullivan [by] Leonard K. Eaton. Cambridge, Mass., MIT Press [1972] xiii, 256 p. illus. 27 cm. Bibliography: p. [240]-242. [NA710.E24] 76-171556 ISBN 0-262-05010-2 14.95
1. Richardson, Henry Hobson, 1838-1886. 2. Sullivan, Louis Henri, 1856-1924. 3. Architecture—United States. 4. Architecture, Modern—19th century—United States. I. Title.

HITCHCOCK, Henry Russell. 720.973
1903-
The architecture of H. H. Richardson and his times. Cambridge, Mass., M.I.T. Pr. [1966, c.1936, 1961] xxvi. 343p. illus., plans. 21cm. (MIT43) Bibl. [NA737.R5H5] 3.95 pap.,
1. Richardson. Henry Hobson. 1838-1886. 2. Architecture—Hist. I. Title. BIP

HITCHCOCK, Henry Russell, 720.973
1903-
The architecture of H. H. Richardson and his times. [Rev. ed.] Hamden, Conn., Archon Bks. [dist. Shoe String Pr.] 1961 [c.1936, 1961] xxvi, 343p. illus., 25cm. Bibl. 61-4984 10.50
1. Richardson, Henry Hobson, 1838-1886. 2. Architecture—Hist. I. Title.

HITCHCOCK, Henry Russell, 720.924
1903-
Richardson as a Victorian architect. [Baltimore, Pub. by Smith College at the Barton-Gillet Co., 1966] 53p. illus., plans. 23cm. (Katharine Asher Engel lects. 1965) Bibl. [NA737.R5H54] 66-6442 2.00 pap.,
1. Richardson, Henry Hobson, 1838-1886. I. Title. II. Series.

O'GORMAN, James F. 720'.92'4
H. H. Richardson and his office, a centennial of his move to Boston, 1874 : selected drawings : [exhibition organized by the Department of Printing and Graphic Arts, Harvard College Library, Fogg Art Museum, Harvard University, October 23-December 8, 1974, Albany Institute of History and Art, January 7-February 23, 1975, Renwick Gallery, Washington, D.C., The National Collection of Fine Arts, Smithsonian Institution, March 21-June 22, 1975 : catalogue] / [James F. O'Gorman]. [Cambridge, Mass.] : Dept. of Printing and Graphic Arts, Harvard College Library, 1974. xii, 220 p., [8] leaves of plates : ill. (some col.) ; 22 x 28 cm. Includes bibliographical references and index. [NA737.R5O35] 74-80839 ISBN 0-914630-00-8
1. Richardson, Henry Hobson, 1836-1886. 2. Artists' preparatory studies. I. Richardson, Henry Hobson, 1838-1886. II. Harvard University. Library. Dept. of Printing and Graphic Arts. III. Harvard University. William Hayes Fogg Art Museum. IV. Albany Institute of History and Art. V. Renwick Gallery. VI. Title.

VAN RENSSELAER, Mariana 720'.924
(Griswold), 1851-1934
Henry Hobson Richardson and his works, by Mrs. Schuyler Van Rensselaer. With a portrait and illus. of the architect's designs. Park Forest, Ill., Prairie School Pr. [1967] ix, 152p. illus., plans, port. 38cm. Reprint of the 1888 ed., with a new introd. List of Henry Hobson Richardson's works: p. [139]-140. [NA737] 66-29041 25.00
I. Richardson, Henry Hobson, 1838-1886. II. Title.

VAN RENSSELAER, 016.720'924
Mariana (Griswold) 1851-1934.
Henry Hobson Richardson and his works. New York, Dover Publications [1969] xv, 152 p. illus., plans, port. 28 cm. "An unabridged republication of the work originally published ... in 1888, to which has been added a new introduction prepared especially for this ... edition by William Morgan." "List of Henry Hobson Richardson's works": p. [139]-140. Bibliographical footnotes. [NA737.R5V3 1969] 68-12915 3.00
1. Richardson, Henry Hobson, 1838-1886.

Richardson, Sam, 1934—

RICHARDSON, Sam, 1934- 709'.2'4
Sight line, snow drifts : Dallas Museum of Fine Arts, March 24-May 2, 1976 / [Sam Richardson]. [Dallas] : The Museum, c1976. [16] p. : ill. ; 22 cm. Bibliography: p. [15] [N6537.R52D34] 76-362661
1. Richardson, Sam, 1934- I. Dallas. Museum of Fine Arts. II. Title.

Richardson, Sam, 1934- —Exhibitions.

SAM Richardson : 709'.2'4
Coordinate line-motion broken by boulder : [exhibition], April 15, May 12, 1977, The Art Gallery, California State University, Fullerton / [catalogue compilation, Jo Ellen Luetto]. Fullerton : The Gallery, c1977. 48 p. : ill. ; 22 cm. Bibliography: p. 22-23. [NB237.R48S25] 77-151407
1. Richardson, Sam, 1934- —Exhibitions. I. Luetto, Jo Ellen. II. California State University, Fullerton. Art Gallery.

Richardson, Samuel, 1689-1761.

SALE, William Merritt, 655.142
1899-
Samuel Richardson: master printer. Ithaca, N.Y., Cornell University Press, 1950. vi, 389 p. illus. 24 cm. (Cornell studies in English, v. 37) Bibliographical references included in "Notes" (p. [356]-377) [Z232.R595S3] 50-10768
1. Richardson, Samuel, 1689-1761. I. Title. II. Series: Cornell University. Cornell studies in English, v. 37 BIP

SALE, William 686.2'092'4 B
Merritt, 1899-
Samuel Richardson : master printer / William M. Sale, Jr. Westport, Conn. : Greenwood Press, [1977?] c1950. vi, 389 p. : ill. ; 23 cm. Reprint of the ed. published by Cornell University Press, Ithaca, N.Y., which was issued as v. 37 of Cornel studies in English. Includes bibliographical references and index. [Z232.R595S3 1977] 77-22446 ISBN 0-8371-9732-5 lib.bdg. : 21.75
1. Richardson, Samuel, 1689-1761. 2. Printers—England—Biography. 3. Printing—England—History. I. Series: Cornell University. Cornell studies in English ; v. 37.

Richier, Xavier, 1922—

LEITCH, David. 364.16'2
The discriminating thief. With a foreword by Milton Esterow. [1st ed.] New York, Holt, Rinehart and Winston [1969, c1968] 182 p. illus. 24 cm. [N8387.L4 1969] 69-10231 5.95
1. Richier, Xavier, 1922- 2. Art thefts—France. I. Title.

Richmond—Buildings.

DULANEY, Paul S. 917.55'451'044
The architecture of historic Richmond [by] Paul S. Dulaney. Charlottesville, University Press of Virginia [1968] 208 p. illus., maps (1 fold. in pocket) 22 cm. Sponsored by Historic Richmond Foundation and others. [NA735.R5D8] 68-14089
1. Richmond—Buildings. 2. Architecture—Richmond. I. Title. BIP

Richmond, Eng. (Surrey)—Description.

RICHMOND, Surrey, as it 942.1'95
was : a selection of Victorian and Edwardian photographs / compiled and annotated by the Historical and Archaeological Section of the Richmond Society. Nelson : Hendon Publishing Co., 1976. 44 p. : ill., facsim., map, ports. ; 21 x 29 cm. [DA690.R5R5] 77-353513 ISBN 0-86067-004-X : £1.40
1. Richmond, Eng. (Surrey)—Description. 2. Richmond, Eng. (Surrey)—Social life and customs. I. Richmond Society. Historical and Archaeological Section.

Richmond, Oliffe, 1919—

RICHMOND, Oliffe, 1919- 730'.92'4
Oliffe Richmond : Commonwealth Art Gallery, 30 January-25 February 1976. London : [The Gallery], [1976] [12] p. : chiefly ill. ; 23 cm. Exhibition catalogue. [NB1105.R5C65] 76-380216 ISBN 0-901554-03-0 : free
1. Richmond, Oliffe, 1919- I. Commonwealth Art Gallery.

Richmond. Washington statue (Houdon's)

HEATON, Ronald E., 1898- 730'.924
The image of Washington; the history of the Houdon statue, by Ronald E. Heaton. Norristown? Pa. [1971] 31 p. illus., facsim. 23 cm. Includes bibliographical references. [F234.R5H4] 75-25222
1. Houdon, Jean Antoine, 1741-1828. 2. Richmond. Washington statue (Houdon's) I. Title.

Ricker, Hiram, & Sons, Inc.

VINCENT, Pal. 748'.8
The Moses bottle. [1st ed.] Poland Spring, Me., Palabra Shop, 1969. 58 p. illus., facsims., group port. 23 cm. Bibliography: p. 58. [NK5440.B6V5] 79-11534
1. Ricker, Hiram, & Sons, Inc. 2. Bottles, American. I. Title.

Rickey, George.

NEW Jersey. State 730'.924
Museum, Trenton.
Sculptures by George Rickey and James Seawright; [exhibition] November 22, 1969-January 11, 1970. [Trenton, 1970] [20] p. illus. 22 cm. Includes bibliographical references. [NB236.N5] 78-632205
1. Rickey, George. 2. Seawright, James, 1936- I. Title.

RICKEY, George 730'.92'4
George Rickey / Nan Rosenthal. New York : H. N. Abrams, 1977. 220 p. : chiefly ill. (some col.) ; 28 x 30 cm. "Films and taped interviews": p. 216-217. Includes index. Bibliography: p. 211-215. [NB237.R5R67] 76-20569 ISBN 0-8109-0433-0 : 37.50
1. Rickey, George. I. Rosenthal, Nan. BIP

RICKEY, George. 730.92'4
George Rickey: sixteen years of kinetic sculpture. [Exhibition at] the Corcoran Gallery of Art, Washington, D.C., September 30-November 20, 1966. [Berne, Printed by Stampfli, 1966?] 1 v. (unpaged) illus., ports. 23 cm. Introductory essay by Peter Selz. "Writings by the artist": p. [10] [NB237.R5S46] 67-68082
I. selz, Peter Howard, 1919- II. Corcoran Gallery of Art, Washington, D.C. III. Title.

Ricoh camera.

COLES, Charles H 770.2
The Ricoh guide; including the '35,' '500,'and the Super Richofles [i. e. Ricohflex] New York, Greenberg [1957] 126p. illus. 20cm. (The Modern camera guide series) [TR263.R5C6] 57-12729
1. Ricoh camera. 2. Photography — Handbooks, manuals, etc. I. Title.

TYDINGS, Kenneth S 771.31
Ricoh guide. Philadelphia, Chilton Co., Book Division, c1960. 128 p. illus. 20 cm. (Modern camera guide series, 484) [TR263.R5T8] 60-9438
1. Ricoh camera. 2. Photography — Handbooks, cameras, etc. I. Title.

Riemenschneider, Tilmann, d. 1531.

NORTH Carolina. Museum of 730.943
Art, Raleigh.
Sculptures of Tilmann Riemenschneider. [Exhibition] Oct. 6-Nov. 11, 1962. Raleigh [1962] 68 p. illus. 26 cm. Errata slip inserted. [NB588.R5N6] 62-64263
1. Riemenschneider, Tilmann, d. 1531. I. Title.

Rietveld, Gerrit Thomas, 1888-1964.

BARONI, Daniele. 749.2'9492
The furniture of Gerrit Thomas Rietveld / Daniele Baroni. 1st U.S. ed. Woodbury, N.Y. : Barron's, 1978, c1977. 178 p. : ill. (some col.) ; 23 x 25 cm. Translation of I mobili di Gerrit Thomas Rietveld. Bibliography: p. 175-178. [NK2570.R43B3713 1977] 77-17883 ISBN 0-8120-5201-3 : 13.95
1. Rietveld, Gerrit Thomas, 1888-1964. 2. Furniture—Netherlands—History—20th century. I. Title. BIP

Rifesser, Joseph, 1921-

GALERIE St. Etienne, 730'.92'4
New York.
Joseph Rifesser: sculpture. [Exhibition] December 1963. New York [1963] 1 v. (chiefly illus. (part. ed.) port.) 22 cm. [NB623.R5G3 1963] 64-55740
1. Rifesser, Joseph, 1921- I. Title.

Rifles.

DILLIN, John Grace Wolfe, 683'.42
1860-
The Kentucky rifle, by John G. W. Dillin. Edited by Kendrick Scofield. 5th ed. York, Pa., G. Shumway, 1967. xx, 202 p. illus., facsims., ports. 31 cm. (Longrifle series) [TS535.D5 1967] 67-28588
1. Rifles. I. Scofield, Kendrick, ed. II. Title.

FOX, Gardner F 623.442
Custom rifles [by Jeff Cooper, pseud. Los Angeles, Trend Books, 1957] 128p. illus. 24cm. (Trend book 153) [TS535.F6] 57-45324

1. Rifles. 2. Gunsmithing. I. Title.

HANSON, Charles E., 1917-   623.442
The plains rifle. Harrisburg, Pa., Stackpole Co. [1960] 171 p. illus. 29 cm. Includes bibliography.
[TS535.H24] 59-14379
1. Rifles. 2. Pistols. I. Title.   BIP

KELVER, Gerald O.   683'.42
Schuetzen rifles; history and loadings, by Gerald O. Kelver. Illustrated with historical photos. Limited ed. Boulder, Colo., Printed by Paddock Pub., 1972. 121 p. illus. 22 cm. Bibliography: p. 120-121.
[TS536.6.S5K45] 72-178329
1. Rifles. I. Title.

SIMMONS, Richard F   623.442
Custom built rifles. [2nd ed.., completely rev.] Harrisburg, Pa., Stackpole Co. 1955 346p. illus. 23 cm. [TS535.s512 1955] 55-851
1. Rifles I. Title.

Rifles—History.

KENTUCKY Rifle   623.4'425
Association.
The Kentucky rifle: a true American heritage in picture. Washington, 1967. 109 p. (chiefly illus.) 32 cm. [TS535.K45] 67-18479
1. Rifles — Hist. I. Title.

Rifles—History.

KAUFFMAN, Henry J. 1908-   623.442
The Pennsylvania-Kentucky rifle. Harrisburg, Pa., Stackpole Co. [1960] 376 p. illus., port., maps, facsims. 29 cm. Bibliography: p. 373-374. [TS535.K33] 60-7972
1. Rifles—History. I. Title.

KINDIG, Joe.   739.7
Thoughts on the Kentucky rifle in its golden age. Mary Ann Cresswell, editor; Samuel E. Dyke [and] Henry J. Kauffman, research; Bluford W. Muir, photographer. [Wilmington, Del.] G. N. Hyatt, 1960. xii, 561 p. illus,, maps. 31 cm. [NK6912.K5] 61-23719
1. Rifles—History. 2. Firearms—Collectors and collecting. I. Cresswell, Mary Ann, ed. II. Title.

Riis, Jacob August, 1849-1914.

RIIS, Jacob   779'.9'9747104
August, 1849-1914.
Jacob A. Riis : photographer & citizen / by Alexander Alland, Sr. ; with pref. by Ansel Adams. Millerton, N.Y. : Aperture, [1974] 220 p. : ill. ; 24 x 28 cm. Includes index. Bibliography: p. 215. [HV4045.R5 1974] 74-21617 ISBN 0-912334-66-5 : 17.50
1. Riis, Jacob August, 1849-1914. 2. Poor—United States. I. Alland, Alexander.

Riley, Bridget, 1931—

DE SAUSMAREZ, Maurice,   759.2
1915-
Bridget Riley. Greenwich, Conn., New York Graphic Society [1970] 128 p. illus. (part col.) 26 cm. Bibliography: p. 126. [N6797.R54D4 1970] 73-119591 ISBN 0-8212-0396-7 14.50
1. Riley, Bridget, 1931-

Rimmer, William, 1816-1879.

BARTLETT, Truman Howe,   709'.24 B
1835-1923.
The art life of William Rimmer, sculptor, painter, and physician. New York, Kennedy Graphics, 1970. ix, xii, 147 p. illus., ports. 29 cm. (Library of American art) A reprint of the 1890 ed. with a new pref. by Leonard Baskin. [NB237.R6B3 1970] 68-27718
1. Rimmer, William, 1816-1879. I. Title.

Rings.

KUNZ, George Frederick,   391'.7
1856-1932.
Rings for the finger; from the earliest known times to the present, with full descriptions of the origin, early making, materials, the archaeology, history, for affection, for love, for engagement, for wedding, commemorative, mourning, etc. New York, Dover Publications [1973, c1917] xviii, 381 p. illus. 22 cm. Reprint of the ed. published by Lippincott, Philadelphia. [GT2270.K86 1973] 78-172181 ISBN 0-486-22226-8 3.50 (pbk.)
1. Rings. 2. Rings (in religion, folk-lore, etc.) I. Title.   BIP

Rings, British.

OMAN, Charles Chichele,   739.27'8
1901-
British rings, 800-1914 [by] Charles Oman. Totowa, N.J., Rowman and Littlefield [1974, c1973] x, 146 p., 96 p. of illus. 4 col. plates. 26 cm. Includes bibliographical references. [NK7455.G7O42 1974b] 73-14843 ISBN 0-87471-449-4 25.00
1. Rings, British. I. Title.

Rio de Janeiro — Descr. — Views.

SMITH, Robert Chester,   759.36
1912-
Franz Fruhbeck's Brazilian journey; a study of some paintings and drawings made in the years 1817 and 1818 and now in the possession of the Hispanic Society of America [by] Robert C. Smith and Gilberto Ferrez. Philadelphia, University of Pennsylvania Press [1960] 128 p. 16 plates, port., map (on lining papers) 29 cm. Bibliographical references included in "Notes." [ND538.F7S6 1960] 58-11748
1. Fruhbeck, Franz Josef, b. 1795. 2. Leopoldina, consort of Pedro I. Emperor of Brazil, 1797-1826. 3. Rio de Janeiro — Descr. — Views. I. Ferrez, Gilberto, joint author. II. Fruhbeck, Franz Josef, b. 1795. Skizze meiner Reise nach Brasilien in Sud-Amerika. III. Title.   BIP

Riopelle, Jean Paul.

OTTAWA. National Gallery   759.11
of Canada.
Jean-Paul Riopelle; painting and sculpture, peinture et sculpture. [Exhibition] the National Gallery of Canada, the Montreal Museum of Fine Arts [and] the Art Gallery of Toronto. [Ottawa, 1962] unpaged, illus. 26 cm. [N6549.R5O8] 63-3193
1. Riopelle, Jean Paul. I. Title.

Rites and ceremonies—New Guinea—Sepik Valley.

NEWTON, Douglas, 1920-   299'.9
Crocodile and cassowary; religious art of the upper Sepik River, New Guinea. New York, Museum of Primitive Art; distributed by New York Graphic Society, Greenwich, Conn., 1971. 112 p. illus., map. 22 x 27 cm. Bibliography: p. 111-112. [GN473.N48] 70-145914 ISBN 0-912294-42-6 12.95
1. Rites and ceremonies—New Guinea—Sepik Valley. 2. Art—Sepik Valley. 3. Ethnology—New Guinea—Sepik Valley. I. Title.

Ritman, Louis, 1889-1963.

RITMAN, Louis, 1889-1963.   759.13
The paintings of Louis Ritman (1889-1963) : [exhibition, 1975]. [Chicago : Signature Galleries], c1975. 37 p. : ill. (some col.) ; 25 cm. Cover title. Includes bibliographical references. [ND237.R565S53] 75-29548
1. Ritman, Louis, 1889-1963. I. Signature Galleries. II. Title.

Rivera, Diego, 1886-1957.

NEW YORK (City). Museum   759.972
of Modern Art.
Diego Rivera. Reprint ed. [New York] Published for the Museum of Modern Art by Arno Press, 1972 [c1931] 64 p. illus. 27 cm. Catalog of an exhibition held at the Museum of Modern Art, New York, from Dec. 23, 1931 to Jan. 27, 1932. "The work of Diego Rivera" (p. 9-35) signed: Frances Flynn Paine. [ND259.R5N4 1972] 74-169310 ISBN 0-405-01569-0
1. Rivera, Diego, 1886-1957. I. Paine, Frances Flynn.

RIVERA, Diego, 1886-1957.   759.972
Diego Rivera; Guanajuato 1886—Mexico City 1957. [New York, Greer, 1971?] [19] p. col. illus. 25 cm. On cover: Portrait of America. Reproductions of 5 panels from the artist's Portrait of America series, which was painted as a gift to the New Workers' School in 1933. English and Spanish. [ND259.R5A36] 75-198230
I. Title: Portrait of America.

RIVERA, Diego, 1886-1957.   759.972
My art, my life; an autobiography [by] Diego Rivera, with Gladys March. [1st ed.] New York, Citadel Press [1960] 318p. illus., ports. 22cm. [ND259.R5A3] 60-15451
I. March, Gladys. II. Title.

WOLFE, Bertram David,   759.972
1896-
The fabulous life of Diego Rivera. New York, Stein and Day [1963] xxi, 457 p. illus., ports. 24 cm Bibliography: p. 433-442. [ND259.R5W.56] 63-20061
1. Rivera, Diego, 1886-1957. I. Title.   BIP

Rivers, Larry, 1923—

HUNTER, Sam, 1923-   709.24
Larry Rivers. New York, H. N. Abrams [1970] 261 p. plates (part col.) 28 x 30 cm. Bibliography: p. 257-261. [N6537.R57H8] 69-12483 ISBN 0-8109-0451-9
1. Rivers, Larry, 1923-

HUNTER, Sam, 1923-   709'.2'4
Larry Rivers. New York, H. N. Abrams [1971?] 294 p. plates (part col.) 28 x 30 cm. "Supplement to the first edition": p. [263]-294. Bibliography: p. 257-261, 294. [N6537.R57H8 1971] 72-197081
1. Rivers, Larry, 1923-

HUNTER, Sam, 1923-   759.13
Larry Rivers. Introd. by Sam Hunter, with a memoir by Frank o'Hara and a statement by the artist. New York, Pub. for the Poses Inst. of Fine Arts, Brandeis Univ., by October House [1965] 92p. illus. (pt. col.) ports. 25cm. Exhibition org. by the Poses Inst. of Fine Arts, Brandeis Univ., with the Detroit Inst. of Arts, the Jewish Mus., the Minneapolis Inst. of Arts, and the Pasadena Art. Mus. Bibl. [ND237.R57H8] 65-20717 8.50
1. Rivers, Larry, 1923- I. Brandeis University, Waltham, Mass. Poses Institute of Fine Arts. II. Title.

HUNTER, Sam, 1923-   709'.2'4
Rivers [by] Sam Hunter. New York, H. N. Abrams [1972] 102 p. illus. (part col.) 21 x 23 cm. (Modern artists) Bibliography: p. [98]-102. [N6537.R57H82] 71-175945 ISBN 0-8109-4424-3 6.75
1. Rivers, Larry, 1923- I. Rivers, Larry, 1923-   BIP

RIVERS, Larry, 1923-   709.24
Larry Rivers, 1965-1970. [Exhibition] December 1970-January 1971, Marlborough Gallery, New York. [New York, Marlborough Gallery, 1971] 44 p. illus. (part col.) 30 cm. "Cat[alogue] no. 281." Bibliography: p. 5. [N6537.R57A48] 72-199946
I. Marlborough Gallery. II. Title.   BIP

RIVERS, Larry, 1923-   741.9'73
Larry Rivers: drawings, 1949-1969. [Chicago? 1970] [36] p. 12 illus. 34 x 41 cm. Caption title. Label mounted on t.p.: Supplied by Worldwide books, inc., Boston. Catalogue, by Carol Selle, of an exhibition held at the Art Institute, Chicago, Mar. 6-Apr. 19, 1970. [NC139.R56S35] 73-21575
I. Selle, Carol O. II. Chicago. Art Institute.

Roads—Design.

†AMERICAN Society of Civil   713
Engineers. Committee on Geometrics and Esthetics of Highway Location and Design.
Practical highway esthetics / prepared by the Committee on Geometrics and Esthetics of Highway Location and Design, Highway Division of the American Society of Civil Engineers, committee members, Roland H. Berger ... [et al.], Frederick W. Cron, principal author. New York : The Society, c1977. 79 p. : ill. ; 28 cm.

Includes bibliographical references. [TE175.A6 1977] 77-155216 14.00
1. Roads—Design. 2. Roads—Location. 3. Roadside improvement. I. Berger, Roland H. II. Cron, Frederick William, 1906- III. Title.

SNOW, William Brewster,   625.72
1910- ed.
The highway and the landscape. New Brunswick, N. J., Rutgers University Press, 1959. 230 p. illus. 22 cm. [TE175.S56] 59-7516
1. Roads—Design. 2. Express highways. 3. Landscape protection. I. Title.

Roads—Design—Bibliography.

FELLEMAN, John P.   016.3092'08 s
The incorporation of esthetics within the comprehensive highway development process / by John P. Felleman, Thomas J. Nieman. Monticello, Ill. : Council of Planning Librarians, 1976. 27 p. ; 29 cm. (Exchange bibliography - Council of Planning Librarians ; no. 1141) Caption title. [Z5942.C68 no. 1141] [Z7295] [TE175] 016.711'73 77-363799 pbk. : 2.50
1. Roads—Design—Bibliography. 2. Roads—Location—Bibliography. 3. Roadside improvement—Bibliography. I. Nieman, Thomas J., joint author. II. Title. III. Series: Council of Planning Librarians. Exchange bibliography ; no. 1141.

Roads—Design—Congresses.

THE Environment & highway   711'.73
design. [Conference] September 22 and 23, 1970, Burlingame, California [proceedings. Edited by L. J. Odell] San Francisco, Federal Highway Administration, Region 7 [1970?] 151 p. 26 cm. [TE175.E57] 71-611269
1. Roads—Design—Congresses. 2. Environmental policy—Congresses. I. Odell, L. J., ed. II. U.S. Federal Highway Administration. Region 7.

Roadside improvement.

AMERICAN Association of State   713
Highway Officials. Operating Committee on Roadside Development.
A guide for highway landscape policy and design. Washington, American Association of State Highway Officials, 1970. ii, 117 p. illus., plans. 27 cm. Bibliography: p. 114-117. [TE177.A47] 74-265614
1. Roadside improvement. I. Title.

CALIFORNIA.   328.794'04 s
Legislature. Assembly. Committee on Natural Resources, Planning, and Public Works.
Highway beautification, beautification and maintenance of the capitol mall, highway and freeway planning, regional planning in the Lake Tahoe basin, the filling of San Francisco Bay. [Sacramento, Assembly of the State of California, 1967] 23 p. 28 cm. (Its Report, pt. 5) (California. Legislature. Assembly. Assembly interim committee reports] 1965-67, v. 25, report 6) [J87.C2 1965-67jd vol. 25, no. 6] [TE177] 711'.73'09794 72-181216
1. Roadside improvement. 2. Roads—California. I. Title.

MASSACHUSETTS.   333.9'1'009744 s
University. Water Resources Research Center.
Enhancement of ecologic and aesthetic values of wetlands associated with interstate highways. Carl A. Carlozzi, principal investigator. Julius Gy. Fabos, Lewis C. Mainzer [and] Roger J. Reed, co-investigators. [Amherst, 1971?] iii l., 114 p. illus. 28 cm. (Its Publication, no. 19) Cover title: Enhancement of ecologic and aesthetic values of water associated with interstate highways. Bibliography: p. 96-114. [TD224.M4M37 no. 19] [TE177] 711'.73 72-610239
1. Roadside improvement. 2. Wetland ecology. 3. Landscape protection. I. Carlozzi, Carl A. II. Bergstrom, Kenneth L. III. Title. IV. Series.

U. S. Bureau of Public   711.73
Roads.
1967 Highway beautification program. Report of the Department of Commerce, together with additional correspondence, to

the United States Congress, pursuant to Public law 89 - 285, Highway beautification act of 1965. Washington, U. S. Govt. Print. Off., 1967. vii, 61 p. 24 cm. (90th Congress, 1st sess. Senate. Document no. 6) Includes bibliography. [[KF5532]]
1. Roadside improvement. 2. Roads—U. S.—Finance. 3. Highway law—U. S. I. Title. II. Title: Highway beautification program.

Roadside improvement—Addresses, essays, lectures.

ROADSIDE development; 711'.73
5 reports. Washington, Highway Research Board, National Research Council, 1969. 58 p. illus. 25 cm. (National Academy of Sciences. Publication 1657.) (Highway research record no. 280) Papers sponsored by the Committee on Roadside Development of the Highway Research Board. Contents.Contents.—Wildlife, an essential consideration determining future highway roadside maintenance policy, by G. B. Joselyn.—The highway roadside as an element in urban design, by J. C. Frederick.—Highway aesthetics: functional criteria for planning and design, by P. L. Hornbeck, R. R. Forster, and M. R. Dillingham.—Water systems for interstate safety rest area: quantity and quality aspects, by R. L. Johnson.—Design of rest area comfort facilities by systems analysis, by H. McCann and G. Maring. Includes bibliographies. [TE7.H5 no. 280] 74-603563 2.00
1. Roadside improvement—Addresses, essays, lectures. I. National Research Council. Highway Research Board. II. Title. III. Series. IV. Series: National Academy of Sciences, Washington, D.C. Publication 1657

Roadside improvement—Great Britain.

DE HAMEL, Bruno. 713'.0941
Roads and the environment / by Bruno de Hamel. London : H.M. Stationery Off., 1976. vii, 10 p. : ill. ; 30 cm. At head of title: Department of the Environment. Bibliography: p. 10. [TE177.D4] 77-360858 ISBN 0-11-550368-4 : £1.50
1. Roadside improvement—Great Britain. I. Great Britain. Dept. of the Environment. II. Title.

Roanoke, Va.—History—Pictorial works.

BRUCE, Carolyn Hale, 1942- 779'.9'9755791
Roanoke : a pictorial history / by Carolyn Hale Bruce. Virginia Beach, Va. : Donning, c1976. p. cm. [F234.R6B73] 76-25541 ISBN 0-915442-15-9 : 14.95
1. Roanoke, Va.—History—Pictorial works. I. Title.

Robbia, Andrea della, 1435?-1525?

MARQUAND, Allan, 1853-1924. 730'.92'4
Andrea della Robbia and his atelier. New York, Hacker Art Books, 1972 [i.e. 1973] 2 v. in 1. illus. 27 cm. Reprint of the 1922 ed. published by Princeton University Press as v. 11 of Princeton monographs in art and archaeology. Bibliography: v. 2, p. [267]-272. [NB623.R713M3 1972] 70-153007 ISBN 0-87817-102-9
1. Robbia, Andrea della, 1435?-1525? I. Title. II. Series: Princeton monographs in art and archaeology, 11.
Set of 8 vols. bound in four selling for 250.00.

Robbia, Della, family.

MARQUAND, Allan, 1853-1924. 730'.92'4
Robbia heraldry. New York, Hacker Art Books, 1972. xviii, 310 p. illus. 27 cm. Reprint of the 1919 ed. published by Princeton University Press, which was issued as v. 7 of Princeton monographs in art and archaeology. Bound with the author's Della Robbias in America. New York, 1972. Bibliography: p. [305]-307. [NB623.R7M3 1972] 73-164574 ISBN 0-87817-101-0
1. Robbia, Della, family. 2. Heraldry—Italy. 3. Terra-cottas, Italian. I. Title. II. Series: Princeton monographs in art and archaeology, 7.

Robbia, Fra Mattia della, b. 1468.

MARQUAND, Allan, 1853-1924. 730'.92'2
The brothers of Giovanni della Robbia: Fra Mattia, Luca, Girolamo, Fra Ambrogio. With an appendix, additions and corrections for all the Della Robbia catalogues. Edited and extended by Frank Jewett Mather, Jr. and Charles Rufus Morey from the manuscript of the late Professor Marquand. New York, Hacker Art Books, 1972. 221 p. illus. 27 cm. Reprint of the 1928 ed. published by Princeton University Press, which was issued as v. 13 of Princeton monographs in art and archaeology. Bound with the author's Benedetto and Santi Buglioni. New York, 1972. Bibliography: p. [207]-208. [NB623.B8M3 1972] 76-153011 ISBN 0-87817-111-8
1. Robbia, Fra Mattia della, b. 1468. 2. Robbia, Luca della, 1475-ca. 1550. 3. Robbia, Girolamo della, 1488-1566. 4. Robbia, Fra Ambrogio della, 1477-ca. 1527. I. Title. II. Series: Princeton monographs in art and archaeology, 13.

Robbia, Giovanni della, 1469-1529?

MARQUAND, Allan, 1853-1924. 730'.92'4
Giovanni della Robbia. New York, Hacker Art Books, 1972 [i.e. 1973] xxiv, 233 p. illus. 27 cm. Reprint of the 1920 ed. published by Princeton University Press, which was issued as v. 8 of Princeton monographs in art and archaeology. Bound with the author's Luca della Robbia. New York, 1972. Bibliography: p. [227]-230. [NB623.R72M3 1972] 73-164573 ISBN 0-87817-103-7
1. Robbia, Giovanni della, 1469-1529? I. Series: Princeton monographs in art and archaeology, 8.
Set of 8 vols. bound in four selling for 250.00.

Robbia, Luca della, 1400?-1482.

CRUTTWELL, Maud. 730'.92'2
Luca & Andrea della Robbia and their successors. With over 150 illus. London, Dent; New York, Dutton, 1902. [New York, AMS Press, 1972] xix, 363 p. illus. 24 cm. Includes bibliographies. [NB623.R7C8 1972] 79-155625 ISBN 0-404-01869-6 12.50
1. Robbia, Luca della, 1400?-1482. 2. Robbia, Andrea della, 1435?-1525? 3. Robbia, Giovanni della, 1469-1529? I. Title.

MARQUAND, Allan, 1853-1924. 730'.92'4
Della Robbias in America. New York, Hacker Art Books, 1972 [i.e. 1973] 168 p. illus. 27 cm. Reprint of the 1912 ed. published by Princeton University Press, which was issued as v. 1 of Princeton monographs in art and archaeology. Bound with the author's Robbia heraldry. New York, 1972. [NB623.R7M3 1972] 73-164570 ISBN 0-87817-101-0
1. Robbia, Luca della, 1400?-1482. 2. Robbia, Andrea della, 1435?-1525? 3. Robbia, Giovanni della, 1469-1529? I. Title. II. Series: Princeton monographs in art and archaeology, 1.
Set of 8 vols. bound in four selling for 250.00.

MARQUAND, Allan, 1853-1924. 730'.92'4
Luca della Robbia. New York, Hacker Art Books, 1972. xxxix, 286 p. illus. 27 cm. Reprint of the 1914 ed. published by Princeton University Press, which was issued as v. 3 of Princeton monographs in art and archaeology. Bound with the author's Giovanni della Robbia. New York, 1972. Includes bibliographical references. [NB623.R72M3 1972] 73-164572 ISBN 0-87817-103-7
1. Robbia, Luca della, 1400?-1482. I. Series: Princeton monographs in art and archaeology, 3.

Robbia, Luca della, 1400?-1482—Juvenile literature.

DOWNER, Marion. 92 (j)
Long ago in Florence; the story of the della Robbia sculpture. Drawings by Mamoru Funai. New York, Lothrop, Lee & Shepard Co. [1968] 31 p. illus. 26 cm. [NB623.R7D6] 68-27707 3.50
1. Robbia, Luca della, 1400?-1482—Juvenile literature. I. Title. BIP

Roberts, Darrah L., Mrs.—Art collections.

ROBERTS, Darrah L. 749'.63
Art glass shades, by Darrah L. Roberts. [Des Moines, Iowa, 1968] 31 p. (incl. cover) 15 x 24 cm. [NK5440.L3R6] 70-1792
1. Roberts, Darrah L., Mrs.—Art collections. 2. Lampshades, Glass—Catalogs. 3. Art nouveau. I. Title. BIP

Roberts, Howard, 1843-1900.

SELLIN, David. 709'.748'11
The first pose / David Sellin. 1st ed. New York : Norton, c1976. 72 p. : ill. ; 22 cm. Contents.Contents.—1876, turning point in American art.—Howard Roberts, Thomas Eakins, and a century of Philadelphia nudes. Includes bibliographical references. [N6535.P5S44 1976] 76-150731 ISBN 0-393-04447-5 : 7.95.
1. Roberts, Howard, 1843-1900. 2. Eakins, Thomas, 1844-1916. 3. Art—Pennsylvania—Philadelphia—History. 4. Art, Modern—19th century—Pennsylvania—Philadelphia—History. I. Title. BIP

Roberts, Tom, 1856-1931.

SPATE, Virginia. 759.994
Tom Roberts. Editorial consultant, John Henshaw. Melbourne, Lansdowne, 1972. 161 p. ill., col. plates. 31 cm. (Australian art library) Aus Bibliography: p. 155-157. [ND1105.R6S62] 74-160483 ISBN 0-7018-0390-8 15.00
1. Roberts, Tom, 1856-1931. I. Roberts, Tom, 1856-1931.

Robinson, Alfred S., 1835 or 6-1878.

DEWITT, John Doyle, 1902- 737.4'0924 B
Alfred S. Robinson, Hartford numismatist, by J. Doyle DeWitt. [Hartford] Connecticut Historical Society, 1968. 28 p. illus. 20 cm. Bibliography: p. 28. [CJ62.R6D4] 78-11034
1. Robinson, Alfred S., 1835 or 6-1878.

Robinson, Beverley Randolph, 1876-1951—Art collections.

UNITED States. Naval Academy, Annapolis. Museum. 769'.4'935940973074013
American naval prints : from the Beverly R. Robinson Collection, U.S. Naval Academy Museum, Annapolis, Maryland / introd. by Roger B. Stein ; circulated by the International Exhibitions Foundation, 1976-1977. [Washington] : The Foundation, c1976. 121 p. : ill. ; 22 x 26 cm. Participating museums: Mariners Museum, Newport News, Va., and five others. [NE957.2.U54 1976] 76-21904 pbk. : 7.00
1. Robinson, Beverley Randolph, 1876-1951—Art collections. 2. Naval prints, American—Exhibitions. 3. Naval battles in art—Exhibitions. I. International Exhibitions Foundation. II. Mariners Museum, Newport News, Va. III. Title.

Robinson, Charles.

ROBINSON, Charles. 741.64'092'2
Charles & William Heath Robinson / edited by David Larkin ; introduction by Leo John De Freitas. London : Constable, 1976. [16] p., [80] p. of plates : chiefly col. ill. ; 31 cm. [NC978.5.R6L37 1976] 77-354820 ISBN 0-09-461480-6 : £4.95
1. Robinson, Charles. 2. Robinson, William Heath, 1872-1944. I. Robinson, William Heath, 1872-1944, joint author. II. Larkin, David.

Robinson, David Moore, 1880-

MYLONAS, George Emmanuel, 1898- ed. 913.38
Studies presented to David Moore Robinson on his seventieth birthday. Saint Louis, Washington University [1951-] v. illus., plates, port., maps. 29 cm. "A list of the published writings of David Moore Robinson": v. 1, p. [xxii]-xii. [N8375.R6M9] 51-13567
1. Robinson, David Moore, 1880- 2. Art, Ancient. 3. Art — Addresses, essays, lectures. I. Title.

Robinson, Edward G., 1893- —Art collections.

ROBINSON, Jane. 759
Edward G. Robinson's world of art, by Jane Robinson. Introd. by Leonard Spigelgass. Epilogue by Edward G. Robinson. [1st ed.] New York, Harper & Row [1971?] x, 117 p. illus. (part col.) 27 cm. (A Cass Canfield book) [N5220.R56R6 1971] 75-160649 ISBN 0-06-013579-4 15.00
1. Robinson, Edward G., 1893- —Art collections. I. Title.

Robinson, Theodore, 1852-1896.

ROBINSON, Theodore, 1852-1896. 759.13
Theodore Robinson, 1852-1896. Introd. and commentary by Sona Johnston. [Baltimore,] Baltimore Museum of Art [1973] xxv, 78 p. illus. (part col.) 22 x 25 cm. Catalog of the exhibition held May 1-June 10, 1973 at the Baltimore Museum of Art, Baltimore, July 12-Aug. 26, 1973, at the Columbus Gallery of Fine Arts, Ohio, Sept. 19-Oct. 28, 1973, at the Worcester Art Museum, Mass., Nov. 19-Dec. 23, 1973, at the Joslyn Art Museum, Omaha, Neb., Jan. 20-Feb. 24, 1974, at the Munson-Williams-Proctor Institute, Utica, New York. [ND237.R67J6] 73-80318 6.25
1. Robinson, Theodore, 1852-1896. I. Johnston, Sona. II. Baltimore. Museum of Art. BIP

Robinson, William Heath, 1872-1944.

LEWIS, John Noel Claude, 1912- 741.5'942
Heath Robinson, artist and comic genius, by John Lewis. Introd. by Nicolas Bentley. New York, Barnes & Noble [1973] 223 p. illus. (part col.) 27 cm. Bibliography: p. 213-219. [NC242.R6L48 1973b] 74-151721 ISBN 0-06-494261-9 15.00
1. Robinson, William Heath, 1872-1944. I. Title.

Robus Hugo.

AMERICAN Federation of Arts 730.973
Hugo Robus, by Lincoln Rothschild. New York [Author, 1083 Fifth Ave., c.1960] 36p. illus. 18cm. 60-3045 2.00; .50 pap.,
1. Robus Hugo. I. Rothschild, Lincoln. II. Title.

Rock craft.

HYDE, Christopher S. 736'.2'028
The complete book of rock tumbling / Christopher S. Hyde & Richard A. Matthews. 1st ed. Radnor, Pa. : Chilton Book Co., c1977. xiii, 182 p. : ill. ; 27 cm. (Chilton's creative crafts series) Includes index. [TT880.H9 1977] 76-51251 ISBN 0-8019-6236-6 : 13.95. ISBN 0-8019-6237-4 pbk. : 7.95
1. Rock craft. I. Matthews, Richard A., joint author. II. Title. BIP

PEAVY, Linda. 745.5
The complete book of rock crafting / by Linda Peavy and Jere Day. New York : Drake Publishers, c1976. p. cm. [TT880.P4] 75-36134 ISBN 0-8473-1053-1 : 12.95
1. Rock craft. I. Day, Jere, joint author. II. Title. BIP

SUBJECT INDEX ROCKWELL, NORMAN, 1894—

SOMMER, Elyse. 745.5
Rock and stone craft. New York, Crown Publishers [1973] 96 p. illus. (part col.) 29 cm. [TT880.S67 1973] 72-96661 ISBN 0-517-50353-0 4.95
1. Rock craft. I. Title. BIP

VANE, Peter K. 745.5
Pebble people, pets & things / Peter K. Vane ; [color photos. by Edward Scibetta, black and white photos. by Peter K. Vane ; ill. by Mel Klapholtz]. New York : Butterick Pub., c1977. 184 p. : ill. (some col.) ; 23 cm. Includes index. [TT880.V33] 77-89711 ISBN 0-88421-038-3 pbk. : 5.95
1. Rock craft. I. Title. BIP

Rock craft—Juvenile literature.

LAURITZEN, Trynitje. 745.5
Painted rock creatures / by Trynitje Lauritzen ; pictures by George Overlie. Minneapolis : Lerner Publications Co., c1976. p. cm. (An Early craft book) Directions for making rocks into unique creatures by painting with enamels or acrylics. Includes suggestions for designs and for naming rock pets. [TT880.L36] 76-13069 ISBN 0-8225-0878-8 lib.bdg. : 3.95
1. Rock craft—Juvenile literature. I. Overlie, George. II. Title. BIP

Rock gardens.

KLABER, Doretta. 712.62
Rock garden plants; new ways to use them around your home. Illustrated by the author. [1st ed.] New York, Holt [1959] 173 p. illus. 22 cm. Includes bibliography. [SB454.K55] 59-7101
1. Rock gardens. I. Title.

Rock gardens, Japanese.

FUKUDA, Kazuhiko. 712
Japanese stone gardens; how to make and enjoy them. Rutland, Vt., C. E. Tuttle Co. [1970] 312 p. (chiefly illus., col. plates, plans) 32 cm. Bibliography: p. 307. [SB458.F84] 73-125562 ISBN 0-8048-0318-8 22.50
1. Rock gardens, Japanese. 2. Gardens—Japan. I. Title.

KRAMER, Jack, 1927- 712'.6
Gardening with stone and sand. Botanical plates by Michael Valdez and Charles Hoeppner. Garden plans by Frank A. Chin Loy. New York, Scribner [1972] 85 p. illus. 28 cm. [SB458.K7] 76-174653 ISBN 0-684-12518-8 5.95
1. Rock gardens, Japanese. 2. Landscape gardening. 3. Plants, Ornamental. I. Title.

Rock music—Pictorial works.

LEIBOVITZ, Annie, comp. 779'.2
Shooting stars, edited by Annie Leibovitz. Designed by Tony Lane. [San Francisco] Straight Arrow Books; [distributed by Quick Fox Inc., New York, 1973] 152 p. (chiefly ports.) 35 cm. "The Rolling Stone book of portraits." [ML89.L23] 72-79031 ISBN 0-87932-036-2 9.95
1. Rock music—Pictorial works. 2. Musicians—Portraits. 3. Photographers. I. Title. II. Title: The Rolling Stone book of portraits.

*MCCARTNEY, Linda 779'2
Linda's pictures : a collection of photographs / photographs and words by Linda McCartney. New York : Alfred A. Knopf, c1976. [155] p. : chiefly ill. ; 33 cm. [ML87] 75-10706 ISBN 0-394-49959-X : 25.00
1. Rock music—Pictorial works. I. Title. BIP

Rock paintings.

MAZONOWICZ, Douglas. 759.01'1
Voices from the stone age; a search for cave and canyon art, written and illustrated by Douglas Mazonowicz. New York, Crowell [1974] viii, 211 p. illus. 26 cm. Bibliography: p. [205]-206. [N5310.M33 1974] 74-8590 ISBN 0-690-00574-1
1. Rock paintings. 2. Cave drawings. I. Title.

Rock paintings—Afghanistan.

AGRESTI, Henri. 732'.2
Rock drawings in Afghanistan. Edited by Henry Field. Miami, Field Research Projects, 1970. 5 l., [9] l. of illus. 28 cm. (Field Research Projects. Occasional paper no. 14) Pref. and captions in English; text in French. [GN799.P4A34] 74-153545
1. Rock paintings—Afghanistan. 2. Afghanistan—Antiquities. I. Title. II. Series.

Rock paintings—Africa.

RITCHIE, Carson I. 759.01'1'096 A.
Rock art of Africa / Carson I. A. Ritchie. South Brunswick : A. S. Barnes, c1977. p. cm. Includes bibliographical references. [N5310.5.A35R57 1977] 76-24614 ISBN 0-498-01753-2 : 25.00
1. Rock paintings—Africa. 2. Africa—Antiquities. I. Title. BIP

Rock paintings—British Columbia.

CORNER, John. 759.01'1
Pictographs (Indian rock paintings) in the interior of British Columbia. Vernon, B.C., J. Corner, R.R. 4, [1968] 131 p. illus. (part col.) port., maps. 23 cm. Bibliography: p. 130-131. [E98.P6C6] 72-383679 unpriced
1. Rock paintings—British Columbia. 2. Indians of North America—British Columbia—Antiquities. 3. British Columbia—Antiquities. I. Title.

Rock paintings—Catalogs.

CERVICEK, Pavel. 016.732'2
Catalogue of the rock art collection of the Frobenius Institute / by Paval Cervicek ; with drawings by Gisela Wittner and photos by Margit Matthews. 1. Aufl. Wiesbaden : Steiner, 1976. xv, 306 p., [99] leaves of plates : ill. ; 24 cm. (Studien zur Kulturkunde ; Bd. 41) Includes bibliographies and index. [GN799.P4C45] 77-356931 ISBN 3-515-01856-5
1. Frankfurt am Main. Frobenius-Institut. 2. Rock paintings—Catalogs. 3. Petroglyphs—Catalogs. I. Frankfurt am Main. Frobenius-Institut. II. Title. III. Series.

Rock paintings—Exhibitions.

PHILLIPSON, D. W. 759.01'1'096894
Prehistoric rock paintings and engravings of Zambia; exhibition catalogue, by D. W. Phillipson. [Livingstone, Zambia, Livingstone Museum] 1972. 70 p. illus. 21 cm. English and French. Bibliography: p. 30. [N5310.5.Z3P47] 72-980294
1. Rock paintings—Exhibitions. 2. Rock paintings—Zambia. 3. Petroglyphs—Exhibitions. 4. Petroglyphs—Zambia. I. Livingstone Museum. II. Title.

Rock paintings—India.

BROOKS, Robert 759.01'1'0954 Romano Ravi, 1905-
Stone age painting in India / Robert R. R. Brooks, Vishnu S. Wakankar. New Haven : Yale University Press, 1976. xi, 116 p. : ill. (some col.) ; 29 cm. Includes index. Bibliography: p. 111-112. [N5310.5.I4B76] 75-43307 ISBN 0-300-01937-8 : 15.00
1. Rock paintings—India. 2. Art, Prehistoric—India. 3. India—Antiquities. I. Wakankar, Vishnu S., joint author. II. Title. BIP

Rock paintings—North America.

GRANT, Campbell, 1909- 709.01'1
Rock art of the American Indian. Written and illustrated by Campbell Grant. New York, Crowell [1967] xiv, 178 p. illus., 23 col. plates. 26 cm. Bibliography: p. 156-170. [E98.P6G7] 67-12402
1. Rock paintings—North America. 2. Petroglyphs—North America. 3. Indians of North America—Antiquities. 4. North America—Antiquities. I. Title.

GRANT, Campbell, 759.01'1'09701 1909-
Rock art of the American Indian / written and illustrated by Campbell Grant. New York : Promontory Press, [1974?] c1967. xiv, 178 p., [8] leaves of plates : ill. (some col.) ; 27 cm. Originally published by Crowell, New York. Includes index. Bibliography: p. 155-170. [E98.P6G7 1974] 73-92815 ISBN 0-88394-026-4 : 12.95
1. Rock paintings—North America. 2. Petroglyphs—North America. 3. Indians of North America—Antiquities. 4. North America—Antiquities. I. Title.

Rockefeller Center, inc., New York.

BALFOUR, Alan. 725'.2'097471
Rockefeller Center : architecture as theater / Alan Balfour. New York : McGraw-Hill, 1977,c1978 p. cm. Includes bibliographical references and index. [NA6233.N5R63] 77-5444 ISBN 0-07-003480-X : 25.00
1. Rockefeller Center, inc., New York. I. Title. BIP

CHAMBERLAIN, Samuel, 917.471 1895- ed.
Rockefeller Center; a photographic narrative. New York, Hastings House [1951] 72 p. (chiefly illus.) 21 cm. [F128.8.R7C5 1951] 51-2633
1. Rockefeller Center, inc., New York. I. Title.

CHAMBERLAIN, Samuel, 917.471 1895- ed.
Rockefeller Center; a photographic narrative. [Rev. ed.] New York, Hastings House [1956] 72p. illus. 21cm. [F128.8.R7C5 1956] 56-11968
1. Rockefeller Center, inc., New York. I. Title.

KRINSKY, Carol 725'.09747'1 Herselle.
Rockefeller Center / Carol Herselle Krinsky. New York : Oxford University Press, 1978. xxiv, 223 p. : ill. ; 24 cm. Includes index. Bibliography: p. 214-217. [NA6233.N5R64] 77-23735 ISBN 0-19-502317-X : 17.50
1. Rockefeller Center, inc., New York. I. Title. BIP

Rockefeller family—Portraits, etc.

THE Rockefeller family 779'.2 *album.* New York : Drake Publishers, 1976. p. cm. [E747.R62] 76-5491 ISBN 0-8473-1195-3 : 4.95
1. Rockefeller family—Portraits, etc.

Rockefeller, John D., 1906- —Art collections.

ASIA Society. 709.5'074'013
Asian art; selections from the Collection of Mr. and Mrs. John D. Rockefeller 3rd. [New York]; distributed by New York Graphic Society [1970] 94 p. plates (part col.) 28 cm. "Catalogue of an exhibition ... shown in the Asia House Gallery in the fall of 1970 as an activity of the Asia Society." [N7262.A8] 72-129577
1. Rockefeller, John D., 1906- —Art collections. 2. Rockefeller, Blanchette Hooker, 1909- —Art collections. 3. Art, Asian—Exhibitions. I. Asia House Gallery, New York. II. Title.

LEE, Sherman E. 730'.095'07401471
Asian art; selections from the Collection of Mr. and Mrs. John D. Rockefeller 3rd [by] Sherman E. Lee. New York, Intercultural Arts Press [1970] [66] p. and slide set (29 col. slides. 2 x 2 in.) 30 cm. At head of title: Asia House Gallery. Lecture materials based on Asian art, the catalogue of an exhibition shown in the Asia House Gallery in the autumn of 1970. Includes bibliographical references. [N7262.L36] 77-25165 30.00
1. Rockefeller, John D., 1906- —Art collections. 2. Rockefeller, Blanchette Hooker, 1909- —Art collections. 3. Art, Asian—Catalogs. I. Asia House Gallery, New York. II. Title. BIP

Rockefeller, Nelson Aldrich, 1908- —Art collections.

MASTERPIECES of 709'.01'107401471 *primitive art / photographs by Lee Boltin ;* text by Douglas Newton ; foreword by Andre Malaraux ; introduction by Nelson A. Rockefeller. New York : Knopf, 1978. p. cm. (The Nelson A. Rockefeller collection) Bibliography: p. [N5310.M286] 78-54888 ISBN 0-394-50057-1 : 30.00
1. Rockefeller, Nelson Aldrich, 1908- —Art collections. 2. Art, Primitive. I. Boltin, Lee. II. Newton, Douglas, 1920- III. Title. IV. Series.

NEW York (City). 707.4'01471 Museum of Modern Art.
Twentieth-century art from the Nelson Aldrich Rockefeller Collection. New York, Museum of Modern Art; distributed by New York Graphic Society, Greenwich, Conn. [1969] 139 p. illus. (part col.) 28 cm. Title on spine: The Nelson Aldrich Rockefeller Collection. Catalog of an exhibition held May 26-Sept. 1, 1969. [N6490.N44] 73-77512 7.50
1. Rockefeller, Nelson Aldrich, 1908- —Art collections. 2. Art, Modern—20th century—Exhibitions. I. Title. II. Title: The Nelson Aldrich Rockefeller Collection.

NEW York 709.04'074'014743 (State). State University, Albany. Art Gallery.
Paintings and sculpture from the Nelson A. Rockefeller Collection. [Albany, 1967] [32] p. (chiefly illus. (part col.)) 25 cm. Cover title. Catalog of an exhibition held Oct. 5-Nov. 17, 1967 at the Art Gallery, State University of New York at Albany. [N6487.A4N46] 77-635003
1. Rockefeller, Nelson Aldrich, 1908- —Art collections. 2. Art, Modern—20th century—Exhibitions. I. Title.

Rockingham pottery.

EAGLESTONE, Arthur 738.3'7 Archibald, 1892-
The Rockingham pottery [by] Arthur A. Eaglestone and Terence A. Lockett. New rev. ed. Rutland, Vt., C. E. Tuttle Co. [1973] 159 p. illus. 23 cm. Bibliography: p. 146. [NK4340.R6E17 1973b] 73-86799 ISBN 0-8048-1121-0 8.50
1. Rockingham pottery. I. Lockett, Terence A., joint author. II. Title.

RICE, Dennis George. 738.2'7
The illustrated guide to Rockingham pottery and porcelain [by] Dennis G. Rice. New York, Praeger [1971] xx, 194 p. illus. (part col.) 26 cm. (The Illustrated guides to pottery and porcelain) Bibliography: p. 186-187. [NK4340.R6R5] 71-121079 18.50
1. Rockingham pottery. 2. Rockingham porcelain. I. Title.

Rockwell, Norman, 1894—

FINCH, Christopher. 759.13
Norman Rockwell's America / Christopher Finch. New York : H. N. Abrams, [1975] 313 p. : ill. (some col.) ; 34 cm. Includes index. [ND237.R68F56] 75-15703 ISBN 0-8109-0454-3
1. Rockwell, Norman, 1894- 2. United States in art. I. Title.

GUPTILL, Arthur Leighton, 759.13 1891-1956.
Norman Rockwell, illustrator. Pref. by Dorothy Canfield Fisher. Biographical introd. by Jack Alexander. [3d ed.] New York, Watson-Guptill Publications [1970] 208 p. illus. (part col.), plan, col. plates, ports. (part col.) 31 cm. [ND237.R68G8 1970] 75-125848 17.50
1. Rockwell, Norman, 1894-

HILLCOURT, William, 1900- 759.13
Norman Rockwell's world of scouting / by William Hillcourt. New York : H. N. Abrams, [1977] p. cm. Includes index. [ND237.R68H54] 77-8491 ISBN 0-8109-1582-0 : 14.95
1. Rockwell, Norman, 1894- 2. Boy Scouts of America—History. 3. Boy Scouts in art. I. Rockwell, Norman, 1894- II. Title. BIP

ROCKWELL, Norman, 1894- 759.13
Norman Rockwell, my adventures as an illustrator, as told to Thomas Rockwell. [1st ed.] Garden City, N. Y., Doubleday,

1960. 436p. illus. 24cm. [ND237.R68R69] 60-6904
I. Rockwell, Thomas, 1963- II. Title.

ROCKWELL, Norman, 1894- 759.13
Norman Rockwell: a sixty year retrospective. With text by Thomas S. Buechner. New York, Abrams [1972] 157 p. illus. (part col.) 30 cm. "Catalogue of an exhibition organized by Bernard Danenberg Galleries, New York," and held from Feb. 11, 1972, to Apr. 15, 1973, at the Fort Lauderdale Museum of the Arts [and others] [ND237.R68B4] 70-38513 ISBN 0-8109-2049-2
I. Bernard Danenberg Galleries. II. Fort Lauderdale Museum of the Arts.

ROCKWELL, Norman, 1894- 759.13
The Norman Rockwell album. [1st ed.] Garden City, N.Y., Doubleday, 1961. 191 p. illus. (part col.) ports., map. 36 cm. [ND237.R68A5] 61-12573

ROCKWELL, Norman, 1894- 759.13
Norman Rockwell, artist and illustrator [by] Thomas S. Buechner. [1st ed.] New York, H. N. Abrams [1970] 328 p. illus. (part col.) 44 cm. [ND237.R68B8] 75-125785
I. Buechner, Thomas S. II. Title.

ROCKWELL, Norman, 1894- 759.13
The Norman Rockwell poster book / edited by Michael Schau. New York : Watson-Guptill Publications, 1976. [46] p. : all col. ill. ; 41 cm. [NC1850.R62S3 1976] 76-365708 ISBN 0-8230-4588-9 : 6.95
1. Rockwell, Norman, 1894- I. Schau, Michael, 1945- II. Title. BIP

ROCKWELL, Norman, 1894- 759.13
The second Norman Rockwell poster book / [with an introd. by Donald Holden]. New York : Watson-Guptill Publications, 1977. [4] p., [20] leaves of plates : col. ill. ; 41 cm. [NC1850.R62S3 1977] 77-151020 ISBN 0-8230-4589-7 : 6.95
1. Rockwell, Norman, 1894- I. Title. BIP

THE Saturday evening post 759.13
Norman Rockwell book. Indianapolis : Curtis Pub. Co., c1977. vii, 152 p. : ill. (some col.) ; 32 cm. [ND237.R68A4 1977] 77-12286 ISBN 0-89387-007-2 : 9.95
1. Rockwell, Norman, 1894- 2. The Saturday evening post—Illustrations. I. Rockwell, Norman, 1894- II. Title: Norman Rockwell book.

WALTON, Donald. 759.13 B
A Rockwell portrait : an intimate biography / by Donald Walton. Kansas City [Kan.] : Sheed Andrews and McMeel, c1978. p. cm. [ND237.R68W34] 78-13076 ISBN 0-8362-6602-1 : 12.95
1. Rockwell, Norman, 1894- 2. Painters—United States—Biography. I. Title. BIP

Rockwell, Norman, 1894- —Collectibles—Catalogs.

MOLINE, Mary. 759.13
Norman Rockwell collectibles value guide : the little Rockwell book / created by Mary Moline for Rumbleseat Press, inc. 1st ed. Van Nuys, Ca. : Rumbleseat Press, 1978. 150 p. : ill. ; 24 cm. Includes index. [NK808.M64] 76-17960 ISBN 0-913444-02-2 pbk. : 8.95
1. Rockwell, Norman, 1894- —Collectibles—Catalogs. I. Title. BIP

Rockwell, Norman, 1894- —Juvenile literature.

ROCKWELL, Norman, 1894- 759.13
Norman Rockwell's Americana ABC / with poems by George Mendoza. New York : H. N. Abrams, [1975] p. cm. The letters of the alphabet are introduced through paintings and poetry on an Americana theme. [ND237.R68M46 1975] 75-8886 ISBN 0-8109-0457-8 : 5.95
1. Rockwell, Norman, 1894- —Juvenile literature. 2. Mendoza, George—Illustrations—Juvenile literature. 3. United States in art—Juvenile literature. 4. Alphabet—Juvenile literature. I. Mendoza, George. II. Title: Americana ABC. BIP

Rocky Mount, N.C.—History—Pictorial works.

†BARRINGER, Bugs, 1911- 779'.9'975646
Rocky Mount : a pictorial history / Bugs Barringer, Dot Barringer, and Lela Chesson. Norfolk, Va. : Donning Co., c1977. 171 p. : ill. ; 29 cm. [F264.R62B37] 77-8620 ISBN 0-915442-31-0 : 14.95
1. Rocky Mount, N.C.—History—Pictorial works. 2. Rocky Mount, N.C.—Description—Views. I. Barringer, Dot, 1920- joint author. II. Chesson, Lela, 1941- joint author. III. Title.

Rocky Mountains—Description and travel—Views.

MUENCH, David. 779'.9'9178
Rocky Mountains / photography: David Muench ; text: David Sumner. Portland, Or. : Graphic Arts Center Pub. Co., [1975] iv, 186 p. : chiefly col. ill. ; 36 cm. [F721.M83] 74-33864 ISBN 0-912856-16-5 : 30.00
1. Rocky Mountains—Description and travel—Views. I. Sumner, David. II. Title. BIP

Rodeos in art.

FORTH Worth Art Museum. 704.94'9'7918
The great American rodeo John Alberty, Terry Allen, Ed Blackburn, George Green, Mimi Gross Grooms, Red Grooms, Joe Ferrell Hobbs, Andy Mann, Robert Rauschenberg, Garry Windgrand, Joe Zucker : an exhibition / organized by the Fort Worth Art Museum. 1st ed. Fort Worth, Tex. : The Museum, c1976. 72, [6] p. : ill. (some col.) ; 24 cm. Catalog of an exhibition held at the Fort Worth Art Museum, Jan. 25-Apr. 11, 1976; Colorado Springs Fine Arts Center, Aug. 1-29, 1976; Witte Memorial Museum, San Antonio, Feb. 5-Apr. 3, 1977. [N6512.F66 1976] 76-4119 10.00
1. Rodeos in art. 2. Art, American—Exhibitions. 3. Art, Modern—20th century—United States—Exhibitions. I. Alberty, John, 1939- II. Colorado Springs. Fine Arts Center. III. Witte Memorial Museum, San Antonio. IV. Title.

Rodin, Auguste, 1840-1917.

DE CASO, Jacques, 1928- 730'.92'4
Rodin's Thinker; significant aspects [by] Jacques de Caso [and] Patricia B. Sanders. [San Francisco] Fine Arts Museums of San Francisco; [distributed by Demia Press, Burlingame, Calif., c1973] 30 p. illus. 21 cm. Bibliography: p. 30. [NB553.R7D37] 74-160954
1. Rodin, Auguste, 1840-1917. Thinker. I. Sanders, Patricia B., joint author. II. Title.

DESCHARNES, Robert. 730'.924
Auguste Rodin [by] Robert Descharnes and Jean-Francois Chabrun. [English translation by Edita Lausanne] New York, Viking Press [1967] 277, [4] p. illus. (part col.), facsims., ports. 30 cm. (A Studio book) Bibliography: p. [278]-[281]. [NB553.R7D43] 67-31963
1. Rodin, Auguste, 1840-1917. I. Chabrun, Jean Francois, 1920- joint author.

ELSEN, Albert Edward, 1927- 730.924
Auguste Rodin: readings on his life and work. Englewood Cliffs, N.J., Prentice [c.1965] 185p. illus. 22cm. Bibl. [NB553.R7E36] 65-17532 3.95 pap.,
1. Rodin, Auguste, 1840-1917. I. Title.

ELSEN, Albert Edward, 1927- 741.9'44
The drawings of Rodin [by] Albert Elsen [and] J. Kirk T. Varnedoe. With additional contributions by Victoria Thorson and Elisabeth Chase Geissbuhler. New York, Praeger Publishers [1972, c1971] 191 p. illus. (part col.) 26 cm. Bibliography: p. 189-191. [NC248.R58E4] 76-159409 13.50
1. Rodin, Auguste, 1840-1917. I. Varnedoe, J. Kirk T. II. Title.

ELSEN, Albert Edward, 1927- 730.944
Rodin. New York, Museum of Modern Art; distributed by Doubleday, Garden City, N.Y, [1963] 228 p. illus. (part col.) ports. 26 cm. Bibliography: p. 214-216. 63-14847
1. Rodin, Auguste, 1840-1917. I. Title.

ELSEN, Albert Edward, 1927- 730.944
Rodin's Gates of hell Minneapolis, University of Minnesota Press [c.1960] 160 p. Bibl. & bibl. notes: p. 145-156 illus., plates, port. 28 cm. 60-14640 7.50
1. Rodin, Auguste, 1840-1917 I. Title. II. Title: Gates of hell

GEISSBUHLER, Elisabeth Chase. 741.944
Rodin; later drawings With interpretations by Antoine Bourdelle. Text and translations by Elisabeth Chase Geissbuhler. Boston, Beacon Press [1963] 105 p. illus., port., facsims. 25 cm. Bibliographical references included in "Notes" (p. 100-102) 63-11390
I. Rodin, Auguste, 1840-1917. II. Bourdelle, Emile Antoine, 1861-1929. III. Title.

JIANU, Ionel. 730/.924
Rodin [par] Ionel Jianou, C. Goldscheider. Paris, Arted, 1967. 118p. plates. 28cm. Errata slip inserted. Issued in a case. Bibl. [NB553.R7J5] 67-107873 12.50
1. Rodin, Auguste, 1840-1917. I. Goldscheider, Cecile. II. Title.
American distributor: Tudor, New York.

RILKE, Rainer Maria, 1875-1926. 730'.92'4
Rodin. Translated by Jessie Lemont and Hans Trausil. With an introd. by Padraic Colum. New York, Haskell House, 1974. xvi, 62 p. illus. 24 cm. Translation of Auguste Rodin. Reprint of the 1946 ed. published by Grey Walls Press, London. [NB553.R7R65 1974] 74-6405 ISBN 0-8383-1913-0
1. Rodin, Auguste, 1840-1917.

RIPLEY, Elizabeth 730.924
Rodin; a biography. [1st ed.] Philadelphia, Lippincott [1966] 72p. illus., ports. 2mcm.7bBibl. [NB553.R7R68] 66-8225 3.75; 3.39 lib. ed.,
1. Rodin, Auguste, 1840-1917. I. Title.

RIPLEY, Elizabeth, 1906- 730.924
Rodin; a biography. [1st ed.] Philadelphia, Lippincott [1966] 72 p. illus., ports. 27 cm. Bibliography: p. 70. [NB553.R7R68] 66-8225
1. Rodin, Auguste, 1840-1917. I. Title.

RODIN, Auguste 1840-1917 730.944
Rodin, by Andre Leclerc[pseud.] New York, Crown [1963] 36p. chiefly illus. 18cm. (Little bks. on great artist) Bibliographical sketch in French, English, German. 63-5634 .69
I. Immerman, Irene. II. Title.

SLATKIN Charles E. Galleries, New York. 707.4
Auguste Rodin, 1840-1917; an exhibition of sculptures and drawings [May 6-June 26, 1963] With an introd. by Leo Steinberg, and catalogue notes by Cecile Goldscheider. Held under auspices ot the Rodin Musuem of Paris New York [1963] 114 p. illus. 27 cm. [NB553.R7S5] 63-17577
1. Rodin, Auguste, 1840-1917. I. Goldscheider, Cecile. II. Paris. Musee Rodin.

SPEAR, Athena Tacha. 730'.924
Rodin sculpture in the Cleveland Museum of Art. [Cleveland] Cleveland Museum of Art [1967] ix, 101 p. 105 illus., port. 24 cm. [NB553.R7S6] 67-28952
1. Rodin, Auguste, 1840-1917. I. Cleveland Museum of Art. II. Title.

SUTTON, Denys. 730.924
Triumphant satyr: the world of Auguste Rodin. [1st Amer. ed.] New York, Hawthorn Books [1967, c1966] 149 p. illus. (part col.) port. 26 cm. Bibliographical footnotes. [NB553.R7S8 1967] 66-20197
1. Rodin, Auguste, 1840-1917. I. Title.

TAILLANDIER, Yvon 709'.44
Rodin. [Tr. from French by Anne Ross] New York, Crown [1967] 94, [2]p. illus. (pt. col) 29cm.) 29cm. Bibl. [NB553.R7T313] 67-4121 3.50
1. Rodin, Auguste, 1840-1917. I. Title. BIP

TIREL, Marcelle. 730'.92'4
The last years of Rodin. Translated by R. Francis. Pref. by Judith Cladel. New York, Haskell House, 1974. 224 p. illus. 20 cm. Translation of Rodin intime; ou, L'envers d'une gloire. Reprint of the 1925 ed. published by R. M. McBride, New York. [NB553.R7T52 1974] 74-16282 ISBN 0-8383-1945-9
1. Rodin, Auguste, 1840-1917. I. Title. BIP

Rodin, Auguste, 1840-1917—Catalogs.

DE CASO, Jacques, 1928- 730'.92'4
Rodin's sculpture : a critical study of the Spreckels Collection, California Palace of the Legion of Honor / Jacques de Caso and Patricia B. Sanders. San Francisco : Fine Arts Museum of San Francisco, 1978, c1977 360 p. : ill. ; 28 cm. Includes indexes. Bibliography: p. 349-351. [NB553.R7A4 1977] 76-45944 ISBN 0-88401-023-6 : 20.00 ISBN 0-88401-022-8 pbk. : 13.95
1. Rodin, Auguste, 1840-1917—Catalogs. 2. Spreckels, Alma de Bretteville, 1886-1968—Art collections—Catalogs. 3. California Palace of the Legion of Honor, San Francisco—Catalogs. I. Sanders, Patricia B., joint author. II. Title.
Available also from Charles E. Tuttle BIP

RODIN Museum, Philadelphia. 730'.924
Handbook, by John L. Tancock. [Philadelphia] Philadelphia Museum of Art, 1969. 103 p. illus., port. 17 cm. [NB87.P45R6] 70-101487
I. Tancock, John L.

Rodrigue, George.

†RODRIGUE, George. 759.13
The Cajuns of George Rodrigue / introd. and commentary by the artist ; translation by Georges and Jacqueline Planel. 1st ed. Birmingham, Ala. : Oxmoor House, c1976. xii, 155 p. : ill. (some col.) ; 25 x 29 cm. English and French. [ND237.R69A44] 76-14111 ISBN 0-8487-0443-6 : 24.95
1. Rodrigue, George. 2. Acadians in Louisiana—Portraits. I. Title.

Rodriguez Tizon, Ventura, 1717-1785.

REESE, Thomas Ford. 720'.92'4
The architecture of Ventura Rodriguez / Thomas Ford Reese. New York : Garland, 1976. 2 v. : ill. ; 21 cm. (Outstanding dissertations in the fine arts) Originally presented as the author's thesis, Yale, 1973, under title: The architecture of Ventura Rodriguez Tizon in the development of the eighteenth century style in Spain. Bibliography: v. 2, p. 414-451. [NA1313.R6R43 1976] 75-23810 ISBN 0-8240-2004-9 lib.bdg. : 80.00
1. Rodriguez Tizon, Ventura, 1717-1785. I. Title. II. Series. BIP

Roentgen, Abraham, 1711-1793.

HUTH, Hans, 1892- 749.2'3
Roentgen furniture : Abraham and David Roentgen, European cabinet-makers / Hans Huth. London ; New York : Sotheby Parke Bernet, 1974 1974. vii, 108 p., 68 leaves of plates : ill. ; 30 cm. Original ed. published in German in 1928 under title: Abraham und David Roentgen und ihre Neuwieder mobelwerkstatt. Includes index. Bibliography: p. 97-99. [NK2554.R6H813] 74-178943 ISBN 0-85667-003-0 : 55.00
1. Roentgen, Abraham, 1711-1793. 2. Roentgen, David, 1743-1807. 3. Furniture, German. I. Title. BIP

Roerich, Nikolai Konstantinovich, 1874-1947.

PAELIAN, Garabed Hagop, 1880- 759.7 B
Nicholas Roerich / Garabed Paelian. Agoura, Calif. : Aquarian Educational Group, [1974] 96 p. : ports. ; 27 cm. Bibliography: p. 93-96. [ND699.R6P35] 74-11757 ISBN 0-911794-09-3 : 6.00
1. Roerich, Nikolai Konstantinovich, 1874-1947. BIP

SUBJECT INDEX ROME—ANTIQUITIES.

Rogers, Bruce, 1870-1957.

ROGERS, Bruce, 1870- 1957. 686.2'092'4
Typographical partnership: ten letters between Bruce Rogers and Emery Walker, 1907-31. Together with an unpublished fragment of Bruce Rogers' Bye-ways of book-making. Edited with an introd. by John Dreyfus. Cambridge, Eng., Printed for the Carl H. Pforzheimer Library at the University Printing House, 1971. xvi, 44 p. 29 cm. "350 copies composed in monotype centaur type." Includes bibliographical references. [Z232.R67A336] 73-163900
1. Rogers, Bruce, 1870-1957. 2. Walker, Emery, Sir, 1851-1933. 3. Type and type-founding. I. Walker, Emery, Sir, 1851-1933. II. Dreyfus, John, ed. III. Carl H. Pforzheimer Library, New York. IV. Title.

WARDE, Frederic, 1894-1939. 016.6554'0924
Bruce Rogers, designer of books, by Frederic Warde. And Bruce Rogers: a bibliography; hitherto unrecorded work 1889-1925, complete works 1925-1936, by Irvin Haas. Port Washington, N.Y., Kennikat Press [1968] 74 p., 15 l., vii, 72 p. illus., facsims. 22 cm. A combined ed. of the works first published in 1925 and 1936. [Z232.R67W2 1968] 67-27640
1. Rogers, Bruce, 1870-1957. I. Haas, Irwin. Bruce Rogers; a bibliography; hitherto unrecorded work, 1889-1925, complete work, 1925-1936.

Rogers, Charles B., 1911—

ROGERS, Charles B., 1911- 759.13
Images of the American West : paintings and haiku / Charles B. Rogers. Millbrae, Calif. : Celestial Arts, 1975. 126 p. : ill. ; 14 x 22 cm. [NX512.R63A47] 74-25838 ISBN 0-89087-010-1 pbk. : 3.95
1. Rogers, Charles B., 1911- 2. Southwest, New, in art. I. Title.

Rogers, Charles Bolles—Art collections.

MCKENZIE, A Dean. 704.948'4'074094183
Greek and Russian icons and other liturgical objects in the Collection of Mr. Charles Bolles Rogers [by] A. Dean MacKenzie. Milwaukee, University of Wisconsin [1965] 44, 35 p. illus. (part col.) 28 cm. Catalog of an exhibition held Nov. 15 to Dec. 10, 1965, Dept. of Art History Gallery, University of Wisconsin, Milwaukee. Bibliography: p. 22. [N7827.M3] 66-65270
1. Rogers, Charles Bolles—Art collections. 2. Icons, Greek. 3. Icons, Russian. I. Wisconsin. University, Milwaukee. Dept. of Art History. II. Title.

Rogers, John, 1829-1904.

BLEIER, Paul. 730'.924
John Rogers' groups of statuary; a pictorial & annotated guide for the collector, by Paul & Meta Bleier. [N. Woodmere? N.Y., 1971] [6], 134 (i.e. 240) p. illus. 15 cm. Bibliography: 2d prelim. page. [NB237.R77B55] 78-31285
1. Rogers, John, 1829-1904. I. Bleier, Meta, joint author. II. Title.

ORTON, Vrest, 1897- 730'.924
The famous Rogers groups; a complete check-list and collectors' manual. [3d ed.] Rockingham, Vt., Vermont Country Store [1968] 40 p. illus. 20 cm. Cover title. [NB237.R77O7 1968] 68-5072
1. Rogers, John, 1829-1904. I. Title.

WALLACE, David H. 730'.924
John Rogers; the people's sculptor, by David H. Wallace. [1st ed.] Middletown, Conn., Wesleyan University Press [1967] xv, 326 p. illus., facsims., ports. 27 cm. "Catalogue of the works of John Rogers": p. 171-280. [NB237.R65W3] 67-24107
1. Rogers, John, 1829-1904.

Rogers, Mondel, 1946—

†ROGERS, Mondel, 1946- 759.13
Old ranches of the Texas plains : paintings / by Mondel Rogers ; foreword by Mitchell A. Wilder. 1st ed. College Station : Texas A & M University, c1976. 124 p., [1] leaf of plates : ill. (some col.) ; 24 x 32 cm. (The Joe and Betty Moore Texas art series ; no. 1) [ND1839.R63A56] 76-17980 ISBN 0-89096-019-4 : 27.50
1. Rogers, Mondel, 1946- 2. Ranches in art. 3. Ranches—Texas—Pictorial works. I. Title. II. Series. BIP

Rogers, Randolph, 1825-1892.

ROGERS, Millard F. 730'.924 B
Randolph Rogers; American sculptor in Rome [by] Millard F. Rogers, Jr. [Amherst] University of Massachusetts Press, 1971. xviii, 237 p. illus. 24 cm. Bibliography: p. [187]-192. [NB237.R66R6] 75-164439 17.50
1. Rogers, Randolph, 1825-1892. I. Title.

Rohm, Robert, 1934—

BOSTON. Museum of Fine Arts. 730'.92'4
Robert Rohm, Christopher Sproat; [catalog of an exhibition] Museum of Fine Arts, Boston, May 15-June 30, 1974. [Boston, 1974] [20] p. illus. 22 x 28 cm. Includes bibliographies. [NB237.R67B67 1974] 74-81242 ISBN 0-87846-082-9
1. Rohm, Robert, 1934- 2. Sproat, Christopher, 1945- I. Title. BIP

Roland, Anthony.

THE Roland collection; 011
award winning films on art. Northfield, Ill. [1973?] 56 p. illus. 15 x 21 cm. [N369.R64R64] 73-179261
1. Roland, Anthony. 2. Art—Film catalogs. 3. Art in moving pictures.

Roland, Henry Montagu—Art collections.

ROLAND, Henry Montagu. 709'04'07402142
The Roland Collection : [catalogue of an exhibition held] 15 September-10 October 1976, Camden Arts Centre, Arkwright Road, London NW3 ... organised by the Arkwright Arts Trust .... [Woking : H. M. Roland, 1976] 48 p. : ill. ; 25 cm. Cover title. [N6488.G7L66] 77-361143 ISBN 0-9504265-1-2 : £0.50
1. Roland, Henry Montagu—Art collections. 2. Art, Modern—20th century—Exhibitions. I. Camden Arts Centre. II. Arkwright Arts Trust. III. Title.

Rollei camera.

EMANUEL, Walter Daniel, 1908- 771.3'1
Rollei 35 guide; how to use the Rollei 35 camera, by W. D. Emanuel. [1st ed.] London, New York, Focal Press; distributed in U.S.A. by Amphoto, New York [1969] 72 p. illus. 17 cm. (The Camera guide) [TR263.R6E55] 73-97258
1. Rollei camera. 2. Photography—Handbooks, manuals, etc. I. Title. II. Series.

Rolleiflex camera.

EMANUEL, Walter Daniel, 1908- 771.3'1
Rolleiflex guide: how to use all the twin-lens 2 1/4 x 2 1/4 Rolleiflex, Rollei-Magic and 1 5/8 x 1 5/8 Rolleiflex models, by W. D. Emanuel. 38th ed. London, New York, Focal Press; distributed in U.S.A. by Amphoto, New York, 1972. 72 p. illus. 17 cm. (Focal camera guide 678) [TR263.R6E5 1972] 74-98704 2.50 (U.S.)
1. Rolleiflex camera. 2. Photography—Handbooks, manuals, etc. I. Title.

HENLE, Fritz, 1909- 771.31
A new guide to Rollei photography, by Fritz Henle with H. M. Kinzer. New York, Viking Press [1965] 118 p. illus. (part col.) ports. 26 cm. (A Studio book) [TR263.R6H46] 65-12576
1. Rolleiflex camera. 2. Photography—Handbooks, manuals, etc. 3. Photography, Artistic. I. Kinzer, Harless Mahlon. II. Title.

TYDINGS, Kenneth S 771.31
Advanced Rolleiflex and Rolleicord guide. Philadelphia, Chilton Co., Book Division, c1960. 127 p. illus. 20 cm. (Modern camera guide series, 632) [TR263.R6T89] 60-15377
1. Rolleiflex camera. 2. Rolleicord camera. 3. Photography — Handbooks, manuals, etc. I. Title.

Roller painting.

STONHAM, F. H. 760
Painting and printmaking with rollers [by] F. H. Stonham. New York, Van Nostrand Reinhold Co. [1972] 124 p. illus. (part col.) 29 cm. Bibliography: p. 121. [ND1536.S76] 70-155896 ISBN 0-442-08015-8
1. Roller painting. 2. Roller printing (Printmaking) I. Title. II. Title: Printmaking with rollers.

Romanesque revival (Architecture)—United States.

TUCCI, Douglass Shand. 720'.92'4
Ralph Adams Cram, American medievalist / by Douglass Shand Tucci. [Boston] : Boston Public Library, 1975. 49 p., [2] fold. leaves of plates : ill. ; 27 cm. Catalogue of an exhibition held at the Boston Public Library. Bibliography: p. 45-49. [NA737.C7T82] 76-358972
1. Cram, Ralph Adams, 1863-1942. 2. Romanesque revival (Architecture)—United States. 3. Gothic revival (Architecture)—United States. I. Boston. Public Library. II. Title. BIP

Romanticism.

PECKHAM, Morse, ed. 709.034
Romanticism; the culture of the nineteenth century. New York, G. Braziller [1965] 351 p. illus. 24 cm. (The Cultures of mankind) [PN603.P38] 65-23181
1. Romanticism. 2. Romanticism in art. BIP

Romanticism—England.

QUENNELL, Peter, 1905- 709'.42
Romantic England; writing and painting, 1717-1851. [1st American ed. New York] Macmillan [1970] 272 p. illus. (part col.), ports. 26 cm. Bibliography: p. 267. [PR447.Q4] 78-119142 11.95
1. Romanticism—England. 2. English literature—18th century—History and criticism. 3. English literature—19th century—History and criticism. 4. Romanticism in art—England. 5. Painting, English—History. I. Title. BIP

Romanticism in art.

ABERDEEN Art Gallery, Aberdeen, Scot. 760'.094'074094125
Romantic art: [catalogue of] a loan exhibition of watercolours, drawings, prints, books [at the] Aberdeen Art Gallery, 13th February to 14th March, 1971. Aberdeen, Aberdeen Art Gallery, 1971. [28] p. 22 cm. Organized by the University of Aberdeen Dept. of History of Art. [N6465.R6A2] 71-596265 ISBN 0-900017-02-3 £0.10
1. Romanticism in art. 2. Art, Modern—19th century—Exhibitions. I. Aberdeen, Scot. University. Dept. of History of Art. II. Title.

BABINSKI, Hubert F., 1936- 809'.933'51
The Mazeppa legend in European romanticism [by] Hubert F. Babinski. New York, Columbia University Press, 1974. 164 p. 23 cm. Bibliography: p. [155]-161. [NX652.M3B32] 74-6152 ISBN 0-231-03825-9 12.00
1. Mazepa, Ivan Stepanovych, Hetman of the Cossacks, 1644-1709, in fiction, drama, poetry, etc. 2. Mazepa, Ivan Stepanovych, Hetman of the Cossacks, 1644-1709—Portraits, caricatures, etc. 3. Mazepa, Ivan Stepanovych, Hetman of the Cossacks, 1644-1709—Songs and music—History and criticism. 4. Romanticism in art. I. Title. BIP

BRION, Marcel, 1895- 709.035
Romantic art. New York, McGraw-Hill [1960] 240p. mounted col. illus., plates. 34cm. 60-12761 25.00
1. Romanticism in art. 2. Art—Hist. 3. Paintings. I. Title.

CALIFORNIA State University, Chico. Art Dept. 700'.9'034
Breaking the chains: romanticism. Exhibition dates: Mar. 18-Apr. 11, Taylor Art Gallery. [Chico, 1973] 60 p. illus. 26 cm. Cover title. Catalog. Bibliography: p. 60. [NX600.R6C34] 73-161973
1. Romanticism in art. 2. Arts—Exhibitions. I. Taylor Art Gallery. II. Title.

CUMMINGS, Frederick J. 709'.42
Romantic art in Britain; paintings and drawings, 1760-1860. Catalogue [by] Frederick J. Cummings, Allen Staley. Essays [by] Robert Rosenblum. Frederick Cummings, Allen Staley. [n. p., Printing: Falcon Pr, 1968] 335p. illus., ports. 23x28cm. Catalog of an exhibition held Jan. 9 to Feb. 18, 1968, at the Detrolt Inst. of Arts. and Mar. 14 to Apr. 21, 1968, at the Philadelphia Mus. of Art. Bibl. [N6766.C8] 68-14543 7.50
1. Romanticism in art. 2. Art. British—Exhibitions. I. Staley, Allen. joint author. II. Detroit. Institute of Arts. III. Philadelphia Museum of Art. IV. Title.
Available from the Detroit Inst. of Arts, Detroit, Mich., or the Philadelphia Museum of Art, Philadelphia, Pa.

NEWTON, Eric, 1893- 709.035
The romantic rebellion. New York, St Martin's [1963, c.1962] 224p. illus. 23cm. 63-9417 5.95
1. Romanticism in art. 2. Art—Hist. I. Title.

ROSENBLUM, Robert. 759.05
Modern painting and the northern romantic tradition : Friedrich to Rothko / Robert Rosenblum. 1st. U.S. ed. New York : Harper & Row, c1975. 240 p. : ill. ; 26 cm. (Icon editions) Includes bibliographical references and index. [ND192.R6R67 1975] 74-6579 ISBN 0-06-438450-0 : 17.50.
1. Romanticism in art. 2. Painting, Modern—19th century. 3. Painting, Modern—20th century. I. Title. BIP

SCHLENOFF, Norman. 759.05
Romanticism and realism. New York, McGraw-Hill [1965] 47 p. illus. and 24 col. slides. 2 x 2 in. (in pocket) 25 cm. (Color slide program of the world's art) [ND547.S35] 65-21592
1. Romanticism in art. 2. Realism in art. 3. Paintings, French. 4. Paintings. 5. Lantern slides. I. Title. II. Series. BIP

SUTHERLAND, Donald, 1915- 701.1
On, romanticism. New York, New York University Press, 1971. ix, 449 p. illus. 24 cm. [NX600.R6S9] 78-145514 ISBN 0-8147-7753-8
1. Romanticism in art. I. Title. BIP

Romanticism in art—England—Addresses, essays, lectures.

IMAGES of Romanticism 700'.9'034
: verbal and visual affinities / edtied by Karl Kroeber and William Walling. New Haven : Yale University Press, 1978. p. cm. Includes index. [NX543.I52] 78-6151 ISBN 0-300-02209-3 : 18.95
1. Romanticism in art—England—Addresses, essays, lectures. 2. Ut pictura poesis (Aesthetics)—Addresses, essays, lectures. 3. Arts, Modern—19th century—England—Addresses, essays, lectures. I. Kroeber, Karl, 1926- II. Walling, William.

Rome—Antiquities.

BLAKE, Marion Elizabeth, 1892-1961. 081 s
Roman construction in Italy from Nerva through the Antonines. Edited and completed by Doris Taylor Bishop. Philadelphia, American Philosophical Society, 1973. xix, 328, [44] p. illus. 30 cm. (Memoirs of the American Philosophical Society, v. 96) Bibliography: p. xiii-xix. [Q11.P612 vol. 96] [D667] 721'.0937'6 72-83463 15.00
1. Rome—Antiquities. 2. Architecture, Roman. 3. Engineering—Rome. I. Bishop, Doris Taylor, ed. II. Title. III. Series: American Philosophical Society, Philadelphia. Memoirs, v. 96. BIP

Rome—Churches.

SHARP, Mary, 1903- 726.5'09'45632
A guide to the churches of Rome. Philadelphia, Chilton Books [1966] xi, 260 p. illus., maps. 23 cm. "A project of Dimension Books." Bibliography: p. 260. [DG816.3.S5] 66-22875
1. Rome—Churches. I. Title. II. Title: The churches of Rome.

Rome (City) Ara Pacis Augustae.

SIMON, Erika. 913.37'6
Ara Pacis Augustae. Greenwich, Conn., New York Graphic Society [1968] 32 p. 32 plates. 23 cm. Bibliography: p. 31-32. [NA323.S5] 68-25742 6.50
1. Rome (City) Ara Pacis Augustae. I. Title.

Rome (City)—Bridges—Ponte San Angelo.

WEIL, Mark S. 730'.945'632
The history and decoration of the Ponte S. Angelo [by] Mark S. Weil. University Park, Pennsylvania State University Press [1974] 160 p. illus. 23 x 29 cm. Bibliography: p. 155-157. [NB620.W44] 72-163216 ISBN 0-271-01101-7 24.50
1. Rome (City)—Bridges—Ponte San Angelo. 2. Sculpture, Baroque—Rome (City) I. Title. BIP

Rome (City)—Churches.

MALE, Emile 726.582
The early churches of Rome. Translated [From the French] by David Buxton. Chicago, Quadrangle Books, 1960[ ] 253p. (bibl. footnotes) illus. 29cm. 60-7082 2.50
1. Rome (City)—Churches. I. Title.

SHARP, Mary, 1903- 726'.5'0945632
A guide to the churches of Rome. Philadelphia, Chilton Books [1966] xi, 260 p. illus., maps. 23 cm. "A project of Dimension Books." London ed. (Evelyn) has title: A traveller's guide to the churches of Rome. Bibliography: p. 260. [DG816.3.S5 1966] 66-22875
1. Rome (City)—Churches. I. Title. II. Title: The churches of Rome.

Rome (City). Colonna Trajana.

ROSSI, Lino. 729'.32
Trajan's column and the Dacian wars. English translation rev. by J. M. C. Toynbee. Ithaca, N.Y., Cornell University Press [1971] 240 p. illus. 23 cm. (Aspects of Greek and Roman life) Bibliography: p. 231-233. [DG59.D3R68] 70-127778 ISBN 0-8014-0594-7 10.00
1. Rome (City). Colonna Trajana. 2. Dacia—History. 3. Rome—Army. I. Title. II. Series. BIP

Rome (City)—Description—Views.

HIND, Arthur Mayger, 760'.0924
1880-1957.
Giovanni Battista Piranesi; a critical study, with a list of his published works and detailed catalogues of the prisons and the views of Rome. New York, Da Capo Press [1967, c1922] xi, 95 p. illus., facsim., port. 26 cm. (Da Capo Press series in graphic art, v. 7) Bibliography: p. [vii]-viii. [NE662.P5H5] 68-16238
1. Piranesi, Giovanni Battista, 1728-1778. 2. Rome (City)—Descr.—Views. I. Title.

INGRES, Jean Auguste 741.9'44
Dominique, 1780-1867.
Ingres in Rome: a loan exhibition from the Musee Ingres, Montauban and American collections. Introd. and catalogue by Hans Naef. Circulated by the International Exhibitions Foundation, 1971. [Meriden, Conn., Printed for the International Exhibitions Foundation by the Meriden Gravure Co., 1971] xiv, 138 p. illus. 22 x 29 cm. "Participating museums: National Gallery of Art, Washington, D.C. [and others]" Based on Naef's Rome vue par Ingres. Bibliography: p. 133-135. [NC248.I5N3] 70-148356
1. Rome (City)—Description—Views. I. Naef, Hans, 1920- II. Musee Ingres. III. International Exhibitions Foundation. IV. United States. National Gallery of Art. V. Title.

SASEK, Miroslav. 914.5632
This is Rome. New York, Macmillan, c1960. 60 p. illus. 32 cm. [ND1946.S2A58] 60-2678
1. Rome (City)—Description—Views. I. Title. BIP

Rome (City)—Fountains.

MORTON, Henry Canova 731.722
Vollam, 1892-
The fountains of Rome [by] H. V. Morton. With 49 color photos. by Mario Carrieri and other illus. New York, Macmillan [1966] 302 p. illus. (part col.) facsims., maps, ports. 26 cm. "A Giniger book." London ed. (Joseph) has title: The waters of Rome. Bibliography: p. 293. [NA9415.R7M6] 66-21983
1. Rome (City)—Fountains. I. Title.

MORTON, Henry Canova 731.722
Vollam, 1892-
The waters of Rome [by] H. V. Morton; with 49 colour photographs by Mario Carrieri. London, Connoisseur; Joseph, 1966. 302 p. col. front., illus. (incl. 46 col.) maps, facsim. 26 cm. (B 66-18917) American ed. (New York, Macmillan) has title: The fountains of Rome. Bibliography: p. 263. [NA9415.R7M6] 66-77121
1. Rome (City) — Fountains. I. Carrieri, Mario, 1932- illus. II. Title.

Rome (City) in art.

COLUMBIA 769'.4'36094563207401471
University. Libraries. Avery Architectural Library.
Catalogue of the Earl of Crawford's "Speculum Romanae magnificentiae," now in the Avery Architectural Library / by Lawrence R. McGinniss, with the assi[s]tance of Herbert Mitchell. New York : The Library, Columbia University, c1976. v, 75 p. ; 23 cm. Includes bibliographical references and index. [NE954.3.I8C64 1976] 77-362421
1. Lafrery, Antoine, 1512-1577. Speculum Romanae magnificentiae. 2. Crawford, David Alexander Robert Lindsay, 28th earl of, 1900- —Library. 3. Columbia University. Libraries. Avery Architectural Library. 4. Rome (City) in art. 5. Prints—Catalogs. I. McGinniss, Lawrence R. II. Mitchell, Herbert. III. Crawford, David Alexander Robert Lindsay, 28th earl of, 1900- IV. Title: Catalogue of the Earl of Crawford's "Speculum Romanae magnificentiae" ... V. Title: Speculum Romanae magnificentiae.

LEVIT, Herschel. 769'.92'4
Views of Rome, then and now / 41 etchings by Giovanni Battista Piranesi ; corresponding photographs and text by Herschel Levit. New York : Dover Publications, 1976. xxvi, [83] p. : ill. ; 38 cm. Bibliography: p. viii. [NE2052.5.P5L57 1976] 76-3237 ISBN 0-486-23339-1 : 6.00
1. Piranesi, Giovanni Battista, 1720-1778. 2. Rome (City) in art. 3. Rome (City)—Description—Views. I. Piranesi, Giovanni Battista, 1720-1778. II. Title. BIP

MICHIGAN. 704.94'9'9145632
University. Graduate Seminar in Museum Practice.
Rome through the eyes of the eighteenth century. Ann Arbor, Mich., University of Michigan Museum of Art [1972] v, 16 p. illus. 22 x 29 cm. Catalogue of an exhibition held at the University of Michigan Museum of Art, Dec. 5, 1971-Jan. 16, 1972; the 10th in a series organized by the Graduate Seminar in Museum Practice. Bibliography: p. iv. [N8214.5.I8M52] 73-170966
1. Rome (City) in art. 2. Art, Modern—17th-18th centuries—Exhibitions. I. Michigan. University. Museum of Art. II. Title.

PIRANESI, Giovanni 760'.092'4
Battista, 1720-1778.
Piranesi : etchings and drawings / selected and with an introd. by Roseline Bacou. Boston : New York Graphic Society, 1975. 200 p. : chiefly ill. ; 28 x 33 cm. Translation of Piranese. Includes index. Bibliography: p. 198. [NE2052.5.P5B3213 1975] 73-9113 ISBN 0-8212-0577-3 : 19.95
1. Piranesi, Giovanni Battista, 1720-1778. 2. Rome (City) in art. I. Bacou, Roseline. BIP

PIRANESI, Giovanni 769'.92'4
Battista, 1720-1778.
Piranesi; [exhibition and catalogue]. Northampton, Mass., Smith College Museum of Art, 1961. 109 p., 57 plates. 16 x 23 cm. [NE2052.5.P5S54] 74-173321
1. Piranesi, Giovanni Battista, 1720-1778. 2. Rome (City) in art. I. Smith College. Museum of Art.

Rome (City). Ospedale di Santo Spirito—History.

HOWE, Eunice 751.7'3'09457405632
D.
The Hospital of Santo Spirito and Pope Sixtus IV / by Eunice D. Howe. New York : Garland Pub., [1978] p. cm. (Outstanding dissertations in the fine arts) Vita. Originally presented as the author's thesis, Johns Hopkins University, 1977. Bibliography: p. [RA989.I9R633 1978] 77-94698 ISBN 0-8240-3230-6 : lib.bdg. : 35.00
1. Rome (City). Ospedale di Santo Spirito—History. 2. Sixtus IV, Pope, 1414-1484—Portraits. 3. Mural painting and decoration, Renaissance—Italy—Rome. 4. Mural painting and decoration, Italian—Italy—Rome. 5. Hospitals—Italy—Design and construction—History. I. Title. II. Series. BIP

Rome (City)—Palaces.

COFFIN, David R. 945'.632'05
The villa in the life of Renaissance Rome / by David R. Coffin. Princeton, N.J. : Princeton University Press, c1978. p. cm. (Princeton monographs in art and archaeology ; 43) Includes index. Bibliography: p. [NA7755.C6] 78-9049 ISBN 0-691-03942-9 : 45.00
1. Rome (City)—Palaces. 2. Architecture, Renaissance—Italy—Rome (City) 3. Palaces—Italy—Rome region. 4. Architecture, Renaissance—Italy—Rome region. 5. Rome (City)—Social life and customs. 6. Rome region, Italy—Social life and customs. I. Title. II. Series. BIP

Rome (City). Pantheon.

MACDONALD, 726'.1'2070945632
William Lloyd.
The Pantheon : design, meaning, and progeny / William L. MacDonald. London : A. Lane, 1976. 160 p. : ill. ; 25 cm. Includes bibliographical references and index. [NA323.M3] 76-373004 ISBN 0-7139-0984-6 : £10.00
1. Rome (City). Pantheon. 2. Classicism in architecture. 3. Neoclassicism (Architecture) I. Title.

Rome (City)—Plazas—Piazza di San Pietro.

KITAO, Timothy K. 720'.92'4
Circle and oval in the Square of Saint Peter's : Bernini's art of planning / Timothy K. Kitao. New York : Published by New York University Press for the College Art Association of America, 1974. xiv, 156 p., [16] leaves of plates : ill. ; 29 cm. (Monographs on archaeology and the fine arts ; 29) A revision of the author's thesis, Harvard, 1966. Includes index. Bibliography: p. 139-148. [NA1123.B28K57 1974] 73-14849 ISBN 0-8147-4557-1
1. Bernini, Giovanni Lorenzo, 1598-1680. 2. Rome (City)—Plazas—Piazza di San Pietro. I. Title. II. Series. BIP

Rome (City)—Sepulchral monuments.

DE TOLNAY, Charles, 1899- 731.76
The tomb of Julius II. Princeton, Princeton University Press, 1954. viii, 200p. plates. 31cm. (His Michelangelo, 4) Bibliography: p. 163-166. [NB623.B9D4] 58-6582
1. Buonarrott, Michel Angelo, 1475-1564. 2. Julius II, Pope, 1443-1513. 3. Rome (City)—Sepulchral monuments. I. Title.

Rome (City). Tempietto.

MURRAY, Peter. 726'.5'0924
Bramante's Tempietto. [Newcastle upon Tyne] University of Newcastle upon Tyne, 1972. 21 p. illus. 24 cm. (Charlton lecture, 53) Includes bibliographical references. [NA1123.B7M82] 73-161098
1. Bramante, Donato, 1444?-1514. 2. Rome (City). Tempietto. I. Title. II. Series.

Rome (City). Villa Medici.

ANDRES, Glenn M. 945'.632
The Villa Medici in Rome / Glenn M. Andres. New York : Garland, 1976. 2 v. : ill. ; 21 cm. (Outstanding dissertations in the fine arts) Originally presented as the author's thesis, Princeton, 1970. Bibliography: v. 2, p. 385-410. [NA7595.M5A52 1976] 75-23778 ISBN 0-8240-1975-X lib.bdg. : 80.00
1. Rome (City). Villa Medici. I. Title. II. Series. BIP

Rome—Hist.—Constantine I, the Great, 306-337—Chronology.

BRUUN, Patrick 737.4937
Studies in Constantinian chronology. New York, Amer. Numismatic Soc., 1961. xi, 116, viiip. illus., map. (Numismatic notes and monographs, no. 146) Bibl. 62-2163 5.00 pap.,
1. Rome—Hist.—Constantine I, the Great, 306-337—Chronology. 2. Numismatics—Rome. I. Title. II. Series.

Rome, N.Y.—Historic houses, etc.

WAITE, Diana S. 917.3'03 s
History of a nineteenth century urban complex on the site of Fort Stanwix, Rome, New York, by Diana Steck Waite. [Albany] New York State Historic Trust, 1972. iii, 73 p. illus. 29 cm. (Selections from the Historic American Buildings Survey, v. 15) On spine: An urban complex on the site of Fort Stanwix. Bibliography: p. 71-73. [NA705.A25 no. 15] [NA735] 917.47'62 73-621326
1. Rome, N.Y.—Historic houses, etc. 2. Architecture, Modern—19th century—Rome, N.Y. 3. Architecture—Details. I. New York State Historic Trust. II. Title. III. Title: An urban complex on the site of Fort Stanwix. IV. Series: Historic American Buildings Survey. Selections, v. 15.

Rome—Pantheon.

*MACDONALD, William L. 726.'1'207
The Pantheon : design, meaning, and progeny. / William L. MacDonald. Cambridge, Mass. : Harvard University Press, c1976. 160 p. : ill., plans ; 24 cm. Includes index. Bibliography: p. 135-146. [NA323] 75-27900 ISBN 0-674-65345-9 : 12.50
1. Rome—Pantheon. I. Title. BIP

Rome—Religion.

STRONG, Eugenie 709'.37
(Sellers)
Apotheosis and after life; three lectures on certain phases of art and religion in the Roman Empire, by Mrs. Arthur Strong. Freeport, N.Y., Books for Libraries Press [1969] xx, 293 p. illus. 23 cm. (Select bibliographies reprint series) Reprint of the 1915 ed. Includes bibliographical references. [DG121.S7 1969] 78-103668 ISBN 8-369-51689-
1. Rome—Religion. 2. Art, Roman. I. Title.

Rome—Social life and customs—Juvenile literature.

RUTLAND, Jonathan. 937
See inside a Roman town / [author, Jonathan Rutland ; ill., Angus McBride, Bernard Robinson, Bill Stallion]. New York : Warwick Press, 1978, c1977. 29 p. : ill. ; 29 cm. (See inside) Includes index.

Roses in art.

DU TILLEUX, Jean, 1903- 738.2'092'4
Roses in porcelain. [Shreveport, La., R. W. Norton Art Foundation, 1973] 16 p. col. illus. 28 cm. Catalog of an exhibition held June 3 to July 15, 1973 at the R. W. Norton Art Gallery, Shreveport, La. [NK4210.D8N67] 73-81397 ISBN 0-913060-02-X
1. Du Tilleux, Jean, 1903- 2. Roses in art. 3. Porcelain, American. I. Norton (R. W.) Art Gallery. II. Title.

Roseville Pottery Company.

ALEXANDER, Donald E. 738.2'7
Roseville; pottery for collectors [by] Donald E. Alexander. [Richmond, Ind., 1970] 78 p. illus. 19 cm. [NK4210.R58A7] 70-282780
1. Roseville Pottery, inc. I. Title. II. Title: Pottery for collectors.

HUXFORD, Sharon. 738.3'7
The collectors encyclopedia of Roseville pottery / by Sharon and Bob Huxford. 1st ed. Paducah, Ky. : Collector Books, c1976. 184 p. : ill. (some col.) ; 29 cm. Includes index. Bibliography: p. 179-182. [NK4210.R58H88] 76-358474 ISBN 0-89145-015-7 : 17.95
1. Roseville Pottery Company. 2. Roseville Pottery, inc. 3. Pottery, American. I. Huxford, Bob, joint author. II. Title. III. Title: Roseville pottery. BIP

PURVIANCE, Louise. 738.3'7
Roseville art pottery in color, by Louise and Evan Purviance and Norris F. Schneider. Des Moines, Iowa, Wallace-Homestead Book Co. [1970] [50] p. illus. (part col.), ports. 23 cm. [NK4210.R58P86] 71-25177 4.95
1. Roseville Pottery Company. 2. Roseville Pottery, inc. I. Purviance, Evan, joint author. II. Schneider, Norris Franz, 1898- joint author. III. Title.

Ross, Charles, 1937—

ROSS, Charles, 1937- 709'.2'4
The substance of light : sunlight dispersion, the solar burns, point source/star space : selected work of Charles Ross : an exhibition organized by the La Jolla Museum of Contemporary Art, February 6-March 14, 1976. La Jolla, Calif. : The Museum, c1976. 36 p. : ill. (some col.) ; 21 x 25 cm. [N6537.R584L34] 76-3296
1. Ross, Charles, 1937- 2. Light in art. I. La Jolla Museum of Contemporary Art. II. Title.

Rossellino, Bernardo, 1409-1464.

SCHULZ, Anne Markham, 1938- 730'.92'4
The sculpture of Bernardo Rossellino and his workshop / Anne Markham Schulz. Princeton, N.J. : Princeton University Press, [1976] c1975. p. cm. Originally presented as the author's thesis, New York University, 1968. [NB623.R83S38 1976] 75-3473 ISBN 0-691-03886-4 : 30.00
1. Rossellino, Bernardo, 1409-1464. I. Title.

Rossetti, Dante Gabriel, 1828-1882.

ANGELI, Helen (Rossetti) 759.2 B
Dante Gabriel Rossetti: his friends and enemies. New York, B. Blom, 1972. xx, 291 p. ports. 21 cm. Reprint of the 1949 ed. [PR5246.A8 1972] 76-184272
1. Rossetti, Dante Gabriel, 1828-1882.

AZECHI, Umetaro, 1902- 762.20952
Japanese woodblock prints: their techniques and appreciation. Tokyo, Toto Shuppan Co.; Rutland, vt., Japan Publications Trading Co. [1963] 104 p. illus. (part col.) mounted samples. 31 cm. Translated from the Japanese ms. by Charles A. Pomeroy. [NE1310.A913] 63-6366
1. Color prints, Japanese. 2. Wood-engraving—Technique. I. Title.

BIRMINGHAM Museums and Art Gallery. 741.9'42
Pre-Raphaelite drawings : Dante Gabriel Rossetti / Andrea Rose. Chicago : University of Chicago Press, 1977. 72 p. ; 23 cm. & microfiche (3 sheets : all ill. ; 11 x 15 cm.) in pocket. (A University of Chicago Press text-fiche) At head of title: Birmingham Museums and Art Gallery. [NC242.R646B57 1977] 77-24058 ISBN 0-226-68840-2 : 23.00
1. Rossetti, Dante Gabriel, 1828-1882. 2. Artists' preparatory studies—Great Britain. 3. Preraphaelitism—Great Britain. I. Rose, Andrea. II. Title.

CAINE, Hall, Sir, 1858-1931. 759.2 B
Recollections of Rossetti. New York, Haskell House Publishers, 1973. ix, 259 p. 23 cm. Reprint of the 1928 ed. [PR5246.C4 1973] 72-6285 ISBN 0-8383-1634-4 11.95
1. Rossetti, Dante Gabriel, 1828-1882. I. Title. BIP

CARY, Elisabeth Luther, 1867-1936. 760'.092'4
The Rossettis : Dante Gabriel and Christina / by Elisabeth Luther Cary. New York : Haskell House, 1974. iv, 310 p. : port. ; 22 cm. Reprint of the 1900 ed. published by Putnam, New York. Includes index. "List of the more important writings of Dante Gabriel Rossetti": p. 277-281. [NX547.6.R67C37 1974] 74-30190 ISBN 0-8383-1943-2 : 17.95
1. Rossetti, Dante Gabriel, 1828-1882. 2. Rossetti, Christina Georgina, 1830-1894. 3. Preraphaelitism—England. I. Title. BIP

CARY, Elisabeth Luther, 1867-1936. 759.2
The Rossettis: Dante Gabriel and Christina. [Folcroft, Pa.] Folcroft Library Editions, 1973 [c1900] p. Reprint of the ed. published by Putnam, New York. "Christian Rossetti's poems": p. "List of the more important writings of Dante Gabriel Rossetti": p. [ND497.R8C3 1973] 73-12547 35.00
1. Rossetti, Dante Gabriel, 1828-1882. 2. Rossetti, Christina Georgina, 1830-1894. 3. Preraphaelitism. I. Title.

DUNN, Henry Treffry, 1838-1899. 759.2
Recollections of Dante Gabriel Rossetti and his circle (Cheyne Walk life). Edited and annotated by the late Gale Pedrick. With a prefatory note by William Michael Rossetti. London, E. Mathews, 1904. [New York, AMS Press, 1971] 96 p. illus., port. 19 cm. Includes bibliographical references. [ND497.R8D8 1971] 73-129379 ISBN 0-404-02222-7
1. Rossetti, Dante Gabriel, 1828-1882. 2. Preraphaelitism. I. Title. BIP

FORD, Ford Madox, 1873-1939. 759.2
Rossetti : a critical essay on his art / by Ford Madox Hueffer [i.e. F. M. Ford]. Folcroft, Pa. : Folcroft Library Editions, 1976. p. cm. Reprint of the 1914 ed. published by Duckworth, London. [ND497.R8F6 1976] 76-40417 ISBN 0-8414-4939-2 lib. bdg. : 20.00
1. Rossetti, Dante Gabriel, 1828-1882. BIP

GRAY, Nicolete. 759.2
Rossetti, Dante, and ourselves. [Folcroft, Pa.] Folcroft Library Editions, 1974. p. cm. Reprint of the 1947 ed. published by Faber and Faber, London. [ND497.R8G7 1974b] 74-11358 10.75
1. Rossetti, Dante Gabriel, 1828-1882. 2. Dante Alighieri, 1265-1321. I. Title. BIP

GRAY, Nicolete, 1911- 759.2
Rossetti, Dante, and ourselves. New York, Haskell House [1974] p. Reprint of the 1947 ed. published by Faber and Faber, London. [ND497.R8G7 1974] 74-6406 ISBN 0-8383-1917-3 10.95 (lib. bdg.)
1. Rossetti, Dante Gabriel, 1828-1882. 2. Dante Alighieri, 1265-1321. I. Title.

GRIEVE, Alastair Ian. 759.2
The art of Dante Gabriel Rossetti: the Pre-Raphaelite period, 1848-50 [by] A. I. Grieve. Hingham, Real World Publications [1973] [4], 31 p. illus., ports. 30 cm. Includes bibliographical references. [ND497.R8G73] 73-164125 ISBN 0-903822-00-8 £1.10
1. Rossetti, Dante Gabriel, 1828-1882. 2. Preraphaelitism—England. I. Title.

KANSAS. University. Museum of Art. 759.2
Dante Gabriel Rossetti and his circle; a loan exhibition of paintings, drawings, and decorative objects by the pre-Raphaelites and their friends, the University of Kansas Museum of Art, November 4 to December 15, 1958. [Lawrence] 1958. unpaged. illus. 23cm. [ND497.R8K2] 59-62664
1. Rossetti, Dante Gabriel, 1828-1882. I. Title.

KNIGHT, Joseph, 1829-1907. 759.2 B
Life of Dante Gabriel Rossetti. Port Washington, N.Y., Kennikat Press [1972] 186, xix p. 21 cm. Reprint of the 1887 ed. "Bibliography, and catalogue of pictures, by John P. Anderson": p. [i]-xix. [PR5246.K5 1972] 73-160765 ISBN 0-8046-1586-1
1. Rossetti, Dante Gabriel, 1828-1882. I. Title. BIP

KNIGHT, Joseph, 1829-1907. 759.2 B
Life of Dante Gabriel Rossetti. Freeport, N.Y., Books for Libraries Press [1972] 186, xix p. 23 cm. Reprint of the 1887 ed., which was issued in series: Great writers. "Bibliography and catalogue of pictures, by John P. Anderson": p. [i]-xix. [PR5246.K5 1972b] 75-38359 ISBN 0-8369-6776-3
1. Rossetti, Dante Gabriel, 1828-1882. I. Title.

KNIGHT, Joseph, 1829-1907. 759.2 B
Life of Dante Gabriel Rossetti. [Folcroft, Pa.] Folcroft Library Editions, 1973. 186, xix p. 20 cm. Reprint of the 1887 ed. published by W. Scott, London, in series: Great writers. "Bibliography and catalogue of pictures, by J. P. Anderson" p.: [i]-xix. [PR5246.K5 1973] 73-12645 ISBN 0-8414-5454-X (lib. bdg.)
1. Rossetti, Dante Gabriel, 1828-1882. I. Title.

MARILLIER, Henry Currie, 1865-1951. 759.2
Rossetti. [Folcroft, Pa.] Folcroft Library Editions, 1973. 112 p. illus. 23 cm. Reprint of the 1906 ed. published by G. Bell, London, in series: Bell's miniature series of painters. [ND497.R8M34 1973] 73-15949 ISBN 0-8414-6066-3 (lib. bdg.)
1. Rossetti, Dante Gabriel, 1828-1882. 2. Preraphaelitism—Great Britain. I. Series: Bell's miniature series of painters.

MEGROZ, Rodolphe Louis, 1891- 759.2 B
Dante Gabriel Rossetti; painter poet of heaven in earth, by R. L. Megroz. New York, Haskell House Publishers, 1971. xi, 339 p. illus. 23 cm. "First published 1929." Bibliography: p. 319-321. [PR5246.M4 1971] 74-173851 ISBN 0-8383-1336-1
1. Rossetti, Dante Gabriel, 1828-1882.

MEGROZ, Rodolphe Louis, 1891- 759.2
Dante Gabriel Rossetti, painter poet of heaven in earth, by R. L. Megroz. London, Faber & Gwyer. St. Clair Shores, Mich., Scholarly Press, 1972. 339 p. 21 cm. Reprint of the 1928 ed. Bibliography: p. 319-321. [PR5246.M4 1972] 75-145173 ISBN 0-403-01101-9
1. Rossetti, Dante Gabriel, 1828-1882. BIP

NICOLL, John. 759.2 B
Dante Gabriel Rossetti / John Nicoll. 1st American ed. New York : Macmillan, 1976, c1975. 175 p. : ill. (some col.) ; 28 cm. Includes bibliographical references and index. [ND497.R8N52 1976] 75-23267 ISBN 0-02-589340-8 : 22.50
1. Rossetti, Dante Gabriel, 1828-1882. 2. Painters—Great Britain—Biography. I. Rossetti, Dante Gabriel, 1828-1882.

ROSSETTI, Dante Gabriel, 1828-1882. 760'.92'4
Dante Gabriel Rossetti 1828-1882. Newcastle festival, 1971; Laing Art Gallery, Newcastle Upon Tyne, 1st October-6th November, 1971. Newcastle upon Tyne, [R. Ward] 1971. 41 p. illus. 27 cm. Introduction by Alastair Grieve. [N6797.R58G74] 72-198444
1. Rossetti, Dante Gabriel, 1828-1882. I. Grieve, Alastair Ian. II. Laing Art Gallery, Newcastle-upon-Tyne.

ROSSETTI, Dante Gabriel, 1828-1882. 759.2 B
Dante Gabriel Rossetti: his family-letters. With a memoir by William Michael Rossetti. [1st AMS ed.] New York, AMS Press [1970] 2 v. facsim., ports. 23 cm. Reprint of the 1895 ed. [PR5246.A43 1970] 70-130231 ISBN 0-404-05434-X
1. Rossetti, Dante Gabriel, 1828-1882. 2. Rossetti family. 3. Artists—Correspondence, reminiscences, etc. I. Rossetti, William Michael, 1829-1919, ed.

ROSSETTI, Dante Gabriel, 1828-1882. 759.2 B
The Rossetti-Leyland letters : the correspondence of an artist and his patron / edited by Francis L. Fennell, Jr. Athens : Ohio University Press, c1978. xxxiv, 111 p. : ports. ; 24 cm. Includes bibliographical references and index. [ND497.R8A3 1978] 75-14552 ISBN 0-8214-0207-2 : 11.00
1. Rossetti, Dante Gabriel, 1828-1882. 2. Painters—England—Correspondence. I. Leyland, Frederick Richard, 1831-1892, joint author. II. Fennell, Francis L. III. Title. BIP

ROSSETTI, William Michael, 1829-1919. 759.2
Dante Gabriel Rossetti as designer and writer. Notes by William Michael Rossetti, including a prose paraphrase of The house of life. London, New York, Cassell, 1889. [New York, AMS Press, 1970] xv, 302 p. port. 19 cm. [ND497.R8R8 1970] 73-144678 ISBN 0-404-05429-3
1. Rossetti, Dante Gabriel, 1828-1882. I. Rossetti, Dante Gabriel, 1828-1882. The house of life. II. Rossetti, William Michael, 1829-1919. The house of life. 1970. III. Title. BIP

ROSSETTI, William Michael, 1829-1919, ed. 759.2
Preraphaelite diaries and letters, edited by William Michael Rossetti. London, Hurst and Blackett, 1900. [New York, AMS Press, 1974] 328 p. illus. 23 cm. Contents.Contents.—Some early correspondence of Dante Gabriel Rossetti, 1835-54.—Madox Brown's diary, etc., 1844-56.—The P.R.B. journal kept by W. M. Rossetti, 1849-53. Includes bibliographical references. [ND467.5.P7R59 1974] 70-148293 ISBN 0-404-08898-8
1. Rossetti, Dante Gabriel, 1828-1882. 2. Brown, Ford Madox. 3. Preraphaelitism—England. I. Title.

RUTTER, Frank Vane Phipson, 1876-1937. 759.2
Dante Gabriel Rossetti : painter & man of letters / by Frank Rutter. New York : AMS Press, [1975] p. cm. Reprint of the 1908 ed. published by G. Richards, London. Includes index. [NX547.6.R67R87 1975] 78-148295 ISBN 0-404-05468-4 : 9.50
1. Rossetti, Dante Gabriel, 1828-1882.

SHARP, William, 1855-1905. 759.2
Dante Gabriel Rossetti; a record and a study. New York, AMS Press [1970] viii, 432 p. front. 23 cm. Reprint of the 1882 ed. [ND497.R8S5 1970] 71-115006
1. Rossetti, Dante Gabriel, 1828-1882. BIP

STEPHENS, Frederic George, 1828-1907. 759.2
Dante Gabriel Rossetti. [Folcroft, Pa.] Folcroft Library Editions, 1974. 96 p. illus. 32 cm. Reprint of the 1897 ed. published by Seeley, London, which was issued as no. 5 of The Portfolio; monographs on artistic subjects. [ND497.R8S8 1974] 74-1476 ISBN 0-8414-7736-1 (lib. bdg.)
1. Rossetti, Dante Gabriel, 1828-1882. I. Series: The Portfolio; monographs on artistic subjects, no. 5.

SURTEES, Virginia. 760'.0924
The paintings and drawings of Dante Gabriel Rossetti (1828-1882): a catalogue raisonn e. Oxford, Clarendon Press, 1971. 2 v. (xvi, 267) p., 225 plates, illus. 30 cm. Contents.Contents.—[1] Text.—[2] Plates. [N6797.R58S9] 70-25419 ISBN 0-19-817174-9 £20.00
1. Rossetti, Dante Gabriel, 1828-1882. I. Title. BIP

WAUGH, Evelyn, 1903-1966. 759.2
Rossetti, his life and works. [Folcroft, Pa.] Folcroft Library Editions, 1973. 232 p. illus. 23 cm. Reprint of the 1928 ed.

SUBJECT INDEX ROUAULT, GEORGES, 1871-1958.

published by Duckworth, London. [ND497.R8W3 1973] 72-6678 ISBN 0-8414-0141-1 15.00
1. Rossetti, Dante Gabriel, 1828-1882.

WOOD, Esther. 700'.942
Dante Rossetti and the Pre-Raphaelite movement. New York, Cooper Square Publishers, 1973. xii, 323 p. illus. 21 cm. Reprint of the 1894 ed. published by S. Low, Marston, London. Includes bibliographical references. [NX543.W66 1973] 72-91205 ISBN 0-8154-0445-X 9.50
1. Rossetti, Dante Gabriel, 1828-1882. 2. Preraphaelitism—England. I. Title.

Rossetti, Dante Gabriel, 1828-1882—Correspondence.

ROSSETTI, Dante Gabriel, 1828-1882. 759.2 B
Dante Gabriel Rossetti and Jane Morris : their correspondence / edited with an introd. by John Bryson, in association with Janet Camp Troxell. Oxford [Eng.] : Clarendon Press, 1976. xx, 219 p. ; ill. ; 25 cm. Includes index. [PR5246.A45] 76-378435 ISBN 0-19-812464-3 : 21.00
1. Rossetti, Dante Gabriel, 1828-1882—Correspondence. 2. Morris, Jane Burden. 3. Poets, English—19th century—Correspondence. I. Morris, Jane Burden.
distributed by Oxford U Pr.

ROSSETTI, William Michael, 1829-1919, comp. 759.2 B
Rossetti papers 1862 to 1870; acompilation by William Michael Rossetti New York, AMS Press [1970] xxiii, 559 p. 23 cm. Reprint of the 1903 ed. Papers and correspondence of D. G., C. G. and W. M. Rossetti. [PR5236.R9A3 1970] 76-130238
I. Rossetti, Dante Gabriel, 1828-1882. II. Rossetti, Christina Georgina, 1830-1894. BIP

Rossetti family.

ROSSETTI, William Michael, 1829-1919. 700'.924 B
Some reminiscences of William Michael Rossetti. New York, AMS Press [1970] 2 v. (xviii, 578 p.) illus., facsims., ports. 23 cm. Reprint of the 1906 ed. [PR5249.R2A8 1970] 75-132386 ISBN 0-404-05440-4
I. Title.

WALLER, Ross Douglas. 700'.92'2 B
The Rossetti family, 1824-1854, by R.D. Waller [Folcroft, Pa] Folcroft Library Editions, 1973. p. Reprint of the 1932 ed. published by the University of Manchester Press, Manchester, which was issued as no. 217 of Publications of the University of Manchester and as no. 21 of Publications of the University of Manchester English series. Bibliography: p. [PR5236.R9W3 1973] 73-15815 ISBN 0-8414-9477-0 (lib. bdg.)
1. Rossetti family. 2. Rossetti, Gabriele Pasquale Giuseppe, 1783-1854. I. Series: Victoria University of Manchester. Publications, no. 217. II. Series: Victoria University of Manchester. Publications. English series, no. 21. BIP

WEINTRAUB, Stanley, 1929- 700'.92'2 B
Four Rossettis : a Victorian biography / Stanley Weintraub. New York : Weybright and Talley, c1976. p. cm. Includes bibliographical references and index. [PR5236.R9W4] 76-21341 ISBN 0-679-40136-9 : 15.00
1. Rossetti family. I. Title. BIP

Rossetti, William Michael, 1829-1919.

ROSSETTI, William Michael, 1829-1919. 700'.92'4 B
The diary of W. M. Rossetti 1870-1873 / edited with an introd. and notes by Odette Bornand. Oxford [Eng.] : Clarendon Press, 1978 xxiii, 302 p., [1] leaf of plates : port. ; 22 cm. Includes bibliographical references and index. [PR5249.R2A799 1977] 78-312738 ISBN 0-19-812458-9 : 26.50
1. Rossetti, William Michael, 1829-1919. 2. Rossetti Family. 3. Critics—England—Biography. 4. Art critics—England—Biography. 5. Poets, English—19th century—Biography. I. Bornand, Odette. II. Title.
Distributed by Oxford University Press, NY BIP

ROSSETTI, William Michael, 1829-1919. 700'.92'4 B
The P.R.B. journal : William Michael Rossetti's diary of the Pre-Raphaelite brotherhood, 1849-1853, together with other Pre-Raphaelite documents / edited from the original manuscript with an introd. and notes by William E. Fredeman. Oxford [Eng.] : Clarendon Press, 1975. xxvii, 282 p. : ill. ; 22 cm. Includes indexes. Bibliography: p. [251]-255. [ND467.5.P7R58 1975] 75-316365 ISBN 0-19-812505-4 : 32.00
1. Rossetti, William Michael, 1829-1919. 2. Preraphaelitism—England. I. Fredeman, William Evan, 1928- II. Title.
Distributed by Oxford University Press, New York. BIP

Rosso, Medardo, 1858-1928.

BARR, Margaret Scolari. 730'.92'4
Medardo Rosso. Reprint ed. [New York] Published for the Museum of Modern Art by Arno Press, 1972 [c1963] 91 p. illus. 28 cm. Bibliography: p. 86-88. [NB623.R8B3 1972] 73-169298 ISBN 0-405-01558-5
1. Rosso, Medardo, 1858-1928.

BARR, Margaret Scolari. 730.945
Medardo Rosso. New York, Museum of Modern Art; distributed by Doubleday, Garden City [c1963] 91 p. illus. (1 col.) ports., facsims. 28 cm. Errata slip inserted. Bibliography: p. 86-88. [NB623.R8B3] 63-19795
1. Rosso, Medardo, 1858-1928. I. Title. BIP

Roszak, Theodore.

WALKER Art Center, Minneapolis. 735.73 927.3
Theodore Roszak [by] H. H. Arnason. Minneapolis, Walker Art Center in collaboration with the Whitney Museum of American Art, New York [1956] 54 p. illus. (part col.) port. 28 cm. "Catalogue of the exhibition": p. 48-50. Bibliography: p. 54. [N6537.R6W3] 57-925
1. Roszak, Theodore. 2. Art, American — Exhibitions. I. Arnason, H. H. II. Title.

Roth, Walter Edmund, 1861?-1933—Library.

UNIVERSITY of Guyana. Library. 016.91'0039'69881
A catalogue of the Roth collection in the University of Guyana Library. Compiled by Carol Collins. Georgetown, 1971. ii, 32 l. 28 cm. (University of Guyana Library series, no. 4) "Select bibliography of the published works of W. E. Roth": leaf ii. [Z1209.U584 1971] 74-160789
1. Roth, Walter Edmund, 1861?-1933—Library. 2. Indians—Bibliography—Catalogs. 3. Australian aborigines—Bibliography—Catalogs. I. Title. II. Series: University of Guyana. Library. University of Guyana Library series, no. 4.

Rothenstein, John Knewstub Maurice, Sir 1901-

ROTHENSTEIN, John Kenwstub Maurice Sir 1901- 708 (B)
Brave day, hideous night; autobiography, 1939-1965 [by] John Rothenstein. [1st ed.] New York, Holt, Rinehart and Winston [1967, c1966] xii, 386 p. illus., ports. 22 cm. [N8375.R67A32] 67-14081
I. Title.

ROTHENSTEIN, John Knewstub Maurice, Sir 1901- 708(B)
Brave day, hideous night; autobiography. 1939-1965 [by] John Rothenstein. [1st ed.] New York, Holt [1967,c.1966] xii, 386p. illus., ports. 22cm. [N8375.R67A32 1967] 67-14081 6.95
I. Title.

SICKERT, Walter, 1860-1942. 759.2
Sickert. London, Beaverbrook Newspapers Ltd. [Chester Springs, Pa., Dufour 1966, c.1961] 5p., 36 illus. (pt. mounted col.) 36cm. (British painters ser.; Express art bk.,) [ND497.S48R6] 64-2167 6.95 bds.,
1. Rothenstein, John Knewstub Maurice, Sir 1901- I. Title.

Rothenstein, Michael, 1908—

ROTHENSTEIN, Michael, 1908- 769'.92'4
Suns & moons; eight color woodcuts, with accompanying poems chosen by the artist. Cambridge [Eng.] Rampant Lions Press, 1972. 1 portfolio. 57 cm. Includes 9 separate leaves with t.p. and 8 color woodcuts issued in a box. Limited ed. of 85 signed and numbered copies. No. 55. [NE1300.8.G72R677] 74-159219
1. Rothenstein, Michael, 1908- I. Title.

Rothenstein, William, Sir, 1872-1945.

BRADFORD, Eng. (Yorkshire). Art Gallery and Museum. 759.2
Sir William Rothenstein, 1872-1945; a centenary exhibition, 5 March-9 April 1972. [Bradford, Eng., 1972] [71] p. illus. 25 cm. Bibliography: p. [7] [ND497.R85B7] 72-185542
1. Rothenstein, William, Sir, 1872-1945. I. Rothenstein, William, Sir, 1872-1945.

CARLISLE, Eng Museum and Art Gallery. 708'.28'5
William Rothenstein; a unique collection. Rothstein's purchases for Carlisle 1933-1942. [Carlisle, Eng., 1972?] 32 p. illus. 21 cm. Cover title. Bibliography: p. 32. [N6767.C27] 72-198132
1. Rothenstein, William, Sir, 1872-1945. 2. Art, British—Catalogs. 3. Art, Modern—19th century—Great Britain. 4. Art, Modern—20th century—Great Britain.

ROTHENSTEIN, William, Sir, 1872-1945. 759.2 B
Men and memories : recollections, 1872-1938 / by William Rothenstein ; edited by Mary Lago. Columbia : University of Missouri Press, 1978. 263 p., [5] leaves of plates : ill. ; 23 cm. Includes index. Bibliography: p. [241]-246. [ND497.R85A2 1978] 77-1470 17.00
1. Rothenstein, William, Sir, 1872-1945. 2. Painters—England—Biography. I. Lago, Mary. II. Title. BIP

SPEAIGHT, Robert, 1904- 759.2
William Rothenstein: the portrait of an artist in his time. London, Eyre & Spottiswoode, 1962 xiii. 443p. illus., ports. 23cm. [N6797.R6S66] 64-1286 7.50
1. Rothenstein, William. Sir 1872-1945. I. Title.
Available from Hillary House in New York.

Rotherham, Eng.—Description—Views.

ROTHERHAM as it was / 942.8'23
[compiled by] Robert G. Neville & John Benson. Nelson : Hendon Publishing Co., 1976. 44 p. : chiefly ill., map, ports. ; 21 x 29 cm. [DA690.R78R67] 77-359068 ISBN 0-902907-90-5 : £1.40
1. Rotherham, Eng.—Description—Views. 2. Rotherham, Eng.—Social life and customs—Pictorial works. I. Neville, Robert G. II. Benson, John.

Rothko, Mark, 1903-1970.

NEW York (City). Museum of Modern Art. 759.13
Mark Rothko [by] Peter Selz. [New York] Published for the Museum of Modern Art by Arno Press, 1972. 44 p. illus. 25 cm. (Museum of Modern Art publications in reprint) Reprint of the 1961 ed. Catalogue of the exhibition held Jan. 18-Mar. 12, 1961. Bibliography: p. 40-41. [ND237.R725N4 1972] 76-169316 ISBN 0-405-01574-7
1. Rothko, Mark, 1903- I. Selz, Peter Howard, 1919-

NEW York. Museum of Modern Art 759.13
Mark Rothko [by] Peter Selz. Garden City, N. Y., dist. Doubleday [1961] 44p. illus. (part col.) Catalogue of the exhibition to be held Jan. 18-Mar. 12, 1961. Bibl. 61-7685 2.25 pap.,
1. Rothko, Mark, 1903- I. Selz, Peter. II. Title. BIP

ROTHKO, Mark, 1903-1970. 759.13
Mark Rothko. 21 giugno - 15 ott., 1970. [New York, Marlborough Gallery, 1970] [64] p. (chiefly col. plates, port.) 31 cm. Label mounted on t.p.: Supplied by Worldwide Books, Boston. At head of title: Comune di Venezia, Museo d'arte moderna Ca' Persaro. "Sotto gli auspici della Biennale internazionale d'arte di Venezia, con la collaborazione delle Gallerie Marlborough, New York, Londra, Roma." [ND237.R725A46] 70-199869
I. Museo d'arte moderna Ca' Pesaro. II. Venice. Biennale d'arte.

ROTHKO, Mark, 1903-1970. 759.13
Mark Rothko, 1903-1970 : a retrospective / Diane Waldman. New York : H. N. Abrams, 1978. 296 p. : ill. (some col.) ; 29 cm. Based on the retrospective exhibition presented at the Guggenheim Museum in 1978. Bibliography: p. 292-295. [ND237.R725A4 1978] 78-58411 ISBN 0-8109-1587-1 : 30.00
1. Rothko, Mark, 1903-1970. 2. Painters—United States—Biography. I. Waldman, Diane. II. Solomon R. Guggenheim Museum, New York.

SELDES, Lee. 759.13 B
The legacy of Mark Rothko / by Lee Seldes. New York : Penguin Books, [1979] p. cm. Includes index. Bibliography: p. [ND237.R725S44 1979] 78-31441 ISBN 0-14-005205-4 pbk. : 4.95
1. Rothko, Mark, 1903-1970. 2. Painters—United States—Biography. I. Title. BIP

SELDES, Lee. 759.13 B
The legacy of Mark Rothko / by Lee Seldes. 1st ed. New York : Holt, Rinehart and Winston, c1978. ix, 372 p. : ill. ; 24 cm. Includes index. Bibliography: p. 357-360. [ND237.R725S44] 76-29921 ISBN 0-03-014751-4 : 14.95
1. Rothko, Mark, 1903-1970. 2. Painters—United States—Biography. I. Title.

Rothmans World Group of Companies—Art collections.

CONTEMPORARY French tapestries. 746.3'9'44
Richmond [1970?] 1 v. (chiefly col. illus.) 21 x 27 cm. Catalog of an exhibition from the Collection of the Rothmans World Group of Companies, presented by the House of Edgeworth at the Virginia Museum of Fine Arts, Nov. 16-Dec. 27, 1970. Label on t.p.: Supplied by Worldwide Books, inc., Boston. "Jean Lurcat, an exhibition of paintings, drawings, and textiles from the T. Catesby Jones Collection of the Virginia Museum, November 16 through December 27, 1970" ([8] p.) inserted at end. [NK3049.A1C6] 78-199985
1. Rothmans World Group of Companies—Art collections. 2. Tapestry, French—Exhibitions. I. Lurcat, Jean, 1892-1966. II. House of Edgeworth. III. Virginia Museum of Fine Arts, Richmond.

Rouault, Georges, 1871-1958.

COURTHION, Pierre. 759.4
Georges Rouault. Including a catalogue of works prepared with the collaboration of Isabelle Rouault. New York, H. N. Abrams [1962] 489 p. illus. (part mounted col.) ports. 30 cm. Bibliography: p. 472-483. [ND553.R66C6] 61-13855
1. Rouault, Georges, 1871-1958.

DYRNESS, William A. 759.4
Rouault: a vision of suffering and salvation [by] William A. Dyrness. Grand Rapids, Eerdmans [1971] 235 p. illus. (1 col.) 24 cm. Includes bibliographical references. [ND553.R66D9] 73-151985 8.95
1. Rouault, Georges, 1871-1958. I. Title.

GETLEIN, Frank. 759.4
Georges Rouault's Miserere [by] Frank and Dorothy Getlein. Milwaukee, Bruce Pub. Co. [1964] ix, 149 p. plates, ports. 23 cm. [NE650.R67G4] 63-19633
1. Rouault, Georges, 1871-1958. 2. Jesus Christ — Art. 3. Jesus Christ — Crucifixion. Getlein, Dorothy, joint author. I. Title.

NEW York. Museum of Modern Art. 759.4
Georges Rouault; paintings and prints, by James Thrall Soby. [New York] Published for the Museum of Modern Art by Arno Press, 1972 [c1947] 141 p. illus. 27 cm. (Museum of Modern Art publications in reprint) Contents.Contents.—Georges

Rouault: paintings and prints, by J. T. Soby.—The technique of Georges Rouault's prints, by C. O. Schniewind.—Notes received from the artist February, 1945.—Illustrations: paintings.—Illustrations: prints.—Catalog of the exhibition held at the museum, 1945.—Text references (p. 133-134)—Bibliography, by H. B. Muller (p. 134-141) [ND553.R66N45 1972] 70-169317 ISBN 0-405-01575-5
1. Rouault, Georges, 1871-1958. I. Soby, James Thrall, 1906-

ROUAULT, Georges, 1871- 759.4
Rouault; introduced by Jacques Lassaigne. With a biographical foreword and bibliographical notes. Geneva, New York, Skira [1953?] unpaged, illus. (in portfolio) 30cm. (Masterpieces of French painting) The New Skira art books. [ND553.R66A57] 51-14802
I. Title.

ROUAULT, Georges, 1871- 759.4
1958.
Georges Rouault. Text by Jacques Maritain. New York, H. N. Abrams [1969] 40 p. illus. (part col.) 33 cm. (Great art of the ages) [ND553.R66M37 1969] 69-19715 ISBN 0-8109-5136-3
I. Maritain, Jacques, 1882-

ROUAULT, Georges, 1871- 759.4
1958.
Georges Rouault. Text by Jacques Maritain. New York, H. N. Abrams [1969] 22 p. illus. (part col.) 33 cm. (The Library of great painters. Portfolio ed.) On cover: Rouault. First ed. published in 1954 under title: Rouault. [ND553.R66M39 1969] 69-14758
I. Maritain, Jacques, 1882-

ROUAULT, Georges, 1871- 759.4
1958.
Georges Rouault / text by Pierre Courthion. New York : H. N. Abrams, [1977] p. cm. (The Library of great painters) Translation of Rouault. Includes index. Bibliography: p. [ND553.R66C6313] 76-53575 ISBN 0-8109-0459-4 : 22.50
1. Rouault, Georges, 1871-1958. I. Courthion, Pierre. BIP

ROUAULT, Georges, 1871- 769'.92'4
1958.
Georges Rouault, the graphic work : [catalogue] / by Alan Wofsy. San Francisco : Alan Wofsy Fine Arts, 1976. 104 p. : ill. (some col.) ; 32 cm. Most of the works described are in the collection of A. Wofsy. The balance is mainly from two major collections in Los Angeles, those of H. P. & J. F. Ullman and the Grunwald Center for Graphic Arts at UCLA. Bibliography: p. 7. [NE650.R67W63 1976] 75-27620 ISBN 0-915346-05-2 : 30.00
1. Rouault, Georges, 1871-1958. I. Wofsy, Alan. II. Title.

ROUAULT, Georges, 1871- 769'.92'4
1958.
The graphic work of Georges Rouault. [Catalog of an exhibition] January 16-February 27, 1972, Art Gallery, University of Notre Dame. [Notre Dame, Ind., Art Gallery, University of Notre Dame, 1972] [24] p. illus. 28 cm. Bibliography: p. [14] [NE650.R67N67] 73-299004
1. Rouault, Georges, 1871-1958. I. Notre Dame, Ind. University. Art Gallery. II. Title.

ROUAULT, Georges, 1871- 759.4
1958.
Rouault. Text and notes by Joshua Kind. New York, Tudor Pub. Co. [1969] 36 p., 92 col. plates. 18 cm. Bibliography: p. 15. [ND553.R66K5] 69-18395
I. Kind, Joshua.

ROUAULT, Georges, 1871- 759.4
1958.
Rouault. Text by Giuseppe Marchiori. New York, Reynal [1967] 34, [86] p. plates (part col.) 36 cm. Bibliography: p. 34. [ND553.R66M33] 67-31964
I. Marchiori, Giuseppe.

ROUAULT, Georges, 1871- 759.4
1958.
Rouault retrospective exhibition, 1953. New York, Museum of Modern Art [1953] 32 p. illus. 26 cm. Catalog of an exhibition held at Cleveland Museum of Art and Museum of Modern Art, New York. Bibliography: p. 32. [ND553.R66C55] 73-171325
1. Rouault, Georges, 1871-1958. I. Cleveland Museum of Art. II. New York (City). Museum of Modern Art. III. Title.

VENTURI, Lionello, 1885- 759.4
1961.
Rouault, biographical and critical study. Translated from the Italian by James Emmons. [New York] Skira [1959] 141 p. mounted col. illus. 19 cm. (The Taste of our time, v. 26) Bibliography: p. 127-129. [ND553.R66V433] 59-7253
1. Rouault, Georges, 1871-1958.

Roulstone, George, 1767-1804.

DOBSON, John, 1924- 070.5'092'4
The lost Roulstone imprints : with a checklist of issues from George Roulstone's Tennessee press, 1793-1804 / by John Dobson. Knoxville : University of Tennessee Library, 1975. xiii, 70 p. : facsims. ; 24 cm. (Occasional publication - University of Tennessee Library ; no. 2) Bibliography: p. 69-70. [Z232.R753D6] 74-16840
1. Roulstone, George, 1767-1804. 2. Printing—History—Tennessee. 3. Legislislative journals—Tennessee—Bibliography. 4. Tennessee—History—Sources—Bibliography. I. Title. II. Series: Tennessee. University. Libraries. Occasional publication ; no. 2.

Rousseau, Henri Julien Felix, 1844-1910.

BOURET, Jean 759.4
Douanier Rousseau. Greenwich, Conn., Fawcett [c.1963] 8, [1]p., 30 plates (incl. ports., pt. col.) 19cm. (Premier art lib., v.4; R173) Bibl. 62-21866 .60 pap.,
1. Rousseau, Henri Julien Felix, 1844-1910. I. Title.

BOURET, Jean. 759.4
Henri Rousseau. [Translated from the French by Martin Leake] Greenwich, Conn., New York Graphic Society [1961] 267 p. illus., 50 col. plates, 29 cm. "Illustrated catalogue...by Andre and Joan Rosselet": p. 175-263. Bibliography: p. 264-266. [ND553.R67B63] 61-15769
1. Rousseau, Henri Julien Felix, 1844-1910.

LEONARD, Sandra E. 759.4
Henri Rousseau and Max Weber [by] Sandra E. Leonard. New York, R. L. Feigen [1970] 94 p. illus., facsims., ports. 25 cm. Bibliography: p. 89-93. [ND553.R67L4] 73-125361
1. Rousseau, Henri Julien Felix, 1844-1910. 2. Weber, Max, 1881-1961.

RICH, Daniel Catton, 1904- 759.4
Henri Rousseau. In collaboration with the Art Institute of Chicago. New York, Museum of Modern Art. Reprint ed. [New York] Published for the Museum of Modern Art by Arno Press, 1969 [c1946] 80 p. illus., facsim. (on lining paper) 27 cm. Bibliography: p. 74-80. [ND553.R67R5 1969] 75-86436
1. Rousseau, Henri Julien Felix, 1844-1910. I. Chicago. Art Institute. II. New York (City). Museum of Modern Art.

ROUSSEAU, Henri Julien 759.4
Felix, 1844-1910.
Henri Rousseau (1844-1910) Text by Alfred Werner. New York, H. N. Abrams [1957] unpaged. illus. 17cm. (The Pocket library of great art, A30) An Abrams art book. [ND553.R67W4] 58-4698
I. Werner, Alfred, 1911- II. Title. III. Series.

ROUSSEAU, Henri Julien 759.4
Felix, 1844-1910.
Henri Rousseau, le douanier / Carolyn Keay. New York : Rizzoli, 1976. 192 p. : ill. (some col.) ; 32 cm. Includes index. Bibliography: p. 185-190. [ND553.R67K4] 76-11994 ISBN 0-8478-0035-0 : 30.00
1. Rousseau, Henri Julien Felix, 1844-1910. I. Keay, Carolyn. II. Title.

SALMON, Andre, 1881- 759.4
Rousseau. [Translated from the French by Paul Colacicchi] New York, H. N. Abrams [1963] 87 p. illus. 19 cm. [ND553.R67S33] 63-8671
1. Rousseau, Henri Jullen Felix, 1844-1910. I. Title.

UHDE, Wilhelm, 1874-1947. 759.4
Five primitive masters. [Translated by Ralph Thompson] New York, Arno Press [1969, c1949] 98 p. illus., port. 27 cm. (Arno series of contemporary art no. 35) [ND552.U3513 1969] 75-91371
1. Rousseau, Henri Julien Felix, 1844-1910. 2. Vivin, Louis, 1861-1936. 3. Bombois, Camille, 1883- 4. Bauchant, Andre, 1873-1958. 5. Louis, Seraphine, 1864-1942. 6. Primitivism in art. I. Title. BIP

VALLIER, Dora. 759.4
Henri Rousseau. New York, H. N. Abrams [1964] 327 p. illus. (part mounted, part col.) facsims., music, ports. 31 cm. Bibliography: p. 323-326. [ND553.R67V33] 62-16467
1. Rousseau, Henri Julien Felix, 1844-1910. BIP

Rousseau, Henri Julien Felix, 1844-1910—Influence.

SVENDSEN, Louis 760'.09'04
Averill.
Rousseau, Redon, and fantasy. [New York, Solomon R. Guggenheim Foundation, 1968] [52] p. col. illus. 26 x 12 cm. Catalog ([8]) p. of works of Exhibition 68/5, May-September, 1968 at the Solomon R. Guggenheim Museum inserted. Bibliographical references included in "Footnotes" (p. [49]-[50]) [N6490.S885] 68-31156
1. Rousseau, Henri Julien Felix, 1844-1910—Influence. 2. Redon, Odilon, 1840-1916—Influence. 3. Art, Modern—20th century—Exhibitions. 4. Fantasy. I. Solomon R. Guggenheim Museum, New York. II. Title.

Rousseau, Henri Julien Felix, 1844-1910—Juvenile literature.

RABOFF, Ernest Lloyd. 759.4
Henri Rousseau, by Ernest Raboff. Garden City, N.Y., Doubleday [1970] [31] p. illus. (part col.), ports. (part col.) 29 cm. (Art for children) (A Gemini-Smith book.) A brief biography of this French artist accompanies color reproductions and analyses of fifteen of his paintings. [ND553.R67R3] 76-93206 3.95
1. Rousseau, Henri Julien Felix, 1844-1910—Juvenile literature. I. Title.

Routh, Dorothy Adler—Art collections.

OGITA, Tomoo. 738.4
Asian cloisonne enamels / by Tomoo Ogita & Richard Petterson. Los Angeles : Dorothy Adler Routh Publications, c1975. xvi, 83 p. : ill. (some col.) ; 29 cm. Published in 1974 under title: Asian cloisonne enamels from the Dorothy Adler Routh Collection. Bibliography: p. 81-82. [NK5015.O34 1975] 75-326567 27.50
1. Routh, Dorothy Adler—Art collections. 2. Cloisonne—China—Catalogs. 3. Cloisonne—Japan—Catalogs. I. Petterson, Richard B., joint author. II. Title.
Distributed by Paragon Books

Row houses—New York (City)—History.

LOCKWOOD, Charles. 917.47'1
Bricks & brownstone; the New York row house, 1783-1929, an architectural & social history. Introd. by James Biddle. [1st ed.] New York, McGraw-Hill [1972] xxv, 262 p. illus. 29 cm. Bibliography: p. [257]-260. [NA7238.N6L66] 72-9000 ISBN 0-07-038310-3 17.95
1. Row houses—New York (City)—History. 2. Brick houses—New York (City) I. Title. II. Title: Brownstone. BIP

Rowe, William, 1941—

ROWE, William, 1941- 745.4'49'24
Exotic alphabets and ornament. New York, Dover Publications [1974] 72 p. of illus. 29 cm. (Dover pictorial archive series) [NK1535.R68A45 1974] 73-93544 ISBN 0-486-22989-0 2.50 (pbk.)
1. Rowe, William, 1941- 2. Art deco. I. Title.

ROWE, William, 1941- 745.4'49'24
Original art deco designs eighty plates New York, Dover Publications [1973] 72 p. (chiefly illus., part col.) 29 cm. (Dover pictorial archive series) [NK1535.R68A52 1973] 73-75281 ISBN 0-486-22567-4 3.00 (pbk.)
1. Rowe, William, 1941- 2. Art deco. I. Title.

Rowland, Benjamin, 1904-1972.

HARVARD University. 759.13
William Hayes Fogg Art Museum.
Benjamin Rowland, Jr., memorial exhibition. [Cambridge, Mass., 1973] [24] p. illus. 25 cm. Catalog of an exhibition held Sept. 28-Oct. 21, 1973, at the Fogg Art Museum. Includes bibliographical references. [ND1839.R67H37 1973] 74-166339
1. Rowland, Benjamin, 1904-1972. I. Rowland, Benjamin, 1904-1972. II. Title.

Rowlandson, Thomas, 1756-1827.

GREGO, Joseph, 1843- 741.9'42
1908.
Rowlandson the caricaturist. [New York] Collectors Editions [1970] 2 v. illus. 29 cm. Reprint of the 1880 ed. published by Chatto and Windus, London. Lists of drawings by Rowlandson: v. 2, p. 412-431. Includes bibliographical references. [NC1479.R8G8 1970] 78-102790 ISBN 0-87681-038-5
1. Rowlandson, Thomas, 1756-1827. 2. English wit and humor, Pictorial. I. Rowlandson, Thomas, 1756-1827. II. Title.

HAYES, John T. 759.2
Rowlandson; watercolours and drawings [by] John Hayes. [London] Phaidon [Distributed in U.S.A. by Praeger, New York, 1972] 214 p. illus. (part col.) 29 cm. Includes bibliographical references. [ND1942.R64H39] 79-190599 ISBN 0-7148-1555-1 25.00 (U.S.)
1. Rowlandson, Thomas, 1756-1827. I. Rowlandson, Thomas, 1756-1827.

KANSAS. University. 709'.42
Museum of Art.
The school for scandal: Thomas Rowlandson's London; as account of his life & times & especially his depictions of the theatre, together with some discussion of the life & works of Richard Brinsley Sheridan of his play The school for scandal as performed at the University Theatre. Lawrence, 1967. 78p. illus. 23cm. (Miscellaneous pubns. of the Museum of Art, no. 66) A catalogue of the exhibition held at the Museum of Art, Univ. of Kan., Feb. 8th-Mar. 12th. Bibl. [NE2180.R68K3] 67-7828 1.50
1. Rowlandson, Thomas, 1756-1827. I. Sheridan, Richard 1751-1816. The school for scandal. II. Title. III. Series: Kansas. University. Brinsley Butler, Museum of Art. Miscellaneous publications, no. 66

PAULSON, Ronald. 769'.92'4
Rowlandson; a new interpretation. New York, Oxford University Press, 1972. 144 p. illus. 26 cm. Includes bibliographical references. [NC1479.R8P38] 72-82673 15.00
1. Rowlandson, Thomas, 1756-1827. BIP

ROWLANDSON, Thomas, 741.9'42
1756-1827.
Drawings by Thomas Rowlandson in the Huntington collection / by Robert R. Wark. San Marino, Calif. : Huntington Library, 1975. ix, 398 p. : ill. ; 27 cm. Includes bibliographical references and indexes. [NC242.R66W29] 74-20036 ISBN 0-87328-065-2 : 20.00
1. Rowlandson, Thomas, 1756-1827. I. Wark, Robert R. II. Henry E. Huntington Library and Art Gallery, San Marino, Calif. III. Title. BIP

ROWLANDSON, Thomas, 1756- 759.2
1827.
The watercolor drawings of Thomas Rowlandson, from the Albert H. Wiggin

Collection in the Boston Public Library, by Arthur W. Heintzelman. New York, Watson-Guptill Publications [1971] 127 p. illus. (part col.) 33 cm. Reprint of the 1947 ed. [ND1942.R64H4 1971] 78-157651 ISBN 0-8230-4602-8 17.50
1. Heintzelman, Arthur William, 1892- II. Boston. Public Library. Albert H. Wiggin Collection. III. Title.

Rowntree, Kenneth.

ROWNTREE, Kenneth. 709'.2'4
Paintings, drawings, and collages / Kenneth Rowntree. Newcastle upon Tyne : Laing Art Gallery, [1977] [16] p. : ill. ; 21 cm. Special exhibition arranged to mark the occasion of the opening of the new galleries by Lord Donaldson, Minister for the Arts, on Wednesday, 15th Dec.-23rd Jan. 1976, Laing Art Gallery. [N6797.R64L34] 77-368355 £0.90
1. Rowntree, Kenneth. I. Laing Art Gallery, Newcastle upon Tyne. II. Title.

Roy, Jamini, 1887—

JAMINI Roy & 709'.54'14074015979
Bengali folk art; a special exhibition of works in the Collection of Mr. & Mrs. Thomas J. Needham of Jacksonville, Florida. [Gainesville, University Gallery, University of Florida, 1971] [44] p. illus. (part col.) 23 cm. Catalogue of an exhibition held at the University Gallery, University of Florida, Mar. 19-Apr. 25, 1971 and at the Jacksonville Art Museum, May 6-30, 1971. [N7307.B4J3] 76-198197
1. Roy, Jamini, 1887- 2. Needham, Thomas J.—Art collections. 3. Folk art—Exhibitions. 4. Folk art—Bengal. I. Roy, Jamini, 1887- II. Florida. University, Gainesville. University Gallery. III. Jacksonville Art Museum.

Royal Ontario Museum.

ROYAL 738.3'0937'0740113541
Ontario Museum.
Roman pottery in the Royal Ontario Museum : a catalogue / John W. Hayes ; with photos. by L. Warren ... [et al.]. Toronto : Royal Ontario Museum, 1976. ix, 125 p. : ill. ; 32 cm. Bibliography: p. vii-viii. [NK3850.R69 1976] 76-375743 ISBN 0-88854-172-4
1. Royal Ontario Museum. 2. Pottery, Roman—Catalogs. 3. Pottery—Toronto—Catalogs. I. Hayes, John W. II. Title.

Royal Pavilion, Art Gallery and Museums.

ROYAL Pavilion, Art 942.2'56
Gallery and Museums.
The Royal Pavilion, Brighton / [Royal Pavilion, Art Gallery and Museums, Brighton] ; [text by David Higginbottom]. [Brighton] : [Royal Pavilion, Art Gallery and Museums], [1976]. [40] p. : col. ill., facsims. ; 30 cm. Cover title. [NA7746.B8R69 1976] 77-355060 ISBN 0-9502372-3-X : £0.45
1. Royal Pavilion, Art Gallery and Museums. I. Higginbottom, David. II. Title.

Royal Society of British Artists, London.

BRADSHAW, Maurice. 759.941
Royal Society of British Artists, members exhibiting, 1931-1946 / [compiled] by Maurice Bradshaw. Leigh-on-Sea : F. Lewis, 1976. [8], 80 p. ; 29 cm. Cover title: R.B.A. exhibitors 1931-1946. [ND468.B722] 76-383755 ISBN 0-85317-044-4 : £14.50
1. Royal Society of British Artists, London. 2. Painting, British—Exhibitions—Catalogs. 3. Painting, Modern—20th century—Great Britain—Exhibitions—Catalogs. I. Royal Society of British Artists, London. II. Title. III. Title: R.B.A. exhibitors 1931-1946.

Rubbing.

BURCH, Mary Lou, 1914- 760
Making leaf rubbings : a hobby for the entire family / by Mary Lou Burch. Brattleboro, Vt. : S. Greene Press, c1979. p. cm. Includes index. Bibliography: p. [TT912.B87] 78-58678 ISBN 0-8289-0334-4 pbk. : 3.50
1. Rubbing. 2. Leaves. 3. Leaf prints. I. Title. II. Title: Leaf rubbings. BIP

FIRESTEIN, Cecily Barth. 760
Rubbing craft : how to rub doors, letterboxes, gravestones, manhole covers and how to use these designs to make jewelry, T-shirts, needlepoint and more / by Cecily Barth Firestein. New York : Quick Fox, c1977. 95 p. : ill. ; 28 cm. Includes index. Bibliography: p. 93-94. [TT912.F57] 76-56570 ISBN 0-8256-3062-2 pbk. : 4.95
1. Rubbing. 2. Handicraft. I. Title. BIP

Rubbing—Juvenile literature.

HETZER, Linda. 745.54
Paper crafts / crafts by Linda Hetzer ; photos. by Steven Mays, ill. by Sally Shimizu and Lynn Matus. Milwaukee : Raintree, c1978. p. cm. Introduces various techniques in block printing, rubbings, and papermaking and includes step-by-step instructions for a selection of projects involving each craft. [TT912.H47] 77-28796 ISBN 0-8172-1186-1 lib.bdg. : 7.93
1. Rubbing—Juvenile literature. 2. Paper making and trade—Juvenile. 3. Relief printing—Juvenile literature. I. Mays, Steven. II. Shimizu, Sally. III. Matus, Lynn. BIP

Rubbings.

ANDREW, Laye. 745.54
Creative rubbings. London, Batsford; New York, Watson-Guptill, 1967. 96 p. illus. 21 1/2 cm. 25/- (B67-24282) [NC915.R8A5] 68-10499
1. Rubbings. I. Title.

JACOBS, G. Walker. 760
Stranger stop and cast an eye; a guide to stones & rubbings, by G. Walker Jacobs. [2d ed. Marblehead, Mass., Oldstone Enterprises, 1972] 52 p. illus. 24 cm. Bibliography: p. 52. [NC915.R8J3 1972] 72-190919
1. Rubbings. I. Title. BIP

JACOBS, G. Walker. 760
Stranger stop and cast an eye; a guide to gravestones & gravestone rubbing [by] G. Walker Jacobs. With photos. and rubbings by the author. [3d ed.] Brattleboro, Vt., S. Greene Press [1973] 123 p. illus. 23 cm. Bibliography: p. 117-118. [NC915.R8J3 1973] 73-82745 ISBN 0-8289-0189-9 4.95
1. Rubbings. 2. Sepulchral monuments—New England. 3. Symbolism in art—New England. I. Title.

SEIDELMAN, James E. 761
The rub book, by James E. Seidelman and Grace Mintonye. Drawings by Lynn Sweat. New York, Crowell-Collier Press [1968] [32] p. illus. (part col.) 22 cm. Jeff has an interesting day as he discovers how to reproduce the texture of things he touches, and makes many rubbings of familiar items around his house. [NC915.R8S4] AC 68
1. Rubbings. I. Mintonye, Grace, joint author. II. Sweat, Lynn, illus. III. Title. BIP

Rubbings—Juvenile literature.

SEIDELMAN, James E. 746.6 (j)
The rub book, by James E. Seidelman and Grace Mintonye. Drawings by Lynn Sweat. New York, Crowell-Collier Press [1968] 1 v. (unpaged) illus. (part col.) 22 cm. [NC915.R8S4] 68-12286
1. Rubbings—Juvenile literature. I. Mintonye, Grace, joint author. II. Sweat, Lynn, illus. III. Title.

Rubbings—Technique.

BODOR, John J. 741.2'9
Rubbings and textures; a graphic technique [by] John J. Bodor. New York, Reinhold [1968] 107 p. (chiefly illus.) 21 cm. (An Art horizons book) (Art horizons series.) Bibliography: p. 106. [NC915.R8B6 1968] 68-16026
1. Rubbings—Technique. I. Title.

Rubens, Peter Paul, Sir, 1577-1640.

AVERMAETE, Roger, 759.9'493 B
1893-
Rubens and his times. Translated by Christine Trollope. [1st American ed.] South Brunswick [N.J.] A. S. Barnes [1968] 218 p. illus., facsims., ports. 22 cm. Translation of Rubens et son temps. [ND673.R9A973 1968] 68-27197 6.00
1. Rubens, Peter Paul, Sir, 1577-1640. I. Title.

BAUDOUIN, Frans. 759.9493 B
Pietro Pauolo Rubens / Frans Baudouin ; translated by Elsie Callander. New York : Abrams, 1977. 405 p. : ill. (some col.) ; 34 cm. Text in English. Includes bibliographical references and indexes. [ND673.R9B238 1977b] 77-82339 ISBN 0-8109-1586-3 : 60.00
1. Rubens, Peter Paul, Sir, 1577-1640. 2. Painters—Belgium—Biography.

BURCKHARDT, Jakob 927.5
Christoph, 1818-1897.
Recollections of Rubens. [Edited, with an introd., by H. Gerson. Translation of Burckhardt's essay by Mary Hottinger. Translation of the selected letters by R. H. Boothroyd and I. Grafe] New York, Phaidon Publishers; distributed by Oxford University Press [1950] xi, 374, [1] p. 143 plates (part col.) 19 cm. "Selected letters of Rubens": p. [191]-249. Bibliography: p. [375] [ND673.R9B784] 50-9158
1. Rubens, Sir Peter Paul, 1377-1640. I. Title.

CABANNE, Pierre. 759.9493
Rubens. [Translated from the French by Oliver Bernard] New York, Tudor Pub. Co. [1967] 286 p. 146 illus. (part col.) 22 cm. (The World of art library) Bibliographical references included in "Text references" (p. 274-276) [ND673] 67-9555
1. Rubens, Peter Paul, Sir, 1577-1640.

CORPUS Rubenianum Ludwig 759.9493
Burchard; an illustrated catalogue raisonne of the work of Peter Paul Rubens based on the material assembled by the late Dr. Ludwig Buuchard in twenty-six parts. Edited by the Nationaal Centrum voor de Plastische Kunsten in de XVIde en XVIIde Eeuw. London, New York, Phaidon, 1968- v. illus. 27 cm. Sponsored by the city of Antwerp. Bibliography: v. 1, p. 13-17. [ND673.R9C63] 73-4996 1500.00 (v. 1)
1. Rubens, Peter Paul, Sir, 1577-1640. I. Burchard, Ludwig, 1886- II. Nationaal Centrum voor de Plastische Kunsten van de XVIde en XVIIde Eeuw.

DE MONTEBELLO, Philippe. 759.9493
Rubens. New York, McGraw-Hill [1968] 48 p. illus., 20 col. slides. 2 x 2 in. (in pockets) 29 cm. (Color slide program of the great masters) [ND673.R9D39] 68-20385
1. Rubens, Peter Paul, Sir, 1577-1640. I. Title. II. Series.

FLETCHER, Jennifer. 759.9'493
Peter Paul Rubens; with fifty plates in full colour. London, New York, Phaidon [1968] 90 p. illus. (part col.) 32 cm. ([Phaidon colour books]) Bibliography: p. 29. [ND673.R9F58] 68-27418 ISBN 0-7148-1340-0
1. Rubens, Peter Paul, Sir, 1577-1640.

GERSON, Noel Bertram, 759.9493 B
1914-
Peter Paul Rubens; a biography of a giant, by Samuel Edwards. New York, D. McKay Co. [1973] 250 p. 22 cm. Bibliography: p. 240. [ND673.R9G46] 72-95157 6.95
1. Rubens, Peter Paul, Sir, 1577-1640.

GLEN, Thomas L. 759.9493
Rubens and the Counter Reformation : studies in his religious paintings between 1609 and 1620 / Thomas L. Glen. New York : Garland Pub., 1977. p. cm. (Outstanding dissertations in the fine arts) Originally presented as the author's thesis, Princeton University, 1975. Bibliography: p. [ND673.R9G535 1977] 76-23621 ISBN 0-8240-2692-6 lib.bdg. : 40.00
1. Rubens, Peter Paul, Sir, 1577-1640. 2. Counter-Reformation in art. I. Title. II. Series. BIP

HELD, Julius Samuel, 759.9493
1905-
The oil sketches of Peter Paul Rubens : a critical catalogue / by Julius S. Held. Princeton, N.J. : Princeton University Press, c1979. p. cm. (Kress Foundation studies in the history of European art ; no. 7) Includes index. Bibliography: p. [ND673.R9A4 1979] 77-2532 100.00
1. Rubens, Peter Paul, Sir, 1577-1640—Catalogs. I. Rubens, Peter Paul, Sir, 1577-1640. II. Title. III. Series. BIP

JAFFE, Andrew 759.9493 B
Michael.
Rubens and Italy / Michael Jaffe. Ithaca, N.Y. : Cornell University Press, 1977. 128 p., [103] leaves of plates : ill. (some col.) ; 29 cm. Includes index. Bibliography: p. 121-123. [ND673.R9J27] 76-20065 ISBN 0-8014-1064-9 : 55.00
1. Rubens, Peter Paul, Sir, 1577-1640. 2. Mannerism (Art)—Italy. 3. Art, Italian. I. Rubens, Peter Paul, Sir, 1577-1640. II. Title. BIP

LEPORE, Mario, 1912- 759.9493 B
The life and times of Rubens; translated [from the Italian] by F. B. Sear. Feltham, New York, Hamlyn, 1970. 2-75 p. illus. (chiefly col.), ports. (chiefly col.). 30 cm. (Portraits of greatness) Illus. on lining papers. [ND673.R9L4513] 79-851769 ISBN 0-600-37511-0 21/-
1. Rubens, Peter Paul, Sir, 1577-1640. I. Title.

MARTIN, John Rupert. 760'.092'4
The decorations for the Pompa Introitus Ferdinandi. London, New York, Phaidon, 1972. [7], 278, [99] p. illus., facsims., col. map. 27 cm. (Corpus Rubenianum Ludwig Burchard, pt. 16) Distributed in the USA by Praeger, New York. Includes bibliographical references. [ND673.R9C63 pt. 16] 72-186634 ISBN 0-7148-1433-4 £13.00
1. Rubens, Peter Paul, Sir, 1577-1640. 2. Fernando, Infante of Spain, 1609-1641. 3. Visits of state—Belgium—Antwerp. 4. Street decoration—Antwerp. I. Title. II. Series.

MARTIN, John Rupert, 759.9492
comp.
Rubens: the Antwerp altarpieces ... [1st ed.] New York, Norton [1969] xiii, 132 p. 37 illus., 4 col. plates. 22 cm. (Norton critical studies in art history) Includes an introductory essay, documents, commentary, and criticism. Bibliography: p. [131]-132. [ND673.R9M33] 68-20828 5.95
1. Rubens, Peter Paul, Sir, 1577-1640. Raising of the Cross. 2. Rubens, Peter Paul, Sir, 1577-1640. Descent from the Cross. I. Title.

PUYVELDE, Leo van, 1882- 759.9493
Rubens. Paris, New-York, Elsevier, 1952. 238p. illus. (part mounted col.) 31cm. (Les Peintres flamands du xviie siecle) Bibliographical references included in 'Notes' (p. [198]-219) [ND673.R9P82] [ND673.R9P82] 927.5 53-1873 53-1873
1. Rubens, Peter Paul, Sir 1577-1640. I. Title. II. Series.

RIPLEY, Elizabeth. 927.5
Rubens, a biography. With drawings and paintings by Rubens. New York, Oxford University Press, 1957. 68, [3]p. illus. 27cm. Bibliography: p.[70] [ND673.R9R5] 57-11450
1. Rubens, Sir Peter Paul, 1577-1640. I. Title.

RIPLEY, Elizabeth, 1906- 927.5
Rubens, a biography. With drawings and paintings by Rubens. New York, Oxford University Press, 1957. 68 [3] p. illus. 27 cm. Bibliography: p. [70] [ND673.R9R5] 57-11450
1. Rubens, Peter Paul, 1577-1640.

RUBENS, Peter Paul, 759.9493
Sir, 1577-1640.
The battle of the Amazons. With an introd. by Leo van Puyvelde. Translated by D.J. Wilson [i.e. Wilton] [1st American ed.] New York, Harper [1950] 14 p. col. illus. 27 x 34 cm. (Form and color) Harper's art library. [ND673.R9P833] 50-5887
I. Puyvelde, Leo van, 1882- II. Title. III. Series: Form and color (New York

RUBENS, Peter Paul, Sir, 1577-1640. 795.9493
Peter Paul Rubens. Text by Julius S. Held. New York, H. N. Abrams [1970] 24 p. illus. (part col.) 33 cm. (Library of great painters. Portfolio ed.) [ND673.R9H45 1970] 69-14759
I. Held, Julius Samuel, 1905-

RUBENS, Peter Paul, Sir 1577-1640. 759.9493
Peter Paul Rubens (1577-1640) Text by Julius S. Held. New York, H. N. Abrams in association with Pocket Books [1954] [74] p. 38 illus. (part col.) 18cm. (The Pocket library of great art, A 17) An Abrams art book. Bibliography: p. [74] [ND673.R9H46] 927.5 54-14561
I. Held, Julius Samuel, 1905- II. Title.

RUBENS, Peter Paul, Sir, 1577-1640. 759.9493
Rubens : 108 reproductions / compiled and with an introd. by Keith Roberts. Oxford : Phaidon ; New York : E. P. Dutton, 1977. [16] p., 96 p. of plates : chiefly ill. (some col.) ; 42 cm. (Giant art paperbacks) [ND673.R9R59] 76-51499 ISBN 0-7148-1796-1 : 7.95
1. Rubens, Peter Paul, Sir, 1577-1640. I. Roberts, Keith, 1937-

STECHOW, Wolfgang, 1896- 759.9493
Rubens and the classical tradition. Cambridge, Published for Oberlin College [Oberlin, Ohio] by Harvard University Press, 1968. xiii, 110 p. illus. 24 cm. (Martin classical lectures, v. 22) Includes bibliographical references. [PA25.M3 vol. 22] 68-54025 6.00
1. Rubens, Peter Paul, Sir, 1577-1640. I. Title. II. Series.

STUBBE, Achilles, 1896- 759.9493
Peter Paul Rubens [by] A. Stubbe. [Editor: Anthony Bosman. Translation: Albert J. Fransella] New York, Barnes & Noble [1966] 90 p. plates (part col.) 18 cm. (Barnes & Noble art series, no. 626) [ND673.R9S88 1966] 66-9088
1. Rubens, Peter Paul, Sir, 1577-1640. I. Title.

THUILLIER, Jacques. 759.9493
Rubens' Life of Marie de Medici. Text by Jacques Thuillier. With a catalogue and a documentary history by Jacques Foucart. [Translated by Robert Erich Wolf] New York, H. N. Abrams [1970] 158 p. illus. (part col.), 50 col. plates (part fold.) 42 cm. Translation of Le storie di Maria de' Medici di Rubens al Lussemburgo. Bibliography: p. 155-[156] [ND673.R9T453] 72-85674 150.00
1. Rubens, Peter Paul, Sir, 1577-1640. Histories of Marie de Medicis. I. Foucart, Jacques, writer on art. II. Title.

VLIEGHE, Hans. 759.9493 s
Saints. [Translated from the Dutch, by P. S. Falla] London, New York, Phaidon [distributed in the USA by Praeger, New York, 1972-73] 2 v. illus. 27 cm. (Corpus Rubenianium Ludwig Burchard, pt. 8) Includes bibliographical references. [ND673.R9C63 pt. 8] [N6973.R9] 759.9493 72-185770 ISBN 0-7148-1505-5 (v. 1) 42.50 (U.S.) (v. 2)
1. Rubens, Peter Paul, Sir, 1577-1640. 2. Christian saints in art. I. Title. II. Series.

WEDGWOOD, Cecily Veronica, Dame, 1910- 759.9493 B
The political career of Peter Paul Rubens / C. V. Wedgwood. London : Thames and Hudson, c1975. 64 p. : ill. ; 22 cm. (Walter Neurath memorial lectures ; 7) Bibliography: p. 62. [ND673.R9W38] 76-365317 ISBN 0-500-55007-7 : 9.25
1. Rubens, Peter Paul, Sir, 1577-1640. 2. Flanders—Foreign relations. I. Title. II. Series.
Distributed by transatlantic Arts. **BIP**

WEDGWOOD, Cicely Veronica, Dame, 1910- 759.9493
The world of Rubens, 1577-1640, by C.V. Wedgwood and the editors of Time-Life Books New York, Time, inc., [1967] 192 p. illus. (part col.) 31 cm. (Time-Life library of art) Bibliography: p. 187. [ND673.R9W4] 67-27679
1. Rubens, Peter Paul, Sir, 1577-1640. I. Time-Life Books. II. Title. **BIP**

WHITE, Christopher. 759.9'493
Rubens and his world. New York, Viking Press [1968] 144 p. illus. (part col.), facsims., ports. (part col.) 24 cm. (A Studio book) [ND673.R9W45 1968] 68-19327
1. Rubens, Peter Paul, Sir, 1577-1640. I. Title.

Rubens, Peter Paul, Sir, 1577-1640—Influence.

BROWN University. Dept. of Art. 760'.0944
Rubenism : an exhibition by the Department of Art, Brown University, and the Museum of Art, Rhode Island School of Design, Bell Gallery, List Art Building, Brown University, Providence, Rhode Island, January 30 through February 23, 1975. [Providence, R.I.] : The Department, [1975] 278 p. : ill. ; 27 cm. "Catalogue number 3." Bibliography: p. 274-275. [N6846.B76 1975] 74-33245 12.00
1. Rubens, Peter Paul, Sir, 1577-1640—Influence. 2. Art, French—Exhibitions. 3. Art, Modern—17th-18th centuries—France—Exhibitions. 4. Romanticism in art—France—Exhibitions. 5. Art, English—Exhibitions. 6. Art, Modern—17th-18th centuries—England—Exhibitions. I. Rhode Island School of Design, Providence. Museum of Art. II. Title.

Rubens, Peter Paul, Sir, 1577-1640—Juvenile literature.

ROBERTO, Brother, 1927- 92
The golden gift; a story of Peter Paul Rubens. Illus. by Carolyn Lee Jagodits. Notre Dame, Ind., Dujarie Press [c1962] 94 p. illus. 24 cm. [ND673.R9R58] 63-1818
1. Rubens, Sir Peter Paul, 1577-1640 — Juvenile literature. I. Title.

Rubin, Reuven, 1893—

RUBIN, Reuven, 1893- 759.95694 B
My life, my art; an autobiography and selected paintings by Reuven Rubin. With an introd. by Haim Gamzu. New York, Funk & Wagnalls [1969] 227 p. plates (part col.), ports. 31 cm. (Sabra books) At head of title: Rubin. [ND979.R8A2] 74-82694 25.00
I. Title.

RUBIN, Reuven, 1893- 759.95694 B
Reuven Rubin, by Sarah Wilkinson. New York, H. N. Abrams [1974] 288 p. illus. (part col.) 28 cm. Bibliography: p. 283-287. [N7279.R82W54] 71-166215 ISBN 0-8109-0463-2
1. Rubin, Reuven, 1893- I. Wilkinson, Sarah. **BIP**

Rubrication.

GOFF, Frederick Richmond, 1916- 655.1'73
Rubrication in American books of the eighteenth century [by] Frederick R. Goff. Worcester, Mass., The Society, 1969. 29-43 p. facsims. 24 cm. "Reprinted from the Proceedings of the American Antiquarian Society for April 1969." [Z258.G64] 74-11802
1. Rubrication. 2. Printing—History—U.S. I. Title.

Rudolph, Paul, 1918—

RUDOLPH, Paul, 1918- 720'.924
The architecture of Paul Rudolph. Introd. by Sibyl Moholy-Nagy. Captions by Gerhard Schwab. With comments by Paul Rudolph. [Translation of the captions into English by Maria Kroll] New York, Praeger [1970] 239 p. illus. (part col.), map, plans, port. 26 cm. [NA737.R8M6] 69-19186 20.00
I. Moholy-Nagy, Dorothea Maria Pauline Alice Sybille (Pietzsch) II. Title.

RUDOLPH, Paul, 1918- 720'.22'2
Paul Rudolph : drawings / edited by Yukio Futagawa ; text by Paul Rudolph ; designed by Gan Hosoya. New York : Architectural Book Pub. Co., [1977] p. cm. English and Japanese. [NA737.R8F87 1977] 77-8680 ISBN 0-8038-0208-0 : 35.00
1. Rudolph, Paul, 1918- I. Futagawa, Yukio, 1932-

Ruggieri, Nick T.

RUGGIERI, Nick T. 759.13
Pennsylvania .... a commemorative portrait / by Nick T. Ruggieri ; text by John M. Baer ; [edited by Marion W. Milliron ; ill. cutlines by Thomas Coolidge]. Harrisburg, Pa. : Patriot-News Co., 1975. 140 p. : col. ill. ; 23 x 28 cm. "A Bicentennial collection of the Harrisburg Patriot-News Company." Includes indexes. [ND1839.R74B33] 75-21055
1. Ruggieri, Nick T. 2. Pennsylvania in art. I. Baer, John M. II. Title.

Rugs.

ALLARD, Mary. 746.7
Rug making: techniques and design. [1st ed.] Philadelphia, Chilton Books [1963] 160 p. illus. 26 cm. [TS1777.A64] 63-10590
1. Rugs. I. Title.

ALLER, Doris, 1909- 746.74
Handmade rugs; written & illustrated by Doris Aller. [1st ed.] Menlo Park, Calif., Lane Pub. Co. [1953] 95 p. illus. 28 cm. (Sunset craft books) [TT850.A42] 53-10325
1. Rugs. 2. Rugs, Hooked. I. Title.

BEITLER, Ethel Jane. 746.7'4
Hooked & knotted rugs. New York, Sterling Pub. Co. [1973] 48 p. illus. 20 cm. (Little craft book series) Discusses the background, materials, equipment, and techniques for making hooked and knooted rugs. Includes suggestions for creating designs. [TT850.B37 1973] 72-95202 2.95
1. Rugs. 2. Hooking. I. Title.

BLAKE, David P. 746.7'4
Making 75 rugs by the square : rugs to work in latchet hook, rya, punch, and gros point / David P. Blake, Charles Barnes & Charles Thompson. New York : Crown Publishers, c1978. vi, 218 p., [4] leaves of plates : ill. ; 27 cm. Includes index. [TT850.B52 1978] 77-10718 ISBN 0-517-52471-6 : 10.95 9.95. ISBN 0-517-52472-4 pbk. : 5.95
1. Rugs. I. Barnes, Charles, joint author. II. Thompson, Charles, 1939- joint author. III. Title. **BIP**

BOWLES, Ella Shannon, 1886- 746.7
Handmade rugs. Garden City, N.Y., Garden City Pub. Co. Detroit, Gale Research Co., 1974. p. Reprint of the 1937 ed. Bibliography: p. [TT850.B67 1974] 77-178620 11.00
1. Rugs. I. Title.

BRINLEY, Rosemary. 746.7
Rugmaking. Edited by Marjorie O'Shaughnessy. New York, Dover Publications [c1952] 87p. illus. 20cm. (Dover-Foyle handbook) [TT850.B7] 53-10111
1. Rugs. I. Title.

CHRISTOPHER, Rosemary Brinley, 1918- 746.7
Rugmaking. Edited by Marjorie O'Shaughnessy. New York, Dover Publications [c1952] 87p. illus. 20cm. (Dover-Foyle handbook) [TT850.C48] 53-10111
1. Rugs. I. Title.

CREATIVE rug making / 746.7'4
edited by Sue Simmons. Chicago : Regnery, 1976. 88 p. : ill. (some col.) ; 30 cm. [TT850.C73 1976] 76-150301 ISBN 0-8092-7999-1 : 6.95
1. Rugs. I. Simmons, Sue.

DROOP, Joan. 746.7
Rugmaking; a practical introduction. Newton Centre, Mass., C. T. Branford Co. [1971] 68 p. illus. 21 cm. Bibliography: p. [66] [TT850.D76] 76-149881 ISBN 0-8231-5026-7
1. Rugs. I. Title. **BIP**

FELCHER, Cecelia. 746.7
The complete book of rug making : folk methods and ethnic designs / Cecelia Felcher ; graphs by Jerome Felcher ; photos. by Daniel Quat ; drawings by Elaine Weinmann. New York : Hawthorn Books, [1975] 208 p. : ill. ; 29 cm. Includes index. Bibliography: p. 203-204. [TT850.F42 1975] 74-22927 ISBN 0-8015-1654-4 : 16.95
1. Rugs. I. Title.

FRANSES, Jack. 746.7
European and oriental rugs for pleasure and investment. New York, Arco Pub. Co. [1970] 176 p. illus., maps, col. plates. 23 cm. [NK2795.F7] 75-123397 5.95
1. Rugs. I. Title.

GALLINGER, Osma Palmer Couch, 1895- 746.7
Rug weaving for everyone, by Osma Couch Gallinger and Josephine Couch Del Deo. Illustrated by Dorothy Helen McCloud and Carolyn Fiedler. Milwaukee, Bruce Pub. Co. [1957] 294 p. illus. 26 cm. [TT850.G3] 57-10825
1. Rugs. I. Del Deo, Josephine Couch, joint author. II. Title.

HANLEY, Hope. 746.7'4
Needlepoint rugs. New York, Scribner [1971] xi, 115 p. illus. 23 cm. Bibliography: p. 113-114. [TT850.H35] 77-162728 ISBN 0-684-12484-X
1. Rugs. 2. Canvas embroidery. I. Title.

HINCHCLIFFE, John. 746.7
Rugs from rags / John Hinchcliffe and Angela Jeffs. Los Angeles : Brooke House, [1977] p. cm. [TT850.H55] 77-6477 ISBN 0-912588-50-0 : 10.95 ISBN 0-912588-22-5 pbk. : 8.95
1. Rugs. 2. Rags. I. Jeffs, Angela, joint author. II. Title.

KAESTNER, Dorothy. 746.7'4
Designs for needlepoint and latch hook rugs / by Dorothy Kaestner. New York : Scribner, [1977] p. cm. Bibliography: p. [TT850.K3] 76-50111 ISBN 0-684-14837-4 : 14.95
1. Rugs. 2. Canvas embroidery—Patterns. I. Title. **BIP**

LANE, Maggie. 746.4'4
Rugs and wall hangings / Maggie Lane. New York : Scribner, [1976] p. cm. Continues the author's Chinese rugs designed for needlepoint. Bibliography: p. [TT850.L3] 76-10177 ISBN 0-684-14670-3 : 15.00
1. Rugs. 2. Wall hangings. I. Title. **BIP**

LAURY, Jean Ray. 746.7
Handmade rugs from practically anything, by Jean Ray Laury and Joyce Aiken. Photos. by Gayle Smalley. Philadelphia, Countryside Press [1971] 94 p. illus. 24 cm. (A Farm journal countryside craft book) [TT850.L33] 77-31633
1. Rugs. I. Aiken, Joyce, joint author. II. Title.

LAURY, Jean Ray. 746.7
Handmade rugs from practically anything, by Jean Ray Laury and Joyce Aiken. Photos. by Gayle Smalley. Philadelphia, Countryside Press; distributed by Doubleday, Garden City, N.Y., [1972] 125 p. illus. 29 cm. [TT850.L33 1972] 70-185588 7.95
1. Rugs. I. Aiken, Joyce, joint author. II. Title.

LEWES, Klares. 677.643
Rug weaving [by] Klares Lewes & Helen Hutton. Neston Centre, Mass., C. T. Branford Co. [1962] 160 p. illus. 23 cm. Includes bibliography. [TT850.L4] 66-2992
1. Rugs. I. Hutton, Helen, joint author. II. Title.

MCBAINE, Susan. 746.7'4
Miniature needlepoint rugs for dollhouses : charted for easy use / Susan McBaine. New York : Dover Publications, 1976. 40 p. : chiefly ill. (some col.) ; 28 cm. (Dover needlework series) [TT850.M28 1976] 76-18406 ISBN 0-486-23388-X pbk. : 1.50
1. Rugs. 2. Canvas embroidery—Patterns. I. Title.

MACBETH, Ann. 746.7
The country woman's rug book. Peoria, Ill., Manual Arts Press. [Leicester, Eng.] Dryad Press. [Kentfield, Calif., N. K. Gregg, 1971] 48 p. illus. 21 cm. (Gregg series of reprints on crafts and hobbies) Reprint of the 1936 ed. [TT850.M3 1971] 73-163523 ISBN 0-912318-11-2
1. Rugs. I. Title. **BIP**

by Florence Starr Taylor. New York, Coward-McCann [1951] 110 p. illus. 26 cm. [TT850.U5] 51-13971
1. Rugs, Hooked. I. Title.

ZARBOCK, Barbara J 746.74
The complete book of rug hooking. Princeton, N.J., Van Nostrand [1961] 120 p. illus. 26 cm. Includes bibliography. [TT850.Z3] 61-16303
1. Rugs, Hooked. I. Title.

ZARBOCK, Barbara J. 746.7'4
The complete book of rug hooking, by Barbara J. Zarbock. 2d ed. New York, Van Nostrand-Reinhold Co. [1969] xii, 128 p. illus. (part col.) 26 cm. Bibliography: p. 119-120. [TT850.Z3 1969] 71-83216
1. Rugs, Hooked. I. Title.

Rugs, Hooked — Anecdotes, facetiae, satire, etc.

REX, Stella (Hay) 746.74088
By hook or crook; illustrated by Rodrigues. [1st ed.] New York, Pageant Press [1951] 61 p. illus. 21 cm. [PN6231.R8R4] 51-14982
1. Rugs, Hooked — Anecdotes, facetiae, satire, etc. I. Title.

Rugs, Hooked—Catalogs.

FROST, Edward Sands, b.1843. 381'.45'74674
Edward Sands Frost's hooked rug patterns. Dearborn, Mich. : Greenfield Village and Henry Ford Museum, c1970. 59 p. : chiefly ill. ; 28 cm. Cover title: Descriptive catalogue of E. S. Frost & Co's. hooked rug patterns. [TT850.F76] 74-196848
1. Rugs, Hooked—Catalogs. I. Edison Institute (Henry Ford Museum and Greenfield Village) Dearborn, Mich. II. Title. III. Title: Descriptive catalogue of E. S. Frost & Co's. hooked rug patterns.

Rugs, Hooked—Exhibitions.

MUSEUM of American Folk Art. 746.7'4'0973
Hooked rugs in the folk art tradition : [exhibition] September 19-November 24, 1974. New York : Museum of American Folk Art, [1974] [41] p. : ill. (some col.) ; 18 x 26 cm. Collection researched and assembled by Kate and Joel Kopp, guest curators. Includes bibliographical references. [NK2812.M87 1974] 74-16921
1. Rugs, Hooked—Exhibitions. 2. Folk art—United States. I. Kopp, Kate. II. Kopp, Joel. III. Title.

Rugs, Hooked—United States.

KOPP, Joel. 746.7'4'0973
American hooked and sewn rugs : folk art underfoot / Joel and Kate Kopp. 1st ed. New York : Dutton, 1975. 128 p. : ill. ; 27 cm. Bibliography: p. 128. [NK2812.K66 1975] 75-24532 ISBN 0-525-05362-X : 15.95. ISBN 0-525-47405-6 pbk. : 8.95
1. Rugs, Hooked—United States. 2. Coverlets—United States. 3. Folk art—United States. I. Kopp, Kate, joint author. II. Title. BIP

Rugs—Iran.

HOUSEGO, Jenny. 746.7'955
Tribal rugs : an introduction to the weaving of the tribes of Iran / Jenny Housego. New York : Van Nostrand Reinhold, 1978. 174 p. : ill. ; 20 x 21 cm. Includes index. Bibliography: p. 21. [NK2809.P4H68 1978] 77-26252 ISBN 0-442-23551-8 : 15.00. ISBN 0-442-23552-6 pbk. : 8.00
1. Rugs—Iran. 2. Rugs, Islamic—Iran. I. Title. BIP

Rugs, Iranian.

AMIR, M. K. Zephyr, 1931- 746.7'9'55
Supreme Persian carpets; oriental carpets, by M. K. Zephyr Amir. Rutland, Vt., C. E. Tuttle [1972] 138 p. col. illus. 34 cm. [NK2809.P4A57 1972b] 74-156770
1. Rugs, Iranian. I. Title.

Rugs, Islamic.

TURKHAN, Kudret H. 746.7'56
Islamic rugs [by] Kudret H. Turkhan. Edited by Lynne Thornton. New York, Praeger [1969] 112 p. illus. (part col.), maps. 25 cm. [NK2809.I8T8] 75-75418 10.00
1. Rugs, Islamic.

Rugs, Islamic—Catalogs.

SPUHLER, Friedrich. 746.7'5'07402176
Islamic carpets and textiles in the Keir Collection / Friedrich Spuhler ; with an introd. by George Wingfield Digby ; translated by George and Cornelia Wingfield Digby. London : Faber and Faber, 1978. 251 p. : ill. (some col.) ; 29 cm. (The Keir collection) Includes bibliographical references and index. [NK2809.I8S6813] 78-310307 ISBN 0-571-09783-9 : 84.95
1. De Unger, Edmund—Art collections—Catalogs. 2. Rugs, Islamic—Catalogs. 3. Textile fabrics, Islamic—Catalogs. I. Title. II. Series.
Distributed by Faber & Faber, Salem, NH

Rugs—Juvenile literature.

ALBERTINE, Sister, S.S.N.D., 1909- 746.7
How to have fun making rugs, by Sister Albertine. Illustrated by Nancy Inderieden. [Mankato, Minn., Creative Education; distributed by Childrens Press, Chicago, 1974] 31 p. illus. (part col.) 25 cm. (Creative education craft series) A brief, easy-to-read history of rugs with instructions on making braided, scrap, or rag rugs. [TT850.A38] 74-14521 ISBN 0-87191-359-3
1. Rugs—Juvenile literature. I. Inderieden, Nancy, illus. II. Title.

BORAWSKA, M. Albertine. 746.7
How to have fun making a rug, by M. Albertine Borawska. Illustrated by Nancy Inderieden. [Mankato, Minn., Creative Education, 1974] p. cm. (Creative education craft series) A brief, easy-to-read history of rugs with instructions on making braided, scrap, or rag rugs. [TT850.B65] 74-14521 ISBN 0-87191-359-3 4.50 (lib. bdg.)
1. Rugs—Juvenile literature. I. Inderieden, Nancy, illus. II. Title. BIP

LEWIS, Anne Gillespie. 746.7
Making rugs / by Anne Gillespie Lewis ; pictures by G. Overlie. Minneapolis : Lerner Publications Co., c1976. p. cm. (An Early craft book) Instructions for making hooked, braided, rya, felt, and other kinds of rugs and wall hangings from inexpensive materials such as discarded nylons, leftover yarn, and carpet remmants. [TT850.L45] 76-13067 lib.bdg. : 3.95
1. Rugs—Juvenile literature. I. Overlie, George. II. Title. BIP

Rugs, Oriental.

CALATCHI, Robert de 746.7'5
Oriental carpets. [Translated from the French by Valerie Howard] Rutland, Vt., C. E. Tuttle Co. [1967] xiii, 223 p. illus. (part col.), map. 36 cm. Translation of Tapis d'Orient. Bibliography: p. 217. [NK2808.C2613] 67-28904 22.50
1. Rugs, Oriental. I. Title.

CAMPANA, P. Michele. 746.7'5
Oriental carpets [by] Michele Campana; [translated from the Italian by Adeline Hartcup] London, New York, Hamlyn, 1969. 3-157 p. 66 col. illus. 20 cm. (Cameo) Originally published as Tappeti d'oriente. Milano, Fabbri, 1966. [NK2808.C2813] 70-437385 15/-
1. Rugs, Oriental. I. Title.

COEN, Luciano. 746.7'5
The oriental rug / Luciano Coen and Louise Duncan. 1st ed. New York : Harper & Row, c1978. p. cm. Includes index. Bibliography: p. [NK2808.C55 1978] 76-5119 ISBN 0-06-010824-X : 35.00
1. Rugs, Oriental. I. Duncan, Louise, joint author. II. Title. BIP

CON, J. M. 746.7'5
Carpets from the Orient, by J. M. Con. Translated from the Dutch by Marieke Clarke. New York, Universe Books [1967, c1966] 63 p. illus., map, plates (part col.) 21 cm. Bibliography: p. 62-63. [NK2808.C613 1967] 65-24048
1. Rugs, Oriental. I. Title.

DILLEY, Arthur Urbane, 1873- 746.75
Oriental rugs and carpets; a comprehensive study. Rev. by Maurice S. Dimand. [Rev. ed.] Philadelphia, Lippincott [1959] xxi, 289 p. 75 plates (part col.) maps. 29 cm. [NK2808.D5 1959] 59-13247
1. Rugs, Oriental. 2. Carpets.

EILAND, Murray L. 746.7'5
Oriental rugs: a comprehensive guide [by] Murray L. Eiland. Greenwich, Conn., New York Graphic Society [1973] 196 p. illus. (part col.) 32 cm. Includes bibliographical references. [NK2808.E44] 72-89825 ISBN 0-8212-0506-4 16.95
1. Rugs, Oriental.

†EILAND, Murray L. 746.7'5
Oriental rugs : a comprehensive guide / by Murray L. Eiland. Rev. and expanded ed. Boston : New York Graphic Society, c1976. 214 p., [24] leaves of plates : ill. (some col.) ; 32 cm. Includes bibliographical references and index. [NK2808.E44 1976] 76-12189 ISBN 0-8212-0643-5 : 24.50
1. Rugs, Oriental. I. Title.

ERDMANN, Kurt, 1901- 746.7509
Oriental carpets: an essay on their history. Tr. by Charles Grant Ellis. New York, Universe Books [1961, c.1960] 78p. illus. 179 plates (part col.) 28cm. Bibl. 60-14504 17.50, bxd.
1. Rugs, Oriental. I. Title.

ERDMANN, Kurt, 1901-1964. 746.7'5
Seven hundred years of Oriental carpets. Edited by Hanna Erdmann and translated by May H. Beattie and Hildegard Herzog. Berkeley, University of California Press [1970] 238 p. illus. (part col.) 32 cm. Translation of Siebenhundert Jahre Orientteppich. Includes bibliographical references. [NK2808.E7513 1970b] 69-12473 40.00
1. Rugs, Oriental. I. Title.

FOKKER, Nicolas, 1908- 746.7'5
Oriental carpets for today. [English translation by Keith Bradfield] Garden City, N.Y., Doubleday [1974, c1973] 135 p. illus. 28 cm. Translation of Orientaliska mattor av idag. [TS1778.F6413 1974] 73-12321 9.95
1. Rugs, Oriental. I. Title.

FORMENTON, Fabio. 746.7'5
Oriental rugs and carpets. [Translated by Pauline L. Phillips] New York, McGraw-Hill [1972] 251, [1] p. illus. 27 cm. Translation of Il libro del tappeto. Bibliography: p. [252] [NK2808.F6613 1972] 71-179881 ISBN 0-07-021540-5 12.95
1. Rugs, Oriental. I. Title. BIP

FORMENTON, Fabio. 746.7'5
Oriental rugs and carpets; [translated from the Italian by Pauline L. Phillips] London, New York, Hamlyn, 1972. 5-252 p. illus. (chiefly col.), maps. 27 cm. Translation of Il libro del tappeto. Bibliography: p. 252. [NK2808.F6613 1972b] 72-188557 ISBN 0-600-02888-7 £3.50
1. Rugs, Oriental. I. Title.

GANS-RUEDIN, Erwin. 746.7'5
The connoisseur's guide to oriental carpets [by] E. Gans-Ruedin. [Translated from the French by Valerie Howard] Rutland, Vt., C. E. Tuttle Co. [1971] 430 p. illus. (part col.) 26 cm. Translation of Connaissance du tapis. Bibliography: p. 426. [NK2808.G2613 1971b] 70-157255 ISBN 0-8048-0988-7 19.50
1. Rugs, Oriental. I. Title.

GANS-RUEDIN, Erwin 746.75
Oriental carpets. Berne. Hallwag [New York, Taplinger c.1965] 8p., 19 col. plates. 19cm. (Orbis pictus, 14) [NK2808.G273] 65-8840 2.50 bds.,
1. Rugs, Oriental. I. Title.

GREGORIAN, Arthur T. 746.7'5
Oriental rugs and the stories they tell [by] Arthur T. Gregorian. [1st ed.] Boston, Nimrod Press [1967] xvii, 230 p. illus. (part col.), maps. 21 x 25 cm. Bibliography: p. 225-230. [NK2808.G58 1967] 67-30362 14.50
1. Rugs, Oriental. I. Title. BIP

HAACK, Hermann. 746.75
Oriental rugs, an illustrated guide. Edited and translated by George and Cornelia Wingfield Digby. Newton, Mass., C. T. Branford Co. [1960] 76 p. illus. 26 cm. Translation of Echte Teppiche. [NK2808.H223] 60-50538
1. Rugs, Oriental. BIP

HAWLEY, Walter Augustus, 1863-1920. 746.7'5
Oriental rugs, antique and modern. [Magnolia, Mass.] [Peter Smith] [1973 c.1970] 320 p. illus., maps, col. plates. 24 cm. (Dover bk. rebound) Originally published in 1913. [NK2808.H3 1970] 79-105665 ISBN 0-486-22366-3 8.00
1. Rugs, Oriental. I. Title.

HOPF, Albrecht 746.75
Oriental carpets and rugs. [Tr. from German by Daphne Woodward] New York, Viking [c.1961, 1962] 140p. 62 col. plates. 28cm. (Studio bk.) 62-11771 22.50
1. Rugs, Oriental. 2. Carpets. I. Title.

IZMIDLIAN, Georges. 746.7'5
Oriental rugs and carpets today / Georges Izmidlian. New York : Hippocrene Books, [1977] p. cm. [NK2808.I95] 77-174 ISBN 0-88254-442-X : 10.95
1. Rugs, Oriental. I. Title. BIP

JACOBSEN, Charles W. 746.75
Oriental rugs, a complete guide. Rutland, Vt., Tuttle [c.1962] 479p. illus. (pt. col.) maps. 27cm. Bibl. 62-14117 10.00, bxd.
1. Rugs, Oriental. I. Title. BIP

JACOBSEN, Charles W 746.75
Oriental rugs, a complete guide. [1st ed.] Tokyo, Rutland, Vt., C. E. Tuttle Co., [1962] 479p. illus. (part col.) maps. 27cm. 'About rug books: p. 144-149. [NK2808.J3113] 62-14117
1. Rugs, Oriental. I. Title.

KESHISHIAN, Mark, 1894- 746.7'5
Guide to Oriental rugs. [Washington, 1970] xvi, 134 p. illus. (part col.), maps, col. port. 32 cm. Bibliography: p. 132. [NK2808.K35] 74-125356
1. Rugs, Oriental. I. Title.

KYBALOVA, Ludmila. 746.7'5
Carpets of the Orient. Text by Ludmila Kybalova and photos. by Dominique Darbois. [Translated by Till Gottheiner] London, New York, P. Hamlyn [1969] 56 p. illus., map, 74 col. plates. 29 cm. [NK2808.K913] 77-481875
1. Rugs, Oriental. I. Darbois, Dominique, illus. II. Title.

LIEBETRAU, Preben. 746.75
Oriental rugs in colour. [Translated from the Danish by Katherine John] New York, Macmillan [1963] 131 p. illus., col. plates, maps. 19 cm. Bibliography: p. 129. [NK2808.L683] 63-18408
1. Rugs, Oriental. I. Title.

MILHOFER, S. A. 746.7'5
The color treasury of oriental rugs / Stefan A. Milhofer ; translated by D. D. Paige. New York : Crowell, c1976. ix, 134 p. : ill. (some col.) : 30 cm. Includes index. [NK2808.M49 1976] 75-28057 ISBN 0-690-01060-5 : 9.95
1. Rugs, Oriental. I. Title.

RAPHAELIAN, Harry M., 1882- 745.52643
The hidden language of symbols in oriental rugs; with introd. by Felix Marti-Ibanez. New York, A. Sivas, 1953. 230 p. illus. 24 cm. [NK2808.R3] 53-5737
1. Rugs, Oriental. 2. Symbolism in art. I. Title.

REED, Stanley, 1912- 746.7'5
Oriental rugs and carpets. New York, Putnam [1967] 120 p. illus. (part col.) 22 cm. (Pleasures and treasures) [NK2808] 67-21989
1. Rugs, Oriental. I. Title.

SCHLOSSER, Ignaz. 746.75
The book of rugs, Oriental and European. New York, Crown [1963] 318 p. illus.

SUBJECT INDEX RUSKIN, JOHN, 1819-1900.

(part col.) maps. 29 cm. Translation of Der schone Teppich in Orient und Okzident. Bibliography: p. 307-309. [NK2808.S333] 62-11812
1. Rugs, Oriental. 2. Rugs. I. Title.

WILLIAMS, Moddie Jeffries. 746.7'5
A primer of facts about Oriental rugs. New York, Carlton Press [1967] 144 p. illus., 24 plates. 21 cm. (A Hearthstone book) Bibliography: p. 140. [NK2808.W5] 67-5866
1. Rugs, Oriental. I. Title.

Rugs, Oriental—Catalogs.

NEW York (City). Metropolitan Museum of Art. 746.7'5
Oriental rugs in the Metropolitan Museum of Art, by M. S. Dimand, curator emeritus of Islamic art. With a chapter and catalogue of rugs of China and Chinese Turkestan by Jean Mailey, associate curator of the textile study room. [New York]; Distributed by New York Graphic Society [Greenwich, Conn., 1973] ix, 353 p. illus. 28 cm. Bibliography: p. 351-353. [NK2808.N37] 73-2846 ISBN 0-87099-124-8 45.00
1. Rugs, Oriental—Catalogs. 2. Rugs—New York (City)—Catalogs. I. Dimand, Maurice Sven. II. Mailey, Jean. III. Title.

SCHLICK, Donald P. 746.7'5
Modern oriental carpets; a buyer's guide, by Donald P. Schlick. Illus. by Yvonne J. Schlick. Rutland, Vt., C. E. Tuttle Co. [1970] 139 p. illus., map, col. plates. 22 cm. Bibliography: p. 139. [NK2808.S32 1970] 72-123896 5.00
1. Rugs, Oriental—Catalogs. I. Title.

Rugs, Oriental—Exhibitions.

DIMAND, Maurice Sven. 746.7'5
The Kevorkian Foundation collection of rare and magnificent oriental carpets: special loan exhibition, a guide and catalog, by Maurice S. Dimand. New York, 1966. [35] p. 17 plates (part col.) 23 cm. [NK2808.D52] 68-1167
1. Rugs, Oriental—Exhibitions. 2. Rugs—Private collections. I. Kevorkian Foundation. II. Title.

GARDINER, Roger F. 746.7'5
Art of the loom; a loan exhibition of Oriental rugs for the month of November, organized and catalogued by Roger F. Gardiner. Chatham, Ont., Thames Art Gallery; supplied by World Wide Books, Boston, 1973. [64] p. illus. 23 cm. Bibliography: p. [63]-[64] [NK2808.G32] 74-167414
1. Rugs, Oriental—Exhibitions. I. Thames Art Gallery. II. Title.

HARVARD University. William Hayes Fogg Art Museum 746.7584074014461
Turkoman rugs. Foreword by Joseph V. McMullan. Introd., notes by Christopher Dunham Reed. Cambridge, Mass., Author [c]1966. 63p. illus. (pt. col.) map. 22x23cm. Catalog of an exhibition held in the Fogg Art Mus., Jan. 26, 1966 through Mar. 6, 1966. [NK2809.T83H3] 66-11620 8.50 bds.,
1. Rugs, Oriental—Exhibitions. I. Reed, Christopher Dunham. II. Title.

LANDREAU, Anthony N., 1930- 746.7
From the Bosporus to Samarkand; flat-woven rugs [by] Anthony N. Landreau [and] W. R. Pickering. Washington, Textile Museum, 1969. 112 p. illus. (part col.) 28 cm. Catalog of a loan exhibition held at the Textile Museum, Washington, D.C., May 25-Sept. 27, 1969, and subsequently circulated by the Smithsonian Institution. Bibliography: p. 111. [NK2808.L27] 71-81238
1. Rugs, Oriental—Exhibitions. I. Pickering, W. R., joint author. II. Washington, D.C. Textile Museum. III. Smithsonian Institution. IV. Title. BIP

O'BANNON, George W. 746.7'5
Oriental rugs from western Pennsylvania collections, 12 January-February 2, 1975 : [notes on the exhibition / by George W. O'Bannon]. Greensburg, Pa. : Westmoreland County Museum of Art, 1975. [84] p. : ill. (some col.) ; 21 cm. Catalog. Bibliography: p. [84] [NK2808.O22] 74-31655
1. Rugs, Oriental—Exhibitions. 2. Rugs—Private collections—Pennsylvania. I. Westmoreland County Museum of Art, Greensburg, Pa. II. Title: Oriental rugs from western Pennsylvania collections ...

Rugs, Oriental—Handbooks, manuals, etc.

JACOBSEN, Charles W. 746.7
Check points on how to buy oriental rugs [by] Charles W. Jacobsen. [1st ed.] Rutland, Vt., C. E. Tuttle Co. [1969] 208 p. illus. (part col.), map. 27 cm. [NK2808.J28] 73-94020 ISBN 0-8048-0714-0 7.50
1. Rugs, Oriental—Handbooks, manuals, etc. I. Title. II. Title: How to buy oriental rugs. BIP

Rugs, Oriental—History.

HUBEL, Reinhard G. 746.7'5
The book of carpets [by] Reinhard G. Hubel. Translated by Katherine Watson. New York, Praeger Publishers [1970] 348 p. illus. (part col.), maps. 24 cm. Translation of Ullstein Teppichbuch. Bibliography: p. 345-346. [NK2800.H813 1970] 71-107152 15.00
1. Rugs, Oriental—History. I. Title.

Rugs, Oriental—Iran—Exhibitions.

BEATTIE, May H. 746.7'55
Carpets of central Persia : with special reference to rugs to Kirman / [by] May H. Beattie. [London] : World of Islam Festival Publishing Co. Ltd, 1976. 104 p., [8] p. of plates : ill. (some col.), map ; 26 cm. Catalogue of an exhibition held 10 Apr.-19 May at the Mappin Art Gallery, Sheffield, and 4 June-11 July at the City Museum and Art Gallery, Birmingham. Technical note, 1 p. inserted. Bibliography: p. 97-104. [NK2809.P4B4] 76-377866 ISBN 0-905035-16-X. ISBN 0-905035-17-8 pbk.
1. Rugs, Oriental—Iran—Exhibitions. 2. Rugs—Iran—Exhibitions. 3. Rugs—Iran—Kerman (City)—Exhibitions. I. Mappin Art Gallery, Sheffield, Eng. II. Birmingham, Eng. Museum and Art Gallery. III. Title.

Rugs, Persian.

EDWARDS, Arthur Cecil, 1881- 745.52643
The Persian carpet; a survey of the carpetweaving industry of Persia. London, Duckworth [1967] xvi, 384p. illus. (pt. col) port., maps. 29cm. [NK2809.P4E3] 54-29181 36.00
1. Rugs, Persian. I. Title.
Available from Humanities, New York. BIP

Rugs, Rumanian.

ZDERCIUC, Boris 746.79498
The hand-woven rugs of Maramures, Rumania. Bucarest, Meridane [dist. New York, Vanous] 1963 27p. illus. (pt. col.) 19cm. Bibl. 64-1057 2.00 pap.,
1. Rugs, Rumanian. I. Title.

Rugs—Spain.

†HISPANIC Society of America. 746.7'946
Rugs of Spain and Morocco / the Hispanic Society of America ; Florence Lewis May. Chicago : University of Chicago Press, 1977. vii, 41 p. ; 23 cm. & microfiche (1 card ; 11 x 15 cm.) in pocket. (A University of Chicago Press text-fiche) Bibliography: p. 39-41. [NK2862.A1H57 1977] 77-9513 ISBN 0-226-69109-8 : 19.00
1. Rugs—Spain. 2. Rugs—Morocco. I. May, Florence Lewis. II. Hispanic Society of America. III. Title. BIP

Rugs, Turkish.

ASIANAPA, Oktay. 709.561
Turkish arts: Seljuk and Ottoman carpets, tiles and miniature paintings. [Translated by Herman Kreider. Rev. by Sheila M. O'Callaghan] Edited, published and printed by Dogan Kardes Yayinlari. Istanbul [1961?] 147 [24] p. illus. (part col.) 17 cm. Label mounted on t. p.: Sole distributors Paragon Book Gallery, New York. Bibliography: p. [166]-[169] [NK2809.T8A83] NE63
1. Rugs, Turkish. 2. Tiles. 3. Miniature painting — Turkey. I. Title.

ASLANAPA, Oktay 709.561
Turkish arts: Seljuk and Ottoman carpets, tiles and miniature paintings. [Tr. from Turkish by Herman Kreider. Rev. by Sheila M. O'Callaghan] Ed., published, printed by Dogan Kardes Yayinlari. Istanbul [dist. New York, Paragon, 1962] 147 [24] p. illus. (pt. col.) 17cm. Bibl. NE 63 3.50 pap.,
1. Rugs, Turkish. 2. Tiles. 3. Miniature painting—Turkey. I. Title.

Rugs, Turkish—Exhibitions.

WASHINGTON, D.C. Textile Museum. 746.7'561'0740153
Turkish rugs. The Rachel B. Stevens Memorial Collection. With an introd. by Joseph V. McMullan. Washington [1972] 63 p. illus. (part col.) 28 cm. Catalogue of an exhibition held at the Textile Museum, Sept. 24-Dec. 9, 1972. [NK2865.A1W37] 73-154450
1. Stevens, Rachel B.—Art collections. 2. Rugs, Turkish—Exhibitions. I. Title. BIP

Rugs, Turkoman.

O'BANNON, George W. 746.7'58
The Turkoman carpet / George W. O'Bannon. London : Duckworth, 1974 [i.e.1975] 168 p. : ill. (some col.), map ; 29 cm. Includes index. Bibliography: p. 164-165. [NK2875.O2] 75-328318 ISBN 0-7156-0256-X : 75.00
1. Rugs, Turkoman. 2. Rugs—Asia, Central. I. Title.
Distributed by Humanities. BIP

Ruins in art.

CUMMER Gallery of Art. 760'.074'0159
Remnants of things past; [an exhibition at] the Museum of Fine Arts, St. Petersburg, Fla., January 8-February 7, 1971 [and] the Cummer Gallery of Art, Jacksonville, Fla., February 16-March 14, 1971. [Jacksonville? 1971] 1 v. (unpaged) illus. 23 x 27 cm. Catalog written by Margaret Koscielny Parker. [N8237.8.R8C85] 71-198213
1. Ruins in art. 2. Art—Exhibitions. I. Parker, Margaret Koscielny. II. St. Petersburg, Fla. Museum of Fine Arts. III. Title.

Rukhin, Evgenii, 1943—

RUKHIN, Evgenii, 1943- 759.7
Eugene Rukhin, a contemporary Russian artist : an exhibition of paintings from private collections in the United States and Canada, August 10 through September 14, 1975 / Moussa M. Domit, Ruth Mayfield, Doris E. Dunlavy. Raleigh : North Carolina Museum of Art, 1975. p. cm. Includes index. [ND699.R83D65] 75-25733 ISBN 0-88259-079-0
1. Rukhin, Evgenii, 1943- 2. Paintings—Private collections—United States. I. Domit, Moussa M. II. Mayfield, Ruth, 1940- III. Dunlavy, Doris E., 1914- IV. North Carolina. Museum of Art, Raleigh. V. Title.

Runge, Philipp Otto, 1777-1810.

BISANZ, Rudolf M. 759.3
German romanticism and Philipp Otto Runge; a study in nineteenth-century art theory and iconography [by] Rudolf M. Bisanz. DeKalb, Northern Illinois University Press, 1970. xi, 144 p. illus. 26 cm. Bibliography: p. 131-139. [ND588.R9B5] 74-98388
1. Runge, Philipp Otto, 1777-1810. I. Title. BIP

Rupee, Indian.

FALCKE, George. 737.49'54
India's 1862 rupees, by George Falcke and Robert L. Clarke. [Iola, Wis., Krause Publications, 1971] 34 p. illus. 23 cm. Includes bibliographical references. [CJ3546.F33] 78-148382
1. Rupee, Indian. I. Clarke, Robert L., joint author. II. Title.

Rush-work.

CANE and rush seating. 684.1'3
Leicester : Dryad Press, [1976?] 16 p. : ill. ; 21 cm. (Dryad leaflet ; 16) Cover title. [TT877.C37] 77-362485 ISBN 0-85219-508-7 : £0.20
1. Rush-work. 2. Furniture—Repairing.

FLORANCE, Norah 746.41
Rush-work. Illus. by Jennie Corbett. Photos. by J. W. Florance. London, G. Bell [dist. New Rochelle, N.Y., Sportshelf, c.1962] 90p. illus. 19cm. (Bell handbk.) 62-4970 3.25 bds.,
1. Rush-work. I. Title.

WHITBOURN, Kathleen. 746.4'1
Introducing rushcraft [by] K. Whitbourn. Photos. by P. R. Whitbourn. Newton Centre, Mass., C. T. Branford Co. [1969] 95 p. illus. (part col.) 22 cm. [TT877.W48 1969b] 70-92277
1. Rush-work. I. Title. BIP

Ruskin, John, 1819-1900.

ASHBEE, Charles Robert, 1863-1942. 745.4'49'42
An endeavour towards the teaching of John Ruskin and William Morris. [Folcroft, Pa.] Folcroft Library Editions, 1973. 52 p. 23 cm. Reprint of the 1901 ed. published by E. Arnold, London. [NK1142.A7 1973] 73-7761 10.00
1. Ruskin, John, 1819-1900. 2. Morris, William, 1834-1896. 3. Guild of Handicraft, London. 4. Essex House Press, London. 5. Arts and crafts movement. I. Title.

BENSON, Arthur Christopher, 1862-1925. 828'.8'09 B
Ruskin : a study in personality / by Arthur Christopher Benson. New York : Haskell House Publishers, [1977.] p. cm. Reprint of the 1911 ed. published by Smith, Elder, London. [PR5263.B4 1976] 76-26 ISBN 0-8383-1921-1 : 13.95
1. Ruskin, John, 1819-1900.

BENSON, Arthur Christopher, 1862-1925. 828'.8'09 B
Ruskin; a study in personality. London, Smith, Elder, 1911. St. Clair Shores, Mich., Scholarly Press, 1973. p. Seven lectures originally delivered at Magdalene College, Cambridge, in 1910. [PR5263.B4 1973] 73-6985 ISBN 0-403-01757-2 19.50
1. Ruskin, John, 1819-1900. I. Title.

COOK, Edward Tyas, Sir, 1857-1919. 700'.924 B
The life of John Ruskin. New York, Haskell House Publishers, 1968. 2 v. illus., ports. 24 cm. Reprint of the 1911 ed. Contents.—v. 1. 1819-1860.—v. 2. 1860-1900. [PR5263.C7 1968] 68-24903
1. Ruskin, John, 1819-1900. I. Title.

COOK, Edward Tyas, Sir, 1857-1919. 709'.24
Studies in Ruskin: some aspects of the work and teaching of John Ruskin. With reproductions of drawings by Mr. Ruskin. Port Washington, N.Y., Kennikat Press [1972] xiv, 334 p. illus. 21 cm. Reprint of the 1890 ed. [PR5263.C75 1972] 71-160751 ISBN 0-8046-1567-5
1. Ruskin, John, 1819-1900. I. Title.

CROW, Gerald H. 828'.8'09 B
Ruskin, by Gerald Crow. [Folcroft, Pa.] Folcroft Library Editions, 1973. 140 p. 24 cm. Reprint of the 1936 ed. published by Duckworth, London, in series: Great lives. Bibliography: p. 140. [PR5263.C8 1973] 73-19678 ISBN 0-8414-3530-8 (lib. bdg.)
1. Ruskin, John, 1819-1900. BIP

DOWNES, Robert Percival, 1842-1924. 828'.8'09
John Ruskin: a study. [Folcroft, Pa.]

Folcroft Library Editions, 1973. 119 p. illus. 23 cm. Reprint of the 1890 ed. published by A. W. Hall, London. [PR5263.D65 1973] 73-7768 ISBN 0-8414-1872-1 (lib. bdg.)
1. Ruskin, John, 1819-1900.

DOWNES, Robert Percival, 1842-1924. 828'.8'09 B
John Ruskin : a study / by R. P. Downes. Norwood, Pa. : Norwood Editions, 1976. p. cm. Reprint of the 1890 ed. published by A. W. Hall, London. [PR5263.D65 1976] 76-4490 ISBN 0-88305-493-0 : 15.00
1. Ruskin, John, 1819-1900.

EARLAND, Ada. 828'.8'09 B
Ruskin and his circle. New York, AMS Press [1971] xi, 340 p. illus., ports. 18 cm. Reprint of the 1910 ed. Bibliography: p. 333-334. [PR5263.E2 1971] 71-129381 ISBN 0-404-02232-4
1. Ruskin, John, 1819-1900. I. Title.

EVANS, Joan, 1893- 709'.24
John Ruskin. New York, Oxford University Press, 1954. 447p. illus., ports. 23cm. Bibliography: p. 424-430. [PR5263.E9] 54-12299
1. Ruskin, John, 1819-1900. I. Title. BIP

EVANS, Joan, 1893- 828'.8'09 B
John Ruskin. New York, Haskell House Publishers, 1970. 447 p. illus., ports. 23 cm. Bibliography: p. 424-430. [PR5263.E9 1970] 70-117998 ISBN 0-8383-1053-2
1. Ruskin, John, 1819-1900.

HARRISON, Frederic, 1831-1923. 820*.9*092
John Ruskin. New York, Macmillan, 1902. Ann Arbor, Mich., Gryphon Books, 1971. vi, 216 p. 22 cm. (English men of letters) [PR5263.H3 1971] 72-78229
1. Ruskin, John, 1819-1900. BIP

HEWISON, Robert, 1943- 709'.2'4 B
John Ruskin : the argument of the eye / Robert Hewison. London : Thames and Hudson, c1976. 228 p. : ill. (some col.) ; 24 cm. Includes index. Bibliography: p. 219-223. [ND497.R88H48 1976c] 77-364352 ISBN 0-500-01148-6 : £7.50
1. Ruskin, John, 1819-1900.

HEWISON, Robert, 1943- 709'.2'4 B
John Ruskin : the argument of the eye / Robert Hewison. Princeton, N.J. : Princeton University Press, c1976. 228 p. : ill. (some col.) ; 24 cm. Includes index. Bibliography: p. 219-223. [ND497.R88H48] 77-352685 ISBN 0-691-03890-2 : 15.00
1. Ruskin, John, 1819-1900.

LEON, Derrick, 1908-1944. 700'.924 B
Ruskin, the great Victorian. [Hamden, Conn.] Archon Books, 1969. xxvi, 595 p. ports. 23 cm. "First published in ... 1949." Bibliography: p. 583-586. [PR5263.L4 1969] 79-8514 12.00
1. Ruskin, John, 1819-1900. I. Title. BIP

MATHER, Marshall, 1851-1916. 828'.8'09
John Ruskin: his life and teaching. 5th ed. [Folcroft, Pa.] Folcroft Library Editions [1973. xxvii, 184 p. port. 23 cm. Reprint of the 1903 ed. published by F. Warne, London and New York. Bibliography: p. [171]-179. [PR5263.M3 1973] 73-14927 9.75
1. Ruskin, John, 1819-1900. I. Title.

ROSENBERG, John D. 828.8
The darkening glass; a portrait of Ruskin's genius. New York, Columbia University Press, 1961. 274 p. illus. 24 cm. Includes bibliography. [PR5263.R6] 61-16678
1. Ruskin, John, 1819-1900. I. Title.

RUSKIN, John, 1819-1900. 828'.8'09 B
The Brantwood diary of John Ruskin, together with selected related letters and sketches of persons mentioned. Edited and annotated by Helen Gill Viljoen. New Haven, Yale University Press, 1971. xv, 632 p. illus. 25 cm. [PR5263.A13 1971] 72-99844 ISBN 0-300-01227-6 25.00
I. Title.

SPIELMANN, Marion Harry, 1858-1948. 828'.8'09 B
John Ruskin; a sketch of his life, his work, and his opinions, with personal reminiscences. [Folcroft, Pa.] Folcroft Library Editions, 1973. p. Reprint of the 1900 ed. published by Cassell, London, New York. [PR5263.S66 1973] 73-15854 ISBN 0-8414-7681-0 (lib. bdg.)
1. Ruskin, John, 1819-1900.

UNRAU, John. 720'.9
Looking at architecture with Ruskin / John Unrau. Toronto ; Buffalo : University of Toronto Press, 1978. 180 p., [2] leaves of plates : ill. (some col.) ; 25 cm. Includes index. Bibliography: p. 172-174. [NA2760.U57] 78-318139 ISBN 0-8020-2284-7 : 15.00
1. Ruskin, John, 1819-1900. 2. Architecture—Composition, proportion, etc. 3. Decoration and ornament, Architectural. 4. Architecture—Psychological aspects. I. Title. BIP

VILJOEN, Helen Gill. 928.2
Ruskin's Scottish heritage, a prelude. Urbana, University of Illinois Press, 1956. 284p. illus., ports., facsims., geneal. table. 24cm. Bibliography: p. [257]-266. [PR5263.V5] 56-8062
1. Ruskin, John, 181g-1900. I. Title. BIP

WALTON, Paul H. 741'.092'4
The drawings of John Ruskin [by] Paul H. Walton. Oxford, Clarendon Press, 1972. x, 134 p., leaf. illus. (incl. 1 col.), map. 29 cm. (Oxford studies in the history of art and architecture) Bibliography: p. [127]-130. [NC242.R8W34] 73-151272 ISBN 0-19-817305-9 24.00
1. Ruskin, John, 1819-1900. I. Title. II. Series.
Distributed by Oxford University Press N.Y. BIP

WHITEHOUSE, John Howard, 1873- ed. 828'.8'09
Ruskin the prophet, and other centenary studies, by John Masefield [and others] Edited by J. Howard Whitehouse. [Folcroft, Pa.] Folcroft Library Editions, 1973. 157 p. 24 cm. Reprint of the 1920 ed. published by G. Allen & Unwin, London. For the most part lectures delivered at the Ruskin exhibition in the Royal Academy, held in co-operation with the Ruskin Centenary Council, 1919. Contents.Contents.—Masefield, J. Ruskin.—Inge, W. R. Ruskin and Plato.—Masterman, C. F. G. Ruskin the prophet.—Binyon, L. John Ruskin.—Hobson, J. A. Ruskin as political economist.—Dale, J. A. Ruskin and Shakespeare.—Whitehouse, J. H. Ruskin and an early friendship (with many unpublished letters).—Whitehouse, J. H. Ruskin and London.—Nevinson, H. W. Some memories of Ruskin. [PR5263.W47 1973] 73-11306 22.50
1. Ruskin, John, 1819-1900. I. Masefield, John, 1878-1967. II. Ruskin Centenary Council, London. III. Title.
Contents Omitted. BIP

WILENSKI, Reginald Howard, 1887- 828'.8'09
John Ruskin; an introduction to further study of his life and work, by R. H. Wilenski. New York, Russell & Russell [1967] 406 p. ports. 22 cm. Reprint of the 1933 ed. Bibliographical footnotes. [PR5263.W476 1967] 66-27182
1. Ruskin, John, 1819-1900.

WILENSKI, Reginald Howard, 1887- 828'.8'09 B
John Ruskin; an introduction to further study of his life and work, by R. H. Wilenski. [Folcroft, Pa.] Folcroft Library Editions, 1974. p. cm. Reprint of the 1933 ed. published by Faber & Faber, London. [PR5263.W476 1974] 74-9725 35.00 (lib. bdg.).
1. Ruskin, John, 1819-1900. BIP

WILENSKI, Reginald Howard, 1887- 828'.8'09 B
John Ruskin : an introduction to further study of his life and work / by R. H. Wilenski. New York : AMS Press, [1978] p. cm. Reprint of the 1933 ed. published by Faber & Faber, London. Includes index. [PR5263.W476 1978] 75-30042 ISBN 0-404-14046-7 : 28.50
1. Ruskin, John, 1819-1900. 2. Authors, English—19th century—Biography.

WINGATE, Ashmore Kyle Paterson, 1881- 828'.8'09 B
Life of John Ruskin, by Ashmore Wingate. [Folcroft, Pa.] Folcroft Library Editions, 1973. p. Reprint of the 1910 ed. published by Walter Scott Pub. Co., London, in series: Great writers. Bibliography: p. [PR5263.W5 1973] 73-12590 20.00
1. Ruskin, John, 1819-1900. I. Title.

Ruskin, John, 1819-1900—Aesthetics.

LADD, Henry Andrews, 1895-1941. 701.17
The Victorian morality of art; an analysis of Ruskin's esthetic. New York, Octagon Books, 1968 [c1932] xi, 418 p. 22 cm. Includes bibliographical references. [N62.R8L3 1968] 68-22298
1. Ruskin, John, 1819-1900—Aesthetics. 2. Art and morals. I. Title. BIP

STEIN, Roger B. 111.8'5'0973
John Ruskin and aesthetic thought in America, 1840-1900 [by] Roger B. Stein. Cambridge, Mass., Harvard University Press, 1967. xviii, 321 p. illus., port. 22 cm. Bibliographical references included in "Notes" (p. [267]-307) [BH221.U53S7] 67-20883
1. Ruskin, John, 1819-1900—Aesthetics. 2. Aesthetics, American. I. Title.

Ruskin, John, 1819-1900—Appreciation.

WHITEHOUSE, John Howard, 1873- 828'.8'09
John Ruskin. New York, Haskell House [1974] p. cm. Reprint of the 1953 ed. printed at the University Press, Oxford, for the Ruskin Society and Friends of Brantwood. [PR5263.W45 1974] 74-8083 ISBN 0-8383-1914-9 7.95
1. Ruskin, John, 1819-1900—Appreciation.

Ruskin, John, 1819-1900—Biography.

LARG, David Glass. 828'.8'09 B
John Ruskin, by David Larg. [Folcroft, Pa.] Folcroft Library Editions, 1974. p. cm. Reprint of the 1933 ed. published by D. Appleton, New York, in series: Appleton biographies. [PR5263.L26 1974b] 74-11438 ISBN 0-8414-5735-2 12.50
1. Ruskin, John, 1819-1900—Biography. I. Series: Appleton biographies.

MASEFIELD, John, 1878-1967. 828'.8'09 B
John Ruskin / by John Masefield. Folcroft, Pa. : Folcroft Library Editions, 1977. p. cm. "Originally delivered by Mr. Masefield as a lecture at the Ruskin Centenary Exhibition held at the Royal Academy in the autumn of 1919." Reprint of the 1920 ed. printed by H. Whitehouse and E. Daws at the Yellowsands Press, Bembridge, Eng. [PR5263.M28 1977] 77-24663 ISBN 0-8414-6213-5 lib. bdg. : 10.00
1. Ruskin, John, 1819-1900—Biography. 2. Authors, English—19th century—Biography. I. Title.

Ruskin, John, 1819-1900—Correspondence.

RUSKIN, John, 1819-1900. 828'.8'09 B
John Ruskin's letters to William Ward : with a short biography of William Ward / by William C. Ward ; and an introd. by Alfred Mansfield Brooks. Norwood, Pa. : Norwood Editions, 1976, c1922. p. cm. Reprint of the ed. published by Marshall Jones Co., Boston. [PR5263.A475 1976] 76-15200 ISBN 0-8482-0163-9 : 20.00
1. Ruskin, John, 1819-1900—Correspondence. 2. Ward, William, 1829-1908. I. Ward, William C. II. Title.

RUSKIN, John, 1819-1900. 828'.8'09 B
John Ruskin's letters to William Ward / with a short biography of William Ward by William C. Ward ; and an introd. by Alfred Mansfield Brooks. Folcroft, Pa. : Folcroft Library Editions, 1974 [c1922] p. cm. Reprint of the ed. published by M. Jones Co., Boston. [PR5263.A475 1974] 74-20802 ISBN 0-8414-3219-8 lib. bdg. : 22.50
1. Ruskin, John, 1819-1900—Correspondence. 2. Ward, William, 1829-1908. I. Ward, William, 1829-1908. II. Ward, William C., ed. III. Title. BIP

RUSKIN, John, 1819-1900. 828'.8'09 B
Letters of John Ruskin to Bernard Quaritch, 1867-1888 / edited by Charlotte Quaritch Wrentmore. Norwood, Pa. : Norwood Editions, 1976. p. cm. Reprint of the 1938 ed. published by B. Quaritch, London. [PR5263.A45 1976] 76-13479 ISBN 0-8482-2855-3 lib. bdg. : 15.00
1. Ruskin, John, 1819-1900—Correspondence. 2. Quaritch, Bernard, 1819-1899. I. Quaritch, Bernard, 1819-1899. II. Title.

RUSKIN, John, 1819-1900. 828'.8'09 B
Letters of John Ruskin to Bernard Quaritch, 1867-1888. Edited by Charlotte Quaritch Wrentmore. [Folcroft, Pa.] Folcroft Library Editions, 1974. vi, 125 p. facsim. 24 cm. Reprint of the 1938 ed. published by B. Quaritch, London. [PR5263.A45 1974] 74-13028 17.50
1. Ruskin, John, 1819-1900—Correspondence. 2. Quaritch, Bernard, 1819-1899. I. Quaritch, Bernard, 1819-1899. II. Wrentmore, Charlotte Quaritch, ed. III. Title.

RUSKIN, John, 1819-1900. 914.5'04'8
Ruskin in Italy: letters to his parents, 1845; edited by Harold I. Shapiro. Oxford, Clarendon Press, 1972. xxii, 263 p., [8] leaves. illus. 23 cm. Includes bibliographical references. [PR5263.A27 1972] 72-192985 ISBN 0-19-812441-4 £6.00 ($20.50 U.S.)
I. Shapiro, Harold I., ed. II. Title.

RUSKIN, John, 1819-1900. 928.2
Ruskin's letters from Venice, 1851-1852 By John Lewis Bradley. New Haven, Yale University Press, 1955. xx. 330p. illus. 24cm. (Yale studies in English, v. 129) The editor's thesis--Yale University.Without thesis statement. 'Daily letters from Ruskin to his father.' Bibliographical footnotes. [PR5263.A37] 55-9436
I. Ruskin, John James. II. Bradley, John Lewis, ed. III. Title. IV. Series.

RUSKIN, John, 1819-1900. 828'.8'09 B
The Winnington letters; John Ruskin's correspondence with Margaret Alexis Bell and the children at Winnington Hall. Edited by Van Akin Burd. Cambridge, Mass., Belknap Press of Harvard University Press, 1969. 739 p. illus. 25 cm. Bibliography: p. 715-716. [PR5263.A28 1969b] 68-28692
I. Bell, Margaret Alexis, 1818-1889. II. Burd, Van Akin, 1914- ed. III. Title. BIP

Ruskin, John, 1819-1900—Criticism and interpretation.

FELLOWS, Jay, 1940- 700'.92'4 B
The failing distance : the autobiographical impulse in John Ruskin / by Jay Fellows. Baltimore : John Hopkins University Press, [1975] xvi, 187 p. ; 23 cm. Includes bibliographical references. [PR5264.F4] 74-24374 ISBN 0-8018-1671-8 : 10.00
1. Ruskin, John, 1819-1900—Criticism and interpretation. I. Title. BIP

Ruskin, John, 1819-1900—Homes and haunts—Coniston, Eng.

WHITEHOUSE, John Howard, 1873- 828'.8'09 B
Ruskin & Brantwood; an account of the exhibition rooms. [Folcroft, Pa.] Folcroft Library Editions, 1973. 43 p. illus. 24 cm. Reprint of the 1937 ed. printed at the University Press, Cambridge, and published by the Ruskin Society. [PR5263.W455 1973] 73-17088 10.00
1. Ruskin, John, 1819-1900—Homes and haunts—Coniston, Eng. 2. Ruskin, John, 1819-1900—Museums, relics, etc. I. Title. BIP

Ruskin, John, 1819-1900—Influence.

GARRIGAN, Kristine Ottesen, 1939- 720'.9
Ruskin on architecture: his thought and

influence. [Madison] University of Wisconsin Press [1973] xv, 220 p. illus. 25 cm. Includes bibliographical references. [NA610.G37] 73-2045 ISBN 0-299-06460-3 20.00
1. Ruskin, John, 1819-1900—Influence. 2. Gothic revival (Architecture) 3. Architecture, Victorian. I. Title.

Russell, Charles Marion, 1864-1926.

AMON Carter Museum of 709'.2'4
Western Art, Fort Worth, Tex.
Charles M. Russell; paintings, drawings, and sculpture in the Amon Carter Museum [by] Frederic G. Renner. [Rev. ed.] New York, H. N. Abrams [1974] 296 p. illus. (part col.) 31 x 35 cm. Bibliography: p. 291-292. [ND237.R75A72 1974] 74-5114 ISBN 0-8109-0466-7
1. Russell, Charles Marion, 1864-1926. 2. The West in art. I. Renner, Frederic Gordon, 1897-

AMON Carter Museum of 709.73
Western Art, Fort Worth, Tex.
Charles M. Russell; paintings, drawings and sculpture in the Amon G. Carter collection: a descriptive catalogue, by Frederic G. Renner. Foreword by Ruth Carter Johnson. Austin, University of Texas Press [1966] xvi, 148 p. illus. (part col.) map., port. 30 cm. Bibliography: p. 143-144. [ND237.R75A72] 65-11152
1. Russell, Charles Marion, 1864-1926. 2. The West in art. I. Renner, Frederic Gordon, 1897-

AMON Carter Museum of 709'.2'4
Western Art, Fort Worth, Tex.
Charles M. Russell: paintings, drawings, and sculpture in the Amon G. Carter Collection; a descriptive catalogue, by Frederic G. Renner. Foreword by Ruth Carter Johnson. Austin, University of Texas Press [1972, c1966] xvi, 148 p. illus. 30 cm. Bibliography: p. 143-144. [ND237.R75A72 1972] 72-192460 ISBN 0-292-73622-3 20.00
1. Russell, Charles Marion, 1864-1926. 2. The West in art. I. Renner, Frederic Gordon, 1897-

†AMON Carter Museum of 709'.2'4
Western Art, Forth Worth, Tex.
Charles M. Russell : paintings, drawings, and sculpture in the Amon Carter Museum / by Frederic G. Renner ; foreword by Ruth Carter Johnson. New concise ed. New York : H. N. Abrams, 1976. 160 p. : ill. (some col.) ; 24 x 28 cm. Includes index. [ND237.R75A72 1976] 76-22656 ISBN 0-8109-2057-3 : 40.00
1. Russell, Charles Marion, 1864-1926. 2. Amon Carter Museum of Western Art, Fort Worth, Tex. 3. The West in art. I. Russell, Charles Marion, 1864-1926. II. Renner, Frederic Gordon, 1897-

GARST, Doris Shannon, 1899- 927.5
Cowboy-artist: Charles M. Russell. New York, Messner [1960] 192 p. 22 cm. Includes bibliography. [ND237.R75G3] 60-7057
1. Russell, Charles Marion, 1864-1926. I. Title.

GARST, Doris Shannon, 709'.24 B
1899-
Cowboy-artist: Charles M. Russell. New York, Messner [1960] 192 p. 22 cm. Includes bibliography. A biography of the painter and sculptor who spent his boyhood yearning to go west, fulfilled his own dream of illustrating the life of the cowboy, and finally won recognition for his realistic portrayal of the Old West. [ND237.R75G3] 92 AC 68
1. Russell, Charles Marion, 1864-1926. I. Title.

LINDERMAN, Frank Bird, 927.5
1868-1938.
Recollections of Charley Russell. Edited by H. G. Merriam, with drawings by Charley Russell. [1st ed.] Norman, University of Oklahoma Press [1963] xxxii, 148 p. illus. (part col.) ports. 23 cm. Bibliographical footnotes. [ND237.R75L5] 63-18074
1. Russell, Charles Marion, 1864-1926. I. Title.

MCCRACKEN, Harold, 1894- 927.5
The Charles M. Russell book; the life and work of the cowboy artist. Garden City, N.Y., Doubleday, [1957] 236 p. illus., col. plates, ports. 35 cm. Bibliographical references included in "Notes" (p. 232-233) [ND237.R75M3] 759.13 57-11431
1. Russell, Charles Marion, 1864-1826. 2. The West in art. BIP

NORTON (R. W.) Art 730'.924
Gallery.
Artistry in silver; an exhibition of sculpture by Charles M. Russell (1864-1926), August 2-30, 1970, the R. W. Norton Art Gallery. Shreveport, La., R. W. Norton Art Foundation [1970] [10] p. (incl. cover) illus. 23 cm. Cover title. [NK7198.R8N6] 78-17945
I. Russell, Charles Marion, 1864-1926. II. Title.

RENNER, Frederic Gordon, 709'.24
1877-
Charles Marion Russell; greatest of all western artists, by Frederic G. Renner. Washington, Potomac Corral, The Westerners, 1968. 24 p. illus., port. 23 cm. (The Great western series, no. 2) [ND237.R75R4] 68-26566
1. Russell, Charles Marion, 1864-1926.

RUSSELL, Austin, 1887- 759.13
C. M. R.: Charles M. Ressell, cowboy artist, a biography. New York, Twayne Publishers [1957] 247p. illus. 23cm. Includes bibliography. [ND237.R75R8] [ND237.R75R8] 927.5 57-2024 57-2024
1. Russell, Charles Marion, 1864-1926. I. Title.

RUSSELL, Austin, 1887- 759.13
C. M. R.: Charles M. Russell, cowboy artist, a biography. New York, Twayne Publishers [1957] 247p. illus. 23cm. Includes bibliography. [ND237.R75R8] 927.5 57-2024
1. Russell, Charles Marion, 1864-1926. I. Title.

RUSSELL, Charles Marion, 741.9'73
1864-1926.
C. M. Russell: boyhood sketchbook, by R. D. Warden. Introd. by Frederic G. Renner. [1st ed.] Bozeman, Mont., Treasure Products [1972] iv, 29 p. illus. 30 cm. Errata slip inserted. [NC139.R87W37] 72-88933
1. Russell, Charles Marion, 1864-1926. 2. The West in art. I. Warden, Robert D. II. Title. III. Title: Boyhood sketchbook.

RUSSELL, Charles Marion, 709'.2'4
1864-1926.
Charles M. Russell : centennial exhibition : [summer 1964 at Hammer Galleries]. New York : Hammer Galleries, [1964] 48 p. : ill. ; 27 cm. Cover title. [N6537.R88H35] 75-318274
1. Russell, Charles Marion, 1864-1926. 2. The West in art. I. Hammer Galleries, New York.

RUSSELL, Charles Marion, 759.13
1864-1926.
The CMR book. Text by John Willard. With foreword by Mike Mansfield. Seattle, Salisbury Press [1970] 64 p. illus. (part col.) 36 cm. Includes bibliographical references. [ND237.R75W54] 78-125897
1. Russell, Charles Marion, 1864-1926. 2. The West in art. I. Willard, John, 1915- II. Title.

RUSSELL, Charles Marion, 759.13
1864-1926.
50 Charles M. Russell paintings of the old American West from the Amon Carter Museum / introd. and commentaries by Louis Chapin. New York : Crown Publishers, c1978. p. cm. "An Artabras book." [ND237.R75A4 1978] 78-2237 pbk. : 7.98
1. Russell, Charles Marion, 1864-1926. 2. Amon Carter Museum of Western Art, Fort Worth, Tex. 3. The West in art—Catalogs. I. Chapin, Louis. II. Amon Carter Museum of Western Art, Fort Worth, Tex. III. Title.

RUSSELL, Charles Marion, 927.5
1864-1926.
Paper talk; illustrated letters of Charles M. Russell. Introd. and commentary by Frederic G. Renner. Fort Worth, Tex., Amon Carter Museum of Western Art [1962] 120p. illus. (part col.) ports., facsims, 30cm. [ND237.R75A33] 62-12663
I. Renner, Frederic Gordon, 1897- II. Amon Carter Museum of Western Art, Fort Worth, Tex. III. Title.

RUSSELL, Charles Marion, 759.13
1864-1926.
The western art of Charles M. Russell / edited by Lanning Aldrich. New York : Ballantine Books, 1975. [95] p. : chiefly col. ill. ; 24 x 29 cm. [ND237.R75A57] 76-359873 ISBN 0-345-24734-5 pbk. : 5.95
1. Russell, Charles Marion, 1864-1926. 2. The West in art. I. Title.

SHELTON, Lola. 927.5
Charles Marion Russell; cowboy, artist, friend New York Dodd, Mead, 1962. 230 p. illus. 24 cm. Includes bibliography. [ND237.R75S5] 61-15986
1. Russell, Charles Marion, 1864-1926. I. Title.

YOST, Karl, 1911- 759.13
An essay toward an iconography of Charles M. Russell. Morrison, Ill. 1956. 135 l. 22 x 36 cm. [ND237.R75Y6] 56-39463
1. Russell, Charles Marion, 1864-1926. I. Title.

YOST, Karl, 1911- 759.13
An essay toward an inconography of Charles M. Russell. Morrison, Ill., 1956. 135l. 22x36cm. [ND237.R75Y6] 56-39463
1. Russell. Charles Marion, 1864-1926. I. Title.

Russell, Charles Marion, 1864-1926—Bibliography.

DYKES, Jefferson 016.709'2'4
Chenowth, 1900-
Russell roundup : a catalog and supplement to the Yost-Renner Russell bibliography / Jeff Dykes. [College Park, Md. : Jeff Dykes/Western Books, 1972?] 2 v. in 1 (92 p.) : ill. ; 23 cm. "Number 24 of 100 numbered and signed copies." [Z8765.485.D94] [ND237.R75] 75-319371
1. Russell, Charles Marion, 1864-1926—Bibliography. I. Yost, Karl, 1911- A bibliography of the published works of Charles M. Russell. II. Title.

Russell, Charles P., 1840-1923—Art collections.

DEERFIELD Academy, 750'.74'014422
Deerfield, Mass.
The Charles P. Russell Collection. Deerfield, American Studies Group, Deerfield Academy [1969] 76 p. illus., ports. 21 x 29 cm. Bibliography: p. 72-74. [N5220.R82D4] 70-23153
1. Russell, Charles P., 1840-1923—Art collections. 2. Paintings—Catalogs. I. Deerfield Academy, Deerfield, Mass. American Studies Group.

Russell, John Peter, 1858-1930.

SALTER, Elizabeth, 759.994 B
1918-
The lost Impressionist : a biography of John Peter Russell / [by] Elizabeth Salter. London : Angus and Robertson, 1976. [11] , 209 p., [16] p. of plates : ill. (some col.), ports. ; 23 cm. Includes index. Bibliography: p. 205-206. [ND1105.R87S24] 76-363397 ISBN 0-207-95566-2 : £5.80
1. Russell, John Peter, 1858-1930. I. Title.

Russia—Descr. & trav.—Views.

REFREGIER, Anton, 1905- 741.973
An artist's journey. New York, Intl. Pubs. [1965] 96p. illus. 29cm. [NC1075.R38] 65-16391 6.95; 3.95 pap.,
1. Russia—Descr. & trav.—Views. 2. Europe, Eastern—Descr. & trav.—Views. I. Title.

Russia—History—19th century—Pictorial works.

RUSSIA in original 779'.9'94708
photographs, 1860-1920 / [compiled by] Marvin Lyons ; edited by Andrew Wheatcroft. New York : Scribner, 1978,c1977. xii, 212 p. : ill. ; 30 cm. Includes index. [DK189.R87] 77-73931 ISBN 0-684-15274-6 : 20.00
1. Russia—History—19th century—Pictorial works. 2. Russia—History—20th century—Pictorial works. I. Lyons, Marvin. II. Wheatcroft, Andrew. BIP

Russia—Intellectual life.

JOHNSON, Priscilla. 701.1
Khrushchev and the arts; the politics of Soviet culture, 1962-1964. Documents selected and edited by Priscilla Johnson and Leopold Labedz. Cambridge [Mass.] M. I. T. Press [1965] xv, 300 p. illus. 25 cm. [DK276.J6] 64-8311
1. Khrushchev, Nikita Sergeevich, 1894-1971. 2. Russia—Intellectual life. I. Title. BIP

Russian literature—History and criticism—Bibliography.

ETTLINGER, Amrei. 016.7'00947
Russian literature, theatre, and art; a bibliography of works in English, published 1900-1945, by Amrei Ettlinger [and] Joan M. Gladstone. Port Washington, N.Y., Kennikat Press [1971] 96 p. 22 cm. "First published in 1945." Supplements P. Grierson's Books on Soviet Russia, 1917-1942, published in 1943. [Z2501.E8 1971] 72-118410
1. Russian literature—History and criticism—Bibliography. 2. Theater—Russia—Bibliography. 3. Art—Russia—Bibliography. 4. Russian literature—Translations into English—Bibliography. 5. English literature—Translations from Russian—Bibliography. I. Gladstone, Joan M., joint author. II. Grierson, Philip. Books on Soviet Russia, 1917-1942. III. Title.

Rustempasa Camii, Istanbul.

DENNY, Walter B. 738.6'09561
The ceramics of the Mosque of Rustem Pasha and the environment of change / Walter B. Denny. New York : Garland Pub., 1977. xi, 424 p. : ill. ; 21 cm. (Outstanding dissertations in the fine arts) A revision of the author's thesis, Harvard University, 1970. Bibliography: p. 241-258. [NK4670.7.T9D46 1977] 76-23612 ISBN 0-8240-2684-5 : 47.50
1. Rustempasa Camii, Istanbul. 2. Tiles, Islamic—Turkey. 3. Tiles, Turkish. 4. Decoration and ornament, Islamic—Turkey. 5. Decoration and ornament—Turkey. 6. Iznik pottery. I. Title. II. Series. BIP

Ryan, Anne, 1889-1954.

RYAN, Anne, 1889-1954. 759.13
Anne Ryan : collages : [exhibition] November 16-December 4, 1974, Marlborough Gallery, Inc. New York : Marlborough, [1974] 28 p. : chiefly ill. (some col.) ; 30 cm. [N6537.R92M37] 75-328499
1. Ryan, Anne, 1889-1954. I. Marlborough Gallery.

RYAN, Anne, 1889-1954. 759.13
Anne Ryan, collages : [exhibition] / text and catalogue by Sarah Faunce. [Brooklyn : Brooklyn Museum, 1974] 32 p. : ill. (some col.) ; 23 cm. "The Brooklyn Museum, March 13-April 21, 1974; National Collection of Fine Arts, Smithsonian Institution, May 24-July 14, 1974." Bibliography: p. 32. [N6537.R92F38] 74-75530
1. Ryan, Anne, 1889-1954. I. Faunce, Sarah. II. Brooklyn Institute of Arts and Sciences. Museum.

Ryder, Albert Pinkham, 1847-1917.

GOODRICH, Lloyd, 1897- 759.13
Albert P. Ryder. New York, G. Braziller, 1959. 128 p. illus. (part col.) port. 26 cm. (The Great American artists series) Bibliography: p. 123-126. [ND237.R8G6] 59-12227
1. Ryder, Albert Pinkham, 1847-1917.

Rye, Eng.—History.

SAVILLE, Malcolm. 942.2'52
Portrait of Rye : with some sketches of places worth visiting within easy reach of the ancient town / by Malcolm Saville ;

with woodcuts by Michael Renton ; with a new poem by Patric Dickinson. East Grinstead : Henry Goulden Ltd, 1976. 93 p. : ill. ; 22 cm. Includes index. Bibliography: p. [91] [DA690.R9S28] 77-367640 ISBN 0-904822-05-2 : £5.00. ISBN 0-904822-06-0 pbk.
1. Saville, Malcolm. 2. Rye, Eng.—History. 3. Rye, Eng.—Description. I. Title.

Ryman, Robert, 1930—

WALDMAN, Diane. 759.13
Robert Ryman. [New York, Solomon R. Guggenheim Foundation, 1972] 1 v. (unpaged) illus. 22 cm. Catalog of the exhibition held at the Solomon R. Guggenheim Museum, New York. "Exhibition 72/2." Includes bibliography. [ND237.R83W3] 78-188506
1. Ryman, Robert, 1930- I. Solomon R. Guggenheim Museum, New York.

Saarinen, Eero, 1910-1961.

HALL, Mildred. 725'.23
The fourth dimension in architecture : the impact of building on man's behavior : Eero Saarinen's administrative center for Deere & Company, Moline, Illinois / by Mildred and Edward Hall. Santa Fe, N.M. : Sunstone Press, [1975]. 45 p. : ill. ; 22 x 28 cm. [NA6233.M64D433] 75-318515 ISBN 0-913270-40-7 : 4.95
1. Saarinen, Eero, 1910-1961. 2. Moline, Ill. Deere and Company Administrative Center. I. Hall, Edward Twitchell, 1914- joint author. II. Title.

SAARINEN, Eero, 1910- 720.973
1961.
Eero Saarinen on his work; a selection of buildings dating from 1947 to 1964 with statements by the architect, edited by Aline B. Saarinen. New Haven, Yale University Press, 1962. 107 p. illus., port., plans. 37 cm. [NA737.S28S2] 62-16241

SAARINEN, Eero, 1910- 720'.924
1961.
Eero Saarinen on his work; a selection of buildings dating from 1947 to 1964 with statements by the architect, edited by Aline B. Saarinen. Rev. ed. New Haven, Yale University Press, 1968. 117 p. illus., plans, port. 37 cm. [NA737.S28S2 1968] 68-5268

TEMKO, Allan. 720.973
Eero Saarinen. New York, G. Braziller, 1962. 127 p. illus., ports., plans. 26 cm. (Makers of contemporary architecture) Bibliography: p. [124]-125. [NA737.S28T4] 62-16266
1. Saarinen, Eero, 1910-1961. I. Title. II. Series. BIP

Saarinen, Eero, 1910-1961—Bibliography.

KUHNER, Robert A. 016.3092'08 s
Eero Saarinen, his life and work / Robert A. Kuhner. Monticello, Ill. : Council of Planning Librarians, 1975. 73 p. ; 28 cm. (Exchange bibliography - Council of Planning Librarians ; 836) Cover title. Includes index. [Z5942.C68 no. 836] [Z8772.4] [NA737.S28] 016.72'092'4 75-321300 pbk. : 7.50
1. Saarinen, Eero, 1910-1961—Bibliography. I. Title. II. Series: Council of Planning Librarians. Exchange bibliography ; 836.

Sacchi, Andrea, called Ouche, 1599?-1661—Catalogs.

†HARRIS, Ann Sutherland. 759.5
Andrea Sacchi : complete edition of the paintings with a critical catalogue / Ann Sutherland Harris. Princeton, N.J. : Princeton University Press, c1977. 264 p., [4] leaves of plates : ill. (some col.) ; 29 cm. Based on the author's thesis, University of London, 1965. Erratum slip inserted. Includes indexes. Bibliography: p. [129]-133. [ND623.S124A4 1977] 77-6101 ISBN 0-691-03117-7 : 50.00
1. Sacchi, Andrea, called Ouche, 1599?-1661—Catalogs. I. Sacchi, Andrea, called Ouche, 1599?-1661. BIP

Sachines, Doukas, 1942—

SACHINES, Doukas, 1942- v. 12
Ducas Sachinis = [Ho kritikos tes technes Dantes Maphphias parousiazei tou Douka Sachine. (romanized form)] / presentato dal critico d'arte Dante Maffia. Firenze : Galleria d'arte internazionale, [1976]. 54 p., [19] leaves of plates : ill. (some col.) ; 30 cm. Introductory text in English, French, German, Greek and Italian. Catalog of an exhibition. [ND603.S2M34] 76-368467
1. Sachines, Doukas, 1942- I. Maffia, Dante. II. Galleria d'arte internazionale. III. Title: Ho kritikos tes technes Dantes Maphphias parousiazei tou Douka Sachine.

Sachs, Paul Joseph, 1878-1965—Art collections.

†HARVARD 741.9'074'01444
University. William Hayes Fogg Art Museum.
Memorial exhibition : works of art from the Collection of Paul J. Sachs (1878-1965) : given and bequeathed to the Fogg Art Museum, Harvard University, Cambridge, Massachusetts. New York : Garland Pub., [1977] c1965. 214 p. : ill. ; 23 cm. "Compiled by Agnes Mongan with the assistance of Mary Lee Bennett." Catalog of the exhibitions held at the Fogg Art Museum, Cambridge, Mass., Nov. 15, 1965-Jan. 15, 1966 and at the New York Museum of Modern Art, Dec. 19, 1966-Feb. 25, 1967. Reprint of the ed. published by William Hayes Fogg Art Museum, Harvard University, Cambridge. [NC25.C35H45 1977] 77-22978 ISBN 0-8240-1961-X : 35.00
1. Sachs, Paul Joseph, 1878-1965—Art collections. 2. Drawing—Exhibitions. I. Mongan, Agnes. II. Bennett, Mary Lee. III. New York (City). Museum of Modern Art. IV. Title.

Sade, Donatien Alphonse Francois, comte, called Marquis de, 1740-1814.

SIXTY erotic 769'.4'260944
engravings from Juliette. New York, Grove Press [1969] [8] p., 60 plates. 29 cm. "The engravings which appear in the present work were reproduced from a copy of the 1797 edition of l'Histoire de Juliette, by the Marquis de Sade." [NE650.S27S5] 74-93846
1. Sade, Donatien Alphonse Francois, comte, called Marquis de, 1740-1814. Histoire de Juliette—Illustrations. I. Sade, Donatien Alphonse Francoise, comte, called Marquis de, 1740-1814. Histoire de Juliette.

Safdie, Moshe, 1938—

SAFDIE, Moshe, 1938- 720'.924
Beyond Habitat. Edited by John Kettle. Cambridge, Mass., M.I.T. Press [1970] 244 p. illus., ports. 24 cm. [NA749.S2A43 1970] 76-130455 ISBN 0-262-19083-4
1. Safdie, Moshe, 1938- I. Title. BIP

SAFDIE, Moshe, 1938- 720'.92'4
For everyone a garden. Edited by Judith Wolin. Cambridge, M.I.T. Press [1974] 1 v. (unpaged) illus., plans. 24 cm. [NA749.S2W64] 73-16432 ISBN 0-262-19108-3
1. Safdie, Moshe, 1938- I. Title.

Sailboats—Juvenile literature.

CREATIVE Educational 745.59'28
Society, Mankato, Minn.
How to have fun building sailboats, by editors of Creative [Educational Society] Illustrated by Harold Henriksen. Mankato, Minn. [distributed by Childrens Press, 1973, c1974] 31 p. illus. (part col.) 25 cm. (Creative craft book) On spine: Sailboats. Instructions for making a model sailboat and simpler sailboats of soap, cork, and milk cartons. [VM359.C7] 73-9707 ISBN 0-87191-250-3
1. Sailboats—Juvenile literature. I. Henriksen, Harold, illus. II. Title. III. Title: Sailboats.

Sailing cards.

FORBES, Allan, 1874- 769.5
The story of clipper ship sailing cards. Worcester, Mass., The Society, 1950. [225]-274 p. illus. (part col.) 25 cm. "Reprinted from the Proceedings of the American Antiquarian Society for October 1949." [NE965.F595] 50-14325
1. Sailing cards. I. Title. II. Title: Clipper ship sailing cards.

FORBES, Allan, 1874- 769.5
Yankee ship sailing cards ... by Allan Forbes and Ralph M. Eastman. Boston, State Street Trust Co. [1948-52] 3v. illus. (part col.) 23cm. Vol. 2 has title: Other Yankee ship sailing cards. [NE965.F6] 48-3704
1. Sailing cards. 2. Shipping—Boston. 3. Ships. I. Eastman, Ralph Mason, 1891- joint author. II. State Street Trust Company, Boston. III. Title.

Sailing ships—Pictorial works.

SMITH, Melbourne. 769'.92'4
Sailing vessels of the Chesapeake; nine original lithographed prints. Annapolis, Md., Admiralty Pub. House [1973] [21] l. (chiefly col. plates) 31 x 42 cm. (His International historical watercraft collection, portfolio no. 1) [VM307.S58] 72-96819 ISBN 0-913544-01-9
1. Sailing ships—Pictorial works. 2. Shipbuilding—Chesapeake Bay—History. I. Title.

Sainsbury, Robert J.—Art collections.

NEW York 709.01'1'07401471
(City). Museum of Primitive Art.
The Robert and Lisa Sainsbury Collection. [New York]; Distributed by the New York Graphic Society [Greenwich, Conn.] 1963. [40] p. (chiefly illus.) 28 cm. Catalogue of an exhibition held at the museum May 15-Sept. 8, 1963. [N5310.N45] 71-19112
1. Sainsbury, Robert J.—Art collections. 2. Sainsbury, Lisa—Art collections. 3. Art, Primitive—Exhibitions. I. Title.

St. Albans Abbey.

ROBERTS, Eileen. 751.7'3'094258
A guide to the medieval murals in St Albans Abbey. [St Albans], Fraternity of the Friends of St Albans Abbey, 1971. 52 p. illus. 21 cm. Bibliography: p. 45. [ND2733.S2R6] 73-167284 ISBN 0-9502514-0-2 £0.30
1. St. Albans Abbey. 2. Mural painting and decoration, Medieval—St. Albans, Eng. 3. Mural painting and decoration—St. Albans, Eng. I. St. Albans Abbey. Fraternity of the Friends of St. Albans Abbey. II. Title.

St. Albans, Eng.—History.

TOMS, Elsie. 942.5'85
The new book of St Albans : an illustrated record / by Elsie Toms. Chesham : Barracuda Books Ltd, 1976. 3-132 p. : ill., facsims., maps, ports. ; 31 cm. Maps on lining papers. Includes index. Bibliography: p. 127-128. [DA690.S13T58] 77-355075 ISBN 0-86023-019-8 : £8.00
1. St. Albans, Eng.—History. I. Title.

Saint-Denis, France (Benedictine abbey).

SUGER, Abbot of 726'.5'0944362
Saint Denis, 1081-1151.
Abbot Suger on the Abbey Church of St.-Denis and its art treasures / edited, translated, and annotated by Erwin Panofsky. 2d ed. / by Gerda Panofsky-Soergel. Princeton, N.J. : Princeton University Press, c1978. p. cm. Latin and English. Includes index. Bibliography: p. [NA5551.S2S8 1978] 78-51186 ISBN 0-691-03936-4 : 22.50. ISBN 0-691-10068-3 pbk. : 9.95
1. Saint-Denis, France (Benedictine abbey). 2. Architecture—Early works to 1800. 3. Art—Early works to 1800. I. Panofsky, Erwin, 1892-1968. II. Panofsky-Soergel, Gerda, 1929- III. Title.

Saint-Denis, France (Benedictine abbey). Apostle Bas-relief.

CROSBY, Sumner McKnight, 731'.54
1909-
The apostle bas-relief at Saint-Denis [by] Sumner McK. Crosby. New Haven, Yale University Press, 1972. xvi, 116 p., 86 p. of illus. 26 cm. (Yale publications in the history of art, 21) Bibliography: p. [98]-110. [NB543.C7] 71-179471 ISBN 0-300-01504-6 10.00
1. Saint-Denis, France (Benedictine abbey). Apostle Bas-relief. I. Title. II. Series. BIP

Saint-Galy, Geza, 1908-

DAVIS, Burke. 738.6
The Saint-Galy tiles of Williamsburg : a narrative history of early Virginia and the restoration of Colonial Williamsburg / text by Burke Davis. Milwaukee : W. H. Brady Co., c1974. 63 p. : ill. (some col.) ; 28 cm. Bibliography: p. 55-56. [NK4670.7.U53S243] 74-17781
1. Saint-Galy, Geza, 1908- 2. Colonial Williamsburg, inc. 3. Williamsburg, Va., in art. 4. Williamsburg, Va.—History—Pictorial works. 5. Williamsburg, Va.—Antiquities. 6. Tiles, American. I. Title.

Saint-Gaudens, Augustus, 1848-1907.

DRYFHOUT, John, 1940- 730'.924
Augustus Saint-Gaudens: the portrait reliefs, the National Portrait Gallery, the Smithsonian Institution. New York, Grossman Publishers, 1969. 1 v. (unpaged) illus., ports. 29 cm. "Catalogue prepared by John Dryfhout and Beverly Cox." Includes bibliography. [NB237.S2D7] 77-101514 10.00
1. Saint-Gaudens, Augustus, 1848-1907. I. Cox, Beverly, joint author. II. National Portrait Gallery, Washington, D.C.

DRYFHOUT, John, 332.4'042'0973
1940-
The 1907 United States gold coinage [by John H. Dryfhout.] Cornish, N.H., Eastern National Park & Monument Association, 1972] 12 p. illus. 28 cm. Caption title. Bibliography: p. 12. [CJ1834.D79] 74-152641
1. Saint-Gaudens, Augustus, 1848-1907. 2. Coins, American. 3. Gold coins. I. Title.

SAINT-GAUDENS, 730'.92'4 B
Augustus, 1848-1907.
The reminiscences of Augustus Saint-Gaudens / edited and amplified by Homer Saint-Gaudens. [New York : Garland Pub., 1976], c1913-. v. : ill. ; 19 cm. (The Art experience in late nineteenth-century America) Reprint of the ed. published by the Century Co., New York, with new introd. [NB237.S2A2 1976] 75-28890 ISBN 0-8240-2247-5 lib.bdg. : 50.00
1. Saint-Gaudens, Augustus, 1848-1907. 2. Sculptors—United States—Biography. I. Saint-Gaudens, Homer, 1880- II. Title. III. Series. BIP

THARP, Louise (Hall) 730'.924 B
1898-
Saint-Gaudens and the gilded era. [1st ed.] Boston, Little, Brown [1969] xii, 419 p. illus., ports. 24 cm. Bibliographical references included in "Notes" (p. [383]-398) [NB237.S2T5] 72-79372 8.50
1. Saint-Gaudens, Augustus, 1848-1907. I. Title.

Saint-Gilles, France (Gard). Church.

STODDARD, Whitney S. 731'.54
The facade of Saint-Gilles-du-Gard; its influence on French sculpture, by Whitney S. Stoddard. [1st ed.] Middletown, Conn., Wesleyan University Press [1973] xxiv, 340 p. illus. 29 cm. Bibliography: p. 325-331. [NB543.S79] 72-3696 ISBN 0-8195-4056-0 40.00
1. Saint-Gilles, France (Gard). Church. 2. Sculpture, Romanesque—Saint Gilles, France (Gard) 3. Sculpture—Saint-Gilles, France (Gard) I. Title.

St. Helens, Eng.—Description—Views.

HART, Roger. 942.7'57'0810222
Vintage St Helens and district / [compiled] by Roger Hart. Nelson : Hendon

Publishing Co., 1976. [44] p. : of ill., ports. ; 21 x 29 cm. [DA690.S1417H37] 77-364058 ISBN 0-86067-007-4 : £1.40
1. St. Helens, Eng.—Description—Views. 2. St. Helens, Eng.—Social life and customs—Pictorial works. I. Title.

St. John's Abbey, Collegeville, Minn.

STODDARD, Whitney S 726.771
Adventure in architecture; building the new Saint John's. Text and pictures by Whitney S. Stoddard, plans by Marcel Breuer. [1st ed.] New York, Longmans, Green, 1958. 127 p. illus., ports., diagrs., plans. 29 cm. [NA5235.C6S8] 57-13215
1. St. John's Abbey, Collegeville, Minn. I. Title.

St. John's Seminary, Collegeville, Minn.

VOIGHT, Robert J 748.5
Symbols in stained glass. St. Paul, North Central Pub. Co., 1957. 55 p. illus. 29 cm. Includes bibliography. [NK5312.C6V6] 57-12093
1. St. John's Seminary, Collegeville, Minn. 2. Glass painting and staining — Collegeville, Minn. 3. Christian art and symbolism. I. Title.

St. John's University, Collegeville, Minn. Monastic Manuscript Microfilm Library.

ST. John's University, 091
Collegeville, Minn. Monastic Manuscript Microfilm Library.
The Monastic Manuscript Microfilm Library: its purpose and progress. [Text by Julian G. Plante. Collegeville? Minn., 1970] [24] p. (incl. cover) illus. (part. col.) 22 x 28 cm. [Z110.R4S24 1970] 74-192167
1. St. John's University, Collegeville, Minn. Monastic Manuscript Microfilm Library. 2. Manuscripts on microfilm. I. Plante, Julian G. II. Title.

St. Joseph's College, Princeton, N. J. Queen of the Miraculous Medal Chapel.

DIRVIN, Joseph I. 726.41
The queen of the Miraculous Medal Chapel, Saint Joseph's College, Princeton, New Jersey. Philadelphia, Central Association of the Miraculous Medal, 1951. 125 p. illus. 17 cm. [NA5235.P75D5] 52-21730
1. St. Joseph's College, Princeton, N. J. Queen of the Miraculous Medal Chapel. I. Title.

St. Lawrence Co., N.Y.—Description and travel—Views—Exhibitions.

ST. Lawrence County 779'.9'974756
Historical Association.
St. Lawrence County history, ... a view from the people : a photographic portrait by those who live here. Canton, N.Y. : St. Lawrence County Historical Association, 1975. 64 p. : chiefly ill. ; 21 cm. [F127.S2S23 1975] 75-13690
1. St. Lawrence Co., N.Y.—Description and travel—Views—Exhibitions. I. Title.

St. Louis—Office buildings—History.

RANDALL, John D. 725'.23'0977866
The art of office buildings; Sullivan's Wainwright & the St. Louis real estate boom [by] John D. Randall. [Springfield, Ill.] 1972. 132 p. illus. 29 cm. Includes bibliographical references. [NA6230.R36] 72-95100
1. St. Louis—Office buildings—History. 2. Urban renewal—St. Louis. I. Title.

St. Louis—Plazas—Lafayette Square.

ST. Louis; City 711'.4'0977866
Plan Commission.
Lafayette Square restoration plan. [St. Louis] 1971. 48 p. illus. 22 x 28 cm. "Preapred in cooperation with the Lafayette Square Restoration Committee and the Lafayette Park Neighborhood Association." [NA9072.S25L337] 73-172335
1. St. Louis—Plazas—Lafayette Square. 2. Architecture—St. Louis—Conservation and restoration. I. Lafayette Square Restoration Committee. II. Lafayette Park Neighborhood Association. III. Title.

Saint Macarius (Monastery)

EVELYN-WHITE, Hugh Gerard, 913.32
d.1924.
The monasteries of the Wadi 'n Natrun. New York, Metropolitan Museum of Art, Egyptian Expedition, 1926-[33. New York] Arno Press, 1973. 3 v. illus. 32 cm. Original ed. issued as v. 2, 4, and 8 of Publications of the Metropolitan Museum of Art, Egyptian Expedition. Contents.Contents.--pt. 1. New Coptic texts from the Monastery of Saint Macarius, edited with an introd. on the Library at the Monastery of Saint Macarius; with an appendix on a Copto-Arabic ms. by G. P. G. Sobhy.—pt. 2. The history of the monasteries of Nitria and Scetis, edited by W. Hauser.—pt. 3. The architecture and archaeology, edited by W. Hauser. Includes bibliographies. [DT73.N28E92] 77-168409 ISBN 0-405-02242-5
1. Saint Macarius (Monastery) 2. Monasteries—Egypt—Natrun Valley. 3. Coptic language—Texts. I. Hauser, Walter, 1893- ed. II. Title. III. Series: New York (City). Metropolitan Museum of Art. Egyptian Expedition. Publications, v. 2 [etc.] BIP

St. Mary's Church, Great Bealings, Eng.

BROWN, Cynthia. 746.9'5
Hassocks for your church : how we made them at Great Bealings / [by] Cynthia Brown. [Great Bealings] : [St. Mary's Church], [1976] 36 p. : ill. ; 12 x 19 cm. [NK9310.B77] 77-364716 ISBN 0-9505054-0-4 : £0.95
1. St. Mary's Church, Great Bealings, Eng. 2. Ecclesiastical embroidery—England—Great Bealings. 3. Canvas embroidery. 4. Kneelers (Church furniture)—England—Bealings. I. Title.

St. Michael and All Angels (Church), Kerry, Wales.

JERMAN, H. Noel. 942.9'51
Kerry : the church and the village / by H. Noel Jerman ; line drawings by Kate Mellor. [Kerry, Montgomeryshire] : [The author], [1976] [1], 44, [1] p. : ill., map ; 21 cm. Caption title. [NA5494.K47J47] 77-363473 ISBN 0-9505399-0-2 : £0.50
1. St. Michael and All Angels (Church), Kerry, Wales. 2. Kerry, Wales. I. Title.

St. Pancras, Eng. (Parish)—Historic houses, etc.

LOVELL, Percy W. 914.21'42
The Parish of St. Pancras [by Percy W. Lovell and William McB. Marcham] London, Published by the London County Council, 1936- [New York, AMS Press, 1971- v. illus. 29 cm. (Survey of London, v. 17, 19,) Contents.—v. 1. The village of Highgate.—v. 2. Old St. Pancras and Kentish Town. Includes bibliographical references. [DA685.S1493L682] 76-37851
1. St. Pancras, Eng. (Parish)—Historic houses, etc. 2. Architecture—St. Pancras, Eng. (Parish) I. Marcham, William McBeath, joint author. II. Series: Joint Publishing Committee Representing the London County Council and the London Survey Committee. Survey of London, v. 17, etc. BIP

St. Paul. State Capitol.

THOMPSON, Neil B., 917.76'581
1921-
Minnesota's State Capitol: the art and politics of a public building, by Neil B. Thompson. St. Paul, Minnesota Historical Society, 1974. 100 p. illus. 27 cm. (Publications of the Minnesota Historical Society) (Minnesota historic sites pamphlet series, no. 9) Includes bibliographical references. [NA4413.S24T45] 74-4326 ISBN 0-87351-085-2 4.50 (pbk.)
1. Gilbert, Cass, 1859-1934. 2. St. Paul. State Capitol. 3. Politics in art. I. Title. II. Series. III. Series: Minnesota Historical Society. Publications. BIP

Saint-Phalle, Niki de, 1930-

SAINT-PHALLE, Niki de, 730'.92'4
1930-
Realisations & [i.e. et] projets d'architectures / de Niki de Saint-Phalle. Paris ; New York : A. Iolas, [1974?] [22] p. (on double leaves) : ill. (some col.) ; 17 x 25 cm. Cover title. Leaves joined to form a continuous strip, 17 x 588 cm., fold. to 17 x 25 cm. [NB553.S32A54] 74-194637
1. Saint-Phalle, Niki de, 1930- I. Title.

Saint-Simeon school of painting.

CUNNINGHAM, Charles 759.4'22
Crehore.
Jongkind and the Pre-Impressionists : painters of the Ecole Saint-Simeon : Smith College Museum of Art, Northampton, Massachusetts, October 15-December 5, 1976, Sterling and Francine Clark Art Institute, Williamstown, Massachusetts, December 17, 1976-February 13, 1977 / Charles C. Cunningham, with Susan D. Peters and Kathleen Zimmerer. [Williamstown, Mass.] : The Institute, c1977. 167 p. : ill. ; 26 cm. Bibliography: p. 163-167. [ND547.5.S24C86] 77-73073
1. Jongkind, Johan Barthold, 1819-1891. 2. Saint-Simeon school of painting. 3. Painting, French—Exhibitions. 4. Painting, Modern—19th century—France—Exhibitions. I. Peters, Susan D., joint author. II. Zimmerer, Kathleen, joint author. III. Smith College. Museum of Art. IV. Sterling and Francine Clark Art Institute, Williamstown, Mass. V. Title.

Saints—Art.

BREESE, Frances, 704.948'2'09789
illus.
New Mexico santos: how to name them. Illus. by Frances Breese. Foreword and captions by E. Boyd. Santa Fe, N. M., Museum of New Mexico [and] International Folk Art Foundation, 1966. 1 v. (chiefly illus.) 26 cm. [NK835.N5N4] 68-6768
1. Saints—Art. 2. Folk art—New Mexico. I. Hall, Elizabeth Boyd (White) 1903- II. International Folk Art Foundation. III. Santa Fe, N. M. Museum of New Mexico. IV. Title.

MEISS, Millard. 759.5
Giovanni Bellini's St. Francis in the Frick Collection. [Princeton] Published for the Frick Collection, New York, by Princeton University Press, 1964. 50 p. plates (part col.) 32 cm. Bibliography: p. 39. Bibliographical references included in "Notes" (p. 43-50) [ND623.B39M37] 63-18639
1. Bellini, Giovanni, d. 1516. 2. Francesco d'Assisi, Saint, 1182-1226. 3. Saints — Art. I. The Frick Collection, New York. II. Title.

MILLS, George Thompson. 704.948'6
The people of the saints [by] George Mills. Colorado Springs, Taylor Museum [1967] 71 p., 32 col. plates. 16 x 17 cm. "Illustrated...from the collection of the Taylor Museum of the Colorado Springs Fine Arts Center." Bibliographical references included in "Footnotes" (p. 63-65) [NK835.N5M5] 68-1617
1. Saints—Art. 2. Folk art—New Mexico. 3. Art, Spanish-American. 4. Colorado Springs. Fine Arts Center. Taylor Museum. I. Title. BIP

TINTORI, Leonetto, 1908- 704.9486
The painting of the life of St. Francis in Assisi. With notes on the arena chapel, and a 1964 appendix, by Leonetto Tintori, Millard Meiss. New York, Norton, [1967,c.1962] xv, 207p. illus. 20cm. (Norton lib., N393) Bibl. [N8080.T55] 1.95 pap.,
1. Francesco d'Assisi, Saint 1182-1226. 2. Assisi, San Francesco (Church) 3. Padua. Madonna dell' Arena (Chapel) 4. Saints—Art. 5. Mural painting and decoration. I. Meiss, Millard, joint author. II. Title.

TINTORI, Leonetto, 1908- 704.9486
The painting of The life of St. Francis in Assisi, with notes on the Arena Chapel, by Leonetto Tintori and Millard Meiss. [New York] New York University Press, 1962. xv, 205 p. illus. 25 cm. At head of title: Conservation Center, Institute of Fine Arts, New York University. Erratum slip inserted. "Selective list of technical studies": p. 187-188. Includes bibliographical references. [N8080.T55] 62-10308
1. Francesco d'Assisi, Saint, 1182-1226. 2. Saints—Art. 3. Assisi. San Francesco (Church) 4. Padua. Madonna dell'Arena (Chapel) 5. Mural painting and decoration, Italian. I. Meiss, Millard, joint author. II. Title.

Saints—Cultus.

BACIGALUPA, Andrea, 1923- 759.13
Santos and saints' days. [1st ed.] Santa Fe, N.M., Sunstone Press, 1972. 32 p. illus. 22 cm. [BX2333.B3] 73-154725 ISBN 0-913270-09-1 2.95
1. Mary, Virgin—Cultus. 2. Saints—Cultus. 3. Santos (Art) I. Title.

Sakkara—Antiquities.

KAMIL, Jill. 932
Sakkara : a guide to the necropolis and the site of Memphis / Jill Kamil. London ; New York : Longman, 1978. p. cm. [DT73.S3K35 1978] 77-27546 ISBN 0-582-78069-1 pbk. : 5.50
1. Sakkara—Antiquities. 2. Memphis, Egypt. 3. Egypt—Antiquities. I. Title. BIP

LAUER, Jean Philippe, 932'.01
1902-
Saqqara : the royal cemetery of Memphis : excavations and discoveries since 1850 / Jean-Philippe Lauer. New York : Scribner, c1976. 248 p. : ill. (some col.) ; 26 cm. Includes index. Bibliography: p. 231-240. [DT73.S3L38 1976b] 75-33508 ISBN 0-684-14551-0 : 25.00
1. Sakkara—Antiquities. 2. Egypt—Antiquities. I. Title.

Sakkara—Tombs.

GABALLA, G. A. 932'.01
The Memphite tomb-chapel of Mose / G. A. Gaballa. Warminster, Eng. : Aris & Phillips ; Forest Grove, Or. : distributed in the USA and Canada by ISBS, c1977. v, 40 p., [32] leaves of plates : ill. ; 31 cm. Includes bibliographical references and indexes. [DT73.S3G32] 78-313344 ISBN 0-85668-088-5 : 36.00
1. Mose, 13th cent. B.C.—Tomb. 2. Sakkara—Tombs. 3. Egyptian language—Inscriptions. 4. Law—Egypt—Sources. 5. Egypt—Antiquities. I. Title. BIP

Salem, Mass.—Description—Views.

CHAMBERLAIN, Samuel, 974.4'5
1895-
A stroll through historic Salem. New York, Hastings House [1969] 122 p. illus. 24 cm. [F74.S1C52 1969] 78-79738 5.95
1. Salem, Mass.—Description—Views. I. Title. BIP

Salem, Mass.—Historic houses, etc.

CHAMBERLAIN, Samuel, 1895- 747.88
Salem interiors; two centuries of New England taste and decoration. Illus. and text by Samuel Chamberlain. New York, Hastings House [1950] 176 p. (chiefly illus.) 25 cm. [NA7238.S3C5] 50-10950
1. Salem, Mass.—Historic houses, etc. 2. Interior decoration. 3. Architecture, Domestic—Salem, Mass. I. Title. BIP

Salem, Mass. John Tucker Daland House.

TOLLES, Bryant Franklin, 974.4'5
1939-
The John Tucker Daland House / by Bryant F. Tolles, Jr. ; foreword by Anne Farnam. Salem, Mass. : Essex Institute, 1978. 27 p., [4] leaves of plates : ill. ; 23 cm. (Historic house booklet series ; no. 7) Includes bibliographical referendes.

[NA7238.S3T64] 76-27382 ISBN 0-88389-065-8 : 2.00
1. Daland, John Tucker, 1795-1858. 2. Salem, Mass. John Tucker Daland House. I. Title. II. Series.
Publisher's address : 132 Essex St., Salem, MA 01970 BIP

Salemme, Attilio, 1911-1955.

BOSTON, Institute of Contemporary Art. 759.13
Attilio Salemme. [Catalogue. Boston, 1956?] 1 v. (unpaged) illus. (part col.) port. 20cm. Includes bibliography (u p. at end) [ND237.S2B6] 61-3210
1. Salemme, Attllio, 1911-1955. I. Title.

WHITNEY Museum of American Art, New York. 759.13
Attilio Salemme. [Exhibition. Whitney Museum of American Art, April 14 -- May 30, 1959. Boston, Institute of Contemporary Art, 1959] unpaged. illus. 20 cm. [ND237.S2W47] 59-3337
1. Salemme, Attilio, 1911-1955. I. Boston. Institute of Contemporary Art. II. Title.

Salinas de los Nueve Cerros site, Guatemala.

DILLON, Brian D. 972.81
Salinas de los Nueve Cerros, Guatemala : preliminary archaeological investigations / by Brian D. Dillon. Socorro, N.M. : Ballena Press, c1977. 94 p. : ill. ; 28 cm. (Ballena Press studies in Mesoamerican art, archaeology, and ethnohistory ; no. 2) Bibliography: p. 60-66. [F1435.1.S24D54] 78-100199 pbk. : 5.95
1. Salinas de los Nueve Cerros site, Guatemala. I. Title. BIP

Salinas, Porfirio.

GODDARD, Ruth, 1912- 759.13
Porfirio Salinas / by Ruth Goddard ; with an introd. by Dewey Bradford. Austin, Tex. : Rock House Press, 1975. 95 p. : ill. (some col.) ; 24 x 32 cm. Includes index. [ND237.S25G62] 75-20743 25.00
1. Salinas, Porfirio. BIP

Salish Indians—Basket making.

FARRAND, Livingston, 1867-1939. 746.4'1
Basketry designs of the Salish Indians / by Livingston Farrand. New York : AMS Press, 1975. p. 391-399, [3] leaves of plates : ill. ; 24 cm. Reprint of the 1900 ed. published in New York, which was issued as v. 2 of Memoirs of the American Museum of Natural History, Anthropology, v. 1, pt. 5, and as v. 1, pt. 5 of Publications of the Jesup North Pacific Expedition. [E99.S2F3 1975] 73-3514 ISBN 0-404-58116-1 : 27.50
1. Salish Indians—Basket making. 2. Indians of North America—Montana—Basket making. I. Title. II. Series: American Museum of Natural History, New York. Memoirs ; v. 2. III. Series: The Jesup North Pacific Expedition. Publications ; v. 1, pt. 5. BIP

Salishan Indians—Pictorial works.

JESUP North Pacific Expedition. 779.9'9'97900497
Ethnographical album of the North Pacific coasts of America and Asia / Jesup North Pacific Expedition. New York : AMS Press, 1975. [9] p., 28 leaves of plates : chiefly ill. ; 24 cm. Reprint of the 1900 ed. published by American Museum of Natural History, New York. [E99.S21J5 1975] 73-3534 ISBN 0-404-58112-9 : 84.50
1. Salishan Indians—Pictorial works. I. American Museum of Natural History, New York. II. Title.

Salmon, Robert, 1775-ca. 1848.

DECORDOVA and Dana Museum and Park, Lincoln, Mass. 707.4*097444
Robert Salmon; the first major exhibition. [Lincoln, Mass., 1967] 1 v. (unpaged) illus. 16 x 23 cm. Catalog of the exhibition held in 1967. [ND237.S26D4] 72-184661
1. Salmon, Robert, 1775-ca. 1848.

WILMERDING, John. 759.2
Robert Salmon, painter of ship & shore. With an introd. by Charles D. Childs. [Salem, Mass.] Peabody Museum of Salem [1971] xvi, 123 p. illus. (part col.) 29 cm. Bibliography: p. 116-118. [ND497.S27W5] 79-153131 ISBN 0-87577-040-1 20.00
1. Salmon, Robert, 1775-ca. 1848. I. Title. BIP

Salomon, Haym, 1740-1785.

BARNARD, Harry, 1906- 731.7'6
"This great triumvirate of patriots"; the inspiring story behind Lorado Taft's Chicago monument to George Washington, Robert Morris, and Haym Salomon. Chicago, Follett [1971] 105 p. illus. 22 cm. [F548.64.G4B3] 72-162791 ISBN 0-695-80272-0 5.95
1. Salomon, Haym, 1740-1785. 2. Washington, George, Pres. U.S., 1732-1799. 3. Morris, Robert, 1734-1806. 4. Chicago. George Washington-Robert Morris-Haym Salomon Monument. I. Title.

Salt Lake City. Temple.

RAYNOR, Wallace Alan. 726.5893
The everlasting spires; a story of the Salt Lake Temple. Salt Lake City, Deseret Book Co. [c1965] 203 p. illus., facsims., plans. 24 cm. Bibliography: p. [193]-196. [BX8685.S35R3] 65-28864
1. Salt Lake City. Temple. I. Title.

Salt shakers.

PETERSON, Arthur Goodwin, 1904- 748'.8
Glass salt shakers: 1,000 patterns, by Arthur G. Peterson. Des Moines, Wallace-Homestead Co. [1970] 196 p. illus. (part col.) 23 cm. "Most of the material in chapters 1 through 9 is the same as in Salt and salt shakers [1960] ... The 1965 supplement, 333 glass salt shakers, is incorporated herein and superseded." Bibliographical footnotes. [NK5440.S3P419] 70-93972
1. Salt shakers. 2. Glassware—Collectors and collecting. I. Title.

PETERSON, Arthur Goodwin, 1904- 748.8
Salt and salt shakers: hobbies for young and old. Washington, Washington College Press [1960] 148p. illus. 23cm. [NK5440.S3P4] 60-5196
1. Salt shakers. 2. Glassware— Collectors and collecting. 3. Condiments. I. Title.

PETERSON, Arthur Goodwin, 1904- 748.8
333 glass salt shakers; a companion to Salt and salt shakers. Takoma Park, Md., Washington Coll. Pr., Columbia Union Coll. [c.1965] 28p. illus. 22cm. [NK5440.S3P42] 65-16175 3.33 pap., plastic bdg.
1. Salt shakers. 2. Glassware—Collectors and collecting. I. Title.

Salt shakers—Collectors and collecting.

LECHNER, Mildred. 748.8
The world of salt shakers / by Mildred and Ralph Lechner. 1st ed. Paducah, Ky. : Collector Books, c1976. vii, 127 p. : col. ill. ; 22 cm. Includes index. [NK5440.S3L42] 77-355655 ISBN 0-89145-025-4 : 7.95
1. Salt shakers—Collectors and collecting. 2. Glassware—United States—Catalogs. I. Lechner, Ralph, joint author. II. Title. BIP

Saltcellars.

NEAL, Logan Wolfe 748.8
Pressed glass salt dishes of the lacy period, 1825-1850, by L. W. & D. B. Neal. [All drawings actual size and scale by D. B. Neal] Philadelphia, Author [c.1962] viii, p., 465p. of illus. 25cm. 62-19102 15.00
1. Saltcellars. 2. Glassware—Collectors and collecting. I. Neal, Dorothy Broom, joint author. II. Title.

NEAL, Logan Wolfe. 748.8
Pressed glass salt dishes of the lacy period, 1825-1850, by L. W. & D. B. Neal. [All drawings actual size and scale by D. B. Neal] Philadelphia [1962] viii p., 465p. of illus. 25cm. [NK5440.S3N4] 62-19102
1. Saltcellars. 2. Glassware— Collectors and collecting. I. Neal, Dorothy Broom, joint author. II. Title.

Saltcellars—Collectors and collecting.

SMITH, Allan B., 1904- 748.8
One thousand individual open salts [by] Allan B. & Helen B. Smith. [Litchfield, Me., Country House, 1972] [109] p. illus. (part col.) 23 cm. On spine: Individual open salts. Bibliography: p. [108] [NK8640.S6] 72-190883
1. Saltcellars—Collectors and collecting. I. Smith, Helen Benner, 1906- joint author. II. Title. III. Title: Individual open salts.

Saltonstall, Nathaniel, 1903-1968—Art collections.

BOSTON. Institute of Contemporary Art. 709'.73
A memorial exhibition; selections from the Nathaniel Saltonstall Collection. [Boston, 1969] [59] p. illus. (part col.) 23 cm. Catalog of the exhibition held Nov. 11-Dec. 14, 1969. [N6512.B58] 78-104038
1. Saltonstall, Nathaniel, 1903-1968—Art collections. 2. Art, American—Exhibitions. 3. Art, Modern—20th century—U.S. I. Title.

Salvini, Roberto.

GIOTTO DI BONDONE, 1266?-1337 759.5
All the paintings of Giotto [2v.] Text by Roberto Salvini. Tr. [from Italian] by Paul Colaicicchi. New York, Hawthorn [1964, c.1963] 2v. (various p.) illus., plates (pt. col.) 19cm. (Complete lib. of world art, 18-19) Bibl. 63-8012 3.95 bds., ea.
1. Salvini, Roberto. I. Title. II. Series.

Samaras, Lucas, 1936—

ALLOWAY, Lawrence 1900- 709.73
Samaras; selected works, 1960-1966. [New York] Pace Gallery [1966] 56 p. illus., port. 23 cm. Bibliography: p. 52. [N6537.S3A6] 66-29375
1. Samaras, Lucas. 1936- I. Title.

SAMARAS, Lucas, 1936- 709.24
Chair transformation. New York, Pace Gallery, 1970. 63 p. of illus. 26 cm. Label mounted on t.p.: Supplied by Worldwide Books, inc., Boston, Mass. [N6537.S3A43] 79-138435
I. Pace Gallery. II. Title.

SAMARAS, Lucas, 1936- 709'.2'4
Lucas Samaras. Exhibition directed by Robert Doty. [New York] Whitney Museum of American Art [1972] [72] p. illus. (part col.) 29 cm. Catalog of the exhibition held Nov. 18, 1972-Jan. 7, 1973, at the Whitney Museum of American Art. Bibliography: p. [64]-[67] [N6537.S3D67] 72-87740
1. Samaras, Lucas, 1936- I. Doty, Robert M. II. Whitney Museum of American Art, New York.

Samothrace—Antiquities.

LEHMANN, Phyllis Lourene (Williams) 1912- 709'.38
Samothracian reflections; aspects of the revival of the antique, by Phyllis Williams Lehmann and Karl Lehmann. [Princeton, N.J.] Princeton University Press [1973] xxiii, 278 p. illus. 27 cm. (Bollingen series, 92) [N6915.L38] 71-163867 ISBN 0-691-09909-X 20.00
1. Ciriaco de' Pizzicolli, of Ancona, 1391-1457? 2. Mantegna, Andrea, 1431-1506. Parnassus. 3. Victoria (Goddess)—Art. 4. Samothrace—Antiquities. 5. Renaissance—Italy. I. Lehmann, Karl, 1894-1960, joint author. II. Title. III. Series.

Samplers.

CHRISTIE, Archibald H., Mrs. 746.4'4
Samplers and stitches; a handbook of the embroiderer's art. With many designs and other illus. by the author. Great Neck, N.Y., Hearthside Press [1971] viii, 152 p. illus. (part col.) 24 cm. Reprint of the 1948 ed. [TT770.C54 1971] 73-151461 6.95
1. Samplers. 2. Embroidery. I. Title. BIP

CHRISTIE, Grace. 746.445
Samplers and stitches; a handbook of the embrioiderers art, by Mrs. Archibalo Christie; with many designs and other illus. by the author. [4th ed.] New York, Hearthside Press [1959] 152p. illus. 24cm. [NK9104.C5 1959] 59-15824
1. Samplers. 2. Embroidery. I. Title.

COLBY, Averil 746.445
Samplers. Newton Center, Mass., Branford [1965, c1964] 266 p. illus. (pt. col.) 26 cm. Bibl. [NK9143.C6] 65-11616 8.95
1. Samplers. I. Title.

DREESMANN, Cecile. 746.4'4
Samplers for today / Cecile Dreesmann. New York : Galahad Books, [1975] c1972. 160 p. : ill. ; 29 cm. Bibliography: p. 158-159. [TT753.D7 1975] 75-12265 ISBN 0-88365-320-6 : 12.50
1. Samplers. 2. Needlework. I. Title.

HUISH, Marcus Bourne, 1845-1921. 746.4'4
Samplers & tapestry embroideries. 2d ed. New York, Dover Publications [1970] xii, 176 p. 101 illus. (8 col.) 22 cm. "An unabridged and corrected republication of the second revised edition (1913)." [NK9143.A1H8 1970] 78-107667
1. Samplers. 2. Embroidery, English. I. Title. BIP

MEULENBELT-NIEUWBURG, Albarta. 746.4'4
Embroidery motifs from old Dutch samplers / compiled by Albarta Meulenbelt-Nieuwburg ; drawings by Albarta Meulenbelt-Nieuwburg, Emmy van Vrijberghe de Coningh, Baukje Zijlstra ; translated by Patricia Wardle, Gillian Downing. New York : Scribner, [1975] c1974. 192 p., [4] leaves of plates : ill. (some col.) ; 25 cm. Translation of Merklapmotieven en hun symboliek. Bibliography: p. 188-189. [TT753.M4713 1975] 73-13367 ISBN 0-684-13678-3 : 12.50
1. Samplers. 2. Embroidery—Patterns. 3. Embroidery, Dutch. I. Title.

Samplers—Germany—Exhibitions.

ALTONAER Museum in Hamburg. v. 12
Stickmustertucher aus dem Besitz des Altonaer Museums : Altonaer Museum, Norddeutsches Landesmuseum, 10. September bis 9. November 1975 : [Ausstellung : Katalog / Gesamtbearbeitung, Gerhard Kaufmann]. [Hamburg : Das Museum, 1975] 54 p., [13] leaves of plates : ill. (some col.) ; 22 cm. Bibliography: p. 22. [NK9150.A1A47 1975] 75-522112
1. Samplers—Germany—Exhibitions. I. Kaufmann, Gerhard. II. Title.

Samplers—Lawrence, Kan.—Exhibitions.

CURRY, David Park. 746.3'074'018165
Stitches in time : samplers in the Museum's collection : [an exhibition] March 2-April 6, 1975 / introd. and catalogue by David Park Curry. [Lawrence] : University of Kansas, Museum of Art, [1975] [48] p. : ill. ; 38 x 15 cm. (Miscellaneous publication of the Museum of Art ; no. 98) Bibliography: p. [46]-[47] [NK9101.L38K362] 75-4278
1. Kansas. University. Museum of Art. 2. Samplers—Lawrence, Kan.—Exhibitions. I. Kansas. University. Museum of Art. II. Title. III. Series: Kansas. University. Museum of Art. Miscellaneous publications ; no. 98.

Samplers—United States.

BOLTON, Ethel (Stanwood) 1873- 746.3'0973
American samplers, by Ethel Stanwood Bolton and Eva Johnston Coe. New York, Dover Publications [1973] xii, 416 p. illus. 24 cm. Reprint of the 1921 ed. published by the Massachusetts Society of the Colonial Dames of America, Boston.

America—Southwest, New. 3. Indians of North America—Religion and mythology. I. Title. BIP

Sani, Alberto.

BERENSON, Bernhard, 1865-1959. 730'.924
Alberto Sani, an artist out of his time. (Un artista fuori del suo tempo) Westport, Conn., Greenwood Press [1972] 115 p. illus. 23 cm. Reprint of the 1950 ed. English and Italian. [NB623.S32B47 1972] 70-138202 ISBN 0-8371-5555-X
1. Sani, Alberto.

Sansovino, Andrea, 1460-1529.

HUNTLEY, George Haydn, 1905- 730'.92'4 B
Andrea Sansovino, sculptor and architect of the Italian Renaissance, by G. Haydn Huntley. Westport, Conn., Greenwood Press [1971, c1935] xvi, 155 p. illus. 24 cm. Bibliography: p. [137]-143. [N6923.S34H8 1971] 78-138152 ISBN 0-8371-5609-2
1. Sansovino, Andrea, 1460-1529.

Santa Barbara, Calif. Museum of Art.

ARCHIVERO I; 759'.074'019491
research papers on works of art in the collection of the Santa Barbara Museum of Art, by Roger C. Burns [and others] Santa Barbara, Calif. [Santa Barbara Museum of Art] 1973. 189 p. illus. (part col.) 27 cm. Includes bibliographies. [N742.S15A95] 73-88840
1. Santa Barbara, Calif. Museum of Art. 2. Paintings—Santa Barbara, Calif. 3. Paintings—Expertising. I. Burns, Rogert C. II. Santa Barbara, Calif. Museum of Art.

SANTA Barbara, Calif. Museum of Art. 730'.922
The collection of Greek and Roman antiquities at the Santa Barbara Museum of Art [by] Mario A. Del Chiaro. [Santa Barbara, Calif., 1962] [32] p. illus. 15 x 24 cm. Cover title. [NB90.S24 1962] 75-309807
1. Santa Barbara, Calif. Museum of Art. 2. Sculpture, Greek—Catalogs. 3. Sculpture, Greco-Roman—Catalogs. 4. Sculpture—Santa Barbara, Calif.—Catalogs. 5. Vase-painting, Greek—Catalogs. 6. Vase-painting—Santa Barbara, Calif.—Catalogs. I. Del Chiaro, Mario Aldo, 1925- II. Title.

SANTA Barbara, Calif. Museum of Art. 741.9'4'074019491
European drawings in the collection of the Santa Barbara Museum of Art / Alfred Moir, editor. [Santa Barbara, Calif.] : The Museum, c1976. 298 p. : ill. ; 28 cm. Includes bibliographical references and index. [NC225.S2 1976] 76-4685
1. Santa Barbara, Calif. Museum of Art. 2. Drawings, European—Catalogs. 3. Drawings—Santa Barbara, Calif.—Catalogs. I. Moir, Alfred. II. Title.

SANTA Barbara, Calif. Museum of Art. 704.94'6
Iconocom: cross-cultural iconography for the community. [Santa Barbara, 1973] 140 p. illus. 22 cm. [N7740.S33 1973] 73-88841
1. Santa Barbara, Calif. Museum of Art. 2. Symbolism in art. 3. Art—Santa Barbara, Calif.—Catalogs. I. Title.

Santa Barbara Mission.

GEIGER, Maynard J., 1901- 726.41
A pictorial history of the physical development of Mission Santa Barbara, from brush hut to institutional greatness, 1786-1963. [Oakland, Calif., Franciscan Fathers of California, c1963] x, 180 p. illus., plans. 28 cm. 500 copies. Copy no. 213. [NA5235.S26G4] 64-911
1. Santa Barbara Mission. I. Title.

Santa Fe, N.M.

STILLMAN, Yedida Kalfon, 1946- 391'.0095694'074018956
Palestinian costume and jewelry / Yedida Kalfon Stillman. 1st ed. Albuquerque : University of New Mexico Press, 1978. p. cm. "Published for the Museum of New Mexico and the International Folk Art Foundation." Includes index. Bibliography: p. [NK7373.7.A1S75] 78-55711 ISBN 0-8263-0490-7 pbk. : 12.50
1. Santa Fe, N.M. Museum of New Mexico—Catalogs. 2. Costume—Palestine—Catalogs. 3. Jewelry—Palestine—Catalogs. I. Santa Fe, N.M. Museum of New Mexico. II. International Folk Art Foundation. III. Title. BIP

Santa Fe, N.M. Museum of New Mexico. Museum of Fine Arts.

SANTA Fe, N.M. Museum of New Mexico. Museum of Fine Arts. 708'.189'56
Handbook of the collections, 1917-1974, Museum of Fine Arts. [Santa Fe] : Museum of New Mexico, [1974] 192 p. : ill. (some col.) ; 26 cm. [N742.S3A55] 74-84236
1. Santa Fe, N.M. Museum of New Mexico. Museum of Fine Arts. 2. Art—Santa Fe, N.M.—Catalogs.

Santa Maria Maddalena dei Pazzi (Church), Florence.

LUCHS, Alison. 726'.5'094551
Cestello, a Cistercian church of the Florentine renaissance / Alison Luchs. New York : Garland Pub. Co., 1977. xix, 443 p. : ill. ; 21 cm. (Outstanding dissertations in the fine arts) Originally presented as the author's thesis, Johns Hopkins University, 1975. Bibliography: p. 421-443. [NA5621.F748L8 1977] 76-23642 ISBN 0-8240-2706-X lib.bdg. : 45.00
1. Santa Maria Maddalena dei Pazzi (Church), Florence. 2. Architecture, Cistercian—Italy—Florence. 3. Art, Italian—Italy—Florence. 4. Art, Renaissance—Italy—Florence. I. Title. II. Series.

Santa Rosa site, Mexico.

BROCKINGTON, Donald Leslie. 970*.4*27
The ceramic history of Santa Rosa, Chiapas, Mexico, by Donald L. Brockington. Provo, Utah, New World Archaeological Foundation, Brigham Young University, 1967. vii, 74 p. illus. 27 cm. (Papers of the New York Archaeological Foundation, no. 23) Bibliography: p. 73-74. [E51.N38 no. 23] [F1219.3.P8] 72-183659
1. Santa Rosa site, Mexico. 2. Indians of Mexico—Pottery. I. Title. II. Series: New World Archaeological Foundation. Papers, no. 23.

Santayana, George, 1863-1952.

SINGER, Irving. 101
Santayana's aesthetics; a critical introduction. Cambridge, Harvard University Press, 1957. ix, 235p. 22cm. Bibliographical references included in 'Notes' (p. [225]-232) Bibliographical footnotes. [B945.S24S55] [B945.S24S55] 701.17 57-9079 57-9079
1. Santayana, George, 1863-1952. 2. Aesthetics. I. Title. BIP

Santos (Art)

ESPINOSA, Jose Edmundo, 1900- 704.948'4
Saints in the valleys; Christian sacred images in the history, life and folk art of Spanish New Mexico [by] Jose E. Espinosa. Rev. ed. [Albuquerque] University of New Mexico Press [1967] xiii, 122 p. illus., map (on lining paper) 28 cm. Bibliography: p. 101-108. [N8080.E8 1967] 67-2675
1. Santos (Art) 2. Folk art—New Mexico. 3. Art, Latin American. I. Title.

NEW Mexico 704.948'2'09789
santos: how to name them. Illus. by Frances Breese. Foreword and captions by E.Boyd. Santa Fe, N.M., Museum of New Mexico [and] International Folk Art Foundation, 1966. 1 v. (chiefly illus.) 26 cm. [NK835.N5N4] 68-6768
1. Santos (Art) 2. Folk art—New Mexico. I. Breese, Frances, illus. II. Hall, Elizabeth Boyd (White) 1903- III. International Folk Art Foundation. IV. Santa Fe., N.M. Museum of New Mexico.

Santos (Art)—New Mexico.

HALL, Elizabeth Boyd (White) 1903- 704.948'2'09789
The New Mexico santero, by E. Boyd. [Santa Fe, Museum of New Mexico Press, 1969] 23, [1] p. illus. 28 cm. Bibliography: p. [24] [N7910.N6H2] 73-628661
1. Santos (Art)—New Mexico. I. Title. BIP

MARTINEZ, Eluid Levi, 1944- 730'.9789
What is a New Mexico santo? / by Eluid Levi Martinez ; [Spanish translation by Julia Rosa Emslie]. Santa Fe, N.M. : Sunstone Press, [1978] p. cm. English and Spanish. [NK835.N5M37] 77-78519 ISBN 0-913270-76-8 pbk. : 2.95
1. Santos (Art)—New Mexico. 2. Folk art—New Mexico. I. Title. BIP

STEELE, Thomas J. 704.948'2'09789
Santos and saints : essays and handbook / by Thomas J. Steele. 1st ed. Albuquerque : Calvin Horn, 1974. viii, 220 p. : ill. ; 24 cm. Includes bibliographical references and index. [N7910.N6S8] 74-75452 ISBN 0-910750-30-0 : 10.00
1. Santos (Art)—New Mexico. 2. Art, Spanish-American—New Mexico. I. Title. BIP

WILDER, Mitchell A. 704.948'2
Santos : the religious folk art of New Mexico : text and photographs / by Mitchell A. Wilder, with Edgar Breitenbach. New York : Hacker Art Books, 1976. 49, [64] p., [32] leaves of plates : ill. ; 32 cm. Reprint of the 1943 ed. published by Taylor Museum of the Colorado Springs Fine Arts Center, Colorado Springs, Colo. Bibliography: p. 48-49 (1st group) [N7910.N6W5 1976] 75-11066 ISBN 0-87817-169-X lib.bdg. : 30.00
1. Santos (Art)—New Mexico. 2. Folk art—New Mexico. 3. Art, Spanish-American—New Mexico. I. Breitenbach, Edgar, joint author. II. Title. BIP

Santos (Art)—Southwest, New—Catalogs.

DENVER. Art Museum. 704.948'2'074018883
Santos of the Southwest; the Denver Art Museum collection. [Text prepared by Mary Jane Downing. Florence B. Haslett, photographer. Denver, Lithography by A. B. Hirschfeld Press, 1969?] 72 p. illus. 26 cm. Bibliography: p. 70. [N7822.D4A75] 72-25362
1. Santos (Art)—Southwest, New—Catalogs. I. Downing, Mary Jane. II. Title.

Sao Paulo, Brazil (City) Museu de Arte.

BARDI, Pietro Maria, 1900- 708.9816
Art treasures of the Sao Paulo Museum and the development of art in Brazil. [Translated from the Italian by John Drummond] New York, Abrams [1956] 296p. illus. (part col.) ports. (part col.) 28cm. [N910.S36B3] 58-9034
1. Sao Paulo, brazil (City) Museu de Arte. 2. Art—Brazil. I. Title.

Sapp, Allen, 1929—

SAPP, Allen, 1929- 759.11
A Cree life : the art of Allen Sapp / introd. by John Anson Warner & Thecla Bradshaw. Vancouver : J. J. Douglas, c1977. 126 p. : ill. (some col.), port. ; 31 cm. Bibliography: p. 121-122. [ND249.S27A4 1977] 78-304465 ISBN 0-88894-149-8 : 24.95
1. Sapp, Allen, 1929- 2. Cree Indians—Pictorial works. I. Title.
Distributed by ISBS

Sara Roby Foundation, New York—Art collections.

AMERICAN Federation of Arts. 759.13'074
Americans: individualists at work, from the Sara Roby Foundation Collection. New York [1972] [16] p. illus. 20 x 23 cm. [ND212.A515] 72-87727
1. Sara Roby Foundation, New York—Art collections. 2. Paintings, American—Exhibitions. 3. Painting, Modern—20th century—United States. I. Title.

Sarcophagi.

HANFMANN, George Maxim Anossov, 1911- 733.176
The Season sarcophagus in Dumbarton Oaks. Cambridge, Harvard University Press, 1951 [i. e. 1952] 2 v. plates. 30 cm. (Dumbarton Oaks studies, 2) "A catalogue of the representations of the Horae and the Seasons in ancient art": v. 2, p. [129]-192. Includes bibliographies. [NB1810.H3] 52-7580
1. Sarcophagi. 2. Seasons in art. 3. Art, Roman. I. Title. II. Series. BIP

Sardis.

HANFMANN, George Maxim Anossov, 1911- 730'.9561
Sculpture from Sardis : the finds through 1975 / George M. A. Hanfmann and Nancy H. Ramage. Cambridge, Mass. : Harvard University Press, 1977. p. cm. (Report - Archaeological Exploration of Sardis ; 2) Bibliography: p. Includes indexes. [NB130.S37H36] 77-21124 ISBN 0-674-79588-1 : 30.00
1. Sardis. 2. Sculpture—Turkey. 3. Turkey—Antiquities. I. Ramage, Nancy H., 1942- joint author. II. Title. III. Series: Archaeological Exploration of Sardis. Report — Archaeological Exploration of Sardis ; 2. BIP

Sargent, John Singer, 1856-1925.

ART Reference Gallery. Art Appraisal Information Division. 709'.2'4
Price profile on all works by John Singer Sargent. Montclair, N.J. [1973] vi, 20 p. 22 cm. [N6537.S32A77] 73-158797 12.00
1. Sargent, John Singer, 1856-1925. 2. Art—Prices. I. Title.

CHARTERIS, Evan Edward, Sir, Hon., 1864-1940. 759.13
John Sargent; with reproductions from his paintings and drawings. New York, B. Blom, 1972. viii, 308 p. illus. 26 cm. Reprint of the 1927 ed. [ND237.S3C4 1972] 71-174842 15.75
1. Sargent, John Singer, 1856-1925. BIP

CHARTERIS, Evan Edward, Hon. Sir, 1864-1940. 759.13
John Sargent, with reproductions from his paintings and drawings. New York, Scribner, 1927. Detroit, Tower Books, 1971. xii, 308 p. illus. 23 cm. Includes bibliographical references. [ND237.S3C4 1971] 70-164163
1. Sargent, John Singer, 1856-1925.

CHICAGO. Art Institute. 759.13
Sargent, Whistler, and Mary Cassatt, by Frederick A. Sweet. [A catalogue of the exhibition] The Art Institute of Chicago, January 14 through February 25, 1954 [and] theMetropolitan Museum of Art, March 25 through May 23, 1954. [Chicago, 1954] 101p. illus. (part col.) ports. 26cm. [ND210.C47] 54-811
1. Sargent, John Singer, 1856-1925. 2. Whistler, James Abbott McNelli, 1834-1903. 3. Cassatt, Mary, 1845-1926. 4. Paintings, American—Exhibitions. I. Sweet, Frederick Arnold, 1903- II. New York. Metropolitan Museum of Art. III. Title.

HOOPES, Donelson F. 759.13
Sargent watercolors, by Donelson F. Hoopes. New York, Watson-Guptill Publications [1970] 87 p. col. illus. 29 cm. Reproductions of watercolors are from the collections of the Metropolitan Museum of Art and the Brooklyn Museum of Art. [ND1839.S32H6 1970] 70-120549 ISBN 0-8230-4640-0 17.50
1. Sargent, John Singer, 1856-1925. I. New

SUBJECT INDEX SCHIELE, EGON, 1890-1918.

York (City). Metropolitan Museum of Art. II. Brooklyn Institute of Arts and Sciences. Museum. III. Title. BIP

JOHN Singer Sargent, 759.13
a biography. [1st ed.] New York, W. W. Norton [1955] xv, 464p. illus. 25cm. Bibliographical references included in 'Notes' (p. 403-426) [ND237.S3M6] 927.5 55-13654
1. Mount, Charles Merrill. II. Sargent, John Singer, 1856-1925.

ORMOND, Richard. 759.13
John Singer Sargent: paintings, drawings, watercolors. [1st U.S. ed.] New York, Harper & Row [1970] 264 p. plates (part col.), ports. (part col.) 32 cm. [ND237.S3O7 1970b] 76-114743 20.00
1. Sargent, John Singer, 1856-1925.

SARGENT, John Singer, 741.973
1856-1925.
Drawings by John Singer Sargent in the Corcoran Gallery of Art. Selected and edited by Ellen Gross and James Harithas. [1st ed.] Alhambra, Calif., Borden Pub. Co. [1967] [64] p. illus. 31 cm. (American museum series) [NC1075.S34G7] 67-26426
I. Gross, Ellen, ed. II. Harithas, James, ed. III. Corcoran Gallery of Art, Washington, D.C. IV. Title. BIP

SARGENT'S Boston, 759.13
with an essay a biographical summary & a complete check list of Sargent's portraits. Boston, Museum of Fine Arts, 1956. 132p. illus. (part col.) ports. 26cm. 'Catalogue of a centennial exhibition, Sargent's Boston, January 3 to February 7, 1956':p. 67-75. [ND237.S3M3] [ND237.S3M3] 927.5 56-1995 56-1995
1. Sargent, John Singer, 1856-1925. 2. Paintings, American—Exhibitions. I. McKibbin, David. II. Boston, Museum of Fine Arts.

Sarony, Napoleon, 1821-1896.

BASSHAM, Ben L. 770'.92'4 [B]
The theatrical photographs of Napoleon Sarony / by Ben L. Bassham. Kent, Ohio : Kent State University Press, c1978. p. cm. Bibliography: p. [TR140.S37B37] 78-4933 ISBN 0-87338-213-7 : 8.50
1. Sarony, Napoleon, 1821-1896. 2. Actors—Portraits. I. Title. BIP

Sarto, Andrea del, 1486-1531.

FREEDBERG, Syndey Joseph 759.5
Andrea del Sarto [v.2] Cambridge, Mass., Belknap Pr., Harvard, 1963. 302p. illus. 29cm. Contents.[2] Catalogue raisonne. Bibl. 63-17198 15.00
1. Sarto, Andrea del, 1486-1531. I. Title.

SHEARMAN, John K G 759.9493'2
Andrea del Sarto [by] John Shearman. Oxford, Clarendon Press, 1965. 2 v. (xi, 466 p.) 181 plates. 29 cm. Includes bibliographies. [ND623.S2S5] 65-22669
1. Sarto, Andrea del, 1486-1531. I. Title.

Satsuma pottery—Catalogs.

ANDACHT, Sandra. 738.3'7
Satsuma : an illustrated guide / by Sandra Andacht. Des Moines : Wallace-Homestead Book Co., c1978. 67, [1] p. : ill. (some col.) ; 23 cm. Bibliography: p. [68] [NK4168.K3A52] 77-80744 ISBN 0-87069-227-5 pbk. : 7.95
1. Satsuma pottery—Catalogs. 2. Pottery, Japanese—Japan—Kagoshima (Prefecture)—Catalogs. I. Title. BIP

Satty, W.

SATTY, W. 769'.924
The cosmic bicycle [by] Satty. 1st ed. San Francisco, Calif., Straight Arrow Books [1971] 1 v. (chiefly illus., part col.) 31 cm. [NE654.S24A43] 78-160454 7.95
I. Title.

SATTY, W. 769'.92'4
Time zone [by] Satty. [San Francisco] Straight Arrow Books; [distributed by Quick Fox, New York, 1973] 155 p. (chiefly illus.) 31 cm. [NE654.S24A57 1973] 73-79877 ISBN 0-87932-028-1 5.95 (pbk.)
1. Satty, W. 2. Photography, Composite. I. Title.

The Saturday evening post—Illustrations.

THE Saturday evening post 759.13
Norman Rockwell book. Indianapolis : Curtis Pub. Co., c1977. vii, 152 p. : ill. (some col.) ; 32 cm. [ND237.R68A4 1977] 77-12286 ISBN 0-89387-007-2 : 9.95
1. Rockwell, Norman, 1894- 2. The Saturday evening post—Illustrations. I. Rockwell, Norman, 1894- II. Title: Norman Rockwell book.

Saville, Malcolm.

SAVILLE, Malcolm. 942.2'52
Portrait of Rye : with some sketches of places worth visiting within easy reach of the ancient town / by Malcolm Saville ; with woodcuts by Michael Renton ; with a new poem by Patric Dickinson. East Grinstead : Henry Goulden Ltd, 1976. 93 p. : ill. ; 22 cm. Includes index. Bibliography: p. [91] [DA690.R9S28] 77-367640 ISBN 0-904822-05-2 : £5.00. ISBN 0-904822-06-0 pbk.
1. Saville, Malcolm. 2. Rye, Eng.—History. 3. Rye, Eng.—Description. I. Title.

Savonarola, Girolamo Maria Francesco Matteo, 1452-1498.

STEINBERG, Ronald M. 709'.45'51
Fra Girolamo Savonarola, Florentine art, and Renaissance historiography / Ronald M. Steinberg. Athens : Ohio University Press, c1977. 151 p. : ill. ; 25 cm. Includes index. Bibliography: p. 142-148. [N6921.F7S377] 76-8304 ISBN 0-8214-0202-1 lib.bdg. : 11.00
1. Savonarola, Girolamo Maria Francesco Matteo, 1452-1498. 2. Art, Renaissance—Italy—Florence. 3. Art, Italian—Italy—Florence. 4. Humanism in art. I. Title.

Saws.

HAINES, Ray Edward. 684
The circular saw [by] Ray E. Haines [and others] New York, Van Nostrand [1952] 118 p. illus. 27 cm. (The Home workshop series) [TT180.H32] 52-5741
1. Saws. 2. Woodwork. 3. Furniture. I. Title.

Sawyier, Paul, 1865-1917.

JILLSON, Willard Rouse, 759.13
1890-
Paul Sawyier: American artist, 1865-1917, a brief biographical sketch. [1st ed.] Lexington, Ky., Keystone Printery, 1961. 50p. illus. 23cm. Includes bibliography. [ND237.S34J5] 61-46579
1. Sawyler, Paul, 1865-1917. I. Title.

JONES, Arthur Frederick, 759.13
1945-
The art of Paul Sawyier / by Arthur F. Jones ; with a foreword by Jaqueline Bull ; color photography by Clyde T. Burke. Lexington : University Press of Kentucky, c1976. xx, 119 p., [32] leaves of plates : ill. (some col.) ; 27 x 34 cm. Includes bibliographical references and index. [ND237.S34J66] 75-41988 ISBN 0-8131-1340-7 : 27.50
1. Sawyier, Paul, 1865-1917. 2. Painters—United States—Biography. I. Title. BIP

JONES, Arthur Frederick, 759.13
1945-
An exhibition of the art of Paul Sawyier / organized by Arthur F. Jones for the University of Kentucky and held at the Art Gallery, Fine Arts Building, November 7 through November 28, 1976. [s.l. : s.n., c1976] [8] p. ; 28 cm. [ND237.S34J67] 77-368158
1. Sawyier, Paul, 1865-1917. I. Sawyier, Paul, 1865-1917. II. Kentucky. University. III. Kentucky. University. Art Gallery. IV. Title.

Scamuzzi, Ernesto.

TURIN. Museo egizio. 709.32
Egyptian art in the Egyptian Museum of Turin: paintings, sculpture, furniture, textiles, ceramics, papyri [by] Ernesto Scamuzzi. [Translated by Barbara Arnett Melchiori. New York, H. N. Abrams [1965] 1 v. (unpaged) mounted col. illus., facsims., plates (some col.), port. 36 cm. Translation of Museo egizio di Torino. Includes bibliography. [N5350.T8] 65-13910
1. Scamuzzi, Ernesto. I. Title.

Scarabs.

WARD, John, 1832-1912. 736.2'0932
The sacred beetle; Egyptian scarabs in art and history. Five hundred examples of scarabs and cylinders: the translations by F. Llewellyn Griffith. San Diego, Calif., Malter-Westerfield Pub. Co. [1968] xviii, 122 p. illus. 22 cm. (Library series) Reprint of the 1902 ed. [NK5561.W3 1968] 68-59305
1. Scarabs. 2. Egypt—Antiquities. I. Title.

Scarborough, Eng.—Description—Views.

VINTAGE Scarborough / 942.8'47
[compiled by] Bryan Berryman. Nelson : Hendon Publishing Co., 1976. [40] p. : of ill., port. ; 21 x 29 cm. "A companion volume to Scarborough as it was." [DA690.S28V56] 76-378406 ISBN 0-902907-93-X : £1.30
1. Scarborough, Eng.—Description—Views. 2. Scarborough, Eng.—Social life and customs—Pictorial works. I. Berryman, Brian.

Scarves.

REINGOLD, Carmel Berman. 391'.4
Fashion forecast: scarves and belts. New York, Grosset & Dunlap [1970] 95 p. illus. 21 cm. [TT507.R4] 75-106314 1.45
1. Scarves. 2. Belts (Clothing) 3. Fashion. I. Title.

Scene painting.

POLUNIN, Vladimir. 751.7'5
The continental method of scene painting / by Vladimir Polunin ; edited by Cyril W. Beaumont. New York : Da Capo Press, 1978. p. cm. (Da Capo series in dance) Reprint of the 1927 ed. published by C. W. Beaumont, London. [ND2885.P6 1978] 77-19083 ISBN 0-306-77578-6 pbk. : 22.50
1. Scene painting. 2. Theaters—Stage-setting and scenery. I. Title. BIP

SCHOLZ, Janos, ed. 751.75
Baroque and romantic stage design; introd. by A. Hyatt Mayor. New York, H. Bittner, 1950 [i.e. 1949] xiii, 24 p., [98] p. of illus. 29 cm. [ND2885.S35] 50-5226
1. Scene painting. I. Title.

SCHOLZ, Janos, ed. 751.75
Baroque and romantic stage design. Introd. by A. Hyatt Mayor. New York, Dutton, 1962 [c.1949] 22p. chiefly illus. (Dutton paperback, D101) Bibl. 2.15 pap.,
1. Scene painting. I. Title.

SCHOLZ, Janos, ed. 751.75
Baroque and romantic stage design. Introd. by A. Hyatt Mayor. [New ed.] New York, Beechhurst Press [1955, c1949] 1v. (chiefly illus.) 29cm. (A Bittner art book) Bibliography: p.22-24. [ND2885.S35 1955] 55-1417
1. Scene painting. I. Title.

VIALE FERRERO. MERCEDES 759.5
La scenografia del'700 e i fratelli Galliari. [in Italian] Torino, Fratelli Pozzo. [dist. New York 52, Benjamin Blom, 4 W. Mt. Eden Ave., 1964, c.1963] 283p. illus., plates (pt. col.) 2830 cm. Bibl. 64-25907 25.00
1. Scene painting. 2. Theaters—Stage-setting and scenery. 3. Galliari family. I. Title.

Scene painting, Roman.

LITTLE, Alan 751.7'5'0937
MacNaughton Gordon.
Roman perspective painting and the ancient stage [by] Alan M. G. Little. [Wheaton, Md., c1971] vi, 50 p. illus. 28 cm. Cover title. Companion volume: A Roman bridal drama at the Villa of the Mysteries. Bibliography: p. [48]-50. [ND2885.L54] 72-180621 3.00
1. Scene painting, Roman. 2. Perspective. I. Title.

Schamberg, Morton Livingston, 1881-1918.

WOLF, Ben. 759.13
Morton Livingston Schamberg; a monograph. Philadelphia, University of Pennsylvania Press [1963] 125 p. illus., ports. 29 cm. Bibliography: p. 125. [ND237.S42W6 1963] 63-21716
1. Schamberg, Morton Livingston, 1881-1918. I. Title.

Schanker, Louis, 1903—

SCHANKER, Louis, 1903- 769'.92'4
Louis Schanker prints, 1924-1971 / essay by Una E. Johnson ; foreword by Jo Miller ; research by Tom Jagger. Brooklyn : Brooklyn Museum, c1974. 55 p. : ill. ; 23 cm. (American graphic artists of the twentieth century ; monograph no. 9) Bibliography: p. 54-55. [NE539.S33J64] 74-15701
1. Schanker, Louis, 1903- I. Johnson, Una E. II. Brooklyn Institute of Arts and Sciences. Museum. III. Title. IV. Series.

Schedel, Hartmann, 1440-1514.

WILSON, Adrian. 093
The Nuremberg Chronicle designs; an account of the new discovery of the earliest known layouts for a printed book: the exemplars for the Nuremberg Chronicle of 1493, with pages from the Latin exemplar reproduced for the first time. San Francisco, Printed for the members of the Roxburghe Club of San Francisco and The Zamorano Club of Los Angeles, 1969. 41 p. facsims. 35 cm. 350 copies printed. [Z241.S31W5] 70-13420
1. Schedel, Hartmann, 1440-1514. Liber chronicarum. I. Title.

Schedel, J. J.—Art collections.

SCHEDEL, J. J. 736'.24'0951
The splendor of jade; four thousand years of the art of Chinese jade carving, by J. J. Schedel. With an introd. by Na Chih-liang. [1st ed.] New York, Dutton, 1974. 221 p. col. illus. 32 cm. (A Dutton visual book) Bibliography: p. 221. [NK5750.S39 1974] 74-9855 35.00
1. Schedel, J. J.—Art collections. 2. Jade art objects—China—Catalogs. I. Title. BIP

Scheyer, Galka E.—Art collections.

NORTON Simon Museum of 709'.04
Art at Pasadena.
The Blue Four Galka Scheyer Collection, Norton Simon Museum of Art at Pasadena : Feininger, Jawlensky, Kandinsky, Klee / edited by Sara Campbell. Pasadena, Calif. : The Museum, [1976] p. cm. [N6868.5.E9N67 1976] 76-13890 ISBN 0-915776-01-4 pbk.
1. Scheyer, Galka E.—Art collections. 2. Norton Simon Museum of Art at Pasadena. 3. Blaue Vier (Group of artists)—Catalogs. 4. Expressionism (Art)—Germany—Catalogs. 5. Art, Modern—20th century—Germany—Catalogs. 6. Art—Pasadena, Calif.—Catalogs. I. Campbell, Sara, 1941- II. Title.

Schiele, Egon, 1890-1918.

BENESCH, Heinrich, 1862- 759.36
1947.
Mein Weg mit Egon Schiele, [Redigiert und bearb. von Eva Benesch] New York, Verlag der Johannespresse, 1965. 39 p. facism. 6 plates, ports. 21 cm. [ND538.S37B4] 66-5782

I. Schiele, Egon 1890-1918. II. Benesch, Eva, ed. III. Title.

BOSTON. Institute of Contemporary Art. 759.36
Egon Schiele, 1890-1918. [Boston, 1960] [56]p. illus. (part col.) 19cm. (Its Exhibition, 3/1960) Catalog of exhibition, Oct. 6-Nov. 6, 1960. Bibliography: p.[17] [N5020.B6127 3/1960] 61-23435
1. Schiele, Egon, 1890-1918. I. Title. II. Series.

COMINI, Alessandra. 760'.092'4
Egon Schiele's portraits / Alessandra Comini. Berkeley : University of California Press, c1974. xxxii, 271 p., [121] leaves of plates : ill. (some col.) ; 29 cm. (California studies in the history of art ; 17) Includes index. Bibliography: p. [255]-260. [ND1329.S34C65] 78-117582 ISBN 0-520-01726-9 : 65.00
1. Schiele, Egon, 1890-1918. I. Title. II. Series. BIP

COMINI, Alessandra. 759.36
Schiele in prison. Greenwich, Conn., New York Graphic Society [1973] 111, [1] p. illus. (part col.) 26 cm. Bibliography: p. [112] [ND511.5.S3C65 1973] 73-79999 ISBN 0-8212-0537-4 12.00
1. Schiele, Egon, 1890-1918. I. Title.
Pbk. 5.95, ISBN 0-8212-0554-4. BIP

KALLIR, Otto, 1894- 759.3
Egon Schiele; oeuvre catalogue of the paintings. Wtih essays by Otto Benesch and Thomas M. Messer. New York, Crown Publishers, 1966. 559 p. illus. (part mounted col.) facisms, ports. 30 cm. Englsih and German. Based on Egon Schiele, Personlichkeit und Werk, by Otto Nirenatein, published in 1930. Bibliography: p. 519-[534] [ND538.S37K3] 66-15123
1. Schiele, Egon, 1890-1918. I. Benesch, Otto, 1896-1964. II. Messer, Thomas M. III. Nirenstein, Otto. Egon Schiele, Persönlichkeit und Werk. IV. Title.

LA Boetie, inc. 760'.09436'07401471
Egon Schiele and his circle. New York [1971] [51] p. illus. (part col.), ports. 22 cm. Catalog of an exhibition held May-June 1971. [N6808.5.E9L3] 78-198239
1. Schiele, Egon, 1890-1918. 2. Art, Austrian—Exhibitions. 3. Expressionism (Art)—Austria. I. Title.

SCHIELE, Egon, 1890-1918. 760'.092'4
The art of Egon Schiele / Erwin Mitsch ; [translated from the German by W. Keith Haughan]. London : Phaidon ; New York : distributed by Praeger, 1975. 267 p. : ill. (some col.) ; 29 cm. Translation of Egon Schiele, 1890-1918. Bibliography: p. 265-267. [ND511.5.S3M5713] 76-12709 ISBN 0-7148-1641-8 : 45.00
1. Schiele, Egon, 1890-1918. 2. Expressionism (Art)—Austria. I. Mitsch, Erwin, 1931- II. Title.

SCHIELE, Egon, 1890-1918. 759.36
Egon Schiele : drawings and water-colours / Erwin Mitsch. New York : Rizzoli, 1976. 120 p. : chiefly ill. (some col.) ; 18 cm. [ND1946.S3M513] 76-13777 ISBN 0-8478-0054-7 : 6.50
1. Schiele, Egon, 1890-1918. I. Mitsch, Erwin, 1931-

SCHIELE, Egon, 1890-1918. 759.36
Egon Schiele / Alessandra Comini. New York : G. Braziller, 1976. 31 p., 95 leaves of plates : ill. (some col.) ; 28 cm. [ND511.5.S3C64] 75-37328 ISBN 0-8076-0819-X : 15.00. ISBN 0-8076-0820-3 pbk. : 8.95
1. Schiele, Egon, 1890-1918. I. Comini, Alessandra.

SCHIELE, Egon, 1890-1918. 760'.0924
Watercolors and drawings; memorial exhibition, October 31-December 14, 1968. The Galerie St. Etienne. New York [1968] 155 p. plates (part col.) 21 cm. [ND1946.S3A58 1968] 79-725
I. Galerie St. Etienne, New York. II. Title.

Schilsky, Eric, 1898-1974.

SCOTTISH Arts Council. 730'.92'4
Eric Schilsky, sculptures and drawings : [catalogue of] a Scottish Arts Council exhibition. [Edinburgh] : The Council, 1976. [17] p. : ill., 2 ports. ; 21 cm. Exhibition held at Scottish Arts Council Gallery, 28 February - 28 March 1976; City Museum and Art Gallery, Dundee, 3 April - 24 April, 1976; Kirkcaldy Museums and Art Gallery, 30 April - 23 May 1976. [NB497.S33S36 1976] 76-368959 ISBN 0-902989-27-8 : £0.30
1. Schilsky, Eric, 1898-1974. I. Schilsky, Eric, 1898-1974. II. Scottish Arts Council Gallery. III. Dundee, Scot. Museum and Art Gallery. IV. Kirkcaldy Museum and Art Gallery.

Schindler, Gustave—Art collections.

DALLAS. Museum of Fine Arts. 732'.2'0967
The Gustave and Franyo Schindler Collection of African sculpture : gift of the McDermott Foundation in honor of Eugene McDermott / John Lunsford, text ; Werner Forman, photos. [Dallas] : Dallas Museum of Fine Arts, 1975. 163 p. : ill. ; 26 cm. Cover title: The Schindler Collection of African sculpture. Bibliography: p. 157-162. [NB1255.W47D34 1975] 75-320691 15.00
1. Schindler, Gustave—Art collections. 2. Schindler, Franyo—Art collections. 3. Sculpture, Primitive—Africa, West—Exhibitions. 4. Sculpture—Africa, West—Exhibitions. 5. Masks, African—Exhibitions. 6. Wood-carving, African—Exhibitions. I. Lunsford, John. II. Title. III. Title: The Schindler Collection of African sculpture.

Schindler, R. M., 1887-1953.

GEBHARD, David. 720'.924
Schindler. Pref. by Henry-Russell Hitchcock. New York, Viking Press [1972, c1971] 216 p. illus., plans. 22 cm. (A Studio book) Bibliography: p. 205-211. [NA737.S5G37 1972] 71-172899 ISBN 0-670-62063-7 7.95
1. Schindler, R. M., 1887-1953.

SCHINDLER, R. M., 1887-1953 720'.92
R. M. Schindler; an exhibition of the architecture of R. M. Schindler. 1887-1953. [Catalogue designed by David Bebhard] [Santa Barbara? Calif., 1967] 111p. illus., plans. 26cm. Organized by David Gebhard for presentation at the Art Gallery, Univ. of Calif., Santa Barbara, March 30 to Apr. 30, 1967 [and at] the Los Angeles County Mus. of Art, fall, 1967. Bibl. [NA737.S5G4] 67-63790 3.00 pap.,
I. Gebhard, David. II. California. University, Santa Barbara, Art Gallery. III. Los Angeles Co., Calif. Museum of Art, Los Angeles. IV. Title.
Available from the Univ. of Calif.

Schinkel, Karl Friedrich, 1781-1841.

PUNDT, Hermann G. 720'.92'4
Schinkel's Berlin; a study in environmental planning [by] Hermann G. Pundt. Cambridge, Harvard University Press, 1972. xviii, 263 p. illus. 26 cm. Bibliography: p. 227-233. [NA1088.S3P86] 75-172325 ISBN 0-674-79095-2 12.50
1. Schinkel, Karl Friedrich, 1781-1841. 2. Architecture—Berlin. 3. Cities and towns—Planning—Berlin. I. Title. BIP

Schinman, Edward P.—Art collections.

EPSTEIN, Jacob, Sir, 1880-1959. 709.24
Jacob Epstein: a catalogue of the Collection of Edward P. Schinman. Edited by Edward P. Schinman and Barbara Ann Schinman. Rutherford [N.J.] Fairleigh Dickinson University Press [1970] 126 p. illus. (part col.), port. 29 cm. Exhibition held at Fairleigh Dickinson University, Feb. 19-Apr. 1, 1967. Bibliography: p. 23-27. [NB497.E6S3] 67-29137 12.50
1. Schinman, Edward P.—Art collections. I. Schinman, Edward P., ed. II. Schinman, Barbara Ann, ed. III. Fairleigh Dickinson University.

Schiwetz, Edward Muegge, 1898—

SCHIWETZ, Edward Muegge, 1898- 759.13 B
Buck Schiwetz' Memories : paintings and drawings / by E. M. Schiwetz ; introductory essay by Leon Hale ; notes by the artist with Robert Calvert. 1st ed. College Station : Texas A & M University Press, c1978. 112 p. : ill. (some col.) ; 24 x 31 cm. ([The Joe and Betty Moore Texas art series ; no. 3]) [N6537.S35A4 1978] 78-6370 ISBN 0-89096-053-4 : 24.50
1. Schiwetz, Edward Muegge, 1898- I. Hale, Leon. II. Title. III. Title: Memories. IV. Series. BIP

Schlegelmilch, Erdmann.

SCHLEGELMILCH, Clifford J. 738.2'7
Handbook of Erdmann and Reinhold Schlegelmilch, Prussia-Germany, and Oscar Schlegemilch, Germany, porcelain marks, my ancestor's [sic] china, by Clifford J. Schlegelmilch. [3d ed. Flint, Mich., 1973] 44 p. illus. (part col.) 26 cm. On cover: R. S. Prussia Schlegelmilch. Previous editions published under title: Handbook of RS Prussia, RS Germany and Oscar Schlegelmilch porcelain marks. [NK4215.S34 1973] 73-171135
1. Schlegelmilch, Erdmann. 2. Schlegelmilch, Reinhold. 3. Schlegelmilch, Oscar. 4. Porcelain—Marks. I. Title.
Publisher's address: 3560 Rue Forest, Flint, Mich. 48504.

SCHLEGELMILCH, Clifford J. 738.2'7
Handbook of R S Prussia, R S Germany and Oscar Schlegelmilch porcelain marks [by Clifford J. Schlegelmilch, in collaboration with Louise J. Schlegelmilch. 2d ed. Flint, Mich., 1971] 32 p. illus., map. 21 cm. [NK4215.S34 1971] 71-25185
1. Schlegelmilch, Erdmann. 2. Schlegelmilch, Reinhold. 3. Schlegelmilch, Oscar. 4. Porcelain—Marks. I. Schlegelmilch, Louise J. II. Title.

SCHLEGELMILCH, Clifford J. 738.2'7
Handbook of R.S. Prussia, R.S. Germany and Oscar Schlegelmilch porcelain marks [by Clifford J. Schlegelmilch] 1st ed. Flint, Mich., Printed by Schultz Print. Co., c1970. 31 p. illus., map. 20 cm. Third ed. published in 1973 under title: Handbook of Erdmann and Reinhold Schlegelmilch, Prussia-Germany, and Oscar Schlegelmilch, Germany, porcelain marks. [NK4215.S34] 72-22490 3.00
1. Schlegelmilch, Erdmann. 2. Schlegelmilch, Reinhold. 3. Schlegelmilch, Oscar. 4. Porcelain—Marks. I. Title.

Schlemmer, Oskar, 1888-1943.

SCHLEMMER, Oskar, 1888-1943. 700'.92'4 B
The letters and diaries of Oskar Schlemmer. Selected and edited by Tut Schlemmer. Translated from the German by Krishna Winston. [1st ed.] Middletown, Conn., Wesleyan University Press [1972] xiii, 425 p. illus. 24 cm. Translation of his Briefe und Tagebucher. [ND588.S2818A3413] 77-184362 ISBN 0-8195-4047-1 19.95
1. Schlemmer, Oskar, 1888-1943. 2. Painters—Germany—Correspondence, reminiscences, etc. BIP

SCHLEMMER, Oskar, 1888-1943. 709'.2'4
Oskar Schlemmer: exhibition, October 22-November 20, 1969, Spencer A. Samuels & Company, ltd. Catalogued by Karin von Maur. [New York, S. A. Samuels, 1969] 180 p. illus. (part col.) 25 cm. Bibliography: p. 167-172. [N6888.S358M3] 72-176974
1. Maur, Karin von, 1938- II. Spencer A. Samuels & Company.

Schmied, Francois Louis, 1873—

RITCHIE, Ward, 1905- 686.2'092'4 B
Francois-Louis Schmied, artist, engraver, printer : some memories and a bibliography / by Ward Ritchie. Tucson : Graduate Library School, University of Arizona, c1976. vi, 41 p. : ill. ; 22 cm. (Bibliographic papers ; no. 1) Bibliography: p. [29]-41. [Z232.S253R58] 76-374430
1. Schmied, Francois Louis, 1873- 2. Printers—France—Biography. 3. Illustrators—France—Biography. 4. Engravers—France—Biography. I. Title.

Schoenhut (A.) Company.

ACKERMAN, Evelyn. 688.7'2
Shoenhut's Humpty Dumpty Circus from A to Z / Evelyn Ackerman and Frederick E. Keller. Los Angeles : Era Industries, c1975. 111 p. : ill. ; 29 cm. Includes bibliographical references. [TS2301.T7A38] 75-23604
1. Schoenhut (A.) Company. 2. Toys—Catalogs. I. Keller, Frederick E., joint author. II. Title. III. Title: Humpty Dumpty Circus from A to Z.

BUSER, M. Elaine. 688.7'2'075
M. Elaine and Dan Buser's guide to Schoenhut's dolls, toys, and circus, 1872-1976. Paducah, Ky. : Collector Books, c1976. 104 p. : ill. (some col.) ; 29 cm. [NK4894.2.S3B98] 76-374765 12.95
1. Schoenhut (A.) Company. 2. Dolls—United States. 3. Toys—United States. I. Buser, Daniel S., joint author. II. Title: M. Elaine and Dan Buser's guide to Schoenhut's dolls, toys, and circus ... III. Title: Guide to Schoenhut's dolls, toys, and circus, 1872-1976.

MANOS, Susan. 688.7'2'075
Schoenhut dolls & toys : a loving legacy / by Susan Manos. 1st ed. Paducah, Ky. : Collector Books, c1976. 96 p. : ill. (some col.) ; 23 cm. Includes index. Bibliography: p. 94. [NK4894.2.S3M35] 76-374764 ISBN 0-89145-012-2 : 8.95
1. Schoenhut (A.) Company. 2. Dolls—United States—Catalogs. 3. Toys—United States—Catalogs. I. Title. BIP

Scholarly publishing—Venice—History—Exhibitions.

STANFORD University. Libraries. Dept. of Special Collections. 070.5'092'2
The Aldine Press, 1494-1598, the first century of scholarly printing. An exhibition of books from libraries in San Francisco Bay area designed to illustrate the contributions of the Aldine Press to Renaissance scholarship and learning [Stanford, Calif.] 1973. [8] p. 31 cm. [Z232.M3S8 1973] 73-161507
1. Manuzio, family of printers, Venice. 2. Scholarly publishing—Venice—History—Exhibitions. 3. San Francisco Bay region—Libraries. I. Title.

Scholder, Fritz, 1937—

ADAMS, Clinton, 1918- 769'.92'4
Fritz Scholder : lithographs / text by Clinton Adams. Boston : New York Graphic Society, [1976] p. cm. Bibliography: p. [NE2312.S36A65] 75-9106 ISBN 0-8212-0689-3 : 17.50. ISBN 0-8212-0690-7 deluxe ed. : 200.00
1. Scholder, Fritz, 1937- I. Scholder, Fritz, 1937-

SCHOLDER, Fritz, 1937- 704.94'9
Indian kitsch : the use and misuse of Indian images / photos. by Fritz Scholder ; foreword by Patrick Houlihan. 1st ed. [Flagstaff, Ariz.] : Northland Press, c1979. [60] p. : chiefly ill. (some col.) ; 24 cm. [TR654.S35] 78-65928 ISBN 0-87358-190-3 : 8.50
1. Scholder, Fritz, 1937- 2. Photography, Artistic. 3. Indians of North America—Pictorial works. 4. Kitsch—United States. I. Title. BIP

SCHOLDER, Fritz, 1937- 759.13
Scholder/Indians. Introd. by Adelyn D. Breeskin. Commentary by Rudy H. Turk. [Flagstaff, Ariz.] Northland Press [1972] x, 115 p. illus. (part col.) 32 cm. Bibliography: p. 113-115. [E99.L9S3] 79-188288 ISBN 0-87358-092-3 17.50
I. Turk, Rudy H. II. Title. BIP

Scholz, Janos—Art collections.

DRAWINGS by seventeenth century Italian masters from the Collection 741.9'45

of Janos Scholz. A faculty-graduate student project, University of California, Santa Barbara. Edited by Alfred Moir. [Santa Barbara, Art Galleries, University of California, 1974] 150 p. illus. 27 cm. Catalog of an exhibition carried out as a project of the Dept. of Art, to be shown at the Art Galleries, University of California, Santa Barbara, and other museums, Feb. 26-Dec. 9, 1974. Bibliography: p. 148-150. [NC255.D72] 73-620185
1. Scholz, Janos—Art collections. 2. Drawings, Italian—Exhibitions. 3. Drawing, Baroque—Italy. I. Moir, Alfred, ed. II. California. University, Santa Barbara. Dept. of Art. III. California. University, Santa Barbara. Art Galleries.

FINCH 741'.0945'7307401471 College, New York. Museum of Art.
In the shadow of Vesuvius; Neapolitan drawings from the Collection of Janos Scholz. New York [1969] 40 p. 57 illus. 23 cm. Foreword signed: Robert L. Manning. "[Catalogue of] a loan exhibition, Feb. 12-April 12, 1969." [NC256.N3F5] 70-17565
1. Scholz, Janos—Art collections. 2. Drawings, Neapolitan—Exhibitions. I. Manning, Robert L. II. Title.

ITALIAN master 741.9'45'075
drawings, 1350-1800 from the Janos Scholz collection / selected and described by Janos Scholz. New York : Dover Publications, 1976. xxiv p., [75] leaves of plates : ill. ; 31 cm. [NC255.I82 1976] 75-19835 ISBN 0-486-23257-3 pbk. : 5.00
1. Scholz, Janos—Art collections. 2. Drawings, Italian—Catalogs. I. Scholz, Janos.

NEW York 741.945'074'01471 (City). New School for Social Research. New School Art Center.
One hundred Italian drawings from the 14th to the 18th centuries from the Janos Scholz collection. New York [1971] 36 p. illus. 17 x 26 cm. (American private collections) Catalogue of an exhibition, Mar.-Apr. 1971. [NC255.N46] 72-192516
1. Scholz, Janos—Art collections. 2. Drawings, Italian—Exhibitions. I. Title.

OBERHUBER, Konrad. 741.9'45
Sixteenth century Italian drawings from the Collection of Janos Scholz [by] Konrad Oberhuber [and] Dean Walker. Washington, National Gallery of Art [1973] xv, 143 p. 28 cm. Catalog of an exhibition held at the National Gallery of Art, Washington, D.C., 23 Sept. to 25 Nov. 1973, and at the Pierpont Morgan Library, New York, 12 Dec. 1973 to 3 Feb. 1974. Includes bibliographical references. [NC255.O23] 73-86478 8.50
1. Scholz, Janos—Art collections. 2. Drawings, Italian—Exhibitions. 3. Drawing, Renaissance—Italy. 4. Drawing, Baroque—Italy. I. Walker, Dean, 1948- joint author. II. United States. National Gallery of Art. III. Pierpont Morgan Library, New York. IV. Title. BIP

Schoneberg, S. C., 1926—

SCHONEBERG, S. C., 1926- 741.9'73
Schoneberg : [drawings, paintings, collages] . [San Francisco? : Schoneberg, 1974] [52] p. (incl. cover) : ill. (some col.) ; 27 cm. Cover title. "Baroque revisited ... (the Schoneberg vision)," by Arthur Secunda: p. [20]-[27] [NC139.S36A555] 74-191752
1. Schoneberg, S. C., 1926-

SCHONEBERG, S. C., 1926- 741.9'73
Schoneberg: [drawings and collages. San Francisco, 1969? c1968] [20] p. (incl. cover) illus. 27 cm. Cover title. [NC139.S36A55] 73-178355
1. Schoneberg, S. C., 1926-

SCHONEBERG, S. C., 1926- 741.9'73
Schoneberg: original drawings. [San Francisco, 1973, c1972] [28] p. (incl. cover) illus. 27 cm. Cover title. [NC139.S36A56] 73-178354
1. Schoneberg, S. C., 1926-

Schongauer, Martin, 15th cent.

FLECHSIG, Eduard, 1864- 709'.2'4
Martin Schongauer. Strasbourg, P. H. Heitz, 1951. 410 p. 41 plates (incl. port.) 24 cm. [NE654.S5F55] A52
1. Schongauer, Martin, 15th cent. I. Title.

SCHONGAUER, Martin, 769'.924 15thcent.
The complete engravings of Martin Schongauer, edited and introduced by Alan Shestack. New York, Dover Publications [1969] xx p., 120 illus. 28 cm. Bibliographical references included in "Notes" (p. xv-xvi) [NE654.S66S5] 68-29580 2.75
I. Shestack, Alan, ed. II. Title.

Schoofs, Rudolf, 1932-

GALERIE Dieter Brusberg, 769.943 Hanover.
Rudolf Schoofs: Gravuren. New York, Geo. Wittenborn. 1960[ ] pagination erratic. illus., port. 30x15cm. 61-89 2.50 pap.,
1. Schoofs, Rudolf, 1932- I. Title.

School architecture—Secondary.

*GT. Brit. Dept. of 727.2 Education and Science
Secondary school design: sixth form and staff. London, H.M.S.O. [New York, Brit. Info., c.]1965. 48p. illus., plans. 30cm. (Its building bulln., 25) 1.50 pap.,
1. School architecture—Secondary. I. Title.

School buildings.

BIRCH, Jack W. 371.9'045
Designing schools and schooling for the handicapped : a guide to the dynamic interaction of space, instructional materials, facilities, educational objectives, and teaching methods / by Jack W. Birch and B. Kenneth Johnstone. Springfield, Ill. : Thomas, [1975] xiii, 229 p. ; 24 cm. Includes index. Bibliography: p. 205-223. [LB3209.B46] 74-23213 ISBN 0-398-03362-5 : 14.50
1. School buildings. 2. Handicapped children—Education. I. Johnstone, Burton Kenneth, 1907- joint author. II. Title. BIP

BUILDING Systems 690.7'08 s Information Clearinghouse.
Building systems planning manual. Menlo Park, Calif., 1971. 47 p. illus. 28 cm. (Its Special report no. 3) Bibliography: p. 21-24. [LB3205.B77 no. 3] [LB3221] 727 73-165264
1. School buildings. 2. School facilities—Planning. I. Title. II. Series.

O'CONNOR, John W. 690.7
A study in school and university building design / John W. O'Connor. 1st ed. New York : Vantage Press, c1974. ix, 318 p. : ill. ; 22 cm. Bibliography: p. 305-318. [LB3221.O35] 75-306198 ISBN 0-533-01035-7 : 12.50
1. School buildings. I. Title.

ORGANIZATION for Economic 727 Cooperation and Development. Programme on Educational Building.
Providing for future change : adaptability and flexibility in school building. Paris : Organisation for Economic Co-operation and Development, 1976. 110 p. : ill. ; 27 cm. Issued also in French under title: Pourvoir aux changements futurs: adaptabilite et flexibilite dans la construction scolaire. [LB3205.O8 1976] 76-373518 ISBN 9-264-11487-4 : 7.00
1. School buildings. I. Title.
Distributed by OECD, Washington, D.C. BIP

OTTO, Karl, architect ed. 727
School buildings. London, pub. for 'The Architect & Building News by Iliffe [1965-66] 2 v. illus., plans. 29cm. Introd. essays in English: text in German and English in v.1. Orig. pub. as Schulbau. Stuttgart, Alexander Koch, 1963. Contents.v.1--Examples and developments in primary and secondary school buildings.--v.2--Technical schools, training; translated [from the German] by Eric Erber [LB3221.O813] 67-70824 20.00 ea.,
1. School buildings. 2. Architecture—Designs and plans. I. Title.
American distributor: Heinman, New York.

ROBSON, Edward Robert, 1835- 727 1917.
School architecture. With an introd. by Malcolm Seaborne. [Leicester] Leicester University Press; [Distributed by Humanities Press, New York, [1972, i.e. 1973] 37, xxiv, 440 p. illus. 24 cm. (The Victorian library) Reprint, with new introd. of the ed. published in 1874 by J. Murray. Bibliography: p. [27]-30. [LB3205.R6 1972] 73-159698 ISBN 0-391-00251-1 14.75
1. School buildings. BIP

ROTH, Alfred, 1903- 371.6
The new schoolhouse. Das neue Schulhaus. La nouvelle ecole. Rev. [i.e. 4th] ed. New York, Praeger [1966] 304p. illus., plans. 25cm. Previous eds. pub. under title: The new school. Bibl. [LB3221.R6 1966] 66-12529 15.00
1. School buildings. I. Title.

TESTA, Carlo, 1939- 371.6'2
New educational facilities : international survey / by Carlo Testa. Boulder, Colo. : Westview Press, [1975] p. cm. English, French, and German. Bibliography: p. [LB3205.T47] 75-23359 ISBN 0-89158-505-2 : 25.00
1. School buildings. 2. School facilities. I. Title. BIP

School buildings—Alaska.

ALASKA. Legislative 373.1'6'0973 Council.
Report on standard building design for schools and other State buildings. Juneau, 1962. 22 p. 28 cm. [LB3218.A6A5] 63-63063
1. School buildings—Alaska.

School buildings—Asia, Southeastern—Bibliography.

SINNAMON, Ian T. 727'.0959
Natural disasters and educational building design : an introductory review and annotated bibliography for the Asian region / by Ian T. Sinnamon. Bangkok : Unesco Regional Office for Education in Asia, 1976. 33 p. : ill. ; 30 cm. (Educational building report ; 4) [Z5815.A77S56] [LB3219.A7842] 77-369016
1. School buildings—Asia, Southeastern—Bibliography. 2. Natural disasters—Asia, Southeastern—Bibliography. I. Title. II. Series. BIP

School buildings—California.

CALIFORNIA. Bureau of 727'.09794 School Planning.
California school buildings, 1960-1965 [Sacramento, California State Department of Education, 1966] viii, 151 p. illus., maps, plans. 27 cm. [LB3218.C2A5] 67-65804
1. School buildings—California. 2. Architecture—Designs and plans. I. Title.

School buildings—Great Britain.

BRITISH school 727'.0941
buildings : designs and appraisals 1964-74 / edited by Colin Ward. London : Architectural Press, 1976. xiv, 249 p. : ill. ; 31 cm. Bibliography: p. 249. [LB3219.G7B74] 76-381278 ISBN 0-85139-085-4 : £15.00
1. School buildings—Great Britain. I. Ward, Colin.

School buildings—Kentucky.

KENTUCKY. Dept. of 727'.09769 Education.
Kentucky public school construction. [Frankfort, 1967] iv, 171 p. illus., plans, port. 28 cm. [LB3218.K4A5] 68-63756
1. School buildings—Kentucky. 2. Architecture—Designs and plans. I. Title.

School buildings—United States.

BARNARD, Henry, 1811- 727'.0973 1900.
School architecture. Edited, with an introd. and notes, by Jean and Robert McClintock. New York, Teachers College Press [1970] xvi, 338 p. illus., plans. 19 cm. (Classics in education, no. 42) Reprint of the 1848 ed. which was an expansion of the author's School-house architecture, published in 1842. [LB3218.A1B28 1970] 72-129262
1. School buildings—U.S. I. Title.

MORISSEAU, James J. 727
The new schools [by] James J. Morisseau. New York, Van Nostrand Reinhold Co. [1972] 128 p. illus. 26 cm. (Design & planning) [LB3221.M68] 70-163489
1. School buildings—United States. 2. Architecture—Designs and plans. I. Title.

PRESTRESSED Concrete 727 Institute.
Schools of prestressed concrete; planning, design, and construction of educational facilities for schools and colleges. [Chicago, 1968] 156 p. illus. 23 x 28 cm. Includes bibliographies. [LB3218.A1P7] 67-30662
1. School buildings—United States. 2. Universities and colleges—United States—Buildings. 3. Prestressed concrete. I. Title.

PROCTOR, Arthur Marcus, 1886- 727
Safeguarding the school board's purchase of architects' working drawings. New York, Bureau of Publications, Teachers College, Columbia University, 1931. [New York, AMS Press, 1972, ie 1973] viii, 138 p. plans. 22 cm. Reprint of the 1931 ed., issued in series: Teachers College, Columbia University. Contributions to education, no. 474. Originally presented as the author's thesis, Columbia. Bibliography: p. 109-113. [LB3221.P7 1972] 73-177168 ISBN 0-404-55474-1 10.00
1. School buildings—Contracts and specifications—United States. 2. Architecture—Designs and plans. I. Title. II. Series: Columbia University. Teachers College. Contributions to education, no. 474. BIP

School buildings—West Hartford, Conn.

MCLEOD, Ferrara 371.6'2'097463 and Ensign.
School renewal. [Washington, 1972] 76 p. illus. 22 x 29 cm. Cover title. A report prepared for the Board of Education of West Hartford, Conn. [LB3218.C7M32] 72-197074
1. School buildings—West Hartford, Conn. I. West Hartford, Conn. Board of Education. II. Title.

School facilities—Design and construction.

BUILDINGS for school and 727'.9
community use : five case studies. Paris : Unesco ; [New York : distributed by Unipub], 1978. 122 p. : ill. ; 27 cm. (Educational studies and documents : New series ; 26) Results of a research project initiated by Unesco. Includes bibliographical references. [LB3221.B84] 77-377719 ISBN 9-231-01441-2 pbk. : 4.00
1. School facilities—Design and construction. 2. School buildings—Community use. 3. School facilities—Extended use. I. United Nations Educational, Scientific and Cultural Organization. II. Title. III. Series.

School facilities—Planning.

†*BUILDINGS for education,* 729 s
culture, and science / edited by Edward D. Mills. 9th ed. Huntington, N.Y. : Krieger Pub. Co., 1976. 193 p. in various pagings : ill. ; 31 cm. (Planning ; v. [2]) Includes bibliographical references and index. [NA2750.P57 1976 vol. 2] 727 77-365512 ISBN 0-88275-381-9 : 22.95
1. School facilities—Planning. I. Mills, Edward David. II. Series: Planning (Huntington, N.Y., Krieger) ; v. [2]

GROSS, Ronald. 727'.1'0973
Educational change and architectural consequences; a report on facilities for individualized instruction [by Ronald Gross and Judith Murphy. New York] Educational Facilities Laboratories [1968] 88 p. illus. (part col.), plans. 26 cm. [LB3205.G7] 68-57806
1. School facilities—Planning. 2. Individualized instruction. I. Murphy, Judith, joint author. II. Educational Facilities Laboratories. III. Title. BIP

School facilities—Planning—Great Britain.

PEARSON, Eric. 727'.1
Trends in school design. New York, Citation Press, 1972. 82 p. illus. 19 cm. (Informal schools in Britain today) Bibliography: p. 79-80. [LB3219.G7P4] 76-168883 ISBN 0-590-09521-8 2.45
1. School facilities—Planning—Great Britain. I. Title. II. Series.

School facilities—Planning—Lancashire, Eng.

PLANS and people; 727'.2'094272
secondary education: the brief and the buildings [prepared by an Advisory Panel for Lancashire Education Committee and the Archdiocese of Liverpool. Preston] Lancashire Education Committee [1973]. [4], v, 42 p. illus., plans. 30 cm. Cover title. Six fold. plans in pockets. [LB3219.G7P55] 74-164435 ISBN 0-9500458-1-0
1. School facilities—Planning—Lancashire, Eng. I. Lancashire, Eng. Education Committee. II. Liverpool (Archdiocese)

School-houses.

ADULT Education Association. Commission on Architecture. 727.97
Architecture for adult education, a graphic guide for those who are planning physical facilities for adult education. [Chicago, 1956] 74p. illus., plans. 22x 28cm. [LB3221.A35] 57-2090
1. School-houses. 2. Education of adults. I. Title.

CAUDILL, William Wayne. 371.62
Toward better school design. N[ew] Y[ork] F. W. Dodge Corp. [c1954] 271p. illus., plans. 30cm. (An Architectural record book) Bibliography: p. [266]-[267] [LB3205.C3] 54-11605
1. School-houses. I. Title.

School-houses—U. S.

ARCHITECTURAL record. 371.62
Schools for the new needs: educational, social, economic. Foreword and introd. by Frank G. Lopez, senior editor. [New York] F. W. Dodge Corp., c1956. xii, 312p. illus., plans. 31cm. (An Architectural record book) [LB3221.A73] 55-12225
1. School-houses—U. S. I. Lopez., Frank G. II. Title.

School libraries—Hawaii.

HAWAII. Office of Library Services. 727'.8'09969
Hawaii State library system planning for school libraries, public libraries [and] community/school libraries. Honolulu, 1968. 7, [22] l. illus., maps, plans. 29 cm. [Z675.S3H32 1968] 70-625634
1. School libraries—Hawaii. 2. Library architecture—Hawaii. I. Title.

School music—Instruction and study.

ANDERSON, William M. 700'.7'1
Music and related arts for the classroom / William M. Anderson and Joy E. Lawrence. Dubuque, Iowa : Kendall/Hunt Pub. Co., c1978. v, 196 p. : ill. ; 24 cm. Includes index. Bibliography: p. 183-184. [MT1.A698] 77-90652 ISBN 0-8403-1824-3 : 11.95
1. School music—Instruction and study. 2. Arts—Study and teaching. I. Lawrence, Joy E., joint author. II. Title.

School music—Instruction and study—U. S.

NATIONAL Education Association of the United States. Research Division. 707
Music and art in the public schools. [Washington, D.C., Author, c.1963] 88p. tables. 28cm. (Its Res. monograph 1963-M3) 63-6374 1.50 pap.,
1. School music—Instruction and study—U. S. 2. Art—Study and teaching—U. S. I. Title. II. Series.

School photography.

LLOYD, Irving. 371.805
Creative school photography: a gallery of picture ideas. 1st ed. Cambridge, Md., American Yearbook Co., 1962. 231 p. illus. 32 cm. [TR680.L5] 62-15771
1. School photography. 2. School yearbooks. I. Title.

LLOYD, Irving. 770'.28
The photo and its use in yearbook journalism. Photos. by Irving Lloyd. [Topeka, American Yearbook Co., 1969] 188 p. (chiefly illus., part col.) 32 cm. [TR818.L55] 72-178812
1. School photography. 2. School yearbooks. 3. Photography, Journalistic. I. Title.

MILLER, Julia Kelley. 770'.28
News and yearbook photography for the student journalist / by Julia Kelley Miller. Kansas City, Mo. : Yearbook House, c1975. 304 p. : ill. (some col.) ; 29 cm. Includes index. Bibliography: p. 297. [TR818.M54] 75-18841
1. School photography. I. Title.

PISCHEL (R. Wallace), inc. 770.2
Creative yearbook photography. Bob Ternavan, editor. [Pasco, Wash.] 1968. 48 p. illus. (part col.) 29 cm. "Pischel photo schedule board" (1 fold. sheet) and forms (1 leaf) inserted. Bibliography: p. 46. [TR820.P56] 68-1672
1. School photography. 2. School yearbooks. I. Ternavan, Bob, ed. II. Title.

SELLMEYER, Ralph. 770'.28
The professional approach to journalistic photography [by] Ralph Sellmeyer [and] Cal Wayne Moore. [Dallas] Taylor Pub. Co. [1972] 119 p. illus. 29 cm. [TR818.S45 1972] 73-179556 ISBN 0-87833-402-5 7.50
1. School photography. I. Moore, Cal Wayne, joint author. II. Title.

School photography — Handbooks, manuals, etc.

SPENCER, Otha Cleo, 1920- 770.28
The art and techniques of yearbook photography [by] Otha C. Spencer. [Wolfe City, Tex., Henington Pub. Co., 1966] 232, [1] p. illus. (part col.) 32 cm. Bibliography: p. [233] [TR820.S66] 66-15929
1. School photography — Handbooks, manuals, etc. 2. School yearbooks — Handbooks, manuals, etc. I. Title.

SPENCER, Otha Cleo, 1920- 770.28
The art and techniques of yearbook photography. Wolfe City, Tex., 75496 Henington Pub. Co., c.1966 232p. [1]p. illus. (pt. col.) 32cm. Bibl. [TR820.S66] 66-15929 12.95
1. School photography—Handbooks, manuals, etc. 2. School yearbooks—Handbooks, manuals, etc. I. Title.

School shops.

BROWN, Robert Dean. 371.6'23
Industrial arts laboratory planning and administration [by] Robert D. Brown. Milwaukee, Bruce Pub. Co. [1968, c1969] vii, 327 p. illus. 24 cm. Includes bibliographies. [TT160.B85] 69-15727
1. School shops. 2. Industrial arts—Study and teaching. I. Title.

TENNESSEE. State Board for Vocational Education. 373.1'6'23
Trade and industrial education, shop layout and equipment list. Nashville, 1968. 1 v. (various pagings) 15 fold. plans. 28 cm. Cover title. On spine: T & I shop layout and equipment list. "008-00073, 05-68-004.5C." [TT170.T45] 75-630663
1. School shops. I. Title. II. Title: T & I shop layout and equipment list.

TEXAS. Education Agency. 371 6'23
A guide for planning industrial arts facilities. Austin, 1970. vi, 41 p. 23 cm. (Its Bulletin 701) Bibliography: p. 33-36. [TT170.T48] 72-634317 1.00
1. School shops. 2. Industrial arts—Study and teaching. I. Title. II. Series.

School yearbooks.

LLOYD, Irving. 779'.092'4
Yearbook photo journalism; a system of pictorial editing. 1st ed. Dallas, Taylor Pub. Co., 1964. 240 p. illus. 31 cm. [TR820.L55] 64-19450
1. School yearbooks. 2. School photography. I. Title.

Schools—Furniture, equipment, etc.

FURNITURE Industry Research Association. 727'.08 s
School furniture : standing and sitting postures / [Furniture Industry Research Association]. London : H.M. Stationery Off., 1976. iv, 28 p. : ill. ; 30 cm. (Building bulletin - Department of Education and Science ; 52) Includes bibliographical references. [LB3219.G7A2 no. 52] [LB3261] 371.6'21 76-375391 ISBN 0-11-270349-6 : £1.20
1. Schools—Furniture, equipment, etc. I. Title. II. Series: Great Britain. Dept. of Education and Science. Building bulletin ; 52.

Schools of architecture-United States-Directories.

**ARCHITECTURE schools* 720.71173
in north america. Karen Collier Hegener, David Clarke, editors. Princeton, N. J. : Peterson's Guides, c1976. 251p. ; 28 cm. [NA2305.V5] 76-23989 ISBN 0-87866-069-0 pbk. : 5.95
1. Schools of architecture-United States-Directories. I. Hegener, Karen Collier, ed. II. Clarke, David, joint ed.

ARCHITECTURE schools 720'.7'1173
in North America / Karen Collier Hegener, David Clarke, editors. Princeton, N.J. : Peterson's Guides, c1976. 251 p. ; 28 cm. [NA2105.A73] 76-23989 ISBN 0-87866-069-0 pbk. : 5.95
1. Schools of architecture—United States—Directories. 2. Schools of architecture—Canada—Directories. I. Hegener, Karen C. II. Clarke, David, 1942-

Schoonover, Frank Earle, 1877-1972.

SCHOONOVER, Frank Earle, 1877-1972. 760'.092'4
The edge of the wilderness : a portrait of the Canadian North / Frank E. Schoonover ; edited by Cortlandt Schoonover. 1st U.S. ed. Secausus [i.e. Secaucus] N.J. : Derbibooks, 1974. 166 p. : ill. (some col.) ; 32 cm. Contents.Contents.—From the day book of the winter expedition of 1903-1904.—From the day book of the summer expedition of 1911.—The Canadian stories: The edge of the wilderness. Breaking trail. The fur harvesters. Bringing the outdoors in. The snow baby.—The Canadian illustrations. [ND237.S4338S36 1974b] 75-312671 ISBN 0-89009-026-2 : 25.00
1. Schoonover, Frank Earle, 1877-1972. 2. Canada, Northern, in art. 3. Indians of North America—Canada, Northern—Pictorial works. 4. Canada, Northern—Description and travel. I. Title.

SCHOONOVER, Frank Earle, 1877-1972. 760'.092'4 B
Frank Schoonover, illustrator of the North American frontier / by Cortlandt Schoonover. New York : Watson-Guptill Publications, 1976. p. cm. Includes index. [ND237.S4338S37] 76-16509 ISBN 0-8230-4655-9 : 35.00
1. Schoonover, Frank Earle, 1877-1972. 2. Indians of North American—Pictorial works. 3. The West in art. 4. Indians of North America—Canada, Northern—Pictorial works. 5. Canada, Northern, in art. I. Schoonover, Cortlandt. II. Title.

Schrag, Karl.

AMERICAN Federation of Arts. 759.13
Karl Schrag, by John Gordon. New York 28, American Federation of Arts, 1083 Fifth Ave. [c.1960] 28p. Bibl.: p. 20-22. illus., plates (part col.) port. 18cm. 60-3241 .50 pap.,
1. Schrag, Karl. I. Gordon, John. II. Title.

KARL Schrag: a catalogue 769'.924
raisonne of the graphic works, 1939-1970. Commentary by Una E. Johnson. Syracuse, N.Y., School of Art, Syracuse University [1971] 131 p. illus. (part col.) 24 cm. "Two trees by the sea," etching engraving, and aquatint in six colors, signed by the author, inserted. No. 17 of 75 copies. Issued in case. Bibliography: p. 131. [NE539.S35K3] 79-30989
1. Schrag, Karl. I. Johnson, Una E. II. Syracuse University. School of Art.

Schreck, Michael.

SCHRECK, Michael. 730'.92'4
Michael Schreck sculptures / by Alfred Werner. Coral Gables, Fla. : University of Miami Press, [1975] p. cm. [NB237.S38W47] 75-17532 ISBN 0-87024-295-4 : 25.00
1. Schreck, Michael. I. Werner, Alfred, 1911- II. Title.

Schreiber, Georges, 1904—

SCHREIBER, Georges, 1904- 759.13
Georges Schreiber: watercolors 1969-1970; exhibition: Nov. 24-Dec. 16, 1970, Kennedy Galleries. [New York, Kennedy Galleries] c1970. [12] p. illus. (part col.) 28 cm. [ND1839.S36A46] 72-198240
I. Kennedy Galleries, inc., New York.

SCHREIBER, Georges, 1904- 759.13
"Symphonic variations 1971-1973"; exhibition of oils, watercolors, and drawings, September 13-29, 1973. New York, Kennedy Galleries [1973] 1 v. (unpaged) illus. 28 cm. [ND1839.S36A55] 73-181602
1. Schreiber, Georges, 1904- 2. Musical instruments in art. I. Title.

Schreyvogel, Charles, 1861-1912.

HORAN, James David, 1914- 759.13
The life and art of Charles Schreyvogel, painter-historian of the Indian-fighting army of the American West [by] James D. Horan. New York, Crown Publishers [1969] 62 p. illus., facsims., 91 plates (incl. ports.; part col.), ports. 32 x 41 cm. Includes bibliographical references. [ND237.S4345H6 1969] 70-93400 25.00
1. Schreyvogel, Charles, 1861-1912. I. Title.

Schuetzen rifles.

PAGE, Warren. 683'.42
The accurate rifle. [New York] Winchester Press [1973] xiii, 238 p. illus. 24 cm. [TS536.6.S3P33] 72-96092 ISBN 0-87691-102-5 8.95
1. Schuetzen rifles. I. Title. **BIP**

ROBERTS, Ned Henry, 1866-1948. 683'.42
The breech-loading single-shot match rifle, by Ned H. Roberts and Kenneth L. Waters. Princeton, N.J., Van Nostrand [1967] xiv, 293 p. illus., port. 26 cm. [TS535.R55] 67-27986
1. Schuetzen rifles. I. Waters, Kenneth L., joint author. II. Title.

Schwartz, Manfred, 1909-1970.

SCHWARTZ, Manfred, 1909-1970. 741.9'73
Manfred Schwartz: the last ten years. [Exhibition] Jan. 17-Feb. 24, 1974, Museum of Art, Rhode Island School of Design, Providence, Rhode Island. [Introd. by J. Patrice Marandel. Providence, Museum of Art, Rhode Island School of Design, 1974] [48] p. illus. (part col.) 18 x 22 cm. [N6537.S36M37] 73-93335 5.50
1. Schwartz, Manfred, 1909-1970. I. Marandel, J. Patrice. II. Rhode Island School of Design, Providence. Museum of Art. III. Title.

Schwarz (F. A. O.) (Firm)

SCHWARZ (F. A. O.) (Firm) 745.59'2'0973
F. A. O. Schwarz toys through the years / text by Marvin Schwartz ; design by Ladislav Svatos. 1st ed. Garden City, N.Y.

SUBJECT INDEX SCREEN PAINTINGS, JAPANESE—EXHIBITIONS.

: Doubleday, [1975] 142 p. : ill. ; 27 cm. [TS2301.T7S37 1975] 73-13096 ISBN 0-385-07136-1 : 6.95.
1. Schwarz (F. A. O.) (Firm) 2. Toys—Catalogs. I. Schwartz, Marvin D. II. Svatos, Ladislav. III. Title. BIP

Schwedler, William, 1942—

SCHWEDLER, William, 1942- 759.13
Schwedler paintings, drawings : February 21-March 15, 1975, Andrew Crispo Gallery. New York : The Gallery, c1975. [40] p. : ill. (some col.) ; 23 x 27 cm. Catalogue of the exhibition: p. [9]-[36] Bibliography: p. [39] [ND237.S4356A84] 76-358250
1. Schwedler, William, 1942- I. Andrew Crispo Gallery. II. Title.

Schweitzer, Gertrude.

SCHWEITZER, Gertrude. 759.13
Gertrude Schweitzer: spring '73 exhibitions, February 23-March 18, Norton Gallery and School of Art, West Palm Beach, Fla., March 31-April 24, Pratt Manhattan Center, New York, May 26-June 17, The New Britain Museum of American Art, New Britain, Conn. [West Palm Beach, Fla., Norton Gallery and School of Art, 1973] [16] p. illus. (part col.) 26 cm. [ND237.S436N67] 74-152316
1. Schweitzer, Gertrude. I. Norton Gallery and School of Art, West Palm Beach, Fla. II. New York (City). Pratt Manhattan Center. III. New Britain Museum of American Art.

Schwiering, Conrad, 1916—

WAKEFIELD, Robert. 759.13 B
Schwiering and the West. [1st ed. Aberdeen, S.D., North Plains Press, 1973] xvii, 207 p. illus. (part col.) 32 cm. [ND237.S4363W34] 73-77752 ISBN 0-87970-128-5 25.00
1. Schwiering, Conrad, 1916- 2. The West in art. I. Title. BIP

Schwitters, Kurt, 1887-1948.

NEW York (City). Museum of Modern Art. 709'.2'4
Kurt Schwitters, works in the museum collections. [New York, c1972] 14 p. illus. 22 cm. Catalogue of an exhibition, July 31-Sept. 10, 1972, Museum of Modern Art, New York. [N6888.S42N48 1972] 73-166447
1. Schwitters, Kurt, 1887-1948.

SCHMALENBACH, Werner, 1917- 759.3
Kurt Schwitters. New York, H. N. Abrams [1970, c1967] 400 p. illus., plates (part col.), ports. 31 cm. "Selected bibliography by Hans Bolliger": p. 372-[394] [ND588.S42S313] 77-82877 ISBN 0-8109-0477-2
1. Schwitters, Kurt, 1887-1948.

STEINITZ, Kate (Trauman) 759.3
Kurt Schwitters; a portrait from life. With Collision, a science-fiction opera libretto in banalities, by Kurt Schwitters and Kate Trauman Steinitz, and other writings. Translations by Robert Bartlett Haas. Introd. by John Coplans and Walter Hopps. Berkeley, University of California Press, 1968. xxviii, 221 p. illus., facsims., ports. 23 cm. "Based on an earlier, briefer publication in German entitled Erinnerungen und Gesprache mit Kurt Schwitters. Zurich, Verlag der Arche, 1963." "Collision" (p. 149-202) is a translation of "Zusammenstoss", an unpublished comic opera from 1928. [PT2638.W896Z8] 68-16360 7.95
1. Schwitters, Kurt, 1887-1948. I. Schwitters, Kurt, 1887-1948. Collision.

Science and the arts.

KRANZ, Stewart. 709'.04
Science and technology in the arts: a tour through the realm of science/art. Edited by Margaret Holton. Interviews edited by Elizabeth S. Fowler, Jr. Designed by Lorraine Hohman, Myron Hall III [and] Jean King. New York, Van Nostrand Reinhold Co. [1974] 335 p. illus. 36 cm. Bibliography: p. 328-332. [NX180.S3K72] 78-167830 ISBN 0-442-24532-7
1. Science and the arts. 2. Technology and the arts. I. Title.

OPPER, Jacob, 1935- 700
Science and the arts; a study in relationships from 1600-1900. Rutherford [N.J.] Fairleigh Dickinson University Press [1973] 226 p. music. 24 cm. Bibliography: p. 205-217. [NX180.S3O66] 70-178042 ISBN 0-8386-1054-4 13.50
1. Science and the arts. 2. Music—Philosophy and aesthetics. BIP

Science fiction-Illustrations.

FANTASTIC science-fiction art, 1926-1954 / edited with an introduction by Lester del Rey New York : Ballantine Books, 1975. [15] p., [40] leaves of plates : col. ill. ; 30 cm. [NC975.F36] 75-333115 ISBN 0-345-24731-0 : 5.95 741.65
1. Science fiction—Illustrations. 2. Magazine covers—United States. I. Del Ray, Lester, 1915

FOSS, Chris. 759.2
Science fiction art / illus. by Chris Foss ; introd. by Brian Aldiss. London : Hart-Davis, MacGibbon, 1976. [4] p., [10] leaves of plates : all ill. ; 46 cm. [ND497.F64A57] 76-363978 ISBN 0-246-10937-8 : £1.95
1. Foss, Chris. 2. Science fiction—Illustrations. I. Title.

FRAZETTA, Frank. 741.9'73
Frank Frazetta / introd. by Betty Ballantine. 1st U.S. ed. New York : Peacock Press/Bantam Books, 1977. [95] p. : chiefly ill. (some col.) ; 29 cm. "Book two." [NC1850.F7A45 1977] 77-77520 7.95
1. Frazetta, Frank. 2. Science fiction—Illustrations. BIP

FRAZETTA, Frank. 741.9'73
Frank Frazetta / introd. by Betty Ballantine. 1st U.S. ed. New York : Peacock Press/Bantam Books, 1978. [93] p. : chiefly ill. (some col.) ; 29 cm. "Book three." [N6537.F75A4 1978] 78-61114 pbk. : 7.95
1. Frazetta, Frank. 2. Science fiction—Illustrations. I. Ballantine, Betty.

FREWIN, Anthony, 1947- comp 741.64.
One hundred years of science fiction illustration, 1840-1890 New York, Pyramid Books [1975c1974] 128p. ill. 29 cm. Bibliography:p.128. [NC960.F73.] 75-305430 ISBN 0-515-03863-6. 4.95 (pbk.)
1. Science fiction-Illustrations. I. Title.

SADOUL, Jacques. 741.65
2000 A.D. : illustrations from the golden age of science fiction pulps / [text by Jacques Sadoul; translated by Eileen B. Hennessy. Chicago : H. Regnery, [1975] p. cm. Translation of Hier, l'an 2000. Includes bibliographical references. [NC968.S2213] 75-15643 ISBN 0-8092-8298-4 ISBN 0-8092-8117-1 pbk.
1. Science fiction—Illustrations. 2. Illustrated periodicals. I. Title.

Science fiction in art.

SCIENCE fiction art / compiled & introduced by Brian Aldiss. New York : Bounty Books, c1975. 128 p. : ill. (some col.) ; 38 cm. Includes index. [NC968.S33] 75-13823 ISBN 0-517-52432-5 : 9.95 741.65
1. Science fiction in art. 2. Science fiction—Illustrations. 3. Illustrated periodicals. I. Aldiss, Brian Wilson, 1925-

Scientific illustration.

PAPP, Charles S. 743
Scientific illustration; theory and practice [by] Charles S. Papp. Dubuque, Iowa, W. C. Brown Co. [1968] xii, 318 p. illus. 29 cm. [Q222.P38] 67-21315
1. Scientific illustration.

Scopas, fl. 4th century B.C.

LATTIMORE, Steven. 733'.3
The marine thiasos in Greek sculpture / by Steven Lattimore. Los Angeles : Institute of Archaeology, University of California, Los Angeles, 1976. 80 p., [16] leaves of plates : ill. ; 30 cm. (Monograph of the Archaeological Institute of America ; no. 9) (Monumenta archaeologica ; v. 3) ISSN 0363-7565) Includes bibliographical references. [NB94.L37] 76-18609 ISBN 0-917956-02-8
1. Scopas, fl. 4th cent. B.C. 2. Sea gods in art. 3. Sculpture, Greek. 4. Sculpture, Hellenistic. I. Title. II. Series. III. Series: Archaeological Institute of America. Monograph ; no. 9. BIP

LEHMANN, Phyllis Lourene Williams, 1912- 733'.3
Skopas in Samothrace [by] Phyllis Williams Lehmann. Northampton, Mass., Smith College, 1973. 85 p. illus. 23 cm. (The Katharine Asher Engel lectures, 1972) Includes bibliographical references. [NB104.L43] 73-88453 5.00
1. Scopas, fl. 4th century B.C. 2. Propylon, Samothrace. I. Title. II. Series.

STEWART, Andrew F. 730'.92'4
Skopas of Paros / by Andrew F. Stewart. Park Ridge, N.J. : Noyes Press, c1977. xvi, 183 p., [28] leaves of plates : ill. ; 29 cm. Includes index. Bibliography: p. 149. [NB104.S73] 77-149 ISBN 0-8155-5051-0 : 32.00
1. Scopas, fl. 4th cent. B.C. 2. Tegea, Greece. Temple of Athena Alea. 3. Marble sculpture, Greek—Greece—Tegea. 4. Tegea, Greece—History. BIP

Scotland—Description and travel—Views.

BLOEMENDAL, Frederik Arnold Herman. 779'.9'9141
Scotland. Text by Margaret Hides. Photography by F. A. H. Bloemendal. New York, Scribner [1973, c1972] 110 p. (chiefly col. illus.) 31 cm. First published in Great Britain under title: Scotland in cameracolour. [DA867.B58 1973] 73-39578 ISBN 0-684-12920-5 9.95
1. Scotland—Description and travel—Views. I. Hides, Margaret.

Scotland in art.

TURNER, Joseph Mallord William, 1775-1851. 741.9'42
Sir Walter Scott countryside : an album of J. W. M. Turner landscapes. Edinburgh : Ramsay Head Press, 1976. [10] leaves : of ill. ; 21 x 30 cm. (Ramsay Head prints ; no. 2) Cover title. Two leaves printed on both sides. [NC242.T9A55 1976] 77-358157 ISBN 0-902859-36-6 : £1.25
1. Turner, Joseph Mallord William, 1775-1851. 2. Scotland in art. I. Title.

Scott, Annette.

SCOTT, Annette. 759.13
Cruising and sketching Baja. [1st ed.] Flagstaff, Northland Press [1974] x, 116 p. illus. 19 x 25 cm. [ND1839.S38A43] 73-93994 ISBN 0-87358-123-7 12.50
1. Scott, Annette. 2. Baja California in art. 3. Baja California—Description and travel. I. Title.

Scott, David, 1806-1849.

SCOTT, William Bell, 1811-1890. 759.941
Memoir of David Scott, R.S.A. : containing his journal in Italy, notes on art, and other papers / by William B. Scott. New York : AMS Press, [1975] p. cm. Reprint of the 1850 ed. published by A. & C. Black, Edinburgh. [ND497.S4S5 1975] 70-144685 ISBN 0-404-05646-6 : 24.50
1. Scott, David, 1806-1849. I. Title. BIP

Scott, Donald, 1879-1967.

SCHAAFSMA, Polly. 913.3'008 s
The rock art of Utah; a study from the Donald Scott Collection, Peabody Museum, Harvard University. Cambridge, Mass., Peabody Museum of Archaeology and Ethnology, Harvard University, 1971. xix, 169 p. illus., col. plate. 28 cm. (Papers of the Peabody Museum of Archaeology and Ethnology, v. 65) Bibliography: p. [165]-169. [E51.H337 vol. 65] [E78.U55] 732'.2 72-173663
1. Scott, Donald, 1879-1967. 2. Indians of North America—Utah—Art. 3. Petroglyphs—Utah. I. Title. II. Series: Harvard University. Peabody Museum of Archaeology and Ethnology. Papers, v. 65. BIP

Scott, George Gilbert, Sir, 1811-1878.

SCOTT, George Gilbert, Sir, 1811-1878. 720'.92'4 B
Personal and professional recollections / by George Gilbert Scott ; edited by his son, G. Gilbert Scott ; with an introd. by John Williams Burgon. New York : Da Capo Press, 1977. xx, 436 p., [1] leaf of plates : port. ; 23 cm. (A Da Capo Press reprint series in architecture and decorative arts) Reprint of the 1879 ed. published by S. Low, Marston, Searle & Rivington, London. [NA997.S4A25 1977] 77-1202 ISBN 0-306-70873-6 : 27.50
1. Scott, George Gilbert, Sir, 1811-1878. 2. Architects—England—Biography. BIP

Scott, Mackay Hugh Baillie, 1865-1945.

KORNWOLF, James D. 720'.92'4 B
M. H. Baillie Scott and the arts and crafts movement; pioneers of modern design [by] James D. Kornwolf. Baltimore, Johns Hopkins Press [1972] xxx, 588 p. illus. 27 cm. Bibliography: p. [561]-570. [NA997.S42K6] 70-135661 ISBN 0-8018-1112-0 27.50
1. Scott, Mackay Hugh Baillie, 1865-1945. I. Title. BIP

Scottish Typographical Association.

GILLESPIE, Sarah C 655.2'062'7
A hundred years of progress; the record of the Scottish Typographical Association, 1853 to 1952. Glasgow, Printed for the Association by R. Maclehose, 1953. 268p. illus. 23cm. [Z120.S36] 54-34163
1. Scottish Typographical Association. I. Title.

Scratchboard drawing.

BACON, Cecil Walter, 1905- 741.29
Scratchboard drawing. London, New York, Studio Publications [1951] 96 p. illus. 26 cm. (The How to do it series, no. 41) [NC915.S4B3] 52-7609
1. Scratchboard drawing.

CUTLER, Merritt Dana, 1898- 741.29
How to cut drawings on scratchboard. New York, Watson-Guptill Publications [1960] 88 p. illus. 27 cm. [NC915.S4C87] 59-15674
1. Scratchboard drawing. I. Title. BIP

CUTLER, Merritt Dana, 1898- 741.2'9
Scratchboard [by] Merritt Cutler. New York, Pitman [1973] 48 p. illus. 20 x 26 cm. (The Pitman art series, 83) [NC915.S4C875] 72-136466 1.25 (pbk.).
1. Scratchboard drawing. I. Title.

Screen paintings, Japanese—Exhibitions.

JAPANESE screens; a loan exhibition, October 22 to November 29, 1964, Wadsworth Atheneum, Hartford, Connecticut. [Hartford, Wadsworth Atheneum, 1964] [20] p. illus. 18 x 26 cm. [ND1052.J36] 74-185428 759.952
1. Screen paintings, Japanese—Exhibitions. I. Wadsworth Atheneum, Hartford.

MURASE, Miyeko. 759.952
Byobu: Japanese screens from New York collections. [New York] Asia Society; distributed by New York Graphic Society [Greenwich, Conn., 1971] 134 p. illus. (part col.) 21 x 27 cm. "An Asia House Gallery publication." Catalog of the exhibition held Jan. 14-Mar. 14, 1971, in the Asia House Gallery, New York. Bibliography: p. 134. [ND1052.M88] 74-134207 ISBN 0-87848-035-8
1. Screen paintings, Japanese—Exhibitions.

2. Screen paintings, Japanese—New York (City) I. Asia Society. II. Title.

Screen process printing.

BIEGELEISEN, Jacob Israel, 1910- 764'.8
Screen printing; a contemporary guide to the technique of screen printing for artists, designers, and craftsmen, by J. I. Biegeleisen. New York, Watson-Guptill Publications [1971] 159 p. illus. (part col.) 29 cm. Includes bibliographical references. [TT273.B498] 79-133979 ISBN 0-8230-4665-6 12.50
1. Screen process printing. I. Title.

BIRKNER, Heinrich. 764.8
Screen printing. [Translated by Kenneth T. Dutfield; adapted by Jane Lassner] New York, Sterling Pub. Co. [1971] 96 p. illus. (part col.) 22 cm. Translation of Siebdruck. An introduction to screen printing describing frame construction, use of stencils and inks, and the application of various printing techniques. [TT273.B5413] 79-151713 ISBN 0-8069-5170-2
1. Screen process printing. I. Title.

CARR, Francis. 655.316
A guide to screen process printing. Edited by Brian Innes and Beatrice Warde. New York, Pitman [1962, c1961] 208 p. illus. 21 cm. (Facts of print series) [TT273.C33] 62-16082
1. Screen process printing. I. Title.

CLEMENCE, Will. 764.8
The beginner's book of screen process printing, written and illustrated by Will Clemence. New York, Pitman Pub. Corp. [1961, c1959] 80 p. illus. 22 cm. [TT273.C5 1961] 61-66492
1. Screen process printing. I. Title.

ELLIOTT, Brian. 764'.8
Silk-screen printing. London, New York, Oxford University Press, 1971. 85 p. illus. 21 cm. (Oxford paperbacks, handbooks for artists, 10) [TT273.E54] 72-32026 ISBN 0-19-289914-7 £1.00 ($3.25 U.S.)
1. Screen process printing.

GARDNER, Andrew B. 764'.8
The artist's silkscreen manual / Andrew B. Gardner. New York : Grosset & Dunlap, c1976. 160 p. : ill. ; 28 cm. Includes index. [TT273.G37] 73-22737 ISBN 0-448-13322-9 lib. bdg. ISBN 0-448-11593-X pbk. : 4.95
1. Screen process printing. I. Title. BIP

KINSEY, Anthony. 764'.8
Introducing screen printing. London. Batsford; New York, Watson Guptill. 1967. 96p. illus. (some col.). 22cm. Bibl. [TT273.K48 1967] 68-10050 6.95 bds.,
1. Screen process printing. I. Title.

KOSLOFF, Albert. 655.316
The art and craft of screen process printing. Illus. by the author. Milwaukee, Bruce Pub. Co. [1960] 173 p. illus. 25 cm. A new, enl. ed. of the author's Mitography. [TT273.K655 1960] 60-8234
1. Screen process printing. I. Title.

KOSLOFF, Albert. 655.32
Photographic screen process printing. Illus. by the author. Cincinnati, Signs of the Times Pub. Co. [1955] 240p. illus. 24cm. [TT273.K657] 55-34479
1. Screen process printing. I. Title.

KOSLOFF, Albert. 655.3'2
Photographic screen process printing. Illus. by the author. 3d ed. Cincinnati, Signs of the Times Pub. Co. [1968] 304 p. illus. 24 cm. [TT273.K657 1968] 77-1238
1. Screen process printing. I. Title.

KOSLOFF, Albert. 667'.38
Textile screen printing / by Albert Kosloff. 2d ed. Cincinnati : Signs of the Times Pub. Co., c1976. 134 p. : ill. ; 24 cm. Includes index. [TT273.K67 1976] 76-150498 ISBN 0-911380-39-6
1. Screen process printing. 2. Textile printing. I. Title.

RAINEY, Sarita R. 686'.2316
Basic silkscreen printmaking [by] Sarita Rainey [and] Burton Wasserman. Worcester, Mass., Davis Publications [1971] 33 p. illus. 20 x 26 cm. (Basic concept series, no. 2) [TT273.R35] 74-171936 ISBN 0-87192-043-3
1. Screen process printing. I. Wasserman, Burton, joint author. II. Title. BIP

SAFF, Donald, 1937- 764
Screenprinting : history and process / Donald Saff, Deli Sacilotto. New York : Holt, Rinehart and Winston, [1978] p. cm. Includes index. Bibliography: p. [TT273.S22] 78-21877 ISBN 0-03-045491-3 : 8.95
1. Screen process printing. I. Sacilotto, Deli, joint author. II. Title. BIP

SCHWALBACH, Mathilda V. 655.3'16
Screen-process printing for the serigrapher & textile designer [by] Mathilda V. Schwalbach & James A. Schwalbach. New York, Van Nostrand Reinhold Co. [1970] 142 p. illus. (part col.), col. plates. 29 cm. Bibliography: p. 140. [TT273.S3] 72-126871
1. Screen process printing. 2. Textile printing. I. Schwalbach, James Alfred, 1912- joint author. II. Title.

SEARLE, Valerie. 764'.8'028
Screen printing on fabric [by] Valerie Searle, Roberta Clayson. London, Studio Vista; New York, Watson-Guptill, 1968. 104p. (Chiefly illus. (some col.)) 19cm. (Pocket how to do it) Bibl. [TT273.S4] 68-13121 2.50
1. Screen process printing. 2. Textile printing. I. Clayson, Roberta. joint author. II. Title.

TERMINI, Maria. 764'.8
Silkscreening / Maria Termini. Englewood Cliffs, N.J. : Prentice-Hall, c1978. x, 182 p., [8] leaves of plates : ill. (some col.) ; 24 cm. (A Spectrum book) (The Art & design series) Includes index. [TT273.T47] 77-10719 ISBN 0-13-809996-0 : 14.95. ISBN 0-13-809988-X pbk. : 6.95
1. Screen process printing. I. Title. II. Series. BIP

TURNER, Silvie, 1946- 746.6
Screen printing techniques / Silvie Turner ; photos. by Graham Murrell. New York : Taplinger Pub. Co., 1976. 120 p., [2] leaves of plates : ill. ; 26 cm. Includes index. Bibliography: p. 116. [TT273.T87 1976b] 75-18636 ISBN 0-8008-7005-0 : 12.50
1. Screen process printing. I. Murrell, Graham. II. Title. BIP

Screen process printing—Dictionaries.

SCREEN Printing Association International. Vocational and Educational Development Committee. 686.2'316'03
Glossary of screen printing. [Falls Church, Va., 1974] 47 p. 28 cm. Caption title. [TT273.S32 1974] 74-166418
1. Screen process printing—Dictionaries. I. Title.

Screen process printing — Study and teaching.

SWENSON, Theodore H 655.316
Industrial arts: silk screen process printing; teachers guide. Prepared by Theodore H. Swenson. New Brunswick, N.J., Vocational Division, Curriculum Laboratory, 1961. 99 p. illus. 28 cm. Bibliography: p. 94-99. [TT273.S9] A62
1. Screen process printing — Study and teaching. I. New Jersey. Division of Vocational Education. Curriculum Laboratory, New Brunswick. II. Title. III. Title: Silk Screen process printing.

Scriber, Bob, 1914—

SCRIVER, Bob, 1914- 730'.92'4
An honest try / by Bob Scriver ; Asger Mikklesen, photography ; Bill Cochran, consultation ; Dean Krakel, "Bob Scriver and the sound of music" ; Don Hedgepeth, "The rodeo story" ; Nick Eggenhofer, ill. 1st ed. Kansas City, Mo. : Lowell Press, [1975] xii, 91 p. : ill. (some col.) ; 32 cm. [NB237.S39M54] 74-32526 ISBN 0-913504-22-X : 25.00 ISBN 0-913504-23-8 deluxe ed. 750.00
1. Scriber, Bob, 1914- I. Mikklesen, Asger, 1904- II. Title. BIP

Scrimshaw.

GILKERSON, William. 736'.6
The scrimshander / by William Gilkerson ; with introd. by Karl Kortum. San Francisco : Troubador Press, [1975] 119 p. : ill. ; 26 cm. Includes index. Bibliography: p. 116. [NK6022.G55] 74-24008 ISBN 0-912300-54-X : 12.95 ISBN 0-912300-53-1 pbk. : 6.95
1. Scrimshaw. I. Title.

Scrimshaws.

BARCELOS, Frank. 736'.6
A showing of scrimshaw. [New Bedford? Mass., 1974] 55 p. col. illus. 26 cm. [NK6022.B36] 74-180369
1. Scrimshaws. I. Title.

BARNES, Clare. 736'.6
John F. Kennedy: scrimshaw collector. Photos. by Alan Fontaine. [1st ed.] Boston, Little, Brown [1969] 129 p. col. illus. 29 cm. Bibliography: p. 127-129. [NK6022.B37] 70-83737 15.00
1. Kennedy, John Fitzgerald, Pres. U.S., 1917-1963—Art collections. 2. Scrimshaws.

BURROWS, Fredrika Alexander. 736'.6
The Yankee scrimshanders. Taunton, Mass., W. S. Sullwold Pub. [1973] 79 p. illus. 23 cm. Bibliography: p. 79. [TT288.B87] 73-80907 2.50 (pbk.)
1. Scrimshaws. 2. Whaling—New England. I. Title.
Publisher's address: 18 Pearl St. Taunton, Mass. 02780 BIP

FLAYDERMAN, E. Norman. 736'.6
Scrimshaw and scrimshanders; whales and whalemen, by E. Norman Flayderman. Edited by R. L. Wilson. New Milford, Conn., N. Flayderman [1972] 291, [14] p. illus. 27 cm. Bibliography: p. [294]-[295] [NK6022.F55] 79-154305 ISBN 0-910598-09-6 19.95
1. Scrimshaws. I. Title. BIP

GILKERSON, William. 736'.6
The scrimshander / by William Gilkerson ; with introd. by Karl Kortum. Rev. ed. San Francisco : Troubador Press, c1978. p. cm. Includes bibliographical references and index. Text and illustrations introduce the history and techniques of whale ivory carving and engraving. Includes contemporary examples of scrimshaw and discusses the future of this art form. [NK6022.G55 1978] 78-18351 ISBN 0-912300-92-2 pbk. : 8.95
1. Scrimshaws. I. Title. BIP

LINSLEY, Leslie. 736'.6
Scrimshaw : a traditional folk art, a contemporary craft / by Leslie Linsley ; photos. by Jon Aron. New York : Hawthorn Books, c1976. ix, 166 p. : ill. ; 29 cm. Bibliography: p. 165-166. [TT288.L56 1976] 75-28700 ISBN 0-8015-6608-8 : 9.95
1. Scrimshaws. I. Title.

RITCHIE, Carson I. A. 736'.6
Scrimshaw, by Carson I. A. Ritchie. New York, Sterling Pub. Co. [1972] 48 p. illus. 20 cm. (Little craft book series) Explains the tools and techniques for carving on hard surfaces, especially teeth, bones, or shells. [TT288.R57 1972] 71-180454 ISBN 0-8069-5194-X
1. Scrimshaws. I. Title.

Scripture, Melanesian.

SCHMITZ, Carl August 730.993
Oceanic sculpture of Melanesia. Photographed by F. L. Kenett. Greenwich, Conn., N.Y. Graphic [c.1962] xv p. illus., map. 38cm. (Acanthus hist. of sculpture, v.4) 62-7574 8.95
1. Scripture, Melanesian. I. Kenett, F. L. II. Title. III. Series.

Scrolls, Japanese.

GROTENHUIS, Elizabeth ten. 759.952
Narrative picture scrolls, by Hideo Okudaira. Translation adapted with an introd. by Elizabeth ten Grotenhuis. [1st ed.] New York, Weatherhill [1973] 151 p. illus. (part col.) 23 cm. (Arts of Japan, 5) Adapted from Emakimono. Bibliography: p. [147]-148. [ND1053.G76 1973] 73-9619 ISBN 0-8348-2710-7 7.95
1. Scrolls, Japanese. 2. Painting, Japanese. 3. Japan—Social life and customs—Pictorial works. I. Okudaira, Hideo, 1905- Emakimono. II. Title.
Pbk., 4.95. BIP

Sculptors, American.

BARTSCHT, Heri Bert. 730'.924
Twenty years of my sculpture; a portfolio of photographs. With an introd. by Roger Ortmayer. Dallas, Printed by Taylor Pub. Co. [1968] 56 p. illus., ports. 24 cm. [NB237.B373A2] 68-59154
I. Title.

BULLARD, Frederic Lauriston, 1873- 923.173
Lincoln in marble and bronze. New Brunswick, Rutgers University Press [1952] xiii, 353 p. illus., ports. 24 cm. "A publication of the Abraham Lincoln Association, Springfleld, Illinois." Includes bibliographies. [E457.6.B88] 52-9189
1. Lincoln, Abraham, Pres. U. S.—Monuments, etc. 2. Sculptors, American. I. Title.

CAFFIN, Charles Henry, 1854-1918. 730'.922
American masters of sculpture: being brief appreciations of some American sculptors and of some phases of sculpture in America. Freeport, N.Y., Books for Libraries Press [1969] xiii, 234 p. illus., ports. 24 cm. (Essay index reprint series) Reprint of the 1903 ed. Contents.Contents.—Augustus Saint-Gaudens.—George Grey Barnard.—John Quincy Adams Ward.—Daniel Chester French.—Frederick Macmonnies.—Paul Weyland Bartlett.—Herbert Adams.—Charles Henry Niehaus.—Olin Levi Warner.—Solon Hannibal Borglum.—Victor David Brenner.—The decorative motive.—The ideal motive. [NB205.C3 1969] 75-84301
1. Sculptors, American. I. Title.

DODD, Loring Holmes, 1879- 730.922
Golden moments in American sculpture. Cambridge, Mass., Dresser, Chapman & Grimes [1967] 127 p. illus., ports. 21 cm. Articles, most of which first appeared in the Worchester gazette and Telegram. Contents.Contents.—The golden age of American sculpture.—George Grey Barnard.—Antoine Louis Barye.—Gutzon Borglum.—Cyrus Dallin.—James Earle Fraser.—Daniel Chester French.—Harriet Frishmuth.—Malvina Hoffman.—Ann Vaughn Hyatt.—Frederick MacMonnies.—Hermon MacNeil.—Paul Manship.—Edward McCartan.—Robert Tait McKenzie.—Carl Milles.—Bashka Paeff.—Attilio Piccirilli.—Frederic Remington.—John Rogers.—Charles Russell.—Augustus Saint Gaudens.—Janet Scudder.—Lorado Taft. [NB236.D6] 67-18350
1. Sculptors, American. 2. Sculpture, American. I. Title.

MCSPADDEN, Joseph Walker, 1874- 730'.922 B
Famous sculptors of America, by J. Walker McSpadden. Freeport, N.Y., Books for Libraries Press [1968] xv, 377 p. illus., ports. 22 cm. (Essay index reprint series) Reprint of the 1924 ed. Bibliography: p. 369-377. [NB236.M3 1968] 68-57331
1. Sculptors, American. 2. Sculpture, American. I. Title. BIP

PROCTOR, Alexander Phimister, 1862-1950. 730'.924
Alexander Phimister Proctor, sculptor in buckskin; an autobiography. Edited and with an introd. by Hester Elizabeth Proctor. Introd. by Vivian A. Paladin. [1st ed.] Norman, University of Oklahoma Press [1971] xvii, 266 p. illus., ports. 19 x 23 cm. [NB237.P74A2] 77-108803 ISBN 0-8061-0912-2 201
A0031778TURNBULL, Grace Hill, 1880-

TURNBULL, Grace Hill, 1880- 927.3
Chips from my chisel, an autobiography. Rindge, N. H., R. R. Smith, 1953. 256p. illus. 25cm. [NB237.T8A3] 53-12776
I. Title.

SUBJECT INDEX SCULPTURE.

Sculptors, American—Los Angeles.

CALIFORNIA. University, Irvine. Art Gallery. 917.47'1'044
Five Los Angeles sculptors: Larry Bell, Tony DeLap, David Gray, John McCracken [and] Kenneth Price [and] sculptors drawings, Los Angeles New York. [Exhibition] January 7th to February 6th, 1966. [Irvine? 1966] 36 p. illus. (part col.) 21 x 23 cm. Includes bibliographies. [NB235.L6C3] 66-63516
1. Sculptors, American—Los Angeles. 2. Sculpture, Modern—Exhibitions. I. Title.

Sculptors—Australia—Biography.

VON BERTOUCH, Ann. 730'.92'4 B
Guy Boyd / [by] Ann von Bertouch [and] Patrick Hutchings. Melbourne : Lansdowne Press, 1976. 136 p. : ill. ; 38 cm. Includes bibliographical references and index. [NB1105.B7V66] 77-350246 ISBN 0-7018-0079-8
1. Boyd, Guy Martin a Beckett, 1923- 2. Sculptors—Australia—Biography. I. Hutchings, Patrick A., joint author. II. Boyd, Guy Martin a Beckett, 1923-

Sculptors, British.

GUNNIS, Rupert. 730.942
Dictionary of British sculptors, 1660-1851 Cambridge, Harvard University Press, 1954. 514p. 32 plates. 26cm. [NB496.G] A55
1. Sculptors, British. 2. Sculpture—Gt. Brit.—Dictionaries. I. Title. BIP

Sculptors, British—Correspondence, reminiscences, etc.

ROBERTS, Eric Samuel. 730'.92'4
The distance enchanted. Sheffield, J. W. Northend, 1954. 123p. illus. 20cm. Reminiscences. [PR6035.O522D5] 55-21114
I. Title.

WOOLNER, Thomas, 1825-1892. 730'.924 B
Thomas Woolner, R.A., sculptor and poet; his life in letters. Written by his daughter Amy Woolner. New York, AMS Press [1971] xviii, 352 p. illus., ports. 23 cm. Reprint of the 1917 ed. "List of writings": p. 346. [NB497.W7A3 1971] 70-158614 ISBN 0-404-07030-2
1. Sculptors, British—Correspondence, reminiscences, etc. I. Woolner, Amy. BIP

Sculptors— Dictionaries.

DICTIONARY of modern sculpture. 730.3 General ed.: Robert Maillard. [Tr. from French by Bettina Wadia] New York, Tudor [c.1962, 1960] 310p. illus. 22cm. 62-6907 7.95
1. Sculptors— Dictionaries. I. Maillard, Robert, ed.

NEW dictionary of modern sculpture. 730'.922 General editor: Robert Maillard. [Translated from the French by Bettina Wadia] New York, Tudor Pub. Co. [1971] 328 p. illus. 24 cm. Translation of Nouveau dictionnaire de la sculpture moderne, first published in 1960 under title: Dictionnaire de la sculpture moderne. [NB50.N6813] 70-153118 ISBN 0-8148-0479-9
1. Sculptors—Dictionaries. I. Maillard, Robert, ed. BIP

Sculptors, French—Correspondence, reminiscences, etc.

LIPCHITZ, Jacques, 1891- 730'.92'4 B
My life in sculpture, by Jacques Lipchitz with H. H. Arnason. New York, Viking Press [1972] xxxiv, 249 p. illus. 22 cm. (The Documents of 20th-century art) "Lipschitz: a documentary review, by Bernard Karpel": p. [233]-249. [NB553.L55A8 1972] 77-184539 ISBN 0-670-50000-3 10.00
1. Sculptors, French—Correspondence, reminiscences, etc. I. Arnason, H. Harvard. II. Title. III. Series. BIP

Sculptors—Great Britain—Correspondence, reminiscences, etc.

EPSTEIN, Jacob, Sir, 1880-1959. 730'.92'4 B
Epstein, an autobiography / Jacob Epstein. [Rev. & extended ed.]. New York : Arno Press, 1975. x, 294 p., [47] leaves of plates : ill. ; 24 cm. (The Modern Jewish experience) Published in 1940 under title: Let there be sculpture. Reprint of the 1955 ed. published by Dutton, New York. Includes index. [NB497.E6A2 1975] 74-27978 ISBN 0-405-06707-0 : 26.00
1. Epstein, Jacob, Sir, 1880-1959. 2. Sculptors—Great Britain—Correspondence, reminiscences, etc. I. Title. II. Series.

Sculptors, Greek.

GARDNER, Ernest Arthur, 1862-1939. 730'.922
Six Greek sculptors. Freeport, N.Y., Books for Libraries Press [1967] xvi, 260 p. illus. 22 cm. (Essay index reprint series) Reprint of the 1910 ed. Contents.Contents.—Characteristics of Greek sculpture.—Early masterpieces.—Myron.—Phidias.—Polyclitus.—Praxiteles.—Scopas.—Lysippus.—Hellenistic sculpture.—Select bibliography (p. 253-254) [NB90.G35 1967] 67-26744
1. Sculptors, Greek. 2. Sculpture, Greek. I. Title. BIP

Sculptors—Ireland—Biography.

MURPHY, Seamus. 736'.5'0924 B
Stone mad / Seamus Murphy ; with illustrations by William Harrington and initial letters by the author. [New and revised ed.]. London : Routledge and Kegan Paul, 1977 [i.e. 1976] x, 229 p. : ill., port. ; 22 cm. [NB497.M8A2 1977] 77-375105 ISBN 0-7100-8542-7 pbk. : 5.00
1. Murphy, Seamus. 2. Sculptors—Ireland—Biography. 3. Stone carving—Ireland. 4. Ireland—Social life and customs. I. Title.
Distributed by Routledge and Kegan Paul, Boston.

Sculptors—Italy—Biography.

HOLDERBAUM, James. 730'.92'4
The sculptor Giovanni Bologna / James Holderbaum. New York : Garland Pub., 1977. p. cm. (Outstanding dissertations in the fine arts) Originally presented as the author's thesis, Harvard, 1959. Bibliography: p. [NB623.B7H64 1977] 76-23626 ISBN 0-8240-2696-9 lib.bdg. : 46.00
1. Bologne, Jean de, 1524-1608. 2. Sculptors—Italy—Biography. I. Title. II. Series. BIP

SCHULZ, Anne Markham, 1938- 730'.92'4 B
Niccolo di Giovanni Fiorentino and Venetian sculpture of the early Renaissance / Anne Markham Schulz. New York : Published by New York State University Press for the College Art Association of America, 1978. p. cm. (Monographs on archaeology and fine arts ; 33) "Digest of documents concerning the life and works of Niccolo di Giovanni Fiorentino": p. [NB623.N515S38] 77-6903 ISBN 0-8147-7786-4 : 22.50
1. Niccolo di Giovanni Fiorentino. 2. Sculptors—Italy—Biography. 3. Sculpture, Renaissance—Italy—Venice. I. College Art Association of America. II. Title. III. Series. BIP

Sculptors—South Africa—Biography.

PILLMAN, Naka. 730'.92'4 B
African portrait : the life and sculpture of Sister Joe Vorster / Naka Pillman. 1st ed. Johannesburg : H. Keartland, 1976. 128 p. : ill. ; 32 cm. [NB1096.V67P54] 77-366429 ISBN 0-949997-31-5
1. Vorster, Joe, 1887-1945. 2. Sculptors—South Africa—Biography. 3. Blacks in art. I. Vorster, Joe, 1887-1945. II. Title.

Sculptors—Spain—Biography.

WITHERS, Josephine. 730'.92'4 B
Julio Gonzalez : sculpture in iron / by Josephine Withers. New York : New York University Press, 1977. p. cm. Includes index. Bibliography: p. [NB813.G6W57] 76-26798 ISBN 0-8147-9171-9 : 40.00
1. Gonzalez, Julio, 1876-1942. 2. Sculptors—Spain—Biography. BIP

Sculptors—United States—Biography.

BALL, Thomas, 1819-1911. 730'.92'4 B
My threescore years and ten : an authobiography / by Thomas Ball. 2d ed. New York : Garland Pub., 1977, c1891. 13, xi, 379 p., [5] leaves of plates ; ill. ; 19 cm. (The Art experience in late nineteenth-century America) Reprint of the 1892 ed. published by Roberts Bros., Boston; with new introd. [NB237.B3A25 1977] 75-28884 ISBN 0-8240-2242-4 : 25.00
1. Ball, Thomas, 1819-1911. 2. Sculptors—United States—Biography. I. Title. II. Series. BIP

CALDER, Alexander, 1898-1976. 709'.2'4 B
Calder : an autobiography with pictures / with a new introd. by Jean Davidson. New York : Pantheon Books, 1977,c1966 288 p., [6] leaves of plates : ill. ; 27 cm. [NB237.C28A2 1966b] 77-5300 ISBN 0-394-42142-6 : 15.95. ISBN 0-394-73408-4 pbk. : 7.95
1. Calder, Alexander, 1898-1976. 2. Sculptors—United States—Biography. I. Title.

COOLEY, Adelaide N. 730'.92'4 B
The monument maker : biography of Frederick Ernst Triebel / Adelaide N. Cooley. 1st ed. Hicksville, N.Y. : Exposition Press, c1978. 32 p., [12] leaves of plates : ill. ; 22 cm. Bibliography: p. 31-32. [NB237.T66C66] 78-103167 ISBN 0-682-49051-2 : 5.95
1. Triebel, Frederick Ernst, 1865-1944. 2. Sculptors—United States—Biography. I. Title. BIP

GLIMCHER, Arnold B. 730'.92'4 B
Louise Nevelson / Arnold B. Glimcher. 2d ed., rev. and enl. New York : Dutton, c1976. 197 p., [5] leaves of plates : ill. (some col.) ; 28 cm. [NB237.N43G55 1976] 76-150542 ISBN 0-525-47439-0 : 11.95
1. Nevelson, Louise, 1900- 2. Sculptors—United States—Biography.

HAYES, Margaret Calder, 1896- 709'.2'2 B
Three Alexander Calders : a family memoir / by Margaret Calder Hayes ; introd. by Malcolm Cowley. Middlebury, Vt. : P. S. Eriksson, c1977. xix, 300 p. : ill. ; 24 cm. Includes index. [NB237.C29H39 1977] 77-79244 ISBN 0-8397-8017-6 : 15.00
1. Calder, Alexander Milne, 1846-1923. 2. Calder, Alexander Stirling, 1870-1945. 3. Calder, Alexander, 1898-1976. 4. Hayes, Margaret Calder, 1896- 5. Sculptors—United States—Biography. 6. United States—Biography. I. Title. BIP

HUNTER, Sam, 1923- 730'.92'4
Isamu Noguchi / by Sam Hunter. New York : Abbeville Press, c1978. p. cm. Includes index. [NB237.N6H86] 78-5288 65.00
1. Noguchi, Isamu, 1904- 2. Sculptors—United States—Biography. BIP

HUTSON, Alice, 1941- 730'.92'4 B
From chalk to bronze : a biography of Waldine Tauch / by Alice Hutson. 1st ed. Austin : Shoal Creek Publishers, c1978. p. cm. Includes index. Bibliography: p. [NB237.T38H87] 78-16000 ISBN 0-88319-037-0 : 15.00
1. Tauch, Waldine, 1892- 2. Sculptors—United States—Biography. I. Title. BIP

REYNOLDS, Donald M. 730'.92'4
Hiram Powers and his ideal sculpture / Donald Martin Reynolds. New York : Garland Pub., 1977. xxvii, 377, 1051-1118 p. : ill. ; 21 cm. (Outstanding dissertations in the fine arts) Originally presented as the author's thesis, Columbia, 1975. "The letters from Appendix A (Unpublished correspondence of Hiram Powers, pp. 378 through 1050) have been withheld at the request of the author. They are qvailable to the reader in the Hiram Powers archives at the National Collection of Fine Arts; Smithsonian Institution, Washington, D.C." Bibliography: p. 1109-1110. [NB237.P7R49 1977] 76-23685 ISBN 0-8240-2720-5 lib.bdg. : 45.00
1. Powers, Hiram, 1805-1873. 2. Sculptors—United States—Biography. I. Title. II. Series. BIP

SAINT-GAUDENS, Augustus, 1848-1907. 730'.92'4 B
The reminiscences of Augustus Saint-Gaudens / edited and amplified by Homer Saint-Gaudens. [New York : Garland Pub., 1976], c1913-. v. : ill. ; 19 cm. (The Art experience in late nineteenth-century America) Reprint of the ed. published by the Century Co., New York, with new introd. [NB237.S2A2 1976] 75-28890 ISBN 0-8240-2247-5 lib.bdg. : 50.00
1. Saint-Gaudens, Augustus, 1848-1907. 2. Sculptors—United States—Biography. I. Saint-Gaudens, Homer, 1880- II. Title. III. Series. BIP

SLIVKA, Rose. 730'.92'4 B
Peter Voulkos : a dialogue with clay / Rose Slivka. 1st ed. Boston : New York Graphic Society, c1978. xvii, 142 p., [12] leaves of plates : ill. ; 31 cm. Bibliography: p. 139-142. [NB237.V64S58 1978] 77-17166 27.50
1. Voulkos, Peter. 2. Sculptors—United States—Biography. I. Title. BIP

Sculptors—United States—Correspondence, reminiscences, etc.

CALDER, Alexander, 1898- 730.924
Calder; an autobiography with pictures. New York, Pantheon Books [1966] 285 p. illus. (part col.) ports. 28 cm. [NB237.C28A2] 66-23203
1. Calder, Alexander, 1898- 2. Sculptors—United States—Correspondence, reminiscences, etc. I. Title.

NEVELSON, Louise, 1900- 730'.92'4 B
Dawns and dusks : taped conversations with Diana Mackown / Louise Nevelson. New York : Scribner, [1976] p. cm. [NB237.N43A23] 76-20634 ISBN 0-684-14781-5 : 9.95
1. Nevelson, Louise, 1900- 2. Sculptors—United States—Correspondence, reminiscences, etc. I. Mackown, Diana. II. Title. BIP

Sculptors—Virginia—Correspondence, reminiscences, etc.

EZEKIEL, Moses, Sir, 1844-1917. 730'.92'4 B
Memoirs from the Baths of Diocletian / Moses Jacob Ezekiel ; edited by Joseph Gutmann and Stanley F. Chyet. Detroit : Wayne State University Press, 1975. 509 p. : ill. ; 26 cm. Includes index. Bibliography: p. 490-493. [NB237.E9A35] 74-28009 ISBN 0-8143-1525-9 : 25.00
1. Ezekiel, Moses, Sir, 1844-1917. 2. Sculptors—Virginia—Correspondence, reminiscences, etc. 3. Sculptors—Rome (City)—Correspondence, reminiscences, etc. I. Gutmann, Joseph, ed. II. Chyet, Stanley F., ed. III. Title.

Sculpture.

BOECK, Urs. 729.5
Sculpture on buildings. [1st American ed.] New York, Universe Books [1961] xxx p., 208p. of illus. 30cm. [NB1137.B6 1961] 61-14471
1. Sculpture. 2. Architecture. I. Title.

CARSTENSON, Cecil C. 731.4'62
The craft and creation of wood sculpture [by] Cecil C. Carstenson. Edited by William S. Brown. New York, Scribner [1971] ix, 179 p. illus. 24 cm. Bibliography: p. 172. [NB1250.C3] 72-162740 ISBN 0-684-12480-7 9.95
1. Sculpture. 2. Wood-carving—Technique. I. Title.

DIVALENTIN, Maria (Messuri) 1911- 730
The everyday pleasures of sculpture, by Maria M. and Louis di Valentin. Introd. by Edward Durell Stone. New York, J. H.

Heineman, 1966. 128p. illus. 26cm. Bibl. [NB1140.D5] 65-24533 8.50 bds.,
1. Sculpture. I. DiValentin, Louis, joint author. II. Title.

FEININGER, Andreas, 1906- 731.824
Maids, madonnas & witches; women in sculpture from prehistoric times to Picasso. Photos. by Andreas Feininger. Introd. by Henry Miller. Text by J. Bon. [Translated from the German by Joan Bradley] New York, Abrams [1961] 194 p. plates. 33 cm. Translation of Frauen und Gottinnen von der Steinzeit bis zu Picasso. [NB1930.F413] 61-13859
1. Sculpture. 2. Women in art. I. Bon, J. II. Title.

GIEDION-WELCKER, Carola. 709'.04'0740153
Contemporary sculpture: an evolution in volume and space. Selective bibliography by Bernard Karpel: Modern art and sculpture. New York, G. Wittenborn [1955] xxxi, 327p. (chief3y illus., ports.) 26cm. (Documents of modern art, v. 12) 'Greatly enlarged and revised edition of 'Modern plastic art. Bibliography: p. [235]-324. [NB198.G] A56
1. Sculpture. I. Kerpel, Bernard, 1911- II. Title. III. Series.

GROSS, Chaim, 1904- 731.22
The technique of wood sculpture. With photos. by Eliot Elisofon and others. New York, Vista House [1957] 136p. illus. 24cm. [NB1250.G7] 57-2375
1. Sculpture. 2. Wood-carving. I. Title. BIP

MEYER, Frederick Robert. 738
Sculpture in ceramic, by Fred Meyer. New York, Watson-Guptill Publications [1971] 156 p. illus. 29 cm. Bibliography: p. 151. [NB1140.M4] 79-152753 ISBN 0-8230-4694-X 10.00
1. Sculpture. I. Title.

NORMAN, Percival Edward. 736.4
Sculpture in wood. London, New York, Studio Publications [1954] 94 p. illus. 26 cm. (How to do it series, 53) [NB1250.N6] 55-14004
1. Sculpture. 2. Wood-carving. I. Title. II. Series.

NORMAN, Percival Edward. 731.462
Sculpture in wood [by] P. Edward Norman. [1st American ed.] New York, Transatlantic Arts, 1966. vi, 70, [36] p. 108 illus. 23 cm. [NB1250.N6 1966] 66-6718
1. Sculpture. 2. Woodcarving—Technique. I. Title.

NORMAN, Percival Edward 731.462
Sculpture in wood [Rev. ed] London, A. Tiranti [Hollywood-by-the-Sea. Fla., Transatlantic, 1964] vi, 70p. 108 illus. 22cm. (Scopas handbk.) 64-55871 5.50
1. Sculpture. 2. Wood-carving—Technique. I. Title.

READ, Herbert Edward, Sir, 1893-1968. 730
The art of sculpture. [New York] Pantheon Books [1956] xxxi, 152 p. 225 plates. 27 cm. (Bollingen series, 35. The A. W. Mellon lectures in the fine arts, 3) Includes bibliographical references. [NB1140.R4] 56-10426
1. Sculpture. I. Title. II. Series: Bolligen series, 35 III. Series: The A. W. Mellon lectures in the fine arts, 3 BIP

RIEGER, Shay. 730'.0924
The stone menagerie. New York, Scribner [1970] [48] p. illus. 27 cm. A sculptor describes in text and photographs the process of creating in stone. [NB1208.R53] 73-121748 4.50
1. Sculpture. 2. Stone carving. I. Title.

RITCHIE, Andrew Carnduff. 735.084
Sculpture of the twentieth century. New York, Museum of Modern Art [1952] 238 p. (chiefly illus.) 26 cm. Bibliography: p. 233-237. [NB198.R5] 53-9361
1. Sculpture. I. Title. BIP

ROGERS, Leonard Robert, 1924- 730
Sculpture [by] L. R. Rogers. London, New York, Oxford U.P., 1969. xiv, 242 p. illus., ports. 21 cm. (The Appreciation of the arts, 2) [NB1140.R6] 74-109896 42/- ($9.75)
1. Sculpture. I. Title.

ROOD, John, 1902- 736.4
Sculpture in wood. Minneapolis, University of Minnesota Press [1950] 179 p. illus. 26 cm. Bibliography: p. 175-176. [NB1250.R59] 50-9725
1. Sculpture. 2. Wood-carving. I. Title. BIP

SCHWARTZ, Paul Waldo. 730'.922
The hand and eye of the sculptor. Text and photos. by Paul Waldo Schwartz. New York, Praeger [1969] ix, 244 p. illus., ports. 27 cm. [NB1135.S3] 79-83348 15.00
1. Sculpture. 2. Art—Psychology. 3. Composition (Art). I. Title.

SEIDELMAN, James. 731.4
Creating with clay, by James Seidelman and Grace Mintonye. Illustrated by Robert William Hinds. New York, Crowell-Collier Press [1967] 56 p. illus. (part col.) 29 cm. An elementary yet comprehensive handbook for clay modeling. Introduces shapes made from slabs, coils, and bricks, and includes instructions for tooling and decorating as well as firing and glazing. [NB1143.S4 1967] AC 67
1. Sculpture. 2. Modeling. I. Mintonye, Grace, joint author. II. Hinds, Robert William, illus. III. Title. BIP

SEYMOUR, Charles, 1912- 735
Tradition and experiment in modern sculpture. Washington, aMerican University Press, 1949 [i.e. 1950] viii, 86 p. illus. 27 cm. [NB198.S4] 49-50355
1. Sculpture. I. Title. BIP

VERHELST, Wilbert, 1923- 731.4
Sculpture: tools, materials, and techniques. Englewood Cliffs, N.J., Prentice-Hall [1973] xiii, 287 p. illus. 28 cm. Bibliography: p. 261-263. [NB1140.V47] 72-10335 ISBN 0-13-796615-6 12.95
1. Sculpture. I. Title.

WILENSKI, Reginald Howard 735
The meaning of modern sculpture. Boston, Beacon [1961] 171p. illus. (Beacon BP, 124) 1.95 pap.,
1. Sculpture. 2. Sculpture, Greek. I. Title. BIP

WILENSKI, Reginald Howard, 1887- 730
The meaning of modern sculpture : an essay on some original sculpture of the present day together with some account of the methods of professional disseminators ... / by R. H. Wilenski. New York : AMS Press, 1978. xx, 171 p., [12] leaves of plates : ill. ; 23 cm. Reprint of the 1932 ed. published by Faber and Faber, London. Includes bibliographical references and index. [NB1135.W5 1978] 75-41297 ISBN 0-404-14757-7 : 17.50
1. Sculpture. 2. Sculpture, Greek. I. Title.

WITTKOWER, Rudolf. 730
Sculpture : processes and principles / Rudolf Wittkower. New York : Harper & Row, c1977. 288 p. : ill. ; 24 cm. (Icon editions) Lectures given at Cambridge University during 1970-71. Includes index. Bibliography: p. [277]-280. [NB1140.W57 1977b] 77-258 ISBN 0-06-430091-9 pbk. : 8.95
1. Sculpture. I. Title. BIP

ZORACH, William, 1887- 731
Zorach explains sculpture, what it means and how it is made. [Rev. ed] New York, Tudor Pub. Co. [1961, c.1947, 1960] 308p. illus. 26cm. 60-15042 4.95
1. Sculpture. I. Title.

Sculpture—Addresses, essays, lectures.

RUSKIN, John, 1819-1900. 730
Aratra Pentelici; seven lectures on the elements of sculpture given before the University of Oxford in Michaelmas term, 1870. With an introd. by Charles Eliot Norton. Brantwood ed. New York, Merrill, 1892. St. Clair Shores, Mich., Scholarly Press, 1972 [c1891] p. (The works of John Ruskin) Contents.Contents.—Of the division of arts.—Idolatry.—Imagination.—Likeness.—Structure.—The school of Athens.—The relation between Michael Angelo and Tintoret. [NB1145.R8 1972] 72-8326 ISBN 0-403-02052-2
1. Sculpture—Addresses, essays, lectures. 2. Sculpture, Greek—Addresses, essays, lectures. I. Title.

Sculpture—Africa.

ELISOFON, Eliot. 730.96
The sculpture of Africa; 405 photographs. Text by William Fagg. Pref. by Ralph Linton. Design by Bernard Quint. New York, Praeger [1958] 256 p. illus., map (on lining papers) 36 cm. (Books that matter) "Bibliographical notes": p. 252-254. [NB1080.E57] 58-8971
1. Sculpture—Africa. I. Flagg, William. BIP

KJERSMEIER, Carl, 1889-1961. 730'.96
Centres de style de la sculpture negre africaine. [Traduction: France Gleizal] New York, Reprinted by Hacker Art Books, 1967. 4 v. in 1. illus. 29 cm. "First published in 1935[-38]" Contents.CONTENTS. -- 1. v. Afrique occidentale francaise. -- 2. v. Guinee portugaise, Sierra-Leone, Liberia, Cote d'or, Togo, Dahomey et Nigeria. -- 3. v. Congo belge. -- 4. v. Cameroun, Afrique equatoriale francaise. Angola, Tanganyika, Rhodesie. Includes bibliographies. [NB1080.K52] 67-70231
1. Sculpture — Africa. 2. Sculpture, Primitive. 3. Negroes in Africa. I. Title.

WINGERT, Paul Stover, 1900- 732.2
The sculpture of Negro Africa. New York, Columbia University Press, 1950. vii, 96 p. illus., plates, map. 24 cm. Bibliography: p. [83]-96. [NB1080.W5] 50-11001
1. Sculpture—Africa. 2. Black art. I. Title.

Sculpture—Africa, West.

ALLISON, Philip. 730'.966
African stone sculpture. New York, Praeger [1968] vii, 71 p. illus., maps. 26 cm. Bibliography: p. 65-69. [NB1097.W4A69] 68-54465 10.00
1. Sculpture—Africa, West. 2. Stone carving—Africa, West. I. Title.

BASCOM, William Russell, 1912- 732'.2
African arts; an exhibition at the Robert H. Lonie Museum of Anthropology of the University of California, Berkeley, April 6,-october 22, 1967. Catalogue by William Bascom. [Berkeley, Printed by the University of California Printing Dept., 1967] 90 p. illus., maps (on lining papers) 24 cm. Bibliography: p. 89-90. [NB1097.W4B3] 67-63353
1. Sculpture—Africa, West. 2. Sculpture, Primitive—Exhibitions. I. California. University. Robert H. Lowie Museum of Anthropology. II. Title.

BEIER, Ulli. 731.7'5'096
African mud sculpture. Cambridge [Eng.] University Press, 1963. 96 p. 77 illus. 24 cm. [NB1097.W4B4] 63-5590
1. Scuipture — Africa, West. I. Title.

BEIER, Ulli 730.96
African mud sculpture. [New York] Cambridge [c.]1963. 96p. 77illus. 24cm. 63-5590 4.95
1. Sculpture—Africa, West. I. Title.

MUSEUM of African Art. 732'.2
African sculpture; an exhibition at Princeton University from the Museum of African Art, February 1971. Washington [1971] 36 p. illus., map. 21 cm. Text by W. L. Hommel. [NB1098.M85] 70-151806
1. Sculpture—Africa, West. 2. Idols and images—Exhibitions. I. Hommel, William L. II. Princeton University. III. Title.

Sculpture—Africa, West—Catalogs.

NEW York (City). Museum of Primitive Art. 732'.2'0966
African tribal sculpture, from the collection of Ernst and Ruth Anspach. Greenwich, Conn., Distributed by the New York Graphic Society, 1967. 30 p. illus. 28 cm. [NB1097.W4N44] 68-402
1. Sculpture—Africa, West—Catalogs. 2. Sculpture—Private collections. I. Anspach, Ernst. II. Anspach, Ruth. III. Title.

Sculpture—Africa, West—Exhibitions.

PENNSYLVANIA. University. University Museum. 730.96
African tribal sculpture, by Margaret Plass. Philadelphia [1956] 57p. illus., fold. map. 23cm. Catalogue of a loan exhibition held from Apr. to Sept. 1956. Bibliography: p. 10-13. [NB1080.P4] 56-59248
1. Sculpture—Africa, West—Exhibitions. 2. Sculpture, Primitive. I. Plass, Margaret. II. Title.

Sculpture, African.

BASCOM, William Russell, 1912- 732'.2'0967
African art in cultural perspective; an introduction, by William Bascom. [1st ed.] New York, Norton [1973] xii, 196 p. illus. 21 cm. Bibliography: p. 189-191. [NB1080.B37 1973] 73-4680 ISBN 0-393-04368-1 6.95
1. Sculpture, African. 2. Sculpture, Primitive—Africa. I. Title.
Pbk. 2.95; ISBN 0-393-09373-1. BIP

*FAGG, William 732.2
African tribal sculptures. New York, Tudor [1966] 2v. (various p.) maps. plates 15cm. (Petite encyclopedia d art. 82 /3) Contents.1. The Niger basin tribes.--2. The Congo basin tribes.
1. Sculpture, African. 2. Sculpture, Primitive. 3. Ethnology—Africa. I. Title. II. Series.

FAGG, William Buller, comp. 730.96
African sculpture, an anthology [by] William Fagg, Margaret Plass [London, Studio Vista] New York, Dutton [c.1964] 157,[3]p. illus. 19cm. (Dutton Vista pictureback, 8) Bibl. 64-56939 1.75 pap.,
1. Sculpture, African. I. Plass, Margaret, joint comp. II. Title.

FAGG, William Buller. 732.2
Tribes and forms in African art [by] William Fagg. New York, Tudor Pub. Co. [1965] 1 v. (various pagings) illus., col. map (on lining papers) 29 cm. Based on the exhibition Africa: 100 Stamme, 100 Meisterwerke, sponsored by the Congress for Cultural Freedom at the Berlin Festival, 1964. Includes bibliography. [NB1080.F32] 65-9192
1. Sculpture, African. 2. Sculpture, Primitive. 3. Ethnology — Africa. I. Title.

NEW York. Museum of Primitive Art. 709.01
Sculpture from Africa in the collection of the Museum of Primitive Art. 1 v. (chiefly illus., map) 21 cm. [NB1080.N427] 66-38231
1. Sculpture, African. 2. Sculpture, Primitive. 3. Sculpture — New York (City) I. Title. II. Title: New York,

NEW York. Museum of Primitive Art. 730.966
Senufo Sculpture from West Africa, by Robert Goldwater [director] Greenwich, Conn., Distributed by New York Graphic Society, 1964. 126 p. illus., map. 29 cm. Bibliography: p. 124-125. [NB1097.W4N4] 63-22414
1. Sculpture, African. 2. Sculpture, Primitive. 3. Senufo (African people) I. Goldwater, Robert John, 1907- II. Title.

PAULME, Denise. 730.96
African sculpture Translated by Michael Ross. New York, Viking Press, 1962. 160p. illus. 22cm. (A Studio book) Translation of Les sculptures de l'Afrique noire. [NNb1080.P313] 61-5480
1. Sculpture, African. 2. Negro art. I. Title.

SEGY, Ladislas. 732.2
African sculpture. With photos. by the author. New York, Dover Publications [1958] 34, [2] p. 163 plates, map. 23 cm. Bibliography: p. [36] [NB1080.S39] 58-5485
1. Sculpture, African. 2. Sculpture, Primitive—Africa. BIP

SEGY, Ladislas. 730.96
African sculpture speaks. New York, A. A. Wyn [1952] 254 p. 277 illus., maps (on lining papers) 20 cm. Bibliography: p. 231-236. [NB1080.S4] 52-6927
1. Sculpture, African. 2. Sculpture, Primitive. I. Title. BIP

SEGY, Ladislas. 732'.2
African sculpture speaks. 3d ed., enl. and fully rev. New York, Hill and Wang [1969] 315 p. illus., maps. 29 cm. Bibliography: p.

281-292. [NB1080.S4 1969] 68-14790 ISBN 0-8090-2351-2 14.95
1. Sculpture, African. 2. Sculpture, Primitive—Africa, West. I. Title.

SEGY, Ladislas. 732'.2'0966
African sculpture speaks / Ladislas Segy. 4th ed., enl. New York : Da Capo Press, 1975. 346 p. : ill. ; 28 cm. (A Da Capo paperback) Includes bibliographies and index. [NB1098.S44 1975] 75-14323 ISBN 0-306-80018-7 pbk. : 6.95
1. Sculpture, African. 2. Sculpture, Primitive—Africa, West. I. Title.

SWEENEY, James Johnson, 1900- comp. 732'.2'0966
African sculpture. Selected, with an introd., by James Johnson Sweeney. [Princeton, N.J.] Princeton University Press [1970, c1964] v, 196 p. (chiefly illus.) 26 cm. (Princeton/Bollingen paperbacks, 201) (Bollingen series) "Extracted from African folktales and sculpture, Bollingen series XXXII, first published in 1952 and in a revised edition in 1964." [NB1098.S93 1970] 78-106801 ISBN 0-691-01763-8
1. Sculpture, African. 2. Sculpture, Primitive—Africa, West. I. Title. II. Series. **BIP**

TROWELL, Kathleen Margaret. 730.96
Classical African sculpture [by] Margaret Trowell. [2d ed.] New York, Praeger [1964] 103 p. maps, 48 plates. 26 cm. Bibliography: p. 90. [NB1080] 64-23110
1. Sculpture, African. 2. Sculpture, Primitive. I. Title.

TROWELL, Kathleen Margaret. 732.2
Classical African sculpture. New York, Praeger [1954] 103 p. 48 plates, maps. 26 cm. (Books that matter) Bibliography: p. 99. Bibliographical footnotes. [NB1080.T7] 54-12094
1. Sculpture, African. 2. Sculpture, Primitive. I. Title.

TROWELL, Kathleen Margaret. 732'.2
Classical African sculpture, by Margaret Trowell. [3rd rev. ed.] New York, Praeger Publishers [1970] 101 p. 48 plates. 26 cm. Bibliography: p. 97. [NB1098.T7 1970b] 76-120024 10.00
1. Sculpture, African. 2. Sculpture, Primitive—Africa, West. I. Title.

Sculpture, African—Africa, Sub-Saharan.

HAAF, Ernst. v. 12
Geburt, Krankheit, Tod in der afrikanischen Kunst / von E. Haaf u. J. Zwernemann. Stuttgart ; New York : Schattauer, 1975. 108 p. : 76 ill. (some col.), fold. col. map ; 21 cm. Bibliography: p. 106-108. [NB1091.65.H32] 76-457882 ISBN 3-7945-0463-1 : DM39.00
1. Sculpture, African—Africa, Sub-Saharan. 2. Sculpture, Primitive—Africa, Sub-Saharan. 3. Childbirth in art. 4. Diseases in art. 5. Death in art. I. Zwernemann, Jurgen, joint author. II. Title.

Sculpture, African—Catalogs.

FAGG, William Buller. 730'.967
African tribal images; the Katherine White Reswick Collection [by] William Fagg. [Cleveland] Cleveland Museum of Art [1968] 1 v. (unpaged) illus., maps. 24 cm. Includes bibliography. [NB1080.F312] 68-31762 9.50
1. Reswick, Katherine White—Art collections. 2. Sculpture, African—Catalogs. I. Cleveland Museum of Art. II. Title.

ROBBINS, Warren M. 730.96
African art in American collections. L'art africain dans les collections americaines, by Warren M. Robbins with the assistance of Robert H. Simmons. Translated into French by Richard Walters. New York, F. A. Praeger, 1966. xv, 237 p. illus., map. 29 cm. In English and French. [NB1080.R6] 66-13681
1. Sculpture, African—Catalogs. I. Title. II. Title: L'art africain dans les collections americaines.

Sculpture, African—Exhibitions.

THE Art of Black Africa; 730'.967'097471
Collection of Jay C. Leff. [Pittsburgh? 1970] [90] p. illus., map. 24 cm. Catalog of an exhibition at Museum of Art, Carnegie Institute, October 24, 1969—January 18, 1970. [NB1080.A76] 74-13622
1. Leff, Jay C.—Art collections. 2. Sculpture, African—Exhibitions. I. Pittsburgh. Carnegie Institute. Museum of Art.

BRAVMANN, Rene A. 732'.2'0966
West African sculpture, by Rene A. Bravmann. Seattle, Published for the Henry Art Gallery by the University of Washington Press [1970] 80 p. illus. 28 cm. (Index of art in the Pacific Northwest, no. 1) "Catalogue for an exhibition held at the Henry Art Gallery, University of Washington, February 8-March 8, 1970." Bibliography: p. 78-79. [NB1097.W4B7] 78-115415 3.95 (pbk.)
1. Sculpture, African—Exhibitions. 2. Sculpture—Africa, West. I. Henry Art Gallery. II. Title. III. Series.

BROOKLYN Institute of Arts and Sciences. Museum. 732'.2'096
African sculpture; the Brooklyn Museum. [Text by Michael Kan. New York, 1970] 63, [1] p. illus. 23 cm. Bibliography: p. [64] [NB1080.B75] 74-122015
1. Sculpture, African—Exhibitions. I. Kan, Michael. II. Title.

[CHICAGO. Art Institute. 732'.2
African sculpture, 1969-1970, Illinois Arts Council; a traveling exhibition organized for the Illinois Arts Council by the Art Institute of Chicago. [Allen Wardell, curator of primitive art. Chicago, Huron Press, 1970] [16] p. illus. 27 cm. Catalog. [NB1048.C46] 76-633609
1. Sculpture, African—Exhibitions. 2. Sculpture, Primitive—Africa, West. I. Wardell, Allen. II. Illinois. Arts Council. III. Title.

FAGG, William Buller. 732'.2
African sculpture; [loan exhibition] circulated by the International Exhibitions Foundation, 1970. [Catalogue] by William Fagg. [Washington, International Exhibitions Foundation, 1970] 156 p. illus. (part col.) 28 cm. Participating museums: National Gallery of Art, William Rockhill Nelson Gallery of Art, and the Brooklyn Museum. Bibliography: p. 153. [NB1080.F304] 76-109185
1. Sculpture, African—Exhibitions. I. International Exhibitions Foundation. II. U.S. National Gallery of Art. III. William Rockhill Nelson Gallery of Art and Mary Atkins Museum of Fine Arts, Kansas City, Mo. IV. Brooklyn Institute of Arts and Sciences. Museum. V. Title.

ITHACA College, Ithaca, N.Y. Museum of Art. 732'.2
The innovative African sculptor. An exhibition presented by Ithaca College Museum of Art, Ithaca, New York. Introd. and descriptive notes by George Nelson Preston. [Ithaca, N.Y., 1970] 60 p. illus. 26 cm. "Ithaca College Museum of Art, November 11-December 21, 1969. The Picker Art Gallery, Colgate University, Hamilton, New York, February 15-March 15, 1970." Bibliography: p. 60. [NB1098.I85] 71-29393
1. Sculpture, African—Exhibitions. 2. Sculpture, Primitive—Africa, West. I. Preston, George Nelson. II. Picker Gallery. III. Title.

MUSEUM of African Art. 732'.2
The deHavenon collection. Washington [1971] 1 v. (unpaged) illus. (part col.) 26 cm. Catalogue of a loan exhibition held at the opening of the museum's enlarged galleries, 1971. [NB1080.M83] 70-198245
1. DeHavenon, Gaston T.—Art collections. 2. Sculpture, African—Exhibitions. 3. Wood-carving, African—Exhibitions. I. Title.

MUSEUM of African Art. 730'.96
The language of African art; a guest exhibition of the Museum of African Art at the Smithsonian Institution, May 24 to September 7, 1970. [Washington, 1970?] [20] p. illus. 21 cm. Cover title. Label mounted on p. [1]: Supplied by Worldwide Books, Boston. "Catalogue is principally the work of Delmar Lipp, editorial associate of the museum." [NB1098.M86] 70-22034
1. Sculpture, African—Exhibitions. 2. Sculpture—Africa, West. 3. Symbolism in art—Africa, West. I. Lipp, Delmar. II. Smithsonian Institution. III. Title.

MUSEUM of African Art. 732'.2'09660740153
Tribute to Africa: the photography and the collection of Eliot Elisofon; a memorial exhibition at the Museum of African Art, June through December, 1974. Washington [1974] 48 p. illus. 28 cm. Catalog. Bibliography: p. 48. [TR140.E4M87 1974] 74-81895
1. Elisofon, Eliot. 2. Sculpture, African—Exhibitions. 3. Photography, Artistic—Exhibitions. I. Elisofon, Eliot. II. Title. **BIP**

NEW York. Museum of Primitive Art. 730.967
African sculpture lent by New York collectors. [Exhibition] summer 1958. New York [1958] unpaged. illus. 28cm. [NB1080.N4] 59-1580
1. Sculpture, African— Exhibitions. I. Title.

NEW York. Museum of Primitive Art. 730.9624
Sculpture from three African tribes: Senufo, Baga, Dogon, spring, 1959. New York [1959] unpaged. illus. 28cm. [NB1080.N43] 59-31932
1. Sculpture, African— Exhibitions. I. Title.

SANTA Barbara, Calif. Museum of Art. 732'.2'0967
Antelopes and elephants, hornbills and hyenas; animals in African art. An exhibition organized by Ronald A. Kuchta, curator. [Santa Barbara, 1973] [48] p. illus. 28 cm. Catalog of the exhibition held Oct. 4-Dec. 2, 1973 at the Santa Barbara Museum of Art, Calif. [NB1098.S27 1973] 73-91900
1. Sculpture, African—Exhibitions. 2. Sculpture, Primitive—Africa, West. 3. Animals in art. I. Title.

SIEBER, Roy, 1923- 730'.967
Sculpture of Black Africa; the Paul Tishman Collection, by Roy Sieber and Arnold Rubin. [Los Angeles, Los Angeles County Museum of Art, 1968] 150 p. illus. (part col.) 31 cm. Catalog of an exhibition held at the Los Angeles County Museum of Art, Oct. 16, 1968-Jan. 5, 1969. Bibliography: p. 150. [NB1097.T5S55] 68-57350
1. Tishman, Paul—Art collections. 2. Sculpture, African—Exhibitions. 3. Sculpture—Africa, West. I. Rubin, Arnold, joint author. II. Los Angeles Co., Calif. Museum, Los Angeles. III. Title.

SIEBER, Roy, 1923- 730'.967
Sculpture of Black Africa; the Paul Tishman Collection, by Roy Sieber and Arnold Rubin. [Washington, 1970] 150, A39 p. illus. (part col.), maps. 30 cm. Catalog of an exhibition circulated by the International Exhibitions Foundation, 1970-71. Participating museums: The High Museum of Art, Atlanta, Georgia and others. Addendum to the catalog compiled by Roy Sieber and Robin Poyner: p. A1-A39. Includes bibliographies. [NB1097.W4S5 1970] 75-124430
1. Tishman, Paul—Art collections. 2. Sculpture, African—Exhibitions. 3. Sculpture—Africa, West. I. Rubin, Arnold, joint author. II. International Exhibitions Foundation. III. High Museum of Art. IV. Title.

Sculpture, American.

ANDERSEN, Wayne V. 730'.973
American sculpture in process, 1930-1970 / Wayne Andersen. Boston : New York Graphic Society, 1975. p. cm. Includes bibliographical references and index. [NB212.A43] 74-21498 ISBN 0-316-03681-1 : 17.50
1. Sculpture, American. 2. Sculpture, Modern—20th century—United States. I. Title. **BIP**

ASHTON, Dore. 730'.973
Modern American sculpture. New York, H. N. Abrams [1968?] 54, [78] p. illus. (part col.) 37 cm. Bibliographical footnotes. [NB212.A8] 68-23168
1. Sculpture, American. 2. Sculpture, Modern—20th century—U.S. I. Title.

CLARK, William J., 1840-1889. 730'.973
Great American sculptures / by William J. Clark, Jr. [New York] : Garland, [1977] 13, 144 p. : ill. ; 26 cm. (The Art experience in late nineteenth-century America) Reprint of the 1878 ed. published by Gebbie & Barrie, Philadelphia; with new introd. [NB210.C58 1977] 75-28869 ISBN 0-8240-2229-7 lib.bdg. : 30.00
1. Sculpture, American. 2. Sculpture, Modern—19th century—United States. 3. Sculptors—United States. I. Title. II. Series. **BIP**

CRAVEN, Wayne. 730'.973
Sculpture in America. New York, Crowell [1978] xx, 722 p. illus. 26 cm. Bibliography: p. 675-690. [NB205.C7] 68-21611 17.50
1. Sculpture, American. I. Title.

DAVIS, Myra Tolmach. 739'.47'24
Sketches in iron: Samuel Yellin, American master of wrought iron, 1885-1940. [Washington, D.C., 1971] [20] p. illus., ports. 23 cm. Published in conjunction with an exhibition held in the Dimock Gallery, George Washington University, Mar. 5-26, 1971. Bibliography: p. [18]-[19] [NK8298.D3Y4] 78-156287
I. Yellin, Samuel, 1885-1940. II. George Washington University, Washington, D.C. III. Title.

HARRIS, Julian Hoke, 1906- 735.73
Julian Hoke Harris. Edited by Joseph F. Morris. [Athens] University of Georgia Press in collaboration with the National Sculpture Society [1955] 59p. (chiefly illus., ports.) 28cm. (The American sculptors series, 16) [NB237.H27M6] 55-8076
I. Title. II. Series.

HOOVER, Francis Louis, 1913- 730'.973
Young sculptors; outstanding sculpture by high school students. Ed. by F. Louis Hoover. Worcester, Mass., Art Resource Pubns [1967] 30 double 1. plates. 31cm. In portfolio. [NB236.H6] 67-17975 4.95
1. Sculpture, American. 2. Youth as artists. I. Title.
Publisher's address 50 Portland St., Worcester, Mass. 01608.

JENNEWEIN, Carl Paul, 1890- 735.73
C Paul Jennewein. [Athens] University of Georgia Press in collaboration with the National Sculpture Society [1950] 61 p. (chiefly illus., ports.) 26 cm. (The American sculptors series, 11) [NB237.J4A43] 50-4461
I. Title. II. Series.

JUDSON, Sylvia (Shaw) 730'.924
For gardens and other places; the sculpture of Sylvia Shaw Judson. Chicago, H. Regnery Co. [1967] 1 v. (chiefly illus.) 28 cm. [NB237.J8A44] 67-25634
I. Title.

LYNCH, John, 1904- 735.291
Mobile design. New York, Studio-Crowell [1955] 126 p. illus. 24 cm. [NB212.L93] 55-7327
1. Sculpture, American. 2. Art, Abstract. I. Title.

NELSON, Jack, 1929(Jan.24)- 730'.92'4
Jack Nelson. Syracuse, Everson Museum of Art [1971] [8] p. illus. 22 cm. Catalog of the exhibition held Dec. 21, 1971-Jan. 21, 1972 at the Everson Museum of Art. [N6537.N4E9] 75-187744
I. Everson Museum of Art of Syracuse and Onondaga County.

NEW York, Metropolitan Museum of Art 730.973
American sculpture; a catalogue of the collection of the Metropolitan Museum of Art [by] Albert Ten Eyck Gardner. Greenwich, Conn., N.Y. Graphic [c.1965] xii, 192p. illus. 25cm. [NB205.N38] 65-10579 7.50
1. Sculpture, American. 2. Sculptors, American. I. Gardner, Albert Ten Eyck, comp. II. Title.

PRIZE-WINNING 731.108
sculpture; bk. 1, 1964 [Fort Lauderdale, Fla., Allied, c.1964] 1v. illus., ports. 34cm. annual. Comp.: 1964. M. Harold. 64-25836 1.95 pap.,
1. Sculpture, American. I. Harold, Margaret, comp.

PRIZE-WINNING sculpture; 735.29
bk. 7, 1967. Ft. Lauderdale, Fla., Allied Pubs. 1967. v. illus., ports. 34cm. annual. Comp. 1964- M. Harold [NB212.P7] 64-25836 1.95 pap.,
1. Sculpture, American. I. Harold, Margaret, comp.

PRIZE-WINNING sculpture; 735.29
bk. 3 1966 [Fort Lauderdale, Fia., Allied Pubns., c.1966] 37p. illus., ports. 34cm. annual. Comp.: 1964-66 M. Harold [NB212.P7] 64-25836 1.95 pap.,
1. Sculpture, American. I. Harold, Margaret, comp.

SCHNIER, Jacques 730'.973
Preston, 1898-
Sculpture in modern America [by] Jacques Schnier. Westport, Conn., Greenwood Press [1972, c1948] ix, 224 p. 139 plates. 26 cm. Bibliography: p. 65-67. [NB205.S35 1972] 70-163549 ISBN 0-8371-6213-0 19.75
1. Sculpture, American. I. Title. **BIP**

THORP, Margaret (Farrand) 730.973
1891-
The literary sculptors. Durham, N. C., Duke University Press 1965. x, 206 p. illus., ports. 25 cm. Bibliography: p. [198]-202. [NB210.T45] 65-13655
1. Sculpture, American. 2. Sculptors, American. I. Title. **BIP**

Sculpture, American—Bibliography.

EKDAHL, Janis. 016.73'0973
American sculpture : a guide to information sources / Janis Ekdahl. Detroit : Gale Research Co., [1976] p. cm. (Art and architecture information guide series ; v. 5) (Gale information guide library) Includes index. [Z5954.U5E37] [NB205] 74-11544 ISBN 0-8103-1271-9
1. Sculpture, American—Bibliography. I. Title.

Sculpture, American—Exhibitions.

CIKOVSKY, Nicolai. 730'.92'2
Nineteenth century American women neoclassical sculptors; [exhibition] Vassar College Art Gallery, April 4 through April 30, 1972. Introd. by William H. Gerdts, Jr. Catalogue by Nicolai Cikovsky, Jr., Marie H. Morrison, and Carol Ockman. [Poughkeepsie, N.Y., Printed by Merchants Press, 1972] [40] p. illus. 26 cm. Cover title: The white, marmorean flock. Bibliography: p. [23]-[25] [NB210.5.N4C5] 72-78318
1. Sculpture, American—Exhibitions. 2. Neoclassicism (Art)—United States. 3. Women sculptors—United States. I. Morrison, Marie H., joint author. II. Ockman, Carol, joint author. III. Gerdts, William H. IV. Vassar College. Art Gallery. V. Title. VI. Title: The white, marmorean flock.

CINCINNATI. 730'.976'074017178
Art Museum.
Contemporary sculpture 1961 : works by artists resident in Ohio, Indiana, Illinois, Michigan, Wisconsin, Minnesota, Kentucky, and Missouri: exhibition Cincinnati Art Museum, January13 February 5, 1961. John Herron Art Institute February 12-March 12, 1961 [Cincinnati : The Museum, 1961?] [20] p. : ill. ; 25 cm. [NB222.C55 1961] 75-313201
1. Sculpture, American—Exhibitions. 2. Sculpture, Modern—20th century—Middle West. I. Art Association of Indianapolis, Indiana. John Herron Art Institute. II. Title.

CONNECTICUT. 730'.973'074014643
University. Museum of Art.
Sculpture in the spring. [Exhibition] April 4 to May 3, 1970. Presented in cooperation with the Sculptors Guild. [Storrs, 1970?] 34 p. (chiefly illus.) 22 cm. [NB212.C65] 73-198164
1. Sculpture, American—Exhibitions. 2. Sculpture, Modern—20th centry—U.S. I. Sculptors' Guild, New York. II. Title.

CONNECTICUT. 730'.0973'074014643
University. Museum of Art.
... small packages: an invitational sculpture competition sponsored by the International Silver Company. Storrs, 1971. 45 p. illus. 23 cm. Catalog of an exhibition. [NB212.C66] 72-183083
1. Sculpture, American—Exhibitions. 2. Sculpture, Modern—20th century—United States. 3. Sculpture—Competitions. I. International Silver Company, Meriden, Conn. II. Title.

DETROIT. 730'.973'074017434
Institute of Arts.
Art in space : some turning points : [exhibition] May 15-June 24, 1973, the Detroit Institute of Arts. [Detroit : Institute of Arts, 1973] [40] p. : ill. ; 30 x 13 cm. Bibliography: p. [37]-[40] [NB212.D47 1973] 75-313096
1. Sculpture, American—Exhibitions. 2. Sculpture, Modern—20th century—United States. 3. Space (Art) I. Title.

GALERIE Chalette, New 730'.973
York.
Structured sculpture. New York [1968] 1 v. (unpaged) illus. (part col.) 18 cm. Catalog of the exhibition held Oct.-Nov. 1968. [NB212.G3] 76-271753
1. Sculpture, American—Exhibitions. 2. Sculpture, Modern—20th century—U.S. I. Title.

GIBSON, Roland, 1902- 730'.973
New New England sculpture; [catalog of] a traveling exhibition. Sponsored by the Roland Gibson Art Foundation. Potsdam, N.Y. [1973] [27] p. illus. 22 cm. Cover title. Exhibition held at Dartmouth College, Sept. 12-Oct. 14, 1973; Currier Gallery of Art, Oct. 17-Nov. 10, 1973; and State University College at Potsdam, N.Y., Nov. 16-Dec. 16, 1973. [NB215.G52] 74-173053
1. Sculpture, American—Exhibitions. 2. Sculpture, Modern—20th century—New England. I. Dartmouth College. II. Currier Gallery of Art, Manchester, N.H. III. New York (State). State University College, Potsdam. IV. Title.

HALL, Michael 730'.973'074017438
D.
American folk sculpture: the personal and the eccentric. [Exhibition compiled by Michael D. Hall] [Bloomfield Hills, Cranbrook Academy of Art, 1971] [28] p. illus. (part col.) 30 cm. Catalog of the exhibition held Nov. 9, 1971-Jan. 2, 1972 at the Cranbrook Academy of Art Galleries, Bloomfield Hills, Mich. [NK805.H3] 75-185009
1. Sculpture, American—Exhibitions. 2. Folk art—United States. 3. Primitivism in art—United States. I. Cranbrook Academy of Art, Bloomfield Hills, Mich. Galleries. II. Title.

HOPE, Henry Radford, 1905- 735.44
The sculpture of Jacques Lipchitz. New York, Museum of Modern Art; [distributed by Simon and Schuster, 1954] 95p. illus., plates, ports. 26cm. 'Catalog of the exhibition': p.90-92. Bibliography: p.93-95. [NB237.L55H6] 54-10937
1. Lipchitz, Jacques, 1891- 2. Sculpture, American—Exhibitions. I. New York. Museum of Modern Art. II. Title.

HOWARD, Cecil, 1888- 735
Cecil Howard. [Athens, Ga.] University of Georgia Press in collaboration with the National Sculpture Society [1950] 50 p. (chiefly illus., ports.) 26 cm. (The American sculptors series, 10) [NB237.H65A43] 50-4509
I. Title. II. Series.

KIENHOLZ, Edward, 1927- 709'.73
Edward Kienholz; an exhibition organized by the Los Angeles County Museum of Art in cooperation with the Museum's Contemporary Art Council [March 30 to May 15, 1966. Los Angeles] Los Angeles County Museum of Art, Lytton Gallery, 1966. 52 p. illus. 29 cm. Bibliography: p. 12-13. [N6537.K48A44] 67-8878
I. Los Angeles Co., Calif. Museum of Art, Los Angeles. II. Los Angeles Co., Calif. Museum of Art, Los Angeles. Contemporary Art Council.

NATIONAL 730'.973'07401471
Sculpture Society, New York.
Sculpture, reliefs, medals : Bicentennial exhibition, National Sculpture Society, at the Equitable Gallery ... April 5 through April 23, 1976 / [exhibition chairman, Charlotte Dunwiddie]. New York : The Society, c1976. 97 p. : chiefly ill. ; 23 cm. [NB212.N35 1976] 76-5939 pbk. : 3.00
1. Sculpture, American—Exhibitions. 2. Sculpture, Modern—20th century—United States—Exhibitions. 3. Medals—United States—Exhibitions. I. Dunwiddie, Charlotte. II. Equitable Gallery. III. Title. IV. Title: Bicentennial exhibition, National Sculpture Society, Equitable Gallery, 1976.
Publisher's address: 75 Rockefeller Plaza.

NEBRASKA Art 730'.973'074018282
Association.
American sculpture; an exhibition organized to inaugurate the Sheldon Sculpture Garden at the University of Nebraska, Lincoln. Presented as its annual exhibition by the Nebraska Art Association, Sept. 11 through Nov. 15, 1970. [Lincoln] 1970. 1 v. (unpaged) illus. (part col.) 26 cm. [NB210.N4] 73-634273
1. Sculpture, American—Exhibitions. 2. Sculpture, Modern—19th century—U.S. 3. Sculpture, Modern—20th century—U.S. I. Nebraska. University. Sheldon Memorial Art Gallery. II. Title.

NORTON (R. W.) 730'.973'074016399
Art Gallery.
American sculpture : a tenth anniversary exhibition, November 7-December 5, 1976 / by R. W. Norton Art Gallery. Shreveport, La. : The Gallery, 1976, i.e.1977 p. cm. Includes index. Bibliography: p. [NB212.N67] 76-50425 ISBN 0-913060-11-9 pbk. : 3.00
1. Sculpture, American—Exhibitions. 2. Sculpture, Modern—20th century—United States—Exhibitions. I. Title. **BIP**

PASADENA, Calif. Art 730'.973
Museum.
New American sculpture [Bontecou, Chamberlain, Higgins, Price, Westermann. Pasadena, Calif., 1964] [24] p. illus. 25 cm. Exhibition held Feb. 11-Mar. 7, 1964. Includes bibliographical references. [NB212.P33] 78-22202
1. Sculpture, American—Exhibitions. 2. Sculpture, Modern—20th century—U.S. I. Title.

PENNSYLVANIA. 730'.973
University. Institute of Contemporary Art.
7 sculptors : Anthony Caro, John Chamberlain, Donald Judd, Alexander Liberman, Tina Matkovic, David Smith, Anne truitt. / Samuel Adams Green, director of exhibitions. Philadelphia, 1969?] 43 p. illus., ports. 19 cm. Cover title. [NB212.P4] 70-263284
1. Sculpture, American—Exhibitions. 2. Sculpture, Modern—20th century—U.S. I. Green, Samuel Adams. II. Title.

PERKINS, Constance M., 730'.973
1913-
Small sculpture from the United States. [Washington, 1970] [28] p. illus. 26 cm. Cover title. Catalog of an exhibition assembled for the United States Information Agency by the International Art Program of Smithsonian Institution. "American prints: new directions," by International Art Program, National Collection of Arts, Smithsonian Institution: p. [13]-[16] [NB212.P45] 79-609457
1. Sculpture, American—Exhibitions. 2. Sculpture, Modern—20th century—U.S. I. Smithsonian Institution. National Collection of Fine Arts. International Art Program. II. Title.

QUEENS 730'.973'0740147243
Museum.
American sculpture, folk & modern : [exhibition] March 12-May 8, 1977. Flushing, N.Y. : Queens Museum, c1977. [24] p. : ill. ; 26 cm. Includes bibliographical references. [NB212.5.P7Q43 1977] 77-150382
1. Sculpture, American—Exhibitions. 2. Primitivism in art—United States—Exhibitions. 3. Folk art—United States—Exhibitions. 4. Sculpture, Modern—20th century—United States—Exhibitions. I. Title.

SHARP, Lewis I. 730'.973
New York City public sculpture by 19th-century American artists. Catalogue by Lewis I. Sharp. Walking tours by David W. Kiehl. [New York] Metropolitan Museum of Art [1974] 68 p. illus. 21 x 23 cm. Catalogue of an exhibition held at the Metropolitan Museum of Art, June 18, 1974. Bibliography: p. 68. [NB210.S48] 74-176071
1. Sculpture, American—Exhibitions. 2. Sculpture, Modern—19th century—United States. 3. Sculpture—New York (City) I. New York (City). Metropolitan Museum of Art. II. Title.

TUCHMAN, Maurice 730'.973
American sculpture of the sixties: exhibition selected and book-catalog ed. by Maurice Tuchman. Sponsored by the Contemporary Art Council. [Los Angeles, 1967] 258p. illus. 28cm. Exhibition to be held at the Los Angeles County Museum of Art Apr. 28-June 25, 1967, and at the Philadelphia Museum of Art Sept. 15-Oct, 29, 1967. Bibl. [NB212.T8] 67-18143 6.00 pap.,
1. Sculpture, American—Exhibitions. I. Los Angeles Co., Calif. Museum of Art, Los Angeles. II. Philadelphia Museum of Art. III. Title.
Available from N.Y. Graphic, Greenwich, Conn. **BIP**

200 years of 730'.973'07401471
American sculpture / Tom Armstrong . . .et. al. . . [Boston] : D. R. Godine, c1976. 350 p. : ill. (some col.) ; 30 cm. "A Bicentennial exhibition organized by the Whitney Museum of American Art, New York, shown from March 16 to September 26, 1976." Includes bibliographies and index. [NB205.T86] 76-1762 ISBN 0-87923-185-8 : 35.00
1. Sculpture, American—Exhibitions. 2. Neoclassicism (Art)—United States—Exhibitions. 3. Sculpture, Modern—19th century—United States—Exhibitions. 4. Sculpture, Modern—20th century—United States—Exhibitions. I. Armstrong, Tom, 1932- II. Whitney Museum of American Art, New York.

VASSAR 730'.973'074014733
College. Art Gallery.
Twenty six by twenty six. [Exhibition] Vassar College Art Gallery, Poughkeepsie, New York, May 1-June 6, 1971. [Poughkeepsie, N.Y., Printed by Lansing-Broas Print. Co., 1971] 1 v. (unpaged) illus., facsims. 27 cm. Catalog. Includes a bibliography. [NB212.V37] 74-163116
1. Sculpture, American—Exhibitions. 2. Sculpture, Modern—20th century—U.S. I. Title. **BIP**

WALKER Art Center, 730'.922
Minneapolis.
14 sculptors : the industrial edge / Peter Alexander and others. An exhibition organized by Walker Art Center, May 29-June 21, 1969, presented at Dayton's 8th floor auditorium, Minneapolis. [Minneapolis, 1969] 53 p. illus. (14 in pocket) 28 cm. Bibliography: p. 46-48. [NB212.W26] 73-87785
1. Sculpture, American—Exhibitions. 2. Sculpture, Modern—20th century—U.S. I. Title.

WALKER Art Center, 730'.922
Minneapolis.
Eight sculptors: the ambiguous image; an exhibition organized by Walker Art Center, Minneapolis, October 22 through December 4, 1966. Introd. and essays on Donald Judd, Robert Morris, Lucas Samaras, H. C. Westermann, by Martin Friedman. Essays on Christo, Claes Oldenburg, George Segal, Ernest Trova, by Jan van der Marck. [Minneapolis, 1966] 40 p. illus. 28 cm. Includes bibliographies. [NB212.W25] 68-1391
1. Sculpture, American—Exhibitions. 2. Sculptors, American. I. Friedman, Martin L. II. Van der Marck, Jan, 1929- III. Title.

WALKER Art 730'.973'074014766
Center, Minneapolis.
Six-state sculpture show. Minneapolis. v. illus. 14x21cm. [NB212.W3] 55-15268
1. Sculpture, American—Exhibitions. I. Title.

descriptions and an introductory essay, by Osvald Siren. New York, Reprinted by Hacker Art Books, 1970. 4 v. in 2. illus., plans. 32 cm. Reprint of the 1925 ed. Includes bibliographical references. [NB1043.S5 1970] 78-78363
1. Sculpture, Chinese. I. Title.

Sculpture—Cincinnati—Catalogs.

CINCINNATI. Art Museum. 730'.74'017178
Sculpture collection of the Cincinnati Art Museum. [Cincinnati, 1970] 166 p. illus. 28 cm. Bibliography: p. 164-165. [NB25.C5A65] 77-132531
1. Sculpture—Cincinnati—Catalogs. I. Title.

Sculpture, Classical.

FURTWANGLER, Adolf, 1853-1907. 733
Greek & Roman sculpture / by A. Furtwangler & H. L. Urlichs ; translated by Horace Taylor. Boston : Longwood Press, 1977. p. cm. Translation of Denkmaler griechischer und romischer Skulptur. Reprint of the 1914 ed. published by J. M. Dent, London, and E. P. Dutton, New York. [NB85.F913 1977] 77-23569 ISBN 0-89341-205-8 lib.bdg. : 35.00
1. Sculpture, Classical. I. Urlichs, Heinrich Ludwig, 1864- joint author. II. Title. BIP

Sculpture, Classical—Catalogs.

HARRISON, Evelyn Byrd. 938'.5 s
Portrait sculpture / by Evelyn B. Harrison. Meriden, Conn. : Meriden Gravure Co., 1961. xiv, 114 p., [25] leaves of plates : ill. ; 21 cm. (The Athenian Agora ; v. 1) Reprint of the 1953 ed. published by the American School of Classical Studies at Athens, Princeton, N.J. Includes indexes. Bibliography: p. [xi]-xiv. [DF287.A23A5 vol. 1] [NB86] 733'.3'09385 75-322652
1. Sculpture, Classical—Catalogs. 2. Portrait sculpture—Catalogs. 3. Athens. Agora. I. Title. II. Series: American School of Classical Studies at Athens. The Athenian Agora ; v. 1.

Sculpture, Classical—Exhibitions.

ART Museum of South Texas. 733
Greek and Roman sculpture from the Boston Museum of Fine Arts : [exhibition] Feburary 7—May 25, 1975, Art Museum of South Texas, Corpus Christi. [Corpus Christi, Tex. : Golden Banner Press, 1975] [31] p. : ill. ; 23 cm. Catalog. Includes bibliographical references. [NB87.B6A77 1975] 75-312721
1. Sculpture, Classical—Exhibitions. 2. Classical antiquities. I. Boston. Museum of Fine Arts. II. Title.

Sculpture, Congo—Catalogs.

DALLAS. Museum of Fine Arts. 730'.9675'0976428
The Clark and Frances Stillman Collection of Congo sculpture: a gift of Eugene and Margaret McDermott to the Dallas Museum of Fine Arts. [Dallas] 1969. 83 p. illus., map. 22 cm. Bibliography: p. 83. [NB1097.C75D3] 73-9373
1. Stillman, Clark, 1907- —Art collections. 2. Stillman, Frances, 1910- —Art collections. 3. Sculpture, Congo—Catalogs. I. Title.

Sculpture, Congo—Exhibitions.

WALKER Art Center, Minneapolis. 730'.967
Art of the Congo; objects from the collection of the Koninklijk Museum voor Midden-Afrika/Musee Royal de l'Afrique Centrale, Tervuren, Belgium. Minneapolis [1967] 71 p. illus., map. 28 cm. Catalogue of an exhibition to be held at Walker Art Center, Nov. 5-Dec. 31, 1967, and five other art museums in U.S. and Canada, from Feb. 6, 1968 to May 4, 1969. Bibliography: p. 71. [NB1097.C75W3] 67-31115
1. Sculpture, Congo—Exhibitions. 2. Masks (Sculpture)—Exhibitions. I. Tervuren, Belgium. Musee royal de l'Afrique centrale. II. Title.

Sculpture—Conservation and restoration.

ANDRE, Jean Michel. 731.4'8
The restorer's handbook of sculpture / Jean-Michel Andre ; [English translation, J. A. Underwood]. New York : Van Nostrand Reinhold, c1977. 130 p. : ill. ; 22 cm. Translation of Restauration des sculptures. Includes index. Bibliography: p. 124-126. [NB1199.A5213] 77-5413 ISBN 0-442-20237-7 : 25.00
1. Sculpture—Conservation and restoration. I. Title. BIP

Sculpture, Coptic.

BECKWITH, John, 1918- 730.962
Coptic sculpture, 300-1300. London, A. Tiranti, 1963. vii, 56p. 147 illus, 20cm. (Chapts. in art ser. v. 37) Bibl. [NB1082.B4] 65-4407 9.00
1. Sculpture, Coptic. I. Title.
Available from Transatlantic, New York.

Sculpture, Cypriote—Catalogs.

BOSTON. Museum of Fine Arts. 730'.09393'7
Art of ancient Cyprus. Boston, 1972. [74] p. illus. 22 cm. Bibliography: p. [73]-[74] [NB130.C8B6] 72-83722 ISBN 0-87846-068-3
1. Sculpture, Cypriote—Catalogs. 2. Pottery, Cypriote—Catalogs. 3. Coins, Cypriote—Catalogs. 4. Art—Boston—Catalogs. I. Title. BIP

Sculpture— Cyrenaica.

ROSENBAUM, Elisabeth 730.9614
A catalogue of Cyrenaican portrait sculpture. New York. Published for the British Academy by Oxford University Press, 1960[,] xvii, 140p. 108 plates. 30cm. Bibl.: p.29-[31] 60-52146 19.35
1. Sculpture— Cyrenaica. 2. Sculpture, Roman. I. Title. II. Title: Cyrenaican portrait sculpture.

Sculpture—Detroit—Catalogs.

DETROIT. Institute of Arts. 730'.074'017434
A check list of ancient, European, American and Canadian sculpture in the Detroit Institute of Arts. Detroit, 1966. 55 p. 28 cm. [NB25.D4I6] 730'.74'017178 75-278333
1. Sculpture—Detroit—Catalogs. I. Title.

DETROIT. Institute of Arts. 730'.74'017434
A check list of ancient, European, American and Canadian sculpture in the Detroit Institute of Arts. [2d ed., rev.] Detroit, 1969. 52 p. 28 cm. [NB25.D416 1969] 72-197550
1. Sculpture—Detroit—Catalogs. I. Title.

Sculpture, Egyptian.

DESROCHES-NOBLECOURT, Christiane, 1913- 732.8
Ancient Egypt; the new kingdom and the Amarna period. Photographed by F. L. Kenett. Greenwich, Conn., New York Graphic Society [c.1960] xv p.33 plates. 38cm. (The Acanthus history of sculpture) 60-10476 6.95 bds.,
1. Sculpture, Egyptian. I. Kenett, F. L. II. Title. III. Series.

JAMES, Thomas Garnet Henry. 732.8
Egyptian sculptures. Introd. by T. G. H. James. New York, New American Library, by arrangement with UNESCO [1966] 24 p. 32 col. plates. 17 cm. (A Mentor-Unesco art book) "MQ694." Includes bibliography. [NB75.J3] 66-31845
1. Sculpture, Egyptian. I. United Nations Educational, Scientific and Cultural Organization. II. Title.

MURRAY, Margaret Alice. 732'.8
Egyptian sculpture. With a pref. by Ernest A. Gardner. Westport, Conn., Greenwood Press [1970] xxiv, 207 p. illus. 23 cm. Reprint of the 1930 ed. [NB75.M8 1970] 74-109802
1. Sculpture, Egyptian. BIP

STEINDORFF, Georg, 1861- 732.8
A royal head from ancient Egypt. Washington, 1951. xv, 30 p. 29 plates. 24 cm. (Freer Gallery of Art occasional papers. v. 1. no. 5) Smithsonian Institution. Publication 4022. "Richard Ettinghausen...prepared the English translation from [the author's]...German draft." Bibliography: p. 28-30. [NB75.S9] 51-60448
1. Sculpture, Egyptian. 2. Portraits, Egyptian. I. Title. II. Series: Freer Gallery of Art, Washington, DC. Occasional papers. v. 1, no. 5 BIP

Sculpture, Egyptian—Exhibitions.

ALDRED, Cyril. 732'.8
Akhenaten and Nefertiti; [Catalog of an exhibition celebrating the 150th anniversary of the Brooklyn Institute of Arts and Sciences] New York, Brooklyn Museum in association with the Viking Press. [1973] 231 p. illus. (part col.) 27 cm. (A Studio book) Bibliography: p. 224-229. [NB75.A57 1973] 73-6065 ISBN 0-670-11139-2 16.95
1. Amenhetep IV, King of Egypt, 1388-1358 B.C.—Art. 2. Nefertiti, Queen of Egypt, 14th cent. B.C.—Art. 3. Sculpture, Egyptian—Exhibitions. 4. Tell el-Amarna. I. Brooklyn Institute of Arts and Sciences. Museum. II. Title.

BECKER-COLONNA, Andieina Leanza. 732'.8'074019461
Ancient Egypt : an exhibition of el-Amarna sculptures and reliefs of the M. A. Mansoor Collection / Andreina Leanza Becker-Colonna ; sponsored by the Department of Classical Archaeology of San Francisco State University and by the Marie Stauffer Sigall Foundation. [San Francisco] : The Department?, c1975. 54 p. : ill. ; 28 cm. Cover title. Bibliography: p. 53-54. [NB75.B35] 75-323831
1. Mansoor, M. A., 1881- —Art collections. 2. Sculpture, Egyptian—Exhibitions. 3. Sculpture—Tell el-Amarna—Exhibitions. 4. Egypt—Antiquities. I. San Francisco State University. Dept. of Classical Archaeology. II. Marie Stauffer Sigall Foundation. III. Title.

BROOKLYN Institute of Arts and Sciences. Museum. 732.8074
Egyptian sculpture of the late period 700 B. C. to A. D. 100. [Brooklyn] 1960. xxxix, 197p. 135 plates. 29cm. 'An exhibition held ... 18 October 1960 to 9 January 1961. Catalogue compiled by Bernard V. Bothmer in collaboration with Herman de Meulenaere and Hans Wolfgang Muller. Bibliography: p.xxvii-xxix. [NB75.B75] 60-14710
1. Sculpture. Egyptian—Exhibitions. I. Title.

SIMPSON, William Kelly. 732'.8'0740147277
The face of Egypt : permanence and change in Egyptian art : from museum and private collections : the Katonah Gallery, March 13-May 15, 1977, Dallas Museum of Fine Arts, June 14-August 28, 1977 / by William Kelly Simpson. Katonah, N.Y. : [Katonah Gallery], c1977. 71 p. : ill. ; 31 cm. Catalog of an exhibition. Bibliography: p. 71. [NB75.S45] 76-52616 3.00
1. Sculpture, Egyptian—Exhibitions. 2. Egypt—Kings and rulers—Portraits—Exhibitions. 3. Gods in art—Exhibitions. 4. Animals in art—Exhibitions. I. Katonah Gallery. II. Dallas. Museum of Fine Arts. III. Title.
Publisher's address: 28 Bedford Rd., Katonah, NY 10536

Sculpture, English.

GARDNER, Arthur, 1878- 730'.942
English medieval sculpture. The original handbook rev. and enl., with 683 photos. New York, Hacker Art Books [1973, i.e. 1974] viii, 351 p. 29 cm. Reprint of the 1951 ed. published by Cambridge University Press, Cambridge, Eng. First ed. published in 1935 under title: A handbook of English medieval sculpture. Bibliography: p. 345-346. [NB463.G27 1973] 78-171421 ISBN 0-87817-110-X 40.00
1. Sculpture, English. 2. Sculpture, Medieval—England. I. Title.

HAMMACHER, Abraham Marie, 1897- 730'.942
Modern English sculpture. Text by A. M. Hammacher. New York, H. N. Abrams [1967?] 162 p. (chiefly plates (part col.)) 37 cm. A critical survey of English sculpture together with reproductions, selected by the author, of representative works of all the artists discussed. Bibliographical references included in "Biographical notes." [NB468.H3 1967b] 66-17272
1. Sculpture, English. 2. Sculpture, Modern—20th century—England. I. Title.

Sculpture, Etruscan.

RICHARDSON, Emeline Hill. 733.4
Etruscan sculptures. Introd. by Emeline Richardson. New York, New American Library, by arrangement with UNESCO [1966] 24 p. illus., 32 col. plates. 17 cm. (A Mentor-Unesco art book) "MQ695." Includes bibliography. [NB110.R48] 66-31705
1. Sculpture, Etruscan. I. United Nations Educational, Scientific and Cultural Organization. II. Title.

Sculpture, European.

MASTERPIECES of European sculpture. 730.94
167 photogravure plates, 10 colour plates from photos. by Martin Hurlimann and others. With a prefatory note by Eric Newton. New York, H. N. Abrams [1959] 54p. plates (part col.) 31cm. [NB450.M3] 59-5998
1. Sculpture, European. I. Hurlimann, Martin, 1897- II. Newton, Eric, 1893-

MERILLAT, Herbert Christian Laing, 1915- 730'.9
Sculpture, West and East: two traditions [by] Herbert Christian Merillat. Illustrated with photos. New York, Dodd, Mead [1973] xii, 272 p. illus. 24 cm. Bibliography: p. 221-224. [NB450.M47] 72-3934 ISBN 0-396-06703-4 12.50
1. Sculpture, European. 2. Sculpture, Oriental. I. Title. BIP

Sculpture, European—History.

MOLESWORTH, Hender Delves, 1907- 730.94
European sculpture from romanesque to neoclassic [by] H. D. Molesworth in collaboration with P. Cannon Brookes. New York, F. A. Praeger [1965] 288 p. illus. (part col.) 22 cm. (Praeger world of art series) Bibliography: p. 269-276. [NB450.M6] 65-16347
1. Sculpture, European—History. I. Title.

Sculpture—Exhibitions.

AMERICAN Federation of Arts. 730.74
Sculpture in silver, from islands in time; an exhibition, Sponsored by the Towle Silversmiths. [New York? 1955] unpaged. illus. 23cm. [NB1240.A4] 59-18072
1. Sculpture—Exhibitions. 2. Silversmithing—Exhibitions. I. Title.

CALIFORNIA. Arts Commission. 730'.74'0194
Perception: an exhibition of sculpture for the sighted and blind. [Sacramento, 1970?] 61 p. illus. 29 cm. Cover title. [NB16.S23C3] 73-637224
1. Sculpture—Exhibitions. 2. Perception. 3. Visual perception. I. Title.

JEWISH Theological Seminary of America. Jewish Museum 735.2907401471
Primary structures: younger American and British sculptors. New York [1966] [51] p. illus. 25 cm. Catalog of an exhibition held at the Jewish Museum, New York, April 27-June 12, 1966. "Selected bibliography [by] Katherine Kline": p. [46] [NB16.N5J45] 66-18742
1. Sculpture — Exhibitions. 2. Art, Modern — 20th cent. — Exhibitions. I. Title.

SUBJECT INDEX SCULPTURE—GREAT BRITAIN.

MICHIGAN. University. Museum of Art. v. 12
Sculpture and sculptors' drawings; [exhibition] March 4 through March 25, 1962. Ann Arbor [1962] unpaged. illus. 28cm. [NB17.A53 1962] 62-63408
1. Sculpture—Exhibitions. I. Title.

SOLOMON R. Guggenheim Museum, New York. 735.29
Modern sculpture from the Joseph H. Hirshhorn collection [Commentary: H. H. Arnason] New York, Author [1963, c.1962] 246p. chiefly illus. 29cm. 62-19719 7.50
1. Sculpture—Exhibitions. 2. Sculpture—Private collections. I. Hirshhorn, Joseph H. II. Arnason, H. H. III. Title.

UNITED States. National Gallery of Art. 709'.4'0740153
Recent acquisitions and promised gifts: sculpture, drawings, prints. [Washington] 1974. 223 p. illus. 30 cm. Catalog of an exhibition held at the National Gallery of Art, June 2-Sept. 2, 1974. [N5020.W52U558 1974] 74-8864 7.95
1. Sculpture—Exhibitions. 2. Drawings—Exhibitions. 3. Prints—Exhibitions. I. Title.

Sculpture, Finnish.

SCHILDT, Goran, 1917- 730'.947'1
Modern Finnish sculpture. New York, Praeger Publishers [1970] 63 p. illus. (part col.) 20 cm. [NB693.S3] 74-98345 4.50
1. Sculpture, Finnish. 2. Sculpture, Modern—20th century—Finland. I. Title.

Sculpture—Florence.

BODE, Wilhelm von, 1845-1929. 730'.945'51
Florentine sculptors of the Renaissance. Translated by Jessie Haynes. 2d ed. rev. by F. L. Rudston Brown. New York, Hacker Art Books, 1969. xii, 258 p. illus. 29 cm. Reprint of the 1928 ed. Translation of Florentiner Bildhauer der Renaissance. [NB621.F6B8 1969] 70-4420
1. Sculpture—Florence. 2. Sculpture, Renaissance—Florence. 3. Sculptors, Italian—Florence. I. Brown, Florence Lucy Rudston, 1875- II. Title. BIP

BODE, Wilhelm von, 1845-1929. 730'.945'51
Florentine sculptors of the Renaissance. Translated by Jessie Haynes. 2d ed. Freeport, N.Y., Books for Libraries Press [1968] xii, 258 p. illus. 26 cm. (Essay index reprint series) Reprint of the 2d ed., rev. by F. L. R. Brown, 1928. Translation of Florentiner Bildhauer der Renaissance. [NB621.F6B8 1968] 68-16912
1. Sculpture—Florence. 2. Sculpture, Renaissance—Florence. 3. Sculptors, Italian—Florence. I. Brown, Florence Lucy Rudston, 1875- II. Title.

Sculpture, Florentine.

AVERY, Charles. 730'.945'51
Florentine Renaissance sculpture. [1st U.S. ed.] New York, Harper & Row [1970] 274 p. illus. 25 cm. (Icon editions) Bibliography: p. 268. [NB621.F6A87 1970b] 78-148429 ISBN 0-06-430300-4 10.00
1. Sculpture, Florentine. 2. Sculpture, Renaissance—Florence. I. Title. BIP

WEIL-GARRIS, Kathleen 1934- 730'.945'51
The Santa Casa di Loreto : problems in cinquecento sculpture / Kathleen Weil-Garris. New York : Garland Pub., 1977. p. cm. (Outstanding dissertations in the fine arts) Bibliography: p. [NB621.L67W44] 76-23653 ISBN 0-8240-2735-3 : 100.00
1. Sculpture, Florentine. 2. Relief (Sculpture)—Italy—Loreto. 3. Sculpture, Renaissance—Loreto, Italy. 4. Mannerism (Art)—Loreto, Italy. 5. Loreto, Italy. Santa casa. I. Title. II. Series. BIP

Sculpture—France.

BRIDAHAM, Lester Burbank. 730'.944
Gargoyles, chimeres, and the grotesque in French Gothic sculpture. 2d ed., rev. and enl. New York, Da Capo Press, 1969. xv, 220 p. illus. 33 cm. (Da Capo Press series in architecture and decorative art, v. 21) Bibliography: p. 217-220. [NB543.B7 1969] 68-27724 37.50
1. Sculpture—France. 2. Sculpture, Gothic—France. 3. Grotesque. 4. Decoration and ornament, Architectural—France. 5. Decoration and ornament, Gothic—France. I. Title. BIP

Sculpture, French.

AUBERT, Marcel, 1884-1962. 730'.944
French sculpture at the beginning of the Gothic period, 1140-1225. New York, Hacker Art Books, 1972. xiii, 119 p. 88 plates. 32 cm. Reprint of the 1929 ed. Includes bibliographical references. [NB543.A8 1972] 75-143337 ISBN 0-87817-057-X 35.00
1. Sculpture, French. 2. Sculpture, Gothic—France. I. Title.

MARCHIORI, Giuseppe. 730.944
Modern French sculpture. [Translated from the Italian by John Ross] New York, H. N. Abrams [1963] 63, [1] p. 12 illus., 81 plates (part col.) 37 cm. Bibliography: p. [64] [NB548.M293] 63-19570
1. Sculpture, French. I. Title.

MILLARD, Charles W. 730'.92'4
The sculpture of Edgar Degas / Charles W. Millard. Princeton, N.J. : Princeton University Press, c1976. p. cm. Includes index. Bibliography: p. [NB553.D4M44] 73-2485 ISBN 0-691-03898-8 : 20.00
1. Degas, Hilaire Germain Edgar, 1834-1917. 2. Sculpture, French. 3. Sculpture, Modern—19th century. I. Degas, Hilaire Germain Edgar, 1834-1917. II. Title. BIP

RICHIER, Germaine, 1904-1959. 730.944
Germaine Richier [by] Jean Cassou. New York, Universe Books [c.1961] [16]p. 32 plates (Universe sculpture series) Captions in French, English, German, Dutch, and Spanish. 60-14503 1.95 pap.,
I. Cassou, Jean, 1897- II. Title.

STAHLY, Francois, 1911- 730.944
Francois Stahly. Introd. by Carola Giedion-Welcker. Ed. by Walter Herdeg. New York, Wittenborn [1962] 83p. (chiefly illus.) 24cm. French, English and German. Bibl. 63-488 6.50
I. Herdeg, Walter, 1908- ed. II. Title.

STODDARD, Whitney S 734.2
The west portals of Saint-Denis and Chartres; sculpture in the Ile de France from 1140 to 1190, theory of origins. Cambridge, Harvard University Press, 1952. xi, 64 p. 40 plates. 36 cm. In portfolio. "A development of [the author's] ...doctoral dissertation, presented at Harvard University in 1941." Bibliography: p. 62-64. [NB543.S8] 52-5043
1. Sculpture, French. 2. Sculpture, Gothic. 3. Saint-Denis, France. Eglise abbatiale de Saint-Denis. 4. Chartres, France. Notre Dame (Cathedral) I. Title.

VITRY, Paul, 1872-1941. 730'.944
French sculpture during the reign of Saint Louis, 1226-1270. New York, Hacker Art Books, 1973. xii, 98 p. 90 plates. 32 cm. "First published in Florence, 1929." Includes bibliographical references. [NB543.V53 1973] 72-80902 ISBN 0-87817-116-9 40.00
1. Sculpture, French. 2. Sculpture, Gothic—France. I. Title.

Sculpture, French—Exhibitions.

MIROLLI, Ruth. 730'.944'074016944
Nineteenth century French sculpture: monuments for the middle class. [Catalogue by Jane Van Nimmen and Ruth Mirolli. Louisville? Ky., 1971?] 244 p. illus. 26 cm. Exhibition held at J. B. Speed Art Museum, Louisville, Ky., Nov. 2-Dec. 5, 1971. "Bibliographical note": p. 26. [NB547.M57] 72-198006
1. Sculpture, French—Exhibitions. 2. Sculpture, Modern—19th century—France. I. Van Nimmen, Jane, 1937- II. Speed Art Museum, Louisville, Ky. III. Title.

Sculpture, French—United States.

BUFFALO Fine Arts Academy. 730'.92'4
Aristide Maillol, with an introd. and survey of the artist's work in American collections, edited by Andrew C. Ritchie. Westport, Conn., Greenwood Press [1972, c1945] 128 p. illus. 26 cm. Bibliography: p. 119-128. [NB553.M3B8 1972] 71-184839 ISBN 0-8371-6329-3 12.00
1. Maillol, Aristide Joseph Bonaventure, 1861-1944. 2. Sculpture, French—United States. I. Ritchie, Andrew Carnduff, ed.

Sculpture—Fresno, Calif.

FRESNO Mall Art Committee. 730'.973
Publicly owned art in Fresno, California. [Fresno, Calif., Fresno County and City Chamber of Commerce, 1973] 32 p. illus. 28 cm. Cover title. [NB235.F73F73] 73-160566
1. Sculpture—Fresno, Calif. 2. Mural painting and decoration—Fresno, Calif. I. Title.

Sculpture. German — Catalogs.

HARDING, Anneliese. 730'.943'074014
German sculpture in New England museums. Boston [Goethe Institute Boston] 1972. 95 p. illus. 28 cm. (Publications of the Goethe Institute Boston, 1) Bibliography: p. 89. [NB561.H35] 72-75439
1. Sculpture, German—Catalogs. 2. Sculpture, German—New England. I. Title. II. Series: Goethe Institute Boston. Publications, 1.

KUHN, Charles Louis. 730.943
German and Netherlandish sculpture, 1280-1800, the Harvard collections, by Charles L. kuhn Cambridge, Harvard University Press, 1965. xiv, 146 p. 1 mounted col. illus., 85 plates. 28 cm. Catalogue of works in the Fogg Art Museum and the Busch-Reisinger Museum at Harvard University. "Selected bibilography on German sculpture": p. 35-40. [NB625.K8] 65-19824
1. Sculpture. German — Catalogs. 2. Sculpture, Belgian — Catalogs. 3. Sculpture, Dutch — Catalogs. 4. Sculpture — Cambridge, Mass. — Catalogs. I. Harvard University. William Hayes Fogg Art Museum. II. Harvard University. Busch-Reisinger Museum of Germanic Culture. III. Title. BIP

Sculpture, Gothic.

BUSCH, Harald, 1904- ed. 734.25
Gothic sculpture. With an introd. by Hans Weigert. Edited by Harald Busch and Bernd Lohse. With commentaries on the illus. by Hans Weigert. [Translated by Peter Gorge] New York, Macmillan, 1963. xxiii p., illus., 201 plates (1 col.) 27 cm. (European sculpture) Legends in English and German. [NB180.B813] 63-14826
1. Sculpture, Gothic. I. Lohse, Bernd, joint ed. II. Series.

BUSCH, Harald, 1904- ed. 734.25
Renaissance sculpture. With an introd. by Hans Weigert; edited by Harald Busch and Bernd Lohse. With commentaries on the illus. by Hans Weigert. [Translated by Peter Gorge] New York, Macmillan, 1964. xxiii p., 224 p. of illus. 27 cm. (European sculpture) Translation of Europaische Plastik der Spatgotik und Renaissance. [NB180.B793] 64-11867
1. Sculpture, Gothic. 2. Sculpture, Renaissance. I. Lohse, Bernd, joint ed. II. Series.

FREEDEN, Max Hermann von, 1913- 734.25
Gothic sculpture, the intimate carvings. Photographed by F. L. Kenett. Greenwich, Conn., N. Y. Graphic [c.1962] xv p. 33 plates. 38cm. (Acanthus hist. of sculpture, v.3) 62-7573 8.95
1. Sculpture, Gothic. I. Title.

MULLER, Theodor, 1905- 735.21
Sculpture in the Netherlands, Germany, France, and Spain: 1400 to 1500; translated from the German by Elaine and William Robson Scott. Harmondsworth, Penguin, 1966. xxiv, 262 p. col. front., 192 plates, maps. 27 cm. (B 66-20656) (The Pelican history of art) In slip case. Bibliography: p. 227-234. [NB180.M82] 66-68067
1. Sculpture, Gothic. 2. Sculpture, Renaissance. I. Title. II. Series. BIP

Sculpture. Gothic — Catalogs.

LOS Angeles Co., Calif. Museum of Art, Los Angeles. 730'.74'017178
Gothic and Renaissance sculptures in the collection of the Los Angeles County Museum: catalogue and guide, by W. R. Valentiner. [Los Angeles] 1951. 184 p. illus. 26 cm. [NB25.L6] 67-4839
1. Sculpture. Gothic — Catalogs. 2. Sculture, Renaissance — Catalogs. 3. Sculpture — Los Angeles — Catalogs. I. Valentiner, Wilhelm Reinhold, 1880-1958. II. Title.

Sculpture, Gothic—Chartres, France.

MARRIAGE, Margaret S. 731'.82'094451
The sculptures of Chartres cathedral. Les sculptures de la cathedrale de Chartres. Text in English and French. Texte francais et anglais. By Margaret and Ernest Marriage. Freeport, N.Y., Books for Libraries Press [1973] p. Reprint of the 1909 ed. published by University Press, Cambridge. Bibliography: p. [NB551.C45M37 1973] 73-6598 ISBN 0-518-19061-7
1. Chartres, France. Notre-Dame (Cathedral) 2. Sculpture, Gothic—Chartres, France. 3. Sculpture—Chartres, France. I. Marriage, Ernest, joint author. II. Title.

Sculpture, Gothic—France.

SAUERLANDER, Willibald. 731'.88'20944
Gothic sculpture in France, 1140-1270. Translated by Janet Sondheimer. Photos. by Max Hirmer. New York, H. N. Abrams [1973, c1972] 527 p. illus. (part col.) 32 cm. Bibliography: p. 515-522. [NB543.S31413 1973] 76-160223 ISBN 0-8109-0147-1 50.00
1. Sculpture, Gothic—France. 2. Sculpture, French. I. Hirmer, Max, 1893- illus. II. Title.

SAUERLANDER, Willibald. 730'.944
Gothic sculpture in France 1140-1270; with photographs by Max Hirmer; translated [from the German] by Janet Sandheimer. London, Thames and Hudson, 1972. 527 p., chiefly illus. (some col.). map. 32 cm. Col. illus. tipped in. Translation of Gotische Skulptur in Frankreich, 1140-1270. Bibliography: p. 515-522. [NB543.S31413] 72-195546 ISBN 0-500-16017-1
1. Sculpture, Gothic—France. 2. Sculpture, French. I. Title.
Available from Abrams, 50.00.

Sculpture—Great Britain.

GARDNER, Arthur, 1878- 734.42
English medieval sculpture. The original handbook rev. and enl. Cambridge [Eng.] University Press, 1951. viii, 351 p. illus. 28 cm. First ed. published in 1935 under title: A handbook of English medieval sculpture. Bibliography: p. 345-346. [NB463.G27 1951] 51-14711
1. Sculpture—Gt. Brit. 2. Sculpture, Medieval. I. Title. BIP

STONE, Lawrence. 735.42
Sculpture in Britain: the Middle Ages. [Baltimore] Penguin Books [1955] xxi, 297p. illus., 192plates. 27cm. (The Pelican history of art, Z9) Bibliography: p. 271-279. [NB463.S8] 55-3485
1. Sculpture—Gt. Brit. 2. Sculpture, Medieval. I. Title. II. Series. BIP

STONE, Lawrence. 730'.942
Sculpture in Britain: the Middle Ages. [2d ed. Harmondsworth, Eng., Baltimore] Penguin Books [1972 i.e. 1973] xxii, 297 p. illus. 27 cm. (The Pelican history of art) Bibliography: p. 271-280. [NB463.S8 1972] 73-161595 ISBN 0-14-056009-2 35.00 (U.S.)

1. Sculpture—Great Britain. 2. Sculpture, Medieval—Great Britain. I. Title. II. Series.

Sculpture, Greco-Roman.

BIEBER, Margarete, 1879- 733
Ancient copies : contributions to the history of Greek and Roman art / Margarete Bieber. New York : New York University Press, 1977. xliv, 302 p., [81] leaves of plates : ill. ; 29 cm. Includes index. Bibliography: p. 275-282. [NB94.B47] 72-95529 ISBN 0-8147-0970-2 : 75.00
1. Sculpture, Greco-Roman. I. Title. BIP

VERMEULE, Cornelius Clarkson, 1925- 733
Greek sculpture and Roman taste : the purpose and setting of Graeco-Roman art in Italy and the Greek Imperial East / Cornelius C. Vermeule III. Ann Arbor : University of Michigan Press, c1977. xii, 137 p., [26] leaves of plates : ill. ; 27 cm. (Jerome lectures ; 12th ser.) Includes index. Bibliography: p. 115-121. [NB115.V47 1977] 77-5783 ISBN 0-472-08940-4 : 18.50
1. Sculpture, Greco-Roman. I. Title. II. Series. BIP

Sculpture—Greece—Hist.

BEAZLEY, John Davidson, Sir 1885- 709.38
Greek sculpture and painting to the end of the Hellenistic period. by J. D. Beazley. Bernard Ashmole. [New York] Cambridge [1966] xviii, 111p. 248 illus. 21cm. First pub. 1932. Bibl. [N5630.B35] 65-14355 7.50
1. Sculpture—Greece—Hist. 2. Vase-painting, Greek—Hist. 3. Painting, Greek—Hist. I. Ashmole, Bernard, 1894- II. Title.

Sculpture, Greek.

ANDERSON, Clarence William, 1891- 733'.3
The miracle of Greek sculpture, with forty-seven drawings, by C. W. Anderson. Introd. by Jean L. Keith. [1st ed.] New York, Dutton [1970] 112 p. illus. 26 cm. Bibliography: p. 112. [NB90.A5 1970] 69-13358 6.95
1. Sculpture, Greek. I. Title.

ASHMOLE, Bernard, 1894- 733'.3
Architect and sculptor in classical Greece. London, Phaidon Press, 1972. [6], 218 p. illus., maps, plans. 28 cm. (Wrightsman lectures; 6th) Includes bibliographical references. [NB94.A83] 73-152837 ISBN 0-7148-1551-9
1. Sculpture, Greek. 2. Olympia. Temple of Zeus. 3. Athens. Parthenon. 4. Halicarnassus. Mausoleum. I. Title. II. Series.
Distributed by New York Graphic 15.00. BIP

ASHMOLE, Bernard, 1894- 730'.922
The classical ideal in Greek sculpture. [Cincinnati] University of Cincinnati, 1964. 47, [36] p. plates, ports. 24 cm. (Lectures in memory of Louise Taft Semple) Bibliographical footnotes. [NB90.A8] 76-282980
1. Sculpture, Greek. 2. Classicism in art. I. Title. II. Series: Cincinnati. University. Lectures in memory of Louise Taft Semple

BARRON, John P. 733.3
Greek sculpture [London, Studio Vista [New York] Dutton [c.1965] 159p. illus., map. 19cm. (Vista pictureback, 11) [NB90.B35] 65-3450 1.75 pap.,
1. Sculpture, Greek. I. Title.

BIEBER, Margarete, 1879- 733'.3
Laocoon; the influence of the group since its rediscovery. Photos. by Ernest Nash. Rev., enl. ed. Detroit, Wayne State Univ. Pr., 1967. 41p. 39 illus. 24cm. Reprint of the 1942 ed. Bibl. [NB94.B48 1967] 67-16850 5.50
1. Sculpture, Greek. 2. Human figure in art. 3. Laocoon. I. Title.

BIEBER, Margarete, 1879- 733.3
The sculpture of the Hellenistic Age. Rev. ed. New York, Columbia [c.1955, 1961] xi, 259p. illus. 31cm. Bibl. 61-66470 27.00
1. Sculpture, Greek. I. Title.

BIEBER, Margarete, 1879- 733.3
The sculpture of the Hellenistic Age. New York, Columbia University Press, 1955. xi, 232p. 713 illus. 31cm. (Columbia bicentennial editions and studies) Bibliography: p.[177]-185. [NB90.B48] 54-57837
1. Sculpture, Greek. I. Title. II. Series.

BOARDMAN, John, 1927- 733'.3
Greek sculpture : the archaic period : a handbook / John Boardman. New York : Oxford University Press, 1978. 252 p. : ill. ; 22 cm. (World of art) Includes bibliographical references and index. [NB90.B62] 77-25202 ISBN 0-19-520046-2 : 12.95. ISBN 0-19-520047-0 pbk. : 6.95
1. Sculpture, Greek. I. Title. II. Series: The World of art.

CARPENTER, Rhys, 1889- 733.3
Greek sculpture, a critical review. [Chicago] University of Chicago Press [c.1960] xiv, 275p. Bibl.: p.255-265. illus., 47 plates. 25cm. 60-14233 6.95
1. Sculpture, Greek. I. Title. BIP

CARPENTER, Rhys, 1889- 733'.3
The sculpture of the Nike Temple parapet. With photos. by Bernard Ashmole. College Park, Md., McGrath Pub. Co., 1971. 83 p. illus. 24 cm. Reprint of the 1929 ed. published for the American School of Classical Studies at Athens. Bibliography: p. 83. [NB91.A7C3 1971] 78-119256 ISBN 0-8434-0126-5
1. Sculpture, Greek. 2. Athens. Temple of Athena Nike. I. American School of Classical Studies at Athens. II. Title.

CASSON, Stanley, 1889-1944. 733'.3
The technique of early Greek sculpture. New York, Hacker Art Books, 1970. xiii p., [1] l., 246 p. illus. 25 cm. Reprint of the 1933 ed. Bibliography: leaf [1]. [NB90.C3 1970] 72-116353 ISBN 0-87817-041-3
1. Sculpture, Greek. 2. Sculpture—Technique. I. Title. BIP

DEVAMBEZ, Pierre, 1902- 733.3
Greek sculpture. Photos. by Robert Descharnes selected and arr. by Sonja Knapp and Jean Imbert. [Tr. by Barbara M. Bell] New York, Tudor Pub. Co. [1961, c.1960] (unpaged) illus. (part mounted col.) 22cm. 61-1513 5.95
1. Sculpture, Greek. I. Descharnes, Robert. II. Title.

FURTWANGLER, Adolf, 1853-1907 733.3
Masterpieces of Greek sculpture; a series of essays on the history of art. [Tr. from German] Ed. by Al. N. Oikonomides. New, enl. ed. Chicago, Argonaut Pubs., 737 N. Michigan Ave., [c.]1964. xvi, 439p. illus., plates. 29cm. Bibl. 64-910 20.00
1. Sculpture, Greek. I. Title.

[GIALOURES, Nikolaos] 1917- 733.3
Classical Greece; the Elgin marbles of the Parthenon [by Nicholas Yalouris]. Photographed by F. L. Kenett. Greenwich, Conn., New York Graphic Society [c.1960] xv p. illus., 33 plates. 38cm. (The Acanthus history of sculpture) 60-10477 6.95 bds.,
1. Sculpture, Greek. 2. Athens, Parthenon. 3. Elgin marbles. I. Kenett, F. L. II. Title. III. Series.

HANFMANN, George Maxim Anossov, 1911- 733
Classical sculpture [by] George M. A. Hanfmann. Greenwich, Conn., New York Graphic Society [1967] 352 p. illus. (part col.), map. 25 cm. (A History of Western sculpture [v. 1]) Bibliography: p. 344-345. [NB85.H3] 67-11105
1. Sculpture, Greek. 2. Sculpture, Roman. I. Title. II. Series.

HARRISON, Evelyn Byrd. 938'.5 s
Archaic and archaistic sculpture / by Evelyn B. Harrison. Princeton, N.J. : American School of Classical Studies at Athens, 1965. xix, 192 p., [34] leaves of plates : ill. ; 32 cm. (The Athenian Agora ; v. 11) Includes indexes. Bibliography: p. [xiii]-xix. [DF287.A23A5 vol. 11] [NB90] 733'.3'09385 75-322659
1. Sculpture, Greek. 2. Athens. Agora. I. Title. II. Series: American School of Classical Studies at Athens. The Athenian Agora ; v. 11. BIP

LANGLOTZ, Ernst, 1895- 733.3
Ancient Greek sculpture of South Italy and Sicily. Photos. by Max Hirmer [Tr. from German by Audrey Hicks] New York, Abrams [1965] 312p. illus., col. plates, maps, plans. 31cm. Bibl. [NB91.18L33] 65-19227 25.00
1. Sculpture, Greek. 2. Sculpture—Italy, Southern. 3. Sculpture—Sicily. I. Hirmer, Max, illus. II. Title.

LULLIES, Reinhard, 1907- 733.3
Greek sculpture. Text and notes by Reinhard Lullies. Photos. by Max Hirmer. [Translated from the German by Michael Bullock. [Rev. ed.] New York, H. N. Abrams [1957] 88p. 264 plates (part col.) 31cm. Includes bibliography. [NB90.L813 1957] 57-4590
1. Sculpture, Greek. I. Hirmer Max. II. Title.

LULLIES, Reinhard, 1907- 733.3
Greek sculpture, Text and notes by Reinhard Lullies. Photos. by Max Hirmer. [Translated from the German by Michael Bullock. 2nd Rev. and enl. ed.] New York, H. N. Abrams [1960] 115p. (Bibl.: p.112-113 and bibl. notes in 'Notes on the plates' p.53-108) illus., 292 plates (part col.) plans 31cm. 60-10887 15.00
1. Sculpture, Greek. I. Hirmer, Max. II. Title.

NEW York. Metropolitan Museum of Art. 733.3
Catalogue of Greek sculptures [by] Gisela M. A. Richter. Cambridge, Published for the Museum by Harvard University Press, 1954. xviii, 123p. illus., 164 plates. 29cm. Includes bibliographical references. [NB90.N4] A 54
1. Sculpture, Greek. 2. Sculpture—New York (City)—Catalogs. I. Richter, Gisela Marie Augusta, 1882- II. Title.

PAYNE, Humfry, 1902-1936 733.3
Archaic marble sculpture from the Acropolis; a photographic catalogue, by Humfry Payne, Gerard Mackworth-Young. Introd. by Humfry Payne. New rev. [i.e.2d] ed. London, Cresset Pr. [dist. Chester Springs, Pa. Dufour, 1965] xiii, 79p. plates. 34cm. Bibl. [NB87.A8P3] 65-3850 12.50
1. Athens, Mouseion tes Akropoleos. 2. Sculpture, Greek. I. Young, Gerard Mackworth, 1884- II. Title.

RICHTER, Gisela Marie Augusta, 1882- 733'.3
Kouroi: archaic Greek youths: a study of the development of the Kouros type in Greek sculpture, by Gisela M. A. Richter; in collaboration with Irma A. Richter; photographs by Gerard Mackworth-Young. 3rd ed. London, New York, Phaidon, 1970. xvii, 365 p. illus. 32 cm. Revision of Kouroi, a study of the development of the Greek kouros from the late seventh to the early fifth century B.C., published in 1942. Distributed in the U.S. by Praeger Publishers. Includes bibliographical references. [NB94.R53 1970] 75-118660 ISBN 0-7148-1459-8 £9/-/-
1. Sculpture, Greek. 2. Human figure in art. I. Richter, Irma Anne. II. Title.

RICHTER, Gisela Marie Augusta, 1882- 733.3
The sculpture and sculptors of the Greeks. New rev. ed. New Haven, Yale University Press, 1950. xxxvi, 625 p. illus., plates, maps. 25 cm. At head of title: The Metropolitan Museum of Art. Bibliography: p. [309]-318. [NB90.R54 1950] 50-10289
1. Sculpture, Greek. 2. Sculptors, Greek. I. New York. Metropolitan Museum of Art. II. Title. BIP

RICHTER, Gisela Marie Augusta, 1882- 733'.3
The sculpture and sculptors of the Greeks, by Gisela M. A. Richter. 4th ed, newly rev. New Haven, Yale University Press, 1970. xvi, 317, [345] p. illus., maps. 29 cm. At head of title: The Metropolitan Museum of Art. Bibliography: p. [261]-270. "Illustrations": p. [1-345] p. (3d group) [NB90.R54 1970] 70-99838 35.00
1. Sculpture, Greek. 2. Sculptors, Greek. I. Title.

RICHTER, Gisela Marie Augusta, 1882- *730.938
Three critical periods in Greek sculpture. Oxford, Clarendon Press, 1951. ix, 86 p. plates. 29 cm. "Lectures delivered at the Dumbarton Oaks Research Library and Collection, Harvard University, 28, 30 March, and 1 April 1949." Includes bibliographies. [NB90.R55] 733.3 52-7629
1. Sculpture, Greek. I. Title.

RIDGWAY, Brunilde Sismondo, 1929- 733'.3
The archaic style in Greek sculpture / by Brunilde Sismondo Ridgway. Princeton, N.J. : Princeton University Press, [1976] p. cm. Includes bibliographies and index. [NB90.R56] 76-19655 ISBN 0-691-03920-8 : 40.00
1. Sculpture, Greek. I. Title. BIP

RIDGWAY, Brunilde Sismondo, 1929- 733'.3
The severe style in Greek sculpture. Princeton, N.J., Princeton University Press, 1970. xviii, 155, [67] p. plates. 29 cm. Includes bibliographical references. [NB90.R57] 77-113008 15.00
1. Sculpture, Greek. I. Title.

Sculpture, Greek—Antioch.

BRINKERHOFF, Dericksen M. 733
A collection of sculpture in classical and early Christian Antioch [by] Dericksen M. Brinkerhoff. New York, Published by New York University Press for the College Art Association of America, 1970. xi, 83 p. illus., ports. 29 cm. (Monographs on Archaeology and the fine arts, 22) Bibliography: p. [73]-83. [NB86.B85] 69-18278
1. Sculpture, Greek—Antioch. 2. Sculpture, Roman—Antioch. 3. Sculpture, Early Christian—Antioch. 4. Sculpture—Antioch. I. College Art Association of America. II. Title. III. Series. BIP

Sculpture, Greek—Catalogs.

CAMBRIDGE. University. Fitzwilliam Museum. 733
A catalogue of the Greek and Roman sculpture in the Fitzwilliam Museum, Cambridge, by Ludwig Budde and Richard Nicholls. Cambridge, Published for the Fitzwilliam Museum at the University Press, 1964. xix, [i], 138 p. 62 plates. 29 cm. Bibliographical references included in "Abbreviations" (p. xix-[xx]) [NB87.C18] 64-55365
1. Sculpture, Greek—Catalogs. 2. Sculpture, Roman—Catalogs. 3. Sculpture—Cambridge, Eng.—Catalogs. I. Budde, Ludwig. II. Nicholls, Richard. III. Title.

CHAMOUX, Francois. 733'.3
Ancient Greek sculpture from the museums of Athens. New York, New American Library [1968] 24 p. 32 col. plates. 17 cm. (A Mentor-Unesco art book) Includes bibliography. [NB90.C47] 79-3167 1.25
1. Sculpture, Greek—Catalogs. 2. Sculpture—Athens—Catalogs. I. Title.

RHODE Island School of Design, Providence. Museum of Art. 733'.074'01452
Classical sculpture, by Brunilde Sismondo Ridgway. [Providence, 1972] 244 p. illus. 28 cm. (Catalogue of the classical collection) Includes bibliographical references. [NB87.P76R457] 72-79496
1. Rhode Island School of Design, Providence. Museum of Art. 2. Sculpture, Greek—Catalogs. 3. Sculpture, Roman—Catalogs. 4. Sculpture—Providence—Catalogs. 5. Classicism in art. I. Ridgway, Brunilde Sismondo, 1929- II. Title.

SANTA Barbara, Calif. Museum of Art. 730'.922
The collection of Greek and Roman antiquities at the Santa Barbara Museum of Art [by] Mario A. Del Chiaro. [Santa Barbara, Calif., 1962] [32] p. illus. 15 x 24 cm. Cover title. [NB90.S24 1962] 75-309807
1. Santa Barbara, Calif. Museum of Art. 2. Sculpture, Greek—Catalogs. 3. Sculpture, Greco-Roman—Catalogs. 4. Sculpture—Santa Barbara, Calif.—Catalogs. 5. Vase-painting, Greek—Catalogs. 6. Vase-

painting—Santa Barbara, Calif.—Catalogs. I. Del Chiaro, Mario Aldo, 1925- II. Title.

Sculpture, Greek—History.

JONES, Henry Stuart, 1867- 1939, ed. 733.3
Select passages from ancient writers illustrative of the history of Greek sculpture, edited with a translation and notes by H. Stuart Jones. New enl. ed. with introd., bibliography, and index by Al N. Oikonomides. Chicago, Argonaut, 1966. xlvii, 265 p. 22 cm. Cover title: Ancient writers on Greek sculpture. Reprint of a work first published in 1895. Bibliography: p. [xli]-xlvii. [NB90.J7 1966] 65-26123
1. Sculpture, Greek—History. I. Oikonomides, Al N. II. Title. III. Title: Ancient writers on Greek sculpture.

MURRAY, Alexander Stuart, 1841-1904. 733'.3
A history of Greek sculpture. Rev. ed. Freeport, N.Y., Books for Libraries Press [1973] p. Reprint of the 1890 ed., published by J. Murray, London. [NB90.M92 1973] 73-6515 ISBN 0-518-19062-5
1. Sculpture, Greek—History. I. Title.

Sculpture, Greek—Influence.

LAWRENCE, Arnold Walter, 1900- 733'.3
Later Greek sculpture, and its influence on East and West, by A. W. Lawrence. New York, Hacker Art Books, 1969. xvii, 158 p. 112 plates. 29 cm. Reprint of the 1927 ed. Bibliography: p. 91-92. [NB90.L36 1969] 68-9005
1. Sculpture, Greek—Influence. I. Title.

Sculpture—Handbooks, manuals, etc.

COLEMAN, Ronald L. 731
Sculpture; a basic handbook for students [by] Ronald L. Coleman. Dubuque, Iowa, W. C. Brown [1968] x. 152p. illus. 29cm. Bibl. [NB1140.C6] 67-21317 7.50
1. Sculpture—Handbooks, manuals, etc. I. Title.

Sculpture—Hartford—Conservation and restoration.

MICHALCZYK, Casimer, 1914- 731.4'8
Restoration of the Genius of Connecticut. [Hartford] C.S.C.P.R.C., 1973. iii, 70 l. illus. 28 cm. Cover title. [NB1200.M52C66] 75-304012
1. Michalczyk, Casimer, 1914- 2. Rogers, Randolph, 1825-1892. Genius of Connecticut. 3. Sculpture—Hartford—Conservation and restoration. I. Connecticut State Capitol Preservation and Restoration Commission. II. Title.

Sculpture—Hatra, Mesopotamia.

INGHOLT, Harald, 1896- 595.78
Parthian sculptures from Hatr;' Orient and Hellas in art and religion. New Haven, The Academy, 1954. 55p. illus., map, plans, 32cm. (Memoirs of the Connecticut Academy of Arts & Science, vol. 12) Bibliographical footnotes. [Q11.C85 vol.12] 54-14655
1. Sculpture—Hatra, Mesopotamia. I. Title. II. Series: Connecticut Academy of Arts and Sciences, New Haven. Memoirs, v. 12

Sculpture—Hawaii—Catalogs.

RADFORD, Georgia. 735'.29'07409969
Sculpture in the sun : Hawaii's art for open spaces / Georgia and Warren Radford ; photos. by Rick Golt. Honolulu : University Press of Hawaii, 1977, c1978. xvii, 100 p. : ill. ; 29 cm. Bibliography: p. 99-100. [NB230.H3R32] 77-92972 ISBN 0-8248-0526-7 pbk. : 7.95
1. Sculpture—Hawaii—Catalogs. 2. Sculpture, Modern—20th century—Hawaii—Catalogs. 3. Environment (Art)—Hawaii—Catalogs. I. Radford, Warren, joint author. II. Golt, R. S. III. Title. BIP

Sculpture, Hawaiian.

COX, J. Halley, 1910- 732'.2'09969
Hawaiian sculpture / J. Halley Cox with William H. Davenport. Honolulu : University Press of Hawaii, [1974] ix, 198 p. : ill. ; 29 cm. Bibliography: p. 195-197. [NB1255.U6C68] 73-151453 ISBN 0-8248-0281-0 : 15.00
1. Sculpture, Hawaiian. 2. Wood-carving, Hawaiian. I. Davenport, William H., 1922- joint author. BIP

Sculpture, Hellenistic.

BROWN, Blanche R. 733'.3
Anticlassicism in Greek sculpture of the fourth century B.C. [by] Blanche R. Brown. New York, Published by New York University Press for the Archaeological Institute of America and the College Art Association of America, 1973. xv, 104 p. 103 illus. 29 cm. (Monographs on archaeology and the fine arts, 26) Bibliography: p. 69-87. [NB94.B76] 72-94082 ISBN 0-8147-0971-0
1. Sculpture, Hellenistic. I. Archaeological Institute of America. II. College Art Association of America. III. Title. IV. Series. BIP

DICKINS, Guy, 1881-1916. 733'.3
Hellenistic sculpture. With a pref. by Percy Gardner. Freeport, N.Y., Books for Libraries Press [1972] xiv, 99 p. illus. 24 cm. Reprint of the 1920 ed. Bibliography: p. [89]-94. [NB90.D5 1972] 72-37 ISBN 0-8369-9960-6
1. Sculpture, Hellenistic. I. Title.

DICKINS, Guy, 1881-1916. 733'.3
Hellenistic sculpture. With a pref. by Percy Gardner. College Park, Md., McGrath Pub. Co., 1971. xiv, 99 p. illus. 24 cm. Reprint of the 1920 ed. "Published works of the author": p. [89]-94. [NB94.D53 1971] 79-119259 ISBN 0-8434-0129-X
1. Sculpture, Hellenistic. I. Title.

Sculpture, Hellenistic—Taranto, Italy (City)

CARTER, Joseph Coleman. 733'.3'09377
The sculpture of Taras / Joseph Coleman Carter. Philadelphia : American Philosophical Society, 1975, c1976. 196 p. : ill. ; 30 cm. (Transactions of the American Philosophical Society ; new ser., v. 65, pt. 7 ISSN 0065-9746s) Includes index.IBibliography: p. 121-123..[NB91.T3C37].75-19514 ISBN 0-87169-657-6 : 18.00
1. Sculpture, Hellenistic—Taranto, Italy (City) 2. Sculpture—Taranto, Italy (City) 3. Taranto, Italy (City)—Antiquities. I. Title. II. Series: American Philosophical Society, Philadelphia. Transactions ; new ser., v. 65, pt. 7. BIP

Sculpture, Hindu.

HARLE, James C. 732'.4
Gupta sculpture : Indian sculpture of the fourth to the sixth centuries A.D. / J. C. Harle. Oxford [Eng.] : Clarendon Press, 1974. xii, 57 p., [40] leaves of plates : ill. ; 29 cm. Bibliography: p. [32]. [NB1002.H33] 75-306296 ISBN 0-19-817322-9 : 19.25
1. Gupta dynasty. 2. Sculpture, Hindu. I. Title.
Distributed by Oxford University Press New York. BIP

Sculpture—History.

ALLEN, Agnes. 730.9
The story of sculpture. Illustrated by Jack Allen. New York, Roy Publishers [1958?] 208p. illus. 21cm. [NB60.A55] 58-5089
1. Sculpture—Hist. I. Title. BIP

AUERBACH, Arnold, 1898- 730.9
A brief history of sculpture. New York, Studio Publications [c1952] 111p. illus. 23cm. First published in London in 1952 under title: Sculpture, a history in brief. [NB60] 53-13485
1. Sculpture—Hist. I. Title.

KOEPF, Hans 730.9
Masterpieces of sculpture from the Greeks to modern times. Ed. by J. E. Schuler. [Tr. from German by Mervyn Savill] New York, Putnam [1966] 92, 108p. illus. (pt. col.) 31cm. [NB60.K613] 66-11339 25.00
1. Sculpture—Hist. I. Title.

KOEPF, Hans. 730.9
Masterpieces of sculpture from the Greeks to modern times. Edited by J. E. Schuler. [Translated from the German by Mervyn Savill] New York, Putnam [1966] 92, 108 p. illus. (part col.) 31 cm. [NB60.K613] 66-11339
1. Sculpture—Hist. I. Title.

PLATTE, Hans. 709'.04'0740153
Plastik. Hamburg, Standard- Verlag [c1957] 1 v. (chiefly plates) 22cm. (Die Kunst des 20. Jahrhunderts) [NB198.P5] 58-22602
1. Sculpture—Hist. 2. Art—Hist.—20th cent. I. Title.

Sculpture—History—20th century.

BERCKELAERS, Ferdinand Louis 730.904
The sculpture of this century [by] Michel Seuphor [pseud. Translated from the French by Haakon Chevalier[New York, G. Braziller. 1960 372p. (3p. bibl.) illus., ports. 24cm. 60-7807 15.00
1. Sculpture—Hist.— 20th cent. I. Title.

GIEDION-WELCKER, Carola 730.904
Contemporary sculpture, an evolution in volume and space. Rev. and enl. ed. New York, G. Wittenborn [1961, c.1960] xxxi, 400 p. illus. 26 cm. (Documents of modern art, v.12) 60-15444 16.50
1. Sculpture—Hist.—20th cent. 2. Sculptors. I. Title. II. Series.

TRIER, Eduard 735.29
Form and space; sculpture of the twentieth century. [Tr. from German by C. Ligota] New York, Praeger [1962, c.1960, 1961] 291p. illus. (pt. col., pt. mounted) 29cm. 62-8371 15.00
1. Sculpture—Hist.—20th cent. I. Title.

Sculpture—History—Juvenile literature.

HAGGAR, Reginald George, 1905- 730.9
Sculpture through the ages. Illus. by the author. New York, Roy [1962, c.1960] 80p. 61-12925 3.25 bds.,
1. Sculpture—Hist.—Juvenile literature. I. Title.

Sculpture—History—Outlines, syllabi, etc.

GAUNT, William 730
The observer's book of sculpture. London, New York, Warne [1966] xii, 132p. 64 plates (incl. 8 col.) maps. 15cm. (Observer's pocket ser. no. 37) Tables on endpapers. [NB61.G3] 66-15684 1.50 bds.,
1. Sculpture—Hist.—Outlines, syllabi, etc. I. Title. II. Series.

JANNEAU, Guillaume, 1887- 730'.9
An introduction to sculpture, from its origins to today, by Guillaume Janneau and Simone Hoog. New York, Golden Press [1970] 240 p. illus. (part col.) 15 cm. (A Golden art guide) On spine: Sculpture, from its origins to today. [NB60.J313] 76-119565 1.95
1. Sculpture—History—Outlines, syllali, etc. I. Hoog, Simone, joint author. II. Title. III. Title: Sculpture, from its origins to today.

Sculpture—Indexes.

CLAPP, Jane. 730'.16
Sculpture index. Metuchen, N.J., Scarecrow Press, 1970 [c1970-71] 2 v. in 3. 22 cm. Contents.Contents.—v. 1. Sculpture of Europe and the contemporary Middle East.—v. 2. Sculpture of the Americas, the Orient, Africa, the Pacific area, and the classical world. 2 v. [NB36.C55] 79-9538 ISBN 0-8108-0249-X (v. 1)
1. Sculpture—Indexes. I. Title. BIP

Sculpture. India.

BARRETT. DOUGLAS. E. 732.4
Farly Cola bronzes [by] Douglas Barrett. [1st ed.] Bombay. Bhulabhai Memorial Inst. 1965. viii. 46p. 102 plates. 35cm. Bibl. [NB1002.B37] SA65 15.00
1. Sculpture. India. 2. Bronzes. India. I. Title.
Available from Wittenborn in New York.

Sculpture, Indic.

BACHHOFER, Ludwig, 1894- 732'.4
Early Indian sculpture. New York, Hacker Art Books, 1972. 2 v. in 1. 161 plates. 32 cm. Reprint of the 1929 ed. Bibliography: p. 125-128. [NB1002.B3 1972] 79-143338 ISBN 0-87817-058-8 50.00
1. Sculpture, Indic. 2. Sculpture, Buddhist—India. I. Title. BIP

FORMAN, Werner. 730'.954
Indian sculpture: masterpieces of Indian, Khmer and Cham art, photographs by W. and B. Forman; text by Marguerite-Marie Deneck [translated from the French by Iris Urwin] Revised ed. London, New York, Hamlyn, 1970. 3-35 p., 238 plates (4 fold.). illus. (some col.) 34 cm. Bibliography: p. [33] [NB1002.F573 1970] 79-861329 ISBN 0-600-02006-1 £3.15
1. Sculpture, Indic. 2. Sculpture, Khmer. 3. Sculpture, Cham. I. Forman, Bedrich. II. Deneck, Marguerite Marie. III. Title.

KRAMRISCH, Stella, 1898- 730
Indian sculpture in the Philadelphia Museum of Art. Philadelphia Univ. of Pa. Pr. [1961, c.1960] 183p. plates (part col.) 32cm. 60-14837 8.00
1. Sculpture, Indic. I. Philadelphia Museum of Art. II. Title. BIP

LANNOY, Richard. 732'.4
The eye of love : in the temple sculpture of India / Richard Lannoy ; with drawings by Harry Baines. New York : Grove Press : distributed by Random House, 1977, c1976 160 p. : ill. ; 24 cm. Bibliography: p. [159]-160. [NB1002.L34] 76-54403 ISBN 0-8021-0137-2 : 12.50
1. Sculpture, Indic. 2. Erotica. 3. Temples—India. I. Title.

LIPPE, Aschwin. 732'.4
The Freer Indian sculptures. Washington, Smithsonian Institution, 1970. xv, 54 p. map, 55 plates (part col.) 31 cm. (Freer Gallery of Art. Oriental studies no. 8) Bibliography: p. 47-49. [NB1002.L56] 71-609901
1. Sculpture, Indic. 2. Sculpture, Hindu. 3. Sculpture, Buddhist—India. I. Freer Gallery of Art, Washington, D.C. II. Title. III. Series: Freer Gallery of Art, Washington, D.C. Oriental studies, no. 8 BIP

RAWSON. PHILIP S. 730.954
Indian sculpture. by Philip Rawson. London. Studio Vista: New York. Dutton. 1966. 160p. front., illus. Bibl. [NB1001.R38] 66-77651 1.95 pap.,
1. Sculpture, Indic. I. Title.

SAHAI, Bhagwant, 1929- 732'.4
Iconography of minor Hindu and Buddhist deities / Bhagwant Sahai. New Delhi : Abhinav Publications, 1975. xiii, 295 p., [14] leaves of plates : ill. ; 25 cm. Running title: Iconography of some important minor Hindu and Buddhist deities. "The present work ... embodies in the main the thesis approved for the degree of Ph.D. by the University of Patna in 1965." Includes index. Bibliography: p. [263]-274. [NB1002.S24] 75-904218 ISBN 0-88386-610-2 : 24.00
1. Sculpture, Indic. 2. Gods, Hindu, in art. 3. Gods, Buddhist, in art. I. Title. II. Title: Iconography of some important minor Hindu and Buddhist deities.
Distributed by South Asia Books. BIP

Sculpture, Indic—Exhibitions.

ANCIENT sculpture from India; a catalog of the exhibition: the M. H. deYoung Memorial Museum, San 730.954

Francisco, May 29-July 19, 1964; Seattle Art Museum Pavilion, August 14-October 4, 1964; the Cleveland Museum of Art, November 25-January 3, 1965; the Metropolitan Museum of Art, New York, February 9-March 21, 1965; the Honolulu Academy of Arts, May 13-June 27, 1965. [Cleveland] Cleveland Museum of Art [1964] [143] p. illus., maps. 23 cm. Introduction by Sherman E. Lee. Bibliography: p. [23] [NB1002.A53] 64-20469
1. Sculpture, Indic—Exhibitions. I. Lee, Sherman E. II. De Young Memorial Museum, San Francisco. III. Cleveland Museum of Art.

CATALOG of an exhibition 730'.954 *of sculpture of India and Thailand.* Lawrence University, Appleton, Wisconsin, Sept. 18-Oct. 27, 1968. [Appleton, Wis., Lawrence University, 1968] 51 p. illus. (part col.) 23 cm. Cover title. Pages 50-51, blank. Contents.Contents.—Part 1: Sculpture of India from the collection of Jack Turner Wilson.—Part 2: Sculpture of Thailand from the collection of John Adams Thierry. Includes bibliographies. [NB1000.C3] 73-729
1. Wilson, Jack Turner—Art collections. 2. Thierry, John Adams, 1913—Art collections. 3. Sculpture, Indic—Exhibitions. 4. Sculpture, Thai—Exhibitions. I. Lawrence University.

LEFEBVRE d'Argence, 730'.959
Rene Yvon.
Indian and South-east Asian stone sculptures from the Avery Brundage Collection [by] Rene-Yvon Lefebvre d'Argence and Terese Tse. [Pasadena, Calif., Pasadena Art Museum, 1969] 116 p. illus. (part col.), map. 23 cm. Catalogue of an exhibition shown at Pasadena Art Museum, Nov. 22, 1969-Feb. 1, 1970 and at four other museums, Feb. 26-Dec. 31, 1970. Bibliography: p. 115-116. [NB1000.L4] 70-93704
1. Brundage, Avery—Art collections. 2. Sculpture, Indic—Exhibitions. 3. Sculpture—Asia, Southeastern—Exhibitions. I. Tse, Terese, joint author. II. Pasadena, Calif. Art Museum. III. Title.

LERNER, Martin. 732'.4
Images of divinity; sculpture from India, Nepal, Thailand, and Cambodia. Selections from the Norton Simon, Inc. Museum of Art and the Norton Simon Foundation. Introd. and catalogue by Martin Lerner. Photographs by Lee Boltin. Foreword by Thomas Hoving. Statement by Norton Simon. [New York] Metropolitan Museum of Art [1974] p. cm. Catalog of an exhibition held at the Metropolitan Museum of Art. [NB1002.L47] 74-989 ISBN 0-87099-088-8
1. Sculpture, Indic—Exhibitions. 2. Sculpture, Nepali—Exhibitions. 3. Sculpture, Thai—Exhibitions. 4. Sculpture, Khmer—Exhibitions. 5. Gods in art. I. Norton Simon, Inc. Museum of Art. II. Norton Simon Foundation. III. New York (City). Metropolitan Museum of Art. IV. Title.

MINNESOTA. University. 730'.954
University Gallery.
Art of India: sculpture and miniature paintings. [Catalogue of the exhibition] June 23-Aug. 23, 1969. Minneapolis [1969] 52 p. illus. 28 cm. [N7302.M5] 72-633833
1. Sculpture, Indic—Exhibitions. 2. Miniature paintings, Indic—Exhibitions. I. Title.

Sculpture, Italian.

CRAWFORD, David 730'.945
Alexander Edward Lindsay, 27th Earl of, 1871-1940.
The evolution of Italian sculpture, by Lord Balcarres. New York, B. Franklin Reprints [1973] xiv, 348 p. illus. 23 cm. (Burt Franklin research & source works series. Art history and reference series, 44) Reprint of the 1909 ed. published by J. Murray, London. Includes bibliographical references. [NB611.C8 1973] 72-81977 ISBN 0-8337-0730-2
1. Sculpture, Italian. I. Title. **BIP**

HASELOFF, Arthur Erich 730'.945
George, 1872-1955.
Pre-Romanesque sculpture in Italy. [Translated from the German by Ronald Boothroyd] New York, Hacker Art Books, 1971. x, 85 p., 80 plates. 32 cm. Reprint of the 1930 ed. Translation of Die Vorromanische Plastik in Italien. Bibliography: p. 73-77. [NB613.H313 1971] 70-116355 ISBN 0-87817-043-X
1. Sculpture, Italian. 2. Sculpture, Medieval—Italy. I. Title.

MACLAGAN, Eric Robert 730.9'45
Dalrymple, 1879-1951.
Italian sculpture of the Renaissance. Westport, Conn., Greenwood Press [1971, c1963] xii, 277 p. illus. 23 cm. (The Charles Eliot Norton lectures, 1927-1928) [NB615.M3 1971] 70-110272 ISBN 0-8371-4498-1
1. Sculpture, Italian. 2. Sculpture, Renaissance—Italy. 3. Sculptors—Italy. I. Title. II. Series. **BIP**

POPE-HENNESSY, John, 730.945
1913-
An introduction to Italian sculpture [pt. 3] 3v. Phaidon, dist. Greenwich, Conn., N.Y. Graphic [c.] 1963. 3v. (various p.) illus. 29cm. Contents.Pt. 3, [v. 1]Italian High Renaissance and Baroque sculpture; text: Pt. 3 [v.2] Plates: Pt. 3 [v.3] Catalogue volume. Bibl. A56 12.50 ea.,
1. Sculpture, Italian. I. Title. II. Title: Italian High Renaissance and Baroque sculpture.

POPE-HENNESSY, John 730'.945
Wyndham 1913-
Essays on Italian sculpture, [by] John Pope-Hennessy. London, New York, Phaidon, 1968. ix, 243 p. illus. 26 cm. Distributors in the U.S.A.: Frederick A. Praeger, New York. Bibliographical references included in "Notes" (p. 212-230) [NB611.P58] 68-18906 ISBN 0-7148-1327-3
1. Sculpture, Italian. 2. Bronzes, Italian. I. Title.

POPE-HENNESSY, John 730'.945
Wyndham, Sir, 1913-
An introduction to Italian sculpture [by] John Pope-Hennessy. 2nd ed. London, New York, Phaidon, 1970-72. 3 v. illus. 29 cm. Contents.Contents.—pt. 1. Italian Gothic sculpture.—pt. 2. Italian Renaissance sculpture.—pt. 3. Italian High Renaissance and Baroque scuplture. [NB614.P6] 71-588143 ISBN 0-7148-1465-2 (pt. 1) £26.50
1. Sculpture, Italian. I. Title.

SALVINI, Roberto 730.945
Modern Italian sculpture. New York, Abrams, [1962] 52p. illus. (pt. col.) 37cm. 62-19130 20.00
1. Sculpture, Italian. I. Title.

Sculpture, Italian—History.

SEYMOUR, Charles, 1912- 730.945
Sculpture in Italy: 1400-1500. Harmondsworth, Penguin, 1966. xxvi, 295 p. col. front., illus., 160 plates, maps, plans, tables, diagrs. 26 1/2 cm. (Pelican history of art) £5/5/- In slip case. Bibliography: p. 253-278. [NB615.S45] 66-73887
1. Sculpture, Italian—Hist. I. Title. II. Series.

SUMMERS, John David. 730'.92'4
The sculpture of Vincenzo Danti : a study in the influence of Michelangelo and the ideals of the Maniera / John David Summers. New York : Garland, 1979, c1970. p. cm. (Outstanding dissertations in the fine arts) Originally presented as the author's thesis, Yale University, 1969. Bibliography: p. [NB623.D35S9 1979] 77-94718 ISBN 0-8240-3252-7 : 50.00
1. Danti, Vincenzo, 1530-1576. 2. Buonarroti, Michel Angelo, 1475-1564—Influence. 3. Mannerism (Art)—Influence. I. Title. II. Series. **BIP**

Sculpture, Italian—History.

GODFREY, Frederick M. 730'.945
Italian sculpture, 1250-1700 [by] F. M. Godfrey. [1st ed.] New York, Taplinger Pub. Co., 1967. vi, 332 p. illus. 22 cm. Bibliography: p. 309-310. [NB614.G6 1967] 67-19693
1. Sculpture, Italian—History. I. Title. **BIP**

1200 years of Italian 730'.945 *sculpture.* Texts by Rossana Bossaglia and others Photos. by Bruno Balestrine. New York, H. N. Abrams [1973] 455 p. illus. (part col.) 35 cm. [NB611.T93] 70-149858 ISBN 0-8109-0204-4 45.00
1. Sculpture, Italian—History. I. Balestrini, Bruno, illus. II. Title: Italian sculpture. Contents omitted.

Sculpture, Jaina.

BHATTACHARYA, Brindavan 732'.4
Chandra, 1893-
The Jaina iconography / B. C. Bhattacharya ; foreword by B. N. Sharma. 2d rev. ed. Delhi : Motilal Banarsidass, 1974. xi, 171 p., [27] leaves of plates : ill. ; 23 cm. Includes quotations in Sanskrit and index. Bibliography: p. [145]-164. [NB1002.B47 1974] 75-900652 21.00
1. Sculpture, Jaina. 2. Gods in art. I. Title. Distributed by Verry **BIP**

Sculpture. Japanese.

"BUNRAKU Kashira no 791.5
Meisaku" Kankokai.
Masterpieces of Japanese puppetry, sculptured heads of the Bunraku Theater. Edited for the Society for the Publication of "Bunraku Puppet-head Masterpieces" by Saito Seijiro, Yamaguchi Hiroichi [and] Yoshinaga Takao. English adaption by Roy Andrew Miller. [1st ed.] Rutland, Vt., C. E. Tuttle Co. [1958] 91 p. illus., 32 col. plates. 37 cm. Translation of Bunraku kashira no meisaku. "Special limited edition of 375 copies... No. 316." [NB1050.B8] 58-7493
1. Sculpture, Japanese. 2. Wood-carving, Japanese. 3. Puppets and puppet-plays—History and criticism. 4. Theater—Japan. I. Saito, Seijiro, 1894- ed. II. Title.

HAGANO, Taizo 730.952
Ancient sculpture of Japan. Photographs by Taizo Nagano; Japanese text by Narashige Matsumoto; Eng. tr. by Tetsuo Kishi; English advice by Dennis Keene; book design by Susumu Masunaka. Mitsumura Suiko Shoin [dist. New York, Perkins Oriental,] c.1963. unpaged. chiefly illus., maps. 20x22cm. J63 7.50
I. Matsumoto, Narashige. II. Title. III. Title: Ancient sculpture of Japan.

MASTERPIECES of Japanese 730.952 *sculpture* Photographed by Yasukichi Irie [others] Introd., text, commentaries by J. Edward Kidder, Jr. Rutland, Vt., Tuttle [c.1961] xvi, 328p. 199 plates (pt. col.) 34cm. Bibl. 61-12426 27.50
1. Sculpture, Japanese. I. Irie, Taikichi, 1905- II. Kidder, Jonathan Edward.

SAUNDERS, Ernest Dale, 730.952
1919-
Mudra; a study of symbolic gestures in Japanese Buddhist sculpture. [New York] Pantheon Books [1960] xxiii, 296p. illus., 26 plates.26cm. (Bollingen series, 58) Bibliography: p. 265-278. [NB1050.S3] 59-13518
1. Sculpture. Japanese. 2. Art, Buddhist. 3. Symbolism in art. 4. Buddha and Buddhism—Rituals. I. Title. II. Series. **BIP**

*WARNER, Langdon. 732.'7
The craft of the Japanese sculptor / by Langdon Warner. New York : Hacker Art Books, 1976. 55p., remainder unpaged : ill. ; 29 cm. Reprint of edition first published in 1936. [NB1052] 75-11049 lib. bdg. : 30.00
1. Sculpture, Japanese. I. Title. **BIP**

WARNER, Langdon, 1881- 730.952
1955.
Japanese sculpture of the Tempyo period; masterpieces of the eighth century. Edited and arr. by James Marshall Plumer. Cambridge, Harvard University Press [1959] xix, 165 p. illus., port., maps. 28 cm. and portfolio (217 plates) 12 cm. Bibliography: p. 155-156. [NB1053.W32] 58-12976
1. Sculpture, Japanese. 2. Art, Buddhist. I. Title.

WARNER, Langdon, 1881- 730.952
1955.
Japanese sculpture of the Tempyo period; masterpieces of the eighth century. Edited and arr. by James Marshall Plumer. [One-volume ed.] Cambridge, Mass., Harvard University Press [1964] xix, 165 p., A-B, 217 p. of illus. maps, ports. 30 cm. Bibliography: p. 155-156. [NB1053.W32] 64-23111
1. Sculpture, Japanese. 2. Art, Buddhist. I. Title. **BIP**

WATSON, William 730.952
Sculpture of Japan, from the fifth to the fifteenth century. New York, Viking Press [1960] 216p. bBibliography: p.216. plates. 38cm. (A Studio book) 60-910 15.00
1. Sculpture, Japanese. 2. Art, Buddhist. I. Title.

Sculpture, Japanese—Kamakura-Momoyama periods, 1185-1600.

MORI, Hisashi, 1916- 732'.7
Sculpture of the Kamakura period. Translated by Katherine Eickmann. [1st English ed.] New York, Weatherhill [1974] 174 p. illus. (part col.) 23 cm. (The Heibonsha survey of Japanese art, v. 11) Translation of Unkei to Kamakura chokoku. [NB1053.4.M6713 1974] 73-88470 ISBN 0-8348-1017-4 10.00
1. Sculpture, Japanese—Kamakura-Momoyama periods, 1185-1600. I. Title.

Sculpture—Juvenile literature.

HILLYER, Virgil Mores, 730.9
1875-1931.
Sculpture, by V. M. Hillyer and E. G. Huey. New ed. designed and rev. by Childrens Press, Chicago. Consultants: Ruth Esserman [and] Everett Saunders. New York, Meredith Press [1966] 126 p. illus. (part col.) 29 cm. (Young people's story of our heritage) Cover title: Young people's story of sculpture. Originally published as a part of the author's A child's history of art. [NB1143.H5] 66-11325
1. Sculpture—Juvenile literature. I. Huey, Edward Greene, 1899- joint author. II. Childrens Press, inc., Chicago. III. Title. IV. Title: Young people's story of sculpture.

LEYH, Elizabeth. 731.4
Children make sculpture. New York, Van Nostrand Reinhold [1972] 96 p. illus. 22 x 26 cm. Describes the use of cardboard, twigs, pebbles, wire, styrofoam, paper, wood, junk, plaster, and clay in making various kinds of sculpture. Also includes a section on carving. [NB1143.L4] 70-155438 ISBN 0-442-04771-1
1. Sculpture—Juvenile literature. 2. Modeling—Juvenile literature. I. Title. **BIP**

MOORE, Lamont 730
The sculptured image; the art of sculpture as seen in monuments to gods, men, and ideas. New York, Watts [1967] viii, 100p. illus. 23cm. [NB1143.M6] 67-17511 2.65
1. Sculpture—Juvenile literature. I. Title.

NAYLOR, Penelope. 730
Sculpture: the shapes of belief. New York, F. Watts [1971] 89 p. illus. 23 cm. (A First book) Bibliography: p. 86-87. Describes the history, significance, and variety of sculpture from ancient times to the present. [NB1143.N3] 76-161070 ISBN 0-531-00752-9
1. Sculpture—Juvenile literature. 2. Art and religion. I. Title.

PAINE, Roberta M. 730
Looking at sculpture [by] Roberta M. Paine. New York, Lothrop, Lee & Shepard [1968] 128 p. illus., map, ports. 29 cm. Bibliography: p. 125. [NB1143.P3] 68-27710 4.95
1. Sculpture—Juvenile literature. I. Title.

RIEGER, Shay. 731.4'56
The bronze zoo. New York, Scribner [1970] [48] p. illus. 27 cm. A sculptor describes the sketching, clay and plaster modeling, and casting processes she used in making eight bronze animals for outdoor parks. [NB1143.R5] 79-106532 3.95
1. Sculpture—Juvenile literature. I. Title.

Sculpture, Khmer.

GITEAU, Madeleine 730.9596
Khmer sculpture and the Angkor civilization. [Tr. from French by Diana Imber] New York, Abrams [1966, c.1965]

301p. illus., map, plans. 24 col. plates. 30cm. Bibl. [NB1015.G5413] 66-10991 25.00
1. Sculpture, Khmer. 2. Khmers. I. Title.

Sculpture, Khmer—Catalogs.

LEE, Sherman E. 732'.4
Ancient Cambodian sculpture [by] Sherman E. Lee. [Photos. by Otto E. Nelson] New York, Intercultural Arts Press [1970- 1 v. (loose leaf) map, 23 col. slides (film, 2 x 2 in.) 30 cm. At head of title: Asia House Gallery. The slides are in pockets in 2 transparent leaves. Slide lecture based on the author's Ancient Cambodian sculpture, catalog of an exhibition shown in the Asia House Gallery in the fall of 1969. Includes bibliography. [NB1015.L42] 73-23458 25.00
1. Sculpture, Khmer—Catalogs. I. Asia House Gallery, New York. II. Title.

Sculpture, Khmer—Exhibitions.

ASIA House Gallery, New York. 730.9596
Khmer sculpture; [with a critical essay by Ad Reinhardt], and a partial account by Chou Ta-kuan of his travels to the city of Angkor in 1296 A. D. New York, c1961] 64p. illus. 21cm. Catalogue of an exhibition. Bibliography: p. 62. [NB1015.A8] 62-4365
1. Sculpture, Khmer—Exhibitions. 2. Cambodia—Soc. life a cust. I. Chou. Ta-kuan, flaulim. Recollections on the customs of Cambodia. II. Title.

LEE, Sherman E. 732'.4
Ancient Cambodian sculpture [by] Sherman E. Lee. [New York] Asia Society; distributed by New York Graphic Society [1969] 115 p. illus. (part col.), map. 27 cm. "An Asia House Gallery publication." Catalog of an exhibition selected by Sherman E. Lee, and shown in the Asia House Gallery in the fall of 1969 as an activity of the Asia Society. Bibliography: p. 114-115. [NB1015.L4] 79-86374
1. Sculpture, Khmer—Exhibitions. I. Asia House Gallery, New York. II. Title.

Sculpture—Life.

WILLETT, Frank 732'.2'096692
Life in the history of West African sculpture, New York McGraw [1967] 232p. illus. (pt. col.) maps. 26 cm. (New aspects of archaeology) [NB1097.W4W5 1967b] 67-141515 9.95
1. Sculpture—Life. 2. Sculpture, Primitive. I. Title. II. Series.

Sculpture, Makonde (Bantu tribe)

KORN, Jorn. 732'.2'0967823
Modern Makonde art / [by] Jorn Korn ; with photographs by Jesper Kirknaes. London ; New York : Hamlyn, 1974. 95 p. : ill. (some col.), ports. ; 30 cm. Bibliography: p. 94. [NB1255.A4K67] 75-312168 ISBN 0-600-36171-3 : £2.50
1. Sculpture, Makonde (Bantu tribe) 2. Sculpture—Africa, East. 3. Wood-carving—Africa, East. 4. Sculptors—Africa, East. I. Kirknas, Jesper, 1943- II. Title.

Sculpture, Makonde (Bantu tribe)—Exhibitions.

OLSON, Gordon L. 732'.2'0967825074017456
Spirits in ebony : woodcarvings of the African Makonde : [exhibition] / narrative by Gordon L. Olson ; layout and cover design by Carl Ulanowicz. [Grand Rapids : Grand Rapids Public Museum, 1977, c1976] 26 p. : ill. ; 28 cm. (Grand Rapids Public Museum publication ; no. 2) Includes bibliographical references. [NB1255.A42O47 1977] 77-361608
1. Sculpture, Makonde (Bantu tribe)—Exhibitions. 2. Sculpture—Africa, East—Exhibitions. 3. Wood-carving—Africa, East—Exhibitions. I. Grand Rapids Public Museum. II. Title. III. Series: Grand Rapids Public Museum. Grand Rapids Public Museum publication ; no. 2.

Sculpture, Medieval.

SALVINI, Roberto. 734
Medieval sculpture. Greenwich, Conn., New York Graphic Society [1970, c1969] 368 p. illus., col. plates. 25 cm. (A History of Western sculpture) Translation from the Italian. Bibliography: p. 361-367. [NB170.S213] 68-12365 13.50
1. Sculpture, Medieval. I. Title. II. Series.

SHERIDAN, Ronald. 731'.88'9
Gargoyles and grotesques : paganism in the medieval church / Ronald Sheridan and Anne Ross. Boston : New York Graphic Society, 1975. 127 p. : ill. ; 29 cm. Includes index. Bibliography: p. 125. [NB170.S47 1975b] 74-21494 ISBN 0-8212-0644-3 : 14.95
1. Sculpture, Medieval. 2. Paganism in art. 3. Church decoration and ornament. I. Ross, Anne, Ph.D., joint author. II. Title.
BIP

Sculpture, Medieval—Exhibitions.

STODDARD, Brooks W. 734'.074'014191
The medieval sculptor; [exhibition catalogue, by Brooks W. Stoddard. Brunswick, Me.] Bowdoin College, Museum of Art, 1971. [30] p. illus. 21 cm. [NB170.S8] 70-288271
1. Sculpture, Medieval—Exhibitions. I. Bowdoin College. Museum of Art. II. Title.

Sculpture, Medieval—India.

DE LIPPE, Aschwin. 732'.4
Indian medieval sculpture / Aschwin De Lippe. Amsterdam ; New York : North-Holland Pub. Co. ; New York : distributors for the U.S.A., Elsevier-Holland, c1978. p. cm. Includes index. Bibliography: p. [NB1002.D45] 77-18869 ISBN 0-444-85086-4 : 63.00
1. Sculpture, Medieval—India. 2. Sculpture, Indic. I. Title.
BIP

Sculpture — Mexico.

WEISMANN, Elizabeth (Wilder) 1908- 730.972
Mexico in sculpture, 1521-1821 Cambridge, Harvard University Press, 1950. 224 p. illus. 27 cm. Bibliography: p. 220-222. [NB253.W4] 50-10816
1. Sculpture — Mexico. I. Title.

WEISMANN, Elizabeth (Wilder) 1908- 730'.972
Mexico in sculpture, 1521-1821. Westport, Conn., Greenwood Press [1971, c1950] 226 p. illus. 27 cm. Reprint ed. includes additions to the bibliography. Bibliography: p. 220-224. [NB253.W4 1971] 75-95137 ISBN 0-8371-2530-8
1. Sculpture—Mexico. I. Title.

WESTHEIM, Paul 732
The sculpture of ancient Mexico. La esculture del Mexico antiguo. Tr. from Spanish into English by Ursula Bernard. Tr. into Spanish from the orig. German by Mariana Frenk [Gloucester, Mass., P. Smith, c.1963] various p. illus. 19cm. (Anchor bk. A335 rebound) Bibl. 3.50
1. Sculpture—Mexico. 2. Indians of Mexico—Art. 3. Mexico—Antiq. I. Title.

WESTHEIM, Paul. 732
The sculpture of ancient Mexico. La escultura del Mexico antiguo. Translated from Spanish into English by Ursula Bernard; translated into Spanish from the original German by Mariana Frank. [1st ed. in the United States of America] Garden City, N.Y., Doubleday, 1963. 69 p., 96 illus. 19 cm. (Anchor books, A335) [F1219.3.A7W43] 63-7697
1. Sculpture — Mexico. 2. Indians of Mexico — Art. 3. Mexico — Antiq. I. Title.

Sculpture, Modern—19th century.

DENNIS, James M. 730'.924
Karl Bitter; architectural sculptor, 1867-1915 [by] James M. Dennis. Madison, Univ. of Wis. Pr., 1967. xiv, 302p. illus., ports. 27cm. Bibl. [NB237.B5D4] 67-20757 12.50
I. Bitter, Karl Theodore Francis, 1867-1915. II. Title.

ELSEN, Albert Edward, 1927- 735'.29
Origins of modern sculpture: pioneers and premises [by] Albert E. Elsen. New York, G. Braziller [1974] ix, 179 p. illus. 27 cm. An enl. and altered version of the introd. to the author's Pioneers of modern sculpture originally published in 1973. Includes bibliographical references. [NB197.E44 1974] 73-90927 ISBN 0-8076-0736-3 12.50
1. Sculpture, Modern—19th century. 2. Sculpture, Modern—20th century. I. Title. Pbk. 4.95; ISBN 0-8076-0737-1.

LICHT, Fred, 1928- 735.2
Sculpture, 19th & 20th centuries. Greenwich, Conn., New York Graphic Society [1967] 352 p. illus. (part col.) 25 cm. (A History of Western sculpture [v. 4]) [NB197.L5] 67-11106
1. Sculpture—Modern—19th century. 2. Sculpture—Modern—20th century. I. Title. II. Series.

STRACHAN, Walter John, 1903- 735'.22
Towards sculpture : drawings and maquettes from Rodin to Oldenburg / W. J. Strachan. Boulder, Colo. : Westview Press, 1976. 263 p. : ill. (some col.) ; 28 cm. Includes index. Bibliography: p. 251. [NB197.S88 1976] 76-14955 ISBN 0-89158-618-0 : 35.00
1. Sculpture, Modern—19th century. 2. Sculpture, Modern—20th century. 3. Artists' preparatory studies. 4. Models (Clay, plaster, etc.) 5. Drawings. I. Title.

TUCKER, William, 1935- 735'.22
Early modern sculpture; Rodin, Degas, Matisse, Brancusi, Picasso, Gonzalez. New York, Oxford University Press, 1974. 174 p. illus. 25 cm. Includes bibliographical references. [NB197.T82 1974] 73-92319 ISBN 0-19-519773-9 15.00
1. Sculpture, Modern—19th century. 2. Sculpture, Modern—20th century. 3. Visual perception. I. Title.

Sculpture, Modern—19th century—Exhibitions.

METAMORPHOSES in 735'.22'07401444 *nineteenth-century sculpture* : [exhibition, November 19, 1975-January 7, 1976, Fogg Art Museum, Harvard University : catalogue] / edited by Jeanne L. Wasserman. [Cambridge, Mass.] : The Museum, 1975. p. cm. Includes bibliographies and index. [NB197.3.M48] 75-31618
1. Sculpture, Modern—19th century—Exhibitions. I. Wasserman, Jeanne L. II. Harvard University. William Hayes Fogg Art Museum.

Sculpture, Modern—19th century—History.

RHEIMS, Maurice. 735'.22
19th century sculpture / Maurice Rheims New York : H.N. Abrams, [1976] p. cm. Translation of La sculpture au XIXe siecle. Includes index. Bibliography: p. [NB197.3.R4513] 75-39871 ISBN 0-8109-0375-X : 37.50
1. Sculpture, Modern—19th century—History. I. Title.

Sculpture, Modern—20th century.

BALDWIN, John, 1922- 731.4
Contemporary sculpture techniques: welded metal and fiberglass. Photographic supervision: Doug Stewart. New York, Reinhold [1967] 120p. illus., col. plates. ports. 27cm. Bibl. [NB1170.B22] 67-14152 10.00
1. Sculpture, Modern—20th cent. 2. Sculpture—Technique. I. Title.

CALLERY, Mary, 1903- 730.973
Sculpture. New York, Dist. Wittenborn [1961] xi, 151p. (chiefly illus.) 27cm. Texts, in English and French, by Philip R. Adams, Christian Zervos. Bibl. by Bernard Karpel 60-15443 10.00
I. Title.

CASSON, Stanley, 1889-1944. 730'.922
XXth century sculptors. Freeport, N.Y., Books for Libraries Press [1967] xii, 130 p. illus. 22 cm. (Essay index reprint series) Reprint of the 1930 ed. Bibliographical footnotes. [NB198.C32 1967] 67-23189
1. Sculpture, Modern—20th cent. 2. Sculptors. I. Title.

CONSAGRA, Pietro, 1920- 730.945
Pietro Consagra [by] Giulio Carlo Argan. [English tr. by Haakon Chevalier. Ins Deutsche ubers. von Felix Baumann] Neuchatel, Switzerland, Editions du Griffon [dist. New York, Universe, 1963, c.1962] 105p. chiefly illus. (pt. col.) 31cm. (Sculpture of the 20th cent.) English & German.bBibl. 63-4123 15.00
I. Argan, Giulio Carlo. II. Title. III. Series: The Sculpture of the twentieth century

FRANK, Jane. 759.13
The sculptural landscape of Jane Frank. Text by Phoebe B. Stanton. South Brunswick [N.J.] A. S. Barnes [1968] 120 p. illus. (part col.) 29 cm. [ND237.F673S7] 68-29877 12.00
I. Stanton, Phoebe B. II. Title.

HOHAUS, Hermann, 1920- 730'.92'4
Sculpture. [Melbourne, Printed by Herald Gravure Printers, for Hermann Hohaus, 1970?] [72] p. illus. 19 cm. English and German. [NB1105.H6A67] 72-193552
I. Title.

KRICKE, Norbert, 1922- 730.943
Kricke [by] John Anthony Thwaites New York, Abrams [c.1964] 75 p. illus., port. 21 x 23 cm. (Mod. artists) Bibl. 64-18893 5.95
I. Thwaites, John Anthony, 1909- II. Title.

MASON, Raymond, 1922- 730'.92'4
Raymond Mason. New York, Pierre Matisse Gallery [1969?] [32] p. illus. 26 cm. English and French. Text by Yves Bonnefoy, translated by Anthony Rudolf. Text in French ([4] p.) laid in. [NB497.M37B66] 73-158487
I. Bonnefoy, Yves.

*TYSOE, Peter 735'.29
Glass, resin and metal construction. London, Mills & Boon [1972, c.1971] 128 p. illus., col. plates. 26 cm. [NB198] ISBN 0-263-51394-7
1. Sculpture, Modern—20th cent. 2. Murals. I. Title.
Dist. by Transatlantic Arts, Levittown, N.Y., for 16.50

Sculpture, Modern—20th century—Exhibitions.

CALIFORNIA. University, Irvine. 709'.04'0740153
Twentieth century sculpture, 1900-1950. [Irvine, 1965] 39 p. illus. 23 cm. Introd. by J. Coplans. Catalogue of an exhibition of sculptures selected from California collections and shown at the University Oct. 2-24, 1965. [NB198.C24] 66-63981
1. Sculpture, Modern—20th cent.—Exhibitions. I. Coplans, John. II. Title.

HON--EN historia. 730/.74/087
Conception: Niki de Saint-Phalle, Jean Tinguely [och] Per Olof Ulvedt. Stockholm, Moderna museet, 1967. American dist.: Wittenborn, New York. 208p., chiefly illus. 37cm. Exhibition held 4.6-4.9 1966, Moderna museet, Stockholm. [NB198.H65] 67-107707 6.00 pap.,
1. Sculpture, Modern—20th cent.—Exhibitions. I. Saint-Phalle, Niki de, 1930- II. Tinguely, Jean, 1925- III. Ultvedt, Per Olof, 1927- IV. Stockholm. Nationalmuseum. Moderna museet. Hon.

NEW York (City) Administration of Recreation and Cultural Affairs. 735'.29
Sculpture in environment; [catalogue of an exhibition. October 1-31, 1967. Graphic design: Amy Stromsten. Photography: Fred W. McDarrah. New York, Seybert--Nicholas Print. Corp., 1967] [50] p. illus., ports. 24 cm. Cover title. Sponsored by the New York City Administration of Recreation and Cultural Affairs for the Cultural Showcase Festival. [NB198.S3515] 68-1084
1. Sculpture, Modern—20th cent.—Exhibitions. I. Title.

RAUH, Emily S, 1933- 730.922
7 for 67; works by contemporary American sculptors: Christo and others. Exhibition at the City Art Mus. of St. Louis, Oct. 1 to Nov. 12, 1967. [St. Louis, 1967] 1v. (unpaged) illus. 24cm. Bibl. [NB198.R39] 67-29858 3.00
1. Sculpture, Modern—20th cent.—Exhibitions. I. St. Louis. City Art Museum. II. Title.

SOLOMON R. Guggenheim 735'.29
Museum, New York.
Guggenheim international exhibition, 1967; sculpture from twenty nations [New York, Solomon R. Guggenheim Foundation, 1967] 148 p. illus. (part col.) 28 cm. "Exhibition 67-4." Catalogue of the exhibition to be held at the Solomon R. Guggenheim Museum, New York, Oct. 20, 1967-Feb. 4, 1968; at three other galleries in Canada, Feb.-Aug. 1968. Bibliography: p. [127]-148. [NB198.S6] 67-30453
1. Sculpture, Modern—20th cent.—Exhibitions. I. Title.

Sculpture, Modern—20th century.

BRCIN, John David, 1899- 730'.924
The sculpture of John David Brcin; being a collection of work by the artist with photographic illustrations chiefly by August Carl Hoffmann. Chicago, 1967. 1 v. (chiefly illus.) 21 cm. [NB237.B68A55] 67-66238
I. Title.

BURNHAM, Jack, 1931- 735'.29
Beyond modern sculpture; the effects of science and technology on the sculpture of this century. New York, G. Braziller [1968] x, 402 p. illus. 25 cm. Bibliography: p. 379-388. [NB198.B84] 68-16106 15.00
1. Sculpture, Modern—20th century. 2. Sculpture—Technique. I. Title. BIP

BUSCH, Julia M., 1940- 735'.29
A decade of sculpture: the 1960s [by] Julia M. Busch. Philadelphia, Art Alliance Press [1974] p. cm. Bibliography: p. [NB198.B86] 72-7855 ISBN 0-87982-007-1 25.00
1. Sculpture, Modern—20th century. 2. Form (Aesthetics) 3. Art and technology. I. Title. BIP

CASSON, Stanley, 1889- 735'.29
1944.
Some modern sculptors. Freeport, N.Y., Books for Libraries Press [1967] x, 119 p. illus. 24 cm. (Essay index reprint series) Reprint of the 1928 ed. [NB198.C3 1967] 67-28746
1. Sculpture, Modern—20th century. I. Title. BIP

COLETTI, Joseph, 1898- 730'.924
The sculpture of Joseph Coletti. Introd. by Alan Priest. New York, Macmillan [1968] xx, 173 p. illus. (part col.) 32 cm. Bibliography: p. 171. [NB237.C57P7] 67-26638
I. Priest, Alan, 1898- ed. II. Title.

DE CREEFT, Jose, 1884- 730'.92'4
The sculpture of Jose de Creeft, by Jules Campos; with a statement on sculpture by the artist. New York, Kennedy Graphics, 1972. 227 p. illus. 28 cm. Bibliography: p. 220-221. [NB237.D4C325] 77-166088 ISBN 0-306-70294-0 30.00
I. Campos, Jules. II. Title. BIP

HAMMACHER, Abraham Marie, 735'.29
1897-
The evolution of modern sculpture; tradition and innovation [by] A. M. Hammacher. New York, H. N. Abrams [1969] 383 p. illus. (part col.) 31 cm. Bibliography: p. 364-373. [NB198.H3] 69-17457
1. Sculpture, Modern—20th century. I. Title.

KRAUSS, Rosalind E. 735'.29
Passages in modern sculpture / Rosalind E. Krauss. New York : Viking Press, [1977] p. cm. Includes index. Bibliography: p. [NB198.K69] 76-41914 ISBN 0-670-54133-8 : 18.95
1. Sculpture, Modern—20th century. I. Title. BIP

KULTERMANN, Udo. 735'.29
The new sculpture; environments and assemblages. New York, F. A. Praeger [1968] 236 p. illus. (part col.), ports. 28 cm. Translation of Neue Dimensionen der Plastik. Bibliography: p. 233-236. [NB198.K813 1968] 68-17366
1. Sculpture, Modern—20th century. I. Title.

LACHAISE, Gaston, 1882- 730.92'4
1935.
The sculpture of Gaston Lachaise. With an essay by Hilton Kramer, and appreciations by Hart Crane [and others] New York, Eakins Press Publishers [1967] 49 [91] p. illus., 86 plates, ports. 29 cm. [NB553.L24K7] 67-17017
I. Kramer, Hilton. II. Title. BIP

LIPTON, Seymour, 1903- 730'.924
Seymour Lipton. Text by Albert Elsen. New York, H. N. Abrams [1970] 244 p. illus. (part col.), ports. 28 cm. Bibliography: p. 241-244. [NB237.L55E4] 74-80823
I. Elsen, Albert Edward, 1927-

LIPTON, Seymour, 1903- 730'.924
Seymour Lipton: recent works. [New York, Marlborough] 1971. 40 p. illus. (part col.), port. 30 cm. Catalog of an exhibition held at the Marlborough Gallery, New York, March 1971. [NB237.L55A56] 70-198120
I. Marlborough Gallery.

MERILLAT, Herbert 735'.29
Christian Laing, 1915-
Modern sculpture : the new old masters / Herbert Christian Merillat. New York : Dodd, Mead, [1974] xii, 171 p., [32] leaves of plates : ill. ; 24 cm. Includes index. Bibliography: p. 162-165. [NB198.M4] 74-6801 ISBN 0-396-06987-8 : 12.50
1. Sculpture, Modern—20th century. I. Title. BIP

PARKS, Charles C., 1922- 730'.924
The sculptures of Charles C. Parks. [Bridgeton, N. J., Cowan Printing, 1967] 84p. (chiefly illus., port.) 31cm. Cover title. [NB237.P27A47] 67-5712 7.00 pap.,
I. Title.

READ, Herbert Edward, 735.29
Sir, 1893-1968.
A concise history of modern sculpture [by] Herbert Read. New York, Praeger [1964] 310 p. illus. (part col.) 22 cm. (Praeger world of art series) "Text references":. 279-282. Bibliography: p. 283-285. [NB198.R4] 64-19789
1. Sculpture, Modern—20th century. I. Title. II. Title: Modern sculpture. BIP

REHMANN, Erwin, 1921- 730'.924
Erwin Rehmann. Texts by Adolf Reinle, Eugen Gomringer and the artist. Tr. by Robert Allen. Neuchatel, Editions du Griffon, 1967. 153p. illus. 30cm. (Sculpture of the 20th cent.) Bibl. [NB853.R36R3] 68-71007 21.50
I. Reinle, Adolf. II. Gomringer, Eugen, 1925- III. Title. IV. Series: The Sculpture of the twentieth century
American distributor: Wittenborn, New York.

RITCHIE, Andrew 735'.29'07401471
Carnduff.
Sculpture of the twentieth century. New York, Museum of Modern Art. [New York] Published for the Museum of Modern Art by Arno Press, 1972 [c1952] 237, 47 p. illus. 27 cm. "Including the exhibition catalogue, Sculpture of the twentieth century, with an introduction by Andrew Carnduff Ritchie." Includes bibliographies. [NB198.R5 1972] 78-169311 ISBN 0-405-01570-4 30.00
1. Sculpture, Modern—20th century. I. New York (City). Museum of Modern Art. II. Title.

ROSENTHAL, Bernard. 730'.924
Sculptures. [Introd. by] Sam Hunter. [New York] M. Knoedler [1968] 24 p. illus. (part col.) 22 cm. Catalog of an exhibition held on Mar. 5-23, 1968, by M. Knoedler & Co., New York. [NB237.R775H8] 68-24154 1.95
I. Hunter, Sam, 1923- II. Knoedler (M.) and Company, inc.

SALERNO, Charles, 1916- 730'.924
Salerno sculpture, by Frances Christoph. New York, Weyhe Gallery [1965?] 58 p. (chiefly illus.) 27 cm. [NB237.S24C35] 65-28928
I. Christoph, Frances. II. Title.

SELZ, Jean. 730.9
Modern sculpture: origins and evolution. Translated by Annette Michelson. New York, G. Braziller, 1963. 292 p. illus. (part col.) 28 cm. Bibliography: p. 279-288. [NB198.S353] 63-14802
1. Sculpture, Modern—20th century. I. Title.

SEYMOUR, Charles, 1912- 735'.29
Tradition and experiment in modern sculpture. New York, Arno Press [1969, c1949] viii, 86 p. illus. 29 cm. (Arno series of contemporary art, no. 34) [NB198.S4 1969] 70-91378
1. Sculpture, Modern—20th century. I. Title.

SHINGU, Susumu, 1937- 730'.92'4
Shingu. Photos. by Yukio Futagawa. Introd. by Edward F. Fry. Commentary by Takahiko Okada. [Translated by Richard Gage] New York, Abrams [1973] 152 p. (chiefly illus., part col.) 28 x 30 cm. [NB1059.S5O3713] 72-3684 ISBN 0-8109-0481-0 35.00
I. Okada, Takahiko, 1939- II. Futagawa, Yukio, 1932- illus.

TAFT, Lorado, 1860-1936. 735'.29
Modern tendencies in sculpture. Freeport, N.Y., Books for Libraries Press [1970] xxvi, 152 p. illus., port. 23 cm. (Essay index reprint series) Reprint of the 1921 ed., published as part of the Scammon lectures for 1917. [NB198.T3 1970] 77-105040
1. Sculpture, Modern—20th century. I. Title. BIP

TRIER, Eduard. 735'.29
Form and space; sculpture of the twentieth century. Rev. ed. New York, Praeger [1968] 339 p. illus. (part col.) 29 cm. Translation of Figur und Raum. [NB198.T683 1968b] 68-14737 17.50
1. Sculpture, Modern—20th century. I. Title.

ZAJAC, Jack, 1929- 730.973
The sculpture of Jack Zajac [by] Henry J. Seldis, Ulfert Wilke. Los Angeles, Galland Press [dist. Wittenborn, 1961c.1960) 74p. illus. 29cm. 61-65474 6.00
I. Seldis, Henry J. II. Wilke, Ulfert, 1907- III. Title.

Sculpture, Modern—20th century—Exhibitions.

7 + 5 sculptors in the 1950's : an exhibition / organized by Phyllis Plous for the Art Galleries. University of California. Santa Barbara 6 January-15February, 1976 Phoenix Art Museum, 5 March - April, 1976 Santa Barbara : The Galleries, c1976. 122 p. : 70 ill. ; 26 cm. Bibliography: p. 119-121. [NB198.S357] 75-620014 735'.29
1. Sculpture, Modern—20th century—Exhibitions. I. Plous, Phyllis. II. California. University, Santa Barbara. Art Galleries. III. Phoenix, Ariz. Art Museum.

ARTS Council of Great 735'.29
Britain.
Sculpture for the collection : purchases by Bryan Kneale [for the] Arts Council of Great Britain : [catalogue of a touring exhibition], 1976. [London] : The Council, 1976. 28 p. : ill. ; 21 cm. [NB198.A75 1976] 76-378351 ISBN 0-7287-0082-4 : £0.75
1. Sculpture, Modern—20th century—Exhibitions. I. Kneale, Bryan, 1930- II. Title.

CHICAGO. Art Institute. 735'.29
Sculpture: a generation of innovation, June 23 - August 27, 1967. [Chicago, 1967] 1 v. (unpaged) illus. 28 cm. [NB198.C5 1967] 74-172639
1. Sculpture, Modern—20th century—Exhibitions. I. Title.

MICHIGAN. 730'.973'074017435
University. School of Art.
First invitational exhibition of sculpture inside & out, University of Michigan School of Art, Ann Arbor, Michigan. [Ann Arbor] : The School, [1975] [89] p. : chiefly ill. ; 23 cm. Cover title. [NB198.M5 1975] 75-624286
1. Sculpture, Modern—20th century—Exhibitions. I. Title. II. Title: Sculpture inside & out.

MONUMENTA : 735'.29
a biennial exhibition of outdoor sculpture, Newport, Rhode Island, August 17 through October 13, 1974 / edited with an introd. by Sam Hunter. Newport, R.I. : Monumenta Newport Inc., [1974] 96 p. : ill. ; 29 cm. [NB198.M7] 74-14395
1. Sculpture, Modern—20th century—Exhibitions. I. Hunter, Sam, 1923- ed. II. Monumenta Newport Inc.

POMODORO, Arnaldo, 1926- 730'.924
Arnaldo Pomodoro: sculpture, 1960-1970. Berkeley, Art Museum, University of California, 1970. A-X illus. (in portfolio) 31 x 23 cm. Title from portfolio. Label on portfolio: Supplied by Worldwide Books, inc., Boston. Exhibit held at the University of California Art Museum, Berkeley, and others. The catalogue appears on verso of illus. F. Bibliography on versos of illus. H and I. [NB623.P588A44] 76-630536
I. California. University. Art Museum. II. Title.

ROSATI, James, 1912- 730'.924
James Rosati: sculpture 1963-1969. An exhibition of the Poses Institute of Fine Arts in cooperation with the Marlborough-Gerson Gallery, New York City, [Waltham? Mass., 1969?] 44 p. illus., port. 30 cm. Label mounted on t.p.: Supplied by Worldwide Books, Boston. Exhibition held at Rose Art Museum, Brandeis University, Waltham, Mass., and others. Bibliography: p. 15. [NB237.R69A49] 72-18607
I. Brandeis University, Waltham, Mass. Poses Institute of Fine Arts. II. Marlborough-Gerson Gallery. III. Brandeis University, Waltham, Mass. Rose Art Museum.

SCULPTURE in 735'.29
environment; [catalogue of an exhibition, October 1-31, 1967. Graphic design: Amy Stromsten. Photography: Fred W. McDarrah. New York, Seybert-Nicholas Print. Corp., 1967] [50] p. illus., ports. 24 cm. Cover title. Sponsored by the New York City Administration of Recreation and Cultural Affairs for the Cultural Showcase Festival. [NB198.S3515] 68-1084
1. Sculpture, Modern—20th century—Exhibitions. I. New York (City). Administration of Recreation and Cultural Affairs.

SOLOMON R. Guggenheim 741.9'73
Museum, New York.
Frederick Kiesler: environmental sculpture. New York (61964] 1 v. (unpaged) illus. (part col.) port. 26 cm. Catalog of "Exhibition 64/3, May-June, 1964." Includes "Towards the endless sculpture [by] Frederick Kiesler." [N6537.K5S6] 64-22277
I. Kiesler, Frederick. II. Title.

SOLOMON R. Guggenheim 735'.29
Museum, New York.
Guggenheim international exhibition sculpture from twenty nations. [New York] [Solomon R. Guggenheim Foundation] [1967] 148 p. illus. (part col.) 28 cm. "Exhibition 67-4." Catalogue of the exhibition to be held at the Solomon R. Guggenheim Museum, New York, Oct. 20, 1967-Feb. 4, 1968; at three other galleries in Canada, Feb.-Aug. 1968. Bibliography: p. [127]-148. [NB198.S6] 67-30453
1. Sculpture, Modern—20th century—Exhibitions. I. Title.

TEANA, Marino, 1920- 730/.924
Marino di Teana. Photos. by Pierre Joly, Vera Cardot. Introd. by Jean Clay. [Tr. from French, by Haakon Chevalier.] Neuchatel, Editions du Griffon, [1967]. 144p. illus. 31cm. (Sculpture of the 20th cent.) Bibl. [NB623.D5C53] 68-70871 16.50
I. Joly, Pierre, writer on art; illus. II. Cardot, Vera. illus. III. Title. IV. Series.
Distributor: Wittenborn, New York.

WALKER Art Center, 730'.922
Minneapolis.
Twentieth century sculpture; selections from the collection. Minneapolis [1969] 96 p. illus. 28 cm. Bibliography: p. 95-96. [NB198.W3] 71-75259
1. Sculpture, Modern—20th century—Exhibitions. I. Title.

1. Sculpture, Renaissance—Spain. 2. Sculpture—Spain. I. Title. BIP

Sculpture, Roman.

FEHL, Philipp P. 733'.3
The classical monument; reflections on the connection between morality and art in Greek and Roman sculpture [by] Philipp Fehl. New York, Published by New York University Press for the College Art Association of America, 1972. xv, 115, [34] p. illus. 29 cm. (Monographs on archaeology and the fine arts, 24) Originally presented as the author's thesis, University of Chicago, 1963. Bibliography: p. 106-115. [NB85.F36 1972] 73-164023 ISBN 0-8147-2554-6
1. Sculpture, Roman. 2. Sculpture, Greek. 3. Art and morals. I. Title. II. Series. BIP

SPENCE, Joseph, 1699-1768. 733'.5
Polymetis. New York, Garland Pub., 1971. vi, 361 p. illus., port. 31 cm. "Facsimile ... made from a copy loaned by Stephen Weissman of Ximenes: Rare Books [originally published in 1755]" Includes bibliographical references. [NB115.S65 1755a] 70-112242
1. Sculpture, Roman. 2. Gods in art. 3. Mythology, Classical. 4. Latin poetry—History and criticism. I. Title. BIP

SPENCE, Joseph, 1699-1768. 733'.5
Polymetis, London, 1747 / Joseph Spence. New York : Garland Pub., 1976. p. cm. (The Renaissance and the gods ; 41) Reprint of the 1747 ed. printed for R. Dodsley, London. Includes index. [NB115.S65 1976] 75-27886 ISBN 0-8240-2090-1 lib. bdg. : 40.00
1. Sculpture, Roman. 2. Gods in art. 3. Mythology, Classical, in art. 4. Latin poetry—History and criticism. I. Title. II. Series.

STRONG, Donald Emrys 733.5
Roman imperial sculpture; an introduction to the commemorative and decorative sculpture of the Roman Empire down to the death of Constantine. London, A. Tiranti [dist. Hollywood-by-the-Sea, Fla., Transatlantic, 1964, c.1961] vii, 104p. illus. 19cm. Bibl. 64-6864 9.00
1. Sculpture, Roman. I. Title.

STRONG, Donald Emrys. 733'.5
Roman imperial sculpture; an introduction to the commemorative and decorative sculpture of the Roman Empire down to the death of Constantine [by] D. E. Strong. [1st American ed.] New York, Transatlantic Arts, 1971. vii, 104 p. 144 plates. 20 cm. Bibliography: p. 81-86. [NB115.S79 1971] 76-166294
1. Sculpture, Roman. I. Title. BIP

STRONG, Eugenie (Sellers) 733'.5
Roman sculpture from Augustus to Constantine. New York, Arno Press, 1969. xvi, 408 p. 130 plates. 23 cm. Reprint of the 1907 ed. "Based upon a series of lectures." [NB115.S8 1969] 79-88825
1. Sculpture, Roman. 2. Sculpture, Greco-Roman. I. Title. BIP

STRONG, Eugenie (Sellers) 733'.5
Roman sculpture from Augustus to Constantine, by Mrs. Arthur Strong. New York, Hacker Art Books, 1971. xvi, 408 p. illus. 24 cm. Reprint of the 1907 ed. Includes bibliographical references. [NB115.S8 1971] 76-116362 ISBN 0-87817-053-7
1. Sculpture, Roman. 2. Sculpture, Greco-Roman. I. Title.

Sculpture, Romanesque.

BUSCH, Harald Walter Robert, 1904- ed. 734.24
Romanesque sculpture, ed. by Harald Busch, Bernd Lohse, Introd. by Hans Weigert. Commentaries on the illus. by Hans Weigert. [Tr. from German by Peter Gorge] London, Batsford, [dist. New York, Macmillan, 1963, c.1962] xxiiip., 180p. of illus. col. front. 27cm. (European sculpture) Captions to the illus. are in German and English. 63-5391 12.95
1. Sculpture, Romanesque. 2. Sculpture, European. I. Lohse, Bernd, joint ed. II. Title. III. Series.

PORTER, Arthur Kingsley, 1883-1933. 734'.24
Romanesque sculpture of the pilgrimage roads. New York, Hacker Art Books, 1966. 10 v. in 3 (v. 2-10 chiefly illus.) 24 cm. Reprint of the 1923 ed. Contents.Contents.—v. 1. Text. List of books referred to p. [343]-356.—v. 2. Burgundy.—v. 3. Tuscany and Apulia.—v. 4. Aquitaine.—v. 5. Catalonia and Aragon.—v. 6. Castile, Asturias, Galicia.—v. 7. Western France.—v. 8. Auvergne and Dauphine.— v. 9. Provence.—v. 10. Ile-de-France. [NB175.P6 1966] 67-4262
1. Sculpture, Romanesque. 2. Christian art and symbolism. 3. Christian pilgrims and pilgrimages. I. Title. BIP

Sculpture, Romanesque—Addresses, essays, lectures.

SCHAPIRO, Meyer, 1904- 709'.02'1
Romanesque art / Meyer Schapiro. New York : G. Braziller, 1976. p. cm. (His Selected papers) Includes index. Contents.Contents.—The aesthetic attitude in Romanesque art.—The Romanesque sculptures of Moissac.—The sculptures of Souillac.—On geometrical schematism in Romanesque art.—From Mozarabic to Romanesque in Silos.—A relief in Rodez and the beginnings of Romanesque sculpture in southern France.—Two Romanesque drawings in Auxerre and some iconographic problems.—New documents on St. Gilles. [NB175.S28] 76-11842 ISBN 0-8076-0853-X
1. Sculpture, Romanesque—Addresses, essays, lectures. 2. Art, Romanesque—Addresses, essays, lectures. I. Title. II. Series.

Sculpture, Romanesque—France.

DESCHAMPS, Paul, 1888- 730'.944
French sculpture of the Romanesque period, eleventh and twelfth centuries. New York, Hacker Art Books, 1972. xiii, 152 p. 96 plates. 32 cm. Reprint of the 1930 ed. Includes bibliographical references. [NB175.D4 1972] 78-143343 ISBN 0-87817-063-4 40.00
1. Sculpture, Romanesque—France. 2. Sculpture—France. 3. Church architecture—France. I. Title. BIP

FORSYTH, Ilene H. 731'.88'550944
The Throne of Wisdom; wood sculptures of the madonna in Romanesque France [by] Ilene H. Forsyth. Princeton, N.J., Princeton University Press [1972] xviii, 226, [64] p. illus. 29 cm. A revision of the author's thesis, Columbia, 1960. Bibliography: p. 209-218. [NB1255.F8F67 1972] 72-166372 ISBN 0-691-03837-6 30.00
1. Mary, Virgin—Art. 2. Sculpture, Romanesque—France. 3. Sculpture, French. 4. Wood-carving, French. I. Title.

Sculpture, Romanesque—Latin Orient.

BARASH, Moshe. 734
Crusader figural sculpture in the Holy Land; twelfth century examples from Acre, Nazareth and Belvoir Castle. New Brunswick, N.J., Rutgers University Press [1971] 237 p. illus. 29 cm. Bibliography: p. 227-234. [NB977.B3] 74-129513 ISBN 0-8135-0680-8 15.00
1. Sculpture, Romanesque—Latin Orient. 2. Sculpture—Latin Orient. I. Title. BIP

Sculpture, Romanesque—Lincoln, Eng.

ZARNECKI, George. 726'.59
Romanesque sculpture at Lincoln Cathedral. Lincoln, Friends of Lincoln Cathedral, 1968. 24 p. 36 plates, illus. 22 cm. (Lincoln Minster pamphlets. Second series no. 2) Bibliographical references included in "Notes" (p. 22-24) [NB471.L5Z3] 79-458153 7/6
1. Lincoln Cathedral. 2. Sculpture, Romanesque—Lincoln, Eng. I. Friends of Lincoln Cathedral. II. Title. III. Series.

Sculpture, Romanesque—Saint-Gilles, France (Gard)

O'MEARA, Carra Ferguson. 730'.944'83
The iconography of the facade of Saint-Gilles-du-Gard / Carra Ferguson O'Meara. New York : Garland Pub., 1977. xi, 221 p., [35] leaves of plates : ill. ; 21 cm. (Outstanding dissertations in the fine arts) Originally presented as the author's thesis, University of Pittsburgh, 1975. Bibliography: p. 195-221. [NB551.S28O46 1977] 76-23668 ISBN 0-8240-2717-5 : 37.50
1. Sculpture, Romanesque—Saint-Gilles, France (Gard) 2. Sculpture—Saint-Gilles, France (Gard) 3. Saint-Gilles, France (Gard). Church. Facade. I. Title. II. Series. BIP

Sculpture, Romanesque—Spain.

PORTER, Arthur Kingsley, 1883-1933. 730'.946
Spanish Romanesque sculpture. New York, Hacker Art Books, 1969. 2 v. in 1. 160 plates. 32 cm. Reprint of the 1928 ed. Includes bibliographical references. [NB803.P6 1969] 73-94903 50.00
1. Sculpture, Romanesque—Spain. 2. Sculpture, Spanish. I. Title. BIP

Sculpture, Romanesque—Toulouse.

SEIDEL, Linda. 730'.944'86
Romanesque sculpture from the Cathedral of Saint-Etienne, Toulouse / Linda Seidel. New York : Garland Pub., 1977, c1964. xii, 187 p., [52] leaves of plates : ill. ; 21 cm. (Outstanding dissertations in the fine arts) Thesis—Harvard, 1964. Bibliography: p. [173]- [NB551.T6S44 1977] 76-23646 ISBN 0-8240-2729-9 lib.bdg. : 37.50
1. Toulouse. Saint-Etienne (Cathedral) 2. Sculpture, Romanesque—Toulouse. 3. Sculpture, French—Toulouse. I. Title. II. Series. BIP

Sculpture—Rome (City)

ENGGASS, Robert, 1921- 730'.945'632
Early eighteenth-century sculpture in Rome : an illustrated catalogue raisonne / Robert Enggass. University Park [Pa.] : Pennsylvania State University Press, 1975, c1976. p. cm. Includes bibliographies. [NB620.E53] 75-16353 ISBN 0-271-01200-5
1. Sculpture—Rome (City) 2. Sculpture, Baroque—Rome (City) I. Title. BIP

MATT, Leonard von 730.94563
Baroque art in Rome. Commentary by Valerio Mariani. New York, Universe Bks. [c.1961] xvi p., 48p. of illus 29cm. (Rome ser.) 61-14582 4.75
1. Sculpture—Rome (City) 2. Sculpture, Baroque. I. Mariani, Valerio, 1899- II. Title.

Sculpture—San Marino, Calif.—Catalogs.

HENRY E. Huntington Library and Art Gallery, San Marino, Calif. 730.979493
Sculpture in the Huntington collection [by] R. R. Wark. [San Marino, 1959] v, 85p. illus. 26cm. (Its Huntington Library publications) Includes bibliographical references. [NB25.H4] 58-10419
1. Sculpture—San Marino, Calif.—Catalogs. I. Wark, R. R. II. Title. III. Series. BIP

Sculpture, Scottish.

RICHARDSON, James S. 730.941
The mediaeval stone carver in Scotland Edinburg, Univ. [dist. Chicago. Aldine, c.1964] 78p. 127 illus. 26cm. 64-14918 10.00
1. Sculpture, Scottish. 2. Sculpture, Medieval. I. Title.

Sculpture, South Asian—Exhibitions.

PAL, Pratapaditya. 732'.4'074019494
The sensuous immortals : a selection of sculptures from the Pan-Asian collection : Los Angeles County Museum of Art, 25 October 1977-15 January 1978 / by Pratapaditya Pal. Los Angeles : Los Angeles County Museum of Art, [1977] p. cm. Includes bibliographical references. [NB1000.P34] 77-2619 ISBN 0-87587-079-1 : 35.00
1. Sculpture—South Asia—Exhibitions. 2. Sculpture—Asia, Southeastern—Exhibitions. I. Los Angeles Co., Calif. Museum of Art, Los Angeles. II. Title. BIP

Sculpture, South Asian—Exhibitions.

OTSUKA, Ronald Y. 732'.4
South Asian sculpture : the Harold P. and Jane F. Ullman Collection : [exhibition], Denver Art Museum, January 11-February 23, 1975 / by Ronald Y. Otsuka and Mary C. Lanius. Denver : The Museum, [1975] [47] p. : ill. ; 22 x 25 cm. Catalog. Includes bibliographical references. [NB1000.O87] 74-30854 ISBN 0-914738-06-2
1. Ullman, Harold P.—Art collections. 2. Ullman, Jane F.—Art collections. 3. Sculpture, South Asian—Exhibitions. I. Lanius, Mary C., joint author. II. Denver. Art Museum. III. Title. BIP

PAL, Pratapaditya. 732'.4'074019494
The divine presence : Asian sculptures from the collection of Mr. and Mrs. Harry Lenart / by Pratapaditya Pal. Los Angeles : Los Angeles County Museum of Art, c1978. 58 p. : ill. ; 26 cm. Catalog of an exhibition held at the Los Angeles County Museum of Art, Aug. 15-Oct. 15, 1978. Bibliography: p. 57. [NB1000.P33] 78-59792 ISBN 0-87587-086-4 pbk. : 4.50
1. Lenart, Harry—Art collections—Exhibitions. 2. Sculpture, South Asian—Exhibitions. 3. Sculpture, Southeast Asian—Exhibitions. 4. Gods in art—Exhibitions. I. Los Angeles Co., Calif. Museum of Art, Los Angeles. II. Title.

PAL, Pratapaditya. 732'.4'074019494
The divine presence : Asian sculptures from the collection of Mr. and Mrs. Harry Lenart / by Pratapaditya Pal. Los Angeles : Los Angeles County Museum of Art, c1978. 58 p. : ill. ; 26 cm. Catalog of an exhibition held at the Los Angeles County Museum of Art, Aug. 15-Oct. 15, 1978. Bibliography: p. 57. [NB1000.P33] 78-59792 ISBN 0-87587-086-4 pbk. : 4.50
1. Lenart, Harry—Art collections—Exhibitions. 2. Sculpture, South Asian—Exhibitions. 3. Sculpture, Southeast Asian—Exhibitions. 4. Gods in art—Exhibitions. I. Los Angeles Co., Calif. Museum of Art, Los Angeles. II. Title. BIP

Sculpture, Spanish.

GOMEZ-MORENO, Manuel, 1870- 730.946
The golden age of Spanish sculpture. Notes on the plates by Maria Elena Gomez Moreno. 88 black and white photos. by F. L. Kenett. 12 colour photos by Paul Pietzsch. Greenwich, Conn., New York Graphic Society [1964] 63 p. 101 plates (part col.) 34 cm. ([The Great masters of the past, 12]) [NB804.G6] 64-21816
1. Sculpture, Spanish. I. Gomez-Moreno, Maria Elena. II. Kenett, F. L. III. Title. IV. Series.

PROSKE, Beatrice Irene (Gilman) 1899- 735.46
Pompeo Leoni; work in marble and alabaster in relation to Spanish sculpture. New York, Hispanic Society of America, 1956. 49p. illus. 23cm. (Hispanic notes & monographs; essays, studies, and brief biographies) [NB813.L4P7] 927.3 56-14493
1. Leoni, Pompeo, d. 1610? 2. Leoni, Leone, 1509-1590. 3. Sculpture, Spanish. I. Title. BIP

Sculpture—Sudan, French.

NEW York (City) Museum of Primitive Art. 730.9662
Bambara sculpture from the Western

SUBJECT INDEX SCULPTURE, THAI—EXHIBITIONS.

Sudan. With an introd. by Robert Goldwater. New York, distributed by University Publishers, 1960. [64] p. (chiefly illus., map.) 29 cm. Bibliography: p. [18-21] [NB1097.S8N4] 60-1451
1. Sculpture—Sudan, French. 2. Sculpture, Primitive. 3. Bambara tribe. I. Goldwater, Robert John, 1907- II. Title.

Sculpture, Swedish.

THORDEMAN, Bengt Johan Neren, 1893- 730.9485
Medieval wooden sculpture; v.5. Stockholm, Almqvist & Wiksell [New York, Wittenborn, 1965, c.1964] 343,8p. (chiefly plates) 29cm. At head of title: Mus. of Natl. Antiquities, Stockholm. Contents.v.5. The museum collection; plates. [NB1255.S9T5] 64-55451 35.00 pap.,
1. Sculpture, Swedish. 2. Wood-carving, Swedish. 3. Sculpture, Medieval. I. Stockholm. Statens historiska museum. II. Title.

THORDEMAN, Bengt Johan Neren, 1893- 730.9485
Medieval wooden sculpture in sweden: v.1. Stockholm, Almqvist & Wiksell [New York, Wittenborn, c.1964] 104p. illus. (pt. col.) ports. 29cm. At head of title: Mus. of Natl. Antiquities, Stockholm. Contents.v.1. Attitudes to the heritage. 64-55451 8.50 pap.,
1. Sculpture, Swedish. 2. Wood-carving, Swedish. 3. Sculpture, Medieval. I. Stockholm. Statens historiska museum. II. Title.

THORDEMAN, Bengt Johan Neren, 1893- 730.9485
Medieval wooden sculpture in Sweden; v.2. Stockholm, Almqvist & Wiksell [New York, Wittenborn, 1966, c.1965] 159p. illus. 29cm. At head of title: Museum of National Antiquities Stockholm. Contents.v.2. Romanesque and Gothic sculpture, by Aron Andersson [NB1255.S9T5] 64-55451 9.50 pap.,
1. Sculpture, Swedish. 2. Wood-carving, Swedish. 3. Sculpture, Medieval. I. Stockholm. Statens historiska museum. II. Title.

Sculpture, Swiss.

JORAY, Marcel. 730
La sculpture moderne en Suisse. Neuchatel, Eds. du Griffon [1955-59- v. plates. 30cm. (Collection L'Art suisse contemporain, no. 12, 14) [NB848.J6] 57-22881 21.50
1. Sculpture, Swiss. I. Title.
American distributor, Wittenborn, N.Y.

Sculpture—Technique.

ANDREWS, Michael F. 731.2
Sculpture and ideas ... for school and camp programs [by] Michael F. Andrews. Englewood Cliffs, N.J., Prentice-Hall [1966] xii, 208 p. illus. 25 cm. Bibliography: p. 193-197. [NB1170.A6] 66-10132
1. Sculpture—Technique. I. Title.

BARJANSKY, Catherine. 731.42
Sculpting made easy; the Barjansky method of figure and portrait sculpture by outline. [1st ed.] Garden City, N. Y., Doubleday, 1964. 95 p. illus. 27 cm. [NB1170.B28] 62-15916
1. Sculpture—Technique. I. Title.

BATTEN, Mark. 731.23
Stone sculpture by direct carving. [London, New York] The Studio Publications [1957] 96 p. illus. 26 cm. (The How to do it series, no. 71) [NB1170.B3] 57-3375
1. Sculpture—Technique. I. Title.

BEECROFT, Glynis. 731.4'6
Carving techniques / Glynis Beecroft ; drawings and photos. by Edwin Beecroft. New York : Watson-Guptill Publications, 1976. 142 p. : ill. ; 26 cm. Includes index. [NB1170.B43 1976] 75-46629 ISBN 0-8230-0568-2 : 10.95
1. Sculpture—Technique. 2. Carving (Art industries) I. Title. BIP

BROMMER, Gerald F. 731.4
Wire sculpture and other three-dimensional construction [by] Gerald F. Brommer. Worcester, Mass., Davis Pubns., 1968. 128p. illus. 26cm. [NB1220.B7] 68-19999 8.50 bds.,
1. Sculpture—Technique. 2. Wire. I. Title. BIP

CLARKE, Geoffrey., 1915- 731
A sculptor's manual [by] Geoffrey Clarke, Stroud Cornock. London, Studio Vista, New York, Reinhold, 1968. 158p. illus. (some col.). 26cm. [NB1170.C53] 68-101814 8.50
1. Sculpture—Technique. 2. Artists' materials. I. Cornock Stroud. joint author. II. Title.

COPNALL, Bainbridge, 1903- 731.4
A sculptor's manual. [1st ed.] Oxford, New York, Pergamon Press [1971] ix, 266 p. illus. (part col.), ports. (part col.) 16 x 22 cm. (The Commonwealth and international library. Painting, sculpture, and fine arts) [NB1140.C64] 76-130368 ISBN 0-08-015577-4
1. Sculpture—Technique. I. Title.

DAINGERFIELD, Marjorie Jay. 731.4
The fun and fundamentals of sculpture. New York, Scribner [1963] 95 p. illus. 24 cm. [NB1170.D3] 63-18749
1. Sculpture—Technique. I. Title.

DIVALENTIN, Maria 731.4
Sculpture for beginners, by Maria and Louis DiValentin. New York, Sterling [c.1965] 160p. illus. 21cm. Pub. in London by Oak Tree Pr. [NB1170.D5] 64-24687 3.95; 3.69 lib. ed.,
1. Sculpture—Technique. I. DiValentin, Louis, joint author. II. Title.

DIVALENTIN, Maria Messuri, 1911- 731.4
Sculpture for beginners, by Maria and Louis DiValentin. New York, Sterling Pub. Co. [1965] 160 p. illus. 21 cm. [NB1170.D5] 64-24687
1. Sculpture — Technique. I. DiValentin, Louis, joint author. II. Title.

DIVALENTIN, Maria (Messuri) 1911- 731.4
Sculpture for beginners, by Maria and Louis DiValentin. [Enl. and rev. ed.] New York, Sterling Pub. Co. [1969] 192 p. illus. (part col.) 21 cm. [NB1150.D5 1969] 74-13089
1. Sculpture—Technique. I. DiValentin, Louis, joint author. II. Title.

ELISCU, Frank. 731.4
Sculpture: techniques in clay, wax, slate. [1st ed.] Photos. of processes by Conrad Brown. Philadelphia, Chilton Co. [1959] 192 p. illus. 27 cm. (Arts and crafts series) [NB1180.E48] 59-7275
1. Sculpture—Technique. 2. Modeling.

GROSS, Chaim, 1904- 730'.92'4
Sculpture in progress [by] Chaim Gross and Peter Robinson. New York, Van Nostrand Reinhold Co. [1972] 63 p. illus. 22 cm. [NB1170.G7] 71-90322
1. Sculpture—Technique. I. Robinson, Peter, 1915- illus. II. Title.

IRVING, Donald J. 731
Sculpture; material and process [by] Donald J. Irving. New York, Van Nostrand [1970] 144 p. illus. (part col.), ports. 27 cm. Bibliography: p. 140-141. [NB1170.I7 1970] 73-90301
1. Sculpture—Technique. 2. Artists' materials.

JOHNSON, Lillian (Bass) 1916- 731.4
Sculpture, the basic methods and materials. New York, D. McKay [1960] 90p. illus. 26cm. Includes bibliography. [NB1170.J6] 60-9563
1. Sculpture—Technique. I. Title.

KELLY, James J. 731.4
The sculptural idea, by James J. Kelly. Minneapolis, Burgess Pub. Co. [1970] xv, 102 p. illus. 19 x 26 cm. Bibliography: p. 101-102. [NB198.K4] 70-99941
1. Sculpture—Technique. 2. Sculpture, Modern—20th century. I. Title. BIP

KELLY, James J. 731.4
The sculptural idea, by James J. Kelly. 2d ed. Minneapolis, Burgess Pub. Co. [1974] xiv, 186 p. illus. 26 cm. Bibliography: p. 183-186. [NB198.K4 1974] 74-77079 ISBN 0-8087-1112-1 5.00 (pbk.)
1. Sculpture—Technique. 2. Sculpture, Modern—20th century. I. Title.

MILLER, Richard McDermott, 1922- 731.8'2
Figure sculpture in wax and plaster. Edited by Gloria Bley Miller. New York, Watson-Guptill Publications [1971] 175 p. illus. 29 cm. [NB1170.M52] 79-125849 ISBN 0-8230-1720-6 10.00
1. Sculpture—Technique. 2. Wax-modeling. I. Title. BIP

MILLS, John W. 731.4
Sculpture in concrete [by] John W. Mills. New York, Praeger [1968] 44 p. illus., plates. 26 cm. [NB1215.M5 1968b] 68-9815 9.95
1. Sculpture—Technique. 2. Concrete. I. Title.

MILLS, John W. 731.4'5
The technique of casting for sculpture [by] John W. Mills. London, Batsford; New York, Reinhold, 1967. 168 p. illus., diagrs. 25 1 2 cm. 55 - (B67-19634) [NB1190.M5] 67-21032
1. Sculpture — Technique. 2. Plaster casts. I. Title.

MILLS, John W. 731.4
The technique of sculpture. New York, Reinhold [c.1965] 168p. illus., ports. 26cm. Bibl. [NB1170.M53] 65-14037 12.00
1. Sculpture—Technique. I. Title. BIP

MILLS, John W. 731.4
The technique of sculpture / John W. Mills. New York : Watson-Guptill Publications, 1976. 168 p. : ill. ; 26 cm. Includes index. Bibliography: p. 162. [NB1170.M53 1976] 75-19461 ISBN 0-8230-5210-9 : 13.95
1. Sculpture—Technique. I. Title.

MULLANEY, Sean. 731.4
Taking up sculpture. New York, Taplinger Pub. Co. [1973, c1971] 142 p. illus. 22 cm. (Taplinger's teach-yourself-crafts series) [NB1170.M8 1973] 72-2201 ISBN 0-8008-7544-3 5.95
1. Sculpture—Technique. I. Title. BIP

MYERS, Bernard 730.9
Sculpture; form and method. London, Studio Vista; New York, Reinhold [c.1965] 95p. illus. (pt. col.) 20cm. (Studio Vista/Reinhold art paperback) [NB1170.M9] 65-24056 2.25 pap.,
1. Sculpture—Technique. 2. Sculpture—Hist. I. Title.

*PAYNE, G. C. 731.4
Adventures with sculpture by G. C. Payne. New York, Frederick Warne and Co. [1973, c1971] 64 p. illus., 26 cm. (Adventures in learning series) London ed. (Kaye & Ward) has title: Fun with sculpture. [NB1170] 72-94536 ISBN 0-7232-6035-4 4.50
1. Sculpture—Technique. I. Title.

PERCY, Hubert Montagu. 731.2
New materials in sculpture; cold casting in metals, glass fibre, polyester resins, vinamold hot melt compunds, cold-cure silastomer flexible moulds, cavityless sand casting [and] vinagel [by] H. M. Percy. With a section on casting in cement fondu by Edward Folkard. 2d ed., rev. and enl. [1st American ed.] New York, Transatlantic Arts, 1966. viii, 152 p. illus. 23 cm. Bibliography: p. vi. [NB1170.P4 1966] 66-6812
1. Sculpture—Technique. 2. Artists' materials. I. Title. BIP

PRESS, Fred. 731.4
Sculpture at your finger tips. Photos. by Burton Berinsky. New York, Reinhold Pub. Corp. [1962] 60p. illus. 27cm. [NB1170.P7] 62-13690
1. Sculpture—Technique. I. Title.

ROOD, John, 1902- 739.14
Sculpture with a torch. Minneapolis, University of Minnesota Press [1963] 108 p. illus. 28 cm. [NB1220.R6 1963] 63-13883
1. Sculpture—Technique. 2. Welding. I. Title. BIP

SLOBODKIN, Louis, 1903- 731
Sculpture; principles and practice. New York, Dover Publications [1973] 255 p. illus. 28 cm. [NB1170.S58 1973] 73-77636 4.00 (pbk.)
1. Sculpture—Technique. I. Title. BIP

STEVENS, Harold. 731
Art in the round; elements and materials of three-dimensional design. New York, Reinhold Pub. Corp. [1965] 160 p. illus. 26 cm. [NB1170.S75] 65-19674
1. Sculpture—Technique. 2. Handicraft. I. Title.

STRUPPECK, Jules. 731
The creation of sculpture. Photos. by the author. New York, Holt [1952] 260 p. illus. 27 cm. [NB1170.S8] 52-7020
1. Sculpture—Technique. I. Title.

SUNSET 731.4
Sculpture with simple materials, by the Sunset edit. staff with Robert and Joan Dawson. Menlo Park Calif., Lane [c.1966] 96p illus. 28cm. (Sunset bk.) [NB1170.S9] 66-15339 1.95 pap.,
1. Sculpture—Technique. I. Title.

†TAWES, William I. 730
Creative sculpture / by William I. Tawes. Cambridge, Md. : Tidewater Publishers, 1976. xii, 250 p., [1] leaf of plates : ill. (some col.) ; 27 cm. Includes index. Bibliography: p. 241-242. [NB1170.T34] 76-10862 ISBN 0-87033-219-8: 10.00
1. Sculpture—Technique. 2. Carving (Art industries) I. Title. BIP

ZAIDENBERG, Arthur, 1903- 731.4
Anyone can sculpt; a book of established and new methods and techniques for amateurs and students. New York, Harper [1952] 157 p. illus. 28 cm. [NB1170.Z3] 52-5480
1. Sculpture—Technique. I. Title. BIP

ZAIDENBERG, Arthur, 1903- 731.4
Anyone can sculpt; a book of established and new methods and techniques for amateurs and students. Rev. ed. New York, Harper & Row [1972] xvi, 181 p. illus. 28 cm. Bibliography: p. 179. [NB1170.Z3 1972] 76-138776 ISBN 0-06-014800-4 8.50
1. Sculpture—Technique. I. Title.

ZAIDENBERG, Arthur, 1903- 731.4
The new and classic sculpture methods. New York, World [1972] 174 p. illus. 28 cm. [NB1170.Z32 1972] 68-15190 ISBN 0-529-00289-2 12.50
1. Sculpture—Technique. I. Title.

Sculpture, Thai—Exhibitions.

BOWIE, Theodore Robert. 732'.4
The sculpture of Thailand / Theodore Bowie, editor ; M. C. Subhadradis Diskul, A. B. Griswold ; photos. by Brian Brake. New York : Arno Press, 1975, [c1972] p. cm. (The Asia Society reprint collection) Catalog of an exhibition held at the Asia House Gallery, fall, 1972, and others. Includes Images of the Buddha by A. B. Griswold (p.) and Catalogue and plates: notes, by M. C. Subhadradis Diskul (p.). Reprint of the ed. published by the Asia Society, New York. [NB1021.B65 1975] 75-6571 ISBN 0-405-06559-0 : 30.00
1. Sculpture, Thai—Exhibitions. 2. Sculpture, Buddhist—Thailand. I. Griswold, Alexander B. II. Subhadradis Diskul, Prince. III. Asia House Gallery, New York. IV. Title. V. Series. BIP

BOWIE, Theodore Robert. 732'.4
The sculpture of Thailand. Theodore Bowie, editor, M. C. Subhadradis Diskul [and] A. B. Griswold. Photos. by Brian Brake. [New York] Asia Society; distributed by New York Graphic Society [1972] 137 p. illus. (part. col.) 28 cm. Catalog of an exhibition held at the Asia House Gallery, fall, 1972, and others. Includes Images of the Buddha by A. B. Griswold (p. 13-25) and Catalogue and plates: notes by M. C. Subhadradis Diskul (p. 31-129) "An Asia House Gallery publication." Bibliography: p. 136-137. [NB1021.B65] 78-186666 ISBN 0-87848-039-0 17.50
1. Sculpture, Thai—Exhibitions. 2. Sculpture, Buddhist—Thailand. I. Subhadradis Diskul, Prince. II. Griswold, Alexander B. III. Asia House Gallery, New York. IV. Title.

Sculpture, Thai—History.

BOISSELIER, Jean. 732'.4
The heritage of Thai sculpture / Jean Boisselier, Jean-Michel Beurdeley. [New York] : J. Weatherhill, [1975] 51 p. cm. Translation of La sculpture en Thailande. Includes index. Bibliography: p. [NB1021.B5713] 75-7515 ISBN 0-8348-0109-4 : 60.00
1. Sculpture, Thai—History. 2. Sculpture, Buddhist—Thailand—History. I. Beurdeley, Michel, joint author. II. Title. BIP

Sculpture—Thailand.

SALMONY, Alfred, 1890-1958. 732'.4
Sculpture in Siam. New York, Hacker Art Books, [1972 i.e.1973] xvi, 51 p. map, 70 plates. 33 cm. Reprint of the 1925 ed. published by E. Benn, London. Bibliography: p. 49-50. [NB1021.S3 1972] 79-143362 ISBN 0-87817-081-2 35.00
1. Sculpture—Thailand. I. Title. BIP

Sculpture—Themes, motives—Exhibitions.

CLEVELAND Museum of Art. 730'.074'017132
Traditions and revisions : themes for the history of sculpture / catalogue, Gabriel P. Weisberg ; introductory essay, H. W. Janson. Cleveland : Cleveland Museum of Art, [1975] p. cm. An exhibition held Sept. 23-Nov. 16, 1975, as a part of a joint program in art history with Case Western Reserve University. [NB16.C55C553 1975] 75-26708 ISBN 0-910386-23-4 pbk. : 4.00
1. Sculpture—Themes, motives—Exhibitions. I. Weisberg, Gabriel P. II. Janson, Horst Woldemar, 1913- III. Case Western Reserve University. IV. Title. Distributed by Kent State University Press.

Sculpture—United States.

ROBINETTE, Margaret A., 1932- 731'.8
Outdoor sculpture : object and environment / by Margaret A. Robinette. New York : Whitney Library of Design, 1976. p. cm. Includes index. Bibliography: p. [NB212.R62] 75-34326 ISBN 0-8230-7406-4
1. Sculpture—United States. 2. Sculpture, Modern—20th century—United States. 3. Art, Municipal—united States. 4. Urban beautification—United States. I. Title. BIP

Sculpture, Yugoslav.

LATTER-DAY Yugoslav sculpture. 730.9497
Text by Miodrag Kolaric [Photos.: T. Dabac, M. Szabo. Dist. New York, Vanous, 1962] 155p. (chiefly illus) 34cm. 62-4927 15.00
1. Sculpture, Yugoslav. I. Kolaric, Miodrag. II. Dabac, Toso.

Sculptures—Technique.

MARKS, Mickey Klar 731.4
Slate sculpturing. Sculptures by Frank Eliscu; photos. by David Rosenfeld. New York, Dial [c.]1963. 44p. illus. 21cm. 63-9780 2.75
1. Sculptures—Technique. I. Title.

Sculpure, Indic.

MUKERJEE, Radhakamal, 1889- 732'.4
The cosmic art of India; symbol (murti), sentiment (rasa) and silence (voga) Bombay, New York Allied Publishers [1965] xvi, 227 p. plates. 26 cm. [NB1002.M78] SA 66
1. Sculpure, Indic. 2. Art, Buddhist. 3. Symbolism in art. I. Title.

Sea Cliff—Description—Views.

BRAYNARD, Frank Osborn, 1916- 741.9'747'245
One square mile; a Sea Cliff sketchbook, by Frank O. Braynard. [Ann Arbor, Priv. print. by Edwards Bros. Press c1967] 144 p. illus. 23 x 29 cm. [F129.S615B7] 67-20405
1. Sea Cliff—Description—Views. I. Title.

Sea gods in art.

LATTIMORE, Steven. 733'.3
The marine thiasos in Greek sculpture / by Steven Lattimore. Los Angeles : Institute of Archaeology, University of California, Los Angeles, 1976. 80 p., [16] leaves of plates : ill. ; 30 cm. (Monograph of the Archaeological Institute of America ; no. 9) (Monumenta archaeologica ; v. 3) ISSN 0363-7565) Includes bibliographical references. [NB94.L37] 76-18609 ISBN 0-917956-02-8
1. Scopas, fl. 4th cent. B.C. 2. Sea gods in art. 3. Sculpture, Greek. 4. Sculpture, Hellenistic. I. Title. II. Series. III. Series: Archaeological Institute of America. Monograph ; no. 9. BIP

Sea in art.

HECKSCHER Museum. 758'.2'07404725
The drama of the sea : [exhibition], Heckscher Museum, Huntington, New York, May 11-June 15, 1975. [Huntington] : The Museum, [1975] 20 p. : ill. ; 28 cm. Catalogue. Introd. signed: Ruth Solomon. [N8240.H42 1975] 75-317475
1. Sea in art. 2. Naval battles in art. 3. Art, Modern—Exhibitions. I. Solomon, Ruth. II. Title.

Miami Art Center. 758'.2'0740159381
The artist and the sea; a group of paintings related to the sea, conchology, and marine archaeology lent by museums and private collections. [An exhibit] March 21 through April 18, 1969. Miami [1969] 16 p. illus. (part col.) 23 cm. [N8240.M5] 75-21282
1. Sea in art. 2. Art—Exhibitions. I. Title.

ROUGH sea / 769'.4'37094207402256
[compiled] by Susan Hiller. Brighton : Gardner Centre Gallery, University of Sussex, 1976. [60] p. : of ill. ; 12 x 17 cm. "This book was produced in conjunction with the exhibition 'Dedicated to the unknown artists', first shown at The Gardner Centre Gallery, University of Sussex in April 1976." [NC1878.S4R68] 77-350736 ISBN 0-9504908-0-6 : £1.00
1. Sea in art. 2. Postal cards—England. I. Hiller, Susan.

Sea in art—Juvenile literature.

GRACZA, Margaret 704.94
The ship and the sea in art. Designed by Robert Clark Nelson. Minneapolis, Lerner c.1965. 64p. illus., (pt. col.) ports. 27cm. [N8240.G7] 64-8203 3.79 bds.,
1. Sea in art—Juvenile literature. 2. Ships in art—Juvenile literature. I. Title. BIP

Seals (Numismatics)— Ancient.

FRANKFORT, Henri, 1897-1954. 929.8
Stratified cylinder seals from the Diyala region. With a chapter by Thorkild Jacobsen. Chicago, University of Chicago Press [1955] xi, 78p. 96 plates (incl. 4 maps, 3 fold.) (The University of Chicago Oriental Institute Publications v.72) 'This publication is one of a group planned to present as a whole the work of the Oriental Institute's Iraq Expedition in the Diyala region. Bibliographical footnotes. [CD5348.F73] 54-11976
1. Seals (Numismatics)— Ancient. 2. Art—Mesopotamia. 3. Design, Decorative. 4. Assyro-Babylonian religion. I. Title. II. Series: Chicago, University. Oriental Institute. Publications, v. 72

Seals (Numismatics)—China.

LAI, T'ien-ch'ang. 737'.6'0951
Chinese seals / T. C. Lai ; introd. by Jiu-fong L. Chang. Seattle : University of Washington PRESS 1976. xx, 200 p., [2] leaves of plates : ill. ; 23 cm. [CD6173.L26] 76-7789 ISBN 00-295-95517-1 : 10.00
1. Seals (Numismatics)—China. I. Title.

TAGUCHI, Nishu 1907- 736.3
Tenkoku, the seal engraving; from hieroglyphs to alphabet, by Nishu Taguchi [Rutland, vt.] Japan Pubns. [c.1964] 59 p. illus. 21 cm. 64-4094 pap., 1.25
1. Seals (Numismatic)—China. I. Title.

WANG, Chi-ch'ien, comp. 737.6
Seals of Chinese painters and collectors of the Ming and Ch'ing periods, reproduced in facsimile size and deciphered, by Victoria Contag, Wang Chi-ch'ien. Introd. by James Cahill. Rev. ed. with supplement. [Hongkong] Hong Kong. Univ. Pr., 1966. lxviii, 729p. illus. 27cm. First ed. pub. in 1940 under Chinese title: Wang's name in characters appeared on the title page. Prefatory matter in English and Chinese; text in Chinese, with trs. in German or English; added t.p.: in Chinese. p. 513-528. Seals of Sung and Yuan painters': American supplement: further seals found on Chinese paintings in American public and private collections': p. [631]-726. 'Source material': p. [xxii]-xxiii. 'Literature': p. xxvii-xxviii. [N45.W3 1966] 66-84760 40.00. bxd.
1. Seals (Numismatics)—China. 2. Artists' marks. 3. Collectors' marks. 4. Painters, Chinese. 5. Painters—Dictionaries—German. 6. Painters—Dictionaries—English. 7. Art—Collectors and collecting. I. Contag, Victoria, joint comp. II. Title. III. Title: Ming Ch'ing hua chia yin chien. American distributor: Oxford Univ. Pr., New York.

Seals (Numismatics)—Crete.

KENNA, V. E. G. 736.3
Cretan seals. with a catalogue of the Minoan gems in the Ashmolean Museum. Oxford [Eng.] Clarendon Press, [dist. New York, Oxford Univ. Press 1960 163p. illus., 23 plates. 32cm. Bibl.: p.[157]-158. Bibl. footnotes. 60-3317 16.80
1. Seals (Numismatics)—Crete. I. Oxford. University. Ashmolean Museum. II. Title. III. Title: Minoan gems in the Ashmolean Museum.

Seals (Numismatics)—Iran.

NEW York (City). Metropolitan Museum of Art. 737'.6
Sasanian stamp seals in the Metropolitan Museum of Art / Christoper J. Brunner. New York : The Museum, 1978. p. cm. Includes indexes. Bibliography: p. [CD6255.N48 1978] 78-2845 ISBN 0-87099-176-0 : 35.00
1. New York (City). Metropolitan Museum of Art. 2. Seals (Numismatics)—Iran. 3. Sassanids. I. Brunner, Christopher J. II. Title.

Seals (Numismatics)—Massachusetts.

FORBES, Allan, 1874- 929.8
Town and city seals of Massachusetts; presenting the official seals of some of the towns and cities of Massachusetts, together with brief historical sketches and local anecdotes. By Allan Forbes and Ralph M. Eastman. Boston, Printed for State Street Trust Co., 1950-51. 2 v. illus. 23 cm. [CD5618.M4F6] 50-12483
1. Seals (Numismatics)—Massachusetts. I. Eastman, Ralph Mason, 1891- joint author. II. Title.

Seals (Numismatics) — Near East.

OXFORD, University. Ashmolean Museum. 737.6
Catalogue of ancient Near Eastern seals in the Ashmolean Museum. Oxford, Clarendon P., 1966- v. illus., plates 28 1/2 cm. vol 1:7/7/- (v. 1: B 66-4703) Contents.v. 1. Cylinder seals [by] Briggs Buchanan. Bibliography: v. 1, p. [xv]-xvii. [CD5210.O9A5] 66-2580
1. Seals (Numismatics) — Near East. I. Buchanan, Briggs. II. Title.

Searle, Ronald, 1920—

SEARLE, Ronald, 1920- 741.59'42
Dick Deadeye [by] Ronald Searle and Gilbert & Sullivan. New York, Harcourt Brace Jovanovich [1974] p. cm. Based on an animated motion picture for which Searle produced artwork for Gilbert and Sullivan characters. [NC1766.G72S42] 74-8141 7.95
1. Searle, Ronald, 1920- I. Gibert, William Schwenck, Sir, 1836-1911. II. Sullivan, Arthur Seymour, Sir, 1842-1900. III. Title.

Season Sarcophagus (Dumbarton Oaks)

HANFMANN, George Maxim Anossov, 1911- 733'.5
The Season sarcophagus in Dumbarton Oaks, by George M. A. Hanfmann. Cambridge, Mass., Harvard University Press, 1951. New York, Johnson Reprint Corp., 1971. 2 v. plates. 30 cm. (Dumbarton Oaks studies, 2) "A catalogue of the representations of the Horae and the Seasons in ancient art": v. 2, p. [129]-192. Includes bibliographies. [NB1810.H3 1971] 71-146800
1. Season Sarcophagus (Dumbarton Oaks) I. Title. II. Series.

Seattle. Art Museum.

SEATTLE. Art Museum. 709'.5'074019777
Asiatic art in the Seattle Art Museum : a selection and catalogue / by Henry Trubner, William Jay Rathbun, Catherine A. Kaputa ; photography by Paul Macapia. Seattle : The Museum, 1973. 300 p. : ill. (some col.) ; 27 cm. Includes bibliographies and index. [N7262.S4 1973] 73-88583
1. Seattle. Art Museum. 2. Art, Oriental—Catalogs. 3. Art—Seattle—Catalogs. I. Trubner, Henry. II. Rathbun, William Jay. III. Kaputa, Catherine A. IV. Title.

SEATTLE, Art Museum. 708.1797
Handbook; selected works from the permanent collections. [Seattle] 1951. 126 p. illus. 20 cm. [N745.A6 1951] 52-28623
I. Title.

Seattle Club of Printing House Craftsmen.

A Half century, 686.2'06'579777
1925-1975 : commemorating fifty years of Craftsmen's activity in Seattle / edited by Bert Hagg. [Seattle] : Seattle Club of Print. House Craftsmen, c1975. 122 p., [1] leaf of plates : ill. ; 25 cm. 500 copies published. [Z120.S5H34] 76-351162
1. Seattle Club of Printing House Craftsmen. I. Hagg, Bert.

Seattle—Markets.

TOBEY, Mark. 759.13
The world of a market. Seattle, University of Washington Press [1964] [15] p. 64 plates (part col.) port. 29 cm. "This book had its origin in an exhibition, 'Mark Tobey and the Seattle Public Market,' held at the Seattle Art Museum in August, 1963." [ND237.T56A57] 64-18427
1. Seattle—Markets. I. Title.

Second Bank of the United States (Portrait gallery)

MILLEY, John C. 704.94'2'0973074014811
Faces of independence : portrait gallery guidebook : Second Bank of the United States, Independence National Historical Park / by John C. Milley. [Philadelphia : Eastern National Park & Monument Association, c1974] [39] p. : ill. (some col.) ; 16 x 23 cm. [N7593.1.M54] 74-21547
1. Second Bank of the United States (Portrait gallery) 2. United States—Biography—Portraits. I. Second Bank of the United States (Portrait gallery) II. Title.

Segal, George, 1924—

SEGAL, George, 1924- 730'.92'4
George Segal. [Text] by Jan van der

Marck. New York, H. N. Abrams 1976 233 p. illus. 28 x 30 cm. Bibliography: p. 228-[230] [NB237.S44V36] 74-13110 ISBN 0-8109-0488-8 :
1. Segal, George, 1924- I. Van der Marck, Jan, 1929- II. Title. BIP

SEGAL, George, 1924- 741.9'73
The private world of George Segal. Organized by Jose L. Barrio-Garay and John Lloyd Taylor. [Milwaukee] Art History Galleries, University of Wisconsin-Milwaukee [1973] [24] p. illus. 22 x 28 cm. Catalogue of an exhibition held Mar. 14-Apr. 10, 1973, Union Art Gallery, University of Wisconsin-Milwaukee and May 1-June 3, 1973, Indianapolis Museum of Art. Catalogue essay "The private world of George Segal" by J. L. Barrio-Garay (p. [5]-[8]) Includes bibliographical references. [N6537.S37B37] 73-77432
1. Segal, George, 1924- I. Barrio-Garay, Jose L. II. Wisconsin. University, Milwaukee. Art History Galleries. III. Wisconsin. University, Milwaukee. Union Art Gallery. IV. Indianapolis Museum of Art. V. Title.

SEGAL, George, 1924- 730'.92'4
Segal : [Sidney Janis presents an exhibition of new work by George Segal, opening Wednesday, March 29, 1967, and continuing until April 22 at 15 East 57 St., New York : catalogue]. [New York : Sidney Janis Gallery, 1967] [16] p. : chiefly ill. ; 28 cm. Cover title. [NB237.S44S52] 75-304408
1. Segal, George, 1924- I. Sidney Janis Gallery.

SEITZ, William Chapin. 730'.92'4
Segal [by] William C. Seitz. New York, Abrams [1972] 95 p. (p. [25]-[86] plates, part col.) 21 x 23 cm. (Modern artists) Bibliography: p. 90-93. [NB237.S44S439] 72-3235 ISBN 0-8109-4420-0 5.95
1. Segal, George, 1924- I. Segal, George, 1924-

Segall, Lasar, 1790-1957.

BARDI, Pietro Maria 759.981
Lasar Segall. [English translation by John Drummond. Milano] Edizioni del milione, 1959 [dist. New York Wittenborn, 1960] 179p. (Bibl.: p.41-[48]) illus. (part col.) ports. 28cm. "Second enlarged edition of that published on [sic] 1951 in Portuguese language and French language, by the Sao Paulo Museum of Art, for the Lasar Segall exhibition." 60-3261 12.50
1. Segall, Lasar, 1790-1957. I. Sao Paulo, Brazil (City) Museu de Arte. II. Title.

Seghers, Daniel, 1590-1661.

BURKE-GAFFNEY, Michael Walter, 1896- 759.9493
Daniel Seghers, 1590-1661, a tercentenary commemoration. [1st ed.] New York, Vantage Press [1961] 54p. illus. 21cm. Includes bibliography. [ND673.S39B8] 62-1559
1. Seghers, Daniel, 1590-1661. I. Title.

Seghers, Hercules, 17th cent.

COLLINS, Leo C. 760'.092'4
Hercules Seghers / by Leo C. Collins. New York : Hacker Art Books, 1978. ix, 149 p., [54] leaves of plates : ill. ; 29 cm. Includes index. Bibliography: p. 135-138. [N6953.S4C64 1978] 77-73729 ISBN 0-87817-209-2 lib bdg :40.00
1. Seghers, Hercules, 17th cent.

HERCULES Seghers. 759.9492
[Chicago] University of Chicago Press [1953] ix, 149p. illus., 111plates. 31cm. Bibliography: p. 135-138. [ND653.S4C6] [ND653.S4C6] 927.5 53-12895 53-12895
1. Seghers, Hercules, 17th cent. I. Collins, Leo C
BIP

Segonzac, Andre Dunoyer de, 1884-1974.

SEGONZAC, Andre Dunoyer de, 1884-1974. 769'.92'4
The graphic art of Andre Dunoyer de Segonzac, 1884-1974 : a tribute, Grunwald Center for the Graphic Arts, January 14-February 23, 1975. Los Angeles : Frederick S. Wright Art Gallery, University of California, [1975] 42 p. : ill. ; 29 cm. Bibliography: p. 40-42. [NE2049.5.S4G78] 76-354449
1. Segonzac, Andre Dunoyer de, 1884-1974. I. Grunwald Center for the Graphic Arts. II. Title.

Seguy, E. A.

SEGUY, E. A. 745.4'49'24
Exotic floral patterns in color / by E.-A. Seguy. New York : Dover Publications, 1974. [5] p., 40 leaves of plates : col. ill. ; 31 cm. Unabridged republication of two of the author's portfolios originally published by C. Massin, Paris: Bouquets et frondaisons, published in 1926 and Suggestions pour etoffes et tapis, published in 1923. [NK9502.2.S43A45] 74-77178 ISBN 0-486-23041-4
1. Seguy, E. A. 2. Design, Decorative—Plant forms. I. Title. BIP

Seibal site, Guatemala.

EXCAVATIONS at Seibal, 972.81
Department of Peten, Guatemala / [Gorgon R. Willey, general editor and project director]. Cambridge, Mass. : Peabody Museum of Archaeology and Ethnology, Harvard Univrsity, 1978. xiii, 250 p. : ill. ; 31 cm. (Memoirs of the Peabody Museum of Archaeology and Ethnology, Harvard University ; v. 14, no. 1-3) Includes bibliographies. [F1435.1.S44E9] 76-53126 ISBN 0-87365-686-5 : 30.00
1. Seibal site, Guatemala. 2. Cancuen site, Guatemala. 3. Itzuan site, Guatemala. I. Willey, Gordon Randolph, 1913- Artifacts. 1978. II. Tortellot, Gair. A reconnaissance of Cancuen. 1978. III. Tourtellot, Gair. A brief reconnaissance of Itzan. 1978. IV. Series: Harvard University. Peabody Museum of Archaeology and Ethnology. Memoirs ; v. 14, no. 1-3.
Contents omitted.

Sekhem-khet, King of Egypt.

GHUNAIM, Muhammad Zakariya. 913.32
The buried pyramid. London, New York, Longmans, Green [1956] 155p. illus. 23cm. American ed. (New York, Rinehart) has title: The lost pyramid. [DT73.S3G5 1956a] 56-14553
1. Sekhem-khet, King of Egypt. 2. Pyramids. I. Title.

Seley, Jason, 1919—

SELEY, Jason, 1919- 730'.92'4
Figures & objects : [exhibition April 6-28, 1974, the Picker Gallery, Dana Arts Center, Colgate University, Hamilton, N.Y.] / Jason Seley. [Hamilton, N.Y. : Picker Gallery], 1974. [16] p. : ill. ; 21 x 22 cm. [NB237.S45P5] 75-316416
1. Seley, Jason, 1919- I. Picker Gallery. II. Title.

Self-portraits.

GASSER, Manuel. 704.942
Self-portraits: from the fifteenth century to the present day. Translated by Angus Malcolm. [1st ed.] New York, Appleton-Century [1963] 302 p. illus., col. plates. 25 cm. [N7592.G313] 63-18195
1. Self-portraits.

SELF-PORTRAITS of great 743'.9'2
artists. Introd. by Stephen Longstreet. [1st ed.] Alhambra, Calif., Borden Pub. Co. [1973] [48] p. (chiefly illus.) 31 cm. (Master draughtsman series) [NC772.S44] 72-84100
1. Self-portraits. 2. Portrait drawing. I. Longstreet, Stephen, 1907-

Self-portraits, American—Exhibitions.

VAN DEVANTER, Ann C. 757'.3'0973
American self-portraits, 1670-1973. Introd. and [exhibition] catalogue by Ann C. Van Devanter and Alfred V. Frankenstein with the assistance of Shirley S. Simpson. [Washington] International Exhibitions Foundation, 1974. 247 p. illus. 28 cm. Exhibition held at the National Portrait Gallery and the Indianapolis Museum of Art. Bibliography: p. 234-244. [ND1311.V36] 73-93138
1. Self-portraits, American—Exhibitions. I. Frankenstein, Alfred Victor, 1906- joint author. II. International Exhibitions Foundation. III. National Portrait Gallery, Washington, D.C. IV. Indianapolis Museum of Art. V. Title. BIP

Self-portraits—Juvenile literature.

LERNER, Sharon 704.94
The self-portrait in art. Designed by Robert Clark Nelson. Minneapolis, Lerner c.1965. 64p. illus., (pt. col.) ports. 27cm. [N7575.L4] 64-8202 3.79 bds.,
1. Self-portraits—Juvenile literature. 2. Artists—Juvenile literature. I. Title. BIP

Self-realization.

RICHARDS, Mary Caroline. 171.3
Centering in pottery, poetry, and the person. [1st ed.] Middletown, Conn., Wesleyan University Press [1964] 159 p. 24 cm. [NK4028.R5A3] 64-22372
1. Self-realization. I. Title. BIP

Selfix camera.

EMANUEL, Walter Daniel, 1908- 770.2
Selfix guide. London, New York, Focal Press [1952] 72 p. illus. 17 cm. (The Camera guide) [TR263.S4E5] 52-65093
1. Selfix camera. 2. Photography—Handbooks manuals, etc. I. Title.

Seligmann, Jacques, 1858-1923.

SELIGMAN, Germain. 706.994
Merchants of art: 1880-1960; eighty years of professional collecting. New York, Appleton-Century-Crofts [1962, c1961] xxi, 294 p. plates, ports. 26 cm. [N8660.S47S4] 61-15096
1. Seligmann, Jacques, 1858-1923. 2. Art—Collectors and collecting. 3. Art dealers. I. Title.

Seligmann, Kurt, 1900-1962.

SELIGMANN, Kurt, 1900-1962. 769'.92'4
Kurt Seligmann; his graphic work. New York, Helen Serger, La Boetie [1973] [36] p. illus. 21 cm. Catalog of an exhibition held March-April 1973. [NE2064.5.S44H44] 73-77328
1. Seligmann, Kurt, 1900-1962. I. Helen Serger, La Boetie, inc.

SPRINGFIELD, Mass. Museum of Fine Arts. 769'.92'4
Kurt Seligmann graphics, with essays by Nicolas Calas [and others] Springfield [1974] 19 p. illus. 15 x 22 cm. Catalogue of an exhibition held May 11-June 16, 1974. [NE2064.5.S44S67 1974] 74-81525
1. Seligmann, Kurt, 1900-1962.

Sendak, Maurice.

SENDAK, Maurice. 741.9'73
Fantasy sketches. Philadelphia, Philip H. & A. S. W. Rosenbach Foundation, 1970. [14] l. (chiefly illus.) 29 cm. "This book was first published on the occasion of an exhibition of original drawings and other materials illustrating the art of Maurice Sendak at the Philip H. & A. S. W. Rosenbach Foundation." [NC139.S4A45] 73-22513
I. Philip H. & A. S. W. Rosenbach Foundation. II. Title.

SENDAK, Maurice. 741.9'42
Pictures by Maurice Sendak. [New York] Harper and Row [1971] [3] p., 20 plates (part col.) in portfolio. 66 cm. Cover title. The artist's selection of 19 pictures from books he has illustrated. "Limited to five hundred copies. Each copy includes a signed reproduction of a previously unpublished pencil drawing of Jennie, the Sealyham terrier who posed for the heroine of Higglety Pigglety Pop!" No. 56. [NC975.5.S44A5 1971] 72-172496
1. Sendak, Maurice. BIP

Sendak, Maurice—Interviews.

SENDAK, Maurice. 741'.0924
Questions to an artist who is also an author; a conversation between Maurice Sendak and Virginia Haviland. Washington, Library of Congress, 1972. 264-280 p. illus. 27 cm. Cover title. Based on a transcript of a discussion held at the Library of Congress, Nov. 16, 1970. Reprinted from the library's Quarterly journal, v. 28, no. 4 (Oct. 1971) [PS3569.E6Q4] 72-3428 ISBN 0-8444-0026-2 0.30
1. Sendak, Maurice—Interviews. I. Haviland, Virginia, 1911- II. United States. Library of Congress. III. Title.

SMITH, Jeffrey Jon. 741'.092'4 B
A conversation with Maurice Sendak / Jeffrey Jon Smith. [Elmhurst? Ill.] : Smith, [1974] [15] p. (incl. cover) : ill. ; 15 x 22 cm. Cover title. "Based on a transcript of a phone conversation ... taped on August 27, 1974." [PS3569.E6Z85] 75-305049
1. Sendak, Maurice—Interviews. I. Sendak, Maurice. II. Title.

Senebtisi.

MACE, Arthur Crittenden, 1874-1928. 913.32'03'1
The tomb of Senebtisi at Lisht, by Arthur C. Mace and Herbert E. Winlock. New York, 1916. [New York] Arno Press, 1973. xxii, 132 p., 35 plates. illus. 32 cm. At head of title: The Metropolitan Museum of Art Egyptian Expedition. Reprint of the ed. which was issued as v. 1 of Publications of the Metropolitan Museum of Art Egyptian Expedition. Bibliography: p. 127-128. [DT73.L6M3 1973] 73-168408 ISBN 0-405-02241-7
1. Senebtisi. 2. Lisht, Egypt—Tombs. I. Winlock, Herbert Eustis, 1884-1950, joint author. II. New York (City). Metropolitan Museum of Art. Egyptian Expedition. III. Title. IV. Series: New York (City). Metropolitan Museum of Art. Egyptian Expedition. Publications, v. 1.

Seneca Indians—Masks.

MATHEWS, Zena Pearlstone. 732'.2
The relation of Seneca false face masks to Seneca and Ontario archeology / Zena Pearlstone Mathews. New York : Garland Pub., 1978. p. cm. (Outstanding dissertations in the fine arts) Bibliography: p. [E99.S3M38] 77-94707 ISBN 0-8240-3239-X : lib.bdg. : 30.00
1. Seneca Indians—Masks. 2. Seneca Indians—Antiquities. 3. Iroquoian Indians—Antiquities. 4. Ontario—Antiquities. I. Title. II. Series. BIP

Sengai, 1751-1837.

SUZUKI, Daisetz Teitaro, 1870-1966. 741.0924
Sengai, the Zen master, by Daisetz T. Suzuki. With editorial and prefatory notes by Eva van Hoboken [and others] Greenwich, Conn., New York Graphic Society [1971] xviii, 191 p. illus. 26 cm. [ND1059.S45S98] 68-25738 ISBN 0-8212-0319-3 10.00
1. Sengai, 1751-1837. BIP

Sepeshy, Zoltan L., 1898-

SYRACUSE University. Joe and Emily Lowe Art Center 759.13
Zoltan Sepeshy; forty years of his work, by Laurence Schmeckebier. Syracuse, N.Y., School of Art, Syracuse Univ. [1966] 83p. illus. 23cm. An exhibition of paintings and drawings executed during the period 1926-1966, org. jtly. by the Sch. of Art, Syracuse Univ., and the Cranbrook Acad. of Art, and held in the galleries of the Joe and Emily Lowe Art Center, Syracuse Univ., March 8-April 3, 1966, and the Cranbrook Mus. of Art, Bloomfield Hills, Mich., April 19-May 8, 1966. [ND237.S438S9] 66-20904 price unreported pap.,
1. Sepeshy, Zoltan L., 1898- I. Schmeckebier, Laurence Eli, 1906- II. Syracuse University. School of Art. III.

Cranbrook Academy of Art, Bloomfield Hills, Mich. IV. Title.

Sepulchral monuments— Bosnia and Herzegovina.

BIHALJI-MERIN, Oto, 1904- 736.5
Bogomil sculpture, essays by Oto Bihalji-Merin, Alojz Benac [Tr.] Photos. by Toso Dabac. New York, Harcourt [1963] xxxvi, [7] p., 80p. of illus. map, 32cm. (Helen & Kurt Wolff bk.) Bibl. 63-3618 8.50
1. Sepulchral monuments— Bosnia and Herzegovina. 2. Sculpture—Bosnia and Herzegovina. 3. Sculpture, Medieval. 4. Bogomiles. I. Benac, Alojz. II. Title.

Sepulchral monuments—Canada—Ontario.

HANKS, Carole. 731'.76'09713
Early Ontario gravestones. Toronto, New York, McGraw-Hill Ryerson [1974] 94 p. illus. 24 cm. [NB1880.C2H36] 73-21056 ISBN 0-07-077765-9
1. Sepulchral monuments—Canada—Ontario. 2. Epitaphs—Ontario. I. Title.

Sepulchral monuments—Direct.

AMERICAN Monument 745.59'22'075 Association.
A complete directory of the monument industry. Buffalo. v. 17cm. Cover title, 19 Directory of the monument industry. [TS2301.M8A5] 55-30817
1. Sepulchral monuments—Direct. I. Title.

THE Monument 745.59'22'075 industry's buying guide.
Quincy, Mass, American Art in Stone. v. 23cm. Editor: 19 E. M. Ford. [TS2301.M8M6] 55-21911
1. Sepulchral monuments—Direct. I. Ford, Eather McDade, ed. II. Title.

Sepulchral monuments—England.

BURGESS, Frederick Bevan 731.76
English churchyard memorials. London, Lutterworth Pr. [New York, Praeger, 1965, c.1963] 325p. illus. 23cm. Bibl. [NB1860.B8] 66-38184 8.50
1. Sepulchral monuments—England. 2. Stone-cutters. 3. Cemeteries—England. I. Title.

ESDAILE, Katharine Ada 730'.942 McDowall.
English monumental sculpture since the Renaissance / by Katharine A. Esdaile. Westport, Conn. : Hyperion Press, [1979] p. cm. Reprint of the 1927 ed. published by Society for Promoting Christian Knowledge, London, in series: The Historic monuments of England. Includes index. [NB1860.E83 1979] 78-59020 ISBN 0-88355-694-4 : lib.bdg. : 19.50
1. Sepulchral monuments—England. I. Title. II. Series: The Historic monuments of England. BIP

Sepulchral monuments—France.

BRUNHOFF, Anne de. 730'.945
Souls in stone : European graveyard sculpture / photographed by Anne de Brunhoff ; with an introd. by Thomas B. Hess. 1st ed. New York : Knopf : distributed by Random House, 1978. x, 96 p. : chiefly ill. ; 22 x 24 cm. [NB1865.B78 1978] 77-20371 ISBN 0-394-73283-9 pbk. : 7.95
1. Sepulchral monuments—France. 2. Sepulchral monuments, Victorial—France. 3. Sepulchral monuments—Italy. 4. Sepulchral monuments, Victorian—Italy. I. Title. BIP

Sepulchral monuments—Great Britain—Lettering.

BARTRAM, Alan. 745.6'197
Tombstone lettering the British Isles / Alan Bartram. London : Lund Humphries ; New York : Watson-Guptill Publications, 1978. [96] p. : ill. ; 20 x 21 cm. [NK3630.3.S46B37 1978] 78-52350 ISBN 0-8230-5380-6 : 8.95
1. Sepulchral monuments—Great Britain—Lettering. I. Title. BIP

Sepulchral monuments—Greece.

GARDNER, Percy, 1846-1937. 913.38
Sculptured tombs of Hellas. Washington, McGrath Pub. Co., 1973. xix, 259 p. illus. 24 cm. Reprint of the 1896 ed. published by Macmillan, London. [NB1370.G2 1973] 74-119263 ISBN 0-8434-0133-8 38.00
1. Sepulchral monuments—Greece. 2. Sculpture, Greek. 3. Funeral rites and ceremonies—Greece. I. Title.

Sepulchral monuments—History.

PANOFSKY, Erwin, 1892- 731.76 1968.
Tomb sculpture; four lectures on its changing aspects from ancient Egypt to Bernini. Edited by H. W. Janson. New York, H. N. Abrams [1964] 319 p. 446 illus. 29 cm. Errata slip inserted. Bibliography: p. 301-310. [NB1800.P3] 64-15235
1. Sepulchral monuments—History. 2. Sculpture. I. Title.

Sepulchral monuments—Japan.

ASIA Society. 730.952
Haniwa. [Exhibition as shown in four American museums, 1960] [New York] [1960] unpaged (chiefly illus.) 21 cm. [NB1667.A8] 60-24383
1. Sepulchral monuments, Japan. 2. Pottery, Japanese. I. Title.

MIKI, Fumio 730.952
Haniwa, the clay sculpture of protohistoric Japan. English adaption [from the Japanese] by Roy Andrew Miller. Rutland, Vt., C. E. Tuttle Co. [1960] 160p. illus., 92 plates (part col.) map, diagrs. 28cm. 60-9286 8.75, half cloth, bxd.
1. Sepulchral monuments—Japan. 2. Terra-cottas, Japanese. I. Miller, Roy Andrew. II. Title.

Sepulchral monuments—Middle States.

SMITH, Elmer Lewis. 731.7'6
Early American grave stone designs; [a pictorial presentation of the often forgotten folk art in the early graveyards of New Jersey, Pennsylvania, Maryland, and in Virginia] by Elmer L. Smith. Witmer, Pa., Applied Arts [1968] 42 p. (chiefly illus.) 28 cm. (Americana dollar publications) Bibliography: p. 42. [NB1856.M5S6] 76-700 1.00
1. Sepulchral monuments—Middle States. 2. Sculpture, American. I. Title.

Sepulchral monuments—New England.

DUVAL, Francis Y. 736'.5'0974
Early American gravestone art in photographs / by Francis Y. Duval and Ivan B. Rigby. New York : Dover Publications, 1978. ix, 133 p. : ill. ; 29 cm. Bibliography: p. 133. [NB1856.N4D8 1978] 78-54867 ISBN 0-486-23689-7 : 6.00
1. Sepulchral monuments—New England. 2. Sepulchral monuments—Middle Atlantic States. I. Rigby, Ivan B., joint author. II. Title. BIP

FORBES, Harriette 731'.549'0974 (Merrifield) 1856-1951.
Gravestones of early New England, and the men who made them, 1653-1800. Princeton, Pyne Press [1973, c1927] 141 p. illus. 28 cm. Reprint of the ed. published by Houghton Mifflin, Boston. [NB1855.F6 1973] 73-79521 6.95
1. Sepulchral monuments—New England. 2. Boston—Sepulchral monuments. 3. Stone-cutters—New England. I. Title.

FORBES, Harriette 731.5'49'0974 (Merrifield) 1856-1951.
Gravestones of early New England, and the men who made them, 1653-1800. New York, Da Capo Press, 1967. 141 p. illus. 27 cm. (Da Capo Press series in architecture and decorative art, v. 4) Reprint of the 1927 ed. [NB1855.F6 1967] 67-27452
1. Sepulchral monuments—New England. 2. Boston—Sepulchral monuments. 3. Stone-cutters—New England. I. Title.

GILLON, Edmund Vincent. 731.76
Early New England gravestone rubbings. New York, Dover Publications [1966] 195 plates, xxvi p. 29 cm. (Pictorial archive series) [NB1856.N4G5 1966] 66-14555
1. Sepulchral monuments—New England. 2. Sculpture, American—New England. 3. Rubbings. I. Title. BIP

GILLON, Edmund Vincent, 731.76 Jr.
Early New England gravestone rubbings [Gloucester, Mass., P. Smith, c.1966] 195 plates. xxvip. 29cm. (Pictorial archives ser. Dover bk., T1380 rebound) [NB1856.N4G5 1966] 5.00
1. Sepulchral monuments—New England. 2. Sculpture, American. I. Title.

LUDWIG, Allan I 731.76
Graven images; New England stonecarving and its symbols, 1650-1815, by Allan L. Ludwig. [1st ed.] Middletown, Conn., Wesleyan University Press [1966] xxxi, 482 p. illus., maps, 29 cm. Includes bibliographical references. [NB1856.N4L8] 66-14665
1. Sepulchral monuments — New England. 2. Sculpture, American. I. Title. BIP

Sepulchral monuments—New York (State)

WASSERMAN, Emily. 736'.5
Gravestone designs; rubbings and photographs from early New York & New Jersey. New York, Dover Publications [1972] 33, xvi p. illus., 135 plates. 29 cm. (Dover pictorial archive series) Bibliography: p. [xi]-xii. [NB1856.N5W37 1972] 79-174493 ISBN 0-486-22873-8 4.00
1. Sepulchral monuments—New York (State) 2. Sculpture, American—New York (State) 3. Sepulchral monuments—New Jersey. 4. Rubbings. 5. Sculpture, American—New Jersey. I. Title.

Sepulchral monuments—Rome.

ALTMANN, Walter, 1873- 733'.5
Die romischen Grabaltare der Kaiserzeit / Walter Altmann. New York : Arno Press, 1975. 306 p. ; 24 cm. (Ancient religion and mythology) Reprint of the 1905 ed. published by Weidmann, Berlin. Includes bibliographical references and indexes. [NB1380.A5 1975] 75-10626 ISBN 0-405-07002-0
1. Sepulchral monuments—Rome. 2. Altars—Rome. 3. Sculpture, Roman. I. Title. II. Series. BIP

Sepulchral monuments, Victorian—Northeastern States.

GILLON, Edmund 731'.76'0974 Vincent.
Victorian cemetery art [by] Edmund V. Gillon, Jr. With 260 photos. by the author. New York, Dover [1972] xiii, 173 p. (chiefly illus.) 28 cm. [NB1856.N6G5 1972] 71-175421 ISBN 0-486-22785-5 4.00
1. Sepulchral monuments, Victorian—Northeastern States. I. Title. BIP

GILLON, Edmund 731'.76'0974 Vincent.
Victorian cemetery art [by] Edmund V. Gillon, Jr. With 260 photos. by the author. Magnolia, Mass, Peter Smith [1973 c1972] xiii 173 p (chiefly illus.) 28 cm. (Dover bk rebound) [NB1856.N6G5 1972] 71-175421 ISBN 0-8446-4549-4 6.75
1. Sepulchral monuments, Victorian—Northeastern States. I. Title.

Sepulchral slabs.

GREENHILL, Frank 736'.5'094 Allen.
Incised effigial slabs : a study of engraved stone memorials in Latin Christendom, c.1100 to c.1700 / F. A. Greenhill ; with line drawings by H. W. Jones. London : Faber and Faber, 1976. 2 v. : ill. ; 29 cm. Errata slips inserted. Includes indexes. Bibliography: v. 1, p. 362-378. [NB1830.G73] 76-363778 ISBN 0-571-10741-9 (v. 1) : £35.00
1. Sepulchral slabs. 2. Stone carving. I. Title. BIP

Serial art—United States—Exhibitions.

CARMEAN, E. A. 709'.73'0740153
American art at mid-century : the subjects of the artist / E. A. Carmean and Eliza E. Rathbone, with Thomas B. Hess. Washington : National Gallery of Art, 1978. 268 p. : ill. (some col.) ; 28 cm. Catalog an exhibition held at the East Building, National Gallery of Art June 1-1978,-Jan. 14, 1979. Includes bibliographical references. [N6512.5.S43C37] 78-4595 18.95
1. Serial art—United States—Exhibitions. 2. Abstract expressionism—United States—Exhibitions. 3. Art, Modern—20th century—United States—Exhibitions. I. Rathbone, Eliza E., 1948- joint author. II. Hess, Thomas B., joint author. III. United States. National Gallery of Art. IV. Title.

Serigraphy.

AUVIL, Kenneth W. 764.8
Serigraphy; silk screen techniques for the artist [by] Kenneth W. Auvil. Englewood Cliffs, N.J., Prentice-Hall [1965] vii, 165 p. illus. 22 cm. Bibliography: p. 158. [NE1843.A8] 65-16337
1. Serigraphy.

BIEGELEISEN, Jacob Israel, 745.7 1910-
Silk screen techniques, by J. I. Biegeleisen and Max Arthur Cohn. New York, Dover Publications [1958] 187 p. illus. 24 cm. "Corrected and expanded version of ... Silk screen stencilling as a fine art." [NE1843.B52 1958] 655.3* 58-3044
1. Serigraphy. I. Cohn, Max Arthur, 1904- joint author. II. Title. BIP

CAZA, Michel. 764'.8
Silk screen printing. [English version by Julian Snelling and Claude Namy] New York, Van Nostrand Reinhold Co. [1974, c1973] 123 p. illus. (part col.) 18 x 21 cm. (Craft and art) Translation of La serigraphie. Bibliography: p. 118. [NE2236.C2913 1974] 73-8469 ISBN 0-442-29992-3 7.95
1. Serigraphy.

CHIEFFO, Clifford T. 764'.8
Silk-screen as a fine art; a handbook of contemporary silk-screen printing [by] Clifford T. Chieffo. New York, Reinhold [1967] 120 p. illus. (part col.) 29 cm. Bibliography: p. 118. [NE1843.C5] 67-14153
1. Serigraphy. I. Title. BIP

EISENBERG, James. 655.3
Silk screen printing. Bloomington, Ill., McKnight and McKnight Pub. Co. [1952] 55 p. illus. 26 cm. [NE1843.E4] 745.7 52-28624
1. Serigraphy. I. Title. BIP

KOSLOFF, Albert. 655.3
Mitography, the art and craft of screen process printing. Illus. by the author. Milwaukee, Bruce Pub. Co. [1952] 134 p. illus. 25 cm. [TT273.K655] 745.7 52-14647
1. Serigraphy. I. Title.

KOSLOFF, Albert. 745.7
Screen process printing. Illus. by the author. Cincinnati, Signs of the Times Pub. Co. [1950] 194 p. illus. 24 cm. [TT273.K66] 51-15339
1. Serigraphy. I. Title.

MACKENZIE, F. W. ed. 745.7
Screen process printing, 1951. Wealdstone, Middlesex. Skinner and Wilkinson [1951] 92 p. illus. 26 cm. [TT273.M3] 655.3 52-2359
1. Serigraphy. I. Title.

MARSH, Roger. 764'.8
Silk screen printing for the artist. [1st American ed.] New York, Transatlantic Arts, 1968. 77 p. illus., 6 col. plates. 23 cm. [NE1843.M3] 71-88657 6.75
1. Serigraphy. I. Title.

SHOKLER, Harry, 1896- 764.8
Artists manual for silk screen print making. [3d ed.] New York, Tudor Pub. Co. [1961, c1960] 178 p. illus. 24 cm. [NE1843.S4 1961] 60-15041
1. Serigraphy. I. Title.

SILK screen printing 655.3
[by] James Eisenberg and Francis J. Kafka.

[2d ed.] Bloomington, Ill., mcKnight & McKnight Pub. Co. [1957] 91p. illus. 26cm. [NE1843.E4 1957] [NE1843.E4 1957] 745.7 57-4589 57-4589
1. Serigraphy. I. Eisenberg, James. II. Kafka, Francis J., joint author.

STEPHENSON, Jessie Bane. 655.3
From old stencils to silk screening; a practical guide. Full basic instruction, with a historical sketch of the craft from the earliest examples to the present-day, and 200 selected designs. London, New York, Scribner, 1953. 239p. illus. 26cm. [TT273.S74] [TT273.S74] 745.7 53-6377 53-6377
1. Serigraphy. I. Title.

Serigraphy—Exhibitions.

VIETZE, Eric. 764'.8'028
How a screen print is made. Selected by Eric Vietze. [Exhibition, 1970-1972] circulated by the American Federation of Arts. [New York, Rapoport Printing, 1970] [31] p. ([12] on fold. sheet) 26 cm. "Catalog designed by M. Shroyer." Includes bibliography. [NE2236.V53] 78-135039
1. Serigraphy—Exhibitions. I. American Federation of Arts. II. Title.

Serigraphy—Yearbooks.

MYTTON-DAVIES, Peter, ed. 655.3
Screen process printing. Wealdstone, Middlesex, Press and Process Publications, 19 v. illus. (part col.) 25cm. annual. Editor: P. Mytton-Davies. [TT273.S35] [TT273.S35] 745.7 54-26312 54-26312
1. Serigraphy—Yearbooks. I. Title.

Serra, Junipero, 1713-1784.

DEGRAZIA, Ted Ettore, 1909- 759.13
The rose and the robe; the travels of Fray Junipero Serra in California. Paintings and text by De Grazia. Foreword by Carl S. Dentzel. Palm Desert, Calif., Best-West Publications [1968] [74] p. illus. (part col.), col. map. 32 cm. [ND237.D3337A52] 75-14535 11.75
1. Serra, Junipero, 1713-1784. I. Title.

Sert, Jose Luis, 1902—

BASTLUND, Knud. 720'.924
Jose Luis Sert; architecture, city planning, urban design. Introd., S. Giedon. New York, Praeger [1967] 244 p. illus. (part col.), plans. 23 x 29 cm. English, German, and French. Bibliography: p. 244. [NA737.S4B3] 66-21768
1. Sert, Jose Luis, 1902- I. Title.

SERT, Jose Luis, 1902- 720'.92'4
Sert, Mediterranean architecture / edited by Maria Lluisa Borras [translated by Kenneth Lyons]. Boston : New York Graphic Society, 1975. 25, 226 p., [3] leaves of plates : chiefly ill. (some col.) ; 21 cm. Translation of Sert, arquitectura mediterranea. Includes index. [NA737.S4A8513] 75-9108 ISBN 0-8212-0675-3 : 19.50
1. Sert, Jose Luis, 1902- 2. Architecture, Domestic—Western Mediterranean. I. Title.

Sesshu, 1420-1506.

COVELL, Jon Etta Hastings Carter, 1910- 759.952
Under the seal of Sesshu / by Jon Carter Covell. New York : Hacker Art Books, 1975. xii, 163 p., [23] leaves of plates : ill. ; 25 cm. Originally presented as the author's thesis, Columbia University, 1941. Reprint of the 1941 ed. privately printed for the author by the De Pamphilis press. "Selective bibliography on Sesshu": p. 159-163. [ND1059.S5C6 1975] 73-82864 ISBN 0-87817-143-6 : 17.50
I. Title. BIP

NAKAMURA, Tanio. 759.952
Sesshu Toyo, 1420-1506. English text by Elise Grilli. [1st English ed.] Tokyo, Rutland, Vt., C. E. Tuttle Co. [1957] 1 v. (unpaged) illus. (part col.) plates (part col.) ports. 18cm. (Kodansha library of Japanese art, no. 10) [ND1059.S5N3] 927.5 57-8792
1. Sesshu, 1420-1506. I. Title. II. Series.

Seton, Ernest Thompson, 1860-1946.

GARST, Doris Shannon, 1899- 925.7
Ernest Thompson Seton, naturalist, by Shannon and Warren Garst. New York, Messner [1959] 192 p. 22 cm. Includes bibliography. [QL31.S45G3] 59-7012
1. Seton, Ernest Thompson, 1860-1946. I. Garst, Warren Edward, 1922- joint author.

Seurat, Georges Pierre, 1859-1891.

CHICAGO. Art Institute. 759.4
Seurat, paintings and drawings. Chicago University of Chicago Press c.1958. 92p. plates (part col.) 26cm. Catalog of the exhibition held at the Art Institute of Chicago, Jan. 16-Mar. 7, 1958. and at the Museum of Modern Art, New York, Mar. 24-Mar 11, 1958. [ND553.S5C5 1958] 58-11956
1. Seurat, Georges Pierre, 1859-1891. I. Rich, Daniel Catton, 1903- ed. II. New York. Museum of Modern Art. III. Title. IV. Title: Edited by Daniel Catton Rich, with an essay on Seurat's drawings by Robert L. Herbert.

COURTHION, Pierre. 759.4
Georges Seurat. Text by Pierre Courthion. [Translated by Norbert Guterman. 1st ed.] New York, H. N. Abrams [1968] 160 p. illus. (part col.) 33 cm. (The Library of great painters) Bibliography: p. 160. [ND553.S5C643] 68-13066
1. Seurat, Georges Pierre, 1859-1891.

HERBERT, Robert L 1929- 741.944
Seurat's drawings. New York, Shorewood [c1962] 194 p. illus. (part col.) ports., facsims. 32 cm. "Began as part of my doctoral thesis, Yale University, 1957." Bibliography: p. 170-172. [NC1135.S45H4] 63-19842
1. Seurat, Georges Pierre, 1859-1891. I. Title.

HOMER, William Innes. 759.4
Seurat and the science of painting. Cambridge, Mass., M. I. T. Press [1964] xvi, 327 p. illus. (part col.) 24 cm. Bibliography: p. 305-317. [ND553.S5H63] 64-15751
1. Seurat, Georges Pierre, 1859-1891. 2. Art and science. I. Title.

HOMER, William Innes. 759.4
Seurat and the science of painting / by William Innes Homer. MA : MIT Press, 1978. 327p. : ill. ; 23 cm. Includes index. Bibliography: p. 305. [ND553.S5H63] ISBN 0-262-58036-5 pbk. : 8.95
1. Seurat, Georges Pierre, 1859-1891. 2. Art and science. I. Title.
L.C. card no. for 1964 MIT Press hardcover ed.: 64-15751. BIP

RICH, Daniel Catton, 1904- 759.4
Seurat and the evolution of "La Grande Jatte." New York, Greenwood Press [1969, c1935] xvi, 63 p. illus., 60 plates. 23 cm. (Studies of meaning in art) Bibliography: p. 53-63. [ND553.S5R5 1969] 69-14055
1. Seurat, Georges Pierre, 1859-1891. Grande Jatte. I. Title. II. Title: "La Grande Jatte." III. Series. BIP

RUSSELL, John, 1919- 759.4
Seurat. New York, F. A. Praeger [1965] 286 p. illus. (part col.) 22 cm. (A Praeger world of art profile) Bibliography: p. 271. [ND553.S5R8] 65-20074
1. Seurat, Georges Pierre, 1859-1891. I. Title. BIP

SEURAT, Georges Pierre, 1859-1891. 741.9'44
The drawings of Georges Seurat. With an introd. by Gustave Kahn. Translated by Stanley Appelbaum. New York, Dover Publications [1971] xviii, 136 p. illus. 31 cm. "Unabridged republication of the illustrations of the two portfolios of Les dessins de Georges Seurat (1859-1891), published in 1928." [NC248.S4K313] 73-131438 ISBN 0-486-22786-3
I. Kahn, Gustave, 1859-1936. II. Title. BIP

SEURAT, Georges Pierre, 1859-1891 759.4
Seurat. Essay by Roger Fry and a foreword & notes by Sir Anthony Blunt. [London] Phaidon Pub.; dist. Greenwich, Conn., N.Y. Graphic [1965] 86p. illus., 50 col. plates. 31cm. [ND553.S5F7] 65-6826 5.95
I. Fry, Roger Eliot, 1866-1934. II. Title.

SEVRAT, paintings and drawings; exhibitionThe Arts Institute of Chicago, January 16-March 7, 1958. The Museum of Modern Art, New York, March 24--May 11, 1958. Edited by Daniel catton Rich. With an essay on Seurat's drawings by Robert L. Herbert. Chicago 1958 92p. illus. (part col.) 26cm. [ND553.S5C5] 927.5 58-299 759.4
I. Chicago. Art Institute. II. Seurat, Georges Pierre, 1859-1891. III. New York. Museum of Modern Art.

Seurat, Georges Pierre, 1859-1891—Influence.

STEADMAN, William E. 760'.094
Homage to Seurat; paintings, watercolors, and drawings by the followers of Seurat, collected by Mr. and Mrs. W. J. Holliday. [Catalog by William E. Steadman] Tucson, University of Arizona Art Gallery [1968] [14] p., 73 plates (part col.) 29 cm. On cover: The Holliday Collection. Text on versos of plates. Includes bibliographies. [N6465.P6S7] 67-65947
1. Seurat, Georges Pierre, 1859-1891—Influence. 2. Holliday, William J., Mrs.—Art collections. 3. Neo-impressionism (Art) 4. Holliday, William J.—Art collections. I. Arizona. University. Art Gallery. II. Title. III. Title: The Holliday Collection.

Seven Wonders of the World—Juvenile literature.

NICHOLLS, Arthur. 930
The seven wonders of the world / by Arthur Nicholls ; illustrated by Zena Flax. Englewood Cliffs, N.J. : Prentice-Hall, 1977, c1976. p. cm. Includes index. An illustrated introduction to the seven wonders of the world discussing the construction and significance of each monument. [N5333.N53 1977] 77-6332 ISBN 0-13-806885-2 lib.bdg. : 5.95
1. Seven Wonders of the World—Juvenile literature. I. Flax, Zena. II. Title.

SILVERBERG, Robert. 709'.012
The Seven Wonders of the Ancient World. Illus. by Paul Williams. [New York] Crowell-Collier Press [1970] 120 p. illus., map. 23 cm. Bibliography: p. 116-117. Reconstructs from ancient sources the Seven Wonders of the ancient World: the Great Pyramid of Egypt; the Hanging Gardens of Babylon, the Statue of Zeus at Olympia, the Temple of Artemis of Ephesus, the Mausoleum of Halicarnassus, The Colossus of Rhodes, and the Lighthouse of Alexandria. [N5333.S44] 70-95298
1. Seven Wonders of the World—Juvenile literature. I. Williams, Paul, 1934- illus. II. Title. BIP

Severn, Arthur, 1842-1931.

BIRKENHEAD, Sheila (Berry) Smith, countess of 1913- 759.2
Illustrious friends; the story of Joseph Severn and his son Arthur. [New York] Reynal [dist. Morrow, 1966, c.1965] xiv, 393p. illus., ports. 25cm. Bibl. [ND497.S43B53] 66-2038 8.50
1. Severn, Arthur, 1842-1931. 2. Severn, Joseph, 1793-1879. I. Title.

Severn, Joseph, 1793-1879.

SHARP, William, 1855-1905. 759.2 B
The life and letters of Joseph Severn. London, S. Low, Marston, 1892. [New York, AMS Press, 1973] xix, 308 p. illus. 23 cm. [ND497.S43S5 1973] 70-175852 ISBN 0-404-07438-3 15.00
1. Severn, Joseph, 1793-1879. BIP

Sevres porcelain.

DAUTERMAN, Carl Christian, 1908- 738.2'7
Sevres. New York, Walker [1969] 84 p. illus. (part col.) 22 cm. (Collectors' blue books) Bibliographical footnotes. [NK4390.D37 1969] 69-15715 4.50
1. Sevres porcelain. I. Title.

Sevres porcelain—Catalogs.

WALLACE Collection. 738.2'7
Sevres porcelain / Wallace Collection ; [text] by R. A. Cecil. London : Trustees of the Wallace Collection, 1976. [4] p., 11 p. of plates (2 fold.) : ill. (chiefly col.) ; 18 cm. [NK4390.W34 1976] 77-361001 ISBN 0-900785-08-X : £0.45
1. Wallace Collection. 2. Sevres porcelain—Catalogs. I. Cecil, R. A. II. Title.

Sewing.

BAKKE, Karen. 746.4'028
The sewing machine as a creative tool / Karen Bakke. Englewood Cliffs, N.J. : Prentice-Hall, c1976. p. cm. (The Creative handcrafts series) (A Spectrum book) Includes index. Bibliography: p. [TT713.B34] 75-26868 ISBN 0-13-807255-8 : 10.95 ISBN 0-13-807248-5 pbk. : 4.95
1. Sewing. 2. Needlework. I. Title. BIP

BISHOP, Edna Bryte. 646.4
Fashion sewing by the Bishop method [by] Edna Bryte Bishop [and] Marjorie Stotler Arch. Pattern sketches by Dorothy L. Davids. Line drawings for chapters 1 and 2 by Anna R. Atene. Photos by Stewart Love. Philadelphia, Lippincott [1962] 233 p. illus. 28 cm. [TT705.B5] 62-16378
1. Sewing. I. Arch, Marjorie Stotler, joint author. II. Title.

BOTSFORD, Shirley J. 746.4'4
Between thimble and thumb / Shirley J. Botsford. 1st ed. New York : Holt, Rinehart, and Winston, c1979. p. cm. [TT705.B67] 78-16332 pbk. : 8.95
1. Sewing. 2. Needlework. I. Title.

BOTSFORD, Shirley J. 746.4'4
Between thimble and thumb / Shirley J. Botsford. 1st ed. New York : Holt, Rinehart, and Winston, c1979. p. cm. [TT705.B67] 78-16332 pbk. : 8.95 12.95
1. Sewing. 2. Needlework. I. Title.

THE Complete book of sewing. Larry Eisinger, consulting editorial director. Dolores Sini, editorial assistant. Lawrence E. Marsh, creative director, Charles A. Levine, art editor. New York, Crown Publishers [1972] 320 p. illus. 29 cm. [TT705.C74] 72-194968 9.95 646.2
1. Sewing. I. Eisinger, Larry, ed.

HANNAN, Watson M 687
The methods of sewing. [New York, Kogos International Corp., 1963] 75 p. illus. 22 cm. [TT713.H35] 63-8142
1. Sewing. 2. Sewing-machines. 3. Clothing trade — Management. I. Title.

HOLLIS, Nesta. 646.2
Successful sewing, a modern guide. With illus. by Winifred Rickwood. New York, Taplinger [1969] 206 p. illus. (part col.) 26 cm. [TT705.H65 1969] 76-84974 8.75
1. Sewing. I. Title.

JONES, Frances Martin. 646.4
Modern sewing; a text and handbook, by Frances Jones. Danville, Ill., Interstate Printers & Publishers [1972] 498 p. illus. 24 cm. [TT518.J65] 71-155248
1. Sewing. 2. Dressmaking. I. Title. BIP

KINSER, Charleen. 746.4
Sewing sculpture / Charleen Kinser. New York : M. Evans, [1977] p. cm. [TT715.K56] 76-56736 ISBN 0-87131-215-8 : 12.50. ISBN 0-87131-236-0 pbk. : 6.95
1. Sewing. 2. Soft sculpture. I. Title. BIP

LOWRIE, Drucella. 646.2
Modern home sewing; a new, complete sewing handbook for beginner and expert, with step-by-step instructions for every sewing job, plus hundreds of short-cuts, designing tips, and money-saving ideas. [New York? 1952] 160, 305 columns. illus. 17 x 23 cm. In 2 pts; pt. 2 previously published separately. [TT705.L59] 52-2157
1. Sewing I. Mager, Sylvia K., 1916- A complete guide to home sewing. II. Title. CONTENTS--Modern machine sewing by

D. Lowrie.--A complete guide to home sewing by S. K. Mager.

MOORE, Marie I., 1914- 646.48
Dress accessories and gifts you can make. Scranton, Laurel Publishers; distributed by Grosset & Dunlap, New York [1952] 120 p. illus. 23 cm. [Books for better living] [TT705.M6] 52-10744
1. Sewing. 2. Needlework. I. Title.

RELIS, Nurie, 1929- 646.4'04
Sewing for fashion design / Nurie Relis and Gail Strauss. Reston, Va. : Reston Pub. Co., c1978. x, 162 p. : ill. ; 24 cm. Includes index. [TT715.R44] 78-8557 ISBN 0-87909-755-8 : 12.95
1. Sewing. 2. Machine sewing. I. Strauss, Gail, joint author. II. Title. BIP

RODA, Janet E. 646.2'1
Fabric decorating for the home / Janet E. Roda. 1st ed. Birmingham : Oxmoor House, c1976. ix, 254 p. : ill. (some col.) ; 25 x 29 cm. [TT715.R6] 76-14112 ISBN 0-8487-0422-3 : 19.95
1. Sewing. 2. Textile fabrics. 3. Interior decoration—Amateurs' manuals.

SCHREIBER, Joanne. 646.2'1
Sewing to decorate your home / by Joanne Schreiber ; ill. by Penny Havard. 1st ed. Garden City, N.Y. : Dolphin Books, c1979. p. cm. Includes index. [TT705.S34] 77-16946 ISBN 0-385-12560-7 : 6.95
1. Sewing. 2. Interior decoration—Amateurs' manuals. I. Title. BIP

SIMONS, Violet Kathleen. 646
Very basic book of sewing, altering, & mending : 999 pictures show you how / by Violet K. Simons ; [drawings by Alan Burton]. New York : Sterling Pub. Co., c1976. 256 p. : ill. ; 23 cm. First published in 1975 under title: The long book of sewing in pictures. Includes index. [TT705.S494 1976] 76-1187 ISBN 0-8069-5358-6 : 6.95. ISBN 0-8069-5359-4 lib.bdg. :
1. Sewing. 2. Dressmaking. 3. Tailoring. I. Title.

TILLING, Meriel. 646.2
The observer's book of sewing / Meriel Tilling ; diagrams by Barbara Firth. London ; New York : F. Warne, 1975. 192 p., 8 p. of plates : ill. (some col.) ; 15 cm. (The Observer's pocket series ; 57) Illustrative matter on lining papers. [TT705.T53] 74-21040 ISBN 0-7232-1542-1 : 2.50
1. Sewing. 2. Dressmaking. 3. Embroidery. I. Title. II. Series. BIP

TIME-LIFE Books. 646.4
The classic techniques, by the editors of Time-Life Books. New York [1973] 208 p. illus. 30 cm. (The Art of sewing) [TT705.T55] 73-85529 6.95
1. Sewing. 2. Embroidery. 3. Knitting. 4. Crocheting. I. Title. BIP

VAN WYKE, Anne. 646.2'1
The craft of soft furnishing / [by] Anne Van Wyke. London : Paul, 1978. 88 p. : ill. ; 23 cm. (The Craftsman's art series) Includes index. [TT715.V36] 78-314636 ISBN 0-09-131670-7 pbk. : 3.95
1. Sewing. 2. House furnishings.
Distributed by Merrimack Book Service, Salem, NH BIP

Sewing—Dictionaries.

CARBONE, Linda. 646.2'03
Dictionary of sewing terminology / by Linda Carbone. New York : Arco, c1977. p. cm. [TT705.C37] 77-2559 ISBN 0-668-04039-4 : 5.95
1. Sewing—Dictionaries. I. Title.

MEYER, Judy A., 1950- 646.4
Sewing dictionary / Judy A. Meyer. South Brunswick [N.J.] : A. S. Barnes, c1978. p. cm. [TT715.M48] 77-84579 ISBN 0-498-02147-5 : 12.00. ISBN 0-498-02306-0 pbk. : 5.95
1. Sewing—Dictionaries. 2. Dressmaking—Dictionaries. 3. Tailoring—Dictionaries. I. Title. BIP

Sewing—Equipment and supplies—Catalogs.

WHOLE sewing catalog / 646.2'1
by the editors of Consumer guide. New York : Simon and Schuster, 1979. p. cm. (A Fireside book) Includes index. [TT715.W53] 78-15439 ISBN 0-671-24385-3 pbk. : 9.95
1. Sewing—Equipment and supplies—Catalogs. 2. Sewing. I. Consumer guide.

Sewing—Study and teaching.

MURDOCH, Katharine, 1884- 646.4
The measurement of certain elements of hand sewing. New York, Teachers College, Columbia University, 1919. [New York, AMS Press, 1973, c1972] 119 p. 22 cm. Reprint of the 1919 ed., issued in series: Teachers College, Columbia University. Contributions to education, no. 103. Originally presented as the author's thesis, Columbia. Includes bibliographical references. [TT708.M87 1972] 73-177097 ISBN 0-404-55103-3 10.00
1. Sewing—Study and teaching. 2. Grading and marking (Students) I. Title. II. Series: Columbia University. Teachers College. Contributions to education, no. 103.

Sex in art.

KORNBERG, Harvey. 741.5'973
The gentleman's alphabet book; [drawings] by Harvey Kornberg, limericks by Donald Hall. New York, Dutton, 1972. [61] p. illus. 23 x 29 cm. [NC139.K67H34 1972] 72-82706 ISBN 0-525-11244-8 5.95
1. Sex in art. I. Hall, Donald, 1928- II. Title.

*KRONHAUSEN, Phyllis, 704'.94'2 comp.
A gallery of erotic art, collected and with text by Drs. Phyllis and Eberhard Kronhausen. New York, Bantam Books [1974] 1v. (chiefly illus.) 18 cm. [NC6490] 2.95 (pbk.)
1. Sex in art. I. Kronhausen, Eberhard, joint comp. II. Title.

MARCADE, Jean. 704.94
Roma amor; essay on erotic elements in Etruscan and Roman art. Geneva, New York, Nagle [1961] 129p. illus. (part col., part mounted3 34cm. [B8217.E6M33] 62-5848
1. Sex in art. 2. Art, Etruscan. 3. Art, Roman. I. Title.

Seymour, David.

SEYMOUR, David. 770'.92'4
David Seymour—"Chim", 1911-1956 / [editors, Cornell Capa, Bhupendra Karia]. New York : Grossman Publishers, 1974. 95 p. : chiefly ill. ; 23 cm. (ICP library of photographers ; v. 3) Bibliography: p. 94-95. [TR140.S46A32 1974] 73-14140 ISBN 0-670-25831-8 : 10.00. ISBN 0-670-25832-6 pbk : 5.95
1. Seymour, David. 2. Photography, Journalistic. I. Series: International Fund for Concerned Photography. ICP library of photographers ; v. 3.

Seymour, John, cabinetmaker.

STONEMAN, Vernon C 749.21446
John and Thomas Seymour, cabinetmakers in Boston, 1794-1816. [1st ed.] Boston, Special Publications, 1959. 393 p. (chiefly plates (part col.) map. facsims.) 32 cm. Bibliography: p. 392-393. [NK2439.S45S73] 58-59566
1. Seymour, Thomas, cabinetmaker. 2. Seymour, John, cabinetmaker. 3. Furniture — Boston. I. Title.

Seymour, Samuel.

MCDERMOTT, John Francis, 595.78 1902-
Samuel Seymour: pioneer artist of the plains and the Rockies Washington 1951. 24 cm. p. 4970509 16 plates) (In Smithsonian Institution. Annual report, 1950 Bibliography: p. 508-500. [Q11.S66 1950] 52-4085
1. Seymour, Samuel. I. Title.

Seymour, Thomas, cabinetmaker.

STONEMAN, Vernon C 749.21446
John and Thomas Seymour, cabinetmakers in Boston, 1794-1816. [1st ed.] Boston, Special Publications, 1959. 393 p. (chiefly plates (part col.) map. facsims.) 32 cm. Bibliography: p. 392-393. [NK2439.S45S73] 58-59566
1. Seymour, Thomas, cabinetmaker. 2. Seymour, John, cabinetmaker. 3. Furniture — Boston. I. Title.

Shafer, L. E., 1907—

SHAFER, L. E., 1907- 709'.2'4
Gus Shafer's West, by L. E. "Gus" Shafer, with the editorial assistance of Donald V. Bates. Foreword by John M. Christlieb. [1st ed.] Kansas City, Mo., Trail West [1973] x, 150 p. illus. (part col.) 29 cm. [N6537.S48A46] 73-85933 ISBN 0-914160-00-1 20.00
1. Shafer, L. E., 1907- 2. The West in art. I. Title.

Shahn, Ben, 1898-1969.

BUSH, Martin H. 759.13
Ben Shahn: The passion of Sacco and Vanzetti, by Martin H. Bush. With an essay and commentary by Ben Shahn. 1st ed. [Syracuse, N.Y.] Syracuse University, 1968. 85 p. illus. (part col.), ports. (part col.) 24 cm. Contents.Contents.—The Sacco-Vanzetti theme, by M. H. Bush.—American painting at mid-century, by B. Shahn.—Selected bibliography (p. 78-85) [NA3860.S49B8] 68-54903
1. Shahn, Ben, 1898- Passion of Sacco and Vanzetti. I. Shahn, Ben, 1898- American painting at mid-century. II. Title: The passion of Sacco and Vanzetti.

MORSE, John D., 1906- 709'.2'4
Ben Shahn. Edited by John D. Morse. New York, Praeger [1972] 228 p. illus. (part col.) 23 cm. (Documentary monographs in modern art) Bibliography: p. 219-226. [N6537.S5M6] 76-178226 13.50
1. Shahn, Ben, 1898-1969. I. Shahn, Ben, 1898-1969.

PRESCOTT, Kenneth Wade, 769'.92'4 1920-
The complete graphic works of Ben Shahn [by] Kenneth W. Prescott. [New York] Quadrangle [1973] xxii, 250 p. illus. (part col.) 25 x 31 cm. Bibliography: p. 230-235. [NE539.S4P73 1973] 73-79928 ISBN 0-8129-0367-6 35.00
1. Shahn, Ben, 1898-1969. I. Shahn, Ben, 1898-1969.

RODMAN, Selden, 1909- 927.59
Portrait of the artist as an American; Ben Shahn: a biography with pictures. New York, Harper [1951] xiv, 180 p. illus. (part col.) ports. 26 cm. [ND237.S465R6] 51-13491
1. Shahn, Ben, 1898- I. Title.

SHAHN, Ben, 1898- 769'.924
The collected prints of Ben Shahn. The catalogue by Kneeland McNulty. An essay & commentary by the artist. Philadelphia, Philadelphia Museum of Art, 1967. x, 150 p. illus. (part. col.) 31 cm. "Published in conjunction with an exhibition of Ben Shahn's Graphics, held at the Philadelphia Museum of Art, November 15-December 31, 1967." Bibliography: p. 144-147. [NE539.S4M3] 68-1113
I. McNulty, Kneeland. II. Philadelphia Museum of Art. III. Title.

SHAHN, Ben, 1898- 916
Graphic work. Text by James Thrall Soby. London, Cory, Adams & Mackay [1965, 1957] 142 p. illus. (part col.) 29 cm. On spine: Ben Shahn: Graphic art. Bibliography: p. 133-141. [NC1075.S47S62 1965] 65-9389
I. Soby, James Thrall, 1906- II. Title.

SHAHN, Ben, 1898-1969. 709'.2'4
Ben Shahn, by Bernarda Bryson Shahn. New York, H. N. Abrams [1972] 373 p. illus. (part col.) 36 cm. Bibliography: p. 357-363. [ND237.S465B79] 72-2170 ISBN 0-8109-0495-0 50.00
I. Bryson, Bernarda.

SHAHN, Ben, 1898-1969. 759.13
Ben Shahn (1898-1969). Exhibition November 6-27, 1971. New York, Kennedy Galleries [1971] 1 v. (chiefly illus.; part col.) 28 cm. [N6537.S5K4] 73-31127
I. Kennedy Galleries, inc., New York.

SHAHN, Ben, 1898-1969. 759.13
Ben Shahn: a retrospective exhibition. [Trenton, New Jersey State Museum, 1969] 1 v. (chiefly illus.) 22 cm. Catalogue of an exhibition held in the New Jersey State Museum, main galleries, Sept. 20-Nov. 16, 1969. Includes bibliography prepared by Peggy Lewis. [ND237.S465A34] 78-629165
I. New Jersey. State Museum, Trenton. II. Title.

SHAHN, Ben, 1898-1969. 760'.0924
Ben Shahn; exhibition: November 5 through November 29, 1969, Kennedy Galleries. New York [1969] [71] p. (chiefly illus. (part col.)) 28 cm. [N6537.S5A42] 79-13417
I. Kennedy Galleries, inc., New York.

SHAHN, Ben, 1898-1969. 741.91
Ben Shahn: his graphic art. Text by James Thrall Soby. New York, G. Braziller, 1957. 139 p. illus. (part col.) 29 cm. "Chronology and bibliography [prepared by Barbara Novak with the assistance of Mr. Shahn and the Downtown Gallery for the Institute of Contemporary Art, Boston]": p. [127]-139. [NC1075.S47S6] 57-12840
I. Soby, James Thrall, 1906-

SHAHN, Ben, 1898-1969. 759.13
The biography of a painting. [New York, Paragraphic Books, 1966] 1 v. (unpaged) illus. 28 cm. [ND237.S465A35] 66-26546
I. Title.

SHAHN, Ben, 1898-1969. 769'.924
The collected prints of Ben Shahn. The catalogue by Kneeland McNulty. An essay & commentary by the artist. Philadelphia, Philadelphia Museum of Art, 1967. x, 150 p. illus. (part col.) 31 cm. "Published in conjunction with an exhibition of Ben Shahn's Graphics, held at the Philadelphia Museum of Art, November 15-December 31, 1967." Bibliography: p. 144-147. [NE539.S4M3] 68-1113
I. McNulty, Kneeland. II. Philadelphia Museum of Art. III. Title.

SHAHN, Ben, 1898-1969. 741'.0924
The drawings of Ben Shahn. October, 1970. New York, Kennedy Galleries [1970] 1 v. (chiefly illus.) 28 cm. [NC139.S48A43] 70-199845
I. Kennedy Galleries, inc., New York. II. Title.

SHAHN, Ben, 1898-1969. 741.9'73
The drawings of Ben Shahn, May 14 to June 4th, 1976, Kennedy Galleries. [New York : Kennedy Graphics], c1976. [64] p. : chiefly ill. ; 28 cm. Includes index. [NC139.S48K45] 76-367904
1. Shahn, Ben, 1898-1969. I. Kennedy Galleries, inc., New York. II. Title.

SHAHN, Ben, 1898-1969. 769'.92'4
For the sake of a single verse ... : from The notebooks of Malte Laurids Brigge / by Rainer Maria Rilke ; lithographs and afterword by Ben Shahn. 1st ed. New York : C. N. Potter ; distributed by Crown Publishers, [1974] [62] p. : chiefly ill. (some col.) ; 30 cm. Text selected from M. D. Herter Norton's English translation of Rilke's Die Aufzeichnungen des Malte Laurids Brigge. [NE2312.S52A45 1974] 73-94241 ISBN 0-517-51205-X : 12.95
1. Shahn, Ben, 1898-1969. 2. Rilke, Rainer Maria, 1875-1926. Aufzeichnungen des Malte Laurids Brigge—Illustrations. I. Rilke, Rainer Maria, 1875-1926. Die Aufzeichnungen des Malte Laurids Brigge. English. Selections. 1974. II. Title. BIP

SHAHN, Ben, 1898-1969. 769'.92'4
For the sake of a single verse ... from The notebooks of Malte Laurids Brigge by Rainer Maria Rilke. [Original lithographs by Ben Shahn. New York, Atelier Mourlot, 1968] 1 portfolio ([61] p., 22 plates) 57 cm. Issued in a case. Signed by the artist. Text selected from M. D. Herter Norton's English translation of Die Aufzeichnungen des Malte Laurids Brigge by R. M. Rilke. [NE2312.S52A45] 73-159471
1. Shahn, Ben, 1898-1969. 2. Rilke, Rainer

Maria, 1875-1926. Aufzeichnungen des Malte Laurids Brigge—Illustrations. I. Rilke, Rainer Maria, 1875-1926. Die Aufzeichnungen des Malte Laurids Brigge. English. Selections. 1968. II. Title.

Shahn, Ben, 1898-1969—Exhibitions.

JOE and Emily Lowe Art Gallery. 760'.092'4
The mural art of Ben Shahn : original cartoons, drawings, prints, and dated paintings, September 28-October 30, 1977 : a loan exhibition / organized by the Joe and Emily Lowe Art Gallery, Sims Hall, College of Visual and Performing Arts, Syracuse University. Syracuse, N.Y. : The Gallery, c1977. [24] p. : ill. ; 28 cm. Bibliography: p. [20] [N6537.S5A4 1977] 78-100275
1. Shahn, Ben, 1898-1969—Exhibitions. 2. Artists' preparatory studies—United States—Exhibitions. I. Shahn, Ben, 1898-1969. II. Title.

SHAHN, Ben, 1898-1969. 759.13
Paintings. Text by James Thrall Soby. New York, G. Braziller, 1963. 144 p. illus. (part col.) 29 cm. Bibliography: p. 139-144. [ND237.S465S62] 63-18187
I. Soby, James Thrall, 1906-

Shakers—Industries.

ANDREWS, Edward Deming, 1894-1964. 749.211
Shaker furniture; the craftsmanship of an American communal sect, by Edward Deming Andrews and Faith Andrews. Photos. by William F. Winter. New York, Dover Publications, 1950 [c1937] xi, 133 p. 48 plates. 28 cm. Bibliography: p. [121]-126. [NK2405.A7 1950] 50-7797
1. Shakers—Industries. 2. Furniture, American. I. Andrews, Faith, joint author. II. Title.

Shakespeare, William, 1564-1616.

ARAGON, Louis, 1897- 741.9'46
Shakespeare [by] Aragon. [Illus. by] Picasso. [Translated from the French by Bernard Frechtman] New York, H. N. Abrams [1966] 124 p. illus. 48 cm. The text was originally a short story with title: Murmure. [NC248.P5A83] 65-21830
1. Shakespeare, William, 1564-1616. 2. Shakespeare, William, 1564-1616—Portraits, etc. I. Picasso, Pablo, 1881- II. Aragon, Louis, 1897- Murmure. III. Title. IV. Title: Murmure.

CHASSERIAU, Theodore, 1819-1856. 769'.944
Othello; fifteen etchings. New York, Walker, 1969. 1 portfolio (8 p., facsim., 15 (i.e. 16) plates) illus. 42 cm. (Philip Hofer books) "The separate plates and title-page are facsimiles of the 1844 edition of Chasseriau's Othello, made from a copy lent by Philip Hofer." [NE2049.5.C48A54] 69-17778
1. Shakespeare, William, 1564-1616. Othello—Illustrations. I. Title. II. Series.

STILL, Colin, 1888- 111.8'5
The timeless theme; a critical theory formulated and applied. [Folcroft, Pa.] Folcroft Library Editions, 1973. viii, 244 p. 29 cm. Reprint of the 1936 ed. published by I. Nicholson & Watson, London. Contents.Contents.—The theory formulated: Art, myth, ritual and experience.—The theory applied: An interpretation of Shakespeare's "Tempest." Includes bibliographical references. [BH39.S83 1973] 73-1310 17.50 (lib. bdg.)
1. Shakespeare, William, 1564-1616. The tempest. 2. Aesthetics. I. Title. BIP

Shakespeare, William, 1564-1616—Illustrations.

WARK, Robert R. 760'.0942
Drawings from the Turner Shakespeare, by Robert R. Wark. With a bibliographical note by Shelley M. Bennett. San Marino, Calif., Henry E. Huntington Library and Art Gallery, 1973. 89 p. illus. 14 x 22 cm. Consists of a guide to some of the drawings (illustrations to Shakespeare) originally collected by T. Turner of Gloucester from approximately 1835-60. The 44 v. set of original drawings is now in the Henry E. Huntington Library. Includes bibliographical references. [PR2883.W3] 73-85885
1. Shakespeare, William, 1564-1616—Illustations. 2. Turner, Thomas, of Gloucester, Eng.—Art collections. 3. Drawings—Catalogs. I. Title. BIP

ZAIDENBERG, Arthur, 1903- 743'.4
How to draw Shakespeare's people. London, New York, Abelard-Schuman [1967] 64 p. illus. 27 cm. [PR2883.Z3] 67-18121
1. Shakespeare, William, 1564-1616—Illustrations. I. Title.

Shakespeare, William, 1564-1616—Portraits, etc.

ARAGON, Louis, 1897- 741.9'46
Shakespeare [by] Aragon. [Illus. by] Picasso. [Translated from the French by Bernard Frechtman] New York, H. N. Abrams [1966] 124 p. illus. 48 cm. The text was originally a short story with title: Murmure. [NC248.P5A83] 65-21830
1. Shakespeare, William, 1564-1616. 2. Shakespeare, William, 1564-1616—Portraits, etc. I. Picasso, Pablo, 1881- II. Aragon, Louis, 1897- Murmure. III. Title. IV. Title: Murmure.

BOADEN, James, 1762-1839. 769'.4'982233
An inquiry into the authenticity of various pictures and prints, which, from the decease of the poet to our own times, have been offered to the public as portraits of Shakspeare ... / by James Boaden. New York : AMS Press, 1975. v, 206 p., [5] leaves of plates : ports. ; 23 cm. Reprint of the 1824 ed. printed for R. Triphook, London. [PR2929.B6 1975] 70-39458 ISBN 0-404-00915-8 : 12.50
1. Shakespeare, William, 1564-1616—Portraits, etc. I. Title: An inquiry into the authenticity of various pictures and prints ...

Shakespeare, William, 1564-1616—Stage history—To 1625.

REYNOLDS, George Fullmer, 1877- 792'.025
Some principles of Elizabethan staging, by George F. Reynolds. [Folcroft, Pa.] Folcroft Press, 1970. 34, 29 p. facsim. 26 cm. "Limited to 150 copies." Reprint of the 1905 ed. Thesis—University of Chicago, 1905. Includes bibliographical references. [PN2091.S8R4 1971b] 72-193209
1. Shakespeare, William, 1564-1616—Stage history—To 1625. 2. Theaters—England—Stage-setting and scenery. I. Title. BIP

REYNOLDS, George Fullmer, 1877- 792'.0942
Some principles of Elizabethan staging / by George F. Reynolds. Norwood, Pa. : Norwood Editions, 1975. 29 p. ; 26 cm. Reprint of the 1905 ed. published by University of Chicago Press, Chicago. Originally presented as the author's thesis, University of Chicago. Includes bibliographical references. [PN2091.S8R4 1975] 75-35556 ISBN 0-88305-593-7 : 8.50
1. Shakespeare, William, 1564-1616—Stage history—To 1625. 2. Theaters—England—Stage-setting and scenery. I. Title.

Shaped canvas.

BOWMAN, Bruce. 751.2
Shaped canvas / by Bruce Bowman. New York : Sterling Pub. Co., c1976. 64 p. : ill. (some col.) ; 22 cm. [ND1505.B68] 76-1183 ISBN 0-8069-5360-8 : 5.95 ISBN 0-8069-5361-6 lib.bdg. :
1. Shaped canvas. 2. Painting—Technique. I. Title. BIP

Sharaff, Irene.

SHARAFF, Irene. 746.9'2'0924 B
Broadway & Hollywood : costumes designed by Irene Sharaff / Irene Sharaff. New York : Van Nostrand Reinhold Co., 1976. 136 p. : ill. (some col.) ; 24 cm. Includes index. [TT505.S5A33] 75-43903 ISBN 0-442-27527-7 : 12.50
1. Sharaff, Irene. 2. Costume design. I. Title.

Sharon, Aryeh, 1900—

SHARON, Aryeh, 1900- v. 12
Kibbutz + Bauhaus : an architect's way in a new land / by Arieh Sharon. Stuttgart : Kramer Verlag, 1976. 267 p. : chiefly ill. ; 29 cm. Text in English, French, and German. Includes index. Bibliography: p. 267. [NA1479.S5A48] 77-365331 ISBN 3-7828-1430-4
1. Sharon, Aryeh, 1900- 2. Architects—Israel—Biography. 3. Architecture—Israel. 4. Architecture, Modern—20th century—Israel. 5. Bauhaus—Influence. I. Title.

Sharon, Mary Bruce, 1878-1961.

SHARON, Mary Bruce, 1878-1961. 759.13
Mary Bruce Sharon, an American primitive. [Washington, Traveling Exhibition Service, Smithsonian Institute, 1973] [25] p. illus. 22 cm. "This exhibition has been organized by Mrs. Sharon's daughter. Henrietta Sharon Aument, and her cousin, John Harvey, and is being circulated by the Traveling Exhibition Service of the Smithsonian Institute, 1974-76." [ND237.S467A95] 73-178353
1. Sharon, Mary Bruce, 1878-1961. 2. Primitivism in art—United States. I. Aument, Henrietta Sharon. II. Harvey, John, 1947- III. Smithsonian Institution. Traveling Exhibition Service. IV. Title.

SHARON, Mary Bruce, 1878-1961. 759.13 B
Scenes from childhood / by Mary Bruce Sharon. 1st ed. New York : Dutton, [1978] p. cm. [ND237.S467A2 1978] 78-4939 ISBN 0-525-38820-6 : 6.95
1. Sharon, Mary Bruce, 1878-1961. 2. Painters—United States—Biography. I. Title. BIP

Sharples, James, 1750?-1811.

KNOX, Katharine (McCook) 741'.092'2 B
The Sharples: their portraits of George Washington and his contemporaries; a diary and an account of the life and work of James Sharples and his family in England and America. New York, Kennedy Graphics, 1972 [c1930] xvi, 133 p. illus. 28 cm. (Library of American Art) [ND497.S445K6 1972] 70-87456 ISBN 0-306-71529-5
1. Sharples, James, 1750?-1811. 2. Sharpless family. 3. Washington, George, Pres. U.S., 1732-1799—Portraits. 4. Portraits, American. I. Title.

Sharps, Christian, 1811-1874.

RYWELL, Martin, 1905- 623.4422
The gun that shaped American destiny. Harriman. Tenn., Pioneer Press [1957] 156p. illus. 24cm. [TS535.R917] 56-12177
1. Sharps, Christian, 1811-1874. 2. Sharps rifle. 3. U. S. Army—Firearms. I. Title.

Sharps rifle.

RYWELL, Martin, 1905- 623.4422
The gun that shaped American destiny. Harriman. Tenn., Pioneer Press [1957] 156p. illus. 24cm. [TS535.R917] 56-12177
1. Sharps, Christian, 1811-1874. 2. Sharps rifle. 3. U. S. Army—Firearms. I. Title.

SELLERS, Frank M. 683'.4
Sharps firearms, by Frank M. Sellers and De Witt Bailey, III. [Denver, Printed by G. Chester's Idea Press, 1969- v. illus. 28 cm. Contents.Contents.— —v. 3, pt. 3. Model 1874 rifles. [TS536.4.S45] 68-16736
1. Sharps rifle. I. Bailey, De Witt, joint author. II. Title. BIP

Shaving mugs—United States—Catalogs.

POWELL, Robert Blake. 738.3'83
Occupational & fraternal shaving mugs of the United States / by Robert Blake Powell. Limited collectors ed. Hurst, Tex. : Powell, c1978. x, 211 p. : chiefly ill. ; 22 cm. [NK4695.S5P69] 77-89674 ISBN 0-9600680-3-1 : 17.50
1. Shaving mugs—United States—Catalogs. I. Title. BIP

Shaving mugs—United States—History.

POWELL, Robert Blake. 738
Antique shaving mugs of the United States. [Hurst, Tex., 1972] xiv, 272 p. illus. 23 cm. "Limited first edition reference book." [NK4695.S5P68] 71-186119 17.95
1. Shaving mugs—United States—History. I. Title. BIP

POWELL, Robert Blake. 738.3'83
Occupational & fraternal shaving mugs of the United States / by Robert Blake Powell. Limited collectors ed. Hurst, Tex. : Powell, c1978. x, 211 p. : chiefly ill. ; 22 cm. [NK4695.S5P69] 77-89674 ISBN 0-9600680-3-1 : 17.50
1. Shaving mugs—United States—Catalogs. I. Title.

Shaw, Robert Gould, 1837-1863.

BURCHARD, John Ely, 1898- 720.943
The voice of the phoenix; postwar architecture in Germany [by] John Burchard. Cambridge,Mass., M.I.T. Press [1966] New York, St Martin's Press [1965] xii, 179 p. illus., plans. 23 x 25 cm. x 168 p. illus. maps. port. 22 cm. Biblographical footnotes. [NA1068.B86] [E513.5 54th.B8] 973.7415 65-24414 65-18643
1. Shaw, Robert Gould, 1837-1863. 2. Architecture — Germany. 3. Architecture, Modern — 20th cent. 4. Massachusetts Infantry. 54th Regt., 1863-1865. 5. U.S. — Hist. — Civil WarPregimental histories — Massachusetts Infantry — 54th. I. Burchard, Peter. II. Title. III. Title: One gallant rush;

Shawnee Pottery Company.

SIMON, Dolores H. 738.3'7
Shawnee pottery in color : [an illustrated value guide] / by Dolores H. Simon. Paducah, Ky. : Collector Books, c1977. 64 p. : ill. ; 22 cm. [NK4210.S52S55] 77-150235 ISBN 0-89145-030-0 : 7.95
1. Shawnee Pottery Company. 2. Pottery, American—Ohio—Zanesville. I. Title.

Shearer, Thomas, fl. 1788.

FASTNEDGE, Ralph, 1913- ed. 749.22
Shearer furniture designs, from the Cabinet-makers' London book of prices, 1788. pref., descriptive notes, by Ralph Fastnedge. London, A. Tiranti [dist. Hollywood-by-the-Sea, Fla., Transatlantic, 1964c.1962] 22p. illus., facism., 17 plates. 26cm. (Master hands ser.) [NK2542.S4F3] 65-1445 6.00 bds.,
1. Shearer, Thomas, fl. 1788. 2. Furniture—London. I. Society of Cabinet-Makers, London. The Cabinet makers'London book of prices. II. Title. BIP

Sheds — Construction and design.

KENT, Lewis Edward. v. 12
Design of a stanchion and truss frame, by Lewis E. Kent and David W. Lazenby. Westminster [1965] 39 p. illus. 28 cm. (British constructional steelwork association. Publication. no. 27) [NUC67-42492]
1. Sheds — Construction and design. 2. Trusses. 3. Framing, Building. I. Lazenby, David W., joint author. II. Title. III. Series.

Sheeler, Charles, 1883-1965.

IOWA. University. Dept. of Art. 759.13
The quest of Charles Sheeler: 83 works honoring his 80th year. [Exhibition] March

17-April 14, 1963. [Iowa City, University of Iowa, 1963] 52 p. illus. 26 cm. Organized by the Dept. of Art, State University of Iowa. Includes bibliography. [ND237.S47I6] 63-63510
1. Sheeler, Charles, 1883- I. Title.

ROURKE, Constance 709'.24 B
Mayfield, 1885-1941.
Charles Sheeler, artist in the American tradition. New York, Kennedy Galleries, 1969 [c1938] 203 p. illus. 26 cm. (Library of American art) [ND237.S47R6 1969] 70-87603
1. Sheeler, Charles, 1883-1965.

SHEELER, Charles, 1833- 760'.0924
1965.
Charles Sheeler. Essays by Martin Friedman, Bartlett Hayes [and] Charles Millard. Washington, Published for the National Collection of Fine Arts by the Smithsonian Institution Press, 1968. 156 p. illus. (part col.) 21 x 27 cm. (Smithsonian publication 4746) Catalog of an exhibition held Oct. 10 to Nov. 24, 1968, at the National Collection of Fine Arts, Jan. 10 to Feb. 16, 1969, at the Philadelphia Museum of Art, Mar. 11 to Apr. 27, 1969, at the Whitney Museum of American Art. Bibliography: p. 106-107. [ND237.S47A43] 68-57069 5.95
I. Smithsonian Institution. National Collection of Fine Arts. II. Philadelphia Museum of Art. III. Whitney Museum of American Art, New York. IV. Title.

SHEELER, Charles, 1883- 759.13
1965.
Charles Sheeler / Martin Friedman. New York : Watson-Guptill Publications, 1975. 224 p. : ill. (some col.) ; 31 cm. Includes index. Bibliography: p. 220-222. [ND237.S47F74 1975] 75-6524 ISBN 0-8230-4799-7 : 29.95
1. Sheeler, Charles, 1883-1965. I. Friedman, Martin L.

Sheet-metal work.

BUDZIK, Richard S. 744.5
Precision sheet metal: blueprint reading [by] Richard S. Budzik. [1st ed.] Indianapolis, H. W. Sams [1969] 127 p. illus. 27 cm. [TS250.B866] 75-86373
1. Sheet-metal work. 2. Drawing-room practice. 3. Engineering drawings. I. Title. BIP

SEPPA, Heikki. 739
Form emphasis for metalsmiths / by Heikki Seppa. Kent, Ohio : Kent State University Press, c1978. p. cm. [TS250.S42] 78-1091 ISBN 0-87338-212-9 pbk. : 9.50
1. Sheet-metal work. 2. Art metal-work. I. Title. BIP

Sheets, Millard, 1907—

SHEETS, Millard, 1907- 759.13
Millard Sheets : [catalogue of the exhibition] Lang Art Gallery, Scripps College, March 27-April 29, 1976. Claremont, Calif. : Galleries of the Claremont Colleges, c1976. 20 p. : ill. ; 23 cm. [ND237.S473L36] 77-353332
1. Sheets, Millard, 1907- I. Lang Art Gallery.

Sheffield, Eng.—Buildings.

VICKERS, John Edward, 914.27'46
1917-
Old Sheffield town: an historical miscellany, by J. Edward Vickers. Wakefield, EP Publishing, 1972. [16], 183 p. illus. 22 cm. [DA690.S54V52] 73-330742 ISBN 0-85409-774-0 £3.00
1. Sheffield, Eng.—Buildings. 2. Sheffield, Eng.—Suburbs and environs. I. Title. BIP

Sheffield plate.

BEDFORD, John, 1907- 739.2'3
Old Sheffield plate [by] John Bedford & Derek Austin. New York, Walker [1967] 63 p. illus. 20 cm. (Collectors' pieces, 11) [NK7250.B4 1967] 67-23843
1. Sheffield plate. I. Austin, Derek, joint author. II. Title.

HAYDEN, Arthur, 739.2'3'742746
1868-1946.
Chats on old Sheffield plate / by Arthur Hayden. Wakefield : E.-P. Publishing, 1973. 302 p., leaf : ill. ; 22 cm. Reprint of 1st ed. London, T. Fisher Unwin, 1920. Includes index. [NK7250.H3 1973] 74-186863 ISBN 0-85409-825-9 : £3.25
1. Sheffield plate. 2. Plate—Collectors and collecting. 3. Hall-marks. I. Title. BIP

HUGHES, George Bernard, 739.2'3'8
1896-
Sheffield silver plate [by] G. Bernard Hughes. New York, Praeger Publishers [1970] 303 p. illus. 26 cm. Bibliography: p. [267] [NK7250.H84 1970] 72-114296 15.00
1. Sheffield plate. I. Title.

ROBERTSON, Richard 739.2383
Austin.
Old Sheffield plate. London, Benn [dist. New York, Dover, 1965] 190p. illus. 21cm. (Practical handbks. for collectors) [NK7250.R6] 57-4785 3.00
1. Sheffield plate. I. Title.

Sheffield plate—Catalogs.

FROST, Thomas 338.4'3739'23742746
William.
The price guide to old Sheffield plate, by T. W. Frost. Woodbridge (Clopton, Woodbridge, Suffolk), The Antique Collector's Club, 1971. [14], 396 p. (chiefly illus.). 22 cm. [NK7250.F7] 72-175520 ISBN 0-902028-07-3 £3.25
1. Sheffield plate—Catalogs. I. Title.

Shelburne, Vt. Museum.

SHELBURNE, Vt. 759.13'074'014317
Museum.
Paintings and drawings at the Shelburne Museum / Nancy C. Muller. Shelburne, Vt. : Shelburne Museum, 1976. 200 p. : ill. (some col.) ; 29 cm. (Forge ahead ; no. 2) Includes index. [N749.A62] 76-367506
1. Shelburne, Vt. Museum. 2. Art—Shelburne, Vt.—Catalogs. 3. Art, American—Catalogs. I. Muller, Nancy C. II. Title. III. Series: The Forge ahead series ; no. 2. BIP

Shell money.

MELANESIAN shell money 390.00993 *in Field Museum collections.* Chicago, 1929; New York, Kraus Reprint, 1968. 64p. (incl. 25 plates) 25cm. (Orig. pub. as pubn 268, Field Mus. of Natural Hist. Anthropological ser., v. 19, no. 1) Bibl. refs. [GN436.2.L4] [GN2.F4 vol. 19, no. 1] 30-7633 3.50 pap.,
1. Shell money. 2. Ethnology—Melanesia. I. Lewis, Albert Buell, 1867- BIP

Shellcraft.

CRITCHLEY, Paula. 745.55
The art of shellcraft / Paula Critchley. New York : Praeger, 1975. 96 p. : ill. ; 27 cm. [TT862.C74 1975] 74-6862 ISBN 0-275-51540-0 : 10.95
1. Shellcraft. I. Title.

ELBERT, Virginie. 745.55
Shell craft for beginners / by Virginie Fowler Elbert. Indianapolis : Bobbs-Merrill, [1977] p. cm. Includes bibliographical references and index. [TT862.E4] 76-54472 ISBN 0-672-52176-8 : 15.00
1. Shellcraft. I. Title.

GOODMAN, Stuart. 745.55
Art from shells; jewelry, sculptures, collages, figurines, collections, by Stuart and Leni Goodman. New York, Crown [1972] 210 p. illus. 27 cm. Bibliography: p. 203. [TT862.G66 1972] 72-84317 ISBN 0-517-50024-8 7.95
1. Shellcraft. I. Goodman, Leni, joint author. II. Title. BIP

KRAUSS, Helen K. 745.55
Shell art; a handbook for making shell flowers, mosaics, jewelry, and other ornaments. New York, Hearthside [c.1965] 128p. illus., plates (pt. col.) 25cm. Bibl. [NK8643.K7] 65-14121 6.95 bds.,
1. Shellcraft. I. Title. II. Title: Handbook for making shell flowers. BIP

KRAUSS, Helen K. 745.55
Shell art : a handbook for making shell flowers, mosaics, jewelry, and other ornaments / Helen K. Krauss. New York : Dover Publications, 1976. 128 p., [4] leaves of plates : ill. (14 col.) ; 22 cm. Includes index. Bibliography: p. 121-122. [NK8643.K7 1976] 75-21356 ISBN 0-486-23255-7 pbk. : 2.50
1. Shellcraft. I. Title.

LOGAN, Elizabeth D. 745.55
Shell crafts, by Elizabeth D. Logan. New York, Scribner [1974] viii, 214 p. illus. 28 cm. Bibliography: p. 205-206. [TT862.L63] 74-2018 ISBN 0-684-13863-8 12.50
1. Shellcraft. I. Title.

NASSIET, Claude. 745.55
Fun with seashells. Illus. by Marc Berthier. Photos: Promophot. New York, Drake Publishers [1974] 62 p. illus. (part col.) 23 cm. Translation of Avec des coquillages. Instructions for creating a variety of objects with seashells. [TT862.N3713] 73-3719 ISBN 0-87749-477-0 3.95
1. Shellcraft. I. Berthier, Marc, illus. II. Title.

PARKER, Anthony. 745.55
Shellcraft. Illustrated by Diana Tull. Boston, C. T. Branford Co. [c1958] 95p. illus. 21cm. [NK8643.P3 1958] 58-59815
1. Shellcraft. I. Title. BIP

POPE, Patricia E., 1949- 745.55
Shellcraft animals / Patricia Pope. St. Petersburg, Fla. : Great Outdoors Pub. Co., [1975] 32 p. : ill. ; 22 cm. [TT862.P66] 75-15906 ISBN 0-8200-0506-1 pbk. : 1.00
1. Shellcraft. I. Title. BIP

POPE, Patricia E., 745.59'42
1949-
Shellcraft earrings / Patricia Pope. St. Petersburg, Fla. : Great Outdoors Pub. Co., [1976] c1975. p. cm. [TT862.P66 1976] 76-5505 ISBN 0-8200-0508-8 pbk. : 1.00
1. Shellcraft. 2. Jewelry making—Amateurs' manuals. 3. Ear-rings. I. Title. BIP

*POWNALL, Glen. 745.55
Shell craft. Wellington, N.Z., Seven Seas, [1975 c1974] 72 p. ill. (part col.) 25 cm. (His creative leisure series.) [TT862] ISBN 0-85467-021-1
1. Shellcraft. I. Title.
Distributed by Int'l Publications Service, Collings, for 5.50.

RITCHIE, Carson I. A. 736'.6
Carving shells and cameos and other marine products: tortoiseshell, coral, amber, jet [by] Carson I. A. Ritchie. [1st American ed.] South Brunswick, A. S. Barnes [1971, c1970] 156 p. illus. 21 cm. [TT862.R57 1971] 71-131905 ISBN 0-498-07817-5 5.95
1. Shellcraft. 2. Carving (Art industries) 3. Cameos. I. Title.

RITCHIE, Carson I. A. 736'.6
Shell carving; history and techniques [by] Carson I. A. Ritchie. South Brunswick, A. S. Barnes [1974] p. Includes bibliographical references. [NK8643.R57] 73-120 ISBN 0-498-07928-7 10.00
1. Shellcraft. I. Title.

STEPHENS, Cleo. 745.55
Shellcraft [by] Cleo M. Stephens. [1st ed.] Radnor, Pa., Chilton Book Co. [1974] xiv, 151 p. illus. 26 cm. Bibliography: p. [147] [TT862.S73 1974] 74-1101 ISBN 0-8019-5886-5 4.95 (pbk.)
1. Shellcraft. I. Title.
Hardbound 9.95, ISBN 0-8019-5885-7. BIP

TRAVERS, Louise 745.55
Allderdice.
The romance of shells, in nature and art. New York, M. Barrows, 1962. 135 p. illus. 24 cm. Includes bibliography. [NK8643.T7] 62-8550
1. Shellcraft. 2. Shells in art. 3. Shells. I. Title.

Shellcraft—Juvenile literature.

CUTLER, Katherine N. 745.55
Creative shellcraft [by] Katherine N. Cutler. Illustrated by Giulio Maestro. New York, Lothrop, Lee & Shepard Co. [1971] 96 p. illus. 25 cm. Bibliography: p. 88. Directions for collecting shells and using them to make a variety of items such as pictures, mobiles, jewelry, ashtrays, and Christmas decorations. [TT862.C87] 73-148484
1. Shellcraft—Juvenile literature. I. Maestro, Giulio, illus. II. Title. BIP

Shelley, Percy Bysshe, 1792-1822.

READ, Herbert Edward, 700'.9
Sir, 1893-1968.
In defence of Shelley & other essays. Freeport, N.Y., Books for Libraries Press [1968] 282 p. 22 cm. (Essay index reprint series) Reprint of the 1936 ed. [PN710.R37 1968] 68-26470
1. Shelley, Percy Bysshe, 1792-1822. 2. Literature, Modern—Addresses, essays, lectures. 3. Art—Addresses, essays, lectures. I. Title. BIP

Shells.

LEEMING, Joseph, 1897- 745.55
1968.
Fun with shells; illustrated by Jessie Robinson. [1st ed.] Philadelphia, Lippincott [1958] 92 p. illus. 24 cm. [NK8643.L4] 58-7535
1. Shells. 2. Handicraft. I. Title. BIP

Shelving (for books)

BRANN, Donald R. 684.1'6
How to construct built-in and sectional bookcases / Donald R. Brann. Rev. ed. Briarcliff Manor, NY : Directions Simplified, 1978. 98 p. : ill. ; 23 cm. (Easi-bild home improvement library ; 664) (Easi-bild simplified directions) Editions of 1969 and 1970 published under title: How to construct built-in bookcases. [TT197.5.B6B72 1978] 78-104637 ISBN 0-87733-664-4 pbk. : 2.50
1. Shelving (for books) 2. Woodwork—Amateurs' manuals. I. Title.

BRANN, Donald R. 684.1'6
How to construct built-in and sectional bookcases, by Donald R. Brann. Rev. ed. Briarcliff Manor, N.Y., Directions Simplified, 1974. 98 p. illus. 23 cm. (Easi-bild home improvement library, 664) (Easi-bild simplified directions) Published in 1969 and 1970 under title: How to construct built-in bookcases. "Easi-bild 664." [TT197.5.B6B72 1974] 74-177208 2.00 (pbk.)
1. Shelving (for books) 2. Woodwork—Amateurs' manuals. I. Title. BIP

LEAVY, Herbert T. 684.1'6
Bookshelves & storage units / by Herbert Leavy. New York : Grosset & Dunlap, 1977. 96 p. : ill. ; 28 cm. (Grosset good life books) Includes index. [TT197.5.B6L4] 76-48002 ISBN 0-448-12995-7 pbk.: 1.95. ISBN 0-448-13424-1 lib. bdg.: 4.99
1. Shelving (for books) 2. Storage in the home. I. Title.

REIF, Rita. 749'.4
Living with books; 116 designs for homes and offices. New York, Arno Press [1968] 119 p. illus. 27 cm. "A New York times book." [NK2740.R4] 68-5112
1. Shelving (for books) I. Title. BIP

REIF, Rita. 749'.4
Living with books; 118 designs for homes and offices. [Newly rev. and updated ed. New York] Quadrangle/New York Times Book Co. [1973, c1968] 123 p. illus. 26 cm. [NK2740.R4 1973] 72-96434 ISBN 0-8129-0365-X 4.95 (pbk.)
1. Shelving (for books) I. Title.

SUNSET. 729.94
Ideas for bookcases & bookshelves. [1st ed.] Menlo Park, Calif., Lane Pub. Co. [1952] 80p. illus. 21cm. [NK2113.S85] 52-10165
1. Shelving (for books) I. Title.

ZEGEL, Jon, 1948- 684.1'6
The shelf book : complete do-it-yourself systems for building shelves in living rooms, kitchens, closets, basements, garages / Jon Zegel. Philadelphia : Running Press, c1977. p. cm. Includes index. Bibliography: p. [TT197.5.B6Z43] 77-12366 ISBN 0-89471-000-1 pbk. : 4.95. ISBN 0-89471-001-X lib. bdg. : 9.80

1. Shelving (for books) 2. Storage in the home. I. Title. BIP

Shen, Chou, 1427-1509

EDWARDS, Richard, 1916- 759.951
The Field of Stones; a study of the art of Shen Chou (1427-1509) Washington, 1962. xxi, 131 p. 50 plates. 36 cm. (Smithsonian Institution. Freer Gallery of Art. Oriental studies no. 5) Smithsonian Institution. Publication 4433. "Catalogue": p. 81-110. Bibliography: p. 112-118. [ND1049.S44E35] 63-60198
1. Shen, Chou, 1427-1509 I. Title. II. Series. III. Series: Freer Gallery of Art, Washington, D.C. Oriental studies no. 5 BIP

Shepard family.

PHILLIPS, John F. C., 1943- 760'.092'2
Shepherd's London / [by] J. F. C. Phillips. London : Cassell, 1976. 116 p. : ill. (some col.), geneal. table, map ; 29 cm. Contains reproductions of works by Thomas Hosmer Shepherd and other members of the Shepherd family. Includes index. Bibliography: p. 110-111. [NC242.S48P48] 77-361079 ISBN 0-304-29675-9 : £5.95
1. Shepard family. 2. London in art. I. Shepherd, Thomas Hosmer. II. Title. BIP

Shepherd, David, 1931—

SHEPHERD, David, 1931- 759.2 B
The man who loves giants : an artist among elephants and engines : David Shepherd's autobiography. New York : Scribner, c1975. 164 p. : ill. (some col.) ; 24 cm. [ND497.S46A25 1975b] 75-21663 ISBN 0-684-14509-X : 12.50
1. Shepherd, David, 1931- 2. Painters—Great Britain—Correspondence, reminiscences, etc. I. Title.

Shepler, Dwight.

SHEPLER, Dwight. 759.13
An artist's horizons. Weston, Mass., Fairfield House, 1973. 148 p. illus. (part col.) 21 x 26 cm. [ND1839.S45A22] 72-95108 ISBN 0-8271-7254-0 14.95
1. Shepler, Dwight. 2. Painters—United States—Correspondence, reminiscences, etc. I. Title.
Distributed by Barre, Mass.

Sheraton, Thomas, 1751-1806.

FASTNEDGE, Ralph, 1913- 749.22
Sheraton furniture. New York, Yoseloff [c.1962] 125p. illus. (pt. col.) 26cm. Bibl. 62-10187 12.50
1. Sheraton, Thomas, 1751-1806. 2. Furniture, English. I. Title.

Sheridan, Clare Consuelo Frewen, 1885-1970—Biography.

LESLIE, Anita. 730'.92'4 B
Clare Sheridan / Anita Leslie. 1st ed. Garden City, N.Y. : Doubleday, 1977. xv, 318 p., [8] leaves of plates : ill. ; 22 cm. Includes index. [PR6037.H465Z7 1977] 76-23773 ISBN 0-385-06745-3 : 10.00
1. Sheridan, Clare Consuelo Frewen, 1885-1970—Biography. 2. Authors, English—20th century—Biography. 3. Artists—Great Britain—Biography. BIP

Shimada, Shujiro, 1907—

JAPANESE ink paintings from American collections : the Muromachi period : an exhibition in honor of Shujiro Shimada / edited by Yoshiaki Shimizu and Carolyn Wheelwright. Princeton, N.J. : Art Museum, Princeton University : distributed by Princeton University Press, c1976. 300 p. : ill. ; 29 cm. Exhibition held Apr. 25-June 13, 1976. Includes index. Bibliography: p. 280-291. [ND2071.J36] 75-33450 ISBN 0-691-03913-5 : 40.00 ISBN 0-691-03918-6 pbk. : 18.00 759.952'074'014967
1. Shimada, Shujiro, 1907- 2. Water-colors, Japanese—Exhibitions. 3. Sumie—Exhibitions. 4. Painting, Japanese—Kamakura-Momoyama periods, 1185-1600. I. Shimizu, Yoshiaki, fl. 1967- II. Wheelwright, Carolyn. III. Princeton University. Art Museum.

Shinn, Everett, 1876-1953.

DESHAZO, Edith. 759.13 B
Everett Shinn, 1876-1953, a figure in his time / by Edith DeShazo ; research assistant, Richard Shaw. 1st ed. New York : C. N. Potter : distributed by Crown Publishers, [1974] xvii, 236 p., [8] leaves of plates: ill. (some col.) ; 29 cm. Includes index. Bibliography: p. 227-230. [N6537.S53D47 1974] 74-77561 ISBN 0-517-51490-7 : 15.00
1. Shinn, Everett, 1876-1953.

SHINN, Everett, 1876-1953. 741.9'73
Everett Shinn, 1873 [sic]-1953. An exhibition organized by the New Jersey State Museum, Edith DeShazo, special consultant, in cooperation with the Delaware Art Museum and the Munson-Williams-Proctor Institute. [Trenton, New Jersey State Museum, 1973] 61 p. illus. 22 cm. Bibliography: p. 21-22. [NC139.S52D47] 73-176059
1. Shinn, Everett, 1876-1953. I. DeShazo, Edith. II. New Jersey. State Museum, Trenton. III. Delaware Art Museum. IV. Munson-Williams-Proctor Institute, Utica, N.Y.

Shino pottery.

FUJIOKA, Ryoichi, 1909- 738.3'7
Shino and oribe ceramics / by Ryoichi Fujioka ; translated and adapted with an introd. by Samuel Crowell Morse. 1st ed. New York : Weatherhill, 1975. p. cm. (Arts of Japan, 10) Translation of Shino to Oribe. Includes index. [NK4340.S5F8313] 74-28220 ISBN 0-8348-2718-2. ISBN 0-8348-2719-0 pbk.
1. Shino pottery. 2. Oribe pottery. I. Morse, Samuel Crowell, tr. II. Title. BIP

FUJIOKA, Ryoichi, 1909- 738'.0952
Shino and Oribe ceramics / Ryoichi Fujioka ; translator, Samuel Crowell Morse. New York : Kodansha International, [1977] p. cm. (Japanese arts library ; v. 1) Translation of Shino to Oribe. Includes index. Bibliography: p. [NK4340.S5F8313] 76-9357 ISBN 0-87011-284-8 : 12.95
1. Shino pottery. 2. Oribe pottery. 3. Pottery, Japanese—Edo period, 1600-1868. I. Title. II. Series.

Shinto shrines—Ise, Japan.

WATANABE, Yasutada, 1922- 726'.1'9561095218
Shinto art: Ise and Izumo shrines. Translated by Robert Ricketts. [1st English ed.] New York, Weatherhill/Heibonsha [1974] 190 p. illus. (part col.) 24 cm. (The Heibonsha survey of Japanese art, v. 3) Translation of Ise to Izumo. [NA6057.I79W3713] 73-88471 ISBN 0-8348-1018-2 10.00
1. Shinto shrines—Ise, Japan. 2. Shinto shrines—Izumo, Japan. I. Title. II. Series.

Ship models.

FREESTON, Ewart C. 745.59'28
Prisoner-of-war ship models, 1775-1825 [by] Ewart C. Freeston. Annapolis, Naval Institute Press [1973] xv, 174 p. illus. 29 cm. Includes bibliographical references. [VM298.F68 1973] 73-77883 ISBN 0-87021-858-1 24.00
1. Ship models. 2. Prisoners of war—Great Britain. 3. Prisons—Great Britain—History. I. Title. BIP

HUBBARD, Donald, 1926- 745.59'28
Ships-in-bottles; a step-by-step guide to a venerable nautical craft. Written and illustrated by Donald Hubbard. [1st ed.] New York, McGraw-Hill [1971] 102 p. illus. 25 cm. [VM298.H77] 72-150461 ISBN 0-07-030827-6 7.95
1. Ship models. I. Title.

LA BERGE, Armand John, 1891- 623.8
Boats, airplanes, and kites. [Rev. ed.] Peoria, Ill., C. A. Bennett Co. [1950] 135 p. illus. 25 cm. [TT160.L3 1950] 51-9021
1. Ship models. 2. Aeroplanes—Models. 3. Kites. I. Title.

NEEDHAM, Jack, 1916- 745.59'28
Modelling ships in bottles. With a foreword by Alan Villiers. [1st American ed.] New York, Collier Books [1973, c1972] 64 p. illus. 25 cm. Bibliography: p. 63-64. [VM298.N4 1973] 72-14074 2.95
1. Ship models. I. Title.

Ship models—Juvenile literature.

WEISS, Harvey. 745.59'28
Ship models and how to build them. New York, Crowell [1973] 66 p. illus. (part col.) 24 cm. Directions for using simple construction methods and tools to make models of a tugboat, sailboat, sternwheeler, submarine, and other types of boats. [VM298.W37] 72-7562 ISBN 0-690-73270-8 4.50
1. Ship models—Juvenile literature. I. Title. BIP

Ships in art.

ANGLO-AMERICAN Art Museum. 760'.0740'6335
Sail and steam in Louisiana waters. [Exhibition] September 19-December 8, 1971. Baton Rouge [1971] 1 v. (unpaged) 43 plates. 21 x 26 cm. [N8230.A5] 74-636727
1. Ships in art. 2. Art, Modern—19th century—Exhibitions. 3. Rivers—Louisiana—Views. I. Title.

AYLWARD, William James, 1875- 741.6396238
Ships and how to draw them. New York, Pitman [1957] unpaged. illus. 20 x 27cm. (Pitman drawing series) [NC825.S5A9 1957] 57-10745
1. Ships in art. 2. Drawing—Instruction. I. Title.

AYLWARD, William James, 1875- 741
Ships and how to draw them. New York, Pitman [1950] [64] p. illus. 20 x 26 cm. (Pitman drawing series) [NC825.S5A9] 50-5524
1. Ships in art. I. Title. BIP

BECK, Stuart E. 741.6396238
How to draw fishing craft. London, New York, Studio Publications [1953] 63p. illus. 18cm. (How to draw) [NC825.S5B4] 53-12402
1. Ships in art. I. Title.

BECK, Stuart E. 741.6396238
How to draw pleasure craft. London, New York, Studio Publications [1954] 62p. illus. 18cm. (How to draw series) [NC825] 55-545
1. Ships in art. I. Title.

BRAYNARD, Frank Osborn, 1916- 741.9'73
The tall ships : official OpSail '76 portfolio / Frank Braynard. New York : Sabine Press, c1976. 1 portfolio ([4] leaves, [20] leaves of plates : 20 ill.) ; 38 cm. [NC139.B73A56] 76-369981
1. Braynard, Frank Osborn, 1916- 2. Ships in art. 3. Operation Sail, '76. I. Operation Sail 1976. II. Title. BIP

COBB, David, 1921- 741.633
Drawing and painting seascape, shipping and waterside scenery. New York, Pitman Pub. Corp. [1953] xvi, 166p. illus. (part mounted, part col.) 29cm. [NC825.S5C6 1953a] 54-2705
1. Ships in art. 2. Sea in art. 3. Marine painting. 4. Drawing—Instruction. I. Title.

EVERS, Carl G. 759.13
The marine paintings of Carl G. Evers / introd. by Ian Ballantine. Toronto ; New York : Peacock Press, 1975. [6] p., [45] leaves of plates : 45 col. ill. ; 23 x 28 cm. [ND1839.E93A45] 75-10068 pbk. : 5.95
1. Evers, Carl G. 2. Ships in art. I. Title.

EVERS, Carl G. 759.13
The marine paintings of Carl G. Evers introduction by Ian Ballantine New York, Charles Scribner's Sons [1975] [6] p., [45] leaves of plates 45 col. ill. 23 x 28 cm. [ND1839.E93A45] 10.00.
1. Evers, Carl C. 2. Ships in Art. I. Title.
L.C. card no. for original edition: 75-10068. BIP

GREENWICH, Eng. National Maritime Museum. 741.91
Van de Velde drawings; a catalogue of drawings in the National Maritime Museum made by the elder and the younger Willem Van de Velde. Cambridge [Eng.] University Press, 1958. ix, 450 p. illus., coats of arms. 32 cm. [NC1055.V4G7 1958] 58-14763
1. Velde, Willem van de, 1610 or 11-1693. 2. Velde, Willem van de, 1633-1707. 3. Ships in art. I. Title.

JACOBSEN, Anita. 759.13
From sail to steam: the story of Antonio Jacobsen, marine artist; an artist's chronicle of the ships that sailed the seas from 1870-1920. Illus. from the Collection of Wilfred W. Sullivan. Staten Island, N.Y., Manor Pub. Co., 1972. 58 p. col. illus. 19 x 27 cm. [ND237.J23J32] 72-83646 14.95
1. Jacobsen, Antonio, 1850-1921. 2. Sullivan, Wilfred W.—Art collections. 3. Ships in art. I. Title.

MAYGER, Chris. 759.2
The marine paintings of Chris Mayger / edited and introduced by David Larkin. London : Pan Books, 1976. [93] p. : chiefly ill. (chiefly col.) ; 29 cm. [ND497.M485A5 1976b] 77-359766 ISBN 0-330-24832-4 : £2.95
1. Mayger, Chris. 2. Ships in art. I. Title.

SCHAEFER, Rudolph J. 759.13
J. E. Buttersworth : 19th-century marine painter / by Rudolph J. Schaefer. Mystic, Conn. : Mystic Seaport, 1975. xxvi, 276 p., [24] leaves of plates : ill. (some col.) ; 31 cm. Errata slip inserted. Includes index. Bibliography: p. 227-231. [ND237.B98S32] 74-82666 ISBN 0-913372-12-9 : 75.00
1. Buttersworth, James Edward, 1817-1894. 2. Ships in art. 3. Schaefer, Rudolph J.—Art collections. I. Title.

STOBART, John. 759.2
Ports & pioneers of the sailing days; new paintings. [New York? 1972] [24] p. illus. (part col.) 26 cm. Catalog of the artist's 4th New York exhibition held Nov. 15-Dec. 9, 1972, at the Kennedy Galleries. [ND497.S797K46] 72-172721
1. Stobart, John. 2. Ships in art. I. Kennedy Galleries, inc., New York. II. Title.

WORSLEY, John, 1919- 743'.8'9.62382
Ships. [1st American ed. New York, Watson-Guptill Publications, 1967, c1962] 56 p. illus. 18 x 20 cm. (Watson-Guptill drawing books) Cover title: Drawing ships. [NC825.S5W6 1967] 65-19013
1. Ships in art. 2. Drawing—Instruction. I. Title. II. Title: Drawing ships.

Ships in art—Juvenile literature.

GRACZA, Margaret Young. 704.94 (j)
The ship and the sea in art. Designed by Robert Clark Nelson. Minneapolis, Lerner Publications Co. [1965] 64 p. illus., ports. 27 cm. [N8240.G7] 64-8203
1. Ships in art—Juvenile literature. 2. Sea in art—Jvenile literature. I. Title.

Ships (in numismatics)

OBOJSKI, Robert. 737.4
Ships & explorers on coins. New York, Sterling Pub. Co. [1970] 48 p. illus. 20 cm. (Topical coin library) Includes a catalogue section. Traces the history of ships and explorers through their representation on the coins of various countries. [CJ161.S5O2] 77-115447
1. Ships (in numismatics) 2. Explorers—Portraits. I. Title.

Ships—Pictorial works.

BEAUTY of ships (The) Introd. essay by Peter Stewart. New York, Pitman [c.1963] 23p., 124. [4] p. of illus. 28cm. 63-23484 7.50 779.962382

1. Ships—Pictorial works. I. Stewart, Peter, writer on ships.

FRERE-COOK, Gervis, ed. 704.94962382
The decorative arts of the mariner. [1st American ed.] Boston, Little, Brown [1966] 296 p. illus. (part col.) maps. 32 cm. [VM307.F7 1966a] 66-20998
1. Ships—Pictorial works. I. Title.

HANSEN, Hans Jurgen, 1921- ed. 725'.99
Art and the seafarer; a historical survey of the arts and crafts of sailors and shipwrights. With contributions by Edward H. H. Archibald [and others] General editor: Hans Jurgen Hansen. Translated by James and Inge Moore. New York, Viking Press [1968] 292, [1] p. illus., plates (part col.) 31 cm. (A Studio book) Translation of Kunstgeschichte der Seefahrt. Bibliography: p. 290-[293] [VM307.H3713 1968b] 68-15485
1. Ships—Pictorial works. 2. Naval architecture—History. I. Archibald, Edward H. H. II. Title.

PEABODY Museum of Salem, Salem, Mass. 760
The marine paintings and drawings in the Peabody Museum, by M. V. and Dorothy Brewington. Salem, 1968. xvii, 530 p. (chiefly illus. (part col.)) 29 cm. [VM307.P4] 68-20837
1. Ships—Pictorial works. I. Brewington, Marion Vernon, 1902- II. Brewington, Dorothy. III. Title.

STEWART, George Peter, 1926- 779.962382
The Beauty of ships. With an introductory essay by Peter Stewart. New York, Pitman [c1963] 23 p., 124, [4] p. of illus. 28 cm. [VM307.B38] 63-23484
1. Ships — Pictorial works. I. Title.

Shipwrecks—Missouri River.

PETSCHE, Jerome E. 913'.031'08 s
The steamboat Bertrand: history, excavation, and architecture, by Jerome E. Petsche. Washington, National Park Service, 1974. p. cm. (Publications in archeology, 11) Bibliography: p. [E51.U75 no. 11] [VM461.5.B47] 917.82'2 72-600352
1. Bertrand (Steamboat) 2. Shipwrecks—Missouri River. I. Title. II. Series.

Shirts, Men's—Pattern design.

KOGOS, Frederick, ed. 646.4
Designing and drafting shirts for men and boys. [New York, Kogos International Corp., 1962] 55 p. illus. 31 cm. [TT675.K6] 62-18569
1. Shirts, Men's—Pattern design. I. Title.

Shisha mirror embroidery.

SIMPSON, Jean, 1942- 746.4'4
Shisha mirror embroidery : a contemporary approach / by Jean Simpson ; [photos. by Don Rasmussen ; ill. by Gwenn Stutzman]. New York : Van Nostrand Reinhold, [1978] p. cm. Includes index. [TT778.S55S56] 78-17836 ISBN 0-442-27641-9 : 12.95
1. Shisha mirror embroidery. I. Title. BIP

Shoes and boots.

STREATFEILD, Noel. 391
The first book of shoes. Pictures by Jacqueline Tomes. New York, F. Watts [1967] 54 p. illus. 23 cm. A brief survey of the history and development of footwear. Examines the influence of shoes on tradition and legend; shows how shoe styles reveal much about their owners; and discusses the shoemaker and his trade. [GT2130.S7] AC 67
1. Shoes and boots. I. Tomes, Jacqueline, illus. II. Title.

Shop fronts.

DEBAIGHTS, Jacques. 729'.1
Shopfronts. Photos. by Michel Nahmias. New York, Architectural Book Pub. Co. [1974] 192 p. illus. 27 cm. [NA6225.D35] 74-18270 ISBN 0-8038-0236-6 36.00
1. Shop fronts. I. Title.

ENGLISH shop fronts from contemporary source books, 1792-1840, including: Designs for shop fronts, by I. & J. Taylor, 1792; A series of designs for shop fronts, by J. Young, 1828; Designs for shop fronts, by J. Faulkner, 1831; Shop fronts and exterior doors, by T. King, n.d.; On the construction and decoration of the shop fronts of London, by N. Whittock, 1840. With a pref. by David Dean. [1st American ed.] New York, Transatlantic Arts, 1970. [12] p., 77 plates. illus. 29 cm. [NA6220.E5] 78-119875 725'.21'0942
1. Shop fronts. BIP

Shopping centers.

BAKER, Geoffrey Harold, 1912- 711.552
Shopping centers; design and operation [by] Geoffrey Baker and Bruno Funaro. New York, Reinhold [1951] 288 p. illus., maps. 30 cm. (Progressive architecture library) [NA9050.B23] 51-12435
1. Shopping centers. I. Funaro. Bruno, 1911- joint author. II. Title. III. Series.

GOSLING, David. 711'.552
Design and planning of retail systems / David Gosling, Barry Maitland. New York : Whitney Library of Design, 1976. 208 p. : ill. ; 31 cm. Includes index. Bibliography: p. 197-202. [HF5430.G67] 75-38806 ISBN 0-8230-7138-3 : 30.00
1. Shopping centers. 2. Shopping centers—Design and construction. 3. Retail trade. I. Maitland, Barry, joint author. II. Title.

GOSLING, David. 711'.552
Design and planning of retail systems / David Gosling and Barry Maitland. London : Architectural Press, 1976. 208 p. : ill. ; 30 cm. Includes index. Bibliography: p. 197-202. [HF5430.G67 1976b] 76-373229 ISBN 0-85139-142-7 : £16.00
1. Shopping centers. 2. Shopping centers—Design and construction. 3. Retail trade. I. Maitland, Barry, joint author. II. Title.

GRUEN, Victor, 1903- 711.552
Shopping towns USA; the planning of shopping centers, by Victor Gruen and Larry Smith. New York, Reinhold Pub. Corp. [1960] 288 p. illus., plans. 27 cm. (Progressive architecture library) Bibliography: p. 279-281. [HF5429.G75] 60-8527
1. Shopping centers. I. Smith, Larry, 1901- joint author. II. Title. BIP

REDSTONE, Louis G. 711'.552
New dimensions in shopping centers and stores [by] Louis G. Redstone. New York, McGraw Hill [1973] xix, 323 p. illus. 28 cm. [NA6218.R43] 73-4021 ISBN 0-07-051368-6 18.95
1. Shopping centers. I. Title. BIP

Shopping centers—Planning.

NORTHEN, R. I. 711'.552
Shopping centres : a developer's guide to planning and design / [by] R. I. Northen, M. Haskoll. Reading : Centre for Advanced Land Use Studies, College of Estate Management, 1977. [8], 89 p. : ill.(some col.), maps, plans ; 30 cm. (Planning for people) [HF5430.N67] 77-373631 ISBN 0-902132-33-4 : £5.50
1. Shopping centers—Planning. 2. Shopping centers—Design and construction. I. Haskoll, M., joint author. II. Title. III. Series.

Shopping malls.

RUBENSTEIN, Harvey M. 711'.552
Central city malls / Harvey M. Rubenstein. New York : Wiley, c1978. p. cm. "A Wiley-Interscience publication." Includes index. Bibliography: p. [HF5430.R8] 78-7536 ISBN 0-471-03098-8 : 20.00
1. Shopping malls. 2. Central business districts. 3. Pedestrian facilities design. 4. City planning. 5. Landscape architecture. I. Title. BIP

Shopping malls—Europe.

PERKIN, George. 711'.552
Streets for pedestrians / [written and compiled by George Perkin]. [Slough, Eng. : Cement and Concrete Assn., 1976] 32 p. : chiefly ill. ; 22 x 30 cm. Cover title. "A Cembureau publication." Text in English, French, German and Italian. [HE336.S5P47] 77-352867
1. Shopping malls—Europe. 2. Pedestrians—Europe. 3. Streets—Europe. I. Title.

Shopping malls—Great Britain.

NORWICH, Eng. City Planning Dept. 711'.552
Norwich: the creation of a foot street [prepared by a study team under] A. A. Wood. Norwich, Norwich City Planning Department, 1969. [5], 28 p., 15 plates (2 fold.) illus., coat of arms, maps (chiefly col.), col. plan. 29 cm. [HF5430.6.G7N65 1969] 70-460861 ISBN 0-901965-00-6 21/-
1. Shopping malls—Great Britain. I. Wood, Alfred Arden. II. Title.

Shoreham Circle (Group of artists)

GLEESON, Larry. 769'.942
Followers of Blake : The Santa Barbara Museum of Art, March 2-April 4, 1976 / Larry Gleeson, editor. [Santa Barbara, Calif.] : Santa Barbara Museum of Art, c1976. 40 p. : ill. ; 26 cm. Bibliography: p. 37-38. [NE628.G56] 76-4928
1. Shoreham Circle (Group of artists) 2. Blake, William, 1757-1827—Influence. 3. Prints, English—Exhibitions. I. Santa Barbara, Calif. Museum of Art. II. Title.

Shoring and underpinning.

PRENTIS, Edmund Astley, 1883- 721.1
Underpinning, its practice and applications, by Edmund Astley Prentis and Lazarus White. 2d ed., rev. and enl. New York, Columbia University Press, 1950. xxiv, 374 p. illus. 25 cm. [TH5281.P7 1950] 50-10640
1. Shoring and underpinning. 2. Foundations. I. White, Lazarus, 1874- joint author. II. Title.

Shosoin, Nara, Japan.

HAYASHI, Ryoichi, 1918- 708'.952'18
The silk road and the Shoso-in / Ryoichi Hayashi; translated by Robert Ricketts New York : Weatherhill, 1975. p. cm. (The Heibonsha survey of Japanese art ; v. 6) Translation of Shiruku Rodo to Shosoin. [N3750.N36H3713] 75-23081 ISBN 0-8348-1022-0 : 12.50
1. Shosoin, Nara, Japan. 2. Silk Road. 3. Art, Ancient—Nara, Japan—History. 4. Art—Nara, Japan—History. I. Title. II. Series. BIP

Shot-guns—History.

HINMAN, Bob. 739.7'4'2
The golden age of shotgunning. [New York] Winchester Press [1971] xiii, 175 p. illus. 24 cm. Bibliography: p. 165-166. [SK274.H56] 72-159432 ISBN 0-87691-043-6 8.95
1. Shot-guns—History. 2. Hunting—North America—History. I. Title. BIP

Show-windows.

BERNARD, Frank J. 659.157
Dynamic display, technique and practice. Cincinnati, Display Pub. Co. [1952] 260 p. illus. 31 cm. [HF5845.B4] 52-2493
1. Show-windows. I. Title.

BUCKLEY, Jim. 659.157
The drama of display; visual merchandising and its techniques. New York, Pellegrini & Cudahy [1953] 224p. illus. (part col.) 29cm. (Visual arts books) [HF5845.B67] 52-9365
1. Show-windows. I. Title.

CASTRO, Nestor. 659.157
The handbook of window display. New York, Architectural Book Pub. Co. [1954] 194 p. illus. 28 cm. [HF5845.C37] 54-6398
1. Show-windows. I. Title: Window display.

FAIRCHILD'S book of window display / [edited] by Shirley Joel. New York : Fairchild Publications, c1973. xi, 181 p. : ill. (part col.) ; 23 cm. Includes index. [HF5845.F32] 72-97757 ISBN 0-87005-101-6 : 15.00 659.1'57
1. Show-windows. I. Joel, Shirley. II. Fairchild Publications, inc., New York. III. Title: Book of window display. BIP

GABA, Lester. 658.855
The art of window display. [New York, Studio Publications in association with Crowell, 1952] 142 p. illus. 26 cm. [HF5845.G3] 52-7383
1. Show-windows. I. Title.

HERDEG, Walter. ed. 659.157
International window display; an international survey of the art of window display with special sections on interior display, mannequin design, display units and paper sculpture. Schaufensterkunst. Etalages. New York, Pellegrini & Cudahy [1951] 276 p. illus. 31 cm. (A Graphis book, 1) [HF5845.H4] 51-14162
1. Show-windows. I. Title. II. Title: Schaufensterkunst. III. Title: Etalages. IV. Series.

HERDEG, Walter, 1908- ed. 659.157
Window display; an international survey of the art of window display. Schaufensterkunst; eine internationale Ubersicht uber die Schaufensterkunst. L'art de l'etalage; repertoire international de l'art de l'etalage. Zurich, Amstutz & Herdeg; [distributed by Praeger, New York, 1961] 282p. illus. 31cm. (Graphis, v. 2) [HF5845.H43] 61-3530
1. Show-windows. I. Title.

INTERNATIONAL window display, Etalages internationaux. Schaufenster-international; 1966. New York, Praeger [1966] 151p. illus. 29cm. biennial. Eds.: 1966- K. Kaspar and L. Mickel. [HF5845.A27] 66-14975 15.00 659.157
1. Show-windows. I. Kaspar, Karl, ed. II. Mickel. Liselotte ed. III. Title: Etalages internationaux. IV. Title: Schaufenster-international.

KROLL, Natasha. 659.157
Window display. London & New York, Studio Publications [1954] 96p. illus. 26cm. (The How to do it series, no. 51) Bibliography: p. 96. [HF5845.K77] 54-11395
1. Show- windows. j(Series: How to do it series (London, The Studio)) I. Title.

LEYDENFROST, Robert J, 1925- 659.157
Window display. Foreword by Gene Moore. New York, Architeetural Book Pub. Co. [1950] 207 p. illus. 28 cm. [The Designing for business series] [HF5845.L48] 50-6963
1. Show-windows. I. Title.

Show-windows—Pictorial works.

WINDOWS / 659.1'57
Michael Emory ; designed by Bea Feitler. Chicago : Contemporary Books, c1977. [126] p. : ill. (some col.) ; 24 x 32 cm. [HF5845.W6 1977] 77-75725 ISBN 0-8092-7819-7 : 25.00
1. Show-windows—Pictorial works. I. Emory, Michael. BIP

Show-windows—United States—History.

MARCUS, Leonard S., 1950- 659.1'57
The American store window / by Leonard S. Marcus. New York : Whitney Library of Design, 1978. p. cm. Includes index. Bibliography: p. [HF5845.M35 1978] 78-18176 ISBN 0-8230-7030-1 : 25.00
1. Show-windows—United States—History. I. Title.
:Distributed by Watson-Guptill Pubns. Inc. New York, N.Y. 10036 BIP

Shreveport, La. Louisiana State Fair Stadium.

GULF South 711'.558'09763
Research Institute.
Louisiana State fair stadium study. Prepared for Louisiana Science Foundation. Baton Rouge, 1967. iv, 48 l. illus., maps. 28 cm. "Final copy, GSRI project no. ES-117-2." Bibliography: leaf 48. [GV416.S5G8] 68-63545
1. Shreveport, La. Louisiana State Fair Stadium. I. Louisiana State Science Foundation. II. Title.

Shrubs—California.

BOLTZ, Howard Owen. 715.3
The landscape use of shrubs and vines, according to form, color, and texture, soil and culture. 1st ed. Saint Louis, Educational Publishers [c1958] 122p. illus. 28cm. [SB435.B58] 60-21774
1. Shrubs—California. 2. Climbing plants. 3. Landscape gardening—California. I. Title.

Shulman, Joseph L.—Art collections.

WADSWORTH 759.94'074'01463
Atheneum, Hartford.
Selections from the Joseph L. Shulman Collection : [catalogue of] an exhibition, 5 March-13 April, 1975 / organized by the Wadsworth Atheneum, Hartford, Connecticut. Hartford, Conn. : The Atheneum, [1975] 47 p. : chiefly ill. (some col.) ; 28 cm. [N6758.W32 1975] 75-313874
1. Shulman, Joseph L.—Art collections. 2. Art, European—Exhibitions. 3. Art, Modern—20th century—Europe—Exhibitions.

Shuptrine, Hubert, 1936—

SHUPTRINE, Hubert, 1936- 759.13
Jericho : the South beheld / Hubert Shuptrine, James Dickey. 1st ed. Birmingham, Ala. : Oxmoor House, 1974. 165 p. : ill. (some col.) ; 33 x 42 cm. [ND1839.S48D53] 74-78763 60.00
1. Shuptrine, Hubert, 1936- 2. Southern States in art. I. Dickey, James. II. Title. BIP

Siberch, John, 1475 or 6-1554?

CRUTCHLEY, Brooke. 686.2'094
Siberch celebrations, 1521-1971; edited by Brooke Crutchley. Cambridge, University Printing House, 1971. xi, 133 p. illus., facsims., music. 25 cm. Bibliography: p. 44. [Z232.S56C7] 72-190735 ISBN 0-903349-00-0 £0.75
1. Siberch, John, 1475 or 6-1554? 2. Printing—History—Addresses, essays, lectures. I. Title.

Sicily in art.

TOWNSEND, Elinor. 741.9'73
Sicily : a sketchbook / by Elinor Townsend. Canaan, N.H. : Phoenix Pub., c1978. 70 p. : ill. (some col.) ; 16 x 24 cm. English and Italian text. Erratum slip tipped in. [NC139.T68A4 1978] 78-15131 ISBN 0-914016-52-0 : 10.00
1. Townsend, Elinor. 2. Sicily in art. I. Title. BIP

Sick children—Juvenile literature.

BASSINGTHWAIGHTE, 745.5'02'40816
Inger, 1937-
Stay in bed book. New York, S. G. Phillips [1975, c1974] p. cm. Projects for children in bed. Includes paper rubbing, weaving, vegetable carving, and making puppets, musical instruments, miniature furniture, and much more. [RJ242.B37 1975] 74-11213 ISBN 0-87599-212-9
1. Sick children—Juvenile literature. 2. Convalescence—Juvenile literature. 3. Handicraft—Juvenile literature. I. Title.

Sickert, Walter, 1860-1942.

LILLY, Marjorie. 759.2
Sickert; the painter and his circle. [1st U.S. ed.] Park Ridge, N.J., Noyes Press [1973, c1971] 176 p. illus. 26 cm. [ND497.S48L5 1973] 72-86251 ISBN 0-8155-5014-6 14.00
1. Sickert, Walter, 1860-1942. I. Title.

SICKERT, Walter Richard, 759.2
1860-1942
Sickert. [by] Lillian Browse. London, Hart-Davis [dist. Chester Springs, Pa., Dufour, 1965, c.1960] 124p. illus., plates (pt. col.) 30cm. Bibl. [ND497.S48B7] 60-50038 12.50
I. Browse, Lillian. II. Title.

SUTTON, Denys. 759.2 B
Walter Sickert : a biography / [by] Denys Sutton. London : Joseph, 1976. 272 p., leaf of plate, [24] p. of plates : ill., ports. ; 24 cm. Includes index. Bibliography: p. 252-262. [ND497.S48S97 1976] 76-373164 ISBN 0-7181-1436-1 : £10.50
1. Sickert, Walter, 1860-1942. 2. Painters—Great Britain—Biography.

WOOLF, Virginia Stephen, 759.2
1882-1941.
Walter Sickert : a conversation / Virginia Woolf. Folcroft, Pa. : Folcroft Library Editions, 1977. p. cm. Reprint of the 1934 ed. published by L. and V. Woolf at the Hogarth Press, London. [ND497.S48W6 1977] 77-24047 ISBN 0-8414-9620-X lib. bdg. : 8.50
1. Sickert, Walter, 1860-1942. I. Title. BIP

Sidewalks—Miscellanea—Juvenile literature.

SOMMER, Robert. 745.5
Sidewalk fossils / text and photos. by Robert Sommer and Harriet Becker. New York : Walker, 1976. [48] p. : ill. ; 27 cm. Examines the various impressions left on sidewalks which are similiar to fossils. Includes instructions for making rubbings and original impressions. [TE280.S65 1976] 75-10056 ISBN 0-8027-6228-X : 5.95 ISBN 0-8027-6233-6 pbk. :
1. Sidewalks—Miscellanea—Juvenile literature. I. Becker, Harriet, joint author. II. Title. BIP

Sidney, Philip, Sir, 1554-1586—Portraits, etc.

JUDSON, Alexander Corbin, 001.3 s
1883-
Sidney's appearance; a study in Elizabethan portraiture, by Alexander C. Judson. Freeport, N.Y., Books for Libraries Press [1971, c1958] xii, 98 p. ports. 23 cm. (Indiana University publications. Humanities series, no. 41) (Biography index reprint series) Bibliography: p. 91-94. [AS36.I385 no. 41 1971] [ND1314.2] 757'.3'0942 73-179730 ISBN 0-8369-8098-0
1. Sidney, Philip, Sir, 1554-1586—Portraits, etc. 2. Portrait painting, British—History. I. Title. II. Series: Indiana. University. Indiana University humanities series, no. 41. BIP

Siegel, Eli, 1902—

AESTHETIC realism: we have 701.1
been there; six artists on the Siegel theory of opposites [by] Ted Van Griethuysen [and others] New York, Definition Press [1969] 119 p. illus. 20 cm. "Material ... originally presented at the Terrain Gallery in New York City on November 18, 1967." [BH221.U54S5] 69-17523 4.95
1. Siegel, Eli, 1902- 2. Realism in art. 3. Aesthetics. I. Van Griethuysen, Ted, 1934- II. Terrain Gallery.

Siena. Palio.

HENRY, Marguerite, 1902- JUV
Gaudenzia, pride of the Palio; illustrated by Lynd Ward. Chicago, Rand McNally [1960] 237 p. illus. (part col.) 25 cm. [PZ7.H394Gau] fic 60-8264
1. Siena. Palio. I. Title.

Sievan, Maurice.

SIEVAN, Maurice. 759.13
Maurice Sievan retrospective [exhibition] March 8 through April 21, 1974. Flushing, N.Y., Queens County Art & Cultural Center [1974] 39 p. illus. (part col.) 23 cm. Cover title: Maurice Sievan. Bibliography: p. 37-39. [ND237.S543Q43] 74-168281
1. Sievan, Maurice. I. Queens County Art & Cultural Center. II. Title.

Sign painting.

DUVALL, Edward J. 659.134
Modern sign painting. Wilmette, Ill., F. J. Drake [1952] 160 p. illus. 21 x 28 cm. [TT360.D8 1952] 52-2718
1. Sign painting. I. Title.

DUVALL, Edward J 659.134
Sign Painting. Serial 6299A-2-Ed. 2. Scranton, International Correspondence Schools, 1962- v. illus. 19 cm. [TT360.D83] 63-1885
1. Sing painting. 2. Lettering. I. International Correspondence Schools, Scranton, Pa. II. Title.

EHR, Syl, 1903- 698.1
Signpainters don't read signs; memories of and reflections on an ancient art. [1st ed.] New York, Exposition Press [1957] 159 p. illus. 21 cm. (A Banner book) [TT360.E47] 56-12368
1. Sign painting. I. Title.

GREGORY, Ralph. v. 12
Better sign painting. Cincinnati, Signs of the Times Pub. Co. [1960] 220p. illus. 24cm. [TT698.128] 60-29913
1. Sign painting. I. Title.

GREGORY, Ralph. 698.1'28
Better sign painting. 2d ed. Cincinnati, Signs of the Times Pub. Co. [1968] 220 p. illus. 24 cm. [TT360.G7 1968] 68-6133
1. Sign painting. I. Title.

GREGORY, Ralph. 667'.9
Ralph Gregory's sign painting techniques; beginner to professional. Illus. by the author. 1st ed. Cincinnati, Signs of the Times Pub. Co. [1973] x, 388 p. illus. 23 cm. Title on spine: Sign painting techniques. [TT360.G72] 73-160520 ISBN 0-911380-29-9
1. Sign painting. I. Title. II. Title: Sign painting techniques.
Publisher's Address: 407 Gilbert Ave; Cincinnati, Ohio 45202

HEARN, Bertie, 1897- 745.6
The art of signwriting. New York, Studio Publications [1954] 114 p. illus. 26 cm. [TT360.H39] 54-8439
1. Sign painting. I. Title: Signwriting.

MATTHEWS, Eric Christian, 745.6
1892-
Sign painting course; a complete self-instruction course for home study for the beginner as well as the full fledged sign man who wants to improve and modernize his techniques. New ed., rev. and enl. Chicago, Nelson-Hall 1958 149 p. illus. 29 cm. [TT360.M373 1958] 58-25474
1. Sign painting. I. Title.

OWEN, Robert E 1913- 745.6
New practical sign painting. Milwaukee, Bruce Pub. Co. [1958] 182p. illus. 25cm. Published in 1948 under title: Practical sign painting. [TT360.O9 1958] 58-12233
1. Sign painting. 2. Lettering. I. Title. II. Title: Practical sign painting.

PROHASKA, Steve 698.128
Sign painting the new way. Cincinnati, Signs of the Times Pub. Co., 407 Gilbert Ave. [1964] 183p. illus. 24cm. [TT360.P7] 65-654 6.00
1. Sign painting. I. Title.

Signac, Paul, 1863-1935.

SIGNAC, Paul, 1863- 769'.92'4
1935.
Catalogue raisonne de l'ouvre grave et lithographie de Paul Signac / E. W. Kornfeld gt P. A. Wick. Berne : Kornfeld et Klipstein, 1974. [66] p. : ill. (some col.) ; 32 cm. [NE2349.5.S53K67] 75-503903 ISBN 3-85773-001-3 : 150F
1. Signac, Paul, 1863-1935. I. Kornfeld, Eberhard W. II. Wick, Peter A. III. Title.

SIGNAC, Paul, 1863-1935. 759.4
Paul Signac, 1863-1935 [par] George Besson. Paris, Braun; agent pour U.S.A.: E. S. Herrmann. New York [1950] [63] p. (p. [15]-[62] illus.) 17 cm. (Collection des maitres) (Collection "Les Maitres") French, English and German. Bibliography: p. [63] [ND553.S55B4] 52-27766
I. Besson, George, 1882- ed. II. Title. III. Series.

Signorelli, Luca, 1441?-1523.

CRUTTWELL, Maud. 759.5
Luca Signorelli. London, G. Bell, 1907. St. Clair Shores, Mich., Scholarly Press, 1972. xi, [84], 144 p. illus. 22 cm. Original ed. issued in series: The Great masters in painting and sculpture. Bibliography: p. [81] (2d group) [ND623.S5C8 1972] 75-131677 ISBN 0-403-00564-7
1. Signorelli, Luca, 1441?-1523. I. Series: The Great masters in painting and sculpture. BIP

Signs and sign-boards.

CONSTANTINE, Mildred. 659.134
Sign language for buildings and landscape [by] Mildred Constantine and Egbert Jacobson. New York, Reinhold Pub. Corp. [1961] 212 p. illus. 27 cm. Includes bibliography. [HF5843.5.C65] 61-13197
1. Signs and sign-boards. 2. Advertising, Outdoor. I. Jacobson, Egbert, 1890- joint author. II. Title.

CROSBY/FLETCHER/FORBES. 744
A sign systems manual. New York, Praeger [1970] 76 p. illus. (part col.) 28 cm. Bibliography: p. 76. [TT360.C78] 75-127416 10.00
1. Signs and sign-boards. 2. Lettering. I. Title.

Signs and sign-boards—Boston.

ASHLEY/MYER/SMITH. 380.3
City signs and lights; a policy study, prepared for the Boston Redevelopment Authority and the U.S. Department of Housing and Urban Development by Signs/Lights/Boston, a project of Ashley/Myer/Smith. [Cambridge? Mass.] 1971. 272 p. illus. (part col.), maps. 23 x 26 cm. Bibliography: p. [263]-272. [HF5843.5.A8] 72-170492
1. Signs and sign-boards—Boston. 2. Traffic signs and signals—Boston. 3. Cities and towns—Planning—Boston. I. Boston Redevelopment Authority. II. United States. Dept. of Housing and Urban Development. III. Title.

Signs and sign-boards—Great Britain.

RICE, Brian. 745.2
The English sunrise [by] Brian Rice and Tony Evans. [New York] Flash Books; [distributed by Quick Fox, 1973] 76 p. illus. 21 cm. [GT3911.43.A2R52 1973] 73-177658 2.95
1. Signs and sign-boards—Great Britain. 2. Sun lore. I. Evans, Tony, joint author. II. Title. BIP

Signs and sign-boards—Hist.

WAGNER, Charles Louis 659.13409
Henry, 1879-
The story of signs; an outline history of the sign arts from the earliest recorded times to the present 'atomic age.' Boston, A. MacGibbon, 1954. 123p. illus. 23cm. [HF5841.W25] 54-7235
1. Signs and sign-boards—Hist. I. Title.

Signs and sign-boards—United States.

MACK, Kathy. 659.13'6
American neon / compiled by Kathy Mack. New York : Universe Books, 1976. 72 p. : chiefly col. ill. ; 20 x 22 cm. [HF5841.M32] 76-15043 ISBN 0-87663-276-2 : 7.95 ISBN 0-87663-950-3 pbk. : 4.95
1. Signs and sign-boards—United States. 2. Electric signs. 3. Neon tubes. I. Title.

Signs and signboards.

NORMAN, Philip, 1842-1931. 929.8
London signs and inscriptions. With an introd. by Henry B. Wheatley. London, E. Stock, 1893. Detroit, Singing Tree Press,

1968. xx, 237 p. illus. 20 cm. (The Camden Library) [DA677.1.N78 1968] 68-22039
1. Signs and signboards. 2. Inscriptions—London. 3. London—Antiquities. I. Title. II. Series. BIP

Signs and symbols.

DREYFUSS, Henry, 1904- 001.56
Symbol sourcebook; an authoritative guide to international graphic symbols. New York, McGraw-Hill [1972] 292 p. illus. 28 cm. Bibliography: p. 252-269. [AZ108.D74] 71-172261 ISBN 0-07-017837-2
1. Signs and symbols. I. Title. BIP

HELFMAN, Elizabeth S. 419
Signs and symbols around the world [by] Elizabeth S. Helfman. New York, Lothrop, Lee & Shepard Co. [1967] 192 p. illus. 24 cm. Bibliography: p. [180]-182. [AZ108.H44] 67-22596
1. Signs and symbols. I. Title. BIP

KOCH, Rudolf, 1876-1934. 652
The book of signs, which contains all manner of symbols used from the earliest times to the Middle Ages by primitive peoples and early Christians, collected, drawn and explained by Rudolf Koch. Translated from the German by Vyvyan Holland. [New York] Dover Publications [1955?] 104 p. illus. 25 cm. "An unabridged republication of the English translation first published ... in 1930." [AZ108.K62 1955] 55-2433
1. Signs and symbols. I. Title. BIP

LEHNER, Ernst, 1895- 031
The picture book of symbols. New York, Wm. Penn Pub. Corp. [1956] 96 p. (chiefly illus.) 29 cm. [AZ108.L38] 56-14454
1. Signs and symbols. I. Title.

LEHNER, Ernst, 1895- 704.946
Symbols, signs & signets. Cleveland, World Pub. Co. [1950] xi, 220, [1] p. (chiefly illus.) 32 cm. Bibliography: p. 217-[221] [AZ108.L4] 50-9861
1. Signs and symbols. I. Title. BIP

LEHNER, Ernst, 1895- 704.94'6
Symbols, signs & signets. New York, Dover Publications [1969, c1950] 220, [1] p. (chiefly illus.) 28 cm. (Dover pictorial archive series) Bibliography: p. 217-[221] [AZ108.L4 1969] 69-16134 3.50
1. Signs and symbols. I. Title.

MODLEY, Rudolf. 001.56
Handbook of pictorial symbols : 3,250 examples from international sources / Rudolf Modley, with the assistance of William R. Myers. New York : Dover Publications, 1976. xiv, 143 p. : chiefly ill. ; 28 cm. (Dover pictorial archive series) Includes index. Bibliography: p. xi. [AZ108.M63 1976] 76-15438 ISBN 0-486-23357-X pbk. : 3.50
1. Signs and symbols. I. Myers, William R., joint author. II. Title. BIP

RAPHAELIAN, Harry M., 1882- 704.946
Signs of life; a pictorial dictionary of symbols. Introd. by Felix Marti-Ibanez. Edited with a pref. by David Sortor. [1st ed.] New York, A. Sivas, 1957. 124 p. illus. 27 cm. [GR950.S5R3] 57-6637
1. Signs and symbols. I. Title.

SHEPHERD, Walter. 001.5'6
Shepherd's glossary of graphic signs and symbols. Compiled and classified for ready reference by Walter Shepherd. New York, Dover Publications [1971] x, 597 p. illus. 23 cm. Bibliography: p. 585-590. [AZ108.S53 1971b] 74-153895 ISBN 0-486-20700-5 15.00
1. Signs and symbols. I. Title. II. Title: Glossary of graphic signs and symbols. BIP

SMITH, Laura J. 769.5
The development of a symbol, designed, written by Laura J. Smith. [New Haven, Conn., 1966] 1v. (unpaged) illus. (pt. col.) 21cm. Thesis (M.F.A.)--Yale. [NK1585.S6] 66-8630 8.50 pap.,
1. Signs and symbols. I. Title.
Distributed by Wittenborn, New York.

Signs and symbols—Congresses.

MEYLAN, E. Paul. 001.56
Symbology : a review of a conference on this topic / by E. Paul Meylan. Los Angeles : Consultants for Product Design, 1959. 26 p. ; 21 cm. Cover title. "A combination of notes and commentary on the fourth Communications Conference of the Art Director's Club of New York." [AZ108.M49] 75-321383
1. Visual Communications Conference, 4th, New York, 1959. 2. Signs and symbols—Congresses. I. Visual Communications Conference, 4th, New York, 1959. II. Title. BIP

Signs and symbols in architecture.

FOLLIS, John, 1923- 720
Architectural signing and graphics / by John Follis and Dave Hammer. New York : Whitney Library of Design, 1979. p. cm. Includes index. Bibliography: p. [NA2500.F63] 79-933 ISBN 0-8230-7051-4 : 32.50
1. Signs and symbols in architecture. 2. Communication in architectural design. I. Hammer, Dave, 1923- joint author. II. Title.

FOLLIS, John, 1923- 720
Architectural signing and graphics / by John Follis and Dave Hammer. New York : Whitney Library of Design, 1979. p. cm. Includes index. Bibliography: p. [NA2500.F63] 79-933 ISBN 0-8230-7051-4 : 32.50
1. Signs and symbols in architecture. 2. Communication in architectural design. I. Hammer, Dave, 1923- joint author. II. Title. BIP

Signs and symbols—Juvenile literature.

LUBELL, Winifred. 001.55'2
Picture signs & symbols, by Winifred & Cecil Lubell. New York, Parents' Magazine Press [1972] 64 p. illus. 24 cm. (A Stepping-stone book) Explains the use of picture signs and symbols as a form of communication. [AZ108.L82] 76-39742 ISBN 0-8193-0577-4 (lib. bdg.) 3.78
1. Signs and symbols—Juvenile literature. I. Lubell, Cecil, joint author. II. Title. BIP

MYLLER, Rolf. 001.56
Symbols & their meaning / text and pictures by Rolf Myller. 1st ed. New York : Athenaum, 1978. [95] p. : ill. (some col.) ; 21 cm. Brief text and illustrations examine the use of symbols for quick and simple communications. [AZ108.M9] 77-17015 ISBN 0-689-30638-5 : 9.95
1. Signs and symbols—Juvenile literature. I. Title. BIP

Siletz Indians—Basket making.

KASNER, Leone Letson. 746.4'1
Siletz : survival for an artifact / by Leone Letson Kasner ; ill. by the author. [s.l. : Kasner, c1976] 114 p. (p. 111-114 blank for "notes") : ill. ; 28 cm. "Sponsored by the Confederated Tribes of Siletz." Includes bibliographical references. [E99.S544K37] 77-374108
1. Siletz Indians—Basket making. 2. Siletz Indians—History. 3. Indians of North America—Oregon—Basket making. I. Title.

Silhouettes.

COKE, Desmond, 1879- 741.7
The art of silhouette. Detroit, Singing Tree Press, 1970. 230 p. illus. 22 cm. "Facsimile reprint of the 1913 edition." [NC910.C65] 73-110809
1. Silhouettes. I. Title. BIP

DECORATIVE silhouettes of the twenties for designers & craftsmen / selected and introduced by Jo Anne C. Day. New York : Dover Publications, 1975. [5] p., 77 leaves of plates : 77 ill. ; 28 cm. (Dover pictorial archive series) [NC910.D24 1975] 73-89255 ISBN 0-486-23152-6 pbk. : 3.00 741.7
1. Silhouettes. I. Day, JoAnne C. BIP

HICKMAN, Peggy. 760
Silhouettes. New York, Walker [1968] 60 p. illus. (part col.), facsims., ports. 20 cm. (Collectors' pieces, 12) [NC910.H47 1968b] 68-14005 3.50
1. Silhouettes. BIP

JACKSON, Emily, 1861- 741.9'4
Ancestors in silhouette, cut by August Edouart. Illustrative notes and biographical sketches by Mrs. F. Nevill Jackson. Boston, Milford House [1973] p. Reprint of the 1921 ed. published by J. Lane, London, and J. Lane Co., New York. [NC910.5.E3J32 1973] 73-5522 ISBN 0-87821-141-1 45.00 (lib. bdg.)
1. Edouart, Augustin Amant Constance Fidele, 1789-1861. 2. Silhouettes. I. Title. BIP

KRAMER, Jack. 741.7
Silhouettes : how to make and use them / by Jack Kramer ; drawings by Michael Valdez ; photos. by Matthew Barr. Boston : Houghton Mifflin, 1977. 143 p. : ill. ; 26 cm. [NC910.K78] 76-44873 ISBN 0-395-25060-9 : 7.95
1. Silhouettes. I. Title. BIP

LALIBERTE, Norman. 741.7
Silhouettes, shadows, and cutouts; history and modern use [by] Norman Laliberte [and] Alex Mogelon. New York, Reinhold Book Corp. [1968] 112 p. illus. (part col.) 21 cm. (An Art horizons book) [NC910.L3] 68-16021
1. Silhouettes. 2. Decoupage. I. Mogelon, Alex, joint author. II. Title. III. Series.

MELCHERS, Bernd, 1886- 736'.98
Traditional Chinese cut-paper designs / collected and edited by Bernd Melchers. New York : Dover Publications, 1978. 64 p. : chiefly ill. ; 24 cm. (The Dover pictorial archive series) Translation of Chinesische schattenschnitte. [NC910.M413] 77-88654 ISBN 0-486-23581-5 pbk. : 2.00
1. Silhouettes. 2. Paper work—China. I. Title. BIP

MORRIS, Floyd. 741.7
272 artistic silhouttes South Holland, Ill., Goodheart-Willcox Co. [1972] 96 p. (chiefly illus.) 28 cm. [NC910.M67] 72-87370 ISBN 0-87006-158-5 (pbk)
1. Silhouettes. I. Title.

Silhouettes—England.

PIPER, David. 741.7'0942
Shades : an essay on English portrait silhouettes / David Piper. New York : Chilmark Press, c1970. 63 p. : 36 ports. ; 28 cm. "This is the fourth of the Clover Hill Editions of the Chilmark Press, and consists of 500 copies, of which this is number 302." Bibliography: p. 63. [NC910.P54] 75-307773
1. Silhouettes—England. I. Title.

Silhouettes—History.

HICKMAN, Peggy. 741.7'09
Silhouettes, a living art / Peggy Hickman ; with a foreword by Roy Strong. New York : St. Martin's Press, 1975. 96 p. : ill. ; 25 cm. Includes index. Bibliography: p. 91. [NC910.H473 1975] 75-4503 8.95
1. Silhouettes—History. I. Title.

Silhouettes—United States.

CARRICK, Alice Van Leer, 1875- 741.7'0973
A history of American silhouettes; a collector's guide, 1790-1840. Rutland, Vt., C. E. Tuttle [1968] xx, 205 p. illus., facsims., ports. 24 cm. Reprint of the 1928 ed. published under title: Shades of our ancestors. Bibliography: p. 193-194. [NC910.C3 1968] 68-21119
1. Silhouettes—United States. 2. United States—Biography—Portraits. 3. Artists, American. I. Title. II. Title: American silhouettes.

EDOUART, Augustin Amant Constance Fidele, 1789-1861. 741.9'4
Auguste Edouart's Silhouettes of eminent Americans, 1839-1844 / Andrew Oliver. Charlottesville : Published for the National Portrait Gallery, Smithsonian Institution, by the University Press of Virginia, 1976. p. cm. "Catalogue of 3,800 named and dated American silhouette portraits by August Edouart" by E. Jackson: p. Includes index. [NC910.5.E3O44] 76-21073 ISBN 0-8139-0632-6 : 22.50
1. Edouart, Augustin Amant Constance Fidele, 1789-1861. 2. Silhouettes—United States. 3. United States—Biography—Portraits. I. Oliver, Andrew, 1906- II. Jackson, Emily, 1861- Catalogue of 3,800 named and dated American silhouette portraits by August Edouart, 1789-1861. 1976. III. Title. IV. Title: Silhouettes of eminent Americans, 1839-1844.
Distributed by University Press of Virginia. BIP

LONDON, Hannah Ruth, 1894- 741.7
Miniatures and silhouettes of early American Jews, by Hannah R. London. Rutland, Vt., C. E. Tuttle [1970] 2 v. in 1. ports. 27 cm. Reprint of the author's Miniatures of early American Jews and Shades of my forefathers. Includes bibliographies. [NC910.L59] 78-87797 ISBN 0-8048-0657-8 15.00
1. Silhouettes—United States. 2. Jews in the United States. 3. United States—Biography—Portraits. I. London, Hannah Ruth, 1894- Miniatures of early American Jews. II. London, Hannah Ruth, 1894- Shades of my forefathers. III. Title. BIP

Silk, Chinese.

HSIN-CHIANG Wei-wu-erh tsu chih ch'u po wu kuan. 746.751
Ssu ch'ou chih lu—Han T'ang chih wu. (Silk road—silks from Han to T'ang.) (Distributor: New York, China Books & Periodicals, 1972) [9] p., 46 col. plates. 36 cm. "(Explanation)" (8 p.) in pocket. [NK8983.A1H75] 72-837198 25.00
1. Silk, Chinese. 2. China—Antiquities. I. Ch'u t'u wen wu chan lan kung tso tsu. II. Title.
L.C. cataloging in Chinese.

Silk manufacture and trade—Europe—Hist.

THORNTON, Peter 746
Baroque and rococo silks [1st Amer. ed.] New York, Taplinger [c.1965] 209p. 120p. of illus. (incl. ports.) 29cm. Bibl. [NK8942.T5] 65-14391 30.00
1. Silk manufacture and trade—Europe—Hist. 2. Silk, European—Hist. 3. Textile design. I. Title. BIP

Silk manufacture and trade—Spain.

MAY, Florence Lewis. 745.524
Silk textiles of Spain, eighth to fifteenth century. Printed by order of the trustees, the Hispanic Society of America. New York, 1957. ix, 286p. illus. (part col.) 26cm. (Hispanic notes & monographs: essays, studies, and brief biographies. Peninsular series) Bibliographical references included in'Notes' (p. 249-266 Bibliography: p. 266-273. [NK8862.M3] 57-59024
1. Silk manufacture and trade—Spain. 2. Textile design. I. Title. II. Series.

Silk pictures—Collectors and collecting.

BAKER, Wilma (Sinclair) Le Van. 927.4552
The silk pictures of Thomas Stevens; a biography of the Coventry weaver and his contribution to the art of weaving, with an illustrated catalogue of his work. [1st ed.] New York, Exposition Press [1957] 147p. illus. (part col.) ports. 24cm. [NK8998.S8B3] 57-9216
1. Stevens, Thomas, 1828-1888. 2. Slik. 3. Textile design. I. Title. BIP

GODDEN, Geoffrey A. 746.3'924
Stevengraphs and other Victorian silk pictures [by] Geoffrey A. Godden. [1st American ed.] Rutherford [N.J.] Fairleigh Dickinson University Press [1971] 492 p. illus. (part col.) 25 cm. [NK9002.G6 1971] 71-144124 ISBN 0-8386-7880-7 35.00
1. Stevens, Thomas, 1828-1888. 2. Silk pictures—Collectors and collecting. I. Title. BIP

SPRAKE, Austin. 746.3'92'4
The price guide to Stevengraphs: Stevengraphs, Stevens silk postcards, bookmarkers. Woodbridge, Antique

Collecters' Club, 1972. [9], 208 p. illus. 21 cm. Includes index. [NK9002.S67] 74-156395 £4.75
1. Stevens, Thomas, 1828-1888. 2. Silk pictures—Collectors and collecting. I. Title.

Silk Road.

HAYASHI, Ryoichi, 1918- 708'.952'18
The silk road and the Shoso-in / Ryoichi Hayashi; translated by Robert Ricketts New York : Weatherhill, 1975. p. cm. (The Heibonsha survey of Japanese art ; v. 6) Translation of Shiruku Rodo to Shosoin. [N3750.N36H3713] 75-23081 ISBN 0-8348-1022-0 : 12.50
1. Shosoin, Nara, Japan. 2. Silk Road. 3. Art, Ancient—Nara, Japan—History. 4. Art—Nara, Japan—History. I. Title. II. Series. BIP

Silk-screen printing.

STEFFEN, Bernard 764.8
Silk screen. Tech. photogs. by Robert Angeloch. New York, Pitman [c.1963] 31p. illus. (pt. col.) 20x26cm. (Pitman art bks., 47) 1.00 pap.,
1. Silk-screen printing. I. Title. BIP

Silva, Jerald.

SILVA, Jerald. 759.13
Jerald Silva and his world. Sacramento, Calif. : E. B. Crocker Art Gallery, c1975. [44] p. : ill. (some col.) ; 27 cm. Catalogue of an exhibition at the Crocker Art Gallery, 1975. [ND1839.S52A48] 75-25216
1. Silva, Jerald. I. Crocker Art Gallery, Sacramento, Calif. II. Title.

Silver articles, American.

SCHWARTZ, Marvin D. 739.2'3'773
Collectors' guide to antique American silver / by Marvin D. Schwartz. 1st ed. New York : Doubleday, [1975] xvii, 174 p. : ill. ; 22 cm. Includes index. Bibliography: p. [169] [NK7112.S38] 74-10012 ISBN 0-385-02926-8 : 7.95
1. Silver articles, American. 2. Silver articles—Collectors and collecting. 3. Silversmithing, American. I. Title.

Silver articles, American—Catalogs.

BOSTON. Museum of Fine Arts. 739.2'3'773074014461
American silver, 1655-1825, in the Museum of Fine Arts, Boston, by Kathryn C. Buhler. Boston; distributed by New York Graphic Society, Greenwich, Conn. [1972] 2 v. (xx, 708 p.) illus. 29 cm. Bibliography: v. 1, p. xv-xx. [NK7112.B577] 75-190547 ISBN 0-87846-064-0 45.00
1. Silver articles, American—Catalogs. I. Buhler, Kathryn C. II. Title. BIP

BUHLER, Kathryn C. 739.2'3'774
American silver, Garvan and other collections in the Yale University Art Gallery, by Kathryn C. Buhler & Graham Hood. New Haven, Published for the Yale University Art Gallery, by the Yale University Press, 1970. 2 v. illus. 27 cm. Contents.Contents.—v. 1. New England.—v. 2. Middle Colonies & the South. Bibliography: v. 1, p. xv-xvi. [NK7112.B79] 77-99821
1. Silver articles, American—Catalogs. I. Hood, Graham, 1936- joint author. II. Garvan, Francis Patrick, 1875-1937. III. Yale University. Art Gallery. IV. Title.

Silver articles, American—Exhibitions.

HOUSTON, Tex. Museum of Fine Arts. 739.2'3'775
Southern silver; an exhibition of silver made in the South prior to 1860. September 27 - November 10, 1968. Houston [1968] [92] p. illus. 28 cm. [NK7112.H68] 68-58525
1. Silver articles, American—Exhibitions. 2. Silversmiths, American—Southern States. I. Title.

NEW Haven Colony Historical Society, New Haven. 739.2'3'722
An exhibition of early silver by New Haven silversmiths. [New Haven] 1967. 99 p. illus. 23 cm. Bibliography: p. 62. [NK7111.N37 1967] 74-187502
1. Silver articles, American—Exhibitions. 2. Silversmiths—New Haven. 3. Hallmarks. I. Title. II. Title: New Haven silversmiths.

NEW York (City). Metropolitan Museum of Art. 739.2'3'7747
An exhibition of early New York silver, by C. Louise Avery. New York, December 8, 1931, through January 31, 1932. [New York] Arno Press, 1974 [c1931] 20 p., 70 p. of illus. 23 cm. [NK7112.N4 1974a] 77-168417 12.00
1. Silver articles, American—Exhibitions. 2. Silversmithing—New York (State) I. Avery, Clara Louise, 1891- II. Title. BIP

Silver articles, American—New York metropolitan area—Catalogs.

CHECKLIST of American silversmiths' work, 1650-1850, in museums in the New York metropolitan area. 739.2'3'773 [New York? 1968] 1 v. (unpaged) 22 cm. "Initiated as a class project for ... [a] course ... offered jointly by the Metropolitan Museum and Columbia University ... expanded with aid from the New York State Council on the Arts and the museum's Friends of the American Wing." Bibliography: p. [5] [NK7103.C5] 68-18952
1. Silver articles, American—New York metropolitan area—Catalogs. 2. Silversmiths, American. I. New York (City). Metropolitan Museum of Art. II. Columbia University.

Silver articles, British.

HAYDEN, Arthur, 1868-1946. 739.2'3
Chats on old silver, by Arthur Hayden. Edited by Cyril G. E. Bunt. Rev., with a new chapter on American silver by Jessie McNab Dennis. New York, Dover Publications [1969] 371 p. illus. 22 cm. [NK7143.H3 1969] 69-17528 3.00
1. Silver articles, British. I. Dennis, Jessie McNab. II. Title. BIP

Silver articles, British—Catalogs.

LAWRANCE, David. 739.2'3'742
English silver from the sixteenth century to the nineteenth century. Melbourne, New York, Oxford University Press [1968] 31 p. plates. 22 cm. (National Gallery booklets) Bibliography: p. 31. [NK7143.A1L3] 78-575686 0.70
1. Silver articles, British—Catalogs. I. Title. II. Series: Victoria, Australia. National Gallery, Melbourne. Booklets

UNTERMYER, Irwin. 739.2'3'742
English and other silver in the Irwin Untermyer Collection. Text by Yvonne Hackenbroch. Rev. ed. [New York] Metropolitan Museum of Art; Distributed by New York Graphic Society, Greenwich, Conn. [1969] xlv, 115 p. 213 illus. 31 cm. (The Irwin Untermyer Collection, 6) Bibliography: p. 111-112. [NK7143.U5 1969] 78-80674 25.00
1. Silver articles, British—Catalogs. 2. Silver articles—Private collections—U.S. I. Hackenbroch, Yvonne. II. New York (City). Metropolitan Museum of Art. III. Title. IV. Series.

Silver articles, British—Dictionaries.

ASH, Douglas. 739.2'3'742
Dictionary of British antique silver. New York, Hippocrene Books [1972] 189 p. illus. 23 cm. Bibliography: p. 189. [NK7143.A66 1972] 72-80991 ISBN 0-88254-007-6 7.95
1. Silver articles, British—Dictionaries. I. Title. BIP

Silver articles—Catalogs.

HUGHES, Graham. 739.2'3
Modern silver, throughout the world, 1880-1967. New York, Crown Publishers [1967] 256 p. 441 illus. (part col.) 28 cm. Bibliography: p. 255. [NK4705.H8] 67-26050
1. Silver articles—Catalogs. 2. Design, Industrial. I. Title.

Silver articles—Collectors and collecting.

COHEN, Hal L. 739.2'3'075
Official guide to silver & silverplate, by Hal L. Cohen. 1st ed. New York, House of Collectibles [1974] 264 p. illus. 18 cm. [NK7104.C63] 73-93244 ISBN 0-87637-328-7 5.00
1. Silver articles—Collectors and collecting. 2. Silverware—Collectors and collecting. I. Title.

CULME, John. 739.2'3'742
Antique silver and silver collecting [by] John Culme [and] John G. Strang. London, New York, Hamlyn, 1973. 96 p. illus. (some col.), col port. 30 cm. Includes index. Bibliography: p. 92. [NK7104.C84] 74-158555 ISBN 0-600-38023-8 £1.95
1. Silver articles—Collectors and collecting. I. Strang, John G., joint author. II. Title.

DELIEB, Eric. 739.2'3'075
Investing in silver. New York, C. N. Potter [1967] 152 p. illus. (part col.) 30 cm. Bibliography: p. 152. [NK7143.D4 1967b] 67-24609
1. Silver articles—Collectors and collecting. 2. Silver articles, British. I. Title.

FREEMAN, Graydon La Verne, 1904- 739.2'3'8
Victorian silver; plated & sterling, hollow & flatware, by Larry Freeman. Watkins Glen, N.Y., Century House [1967] 400 p. illus. 24 cm. Bibliography: p. 396-399. [NK7110.F7] 66-12052
1. Silver articles—Collectors and collecting. 2. Civilization, Modern—19th century. I. Title.

MCCLINTON, Katherine (Morrison) 739.2'3'773
Collected American 19th century silver New York, Scribner [1968] viii, 280 p. illus. 27 cm. Bibliography: p. 274-276. [NK7103.M22] 68-27787 12.50
1. Silver articles—Collectors and collecting. 2. Silver articles, American. I. Title.

SNELL, Doris Jean. 739.2'3'773
100 silver collectibles. [1st ed.] Des Moines, Wallace-Homestead Book Co., c1973] [7] p., 53 plates. illus. 23 cm. Cover title. [NK7112.S64] 74-160952
1. Silver articles—Collectors and collecting. 2. Silver articles—United States—Catalogs. I. Title.

Silver articles, English.

BANISTER, Judith. 739.2'3'742
Collecting antique silver / Judith Banister. New York : Galahad Books, [1974] c1972. 128 p. : ill. ; 21 cm. Includes index. [NK7143.B33 1974] 74-184819 4.95
1. Silver articles, English. 2. Silver articles—Collectors and collecting. I. Title.

Silver articles, English—Exhibitions.

TEXAS. University at Austin. Art Museum. 739.2'3'7420740164
One hundred years of English silver, 1660-1760. [Austin, Printed by the Printing Division of the University of Texas, 1969?] 1 v. (unpaged) illus., col. plate. 22 cm. Catalog of an exhibition held at the Art Museum, University of Texas, Sept. 21-Oct. 22, 1969, and at Fort Worth Art Center-Museum, Fort Worth, Tex., Nov 2-30, 1969. Co-sponsors: the University Art Museum, Fort Worth Art Center [and] the Hoblitzelle Foundation. Includes bibliography. [NK7143.L57T48] 79-23533
1. Silver articles, English—Exhibitions. 2. Silversmithing—Gt. Brit.—London. I. Fort Worth Art Center-Museum. II. Title.

Silver articles, Georgian.

BANISTER, Judith. 739.2'3'742
Late Georgian and Regency silver. Feltham, Hamlyn, 1971. 63 p. illus. 19 cm. (Country Life collectors' guides) [NK7143.B346] 70-850886 ISBN 0-600-43203-3 £0.65
1. Silver articles, Georgian. 2. Silver articles, Regency. I. Title.

BANISTER, Judith. 739.2'3'742
Mid Georgian silver. [London] [Hamlyn] 1972. 64 p. illus. 19 cm. (Country Life collectors' guides) Caption title. [NK7143.B348] 73-153158 ISBN 0-600-43129-0
1. Silver articles, Georgian. I. Title.
Distributed by Transatlantic, 2.95. BIP

Silver articles, Irish—Exhibitions.

DUBLIN. University. Exhibitions Committee of Trinity College. 739.2'3'7415
Irish silver; an exhibition of Irish silver from 1630-1820 at Trinity College, Dublin, October 24 to December 29, 1971. [Dublin, Trinity College, 1971] 56 p. illus. 24 cm. Annotated and catalogued by I. Delamer. Bibliography: p. 6. [NK7146.A1D82] 72-198385
1. Silver articles, Irish—Exhibitions. I. Delamer, Ida. II. Dublin. University. III. Title.

Silver articles, Victorian—Catalogs.

HARRIS, Ian, 1937- 739.2'3'742
The price guide to Victorian silver. Woodbridge, Antique Collectors' Club, 1971. [12], 276 p. (chiefly illus.) 22 cm. (Price guide series) [NK7109.8.H37] 73-152797 £2.95
1. Silver articles, Victorian—Catalogs. I. Title.

Silver boxes, British.

DELIEB, Eric. 739.2'3'84
Silver boxes. Photos. by Michael Plomer. New York, C. N. Potter [1968] 119 p. illus. (part col.) 31 cm. [NK7143.D42 1968b] 68-31838 10.00
1. Silver boxes, British. I. Title.

Silver coins.

DAVENPORT, John Stewart, 1907- 737.4
Larger size silver coins of the world [by] John S. Davenport [and] Tyge Sondergaard. [2d ed.] Galesburg, Ill., 1972. viii, 186 p. illus. 29 cm. A new ed. of Oversize multiple talers of the Brunswick Duchies and Saxe-Lauenburg, with additions and corrections, first published in 1956. Bibliography: p. 185-186. [CJ1546.D38 1972] 72-181955
1. Silver coins. 2. Taler. I. Sondergaard, Tyge, joint author. II. Title.

Silver halide crystals—Congresses.

INTERNATIONAL Colloquium on the Physics and Chemistry of the Silver Halide Crystal, University of Montreal, 1972. 548
Physics and chemistry of the silver halide crystal; [reports from] an international symposium sponsored by the Society of Photographic Scientists and Engineers and the University of Montreal. Edited by Deane R. White. [Washington] Society of Photographic Scientists and Engineers [1973] iv, 204 p. illus. 30 cm. "Reprinted papers from Photographic science and engineering, volume 17, 1973." Includes bibliographical references. [TR280.I57 1972] 73-176455
1. Silver halide crystals—Congresses. 2. Photographic emulsions—Congresses. I. White, Deane Rowland, 1902- ed. II. Society of Photographic Scientists and Engineers. III. Montreal. Universite. IV. Title.

PREPRINTS of papers for the physics and chemistry of the silver halide crystal, 548 an international colloquium at the University of Montreal. [Washington, Society of Photographic Scientists and Engineers, 1972] vi, 326 p. illus. 23 cm. On cover: Physics and chemistry of the silver halide crystal. "Sponsored by the University of Montreal and the Society of

Photographic Scientists and Engineers." Includes bibliographical references. [TR280.P73] 72-170666
1. Silver halide crystals—Congresses. 2. Photographic emulsions—Congresses. I. Montreal. Universite. II. Society of Photographic Scientists and Engineers. III. Title: Physics and chemistry of the silver halide crystal.

Silver-plated ware—England—Catalogs.

CAMBRIDGE. 739.2'3'74207402659 University. Selwyn College.
Catalogue of the silver plate of Selwyn College, Cambridge / ... written ... by P. C. Gray. [Cambridge] : [Selwyn College], [1976] [2], 36 leaves ; 30 cm. Cover title. [NK7240.C35 1976] 77-362492 ISBN 0-9505033-0-4
1. Cambridge. University. Selwyn College. 2. Silver-plated ware—England—Catalogs. I. Gray, Percy Charles. II. Title.

Silver-plated ware—United States.

FREEMAN, Graydon La 739.2'3'773 Verne, 1904-
Early American plated silver, by Larry Freeman. Watkins Glen, N.Y., Century House [1973] 160 p. illus. 22 cm. [NK7240.F7 1973] 72-97475 5.95
1. Silver-plated ware—United States. I. Title. BIP

Silver-plated ware, Victorian—Catalogs.

VICTORIAN 739.2'3'77467 *silverplated holloware;* tea services, caster sets, ice water pitchers, card receivers, napkin rings, knife rests, toilet sets, goblets, cups, trays and waiters, epergnes, butter dishes, pickle casters, salts, tureens, communion services. Compiled by the editors of the Pyne Press. [1st ed.] Princeton [N.J.] Pyne Press [1972] 156 p. illus. 28 cm. (American historical catalog collection) Contains reproductions of the important plates from catalogs of Rogers Brothers Mfg. Co., 1857; Meriden Britannia Co., 1867; and Derby Silver Co., 1883. [NK7240.V52] 72-76873 ISBN 0-87861-019-7 4.95
1. Silver-plated ware, Victorian—Catalogs. 2. Silver-plated ware, Victorian—United States. I. Pyne Press. II. Rogers Brothers Manufacturing Company. III. Meriden Britannia Company. IV. Derby Silver Company. V. Title. VI. Series.

Silver-plated ware, Victorian—United States.

SNELL, Doris Jean. 739.2'3'773
Victorian silverplated flatware / by Doris Jean Snell. 1st ed. Des Moines : Wallace-Homestead Book Co., [1975] [7] p., [26] leaves of plates : chiefly ill. ; 23 cm. [NK7240.S63] 75-1572 ISBN 0-87069-114-7
1. Silver-plated ware, Victorian—United States. 2. Silverware, American—Catalogs. I. Title.

Silversmithing.

BOVIN, Murray. 730
Silversmithing and art metal, for schools, tradesmen, craftsmen. Forest Hills, N. Y. [c1963] 151 p. illus. 27 cm. [NK7104.B6] 64-2766
1. Silversmithing. 2. Art metal-work. I. Title. BIP

BUHLER, Kathryn C 739.23
Mount Vernon silver. Mount Vernon, Va., Mount Vernon Ladies' Association of the Union, 1957. 75p. illus., coat of arms, facsims. 22cm. [NK7103.B8] 57-4506
1. Silversmithing. 2. Art objects—Private collections. 3. Mount Vernon. I. Title.

GOODDEN, Robert. 739.2'3
Silversmithing [by] Robert Goodden, Philip Popham. London, New York, Oxford University Press, 1971. 128 p. illus. 21 cm. (Oxford paperbacks, handbooks for artists, 12) Bibliography: p. 123. [NK7104.G66 1971] 72-175094 ISBN 0-19-289915-5 £1.50
1. Silversmithing. I. Popham, Philip, joint author. BIP

SMITH, Keith, 1929- 739.27
Practical silver-smithing and jewelry / Keith Smith. New York : Van Nostrand Reinhold, [1975] p. cm. Includes index. Bibliography: p. [TS730.S46 1975] 75-9988 ISBN 0-442-27791-1 : 12.95
1. Silversmithing. 2. Jewelry making. I. Title. II. Title: Silver-smithing and jewelry. BIP

ZIEK, Nona. 739.27
Making silver jewelry. Illus. by Marjorie Sablow. Photography by Marga Kassimir. New York, Lancer Books [1973] 237 p. illus. 20 cm. (A Lancer Larchmont book) Bibliography: p. 237. [TS741.Z52] 73-157926 1.95
1. Silversmithing. 2. Jewelry making—Amateurs' manuals. I. Title.

ZIEK, Nona. 737-27
Making silver jewelry / Nona Ziek ; illustrations by Marjorie Sablow ; photography by Marga Kassir. New York : Berkley Pub. Corp., 1977c1973. 237p. : ill. ; 20 cm. (A Berkley Windhover Book) Bibliography: p. 236-237. [TS741.Z52] ISBN 0-425-03486-0 pbk. : 2.95
1. Silversmithing. 2. Jewelry making-amateur's manuals. I. Title.
L.C. cad no. for 1973 Lancer Books ed.: 73-157926. BIP

Silversmithing, American.

AVERY, Clara Louise, 739.2'3'773 1891-
Early American silver, by C. Louise Avery. New York, Russell & Russell [1968, c1930] xliv, 384 p. illus., facsim. 22 cm. "A revised edition is not here proposed ... [but] a supplement to the original bibliography has been added." Bibliography: p. 361-370. [NK7112.A8 1968] 68-15093
1. Silversmithing, American. I. Title.

DEGRAZIA, Ted Ettore, 739.2'092'4 1909-
De Grazia Moods in gold, silver, precious gems, and cookies. Artist proof ed. Tucson, Ariz. : De Grazia Gallery in the Sun, [1974] 47 p. : ill. (some col.) ; 32 cm. [NK7198.D43A44] 74-190646
1. DeGrazia, Ted Ettore, 1909- 2. Silversmithing, American. I. Title: Moods in gold, silver, precious gems, and cookies.

KAUFFMAN, Henry J., 739.2'3'773 1908-
The colonial silversmith; his techniques & his products [by] Henry J. Kauffman. Drawings by Dorothy Briggs. [Camden, N.J.] T. Nelson [1969] 176 p. illus. (part col.) 27 cm. Bibliography: p. 173. [NK7103.K35] 71-101526 12.50
1. Silversmithing, American. 2. Silversmiths—United States. 3. Silverwork—United States. I. Title.

KAUFFMAN, Henry J., 739.2'3'773 1908-
The colonial silversmith : his techniques & his products / Henry J. Kauffman ; drawings by Dorothy Briggs. New York : Galahad Books, [1974] c1969. 176 p. : ill. ; 27 cm. Includes index. Bibliography: p. 173. [NK7112.K38 1974] 73-90836 ISBN 0-88365-136-X : 12.50
1. Silversmithing, American. 2. Silversmiths—United States. 3. Silver articles, American. I. Title.

Silversmithing, Byzantine.

DODD, Erica Cruikshank. 739.2388
Byzantine silver stamps. With an excursus on the comes sacrarum largitionum by J. P. C. Kent. Washington, Dumbarton Oaks Research Library and Collection, trustees for Harvard University; [distributed by J. J. Augustin, Locust Valley, N.Y., 1961. xix, 283 p. 103 plates, map, tables. 30 cm. (Dumbarton Oaks studies, 7) Part of illustrative matter fold. in pocket. "Originally part of a doctoral thesis submitted to London University in the summer of 1958 under the title "Studies in early Byzantine silver."" Bibliography: p. 279-280. Bibliographical footnotes. [NK7210.D6] 61-16953
1. Silversmithing. Bysantine. 2. Hall-marks. I. Title. II. Title: Supplement I. New stamps from the reigns of Justin II and Constans II. III. Series. BIP

Silversmithing, Colonial—North America—Congresses.

WINTERTHUR Conference 739.2'3'773 on Museum Operation and Connoisseurship, 14th, 1968.
Spanish, French, and English traditions in the colonial silver of North America. Winterthur, Del., Henry Francis du Pont Winterthur Museum [1969] 109 p. illus. 28 cm. (Winterthur Conference report, 1968) At head of title: Major addresses and exhibition catalogue. [NK7111.W55 1968a] 71-14542
1. Silversmithing, Colonial—North America—Congresses. 2. Silversmithing, Colonial—Foreign influences—Congresses. I. Henry Francis du Pont Winterthur Museum. II. Title. III. Series: Winterthur Conference on Museum Operations and Connoisseurship. Report, 1968

Silversmithing—Denmark.

HIORT, Esbjorn. 739.23
Modern Danish silver. Modern dansk solv. New York, Museum Books, 1954. 121p. illus. 31cm. English, French, German, and Danish. [NK7158.H5] 55-1951
1. Silversmithing—Denmark. I. Title.

Silversmithing— Exhibitions.

BROOKLYN Institute of Arts 739.2 and Sciences. Museum.
Elias Pelletreau, Long Island silversmith, and his sources of design. [Exhibition. Brooklyn, 1959] unpaged. illus. 23cm. [NK7198.P38B7] 59-31924
1. Pelletreau, Elias, 1726-1810. 2. Silversmithing— Exhibitions. I. Title.

MINNEAPOLIS. Institute 739.230838 of Arts.
French, English, and American silver; a loan exhibition in honor of Russell Russell A. Plimpton, June 9 to July 15, 1956. [Texts by Kathryn C. Buhler. Minneapolis, 1956] 80p. 51 illus. 26cm. 'Catalogue': p. 60-79. [NK7101.M5Mz5] 56-3809
1. Silversmithing—Exhibitions. I. Buhler, Kathryn C. II. Title.

NORTON (R.W.) Art 739.2'3 Gallery.
American silver and pressed glass: a collection in the R. W. Norton Art Gallery. [1st ed.] Shreveport, La., 1967] 68 p. illus. 28 cm. On cover: A special Holiday in Dixie exhibition of American silver and pressed glass, April 21 30, 1967. Bibliography: p. 67. [NK7103.N6] 67-24712
1. Silversmithing — Exhibitions. 2. Silversmithing — U.S. 3. Hallmarks. 4. Pressed glass. 5. Glassware, American — Exhibitions. I. Title. BIP

NORTON (R.W.) Art Gallery 739.2'3
American silver and pressed glass; a collection in the R. W. Norton Art Gallery. [1st ed. Shreveport, La., 1967] 68p. illus. 28cm. On cover: A special Holiday in Dixie exhibiton of American silver and pressed glass, April 21-30, 1967. Bibl. [NK7103.N6] 67-4477 1.60 pap.,
1. Silversmithing — Exhibitions. 2. Silversmithing — U. S. 3. Hallmarks. 4. Pressed glass. 5. Glassware, American — Exhibitions. I. Title.
700 Block of Cresswell Ave., Shreveport, La., 71106.

PORTLAND, Or. Art 739.2383 Museum.
The Lipton collection; antique English silver designed for the serving of tea. Catalog of exhibition, February 5 to March 7, 1954, Portland Art Museum, Portland, Oregon. [Portland, 1954] 106p. illus. 18x19cm. [NK7101.P65P6] 55-18276
1. Sliveramithing—Exhibitions. 2. Stiversmithing—Gt. Brit. 3. Tea. I. Lipton (Thomas J.) inc. II. Title.

Silversmithing—France.

DAVIS, Frank, 1892- 739.2'3'744
French silver, 1450-1825. New York, Praeger [1970] 104 p. illus., plates, ports. 25 cm. (Collectors handbook) "Books that matter." Bibliography: p. 99-100. [NK7149.D33 1970] 70-108244 12.50
1. Silversmithing—France. 2. Silver articles, French. I. Title.

Silversmithing—Gt. Brit.

BANISTER, Judith 739.23742
English silver. [1st Amer. ed.] New York, Hawthorn [1966, c.1965] 251p. illus. 20cm. Bibl. [NK7143.B34 1966] 66-16161 4.95
1. Silversmithing—Gt. Brit. I. Title.

DENNIS, Jessie McNab. 739.2
English silver. New York, Walker [1970] 83, [1] p. illus. (part col.) 23 cm. (Collector's blue books) Bibliography: p. [84] [NK7143.D43] 74-87071 4.50
1. Silversmithing—Gt. Brit. 2. Goldsmithing—Gt. Brit. I. Title.

HOBLITZELLE, Karl, 1879- 739.23
The Esther Thomas Hoblitzelle collection of English silver, by Mary L. Kennedy. Photos. by Gillis King. Designed by Warren Hunter. Austin, Tex., 1957. xix, 196p. illus. (part mounted col.) mounted col. port. 33cm. 'An address by Dr. Harry H. Ransom ... at a dinner given by the University of Texas to honor the publication ... July 30, 1957' (5 p.) inserted. Bibliography: p. 193-194. [NK7143.H6] 58-107
1. Silversmithing—Gt. Brit. I. Hoblitzelle, Esther (Thomas) II. Kennedy, Mary L. III. Title.

HUGHES, George Bernard, 720'.924 1896-
Three centuries of English domestic silver, 1500-1820 [by] Bernard and Therle Hughes. New York, W. Funk, 1952. 248p. illus., plates. 23cm. [NK7143.H] A53
1. Silversmithing—Gt. Brit. I. Hughes, Therle, joint author. II. Title.

HUGHES, George 739.2'3'742 Bernard, 1896-
Three centuries of English domestic silver, 1500-1820 [by] Bernard and Therle Hughes New York, F. A. Praeger [1968] 248 p. illus. 24 cm. [NK7143.H83 1968] 68-21582
1. Silversmithing—Great Britain. 2. Silverware, English. I. Hughes, Therle, joint author. II. Title.

MILES, Elizabeth B 720'.924
The English silver pocket nutmeg grater; a collection of fifty examples from 1693 to 1816, by Elizabeth B. Miles. [Shaker Heights? Ohio, 1966] 81 p. illus. 23 cm. [NK7143.M5] 67-740
1. Silversmithing — Gt. Brit. 2. Nutmeg Graters. I. Title.

PRESTON, Arthur 739.2374229 Edwin.
The Abingdon Corporation plate, some notes on the Abingdon plate and kindred treasures, and on the donors and the occasions of the gifts. Edited by Agnes C. Baker. Oxford, Printed at the University Press by C. Batey, 1958. 84p. illus. 22cm. [NK7143.P7] 59-49101
1. Silversmithing—Gt. Brit. 2. Art objects—Abingdon, Eng. I. Title.

STONE, Jonathan. 739.23742
English silver of the eighteenth century. New York, October House [1965] viii, 72 p. illus. (part col.) 21 cm. (Collectors guidebooks) Bibliography: p. 50. [NK7143.S7] 65-23429
1. Silversmithing — Gt. Brit. I. Title. II. Series. BIP

UNTERMYER, Irwin 739.23742
English and other silver in the Irwin Untermyer collection. Text by Yvonne Hackenbroch. New York, Metropolitan Mus. of Art [1964] xxx, 96p. illus., 201 plates, ports. 31cm. (Irwon Untermyer collection, 6) Bibl. 64-1259 25.00
1. Silversmithing—Gt. Brit. 2. Silversmithing—Private collections. I. Hackenbroch, Yvonne. II. Title. III. Series.

WARDLE, Patricia. 739.23742
Victorian silver and silver-plate. Foreword by Hugh Wakefield. New York, T. Nelson [c1963] 238 p. illus. plates 25 cm. (The Victorian collector series) Bibliography: p. 227-228. [NK7143.W27] 63-20988

N.Y., Author, 790 Lebrun Rd. [c.1964] 228p. illus. 24cm. Bibl. [NK7112.D3] 65-1645 35.00, lim. ed.
1. Silversmiths, American—New York (State) 2. Hallmarks. I. Title.

Silversmiths, American—Rhode Island—Directories.

FREDYMA, Paul J. 739.2'3'7745
A directory of Rhode Island silversmiths and their marks [by] Paul J. and Marie-Louise Fredyma. [Hanover, N.H., c1972] v, 21 p. 23 cm. Five hundred copies printed. Bibliography: p. 20-21. [NK7110.F69] 72-86690
1. Silversmiths, American—Rhode Island—Directories. 2. Hall-marks. I. Fredyma, Marie-Louise, joint author. II. Title.

Silversmiths, American—South Carolina.

BURTON, E. Milby. 739.2'3'7757
South Carolina silversmiths, 1690-1860, by E. Miloy Burton Rutland, Vt., C. Tuttle Co. [1968] xvii, 311 p. illus., facsims., ports. 24 cm. (Contributions from the Charleston Museum, 10) Reprint of 1942 ed. Bibliography: p. [291]-302. [NK7112.B8 1968] 68-25892
1. Silversmiths, American—South Carolina. I. Title. II. Series: Charleston Museum, Charleston, S.C. Contributions from the Charleston Museum, 10

Silversmiths—Boston—Directories.

FREDYMA, Paul J. 739.2'3'722
A directory of Boston silversmiths and watch and clock makers / Paul J. and Marie-Louise Fredyma. Hanover, N.H. : Fredyma, 1975. iv, 46 p. ; 23 cm. Includes bibliographical references. [NK7112.F66] 75-3654
1. Silversmiths—Boston—Directories. 2. Clock and watch makers—Boston—Directories. I. Fredyma, Marie-Louise, joint author. II. Title. III. Title: Boston silversmiths.

Silversmiths. Canadian.

LANGDON, John Emerson. 739.23771
Canadian silversmiths; their marks, 1667-1867. Lunenburg, Vt., Priv. print., Stinehour Press [1960] 190p. illus., facsim. 24cm. 'Limited to 500 copies.' Bibliography: p. 175-179. [NK7113.L3] 60-2484
1. Silversmiths. Canadian. 2. Hall-marks. I. Title.

Silversmiths—Connecticut—Directories.

FREDYMA, John J. 739.2'3'7746
A directory of Connecticut silversmiths and watch and clock makers [by] John J. Fredyma. [Hanover, N.H., P. J. Fredyma and M-L. Fredyma, 1973] iv, 60 p. 23 cm. Five hundred copies printed. Bibliography: p. 59-60. [NK7110.F68] 73-92353
1. Silversmiths—Connecticut—Directories. 2. Clock and watch makers—Connecticut—Directories. I. Title. II. Title: Connecticut silversmiths and watch and clock makers.

Silversmiths—Great Britain.

VICTORIA and Albert 739.23742
Museum, South Kensington
English Silversmiths' work. civil and domestic: an introduction-by Charles Oman London, H.M.S.O. New York British Info., 1966. c.1965 [5]. 16p. front., 192 plates (incl. facsim.) 26cm. [NK 7143.V492] 66-2654 8.40
1. Oman, Charles Chichele, 1901- 2. Silversmiths'—Gt. Brit. I. Oman, Charles Chichele, 1901- II. Title.

Silversmiths—Lancaster, Pa.

GERSTELL, Vivian S. 739.2'3'722
Silversmiths of Lancaster, Pennsylvania, 1730-1850 [by] Vivian S. Gerstell. [Lancaster] Lancaster County Historical Society, 1972. ix, 145 p. illus. 24 cm. Bibliography: p. 143-145. [NK7111.G47] 72-86855
1. Silversmiths—Lancaster, Pa. 2. Silversmithing—Pennsylvania—Lancaster. I. Title. BIP

Silversmiths—Maine—Directories.

FREDYMA, 338.4'7'73923025741
James P.
A directory of Maine silversmiths and watch and clock makers [by] James P. Fredyma. [Hanover, N.H., c1972] v, 26 p. 23 cm. Five hundred copies printed. Includes bibliographical references. [TS730.F7] 72-94414 4.25
1. Silversmiths—Maine—Directories. 2. Clock and watch makers—Maine—Directories. I. Title.

Silversmiths—Maryland.

PLEASANTS, Jacob 739.2'3'7752
Hall, 1873-1957.
Maryland silversmiths, 1715-1830, with illustrations of their silver and their marks and with a facsimile of the design book of William Faris, by J. Hall Pleasants and Howard Sill. And including a publisher's foreword by Robert Alan Green. Harrison, N.Y., R. A. Green, 1972 [c1930] xiv, 324 p. illus. 29 cm. [NK7112.P6 1972] 72-195417 ISBN 0-9600266-2-2
1. Silversmiths—Maryland. I. Sill, Howard, 1868?-1927. II. Faris, William, 1728-1804. III. Title. BIP

Silversmiths—Massachusetts—Boston—Biography.

LEIGHTON, 739.2'3'724 B
Margaretha Gebelein.
George Christian Gebelein, Boston silversmith, 1878-1945 : a biographical sketch / by Margaretha Gebelein Leighton, in collaboration with Esther Gebelein Swain and J. Herbert Gebelein. Boston : [Gebelein], 1976. xix, 118 p., [4] leaves of plates : ill. ; 25 cm. Includes bibliographical references. [NK7198.G35L44] 76-52871
1. Gebelein, George Christian, 1878-1945. 2. Silversmiths—Massachusetts—Boston—Biography. 3. Silverwork—Massachusetts—Boston. I. Swain, Esther Gebelein, joint author. II. Gebelein, J. Herbert, joint author. III. Title.

Silversmiths—Mobile, Ala.

SMITH, Sidney 739.2'3'776122
Adair.
Mobile silversmiths and jewelers, 1820-1867. [Mobile, Ala.] Historic Mobile Preservation Society [1970] [15] p. illus., port. 23 cm. Bibliography: p. [13] [NK7112.S48] 79-23462
1. Silversmiths—Mobile, Ala. 2. Jewelers—Mobile, Ala. I. Title.

Silversmiths—New Hampshire—Directories.

FREDYMA, Paul J. 739.2'3'025742
A directory of New Hampshire silversmiths and their marks [by] Paul J. and Marie-Louise Fredyma. [Orford, N.H., Equity Pub. Corp., c1971] 17 p. 24 cm. "Limited to 500 copies." Bibliography: p. 15-17. [NK7112.F68] 75-183142
1. Silversmiths—New Hampshire—Directories. 2. Hall-marks. I. Fredyma, Marie-Louise, joint author. II. Title.

FREDYMA, Paul J. 739.2'3'025742
A directory of New Hampshire silversmiths and watch and clock makers / Paul J. and Marie-Louise Fredyma. Hanover, N.H. : Fredyma, 1977. iv, 48 p. ; 23 cm. "Edition limited to 500 copies." Includes bibliographical references. [NK7112.F683] 77-2117
1. Silversmiths—New Hampshire—Directories. 2. Clock and watch makers—New Hampshire—Directories. I. Fredyma, Marie-Louise, joint author. II. Title.

Silversmiths—North Carolina.

CUTTEN, George 739.2'3'722 B
Barton, 1874-1962.
Silversmiths of North Carolina, 1696-1850. Rev. by Mary Reynolds Peacock. Raleigh, North Carolina Dept. of Cultural Resources, Division of Archives and History, 1973. xxvi, 140 p. illus. 24 cm. Includes bibliographical references. [NK7112.C84 1973] 74-154315
1. Silversmiths—North Carolina. I. Peacock, Mary Reynolds. II. Title.

Silversmiths—Philadelphia.

FALES, Martha 338.4'7'73923722 B
Gandy.
Joseph Richardson and family, Philadelphia silversmiths. [1st ed.] Middletown, Conn., Published for the Historical Society of Pennsylvania by Wesleyan University Press [1974] xviii, 340 p. illus. 28 cm. Bibliography: p. [312]-320. [TS730.F34] 74-5911 ISBN 0-8195-4076-5 17.50
1. Richardson family. 2. Silversmiths—Philadelphia. I. Pennsylvania. Historical Society. II. Title.

Silversmiths—United States.

CURRIER, Ernest M., 739.2'0278
1867-1936.
Marks of early American silversmiths, with notes on silver, spoon types & list of New York City silversmiths 1815-1841, by Ernest M. Currier; illustrated with many of his original drawings. Edited with introductory note by Kathryn C. Buhler and including a publisher's foreword by Robert Alan Green. Harrison, N.Y., R. A. Green, 1970. ix, 179 p. illus., facsims., port. 29 cm. Reprint of the 1938 ed. Bibliography: p. 177-179. [NK7112.C78 1970] 74-111387
1. Silversmiths—United States. 2. Hall-marks. I. Buhler, Kathryn C., ed. II. Title.

GREEN, Robert Alan. 739.2'3'0278
Marks of American silversmiths / by Robert Alan Green. 1st ed. Harrison, N.Y. : Green, c1977. x, 245 p. : ill. ; 23 cm. Includes index. [NK7112.G73] 76-57343 ISBN 0-9600266-5-7 : 25.00
1. Silversmiths—United States. 2. Hall-marks. I. Title. BIP

RAINWATER, Dorothy T. 708.152'6
American silver manufacturers [by] Dorothy T. Rainwater. Hanover, Pa., Everybodys Press [1966] xi, 223 p. illus. 24 cm. Half title: American silver manufacturers, their marks, trademarks and history. "Family tree of the American silverware industry: 1815-1965" on lining papers. Beginning with the 1975 ed. published under title: Encyclopedia of American silver manufacturers. Bibliography: p. 215-223. [NK7112.R3] 66-23531
1. Silversmiths—United States. 2. Hall-marks. I. Title.

RAINWATER, Dorothy T. 739.2'3'773
Encyclopedia of American silver manufacturers / Dorothy T. Rainwater. New York : Crown Publishers, c1975. 222 p. : ill. ; 24 cm. Edition for 1966 published under title: American silver manufacturers. Bibliography: p. 217-222. [NK7112.R3 1975] 75-18953 ISBN 0-517-52145-8 : 7.95
1. Silversmiths—United States. 2. Hall-marks. I. Title. BIP

Silversmiths—Vermont—Directories.

FREDYMA, Paul J. 739.2'3'722
A directory of Vermont silversmiths and watch and clock makers / Paul J. Fredyma, Marie-Louise Fredyma. Hanover, N.H. : Fredyma, 1974. iv, 58 p. ; 23 cm. "Edition limited to 500 copies." Bibliography: p. 57-58. [NK7112.F69] 74-83829
1. Silversmiths—Vermont—Directories. 2. Clock and watch makers—Vermont—Directories. I. Fredyma, Marie-Louise, joint author. II. Title.

Silverware, American.

TURNER, Noel D. 739.2'283
American silver flatware, 1837-1910, by Noel D. Turner. South Brunswick, A. S. Barnes [1972] 473 p. illus. 29 cm. Bibliography: p. 413-422. [NK7112.T8] 68-27217 ISBN 0-498-06580-4 20.00
1. Silverware, American. 2. Hall-marks. I. Title. BIP

Silverware, American—Catalogs.

RAINWATER, Dorothy 739.2'3'773
T., comp.
Sterling silver holloware: tea and coffee service, pitchers and ewers, bookmarks, ash trays, candelabra, salts and peppers, desk sets and dressing sets, berry bowls, napkin rings, cups, tea balls and bells, trays, flasks, match safes. Edited, with an historical introd. by Dorothy T. Rainwater. [1st ed. Princeton, N.J., Pyne Press; Distributed by Scribner, New York, 1973] 1 v. (various pagings) illus. 29 cm. (American historical catalog collection) Reprint of three catalogs: Gorham Manufacturing Company, 1888 and Gorham Martele, 1900, published in New York; Unger Brothers, 1904, published in Newark, N.J. Bibliography: p. 16. [NK7198.G76R34 1973] 72-95726 ISBN 0-87861-040-5 6.95
1. Gorham Manufacturing Company. 2. Unger Brothers. 3. Silverware, American—Catalogs. I. Gorham Manufacturing Company. II. Unger Brothers. III. Title. IV. Series.

Silverware—Collectors and collecting.

BRUNNER, Herbert, 739.2'3'075
1922-
Old table silver; a handbook for collectors and amateurs. Translated by Janet Seligman. [1st American ed.] New York, Taplinger Pub. Co. [1967, c1964] 223 p. illus., facsim. (on lining papers) plates (part col.) 25 cm. Translation of Altes Tafelsilber. Bibliography: p. 160-163. [NK7105.B713 1967] 67-16593
1. Silverware—Collectors and collecting. I. Title. BIP

Silverware—Exhibitions.

NEW York (City). 739.2'3'773
Metropolitan Museum of Art.
Catalogue of an exhibition of silver used in New York, New Jersey, and the South. With a note on early New York silversmiths by R. T. Haines Halsey, New York, November 6 to December 31, 1911. [New York] Arno Press, 1974. xxxvi, 97 p. illus. 23 cm. Cover title: Exhibition of silver used in New York, New Jersey, and the South. Reprint of the 1911 ed. published by the Gillis Press, New York. [NK7112.N4 1974] 72-168421 ISBN 0-405-02259-X 14.00
1. Silverware—Exhibitions. 2. Silversmithing—New York (State) 3. Silversmithing—New Jersey. 4. Silversmithing—Southern States. I. Halsey, Richard Townley Haines, 1865-1942. II. Title. III. Title: Exhibition of silver used in New York, New Jersey, and the South. BIP

Silverwood Lake, Calif.

CALIFORNIA. 711'.558'0979495
Dept. of Water Resources.
Silverwood Lake recreation development plan. [Sacramento] 1970. 14 p. map. 28 cm. (Its Bulletin no. 117-10) [GV54.C2S53] 70-635107 1.00
1. Silverwood Lake, Calif. 2. Outdoor recreation—California—San Bernardino Co. I. Title. II. Series.

Silverwork.

HOLDEN, Geoffrey. 739.23
The craft of the silversmith. London, New York, Studio Publications [1954] 96 p. illus. 26 cm. (The How to do it series, no. 55) [NK7104.H606] 55-14098
1. Silverwork. I. Title. II. Series: How to do it series (London, The Studio) no. 55

STEAKLEY, Douglas, 739.2'3'4
1944-
Holloware techniques / by Douglas

Steakley. New York : Watson-Guptill Publications, 1979. p. cm. Includes index. Bibliography: p. [TS730.S74 1979] 78-27867 ISBN 0-8230-2322-2 : 15.00
1. Silverwork. 2. Metal-work. I. Title.

STEAKLEY, Douglas, 1944- 739.2'3'4
Holloware techniques / by Douglas Steakley. New York : Watson-Guptill Publications, 1979. p. cm. Includes index. Bibliography: p. [TS730.S74 1979] 78-27867 ISBN 0-8230-2322-2 : 15.00
1. Silverwork. 2. Metal-work. I. Title. BIP

Silverwork—Amateurs' manuals.

HUMEZ, Nicholas D. 739.2'3
Silversmithing : a basic manual / Nicholas D. Humez. 1st ed. Boston : Little, Brown, c1976. 178 p. : ill. ; 22 cm. (Little, Brown craft series) Bibliography: p. 174-177. [TS730.H85] 76-1993 ISBN 0-316-38151-9 : 4.95
1. Silverwork—Amateurs' manuals. I. Title. BIP

Silverwork, Classical—Exhibitions.

OLIVER, Andrew, 1936- 739.2'3'738074013
Silver for the gods : 800 years of Greek and Roman silver : The Toledo Museum of Art, Toledo, Ohio, October 9-November 20, 1977, The William Rockhill Nelson Gallery of Art and Atkins Museum of Fine Arts, Kansas City, Missouri, December 11, 1977-January 22, 1978, The Kimbell Art Museum, Fort Worth, Texas, February 18-April 2, 1978. / Catalogue by Andrew Oliver, Jr. ; exhibition organized by Kurt T. Luckner. [Toledo, Ohio] : Toledo Museum of Art, c1977. 175 p. : ill. ; 23 cm. Includes bibliographical references. [NK7107.3.O44] 77-79207
1. Silverwork, Classical—Exhibitions. I. Toledo. Museum of Art. II. William Rockhill Nelson Gallery of Art and Mary Atkins Museum of Fine Arts, Kansas City, Mo. III. Kimbell Art Museum. IV. Title.

Silverwork—Collectors and collecting.

SILVER / 739.2'3'075
compiled and edited by Tony Curtis. Galashiels : Lyle Publications, 1976. 126 p. : chiefly ill. ; 16 cm. (Antiques and their values) Includes index. [NK7105.S55] 76-382250 ISBN 0-902921-52-5 : £1.50
1. Silverwork—Collectors and collecting. 2. Silverwork—Prices. I. Curtis, Tony.

Silverwork, Colonial—New Mexico.

BOYLAN, Leona Davis. 739.2'3'78
Spanish colonial silver / Leona Davis Boylan. Santa Fe : Museum of New Mexico Press, c1974. vii, 202 p. : ill. ; 27 cm. Includes index. Bibliography: p. 159-162. [NK7112.B63] 74-82799 ISBN 0-89013-065-5 : 12.00. ISBN 0-89013-066-3 pbk.
1. Silverwork, Colonial—New Mexico. 2. Silverwork—New Mexico. 3. Silverwork—Spain. 4. Hall-marks. I. Title. BIP

Silverwork—Connecticut.

BOHAN, Peter J. 739.2'3
Early Connecticut silver, 1700-1840, by Peter Bohan and Philip Hammerslough. [1st ed.] Middletown, Conn., Wesleyan University Press [1970] xi, 288 p. illus., facsims., ports. 29 cm. Bibliography: p. 279-283. [NK7110.B6] 76-82543 ISBN 0-8195-4008-0 25.00
1. Silverwork—Connecticut. 2. Silversmiths—Connecticut. 3. Hall-marks. I. Hammerslough, Philip H., joint author. II. Title. BIP

Silverwork—Delaware.

DELAWARE Historical Society. 739.2'3'724
Bancroft Woodcock, silversmith : March 9, 1976 through April 15, 1976, the Historical Society of Delaware. Wilmington : The Society, c1976. [40] p. : ill. ; 21 cm. [NK7198.W66D44 1976] 76-367795 5.00
1. Woodcock, Bancroft, 1732-1817? 2. Silverwork—Delaware. I. Woodcock, Bancroft, 1732-1817? II. Title.

Silverwork—England.

CHADWICK, Oliver. 739.2'3'742
English silver / by Oliver Chadwick. London : Merlin Press, [1976] 75 p., 16 p. of plates : ill. ; 21 cm. [NK7143.C45] 76-377772 ISBN 0-85036-136-2 : £2.40
1. Silverwork—England. I. Title.

Silverwork—Exhibitions.

LOS Angeles Co., Calif. Museum of Art, Los Angeles. 739.2'3'074019494
Monumental silver : selections from the Gilbert Collection : [catalog] : Los Angeles County Museum, 28 April-10 July 1977 / William Ezelle Jones. Los Angeles : Los Angeles County Museum of Art, c1977. 118 p. : ill. (some col.) ; 26 cm. Bibliography: p. 117-118. [NK7101.L75L674] 76-57976 ISBN 0-87587-077-5 pbk. : 5.50
1. Gilbert, Arthur, 1913- —Art collections. 2. Silverwork—Exhibitions. 3. Hall-marks. I. Jones, William Ezelle. II. Title. BIP

Silverwork—Great Britain—History.

BANISTER, Judith. 739.2'3'742
English silver. London, New York [etc.] Hamlyn, 1969. 157 p. 71 col. illus. 20 cm. (Cameo) Originally published as 'Gli argenti inglesi'. Milano, Fabbri, 1966. [NK7143.B3433] 73-437753 ISBN 0-600-01227-1 15/-
1. Silverwork—Great Britain—History. 2. Silverwork—England. I. Title.

TAYLOR, Gerald, 1923- 739.23742
Silver through the ages. New York, Barnes & Noble [1965, c1963] 301 p. illus., plates. 21 cm. (The Belle sauvage library) First published in 1956 under title: Silver. Bibliography: p. 285-297. [NK7143.T3 1965] 65-1198
1. Silverwork—Gt. Brit.—History. I. Title.

Silverwork—History.

CAME, Richard. 739.209
Silver. New York, Putnam [1961] 128 p. illus. (part col.) 22 cm. (Pleasures and treasures) [NK7106.C3] 61-12197
1. Silverwork—History. 2. Goldwork—History.

Silverwork—Ireland.

BENNETT, Douglas. 739.2'3'7415
Irish silver / [by] Douglas Bennett. Norwich : Jarrold and Sons, 1976. [28] p. (2 fold.) : ill. (some col.) ; 25 cm. (The Irish heritage series ; 7) Caption title. [NK7146.B47] 77-366837
1. Silverwork—Ireland. I. Title. II. Series.

Silverwork—Malaysia—Straits Settlements.

HO, Wing Meng. 739.2'3'7595
Straits Chinese silver / Ho Wing Meng. Singapore : University Education Press, c1976. 268 p., [4] leaves of plates : 158 ill. (some col.) ; 22 cm. Includes bibliographical references. [NK7179.A3S743] 76-940777
1. Silverwork—Malaysia—Straits Settlements. 2. Silverwork—China. I. Title.

Silverwork—Maryland—Catalogs.

BALTIMORE. Museum of Art. 739.2'3'775207401526
Eighteenth and nineteenth century Maryland silver in the collection of the Baltimore Museum of Art / text by Jennifer Faulds Goldsborough ; edited by Ann Boyce Harper. Baltimore : The Museum, 1975. ix, 204 p. : ill. ; 26 cm. "A project supported by the Stieff Company, Baltimore." Bibliography: p. 201-204. [NK7112.B26 1975] 75-15344
1. Baltimore. Museum of Art. 2. Silverwork—Maryland—Catalogs. I. Goldsborough, Jennifer F. II. Title: Eighteenth and nineteenth century Maryland silver ... III. Title: Maryland silver. BIP

Silverwork—Mexico.

ANDERSON, Lawrence Leslie, 1894- 739.2'3'772
The art of the silversmith in Mexico, 1519-1936 / by Lawrence Anderson. New York : Hacker Art Books, 1975. 2 v. (460 p., [185] leaves of plates) in 1 : ill. ; 27 cm. Reprint of the 1941 ed. published in 2 v. by Oxford University Press, New York. Includes index. Bibliography: p. [435]-451. [NK7114.A1A7 1975] 73-81683 ISBN 0-87817-139-8 : 75.00
1. Silverwork—Mexico. 2. Silversmiths—Mexico. 3. Hall-marks. I. Title. BIP

Silverwork, Minoan.

DAVIS, Ellen N., 1937- 739.2'0938
The Vapheio cups and Aegean gold and silver ware / Ellen N. Davis. New York : Garland Pub., 1977. xxvii, 390 p., [69] leaves of plates : ill. ; 21 cm. (Outstanding dissertations in the fine arts) A revision of the author's thesis, New York University, 1973. Bibliography: p. 357-383. [NK7107.3.D38 1977] 76-23609 ISBN 0-8240-2681-0 lib.bdg. : 45.00
1. Silverwork, Minoan. 2. Goldwork, Minoan. 3. Silverwork, Mycenean. 4. Goldwork, Mycenean. 5. Drinking vessels—Aegean Sea region. 6. Aegean Sea region—Antiquities. I. Title. II. Series. BIP

Silverwork—Oman.

HAWLEY, Ruth. 739.2'3'09535
Omani silver / by Ruth Hawley. London ; New York : Longman, 1977. p. cm. [NK7173.6.O45H38] 77-20799 ISBN 0-582-78070-5 pbk. : 6.00
1. Silverwork—Oman. I. Title.

Silverwork—Quebec (Province)—Catalogs.

DETROIT. Institute of Arts. 739.2'3'7714074017434
Quebec and related silver at the Detroit Institute of Arts : [catalogue] / by Ross Allan C. Fox. Detroit : Published for Founders Society, Detroit Institute of Arts by Wayne State University Press, 1977. p. cm. Includes bibliographical references and index. [NK7113.A3Q33] 77-4850 ISBN 0-8143-1575-5 : 17.50
1. Detroit. Institute of Arts. 2. Silverwork—Quebec (Province)—Catalogs. 3. Church plate—Quebec (Province)—Catalogs. 4. Silversmiths—Quebec (Province)—Biography. I. Fox, Ross Allan C., 1945- II. Founders Society. III. Title. BIP

Silverwork—Sweden.

ANDREN, Erik, 1904- 739.23
Swedish silver; translated from the Swedish by Lillian Ollen. New York, Barrows [1950] 160 p. 101 illus. 15 cm. (Collectors' little-book library) [NK7161.A612] 50-8711
1. Silverwork—Sweden. I. Title.

Silverwork—U.S.

BUHLER, Kathryn C. 739.23
American silver. Cleveland, World Pub. Co. [1950] 64 p. illus., col. plates, port. 20 cm. (The American arts library, 1586) Bibliography: p. 64. [NK7112.B78] 50-58064
1. Silverwork—U.S. I. Title.

STOW, Millicent. 739.23
American silver. New York, Barrows [1950] 170 p. illus. 15 cm. (Collectors' little-book library) "Books to read": p. 151-153. [NK7112.S8] 50-8735
1. Silverwork—U.S. I. Title.

Silverwork—United States—Exhibitions.

ANGLO-AMERICAN Art Museum. 739.2'3'776226
The Anglo-American Art Museum in cooperation with the Pilgrimage Garden Club of Natchez presents Natchez-made silver of the ninteenth century; [exhibition] January 4-March 5, 1970. Baton Rouge, La. [1970] 48 p. illus. 21 x 26 cm. [NK7111.A7] 77-631737
1. Silverwork—United States—Exhibitions. 2. Silversmiths—Natchez, Miss. I. Pilgrimage Garden Club of Natchez. II. Title: Natchez-made silver of the nineteenth century.

Silverwork—United States—History—19th century.

CARPENTER, Charles Hope, 1916- 739.2'3'77471
Tiffany silver / by Charles H. Carpenter, Jr., with Mary Grace Carpenter. New York : Dodd, Mead, [1978] p. cm. Includes index. Bibliography: p. [NK7198.T5C37] 78-12273 ISBN 0-396-07547-9 : 25.00
1. Tiffany and Company, New York. 2. Silverwork—United States—History—19th century. 3. Silverwork—United States—History—20th century. I. Carpenter, Mary Grace, joint author. II. Title. BIP

Silverwork—United States—History—Catalogs.

LUCKEY, Carl F. 739.2'3'773
Official price guide to silver-silverplate and their makers, 1865-1920 / by Carl F. Luckey. New ed. Florence, Ala. : House of Collectibles, c1978. v, 251 p. : ill. ; 18 cm. Includes index. Bibliography: p. 54-56. [NK7112.L8 1978] 77-94795 ISBN 0-87637-338-4 : 6.95
1. Silverwork—United States—History—Catalogs. 2. Silver-plated ware—United States—History—Catalogs. 3. Silversmiths—United States—Registers. 4. Silverwork—Great Britain—History—Catalogs. 5. Silver-plated ware—Great Britain—History—Catalogs. 6. Silversmiths—Great Britain—Registers. 7. Hall-marks. I. Title.
Publisher's address : 771 Kirkman Rd., Suite 100, Orlando, FL 32811

Simbari, Nicola.

SIMBARI, Nicola. 759.5
Simbari / commentary by Stuart Preston. New York : Simon and Schuster, c1975. 363 p., [2] leaves of plates : 258 ill. (185 col.) ; 34 cm. "Bibliography": p. 363. [ND623.S533P73] 75-4416 ISBN 0-671-22097-7 : 40.00
1. Simbari, Nicola. I. Preston, Stuart.

Simmons, Edward, 1852—

SIMMONS, Edward, 1852- 759.13 B
From seven to seventy : memories of a painter and a Yankee / by Edward Simmons ; with an interruption by Oliver Herford. New York : Garland Pub., 1976, c1922. p. cm. (The Art experience in late nineteenth-century America) Reprint of the ed. published by Harper, New York. [ND237.S55A23 1976] 75-28891 ISBN 0-8240-2248-3 lib.bdg. : 25.00
1. Simmons, Edward, 1852- 2. Painters—United States—Biography. I. Title. II. Series.

Simon, Norton—Art collections.

PARKE-BERNET Galleries, inc., New York. 380.1'45'7 s
Chinese porcelain, Italian majolica, European porcelain, Gothic & Renaissance sculpture, works of art, Italian Renaissance & French furniture, French 18th century decorations, old master paintings, oriental carpets and rugs, Gothic & 18th century tapestries and tapestry suites. Property of the Norton Simon Foundation, formerly in the inventory of Duveen Brothers, New York & old master drawings and paintings from the private Collection of Norton Simon. Public auction Friday and Saturday, May 7 and 8 at 2 p.m. New

York, 1971. 217 p. illus. (part. col.) 28 cm. "Sale number 3204." Errata slip inserted. "Price list 3204, Simon works of art & furniture ..." ([3] p. 22 cm.) in pocket. [Z999.P23 no. 3204] [N5220] 707'.4'01471 72-195333
1. Simon, Norton—Art collections. 2. Art—Exhibitions. I. Norton Simon Foundation.

Simonds, Charles.

CHARLES Simonds : 709'.2'4
[an exhibition at the Albright-Knox Art Gallery, June 11-July 17, 1977]. [Buffalo] : Buffalo Fine Arts Academy, c1977. 16 p. : ill. ; 18 x 28 cm. Cover title. Includes exhibition catalog. Bibliography: p. 16. [N6537.S55C47] 77-81577 ISBN 0-914782-14-2 pbk. : 2.00
1. Simonds, Charles. I. Simonds, Charles. II. Albright-Knox Art Gallery. III. Buffalo Fine Arts Academy.

Sinai. Saint Catharine (Basilian monastery)

FORSYTH, George H. 726'.7'09531
The Monastery of Saint Catherine at Mount Sinai: the church and fortress of Justinian. Plates. By George H. Forsyth and Kurt Weitzmann, with Ihor Sevcenko and Fred Anderegg. Ann Arbor, University of Michigan Press [1973] 20 p., 198 p. of illus. (part col.) 36 cm. [NA6084.S5F67] 68-29257 ISBN 0-472-33000-4 37.50 45.00 (after Dec. 31, 1973)
1. Sinai. Saint Catharine (Basilian monastery) I. Weitzmann, Kurt, 1904- II. Title. III. Title: The church and fortress of Justinian. BIP

WEITZMANN, Kurt, 1904- 755'.2
The Monastery of Saint Catherine at Mount Sinai, the icons / photos. by John Galey. Princeton, N.J. : Princeton University Press, [1975- p. cm. Includes index. Contents.Contents.—1. Weitzmann, K. From the sixth to the tenth century. [N8189.E32S558] 75-3482 ISBN 0-691-03543-1 : 75.00
1. Sinai. Saint Catharine (Basilian monastery) 2. Icons, Byzantine—Sinai—Catalogs. 3. Icons—Sinai—Catalogs. I. Galey, John. II. Title.

Sinan, Koca, mimar, 1490-1588.

STRATTON, Arthur. 720'.924
Sinan. New York, Scribner [1971, c1972] 299 p. illus. 24 cm. Bibliography: p. [283]-285. [NA1373.S5S8] 70-162777 ISBN 0-684-12582-X 12.95
1. Sinan, Koca, mimar, 1490-1588.

Sinclaire, Henry Purdon.

FARRAR, Estelle 748.2'913
Sinclaire.
H. P. Sinclaire, Jr., glassmaker. Garden City, N.Y., Farrar Books, 1974-75. 2 v. illus. 26 cm. Contents.—v. 1. The years before 1920.—v. 2. The manufacturing years. Includes bibliographies. [NK5198.S45F37] 74-168304
1. Sinclaire, Henry Purdon. 2. Glassware, American. I. Title.

Singer, Paul, 1911-

BRADY, Seamus 769.560924
Doctor of millions. [Tralee, Ire.] Anvil Bks. [1965] 176p. 19cm. [HE6207.S5B7] 66-54218 1.25 pap.,
1. Singer, Paul, 1911- I. Title.
Available from Sport Shelf, New Rochelle, N.Y.

Single-lens reflex cameras.

BATES, G. Gordon 771.3
35 mm single lens reflex manual. London, Fountain Pr. [dist. New York, Morgan & & Morgan, c. 1964] 255p. illus. 22cm. 64-6909 7.95
1. Single-lens reflex cameras. I. Title.

JACOBS, Lou. 770'.28
How to take great pictures with your SLR / Lou Jacobs, Jr. Tucson, Az. : H. P. Books, 1974. 223 p. : ill. (some col.) ; 28 cm. (The New photo series ; 3) Caption title. [TR261.J32] 74-82515 ISBN 0-912656-26-3 : 5.95
1. Single-lens reflex cameras. 2. Photography—Handbooks, manuals, etc. I. Title. BIP

JACOBS, Lou. 770'.28
How to take great pictures with your SLR / Lou Jacobs, Jr. Tucson, AZ : H. P. Books, c1978. 224 p. : ill. (some col.) ; 28 cm. (The New photo series ; 3) Includes index. [TR261.J32 1978] 78-105163 ISBN 0-912656-26-3 : 5.95
1. Single-lens reflex cameras. 2. Photography—Handbooks, manuals, etc. I. Title.

KEPPLER, Herbert 770.28
Keppler on the eye level reflex; text and photos. by Herbert Keppler. [New York, Amphoto, 1961,c. 1960] 164p. 25cm. 61-8771 4.95bds.,
1. Single-lens reflex cameras. 2. Photography—Handbooks, manuals, etc. I. Title. II. Title: Eye level reflex..

LONDON, Barbara, 1936- 770'.282
A short course in photography / Barbara London. New York : Van Nostrand Reinhold Co., [1979] p. cm. Includes index. Bibliography: p. [TR261.L66] 78-23910 ISBN 0-442-26611-1 pbk. : 9.00 ISBN 0-442-26615-4 : 14.95
1. Single-lens reflex cameras. 2. Photography—Handbooks, manuals, etc. I. Title. BIP

NEWCOMBE, Henry Sainsbury, 770.2
1901-
Photography with the eye-level reflex [by] H. S. Newcombe. [1st ed.] London, New York, Focal [1964] 247p. illus. (pt. col.) 22cm. [TR261.N45 1964] 68-127244 6.95
1. Single-lens reflex cameras. 2. Photography—Handbooks, manuals, etc. . I. Title.

NEWCOMBE, Henry Sainsbury, 771.3
1901-
Photography with the eye-level reflex [by] H. S. Newcombe. 2nd ed. London, New York, Focal 1966 [i.e. 1967]. 247p. illus. (some col.), tables, diagrs. 22cm. [TR261.N45 1967] 68-94813 6.95
1. Single-lens reflex cameras. 2. Photography—Handbooks, manuals, etc. I. Title. II. Title: The eye-level reflex.
Distributed by Amphoto, New York.

SHIPMAN, Carl. 770'.28
SLR photographers handbook / by Carl Shipman. Tucson, Ariz. : H. P. Books, c1977. 160 p. : ill. (some col.) ; 28 cm. Includes index. [TR261.S54] 77-10176 ISBN 0-912656-72-7 : 9.95 ISBN 0-912656-59-X pbk. : 5.95
1. Single-lens reflex cameras. 2. Photography—Handbooks, manuals, etc. I. Title. BIP

WAHL, Paul Francis, 1922- 771.31
Single lens reflex guide. Philadelphia, Chilton Co., Book Division, e1959. 149 p. illus. 20 cm. (The Modern camera guide series, 56) [TR261.W3] 58-14332
1. Single-lens reflex cameras. I. Title.

WAHL, Paul Francis, 1922- 771.31
Single lens reflex guide. Rev. 2d print. Philadelphia, Chilton Co., Book Division, 1960. 127 p. illus. 20 cm. (Modern camera guide series, 378) [TR261.W3] 60-52192
1. Single-lens reflex cameras. I. Title.

Siqueiros, David Alfaro.

SIQUEIROS, David Alfaro. 759.972
David Alfaro Siqueiros: paintings, 1935-1967; a loan exhibition from the collections of Dr. Alvar Carrillo Gil and Mr. and Mrs. Albert A. Mitchell, February 5-April 5, 1970. New York, Art Gallery, Center for Inter-American Relations [1970] 27 p. illus. (part col.) 21 cm. [ND259.S56C46] 78-23565
1. Siqueiros, David Alfaro. 2. Carrillo Gil, Alvar—Art collections. 3. Mitchell, Albert A.—Art collections. 4. Mitchell, Albert A., Mrs.—Art collections. I. Center for Inter-American Relations. Art Gallery.

Sirak, Howard D.,—Art collections.

THE Sirak 709'.04'074016944
Collection. [Louisville, Ky., J. B. Speed Art Museum, 1968] [71] p. illus. (part col.) 28 cm. A catalogue of an exhibition of paintings and sculpture owned by Dr. and Mrs. Howard D. Sirak of Columbus, Ohio, held at the J.B. Speed Art Museum, Oct. 22-Dec. 1, 1968. Cover title. [N6487.L68S637] 74-153376
1. Sirak, Howard D.,—Art collections. 2. Art, Modern—20th century—Exhibitions. I. Speed Art Museum, Louisville, Ky.

Sisley, alfred, 1839-1899.

COGNIAT, Raymond, 1896- 759.4' B
Sisley / by Raymond Cogniat ; [translated by Jeanine Warnod]. New York : Crown Publishers, c1978. p. cm. Bibliography: p. [ND553.S62C6313] 77-26315 ISBN 0-517-53321-9 : 5.95
1. Sisley, Alfred, 1839-1899. 2. Painters—France—Biography. 3. Impressionism (Art)—France. BIP

DAULTE, Francois 759.2
Sisley: landscapes. [Tr. from French by Diana Imber] New York 20. French & European Pubns., 610 Fifth Ave. [1963] 61p. mounted col. illus. 21cm. (Rhythm & colour, 1) Bibl. 63-3613 3.95
1. Sisley, alfred, 1839-1899. I. Title.

Sitte, Camillo, 1843-1903. Der Stadte-Bau nach seinen kunstlerischen Grundsatzen.

COLLINS, George 711.40924
Roseborough, 1917-
Camillo Sitte and the birth of modern city planning, by George R. Collins and Christiane Crasemann Collins. New York, Random House [1965] x, 232 p. illus., plans, 16 plates, port. 21 cm. (Columbia University studies in art history and archaeology, no. 3) "Companion volume to ... City planning according to artistic principles, by Camillo Sitte." Bibliography: p. 199-221. [NA9030.S63C6 1965] 64-15893
1. Sitte, Camillo, 1843-1903. Der Stadte-Bau nach seinen kunstlerischen Grundsatzen. 2. Cities and towns—Planning. I. Collins, Christiane Crasemann joint author. II. Title. III. Series.

Sitte, Willi.

SITTE, Willi. 741.973
Willi Sitte : Gemalde und Zeichnungen, 1950-1974 : [Ausstellung] Kunstverein in Hamburg, 12. April bis 18. Mai 1975. Hamburg : Kunstverein, [1975?] 108 p. : ill. (some col.) ; 24 cm. Bibliography: p. 101-103. [ND588.S474K86] 75-510364
1. Sitte, Willi. I. Kunstverein in Hamburg.

Skirts.

HEINEMANN, Gisella. 646.4'3
Skirts : sew your own! / Gisella Heinemann ; illustrated by the author. 1st ed. New York : McGraw-Hill, 1978. xi, 116 p. : ill. ; 28 cm. (McGraw-Hill paperbacks) [TT540.H44] 78-1342 ISBN 0-07-027940-3 pbk. : 7.95
1. Skirts. I. Title. BIP

Skyscrapers.

ARREGER, Hans. 720
Highrise building and urban design [by] Hans Aregger and Otto Glaus.[Translated from the German by Maria Kroll] New York, F. A. Praeger [1967] 199 p. illus., plans. 29 cm. [NA6230.A7313] 67-18826
1. Skyscrapers. 2. Architecture—Designs and plans. 3. Cities and towns—Planning. I. Glaus, Otto, joint author. II. Title.

BOSSOM OF MAIDSTONE, Alfred 725.2
Charles Bossom, baron, 1881-
Building to the skies; the romance of the skyscraper [by] Alfred C. Bossom. London, The Studio; New York, Studio Publications, 1934. 152 p. plates. port. 26 cm. [NA6230.B6] 35-8573
1. Skyscrapers. I. Title.

RIEDMAN, Sarah Regal, 725.232
1902-
Let's take a trip to a skyscraper. Illus. by John Teppich. New York, Abelard-Schuman [1955] 126p. illus. 25cm. [NA6230.R5] 55-8541
1. Skyscrapers. 2. Art—Juvenile literature. I. Title.

Skyscrapers—Juvenile literature.

GOLDIN, Augusta R. 690'.5'23
Let's go to build a skyscraper, by Augusta Goldin. Illustrated by William Hart. New York, Putnam [1974] 43 p. illus. (part col.) 21 cm. (Let's go series) Describes each step in the planning and construction of a modern skyscraper. [TH1615.G64 1974] 77-189239 ISBN 0-399-60857-5 2.86 (lib. bdg.)
1. Skyscrapers—Juvenile literature. I. Hart, William, 1944- illus. II. Title. BIP

HARMAN, Carter. 690.5'23
A skyscraper goes up. Illustrated with photos. New York, Random House [1973] 137 p. illus. 26 cm. A step-by-step account of building a fifty-four story office tower from planning to a view of the completed structure. [TH1615.H37] 72-11059 ISBN 0-394-82147-5 4.95
1. Skyscrapers—Juvenile literature. I. Title.
Library edition 5.49; ISBN 0-394-92147-x. BIP

PEET, Creighton, 1899- 725.23
The first book of skyscrapers. New York, Watts [c.1964] 63p. illus., plans. 23cm. (First bks.) 64-17781 2.65
1. Skyscrapers—Juvenile literature. I. Title. BIP

Skyscrapers—United States.

MUJICA, Francisco. 725'.97
History of the skyscraper / by Francisco Mujica. New York : Da Capo Press, 1977. p. cm. (Architecture and decorative art) Reprint of the 1929 ed. published by Archaeology & Architecture Press, Paris, New York. [NA6231.M8 1977] 76-57764 ISBN 0-306-70862-0 lib.bdg. : 75.00
1. Skyscrapers—United States. 2. Architecture—United States. I. Title. BIP

Slate sculpture.

ELISCU, Frank. 731.4'63
Slate and soft stone sculpture. Photos. by David Rosenfeld. [1st ed.] Philadelphia, Chilton Book Co. [1972] 145 p. illus. 27 cm. [NB1210.S55E44] 72-4403 ISBN 0-8019-5643-9
1. Slate sculpture. 2. Sculpture. I. Rosenfeld, David, 1907- illus. II. Title.

Slavic imprints—United States.

LOVEJOY Library. 016.9147'03
Slavic-American imprints: a classified catalog of the collection at Lovejoy Library, Southern Illinois University at Edwardsville. Edited by Stanley B. Kimball. Cataloged by Rudolph Wierer and Milton Moore. [1st ed. Edwardsville, University Graphics and Publications, Southern Illinois University at Edwardsville] 1972. viii, 242 p. 28 cm. (Southern Illinois University Carbondale-Edwardsville. The Libraries. Bibliographic contributions, no. 7) Cover title. [Z2483.L68 1972] 73-620974 4.00
1. Slavic imprints—United States. I. Kimball, Stanley Buchholz, ed. II. Wierer, Rudolf. III. Moore, Milton, 1921- IV. Title. V. Series: Southern Illinois University. University Libraries. Bibliographic contributions, no. 7.

Sleepy Eye, Chief of the Lower Sisseton Sioux, d. 1859—Portraits, caricatures, etc.

MEUGNIOT, Elinor. 745'.09776'31
Old Sleepy Eye. [1st ed. Tulsa, Okla., D. L. Hill, 1973] 46 p. illus. 22 cm. [NK808.M48] 73-173445 4.95
1. Sleepy Eye, Chief of the Lower Sisseton Sioux, d. 1859—Portraits, caricatures, etc. 2. Art objects—Collectors and collecting—United States. I. Title. BIP

SUBJECT INDEX SMITH, DAVID, 1906-1965.

Slides (Photography)

BURDEN, Ernest E., 1934- 720.28
Visual presentation : a practical manual for architects & engineers / Ernest Burden. [New York : Big G Press], c1977. 88 p. : ill. ; 22 x 29 cm. Includes index. Bibliography: p. 84. [TR505.B87] 77-73661 21.95
1. Slides (Photography) 2. Visual education. I. Title. BIP

EASTMAN Kodak Company. 770'.28
Motion Picture and Audiovisual Markets Division.
Planning and producing slide programs. Rochester, N.Y. : Motion Picture and Audiovisual Markets Division, Eastman Kodak Co., c1975. 68 p., [1] fold. leaf of plates : ill. ; 29 cm. (Kodak publication ; no. S-30) Cover title. [TR505.E27 1975] 74-30830 ISBN 0-87985-150-3 pbk. : 3.25
1. Slides (Photography) I. Title. BIP

Slides (Photography)—Copying.

MIKE Q. 770'.283
The manual of slide duplicating / Mike and Pat Q. Garden City, N.Y. : Amphoto, c1978. 160 p., [8] leaves of plates : ill. ; 26 cm. Includes index. [TR505.M54] 78-1878 ISBN 0-8174-2426-1 : 12.95
1. Slides (Photography)—Copying. I. Pat Q, joint author. II. Title. BIP

Slides (Photography)—Exhibitions.

MELCHERT, Jim, 1930- 779'.092'4
Jim Melchert : points of view slide projection pieces : [exhibition, San Francisco Museum of Art, November 14-December 21, 1975]. [San Francisco] : San Francisco Museum of Art, c1975. 48 p. : ill. ; 21 x 28 cm. Includes bibliographical references. [TR505.M44] 75-28744
1. Slides (Photography)—Exhibitions. I. San Francisco. Museum of Art.

Slipware, English.

COOPER, Ronald G. 738.3'7
English slipware dishes, 1650-1850 [by] Ronald G. Cooper. [1st American ed.] New York, Transatlantic Arts, 1968. vi, 144, [160] p. 333 illus. (incl. facsim., maps, plates (part col.)) 26 cm. Bibliography: p. 124. [NK4085.C585 1968b] 68-31967 ISBN 0-85458-070-0
1. Slipware, English. I. Title. BIP

Silversmithing—U. S.

FISHER, Leonard Everett 739.2
The silversmiths. Written, illus. by Leonard Everett Fisher. New York, Watts [c.1964] 46p. illus. 23cm. (His Colonial Amer. craftsmen) 64-17792 2.65
1. Sliversmithing—U.S. I. Title. BIP

Sloan, John, 1871-1951.

BROOKS, Van Wyck, 1886- 759.13
John Sloan; a painter's life. [1st ed.] New York, Dutton, 1955. 246p. illus. 23cm. [ND237.S57B7] 927.5 55-5350
1. Sloan, John, I. Title.

GOODRICH, Lloyd, 1897- 759.13
John Sloan, 1871-1951. [Text by Lloyd Goodrich. Research by Rosalind Irvine] Whitney Museum of American Art, New York, January 10-March 2, 1952. The Corcoran Gallery of Art, Washington, March 15-April 20, 1952. The Toledo Museum of Art, Toledo, May 4-June 8, 1952. [New York, Whitney Museum of American Art, 1952] 87 p. illus. (part col.) 26 cm. "Selected bibliography": p. 78-80. [ND237.S57G] A52
1. Sloan, John, 1871-1951. I. Title.

JOHN Sloan. [759.13]
New York, Published for the Whitney Museum of American Art by the Macmillan Co., 1952. 80 p. illus. 26 cm. Includes bibliography. [ND237.S57G6] 927.5 52-7168
1. Sloan, John, 1871-1951. I. Goodrich, Lloyd, 1897-

MORSE, Peter. 769'.924
John Sloan's prints; a catalogue raisonne of the etchings, lithographs, and posters. By Peter Morse. With a foreword by Jacob Kainen. New Haven, Yale University Press, 1969. x, 406 p. illus., ports. 24 cm. Bibliography: p. 393-394. [NE539.S55M6] 79-84676 50.00
1. Sloan, John, 1871-1951. BIP

ST. John, Bruce. 760'.0924
John Sloan. New York, Praeger [1971] 156 p. illus. (part col.), ports. (part col.) 27 cm. (American art & artists) Bibliography: p. 150-152. [N6537.S57S3] 74-117478 15.00
1. Sloan, John, 1871-1951. I. Title. II. Series.

SCOTT, David W., 1916- 759.13
John Sloan / by David Scott. New York : Watson-Guptill, 1975. 223 p. : ill. (some col.) ; 32 cm. Includes index. Bibliography: p. 215-219. [ND237.S57S36] 75-6694 ISBN 0-8230-4869-1 : 25.00
1. Sloan, John, 1871-1951. I. Sloan, John, 1871-1951.

SLOAN, John, 1871-1951. 759.13
John Sloan, 1871-1951; his life and paintings [by] David W. Scott; his graphics [by] E. John Bullard. Washington, National Gallery of Art, 1971. 215 p. illus. (part col.), ports. 27 cm. Exhibition held at National Gallery of Art, Sept. 18 - Oct. 31, 1971; Georgia Museum of Art, Athens, Nov. 20, 1971 - Jan. 16, 1972; etc. "Books illustrated by John Sloan": p. 210. [ND237.S57U5] 76-158452 ISBN 0-8435-2026-4
I. U.S. National Gallery of Art.

SLOAN, John, 1871-1951. 769'.92'4
John Sloan etchings : exhibition, December 8th, 1974-January 11th, 1975. [Cold Spring Harbor, N.Y. : Harbor Gallery, 1974] 40 p. : chiefly ill. ; 22 cm. [NE2012.S56H37] 75-301751
1. Sloan, John, 1871-1951. I. Harbor Gallery. II. Title.

SLOAN, John, 1871-1951. 769.'924
A selection of etchings by John Sloan. Introductory essay by Peter Morse. Columbia, University of Missouri Press [1967] 62 p. (chiefly illus.) 28 cm. "From the Philadelphia Museum of Art, exhibited in the Gallery of the Department of Art, University of Missouri, Columbia, March 3-24, 1967." [NE2210.S472M6] 67-22228
I. Philadelphia Museum of Art. II. Missouri. University. Dept. of Art. Gallery. III. Title. BIP

SLOAN, John, 1871-1951. 759.13
The Sloan exhibit, a double centennial: paintings by John Sloan, born 1871 ... on exhibit at Lock Haven State College, founded 1870. [Lock Haven, Pa., 1970] 36 p. illus. 26 cm. [ND237.S57A55] 72-633703
I. Pennsylvania. State College, Lock Haven. II. Title.

Sloan, John, 1871-1951—Catalogs.

SLOAN, John, 1871-1951. 769'.92'4
New York etchings (1905-1949) / John Sloan ; edited by Helen Farr Sloan. New York : Dover Publications, c1978. xi p., [33] leaves of plates : chiefly ill. ; 29 cm. [NE2012.S56A4 1978] 77-94929 ISBN 0-486-23651-X : 4.00
1. Sloan, John, 1871-1951—Catalogs. 2. New York (City) in art—Catalogs. I. Sloan, Helen Farr, 1911- II. Title. BIP

Sloane, Eric.

SLOANE, Eric. 741.9'73
Recollections in black and white / by Eric Sloane. New York : Walker, 1974. 64 p. : ill. ; 23 x 29 cm. [NC139.S56A27 1974] 73-90383 ISBN 0-8027-0461-1 : 10.00
1. Sloane, Eric. 2. United States in art. I. Title. BIP

SLOANE, Eric. 741'.092'4 B
Recollections in black and white / by Eric Sloane. Enl., portfolio ed. New York : T. Y. Crowell, c1978. 95 p. : ill. ; 23 x 29 cm. "A Funk and Wagnalls book." [NC139.S56A4 1978] 78-4769 ISBN 0-308-10347-5 : 10.95
1. Sloane, Eric. I. Title.

Smart, John, 1741-1811.

FOSKETT, Daphne 927.5
John Smart: the man and his miniatures. New York, October House, [1965, c.1964] xviii, 100 p. geneal, tables (Fold.), plates (pt. col.) 21 cm. Collectors guidebks.) Bibl. [ND1337.G8S63] 65-11509 7.50 bds.,
1. Smart, John, 1741-1811. I. Title. BIP

Smibert, John, 1688-1751.

FOOTE, Henry Wilder, 1875- 927.5
John Smibert, painter; with a descriptive catalogue of portraits, and notes on the work of Nathaniel Smibert. Cambridge, Harvard University Press, 1950. vii, 292 p. ports. 25 cm. Bibliography: p. [275]-278. [ND237.S59F6] 50-9807
1. Smibert, John, 1688-1751. 2. Smibert, Nathaniel, 1734 or 5-1756. I. Title.

FOOTE, Henry Wilder, 759.13 B
1875-
John Smibert, painter; with a descriptive catalogue of portraits and notes on the work of Nathaniel Smibert. New York, Kennedy Galleries, 1969 [c1950] vii, 292 p. illus., ports. 24 cm. (Library of American art) Bibliography: p. [277]-278. [ND237.S59F6 1969] 78-87537
1. Smibert, John, 1688-1751. 2. Smibert, Nathaniel, 1734 or 5-1756.

SMIBERT, John, 1688-1751. 759.13
The notebook of John Smibert. With essays by Sir David Evans, John Kerslake, and Andrew Oliver, and with Notes relating to Smibert's American portraits by Andrew Oliver. Boston, Massachusetts Historical Society, 1969. vi, 131 p. facsims., maps (on lining papers) 26 cm. Includes actual-size facsims. of the notebook pages with MS notes as well as the blank pages necessary for logical sequence, and a transcription. The notebook is preserved in the Public Record Office, London, in the class of records known as Chancery Masters' Exhibits, Richards. Bibliographical footnotes. [ND237.S59A52] 69-19752
1. Smibert, John, 1688-1751. I. Evans, David Lewis, Sir, 1893- II. Kerslake, John F. III. Oliver, Andrew, 1906- IV. Massachusetts Historical Society. V. Gt. Brit. Public Record Office. VI. Title. BIP

Smith and Wesson firearms.

†JINKS, Roy 338.4'7'683400974426
G., 1936-
History of Smith & Wesson : no thing of importance will come without effort / by Roy G. Jinks. North Hollywood, Calif. : Beinfeld Pub. Co., 1977. xiii, 290 p. : ill. ; 24 cm. Includes bibliographical references and index. [TS533.3.M4J56] 77-78796 ISBN 0-917714-14-8 : 15.95
1. Smith and Wesson, inc., Springfield, Mass. 2. Smith and Wesson firearms. I. Title.

Smith and Wesson, inc., Springfield, Mass.

†JINKS, Roy 338.4'7'683400974426
G., 1936-
History of Smith & Wesson : no thing of importance will come without effort / by Roy G. Jinks. North Hollywood, Calif. : Beinfeld Pub. Co., 1977. xiii, 290 p. : ill. ; 24 cm. Includes bibliographical references and index. [TS533.3.M4J56] 77-78796 ISBN 0-917714-14-8 : 15.95
1. Smith and Wesson, inc., Springfield, Mass. 2. Smith and Wesson firearms. I. Title.

NEAL, Robert J., 1933- 623.443
Smith and Wesson, 1857-1945 [by] Robert J. Neal and Roy G. Jinks. South Brunswick [N.J.] A. S. Barnes [1966] 360 p. illus., facsims., ports. 26 cm. Bibliography: p. 354-355. [TS537.N35 1966] 66-12902
1. Smith and Wesson, inc., Springfield, Mass. 2. Pistols. 3. Revolvers. I. Jinks, Roy G., 1936- joint author. BIP

PARSONS, John E. 623.4434
Smith & Wesson revolvers; the pioneer single action models. New York, Morrow, 1957. 242 p. illus., ports., facsims., tables. 25 cm. "Correspondence with Colonel Schofield": p. 177-214. Bibliographical references included in "Notes" (p. 217-227) Bibliography: p. 231-234. [TS537.P32] 57-8596
1. Smith and Wesson, Inc., Springfield, Mass. 2. Revolvers.

Smith, Clark Ashton, 1893-1961.

RICKARD, Dennis. 730'.92'4
The fantastic art of Clark Ashton Smith, by Dennis Rickard. Introd. by Gahan Wilson. Baltimore, Mirage Press, 1973. 25, [35] p. illus. 28 cm. [N6537.S615R52] 72-85409 ISBN 0-88358-013-6 3.75 (pbk.)
1. Smith, Clark Ashton, 1893-1961. I. Smith, Clark Ashton, 1893-1961. II. Title.

Smith, Cyrus Rowlett, 1899- —Art collections.

TEXAS. University at 759.13
Austin. Art Museum.
Paintings from the C. R. Smith Collection. [Austin, 1970] xii, 40 p. illus. (part col.) 21 x 22 cm. Catalog of an exhibition presented jointly by the University Art Museum and the Humanities Research Center of the University of Texas, Dec. 4, 1969-Jan. 15, 1970. [ND210.T48] 73-171236
1. Smith, Cyrus Rowlett, 1899- —Art collections. 2. The West in art. 3. Paintings, American—Exhibitions. 4. Painting, Modern—19th century—United States. I. Texas. University at Austin. Humanities Research Center. II. Title. BIP

Smith, David, 1906-1965.

ALANDER, Kyosti, ed. 720.924
Viljo Revell: works and projects. Bauten und Projekte. New York, Praeger [1967] 119p. illus., plans. 23x26cm. [NA1199.R4A63] 66-20425 10.00
I. Revell, Viljo, 1910-1964. II. Title.

CONE, Jane Harrison 730.924
David Smith, 1906-1965; a retrospective exhibition [Cambridge? 1966] ix, 107p. illus. 23cm. Catalog of exhibitions held at the Fogg Art Mus., Harvard, Sept. 28-Nov. 15, 1966 and at the Washington Gallery of Modern Art, Jan. 7-Feb. 26, 1967. Bibl. [NB237.S567C6] 66-29123 8.00
1. Smith, David, 1906-1965. I. Harvard University, William Hayes Fogg Art Museum. II. Washington, D. C. Gallery of Modern Art. III. Title.
Available from New York Graphic, Greenwich, Conn.

KRAUSS, Rosalind E. 730'.92'4
The sculpture of David Smith : a catalogue raisonne / Rosalind E. Krauss. New York : Garland Pub., 1977. ix, 158 p., [197] leaves of plates : ill. ; 23 cm. (Garland reference library of the humanities ; v. 73) Bibliography: p. 150-158. [NB237.S567K69] 76-24753 ISBN 0-8240-9924-9 lib.bdg. : 60.00
1. Smith, David, 1906-1965. I. Title. BIP

SMITH, David, 1906-1965. 720'.924
David Smith, by David Smith; text and photos. by the author. Ed. by Cleve Gray. New York, Holt [1972] 176 p. illus. (pt. col.) facsims. port. 28 cm. (Holt pbk., 38) Bibl. [NB237.S567G7] 68-18582 ISBN 0-03-091563-5 pap., 9.95
I. Gray, Cleve, ed. II. Title.

SMITH, David, 1906- 730.973
Voltron. Text by Giovanni Carandente. Voltri photos. by Ugo Mulas. Bolton photos. by David Smith. [Philadelphia] Institute of Contemporary Art, University of Pennsylvania; distributed by H. N. Abrams, New York [1964] 78 p. (chiefly illus., ports.) 37 cm. Bibliography: p. [77] [NB237.S567C3] 64-25938
I. Carandente, Giovani. II. Title.

SMITH, David, 1906-1965 730'.924
David Smith. Text, photos. by the author. Ed. by Cleve Gray. New York, Holt [1968] 176p. illus. (pt. col.) facsims., port. 29cm. Bibl. [NB237.S567G7] 68-18582 22.95
I. Gray, Cleve. ed. II. Title.

SMITH, David, 1906- 730'.92'4
1965.
David Smith. Edited by Garnett McCoy.

New York, Praeger [1973] 231 p. illus. (part col.) 23 cm. (Documentary monographs in modern art) Bibliography: p. 225-228. [NB237.S567M32] 72-88672 13.50
1. Smith, David, 1906-1965. I. McCoy, Garnett, ed.

SMITH, David, 1906-1965. 730'.92'4
David Smith: a memorial exhibition, Los Angeles County Museum of Art, November 3, 1965, to January 30, 1966. [Los Angeles? Printed for the Los Angeles County Museum of Art by Koltun Bros. Lithography, 1965] 50 p. (chiefly illus.) 26 cm. Bibliography: p. 43-46. [NB237.S567L67] 73-159105
I. Los Angeles Co., Calif. Museum of Art, Los Angeles.

SOLOMON R. Guggenheim Museum, New York. 730'.924
David Smith, by Edward F. Fry. [New York, Solomon R. Guggenheim Foundation, 1969] 182 p. illus. (part col.) 29 cm. Catalog prepared for a retrospective loan exhibition held in 1969 at the Solomon R. Guggenheim Museum, New York, the Dallas Museum of Fine Arts, and the Corcoran Gallery, Washington, D. C. "Exhibition 69/2." "A Van Nostrand Reinhold book."—Book jacket. Bibliography: p. 170-182. [NB237.S567S6] 73-77748 12.50
1. Smith, David, 1906-1965. I. Fry, Edward F. II. Dallas. Museum of Fine Arts. III. Corcoran Gallery of Art, Washington, D.C.

Smith, Eugene Randolph, 1876- —Art collections.

SMITH, Grace Howard. 739.27'8
Watch keys as jewelry; collecting experiences of a husband and wife [by] Grace Howard Smith & Eugene Randolph Smith. [1st ed. Syracuse, N.Y.] Syracuse University [1967] 135 p. illus. (part col.) 24 cm. [NK7503.S6] 67-16847 15.00
1. Smith, Eugene Randolph, 1876- —Art collections. 2. Watch keys—Catalogs. I. Title.

Smith, Gordon A., 1919—

SMITH, Gordon A., 1919- 759.11
Gordon Smith : [exhibit held at] the Vancouver Art Gallery, April 16th to May 24th, 1976. [Vancouver, B.C. : Vancouver Art Gallery, 1976] [36] p. : ill. (part col.) ; 28 cm. Bibliography: p. [36] [ND497.S564V36] 76-379631
1. Smith, Gordon A., 1919- 2. Vancouver Art Gallery.

Smith, Hassel, 1915—

SMITH, Hassel, 1915- 759.13
Hassel Smith : paintings, 1954-1975 : [exhibition] / organized by San Francisco Museum of Art, October 3-November 16, 1975. [San Francisco, Calif.] : San Francisco Museum of Art, c1975. [16] p. : col. ill. ; 31 cm. Bibliography: p. [15] [ND237.S598S26] 75-22613
1. Smith, Hassel, 1915- I. San Francisco. Museum of Art.

Smith, Jessie Willcox, 1863-1935.

SCHNESSEL, S. Michael. 741.9'73 B
Jessie Willcox Smith / S. Michael Schnessel. New York : Crowell, [1977] 224 p. : ill. (some col.) ; 29 cm. Includes bibliographical references and index. [NC975.5.S64S36] 77-3530 ISBN 0-690-01493-7 : 22.95
1. Smith, Jessie Willcox, 1863-1935. **BIP**

Smith, John Frederick.

CALLAHAN, Sean. 770
J. Frederick Smith : photographing sensuality / text by Sean Gallahan, with the editors of Alskog, inc. [New York] : Crowell, [1975] p. cm. (Masters of contemporary photography) [TR654.C32] 75-12934 ISBN 0-690-00781-7 : 8.95 ISBN 0-690-00782-5 pbk. : 4.95
1. Smith, John Frederick. 2. Photography, Artistic. I. Title.

Smith, Joseph Edward, 1858-1936.

SMITH, Joseph Edward, 1858-1936. 978.9'62 s
Socorro photographer, Joseph Edward Smith, 1858-1936 / compiled by John DeWitt McKee and Spencer Wilson. Socorro, N.M. : Socorro County Historical Society, 1974, c1975. 54 p. : chiefly ill. ; 28 cm. (Publications in history ; v. 8) [F802.S6S65 vol. 8] 779'.9'91789620924 75-309599 4.95
1. Smith, Joseph Edward, 1858-1936. 2. Socorro Co., N.M.—Description and travel—Views. I. McKee, John DeWitt, 1919- II. Wilson, Spencer. III. Title. IV. Series: Socorro County Historical Society. Publications in history ; v. 8.

Smith, Joseph Lindon, 1863-1950.

SMITH, Corinna Haven (Putnam) 920.7
Interesting people; eighty years with the great and near-great, by Corinna Lindon Smith. [1st ed.] Norman, University of Oklahoma Press [1962] 456 p. illus. 24 cm. [ND237.S6S5] 62-11273
1. Smith, Joseph Lindon, 1863-1950. I. Title. **BIP**

Smith, Leon Polk.

SAN Francisco. Museum of Art. 759.13
Leon Polk Smith; an exhibition. Organized by the San Francisco Museum of Art, San Francisco, California, May 21-June 30, 1968. [San Francisco, 1968] 24 p. illus. (part col.) 24 cm. Introductory essay by L. Alloway. Catalogue of an exhibition of the Poses Institute of Fine Arts, Rose Art Museum, Brandeis University, Waltham, Mass., Apr. 15-May 8, 1968. Includes bibliographies. [ND237.S62S3] 68-26720
1. Smith, Leon Polk. I. Alloway, Lawrence, 1900- II. Brandeis University, Waltham, Mass. Poses Institute of Fine Arts. III. Brandeis University, Waltham, Mass. Rose Art Museum. IV. Title.

SAN Francisco. Museum of Art. 759.13
Leon Polk Smith; an exhibition. Organized by the San Francisco Museum of Art, San Francisco, California, May 21-June 30, 1968. [San Francisco, 1968] 24 p. illus. (part col.) 24 cm. Introductory essay by L. Alloway. Catalogue of an exhibition of the Poses Institute of Fine Arts, Rose Art Museum, Brandeis University, Waltham, Mass., Apr. 15-May 8, 1968. Includes bibliographies. [ND237.S62S3] 68-26720
1. Smith, Leon Polk. I. Alloway, Lawrence, 1900- II. Brandeis University, Waltham, Mass. Poses Institute of Fine Arts. III. Brandeis University, Waltham, Mass. Rose Art Museum.

Smith, Pamela Colman.

PARSONS, Melinda Boyd. 760'.092'4
To all believers : the art of Pamela Colman Smith : [exhibition] Delaware Art Museum, September 11-October 19, 1975, The Art Museum, Princeton University, November 4-December 7, 1975 / by Melinda Boyd Parsons. [Newark : University of Delaware?], c1975. [28] p. : ill. ; 24 x 29 cm. Bibliography: p. [26] [N6537.S617P37] 75-22968
1. Smith, Pamela Colman. 2. Symbolism in art. I. Smith, Pamela Colman. II. Delaware Art Museum. III. Princeton University. Art Museum. IV. Title.

Smith, Russell, 1812-1898.

LEWIS, Virginia Elnora, 1907- 759.13
Russell Smith, romantic realist. [Pittsburgh] University of Pittsburgh Press [1957, c1956] xix, 348p. plates, ports. 24cm. Bibliography: p. 327-333. [ND237.S632L4] [ND237.S632L4] 927.5 56-6427 56-6427
1. Smith, Russell, 1812-1898. I. Title.

LEWIS, Virginia Elnora, 1907- 759.13
Russell Smith, romantic realist. [Pittsburgh] University of Pittsburgh Press [1957, c1956] xix, 348p. plates, ports. 24cm. Bibliography: p.327-333. [ND237.S632L4] 927.5 56-6427
1. Smith, Russell, 1812-1896. I. Title.

Smith, Tony, 1912—

MARYLAND. University. Art Gallery. 759.13
Tony Smith, painting and sculpture; [catalog of the exhibition] University of Maryland Art Gallery, February 8 to March 8, 1974. Foreword by Eleanor Green. [College Park, Md., 1974] 24 p. illus. (part col.) 22 cm. Includes bibliographical references. [ND237.S6323M37 1974] 74-75820
1. Smith, Tony, 1912- I. Smith, Tony, 1912- II. Green, Eleanor, 1929- III. Title.

SMITH, Tony, 1912- 730'.92'4
Tony Smith [by] Lucy R. Lippard. New York, H. N. Abrams [1972] 86 p. illus. 21 x 23 cm. (Modern artists) Bibliography: p. 85-86. [NB237.S569L49] 77-37854 ISBN 0-8109-4415-4 6.75
I. Lippard, Lucy R.

SMITH, Tony, 1912- 730'.92'4
Tony Smith: two exhibitions of sculpture. [Hartford? 1966?] 1 v. (unpaged) illus. 20 x 28 cm. Catalog of an exhibition held Nov. 8 to Dec. 31, 1966, at the Wadsworth Atheneum, Hartford, and an exhibition held Nov. 22, 1966 to Jan. 6, 1967, at the Institute of Contemporary Art, University of Pennsylvania. [NB237.S569A57] 68-840
I. Wadsworth Atheneum, Hartford. II. Pennsylvania. University. Institute of Contemporary Art. III. Title.

SMITH, Tony, 1912- 730'.92'4
Tony Smith: recent sculpture. Foreword by Martin Friedman. Interview by Lucy Lippard. New York, M. Knoedler [1971] 34 p. illus. (part col.) 22 cm. Exhibition held Mar. 23-Apr. 24, 1971, at M. Knoedler & Co., New York. [NB237.S569L5] 72-194164
I. Lippard, Lucy R. II. Knoedler (M.) and Company, inc.

SMITH, Tony, 1912- 730'.92
Tony Smith: two exhibitions of sculpture. [Hartford? 1966?] 1 v. (unpaged) illus. 20 x 28 cm. Catalog of an exhibition held Nov. 8 to Dec. 31, 1966, at the Wadsworth Atheneum, Hartford, and an exhibition held Nov. 22, 1966 to Jan. 6, 1967, at the Institute of Contemporary Art, University of Pennsylvania. [NB237.S569A57] 730'.92'4 68-840
I. Wadsworth Atheneum, Hartford. II. Pennsylvania. University. Institute of Contemporary Art.

Smithson, Robert.

SMITHSON, Robert. 741.9'73
Robert Smithson: drawings. April 19-June 16, 1974. The New York Cultural Center in association with Fairleigh Dickinson University ... New York. [New York, New York Cultural Center, 1974] 95 p. illus. 28 cm. Bibliography: p. 93-95. [NC139.S57N48] 74-79018
1. Smithson, Robert. I. New York Cultural Center. II. Fairleigh Dickinson University.

Smithsonian Institution.

DESAUTELS, Paul E. 736.2'074'0153
Gems in the Smithsonian, [by] Paul E. Desautels. Washington, Smithsonian Institution Press, 1972. 63 p. illus. (chiefly col.) 27 cm. 1965 ed. issued under title: Gems in the Smithsonian Institution. [NK5510.W3D4 1972] 76-39489 ISBN 0-87474-117-3 6.95
1. Smithsonian Institution. 2. Gems. I. Title.

GURNEY, Gene. 069.09753
The Smithsonian Institution, a picture story of its buildings, exhibits, and activites. Pref. by S. Dillon Ripley. New York, Crown [1964] 126 p. illus., plans, ports. 28 cm. [Q11.S8G85] 64-23813
1. Smithsonian Institution.

HELLMAN, Geoffrey Theodore, 1907- 506'.1'753
The Smithsonian : octopus on the Mall / by Geoffrey T. Hellman. Westport, CT : Greenwood Press, 1978, c1967. 224 p. : ill. (on lining papers) ; 23 cm. Reprint of the ed. published by Lippincott, Philadelphia. Includes index. [Q11.S8H4 1978] 77-16190 ISBN 0-313-20019-X lib.bdg. : 17.75
1. Smithsonian Institution. I. Title.

HELLMAN, Geoffrey Theodore, 1907- 506'.1'753
The Smithsonian octopus on the Mall, by Geoffrey T. Hellman. [1st ed.] Philadelphia, Lippincott [1967] 224 p. 22 cm. [Q11.S8H4] 67-20172
1. Smithsonian Institution. I. Title.

NEAL, Harry Edward, 1906- 506.173
Treasures by the millions; the story of the Smithsonian Institution. New York, Messner [1961] 192 p. illus. 22 cm. [Q11.N297] 61-7999
1. Smithsonian Institution. I. Title.

OEHSER, Paul Henry, 1904- 506'.1'73
The Smithsonian Institution [by] Paul H. Oehser. New York, Praeger [1970] xiii, 275 p. illus., ports. 22 cm. (Praeger library of U.S. government departments and agencies, no. 21) Bibliography: p. 264-268. [Q11.S8O39 1970] 74-95682 8.95
1. Smithsonian Institution.

SMITHSONIAN Institution. 595.78
Brief guide to the Smithsonian Institution: National Museum, National Collection of Fine Arts, National Air Museum, Freer Galery, National Zoological Park. Washington [1962?] 74 p. illus. 18 cm. (Its Publ[ication] no. 4507) [Q11.S8A45 1962] 63-60290
I. Title.

SMITHSONIAN Institution. Archives. 016.5061'753
Preliminary guide to the Smithsonian Archives. [Washington] Smithsonian Institution Press, 1971. 72 p. 26 cm. (Archives and special collections of the Smithsonian Institution, no. 1) [Q11.S8A48] 70-170087
I. Title. II. Series: Smithsonian Institution. Archives and special collections, no. 1.

SMITHSONIAN Institution. Office of Education and Training. 507.2'073
Smithsonian research opportunities: fine arts, history, science, 1967-1968. Washington, 1966. vi, 153 p. illus. 23 cm. (Smithsonian publication 4691) [Q11.S8A5] 67-60377
1. Smithsonian Institution. 2. Research—United States I. Title.

SMITHSONIAN Institution. Office of Public Affairs. 069'.09'753
Increase and diffusion : a brief introduction to the Smithsonian Institution. Washington : Office of Public Affairs, Smithsonian Institution, 1975. 86 p. : ill. ; 26 cm. Bibliography: p. 81-82. [Q11.S8A55 1975] 75-602190
1. Smithsonian Institution. I. Title.

SMITHSONIAN Institution. Office of Public Affairs. 069'.09'753
Increase and diffusion; a brief introduction to the Smithsonian Institution, Washington, D.C.; Washington, 1970. 87 p. 26 cm. Bibliography: p. 85-86. [Q11.S8A55] 70-607143
1. Smithsonian Institution. I. Title.

UNITED States. General Accounting Office. 353'.007'232
Improvement needed in financial management activities of the Smithsonian Institution, Washington, D.C.; report to the Congress by the Comptroller General of the United States. [Washington, 1970] 4, 37 p. 27 cm. Cover title. "B-133332." Publication date stamped on t.p. [Q11.S8U55] 70-608093
1. Smithsonian Institution. I. Title.

Smithsonian Institution—History.

OEHSER, Paul Henry, 1904- 506'.1'73
Sons of science; the story of the Smithsonian Institution and its leaders [by] Paul H. Oehser. New York, Greenwood Press, 1968 [c1949] xvii, 220 p. illus., ports. 23 cm. Bibliography: p. 205-208. [Q11.S8O4 1968] 69-10144
1. Smithsonian Institution—History. I. Title. **BIP**

SMITHSONIAN 069'.09753
Institution.
The Smithsonian experience : science, history, the arts ... the treasures of the nation. Washington : The Smithsonian Institution ; New York : distributed to the trade by Norton, 1977. 255 p. : ill. (some col.) ; 28 cm. Includes index. [Q11.S8S8 1977] 77-9213 19.95
1. *Smithsonian Institution—History.* I. Title.

TRUE, Webster Prentiss, 1892- 506
The Smithsonian, America's treasure house. New York, Sheridan House [1950] 306 p. illus., ports. 22 cm. [Q11.S8T68] 50-14651
1. *Smithsonian Institution—History.*

Smithsonian Institution—Juvenile literature.

THOMSON, Peggy. 069'.09753
Museum people / by Peggy Thomson ; ill. by Joseph Low. Englewood Cliffs, N.J. : Prentice-Hall, c1977. p. cm. Includes index. Bibliography: p. Uses interviews with curators, research scientists, technicians, and zookeepers to present life behind the scenes at the Smithsonian Institution. [Q11.S8T47] 77-3175 ISBN 0-13-606889-8 : 8.95
1. *Smithsonian Institution—Juvenile literature.* I. Low, Joseph, 1911- II. Title.
BIP

Smithsonian Institution. National Collection of Fine Arts.

SMITHSONIAN Institution. 708.153
National Collection of Fine Arts.
National Collection of Fine Arts, Smithsonian Institution, Washington, D.C. [Washington, 1967] [19] p. illus. 24 cm. (Smithsonian publication 4698) [N857.A85] 67-61361
1. *Smithsonian Institution. National Collection of Fine Arts.* I. Title.

Smithsonian Institution—Pictorial works.

WIDDER, Robert B. 507.40153
A pictorial treasury of the Smithsonian Institution, by Robert B. Widder [1st ed.] Philadelphia, Chilton [1966] 272p. illus. (pt. col.) 31cm. [Q11.S8W5] 66-23965 20.00
1. *Smithsonian Institution—Pictorial works.* I. Title.

Smocking.

FISHER, Katharine. 746.4'4
The craft of smocking / by Katharine Fisher and Elizabeth Kay. New York : Scribner, [1979] p. cm. Includes index. [TT840.F56] 78-27335 ISBN 0-684-16082-X pbk. : 6.95
1. *Smocking.* I. Kay, Elizabeth, joint author. II. Title.
BIP

THOM, Margaret. 746.4'4
Smocking in embroidery. [New York] Drake Publishers [1972] 96 p. illus. 23 cm. [TT840.T54] 70-180128 ISBN 0-87749-171-2 5.95
1. *Smocking.* I. Title.

Smoky Hill Trail in art.

CURREY, Thomas Lane, 1922- 759.13
The Smoky Hill Trail / paintings, Thomas Lane Currey ; narrative, Betty Radcliffe Jackson. Colby, Kan. : H. F. Davis Memorial Library, Colby Community College, c1976. [40] p. : ill. (some col.) ; 29 x 37 cm. (Western plains heritage publications ; no. 3) [ND1839.C87J33] 77-360307
1. *Currey, Thomas Lane, 1922-* 2. *Smoky Hill Trail in art.* 3. *Smoky Hill Trail, Kan. and Colo.* I. Jackson, Betty Radcliffe. II. Title. III. Series.

Smythson, Robert, 1534 or 5-1614.

GIROUARD, Mark, 1931- 720'.924
Robert Smythson and the architecture of the Elizabethan era. South Brunswick [N.J.] Barnes [1967] 232 p. illus., plans. 26

cm. Bibliographical footnotes. [NA997.S6G5 1967] 67-13084
1. *Smythson, Robert, 1534 or 5-1614.* 2. *Architecture—England.* I. Title.

Snidow, Gordon, 1936—

SNIDOW, Gordon, 1936- 709'.73
Gordon Snidow, chronicler of the contemporary West. Foreword by Sam Gilluly. Introd. by Don Hedgpeth. [1st ed. Flagstaff, Ariz.] Northland Press [1973] x, 68 p. illus. (part col.) 21 x 25 cm. Catalog of an exhibition held at the Montana Historical Society, 6 Apr. thru 22 May, 1973. [N6537.S62M66] 73-78005 ISBN 0-87358-117-2 6.50 (pbk.)
1. *Snidow, Gordon, 1936-* 2. *The West in art.* I. Montana Historical Society. II. Title.

Snodland, Eng.—City planning.

KENT, Eng. 711'.4'09422372
Planning Dept.
Snodland informal district plan / [Kent County Planning Department]. Maidstone : Kent County Council, 1976. [7], 25 p., [2] fold. leaves of plates : ill., col. maps ; 30 cm. [HT169.G72S594] 77-362350 £1.35
1. *Snodland, Eng.—City planning.* 2. *Architecture—England—Snodland— Conservation and restoration.* I. Title.

Snow sculpture.

HASKINS, James, 1941- 736'.94
Snow sculpture and ice carving, by Jim Haskins. New York, Macmillan [1974] 91 p. illus. 29 cm. [NK6030.H37] 72-20992 ISBN 0-02-548880-5
1. *Snow sculpture.* 2. *Ice carving.* I. Title.
BIP

Snuff boxes and bottles.

BLAKEMORE, Kenneth. 745.1
Snuff boxes / Kenneth Blakemore. London : F. Muller, 1976. 176 p., [16] leaves of plates : ill. (some col.) ; 26 cm. Includes index. Bibliography: p. 171. [NK9507.B56 1976] 76-381653 ISBN 0-584-10269-0 : £7.50
1. *Snuff boxes and bottles.* I. Title. BIP

HILL, Henry D., 1899- 739.2284
Antique gold boxes, their lore and their lure, by Henry [Berry-Hill, pseud.] and Sidney Berry-Hill [pseud.] New York, Abelard Press [1953] xiii, 223 p. illus. (part col.) 29 cm. Bibliography: p. 221-223. [NK9507.H45] 53-6806
1. *Snuff boxes and bottles.* I. Hill, Sidney, 1903- joint author. II. Title.

LE CORBEILLER, Clare. 730
European and American snuff boxes, 1730-1830. New York, Viking Press [1966] viii, 120 p. illus., fasims., col. plates, port. 31 cm. (A Studio book) Bibliography: p. 99-105. [NK9507.L4] 66-16384
1. *Snuff boxes and bottles.* I. Title.

PERRY, Lilla S. 704.949
Chinese snuff bottles; the adventures & studies of a collector. Rutland, Vt., C. E. Tuttle Co. [1961, c.1960] 158p. illus. (part col.) 26x27cm. Bibl. 60-12196 silk bdg., bxd., 12.50
1. *Snuff boxes and bottles.* 2. *Art objects, Chinese.* I. Title. BIP

Snuff boxes and bottles, Chinese.

HITT, Henry C. 745.1
Old Chinese snuff bottles; notes, with a catalogue of a modest collection / by Henry C. Hitt. 1st Tuttle ed. Rutland, Vt. : Tuttle, 1978. xii, 121 p. : ill. (some col.) ; 22 cm. Includes index. Bibliography: p. 106-107B. [NK9507.H5 1978] 76-44088 ISBN 0-8048-1220-9 : 10.00
1. *Snuff boxes and bottles, Chinese.* 2. *Snuff boxes and bottles—Collectors and collecting.* I. Title. BIP

Snuff boxes and bottles—Collectors and collecting.

STEVENS, Bob C. 745.1
The collector's book of snuff bottles / by Bob C. Stevens. 1st ed. New York :

Weatherhill, 1976. xvi, 312 p. : col. ill. ; 31 cm. Includes indexes. Bibliography: p. 293-301. [NK9507.S8] 76-884 ISBN 0-8348-0119-1 : 75.00
1. *Snuff boxes and bottles—Collectors and collecting.* I. Title.
BIP

Soane, John, Sir, 1753-1837.

DIXON, Hugh. 720'.92'4
Soane and the Belfast Academical Institute / Hugh Dixon. [Ballycotton, Ire. : Gifford & Craven, c1976] 12 p. : ill. ; 25 cm. (Gatherum ; 8) Cover title. Includes bibliographical references. [NA997.S7D58] 77-351088 £0.45
1. *Soane, John, Sir, 1753-1837.* 2. *Belfast. Royal Belfast Academical Institution.* I. Title.

DU PREY, Pierre de la 720'.92'4 B
Ruffiniere.
John Soane's architectural education, 1753-80 / Pierre de la Ruffiniere du Prey. New York : Garland Pub., 1977, i.e.1978 xxxv, 565, 299 p. : ill. ; 22 cm. (Outstanding dissertations in the fine arts) Originally presented as the author's thesis, Princeton, 1972. Bibliography: p. 557-565. [NA997.S7D86 1977] 76-23615 ISBN 0-8240-2686-1 lib.bdg. : 62.50
1. *Soane, John, Sir, 1753-1837.* 2. *Architects—Education—England.* 3. *Architects—England—Biography.* I. Title. II. Series. BIP

Soap sculpture.

GABA, Lester. 736'.95'028
Soap sculpture. New York, F. Watts [1968, c1969] 63 p. illus. 23 cm. [NB1270.S6G34] 69-11141 2.95
1. *Soap sculpture.*

Social perception—Case studies.

WILLATS, Stephen, 1943- 700'.92'4
Art and social function : three projects / [by] Stephen Willats. London : Latimer New Dimensions, 1976. [4], 51 p., [68] p. of plates : ill., facsims., forms, maps ; 24 cm. [HM291.W49] 77-363790 £6.50
1. *Social perception—Case studies.* 2. *Social interaction—Case studies.* 3. *Art and society—Case studies.* I. Title.

Social realism—United States.

SHAPIRO, David, 1916- 759.13
comp.
Social realism: art as a weapon. Edited and introduced by David Shapiro. New York, Ungar [1973] xii, 340 p. illus. 25 cm. (Critical studies in American art) Bibliography: p. 323-332. [N6512.5.S57S48] 72-80263 ISBN 0-8044-3264-3 12.00
1. *Social realism—United States.* 2. *Art, Modern—20th century—United States.* I. Title. II. Series.

Socialism and art.

BERGER, John. 709'.47
Art and revolution; Ernst Neizvestny and the role of the artist in the U.S.S.R. [1st American ed.] New York, Pantheon Books [1969] 191 p. illus. 21 cm. [NB699.N4B4 1969] 68-26045 1.95
1. *Neizvestnyi, Ernest, 1926-* 2. *Socialism and art.* I. Title.

BERGER, John. 730'.924
Art and revolution: Ernst Neizvestny and the role of the artist in the U.S.S.R. Harmondsworth, Penguin, 1969. 191 p. 89 illus., facsim., 5 ports. 20 cm. (Pelican books, A 1078) Bibliographical footnotes. [NB699.N4B4 1969c] 74-525631 12/-
1. *Neizvestnyi, Ernest, 1926-* 2. *Socialism and art.* I. Title.

EGBERT, Donald Drew, 335.43'8'7
1902
Socialism and American art in the light of European utopianism, Marxism, and anarchism. Princeton, N.J., Princeton University Press, 1967. x, 159 p. illus. 21 cm. (Princeton paperbacks, 103) Bibliographical footnotes. [HX521.E35] 67-30480

1. *Socialism and art.* 2. *Art, American—Hist.* I. Title.

Socialism and the arts.

BAXANDALL, Lee, comp. 701
Radical perspectives in the arts, edited by Lee Baxandall. [Harmondsworth, Eng.] Penguin [1972] 388 p. 18 cm. [HX521.B38] 72-191687 ISBN 0-14-021423-2
1. *Socialism and the arts.* 2. *Art and society.* I. Title. BIP

LEAGUE of Socialist Artists. 700
Essays on art and imperialism ; art and socialism / League of Socialist Artists. London : M. Scott, [1976] 26 p. ; 30 cm. Cover title. "Based on lectures given in the 1972 League of Socialist Artists lecture programme by Maureen Scott and Mike Baker." [HX521.L38 1976] 76-381605 ISBN 0-9501540-6-7 : £0.50
1. *Socialism and the arts.* I. Scott, Maureen. II. Baker, Mike. III. Title.

Socialism and the arts—Addresses, essays, lectures.

EGBERT, Donald Drew, 1902- 700.9
Social radicalism and the arts, Western Europe; a cultural history from the French Revolution to 1968. [1st ed.] New York, Knopf, 1970. xxxiii, 821, liii p. illus. 25 cm. Includes bibliographical references. [HX521.E34] 74-79351 15.00
1. *Socialism and the arts—Addresses, essays, lectures.* 2. *The arts—Europe— Addresses, essays, lectures.* I. Title.

Socialist realism in art—Russia.

THOMSON, Boris. 700'.947
Lot's wife and the Venus of Milo : conflicting attitudes to the cultural heritage in modern Russia / Boris Thomson. Cambridge ; New York : Cambridge University Press, 1978. 171 p. ; 23 cm. Includes index. Bibliography: p. [167]-168. [NX556.A1T48] 77-77703 ISBN 0-521-21677-X : 14.95
1. *Socialist realism in art—Russia.* 2. *Socialist realism in literature.* 3. *Communism and art—Russia.* 4. *Arts, Modern—20th century—Russia.* I. Title. BIP

Societe Anonyme.

SOCIETE 709'.04'07401471
Anonyme.
Societe Anonyme (the first museum of modern art, 1920-1944) : selected publications. [New York] : Arno Press, 1972- v. : ill. ; 14-19 cm. (Arno series of contemporary art) Contents.Contents.— 1. Documents.—v. 2. Pamphlets.—v. 3. Monographs. [N6487.N4S627 1972] 70-138690
1. *Societe Anonyme.*

Society emblems—Catalogs.

IRONS, Charles F. 737.2
Illustrated catalogue of solid gold society emblems, pins, and charms, manufactured by Charles. F. Irons. Providence, R. I., 1885. Detroit, Repub. by Gale, 1966. 194p. illus. (Assn. ref. ser.) [TS761.I7 1966] 66-20614 6.50
1. *Society emblems—Catalogs.* I. Title.

Society of Arts and Crafts, Detroit.

ARTS and crafts in 707'.4'017434
Detroit 1906-1976 : the movement, the society, the school : the Detroit Institute of Arts, November 26, 1976-January 16, 1977 : exhibition / sponsored by Founders Society Detroit Institute of Arts and the Center for Creative Studies—College of Art and Design. Detroit : The Institute, c1976. 296 p. : ill. (some col.) ; 26 cm. Bibliography: p. 265-293. [NK1137.A77] 77-358697
1. *Society of Arts and Crafts, Detroit.* 2. *Society of Arts and Crafts, Detroit. Art School.* 3. *Arts and crafts movement— Exhibitions.* I. Detroit. Institute of Arts.

COLBY, Joy Hakanson. 745.062774
Art and a city; a history of the Detroit Society of Arts & Crafts. Detroit, Wayne State University Press, 1956. 84p. illus. 26cm. [NK1136.D43] 56-10573
1. Society of Arts and Crafts, Detroit. I. Title.

Society of Naval Architects and Marine Engineers, New York—Bibliography.

SOCIETY of Naval Architects and Marine/Engineers, New York. 016.6238
Index of SNAME publications, 1961-1973. New York : The Society, [1974] 86 p. ; 28 cm. [Z6834.S5S6 1974] 74-191731 ISBN pbk. : 3.00
1. Society of Naval Architects and Marine Engineers, New York—Bibliography. 2. Naval architecture—Indexes. 3. Marine engineering—Indexes. I. Title.

Society of Printers, Boston.

NASH, Ray, 1905- 655.062744
Printing as an art. [A history of the Society of Printers, Boston, 1905-1955] Cambridge, Published for the Society of Printers by Harvard University Press, 1955. xi, 141 p. illus. 25 cm. Bibliographical footnotes. [Z120.S728] 55-7446
1. Society of Printers, Boston. I. Title.

Socorro Co., N.M.—Description and travel—Views.

SMITH, Joseph Edward, 1858-1936. 978.9'62 s
Socorro photographer, Joseph Edward Smith, 1858-1936 / compiled by John DeWitt McKee and Spencer Wilson. Socorro, N.M. : Socorro County Historical Society, 1974, c1975. 54 p. : chiefly ill. ; 28 cm. (Publications in history ; v. 8) [F802.S6S65 vol. 8] 779'.9'91789620924 75-309599 4.95
1. Smith, Joseph Edward, 1858-1936. 2. Socorro Co., N.M.—Description and travel—Views. I. McKee, John DeWitt, 1919- II. Wilson, Spencer. III. Title. IV. Series: Socorro County Historical Society. Publications in history ; v. 8.

Sodoma, Giovanni Antonio Bazzi, known as, 1477?-1549.

HAYUM, Andree. 759.5
Giovanni Antonio Bazzi—"Il Sodoma" / Andree Hayum. New York : Garland Pub., 1976. xvii, 335 p. : ill. ; 21 cm. (Outstanding dissertations in the fine arts) Reprint of the author's thesis, Harvard, 1968. Bibliography: p. 278-286. [ND623.S6H38 1976] 75-23794 ISBN 0-8240-1989-X lib.bdg. : 27.50
1. Sodoma, Giovanni Antonio Bazzi, known as, 1477?-1549.

Sofia. Natsionalna khudozhestvena galeriia.

SOFIA. Natsionalna khudozhestvena galeriia. Branch for Medieval Bulgarian Pictorial Art. 704.948'2
Old Bulgarian art / K. Paskaleva ; [translator, Marguerite Alexieva]. [Sofia] : Sofia Press, 1976. 57 p. : chiefly col. ill. ; 20 x 22 cm. On cover: National Art Gallery. Plan of gallery: [1] leaf inserted. [N8189.B8S63 1976] 77-458444
1. Sofia. Natsionalna khudozhestvena galeriia. 2. Icons, Bulgarian—Catalogs. 3. Icons—Bulgaria—Sofia—Catalogs. I. Paskaleva, Kostadinka Georgieva. II. Title.

Soft sculpture.

MEILACH, Dona Z. 745.5
Soft sculpture and other soft art forms, with stuffed fabrics, fibers, and plastics, by Dona Z. Meilach. New York, Crown Publishers [1974] viii, 248 p. illus. (part col.) 27 cm. Bibliography: p. 244-245. [NB1203.M44 1974] 73-91153 8.95
1. Soft sculpture. I. Title. BIP

WOOSTER, Ann-Sargent, 1946- 745.5
Techniques of fabric sculpture. New York, Drake Publishers [1974] p. cm. [NB1203.W66] 74-6459 ISBN 0-87749-671-4 12.95
1. Soft sculpture. I. Title.

Soft toy making.

BRADSHAW-SMITH, Gillian. 745.59'24
Adventures in toy-making / Gillian Bradshaw-Smith ; illustrated with drawings by the author and with photos. by Bob Hanson. 1st ed. New York : Taplinger Pub. Co., 1976. 128 p., [4] leaves of plates : ill. (some col.) ; 25 cm. [TT174.3.B7 1976] 75-903 ISBN 0-8008-0102-4 : 9.95
1. Soft toy making. I. Hanson, Bob. II. Title. BIP

CHAPPELL, Phyllis. 745.59'24
Soft toy making. New York, Drake Publishers [1971] 128 p. illus. 26 cm. [TT174.3.C48 1971] 73-173737 ISBN 0-87749-131-3 5.95
1. Soft toy making.

DAVIDSON, Delphine. 745.59'2
Introducing soft toy making. Newton Centre, Mass., C. T. Branford [1969] 79 p. illus. (part col.) 22 cm. Bibliography: p. 78. [TT157.D38 1969] 78-75771
1. Soft toy making. I. Title. BIP

DE SARIGNY, Rudi. 745.59'24
How to make and design stuffed toys / Rudi de Sarigny. New York : Dover Publications, 1978, c1971. 239 p. : ill. ; 28 cm. Reprint, with corrections, of the 1971 ed. published by Mills & Boon, London, under title: Good design in soft toys. Includes bibliographical references. [TT174.3.D4 1978] 77-92482 ISBN 0-486-23625-0 : 5.00
1. Soft toy making. I. Title. BIP

DOYLE, Ruth Moses. 745.59'24
Soft toys made with love ... and the help of 30 full-size patterns / Ruth Moses Doyle. East Dennis, MA : East Dennis Pub. Co., c1975. 95 p. : ill. ; 36 cm. [TT174.3.D68] 74-82109
1. Soft toy making. I. Title. BIP

DYER, Anne. 745.59'2
Design your own stuffed toys. [U.S. ed.] Newton, Mass., C. T. Branford Co. [1970, c1969] 117 p. illus. 26 cm. [TT157.D9 1970] 75-105680
1. Soft toy making. I. Title. BIP

FORSTER, Marianne. 745.59'24
Making furry toys. New York, Drake Publishers [1973] 120 p. illus. 20 cm. Photographs, patterns, and working drawings accompany instructions for making a variety of stuffed animal toys from a wide range of furs and fabrics. [TT174.3.F67] 73-5257 5.95
1. Soft toy making. I. Title. BIP

FREMLIN-KEY, Hermyone. 745.59'24
Toys and gifts for you to make. Newton, Mass., C. T. Branford Co. [1970] 94 p. illus. (part col.) 26 cm. [TT157.F75 1970] 70-108784
1. Soft toy making. I. Title. BIP

FREMLIN-KEY, Hermyone. 745.59'24
Toys with a theme / Hermyone Fremlin-Key. London : Mills and Boon, 1974. 79 p., [4] p. of plates : ill. (some col.) ; 26 cm. Label mounted on t.p.: Transatlantic Arts, Inc., Levittown, New York, sole distributor for the U.S.A. Step-by-step instructions for making soft toy and puppet characters that are introduced in a short story at the beginning of the book. [TT174.3.F73 1974] 75-318169 ISBN 0-263-05483-7 : 8.50
1. Soft toy making. 2. Puppets and puppet-plays. I. Title. BIP

GORGE, Alice A. 745.59'22
Creative toymaking [by] Alice A. Gorge. New York, Drake [1973] 64 p. illus. (part col.) 24 cm. Instructions for making toys and puppets from such materials as dishcloths, towels, and felt using only needle, thread, and scissors. [TT174.3.G67] 73-5854 ISBN 0-87749-545-9 4.95
1. Soft toy making. I. Title.

GREENAWAY, Gladys. 745.59'24
Toy making [by] Gladys and Kathryn Greenaway. New York, Drake Publishers [1974, c1973] 96 p. illus. (part col.) 26 cm. Published in 1973 under title: Soft toy making. [TT174.3.G73 1974] 73-10902 ISBN 0-87749-563-7 6.95
1. Soft toy making. I. Greenaway, Kathryn, joint author. II. Title.

HUTCHINGS, Margaret. 745.59'22
Patchwork playthings : with full-size templates / Margaret Hutchings ; line drawings by the author. New York : Dover Publications, 1976. 48 p., [2] leaves of plates : ill. ; 28 cm. (Dover needlework series) [TT174.3.H87 1976] 75-21354 ISBN 0-486-23247-6 pbk. : 1.75
1. Soft toy making. 2. Christmas decorations. 3. Patchwork. I. Title.

HUTCHINGS, Margaret. 745.59'24
Teddy bears and how to make them / Margaret Hutchings ; with ill. by the author. New York : Dover Publications, 1977, c1964. 283 p., [8] leaves of plates ; 28 cm. Reprint of the ed. published by Mills & Boon, London, under title: The book of the teddy bear. Bibliography: p. 281. [TT174.3.H86 1977] 77-70049 ISBN 0-486-23487-8 pbk. : 5.00
1. Soft toy making. 2. Teddy bears. I. Title. BIP

LOCKWOOD, Gillian. 745.59/24
Making soft toys. London, Studio Vista; New York, Watson-Guptill [1967] 104p. front., illus. (some col.), diagrs. 19cm. [TT157.L55] 67-13737 1.95 bds.,
1. Soft toy making. I. Title.

MORTON, Brenda. 745.59'24
Do-it-yourself dinosaurs; imaginative toycraft for beginners. With drawings by Juliet Renny and photos. by Stephen Moreton-Prichard. New York, Taplinger Pub. Co. [1974, c1973] 149 p. illus. 22 cm. Instructions for making many kinds of dinosaurs and other prehistoric creatures from such materials as thread, pipe cleaners, and felt. [TT174.3.M66 1974] 73-1765 ISBN 0-8008-2263-3 6.95
1. Soft toy making. I. Renny, Juliet, illus. II. Moreton-Prichard, Stephen, illus. III. Title. BIP

MORTON, Brenda. 688.7'2
Floppy toys. With drawings by Juliet Renny and photos, by Stephen Moreton-Prichard. New York, Taplinger Pub. Co. [1971] 136 p. illus. 22 cm. Instructions and diagrams for making sixteen floppy toys from remnant materials. Includes a photograph of each finished toy. [TT157.M64 1971] 78-126981 ISBN 0-8008-2770-8 5.95
1. Soft toy making. I. Renny, Juliet, illus. II. Moreton-Prichard, Stephen, illus. III. Title. BIP

MORTON, Brenda. 745.59'24
Mascot toys; simple toys to make from sponges. With diagrams by Christopher Wright and photos. by Stephen Moreton-Prichard. [1st ed.] New York, Taplinger Pub. Co. [1969] 79 p. illus. 22 cm. Gives easy instructions and diagrams for making fifteen toys by covering foam sponges. Includes a photograph of each finished toy. [TT157.M66 1969] 69-18369 4.50
1. Soft toy making. I. Wright, Christopher, illus. II. Moreton-Prichard, Stephen, illus. III. Title. BIP

MORTON, Brenda. 745.59'2
Soft toys made easy. With drawings by Juliet Renny and photos. by Stephen Moreton-Prichard. New York, Taplinger Pub. Co. [1972] 119 p. illus. 22 cm. Photographs and line drawings accompany instructions for making simple and quickly completed soft toys from a variety of fabrics. [TT174.3.M67 1972] 79-184412 ISBN 0-8008-7245-2 6.95
1. Soft toy making. I. Renny, Juliet, illus. II. Moreton-Prichard, Stephen, illus. III. Title. BIP

MORTON, Brenda. 745.59'24
Your book of knitted toys. With drawings by Juliet Renny. New York, Taplinger Pub. Co. [1973] 78 p. illus. 22 cm. Instructions for creating a variety of toys with simple knitting stitches. [TT174.3.M68 1973b] 72-11090 ISBN 0-8008-8757-3 4.95
1. Soft toy making. 2. Knitting—Patterns. I. Renny, Juliet, illus. II. Title. BIP

*POWNALL, Glen. 745.59'24
Soft toys. Wellington, N.Z., Seven Seas, [1975 c1974] 80 p. ill. (part col.) 25 cm. (His creative leisure series.) [TT174.3] ISBN 0-85467-008-4
1. Soft toy making. I. Title.
Distributed by Int'l Publications Service, Collings for 5.50.

ROTH, Charlene Davis, 1945- 745.59'24
The art of making cloth toys. [1st ed.] Radnor, Pa., Chilton Book Co. [1974] xii, 210 p. illus. 26 cm. [TT174.3.R67 1974] 74-865 ISBN 0-8019-5870-9 9.95
1. Soft toy making. I. Title.
Pbk. 4.95, ISBN 0-8019-5871-7. BIP

RUSSELL, Joan. 745.59'24
The Woman's day book of soft toys and dolls. New York, Simon and Schuster [1975] 255 p. illus., (part col.) 29 cm. [TT174.3.R87] 75-16354 ISBN 0-671-22085-3 9.95
1. Soft toy making. 2. Dollmaking. I. Title. BIP

STAPLES, Caroline M. 746.4
The yarn animal book / by Caroline M. Staples. New York : Simon and Schuster, c1976. p. cm. [TT174.3.S73] 76-20465 ISBN 0-671-22336-4 : 9.95
1. Soft toy making. 2. Needlework. I. Title. BIP

TYLER, Mabs. 745.59'2
The big book of soft toys. Photos. by Gina Harris. Line illus. by John Kingsford. New York, McGraw-Hill [1973, c1972] 256 p. illus. (part col.) 26 cm. [TT174.3.T92] 72-6420 ISBN 0-07-062952-8 8.95
1. Soft toy making. I. Title.

VAN GILDEN, Amy 745.59'22
Felt toymaking: advanced techniques. New York, Drake Publishers [1974] p. [TT174.3.V36] 74-6077 ISBN 0-87749-672-2 9.95
1. Soft toy making. 2. Felt work. I. Title.

WEAVER, Janet. 745.59'24
The huggables : how to make large stuffed animals / Janet and Alice Weaver. Dayton, Ohio : Lorenz Press, c1977. 67 p., 68-111 fold. leaves : ill. ; 30 cm. [TT174.3.W4] 77-357843 ISBN 0-89328-004-6 pbk. : 6.95
1. Soft toy making. I. Weaver, Alice, joint author. II. Title. BIP

Soft toy making—Juvenile literature.

TYLER, Mabs. 745.59'2
Let's make soft toys. New York, Van Nostrand Reinhold [1972] c1971. 32 p. illus. (part col.) 21 cm. (Starting points) Instructions for making different kinds of toys from felt and other soft material. [TT174.3.T93] 77-188511 pap. 1.45
1. Soft toy making—Juvenile literature. I. Title.

WRIGLEY, Elsie. 745.59'24
Soft toys / written and illustrated by Elsie Wrigley. New York : F. Warne, 1978, c1977. [32] p. : ill. ; 20 cm. Easy-to-follow instructions for soft toys made from household items. [TT174.3.W74 1978] 77-81969 ISBN 0-7232-2000-X : 3.95
1. Soft toy making—Juvenile literature. I. Title. BIP

WRIGLEY, Elsie. 746.4
Wool toys / written and illustrated by Elsie Wrigley. New York : F. Warne 1978. [32] p. : col. ill. ; 20 cm. Easy-to-follow instructions for soft toys made from yarn. [TT174.3.W75 1978] 77-81970 ISBN 0-7232-1998-2 : 3.95
1. Soft toy making—Juvenile literature. I. Title. BIP

Solar heating.

SOLAR dwelling design concepts. New York : Drake Publishers, [1977] p. cm. [TH7413.S6] 77-6919 ISBN 0-8473-1574-6 pbk. : 6.95 728
1. Solar heating. 2. Solar houses—Design and construction. BIP

SOLARIA : 721
... on the threshold of environmental renaissance / written by Edmund Scientific Co. ... [et al.]. Barrington, N.J. : The Company, 1975. 57 p., 10 fold. leaves of plates : ill. ; 28 cm. "No. 9469." [TH7413.S63] 75-10732 24.95

1. Solar heating. 2. Solar houses.

Solar heating—Congresses.

WORKING Conference on Solar Effects on Building Design, National Academy of Sciences, 1975. 729
Solar radiation considerations in building planning and design : proceedings of a working conference / Committee on Solar Energy in the Heating and Cooling of Buildings, Building Research Advisory Board, Commission on Sociotechnical Systems, National Research Council. Washington : National Academy of Sciences, 1976. xi, 179 p. : ill. ; 28 cm. Includes bibliographical references. [TH7413.W65 1975] 76-25753 ISBN 0-309-02516-8 pbk. : 8.75
1. Solar heating—Congresses. 2. Architecture and solar radiation—Congresses. I. National Research Council. Committee on Solar Energy in the Heating and Cooling of Buildings. II. Title. BIP

Solar houses.

PRACTICAL guide to solar homes / by the editors of Hudson home guides. New York : Van Nostrand Reinhold Co., 1978, c1977. 143 p. : ill. (some col.) ; 29 cm. Bibliography: p. 140. [TH7414.P7 1978] 77-93914 ISBN 0-442-22594-6 : 10.95 728.3'7
1. Solar houses. I. Hudson home guides. II. Solar home.

WRIGHT, David, 1941- 728
Natural solar architecture : a passive primer / by David Wright ; technical advice, Jeffrey Cook ; ill., Dennis A. Andrejko. New York : Van Nostrand Reinhold Co., c1978. 245 p. : ill. ; 22 x 38 cm. Includes index. Bibliography: p. 240-243. [NA2542.S6W74] 77-28541 ISBN 0-442-29585-5 : 14.95 ISBN 0-442-29586-3 pbk. : 7.95
I. Title. BIP

Solar houses—North America.

SHURCLIFF, William A. 721
Solar heated buildings of North America : 120 outstanding examples / William A. Shurcliff. Harisville, N.H. : Brick House Pub. Co., c1978. xv, 295 p. : ill. ; 28 cm. Includes index. [TH7414.S48] 78-57234 ISBN 0-931790-00-X : 8.95
1. Solar houses—North America. 2. Solar heating. I. Title.

Solder and soldering.

ALLEN, B. M. 671.5'6
Soldering and welding / B. M. Allen. New York : Drake Publishers, 1975, c1970. 120 p. : ill. ; 23 cm. (A Drake home craftsman's book) First published in 1969 under title: Soldering handbook. Includes index. [TT267.A395 1975] 75-330723 ISBN 0-8473-1120-1 : 4.95
1. Solder and soldering. 2. Welding. I. Title. BIP

AMERICAN Society for Testing Materials. 671.56
Symposium on solder, presented at the fifty-ninth annual meeting American Society for Testing Materials, Atlantic City, N. J., June 19-20, 1956. Philadelphia [1957] v, 190p. illus., diagrs., tables. 23cm. (Its Special technical publication no. 189) Includes bibliographies. [TT267.A5 1956] 57-2317
1. Solder and soldering. I. Title. II. Series.

AMERICAN Welding Society. Committee on Brazing and Soldering. 671.5'6
Soldering manual / prepared by AWS Committee on Brazing and Soldering under the direction of AWS Technical Activities Committee ; approved by AWS Board of Directors, April 1, 1977. 2d ed., rev. Miami, Fla. : American Welding Society, c1978. ix, 149 p. : ill. ; 25 cm. Includes bibliographical references and index. [TT267.A55 1978] 77-90783 ISBN 0-87171-151-6 : 15.00
1. Solder and soldering. I. American Welding Society. Technical Activities Committee. II. Title. BIP

BRIGHTMAN, Robert. 621.9
101 practical uses for propane torches / Robert Brightman ; illustrated by Henry Clark. 1st ed. Blue Ridge Summit, Pa. : G/L Tab Books, [1978] c1977. 142 p. : ill. ; 22 cm. Includes index. [TT267.B69] 78-2788 6.95
1. Solder and soldering. 2. Brazing. 3. Welding. I. Title. II. Title: Propane torches.

DEZETTEL, Louis M. 671.5'6
ABC's of electrical soldering, by Louis M. Dezettel. [1st ed.] Indianapolis, H. W. Sams [1968] 128 p. illus. 22 cm. [TT267.D43] 68-21312
1. Solder and soldering. I. Title.

†DEZETTEL, Louis M. 671.5'6
Electrical soldering : a revision of ABC's of Electrical soldering / by Louis M. Dezettel. 2d ed. Indianapolis : H. W. Sams, c1976. 144 p. : ill. ; 22 cm. [TT267.D44 1976] 76-42878 ISBN 0-672-21411-3 : 4.95
1. Solder and soldering. I. Title. BIP

INDIUM Corporation of America. 671.56
Intermediate Indalloy solders. New York [1954] 58p. illus. 23cm. [TT267.I58] 55-58362
1. Solder and soldering. 2. Indium. I. Title. II. Title: Indalloy solders.

KESTER Solder Company. 671.56
Solder, its fundamentals and usage, by Clifford L. Barber, research director. [Chicago, 1954] 78p. illus. 23cm. [TT267.K4] 54-32001
1. Solder and soldering. I. Barber, Clifford L. II. Title.

MANKO, Howard H. 671.56
Solders and soldering; materials, design, production, and analysis for reliable bonding. New York, McGraw-Hill [1964] xv, 323 p. illus., diagrs., tables. 23 cm. [TT267.M26] 63-20268
1. Solder and soldering. BIP

Soldiers in art.

FORTE, Nancy 704.94
The warrior in art. Designed by Wendell Carroll. Minneapolis, Lerner [1966] 72p. illus. (pt. col.) 27cm. [N826b.F6] 65-29039 3.95 lib.ed.,
1. Soldiers in art. I. Title. BIP

SASSER, Elizabeth Skidmore, 1919- 704.94'9'355
The soldier in French literature and art, 1800-1848 [by] Elizabeth S. Sasser [and] Harold L. Simpson. [Lubbock, Tex.] 1969. 18 p. 23 cm. (Research bulletin of Texas Technological College, v. 1, no. 1) Bibliographical footnotes. [NX549.S25] 76-628485
1. Soldiers in art. 2. The arts, French. I. Simpson, Harold L., 1925- joint author. II. Title. III. Series: Texas Technological College, Lubbock. Research bulletin, v. 1, no. 1

Soleri, Paolo, 1919—

WALL, Donald. 720'.924
Documenta; the Paolo Soleri retrospective. Commentary and graphics by Donald Wall. [Washington, Corcoran Gallery of Art, 1970] [84] p. (incl. cover) illus. 25 cm. and case (16 rolls of illus.) 28 cm. Title from label on case. Catalog of an exhibition held at the Corcoran Gallery of Art, Feb. 20-Apr. 5, 1970. [NA1123.S6W3] 72-114986
1. Soleri, Paolo, 1919- I. Corcoran Gallery of Art, Washington, D.C. II. Title.

WALL, Donald. 711'.4
Visionary cities: the arcology of Paolo Soleri. Commentary and graphics [by] Donald Wall. Graphics associate: W. Borek. New York, Praeger Publishers [1971] 1 v. (unpaged) illus. 26 cm. [NA9085.S6W3 1971] 75-144350 25.00
1. Soleri, Paolo, 1919- I. Title.

WALL, Donald. 711'.4
Visionary cities: the arcology of Paolo Soleri. [Commentary: D. Wall. Graphics: D. Wall and W. Borek. 1st ed. New York, Praeger, 1970] 1 v. (unpaged) illus. 25 cm. Cover title. [NA9085.S6W3] 70-128102 5.95
1. Soleri, Paolo, 1919- I. Title.

Soleri, Paolo, 1919- —Bibliography.

WILCOXEN, Ralph. 016.720'924
Paolo Soleri: a bibliography. Monticello, Ill., Council of Planning Librarians, 1969. 24 l. 29 cm. (Council of Planning Librarians. Exchange bibliography, 88) Cover title. [Z5942.C68 no. 88] 79-10608
1. Soleri, Paolo, 1919- —Bibliography. I. Title. II. Series.

Solman, Joseph, 1909—

SOLMAN, Joseph, 1909- 769'.92'4
The monotypes of Joseph Solman / introd. by Una E. Johnson ; with technical notes by the artist on the making of the prints. New York : Da Capo Press, 1977. [96] p. : chiefly col. ill. ; 22 x 29 cm. Bibliography: p. [96]. [NE2246.S64A5] 77-9923 ISBN 0-306-77425-9 lib.bdg. : 18.95
1. Solman, Joseph, 1909- 2. Monotype (Engraving)—Technique. I. Title. BIP

Solomon R. Guggenheim Museum, New York.

GUGGENHEIM, Solomon R., Foundation 708.1471
The Solomon R. Guggenheim Museum. Architect: Frank Lloyd Wright. New York [dist. Horizon Press] [c.1960] 72p. (chiefly illus., ports., one foldout) 26cm. 60-13748 3.95
1. Wright. Frank Lloyd, 2. Solomon R. Guggenheim Museum, New York. I. Title.

SOLOMON R. Guggenheim Foundation. 708.1471
The Solomon R. Guggenheim Museum. Architect: Frank Lloyd Wright. New York [1960] 72 p. (chiefly illus., ports.) 26 cm. [N620.S63S6] 60-16748
1. Solomon R. Guggenheim Museum, New York. 2. Wright, Frank Lloyd, 1869-1959. I. Title.

Solomon R. Guggenheim Museum, New York—Juvenile literature.

HOLLINGSWORTH, Alvin C. 708.1471
I'd like the Goo-gen-heim. Written and illustrated by A. C. Hollingsworth. Chicago, Reilly & Lee Books [1970] [48] p. col. illus. 18 x 21 cm. A little boy wanders into the Guggenheim art museum in New York and finds it an exciting experience. [PZ9.H7Id] 76-102874 4.50
1. Solomon R. Guggenheim Museum, New York—Juvenile literature. I. Title.

Solomon, Syd, 1917—

SOLOMON, Syd, 1917- 759.13
Syd Solomon : a retrospective showing, December 5, 1974-January 19, 1975, John and Mable Ringling Museum of Art, Sarasota, Florida, Februrary 6, 1975-March 16, 1975, New York Cultural Center, New York, New York. [Sarasota, Fla. : Ringling Museum of Art, 1974] 44 p. : ill. (some col.) ; 29 cm. Bibliography: p. 43-44. [ND237.S6329J65] 75-326503
1. Solomon, Syd, 1917- I. John and Mable Ringling Museum of Art, Sarasota, Fla. II. New York Cultural Center.

Sommer, Frederick, 1905—

PHILADELPHIA College of Art. 779'.0924
Frederick Sommer; an exhibition of photographs at Philadelphia College of Art, November 1 through November 30, 1968. [Philadelphia, 1968] 27 p. plates, ports. 32 cm. [TR647.S62P45] 76-286099
1. Sommer, Frederick, 1905- 2. Photography, Artistic—Exhibitions.

Sommer, William, 1867-1949.

AKRON, Ohio. Art Institute. 759.13
William Sommer retrospective [exhibition] Akron Art Institute, October 25-November 29, 1970. Akron [1970?] 65 p. illus. (part col.) 18 x 22 cm. [N6537.S63A78] 72-182614
1. Sommer, William, 1867-1949. I. Title.

THE William Sommer memorial exhibition; catalogue of an exhibition of works by William Sommer held November first through December tenth in the Cleveland Museum of Art, 1950. [Cleveland, 1950] 98 p. illus., port. 26 cm. [ND237.S633C6] 759.13 50-11266 [927.5]
1. Sommer, William, 1867-1949. 2. Paintings. American—Exhibitions. I. Cleveland Museum of Art.

Sonfist, Alan.

SONFIST, Alan. 709'.2'4
Autobiography of Alan Sonfist : a self-presentation by Alan Sonfist published in connection with an exhibition of his works at the Herbert F. Johnson Museum of Art, Cornell University, March 19-May 4, 1975. [Ithaca, N.Y. : Herbert F. Johnson Museum of Art, Cornell University, c1975] [32] p. : ill. ; 22 x 28 cm. Includes bibliography. [N6537.S64A22] 75-12049
1. Sonfist, Alan. I. Herbert F. Johnson Museum of Art. II. Title.

Sonnenberg, Benjamin, 1901- —Art collections.

STAMPFLE, Felice. 743.9'2'07401471
Artists and writers; nineteenth and twentieth century portrait drawings from the collection of Benjamin Sonnenberg. Catalogue by Felice Stampfle and Cara Dufour. With an introd. by Brendan Gill. [Exhibition held at] the Pierpont Morgan Library, New York, May 13 to July 30, 1971. [New York, 1971] 52 p., 64 plates. 28 cm. Includes bibliographies. [NC31.S6S8] 73-161537 ISBN 0-87598-004-X
1. Sonnenberg, Benjamin, 1901- —Art collections. 2. Portrait drawing—Exhibitions. 3. Artists—Portraits. I. Dufour, Cara, joint author. II. Pierpont Morgan Library, New York. III. Title.

Sorensen, Lewis, 1910—

SORENSEN, Lewis, 1910- 745.59'22
Lewis Sorensen's Doll scrapbook / by Lewis Sorensen ; compiled and edited by Don Thorup. A collector's ed. Alhambra, Calif. : Thor Publications, 1976- v. : ill. (some col.) ; 29 cm. [NK4894.2.S65A43] 76-7692
1. Sorensen, Lewis, 1910- 2. Dolls—United States. 3. Dolls—Collectors and collecting—United States. I. Title. II. Title: Doll scrapbook.

Sotatsu, d. 1643.

GRILLI, Elise. 759.952
Tawaraya Sotatsu (active early 17th century) Edited by Ichimatsu Tanaka; English text by Elise Grilli. [1st English ed.] Tokyo, Rutland, Vt., C. E. Tuttle Co. [1956] 86p. illus. (part col.) 18cm. (Kodansha library of Japanese art, no. 6) Title also in Japanese on t. p. 'For theJapanese-language edition ... Professor Ichimatsu Tanaka provided ... [the] text ... Though the present book contains the same selection and arrangement of plates as originally made by Professor Tanaka, with his approval I [i. e. Elise Grilli] have written an entirely new text.' Bibliography: p. 86. [ND1059.S6G7] 927.5 56-8491
1. Sotatsu, d. 1643. I. Tanaka, Ichimatsu, 1895- II. Title. III. Series.

Sotheby, firm. auctioneers, London.

WILSON, Philip, 1940- ed. 702
Art at auction, the year at Sotheby's & Parke-Bernet, 1966-67; the two hundred and twenty-third season.. [Edited by Philip Wilson assisted by Alison Brand. 1st ed.] New York, American Heritage Pub. Co.; distributed by the Viking Press [1967] 432 p. illus. (part col.) 28 cm. [N8640.A7 1967] 67-30652
1. Sotheby, firm. auctioneers, London. 2. Parke-Bernet Galleries, inc.,New York. 3. Art—Catalogs. I. Brand, Alison ed. II. Title.

Soto, Jesus Raphael, 1923—

CLAY, Jean. 730'.92'4
Soto. New York, H. N. Abrams [1974] p. [NB439.S6C55] 74-8620 ISBN 0-8109-4421-9 7.50
1. Soto, Jesus Raphael, 1923- I. Soto, Jesus Raphael, 1923-

SOTO, Jesus Raphael, 1923- 730'.92'4
Soto : a retrospective exhibition : The Solomon R. Guggenheim Museum, New York. New York : Solomon R. Guggenheim Foundation, 1974. 136 p. : ill. (some col.) ; 26 cm. English, French or Spanish. Bibliography: p. 132-135. [NB439.S6S64] 74-16856 pbk. : 6.50
1. Soto, Jesus Raphael, 1923- I. Solomon R. Guggenheim Museum, New York.

Sottsass, Ettore, 1917—

SOTTSASS, Ettore, 1917- 720'.92'4
Sottsass's scrap-book : disegni e note / di Ettore Sottsass jr. ... ; a cura di ... Federica Di Castro. Milano : Casabella, [1976] 148 p. : ill. (some col.) ; 23 x 24 cm. (Documenti di Casabella) English and Italian. Bibliography: p. 144-147. [NA1123.S66D5] 77-354457 L15000
1. Sottsass, Ettore, 1917- I. Di Castro, Federica. II. Title.

Soulages, Pierre, 1919-

JUIN, Hubert. 759.4
Soulages. Translated by Haakon Chevalier. New York, Grove Press [1960, c1959] 64p. illus. 21cm. [ND553.S66J83] 59-12071
1. Soulages, Pierre, 1919- I. Title.

SOULAGES, Pierre, 1919- 759.4
Soulages: paintings since 1963 [by] James Johnson Sweeney [New York] M. Knoedler [1968] 31 p. illus. (part col.) port. 22 cm. Catalog of an exhibition held at M. Knoedler & Co., inc., New York, Feb. 6-24, 1968; Museum of Art, Carnegie Institute, Pittsburgh, Mar. 7-Apr. 7, 1968; Albright-Knox Art Gallery, Buffalo, May 6-June 2, 1968. Bibliography: p. 14. [ND553.S66S9] 68-14004
I. Sweeney, James Johnson, 1900- II. Knoedler (M.) and Company, inc. III. Pittsburgh. Carnegie Institute. Museum of Art. IV. Albright-Knox Art Gallery. V. Title.

Soundproofing.

DAY, Brian Frederick. 693.8'34
Building acoustics, edited by B. F. Day, R. D. Ford, and P. Lord. Amsterdam, New York, Elsevier, 1969. vii, 120 p. illus. 22 cm. Bibliography: p. 115. [TH1725.D38] 73-95655 unpriced
1. Soundproofing. 2. Architectural acoustics. I. Ford, R. D., joint author. II. Lord, Peter, joint author. III. Title.

Soundproofing—Congresses.

BUILDING acoustics, 729'.29
editors: T. Smith [and others] Newcastle upon Tyne, Oriel Press, 1971. vii, 242 p. illus. 23 cm. (British Acoustical Society. Special volumes no. 2) Proceedings of a conference held at the University of Newcastle upon Tyne 8-10 April 1970. Includes bibliographies. [TH1725.B84] 79-127066 ISBN 0-85362-130-6 £3.75
1. Soundproofing—Congresses. 2. Architectural acoustics—Congresses. I. Smith, Trevor, ed. II. Title. III. Series.

South Africa—Race relations—Pictorial works.

MAGUBANE, Peter. 779.9'9'96806
Magubane's South Africa / by Peter Magubane ; with a foreword by Andrew Young. 1st ed. New York : Knopf : distributed by Random House, 1978. 115 p. : chiefly ill. ; 31 cm. [DT763.M316 1978] 77-20350 ISBN 0-394-50016-4 : 12.95. ISBN 0-394-73565-X pbk. : 7.95
1. South Africa—Race relations—Pictorial works. 2. South Africa—Social conditions—Pictorial works. I. Title. II. Title: South Africa. BIP

South African National Gallery, Cape Town.

SOUTH African 759.2'074'09687
National Gallery, Cape Town.
English and South African watercolours in the South African National Gallery. [Cape Town : South African National Gallery, 1976] [24] p. : ill. ; 27 x 13 cm. Cover title. Bibliography: p. [24] [ND1928.S68 1976] 77-362556 ISBN 0-620-01748-1 : 0.50
1. South African National Gallery, Cape Town. 2. Water-color painting, English—Catalogs. 3. Water-color painting, South African—Catalogs. 4. Water-color painting—South Africa—Cape Town—Catalogs. I. Title.

Southbridge, Mass.—Description—Views.

A New England town in early photographs : 974.4'3
149 illustrations of Southbridge, Massachusetts, 1878-1930 / selected and edited by Edmund V. Gillon, Jr. ; introd. and captions by Arthur J. Kavanagh. New York : Dover Publications, 1976. 170 p. : ill. ; 24 cm. [F74.S73N48 1976] 76-380345 ISBN 0-486-23286-7 pbk. : 5.00
1. Southbridge, Mass.—Description—Views. 2. Southbridge, Mass.—Social life and customs—Pictorial works. I. Gillon, Edmund Vincent. II. Kavanagh, Arthur J. BIP

Southern States—Antiq.

HOUSTON, Tex. Museum of Fine Arts 970.466
Spiro and Mississippian antiquities from the McDannald Collection [Catalogue. Houston, Tex., Author [1965] 58p. illus., map (on lining papers) 18cm. [E78.S65H65] 65-24455 3.00 pap.,
1. Spiro Mound. 2. Southern States—Antiq. 3. Indians of North America—Southern States—Antiq. I. Title.

Southern States—Description and travel—Views.

HINDS, Will, 1936- 759.13
Will Hinds: artist of the Deep South. Shreveport, La., R. W. Norton Art Gallery [1972] 20 p. illus. 22 x 28 cm. Catalog of an exhibition held at the R. W. Norton Art Gallery, Shreveport, La., Jan. 16-Feb. 20, 1972. [ND237.H63N6] 79-187911 ISBN 0-9600182-6-3
1. Southern States—Description and travel—Views. I. Norton (R. W.) Art Gallery.

TROVAIOLI, August P. 759.13
William Aiken Walker, southern genre painter [by] August P. Trovaioli and Roulhac B. Toledano. Baton Rouge, Louisiana State University Press [1972] xviii, 142 p. illus. (part col.) 29 cm. Bibliography: p. [133]-138. [ND237.W314T76] 72-79340 ISBN 0-8071-0234-2 15.00
1. Walker, William Aiken, 1838-1921. 2. Southern States—Description and travel—Views. I. Toledano, Roulhac, joint author.

Southern States in art.

LOONEY, Ben Earl. 759.13
Watercolors of Dixie / by Ben Earl Looney. Baton Rouge : Claitor's Pub. Div., c1974. 90 p. : ill. (some col.) ; 23 x 29 cm. [ND1839.L63A57] 74-21848 13.95
1. Looney, Ben Earl. 2. Southern States in art. I. Title. BIP

SHUPTRINE, Hubert, 1936- 759.13
Jericho : the South beheld / Hubert Shuptrine, James Dickey. 1st ed. Birmingham, Ala. : Oxmoor House, 1974. 165 p. : ill. (some col.) ; 33 x 42 cm. [ND1839.S48D53] 74-78763 60.00
1. Shuptrine, Hubert, 1936- 2. Southern States in art. I. Dickey, James. II. Title. BIP

Southwark, Eng. Globe Theatre.

SMITH, Irwin, 1892- 725.822
Shakespeare's Globe Playhouse; a modern reconstruction in text and scale drawings, by Irwin Smith. Based upon the reconstruction of the Globe by John Cranford Adams. Introd. by James G. McManaway. New York, Scribners [1962, c.1956] xxiii, 240p. illus. (pt. col.) 26cm. Bibl. 10.00
1. Southwark, Eng. Globe Theatre. I. Adams, John Cranford, 1903- II. Title.

SMITH, Irwin, 1892- 725.822
Shakespeare's Globe Playhouse; a modern reconstruction in text and scale drawings, by Irwin Smith. Based upon the reconstruction of the Globe by John Cranford Adams. With an introd. by James G. McManaway. New York, Scribner [1956] xxiii, 240 p. illus., plans (part col.) 26 cm. Erratum slip inserted. Bibliography: p. 225-228. [NA6840.G7S5] 56-6150
1. Southwark, Eng. Globe Theatre. I. Adams, John Cranford, 1903- II. Title. BIP

Southwest New—Antiq.

BRETERNITZ, David A. 917.91'03
An appraisal of tree-ring dated pottery in the Southwest [by] David A. Breternitz. Tuccon, Univ. of Ariz. Pr. [c.1966] vii, 128p. illus., map. 27cm. (Anthropological paps. of the Univ. of Ariz., no. 10) Based on a thesis, Univ. of Ariz., Tucson. Bibl. [E78.S7B7] 66-64118 5.00 pap.,
1. Southwest New—Antiq. 2. Indians of North America—Southwest, New—Antiq. 3. Indians of North America—Pottery. 4. Dendrochronology. I. Title. II. Series: Arizona. University. Anthropological papers, no. 10

Southwest, New—Description and travel—Views.

HINE, Robert V., 1921- 760'.09791
Bartlett's West; drawing the Mexican boundary [by] Robert V. Hine. New Haven, Published for the Amon Carter Museum, Fort Worth [by] Yale University Press, 1968. xv, 155 p. illus. (part col.), map, col. port. 19 x 26 cm. (Yale Western Americana series, 19) The illustrations are chiefly from the John Russell Bartlett papers in the John Carter Brown Library, Brown University. Bibliography: p. 95-96. [ND1839.B3H5] 68-13910
1. Bartlett, John Russell, 1805-1886. 2. Southwest, New—Description and travel—Views. I. Amon Carter Museum of Western Art, Fort Worth, Tex. II. Brown University. John Carter Brown Library. III. Title. IV. Series. BIP

VROMAN, Adam Clark, 1856-1916. 779.9979
Photographer of the Southwest, Adam Clark Vroman, 1856-1916. Edited by Ruth I. Mahood, with the assistance of Robert A. Weinstein. Introd. by Beaumont Marshall. [Los Angeles] Ward Ritchie Press, 1961. 127 p. (chiefly illus., plates, ports.) 30 cm. Bibliographical footnotes. [TM140.V7A3] 61-17935
1. Southwest, New—Description and travel—Views. I. Mahood, Ruth Ione, ed. II. Title.

Southwest, New, in art.

BABBITT, Bruce E. 759.13
Color and light; the southwest canvases of Louis Akin, by Bruce E. Babbitt. [1st ed.] Flagstaff, Ariz., Northland Press [1973] xiv, 76 p. illus. 27 cm. Bibliography: p. 75-76. [ND237.A28B32] 73-79778 ISBN 0-87358-111-3 12.50
1. Akin, Louis, 1868-1913. 2. Southwest, New, in art. I. Title.

CISNEROS, Jose, 1910- 741.9'73
Faces of the borderlands : twenty-one drawings / by Jose Cisneros, with text by the artist. [El Paso] : Texas Western Press, c1977. [58] p. : ill. ; 23 cm. (Southwestern studies ; monograph no. 52) Bibliography: p. [58] [NC139.C56A45] 77-359189 ISBN 0-87404-111-2 : 3.00
1. Cisneros, Jose, 1910- 2. Southwest, New, in art. I. Title. II. Series: Southwestern studies (El Paso, Tex.) ; monograph no. 52. BIP

MILLS, Donald, 1896- 741.9'73
Southwest impressions, by Mills. Glorieta, N.M., Rio Grande Press [1973] 125 p. (chiefly illus., part col.) 29 cm. [NC139.M54A55] 73-17268 ISBN 0-87380-090-7 10.00
1. Mills, Donald, 1896- 2. Southwest, New, in art. I. Title.

NESTLER, Al. 917.91'04
Al Nestler's Southwest; the rugged and beautiful Southwest, interpreted by one of Arizona's foremost painters. With a pref. by Robert McLeod. Flagstaff, Ariz., Northland Press, 1970. xii, 92 p. plates (part col.) 24 x 29 cm. [ND237.N447A4] 70-121017 ISBN 0-87358-052-4 12.50
1. Southwest, New, in art. I. Title. BIP

PURCELL, Roy, 1936- 769'.92'4
The wayfarer : poetry and etchings / by Roy Purcell. Millbrae, Calif. : Celestial Arts, 1975. [96] p. : ill. ; 22 cm. [NE2012.P87A58] 74-25836 ISBN 0-89087-007-1 : 4.95
1. Purcell, Roy, 1936- 2. Southwest, New, in art. 3. Self-realization in art. I. Title.

ROGERS, Charles B., 1911- 759.13
Images of the American West : paintings and haiku / Charles B. Rogers. Millbrae, Calif. : Celestial Arts, 1975. 126 p. : ill. ; 14 x 22 cm. [NX512.R63A47] 74-25838 ISBN 0-89087-010-1 pbk. : 3.95
1. Rogers, Charles B., 1911- 2. Southwest, New, in art. I. Title.

Southworth, Albert Sands, 1811-1894.

SOBIESZEK, Robert A., 1943- 779'.2'0924
The spirit of fact : the daguerreotypes of Southworth & Hawes, 1843-1862 / Robert A. Sobieszek and Odette M. Appel ; with research assistance by Charles R. Moore. Boston : D. R. Godine, c1976. xxv, 163 p. : ill. ; 28 x 32 cm. Catalogue of an exhibition held at the International Museum of Photography at the George Eastman House, Rochester, Feb.-June 1976; at the National Portrait Gallery, Washington, July-Dec. 1976; and at the Museum of Fine Arts, Boston, Jan.-Feb. 1977. Bibliography: p. 161-163. [TR365.S6] 75-43054 ISBN 0-87923-179-3 : 27.50
1. Southworth, Albert Sands, 1811-1894. 2. Hawes, Josiah Johnson, 1808-1901. 3. Daguerreotype—Exhibitions. I. Appel, Odette M., joint author. II. Moore, Charles R. III. International Museum of Photography at George Eastman House. IV. National Portrait Gallery, Washington, D.C. V. Boston. Museum of Fine Arts. VI. Title. BIP

Soutine, Haim, 1894-1943.

COGNIAT, Raymond, 1896- 759.4
Soutine. [Translated by Eileen B. Hennessy] New York, Crown [1974, c1973] 87 p. illus. (part col.) 29 cm. Bibliography: p. 83. [ND553.S7C6213] 73-84255 ISBN 0-517-51136-3 3.95
1. Soutine, Haim, 1894-1943. BIP

NEW York (City) Museum of Modern Art. 759.4
Soutine, by Monroe Wheeler. New York, Museum of Modern Art, in collaboration with the Cleveland Museum of Art [1950] 115 p. illus., col. plates, ports. 26 cm. "Catalog of the exhibition" p. 112-114. Bibliography, by H. B. Muller: p. 114-115. [ND553.S7N4] 927.5 50-11267
1. Soutine, Haim, 1894-1943. 2. Paintings, French—Exhibitions. I. Cleveland Museum of Art. II. Wheeler, Monroe, 1899-

SOUTINE, Haim, 1894-1943. 759.4
Chaim Soutine, 1893-1943 by Maurice Tuchman. [Los Angeles] Los Angeles County Museum of Art [1968] 152 p. 116 illus. (part col.), ports. 28 cm. Catalog of an exhibition held Feb. 20 to April 14, 1968, at the Los Angeles County Museum of Art. Bibliography: p. 146-150. [ND553.S7T8] 68-17297
I. Tuchman, Maurice. II. Los Angeles Co., Calif. Museum, Los Angeles.

SOUTINE, Haim, 1894-1943. 759.4
Soutine. [Introd.] by Marcellin Castaing and [text by] Jean Leymarie. [Translated by John Ross] New York, Abrams, [1964] 93 p. illus. (part mounted col.) facsims., ports. 36 cm. ([The Library of great painters]) Bibliography: p. 93. [ND553.S7C3] 64-11572
I. Castaing, Marcellin. II. Leymarie, Jean.

WERNER, Alfred, 1911- 759.4
Chaim Soutine / text by Alfred Werner. New York : H. N. Abrams, 1977. 167 p. : ill. (some col.) ; 34 cm. (The Library of great painters) Includes index. Bibliography: p. 163. [ND553.S7W4] 77-1249 ISBN 0-8109-0468-3 : 25.00
1. Soutine, Haim, 1894-1943. 2. Painters—France—Biography. I. Soutine, Haim, 1894-1943.

WHEELER, Monroe, 1899- 759.4
Soutine. [New York] Published for the Museum of Modern Art by Arno Press, 1966 [c1950] 115, [1] p. illus., port. 27 cm. Prepared for a loan exhibition held at the Museum of Modern Art, New York, Oct. 31, 1950 to Jan. 7, 1951, and at the Cleveland Museum of Art, Jan. 30 to Mar. 18, 1951. "Catalog of the exhibition": p. 112-114. Bibliography: p. 114-[116] [ND553] 66-26125
1. Soutine, Haim, 1894-1943. I. New York (City) Museum of Modern Art. II. Cleveland Museum of Art. BIP

Souvenirs (Keepsakes)—Collectors and collecting.

HENDERSON, Ian Thomson. 738'.0941
Pictorial souvenirs of Britain / [by] Ian T. Henderson. Newton Abbot ; North Pomfret, Vt. : David & Charles, 1974 [i.e.,1975] 160 p. : ill. ; 25 cm. Includes index. [NK4230.H46] 74-83321 ISBN 0-7153-6660-2 : 15.95
1. Souvenirs (Keepsakes)—Collectors and collecting. 2. Pottery—Collectors and collecting. 3. Porcelain—Collectors and collecting. 4. Great Britain in art. I. Title. BIP

Sovereign (Coin)

DUVEEN, Geoffrey Edgar, Sir 1883- 737.4942
The history of the gold sovereign [by] Geoffrey Duveen, H. G. Stride. New York, Oxford [c.]1962. 112p. illus. 22cm. Bibl. 62-4674 4.80
1. Sovereign (Coin) I. Stride, H. G., joint author. II. Title. III. Title: The gold sovereign.

Soyer, Raphael, 1899—

GOODRICH, Lloyd, 1897- 759.13
Raphael Soyer. New York, Published for the Whitney Museum of American Art by F. A. Praeger [1967] 77 p. illus. (part col.) 28 cm. "Published on the occasion of the ... retrospective exhibition of Raphael Soyer's work, organized by the Whitney Museum of American Art in the fall of 1967, and shown ... in six other museums." Bibliography: p. 72-74. [ND237.S636G6] 67-28775
1. Soyer, Raphael, 1899- I. Whitney Museum of American Art, New York.

SOYER, Raphael, 1899- 759.13 B
Diary of an artist / by Raphael Soyer. Washington : New Republic Books, c1977. p. cm. [ND237.S636A226] 77-4798 ISBN 0-915220-29-6 : 15.00
1. Soyer, Raphael, 1899- 2. Painters—United States—Biography. I. Title. BIP

SOYER, Raphael, 1899- 760'.0924
Drawings and watercolors. [Text] by Joseph K. Foster. New York, Crown Publishers [1968] 26 p., 124 plates (part col.) illus., port. 29 cm. [NC1075.S713F6] 68-29114 10.00
I. Foster, Joseph K.

SOYER, Raphael, 1899- 759.13
Paintings and drawings. Text by Walter K. Gutman. Pref. by Jerome Klein. Comments on art by Raphael Soyer. New York, Shorewood Pub. Co. [1961] 192 p. illus. plates (part col.) 29 cm. Label mounted on t. p.: New York. Tudor Pub. Co. [ND237.S636G8] 60-53512
I. Gutman, Walter Knowlton, 1903- II. Title.

SOYER, Raphael, 1899- 769'.924 (B)
Raphael Soyer; fifty years of printmaking, 1917-1967. Edited by Sylvan Cole, Jr. With a foreword by Jacob Kainen. New York, Da Capo Press, 1967. xiii, 257 p. illus. 29 cm. [NE539.S6C6] 67-29917
I. Cole, Sylvan, ed. II. Title.

SOYER, Raphael, 1899- 759.13
Raphael Soyer, by Lloyd Goodrich. New York, H. N. Abrams [1972] 349 p. illus. (part col.) 39 cm. Bibliography: p. 339-342. [ND237.S636G62] 72-2169 ISBN 0-8109-0486-1 50.00
I. Goodrich, Lloyd, 1897-

SOYER, Raphael, 1899- 741.9'73
Raphael Soyer; an exhibition of drawings and watercolors, 5 May through 5 June 1968. Athens, Georgia Museum of Art, the University of Georgia [1968] 1 v. (unpaged) illus. 28 cm. [NC139.S633G46] 74-187164
1. Soyer, Raphael, 1899- I. Georgia Museum of Art.

SOYER, Raphael, 1899- 769'.924 B
Raphael Soyer; fifty years of printmaking, 1917-1967. Edited by Sylvan Cole, Jr. With a foreword by Jacob Kainen. New York, Da Capo Press, 1967. xiii, 257 p. illus. 29 cm. [NE539.S6C6] 67-29917
I. Cole, Sylvan, ed.

SOYER, Raphael, 1899- 759.13
Self-revealment; a memoir. New York, Maecenas Press [1969] 116, [3] p. illus. (part col.) 30 cm. "Books about Raphael Soyer": p. [119] [ND237.S636A24] 74-85582 2.50
I. Title.

Space (Architecture)

ASHIHARA, Yoshinobu, 1918- 729
Exterior design in architecture. New York, Van Nostrand Reinhold [1970] 143 p. illus., plans. 26 cm. Includes bibliographical references. [NA2765.A8] 72-90317
1. Space (Architecture) 2. Architectural design. I. Title.

GIEDION, Sigfried, 1888-1968. 729'.1
Architecture and the phenomena of transition; the three space conceptions in architecture. Cambridge, Mass., Harvard University Press, 1971. 311 p. illus. (part col.), plans. 26 cm. Translation of Architektur und das Phanomen des Wandels. Includes bibliographical references. [NA2765.G513 1971] 71-95921 ISBN 0-674-04337-5 18.50
1. Space (Architecture) 2. Architecture—Composition, proportion, etc. I. Title.

HEJDUK, John, 1929- 729
Three projects. [New York] Cooper Union School of Art and Architecture [1969] 1 case ([11] p., 24 plates (2 col.)) 47 cm. Caption title. "Copies: 500." [NA2765.H45] 72-169238
1. Space (Architecture) 2. Architecture—Designs and plans. I. Title.

LAM, William M. C. 729'.28
Perception and lighting as formgivers for architecture / William M. C. Lam ; edited by Christopher Hugh Ripman. New York : McGraw-Hill, c1977. ix, 310 p. : ill. (some col.) ; 29 cm. Includes index. Bibliography: p. 302-307. [NA2765.L35] 76-2554 ISBN 0-07-036094-4 : 32.50
1. Space (Architecture) 2. Visual perception. 3. Light in architecture. I. Title. BIP

MOORE, Charles Willard, 1925- 729
Dimensions : space, shape & scale in architecture / Charles Moore, Gerald Allen. New York : Architectural Record Books, c1976. viii, 183 p. : ill. ; 24 cm. Includes bibliographical references and index. [NA2765.M66] 76-28406 ISBN 0-07-002336-0 12.95
1. Space (Architecture) 2. Architecture—Composition, proportion, etc. 3. Visual perception. 4. Harmony (Aesthetics) I. Allen, Gerald, joint author. II. Title.
Distributed by McGraw Hill BIP

NORBERG-SCHULZ, Christian. 720'.1
Existence, space & architecture. New York, Praeger [1971] 120 p. illus., plans. 22 cm. Bibliography: p. 116-118. [NA2765.N67 1971] 70-128598 7.50
1. Space (Architecture) I. Title.

SEVERINO, Renato. 729'.23
Equipotential space; freedom in architecture. New York, Praeger [1970] vii, 141 p. illus., plans. 25 cm. [NA2765.S48 1970] 70-124863 12.50
1. Space (Architecture) 2. Modular coordination (Architecture) I. Title. BIP

STIBBS, Richard. 729'.28
The prediction of surface luminances in architectural space / [by] Richard Stibbs ; ... prepared under the sponsorship of the Department of Health and Social Security. Cambridge (16 Brooklands Ave., Cambridge) : University of Cambridge Department of Architecture, 1971. [5], 18 p. : ill. ; 30 cm. (Land use and built form studies : working paper ; no. 54) Includes bibliographical references. [NA2765.S84] 75-309533 ISBN 0-903248-40-9 : £0.50
1. Space (Architecture) 2. Light in architecture. 3. Architecture—Mathematical models. I. Title. II. Series.

UNITED States. 725'.1'0973
General Accounting Office.
Need for improving reviews of designs of Federal buildings to achieve better utilization of space; report to the Congress [on the] Public Buildings Service, General Services Administration by the Comptroller General of the United States. [Washington] 1968. 19 p. 27 cm. Cover title. "B-156512." Publication date stamped on t.p. [NA4208.A39] 68-61618
1. United States. Public Buildings Service. 2. United States. General Services Administration. Washington National Records Center. 3. Space (Architecture) I. Title.

ZEVI, Bruno, 1918- 720
Architecture as space; how to look at architecture. Edited by Joseph A. Barry; translated by Milton Gendel. New York, Horizon Press [1957] 288 p. illus., diagrs., plans. 26 cm. Translation of Saper vedere l'architettura. Bibliography: p. 245-271. [NA2500.Z413] 57-7362
1. Space (Architecture) I. Title. BIP

Space (Architecture)—Computer programs.

LEE, Kaiman. 729'.028'54
Evaluation, synthesis, and development of an interactive approach to space allocation / by Kaiman Lee. Boston : Environmental Design & Research Center, [1974] 45 leaves ; 29 cm. Cover title: Interactive space allocation. Bibliography: leaf 45. [NA2765.L43] 74-187884 12.00
1. Space (Architecture)—Computer programs. I. Title. II. Title: Interactive space allocation.

LEE, Kaiman. 729'.028'54
Evaluation, systhesis, and development of an interactive approach to space allocation / by Kaiman Lee. 2d ed. Boston : Environmental Design & Research Center, c1975. 56 leaves : ill. ; 29 cm. Cover title: Interactive space allocation. Bibliography: leaf 51. [NA2765.L43 1975] 76-352600
1. Space (Architecture)—Computer programs. I. Title. II. Title: Interactive space allocation.

Space (Architecture)—Data processing.

LEE, Kaiman. 729'.01'83
Computer aided space planning / Kaiman Lee. Boston : Environmental Design & Research Center, c1976. 100 leaves : ill. ; 29 cm. Bibliography: leaves 98-100. [NA2728.L432] 76-366704 ISBN 0-915250-20-9 : 30.00
1. Space (Architecture)—Data processing. 2. Architectural design—Data processing. I. Title. BIP

Space (Architecture)—Philosophy.

VEN, Cornelis van de. 720'.1
Space in architecture : the evolution of a new idea in the theory and history of the modern movements / Cornelis van de Ven. Assen : Van Gorcum, 1978. xv, 278 p. : ill. ; 24 cm. Originally presented as the author's thesis, Eindhoven. Includes index. Bibliography: p. 263-269. [NA2765.V46 1978] 78-310431 ISBN 9-02-31522-2 pbk. : 22.50
1. Space (Architecture)—Philosophy. 2. Architecture, Modern—19th century—History. 3. Architecture, Modern—20th century—History. I. Title.
Distributed by Humanities Press, Atlantic Highlands, NJ BIP

Space (Art)

GOLDING, John. 730'.92'4
Boccioni's Unique forms of continuity in space. [Newcastle upon Tyne] University of Newcastle upon Tyne, 1972. 32 p. illus. 25 cm. (Charlton lecture 54) Includes bibliographical references. [NB623.B65G64] 73-168650 £1.00
1. Boccioni, Umberto, 1882-1916. 2. Space (Art) I. Title. II. Series.

HARBISON, Robert. 700
Eccentric spaces / Robert Harbison. 1st ed. New York : Knopf, 1977. xii, 177 p. ; 25 cm. Includes bibliographical references and index. [NX650.S8H37 1977] 76-24460 ISBN 0-394-40719-9 : 8.95
1. Space (Art) 2. Arts. I. Title. BIP

MCLUHAN, Herbert Marshall. 700'.1
Through the vanishing point; space in poetry and painting [by] Marshall McLuhan and Harley Parker. [1st ed.] New York, Harper & Row [1968] xxiv, 267 p. illus. 22 cm. (World perspectives, v. 37) [NX650.S8M32] 68-15964
1. Space (Art) 2. Arts. I. Parker, Harley, joint author. II. Title. III. Series. BIP

WINTER, John F. 700'.944
Visual variety and spatial grandeur; a study of the transition from the sixteenth to the seventeenth century in France, by John F. Winter. Chapel Hill, U.N.C. Dept. of Romance Languages; [distributed by International Scholarly Book Service, Portland, Or.] 1974. 126 p. illus. 23 cm. (North Carolina studies in the Romance languages and literatures, no. 140) Includes bibliographical references. [NX549.A1W56] 74-10611 ISBN 0-88438-940-5
1. Space (Art) 2. Arts, Renaissance—France. 3. Arts, Baroque—France. 4. Arts—France. I. Title. II. Series. BIP

Space (Art)—Juvenile literature.

BROMMER, Gerald F. 701'.8
Space / Gerald F. Brommer. Worcester, Mass. : Davis Publications, [1974] 80 p. : ill. ; 26 cm. (Elements of design) Includes index. Text and photographs explore spatial concepts and ways in which one may become aware of and use space as a design element. [N7430.7.B76] 75-321020 ISBN 0-87192-062-X
1. Space (Art)—Juvenile literature. 2. Visual perception—Juvenile literature. I. Title. II. Series. BIP

KAMPMANN, Lothar. 709'.04
Creating with space and construction. New York, Van Nostrand Reinhold [1973] 76 p. illus. (part col.) 21 cm. (Art media series) Translation of Raume und Konstruktionen. Explains the fundamental concepts of space and three-dimensional structure and suggests a variety of projects using simple materials. [N7430.7.K3513] 72-2791 ISBN 0-442-24248-4 5.95
1. Space (Art)—Juvenile literature. I. Title.

Space frame structures.

INTERNATIONAL Conference on Space Structures, University of Surrey, 1966. 721
Space structures; a study of methods and developments in three-dimensional construction. Edited by R. M. Davies. New York, Wiley [1967] xviii, 1233 p. illus. 31 cm. English or French. Includes bibliographies. [TH1635.I5 1966ab] 68-4691 ISBN 0-632-01230-7
1. Space frame structures. I. Davies, Robert Mervyn, ed.

Space-perception.

SPAZIO dell'immagine (Lo) 701.8
[di] Umbro Apollonio [et al. Venezia] Alfieri edizioni d arte Stamped on t.p.: American dist.: Wittenborn, N.Y. [1967] 116p. illus. 23x24cm. Page [4] of cover has title: The space of image. Italian and English. Questo libro e stato realizzato in occasione della mostra 'Lo spazio dell'immagine' che e aperta dal 2 luglio at

1 ottobre 1967 a Palazzo Trici, Foligno. sotto gli auspici dell'Azienda autonoma di soggiorno. Notizie sugli artisti p. 109-116) in Italian only. p5.00 pap., [N7430.S67] 67-68445
1. Space-perception. 2. Art—Technique. I. Apollonio, Umbro, 1911- II. Title: The space of image.

Space perception—Bibliography.

BARTHOLOMEW, Robert.   016.3092 s
Spatial perception of the physical environment / Robert Bartholomew. Monticello, Ill. : Council of Planning Librarians, 1976. 15 p. ; 28 cm. (Exchange bibliography ; 1047) Cover title. [Z5942.C68 no. 1047] [Z7204.S76] [BF469] 153.7'52 77-372933 1.50
1. Space perception—Bibliography. 2. Environmental psychology. I. Title. II. Series: Council of Planning Librarians. Exchange bibliography ; 1047.

Space photography.

DICKSON, Paul.   778.3'5
Out of this world / by Paul Dickson. New York : Delacorte Press, c1977. p. cm. [TR713.D5] 77-21740 ISBN 0-440-06568-2 : 19.95
1. Space photography. I. Title.   BIP

GENERAL Electric   778.3'53
Company. Missile and Space Division.
Photographs from space. [Philadelphia, General Electric, Valley Forge Space Technology Center, 1967] 87 p. (chiefly illus.) 22 cm. Cover title. [TR713.G4] 70-3892
1. Space photography. I. Title.

Spain—Description and travel—1951- —Views.

CHRISTOPHER, Peter.   779'.9'946
Images of Spain / photos. by Peter Christopher ; text by Mordecai Richler. New York : Norton, c1977. 191 p. : ill. : 32 cm. [DP22.C52] 77-153476 27.50
1. Spain—Description and travel—1951- —Views. I. Richler, Mordecai, 1931- II. Title.

Spain—Hist.—Napoleonic Conquest, 1808-1813—Pictorial works.

GOYA y Lucientes,   769'.924
Francisco Jose de, 1746-1828
The disasters of war. New introd. by Philip Hofer. New York, Dover [1967] 12p. 83 plates. 21 x 24cm. Tr. of Los desastres de la guerra. With 3 extra plates and some new material. [NE2195.G78D43 1967] 67-15964 1.75 pap.,
1. Spain—Hist.—Napoleonic Conquest, 1808-1813—Pictorial works. I. Title.   BIP

GOYA y Lucientes,   769'.924
Francisco Jose de, 1746-1828
The disasters of war. New introd. by Philip Hofer [Magnolia Mass., Peter Smith 1968] 12p. 83 plates. 21x24cm. (Dover bk. rebound) Tr. of Los desastres de la guerra. With 3 extra plates and some new material [NE2195.G78D43 1967] 4.00
1. Spain—Hist.—Napoleonic Conquest, 1808-1813—Pictorial works. I. Title.

Spain—History—Pictorial works.

SMITH, Bradley.   759.6
Spain; a history in art. New York, Simon and Schuster, 1966. 296 p. col. illus. 33 cm. (A Gemini book) Bibliography: p. 294-296. [N7101.S55] 66-19432
1. Spain—History—Pictorial works. 2. Art, Spanish—History. I. Title.

SMITH, Bradley.   759.6
Spain, a history in art. Garden City, N.Y., Doubleday [1971] 296 p. col. illus. 33 cm. (A Gemini-Smith book) Bibliography: p. 294-296. [N7101.S55 1971] 70-27089
1. Spain—History—Pictorial works. 2. Art, Spanish—History. I. Title.

Spanish America—Intellectual life— Congresses.

TEXAS. University. College   709.8
of Fine Arts.
Proceedings of the conference on Latin-American fine arts, June 14-17, 1951. Cosponsored by the College of Fine Arts and the Institute of Latin-American Studies, the University of Texas. Austin, University of Texas Press, 1952. xi, 132p. illus., ports. 24cm. (Latin-American studies, 13) Bibliographical footnotes. [F1401.T45 no.13] 53-62101
1. Spanish America—Intellectual life—Congresses. I. Texas. University.Institute of Latin-American Studies. II. Title. III. Series: Texas. University. Institute of Latin-American Studies. Latin-American studies, 13

Spanish missions of California — Views.

DEAKIN, Edwin.   759.13
A gallery of California mission paintings. Edited by Ruth I. Mahood. Additional texts by Paul Mills and Donald C. Cutter. Produced by the staff of the History Division, Los Angeles County Museum of Natural History. Los Angeles, W. Ritchie Press, 1966. 58 p. col. illus. 21 x 24 cm. (Los Angeles County Museum of Natural History. History Division. Bulletin no. 3) [F862.M6D4] 66-265194
1. Spanish missions of California — Views. I. Mills, Paul Chadbourne, 1924- II. Cutter, Donald C. III. Mahood, Ruth Ione, ed. IV. Title. V. Series. VI. Series: Los Angeles Co., Calif. Museum of Natura History. History Division. Bulletin no. 3

Spanish missions of Texas—Views.

SCHIWETZ, Edward Muegge,   759.13
1898-
Six Spanish missions in Texas; a portfolio of paintings by E. M. Schiwetz. Historical notes by Robert S. Weddle. Austin, University of Texas Press [1968] 1 portfolio ([4] p., 6 col. plates) 58 cm. [ND237.S4312W4] 68-23428
1. Spanish missions of Texas—Views. I. Weddle, Robert S.

Spatialism (Art)—Exhibitions.

AMERICAN Federation of   759.13
Arts.
Inverse illusionism. [Edited by Catherine M. Perebinossoff. New York, 1971] [16] p. illus. 23 cm. "AFA exhibition number 71-10." [ND212.5.S6A7] 75-169112
1. Spatialism (Art)—Exhibitions. 2. Painting, Modern—20th century—U.S. I. Perebinossoff, Catherine M., ed. II. Title.   BIP

BLACK, Carl, 1938-   759.3
Two visions of space: Herbert Bayer [and] Ingeborg Ten Haeff. [Yonkers, N.Y., 1969] [40] p. illus., ports. 22 cm. Cover title. Exhibition held Nov. 9-Dec. 7, 1969 at the Hudson River Museum. [N6494.S7B55] 73-22757
1. Bayer, Herbert, 1900- 2. Ten Haeff, Ingeborg. 3. Spatialism (Art)—Exhibitions. I. Hudson River Museum at Yonkers, Yonkers, N.Y. II. Title.

CORCORAN Gallery   709'.73'0740153
of Art, Washington, D.C.
Andre, Leva, Long : [catalogue of the exhibition], Corcoran Gallery of Art, December 11, 1976-January 30, 1977. [Washington] : The Gallery, [1977] 32 p. : ill. ; 22 x 27 cm. Includes bibliographies. [N6494.S7C67 1977] 77-73028
1. Andre, Carl, 1935- 2. Leva, Barry, 1941- 3. Long, Richard. 4. Spatialism (Art)—Exhibitions. I. Title.

LICHT, Jennifer.   730'.922
Spaces. New York, Museum of Modern Art [1969] [36] p. illus. 22 x 28 cm. Catalog of the exhibition held Dec. 30, 1969-Mar. 1, 1970, at the Museum of Modern Art, New York. Includes bibliographical references. [N6494.S7L5] 72-100678
1. Spatialism (Art)—Exhibitions. I. New York. Museum of Modern Art. II. Title.

Speed Art Museum, Louisville, Ky.

BUTLER, Reginald Cotterell,   579.9
1913-
Reg Butler; a retrospective exhibition: J. B. Speed Art Museum, Louisville, Kentucky, October 22 through December 1, 1963. [Louisville, 1963] c1 v. (unpaged) illus., ports. 28 cm. Includes bibliography. [NB497.B8A55] 67-7785 94
1. Speed Art Museum, Louisville, Ky. I. Title.

SPEED Art Museum,   708'.169'44
Louisville, Ky.
J. B. Speed Art Museum handbook. [Edited by John F. Martin. Louisville, Ky., 1973] 160 p. illus. 22 cm. [N582.L8A58] 73-161440 2.75
1. Speed Art Museum, Louisville, Ky. I. Martin, John Franklin, 1948- II. Title.

Speicher, Eugene Edward, 1883-

BUFFALO Fine Arts Academy.   759.13
Eugene Speicher; a retrospective exhibition of oils and drawings, 1908-1949. September 29-October 26, 1950. Buffalo, Buffalo Fine Arts Academy, Albright Art Gallery [1950] 26 p. 23 plates. 26 cm. "Eugene Speicher," by Charles E. Burchfield": p. 9-12. Catalogue: p. 15-23. Bibliography: p. 14. [ND237.S64B8] 51-823
1. Speicher, Eugene Edward, 1883- 2. Paintings, American—Exhibitions. 3. Drawings, American—Exhibitions. I. Title.

Speight, Francis, 1896—

NORTH Carolina. Museum of   759.13
Art, Raleigh.
Francis Speight; a retrospective exhibition, February 16-March 26, 1961. Raleigh [1961] [40]p. illus., port. 26cm. [ND237.S643N6] 61-63138
1. Speight, Francis, 1896- I. Title.

Spencer, Stanley, 1891-1959.

ROTHENSTEIN, Elizabeth   759.42
(Smith)
Stanley Spencer. [London, Beaverbrook Newspapers, Chester Springs, Pa., Dufour, 1966, c.1962] 1 v. (unpaged) illus., col. plates. 36cm. ([British painters ser., Express art bk]) Caption title. [ND497.S75R58] 66-3361 6.00 bds.,
1. Spencer, Stanley, 1891-1959. I. Title.

Spencer, Stanley, Sir, 1891-1959.

CARLINE, Richard.   759.2 B
Stanley Spencer at war / Richard Carline. London ; Boston : Faber and Faber, 1978. 224 p : ill. ; 23 cm. Includes bibliographical references and index. [ND497.S75C37] 79-300467 ISBN 0-571-11028-2 : 21.95
1. Spencer, Stanley, Sir, 1891-1959. 2. Painters—Great Britain—Biography. I. Title.
Dist. by merrimack, Salem, NH 03079   BIP

SPENCER, Stanley, Sir,   741.9'42
1891-1959.
Stanley Spencer, the Astor Collection / [text] by Carolyn Leder. London : Thomas Gibson Publishing Ltd., 1976. 103 p. : chiefly ill. ; 31 cm. Bibliography: p. 17-20. [NC242.S65L42 1976] 77-361637
1. Spencer, Stanley, Sir, 1891-1959. 2. Astor, William Waldorf, 3d Viscount Astor, 1907-1966—Art collections. I. Leder, Carolyn.

Sperakis, Nicholas, 1943—

SPERAKIS, Nicholas,   769'.92'4
1943-
Woodcuts / Nicholas Sperakis. New York : Smyrna Press, c1976. 94 p. : chiefly ill. ; 28 cm. [NE1112.S68A58] 76-380368 3.95
1. Sperakis, Nicholas, 1943- I. Title.   BIP

Sperry, Mrs. Leonard M.—Art collections.

NATZLER, Otto.   738'.0922
Gertrud and Otto Natzler: ceramics. Catalog of the Collection of Mrs. Leonard M. Sperry, and a monograph, by Otto Natzler. [Los Angeles] Los Angeles County Museum of Art, 1968. 80 p. illus., col. plates. 28 cm. Cover title: Natzler ceramics. [NK4200.N32] 68-57263
1. Sperry, Mrs. Leonard M.—Art collections. I. Natzler, Gertrud. II. Los Angeles Co., Calif. Museum of Art, Los Angeles. III. Title.

Spinning.

FANNIN, Allen.   746.1'2
Handspinning art & technique. New York, Van Nostrand Reinhold [1970] 208 p. illus. 27 cm. [TS1480.F35] 76-126872
1. Spinning. I. Title.

Spiral Press inc., New York.

BLUMENTHAL,   338.7'65'557074
Joseph, 1897-
The Spiral Press; an exhibition of selected books and ephemera designed and printed at the Spiral Press in New York from 1926 to 1968. With an introductory commentary by Joseph Blumenthal. [New York, 1968] 38, [31] p. illus. 28 cm. "Shown at the Royal Library of Belgium in Brussels, May-June 1968, and at the Meermanno-Westreenianum Museum in The Hague, September-October 1968." [Z232.S75B55] 68-20133
1. Spiral Press inc., New York. 2. Bibliographical exhibitions. I. Spiral Press, inc., New York. II. Brussels. Bibliotheque royale de Belgique. III. Hague. Museum Meermanno-Westreenianum.

Spiro Mound.

HAMILTON, Henry W.   739'.511
Spiro Mound copper / by Henry W. Hamilton, Jean Tyree Hamilton, Eleanor F. Chapman. [Columbia] : Missouri Archaeological Society, 1974. xii, 212 p. : ill. ; 23 cm. (Memoir - Missouri Archaeological Society ; no. 11) Bibliography: p. 194-200. [E78.M8M48a no. 11] [E78.O45] 74-31740
1. Spiro Mound. 2. Indians of North America—Southern States—Metal-work. 3. Caddoan Indians—Metal-work. I. Hamilton, Jean Tyree, joint author. II. Chapman, Eleanor F., joint author. III. Title. IV. Series: Missouri. State Archaeological Society. Memoir ; no. 11.

HOUSTON, Tex. Museum of   970.466
Fine Arts
Spiro and Mississippian antiquities from the McDannald Collection [Catalogue. Houston, Tex., Author [1965] 58p. illus., map (on lining papers) 18cm. [E78.S65H65] 65-24455 3.00 pap.,
1. Spiro Mound. 2. Southern States—Antiq. 3. Indians of North America—Southern States—Antiq. I. Title.

Spiro site, Okla.

PHILLIPS, Philip, 1900-   736'.6
Pre-Columbian shell engravings : from the Craig Mound at Spiro, Oklahoma / Philip Phillips, James A. Brown, with the collaboration of Eliza McFadden, Barbara C. Page, and Jeffrey P. Brain. Cambridge, Mass. : Peabody Museum Press, 1978 v. : ill. ; 47 cm. Includes index. [E78.O45P44] 74-77557 ISBN 0-87365-777-2 lib.bdg. : 180.00 pbk. : 25.00
1. Spiro site, Okla. 2. Indians of North America—Oklahoma—Shell engraving. 3. Shell engraving—Oklahoma. I. Brown, James Allison, 1934- joint author. II. Title.

Spitzweg, Karl, 1808-1885.

SPITZWEG, Karl, 1808-1885.   759.3
Carl Spitzweg / hrsg. von Siegfried Wichmann ; [translation into English by Hannelore Koob and Anneliese Klein, traduction francaise par Denise Baumann]. New York : Rizzoli, [c1976] 97 p. : chiefly ill. (some col.) ; 25 cm. English, French,

and German. [ND588.S6W45 1976b] 77-353152 ISBN 0-8478-0028-8 : 16.50
1. Spitzweg, Karl, 1808-1885. I. Wichmann, Siegfried, 1921-

Spode family.

BEDFORD, John, 1907- 738.2'7
Old Spode china. New York, Walker [1969] 64 p. illus. (part col.), facsims. 20 cm. (Collectors' pieces 17) [NK4087.S6B38 1969] 72-84598 3.50
1. Spode family. 2. Staffordshire pottery. I. Title.

WHITER, Leonard. 738.2'7
Spode; a history of the family, factory, and wares from 1733 to 1833. New York, Praeger [1970] xiii, 246 p. illus., facsims., col. plates, ports. 29 cm. Includes bibliographical references. [NK4087.S6W48 1970] 72-116641 32.50
1. Spode family. 2. Staffordshire pottery. I. Title.

Sponged ware—Collectors and collecting.

ROBACKER, Earl Francis. 738.3'7
Spatterware and sponge : hardy perennials of ceramics / by Earl F. and Ada F. Robacker. South Brunswick [N.J.] : A. S. Barnes, c1978. p. cm. Includes index. Bibliography: p. [NK4340.S65R62] 77-74112 ISBN 0-498-02086-X : 20.00
1. Sponged ware—Collectors and collecting. I. Robacker, Ada F., 1905- joint author. II. Title. BIP

Spoons.

HARDT, Anton 739.2383
Adventuring further in souvenir spoons, with a first glimpse of the Tiffany souvenir spoons. New York, N.Y., 10014 335 Bleecker St., [Author. 1966, c.]1965. xi,107p illus. 31cm. [NK7235.H29] 65-28707 9.95
1. Spoons. 2. Silversmithing—U.S. 3. Tiffany and Company. New York. I. Title.

HARDT, Anton, comp. 739.2'3'02573
Souvenir spoons of the 90's as pictured and described in The Jeweler's circular & the James catalogue in 1891. New York, 1962. 269 p. illus. 23 cm. Facsimile reprint of Souvenir spoons of America, and of parts of G. B. James' Souvenir spoons. [NK7235.H3] 62-53506
1. Spoons. 2. Silversmithing — U.S I. James, George B., Jr. Souvenir spoons. II. The Jewelers' circular-keystone. Souvenir spoons of America. III. Title.

STUTZENBERGER, Albert, 739.2383
1901-
The American story in spoons; with an historical sketch of the spoon through the ages. [Louisville? Ky., 1953] 535p. illus. 24cm. 'A Bookmaster book.' [NK7235.S88] 53-38656
1. Spoons. 2. Silversmithing—U. S. I. Title.

Spoons, American.

HARDT, Anton. 739.2'3'83
A third harvest of souvenir spoons. New York, 1969. x, 141 p. illus. 26 cm. [NK7235.H32] 79-97010
1. Spoons, American. I. Title. BIP

RAINWATER, Dorothy T. 739.2'3'83
American spoons; souvenir and historical [by] Dorothy T. Rainwater and Donna H. Felger. [Camden, N.J.] T. Nelson [1969, c1968] 416 p. illus. (part col.) 26 cm. Bibliography: p. 412-413. [NK7235.R3] 70-77266 15.00
1. Spoons, American. 2. Spoons—Collectors and collecting. I. Felger, Donna H., joint author. BIP

Spoons—Collectors and collecting.

RAINWATER, Dorothy T. 739.2'3'83
A collector's guide to spoons around the world / by Dorothy T. Rainwater and Donna H. Felger ; photographs by H. Ivan Rainwater. Hanover, Pa. : Everybodys Press, c1976. x, 405 p. : ill. ; 27 cm. Includes index. Bibliography: p. 396-400.

[NK7235.R325] 76-46719 ISBN 0-8407-4328-9 : 19.95
1. Spoons—Collectors and collecting. I. Felger, Donna H., joint author. II. Title. BIP

Spoons—Europe.

EMERY, John. 745.1
European spoons before 1700 / [by] John Emery. Edinburgh : Donald, 1976. ix, 205 p. : ill., port. ; 26 cm. Includes index. Bibliography: p. 200-202. [NK7235.E46] 76-371999 ISBN 0-85976-012-X : £12.50
1. Spoons—Europe. I. Title.

Spoons—United States.

STUTZENBERGER, 739.2'3'773
Albert, 1901-
American historical spoons; the American story in spoons. Rutland, Vt., C.E. Tuttle Co. [1971] xviii, 535 p. illus. 23 cm. First ed., 1953, published under title: The American story in spoons. Bibliography: p. 512-530. [NK7235.S88 1971] 72-116483 ISBN 0-8048-0903-8 10.00
1. Spoons—United States. I. Title. BIP

Spoons—United States—Collectors and collecting.

†HARDT, Anton. 739.2'3'773
New discoveries in historical spoons : souvenirs of United States and Canada / by Anton Hardt. New York : Greenwich Press, c1977. xi, 175 p. : ill. ; 27 cm. Includes bibliographical references. [NK7235.H296] 77-93455 ISBN 0-911708-05-7 : 17.95
1. Spoons—United States—Collectors and collecting. 2. Spoons—Canada—Collectors and collecting. I. Title.
Publisher's address : 335 Bleecker St., NY 10014 BIP

Sporting goods.

LACEY, John L. 680
Make your own outdoor sports equipment. New York, Putnam [1955] 128 p. illus. 21 cm. [TT157.L2] 55-5785
1. Sporting goods. 2. Handicraft. I. Title. II. Title: Sports equipment.

Sporting prints.

CADFRYN-ROBERTS, John, 769.942
ed.
British sporting prints [features the work of James Pollard, F.C. Turner, Henry Alken] London, Ariel Pr. [dist. Princeton, N.J., Van Nostrand, 1965, c.1963] 13p. 24 col. plates. 25cm. (Golden Ariels, no. 2) [NE960.C3] 65-1599 3.95 bds.,
1. Sporting prints. 2. Engraving, British. I. Title.

Sporting prints, English.

WILDER, F. L. 769'.4'97960942
Sporting prints / F. L. Wilder. New York : Viking Press, 1974. 224 p. : col. ill. ; 31 cm. (A Studio book) [NE628.3.W54] 74-3519 ISBN 0-670-66474-X : 37.50
1. Sporting prints, English. I. Title.

Sports—Canada—History—Pictorial works.

DUNBAR, Nancy J. 704.94'9'7960971
Images of sport in early Canada = Images du sport dans le Canada d'autrefois / compiled by Nancy J. Dunbar ; introd. by Hugh MacLennan. Montreal : McCord Museum, McGill University, 1976. 95 p. : chiefly ill. (some col.) ; 28 cm. English and French. [GV585.D94] 76-378551 ISBN 0-7735-0246-7. ISBN 0-7735-0244-0 pbk.
1. Sports—Canada—History—Pictorial works. 2. Sports in art. I. McCord Museum. II. Title. III. Title: Images du sport dans le Canada d'autrefois. BIP

Sports in art.

BAILLIE-GROHMAN, 704.94'9'796
William Adolph, 1851-1921.
Sport in art; an iconography of sport

during four hundred years from the beginning of the fifteenth to the end of the eighteenth centuries. New York, B. Blom [1969, c1925] xxiii, 422 p. illus. 34 cm. Bibliographical footnotes. [N8250.B3 1969] 69-18532
1. Sports in art. 2. Sporting prints. I. Title.

GROTH, John, 1908- 741.9'73
John Groth's world of sport. Foreword by Arnold Gingrich. Text by Pat Smith. [New York] Winchester Press [1970] 152 p. illus. (part col.) 23 x 32 cm. [NC139.G75S6] 72-127958 ISBN 0-87691-013-4 25.00
1. Sports in art. I. Smith, Pat, 1937- II. Title. III. Title: World of sport.

NOAKES, Aubrey. 758.8
Sportsmen in a landscape. Philadelphia, Lippincott [1954] 224p. illus. (part col.) 23cm. [N8250] 54-14220
1. Sports in art. I. Title. BIP

NOAKES, Aubrey. 754
Sportsmen in a landscape. Freeport, N.Y., Books for Libraries Press [1971, c1954] 224 p. illus., ports. 23 cm. (Essay index reprint series) [ND1385.N6 1971] 72-134122 ISBN 0-8369-2005-8
1. Sports in art. 2. Landscape painting. I. Title.

REMINGTON, Frederic, 1861- 759.13
1909.
Frederic Remington's own outdoors. With an introd. by Harold McCracken. Edited by Douglas Allen. New York, Dial Press, 1964. 190 p. illus., ports. 26 cm. [ND237.R36A7] 63-19938
1. Sports in art. 2. Sports stories. I. Title.

SCOTT, Martha B. 704.94'9'796
The artist and the sportsman; catalogue, by Martha B. Scott. New York, Renaissance Editions [1968] 95 p. illus. (part col.) 26 cm. Catalogue of an exhibition of the National Art Museum of Sport, Madison Square Garden Center, Gallery of Art, New York, Apr. 18-June 16, 1968. [N8250.S36] 68-25491
1. Sports in art. 2. Art—Exhibitions. I. National Art Museum of Sport. II. Title.

SHISSLER, Barbara 704.94979
Johnson
Sports and games in art. Designed by Wendell Carroll. Minneapolis. Lerner [1966] 72p. illus. (pt. col.) 27cm. (Fine art bks. for young people) [N8250.S46] 65-29038 3.95 lib. ed.,
1. Sports in art. 2. Games in art. I. Title. BIP

SPORTS illustrated 704.949796
(Chicago)
Sport in art, from American collections assembled for an Olympic year. [New York? 1955] unpaged. illus. 23cm. Catalog of an exhibition presented by Sports illustrated and the American Federation of Arts. [N8250.S65] 57-3264
1. Sports in art. 2. Art—Exhibitions. I. American Federation of Arts. II. Title.

WALKER, Stella A. 759.2
Sporting art, England 1700-1900 [by] Stella A. Walker. New York, C. N. Potter; distributed by Crown Publishers [1972] 200 p. illus. (part col.) 30 cm. Bibliography: p. 191-192. [N6764.W3] 70-187507 15.00
1. Sports in art. 2. Art, English. 3. Art, Modern—Great Britain. I. Title.

Sprang.

COLLINGWOOD, Peter, 1922- 746.1'4
The techniques of sprang; plaiting on stretched threads. New York, Watson-Guptill Publications [1974] 292 p. illus. 25 cm. Bibliography: p. [279]-287. [TT840.C593 1974] 73-17319 ISBN 0-8230-5220-6 25.00
1. Sprang. I. Title. BIP

Spray painting.

CREWDSON, Frederick Mason, 698.1
1893-
Spray painting for the amateur, including wood finishing ... Wilmette, Ill., F. J. Drake [1952] 80 p. illus. 22 cm. (Drake's handyman series) [TT305.C83] 52-40988
1. Spray painting. I. Title.

Spreckelsen, Margrit von.

SPRECKELSEN, Margrit von. 741.943
Margrit v. Spreckelsen : Ölbilder, Zeichnungen : [Ausstellung in der Galerie Brockstedt, Hamburg, Feb.-März 1975 : Katalog]. Hamburg : Galerie Brockstedt, [1975?] [8] p., [16] leaves of plates : ill. (some col.) ; 12 x 21 cm. [ND588.S615G35] 75-504831
1. Spreckelsen, Margrit von. I. Galerie Brockstedt. II. Title.

Springfield, Ill. Bannerstone House.

CAVANAUGH, Tom R., 1923- 728.8
Bannerstone House; a Frank Lloyd Wright house, Springfield, Illinois, by Tom R. Cavanaugh and Payne E. L. Thomas. With photos. by Herbert Georg Studio. Springfield, Ill., C. C. Thomas [1970] vi, 41 p. illus., plan. 22 cm. Bibliography: p. 39-41. [NA7238.S65C3] 79-113787
1. Springfield, Ill. Bannerstone House. I. Thomas, Payne Edward Lloyd, 1919- joint author. II. Wright, Frank Lloyd, 1867-1959. III. Title. BIP

Springfield, Mass. — Historic houses, etc.

TOMLINSON, Juliette, 974.426
1921-
Ten famous houses of Springfield. Springfield, Mass., Connecticut Valley Historical Museum [1952] unpaged. illus. 25 cm. [F74.S8T65] 52-32406
1. Springfield, Mass. — Historic houses, etc. I. Title.

Springfield, Mass. Museum of Fine Arts.

SPRINGFIELD, Mass. 708'.144'26
Museum of Fine Arts.
Handbook. [A fortieth anniversary publication. 4th ed.] Springfield [1973] 71 p. illus. (part col.) 28 cm. "The 1973 handbook is the fourth pictorial survey of the Museum of Fine Arts collections acquired by purchase and gift since 1963." [N773.A6 1973] 74-160799
1. Springfield, Mass. Museum of Fine Arts. 2. Art—Springfield, Mass.—Catalogs. I. Title.

Spruce, Everett.

AMERICAN Federation of 759.13
Arts.
Everett Spruce, by John Palmer Leeper. New York 28, Amer. Federation of Arts, 1083 Fifth Ave. [c.1959] 28p. Bibl.: p. 21-23. and Bibl. notes) illus. (part col.) port 18cm. Catalog of retrospective exhibition circulated by the federation. 60-2727 2.00; .50 pap.,
1. Spruce, Everett. I. Leeper, John Palmer. II. Title.

Square in art.

ANUSZKIEWICZ, Richard. 759
The square in painting, selected by Richard Anuszkiewicz. [New York, 1969] [24] p. illus. 21 cm. Catalog of a loan exhibition organized and circulated 1968-69 by the American Federation of Arts. "Exhibition number 68-4." [N6494.A2A5] 75-78783
1. Square in art. 2. Art, Abstract—Exhibitions. I. American Federation of Arts. II. Title.

Squirrels—Pictorial works.

BEWICK, Thomas, 1753- 769'.92'4
1828.
Squirrels / [by] Thomas Bewick. London : Merrion Press, 1976. Fold. leaf : of ill. ; 12 x 15 cm. (Wood engravings by the English engraver Thomas Bewick, 1753-1828) [QL737.R68B48 1976] 77-356210 ISBN 0-903560-12-7 : £0.90
1. Squirrels—Pictorial works. I. Title.

Stables.

BRANN, Donald R. 728'.9
How to build a stable and a red barn tool house, by Donald R. Brann. Briarcliff

Manor, N.Y., Directions Simplified, 1973. 178 p. illus. 23 cm. (Easi-bild, 679) [TH4930.B7] 72-88710 2.50 (pbk.)
1. Stables. 2. Farm shops. I. Title. BIP

Stack, Frank.

STACK, Frank. 769'.92'4
Etchings & lithographs / Frank Stack ; introd. by Sidney Larson. Columbia, Mo. : Singing Wind Publications, c1976. [9] p., [30] leaves of plates : ill. ; 31 cm. [NE2012.5.S8L37] 76-365644
1. Stack, Frank. I. Larson, Sidney. II. Title.

Stadia—Bibliography.

STARBUCK, James C. 016.3092'08 s
Stadiums : a bibliography / James C. Starbuck. Monticello, Ill. : Council of Planning Librarians, 1974. 24 p. ; 28 cm. (Exchange bibliography - Council of Planning Librarians ; 681) Cover title. [Z5942.C68 no. 681] [Z7514.S75] [NA6860] 016.725'827 75-314185 2.50
1. Stadia—Bibliography. I. Title. II. Series: Council of Planning Librarians. Exchange bibliography ; 681.

Stael, Nicolas de, 1914-1955.

DE Stael; 759.4
a retrospective exhibition held during 1965-1966 in Rotterdam, Zurich, Boston, Chicago [and] New York. [Boston, Museum of Fine Arts, 1965] 1 v. (chiefly illus. (part col.)) 25 cm. Catalog of the exhibition held at the Museum of Fine Arts, Boston, the Art Institute of Chicago, and the Guggenheim Museum, New York. Includes bibliography. [ND553.S8D4] 65-26638
1. Stael, Nicolas de, 1914-1955. I. Boston. Museum of Fine Arts.

STAEL, Nicolas de, 1914-1955. 759.4 B
Nicolas de Stael / by Guy Dumur ; translated by Fintan O'Connell ; photography by Henry B. Beville ... [et al.]. New York : Crown Publishers, c1976. p. cm. [ND553.S8D8413] 76-27652 ISBN 0-517-52611-5 : 4.95
1. Stael, Nicolas de, 1914-1955. 2. Painters—France—Biography. I. Dumur, Guy, 1921- II. Title.

SUTTON, Denys. 759.4
Nicolas de Stael. Notes on painting, by Nicolas de Stael; translated from the French by Rita Barisse. Photos, by Luc Joubert. New York, Grove Press [1960, c1959] 72 p. illus. 21 cm. Includes bibliography. [N1)553.S8S83] 59-12073
1. Stael, Nicolas de, 1914-1955. I. Title.

Staff (Sticks, canes, etc.)

STEIN, Kurt. 391'.44
Canes & walking sticks. York, Pa., Liberty Cap Books [1974] 175 p. illus. 23 cm. Bibliography: p. 170. [TS2301.C3S83] 71-186939 ISBN 0-87387-067-0 14.00
1. Staff (Sticks, canes, etc.) I. Title.
Pbk. 8.00, ISBN 0-87387-038-7. BIP

Staffordshire pottery.

BEDFORD, John, 1907- 738.37
Staffordshire pottery figures. New York, Walker [1965, c1964] 62 p. illus., col. plates. 19 cm. (His Collectors' pieces, 3) [NK4087.S6B4 1965] 65-22128
1. Staffordshire pottery. 2. Pottery—Collectors and collecting. I. Title.

CAMEHL, Ada Walker. 738.3'7
The blue-china book; early American scenes and history pictured in the pottery of the time. With a new introd. and checklist of British blue-china potters by Geoffrey A. Godden. New York, Dover Publications [1971] xliii, 327 p. illus. 22 cm. Reprint of the 1916 ed. [NK4087.S6C27 1971] 73-145884 ISBN 0-486-22749-5 5.00
1. Staffordshire pottery. 2. United States in art. I. Title. BIP

GREASER, Arlene. 738.3
Homespun ceramics; a study of spatterware, by Arlene and Paul H. Greaser. 3d ed. enl. Allentown, Pa., Printed by A.B.E. Print Co. [1967] 123 p. illus. (part col.) 24 cm. Bibliography: p. 120-123. [NK4087.S6G7] 67-31449
1. Staffordshire pottery. I. Greaser, Paul H., joint author. II. Title. BIP

HALL, John. 738.3'7
Staffordshire portrait figures. [1st American ed.] New York, World Pub. Co. [1972] 80 p. col. illus. 22 cm. Bibliography: p. 80. [NK4087.S6H19 1972] 78-174711 5.95
1. Staffordshire pottery. I. Title.

HALSEY, Richard 738.3'09424'6
Townley Haines, 1865-1942.
Pictures of early New York, on dark blue Staffordshire pottery, together with pictures of Boston and New England, Philadelphia, the South and West. With a new introd. by Marvin D. Schwartz. New York, Dover Publications [1974] xxiv, 326 p. illus. 24 cm. Reprint of the 1899 ed. published by Dodd, Mead, New York. [NK4087.S6H2 1974] 73-77376 ISBN 0-486-21950-X 5.00 (pbk.).
1. Staffordshire pottery. 2. New York (City)—History. I. Title.

LARSEN, Ellouise Baker. 738.27
American historical views on Staffordshire china. New rev. and enl. ed. Garden City, N. Y., Doubleday, 1950. xxx, 317 p. illus., col. plates, map. 29 cm. Bibliography: p. [297]-299. [NK4087.S6L3 1950] 50-11741
1. Staffordshire pottery. 2. U. S.—Hist.—Pictorial works. I. Title. BIP

LARSEN, Ellouise Baker. 738.3'7
American historical views on Staffordshire china / Ellouise Baker Larsen. 3d ed. New York : Dover Publications, 1975. xxx, 345 p. : ill. ; 28 cm. Includes index. Bibliography: p. [297]-299. [NK4087.S6L3 1975] 74-22896 ISBN 0-486-23088-0 : 12.50 ISBN 0-486-23055-4 pbk. : 8.00
1. Staffordshire pottery. 2. United States—History—Pictorial works. 3. United States in art. I. Title.

LITTLE, Wilfred Laurence. 738.3'7
Staffordshire blue: underglaze blue transfer-printed earthenware [by] W. L. Little. New York, Crown Publishers [1969] 160, [64] p. illus. 26 cm. Bibliography: p. 7-8. [NK4087.S6L56 1969b] 68-31784 10.00
1. Staffordshire pottery. I. Title.

MOUNTFORD, Arnold Robert. 738.3'7
The illustrated guide to Staffordshire salt-glazed stoneware [by] Arnold R. Mountford. New York, Praeger [1971] xxi, 88 p. plates (part col.), map. 26 cm. (The Illustrated guides to pottery and porcelain) Bibliography: p. 78-79. [NK4087.S6M6 1971b] 73-151804 20.00
1. Staffordshire pottery. I. Title.

PUGH, Patterson David 738.3'7
Gordon.
Staffordshire portrait figures and allied subjects of the Victorian era [by] P. D. Gordon Pugh. New York, Praeger [1971] xi, 657 p. illus. (part col.) 26 cm. Bibliography: p. 645-647. [NK4087.S6P8] 70-107220 45.00
1. Staffordshire pottery. I. Title.

SHAW, Simeon. 738'.09424'6
History of the Staffordshire potteries. New York, Praeger [1970] viii, 244 p. facsim. 20 cm. Reprint of the 1829 ed. [NK4087.S6S5 1970] 79-117392 7.50
1. Staffordshire pottery. 2. Potters—England. I. Title.

WHITER, Leonard. 738.2'7
Spode; a history of the family, factory, and wares from 1733 to 1833. New York, Praeger [1970] xiii, 246 p. illus., facsims., col. plates, ports. 29 cm. Includes bibliographical references. [NK4087.S6W48 1970] 72-116641 32.50
1. Spode family. 2. Staffordshire pottery. I. Title.

WILLIAMS, Petra. 738.3'7
Staffordshire, romantic transfer patterns : cup plates and early Victorian china / Petra Williams ; layout and photographic ill. for the text by Marguerite R. Weber. Jeffersontown, Ky. : Fountain House East, c1978. 763 p. : ill. ; 24 cm. Includes index. Bibliography: p. 747. [NK4087.S6W49] 78-55047 ISBN 0-914736-05-1 : 15.95
1. Staffordshire pottery. 2. Plates (Tableware) 3. Pottery—19th century—England. I. Weber, Marguerite R. II. Title. BIP

Staffordshire pottery—Catalogs.

ARMAN, David. 738.3'7
Historical Staffordshire : an illustrated check list / by David and Linda Arman. Danville, Va. : Arman Enterprises, c1974. 244 p. : ill. ; 23 cm. Includes index. Bibliography: p. 237. [NK4087.S6A74] 74-18756 15.00
1. Staffordshire pottery—Catalogs. I. Arman, Linda, joint author. II. Title. BIP

Staffordshire pottery—Collectors and collecting.

OLIVER, Anthony. 738.3'7
The Victorian Staffordshire figure; a guide for collectors. New York, St. Martin's Press [1972, c1971] 179 p. illus. (part col.) 26 cm. Bibliography: p. 173. [NK4087.S6O45 1972] 72-78433 12.50
1. Staffordshire pottery—Collectors and collecting. 2. Portraits, English. I. Title.

TURNER, H. A. B. 738.3'8
A collector's guide to Staffordshire pottery figures [by] H. A. B. Turner. New York, Emerson Books [1971] 294 p. illus. (part col.), geneal. tables. 24 cm. Includes bibliographical references. [NK4087.S6T8] 70-138391 ISBN 0-87523-175-6 13.50
1. Staffordshire pottery—Collectors and collecting. I. Title. BIP

Staffordshire pottery—Indexes.

JONES, Charles 738'.09424'6
Allen, 1917-
This 'n that and where it's at in early Staffordshire tableware; an index of published illustrations, by Charles A. Jones. New York [1973] vi, 42 p. 22 cm. [NK4087.S6J66] 74-154463
1. Staffordshire pottery—Indexes. I. Title. II. Title: Early Staffordshire tableware.

Stafforshire pottery.

BEDFORD, John, 1907- 738.2'7
Old Spode china. New York, Walker [1969] 64 p. illus. (part col.), facsims. 20 cm. (Collectors' pieces 17) [NK4087.S6B38 1969] 72-84598 3.50
1. Spode family. 2. Stafforshire pottery. I. Title.

Staffs (Sticks, canes, etc.)

BOOTHROYD, Albert Edward. 391'.44
Fascinating walking sticks [by] A. E. Boothroyd; photographs by Edward Morgan. [Ipswich, Viking Antiques] 1970. 205 p. illus. 23 cm. [GT2220.B6] 72-195346 ISBN 0-9501474-0-0 £2.50
1. Staffs (Sticks, canes, etc.) I. Title.

FENTON, William Nelson, 970.3
1908-
The roll call of the Iroquois chiefs; a study of mnemonic cane from the Six Nations Reserve. Washington, Smithsonian Institution, 1950. iv. 73 p. plates. facsims. 25 cm. (Smithsonian miscellaneous collections, v. 111, no. 15) Publication 3995. Bibliography: p. 70-73. [Q11.S7 vol. 111, no. 15] 50-60282
1. Staffs (Sticks, canes, etc.) 2. Iroquois Indians—Rites and ceremonies. I. Title. II. Series: Smithsonian Institution, Smithsonian miscellaneous collections, v. 111, no. 15 BIP

Stage-lighting.

BELLMAN, Willard F. 792'.025
Lighting the stage; art and practice [by] Willard F. Bellman. San Francisco, Chandler Pub. Co. [1967] xii, 348 p. illus. (part col.) 26 cm. Bibliography: p. 341-342. [PN2091.E4B39] 67-10210
1. Stage-lighting. I. Title. BIP

BELLMAN, Willard F. 792'.025
Lighting the stage: art and practice [by] Willard F. Bellman. 2d ed. New York, Chandler Pub. Co. [1974] xv, 480 p. illus. 25 cm. Bibliography: p. 474-476. [PN2091.E4B39 1974] 73-18363 ISBN 0-8102-0040-6 15.00
1. Stage lighting. I. Title.

BENTHAM, Frederick. 792'.025
The art of stage lighting. New York, Taplinger Pub. Co. [1969, c1968] xix, 447 p. illus. 23 cm. Bibliographical footnotes. [PN2091.E4B398 1969] 69-17081 14.95
1. Stage lighting. I. Title. BIP

BENTHAM, Frederick. 792'.025
The art of stage lighting / Frederick Bentham. 2d ed., rev. and expanded. New York : Theatre Arts Books, 1976. 361 p. : ill. ; 26 cm. (Theatre and stage series) Includes bibliographical references and index. [PN2091.E4B398 1976] 77-351421 ISBN 0-87830-009-0 : 16.95
1. Stage lighting. I. Title.

BONGAR, Emmet W. 792'.025
Practical stage lighting [by] Emmet Bongar. [1st ed.] New York, R. Rosen Press [1971] 123, [1] p. illus. 29 cm. (The Theatre student) Bibliography: p. [124] Explains the purposes, electrical techniques, and equipment of stage lighting for all kinds of productions and stages. Includes information on special effects, care of instruments, cue sheets, and obtaining or making equipment. [PN2091.E4B57] 70-125194 ISBN 0-8239-0224-2 5.97
1. Stage lighting. I. Title.

BOWMAN, Wayne, 1914- 792.92
Modern theatre lighting. Illustrated by Jean Bowman. New York, Harper [1957] 228p. illus. 22cm. [PN2091.E4B6] 57-10574
1. Stage lighting. I. Title.

GILLETTE, J. Michael. 792'.025
Designing with light : an introduction to stage lighting / J. Michael Gillette. 1st ed. Palo Alto, Calif. : Mayfield Pub.Co., 1978. vi, 195 p. : ill. ; 23 cm. Includes index. Bibliography: p. 191-192. [PN2091.E4G5] 78-51945 ISBN 0-87484-420-7 pbk. : 7.95
1. Stage lighting. I. Title. BIP

HARTMANN, Louis. 792'.025
Theatre lighting; a manual of the stage switchboard. Foreword by David Belasco. New York, DBS Publications [1970] xiii, 138 p. illus. 20 cm. Reprint of the 1930 ed. Bibliography: p. 114-118. [PN2091.E4H3 1970] 70-115696
1. Stage lighting. I. Title. BIP

MCCANDLESS, Stanley 792.025
Russell.
A method of lighting the stage. 4th ed. amended and rev. New York, Theatre Arts Books [1958] 143 p. illus. 21 cm. [PN2091.E4M3 1958] 58-10331
1. Stage lighting. BIP

PILBROW, Richard. 792'.025
Stage lighting. Foreword by Laurence Olivier. New York, Von [sic] Nostrand Reinhold [1970] 151 p. illus. (part col.) 26 cm. Bibliography: p. 151. [PN2091.E4P5 1970b] 70-125596
1. Stage lighting. BIP

REID, Francis. 792'.025
The stage lighting handbook / Francis Reid. New York : Theatre Arts Books, 1976. 129 p. : ill. ; 24 cm. Includes index. [PN2091.E4R4] 76-8319 ISBN 0-87830-156-9 : 10.45
1. Stage lighting. I. Title. BIP

ROSENTHAL, Jean, 1912- 792'.025 B
The magic of light: the craft and career of Jean Rosenthal, pioneer in lighting for the modern stage [by] Jean Rosenthal and Lael Wertenbaker. Illus. by Marion Kinsella. [1st ed.] Boston, Little, Brown [1972] ix, 256 p. illus. 27 cm. Bibliography: p. 249-250. [PN2091.E4R68] 72-6465 ISBN 0-316-93120-9 15.00
1. Stage lighting. I. Wertenbaker, Lael Tucker, 1909- joint author. II. Title. BIP

RUBIN, Joel E 792.92
Theatrical lighting practice, by Joel E. Rubin and Leland H. Watson. [New York, Theatre Arts Books, c1954] 142p. illus. 25cm. Includes bibliographies. [PN2091.E4R8] 55-384
1. Stage lighting. I. Watson, Leland H., joint author. II. Title.

SELLMAN, Hunton Dade. 792'.025
Essentials of stage lighting [by] Hunton D. Sellman. New York, Appleton-Century-Crofts [1972] xiv, 214 p. illus. 27 cm. Bibliography: p. 205-207. [PN2091.E4S4] 75-187988 ISBN 0-390-79553-4 9.95
1. Stage lighting. I. Title. **BIP**

Stage lighting—Drawings.

WARFEL, William B. 792'.025
Handbook of stage lighting graphics [by] William B. Warfel. [2d ed., rev. and enl.] New York, Drama Book Specialists [1973, c1974] 41 p. illus. 28 cm. [PN2091.E4W3] 73-16421 ISBN 0-910482-47-0 4.95
1. Stage lighting—Drawings. I. Title. **BIP**

Stage lighting—History.

BERGMAN, Gosta Mauritz, 1905-1975. 792'.025
Lighting in the theatre / by Gosta M. Bergman. Stockholm : Almqvist & Wiksell International ; Totowa, N.J. : Rowman and Littlefield, 1977. 426 p. : ill. ; 24 cm. Includes index. Bibliography: p. 413-421. [PN2091.E4B45 1977] 77-372895 ISBN 0-87471-602-0 (Rowman) : 47.50
1. Stage lighting—History. I. Title. **BIP**

PENZEL, Frederick, 1948- 792'.025
Theatre lighting before electricity / by Frederick Penzel. Middletown, Conn. : Wesleyan University Press, [1978] p. cm. Includes index. Bibliography: p. [PN2091.E4P44] 77-14840 ISBN 0-8195-5021-3 : 16.00
1. Stage lighting—History. I. Title. **BIP**

Stage lighting—Terminology.

WEHLBURG, Albert F. C. 792'.025
Theatre lighting : an illustrated glossary / by Albert F. C. Wehlburg. New York : Drama Book Specialists, [1975, i.e.1976] p. cm. [PN2091.E4W4] 75-19332 ISBN 0-910482-69-1 spiral bdg. : 7.95
1. Stage lighting—Terminology. I. Title.

Stage management.

BECK, Roy A. 792'.025
Stagecraft / Roy A. Beck. Skokie, Ill. : National Textbook Co., c1975. 81 p. : ill. ; 23 cm. (Theater arts series) Bibliography: p. 78. [PN2085.B4] 76-359616
1. Stage management. I. Title.

HOGGETT, Chris. 792'.025
Stage crafts / Chris Hoggett. New York : St. Martin's Press, c1976. p. cm. Includes index. Bibliography: p. [PN2085.H6 1976] 76-10554 12.50
1. Stage management. I. Title. **BIP**

WELKER, David Harold. 792'.025
Stagecraft : a handbook for organization, construction, and management / David Welker. Boston : Allyn and Bacon, c1977. xviii, 423 p. : ill. ; 26 cm. Includes index. [PN2085.W4] 76-25534 ISBN 0-205-05589-3 : 17.95
1. Stage management. I. Title.

Stage management—Terminology.

BAKER, James W., 1932- 792'.02
Elements of stagecraft / by James W. Baker. Sherman Oaks, CA : Alfred Pub. Co., c1978. xii, 241 p. : ill. ; 26 cm. Includes index. [PN2086.B3] 77-25899 ISBN 0-88284-053-3 pbk. : 8.95
1. Stage management—Terminology. I. Title. **BIP**

Staircases—Durham, Eng.

JOHNSON, Francis Frederick. 729'.39
Historic staircases in Durham City, by Francis F. Johnson. Durham, City of Durham Trust, 1970. 48 p., 8 plates. illus. 21 cm. [NA3060.J64] 75-545885 ISBN 0-902776-00-2 15/-
1. Staircases—Durham, Eng. I. Title.

Stallknecht, Alice, 1880-1973.

STALLKNECHT, Alice, 1880-1973. 759.13
A New England town : a portrait / by Alice Stallknecht, 1880-1973 ; foreword, William C. Agee ; contributors, LLoyd Goodrich ... [et al.]. Houston, Tex. : [Museum of Fine Arts], c1977. 24 p. : ill. ; 22 x 28 cm. Catalogue of an exhibition to be held in the Municipal Art Gallery, Los Angeles, Mar. 27-Apr. 17, 1977; the Museum of Fine Arts, Houston, May 4-June 5, 1977; and the National Portrait Gallery, Washington, D.C., Oct. 15-Nov. 27, 1977. [ND237.S6465L67] 77-72067
1. Stallknecht, Alice, 1880-1973. 2. Chatham, Mass., in art. I. Los Angeles Municipal Art Gallery. II. Houston, Tex. Museum of Fine Arts. III. National Portrait Gallery, Washington, D.C. IV. Title.

Stamnos.

PHILIPPAKE, Varvara. 738.3'83
The Attic stamnos, by Barbara Philippaki. Oxford, Clarendon P., 1967. xxii, 171 p. illus., 64 plates. 29 cm. (Oxford monographs on classical archaeology) [NK4650.S8P5 1967] 67-77632
1. Stamnos. 2. Vase-painting, Greek. I. Title. II. Series.

Stamos, Theodoros, 1922—

STAMOS, Theodoros, 1922- 759.13
Stamos / Ralph Pomeroy. New York : Abrams, [1974] 273 p. : 215 ill. (some col.) ; 29 x 30 cm. Bibliography: 271-273. [ND237.S647P65] 77-160155 ISBN 0-8109-0487-X : 35.00.
1. Stamos, Theodoros, 1922- I. Pomeroy, Ralph, 1926- **BIP**

Stamped envelopes.

UNITED Postal Stationery Society. 769'.5
The postal stationery of the possessions and administrative areas of the United States: Canal Zone, Cuba, Hawaii, Philippines, Puerto Rico, Ryukyu Islands, Danish West Indies. 2d ed. [Rochester, N.Y.] 1971. 268 p. illus. 23 cm. Cover title: The postal stationery of the United States possessions and administrative areas. 1957 ed. published under title: The postal stationery of the possessions of the United States. [HE6185.U6U54 1971] 74-175296 6.50
1. Stamped envelopes. 2. Postal cards—United States. I. Title.

UNITED Postal Stationery Society. 383.4973
The postal stationery of the possessions of the United States, including Canal Zone, Hawaii, Cuba, Philippines [and] Puerto Rico. George C. Slawson, editor. Editorial committee: C. Warner Bates [and others] Albany, Or., Van Dahl Publications, c1957. 70 p. illus. 23 cm. [HE6185.U6U54] 58-35042
1. Stamped envelopes. 2. Postal cards. I. Slawson, George Clark, 1905 ed. II. Title.

Stanford University. Libraries.

LENKEY, Susan V. 016.093
Stanford incunabula, 1975 : a descriptive catalog / compiled by Susan V. Lenkey. [Stanford, Calif. : Leland Stanford Junior University, 1975] 92 p. : ill. ; 28 cm. [Z240.L455] 75-321801
1. Stanford University. Libraries. 2. Incunabula—Bibliography—Catalogs. I. Stanford University. II. Title.

Stanford University. Stanford Memorial Church.

STANFORD University. Publications Service. 917.94'73
Stanford Memorial Church / prepared by the Stanford University Publications Service. 2d ed. [Stanford, Calif.] : The University, [1974] 27 p., [2] leaves of plates : ill. (some col.) ; 23 cm. [NA5235.S72S72 1974] 74-195997
1. Stanford University. Stanford Memorial Church. I. Title.

Stark, Otto, 1859-1926.

OTTO Stark, 1859-1926 : 759.13
[exhibition], Indianapolis Museum of Art, April 13-May 15, 1977 / by Leland G. Howard. Indianapolis : The Museum, c1977. 72 p. : ill. (some col.) ; 26 cm. Includes bibliographical references. [ND237.S66H68] 77-151480
1. Stark, Otto, 1859-1926. I. Stark, Otto, 1859-1926. II. Indianapolis Museum of Art.

Starkweather, Frank—Art collections.

STARKWEATHER, Frank. 730.9*6
Traditional Igbo art, 1966; an exhibition of wood sculpture carved in 1965-66, from the Frank Starkheather Collection, August 15 through Octber 27, 1968. [Ann Arbor] University of Michigan [1968] [64] p. illus., col. map. 19 x 26 cm. Sponsored by the Dept. of Anthropology and the Museum of Art, University of Michigan. Bibliography: p. [60]-[64] [NB1255.N5S8] 68-66438
1. Starkweather, Frank—Art collections. 2. Art, Ibo—Exhibitions. I. Michigan. University. Dept. of Anthropology. II. Michigan. University. Museum of Art. III. Title.

Starr, John W., 1925- —Art collections.

WILLIAM Rockhill Nelson Gallery of Art and Mary Atkins Museum of Fine Arts, Kansas City, Mo. 757'.7'09420740178411
The Starr Collection of miniatures in the William Rockhill Nelson Gallery. With introd. by Graham Reynolds. Kansas City, 1971. 84 p. illus. (part col.) 25 cm. "The basic structure of this catalogue is patterned after ... [Reynold's] book English portrait miniatures." [ND1337.G7W47] 72-177685
1. Starr, John W., 1925- —Art collections. 2. Portrait miniatures—Great Britain—Catalogs. 3. Miniature painting—Kansas City, Mo.—Catalogs. I. Reynolds, Graham. II. Title.

State encouragement of science, literature and art.

UNITED States. Library of Congress. Education and Public Welfare Division. 338.4'7'7
Survey of United States and foreign government support for cultural activities [by Lilla M. Pearce] Washington, U.S. Govt. Print. Off., 1971. xi, 245 p. forms. 24 cm. At head of title: 92d Congress, 1st session. Committee print. "Prepared for the Special Subcommittee on Arts and Humanities of the Committee on Labor and Public Welfare, United States Senate." [NX720.U5] 70-614904
1. State encouragement of science, literature and art. I. Pearce, Lilla M. II. United States. Congress. Senate. Committee on Labor and Public Welfare. Special Subcommittee on Arts and Humanities. III. Title.

State encouragement of science, literature, and art—New York (State)

NEW York (State). Commission on Cultural Resources. 338.4'7'7
State financial assistance to cultural resources; report. [New York] 1971. xii, 163 p. illus. (part col.) 23 cm. [NX742.N7A57] 77-634771
1. State encouragement of science, literature, and art—New York (State) 2. The arts—New York (State)—Finance. I. Title.

State encouragement of science, literature, and art—U.S.

SCOTT, Mellier Goodin, 1906- 700'.61
The states and the arts; the California Arts Commission and the emerging federal-state partnership, by Mel Scott. Berkeley, Institute of Governmental Studies, University of California, 1971. xiv, 129 p. 23 cm. Bibliography: p. 127-129. [NX26.C33S3] 70-633156 ISBN 0-87772-075-4 3.00
1. California. Arts Commission. 2. State encouragement of science, literature, and art—U.S. I. Title.

State of Liberty, New York.

LUDMANN, Oscar Henry, 1900- 730.924
Quand? Or, Liberty nee Bartholdi, by Oscar H. Ludmann. [1st ed.] New York, Vantage Press [1965] 251 p. ports. 21 cm. [NB553.B3LS] 65-20120
1. Bartholdi, Frederic Auguste, 1834-1904. 2. State of Liberty, New York. I. Title. II. Title: Liberty nee Bartholdi.

Statue of Liberty, New York.

GSCHAEDLER, Andre. 730.924
True light on the Statue of Liberty and its creator. [1st ed.] Narberth, Pa., Livingston Pub. Co. [1966] xiii, 186 p. illus., ports. 23 cm. "Sources": p. 171-173. [NB553.B3G8] 65-28279
1. Bartholdi, Frederic Auguste, 1834-1904. 2. Statue of Liberty, New York. I. Title.

HANDLIN, Oscar, 1915- 325.73
Statue of Liberty, by Oscar Handlin and the editors of the Newsweek Book Division. New York, Newsweek [1971] 172 p. illus. (part col.) 30 cm. (Wonders of man) Bibliography: p. 168. [F128.64.L6H3] 77-136435
1. Statue of Liberty, New York. 2. U.S.—Emigration and immigration—History. I. Newsweek, inc. Book Division. II. Title.

PAULI, Hertha Ernestine, 1909- 974.71
I lift my lamp; the way of a symbol, by Hertha Pauli and E. B. Ashton. Port Washington, N.Y., I. J. Friedman [1969, c1948] ix, 368 p. 22 cm. (Empire State historical publications series, no. 65) [F128.64.L6P3 1969] 70-83481
1. Statue of Liberty, New York. I. Basch, Ernst, 1909- joint author. II. Title. III. Series: Empire State historical publication no. 65 **BIP**

PRICE, Willadene. 730.944
Bartholdi and the Statue of Liberty. Chicago, Rand McNally [1959] 188 p. illus. 22 cm. [NB553.B3P7] 59-10473
1. Bartholdi, Frederic Auguste, 1834-1904. 2. Statue of Liberty, New York.

ROMIGH, Philip S. 731'.76'097471
Fort Wood: Statue of Liberty National Monument, New York, by Philip S. Romigh. Denver, Historic Preservation Team, Denver Service Center, National Park Service, 1973. v, 47 p. illus. 27 cm. "Historic structure report, architectural data section." "NPS 720." Bibliography: p. 29. [F128.64.L6R65] 74-602011
1. Statue of Liberty, New York. I. Title.

SMARIDGE, Norah. 917.471
The tallest lady in the world: the Statute of Liberty. Illustrated by Leonard Vosburgh. [1st ed.] New York, Hawthorn Books [1967] 94 p. illus. 21 cm. Describes the inspiration, financing, construction, ocean voyage, and rebuilding of Auguste Bartholdi's statue, the gift of France, which has become the gatepost of the New York City harbor. [F128.64.L6S6] AC 67
1. Statue of Liberty, New York. I. Vosburgh, Leonard, illus. II. Title.

TRACHTENBERG, Marvin. 730'.92'4
The Statue of Liberty. New York, Viking Press, 1976. 224 p. illus. 23 cm. Includes bibliographical references. [NB553.B3T72] 74-19306 ISBN 0-670-66854-0 : 10.95
1. Bartholdi, Frederic Auguste, 1834-1904. 2. Statue of Liberty, New York. I. Title. **BIP**

TRACHTENBERG, Marvin. 730'.92'4
The Statue of Liberty / Marvin Trachtenberg. New York : Penguin Books, 1977. 224 p. : ill. ; 23 cm. Includes bibliographical references and index. [NB553.B3T72 1977] 77-5624 ISBN 0-14-004513-9 pbk. : 5.95
1. Bartholdi, Frederic Auguste, 1834-1904. 2. Statue of Liberty, New York. I. Title.

Statue of Liberty, New York—Juvenile literature.

SMARIDGE, Norah.　　917.471 (j)
The tallest lady in the world: the Statue of Liberty. Illustrated by Leonard Vosburgh. [1st ed.] New York, Hawthorn Books [1967] 94 p. illus. 21 cm. [F128.64.L6S6] 67-5130
1. Statue of Liberty, New York—Juvenil literature. I. Vosburgh, Leonard W., illus. II. Title.

Statue of Liberty, New York—Juvenile literature.

KRASKE,　　731'.76'0944097471
Robert.
The Statue of Liberty comes to America. Illustrated by Victor Mays. Champaign, Ill., Garrard Pub. Co. [1972] 95 p. illus. (part col.) 23 cm. Recounts the planning, building, and transporting of the gigantic statue that was France's gift to the United States. [F128.64.L6K7] 74-171412 ISBN 0-8116-6505-4 2.79
1. Statue of Liberty, New York—Juvenile literature. I. Mays, Victor, 1927- illus. II. Title.　　BIP

MERCER, Charles E.　　974.7'1
Statue of Liberty / by Charles Mercer. New York : Putnam, [1979] p. cm. Includes index. Presents the story behind the building of the colossal statue in New York Harbor, France's gift to the U.S. commemorating friendship and symbolizing freedom. [F128.64.L6M44] 78-21305 ISBN 0-399-20670-1 : 8.95
1. Statue of Liberty, New York—Juvenile literature. I. Title.　　BIP

MILLER, Natalie.　　974.71
The story of the Statue of Liberty. Illus. by Lucy and John Hawkinson. Chicago, Childrens Press [1965] 30 p. col. illus. 25 cm. (Cornerstones of freedom) [F128.64.L6M5] 65-12216
1. Statue of Liberty, New York—Juvenile literature. I. Title.　　BIP

NASON, Thelma Campbell.　　917.471
Our Statue of Liberty [by] Thelma Nason. Illustrated by Adolph Le Moult. Chicago, Follett Pub. Co. [1969] 32 p. col. illus. 21 cm. Describes how the Statue of Liberty was conceived, constructed, and transported to the Unitd States. [F128.64.L6N3] 69-10260 1.00
1. Statue of Liberty, New York—Juvenile literature. I. Le Moult, Adolph, illus. II. Title.　　BIP

PATTERSON, Lillie.　　917.471
Meet Miss Liberty. Illustrated with historic engravings and photos. New York, Macmillan, 1962. 162 p. illus. 22 cm. [F128.64.L6P28] 62-10645
1. Statue of Liberty, New York—Juvenile literature. I. Title.　　BIP

PAULI, Hertha Ernestine,　　731.86
1909-
Gateway to America; Miss Liberty's first hundred years. Illus. by Leonard Vosburgh. New York, McKay [c.1965] 70p. illus. 22cm. [F128.64.L6P29] 65-23833 2.95
1. Statute of Liberty, New York—Juvenile literature. I. Title.

Steadman, Ralph.

STEADMAN, Ralph.　　741.9'42
Cherrywood cannon / Ralph Steadman ; based on a story told to him by Dimitri Sidjanski. New York : Paddington Press : distributed by Grosset & Dunlap, c1978. [48] p. : ill. (some col.) ; 31 cm. An illustrated Montenegrin folktale with 24 original illustrations in pen and ink. [NC242.S73A4 1978] 77-16163 pbk. : 7.95
1. Steadman, Ralph. 2. Tales, Montenegrin—Illustrations. I. Damjan, Mischa, pseud. II. Title.

Steamboats.

GREAT Lakes steam　　741.973
vessels. Drawings by Samuel Ward Stanton. [dist. Upper Montclair, N.J., H.

Kneeland Whiting, 63 Beverly Rd. c.1962] 48p. illus. 22x28cm. 2.25 pap.,

HUGHES, Jesse P　　741.639623823
1877-
Cap'n Hughes steamboat sketchbook. Cincinnati, Picture Marine Pub. Co. [1951] unpaged. illus. 22x29cm. [NC1075.H775A44] 53-248846
1. Steamboats. I. Title.

Stebbins, Nathaniel Livermore, 1847—

BUNTING, William　　779'.37'0924
Henry, 1945-
Steamers, schooners, cutters, and sloops; the marine photographs of N. L. Stebbins taken from 1884 to 1907. Selected and annotated by W. H. Bunting. [Boston] Published for Society for the Preservation of New England Antiquities, by Houghton Mifflin Co., 1974. 126 p. illus. 23 x 29 cm. Includes bibliographical references. [TR670.5.B86] 74-12034 ISBN 0-395-19895-X 12.50
1. Stebbins, Nathaniel Livermore, 1847- 2. Photography of ships. 3. Steamboats. 4. Sailing ships. I. Stebbins, Nathaniel Livermore, 1847- illus. II. Title.

Steel sculpture.

ZAIDENBERG, Arthur, 1903-　　731.4
Sculpting in steel and other metals. [1st ed.] Radnor, Pa., Chilton Book Co. [1974] xviii, 137 p. illus. 26 cm. Bibliography: p. 134. [NB1240.S7Z34 1974] 74-1086 ISBN 0-8019-5829-6 12.50
1. Steel sculpture. 2. Metal sculpture. I. Title.　　BIP

Steele, Theodore C., 1847-1926.

STEELE, Selma N.　　759.13
The house of the singing winds; the life and work of T. C. Steele [by] Selma N. Steele, Theodore L. Steele [and] Wilbur D. Peat. Indianapolis, Indiana Historical Society, 1966. x, 209 p. illus. (part col.), col. plates. 26 cm. Bibliographical footnotes. [ND237.S68S7] 67-7939
1. Steele, Theodore C., 1847-1926. I. Steele, Theodore L. II. Peat, Wilbur David, 1898- III. Title.

Steer, Philip Wilson, 1860-1942.

LAUGHTON, Bruce.　　759.2
Philip Wilson Steer, 1860-1942. Oxford, Clarendon Press, 1971. xix, 167, [102] p. illus. (some col.), ports. 30 cm. (Oxford studies in the history of art and architecture) Bibliography: p. 159-161. [ND497.S78L3] 72-181003 ISBN 0-19-817182-X £8.00
1. Steer, Philip Wilson, 1860-1942. I. Title. II. Series.

Stefan, Ross, 1934—

GOODMAN, John K.　　759.13 B
Ross Stefan, an impressionistic painter of the contemporary Southwest / by John K. Goodman ; with a foreword by Clay Lockett. 1st ed. [Flagstaff, Ariz.] : Northland Press, c1977. xii, 91 p. : ill. (some col.) ; 31 cm. [ND237.S6825G66] 77-79013 ISBN 0-87358-168-7 : 25.00
1. Stefan, Ross, 1934- 2. Painters—United States—Biography. 3. Southwest, New, in art. 4. Indians of North America—Southwest, New—Pictorial works.

Steichen, Edward, 1879-1973.

NEW York. Museum of Modern　　779
Art.
Steichen the photographer. Texts by Carl Sandburg [and others] Biographical outline by Grace M. Mayer. Garden City, N. Y., Distributed by Doubleday [1961] 80p. plates, ports. 25cm. A selected bibliography by Bernard Karpel': p. 76-80. [TR140.S68N4] 61-12288
1. Steichen, Edward, 1879- 2. Photography, Artistic. 3. Photographs. I. Sandburg, Carl, 1878 II. Title.

STEICHEN, Edward,　　779'.092'4
1879-1973.
Steichen : the master prints 1895-1914, the

symbolist period / Dennis Longwell. New York : Museum of Modern Art ; Boston : distributed by New York Graphic Society, c1978. 180 p. : ill. (some col.) ; 29 cm. Includes index. Bibliography: p. 175-177. [TR654.S72 1978] 77-90995 ISBN 0-87070-581-4 : 35.00
1. Steichen, Edward, 1879-1973. 2. Photography, Artistic. I. Longwell, Dennis. II. New York (City). Museum of Modern Art.　　BIP

Stein, David.

STEIN, Anne-Marie.　　751.5'8'0924 B
Three Picassos before breakfast; memoirs of an art forger's wife, by Anne-Marie Stein, as told to George Carpozi, Jr. New York, Hawthorn Books [1973] 192 p. illus. 25 cm. [ND553.S855S83 1973] 72-7784 6.95
1. Stein, David. 2. Forgery of works of art. I. Carpozi, George. II. Title.

Steinberg, Saul.

STEINBERG, Saul　　741.59
The catalogue. Cleveland, World [c.1945-1962] unpaged. chiefly illus. 28cm. (Meridian bks., M147) 2.75 pap.,
I. Title.

STEINBERG, Saul.　　741.5973
The catalogue; [a selection of drawings reprinted from The art of living, The passport, and The labyrinth] Cleveland, world Pub. Co. [1962] unpaged. illus. 28 cm. (Meridian books, M147) [NC1429.S588A45] 62-18678
I. Title.

STEINBERG, Saul.　　741.5973
The new world [by] Steinberg. [1st ed.] New York, Harper & Row [1965] 1 v. (chiefly illus.) 32 cm. [NC1429.S588A52] 65-21379
I. Title.

STEINBERG, Saul.　　741.5'973
The passport / Saul Steinberg ; introd. by John Hollander. New York : Random House, [1979] p. cm. [NC1429.S588A4 1979] 78-21836 ISBN 0-394-50528-X : 17.95
1. American wit and humor, Pictorial. I. Title.　　BIP

STEINBERG, Saul.　　760'.092'4
Saul Steinberg / [commentary] by Harold Rosenberg. 1st ed. New York : Knopf, c1978. 256 p. : ill. (some col.) ; 27 x 28 cm. "A John L. Hochman book." Published in conjunction with a major exhibition organized by the Whitney Museum of American Art and held in various cities, Apr. 14, 1978-Apr. 30, 1979. Bibliography: p. 250-256. [N6537.S7A4 1978] 77-20349 ISBN 0-394-50136-5 : 25.00 ISBN 0-394-73591-9 pbk. : 10.95
1. Steinberg, Saul. I. Rosenberg, Harold. II. Whitney Museum of American Art.　　BIP

Steiner, Michael, 1945—

STEINER, Michael, 1945-　　730'.92'4
Michael Steiner; March 22-April 28, 1974, Museum of Fine Arts, Boston. [Boston, Museum of Fine Arts, 1974] [24] p. illus. 22 x 26 cm. Exhibition catalog written by Kenworth Moffett. Bibliography: p. [24] [NB237.S58M63] 74-77931 ISBN 0-87846-079-9
1. Steiner, Michael, 1945- I. Moffett, Kenworth. II. Boston. Museum of Fine Arts.

STEINER, Michael, 1945-　　730'.924
Michael Steiner. May-June, 1970. New York, Marlborough Gallery [1970] 28 p. (chiefly illus. (part col.), port.) 30 cm. Label mounted on t.p.: Supplied by Worldwide Books, inc., Boston. "Cat[alogue] no. 274." [NB237.S58A5] 70-18396
I. Marlborough Gallery.

Steiner, Ralph, 1899—

STEINER, Ralph, 1899-　　770'.92'4 B
A point of view / Ralph Steiner. 1st ed. Middletown, Conn. : Wesleyan University Press, c1978. xii, 144 p. : ill. ; 27 cm.

[TR140.S683A34] 77-20513 ISBN 0-8195-5019-1 : 20.00
1. Steiner, Ralph, 1899- 2. Photographers—United States—Biography.
I. Title.　　BIP

Steinlen, Theophile Alexandre, 1859-1923.

SLATKIN (CHARLES E.)　　741.944
GALLERIES, New York.
Theophile-Alexandre Steinlen; an exhibition of drawings, pastels, watercolors, October 18th to November 16th, 1963 [Introd. by Alain de Leiris] New York, 115 E. 92 St. Author, [c.1963] [96]p. illus. 27cm. Bibl. 63-22086 2.50
1. Steinlen, Theophile Alexandre, 1859-1923. I. Leiris, Alain de. II. Title.

Steins.

DIMSDLE, June.　　738
Steins and prices. Kansas City? Mo. [1970] 104 p. illus. 22 cm. [NK8647.D55] 70-13700 6.95
1. Steins. I. Title.

Steins—Mettlach, Ger.—Catalogs.

FENWICK, Paul E.　　745.1
Mettlach steins : prices and description of 1,041 steins, over 500 steins illustrated / Paul E. Fenwick. 1st ed. [Lee, Mass.] : Fenwick, [1974] 116 p. : ill. ; 22 cm. Pages 113-115 blank for "Notes". [NK4100.M47F46] 74-195090 5.95
1. Steins—Mettlach, Ger.—Catalogs. I. Title.

Stele (Archeology)

RICHTER, Gisela Marie　　733.3
Augusta, 1882-
The archaic gravestones of Attica. With 216 illus., including 108 from photos. by Alison Frantz, and an appendix with epigraphical notes by Margherita Guarducci. [New York] Phaidon Publishers; distributed by New York Graphic Society, Greenwich, Conn. [1961] viii, 184p. illus., plates. 31cm. Bibliography: p. 57-58. [NB1370.R5] 61-19870
1. Stele (Archeology) 2. Sculpture, Greek. 3. Sepulchral monuments—Greece—Attics. I. Title.

Stella, Frank.

RICHARDSON, Brenda.　　759.13
Frank Stella : the black paintings : [exhibition, November 23, 1976-January 23, 1977] / by Brenda Richardson, with assistance from Mary Martha Ward. Baltimore : Baltimore Museum of Art, c1976. xiv, 90 p. : ill. ; 28 cm. Bibliography: p. 85-87. [ND237.S683R47] 76-48793 10.00
1. Stella, Frank. 2. Black in art. I. Stella, Frank. II. Ward, Mary Martha, joint author. III. Baltimore. Museum of Art.

ROSENBLUM, Robert.　　759.13
Frank Stella. (Harmondsworth, Eng., Penguin Books, 1971) 62 p. illus. (part col.) 23 cm. (Penguin new art 1) Includes bibliographical references. [ND237.S683R6] 72-109890 ISBN 0-14-070621-6 3.50 (U.S.)
1. Stella, Frank.

RUBIN, William Stanley.　　759.13
Frank Stella [by] William S. Rubin. New York, Museum of Modern Art; distributed by New York Graphic Society, Greenwich, Conn. [1970] 174 p. illus. (part col.), port. 27 cm. Bibliography: p. 161-170. [ND237.S683R8] 75-100684
1. Stella, Frank.

Stella, Giuseppe Carlo, 1877-1946.

BAUR, John Ireland Howe,　　759.13
1909-
Joseph Stella [by] John I. H. Baur. Research by Irma B. Jaffe. New York, Praeger [1971] 154 p. illus. (part col.) 27 cm. (American art & artists) Bibliography: p. 145-149. [N6537.S73B38] 74-125486 15.00

collections of William Culp Darrah and Richard Russack. 1st ed. Garden City, N.Y. : Doubleday, 1977. 109 p. : chiefly ill. ; 26 cm. [TR780.A4] 76-23805 pbk. : 3.95
1. Stereoscopic views. 2. Wit and humor, Pictorial. I. Darrah, William Culp, 1909- II. Russack, Richard. III. Title: Our country victorious and now a happy home.

DARRAH, William Culp, 1909- 778.40973
Stereo views, a history of stereographs in America and their collection. [Gettysburgh, Pa., Author, Rt. 1. c.1964] xii, 255p. illus., facsims. 24cm. Bibl. [TR780.D34] 65-1535 6.00
1. Stereoscopic views. I. Title.

Sterling and Francine Clark Art Institute, Williamstown, Mass.

STERLING and Francine Clark Art Institute, Williamstown, Mass. 750'.74'01441
List of paintings in the Sterling and Francine Clark Art Institute. [Williamstown, c1972] 144 p. illus. 25 cm. "A chronological list of the publications of the Sterling and Francine Clark Art Institute": p. 142-144. [N867.A6] 72-90682
1. Sterling and Francine Clark Art Institute, Williamstown, Mass. 2. Paintings—Williamstown, Mass.—Catalogs. I. Title.

Stern, Alec, 1904—

STERN, Alec, 1904- 769'.92'4
Etchings of Israel, land of the Bible / [Alec Stern]. Studio ed. San Mateo, Calif. : Studio of Alec Stern, [1974] 175 p. : ill. ; 29 cm. [NE2012.S73A45] 74-191739
1. Stern, Alec, 1904- 2. Israel in art. I. Title.

Stern, Bert.

CORNFIELD, Jim. 770'.92'4
The photo illustration, Bert Stern / text by Jim Cornfield, with the editors of Alskog, inc. [New York] : T. Y. Crowell, [1974] 95 p. : ill. (some col.) ; 29 cm. (Masters of contemporary photography) [TR140.S687C67] 74-8228 ISBN 0-690-00617-9 : 7.95. ISBN 0-690-00618-7 pbk. : 3.95
1. Stern, Bert. 2. Photography, Commercial. I. Stern, Bert. II. Alskog, inc. III. Title.

Stern, Josef, 1923—

STERN, Josef, 1923- 741.9'5694
The drawings of Jossi Stern / introd. by Stephen Longstreet. 1st ed. Alhambra, Calif. : Borden Pub. Co., c1974. [48] p. : ill. ; 31 cm. (Master draughtsman series) [NC320.Z9S83] 74-24406
1. Stern, Josef, 1923- I. Title. **BIP**

Sternberg, Harry, 1904—

STERNBERG, Harry, 1904- 769'.92'4
Harry Sternberg : a catalog raisonne of his graphic work : [exhibition] : Edwin A. Ulrich Museum of Art, Wichita State University, Wichita, Kansas / by James C. Moore ; with annotations by Harry Sternberg. Wichita, Kan. : The Museum, c1975. 95 p. : ill. ; 23 cm. "Biographical data of Harry Sternberg": p. 94. Bibliography: p. 95. [NE539.S73E38] 75-26036
1. Sternberg, Harry, 1904- 2. United States in art. I. Edwin A. Ulrich Museum of Art. II. Moore, James Collins, 1941-

Sternbergs, Janis.

STERNBERGS, Janis. 709'.2'4
Images in sand / Janis Sternbergs. Lexington : University Press of Kentucky, c1977. [109] p. : chiefly ill. (some col.) ; 23 cm. [N6537.S733A47] 76-46030 ISBN 0-8131-1354-7 : 12.95
1. Sternbergs, Janis. I. Title. **BIP**

Sterne, Hedda, 1916—

HEDDA Sterne : 759.13
retrospective, April 24 through June 26, 1977, Montclair Art Museum, Montclair, New Jersey. Montclair : The Museum, c1977. 36 p. : ill. ; 27 cm. Catalog of an exhibition. [N6537.S736M664] 77-152872
1. Sterne, Hedda, 1916- I. Sterne, Hedda, 1916- II. Montclair, N.J. Art Museum.

Stettheimer, Florine, 1871-1944.

STETTHEIMER, Florine, 1871-1944. 759.13
Florine Stettheimer: an exhibition of paintings, watercolors, drawings. New York, Columbia University, 1973. 59 p. illus. (part col.) 29 cm. Catalog of an exhibition held at the Low Memorial Library, Columbia University, Feb. 8-Mar. 8, 1973. [ND237.S75C64] 73-158912 7.50 (pbk.)
1. Stettheimer, Florine, 1871-1944. I. Columbia University. Libraries.

TYLER, Parker. 927.5
Florine Stettheimer: a life in art. New York, Farrar, Straus [1963] xiv, 194 p. illus. (part col.) ports. 30 cm. [ND237.S75T9] 63-19561
1. Stettheimer, Florine, 1871-1944. I. Title.

Steuben Glass, inc.

HOTCHKISS, John F. 748.2913085
Steuben glass. Rochester, N.Y., Author, 89 Sagamore Dr. [c.1964] 103p. illus. (pt. col.) facsim., port. 23cm. Vol. 1 includes a reduced size copy of the 1932 catalogue, Steuben hand-blown glassware, pub. by Steuben Div., Corning Glass Works, with price code letters added to show 1964 price ranges [NK5198.C3H6] 65-1047 5.00 pap.,
1. Carder, Frederick. 2. teuben glass; index & price guide 3. Steuben Glass, Inc. 4. Glassware, American—Catalogs. I. Steuben Glass, Inc. Steuben hand-blown glassware. II. Title.

PERROT, Paul N. 748.2'9147'83
Steuben: seventy years of American glassmaking [by] Paul N. Perrot, Paul V. Gardner [and] James S. Plaut. New York, Praeger [1974] 172 p. illus. (part col.) 26 cm. Catalog of the exhibition held at the Toledo Museum of Art and various other museums throughout the United States beginning Nov. 1974 and lasting two years. [NK5101.T62T647] 74-6730 ISBN 0-275-44320-5 15.00
1. Steuben Glass, inc. 2. Glassware, American—Exhibitions. I. Gardner, Paul Vickers, 1908- II. Plaut, James Sachs, 1912- III. Toledo. Museum of Art. IV. Title.

PLAUT, James Sachs, 1912- 748.2'9147'83
Steuben glass; a monograph by James S. Plaut. 3d rev. and enl. ed. New York, Dover Publications [1972] xi, 111 p. illus. 29 cm. [NK5112.P56 1972] 72-78376 ISBN 0-486-22892-4 3.50
1. Steuben Glass, inc. 2. Glassware, American. I. Title. **BIP**

STEUBEN Glass, inc. 748.2'9147'83
Five masterworks. [1st ed. New York, 1972] 27 p. col. plates. 32 cm. "The artists": p. 27. [NK5112.S762 1972] 74-152329
1. Steuben Glass, inc. 2. Cut glass, American. 3. Engraved glass—United States.

Stevens, Rachel B.—Art collections.

WASHINGTON, D.C. Textile Museum. 746.7'561'0740153
Turkish rugs. The Rachel B. Stevens Memorial Collection. With an introd. by Joseph V. McMullan. Washington [1972] 63 p. illus. (part col.) 28 cm. Catalogue of an exhibition held at the Textile Museum, Sept. 24-Dec. 9, 1972. [NK2865.A1W37] 73-154450
1. Stevens, Rachel B.—Art collections. 2. Rugs, Turkish—Exhibitions. I. Title. **BIP**

Stevens, Samuel Dale, 1859-1922—Art collections.

NORTH Andover Historical Society. 709'.73'07401445
The Collection of Samuel Dale Stevens (1859-1922) arranged and presented by the North Andover Historical Society; catalogue by the North Andover Historical Society. North Andover, Mass., Advance Reproductions Corp., 1971. iv, 66 p. illus. 23 cm. Cover title: Catalogue of the Samuel Dale Stevens exhibition. [NK805.N6] 73-32037
1. Stevens, Samuel Dale, 1859-1922—Art collections. 2. Art objects, American—Exhibitions. I. Title. II. Title: Catalogue of the Samuel Dale Stevens exhibition.

Stevens, Thomas, 1828-1888.

BAKER, Wilma (Sinclair) Le Van. 927.4552
The silk pictures of Thomas Stevens; a biography of the Coventry weaver and his contribution to the art of weaving, with an illustrated catalogue of his work. [1st ed.] New York, Exposition Press [1957] 147p. illus. (part col.) ports. 24cm. [NK8998.S8B3] 57-9216
1. Stevens, Thomas, 1828-1888. 2. Slik. 3. Textile design. I. Title. **BIP**

GODDEN, Geoffrey A. 746.3'924
Stevengraphs and other Victorian silk pictures [by] Geoffrey A. Godden. [1st American ed.] Rutherford [N.J.] Fairleigh Dickinson University Press [1971] 492 p. illus. (part col.) 25 cm. [NK9002.G6 1971] 71-144124 ISBN 0-8386-7880-7 35.00
1. Stevens, Thomas, 1828-1888. 2. Silk pictures—Collectors and collecting. I. Title. **BIP**

SPRAKE, Austin. 746.3'92'4
The price guide to Stevengraphs: Stevengraphs, Stevens silk postcards, bookmarkers. Woodbridge, Antique Collecters' Club, 1972. [9], 208 p. illus. 21 cm. Includes index. [NK9002.S67] 74-156395 £4.75
1. Stevens, Thomas, 1828-1888. 2. Silk pictures—Collectors and collecting. I. Title.

Stevens, William Lester, 1888-1969.

STEVENS, William Lester, 1888-1969. 759.13
W. Lester Stevens, N.A., 1888-1969 : [catalogue]. Greenfield, Mass. : Greenfield Community College Foundation, 1977. 32 p. : ill. ; 29 cm. Exhibition held at Greenfield Community College. Includes index. Bibliography: p. 28. [ND237.S755G73] 77-368159
1. Stevens, William Lester, 1888-1969. I. Greenfield Community College.

Stewart, Dresden Blake, 1881—

JARCHOW, Merrill E., 1910- 712'.092'4 B
In search of fulfillment : episodes in the life of D. Blake Stewart / by Merrill E. Jarchow. [St. Paul] : North Central Pub. Co., 1974. ix, 86 p. : ill. ; 22 cm. [SB470.S67J37] 74-19986
1. Stewart, Dresden Blake, 1881- 2. Carleton College, Northfield, Minn. I. Title.

Stickley, Gustav, 1858-1942.

FREEMAN, John Crosby 749.2130924
The forgotten rebel; Gustav Stickley and his craftsman mission furniture. Watkins Glen, N.Y., Century House [1965, c.1966] 112p. illus., ports. 27cm. Includes author and subject indexes to the Craftsman magazine. Bibl. [NK2439.S8F7] 65-28083 price unreported lim. ed.,
1. Stickley, Gustav, 1858-1942. I. The Craftsman (Indexes) II. Title. **BIP**

Stiegel, Henry William, 1729-1785.

HUNTER, Frederick William, 1865-1919. 748.2
Stiegel glass. Introd. and notes by Helen McKearin. Illustrated with 12 plates in color from autochromes by J. B. Kerfoot and with 159 halftones. New York, Dover Publications, 1950 [i.e. 1951] xxii, 272 p. illus., plates (part col.) maps, facsims. 28 cm. Bibliography: p. 263-265. [NK5112.H8 1951] 51-9160
1. Stiegel, Henry William, 1729-1785. 2. Glass manufacture—U.S. 3. Glassware—U.S. I. Title. **BIP**

Stieglitz, Alfred, 1864-1946.

AMERICA & Alfred Stieglitz : a collective portrait / edited by Waldo Frank ... [et al.] ; with a new introd. by Dorothy Norman. New York : Octagon Books, 1975, c1934. xvi, 339 p., 32 leaves of plates : ill. ; 24 cm. Reprint of the 1st ed. published by Doubleday, Doran, Garden City, N.Y.; with a new introd. Includes index. Bibliography: p. 319-322. [TR140.S7A7 1975] 75-11881 ISBN 0-374-96117-4 : 17.00 779'.092'4
1. Stieglitz, Alfred, 1864-1946. 2. Photography, Artistic. I. Frank, Waldo David, 1889-1967.

BOSTON. Museum of Fine Arts. 779
Alfred Stieglitz: photographer, by Doris Bry. Boston; [Distributed by October House, New York, 1965] 28 p. 62 plates. 28 cm. Contents.Contents.—The Alfred Stieglitz collection in the Museum of Fine Arts.—Alfred Stieglitz: photographer, by D. Bray.—Chronology.—Bibliography (p. 25-26)—Catalogue. [TR140.S7B6] 65-24359
1. Stieglitz, Alfred, 1864-1946. 2. Photography, Artistic. I. Bry, Doris.

GEORGE Eastman House, Rochester, N.Y. 770'.1
Photo-secession : Stieglitz and the fine-art movement in photography / Robert Doty ; with a foreword by Beaumont Newhall. New York : Dover Publications, 1978. 139 p. : ill. ; 28 cm. Reprint of the 1960 ed. published by George Eastman House, New York, which was issued as George Eastman House monograph no. 1. Bibliography: p. 135-136. [TD650.G36 1978] 77-20467 ISBN 0-486-23588-2 : 5.00
1. Stieglitz, Alfred, 1864-1946. 2. Photography, Artistic. I. Doty, Robert M. II. Title. III. Series: George Eastman House monograph ; no. 1. **BIP**

NORMAN, Dorothy, 1905- 779
Alfred Stieglitz; introduction to an American seer. New York, Duell, Sloan and Pearce [1960] 66 p. illus., ports. 24 cm. [TR140.S7N6] 60-12836
1. Stieglitz, Alfred, 1864-1946. I. Title. **BIP**

NORMAN, Dorothy, 1905- 779'.092'4 B
Alfred Stieglitz: an American seer. [1st ed.] New York, Random House [1973] 253 p. illus. 31 cm. "An Aperture book." Bibliography: p. 243-249. [TR140.S7N59] 74-529 ISBN 0-394-48809-1 35.00
1. Stieglitz, Alfred, 1864-1946. I. Stieglitz, Alfred, 1864-1946.

SELIGMANN, Herbert Jacob, 1891- 779.0924
Alfred Stieglitz talking; notes on some of his conversations, 1925-1931. Foreword by Herbert J. Seligmann. New Haven [Conn.] Yale University Library, [c.]1966. ix, 149p. 24cm. [TR140.S7S4] 66-21942 7.50
1. Stieglitz, Alfred, 1864-1946. 2. Artists—Correspondence, reminiscences, etc. I. Stieglitz, Alfred, 1864-1946. II. Title.

Stieglitz, Alfred, 1864-1946—Art patronage.

HOMER, William Innes. 709'.73
Stieglitz and the American avant-garde / William Innes Homer. 1st ed. Boston : New York Graphics Society, c1977. p. cm. Bibliography: p. [N5220.S858H65 1977] 76-50068 ISBN 0-8212-0676-1 : 17.50
1. Stieglitz, Alfred, 1864-1946—Art patronage. 2. Art, American. 3. Art, Modern—20th century—United States. 4. Photography, Artistic. 5. Artists—United States—Biography. I. Title.

SUBJECT INDEX STOCKHOLM. NATIONALMUSEUM.

Stieglitz Group.

YOUNG, Mahonri Sharp, 1911- 759.06
Early American moderns; painters of the Stieglitz Group. New York, Watson-Guptill Publications [1974] 159 p. illus. (part col.) 32 cm. Bibliography: p. 156-157. [ND212.5.S75Y67] 74-9909 ISBN 0-8230-1598-X 24.50
1. Stieglitz Group. 2. Stieglitz, Alfred, 1864-1946—Art patronage. 3. Painting, Modern—20th century—United States. I. Title.

Still, Clyfford, 1904—

STILL, Clyfford, 1904- 759.13
Clyfford Still. New York, Marlborough-Gerson Gallery [1969] 89 p. (chiefly col. plates) 30 cm. Catalog of the exhibition held Oct.-Nov. 1969, at the Marlborough-Gerson Gallery, New York. [ND237.S78A43] 76-18395
I. Marlborough-Gerson Gallery.

STILL, Clyfford, 1904- 759.13
Clyfford Still. [San Francisco] : San Francisco Museum of Modern Art, 1976. 141 p. : ill. (some col.) ; 31 cm. Catalog of an exhibition of C. Still's gift to the San Francisco Museum of Modern Art, held in early 1976. Bibliography: p. 139. [ND237.S78S25] 75-35088
1. Still, Clyfford, 1904- I. San Francisco. Museum of Modern Art.

Still-life in art.

HAMM, Jack. 743'.8'35
Still-life drawing and painting / by Jack Hamm. New York : Grosset & Dunlap, c1976. 120 p. : ill. ; 28 cm. Includes index. Instructions for drawing and painting still-life art, beginning with basic skills and progressing to advanced techniques. [N8251.S3H35] 75-37308 ISBN 0-448-11526-3 : 4.95
1. Still-life in art. 2. Art—Technique. I. Title. BIP

Still-life painting.

BERGSTROM, Ingvar. 758.4
Dutch still-life painting in the seventeenth century. Translated by Christina Hedstrom and Gerald Taylor. [1st American ed.] New York, T. Yoseloff [1956] xix, 330p. illus. (part col.) 29cm. Translation of Studier I hollandskt stillebenmaleri under 1600-talet. Bibliography: p.317-325. [ND1390.B42] 56-14629
1. Still-life painting. 2. Painting, Dutch. I. Title.

BOHROD, Aaron 759.13
A decade of still life. Madison, Univ. of Wis. Pr., 1966. xiii, 298p. illus. (pt. col.) 32cm. Autobiographical. [ND237.A2B6] 66-10492 20.00
I. Title. BIP

FINCH College, New York. Museum of Art. 758'.4'07401471
Still life painters, Pieter Aertsen, 1508-1575 to Georges Braque, 1882-1963; a loan exhibition, opening February 2, 1965. [Catalogue prepared by Robert L. Manning] New York [1965?] [48] p. illus. 23 cm. [ND1390.F53] 74-280416
1. Still-life painting. 2. Paintings—Exhibitions. I. Manning, Robert L. II. Title.

GWYNNE-JONES, Allan, 1892- 751.45
Introduction to still-life. London, New York, Staples Press [1954] xx, 72p. 68 plates. 24cm. Bibliographical footnotes. [ND1390.G90758.4] 55-24578
1. Still-life painting. I. Title.

SCHAAD, Bentley 758.4
The realm of contemporary still life painting. New York, Reinhold [1962] 127p. illus. (pt. col.) port. 31cm. 62-19485 12.00
1. Still-life painting. 2. Painting—Technique. I. Title.

STERLING, Charles, 1901- 758.4
Still life painting from antiquity to the present time. [A new rev. ed. Translated by James Emmons] New York, Universe Books [1959] 164 p. illus., 125 plates (part col.) 27 cm. Bibliography: p. 151-[158] [ND1390.S713] 59-13045
1. Still life painting. I. Title.

WALTER, Start 751.45
Still life painting. New York, Reinhold [1961, c.1960] 63p. illus. (part col.) 61-11309 2.95 bds.,
1. Still-life painting. I. Title.

Still-life painting, American.

BORN, Wolfgang, 1893- 758'.4'0973
Still-life painting in America. New York, Hacker Art Books, 1973 [i.e. 1974] xiv, 54 p., 134 p. of illus. 31 cm. Includes bibliographical references. [ND1390.B6 1974] 77-147035 ISBN 0-87817-092-8 25.00
1. Still-life painting, American. I. Title. BIP

GERDTS, William H. 758'.4'0973
American still-life painting [by] William H. Gerdts and Russell Burke. New York, Praeger [1971] 263 p. illus. (part col.) 29 cm. (American art & artists) Bibliography: p. 257-259. [ND1392.G47] 78-149966 25.00
1. Still-life painting, American. I. Burke, Russell, joint author. II. Title. III. Series.

GERDTS, William H. 758'.4'0973
A century of American still-life painting, 1813-1913. Selected by William H. Gerdts. [New York, American Federation of Arts, c1966] 1 v. (unpaged) illus. 29 cm. "Organized and circulated by the American Federation of Arts." Contains "Nature's bounty and man's delight, by William H. Gerdts" (an essay which originally appeared in the catalog for the exhibition, Nature's bounty and man's delight, shown at the Newark Museum, June 15-September 28, 1958) and a catalog. [ND210.G4] 77-7755
1. Still-life painting, American. I. American Federation of Arts. II. Title.

Still-life painting, American—Catalogs.

KENNEDY Galleries, inc., New York. 708.147'1 s
American still lifes: 19th and 20th centuries. New York [1971] 66-127 p. illus. 23 cm. (The Kennedy quarterly, v. 11, no. 2) [N8640.K4 vol. 11, no. 2] [ND1392.5] 758'.4 72-180810 2.00
1. Still-life painting, American—Catalogs. I. Title. II. Series.

Still-life painting, American—Exhibitions.

BRINDLE, John V. 758'.4'0973074014886
American cornucopia : 19th century still lifes and studies : a bicentennial exhibition presented by the Hunt Institute for Botanical Documentation, Carnegie-Mellon University, Pittsburgh, Pennsylvania, 5 April-30 July, 1976 : catalogue / by John V. Brindle and Sally Secrist ; introd. by William H. Gerdts. [Pittsburgh] : Hunt Institute for Botanical Documentation, [1976] 48 p. : ill. (some col.) ; 23 cm. Includes index. [ND2291.B74] 77-354770 ISBN 0-913196-18-5
1. Still-life painting, American—Exhibitions. 2. Paintings, Modern—19th century—United States—Exhibitions. I. Secrist, Sally, joint author. II. Hunt Institute for Botanical Documentation. III. Title.

Still-life painting—Technique.

THE art of still life painting. 751.4
[Designed and edited by Walter Brooks. New York, Western Pub. Co., 1972] 48 p. illus. 32 cm. (A Grumbacher library book) [ND1390.A87] 70-184643 1.00
1. Still-life painting—Technique. I. Brooks, Walter, 1921-

DAVIES, Ken, 1926- 758'.4
Painting sharp focus still lifes : trompe l'oeil oil techniques / by Ken Davies and Ellye Bloom. New York : Watson-Guptill Publications, 1975. p. cm. Includes index. [ND1390.D35 1975] 75-20196 ISBN 0-8230-3856-4 : 15.95
1. Still-life painting—Technique. 2. Trompe l'oeil painting. I. Bloom, Ellye, 1929- joint author. II. Title. BIP

RYAN, Adrian. 751.4'5
Still life painting techniques / Adrian Ryan. London : Batsford, 1978. 120 p., [2] leaves of plates : ill. (some col.) ; 26 cm. Includes index. Bibliography: p. 115. [ND1390.R9] 78-312297 ISBN 0-7134-0635-6 : 12.50
1. Still-life painting—Technique. I. Title. Distributed by Hippocrene Books, New York, NY 10016 BIP

TAUBES, Frederic, 1900- 751.4
The technique of still life painting. New York, Watson-Guptill Publications [1968] 142 p. illus. (part col.) 29 cm. [ND1390.T3] 68-27550 12.50
1. Still-life painting—Technique. I. Title.

Still-life paintings—Exhibitions.

FISHER, M. Roy. 758'.4'07401471
The object as subject : still life paintings from the seventeenth to the twentieth century : [catalogue of a loan exhibition, April 4th-May 3rd, 1975]. New York : Wildenstein, [1975] [6] p. ; 28 cm. Cover title. Text on p. [2]-[3] of cover. "A note on still life [by] M. R. F.": p. [2]-[3] [ND1390.F57] 75-318678
1. Still-life paintings—Exhibitions. I. Wildenstein and Company, inc., New York. II. Title.

WADSWORTH Atheneum, Hartford. 754
Harvest of plenty, de gustibus; an exhibition of banquets and eating scenes, harvests and the fruits of the harvests. [Hartford, 1963] 12 p. illus. 23 cm. Page 12 blank for "Notes." Catalog of the exhibition held Oct. 24-Dec. 1, 1963. [ND1390.W28] 73-156742
1. Still-life paintings—Exhibitions. 2. Genre paintings—Exhibitions. I. Title.

Stillman, Ary, 1891-1967.

HIRSCH, Richard Teller. 759.13
Ary Stillman, 1891-1967; a retrospective exhibition [held at] the Museum of Fine Arts, Houston, February 23-March 26, 1972. [Houston, Tex., Museum of Fine Arts, 1972] 48 p. illus. (part col.) 28 cm. Introd. and catalogue by R. T. Hirsch. [ND237.S79H56] 78-190100
1. Stillman, Ary, 1891-1967. I. Houston, Tex. Museum of Fine Arts.

Stillman, Clark, 1907- —Art collections.

DALLAS. Museum of Fine Arts. 730'.9675'0976428
The Clark and Frances Stillman Collection of Congo sculpture: a gift of Eugene and Margaret McDermott to the Dallas Museum of Fine Arts. [Dallas] 1969. 83 p. illus., map. 22 cm. Bibliography: p. 83. [NB1097.C75D3] 73-9373
1. Stillman, Clark, 1907- —Art collections. 2. Stillman, Frances, 1910- —Art collections. 3. Sculpture, Congo—Catalogs. I. Title.

Stine, Richard.

STINE, Richard. 741.9'73
Richard Stine's Non-pointless pencil book. New York : Harcourt Brace Jovanovich, c1978. [64] p. : all ill. ; 16 x 23 cm. (A Harvest/HBJ book) [NC139.S73A4 1978] 78-889 ISBN 0-15-679167-6 pbk. : 2.95
1. Stine, Richard. I. Title. II. Title: Non-pointless pencil book.

Stirling, James Frazer.

HODGETTS, Craig. 745'.05 s
Inside James Stirling / Craig Hodgetts. Minneapolis : Walker Art Center, c1976. 36 p., [1] fold. leaf of plates : ill. ; 28 cm. (Issues in architecture ; 2) Bibliography: p. 36. [NK1.E9 no. 100] [NA997.S78] 720'.92'4 77-150324 1.60
1. Stirling, James Frazer. I. Title. II. Series. III. Design quarterly ; 100

STIRLING, James Frazer. 720'.92'4
James Stirling : buildings & projects, 1950-1974 / introd. by John Jacobus ; layout by Leon Krier and James Stirling. New York : Oxford University Press, 1975. 183 p. : ill. ; 24 x 29 cm. Caption titles in English and German. [NA997.S78A44] 75-317127 30.00
1. Stirling, James Frazer. BIP

Stix, Marguerite.

MCLANATHAN, Richard B. K. 709'.2'4
The art of Marguerite Stix / by Richard McLanathan. New York : H. N. Abrams, [1977] p. cm. Includes index. Bibliography: p. [N6811.5.S76M32] 77-9089 ISBN 0-8109-1620-7 : 45.00
1. Stix, Marguerite. I. Title. BIP

Stoas.

COULTON, John James. 722'.8
The architectural development of the Greek stoa / by J. J. Coulton. Oxford [Eng.] : Clarendon Press, 1976. xviii, 308 p., [5] leaves of plates : ill. ; 29 cm. (Oxford monographs in archaeology) Based on author's thesis. Includes bibliographical references and indexes. [NA278.S85C68] 77-364961 ISBN 0-19-813215-8 : 39.00
1. Stoas. 2. Greece—Antiquities. I. Title. II. Series. BIP

Stobart, John.

STOBART, John. 759.2
Ports & pioneers of the sailing days; new paintings. [New York? 1972] [24] p. illus. (part col.) 26 cm. Catalog of the artist's 4th New York exhibition held Nov. 15-Dec. 9, 1972, at the Kennedy Galleries. [ND497.S797K46] 72-172721
1. Stobart, John. 2. Ships in art. I. Kennedy Galleries, inc., New York. II. Title.

Stock, Joseph Whiting, 1815-1855.

STOCK, Joseph Whiting, 1815-1855. 759.13 B
The paintings and the journal of Joseph Whiting Stock / edited by Juliette Tomlinson ; with a checklist of his works compiled by Kate Steinway. Middletown, Conn. : Wesleyan University Press, [1976] p. cm. Includes index. Bibliography: p. [ND1329.S69A25] 76-7189 ISBN 0-8195-4098-6 : 30.00
1. Stock, Joseph Whiting, 1815-1855. 2. Portrait-painters—United States—Correspondence, reminiscences, etc. 3. Primitivism in art—United States. I. Tomlinson, Juliette, 1921- II. Title. BIP

Stockfleth, Julius, 1857-1935.

STOCKFLETH, Julius, 1857-1935. 759.13
Julius Stockfleth, Gulf Coast marine and landscape painter / by James Patrick McGuire ; introduction by Eric Steinfeldt. San Antonio : Trinity University Press, 1976. xii, 161 p. : chiefly ill. (some col.) ; 23 x 27 cm. "Published in conjunction with an exhibition of paintings and drawings by Julius Stockfleth in December, 1976 at the Rosenberg Library, Galveston, Texas." Bibliography: p. 15-16. [N6537.S75M32 1976] 76-29876 ISBN 0-911536-67-1 pbk. : 10.00
1. Stockfleth, Julius, 1857-1935. 2. Gulf coast (United States) in art. I. McGuire, James Patrick. II. Rosenberg Library, Galveston. III. Title.

Stockholm. Nationalmuseum.

STOCKHOLM. Nationalmuseum. Moderna museet. v. 12
Katalogen over Moderna museets samlingar av svensk och internationell 1900 -talskonst = Catalogue of the Modern Museum's collection of Swedish and international 20th century art / red. o. arbetsgrupped. staff, Birgitta Arvas ... [et al.] ; overs. / transl., Steven Wentworth, Keith Bradfield. Stockholm : Moderna mus., 1976. 196 p. : ill. ; 21 x 30 cm. Introd. and list of exhibitions held at Moderna museet, 1956-1976 in Swedish and English. [N7088.S76 1976] 77-470872 ISBN 9-17-100097-6 : kr35.00

1. Stockholm. Nationalmuseum. Moderna museet. 2. Art, Swedish—Catalogs. 3. Art, Modern—20th century—Sweden—Catalogs. 4. Art, Modern—20th century—Catalogs. 5. Art—Sweden—Stockholm—Catalogs. I. Arvas, Birgitta. II. Title. III. Title: Catalogue of the Modern Museum's collection of Swedish and international 20th century art.

Stoddard, Seneca Ray, 1844-1917.

DE SORMO, Maitland C. 770'.92'4 B
Seneca Ray Stoddard; versatile camera-artist, by Maitland C. De Sormo. Saranac Lake, N.Y., Adirondack Yesteryears [1972] 190 p. illus. 27 cm. [TR140.S73D47] 72-90586 10.50
1. Stoddard, Seneca Ray, 1844-1917. I. Title. BIP

Stokes, Isaac Newton Phelps, 1867-1944—Art collections.

NEW York (City). Public Library. 769.973
American historical prints: early views of American cities, etc. from the Phelps Stokes and other collections, by I. N. Phelps Stokes and Daniel C. Haskell. New York, New York Public Library, 1933. Detroit, Gale Research Co., 1972. xxxiii, 235 p. illus. 23 cm. [NE954.2.N39 1972] 77-180284 ISBN 0-8103-3950-1
1. Stokes, Isaac Newton Phelps, 1867-1944—Art collections. 2. Prints—New York (City)—Catalogs. 3. Drawings—New York (City)—Catalogs. 4. America—Description and travel—Views. 5. America—Description and travel—Maps, Early. 6. America—History—Pictorial works. I. Stokes, Isaac Newton Phelps, 1867-1944. II. Haskell, Daniel Carl, 1883-III. Title.

Stone carving.

BATTEN, Mark. 731.463
Direct carving in stone. [1st American ed. Rev. and enl. ed.] New York, Transatlantic Arts, 1966. vi, 153 p. illus. 23 cm. First ed. published in 1957 under title: Stone sculpture by direct carving. [NB1170.B3 1966] 67-31913
1. Stone carving. I. Title.

MEILACH, Dona Z. 731.4'63
Contemporary stone sculpture; aesthetics, methods, appreciation, by Dona Z. Meilach. New York, Crown Publishers [1970] xi, 211 p. illus. (part col.), ports. 27 cm. [NB1208.M44 1970] 71-108070 7.95
1. Stone carving. I. Title. BIP

MURPHY, Seamus 730.924
Stone mad; with illustrations by William Harrington and initial letters by the author. New ed. rev. London, Routledge & K. Paul, 1966. x, 229p. front., illus. (incl. port.) 23cm. [NB497.M8A2 1966] 66-78754 6.00
1. Stone carving. 2. Ireland—Soc. life & cust. I. Title.
American distributor: Hillary House, New York. BIP

SUSINI, Giancarlo. 736'.5'0937
The Roman stonecutter; an introduction to Latin epigraphy. Edited with an introd. by E. Badian; translated by A. M. Dabrowski. Totowa, N.J., Rowman and Littlefield [1973] ix, 84 p. illus. 23 cm. Translation of Il lapicida romano. Includes bibliographical references. [NK8705.S9713] 73-6538 ISBN 0-87471-196-7 7.50
1. Stone carving. 2. Inscriptions, Latin. 3. Lettering. I. Title. BIP

Stone, Harris, 1934—

STONE, Harris, 1934- 720'.92'4
Workbook of an unsuccessful architect. New York, M[onthly] R[eview Press, 1974, c1973] 192 p. illus. 25 cm. Includes bibliographical references. [NA737.S67A27] 73-8052 ISBN 0-85345-294-6 8.95
1. Stone, Harris, 1934- 2. Architects—United States—Correspondence, reminiscences, etc. I. Title.

STONE, Harris, 1934- 720.924
Workbook of an unsuccessful architect. New York, Monthly Review Press [1974, c1973] 192 p. illus. 24 cm. Includes bibliographical references. [NA737.S67A27] ISBN 0-85345-294-6 3.45 (pbk.)
1. Stone, Harris, 1934- 2. Architects—U.S.—Correspondence, reminiscences, etc. I. Title.
L.C. card number for cloth edition: 73-8052.

Stone, Ida Mae, 1867-1932.

STONE, Ida Mae, 1867-1932. 741.9'68'2
Sketches : published on the occasion of Johannesburg's ninetieth birthday / by Ida Mae Stone and Harry Clayton ; edited by Anna H. Smith. Johannesburg : Published for the Africana Museum by Ad. Donker, 1976. 208 p. : chiefly ill. ; 16 x 25 cm. Includes index. Bibliography: p. 204. [NC368.6.S63S833] 77-357717 ISBN 0-949937-27-4
1. Stone, Ida Mae, 1867-1932. 2. Clayton, Harry, 1864-1938. 3. Johannesburg in art. I. Clayton, Harry, 1864-1938.

Stone implements.

BORDAZ, Jacques. 621.9'08'09012
Tools of the old and new stone age. Photos. by Lee Boltin. [1st ed.] Garden City, N.Y., Published for the American Museum of Natural History [by] the Natural History Press [1970] xii, 145 p. illus. 22 cm. "Portions of this book are based on two articles written by the author which appeared in Natural history magazine in January and February, 1959." Bibliography: p. [112]-141. [GN446.1.B67] 76-103733 5.95
1. Stone implements. I. American Museum of Natural History, New York. II. Title.

CRABTREE, Don E. 970.1 s
An introduction to flintworking, by Don E. Crabtree. With editorial assistance of Guy Muto, Christine Lovgren [and] Earl H. Swanson; and illus. by Mary Keeler. [Pocatello, Idaho State University Museum, 1972] 98 p. illus. 28 cm. (Occasional papers of the Idaho State University Museum, no. 28) Errata sheet inserted. [E78.I18I4 no. 28] [GN446.1] 621.9'08 72-612039 4.00 (pbk)
1. Stone implements. I. Title. II. Series: Idaho. State University, Pocatello. Museum. Occasional papers, no. 28.
Contents Omitted.

MEWHINNEY, Hubert. 571.15
A manual for Neanderthals. Austin, University of Texas Press [1957] 122 p. illus. 24 cm. [GN446.1.M5] 57-8821
1. Stone implements. I. Title.

Stone implements—Congresses.

STONE tools as cultural markers : change, evolution and complexity / edited by R. V. S. Wright. Canberra : Australian Institute of Aboriginal Studies ; New Jersey : Humanities Press, 1977. 400 p. : ill. ; 30 cm. (Prehistory and material culture series ; no. 12) Papers presented to a symposium at the 1974 meeting of the Australian Institute of Aboriginal Studies. Includes bibliographical references and indexes. [GN434.S76] 77-93952 ISBN 0-391-00835-8 : 33.50 ISBN 0-391-00836-6 pbk. : 23.75 301.21
1. Stone implements—Congresses. 2. Stone implements—Australia—Congresses. I. Wright, R. V. S. II. Australian Institute of Aboriginal Studies, Canberra. III. Title. IV. Series. BIP

Stone, Reynolds.

†STONE, Reynolds. 769'.92'4
Reynolds Stone : engravings / with an introd. by the artist and an appreciation by Kenneth Clark. Brattleboro, Vt. : S. Greene Press, c1977. xli, 151 p. : chiefly ill. ; 30 cm. Bibliography: p. xl-xli. [NE1147.6.S8A4 1977a] 77-80334 ISBN 0-8289-0321-2 : 65.00
1. Stone, Reynolds. I. Title. BIP

Stonehenge.

BERGSTROM, Theo. 779'.9'936219
Stonehenge / photographed by Theo Bergstrom ; text by Lance Vatcher. Rev. and enl. ed. London : Bergstrom and Boyle Books ; New York : Two Continents, 1977. [93] p. : chiefly ill. ; 23 cm. [DA142.B45 1977] 78-318520 ISBN 0-8467-0323-8 (Two Continents) : 4.95
1. Stonehenge. I. Vatcher, Lance. II. Title. BIP

Storage in the home.

SUNSET. 684.1'6
Sunset ideas for storage; bookshelves, cupboards, cabinets, by the editorial staff of Sunset books. [2d ed.] Menlo Park, Calif. Lane Books [1966] 128 p. illus. 28 cm. First ed. published in 1958 under title: Sunset ideas for storage in your home. [TT197.5.B8S8 1966] 66-24884
1. Storage in the home. 2. Built-in furniture. I. Title.

SUNSET. 684.2
Sunset ideas for storage in your home, by the editorial staff of Sunset books. [1st ed.] Menlo Park, Calif. Lane Pub. Co. [1958] 128 p. illus. 28 cm. [TT197.5.B8S8] 58-13246
1. Storage in the home. 2. Built-in furniture. I. Title.

Store fixtures.

BEAUDET, Richard S v. 12
Retail planning standards. Los Angeles, Retail Planning Service, c1966. 1 v. (unpaged, chiefly illus.) 29 cm. [NUC68-44567]
1. Store fixtures. 2. Department stores. 3. Stores, Retail. I. Retail Planning Service. II. Title.

Stores, Retail.

ARCHITECTURAL record. 725.21
Stores and shopping centers. Edited by James S. Hornbeck, senior editor. New York, McGraw-Hill [1962] viii, 181 p. illus., diagrs. 30 cm. (Dodge books) [NA6220.A75] 62-20520
1. Stores, Retail. 2. Shopping centers. 3. Architecture — Designs and plans. I. Hornbeck, James S., ed. II. Title.

FERNANDEZ, Jose Antonio, 1898- 725.213
The specialty shop, a guide. with a foreword by Leopold Arnaud. Rev. ed. New York, Architectural Book Pub. Co. [c1955] 304p. illus., plans. 28cm. ['Designing for business' series] [NA6220.F4 1955] 55-633
1. Stores, Retail. I. Title.

KETCHUM, Morris, 1904- 725.213
Shops & stores. Rev. ed. New York, Reinhold Pub. Corp. [1957] 263p. illus. (part col.) 30cm. (Progressive architecture library) Bibliography: p.257. [NA6220.K4 1957] 57-11778
1. Stores, Retail. 2. Architecture—U. S. I. Title.

Stories without words.

WARD, Lynd Kendall, 1905- 769'.92'4
Gods' man : a novel in woodcuts / by Lynd Ward. New York : St. Martin's Press, 1978. [118] p. : chiefly ill. ; 20 cm. [NE1112.W37A4 1978] 77-91889 ISBN 0-312-33100-2 : 7.95. ISBN 0-312-33101-0 pbk. : 4.95
1. Ward, Lynd Kendall, 1905- 2. Stories without words. I. Title. II. Title: A novel in woodcuts.

Storr, Paul, 1771-1844.

PENZER, Norman Mosley, 1892- 739.2'092'4
Paul Storr, 1771-1844, silversmith and goldsmith, [by] N. M. Penzer. Feltham, New York, Spring Books, 1971 [c1954] 5-292 p. illus., facsim., geneal. tables, maps, port. 31 cm. Originally published in 1954 under title: Paul Storr, the last of the goldsmiths. Includes bibliographical references and index. [NK7198.S85P4 1971] 73-169542 ISBN 0-600-37960-4 £4.25
1. Storr, Paul, 1771-1844.

Story, Ala—Art collections.

CALIFORNIA. University, Santa Barbara. Art Gallery. 769
The Ala Story Print Collection of the Art Gallery, University of California at Santa Barbara. [Exhibition] March 9 through March 26, 1967. [Santa Barbara, 1967] 11 p. 5 illus. 26 cm. Catalogue. Bibliography: p. 11. [NE42.S3C32] 67-63593
1. Story, Ala—Art collections. 2. Prints—Exhibitions. I. Title.

SANTA Barbara, Calif. Museum of Art. 760'.09'04074019491
The Ala Story Collection of the Santa Barbara Museum of Art; exhibited on the occasion to the museum's thirtieth anniversary, June 6, 1971. [Santa Barbara, 1971] 167 p. illus., ports. 24 cm. [N6487.S25S25] 79-164744
1. Story, Ala—Art collections. 2. Art, Modern—20th century—Exhibitions. I. Title.

Story, William Wetmore, 1819-1895.

JAMES, Henry, 1843-1916. 927.3
William Wetmore Story and his friends; from letters, diaries, and recollections. New York, Grove Press [1957?] 2v. in 1. 22cm. [NB237.S7J3] 57-5157
1. Story, William Wetmore, 1819-1895. I. Title. BIP

JAMES, Henry, 1843-1916. 709'.24 B
William Wetmore Story and his friends; from letters, diaries, and recollections. New York, Kennedy Galleries, 1969. 2 v. in 1. ports. 24 cm. (Library of American art) Reprint of the 1903 ed. [NB237.S7J3 1969] 69-18460
1. Story, William Wetmore, 1819-1895. I. Title.

Stoss, Veit, d. 1533.

BURKHARD, Arthur. 730'.92'4
The Cracow Altar of Veit Stoss. [Cambridge, Mass., 1972] 26 p. illus. 25 cm. Includes bibliographical references. [NB588.S8B87] 73-150441
1. Stoss, Veit, d. 1533. Cracow Altar. 2. Krakow. Kosciol Mariacki. I. Title.

Stoves.

BACON, Richard M. 738.8
The forgotten art of building and using a brick bake oven : a practical guide : how to date, renovate, and use an existing brick oven and how to construct a new one from scratch / Richard M. Bacon. 1st ed. Dublin, N.H. : Yankee, inc., 1977. 62 p., [1] leaf of plates : ill. ; 23 cm. [TX657.O57B3] 77-74809 ISBN 0-911658-76-9 pbk. : 2.50
1. Stoves. 2. Fireplaces. 3. Building, Brick. I. Title. II. Title: Brick bake. BIP

MERCER, Henry Chapman, 1856-1930. 739.47
The Bible in iron: pictured stoves and stoveplates of the Pennsylvania Germans; notes on colonial firebacks in the United States, the ten-plate stove, Franklin's fireplace, and the tile stoves of the Moravians in Pennsylvania and North Carolina, together with a list of colonial furnaces in the United States and Canada. Rev., corr. and enl. by Horace M. Mann. With further amendments and additions by Joseph E. Sandford, editor. [3d ed.] Doylestown, Pa., Bucks County Historical Society, 1961. xvi, 256p. plates. 28cm. Bibliography: p. 143-149. [NK8212.P4M4 1961] 61-15473
1. Stoves. 2. Stove- plates. 3. Christian art and symbolism. 4. Germans in Pennsylvania. I. Title.

REID, Jo, 1944- 749'.62
Stove book / Jo Reid and John Peck. New York : St. Martin's Press, 1977. [84] p. : all col. ill. ; 21 cm. [TH7435.R44 1977] 77-73016 ISBN 0-312-76376-X pbk. : 5.95

1. Stoves. I. Peck, John, 1943- joint author. II. Title. BIP

Stowe House. Gardens.

GILPIN, William, 1724-1804. 712'.6'0942593
A dialogue upon the gardens of the right honourable the Lord Viscount Cobham at Stow in Buckinghamshire / William Gilpin ; introd. by John Dixon Hunt. [Los Angeles] : William Andrews Clark Memorial Library, University of California, Los Angeles, 1976. ix, 60 p. ; 22 cm. (Publicaton - Augustan Reprint Society ; no. 176) On cover: A dialogue upon the gardens at Stow. [SB466.G8S764 1976] 76-622992
1. Stowe House. Gardens. 2. Cobham, Richard Temple, 1st Viscount, 1669?-1749. 3. Landscape gardening—Early works to 1800. I. Title: A dialogue upon the gardens of the right honourable the Lord Viscount Cobham ... II. Title: A dialogue upon the gardens at Stow. III. Series: Augustan Reprint Society. Publication ; no. 176.

Strahan, William, 1715-1785.

COCHRANE, James Aikman 920.4
Dr. Johnson's printer; the life of William Strahan. Cambridge, Mass., Harvard [c.] 1964. xiii, 225p. illus., facsims., geneal. table, port. 23cm. Bibl. [Z232.S887C6] 65-7048 6.00
1. Strahan, William, 1715-1785. I. Title.

COCHRANE, James Aikman. 926.55
Dr. Johnson's printer; the life of William Strahan, by J. A. Cochrane. London, Routledge & K. Paul [1964] xiii, 225 p. facsims., geneal. table, port. 23 cm. Bibliographical footnotes. [Z232.S887C6 1964a] 65-68018
1. Strahan, William, 1715-1785. I. Title.

Strand, Paul, 1890-1976.

LONDON. National Portrait Gallery. 779'.092'4
Paul Strand : [catalogue of] a retrospective exhibition of his photographs, 1915-68 / [organized by the] National Portrait Gallery in association with the Arts Council of Great Britain. London : the Gallery, 1976. [16] p. : ill., ports. ; 26 cm. Exhibition arranged by the Philadelphia Museum of Art and on view at the National Portrait Gallery annex 30 January -4 April, 1976. [TR647.S85L66 1976] 77-366432 ISBN 0-904017-05-2 : £0.50
1. Strand, Paul, 1890-1976. 2. Photography, Artistic—Exhibitions. I. Arts Council of Great Britain. II. Philadelphia Museum of Art.

Strater, Henry, 1896—

STRATER, Henry, 1896- 759.13
Paintings, 1968-1972, together with earlier works, 1920-1967; also various drawings. New York, Frank Rehn Gallery, 1973. 95 p. illus. (part col.), ports. 24 cm. [ND237.S795A54] 72-93044
1. Strater, Henry, 1896-

Stratford Hall, Westmoreland Co., Va. 2 Box.

SMITH, Archibald Gray, 1890- 715'.3
The boxwood at Stratford Hall [by] A. G. Smith, Jr. Drawings by Walker Reed Muse. [Stratford? Va., 1966] ix, 64 p. illus. 24 cm. Prepared at the request of the Robert E. Lee Memorial Foundation. [SB466.U7S8] 66-18968
1. Stratford Hall, Westmoreland Co., Va. 2 Box. I. Robert E. Lee Memorial Foundation, inc. II. Title.

Straus, Irma N.—Art collections.

PARKE-BERNET Galleries, inc., New York. 380.1'45'7 s
Highly important old master drawings including examples of Francois Boucher [and others]. Collected by Irma N. Straus and Jesse Isidor Straus ... Public auction, Wednesday evening, October 21 at 8 p.m. New York, 1970. 94 p. illus. 28 cm. On cover: The Irma N. Straus Collection of old master drawings. "Sale number 3096." [Z999.P23 no. 3096] [NC80] 741.9'4'0740471 74-189761 7.00
1. Straus, Irma N.—Art collections. 2. Straus, Jesse Isidor, 1872-1936—Art collections. 3. Drawings—Exhibitions. I. Title. II. Title: Old master drawings.

Straw work.

HIBBS, Ruth. 746.4'1
Straw sculpture: techniques and projects. New York, Drake Publishers [1974] p. [TT876.H5] 74-6117 ISBN 0-87749-676-5 9.95
1. Straw work. I. Title.

LAMBETH, Minnie. 746.4'1
Straw craft : more golden dollies / [by] M. Lambeth. London : J. Baker, 1974. 72 p. : ill. ports. ; 26 cm. Label mounted on t.p.: Transatlantic Arts, inc., New York, sole distributor for the U.S.A. Bibliography: p. [72] [TT876.L35] 74-184830 ISBN 0-212-97010-0 : 8.75
1. Straw work. I. Title. BIP

RENDELL, Joan. 746.4'1
Your book of corn dollies / [by] Joan Rendell. London : Faber, 1976. 48 p. : ill., ports. ; 16 x 22 cm. (The Your book series) [TT876.R46] 76-376019 ISBN 0-571-10841-5 : 4.95
1. Straw work. 2. Corn dollies. I. Title.
Distributed by Faber and Faber, Salem, New Hampshire Distributed by Faber and Faber, Salem, New Hampshire BIP

SANDFORD, Lettice 746.41
Decorative straw work and corn dollies [by] Lettice Sandford, Philla Davis. Drawings by Philla Davis. [London] Batsford [New Rochelle, N.Y., Leisure Time Bks., 1965, c.1964] 135p. illus. 23cm. Bibl. [TT880.S3] 65-4615 6.75
1. Straw work. I. Davis, Philla, joint author. II. Title.

SANDFORD, Lettice. 745.5
Straw work and corn dollies / Lettice Sandford. New York : Viking Press, 1975, c1974. 96 p. : ill. ; 21 cm. (A Studio book) Bibliography: p. 95-96. [TT876.S34 1975] 74-15660 ISBN 0-670-67813-9 : 8.95
1. Straw work. 2. Corn dollies. I. Title. BIP

SVINICKI, Eunice. 746.4'1
Making nice things out of straw : a step-by-step crafts book using straw and cornhusks / Eunice Svinicki. New York : McKay, 1978,c1979 p. cm. [TT876.S94] 77-90452 ISBN 0-679-20452-0 : 7.95
1. Straw work. 2. Cornhusk craft. I. Title. BIP

Straw work—Exhibitions.

KAHLENBERG, Mary Hunt. 746.4'1
Grass : Los Angeles County Museum of Art, October 14, 1976—January 2, 1977 / Mary Hunt Kahlenberg. Los Angeles : The Museum, c1976. [28] p. : ill. ; 23 x 26 cm. Catalogue of an exhibition to be held also at the Institute for the Arts, Rice University, Houston, Tex., Jan. 25-Mar. 13, 1977; the Museum of Contemporary Crafts of the American Crafts Council, New York, Apr. 5-June 19, 1977; and the Renwick Gallery of the National Collection of Fine Arts, Washington, D.C., Aug. 5, 1977-Feb. 20, 1978. [TT876.K33] 76-382198 ISBN 0-87587-075-9
1. Straw work—Exhibitions. I. Los Angeles Co., Calif. Museum of Art, Los Angeles. II. Title.

Strawberry Hill Press.

HAVENS, Munson Aldrich, 1873- 070.5'092'4
Horace Walpole and the Strawberry Hill Press, 1757-1789 / by Munson Aldrich Havens. Norwood, Pa. : Norwood Editions, 1975 [c1901] p. cm. Reprint of the ed. published by L. Buddy, 3d, Canton, Pa. "Publications of the Strawberry Hill Press": p. [Z232.S9H2 1975] 75-30626 ISBN 0-88305-284-9 lib. bdg. : 15.00
1. Strawberry Hill Press. 2. Walpole, Horace, 4th Earl of Oxford, 1717-1797. I. Title. BIP

HAZEN, Allen Tracy, 1904- 094
A bibliography of the Strawberry Hill Press; with a record of the prices at which copies have been sold, including a new supplement, by A. T. Hazen; together with a bibliography and census of the detached pieces, by A. T. Hazen and J. P. Kirby. [New ed.] Folkestone [Eng.] Dawsons of Pall Mall, 1973. xxxiv, 300 p. illus. 25 cm. The bibliography is based in large part on the Walpolian collection of W. S. Lewis, who has written the preface. [Z232.S9H25 1973] 74-155393 ISBN 0-7129-0571-5 £7.50
1. Strawberry Hill Press. 2. Books—Prices. I. Kirby, John Pendy. II. Lewis, Wilmarth Sheldon, 1895- III. Title.
Distributed by Barnes and Noble, 25.00 BIP

Strazetelski, Stanislaw, 1895-

POLISH Institute of Arts and Sciences in America. 330.9'73 s
The Polish Institute of Arts and Sciences in America: origin and development, by Stanislaw Strzetelski, director. New York, 1960. 54p. 23cm. [AS36.P8434] 60-36044
1. Strazetelski, Stanislaw, 1895- I. Title.

Street art—United States.

ENVIRONMENTAL Communication (Firm). 751.7'3'0973
Big art : a visual document of American wall art, murals, and supergraphics / Environmental Communications. Philadelphia : Running Press, c1977. p. cm. [ND2608.E58 1977] 77-14043 ISBN 0-89471-006-0 pbk. : 5.95. ISBN 0-89471-007-9 lib. bdg. : 15.90
1. Street art—United States. 2. Mural painting and decoration—20th century—United States. I. Title. BIP

Street, George Edmund, 1824-1881.

STREET, Arthur Edmund, 1855- 720'.92'4 B
Memoir of George Edmund Street, R.A., 1824-1881. New York, B. Blom, 1972. 441 p. port. 21 cm. Reprint of the 1888 ed. Includes lectures given before students of the Royal Academy in the spring of 1881. [NA997.S8S8 1972] 70-173141
1. Street, George Edmund, 1824-1881. 2. Architecture—Addresses, essays, lectures. BIP

Street names—Great Britain—Lettering.

BARTRAM, Alan. 745.6'197
Street name lettering in the British Isles / Alan Bartram. 1st ed. London : Lund Humphries ; New York : Watson-Guptill Publications, 1978. 106 p. : ill. ; 20 x 21 cm. [NK3630.3.S77B37] 78-52296 ISBN 0-8230-4930-2 (Watson) : 8.95
1. Street names—Great Britain—Lettering. I. Title. BIP

Streeter, Tal.

STREETER, Tal. 730'.92'4
Kites: red line in the sky [exhibition] April 30 - May 28, 1972. [Lawrence] University of Kansas Museum of Art [1972] [12] p. illus. 24 cm. ([Kansas. University. Museum of Art] Miscellaneous publication, no. 86) [NB237.S76K36] 72-611767
1. Streeter, Tal. 2. Kites. I. Kansas. University. Museum of Art. II. Title. III. Series: Kansas. University. Museum of Art. Miscellaneous publications, no. 86.

Streeton, Arthur, Sir, 1867-1943.

GALBALLY, Ann. 709'.24
Arthur Streeton. [Melbourne] Lansdowne [1969] 87 p. illus., 32 col. plates. 27 cm. (Australian art library) Bibliography: p. 87. [ND1105.S7G3] 73-467371 8.50
1. Streeton, Arthur, Sir, 1867-1943. I. Title.

GALBALLY, Ann. 759.994
Arthur Streeton. Melbourne, New York, Oxford University Press, 1972. 30 p. illus. 19 cm. (Great Australians) Bibliography: p. 30. [ND1105.S7G32] 73-158518 ISBN 0-19-550415-1 0.70
1. Streeton, Arthur, Sir, 1867-1943.

GALBALLY, Ann. 759.9'94
Arthur Streeton. [2nd ed. Melbourne] Lansdowne [1971] 123, [4] p. illus., 79 col. plates. 26 cm. (Australian painting studio series) Bibliography: p. 121-122. [ND1105.S7G3 1971] 72-175379 ISBN 0-7018-0234-0 4.50
1. Streeton, Arthur, Sir, 1867-1943.

Streets—Great Britain—Accessories.

WARREN, Geoffrey. 717
Vanishing street furniture / Geoffrey Warren. Newton Abbot ; North Pomfret, Vt. : David & Charles, 1978. 159 p. : ill. ; 26 cm. Includes index. Bibliography: p. 153-154. [TE57.W37] 77-85020 ISBN 0-7153-7482-6 : 17.95
1. Streets—Great Britain—Accessories. I. Title. BIP

Strickland, William, 1787-1854.

GILCHRIST, Agnes Eleanor (Addison), 1907- 720.81
William Strickland, architect and engineer, 1788-1854. Philadelphia, University of Pennsylvania Press, 1950. xvii, 145 p. 51 plates (incl. ports., plans) 29 cm. Includes bibliographies. [NA737.S68G5] 51-515
1. Strickland, William, 1787-1854. 2. Architecture—U. S. I. Title.

GILCHRIST, Agnes Eleanor (Addison) 1907- 720.81
William Strickland, architect and engineer, 1788-1854. Philadelphia, University of Pennsylvania Press, 1950. [n. p.] 1954. xvii, 145p. 51plates (incl. ports., plans) 29cm. 16p. illus. ports. 29cm. 'Documentary supplement, Journal of the Society of Architectural Historians, XIII, 3.' Includes bibliographies. [NA737.S68G5] 51-515
1. Strickland, William, 1787-1854. 2. Architecture—U. S. I. Society of Architectural Historians, Journal. Supplement. II. Title. III. Title: — Additions.

GILCHRIST, Agnes Eleanor (Addison) 1907- 720'.924 B
William Strickland, architect and engineer, 1788-1854, by Agnes Addison Gilchrist. enl.ed. New York, Da Capo Press, 1969. 1 v. (various pagings) illus., plans, ports. 29 cm. (A Da Capo Press reprint edition) "An unabridged republication of the first edition, published in ... 1950 ... It includes as a supplement three articles about Strickland prepared by Mrs. Gilchrist [and first published in 1953-54]" Includes bibliographical references. [NA737.S68G5 1969] 69-13714 20.00
1. Strickland, William, 1787-1854. 2. Architecture—U.S. BIP

String craft.

FARNWORTH, Warren. 745.5
Pin and thread art / Warren Farnworth. New York : Taplinger Pub. Co., 1975. 94 p. : chiefly ill. ; 21 cm. [TT880.F37 1975] 74-29203 ISBN 0-8008-6452-2 : 8.95
1. String craft. 2. Wire craft. 3. Nail craft. I. Title. BIP

44 string and nail art projects / edited by Vivien Bowler. New York : Crown Publishers, 1975, c1974. 96 p. : ill. (some col.) ; 30 cm. [TT880.F67 1975] 75-520 ISBN 0-517-51887-2 : 6.95 745.5
1. String craft. 2. Nail craft. I. Bowler, Vivien.

GAUTARD, Raymond. 746.3
The beautiful string art book : 100 projects you can create / [edited and written by Raymond Gautard ; designs, D. Ligocki ... et al.]. New York : Sterling Pub. Co., 1978. 161 p. : ill. (some col.) ; 26 cm. Includes index. [TT880.G39 1978] 78-111376 ISBN 0-8069-5386-1 : 16.95 ISBN 0-8069-5387-X lib.bdg. : 14.79
1. String craft. I. Ligocki, D. II. Title. BIP

KREISCHER, Lois. 745.5
String art pattern book / by Lois Kreischer. New York : Crown, c1976- p. cm. [TT880.K73 1976] 75-33972 ISBN 0-517-52396-5 pbk. : 3.95
1. String craft. I. Title.

LEEMING, Joseph, 1897- 1968. 746'.04'71
Fun with string; a collection of string games, useful braiding & weaving, knot work & magic with string and rope. Illustrated by Charles E. Pont. New York, Dover Publications [1974] xii, 161 p. illus. 22 cm. Reprint of the 1940 ed. published by F. A. Stokes Co., New York. Bibliography: p. 161. [TT880.L47 1974] 74-75260 ISBN 0-486-23063-5 1.75 (pbk.)
1. String craft. 2. String-figures. 3. Knots and splices. 4. Braid. I. Title. BIP

RISTING, Fran. 746.3
String art / by Fran Risting. New York : Drake Publishers, [1975] p. cm. [TT880.R57] 74-22592 ISBN 0-87749-794-X : 9.95. ISBN 0-87749-816-4 pbk. : 4.95
1. String craft. I. Title.

*RIVIERE, Marie-Claude. 745.5
Pin pictures, with wire and thread. New York, Sterling, 1975. 48 p. ill. (part col) 19 cm. (Little craft book series) Includes index. [TT880] 75-14521 ISBN 0-8069-5340-3 3.75.
1. String craft. 2. Nail craft. 3. Wire craft. I. Title. BIP

SAEGER, Glen. 746'.04'71
String things you can create. New York, Sterling Pub. Co. [1973] 48 p. illus. 20 cm. (Little craft book series) Introduces the tools, materials, and techniques for creating a variety of articles with string. [TT880.S26 1973] 72-95217 ISBN 0-8069-5263-6 2.69 (lib. ed.)
1. String craft. I. Title.
Cloth edition 2.95; ISBN 0-8069-5262-8. BIP

SHARPTON, Robert E. 746.3
Designing pictures with string / Robert E. Sharpton ; designs and drawings by the author ; photos. by Barbara A. Greadington. Buchanan, N.Y. : Emerson Books, [1974] 121 p. : ill. ; 21 cm. [TT880.S5] 74-81896 ISBN 0-87523-183-7 : 6.95
1. String craft. I. Title. BIP

SHARPTON, Robert E. 746'.04'71
String art : step-by-step / Robert E. Sharpton. 1st ed. Radnor, Pa. : Chilton Book Co., [1975] xvi, 137 p., [4] leaves of plates : ill. (some col.) ; 27 cm. (Chilton's creative crafts series) [TT880.S53 1975] 75-4191 ISBN 0-8019-6131-9 : 12.50. ISBN 0-8019-6132-7 pbk. : 5.95
1. String craft. I. Title. BIP

String craft—Juvenile literature.

CAURO, Roland. 746.3
Stringcraft / by Roland & Dominique Cauro ; [translated by Anne E. Kallem]. New York : Sterling Pub. Co., c1976. 48 p. : ill. (some col.) ; 20 cm. (Little craft book series) Translation of Tout l'art des fils tendus. Includes index. Introduces the basic techniques and materials of string art and provides several original project patterns. [TT880.C3513 1976] 76-1181 ISBN 0-8069-5364-0 : 3.75 ISBN 0-8069-5365-9 lib.bdg. :
1. String craft—Juvenile literature. I. Cauro, Dominique, joint author. II. Title. BIP

FLETCHER, Helen Jill, 1910- 746'.04'71
String projects. Illustrated by Francoise Webb. [1st ed] Garden City, N.Y., Doubleday [1974] 62 p. illus. 22 cm. (Crafts for children) Instructions for making belts, pictures, puzzles, a bulletin board, basketball hoop, and other useful or decorative items from string. [TT880.F59] 73-15338 ISBN 0-385-06371-7 4.95
1. String craft—Juvenile literature. I. Webb, Francoise, illus. II. Title.
Library binding 5.70, ISBN 0-385-02366-9. BIP

MORIN, Claude. 746'.04'71
Braided cord animals you can make / by Claude Morin ; drawings by Wiegeist ; photographs by Jean-Pierre Tesson ; [translated by Maxine Hobson]. New York : Sterling Pub. Co., c1976. 32 p. : ill. (some col.) ; 22 cm. (Easy craft series) Translation of La ficelle tressee. Step-by-step directions for basic braiding techniques and several braided cord projects. [TT880.M6613 1976] 76-19816 ISBN 0-8069-5400-0 : 3.95 ISBN 0-8069-5401-9 lib. bdg. : 3.99
1. String craft—Juvenile literature. 2. Cordage—Juvenile literature. 3. Zoological models—Juvenile literature. I. Wiegeist. II. Tesson, Jean-Pierre. III. Title. IV. Title: Animals you can make. BIP

SAEGER, Glen. 746'.04'71
String designs / by Glen Saeger. New York : Sterling Pub. Co., [1975] 48 p. : ill. (some col.) ; 20 cm. (Little craft book series) Includes index. Introduces the tools and techniques for creating a variety of string designs that may be incorporated into different objects. [TT880.S25] 74-31703 ISBN 0-8069-5320-9 : 3.75 3.75 ISBN 0-8069-5321-7 lib.bdg. : 3.99 3.99
1. String craft—Juvenile literature. I. Title. BIP

STRING art encyclopedia. 746'.04'71
New York : Sterling Pub. Co., c1976. 128 p., [12] leaves of plates : ill. ; 27 cm. Includes index. Introduces the basic techniques and materials of string art and provides instructions for producing original project designs. [TT880.S76] 76-1184 ISBN 0-8069-5362-4 : 8.95 ISBN 0-8069-5363-2 lib.bdg. :
1. String craft—Juvenile literature. I. Sterling Publishing Company, inc., New York. BIP

String-figures.

BALL, Walter William Rouse, 1850-1925. 793'.9
Fun with string figures. New York, Dover Publications [1971] viii, 80 p. 21 cm. "Unabridged republication of the third edition of the work first published ... in 1920 under title: An introduction to string figures." Includes bibliographical references. Discusses the history of string figures and gives directions for making cat's cradle, the ebbing tide, and many other designs. [GV1218.S8B35 1971] 76-173664 ISBN 0-486-22809-6 1.00
1. String figures. I. Title. BIP

HADDON, Kathleen. 793'.9
Artists in string : string figures ; their regional distribution and social significance / by Kathleen Haddon (Mrs. O. H. T. Rishbeth) ; with a foreword by J. L. Myres. New York : AMS Press, [1979] p. cm. Reprint of the 1930 ed. published by Methuen, London. Includes index. Bibliography: p. [GN455.S9H25 1979] 75-32823 ISBN 0-404-14127-7 : 14.95
1. String-figures. I. Title. BIP

RANSOM, William Richard, 1876- 793.9
Pastimes with string and paper. Profusely illustrated, 720 diagrs. by Edwin A. Hoadley and the author. Boston, Christopher Pub. House [1963] 151 p. illus. 23 cm. [GV1218.S8R3] 63-16993
1. String-figures. 2. Paper work. I. Title. BIP

SEYD, Mary. 745.59
Designing with string. London, Batsford; New York, Watson-Guptill, 1967. 96p. illus., 2 col. plates. 22cm. Bibl. [TT880.S48] 68-10049 5.95 bds.,
1. String-figures. 2. College. 3. Handicraft. I. Title.

String-figures—Juvenile literature.

HELFMAN, Harry Carmozin, 1910- 793 (j)
Strings on your fingers; how to make string figures [by] Harry and Elizabeth Helfman. Illustrated by William Meyerriecks. New York, Morrow, 1965. 47, [1] p. col. illus. 24 cm. Bibliography: p. [48] [GV1218.S8H4] 65-11329
1. String-figures—Juvenile literature. I. Helfman, Elizabeth S., joint author. II. Title. BIP

KALTER, Joanmarie. 793'.9
String figures : cat's cradle, Jacob's ladder, two stars, magic carpet, an apache door, two coyotes, many stars, and many more / Joanmarie Kalter. New York : Drake, 1978. 141 p. : ill. ; 23 cm. Instructions for string games using one or two hands and one or two people. [GV1218.S8K34] 77-87468 ISBN 0-8473-1660-2 pbk. : 4.95
1. String figures—Juvenile literature. 2. Indians of North America—Games—Juvenile literature. I. Title.

Strother, David Hunter, 1816-1888.

EBY, Cecil D. 741'.092'4 B
"Porte Crayon": the life of David Hunter Strother, by Cecil D. Eby, Jr. Westport, Conn., Greenwood Press [1973] xi, 258 p. illus. 22 cm. Reprint of the 1960 ed. Bibliography: p. [239]-251. [E175.5.S87E2 1973] 72-11235 ISBN 0-8371-6638-1 12.00
1. Strother, David Hunter, 1816-1888. I. Title.

Structural design.

SALVADORI, Mario George, 1907- 729'.3
Structural design in architecture [by] Mario Salvadori [and] Matthys Levy. With example and problem solutions by John J. Farrell. Englewood Cliffs, N.J., Prentice-Hall [1967] xv, 457 p. illus., maps. 24 cm. [TH845.S32] 67-10751
1. Structural design. I. Levy, Matthys, joint author. II. Title. BIP

ZUK, William. 729
Kinetic architecture [by] William Zuk and Roger H. Clark. New York, Van Nostrand Reinhold [1970] 163 p. illus., plans. 23 x 29 cm. Includes bibliographical references. [TA658.2.Z85] 74-108655
1. Structural design. I. Clark, Roger H., joint author. II. Title.

Structural drawing.

SHAH, Motichand Gulabchand, 1927- 744.4'24
Principles of building drawing, by M. G. Shah, C. M. Kale. New York, Asia Pub. [c.1966] 111p. illus., plans. 42cm. Bibl. [T355.S5] 65-16039 7.25 pap.,
1. Structural drawing. I. Kale, Chandrashekhar Mahadoe, 1934- joint author. II. Title.
Distributed by Taplinger, New York.

Structural dynamics.

BUFFA, Anthony J. 721'.01'52
Physics for modern architecture / by A. J. Buffa, Jr. and D. W. Hafemeister. [San Luis Obispo, Calif. : Buffa, 1974] i, 204 p. : ill. ; 22 cm. Includes bibliographical references. [TA654.B77] 74-21171 4.70
1. Structural dynamics. 2. Vibration. 3. Physics. 4. Architecture. I. Hafemeister, D. W., joint author. II. Title.

Structural engineering—Tables, calculations, etc.

GUIDELINES Publications. 721'.021'2
Architectural rules of thumb. Orinda, Calif. : Guidelines Publications, 1975, c1974. 60 p. ; 28 cm. Includes index. [TA635.G84 1975] 75-322629
1. Structural engineering—Tables, calculations, etc. 2. Building—Tables, calculations, etc. I. Title.

Struss, Karl, 1886—

STRUSS, Karl, 1886- 779'.092'4
Karl Struss, man with a camera : the artist-photographer in New York and Hollywood ... Cranbrook Academy of Art/Museum ... [et al.] / [exhibition organized, and catalogue prepared, researched, written, and edited by Susan and John Harvith]. Bloomfield Hills, Mich. : The Museum, c1976. viii, 104 p. : ill. ; 26 cm. Bibliography: p. 103-104. [TR647.S88A44] 76-1404
1. Struss, Karl, 1886- 2. Photography, Artistic—Exhibitions. 3. Cinematographers—Correspondence, reminiscences, etc. I. Harvith, Susan. II. Harvith, John. III. Cranbrook Academy of Art, Bloomfield Hills, Mich. Museum. IV. Title.

Stryker, Roy Emerson, 1893—

HURLEY, Forrest Jack. 779'.9'917303916
Portrait of a decade; Roy Stryker and the development of documentary photography in the thirties [by] F. Jack Hurley. Photographic editing by Robert J. Doherty. Baton Rouge, Louisiana State University Press [1972] ix, 196 p. illus. 29 cm. Bibliography: p. 189-193. [TR820.5.H87] 72-79331 ISBN 0-8071-0235-0 12.95
1. Stryker, Roy Emerson, 1893- 2. United States. Farm Security Administration. 3. Photography, Documentary. I. Title. BIP

HURLEY, Forrest Jack. 779'.9'973916
Portrait of a decade : Roy Stryker and the development of documentary photography in the thirties / F. Jack Hurley ; photographic editing by Robert J. Doherty. New York : Da Capo Press, [1977] c1972. ix, 196 p. : ill. ; 28 cm. (A Da Capo paperback) Includes index. Bibliography: p. 189-193. [TR820.5.H87 1977] 76-51427 ISBN 0-306-80058-6 pbk. : 6.95
1. Stryker, Roy Emerson, 1893- 2. United States. Farm Security Administration. 3. Photography, Documentary. I. Title.

Stuart, Gilbert, 1755-1828.

FLEXNER, James Thomas, 1908- 927.5
Gilbert Stuart; a great life in brief. [1st ed.] New York, Knopf, 1955. 197p. 23cm. (Great lives in brief; a new series of biographies) [ND237.S8F5] [ND237.S8F5] 759.13 55-6218 55-6218
1. Stuart, Gilbert, 1755-1828. I. Title.

GILBERT Stuart, portraitist of the young republic, 1755-1828. 759.13
[Meridan, Conn., Printed by the Meridan Gravure Co.] 1967. 115 p. 26 cm. Exhibition held at the National Gallery, June 28-Aug. 20, and at the Museum of Arts, Rhode Island School of Desing, Sept. 9-Oct. 15, 1967. Bibliography: p. 114. [ND237.S8A46] 67-23954
1. Stuart, Gilbert, 1775-1828. I. United States. National Gallery of Art. II. Rhode Island School of Design, Providence. Museum of Art.

MASON, George Champlin, 1820-1894. 759.13 B
The life and works of Gilbert Stuart. With selections from Stuart's portraits reproduced on steel and by photogravure. New York, B. Franklin Reprints [1974] x, 286 p. ports. 26 cm. (Burt Franklin research & source works series. Art history & reference series, 48) Reprint of the 1879 ed. published by Scribner, New York. [ND1329.S7M37 1974] 72-82298 ISBN 0-8337-5236-7
1. Stuart, Gilbert, 1755-1828. 2. Portraits—Catalogs. I. Title. BIP

MORGAN, John Hill, 1870-1945. 759.13
Gilbert Stuart and his pupils. Together with the complete notes on painting, by Matthew Harris Jouett, from conversations with Gilbert Stuart in 1816. New York, Kennedy Galleries, 1969 [c1939] 102 p. illus., ports. 24 cm. (Library of American art) Includes bibliographical references. [ND237.S8M6 1969] 72-96440
1. Stuart, Gilbert, 1755-1828. 2. Portrait painters, American. 3. Portraits, American. I. Jouett, Matthew Harris, 1788-1827. II. Title. BIP

MOUNT, Charles Merrill. 927.5
Gilbert Stuart, a biography. [1st ed.] New York, W. W. Norton [1964] 384 p. illus., ports. 25 cm. "The works of Gilbert Stuart": p. [357]-379. Bibliographical references included in "Notes" (p. [333]-356) [ND237.S8M65] 63-15881
1. Stuart, Gilbert, 1755-1828.

PENNSYLVANIA Academy of the Fine Arts, Philadelphia. 759.13
Portraits by Gilbert Stuart, 1755-1828. Philadelphia [1963?] 19 p. 25 port. 22 cm. Cover title. Catalogue of an exhibition, Nov. 7-Dec. 1, 1963. "Gilbert Stuart at Philadelphia, 1795-1803, by Charles Merrill Mount": p. 3-14. [ND1329.S7P4] 76-253724
1. Stuart, Gilbert, 1755-1828. I. Mount, Charles Merrill. II. Title.

WHITLEY, William Thomas, 1858-1942. 759.13 B
Gilbert Stuart. New York, Kennedy Galleries, 1969. xiv, 240 p. illus., port. 27 cm. (Library of American art) Reprint of the 1932 ed. Bibliography: p. [227]-228. [ND237.S8W5 1969] 77-87680
1. Stuart, Gilbert, 1755-1828.

WHITLEY, William Thomas, 1858-1942. 759.13
Gilbert Stuart. Cambridge, Mass., Harvard University Press, 1932. [New York, AMS Press, 1971] xiv, 240 p. ports. 24 cm. Bibliography: p. [227]-228. [ND237.S8W5 1971] 79-155223 ISBN 0-404-06941-X
1. Stuart, Gilbert, 1755-1828. BIP

Stubbs, George, 1724-1806.

TATE Gallery, London. 599'.04'0222
George Stubbs, anatomist and animal painter / [by] Judy Egerton ; [photographs by A. C. Cooper Ltd. et al.]. London : Tate Gallery Publications, 1976. 64 p., plate : ill., port. ; 25 cm. Published for an exhibition held at the Tate Gallery, 25 Aug.-3 Oct., 1976. Distributed in France and Italy by Idea Books, Paris and Milan. Includes reprint of an article by B. Taylor written for the Arts Council's exhibition catalogue, 1958 and excerpts from O. Humphry's ms. Memoir of George Stubbs. Includes bibliographical references. [QL31.S82T37 1976] 77-359204 ISBN 0-905005-55-4. ISBN 0-905005-50-3 pbk.
1. Stubbs, George, 1724-1806. 2. Tate Gallery, London. 3. Anatomy—Exhibitions. 4. Animal painting and illustration—Exhibitions. 5. Anatomists—England—Biography. I. Stubbs, George, 1724-1806. II. Egerton, Judy. III. Taylor, Basil. IV. Humphry, Ozias, 1743-1810.

Stubbs, George, 1724-1806—Catalogs.

STUBBS, George, 1724-1806. 759.2
Stubbs / [text by] William Gaunt. Oxford : Phaidon, 1977. 16 p., 28 p. of plates : chiefly col. ill. ; 32 cm. Bibliography: p. 14. [ND497.S93A4 1977] 78-313922 ISBN 0-7148-1808-9 : 7.95
1. Stubbs, George, 1724-1806—Catalogs. 2. Animals in art—Catalogs. I. Gaunt, William, 1900- BIP

Stucco—Iran.

THOMPSON, Deborah. 730'.955'25
Stucco from Chal Tarkhan-Eshqabad near Rayy / [by] Deborah Thompson ; including illustrations of the excavated ostraca from the same site. Warminster : Aris and Phillips, 1976. xvi, 329 p., [36] p. of plates, [6] leaves of plates (5 fold.) : ill., map, plans ; 31 cm. (Colt Archaeological Institute publications) Label mounted on verso of t.p.: Exclusive distributor, ISBS, Inc., Forest Grove, Or. Includes index. Bibliography: p. [v]-viii. [NA3574.C52T56] 77-362903 ISBN 0-85668-062-1 : 42.00
1. Stucco—Iran. 2. Architecture, Sassanid. 3. Chal Tarkhan-Eshqabad site, Iran. 4. Iran—Antiquities. I. Title. II. Series: Colt Archaeological Institute. Publications. BIP

Stucco—Italy—Vatican City.

SMITH, Graham, 1942- 726'.5'0945634
The Casino of Pius IV / Graham Smith. Princeton, N.J. : Princeton University Press, c1976. p. cm. Includes index. Bibliography: p. [N6920.S54] 76-3017 ISBN 0-691-03915-1 : 20.00
1. Vatican City. Casino di Pio IV. 2. Stucco—Italy—Vatican City. 3. Mural painting and decoration, Renaissance—Vatican City. 4. Mural painting and decoration—Vatican City. 5. Symbolims in art—Vatican City. I. Title. BIP

Student housing.

MULLINS, William. 727'.38
Student housing: architectural and social aspects [by] William Mullins and Phyllis Allen. New York, Praeger Publishers [1971] vii, 248 p. illus., maps, plans. 29 cm. Bibliography: p. 244. [LB3227.M84 1971b] 76-159965 25.00
1. Student housing. I. Allen, Phyllis, joint author.

Stuempig, Walter, 1914-1970.

PENNSYLVANIA Academy of the Fine Arts, Philadelphia. 759.13
Walter Stuempfig memorial exhibition. Philadelphia [1972] 1 v. (unpaged) illus. 27 cm. Catalog of the exhibition held Mar. 14-Apr. 9, 1972. [ND237.S83P4] 70-190480
1. Stuempig, Walter, 1914-1970. I. Title.

Stump work.

BAKER, Muriel L. 746.4'4
Stumpwork : the art of raised embroidery / by Muriel Baker. New York : Scribner, c1978. 116 p., [4] leaves of plates : ill. (some col.) ; 29 cm. Includes index. Bibliography: p. 113. [TT778.S75B34] 612'.398 77-13204 ISBN 0-684-15360-2 : 16.95
1. Stump work. I. Title. BIP

Stupas—Asia, Southeastern.

GOVINDA, Anagarika Brahmacari. 726'.1'430954
Psycho-cosmic symbolism of the Buddhist stupa / Lama Anagarika Govinda. Emeryville, Calif. : Dharma Pub., c1976. xviii, 102 p. : ill. ; 21 cm. Consists of the author's Some aspects of stupa symbolism, to which is added an article originally published in 1950 in Marg under title: Solar and lunar symbolism in the development of stupa architecture. Includes bibliographical references and index. [NA6000.G68] 76-797 ISBN 0-913546-35-6 : 8.95. ISBN 0-913546-36-4 pbk. : 4.95
1. Stupas—Asia, Southeastern. 2. Buddhist art and symbolism—Asia, Southeastern. 3. Stupas—Tibet. 4. Buddhist art and symbolism—Tibet. I. Govinda, Anagarika Brahmacari. Some aspects of stupa symbolism. c1976. II. Title. BIP

Sturbridge, Mass.—Descr.—Views.

CHAMBERLAIN, Samuel, 1895- 917.443
Old Sturbridge Village, a photographic impression. New York, Hastings House [1951] 68 p. illus. 24 cm. [F74.S93C45] 51-12279
1. Sturbridge, Mass.—Descr.—Views. I. Title.

CHAMBERLAIN, Samuel, 1895- 917.443
A tour of Old Sturbridge Village [Rev. ed.] NewYork, Hastings [c.1955-1965] 72p. (chiefly illus.) 21cm. [F74.S93C46] 55-9058 1.25 pap.,
1. Sturbridge, Mass.—Descr.—Views. I. Title. BIP

Sturbridge, Mass.—Description.

FENNELLY, Catherine, 1918- 974.4'3
Old Sturbridge village in color / text and notes on the illustrations by Catherine Fennelly ; photos. by Donald S. Eaton. New York : Hastings House, 1978. p. cm. (Profiles of America) [F74.S93F46] 78-2337 ISBN 0-8038-5389-0 : 5.95
1. Sturbridge, Mass.—Description. 2. Sturbridge, Mass.—History. I. Title. BIP

Sturbridge, Mass.—Juvenile literature.

BOWEN, Gary. 974.4'3
My village, Sturbridge / story by Gary Bowen ; wood engravings designed by Gary Bowen and engraved by Randy Miller. New York : Farrar, Straus and Giroux, [1977] p. cm. Wood engravings and accompanying descriptions highlight Sturbridge, Massachusetts, as seen by an apprentice in a printing office. [F74.S93B68] 77-10059 ISBN 0-374-35110-4 : 5.95
1. Sturbridge, Mass.—Juvenile literature. I. Miller, Randy. II. Title. BIP

Sturges, Dwight Case, 1874-1940.

STURGES, Dwight Case, 1874-1940. 769'.92'4 B
Dwight C. Sturges, etcher of an era / by Natalie Sturges Butler ; with photographic reproductions by D. Richard Sturges ; and a foreword by Erwin D. Canham. 1st ed. Freeport, Me. : B. Wheelwright Co., [1974] 127 p. : chiefly ill. ; 28 cm. "List of Dwight C. Sturges' prints": p. 124-126. "Dwight C. Sturges' works in permanent collections": p. 126-127. [NE2012.S75B57] 74-20198 ISBN 0-87027-154-7 : 12.95. ISBN 0-87027-155-5 pbk. 7.95
1. Sturges, Dwight Case, 1874-1940. I. Butler, Natalie Sturges, 1908- II. Title.

Sturtevant, Elaine.

STURTEVANT, Elaine. 709'.2'4
Studies for Warhol's marilyns'; Beuys Actions and Objects Duchamp's; etc., including film. [Edited and produced by Judson Rosebush. Concept and design by Elaine Sturtevant. Syracuse, N.Y.] Everson Museum, 1973. [52] l. (chiefly illus.) 28 cm. [N6537.S78R67] 73-92281
1. Sturtevant, Elaine. I. Rosebush, Judson. II. Everson Museum of Art of Syracuse and Onondaga County. III. Title.
Publisher's Address: Corner of South State and Harrison, Syracuse, N.Y.

Style, Literary.

SPENCER, Herbert, 1820-1903. 701.17
Literary style and music, including two short essays on gracefulness and beauty. Port Washington, N.Y., Kennikat Press [1970] x, 119 p. 19 cm. (Essay and general literature index reprint series) Reprint of the 1951 ed. [B1652.A5 1970] 78-91057
1. Style, Literary. 2. Music. 3. Aesthetics. I. Title. BIP

Subercaseaux Errazuriz, Pedro.

SUBERCASEAUX Errazuriz, Pedro. 759.983
Saint Francis of Assisi / from the water colors of P. Subercaseaux Errazuriz ; introd. by Johannes Joergensen. Chicago : Franciscan Herald Press, 1976. xviii, 198 p. : ill. ; 31 cm. Published in 1925 under title: Saint Francois d'Assise. French and English. [ND1903.S9A5613 1976] 76-57685 ISBN 0-8199-0615-8 : 25.00
1. Subercaseaux Errazuriz, Pedro. 2. Francesco d'Assisi, Saint, 1182-1226—Art.

Subleyras, Luigi, 1743-1814.

SUBLEYRAS, Luigi, 1743-1814. 371.1'02'0207
A visit to Rome in 1764. Cambridge, Mass., Fogg Art Museum and Harvard College Library [1956] 13 [19] p. illus. 20 cm. (Fogg Museum picture book no. 5) Prepared by the Dept. of Printing and Graphic Arts, Harvard Library for the Boston Museum of Fine Arts, and others. The "Foreword" is an introductory essay by Philip Hofer. Reproduces the original t.p. and a selection of the author's sonnets with illustrations principally by Etienne de la Vallee-Poussin. The complete work was first published in 1764 under title: Nella venuta in Roma di madama Le Comte e dei signori Watelet e Copette. Bibliography: p. [31] [N527.A55 no. 5] 70-16296
1. Subleyras, Luigi, 1743-1814. Nella Venuta in Roma di madama Le Comte e dei signori Watelet e Copette.—Illustrations. I. Hofer, Philip, 1898- II. La Vallee-Poussin, Etienne de, ca. 1733-ca. 1793, illus. III. Harvard University. Library. Dept. of Printing and Graphic Arts. IV. Title. V. Series: Fogg picture book no. 5

Suburban homes.

BARDESCHI, Marco Dezzi 728.84'0945
Italian villas today. Ed. by Giulio Segoloni. [1st Amer. ed.] Bologna, Edizioni C. E. L. I., New York, Transatlantic [1967] 241p. illus. (pt. col.), plans. 29cm. Text in Italian: summaries in English, French, German and Spanish. [NA7594.B353 1967] 67-31915 18.50
1. Suburban homes. 2. Architecture, Domestic—Italy. I. Segoloni, Giulio. II. Title. BIP

BRISEUX, Charles, d.1754 728.8'3
L'art de batir des maisons de campagne ou l'on traite de leur distribution, de leur construction, & de leur decoration, par le Sieur C. E. Briseux. Farnborough (Hants), Gregg. 1966 [i.e.1967] 2v. 30cm. Facsim. reprint of the 1761 ed. [NA7560.B7 1761b] 67-82578 154.00 set,
1. Suburban homes. 2. Architecture, Domestic—Designs and plans. I. Title.
Available from the publisher's Ridgewood, N.J. office.

POLLMAN, Richard B., 1914- 728.3
117 low cost homes, by Richard B. pollman. Detroit, Home Planners [1970] 71 p. illus., plans. 28 cm. (Designs for convenient living book no. 75) [NA7570.P59] 78-289211 1.00
1. Suburban homes. 2. Architecture, Domestic—Designs and plans. I. Home Planners, inc., Detroit. II. Title.

WHEELER, Gervase. 728.6'0973
Homes for the people in suburb and country; the villa, the mansion, and the cottage. New York, Arno Press, 1972 [c1855] x, 443 p. illus. 23 cm. (Technology and society) [NA7207.W48 1972] 72-5085 ISBN 0-405-04733-9
1. Suburban homes. 2. Country homes. I. Title. II. Series. BIP

Suburban homes—Essex, Eng. (County)

ESSEX, Eng. County Planning Dept. 711'.58'094267
A design guide for residential areas; County Council of Essex [Planning Department] Chelmsford, Essex County Council [Planning Department] 1973. 134 p. illus. (some col.), plans. 31 cm. Bibliography: p. 134. [NA7572.E87 1973] 74-168509 ISBN 0-901355-46-1 £4.50
1. Suburban homes—Essex, Eng. (County) 2. Architecture, Domestic—Designs and plans. I. Title.

Suburban homes—U.S.

POLLMAN, Richard B., 1914- 728.3
155 homes, by Richard B. Pollman New York, Published by Universal Pub. and Distributing Corp. for Home Planners, inc., c1971. 133 p. illus. 28 cm. (Designs for convenient living, book no. 80. Design series, v. 4) [NA7571.P64] 72-200269 1.25
1. Suburban homes—U.S. 2. Architecture, Domestic—Designs and plans. I. Home Planners, inc., Detroit. II. Title.

POLLMAN, Richard B., 1914- 728.3
166 low and medium cost homes, by Richard B Pollman. [New York, Published by Universal Pub. and Distributing Corp. for Home Planners, inc., c1971] 95 p. illus. 28 cm. (Designs for convenient living, book no. 79) At head of title: Home Planners. Cover title. [NA7571.P642] 72-200270 1.00
1. Suburban homes—U.S. 2. Architecture, Domestic—Designs and plans. I. Home Planners, inc., Detroit. II. Title.

Suffolk Co., N.Y., in art.

BECCA, R. G. 741.9'73
Suffolk County family album of art / R. G. Becca. Huntington, N.Y. : R. E. Krieger Pub. Co., 1977. p. cm. [NC139.B416A55] 77-8645 ISBN 0-88275-574-9 pbk. : 4.95
1. Becca, R. G. 2. Suffolk Co., N.Y., in art. I. Title.

Suiseki—British Colombia.

HUTCHINSON, Bill. 730
Suiseki in British Columbia / Bill and Julie Hutchinson. Victoria, B.C. : B. & J. Hutchinson, c1976. 52 p. : chiefly ill. ; 28 cm. [NK8715.H87] 77-364155
1. Suiseki—British Colombia. I. Hutchinson, Julie, joint author. II. Title.

Sulgrave Manor House.

VEIT, Gerald Michel. 942.55
Sulgrave Manor; an illustrated survey of the Northamptonshire home of George Washington's ancestors. Derby, Designed and produced by English Life Publications [1953] unpaged. illus. 14x22cm. 'Based ... on 'Sulgrave Manor and the Washingtons,' by Mr. H. Clifford Smith.' [DA690.S943V4] 54-43682
1. Sulgrave Manor House. I. Title.

Sullivan, Louis Henri, 1856-1924.

BRAGDON, Claude Fayette, 1866-1946. 720
Architecture and democracy. Freeport, N.Y., Books for Libraries Press [1971, c1918] 213 p. illus. 23 cm. (Essay index reprint series) Contents.Contents.—Architecture and democracy.—Ornament from mathematics.—Harnessing the rainbow.—Louis Sullivan, prophet of democracy.—Color and ceramics.—Symbols and sacraments.—Self-education. [NA2560.B7 1971] 70-156617 ISBN 0-8369-2386-3
1. Sullivan, Louis Henri, 1856-1924. 2. Architecture—Addresses, essays, lectures. 3. Architecture—United States. 4. Decoration and ornament. I. Title. BIP

BUSH-BROWN, Albert. 720.973
Louis Sullivan. New York, G. Braziller, 1960. 128 p. plates, ports. 26 cm. (The Masters of world architecture series) "Selected bibliography of books and articles written by Louis Sullivan": p. 120. "Selected bibliography of Louis Sullivan": p. 121-122. [NA737.S9B8] 60-13306
1. Sullivan, Louis Henry, 1856-1924. I. Title. II. Series. BIP

CONNELY, Willard, 1888- 720.973
Louis Sullivan as he lived; the shaping of American architecture, a biography. New York, Horizon Press, 1960. 322 p. illus. 25 cm. Includes bibliography. [NA737.S9C6] 60-8160
1. Sullivan, Louis Henry, 1856-1924. 2. Architecture—U.S.

MORRISON, Hugh Sinclair, 1905- 720'.924 B
Louis Sullivan, prophet of modern architecture, by Hugh Morrison. Westport, Conn., Greenwood Press [1971, c1935] 391 p. illus. 23 cm. "Dankmar Adler, a biographical sketch": p. 283-293. Includes bibliographies. [NA737.S9M6 1971] 78-139141 ISBN 0-8371-5757-9
1. Sullivan, Louis Henri, 1856-1924. 2. Adler, Dankmar, 1844-1900. 3. Architecture—United States.

PAUL, Sherman. 927.2
Louis Sullivan, an architect in American thought. Englewood Cliffs, N. J., Prentice-Hall [1962] 176p. illus. 21cm. (A Spectrum book, S47) Includes bibliography. [NA737.S9P3] 62-19991
1. Sulivan, Louis Henry, 1856-1924. I. Title.

SULLIVAN, Louis Henry, 1856-1924. 927.2
The autobiography of an idea. Foreword by Claude Bragdon. With a new introd. by Ralph Marlowe Line, and 35 illus. of Sullivan's works selected and photographed by Ralph Marlowe Line for this ed. New York, Dover Publications, 1956. 329 p. illus. 21 cm. [NA737.S9A3 1956] 57-28992
I. Title.

SULLIVAN, Louis Henry, 1856-1924. 927.2
The autobiography of an idea. Foreword by Claude Bragdon. With a new introd. by Ralph Marlowe Line, and 35 illus. of Sullivan's works selected and photographed by Ralph Marlowe Line for this ed. New York, Dover Publications, 1956. 329p. illus. 21cm. [NA737.S9A3 1956] 57-2899
I. Title. BIP

SZARKOWSKI, John. 720.973
The idea of Louis Sullivan. Minneapolis, University of Minnesota Press [1956] 161 p. illus., ports. 32 cm. [NA737.S9S9] 720 56-11616
1. Sullivan, Louis Henry, 1856-1924. I. Title.

WRIGHT, Frank Lloyd, 1867-1959. 720'.924
Genius and the mobocracy. [Enl. ed.] New York, Horizon Press [1971] 247 p. illus., plan. 26 cm. [NA737.S9W7 1971] 79-132328 ISBN 0-8180-0022-8 20.00
1. Sullivan, Louis Henri, 1856-1924. I. Title. BIP

Sullivan, Louis Henri, 1856-1924— Juvenile literature.

KAUFMAN, Mervyn D. 720'.924 B
Father of skyscrapers; a biography of Louis Sullivan, by Mervyn Kaufman. [1st ed.] Boston, Little, Brown [1969] x, 171 p. illus., ports. 24 cm. A biography of the architect who helped lead the revolt against the established European school of architecture in America. [NA737.S9K3] 92 77-77450 4.95
1. Sullivan, Louis Henri, 1856-1924—Juvenile literature. I. Title.

Sully, Thomas, 1783-1872.

BIDDLE, Edward. 759.13 B
The life and works of Thomas Sully, by Edward Biddle and Mantle Fielding. New York, Kennedy Graphics, 1970. viii, 411 p. illus., facsim., ports. 27 cm. (Library of American art) Reprint of the 1921 ed. [ND237.S9B5 1970] 74-77716
1. Sully, Thomas, 1783-1872. I. Fielding, Mantle, 1865-1941, joint author. II. Title. BIP

Sulphides (Art)

JOKELSON, Paul, 1905- 748.2
Sulphides; the art of cameo incrustation. [New York] Nelson [1968] 159 p. illus. 26 cm. Bibliography: p. 147. [NK5440.S8J6] 68-25513
1. Sulphides (Art) I. Title.

Sultan, S. M., 1924—

SULTAN, S. M., 1924- 759.9549'2
S. M. Sultan / [edited by Muhammad Sirajul Islam]. [Dacca] : Bangladesh Shilpakala Academy, 1976. [32] p. : chiefly ill. ; 19 cm. ([Contemporary art series of Bangladesh ; 1]) Imprint date in ms. Series statement from jacket. [ND1010.8.B353S847] 77-900949 Tk20.00
1. Sultan, S. M., 1924- I. Title. II. Series.

Sumie.

AIDA, Kohei. 751.4'25
Japanese brush painting in color. [Tokyo] Japan Publications [1973] 103 p. illus. 31 cm. [ND2462.A29] 73-78182 ISBN 0-87040-225-0 11.00
1. Sumie. I. Title.
Distributed by Japan Publications, San Francisco. BIP

HOLMES, Stewart Walker. 759.951
Zen art for meditation, by Stewart W. Holmes and Chimyo Horioka. Rutland, Vt., C.E. Tuttle Co. [1973] 115 p. illus. 24 cm. [ND2462.H64] 73-78279 ISBN 0-8048-1113-X 10.00
1. Sumie. 2. Painting, Zen. 3. Haiku. I. Horioka, Chimyo, joint author. II. Title. BIP

MATSUSHITA, Takaaki, 1909- 751.4'25
Ink painting. Translated and adapted with an introd. by Martin Collcutt. [1st ed.] New York, Weatherhill [1974] 143 p. illus. (part col.) 23 cm. (Arts of Japan, 7) Translation of Suibokuga. Bibliography: p. [140] [ND2462.M413] 73-88476 ISBN 0-8348-2712-3 10.00
1. Sumie. I. Collcutt, Martin. II. Title.
Pbk. 7.95; ISBN 0-8348-2713-1. BIP

MIKAMI, Takahiko 751.425
T. Mikami's Sumi painting; study of Japanese brush painting. Tokyo, Shufunotomo [Rutland, Vt., Japan Pubns.] c.1965. 49p. (chiefly illus.) 26cm. [ND2462.M5] 65-4252 2.00 pap.,
1. Sumie. I. Title. II. Title: Sumi painting.

OI, Motoi, 1910- 751.425
Brush control research progress report, 1968 [Tokyo, Japan House of Art, dist. Rutland, Vt., Japan Pubns., 1963] 64p. illus. 29cm. 63-23946 5.00
1. Sumie. I. Title.

SIUDZINZKI, Paul. 751.4'25
Sumi-e : a meditation in ink / Paul Siudzinski. New York : Drake, 1978. xi, 114 p., : ill. ; 26 cm. [ND2462.S58] 77-87475 pbk. : 5.95
1. Sumie. I. Title. BIP

SOLLIER, Andre. 751.4'25
Introduction to Sumi-e: the Zen way of the brush, by Andre Sollier. Melbourne, Georgian House, 1972. 83 p. (chiefly illus.) 36 cm. [ND2462.S64] 73-158656 ISBN 0-85585-491-X 6.95
1. Sumie. I. Title.

YAMADA, Sadami, 1915- 751.425
Complete Sumie techniques complete instructions for painting over 200 subjects including flowers, trees, animals, fish, and landscapes. [Translation by Transearch, under the direction of Charles Pomeroy] Rutland, Vt., Japan Publications Trading Co. [1966] 151 p. illus. 31 cm. "A compilation of ... Sumi-e in three weeks, Floral sumi-e in three weeks, Animal sumi-e in three weeks, and Landscape sumi-e in three weeks." [ND2462.Y2816] 66-24010
1. Sumie. I. Title. BIP

YAMADA, Sadami, 1915- 751.425
Floral sumi-e in three weeks. [Tr. by Transearch, under the direction of Charles Pomeroy. Rutland, Vt., Japan Pubns. [c.1965] 33p. [incl. cover) illus., port. 30cm. Cover title [ND2462.Y293] 65-27099 1.50 pap.,
1. Sumie. 2. Flower painting and illustration. I. Title. BIP

YAMADA, Sadami. 1915- 751.425
Landscape sumie in three weeks. [Tr. by Transearch, under the direct. of Charles Pomeroy. Rutland, Vt., Japan Pubns., c.1966. 37p. (incl. cover) illus., port. 30cm. Cover title. [ND2462. Y2983] 65-27102 1.50 pap.,
1. Sumie. 2. Landscape painting—Technique. I. Title. BIP

YAMADA, Sadami, 1915- 751.425
Sumi-e in three weeks. Tr. [from Japanese] by Charles Pomeroy, Charles S. Terry. Rutland, Vt., Japan Pubns., c.1964. 33p. illus. 30cm. 64-17024 1.50 pap.,
1. Sumie. I. Title. BIP

Summer homes.

BARRAN, Fritz Richard 728.7
Ferienhauser; Wochenend- und Ferienhauser, Jagdhutten, Wohnboote. Eine Auswahl von 63 Beispielen aus 13 Landern. [Summer houses; summer houses and weekend retreats, hunting cottages, houseboats. Maison de vacances; maisons de weekend et de vacances, pavillons de chasse, bateaux habitables. Die Ubersetzung der Texte besorgten Hans Heinz Kaufmann (englisch) and George Riedel (franzosisch) dist. New York 24, George Efron, 41 W. 83 St., 1962, c.1961] 120p. illus. 30cm. 62-1838 12.50
1. Summer homes. 2. Architecture, Domestic—Designs and plans. I. Title. II. Title: Summer houses.

HAGUE, William E. 728'.7
Your vacation home: how to plan it, how to live in it, by William E. Hague. Garden City, N.Y., Doubleday [1972] x, 178 p. illus. 24 cm. [NA7574.H3] 71-182999 6.95
1. Summer homes. 2. Interior decoration. I. Title.

HOLMES, David. 728'.7
Planning your vacation home. Garden City, N.Y., Doubleday [1970] 71 p. illus., col. plates. 24 cm. (The Doubleday home decorating program) [TH4835.H55] 75-13964
1. Summer homes. I. Title.

KASPAR, Karl. 728'.7
Vacation houses; an international survey. New York, Praeger [1967] 167 p. illus., plans. 29 cm. [NA7574.K3] 67-17762
1. Summer homes. 2. Architecture, Domestic—Designs and plans. I. Title.

LANG, Andy, 1909- 728.7
Vacation dream homes / Andy Lang. Maplewood, N.J. : Hammond, [1975] 96 p. : ill. ; 28 cm. [NA7574.L36] 75-2421 ISBN 0-8437-3250-4
1. Summer homes. 2. Summer homes—Designs and plans. I. Title.

MCNERTNEY, Gerald. 1923- 728.7
Cabana. [Cranbury N.J.] A. S. Barnes [c1965] 1 v. (unpaged) illus., plans. 28cm. [NA7575.M2] 65-24457 5.95
1. Summer homes. 2. Architecture, Domestic—Designs and plans. I. Title.

POLLMAN, Richard B., 1914- 728'.7
151 vacation homes, by Richard B. Pollman. [New York, Published by Universal Pub. and Distributing Corp. for Home Planners, inc., Detroit, 1968] 128 p. illus. (part col.), plans. 28 cm. (Designs for convenient living living, book no. 67) Cover title. At head of title: Home Planners. [NA7574.P6 1968] 77-13438 1.00
1. Summer homes. 2. Architecture, Domestic—Designs and plans. I. Home Planners, inc., Detroit. II. Title.

POLLMAN, Richard B., 1914- 728'.7
151 vacation homes; a pictorial presentation of homes for leisure-living, created by RichardB. Pollman. New York, Grosset & Dunlap [1968] viii, 118 p. illus. (part col.), plans (part col.) 28 cm. On cover: 151 leisure-time vacation homes. [NA7574.P6] 68-19197
1. Summer homes. 2. Architecture, Domestic—Designs and plans. I. Title. II. Title: 151 leisure-time vacation homes.

POLLMAN, Richard B., 1914- 728'.7
156 vacation homes, by Richard B. Pollman New York, Published by Universal Pub. and Distributing Corp. for Home Planners [1971] 128 p. illus. (part col.) 28 cm. (Designs for convenient living, book no. 78) At head of title: Home Planners. [NA7574.P63] 70-30306 1.25
1. Summer homes. I. Home Planners, inc., Detroit. II. Title. III. Title: Vacation homes.

Summer homes—Designs and plans.

UNITED States. Dept. of Agriculture. 690'.8'7
Vacation homes and cabins : 16 complete plans / prepared by the United States Department of Agriculture. New York : Dover Publications, 1978. 105 p. : ill. ; 31 cm. Abridged and slightly altered republication of portions of Agriculture handbook no. 438, Recreational buildings and facilities, prepared by the Agricultural Research Service, and of various working drawings published on various dates. [TH4835.U54 1978] 77-99250 ISBN 0-486-23631-5 : 3.00
1. Summer homes—Designs and plans. I. United States. Agricultural Research Service. Recreational buildings and facilities. II. Title. BIP

Summer homes—Europe.

WOLGENSINGER, Bernard. 728'.7
Vacation houses in Europe [by] Bernard Wolgensinger [and] Jacques Debaigts. Photos by Michel Nahmias. [Translated from the French by Gabriel Otvos] Rutland, Vt., C. E. Tuttle Co. [1968] 159 p. illus. (part col.), plans. 27 cm. English, French, and German. [NA7574.W6] 69-13512 15.00
1. Summer homes—Europe. 2. Architecture, Domestic—Designs and plans. I. Debaigts, Jacques, joint author. II. Nahmias, Michel, illus. III. Title.

WOLGENSINGER, Bernard. 728'.7
Villas in the sun [by] Bernard Wolgensinger. Photos. by Michel Nahmias. [Translated from the French by Douglas-J. Gillam] Rutland, Vt., C. E. Tuttle [1971] 156 p. illus. (part col.) 27 cm. Translation of Maisons de vacances au soleil. English, French, and German. [NA7574.W58 1971c] 75-152109 ISBN 0-8048-0989-5 17.50
1. Summer homes—Europe. 2. Architecture, Domestic—Designs and plans. I. Nahmias, Michel, illus. II. Title.

Summer houses.

SPORTS afield second 728'.7
homes. [New York, Hearst Corp.] v. illus. (part col.), plans. 28 cm. [NA7575.S57] 68-4874
1. Summer houses. 2. Architecture, Domestic—Designs and plans.

Sun in art.

KOMAROFF, 704.94'9'398362
Katherine.
Sky gods : the Sun and Moon in art and myth / by Katherine Komaroff. New York : Universe Books, 1974. 86 p. : ill. (some col.) ; 30 cm. [N8251.S6K65] 73-80052 ISBN 0-87663-187-1 : 7.95
1. Sun in art. 2. Sun lore. 3. Moon in art. 4. Moon (in religion, folk-lore, etc.) I. Title. BIP

Sundt-Hansen, Carl, 1841-1907.

SoRBY, Hild, 1943- 704.9424
Carl Sundt-Hansen, 1841-1907 / Hild Sorby. [Stavanger] : Stavanger lithografiske anstalt, 1976. 86 p. : ill. ; 28 cm. Summary in English. Bibliography: p. 86. [ND773.S85S67] 77-475562 ISBN 8-299-04301-8 : kr195.00
1. Sundt-Hansen, Carl, 1841-1907. I. Sundt-Hansen, Carl, 1841-1907.

Landscape gardening.

SUNSET. 712.6
Ideas for entryways and front gardens, by the editors of Sunset books and Sunset magazine. [1st ed.] Menlo Park, Calif., Lane Book Co. [1961] 80 p. illus. 27 cm. [SB476.S79] 61-6903
1. (A Sunset book, 317) 2. Landscape gardening. I. Title. II. Title: Entryways and front gardens.

Superman (Comic strip)

SUPERMAN; from the 741.59
thirties to the seventies. Introd. by E. Nelson Bridwell. New York, Crown Publishers [1971] 386 p. illus. (part col.) 28 cm. Bibliography: p. 385-386. [NC1426.3.S9S9 1971] 77-175018 10.00
1. Superman (Comic strip)

Superstition Mountains, Ariz.—Views.

DEGRAZIA, Ted Ettore, 759.13
1909-
De Grazia and his mountain, the Superstition. Artist proof ed. Tucson, Ariz., De Grazia Gallery in the Sun, 1972. 60 p. illus. (part col.) 32 cm. "First printing limited." [ND237.D3337A24] 72-192227 12.50
1. Superstition Mountains, Ariz.—Views. I. Title.

Surrealism.

ALEXANDRIAN, Sarane. 709'.04
Surrealist art. Translated from the French by Gordon Clough. New York, Praeger [1970] 256 p. illus. (part col.) 21 cm. (Praeger world of art paperbacks, P-247) Translation of L'art surrealiste. Bibliography: p. 243-244. [N6494.S8A413] 70-92584 3.95
1. Surrealism. I. Title.

ALQUIE, Ferdinand. 149.9
The philosophy of surrealism. Translated by Bernard Waldrop. Ann Arbor, University of Michigan Press [1965] viii, 196 p. 22 cm. Bibliographical references included in "Notes" (p. 173-196) [BH301.S75A43] 65-20352
1. Surrealism. I. Title.

BRETON, Andre, 1896-1966. 700'.1
Manifestoes of surrealism. Translated from the French by Richard Seaver and Helen R. Lane. Ann Arbor, University of Michigan Press [1969] xi, 304 p. 22 cm. Translation of Les manifestes du surrealisme. Bibliographical footnotes. [BH301.S75B683 1969] 68-29273 8.50
1. Surrealism. 2. Arts, Modern—20th century. I. Title. BIP

BRETON, Andre, 1896-1966. 759.06
Surrealism and painting / Andre Breton ; translated from the French by Simon Watson Taylor. 1st U.S. ed. New York : Harper & Row, 1972. 415 p. : ill. ; 26 cm. (Icon editions ; IN-24) Translation of Le surrealisme et la peinture. Includes bibliographical references and index. [ND196.S8B7313 1972b] 70-188930 ISBN 0-06-430407-8. ISBN 0-06-430024-2 pbk. : 7.95
1. Surrealism. 2. Painting, Modern—20th century. I. Title. BIP

BRETON, Andre, 1896- 709'.04
1966.
What is surrealism? Translated by David Gascoyne. New York, Haskell House Publishers, 1974. 90 p. illus. 20 cm. Translation of Qu'est-ce que le surrealisme? Reprint of the 1936 ed. published by Faber & Faber, London, which was issued as no. 43 of Criterion miscellany. [NX600.S9B7213 1974] 74-6446 ISBN 0-8383-1709-X 7.95 (lib. bdg.).
1. Surrealism. I. Title. II. Series: Criterion miscellany no. 43. BIP

CARROUGES, Michel, 1910- 759.06
Andre Breton and the basic concepts of surrealism / by Michel Carrouges ; translated by Maura Prendergast. University : University of Alabama Press, [1974] 294 p. ; 22 cm. (Studies in the humanities : Philosophy) Translation of Andre Breton et les donnees fondamentales du surrealisme. Includes index. Bibliography: p. 284-289. [NX600.S9C3313] 73-21060 ISBN 0-8173-7316-0 : 10.00
1. Breton, Andre, 1896-1966. 2. Surrealism. I. Title. II. Series: Studies in the humanities (University, Ala.) : Philosophy. BIP

CLURMAN, Irene. 759.9493
Surrealism and the painting of Matta and Magritte. Stanford, Calif. [Humanities Honors Program, Stanford University] 1970. viii, 45 p. illus. 23 cm. (Stanford honors essay in humanities, no. 14) Bibliography: p. 42-45. [NX600.S9C55] 70-134703
1. Matta Echaurren, Roberto Sebastian, 1911- 2. Magritte, Rene, 1898-1967. 3. Surrealism. I. Title. II. Series.

DUPLESSIS, Yves, 1912- 709.04
Surrealism. Translated by Paul Capon. New York, Walker [1963, c1962] 158 p. 21 cm. (A Sun book, SB-8. Literature and the arts) [BH301.S75D83 1963] 62-12752
1. Surrealism. BIP

DUPLESSIS, Yves, 1912- 700'.9'04
Surrealism / by Yves Duplessis ; translated by Paul Capon. Westport, Conn. : Greenwood Press, 1978, c1962. 158 p. ; 23 cm. Translation of Surrealisme. Reprint of the ed. published by Walker, New York in series : A Sun book. [NX600.S9D8413 1978] 77-17880 ISBN 0-313-20110-2 lib.bdg. : 13.00
1. Surrealism. 2. Arts, Modern—20th century. I. Title.

FOWLIE, Wallace, 1908- 701.16
Age of surrealism. [New York] Swallow Press, 1950. 203 p. 22 cm. Bibliography: p. 193-197. [BH301.S75F6] 50-10630
1. Surrealism. I. Title. BIP

FOWLIE, Wallace, 1908- 709.04
Age of surrealism. Bloomington, Indiana University Press [1960] 215 p. illus. 21 cm. (A Midland book, MB24) [BH301.S75F6 1960] 60-8309
1. Surrealism. I. Title.

FOWLIE, Wallace. Adams 709.04
Age of surrealism. Bloomington, Indiana University Press [dist. Gloucester, Mass., Peter Smith, c.1950, 1960] 215p.Bibl.: p.[205]-209. illus. 21cm. (A Midland book, MB24, paperback, rebound in cloth) 3.50
1. Surrealism. I. Title.

GAUNT, William, 1900- 759.06
The surrealists. New York, Putnam [1972] 272 p. col. illus. 32 cm. Bibliography: p. 260. [ND196.S8G38] 72-75027
1. Surrealism. 2. Painting, Modern—20th century. I. Title. BIP

HASLAM, Malcolm. 700'.9'04
The real world of the surrealists / Malcolm Haslam ; introd. by Barbara Rose. New York : Rizzoli, 1978. 264 p. : ill. (some col.) ; 29 cm. Includes index. Bibliography: p. 257. [NX600.S9H37] 78-102303 ISBN 0-8478-0151-9 : 35.00
1. Surrealism. 2. Arts, Modern—20th century. I. Title.

JEAN, Marcel. 759.06
The history of surrealist painting, by Marcel Jean, with the collaboration of Arpad Mezei. Translated from the French by Simon Watson Taylor. New York, Grove Press [1960] 383 p. illus. (part col.) ports. 25 cm. Bibliographical footnotes. [ND1265.J483] 60-11094
1. Surrealism. 2. Paintings. I. Title: Surrealist painting.

JOSEPHSON, Matthew, 1899- 818.52
Life among the surrealists, a memoir. [1st ed.] New York, Holt, Rinehart and Winston [1962] 403p. illus. 22cm. Includes bibliography. [BH301.S75J6] 62-7704
1. Surrealism. I. Title.

LEVY, Julien, comp. 701
Surrealism. New York, Black Sun Press, 1936. [New York] Arno/Worldwide [1968] 191 p. illus. 25 cm. Bibliography: p. 32. [BH301.S75L4 1968] 68-9469 12.95
1. Surrealism. BIP

LIPPARD, Lucy R., comp. 709'.04
Surrealists on art. Edited by Lucy R. Lippard. Englewood Cliffs, N.J., Prentice-Hall [1970] x, 213 p. 21 cm. (A Spectrum book) Includes bibliographical references. [NX600.S9L5] 78-104858 5.95
1. Surrealism. I. Title.

LUZWICK, Dierdre. 741.9'73
The surrealist's Bible : a collection of charcoal drawings / by Dierdre Luzwick. Middle Village, N.Y. : Jonathan David, c1976. 118 p. : ill. ; 29 cm. [NC139.L89A58] 75-44001 ISBN 0-8246-0206-4 : 12.95
1. Luzwick, Dierdre. 2. Bible—Pictures, illustrations, etc. 3. Surrealism. I. Title. BIP

MATTHEWS, J. H. 700'.9'04
The imagery of surrealism / John Herbert Matthews. 1st ed. [Syracuse, N.Y.] : Syracuse University Press, 1977. p. cm. Includes index. Bibliography: p. [NX600.S9M37] 77-7927 ISBN 0-8156-2183-3 : 25.00
1. Surrealism. 2. Arts, Modern—20th century. I. Title. BIP

MATTHEWS, J. H. 709.04
An introduction to surrealism. University Park, Pa., State Univ. Pr. [c.1965] 192p. 23cm. Bibl. [BH301.S75M3] 64-8083 5.00 bds.,
1. Surrealism. I. Title.

NADEAU, Maurice. 709.04
The history of surrealism. Translated from the French by Richard Howard. With an introd. by Roger Shattuck. New York, Macmillan [1965] 351 p. illus. 22 cm. Bibliography: p. 319-335. [BH301.S75N33] 65-23834
1. Surrealism. I. Title.

READ, Herbert Edward, 700'.9'04
Sir, 1893-1968, ed.
Surrealism. Edited with an introd. by Herbert Read. Contributions by Andre Breton [and others] New York, Praeger [1971] 251 p. illus. 26 cm. [NX600.S9R42 1971] 79-131355 15.00
1. Surrealism. I. Breton, Andre, 1896-1966.

SANDROW, Nahma. 700'.944'36
Surrealism: theater, arts, ideas. New York, Harper & Row [1972] ix, 124, 4 p. illus. 21 cm. (Harper torchbooks, TB 1599) Bibliography: p. [113]-117. [NX600.S9S25 1972] 77-159629 ISBN 0-06-131599-0 1.95 (pbk.)
1. Surrealism. I. Title.

SCHNEEDE, Uwe M. 759.06
Surrealism [by] Uwe M. Schneede. Translated by Maria Pelikan. New York, H. N. Abrams [1974] 144 p. illus., 41 col. plates. 33 cm. (The Library of great art movements) Translation of Malerei des Surrealismus. Bibliography: p. 139-142. [NX600.S9S2813] 74-2302 ISBN 0-8109-0499-3
1. Surrealism. I. Title.

SPACE and dream 709.04
[by] Robert Goldwater. New York, Walker [1968, c1967] 80 p. illus. (part col.) 22 cm. "Almost all of the works reproduced were ... loaned to M. Knoedler and Company for the exhibition held from December 5 through December 29, 1967." Includes bibliographical references. [N6494.S8S6] 67-30381 6.50
1. Surrealism. I. Goldwater, Robert John, 1907- II. Knoedler (M.) and Company, inc.

SURREALISM pro and 700'.9'04
con. [New York] Gotham Book Mart, 1973. 77 p. 23 cm. These essays originally appeared in New directions in prose & poetry, 1940, edited by J. Laughlin. Contents.Contents.—Calas, N. The meaning of surrealism. Surrealist pocket dictionary. Toward a third surrealist manifesto.—Muller, H. J. Surrealism: a dissenting opinion.—Burke, K. Surrealism. [NX600.S9S89] 72-87890 ISBN 0-910664-26-9 2.50
1. Surrealism. I. Calas, Nicolas. II. Muller, Herbert Joseph, 1905- III. Burke, Kenneth, 1897-
Publisher's Address: 41 W 47th Street N.Y. 10036. BIP

†TOMKINS, Calvin, 1925- 709'.04
The world of Marcel Duchamp, 1887-1968 / by Calvin Tomkins and the editors of Time-Life Books. Rev. Alexandria, Va. : Time-Life Books ; Morristown, N.J. : school and library distribution by Silver Burdett Co., c1977. 192 p. : ill. (some col.) ; 31 cm. (Time-Life library of art) Includes index. Bibliography: p. 185. [N6853.D8T6 1977] 77-153784 ISBN 0-8094-0236-X : 10.95
1. Duchamp, Marcel, 1887-1968. 2. Surrealism. I. Time-Life Books. II. Title.

WALDBERG, Patrick. 759.06
Surrealism. New York, McGraw-Hill [1966?] 127 p. illus., facsims., plates (part col.) parts. 22 cm. Bibliography: p. 117-119. [ND1265.W253 1966] 65-24531
1. Surrealism. 2. Paintings. BIP

WALDBERG, Patrick. 759.06
Surrealism. Translated from the French by Stuart Gilbert. [Geneva?] Skira; [distributed in the U.S. by World Pub. Co. Cleveland, 1962] 149 p. mounted illus. (part col.) 19 cm. (The Taste of our time, 37) Bibliography: p. 135-[137] [ND1265.W253] 62-10989
1. Surrealism. 2. Paintings. I. Title.

WALDBERG, Patrick. 709'.04
Surrealism / Patrick Waldberg. New York : Oxford University Press, 1978, c1965. p. cm. (The World of art) Reprint of the ed. published by Thames & Hudson, London. Includes index. Bibliography: p. [N6494.S8W32 1978] 78-7516 ISBN 0-19-520070-5 pbk. : 7.95
1. Surrealism. 2. Art, Modern—20th century. I. Title. II. Series.

Surrealism—Addresses, essays, lectures.

THE Autobiography of 700'.9'04
surrealism / edited by Marcel Jean. New York : Viking Press, [1977] p. cm. (The Documents of 20th century art) Includes index. Bibliography: p. [NX600.S9A95] 76-46637 ISBN 0-670-14235-2 : 20.00
1. Surrealism—Addresses, essays, lectures. 2. Arts, Modern—20th century—Addresses, essays, lectures. I. Jean, Marcel. II. Series.

CARRA, Massimo, 1922- 750'.1
comp.
Metaphysical art [compiled by] Massimo

Carra, with Patrick Waldberg and Ewald Rathke. Translation and historical foreword by Caroline Tisdall. New York, Praeger Publishers [1971] 216 p. illus. 22 cm. Translation of Metafisica. Bibliography: p. 207-208. [N6494.S8C313] 79-116640 8.50
1. Surrealism—Addresses, essays, lectures. I. Waldberg, Patrick. II. Rathke, Ewald. III. Title.

Surrealism—Bibliography—Catalogs.

CHICAGO. Art Institute. 016.700'9'04
Surrealism & its affinities: the Mary Reynolds collection; a bibliography compiled by Hugh Edwards. Chicago [1973] 147 p. illus. 26 cm. [Z5936.S8C45 1973] 73-132025
1. Reynolds, Mary Louise—Art collections. 2. Surrealism—Bibliography—Catalogs. I. Edwards, Hugh L. II. Title.

Surrealism—Exhibitions.

DURHAM Surrealist Festival, 1968. 759
Durham Surrealist Festival [Nov. 18-Dec. 6, 1968]; organized by Ian Barker and Andrew Lanyon: catalogue/compendium. [Durham, I. Barker] 1969. [2], 49 p. illus., ports. 23 cm. [NX600.S9D8] 79-199133 8/6
1. Surrealism—Exhibitions. I. Barker, Ian. II. Lanyon, Andrew. III. Title.

JOHN and Mable Ringling Museum of Art, Sarasota, Fla. 709'.04
After surrealism: metaphors & similes [Exhibition] November 17-December 10, 1972. [Catalogue] Sarasota [1972?] 32 p. illus. 28 cm. Bibliography: p. 30-31. [N6512.5.S9J63 1972] 75-303857
1. Surrealism—Exhibitions. 2. Surrealism—United States. 3. Art, Modern—20th century—United States. I. Title.

SANTA Barbara, Calif. Museum of Art. 759.06
Harbingers of surrealism; [catalogue of an exhibition. Santa Barbara, 1966] [26] p. illus. 27 cm. Cover title. [N6494.S8S25 1966] 74-184327
1. Surrealism—Exhibitions. 2. Art, Modern—20th century. I. Title.

SURREALISM in art, 709'.04
February 5-March 6, 1975. New York : M. Knoedler, c1975. 63 p. : chiefly ill. (some col.) ; 22 cm. "Catalogue of the exhibition": p. 60-63. [N6494.S8S87] 76-353217
1. Surrealism—Exhibitions. 2. Art, Modern—20th century—Exhibitions. I. Knoedler (M.) and Company, inc.

THE 759.06'074'0471
Surrealists: [exhibition] November 11-December 21, 1969, Byron Gallery ... New York. [New York, Byron Gallery, 1969] 132 p. (chiefly illus. (part col.)) 21 cm. Label on t.p.: Worldwide Books, inc., Boston. [N6494.S8S9] 71-18671
1. Surrealism—Exhibitions. I. Byron Gallery.

Surrealism—France.

GERSHMAN, Herbert S. 111.8'5
The surrealist revolution in France [by] Herbert S. Gershman. Ann Arbor, University of Michigan Press [1969] xii, 255 p. illus., port. 24 cm. Bibliographical references included in "Notes" (p. [173]-247) [BH301.S75G44 1969] 68-29263 8.50
1. Surrealism—France. I. Title. BIP

GERSHMAN, Herbert S. 111.8'5
The surrealist revolution in France [by] Herbert S. Gershman. Ann Arbor, University of Michigan Press [1974, c1969] viii, 253 p. 21 cm. (Ann Arbor paperbacks) Bibliographical references included in "Notes." [BH301.S75G44] ISBN 0-472-06188-7 3.45 (pbk.)
1. Surrealism—France. I. Title.
L.C. card number for original ed.: 68-29263.

Surrealism—France—Bibliography.

GERSHMAN, Herbert S. 016.8408'015
A bibliography of the surrealist revolution in France [by] Herbert S. Gershman. Ann Arbor, University of Michigan Press [1969] 57 p. 24 cm. [Z5939.G38] 68-31128 4.50
1. Surrealism—France—Bibliography. I. Title. II. Title: The surrealist revolution in France.

Sussman, Richard, 1908-1971.

WALKER Art Center, Minneapolis. 759.13
Richard Sussman: watercolors and brush drawings; a memorial exhibition. [Minneapolis, 1973] [8] p. illus. 28 cm. Catalog of an exhibition presented at the Walker Art Center, Minneapolis, Nov. 19-Dec. 24, 1972; Carleton College, Northfield, Minn., Mar. 11-Apr. 15, 1973; and the Tweed Museum of Art, Duluth, Apr. 25-May 27, 1973. [ND1839.S95W34] 73-173338
1. Sussman, Richard, 1908-1971. I. Sussman, Richard, 1908-1971. II. Carleton College, Northfield, Minn. III. Tweed Museum of Art.

Sutcliffe, Frank, 1853-1941.

HILEY, Michael. 770'.92'4 B
Frank Sutcliffe, photographer of Whitby / Michael Hiley. Boston : D. R. Godine, c1974. 224 p. : ill. ; 30 cm. (Godine photographic monographs) Includes bibliographical references and index. [TR140.S74H55 1974b] 74-81519 ISBN 0-87923-105-X : 27.50
1. Sutcliffe, Frank, 1853-1941. 2. Photography, Artistic. I. Title.

Sutherland, David McBeth, 1883-1973.

ABERDEEN Art Gallery, Aberdeen, Scot. 759.9411
D. M. Sutherland MC, LLD, RSA, 1883-1973 : [catalogue of an exhibition held at] Aberdeen Art Gallery ... 5-26 October, 1974 ... [and elsewhere]. Aberdeen : Aberdeen Art Gallery, 1974. [31] p. : ill. (some col.), port. ; 20 x 21 cm. Bibliography: p. [17] [ND497.S94A67 1974] 75-315099 £0.50
1. Sutherland, David McBeth, 1883-1973. I. Sutherland, David McBeth, 1883-1973.

Sutherland, Graham Vivian, 1903—

COOPER, Douglas 759.2
The work of Graham Sutherland. New York, McKay [1962, c.1961] 97p. illus. (pt. col.) 30cm. Bibl. 15.00
I. Sutherland, Graham, 1903- II. Title.

SUTHERLAND, Graham Vivian, 1903- 759.2
Graham Sutherland / text by Francesco Arcangeli ; translated by Helen Barolini. New York : H. N. Abrams, [1975] p. cm. Includes index. Bibliography: p. [ND497.S95A8913] 75-14028 ISBN 0-8109-0235-4 : 37.50
1. Sutherland, Graham Vivian, 1903- I. Arcangeli, Francesco, 1915-

SUTHERLAND, Graham Vivian. 1903- 759.2
The work of Graham Sutherland. Text by Douglas Cooper. [1st ed.] London, Lund, Humphries [1961] 97 p. illus., plates (part col.) port. 30 cm. Errata slip inserted. "A selective bibliography on Graham Sutherland, by Bernard Karpel":p. 85-93. [ND497.S95C6] 62-4067
I. Cooper, Douglas, 1911- II. Title.

Sutton Manor.

LECONFIELD, Hugh Archibald Wyndham, baron, 1877- 942.25
Sutton and Duncton Manors. London, New York, Oxford University Press, 1956. 107p. illus., maps (2 fold.) 23cm. Bibliographical footnotes. [DA690.S9606L4] 57-1033
1. Sutton Manor. 2. Duncton Manor. I. Title.

Swann, Don, 1889—

SWANN, Don, 1889- 769'.92'4
Colonial and historic homes of Maryland : one hundred etchings / by Don Swann ; text by Don Swann, Jr. ; foreword by F. Scott Fitzgerald. Baltimore : Johns Hopkins University Press, [1975] 211 p. : ill. ; 29 cm. Includes index. [NE2012.S92A43 1975] 75-9722 ISBN 0-8018-1727-7 : 35.00
1. Swann, Don, 1889- 2. Architecture, Domestic, in art. 3. Historic buildings—Maryland—Pictorial works. 4. Architecture, Colonial—Maryland—Pictorial works. I. Swann, Don, 1911- joint author. II. Title. BIP

Sweaters.

BROWN, Gail. 646.4'5
The super sweater idea book : hundreds of new and exciting ways to turn sweater fabrics into unique fashions, home accessories, and gifts / Gail Brown and Gail Hamilton. New York : Butterick Pub., c1978. 216 p. : ill. ; 23 cm. Includes index. [TT825.B76] 77-92584 ISBN 0-88421-035-9 : 6.95
1. Sweaters. I. Hamilton, Gail, 1950-joint author. II. Title. BIP

DALE Yarn Company. 746.9'2
Knit your own Norwegian sweaters : complete instructions for 50 authentic sweaters, hats, mittens, gloves, caps, etc. / by Dale Yarn Company. New York : Dover Publications, 1974. xii, 58 p. : ill. ; 29 cm. "An expanded and revised version of the 1966 edition of "Knit it yourself" published by J. W. Cappelens Forlag in Oslo, Norway." [TT825.D33 1974] 73-94350 ISBN 0-486-23031-7 pbk. : 2.50
1. Sweaters. I. Title. BIP

GLASSMAN, Judith. 746.9'2
The sweater book : 35 original sweater patterns for men, women, and children / Judith Glassman. New York : Quick Fox, c1976. 95 p., [4] leaves of plates : ill. ; 28 cm. [TT825.G54] 76-8069 ISBN 0-8256-3061-4 pbk. : 4.95
1. Sweaters. I. Title. BIP

Sweden—Social life and customs—Pictorial works—Juvenile literature.

LARSSON, Carl Olof, 1853-1919. 759.85
A home / Carl Larsson, with paintings by Carl Larsson ; and a text by Lennart Rudstrom ; translated by Lone Thygesen-Blecher. 1st American ed. New York : Putnam, 1974. [31] p. : col. ill. ; 24 x 32 cm. Translation of Ett hem. Sixteen of Larsson's watercolors of his home and family are accompanied by text explaining the pictures and something of the life of this great Swedish artist. [ND1998.L3R82] 73-91718 ISBN 0-399-20400-8 : 5.95.
1. Larsson, Carl Olof, 1853-1919—Juvenile literature. 2. Sweden—Social life and customs—Pictorial works—Juvenile literature. I. Rudstrom, Lennart. II. Title.

Sweerts, Emanuel, b. 1552.

SWEERTS, Emanuel, b.1552. 769'.92'4
Early floral engravings : all 110 plates from the 1612 "Florilegium" / by Emanuel Sweerts ; edited by E. F. Bleiler. New York : Dover Publications, c1976. 233 p. in various pagings : ill. ; 32 cm. (Dover pictorial archive series) Includes index. [QK98.S95 1976] 73-76963 ISBN 0-486-23038-4 pbk. : 6.00
1. Sweerts, Emanuel, b. 1552. Florilegium Emanuelis Sweerti—Illustrations. 2. Botany—Pictorial works. 3. Botany—Pre-Linnean works. 4. Botanical illustration. I. Bleiler, Everett Franklin, 1920- II. Title. BIP

Swenson, Gene, 1934-1969—Art collections.

KANSAS. University. Museum of Art. 704.9'2 s
Gene Swenson: retrospective for a critic. [Lawrence, Kan., 1971] 104 p. illus. (part col.) 26 cm. (Its Register, v. 4, nos. 6-7) Catalog of an exhibition held Oct. 24-Dec. 5, 1971. Bibliography: p. 83. [N582.L25A35 vol. 4, no. 6-7] [N6512.5.P6] 709'.2'4 76-198477
1. Swenson, Gene, 1934-1969—Art collections. 2. Pop art—Exhibitions. 3. Art, Modern—20th century—U.S. I. Title. II. Series.

Switzerland in art.

MULLER, Jorg. 741.9'494
The changing city / Jorg Muller. 1st American ed. New York : Atheneum Publishers, c1977. 8 fold. leaves in portfolio : all col. ill. ; 33 cm. Translation of Hier Fallt ein Haus, dort steht ein Kran und ewig droht der Baggerzahn oder Die Veranderung der Stadt. Cover title. "A Margaret K. McFlderry book." [NC293.M82A4313 1977] 76-46646 ISBN 0-689-10782-X : 9.95
1. Muller, Jorg. 2. Switzerland in art. 3. Landscape in art. I. Title. BIP

MULLER, Jorg. 741.9'494
The changing countryside / Jorg Muller. 1st American edition. New York : Atheneum Publishers, 1977. 7 fold. leaves in portfolio : all. col. ill. ; 33 cm. Translation of Alle Jahre wieder saust der Presslufthammer nieder oder Die Veranderung der Landschaft. "A Margaret K. McElderry book." [NC293.M82A4213 1977] 76-46647 ISBN 0-689-10783-8 : 9.95
1. Muller, Jorg. 2. Switzerland in art. 3. Landscape in art. I. Title. BIP

Sword.

FIELD Museum of Natural History. Chicago. 739.72
Japanese sword mounts in the collections of Field Museum, by Helen C. Gunsaulus, asst. curator of Japanese ethnology. Chicago, 1923; New York, Kraus Reprint, 1968. 256p. illus. 25cm. (Orig. pub. as pubn. 216 Field Mus. of Natural Hist. Anthropological ser., v. 16) [GN2.F4 vol. 16] 24-4950 12.00
1. Sword. 2. Decoration and ornament, Japanese. I. Gunsaulus, Helen Cowen. II. Title.

Sword guards—Japan—Catalogs.

PEABODY Museum of Salem, Salem, Mass. 739.7'2
The Peabody Museum collection of Japanese sword guards : with selected pieces of sword furniture : [catalogue] / by John D. Hamilton ; photos. by Mark Sexton. Salem, Mass. : The Museum, 1975. xliii i.e. [86] p. : ill. (some col.) ; 29 cm. Cover title: Japanese sword guards. Includes index. [NK6784.A1P4 1975] 74-7603 ISBN 0-87577-041-X
1. Peabody Museum of Salem, Salem, Mass. 2. Sword guards—Japan—Catalogs. I. Hamilton, John D., 1935- II. Title: Japanese sword guards.

Swords.

HAYWARD, John Forrest, 1916- 739.7
Swords & daggers [2d ed.] London, H. M. S. O. [dist. New York, Brit. Info., c.1963] 12p. 46 plates. 22cm. (Victoria and Albert Mus. [South Kensington] Illus. bklet. no. 3) 64-112 1.00 pap.,
1. Swords. 2. Daggers I. Title. II. Series.

NEUMANN, George C. 355.8'2
Edged weapons of the American Revolution, 1775-1783 / [by George C. Neumann] Washington : American Defense Preparedness Association, 1975. 16 p. : ill. ; 26 cm. Bibliography: p. 16. [U855.N42] 75-306740
1. Swords. 2. Bayonets. 3. Spears. 4. United States—History—Revolution, 1775-1783—Supplies. I. Title.

NEUMANN, George C. 355.8'2
Swords & blades of the American Revolution, by George C. Neumann. Drawings by George C. Woodbridge. [Harrisburg, Pa.] Stackpole Books [1973] 288 p. illus. 32 cm. Bibliography: p. 280-284. [U855.N43] 72-12665 ISBN 0-8117-1720-8 24.95
1. Swords. 2. United States—History—Revolution—Supplies.

NEUMANN, George C. 355.8'2
Swords & blades of the American

Revolution / by George C Neimann drawings by George C Woodbridge Harrisburg, Pa. : Promontory Press, [1976?] c1973. 288 p. : ill. ; 32 cm. Includes index. Bibliography: p. 280-284. [U855.N43 1976] 76-359 ISBN 0-88394-041-8 : 24.95
1. Swords. 2. Arms and armor. 3. United States—History—Revolution—1775-1783—Supplies. I. Title.

OAKESHOTT, R Ewart. 355.82
The sword in the age of chivalry [by] R. Ewart Oakeshott. With drawings by the author. New York, Praeger [1965, c1964] 152 p. illus., 49 plates (1 col.) 26 cm. Bibliography: p. 144-145. [U854.O2] 65-14185
1. Swords. I. Title.

PETERSON, Harold Leslie, 1922- 739.72
American silver mounted swords, 1700-1815; a catalog of an exhibition held at the Corcoran Gallery of Art. Photography by Bluford W. Muir; mark drawings by Gugmund Vigtel. Washington, 1955. 58p. illus. 23cm. 'A supplement to the chapter on silver hilted swords in [the author's] The American sword, 1775-1945.' [NK6712.P4] 55-35735
1. Swords. I. Corcoran Gallery of Art, Washington, D. C. II. Title.

VALENTINE, Eric. 739.7'2
Rapiers; an illustrated reference guide to the rapiers of the 16th and 17th centuries, with their companions. Photos by Edward Perry [Harrisburg, Pa.] Stackpole Books [1968] 74 p. illus. 22 cm. (Stackpole arms and armor) Bibliography: p. 69-72. [U855.V3] 68-17217
1. Swords. I. Title.

WAGNER, Eduard, major. 739.7/2
Cut and thrust weapons; tr. by Jean Layton. London, Spring Bks [1967] 3-491p. col. front., illus. (some col.). 35cm. Bibl. [U850.W33] 67-112910 17.50
1. Swords. 2. Sabers. I. Title.
American distributor: Tudor, New York.

WILKINSON, Frederick John, 1922- 739.7'2
Swords & daggers, by Frederick Wilkinson. [1st American ed.] New York, Hawthorn Books [1968, c1967] 256 p. illus. 20 cm. "Books and collections": p. 79-86. [NK6704.W5 1967b] 68-14386
1. Swords. 2. Daggers. I. Title.

YUMOTO, John M 739.72
The samuri sword, a handbook. Rutland, Vt., C. E. Tuttle Co. [1958] 191 p. illus. 23 cm. Includes bibliography. [NK6784.Y8] 58-7497
1. Swords. 2. Arms and armor, Japanese. I. Title.

Swords, American.

ALBAUGH, William A. 1908- 739.7'2
A photographic supplement of confederate swords [Washington? 1963] xv, 205 p. illus. ports. 26 cm. [U856.C6A43] 64-1469
1. Swords. American. I. Title. II. Title: Confederate swords.

PETERSON, Harold Leslie, 1922- 739.72
The American sword, 1775-1945; a survey of the swords worn by the uniformed forces of the United States from the Revolution to the close of World War II, by Harold L. Peterson. With an introd. by Stephen V. Grancsay. New rev. ed. Philadelphia, Ray Riling Arms Books Co., 1965. xvi, 286, 60 p. illus., ports. 24 cm. Includes, with special t. p., the author's American silver mounted swords, 1700-1815, a catalog of an exhibition held at the Corcoran Gallery of Art (60 p., 3d group) [U856.U6P4] 65-25409
1. Swords, American. I. Title. II. Title: American silver mounted swords, 1700-1815.

Swords, Anglo-Saxon.

DAVIDSON, Hilda Roderick (Ellis) 739.7
The sword in Anglo-Saxon England: its archaeology and literature. [New York] Oxford [c.]1962[ ] xxvii, 237p. illus., maps. Bibl. 62-2704 8.80
1. Swords, Anglo-Saxon. 2. Swords in literature. I. Title.

Swords, British.

ANNIS, P. G. W. 739.7'2
Naval swords: British and American naval edged weapons, 1660-1815, by P. G. W. Annis. [Harrisburg, Pa.] Stackpole Books [1970] 80 p. illus., ports. 23 cm. (Stackpole arms and armour) Bibliography: p. 77. [U855.A55] 75-114732 ISBN 0-8117-1104-8 4.95
1. Swords, British. 2. Swords, American. I. Title.

LATHAM, John Wilkinson. 739.7'2
British military swords from 1800 to the present day. New York, Crown Publishers [1967, c1966] xii, 91 p. illus., coats of arms. 26 cm. Bibliography: p. 57. [U856.G7L3 1967] 67-26322
1. Swords, British. I. Title.

Swords—Collections.

SOCIETY of the Cincinnati. Museum. 739.72
Sword and firearm collection of the Society of the Cinncinnati in the Anderson House Museum, Washington, D.C., with biographical sketches of the original owners, by John Brewer Brown. Photos, by Lowell A. Kenyon. Washington, Society of the Cincinnati, 1965. xiv, 120 p. illus., facism. 24 cm. A revision and updating of a manuscript copy of Sword and firearm collection of the museum prepared in 1955 by Edward Morris Davis III. [U850.S64] 65-25758
1. Swords—Collections. 2. Firearms—Collections. I. Brown, John Brewer. II. Davis, Edward Morris, 1904- III. Title.

Swords—History.

WILKINSON-LATHAM, Robert. 623.4'41
Swords in color : including other edged weapons / Robert Wilkinson-Latham ; special photography by John Searle Austin ; colour drawings by Peter Sarson and Tony Bryan. New York : Arco Pub. Co., 1978, c1977. 227 p. : ill. (some col.) ; 19 cm. (Arco color series.) Includes index. [U852.W53 1978.] 77-13385 ISBN 0-668-04475-6 : 8.95 ISBN 0-668-04486-1 pbk. : 6.95
1. Swords—History. 2. Arms and armor—History. I. Title.

Swords, Japanese.

DOBREE, Alfred. 739.7'2
Japanese sword blades. [Rev. 2d ed.] York, Pa., G. Shumway [1971] 73 p. illus. 22 cm. Includes bibliographical references. [U856.J3D6 1971] 72-161471 ISBN 0-87387-034-4
1. Swords, Japanese. I. Title. BIP

ROBINSON, Basil William. 739.7
The arts of the Japanese sword. [1st ed.] Rutland, Vt., C. E. Tuttle Co. [1961] 110 p. illus., 100 plates (part col.) map. 23 cm. (The Arts of the East) [NK6784.R6 1961] 62-573
1. Swords, Japanese. I. Title. II. Series. BIP

Swords, Scottish.

WALLACE, John, 1929- 739.7'2
Scottish swords and dirks; an illustrated reference guide to Scottish edged weapons. [Harrisburg, Pa.] Stackpole Books [1970] 80 p. illus. 22 cm. (Stackpole arms and armour) Includes bibliographical references. [NK6645.A1W3 1970b] 76-134899 ISBN 0-8117-1509-4 4.95
1. Swords, Scottish. 2. Daggers, Scottish. I. Title.

Swordsmiths. Japanese.

HAWLEY, Willis Meeker, 1896- 739.72
Japanese swordsmiths; 13,500 names used by about 12,000swordsmiths from 700 to 1900 A.D. Comp. pub. by W. M. Hawley. [Hollywood, Calif.] 1966. v. 21cm. [NK6784.H43] 66-7951 15.00
1. Swordsmiths. Japanese. I. Title.
8200 Gould Ave., Hollywood, Calif., 90046.

Sydney. Opera House.

BAUME, Michael. 725/.822
The Sydney Opera House affair. Epilogue by Peter Hall. [Melbourne] Nelson [(Australia) 1967] xiii, 174p. illus., diagrs., port. 23cm. [NA6840.A79S9] 67-112485 5.95 bds.,
1. Sydney. Opera House. I. Title.
American distributor: Tri-Ocean, San Francisco.

SMITH, Vincent. 725'.822'09944
The Sydney Opera House / [by] Vincent Smith. Sydney ; New York : Hamlyn, 1974. 160 p. : ill. (part col.) ; 29 cm. [NA6840.A79S975] 75-320507 ISBN 0-600-07232-0 : 4.95
1. Sydney. Opera House.

Symbolic inversion—Congresses.

FORMS of Symbolic Inversion Symposium, Toronto, 1972. 301.2'1
The reversible world : symbolic inversion in art and society : [papers] / edited and with an introd. by Barbara A. Babcock. Ithaca : Cornell University Press, 1978. 302 p. : ill. ; 22 cm. (Symbol, myth, and ritual series) Symposium held at the 1972 meetings of the American Anthropological Association. Includes bibliographies and index. [GN462.5.F67 1972] 77-3113 ISBN 0-8014-1112-2 : 15.00
1. Symbolic inversion—Congresses. 2. Symbolism in literature—Congresses. 3. Ethnology—Congresses. I. Babcock, Barbara A., 1943- II. American Anthropological Association. III. Title. BIP

Symbolism.

FINGESTEN, Peter. 704.948
The eclipse of symbolism. [1st ed.] Columbia, S.C., University of South Carolina Press [1970] 172 p. illus. 21 cm. Includes bibliographical references. [BL603.F55] 77-86194 6.95
1. Symbolism. I. Title. BIP

GOBLET d'Alviella, Eugene Felicien Albert, comte, 1846-1925. 246
The migration of symbols. With an introd. by Sir George Birdwood. New York, B. Franklin [1972] xxiii, 277 p. illus. 23 cm. (Burt Franklin: research & source works series. Art history & reference series, 36) Reprint of the 1894 ed. [BL603.G6 1972] 76-154638 ISBN 0-8337-0762-0
1. Symbolism. I. Title. BIP

THE golden well; [291.37]
an anatomy of symbols. New York, Sheed and Ward, 1950. xiv, 191 p. 21 cm. Bibliographical footnotes. [BF1623.S9D6 1950a] 704.946 50-10712
1. Symbolism. I. Donnelly, Dorothy (Boillotat), 1903-

Symbolism (Art movement)

DELEVOY, Robert L. 700'.9'034
Symbolists and symbolism / by Robert L. Delevoy ; [translated from the French by Barbara Bray, Elizabeth Wrightson, and Bernard C. Swift]. New York : Skira, 1978. 247 p. : ill. (some col.) ; 36 cm. Translation of Journal du symbolisme. Includes index. Bibliography: p. 195-225. [N6465.S9D4413] 77-79717 ISBN 0-8478-0141-1
1. Symbolism (Art movement) 2. Art, Modern—19th century. I. Title.
Distributed by Rizzoli Intl., 715 Fifth Ave., New York, NY 10019 BIP

SYMBOLISTS & decadents / 759.05
[compiled, and with introd. by] John Christian. New York : St. Martin's Press, 1978, c1977. [88] p. : chiefly col. ill. ; 28 cm. [N6465.S9S95 1978] 77-9152 ISBN 0-312-78193-8 pbk. : 5.95
1. Symbolism (Art movement) 2. Art nouveau. 3. Art, Modern—19th century. I. Christian, John. BIP

Symbolism (Art movement)—France.

JULLIAN, Philippe. 760'.094
The symbolists / Philippe Jullian ; [translated by Mary Anne Stevens]. 2d ed. Oxford : Phaidon ; New York : E. P. Dutton, 1977, c1973. 240 p. : ill. (some col.) ; 24 cm. Includes bibliographical references and index. [NX549.A1J8413 1977] 76-62645 ISBN 0-7148-1739-2 : 8.95
1. Symbolism (Art movement)—France. 2. Arts, Modern—19th century—France. 3. Symbolism (Art movement)—Belgium. 4. Arts, Modern—19th century—Belgium. I. Title.

Symbolism—Dictionaries.

COOPER, J. C., fl.1972- 301.2'1
An illustrated encyclopaedia of traditional symbols / J. C. Cooper. London : Thames and Hudson, c1978. 208 p. : ill. ; 25 cm. Bibliography: p. 203-207. [BL603.C66] 78-55429 ISBN 0-500-01201-6 : 14.95
1. Symbolism—Dictionaries. 2. Signs and symbols—Dictionaries. I. Title.
Distributed by Norton, NYC BIP

Symbolism in architecture—Scotland—Orkney.

WORDEN, Ian P. 726'.5'0941132
The round church of Orphir, Orkney / by Ian P. Worden. Cambridge : Institute of Geomantic Research, 1976. 5 p., plate : ill., plan ; 30 cm. (Occasional paper - Institute of Geomantic Research ; no. 6 ISSN 0308-1966s) [NA5481.O74W67]177-373205.ISBN 0-905376-04-8
I. Orphir Church. 2. Symbolism in architecture—Scotland—Orkney. I. Title. II. Series: Institute of Geomantic Research. Occasional paper — Institute of Geomantic Research ; no. 6.

Symbolism in art.

BAILEY, Henry Turner, 1865-1931. 701
Symbolism for artists: creative and appreciative, by Henry Turner Bailey and Ethel Pool. Worcester, Mass., Davis Press, 1925. Detroit, Gale Research Co., [1973 c.1972] 239 p. illus. 18 cm. Bibliography: p. 228-230. [N7740.B25 1972] 68-18018 11.00
1. Symbolism in art. I. Pool, Ethel, joint author. II. Title.

CHAVANNES, Edouard, 1865-1918. 745'.0951
The five happinesses: symbolism in Chinese popular art. Translated, annotated, and illustrated by Elaine Spaulding Atwood. With a foreword by Arthur W. Hummel. [1st English ed.] New York, Weatherhill [1973] 152 p. illus. 26 cm. Translation of De l'Expression des voeux dans l'art populaire chinois. "Selected bibliography of works by Edouard Chavannes": p. 149-150. Bibliography: p. 151-152. [N7740.C4413] 72-92098 ISBN 0-8348-0076-4 10.95
1. Symbolism in art. 2. Folk art—China. I. Atwood, Elaine Spaulding, ed. II. Title.

IMPRESSIONISM, its forerunners and influences; 759'.05
general editor Francesco Abbate; translated [from the Italian] by W. J. Strachan. London, New York, Octopus Books Ltd, 1972. 158 p. chiefly 83 col. illus. 20 cm. Translation of L'Ottocento in Europa. Simbolismo e impressionismo. Bibliography: p. 154. [N6465.S9I4613] 73-151617 ISBN 0-7064-0069-0 £0.99
1. Symbolism in art. 2. Impressionism (Art) 3. Art, Modern—19th century. I. Abbate, Francesco, ed.

KATZENELLENBOGEN, Adolf Edmund Max, 1901- 704.948
Allegories of the virtues and vices in mediaeval art from early Christian times to the thirteenth century [by] Adolf Katzenellenbogen. [Translated by Alan J. P. Crick] New York, W. W. Norton [1964] vii, 102, xiviii p. illus., facsims. 20 cm. (The Norton library, N243) Bibliographical footnotes. [N7740.K313] 65-1559
1. Symbolism in art. 2. Virtues in art. 3. Vices in art. 4. Art. Medieval. I. Title.

LUCIE-SMITH, Edward. 709'.03'4
Symbolist art. New York, Praeger [1972] 216 p. illus. (part col.) 22 cm. Bibliography: p. 209. [N6465.S9L8 1972b] 72-77068 10.00
1. Symbolism in art. 2. Art, modern—19th century. BIP

ROTHSCHILD, Lincoln, 1902- 709
Forms and their meaning in Western art / by Lincoln Rothschild. South Brunswick : A.S. Barnes and Co., c1976. p. cm. Includes index. Bibliography: p. [N7565.R67] 74-9298 ISBN 0-498-01608-0 : 15.00
1. Symbolism in art. 2. Art—Themes, motives. 3. Form (Aesthetics) 4. Art—Philosophy. I. Title. BIP

SANTA Barbara, Calif. 704.94'6
Museum of Art.
Iconocom: cross-cultural iconography for the community. [Santa Barbara, 1973] 140 p. illus. 22 cm. [N7740.S33 1973] 73-88841
1. Santa Barbara, Calif. Museum of Art. 2. Symbolism in art. 3. Art—Santa Barbara, Calif.—Catalogs. I. Title.

VOIGT, Robert J 246
Symbols in Christian art. Somerset, Ohio, Rosary Pfess [1950] 52 p. illus. 18 cm. [N7740.V58] 50-746
1. Symbolism in art. I. Title.

WHITTICK, Arnold, 1898- 745'.4
Symbols for designers; a handbook on the application of symbols and symbolism to design, for the use of architects, sculptors, ecclesiastical and memorial designers, commercial artists, and students of symbolism. Foreword by Sir Herbert Baker. London, C. Lockwood, 1935. Detroit, Gale Research Co., 1972. xv, 168 p. illus. 22 cm. Includes bibliographical references. [N7740.W5 1972] 71-175760
1. Symbolism in art. 2. Design, Decorative. I. Title. BIP

WHITTLESEY, Eunice S. 704.94
Symbols and legends in Western art; a museum guide [by] E. S. Whittlesey. New York, Scribner [1972] ix, 367 p. illus. 21 cm. Bibliography: p. ix. [N7740.W53] 71-162764 ISBN 0-684-12583-8 7.95
1. Symbolism in art. 2. Symbolism—Dictionaries—English. 3. Art and mythology. 4. Mythology—Dictionaries—English. I. Title.

WINGFIELD-DIGBY, George 769.2
Frederick 1911-
Symbol and image in William Blake. Oxford, Clarendon Press, 1957. xx, 143 p. 77 illus. 25 cm. "Based on The gates of Paradise [by William Blake] and the newly found picture at Arlington Court, with reference to nearly sixty other designs and paintings by him, all of which are reproduced here." Bibliographical references included in "Notes" (p. 128-129) Bibliography: p. 130-133. [NE642.B5W5] 58-298
1. Blake, William, 1757-1827. 2. Blake, William, 1757-1827. For the sexes: The gates of Paradise. 3. Symbolism in art. I. Title.

Symbolism in art—Bibliography.

ANDERSON, David L., 1937- 016.7
Symbolism : a bibliography of symbolism as an international and multi-disciplinary movement / compiled and edited by David L. Anderson, with Georgia S. Maas and Diane-Marie Savoye. New York : New York University Press, 1975. xxi, 160 p. ; 26 cm. Includes index. [Z5936.S9A52] [NX600.S95] 74-17460 ISBN 0-8147-0555-3 : 12.50
1. Symbolism in art—Bibliography. 2. Arts—Bibliography. I. Maas, Georgia S., joint author. II. Savoye, Diane-Marie, joint author. III. Title. BIP

Symbolism in art—France.

JULLIAN, Philippe. 760'.0944
The symbolists. [Translated by Mary Anne Stevens. New York] Phaidon; [distributed by Praeger Publishers, 1973] 240 p. illus. (part col.) 29 cm. Includes bibliographical references. [NX549.A1J8413] 72-89483 ISBN 0-7148-1590-X 29.50
1. Symbolism in art—France. 2. Symbolism in art—Belgium. I. Title. BIP

Symmetry.

HUFF, William S. 701'.8 s
Symmetry; an appreciation of its presence in man's consciousness. Text: William S. Huff. Design: Tomas Gonda. [Pittsburgh? 1967- v. illus. 22 x 24 cm. Includes bibliographical references. [NC745.H8] 73-166439
1. Symmetry. I. Gonda, Tomas.

MACGILLAVRY, Caroline 769'.92'4
Henriette, 1904-
Fantasy & symmetry : the periodic drawings of M. C. Escher / Caroline H. MacGillavry. New York : H. N. Abrams, [1976] xi, 84 p. : ill. (some col.) ; 27 cm. Reprint of the 1965 ed. published for International Union of Crystallography by A. Oosthoek's Uitgeversmaatschappij, Utrecht under title: Symmetry aspects of M. C. Escher's periodic drawings. Includes index. Bibliography: p. xi, [NC745.M3 1976] 75-39835 ISBN 0-8109-0850-6 : 15.00
1. Escher, Maurits Cornelis, 1898- 2. Symmetry. 3. Colors. I. Title. BIP

RAZZELL, Arthur G. 741.4
Symmetry, by Arthur G. Razzell and K. G. O. Watts. Illustrated by Ellen Raskin. [1st ed. in the U.S.A.] Garden City, N.Y., Doubleday [1968] 47 p. illus. (part col.) 22 cm. (Exploring mathematics) Discusses the use of symmetry in design and nature and describes bilateral symmetry, rotational symmetry, the axes of symmetry, and symmetry in various shapes. [NC745.R3 1968] AC 68
1. Symmetry. 2. Proportion. I. Watts, Kenneth George Oliver, joint author. II. Raskin, Ellen, illus. III. Title.

Symmetry (Biology)

HUFF, William S. 701'.8 s
Man's observation of the natural environment. Text: William S. Huff. Design: Tomas Gonda. [Pittsburgh? 1972?] [26] p. illus. 22 x 24 cm. (His Symmetry, v. 5) Includes bibliographical references. [NC745.H8 vol. 5] [QH351] 704.94'9'5001 73-166436
1. Symmetry (Biology) I. Gonda, Tomas. II. Title. III. Series.

Synagogue architecture.

DE BREFFNY, Brian. 296.6'5
The synagogue / Brian de Breffny ; photography by George Mott. 1st American ed. New York : Macmillan, 1978. 215 p. : ill. ; 28 cm. Includes bibliographical references and index. [NA4690.D4 1978] 78-7583 18.95
1. Synagogue architecture. 2. Synagogues—History. I. Title. BIP

NATIONAL 726'.3'097307401444
Conference and Exhibit on Synagogue Architecture and Art.
Proceedings. New York, Union of American Hebrew Congregations. v. 28cm. Each vol. has also a distinctive title: 1957, The American synagogue, a progress report. [NA4690.N3] 58-46291
1. Synagogue architecture. I. Union of American Hebrew Congregations. II. Title. III. Title: The American synagogue, aprogress report.

Synagogue architecture—Bibliography.

BLACK, Linda Perlis. 016.3092 s
Synagogue architecture and planning : an annotated bibliography / Linda Perlis Black. Monticello, Ill. : Council of Planning Librarians, 1978. 24 p. ; 28 cm. (Exchange bibliography - Council of Planning Librarians ; 1469) Cover title. [Z5942.C68 no. 1469] [Z5943.S9] [NA4690] 016.726'3 78-103394 2.50
1. Synagogue architecture—Bibliography. I. Title. II. Series: Council of Planning Librarians. Exchange bibliography ; 1469.

Synagogue architecture — Europe.

WISCHNITZER, Rachel 726.3094
(Bernstein) 1885-
The architecture of the European synagogue, by Rachel Wischnitzer. [1st ed.] Philadelphia, Jewish Publication Society of America, 1964. xxxii, 312 p. illus. 19 x 27 cm. Bibliography: p. 299-300. [NA4690.W49] 64-16754
1. Synagogue architecture — Europe. 2. Synagogues — Europe. I. Title.

Synagogue architecture—Illinois—Exhibitions.

FAITH & 726'.3'09773074017311
form : an exhibition / organized by the Maurice Spertus Museum of Judaica ; introductory material, Arthur M. Feldman, Grace Cohen Grossman. Chicago : Spertus College Press, 1976. 101 p. : ill. ; 22 x 28 cm. Contents.Contents.—Gutstein, M. A. The roots and the branches.—Rader, L. W. Synagogue architecture in Illinois. Includes bibliographical references. [NA5230.I3F34] 77-356182
1. Maurice Spertus Museum of Judaica. 2. Synagogue architecture—Illinois—Exhibitions. 3. Jews in Chicago—History. I. Maurice Spertus Museum of Judaica. II. Gutstein, Morris Aaron, 1905- The roots and the branches. 1976. III. Rader, Lauren Weingarden. Synagogue architecture in Illinois. 1976.

Synagogue architecture—Spain.

HALPERIN, Don A. 726'.3'0946
The ancient synagogues of the Iberian peninsula, by Don A. Halperin. Gainesville, University of Florida Press, 1969. 86 p. illus., plans. 23 cm. (University of Florida monographs. Social sciences, no. 38) Bibliography: p. 85-86. [NA4690.H3] 78-625777 2.00
1. Synagogue architecture—Spain. 2. Synagogue architecture—Portugal. I. Title. II. Series: Florida. University, Gainesville. University of Florida monographs. Social sciences, no. 38 BIP

Synagogue architecture—U. S.

JEWISH Theological 726.30973
Seminary of America. Jewish Museum.
Recent American synagogue architecture [Exhibition] organized by Richard Meier. [New York, Author 1963] 63p. illus., facsim., plans. 24cm. Bibliography. 63-22379 2.00
1. Synagogue architecture—U. S. I. Title.
Contents omitted.

WISCHNITZER, Rachel 726.3
(Bernstein) 1885-
Synagogue architecture in the United States; history and interpretation. Philadelphia, Jewish Publication Society of America, 1955. 204p. illus. 23x29cm. (The Jacob R. Schiff library of Jewish contributions to American democracy) Includes bibliographies. [NH4690.W5] 55-8422
1. Synagogue architecture—U. S. I. Title.

Synagogue architecture—United States—Exhibitions.

TWO hundred 726'.3'097307401444
years of American synagogue architecture : [exhibition], the Rose Art Museum, Brandeis University, Waltham, Massachusetts, [March 30 to May 2, 1976] . Waltham, Mass. : American Jewish Historical Society, c1976. 63 p. : ill. ; 25 cm. Bibliography: p. 55-63. [NA4690.T86] 76-15469
1. Brandeis University, Waltham, Mass. Rose Art Museum. 2. Synagogue architecture—United States—Exhibitions. 3. United States—Religious life and customs—Exhibitions. I. Brandeis University, Waltham, Mass. Rose Art Museum. II. American Jewish Historical Society. BIP

Synagogue art, American.

KAMPF, Avram. 704.94896
Contemporary synagogue art; developments in the United States, 1945-1965. New York, Union of American Hebrew Congregations [1966] Westminster, Md., Newman Press, 1966. vii, 276 p. illus. 29 cm. x. 96 p. 22 cm. Bibliography: p. 261-263. [N7415.K35] [BV30,K313] 263.9 65-25202 66-20035
1. Synagogue art, American. 2. Synagogue architecture — U.S. 3. Church year. I. Kampmann, Theoderich. II. Title. III. Title: The year of the church; BIP

Synagogue art—Venice—Exhibitions.

JEWISH art treasures 709'.45'31
in Venice. [Edited by the Venice Jewish Community] New York, International Fund for Monuments [1973?] 94 p. illus. (part col.) 24 cm. Added t.p.: Tesori d'arte ebraica a Venezia; text in English and Italian. [NK1672.J48] 74-177364
1. Synagogue art—Venice—Exhibitions. 2. Synagogues—Venice—Exhibitions. 3. Jews in Venice. I. Comunita israelitica di Venezia.

Synagogues—Addresses, essays, lectures.

GUTMANN, Joseph, comp. 726'.3
The synagogue : studies in origins, archaeology, and architecture / selected with a prolegomenon by Joseph Gutmann. New York : Ktav Pub. House, [1975] xxxi, 359 p. : ill. ; 24 cm. (The Library of Biblical studies) English or German. Bibliography: p. xxx-xxxi. [BM653.G87] 74-34065 ISBN 0-87068-265-2 : 25.00
1. Synagogues—Addresses, essays, lectures. 2. Synagogue architecture—Addresses, essays, lectures. I. Title. II. Series.
Contents omitted.

Synchromism (Art)—United States.

LEVIN, Gail, 1948- 759.13
Synchromism and American color abstraction, 1910-1925 / Gail Levin. 1st ed. New York : G. Braziller, c1978. 144 p. : ill. (some col.) ; 28 cm. Issued in conjunction with an exhibition of the same name organized by the Whitney Museum of American Art. Bibliography: p. 133-136. [ND212.5.S9L48 1978] 77-21051 ISBN 0-8076-0882-3 : 20.00. ISBN 0-8076-0883-1 pbk. : 10.95
1. Synchromism (Art)—United States. 2. Painting, American. 3. Painting, Abstract—United States. I. Whitney Museum of American Art, New York. II. Title. BIP

T-shirts.

KNEITEL, Ken. 391
The great American T-shirt / by Ken Kneitel, Bill Maloney, Andrea Quinn ; photos. by Andrea Quinn. New York : New American Library, 1976. 95 p. : ill. ; 28 cm. "A Push Pin Press book." [TT675.K58] 76-23479 pbk. : 5.95
1. T-shirts. I. Maloney, Bill, joint author. II. Quinn, Andrea, joint author. III. Title.

PLATT, Charles, 1949- 746.6
T-shirting : a do-it-yourself guide to getting it on your chest / by Charles Platt ; photos. by Bernard Glickman. New York : Hawthorn Books, c1975. xii, 162 p. : ill. ; 24 cm. Includes index. [TT675.P57 1975] 75-25307 ISBN 0-8015-7484-6 : 4.95
1. T-shirts. 2. Textile crafts. I. Title.

Tabaguet, Jean Baptiste, fl. 1590.

BUTLER, Samuel, 1835- 914.5'17
1902.
Ex vote. [1st AMS ed.] New York, AMS Press [1968] xxiv, 229 p. illus. 24 cm. (The Shrewsbury edition of the works of Samuel Butler, v. 9) Reprint of the 1924 ed. [PR4349.B7 1968 vol. 9] [N6921.V35] 72-187991
1. Tabaguet, Jean Baptiste, fl. 1590. 2. Varallo, Italy. Nuova Gerusalemme (Shrine) 3. Art—Varallo, Italy. I. Title.

Table setting and decoration.

CYPHERS, Emma Hodkinson, 635.9663
ed.
Fruit and vegetable arrangements. New

SUBJECT INDEX TANGE, KENZO, 1913—

York, Hearthside Press [1955] 128 p. illus. 25 cm. [SB449.3.F7C9] 55-10244
1. Table setting and decoration. 2. Fruit. 3. Vegetables. I. Title. BIP

CYPHERS, Emma Hodkinson. 745.92'6
Fruit and vegetable arrangements. Rev. New York, Hearthside Press [1963] 128 p. illus (part col.) 25 cm. [SB449.3.F7C9 1963] 63-21900
1. Table setting and decoration. 2. Fruit. 3. Vegetables. I. Title.

Tables—History—Juvenile literature.

RECORD, Nancy A. 749'.3
Come to the table. Written and illustrated by Nancy A. Record. Minneapolis, Lerner Publications Co. [1972] 55 p. illus. 25 cm. Text and illustrations trace the history of table design from ancient Greece to twentieth-century Scandinavia. [NK2740.R38] 73-128801 ISBN 0-8225-0274-7
1. Tables—History—Juvenile literature. I. Title. BIP

Tables—Ontario.

INGOLFSRUD, Elizabeth. 749'.3
All about Ontario tables / Elizabeth Ingolfsrud. Toronto : House of Grant (Canada), c1976. 63 p. : ill. ; 23 cm. [NK2740.I55] 77-366628 ISBN 0-460-90087-0 : 3.50
1. Tables—Ontario. I. Title.

Tabuena. Romeo.

ARGUILLA, Lyd 759.9914
Tabuena. Manila. Philippine Art Gallery [dist. Detroit. Cellar Bkshop., 1964.c.1960] 48p. illus. 32 col. plates. port. 21cm. Appraisal based on a ten-year retrospective exhibition of Tabuena's works, from 1949 to 1959. at the Philippine Art Gallery in coop with the Cultural Div.. Dept. of Foreign Affairs and the Asia Found. 64-7133 6.00 bds.,
1. Tabuena. Romeo. 2. Manila. Philippine Art Gallerv. I. Title.

Tack, Augustus Vincent, 1870-1949.

GREEN, Eleanor, 1929- 759.13
Augustus Vincent Tack, 1870-1949: twenty-six paintings from the Phillips Collection. [Austin? Tex., 1972] 39 p. illus. (part col.) 25 cm. Catalog of an exhibition held August 27-October 3, 1972: University Art Museum, the University of Texas at Austin; October 19-November 19, 1972: University of Maryland Art Gallery. Bibliography: p. 34-35. [ND237.T32G73] 72-170609
1. Tack, Augustus Vincent, 1870-1949. I. Tack, Augustus Vincent, 1870-1949. II. Phillips Collection, Washington, D.C. III. Texas. University at Austin. Art Museum. IV. Maryland. University. Art Gallery.

Tahiti.

GAUGUIN, Paul, 1848-1903. 759.4 B
Noa Noa / by Paul Gauguin ; translated from the French by O. F. Theis. Danbury, CT : Archer Editions Press, 1976, c1919. 148 p., [9] leaves of plates : ill. ; 21 cm. Reprint of the ed. published by N. L. Brown, New York. [ND553.G27A25 1976] 76-16128 ISBN 0-89097-006-8 : 15.00
1. Gauguin, Paul, 1848-1903. 2. Tahiti. 3. Painters—France—Correspondence, reminiscences, etc. I. Title. BIP

GAUGUIN, Paul [Eugene Henry Paul Gauguin] 759.4
Noa noa; voyage to Tahiti. [Tr. from the orig. French ms. by Jonathan Griffin. Postscript by Jean Loize] New York, Reynal [dist. Morrow, 1962] 36p. plates (pt. col.) 32cm. A63 13.95
1. Tahiti. I. Title.

Tahiti in art.

FIELD, Richard S. 759.4
Paul Gauguin : the paintings of the first voyage to Tahiti / Richard S. Field. New York : Garland Pub., 1977, i.e.1978 415, [15] p., [44] leaves of plates : ill. ; 21 cm. (Outstanding dissertations in the fine arts) Originally presented as the author's thesis, Harvard, 1963. Includes bibliographies. [ND553.G27F53 1977] 76-23617 ISBN 0-8240-2688-8 lib.bdg. : 45.00
1. Gauguin, Paul, 1848-1903. 2. Tahiti in art. 3. Tahiti—Description and travel—Views. I. Title. II. Series.

Tait, Arthur Fitzwilliam, 1819-1905.

TAIT, Arthur Fitzwilliam, 1819-1905. 759.13
A. F. Tait: artist in the Adirondacks; an exhibition of paintings and other works by the sporting and animal artist Arthur Fitzwilliam Tait (1819-1905). [Blue Mountain Lake, N.Y., Adirondack Museum, 1974] 73 p. illus. (1 col.) 21 x 23 cm. Catalogue of an exhibition held at the Adirondack Museum, June 15-Oct. 15, 1974. [ND237.T323A65] 74-182318 ISBN 0-910020-30-2
1. Tait, Arthur Fitzwilliam, 1819-1905. 2. Adirondack Mountains in art. I. Adirondack Museum, Blue Mountain Lake, N.Y.

Tajin, Mexico.

KAMPEN, Michael Edwin. 917.2'6
The sculptures of El Tajin, Veracruz, Mexico. Gainesville, University of Florida Press, 1972. ix, 195 p. illus. 27 cm. Bibliography: p. 191-195. [F1219.1.T2K35] 71-119809 ISBN 0-8130-0306-7 12.50
1. Tajin, Mexico. 2. Indians of Mexico—Sculpture. I. Title. BIP

Takis, pseud.

ANDERSEN, Wayne V. 730'.92'4
Takis evidence of the unseen [by] Wayne Andersen. With commentaries by Marcel Duchamp [and others. Cambridge, Mass., MIT Press, 1968?] 33 p. illus. 29 cm. "Published on the occasion of the Takis exhibition: Hayden Gallery, Massachusetts Institute of Technology, Cambridge, Massachussetts, November 15 to December 8, 1968 [and] Howard Wise Gallery, New York, February 1 to February 22, 1969." Bibliography: p. 33. [NB603.T3A83] 68-59250
1. Takis, pseud. I. Hayden Gallery. II. Howard Wise Gallery. III. Title.

Talbot, William Henry Fox, 1800-1877.

ARNOLD, Harry John Philip, 1932- 770'.92'4 B
William Henry Fox Talbot : pioneer of photography and man of science / [by] H. J. P. Arnold. London : Hutchinson, 1977. 383 p., leaf of plate, [48] p. of plates : ill. (some col.), col. coat of arms, facsims., geneal. tables, ports. (some col.) ; 26 cm. Includes bibliographies and index. [TR140.T3A76] 78-320092 ISBN 0-09-129600-5 : 31.95
1. Talbot, William Henry Fox, 1800-1877. 2. Photographers—England—Biography.
Distributed by Merrimack Book Service BIP

BUCKLAND, Gail. 770'.92'4 B
Fox Talbot and the invention of photography / Gail Buckland. New York : Camera/Graphic Press, [1978] p. cm. Includes bibliographical references and index. [TR140.T3B8] 78-4405 ISBN 0-918696-07-0 : 37.50
1. Talbot, William Henry Fox, 1800-1877. 2. Photography—History. 3. Photographers—England—Biography. I. Title. BIP

HANNAVY, John. 770'.92'4 B
Fox Talbot : an illustrated life of William Henry Fox Talbot, "Father of modern photography," 1800-1877 / John Hannavy. Princes Risborough : Shire Publications, 1976. 48 p. : ill., facsims., ports. ; 21 cm. (Lifelines ; 38) Includes index. Bibliography: p. 46. [TR140.T3H36] 76-383859 ISBN 0-85263-319-X : £0.60
1. Talbot, William Henry Fox, 1800-1877. 2. Photographers—England—Biography.

TALBOT, William Henry Fox, 1800-1877. 779'.092'4
William H. Fox Talbot, inventor of the negative-positive process [by] Andre Jammes. [English translation by Maureen Oberli-Turner] New York, Macmillan [1973] 96 p. plates. 28 cm. (Photography: men and movements, v. 2) Includes bibliographical references. [TR651.T3413] 73-10789 10.95
1. Talbot, William Henry Fox, 1800-1877. 2. Photography, Artistic. 3. Calotype. I. Jammes, Andre.

Taler.

DAVENPORT, John Stewart, 1907- 737.49'43
German church and city talers, 1600-1700, by John S. Davenport Galesburg, Ill., 1967. 349 p. illus. 24 cm. Bibliography: p. 345-348. [CJ2745.D25] 68-719
1. Taler. I. Title.

DAVENPORT, John Stewart, 1907- 737.4'9'43
German church and city talers, 1600-1700 / by John S. Davenport. [2d ed.]. Galesburg, Ill. : Davenport, 1975. 351 p. : ill. ; 24 cm. Bibliography: p. 345-348. [CJ2715.D25 1975] 76-359674
1. Taler. 2. Coins, German. 3. Germany—History, Local. 4. Germany, West—History, Local. 5. Germany, East—History, Local. I. Title.

Tales, Montenegrin—Illustrations.

STEADMAN, Ralph. 741.9'42
Cherrywood cannon / Ralph Steadman ; based on a story told to him by Dimitri Sidjanski. New York : Paddington Press : distributed by Grosset & Dunlap, c1978. [48] p. : ill. (some col.) ; 31 cm. An illustrated Montenegrin folktale with 24 original illustrations in pen and ink. [NC242.S73A4 1978] 77-16163 pbk. : 7.95
1. Steadman, Ralph. 2. Tales, Montenegrin—Illustrations. I. Damjan, Mischa, pseud. II. Title.

Tall buildings.

AREGGER, Hans. 720
Highrise building and urban design [by] Hans Aregger and Otto Glaus. [Translated from the German by Maria Kroll] New York, F. A. Praeger [1967] 199 p. illus., plans. 29 cm. Translation of Hochhaus and Stadtplanung. [NA6230.A7313] 67-18826
1. Tall buildings. 2. Architecture—Designs and plans. 3. Cities and towns—Planning. I. Glaus, Otto, joint author. II. Title.

ROSMAN, Riko. 721
Statik und Dynamik der Scheibensysteme des Hochbaues; praktische Berechnungsverfahren fur Systeme aus gekoppelten vollen Scheiben, gegliederten Scheiben und Stockwerkrahmen. Berlin, New York, Springer-Verlag, 1968. xvi, 317p. illus. 24cm. Bibl. [TH845.R64] 68-13324 17.25
1. Tall buildings. 2. Structural frames. 3. Walls. I. Title.

Tall buildings—Congresses.

TALL buildings; 721
the proceedings of a symposium on tall buildings with particular reference to shear wall structures. Held in the Dept. of Civil Engineering, University of Southampton, April 1966. Edited by A. Coull and B. Stafford Smith. Oxford, New York, Symposium Publications Division, Pergamon Press [1967] xx, 607 p. illus. 24 cm. Sponsored by the University of Southampton and the Civil Engineering Research Association. Includes bibliographies. [TH845.T27 1967] 66-17929
1. Tall buildings—Congresses. 2. Structure, Theory of—Congresses. 3. Walls—Congresses. I. Coull, A., ed. II. Smith, Bryan Stafford, ed. III. Southampton, Eng. University. IV. Civil Engineering Research Association.

Tall buildings—Psychological aspects—Congresses.

HUMAN response to tall buildings / edited by Donald J. Conway. 301.31
Stroudsburg, Pa. : Dowden, Hutchinson & Ross, c1977. xii, 362 p. : ill. ; 24 cm. (Community development series ; CDS/34) Proceedings of a conference sponsored by the Office of Research Programs, American Institute of Architects, and the Joint Committee on Tall Buildings and held in the Fall of 1974. Includes bibliographical references and index. [NA6231.5.H85] 76-58917 ISBN 0-87933-268-9 : 25.00
1. Tall buildings—Psychological aspects—Congresses. 2. Architecture—Human factors—Congresses. I. Conway, Donald, 1931- II. American Institute of Architects. Office of Research Programs. III. Joint Committee on Tall Buildings. BIP

Talleur, John, 1925—

KANSAS. University. Museum of Art. 769'.924
John Talleur; recent work. [Lawrence, 1966?] 19 p. illus. 20 cm. (Miscellaneous publications of the Museum of Art, no. 63) Catalog of an exhibition held Nov. 4-Dec. 1, 1966, and checklist of the artist's prints. [NE539.T3K3] 68-64673
1. Talleur, John, 1925- I. Title. II. Series: Kansas. University. Museum of Art. Miscellaneous publications, no. 63

Tamaulipas, Mexico—Antiq.

MACNEISH, Richard S 970.4721
Preliminary archacological investigations in the Sierra de Tamaulipas, Mexico. Philadelphia, American Philosophical Society, 1958. 210p. illus., maps. 30cm. (Transactions of the American Philosophical Society, new ser., v. 48, pt. 6) Bibliography: p.204-206. [Q11.P6 n. s, vol. 48, pt. 6] 58-14489
1. Tamaulipas, Mexico—Antiq. 2. Indians of Mexico—Antiq. I. Title. II. Series: American Philosophical Society, Philadelphia. Transactions, new ser., v. 48, pt. 6

Tamayo, Rufino, 1899—

GENAUER, Emily, 1910- 759.972
Rufino Tamayo. New York, Abrams [1974] 175 p. illus. (part col.) 28 x 30 cm. Bibliography: p. 173-175. [ND259.T3G4] 74-2150 ISBN 0-8109-0500-0
1. Tamayo, Rufino, 1899- I. Tamayo, Rufino, 1899- BIP

TAMAYO, Rufino, 1899- 759.972
Tamayo. A commentary by the artist [and] an essay by James B. Lynch, Jr. Phoenix, Ariz., Phoenix Art Museum, 1968. xiii, 117 p. illus. (part col.), ports. 23 cm. Exhibition held at the Phoenix Art Museum, co-sponsored by the Friends of Mexican Art. [ND259.T3L8] 68-23580
I. Lynch, James B. II. Phoenix, Ariz. Art Museum. III. Friends of Mexican Art.

Tamburi, Orfeo, 1910—

TAMBURI, Orfeo, 1910- 741.9'45
London by Orfeo Tamburi. Verona, Edizione d'arte Ghelfi, 1972. 16, [45] p. illus. (part col.) 15 cm. Introduction by Vera Lindsay. [NC257.T35L56] 73-167826
1. Tamburi, Orfeo, 1910- 2. London in art. I. Lindsay, Vera. II. Title.

TAMBURI, Orfeo, 1910- 741.9'45
Squares et jardins. Introduction par Nino Frank. Verona, Edizioni d'arte Ghelfi, 1970. 15 p. illus., 16 plates. 13 cm. [NC257.T35A55] 74-159561
1. Tamburi, Orfeo, 1910- 2. Paris in art. I. Title.

Tange, Kenzo, 1913—

BOYD, Robin. 720.952
Kenzo Tange. New York, G. Braziller, 1962. 125p. illus., port., plans. 26cm. (Makers of contemporary architecture) 'Creation in present-day architecture and the Japanese traidtion, by Kenro Tange. [Reprinted in Bibliography: p. [120]-[121] [NA1559.T33B6] 62-16267
1. Tange, Kenzo, 1913- I. Title. II. Series. BIP

RIANI, Paolo. 720'.92'4
Kenze Tange [translated from the Italian]. London, New York, Hamlyn, 1970. 96 p.

illus. (some col.), plans (some col.), ports. 32 cm. (Twentieth-century masters) "Distributed in the United States of America, by Crown Publishers, Inc." Bibliography: p. 95-96. [NA1559.T33R513] 72-181876 ISBN 0-600-35302-8 £2.25
1. Tange, Kenzo, 1913-

TANGE, Kenzo, 1913- 720'.924
Kenzo Tange, 1946-1969; architecture and urban design. Edited by Udo Kultermann. New York, Praeger Publishers [1970] 304 p. illus., maps (part col.), plans (part col.) 29 cm. Text in English, French and German. "Contains buildings ... selected from the Japanese editions: Reality and creation (Kenzo Tange 1946-1958) and Technology and humanity (Kenzo Tange 1955-1964). It also contains parts of ... [the author's] work Architecture and city (Kenzo Tange 1946-1970) which is being prepared for forthcoming publication." Bibliography: p. 302-303. [NA1559.T33K8 1970] 70-111288
I. Kultermann, Udo, ed.

Tanguy, Yves, 1900-1955.

NEW York (City) Museum of Modern Art. 759.4
Yves Tanguy; [exhibition and catalogue] by James Thrall Soby. New York, [1955] 71 p. illus., plates (part col.) ports. 25 cm. Bibliography: p. 69-70. [ND553.T26N4] 55-11796
1. Tanguy, Yves, 1900-1955. 2. Paintings, French—Exhibitions. I. Soby, James Thrall, 1906-

NEW York (City). Museum of Modern Art. 759.4
Yves Tanguy; [exhibition and catalogue] by James Thrall Soby. Reprint ed. [New York] Published for the Museum of Modern Art by Arno Press, 1972 [c1955] 71 p. illus. 25 cm. Bibliography: p. 69-70. [ND553.T26N4 1972] 75-169321 ISBN 0-405-01579-8
1. Tanguy, Yves, 1900-1955. I. Soby, James Thrall, 1906-

TANGUY, Yves 1900-1955. 709.44
Yves Tanguy. Un recueil de ses oeuvres. A summary of his works. New York, P. Matisse, [dist. Wittenborn, c.]1963. 230 p. illus. (pt. col.) ports. (1 mounted col.) plates (pt. col.) facsims. 30 cm French and English. 63-4602 37.50, lim. ed.
I. Title.
Contents omitted.

TANGUY, Yves, 1900-1955. 759.4
Yves Tanguy : [catalog of an exhibition] November 7-December 7, 1974. New York : Acquavella Galleries, 1974. [23] p., [26] leaves of plates : ill. (some col.) ; 28 cm. Bibliography: p. [75] [ND553.T26A65] 74-84158
1. Tanguy, Yves, 1900-1955. I. Acquavella Galleries.

Taniguchi, Buson, 1716-1784.

FRENCH, Calvin L. 759.952
The poet-painters, Buson and his followers : an exhibition, the University of Michigan Museum of Art, Ann Arbor, January 9-February 17, 1974 ; the Seattle Art Museum, Washington, March 28-May 12, 1974 ; the Asia House Gallery, New York, October 3-December 1, 1974 / organized by Calvin L. French, in collaboration with Stephen Addiss ... [et al.]. [Ann Arbor] : University of Michigan Museum of Art, 1974. xv, 179 p., [3] leaves of plates : ill. (some col.) ; 31 cm. Catalog. Bibliography: p. 178-179. [ND1053.5.F73] 74-623083
1. Taniguchi, Buson, 1716-1784. 2. Taniguchi, Buson, 1716-1784—Influence. 3. Paintings, Japanese—Exhibitions. 4. Painting, Japanese—Edo period, 1600-1868. I. Michigan. University. Museum of Art. II. Seattle. Art Museum. III. Asia House Gallery, New York. IV. Title.

Tankas (Tibetan scrolls)

BRYNER, Edna. 759.9515
Thirteen Tibetan tankas. [Indian Hills, Colo.] Falcon's Wing Press [1957 c1956] xxv, 153p. illus. 28cm. 'Three Jatakas from the Kanjur': p.112-144. Bibliographical references included-in 'Notes' (p.147-153) [ND1046.T5B78] 55-11367
1. Tankas (Tibetan scrolls) 2. Art, Buddhist. 3. Jatakas. I. Kanjur. II. Title. III. Title: Tibetan tankas.

LAUF, Detlef Ingo. 704.948'9'4392309515
Secret revelation of Tibetan thangkas = Verborgene Botschaft tibetischer Thangkas : picture meditation and interpretation of Lamaist cult paintings : this work is based on the John Gilmore Ford Collection / Detlef-Ingo Lauf ; [ins Engl. ubertr. von J. A. Underwood]. Freiburg im Breisgau : Aurum-Verlag, 1976. 167 p. : numerous ill. (some col.) ; 30 cm. Parallel German text with English translation. Includes bibliographical references. [N8193.3.L356T54] 77-552535 ISBN 3-591-08025-X : DM85.00
1. Tankas (Tibetan scrolls) 2. Art, Lamaist—Tibet. 3. Buddhist art and symbolism—Tibet. I. Ford, John Gilmore, 1928- II. Title. III. Title: Verborgene Botschaft tibetischer Thangkas.

Tannahill, Robert Hudson—Art collections.

DETROIT. Institute of Arts. 708.174'34
The Robert Hudson Tannahill bequest to the Detroit Institute of Arts; a catalogue issued on the occasion of the exhibition "A collector's treasure: the Tannahill bequest", May 13-August 13, 1970. [Edited by Graham Hood. Detroit, 1970] 209 p. illus. (part col.) 29 cm. [N5220.T35] 71-122774
1. Tannahill, Robert Hudson—Art collections. 2. Art—Exhibitions. I. Hood, Graham, 1936- ed. BIP

DETROIT. Institute of Arts. 708.174'34
The Robert Hudson Tannahill gifts to the Detroit Institute of Arts; a catalogue issued on the occasion of the opening of the Robert Hudson Tannahill Wing of American Art, June 1, 1969. [Edited by Graham Hood. Detroit, 1969] 75 p. illus. 28 cm. [N5220.T35D42] 74-25289
1. Tannahill, Robert Hudson—Art collections. I. Hood, Graham, 1936-

Tanner, Henry Ossawa, 1859-1937.

MATHEWS, Marcia M. 759.13 B
Henry Ossawa Tanner, American artist [by] Marcia M. Mathews. Chicago, University of Chicago Press [1969] xvii, 261 p. illus. (part col.), ports. 23 cm. (Negro American biographies and autobiographies) Bibliographical footnotes. [ND237.T33M3] 69-19279
1. Tanner, Henry Ossawa, 1859-1937. I. Title. II. Series.

Tanning—Juvenile literature.

FISHER, Leonard Everett. 745.53
The tanners. Written & illustrated by Leonard Everett Fisher. New York, F. Watts [1966] 43 p. illus. 23 cm. (His Colonial American craftsmen) [TS965.5.F5] 66-6518
1. Tanning—Juvenile literature. I. Title. BIP

Tao-chi, 1630-1707.

†CHOU, Ju-hsi. 759.951
The Hua-yu-lu and Tao-chi's theory of painting / by Ju-hsi Chou. Tempe : Center for Asian Studies, Arizona State University, 1977. 49 p. ; 23 cm. (Occasional paper - Center for Asian Studies, Arizona State University ; no. 9) Includes bibliographical references. [ND1049.T3C47] 77-623250 1.25
1. Tao-chi, 1630-1707. Hua yu lu. 2. Painting, Chinese. 3. Painting—Technique. I. Title. II. Series: Arizona. State University, Tempe. Center for Asian Studies. Occasional paper ; no. 9.

FU, Marilyn. 759.951
The wilderness colors of Tao-chi. Introd., commentary, and translations by Marilyn Fu and Wen Fong. [New York] Metropolitan Museum of Art [1973] [43] p. 12 col. plates. 36 cm. Issued in case. Bibliography: p. [41] [ND1049.T3F78] 73-9618 ISBN 0-87099-078-0 12.50
1. Tao-chi, 1630-1707. I. Fong, Wen, joint author. II. Tao-chi, 1630-1707. III. Title. BIP

TAO-CHI, 1630-1707. 759.951
Returning home : Tao-chi's album of landscapes and flowers / introd. and commentaries by Wen Fong. New York : G. Braziller, 1976. p. cm. [ND1049.T3F66] 76-15911 ISBN 0-8076-0827-0 : 17.50
1. Tao-chi, 1630-1707. I. Fong, Wen. II. Title. BIP

Taos, N.M., in art.

DENVER. Art Museum. 759.13
Picturesque images from Taos and Santa Fe; an exhibition sponsored by the First National Bank of Denver and the Denver Art Museum, January 12-March 17, 1974. [Catalogue edited and designed by Cile M. Bach and Marlene Chambers. Denver, 1974] 215 p. illus. (part col.) 24 x 31 cm. Catalog prepared by P. Trenton. Bibliography: p. 214. [ND212.D46 1974] 74-173648
1. Taos, N.M., in art. 2. Santa Fe, N.M., in art. 3. Paintings, American—Exhibitions. 4. Painting, Modern—20th century—United States. I. Bach, Cile M. II. Chambers, Marlene. III. Trenton, Pat. IV. First National Bank of Denver. V. Title. BIP

Tapa.

ARKINSTALL, Patricia Lorraine. 390
A study of bark cloth from Hawaii, Samoa, Tonga and Fiji: an exploration of the regional development of distinctive styles of bark cloth and its relationship to other cultural factors. [Ithaca? N.Y.] 1966. xiii, 220 l. illus., 78 plates (part col.) 29 cm. Vita. Theses (M.Sc.)—Cornell University. Bibliography: leaves 211-220. [GN432.A7] 67-6181
1. Tapa. I. Title.

KOOIJMAN, S. 746'.04'1
Tapa in Polynesia [by] Simon Kooijman. Honolulu, Hawaii, Bishop Museum Press, 1972. xiv, 498 p. illus. 26 cm. (Bernice P. Bishop Museum bulletin 234) Bibliography: p. [481]-494. [GN432.K6] 77-178296 ISBN 0-910240-13-2 18.50
1. Tapa. 2. Polynesians. I. Title. II. Series: Bernice Pauahi Bishop Museum, Honolulu. Bulletin 234. BIP

Tapestry.

BEUTLICH, Tadek. 746.3
The technique of woven tapestry. London, Batsford; New York, Watson-Guptill, 1967. 128 p. col. front., illus., 2 col. plates, diagrs. 25 1/2 cm. Bibliography: p. 121-122. [TT850.B42] 66-24382
1. Tapestry. I. Title.

VAN DOMMELEN, David B. 747.3
Decorative wall hangings; art with fabric. [New York] Funk & Wagnalls Co. [1962] 178 p. illus. 28 cm. Includes bibliography. [TS1780.V3] 62-18327
1. Tapestry. 2. Needlework. 3. Textile design. I. Title. II. Title: Wall hangings.

Tapestry, American.

CALDER, Alexander, 1898- 746.3'92'4
Aubusson tapestries, with a selection of mobiles. [Chicago] 1972?] [9] p. (chiefly col. illus.) 21 cm. Cover title. Catalog of an exhibition held at the Arts Club of Chicago, Nov. 15-Dec. 30, 1972. [NK3012.A3C32] 73-171211
1. Calder, Alexander, 1898- 2. Tapestry, American. I. Arts Club of Chicago. II. Title.

DUKE University, Durham, N.C. Art Museum. 746.3'92'4
Silvia Heyden; recent tapestries. [Exhibition] 11 March-23 April, 1972, Duke University Museum of Art. Durham, N.C. [1972] vi, 65 p. illus. 22 cm. Bibliography: p. 63-64. [NK3064.A3H43] 72-75876
I. Heyden, Silvia, 1927-

KAUFMANN, Ruth. 746.3'9'73
The new American tapestry. New York, Reinhold Book Corp. [1968] 104 p. illus. (part col.) 32 cm. [TT849.K38] 67-14157
1. Tapestry, American. I. Title.

LEVI-STRAUSS, Monique. 746.3'973
Sheila Hicks. New York, Van Nostrand Reinhold Co. [1974] p. [NK3012.A3H524] 74-4529 ISBN 0-442-24766-4 15.00
1. Hicks, Sheila, 1934- 2. Tapestry, American.

Tapestry, Chinese—Exhibitions.

MAILEY, Jean. 746.3
Chinese silk tapestry: k'o-ssu from private and museum collections. New York, China Institute in America [1971] 60 p. illus. 23 cm. Catalog of the exhibition held Mar. 24-May 27, 1971, at the China House Gallery. Bibliography: p. [6] [NK3083.A1M3] 70-157668
1. Tapestry, Chinese—Exhibitions. I. China Institute in America. II. Title.

Tapestry, Coptic.

COPTIC textile designs / [selected by] M. Gerspach. New York : Dover Publications, 1975. 83 p. : all ill. ; 24 cm. (Dover pictorial archive series) "Contains all the illustrations from the work Les tapisseries coptes ... The original text has been omitted and replaced by a new publisher's note." [NK3088.C66C66 1975] 75-12362 ISBN 0-486-22849-5 : 2.00 746.3932
1. Tapestry, Coptic. I. Gerspach, Edouard, 1833-1906. II. Gerspach, Edouard, 1833-1906. Les tapisseries coptes. BIP

LENZEN, Victor Fritz 746.3962
The triumph of Dionysos on textiles of late antique Egypt. Berkeley, University of California Press, 1960. 37p. Bibl. footnotes. illus. 26cm. (University of California publications in classical archaeology, v. 5, no. 1) 60-63404 1.50 pap.,
1. Tapestry, Coptic. 2. Dionysus. I. Title. II. Series: California. University. University of California publications in classical archaeology, v. 5, no. 1

Tapestry, Czech.

KYBALOVA, Ludmila 746.39437
Contemporary tapestries from Czechoslovakia [Tr. by Alga Kuthanova] London, A. Wingate [dist. Big Sur., Calif., Craft & Hobby Bk. Serv., 1965, c.1963] 93,[1]p. illus. (pt. col.) 27cm. Rusume en French. [NK3048.K8913] 65-9808 5.95
1. Tapestry, Czech. I. Title.

KYBALOVA, Ludmila 746.39437
Moderne Gobelins in der Tschechoslowakei, Fotografien von Ladislav Neubert. [Deutsch von Eva Buresch. Praha] Artia [dist. New York, Vanous, c.1964] 89p. 82 illus. (pt. col.) 27cm. [NK3048.K915] 65-965 6.00
1. Tapestry, Czech. 2. Gobelin tapestry. I. Title.

Tapestry — Exhibitions.

ALLENTOWN, Pa. Art Museum. 746.3
Great periods of tapestry. [Exhibition] Allentown Art Museum, February 3-28, 1961. [Allentown, 1961] 4, [61] p. 31 illus. 23 x 29 cm. In a box. Includes bibliographies. [NK2980.A43] 66-5817
1. Tapestry — Exhibitions. I. Title.

FINE Arts Museums of San Francisco. 746.3'074'019461
Five centuries of tapestry from the Fine Arts Museums of San Francisco : [catalogue] / Anna G. Bennett. [San Francisco] : The Museums, c1976. v, 253 p. : ill. (some col.) ; 31 cm. Errata sheet inserted. Exhibition held at the California Palace of the Legion of Honor, San Francisco, Nov. 20, 1976-Jan. 30, 1977. Bibliography: p. 246-249. [NK2980.S26F563] 76-24162 ISBN 0-88401-019-8 pbk. : 9.95
1. Tapestry—Exhibitions. I. Bennett, Anna G. II. California Palace of the Legion of Honor, San Francisco. III. Title.

ATTENBOROUGH, Bessie M. 746.4'3
The craft of tatting, by Bessie M. Attenborough. [U.S. ed.] Newton Centre, Mass., C. T. Brandford Co. [1972] 104 p. illus. 21 cm. Bibliography: p. 104. [TT840.A85 1972] 72-83841 Price not set
1. Tatting. I. Title.
BIP

AULD, Rhoda L. 746.4'3
Tatting; the contemporary art of knotting with a shuttle [by] Rhoda L. Auld. Drawings by James Wood. Photos. by Lawrence Auld. New York, Van Nostrand Reinhold Co. [1974] 128 p. illus. 24 cm. Bibliography: p. [126] [TT840.A87] 73-14011 ISBN 0-442-20378-0 8.95
1. Tatting.

KLIOT, Jules. 746.4'36
Tatting : designs from Victorian lace craft / edited by Jules & Kaethe Kliot. Berkeley, Calif. : Some Place Publications, [c1978] 64 p. : ill. ; 28 cm. Cover title. [TT840.K58] 79-107529 ISBN 0-916896-13-7 pbk. : 5.25
1. Tatting. I. Kliot, Kaethe, joint author. II. Title.

MORGAN, Lael. 746.4'36
Tatting : a new look at the old art of making lace / by Lael Morgan. 1st ed. Garden City, N.Y. : Doubleday, 1977. p. cm. Bibliography: p. [TT840.M63] 76-2808 ISBN 0-385-07707-6 pbk. : 5.50
1. Tatting. I. Title.

NICHOLLS, E. A. 746.43
A new look in tatting; flowers. leaves. and picture composition. Newton, Mass., C. T. Branford Co. [1959] 48p. illus. (part col.), diagrs 25cm. 60-2087 4.95
1. Tatting. I. Title.

NICHOLLS, Elgiva 746.43
Tatting. New York. Taplinger [1965, c.1962] 128p. illus. 26cm. (Embroidery handbks., no. 5) Vista bks. Bibl. [TT840.N55] 65-22993 4.95
1. Tatting. I. Title.

NICHOLLS, Elgiva A. 746.4'36
Tatting techniques : old revivals and new experiments / Elgiva Nicholls. New York : Scribner, c1976. 119 p., [2] leaves of plates : ill. (some col.) ; 26 cm. [TT840.N56] 75-29906 ISBN 0-684-14591-X : 9.95
1. Tatting. I. Title.

NICHOLLS, Elgiva A. 746.4'36
Tatting techniques : old revivals and new experiments / Elgiva Nicholls. London : Mills & Boon, 1976. 119 p., [2] leaves of plates : ill. ; 26 cm. [TT840.N56 1976b] 76-369302 ISBN 0-263-05907-3 : £3.80
1. Tatting. I. Title. BIP

THE Priscilla tatting book. No. 2. 746.4'3
Tatting patterns / [edited by] Julia E. Sanders. New York : Dover Publications, 1977. 48 p. : ill. ; 28 cm. (Dover needlework series) Reprint of the Priscilla tatting book, no. 2, published by the Priscilla Pub. Co., Boston, in 1915. [TT840.P7 1977] 77-77046 ISBN 0-486-23554-8 pbk. : 1.50 ($1.75 Can)
1. Tatting. I. Sanders, Julia Elma, 1844- BIP

*VONN, Leo 746.4'3
Tatting; a historic lacemaking method: fundamentals and patterns. New York, Vantage [1967] 69p. illus. 21cm. 3.50 bds.,
1. Tatting. 2. Lacemaking. I. Title.

WALLER, Irene. 746.4'36
Tatting : a contemporary art form / Irene Waller. Chicago : H. Regnery Co., 1974. 96 p. : ill. ; 26 cm. Includes index. Bibliography: p. 91-92. [TT840.W34 1974] 73-20930 ISBN 0-8092-8394-8 : 7.95
1. Tatting.

Tatting—Patterns.

BLOMQVIST, Gun, 1933- 746.4'36
Tatting; patterns & designs [by] Gun Blomqvist & Elwy Persson. New York, Van Nostrand Reinhold Co. [1974] 96 p. illus. 23 cm. Translation of Frivoliteter. [TT840.B4513] 74-5940 ISBN 0-442-30041-7 6.50
1. Tatting—Patterns. I. Persson, Elwy, joint author. II. Title.

Tattooing.

BURCHETT, George, 1872-1953. 391.7
Memoirs of a tattooist, from the notes, diaries, and letters of the late 'King of TattOoists,' George Burchett. Compiled and edited by Peter Leighton. [1st American ed.] New York, Crown Publishers [1958] 222p. illus. 23cm. [GN419.3.B8 1958a] 58-12872
1. Tattooing. I. Title.

HAMBLY, Wilfrid Dyson, 1886- 391'.65
The history of tattooing and its significance, with some account of other forms of corporal marking. London, H. F. & G. Witherby, 1925. Detroit, Gale Research Co., 1974. p. cm. [GN419.3.H3 1974] 73-174052 ISBN 0-8103-4024-0 15.00
1. Tattooing. 2. Body-marking. I. Title.

SCUTT, R. W. B. 391'.65
Art, sex and symbol; the mystery of tattooing [by] R. W. B. Scutt and Christopher Gotch. South Brunswick, A. S. Barnes [1974] 205 p. illus. 29 cm. Bibliography: p. 199-200. [GT2345.S38] 73-10526 ISBN 0-498-01343-X 20.00
1. Tattooing. I. Gotch, Christopher, joint author. II. Title. BIP

Tattooing—Pictorial works.

FELLOWES, C. H. 741.9'24
The tattoo book, by C. H. Fellowes. With an introd. by William C. Sturtevant. [1st ed.] Princeton, Pyne Press [1971] x, [16] p., 116 p. of illus. 24 cm. [GN419.3.F44] 73-146211 ISBN 0-87861-001-4 8.95
1. Tattooing—Pictorial works. I. Title.

HEAVILY tattooed men and 391'.65
women / compiled and edited by Spider Webb ; introd. by Marcia Tucker. New York : McGraw-Hill, c1976. 100 p. : chiefly ill. ; 25 cm. (McGraw-Hill paperbacks) Includes bibliographical references. [GT2345.H42] 75-45188 ISBN 0-07-068790-0 pbk. : 5.95
1. Tattooing—Pictorial works. I. Webb, Spider. II. Tucker, Marcia. BIP

Tauch, Waldine, 1892—

HUTSON, Alice, 1941- 730'.92'4 B
From chalk to bronze : a biography of Waldine Tauch / by Alice Hutson. 1st ed. Austin : Shoal Creek Publishers, c1978. p. cm. Includes index. Bibliography: p. [NB237.T38H87] 78-16000 ISBN 0-88319-037-0 : 15.00
1. Tauch, Waldine, 1892- 2. Sculptors—United States—Biography. I. Title. BIP

Tawaraya, Sotatsu, d. 1643.

MIZUO, Hiroshi, 1930- 759.952
Edo painting: Sotatsu and Korin. Translated by John M. Shields. [1st English ed.] New York, Weatherhill [1972] 162 p. illus. (part col.) 24 cm. (The Heibonsha survey of Japanese art [18]) Translation of Sotatsu to Korin. [ND1053.5.M5913] 72-79122 ISBN 0-8348-1011-5 7.95
1. Tawaraya, Sotatsu, d. 1643. 2. Ogata, Korin, 1658-1716. 3. Hon'ami, Koetsu, 1558-1637. 4. Ogata, Kenzan, 1663-1743. 5. Painting, Japanese—History. I. Title. II. Series. BIP

Tawney, Lenore.

TAWNEY, Lenore. 709'.2'4
Lenore Tawney : an exhibition of weaving, collage, assemblage : Art Gallery, California State University, Fullerton, November 14th to December 11th, 1975. [Fullerton] : Art Gallery, California State University, Fullerton, c1975. 50 p. : ill. (some col.) ; 23 cm. Bibliography: p. 11-12. [N6537.T38C34] 76-351427
1. Tawney, Lenore. I. California State University, Fullerton. Art Gallery.

Tchelitchew. Pavel. 1898-1957.

NEW York (City). Museum of Modern Art. 759.7
Tchelitchew; paintings, drawings, by James Thrall Soby. New York, Museum of Modern Art. New York, Published for the Museum of Modern Art by Arno Press, 1972 [c1942] 100 p. illus. 27 cm. (Museum of Modern Art publications in reprint) Bibliography: p. 98-100. [ND699.T4N4 1972] 77-169319 ISBN 0-405-01577-1 14.00
1. Tchelitchew, Pavel, 1898-1957. I. Soby, James Thrall, 1906- BIP

NEW York. Gallery of Modern Art 759.7
Pavel Tchelitchew: an exhibition in the Gallery of Modern Art, 20 March through 19 April 1964. New York 19. Found. for Mod. Art. 2 Columbus Circle [c.1964] 69p. illus. 2ix28cm. Bibl. 64-4419 4.25 pap.,
1. Tchelitchew. Pavel. 1898-1957. I. Title.

TCHELITCHEW, Pavel, 1898-1957. 741.9'47
Drawings. Edited by Lincoln Kirstein. New York, Hacker Art Books, 1970 [i.e. 1971] 22 p., 48 plates. 32 cm. Reprint of the 1947 ed. [NC269.T35K5 1971] 70-116363 ISBN 0-87817-046-4 10.00
I. Kirstein, Lincoln, 1907- ed.

TYLER, Parker. 759.7
The divine comedy of Pavel Tchelitchew; a biography. New York, Fleet Pub. Corp. [1967] viii, 504 p. illus. (part col.) ports. 26 cm. Includes bibliographies. [ND699.T4T9] 66-25989
1. Tchelitchew, Pavel, 1898-1957. I. Title. BIP

Teapots.

BEDFORD, John, 1907- v. 12
Talking about teapots; and thus about porcelain, pottery, silver, Sheffield plate, etc. London, M. Parrish [1964] 159, [1] p. illus. (part col.) 21 cm. Bibliography: p. [160] [NK8730.B4] 66-4850
1. Teapots. I. Title.

Technical drawing.

FLEMING, Joseph W., 1888- 744.4
Applied drawing and sketching [by] Joseph W. Fleming, Dewey F. Barich [and] L. C. Smith. 2d ed. Chicago, American Technical Society, 1953. 150 p. illus. 28 cm. [T353.F58 1953] 53-11881
1. Technical drawing. I. Title.

Technical illustration.

GIBBY, Joseph Clifford. 744.4'22
Technical illustration; procedure and practice. 3d ed. Chicago, American Technical Society [1970] 352 p. illus., port. 26 cm. [T11.8.G5 1970] 77-89563
1. Technical illustration.

HICKS, Harmon T. 604.2
Technical illustration, by Harmon T. Hicks and James D. Morrow. Serial 6638A. [Ed. 1] Scranton, International Correspondence Schools, c1966- v. illus. 23 cm. [T11.8.H5] 67-5337
1. Technical illustration. I. Morrow, James D., joint author. II. International Correspondence Schools, Scranton, Pa.

MAGNAN, George A. 744
Using technical art; an industry guide [by] George A. Magnan. New York, Wiley-Interscience [1970] xiii, 237 p. illus. 28 cm. (Wiley series on human communication) [T11.8.M34] 79-93945 ISBN 0-471-56335-8
1. Technical illustration. I. Title.

MORRIS, George E., 1937- 604'.2
Technical illustrating [by] George E. Morris. Englewood Cliffs, N.J., Prentice-Hall [1975] xi, 244 p. : ill. ; 25 cm. Includes bibliographical references. [T11.8.M67] 74-13565 ISBN 0-13-898155-8 10.95
1. Technical illustration. I. Title. BIP

NICYPER, Raymond, 1919- 604'.2
Scale drawing. Westport, Conn., Graphicraft [1973] 72, [78] p. illus. 29 x 38 cm. (Graphics underlay guides, 1) Bibliography: p. 69 (1st group) [T11.8.N5] 73-76377
1. Technical illustration. I. Title. II. Series.

THOMAS, T. A. 744.4'29
Technical illustration [by] T. A. Thomas. Foreword by Carl L. Svenson. 2d ed. New York, McGraw-Hill [1968] ix, 203 p. illus. 29 cm. Bibliography: p. 197. [T357.T5 1968] 68-14341
1. Technical illustration.

THOMAS, T. A. 604'.2'4
Technical illustration / T. A. Thomas. 3d ed. New York : Gregg Division, McGraw-Hill, c1978. viii, 280 p. : ill. ; 28 cm. Includes index. Bibliography: p. 273. [T11.8.T47 1978] 77-9946 ISBN 0-07-064228-1 : 13.95
1. Technical illustration. I. Title.

Technical illustration—Estimates.

SOCIETY for Technical Communication. 604'.2'4
Estimating illustration costs : a guide. Washington : Society for Technical Communication, 1974, c1973. iv, 36 p. : ill. ; 28 cm. Includes index. [T11.8.S65 1974] 75-322631 ISBN 0-914548-07-7
1. Technical illustration—Estimates. I. Title.

Technical illustration—Problems, exercises, etc.

THOMAS, T. A. 604'.2'076
Problems in technical illustration [by] T. A. Thomas. New York, McGraw-Hill [1972] vi, 6 p., [74] leaves of illus. 28 cm. "This workbook is designed to be used in conjunction with [the author's] Technical illustration." [T11.8.T46] 73-168188 ISBN 0-07-064227-3 3.50
1. Technical illustration—Problems, exercises, etc. I. Title. II. Title: Technical illustration.

Teddy bears.

BULL, Peter. 688.724
The teddy bear book. New York, Random House [1975 c1970] 208 p. ill. 28 cm. [GV1220.7.B83] ISBN 0-394-73080-1 6.95 (pbk.)
1. Teddy bears. I. Title.
L.C. card no. for original edition: 77-85556. BIP

BULL, Peter, 1912- 688.7'24
The teddy bear book. [1st American ed.] New York, Random House [1970] 207 p. illus., facsims., ports. 29 cm. 1969 ed. published under title: Bear with me. [GV1220.7.B83 1970] 77-85556 10.00
1. Teddy bears. I. Title.

Tehuacan Valley—Antiquities.

TEHUACAN Archaeological-Botanical Project. 732.2
The prehistory of the Tehuacan Valley. Edited by Douglas S. Byers. Austin, Published for the Robert S. Peabody Foundation, Phillips Academy, Andover [Mass., by the] University of Texas Press [1967- v. illus., maps. 29 cm. Contents.CONTENTS.--v. 1. Environment and subsistence, edited by D. S. Byers.--v. 2. Nonceramic artifacts, by R. S. MacNeish, A. Neiken-Terner, and I. W. Johnson. Includes bibliographies. [F1219.1.]
1. Tehuacan Valley—Antiq. 2. Indians of Mexico—Tehuacan Valley—Antiq. Ethnobotany. 3. Maize—Hist. 4. Botany—Mexico—Tehuacan Valley. I. Byers, Douglas S., 1903- ed. II. Phillips Academy, Andover, Mass. Robert S. Peabody Foundation for Archaeology. III. Title. IV. Title: 224T4 BIP

TEHUACAN Archaeological-Botanical Project. 970.4'2'4
The prehistory of the Tehuacan Valley. Edited by Douglas S. Byers. Austin, Published for the Robert S. Peabody Foundation, Phillips Academy, Andover [Mass., by the] University of Texas Press [1967- v. illus., maps. 29 cm.

Contents.Contents.—v. 1. Environment and subsistence, edited by D. S. Byers.—v. 2. Nonceramic artifacts, by R. S. MacNeish, A. Nelken-Terner, and I. W. Johnson.—v. 3. Ceramics, by R. S. MacNeish, F. A. Peterson, and K. V. Flannery.—v. 4. Chronology and irrigation, edited by F. Johnson. Includes bibliographies. [F1219.1.T224T4] 67-17873 ISBN 0-292-70068-7 (v. 3) 15.00 (v. 4)
1. Tehuacan Valley—Antiquities. 2. Indians of Mexico—Tehuacan Valley—Antiquities. 3. Ethnobotany. 4. Botany—Mexico—Tehuacan Valley. I. Byers, Douglas S., 1903- ed. II. Phillips Academy, Andover, Mass. Robert S. Peabody Foundation for Archaeology. III. Title.

Teikoku Hoteru.

JAMES, Cary, 1935- 728.5'0924
The Imperial Hotel; Frank Lloyd Wright and the architecture of unity. Rutland, Vt., C. E. Tuttle Co. [1968] 46, [79] p. illus., 6 fold. plans. 27 cm. "Quotations from Frank Lloyd Wright": p. 23-46. Bibliography: p. [125] [NA737.W7J33] 68-25888 7.50
1. Wright, Frank Lloyd, 1867-1959. 2. Teikoku Hoteru. I. Title.

Telephotography

LAHUE, Kalton C. 778.3'22
Telephoto photography / by Kalton C. Lahue. Los Angeles : Petersen Pub. Co., c1977. 80 p. : ill. (some col.) ; 28 cm. (Petersen's how-to photographic library) [TR770.L27] 77-74103 ISBN 0-8227-4021-4 pbk. : 3.95
1. Telephotography. I. Title. BIP

SIMMONS, Robert, 1931- 778.32
Fullname:RobertPrestonSimmons
Telephoto and wide-angle photography. Philadelphia, Chilton Co., Book Division, c1959. 155 p. illus. 20 cm. (Modern camera guide series, 408) [TR770.S5] 59-9635
1. Telephotography 2. Wide-angle Hotography. I. Title.

Tempera painting.

ALBENDA, Pauline. 751.4'3
Creative painting with tempera; a guide to developmental learning in painting. New York, Van Nostrand Reinhold [1970] 95 p. 114 illus. (8 col.) 21 cm. [ND2470.A4] 70-110055
1. Tempera painting. I. Title.

ROMBERG, Jenean. 751.4'3
Let's discover tempera. New York, The Center for Applied Research in Education [1974] 64 p. illus. 28 cm. (Her Arts and crafts discovery units) [ND2465.R65] 74-14625 ISBN 0-87628-529-9
1. Tempera painting. I. Title. BIP

THOMPSON, Daniel Varney, 751.43
1902-
The practice of tempera painting. Illus. by Lewis E. York. New York, Dover [1962, c.1936] 141p. 22cm. (T343) 63-299 1.50 pap.,
1. Tempera painting. I. Title. BIP

VICKREY, Robert, 1926- 751.4'3
New techniques in egg tempera, by Robert Vickrey and Diane Cochrane. New York, Watson-Guptill Publications [1973] 159 p. illus. (part col.) 22 x 29 cm. [ND2468.V52] 73-7760 ISBN 0-8230-3170-5 15.00
1. Tempera painting. I. Cochrane, Diane, joint author. II. Title. BIP

Tempesta, Antonio, 1555-1630.

TEMPESTA, Antonio, 769'.92'4
1555-1630.
Metamorphoseon ... Ovidianarum / Antonio Tempesta. New York : Garland Pub., 1976. p. cm. (The Renaissance and the gods ; no. 19) Reprint of the 1606 ed. published in Amsterdam. [NE662.T45O94 1976] 75-27861 ISBN 0-8240-2067-7 lib.bdg. : 30.00
1. Tempesta, Antonio, 1555-1630. 2. Ovidius Naso, Publins. Metamorphoses—Illustrations. I. Ovidius Naso, Publius. Metamorphoses. II. Title. III. Series.

Temple Newsam House, Leeds, Eng.

TEMPLE Newsam 738.3'0942'07402819
House, Leeds, Eng.
Creamware and other English Pottery at Temple Newsam House, Leeds : a catalogue of the Leeds Collection / by Peter Walton. Bradford [Eng.] : Manningham Press, c1976. xi, 293 p. : ill. (some col.) ; 30 cm. Includes index. Bibliography: p. 281-284. [NK4085.T4 1976] 77-356357 ISBN 0-905564-00-6 : £28.00
1. Temple Newsam House, Leeds, Eng. 2. Pottery, English—Catalogs. 3. Pottery—England—Leeds—Catalogs. I. Walton, Peter. II. Title.

Temple, Shirley, 1928- —Collectibles.

SMITH, Patricia 791.43'028'0924
R.
Shirley Temple dolls and collectibles / by Patricia R. Smith ; all photos. by Dwight F. Smith, unless noted ; editor, Karen Penner. Paducah, Ky. : Collector Books ; New York : distributed by Crown Publishers, c1977. vi, 144 p. : ill. ; 29 cm. [NK808.S6] 77-153173 ISBN 0-89145-053-X : 17.95
1. Temple, Shirley, 1928- —Collectibles. 2. Dolls—United States—Collectors and collecting. I. Penner, Karen. II. Title. BIP

Temples—Asia, Southeastern.

LOUIS-FREDERICK pseud. 726.10959
The art of Southeast Asia: temples and sculpture. Foreword by Jeannine Auboyer. [Translated from the French by Arnold Rosin] New York, H. N. Abrams [1965?] 434 p. illus., maps, plans. 32 cm. Translation of Sud-Est asiatique: ses temples, ses sculptures. Bibliography: p. 425-427. [NA5960.L653] 65-19228
1. Temples—Asia, Southeastern. 2. Sculpture—Asia, Southeastern. I. Title.

Temples, Buddhist—China.

PRIP-MOLLER, 726'.7799'430951
Johannes, 1889-1943
Chinese Buddhist monasteries; their plan and its function as a setting for Buddhist monastic life. [2d ed.] Hong Kong, Hong Kong Univ. Pr. [1967] 396p. illus. (pt. col.), facsims., map, plans (pt. col.), ports. 39cm. Buddhist hymn with music: p. 357. [NA6040.P7 1967] 68-2487 50.00
1. Temples, Buddhist—China. 2. Monasticism and religious orders, Buddhist. I. Title.
Available from Oxford Univ. Pr., New York.

Temples—Cambodia—Angkor.

KRASA, Miloslav 726.14
The temples of Angkor; monuments to a vanished empire. Photos. by Jan Cifra. [Tr. by Joy Turner] London. A. Wingate [dist. New York, Tudor, 1964, c. 1963] 211, [61] p. illus., plates, port., col. maps (pt. fold) 28cm. Bibl. 64-1799 9.95
1. Temples—Cambodia—Angkor. 2. Sculpture—Angkor, Cambodia. 3. Art, Khmer. I. Title.

Temples—Egypt.

MURRAY, Margaret 726'.1'931
Alice.
Egyptian temples / by Margaret A. Murray. New York : AMS Press, 1977. x, 246 p., [32] leaves of plates : ill. ; 23 cm. Reprint of the 1931 ed. published by S. Low, Marston, London. Includes index. Bibliography: p. 239. [NA215.M8 1977] 75-41203 ISBN 0-404-14708-9 : 18.50
1. Temples—Egypt. 2. Egypt—Antiquities. I. Title. BIP

OTTO, Eberhard, 1913- 709'.32
Ancient Egyptian art: the cults of Osiris and Amon. Photos. by Max Hirmer. [Translated by Kate Bosse Griffiths] New York, Abrams [1967] 144 p. illus. (part col.), maps, plans. 27 cm. Translation of Osiris und Amon: Kult und heilige Statten. Bibliography: p. 143-144. [DT62.T4O83 1967] 67-26469
1. Temples—Egypt. 2. Osiris. 3. Amon (Egyptian deity) I. Title.

Temples—Egypt—Abu Sunbul.

MACQUITTY, William. 913.32031
Abu Simbel. Foreword by I. E. S. Edwards. New York, Putnam [1965] 192 p. illus. (part col.) map. 26 cm. [NA261.A17M2] 65-19561
1. Temples—Egypt—Abu Sunbul. 2. Abu Simbel, Egypt.

Temples, Greek.

AYRTON, Elizabeth. 726.1
The Doric temple. Photos. by Serge Moulinier. New York, C. N. Potter [c1961] xiv, 227 p. illus., plates. 28 cm. [NA275.A9] 61-14830
1. Temples, Greek. 2. Columns, Doric. I. Title.

BERVE, Helmut, 1896- 722.8
Greek temples, theatres, and shrines. Texts by Helmut Berve, Gottfried Gruben. Photos. by Max Hirmer. New York, Abrams [1963] 508p. illus. 176 plates, maps, plans. 31cm. (36 mounted col.) Bibl. 62-19131 30.00
1. Temples, Greek. 2. Theatres—Greece. 3. Shrines—Greece. 4. Architecture, Greek. I. Gruben, Gottfried. II. Hirmer, Max. III. Title.

GRINNELL, Isabel 726'.1'208
Hoopes.
Greek temples. New York, 1943. [New York] Arno Press, 1974. xxi, 59 p. illus. 32 cm. At head of title: The Metropolitan Museum of Art. Includes bibliographies. [NA275.G7 1974] 79-168420 ISBN 0-405-02258-1 20.00
1. New York (City). Metropolitan Museum of Art. 2. Temples, Greek. I. New York (City). Metropolitan Museum of Art. BIP

MELAS, Evi, 1930- 913.38
The Greek experience; a companion guide to the major architectural sites and an introduction to ancient history and myth. Edited by Evi Melas. [Translated from the German by F. Maxwell Brownjohn] New York, Dutton, 1974 [c1973] 216 p. illus. 22 cm. Translation of Tempel und Statten der Gotter Griechenlands. [NA275.M413 1974] 73-10484 ISBN 0-525-11810-1 9.50
1. Temples, Greek. 2. Gods in art. I. Title.

†TOMLINSON, Richard 726'.1'208
Allan.
Greek sanctuaries / R. A. Tomlinson. New York : St. Martin's Press, 1976. 150 p., [14] leaves of plates (2 fold.) : ill. ; 26 cm. Includes bibliographical references and index. [NA275.T65 1976b] 76-27588 16.95
1. Temples, Greek. I. Title. BIP

Temples, Hindu.

MICHELL, George. 726'.1'450954
The Hindu temple : an introduction to its meaning and forms / George Michell. London : Elek, 1977. 192 p. : ill. ; 25 cm. Includes indexes. Bibliography: p. [185]-186. [BL1227.A1M52 1977] 78-301590 ISBN 0-236-40088-6 : 22.50
1. Temples, Hindu. I. Title.
Available from Harper Row BIP

MICHELL, George. 726'.1'45
The Hindu temple : an introduction to its meaning and forms / George Michell. 1st U.S. ed. New York : Harper & Row, c1977. 192 p. : ill. ; 25 cm. (Icon editions) Includes index. Bibliography: p. [185]-186. [NA6002.M52 1977] 77-82075 ISBN 0-06-435750-3 : 22.50
1. Temples, Hindu. 2. Symbolism in architecture—India. I. Title.

Temples, Hindu—India.

BALASUBRAHMANYAM, S. R.
726'.1'45
Early Chola art [by] S. R. Balasubrahmanyam. Bombay, New York, Asia Pub. House [c1966- v. illus., facsims., map, plans. 25 cm. v. 1: Rs60 Bibliographical footnotes. [NA6002.B3] S A
1. Temples, Hindu—India. 2. Cholas. I. Title. BIP

Temples—India.

FERGUSSON, James, 1808- 726'.1'4
1886.
Archaeology in India, with especial reference to the works of Babu Rajendralala Mitra / James Fergusson. New Delhi : K. B. Publications, 1974. vii, 115 p. : ill. ; 23 cm. "Ist Indian reprint." First published in 1884. Includes bibliographical references. [NA6002.F44 1974] 74-904007 10.00
1. Mitra, Rajendralala, Raja, 1824-1891. 2. Temples—India. 3. Cave temples—India. I. Title.
Distributed by South Asia Books.

LOUIS-FREDERIC, pseud. 726.10954
The art of India: temples and sculpture. Introd. by Jean Naudou. [Translated from the French by Eva M. Hooykaas and A. H. Christie] New York, H. N. Abrams [1960] 464p. illus., maps, plans. 32cm. 59-12873 17.50
1. Temples—India. 2. Sculpture—India. I. Title.

MEHTA, Rustam 726'.1'40954
Jehangir, 1912-
Masterpieces of Indian temples / introd. and notes on plates by Rustam J. Mehta. Bombay : D. B. Taraporevala Sons, 1974i.e.1976 67, 100 p. (chiefly ill.) ; 29 cm. [NA6002.M44] 75-901641 15.00
1. Temples—India. I. Title.
Distributed by International Pubns. Service, New York. BIP

MONOD-BRUHL, Odette. 722.41
Indian temples; 135 photographs chosen and annotated. With a pref. by Sylvain Levi. [English translation by Roy Hawkins. 2d ed. London] Oxford University Press [1952, c1951] 1v. illus. 25cm. Translation of Aux Indes; sanctuaires. [NA6001.M6513 1952] 53-6574
1. Temples—India. 2. Sculpture—India. I. Title.

Temples—India—Bengal.

DATTA, Bimal 726'.1'45095414
Kumar, 1920-
Bengal temples / Bimal Kumar Datta ; with a foreword by Suniti Kumar Chatterji. New Delhi : Munshiram Manoharlal Publishers, 1975, c1974. x, 88 p., [14] leaves of plates : ill., map ; 25 cm. Includes bibliographical references and index. [NA6007.B4D38 1975] 75-904212 16.00
1. Temples—India—Bengal. I. Title.
Distributed by South Asia Books, Columbia, Mo. BIP

Temples—India—South India.

SRINIVASAN, K. R., 726'.1'409548
1910-
Temples of South India. New Delhi, National Book Trust, India; [chief stickists in India: India Book House, Bombay, 1972] 223 p. illus. (pt. col.) 21 cm. (India—the land and people) [NA6007.S6S67] 72-906086
1. Temples—India—South India. I. Title.
Available from Verry, Mystic, Conn., for 3.75. ISBN 0-8426-0511-8.

VENKATARAMAN, 726'.1'509548
Balasubrahmanyam, 1925-
Temple art under the Chola queens / B. Venkataraman. Faridabad : Thomson Press (India), Publication Division, 1976. xx, 154 p., 28 leaves of plates : ill. ; 25 cm. Includes index. Bibliography: p. 126. [NA6007.S6V46] 76-904390 Rs80.00
1. Temples—India—South India. 2. Architecture, Chola. I. Title.

Temples—Japan—Nara (City)

OOKA, Minoru, 726'.1'43095218
1900-
Temples of Nara and their art. Translated by Dennis Lishka. [1st English ed.] New York, Weatherhill [1973] 184 p. illus. (part col.) 24 cm. (The Heibonsha survey of Japanese art, v. 7) Translation of Nara no tera. [NA6057.N3O5513] 72-78601 ISBN 0-8348-1010-7 8.95

1. Temples—Japan—Nara (City) 2. Temples, Buddhist—Japan—Nara (City) I. Title. II. Series. BIP

Temples, Mormon.

ANDREW, Laurel B. 726'.58'9373
The early temples of the Mormons : the architecture of the Millennial Kingdom in the American West / Laurel B. Andrew. Albany : State University of New York Press, 1977. p. cm. Includes bibliographical references. [NA4829.M67A53] 77-23971 ISBN 0-87395-358-4 : 15.00
1. Temples, Mormon. BIP

Temples, Roman—Gt. Brit.

LEWIS, Michael Jonathan Tauton 726.1207
Temples in Roman Britian, by M. J. T. Lewis Cambridge, Cambridge., 1966. xvi, 218p. illus., 4 plates, maps, plans, tables, diagrs. 26cm. (Cambridge classical studies) Bibl. [NA323.L4] 66-2517 9.50
1. Temples, Roman—Gt. Brit. I. Title. II. Series.

Temples, Roman—Lebanon.

TAYLOR, George. 726'.1'207095692
The Roman temples of Lebanon; a pictorial guide. [Beirut, Dar el-Machreq Pub., 1967] Imprint covered by label: Argonaut, Chicago. 133p. illus. 28cm. English & French. Bibl. ref. [NA335.L37T3] 68-3544 price unreported
1. Temples, Roman—Lebanon. I. Title. BIP

Temptation.

*LARKIN, David comp. 753
Temptation 1st ed. New York, Peacock Press/Bantam Book [1975] [90 p.] (Chiefly ill., plates), 30 cm. [ND1422] 5.95 (pbk.)
1. Temptation. I. Title. BIP

Tennent, Madge.

CHARLOT, Jean, 1898- 759.13
The Donald Angus Collection of oil paintings by Madge Tennent; [exhibition] Contemporary Arts Center of Hawaii, February 22 to March 15. [Catalog by Jean Charlot. Honolulu, Contemporary Arts Center of Hawaii? 1968?] [10] p. illus. 25 cm. [ND237.T383C44] 75-314180
1. Tennent, Madge. 2. Angus, Donald—Art collections. I. Contemporary Arts Center of Hawaii. II. Title.

Tennessee — Antiq.

LEWIS, Thomas McDowell Nelson, 1896- 913.768
Hiwasse island, an archaeological account of four Tennessee Indian peoples, by Thomas M. N. Lewis and Madeline Kneberg, partially based on field reports by Charles H. Nash. Knoxville, Tenn., The University of Tennessee press, 1946. x, 188 p. col. front., illus., plates, maps, plans, diagrs. 26 1/2 cm. "Literature cited"; p. 180-183. [E78.T3L4] 46-7196
1. Tennessee — Antiq. 2. Indians of North America — Tennessee. Hiwasse Island. I. Lewis, Madeline Kneberg, 1903- joint author. II. Nash, Charles h. III. Title.

Tennyson, Alfred Tennyson, Baron, 1809-1892—Illustrations.

LAYARD, George Somes, 1857-1925. 760'.92'2
Tennyson and his pre-Raphaelite illustrators : a book about a book / by George Somes Layard. Folcroft, Pa. : Folcroft Library Editions, 1978. p. cm. Reprint of the 1894 ed. published by E. Stock, London. Contents.Contents.—Introductory.—As to the origin of 'P.R.P.'—Millais.—Holman Hunt.—Rossetti. [PR5577.L3 1978] 78-12687 ISBN 0-8414-5755-7 lib. bdg. : 12.50
1. Tennyson, Alfred Tennyson, Baron, 1809-1892—Illustrations. 2. Preraphaelitism. I. Title. BIP

Tents.

FAEGRE, Torvald. 728
Tents : architecture of the nomads / Torvald Faegre ; illustrated by the author. Anchor Books ed. Garden City, N.Y. : Anchor Press/Doubleday, 1979. vi, 167 p. : ill. ; 28 cm. Bibliography: p. 165-167. [GN414.3.T45F33] 77-25588 ISBN 0-385-11656-X pbk. : 5.95
1. Tents. 2. Nomads. I. Title. BIP

Teotihuacan, Mexico.

PASZTORY, Esther. 970 s
The iconography of the Teotihuacan Tlaloc / Esther Pasztory. Washington : Dumbarton Oaks, Trustees for Harvard University, 1974. 22 p. : ill. ; 27 cm. (Studies in pre-Columbian art and archaeology ; no. 15) Errata slip inserted. Bibliography: p. 21-22. [E51.S85 no. 15] [F1219.1.T27] 704.94'7'09725 74-16543 2.00
1. Teotihuacan, Mexico. 2. Indians of Mexico—Religion and mythology. 3. Indians of Central America—Religion and mythology. I. Title. II. Series. BIP

PASZTORY, Esther. 759.01'1
The murals of Tepantitla, Teotihuacan / Esther Pasztory. New York : Garland Pub., 1976. 392 p., [2] fold leaves of plates : ill. ; 21 cm. (Outstanding dissertations in the fine arts) Originally presented as the author's thesis, Columbia University, 1972. Bibliography: p. 260-275. [F1219.1.T27P35 1976] 75-23806 ISBN 0-8240-2000-6 lib.bdg. : 30.00
1. Teotihuacan, Mexico. 2. Indians of Mexico—Art. 3. Indians of Mexico—Religion and mythology. I. Title. II. Series.

SANDERS, William T. 972*.5*004*97
The cultural ecology of the Teotihuacan Valley; a preliminary report of the results of the Teotihuacan Valley Project, by William T. Sanders. [University Park, Pa.] Dept. of Sociology & Anthropology, Pennsylvania State University, 1965. x, 209, [9] p. illus., maps. 29 cm. Bibliography: [9] p. at end. [F1219.1.T27S2] 72-187228
1. Teotihuacan, Mexico. 2. Anthropogeography—Mexico—Teotihuacan. 3. Indians of Mexico—Antiquities. I. Pennsylvania. State University. Dept. of Sociology and Antropology. II. Title.

Teotihuacan, Mexico. Pyramid of the Sun.

MILLON, Rene Francis. 970.425
The Pyramid of the Sun at Teotihuacan, 1959 investigations [by] Rene Millon, Bruce Drewitt, and James A. Bennyhoff. Philadelphia, American Philosophical Society, 1965. 93 p. illus., plans. 30 cm. (American Philosophical Society [Philadelphia] Transactions, new ser., v. 55, pt. 6) Bibliography: p. 40-41. [Q11.P6] [F1219.1.T27M82] 65-23434
1. Teotihuacan, Mexico. Pyramid of the Sun. 2. Excavations (Archaeology) — Mexico — Teotihuacan. I. Drewitt, Bruce, joint author. II. Bennyhoff, James Allen, 1926- joint author. III. American Philosophical Society, Philadelphia. IV. Title. V. Series.

Tepexi El Viejo site, Mexico.

GORENSTEIN, Shirley. 917.2'7
Tepexi el Viejo: a postclassic fortified site in the Mixteca-Puebla region of Mexico. Philadelphia, American Philosophical Society, 1973. 75 p. illus. 30 cm. (Transactions of the American Philosophical Society, new ser., v. 63, pt. 1) Bibliography: p. 70-72. [F1219.1.P9G67] 73-75472 ISBN 0-87169-631-2 pap. 3.50
1. Tepexi El Viejo site, Mexico. I. Title. II. Series: American Philosophical Society, Philadelphia. Transactions, new ser., v. 63, pt. 1.

Teresa, Saint, 1515-1582.

PETERSSON, Robert Torsten. 701.15
The art of ecstasy; Teresa, Bernini, and Crashaw [by] Robert T. Petersson. [1st American ed.] New York, Atheneum, 1970. xv, 183 p. illus., col. plate. 25 cm. Includes bibliographical references. [NX652.T4P4 1970b] 79-108825 8.95
1. Teresa, Saint, 1515-1582. 2. Bernini, Giovanni Lorenzo, 1598-1680. 3. Crashaw, Richard, 1613?-1649. 4. Ecstasy. I. Title. BIP

Terra-cotta sculpture—Technique.

LUCCHESI, Bruno, 1926- 731.4
Terracotta / sculpture by Bruno Lucchesi ; text and photographs by Margit Malmstrom. New York : Watson-Guptill Publications, 1977. 155 p. : ill. ; 29 cm. Includes index. [NB1265.L82 1977] 77-1702 ISBN 0-8230-5320-2 : 17.95
1. Terra-cotta sculpture—Technique. I. Malmstrom, Margit. II. Title. BIP

Terra-cottas—America.

MONTI, Franco. 732'.2
Precolumbian terracottas; [translated by Margaret Crosland from the Italian]. London, New York, Hamlyn, 1969. 3-158 p. col. illus. 20 cm. (Cameo) Translation of Terrecotte precolombiane. [E59.A7M633] 76-482305 15/-
1. Terra-cottas—America. 2. Indians—Art. I. Title.

Terra-cottas, Classical.

CHESTERMAN, James. 733'.3
Classical terracotta figures / James Chesterman ; with a foreword by R. A. Higgins. Woodstock, N.Y. : Overlook Press, 1975, c1974. 99 p. : ill. ; 27 cm. Includes index. Bibliography: p. 90-91. [NB153.C45 1975] 75-10550 ISBN 0-87951-037-4 : 12.95
1. Terra-cottas, Classical. I. Title. BIP

Terra-cottas, French—Exhibitions.

RAGGIO, Olga, 1926- 730'.944'07401471
The fire and the talent : a presentation of French terracottas : a special exhibition in the Velez-Blanco Patio / catalogue by Olga Raggio ; [text photos., Allan Rodney]. New York : Metropolitan Museum of Art, c1976. [23] p. : ill. ; 23 cm. [NB1265.R33] 76-370913
1. Terra-cottas, French—Exhibitions. 2. Sculpture, French—Exhibitions. 3. Sculpture, Rococo—France—Exhibitions. 4. Sculpture, Modern—19th century—France—Exhibitions. I. New York (City). Metropolitan Museum of Art. II. Title.

Terra-cottas, Greek.

HIGGINS, Reynold Alleyne 738.3'8'0938
Greek terracottas [by] R. A. Higgins. London, Methuen, 1967. 169p. col. front., illus., 68 plates (incl. 4 col.), map, tables. 29cm. (Methuen's handbks. of archaeology) Bibl. [NB155.H5] 67-31958 26.50
1. Terra-cottas, Greek. I. Title.
American distributor: Barnes & Noble, New York.

VAN BUREN, Elizabeth (Douglas). 726'.1'20938
Greek fictile revetments in the archaic period, by E. Douglas Van Buren. Washington, McGrath Pub. Co., 1973. xx, 208 p. illus. 27 cm. Reprint of the 1926 ed. published by J. Murray, London. Includes bibliographical references. [NA270.V3 1973] 73-129561 ISBN 0-8434-0150-8 65.00
1. Terra-cottas, Greek. 2. Architecture, Greek. 3. Temples—Greece. I. Title.

WEBSTER, Thomas Bertram Lonsdale, 1905- 733
Greek terracottas / T. B. L. Webster. Harmondsworth, Eng. : Penguin Books, 1950. 35, [27] leaves of plates : ill. ; 19 cm. (The King penguin books ; 54) Bibliography: p. [31]. [NB155.W42] 74-190944
1. Terra-cottas, Greek.

YOUNG, John Howard. 738.84
Terracotta figurines from Kourion in Cyprus, by John Howard Young and Suzanne Halstead Young. Philadelphia, University Museum, University of Pennsylvania, 1955. x, 260p. illus., 74 plates, port., maps, plan. 28cm. (Museum monographs) Bibliography: p. ix-x. [NB159.C9Y6] 56-58743
1. Terr-acottas—Cyprus. I. Young, Suzanne Haistead, joint author. II. Title. III. Series: Pennsylvania. University. University Museum, Museum monographs BIP

Terra-cottas, Greek—Sicily.

VAN BUREN, Elizabeth (Douglas) 726'.1'0938
Archaic fictile revetments in Sicily and Magna Graecia, by E. Douglas Van Buren. Washington, McGrath Pub. Co., 1973. xx, 168 p. illus. 27 cm. Reprint of the 1923 ed. [NB158.5.S52V36 1973] 75-119282 ISBN 0-8434-0149-4 45.00
1. Terra-cottas, Greek—Sicily. 2. Terra-cottas, Greek—Magna Graecia. 3. Temples, Greek—Sicily. 4. Temples,Greek—Magna Graecia. 5. Sicily—Antiquities, Greek. 6. Magna Graecia—Antiquities, Greek. I. Title.

Terra-cottas, Mexican—Catalogs.

ALBERS, Anni. 732.2
Pre-Columbian Mexican miniatures: the Josef and Anni Albers collection. Foreword by Ignacio Bernal. Introductory text by Michael D. Coe. Photos. by John T. Hill. New York, Praeger [1970] [32] p. illus., map, 84 plates. 32 cm. Bibliography: p. [23] [F1219.3.A7A38 1970] 70-99925 15.00
1. Albers, Josef—Art collections—Catalogs. 2. Albers, Anni—Art collections—Catalogs. 3. Terra-cottas, Mexican—Catalogs. 4. Indians of Mexico—Sculpture. I. Coe, Michael D. II. Title.

Terra-cottas—Rome.

GRANDJOUAN, Claireve. 938'.5 s
Terracottas and plastic lamps of the Roman period / by Claireve Grandjouan. Princeton, N.J. : American School of Classical Studies at Athens, 1961. xii, 106 p., [17] leaves of plates : ill. ; 31 cm. (The Athenian Agora ; v. 6) Includes index. Bibliography: p. [xi]-xii. [DF287.A23A5 vol. 6] [NB159.R6] 738.8 75-322658
1. Terra-cottas—Rome. 2. Lamps—Rome. 3. Athens. Agora. I. Title. II. Series: American School of Classical Studies at Athens. The Athenian Agora ; v. 6.

Terrazzo.

NATIONAL Terrazzo and Mosaic Association. 729.7
Catalogue and design book ... 3d ed. Washington, Published jointly by the National Terrazzo & Mosaic Association and the Manufacturers Division of N. T. & M. Association, c1951. 136 p. illus. (part col.) 30 cm. "A. I. A. file no. 23E." [NA3840.N3] 51-33642
1. Terrazzo. I. Mosaics. II. Title.

Terrill, Irv—Art collections.

TERRILL, Frances M. 621.319'37
Porcelain insulators photographed & priced, by Frances M. Terrill. Photos. by Paula Short from the Collection of Irv Terrill. Photos. by Bill Kuhar from his collection. Portland, Or. [1972] 116 p. illus. 22 cm. (Old insulator collector's library, book 6) [NK5440.E4T39] 72-169526 3.00
1. Terrill, Irv—Art collections. 2. Electric insulators and insulation—Catalogs. I. Short, Paula, illus. II. Kuhar, Bill, illus. III. Title. IV. Series.

Teton Mountains—Description and travel—Views.

KERSWILL, Roy. 759.2
Rendezvous '72: Kerswill. Introd. by Charles A. Ross. Captions and commentaries by Roy Kerswill. Biographical information on Roy Kerswill by Jim Bardens. [Jackson, Wyo., Heritage Art-May Enterprises, 1972] [31] p. illus.

York : Crown Publishers, [1975] 96 p., [2] leaves of plates : ill. ; 29 cm. Includes index. [TT699.R39 1975] 75-1465 ISBN 0-517-51652-7 pbk. : 5.95
1. Textile crafts. 2. Rugs. 3. Carpets. I. Moyer, Kathryn Robinette, joint author. II. Title.

SOMMER, Elyse. 746
Inventive fiber crafts / Elyse Sommer ; Mike Sommer, photographer. Englewood Cliffs, N.J. : Prentice-Hall, c1977. xiii, 173 p., [4] leaves of plates : ill. ; 23 cm. (A Spectrum book : The Creative handcrafts series ; S-CR-9) Bibliography: p. 169-170. [TT699.S63] 76-45979 ISBN 0-13-502468-4 : 14.95 pbk. : 6.95
1. Textile crafts. I. Sommer, Mike. II. Title. BIP

SOMMER, Elyse. 746
Wearable crafts : creating clothing, body adornments, and jewelry from fabrics and fibers / by Elyse and Mike Sommer. New York : Crown Publishers, c1976. viii, 246 p. [4] leaves of plates : ill. ; 27 cm. Includes index. Bibliography: p. 234-236. [TT699.S64 1976] 75-40250 ISBN 0-517-52395-7 : 10.95 ISBN 0-517-52518-6 pbk. : 5.95
1. Textile crafts. 2. Clothing and dress. 3. Jewelry making—Amateurs' manuals. I. Sommer, Mike, joint author. II. Title. BIP

TEXTILE crafts / 746
edited by Constance Howard. New York : Scribner, c1978. 304 p. : ill. (some col.) ; 26 cm. Includes index. Bibliography: p. 295-298. [TT699.T49] 77-83675 ISBN 0-684-15507-9 : 19.95
1. Textile crafts. I. Howard, Constance. BIP

VANDERBILT, Gloria, 1924- 745.5
McCall's Gloria Vanderbilt designs for your home / edited by Phyllis Hingston Roderick. New York : Simon and Schuster, c1977. p. cm. [TT699.V36] 77-2281 ISBN 0-671-22637-1 : 12.50
1. Textile crafts. 2. Handicraft. 3. Interior decoration—Amateurs' manuals. I. Roderick, Phyllis Hingston. II. Title. III. Title: Designs for your home.

WALLER, Irene. 746.4
Designing with thread; from fibre to fabric. New York, Viking Press [1973] 183 p. illus. (part col.) 29 cm. (A Studio book) Bibliography p. 176-180. [TT699.W34] 72-12059 ISBN 0-670-26931-X 14.95
1. Textile crafts. 2. Textile design. I. Title.

WILLIAMS, Barbara. 746
26 lively letters : making an ABC quiet book / by Barbara Williams and Carol Grundmann. 1st ed. New York : Taplinger Pub. Co., 1977. 96 p. : ill. ; 25 cm. [TT699.W54 1977] 76-13328 ISBN 0-8008-7918-X : 9.95
1. Textile crafts. 2. Alphabets. 3. Books. I. Grundmann, Carol, joint author. II. Title.

Textile crafts—Africa.

DENDEL, Esther Warner, 1910- 746
African fabric crafts : sources of African design and technique / Esther Warner Dendel ; with drawings and photos. by Jo Dendel. 1st ed. New York : Taplinger Pub. Co., 1974. 160 p., [4] leaves of plates : ill. ; 25 cm. Bibliography: p. 160. [TT699.D45 1974] 72-6627 ISBN 0-8008-0150-4 : 10.95
1. Textile crafts—Africa. I. Title. BIP

Textile crafts—Bibliography.

AMERICAN Crafts Council. 016.746
Research & Education Dept.
Bibliography, fiber / [The Research & Education Department, American Crafts Council]. New York : The Council, c1975. 48 p. ; 28 cm. [Z6151.A46 1975a] [TT699] 75-327021 ISBN 0-88321-014-2 pbk. : 6.00
1. Textile crafts—Bibliography. I. Title. II. Title: Fiber.

AXFORD, Lavonne B. 016.7461
Weaving, spinning, and dyeing / Lavonne Brady Axford. Littleton, Colo. : Libraries Unlimited, 1975. 148 p. ; 24 cm. (Spare time guides ; no. 7) Includes index. [Z6153.T4A94] [TT699] 75-16436 ISBN 0-87287-080-4 lib.bdg. : 11.50
1. Textile crafts—Bibliography. 2. Textile crafts—Equipment and supplies—Directories. 3. Publishers and publishing—Directories. I. Title. BIP

Textile design.

ALBERS, Anni. 746
On designing. [New Haven, Pellango Press, c1959] 70p. illus. 21cm. [TS1475.A4] 59-15929
1. Textile design. I. Title. BIP

ALBERS, Anni. 746
On designing. [2d ed.] Middletown, Conn., Wesleyan University Press [1962, c1961] 80 p. illus. 21 cm. [TS1475.A4 1962] 62-12321
1. Textile design. I. Title.

CONRAN, Terence. 745.52
Printed textile design. London, New York, Studio Publications [1957] 95 p. illus. 26 cm. (The How to do it series, no. 74) [NK8804.C6] 58-570
1. Textile design. 2. Textile printing. I. Title.

HARTUNG, Rolf. 746.6
More creative textile design: color and texture. New York, Reinhold Pub. Corp. [1965, c1964] 96 p. illus. (part col.) 21 cm. ([Creative play series]) Translation of Textiles Werken: Farbe and Gewebe. [NK9500.H313] 65-13368
1. Textile design. 2. Textile printing. 3. Dyes and dyeing—Textile fibers. I. Title. II. Title: Creative textile design.

HARTUNG, Rolf. 746.6
More creative textile design: color and texture. New York, Van Nostrand Reinhold [1972, c1964] 96 p. illus. (part col.) 20 x 21 cm. (Creative play series) Translation of Textiles Werken: Farbe und Gewebe. [TP930.H3313 1972] 72-184849 5.95
1. Textile design. 2. Textile printing. 3. Dyes and dyeing—Textile fibers. I. Title. II. Title: Creative textile design.
Pap. 3.95

JOHNSTON, Meda Parker. 746.6
Design on fabrics [by] Meda Parker Johnston [and] Glen Kaufman. New York, Reinhold [1967] 155 p. illus. (part col.) 29 cm. Bibliography: p. 153. [NK9500.J6] 66-22689
1. Textile design. 2. Textile printing. I. Kaufman, Glen, joint author. II. Title.

KYBAL, Antonin 746.109437
Modern textile designer: Antonin Kybal [by] Jan Spurny. [Tr. by Roberta Finlayson Samsour. Prague] Artia [dist. New York, Vanous, 1962, c.1960] 22p. illus. (pt. col.) 27cm. A62 6.50
I. Spurney, Jan. II. Title.

WARD, Michael, 1934- 746
Art and design in textiles. New York, Van Nostrand [1973] 112 p. illus. 27 cm. Bibliography: p. 110. [TS1475.W28] 77-39891 ISBN 0-442-29956-7 9.95
1. Textile design. I. Title.

Textile design—Exhibitions.

BOSTON. Museum of Fine 745.4
Arts.
Nancy Graves Cabot: in memoriam; sources of design for textiles and decorative arts. Boston [1973] 42 p. illus. 25 cm. Catalog of an exhibition held Sept. 19-Dec. 2, 1973. Includes bibliographies. [NK8801.B67B67 1973] 74-151218
1. Textile design—Exhibitions. 2. Textile design—History—Sources. 3. Cabot, Nancy Graves. I. Cabot, Nancy Graves. II. Title.

CONSTANTINE, Mildred. 746.3'922
Wall hangings, by Mildred Constantine and Jack Lenor Larsen. New York, Museum of Modern Art [1969] [48] p. (chiefly illus.) 29 cm. Catalog of an exhibition, Feb. 25-May 4, 1969. [NK8801.N4M83] 70-77514
1. Textile design—Exhibitions. 2. Textile industry and fabrics—Exhibitions. I. Larsen, Jack Lenor, joint author. II. New York (City). Museum of Modern Art. III. Title.

Textile dyeing.

BATTENFIELD, Jackie. 746.6
Ikat technique / Jackie Battenfield. New York : Van Nostrand Reinhold, 1978. 100 p. : ill. ; 24 cm. Includes index. Bibliography: p. 97. [TT853.B37] 77-8669 ISBN 0-442-20595-3 : 10.95
1. Textile dyeing. 2. Ikat. I. Title. BIP

YAMAZAKI, Akira 746.10952
Nippon hand weaves in 'Kusakizome' dyes; handbook of Japanese weaves in natural plant dyes. [Los Angeles, Perkins Oriental Books. 1959] 59p. illus. mounted samples 29cm. Issued in folding case. 25.00 lim. ed.,
I. Title. II. Title: Nippon hand weaves in 'Kusakimoze' dyes.

Textile fabrics.

FLEMMING, Ernst Richard, 745.52
1866-
Encyclopaedia of textiles; decorative fabrics from antiquity to the beginning of the 19th century, including the Far East and Peru [by] Renate Jacques [and] Ernst Flemming. New York, Praeger [1958] xxx p. 304 plates (16 col.) 30 cm. (Books that matter) A translation of Flemming's Das Textilwerk by R. Jaques, with revisions and new material. [NK8804.F5 1958] 58-8171
1. Textile fabrics. I. Jacques, Renate, ed. and tr.

LARSEN, Jack Lenor. 746.9
Fabrics for interiors : a guide for architects, designers, and consumers / by Jack Lenor Larsen and Jeanne Weeks. New York : Van Nostrand Reinhold Co., [1975] p. cm. Bibliography: p. [TS1767.L37] 75-9117 ISBN 0-442-24683-8 : 14.95 ISBN 0-442-24684-6 pbk. : 7.95 pbk.
1. Textile fabrics. 2. Interior decoration. I. Weeks, Jeanne G., joint author. II. Title. BIP

TAYLOR, Lucy D. 646.1
Know your fabrics; standard decorative textiles and their uses. New York, Wiley [1951] 396 p. illus. 25 cm. [NK8904.T3] 51-13154
1. Textile fabrics. I. Title.

Textile fabrics, Ancient.

VOLBACH, Wolfgang 746.1
Friedrich, 1892-
Early decorative textiles [by] W. Fritz Volbach; [translated from the Italian by Yuri Gabriel]. London, New York, Hamlyn, 1969. 3-157 p. 71 col. illus. 20 cm. (Cameo) Originally published as Il tessuto nell'arte antica. Milano, Fabbri, 1966. [NK8907.V613] 79-437236 ISBN 0-600-01242-5 15/-
1. Textile fabrics, Ancient. 2. Decoration and ornament, Ancient. I. Title.

Textile fabrics—Collectors and collecting—Congresses.

IRENE Emery Roundtable 746'.028
on Museum Textiles, Washington, D.C., 1974.
Archaeological textiles : 1974 proceedings / Irene Emery Roundtable on Museum Textiles ; edited by Patricia L. Fiske. Washington : Textile Museum, c1975. iii, 211 p. : ill. ; 28 cm. Includes bibliographies. [TS1306.A1I73 1974] 75-21585
1. Textile fabrics—Collectors and collecting—Congresses. 2. Textile fabrics, Ancient—Congresses. I. Emery, Irene. II. Fiske, Patricia L. III. Washington, D.C. Textile Museum. IV. Title.

Textile fabrics—Exhibitions.

HONOLULU Academy 746'.074'0996931
of Arts.
A festival of fibers : masterworks of textile art from the collection of the Honolulu Academy of Arts : a fiftieth anniversary exhibition, October 14 through November 20, 1977 : [catalogue] / introd. by Adolph S. Cavallo. [Honolulu] : The Academy, c1977. 75 p. : ill. (some col.) ; 26 cm. [NK8801.H6H664] 77-155961
1. Textile fabrics—Exhibitions. I. Cavallo, Adolph S. II. Title.

LOS Angeles Co., 746'.074'019494
Calif. Museum of Art, Los Angeles.
Fabric and fashion : twenty years of Costume Council gifts : [exhibition], Los Angeles County Museum of Art, May 14-September 8, 1974 / Mary Hunt Kahlenberg. [Los Angeles] : The Museum, [1974] [40] p. : ill. ; 26 cm. Bibliography: p. [39] [NK8801.L72M874 1974] 76-353427
1. Textile fabrics—Exhibitions. 2. Costume—Exhibitions. I. Kahlenberg, Mary Hunt. II. Costume Council. III. Title.

Textile fabrics—France.

LUBELL, Cecil. 746.3'944'07444
France : an illustrated guide to textile collections in French museums / editor, Cecil Lubell. New York : Van Nostrand Reinhold, c1977. p. cm. (Textile collections of the world ; v. 3) Includes index. [NK8849.L82] 77-1628 ISBN 0-442-24894-6 : 30.00
1. Textile fabrics—France. 2. Museums—France. I. Title. II. Series.

Textile fabrics in interior decoration.

HICKS, David. 747'.5
David Hicks on decoration—with fabrics. [1st American ed. New York?] World Pub. [1971] 1 v. (chiefly illus., part col.) 32 cm. [NK2115.5.F3H5 1971] 70-156305 15.00
1. Textile fabrics in interior decoration. I. Title. II. Title: On decoration—with fabrics.

LEWIS, Alfred Allan. 747
Decorating with fabric / by Alfred Allan Lewis ; photographed by Helen Buttfield. New York : Grosset & Dunlap, c1974. ix, 147 p., [8] leaves of plates : ill. (some col.) ; 29 cm. [NK2004.3.P47L48] 73-15128 ISBN 0-448-01303-7 : 15.00
1. Perez, Luis, 1934- 2. Textile fabrics in interior decoration. I. Title.

Textile fabrics—Indonesia.

KAHLENBERG, Mary Hunt. 746'.09598
Textile traditions of Indonesia / Mary Hunt Kahlenberg. Los Angeles : Los Angeles County Museum of Art, c1977. 116 p. : ill. ; 26 cm. Bibliography: p. 114-116. [NK8880.A1K33] 77-17884 ISBN 0-87587-083-X pbk. : 1.50
1. Textile fabrics—Indonesia. 2. Folk art—Indonesia. I. Los Angeles Co., Calif. Museum of Art, Los Angeles. II. Title.

Textile fabrics—Italy.

SANTANGELO, Antonino. 746
A treasury of great Italian textiles. [Translated by Peggy Craig] New York, H. N. Abrams [1964] 239 p. illus. (part mounted, part col.) 31 cm. Translation of Tessuti d'arte italiane dal XII al XVIII secolo. Bibliography: p. 235-237. [NK8852.S313] 64-14691
1. Textile fabrics—Italy. 2. Church vestments. 3. Altar-cloths. I. Title.

Textile fabrics—Peru.

HARCOURT, Raoul d'. 746.10985
Textiles of ancient Peru and their techniques. Edited by Grace G. Denny and Carolyn M. Osborne; translated by Saide Brown. Seattle, University of Washington Press, 1962. xvii, 186 p. 117 plates. 32 cm. Bibliography: p. 141-146. [F3429.3.T3H33] 62-17150
1. Textile fabrics—Peru. 2. Indians of South America—Textile industry and fabrics. I. Title. BIP

Textile fabrics—Soemba.

ADAMS, Marie Jeanne. 746'.0992'3
System and meaning in East Sumba textile design; a study in traditional Indonesian art. [New Haven, Conn., Yale University Southeast Asia Studies; distributed by Cellar Book Shop, Detroit, 1969] ix, 248 p. illus., map. 23 cm. (Yale University. Southeast Asia Studies. Cultural report

SUBJECT INDEX TEXTILE INDUSTRY AND

series, no. 16) Bibliography: p. [233]-248. [NK8879.A63] 70-78298
1. Textile fabrics—Soemba. 2. Textile design. I. Title. II. Series: Yale University. Graduate School. Southeast Asia Studies. Cultural report series, no. 16

Textile fabrics—United States.

†UNITED States & 746'.074'013
Canada : an illustrated guide to the textile collections in United States and Canadian museums / editor, Cecil Lubell ; with essays on the traditions of North American textile design by Andrew Hunter Whiteford (North American Indians), Robert Riley (United States), Dorothy K. Burnham (Canada). New York : Van Nostrand Reinhold Co., c1976. 336 p. : ill. (some col.) ; 29 cm. (Textile collections of the world ; v. 1) Includes index. [NK8812.U54] 75-30412 ISBN 0-442-24896-2 : 30.00
1. Textile fabrics—United States. 2. Textile fabrics—Canada. 3. Indians of North America—Textile industry and fabrics. 4. Art—United States—Galleries and museums. 5. Art—Canada—Galleries and museums. I. Lubell, Cecil. II. Whiteford, Andrew Hunter. Fabrics of the North American Indians. 1976. III. Riley, Robert. The traditions of American textile design. 1976. IV. Burnham, Dorothy K. Canadian textile traditions. 1976. V. Series.

Textile fabrics—Washington, D.C.—Catalogs.

WASHINGTON, D.C. 746'.074'0153
Textile Museum.
Masterpieces in the Textile Museum / essays and captions by Louise W. Mackie and Ann P. Rowe ; foreword by Andrew Oliver, Jr. Washington : The Museum, c1976. 46 p. : ill. ; 28 cm. [NK8902.W37W378 1976] 76-7310
1. Washington, D.C. Textile Museum. 2. Textile fabrics—Washington, D.C.—Catalogs. I. Mackie, Louise W. II. Rowe, Ann P. III. Title. BIP

Textile factories—New England—History.

HISTORIC American 917.3'03 s
Buildings Survey.
The New England textile mill survey. Washington, 1971. ix, 176 l. illus. 28 cm. (Selections from the Historic American Buildings Survey no. 11) Includes bibliographies. [NA705.A25 no. 11] [TH4521] 677'.028 72-600981
1. Textile factories—New England—History. I. Title. II. Series: Historic American Buildings Survey. Selections, no. 11.

Textile industry and fabrics.

BIRRELL, Verla Leone, 1903- 746
The textile arts; a handbook of weaving, braiding, printing, and other textile techniques [by] Verla Birrell. New York, Schocken Books [1973, c.1959] xvi, 512 p. illus. 24 cm. (Schocken Book, SB390) The 1959 edition had subtitle: A handbook of fabric structure and design processes. Includes bibliography. [NK8804.B5] ISBN 0-8052-0390-7 7.95 (pbk.)
1. Textile industry and fabrics. 2. Handicrafts. I. Title. BIP

BIRRELL, Verla Leone, 1903- 746
The textile arts, a handbook of fabric structure and design processes: ancient and modern weaving, braiding, printing, and other textile techniques. New York, Harper [1959] 514 p. illus. 26 cm. (Harper's home economics series) Includes bibliography. 58-8363
1. Textile industry and fabrics. I. Title.

Textile industry and fabrics—Africa.

PLUMER, Cheryl. 746'.0967
African textiles; an outline of handcrafted sub-Saharan fabrics. [East Lansing] African Studies Center, Michigan State University, 1971 [c1970] xiv, 146 p. map (on lining paper) 23 cm. Bibliography: p. 133-146. [TS1415.P55] 76-633408 4.00
1. Textile industry and fabrics—Africa. I. Title.

Textile industry and fabrics, African.

SIEBER, Roy, 1923- 745'.0967
African textiles and decorative arts. New York, Museum of Modern Art; distributed by New York Graphic Society, Greenwich, Conn. [1972] 239 p. illus. (part col.) 29 cm. Issued in connection with the exhibition to be held at the Museum of Modern Art, New York, Oct. 11, 1972-Jan. 31, 1973, the Los Angeles County Museum of Art, March 20-May 31, 1973, the M. H. de Young Memorial Museum, San Francisco, July 2-Aug. 31, 1973, and the Cleveland Museum of Art, Oct 3-Dec. 2, 1973. Bibliography: p. 229-238. [NK8887.S53 1972] 72-76268 ISBN 0-87070-228-9 15.00
1. Textile industry and fabrics, African. 2. Decoration and ornament, African. I. New York (City). Museum of Modern Art. II. Title. BIP

Textile industry and fabrics, American—Exhibitions.

AMERICAN Crafts Council. 746.4
Museum of Contemporary Crafts.
Sewn, stitched & stuffed. Dana Boussard [and others]. New York [1973] [24] p. illus. 22 cm. Catalog of the exhibition held at the Museum of Contemporary Crafts of the American Crafts Council, April 12-June 10, 1973. [NK8804.A46] 73-77895 ISBN 0-88321-002-9
1. Textile industry and fabrics, American—Exhibitions. 2. Needlework—United States. I. Boussard, Dana, 1944- II. Title.

Textile industry and fabrics—Bibliography.

CHARLOTTE, N. C. Public 016.677
Library of Charlotte and Mecklenburg County.
Textiles; a bibliography of the materials in the 'Textile collection' at the Public Library of Charlotte and Mecklenburg County, compiled by Mae S. Tucker, textile literature specialist. Charlotte, 1952. 49p. 23cm. 'Published as a service to the textile industry of North Carolin,, a cooperative project of the Public Libraries and the North Carolina Library Commission.' [Z7914.T3C48] 53-18486
1. Textile industry and fabrics—Bibl.—Catalogs. I. Tucker, Mae S. II. Title.

Textile industry and fabrics—Bibliography.

HALL, David M. 016.677
Guide to literature on textile engineering & textile science. Compiled by David M. Hall, Nicholas Achee, Jr. and Caroline C. Persons. Washington, American Society for Engineering Education, 1972. 19 p. 22 cm. [Z7914.T3H35] 72-189841 1.00
1. Textile industry and fabrics—Bibliography. I. Achee, Nicholas, joint author. II. Persons, Caroline C., joint author. III. Title.

KOPYCINSKI, Joseph V 016.677
Textile industry: information sources; an annotated guide to the literature of textile fibers, dyes and dyeing, design and decoration, weaving, machinery, and other subjects [by] Joseph V. Kopycinski. Foreword by Kenneth R. Fox. Detroit, Gale Research Co. [c1964] 194 p. 23 cm. (Management information guide, 4) [Z7914.T3K6] 64-25644
1. Textile industry and fabrics — Bibl. I. Title. II. Series. BIP

Textile industry and fabrics—Conservation and restoration.

LEENE, Jentina Emma. 746'.028
Textile conservation. Edited by Jentina E. Leene. Washington, Smithsonian Institution [1972] 275 p. illus. 25 cm. Published in conjunction with the International Institute for Conservation of Historic and Artistic Works. Includes bibliographical references. [NK8804.L36] 74-179287 15.00
1. Textile industry and fabrics—Conservation and restoration. I. International Institute for Conservation of Historic and Artistic Works. II. Title.

Textile industry and fabrics—Egypt.

WASHINGTON, D. C. Textile 745.52
Museum.
Catalogue of dated tiraz fabrics: Umayyad, Abbasid, Fatimid, by Ernst Kuhnel. Technical analysis, by Louisa Bellinger. Washington, National Pub. Co., 1952. vii, 137p. illus., 52 plates, maps (on lining papers) 31cm. (Its Catalogue raisonne) Bibliography: p. 129-131. [NK8988.W38] 53-1605
1. Textile industry and fabrics—Egypt. I. Kuhnel, Ernst, 1882- II. Title. III. Title: Dated tiraz fabrics. BIP

Textile industry and fabrics, English.

MONTGOMERY, Florence M. 746.6
Printed textiles; English and American cottons and linens 1700-1850 [by] Florence M. Montgomery. New York, Viking Press [1970] 379 p. illus., col. plates. 29 cm. (A Winterthur book) "Catalogue": p. 111-359. In the catalogue section, more than 400 examples of printed textiles from the Winterthur Museum Collection are described in detail. Bibliography: p. 361-371. [NK8843.A2M6 1970] 69-17973 16.95
1. Textile industry and fabrics, English. 2. Textile industry and fabrics, American. I. Henry Francis du Pont Winterthur Museum. II. Title.

Textile industry and fabrics—Europe—History.

WEIBEL, Adele Coulin. 745.52
Two thousand years of textiles; the figured textiles of Europe and the Near East. New York, Published for the Detroit Institute of Arts [by] Pantheon Books, 1952. xii, 169p. plates (part col.) 31cm. Bibliography: p. 165-167. [NK8842.W43] 52-7395
1. Textile industry and fabrics—Europe—Hist. 2. Textile industry and fabrics—Near East—Hist. 3. Textile industry and fabrics—Catalogs. I. Detroit. Institute of Arts. II. Title.

WEIBEL, Adele Coulin. 746.1'07
Two thousand years of textiles; the figured textiles of Europe and the Near East. New York, Hacker Art Books, 1972 [c1952] xii, 169 p. 331 plates (part col.) 32 cm. Bibliography: p. 165-167. [NK8842.W43 1972] 77-143367 ISBN 0-87817-086-3 60.00
1. Textile industry and fabrics—Europe—History. 2. Textile industry and fabrics—Near East—History. 3. Textile industry and fabrics—Catalogs. I. Title. BIP

Textile industry and fabrics, European.

CHICAGO. Art Institute. 746
Masterpieces of Western textiles from the Art Institute of Chicago. [By] Christa Charlotte Mayer. [Chicago] 1969. 224 p. illus., col. plates. 26 cm. Bibliography: p. 223-224. [NK8842.C45] 69-18743
1. Textile industry and fabrics, European. I. Mayer, Christa Charlotte. II. Title.

Textile industry and fabrics — Exhibitions.

LOS Angeles Co., 739.27'074
Calif. Museum, Los Angeles.
Painted and printed textiles from A. D. 800 to 1961 [Pasadena, Calif., Printed by G. Dahlstrom, 1961?] 63 p. illus. 27 cm. Catalog of a loan exhibition held in the Los Angeles County Museum, June -- Sept., 1961. Introduction by Stefania P. Holt and Eugene I. Holt. [NK8801.L72P3] 67-4955
1. Textile industry and fabrics — Exhibitions. 2. Textile painting. 3. Textile printing. I. Holt, Stefania P. II. Holt, Eugene I. III. Title.

LOS Angeles Co., Calif. 746.1
Museum of Art, Los Angeles.
Velvets East & West from the 14th to the 20th century. [Los Angeles, 1966] 63 p. illus. 17 cm. "An exhibition assembled from the collection of the Los Angeles County Museum of Art, Lytton Gallery: March-May 1966." Bibliography: p. [15] [NK8901.L62] 67-4644
1. Textile industry and fabrics—Exhibitions. 2. Velvet. I. Title.

Textile industry and fabrics—History.

BLUM, Herman, 1884- v. 12
Where did the loom get its brain? [Philadelphia? 1962] 55p. illus. 26cm. Includes bibliography. [NK8906.B6] 62-5547
1. Textile industry and fabrics—Hist. 2. Indians of South America—Textile industry and fabrics. 3. Incas. 4. Textile industry and fabrics, Coptic. 5. Indians—Origin. I. Title.

CLARKE, Leslie J. 746'.09
The craftsman in textiles [by] Leslie J. Clarke. New York, Praeger [1968] 144 p. illus. 23 cm. L.C. copy imperfect: p. 145-160 wanting. [TS1315.C55 1968] 68-28338 5.95
1. Textile industry and fabrics—History. 2. Textile design—History. I. Title.

Textile industry and fabrics—India.

NEW York. Museum of Modern 745.52
Art.
Textiles and ornaments of India; a selection of designs, edited, with a foreword, by Monroe Wheeler [director of the exhibition] Texts by Pupul Jayakar and John Irwin. New York [1956] 95p. illus. (part col.) col. port. 26cm. Based on an exhibition held at the Museum of Modern Art in 1955. 'Selected bibliography of Indian textiles': p. 91-93. [NK8976.N4] 56-8578
1. Textile industry and fabrics—India. 2. Art industries and trade—India. 3. Design, Decorative. I. Wheeler, Monroe, ed. II. Title. BIP

OSUMI, Tamezo, 1881- 746.10954
Printed cottons of Asia; the romance of trade textiles. Rev., adapted from an English tr. by George Saito. Rutland, Vt., Tuttle [c.1963] 186p. mounted col. illus. 36cm. Bibl. 63-11827 25.00
1. Textile industry and fabrics—India. 2. Textile industry and fabrics—Japan. 3. Textile design. I. Title.

Textile industry and fabrics, Indic.

NEW York (City). Museum 746.3'954
of Modern Art.
Textiles and ornaments of India; a selection of designs. Edited, with a foreword, by Monroe Wheeler. Texts by Pupul Jayakar and John Irwin. Reprint ed. [New York] Published for the Museum of Modern Art by Arno Press, 1972 [c1956] 93 p. illus. 26 cm. (Museum of Modern Art publications in reprint) Based on an exhibition held at the Museum of Modern Art in 1955. "Selected bibliography of Indian textiles by John Irwin": p. 91-93. [NK8976.A1N4 1972] 75-169305 ISBN 0-405-01564-X
1. Textile industry and fabrics, Indic. 2. Art industries and trade, Indic. 3. Design, Decorative—India. I. Wheeler, Monroe, 1899- ed. II. Title.

Textile industry and fabrics—Indonesia—Exhibitions.

SOLYOM, Garrett. 915'.03 s
Textiles of the Indonesian Archipelago [by] Garrett and Bronwen Solyom. [Honolulu] University Press of Hawaii [1973] 51 p. 32 plates. (part col.) 23 cm. (Asian studies at Hawaii, no. 10) Catalog of an exhibition held at the Honolulu Academy of Arts, Jan. 15-Apr. 15, 1973. Bibliography: p. 18-22. [DS3.A2A82 no. 10] [TS1306.U452] 746'.09598 72-97100 ISBN 0-8248-0268-3 4.75 (pbk.)
1. Textile industry and fabrics—

Indonesia—Exhibitions. I. Solyom, Bronwen, joint author. II. Honolulu Academy of Arts. III. Title. IV. Series.

Textile industry and fabrics, Indonesian.

LANGEWIS, Laurens 746.3991
Decorative art in Indonesian textiles [by] Laurens Langewis, Frits A. Wagner. Amsterdam. C. P. J. van der Peet. [New York. Heinman, 1965. c.1964] 67p. 230p. illus. (pt. col.) 33cm. Bibl. [NK8879.L3] 65-6590 45.00
1. Textile industry and fabrics, Indonesian. 2. Textile design. I. Wagner, Frits A., joint author. II. Title.

Textile industry and fabrics—Iran.

UEMURA, Rohuro, 1894- 746.10955 ed.
Persian weaving and dyeing. [2 v.] Kyoto, Unsodo Pub. Co. [dist. New York, Perkins Oriental, c.1962] 2 v. (unpaged) 100 col. plates. 43cm. Colophon inserted at end of v.2. In portfolio. In Japanese; English t.p., table of contents, introd. contained on 3 unbound leaves. J62 100.00 set,
1. Textile industry and fabrics—Iran. 2. Textile industry and fabrics, Oriental. I. Nakajima, Yasunosuko, joint ed. II. Title. III. Title: Persian weaving & dying. Perusha no senshoku.

Textile industry and fabrics, Iranian — Exhibitions.

LOS Angeles Co., Calif. 746.10955
Museum, Los Angeles.
Woven treasures of Persian art; Persian textiles from the 6th to the 19th century. Exhibition: Los Angeles County Museum, April-May 1959. [Los Angeles, 1959] 65 p. illus. 27 cm. [NK8974.L6] 59-3092
1. Textile industry and fabrics, Iranian — Exhibitions. I. Title.

Textile industry and fabrics — Japan.

YAMANOBE, Tomoyuki, 1904- 745.52
Textiles. English adaption by Lynn Katoh. [1st English ed.] Tokyo, Rutland, Vt., C. E. Tuttle Co. [1957] 70 p. illus. (part mounted, part col.) 20 cm. (Arts & crafts of Japan, no. 2) [NK8884.Y3] 57-10686
1. Textile industry and fabrics — Japan. 2. Kimonos. I. Katch, Lyy, tr. II. Title. III. Series.

Textile industry and fabrics, Maori.

SIMMONS, D. R. 919.31'57
The Lake Hauroko burial and the evolution of Maori clothing [by] D. R. Simmons. Dunedin, N.Z., Otago Museum Trust Board, 1968. 40 p. illus. 25 cm. (Records of the Otago Museum. Anthropology, no. 5) Caption title. Bibliography: p. 18. [GN432.S5] 72-871978
1. Textile industry and fabrics, Maori. 2. Funeral rites and ceremonies, Maori. I. Title. II. Series: Otago Museum. Records. Anthropology, no. 5

Textile industry and fabrics, Nigerian.

HARRELL, Janet E. 746'.09669
Classification and documentation of the Eicher Collection of selected Nigerian textile fabrics, by Janet E. Harrell. [East Lansing] 1967 [c1968] v, 113 l. illus. 28 cm. Thesis (M.A.)—Michigan State University. Bibliography: leaves 110-113. [NK8889.6.N5H3] 79-23726
1. Eicher, Joanne B.—Art collections. 2. Textile industry and fabrics, Nigerian. I. Title.

Textile industry and fabrics, Rumanian.

PETRESCU, Paul 745.449498
Romanian textiles, by Paual Petrescu and Nicolae Rodna, photographs by Gheorghe Serban. Leigh-on-Sea (Essex). London, F. Lewis, 1966. 3-23p. 48 plates. 29cm. (Survev of world textiles, no. 20) [NK88404-S8no. 20] 66-73850 22.00
1. Textile industry and fabrics, Rumanian. 2. Decoration and ornament, Rumanian. I. Rodna, Nicolae, joint author. II. Title.
Available from Textile Bk. Serv., New York.

Textile industry and fabrics, Slovak.

SELECKA, Zuzka 746.1
[Folk textiles from the Zvolen region] Bratislava, Osveta [dist. New York, Vanous, 1964, c.] 1963. 211p. (chiefly illus., pt. col.) 25cm. t.p. and text in Slovakian. Summaries in Russian, French, English, German. Bibl. 63-59238 12.00
1. Textile industry and fabrics, Slovak. 2. Embroidery, Slovak. I. Title.

Textile industry and fabrics—Sturbridge, Mass.—Catalogs.

OLD Sturbridge Village, 746.6
Sturbridge, Mass.
Printed cottons at Old Sturbridge Village, by Paula Sampson Preston. [Sturbridge, Mass., 1969] 36 p. illus. 22 cm. (Old Sturbridge Village booklet series, 28) [NK8802.S8O45] 77-16054
1. Textile industry and fabrics—Sturbridge, Mass.—Catalogs. I. Preston, Paula Sampson. II. Title. III. Series.

Textile industry and fabrics—Testing—Bibl.

HORIGAN, Francis D, 016.6770287
1910-
The serviceability of fabrics; a literature survey prepared by Francis D. Horigan and Cary R. Sage. Philadelphia, Technical Library, QM Research and Development Laboratories, 1950. 52 p. 27 cm. (Bibliographic series, no. 13) [Z7914.T3H63] 50-60668
1. Textile industry and fabrics—Testing—Bibl. I. Sage, Cary R., 1884- joint author. II. Title. III. Series: U. S. Quartermaster Corps. Research and Development Laboratories. Technical Library. Bibliographic series, no. 13

Textile industry—Bibliography.

RALSTON, Valerie H. 016.677
Textile reference sources : a selective bibliography / by Valerie H. Ralston. Storrs : University of Connecticut Library, 1973. 47 p. ; 21 cm. (Reference bibliography series ; no. 1) Includes index. [Z7914.T3R28] [TS1449] 75-621194
1. Textile industry—Bibliography. 2. Textile fabrics—Bibliography. 3. Textile fibers—Bibliography. I. Title. II. Series.

Textile museums—Great Britain—Directories.

LUBELL, Cecil. 746'.074'0941
United Kingdom-Ireland : an illustrated guide to the textile collections in the United Kingdom and Ireland / editor, Cecil Lubell. New York : Van Nostrand Reinhold, c1976. 240 p. : ill. (some col.) ; 29 cm. (Textile collections of the world ; v. 2) On spine: United Kingdom and Ireland. Includes index. [TS1306.G7L8] 74-31999 ISBN 0-442-24895-4
1. Textile museums—Great Britain—Directories. 2. Textile museums—Ireland—Directories. I. Title. II. Series.

Textile painting.

ASHTON, Pearl Fulton, 745.52
1903-
Everyone can paint fabrics. New York, Studio Publications in association with Crowell [1952] 163 p. illus. 24 cm. [NK9505.A7] 52-7381
1. Textile painting. I. Title.

BROWNLEY, Albert, 1907- 745.52
How to paint and stencil textiles. 4th ed. [rev. and enl.] Brooklyn, Alby Studio, 1952. 101p. illus., ports. 22cm. [NK9500.B7 1952] 52-9212
1. Textile painting. 2. Stencil work. I. Title.

EADES, Bascomb Galloway, 745.52
1924-
Fabric painting, a handbook on technique; with 83 designs for amateur and professional. Illustrated by the author. [2d ed., rev. and enl.] New York, Exposition Press [1956] 89p. illus. 21cm. (A Banner book) [NK9505.E3 1956] 55-5716
1. Textile painting. 2. Design, Decorative. I. Title.

EADES, Bascomb Galloway, 746.6
1924-
Painted warps, a handbook on technique with designs for amateur and professional, by B. G. Eades. Illus., by the author [Dallas, Author, 1503 Cedar Hill Ave., c.1964] 34 1. illus. 28cm. 64-6663 3.50, lim. ed. pap., plastic bdg.
1. Textile painting. 2. Weaving. I. Title.

WING, Marge. 746.6
How to paint on fabric : freehand, tracing, stamping, and stencil methods for beginner and advanced craftsman / by Marge Wing, with N. Mahr, L. Young, and G. G. Grimshaw. New York : Crown Publishers, c1977. 96 p., [4] leaves of plates : ill. ; 29 cm. Includes index. [TT851.W56 1977] 76-27883 ISBN 0-517-5266-3-8 : 6.95 ISBN 0-517-52664-6 pbk. : 4.95
1. Textile painting. I. Title.

Textile printing.

AATCC Textile Printing 667'.38
Symposium, New York, N.Y., 1978.
Printing symposium : meeting the challenge of the 80's / sponsored by the Printing Technology Committee of the American Association of Textile Chemists and Colorists, January 11-13, 1978, at the Hotel Roosevelt, New York City. [Research Triangle Park, N.C.] : The Association, c1978. iii, 89 p. : ill. ; 29 cm. Includes bibliographical references. [TP930.A15 1978] 78-102461 40.00
1. Textile printing—Congresses. I. American Association of Textile Chemists and Colorists. Printing Technology Committee. II. Title. III. Title: Meeting the challenge of the 80's.
Publisher's address: P.O. Box 12215, Research Triangle Park NC 27709

AHLBERG, Gudrun. 746.6
Block and silk screen printing, by G. Ahlberg and O. Jarneryd. New York, Sterling Pub. Co. [1961] 91 p. illus. 22 cm. (Sterling craft books) Translation of Tygtryck. [NK9500.A413] 60-14324
1. Textile printing. I. Jarneryd, O., joint author. II. Title.

ALBECK, Pat. 746.6
Printed textiles. London, New York [etc.] Oxford U.P., 1969. 96 p. illus. 21 cm. (Oxford paperbacks, handbooks for artists, 5) [TP930.A36] 75-382854 15/-
1. Textile printing. 2. Textile design. I. Title. BIP

ALLIED Chemical 667'.38
Corporation, Fibers Division.
Fabric printing. [New York, 1968] 45 p. illus. (part col.) 29 cm. [TP930.A4] 68-19050
1. Textile printing. I. Title.

BYSTRoM, Ellen. 746.6
Printing on fabric; basic techniques. New York, Van Nostrand Reinhold [1971, c1967] 96 p. illus. (part col.) 23 cm. Translation of Stoftryk. [TP930.B9513] 76-123381 ISBN 0-442-01240-3 4.50
1. Textile printing. I. Title.

CLARKE, W. 667'.38
An introduction to textile printing : a practical manual for use in laboratories, colleges, and schools of art / W. Clarke. 4th ed. New York : Wiley, 1974. 288 p. ; 23 cm. First-2d ed. prepared by Dyestuffs Division, Imperial Chemical Industries, ltd. "A Halsted Press book." Includes bibliographical references. [TP930.C583 1975] 75-5662 ISBN 0-470-65343-4 : 14.95
1. Textile printing. I. Imperial Chemical Industries, ltd. Dyestuffs Division. An introduction to textile printing. II. Title. BIP

ERICKSON, Janet Doub. 746.6
Block printing on textiles; a complete guide. [New York] Watson-Guptill, 1961. 168 p. illus. 26 cm. [NK9500.E7] 61-7021
1. Textile printing. 2. Textile design. 3. Linoleum block-printing. I. Title. BIP

ERICKSON, Janet Doub. 746.6
Block printing on textiles, by Janet Erickson. New ed. [New York] Watson-Guptill Publications, 1974 [c1961] 168 p. illus. 26 cm. [TT852.E74 1974] 74-165122 ISBN 0-8230-0501-1 10.95
1. Textile printing. 2. Textile design. 3. Linoleum block-printing. I. Title.

GAINES, Patricia Ellisor. 746.6
The fabric decoration book / by Patricia Ellisor Gaines ; photos. by George Butler. New York : Morrow, [1975] 207 p. : ill. ; 29 cm. Includes index. Bibliography: p. 201. [TT852.G34] 75-4543 ISBN 0-688-02903-5 : 16.95
1. Textile printing. 2. Textile painting. 3. Dyes and dyeing—Textile fibers. I. Title. BIP

GOOCH, Peter H. 746.6
Ideas for fabric printing and dyeing / Peter H. Gooch. New York : Scribner, [1975] c1974. 96 p., [4] leaves of plates : ill. (some col.) ; 21 cm. Bibliography: p. 94-95. [TT852.G66 1975] 74-4816 ISBN 0-684-14066-7 : 7.95
1. Textile printing. 2. Dyes and dyeing—Textile fibers. I. Title.

HEIN, Gisela. 746.6
Printing fabric by hand: beginning techniques. New York, Van Nostrand Reinhold Co. [1972] 79 p. illus. 22 cm. Translation of Stoffdrucken. The fundamentals of printing on cloth with explanations of how to make stamps from and apply coloring agents with such materials as potatoes, clay, and cork. [TP930.H3713 1972b] 77-178698 ISBN 0-442-23289-6 4.95
1. Textile printing. I. Title.

JACOBS, Fred F. 667.3
Textile printing: materials, methods, and formulae. New York, Chartwell House, 1952. 219 p. illus. 22 cm. [TP930.J3] 52-3618
1. Textile printing. I. Title.

KAFKA, Francis J 746.6
The hand decoration of fabrics. [1st ed.] Bloomington, Ill. McKnight & McKnight Pub. Co. [1959] 198p. illus. 24cm. [NK9500.K3] 58-13984
1. Textile printing. 2. Textile design. I. Title. BIP

KAFKA, Francis J. 746.6
The hand decoration of fabrics [by] Francis J. Kafka. New York, Dover Publications [1973, c1959] 198 p. illus. 23 cm. Reprint of the ed. published by McKnight & McKnight Pub. Co., Bloomington, Ill. Includes bibliographies. [NK9500.K3 1973] 73-80948 ISBN 0-486-21401-X 3.00 (pbk.)
1. Textile printing. 2. Textile design. I. Title.

KOSLOFF, Albert. 667.38
Textile screen printing. Illus. by the author. Cincinnati, Signs of the Times Pub. Co. [1966] 131 p. illus. 24 cm. [TP930.K65] 66-2899
1. Textile printing. I. Title. BIP

KUEHNEMANN, Ursula. 746.6
Textile printing and painting made easy. New York, Taplinger Pub. Co. [1967] 111 p. illus. (part col.) 22 cm. Translation of Stoffdruck, Stoffmalerei gar nicht schwer. [NK9505.K813 1967] 67-11517
1. Textile printing. 2. Textile painting. I. Title. BIP

LAMMER, Jutta 746.6
Print your own fabrics [Tr. from German] New York, Watson-Guptill [1966] c.1964, 1965. 59p. illus. (pt. col.) 20cm. [NK9500.L313] 65-21695 3.50 bds.,
1. Textile printing. 2. Textile design I. Title.

LAUTERBURG, Lotti. 746.6
Fabric printing. New York, Reinhold Pub. Corp. [1963, c1959] 112 p. illus. 26 cm. [TP930.L333 1963] 62-13454
1. Textile printing. I. Title.

MONK, Kathleen. 746.6
Fun with fabric printing. New York, Taplinger Pub. Co. [1969] 119 p. illus. (part col.) 26 cm. [TP930.M6 1969] 69-11224 8.50
1. Textile printing. I. Title. BIP

PETTIT, Florence Harvey. 745.52
Block printing on fabrics; with illus. by the author and photos. by Lucia Nebel. New York, Hastings House [1952] 146 p. illus. 26 cm. [NK9500.P4] 52-11809
1. Textile printing. 2. Textile design. I. Title.

PROUD, Nora. 746.6
Introducing textile printing. London, Batsford; New York, Watson-Guptill, 1968. 88p. chiefly illus. (2 col.), 2 plates. 22 x 21cm. Bibl. [TP930.P69 1968] 68-10202 6.95 bds.,
1. Textile printing. I. Title.

PROUD, Nora. 746.6
Textile printing and dyeing. New York, Reinhold [1965] 118 p. illus. (part col.) 22 cm. [TP930.P7] 65-24057
1. Textile printing. 2. Dyes and dyeing—Textile fibers. I. Title.

RUSS, Stephen. 746.6
Fabric printing by hand. New York, Watson-Guptill Publications [1965] 112 p. illus., 32 plates (part col.) 26 cm. Bibliography: p. 106-107. [NK9500.R8 1965] 64-21986
1. Textile printing. I. Title.

SCOTT, Guy. 667'.38
Transfer printing onto man-made fibres / Guy Scott. Newton Centre, Mass. : C. T. Branford Co., 1977. 144 p., [2] leaves of plates : ill. (some col.) ; 23 cm. Includes bibliographical references and index. [TT852.S37 1977b] 77-152472 ISBN 0-8231-7036-5 : 11.75
1. Textile printing. 2. Transfer-printing. I. Title. BIP

SMITH, Allan. 745.52
Fabric printing. With 28 plates by the author. London, New York, Warne [1953] 88p. illus. 22cm. [NK9500.S5] 53-2444
1. Textile printing. I. Title.

STOREY, Joyce. 667'.38
The Thames and Hudson manual of dyes and fabrics / Joyce Storey. London : Thames and Hudson, c1978. 192 p. : ill. (some col.) ; 25 cm. (The Thames and Hudson manuals) Includes index. Bibliography: p. 185. [TP930.S919] 77-92267 ISBN 0-500-67016-1 : 14.95
1. Textile printing. 2. Dyes and dyeing—Textile fibers. I. Title. II. Title: Manual of dyes and fabrics.
Distributed by W. W. Norton, New York, NY 10036 BIP

STOREY, Joyce. 667'.38
Van Nostrand Reinhold manual of textile printing. New York, Van Nostrand Reinhold Co. [1974] 188 p. illus. (part col.) 25 cm. Bibliography: p. 185. [TP930.S93 1974] 73-19427 ISBN 0-442-27914-0 10.95
1. Textile printing. I. Title. II. Title: Textile printing.

Textile printing—History.

PETTIT, Florence Harvey. 667'.26
America's indigo blues; resist-printed and dyed textiles of the eighteenth century, by Florence H. Pettit. With 106 photos., 8 color plates, and 44 woodcuts, engravings, and drawings. New York, Hastings House [1974] 251 p. illus. (part col.) 26 cm. Bibliography: p. 237-241. [TP930.P468 1974] 74-10778 ISBN 0-8038-0376-1
1. Textile printing—History. 2. Dyes and dyeing—Textile fibers—History. 3. Indigo—History. 4. Textile fabrics, American—History. I. Title. BIP

PETTIT, Florence Harvey. 677
America's printed & painted fabrics, 1600-1900, by Florence H. Pettit. Twenty-six drawings by the author. New York, Hastings House [1970] 256 p. illus. (part col.), facsims. 26 cm. Bibliography: p. 245-247. [TP930.P47 1970] 76-113770 20.00
1. Textile printing—History. 2. Textile painting—History. 3. Textile industry and fabrics, American—History. I. Title. BIP

ROBINSON, Stuart. 667'.38'09
A history of printed textiles. Cambridge, Mass., M.I.T. Press [1969] 152 p. illus. (part col.), maps. 26 cm. Bibliography: p. 124-136. [TP930.R78 1969] 71-98040
1. Textile printing—History. I. Title. BIP

Textile research—Bibl.

PRINCETON, N. J. 016.553'635
Textile Research Institute.
Review of textile research and development during 1954. Princeton, 1955. 68p. 27cm. 'The sixth in a series published annually by Textile Research Institute. The five previous surveys ... were published as part of the May issue of Textile research journal.' [Z7914.T3P7] 56-758
1. Textile research—Bibl. I. Title.

Textiles—Canadian—Hist.

THOMPSON, J. H. 746.10971
Canadian textiles. New York, Textile Bk. Serv., 257 Park Ave., 1963. 18p., 114p. of plates, 26cm. 19.00
1. Textiles—Canadian—Hist. I. Title. BIP

Textiles, French—History.

*SCHWARTZ, P. R. 746.0944
A century of French fabrics, 1850-1950, by P. R. Schwartz, R. De Micheaux. NewYork, Textile Bk. Serv., 1964. 11p. 72 plates. 30cm. 19.50
1. Textiles, French—History. I. De Micheaux, R., joint author. II. Title. BIP

Textiles—Persian—Hist.

BUNT, Cyril G. E. 746.10955
Persian fabrics. New York, Textile Bk. Serv., 257 Park Ave., So., 1963. 9p., 55p. of plates. 19.00
1. Textiles—Persian—Hist. I. Title. BIP

Texture (Art)—Juvenile literature.

HORN, George F. 701'.8
Texture : a design element / George F. Horn. Worcester, Mass. : Davis Publications, [1974] 72 p. : ill. ; 26 cm. (Elements of design) Text and photographs explore the textures of our natural and man-made environment through such things as art objects, buildings, grass, a quarry, and a turtle. [N7430.5.H67] 75-321023
1. Texture (Art)—Juvenile literature. 2. Visual perception—Juvenile literature. I. Title. II. Series. BIP

Texture painting.

MILLS, John FitzMaurice, 751.49
1917-
Acrylic painting [New York] Pitman [c.1965] ix, 126p. illus. (pt. col.) ports. 26cm. [ND1260.M54] 66-517 12.50
1. Texture painting. 2. Painting—Technique. I. Title.

*RUSSELL, Jack L. 751.49
Poured plastic painting, by Jack L. Russell. Corpus Christi, Texas, Jack L. Russell, [1975] 127 p. ill. 22 cm. [ND1618] 1.95 (pbk.)
1. Texture Painting. I. Title.
Pub. address: 222 Riviera Corpus Christi, Texas 78418

Thatcher Glass Manufacturing Company. McKee Division.

GROSS, Vicki. 748.2'9148'81
That collectible McKee; in color, by Vicki and Mike Gross. [Hillsboro, Or., 1973] 35 p. col. illus. 23 cm. Cover title. [NK5198.T45G76] 73-164585 4.95
1. Thatcher Glass Manufacturing Company. McKee Division. 2. Glassware—United States—Catalogs. I. Gross, Mike, joint author. II. Title. III. Title: McKee in color.

STOUT, Sandra 748.2'9148'81
McPhee.
The complete book of McKee glass / by Sandra McPhee Stout. North Kansas City, Mo. : Trojan Press, 1972. 456 p. : chiefly ill. ; 29 cm. & handbooks (107 p. ; 22 cm.) Includes index. Bibliography: p. 451. [NK5198.T45S85] 72-89735 19.50
1. Thatcher Glass Manufacturing Company. McKee Division. 2. Glassware—United States—Catalogs. I. Title.

Thaw, Eugene V.—Art collections.

STAMPFLE, 741.9'4'07401471
Felice.
Drawings from the collection of Mr. & Mrs. Eugene V. Thaw : catalogue / by Felice Stampfle & Cara D. Denison ; with an introd. by Eugene V. Thaw. New York : The Pierpont Morgan Library, 1975. 105 p., [62] leaves of plates : ill. (some col.) ; 28 cm. Catalog of the exhibition held Dec. 10, 1975-Feb. 15, 1976 at the Pierpont Morgan Library, New York; Mar. 16-May 2, 1976 at the Cleveland Museum of Art; May 28-July 5, 1976 at the Art Institute of Chicago; and Aug. 6-Sept. 17, 1976 at the National Gallery of Canada, Ottawa. Includes bibliographies and index. [NC15.N56P538] 75-38424 ISBN 0-87598-052-X : 16.50
1. Thaw, Eugene V.—Art collections. 2. Drawings—Exhibitions. I. Denison, Cara D., joint author. II. Thaw, Eugene V. III. Pierpont Morgan Library, New York. IV. Title.

Thawan Duchanee, 1939-

THAWAN Duchanee, 1939- 741.9'593
Forms of man : the Buddhist vision of Thawan Duchanee / commentary by Russell Marcus. Bangkok ; Ojai, Calif. : Books Marcus, 1974. 72 p. : chiefly ill. (some col.) ; 26 cm. [N7323.T46M37] 74-84663 18.00
1. Thawan Duchanee, 1939- 2. Art, Buddhist. 3. Symbolism in art. I. Marcus, Russell. II. Title. BIP

Thaxter, Celia Laighton, 1835-1894.

THAXTER, Celia 635'.09741'95
Laighton, 1835-1894.
An island garden / by Celia Thaxter ; illustrated by Childe Hassam ; with a new introd. by John M. Kingsbury. Bowie, MD : Heritage Books, 1978. xiii, ix, 130 p., [15] leaves of plates : ill. ; 23 cm. Reprint of the 1894 ed. published by Houghton, Mifflin, Boston. Includes index. [SB466.U7T6 1978] 78-3464 ISBN 0-917890-06-X : 15.00
1. Thaxter, Celia Laighton, 1835-1894. 2. Gardens—Maine—Appeldore Island, Kittery. 3. Appledore Island, Kittery, Me.—Description. I. Title. BIP

Thayer, Abbott Handerson, 1840-1921.

WHITE, Nelson C 927.5
Abbott H. Thayer, painter and naturalist. [Hartford] Connecticut Printer, 1951. xxi, 277 p. ports., plates (part col.) 28 cm. Bibliography: p.265-269 [ND237.T5W5] 51-7151
1. Thayer, Abbott Handerson, 1840-1921. I. Title. BIP

Theater.

WHITWORTH, Geoffrey Arundel, 792
1883-
Theatre in action. New York, B. Blom, 1972 [c1939] 128 p. illus. 32 cm. [PN2091.S8W47 1972] 76-175894
1. Theater. 2. Theaters—Stage-setting and scenery. 3. Drama—20th century—History and criticism. I. Title. BIP

Theater—Great Britain—History.

SHARP, Robert 772'.0942
Farquharson, 1864-1945.
A short history of the English stage, from its beginnings to the summer of the year 1908. London, Walter Scott Pub. Co., 1909. [Folcroft, Pa.] Folcroft Library Editions, 1973. p. [PN2581.S4 1973] 73-4181 ISBN 0-8414-7520-2 25.00
1. Theater—Great Britain—History. I. Title.

Theater in art.

KAHAN, Gerald. 769'.92'4
Jacques Callot : artist of the theatre / Gerald Kahan. Athens : University of Georgia Press, c1976. xiii, 118 p. : ill. ; 22 x 29 cm. Bibliography: p. 117-118. [NE2049.5.C3K33] 73-76787 ISBN 0-8203-0345-3 : 15.00
1. Callot, Jacques, 1592-1635. 2. Theater in art. BIP

Theater—Pictorial works.

WALDMAN, Max. 779'.9'792
Waldman on theater. With an introd. by Clive Barnes and a pref. by Peter Bunnell. Garden City, N.Y., Doubleday, 1971. 185 p. illus. 27 cm. [PN2111.W3] 72-160892 10.00
1. Theater—Pictorial works. I. Title.

Theater—U.S.—Caricatures and cartoons.

HIRSCHFELD, Albert. 741.5973
The American theatre as seen by Hirschfeld. New York, G. Braziller, 1961. unpaged (chiefly illus.) 25 x 30 cm. [NC1429.H527A48] 61-15495
1. Theater—U.S.—Caricatures and cartoons. I. Title.

Theaters—Construction.

ALOI, Roberto 725.822
Architetture per lo spettacolo. Con un saggio dell'architetto Agnoldomenico Pica. Didascalie in italiano. francese. inglese, tedesco. Milano, Hoepli. Label mounted on t.p.: W. S. Heinman, New York, 1958. lxiv. 504p. (chiefly illus. (pt. col.) plans) 28cm. (Esempi di architettura di tutto il mondo, 14) [NA6821.A4] 67-1025 30.00
1. Theaters— Construction. I. Title.

AMERICAN Federation of 725.82
Arts
The ideal theater: eight concepts. Exhibition of designs and models resulting from the Ford Foundation, Program for Theater Design. Prepared, circulated by the Amer. Federation of Arts, January, 1962--January, 1964. [New York, Author, 1962] 137p. illus. 26cm. 62-6123 2.00
1. Theaters—Construction. I. Title.

AMERICAN Federation of 725.82
Arts
The ideal theater: eight concepts. An exhibition of designs and models resulting from the Ford Found. Program for Theater Design. Prepared and circulated by the American Federation of Arts. [2d ed.] New York [October House, 1964, c.1962] 137p. illus., plans. 26cm. 64-25353 7.50; 2.00 pap.,
1. Theaters—Construction. I. Title.

BURRIS-MEYER, Harold, 725.82
1902-
Theatres and auditoriums, by Harold Burris-Meyer and Edward C. Cole. 2d ed. New York, Reinhold Pub. Corp. [1964] vii, 376 p. illus., plans 27 cm. [NA6821.B8] 64-8896
1. Theaters — Construction. 2. Auditorims. I. Cole, Edward Cyrus, joint author. II. Title. BIP

BURRIS-MEYER, Harold, 725'.822
1902-
Theatres and auditoriums / by Harold Burris-Meyer and Edward C. Cole. 2d ed. Huntington, N.Y. : R. E. Krieger Pub. Co., 1975. vii, 470 p. : ill. ; 27 cm. Reprint of the 1964 ed., published by Reinhold, New York; with new suppl. Includes indexes. Bibliography: p. 449-451. [NA6821.B8 1975] 75-17792 ISBN 0-88275-170-0 : 29.50
1. Theaters—Construction. 2. Auditoriums. I. Cole, Edward Cyrus, joint author. II. Title.

IZENOUR, George C. 725'.822
Theater design / by George C. Izenour ; with two essays on the room acoustics of multiple-use by Vern O. Knudsen and Robert B. Newman ; foreword by Alois M. Nagler. New York : McGraw-Hill, c1977. xxxiii, 631 p. : ill. ; 30 x 31 cm. Includes indexes. Bibliography: p. 612-615. [NA6821.I94] 76-56258 ISBN 0-07-032086-1 : 49.50
1. Theaters—Construction. I. Knudsen, Vern Oliver, 1893-1974, joint author. II. Newman, Robert B., joint author. III. Title. BIP

JOSEPH, Stephen, ed. 725.82
Actor and architect, by Tyrone Guthrie [and others] Edited by Stephen Joseph. [Toronto] University of Toronto Press [1964] xii, 118 p. illus., plans. 23 cm. Includes the talks given at Manchester University during the 1962 Theatre Week, sponsored by the Dept. of Drama. [NA6821.J6] 65-1381
1. Theaters — Construction. 2. Theater. I. Guthrie, Sir Tyrone, 1900- II. Victoria University of Manchester. Dept. of Drama. Title. III. Title. BIP

RISSER, Arthur C. 725.822
The educational theatre building and its equipment; report of a study project conducted by Arthur C. Risser. [Wichita? Kan.] 1965. 1 v. (various pagings) mounted illus., plans. 29 cm. Includes bibliography. [NA6602.T5R5] 65-29840
1. Theaters — Construction. 2. Architecture — Designs and plans. 3. Universities and colleges — Buildings. I. Title.

SCHUBERT, Hannelore, 725'.822
1927-
The modern theater; architecture, stage design, lighting. Translated by J. C. Palmes. New York, Praeger [1971] 222 p. illus. 29 cm. Translation of Moderner Theaterbau. Bibliography: p. 219. [NA6821.S3813] 74-111072 35.00
1. Theaters—Construction. 2. Architecture, Modern—20th century. I. Title.

SEXTON, Randolph 725'.822'0973
Williams, 1884-
American theatres of today : illustrated with plans, sections, and photographs of exterior and interior details of modern motion picture and legitimate theatres throughout the United States / by R. W. Sexton and B. F. Betts ; with a foreword by S. L. Rothafel. Vestal, N.Y. : Vestal Press, c1977. x, 175, 167 p. : ill. ; 29 cm. Reprint of the 1927-1930 ed. published by Architectural Book Pub. Co., New York ; with new foreword. Includes index. [NA6830.S4 1977] 77-24013 ISBN 0-911572-15-5 : 35.00
1. Theaters—Construction. 2. Moving-picture theaters—United States. I. Betts, Benjamin Franklin, 1888- joint author. II. Title. BIP

SILVERMAN, Maxwell. 725.822
Contemporary theatre architecture; an illustrated survey. A checklist of publications 1946-1964, by Ned A. Bowman. [1st ed.] New York, New York Public Library [1965] [80] p. illus., plans. 37 cm. [NA6821.S55] 65-12942
1. Theaters—Construction. 2. Theaters—Construction—Bibl. I. Bowman, Ned Allan, 1932- II. Title. BIP

SOUTHERN, Richard 792.025
Prosnenium and sight-lines: a complete system of scenery planning and a guide to the laying out of stages for scene-designers, stage-managers, theatre architects and engineers, theatrical history and research workers. and those concerned with the planning of stages for small halls [Rev. ed.] New York, Theater Arts [1965.c.1964] 235p. illus. 23cm. [PN2091.S8S63] 64-24583 5.95
1. Theaters—Construction. 2. Theaters—Stage-setting and scenery. I. Title.

THEATRE architecture & 725'.822
stage machines. Engravings from the Encyclopedie, ou Dictionnaire raisonne des sciences, des arts, et des metiers. Edited by Denis Diderot and Jean le Rond d'Alembert. [New ed.] New York, B. Blom, 1969. [22] p., 89 plates. 35 cm. Eighty of the 89 plates reproduced are taken from the 10th v. of the series of plates published at Paris between 1762 and 1772 under title Recueil de planches, sur les sciences, les arts liberaux, et les arts mechaniques, avec leur explication. Nine plates are reproduced from Supplement a l'Encyclopedie published at Amsterdam, 1776-77. Text in French with introductory material in English. [NA6820.E5 1969 fol.] 68-21210
1. Theaters—Construction. 2. Architecture—Early works to 1800. I. Diderot, Denis, 1713-1784, ed. II. Alembert, Jean Lerond d', 1717-1783, ed.

Theaters—Construction—Bibliography.

STODDARD, Richard. 016.725'822
Theatre architecture : a guide to information sources / Richard Stoddard. Detroit : Gale Research Co., [1978] p. cm. (Performing arts information guide series ; v. 5) Includes indexes. [Z5784.S8S82] [NA6821] 78-14820 ISBN 0-8103-1426-6 : 18.00
1. Theaters—Construction—Bibliography. I. Title.

Theaters—Construction—Congresses.

INTERNATIONAL Federation 792'.025
for Theatre Research.
Innovations in stage and theatre design. Edited by Francis Hodge. [New York] American Society for Theatre Research [1972] 165 p. illus. 23 cm. Papers presented at the sixth congress of the International Federation for Theatre Research, held Oct. 6-10, 1969, at Lincoln Center, New York. Sponsored by the American Society for Theatre Research and the Theatre Library Association. Includes bibliographical references. [NA6821.I57] 72-80767 5.00
1. Theaters—Construction—Congresses. 2. Theaters—Stage-setting and scenery—Congresses. I. Hodge, Francis, ed. II. American Society of Theatre Research. III. Theatre Library Association. IV. Title.

Theaters—Construction—History.

MULLIN, Donald C. 725'.822
The development of the playhouse; a survey of theatre architecture from the Renaissance to the present [by] Donald C. Mullin. Berkeley, University of California Press, 1970. xvi, 197 p. illus., plans. 29 cm. Bibliography: p. 187-191. [NA6821.M83] 77-84532 15.00
1. Theaters—Construction—History. I. Title.

TIDWORTH, Simon. 725'.822'09
Theatres; an architectural and cultural history. New York, Praeger Publishers [1973] 224 p. illus. 26 cm. Bibliography: p. 213-214. [NA6821.T48 1973] 72-165856 18.50
1. Theaters—Construction—History. 2. Theater—History. I. Title.

Theaters—Construction—United States.

MIELZINER, Jo, 1901- 725'.822
The shapes of our theatre. Edited by C. Ray Smith. [1st ed.] New York, C. N. Potter; distributed by Crown Publishers [1970]. 160 p. illus. 27 cm. [NA6830.M53 1970] 70-111343 6.95
1. Theaters—Construction—United States. I. Title.

Theaters—England—Construction.

LEACROFT, Richard. 725'.822'0942
The development of the English playhouse. Ithaca, N.Y., Cornell University Press [1973] xiii, 354 p. illus. 29 cm. Bibliography: p. [338]-345. [NA6840.G7L4] 72-6713 ISBN 0-8014-0750-8 27.50
1. Theaters—England—Construction. 2. Theater—England. I. Title.

Theaters—England—Stage-setting and scenery.

REYNOLDS, George 792'.025
Fullmer, 1877-
Some principles of Elizabethan staging, by George F. Reynolds. [Folcroft, Pa.] Folcroft Press, 1970. 34, 29 p. facsim. 26 cm. "Limited to 150 copies." Reprint of the 1905 ed. Thesis—University of Chicago, 1905. Includes bibliographical references. [PN2091.S8R4 1971b] 72-193209
1. Shakespeare, William, 1564-1616—Stage history—To 1625. 2. Theaters—England—Stage-setting and scenery. I. Title. BIP

REYNOLDS, George 792'.0942
Fullmer, 1877-
Some principles of Elizabethan staging / by George F. Reynolds. Norwood, Pa. : Norwood Editions, 1975. 29 p. ; 26 cm. Reprint of the 1905 ed. published by University of Chicago Press, Chicago. Originally presented as the author's thesis, University of Chicago. Includes bibliographical references. [PN2091.S8R4 1975] 75-35556 ISBN 0-88305-593-7 : 8.50
1. Shakespeare, William, 1564-1616—Stage history—To 1625. 2. Theaters—England—Stage-setting and scenery. I. Title.

Theaters—Europe.

FILIPPI, Joseph de. 792.09
Parallele des principaux theatres modernes de l'Europe et des machines theatrales francaises, allemandes et anglaises. Dessins par Clement Contant Texte par Joseph de Filippi. New York, Blom, 1968. 163p., 134 plates (incl. plans) 34cm. First pub. 1860. [NA6821.F5 1968] 68-21209 75.00
1. Theaters—Europe. 2. Theaters—Construction. I. Contant, Clement. II. Title.

SACHS, Edwin O, 725'.822'094
1870-1919
Modern opera houses and theatres, by Edwin O. Sachs, Ernest A. E. Woodrow. [New York, Blom, 1968] 3 v. illus., plans., 34cm. Reprint of 1896-98 ed. [NA6821.S22 1968] 67-12461 36.66
1. Theaters—Europe. 2. Theaters—Construction. 3. Theaters—Fires and fire prevention. 4. Theaters—Safety measures. I. Woodrow, Ernest A. E. joint author. II. Title. BIP

Theaters—Europe—Construction.

DUMONT, Gabriel 725'.822'094
Pierre Martin, ca.1720-ca.1790.
Parallele de plans de plus belles salles de spectacles d'Italie et de France, avec des details de machines theatrales. New York, B. Blom, 1968. [87] p. (chiefly illus., plans) 34 cm. Composite ed. contains the entire set of plates from 1774 Paris ed. (reproduced from a copy in the possession of the Royal Institute of British Architects) and, in an appendix, 16 plates and a port. of the author from an ed. of his collected works, Recueil de plusieurs parties de l'architecture, published in Paris, ca. 1770 (reproduced from a copy in the Avery Architectural Library, Columbia University) [NA6820.D8 1968] 68-17155
1. Theaters—Europe—Construction. I. Title.

Theaters—Great Britain—Stage-setting and scenery.

ROSENFELD, Sybil 792'.025'0942
Marion, 1903-
A short history of scene design in Great Britain [by] Sybil Rosenfeld. Totowa, N.J., Rowman and Littlefield [1973] xviii, 214 p. illus. 22 cm. (Drama and theatre studies) Bibliography: p. 198-205. [PN2091.S8R59 1973] 73-1621 ISBN 0-87471-178-9 10.50
1. Theaters—Great Britain—Stage-setting and scenery. I. Title. BIP

Theaters—Illinois—Urbana—Construction.

KRANNERT Center 790.2'06'277366
for the Performing Arts.
Krannert Center for the Performing Arts: the concept and the design. [Urbana, Ill., 1969 or 70] 75 p. illus. 31 cm. [NA6813.U6U73 1969] 74-172944
1. Krannert Center for the Performing Arts. 2. Theaters—Illinois—Urbana—Construction.

Theaters—Italy—Stage-setting and scenery—History—Sources.

THE Italian baroque 792'.025'0945
stage : documents / by Giulio Troili ... [et al.] ; translated and with commentary by Dunbar H. Ogden. Berkeley : University of California Press, c1978. xi, 187 p. : facsims. ; 29 cm. Includes bibliographical references and indexes. [PN2091.S8I75] 75-7197 ISBN 0-520-03006-0 : 20.00
1. Theaters—Italy—Stage-setting and scenery—History—Sources. 2. Architecture, Baroque—Italy—History—Sources. 3. Scene painting—Italy—History—Sources. 4. Perspective—Early works to 1800. I. Troili, Giulio, 1613-1685. II. Ogden, Dunbar H.

Theaters—Models.

ALLPORT, Alan. 792'.0292'8
Model theatres, and how to make them / Alan J. Allport. New York : Scribner, 1978. 96 p. : ill. ; 24 cm. Includes index. [PN2091.M6A5] 77-93901 ISBN 0-684-15723-3 : 7.95
1. Theaters—Models. I. Title.

PAYNE, Darwin Reid. 792'.025'0228
Materials and craft of the scenic model / Darwin Reid Payne. Carbondale : Southern Illinois University Press, c1976. xix, 116 p. : ill. ; 19 x 26 cm. Includes index. Bibliography: p. 107-110. [PN2091.M6P37] 76-15230 ISBN 0-8093-0778-2 : 10.00. ISBN 0-8093-0783-9 pbk. : 4.85
1. Theaters—Models. I. Title. BIP

WILLIAMS, Guy R. 792
Making a miniature theatre [by] Guy R. Williams. [1st Amer. ed.] Boston, Plays. [1967] 79p. illus. 26cm. [PN2091.M6W51967] 67-30038 4.95 bds.,
1. Theaters—Models. I. Title.

Theaters—Rome.

HANSON, John Arthur. 725.82
Roman theater-temples. Princeton, N. J., Princeton University Press, 1959. 112p. illus. 31cm. (Princeton monograph in art and archaeology, 33) [NA325.T5H3] 58-13936
1. Theaters—Rome. 2. Tempels, Roman. I. Title. BIP

HANSON, John 725'.822'0937
Arthur.
Roman theater temples / by John Arthur Hanson. Westport, Conn. : Greenwood Press, 1978, c1959. 112 p., [8] leaves of plates : ill. ; 29 cm. Reprint of the ed. published by Princeton University Press, Princeton, N.J., which was issued as no. 33 of Princeton monographs in art and archaeology. Includes index. Bibliography: p. 103-107. [NA325.T5H3 1978] 78-5510 ISBN 0-313-20477-2 lib.bdg. : 21.00 lib.bdg. : 21.00
1. Theaters—Rome. 2. Temples, Roman. I. Title. II. Series: Princeton monographs in art and archaeology ; 33.

Theaters—Russia—Stage-setting and scenery—Exhibitions.

STAGE designs and 792'.025'0947
the Russian avant-garde, 1911-1929 : a loan exhibition of stage and costume designs from the collection of Mr. and Mrs. Nikita D. Lobanov-Rostovsky / introd. and catalogue by John E. Bowlt. Washington : International Exhibitions Foundation, c1976. 84 p. : ill. ; 29 cm. "Circulated by the International Exhibitions Foundation, Washington, D.C. ... 1976-1978." Bibliography: p. 84. [PN2091.S8S69] 76-24947
1. Theaters—Russia—Stage-setting and scenery—Exhibitions. I. Bowlt, John E. II. International Exhibitions Foundations.

Theaters—Spain—Stage-setting and scenery.

SHOEMAKER, William 792'.0946
Hutchinson, 1902-
The multiple stage in Spain during the fifteenth and sixteenth centuries. Westport, Conn., Greenwood Press [1973] xi, 150 p. 22 cm. Reprint of the 1935 ed. Originally presented as the author's thesis, Princeton, 1933. Bibliography: p. 127-136. [PN2087.S7S5 1973] 78-137076 ISBN 0-8371-5539-8 8.50
1. Theaters—Spain—Stage-setting and scenery. 2. Spanish drama—Early to 1500—History and criticism. 3. Spanish drama—Classical period, 1500-1700—History and criticism. I. Title. BIP

Theaters—Stage-setting and scenery.

BAY, Howard. 791
Stage design. New York, Drama Book

Specialists [1974] p. [PN2091.S8B325] 73-15948 ISBN 0-910482-46-2 12.50
1. Theaters—Stage-setting and scenery. 2. Moving-pictures—Setting and scenery. 3. Television—Stage-setting and scenery. I. Title.

BRYSON, Nicholas L. 792'.025
Thermoplastic scenery for theatre, by Nicholas L. Bryson. [1st ed.] New York, Drama Book Specialists/Publishers [1972- v. illus. 28 cm. Contents.Contents.—v. 1. Vacuum forming. [PN2091.S8B69] 72-78908 7.95
1. Theaters—Stage-setting and scenery. 2. Thermoplastics. I. Title.

BUERKI, F. A. 792.02*
Stagecraft for nonprofessionals. [2d ed.] Madison, University of Wisconsin Press, 1955. 131 p. illus. 24 cm. [PN2091.S8B74 1955] 55-9299
1. Theaters—Stage-setting and scenery. 2. Amateur theatricals. I. Title. BIP

BURRIS-MEYER, Harold, 1902- 694
Scenery for the theatre; the organization, processes, materials, and techniques used to set the stage [by] Harold Burris-Meyer and Edward C. Cole. Contributing authors: Nicholas L. Bryson [and others] Rev. ed. Boston, Little, Brown [1971] xix, 518 p. illus. 27 cm. Bibliography: p. 495-499. [PN2091.S8B8 1971] 72-154968 32.00
1. Theaters—Stage-setting and scenery. I. Burrismeyer harold 1902 II. Cole, Edward Cyrus, joint author. III. Title. BIP

CHENEY, Sheldon, 1886- 792'.025
Stage decoration. New York, B. Blom [1966] xxii, 138 p., 127 plates. 26 cm. Reprint of the 1928 ed. [PN2091.S8C5 1966] 66-29421
1. Theaters—Stage-setting and scenery. I. Title. BIP

COREY, Irene. 792'.02
The mask of reality; an approach to design for theatre. Anchorage, Ky., Anchorage Press [1968] 124 p. illus. (part col.) 29 cm. Bibliography: p. 113. [PN2091.S8C627] 71-451
1. Theaters—Stage-setting and scenery. 2. Make-up, Theatrical. 3. Costume. I. Title. BIP

CORRY, Percy. 792.025
Planning the stage. New York, Pitman Pub. Corp. [1961] 148 p. illus. 26 cm. (Theatre and stage series) [PN2091.S8C64] 61-65455
1. Theaters—Stage-setting and scenery. 2. Theaters—Construction. I. Title.

CRAIG, Edward Gordon, 1872-1966. 792'.025
Scene. Forward, introductory poem by John Masefield. New York, B. Blom [1968] xi, 27p., 19 plates. illus., plan. 31cm. Reprint of the 1923 ed. [PN2091.S8C67 1968] 65-20498 12.50
1. Theaters—Stage-setting and scenery. I. Title. BIP

CRAIG, Edward Gordon, 1872-1966. 363.31
Towards a new theatre; forty designs for stage scenes with critical notes by the inventor Edward Gordon Craig. New York, B. Blom, 1969. 89 p. illus. 35 cm. Reprint of the 1913 ed. [PN2091.S8C7 1969] 68-56531
1. Theaters—Stage-setting and scenery. I. Title.

FRIEDERICH, Willard J. 792
Scenery design for the amateur stage [by] Willard J. Friederich [and] John H. Fraser. New York, Macmillan [1950] xvii, 262 p. illus. 22 cm. Bibliography: p. 251-254. [PN2091.S8F7] 50-14785
1. Theaters—Stage-setting and scenery. I. Fraser, John H. joint author. II. Title.

FUERST, Walter Rene. 792'.025
Twentieth-century stage decoration [by] Walter Rene Fuerst and Samuel J. Hume. With introd. by Adolphe Appia. New York, B. Blom [1967] 2 v. in 1. illus. (part col.), plans. 28 cm. "Unabridged and corrected republication of the work originally published...in 1929." Contents.--v. Text.--v. Illustrations. Bibliography: v. 1, p. 167-178. [PN2091.S8F8] 67-28846
1. Theaters—Stage-setting and scenery. I. Hume, Samuel James, 1885- joint author. II. Title.

GALLI da Bibiena, Giuseppe, 1696-1757. 720.945
Architectural and perspective designs dedicated to His Majesty Charles VI, Holy Roman Emperor, by Giuseppe Galli Bibiena. With an introd. by A. Hyatt Mayor. New York, Dover Publications [1964] vi p., 53 plates (incl. plans, port.) 34 cm. "Unaltered, unabridged reprint of original (1740) edition." [NA1123.G32A433] 64-16330
1. Theaters—Stage-setting and scenery. 2. Architecture, Baroque. I. Mayor, Alpheus Hyatt, 1901- II. Title.

GALLI DA BIBIENA, Giuseppe, 1696-1757 720.945
Architectural and perspective designs dedicated to His Majesty Charles VI, Holy Roman Emperor. Introd. by A. Hyatt Mayor [Gloucester, Mass., P. Smith, 1965, c.1964] vi, 53p. (incl. plans, port) 34cm. Unaltered, unabridged reprint of the ed. of 1740 (Dover bk. rebound [NA1123.G32A433] 5.50
1. Theaters—Stage-setting and scenery. 2. Architecture, Baroque. I. Mayor, Alpheus Hyatt, 1901- II. Title. BIP

GILLETTE, Arnold S. 792'.025
An introduction to scenic design [by] A. S. Gillette. New York, Harper & Row [1967] viii, 210 p. illus., plans, 27 cm. Bibliography: p. [205]-206. [PN2091.S8G49] 67-11649
1. Theaters—Stage-setting and scenery. I. Title. II. Title: Scenic design.

JOSEPH, Stephen. 792
New theatre forms. New York, Theatre Arts Books [1968] xvi, 144 p. illus., 10 plates. 22 cm. (Theatre and stage series) Includes bibliographical references. [PN2085.J6 1968b] 68-13407
1. Theaters—Stage-setting and scenery. I. Title.

LOBANOV-ROSTOVSKY, Nikita D. 792'.02'07407
Russian stage and costume designs for the ballet, opera, and theatre; Russian stage and costume designs: a loan exhibition from the Lobanov-Rostovsky, Oenslager and Riabov collections. [Washington? 1967] 63. [1] p. illus. 28cm. "Circulated by the International Exhibitions Foundation, 1967-1969." Bibliography: p. [64] [PN2091.S8R8] 67-7342
1. Theaters—Stage-setting and scenery. 2. Costume. I. Oenslager, Donald, 1902- II. Riabov, George. III. International Exhibitions Foundation. IV. Title.

MOTLEY, pseud. 792'.025
Theatre props / Motley. 1st U.S. ed. New York : Drama Book Specialists/Publishers, 1975. 128 p. : ill. ; 26 cm. Includes index. Bibliography: p. 121. [PN2091.S8M73] 75-6786 ISBN 0-910482-66-7
1. Theaters—Stage-setting and scenery. I. Title. BIP

MOUSSINAC, Leon, 1890-1964. 792'.02
The new movement in the theatre; a survey of recent developments in Europe and America. With an introd. by R. H. Packman and a foreword by Gordon Craig. New York, B. Blom [1967] xi, 23 p. illus. (part col.), 128 plates (part col.) 39 cm. First published in 1931. Bibliography: p. 21-22. [PN2091.S8M76 1967] 65-19619
1. Theaters—Stage-setting and scenery. 2. Costume. I. Title.

NELMS, Henning, 1900- 792'.025
Scene design; a guide to the stage. New York, Sterling Pub. Co. [1970] 96 p. illus., plans. 29 cm. [PN2091.S8N36] 72-115443
1. Theaters—Stage-setting and scenery. I. Title. BIP

NELMS, Henning, 1900- 792'.025
Scene design : a guide to the stage / written and illustrated by Henning Nelms. New York : Dover Publications, 1975, c1970. 96 p. : ill. ; 28 cm. Reprint of the ed. published by Sterling Pub. Co., New York. Includes index. [PN2091.S8N36 1975] 74-25249 ISBN 0-486-23153-4 pbk. : 2.75
1. Theaters—Stage-setting and scenery. I. Title.

OENSLAGER, Donald, 1902- 792.025
Scenery then and now. New York, Russell & Russell [1966, c1936] xiv, 265 p. illus. 25 cm. [PN2091.S804 1966] 66-24741
1. Theaters—Stage-setting and scenery. 2. Theater—History. I. Title.

PARKER, Wilford Oren. 792.025
Scene design and stage lighting [by] W. Oren Parker [and] Harvey K. Smith. New York, Holt, Rinehart and Winston [1963] 376 p. illus. 26 cm. Includes bibliography. [PN2091.S8P3] 63-8109
1. Theaters—Stage-setting and scenery. 2. Stage-lighting. I. Smith, Harvey Kennedy, joint author. II. Title. BIP

PARKER, Wilford Oren. 792'.025
Scene design and stage lighting [by] W. Oren Parker [and] Harvey K. Smith. 2d ed. New York, Holt, Rinehart and Winston [1968] xiv, 496 p. illus. 26 cm. Bibliography: p. 485-489. [PN2091.S8P3 1968] 68-16792
1. Theaters—Stage-setting and scenery. 2. Stage lighting. I. Smith, Harvey Kennedy, joint author. II. Title.

PARKER, Wilford Oren. 792'.025
Scene design and stage lighting [by] W. Oren Parker [and] Harvey K. Smith. 3d ed. New York, Holt, Rinehart and Winston [1974] x, 597 p. illus. 27 cm. Bibliography: p. 578-585. [PN2091.S8P3 1974] 73-22399 ISBN 0-03-089446-8 11.95
1. Theaters—Stage-setting and scenery. 2. Stage lighting. I. Smith, Harvey Kennedy, joint author. II. Title.

PAYNE, Darwin Reid. 792'.025
Design for the stage; first steps. With 117 drawings by the author and 16 photos. Carbondale, Southern Illinois University Press [1974] xx, 265 p. illus. 24 cm. Includes bibliographies. [PN2091.S8P35] 74-3090 ISBN 0-8093-0654-9 15.00
1. Theaters—Stage-setting and scenery. I. Title.
Pbk. 7.95, ISBN 0-8093-0669-7. BIP

PHILIPPI, Herbert. 792
Stagecraft and scene design. [Boston] Houghton Mifflin [1953] 448p. illus. 23cm. [PN2091.S8P48] 53-6010
1. Theaters—Stage-setting and scenery. I. Title. BIP

ROWELL, Kenneth. 792'.025
Stage design. London, Studio Vista; New York, Reinhold [1968] 96p. illus. (pt. col.) 20cm. (Studio Vista/Reinhold art paperback) [PN2091.S8R63] 67-30535 5.50; 2.75 pap.,
1. Theaters—Stage-setting and scenery. I. Title.

SELDEN, Samuel, 1899- 792'.025
Essentials of stage scenery [by] Samuel Selden and Tom Rezzuto. [New York, Appleton-Century-Crofts [1972] xv, 263 p. illus. 27 cm. Based on the first part of Stage scenery and lighting, by S. Selden and H. D. Sellman. Bibliography: p. 257-258. [PN2091.S8S44] 70-182307 ISBN 0-390-79351-5
1. Theaters—Stage-setting and scenery. I. Rezzuto, Tom, joint author. II. Title. BIP

SELDEN, Samuel, 1899- 792'.025
Stage scenery and lighting, by Samuel Selden and Hunton D. Sellman. 3d ed. New York, Appleton-Century-Crofts [1959] 394 p. illus. 24 cm. [PN2091.S8S45 1959] 58-12371
1. Theaters—Stage-setting and scenery. 2. Stage lighting. 3. Scene painting. I. Sellman, Hunton Dade, joint author. II. Title. BIP

SERLIO, Sebastiano, 1475-1552. 792.025
The Renaissance stage: documents of Serlio, Sabbattini and Furttenbach. Translated by Allardyce Nicol, John H. McDowell [and] George R. Kernodle. Edited by Barnard Hewitt. Coral Gables, Fla., University of Miami Press, 1958. ix, 256 p. illus. diagrs., plans. 25 cm. (Books of the theatre series, no. 1) "The present translations grew out of Allardyce Nicoll's seminars in theatre history at Yale in the years 1934-1936." Bibliographical footnotes. [PN2091.S8S48] 58-14141
1. Theaters — Stage-setting and scenery. 2. Theater — Italy — Hist. I. Furtenbach, Joseph, 1591-1667. II. Sabbattini, Nicola, fl. 1638. III. Hewitt, Barnard Wolcott, 1906- ed. IV. Title. V. Series.

SHERINGHAM, George, 1884-1937. 792'.025
Design in the theatre. Commentary by George Sheringham and James Laver, together with literary contributions by E. Gordon Craig, Charles B. Cochran, and Nigel Playfair. New York, B. Blom, 1971. vii, 31 p., [120] p. of illus. 26 cm. Reprint of the 1927 ed. Bibliography: p. 30-31. [PN2091.S8S5 1971] 72-175893
1. Theaters—Stage-setting and scenery. 2. Costume. I. Laver, James, 1899- II. Title. BIP

SIMONSON, Lee, 1888- 792
The art of scenic design; pictorial analysis of stage setting and its relation to theatrical production. New York, Harper [1950] 174 p. illus. (part col.) diagrs., plans. 32 cm. Bibliographical footnotes. [PN2091.S8S525] 50-7282
1. Theaters—Stage-setting and scenery. BIP

SIMONSON, Lee, 1888- 792'.025
The art of scenic design; a pictorial analysis of stage setting and its relation to theatrical production. Westport, Conn., Greenwood Press [1973, c1950] 174 p. illus. 31 cm. Reprint of the ed. published by Harper, New York. Includes bibliographical references. [PN2091.S8S525 1973] 72-6182 ISBN 0-8371-6481-8 21.50
1. Theaters—Stage-setting and scenery. I. Title.

SIMONSON, Lee, 1888- 792
The stage is set / Lee Simonson. Plainview, N.Y. : Books for Libraries Press, 1975 [c1932] p. cm. (Essay index reprint series) Reprint of the ed. published by Harcourt, Brace, New York. Bibliography: p. [PN2091.S8S536 1975] 75-14368 ISBN 0-518-10206-8 : 39.50
1. Theaters—Stage-setting and scenery. 2. Theater. I. Title. BIP

SIMONSON, Lee, 1888- ed. 792'.025
Theatre art, edited and with an introd. by Lee Simonson. Contributions by Allardyce Nicoll [and others] New York, Cooper Square Publishers, 1969 [i.e. 1970] 66 p., [76] p. (chiefly illus.) 26 cm. Reprint of the 1934 ed. [PN2091.S8S54 1970] 74-79205 7.50
1. Theaters—Stage-setting and scenery. 2. Costume. I. Nicoll, Allardyce, 1894- II. Title. BIP

STAHL, LeRoy. 792.02
The simplified stagecraft manual. Minneapolis, T. S. Denison [c1962] 218 p. illus. 22 cm. [PN2091.S8S7] 62-18838
1. Theaters — Stage-setting and scenery. 2. Costume. 3. Make-up, Theatrical. I. Title.

STELL, W. Joseph. 792'.025
The theatre student: scenery [by] W. Joseph Stell. [1st ed.] New York, Richards Rosen Press [1970] 256 p. illus. 29 cm. (The Theatre student series) Bibliography: p. 255-256. [PN2091.S8S73] 70-75264 7.97
1. Theaters—Stage-setting and scenery. I. Title.

WARRE, Michael. 792.025
Designing and making stage scenery. Foreword by Peter Brook. [New York] Reinhold [1966] 104 p. illus. (part col.) plans. 26 cm. Bibliography: p. 99. [PN2091.S8W34] 66-23646
1. Theaters—Stage setting and scenery. I. Title.

WELKER, David Harold. 792'.025
Theatrical set design, the basic techniques [by] David Welker. Boston, Allyn and Bacon [1969] xi, 349 p. illus. 26 cm. [PN2091.S8W38] 69-15463
1. Theaters—Stage-setting and scenery. I. Title. BIP

WILFRED, Thomas, 1889- 792.025
Projected scenery, a technical manual. New York, Drama Bk. Shop, 150 W. 52 St. [c.1965] 59p. illus., plans. 28cm. Bibl. [PN2091.S8W54] 65-21802 5.50, pap., plastic bdg.
1. Theaters—Stage-setting and scenery. I. Title. BIP

Theaters—Stage setting and scenery.

BABLET, Denis. 792.0250924
Edward Gordon Craig. Translated by Daphne Woodward. [New York] Theatre

Arts Books [1966] ix, 207 p. illus., ports. 23 cm. Includes bibliographical references. [PN2091.S8B223 1966a] 66-23134
1. Craig, Edward Gordon, 1872-1966. 2. Theaters—Stage-setting and scenery. BIP

BOYLE, Walden P 792.92
Central and flexible staging; a new theater in the making. Drawings by John H. Jones. Berkeley, University of California Press, 1956. 117p. illus. 15x22cm. [PN2085.B6] 56-5301
1. Theaters—Stage-setting and scenery. 2. Theater—Production and direction. 3. Arena theater. I. Title.

BRUDER, Karl C. 792'.025
The theatre student: properties and dressing the stage [by] Karl C. Bruder. [1st ed.] New York, Richards Rosen Press [1969] 117 p. illus. 29 cm. (The Theatre student series) [PN2091.S8B68] 68-21661 ISBN 8-239-01505- 5.97
1. Theaters—Stage-setting and scenery. I. Title.

CORNBERG, Sol, 1910- 792.92
A stage crew handbook, by Sol Cornberg and Emanuel L. Gebauer. Drawings by Jack Forman. Rev. ed. New York, Harper [c1957] 291p. illus. 22cm. [PN2091.S8C63 1957] 56-11926
1. Theaters—Stage-setting and scenery. I. Gebaner, Emannel Lawrence, 1895- joint author. II. Title. BIP

FUERST, Walter Rene. 792'.025'0904
Twentieth-century stage decoration [by] Walter Rene Fuerst and Samuel J. Hume. With an introd. by Adolphe Appia. New York, Dover Publications [1967] 2 v. illus. (part col.), plans. 27 cm. "Unabridged and corrected republication of the work originally published...in 1929." Contents.--v. 1. Text.--v. 2. Illustrations. Bibliography: v. 1, p. 167-178. [PN2091.S8F8] 65-24021
1. Theaters—Stage-setting and scenery. I. Hume, Samuel James, 1885- joint author. II. Title.

FUERST, Walter Rene. 792'.025
Twentieth-century stage decoration [by] Walter Rene Fuerst and Samuel J. Hume. With an introd. by Adolphe Appia. New York, B. Blom [1967] 2 v. in 1. illus. (part col.), plans. 28 cm. "Unabridged and corrected republication of the work originally published ... in 1929." Contents.Contents.—v. 1. Text.—v. 2. Illustrations. Bibliography: v. 1, p. 167-178. [PN2091.S8F8 1967] 67-28846
1. Theaters—Stage-setting and scenery. I. Hume, Samuel James, 1885- joint author. II. Title.

FUERST, Walter Rene. 792'.025'0904
Twentieth-century stage decoration [by] Walter Rene Fuerst and Samuel J. Hume. With an introd. by Adolphe Appia. New York, Dover Publications [1967] 2 v. illus. (part col.), plans. 27 cm. "Unabridged and corrected republication of the work originally published ... in 1929." Contents.Contents.—v. 1. Text.—v. 2. Illustrations. Bibliography: v. 1, p. 167-178. [PN2091.S8F8 1967b] 65-24021
1. Theaters—Stage setting and scenery. I. Hume, Samuel James, 1885- joint author. II. Title.

GILLETTE, Arnold S. 792'.025
Stage scenery: its construction and rigging [by] A. S. Gillette. 2d ed. New York, Harper & Row [1972] xvi, 429 p. illus. 27 cm. Bibliography: p. 415-416. [PN2091.S8G5 1972] 72-77232 ISBN 0-06-042331-5 9.95
1. Theaters—Stage-setting and scenery. I. Title.

HAINAUX, Rene. 792'.025'09047
Stage design throughout the world, 1970-75 / Rene Hainaux. New York : Theatre Arts Books, 1976. 158 p. : ill. (some col.) ; 31 cm. Captions in English and French. Includes indexes. Bibliography: p. 158. [PN2091.S8H22] 75-7879 ISBN 0-87830-133-X : 42.95
1. Theaters—Stage-setting and scenery. 2. Theater—Pictorial works. I. Title. BIP

HAINAUX, Rene. 792'.025'09047
Stage design throughout the world, 1970-75 / [edited by] Rene Hainaux ; [translated from the French by Michael Nash]. London : Harrap, 1976. 159 p. (2 fold.) : chiefly ill. (some col.), plans ; 31 cm. Captions in English and French. Includes indexes. Bibliography: p. 158. [PN2091.S8H22 1976] 77-350299 ISBN 0-245-52946-2 : £20.00
1. Theaters—Stage-setting and scenery. 2. Theater—Pictorial works. I. Title.

HAINAUX, Rene, comp. 792'.025
Stage design throughout the world since 1960. Text and illus. collected by the national centres of the International Theatre Institute. Chosen and presented by Rene Hainaux, with the collaboration of Yves-Bonnat. Foreword by Paul-Louis Mignon. New York, Theatre Arts Books [1973, c1972] 239 p. (chiefly illus. (part col.)) 31 cm. Bibliography: p. 227-230. [PN2091.S8H23 1973] 72-87117 ISBN 0-87830-129-1 39.95
1. Theaters—Stage-setting and scenery. 2. Theater—Pictorial works. I. Bonnat, Yves, joint comp. II. International Theatre Institute. III. Title. BIP

HAKE, Herbert V 792.0250924
Here's how! A basic stagecraft book. Illustrated by the author. Rev. ed. Evanston, Ill., Row, Peterson, 1958. 128p. illus. 32cm. Bibliography: p.125. [PN2091.S8H] A 58
1. Theaters— Stage-setting and scenery. I. Title.

INTERNATIONAL Theatre Institute. 792.0250924
Stage design throughout the world since 1935, Texts and illus. collected by the national centres of the International Theatre Institute; chosen and presented by Rene Hainaux with the technical advice of Yves-Bonnat, A sketch to serve as foreword by Jean Cocteau; pref, by Kenneth Rae. New York, Theatre Arts Books [1956] 219p. illus. (part col.) 31cm. (Its Publications) [PN2091.S] A58
1. Theaters—Stage setting and scenery. 2. Theater—Pictorial works. I. Hainaux, Roud, ed. II. Title.

INTERNATIONAL Theatre Institute. 792.025
Stage design throughout the world since 1950. Texts and illus. collected by the national centres of the International Theatre Institute, chosen and presented by Rene Hainaux, with the technical advice of Yves-Bonnat. Foreword by Paul-Louis Mignon. New York, Theatre Arts Books [1964] 276 p. (chiefly illus. (part col.)) 31 cm. (Its Publications) [PN2091.S8I53] 63-20345
1. Theaters — Stage-setting and scenery. 2. Theater — Pictorial works. I. Hainaux, Rene, ed. II. Title. BIP

KENTON, Warren 792.025
Stage properties and how to make them. London, I. Pitman [New Rochelle, N.Y., SportShelf, 1966, c.1964] vii, 119p. illus. 23cm. (Theatre and stage ser.) [PN2091.S8K4] 66-38203 6.75
1. Theaters—Stage-setting and scenery. I. Title. BIP

KENTON, Warren. 792'.025
Stage properties and how to make them. New York, Drama Book Specialists, [1974, c1964] vii, 119 p. illus. 23 cm. Reprint of the ed. published by Pitman, London, in series: Theatre and stage series. [PN2091.S8K4 1974] 74-8065 ISBN 0-910482-53-5
1. Theaters—Stage-setting and scenery. I. Title.

LAMBOURNE, Norah. 792.025
Staging the play. [New York] Studio Publications [1956] 95p. illus. 26cm. (The How to do it series, 62) Includes bibliographies. [PN2091.S8L27] 56-14210
1. ttheaters—Stage setting and scienery. I. Title.

LARSON, Orville Kurth, 1914- ed. 792'.025
Scene design for stage and screen : readings on the aesthetics and methodology of scene design for drama, opera, musical comedy, ballet, motion pictures, television, and arena theatre / edited and introduced by Orville K. Larson. Westport, Conn. : Greenwood Press, 1976, c1961. xviii, 334 p. : ill. ; 23 cm. Reprint of the ed. published by Michigan State University Press, East Lansing. [PN2091.S8L29 1976] 76-10460 ISBN 0-8371-8320-0 lib. bdg. : 19.75
1. Theaters—Stage-setting and scenery. I. Title. BIP

MORGAN, Harry, 1937- 792'.025
Perspective drawing for the theatre / Harry Morgan. New York : Drama Book Specialists, [1978] p. cm. Bibliography: p. [PN2091.S8M698] 78-21075 ISBN 0-910482-87-X : 12.50
1. Theaters—Stage-setting and scenery. 2. Drawing—Technique. 3. Perspective. I. Title. BIP

PECKTAL, Lynn. 792'.025
Designing and painting for the theatre / by Lynn Pecktal. New York : Holt, Rinehart and Winston, [1975] p. cm. Includes index. [PN2091.S8P37] 74-31271 ISBN 0-03-012276-7 : 15.95
1. Theaters—Stage-setting and scenery. I. Title. BIP

RISSER, Arthur C. 792.0250924
A theatre in a multi-purpose room. Wichita, Kan., c1962. xii, 64 l. illus., plans. 28 cm. Bibliography: leaves 59-60. [PN2091.S8R5] 62-44883
1. Theaters — Stage-setting and scenery. 2. Schools — Furniture, equipment, etc. I. Title.

TEXAS. University. Humanities Research Center. 792.025
An exhibition of designs for the theatre by Eugene Berman. [Austin] Research Center, University of Texas, 1960. unpaged. illus. 25 cm. [ND2885.T4] 60-63789
1. Berman, Eugene, 1899- 2. Theaters — Stage-setting and scenery. I. Title.

Theaters—Stage-setting and scenery—Bibliography.

STODDARD, Richard. 016.792'025
Stage scenery, machinery, and lighting : a guide to information sources / Richard Stoddard. Detroit : Gale Research Co., c1977. xi, 274 p. ; 23 cm. (Performing arts information guide series ; v. 2) (Gale information guide library) Includes indexes. [Z5784.S8S79] [PN2091.S8] 76-13574 ISBN 0-8103-1374-X : 18.00
1. Theaters—Stage-setting and scenery—Bibliography. 2. Stage machinery—Bibliography. 3. Stage lighting—Bibliography. I. Title. BIP

Theaters—Stage-setting and scenery. Costume.

MOUSSINAC, Leon, 1890- 792/.02
The new movement in the theatre; a survey of recent developments in Europe and America. Introd. by R. H. Packman; foreword by Gordon Craig. New York, Blom [1967] xi, 23p. illus. (pt. col.) 128 plates (pt. col.) 39cm. First pub in 1931. Bibl. [PN2091.S8.M76 1967] 65-19619 35.00
1. Theaters—Stage-setting and scenery. Costume. I. Title. BIP

Theaters—Stage-setting and scenery—Exhibitions.

MONTEVERDI, Mario. 792'.025'094521
La Scala: 400 years of stage design from the Museo teatrale alla Scala, Milan. Catalogue and introd. by Mario Monteverdi. [Washington, International Exhibitions Foundation, 1971] 91 p. (p. 33-91 illus.) 22 x 26 cm. Catalogue of an exhibition circulated by the International Exhibitions Foundation, 1970-71. Participating museums: National Gallery of Art, Washington, D. C., and others. [PN2091.S8M67] 74-174710
1. Theaters—Stage-setting and scenery—Exhibitions. I. International Exhibitions Foundation. II. U.S. National Gallery of Art. III. Title.

OENSLAGER, Donald, 1902- 743'.9'9792025
Four centuries of scenic invention : drawings from the collection of Donald Oenslager / introd. and catalogue by Donald Oenslager. [Washington?] : International Exhibitions Foundation, 1974. 187 p. : ill. ; 22 x 26 cm. [PN2091.S8O35] 74-21958
1. Theaters—Stage-setting and scenery—Exhibitions. I. International Exhibitions Foundation. II. Title.

PHILADELPHIA College of Art. 792'.025
Artists' sets and costumes : recent collaborations between painters and sculptors and dance, opera, and theater : [exhibition], Philadelphia College of Art, October 31-December 17, 1977. [Philadelphia] : The College, [1977] 49 p. : ill. (some col.) ; 26 cm. [PN2091.S8P48 1977] 77-92371
1. Theaters—Stage-setting and scenery—Exhibitions. 2. Costume—Exhibitions. 3. Group work in art—Exhibitions. I. Title.

SCHOLZ, Janos. 741.9'4'074019454
XVIII and XIX century stage designs from the Mayr-Fajt collection. New York, Seiferheld [1962] [47] p. illus. 22 cm. ([Seiferheld Gallery] Catalogue no. 5) Catalog for the exhibition, Seiferheld Gallery, April, 1962; University of Michigan Museum of Art, summer, 1962; Princeton University Art Museum, October, 1962. Bibliography: p. [27] [NC15.N56] 67-9828
1. Theaters—Stage-setting and scenery—Exhibitions. 2. Drawings—Private collections. I. Seiferheld Gallery. II. Michigan. University. Museum of Art. III. Princeton University. Art Museum. IV. Title.

Theaters—Stage-setting and scenery—History.

OENSLAGER, Donald, 1902- 792'.025'09
Stage design : four centuries of scenic invention / Donald Oenslager ; illustrated with drawings for the theatre from his collection. New York : Viking Press, 1975. 303 p. : ill. (some col.) ; 31 cm. (A Studio book) Includes index. Bibliography: p. 291-296. [PN2091.S8O45] 74-6999 ISBN 0-670-66679-3 : 25.00
1. Theaters—Stage-setting and scenery—History. I. Title.

RUSSELL, Douglas A. 792'.025
Theatrical style : a visual approach to the theatre / Douglas A. Russell. 1st ed. Palo Alto, Calif. : Mayfield Pub. Co., 1976. ix, 237 p. : ill. ; 23 cm. Includes index. Bibliography: p. 221-228. [PN2091.S8R77] 75-21072 ISBN 0-87484-226-3 : 7.95
1. Theaters—Stage-setting and scenery—History. I. Title. BIP

Theaters—Stage-setting and scenery—Illustrations.

COOPER, Douglas, 1911- 760'.0924
Picasso theatre. New York, H. N. Abrams [1968] 360 p. illus. (part col.), facsims. 30 cm. Includes facsims. of MS. letters, etc. of Picasso, E. Satie, and J. Cocteau. Bibliography: p. 359-360. [ND2885.C6413] 68-18127
1. Picasso, Pablo, 1881- 2. Theaters—Stage-setting and scenery—Illustrations. I. Title.

GALLIARI, Gaspare, 1761-1823. 792'.025
Numero XXIV invenzioni teatrali. Introd. by Denise Addis. New York, B. Blom, 1970. 10 p., 24 plates. 27 x 33 cm. Galliari's stage designs were first documented in 1803 by engravings, by various artists. [PN2091.S8G35 1970] 68-21215
1. Theaters—Stage-setting and scenery—Illustrations. I. Addis, Denise. II. Title. III. Title: Invenzioni teatrali.

JONES, Robert Edmond, 1887-1954. 741.9'73
Drawings for the theatre. [2d ed.] New York, Theatre Arts Books [1970] 24 p. 35 plates. 29 cm. "Introduction to the second edition [by Donald Oenslager]": p. 9-21. [PN2091.S8J6 1970] 78-85670 13.50
1. Theaters—Stage-setting and scenery—Illustrations. I. Oenslager, Donald, 1902- II. Title. BIP

PIPER, John, 1903- 759.2
Paintings, drawings & theatre designs, 1932-1954. Arr. and with an introd. by S. John Woods. New York, C. Valentin, 1955. 160p. 242 illus. (part col.) port.

SUBJECT INDEX THEOTOCOPULI, DOMINICO, CALLED

33cm. Books and articles by or illustrated by John Piper: p. 156-157. Bibliography: p. 158. [ND497.P] A56
I. Woods, Sydney John, 1915- II. Title.

Theaters—Stage-setting and scenery—Juvenile literature.

YERIAN, Cameron John. 792'.025
Stages, scenery, & props / Cameron and Margaret Yerian, editors. Chicago : Childrens Press, [1975] 46 p. : col. ill. ; 25 cm. "Fun time." Includes index. Illustrated instructions for making scenery and props and using them effectively in theatrical productions. [PN2091.S8Y4 1975] 74-31148 lib.bdg. : 5.25
1. Theaters—Stage-setting and scenery—Juvenile literature. I. Yerian, Margaret, joint author. II. Title.

Theaters—Sweden.

BEIJER, Agne. 725'.822
Court theatres of Drottningholm and Gripsholm. New York, B. Blom, 1972. 39, [126] p. of illus. 31 cm. Translation of Slottsteatrarna pa Drottningholm och Gripsholm. [NA6840.S9B412 1972] 77-180032
1. Theaters—Sweden. 2. Theaters—Decoration. 3. Theaters—Stage-setting and scenery. I. Title. BIP

Theaters—United States—Construction.

AMERICAN Theatre Planning Board. 725'.822
Theatre check list; a guide to the planning and construction of proscenium and open stage theatres. Prepared by and published for the American Theatre Planning Board. With drawings by Ming Cho Lee. [1st ed.] Middletown, Conn., Wesleyan University Press [1969] 71 p. illus. 23 x 27 cm. [NA6830.A7] 69-19619 3.95
1. Theaters—United States—Construction. I. Title. BIP

MCNAMARA, Brooks. 725'.822
The American playhouse in the eighteenth century. Cambridge, Mass., Harvard University Press, 1969. xviii, 174 p. illus. (part col.), map. 21 cm. Bibliographical references included in "Notes" (p. 157-170) [NA6830.M3] 68-54021 9.95
1. Theaters—United States—Construction. 2. Theater—United States—History. I. Title. BIP

THEATRE design 75 725'.822'0973
: a project of the Theatre Architecture Commission / edited by Peter H. Frink. New York : United States Institute for Theatre Technology, c1975. 79 p. : ill. ; 26 cm. "Drawings and photos ... reproduced from the display panels which were shown at the national conference of the United States Institute for Theatre Technology ... Anaheim, California, March 1975." [NA6830.T43] 76-355778
1. Theaters—United States—Construction. I. United States. Institute for Theatre Technology. II. Frink, Peter H. III. Theatre Architecture Commission.

Theaters—United States—History.

YOUNG, William C., 1928- 792'.0973
Famous American playhouses, 1716-1899 [by] William C. Young. Chicago, American Library Association, 1973. xxii, 327 p. illus. 26 cm. (His Documents of American theater history, v. 1) Bibliography: p. 313-316. [NA6830.Y67] 72-9837 ISBN 0-8389-0136-0
1. Theaters—United States—History. 2. Theater—United States—History. I. Title.
Part of a 2 volume set sold for 50.00.

YOUNG, William C., 1928- 792'.0973
Famous American playhouses, 1900-1971 [by] William C. Young. Chicago, American Library Association, 1973. xii, 297 p. illus. 27 cm. (His Documents of American theater history, v. 2) Bibliography: p. 285-286. [NA6830.Y68] 73-657 ISBN 0-8389-0137-9 25.00
1. Theaters—United States—History. 2. Theater—United States—History. I. Title.

Theaters—United States—Stage-setting and scenery.

MCNAMARA, Brooks 792
Theatres, spaces, environments : 18 projects / Brooks McNamara, Jerry Rojo, Richard Schechner. New York : Drama Book Specialists, [1975, i.e.1976] p. cm. [PN2091.S8M24] 75-29018 ISBN 0-910482-63-2 : 18.50
1. Theaters—United States—Stage-setting and scenery. 2. Theaters—United States—Construction. I. Title. BIP

Theatrical posters, American.

LEDGER Job Office. 769'.5
Specimens of show printing; being facsimiles in miniature of poster cuts, comprising colored and plain designs. [Hollywood, Calif., Cherokee Books, 1966] 264, 500-519 p. (chiefly illus.) 29 cm. Cover title: Early American theatrical posters. Reprint of the work originally published in 1869, by the Ledger Job Office, Philadelphia. [PN2226.L4 1966] 79-241171
1. Theatrical posters, American. I. Title. II. Title: Early American theatrical posters.

Theatrical posters, French.

†100 years of 769'.4'979270944361
posters of the Folies Bergere and music halls of Paris / compiled by Alain Weill. New York : Images Graphiques, c1977. 112 p. : chiefly ill. (some col.) ; 41 cm. (Poster art library) Bibliography: p. 5. [ML1727.8.P2O58] 77-75348 ISBN 0-89545-002-X : 19.95 ISBN 0-89545-001-1 pbk. : 8.95
1. Paris. Folies-Bergere. 2. Theatrical posters, French. I. Weill, Alain, 1946-

Thebes, Egypt.

THE Akhenaten Temple 932'.01
Project. Warminster, Eng. : Aris & Phillips ; Forest Grove, Ore. : Distributed by International Scholarly Book Services, c1976- v. : ill. ; 31 cm. At head of title: University Museum. University of Pennsylvania. "Founder; project director 1965-1972: Ray Winfield Smith. Project director since 1972: Donald B. Redford." Includes indexes. Contents.Contents.—v. 1. Smith, R. W. and Redford, D. B. Initial discoveries. Bibliography: v. 1, p. 159-170. [DT73.T3A37] 77-378471 ISBN 0-85668-034-6 (v. 1) : 35.00
1. Amenhetep IV, King of Egypt, 1388-1358 B.C. 2. Thebes, Egypt. I. Smith, Ray Winfield. II. Redford, Donald B. III. Pennsylvania. University. University Museum.

KAMIL, Jill. 932
Luxor : a guide to ancient Thebes / Jill Kamil ; photos. by Alistair Duncan and George Allen ; plans by Hassan Ibrahim. 2d ed. London ; New York : Longman, 1976, c1973. p. cm. [DT73.T3K35 1976] 75-42256 ISBN 0-582-78065-9 pbk. : 4.50
1. Thebes, Egypt. I. Title. BIP

KAMIL, Jill. 913.32
Luxor: a guide to ancient Thebes; photographs by Alistair Duncan and George Allen, plans by Hassan Ibrahim. [London] Longman, 1973. 175 p. illus., maps (incl. 1 col.), plans. 19 cm. [DT73.T3K35] 74-176416 ISBN 0-582-78028-4
1. Thebes, Egypt. I. Title.
Distributed by Longman, New York, 3.00 (pbk.)

Thebes, Egypt — Antiq.

THOMAS, Elizabeth, 1909-. 913.32031
The royal necropolis of Thebes. Princeton, [N.J.] 1966. xii, 298 p. illus., maps. 44 cm. 90 copies. Includes bibliographies. [NA216.T48T48] 67-88
1. Thebes, Egypt — Antiq. 2. Temples — Egypt — Thebes. I. Title.

Thebes, Egypt—Tombs.

DAVIES, Norman de Garis, 1865-1941. 913.32'03'1
The tomb of Ken-Amun at Thebes. With plates in color by Norman de Garis Davies, H. R. Hopgood, and Nina de Garis Davies. New York, 1930. [New York] Arno Press, 1973. 2 v. in 1. illus. 32 cm. Reprint of the ed. published by the Museum, which was issued as v. 5 of the Publications of the Metropolitan Museum of Art Egyptian Expedition. At head of title: The Metropolitan Museum of Art Egyptian Expedition. All the plates in this reprint are in black and white. Includes bibliographical references. [DT73.T3D29 1973] 78-168401 ISBN 0-405-02235-2 39.00
1. Ken-Amun. 2. Thebes, Egypt—Tombs. I. Title. II. Series: New York (City). Metropolitan Museum of Art. Egyptian Expedition. Publications, v. 5.

DAVIES, Norman de Garis, 1865-1941. 913.32'03'1
The tomb of Nefer-hotep at Thebes, by Norman de Garis Davies. With plates in color by Nina de Garis Davies. New York, 1933. [New York] Arno Press, 1973. 2 v. in 1. illus., 68 plates. 31 cm. At head of title: The Metropolitan Museum of Art Egyptian Expedition. Plates in reprint ed. are in black and white. Reprint of the ed. which was issued as v. 9 of the Publications of the Metropolitan Museum of Art Egyptian Expedition. Includes bibliographical references. [DT73.T3D316 1973] 71-168402 39.00
1. Nefer-hotep. 2. Thebes, Egypt—Tombs. I. Davies, Nina M. (Cummings) illus. II. New York (City). Metropolitan Museum of Art. Egyptian Expedition. III. Title. IV. Series: New York (City). Metropolitan Museum of Art. Egyptian Expedition. Publications, v. 9. BIP

DAVIES, Norman de Garis, 1865-1941. 913.32
The tomb of Rekh-mi-Re' at Thebes. New York, 1943. [New York] Arno Press, 1973 [c1944] 2 v. in 1. (ix, 118 p. 122 plates) 32 cm. Reprint of the ed. published as vol. 11 of Publications of the Metropolitan Museum of Art, Egyptian Expedition. At head of title: The Metropolitan Museum of Art, Egyptian Expedition. Bibliography: p. 107-109. [DT73.T3D32 1973] 75-168403 ISBN 0-405-02267-0
1. Rekhmara, Vizir of Upper Egypt, ca. B.C. 1471-1448. 2. Thebes, Egypt—Tombs. 3. Mural painting and decoration, Egyptian—Thebes. I. Title. II. Series: New York (City). Metropolitan Museum of Art. Egyptian Expedition. Publications, v. 11. BIP

WINLOCK, Herbert Eustis, 1884-1950. 913.32'03'1
The tomb of Queen Meryet-Amun at Thebes. Photos. by Harry Burton. Plans by Walter Hauser and catalogue by Charlotte R. Clark. New York, 1932. [New York] Arno Press, 1973. xi, 96 p., 46 plates. illus. 32 cm. Reprint of the ed. published by the Museum, which was issued as v. 6 of the Publications of the Metropolitan Museum of Art Egyptian Expedition. At head of title: The Metropolitan Museum of Art Egyptian Expedition. Includes bibliographical references. [DT73.T3W5 1973] 70-168415 ISBN 0-405-02253-0
1. Meryet-Amun, Queen, consort of Amenhctep II, King of Egypt. 2. Thebes, Egypt—Tombs. I. Title. II. Series: New York (City). Metropolitan Museum of Art. Egyptian Expedition. Publications, v. 6.

TheCraftsman—Illustrations.

THE Craftsman : 700
an anthology / edited by Barry Sanders. Santa Barbara, Calif. : Peregrine Smith, 1978. xvi, 328 p. : ill. ; 28 cm. A collection of articles, photos, and drawings from the Craftsman. [NK1141.C7] 78-15909 ISBN 0-87905-029-2 pbk. : 9.95
1. TheCraftsman—Illustrations. 2. Art industries and trade—United States. 3. Arts and crafts movement. I. Sanders, Barry. II. The Craftsman. BIP

Theodore Roosevelt National Memorial Park.

U.S. Office of Archeology and Historic Preservation. Division of History. 747.2784
Furnishing plan for a Badlands ranch house, Theodore Roosevelt National Memorial Park, North Dakota. [Washington] 1969. vi, 75 l. illus. 26 cm. Bibliography: leaves 72-75. [F642.T5A55] 70-608873
1. Theodore Roosevelt National Memorial Park. 2. Ranch life—North Dakota. I. Title.

Theomin Gallery.

BORRIE, John. 919.315'7
Olveston. Dunedin, Theomin Gallery [Management Committee, 1968] 23 p. illus. (part col.), ports. 22 cm. "Reprinted 1969." [N3978.4.B6] 72-195345
1. Theomin Gallery. I. Theomin Gallery. Management Committee. II. Title.

Theotocopuli, Domenico, called El Greco, d.1614.

ANDRES, Stefan Paul, 1906- 759.6
El Greco malt den Grossinquisitor [von] Stefan Andres. Edited by Richard C. Clark, Ilse Reiling. Englewood Cliffs, N. J., Prentice [1968] 70p. 21cm. (Prentice German ser.) [ND813.T4A74] 67-27065 1.75 pap.,
1. Theotocopuli, Dominico, called El Greco, d. 1614. I. Clark, Richard C. ed. II. Reiling, Ilse. ed. III. Title.

BYRON, Robert, 1905-1941. 759.9'4
The birth of Western painting; a history of colour, form, and iconography, illustrated from the paintings of Mistra and Mount Athos, of Giotto and Duccio, and El Greco, by Robert Byron and David Talbot Rice. New York, Hacker Art Books, 1968. xvi, 236 p. 94 plates. 29 cm. Reprint of the 1930 ed. Bibliography: p. 220-226. [ND53.B9 1968] 68-9002
1. Theotocopuli, Dominico, called El Greco, d. 1614. 2. Painting, Byzantine. 3. Christian art and symbolism. 4. Mural painting and decoration, Byzantine. 5. Paintings—Athos, Mount. 6. Paintings—Mistra, Greece. I. Rice, David Talbot, 1903- joint author. II. Title.

DIEHL, Gaston. 759.6
El Greco. Translated from the French by Anne Ross. New York, Crown Publishers [1967] 46 p. illus. (part col.) 19 cm. (Basic art library) [ND813.T4D53] 68-506
1. Theotocopuli, Dominico, called El Greco, d. 1614.

GUDIOL i Ricart, Josep. 759.6
Domenikos Theotokopoulos, El Greco, 1541-1614, by Jose Gudiol. Translated from the Spanish by Kenneth Lyons. New York, Viking Press, 1973. 374 p. illus. (part col.) 30 cm. Bibliography: p. 361-364. [ND813.T4G7813] 73-381 38.50
1. Theotocopuli, Domenico, called El Greco, d. 1614.

KELEMEN, Pal. 759.6
El Greco revisted: Candia, Venice, Toledo. New York, Macmillan, 1961. xii, 176 p. plates, maps (on lining papers) 30 cm. Bibliography: p. 162-171. [ND813.T4K44] 61-13343
1. Theotocopuli, Dominico, called El Greco, d. 1614. I. Title.

PRESTON, Stuart. 927.5
El Greco. 46 reproductions, including 12 in full color. [1st ed.] New York, Beechhurst Press [1953] 61. [2]p. illus. (part col.) 36cm. Bibliography: p. [63] [ND813.T4P7] 53-13337
1. Theotocopuli, Dominico, called El Greco, d. 1614. I. Title.

PUPPI, Lionello. 759.6
El Greco. [Tr. from Italian by Eva Pirie. 1st Amer. ed.] New York, Grosset [1967] 39, [78]p. illus. (pt. col.) 18cm.E(New Grosset art lib., 5) On cover: El Greco: the life and work of the artist. [ND813.T4P83 1967] 67-25789 1.25 pap.,

1. Theotocopuli, Dominico, called El Greco. d. 1614. I. Title.

THEOTOCOPULI, Dominico, called El Greco, d.1614. 759.6
El Greco: the expressionism of his final years. Text, by Enrique Lafuente Ferrari. Appendix by Jose Manuel Pita Andrade. Translated by Robert Erich Wolf. New York, H.N. Abrams [1975, c1969] 169 p. illus. (part col.), 50 col. plates. 41 cm. Translation of Il Greco di Toledo e il suo espressionismo estremo. Bibliography: p. 163-164. [ND813.T4L2713 1975] 72-6411 ISBN 0-8109-0101-3
I. Theotocopuli, Dominico, called El Greco, d. 1614. II. Lafuente Ferrari, Enrique. III. Pita Andrade, Jose Manuel. IV. Title.

THEOTOCOPULI, Dominico, called El Greco, d.1614. 759.6
El Greco (Domenicos Theotocopoulos) Text by Leo Bronstein. 1st ed. New York, H. N. Abrams, 1950. 126 p. illus., col. plates. 34 cm. (The Library of great painters) [ND813.T4B7] 50-12757
I. Bronstein, Leo.

THEOTOCOPULI, Dominico, called El Greco, d.1614. 759.6
El Greco (Domenicos Theotocopoulos) Text by John F. Matthews. New York, H. N. Abrams [1970] 24 p. illus. (part col.) 33 cm. (The Library of great painters. Portfolio ed.) [ND813.T4M1492 1970] 69-14749
I. Matthews, John F., 1918-

THEOTOCOPULI, Dominico, called El Greco, d. 1614 759.6
El Greco, by Andre Leclerc. New York, Crown [1965] 36p. (chiefly illus. (pt. col.) 18cm. (Little bks. on great artists) Biographical sketch in French, English, and German. [ND813.T4L38] 65-3291 .69 pap.,
I. Leclerc, Andre. II. Title.

VALLENTIN, Antonina, 1893-1957. 927.5
El Greco; translated from the French by Andrew Revai and Robin Chancellor. [1st American ed.] Garden City, N. Y., Doubleday, 1955 [c1954] 316 p. plates. 25 cm. Bibliography: p. [297]-301. Bibliographical footnotes. [ND813.T4V355 1955] 55-7010
1. Theotocopuli, Dominico, called El Greco, d. 1614.

WENTINCK, Charles 759.6
El Greco [Tr.: Albert J. Fransella] New York, Barnes & Noble [1964, c.1963] 89p. illus. (pt. col.) ports. 18cm. (Barnes & Noble art ser., no. 616) 64-1800 .75 pap.,
1. Theotocopuli, Dominico, called El Greco, d. 1614. I. Title.

WETHEY, Harold Edwin. 759.6
El Greco and his school. Princeton, N.J., Princeton University Press, 1962. 2 v. plates. 29 cm. Contents.1. Text and plates. -- 2. Catalogue raisonne. Includes bibliographical references. [ND813.T4W4] 61-7427
1. Theotocopull, Dominico, called El Greco, d. 1614. 2. Artists, Italian. I. Title.

Thermoplastics.

JACQUEZ, Albert F 1895- 764.8
Thermo-plastic painting. [Chicago? 1960] 98p. illus. 23cm. [TT273.J3] 60-16835
1. Thermoplastics. 2. Screen process printing. I. Title.

Theus, Jeremiah, 1719 (ca.)-1774.

JEREMIAH Theus, 759.13
colonial artist of Charles Town. Columbia, University of South Carolina Press, 1953. xviii, 218p. 51 ports. 23cm. 'A contribution of the National Society of the Colonial Dames of America in the State of South Carolina.' Bibliography: p. 187- 189. [ND237.T53M5] 927.5 53-13304
1. Theus, Jeremiah, 1719 (ca.)-1774. I. Middleton, Margaret Simons.

Thiebaud, Wayne.

COPLANS, John. 759.13
Wayne Thiebaud. [Pasadena? Calif., Pasadena Art Museum, 1968] 66 p. illus. (part col.) 24 cm. "Sponsored by the Art Alliance of Pasadena Art Museum, in collaboration with Walker Art Center, Minneapolis [and other museums]" "Catalogue of the exhibition": p. 56-62. Bibliography: p. 45-54. [ND237.T5515C6] 68-21588
1. Thiebaud, Wayne. I. Pasadena, Calif. Art Museum. Art Alliance.

THIEBAUD, Wayne. 759.13
Recent works. [Exhibition] E. B. Crocker Art Gallery, Sacramento, California, January 9, February 8, 1970. [Sacramento, Printed by Cal-Central Press, 1970?] [22] p. illus., port. 23 cm. [ND237.T5515A54] 72-17721
I. Crocker Art Gallery, Sacramento, Calif. II. Title.

THIEBAUD, Wayne. 769'.924
Wayne Thiebaud; graphics, 1964-1971. New York, Parasol Press [1971] [40] p. (chiefly illus. (part col.)) 31 cm. Catalogue of an exhibition organized by Parasol Press. "Participating museums:Whitney Museum of American Art, New York [and others]" [NE539.T5A57] 73-162830
I. Parasol Press. II. Whitney Museum of American Art, New York.

Thimbles.

HOLMES, Edwin F. 646.1'9
Thimbles / [by] Edwin F. Holmes. Dublin : Gill and Macmillan, 1976. [9], 150 p. : ill. (some col.) ; 25 cm. Includes index. Bibliography: p. 146. [NK9505.7.H64] 76-381724 ISBN 0-7171-0762-0 : £13.00
1. Thimbles. I. Title.

Thimbles—Collectors and collecting.

RATH, Jo Anne, 1947- 646.1'9
Antique and unusual thimbles / Jo Anne Rath. South Brunswick, [N.J.] : A. S. Barnes, c1978. p. cm. Includes index. Bibliography: p. [NK9505.7.R37 1978] 76-57474 ISBN 0-498-02065-7 : 15.00
1. Thimbles—Collectors and collecting. I. Title.

Thollander, Earl.

THOLLANDER, Earl. 741.9'73
Barns of California : a collection / by Earl Thollander. 1st ed. San Francisco : California Historical Society, [1974] ca. 150 p. : ill. ; 32 cm. [NC139.T47A42] 74-78099 15.95
1. Thollander, Earl. 2. Barns—California—Pictorial works. 3. Barns in art. I. Title. BIP

Thomas a Becket, Saint, Abp. of Canterbury, 1118?-1170—Art.

BORENIUS, Tancred, 1885-1948. 704.948'6
St. Thomas Becket in art. Port Washington, N.Y., Kennikat Press [1970] xix, 122 p. illus. 24 cm. Reprint of the 1932 ed. Bibliography: p. 115-116. [N8080.B6 1970] 70-102835
1. Thomas a Becket, Saint, Abp. of Canterbury, 1118?-1170—Art. I. Title.

Thomas, Hylton, 1912-1969—Art collections.

MINNESOTA. University. University Gallery. 708.1'76'579
The Hylton A. Thomas Collection; paintings, drawings, prints, furniture and decorative arts objects bequeathed to the University Gallery, University of Minnesota. [Prepared by Charles Helsell] Minneapolis [1971] 69 p. illus. 21 x 21 cm. Catalog of an exhibition held April 1 through May 16, 1971, University Gallery, University of Minnesota. Errata slip inserted. [N5220.T48M5] 74-198471
1. Thomas, Hylton, 1912-1969—Art collections. 2. Art—Exhibitions. I. Helsell, Charles. II. Title.

Thompson, Dorothy, 1894-1961—Manuscripts.

SYRACUSE University. Library. Manuscript Collections. 016.813*5
Dorothy Thompson, an inventory of her papers in Syracuse University Library. Compiled by Stephanie Leon [and] Susan D'Angelo. With introd. by Lisa Sergio. Syracuse, N.Y., 1966. xiii, 144 p. front. 28 cm. (Its Manuscript inventory series. Inventory no. 9) [Z] [Z6621.S9943 no. 9] 72-184008
1. Thompson, Dorothy, 1894-1961—Manuscripts. I. Leon, Stephanie. II. D'Angelo, Susan. III. Title. IV. Series: Syracuse University. Library. Manuscript Collections. Manuscript register series, register no. 9.

Thompson (J. Walter) Company.

ADVERTISING age. v. 12
The centennial of the J. Walter Thompson Company; commemorating 100 years of American advertising. Chicago, Advertising Publications, c1964. 202 p. Published as the December 7, 1964 (v. 35, no. 49, section 2 issue of the Advertising age) [NUC66-69160]
1. Thompson (J. Walter) Company. I. Title.

Thompson, James Harrison Wilson, b. 1906—Art collections.

BRAKE, Brian. 709.5'9
The house on the klong; the Bangkok home and Asian art collection of James Thompson. Photos.: Brian Brake. Text: William Warren. New York, Walker/Weatherhill [1969, c1968] 87 p. (chiefly illus. (part col.), plan, ports.) 27 cm. "A Weathermark edition." [N7311.B7 1969] 68-20640 7.50
1. Thompson, James Harrison Wilson, b. 1906—Art collections. 2. Art, Southeast Asian—Catalogs. 3. Bangkok, Thailand. House on the Klong. I. Warren, William, 1930- II. Title.

Thomson, Tom, 1877-1917.

LITTLE, William T. 759.11
The Tom Thomson mystery [by] William T. Little. Toronto, New York, McGraw-Hill [1970] xv, 239 p. illus., facsims., map, ports. 23 cm. [ND249.T5L5] 75-119483 ISBN 0-07-092655-7
1. Thomson, Tom, 1877-1917. I. Title.

LITTLE, William T. 759.11 B
The Tom Thomson mystery / William T. Little. Toronto ; New York : McGraw-Hill Ryerson, [1973], c1970. xv, 239 p., [4] leaves of plates : ill., map, ports. ; 22 cm. Includes bibliographical references. [ND249.T5L5 1973] 75-302304 ISBN 0-07-077355-6 : 3.95
1. Thomson, Tom, 1877-1917. I. Title.

Thon, William.

GRUSKIN, Alan D., 1904- 759.13
The painter and his techniques: William Thon, by Alan D. Gruskin. Notes by the artist. New York, Viking [c.1964] 151p. illus., col. plates, ports. 29cm. (Studio bk.) 64-13302 8.50
1. Thon, William. 2. Painting—Technique. I. Title.

GRUSKIN, Alan D 1904- 759.13
The painter and his techniques: William Thon, by Alan D. Gruskin. With notes by the artist. New York, Viking Press [1964] 151 p. illus., col. plates, ports. 29 cm. (A Studio book) "Paintings by William Thon": p. 147-151. [ND237.T553G7] 64-13302
1. Thon, William. 2. Painting — Technique. I. Title.

Thonet, Michael, 1796-1871.

BUCHWALD, Hans H. 749'.3
Form from process—the Thonet chair; an exhibition of historic bentwood furniture from the collection of John Sailer, Vienna. Carpenter Center for the Visual Arts, Harvard University, Cambridge, Mass., fall and winter 1967. Catalogue and research by Hans H. Buchwald. Design and graphic by Toshihiro Katayama. [Cambridge? 1967] 64 p. illus., port. 23 cm. Bibliography: p. [61]-64. [NK2546.T5B8] 68-1205
1. Thonet, Michael, 1796-1871. 2. Chairs—Exhibitions. 3. Chairs—Private collections. I. Sailer, John. II. Harvard University. Carpenter Center for the Visual Arts. III. Title.

Thore, Theophile Etienne Joseph, 1807-1869.

JOWELL, Frances Suzman. 709'.2'4 B
Thore-Burger and the art of the past / Frances Suzman Jowell. New York : Garland Pub., 1977. xxiii, 409 p., [24] leaves of plates : ill. ; 21 cm. (Outstanding dissertations in the fine arts) Originally presented as the author's thesis, Harvard, 1971. Bibliography: p. 394-406. [N7483.T53J68 1977] 76-23632 ISBN 0-8240-2701-9 lib.bdg. : 45.00
1. Thore, Theophile Etienne Joseph, 1807-1869. 2. Art historians—France—Biography. I. Title. II. Series.

Thornhill, James, Sir, 1675-1734.

BROCKLEBANK, Joan. 741.9'42
Sir James Thornhill of Dorset, 1675-1734 : [catalogue of the] tercentenary exhibition [held at the] Dorset County Museum, Dorchester, 7th June-12th July 1975 / [written and compiled by Joan Brocklebank]. Dorchester : Dorset Natural History and Archaeological Society, 1975. 40 p., [12] p. of plates : ill., ports. ; 25 cm. At head of title: Dorset Natural History & Archaeological Society. Bibliography: p. 4-5. [ND497.T66B76] 76-353691 ISBN 0-900341-04-1 : £1.20
1. Thornhill, James, Sir, 1675-1734. I. Thornhill, James, Sir, 1675-1734. II. Dorset County Museum. III. Dorset Natural History and Arcaological Society.

Thornton, William, 1759-1828.

PETER, Armistead. 975.3
Tudor Place: designed by Dr. William Thornton and built between 1805 and 1816 for Thomas and Martha Peter; described by their descendant Armistead Peter, 3rd, the present owner. With an introd. by Walter Muir Whitehill and a Commentary on Dr. Thornton by Frederick Doveton Nichols. Georgetown [Washington] 1969. xii, 97 p. illus. (part col.), map (on lining paper), plans, ports. (part col.) 47 cm. [F204.T8P4] 74-89802
1. Thornton, William, 1759-1828. 2. Tudor Place, Washington, D.C. I. Nichols, Frederick Doveton. II. Title.

Throwing-sticks.

KELLAR, James H 398.2'09701
The atlatl in North America. Indianapolis, Indiana Historical Society, 1955. 281-352p. illus., maps. 26cm. (Indiana Historical Society. Prehistory research series, v. 3. no. 3) Bibliography: p.344-352. [E98.A65K4] 55-4631
1. Throwing-sticks. I. Title. II. Series.

Thubron, Harry, 1915—

THUBRON, Harry, 1915- 709'.2'4
Harry Thubron : [catalogue of an exhibition held at the] Serpentine Gallery, Kensington Gardens, London W2, 23 October-21 November 1976 / [introduction by Martin Shuttleworth]. [London] : Arts Council of Great Britain, [1976]. [20] p. : chiefly ill. (some col.) ; 25 cm. [N6797.T47A77] 77-364482 ISBN 0-7287-0105-7 : £1.35
1. Thubron, Harry, 1915- I. Arts Council of Great Britain. II. Title.

Thuin, Raoul Charles de.

THE Yucatan affair : 769'.562
the work of Raoul Ch. de Thuin, philatelic counterfeiter / James M. Chemi, editor-in-chief, James H. Beal and James T. De Voss, associate editors ; detailed and compiled through the assistance of an outstanding specialist editorial staff.

York, Universe Bks. [1964] 136p. illus. 21cm. Bibl. 64-10344 2.75; 1.95 pap.,
1. Tiles. 2. Pottery, Dutch. I. Title.

SOUTHWELL, B. C. 738.6
Making and decorating pottery tiles, by B. C. Southwell. New York, Watson-Guptill Publications [1972] 126 p. illus. 26 cm. Bibliography: p. [127] [TP837.S65] 72-3489 ISBN 0-8230-2988-3
1. Tiles. 2. Glazing (Ceramics) I. Title.

Tiles, Dutch.

JONGE, Caroline Henriette de, 1886- 738.6
Dutch tiles [by] C. H. de Jonge. Translated by P. S. Falla. New York, Praeger [1971] viii, 337 p. illus. 25 cm. Translation of Nederlandse tegels. "Literature and collections": p. 131-137. [NK4670.7.N4J613] 70-150699 20.00
1. Tiles, Dutch.

Tiles—Egypt.

HAYES, William Christopher, 1903-1963. 738.6'0932
Glazed tiles from a palace of Ramesses II at Kantir. New York, Metropolitan Museum of Art, 1937. [New York] Arno Press, 1973. 46 p., 13 plates. illus. 29 cm. Reprint of the ed. issued as no. 3 of the Papers of the Metropolitan Museum of Art. Bibliography: p. 43-44. [NK4670.7.E32K33 1973] 72-168405 ISBN 0-405-02238-7 13.00
1. Kantir, Egypt. Temple of Ramesses II. 2. Tiles—Egypt. 3. Egypt—Antiquities. I. New York (City). Metropolitan Museum of Art. II. Title. III. Series: New York (City). Metropolitan Museum of Art. Papers, no. 3. BIP

Tiles, Islamic—Turkey.

DENNY, Walter B. 738.6'09561
The ceramics of the Mosque of Rustem Pasha and the environment of change / Walter B. Denny. New York : Garland Pub., 1977. xi, 424 p. : ill. ; 21 cm. (Outstanding dissertations in the fine arts) A revision of the author's thesis, Harvard University, 1970. Bibliography: p. 241-258. [NK4670.7.T9D46 1977] 76-23612 ISBN 0-8240-2684-5 : 47.50
1. Rustempasa Camii, Istanbul. 2. Tiles, Islamic—Turkey. 3. Tiles, Turkish. 4. Decoration and ornament, Islamic—Turkey. 5. Decoration and ornament—Turkey. 6. Iznik pottery. I. Title. II. Series. BIP

Tiles—Kutahya, Turkey (City)—Catalogs.

CARSWELL, John, 1931- 738.3'7
Kutahya tiles and pottery from the Armenian Cathedral of St. James, Jerusalem [by] John Carswell, C. J. F. Dowsett. Oxford, Clarendon Press, 1972. 2 v. (xvi, 112, 46 p., leaf; xvi, 179, 43 p., leaf) illus. (some col.), map, plans. 34 cm. Contents.Contents.—v. 1. The pictorial tiles and other vessels, including a catalogue of inscribed and dated Armenian pottery, by J. Carswell. An edition of the Armenian texts, with a translation and notes, by C. J. F. Dowsett.—v. 2. Carswell, J. A historical survey of the Kutahya industry. A catalogue of the decorative tiles. Bibliography: v. 2, p. 97-98. [NK4670.7.T92K832] 73-151909 ISBN 0-19-817176-5 £28.00
1. Jerusalem. Sowrb Hakob Mayr Tachar. 2. Tiles—Kutahya, Turkey (City)—Catalogs. 3. Kutahya pottery—Catalogs. I. Dowsett, C. J. F. II. Title.

Tiles, Spanish.

FROTHINGHAM, Alice Wilson. 738.6
Tile panels of Spain, 1500-1650. New York, Printed by order of the trustees, Hispanic Society of America, 1969. xv, 106, [140] p. 178 illus., 6 col. plates. 27 cm. (Hispanic notes & monographs; essays, studies, and brief biographies. Peninsular series) Includes bibliographical references. [NK4670.F85] 71-5770 30.00
1. Tiles, Spanish. I. Title. II. Series. BIP

Tiles—Zanesville, Ohio.

WIRES, E. Stanley. 738.6
Zanesville decorative tiles, by E. Stanley Wires, Norris F. Schneider [and] Moses Mesre. Zanesville, Ohio, 1972. 32 p. illus. 23 cm. Bibliography: p. 32. [NK4670.7.U52Z38] 72-189301
1. American Encaustic Tiling Company. 2. Tiles—Zanesville, Ohio. I. Schneider, Norris Franz, 1898- joint author. II. Mesre, Moses, joint author. III. Title.

Tillim, Sidney, 1925—

TILLIM, Sidney, 1925- 741.9'73
Drawings by Sidney Tillim : an exhibition organized by the Edmonton Art Gallery, February 20-March 15, 1976. Edmonton : Edmonton Art Gallery, 1976. [16] p. : ill. ; 28 cm. [NC139.T54E33] 77-357807
1. Tillim, Sidney, 1925- I. Edmonton Art Gallery. II. Title.

Tillou, Peter H.—Art collections.

NINETEENTH-CENTURY folk 759.13
painting : our spirited national heritage : works of art from the Collection of Mr. and Mrs. Peter Tillou / selection and catalogue by Peter H. Tillou ; organized by Paul F. Rovetti. Storrs : William Benton Museum of Art, University of Connecticut, 1974, c1973 x, 209, [1] p. : ill. (some col.) ; 27 cm. Bibliography: p. 207-[210] [N6510.5.P7N55] 72-96934 17.50
1. Tillou, Peter H.—Art collections. 2. Art, American—Catalogs. 3. Primitivism in art—United States. 4. Art, Modern—19th century—United States. I. Rovetti, Paul F. II. William Benton Museum of Art. BIP

WHERE liberty 759.13'074'014797
dwells : 19th-century art by the American people : works of art from the Collection of Mr. and Mrs. Peter Tillou / catalogue by Peter H. Tillou ; introd., Robert P. Buck, Jr. [Buffalo, N.Y. : Albright-Knox Art Gallery], c1976. 114 p. : ill. (some col.) ; 26 cm. "Exhibition schedule: January 17-February 22, 1976, Albright-Knox Art Gallery, Buffalo, New York; July 25-August 29, 1976, Milwaukee Art Center, Milwaukee, Wisconsin; January 14-February 20, 1977, Pennsylvania Academy of Fine Arts, Philadelphia, Pennsylvania; April 3-May 29, 1977, Munson-Williams-Proctor Institute, Utica, New York." Bibliography: p. 111-114. [ND210.5.P7W45] 76-362663
1. Tillou, Peter H.—Art collections. 2. Paintings, American—Exhibitions. 3. Primitivism in art—United States—Exhibitions. 4. Paintings, Modern—19th century—United States—Exhibitions. I. Albright-Knox Art Gallery.

Tilson, Joe, 1928—

TILSON, Joe, 1928- 709'.2'4
Tilson, "alchera" : notes for country works : [an exhibition held at] Marlborough Fine Art (London) Ltd. [and] Marlborough Graphics Ltd., April-May 1976. London : Marlborough Fine Art (London) Ltd, [1976] [40] p. : chiefly ill. ; 30 cm. "Cat. no. 357." [N6797.T5M37] 76-380639 ISBN 0-900955-19-8 : £1.50
1. Tilson, Joe, 1928- I. Marlborough Fine Art, ltd., London. II. Marlborough Graphics Ltd. III. Title.

Timberlake, Bob.

TIMBERLAKE, Bob. 759.13
Bob Timberlake: paintings and watercolors. Shreveport, La., R. W. Norton Art Gallery [1974] 26 p. illus. (part col.) 28 cm. Cover title. Catalog of an exhibition held at the R. W. Norton Art Gallery March 31-May 12, 1974. [ND1839.T56N67] 74-5029 ISBN 0-913060-04-6 2.75 (pbk.)
1. Timberlake, Bob. I. Norton (R. W.) Art Gallery. II. Title.

Time-Life Books.

WALLACE, Robert, 1919- 759.9492 B
The world of Van Gogh, 1853-1890, by Robert Wallace and the editors of Time-Life Books New York, Time-Life Books [1969] 192 p. illus. (part col.), ports. 32 cm. (Time-Life library of art) Bibliography: p. 184. [ND653.G7W34] 70-78988
1. Gogh, Vincent van, 1853-1890. 2. Time-Life Books. I. Title. BIP

Times-Sotheby Index of Fine Art Prices.

KEEN, Geraldine, 1940- 338.4'3'76
Money and art; a study based on the Times-Sotheby Index. [1st Amer. ed.] New York, Putnam [1971] 286 p. illus. (part col.) 26 cm. Bibliography: p. 272. [N8675.K4 1971] 77-135261 20.00
1. Times-Sotheby Index of Fine Art Prices. 2. Art—Prices. I. Title.

Tims Ford Lake—Antiquities.

FAULKNER, Charles H. 970.4'68'63
Archaeological investigations in the Tims Ford Reservoir, Tennessee, 1966. Edited by Charles H. Faulkner. Contributions by Travis W. Binion, Jr. [and others] Knoxville, Dept. of Anthropology, University of Tennessee, 1968. vii, 276 p. illus., maps. 28 cm. "Submitted in accordance with National Park Service contract 14-10-0131-1631." Bibliography: p. 269-276. [E78.T3F28] 68-66796
1. Tims Ford Lake—Antiquities. 2. Indians of North America—Tennessee—Antiquities. I. Binion, Travis W. II. Tennessee. University. Dept. of Anthropology. III. U. S. National Park Service. IV. Title.

Tin containers—Catalogs.

DAVIS, Marvin. 688'.4
Tobacco tins; pictures and prices of over 150 tobacco tins by Marvin & Helen Davis. Photography by Terry Skibby, sketches by Don Davis & Vicki Dedrick. Medford, Or., Printed by Grandee Print. Center, 1970. 61 p. illus. (part col.) 22 cm. [NK8425.D3] 79-23813 3.75
1. Tin containers—Catalogs. 2. Tin containers—Collectors and collecting. I. Davis, Helen, joint author. II. Title.

Tin containers—Collectors and collecting.

CLARK, Hyla. 673'.6
The tin can book : the can as collectible art, advertising art, & high art / by Hyla M. Clark. New York : New American Library, c1977. 128 p. : ill. ; 26 cm. Bibliography: p. 36. [NK8425.C55] 76-52265 pbk. : 6.95
1. Tin containers—Collectors and collecting. 2. Tin containers—Catalogs. 3. Tin cans. I. Title. BIP

Tin-plate.

COOK, Sherman Robley. 745.56
Tin things we like to make. Milwaukee, Bruce Pub. Co. [1952] 105p. illus. 24cm. [TT205.C72] 53-322
1. Tin-plate. 2. Handicraft. I. Title.

Tin toys—History.

PRESSLAND, David. 688.7'2
The art of the tin toy / David Pressland. New York : Crown Publishers, c1976. 224 p. : ill. ; 28 x 34 cm. Includes index. [TS2301.T7P73] 76-8387 ISBN 0-517-52610-7 : 32.50
1. Tin toys—History. I. Title. BIP

Tinguely, Jean, 1925—

HULTE'N, Karl Gunnar Pontus, 1924- 730.924
Jean Tinguely : "me'ta" / K. G. Pontus Hulte'n. Boston : New York Graphic Society [1976c1975] 364p. : ill. ; 30 cm. Includes bibliographical references and index. [NB853.T5H84] ISBN 0-8212-0547-1 : 35.00
1. Tinguely, Jean, 1925- I. Title.
L. C. card no. for original edition: 73-80231.

Tinsley, William, 1804-1885.

FORBES, John Douglas, 1910- 927.2
Victorian architect; the life and work of William Tinsley. Bloomington, Indiana University Press, 1953. xiv, 153p. illus., ports., map. 25cm. 'Bibliographical note':p. 140-146. [NA737.T5F6] 53-10024
1. Tinsley, William, 1804-1885. I. Title.

Tinsmithing.

FOWLER, Earl P. 745.56
Can crafts / Earl Fowler ; drawings by Joan Holmes. Radnor, Pa. : Chilton Book Co., c1977. x, 163 p., [4] leaves of plates : ill. ; 27 cm. (Chilton's creative crafts series) [TT266.F67 1977] 77-3522 ISBN 0-8019-6233-1 : 12.50 ISBN 0-8019-6234-X pbk. : 6.95
1. Tinsmithing. 2. Tin cans. I. Title. BIP

HOWARD, Sylvia W. 745.56
Tin-can crafting, by Sylvia W. Howard. Illus. by Harold S. Howard. Photos. by Kenneth Wolfsen. Rev. ed. New York, Sterling Pub. Co. [1964] 64 p. illus. 29 cm. [NK8425.H6 1964] 64-24689
1. Tinsmithing. 2. Art metal-work. I. Title.

SARGENT, Lucy. 745.56
Tincraft. Design and drawings by the author. Flower arrangements by Marianna Brockway. Photos. by George C. Bradbury. New York, Simon and Schuster [1972] 200 p. illus. (part col.) 29 cm. "Sources of supply": p. 195. [TT266.S37] 72-83921 ISBN 0-671-21225-7 9.95
1. Tinsmithing. 2. Tin cans. I. Title.

TIN-CAN crafting. 745.56
Illus. by Harold S. Howard. Photographs by Kenneth Wolfsen. New York, Sterling Pub. Co. [1959] 64p. illus. 29cm. [NK8425.H6] 59-13004
1. Tinsmithing. 2. Art metal-work.

Tinsmithing—Juvenile literature.

SARGENT, Lucy. 745.56
A beginner's book of tincraft / Lucy Sargent ; designs and drawings by the author, photos. by Bradbury/McCormick. New York : Dodd, Mead, c1976. 157 p. : ill. ; 25 cm. Includes index. Directions for making chimes, mobiles, ornaments, jewelry, and other decorative and functional objects out of tin cans. Includes all the techniques necessary for dealing with the medium. [TT266.S36] 76-12506 ISBN 0-396-07354-9 : 5.95
1. Tinsmithing—Juvenile literature. 2. Tin cans—Juvenile literature. I. Title. BIP

Tintoretto, Jacopo Robusti, known as, 1512-1594.

NEWTON, Eric, 1893- 759.5
Tintoretto. London, New York, Longmans, Green [1952] xv. 250 p. plates, 26 cm. Erratum slip mounted on p. 216. Bibliography: p. 234. [ND623.T6N44] 52-2512
1. Tintoretto, Jacopo Robusti, known as, 1512-1594. I. Title. BIP

NEWTON, Eric, 1893-1965 759.5
Tintoretto. Westport, Conn., Greenwood Press [1972, c1952] xv, 250 p. front., 76 plates. 23 cm. Bibliography: p. 234. [ND623.T6N44 1972] 70-110275 ISBN 0-8371-4501-5
1. Tintoretto, Jacopo Robusti, known as, 1512-1594.

TINTORETTO, Jacopo Robusti, known as, 1512-1594. 741.9'45
The drawings. Introd. by Stephen Longstreet. [1st ed.] Alhambra, Calif., Borden Pub. Co. [1967] 1 v. (chiefly illus.) 31 cm. (Master draughtsman series) [NC1055.T47L6] 67-9820
I. Longstreet, Stephen, 1907- ed. II. Title.

TINTORETTO, Jacopo Robusti, known as, 1512-1594. 741.945
Drawings by Tintoretto, by Giuseppe Delogu. Translated by Clara Bargellini. New York, Dover Publications [1969] 11 p., 32 plates. 28 cm. (The Great masters of drawing) Bibliography: p. 9-10. [NC1055.T47D413] 68-27838 1.50
I. Delogu, Giuseppe, 1898- II. Title.

TINTORETTO, Jacopo Robusti, known as, 1512-1594. 759.5
Tintoretto. Text by Margaretta M. Salinger. New York, H. N. Abrams [1971] 24 p. illus. (part col.) 33 cm. (The Library of great painters. Portfolio ed.) [ND623.T6S3 1971] 74-130291 ISBN 0-8109-3060-9
I. Salinger, Margaretta M., 1907-

Tinware.

GOULD, Mary Earle. 739.532
Antique tin & tole ware: its history and romance. With a foreword by R. W. G. Vail. [1st ed.] Rutland, Vt., C. E. Tuttle Co. [1958] 136 p. illus. 29 cm. [NK8425.G6] 57-8796
1. Tinware. 2. Implements, utensils, etc.—U.S. I. Title. **BIP**

POWERS, Beatrice Farnsworth. 739.532
Early American decorated tinware, with designs and practical directions by Beatrice Farnsworth Powers and Olive Floyd. Foreword by Kathryn C. Buhler. New York, Hastings House [1957] 267p. illus. (part col.) facsims. 29cm. Bibliography: p.254-262. [NK8425.P6] 57-14085
1. Tinware. 2. Decoration and ornament—U. S. I. Floyd, Olive Beatrice, joint author. II. Title.

SMITH, Elmer Lewis. 739'.532
Tinware yesterday and today / compiled and edited by Elmer L. Smith ; photography by Melvin J. Horst. Lebanon, Pa. : Applied Arts Publishers, [1974] 40 p. : ill. ; 28 cm. (Americana books) [TS619.S56] 74-187930 1.25
1. Tinware. 2. Tinsmithing. I. Title.

Tinware, American.

COFFIN, Margaret. 739'.532'0973
The history & folklore of American country tinware, 1700-1900. [Camden, N. J.] T. Nelson [1968] 226 p. illus., facsims., ports. 26 cm. Bibliography: p. 212-215. [NK8425.C6] 68-25512 12.50
1. Tinware, American. 2. Tinsmiths, American. 3. Decoration and ornament—U.S. I. Title.

COFFIN, Margaret. 739'.532'0973
The history & folklore of American country tinware, 1700-1900 / Margaret Coffin. New York : Galahad Books, [1974] c1968. 226 p. : ill. ; 26 cm. On spine: American country tinware. Includes index. Bibliography: p. 212-215. [NK8425.C6 1974] 73-88482 ISBN 0-88365-126-2 : 12.50
1. Tinware, American. 2. Tinsmiths—United States. 3. Decoration and ornament—United States. I. Title. II. Title: American country tinware.

Tinware—Collectors and collecting.

DE VOE, Shirley Spaulding, 1899- 739'.532'09746
The tinsmiths of Connecticut. [1st ed.] Middletown, Conn., Published for the Connecticut Historical Society [by] Wesleyan University Press [1968] xxiv, 200 p. illus., facsims. 26 cm. Bibliography: p. 195-200. [NK8425.D4] 68-16010
1. Tinware—Collectors and collecting. 2. Tinsmiths—Connecticut. I. Connecticut Historical Society, Hartford. II. Title.

Tinware, Victorian—Catalogs.

COX, Ralph. 739'.532'0942
Victorian tinware, with notes on a nineteenth century catalogue. Stamford, Stamford Properties Ltd., 1970. 3-96 p. illus. 23 cm. Includes a facsimile reprint of J. H. Hopkins & Son's catalogue for 1862. [NK8425.C65] 74-852868 ISBN 0-9501128-0-1 £1.05
1. Tinware, Victorian—Catalogs. I. Hopkins (J. H.) & Son. II. Title.

Tishman, Paul—Art collections.

SIEBER, Roy, 1923- 730'.967
Sculpture of Black Africa; the Paul Tishman Collection, by Roy Sieber and Arnold Rubin. [Los Angeles, Los Angeles County Museum of Art, 1968] 150 p. illus. (part col.) 31 cm. Catalog of an exhibition held at the Los Angeles County Museum of Art, Oct. 16, 1968-Jan. 5, 1969. Bibliography: p. 150. [NB1097.T5S55] 68-57350
1. Tishman, Paul—Art collections. 2. Sculpture, African—Exhibitions. 3. Sculpture—Africa, West. I. Rubin, Arnold, joint author. II. Los Angeles Co., Calif. Museum, Los Angeles. III. Title.

SIEBER, Roy, 1923- 730'.967
Sculpture of Black Africa; the Paul Tishman Collection, by Roy Sieber and Arnold Rubin. [Washington, 1970] 150, A39 p. illus. (part col.), maps. 30 cm. Catalog of an exhibition circulated by the International Exhibitions Foundation, 1970-71. Participating museums: The High Museum of Art, Atlanta, Georgia and others. Addendum to the catalog compiled by Roy Sieber and Robin Poyner: p. A1-A39. Includes bibliographies. [NB1097.W4S5 1970] 75-124430
1. Tishman, Paul—Art collections. 2. Sculpture, African—Exhibitions. 3. Sculpture—Africa, West. I. Rubin, Arnold, joint author. II. International Exhibitions Foundation. III. High Museum of Art. IV. Title.

Title-page.

DE VINNE, Theodore Low, 1828-1914. 686.2'2
The practice of typography; a treatise on title-pages, with numerous illustrations in facsimile and some observations on the early and recent printing of books. New York, Haskell House Publishers, 1972. xx, 485 p. facsims. 23 cm. [Z242.T6D6 1972] 68-25308 ISBN 0-8383-0935-6
1. Title-page. I. Title. II. Title: A treatise on title-pages.

JOHNSON, Alfred Forbes. 686.2'252
One hundred title-pages, 1500-1800, selected and arr. with an introd. and notes by A. F. Johnson. London, J. Lane. New York, Haskell House Publishers [1973] p. Reprint of the 1928 ed. [Z242.T6J6 1973] 73-2690 ISBN 0-8383-1693-X
1. Title-page. 2. Printing—Specimens. I. Title.

JOHNSON, Alfred Forbes, comp. 686.2'252
One hundred title-pages, 1500-1800. Selected and arr. with an introd. and notes by A. F. Johnson. Boston, Milford House [1972] p. Reprint of the 1928 ed. [Z242.T6J6 1972] 72-11691 ISBN 0-87821-014-8 35.00
1. Title-page. 2. Printing—Specimens. I. Title. **BIP**

JOHNSON, Alfred Forbes, comp. 686.2'252
One hundred title-pages, 1500-1800 / selected and arr. with an introd. and notes by A. F. Johnson. Boston : Longwood Press, 1977. xxiv, 100 leaves : ill. ; 29 cm. Reprint of the 1928 ed. published by J. Lane, London. Includes index. [Z242.T6J6 1977] 77-13524 ISBN 0-89341-228-7 lib.bdg. : 35.00
1. Title-page. 2. Printing—Specimens. I. Title.

NESBITT, Alexander, 1901- ed. 655.25
200 decorative title-pages New York, Dover [c.1964] 1v. (chiefly facsims.) 29cm. (T1264) Bibl. [Z242. N4] 64-16334 2.75 pap.,
1. Title-page. I. Title.

POLLARD, Alfred William, 1859-1944. 686.2'252
Last words on the history of the title-page, with notes on some colophons and twenty-seven fac-similes of title-pages. New York, B. Franklin [1971] 39 p. facsims. 27 cm. (Burt Franklin research & source works series, 668) Reprint of the 1891 ed. [Z242.T6P7 1971] 74-143649 ISBN 0-8337-2796-6
1. Title-page. 2. Printing—History. 3. Colophons. I. Title. **BIP**

Title-page—Standards—United States.

AMERICAN National Standards Institute. 070.5'3
American national standard for title leaves of a book. Secretariat: Council of National Library Association. Approved March 31, 1971. [New York, 1971] 8 p. 28 cm. "Z39.15-1971." [Z242.T6A44] 72-185622
1. Title-page—Standards—United States. I. Council of National Library Associations. II. Title. **BIP**

Titon du Tillet, Evrard, 1677-1762.

COLTON, Judith, 1943- 709'.2'4
The Parnasse francois : Titon du Tillet and the origins of the monument to genius / Judith Colton. New Haven : Yale University Press, 1979. p. cm. (Yale publications in the history of the art ; 27) Includes index. [N6853.T48C64] 78-9878 ISBN 0-300-02270-0 : 25.00
1. Titon du Tillet, Evrard, 1677-1762. Parnasse francois. 2. Artists' preparatory studies—France. I. Title. II. Series. **BIP**

Tivoli, Italy. Villa d'Este.

COFFIN, David R. 728.84094563
The Villa d'Este at Tivoli. Princeton, N.J., Published for the Dept. of Art and Archaeology, Princeton University [by] Princeton University Press, [c.]1960. xvi, 186 p. Bibliographical footnotes. 143 illus. (incl. map, plans) 31 cm (Princeton monographs in art and archaeology, 34) 60-5744 17.50 buck.,
1. Tivoli, Italy. Villa d'Este. I. Title. II. Series.

Tiziano Vecelli, 1477-1576.

BALLARIN, Alessandro. 759.5
Titian. [The life and work of the artist, illustrated with 80 full-color plates. Translated from the Italian by Pearl Sanders. 1st American ed.] New York, Grosset & Dunlap [1968] 40 p. illus., col. plates. 18 cm. (The New Grosset art library, 14) Bibliography: p. 35. [ND623.T7B313 1968b] 68-26685
1. Tiziano, Vecelli, 1477-1576. I. Tiziano, Vecelli, 1477-1576. II. Title.

BORTOLON, Liana. 759.5
The life and times of Titian; text by Liana Bortolon, translator [from the Italian] Clara Green. London, New York [etc.] Hamlyn, 1968. 75 p. illus. (some col.), facsims. 30 cm. (Portraits of greatness) Illus. on lining papers [ND623.T7B73] 70-396965 17/6
1. Tiziano Vecelli, 1477-1576. I. Title.

CECCHI, Dario, 1918- 759.5
Titian. Translated from the Italian by Nora Wydenbruck. New York, Farrar, Straus and Cudahy [1958] 232p. illus. 22cm. [ND623.T7C43] [ND623.T7C43] 927.5 58-5962 58-5962
1. Tiziano Vecelli, 1477-1576. I. Title.

CECCHI, Dario, 1918- 759.5
Titian. Translated from the Italian by Nora Wydenbruck. Freeport, N.Y., Books for Libraries Press [1973] (Biography index reprint series) Translation of Tiziano. Reprint of the 1958 ed. [ND623.T7C43 1973] 72-13188 ISBN 0-8369-8143-X
1. Tiziano, Vecelli, 1477-1576.

FISHER, M. Roy. 759.5 B
Titian's assistants during the later years / M. Roy Fisher. New York : Garland Pub., 1977. xxii, 148, 133 p. : ill. ; 21 cm. (Outstanding dissertations in the fine arts) Originally presented as the author's thesis, Harvard, 1958. Bibliography: p. 141-148. [ND623.T7F53 1977] 76-23618 ISBN 0-8240-2689-6 lib.bdg. : 40.00
1. Tiziano Vecelli, 1477-1576. 2. Apprentices—Italy—Venice—Biography. I. Title. II. Series. **BIP**

GOULD, Cecil Hilton Monk, 1918- 759.5
Titian [by] Cecil Gould. London, New York, Hamlyn [1969] 40, 52 p. col. illus. 28 cm. (Colour library of art) [ND623.T63G6] 74-20408
1. Tiziano, Vecelli, 1477-1576. I. Tiziano, Vecelli, 1477-1576.

GOULD, Cecil Hilton Monk, 1918- 759.5
Titian as portraitist / Cecil Gould. London : National Gallery, 1976. 40 p. : ill., ports. ; 30 cm. [ND1329.T55G68] 77-359765 ISBN 0-901791-63-6 : £0.95
1. Tiziano Vecelli, 1477-1576. I. Tiziano Vecelli, 1477-1576. II. Title.

PANOFSKY, Erwin, 1892-1968. 759.5
Problems in Titian, mostly iconographic. [New York] New York University Press [1969] xv, 208 p. 143 illus. 28 cm. (The Wrightsman lectures, 2) Includes bibliographical references. [ND623.T7P32 1969] 68-16828 ISBN 0-7148-1325-7 12.50
1. Tiziano Vecelli, 1477-1576. I. Title. II. Series. **BIP**

POPE, Arthur, 1880- 759.5
Titian's Rape of Europa; a study of the composition and the mode of representation in this and related paintings. Cambridge, Mass. Published for the Isabella Stewart Gardner Museum by Harvard University Press [1961, c.1960] xi, 62p. illus., col. plates, port. 26cm. Bibl. 60-11562 7.50
1. Tiziano Vecelli, 1477-1576. I. Isabella Stewart Gardner Museum, Boston. II. Title. III. Title: Rape of Europa. **BIP**

ROSAND, David. 759.5
Titian / text by David Rosand. New York : Abrams, [1978] 158 p. : ill. (some col.) ; 33 cm. (Library of great painters) Includes index. Bibliography: p. 158. [ND623.T7R595] 77-11042 ISBN 0-8109-1654-1 : 25.00
1. Tiziano, Vecelli, 1477-1576.

ROSAND, David. 769'.945'31
Titian and the Venetian woodcut : a loan exhibition / introduction and catalogue by David Rosand, Michelangelo Muraro ; organized and circulated by International Exhibitions Foundation, 1976-1977. Washington : The Foundation, c1976. 315 p. : ill. ; 22 x 26 cm. Held at the National Gallery of Art, the Dallas Museum of Fine Arts, and the Detroit Institute of Arts. Bibliography: p. 28-31. [NE1152.4.V46R67] 77-351487
1. Tiziano Vecelli, 1477-1576. 2. Wood-engraving, Venetian—Exhibitions. I. Muraro, Michelangelo, joint author. II. International Exhibitions Foundation. III. United States. National Gallery of Art. IV. Dallas. Museum of Fine Arts. V. Detroit. Institute of Arts. VI. Title. **BIP**

SPECK, Douglas. 759.5
The authenticity of a Titian painting / by Douglas Speck. Minneapolis : T. S. Denison, c1976. ix, 92 p. : ill. ; 24 cm. Includes bibliographical references and index. [ND623.T7S64] 75-32867
1. Tiziano Vecelli, 1477-1576. Madonna and Child with rabbit. 2. Paintings—Expertising. I. Title.

SPENCER, John Richard. 759.5
Titian [by] John R. Spencer. New York, McGraw-Hill [1968] 48 p. illus., 20 col. slides (in pockets), port. 29 cm. (Color slide program of the great masters) [ND623.T7S65] 68-26568
1. Tiziano Vecelli, 1477-1576. 2. Lantern slides—Catalogs. I. Title. II. Series.

SUTTON, Denys 759.5
Titian. New York, Barnes & Noble [1964, c.1963] 20p. illus. (pt. col.) ports. 18cm. (Barnes & Noble art ser., no. 613) 64-1802 .75 pap.,
1. Tiziano Vecelli, 1477-1576. I. Title.

TIZIANO Vecelli, 1477-1576. 759.5
Titian (c. 1490-1576) Text by Marco

Valsecchi New York, H. N. Abrams [1963] 79 p. 41 illus. (part col.) 17 cm. (The Pocket library of great art, A40) Bibliography: p. 79. [ND623.T7V3] 62-8377
I. Valsecchi, Marco.

TIZIANO Vecelli, 1477-1576.   759.5
Titian (Tiziano Vecellio) Text by Theodore Rousseau, Jr. New York, H. N. Abrams [1970] 24 p. illus., col. plates. 33 cm. (The Library of great painters. Portfolio ed.) [ND623.T7R62 1970] 69-14760
I. Rousseau, Theodore, 1912-

TIZIANO VECELLI, 1477-1576   759.5
All the paintings of Titian. pts. 1-4. Text by Francesco Valcanover. Tr. from the Italian by Sylvia J. Tomalin. New York, Hawthorn [1965, c.1960] 4v. (various p.) plates (pt. col.) 18cm. Complete lib. of world art) Bibl. [ND623.T7V283] 64-25276 3.95 ea.,
I. Valcanover, Francesco. II. Title. III. Series.
Contents omitted.

WILLIAMS, Jay, 1914-   759.5
The world of Titian, c. 1488-1576, by Jay Williams and the editors of Time-Life Books New York, Time-Life Books [1968] 192 p. illus. (part col.) 31 cm. (Time-Life library of art) In case. Bibliography: p. 187. [ND623.T7W5] 68-28257
I. Tiziano Vecelli, 1477-1576. II. Time-Life Books. III. Title.

Tiziano Vecelli, 1477-1576—Juvenile literature.

RIPLEY, Elizabeth,   927.5'945
1906-
Titian, a biography. Philadelphia, Lippincott [1962] 68 p. illus. 27 cm. Includes bibliography. [ND623.T7R56] 62-13146
I. Tiziano Vecelli, 1477-1576—Juvenile literature.

Tlapacoyan, Mexico (Mexico)—Antiq.

WEAVER, Muriel Porter.   970.4'25
Tlapacoya pottery in the Museum collection. New York, Museum of the American Indian, Heye Foundation, 1967. xi, 48 p. illus., maps, 41 plates. 17 cm. (Indian notes and monographs; a series of publications relating to the American aborigines, no. 56) Bibliography: p. 42-45. [E51.N45] 67-27950
1. Tlapacoyan, Mexico (Mexico)—Antiq. 2. Mexico (State)—Antiq. 3. Indians of Mexico—Mexico (State)—Antiq. 4. Indians of Mexico—Pottery. I. Title. II. Series: New York (City) Museum of the American Indian, Heye Foundation. Indian notes and monographs; a series of publications relating to the American aborigines. Miscellaneous, no. 56

Tlingit Indians—Wood-carving.

KAIPER, Dan.   970'.004'97
Tlingit, their art, culture, & legends / Dan & Nan Kaiper. Saanichton, B.C. ; Seattle : Hancock House, 1978. 95 p. : ill. ; 22 cm. Introduces the daily life, arts, crafts, and legends of the Tlingit Indians of southeastern Alaska. [E99.T6K3] 79-302001 ISBN 0-88839-010-6 pbk. : 4.00
1. Tlingit Indians—Social life and customs. 2. Tlingit Indians—Art. 3. Tlingit Indians—Legends. 4. Indians of North America—Northwest coast of North America—Art. 5. Indians of North America—Northwest coast of North America—Legends. I. Kaiper, Nan, joint author. II. Title.

PECK, Raymond E.   736'.4
Tlingit designs and carving manual / written and designed by Raymond E. Peck, Aan-Ta-t'Lootl. Seattle : Superior Pub. Co., 1978. p. cm. [E99.T6R38] 78-11887 ISBN 0-87564-861-4 pbk. : 5.95
1. Tlingit Indians—Wood-carving. 2. Indians of North America—Alaska—Wood-carving. I. Title.   BIP

Tobacco in art.

NORTH Carolina.   704.9493941
Museum of Art, Raleigh.
Tobacco and smoking in art; an exhibition, October 14 through December 4, 1960. [Catalogue by James B. Byrnes, with special section by Paul Wescher] Raleigh [1960] 152p. illus. 26cm. 'Early literature on tobacco;. p. 149-150. Bibliography: p.151. [N8253.T6N6] 60-16360
1. Tobacco in art. 2. Smoking in art. 3. Art—Exhibitions. I. Title.

Tobacco package labels—Catalogs.

SCHILD, Gary.   741.6'9
Tobacco tin tags; a listing of over 3000 tobacco tags with more than 200 illustrations. Westbrook, Conn., 1972. 86 p. illus. 22 cm. Bibliography: p. 85. [NC1883.5.S35] 72-194076 4.00 (pbk)
1. Tobacco package labels—Catalogs. I. Title.

Tobae ogi no mato (Cartoons)

A Cure for gloom;   741.5952
being the full set of "Fan-target Toba pictures" as first published at Osaka, Japan, in 1720 plus fables with & without morals. Edited by Meredith Weatherby. [1st U.S. ed.] New York, Walker/Weatherhill [1968] 68 p. col. illus. 24 cm. "A Weathermark edition." [NC1703.3.T65C8 1968] 68-15700 2.95
1. Tobae ogi no mato (Cartoons) 2. Japanese wit and humor, Pictorial. I. Weatherby, Meredith. II. Title: Fan-target Toba pictures.

Tobey, Mark.

ROBERTS, Colette (Levy)   759.13
Mark Tobey. Drawings by Mark Tobey. New York, Grove Press 1960 [c.1959] 63p. illus., plates (part col.) 21cm. (Evergreen gallery bk. no. 4) 59-12070 3.95; 1.95 pap.,
I. Tobey, Mark. I. Title.

SEITZ, William Chapin.   759.13
Mark Tobey. New York, Museum of Modern Art; distributed by Doubleday, Garden City, N.Y. [1962] 112 p. illus. (part col.) ports. 22 x 24 cm. Catalogue of an exhibition to be held at the Museum of Modern Art, Sept. 12-Nov. 4, 1962, the Cleveland Museum of Art, Dec. 11, 1962-Jan. 13, 1963, and the Art Institute of Chicago, Feb. 22-Mar. 24, 1963: p. 107-110. "Selected bibliography, by Inga Forslund": p. 100-105. [ND237.T56S4] 62-18507
1. Tobey, Mark. I. New York (City). Museum of Modern Art.

TOBEY, Mark.   759.13
Mark Tobey : a retrospective exhibition from Northwest collections : [Seattle Art Museum, September 11 through November 1, 1959 : catalog / Edward B. Thomas]. [Seattle : The Museum, 1959] [54] p. : ill. ; 28 cm. [ND1839.T6T48] 75-313508
1. Tobey, Mark. I. Thomas, Edward B., 1920- II. Seattle. Art Museum.

TOBEY, Mark.   759.13
Mark Tobey retrospective. [Dallas? 1968] [56] p. illus. (part col.) 26 cm. "Exhibition dates: 20 March through 21 April, 1968, Dallas Museum of Fine Arts." [ND237.T56D3] 68-2968
I. Dallas. Museum of Fine Arts. II. Title.

TOBEY, Mark.   759.13
Tobey [by] Wieland Schmied. [Translated from the German by Margaret L. Kaplan] New York, Abrams [c1966] 85 p. (chiefly plated) 21 x 22 cm. (Modern artists) Bibliography: p. 82-83. [ND237.T56S323] 66-15214
I. Schmied, Wieland, 1929- II. Title.   BIP

TOBEY, Mark.   759.13
Tobey's 80: a retrospective. Foreword by Richard E. Fuller. Introd. by Betty Bowen. Seattle, Seattle Art Museum [1970] [32] p. illus., ports., 80 plates (part col.) 28 cm. "Prepared as the catalogue for an exhibition held at the Seattle Art Museum, December 3-January 31, 1971." [ND237.T56A56] 78-142756 15.00
I. Seattle. Art Museum. II. Title.

Toby jugs.

BEDFORD, John, 1907-   738
Toby jugs. New York, Walker [1968] 64 p. illus. (part col.) 20 cm. (Collectors' pieces, 14) "Dear Tom, this brown jug" (song) p. [20-21]. [NK4695.T6B4] 68-27555 2.95
1. Toby jugs.

Tockholes, Eng.—Description.

BIRTILL, George.   942.7'615
Heather in my hat / by George Birtill. Chorley : Nelson Brothers, 1976. 115 p. : ill., maps ; 22 cm. [DA690.T626B57] 77-350841 ISBN 0-9500615-3-0 : £1.00
1. Tockholes, Eng.—Description. I. Title.

Todaiji, Nara, Japan.

KOBAYASHI, Takeshi, 1903-   732'.7
1969.
Nara Buddhist art, Todai-ji / by Takeshi Kobayashi ; translated and adapted by Richard L. Gage. 1st English ed. New York : Weatherhill, 1975. 157 p. : ill. (some col.) ; 24 cm. (Heibonsha survey of Japanese art ; v. 5) Translation of Todai-ji no Daibutsu. [NB1057.N36K6213] 74-22034 ISBN 0-8348-1021-2 : 12.50
1. Todaiji, Nara, Japan. 2. Sculpture, Buddhist—Nara, Japan (City) 3. Sculpture—Nara, Japan (City) I. Title. II. Series.

Tofel, Jennings, 1891-1959.

GRANICK, Arthur.   759.13
Jennings Tofel / Arthur Granick. New York : H. N. Abrams, [1976] p. cm. Includes index. Bibliography: p. [ND237.T575G72] 76-10752 ISBN 0-8109-1652-5 : 37.50
1. Tofel, Jennings, 1891-1959. I. Tofel, Jennings, 1891-1959.   BIP

Tokaido.

ANDO, Hiroshige, 1797-   769.952
1858
Down the Emperor's Road with Hiroshige. Ed. by Reiko Chiba. Rutland, Vt., Tuttle [c.1965] 72p. (on double leaves) illus. (pt. col.) col. map. 10 x 15cm. [NE1325.A5A53] 65-18959 2.95 bxd.
1. Tokaido. I. Chiba, Reiko, ed. II. Title.   BIP

ANDO, Hiroshige, 1797-1858   769.9
The fifty-three stages of the Tokaido [Ed. by Ichitaro Kondo. English adaptation by Charles S. Terry] Honolulu, East-West Ctr. Pr. [1965, c.1960] 1v. (various p. chiefly col. illus.) col. maps. 22x30cm. 65-8367 10.50
1. Tokaido. I. Kondo, Ichitaro, 1910-1961, ed. II. Title.

Tokaido in art.

ANDO, Hiroshige, 1797-   769.952
1858.
Hiroshige; the 53 stations of the Tokaido, by Muneshige Narazaki. English adaptation by Gordon Sager. Tokyo, Palo Alto, Calif., Kodansha International [1969] 92 p. map, col. plates. 26 cm. (Masterworks of Ukiyo-e, 10) [NE1325.A5A53 1969] 79-82655 ISBN 0-87011-100-0 3.50
1. Ando, Hiroshige, 1797-1858. 2. Tokaido in art. I. Narazaki, Muneshige, 1904- II. Title. III. Title: The 53 stations of the Tokaido. IV. Series.

Tokaido in art—Exhibitions.

†UTAGAWA, Kuniyoshi,   769'.92'4
1798-1861.
Along the Tokaido : twelve views by Utagawa Kuniyoshi : [exhibition] / by Amy Poster. Brooklyn, N.Y. : Brooklyn Museum, Division of Publications and Marketing Services, c1977. 32 p. : col. ill. ; 24 x 33 cm. Held at the Brooklyn Museum, Feb. 3-June 3, 1977. Bibliography: p. 32. [NE1325.U78A4 1977] 76-51935 ISBN 0-87273-060-3 pbk. : 4.95
1. Utagawa, Kuniyoshi, 1798-1861. 2. Tokaido in art—Exhibitions. I. Poster,

Amy. II. Brooklyn Institute of Arts and Sciences. Museum. III. Title.   BIP

Tokaido—Views.

ANDO, Horoshige, 1797-   761.283084
1858
Tokaido in prints and poetry. Edited by Reiko Chiba. Tokyo, Rutland, Vt., C.E. Tuttle Co. [1957] [70]p. (on double leaves) mounted col. illus., map. 10x15cm. In case. [NE1325.A5C5] 57-11672
1. Tokaido—Views. 2. Japanese poetry—Translations into English. 3. English poetry—Translations from Japanese. I. Chiba, Reiko, ed. II. Title.

Tokens.

SMITH, Kenneth E.   737'.3
Catalogue of world transportation tokens and passes except North America. Compiled and edited by Kenneth E. Smith. 1st ed. [Boston] American Vecturist Association; distributed through K. E. Smith, Redonda Beach, Calif., 1967. xviii, 268 p. illus. 24 cm. [CJ5350.S6] 67-4275
1. Tokens. I. Title.

Tokens—Alaska.

GOULD, Maurice M.   737.49798
Alaska's coinage through the years; an illustrated catalog ... by Maurice M. Gould and Kenneth Bressett. Racine, Wis., Whitman Pub. Co. [1960] 46 p. illus. 20 cm. [CJ4909.A4G6] 60-3075
1. Tokens—Alaska. I. Bressett, Kenneth, joint author. II. Title.

GOULD, Maurice M.   737.49798
Alaska's coinage through the years; an illustrated catalog listing tokens used as money by pioneer Alaskans, plus commemorative medals, souvenir tokens, and medals, by Maurice M. Gould [and others] Rev. 2d ed. Racine, Wis., Whitman Pub. Co., 1965. 175, [1] p. illus. 20 cm. Bibliography: p. [176] [CJ4909.A4G6 1965] 66-843
1. Tokens—Alaska. I. Title.

Tokens—California.

ALBUM, Stephen.   737'.3'09794
Catalogue of California merchants tokens. Berkeley, Calif., 1971 [c1972- v. illus. 24 cm. Vol. 2 has title: Catalogue of California trade tokens. [CJ4909.C3A63] 72-182965 12.50 (v. 2)
1. Tokens—California. I. Title.

Tokens—Catalogs.

FEISEL, Duane H.   737'.3
Feisel's catalogue of parking tokens of the world. Compiled and edited by Duane H. Feisel. 2d ed. Palo Alto, CA, 1973. xx, 243 p. illus. 23 cm. [CJ5350.F4 1973] 73-77898
1. Tokens—Catalogs. 2. Automobile parking. 3. Parking meters. I. Title. II. Title: Catalogue of parking tokens of the world. III. Title: Parking tokens of the world.

Tokens—Colorado.

WRIGHT, Jim, 1920-   737.4'9'788
Colorado merchants' tokens, by Jim Wright, Lee Nott [and] Don Cary. [Westminster, Colo., 1973] iv, 219 p. illus. 22 cm. [CJ4909.C6W74] 74-150397
1. Tokens—Colorado. I. Nott, Lee, joint author. II. Cary, Don, joint author. III. Title.

Tokens — Germany.

LAMB, Robert A   737.3
Catalogue of German war tokens; the municipal issues, 1914-1921, by Robert A. Lamb. [Rev. ed. Tucson? Ariz., 1966] 143 p. illus. 20 cm. Bibliography: p. 143. [CJ5082.L3] 66-6416
1. Tokens — Germany. 2. European War, 1914-1918 — Numismatics. I. Title.

Park : distributed by Pennsylvania State University Press, 1976. 396 p. : ill. (some col.) ; 27 cm. [ND450.T64 1976] 76-24500 ISBN 0-271-01249-8 : 22.50. ISBN 0-271-01248-X pbk. : 12.50
1. Toledo. Museum of Art. 2. Painting, European—Catalogs. 3. Painting—Ohio—Toledo—Catalogs. I. Title.

TOLEDO. Museum of   738.3'82'093 s
Art.
The Toledo Museum of Art / Cedric G. Boulter and Kurt T. Luckner. Toledo : The Museum, c1976. 1 portfolio (55 p., 60 leaves of plates) : ill. ; 33 cm. (Corpus vasorum antiquorum : United States of America ; fasc. 17 : The Toledo Museum of Art ; fasc. 1) At head of title: Union academique internationale. Includes bibliographical references and index. [NK4640.C6U5 fasc. 17, fol.] [NK4623.T57] 738.3'82'0938074017113 77-12415
1. Toledo. Museum of Art. 2. Vases, Greek—Catalogs. 3. Vases—Ohio—Toledo—Catalogs. I. Boulter, Cedric G., 1912- II. Luckner, Kurt T. III. Series: Corpus vasorum antiquorum : United States of America : fasc. 17.

Tolstoi, Lev Nikolaevich, graf, 1828-1910.

GARROD, Heathcote William,   701
1878-1960.
Tolstoi's theory of art. [Folcroft, Pa.] Folcroft Library Editions, 1974. p. cm. Reprint of the 1935 ed. published by Clarendon Press, Oxford, which was issued in series: The Taylorian lecture, 1935. [N70.T78G3 1974] 74-13080 ISBN 0-8414-4539-7 (lib. bdg.)
1. Tolstoi, Lev Nikolaevich, graf, 1828-1910. Chto takoe iskusstvo. I. Title. II. Series: The Taylorian lecture, 1935.   BIP

Toltecs.

DAVIES, Nigel, 1920-   972
The Toltecs, until the fall of Tula / by Nigel Davies. 1st ed. Norman : University of Oklahoma Press, c1977. xviii, 533 p. : ill. ; 24 cm. (The Civilization of the American Indian series) Includes index. Bibliography: p. 485-517. [F1219.D2783] 76-62513 ISBN 0-8061-1394-4 : 14.95
1. Toltecs. 2. Mexico—Antiquities. I. Title. II. Series.

Tomahawks.

PETERSON, Harold Leslie,   739.72
1922-
American Indian tomahawks. Appendix, The blacksmith shop, by Milford G. Chandler. [New York, N. Y.] 10032, Bway 155 St., Heye Found., Mus. of the Amer. Indian, 1965 viii,142p. illus., plates (pt. col.) ports. 26cm. (Contributions from the Mus. of the Amer. Indian, Heye Found. v. 19) Bibl. [E51.N42vol.19] 65-17277 8.50 pap.,
1. Tomahawks. I. Title. II. Series: New York. Museum of the American Indian, Heye Foundation. Contributions, v. 19 BIP

PETERSON, Harold Leslie,   739.7'2
1922-
American Indian tomahawks, by Harold L. Peterson. With an appendix, The blacksmith shop, by Milford G. Chandler. [Rev. ed. New York] Museum of the American Indian, Heye Foundation, 1971. viii, 142, [99] p. illus. 27 cm. (Contributions from the Museum of the American Indian, Heye Foundation, v. 19) Bibliography: p. 78-81. [E51.N42 vol. 19, 1971] [E98.A65] 73-125345 10.00
1. Tomahawks. I. Title. II. Series: New York (City). Museum of the American Indian, Heye Foundation. Contributions, v. 19.

Tombs—Japan.

KIDDER, Jonathan Edward.   730.952
Early Japanese art; the great tombs and treasures [by] J. Edward Kidder. Princeton, N.J., Van Nostrand [1964] 354 p. 113 illus., maps, col. plates. 25 cm. Bibliography: p.   [348]-[351]
[GN796.J3K5] 64-57443
1. Tombs—Japan. I. Title.

Tombs—Sudan, Egyptian.

DUNHAM, Dows, 1890-   913.3978
The royal cemeteries of Kush. Cambridge, Mass., Published for the Museum of Fine Arts by Harvard University Press, 1950- v. illus., plates, maps (part fold.) 35 cm. Contents.v. 1. El Kurru. Bibliographical footnotes. [DT73.K8D8] 51-9344
1. Tombs—Sudan, Egyptian. 2. Sudan, Egyptian—Antiq. I. Title.

Tomioka. Tessai, 1837-1924.

ODAKANE, Taro, 1909-   759.952
Tessai, master of the literati style. Tr. [from Japanese] adaption by Money L. Hickman. Tokyo, Kodansha Intl.; dist. Rutland, Vt. Japan Pubns. [1964,c 1965] 124p. illus., col. plates. port. 29cm. 63-11763 10.00
1. Tomioka. Tessai, 1837-1924. I. Title.

Tomlin. Bradley Walker, 1899-1953.

BAUR, John Ireland Howe,   759.13
1909-
Bradley Walker Tomlin. [Research by Rosalind Irvine] With notes on the artist by Philip Guston [and others] New York, Published for the Whitney Museum of American Art by Macmillan, 1957. 62p. illus., plates (part col.) port. 27cm. 'The result of a retrospective exhibition of painting by Bradley Walker Tomlin, organized by the Art Galleries of the University of California, Los Angeles, in association with the Whitney Museum of American Art, where it opened in September, 1957.'--p. 62. 'Catalogue of the exhibition': p. 58-59. Bibliography: p. 60-61. [ND237.T58B3] 57-14769 927 57-14769
1. Tomlin. Bradley Walker, 1899-1953. I. Whitney Museum of American Art, New York. II. Title.

BRADLEY Walker Tomlin.   759.13
[Research by Rosalind Irvine] With notes on the artist by Philip Guston [and others] New York, Published for the Whitney Museum of American Art by Macmillan, 1957. 62p. illus., plates (part col.) port. 27cm. 'The result of a retrospective exhibition of paintings by Bradley Walker Tomlin, organized by the Art Galleries of the University of California, Los Angeles, in association with the Whitney Museum of American Art, where it opened in September, 1957.'--p. 62. 'Catalogue of the exhibition': p. 58-59. Bibliography: p. 60-61. [ND237.T58B3] [ND237.T58B3] 927.5 57-14769 57-14769
1. Tomlin, Bradley Walxer, 1899-1953. I. Baur, John Ireland Howe, 1909- II. Whitney Museum of American Art, New York.

TOMLIN, Bradley Walker,   759.13
1899-1953.
Bradley Walker Tomlin : a retrospective view. Garden City, N.Y. : Whaler Press, c1975. 164 p. : ill. (some col.) ; 26 cm. Catalog of a traveling exhibition, April 1975-May 1976, organized by the Emily Lowe Gallery, Hofstra University, Hempstead, and the Albright-Knox Art Gallery, Buffalo. Bibliography: p. 156-159. [ND237.T58E44] 75-29510 ISBN 0-914782-03-7
1. Tomlin, Bradley Walker, 1899-1953. I. Emily Lowe Gallery. II. Albright-Knox Art Gallery.

Tomlinson, Charles, 1927—

TOMLINSON, Charles,   760'.092'4
1927-
In black and white : the graphics of Charles Tomlinson / with an introduction by Octavio Paz. Cheadle : Carcanet New Press, 1976. 26 p., 53 p. of plates : ill. ; 23 cm. [NE642.T65A47] 76-363759 ISBN 0-85635-117-2 : £3.25
1. Tomlinson, Charles, 1927- I. Title.   BIP

T●●●● ●homas, 1639-1713.

SY●●●●S, Robert Wemyss,   926;8111
18●●
Thom●● ●ompion, his life & work. London, New York, Batsford [1951] xvi, 320 p. illus. (part col.) ports. 30 cm. [NK7417.T6S8] 52-35554
1. Tompion, Thomas, 1639-1713. 2. Clocks and watches — England. I. Title.

SYMONDS, Robert   681'.11'0924
Wemyss, 1899-1958.
Thomas Tompion: his life and work [by] R. W. Symonds. London, New York, Spring Books, 1969. viii, 320 p., 3 plates (2 fold.). illus. (incl. 4 col.), facsims., map, ports. 30 cm. Includes bibliographical references. [NK7497.T6S9 1969] 72-522090 63/-
1. Tompion, Thomas, 1639-1713.

Tonala ruin, Mexico.

TONALA, Mexico,   972.7
an archaeological survey. Santa Fe, N. M., School of American Research, 1953. xvi, 126p. illus., maps (part fold.) diagrs. 28cm. (Monographs of the School of American Research, no. 16) '500 copies.' Bibliography: p. 123-126. [F1219.1.T65F4] [F1219.1.T65F4] 913.727 53-38378 53-38378
1. Tonala ruin, Mexico. I. Ferdon, Edwin N 1913- II. Series: Santa Fe, N. M. Schools of American Research. Monographs, no. 16

Tonalism—United States.

CORN, Wanda M.   759.13'074'019461
The color of mood: American tonalism, 1880-1910 [by] Wanda M. Corn. San Francisco, M. H. De Young Memorial Museum, 1972. 46 p. illus., 14 plates (part col.) 23 cm. Erratum slip inserted. Catalogue of an exhibition held at the California Palace of the Legion of Honor, San Francisco, Jan. 22-Apr. 2, 1972. Bibliography: p. 26-27. [N6510.5.T6C6] 70-188449
1. Tonalism—United States. 2. Paintings, American—Exhibitions. 3. Photography, Artistic—Exhibitions. I. De Young Memorial Museum, San Francisco. II. California Palace of the Legion of Honor, San Francisco. III. Title.

Tongue (in religion, folk-lore, etc.)

COMPTON, Carl B.   704.94'2
The protruding tongue, by Carl B. Compton. El Paso, Tex., El Paso Archaeological Society, 1971. ii, 16 p. illus. 28 cm. ([El Paso Archaeological Society] Special report no. 10) Bibliography: p. 15-16. [GR489.C55] 74-152455
1. Tongue (in religion, folk-lore, etc.) I. Title. II. Series.

Tonque Pueblo.

BARNETT, Franklin.   970.3
Tonque Pueblo; a report of partial excavation of an ancient Pueblo IV Indian ruin in New Mexico. With foreword by Marjorie F. Lambert. Albuquerque, N.M., Albuquerque Archaeological Society, 1969. xv, 237 p. illus., plans. 28 cm. Bibliography: p. 233-237. [E78.N65B23] 70-8536
1. Tonque Pueblo.

Tonson, Jacob, 1656?-1736.

GEDULD, Harry M.   655.4'24
Prince of publishers; a study of the work and career of Jacob Tonson [by] Harry M. Geduld. Bloomington, Indiana University Press, 1969. 245 p. illus., facsims., ports. 23 cm. (Indiana University humanities series, no. 66) Bibliographical references included in "Notes" (p. 203-235) [AS36.I385 no. 66] 68-64121 6.75
1. Tonson, Jacob, 1656?-1736. I. Title. II. Series: Indiana. University. Indiana University humanities series, no. 66

Toole, John, 1815-1860.

O'NEAL, William Bainter   759.13
Primitive into painter; life and letters of

John Toole. Charlottesville, University of Virginia Press [c.]1960. 113p. 12 plates. 31cm. Bibl.: p.104-105. 60-16871 10.00
1. Toole, John, 1815-1860. I. Title.

Tools.

HOW to get the most out of   621.9
your tools. Middle Village, N.Y., Jonathan David Publishers [1974] 173 p. illus. 22 cm. Based on a book originally published by the Bureau of Naval Personnel under title: Tools and their uses. [TT153.H69] 74-16107 8.95; 6.95 (lib. bdg.)
1. Tools.   BIP

MCSHANE, Robert.   621.9
Portable electric tools and how to use them. [Chicago] Popular Mechanics Press [c1952] 96p. illus. 24cm. (Popular mechanics craftsman's library) [TT153.M2] 53-1024
1. Tools. 2. Electric apparatus and appliances. I. Title.

YATES, Raymond Francis,   621.9
1895-
The boys' book of tools. New York, Harper [1957] 173 p. illus. 22 cm. [TT160.Y35] 57-5358
1. Tools. I. Title.   BIP

Tools—Handbooks, manuals, etc.

CLARK, Stephen, 1948-   621.9
The complete illustrated tool book / edited by Stephen Clark and Daniel Lyman. New York : Galahad Books, c1974. 413 p. : ill. ; 24 cm. Published by Pathfinder Publications under title: The incredible illustrated tool book. Includes index. [TT153.C57 1974b] 75-308806 ISBN 0-88365-262-5 : 12.50
1. Tools—Handbooks, manuals, etc. I. Lyman, Daniel, 1950- joint author. II. Title. III. Title: Tool book.

CLARK, Stephen, 1948-   621.9
The incredible illustrated tool book. Edited by Stephen Clark and Daniel Lyman. Boston, Pathfinder Publications [1974] viii, 413 p. illus. 19 cm. "A Pathmark book." [TT153.C57] 74-80451 ISBN 0-913390-05-4 2.50 (pbk.).
1. Tools—Handbooks, manuals, etc. I. Lyman, Daniel, 1950- joint author. II. Title.   BIP

Tools—Hist.

BURNS, William Aloysius,   621.909
1909-
Man and his tools. Pictures by Paula Hutchison. New York, McGraw-Hill [1956] 158p. illus. 24cm. (A McGraw-Hill-American Museum of Natural History publication) [GN799.T6B8] 55-12095
1. Tools—Hist. I. Title.

OAKLEY, Kenneth Page, 1911-   571
Man the tool-maker. [Chicago] University of Chicago Press [1957] 159p. illus. 21cm. (Phoenix books, P20) [GN799.T6O2 1957] 57-14058
1. Tools—Hist. 2. Implements, utensils, etc. I. Title.   BIP

Toothpick holders—Collectors and collecting.

HEACOCK, William.   745.1
1000 toothpick holders : a collector's guide / byWilliam Heacock; sponsored by the National Toothpic k Holder Collectors' Society; photography by Richardson Printing Corporation. Marietta, Ohio : Antique Publications, c1977. 112 p. : ill. (some col.) ; 23 cm. Includes index. Bibliography: p. 14. [NK9508.H4] 77-152994 ISBN 0-915410-10-9 : 10.95
1. Toothpick holders—Collectors and collecting. I. National Toothpick Holder Collectors' Society. II. Title.

MIGHELL, Florence.   748.8
A collectors book on toothpick holders. Des Moines, Printed by Wallace-Homestead, c1973. [33] p. illus. 23 cm. [NK9508.M53] 74-168258
1. Toothpick holders—Collectors and collecting. I. Title.   BIP

Top.

GOULD, Douglas W. 688.7'28
The top: universal toy, enduring pastime [by] D. W. Gould. [1st ed.] New York, Clarkson N. Potter; distributed by Crown Publishers [1973] xi, 271 p. illus. 24 cm. Bibliography: p. 246-269. [TS2301.T7G68 1973] 79-169050 ISBN 0-517-50416-2 7.50
1. Top.

Top — Juvenile literature.

KETTELKAMP, Larry. j 796.1
Spinning tops. [New York] Morrow, 1966. 63 p. col. illus. 24 cm. [GV1218.T5K4] 66-10307
1. Top — Juvenile literature. I. Title. BIP

Topanga Canyon, Calif.

TREGANZA, Adan Eduardo, 1916- 970.49493
The Topanga culture; final report on excavations, 1948, by A. E. Treganza and A. Bierman. [Berkeley, University of California Press, 1958] iv, 45-86 p. illus., maps, tables. 28 cm. (Anthropological records, v. 20, no. 2) Bibliography: p. 76. [E51.A58 vol. 20, no. 2] A 58
1. Topanga Canyon, Calif. 2. California — Antiq. I. Bierman, Agnes, joint author. II. Title. III. Series.

TREGANZA, Adan Eduardo, 1916- 913.794
The Topanga culture; first season's excavation of the Tank Site, 1947, by A. E. Treganza and C. G. Malamud. [Berkeley, University of California Press, 1950] iii, 129-157 p. illus., fold. map. 28 cm. (Anthropological records 12:4) Bibliography: p. 153 [E51.A58] A 50
1. Topanga Canyon, Calif. 2. California — Antiq. I. Malamud, Consuelo Gorn, 1923- joint author. II. Title. III. Series.

Topiary work.

HADFIELD, Miles. 635.97'6
Topiary and ornamental hedges: their history and cultivation. New York, St. Martin's Press [1971] 100 p. illus. 26 cm. Bibliography: p. 95-96. [SB463.H33] 71-154677 12.50
1. Topiary work. 2. Hedges. I. Title.

ISHIMOTO, Tatsuo. 712
The art of shaping, shrubs, trees, and other plants, by Tatsuo and Kiyoko Ishimoto. New York, Crown Publishers [1966] 125 p. illus. 24 cm. [SB463.I73] 66-26185
1. Topiary work. I. Ishimoto, Kiyoko, joint author. II. Title.

Topiary work—Juvenile literature.

KRAMER, Jack, 1927- 635.9'65
Plant sculptures : making miniature indoor topiaries / Jack Kramer ; photos. by Matthew Barr ; drawings by Tom Adams. 1st ed. New York : Morrow, 1978. 63 p. : ill. ; 24 cm. Includes index. Discusses how the art of topiary can be performed indoors with house plants and gives instruction for ten projects. [SB463.K7] 78-2524 ISBN 0-688-22144-0 : 5.95 ISBN 0-688-32144-5 lib.bdg. : 5.49
1. Topiary work—Juvenile literature. 2. Indoor gardening—Juvenile literature. I. Barr, Matthew. II. Adams, Tom. III. Title. BIP

Torii, Kiyonaga, 1752-1815.

TAKAHASHI, Seiichiro, 1884- [761.283] 927.6
Torii Kiyonaga, 1752-1815. English adaptation by Thomas Kaasa. [1st English ed.] Tokyo, Rutland, Vt., C. E. Tuttle Co. [1956] 1 v. (unpaged) plates (Art col.) 17 cm. (Kodansha library of Japanese art, no. 8) Bibliography: last page in book. [NE1325.T63T3] 56-13411
1. Toric, Kiyonaga, 1752-1815. I. Title. II. Series.

TORII, Kiyonaga, 1752-1815. 769.952
Kiyonaga, by Muneshige Narazaki. English translation by John Bester. Tokyo, Palo Alto, Calif., Kodansha International [1969] 88 p. col. plates. 26 cm. (Masterworks of Ukiyo-e, 9) [NE1325.T63N313] 72-82656 ISBN 0-87011-099-3 3.50
I. Narazaki, Muneshige, 1904- II. Title. III. Series. BIP

Torksey China Factory.

EXLEY, Clifford Landseer. 338.4'7'6665
A history of the Torksey and Mansfield china factories, by C. L. Exley. Lincoln, G. R. G. Exley, 1970. 82 p. illus. (1 col.), geneal. table, map, plan. 22 cm. Bibliography: p. 80-82. [NK4210.T64E94] 74-163281 ISBN 0-9501465-0-1 25/-
1. Torksey China Factory. 2. Mansfield China Factory. 3. Porcelain, English. I. Title. BIP

Torquay, Eng.—Description—Views.

MEADFOOT-WELLSWOOD and Area Residents' Association. 942.3'595
The charm of Torquay / Meadfoot-Wellswood and Area Residents' Association. Torquay : The Association, [1976] [24] p. : chiefly ill., col. map ; 21 x 26 cm. Cover title. [DA690.T69M4 1976] 77-362751 ISBN 0-905854-01-2 : £0.65
1. Torquay, Eng.—Description—Views. 2. Historic buildings—England—Torquay—Pictorial works. 3. Torquay, Eng.—Buildings—Pictorial works. I. Title.

Torres-Garcia, Joaquin, 1874-1949.

DUNCAN, Barbara, 1921- 759.6
Joaquin Torres-Garcia, 1874-1949 : chronology and catalogue of the family collection : exhibition held at the University of Texas at Austin Art Museum, Archer M. Huntington Galleries, 13 October-24 November 1974 / [by Barbara Duncan]. [Austin] : The Art Museum, [1974] 148 p. : ill. (some col.) ; 25 cm. Includes bibliographical references. [ND429.T6D86] 74-24335
1. Torres-Garcia, Joaquin, 1874-1949. I. Texas. University at Austin. Art Museum.

TORRES-GARCIA, Joaquin 1874-1949. 759.6
Joaquin Torres-Garcia, 1874-1949. [Providence, Museum of Art, Rhode Island School of Design, 1970] 139 p. illus. (part col.) 26 cm. Catalogue of an exhibition held at the National Gallery of Canada, the Solomon R. Guggenheim Museum, and the Museum of Art, Rhode Island School of Design. Bibliography: p. 121-137. [N6729.T6O8] 74-130023
1. Ottawa. National Gallery of Canada. II. Solomon R. Guggenheim Museum, New York. III. Rhode Island School of Design, Providence. Museum of Art.

Torres, Horacio, 1924—

TORRES, Horacio, 1924- 759.9895
Horacio Torres. Museum of Fine Arts, Boston, Massachusetts, January 9-March 3, 1974. [Text by Kenworth Moffett. Boston, Museum of Fine Arts, 1974] [24] p. (chiefly illus. (part col.)) 26 cm. Catalog of the exhibition. [ND429.T58M63] 73-93679
1. Torres, Horacio, 1924- I. Moffett, Kenworth. II. Boston. Museum of Fine Arts.

Toshusai Sharaku, fl. 1794.

SUZUKI, Juzo, 1919- 769'.924
Sharaku, translation by John Bester. [1st ed.] Tokyo, Palo Alto, Calif., Kodansha International [1968] 96 p. col. illus., ports. 27 cm. (Masterworks of ukiyo-e, 2) [NE1325.T65S9] 68-13740 unpriced
1. Toshusai Sharaku, fl. 1794. 2. Actors—Japan—Portraits. I. Title. II. Series. BIP

Tote bags.

AIKEN, Joyce. 646.4'8
The total tote bag book : designer totes to craft and carry / Joyce Aiken and Jean Ray Laury. 1st ed. New York : Taplinger Pub. Co., 1976. p. cm. Includes index. [TT667.A35 1976] 76-11058 ISBN 0-8008-7793-4 : 9.95
1. Tote bags. I. Laury, Jean Ray, joint author. II. Title. BIP

MACKALL, Lucy. 646.4'8
Lucy's Bag book / by Lucy Mackall ; photos. by Carol E. Harper ; ill. by Judy Maiewski and Lucy Mackall. Boston : Houghton Mifflin, 1978. 144 p., [2] leaves of plates : ill. ; 25 cm. [TT667.M3] 77-16031 ISBN 0-395-26302-6 : 12.95 pbk. : 6.95
1. Tote bags. 2. Handbags. I. Title. II. Title: Bag book. BIP

Totem poles—Northwest coast of North America—Pictorial works.

ALLEN, D. fl.1977- 736'.4
Totem poles of the Northwest / by D. Allen. [Saanichton, B.C. ; Seattle : Hancock House, c1977] 32 p. : ill. (some col.) ; 22 cm. [E98.T65A43] 77-379664 ISBN 0-919654-83-5 : 2.50
1. Totem poles—Northwest coast of North America—Pictorial works. I. Title.

Totems.

BRINDZE, Ruth, 1903- 970.6572
The story of the totem pole. Illus. by Yeffe Kimball. New York, Vanguard Press [1951] 62 p. illus. 24 cm. [E98.T65B7] 51-8370
1. Totems. 2. Indians of North America—Northwest, Pacific. I. Title. BIP

GARFIELD, Viola Edmundson, 1899- 970.67364
The wolf and the raven; totem poles of southeastern Alaska, by Viola E. Garfield and Linn A. Forrest. [Rev. ed.] Seattle, University of Washington Press, 1961. ix, 148, [6] p. illus., map 23 cm. Bibliography: p. [153]-[154] [E98.T65G32 1961] 61-59889
1. Totems. 2. Indians of North America—Northwest, Pacific. I. Forrest, Linn Argyle, 1905- joint author. II. Title. BIP

KEITHAHN, Edward Linnaeus, 1900- 970.498
Monuments in cedar. [1st ed.] Seattle, Superior Pub. Co., 1963. 160 p. illus. (part col.) ports., map. 27 cm. Bibliography: p. 157-158. [E98.T65K4] 63-15216
1. Totems. 2. Indians of North America — Northwest, Pacific. I. Title. BIP

Toulouse-Lautrec Monfa, Henri Marie Raymond de, 1864-1901.

THE best untold; 759.13
a book of paintings. [New York, Blue Heron Press, 1953] 1v. (chiefly illus.) 29cm. [ND237.B55A43] [ND237.B55A43] 927.5 54-112 54-112
I. Biberman, Edward, 1904-

BOURET, Jean. 759.4
The life and work of Toulouse-Lautrec; court painter to the wicked. [Translated from the French by Daphne Woodward] New York, H. N. Abrams [1966] 270 p. illus. (part col.) facsims. ports. 21 cm. Translation of Toulouse-Lautrec. [ND553.T7B613] 66-13667
1. Toulouse-Lautrec Monfa, Henri Marie Raymond de, 1864-1901. I. Title.

COGNIAT, Raymond, 1896- 759.4
Lautrec. [Translated from the French by Anne Ross] New York, Crown Publishers [1966] 43 p. illus. (part col.) 19 cm. (Basic art library) [ND553.T7C543] 66-26178
1. Toulouse-Lautrec Monfa, Henri Marie Raymond de, 1864-1901.

FERMIGIER, Andre. 759.4 B
Toulouse-Lautrec. Translated by Paul Stevenson. New York, Praeger [1969] 255 p. illus. (part col.) 22 cm. (A Praeger world of art profile) Bibliography: p. 247-248. [ND553.T7F413] 75-82149 7.50
1. Toulouse-Lautrec Monfa, Henri Marie Raymond de, 1864-1901.

FRYBERGER, Betsy Geraghty. 769'.92'4
Toulouse-Lautrec: prints and drawings from the collection of Mr. and Mrs. Sherman Butler. Catalogue by Betsy Geraghty Fryberger. [Stanford, Calif., Dept. of Art, Stanford University, 1971?] 42 p. illus. (part col.) 22 cm. (Stanford art book 13) "Stanford Art Gallery, Stanford University, December 18, 1971 to February 20, 1972." [NE2349.5.T68F78] 72-198464
1. Toulouse-Lautrec Monfa, Henri Marie Raymond de, 1864-1901. 2. Butler, Sherman—Art Collections. I. Stanford University. Thomas Welton Stanford Art Gallery. II. Title. III. Series.

HANSON, Lawrence. 759.4
The tragic life of Toulouse-Lautrec [by] Lawrence and Elisabeth Hanson. N[ew] Y[ork] Random House [1956] x, 277p. plates, ports. 24cm. Bibliography: p.264-270. [ND553.T7H3] 927.5 56-5208
1. Tculcuse-Lautrec Monfa, Henri Marie Raymond de, 1864-1901. I. Hanson, Elisabeth M., joint author. II. Title.

HANSON, Lawrence. 759.4
The tragic life of Toulouse-Lautrev [by] Lawrence and Elisabeth Hanson. N[ew] Y[ork] Random House [1956] x, 277p. plates, ports. 24cm. Bibliography: p. 264-270. [ND553.T7H3] 927.5 56-5208
1. Toulouse-Lautrec Monfa, Henri Marie Raymond de, 1864-1901. I. Hanson, Elisabeth M., joint author. II. Title.

HORWITZ, Sylvia L. 759.4
Toulouse-Lautrec: his world, by Sylvia L. Horwitz, with photos. of the artist and his work. [1st ed.] New York, Harper & Row [1973] 215 p. illus. 22 cm. Bibliography: p. 209-210. [ND553.T7H66 1973] 73-5484 ISBN 0-06-022592-0 4.95
1. Toulouse-Lautrec Monfa, Henri Marie Raymond de, 1864-1901.
Library binding 4.79, ISBN 0-06-022593-9.

HUISMAN, Philippe. 759.4
Lautrec by Lautrec [by] P. Huisman [and] M. G. Dortu. [Translated and edited by Corinne Bellow] New York, Viking Press [1964] 274 p. illus. (part col., part mounted) maps, col. plates. ports. (part col.) 31 cm. (A Studio book) Bibliography: p. 247. [ND553.T7H783] 64-20855
1. Toulouse-Lautrec Monfa, Henri Marie Raymond de, 1864-1901. I. Dortu, M. G. joint author. II. Title.

HUISMAN, Philippe. 759.4
Toulouse-Lautrec [by] Philippe Huisman [and] M. G. Dortu. [1st U.S. ed.] Garden City, N.Y., Doubleday [1973] 95 p. illus. (part col.) 34 cm. (The Great impressionists) Bibliography: p. 94. [ND553.T7H79 1973] 73-82255 ISBN 0-385-08374-2 9.95
1. Toulouse-Lautrec Monfa, Henri Marie Raymond de, 1864-1901. I. Dortu, M. G., joint author.

JEDLICKA, Gotthard, 1899- 759.4
Henri de Toulouse-Lautrec. [Tr.: Joan Erskine] New York, Barnes & Noble [1962, c.1961] 85p. illus. (pt. col.) 18cm. (Barnes & Noble art ser. 62-52815 .75 pap.,
1. Toulouse-Lautrec Monfa, Henri Marie Raymond de, 1864-1901. I. Title.

JULIEN, Edouard 759.4
Lautrec. [Translated from the French by Helen C. Slonim] New York, Crown Publishers, 1959 [ ] llus. (part mounted col.) col. plates. 29cm. 95p. b(bibl.) 59-65436 2.95 bds.,
1. Toulouse-Lautrec Monfa, Henri Marie Raymond de, 1864-1901. I. Title.

KELLER, Horst. 760'.0924
Toulouse-Lautrec: painter of Paris. [Translated from German by Erika Bizzarri] New York, H. N. Abrams [1969, c1968] 108 p. illus. (part col.), ports. (part col.) 30 cm. Translation of Henri de Toulouse-Lautrec. [ND553.T7K413] 69-12478
1. Toulouse-Lautrec Monfa, Henri Marie Raymond, de, 1864-1901. I. Title.

LOFTUS, John. 760'.0924
Toulouse-Lautrec. New York, McGraw-Hill [1969] 47 p. illus., 20 col. slides (in pockets) 29 cm. (Color slide program of the great masters) [ND553.T7L6] 79-91810
1. Toulouse-Lautrec Monfa, Henri Marie Raymond de, 1864-1901. I. Title. II. Series.

NEBBIA, Ugo, 1882- 759.4
Toulouse-Lautrec. Tr. by Cesare Foligno. New York, Crown [1966] 26p. illus., 10

col. plates. 31cm. (Folio art bks.) [ND553.T7N363] 66-3968 1.45 pap.,
1. Toulouse-Lautrec Monfa, Henri Marie Raymond, de, 1864-1901. I. Title.

NEW York (City). 759.4'074'01471
Museum of Modern Art.
Lautrec: Redon. Reprint ed. [New York] Arno Press, 1969. 29 p., 39 plates. 27 cm. At head of title: Tenth loan exhibition. February 1-March 2, 1931. Introduction signed: J. A. [i.e. Jere Abbott] [ND552.N4 1969] 71-86435
1. Toulouse-Lautrec Monfa, Henri Marie Raymond de, 1864-1901. 2. Redon, Odilon, 1840-1916. I. Abbott, Jere. BIP

PERRUCHOT, Henri, 1917- 759.4
T-Lautrec. Tr. by Humphrey Hare. New York, Collier [1962, c.1958, 1960] 350p. illus. 18cm. (BS124Y) Bibl. 1.50 pap.,
1. Toulouse-Lautrec Monfa, Henri Marie Raymond de, 1864-1901. I. Title.

PERRUCHOT, Henri, 1917- 759.4
T-Lautrec. Translated by Humphrey Hare. [1st American ed.] Cleveland, World Pub. Co. [1961, c1960] 317 p. illus. 23 cm. (His Art and destiny) Translation of La vie de Toulouse Lautrec. Includes bibliography. [ND553.T7P413] 61-6334
1. Toulouse-Lautrec Monfa, Henri Marie Raymond de, 1864-1901.

POLASEK, Jan. 741.9'44
Toulouse-Lautrec : drawings introd. and commentary by Jan Polasek. New York : St. Martin's Press, 1976, c1975. 50, [1] p., 62, xx leaves of plates : 82 ill. (some col.) ; 32 cm. Bibliography: p. [51] [NC248.T63P642 1976] 74-83976 15.95
1. Toulouse-Lautrec Monfa, Henri Marie Raymond de, 1864-1901. I. Toulouse-Lautrec Monfa, Henri Marie Raymond de, 1864-1901.

SYMONS, Arthur, 1865- 709'.44
1945.
From Toulouse-Lautrec to Rodin; with some personal impressions. Freeport, N.Y., Books for Libraries Press [1968] vii, 242 p. facsims., port. 23 cm. (Essay index reprint series) Reprint of the 1929 ed. Contents.Contents.—Henri de Toulouse-Lautrec.—On the genius of Degas.—Constantin Guys.—Honore Daumier.—Jean Louis Forain.—The paintings of Henry de Groux.—Simeon Solomon.—Monticelli.—Gustave Moreau.—Odilon Redon.—Aubrey Beardsley.—Whistler and Manet.—Auguste Rodin. [N6450.S87 1968] 68-20342
1. Toulouse-Lautrec Monfa, Henri Marie Raymond de, 1864-1901. 2. Art, Modern—19th century—History. 3. Artists, French. I. Title.

TAPIE de Celeyran, Mary. 759.4
Our cousin Lautrec. [Translated from the French by Mildred Sherrod Bissinger. 1st ed.] Kentfield [Calif., 1967] 63 p. 10 illus. 26 cm. "Two hundred and fifty copies comprise this edition." Translation of Notre oncle Lautrec. [ND553.T7T33] 68-156
1. Toulouse-Lautrec Monfa, Henri Marie Raymond de, 1864-1901. I. Title.

THOMSON, Richard. 760'.092'4 B
Toulouse-Lautrec / Richard Thomson. 1st U.S. ed. New York : Two Continents, c1977. p. cm. (The Oresko art book series) Includes index. Bibliography: p. [ND553.T7T47 1977] 77-21483 ISBN 0-8467-0372-6 : 15.95 9.95
1. Toulouse-Lautrec Monfa, Henri Marie Raymond de, 1864-1901. 2. Painters—France—Biography. I. Title. II. Series.

TIETZE, Hans, 1880- 927.5
Toulouse Lautrec. [1st ed.] New York, Beechhurst Press [1953] 61, [2] p. illus. (part col.) port. 36 cm. Bibliography: p. [63] [ND553.T7T5] 53-13338
1. Toulouse-Lautrec Monfa, Henri Marie Raymond de, 1864-1901.

TOULOUSE-LAUTREC Monfa, 741.9'44
Henri Marie Raymond de, 1864-1901.
Book covers and brochures. [Cambridge] Dept. of Printing and Graphic Arts, Harvard College Library, 1972. 63 p. illus. 20 cm. Bibliography: p. 63. [NC980.5.T68H37] 73-154810
1. Toulouse-Lautrec Monfa, Henri Marie Raymond de, 1864-1901. I. Harvard University. Library. Dept. of Printing and Graphic Arts.

TOULOUSE-LAUTREC 760'.092'4
Monfa, Henri Marie Raymond de, 1864-1901.
Toulouse Lautrec / Richard Shone. New York : St. Martin's Press, 1977. p. cm. [N6853.T6S55] 77-71077 ISBN 0-312-80989-1 pbk. : 5.95
1. Toulouse-Lautrec Monfa, Henri Marie Raymond de, 1864-1901. I. Shone, Richard.

TOULOUSE-LAUTREC 704.94'7918'2
MONFA, Henri Marie Raymond de, 1864-1901.
One hundred ten unpublished drawings. Boston, Boston Book and Art Shop [1955] 1v. (unpaged) illus. 24 x 33cm. Reproductions from Lautrec's sketchbook in the Albert H. Wiggin Collection in the Boston Public Library. Edited with introd., by A. W. Heintzelman and M. R. D. Heintzelman. In case. [NC1135.T6A53] 55-9576
I. Title.

Toulouse-Lautrec Monfa, Henri Marie Raymond de, 1864-1901—Catalogs.

TOULOUSE-LAUTREC 760'.092'4
Monfa, Henri Marie Raymond de, 1864-1901.
Toulouse-Lautrec / [text by] Edward Lucie-Smith. Oxford : Phaidon, 1977. 16 p., 48 p. of plates : chiefly col. ill., col. ports. ; 31 cm. Bibliography: p. 14. [ND553.T7A4 1977] 77-80135 ISBN 0-7148-1802-X : 7.95
1. Toulouse-Lautrec Monfa, Henri Marie Raymond de, 1864-1901—Catalogs. I. Lucie-Smith, Edward.
Distributed by Dutton, New York

Toulouse-Lautrec Monfa, Henri Marie Raymond de, 1864-1901—Juvenile literature.

RABOFF, Ernest Lloyd. 759.4
Henri de Toulouse-Lautrec, by Ernest Raboff. Garden City, N.Y., Doubleday [1970] [31] p. illus. (part col.), ports. (part col.) 29 cm. (Art for children) (A Gemini-Smith book) A brief biographical sketch of the nineteenth-century artist accompanies examples and discussions of his works. [ND553.T7R3] 70-93207 3.95
1. Toulouse-Lautrec Monfa, Henri Marie Raymond de, 1864-1901—Juvenile literature. I. Title.

Toulouse—Lautrec Monfa, Henri Marle Raymond de, 1864-1901.

JOYANT, Maurice. 741'.0924
Henri de Toulouse-Lautrec. New York, Arno Press [1968] 2 v. illus., ports. 27 cm. (Arno series of contemporary art, no. 9) "Reprint edition complete in two volumes." Originally published 1926-27. Includes facsimile of original t.p. "Essai de catalogue chronologique des dessins, pastels, aquarelles, et ceramiques": v. 2, p. [175]-[245] Bibliography: v. 2, p. 265-[274] [NC1135.T6J62 1968] 68-9233
I. Toulouse-Lautrec Monfa, Henri Marie Raymond de, 1864-1901. BIP

LAWRENCE, Jacob, 1917- 759.13
The Toussaint L'Ouverture series; [exhibition] December 8-30, 1968, the Art Gallery, Fisk University. [Nashville, 1968] [9] p. illus., port. 23 cm. "Exhibited on the occasion of the visit of Jacob Lawrence to Fisk University as visiting Scholar in Art, December 8-10, 1968." [ND237.L29A58] 72-626270
I. Fisk University, Nashville, Art Gallery. II. Title.

PHILADELPHIA Museum of Art. 759.4
Toulouse-Lautrec; exhibition organized in collaboration with the Albi Museum. Philadelphia Museum of Art, October 29-December 11, 1955; the Art Institute of Chicago, January 2-February 15, 1956. [Philadelphia, 1955] 112p. (chiefly illus. (part col.)) 26c4. [N6853.T6P4] [N6853.T6P4] 927.5 56-1888 56-1888
1. Toulouse—Lautrec Monfa, Henri Marle Raymond de, 1864-1901. 2. Art, French—Exhibitions. I. Chicago. Art Institute. II. Title.

TOULOUSE-LAUTREC Monfa, 759.4
Henri Marie Raymond de, 1864-1901.
Henri de Toulouse-Lautrec. Text by Douglas Cooper. New York, H. N. Abrams [1969?] 40 p. illus. (part col.) 33 cm. (Great art of the ages) [ND553.T7C563] 72-191691 ISBN 0-8109-5139-8
I. Cooper, Douglas, 1911-

TOULOUSE-LAUTREC Monfa, 759.4
Henri Marie Raymond de, 1864-1901.
Henri de Toulouse-Lautrec. Text by Douglas Cooper. New York, H. N. Abrams [1970?] 24 p. illus. (part col.) 33 cm. (The Library of great painters. Portfolio ed.) [ND553.T7C56 1970] 69-14761
I. Cooper, Douglas, 1911-

TOULOUSE-LAUTREC Monfa, 760'.0924
Henri Marie Raymond de, 1864-1901.
Henri de Toulouse-Lautrec. Text by Douglas Cooper. New York, H. N. Abrams [1969?] 152 p. illus. (part col.) 34 cm. (The Library of great painters.) Bibliography: p. 152. [N6853.T6C6 1969] 69-19716
I. Cooper, Douglas, 1911-

TOULOUSE-LAUTREC Monfa, 759.4
Henri Marie Raymond de, 1864-1901.
Henri de Toulouse-Lautrec. Text by Douglas Cooper. New York, H. N. Abrams [1952] 24 p. illus. (part mounted col.) 33 cm. (The Library of great painters. Portfolio ed.) "An Abrams art book." [ND553.T7C56] 927.5 53-225
I. Cooper, Douglas, 1911-

TOULOUSE-LAUTREC Monfa, 760'.0924
Henri Marie Raymond de, 1864-1901.
Toulouse-Lautrec, by F. Novotny. [Translated from the German by Michael Glenney. New York] Phaidon; [Distributors in the U.S.: Praeger, 1969] 198, [2] p. illus. (part col.) 32 cm. Bibliography: p. [199] [ND553.T7N613] 69-19808 18.00
I. Novotny, Fritz, 1902- II. Title.

TOULOUSE-LAUTREC Monfa, 759.4
Henri Marie Raymond de, 1864-1901.
Toulouse-Lautrec. Introd. by Andre Chastel. New York, New American Library, by arrangement with UNESCO [1966] 24 p. illus., port., 30 col. plates. 17 cm. (A Mentor-Unesco art book) "MQ699." Includes bibliography. [ND553.T7A55] 66-31708
I. Chastel, Andre, 1912- II. United Nations Educational, Scientific and Cultural Organization. III. Title.

Toulouse. Saint-Etienne (Cathedral)

SEIDEL, Linda. 730'.944'86
Romanesque sculpture from the Cathedral of Saint-Etienne, Toulouse / Linda Seidel. New York : Garland Pub., 1977, c1964. xii, 187 p., [52] leaves of plates : ill. ; 21 cm. (Outstanding dissertations in the fine arts) Thesis—Harvard, 1964. Bibliography: p. [173]- [NB551.T6S44 1977] 76-23646 ISBN 0-8240-2729-9 lib.bdg. : 37.50
1. Toulouse. Saint-Etienne (Cathedral) 2. Sculpture, Romanesque—Toulouse. 3. Sculpture, French—Toulouse. I. Title. II. Series. BIP

Tourist camps, hostels, etc.

ARCHITECTURAL record. 728.5084
Motels, hotels, restaurants, and bars. 2nd ed. [New York] F. W. Dodge Corp. [c.1960] v, 327 p. Bibliography: p. 317-321. illus., plans. 31 cm. 59-15178 9.75
1. Tourist camps, hostels, etc. 2. Hotels, taverns, etc. 3. Restaurants, lunch rooms, etc.

TOURIST court journal. 728.53
Tourist court plan book, prepared by the staff of Tourist court journal. 2d ed. Temple, Tex., [1950] 80 p. illus., 52 plans. 31 cm. [NA8470.T6] 50-32511
1. Tourist camps, hostels, etc. I. Title.

Tournachon, Felix, 1820-1910.

TOURNACHON, Felix, 779'.2'0924
1820-1910.
Nadar / Nigel Gosling. London : Secker & Warburg, 1976. 298 p. : ill. ; 31 cm. Includes index. [TR681.F3T68 1976] 77-355116 ISBN 0-436-18610-1 : £9.75
1. Tournachon, Felix, 1820-1910. 2. Photography—Portraits. 3. France—Biography—Portraits. I. Gosling, Nigel.

TOURNACHON, Felix, 779'.2'0924
1820-1910.
Nadar / Nigel Gosling. 1st American ed. New York : Knopf : distributed by Random House, 1976. 298 p. : ill. ; 31 cm. Includes index. [TR681.F3T68 1976b] 76-27546 ISBN 0-394-41106-4 : 25.00
1. Tournachon, Felix, 1820-1910. 2. Photography—Portraits. 3. France—Biography—Portraits. 4. Photographers—France—Biography. I. Gosling, Nigel. II. Title.

Towers.

BRONOWSKI, Heinz. 914.04'55
Towers & turrets of Europe. Photography: Heinz Bronowski. Text: Gunter Meissner. New York, Hart Pub. Co. [1974, c1972] 134 p. illus. 23 cm. [NA2930.B6913] 73-76795 7.95
1. Towers. 2. Gates. I. Meissner, Gunter. II. Title.

WEBSTER, David, 1930- 624'.177
Towers. [1st ed.] Garden City, N.Y., Published for the American Museum of Natural History [by] the Natural History Press, 1971. 117 p. illus. 25 cm. [TH2180.W42] 78-132317 4.95
1. Towers. I. Title.

Towers—England.

FISHER, Ernest Arthur. 726'.597
Anglo-Saxon towers; an architectural and historical study, by E. A. Fisher. New York, A. M. Kelley [1969] 208 p. illus., plans, 5 maps. 23 cm. Bibliography: p. 193-195. [NA2930.F5] 76-77876
1. Towers—England. 2. Architecture, Anglo-Saxon. I. Title. BIP

Towner, Donald C.

TOWNER, Donald C. 759.942
Donald Towner : a retrospective exhibition of paintings and watercolours. Leeds : Temple Newsam House, 1976. [12] p. : chiefly ill. ; 23 cm. Cover title. Catalogue of an exhibition held at the Stable Court Exhibition Galleries, Temple Newsam, Leeds, 11th Aug.-25th Sept., 1976. [ND497.T753T45] 77-361144
1. Towner, Donald C. I. Temple Newsam House, Leeds, Eng.

Townsend, Elinor.

TOWNSEND, Elinor. 741.9'73
Sicily : a sketchbook / by Elinor Townsend. Canaan, N.H. : Phoenix Pub., c1978. 70 p. : ill. (some col.) ; 16 x 24 cm. English and Italian text. Erratum slip tipped in. [NC139.T68A4 1978] 78-15131 ISBN 0-914016-52-0 : 10.00
1. Townsend, Elinor. 2. Sicily in art. I. Title. BIP

Townsend, William, 1909-1973.

TOWNSEND, William, 1909- 759.2 B
1973.
The Townsend journals : an artist's record of his times, 1928-51 / edited by Andrew Forge. London : Tate Gallery Publications, 1976. 3-98 p. : ill., ports. ; 26 cm. Includes index. [ND497.T755A55 1976] 77-358156 ISBN 0-900874-97-X : £3.50
1. Townsend, William, 1909-1973. 2. Painters—Great Britain—Biography. 3. Great Britain—Social life and customs—20th century. I. Title.

Toy making.

CANEY, Steven. 745.59'2
Steven Caney's Toy book / [ill., Arielle Mather, photos., Steven Caney]. New

York : Workman Pub. Co., 1974, c1972. 175 p. : ill. ; 21 x 23 cm. Directions for making fifty-one toys and games from easily available materials. [TT174.C36 1974] 75-8814 ISBN 0-911104-15-1. ISBN 0-911104-17-8 pbk. : 3.95
1. Toy making. I. Title. II. Title: Toy book.

DOUGLASS, Winsome. 745.59'2
Toys for your delight. London, Mills & Boon [1973, c.1957] 208 p. illus., col. plate. 26 cm. [TS2301.T7D6] 57-45064
1. Toy-making. 2. Soft toy-making. I. Title.
Available from Transatlantic Arts, Levittown, NY for 9.95. **BIP**

FREDERICK, Filis. 687.7'2
Design and sell toys, games, & crafts / Filis Frederick. Radnor, Pa. : Chilton Book Co., c1977. ix, 165 p. : ill. ; 27 cm. Includes index. Bibliography: p. 155-160. [TT174.F73 1977] 76-55417 ISBN 0-8019-6223-4 : 12.50
1. Toy making. 2. Games. 3. Handicrafts. 4. Toys—Marketing. 5. Games—Marketing. 6. Handicraft—Marketing. I. Title. **BIP**

HUTCHINGS, Margaret. 745.5
Nature's toyshop / written and illustrated by Margaret Hutchings ; photographs by Eve Legg. London : Mills and Boon, 1975. 128 p., 8 p. of plates : ill. (some col.) ; 29 cm. Bibliography: p. 128. [TT174.H85 1975] 76-363431 ISBN 0-263-05595-7 : 9.75
1. Toy making. 2. Nature craft. I. Title.
Distributed by Transatlantic Arts. **BIP**

LAURY, Jean Ray. 745.59'2
Handmade toys and games : a guide to creating your own / by Jean Ray Laury and Ruth Milliken Law. 1st ed. Garden City, N.Y. : Doubleday, 1975. 160 p., [4] leaves of plates : ill. ; 29 cm. [TT174.L38] 73-81124 ISBN 0-385-07180-9 : 9.95
1. Toy making. 2. Games. I. Law, Ruth Milliken, joint author. II. Title.

MCLAREN, Esme 745.5924
The craft of stuffed toys, Newton, Mass., Branford [c.1961] 124p. illus. 26cm. (Bell handbk.) 5.50
I. Title.

MOLONEY, Joan. 745.59'2
Making children's toys. New York, Drake Publishers [1972] p. [TT174.M64] 72-1259 ISBN 0-87749-255-7
1. Toy making. I. Title.

SWAN, Sara. 745.59'2
Home-made baby toys / Sara K. Swan ; drawing and design by Jim Swan ; photographs by Bill Cahill. Boston : Houghton Mifflin, 1977. 126 p. : ill. ; 28 cm. [TT174.S9] 76-48148 ISBN 0-39525101-X : 8.95 ISBN 0-395-25410-8 pbk. : 4.95
1. Toy making. I. Swan, Jim. II. Title. **BIP**

Toy making—Amateurs' manuals.

HENDERSON, Marjorie. 745.59'2
Naturally powered old time toys : how to make sun yachts, sail cars, a monkey on a string, and other moving toys / Marjorie Henderson and Elizabeth Wilkinson ; with crafts illustrated by Martha Weston and photographed by Tom Liden. 1st ed. Philadelphia : Lippincott, c1978. 128 p. : ill. ; 29 cm. [TT174.H45] 78-8556 ISBN 0-397-01308-6 : 12.95 ISBN 0-397-01316-7 pbk. : 6.95
1. Toy making—Amateurs' manuals. I. Wilkinson, Elizabeth, 1926- joint author. II. Title. **BIP**

HUTCHINGS, Margaret. 745.59'24
Toys from the tales of Beatrix Potter. With sections on the baskets by Eve Legg, and the furniture and accessories by Richard Hutchings. Photography by Eve Legg. New York, F. Warne [1974, c1973] 314 p. illus. 26 cm. [TT174.H87 1974] 73-75922 ISBN 0-7232-6098-2 15.00
1. Potter, Beatrix, 1866-1943. 2. Toy making—Amateurs' manuals. I. Legg, Evelyn. II. Hutchings, Richard. III. Title. **BIP**

PETERSON, Franklynn. 745.59'2
Children's toys you can build yourself / Franklynn Peterson. Englewood Cliffs, N.J. : Prentice-Hall, c1978. 143 p. : ill. ; 18 x 24 cm. Includes index. [TT174.P47] 77-28948 ISBN 0-13-132613-9 : 9.95 pbk. : 5.95
1. Toy making—Amateurs' manuals. I. Title. **BIP**

SCHNACKE, Dick. 745.59'2'0973
American folk toys; 85 American folk toys and how to make them. New York, Putnam [1973] 219 p. illus. 29 cm. [TT174.S36 1973] 72-97311 ISBN 0-399-11125-5 9.95
1. Toy making—Amateurs' manuals. 2. Toys—United States. 3. Folk art—United States. I. Title.

SCHNACKE, Dick. 745.59'2'0973
American folk toys; how to make them. Baltimore, Md., Penguin Books [1974, c1973] 160 p. illus. 23 cm. [TT174.S36 1974] ISBN 0-14-046209-O 3.50 (pbk.)
1. Toy making—Amateurs' manuals. 2. Toys—United States. 3. Folk art—United States. I. Title.
L.C. card no. for original ed.: 72-97311. **BIP**

Toy making—Juvenile literature.

†AMERY, Heather. 745.59'2
The knowhow book of action toys / [written and devised by Heather Amery ; contributors, Christopher Carey ... et al. ; designed by David Armitage and Patricia Lee ; illustrated by Neil Ross]. New York : Corwin Books, c1976. 47 p. : col. ill. ; 29 cm. (The Knowhow books) Includes index. Directions for making toys, machines, models, and games, most of which can be constructed with materials found at home. [TT174.A47] 76-19812 ISBN 0-8069-8056-7 : 4.50 ISBN 0-8069-8057-5 lib.bdg. : 4.89
1. Toy making—Juvenile literature. 2. Handicraft—Juvenile literature. I. Ross, Neil. II. Title. III. Title: Action toys. **BIP**

HANDMADE toys and games 745.59'2 / Cameron and Margaret Yerian, editors ; [contributors, Nancy Muhlbach ... et al.]. Chicago : Childrens Press, [1975] 45 p. : col. ill. ; 24 cm. (Fun time activities) Includes index. Simple instructions for making such toys and games as a periscope, monster checkers, rubber tire swing and box submarine with control panel and torpedoes. [TT174.H36] 75-16458 ISBN 0-516-01327-0 lib.bdg. : 6.60
1. Toy making—Juvenile literature. 2. Games—Juvenile literature. I. Yerian, Cameron John. II. Yerian, Margaret. III. Muhlbach, Nancy.

JOSEPH, Joan. 745.59'2
Folk toys around the world and how to make them. Illustrated by Mel Furukawa. Working drawings and instructions by Glen Wagner. New York, Parents' Magazine Press [1972] 96 p. illus. (part col.) 24 cm. Includes bibliographies. Introduces toys from various countries, gives directions for constructing them, and discusses the materials needed. [TT174.J67] 72-1127 ISBN 0-8193-0598-7 4.19 (lib. bdg.)
1. Toy making—Juvenile literature. I. Furukawa, Mel, illus. II. Title. **BIP**

LAMARQUE, Colette. 745.59'2
Make an animal; from practically anything. New York, Drake Publishers [1973, c1972] 62 p. col. illus. 23 cm. Translation of Les animaux familiers. Instructions for making toy animals from a variety of household items. [TT174.L3513 1973] 73-3262 ISBN 0-87749-483-5 3.95
1. Toy making—Juvenile literature. I. Title.

LOPSHIRE, Robert. 745.59'2
How to make snop snappers and other fine things / Robert Lopshire. New York : Greenwillow Books, c1977. 54 p. : ill. ; 22 cm. (Greenwillow read-alone books) Easy-to-read text and illustrations describe games, toys, and handicrafts which can be easily made. [TT174.L66] 76-18760 ISBN 0-688-80066-1 : 5.95 ISBN 0-688-84066-3 lib. bdg. : 5.21
1. Toy making—Juvenile literature. 2. Games—Juvenile literature. I. Title. **BIP**

Toy pistols—Collectors and collecting.

BEST, Charles W. 745.59'282
Cast iron toy pistols, 1870-1940; a collector's guide, by Charles W. Best. [1st ed.] Englewood, Colo., Rocky Mountain Arms & Antiques [1973] 217 p. illus. 29 cm. [TS532.4.B47] 73-174827 15.00
1. Toy pistols—Collectors and collecting. I. Title. **BIP**

Toys.

ACCORSI, William. 745.59'2
Toy sculpture. New York, Reinhold Book Corp. [1968] 88 p. illus. (part col.) 21 cm. (An Art horizons book) [NK9509.A35] 68-16024
1. Toys. I. Title.

CHAPPELL, Phyllis 745.5924
Make your own soft toys. [Dist. Newton Centre, Mass., Branford, 1962, c.1961] 95p. illus. 61-1147 2.50 bds.,
1. Toys. 2. Handicraft. I. Title. II. Title: Soft toys.

DAVIS, Charlotte L. 745.592
Toys to sew, by Charlotte L. Davis and Jessie Robinson. Philadelphia, Lippincott [c.1961] 96p. illus. 61-7977 3.80
1. Toys. 2. Sewing. I. Robinson, Jessie, joint author. II. Title.

FOLEY, Daniel J. 649.55
Toys through the ages, Dan Foley's story of playthings filled with history, folklore, romance & nostalgia; a book for all ages. Line drawings [by] Charlotte Edmands Bowden. Photos. [by] Richard Merrill and others. [1st ed.] Philadelphia, Chilton Books [1962] 145 p. illus. 27 cm. Includes bibliography. [TS2301.T7F6] 62-19876
1. Toys. I. Title.

GOERDELER, Pearl Pomeroy. 649.55
Yarn animals you can make; the new art of wool sculpture for fun and profit. [1st ed.] Garden City, N. Y., Doubleday [c1951] 70p. illus. 25cm. Includes 'wool sculpture loom' in box attached to cover. [TS2301.T7] 53-2789
1. Toys. 2. Yarn. I. Title.

HUTCHINGS, Margaret 745.5924
The book of the teddy bear. Illus. by the author. [Newton Centre] Mass., Branford [1965. c.1964] 283p. illus. (pt. col.) 26cm. Bibl. [TS2301.T7H77] 65-11100 7.50 bds.,
1. Toys. I. Title. II. Title: The teddy bear.

HUTCHINGS, Margaret. 745.592
Modern soft toy making. [U.S. ed.] Newton Centre, Mass., C. T. Branford Co. [1960, c1959] 243 p. illus. 26 cm. [TS2301.T7H8] 60-2771
1. Toys. I. Title.

HUTCHINGS, Margaret. 745.5922
Patchwork playthings. Line drawings by the author. London, Mills & Boon covered by label: Newton, Mass., C. T. Branford Co. [1961] 59p. illus. 23cm. [TS2301] 61-4550
1. Toys. 2. Patchwork. I. Title.

JACKSON, Sheila 745.592
Simple toymaking London. Studio Vista; New York. Watson-Guptill [c.1966] 95p. illus., 8 plates (incl. 4 col.) diagrs. 19cm. [TS2301.T7J3 1966] 66-13008 1.95 bds.,
1. Toys. 2. Handicraft. I. Title.

KUNZ, Robert. 745.592
101 toys children can make / by Robert and Katherine Kunz. New York, Sterling Pub. Co. [1959] 124p. illus. 21cm. [TS2301.T7K83] 59-12984
1. Toys. I. Kunz, Katharine, joint author. II. Title.

LAWSON, Arthur H. 688.7
Homemade toys for fun and profit; illustrated by Walter Frame and Hamilton Greene. New York, McKay [1953] 178 p. illus. 21 cm. [TS2301.T7L3] 53-7553
1. Toys. I. Title.

LOUISIANA 688.7'2'0740163355
State Museum, New Orleans.
Playthings of the past; 19th and early 20th century toys from the Collection of the Louisiana State Museum. [New Orleans, 1969] xi, 25 p. illus. (part col.) 22 x 26 cm. Bibliography: p. 21. [NK9509.4.N44L62] 70-632531
1. Toys. I. Title.

NORMAN, Percival Edward. 684
Wooden toys for boys. With explanatory drawings by the author. London, New York, Studio Publications [1955] 64p. illus. 18cm. (Make it yourself) [TT185] 56-13865
1. Toys. 2. Woodwork. I. Title.

POPULAR Mechanics Press, 680
Chicago.
Toys you can make; an exciting collection of 140 attractive and easy-to-make toys for children of all ages ... Prepared by the editors of Popular Mechanics Press [Chicago, 1953] 160p. illus. 24cm. [TT157.P63] 53-9419
1. Toys. 2. Handicraft. I. Title.

REES, Elizabeth Lodge. 649.55
A doctor looks at toys. Illustrated by Marilyn Poore. Springfield, Ill., Thomas [1961] 188p. illus. 24cm. Includes bibliography. [TS2301.T7R42] 61-11664
1. Toys. I. Title.

SAYER, Philip. 688.7'28
Making Victorian kinetic toys / Philip and Caroline Freeman Sayer. New York : Taplinger Pub. Co., 1977. 80 p. : ill. ; 22 cm. Bibliography: p. 79. [TS2301.T7S28] 76-55034 ISBN 0-8008-5082-3 : 6.95
1. Toys. 2. Moving-pictures. 3. Animation (Cinematography) I. Sayer, Caroline Freeman, joint author. II. Title. **BIP**

SNOOK, Barbara. 688.72
Creative soft toys. Newton Centre, Mass., C.T. Branford [1964] 111 p. illus. 23 cm. Bibliography: p. 107. [TT157.S55] 64-15196
1. Toys. I. Title.

*SONOBE, Kiyoshi, 745.5920952
1921-
Japanese toys; playing with history. photographs by Kivushi Sonobe. Orig. text by Kazuya Sakamoto, Tekiho Nishizawa. adapted by Charles A. Pomery. Tokyo, Bijutsu Shuppan-sha, Rutland, Vt., Tuttle [c.1965] 516p. (chiefly illus., maps. plates, pt. col.) 26cm. [NK493.36213] 65-23711 17.50
1. Toys. 2. Folk art—Japan. I. Sakamoto, Kazuya. II. Nishizawa, Tekiho. III. Pomeroy, Charles A., ed. and tr. IV. Title.

SONOBE, Kiyoshi, 1921- 745.592
Rustic toys of modern Japan, pt. 1. Photographed by Kiyoshi Sonobe. Text by Kazuya Sakamoto, Tekiho Nishizawa. Japan/Intl. ed. with English introd., text, summary, commentaries. Tokyo, Bijutsu Shuppan-sha [dist. New York, Perkins Oriental, c.1962] 91p. illus. (pt. col.) col. map. 26cm. Contents.pt. 1, Tohoku District. J62 3.90 bds.,
1. Toys. 2. Folk art—Japan. I. Sakamoto, Kazuya. II. Nishizawa, Tekiho. III. Title.

TODD, Leonard. 745.59'2
Trash can toys and games. Drawings by Chas. B. Slackman. Photos. by Carl Fischer. New York, Viking Press [1974] 112 p. illus. 17 x 28 cm. "A Subsistence Press book." [TT174.T62 1974] 73-3953 ISBN 0-670-72433-5 6.95
1. Toys. 2. Games. 3. Handicraft. I. Title.

TODD, Leonard. 745.59'2
Trash can toys and games / by Leonard Todd ; drawings by Chas. B. Slackman ; photos. by Carl Fischer. New York : Penguin Books, 1976, c1974. p. cm. (A Penguin handbook) Reprint of the ed. published by Viking Press, New York. [TT174.T62 1976] 76-14480 ISBN 0-14-046250-3 pbk. : 2.50
1. Toys. 2. Games. 3. Handicraft. I. Title.

WILCOX, Joy 745.59'2
Printed rag toys. London, Batsford, 1967. 96p. illus., 2 col. plates, diagrs. 23cm. Bibl. [TT157.W53] 67-78946 3.95
1. Toys. 2. Handicraft. I. Title.
American distributor Branford, Newton Center, Mass. **BIP**

Toys—Catalogs.

ACKERMAN, Evelyn. 688.7'2
Shoenhut's Humpty Dumpty Circus from A to Z / Evelyn Ackerman and Frederick E. Keller. Los Angeles : Era Industries, c1975. 111 p. : ill. ; 29 cm. Includes bibliographical references. [TS2301.T7A38] 75-23604
1. Schoenhut (A.) Company. 2. Toys—Catalogs. I. Keller, Frederick E., joint

author. II. Title. III. Title: Humpty Dumpty Circus from A to Z.

BROWN, George W., 688.7'2'029
1830-1889.
The George Brown toy sketchbook. Edited, with an introd., by Edith F. Barenholtz. [1st ed.] Princeton, Pyne Press [1971] xvi p., illus., 58 col. plates, port. 37 cm. "A collectors imprint edition." [TS2301.T7B7] 70-146210 ISBN 0-87861-000-6
1. Toys—Catalogs. I. Title.

DESIGN Council. 688.7'2
The Design Centre guide to play equipment for young children / [Design Council ; editor, Cassie Peterson]. 2d ed. London : Published by the Design Council in collaboration with the Pre-School Playgroups Association, 1976. 32 p. : ill. ; 20 x 21 cm. [TS2301.T7D46 1976] 77-373516 ISBN 0-85072-040-0 : £0.60
1. Toys—Catalogs. I. Peterson, Cassie. II. Title.

GEORG Hieronimus 688.7'2'029
Bestelmeier (Firm)
The amazing catalog of the esteemed firm of George Hieronimus Bestelmeier; selective excerpts from editions 1793 and 1807. [Assembled and designed by Daniel S. Jacoby. New York, Merrimack Pub. Corp., 1971] 82 p. (chiefly illus.) 21 x 23 cm. Cover title. [TS2301.TG43] 70-27030 5.00
1. Toys—Catalogs. I. Jacoby, Daniel S., comp. II. Title.

HARMAN, Kenny. 688.7'2
Comic strip toys / by Kenny Harman. Des Moines : Wallace-Homestead Book Co., [1975] 119 p., [4] leaves of plates : ill. (some col.) ; 28 cm. [TS2301.T7H32] 74-84523 ISBN 0-87069-078-7
1. Toys—Catalogs. 2. Toys—Collectors and collecting. I. Title.

SCHWARZ (F. A. O.) 745.59'2'0973
(Firm)
F. A. O. Schwarz toys through the years / text by Marvin Schwartz ; design by Ladislav Svatos. 1st ed. Garden City, N.Y. : Doubleday, [1975] 142 p. : ill. ; 27 cm. [TS2301.T7S37 1975] 73-13096 ISBN 0-385-07136-1 : 6.95.
1. Schwarz (F. A. O.) (Firm) 2. Toys—Catalogs. I. Schwartz, Marvin D. II. Svatos, Ladislav. III. Title. **BIP**

Toys—Collectors and collecting.

†CADBURY, Betty. 688.7'2'075
Playthings past : a collector's guide to antique toys / Betty Cadbury. New York : Praeger, [1976] p. cm. Includes index. Bibliography: p. [NK9509.C32] 76-10051 ISBN 0-275-23190-9 : 10.95
1. Toys—Collectors and collecting. I. Title.

COOK, Catherine. 688.7'2
Fascinating tin toys for girls, 1820-1920 / by Catherine Cook and Edith Morris. Oak Bluffs, Mass. : E. Morris, [1975] 64 p. : ill. ; 23 cm. Bibliography: p. 64. [TS2301.T7C66] 75-312004
1. Toys—Collectors and collecting. 2. Tinware—Collectors and collecting. I. Morris, Edith, joint author. II. Title.

HERTZ, Louis 745.59'2'075
Heilbroner.
The toy collector [by] Louis H. Hertz. New York, Funk & Wagnalls [1969] vii, 304 p. illus. (part col.) 24 cm. Bibliography: p. 277-278. [NK9509.H4] 68-22167 9.95
1. Toys—Collectors and collecting. I. Title.

KING, Eileen. 688.7'2'075
The encyclopedia of toys / by Eileen King. New York : Crown Publishers, 1978. p. cm. [NK9509.K56] 78-6851 ISBN 0-517-53027-9 : 15.95
1. Toys—Collectors and collecting. I. Title. **BIP**

Toys—History.

CULFF, Robert. 688.7'2'09
The world of toys. Feltham, Hamlyn, 1969. 5-140 p. (chiefly illus. (some col.)) 29 cm. Illus. on lining papers. [NK9509.C84] 76-497294 25/-
1. Toys—History. I. Title.

FRASER, Antonia 688.7209
(Pakenham) Lady 1932-
A history of toys, by Antonia Fraser. [New York] Delacorte Press [1966] 256 p. illus. (part col.) 29 cm. Bibliography: p. 249-250. [GV1218.5.F7] 66-20120
1. Toys—Hist. I. Title.

FRASER, Antonia 688.7'2'09
(Pakenham) Lady, 1932-
A history of toys. [New ed.]. London, New York, Spring Books, 1972. 256 p. illus. (some col.), facsims. 29 cm. Bibliography: p. 249-250. [GV1218.5.F7 1972] 72-170632 ISBN 0-600-34387-1 £2.25
1. Toys—History. I. Title.

HILLIER, Mary 745.59209
Pageant of toys [1st Amer. ed.] New York, Taplinger [1966,c.1965] 155p. illus., 4 col. plates. 26cm. Bibl. [NK4894.A2H5] 66-10348 10.00
1. Toys—Hist. I. Title.

MOFFET, Martha. 745.59'2
A treasury of antique toys. New York, Drake Publishers [1973] p. [NK9509.M63] 73-5614 ISBN 0-87749-518-1 7.95
1. Toys—History. I. Title.

REMISE, Jac. 688.7'2
The golden age of toys [by] Jac Remise, Jean Fondin. English text by D. B. Tubbs. [Lausanne] Edita; dist. by N. Y. Graphic Greenwich, Conn. [1967] 252p. illus. (pt col.) 31cm. [GV1218.5.R4] 67-27009 27.50, bxd.
1. Toys—Hist. I. Fondin, Jean. joint author. II. Title.

SHISHIDO, Misako 745.592
The folk toys of Japan [Tr. by Tatsuo Shibata] Rutland, Vt., Japan Pubns. [c.1963] 71p. illus. (pt. col.) 27cm. 63-22034 3.95
1. Toys—Hist. 2. Folk art-Japan. I. Title.

WHITE, Gwen. 745.59'2'09
Antique toys and their background. New York, Arco [1971] 260 p. illus. 26 cm. Bibliography: p. 254-255. [NK9509.W5 1971b] 74-153651 ISBN 0-668-02484-4 19.95
1. Toys—History. I. Title. **BIP**

Toys—Juvenile literature.

MUELLER, Robert E. 745.592
Inventor's notebook; entirely new do-it-yourself toy inventions, with woodcuts by the author. New York, John Day [c.1963] 64p. illus. (pt. col.) 23cm. 63-15920 3.50; 3.29 lib. ed.,
1. Toys—Juvenile literature. 2. Handicraft—Juvenile literature. I. Title.

MUELLER, Robert E 745.592
Inventor's notebook; entirely new do-it-yourself toy inventions, with woodcuts by the author. New York, John Day Co. [1963] 64 p. illus. (part col.) 23 cm. [TT157.M77] 63-15920
1. Toys — Juvenile literature. 2. Handicraft — Juvenile literature. I. Title.

WALTNER, Willard. 745.592
Hobbycraft toys & games [by] Willard & Elma Waltner. New York, Lantern Press [1965] 138 p. illus. 24 cm. [TT157.W352] 65-12601
1. Toys — Juvenile literature. 2. Handcraft — Juvenile literature. I. Waltner, Elma, joint author. II. Title. **BIP**

Toys, Mechanical.

HILLIER, Mary. 668.7'25
Automata & mechanical toys : and illustrated history / by Mary Hillier. London : Jupiter, 1976. 200 p. : ill. (some col.) ; 26 cm. Includes index. Bibliography: p. 196-197. [TS2301.T7H54] 77-357415 ISBN 0-904041-32-8 : £5.95
1. Toys, Mechanical. I. Title.

WELTENS, Arno. 688.7'28
Mechanical tin toys in colour / [by] Arno Weltens ; [translated from the Dutch]. Poole : Blandford Press, 1977. 176 p. : ill. (some col.), facsims. ; 20 cm. Translation

of Mechanisch blikken speelgoed. Includes indexes. Bibliography: p. 171. [NK9509.W4413] 78-314797 ISBN 0-7137-0848-4 : 8.95
1. Toys, Mechanical. I. Title. Distributed by Sterling Pub., 2 Park Ave., New York, NY 10016

Toys—Pictorial works.

BOTTO, Ken, 779'.9'688720924
1937-
Past joys / Ken Botto. San Francisco : Chronicle Books, c1978. 96 p. : chiefly col. ill. ; 23 x 30 cm. "Prism editions." [TS2301.T7B65] 78-7999 ISBN 0-87701-116-8. ISBN 0-87701-115-X pbk. : 12.95
1. Toys—Pictorial works. 2. Toys—Collectors and collecting. I. Title. **BIP**

Toys—United States—History— Juvenile literature.

LOEPER, John J. 688.7'2'09
The shop on High Street : the toys and games of Early America / John J. Loeper. 1st ed. New York : Atheneum, 1978. 112 p. : ill. ; 24 cm. Bibliography: p. 111-112. Describes toys and games available in America during the period from 1760 to 1815. [GV1218.5.L63 1978] 77-24737 ISBN 0-689-30622-9 : 6.95 6.95
1. Toys—United States—History—Juvenile literature. 2. Games—United States—History—Juvenile literature. I. Title. **BIP**

Trabzon, Turkey (City) Ayasofya Kilisei.

RICE, David Talbot, 709'.565
1903-
The church of Haghia Sophia at Trebizond ed. by David Talbot Rice. Edinburgh, Edinburgh Univ. Pr. for the Russell Trust, 1968. xxi, 275p. 89 plates, illus. (some col. 1 fold. col. in pocket), plan. 31cm. Notes & refs. [NA5871.T7R5 1968] 68-19880 30.00
1. Trabzon, Turkey (City) Ayasofya Kilisei. I. Title.
Available from Aldine, Chicago.

Trade-marks.

KAMEKURA, Yusaku, 1915- 741.69
Trademarks and symbols of the world. Pref. by Paul Rand. New York, Reinhold Pub. Corp. [1965] 291 p. (chiefly illus. (part col.)) 29 cm. [NE965.K32] 65-24055
1. Trade-marks. I. Title.

KAMEKURA, Yusaku, 1915- 741.6
Trademarks of the world. With a pref. by Paul Rand. New York, G. Wittenborn [1956?] 164, 34 p. illus. 26 x 27 cm. Bibliography: p. 2 (2d group) [NE965.K3] 57-2141
1. Trade-marks. I. Title.

KAMEKURA, Yusaku, 1915- 741.6
Trademarks of the world. With a pref. by Paul Rand. Tokyo, David Pub. Co.; New York, G. Wittenborn [1956] 192, 34p. illus. 26x27cm. Bibliography: p. 2 (2d group) [NE965] 57-231
1. Trade-marks. I. Title.

3 X TRADEMARKS. 745.4
[Stuttgart, Verlag Gerd Hatje] Amer. distributor: Wittenborn, New York [1967] 1v. (unpaged) illus. (pt. col.) 30cm. English, French and German. [T325.T52] 67-108729 7.50 pap.,
1. Trade-marks.

WILDBUR, Peter, comp. 741.6?
Trademarks; a handbook of international designs. London, Studio Vista; New York, Reinhold [1966] 96 p. illus. (some col.) 20 cm. (Introductory handbooks to art and design) 12/6 (B66-10501) [NC997.W495] 66-15636
1. Trade-marks. I. Title.

WILSON, Robert 683'.4'00275
Lawrence, 1939-
The rampant colt; the story of a trademark [by] R. L. Wilson. Spencer, Ind., T. Haas [1969] v, 107 p. illus., ports. 27 cm. Bibliography: p. 107. [TS533.2.W56] 79-15509
1. Colt Industries, inc. 2. Trade-marks. I. Title.

Trade-marks—Caricatures and cartoons.

ZIRALDO. 741.5'981
Trademarks / by Ziraldo. Los Angeles : Price/Stern/Sloan Publishers, 1978. p. cm. "A Price/Stern/Sloan special." [NC1460.Z5A4 1978] 78-15550 ISBN 0-8431-0453-8 pbk. : 1.25
1. Trade-marks—Caricatures and cartoons. 2. Brazilian wit and humor, Pictorial. I. Title. **BIP**

Trade-marks—United States.

CARTER, David E. 745.2
Designing corporate symbols / David E. Carter. Ashland, Ky. : Century Communications, [1975] 150 p. : ill. ; 20 cm. [T223.V2C33] 74-29013
1. Trade-marks—United States. I. Title. **BIP**

Trade-unions and the arts—Great Britain.

TRADES Union 338.4'7'700941
Congress.
The TUC working party report on the arts. London : T.U.C., [1976] [2], 44 p. ; 24 cm. (A TUC consultative document) Cover title. [NX180.T7T7 1976] 77-364708 ISBN 0-900878-47-9 : £0.50
1. Trade-unions and the arts—Great Britain. I. Title.

Traffic engineering.

SEMINAR on Urban Highway 711.7
Planning and its Relation to General Urban Development, University of California, 1960.
Notes from the seminar, urban highway planning and its relation to general urban development. Berkeley, University of California [1961] vii, 125p. diagrs. 28cm. At head of title: Institute of Transportation and Traffic Engineering. Proceedings. 'Presented ... by the Institute of Transportation and Traffic Engineering and the American Association of State Highway Officials.' [HE333.S4 1960] 62-62527
1. Traffic engineering. 2. Cities and towns—Planning. I. Title. II. Title: Urban highway planning and its relation to general urban development.

WOHL, Martin. 711'.73
Traffic system analysis [by] Martin Wohl [and] Brian V. Martin. New York, McGraw-Hill [1967] xvi, 558 p. illus. 23 cm. (McGraw-Hill series in transportation) Includes bibliographies. [HE333.W58] 67-26355
1. Traffic engineering. I. Martin, Brian V., joint author. II. Title.

Trailer camps.

ASBURY, Norman G. 711'.58
A formula for determining the feasibility of mobile housing developments by N. G. Asbury. Chicago, Mobile Homes Manufacturers Association [1971] 116 p. form, plans. 27 cm. [TX1105.A82] 79-149646
1. Trailer camps. I. Title.

Tramp art—United States.

FENDELMAN, Helaine W. 736'.4'0973
Tramp art : an itinerant's folk art / Helaine W. Fendelman. 1st ed. New York : E. P. Dutton, 1975. 127 p., [4] leaves of plates : ill. (some col.) ; 21 cm. Bibliography: p. 125-127. [NK9712.F46 1975] 75-333029 ISBN 0-525-47407-2 : 6.95
1. Tramp art—United States. 2. Wood-carving—United States. 3. Folk art—United States. I. Title. **BIP**

Transcendentalism (New England)

MILLER, Frederick De Wolfe. 928.1
Christopher Pearse Cranch and his caricatures of New England transcendentalism. Cambridge, Harvard University Press, 1951. xi, 81 p. illus. 22 cm. Bibliography [and] notes": p. [67]-77. [PS1449.C8Z8] 51-10752

2d ed. New York, Dover Publications [1965] xvi, 347 p. illus., map, plates. 22 cm. Bibliography: p. 827-836. [NC810.C75 1965] 65-26015
1. Trees in art. I. Title.

HAYES, Colin.   743'.7
Trees. [1st American ed. New York, Watson-Guptill Publications, 1967, c1963] 56 p. illus. 19 x 20 cm. (Watson-Guptill drawing books) [NC810] 76-4592
1. Trees in art. I. Title.

PERARD, Victor Semon, 1870-
Drawing trees, and introducing landscape composition. Cover illus. by Jack Markow. New York, Pitman Pub. [1955] unpaged. illus. 20x26cm. (Pitman drawing series) [NC825.S5P4 1957] 55-12075
1. Trees in art. 2. Landscape drawing. I. Title.

PERARD, Victor Semon, 1870-   743.7
1957.
Drawing trees and introducing landscape composition. Cover illus. by Jack Markow. New York, Pitman [1959] unpaged. illus. 20x26cm. (Pitman art series, 18) [NC810.P4 1959] 59-12583
1. Trees in art. 2. Landscape drawing. I. Title.

PITZ, Henry Clarence,   743.72
1895-
Drawing trees. New York, Watson-Guptill Publications, 1956. 127p. illus. 27cm. [NC810.P5] 56-13778
1. Trees in art. 2. Drawing—Instruction. I. Title.

PITZ, Henry Clarence,   743'.7
1895-
How to draw trees, by Henry C. Pitz. [2d ed] New York, Watson-Guptill Publications [1972] p. First ed. published in 1956, under title: Drawing trees. Bibliography: p. [NC810.P5 1972] 77-187916 ISBN 0-8230-1441-X
1. Trees in art. 2. Drawing—Instruction. I. Title.   BIP

Trees—Middle West—Pictorial works.

MCCURDY, Dwight R.,   715'.2'0977
1937-
How to choose your tree; a guide to parklike landscaping in Illinois, Indiana, and Ohio, by Dwight R. McCurdy, William Greg Spangenberg, and Charles Paul Doty. Carbondale, Southern Illinois University Press [1972] x, 245 p. illus. 27 cm. Bibliography: p. 243-245. [SB435.M143] 74-156791 ISBN 0-8093-0514-3 10.00
1. Trees—Middle West—Pictorial works. 2. Ornamental trees—Middle West—Pictorial works. I. Spangenberg, William Greg, joint author. II. Doty, Charles Paul, joint author. III. Title.   BIP

Trees—Pictorial works.

FEININGER, Andreas, 1906-   779'.34
Trees / Andreas Feininger. New York : Penguin Books, 1978. 116 p., [80] leaves of plates : ill. (some col.) ; 27 cm. Includes index. [QK475.5.F44 1978] 77-17805 ISBN 0-14-004747-6 pbk. : 7.95
1. Trees—Pictorial works.

Treganza, Adan Eduardo, 1916-1968.

CONTRIBUTIONS to the   917.94'62
archaeology of Point Reyes National Seashore; a compendium in honor of Adan E. Treganza. Edited by Robert E. Schenk. [San Francisco, Treganza Anthropology Museum] 1970. xvii, 321 p. illus. 28 cm. (Treganza Museum. Papers, no. 6) Contents.—Kawahar, S. A survey of the physical setting of the Point Reyes Peninsula area, Marin County, California.—Mannion, L. and Mannion, M. C. Abstracts from the Kelly manuscript: Coast Miwok material culture.—Moratto, M. J. A history of archaeological research at Point Reyes, California.—Edwards, R. L. A settlement pattern hypothesis for the Coast Miwok based on an archaeological survey of Point Reyes Seashore.—King, T. F. and Upson, W. F. Protohistory on Limantour Sandspit: archaeological investigations at 4-Mrn-216 and 4-Mrn-

298.—Henn, W. G. Faunal analysis of 4-Mrn-216, a seasonal site on Limantour Sandspit, Point Reyes National Seashore.—Wilson, S. C. Faunal analysis of 4-Mrn-298W: a perspective of 4-Mrn-216.—Von der Porten, E. P. The porcelains and terra cottas of Drakes Bay.—Moratto, a compendium in honor of Adan E. Treganza. Edited by Robert E. Schenk. [San Francisco, Treganza Anthropology Museum] 1970. xvii, 321 p. illus. 28 cm. (Treganza Museum. Papers, no. 6) Contents.—Kawahar
1. Treganza, Adan Eduardo, 1916-1968. 2. Indians of North America—California—Marin Co.—Antiquities. 3. Point Reyes National Seashore—Antiquities. I. Treganza, Adan Eduardo, 1916-1968. II. Schenk, Robert E., 1944-1970, ed. III. Series: Treganza Anthropology Museum. Papers, no. 6.

Treiman, Joyce.

TREIMAN, Joyce.   759.13
Joyce Treiman, 1943-1977 / text by Lester D. Longman, with an essay by E. Maurice Bloch. Los Angeles : Hennessey & Ingalls, 1978. p. cm. Catalog of an exhibition and the artist's works. Bibliography: p. [ND237.T63L66] 77-14058 ISBN 0-912158-81-6 pbk. : 7.95
1. Treiman, Joyce. I. Longman, Lester Duncan, 1905- II. Bloch, E. Maurice. III. Title.   BIP

Tremissis.

TOMASINI, Wallace John,   737.4936
1926-
The barbaric tremissis in Spain and Southern France: Anastasius to Leovigild. New York, Amer. Numismatic, Bway & 155 St., 1964. xxv, 302p. illus., 46 plates. 23cm. (Numismatic notes and monographs. no. 152) Bibl. [CJ1657.T6] 65-2826 7.50 pap.,
1. Tremissis. I. Title. II. Series.

Trenton. Battle Monument.

THE Trenton   069'.09749'66 s
Battle Monument Eakins bronzes. Edited by Zoltan Buki [and] Suzanne Corlette. Trenton, New Jersey State Museum, 1973. 85 p. illus. 22 cm. (New Jersey State Museum. Bulletin 14) Contents.Contents—The Battle of Trenton.—The Trenton Battle Monument.—The Eakins bronzes.—Thomas Eakins, a chronology. Includes bibliographical references. [NB237.E17] 730'.92'4 75-188488
1. Eakins, Thomas, 1844-1916. 2. Trenton. Battle Monument. 3. Trenton, Battle of, 1776. I. Buki, Zoltan, ed. II. Corlette, Suzanne, ed. III. Series: New Jersey. State Museum, Trenton. Bulletin 14.

Trevelyan, Theodore Macaulay, 1906-1911.

TREVELYAN, Janet Penrose   942.3'74
(Ward) 1879-
Two stories, by Janet Trevelyan (Mrs. G. M. Trevelyan) London, New York, Longmans, Green [1954] 222p. illus. 23cm. [CT788.T78T7] 54-3999
1. Trevelyan, Theodore Macaulay, 1906-1911. 2. London—playgrounds. I. Title. Contents omitted.

Trevisani, Francesco, 1656-1746.

DIFEDERICO, Frank R.   759.5
Francesco Trevisani, eighteenth-century painter in Rome : a catalogue raisonne / by Frank R. DiFederico. Washington : Decatur House Press, c1977. xvi, 124 p., [55] leaves of plates : ill. ; 26 cm. (Art history series ; 1) Includes index. Bibliography: p. 103-108. [ND623.T924D53] 76-30904 ISBN 0-916276-02-3 : 50.00
1. Trevisani, Francesco, 1656-1746. 2. Painting, Modern—17th-18th centuries—Italy—Rome (City) 3. Painting—Italy—Rome (City) I. Title.

The Tribal eye.

ATTENBOROUGH, David,   709'.01'1
1926-
The tribal eye / David Attenborough. New York : Norton, c1976. 144 p., [12] leaves of plates : ill. (some col.) ; 27 cm. Includes index. Bibliography: p. 142. [N5311.A87 1976] 77-150030 ISBN 0-393-04466-1 : 14.95
1. The Tribal eye. 2. Art, Primitive. 3. Ethnology. I. Title.

Triebel, Frederick Ernst, 1865-1944.

COOLEY, Adelaide N.   730'.92'4 B
The monument maker : biography of Frederick Ernst Triebel / Adelaide N. Cooley. 1st ed. Hicksville, N.Y. : Exposition Press, c1978. 32 p., [12] leaves of plates : ill ; 22 cm. Bibliography: p. 31-32. [NB237.T66C66] 78-103167 ISBN 0-682-49051-2 : 5.95
1. Triebel, Frederick Ernst, 1865-1944. 2. Sculptors—United States—Biography. I. Title.   BIP

Trimm, Wayne.

TRIMM, Wayne.   759.13
The beauty of birds. With original paintings by Wayne Trimm. Poetry selected by J. W. Dunn. Norwalk, Conn., C. R. Gibson Co. [1974] 39 p. col. illus. 28 cm. [ND1839.T73D86] 73-88088 ISBN 0-8378-1864-8 5.95
1. Trimm, Wayne. 2. Birds in art. 3. English poetry (Selections: Extracts, etc.) 4. American poetry (Selections: Extracts, etc.) I. Dunn, J. W., comp. II. Title.

Trinity Cathedral, Phoenix, Ariz.

LINCOLN, Joseph   748.5'9191'73
Colville.
The windows of Trinity Cathedral. [1st ed. Flagstaff, Ariz.] Northland Press [1973] vii, 81 p. illus. (part col.) 26 cm. [NK5312.L56] 73-78003 ISBN 0-87358-106-7
1. Trinity Cathedral, Phoenix, Ariz. 2. Glass painting and staining—Phoenix, Ariz. I. Title.

Trique Indians—Textile industry and fabrics.

HIATT, June.   746.9'2
The weavings of San Andreas Chicahuaxtla, Mexico / by Jane Hiatt. San Francisco : California State University, 1972. vi, 66 leaves : ill. ; 28 cm. (Treganza Anthropology Museum papers ; no. 10) Bibliography: leaf 66. [F1221.T7H52] 75-621684
1. Trique Indians—Textile industry and fabrics. 2. Indians of Mexico—Textile industry and fabrics. 3. San Andreas Chicahuaxtla, Mex. I. Title. II. Series: Treganza Anthropology Museum. Papers ; no. 10.

Trivets.

HANDKENSON, Dick   739.4773
Trivets. Maple Plain, Minn., Olde Street Lamn Shop, c.1963. 107p. (chiefly illus.) 23cm. 63-49107 4.75, pap., plastic bdg.
1. Trivets. I. Title.   BIP

Trivets—Catalogs.

HANKENSON, Dick.   739'.48
Trivets; old and re-pro. Maple Plain, Minn., c1968. xi, 144 p illus., port. 23 cm. [NK9540.H3] 70-25112
1. Trivets—Catalogs. I. Title.

Troger, Fritz, 1894-

TROGER, Fritz, 1894-   741.973
Fritz Troger : das fruhe Werk, 1923-1936 : 1974-1975, Genossenschaft "Kunst der Zeit", Dresden ... [et al.]. Dresden : Die Genossenschaft, [1975?] [20] p. : chiefly ill. (some col.) ; 22 cm. Catalog of an exhibition. [ND588.T838G46] 75-510751
1. Troger, Fritz, 1894- I. Genossenschaft Bildender Kunstler "Kunst der Zeit".

Trolls in art—Juvenile literature.

BAUER, John Albert, 1882-   759.85
1918.
In the troll wood / ill. by John Bauer ; text by Olive Jones. Toronto ; New York : Methuen, [1978] p. cm. Fifteen full-page illustrations of the strange haunting world of the trolls accompanied by a simple descriptive text. [ND793.B33A4 1978] 77-18419 ISBN 0-458-93240-X : 8.95
1. Bauer, John Albert, 1882-1918—Juvenile literature. 2. Trolls in art—Juvenile literature. I. Jones, Olive. II. Title.   BIP

Trompe l'oeil painting.

MASTAI, Marie-Louise   759
d'Otrange.
Illusion in art : trompe l'oeil : a history of pictorial illusionism / by M. L. d'Otrange Mastai. New York : Abaris Books, 1975. 379 p., [11] leaves of plates : ill. (some col.) ; 29 cm. Includes indexes. Bibliography: p. 376-379. [ND1390.M37] 74-6501 ISBN 0-913870-03-X : 39.50
1. Trompe l'oeil painting. I. Title.   BIP

Trompe l'oeil painting—History.

BATTERSBY, Martin.   759
Trompe l'oil = The eye deceived / Martin Battersby. New York : St. Martin's Press, 1974. 158 p., [8] leaves of plates : ill. (some col.) ; 32 cm. Includes index. [ND1471.B37 1974] 73-89208 ISBN 0-85670-055-X : 25.00
1. Trompe l'oil painting—History. I. Title. II. Title: The eye deceived.

Trousers.

FISHER, Margaret, 1947-   646.4'3
Palm leaf patterns / by Margaret Fisher. San Francisco : Panjandrum Press, 1977c1976   p. cm. Bibliography: p. [TT605.F57] 76-57189 ISBN 0-915572-20-6 pbk. : 4.95
1. Trousers. 2. Yoga, Hatha 3. Dancing. 4. Movement, Aesthetics of. I. Title.   BIP

Trova, Ernest T., 1927—

KULTERMANN, Udo.   730'.92'4
Trova / Udo Kultermann. New York : H. N. Abrams, 1978. 219 p. : ill. (some col.) ; 28 x 30 cm. ([Contemporary artists series]) Includes index. Bibliography: p. 213-[215] [NB237.T67K84] 77-1915 ISBN 0-8109-0502-7 : 45.00
1. Trova, Ernest T., 1927- I. Title. II. Series.   BIP

TROVA, Ernest T., 1927-   709'.2'4
Artist slain: picture yearbook 1973. Trova 1947/1972: other works/other times. Editor: James Ropiequet Schmidt. [St. Louis? 2:30 Productions] c1973. 1 v. (chiefly illus.) 23 cm. [N6537.T7A42] 73-75115 5.00
1. Trova, Ernest T., 1927- I. Title.

TROVA, Ernest T., 1927-   730'.924
Trova: new sculpture. [New York, 1971] [32] p. (incl. cover) illus., ports. 23 cm. Exhibition held January 9 to February 3, 1971, at the Pace Gallery, New York. Bibliography: p. [30]-[31] [NB237.T67A57] 73-150527
I. Pace Gallery.

TROVA, Ernest T., 1927-   730'.924
Trova; selected works, 1953-1966, by Lawrence Ailoway. [New York] Pace Gallery [1966] 59 p. illus. 23 cm. Bibliography: p. 53-55. [NB237.T67A7] 67-17476
I. Alloway, Lawrence, 1926-

TROVA, Ernest T., 1927-   730'.92'4
Trova: the profile cantos. New York, Pace Gallery [1973] [20] p. illus. 22 x 28 cm. Exhibition held at the Pace Gallery, Apr. 7-May 2, 1973. Bibliography: p. [20] [NB237.T67P32] 73-79498
1. Trova, Ernest T., 1927- I. Pace Gallery. II. Title.

bibliographical references. [ND497.T8G28 1972] 72-161061 ISBN 0-670-73289-3 7.50
1. Turner, Joseph Mallord William, 1775-1851. Rain, steam and speed. I. Title.

GATT, Giuseppe. 759.2
Turner. [1st American ed. Translated from the Italian by Pearl Sanders and Caroline Beamish] New York, Grosset & Dunlap [1967, c1968] 39, [80] p. illus. (part col.) 18 cm. (The New Grosset art library, 9) On cover: Turner; the life and work of the artist. Bibliography: p. 26-27. [ND497.T8G313 1968b] 68-12743
1. Turner, Joseph Mallord William, 1775-1851.

GRAHAM, Douglas J. M. 769'.92'4
Turner and Moran / by Douglas J. M. Graham. [Denver : Turner Museum], c1977. [17] p. ; 22 cm. "Catalogue of the exhibition celebrating the opening of the Museum on April 23, 1977, Turner's 202nd birthday, and on April 24, 1977." [N6797.T88G7] 77-151013 2.00
1. Turner, Joseph Mallord William, 1775-1851. 2. Moran, Thomas, 1837-1926. I. Turner Museum. II. Title.

HERRMANN, Luke. 760'.0924
Ruskin and Turner; a study of Ruskin as a collector of Turner, based on his gifts to the University of Oxford; incorporating a catalogue raisonne of the Turner drawings in the Ashmolean Museum. New York, F. A. Praeger [1969, c1968] 108 p. 52 plates (4 col.) 26 cm. Bibliography: p. 17. [NC1115.T82H4 1969] 69-12954 11.50
1. Turner, Joseph Mallord William, 1775-1851. 2. Ruskin, John, 1819-1900—Art collections. I. Oxford. University. Ashmolean Museum. II. Title. BIP

HIRSH, Diana. 759.2
The world of Turner, 1775-1851, by Diana Hirsh and the editors of Time-Life Books New York, Time-Life Books [1969] 192 p. illus. (part col.) 32 cm. (Time-Life library of art) Bibliography: p. 187. [ND497.T8H64] 73-78989
1. Turner, Joseph Mallord William, 1775-1851. I. Time-Life Books. II. Title. BIP

KITSON, Michael. 759.2
J. M. W. Turner [by] Michael Kitson. New York, Barnes & Noble [1964] 90 p. illus. (part col.) 18 cm. (Barnes & Noble art series, no. 618) [ND497.T8K5] 64-56938
1. Turner, Joseph Mallord William, 1775-1851. I. Title.

LINDSAY, Jack, 1900- 759.2
J. M. W. Turner: his life and work; a critical biography. [Greenwich, Con..] New York Graphic Society [1966] 275 p. illus. (part col.) 25 cm. Bibliography: p. 265-270. [ND497.T8L5 1966] 66-15798
1. Turner, Joseph Mallord William, 1775-1851.

LINDSAY, Jack, 1900- 759.2 B
J. M. W. Turner: his life and work; a critical biography. New York, Harper & Row [1971, c1966] 275 p. illus. 24 cm. (Icon editions, IN-4) Bibliography: p. 265-270. [ND497.T8L5 1971] 73-148425 ISBN 0-06-435350-8 3.95
1. Turner, Joseph Mallord William, 1775-1851.

NEW York. Museum of Modern Art. 759.2
Turner: imagination and reality [by] Lawrence Gowing. New York; Distributed by Doubleday, Garden City, N.Y. [1966] 64 p. illus. (part col.) 25 cm. Catalog of an exhibition held at the Museum of Modern Art, New York. Bibliography: p. 63-64. [ND497.T8N4] 66-16676
1. Turner, Joseph Mallord William, 1775-1851. I. Gowing, Lawrence. II. Title.

NOTRE Dame, Ind. University. Art Gallery 759.2
Turner in Indiana; pencil sketches, watercolor drawings, and some oils and engraved works of Joseph Mallord William Turner, R.A., P.P. (1775-1851) [Exhibition] Feb. 3 to 24, 1963. [Notre Dame, Ind., Author, 1963] vi, 58p. illus., port. 25cm. On cover: Collection of Mr. and Mrs. Kurt F. Pantzer. 63-14096 apply
1. Turner, Joseph Mallord William, 1775-1851. I. Pantzer, Kurt Friedrich, 1892- II. Title.

REYNOLDS, Graham. 759.2 B
Turner. New York, H. N. Abrams [1969?] 216 p. illus. (part col.) 22 cm. Includes bibliographical references. [ND497.T8R4 1969b] 69-14192
1. Turner, Joseph Mallord William, 1775-1851. BIP

ROTHENSTEIN, John Knewstub Maurice, Sir 1901- 759.2
Turner, by John Rothenstein, Martin Butlin. New York, Braziller [c.1964] ix, 94p., 128p. of illus. 24 mounted col. illus. 32cm. Bibl. 64-23604 20.00
1. Turner, Joseph Mallord William, 1775-1851. I. Butlin, Martin, joint author. II. Title.

SELZ, Jean. 759.2
Turner / by Jean Selz ; [translated by Eileen B. Hennessey]. New York : Crown Publishers, c1975. 96 p. : ill. (some col.) ; 29 cm. Bibliography: p. 95. [ND497.T8S4413] 75-13767 ISBN 0-517-52361-2 : 4.95
1. Turner, Joseph Mallord William, 1775-1851. I. Turner, Joseph Mallord William, 1775-1851.

TURNER, Joseph Mallard William, 1775-1851. 759.2
Twelve watercolours in the British Museum / J. M. W. Turner. London : British Museum Publications, c1976. [24] p. : col. ill. ; 21 x 31 cm. Cover title. [ND1942.T8B75] 77-363029 ISBN 0-7141-0752-2
1. Turner, Joseph Mallard William, 1775-1851. 2. British Museum. I. British Museum. II. Title.

TURNER, Joseph Mallord William, 1775-1851. 759.2
J. M. W. Turner / text by John Walker. New York : H. N. Abrams, [1976] p. cm. (The Library of great painters) Includes index. Bibliography: p. [ND497.T8W34] 76-4090 ISBN 0-8109-0513-2 : 22.50
1. Turner, Joseph Mallord William, 1775-1851. I. Walker, John, Dec. 24, 1906-

TURNER, Joseph Mallord William, 1775-1851. 759.2
Joseph Mallord William Turner. Text by John Rothenstein. New York, H. N. Abrams [1971] 24 p. illus. (part col.) 33 cm. (The Library of great painters. Portfolio ed.) [ND497.T8R62] 70-130290 ISBN 0-8109-3065-X
I. Rothenstein, John Knewstub Maurice, Sir, 1901-

TURNER, Joseph Mallord William, 1775-1851. 741.9'42
Sir Walter Scott countryside : an album of J. W. M. Turner landscapes. Edinburgh : Ramsay Head Press, 1976. [10] leaves : of ill. ; 21 x 30 cm. (Ramsay Head prints ; no. 2) Cover title. Two leaves printed on both sides. [NC242.T9A55 1976] 77-358157 ISBN 0-902859-36-6 : £1.25
1. Turner, Joseph Mallord William, 1775-1851. 2. Scotland in art. I. Title.

TURNER, Joseph Mallord William, 1775-1851. 759.2
Turner : paintings, watercolors, prints & drawings / [text by] Luke Herrmann. Boston : New York Graphic Society, 1975. 240 p. : chiefly ill. (some col.) ; 29 cm. Includes index. Bibliography: p. 236-237. [ND497.T8H42 1975b] 75-9101 ISBN 0-8212-0657-5 : 37.50
1. Turner, Joseph Mallord William, 1775-1851. I. Herrmann, Luke.

TURNER, Joseph Mallord William, 1775-1851. 759.2
Turner sketches, 1802-20; romantic genius [by] Gerald Wilkinson. [New York] Watson-Guptill Publications [1974] 189 p. illus. (part col.) 28 cm. Includes bibliographical references. [ND1942.T8W54 1974] 73-20483 ISBN 0-8230-5473-X 17.50
1. Turner, Joseph Mallord William, 1775-1851. I. Wilkinson, Gerald. II. Title.

TURNER, Joseph Mallord William, 1775-1851. 759.2
Turner's early sketchbooks; drawings in England, Wales and Scotland from 1789 to 1802. Selected, with notes, by Gerald Wilkinson. New York, Watson-Guptill Publications [1972] 157 p. illus. (part col.) 29 cm. 176 drawings selected from the Turner Bequest in the Dept. of Prints and Drawings, British Museum. Bibliography: p. 156. [NC242.T9B7] 78-161198 ISBN 0-8230-5472-1 15.00
I. British Museum. #Dept. of Prints and Drawings II. Title.

Turner, Joseph Mallord William, 1775-1851—Addresses, essays, lectures.

RUSKIN, John, 1819-1900. 720
Lectures on architecture and painting, delivered at Edinburgh in Novermber 1853. With an introd. by Charles Eliot Norton. Brantwood ed. New York, Merrill, 1892. St. Clair Shores, Mich., Scholarly Press, 1972. p. (The works of John Ruskin) [N7445.2.R78 1972] 72-8233 ISBN 0-403-02051-4
1. Turner, Joseph Mallord William, 1775-1851—Addresses, essays, lectures. 2. Architecture—Addresses, essays, lectures. 3. Preraphaelitism—Addresses, essays, lectures. I. Title.

Turning.

CRAMLET, Ross C. 684.08
Wood turning visualized. Milwaukee, Bruce [c.1966] viii, 111p. illus. 27cm. [TT201.C7] 66-17717 2.96 pap.,
1. Turning. 2. Woodwork. I. Title. BIP

CRAMLET, Ross C. 684'.08
Woodturning visualized / Ross C. Cramlet. 2d ed. Beverly Hills, Calif. : Bruce, 1973. 117 p. : ill. ; 28 cm. Includes index. [TT201.C7 1973] 73-81378
1. Turning. 2. Woodwork. I. Title.

ENSINGER, Earl W. 684'.083
Problems in artistic wood turning / Earl W. Ensinger. Woburn, Mass. : Woodcraft Supply Corp., 1978, c1954. 71 p. : ill. ; 20 x 26 cm. Reprint of the ed. published by Bruce Pub. Co., Milwaukee; with additional reading. Includes index. [TT203.E6 1978] 78-60054 ISBN 0-918036-07-0 pbk. : 7.50
1. Turning. 2. Woodwork (Manual training) I. Title. BIP

GUSTAVSSON, Ragnar. 684.08'3
Creating in wood with the lathe [by] Ragnar Gustavsson and Olle Olson. [Edited in English by Clara Fried Zwiebel] New York, Reinhold Book Corp. [1968] 92 p. illus. 23 cm. (Reinhold Scandinavian craft series) Translation of Svarva i tra. [TT201.G813] 66-24541
1. Turning. I. Olson, Olle, joint author. II. Title. BIP

HAINES, Ray Edward. 674.43
The wood-turning lathe [by] Ray E. Haines [and others] New York, Van Nostrand [1952] 132 p. illus. 27 cm. (The Home workshop series) [TT202.H3] 52-5742
1. Turning. 2. Lathes. I. Title.

HOLTZAPFFEL, John Jacob. 684'.083 s
Hand or simple turning : principles and practice / John Jacob Holtzapffel. New York : Dover Publications, 1976. xv, 592 p. : ill. ; 25 cm. (Series: Holtzapffel, Charles, 1806-1847. Turning and mechanical manipulation ; v. 4.) Reprint of the 1881 ed. published by Holtzapffel, London, which was issued as v. 4 of Turning and mechanical manipulation, by C. Holtzapffel. Includes index. [TT201.H628 1973 vol. 4] 684'.083 76-10911 ISBN 0-486-23365-0 : 15.00
1. Turning. I. Title. II. Series. BIP

HOLTZAPFFEL, John Jacob. 745.51
The principles and practice of ornamental or complex turning. With a new introd. by Robert Austin. New York, Dover Publications [1973] xxv, 656 p. illus. 24 cm. Reprint of the 1894 ed. published by Holzapffel, London, as vol. 5 of Turning and mechanical manipulation, by C. Holzapffel. Bibliography: p. ix. [TT201.H63 1973] 72-95048 ISBN 0-486-22965-3 15.00
1. Turning. 2. Industrial arts. I. Holzapffel, Charles, 1806-1847. Turning and mechanical manipulation. II. Title. BIP

MILTON, Archie Seldon, 1887- 371.426884
Fundamental wood turning [by] Archie S. Milton [and] Otto K. Wohlers. Milwaukee, Bruce Pub. Co. [1953] 143 p. illus. 25 cm. First published in 1919 under title: A course in wood turning. [TT202.M6 1953] 53-3855
1. Turning. 2. Woodwork. I. Wohlers, Otto K., 1893- joint author.

NISH, Dale, 1932- 684'.083
Creative woodturning ; a how-to book for lathe craftsmen / by Dale Nish. [Provo, Utah] : Brigham Young University Press, [1975] p. cm. [TT201.N56] 75-6952 ISBN 0-8425-1557-7 : 10.95 pbk. : 6.95 ISBN 0-8425-1429-5
1. Turning. I. Title.

NISH, Dale L., 1932- 684'.083
Creative woodturning / by Dale L. Nish. Provo, Utah : Brigham Young University Press, [1975] vii, 248 p. : ill. ; 28 cm. Includes index. [TT201.N56] 75-6952 ISBN 0-8425-0469-9 ISBN 0-8425-1557-7 pbk. ISBN 0-8425-0472-9 (special)
1. Turning. I. Title. BIP

PAIN, Frank. 684'.08
The practical wood turner, by F. Pain. New York, Drake Publishers [1974] p. cm. [TT201.P3 1974] 74-6436 ISBN 0-87749-705-2 3.95 (pbk.)
1. Turning. I. Title. BIP

PAIN, Frank. 684
The practical wood turner: use of gouge and chisel, faceplate turning, chucking, parting, boring, special work, etc. Philadelphia, Lippincott [1957] 166p. illus. 23cm. (Woodworker handbooks) [TT201.P3] 57-13740
1. Turning. I. Title.

PETERS, Geoff. 684.8
Woodturning. [New York] Arc Books [1962, c1961] 152p. illus. 18cm. [TT202.P4] 62-17578
1. Turning. I. Title. BIP

REBHORN, Eldon. 684.08'3
Woodturning. Bloomington, Ill., McKnight & McKnight [1970] xii, 158 p. illus. 24 cm. [TT201.R4] 76-86471
1. Turning. I. Title. BIP

STOKES, Gordon. 684'.083
Beginner's guide to woodturning / Gordon Stokes. London : Pelham Books, c1974. 126 p. : ill. ; 23 cm. Label on t.p.: Transatlantic Arts, Inc., Levittown, N.Y., sole distributor for the U.S.A. Includes index. [TT201.S74 1974] 76-351049 ISBN 0-7207-0637-8 : 9.50
1. Turning. I. Title. BIP

STOKES, Gordon. 745.51
Modern wood turning. New York, Drake Publishers [1973] 128 p. illus. 22 cm. Discusses techniques, tools, and equipment used in shaping wood in a lathe. [TT201.S75] 72-11265 ISBN 0-87749-295-6 6.95
1. Turning. I. Title. BIP

STOKES, Gordon. 684'.083
Woodturning for pleasure / Gordon Stokes. London : Evans Brothers, c1976. 112 p. : ill. ; 22 cm. Includes index. [TT201.S76] 76-377562 ISBN 0-237-44792-4 : £4.50
1. Turning. I. Title.

Turtles in art.

FISCHER, Henry George. 704.94'32
Ancient Egyptian representations of turtles [by] Henry G. Fischer. New York, Metropolitan Museum of Art [1968] 34 p. illus., 21 plates (part col.) 32 cm. (New York. Metropolitan Museum of Art Papers, no. 13) Bibliographical footnotes. [N5350.F5] 66-28189
1. Turtles in art. 2. Art, Egyptian. I. Title. II. Series.

Tutankhamen, King of Egypt.

ROSS, Robert Horace. 746.4'4
Treasures of Tutankhamun in needlepoint / by Robert Horace Ross ; photos. by Edward L. Wintringham. 1st ed. New York : Morrow, c1978. 86 p. : ill. ; 29 cm. [TT778.C3R67] 78-10342 ISBN 0-688-03430-6 : 15.00 ISBN 0-688-08430-3 pbk. : 8.95 pbk.
1. Tutankhamen, King of Egypt. 2. Canvas

embroidery—Patterns. I. Title. II. Title: Tutankhamun in needlepoint.

Tutankhamen, King of Egypt—Tomb.

BRACKMAN, Arnold C. 932'.01'0924
The search for the gold of Tutankhamen / Arnold C. Brackman. New York : Van Nostrand Reinhold Co., 1978. p. cm. Includes index. [DT87.5.B66 1978] 78-16289 ISBN 0-442-80364-8 : 8.95
1. Tutankhamen, King of Egypt Tomb. 2. Excavations (Archaeology)—Egypt. 3. Egypt—Antiquities. I. Title. **BIP**

†BURTON, Harry, 1879-1940. 779'.9'932010924
The discovery of Tutankhamun's tomb / text by Howard Carter ; photos. by Harry Burton ; edited by Polly Cone. New York : Metropolitan Museum of Art : distributed by Grosset & Dunlap, 1977, c1976. xxvii, 82 p. : ill. ; 28 cm. "Originally published as Wonderful things." Much of the text is abridged and adapted from The tomb of Tut-ankh-Amen, by H. Carter and A. C. Mace. Published on the occasion of the exhibition, Treasures of Tutankhamun, at the National Gallery of Art, Washington. D.C., and other museums, 1976-1979. [DT87.5.B87 1977] 77-84859 ISBN 0-448-14554-5. ISBN 0-448-14546-4 pbk. : 5.95
1. Tutankhamun, King of Egypt—Tomb. 2. Excavations (Archaeology)—Egypt. 3. Egypt—Antiquities. I. Carter, Howard, 1873-1939. II. Cone, Polly. III. Carter, Howard, 1873-1939. The tomb of Tut-ankh-Amen. IV. New York (City). Metropolitan Museum of Art. V. Title. **BIP**

EDWARDS, Iorwerth Eiddon Stephen. 709'.32
Tutankhamun, his tomb and its treasures / I. E. S. Edwards ; black and white photos. by Harry Burton, color photos. by Lee Boltin. 1st ed. New York : Metropolitan Museum of Art : distributed by Random House, c1976. ca. 250 p. : ill. (some col.) ; 29 cm. "Published on the occasion of the exhibition Treasures of Tutankhamun at the National Gallery of Art, Washington, D.C., Field Museum of Natural History and the Oriental Institute of the University of Chicago, New Orleans Museum of Art, Los Angeles County Museum of Art, Seattle Art Museum, and the Metropolitan Museum of Art, 1976-1979." [DT87.5.E347 1976] 76-49330 ISBN 0-394-41170-6 : 35.00
1. Tutankhamen, King of Egypt—Tomb. 2. Art objects, Egyptian—Exhibitions. 3. Egypt—Antiquities—Exhibitions. I. Burton, Harry, 1879-1940. II. Boltin, Lee. III. New York (City). Metropolitan Museum of Art. IV. Title.

EDWARDS, Iorwerth Eiddon Stephen. 739.27'0932
Tutankhamun's jewelry / I. E. S. Edwards. New York : Metropolitan Museum of Art, [1976] p. cm. Bibliography: p. [DT87.5.E35] 76-41859 ISBN 0-87099-155-8 pbk. : 4.95
1. Tutankhamen, King of Egypt—Tomb. 2. Jewelry—Egypt. 3. Egypt—Antiquities. I. Title. **BIP**

SILVERMAN, David P. 709'.32
Treasures of Tutankhamen / David P. Silverman. New York : Abbeville Press, [1978] p. cm. [DT87.5.S45] 78-12357 ISBN 0-89659-022-4 : 17.95
1. Tutankhamen, King of Egypt—Tomb. 2. Egypt—Antiquities. 3. Art objects, Egyptian. I. Title.

Tuti'namah—Illustrations—Exhibition.

CHANDRA, Pramod. 745.6'7'0954
The Cleveland Tuti-nama manuscript and the origins of Mughal painting / by Pramod Chandra and Daniel J. Ehnbom. [Cleveland] : Cleveland Museum of Art, 1976. 88 p. : ill. ; 24 cm. Catalog of an exhibition at the Cleveland Museum of Art, Nov. 9-Dec. 19, 1976, and at the David and Alfred Smart Gallery, University of Chicago, Jan. 12-Feb. 27, 1977. Bibliography: p. 57-58. [ND3399.T9C47] 76-46258
1. Tuti'namah—Illustrations—Exhibition. 2. Illumination of books and manuscripts, Mogul—Exhibitions. I. Ehnbom, Daniel J., joint author. II. Cleveland Museum of Art. III. David and Alfred Smart Gallery. IV. Title.

Tuttle, Richard, 1941—

DALLAS. Museum of Fine Arts. 730.924
Richard Tuttle. [Dallas, 1971] 1 v. (unpaged) illus., port. 22 cm. [N6537.T8D3] 79-22394
1. Tuttle, Richard, 1941-

Twardowicz, Stanley, 1917—

HECKSCHER Museum. 759.13
Stanley Twardowicz. Huntington, N.Y. [1974] 12 p. illus. 28 cm. Catalogue of an exhibition held Apr. 7-May 26, 1974. [ND237.T853H43] 74-78946
1. Twardowicz, Stanley, 1917-

Twentieth century—Pictorial works.

SALOMON, Erich. 779'.9'901904
Portrait of an age. Selected by Han de Vries and Peter Hunter-Salomon. Biography and notes by Peter Hunter-Salomon. Photographic layout by Han de Vries. Translated by Sheila Tobias. New York, Macmillan [1967] xiv, 221 p. (chiefly illus., ports.) 29 cm. Bibliography: p. 218. [D426.S213] 66-29845
1. Twentieth century—Pictorial works. I. Vries, Han de, ed. II. Hunter-Salomon, Peter, ed. III. Title. **BIP**

YEAR. 909.82
Turbulent 20th century; the dramatic story of the 20th century in 1,500 pictures, 75,000 words: a permanent record of all the important national and world events. [New York, 1957] 255 p. illus. 29 cm. "Originally published in 1950 as Year's special mid-century edition." [D426.Y4] 57-14501
1. Twentieth century — Pictorial works. I. Title.

Twigg, Jhn, 1732-1790.

*NEAL, W. Keith 683.4009'42'073
Great British gunmakers, 1740-1790; the history of John Twigg and the Packington guns [by] W. Keith Neal&D.H.L. Back. [Totowa, N.J.] Sotheby Parke Bernet Publications, [1975] 196p. ill(part col.) 30cm. Includes index. [TS532.4] ISBN 0-85667-015-4 70.00
1. Twigg, Jhn, 1732-1790. 2. Firearms-history. I. Back, D.H.L. joint author. II. Title. **BIP**

Twin-lens cameras.

TYDINGS, Kenneth S 771.315
The modern twin-lens reflex camera guide. New York, Greenberg, c1953. 128p. illus. 20cm. (The Modern camera guide series) [TR147.T9] 52-5625
1. Twin-lens cameras. 2. Photography—Handbooks, manuals, etc. I. Title.

Twinrocker Handmade Paper Mill.

INDIANAPOLIS Museum of Art. 760'.028
Works on Twinrocker handmade paper : an exhibition organized by the Indianapolis Museum of Art, 15 April-25 May, 1975. [Indianapolis] : The Museum, [1975] [15] p. : ill. ; 26 cm. Includes checklist of exhibition. [TS1083.U61535 1975] 75-7928
1. Twinrocker Handmade Paper Mill. 2. Paper—Exhibitions. I. Title.

Twombly, Cy, 1928—

TWOMBLY, Cy, 1928- 709'.2'4
Cy Twombly : paintings, drawings, constructions, 1951-1974 : [exhibition] Institute of Contemporary Art, University of Pennsylvania, Philadelphia, March 15 to April 27, 1975 [San Francisco Museum of Art, San Francisco, California, May 9 to June 22, 1975]. [Philadelphia] : The Institute, [1975] 63 p. : ill. ; 23 x 27 cm. Catalog. Bibliography: p. 57-61. [N6537.T96P46] 75-320692 ISBN 0-88454-016-2
1. Twombly, Cy, 1928- I. Pennsylvania. University. Institute of Contemporary Art. II. San Francisco. Museum of Art.

Tworkov, Jack, 1900-

BRYANT, Edward. 759.13
Jack Tworkov. New York, Published for the Whitney Museum of American Art by Praeger, 1964. 56 p. illus. (part col.) ports. 24 cm. Bibliography: p. 54-56. [ND237.T88B7] 64-13388
1. Tworkov, Jack, 1900- I. Title.

TWORKOV, Jack, 1900- 759.13
Jack Tworkov : recent paintings and drawings : University Art Galleries, University of California, Santa Barbara, January 5-February 6, 1977 : [exhibition] / sponsored by the Art Affiliates, UCSB. [Santa Barbara : University Art Galleries, University of California], c1977. [30] p. : col. ill. ; 22 cm. Includes bibliographical references. [N6537.T97C34] 76-620096
1. Tworkov, Jack, 1900- I. California. University, Santa Barbara. Art Galleries.

Type and type-founding.

ANNENBERG, Maurice, 1907- 686.2'24
Type foundries of America and their catalogs / compiled and written by Maurice Annenberg. Baltimore : Maran Print. Services, 1975. 245 p. : ill. ; 29 cm. Bibliography: p. 244. [Z250.A2A55] 73-94198 30.00
1. Type and type-founding. 2. Printing—History—United States. 3. Printing—Specimens. I. Title. **BIP**

BIGELOW, Marybelle S 411
Alphabets and design; a text on lettering and techniques for the beginning student in the field of graphic communication [by] M. S. Bigelow. [San Diego? 1965] x. 228 p. illus. 28 cm. [Z250.B566] 65-8429
1. Type and type-founding. 2. Alphabet. I. Title.

BIGELOW, Marybelle S. 655.2'4
Alphabets and design; a text for beginning students in graphic design [by] M. S. Bigelow. Minneapolis, Burgess Pub. Co. [1967] vi, 252 p. illus. (part col.) 27 cm. Bibliography: p. 247-248. [Z250.B566 1967] 68-263
1. Type and type-founding. 2. Alphabet. I. Title.

BIGGS, John R. 411
An approach to type. New York, Pellegrini & Cudahy, 1952. 152p. illus. 25cm. Bibliography: p.79-82. [Z250.B] A53
1. Type and type-founding. I. Title.

CRAIG, James, 1930- 686'.224
Designing with type; a basic course in typography. Edited by Susan E. Meyer. [1st ed.] New York, Watson-Guptill [1971] 175 p. illus. 32 cm. Bibliography: p. 168-169. [Z250.C88] 70-159564 ISBN 0-8230-1320-0 10.95
1. Type and type-founding. I. Title. **BIP**

DAIR, Carl. 655.25
Design with type. New York, Pellegrini & Cudahy [1955 128 p. illus. 14 x 23 cm. [Z246.D23] 52-5900
1. Type and type-founding. 2. Printing. Practical. I. Title. **BIP**

DAIR, Carl. 655.25
Design with type. [Toronto] University of Toronto Press [1967] vi, 162 p. illus. 21 cm. Reprint of the 1952 ed. Bibliography: p. [152]-153. [Z246.D23 1967] 66-23932
1. Type and type-founding. 2. Printing, Practical. I. Title.

DENMAN, Frank. 655.23
The shaping of our alphabet; a study of changing type styles. [1st ed.] New York, Knopf, 1955. 228 p. illus., facsims. 25 cm. [Z250.D46] 53-6850
1. Type and type-founding. I. Title.

FOURNIER, Pierre Simon, 1712-1768 686.22
Fournier on typefounding; the text of the manual typographique (1764-1766). translated into English and edited with notes by Harry Carter. New ed. with a forward and supplementary bibliography & reference by the translator. New York, B. Franklin [1973] xlvii, ii, 323 p. illus., 23 cm. (Burt Franklin bibliography & reference series 468. Art history and reference series 41) Reprint of the 1930 ed. published by Soncino Press, London. Includes bibliographies [Z250.F7813 1973] 78-150161 28.50
1. Type and type—Founding. 2. Printing Specimens. I. Carter, Harry Graham ed. II. Title. **BIP**

FRANKLIN, Colin. 686.2'092'4
Emery Walker; some light on his theories of printing and on his relations with William Morris and Cobden-Sanderson. Cambridge [Eng.] 1973. vii, 35 p. illus. 30 cm. Part of illustrative matter in pocket. "Five hundred copies printed." [Z232.W17F7] 74-181285
1. Walker, Emery, Sir, 1851-1933. 2. Morris, William, 1834-1896. 3. Cobden-Sanderson, Thomas James, 1840-1922. 4. Type and type-founding.

GREENWOOD, Gillian, ed. 655.24
A new book of alphabets. Selected by Gillian Greenwood. New York, Reinhold [c.1965] 80p. 19cm. [Z250.G8] 65-20125 2.50 bds.,
1. Type and type-founding. 2. Printing—Specimens. I. Title.

HLASTA, Stanley C. 655.24
Printing types & how to use them. Pittsburgh, Carnegie Press [1950] x, 304 p. 26 cm. [Z250.H67] 50-8940
1. Type and type-founding. I. Title.

KARCH, Robert Randolph, 1902- 655.24
How to recognize type faces. Bloomington, Ill., McKnight & McKnight [1952] 265 p. illus. 23 cm. [Z250.K15] 52-12914
1. Type and type-founding. 2. Printing—Specimens. I. Title. II. Title: Type faces.

KARCH, Robert Randolph, 1902- 655.24
How to recognize type faces. [2d ed.] Bloomington, Ill., McKnight & McKnight [1959] 264 p. 23 cm. [Z250.K15 1959] 59-2681
1. Type and type-founding. 2. Printing—Specimens. I. Title. II. Title: Type faces.

KRIMPEN, Jan van, 1892-1958. 686.2'24
A letter to Philip Hofer on certain problems connected with the mechanical cutting of punches. A facsim. reproduction, with an introd. and commentary by John Dreyfus. Cambridge, Mass., Dept. of Print. and Graphic Arts, Harvard College Library, 1972. 101 p. illus. 26 cm. (Studies in the history of calligraphy and printing, 4) Facsim. of the Harvard College Library Ms. Typ 410. Includes bibliographies. [Z250.K67 1972a] 73-104909 15.00
1. Krimpen, Jan van, 1892-1958. 2. Hofer, Philip, 1898- 3. Type and type founding. I. Hofer, Philip, 1898- II. Dreyfus, John, ed. III. Title. IV. Series.

LAWSON, Alexander S. 686.2'24
Printing types; an introduction [by] Alexander Lawson. Boston, Beacon Press [1974, c1971] 119 p. illus. 22 cm. [Z250.L35] 70-136232 ISBN 0-8070-6659-1. 2.95 (pbk.)
1. Type and type—Founding. I. Title. **BIP**

LEWIS, John Noel Claude, 1912- 686.2'24
Typography: design and practice / John Lewis. New York : Taplinger Pub. Co., 1978. 144 p. : ill. ; 28 cm. (A Pentalic book) [Z250.L593 1978] 78-52798 ISBN 0-8008-7921-X : 17.50. ISBN 0-8008-7922-8 pbk. : 11.95
1. Type and type-founding. 2. Printing. I. Title.

LEWIS, John Noel Claude, 1912- 655.2
Typography, basic principles: influences and trends since the 19th century [by] John Lewis. New York, Rheinhold [1964] 96 p. illus. (part col.) facsims. 20 cm. (Studio paperbacks) [Z250.L59] 64-14630
1. Type and type founding. I. Title.

LIEBERMAN, J. Ben. 686.2'24
Type and typefaces / by J. Ben Lieberman. 2d ed. New Rochelle, N.Y. : Myriade Press, 1978,c1977. p. cm. (A Treasury of

typography book) First published in 1967 under title: Types of typefaces and how to recognize them. Includes index. [Z250.L6 1977] 77-24401 ISBN 0-918142-01-6 : 14.95
1. Type and type-founding. 2. Printing—Specimens. I. Title. BIP

LIEBERMAN, J. Ben. 655.2'4
Types of typefaces and how to recognize them, by J. Ben Lieberman. New York, Sterling Pub. Co. [1967] 132 p. illus. 29 cm. Bibliography: p. 95-96. [Z250.L6] 66-25820
1. Type and type-founding. 2. Printing—Specimens. I. Title.

MORES, Edward Rowe, 1730-1778. 655.142
A dissertation upon English typographical founders and founderies (1778) With a catalogue and specimen of the typefoundry of John James (1782) Edited with an introd. and notes by Harry Carter & Christopher Ricks. London, Oxford University Press, 1961 [i.e. 1962] lxxx, 145p. illus., ports., typog. specimens. 26cm. Bibliographical footnotes. [Z250.M84 1962] 62-1486
1. Type and type-founding. 2. Printing-Hist.—Gt. Brit. 3. Printing— Specimens. I. Title.

MORISON, Stanley, 1889-1967. 686.2'24
A tally of types. With additions by several hands. Edited by Brooke Crutchley. [New ed.] Cambridge [Eng.] University Press, 1973. 137 p. 27 cm. [Z232.C17M6 1973] 72-90486 ISBN 0-521-20043-1 14.95
1. Cambridge University Press. 2. Type and type-founding. I. Title.
Distributed by Cambridge University Press N.Y; 5.95 (pbk.); ISBN 0-521-09786-X. BIP

OXFORD University Press. 686'.224
Notes on a century of typography at the University Press, Oxford, 1693-1794, by Horace Hart. [1st ed. reprinted ; with an introduction and additional notes by Harry Carter. Oxford, Clarendon Press, 1970. ix, 16, xvi, 203 p., plate. illus. facsims., port. 33 cm. Includes bibliographical references. [Z232.O98A55] 70-24174 ISBN 0-19-818138-8 £10.00
1. Fell, John, Bp. of Oxford, 1625-1686. 2. Type and type-founding. 3. Printing—Specimens. I. Hart, Horace, 1840-1916. II. Title. BIP

ROGERS, Bruce, 1870-1957. 686.2'092'4
Typographical partnership: ten letters between Bruce Rogers and Emery Walker, 1907-31. Together with an unpublished fragment of Bruce Rogers' Bye-ways of book-making. Edited with an introd. by John Dreyfus. Cambridge, Eng., Printed for the Carl H. Pforzheimer Library at the University Printing House, 1971. xvi, 44 p. 29 cm. "350 copies composed in monotype centaur type." Includes bibliographical references. [Z232.R67A336] 73-163900
1. Rogers, Bruce, 1870-1957. 2. Walker, Emery, Sir, 1851-1933. 3. Type and type-founding. I. Walker, Emery, Sir, 1851-1933. II. Dreyfus, John, ed. III. Carl H. Pforzheimer Library, New York. IV. Title.

ROSEN, Ben. 655.24
Type and typography, the designers type book. New York, Reinhold Pub. Corp. [1963] 406 p. illus., ports., facsims., typog. specimens. 30 cm. Bibliography: p. 405. [Z250.R79] 63-19221
1. Type and type-founding. I. Title. BIP

TINKER, Miles Albert, 1893- 655.2
Legibility of print. Ames, Iowa State University Press [c1963] ix, 329 p. illus., tables. 22 cm. Bibliography: p. 267-322. [Z250.A4T5] 63-16674
1. Type and type-founding. I. Title. BIP

TSCHICHOLD, Jan, 1902- 655.24
Treasury of alphabets and lettering; a source book of the best letter forms of past and present for sign painters, graphic artists, commercial artists, typographers, printers, sculptors, architects, and schools of art and design. [Tr. from German] New York. Reinhold. [1966] 236p. illus., plates. 33cm. [Z250.T883] 63-19222 16.50
1. Type and type-founding. 2. Alphabets. 3. Printing—Specimens. I. Title.

U.S. Government Printing Office. 655.24
Specimens of type faces in the United States Government Printing Office. Washington [1962?] viii, 340 p. (p. 335-340 blank for "Notes") 24 cm. At head of title: For office use only. [Z250.U57 1962] 62-5405
1. Type and type-founding. 2. Printing—Specimens.

U.S. Government Printing Office. 655.2'4
Specimens of type faces: United States Government Printing Office. Washington, 1969- 1 v. (loose-leaf) 28 cm. Previous editions issued under title: Specimens of type faces in the United States Government Printing Office. [Z250.U572] 79-604651 5.00
1. Type and type-founding. 2. Printing—Specimens. I. Title.

UPDIKE, Daniel Berkeley, 1860-1941. 655.24
Printing types, their history, forms, and use; a study in survivals. [3d ed.] Cambridge, Mass., Belknap Press, 1962. 2 v. illus., facsims. 25 cm. Bibliographical references included in "Supplementary notes" (v. 1, p. [277]-292; v. 2, p. [277]-296) [Z250.A2U6] 62-5866
1. Type and type-founding. 2. Printing — Hist. 3. Printing — Specimens. I. Title.

ZAPF, Hermann. 655.2'4
About alphabets; some marginal notes on type design. [Translated by Paul Standard. Rev. ed.] Cambridge, M.I.T. Press [1970] 142 p. illus., port. 19 cm. Autobiographical. Bibliography: p. 90-108. [Z250.A2Z36 1970] 72-110238
1. Type and type-founding. 2. Printing—Specimens. I. Title. BIP

Type and type-founding—Direct.

TYPE face directory. 655.24'03
New York, Typographers Assn. of New York City [1967] v, 23cm. Issued for the readers of Printing. [Z250.T96] 57-50867 2.00 pap.,
1. Type and type-founding—Direct.

Type and type-founding—Display type.

ART nouveau display alphabets : 686.2'24 100 complete fonts / selected and arranged by Dan X. Solo from the Solotype typographers catalog. New York : Dover Publications, 1976. 100 p. ; 28 cm. (Dover pictorial archive series) [Z250.A77 1976] 76-18408 ISBN 0-486-23386-3 pbk. : 3.00
1. Type and type-founding—Display type. 2. Decoration and ornament—Art nouveau. 3. Alphabets. I. Solo, Dan X.

BUTLER, Kenneth B 655.24
Practical handbook on display typefaces ofr publication layout, by Kenneth B. Butler and George C. Likeness. Mendota, Ill., Butler Typo-Design Research Center [1959] 175p. illus. 29cm. (His A series of handbooks, no. 6) Bibliography: p. 175. [Z250.B97] 59-1948
1. Type and type-founding—Display type. I. Likeness, George C., joint author. II. Title. III. Title: Display typefaces for publication layout.

Type and type-founding—History.

BREWER, Roy, 1924- 686.2'24
Eric Gill: the man who loved letters. Totowa, N.J., Rowman and Littlefield [1973] x, 86 p. illus. 26 cm. (The Ars typographica library) [Z250.A2G53] 73-7724 ISBN 0-87471-148-7 15.00
1. Gill, Eric, 1882-1940. 2. Type and type-founding—History. I. Title.

CARTER, Harry Graham. 655.2
A view of early typography up to about 1600, by Harry Carter. Oxford, Clarendon P., 1969. xii, 137 p. 45 plates. illus., facsims., col. map. 23 cm. (The Lyell lectures, 1968) Bibliographical footnotes. [Z250.A2C36] 78-444244 42/-
1. Type and type-founding—History. I. Title. II. Series.

GOUDY, Frederic William, 1865-1947. 686.2'24
Typologia : studies in type design & type making, with comments on the invention of typography, the first types, legibility, and fine printing / Frederic W. Goudy. Berkeley : University of California Press, 1977. xviii, 170 p. : ill. ; 24 cm. Reprint of the 1940 ed. published by University of California, Berkeley. [Z250.A2G6 1977] 78-305196 ISBN 0-520-03308-6 : 15.00
1. California. University. Press. 2. Type and type-founding—History. 3. Printing—History. 4. Printing—Specimens. I. Title. BIP

GRAY, Nicolete, 1911- 686.2'24
Nineteenth century ornamented typefaces / Nicolete Gray, with a chapter on Ornamented types in America by Ray Nash. Berkeley : University of California Press, 1976. 238 p. : ill. ; 29 cm. On cover: ABCD types. Edition of 1938 published under title: xixth century ornamented types and title pages. Includes index. Bibliography: p. 231-232. [Z250.A2G7 1976] 75-17294 ISBN 0-520-03074-5 : 42.50
1. Type and type-founding—History. 2. Title-page. 3. Printing—Specimens—Bibliography. I. Title. BIP

GRAY, Nicolete, 1911- 686.2'24'09034
Nineteenth century ornamented typefaces / [by] Nicolete Gray. New ed. / with a chapter on ornamented types in America by Ray Nash. London : Faber, 1976. [6], 238 p. : ill., facsims. (some col.) ; 29 cm. Originally published in 1938 under title: xixth century ornamented types and title pages. Includes index. Bibliography: p. 231-232. [Z250.A2G7 1976b] 77-357023 ISBN 0-571-10217-4 : £20.00
1. Type and type-founding—History. 2. Title-pages. 3. Printing—Specimens—Bibliography. I. Nash, Ray, 1905- joint author. II. Title.

KELLY, Rob Roy, 1925- 655.2'4
American wood type, 1828-1900; notes on the evolution of decorated and large types and comments on related trades of the period. New York, Van Nostrand Reinhold Co. [1969] 350 p. illus. 32 cm. Bibliography: p. 337-342. [Z250.A2K4] 68-16030
1. Type and type-founding—History. 2. Printing—History—U.S. I. Title. II. Title: Wood type, 1828-1900. BIP

MINNEAPOLIS. Institute of Arts. 411
Letters: hand script and type design. [Exhibition] Jan. 16 through Feb. 24 1963. [Minneapolis, 1963] unpaged. illus. 28 cm. [Z250.A2M68] 63-5986
1. Type and type-founding — Hist. I. Title.

PETERS, John Edward. 686.2'21
The type punches at Columbia University; an inventory by John Peters & Peter M. VanWingen. [New York] School of Library Service, Columbia University, 1974. 40 p. illus. 23 cm. Bibliography: p. 13-16. [Z250.A2P47] 74-180508 1.50.
1. Columbia University. 2. Type and type-founding—History. I. VanWingen, Peter M., joint author. II. Title.

SILVER, Rollo Gabriel, 1909- 655.210973
Typefounding in America, 1787-1825 [by] Rollo G. Silver. Charlottesville. Published for the Bibliographical Society of the University of Virginia [by the] University Press of Virginia [1965] xiii, 139 p. illus., facsims. 23 cm. Bibliographical footnotes. [Z250.A2S5] 65-19396
1. Type and type-founding—Hist. 2. Printing—Hist.—U. S. I. Title.

Type and type-founding—Irish type.

LYNAM, Edward. 655.2'4
The Irish character in print, 1571-1923. Introd. by Alf MacLochlainn. New York, Barnes & Noble [1969, c1968] x, 40, [7] p. illus. 23 cm. "First published 1924, in the Library ... 4th series, Vol. IV, no. 4, March." "Illustrations supplement": [7] p. at end. [Z251.I7L9] 73-4890
1. Type and type-founding—Irish type. I. Title.

Type and type-founding—Italic type.

DREYFUS, John. 655.2
Italic quartet; a record of the collaboration between Harry Kessler, Edward Johnston, Emery Walker and Edward Prince in making the Cranach Press italic. Cambridge, University Printing House, 1966. vii, 50 p. illus., facsims., ports. 26 cm. Limited ed. of 500. "A note on sources" (p. 49-50) [Z250.5.I8D7] 79-366374
1. Type and type-founding—Italic type. 2. Type designers. I. Title.

Type and type-founding—Mathematical symbols.

WILLIAM Byrd Press, inc., Richmond. 655.25
Mathematics in type. Richmond [1954] 58p. illus. 25cm. [Z250.6.M3W5] 55-693
1. Type and type-founding—Mathematical symbols. I. Title.

Type and type-founding — Oriental types.

NITENSON, Edward. 655.2'4
Military typesetting equipment and systems for Indo-Aryan and Dravidian languages (Hindi, Marathi, Bengali, Punjabi, Gujarati, Malayalam, Tamil and Telugu) 1961-1963. Natick, Mass., U.S. Army Natick Laboratories, Mechanical Engineering Division, 1964. vi, 78, 2 p. illus., map. 28 cm. (U.S. Army Natick Laboratories, Natick, Mass. Mechanical Engineering Division. Technical report) Bibliography: p. 45-46. [Z251.O6N5] 64-61976
1. Type and type-founding — Oriental types. I. Title.

Type and type-founding—Script type.

HUTCHINGS, Reginald Salis, 1915- 655.24
A manual of script typefaces; a definitive guide to series in current use, selected and arranged with an introd., commentaries and appendices. London, Cory Adams & Mackay; New York, Hastings [c.1965] 92p. 26cm. Bibl. [Z250.5S4H8] 65-28307 6.95
1. Type and type-founding—Script type. I. Title.

Type and type founding—United States—History.

KELLY, Rob Roy, 1925- 686.2'24
American wood type, 1828-1900 : notes on the evolution of decorated and large types and comments on related trades of the period / Rob Roy Kelly. New York : Da Capo Press, 1977, c1969. 350 p. : ill. ; 31 cm. (A Da Capo paperback) Reprint of the ed. published by Van Nostrand Reinhold, New York. Includes index. Bibliography: p. 337-342. [Z250.A2K4 1977] 76-51389 ISBN 0-306-80059-4 pbk. : 8.95
1. Type and type founding—United States—History. 2. Printing—United States—History. I. Title.

Type and type-setting.

DAVIS, Alec. 655.24
Type in advertising. Leicester [Eng.] Raithby, Lawrence [1951] 80p. illus. 22cm. Includes bibliography. [Z250.D215] 52-67946
1. Type and type-setting. 2. Advertising layout and tupography. I. Title.

Type and typesetting—Arabic type.

BRANDEIS University, Waltham, Mass. Library. 686.2'24
Typographia Arabica; the development of Arabic printing as illustrated by Arabic type specimens. Exhibition held at the Rapaporte Treasure Hall [Feb. 1, 1971-Mar. 1, 1971] Waltham, 1971. iii, 43 l. illus. 29 cm. Bibliography: leaf 42. [Z251.A6B7] 72-196276
1. Type and typesetting—Arabic type. I. Title.

Type designers—Biography.

GRANNIS, Chandler B., comp. 686.2'2'0922 B
Heritage of the graphic arts; a selection of lectures delivered at Gallery 303, New York City under the direction of Dr. Robert L. Leslie. Edited by Chandler B. Grannis. New York, Bowker, 1972. xii, 291 p. illus. 26 cm. Includes bibliographical references. [Z250.A2G65] 69-19210 ISBN 0-8352-0213-5 17.50
1. Type designers—Biography. 2. Private presses—Addresses, essays, lectures. I. Title. BIP

Type designers—England—Biography.

JONES, Herbert, 1905- 686.2'2'0924 B
Stanley Morison displayed : an examination of his early typographic work / by Herbert Jones ; foreword by William Emrys Williams. London : F. Muller, 1976. 127 p. : ill. ; 26 cm. Includes bibliographical references and index. [Z250.A2M688 1976] 76-374574 ISBN 0-584-10352-2 : £8.50
1. Morison, Stanley, 1889-1967. 2. Type designers—England—Biography. 3. Printers—England—Biography. 4. Printing—Specimens. I. Morison, Stanley, 1889-1967. II. Title.

Type measurements—American point system—History.

HOPKINS, Richard L. 686.2'24
Origin of the American point system for printers' type measurement / by Richard L. Hopkins. Terra Alta, W. Va. : Hill & Dale Press, c1976. 100 p., [2] fold. leaves of plates : ill. ; 24 cm. Includes index. Bibliography: p. [91]-96. [Z250.A2H57] 76-375517
1. Type measurements—American point system—History. 2. Type and type-founding—History. I. Title. II. Title: The American point system for printers' type measurement.

Type ornaments.

ANNENBERG, Barnet. 686.2'24
Maran borders and decorations. Baltimore, Maran Print. Services, 1971. 144 p. illus. 29 cm. [Z250.3.A55] 73-161868
1. Type ornaments. 2. Printing—Specimens. I. Title.

BRUCE'S (George) Son and Company, New York. 686.2'24
Victorian frames, borders, and cuts from the 1882 type catalog of George Bruce's Son and Co. New York : Dover Publications, 1976. 123 p. : all ill. ; 29 cm. (Dover pictorial archives series) Selected from Specimens of printing types made at Bruce's New York Type-Foundry, published by G. Bruce's Son and Co. in 1882, and originally published in 1818 under title: A specimen of printing types. [Z250.3.B782 1976] 75-46418 ISBN 0-486-23320-0 pbk. : 3.00
1. Type ornaments. 2. Decoration and ornament—Victorian style. I. Title: Victorian frames, borders, and cuts from the 1882 type catalog ... BIP

CONNER, firm, type-founders, New York (1888. James Conner's sons) 686.2'24
Specimens of electrotype cuts, and corners, and ornaments, & tints, etc., etc. & etc. Hastings-on-Hudson, N.Y., Morgan & Morgan [1972, c1888] 200 p. (chiefly illus.) 36 cm. At head of title: James Conner's Sons, United States Type Foundry, New York City. "Facsimile edition." [Z250.3.C65 1972] 77-118674 ISBN 0-87100-007-5 17.50
1. Type ornaments. I. Title.

RYDER, John, 1917- 686.2'24
Flowers & flourishes : including a newly annotated edition of A suite of fleurons / John Ryder. London : Bodley Head for Mackays, 1976. 168 p. : ill. ; 26 cm. Includes reprint of the 1956 "third impression revised in the author's hand, 1975" ed. of A suite of fleurons. Bibliography: p. [151] [Z250.3.R93 1976] 76-367735 ISBN 0-370-11308-X : £8.00
1. Type ornaments. I. Ryder, John, 1917- A suite of fleurons. 1976. II. Title. BIP

SCHERER, Roman A. G. 686.2'24
Art nouveau & early art deco type & design, from the Roman Scherer catalogue. Edited by Theodore Menten. New York, Dover Publications [1972] 87 p. illus. 29 cm. (Dover pictorial archive series) "A new selection of pages from the catalogue (n.d.; accompanying price list dated 1908) of Roman Scherer, a manufacturer of wood type in Lucerne, Switzerland." [Z250.3.R64] 75-189434 ISBN 0-486-22825-8 2.50
1. Type ornaments. 2. Type and type-founding—Display type. 3. Decoration and ornament—Art nouveau. 4. Art deco. I. Menten, Theodore, ed. II. Title.

Type-setting.

AVIS, Frederick Compton. 655.25
Printers' arithmetic. New York, Philosophical Library [1956] 148p. illus. 19cm. [Z245.A888] 57-3137
1. Type-setting. I. Title.

PRINTING Industry of America. 655.25
A composition manual. [Washington, c1953] 311p. illus. 29cm. (PIA tools of industry series) [Z253.P96] 54-34224
1. Type-setting. I. Title.

TSCHICHOLD, Jan, 1902- 655.2'5
Asymmetric typography. Translated by Ruari McLean. New York, Reinhold Pub. Corp. [1967] 94 p. illus. (part col.) facsims., ports. 24 cm. Translation of Typographische Gestaltung. [Z253.T873] 66-24550
1. Type-setting. 2. Printing, Practical. 3. Printing—Specimens. I. Title.

WOOLDRIDGE, D. 686'.225
Letter assembly in printing, by D. Wooldridge. New York, Hastings House [1972] ix, 301 p. illus. 24 cm. (The Library of printing technology) (Visual communication books) Bibliography: p. 295-296. [Z253.W9] 70-178849 ISBN 0-8038-4274-0 17.50
1. Type-setting. I. Title.

WOOLDRIDGE, Dennis. 686.2'25
Letter assembly in printing, by D. Wooldridge. London, New York, Focal Press, 1972. ix, 301 p. illus. 24 cm. (The Library of printing technology) Bibliography: p. 295-296. [Z253.W9 1972b] 72-189604 ISBN 0-240-50745-2 £4.00
1. Type-setting. 2. Printing, Practical—Make-up. I. Title. BIP

Type-setting—Handbooks, manuals, etc.

MORTON, Alan. 655.2'5
Mechanical composition. [1st ed. Oxford, New York] Pergamon Press [1969] 3 v. illus. 22 cm. (Library of industrial and commercial education and training. Printing division) Contents.Contents.—pt. 1. Line composition.—pt. 2. The monotype keyboard.—pt. 3. Monotype caster and metallurgy. [Z253.M79] 69-20483
1. Type-setting—Handbooks, manuals, etc. 2. Type-setting machines. I. Title. BIP

Type-setting machines.

CURRY, Harold A 655.283
Linecasting keyboard operation, I, prepared by Harold A. Curry. New Burnswick, N.J., Curriculum Laboratory, 1966. 99, 13 p. illus. 28 cm. At head of title: Dept. of Vocational-Technical Education, Rutgers, The State University, Graduate School of Education. Prepared for students of the Marie Katzenbach School for the Deaf. [Z249.C8] A66
1. Type-setting machines. 2. Linotype. 3. Intertype. I. New Jersey. Division of Vocational Education. Curriculum Laboratory, New Burnswick. II. Title.

GARDNER, Christina. 655.2'8
Typesetting with IBM Executive typewriters. Santa Rosa, Calif., Gardner Printing [1967] 180 p. illus. 24 cm. "Sources for further information": p. 178. [Z253.G28] 67-23147
1. Type-setting machines. I. Title. II. Title: IBM Executive typewriters.

Type-setting machines—History.

HUSS, Richard E. 686.2'25'028
The development of printers' mechanical typesetting methods, 1822-1925 [by] Richard E. Huss. Charlottesville, Published for the Bibliographical Society of the University of Virginia by the University Press of Virginia [1973] 307 p. illus. 24 cm. Bibliography: p. 297-298. [Z253.H87] 77-190498 ISBN 0-8139-0336-X 17.50
1. Type-setting machines—History. I. Virginia. University. Bibliographical Society. II. Title. BIP

THOMPSON, John Smith, 1872- 686.2'254
History of composing machines, by John S. Thompson. New York, Arno Press, 1972 [c1904] 200 p. illus. 23 cm. (Technology and society) [Z253.T46 1972] 72-5077 ISBN 0-405-04726-6
1. Type-setting machines—History. I. Title. II. Series. BIP

Type specimens (Natural history)

FLORIDA. University, Gainesville. State Museum. Dept. of Natural Sciences. 574'.08 s
Catalogue of type specimens in the Department of Natural Sciences, Florida State Museum / Carter R. Gilbert, ed. Gainesville : University of Florida, 1974. p. 102-120 ; 23 cm. (Bulletin of the Florida State Museum : Biological sciences ; v. 18, no. 2) Cover title. [QH1.F6 vol. 18, no. 2] [QH70.U62] 591'.074'015979 75-621767 1.75
1. Florida. University, Gainesville. State Museum. Dept. of Natural Sciences. 2. Type specimens (Natural history) I. Gilbert, Carter Rowell, 1930- II. Title. III. Series: Florida. University, Gainesville. State Museum. Bulletin. Biological sciences ; v. 18, no. 2.

Typographical Association.

MUSSON, Albert Edward, 1920- 331.88155
The Typographical Association; origins and history up to 1949. London, New York, Oxford University Press, 1954. 559 p. 26 cm. [Z120.M87] 56-347
1. Typographical Association. I. Title.

MUSSON, Alfred Edward. 331.88155
The Typographical Association; origins and history up to 1949. London, New York, Oxford University Press, 1954. 550p. 26cm. [Z120.M87] 56-347
1. Typographical Association. I. Title.

Tyrrhenian Sea-Description and travel.

DENHAM, Henry Mangles. 910.0316383
The Tyrrhenian sea : a sea-guide to its coasts and islands / H. M. Denham. New York : W. W. Norton [1976c1969] xiii, 198p. : ill. maps ; 24 cm. Includes index. [DG975.T8D4] ISBN 0-393-03196-9 : 12.95
1. Tyrrhenian Sea-Description and travel. 2. Yachts and yachting-Italy. I. Title.
L. C. card no. for original edition: 76-421579.

Uchiyama, Ukai, 1907-

THOMPSON, Kay Morrissey. 751.425
The art and technique of sumi-e; Japanese ink-painting as taught by Ukai Uchiyama. [1st ed.] Tokyo, Rutland, Vt., C. E. Tuttle Co. [1960] 71 p. illus. 30 x 31 cm. [ND1055.T45] 60-10951
1. Uchiyama, Ukai, 1907- 2. Painting, Japanese. 3. Painting — Technique. I. Title. BIP

Udinotti, Agnese, 1940—

UDINOTTI, Agnese, 1940- 730'.92'4
Udinotti. [1st ed.] Flagstaff, Ariz., Northland Press [1973] xiv, 78 p. illus. 25 x 26 cm. [NB237.U34A56] 73-78001 ISBN 0-87358-107-5 10.50
1. Udinotti, Agnese, 1940-

Uelsmann, Jerry, 1934—

UELSMANN, Jerry, 1934- 779'.092'4
Silver meditations / Jerry N. Uelsmann ; introd. by Peter C. Bunnell. Dobbs Ferry, N.Y. : Morgan & Morgan, 1977, c1975. ca. 150 p. : chiefly ill. ; 27 cm. Includes bibliography. [TR685.U36 1977] 75-7850 ISBN 0-87100-087-3 : 10.95
1. Uelsmann, Jerry, 1934- 2. Photography, Composite. I. Title. BIP

Ugolino da Siena, 14th cent.

UGOLINO da Siena, 14thcent. 708'.44'1 s
Heptaptych : [Madonna and Child, with saints Francis, Andrew, Paul, Peter, Stephen, and Louis of Toulouse] / Ugolino da Siena. Williamstown, Mass. : Sterling and Francine Clark Art Institute, [1962] 15 p., [7] leaves of plates : 14 ill. ; 25 cm. (Exhibit - Sterling and Francine Clark Art Institute ; 20) Plate 14 on p. [3] of cover. Exhibition held September 1962. Includes bibliographical references. [N867.A27 no. 20] [ND623.U45] 759.5 75-314961
1. Ugolino da Siena, 14th cent. Madonna and Child, with saints Francis, Andrew, Paul, Peter, Stephen and Louis of Toulouse. I. Title. II. Series: Sterling and Francine Clark Art Institute, Williamstown, Mass. Exhibit ; 20.

Ukiyoe.

KIKUCHI, Sadao, 1924- 769.952
A treasury of Japanese wood block prints (ukiyo-e). Translated by Don Kenny. New York, Crown Publishers [1969] 423 p. illus. (part col.) 35 cm. [NE1310.K513] 68-9073 17.50
1. Ukiyoe. 2. Color prints, Japanese. I. Title.

LANE, Richard Douglas, 1926- 769'.952
Images from the floating world : the Japanese print : including an illustrated dictionary of ukiyo-e / Richard Lane. New York : Putnam, c1978. 364 p. : ill. (some col.) ; 29 cm. Includes indexes. Bibliography: p. 356-360. [NE1321.8.L36 1978] 78-53445 ISBN 0-399-12193-5 : 60.00
*1. Ukiyoe. 2. Color prints, Japanese—Edo period, 1600-1868. 3. Color prints, Japanese—Meiji period, 1868-1912. 4. Japan—Social life and customs—Pictorial works. 5. Ukiyoe—Dictionaries. I. Title.*BIP

SUZUKI, Juzo, 1919- 769'.922
"The decadents," by Juzo Suzuki and Isaburo Oka; translation by John Bester. Tokyo, Palo Alto, Calif., Kodansha International [1969] 95 p. col. plates. 26 cm. (Masterworks of ukiyo-e, 8) [NE1310.S9613] 69-16370 3.50 (pbk)
1. Ukiyo-e. 2. Color prints, Japanese. 3. Wood-engravers—Japan. I. Oka, Isaburo, 1914- joint author. II. Title. III. Series.

TAKAHASHI, Seiichiro, 1884- 769'.952
Traditional woodblock prints of Japan. Translated by Richard Stanley-Baker. [1st ed.] New York, Weatherhill [1972] 175 p. illus. (part col.) 24 cm. (The Heibonsha survey of Japanese art [22]) Translation of Edo no ukiyoeshi. [NE1310.T2913] 74-162683 ISBN 0-8348-1002-6 7.95
1. Ukiyoe. 2. Color prints, Japanese. I. Title. II. Series. BIP

Ukiyoe — Exhibitions.

CORNELL University. Andrew Dickson White Museum of Art. 759.951
Japanese painters of the floating world; [exhibition] Commentary, notes by Martie W. Young, Robert J. Smith. [Ithaca, N. Y., Off. of Univ. Pubns., Cornell Univ., 1966, i.e, 1967] 112p. map, plates (pt. col.) 26cm. Presented by the Andrew Dickson White Museum of Art, Cornell Univ. & the Munson-Williams-Proctor Inst., Utica, held April June, 1966. Bibl. [N5020.I83] 66-19504 2.00 pap.,
1. Ukiyoe — Exhibitions. I. Munson-Williams-Proctor Institute, Utica, N. Y. II.

Young, Martie Wing. III. Smith, Robert John, 1927- IV. Title.

MICHIGAN. University. 769'.952
Graduate Seminar in Museum Practice.
Japanese prints: traditions in costume. Ann Arbor, University of Michigan Museum of Art [1967?] 47 p. illus. 26 cm. Catalog of an exhibition held at the University of Michigan Museum of Art, Dec. 2, 1967-Mar. 3, 1968 by the class of 1967; the 6th in a series organized annually by the Graduate Seminar in Museum Practice (History of art 607) [NE1315.M5] 77-64
1. Ukiyoe—Exhibitions. I. Michigan. University. Museum of Art. II. Title.

Ukiyoe—History.

NARAZAKI, Muneshige, 1904- 759.951
Early paintings. English adaptation by Charles A. Pomeroy. [1st ed.] Tokyo, Palo Alto, Calif., Kodansha International [1968] 96 p. col. plates. 26 cm. (Masterworks of Ukiyo-E, 1) [ND1053.N37] 68-17455 3.50
1. Ukiyoe—History. 2. Screen paintings, Japanese. 3. Scrolls, Japanese. I. Title. II. Series.

WHITFORD, Frank. 769'.952
Japanese prints and Western painters / Frank Whitford. 1st American ed. New York : Macmillan, 1977. 264 p. : ill. (some col.) ; 28 cm. Includes index. Bibliography: p. 257-261. [NE1321.W47] 76-45182 ISBN 0-02-627180-X : 29.95
1. Ukiyoe—History. 2. Color prints, Japanese—History. 3. Prints, European—Japanese influences. I. Title. BIP

Ullman, Harold P.—Art collections.

OTSUKA, Ronald Y. 732'.4
South Asian sculpture : the Harold P. and Jane F. Ullman Collection : [exhibition], Denver Art Museum, January 11-February 23, 1975 / by Ronald Y. Otsuka and Mary C. Lanius. Denver : The Museum, [1975] [47] p. : ill. ; 22 x 25 cm. Catalog. Includes bibliographical references. [NB1000.O87] 74-30854 ISBN 0-914738-06-2
1. Ullman, Harold P.—Art collections. 2. Ullman, Jane F.—Art collections. 3. Sculpture, South Asian—Exhibitions. I. Lanius, Mary C., joint author. II. Denver. Art Museum. III. Title. BIP

Umbrellas and parasols.

CRAWFORD, T. S. 391'.44
A history of the umbrella [by] T. S. Crawford. New York, Taplinger Pub. Co. [1970] 220 p. illus., facsims., ports. 23 cm. Bibliography: p. 202-211. [GT2210.C7] 79-108273 8.50
1. Umbrellas and parasols. I. Title. BIP

Umbria — Descr. & trav. — Views.

KELLER, Harald, 1903- 914.565
Umbria, the heart of Italy. 145 photos. by Konrad Helbig, incl. 5 in color. [Translated from the German by Michael Heron] New York, Viking Press [1961] 215 p. plates (part col.) map. 31 cm. (A studio book) Translation of Umbrien; Landschaft und Kunst. Bibliography: p. 211-212. [DG975.U5K413 1961] 61-10423
1. Umbria — Descr. & trav. — Views. I. Heibig, Konrad, pseud. II. Title.

Underdeveloped areas—Housing.

SEELIG, Michael Y., 1938- 720'.9172'4
The architecture of self-help communities : the first International competition for the urban environment of developing countries / by Michael Y. Seelig. New York : Architectural Record Books, c1978. ix, 205 p. : ill. ; 23 x 29 cm. Sponsored by the International Architectural Foundation. Bibliography: p. 200-205. [NA7540.S43] 77-15116 ISBN 0-07-0999901-5 : 25.00
1. Underdeveloped areas—Housing. 2. Underdeveloped areas—Squatters. 3. Architects and community. 4. Architecture—Competitions. I. International Architectural Foundation. II. Title. BIP

Underwater archaeology.

PETERSON, Mendel L 743'.8'9913031
History under the sea; a handbook for underwater exploration, by Mendel Peterson. Washington, Smithsonian Insitution, 1965. xiii, 108 p. front., map, 50 plates. 28 cm. (Smithsonian publication 4538) Bibliography: p. 95-105. [CC77.P4] 65-61491
1. Underwater archaeology. I. Title. II. Title: Underwater exploration.

Underwear.

EWING, Elizabeth. 391'.42
Underwear: a history. With illus. by Jean Webber. New York, Theatre Arts Books [1972] 160 p. illus. 26 cm. First published in London under title: Fashion in underwear. Includes bibliography. [GT2073.E9 1972] 74-183308 ISBN 0-87830-145-3
1. Underwear. I. Title.

Underwear—History.

EWING, Elizabeth. 391'.42
Dress and undress : a history of women's underwear / Elizabeth Ewing. New York : Drama Book Specialists, [1978] p. cm. [GT2073.E89] 78-16819 ISBN 0-89676-000-6 : 12.95
1. Underwear—History. 2. Lingerie—History. I. Title. BIP

Ungerer, Tomi, 1931—

UNGERER, Tomi, 1931- 741.9'73
The poster art of Tomi Ungerer. Edited by Jack Rennert. New York, Darien House [1971] 208 p. illus. (part col.) 32 cm. [NC1850.U5A54] 71-162275 ISBN 0-8212-0374-6 15.00
1. Ungerer, Tomi, 1931- I. Title.

UNGERER, Tomi, 1931- 741.9'73
The poster art of Tomi Ungerer. Edited by Jack Rennert. New York, Dover Publications [1973, c1971] 208 p. illus. (part col.) 31 cm. Reprint of the ed. published by Darien House, New York. [NC1850.U5A54 1973] 73-76870 ISBN 0-486-21638-1 6.00
1. Ungerer, Tomi, 1931- I. Title.

Unicorn and the maiden (Art object)

STEUBEN Glass, inc. 748'.8
The Unicorn and the maiden. Glass design by Donald Pollard. Engraving design by Alexander Seidel. Engraving executed by Ladislav Havlik and Peter Schelling. Goldwork by Louis Feron. [Special commemorative ed. New York, 1971] 35 p. illus. 27 cm. [NK5198.S7P65] 74-173685 ISBN 0-911442-04-9
1. Unicorn and the maiden (Art object) I. Pollard, Donald. II. Seidel, Alexander. III. Title.

Unicorns in art.

FRANCIS, Harley, 1940- 741.9'73
The night blooming delirious : a suite of drawings and poems / by Harley Francis, II. New York : Studio 3000, [1975] [54] p. : ill. ; 21 cm. [NC139.F715A53] 75-1203 ISBN 0-915100-03-7 pbk. : 2.00
1. Francis, Harley, 1940- 2. Unicorns in art. I. Title.

Union College, Schenectady.

FEIGENBAUM, Rita. 757'.9'0973
American portraits, 1800-1850; a catalogue of early portraits in the collections of Union College Schenectady, N.Y., Union College Press, 1972. xxv, 155 p. ports. (1 col.) 24 cm. Originally presented as the author's thesis (M.A.) Union College, 1966-67. Bibliography: p. 143-150. [ND1311.2.F4 1972] 71-173916 ISBN 0-912756-01-2 10.95
1. Union College, Schenectady. 2. Portraits, American—Catalogs. 3. Portraits—Schenectady—Catalogs. I. Union College, Schenectady. II. Title. BIP

Union postale universelle.

TYRRELL, M. William. 769'.563
The Universal Postal Union, members & stamps, 1874-1974 / edited by M. William Tyrrell. Albany, Or. : Van Dahl Publications, [1974] 354 p. : ill. ; 25 cm. Includes index. [HE6271.T93] 74-19565 10.00
1. Union postale universelle. 2. Commemorative postage stamps. I. Title.

United Art Glass Company.

POWELL, Edith Hopps. 748.2'9194'61
San Francisco's heritage in art glass / by Edith Hopps Powell ; photography, by Brian Moran. 1st ed. Seattle : Salisbury Press Book, c1976. [87] p. : ill. (some col.) ; 35 cm. [NK5112.P68] 76-2527 ISBN 0-87564-013-3 : 27.95
1. United Art Glass Company. 2. Glassware—California—San Francisco. 3. Decoration and ornament—Art nouveau. I. Moran, Brian. II. Title. BIP

United Federation of Doll Clubs—Congresses.

UNITED Federation of Doll Clubs. 745.59'22
Silver anniversary convention / United Federation of Doll Clubs, inc. Lincoln, Neb. : The Federation, [1974] 206 p., (p. 127-204 advertisements), [1] leaf of plates : ill. ; 29 cm. Pages 205-206, blank for "Notes." Transactions of the convention held in Miami Beach, Aug. 5-11, 1974. [NK4893.U54 1974] 74-79033
1. United Federation of Doll Clubs—Congresses. 2. Dolls—Collectors and collecting—Congresses.

Unjted Nations Educational, Scientific and Cultural Organization.

UNITED Nations Educational, Scientific and Cultural Organization. 016.759
Catalogue de reproductions de peintures 1860 a 1973 et quinze plans d'expositions = Catalogue of reproductions of paintings 1860 to 1973 with fifteen projects for exhibitions. 10. ed. mise a jour. Paris : Unesco, 1974 [i.e.,1975] 343 p. : ill. ; 23 cm. French, English, and Spanish. "SHC.73/XI. II 1/AFS." Includes indexes. [ND189.U54 1974] 75-508403 ISBN 92-3-001123-1 pbk. : 13.20
1. United Nations Educational, Scientific and Cultural Organization. 2. Paintings, Modern—19th century—Catalogs. 3. Paintings, Modern—20th century—Catalogs. 4. Paintings—Catalogs. I. Title. II. Title: Catalogue of reproductions of paintings 1860 to 1973 ...
Distributed by Unipub Distributed by Unipub.

United Nations peace rug.

CRENSHAW, Catherine. 746.7'4
The United Nations peace rug / Catherine and Charles Lawrence Crenshaw ; book design by Thomas F. Ford. Inman, S.C. : C.L. Crenshaw, c1975. ca 150 p. : col. ill. ; 29 cm. [NK9212.C73] 76-355017
1. American Needlepoint Guild. 2. United Nations peace rug. I. Crenshaw, Charles Lawrence, joint author. II. Title.

United Nations—Postal service.

CONWAY, Herbert E. 769'.56
25 years of philatelic highlights / United Nations Postal Administration. 1st ed. New York : UN, 1976. 59 p. : ill. ; 23 cm. [HE6224.C75] 76-366546 2.50
1. United Nations—Postal service. 2. Postage-stamps—Catalogs. I. United Nations. Postal Administration. II. Title.

HARRIS (H. E.) and Company, Boston. 769'.569'7
Stamps of the United States, United Nations and British North America; plus: Confederate States, U.S. possessions, Americana; albums and accessories. Comprehensive U.S. stamp identifier. Boston, 1971. 192 p. (p. 168-192 advertisements) illus. 21 cm. First published in 1943 under title: United States stamps, U.S. possessions, and British North America. [HE6185.U5H35 1971] 70-23607 1.00
1. United Nations—Postal service. 2. Postage-stamps—U.S.—Catalogs. 3. Postage-stamps—Canada—Catalogs. I. Title.

HARRIS (H. E.) and Company, Boston. 769'.56973
Stamps of the United States, United Nations, and Canada and provinces ... Boston, 1974. 216 p. illus. 21 cm. [HE6185.U5H35 1974] 74-165246 1.00
1. United Nations—Postal service. 2. Postage-stamps—United States—Catalogs. 3. Postage-stamps—Canada—Catalogs. I. Title.

KELEN, Emery, 1896- 769
Stamps tell the story of the United Nations. [1st ed.] New York, Meredith Press [1968] 95 p. illus. 24 cm. Presents the stamps issued by the United Nations, the only international body which issues its own stamps, explaining the aspects of the U.N. and its missions that each stamp honors. Arranged in sections by the subjects of the stamps, for example, the main organs of the U.N., peace-keeping operations, or technical assistance. [JX1977.8.P8K4] AC 68
1. United Nations—Postal service. 2. Postage stamps. I. Title.

WOLKE, Otto. 769'.5691
The 1951 definitives, air mail issues and reprints : the first U.N. definitive issues : a photographic guide to assist in understanding the various printings of the 1951 series of United Nations regular and air mail definitive stamps / [by Otto Wolke.] Brooklyn : United Nations Study Unit of the American Topical Association, [1974] 96 p. : ill., facsims. ; 25 cm. [HE6246.W64] 75-302494
1. United Nations—Postal service. I. Title.

United States—Aerial photographs—Bibliography.

UNITED States. National Archives. 016.6314
Aerial photographs in the National Archives. Compiled by Charles E. Taylor and Richard E. Spurr. Washington, 1971. vii, 106 p. 27 cm. (Its Special list no. 25) [Z6027.U5U6 1971] 75-174520
1. United States. National Archives. 2. United States—Aerial photographs—Bibliography. I. Taylor, Charles Edward, 1928- comp. II. Spurr, Richard E., comp. III. Title. IV. Series.

UNITED States. National Archives. 016.6314
Aerial photographs in the National Archives. Compiled by Charles E. Taylor and Richard E. Spurr. Washington, National Archives and Records Service, 1973. vii, 106 p. 27 cm. (Its Special list no. 25) "Revision of the list first published in 1971." [Z6027.U5U6 1973] 73-602746
1. United States. National Archives. 2. United States—Aerial photographs—Bibliography. I. Taylor, Charles Edward, 1928- II. Spurr, Richard E. III. Title. IV. Series.

United States—Antiquities.

CALDWELL, Joseph Ralston, 1916- 595.78
Trend and tradition in the prehistory of the eastern United States. Springfield, Published jointly by Illinois State Museum and American Anthropological Association. 1958. xiv, 88p. illus., maps. 25cm. (Illinois, State Museum [Springfield] Scientific papers, v. 10) American Anthropological Association Memoir 88. Bibliography: p. 82-88. [Q11.I352 vol.10] A59
1. U. S.— Antiq. 2. Indians of North America—Culture. 3. Social change. I. Title. II. Series. III. Series: American Anthropological Association, Memoir 88

CURRY, Hilda Jane, 1920- 970.6738
Negative painted pottery of Angel Mounds Site in Driver, Harold Edson, 1907- Hoof rattles and girls' puberty rites in North and South America. Baltimore, Indiana Univ. [1950] [GN4.I5 memoir 4-5] A 50

I. Title.

NOEL Hume, Ivor. 917.3'03
A guide to artifacts of colonial America. [1st ed.] New York, Knopf, 1970 [c1969] xviii, 323, vi p. illus. 25 cm. Includes bibliographies. [E159.5.N6] 76-79314 10.00
1. U.S.—Antiquities. I. Title. II. Title: Artifacts of colonial America. BIP

SOUTH, Stanley A. 970
Method and theory in historical archeology / Stanley South. New York : Academic Press, c1977. xxiii, 345 p. : ill. ; 24 cm. (Studies in archeology) Includes bibliographies and index. [E159.5.S65] 75-40616 ISBN 0-12-655750-0 : 24.50
1. United States—Antiquities. 2. Indians of North America—Antiquities. 3. Archaeology—Methodology. I. Title. BIP

United States—Antiquities—Addresses, essays, lectures.

RESEARCH strategies in 930'.1'028
historical archeology / edited by Stanley South. New York : Academic Press, c1977. xxvii, 345 p. : ill. ; 25 cm. (Studies in archeology) Includes bibliographies and index. [E159.5.R47] 76-43377 ISBN 0-12-655760-8 : 19.50
1. United States—Antiquities—Addresses, essays, lectures. 2. Archaeology—Methodology—Addresses, essays, lectures. I. South, Stanley A.

United States—Antiquities—Bibliography.

PETSCHE, Jerome E. 016.9301
Bibliography of salvage archeology in the United States, compiled by Jerome E. Petsche. With a foreword by Joan O. Brew. Lincoln, Neb., 1968. iv, 162 p. 26 cm. (River Basin Surveys. Publications in salvage archaeology, no. 10) [Z1208.U5P4] 68-67086
1. United States—Antiquities—Bibliography. 2. Excavations (Archaeology)—United States—Bibliography. I. Title. II. Title: Salvage archaeology in the United States. III. Series.

United States—Antiquities—Collection and preservation.

MCHARGUE, Georgess. 930'.1
A field guide to conservation archaeology in North America / by Georgess McHargue and Michael Roberts ; with an introd. by Thomas F. King ; drawings by Georgia Lee ; charts and maps by Barbara Page. Philadelphia : Lippincott, c1977. p. cm. Includes bibliographical references and index. [E159.5.M32] 77-21558 ISBN 0-397-31724-7 : 8.95 ISBN 0-397-31725-5 pbk. : 4.95
1. United States—Antiquities—Collection and preservation. 2. Indians of North America—Antiquities. I. Roberts, Michael, 1937- joint author. II. Title. BIP

United States—Antiquities—Collection and preservation—Congresses.

WINTERTHUR Conference, 21st, 973
1975.
Material culture and the study of American life / edited by Ian M. G. Quimby. 1st ed. New York : Published for the Henry Francis du Pont Winterthur Museum, Winterthur, Del. [by] Norton, 1978,c1977 xi, 250 p. : ill ; 22 cm. Includes bibliographical references and index. [E159.5.W56 1975] 77-10894 ISBN 0-393-05661-9 : 12.95
1. United States—Antiquities—Collection and preservation—Congresses. 2. Museum conservation methods—Congresses. 3. Indians of North America—Southwest, New—Antiquities—Collection and preservation—Congresses. I. Quimby, Ian M. G. II. Title.

United States—Antiquities—Congresses.

CONFERENCE on Historic 970.01
Site Archaeology, 13th, Morgantown, W. Va., 1972.
The Conference on Historic Site Archaeology papers, 1972 : volume 7 ... / Stanley South, editor. Columbia, S.C. : Institute of Archaeology and Anthropology, University of South Carolina, 1974. xii, 336 p. : ill. ; 28 cm. Part of illustrative matter fold. in pocket. Includes bibliographies. [E159.5.C66 1972] 75-622778 8.00
1. United States—Antiquities—Congresses. 2. Archaeology—Methodology—Congresses. I. South, Stanley A. II. Title. III. Title: Historic site archaeology papers, 1972.

U.S. Architect of the Capitol.

U.S. General 338.4'7'690511
Accounting Office.
Examination of construction and related costs: Rayburn House Office Building; report to the Congress of the United States [on the] House Office Building Commission [and the] Architect of the Capitol by the Comptroller General of the United States. [Washington] 1967. 2 l., 193 l. illus. 27 cm. [JK1618.A53] 67-61103
1. U.S. Architect of the Capitol. 2. U.S. Congress. House. Commission on Construction of House Office Building. 3. Washington, D.C. Capitol. House Office Building. I. Title.

U. S.—Army—Firearms.

LEWIS, Berkeley R 623.44
Small arms and ammunition in the United States service. Washington, Smithsomian Institution, 1956. viii, 338p. illus., 52 plates. 24cm. (Smithsonian miscellaneouc collections, v.129, whole vol.) Smithsonian Institution, Publication 4254. Bibliography: p. 319-327. [Q11.S7 vol. 129] 56-61921
1. U. S.—Army—Firearms. 2. Firearms—Hist. 3. Cartridges. I. Title. II. Series: Smithsonian Institution. Smithsonian miscellaneous collections, v. 129

United States. Army—Photographers.

UNITED States. Dept. 355'.008 s
of the Army.
Army pictorial techniques, equipments and systems, still photography. [Washington] 1969. 1 v. (various pagings) illus. (part col.), maps. 27 cm. (Its Technical manual TM11-401-2) Cover title. "Supersedes so much of TM11-401, 10 December 1953, including C1, 28 June 1961, as pertains to still photography." [U408.3.A13 TM11-401-2] [UG476] 770'.28 78-605727
1. United States. Army—Photographers. 2. Photography, Military—Handbooks, manuals, etc. I. Title. II. Series: United States. Dept. of the Army. Training publication TM11-401-2.

U.S. Army—Uniforms—History.

CHAPPELL, Gordon. 355.8'1
Summer helmets of the U.S. Army, 1875-1910. [Cheyenne] Wyoming State Archives and Historical Dept., 1967. 35 p. illus., ports. 23 cm. (Wyoming State Museum monograph no. 1) Bibliographical references included in "Notes and sources" (p. 30-31) [AM101.W915 no. 1] 68-64313 1.25
1. U.S. Army—Uniforms—History. 2. Helmets. I. Title. II. Series: Wyoming. State Museum, Cheyenne. Monograph no. 1

United States—Biography.

AMERICAN Academy of Arts and 061
Letters.
Commemorative tributes of the American Academy of Arts and Letters. New York, 1942-51. 2v. 22cm. Vol. 1: 500 copies. Contents.[v.1]1905-1941.-- [v.2]1942-1951. [AS36.A484A15] 42-22390
1. U. S.—Biog. 2. Authors, American. 3. Artists, American. I. Title.

United States—Biography—Portraits.

TOLMAN, Ruel [759.13] 927.5
Pardee, 1878-
The life and works of Edward Greene Malbone, 1777-1807. With an introd. by Theodore Bolton, and a foreword by John Davis Hatch, Jr. New York, New-York Historical Society, 1958. xxiii, 322 p. illus., col. ports., facsims. 25 cm. (The John Divine Jones Fund series of histories and memoirs, 13) Bibliography: p. 280-288. [ND1337.U6M32] 58-2879
1. Malbone, Edward Greene, 1777-1807. 2. U.S. — Biog. — Portraits. I. Title. II. Series: New York Historical Society. The John Divine Jones Fund series of histories and memoirs, 13 BIP

United States—Biography.

AINSWORTH, Katherine, 759.13 B
1908-
The man who captured sunshine : episodes in the life of John W. Hilton, botanist, gemologist, zoologist, and gifted painter of the desert scene / as garnered during long years of friendship by Katherine Ainsworth. Palm Springs, Calif. : ETC Publications, c1978. xiv, 274 p., [8] leaves of plates : ill. (some col.) ; 24 cm. Includes index. [CT275.H59914A46] 77-21823 ISBN 0-88280-054-X : 15.00
1. Hilton, John W. 2. United States—Biography. I. Title. BIP

AMERICAN Academy of Arts 700'.922
and Letters.
Commemorative tributes of the American Academy of Arts and Letters, 1905-1941. Freeport, N.Y., Books for Libraries Press [1968, c1942] 432 p. 22 cm. (Essay index reprint series) [AS36.A484A16] 68-20286
1. United States—Biography. 2. Authors, American. 3. Artists, American. I. Title.

United States—Biography—Portraits.

GILL, Brendan, 1914- 779'.2'0924
Happy times. Text by Brendan Gill. Photos. by Jerome Zerbe. [1st ed.] New York, Harcourt Brace Jovanovich [1973] 288 p. illus. 32 cm. [TR140.Z47G54] 74-157920 ISBN 0-15-138480-0 25.00
1. Zerbe, Jerome, 1904- 2. United States—Biography—Portraits. I. Zerbe, Jerome, 1904- illus. II. Title.

HORAN, James David, 1914- 927.7
Mathew Brady, historian with a camera. Picture collation by Gertrude Horan. New York, Crown Publishers [1955] xix, 244 p. illus., ports., map. 32 cm. "A picture album": p. [91]-[228] "A pictorial bibliography of Brady pictures": p. 235-238. Includes bibliographies. [TR140.B7H6] 55-10171
1. Brady, Mathew B., 1823 (ca.)-1896. 2. United States—Biography—Portraits. 3. United States—History—Pictorial works. 4. Photography—History—United States.

MILLEY, 704.94'2'0973074014811
John C.
Faces of independence : portrait gallery guidebook : Second Bank of the United States, Independence National Historical Park / by John C. Milley. [Philadelphia : Eastern National Park & Monument Association, c1974] [39] p. : ill. (some col.) ; 16 x 23 cm. [N7593.1.M54] 74-21547
1. Second Bank of the United States (Portrait gallery) 2. United States—Biography—Portraits. I. Second Bank of the United States (Portrait gallery) II. Title.

United States. Bureau of Reclamation—Art collections.

UNITED States. Bureau of 759.13
Reclamation.
The American artist and water reclamation; a selection of paintings from the Collection of the Bureau of Reclamation. [Washington, U.S. Govt. Print. Off., 1973] 73 p. (chiefly illus.) 24 x 30 cm. Catalog of an exhibition circulated by the Traveling Exhibition Service, Smithsonian Institution. [N6512.U47 1973] 73-603115 1.75
1. United States. Bureau of Reclamation—Art collections. 2. Art, American—Exhibitions. 3. Art, Modern—20th century—United States. 4. Water reuse in art. I. Smithsonian Institution. Traveling Exhibition Service. II. Title.

United States. Capitol.

UNITED States. Congress. 725
House. Committee on Public Works. Subcommittee on Public Buildings and Grounds.
Building design for the physically handicapped. Comprehensive plan for the U.S. Capitol grounds. Hearings, Ninetieth Congress, second session, on H.R. 6589 and S. 222 ... [and] H.J. Res. 914 and S.J. Res. 74 ... March 19, 1968. Washington, U.S. Govt. Print. Off., 1968. v, 139 p. 24 cm. "90-25." [NA2545.P5U5] 68-61572
1. United States. Capitol. 2. Architecture and the physically handicapped. I. Title. II. Title: Comprehensive plan for the U.S. Capitol grounds.

United States—Centennial celebrations, etc.—Collectibles.

GORES, Stan. 745.1
1876 Centennial collectibles and price guide ; including a history of the Centennial exhibition, with comments on the famous Gillinder & Sons glassworks and a comprehensive report on centennial items of value to antique dealers and collectors. 1st ed. Fond du Lac, Wi[s.] Haber Print. Co. [1974] 163 p. illus. 23 cm. [NK1125.G643] 74-82544
1. Philadelphia. Centennial Exhibition, 1876. 2. United States—Centennial celebrations, etc.—Collectibles. I. Title.

ROSSEN, Howard M., 745.1'075
1936-
Columbian World's Fair collectibles, Chicago (1892-1893) / by Howard M. Rossen and John M. Kaduck. 1st ed. Des Moines : Wallace-Homestead Book Co., c1976. xi, 149 p. : ill. ; 29 cm. Includes index. Bibliography: p. 148. [NK1125.R69] 77-360322 ISBN 0-87069-157-0 : 9.95
1. Chicago. World's Colombian Exposition, 1893. 2. United States—Centennial celebrations, etc.—Collectibles. I. Kaduck, John M., joint author. II. Title.

U. S.—Civilization— Pictorial works.

OSBORN, Robert Chesley, 741.5973
1904-
The vulgarians. [Greenwich, Conn.,] New York Graphic Society [1960. 95]p. illus. (part col.) 21x27cm. 60-13466 3.95 bds.,
1. U. S.—Civilization— Pictorial works. 2. National characteristics, American. I. Title.

UNITED States. Library 779'.9'973
of Congress.
America's yesterdays : images of our lost past discovered in the photographic archives of the Library of Congress / by Oliver Jensen. New York : American Heritage Pub. Co. : distribution by Simon and Schuster, c1978. 352 p. : ill. ; 35 cm. Includes index. [E169.1.U7147 1978] 78-110957 ISBN 0-8281-3074-4 : 29.95
1. United States—Civilization—Pictorial works. 2. United States—Description and travel—Views. I. Jensen, Oliver Ormerod, 1914- II. Title.

U.S. Copyright Office. Catalog of copyright entries.

ROGERS, Joseph William, 015.73
1906-
U.S. national bibliography and the copyright law; an historical study. Foreword by Verner W. Clapp. New York, Bowker, 1960. xii, 115 p. 23 cm. Bibliographical references included in "Notes" (p. 97-107) [Z1216.R6] 60-15545
1. U.S. Copyright Office. Catalog of copyright entries. 2. Bibliography, National—American. I. Title.

United States. Custom House, New York.

GILL, Brendan, 725'.14'097471
1914-
The U.S. Custom House on Bowling Green / by Brendan Gill. New York : New York

Landmarks Conservancy, c1976. 28 p. : ill. ; 28 cm. [NA4465.U62N4834] 76-373987
1. United States. Custom House, New York. I. New York Landmarks Conservancy. II. Title.

United States—Description and travel—Views.

EASTMAN, Seth, 1808-1875. 741.973
A Seth Eastman sketchbook, 1848-1849. Introd. by Lois Burkhalter. Austin, Pub. for the Marion Koogler McNay Art Inst., San Antonio by the Univ. of Texas Pr. [c.1961] xxvi p., 68p. of illus. map. 29cm. 61-12913 7.50
1. U.S.—Descr. & trav.—Views. I. Marion Koogler McNay Art Institute, San Antonio. II. Title.

U.S.—Description and travel—Views.

CURRIER, Nathaniel, 1813-1888. 769'.924
Currier & Ives chronicles of America. Edited by John Lowell Pratt. Introd. by A. K. Baragwanath. Color plates reproduced from the original hand colored stone prints by N. Currier and Currier & Ives. Maplewood, N. J., Hammond [1968] 256 p. illus. (part col.), col. map. 32 cm. [NE2415.C7P7] 68-13933 14.95
1. U.S.—Description and travel—Views. I. Pratt, John Lowell, ed. II. Currier and Ives, joint author. III. Title. IV. Title: Chronicles of America.

EVANS, Walker, 1903-1975. 779'.9'973916
American photographs / Walker Evans ; with an essay by Lincoln Kirstein. New York : East River Press, 1975, c1938. 192 p. : ill. ; 23 cm. Reprint of the ed. published by the Museum of Modern Art, New York. [E169.E85 1975] 75-20144 ISBN 0-89172-001-4 pbk. : 7.50
1. United States—Description and travel—Views. I. Kirstein, Lincoln, 1907- II. Title. BIP

KENNEDY Galleries, inc., New York. 758'.1'0973
An artists' gazeteer; portraits of places in 19th century American art. New York [1971] 176-234 p. illus. 23 cm. (The Kennedy quarterly, v. 10, no. 4) [N8640.K4 vol. 10, no. 4] 76-26423 2.00
1. U.S.—Description and travel—Views. 2. Paintings, American. 3. Painting, Modern—19th century—U.S. I. Title. II. Series.

KENNEDY Galleries, inc., New York. 759.1
The eye of the traveler; an historical & artistic perspective of the American & Canadian frontiers in the work of outstanding 19th century artists. [New York] 1963. 64 p. illus. 23 cm. (The Kennedy quarterly, v. 4, no. 1) [N8640.K4 vol. 4, no. 1] 77-11555
1. U.S.—Description and travel—Views. 2. Canada—Description and travel—Views. 3. Paintings, Modern—19th century—Catalogs. I. Title. II. Series.

SLOANE, Eric. 917.3
I remember America. New York, Funk & Wagnalls, 1971. 184 p. illus. (part col.) 29 x 37 cm. [ND237.S58A2] 72-162582 35.00
1. U.S.—Description and travel—Views. I. Title. BIP

WEIDENAAR, Reynold H., 1915- 741.9'73
Our changing landscape [by] Weidenaar. Cape Cod, Wake-Brook House [1970] 80 p. illus. 29 cm. [NC139.W4A56] 79-138364 ISBN 0-87482-026-X
1. U.S.—Description and travel—Views. I. Title.

United States. Farm Security Administration.

EVANS, Walker, 1903-1975. 779'.092'4
Walker Evans : photographs : [catalogue of] an exhibition circulated under the auspices of the International Council of the Museum of Modern Art, New York [held at the] Museum of Modern Art, Oxford, 18 September-31 October 1976. [London] : Arts Council of Great Britain, 1976. [16] p. : ill., 2 ports. ; 21 cm. [TR820.5.E9 1976] 77-364475 ISBN 0-7287-0110-3 : £0.65
1. United States. Farm Security Administration. 2. Evans, Walker, 1903-1975. 3. Photography, Documentary—Exhibitions. I. International Council of the Museum of Modern Art, New York. II. Museum of Modern Art, Oxford.

SHAHN, Ben, 1898-1969. 779'.9'9173039160924
Ben Shahn, photographer; an album from the thirties. Edited, with an introd., by Margaret R. Weiss. New York, Da Capo Press, 1973. [9] p., 82 plates. 22 x 27 cm. [TR653.S5 1973] 77-75271 ISBN 0-306-71312-8 10.00
1. United States. Farm Security Administration. 2. Photography, Artistic. 3. United States—Description and travel—Views. I. Weiss, Margaret R., ed. II. Title.

SHAHN, Ben, 1898-1969. 779'.9'9739170924
The photographic eye of Ben Shahn / edited by Davis Pratt. Cambridge, Mass. : Harvard University Press, 1975. xiii, 147 p. : all ill. ; 25 x 27 cm. [TR820.5.S48 1975] 75-18543 15.00
1. United States. Farm Security Administration. 2. Photography, Documentary. I. Title. BIP

STRYKER, Roy Emerson, 1893- 779'.9'973917
In this proud land : America, 1935-1943, as seen in the FSA photographs / Roy Emerson Stryker and Nancy Wood. New York : Galahad Books, c1973. 191 p. : chiefly ill. ; 32 cm. Bibliography: p. 189. [TR820.5.S87] 75-12259 ISBN 0-88365-313-3 : 20.00
1. United States. Farm Security Administration. 2. Photography, Documentary. I. Wood, Nancy C., joint author. II. Title. BIP

STRYKER, Roy Emerson, 1893- 779'.9'973917
In this proud land : America, 1935-1943, as seen in the FSA photographs / Roy Emerson Stryker and Nancy Wood. Boston : New York Graphic Society, 1975, c1973. 191 p. : ill. ; 31 cm. Bibliography: p. 189. [TR820.5.S87 1975] 73-78792 ISBN 0-8212-0673-7 pbk : 8.95
1. United States. Farm Security Administration. 2. Photography, Documentary. I. Wood, Nancy C., joint author. II. Title.

U.S. — For. rel. — Russia.

TUCKER, Robert C 327.720947
A preface to U.S. policy toward Russia. Santa Monica, Calif., Rand Corporation, 1958. ix, 135 l. 29 cm. ([Rand Corporation. Paper] P-1341) [AS36.R28 no. 1341] 58-40258
1. U.S. — For. rel. — Russia. 2. Russia — For. rel. — U.S. 3. Russia — For. rel. — 1915- I. Title. II. Series.

U.S. — Hist. — Civil War — Pictorial works.

JOINVILLE, Francois Ferdinand Philippe Louis Marie d'Orleans, Prince de, 1818-1900 759.4
A Civil War album of painting, by the Prince de Joinville, Pref. by the Comte de Paris. Texts by Andre Maurois. General James M. Gavin. New York, Atheneum. [c.]1964. 33p. 20 col. plates. 25x33cm. 64-13136 25.00; 25, 19.95 before Dec.
1. U. S.—Hist.—Civil War—Pictorial works. 2. U. S.—Hist.—Civil War—Foreign participants. I. Maurois, Andre, 1885- II. Gavin, James Maurice, 1907- III. Title.

U.S. National Gallery of Art. 743.899737
The Civil War: a centennial exhibition of eyewitness drawings. Washington, 1961. 153 p. illus., 26 cm. Bibliography: p. 100. [NC107.A55] 61-60315
1. U.S. — Hist. — Civil War — Pictorial works. 2. Drawings, American — Exhibitions. 3. Water colors, American — Exhibitions. I. Title.

U. S.—Hist.—Humor, caricatures, etc.

DARLING, Jay Norwood, 1876-1962. 741.5973
Ding's half century. Ed. by John M. Henry. New York, Duell [dist. Meredith, c.1962] 180p. illus. 25cm. 62-8519 3.95
1. U. S.—Hist.—Humor, caricatures, etc. 2. World politics—Humor, caricatures, etc. I. Title.

U.S.—Historic buildings.

FOLSOM, Merrill. 917.3
Great American mansions and their stories. New York, Hastings House [1963] ix, 310 p. illus., ports. 26 cm. [E159.F65] 63-19792
1. U.S.—Historic buildings. 2. Architecture, Domestic—U.S. I. Title. BIP

PRATT, Dorothy. 728.084
The second treasury of early American homes, by Dorothy and Richard Pratt. New, rev. and enl. ed. New York, Hawthorn Books [1959] 143 p. col. illus. 35 cm. Earlier ed. by Richard Pratt, published in 1954. [NA7205.P684] 59-12179
1. U.S.—Historic buildings. 2. Architecture, Domestic—U.S. I. Pratt, Richard, joint author. II. Title. III. Title: Treasury of early American homes.

PRATT, Richard. 917.303
Houses, history, and people. New York, M. Evans; distributed in association with Lippincott, Philadelphia [1965] 240 p. illus. (part col.), maps, ports. 29 cm. [E159.P7] 65-21773
1. U.S.—Historic buildings. I. Title.

PRATT, Richard. 728.084
The second treasury of early American homes, by Richard Pratt, in collaboration with Dorothy Pratt. [1st ed.] New York, Hawthorn Books [1954] 144 p. col. illus. 35 cm. [NA7205.P72] 54-10656
1. U.S.—Historic buildings. 2. Architecture, Domestic—U.S. I. Title. II. Title: Treasury of early American homes.

U.S. Dept. of Housing and Urban Development. 728'.0973
Preserving historic America. [Washington] [For sale by the Superintendent of Documents, U. S. Govt. Print. Off.] 1966. 80 p. illus. 24 x 29 cm. Bibliography: p. 79. [E159.U528] 66-62042
1. U.S.—Historic buildings. 2. Monuments—U.S.—Preservation. 3. Architecture—Conservation and restoration. 4. Urban renewal—U.S. I. Title.

United States—Historic houses, etc.

AMERICA the Beautiful Fund. 917.3'03
Old Glory; a pictorial report on the grass roots history movement, and The first hometown history primer. [Washington, 1973] 191 p. illus. 24 x 29 cm. "Warner Paperback Library edition." [E159.A38 1973] 73-180411 ISBN 0-446-70131-9 4.95
1. United States—Historic houses, etc. 2. Architecture—United States—Conservation and restoration. 3. United States—History, Local. 4. Collectors and collecting. 5. Handicraft—United States. 6. Genealogy. I. America the Beautiful Fund. The first hometown history primer. 1973. II. Title.

BROWN, Sheldon S., 1937- 917.3'04'92
Remade in America; the grand tour of Europe and Asia within the U.S.A., by Sheldon S. Brown. Salem, Or., Old Time Bottle Pub. Co. [1972] 384 p. illus. 29 cm. [E159.B89] 72-79470 ISBN 0-911068-08-2 20.00
1. United States—Historic houses, etc. 2. Monuments—United States. I. Title. BIP

CARPENTER, Ralph E 973
The fifty best historic American houses, Colonial and Federal, now furnished and open to the public. New York, Dutton, 1955. 112p. illus. 22cm. (A Mowbra Hall Press book) [E159.C3] 55-10288
1. U. S.—Historic houses, etc. I. Title.

COLEMAN, Laurence Vail, 1893- 069'.9'917303
Historic house museums. With a directory. Washington, American Association of Museums, 1933. Detroit, Gale Research Co., 1973. xii, 187 p. illus. 22 cm. Bibliography: p. 160-165. [E159.C724 1972] 71-175318 15.00
1. United States—Historic houses, etc. 2. Museums. I. American association of Museums. II. Title. BIP

DEVLIN, Harry. 728
To grandfather's house we go; a roadside tour of American homes. New York, Parents' Magazine Press [1967] [48] p. illus. (part col.) 28 cm. Presents twenty-two styles of American homes popular at various periods in our history. Includes Neo-Jacobean, Romanesque, Hansel and Gretel Gothic, Victorian Rosetta Stone and many others that are nostalgically remembered as "grandfather's house." [E159.D4] AC 67
1. United States—Historic houses, etc. 2. Dwellings. I. Title. BIP

FOLSOM, Merrill. 728.8'0973
More great American mansions and their stories. New York, Hastings House [1967] x, 276 p. illus. 26 cm. [E159.F66] 67-5867
1. United States—Historic houses, etc. 2. Architecture, Domestic—United States. I. Title. BIP

HAAS, Irvin. 973
America's historic houses and restorations. [1st ed.] New York, Hawthorn Books [1967, c1966] 271 p. illus. (part col.) 29 cm. [E159.H12] 66-22320
1. United States—Historic houses, etc. 2. Architecture—United States—Conservation and restoration. I. Title.

HISTORIC American Buildings Survey. 720'.973
Preservation through documentation. Washington, Library of Congress; [for sale by the Supt. of Docs., Govt. Print. Off., 1968] [16] p. illus. 27 cm. Cover title. Reproductions of measured drawings and photographs exhibited at the Library of Congress, Sept. 25, 1968 to Jan. 1, 1969, together with descriptive notes. "Preprint from the Quarterly journal of the Library of Congress, October 1968." [E159.H68] 68-62342 0.25
1. U.S.—Historic houses, etc. 2. Architecture—Conservation and restoration. I. U.S. Library of Congress. II. Title.

JONES, Cranston. 923.173
Homes of the American Presidents. Photographer and picture editor: William H. Schleisner. New York, McGraw-Hill [1962] 232p. illus. 29cm. Includes bibliography. [E159.J6] 62-19158
1. U. S.—Historic houses, etc. 2. Presidents—U. S.—Biog. I. Title.

NICHOLSON, Arnold. 728.0973
American houses in history. New York, Viking Press [1965] 260 p. illus. (part col.) ports. 28 cm. (A Studio book) Bibliography: p. 256-257. [E159.N5] 65-20157
1. U.S. — Historic houses, etc. 2. Architecture, Domestic — U.S. I. Title.

PRATT, Dorothy. 728.0973
The treasury of early American homes, by Dorothy and Richard Pratt. New, rev. and enl. ed. New York, Hawthorn Books [1959] 144p. col. illus. ports. 36cm. Earlier ed. by Richard Pratt, published in 1949. [NA7205.P685] 59-12178
1. U. S.—Historic houses, etc. 2. Architecture, Domestic—U. S. I. Pratt, Richard, joint author. II. Title.

PRATT, Richard. 973
The golden treasury of early American houses. [1st ed.] New York, Hawthorne Books [1967] 278 p. col. illus. 35 cm. [E159.P68] 67-20791
1. United States—Historic houses, etc. I. Title.

UNITED States Conference of Mayors. Special Committee on Historic Preservation 720.973
With heritage so rich: a report. Albert Rains, chairman. Laurance G. Henderson. director. New York, Random [c.1966] xvi. 230p. plates (pt. col.) 26cm. Bibl. [E159.U527] 66-17835 10.00
1. U.S.—Historic houses, etc. 2. Architecture—Conservation and

SUBJECT INDEX UNITED STATES IN

restoration. 3. Monuments—U.S.—Preservation. I. Title.

VANDERBILT, Cornelius, 1898- 917.3
The living past of America; pictorial treasury of our historic houses and villages that have been preserved and restored. New York, Crown Publishers [1955] xiv, 234 p. illus. 29 cm. [E159.V35] 55-7242
1. United States—Historic houses, etc. I. Title.

WALLER, Herbert H 917.3
Famous historical places in the United States; descriptive views. 2d print. with additions. Boston, Meador Pub. Co., 1956. 312 p. illus. 21 cm. [E159.W3 1956] 56-1676
1. U.S. — Historic houses, etc. I. Title.

WILLIAMS, Henry Lionel 728.80973
Great houses of America. by Henry Lionel Williams, Ottalie K. Williams. [1st ed.] New York Putnam [1966] 295p. illus. (pt. col.) plans, ports, 33cm. [E159.W5] 66-19625 20.00
1. U. S.—Historic houses. etc. 2. Architecture Domestic—U. S. I. Williams, Ottalie Krocher, 1901- joint author. II. Title.

U.S.—Historic houses, etc.— Juvenile literature.

DEVLIN, Harry. 728'.0973
To grandfather's house we go; a roadside tour of American homes. New York, Parents' Magazine Press [1967] 1 v. (unpaged) illus. (part col.) 28 cm. [E159.D4] 67-18474
1. U.S.—Historic houses, etc.— Juvenile literature. I. Title.

United States—Historic houses, etc.—Pictorial works.

GREIFF, Constance M. 917.8'04'3
Lost America: from the Mississippi to the Pacific. Edited by Constance M. Greiff. With a foreword by James Biddle. [1st ed.] Princeton [N.J.] Pyne Press [1972] x, 243 p. illus. 29 cm. A companion volume to Lost America: from the Atlantic to the Mississippi. [E159.G72] 72-79151 ISBN 0-87861-033-2 17.95
1. United States—Historic houses, etc.—Pictorial works. 2. The West—Historic houses, etc.—Pictorial works. I. Title.

U. S.—Historical houses, etc.

FINCH, Elfreda. 973
Flowers and furniture in America's historic homes, annotated by Elfreda Finch. Foreword by Angela Place. New York, Hearthside Press [1967] 117 p. illus. (part col.) 29 cm. [E159.F55] 67-27170
1. U. S.—Historical houses, etc. 2. Gardens—U. S.—Hist. I. Title.

United States—History—1933-1945—Pictorial works.

PATRI, Giacomo, 1898- 769'.92'4
White collar : a novel in linocuts / Giacomo Patri. Millbrae, Calif. : Celestial Arts, 1975. 127 p. : chiefly ill. ; 22 cm. [NE1336.P38A58] 75-9440 ISBN 0-89087-180-9 : 8.95. ISBN 0-89087-101-9 pbk. : 4.95
1. Patri, Giacomo, 1898- 2. United States—History—1933-1945—Pictorial works. 3. United States in art. I. Title.

United States—History—1945-1953—Pictorial works.

ARNOLD, Eve. 779'.9'9739
Flashback! : The 50's / Eve Arnold. 1st ed. New York : Knopf, 1978. 149 p. : ill. ; 27 cm. [E813.A83 1978] 78-54901 ISBN 0-394-50043-1 : 12.95
1. Arnold, Eve. 2. United States—History—1945-1953—Pictorial works. 3. United States—History—1953-1961—Pictorial works. I. Title. BIP

United States—History—Civil War, 1861-1865—Art and the war.

FORBES, Edwin, 1839-1895. 769'.92'4
Life studies of the great army / by Edwin Forbes. [1st ed.]. [San Francisco] : Dunderave, 1976, [c1975] 1 portfolio, ([3] leaves, 40 leaves of plates : 40 ill.) ; 38 cm. Cover title. Ed. statement from label mounted on verso of cover. [NE2012.F67A49 1976] 77-151132
1. Forbes, Edwin, 1839-1895. 2. United States—History—Civil War, 1861-1865—Art and the war. I. Title.

GROSSMAN, Julian. 760'.092'4
Echo of a distant drum: Winslow Homer and the Civil War. New York, H. N. Abrams [1974] 203 p. illus. (part col.) 28 x 30 cm. Bibliography: p. 201-203. [N6537.H58G76] 74-5363 ISBN 0-8109-0225-7
1. Homer, Winslow, 1836-1910. 2. United States—History—Civil War, 1861-1865—Art and the war. I. Homer, Winslow, 1836-1910. II. Title.

United States—History—Civil War, 1861-1865—Iconography.

KENNEDY Galleries, inc., New York. 708.1
Artists of the Civil War [Written and edited by Rudolf Wunderlich] New York, 1961. 2 pts. illus. 24 cm. (The Kennedy quarterly, v. 2, no. 2) Cover title. Part 2 has title: The Civil War in prints. [N8640.K4 vol. 2, no. 2] 68-5497
1. United States—History—Civil War, 1861-1865—Iconography. 2. Art, American—Catalogs. I. Wunderlich, Rudolf. II. Title. III. Title: The Civil War in prints. IV. Series.

United States—History—Civil War, 1861-1865—Pictorial works.

FORBES, Edwin, 1839-1895. 767
A Civil War artist at the front; Edwin Forbes' Life studies of the great army. Edited by William Forrest Dawson. New York, Oxford University Press, 1957. [94] p. illus. 21 x 27 cm. The reproductions of Forbes' etchings are accompanied by the editor's descriptive text. [NE2195.F6D33 1957] 57-10387
1. United States—History—Civil War, 1861-1865—Pictorial works. I. Dawson, William Forrest, ed. II. Title.

RAY, Frederic. 741.9'73
Alfred R. Waud, Civil War artist / Frederic E. Ray. New York : Viking Press, 1974. 192 p. : ill. ; 28 cm. (A Studio book) Includes (p. [73]-[183]) a selection of Waud's sketches, chiefly from the collection in the Library of Congress, together with a smaller sampling of those of his brother, William Waud. Includes index. Bibliography: p. 188-189. [NC139.W38R39 1974] 73-20667 ISBN 0-670-11260-7 : 16.95
1. Waud, Alfred Rudolph, 1828-1891. 2. United States—History—Civil War, 1861-1865—Pictorial works.

United States—History, Comic, satirical, etc.

SYRACUSE University. Library. Manuscript Collections. 741.5'9'73
American political cartoons, 1865-1965, by Martin H. Bush. An exhibition of political and editorial cartoons organized by the Manuscript Collections, Carnegie Library, Syracuse University, with the cooperation of the Samuel I. Newhouse School of Journalism and the School of Art, and held in the lobby of the Carnegie Library, June 1966. [Syracuse, N.Y., 1966] 55 p. illus. 23 cm. [NC1427.S95] 66-29379
1. United States—History, Comic, satirical, etc. 2. Caricatures and cartoons—Exhibitions. I. Bush, Martin H. II. Title.

United States—History—Pictorial works.

RAY, Frederic, comp. 759.13
O! say can you see; the story of America through great paintings. Compiled and narrated by Frederic Ray. Color reproductions by Edward Wilson. Introd. by Robert H. Fowler. Epilogue by Charles C. Sellers. [Harrisburg, Pa.] Stackpole Books [1970] 189 p. illus., col. plates, ports. 34 cm. "A National Historical Society book." [ND205.R37] 70-100349 ISBN 0-8117-1185-4 29.95
1. United States—History—Pictorical works. 2. Paintings, American. I. National Historical Society. II. Title.

United States—History—Revolution, 1775-1783—Biography.

THE face of liberty : 757'.9
founders of the United States / by James Thomas Flexner ; biographies of sitters and painters by Linda Bantel Samter ; in cooperation with the Amon Carter Museum of Western Art, Fort Worth, Texas. 1st ed. New York : Potter : distributed by Crown Publishers, c1975. x, 310 p. : ill. (some col.) ; 29 cm. Includes a catalog of an art exhibition held at Amon Carter Museum of Western Art, Fort Worth, Tex. Includes index. Bibliography: p. [288]-304. [E206.F32 1975] 75-30662 ISBN 0-517-52491-0 : 15.95
1. United States—History—Revolution, 1775-1783—Biography. 2. United States—History—Revolution, 1775-1783—Portraits—Exhibitions. 3. Portraits, American—Exhibitions. 4. Painters—United States—Biography. I. Flexner, James Thomas, 1908- II. Samter, Linda Bantel. III. Amon Carter Museum of Western Art, Fort Worth, Tex. BIP

United States—History—Revolution, 1775-1783—Collectibles—Dictionaries.

NEUMANN, George C. 973.3'075
Collector's illustrated encyclopedia of the American Revolution / George C. Neumann and Frank J. Kravic ; drawings by George C. Woodbridge. Harrisburg, Pa. : Stackpole Books, [1975] 286 p. : ill. ; 29 cm. Bibliography: p. 283-286 [NK806.N37] 75-6897 ISBN 0-8117-0394-0 : 17.95
1. United States—History—Revolution, 1775-1783—Collectibles—Dictionaries. I. Kravic, Frank J., joint author. II. Woodbridge, George C. III. Title.

United States—History—Revolution, 1775-1783—Naval operations—Pictorial works.

POWELL, Nowland Van. 759.13
The American navies of the Revolutionary War : paintings / by Nowland Van Powell ; with descriptive notes by the artist ; introd. by Richard B. Morris. New York : Putnam, [1974] 126, [2] p. : col. ill. ; 28 x 34 cm. Bibliography: p. [128] [ND237.P819A43 1974] 73-78625 ISBN 0-399-11183-2 : 20.00
1. Powell, Nowland Van. 2. United States. Navy—History—Revolution, 1775-1783—Pictorial works. 3. United States—History—Revolution, 1775-1783—Naval operations—Pictorial works. I. Title. BIP

United States—History—Revolution, 1775-1783—Posters.

A Little rebellion now & then. 769'.4'99733
Santa Cruz, Calif. : William James Assoc., 1976. 1 portfolio ([2] p., 14 broadsides) : ill. ; 56 cm. Broadsides contributed by various printers, chiefly American, and containing words of the Founding Fathers. Of 16 broadsides listed on title leaf, 2 were not issued. "Two hundred copies printed." [E209.L58] 77-362991
1. United States—History—Revolution, 1775-1783—Posters. 2. United States—History—Revolution, 1775-1783—Propaganda. 3. Broadsides.

United States in art.

AMERICA'S great adventure : 758
the spirit of freedom. Fort Atkinson, Wis. : Home Library Pub. Co., c1976. 96 p. : col. ill. ; 32 p. [NX503.A53] 76-371685 ISBN 0-87294-091-8 : 4.98
1. United States in art. 2. Arts, American. I. Home Library Publishing Company.

CLARK, Bill, 1926- 741.9'73
Passing America. Pre-publication limited ed. Knoxville, TN : B. Clark, c1976. 44 leaves : all ill. ; 36 cm. Cover title. [NC139.C57A53 1976] 77-670029
1. Clark, Bill, 1926- 2. United States in art. I. Title.

DEAK, Gloria-Gilda, 1930- 704.94'9'973
American views : prospects and vistas / Gloria-Gilda Deak ; with an introd. by James Thomas Flexner. New York : Viking Press, [1976] p. cm. (A Studio book) Includes bibliographical references and index. [N8214.5.U6D42] 76-40041 ISBN 0-670-12091-X : 19.95
1. United States in art. 2. Art, American. I. Title. BIP

FINCH, Christopher. 759.13
Norman Rockwell's America / Christopher Finch. New York : H. N. Abrams, [1975] 313 p. : ill. (some col.) ; 34 cm. Includes index. [ND237.R68F56] 75-15703 ISBN 0-8109-0454-3
1. Rockwell, Norman, 1894- 2. United States in art. I. Title.

HENDRICKS, Gordon. 759.13
Albert Bierstadt: painter of the American West. [Text by] Gordon Hendricks. New York, H. N. Abrams [1974] 360 p. illus. (part col.) 28 cm. Published in association with the Amon Carter Museum of Western Art. Bibliography: p. 353-354. [ND237.B585H42] 73-14954 ISBN 0-8109-0151-X
1. Bierstadt, Albert, 1830-1902. 2. United States in art. 3. Landscape in art. I. Amon Carter Museum of Western Art, Fort Worth, Tex.

HONOUR, Hugh. 704.94'9'973
The new golden land : European images of America from the discoveries to the present time / by Hugh Honour. 1st ed. New York : Pantheon Books, 1976 c1975 299 p. : ill. (some col.) ; 28 cm. Includes bibliographical references and index. [N8214.5.U6H58 1976] 75-22463 ISBN 0-394-73084-4 pbk. : 8.95
1. United States in art. 2. Art, European. I. Title. BIP

HONOUR, Hugh. 704.94'9'973
The new golden land : European images of America from the discoveries to the present time / Hugh Honour. London : Allen Lane, 1976. vii, 301 p. : ill. (some col.), facsims., maps (chiefly col.), ports. (some col.) ; 29 cm. Includes bibliographical references and index. [N8214.5.U6H58 1976] 77-355328 ISBN 0-7139-0959-5 : £12.50
1. United States in art. 2. Art, European. I. Title.

NORTON, Bettina A. 760'.092'4
Edwin Whitefield—North American scenery, faithfully delineated / Bettina A. Norton. Barre, Mass. : Barre Publishers, 1974, c1975. p. cm. Bibliography: p. [NC242.W54N67] 72-95109 ISBN 0-517-51731-0
1. Whitefield, Edwin, b. 1816. 2. United States in art. 3. Canada in art. I. Title.

PRATT, John Lowell, comp. 769'.924
Currier & Ives chronicles of America; color plates reproduced from the original hand colored stone prints by N. Currier and Currier & Ives. Edited by John Lowell Pratt. Introd. by A. K. Baragwanath. Maplewood, N.J., Hammond [1968] 256 p. illus. (part col.), col. map. 32 cm. [NE2312.C8P72 1968] 68-13933 14.95
1. Currier (N.) (Firm) 2. United States in art. I. Currier (N.) (Firm) II. Currier and Ives. III. Title. IV. Title: Chronicles of America.

PRATT, John Lowell, comp. 769'.973
Currier & Ives chronicles of America : color plates reproduced from the original hand colored stone prints by N. Currier and Currier & Ives / edited by John Lowell Pratt ; introd. by A. K. Baragwanath. [New York] : Promontory Press, [1974?] c1968. 256 p. : chiefly col. ill. ; 32 cm. Includes index. [NE2312.C8P72 1974] 74-77002 ISBN 0-88394-031-0 : 17.50
1. Currier (N.) (Firm) 2. United States in art. I. Currier (N.) (Firm) II. Currier and

Ives. III. Title. IV. Title: Chronicles of America.

SLOANE, Eric.   741.9'73
Recollections in black and white / by Eric Sloane. New York : Walker, 1974. 64 p. : ill. ; 23 x 29 cm. [NC139.S56A27 1974] 73-90383 ISBN 0-8027-0461-1 : 10.00
1. Sloane, Eric. 2. United States in art. I. Title.   BIP

SMITHSONIAN   704.94'9'9730740153
Institution. National Collection of Fine Arts.
America as art : [catalog of the exhibition] April 30-November 7, 1976, National Collection of Fine Arts, Smithsonian Institution, Washington, D.C. [Washington] : National Collection of Fine Arts, [1976] [46] p. : ill. ; 26 cm. Cover title. [N8214.5.U6S6 1976] 76-370468
1. United States in art. 2. Art, American—Exhibitions. 3. Art, European—Exhibitions. I. Title.

STERNBERG, Harry, 1904-   769'.92'4
Harry Sternberg : a catalog raisonne of his graphic work : [exhibition] : Edwin A. Ulrich Museum of Art, Wichita State University, Wichita, Kansas / by James C. Moore ; with annotations by Harry Sternberg. Wichita, Kan. : The Museum, c1975. 95 p. : ill. ; 23 cm. "Biographical data of Harry Sternberg": p. 94. Bibliography: p. 95. [NE539.S73E38] 75-26036
1. Sternberg, Harry, 1904- 2. United States in art. I. Edwin A. Ulrich Museum of Art. II. Moore, James Collins, 1941-

United States in art—Catalogs.

CURRIER and Ives.   769'.92'4
50 Currier & Ives favorites, from the Museum of the City of New York / introd. and commentary by A. K. Baragwanath. New York : Crown Publishers, [1978] 104 p. : col. ill. ; 38 cm. "An Artabras book." [NE2312.C8A4 1978] 78-2205 ISBN 0-89660-007-6 pbk. : 7.98
1. Currier and Ives—Catalogs. 2. New York (City). Museum of the City of New York. 3. United States in art—Catalogs. 4. Lithography—19th century—United States—Catalogs. I. Baragwanath, A. K. II. New York (City). Museum of the City of New York. III. Title.

United States in art—Juvenile literature.

HAPPY birthday America!   700'.973
from your sons and daughters / designed and edited by David Melton. Independence, Mo. : Independence Press, c1976. p. cm. art, prose, and poetry by elementary school children are brought together with the writings of the founding fathers on the occasion of our bicentennial. [NX503.H36] 76-5791 ISBN 0-8309-0162-0
1. United States in art—Juvenile literature. 2. Children's art—United States. 3. Children's writings, American. I. Melton, David.

ROCKWELL, Norman, 1894-   759.13
Norman Rockwell's Americana ABC / with poems by George Mendoza. New York : H. N. Abrams, [1975] p. cm. The letters of the alphabet are introduced through paintings and poetry on an Americana theme. [ND237.R68M46 1975] 75-8886 ISBN 0-8109-0457-8 : 5.95
1. Rockwell, Norman, 1894- —Juvenile literature. 2. Mendoza, George—Illustrations—Juvenile literature. 3. United States in art—Juvenile literature. 4. Alphabet—Juvenile literature. I. Mendoza, George. II. Title: Americana ABC.   BIP

United States. Library of Congress.

UNITED States. Library of   686.2'3
Congress.
Color and the graphic arts : selections from an exhibition at the Library of Congress, October 1974 through March 1975. [Washington : The Library, 1975] 190-206 p. : ill. ; 27 cm. "Reprinted from the Quarterly journal of the Library of Congress, volume 31, number 4, October 1974." [Z258.U57 1975] 74-31445 ISBN 0-8444-0152-8

1. United States. Library of Congress. 2. Color-printing—Exhibitions. 3. Color prints—Exhibitions. I. Title.

United States. Library of Congress. Geography and Map Division.

UNITED States. Library of   016.526
Congress. Geography and Map Division.
The bibliography of cartography. Boston, G. K. Hall, 1973. 5 v. 37 cm. A reproduction of a card bibliography in the Geography and Map Division, which contains an estimated 90,000 entries for works published from the early 19th century through 1971. [Z6028.U49 1973] 73-12977 ISBN 0-8161-1008-5 490.00
1. United States. Library of Congress. Geography and Map Division. 2. Cartography—Bibliography—Catalogs. I. Title.   BIP

United States. Library of Congress. Manuscript Division.

UNITED States. Library of   016.091
Congress. Manuscript Division.
Hans P. Kraus Collection of Hispanic American manuscripts; a guide, by J. Benedict Warren. Washington, Library of Congress, 1974. x, 187 p. illus. 25 cm. Bibliography: p. 165-171. [Z6621.U58K7] 74-1097 ISBN 0-8444-0118-8
1. United States. Library of Congress. Manuscript Division. 2. Kraus, Hans Peter, 1907- —Library. 3. Manuscripts, Spanish American—Catalogs. 4. Manuscripts—United States—Catalogs. 5. Latin America—History—Sources. I. Warren, J. Benedict. II. Title.

United States. National Archives.

UNITED States. National   016.6314
Archives.
Aerial photographs in the National Archives. Compiled by Charles E. Taylor and Richard E. Spurr. Washington, 1971. vii, 106 p. 27 cm. (Its Special list no. 25) [Z6027.U5U6 1971] 75-174520
1. United States. National Archives. 2. United States—Aerial photographs—Bibliography. I. Taylor, Charles Edward, 1928- comp. II. Spurr, Richard E., comp. III. Title. IV. Series.

UNITED States. National   016.6314
Archives.
Aerial photographs in the National Archives. Compiled by Charles E. Taylor and Richard E. Spurr. Washington, National Archives and Records Service, 1973. vii, 106 p. 27 cm. (Its Special list no. 25) "Revision of the list first published in 1971." [Z6027.U5U6 1973] 73-602746
1. United States. National Archives. 2. United States—Aerial photographs—Bibliography. I. Taylor, Charles Edward, 1928- II. Spurr, Richard E. III. Title. IV. Series.

UNITED States.   016.911'777
National Archives.
Cartographic records relating to the Territory of Iowa, 1838-1846. Compiled by Laura E. Kelsay and Frederick W. Pernell. Washington, 1971. vii, 27 p. 27 cm. (Its Special list no. 27) [Z6027.U5U6 1971a] 70-175627
1. United States. National Archives. 2. Iowa—Maps—Bibliography—Catalogs. I. Kelsay, Laura E. II. Pernell, Frederick W. III. Title. IV. Series.

United States. National Gallery of Art.

ADVENTURE in art :   750'.74'0153
the National Gallery, Washington, D.C. / [compiled by Marian King]. New York : H. N. Abrams, [1978] p. cm. Includes index. Bibliography: p. [N856.A513] 77-20926 ISBN 0-8109-1769-6 : 14.95 ISBN 0-8109-2167-7 pbk. : 7.95
1. United States. National Gallery of Art. 2. Art—Washington, D.C. I. King, Marian. II. United States. National Gallery of Art.

FINLEY, David E.   708'.153
A standard of excellence: Andrew W. Mellon founds the National Gallery of Art at Washington, by David Edward Finley. Washington, Smithsonian Institution Press, 1973. xii, 193 p. illus. 24 cm. (Smithsonian

publication no. 4825) [N856.F56] 73-5676 ISBN 0-87474-132-7
1. United States. National Gallery of Art. 2. Mellon, Andrew William, 1855-1937. I. Title.

GREAT masters of   759.4'074'0153
French impressionism / introd. by J. Carter Brown ; commentaries by Diane Kelder. New York : Crown, [1978] 158 p., [1] leaf of plates : col. ill. ; 28 cm. "An Artabras book." The paintings reproduced are from The National Gallery of Art, Washington.   [ND547.5.I4G73]   78-862 ISBN 0-89660-030-0 : 17.95
1. United States. National Gallery of Art. 2. Impressionism (Art)—France. 3. Painting, French. 4. Painting, Modern—19th century—France. 5. Painting—Washington, D.C. I. Kelder, Diane. II. United States. National Gallery of Art. BIP

UNITED States.   759.4'074'0153
National Gallery of Art.
European paintings : an illustrated summary catalogue. Washington, 1975. 417 p. illus. 24 cm. [N856.A6917] 74-16421
1. United States. National Gallery of Art. 2. Paintings—Washington, D.C.—Catalogs. I. Title.

UNITED States. National   016.09
Gallery of Art.
Medieval & Renaissance miniatures from the National Gallery of Art : [catalogue] / compiled by Carra Ferguson, David S. Stevens Schaff, Gary Vikan ; under the direction of Carl Nordenfalk ; edited by Gary Vikan. [Washington] : The Gallery, 1975. xxvi, 196 p., 5 leaves of plates : ill. (some col.) ; 28 cm. Fourth exhibition from the Lessing J. Rosenwald collection, held Jan. 26-June 1, 1975. Includes bibliographical references and index. [ND2920.U54 1975] 74-28397
1. United States. National Gallery of Art. 2. Illumination of books and manuscripts, Medieval—Catalogs. 3. Illumination of books and manuscripts, Renaissance—Catalogs. 4. Illumination of books and manuscripts—Washington, D.C.—Catalogs. I. Nordenfalk, Carl Adam Johan, 1907- II. Rosenwald, Lessing Julius, 1891- III. Title.   BIP

WALKER, John.   750.74
National Gallery of Art, Washington, D.C. New York, Abrams, [1965] 339p. illus. col. plates. 21cm. (Abrams art paperback) [N856.W33] 63-15446 4.95 pap.,
1. U.S. National Gallery of Art. 2. Paintings—Washington, D.C. I. Title.

WALKER, John,   759.0838
Dec.24,1906-
National Gallery of Art, Washington. New York, H. N. Abrams [1956] 60 p. illus. (23 mounted col.) 39 cm. (Great peaintings of the world) An abrams art book. [N856.W3] 56-3227
1. U.S. National Gallery of Art. 2. Paintings — Washington, D.C. I. Title. BIP

WALKER, John,   759.0838
Dec.24,1906-
National Gallery of Art, Washington. New York, H.N. Abrams [1956] 60p. illus. (23 mounted col.) 39cm. (Great paintings of the world) An Abrams art book. [N656.W3] 56-3227
1. U.S. National Gallery of Art. 2. Paintings—Washington, D.C. I. Title.

WALKER, John,   750.74
Dec.24,1906-
National Gallery of Art, Washington, D.C. New York, H. N. Abrams [1963] 347 p. illus., col. plates, diagrs. 21 cm. [N856.W33] 63-15446
1. United States. National Gallery of Art. 2. Paintings—Washington, D.C.

WALKER, John,   708'.153
Dec.24,1906-
National Gallery of Art, Washington, D.C. New York, H. N. Abrams [1975] p. cm. [N856.W33 1975] 74-10716 ISBN 0-8109-0336-9 25.00
1. United States. National Gallery of Art. 2. Paintings—Washington, D.C. I. Title.

United States. National Gallery of Art. East Building.

MCLANATHAN, Richard B.   708'.153
K.
East Building, National Gallery of Art : a profile / [compiled and written by Richard B. K. McLanathan]. Washington : National Gallery of Art, c1978. 96 p. : ill. (some col.) ; 30 cm. [N856.M27] 78-606059 4.00
1. United States. National Gallery of Art. East Building. I. Title.

U. S. National Gallery of Art. Widener Collection.

CHRISTENSEN, Erwin   709.02
Ottomar, 1890-
Objects of medieval art from the Widener Collection. Washington, National Gallery of Art, Smithsonian Institution, 1952. 32 p. illus. 23 cm. (National Gallery of Art handbook, 3) Bibliography: p. 31-32. [N5963.C53] 52-3889
1. Art, Medieval. 2. U. S. National Gallery of Art. Widener Collection. I. Title. II. Series: U. S. National Gallery of Art. National Gallery of Art handbook, 3

U.S. National Park Service.

SUTTON, Ann   719.3206173
Guarding the treasured lands: the story of the National Park Service, by Ann and Myron Sutton. Philadelphia, Lippincott [c.1965] 160p. illus., ports. 22cm. Bibl. [E160.S8] 65-13436 3.75
1. U.S. National Park Service. I. Sutton, Myron, joint author. II. Title.   BIP

United States. Penitentiary, Alcatraz Island, Calif.

MERCER, John D.   779'.9'979461
Island of the Pelicans : a photographic essay of the Island of Alcatraz / by John D. Mercer ; introd. by Patricia Mercer. Sonoma, Ca. : Creative Eye Press, c1976. 45 p. : ill. ; 22 cm. [TR654.M463] 75-39153 ISBN 0-916480-01-1
1. United States. Penitentiary, Alcatraz Island, Calif. 2. Photography, Artistic. 3. Alcatraz Island, Calif.—Description—Views. I. Title.   BIP

U. S.—Pol. & govt.—Caricatures and cartoons.

ODELL, Rice.   328.33084
The Congressman's coloring book, by Rice Odell and Joaquin De Alba. [Washington, Hennage Lithograph Co., 1962] unpaged. illus. 36cm. [NC1429.O3A43] 62-52716
1. U. S.—Pol. & govt.—Caricatures and cartoons. 2. U. S.—Pol. & govt.—Anecdotes, facetiae, satire, etc. I. De Alba, Joqquin, joint author. II. Title.

United States—Politics and government—1963-1969—Posters—Exhibitions.

KUNZLE, David.   769'.5
American posters of protest, 1966-70. Foreword by Paul Mocsanyi [New York, New School Art Center, 1971] 81 p. illus., ports. 20 cm. (Art as a political weapon, 6th) Catalogue prepared for an exhibition held at the New School Art Center, New York City, Oct. 12-Dec. 4, 1971. Bibliography: p. 78-79. [E846.K82 1971b] 74-173498
1. United States—Politics and government—1963-1969—Posters—Exhibitions. 2. United States—Politics and government—1969- —Posters—Exhibitions. 3. American wit and humor, Pictorial—Exhibitions. I. New York (City). New School for Social Research. New School Art Center. II. Title. III. Series.

KUNZLE, David.   769'.5
Posters of protest; the posters of political satire in the U.S. 1966-1970. [Goleta, Calif., Printed by Triple R Press, 1971] 160 p. illus., ports. 20 cm. Prepared for an exhibition held at the Art Galleries, University of California, Santa Barbara, Feb. 23-Mar. 28, 1971. Bibliography: p. 41-42. 79-630002
1. United States—Politics and government—1963-1969—Posters—

Exhibitions. 2. United States—Politics and government—1969- —Posters—Exhibitions. 3. American wit and humor, Pictorial—Exhibitions. I. California. University, Santa Barbara. Art Galleries. II. Title.

United States—Politics and government—1974-1977—Caricatures and cartoons.

SZEP, Paul Michael.   741.5'973
"...them damned pictures" : editorial cartoons / by Szep. Boston : Boston globe, 1977. [112] p. : all ill. ; 23 x 29 cm. Cartoons originally published in the Boston globe, Jan. 3, 1975-Sept. 14, 1977. [E865.S93] 77-154785 2.95
1. Carter, Jimmy, 1924- —Cartoons, satire, etc. 2. United States—Politics and government—1974-1977—Caricatures and cartoons. 3. United States—Politics and government—1977- —Caricatures and cartoons. 4. World politics—1975-1985—Caricatures and cartoons. 5. American wit and humor, Pictorial. I. Title.

United States—Politics and government—1974- — Caricatures and cartoons.

LURIE, Ranan R., 1932-   741.5'973
Pardon me, Mr. President! / Ranan R. Lurie ; foreword by Harry Reasoner. New York : Quadrangle/New York Times Book Co., [1975] 224 p. : chiefly ill. ; 28 cm. [E865.L87] 75-309087 ISBN 0-8129-6255-9 pbk. : 4.95
1. United States—Politics and government—1974- —Caricatures and cartoons. 2. United States—Politics and government—1969-1974—Caricatures and cartoons. 3. World politics—1965- —Caricatures and cartoons. 4. American wit and humor, Pictorial. I. Title.   BIP

United States—Public buildings.

CRAIG, Lois A.   725'.1'0973
The Federal presence : architecture, politics, and symbols in United States government building / Lois A. Craig and the staff of the Federal Architecture Project. Cambridge, Mass. : MIT Press, c1978.   p.   cm. Includes index. Bibliography: p. [NA4205.C7] 78-15366 ISBN 0-262-03057-8 : 37.50
1. United States—Public buildings. 2. Architecture and state—United States. I. Federal Architecture Project. II. Title. BIP

UNITED States.   725'.1'0973
Congress. Senate. Committee on Public Works. Subcommittee on Public Buildings and Grounds.
The need for architectural improvement in the design of Federal buildings : hearing before the Subcommittee on Buildings and Grounds of the Committee on Public Works, United States Senate, ninety-fifth Congress, first session, January 24, 1977. Washington : U.S. Govt. Print. Off., 1977. iii, 148 p. : ill. ; 24 cm. "Serial no. 95-H2." [KF26.P866 1977] 77-602115
1. United States—Public buildings. I. Title.

United States. Public Buildings Service.

UNITED States.   725'.1'0973
General Accounting Office.
Need for improving reviews of designs of Federal buildings to achieve better utilization of space; report to the Congress [on the] Public Buildings Service, General Services Administration by the Comptroller General of the United States. [Washington] 1968. 19 p. 27 cm. Cover title. "B-156512." Publication date stamped on t.p. [NA4208.A39] 68-61618
1. United States. Public Buildings Service. 2. United States. General Services Administration. Washington National Records Center. 3. Space (Architecture) I. Title.

United States—Rural conditions—Pictorial work.

A Vision shared   779'.9'3091730917 : a classic portrait of America and its people, 1935-1943 / Text by Hank O'Neal ; foreword by Bernarda Shahn ; afterword by Paul S. Taylor ; photos. & comments by John Collier ... [etc.]. New York : St. Martin's Press, c1976. 309 p. : ill. ; 33 cm. A collection of photos. taken by the photographers of the U.S. Farm Security Administration. Includes index. [HN57.V54] 76-5381 6.95 lib.bdg. : 6.84
1. United States—Rural conditions—Pictorial work. 2. Photography, Documentary. 3. Photographers—United States—Biography. I. O'Neal, Hank. II. Collier, John, 1913- III. United States. Farm Security Administration.   BIP

United States—Rural conditions—Pictorial works—Catalogs.

DA Capo Press.   779'.9'3092630973
Walker Evans: photographs for the Farm Security Administration, 1935-1938; a catalog of photographic prints available from the Farm Security Administration collection in the Library of Congress. Introd. by Jerald C. Maddox New York, 1973. p. [HN57.D22] 74-149598
1. United States—Rural conditions—Pictorial works—Catalogs. 2. Photographs—Catalogs. I. Evans, Walker, 1903- II. Maddox, Jerald C. III. United States. Farm Security Administration. IV. United States. Library of Congress. V. Title.

UNITED States.   779'.9'3092630973
Library of Congress. Prints and Photographs Division.
Walker Evans, photographs for the Farm Security Administration, 1935-1938 : a catalog of photographic prints available from the Farm Security Administration collection in the Library of Congress / introd. by Jerald C. Maddox New York : Da Capo Press, 1975, c1973. xiv, [244] p. : chiefly ill. ; 27 cm. (A Da Capo paperback) [HN57.U555 1975] 74-23992 ISBN 0-306-80008-X : 8.95.
1. United States—Rural conditions—Pictorial works—Catalogs. 2. Photographs—Catalogs. I. Evans, Walker, 1903- II. United States. Farm Security Administration. III. Title.

United States—Seal.

EDWARDS, Floyd M.   929.8
Symbolism of the Great Seal of the United States. As interpreted by Floyd M. Edwards. San Francisco, Falcon Publishers [1972] 36 p. illus. 18 cm. [CD5610.E38] 74-157732
1. United States—Seal. I. Title.

PRICE, P W 1895-   929.8
The great seal; key to our destiny; a study fo its message [1st ed.] New York, Exposition Press [1952] 100 p. illus. 21 cm. [CD5610.P75] 52-8639
1. United States—Seal. I. Title.

United States—Social conditions—Pictorial works.

GUTMAN, Judith Mara.   770.924
Lewis W. Hine, and the American social conscience. New York, Walker [1967] 156 p. illus., ports. 25 cm. Bibliography: p. 52-60. [TR140.H52G8] 67-23089
1. Hine, Lewis Wickes, 1874-1940. 2. United States—Social conditions—Pictorial works. I. Title.

HINE, Lewis Wickes,   770.'92'4
1874-1940.
Lewis W. Hine, 1874-1940 : two perspectives / by Judith Mara Gutman; [editors: Cornell Kapa, Judith Mana Gutman,Bhupendra Kania]. New York : Grossman Publishers, 1974. 84 p. : ill. ; 23 cm. (ICP library of photographers ; v. 4) Bibliography: p. 82-83. [TR140.H52G82 1974] 72-11010 ISBN 0-670-42742-X : 10.00. ISBN 0-670-42743-8 pbk. : 5.95
1. Hine, Lewis Wickes, 1874-1940. 2. United States—Social conditions—Pictorial works. I. Gutman, Judith Mara. II. Series: International Fund for Concerned Photography. ICP library of photographers ; v. 4.

MELTZER, Milton,   778.9'9'309173
1915-
The eye of conscience; photographers and social change, with 100 photographs by noted photographers, past and present, by Milton Meltzer and Bernard Cole. Chicago, Follett Pub. Co. [1974] 192 p. illus. 21 x 24 cm. Bibliography: p. 188-189. [HN57.M35] 73-90055 ISBN 0-695-80445-6 6.95; 6.98 (lib. bdg.).
1. United States—Social conditions—Pictorial works. 2. Poor—United States—Pictorial works. I. Cole, Bernard, joint author. II. Title.

United States—Social life and customs—1918-1945—Pictorial works.

ROTHSTEIN, Arthur,   779'.9'973917
1915-
The depression years / as photographed by Arthur Rothstein. New York : Dover Publications, c1978. 119 p. : all ill. ; 28 cm. (The Dover pictorial archive series) [E169.R84 1978] 77-91384 ISBN 0-486-23590-4 : 5.00 ($5.95 Can)
1. United States—Social life and customs—1918-1945—Pictorial works. I. Title. BIP

United States—Social life and customs—1945-1970—Pictorial works.

FRANK,   779'.9'917303920924
Robert.
The Americans; photographs. Introd. by Jack Kerouac. [Rev. and enl. ed.] New York, Grossman, 1969. v.i p., [189] p. of illus. 20 x 22 cm. "An Aperture book." [E169.02.F7 1969] 72-86107 8.50
1. United States—Social life and customs—1945-1970—Pictorial works. I. Title.

United States—Social life and customs—1945- —Pictorial works.

FRANK, Robert.   779'.9'97392
The Americans / Robert Frank ; introd. by Jack Kerouac. Millerton, N.Y. : Aperture, c1978. 176 p. : chiefly ill. ; 25 x 30 cm. [E169.02.F713 1978] 78-66672 ISBN 0-89381-033-9 : 25.00
1. United States—Social life and customs—1945- —Pictorial works. 2. United States—Description and travel—1960- —Views. I. Title. BIP

U.S.—Social life and customs—19th century.

GOODRICH, Lloyd, 1897-   741.973
Winslow Homer's America. New York, Tudor Pub. Co. [1969] 192 p. illus. 25 x 32 cm. [NC139.H6G6] 66-19318
1. Homer, Winslow, 1836-1910. 2. U.S.—Social life and customs—19th century. I. Title.

United States. Supervising Architect of the Treasury Department.

SMITH, Darrell   353.008'62
Hevenor.
The Office of the Supervising Architect of the Treasury; its history, activities, and organization. Baltimore, Johns Hopkins Press, 1923. [New York, AMS Press, 1974] xii, 138 p. 23 cm. Original ed. issued as no. 23 of Service monographs of the United States Government. Bibliography: p. 133-136. [NA4205.A1S58 1974] 72-3031 ISBN 0-404-57123-9 10.00
1. United States. Supervising Architect of the Treasury Department. I. Title. II. Series: Brookings Institution, Washington, D.C. Institute for Government Research. Service monographs of the United States Government, no. 23. BIP

United States. Veterans Administration.

U.S. General Accounting   725'.59
Office.
Need for Veterans Administration to acquire hospital sites before developing working drawings and specifications for construction of hospitals; report to the Congress by the Comptroller General of the United States. [Washington, 1969] 36 p. illus. 27 cm. Cover title. [UH473.A54 1969] 79-602220
1. U.S. Veterans Administration. 2. Hospitals, Military—U.S.—Design and construction. I. Title.

UNITED States. General   725'.51
Accounting Office.
Need to improve reviews of drawings and specifications prepared by architect-engineers before solicitation of hospital construction bids; report to the Congress [on the] Veterans Administration, by the Comptroller General of the United States. [Washington, 1968] 47 p. 27 cm. Cover title. [RA967.5.U6U54 1968] 68-62737
1. United States. Veterans Administration. 2. Hospitals—Specifications. 3. Hospitals, Military—United States—Design and construction. I. Title.

United States. Work Projects Administration.

MELTZER, Milton, 1915-   700.973
Violins and shovels : the WPA arts projects / by Milton Meltzer. New York : Delacorte Press, [1976] p. cm. Includes index. Bibliography: p. Examines art projects run during the 1930's which were funded by the Work Projects Administration. [NX735.M44] 75-32916 ISBN 0-440-09316-3 : 6.95
1. United States. Work Projects Administration. 2. Federal aid to the arts—United States. 3. Arts, Modern—20th century—United States. I. Title. BIP

NEW Muse   709.'73'074014723
Community Museum of Brooklyn.
The Black artists in the WPA, 1933-1943 : [an exhibition of drawings, paintings, and sculpture, February 15-March 30, 1976 / Charlene Claye Van Derzee, curator, George Carter, assistant curator]. [1st ed.]. [Brooklyn, N.Y. : New Muse Community Museum of Brooklyn, 1976] [23] p. : ill. ; 21 cm. Cover title. [N6538.N5N37 1976] 76-3078
1. United States. Work Projects Administration. 2. Afro-American art—Exhibitions. 3. Art, Modern—20th century—United States—Exhibitions. 4. Politics in art. I. Van Derzee, Charlene Claye. II. Carter, George, 1931- III. Title.

U.S. Work Projects Administration—History.

MCDONALD, William   700.973
Francis, 1898-
Federal relief administration and the arts; the origins and administrative history of the arts projects of the Works Progress Administration [by] William F. McDonald. [Columbus] Ohio State University Press [1969] xiv, 869 p. 25 cm. Includes bibliographies. [NX735.M3] 68-31422 17.50
1. U.S. Work Projects Administration—History. 2. The arts—U.S. I. Title. BIP

Universities and colleges—Buildings.

AMERICAN Association of   371.62
Colleges for Teacher Education. Committee on Studies.
Physical facilities analysis for colleges and universities; a handbook of techniques, by Donald A. Jones [consultant] For the Subcommittee on Physical Facilities, Committee on Studies. [Oneonta, N. Y.] American Association of Colleges for Teacher Education [1958] 211p. illus. 29cm. [NA6600.A6] 57-13047
1. Universities and colleges—Buildings. I. Jones, Donald A. II. Title.

EDUCATIONAL Facilities   727.3
Laboratories.
New building on campus; six designs for a college communications center; a report. [New York, 1963] 1 v. (unpaged) illus., diagrs. 22 x 29 cm. (Case studies of educational facilities, 7) [NA6600.E2] 63-23344
1. Universities and colleges—Buildings. 2. Architecture—Competitions. I. Rensselaer Polytechnic Institute, Troy, N.Y. II. Title. III. Title: Six designs for a college communications center. IV. Series.

RENSSELAER Polytechnic   727.3
Institute, Troy, N.Y. School of Architecture.
New spaces for learning: designing college facilities to utilize instructional aids and media [by] Harold D. Hauf [others] Rev. [Troy] 1966. 137p. illus., plans. 28cm. Report of a res. project carried out under

the code name Project DASFEE: design of auditorium-studio facilities for engin. educ. [NA6600.R4 1966] 66-25153 gratis
1. Universities and colleges—Buildings. 2. Architecture—Designs and plans. I. Hauf. Harold Dana. II. Title.

Universities and colleges—United States.

CAMPUS buildings that work. [Philadelphia, North American Pub. Co., c1972] 242 p. illus. 31 cm. [NA6603.C35] 72-9582 727'.3
1. Universities and colleges—United States. 2. Architecture—Designs and plans. I. North American Publishing Company, Philadelphia.

Universities and colleges — U.S. — Buildings.

AMERICAN Institute of Physics. 378.1962
Physics buildings today. New York [1965] 64 p. illus., plans. 22 x 28 cm. A supplement to Modern physics buildings: design and function, a report by the American Association of Physics Teachers and the American Institute of Physics. "A project of the American Institute of Physics supported by a grant from Educational Facilities Laboratories, inc. Pub. R-180." [NA6751.A55] 66-5834
1. Universities and colleges — U.S. — Buildings. 2. Physical laboratories. 3. Architecture — Designs and plans. I. American Association of Physics Teachers. Modern physics buildings: design and function. II. Title.

Universities and colleges—United States—Curricula.

MORRISON, Jack, 1912- 700'.71'173
The rise of the arts on the American campus. New York, McGraw-Hill [1973] xviii, 223 p. 24 cm. "Thirteenth of a series of profiles sponsored by the Carnegie Commission on Higher Education." Bibliography: p. 169-171. [LB2361.5.M67] 72-10456 ISBN 0-07-010055-1 8.95
1. Universities and colleges—United States—Curricula. 2. The arts—Study and teaching—United States. I. Carnegie Commission on Higher Education. II. Title. BIP

University of North Dakota pottery.

BARR, Margaret Libby. 738'.09784'16
University of North Dakota pottery : the Cable years / Margaret Libby Barr, Donald Miller, Robert Barr. [s.l. : s.n.], 1977 (Fargo, N.D. : Knight Print. Co.) viii, 51 p. : ill. (some col.) ; 23 cm. Bibliography: p. 37. [NK4340.U54B37] 77-153043
1. Cable, Margaret Kelly. 2. University of North Dakota pottery. 3. Pottery—20th century—North Dakota. I. Miller, Donald, 1944- joint author. II. Barr, Robert, 1939- joint author. III. Title.

Untermyer, Irwin—Art collections.

NEW York (City). Metropolitan Museum of Art. 745'.094'07401471
Highlights of the Untermyer Collection of English and continental decorative arts. New York : Metropolitan Museum of Art, c1977. 216 p. : ill. ; 28 cm. [NK613.N48M476 1977] 77-12235 ISBN 0-87099-169-8 : 12.50
1. Untermyer, Irwin—Art collections. 2. Art, Decorative—Exhibitions. I. Title. BIP

Unwin brothers, ltd., printers, London.

UNWIN, Philip. 338.7'61'68620942
The printing Unwins : a short history of Unwin brothers, the Gresham Press, 1826-1976 / by Philip Unwin. London : Published for Unwin Brothers by Allen & Unwin, 1976. 159 p., [9] leaves of plates : ill. ; 24 cm. Includes index. Bibliography: p. 149. [Z232.U74U58] 76-374337 ISBN 0-04-655013-5 : 12.95
1. Unwin brothers, ltd., printers, London. I. Title.
Distributed by Allen & Unwin, Reading, MA BIP

Upholstery.

BAST, Herbert. 684
Making upholstered furniture. Milwaukee, Bruce Pub. Co. [1951] 162 p. illus. 28 cm. [TT198.B32] 52-268
1. Upholstery. I. Title.

BAST, Herbert. 684.1
Modernizing and repairing upholstered furniture. Milwaukee, Bruce Pub. Co. [1956] 73 p. illus. 27 cm. [TT198.B325] 56-4839
1. Upholstery. I. Title.

BERGEN, John, 1915- 684.1
All about upholstering, by John Bergen; illustrated by Lou Burrows and Eldon Shiel. [Chicago] Popular Mechanics Press [1952] 176 p. illus. 24 cm. [TT198.B4] 52-4517
1. Upholstery. I. Title.

BERGEN, John, 1915- 684.12
All about upholstering. Illustrated by Lou Burrows and Eldon Shiel. New York, Hawthorn Books [1963, c1962] 224 p. illus. (part col.) 24 cm. [TT198.B4 1963] 62-16131
1. Upholstery. I. Title. BIP

BEVIN, Arthur. 645.4
Upholstery. [New York] Arc Books [1962, c1961] 158 p. illus. 19 cm. [TT198.B44] 62-17580
1. Upholstery. BIP

BLANDFORD, Percy W. 684.1'2
The upholsterer's Bible / Percy W. Blandford. 1st ed. Blue Ridge Summit, Pa. : G/L Tab Books, 1978. 513 p. : ill. ; 22 cm. Includes index. [TT198.B53] 77-18914 ISBN 0-8306-9986-4 : 12.95. ISBN 0-8306-1004-9 pbk. : 7.95
1. Upholstery. I. Title. BIP

BRUMBAUGH, James E. 645'.4
Upholstering, by James E. Brumbaugh. [1st ed.] Indianapolis, T. Audel [1972] 390 p. illus. 22 cm. [TT198.B74] 72-83060 ISBN 0-672-23189-1 5.95 ($7.25 Can.)
1. Upholstery. I. Title. BIP

CHICAGO. Commercial Trades Institute. 684.1
Practical upholstering [by] Commercial Trades Institute instructional staff. New York, McGraw-Hill, 1953. 296 p. illus. 24 cm. [TT198.C4] 52-11506
1. Upholstery. I. Title.

CHRISTOPHER, Frederick John. 645.4
Upholstering. Editor: W. I. Van der Poel, Jr. [New York] Dover Publications, c1954. 128p. illus. 19cm. (A Dover-Foyle handbook) [TT198] 56-2388
1. Upholstery. I. Title.

DANIEL, William Joseph, 1901- 684
Your drapery workroom guide; a practical manual on drapery, upholstery and slipcover workroom procedure. New York, Fairchild Publications [1950] 64 p. illus. 23 cm. First published in 1948 under title: Your workroom encyclopedia. [TT390.D3 1950] 50-7638
1. Upholstery. I. Title.

DI BERNARDO, D Joseph. 684.1
Making your home furnishings. New York, Van Nostrand [1952] 242 p. illus. 24 cm. [TT198.D5] 52-5740
1. Upholstery. I. Title.

FLITMAN, Malcolm. 645'.4
Upholstering. New York, Drake Publishers [1972] 96 p. illus. 21 cm. [TT198.F63 1972b] 72-193769 ISBN 0-87749-210-7 6.95
1. Upholstery. I. Title. BIP

HARDY, Kay, 1902- 684.1
How to upholster furniture. Sketches by the author. New York, Funk & Wagnalls [1952] 182 p. illus. 26 cm. "A Kay Hardy home primer." [TT198.H337] 52-13940
1. Upholstery. I. Title.

HOWES, C. 684.1'2
Practical upholstery / C. Howes. New York : Drake Publishers, 1978, c1973. 127 p. : ill. ; 22 cm. (A Drake home craftsman's book) Includes index. [TT198.H68 1978] 77-18394 ISBN 0-8473-1690-4 pbk. : 4.95
1. Upholstery. I. Title. BIP

LEAVY, Herbert T. 684.1'2
How to upholster your own furniture / by Herbert T. Leavy. New York : Drake Publishers, [1976] p. cm. (Pro way series ; 1) [TT198.L4] 76-16393 ISBN 0-8473-1295-X : 8.95. ISBN 0-8473-1346-8 pbk. : 4.95
1. Upholstery. I. Title.

LUNA, Benjamin C. 645'.4
Upholstery: refinishing and restyling [by] Benjamin C. Luna. Chicago, American Technical Society [1969] 202 p. illus. 24 cm. [TT198.L8] 68-27147
1. Upholstery. BIP

MCDONALD, Robert J. 684.1'2
Upholstery repair and restoration / Robert J. McDonald. New York : Scribner, 1978,c1977. 168 p., [2] leaves of plates : ill. (some col.) ; 26 cm. Includes index. [TT198.M3 1977] 77-80142 ISBN 0-684-15335-1 : 12.50
1. Upholstery. I. Title. BIP

MINNESOTA Mining and Manufacturing Company. Automotive-Hardware Trades Division. 684.1'2
The home pro reupholstering guide / [Automotive-Hardware Trades Division, 3M Company]. [St. Paul : The Division, 1975] i, 172 p. : ill. ; 13 x 21 cm. (Its The home pro guide series) "Cat. no. 9755." [TT198.M5 1975] 74-82968
1. Upholstery. I. Title.

MORTON, Will. 645'.4
Mending and restoring upholstery and soft furnishings / Will Morton and Nellie Richardson. 1st American ed. South Brunswick, [N.J.] : A. S. Barnes, 1976, c1973. 158 p. : ill. ; 22 cm. Includes index. [TT198.R5 1976] 75-20592 ISBN 0-498-01742-7 : 7.95
1. Upholstery. 2. Drapery. 3. Coverlets. I. Richardson, Nellie, joint author. II. Title. BIP

PARKER, Page, 1913- 645.4
Upholstering at home; how to create, repair, and remodel upholstered furnishings, by Page Parker and J. G. Fornia. New York, Greenberg [1951] 422 p. illus. 24 cm. [TT198.P34] 51-9298
1. Upholstery. I. Fornia, Joseph G., joint author. II. Title.

PARKER, Page, 1913- 684.1'2
Upholstering for everyone / Page Parker, J. G. Fornia, Alice Fornia, with Ben Adams ; drawings by G. P. Parker ; photos. by J. R. Walsh and G. P. Parker. Reston, Va. : Reston Pub. Co., c1976. xiv, 674 p. : ill. ; 24 cm. Includes index. [TT198.P344] 76-3665 ISBN 0-87909-857-0 : 14.95
1. Upholstery. I. Fornia, Joseph G., joint author. II. Fornia, Alice, joint author. III. Title. BIP

SERGIO, Lisa, 1905- 684.1'2
You can upholster! : A do-it-yourself guide / Lisa Sergio ; illustrated by Lisbeth Loughran. 1st ed. Philadelphia : Lippincott, c1978. 186 p. : ill. ; 25 cm. Includes index. [TT198.S47] 77-21195 ISBN 0-397-01121-0 : 8.95
1. Upholstery. I. Loughran, Lisbeth. II. Title. BIP

TIERNEY, William Francies 1915 684.12
Modern upholstering methods, [by] William F. Tierney, [1st ed.] Bloomington, Ill., McKnight & McKnight Pub. Co., [1965] 152 p. illus. 27 cm. [TT198.T5] 65-19549
1. Upholstery. 2. Furniture — Repairing. I. Title. BIP

TORELLI, Michael E. 684.1'2
Reupholstering for the home craftsman / Michael E. Torelli and Ellen K. Haggerty ; drawings by Dennis Griffin. Radnor, Pa. : Chilton Book Co., c1977. p. cm. Includes index. [TT198.T67] 77-4586 ISBN 0-8019-6568-3 : 14.95. ISBN 0-8019-6569-1 pbk. : 9.95
1. Upholstery. I. Haggerty, Ellen K., joint author. II. Title. BIP

WAGNER, Dorothy, 1907- 747
Upholstery, drapes, and slip covers; how to repair and make them yourself. New York, W.H. Wise, 1955. 246p. 24cm. [TT198.W3] [TT198.W3] 645.48 55-1040 55-1040
1. Upholstery. I. Title.

Upholstery trade — Direct.

UPHOLSTERING. 747
Directory of supply sources for the furniture manufacturer, furniture designer, fabric and supply jobber. [New York, Hall Pub. Co.] v. 23 cm. annual. [TT198.U55] 58-32669
1. Upholstery trade — Direct. I. Title.

Upjohn, Richard, 1802-1878.

UPJOHN, Everard Miller, 1903- 720'.924 B
Richard Upjohn, architect and churchman, by Everard M. Upjohn. New York, Da Capo Press, 1968 [c1939] xvii, 243 p. illus., plans, port. 24 cm. (Da Capo Press series in architecture and decorative art, v. 15) Bibliography: p. [227]-228. [NA737.U6U6 1968] 68-26119
1. Upjohn, Richard, 1802-1878. 2. Church architecture—United States.

Upper classes in art.

LUCIE-SMITH, Edward. 759'.05
How the rich lived : the painter as witness 1870-1914 / Edward Lucie-Smith and Celestine Dars. New York : Paddington Press, c1976. 247 p., [4] leaves of plates : ill. ; 29 cm. Includes index. [ND1450.L8] 75-22955 ISBN 0-8467-0108-1 : 16.95
1. Upper classes in art. 2. Narrative painting. 3. Naturalism in art. 4. Painting, Modern—19th century. I. Dars, Celestine, joint author. II. Title.

Urban beautification.

DOBER, Richard P. 711'.4
Environmental design [by] Richard P. Dober. New York, Van Nostrand Reinhold [1969] 278 p. illus., maps, plans. 23 x 29 cm. [NA9052.D6] 79-81351
1. Urban beautification. 2. Cities and towns—Planning. I. Title. BIP

DOBER, Richard P. 711'.4
Environmental design / Richard P. Dober. Huntington, N.Y. : R. E. Krieger Pub. Co., 1975. p. cm. Reprint of the 1969 ed. published by Van Nostrand Reinhold, New York. [NA9052.D6 1975] 75-11961 ISBN 0-88275-331-2 : 19.95
1. Urban beautification. 2. Cities and towns—Planning. I. Title.

MALT, Harold Lewis. 711'.4
Furnishing the city. New York, McGraw-Hill [1970] vii, 254 p. illus. 24 cm. Bibliography: p. 244-246. [NA9052.M3] 76-86088
1. Urban beautification. 2. Cities and towns—Planning—1945- I. Title. BIP

NATIONAL Council of State Garden Clubs. 712'.5
Action blueprint for civic development. Compiled and edited by Mrs. Howard S. Kittel. St. Louis [1969] vi, 122 p. illus. 23 cm. [NA9052.N3] 79-284652
1. Urban beautification. I. Kittel, Mary Badham. II. Title.

RUDOFSKY, Bernard, 1905- 711'.74
Streets for people; a primer for Americans. Photos. by the author. [1st ed.] Garden City, N.Y., Doubleday [1969] 351 p. illus. (part col.), music. 27 cm. Bibliography: p. [343]-348. [NA9053.S7R8] 76-78735 14.95
1. Urban beautification. 2. Streets. I. Title. BIP

SITTE, Camillo, 1843-1903. 711'.4
The art of building cities : city building according to its artistic fundamentals / by Camillo Sitte ; translated by Charles T. Stewart. Westport, Conn. : Hyperion Press, [1979, c1945] p. cm. Translation of Der Stadte—Bau. Reprint of the ed. published by Reinhold Pub. Corp., New York. Includes index. [NA9052.S5813 1979] 78-14144 ISBN 0-88355-817-3 : 19.50

cm. Bibliography: p. 141. [NC1860.S8 1969] 69-12898 12.50
1. Valentines—History. I. Title.

Valette, Adolphe, 1876-1942.

VALETTE, Adolphe, 1876-1942. 760'.092'4
Adolphe Valette : [exhibition] / Manchester City Art Gallery, 6 October-14 November 1976. [Manchester, Eng.] : Manchester City Art Gallery, 1976. 47 p. : ill. (some col.) ; 20 cm. "Catalogue no. 60." Includes index. [ND553.V3264M36] 77-364481 ISBN 0-901673-09-9
1. Valette, Adolphe, 1876-1942. I. Manchester, Eng. Art Gallery.

Vallotton, Felix Edouard, 1865-1925.

VALLOTTON, Felix Edouard, 1865-1925. 760'.09494
Felix Vallotton (1865-1925); a retrospective exhibition of paintings, drawings, woodcuts, and engravings. New York, Hirschl and Adler Galleries [1970?] [30] p. illus. (part col.), ports. 26 cm. Catalog of the exhibition held Apr. 7-25, 1970, at the Hirschl & Adler Galleries, New York. [ND853.V3A44] 74-18610
I. Hirschl & Adler Galleries.

VON KIRSCHEN, Ivo. 769'.92'4
The graphic art of Vallotton & the Nabis [catalogue of an exhibition] Kovler Gallery: Chicago, May-July 1970; Museum of Art, University of Iowa, Iowa City, August-September 1970. [Chicago, Kovler Gallery, 1970] 80 p. illus. 23 cm. Contains translations from French to English by Marina Wolkonsky. Bibliography: p. 76-79. [NE710.V3V66] 70-118825
1. Vallotton, Felix Edouard, 1865-1925. 2. Nabi. I. Kovler Gallery. II. Iowa. University. Museum of Art. III. Title.

Valmiki.

VEQUAUD, Yves. 755'.9'45095412
Women painters of Mithila / Yves Vequaud. London : Thames and Hudson, 1977. 112 p. : chiefly ill. (some col.) ; 28 cm. Translation of L'art du Mithila. [ND1007.M55V4613 1977b] 78-308556 ISBN 0-500-27093-7 : 8.95
1. Valmiki. Ramayana—Illustrations. 2. Mahabharata—Illustrations. 3. Painting, Indic—India—Mithila. 4. Painting—India—Mithila. 5. Painting, Hindu—India—Mithila. 6. Hindu symbolism. 7. Symbolism in art—India—Mithila. I. Title. Distributed by W. W. Norton, New York, NY 10036 BIP

Van Briggle, Artus, 1869-1904.

BOGUE, Dorothy McGraw. 738.3'0924
The Van Briggle story. [Colorado Springs, Printed by Dentan-Berkeland Print. Co.] 1968. 53 p. illus., ports. 22 cm. Bibliography: p. 50-52. [NK4210.V35B6] 68-56344 2.00
1. Van Briggle, Artus, 1869-1904. I. Title.

Van Ess, Warren A., 1935—

VAN ESS, Warren A., 1935- 741.9'73
A world of his own; the artwork of Warren A. Van Ess. Grand Rapids, W. B. Eerdmans Pub. Co. [1974] 71 p. illus. (part col.) 20 x 24 cm. [NC139.V36A57] 74-4372 ISBN 0-8028-3447-7 5.00
1. Van Ess, Warren A., 1935- I. Title.

Van Rensselaer family—Art collections.

BLACKBURN, Roderic H. 929'.2'0973
Cherry Hill : the history and collections of a Van Rensselaer family / Roderic H. Blackburn. [Bethlehem, N.Y. : Historic Cherry Hill], c1976. viii, 176 p. : ill. ; 28 cm. Bibliography: p. 175-176. [N5220.V34B57] 75-44844
1. Van Rensselaer family—Art collections. 2. Van Rensselaer family. I. Historic Cherry Hill (Corporation) II. Title. BIP

Vanbrugh, John, Sir, 1664-1726.

WHISTLER, Laurence, 1912- 720'.92'4 B
Sir John Vanbrugh, architect & dramatist, 1664-1726 / Laurence Whistler. Millwood, N.Y. : Kraus Reprint Co., 1978. p. cm. Reprint of the 1938 ed. published by Cobden-Sanderson, London. Includes index. Bibliography: p. [NA997.V3W5 1978] 78-3501 ISBN 0-527-95850-6 : 8.00
1. Vanbrugh, John, Sir, 1664-1726. 2. Architecture—England. 3. Theater—England. BIP

Vanderbilt, Gloria, 1924—

VANDERBILT, Gloria, 1924- 700'.92'4 B
Woman to woman / by Gloria Vanderbilt. 1st ed. Garden City, N.Y. : Doubleday, 1979. p. cm. [N6537.V33A2 1979] 77-25612 ISBN 0-385-13645-5 : 14.95
1. Vanderbilt, Gloria, 1924- 2. Artists—United States—Biography. I. Title. BIP

Vanderbilt, William Henry,

SHINN, Earl, 1837-1886. 338.4'3745'10973
Mr. Vanerbilt's house and collection. DescribedbyEdward Strahan [pseud.] Japan ed. Boston, G. Barrie [c1883-84] 4v. illus., plates (part col.) 65cm. 'Five hundred copies . . . have been printed . . . No. 35.; [N5220.S54] 54-48277
1. Vanderbilt, William Henry, 2. Art—Private collections. 3. Art—New York (City) I. Title.

Vanderlyn, John, 1775-1852.

SCHOONMAKER, Marius, 1811-1894. 927.5
John Vanderylyn, artist, 1775-1852; biography. Kingston, N.Y., Senate House Association, 1950. vi, 77 p. 24 cm. [ND237.V15S35] 50-31190
1. Vanderlyn, John, 1775-1852. I. Title.

VANDERLYN, John, 1775-1852. 741.9'73
The works of John Vanderlyn, from Tammany to the Capitol, by Kenneth C. Lindsay. [Binghamton, N.Y.] University Art Gallery, State University of New York at Binghamton; [supplied by Worldwide Books, Boston, 1970] xiii, 155 p. illus. 26 cm. Catalogue of a loan exhibition held Oct. 11-Nov. 9, 1970 at the University Art Gallery, State University of New York at Binghamton. Bibliography: p. 155. [ND237.V15L5] 73-636428
I. Lindsay, Kenneth Clement, 1919- II. New York (State). State University at Binghamton. University Art Gallery.

Vanes.

BUCHERT, Ilse. 745.59
Weathercocks and weathercreatures; some examples of early American folk art from the collection of the Shelburne Museum, Vermont. by Ilse Buchert and Alexander Nesbitt. Newport, R.I., Third & Elm Press, 1970. [46] p. col. illus. 18 x 24 cm. 160 copies printed. [NK9585.B8] 73-26074
1. Vanes. 2. Folk art—U.S. I. Nesbitt, Alexander, 1901- joint author. II. Shelburne, Vt. Museum. III. Title.

KENNETH Lynch & Sons. 739'.4773
Weathervanes / by Kenneth Lynch ; [ill. by Andrew D. Crowell, Sr.]. 1st ed. Canterbury, Conn. : Canterbury Pub. Co., c1971. 95 p. : chiefly ill. ; 37 cm. (The Architectural handbook series) Includes index. [NK9585.K46 1971] 72-142540 5.00
1. Vanes. I. Lynch, Kenneth. II. Crowell, Andrew Durkee, 1899- III. Title.

Vanes—New England.

KAYE, Myrna. 739'.4774
Yankee weathervanes. Illustrated with drawings by Corinne Pascoe. [1st ed.] New York, Dutton, 1975. xvii, 236 p. illus. 22 cm. Bibliography: p. 227-230. [NK9585.K39] 74-19245 12.95
1. Vanes—New England. I. Title.

Vanes—United States.

KLAMKIN, Charles. 739'.4773
Weather vanes; the history, design, and manufacture of an American folk art. New York, Hawthorn Books [1973] ix, 209 p. illus. 29 cm. Bibliography: p. 201. [NK9585.K54 1973] 73-352 11.95
1. Vanes—United States. 2. Folk art—United States. I. Title.

Vanity fair.

LONDON. National Portrait Gallery. 741.5'942'07402132
Catalogue of original Vanity fair cartoons in the National Portrait Gallery / by Richard Ormond. London : The Gallery, 1976. 20 p. ; 21 cm. Cover title: Original Vanity fair cartoons in the National Portrait Gallery. Published to coincide with the Vanity fair exhibition, held at the National Portrait Gallery, July to Aug., 1976. Includes index. [NC1478.V36L66 1976] 77-369105 ISBN 0-904017-09-5 : £0.10
1. Vanity fair. 2. Biography—19th century—Caricatures and cartoons—Catalogs. I. Ormond, Richard. II. Title. III. Title: Original Vanity fair cartoons in the National Portrait Gallery.

ORMOND, Richard. 741.5'942'07402132
Vanity Fair : an exhibition of original cartoons / introduction by Eileen Harris ; catalogue by Richard Ormond. London : National Portrait Gallery, 1976. 2-31 p. : ill., ports. ; 30 cm. "Published for the exhibition held at the National Portrait Gallery from 9 July to 30 August 1976." [NC1478.V36O75] 77-359299 ISBN 0-904017-06-0 : £1.00
1. Vanity fair. 2. Caricatures and cartoons—England—Exhibitions. I. London. National Portrait Gallery. II. Title.

Varallo, Italy. Nuova Gerusalemme (Shrine)

BUTLER, Samuel, 1835-1902. 914.5'17
Ex voto. [1st AMS ed.] New York, AMS Press [1968] xxiv, 229 p. illus. 24 cm. (The Shrewsbury edition of the works of Samuel Butler, v. 9) Reprint of the 1924 ed. [PR4349.B7 1968 vol. 9] [N6921.V35] 72-187991
1. Tabaguet, Jean Baptiste, fl. 1590. 2. Varallo, Italy. Nuova Gerusalemme (Shrine) 3. Art—Varallo, Italy. I. Title.

Vargas, Alberto.

AUSTIN, Reid. 759.13
Alberto Vargas / by Reid Austin and Alberto Vargas. New York : Harmony Books, 1978, c1977 p. cm. Includes index. Bibliography: p. [ND1839.V35A96] 77-3274 ISBN 0-517-53047-3 : 14.95
1. Vargas, Alberto. I. Vargas, Alberto, joint author.

Varney, Carleton.

VARNEY, Carleton. 747'.8'83
Carleton Varney decorates from A to Z : an encyclopedia of home decoration / by Carleton Varney. Indianapolis : Bobbs-Merrill, [1977] p. cm. [NK2004.3.V37A43] 77-76890 ISBN 0-672-51863-5 : 17.50
1. Varney, Carleton. 2. Interior decoration—United States. I. Title. BIP

Varnham, Warner.

MUSEUM of the American China Trade. 741.9'42
Warner Varnham: a visual diary of China and the Philippines, 1835 to 1843. Catalogue of an exhibition of drawings and watercolors, May through October 1973, with a checklist of other known works. Milton, Mass., 1973. viii, 23 p. illus. 28 cm. Cover title: Warner Varnham: exhibition of drawings and watercolors. Includes bibliographical references. [NC242.V33M87 1973] 74-157055
1. Varnham, Warner. 2. China in art. 3. Philippine Islands in art. I. Varnham, Warner. II. Title. III. Title: A visual diary of China and the Philippines, 1835 to 1843.

Varnish and varnishing.

FELLER, Robert L. 751.6
On picture varnishes and their solvents [by] Robert L. Feller, Nathan Stolow [and] Elizabeth H. Jones. Rev. and enl. ed. Cleveland, Press of Case Western Reserve University, 1971. xxi, 251 p. illus. 23 cm. "Based on the principal papers presented at a Seminar on Resinous Surface Coatings sponsored by the Intermuseum Conservation Association, Oberlin, Ohio." Includes bibliographies. [ND1530.F4 1971] 77-99229 ISBN 0-8295-0181-9 6.50
1. Varnish and varnishing. 2. Artists' materials. I. Stolow, Nathan. II. Jones, Elizabeth H. III. Title.

Vasarely, Victor, 1908—

DIEHL, Gaston. 759.4
Vasarely. [Translated from the French by Eileen B. Hennessy] New York, Crown Publishers [1972] 95 p. illus. (part col.) 29 cm. Bibliography: p. 93-94. [ND553.V35D513] 71-125043 3.95
1. Vasarely, Victor, 1908- BIP

JORAY, Marcel. 759.4
Vasarely / by Marcel Joray ; transl. from the French by Haakon Chevalier. Neuchatel : Editions du Griffon, 1976. 128 p. : ill. (some col.) ; 16 cm. [ND553.V35J59] 77-468162 18.00F
1. Vasarely, Victor, 1908- I. Vasarely, Victor, 1908-

VASARELY, Victor, 1908- 759.4
Planetary folklore. Photography by Stefan Moses. Design by Peter Wilhelm. [Translation into English by Cedric Hentschel. Greenwich, Conn.] New York Graphic Society [1973] 88 p. illus. (part col.) 25 cm. Text in English, French, and German First published in Munich under title: Farbwelt. [ND553.V35A4513] 73-86480 ISBN 0-8212-0584-6 15.00
I. Moses, Stefan. II. Wilhelm, Peter Jurgen.

VASARELY, Victor, 1908- 759.39
Vasarely. [New York, Gimpel & Weitzenhoffer, 1970] 20 p. illus. (part col.), port. 21 cm. [ND553.V35A59] 74-199846
I. Gimpel & Weitzenhoffer. BIP

VASARELY, Victor, 1908- 759.4
Vasarely: duo exhibition recent works. [New York? 1972] [28] p. illus. (part col.) 27 cm. Exhibition held concurrently at Galerie Denise Rene and Sidney Janis Gallery, New York, April, 1972. [ND553.V35G283] 72-198256
I. Galerie Denise Rene. II. Sidney Janis Gallery.

Vasari, Giorgio, 1511-1574.

BOASE, Thomas Sherrer Ross, 1898-1974. 709'.2'4 B
Georgio Vasari : the man and the book / T. S. R. Boase. [Princeton, N.J.] : Princeton University Press, 19978,c1977 p. cm. (Bollingen series ; XXXV : 20) (The A. W. Mellon lectures in the fine arts ; 20) Based on 6 lectures given at the National Gallery of Art in Washington in Feb. and Mar. 1971. Includes index. Bibliography: p. [N7483.V37B6] 77-4763 ISBN 0-691-09905-7 : 22.50
1. Vasari, Giorgia, 1511-1574. 2. Art historians—Italy—Biography. I. Title. II. Series. III. Series: Bollingen series ; 35.

NOTRE Dame, Ind. University. Art Gallery. 709'.455'1074013
The age of Vasari; a loan exhibition under the high patronage of His Excellency, Egidio Ortona, the Ambassador of Italy to the United States [at] Art Gallery, University of Notre Dame, Notre Dame, Indiana, February 22-March 31, 1970 [and] University Art Gallery, State University of New York at Binghamton, April 12-May 10, 1970. [Notre Dame, Ind., 1970] 202 p. illus. (part col.), facsims. 26 cm. Includes bibliographical references. [N6921.N55N6] 77-632509
1. Vasari, Giorgio, 1511-1574. 2. Art, Florentine—Exhibitions. 3. Mannerism

(Art)—Florence. I. New York (State). State University at Binghamton. University Art Gallery. II. Title.

RUD, Einar, 1892- 759.5
Vasari's life and Lives; the first art historian [Tr. from Danish by Reginald Spink] Princeton, N.J., Van Nostrand [1964, c.1961, 1963] 184p. illus., ports. 24cm. Bibl. 64-3861 7.50
1. Vasari, Giorgio, 1511-1574. 2. Vasari, Giorgio, 1511-1574. Le vite de' piu eccellenti pittori, scultori e architetti. I. Title.

Vase-painting, Etruscan.

BEAZLEY, J. D. 738.38
Etruscan vase painting / by J. D. Beazley. New York : Hacker Art Books, 1976. xvi, 351 p., remainder unpaged : ill. ; 29 cm. Includes addenda and indices. Reprint of the edition first published in 1947 by Oxford U. Pr. [NK4645] 75-11054 ISBN 0-87817-182-7 lib.bdg. : 40.00
1. Vase-painting, Etruscan. I. Title. **BIP**

Vase-painting, Etruscan—Cerveteri, Italy.

DEL CHIARO, Mario Aldo, 1925- 738.3'82'09375
Etruscan red-figured vase-painting at Caere / Mario A. Del Chiaro. Berkeley : University of California Press, c1974. xiv, 160 p., [24] leaves of plates : ill. ; 26 cm. Includes bibliographical references and index. [NK4654.D38] 73-85785 ISBN 0-520-02578-4 : 22.50
1. Vase-painting, Etruscan—Cerveteri, Italy. 2. Vase-painting—Cerveteri, Italy. 3. Cerveteri, Italy—Antiquities. I. Title. **BIP**

Vase-painting, Greek.

BEAZLEY, John Davidson. 738.38
Attic black-figure vase-painter / by J.D. Beazley. New York : Hacker Art Books, 1978. xvi, 851p. ; 25 cm. Includes bibliographical references. [NK4648.B415] 40.00
1. Vase-painting, Greek. 2. Vases, Greek. I. Title.
L.C. card no. for 1956 Clarendon Press ed.: 56-13762. Book carries L.C. card no.: 75-44909.

BEAZLEY, John Davidson, 1885- 738.38
Attic black-figure vase-painters. Oxford, Clarendon Press, 1956. xvi, 851p. 24cm. Includes bibliographical references. [NK4648.B415] 56-13762
1. Vase- painting, Greek. 2. Vases, Greek. I. Title. II. Title: Black-figure vase-painters. **BIP**

BEAZLEY, John Davidson, Sir 1885- 738.382
Attic red-figure vase-painters. 2d ed. Oxford, Clarendon Press, 1963. 3 v. (lvi, 2036 p.) 24 cm. Bibliography: p. [liii]-lvi. [NK4649.B44] 64-714
1. Vase-painting, Greek. 2. Vases, Greek. I. Title. **BIP**

BEAZLEY, John Davidson, Sir, 1885-1970. 738.3'82'09385
Attic black-figure vase-painters / by J. D. Beazley. New York : Hacker Art Books, 1978. xvi, 851 p. ; 25 cm. Reprint of the 1956 ed. pulished by Clarendon Press, Oxford. Includes bibliographical references and indexes. [NK4648.B415 1978] 75-44909 ISBN 0-87817-191-6 : lib.bdg. : 40.00
1. Vase-painting, Greek. 2. Vases, Greek. I. Title.

BEAZLEY, John Davidson, Sir, 1885-1970. 738.3'82'0938
Paralipomena: additions to Attic black-figure vase-painters and to Attic red-figure vase-painters (second edition), by J. D. Beazley. Oxford, Clarendon Press, 1971. xix, 679 p. 24 cm. [NK4648.B43] 77-861524 ISBN 0-19-813152-6 £9.00
1. Vase-painting, Greek. 2. Vases, Greek. I. Beazley, John Davidson, Sir, 1885-1970. Attic black-figure vase-painters. II. Beazley, John Davidson, Sir, 1885-1970. Attische Vasenmaler des rotfigurigen Stils. III. Title.

BUSCHOR, Ernst, 1886-1961. 738.3'82
Greek vase-painting / Ernst Buschor ; [translated by G. C. Richards]. New York : Hacker Art Books, 1978. xii, 179, xciv p. : ill. ; 25 cm. Translation of Griechische Vasenmalerei. Reprint of the 1922 ed. published by Dutton, New York. Includes indexes. [NK4645.B8713 1978] 77-73882 ISBN 0-87817-217-3 : 30.00
1. Vase-painting, Greek. I. Title.

FOLSOM, Robert Slade. 738.3'82'0938
Attic black-figured pottery / by Robert S. Folsom. Park Ridge, N.J. : Noyes Press, [1975] xvi, 171 p. : ill. ; 25 cm. (Noyes classical studies) Includes index. Bibliography: p. 163-166. [NK4648.F6] 75-13568 ISBN 0-8155-5035-9 : 9.95
1. Vase-painting, Greek. 2. Vases, Greek. I. Title. **BIP**

HANNESTAD, Lise. 080 s
The followers of the Paris Painter / Lise Hannestad ; with a contribution by Anja Drukker. København : Det Kongelige Danske Videnskabernes Selskab : kommissionaer Munksgaard, 1976. 95 p., [30] leaves of plates : ill. ; 25 cm. (Historisk-filosofiske meddelelser - Det Kongelige Danske Videnskabernes Selskab ; 47,4) Includes bibliographical references. [AS281.D214 bd. 47, nr. 4] [NK4645] 738.3'82'0938 77-358121 ISBN 8-7730-4052-5 : kr126.50
1. Vase-painting, Greek. 2. Decoration and ornament—Greece. I. Title. II. Series: Danske videnskabernes selskab, Copenhagen. Historisk-filosofiske meddelelser ; 47,4.

HENLE, Jane Elizabeth, 1913- 738.3'82'0938
Greek myths; a vase painter's notebook [by] Jane Henle. Bloomington, Indiana University Press [1973] v, 247 p. illus. 24 cm. Bibliography: p. 200-224. [NK4645.H36 1973] 72-75639 ISBN 0-253-32635-4 3.50
1. Vase-painting, Greek. 2. Gods in art. I. Title. **BIP**

MERTENS, Joan R. 738.3'82'0938
Attic white-ground : its development on shapes other than lekythoi / Joan R. Mertens. New York : Garland Pub., 1977. 243 p., [21] leaves of plates : ill. ; 21 cm. (Outstanding dissertations in the fine arts) Thesis—Harvard, 1972. Includes index. Bibliography: p. 225-235. [NK4649.5.M47 1977] 76-23641 ISBN 0-8240-2711-6 : 35.00
1. Vase-painting, Greek. 2. Vases, Greek. 3. Slipware—Greece. I. Title. II. Series. **BIP**

NOBLE, Joseph Veach, 1920- 738.15
The techniques of painted Attic pottery. New York. Watson-Guptill [c.1965] xvi,217p. illus. (pt. col.) 32cm. Pub. in cooperation with the Metropolitan Mus. of Art. Bibliographical footnotes. [NK4645.N6] 65-25311 17.50
1. Vase-painting, Greek. 2. Vases, Greek. I. New York (City) Metropolitan Museum of Art. II. Title.

PAYNE, Humfry, 1902-1936. 759.938
Necrocorinthia; a study of Corinthian art in the archaic period. College Park, Md., McGrath Pub. Co., 1971. xii, 363, 53 p. illus. 27 cm. Reprint of the 1931 ed. Includes bibliographical references. [N5655.P3 1971] 78-119272 ISBN 0-8434-0141-9
1. Vase-painting, Greek. 2. Corinth, Greece—Antiquities. I. Title.

RICHTER, Gisela Marie Augusta, 1882- 738.382
Attic red-figured vases, a survey. Rev. ed. New Haven, Yale University Press, 1958. 209p. illus. 25cm. At head of title: Metropolitan Museum of Art. Includes bibliography. [NK4649.R5 1958] 58-11406
1. Vase-painting, Greek. 2. Vases, Greek. I. Title.

SCHEFOLD, Karl 704.947
Myth and legend in early Greek art; [Tr. from German by Audrey Hicks] New York, Abrams [1966] 200p. illus. (6 mounted col.) geneal. tables, map. plates. 27cm. Bibl. [NK4645S3313] 66-13271 12.50
1. Vase-painting, Greek. 2. Mythology, Greek. I. Title.

Vase painting, Greek—Athens.

WEBSTER, Thomas Bertram Lonsdale, 1905- 738.3'82'0938
Potter and patron in classical Athens [by] T. B. L. Webster. London, Methuen, [1973 c1972] xvi, 312, 16 p. illus. 23 cm. "Distributed in the USA by Harper & Row Publishers, Inc., Barnes & Noble Import Division." Includes bibliographical references. [NK4648.W4 1972] 73-159352 ISBN 0-416-75630-1 17.50
1. Vase painting, Greek—Athens. 2. Potters—Athens. 3. Art patronage—Athens. I. Title.

Vase-painting, Greek—History.

BENSON, Jack Leonard. 738.3'0938
Horse, bird & man; the origins of Greek paintings [by] J. L. Benson. Amherst, University of Massachusetts Press, 1970. xxx, 182, xli, p. illus. 29 cm. Includes bibliographical references. [NK4645.B46] 70-95787 20.00
1. Vase-painting, Greek—History. 2. Horses in art. 3. Birds in art. 4. Human figure in art. I. Title. **BIP**

Vase-painting, Italian.

TRENDALL, Arthur Dale, 1909- 738.3820945
South Italian vase painting [by] A.D. Trendall. London, British Museum, 1966. 32p. 21 plates (in. 4 col.) map. 22cm. Bibl. [NK4657.18T7] 66-71691 1.00 pap.,
1. Vase-painting, Italian. I. Title.
Available from British Info., New York.

Vases, Ancient—California—Los Angeles—Catalogs.

CORPUS vasorum antiquorum. United States of America. The Los Angeles County Museum of Art. 738.3'82'093 s
Berkeley : University of California Press, 1977- v. : ill. ; 34 cm. (Corpus vasorum antiquorum : United States of America ; fasc. 18) At head of title: Union academique internationale. Vol. 1. edited by P. M. Packard and P. A. Clement. Issued in portfolio. Includes bibliography and index. [NK4640.C6U5 fasc. 18] 738.3'82'093074019494 74-84142 ISBN 0-520-02850-3 : 30.00
1. Los Angeles Co., Calif. Museum of Art, Los Angeles. 2. Vases, Ancient—California—Los Angeles—Catalogs. 3. Vases—California—Los Angeles—Catalogs. I. Packard, Pamela M. II. Los Angeles Co., Calif. Museum of Art, Los Angeles. III. Series.

Vases, Ancient—Catalogs.

CLEVELAND Museum of Art. 738.3'82'074017132
The Cleveland Museum of Art [by] Cedric G. Boulter. Princeton, N.J., Princeton University Press, 1971- v. 48 plates. 34 cm. (Corpus vasorum antiquorum. United States of America, fasc. 15, Cleveland Museum of Art, fasc. 1,) At head of title: Union Academique Internationale. Issued in portfolio. Includes bibliographical references. [NK4640.C6U5 fasc. 15, etc.] 70-148348 ISBN 0-691-03540-7 15.00
1. Vases, Ancient—Catalogs. 2. Vases—Cleveland—Catalogs. I. Boulter, Cedric G., 1912- II. Series: Corpus vasorum antiquorum. United States of America, fasc. 15,

Vases—Baltimore.

ROBINSON, David Moore, 1880- 380.1'45'7
The Robinson collection, Baltimore, Md., by David Moore Robinson with the assistance of Mary W. McGehee. Cambridge, Harvard University Press, 1934-38. 3v. 150 plates (part col.) 33cm. (Corpus vasorum antiquorum. United States of America, fasc. 4, 6-7. The Robinson collection, Baltimore, Md., fasc. 1-) At head of title: Union academique internationale. Vols. 2-3: With the assistance of Sarah Elizabeth Efreeman. issued in portfollos. Includes bibliographical references. [NK4640.C6U5 fasc. 4, etc.] A 54
1. Vases—Baltimore. I. Title. II. Series: Corpus vasorum antiquorum. United States of America, fasc. 4, etc.

Vases—Crete—Catalogs.

WARREN, Peter. 736'.5
Minoan stone vases. London, Cambridge U.P., 1969. xiv, 280 p., 120 plates. illus. 26 cm. (Cambridge classical studies) Bibliography: p. 231-240. [NK4646.W3] 69-13794 8/-/-
1. Vases—Crete—Catalogs. 2. Vases, Greek—Crete. I. Title. **BIP**

Vases, Etruscan

MATTEUCIG, Giacinto. 738.38
Poggio Buco, the necropolis of Statonia. Berkeley University of California Press, 1951. xiii, 117 p. illus., 24 plates, maps. 28 cm. bibliography:p. xi-xiii. [NK4645.M3] 51-10295
1. Vases, Etruscan 2. Statonia, Italy. I. Title.

MATTEUCIG, Giacinto. 738.3'82'09375
Poggio Buco, the necropolis of Statonia. Westport, Conn., Greenwood Press [1972, c1951] xiii, 117 p. illus. 26 cm. Bibliography: p. xi,xiii. [NK4654.M3 1972] 71-163552 ISBN 0-8371-6212-2 9.00
1. Vases, Etruscan. 2. Statonia—Antiquities. I. Title.

Vases—Greece.

BOARDMAN, John, 1927- 738.3'82'09385
Athenian black figure vases. New York, Oxford University Press, 1974. 252 p. illus. 22 cm. Bibliography: p. 235-241. [NK4648.B62 1974] 73-89034 10.00
1. Vases—Greece. 2. Vase-painting, Greek. I. Title. **BIP**

Vases—Greece—Catalogs.

BRANN, Eva T. H. 938'.5 s
Late geometric and protoattic pottery, mid 8th to late 7th century B.C. / Princeton, N.J. : American School of Classical Studies at Athens, 1962. xiv, 134 p., [23] leaves of plates : ill. ; 31 cm. (The Athenian Agora ; v. 8) Includes indexes. Bibliography: p. [xiii]-xiv. [DF287.A23A5 vol.8] [NK4647] 738.3'0938'5 75-322663
1. Vases—Greece—Catalogs. 2. Athens. Agora. I. Title. II. Title: t III. Series: American School of Classical Studies at Athens. The Athenian Agora ; v. 8.

OXFORD. University. Ashmolean Museum. 738.3'82'0938507402574
Oxford, Ashmolean Museum / by John Boardman. London ; New York : Published for the British Academy by Oxford University Press, 1975- v. : ill. ; 31 cm. (Corpus vasorum antiquorum : Great Britain ; fas. 14 : Oxford ; fas. 3) At head of title: Union academique internationle. Issued in portfolio. Includes bibliographical references and indexes. [NK4623.5.G7O926 1975] 76-354773 ISBN 0-19-725953-7 (v. 1) : 47.00 (U.S.) (v. 1)
1. Oxford. University. Ashmolean Museum. 2. Vases—Greece—Catalogs. 3. Vases—England—Oxford—Catalogs. I. Boardman, John, 1927- II. Title. III. Series: Corpus vasorum antiquorum : Great Britain ; fas. 14.

SPARKES, Brian A. 938'.5 s
Black and plain pottery of the 6th, 5th, and 4th centuries B.C. / by Brian A. Sparkes and Lucy Talcott. Princeton, N.J. : American School of Classical Studies at Athens, 1970. 2 v. (xviii, 472 p., [63] leaves of plates) : ill. ; 32 cm. (The Athenian Agora ; v. 12) Includes bibliographical references and indexes. [DF287.A23A5 vol. 12] [NK4648] 738.3'0938'5 75-322660
1. Vases—Greece—Catalogs. 2. Athens. Agora. I. Talcott, Lucy, joint author. II. Title. III. Series: American School of Classical Studies at Athens. The Athenian Agora ; v. 12. **BIP**

Vases, Greek.

ARIAS, Paolo Enrico 738.382
A History of one thousand years of Greek vase painting. Text, notes by P. E. Arias. Photos. by Max Hirmer. Tr., rev. by B. Shefton. History of one thousand years of Greek vase painting. New York, Abrams [1963] 410p. mounted col. illus., plates. 32cm. Bibl. 61-13857 30.00
1. Vases, Greek. 2. Vase-painting, Greek. I. Hirmer, Max. II. Title. III. Title: 1000 years of Greek vase painting.

BEAZLEY, John Davidson, 1885- 738.38
The development of Attic black-figure. Berkeley, University of California Press, 1951. xiv, 127 p. 49 plates. 27 cm. (Sather classical lectures, v. 24) Bibliographical references included in "Notes" (p. [101]-119) [NK4648.B42] 51-61810
1. Vases, Greek. I. Title. II. Title: Attic black-figure. III. Series. BIP

CAMBITOGLOU, Alexander. 738.382
Apulian red-figured vase-painters of the plain style, by Alexander Cambitoglou and A. D. Trendall. [n. p.] Archaeological Institute of America, 1961. xv, 103 p. 41 plates. 33 cm. (Monographs on archaeology and fine arts, 10) In portfolio. Stamped on cover: Stechert-Hafner Service Agency, New York. [NK4649.C3] 64-2458
1. Vases, Greek. 2. Vase-painting, Greek. I. Trendall, Arthur Dale, 1909- joint author. II. Title. III. Series.

FOLSOM, Robert Slade. 738.3'82'0938
Attic red-figured pottery / by Robert S. Folsom. Park Ridge, N.J. : Noyes Press, c1976. 219 p. : ill. ; 24 cm. (Noyes classical studies) Includes index. Bibliography: p. 210-212. [NK4649.F64] 76-41132 ISBN 0-8155-5049-9 : 9.95
1. Vases, Greek. 2. Vase-painting, Greek. I. Title. BIP

RICHTER, Gisela Marie Augusta, 1882-1972. 738.3'82'09385
Shapes and names of Athenian vases, by Gisela M. A. Richter and Marjorie J. Milne. Washington, McGrath Pub. Co., 1973 [c1935] xxiii, 32, [59] p. illus. 24 cm. At head of title: The Metropolitan Museum of Art. Reprint of the ed. published by Plantin Press, New York. Bibliography: p. xvii-xxiii. [NK4645.R63 1973] 76-119277 ISBN 0-8434-0145-1 45.00
1. Vases, Greek. I. Milne, Marjorie Josephine, 1896- joint author. II. New York (City). Metropolitan Museum of Art. III. Title.

VON BOTHMER, Dietrich, 1918- 738.382
Attic black-figured amphorae [New York] Metropolitan Mus. of Art [c.1963] x, 45p. illus. and port. (48 plates) 33cm. (Corpus vasorum antiquorum. U.S. of Amer., fasc. 12. Metropolitan Mus. of Art, New York, fasc. 3) At head of title: Union academique internationale. Bibl. 63-17995 15.00, portfolio
1. Vases, Greek. 2. Vases—New York (City) I. New York. Metropolitan Museum of Art. II. Title. III. Series: Corpus vasorum antiquorum. United States of America, fasc. 12

Vases, Greek — Catalogs.

ASHMEAD, Ann Harnwell. 738.3'82'0938
Attic red-figured vases [by] Ann Harnwell Ashmead and Kyle Meredith Phillips, Jr. Princeton, N.J., Princeton University Press, 1971. 64 p. 42 plates 34 cm. (Corpus vasorum antiquorum. United States of America, fasc. 13. The Ella Riegel Memorial Museum, Bryn Mawr College, fasc. 1) At head of title: Union academique internationale. Issued in portfolio. Includes bibliographical references. [NK4640.C6U5 fasc. 13] 77-112993 ISBN 0-691-03535-0
1. Vases, Greek—Catalogs. I. Phillips, Kyle Meridith, joint author. II. Ella Riegel Memorial Museum. III. Title. IV. Series: Corpus vasorum antiquorum. United States of America, fasc. 13

HOPPIN, Joseph Clark, 1870-1925. 738.3'82'0938
A handbook of Attic red-figured vases, signed by or attributed to the various masters of the sixth and fifth centuries B.C. Washington, McGrath Pub. Co., 1973 [c1919] 2 v. illus. 24 cm. Reprint of the ed. published by Harvard University Press, Cambridge, Mass. [NK4649.H6 1973] 71-119265 ISBN 0-8434-0135-4
1. Vases, Greek—Catalogs. I. Title.

NEUMAYER, Heinrich, 738.3'82'0938
Greek vase-painting. Tr. by J. R. Foster. With 20 colour illus. New York, Crown [1967] 56p. illus., 20 col. plates. 19cm. (Movements in world art) Tr. of Griechische Vasen. Bibl. [NK4645.N493 1967] 67-15643 .95 pap.,
1. Vases, Greek — Catalogs. I. Title.

TOLEDO. Museum of Art. 738.3'82'093 s
The Toledo Museum of Art / Cedric G. Boulter and Kurt T. Luckner. Toledo : The Museum, c1976. 1 portfolio (55 p., 60 leaves of plates) : ill. ; 33 cm. (Corpus vasorum antiquorum : United States of America ; fasc. 17 : The Toledo Museum of Art ; fasc. 1) At head of title: Union academique internationale. Includes bibliographical references and index. [NK4640.C6U5 fasc. 17, fol.] [NK4623.T57] 738.3'82'0938074017113 77-12415
1. Toledo. Museum of Art. 2. Vases, Greek—Catalogs. 3. Vases—Ohio—Toledo—Catalogs. I. Boulter, Cedric G., 1912- II. Luckner, Kurt T. III. Series: Corpus vasorum antiquorum : United States of America : fasc. 17.

Vases, Greek—Corinth, Greece.

AMYX, Darrell Arlynn, 1911- 938'.7 s
Archaic Corinthian pottery and the Anaploga well / by D. A. Amyx and Patricia Lawrence. Princeton, N.J. : American School of Classical Studies at Athens, 1974. p. cm. (Corinth, results of excavations conducted by the American School of Classical Studies at Athens ; v. 7, pt. 2) Includes bibliographical references and indexes. [DF261.C65A6 vol. 7, Pt. 2] [NK4647] 738.3'82'09387 75-4551 ISBN 0-87661-072-6
1. Vases, Greek—Corinth, Greece. 2. Vases—Corinth, Greece. 3. Corinth, Greece—Antiquities. I. Lawrence, Patricia, 1934- joint author. II. Title. III. Series: American School of Classical Studies at Athens. Corinth ; v. 7, pt. 2. BIP

Vases, Greek—Exhibitions.

BUITRON, Diana M. 738.3'82'0938507401444
Attic vase painting in New England collections, by Diana M. Buitron. [Cambridge, Mass.] Fogg Art Museum, Harvard University [1972] 152 p. illus. 22 x 25 cm. Errata slip inserted. Catalog of an exhibition held at the Fogg Art Museum March 1-Apr. 5, 1972. Includes bibliographies. [NK4623.C3H32] 70-189142
1. Vases, Greek—Exhibitions. 2. Vases, Greek—New England. I. Harvard University. William Hayes Fogg Art Museum. II. Title.

Vases, Greek—Greece.

COHEN, Beth. 738.3'82'09385
Attic bilingual vases and their painters / Beth Cohen. New York : Garland Pub., 1978. p. cm. (Outstanding dissertations in the fine arts) Originally presented as the author's thesis, New York University, 1977. Includes index. Bibliography: p. [NK4649.5.A86 1978] 77-94689 ISBN 0-8240-3220-9 : lib.bdg. : 65.00
1. Vases, Greek—Greece. 2. Vase painters—Greece. 3. Vase-painting, Greek. I. Title. II. Series. BIP

Vases—London—Catalogs.

OXFORD. University. Ashmolean Museum. Dept. of Antiquities 738.3
Select exhibition of Sir John and Lady Beazley's gifts to the Ashmolean Museum, 1912-1966. London, Oxford Univ. Pr., for the Ashmolean Mus., 1967. 188p. 84 plates. 25cm. The published writings of Sir John Beazley: p. 177-188. [NK4623.O8A5] 67-87519 6.40 pap.,
1. Vases—London—Catalogs. 2. Pottery—London—Catalogs. I. Beazley, John Davidson, Sir 1885- II. Beazley, Marie Bloomfield, Lady. III. Title. Available from the publisher's New York Office.

Vases—Lucania.

TRENDALL, Arthur Dale, 1909- 738.3'82'09377
The red-figured vases of Lucania, Campania and Sicily, by A. D. Trendall, Oxford, Clarendon Pr., 1967. 2v 29cm. (Oxford monographs on classical archaeology) Bibl. [NK4649.T72] 67-97297 50.40 set
1. Vases—Lucania. 2. Vases—Campania. 3. Vases—Sicily. I. Title. II. Series. Available from Oxford Univ. Pr., New York. BIP

Vases—New York (City)—Catalogs.

NEW York, Metropolitan Museum of Art 738.382
Inscribed Hadra vases in the Metropolitan Museum of Art [by] Brian F. Cook. New York. Author [c.1966] 36, [19]p. illus., port. 32cm. (New York, Metropolitan Mus. of art Papers. no. 12) Catalog of a collection given to the mus. in 1890 by E. E. Farman. Bibl. [NK4623.N55N4] 66-12766 8.50; 5.00 pap.,
1. Vases—New York (City)—Catalogs. 2. Vases, Greek. I. Cook, Brain F. II. Farman, Elbert Eli, 1831-1911. III. Title. IV. Series.

Vases—Reading. Eng.

URE, Percy Neville, 1879-1950. v. 12
University of Reading, by Percy Neville Ure and Annie Dunman Ure. Published for the British Academy and the University of Reading. London, Oxford University Press, 1954- v. plates. 33cm. (Corpus vasorum antiquorum. Great Britain, fasc, 12-Reading fasc. 1-) (Series Corpus vasorum antiquorum, Great Britain, fasc. 12etc.) At head of title: Union academique internationale. issued in portfolio. [NK4640.C6G7 fasc.12] A55
1. Vases—Reading. Eng. I. Reading, Eng. University. II. Ure, Annie Dunman (Hunt) III. Title. IV. Series.

Vases, Roman.

CALLENDER, M. H. 738.382093
Roman amphorae, with index of stamps. New York, Oxford [c.]1965 xxix, 323p. illus., maps, plates. 29cm. (Univ. of Durham pubns.) Title (Series: Durham, Eng. University. Publications) [NK4654.C3] 65-9789 33.60
1. Vases, Roman. I. Title. II. Series.

CALLENDER M H 738.382093
Roman amphorae, with index of stamps, by M. H. Callender. London, New York, Oxford University Press, 1965. xxix, 323 p. illus., maps, plates. 29 cm. (University of Durham publications) "Abbreviations and bibliography": p. [xi]-sviii. [NK4654.C3] 65-9789
1. Vases, Roman. I. Title. II. Series. III. Series: Durham, Eng. University. Publications

Vassos, John, 1898—

VASSOS, John, 1898- 759.13
Contempo, Phobia, and other graphic interpretations / John Vassos ; with a foreword by P. K. Thomajan. New York : Dover Publications, 1976. xi, 115 p. : chiefly ill. ; 31 cm. (Dover art collections) [NC975.5.V37A43 1976] 76-696 ISBN 0-486-23338-3 pbk. : 4.50
1. Vassos, John, 1898- I. Title. BIP

Vatican.

IPSER, Karl. 709.456
Vatican art; with 160 illus. Translated from the German 'Die Kunstwerke des Vatikans' by Doireann MacDermott. New York, Philosophical Library [1953] 198p. illus. 25cm. [N2940.I413] 53-11503
1. Vatican. 2. Art—Rome. 3. Christian art and symbolism. I. Title.

LETAROUILLY, Paul Marie 1795-1885 726.640945632
The Vatican buildings [2v. in one] Pref. by A. E. Richardson. London, A. Tiranti [dist. Hollywood-by-the-Sea, Fla., Transatlantic, 1964, c.]1963. (various p.) plates, diagrs., plans. 29cm. (Precepts of art, 4) English and French. Contents.contents—1. The Pontifical Palace. 2. Belvedere. 3. Loggias. 4. Stanze. 5. Villa Pia. 6. Clementino and Chiaramonti. 7. Piazza of St. Peter. A54 19.50
1. Vatican. 2. Architecture—Rome. I. Title. II. Series.

NOGARA, Bartolomeo, 1868- 709.456
Art treasures of the Vatican. New York, Tudor Pub. Co. [1950] 308 p. illus. (part col.) 28 cm. English, Spanish, French, and Italian. [N2940.N59] 50-10579
1. Vatican. 2. Art — Rome. 3. Christian art and symbolism. I. Title.

Vatican. Biblioteca vaticana. Museo sacro.

MATT, Leonard von. 708.56'34
Art treasures of the Vatican Library. [Photos. by] Leonard von Matt. Text by Georg Daltrop and Adriano Prandi. [Translated by Robert Allen] New York, H. N. Abrams [1970] 182 p. illus. (part col.) 33 cm. Translation of Die Kunstsammlungen der Biblioteca apostolica vaticana Rom. Relates to the collections of the Museo sacro and of the Museo profano. [N2941.M313] 74-125782 ISBN 8-10-905280-
1. Vatican. Biblioteca vaticana. Museo sacro. 2. Vatican. Biblioteca vaticana. Museo profano. I. Daltrop, Georg. II. Prandi, Adriano. III. Title.

Vatican. Cappella paolina.

DE TOLNAY, Charles [Name originally: Vagujhelyi Tolnai Karoly.] 709.45
The final period: Last Judgment, frescoes of the Pauline Chapel, last Pietas. Princeton, N.J., Princeton University Press, [c.]1960. 271p. bBibliography: p.231-[236] plates. 31cm. (His Michelangelo, 5) 58-7125 30.00 buck.,
1. Buonarroti, Michel Angelo, 1475-1564. 2. Vatican. Cappella paolina. 3. Vatican, Cappela sistina. I. Title.

Vatican. Cappella sistina.

BUONARROTI, Michel Angelo, 1475-1564. 759.5
The Sistine Chapel. [Text by] D. Redig de Campos. New York, Reynal [1963] [11] p., 44 plates (18 col.) 41 cm. [ND623.B92R413] 64-2991
1. Vatican. Cappella sistina. I. Redig de Campos, Dioclecio.

FEIN, H. Otto, 1913- illus. 726.60945632
The Sistine Chapel before Michelangelo; religious imagery and papal primacy. Photos of the frescoes by H. O. Fein. Oxford, Clarendon Pr. [New York, Oxford, c.]1965. xiii, 128p. illus. 44 plates. 29cm. (Oxford-Warburg studies) Bibl. [N2950.E8] 65-9047 12.00
1. Vatican. Cappella sistina. 2. Mural painting and decoration—Vatican City. I. Fein, H. Otto, illus. II. Title.

HOHL, Reinhold 759.5634
The Sistine Chapel; the frescoes of the Sistine Chapel in Rome English tr. by Britta M. Charleston [New York, Taplinger, c.1966] 16p. 31 col. plates. 19cm. (Orbis pictus, 16/17) [NA2950. H613] 66-2011 3.25 bds.,
1. Vatican. Cappella sistina 2. Mural painting and decoration—Vatican City. I. Title.

SUBJECT INDEX VELAZQUEZ, DIEGO RODRIGUEZ

SALVINI, Roberto. 708.456'34
The Sistine Chapel. Text by Roberto Salvini. Appendix by Ettore Camesasca. With an essay by C. L. Ragghianti. New York, H. N. Abrams [1971] 2 v. illus. (part col.), plans, col. plates (part fold.) 41 cm. Issued in case. Translation of La Cappella sistina in Vaticano. Contents.Contents.—v. 1. Text and illustrations.—v. 2. Plates. Bibliography: v. 1, p. 298-[304] [N2950.S313] 77-117512 ISBN 0-8109-0479-9
1. Vatican. Cappella sistina. 2. Mural painting and decoration—Vatican City. I. Camesasca, Ettore, 1922-

TURCIO, Genesio 759.5
The Sistine Chapel. Tr. [from Italian] by Gino Veloccia. Rome, A. Belardetti [dist. New York, Heinman, 1963] 15p. 43 plates (pt. fold., pt. col.) 30cm. (Art and faith visions, 1) 63-25306 6.00 bds.,
1. Vatican. Cappella sistina. 2. Mural painting and decoration—Vatican City I. Title. II. Series.

Vatican City. Casino di Pio IV.

SMITH, Graham, 726'.5'0945634
1942-
The Casino of Pius IV / Graham Smith. Princeton, N.J. : Princeton University Press, c1976. p. cm. Includes index. Bibliography: p. [N6920.S54] 76-3017 ISBN 0-691-03915-1 : 20.00
1. Vatican City. Casino di Pio IV. 2. Stucco—Italy—Vatican City. 3. Mural painting and decoration, Renaissance—Vatican City. 4. Mural painting and decoration—Vatican City. 5. Symbolims in art—Vatican City. I. Title. BIP

Vatican City. Colonna di Antonino Pio.

VOGEL, Lise. 731'.76'0945634
The column of Antoninus Pius. Cambridge, Harvard University Press, 1973. xiv, 220 p. illus. 20 x 28 cm. (Loeb classical monographs) Revision of the author's thesis, Harvard, 1968. [NA9340.V3V63 1973] 74-173409 ISBN 0-674-14325-6 16.00
1. Vatican City. Colonna di Antonino Pio. I. Title. II. Series. BIP

Vatican City. San Peitro in Vaticano (Basilica)

MATT, Leonard von 726.582
St. Peter's. Introd. by Dieter von Balthasar. New York, Universe [1962] xi p. illus. 29cm. (His Roma ser.) 62-12008 4.75
1. Vatican City. San Peitro in Vaticano (Basilica) I. Balthasar, Dieter von. II. Title.

Vatican City. San Pietro in Vaticano (Basilica)

BERGERE, Thea. 726.50945634
The story of St. Peter's [by] Thea and Richard Bergere. Illustrated with photos., prints, and with drawings by Richard Bergere. New York, Dodd, Mead [1966] 128 p. illus., plans. 28 cm. Bibliography: p. 123. [NA5620.S9B4] 66-9799
1. Vatican City. San Pietro in Vaticano (Basilica) I. Bergere, Richard, joint author. II. Title.

LAVIN, Irving, 1927- 730'.924
Bernini and the crossing of Saint Peter's. New York, Published for the College Art Association of America, by New York University Press, 1968. vii, 94 p. illus., plans. 28 cm. (Monographs on archaeology and the fine arts, 17) Includes bibliographical references. [NA1123.B5L3] 68-22570
1. Bernini, Giovanni Lorenzo, 1598-1680. 2. Vatican City. San Pietro in Vaticano (Basilica) I. The College Art Association of America. II. Title. III. Series.

LEES-MILNE, James. 726'.6'0945634
Saint Peter's; the story of Saint Peter's Basilica in Rome. Boston, Little, Brown [1967] 336 p. illus., col. plates 26 cm. Bibliography: p. 328. [DG816.3L4 1967b] 67-16263
1. Vatican City. San Pietro in Vaticano (Basilica) I. Title.

TOYNBEE, Jocelyn M C 726.82
The shrine of St. Peter and the Vatican excavations, by Jocelyn Toynbee and John Ward Perkins. London, New York, Longmans, Green [1956] xxii, 293 p. plates, plans. 26 cm. [NA5620.S9T6] 56-1914
1. Peter, Saint, apostle — Tomb. 2. Vatican City. San Pietro in Vaticano (Basilica) I. Ward-Perkins, John Bryan, 1912- joint author. II. Title.

TOYNBEE, Jocelyn M C 726.82
The shrine of St. Peter and the Vatican excavations, by Jocelyn Toynbee and John Ward Perkins. New York, Pantheon Books [1957] xxii, 293 p. plates, plans. 26 cm. Includes bibliographical references. [NA5620.S9T6] 56-13363
1. Peter, Saint, apostle — Tomb. 2. Vatican City. San Pietro in Vaticano (Basilica) I. Ward-Perkins, John Bryan, 1912- joint author. II. Title. BIP

TOYNBEE, Jocelyn MC 726.82
The shrine of St. Peter and the Vatican excavations, by Jocelyn Toynbee and John Ward Perkins. London, New York, Longmans, Green [1956] xxii, 293p. plates plans. 26cm. [NA5620.S9T6] 56-1914
1. Vatican City. San Pietro in Vaticano (Bastilca) 2. Peter, Saint, apostle—Tomb. I. Ward-Perkins, John Bryan, 1912- joint author. II. Title.

Vatican. Loggie.

RAPHAEL, 1483-1520. 759.5
The Raphael Bible [compiled by] Rumer Godden. New York, Viking Press [1970] 248 p. illus. (part col.), geneal. tables, maps, ports. 17 x 25 cm. (A Studio book) Bible passages taken from the Knox translation. Includes bibliographical references. [ND623.R2G58] 70-101783 ISBN 0-670-58943-8 8.95
1. Vatican. Loggie. 2. Bible—Pictures, illustrations, etc. I. Godden, Rumer, 1907- II. Title.

Vaults (Architecture)

WARD, Clarence, 1884- 726'.59
Mediaeval church vaulting. Princeton, Princeton University Press, 1915. [New York, AMS Press, 1973] ix, 192 p. illus. 24 cm. Original ed. issued as no. 5 of Princeton monographs in art and archaeology. Bibliography: p. 185-186. [NA5453.W3 1973] 72-177847 ISBN 0-404-06836-7 10.00
1. Vaults (Architecture) 2. Church architecture. 3. Architecture, Medieval. I. Title. II. Series: Princeton monographs in art and archaeology, 5. BIP

Vegetable carving.

WEINBERG, Julia. 745'.59'43
Gourmet bouquet / Julia Weinberg. New York : Butterick Pub., c1978. 159 p., [6] leaves of plates : ill. (some col.) ; 27 cm. [TX652.W38] 77-608283 ISBN 0-88421-042-1 : 9.95
1. Vegetable carving. 2. Artificial flowers. I. Title. BIP

Vehicles in art—Juvenile literature.

AMES, Lee J. 743'.8'93805
Draw 50 vehicles : selections from Draw 50 boats, ships, trucks, and trains and Draw 50 airplanes, aircraft, and spacecraft / by Lee J. Cramer Garden City, N.Y. : Doubleday, 1978. p. cm. "A Zephyr book." Step-by-step instructions for drawing 50 different vehicles. [NC825.V4A46] 77-94862 ISBN 0-385-14154-8 pbk. : 1.95
1. Vehicles in art—Juvenile literature. 2. Drawing—Instruction—Juvenile literature. I. Title.

Vehicles—Pictorial works.

CURRO, Evelyn Malone. 769'.924
The American eye of Evelyn Curro. Foreword by Evelyn Curro. New York, Chelsea House, 1970. xiii, xvi p. 87 plates (part col.) 24 x 32 cm. [N6537.C8A42] 79-111924 25.00
1. Vehicles—Pictorial works. I. Title.

Velarde, Pablita, 1918- —Juvenile literature.

NELSON, Mary Carroll. 759.13 B
Pablita Velarde. Minneapolis, Dillon Press [1971] 58 p. illus. 24 cm. A biography of a Pueblo Indian artist whose prize winning-work reflects the heritage of the American Indian. [E99.T35V45] 92 77-140992 ISBN 0-87518-037-X
1. Velarde, Pablita, 1918- —Juvenile literature. I. Title. BIP

Velazquez, Diego Rodriguez de Silva y, 1599-1660.

BERUETE, Aureliano de, 759.6
1845-1912.
Velazquez, by Aureliano de Beruete y Moret. [Translated by Hugh E. Poynter] Freeport, N.Y., Books for Libraries Press [1971] xxxi, 172 p. illus. 27 cm. "First published 1906." "List of authentic paintings by Velazquez, arranged according to countries and galleries": p. 149-156. [ND813.V4B513 1971] 77-37330 ISBN 0-8369-6677-5
1. Velazquez, Diego Rodriguez de Silva y, 1599-1660.

BROWN, Dale. 759.6
The world of Velazquez, 1599-1660, by Dale Brown and the editors of Time-Life Books. New York, Time-Life Books [1969] 192 p. illus. (part col.), map, ports. (part col.) 31 cm. (Time-Life library of art) Bibliography: p. 187. [ND813.V4B88] 77-84575
1. Velazquez, Diego Rodriguez de Silva y, 1599-1660. I. Time-Life Books. II. Title. BIP

GUDIOL i Ricart, Josep. 759.6
Velazquez, 1599-1660 / by Jose Gudiol; translated from the Spanish by Kenneth Lyons. New York : Viking Press, 1974. 355 p. : ill. (some col.) ; 30 cm. (A Studio book) Includes indexes. Bibliography: p. 353-355. [ND813.V4G8213 1974b] 74-7000 ISBN 0-670-74394-1 : 45.00
1. Velazquez, Diego Rodriguez de Silva y, 1599-1660. I. Velazquez, Diego Rodriguez de Silva y, 1599-1660.

KAHR, Madlyn Millner. 759.6 B
Velazquez : the art of painting / Madlyn Millner Kahr. 1st ed. New York : Harper & Row, c1976. xii, 233 p. : ill. ; 24 cm. (Icon editions) Includes index. Bibliography: p. [221]-225. [ND813.V4K24 1976] 75-39563 ISBN 0-06-433575-5 : 12.50
1. Velazquez, Diego Rodriguez de Silva y, 1599-1660. 2. Painters—Spain—Biography.

LAFUENTE Ferrari, Enrique. 759.6
Velazquez; biographical and critical study. Translated by James Emmons from the French version of the original Spanish. Lausanne] Skira; [distributed in the U.S. by World Pub. Co., Cleveland, 1960] 128 p. mounted col. illus., port. 19 cm. (The Taste of our time, v. 33) Bibliography: p. 117-[120] [ND813.V4L33] 60-8731
1. Velazquez, Diego Rodriguez de Silva y, 1599-1660.

LOPEZ-REY, Jose. 759.6
Velazquez' work and world. Greenwich, Conn., New York Graphic Society [1968] 172 p. illus. (part col.) 29 cm. Includes bibliographies. [ND813.V4L627 1968b] 70-5436 20.00
1. Velazquez, Diego Rodriguez de Silva y, 1599-1660. I. Title.

MULLER, Joseph Emile. 759.6 B
Velazquez / Joseph-Emile Muller. London : Thames and Hudson, 1976. 264 p. : ill. (some col.) ; 21 cm. "Translated from the French by Jane Brenton." Includes index. Bibliography: p. 251. [ND813.V4M7413 1976b] 76-380215 ISBN 0-500-18152-7 : £3.95
1. Velazquez, Diego Rodriguez de Silva y, 1599-1660.

MULLER, Joseph Emile. 759.6 B
Velazquez / Joseph-Emile Muller ; [translated from the French by Jane Brenton]. London : Thames and Hudson, 1976. 264 p. : ill. (some col.) ; 22 cm. Translation of Velazquez. Label mounted on t.p.: Transatlantic Arts, Levittown, N.Y. sole distributor for the U.S.A. Includes index. Bibliography: p. 251. [ND813.V4M7413 1976] 76-378650 ISBN 0-500-18152-7 : 12.95 ISBN 0-500-20147-1 pbk. : 6.95
1. Velazquez, Diego Rodriguez de Silva y, 1599-1660. 2. Painters—Spain—Biography.

ORTEGA y Gasset, Jose, 759.6
1883-1955.
Velazquez, Goya and the dehumanization of art. Translated by Alexis Brown. With an introd. by Philip Troutman. New York, W. W. Norton [1972] 142 p. illus. 26 cm. Bibliography: p. 137. [ND813.V4O69413 1972] 74-177440 ISBN 0-393-04358-4 17.50
1. Velazquez, Diego Rodriguez de Silva y, 1599-1660. 2. Goya y Lucientes, Francisco Jose de, 1746-1828. 3. Art—Philosophy. I. Title.

PICASSO, Pablo, 1881- 759.6
Picasso: variations on Velazquez' painting "The maids of honor" and other recent works. With a personal reflection by Jaime Sabartes. New York, H. N. Abrams [1959] [24] p., 58 col. plates., mounted illus. (part col.) 39 cm. Translation of Les menines et la vie. [ND553.P5S3173] 59-8095
1. Velazquez, Diego Rodriguez de Silva y, 1599-1660. I. Sabartes, Jaime, 1881- II. Title: Variations on Velazquez' painting "The maids of honor."

RIPLEY, Elizabeth 759.6
Velazquez, a biography. Philadelphia, Lippincott [c.1965] 72p. illus. 27cm. Bibl. [ND813.V4R55] 65-21846 3.75; 3.69 lib. ed.,
1. Velazquez, Diego Rodriguez de Silva y, 1599-1660. I. Title.

RIPLEY, Elizabeth, 1906- 759.6
Velazquez, a biography. [1st ed.] Philadelphia, Lippincott [1965] 72 p. illus. 26 cm. Bibliography: p. 70. [ND813.V4R55] 65-21846
1. Velazquez, Diego Rodriguez de Silva y, 1599-1660. I. Title.

SERULLAZ, Maurice. 759.6
Velazquez / text by Maurice Serullaz, with the collaboration of Christian Pouillon. New York : H. N. Abrams, [1978] p. cm. (The Library of great painters) Includes index. Bibliography: p. [ND813.V4S4513] 78-2555 ISBN 0-8109-1712-2 : 25.00
1. Velazquez, Diego Rodriguez de Silva y, 1599-1660. I. Pouillon, Christian, joint author.

SUTTON, Denys. 759.6
Diego Velasquez. New York, Barnes & Noble [1967, c1966] 89 p. 54 illus. (part col.) 18 cm. (Barnes & Noble art series, no. 627) [ND813.V4S95] 67-3091
1. Velazquez, Diego Rodriguez de Silva y, 1599-1660. I. Title.

VELAZQUEZ, Diego Rodriguez 759.6
de Silva y, 1599-1660.
Diego Velazquez. Text by Margaretta Salinger. New York, H. N. Abrams [1970] 24 p. illus. 33 cm. (The Library of great painters. Portfolio ed.) [ND813.V4S27 1970] 69-14764
I. Salinger, Margaretta M., 1907-

VELAZQUEZ, Diego Rodriguez 759.6
de Silva y, 1599-1660.
Diego Velazquez (1599-1660) Text by Margaretta Salinger. New York, H. N. Abrams in association with Pocket Books [1954] [74] p. 43illus. (part col.) 18cm. (The Pocket library of great art, A19) An Abrams art book. Bibliography: p. [74] [ND813.V4S275] [ND813.V4S275] 927.5 54-14622 54-14622
I. Salinger, Margaretta. II. Title.

VELAZQUEZ, Diego Rodriguez 759.6
de Silva y 1599-1660
Velazquez, by Xavier de Salas. [New York] Phaidon dist. Greenwich, Conn., N. Y. Graphic [c.1962] 75p. 51 col. plates. 32cm. 62-51949 5.95
I. Salas, Xavier de. II. Title.

VELAZQUEZ, Diego 759.6
Rodriguez de Silva y, 1599-1660.
Velazquez. [Prepared under the direction of Alfred E. Herzer. Selection of the

reproductions by F. J. Sanchez Canton. The introd. and interleaving texts were written by Jose Ortega y Gasset. Translation by C. David Ley] New York, Random House [1953] lxxxiii p. 105 plates (part col.) 29 cm. [ND813.V4O68] 53-9707
1. Ortega y Gasset, Jose, 1883-1955.

WHITE, Jon Ewbank 759.6 B
Manchip, 1924-
Diego Velazquez; painter and courtier, by Jon Manchip White. Chicago, Rand McNally [1969] xxiii, 180 p. illus., ports. (part col.) 23 cm. Bibliography: p. 173-174. [ND813.V4W6 1969b] 69-11132 6.95
1. Velazquez, Diego Rodriguez de Silva y, 1599-1660.

Velazquez, Diego Rodriguez de Silva y, 1599-1660—Juvenile literature.

RABOFF, Ernest Lloyd. 759.6
Diego Rodriguez de Silva y Velasquez, by Ernest Raboff. Edited by Bradley Smith. Garden City, N.Y., Doubleday [1970] [31] p. illus. (part col.), ports. (part col.) 29 cm. (Art for children) (A Gemini Smith book.) A brief biographical sketch of the sixteenth-century Spanish painter accompanies color reproductions and discussions of some of his works. [ND813.V18R3] 74-121783 3.95
1. Velazquez, Diego Rodriguez de Silva y, 1599-1660—Juvenile literature. I. Title.

Velde, Willem van de, 1610 or 11-1693.

GREENWICH, Eng. National 741.91
Maritime Museum.
Van de Velde drawings; a catalogue of drawings in the National Maritime Museum made by the elder and the younger Willem Van de Velde. Cambridge [Eng.] University Press, 1958. ix, 450 p. illus., coats of arms. 32 cm. [NC1055.V4G7 1958] 58-14763
1. Velde, Willem van de, 1610 or 11-1693. 2. Velde, Willem van de, 1633-1707. 3. Ships in art. I. Title.

Velvet.

BURNHAM, Harold B 746.1
Chinese velvets, a technical study. Toronto, University of Toronto Press, 1959. 64p. illus. 26cm. (Art and Archaeology Division, Royal Ontario Museum, Toronto. Occasional paper 2) Bibliographical references included in 'Notes' (p. 26-29) [NK8983.B8] 60-38974
1. Velvet. 2. Textile industry and fabrics—China. I. Title. II. Series: Toronto. Royal Ontario Museum. Art and Archaeology Division. Occasional paper 2

Venice. Biennale d'arte.

ALLOWAY, Lawrence, 1926- 708.5'31
The Venice Biennale, 1895-1968; from salon to goldfish bowl. Greenwich, Conn., New York Graphic Society [1968] 202 p. 95 illus. 24 cm. Bibliography: p. 191. [N5073.V4A7] 68-13051 7.50
1. Venice. Biennale d'arte. I. Title.

Venice. Chiesa del Redentore.

TIMOFIEWITSCH, 726'.5'094531
Wladimir.
The Chiesa del Redentore [by] Wladimir Timofiewitsch. University Park, Pennsylvania State University Press [1971] 78, [99] p. illus. (part col.), plans. 35 cm. (Corpus Palladianum, v. 3) Bibliography: p. [71]-72. [NA5621.V43T5313] 76-79838 ISBN 0-271-00090-2 17.50
1. Venice. Chiesa del Redentore. I. Title. II. Series. BIP

Venice — Descr. — Views.

BRUNETTI, Mario. 709.45
Venice; text by Mario Brunetti [and others] Translated by James Emmons. [New York] Skira [1956] 153 p. mounted col. illus. 19 cm. (The Taste of our time, 17) [ND621.V5V42] 56-7922
1. Venice — Descr. — Views. 2. Paintings. 3. Painting — Venice — Hist. I. Title.

BUSSE, Fritz 741.943
Venice; impressions drawn by Fritz Busse. Written by A. Hyatt Mayor. New York, Arts, inc. [667 Madison Ave., 1961] 79p. illus. (part col.) 23x24cm. (Golden Griffin books) 60-15645 5.95 bds.,
1. Venice—Descr.—Views. I. Mayor, Alpheus Hyatt, 1901- II. Title.

Venice—Description—Views.

VENICE; 709.45
text by Mario Brunetti [and others] Translated by James Emmons. [New York] Skira [1956] 153 p. mounted col. illus. 19 cm. (The Taste of our time, 17) [ND621.V5V42] 56-7922
1. Venice—Description—Views. 2. Paintings. 3. Painting—Venice—History. I. Brunetti, Mario.

Venice in art.

CANAL, Antonio, called 769'.924
Canaletto, 1697-1768.
Views of Venice, by Canaletto. Engr. by Antonio Visentini. Introd. and descriptive texts by J. G. Links. New York, Dover Publications [1971] 90 p. illus., facsims., map, ports. 35 cm. "Contains all 38 views ... originally published ... 1742, in the work variously titled Prospectus magni canalis Venetiarum ... and Urbis Venetiarum prospectus celebriores ..." Includes bibliographical references. [NE1714.C27] 77-113990 ISBN 0-486-22627-1
1. Venice in art. I. Visentini, Antonio, 1688-1782. II. Links, J. G. III. Title.

Venice—Palaces.

LAURITZEN, Peter. 728.8'2'094531
Palaces of Venice / Peter Lauritzen, Alexander Zielcke. New York : Viking Press, [1978] p. cm. (A Studio book) Includes index. Bibliography: p. [NA7755.L34] 78-9018 ISBN 0-670-53724-1 : 35.00
1. Venice—Palaces. I. Zielcke, Alexander, 1945- joint author. II. Title. BIP

Venice. Palazzo ducale.

PIGNATTI, Terisio, 1920- 728.82
The Doges Palace. New York, Reynal; [distributed by] Morrow [1965] 11 p., 88 plates (part col.) 41 cm. Bibliography: p. 11. [NA7756.V5P5] 65-28964
1. Venice. Palazzo ducale.

Venice. Palazzo ducale. Arco Foscari.

PINCUS, Debra. 725'.96
The Arco Foscari : the building of a triumphal gateway in fifteenth century Venice / Debra Pincus. New York : Garland Pub., 1976. xii, 574 p. : ill. ; 21 cm. (Outstanding dissertations in the fine arts) Reprint of the author's thesis, New York University, 1974. Bibliography: p. 462-482. [NA9370.V46P56 1976] 75-23808 ISBN 0-8240-2002-2 lib.bdg. : 21.00
1. Venice. Palazzo ducale. Arco Foscari. I. Title. II. Series.

Venice. San Marco (Basilica)

TOESCA, Pietro, *738.5 729.7
1877-
Mosaics of St. Mark's. Text by Pietro Toesca and Ferdinando forlati. [Translated by Joyce Templeton and Gustina Scaglia] Greenwich, Conn., New York Graphic Society [1958] 50, [4] p. illus. (part mounted col.) 41 col. plates. 39 cm. [The Great masters of the past, 5] Bibliography: p. [51] [NA5621.V5T6] 58-5316
1. Venice. San Marco (Basilica) 2. Mosaics. I. Foriati, Ferdinando. II. Title. III. Series.

YAGER, Rosemary, 1909- 733.3
The four bronze horses. Woodcuts by Charles H. Joslin. Caldwell, Idaho, Caxton Printers, 1959. 224 p. illus. 22 cm. [NA5621.V5Y2] 58-5329
1. Venice. San Marco (Basilica) 2. Sculpture, Greek. 3. Bronzes, Greek. I. Title.

Venturi and Rauch.

VENTURI and Rauch. 728.3'7
Vanna Venturi house, Chestnut Hill, Philadelphia, Pennsylvania, 1962 : Peter Brant house, Greenwich, Connecticut, 1973 : Carll Tucker III house, Westchester County, New York, 1975 / Venturi and Rauch ; edited and photographed by Yukio Futagawa ; text by Paul Goldberger. Tokyo : A.D.A. Edita, 1976. 40 p. : ill. (some col.), plans : 37 cm. (Global architecture ; 39) Title also in Japanese. Text in English and Japanese. [NA737.V46F87] 76-377426
1. Venturi and Rauch. 2. Carll Tucker III house, New York (State) 3. Philadelphia. Vanna Venturi house. 4. Greenwich, Conn. Peter Brandt house. I. Futagawa, Yukio, 1932- II. Goldberger, Paul. III. Title.

Venus (Goddess)—Art.

BRINKERHOFF, 731'.88'92211
Dericksen M.
Hellenistic statues of Aphrodite : studies in the history of their stylistic development / by Dericksen Morgan Brinkerhoff. New York : Garland Pub., 1978. p. cm. (Outstanding disserations in the fine arts) Originally presented as the author's thesis, Harvard, 1958. Bibliography: p. [NB163.V5B74 1978] 77-94688 ISBN 0-8240-3217-9 : lib.bdg. : 20.00
1. Venus (Goddess)—Art. 2. Sculpture, Hellenistic. I. Title. II. Series. BIP

Verdak, George—Art collections.

†ERAS of the dance : 760
the George Verdak Collection, Montgomery Museum of Fine Arts, December 10, 1976, through January 13, 1977, Huntsville Museum of Art, April 11, 1976, through May 22, 1976. [Montgomery, Ala] : Montgomery Museum of Fine Arts, c1976. 90 p. : ill. ; 24 cm. On spine: The George Verdak Collection. Exhibition catalog. [N8217.B35E73] 76-52823 ISBN 0-89280-004-6 pbk. : 6.50
1. Verdak, George—Art collections. 2. Ballet in art—Exhibitions. 3. Art—Exhibitions. I. Montgomery Museum of Fine Arts. II. Huntsville Museum of Art. III. Title: The George Verdak Collection.

Vereinigung Bildender Kunstler "Wiener Secession."

POWELL, Nicolas. 709'.436'13
The sacred spring : the arts in Vienna, 1898-1918 / by Nicolas Powell ; with an introd. to the cultural background by Adolf Opel. Greenwich, Conn. : New York Graphic Society, 1974. 224 p. : ill. (some col.) ; 29 cm. Includes bibliographical references and index. [NX600.W53P68 1974] 74-78460 ISBN 0-8212-0619-2 : 25.00
1. Vereinigung Bildender Kunstler "Wiener Secession." 2. Arts—Vienna. I. Title.

VERGO, Peter. 709'.436'13
Art in Vienna 1898-1918 : Klimt, Kokoschka, Schiele and their contemporaries / Peter Vergo. London : Phaidon, 1975. 256 p. : ill. (some col.) ; 29 cm. Distributed in the U.S.A. by Praeger Publishers, Inc., New York. Includes index. Bibliography: p. 250-251. [NX600.W53V47 1975] 75-722 ISBN 0-7148-1600-0 : 27.50
1. Vereinigung Bildender Kunstler "Wiener Secession." 2. Arts, Modern—20th century—Vienna.

WAISSENBERGER, Robert. 709'.04
Vienna Secession / Robert Waissenberger. New York : Rizzoli, 1977. 144 p. : ill. (some col.) ; 32 cm. Translation of Die Wiener Secession. Includes indexes. Bibliography: p. 121-123. [N6494.5.W5W3413 1977] 77-76929 ISBN 0-8478-0114-4 : 35.00
1. Vereinigung Bildender Kunstler "Wiener Secession." I. Title. BIP

Verlys of America, inc.

MCPEEK, Carole. 748.2'9171'54
Verlys of America decorative glass, 1935-1951 [by] Carole and Wayne McPeek. 1st ed. Newark, Ohio, Printed by Newark Leader Print. Co. [1972] 66 p. illus. 19 x 26 cm. [NK5198.V4M3] 72-189964 7.50
1. Verlys of America, inc. 2. Glassware, American—Catalogs. I. McPeek, Wayne, joint author. II. Title. BIP

Vermeer, Johannes, 1632-1675.

BRION, Marcel, 1895- 759.9492
Vermeer. [Tr. from French by Sally Marks] New York, Abrams [1963] 87p. illus. 19cm. 63-8670 1.95
1. Vermeer, Johannes, 1632-1675. I. Title.

GOWING, Lawrence. 759.9492
Vermeer / by Lawrence Gowing. New ed. New York : Harper & Row, c1970. 160 p., [40] leaves of plates : ill. ; 23 cm. (Icon editions ; IN-66) Includes index. [ND653.V5G6 1970b] 75-320305 ISBN 0-06-430066-8
1. Vermeer, Johannes, 1632-1675.

GOWING, Lawrence Burnett 759.9492
Jan Vermeer. New York, Barnes & Noble [1962, c.1961] 85p. illus. (part col.) 18cm. (Barnes & Noble art ser.) 62-52817 .75 pap.,
1. Vermeer, Johannes, 1632-1675. I. Title.

KONINGSBERGER, Hans. 759.9492
The world of Vermeer, 1632-1675, by Hans Koningsberger and the editors of Time-Life Books. New York, Time, inc. [1967] 192 p. illus., col. plates. 31 cm. (Time-Life library of art) Bibliography: p. 187. [ND653.V5K6] 67-15299
1. Vermeer, Johannes, 1632-1675. I. Time-Life Books. II. Title. BIP

LUCAS, Edward Verrall, 759.9492
1868-1938.
Vermeer the magical. Freeport, N.Y., Books for Libraries Press [1971] xii, 47 p. illus. 23 cm. Reprint of the 1929 ed. [ND653.V5L84 1971] 79-37352 ISBN 0-8369-6699-6
1. Vermeer, Johannes, 1632-1675. I. Title. BIP

SWILLENS, P T A [927.5] 759.9492
Johannes Vermeer, painter of Delft, 1632-1675. [Translated from the Dutch ms. by C. M. Breuning-Williamson] Utrect, Spectrum Publishers; New York, Studio Publications, 1950. 221 p. 80 plates. 25 cm. Bibliography: p. 203-208. [ND653.V5S85] 51-8543
1. Vermeer, Johannes, I. Title.

VERMEER, Johannes, 1632- 759.9492
1675.
All the paintings of Jan Vermeer. Text by Vitale Bloch. Translated from the Italian by Michael Kitson. New York, Hawthorn Books [1963] 49 p. plates (part col.) 18 cm. (The Complete library of world art, v. 15) "Bibliographical note": p. 49. [ND653.V5B393] 62-16585
I. Bloch, Vitale.

VERMEER, Johannes, 1632- 759.9492
1675.
The complete paintings of Vermeer. Introd. by John Jacob. Notes and catalogue by Piero Bianconi. New York, H. N. Abrams [1970] 104 p. illus., 64 col. plates. 32 cm. (Classics of the world's great art) Translation of L'opera completa di Vermeer. [ND653.V5B3853] 70-85179 ISBN 0-8109-5524-5
I. Bianconi, Piero, 1899- ed. II. Title.

WRIGHT, Christopher, 759.9492
1945-
Vermeer / Christopher Wright. London : Oresko Books, c1976. 87 p. : ill. (some col.) ; 30 cm. Label on p. 4 of cover: Two Continents Pub. Group, New York. Bibliography: p. 82-83. [ND653.V5W74] 77-362547 ISBN 0-905368-04-5
1. Vermeer, Johannes, 1632-1675. BIP

Vermont—Biography—Portraits.

LITTLE, Nina Fletcher, 759.13
1903-
Asahel Powers; painter of Vermont faces. [Catalog of an exhibition] Abby Aldrich

Rockefeller Folk Art Collection, Williamsburg, Virginia, October 14-December 2, 1973. [Williamsburg, Va., Colonial Williamsburg Foundation, 1973] 49 p. illus. 21 x 26 cm. Includes bibliographical references. [ND1329.P68L57] 73-86269 ISBN 0-87935-015-6 4.00 (pbk.)
1. Powers, Asahel, 1759-1841. 2. Vermont—Biography—Portraits. I. Abby Aldrich Rockefeller Folk Art Collection, Williamsburg, Va.

Vermont—Description and travel—Views.

HILL, Ralph Nading, 1917- 778'.9'9743
Vermont album; a collection of early Vermont photographs, with text by Ralph Nading Hill. Brattleboro, Vt., S. Greene Press in association with Vermont life magazine and the Vermont Historical Society [1974] 144 p. illus. 28 cm. [F50.H52] 74-13090 ISBN 0-8289-0218-6
1. Vermont—Description and travel—Views. 2. Vermont—Social life and customs—Pictorial works. I. Title. BIP

Vermont—Historic houses, etc.

CONGDON, Herbert Wheaton, 1876-1965. 720'.9743
Old Vermont houses. Illus. by the author, selected from the Wilbur Library collection. Peterborough, N.H., Noone House, 1968. xix, 192, vii p. illus. 25 cm. "An outgrowth of the Old Buildings Project initiated by the Robert Hull Fleming Museum and sponsored by the James Benjamin Wilbur Library Fund, both of the University of Vermont." [NA7235.V4C6 1968] 68-22885
1. Vermont—Historic houses, etc. 2. Architecture, Domestic—Vermont. 3. Architecture—Details. I. Title. BIP

Verner, Elizabeth O'Neill, 1884—

BUSSMAN, Marlo Pease. 741'.0924 B
Born Charlestonian; the story of Elizabeth O'Neill Verner. [Columbia, S.C., Lithographed by State Print. Co., 1969] 120 p. illus. 29 cm. [NE2210.V4B8] 73-6146
1. Verner, Elizabeth O'Neill, 1884- I. Title.

Vernet, Joseph, 1714-1789.

GREATER London Council. 759.4
Claude-Joseph Vernet, 1714-1789 / Greater London Council, The Iveagh Bequest ; [catalogue by Philip Conisbee]. London : The Council, 1976. [104] p. : ill. ; 30 cm. [N6853.V43G73 1976] 77-354086 ISBN 0-7168-0818-8 : £1.60
1. Vernet, Joseph, 1714-1789. I. Vernet, Joseph, 1714-1789. II. Conisbee, Philip. III. Iveagh Bequest, Hampstead, Eng.

Veronese, Paolo Cagliari, known as, 1528-1588.

ORLIAC, Antoine. 759.5
Veronese, translated from the French by Mary Chamot. [Edited by Andre Gloeckner] London, New York, Hyperion Press [1950?] 167 p. (p. 33-160 plates (part col.)] illus. 33 cm. Bibliography: p. 164. [ND623.V5O] A 51
1. Veronese, Paolo Cagliari, known as, 1528-1588. I. Title.

Veronesi, Luigi, 1908—

VERONESI, Luigi, 1908- 741.9'45
Veronesi : disegni / Osvaldo Patani. [s.l.] : Edizioni della seggiola, 1976. 131 p. : ill. ; 29 cm. (Documenti del disegno ; 2) English, French and Italian. Bibliography: p. 131. [NC257.V43P37] 77-479199
1. Veronesi, Luigi, 1908- I. Patani, Osvaldo. II. Title. III. Series.

Verrocchio, Andrea del, 1435?-1488.

SEYMOUR, Charles, 1912- 730'.92'4
The sculpture of Verrocchio. Greenwich, Conn., New York Graphic Society [1971] 192 p. illus. 26 cm. Bibliography: p. 185-188. [NB623.V5S48 1971b] 77-154326 ISBN 0-8212-0375-4 13.50
1. Verrocchio, Andrea del, 1435?-1488. I. Title.

Versailles.

KEMP, Gerald van der. 708'.4'366
Versailles / Gerald Van der Kemp. New York : Vendome Press : distributed by Viking Press, c1978. 255 p. : ill. (some col.) ; 23 cm. Includes index. Bibliography: p. 252. [NA7736.V5K4613] 78-8248 ISBN 0-670-74522-7 : 40.00
1. Versailles. I. Title. BIP

KEMP, Gerald van der. 725.17
Versailles and the Trianons [by] G. van der Kemp [and] J. Levron. Translated by Ethel Whitehorn. Cover design by Chapelain-Midy. 184 heliogravre illus. Fair Lawn, N.J., Essential Books, 1958. 237 p. illus., plans. 23 cm. [Les Beaux pays] Bibliography: p. [6] [DC801.V56K43] 58-4078
1. Versailles. I. Levron, Jacques, 1906- joint author.

Versailles. Musee national.

CHICAGO. Art Institute. v. 12
Treasures of Versailles; a loan exhibition from the French Government. Organized by the Art Institute of Chicago. [Chicago, 1962] [96]p. illus. 20x26cm. Catalogue of the exhibition to be held at the Art Institute of Chicago and other places during 1962-1963. [N2180.C5] 62-21225
1. Versailles. Musee national. 2. Art, French—Exhibitions. I. Title.

Vever, Henri, 1854-1943—Art collections.

HILLIER, Jack Ronald. 769'.952'074
Japanese prints & drawings from the Vever Collection / Jack Hillier. New York : Rizzoli International, 1976. 3 v. (xix, 1034 p.) : ill. (some col.) ; 34 cm. Based on catalogs prepared for sales held in 1974 and 1975 at Sotheby, London. Includes index. Bibliography: p. 1029-1034. [NE1318.F8V483 1976] 76-14044 ISBN 0-85667-025-1 : 195.00
1. Vever, Henri, 1854-1943—Art collections. 2. Color prints, Japanese—Catalogs. 3. Drawing, Japanese—Catalogs. 4. Ukiyoe—Catalogs. I. Title. BIP

Vicenza. Loggia del capitaniato.

VENDITTI, Arnaldo. 720'.92'4
The Loggia del Capitaniato. With a note on the pictorial decoration by Franco Barbieri. University Park, Pennsylvania State University Press [1971] 84 p. illus. (part col.) 35 cm. (Corpus Palladianum, v. 4) Includes bibliographies. [NA7595.V47V413] 72-79837 ISBN 0-271-00089-9 16.50
1. Palladio, Andrea, 1508-1580. 2. Vicenza. Loggia del capitaniato. I. Barbieri, Franco. II. Title. III. Series. BIP

Vicenza. Palazzo da Porto Festa.

FORSSMAN, Erik. 728.8'2
The Palazzo da Porto Festa in Vicenza / Erik Forssman ; translated by Catherine Enggass. University Park : Pennsylvania State University Press, [1975] p. cm. (Corpus Palladianum ; v. 8) Includes index. Bibliography: p. [NA7756.V578F6713] 75-20027 ISBN 0-271-01202-1
1. Vicenza. Palazzo da Porto Festa. 2. Palladio, Andrea, 1508-1580. I. Title. II. Series.

Vickrey, Robert, 1926—

VICKREY, Robert, 1926- 759.13
Robert Vickrey. [Tucson, Ariz., Walker Lithocraft Print., 1973] 96 p. illus. (part col.) 30 x 37 cm. Catalog of an exhibition held at the University of Arizona Museum of Art, Feb. 17-Apr. 1, 1973, and at the Fine Arts Gallery of San Diego, May 19-July 8, 1973. [ND1839.V52A89] 73-75364
1. Vickrey, Robert, 1926- I. Arizona. University. Museum of Art. II. San Diego, Calif. Fine Arts Gallery. BIP

Victoria and Albert Museum, South Kensington.

CONWAY, Moncure Daniel, 1832-1907. 709'.42
Travels in South Kensington / Moncure Daniel Conway. New York : Garland Pub., 1977. 234 p. : ill. ; 23 cm. (The Aesthetic movement & the arts and crafts movement) Reprint of the 1882 ed. published by Trubner, London. [N1150.C7 1977] 76-17754 ISBN 0-8240-2457-5 lib.bdg. : 35.00
1. Victoria and Albert Museum, South Kensington. 2. Art, Decorative—England. 3. Architecture—England. 4. Suburban homes—England—Bedford Park. I. Title. II. Series. BIP

VICTORIA and Albert Museum, South Kensington. 708'.21'34 s
The history of the Victoria and Albert Museum / [prepared by C. H. Gibbs-Smith and Katharine Dougharty]. 2nd ed. / [revised by John Physick]. London : H.M.S.O., 1976. 32 p. : ill., plan, ports. ; 16 cm. (Small picture book ; no. 31) Obtainable in the United States of America from Pendragon House, Palo Alto, Calif. [N1150.A73 no. 31] 708'.21'34 77-351084 ISBN 0-11-290218-9 : £0.65
I. Gibbs-Smith, Charles Harvard, 1909- II. Dougharty, Katharine. III. Physick, John. IV. Title. V. Series: Victoria and Labert Museum, South Kensington. Small picture book ; no. 31.

Victoria and Albert Museum, South Kensington—Catalogs.

VICTORIA and Albert Museum, South Kensington. 932'.0074'02134
Egyptian objects in the Victoria and Albert Museum / Barbara Adams. Warminster, Eng. : Aris & Phillips, 1977. 61 p. ; 30 cm. (Egyptology today ; no. 3) Includes bibliographical references. [DT59.S68V52 1977] 78-320285 ISBN 0-85668-103-2 : 19.50
1. Victoria and Albert Museum, South Kensington—Catalogs. 2. Egypt—Antiquities—Catalogs. I. Adams, Barbara G. II. Title. III. Series.
Distributed by International Scholarly Book Services Inc., P. O. Box 555 Forest Grove, OR BIP

Victoria and Albert Museum, South Kensington. Constantine Alexander Ionides Collection.

BOARDMAN, John, 1927- 736'.2'0938
Engraved gems; the Ionides collection. Photos. by Robert L. Wilkins. Evanston, [Ill.] Northwestern University Press, 1968. 114 p. illus. (part col.) 26 cm. Bibliography: p. 111-112. [NK5510.L6B6 1968b] 68-17325
1. Victoria and Albert Museum, South Kensington. Constantine Alexander Ionides Collection. I. Title. BIP

Victoria and Albert Museum, South Kensington. National Art Library.

VICTORIA and Albert Museum, South Kensington. National Art Library. 016.7819'1
Musical instruments : a list of books and articles in the National Art Library / compiled by Michael I. Wilson. [Rev., enl. and updated ed.]. [London] : Victoria and Albert Museum, 1976. iv, 126 p. : ill. ; 30 cm. Earlier eds. published under title: A bibliography of books on musical instruments in the Library of the Victoria and Albert Museum. [ML136.L8V55 1976] 77-368392
1. Victoria and Albert Museum, South Kensington. National Art Library. 2. Musical instruments—Bibliography—Catalogs. I. Wilson, Michael I. II. Title.

Victoria, Australia—Dwellings.

CANTLON, Maurice, 1926- 720.9'94'5
Homesteads of Victoria 1836-1900. With a foreword by E. Graeme Robertson. Melbourne, Georgian House [1967] xx, 108 p. illus., map. 25 x 33 cm. Bibliography: p. 104. [NA7470.V5C3] 73-397127 20.00
1. Victoria, Australia—Dwellings. 2. Architecture, Domestic—Victoria, Australia. I. Title.

Victoria, Australia. National Gallery, Melbourne.

COX, Leonard Bell. 708.994'5
The National Gallery of Victoria, 1861 to 1968; a search for a collection, by Leonard B. Cox. [Melbourne] National Gallery of Victoria [1970?] xxviii, 486 p. illus., ports. 24 cm. "Errata": 1 p., inserted. Bibliography: p. 458-461. [N3948.C6] 76-595123 ISBN 0-85848-000-X 12.00
1. Victoria, Australia. National Gallery, Melbourne. I. Title.

HOFF, Ursula. 708'.9945
The National Gallery of Victoria; with an introd. by Eric Westbrook. London, Thames and Hudson [1973, i.e.1974] 216 p. illus. 22 cm. [N3948.H62 1973] 73-180557 ISBN 0-500-18139-X
1. Victoria, Australia. National Gallery, Melbourne. 2. Art—Melbourne—Catalogs. I. Title.
Distributed by Transatlantic Arts, 11.00; 5.95 (pbk.)

LINDSAY, Daryl, 1890- 708.994
The Felton bequest, an historical record, 1904-1959. New York, Oxford [1964] x, 105p. illus., plates, ports. 23cm. 64-3451 5.50
1. Felton, Alfred, 1831-1904. 2. Victoria, Australia. National Gallery, Melbourne. I. Title. BIP

NATIONAL Gallery Society of Victoria. 708.994'5
Guide [to National Gallery of Victoria] [Melbourne, 1968] 31 p. illus., plans. 18 cm. Cover title. [N3948.N37] 78-441364 unpriced
1. Victoria, Australia. National Gallery, Melbourne. I. Title.

PHILIPP, Franz Adolf, ed. 759
In honour of Daryl Lindsay; essays and studies, ed. by Franz Phillipp, June Stewart. Melbourne, New York, Oxford [1965] xxi, 246p. plates, port. 28cm. Bibl. [N3948.P45] 65-3245 16.40
1. Lindsay, Sir Daryl, 1890- 2. Victoria, Australia. National Gallery. Melbourne. 3. Art—Galleries and museums. 4. Art—Australia—Addresses, essays, lectures. I. Stewart, June, joint ed. II. Lindsay, Daryl, Sir 1890- III. Title.

TENNISON, Patrick. 708.994'5
Meet the gallery; a literary and visual introduction to Victoria's new National Gallery, by Patrick Tennison, writer, & Les Gray, photographer. Melbourne, Sun Books [1968] 68, [16] p. illus. (part col.) 19 cm. [N3948.T45] 77-356078 1.00
1. Victoria, Australia. National Gallery, Melbourne. I. Gray, Les. II. Title.

VICTORIA, Australia. National Gallery, Melbourne. 709'.94'07409945
Freedom from prejudice : an introduction to the Australian Collection in the National Gallery of Victoria / [by] Brian Finemore ; selected and compiled by Jennifer Phipps ; consulting editor, Stephen Murray-Smith. Melbourne : National Gallery of Victoria, 1977. 144 p. : ill. (some col.) ; 25 cm. Includes index. Bibliography: p. 136-138. [N7400.V52 1977] 78-301525 ISBN 0-7241-0031-8
1. Victoria, Australia. National Gallery, Melbourne. 2. Art, Australian—Catalogs. 3. Art—Australia—Victoria—Catalogs. I. Finemore, Brian. II. Phipps, Jennifer. III. Title.

VICTORIA, Australia. National Gallery, Melbourne. 727.7'0994'5
National Gallery of Victoria; photographs, plans and factual descriptions. [Melbourne, 1968] 50 p. illus. (part col.) diagrs. 31 cm. Cover title: Victorian Arts Centre; art gallery. [N3948.A85] 73-464546 unpriced

I. Title. II. Title: Victorian Arts Centre.

WESTBROOK, Eric. 708.994'5
Birth of a gallery. [Melbourne] Macmillan of Australia [1968] 79 p. illus. 31 cm. [N3948.W4] 68-138199 10.00 Aust.
1. Victoria, Australia. National Gallery, Melbourne. I. Title.

Victoria (Goddess)

BELLINGER, Alfred Raymond, 1892- 737.493
Victory as a coin type, by Alfred Bellinger, Marjorie Alkins Berlincourt. New York, Amer. Numismatic Soc. [1963] 68, XIII p. illus. 23cm. (Numismatic notes and monographs, no. 149) 63-2516 4.00 pap.,
1. Victoria (Goddess) 2. Coins, Ancient. I. Berlincourt, Marjorie Alkins, joint author. II. Title.

Video art.

VIDEO by artists / 709'.2'2
edited by Peggy Gale. [Toronto] : Art Metropole, 1976. 223 p. : ill. ; 27 cm. Bibliography: p. 216-223. [PN1992.8.V5V53] 77-368383
1. Video art. I. Gale, Peggy.

Video art—Addresses, essays, lectures.

NEW artists video : 709'.04
a critical anthology / edited by Gregory Battcock. 1st ed. New York : Dutton, c1978. xxii, 198 p. : ill. ; 21 cm. Includes bibliographical references and index. [PN1992.8.V5N37] 77-73146 ISBN 0-525-47461-7 : 8.95
1. Video art—Addresses, essays, lectures. I. Battcock, Gregory, 1937- BIP

Video art—Exhibitions.

PENNSYLVANIA. University. Institute of Contemporary Art. 709'.04
Video art: [exhibition] : Institute of Contemporary Art, University of Pennsylvania, Philadelphia, Pennsylvania, January 17 to February 28, 1975. Philadelphia : The Institute, c1975. 116 p. : ill. ; 22 x 28 cm. Bibliography: p. 107-115. [PN1992.8.V5P4 1975] 75-326775 ISBN 0-88454-014-6
1. Video art—Exhibitions. I. Title.

Video tape recorders and recording.

MURRAY, Michael, 1932- 778.59
The videotape book : a basic guide to portable TV production / Michael Murray. New York : Taplinger Pub. Co., 1975, c1974. 248 p. : ill. ; 21 cm. Includes index. Bibliography: p. 242-244. [TK6655.V5M87 1975] 75-8413 ISBN 0-8008-8020-X : 9.95
1. Video tape recorders and recording. I. Title. BIP

Vieira da Silva, Marie Helena, 1908-

VIEIRA da Silva, Marie Helena, 1908- 759.4
Vieira da Silva : paintings, 1967-1971 : [exhibition, M. Knoedler & Co., inc., New York, May 4-June 5, 1971] / John Rewald. New York : M. Knoedler, c1971. 36 p. : ill. (some col.) ; 22 cm. [ND553.V53R48] 75-518484
1. Vieira da Silva, Marie Helena, 1908- I. Rewald, John, 1912- II. Knoedler (M.) and Company, inc.

Vienna. Albertina.

BENESCH, Otto, 1896-1964. 741.94
Master drawings in the Albertina: European drawings from the 15th to the 18th century, by Otto Benesch in collaboration with Eva Benesch; [translated from the German by R. Rickett and M. Schon; revised by Felice Stamfle and Ruth Kramer]. London, Evelyn, Adams & Mackay, 1967. 379 p. 258 illus. (col.), 2 plates, facsims. 30 1/2 cm. (B67-17552) Translation of Meisterzeichnungen der Albertina. Bibliography: p. [318] [NC225.B413] 67-99891
1. Vienna. Albertina. 2. Drawings, European — Catalogs. 3. Drawings — Vienna — Catalogs. I. Benesch, Eva, joint author. II. Title.

KOSCHATZKY, Walter. 760'.094'0943613
The Albertina in Vienna ([by] Walter Koschatzky [and] Alice Strobl. Translated by Hans Suesserott. Photographs: Erich Lunemann) (Vienna, Federal Chancellery, Federal Press & Information Department [1968]) 35 p. illus., ports. 19 cm. Cover title. On cover: Infor-Austria. [N1670.K6713] 76-439082 N.T.
1. Vienna. Albertina I. Strobl, Alice. II. Title. III. Title: Infor-Austria: the Albertina in Vienna.

Vienna. Kunsthistorisches Museum. Gemalde-Galerie.

ART History 759.94'09436'13
Museum, Vienna. Picture Gallery. [Texts by: Giorgio T. Faggin and others] New York, Newsweek [1969] 171 p. col. illus., plans. 30 cm. (Great museums of the world) Bibliography: p. 168. [N1680.A964] 69-19064
1. Vienna. Kunsthistorisches Museum. Gemalde-Galerie. I. Faggin, Giorgio T. II. Series: Great museums of the world (New York, Newsweek)

HEINZ, Gunther. 759.94'074'03613
The Picture Gallery in the Kunsthistorischen Museum Vienna. [Translated from the German by James Brockway] New York, Meredith Press [1970, c1966] 160 p. illus. (part col.) 28 cm. (Great galleries series) Translation of Die Gemaldegalerie im Kunsthistorischen Museum Wien. [N1680.H413 1970] 70-15607 8.95
I. Vienna. Kunsthistorisches Museum. Gemalde-Galerie. II. Title.

PICTURE Gallery 759.94'074'03613
of the Art History Museum, Vienna; [texts by Giorgio T. Faggin and others]; [translated from the Italian]. London, New York, Hamlyn, 1970. 5-172 p. col. illus., plans. 30 cm. (Great museums of the world) Translation of Kunsthistorisches Museum. Bibliography: p. 168. [N1680.K813] 73-161729 ISBN 0-600-35301-X £2.00
1. Vienna. Kunsthistorisches Museum. Gemalde-Galerie. I. Faggin, Giorgio T.

Vietnam—Description and travel—Views.

NIELSEN, Jon, 1912- 915.97
Artist in South Vietnam, by Jon Nielsen, with Kay Nielsen. New York, J. Messner [1969] 64 p. illus. 26 cm. A cartoonist, sent to South Vietnam to entertain the troops, records in sketches his impressions of the people, the land, farm life, Tet, old Vietnam, Saigon, and the influence of United States soldiers. [NC1075.N5N5] 79-81394 4.64
1. Vietnam—Description and travel—Views. I. Nielsen, Kay, 1923- II. Title.

Vietnamese Conflict, 1961-1975—Pictorial works.

WATERHOUSE, Charles H. 741.9'73
Vietnam sketchbook; drawings from delta to DMZ, by Charles Waterhouse. Rutland, Vt., C. E. Tuttle Co. [1968] 126 p. (chiefly illus.) 21 cm. [DS557.A61W3] 68-21114
1. Vietnamese Conflict, 1961-1975—Pictorial works. I. Title. BIP

View cameras.

SHAMAN, Harvey. 770'.28
The view camera : operations and techniques / Harvey Shaman. Garden City, N.Y. : American Photographic Book Pub. Co., c1977. 127 p., [4] leaves of plates : ill. (some col.) ; 28 cm. [TR258.S45] 75-42770 ISBN 0-8174-0598-4 : 7.95
1. View cameras. I. Title. BIP

STROEBEL, Leslie D. 770'.28
View camera technique [by] Leslie Stroebel. 2nd ed. revised. London, New York, Focal Press, 1972. 311 p. illus. 25 cm. Includes index. [TR258.S7 1972] 74-180790 ISBN 0-240-44854-5 £3.75
1. View cameras. 2. Photography—Handbooks, manuals, etc. I. Title. BIP

STROEBEL, Leslie D. 770.28
View camera techniques [by] Leslie Stroebel. London, New York, Focal P. [1967] 311 p. illus., diagrs. 25 cm. (B 67-11634) [TR258.S7] 67-99142
1. View cameras. 2. Photography — Handbooks, manuals, etc. I. Title.

STROEBEL, Leslie D. 770.282
View camera techniques [by] Leslie Stroebel. New York, Hastings House [1967] 311 p. illus. 25 cm. (Communication art[s] books) [TR258.S7] 67-16907
1. View cameras. 2. Photography—Handbooks, manuals, etc. I. Title.

WAHL, Paul Francis, 1922- 771.31
Press-view camera technique. Philadelphia, Chilton Co., Book Division, e1962. 128 p. illus. 20 cm. (Modern camera guide series, 655) [TR258.W3] 62-12584
1. View cameras. 2. Photography — Handbooks, manuals, etc. I. Title.

Views.

BISCHOF, Werner Adalbert, 1916-1954. 779
The world of Werner Bischof; a photographer's odyssey. Text by Manuel Gasser; translated by Paul Steiner. New York, Dutton, 1959. 1 v. (unpaged) illus. (part col.) 76 plates (part col.) 29 cm. Translation of Unterwegs. [G139.B513] 59-4484
1. Views. 2. Photography, Artistic. I. Gasser, Manuel. II. Title.

Vigeland, Gustav, 1869-1943.

HALE, Nathan Cabot. 730'.924 B
Embrace of life; the sculpture of Gustav Vigeland. Text by Nathan Cabot Hale. Photos. by David Finn. New York, H. N. Abrams [1969] 363 p. illus. (part col.) 28 x 30 cm. Bibliography: p. 363. [NB773.V5H3] 68-13067
1. Vigeland, Gustav, 1869-1943. I. Finn, David, illus. II. Title.

Vigni, Giorgio.

ANTONELLO da Messina, 1430?-1479. 759.5
All the paintings of Antonello da Messina. Text by Giorgio Vigni. Translated from the Italian by Anthony Firmin O'Sullivan. New York, Hawthorn Books [1963] 42 p. illus., 84 plates (4 col.) 18 cm. (The Complete library of world art, v. 14) Bibliography: p. 42. [ND623.A6V53] 63-8013
1. Vigni, Giorgio. I. Title. II. Series.

Vignola, Giacomo Barozzio, known as, 1507-1573.

WARE, William Robert, 1832-1915. 729
The American Vignola / by William R. Ware ; with introductory notes by John Barrington Bayley and Henry Hope Reed. New York : Norton, c1977. xiii, 124 p., [10] leaves of plates : ill. ; 29 cm. (The Classical America series in art and architecture) "Part I is based on the fourth ed. of 1905 and Part II on the 1st ed. of 1906-both published by the International Textbook Co. of Scranton, Pennsylvania." [NA2815.W3 1977] 77-150899 ISBN 0-393-04457-2 : 10.00. ISBN 0-393-00839-8 pbk. : 3.95
1. Vignola, Giacomo Barozzio, known as, 1507-1573. 2. Architecture—Orders. 3. Architecture, Classical. 4. Architecture—Details. I. Title. II. Series. BIP

Villanueva, Carlos Raul.

MOHOLY-NAGY, Dorothea Maria Pauline Alice Sibylle (Pietzsch) 720.987
Carlos Raul Villanueva and the architecture of Venezuela [Tr. into Spanish by Clara Diament de Sujo] New York, Praeger [1964] 179p. illus. (pt. col.) facsims., maps, port. 23x26cm. Bibl. 64-16683 12.50
1. Villanueva, Carlos Raul. 2. Architecture—Venezuela. 3. Architecture, Modern—20th cent. I. Title.

Villas.

ALOI, Roberto 728.6
Ville d'oggi. Con un saggio di Agnoldomenico Pica. Testo e didascalie in italiano e inglese. Milano, Hoepli [New York, Heinman, 1966, c.1964] xiv, 445p. (chiefly illus. (pt. col.) plans) 28cm. [NA7580.A5] 66-4576 30.00
1. Villas. 2. Architecture, Domestic—Designs and plans. I. Pica, Agnoldomenico, 1907- II. Title.

Villodas, Ricardo de, 1849-1904.

BOWLES, Thomas A. 759.6 B
Ricardo de Villodas, 1846-1904 : collection, catalogue, and biography : inaugural exhibition, Huntsville Museum of Art, Von Braun Civic Center, March 15-30 April, 1975 / prepared by Thomas A. Bowles, III. [Huntsville, Ala.] : Huntsville Museum of Art, 1975. 39 p., [10] leaves of plates : ill. ; 25 cm. [ND813.V54B68] 75-312707
1. Villodas, Ricardo de, 1849-1904. I. Villodas, Ricardo de, 1846-1904. II. Huntsville Museum of Art.

Villon, Jacques, 1875-1963.

BOSTON. Museum of Fine Arts. 769.944
Jacques Villon, master of graphic art (1875-1963) New York, October House [1964] 89 p. illus. (part col.) 30 cm. Catalogue of the exhibition: p. 37-89. Pref. in English and French. Errata slip mounted on p. [1] Bibliography: p. 36. [NC248.V54B6] 64-17722
1. Villon, Jacques, 1875-1963. I. Title.

BOSTON. Institute of Contemporary Art. [759.084]
Jacques Villon, Lyonel Feininger, with Reflections on painting by Jacques Villon and critical essays by George Heard Hamilton, Thomas B. Hess, and Frederick S. Wight. New York, Published for the Institute of Contemporary Art, Boston, by Chanticleer Press [1949 or 50] 46 p. illus., ports. 25 cm. "Catalogue of the exhibition": p. 44-46. Bibliography: p. 13, 35 [ND553.V54B6] 927.5 50-12672
1. Villon. Jacques, 1875- 2. Feininger, Lyonel Charles Adrian, 1871- 3. Paintings, French—Exhibitions. 4. Paintings, American—Exhibitions. I. Title.

JACQUES Villon, master 769'.924
printmaker. An exhibition at R. M. Light & Co., Helene C. Seiferheld Gallery inc., New York, February, 1964. With an introd. by Francis Steegmuller. [New York, Printed by High Grade Press, 1964] [54] p., [30] of illus., ports. 21 cm. (Seiferheld Gallery. [Catalogue] no. 14) [NE650.V5S7] 77-13087
1. Villon, Jacques, 1875-1963. I. Steegmuller, Francis, ed. II. Seiferheld Gallery.

VILLON, Jacques, 1875-1963. 760'.092'4
Jacques Villon / edited by Daniel Robbins. Cambridge, Mass. : Fogg Art Museum, Harvard University 1976. 223 p. : ill. (some col.) ; 29 cm. Catalogue of an exhibition held at the Fogg Art Museum, Jan. 17-Feb. 29, 1976, and at the Roy R. Neuberger Museum at Purchase, N.Y., Mar. 23-May 23, 1976. Bibliography: p. 208-222. [ND553.V54R62] 75-43627 ISBN 0-87923-180-7
1. Villon, Jacques, 1875-1963. I. Robbins, Daniel. II. Harvard University. William Hayes Fogg Art Museum. III. Neuberger Museum.

VILLON, Jacques, 1875-1963. 769'.92'4
Master of graphic art: Jacques Villon, 1875-1963; a representative exhibition of the first thirty years of the artist's graphic work: 1891-1921, November-December 1967. Chicago, International Galleries [1967] 47 p. illus. 25 cm. [NE2049.5.V54I58] 75-304479

1. Villon, Jacques, 1875-1963. I. International Galleries. II. Title.

Vinegar bottles—Catalogs.

SMITH, Levin J. 748'.8
White House vinegar book. Levin J. Smith, author. [Independence, Va.] 1971- v. illus. 22 cm. Cover title. [NK5440.B6S6] 76-29669 3.00
1. Vinegar bottles—Catalogs. I. Title.

Violence in art.

FRASER, John. 301.6'33
Violence in the arts. [London] Cambridge University Press [1974] xii, 192 p. 21 cm. Includes bibliographical references. [NX650.V5F72] 73-84319 ISBN 0-521-20331-7
1. Violence in art. I. Title. BIP

Violin makers—Biography.

STOEVING, Paul, 1861-1948. 787'.1
The violin: its famous makers and players. Westport, Conn., Greenwood Press [1970] 100 p. music. 23 cm. Reprint of the 1928 ed. [ML850.S8 1970] 71-109855 ISBN 0-8371-4346-2
1. Violin makers—Biography. 2. Violinists, violoncellists, etc.—Biography. 3. Violin—History. I. Title.

Virginia—Historic houses, etc.

DIETZ, Frieda Meredith. 728.8
Photographic studies of old Virginia homes & gardens. [3d and enl. ed.] Richmond, Dietz Press [1953] 67p. (chiefly illus.) 21cm. [NA7235.V5D5 1953] 53-9378
1. Virginia—Historic houses, etc. 2. Architecture, Domestic—Virginia. 3. Gardens—Virginia. I. Title.

ROTHERY, Agnes Edwards, 1888- 728
Houses Virginians have loved. Illustrated with photos. New York, Rinehart [1954] 319 p. illus. 26 cm. [NA7235.V5R6] 54-9125
1. Virginia—Historic houses, etc. I. Title.

Virginia—Historic houses, etc.—Pictorial works.

ATALAY, Bulent. 741.9'561
The lands of Washington: impressions in ink. [Fredericksburg, Va., 1972] 2 v. (chiefly plates) 36 x 44 cm. Cover title. Volume 2 has special title: Fredericksburg. "First printing—300 copies." Bibliography: v. 1, p. [4]; v. 2, p. 4. [NC296.A92A49] 72-89545
1. Virginia—Historic houses, etc.—Pictorial works. I. Title.

Virginia Museum of Fine Arts, Richmond.

VIRGINIA Museum of Fine Arts, Richmond. 709'.01
Ancient art in the Virginia Museum. [Richmond, Va., 1973] 142 p. illus. (part col.) 25 cm. Includes bibliographical references. [N5335.R53A52] 73-78574 10.95
1. Virginia Museum of Fine Arts, Richmond. 2. Art, Ancient—Catalogs. 3. Art—Richmond—Catalogs. I. Title.

VIRGINIA Museum of Fine Arts, Richmond. 708.155
Roster of members. [Richmond?] v. 23 cm. annual. Included also in its Publications, 1936/38- [N716.V45A33] 50-56350
I. Title.

VIRGINIA Museum of Fine Arts, Richmond. 708'.155'451
Treasures in the Virginia Museum / [Pinkney L. Near, curator and author]. Richmond : Virginia Museum, [1974] 124 p. : col. ill. ; 31 cm. [N716.M8A7] 74-80700 ISBN 0-8139-0600-8 : 13.95
1. Virginia Museum of Fine Arts, Richmond. 2. Art—Richmond—Catalogs. I. Near, Pinkney L. II. Title.

Virginia. University. Library.

O'NEAL, William Bainter. 016.7
A fine arts library : Jefferson's selections for the University of Virginia together with his architectural books at Monticello : an exhibition sponsored by the Alderman Library & the Committee on the Bicentennial, February-May 1976 : catalogue / compiled by William B. O'Neal. Charlottesville : University of Virginia, 1976. 18 p., 38 leaves of plates : ill., facsims. ; 26 cm. [Z5939.O49] [N5300] 76-383681
1. Virginia. University. Library. 2. Jefferson, Thomas, Pres. United States., 1743-1826. 3. Art—Bibliography—Catalogs. 4. Architecture—Bibliography—Catalogs. I. Virginia. University. Library. II. Title.

O'NEAL, William Bainter. 016.7
Jefferson's fine arts library : his selections for the University of Virginia, together with his own architectural books / William Bainter O'Neal. Charlottesville : University Press of Virginia, 1976. xviii, 409 p. : ill. ; 26 cm. Based on the author's earlier ed. published under title: Jefferson's fine arts library for the University of Virginia, with additional notes on architectural volumes known to have been owned by Jefferson. Includes bibliographical references and index. [Z5939.O5] [N5300] 75-33229 ISBN 0-8139-0647-4 : 20.00
1. Virginia. University. Library. 2. Jefferson, Thomas, Pres. U.S., 1743-1826. 3. Art—Bibliography—Catalogs. 4. Architecture—Bibliography—Catalogs. I. Title. BIP

Vishniac, Roman, 1897—

VISHNIAC, Roman, 1897- 770'.92'4 B
Roman Vishniac / editors, Cornell Capa, Bhupendra Karia]. New York : Grossman Publishers, 1974. 95 p. : ill., (some col.) ; 23 cm. (ICP library of photographers ; v. 6) Bibliography: p. 94. [TR140.V48V57 1974] 72-11009 ISBN 0-670-60390-2 : 15.00. ISBN 0-670-60391-0 pbk : 7.95
1. Vishniac, Roman, 1897- 2. Jews in Poland—Pictures, illustrations, etc. 3. Photomicrography. I. Series: International Fund for Concerned Photography. ICP library of photographers ; v. 6.

Visits of state—Belgium—Antwerp.

MARTIN, John Rupert. 760'.092'4
The decorations for the Pompa Introitus Ferdinandi. London, New York, Phaidon, 1972. [7], 278, [99] p. illus., facsims., col. map. 27 cm. (Corpus Rubenianum Ludwig Burchard, pt. 16) Distributed in the USA by Praeger, New York. Includes bibliographical references. [ND673.R9C63 pt. 16] 72-186634 ISBN 0-7148-1433-4 £13.00
1. Rubens, Peter Paul, Sir, 1577-1640. 2. Fernando, Infante of Spain, 1609-1641. 3. Visits of state—Belgium—Antwerp. 4. Street decoration—Antwerp. I. Title. II. Series.

Visual Communications Conference, 4th, New York, 1959.

MEYLAN, E. Paul. 001.56
Symbology : a review of a conference on this topic / by E. Paul Meylan. Los Angeles : Consultants for Product Design, 1959. 26 p. ; 21 cm. Cover title. "A combination of notes and commentary on the fourth Communications Conference of the Art Director's Club of New York." [AZ108.M49] 75-321383
1. Visual Communications Conference, 4th, New York, 1959. 2. Signs and symbols—Congresses. I. Visual Communications Conference, 4th, New York, 1959. II. Title. BIP

Visual discrimination.

PRINCE, Jack Harvey. 411
Studies of visual acuity and reading in relation to letter and word design. [Columbus] Ohio State University [1960] 179l. illus., tables. 28cm. (Ohio, State University [Columbus] Institute for Research in Vision. Publication no. 1) Cover title. Bibliography: leaf 179. [Z250.A4P7] A61
1. Visual discrimination. 2. Type and type-founding. 3. Printing, Practical. I. Title. II. Series.

Visual perception.

ARNHEIM, Rudolf. 701
Visual thinking. Berkeley, University of California Press [1969] xi, 345 p. illus. (part col.) 26 cm. Bibliography: p. 325-338. [N70.A693] 71-76335 11.50
1. Visual perception. 2. Art—Philosophy. I. Title. BIP

CLIFTON, Jack. 751.4
The eye of the artist. Westport, Conn., North Light Publishers; distributed by Watson-Guptill Publications, New York [1973] 160 p. illus. (part col.) 23 x 29 cm. [N7430.5.C55] 73-82101 ISBN 0-8230-1620-X 15.00
1. Visual perception. 2. Art—Technique. I. Title.

DE LUCIO-MEYER, J. J. 701'.17
Visual aesthetics / J. J. de Lucio-Meyer. 1st U.S. ed. New York : Harper & Row, 1974, c1973. 239 p. : ill. ; 20 x 21 cm. (Icon editions) Includes index. Bibliography: p. 237. [N7430.5.D4 1974] 74-120 ISBN 0-06-435665-5 : 15.00. ISBN 0-06-430052-8 pbk. : 7.95
1. Visual perception. 2. Aesthetics. I. Title. BIP

GATTO, Joseph A. 701'.8
Exploring visual design / Joseph A Gatto, Albert W. Porter, Jack Selleck ; consultants, Gerald F. Brommer, George F. Horn. Worcester, Mass. : Davis Publications, c1978. 224 p. : ill. (some col.) ; 25 cm. Includes index. Bibliography: p. 215. Discusses the elements and principles of design as reflected in various art forms and in daily life. [N7430.G323] 78-55398 ISBN 0-87192-101-4 : 14.50
1. Visual perception. 2. Art—Composition, proportion, etc. I. Porter, Albert W., joint author. II. Selleck, Jack, joint author. III. Title. BIP

HARRIS, Ned. 701'.8
Form and texture; a photographic portfolio. New York, Van Nostrand Reinhold [1974] 144 p. illus. 20 cm. [N7430.5.H37] 73-16706 ISBN 0-442-23157-1 7.95
1. Visual perception. 2. Composition (Art) 3. Texture (Art) I. Title. BIP

HOBBS, Jack A. 701'.15
Art in context / Jack A. Hobbs. New York : Harcourt Brace Jovanovich, [1975] xii, 324 p., [16] leaves of plates : ill. (some col.) ; 23 cm. Includes index. Bibliography: p. 311-314. [N7430.5.H62] 74-22510 ISBN 0-15-503469-3 pbk. : 7.95
1. Visual perception. 2. Art—Psychology. I. Title. BIP

LANG, Gerhard, 1916- 686.2'2
The word so visual. [Clarks Green, Pa.] Apricot Press [1973] viii, 64 p. (chiefly illus.) 29 cm. "First edition limited to one hundred numbered copies. [No.] 99." [NK1535.L33A57] 73-77101
1. Lang, Gerhard, 1916- 2. Visual perception. I. Title.

LEEMANN, Fred. 709
The curious magic of anamorphic art : the perception of appearance and reality / text by Fred Leemann ; concept, production, and photos. by Joost Elffers and Michael Schuyt ; translation by Ellyn Childs Allison and Margaret Kaplan. New York : H. N. Abrams, 1976. p. cm. German translation has title: Anamorphosen. [N7430.5.L4313] 76-3736 ISBN 0-8109-9019-9 : 9.85
1. Visual perception. 2. Optical illusions. 3. Perspective. I. Elffers, Joost. II. Schuyt, Michael. III. Title.

MARCOUSE, Renee. 701
Using objects: visual awareness and visual learning. New York, Van Nostrand Reinhold [1974] p. cm. Includes bibliographical references. [N7430.5.M29] 74-4036 ISBN 0-442-30022-0 4.95 (pbk.).
1. Visual perception. 2. Visual education. I. Title.

NELSON, George, 1908- 701'.1
How to see : visual adventures in a world God never made / George Nelson. 1st ed. Boston : Little Brown, c1977. 232 p. : ill. ; 23 x 24 cm. [N7430.5.N44] 77-74658 ISBN 0-316-60311-2 : 9.95
1. Visual perception. I. Title. BIP

PALMER, Frederick. 700'.1
Visual awareness. London, Batsford, 1972. 88 p. [4 leaves], illus. (some col.), coat of arms, map, plan. 21 cm. (Arts and crafts books) Illus. on lining papers. Bibliography: p. 87-88. [N7430.5.P34] 72-197125 ISBN 0-7134-2299-8
1. Visual perception. 2. Aesthetics. I. Title. Available from Transatlantic Arts, Levittown, N.Y., for 8.50.

WAYS of seeing; 759.94
a book made by John Berger [and others] New York, Viking Press [1973, c1972] 160 p. illus. 21 cm. "A Richard Seaver Book." "Based on the television series with John Berger." Includes bibliographical references. [N7430.5.W39 1973] 73-3502 ISBN 0-670-75273-8 6.95
1. Visual perception. 2. Art—Technique. I. Berger, John. BIP

Visual perception—Addresses, essays, lectures.

VISION and artifact / 701'.15
Mary Henle, editor ; foreword by Rudolf Arnheim. New York : Springer Pub. Co., c1976. xviii, 186 p. : ill. ; 24 cm. Contents.Contents.—Visual perception: Held, R. Single vision with doubled images. Metelli, F. What does "more transparent" mean? Kanizsa, G. and Gerbino, W. Convexity and symmetry in figure-ground organization. Kennedy, J. M. Attention, brightness, and the constructive eye. Jameson, D. and Hurvich, L. M. From contrast to assimilation. Wallach, H. The apparent rotation of pictorial scenes. Gibson, J. J., et al. The change from visible to invisible.—Visual thinking: Schaefer-Simmern, H. Basic structures in the earliest beginnings of artistic activity. Nash, E. Hidden visual patterns in Roman architecture and ruins. Gardner, H. Illuminating comparisons in the arts.—Artifact : Sekler, E. F. Le Corbusier's use of a "pictorial word" in his tapestry La femme et le moineau. Teuber, M. L. Blue night by Paul Klee. Zucker, W. M. The representation of the invisible. Hess, W.ary Henle, editor ; foreword by Rudolf Arnheim. New York : Springer Pub. Co., c1976. xviii, 186 p. : ill. ; 24 cm. Contents.Co
1. Arnheim, Rudolf. 2. Visual perception—Addresses, essays, lectures. 3. Optical illusions—Addresses, essays, lectures. 4. Art—Psychology—Addresses, essays, lectures. I. Henle, Mary, 1913- II. Arnheim, Rudolf. BIP

Visual perception—Bibliography.

LIEBER, Stanley R. 016.3092'08 s
A working bibliography on geographic and psychological perception and related subjects [by] Stanley R. Lieber. [Monticello, Ill., Council of Planning Librarians] 1972. 25 p. 28 cm. (Council of Planning Librarians. Exchange bibliography 299) Cover title. [Z5942.C68 no. 299] [Z7204.V55] 016.1537 74-173260 2.50
1. Visual perception—Bibliography. 2. Environmental psychology—Bibliography. I. Title. II. Series.

Visual perception—Juvenile literature.

WASSERMAN, Burton. 700
Exploring the visual arts / Burton Wasserman. Worcester, Mass. : Davis Publications, c1976. 192 p. : ill. (some col.) ; 27 cm. Includes index. Bibliography: p. [182]-185. Discusses contemporary application of different art media including drawing, architecture, sculpture, printmaking, painting, and crafts. [N7430.5.W37] 76-19938 ISBN 0-87192-085-9 : 13.95
1. Visual perception—Juvenile literature. 2. Form (Aesthetics)—Juvenile literature. 3. Art—Technique—Juvenile literature. I. Title. BIP

Vitale da Bologna, fl. 1329-1359.

GNUDI, Cesare 759.5
Vitale da Bologna Bolognese painting in the fourteenth century [Tr. from Italian by Olga Ragusa] New York, Abrams [1965] 80p. illus. (pt. col., pt. mounted) plates (pt. col.) 38cm. Bibl. [ND623.V66G53] 64-11579 25.00
1. Vitale da Bologna, fl. 1329-1359. I. Title.

Vives-Atsara, Jose, 1919—

WEST, Nancy Glass, 1940- 759.6 B
Jose Vives-Atsara, his life and his art / by Nancy Glass West Austin, Tex. : Shoal Creek Publishers, c1976. p. cm. Includes index. Bibliography: p. [ND813.V58W47] 76-47664 ISBN 0-88319-027-3 : 50.00
1. Vives-Atsara, Jose, 1919- 2. Painters—Spain—Biography.

Vivolo, John, 1886—

LAFFAL, Ken. 736'.4'0924 B
Vivolo and his wooden children / text and photography, Ken Laffal. Essex ; Conn. : Gallery Press, c1976. 144 p. : ill. (some col.) ; 24 cm. [NK9798.V58L33] 76-11492 ISBN 0-913622-04-4 : 11.95
1. Vivolo, John, 1886- 2. Wood-carving—United States. 3. Primitivism in art—United States. I. Vivolo, John, 1886- II. Title. BIP

Vlaminck, Maurice de, 1876-1958.

SELZ, Jean. 759.4
Vlaminck. [Translated from the French by Graham Snell] New York, Crown Publishers [1963] 94 p. illus. (part mounted, poart col.) col. ports. 29 cm. Erratum slip inserted. Bibliography: p. 94-[95] [ND553.V6S43] 63-3674
1. Vlaminck, Maurice de, 1876-1958. BIP

VLAMINCK, Maurice de, 1876- 759.4
1958.
Maurice Vlaminck. Text by Alfred Werner. New York, H. N. Abrams [1971] 24 p. illus. (part col.) 33 cm. (The Library of great painters. Portfolio ed.) First published in 1959 under title: Vlaminck, 1876-1958. [ND553.V6W4 1971] 75-130286 ISBN 0-8109-3074-9
I. Werner, Alfred, 1911-

VLAMINCK, Maurice de, 1876- 759.4
1958.
Maurice Vlaminck. Text by Alfred Werner. New York, H. N. Abrams [1971] 24 p. illus. (part col.) 33 cm. (The Library of great painters. Portfolio ed.) First published in 1959 under title: Vlaminck, 1876-1958. [ND553.V6W4 1971] 75-130286 ISBN 0-8109-3074-9
I. Werner, Alfred, 1911-

VLAMINCK, Maurice de, 1876- 759.4
1958.
Vlaminck, 1876-1958. Text by Alfred Werner. [New York, Abrams, 1950] [36] p. illus. (part mounted. col.) 37 cm. (An Abrams art book) Caption title. [ND553.V6W4] 59-11631
I. Werner, Alfred, 1892- II. Title.

VLAMINCK, Maurice de, 1876- 759.4
1958.
Vlaminck (1876-1958) his Fauve period (1903-1907). [New York, Perls Galleries, 1968] 35 p. illus. (part col.) 24 cm. "A loan exhibition for the benefit of the New York Studio School, April 9-May 11, 1968, Perls Galleries." [ND553.V6P42] 72-203303
I. Perls Galleries. II. Title.

VLAMINCK, Maurice de, 769'.92'4
1876-1958.
Vlaminck, master of graphic art : a retrospective exhibition of graphic works, 1905-1926. Chicago : R. S. Johnson-International Gallery, 1975. 46 p. : ill. ; 25 cm. Bibliography: p. 39-40. [NE650.V55J63] 75-4141
1. Vlaminck, Maurice de, 1876-1958. I. Johnson (R. S.)-International Gallery. II. Title.

Voet, Simon, 1590-1649.

CRELLY, William R. 759.4
The painting of Simon Vouet. New Haven, Conn., Yale [c.]1962. xiii, 315p. illus. 29cm. (Yale pubns. in the hist. of art, 14) Bibl. 62-8242 20.00
1. Voet, Simon, 1590-1649. I. Title.

Vogue.

PACKER, William. 741.65
Vogue covers : the complete drawn covers, 1909-1930 / by William Packer. New York : Harmony Books, [1979] p. cm. [NC974.3.A78P32] 79-10205 ISBN 0-517-53838-5 : 6.95
1. Magazine covers. 2. Decoration and ornament—Art nouveau. 3. Art deco. 4. Vogue—Illustrations. I. Title.

VOGUE covers, 1900-1970 741.67
/ introd. by Grace Mirabella. New York : Harmony Books, c1978. 47 p. : chiefly ill. (some col.) ; 39 cm. (A Poster book) [NC1849.F38V64 1978] 78-73357 ISBN 0-517-53585-8 : 6.95
1. Vogue. 2. Fashion—Posters. I. Vogue.

YOXALL, Harold 659.193910924
Waldo
A fashion of life [by] H. W. Yoxall. London, Heinemann, 1966. ix, 269p. front., 8 plates (incl. ports.) 23cm. [TT505.Y6A3] 66-66153 6.50
1. Vogue. I. Title.
American distributor Taplinger in New York.

YOXALL, Harold 659.1'9'39100924
Waldo.
A fashion of life [by] H. W. Yoxall. [1st American ed.] New York, Taplinger Pub. Co. [1967] viii, 269 p. illus., ports. 23 cm. Autobiographical. [TT505.Y6A3 1967] 67-12613
1. Yoxall, Harold Waldo. 2. Vogue. I. Title.

Voightlander camera.

COOPER, Joseph David, 771.31
1917-
Voigtlander Bessamatic guide. New York, Universal Photo Bks. [dist. Amphoto, c. 1961] 128p. illus. 61-14255 1.95 pap.,
1. Voigtlander camera. 2. Photography—Handbooks, manuals, etc. I. Title.

TYDINGS, Kenneth S 770.2
The Voigtlander 35 mm guide. New York, Greenberg, c1952. 128p. illus. 20cm. (The Modern camera guide series) [TR263.V6T9] 52-9284
1. Voigtlander camera. 2. Photography—Handbooks, manuals, etc. I. Title.

TYDINGS, Kenneth S. 771.31
Voigtlander 35mm guide. Rev. Philadelphia, Chilton Co., c.1952, 1960. 127p. illus. (Modern camera guide series, 289) 61-8336 1.95 pap.,
1. Voigtlander camera. 2. Photography—Handbooks, manuals, etc. I. Title.

TYDINGS, Kenneth S 771.31
Voightlander 35mm guide rev. Philadelphia, Chilton Co., Book Division, c1960. 127 p. illus. 20 cm. (Modern camera guide series, 289) [TR263.V6T9] 61-8336
1. Voigtlander camera. 2. Photography — Handbooks, manuals, etc. I. Title.

Volkswagen automobile—Caricatures and cartoons.

THINK small; 741.59
[cartoons and text by] Charles Addams [and others. Introd. by Herb Valen] New York, Golden Press [1967] 1 v. (unpaged) illus., ports. 18 x 21 cm. [NC1428.T45] 68-2464
1. Volkswagen automobile—Caricatures and cartoons. 2. American wit and humor, Pictorial. I. Addams, Charles, 1912- II. Valen, Herb.

Vollard, Ambroise, 1867-1939.

JOHNSON, Una E. 769'.944'074013
Ambroise Vollard, editeur : prints, books, bronzes / Una E. Johnson. New York : Museum of Modern Art ; Boston : distributed by New York Graphic Society, c1977. 176 p. : ill. (come col.) ; 24 cm. Published in 1944 under title: Ambroise Vollard, editeur, 1867-1939. Catalogue of an exhibition held at the Museum of Modern Art, New York, June 9-Sept. 6, 1977 and at the Art Gallery of Ontario, Toronto, the Krannert Art Museum, University of Illinois at Champaign, and the Toledo Museum of Art. "Catalogue raisonne": p. 125-171. Bibliography: p. 172-176. [NE647.3.J63 1977] 77-70042 ISBN 0-87070-062-6 : 17.50.
1. Vollard, Ambroise, 1867-1939. 2. Prints, Frech—Exhibitions. 3. Prints—19th century—France—Exhibitions. 4. Prints—20th century—France—Exhibitions. 5. Illustration of books—France—Exhibitions. 6. Bronzes—France—Exhibitions. I. New York (City). Museum of Modern Art. II. Title.

PICASSO, Pablo, 1881- 769.9
Picasso for Vollard [Milton S. Fox, ed. Introd. by Hans Bolliger, tr. from German by Norbert Guterman] New York, Abrams [1965, c.1956] xxii p. 100 plates. 28cm. Bibl. A57 12.50
1. Vollard, Ambroise, 1867-1939. I. Bolliger, Hans. II. Fox, Milton S., 1904- ed. III. Title.

VOLLARD, Ambroise, 1867- 706'.5 B
1939.
Recollections of a picture dealer / Ambroise Vollard ; translated from the French by Violet M. Macdonald. New York : Dover Publications, 1978. 326 p., [18] leaves of plates : ill. ; 22 cm. Translation of Souvenirs d'un marchand de tableaux. Includes index. [N8660.V6A2 1978b] 77-88948 ISBN 0-486-23582-3 : 4.50
1. Vollard, Ambroise, 1867-1939. 2. Art dealers—France—Biography. I. Title. BIP

VOLLARD, Ambroise, 1867- 706'.5 B
1939.
Recollections of a picture dealer / Ambroise Vollard ; with a new foreword by Una E. Johnson ; [translated from the French by Violet M. MacDonald]. New York : Hacker Art Books, 1978. xv, 326 p., [16] leaves of plates : ill. ; 25 cm. Translation of Souvenirs d'un marchand de tableaux. Includes index.. [N8660.V6A2 1978] 77-76778 ISBN 0-87817-218-1 : lib.bdg. : 30.00
1. Vollard, Ambroise, 1867-1939. 2. Art dealers—France—Biography. 3. Art—Collectors and collecting. 4. Art—Anecdotes, facetiae, satire, etc. I. Title.

Volpe, Robert, 1942—

ADAMS, Laurie. 364.1'62
Art cop Robert Volpe, art crime detective / by Laurie Adams. New York : Dodd, Mead, [1974] xi, 240 p., [4] leaves of plates : ill. ; 24 cm. Includes index. [N8795.5.V64A32] 74-15238 ISBN 0-396-07027-2 : 8.95
1. Volpe, Robert, 1942- 2. Art thefts—New York (City) I. Title.

Voltaire, Francoise Marie Arouet de, 1694-1778.

BESTERMAN, Theodore, 1904- 709
Voltaire on the arts; unity and paradox. Oxford, Clarendon Press, 1974. 24 p. 22 cm. (The Zaharoff lecture for 1973) Includes bibliographical references. [NX640.V64B47] 74-180229 ISBN 0-19-952240-5 £0.75
1. Voltaire, Francoise Marie Arouet de, 1694-1778. 2. Art criticism. I. Title. II. Series: The Zaharoff lecture, 1973.

Von Schleinitz, Rene—Art collections.

MILWAUKEE. Art 759.3'074'07595
Center.
Paintings from the Von Schleinitz Collection; German genre paintings of the 19th century. Milwaukee [1969?] 1 v. (unpaged) plates (part col.) 20 cm. Catalog of the exhibition held Sept. 13-Oct. 13, 1969 at the Milwaukee Art Center. [ND1452.G3M5] 78-18741
1. Von Schleinitz, Rene—Art collections. 2. Genre paintings, German—Exhibitions. I. Title.

Von Schmidt, Harold, 1893—

REED, Walt. 741'.092'4
Harold von Schmidt draws and paints the Old West. Foreword by Dean Krakel. Introd. by Harold McCracken. [1st ed.] Flagstaff [Ariz.] Northland Press [1972] xvii, 230 p. illus. (part col.) 32 cm. Bibliography: p. 225-230. [ND237.V66R44] 72-76376 ISBN 0-87358-095-8 40.00
1. Von Schmidt, Harold, 1893- 2. The West in art. I. Von Schmidt, Harold, 1893- Harold von Schmidt draws and paints the Old West. 1972. II. Title. BIP

VON SCHMIDT, Harold, 1893 759.13
The Western art of Harold Von Schmidt / edited and with an introd. by Walt Reed. 1st U.S. ed. New York : Peacock Press/Bantam Book, 1976. [8] p., 44 leaves of plates : col. ill. ; 23 x 28 cm. [ND237.V66R45] 75-38078 6.95
1. Von Schmidt, Harold, 1893- 2. The West in art. I. Reed, Walt. II. Title.

Vorobev, Marevna, 1892—

VOROBEV, Marevna, 700'.944'361
1892-
Life with the painters of La Ruche [by] Marevna. [Translation from the original Russian by Natalia Heseltine. 1st American ed.] New York, Macmillan [1974] x, 213 p. illus. 22 cm. [ND553.V67A2413 1974] 73-10564 6.95
1. Vorobev, Marevna, 1892- 2. Painters—France—Correspondence, reminiscences, etc. I. Title. BIP

Vorster, Joe, 1887-1945.

PILLMAN, Naka. 730'.92'4 B
African portrait : the life and sculpture of Sister Joe Vorster / Naka Pillman. 1st ed. Johannesburg : H. Keartland, 1976. 128 p. : ill. ; 32 cm. [NB1096.V67P54] 77-366429 ISBN 0-949997-31-5
1. Vorster, Joe, 1887-1945. 2. Sculptors—South Africa—Biography. 3. Blacks in art. I. Vorster, Joe, 1887-1945. II. Title.

Vorticism—Great Britain.

WEES, William C. 700'.942
Vorticism and the English avantgarde, [by] William C. Wees. Manchester, Manchester University Press, 1972. xi, 273, [24] p. illus., facsims. 26 cm. Bibliography: p. [245]-262. [N6768.5.V6W4 1972b] 72-195821 ISBN 0-7190-0504-3
1. Vorticism—Great Britain. 2. Art, Modern—20th century—Great Britain. I. Title.
Available from Univ. of Toronto Pr., 15.00, 0-8020-1763-0. BIP

Vorticism—Great Britain—History.

CORK, Richard. 709'.41
Vorticism and abstract art in the first machine age / Richard Cork. Berkeley : University of California, c1976- v. : ill. (some col.) ; 34 cm. Includes index. Contents.Contents.—v. 1. Origins and development. [N6768.5.V6C67] 75-37227 ISBN 0-520-03154-7 (v. 1) : 65.00
1. Vorticism—Great Britain—History. 2. Art, Abstract—Great Britain—History. 3. Art, Modern—20th century—Great Britain—History. I. Title.

CORK, Richard. 709'.42
Vorticism and abstract art in the first machine age / Richard Cork. London : G. Fraser, 1976- v. : ill. (some col.) ; 34 cm. Contents.Contents.—v. 1. Origins and development. Includes bibliographical references and index. [N6768.5.V6C67 1976b] 76-372732 ISBN 0-900406-24-0 (v. 1) : £29.00 (v. 1)
1. Vorticism—Great Britain—History. 2. Art, Abstract—Great Britain—History. 3. Art, Modern—20th century—Great Britain—History. I. Title.

Wall hangings—Exhibitions.

DESIGNER/CRAFTSMAN Guild. 746.3'0973
Con-tex-ture; invitational weaving exhibition, April 13-May 18, 1974, the Gallery, Fort Wayne Public Library Fort Wayne [1974] [84], 10 p. illus. 21 cm. Bibliography: p. 1-10 (2nd group) [NK3012.A1D47 1974] 74-77443
1. Wall hangings—Exhibitions. 2. Wall hangings—United States. I. Fort Wayne. Public Library. II. Title.

FIBER structures / introd. by Irene Emery. New York : Van Nostrand Reinhold, 1976. 103 p. : ill. (some col.) ; 24 cm. Exhibition held June 18-July 31, 1976, at the Heinz Gallery of the Museum of Art, Carnegie Institute, in conjunction with Convergence '76, the biennial convention of the Handweavers Guild of America. [NK3180.P573F52] 76-3718 ISBN 0-442-23101-6 pbk. : 8.95 746.3'074'014886
1. Wall hangings—Exhibitions. 2. Tapestry—Exhibitions. 3. Soft sculpture—Exhibitions. I. Emery, Irene. II. Pittsburgh. Carnegie Institute. Museum of Art. Heinz Gallery. III. Handweavers Guild of America.

Wall hangings, Hindu—Rajasthan, India.

SKELTON, Robert. 746'.3'954'4
Rajasthani temple hangings of the Krishna cult from the Collection of Karl Mann, New York. Author and guest director: Robert Skelton. An exhibition organized by the American Federation of Arts. [New York, American Federation of Arts, 1973] 112 p. illus. (part col.) 26 cm. Bibliography: p. 109-110. [NK1677.S55] 72-87726 6.00
1. Mann, Karl—Art collections. 2. Wall hangings, Hindu—Rajasthan, India. 3. Wall hangings, Hindu—New York (City) 4. Wall hangings—New York (City)—Catalogs. I. American Federation of Arts. II. Title.

Wall-paper.

ACKERMAN, Phyllis, 1893- 745.54
Wallpaper; its history, design, and use. New York, F. A. Stokes Co., 1923. Detroit, Gale Research Co., 1974. p. cm. Bibliography: p. [NK3395.A3 1974] 74-19309 ISBN 0-8103-4075-5
1. Wall-paper.

KATZENBACH, Lois. 745.54
The practical book of American wallpaper, by Lois and William Katzenbach; with an introd. by Nancy V. McClelland. [1st ed.] Philadelphia, Lippincott [1951] ix, 142 p. illus., col. samples. 29 cm. [NK3412.K3] 51-10280
1. Wall-paper. I. Katzenbach, William. joint author. II. Title.

WALLPAPER Council. 747.35
Selling wallpaper; a study of the fundamental knowledge required for selling wallpaper successfully, prepared under the supervision of Wallpaper Council. Albany, Delmar Publishers [1956] 89 p. illus. 27 cm. [TH8461.W3] 57-38
1. Wall-paper. I. Title.

Wall-paper—History.

GREYSMITH, Brenda. 769'.5
Wallpaper / Brenda Greysmith. 1st American ed. New York : Macmillan, 1976. 208 p. : ill. (some col.) ; 29 cm. Includes index. Bibliography: p. 202-204. [NK3400.G73 1976] 76-3384 27.50
1. Wall-paper—History. I. Title. BIP

Wall-paper—New York (City)—Catalogs.

COOPER Union for the Advancement of Science and Art, New York. Museum for the Arts of Decoration. v. 12
Wallpaper; a picture-book of examples in the collection of the Cooper Union Museum New York, [1961?] 32 p. illus. 25 cm. "Reprinted from the Cooper Union Museum Chronicle, vol. 3, n. 1-3, October, 1961." [NK3385.C6] 75-200002
1. Wall-paper—New York (City)—Catalogs.

Wallace Collection.

WALLACE Collection. 738.2'7
Sevres porcelain / Wallace Collection ; [text] by R. A. Cecil. London : Trustees of the Wallace Collection, 1976. [4] p., 11 p. of plates (2 fold.) : ill. (chiefly col.) ; 18 cm. [NK4390.W34 1976] 77-361001 ISBN 0-900785-08-X : £0.45
1. Wallace Collection. 2. Sevres porcelain—Catalogs. I. Cecil, R. A. II. Title.

Wallace Collection, London.

WALLACE Collection, London. 738'.074'02132
Catalogue of ceramics / Wallace Collection. London : Trustees of the Wallace Collection, 1976- v. : ill. (some col.) ; 24 cm. Includes indexes. Contents.Contents.—v. 1 Norman, A. V. B. Pottery, maiolica, faience, stoneware. Bibliography: v. 1, p. 386-406. [NK3745.G7W348 1976] 77-361360 ISBN 0-900785-06-3 : (v. 1) : £4.00
1. Wallace Collection, London. 2. Pottery—England—London—Catalogs. I. Norman, A. Vesey B. II. Title.

Wallach family—Portraits.

NOREN, Catherine. 929'.2
The camera of my family / Catherine Hanf Noren. 1st ed. New York : Knopf : distributed by Random House, 1976. 240 p. : chiefly ill. ; 24 x 29 cm. [TR680.N68 1976] 75-36805 ISBN 0-394-48838-5 : 20.00
1. Wallach family—Portraits. 2. Photography—Portraits. I. Title. BIP

NOREN, Catherine. 779'.2'07401471
The camera of my family. [Catalogue of exhibition] April 11, 1973-September 3, 1973, Jewish Museum, New York. [New York, Jewish Museum, 1973] [12] p. illus. 24 cm. [TR680.N67] 73-78651
1. Wallach family—Portraits. 2. Photography—Portraits—Exhibitions. I. Jewish Theological Seminary of America. Jewish Museum. II. Title.

Walls.

ELME, John. 747'.3
All about walls. Illustrated by Joseph Bertelli. New York, Popular Library [1969] 182 p. illus. (part col.) 18 cm. On cover: Syroco's guide to decorating with accessories. [NK2119.E4] 73-88549 0.95
1. Walls. 2. Interior decoration. I. Title.

HUNT, William Dudley. 721.2
The contemporary curtain wall: its design, fabrication, and erection. New York, F. W. Dodge Corp. [1958] 454p. illus. 26cm. [TH2231.H8] 58-13444
1. Walls. I. Title.

SCHAAL, Rolf 729.31
Curtain walls; design manual. Tr. [from German] by Thomas E. Burton. New York, Reinhold [c.1961, 1962] 248p. illus., 27cm. Bibl. 62-19482 16.50
1. Walls. 2. Building. I. Title.

VAN DOMMELEN, David B 729.31
Walls: enrichment and ornamentation, by David Van Dommelen. [New York] Funk & Wagnalls [1965] xi, 116 p. illus. 28 cm. Bibliography: p. 114. [NA2940.V3] 65-15316
1. Walls. 2. Decoration and ornament, Architectural. I. Title.

WADE, Carlson. 747'.8'83
Wall decorating / Carlson Wade. New York : A. S. Barnes, c1977. p. cm. [NK2119.W32] 75-20608 ISBN 0-498-01754-0 : 15.00
1. Walls. 2. Interior decoration. I. Title. BIP

Walls—Congresses.

PRODUCERS' Council. New York Chapter. 721.2
Proceedings of seminar held January 29, 1957 on the subject curtain wall dos and donts Editor: Ernest J. Boldue, Jr [New York, 1957?] 81p. illus. 28cm. Cover title. [TH2231.P7 1957] 59-37670
1. Walls—Congresses. I. Bolduc, Ernest J., ed. II. Title.

Walls—Exhibitions.

JEWISH Theological Seminary of America. Jewish Museum. 729'.31
Using walls (outdoors). [New York, 1970] [20] p. illus. 26 cm. Catalog of the exhibition held at the Jewish Museum, New York May 13-June 21, 1970. "The bulk of this exhibition is composed of work by City Walls, inc. and Smokehouse Associates." [NA9053.W3J4] 77-125484
1. Walls—Exhibitions. 2. Urban beautification—New York (City) I. City Walls, inc. II. Smokehouse Associates. III. Title.

Wally, George B.—Art collections.

FIRST Museum of Blind Arts and Sciences. 741.9'24
Drawings and paintings by the blind in perspective : catalogue of the Wally Collection : First Museum of Blind Arts and Sciences, Caguas, Puerto Rico, 1976 / [compiled, designed, edited by G. B. Wally]. Caguas, P.R. : World Research Center for the Blind, 1976. 151 p., [3] leaves of plates : ill. (some col.) ; 28 cm. "First edition, illustrated by the blind." [NC17.P9C333] 76-28871
1. Wally, George B.—Art collections. 2. Drawing—Exhibitions. 3. Painting—Exhibitions. 4. Perspective. 5. Artists, Blind. I. Wally, George B. II. Title.

Walter, Paul F.—Art collections.

LOS Angeles Co., Calif. Museum of Art, Los Angeles. 741.9'54'074019494
The sensuous line : Indian drawings from the Paul F. Walter Collection / by Pratapaditya Pal and Catherine Glynn. Los Angeles : Los Angeles County Museum of Art, c1976. 72 p. : ill. ; 26 cm. Catalog of an exhibition. Bibliography: p. 72. [NC327.L67 1976] 76-18934 ISBN 0-87587-071-6 pbk. : 4.00
1. Walter, Paul F.—Art collections. 2. Drawing, Indic—Exhibitions. I. Pal, Pratapaditya. II. Glynn, Catherine, 1946- III. Title.

Walters Art Gallery, Baltimore.

DER NERSESSIAN, Sirarpie. 091'.09752'6
Armenian manuscripts in the Walters Art Gallery. Baltimore, The Trustees, 1973. x, 111 p., 243 p. of illus. 8 col. plates. 39 cm. Bibliography: p. 93-97. [ND3245.A7D47] 74-177384
1. Walters Art Gallery, Baltimore. 2. Illumination of books and manuscripts, Armenian—Catalogs. 3. Illumination of books and manuscripts—Baltimore—Catalogs. I. Walters Art Gallery, Baltimore. II. Title. BIP

WALTERS Art Gallery, Baltimore. 745.6'7'095662
An introduction to Armenian manuscript illumination : selections from the collection in the Walters Art Gallery / by Sirarpie Der Nersessian. Baltimore : The Gallery, 1974. [12] p., [18] leaves of plates : ill. (some col.) ; 27 cm. (A Walters Art Gallery picture book) [ND3245.A7W34 1974] 75-309486
1. Walters Art Gallery, Baltimore. 2. Illumination of books and manuscripts, Armenian. I. Der Nersessian, Sirarpie, 1896- II. Title. III. Series. BIP

WALTERS Art Gallery, Baltimore. 759.5'074'01526
Italian paintings in the Walters Art Gallery / by Federico Zeri ; with condition notes by Elisabeth C. G. Packard ; edited by Ursula E. McCracken. Baltimore : Walters Art Gallery, 1976. 2 v. (xx, 647 p., [158] leaves of plates) : ill. (some col.) ; 28 cm. Includes bibliographical references and indexes. [ND611.W34 1976] 75-28513 75.00
1. Walters Art Gallery, Baltimore. 2. Paintings, Italian—Catalogs. 3. Paintings—Baltimore—Catalogs. I. Zeri, Federico. II. Title. BIP

Walthamstow, Eng.—Description—Views.

WALTHAM Forest since 1940 : photographs of the period / compiled by W. G. S. Tonkin. London : Walthamstow Antiquarian Society, 1976. 56 p. : ill., facsim., map, ports. ; 21 cm. (Monograph - Walthamstow Antiquarian Society ; new ser., no. 18) [DA690.W233W29] 77-376051 ISBN 0-85480-031-X : £0.65 942.1'72'0850222
1. Walthamstow, Eng.—Description—Views. I. Tonkin, W. G. S. II. Series: Walthamstow Antiquarian Society. Monograph — Walthamstow Antiquarian Society ; new ser., no. 18.

Wang, Wei, 699-759.

WALMSLEY, Lewis Calvin, 1897- 700'.924
Wang Wei, the painter-poet, by Lewis Calvin & Dorothy Brush Walmsley. [1st ed.] Rutland, Vt., C. E. Tuttle Co. [1968] 182 p. illus., maps, ports. 22 cm. Bibliography: p. 153-160. [ND1049.W33W3] 68-21117 6.00
1. Wang, Wei, 699-759. 2. Paintings, Chinese. I. Walmsley, Dorothy Brush, 1894-1968, joint author. II. Title. BIP

Wangford, Eng.—City planning.

WAVENEY, Eng. District Council. Planning and Building Control Dept. 711'.4'0942641
Wangford draft village plan / [Waveney District Council Planning and Building Control Department]. Lowestoft : [The Department], 1976. [1], 7 p., 3 leaves of plates : 3 maps ; 30 cm. Cover title. [HT169.G72W3158] 77-355115 ISBN 0-9504522-1-1 : £0.25
1. Wangford, Eng.—City planning. 2. Architecture—England—Wangford—Conservation and restoration. I. Title.

Wappo Indians.

HEIZER, Robert Fleming, 1915- ed. 979.4
The archaeology of the Napa region. [Berkeley, University of California Press, 1953] v, 225-358p. illus., maps (1 fold.) tables. 28cm. (Anthropological records, v. 12, no. 6) Bibliography: p. 327-331. [E51.A58 vol. 12, no. 6] 913.794 A54
1. Wappo Indians. 2. Patwin Indians. 3. Napa Co., Calif.—Antiq. 4. Excavations (Archaeology)—California. I. Title. II. Series.

War.

BELLUM; two statements on the nature of war: An essay on war, written in 1545 by Erasmus. Fifty etchings, created in 1923 & 1924 by Otto Dix. Barre, Mass., Imprint Society, 1972. 42, [5] p., 50 plates. 31 cm. "The first publication of Bellum [by Erasmus] was as Adagium 3001, under the title Dulce bellum inexpertis, in the Froben edition of 1515... It was first published as an independent work by Froben in April 1517." The 50 etchings by Dix were published as Der Krieg. Captions in German, with English translations. [U21.2.B39] 70-182228 ISBN 0-87636-024-X 45.00 769'.92'4
1. War. 2. European War, 1914-1918—Pictorial works. I. Imprint Society, Barre, Mass. II. Erasmus, Desiderius, d. 1536. Bellum. English. 1972. III. Dix, Otto, 1891-1969. Der Krieg. 1972.

War—Caricatures and cartoons.

DAUMIER, Honore Victorian, 1808-1879. 741.5'944
Daumier on war : 64 print reproductions after the original lithographs / with and introd. by Hans Rothe. New York : Da Capo Press, 1977. 64 leaves : chiefly ill. ; 28 cm. (A Da Capo paperback) "Republication of the edition published in Leipzig in 1926 under the title Daumier

SUBJECT INDEX WARREN, ROBERT HALL—ART

und der Krieg. The introduction ... translated ... by John Matzka. The captions were adopted from both the Leipzig edition and the authoritative French catalogue of Daumier's lithographs published by Hazard and Delteil in 1904." [NC1499.D3R6513] 77-9349 ISBN 0-306-80079-9 : 6.95
1. War—Caricatures and cartoons. 2. French wit and humor, Pictorial. I. Rothe, Hans, 1894- II. Title. BIP

War in art.

BAYNES, Ken. 704.94'9'9047
War. [1st ed.] Boston, Boston Book and Art [1970] 96 p. illus. (part col.), ports. 23 x 27 cm. (Art and society 1) Exhibition organized by K. Baynes for the Welsh Arts Council and opened at Glynn Vivian Art Gallery, Swansea, Wales, in Feb. 1969. [NX650.W3B38] 78-129443 9.50
1. War in art. 2. The arts—Exhibitions. I. Welsh Arts Council. II. Glynn Vivian Art Gallery. III. Title. IV. Series: Art and society (London) 1

DE SILVA, Anil, ed. 704.949399
War and peace. [Editors: Anil de Silva, and others] Greenwich, Conn., New York Graphic Society [1965] 64 p. illus., plates (part col.) 32 cm. (Man through his art, v. 1) First American ed. "Published ... with the sponsorship of the World Confederation of Organizations of the Teaching Profession." Includes bibliographies. [N8260.W35] 65-3851
1. War in art. 2. Peace in art. I. World Confederation of Organizations of the Teaching Profession. II. Title. III. Series.

HODGSON, Pat. 741.65
The war illustrators / compiled and written by Pat Hodgson. 1st American ed. New York : Macmillan, 1977. 191 p. : ill. ; 26 cm. Includes index. Bibliography: p. 31-32. [NC968.5.W35H6 1977] 76-47458 ISBN 0-02-552000-8 : 12.95
1. War in art. 2. Magazine illustration—Great Britain. 3. Magazine illustration—United States. 4. War correspondents—Great Britain. 5. War correspondents—United States. I. Title. BIP

PARSONS School of Design, New York. 769'.973
My God! We're losing a great country; art and society. An exhibition for peace, designed by the students of Parsons School of Design. Presented by the New School Art Center, New York, June 9-July 11, 1970. [New York, New School Art Center, 1970] 1 v. (chiefly illus.) 25 cm. [N330.N52P36] 74-21298
1. War in art. 2. Art, American—Exhibitions. I. New York (City). New School for Social Research. New School Art Center. II. Title.

WORLD Confederation of Organizations of the Teaching Profession. 704.949399
War and peace [First Amer. ed.] [Eds.: Anil de Silva, Otto von Simson] Greenwich, Conn., N.Y., Graphic [1964] 64p. illus. (pt. col.) 32cm. (Man through his art, v.1.) Bibl. [N8260.W6] 65-3851 7.95
1. War in art. 2. Peace in art. I. De Silva, Anil, ed. II. Simson, Otto Georg von, 1912- ed. III. Title. IV. Series.

War in art—Catalogs.

ARMS and the artist : 760
106 reproductions / selected & introduced by Denis Thomas. Oxford : Phaidon Press ; New York : E. P. Dutton, 1977. 96 p. : chiefly col. ill. ; 41 cm. (Giant art paperbacks) [N8260.A75 1977] 77-75317 ISBN 0-7148-1773-2 pbk. : 8.95
1. War in art—Catalogs. 2. Art—Catalogs. I. Thomas, Denis.

War photographers.

HOOD, Robert E. 770'.922
12 at war; great photographers under fire, New York, Putnam [1967] 159 p. illus., ports. 23 cm. Contents.Contents.—The dangerous profession.—Roger Fenton at Balaklava.—Matthew Brady; the eye of history.—The intrepid Jimmy Hare.—Andre Kertesz; the joy of discovery.—The compleat Bourke-White.—The long apprenticeship of Edward Steichen.—Carl Mydans; the mind and the hand.—David Douglas Duncan; vagabond at war.—The cool war of Horst Faas.—David Seymour; the children of Chim.—The elusive Cartier-Bresson.—Death comes to Capa. [TR139.H6] 67-24157
1. War photographers. I. Title.

War photographers—Canada.

ROBERTSON, Peter. 770'.92'2
Irreductible verite; les photographes militaires canadiens depuis 1885. Relentless verity; Canadian military photographers since 1885. [Toronto] University of Toronto Press [1973] 233 p. illus. 26 cm. (The Public Archives of Canada series, 2) English or French. [TR139.R53] 73-85092 ISBN 0-8020-2099-2 10.95
1. War photographers—Canada. 2. Canada—Armed Forces—Pictorial works. I. Title. II. Title: Relentless verity. III. Series: Canada. Public Archives. The Public Archives of Canada series, 2.

Ward, Lemuel T.

BERKEY, Barry R. 745.59'3 B
Pioneer decoy carvers : a biography of Lemuel and Stephen Ward / Barry Robert Berkey, Velma Berkey, Richard Eric Berkey. Cambridge, Md. : Tidewater Publishers, 1977. p. cm. Includes index. Bibliography: p. [NK9797.B47] 77-13075 ISBN 0-87033-243-0 : 17.50
1. Ward, Lemuel T. 2. Ward, Stephen Wesley, 1895-1976. 3. Wood-carvers—United States—Biography. 4. Decoys (Hunting) I. Berkey, Velma A., joint author. II. Berkey, Richard, 1964- joint author. III. Title. BIP

Ward, Lynd Kendall, 1905—

WARD, Lynd Kendall, 1905- 769'.92'4
Gods' man : a novel in woodcuts / by Lynd Ward. New York : St. Martin's Press, 1978. [118] p. : chiefly ill. ; 20 cm. [NE1112.W37A4 1978] 77-91889 ISBN 0-312-33100-2 : 7.95. ISBN 0-312-33101-0 pbk. : 4.95
1. Ward, Lynd Kendall, 1905- 2. Stories without words. I. Title. II. Title: A novel in woodcuts.

WARD, Lynd Kendall, 1905- 769'.92'4
Storyteller without words; the wood engravings of Lynd Ward. With text by the artist. New York, Abrams [1974] 310, [73] p. (chiefly illus.) 28 cm. Bibliography: p. [383] [NE1112.W37A57] 70-163308 ISBN 0-8109-0541-8 25.00
1. Ward, Lynd Kendall, 1905- 2. Wood-engravings, American. I. Title.

Wardrop, John Oliver, Sir, 1864-1948.

OXFORD. University. Bodleian Library. 018'.1
Catalogue of the Wardrop Collection and of other Georgian books and manuscripts in the Bodleian Library [by] David Barrett. [Oxford] Published for the Marjory Wardrop Fund by Oxford University Press, 1973. 354 p. 26 cm. [Z2514.G3O95] 73-161993 ISBN 0-19-920028-9
1. Wardrop, John Oliver, Sir, 1864-1948. 2. Wardrop, Marjory Scott, 1869-1909. 3. Georgia (Transcaucasia)—Bibliography—Catalogs. 4. Manuscripts, Georgian—Bibliography—Catalogs. I. Barrett, David. Distributed by Oxford University Press N.Y. 48.00 BIP

Waregas.

BIEBUYCK, Daniel P., 1925- 916.75'1'033
Lega culture; art, initiation, and moral philosophy among a Central African people [by] Daniel Biebuyck. Berkeley, University of California Press [1973] xxiii, 268 p. illus. 26 cm. Bibliography: p. 241-251. [DT650.B5 1973] 71-165226 ISBN 0-520-02085-5 20.00
1. Waregas. I. Title.

Waregas—Rites and ceremonies.

BIEBUYCK, Daniel P., 1925- 394
Symbolism of the Lega stool / Daniel P. Biebuyck. An ethnoscientific approach to Akan arts and aesthetics / D. M. Warren and J. Kweku Andrews. Philadelphia : Institute for the Study of Human Issues, c1977. p. cm. (Working papers in the traditional arts ; 2-3) Includes bibliographies. [DT650.W37B53] 77-14571 ISBN 0-915980-81-9 pbk. : 3.95
1. Waregas—Rites and ceremonies. 2. Stools—Social aspects—Zaire. 3. Art, Akan. 4. Classification, Primitive—Ghana. 5. Akan language—Glossaries, vocabularies, etc. I. Warren, Dennis M. An ethnoscientific approach to Akan arts and aesthetics. 1977. II. Title. III. Series.

Warehouses—Japan.

ITO, Teiji, 1922- 725'.35'0952
Kura; design and tradition of the Japanese storehouse [by] Teiji Itoh. Adapted by Charles S. Terry; photographs by Kiyoshi Takai. [1st ed.] Tokyo, New York, Kodansha International in cooperation with Tankosha, Kyoto [distributors: Harper & Row, New York; Japan Publications Trading Co., Tokyo, 1973] 251 p. illus. (part col.). 34 cm. Translation with revisions of Nihon no kura. [NA6340.I8613] 73-81112 ISBN 0-87011-217-1 50.00 (U.S.)
1. Warehouses—Japan. 2. Architecture, Industrial—Designs and plans. 3. Decoration and ornament, Architectural—Japan. I. Terry, Charles S. II. Takai, Kiyoshi, 1938- illus. III. Title.

Warfare, Primitive.

LOWMAN, Cherry. 739.7'5
Displays of power: art and war among the Marings of New Guinea. With a design analysis of Maring shields by Alexander Alland, Jr. [New York, Museum of Primitive Art] 1973. 47 p. illus. 28 cm. (The Museum of Primitive Art: studies no. 6) Bibliography: p. 47. [GN497.L67] 72-97162 ISBN 0-912294-43-4 7.50
1. Warfare, Primitive. 2. Maring (New Guinea people) 3. Shields. I. Alland, Alexander, 1931- II. Title. III. Series: New York (City). Museum of Primitive Art. Studies, no. 6.

Warhol, Andy, 1928—

ANDY WARHOLS, index (book) 709.73
With the assistance of Stephen Shore [others] and particularly David Paul. Several photos. by Nat Finkelstein. Factory fotos by Billy Name. New York, Random 1967. 1 v. (unpaged) illus. (pt. col., pt. fold.) 28cm. (Black star bk.) [N6537.W28A8] 67-22621 12.95; 4.95 pap.,
I. Warhol, Andy, 1930-

COPLANS, John. 709'.24
Andy Warhol, by John Coplans with contributions by Jonas Mekas and Calvin Tomkins. [Greenwich, Conn.] New York Graphic Society [1970] 160 p. illus., plates (part col.) 29 cm. Bibliography: p. 157-160. [N6537.W28C6] 78-115841 10.00
1. Warhol, Andy, 1930- I. Mekas, Jonas. II. Tomkins, Calvin, 1925-

CRONE, Rainer, 1942- 759.13
Andy Warhol. [Translated from German by John William Gabriel.] New York, Praeger [1970] 331 p. illus. 29 cm. [N6537.W28C713 1970] 76-129866 22.95
1. Warhol, Andy, 1928-

WARHOL, Andy, 1928- 760'.0924
Andy Warhol: his early works, 1947-1959. Compiled by Andreas Brown. New York, Gotham Book Mart Gallery, 1971. 72 p. illus., facsims., ports. 23 x 31 cm. Catalog of the exhibition held May 26-June 26, 1971. [N6537.W28B7] 76-27439 6.50
I. Brown, Andreas, comp. II. Gotham Book Mart & Gallery. III. Title.

WARHOL, Andy, 1928- 700'.92'4 B
The philosophy of Andy Warhol from A to B and back again. 1st ed. New York : Harcourt Brace Jovanovich, 1975. 241 p.; 22 cm. [NX512.W37A28] 74-31107 ISBN 0-15-189050-1 7.95
1. Warhol, Andy, 1928- I. Title. BIP

WARHOL, Andy, 1928- 700'.92'4 B
The philosophy of Andy Warhol : from A to B and back again. New York : Harcourt Brace Jovanovich, 1977, c1975. 241 p. ; 19 cm. (Harbrace paperbound library ; HPL 75) [NX512.W37A28 1977] 76-40899 ISBN 0-15-671720-4 pbk. :2.95
1. Warhol, Andy, 1928- I. Title.

WARHOL, Andy, 1930- 759.13'074
Andy Warhol. [Stockholm?, 1968] Label mounted on verso of t.p.: Supplied by Worldwide Bks. New York. 1 v. (chiefly illus.) 27cm. Pub. on the occasion of the Andy Warhol exhibition at Moderna Museet in Stockholm, February-March 1968. [PN1998.A3W27] 68-30076 4.95
I. Stockholm Nationalmuseum. Moderna Museet. II. Title.
Distributor's address: 250 W. 57th St., New York. N.Y. 10019.

WILCOCK, John. 709'.24 B
The autobiography and sex life of Andy Warhol, by John Wilcock and a cast of thousands. Photos by Shunk-Kender except where indicated. New York, Other Scenes Inc. [1971] 1 v. (unpaged) illus., ports. 28 cm. [NX93.W37W5] 78-25787 5.00
1. Warhol, Andy, 1928- I. Title.

Warner Brothers Cartoons, inc.

PUTTERMAN, Barry. 791.43'7
Merrie melodies and Loony tunes : a critical history of Warner Brothers cartoons, 1930-1964 / by Barry Putterman. New York : Revisionist Press, 1976. p. cm. (Revisionist Press cinema series) Bibliography: p. [NC1766.U52W376] 76-45098 ISBN 0-87700-247-9 lib.bdg. : 34.95
1. Warner Brothers Cartoons, inc. I. Title.

Warner Brothers Company, Bridgeport, Conn.

PEACE, Arthur W 338.47687
The future out of the past; an illustrated history of the Warner Brothers Company on its 90th anniversary. With the histories of the corporate family: C. F. Hathaway, Puritan Sportswear, and Warner Packaging. [Compiled and written by Arthur W. Peace. Bridgeport? Conn.] 1964. 110 p. illus. (part col.) facsims., ports. 29 cm. [TT497.P36] 64-17417
1. Warner Brothers Company, Bridgeport, Conn. I. Title.

Warner family.

BALTIMORE. Municipal Museum. 739.2'3'77526
The Warner family: silversmiths to Baltimore. Baltimore, The Peale Museum, 1971. [19] p. illus., ports. 22 cm. "This publication is the result of an exhibition held at the Peale Museum, February through March, 1971." [NK7198.W3B3] 70-31914
I. Warner family. I. Title.

Warner, Langdon, 1881-1955.

BOWIE, Theodore Robert 709.24(B)
Langdon Warner through his letters, ed. by Theodore Bowie. Bloomington, Indiana Univ. Pr., 1966. xii. 225p. illus., map, ports. 23cm. [N8375.W35B6] 66-63378 6.75
1. Warner, Langdon, 1881-1955. I. Title.

Warren, Robert Hall—Art collections.

OXFORD. University. Ashmolean Museum. 738.3'7
English Delftware pottery in the Robert Hall Warren Collection, Ashmolean Museum, Oxford [by] Anthony Ray. With a pref. by Nigel Warren. [1st American ed.] Boston, Boston Book & Art Shop [1968] 248 p. 118 illus., geneal. tables, 8 col. plates. 26 cm. Bibliography: p. 240-242. [NK3740.W35 1968b] 70-12857 20.00
1. Warren, Robert Hall—Art collections. 2. Delftware—England—Catalogs. I. Ray, Anthony. II. Title.

Warrener, William Tom, 1861-1934.

USHER Gallery. 759.2
William Tom Warrener, 1861-1934, "L'Anglais au Moulin Rouge" : [catalogue of an exhibition held July 13th-September 8th, 1974, at the Usher Gallery, Lindum Road, Lincoln] Lincoln : The Gallery, [1974] [16] p., [4] p. of plates : col. ill. ; 17 x 22 cm. [ND497.W258U83 1974] 75-323660 ISBN 0-903927-03-9 : £0.45
1. Warrener, William Tom, 1861-1934. I. Warrener, William Tom, 1861-1934.

Warrington, Eng.—Antiquities.

ARCHAEOLOGICAL Surveys Ltd. 942.7'19
The archaeology of Warrington's past / Archaeological Surveys Ltd under the direction of Shelagh Grealey .... Warrington : Warrington Development Corporation, 1976. 100 p. ([10] fold.), [6] fold. leaves of plates, [8] fold. p. of plates : ill., maps (some col.), plans ; 31 cm. Prepared for Warrington New Town Development Corporation. Ill. on lining papers. Bibliography: p. 100. [DA690.W28A73 1976] 77-362923 ISBN 0-9500777-3-9 : £10.00
1. Warrington, Eng.—Antiquities. I. Grealey, Shelagh. II. Warrington New Town Development Corporation. III. Title.

Warsaw—History—Uprising of 1943—Pictorial works.

KALISZAN, Jozef, 1927- 741.9'438
The Warsaw Ghetto; drawings. Compiled and edited by Czeslaw Z. Banasiewicz. New York, T. Yoseloff [1968] 111 p. illus. (part col.), port. 31 cm. [N6999.K3B3] 68-14822 10.00
1. Warsaw—History—Uprising of 1943—Pictorial works. I. Banasiewicz, Czeslaw Z., 1934- ed. II. Title.

Warwick, Eng. St. Mary's Church. Beauchamp Chapel.

DUGDALE, William Francis Stratford, Sir bart., 1872- ed. 726.5
The restoration of the Beauchamp Chapel at St. Mary's Collegiate Church, Warwick, 1674-1742. Oxford, Printed [at University Press] for presentation to the members of the Roxburghe Club, 1956. xvi, 104 p. plates (part col.) ports. (part col.) diagr., geneal. tables. 29cm. Bibliography: p. [92] [NA5471.W33D8] 57-2733
1. Warwick, Eng. St. Mary's Church. Beauchamp Chapel. I. Title.

Warwick, Eng. (Warwickshire)—Description.

FIELD, William, 1768-1851. 914.24'8
An historical and descriptive account of the town and castle of Warwick and of the neighbouring spa of Leamington. [1st ed.] republished; with a foreword by Philip Styles. Wakefield, S. R. Publishers, 1969. xiv, 444, 28 p., 4 plates. 4 illus. 23 cm. ([County history reprints]) Reprint of 1st ed., Warwick, Sharpe, 1815. Includes bibliographical references. [DA690.W3F4 1969] 71-499429 84/-
1. Warwick, Eng. (Warwickshire)—Description. 2. Warwick Castle. 3. Leamington, Eng.—Description. I. Title.

Washington, D.C.—Biography—Portraits.

BUNDESEN, Lynne. 779'.9'920073
Us, people of Washington, D.C : a photostory / by Lynne Bundesen. Washington : Acropolis Books, c1976. 193 p. : chiefly ill., ports. ; 22 x 24 cm. [F193.B86] 76-39648 ISBN 0-87491-176-1 : 35.00.
1. Washington, D.C.—Biography—Portraits. I. Title.

Washington, D.C.—Buildings.

SCHMIDT, Lorraine H. 917.53'04
Washington - the design of the Federal City. [Compiled and written by Lorraine H. Schmidt. Washington, National Archives Trust Fund Board, National Archives and Records Service, 1972] 80 p. illus. 23 cm. (National Archives publication no. 73-1) "Based on a 1971 exhibit in the National Archives Building." [F195.S35] 72-600179
1. Washington, D.C.—Buildings. 2. Washington, D.C.—History. I. Title. II. Series.

UNITED States. Commission of Fine Arts. 725'.2'09753
Georgetown commercial architecture: M Street, Northwest Washington, District of Columbia. Issued jointly by the Commission of Fine Arts and the Historic American Buildings Survey. Arlington, Va., Washington Planning and Service Center, National Park Service, 1967. 130 l. illus. 28 cm. (Historic American Buildings Survey. Selections, no. 2) [NA705.A25 no. 2] 68-60362
1. Washington, D.C.—Buildings. 2. Architecture—Washington, D.C. I. Title. II. Series.

Washington, D.C. Capitol.

BROWN, Glenn, 1854-1932. 725'.11'09753
History of the United States Capitol. New York, Da Capo Press, 1970. 2 v. (xxi, 255 p.) in 1. illus., plans, ports. 29 cm. (Da Capo Press series in architecture and decorative art, v. 34) "An unabridged republication in one volume of the two-volume first edition, published ... in 1900 and 1903." Originally published as Senate document no. 60 of the 56th Congress, 1st session. Contents.Contents.—v. 1. The old Capitol, 1792-1850. v. 2. [1850-1900].—Bibliography (p. [224]-237) [F204.C2B82] 71-77734
1. Washington, D.C. Capitol. I. Title. BIP

MURDOCK, Myrtle M (Cheney) 917.53
National Statuary Hall in the Nation's Capitol. Washington, Monumental Press, 1955. 128p. illus. 28cm. [NB235.W3M8] 55-1697
1. Washington, D. C. Capitol. 2. Sculpture—Washington, D. C. I. Title.

NORTON, Paul F. 725'.11'09753
Latrobe, Jefferson, and the National Capitol / Paul F. Norton. New York : Garland Pub., 1977. 362, 68 p. : ill. ; 21 cm. (Outstanding dissertations in the fine arts) Originally presented as the author's thesis, Princeton, 1952. Bibliography: p. 353-356. [NA4413.W37N67 1977] 76-23662 ISBN 0-8240-2716-7 lib.bdg. : 40.00
1. Latrobe, Benjamin Henry, 1764-1820. 2. Jefferson, Thomas, Pres. U.S., 1743-1826. 3. Washington, D.C. Capitol. I. Title. II. Series. BIP

Washington, D.C. Capitol. House Office Building.

U.S. General Accounting Office. 338.4'7'690511
Examination of construction and related costs: Rayburn House Office Building; report to the Congress of the United States [on the] House Office Building Commission [and the] Architect of the Capitol by the Comptroller General of the United States. [Washington] 1967. 2 l., 193 l. illus. 27 cm. [JK1618.A53] 67-61103
1. U.S. Architect of the Capitol. 2. U.S. Congress. House. Commission on Construction of House Office Building. 3. Washington, D.C. Capitol. House Office Building. I. Title.

U.S. General Accounting Office. 338.4'7'69051109753
Rayburn House Office Building. Letter from the Comptroller General of the United States transmitting a report to the Congress of the United States, pursuant to Public law 88-454, 78 Stat. 551, on the examination of construction and related costs, Rayburn House Office Building. Washington, U.S. Govt. Print. Off., 1967. ix, 193 p. illus., plan. 24 cm. (90th Congress, 1st session. Senate. Document no. 20) [JK1618.A55] 67-61437
1. Washington, D.C. Capitol. House Office Building. I. Title. II. Series: U.S. 90th Congress, 1st session, 1967. Senate. Document no. 20

Washington, D.C. Capitol—Juvenile literature.

PROLMAN, Marilyn. 975.3
The story of the Capitol. Illus. by Bob O'Malley. Chicago, Childrens Press [1969] 30 p. col. illus. 25 cm. (Cornerstones of freedom) Traces the conception and growth of the United States Capitol from the contest to determine a design for the building to its refacing in 1961. [F204.C2P7] 69-14681
1. Washington, D.C. Capitol—Juvenile literature. I. O'Malley, Robert, illus. II. Title. BIP

Washington, D.C. Capitol. Senate Office Building.

UNITED States. Congress. Senate. Committee on Public Works. Subcommittee on Public Buildings and Grounds. 353.007'12'09753
Senate office space. Hearing, Ninetieth Congress, first session. August 3, 1967. Washington, U.S. Govt. Print. Off., 1967. iii, 46 p. 24 cm. [JK1617.A55] 67-62352
1. Washington, D.C. Capitol. Senate Office Building. I. Title.

Washington. D.C. Cathedral of St. Peter and St. Paul.

FELIER, Richard T. 726.609753
For Thy great glory [by] Richard T. Feller. Marshall W. Fishwick [Culpeper. Va., 305 E. Culpeper St., Community Pr., 1965] 111p. 246 illus. (pt. col.) plans. ports. 28cm. Bibl. [NA5235.W3F4] 65-16139 15.00
1. Washington. D.C. Cathedral of St. Peter and St. Paul. I. Fishwick. Marshall William, joint author. II. Title.

MONTGOMERY, Nancy S. 746.4'4
Stitches for God : the story of Washington Cathedral needlepoint / Nancy S. Montgomery. Washington : Cathedral Church of Saint Peter and Saint Paul, [1974] 32 p. : ill. (some col.) ; 23 cm. [NK9310.M66] 74-84715
1. Washington, D.C. Cathedral of St. Peter and St. Paul. 2. Ecclesiastical embroidery—Washington, D.C. 3. Canvas embroidery. I. Title.

Washington, D.C. Cedar Hill.

HINDS, James R. 973.8'092'4 B
Frederick Douglass home, Cedar Hill, by James R. Hinds. [Washington] Division of History, Office of Archeology and Preservation, 1968. iv, 45 l. illus. 27 cm. "Historic structures report, part II (historical data)" Bibliography: leaves 34-36. [F204.C4H5] 73-27737
1. Washington, D.C. Cedar Hill. I. Title.

TOOGOOD, Anna Coxe. 973.8'0924
Frederick Douglass Home, Cedar Hill. [Washington] Division of History, Office of Archeology and Historic Preservation, 1968. iv, 58 l., [36] p. illus. 27 cm. "Historic grounds report, historical data section." Bibliography: leaves 54-56. [F204.C4T6] 77-612463
1. Douglass, Frederick, 1817?-1895. 2. Washington, D.C. Cedar Hill. I. Title.

Washington, D. C.—Churches.

BROWN, Lillian Brooks. 277.53
Churches of the Presidents, a television series. Presented under the auspices of the Dept. of Radio and Television of the Washington Federation of Churches. [Washington? 1955] unpaged. illus. 22cm. [F203.2.A1B7] 55-4016
1. Washington, D. C.— Churches. 2. Presidents—U. S.—Religion. I. Churches of the Presidents (Television program) II. Title.

JONES, Olga Anna. 975.3
Churches of the Presidents in Washington; visits to fifteen national shrines. With a foreword by Edward L. R. Elson. [1st ed.] New York, Exposition Press [1954] 109p. illus. 21cm. [F203.2.J6] 54-7289
1. Washington, D. C.—Churches. 2. Presidents—U. S.—Religion. I. Title.

JONES, Olga Anna. 277.53
Churches of the Presidents in Washington; visits to sixteen national shrines. Foreword by Edward L. P. Elson. [2d enl. ed.] New York, Exposition Press [1961] 128p. illus. 21cm. [F203.2.A1J63 1961] 61-66359
1. Washington, D. C.—Churches. 2. Presidents—U. S.—Religion. I. Title.

Washington, D.C. Dept. of State Building.

UNITED States. Dept. of State. 745.1
Diplomatic reception rooms. Washington, 1966. 32 p. illus. 27 cm. Cover title. [NK460.D6A53] 66-62595
1. Washington, D.C. Dept. of State Building. 2. Decoration and ornament—Washington, D.C.—Catalogs. 3. Furniture—Washington, D.C.—Catalogs. I. Title.

U.S. Dept. of State. 747.2153
Guidebook to diplomatic reception rooms. Washington, 1970. 61 p. illus., ports. 27 cm. Cover title. [NK460.W3D4] 79-607085
1. Washington, D.C. Dept. of State Building. 2. Decoration and ornament—Washington, D.C.—Catalogs. 3. Furniture—Washington, D.C.—Catalogs. I. Title.

U.S. Dept. of State. 917.53'04'4
Guidebook to diplomatic reception rooms. Washington, 1971. iii, 88 p. illus., ports. 27 cm. Cover title. [NK460.W3D4 1971] 74-611705
1. Washington, D.C. Dept. of State Building. 2. Decoration and ornament—Washington, D.C.—Catalogs. 3. Furniture—Washington, D.C.—Catalogs. I. Title.

Washington, D.C.—Description—Views.

BUSSE, Fritz. 741.91
Washington city on the Potomac. Sketches by Fritz Busse; text by Russel Baker. New York, Arts, inc. [1958] 1v. (chiefly illus. (part col.) 18x21cm. [NC1145.B87B3] 58-11264
1. Washington, D. C.—Descr.—Views. I. Baker, Russell. II. Title.

Washington, D.C.—Description—1951-

REYNOLDS, Robert, 1925- 779.9'91753
Washington, D.C. Photography by Robert Reynolds. Text by Thomas K. Worcester. [Portland, Or., C. H. Belding, 1972] iv, 188 p. col. illus. 36 cm. [F200.R48] 72-78004 ISBN 0-912856-08-4 25.00
1. Washington, D.C.—Description—1951- 2. Washington, D.C.—Description—Views. I. Worcester, Thomas K.

Washington, D.C.—Description—1951- —Views.

BROWNING, Mary Eleanor. 975.3'04
Washington, D.C. in color : a collection of color photographs / by Mary Eleanor Browning ; with an introductory text and notes on the illustrations by Barbara J. Stewart. New York : Hastings House, [1977] p. cm. (Profiles of America) [F195.B76] 77-13753 ISBN 0-8038-8083-9 : 5.95
1. Washington, D.C.—Description—1951- —Views. I. Stewart, Barbara J. II. Title. BIP

GURNEY, Gene. 917.53'04'40222
The official Washington, D.C. directory : a pictorial guide / Gene Gurney and Harold Wise. New York : Crown Publishers, c1977. 243 p. : ill. ; 29 cm. Edition of 1969 published under title: Beautiful Washington, D.C. Includes index. Brief historical commentaries on Washington, D.C., and some of its major buildings accompany four hundred black and white photographs of the parks, monuments, buildings, and statues of the city and nearby sites in Maryland and Virginia. [F195.G87 1977] 77-2853 ISBN 0-517-53029-5 : 10.00 pbk. : 5.95
1. Washington, D.C.—Description—1951-

—Views. I. Wise, Harold, joint author. II. Title. BIP

Washington, D.C.—Description—Views.

GURNEY, Gene. 917.53'0022'2
Beautiful Washington, D.C.; a picture story of the Nation's Capital. With special photography by Harold Wise. New York, Crown Publishers [1969] 213 p. illus., map (on lining papers), plans. 28 cm. Brief historical commentaries on Washington, D.C. and some of its major buildings accompany four hundred black and white photographs of the parks, monuments, buildings, and statues of the city and nearby sites in Maryland and Virginia. [F195.G87 1969] 74-75056 5.95
1. Washington, D.C.—Description—Views. I. Wise, Harold, illus. II. Title.

HISTORIC photographs of 975.3'03
Washington, D.C. N[ew] Y[ork] : Eakins, c1976. 1 folder : ill. ; 16 x 87 cm. fold. to 16 x 11 cm. (Eakins pocket album ; 5) Cover title. [F195.H54] 77-374216 1.95
1. Washington, D.C.—Description—Views.

SASEK, Miroslav. 917.53'04'4
This is Washington, D.C. [by] M. Sasex. Abridged ed. New York, Collier Books, [1973] 43 p. col. illus. 23 cm. [ND1946.S2A594] 69-13394 pap., 0.95
1. Washington, D.C.—Description—Views. 2. Washington, D.C.—Juvenile literature. I. Title. BIP

Washington, D.C.—Dwellings.

MILLER, Hope Ridings. 975.3
Great houses of Washington, D.C. Photography by Charles Baptie. Conceived and produced by Whitehall, Hadlyme & Smith, inc. New York, C. N. Potter; distributed by Crown Publishers [1969] vi, 208 p. illus. (part col.) 31 cm. Bibliography: p. 206-208. [F195.M53 1969] 69-13415 25.00
1. Washington, D.C.—Dwellings. I. Title.

Washington, D.C. — Historic houses, etc.

FOLEY, Connie. 917.53
River, port & capital; the architectural and natural landmarks of Washington. [Exhibit sponsored by the National Park Service and others. Narrative by Connie Foley. Washington? 1965] 1 v. (unpaged) illus., maps. 26 cm. Cover title. [F195.F6] 66-60187
1. Washington, D.C. — Historic houses, etc. 2. Architecture — Washington, D.C. Washington, D.C. — Descr. — Views. I. U.S. National Park Service. II. Title. III. Title: The architectural and natural landmarks of Washington.

PETER, Grace (Dunlop) 975.3
Cleveland Park, an early residential neighborhood of the Nation's capital, by Grace Dunlop Peter and Joyce D. Southwick. Washington, Cleveland Park Community Library Committee, 1958. iv, 60p. illus., ports., fold. map. 23cm. Bibliography: p. 53-55. [F195.P45] 59-31018
1. Washington. D. C.—Historic houses, etc. I. Southwick, Joyce D., joint author. II. Title.

Washington, D.C.—Historic houses, etc.—Conservation and restoration—Congresses.

WASHINGTON Preservation 069'.53
Conference, Smithsonian Institution Museum of Natural History, 1972.
Proceedings. [Washington, 1972] 210 p. illus. 28 cm. Sponsored by Latrobe Chapter of the Society of Architectural Historians and the National Trust for Historic Preservation. Bibliography: p. 209-210. [F195.W66 1972] 74-173194
1. Washington, D.C.—Historic houses, etc.—Conservation and restoration—Congresses. 2. Cities and towns—Planning—Washington, D.C.—Congresses. I. Society of Architectural Historians. Latrobe Chapter, Washington, D.C. II. National Trust for Historic Preservation in the United States.

Washington, D.C.—History—Pictorial works.

EWING, Charles, 975.3'0022'2
1918-
Yesterday's Washington, D.C. / Charles Ewing. Miami : E. A. Seemann Pub., [1976] p. cm. (Seemann's historic cities series ; no. 24) Includes index. [F195.E94] 76-10376 ISBN 0-912458-68-2 : 9.95
1. Washington, D.C.—History—Pictorial works. 2. Washington, D.C.—Description—Views. I. Title. BIP

Washington, D.C.—L'Enfant plan.

CAEMMERER, Hans Paul, 1884- 975.3
The life of Pierre Charles L'Enfant, planner of the city beautiful, the city of Washington. Based on original sources. Washington, National Republic Pub. Co., 1950. xxvi, 480 p. illus., ports., maps, 24 cm. Bibliography: p. 472-473. [F195.L53] 51-804
1. L'Enfant, Pierre Charles, 1755-1825. 2. Washington, D. C.—L'Enfant plan. I. Title. BIP

CAEMMERER, Hans Paul, 711'.0924 B
1884-1962.
The life of Pierre Charles L'Enfant. New York, Da Capo Press, 1970 [c1950] xxvi, 480 p. illus., facsims., maps, plans, ports. 24 cm. (Da Capo press series in architecture and decorative art, v. 33) Bibliography: p. 472-473. [F195.L53 1970] 71-87546
1. L'Enfant, Pierre Charles, 1755-1825. 2. Washington, D.C.—L'Enfant plan.

Washington, D.C. Lincoln Memorial.

FURBEE, Leonard J. 917.53
Twenty-four years with Lincoln [by] Leonard J. Furbee. Illustrated with photos. [1st ed.] New York, Vantage Press [1968] 81 p. illus., ports. 21 cm. Bibliography: p. 73-78. [F203.4.L73F8] 68-3269
1. Washington, D.C. Lincoln Memorial. I. Title.

GORDON, Suzanne, 1945- 917.53
In this temple; a guide book to the Lincoln Memorial. Washington, Museum Press [1973] 48 p. illus. (part col.) 23 cm. Bibliography: p. 47. [F203.4.L73G67] 73-76087
1. Washington, D.C. Lincoln Memorial. I. Title.

MAHANNA, John G. W. 917.53
The seated Lincoln, by John G. W. Mahanna. Edited by Keith Wiesley. Washington, BB & W Pub. Co. [1968] 48 p. illus., ports. 23 cm. [F203.4.L73M17] 68-9723 1.00
1. Washington, D.C.—Lincoln Memorial. I. Title.

Washington, D.C. Lincoln Memorial—Juvenile literature.

MILLER, Natalie 975.3
The story of the Lincoln Memorial. Illus by Tom Dunnington. [Chicago] Childrens [1966] 30p. col. illus. 25cm. (Her Cornerstones of freedom) [F203.4.L73M5] 66-7725 1.95; 2.50 lib. ed.,
1. Washington, D.C. Lincoln Memorial—Juvenile literature. I. Title. BIP

Washington, D.C. Memorial Continental Hall.

DAUGHTERS of the 975.8273
American Revolution.
In Washington; the National Society Daughters of the American Revolution. [Editorial supervision by Mrs. Robert V. H. Duncan. Washington 1965] 118 p. illus. (part. col.) facsims., ports. 26 cm. "Diamond anniversary 1890-1965." [F204.M5D3] 65-19791
1. Washington, D.C. Memorial Continental Hall. 2. Daughters of the American Revolution — Hist. I. Duncan, Marion (Moncure) ed. II. Title.

Washington, D.C.—Monuments.

CREIGHTON, Thomas Hawk 725.94
The architecture of monuments; the Franklin Delano Roosevelt Memorial competition. New York, Reinhold [c.1962] 192p. illus. 24cm. 62-8989 6.95 bds.,
1. Roosevelt, Franklin Delano, Pres. U.S.—Monuments, etc. 2. Washington, D.C.—Monuments. 3. Monuments. I. Title. II. Title: Franklin Delano Roosevelt Memorial competition.

GOODE, James M. 917.53
The outdoor sculpture of Washington, D.C. A comprehensive historical guide [by] James M. Goode. [1st ed.] Washington, Smithsonian Institution Press [distributed by G. Braziller] 1974. 615 p. illus. 29 cm. (Smithsonian Institution Press publication no. 4829) Bibliography: p. 609-615. [NB235.W3G66] 74-5111 15.00
1. Washington, D.C.—Monuments. I. Title. Distributed by George Braziller for 15.00; pbk. 4.95, ISBN 0-87474-13-6

MURDOCK, Myrtle M (Cheney) 917.53
Your memorials in Washington. Washington, Monumental Press, 1952. 193p. illus. 24cm. Includes bibliography. [F203.4.A1M8] 53-378
1. Washington, D. C.— Monuments. I. Title.

Washington, D.C., National Gallery of Art.

*CINOTTI, Mia comp. 708.153
The National Gallery of Art of Washington and its paintings edited by Mia Cinotti, with a foreword by J. Carter Brown New York, Arco Publishing Co. [1975] 111 p. col. ill 31 cm. (Great galleries of the world) [N856] 9.95
1. Washington, D.C., National Gallery of Art. I. Title.

U.S. National Gallery of 708.153
Art.
A brief guide to the National Gallery of Art of the United States of America. Washington [1967] 30 p. illus., ports. 24 cm. [N856.A82] 70-13365
I. Title.

Washington, D.C.—Parks.

AUDUBON Society of the 917.53
District of Columbia.
Washington, city in the woods. [Edited by Shirley A. Briggs. Washington? 1954] 56p. illus., maps. 23cm. 'Originally assembled for the Audubon Society's exhibit, with the same title, held in May 1953. Most of it was then printed in Atlantic naturalist, vol.9, nos. 1 and 2.' [SB483.W3A8] 54-2236
1. Washington, D. C.—Parks. 2. Parks—Maryland. 3. Natural history—Washington, D. C 4. Natural history—Maryland. I. Briggs, Shirley Ann, 1918- ed. II. Title.

UNITED States. 333.7'8'09753
National Park Service.
Reservation list; National Capital parks. [Washington, 1973] 65 p. 27 cm. Cover title. [F203.5.A1U47 1973] 74-600806
1. Washington, D.C.—Parks. I. Title.

Washington, D.C.—Parks—Franklin Park.

OLSZEWSKI, George J. 917.53
Franklin Park, Washington, D.C., by George J. Olszewski. [Washington] U.S. Office of History and Historic Architecture, Eastern Service Center, 1970. v, 53 l. illus., maps, plans. 27 cm. Bibliography: leaves 52-53. [F203.5.F7O4] 78-608903
1. Washington, D.C.—Parks—Franklin Park. I. United States. Office of History and Historic Architecture. Eastern Service Center. II. Title.

Washington, D. C.—Parks—Hist.

U. S. Office of National 917.53
Capital Parks.
A history of National Capital parks, by Cornelius W. Heine, historian. [Washington?] 1953. vii, 161p. illus., maps. 27cm. Bibliography: p. 159-161. [SB483.W3A44 1953] 53-61048
1. Washington, D. C.—Parks—Hist. I. Heine, Cornelius W. II. Title.

Washington, D.C.—Parks—Lafayette Park.

DONALDSON, Frances 917.53
Gertrude (Flaacke) 1891-
The President's Square; the Cosmos Club's and other historic homes on Lafayette Square, by Frances F. Donaldson. [1st ed.] New York, Vantage Press [1968] 173 p. illus., facsims., ports. 21 cm. Bibliography: p. 171-173. [F203.5.L2D6] 68-18879
1. Washington, D.C.—Parks—Lafayette Park. 2. Washington, D.C.—Dwellings. I. Title.

OLSZEWSKI, George J. 975.3
Lafayette Park, Washington, D.C., by George J. Olszewski. Washington, U.S. National Park Service, 1964. xii, 65 p. illus., maps, plans. 26 cm. (U.S. National Park Service. National Capital Region. Historical research series, no. 1) Bibliography: p. 64-65. [F203.5.L2O4] 65-60046
1. Washington, D.C.—Parks—Lafayette Park. I. Title. II. Series.

Washington, D.C.—Parks—Lincoln Park.

OLSZEWSKI, George J. 917'.53
Lincoln Park, Washington, D.C., by George J. Olszewski. [Washington] Division of History, Office of Archeology and Historic Preservation, 1968. vii, 57 l. illus., plans. 26 cm. Bibliography: leaves 56-57. [F203.5.L5O4] 70-612464
1. Washington, D.C.—Parks—Lincoln Park. I. U.S. Office of Archeology and Historic Preservation. Division of History. II. Title.

Washington, D.C.—Parks—Potomac Park.

CHAPPELL, Gordon S. 917.53
East and West Potomac Parks: a history, by Gordon Chappell. Denver, Colo., Denver Service Center, Historic Preservation Team, National Park Service, 1973. iii, 178 p. 27 cm. (Historic resource study) Includes bibliographical references. [F203.5.P86C45] 73-602580
1. Washington, D.C.—Parks—Potomac Park. I. United States. National Park Service. Denver Service Center. Historic Preservation Team. II. Title. III. Series.

Washington, D.C.—Parks—President's Park South.

OLSZEWSKI, George J. 917.53
The President's Park South, Washington, D.C., by George J. Olszewski. [Washington] Office of History and Historic Architecture, Eastern Service Center, 1970. viii, 69, [122] p. illus., maps, plans. 26 cm. Bibliography: p. 67-69 (1st group) [F203.5.P9O4] 70-612500
1. Washington, D.C.—Parks—President's Park South. I. U.S. Office of History and Historic Architecture. Eastern Service Center. II. Title.

Washington, D.C.—Parks—The Mall.

OLSZEWSKI, George J. 917.53
History of the Mall, Washington, D.C., by George J. Olszewski. Washington, U.S. Office of History and Historic Architecture, Eastern Service Center, 1970. ix, 115, [64] p. illus. 27 cm. Bibliography: p. 106-111. [F203.5.M2O4] 77-614886
1. Washington, D.C.—Parks—The Mall. I. Title.

Washington, D.C.—Plazas—Farragut Square.

OLSZEWSKI, George J. 917'.53
Farragut Square, Washington, D.C., by George J. Olszewski. [Washington] Division of History, Office of Archeology & Historic Preservation, 1968. vi, 44 l. illus., group port., plans. 26 cm. Bibliography: leaves 42-44. [F203.5.F3O4] 73-612462
1. Washington, D.C.—Plazas—Farragut Square. I. U.S. Office of Archeology and Historic Preservation. Division of History. II. Title.

Washington, D.C.—Plazas—Judiciary Square.

STANLEY, Joan H. 917.53
Judiciary Square, Washington, D.C., a park history, by Joan H. Stanley. [Washington?] Division of History, U.S. Office of Archeology and Historic Preservation, 1968. i, 108 p. illus. 26 cm. Bibliography: p. 104-108. [F203.5.J8S8] 71-601788
1. Washington, D.C.—Plazas—Judiciary Square. I. U.S. Office of Archeology and Historic Preservation. Division of History. II. Title.

Washington, D.C.—Plazas—Logan Circle.

TURNER Associates. 917.53
The Logan Circle historic preservation area; a report prepared for the District of Columbia Redevelopment Land Agency [by] Turner Associates, P. C. and Nicholas Satterlee and Associates. [Washington] 1973. 113 p. illus. 22 x 37 cm. Includes bibliographical references. [NA7238.W3T87 1973] 73-623463
1. Washington, D.C.—Plazas—Logan Circle. 2. Architecture, Domestic—Washington, D.C.—Conservation and restoration. 3. Washington, D.C.—Historic houses, etc. I. Nicholas Satterlee and Associates. II. District of Columbia Redevelopment Land Agency. III. Title.

Washington, D.C.—Plazas—Mt. Vernon Square.

OLSZEWSKI, George J. 917.53
Mt. Vernon Square, Washington, D.C., by George J. Olszewski. [Washington] Office of History and Historic Architecture, Eastern Service Center, 1970. v, 64 l. illus., plans. 26 cm. Bibliography: p. 63-64. [F203.5.M6O4] 77-609959
1. Washington, D.C.—Plazas—Mt. Vernon Square. I. Title.

Washington, D.C.—Statues.

THE Statues of 917.53'03
Washington, D.C.: see it all. [Vienna, Va., J. H. Meierdierck, 1969] 32 p. illus. 13 cm. [F203.4.A1S73] 74-256440
1. Washington, D.C.—Statues.

Washington, D.C.—Streets.

CAMBRIDGE Seven 711'.73
Associates.
Report to the U.S. Commission of Fine Arts on the environmental design of streets in Washington, D.C. Cambridge, Mass. [196-] [44] p. illus. (part col.), maps (part col.) 26 cm. [NA9053.S7C3] 72-601571
1. Washington, D.C.—Streets. 2. Urban beautification—Washington, D.C. I. U.S. Commission of Fine Arts. II. Title. III. Title: The environmental design of streets in Washington, D.C.

Washington, D.C.—Streets—Pennsylvania Avenue.

CABLE, Mary. 975.3
The Avenue of the Presidents. Foreword by Nathaniel Alexander Owings. Boston, Houghton Mifflin, 1969. xxii, 248 p. illus., map (on lining papers), plans, ports. 27 cm. Bibliography: p. [237]-240. [F203.7.P4C3] 69-13006 12.50
1. Washington, D.C.—Streets—Pennsylvania Avenue. I. Title.

U.S. Library of Congress. 711'.5
The grand design; an exhibition tracing the evolution of the L'Enfant plan and subsequent plans for the development of Pennsylvania Avenue and the Mall area, organized jointly by the Library of Congress and the President's Temporary Commission on Pennsylvania Avenue. Washington, 1967. 25 p. (chiefly plates (incl. maps, plans)) 21 x 27 cm. Catalog of the exhibition held in the Library of Congress, Nov. 9, 1966-Apr. 16, 1967. [NA9127.W2A527] 67-60041
1. Washington, D.C.—Streets—Pennsylvania Avenue. 2. Washington, D.C.—Streets—Mall. 3. Cities and towns—Planning—Exhibitions. I. U.S. President's Temporary Commission on Pennsylvania Avenue. II. Title.

Washington, D.C.—Streets—Pennsylvania Avenue—History.

ENYART, Byron K. 975.3
A mile of glory : Pennsylvania Avenue from the Capitol to the White House / Byron K. Enyart. 1st ed. New York : Vantage Press, c1976. 104 p., [9] leaves of plates : ill. ; 21 cm. Bibliography: p. 103-104. [F203.7.P4E59] 76-372541 ISBN 0-533-02352-1 : 4.95
1. Washington, D.C.—Streets—Pennsylvania Avenue—History. I. Title.

Washington, D.C. Textile Museum.

WASHINGTON, D.C. 746'.074'0153
Textile Museum.
Masterpieces in the Textile Museum / essays and captions by Louise W. Mackie and Ann P. Rowe ; foreword by Andrew Oliver, Jr. Washington : The Museum, c1976. 46 p. : ill. ; 28 cm. [NK8902.W37W378 1976] 76-7310
1. Washington, D.C. Textile Museum. 2. Textile fabrics—Washington, D.C.—Catalogs. I. Mackie, Louise W. II. Rowe, Ann P. III. Title. BIP

Washington, D.C. Union Station.

OLSZEWSKI, George J. 385'.31
Construction history of Union Station, Washington, D.C., by George J. Olszewski. [Washington] U.S. Office of History and Historic Architecture, Eastern Service Center, 1970. x, 194, [137] p. illus., plans, 12 plates. 26 cm. Bibliography: p. 187-190. [F204.U5O44] 72-608521
1. Washington, D.C. Union Station. I. U.S. Office of History and Historic Architecture. Eastern Service Center. II. Title.

Washington, D.C. White House.

AIKMAN, Lonnelle. 917.53'03
The living White House. Foreword by Mrs. Richard M. Nixon. [3d ed.] Washington, White House Historical Association with the cooperation of the National Geographic Society [1970] 147 p. illus. (part col.), ports. (part col.) 27 cm. [F204.W5A5 1970] 76-140074 2.75
1. Washington, D.C. White House. 2. Presidents—U.S. I. White House Historical Association. II. National Geographic Society, Washington, D.C. III. Title.

AIKMAN, Lonnelle. 975.3
The living White House / text by Lonnelle Aikman ; foreword by Mrs. Gerald R. Ford. 5th ed. Washington : White House Historical Association, c1975. 147 p. : ill. (some col.) ; 26 cm. "Published ... with the cooperation of the National Geographic Society and its Special Publications Division." Includes index. [F204.W5A5 1975] 76-350127
1. Washington, D.C. White House. 2. Presidents—United States. I. White House Historical Association. II. Title.

AIKMAN, Lonnelle. 973
The living White House, by Lonnelle Aikman. Foreword by Mrs. Lyndon B. Johnson, introd. by Bruce Catton. [1st ed.] Washington, White House Historical Association with the cooperation of the National Geographic Society, Special Publications Division [1966] 143 p. illus. (part col.) 26 cm. [F204.W5A5] 66-30559
1. Washington, D.C. White House. 2. Presidents—United States. I. White House Historical Association. II. National Geographic Society, Washington, D.C. III. Title.

AIKMAN, Lonnelle. 917.53'03
The living White House. Foreword by Mrs. Richard M. Nixon. [4th ed.] Washington, White House Historical Association with the cooperation of the National Geographic Society and its Special Publications Division [1973] 147 p. illus. (part col.) 26 cm. [F204.W5A5 1973] 73-168291
1. Washington, D.C. White House. 2. Presidents—United States. I. White House Historical Association. II. National Geographic Society, Washington, D.C. Special Publications Division. III. Title.

HURD, Charles, 1903- 975.3
The White House story. New York, Hawthorn [c.1966] 240p. illus., ports. 29cm. [F204.W5H82] 66-15233 8.95
1. Washington, D. C. White House. 2. Presidents—U. S. I. Title.

LEEMING, Joseph, 1897-1968. 975.3
The White House in picture and story. New York, G. W. Stewart [1953] 95 p. illus. 26 cm. [F204.W5L5] 53-6172
1. Washington, D. C. White House. I. Title.

LEISH, Kenneth W. 917.53
The White House, by Kenneth W. Leish and the editors of the Newsweek Book Division. New York, Newsweek [1972] 170, [1] p. illus. (part col.) 30 cm. (Wonders of man) Bibliography: p. [171] [F204.W5L53] 72-178706 ISBN 0-88225-020-5
1. Washington, D.C. White House. 2. Presidents—United States—Biography. 3. Washington, D.C.—Social life and customs. I. Newsweek, inc. Book Division. II. Title.

MCCONNELL, Jane (Tompkins) 975.3
1898-
The White House; a history with pictures [by] Jane and Burt McConnell. New York, Studio Publications [1954] 80p. illus. (part col.) ports. 29cm. Bibliography: p. 77-78. [F204.W5M3] 54-5622
1. Washington, D. C. White House. I. McConnell, Burt Morton, 1888- joint author. II. Title.

MONTGOMERY, Ruth Shick, 745.92
1912-
Flowers at the White House; an informal tour of the home of the Presidents of the United States, by Ruth Montgomery. New York, M. Barrows; distributed by W. Morrow, 1967. 104 p. illus. (part col.) plan. 27 cm. [SB449.M58 1967] 67-15160
1. Washington, D. C. White House. 2. Flower arrangement. I. Title.

SHELTON, Isabelle. 975.3
The White House: today and yesterday. [New York, Fawcett Publications, 1962] 127 p. illus. 22 cm. (A Fawcett special edition) [F204.W5S5] 62-53265
1. Washington, D. C. White House. I. Title.

U.S. Committee for 690.5'17'09753
the Preservation of the White House.
Report of the Committee for the Preservation of the White House, 1964-1969. [Washington, 1969] [16] p. illus. 28 cm. Cover title. [F204.W5A39] 75-601762
1. Washington, D.C. White House.

THE White House; 917.53
an historic guide. [11th rev. ed.] Washington, White House Historical Association [1973] 159 p. illus. (part col.) 26 cm. Bibliography: p. 159. [F204.W5W6 1973] 73-90552 1.75 (pbk.)
1. Washington, D.C. White House. I. White House Historical Association.

THE White House : 917.53
an historic guide / White House Historical Association, with the cooperation of the National Geographic Society. 12th ed. Washington : The Association, 1975. 159 p. : ill. ; 26 cm. Includes index. Bibliography: p. 159. [F204.W5W6 1975] 75-315855 2.10 (pbk)
1. Washington, D.C. White House. I. White House Historical Association. II. National Geographic Society, Washington, D.C.

THE White House : 975.3
an historic guide / White House Historical Association, with the cooperation of the National Geographic Society. 13th ed. Washington : The Association, 1977. 159 p. : ill. (some col.) ; 26 cm. Includes index. Bibliography: p. 159. [F204.W5W6 1977] 77-152701 2.10
1. Washington, D.C. White House. I. White House Historical Association. II. National Geographic Society, Washington, D.C.

WHITE House Historical 917.53
Association.
The White House; an historic guide. Washington, 1962. 129 p. illus. (part col.) map. 26 cm. [F204.W5W6] 62-18058
1. Washington, D.C. White House. I. Title.

WOLFF, Perry Sidney, 1921- 917.53
A tour of the White House with Mrs. John F. Kennedy. [1st ed.] Garden City, N.Y., Doubleday, 1962. 258 p. illus. (part col;) ports., plans, facsims. 29 cm. Based on the television program A tour of the White House with Mrs. John F. Kennedy, with additional information, photos, and sketches. Includes bibliography. [F204.W5W73] 62-18608
1. Washington, D.C. White House. 2. Presidents — U.S. — Wives. I. Kennedy, Jacqueline (Bouvier) 1929- II. A tour of the White House with Mrs. John F. Kennedy (Television program) III. Title.

Washington, D. C. White House—Juvenile literature.

JONES, Lois Perry 917.53
The first book of the White House: home, office, museum. Illus. by Leonard Everett Fisher. New York, Watts [c.1965] 56p. illus. 23cm. [F204.W5J75] 65-11383 2.65; 1.98 lib. ed.,
1. Washington, D.C. White House—Juvenile literature. I. Fisher, Leonard Everett, illus. II. Title.

MILLER, Natalie 917.53
The story of the White House, Illus. by John Hawkinson. [Chicago] Children [1966] 1v. (unpaged) col. illus. 25cm. (Her Cornerstones of freedom) [F204.W5M55] 66-7456 1.75; 2.50 lib. ed.,
1. Washington, D. C. White House—Juvenile literature. I. Title.

PHELAN, Mary Kay. 917.53
The White House. Illustrated by Ed Emberley. [1st ed.] New York, Holt, Rinehart and Winston [1962] unpaged. illus. 22cm. (Books to begin on) [F204.W5P5] 62-10354
1. Washington, D. C. White House—Juvenile literature. I. Title.

Washington, Eng. (Durham). Parish—History—Pictorial works.

ARBUCKLE, William 914.28'1
Robert.
Washington: a pictorial history; edited by W. R. Arbuckle. Washington (Co. Durham), 'Northern Notes', 1969. 32 p. illus., coat of arms, facsims., maps, plans, ports. 26 cm. [DA690.W32A7] 73-541087
1. Washington, Eng. (Durham). Parish—History—Pictorial works. I. Title.

Washington, George, Pres. U.S., 1732-1799—Inauguration.

SMITH, Thomas Edward 917.47'1'033
Vermilye, 1857-1922.
The city of New York in the year of Washington's inauguration, 1789. Introd. by Joseph Veach Noble. Riverside, Conn., Chatham Press [1973] 244 p. illus. 23 cm. Facsim. reprint of the 1889 ed. printed for the author by Trow's Print. and Bookbinding Co., New York, with a new selection of period illustrations. [F128.44.S67 1889a] 72-92013 ISBN 0-85699-057-4 2.95 (pbk.)
1. Washington, George, Pres. U.S., 1732-1799—Inauguration. 2. New York (City)—History—1775-1865. 3. New York (City)—Description. I. Title.

Washington, George, Pres. U.S., 1732-1799—Juvenile literature.

COOPER, Michael, 1943- 745.59'41
Things to make and do for George Washington's birthday / by Michael Cooper. New York : Watts, 1979. p. cm. (A Things to make and do book) A collection of games, recipes, and craft projects suitable for George Washington's birthday celebrations. Includes a brief account ofWashington's life. [TT160.C67] 78-11709 ISBN 0-685-65724-8 lib. bdg. : 6.90
1. Washington, George, Pres. U.S., 1732-1799—Juvenile literature. 2. Handicraft—Juvenile literature. 3. Cookery—Juvenile literature. 4. Games—Juvenile literature. 5.

biographical sources": v. 3, p. 283-325. [ND1928.H372] 67-31910
1. Water-color painting—Great Britain—History. 2. Water-colors, British. I. Title.

Water-color painting—History.

KOSCHATZKY, Walter. 751.4'22'09
Watercolor: history and technique. [Translated from the German by Mary Whittall] New York, McGraw-Hill [1970] 128 p. illus., 24 col. plates (incl. port.) ports. 28 cm. Translation of Das Aquarell. Bibliography: p. 124-125. [ND1760.K613 1970b] 72-87837 12.95
1. Water-color painting—History. 2. Water-color painting—Technique. I. Title.

REYNOLDS, Graham. 759
A concise history of watercolours / Graham Reynolds. New York : Oxford University Press, 1978, c1971. 216 p. : ill. (some col.) ; 21 cm. (World of art) Reprint of the ed. published by Thomas and Hudson, London. Includes index. Bibliography: p. 198. [ND1760.R4 1978] 77-26338 ISBN 0-19-520051-9 pbk. : 6.95
1. Water-color painting—History. I. Title. II. Series.

Water-color painting, Japanese.

TANAKA, Ichimatsu, 1895- 759.952
Japanese ink painting: Shubun to Sesshu. Translated by Bruce Darling. [1st English ed.] New York, Weatherhill [1972] 174 p. illus. (part col.) 24 cm. (The Heibonsha survey of Japanese art, 12) Translation of Shubun kara Sesshu e. [ND2071.T313] 73-183522 ISBN 0-8348-1005-0 7.95
1. Water-color painting, Japanese. 2. Sumie. I. Title. II. Series.

Water-color painting—Norwich, Eng.

CLIFFORD, Derek Plint 751.422
Watercolours of the Norwich School [London] Cory, Adams & Mackay [dist. New York, Taplinger, c.1965] xviii, 89, [89]p. illus., 8 col. plates. 26cm. Bibl. [ND1932.N6C5] 65-9075 22.50
1. Water-color painting—Norwich, Eng. 2. Water-colors, English. 3. Landscape painting—Norwich, Eng. I. Title.

Water-color painting—Study and teaching.

REEP, Edward, 1918- 751.4'22
The content of watercolor. New York, Van Nostrand Reinhold Co. [1969] 143 p. illus. (part col.) 29 cm. Bibliography: p. 141. [ND2110.R35] 69-15899
1. Water-color painting—Study and teaching. I. Title.

Water-color painting—Technique.

BARBOUR, Arthur J., 1926- 751.4'22
Painting the seasons in watercolor / by Arthur J. Barbour. New York : Watson-Guptill Publications, 1975. 159 p. : ill. (some col.) ; 29 cm. Includes index. Bibliography: p. 156. [ND2420.B35 1975] 74-34136 15.95
1. Water-color painting—Technique. 2. Seasons in art. I. Title. BIP

BARBOUR, Arthur J., 1926- 751.4'22
Watercolor : the wet technique / by Arthur J. Barbour. New York : Watson-Guptill Publications, 1978. 143 p. : ill. (some col.) ; 32 cm. Includes index. Bibliography: p. 141. [ND2420.B36 1978] 77-27827 ISBN 0-8230-5681-3 : 18.50
1. Water-color painting—Technique. I. Title.

BETTS, Edward H., 1920- 751.4'22
Master class in watercolor / by Edward Betts. New York : Watson-Guptill, 1975. 237 p. : ill. (some col.) ; 29 cm. Includes index. Bibliography: p. 237. [ND2420.B47 1975] 75-15873 ISBN 0-8230-3013-X
1. Water-color painting—Technique. I. Title. BIP

BLAKE, Wendon. 751.4'22
Acrylic watercolor painting. [Edited by Heather Meredith] New York, Watson-Guptill [1970] 175 p. illus. (32 col.) 29 cm. Bibliography: p. 172. [ND2420.B55] 72-115932 ISBN 0-8230-4640-0 15.00
1. Water-color painting—Technique. 2. Polymer painting. I. Title. BIP

BLAKE, Wendon. 751.4'22
The watercolor painting book / by Wendon Blake ; paintings by Claude Croney. New York : Watson-Guptill Publications, c1978. 256 p. : ill. (some col.) ; 32 cm. [ND2420.B56 1978] 77-19322 ISBN 0-8230-5672-4 : 22.50
1. Water-color painting—Technique. I. Croney, Claude. II. Title. BIP

BRANDT, Rexford Elson, 1914- 751.422
Watercolor landscape. New York, Reinhold Pub. Corp. [1963] 160 p. illus. (part col.) 27 cm. Erratum slip inserted. [ND2240.B69] 63-14880
1. Water-color painting—Technique. 2. Landscape painting—Technique. I. Title.

BRANDT, Rexford Elson, 1914- 751.42
Watercolor landscape in fifteen lessons; a handbook for the student-painter covering the visualization, planning,and painting of landscape and marine subjects in watercolor as taught at Chouinard Art Institute and at the Brandt-Dike Summer School. [Corona del Mar, Calif.] [1953] 57 p. illus. 18 x 26 cm. [ND2240.B7] 53-20207
1. Water-color painting—Technique. 2. Landscape painting. I. Title.

BRANDT, Rexford Elson, 1914- 751.42
Watercolor technique in 15 lessons. 5th ed. [Corona del Mar, Calif., 1956] 103p. illus. 19x26cm. First ed. published in 1949 under title: Watercolor with Rex Brandt. [ND2135.B78 1956] 56-7864
1. Water-color painting-Technique. I. Title.

BRANDT, Rexford Elson, 1914- 751.422
Watercolor technique in 15 lessons. 6th ed., rev. New York, Reinhold Pub. Corp. [1963] 102 p. illus. 18 x 25 cm. First ed. published in 1949 under title: Watercolor with Rex Brandt. [ND2135.B78 1963] 63-14882
1. Water-color painting—Technique. I. Title.

BRANDT, Rexford Elson, 1914- 751.4'22
Watercolor techniques and methods : the twenty basic lessons adapted from The winning ways of watercolor for easy student and studio use / Rex Brandt. New York : Van Nostrand Reinhold Co., c1977. 128 p. : ill. (some col.) ; 28 cm. Includes index. [ND2430.B7 1977] 77-153756 ISBN 0-442-21405-7 pbk. : 8.95
1. Water-color painting—Technique. I. Brandt, Rexford Elson, 1914- The winning ways of water color. II. Title. BIP

BROMMER, Gerald F. 751.4'22
Transparent watercolor; ideas and techniques [by] Gerald F. Brommer. Worcester, Mass., Davis Publications [1973] 127 p. illus. 27 cm. Bibliography: p. 124-125. [ND2430.B76] 72-97154 ISBN 0-87192-054-9 10.95
1. Water-color painting—Technique. I. Title.

BROOKS, Leonard, 1911- 751.42
Watercolor, a challenge. New York, Reinhold [1957] 160p. illus. 27cm. Includes bibliography. [ND2133.B64] 57-6540
1. Water-color painting—Technique. 2. Painting— Technique. I. Title.

BROOKS, Leonard, 1911- 751.42
Watercolor, a challenge. New York, Reinhold [1957] 160 p. illus. 27 cm. Includes bibliography. [ND2133.B64] 57-6540
1. Water-color painting—Technique. 2. Painting—Technique. I. Title.

BROOKS, Walter, 1921- ed. 751.422
The art of watercolor painting: still life, landscape, seascape. [Designed and edited by Walter Brooks. New York, 1966] 46 p. illus. (part col.) 32 cm. (A Grumbacher library book) [ND2133.B65] 66-18999
1. Water-color painting—Technique. I. Title. II. Title: Watercolor painting.

BROOKS, Walter, 1921- 751.4'22
Creative ways with watercolor painting. Designed and edited by Walter Brooks. [Demonstrations by Attilio Sinagra and Walter Brooks] New York, Golden Press [1974] 32 p. illus. (part col.) 29 cm. (The Golden Press Art instruction series) [ND2420.B76] 73-88430 1.25 (pbk.).
1. Water-color painting—Technique. I. Sinagra, Attilio, illus. II. Title. BIP

CAMPANA, Domestic Mathews, 1871- 751.42
The teacher of water color painting; art text book. 10th ed. Chicago, c1955. 115p. illus. 20cm. (Campana's popular art library) [ND2135.C3 1955] 57-48470
1. Water-color painting—Technique. I. Title. BIP

CHOATE, Chris. 751.422
Architectural presentation in opaque watercolor, theory and technique. New York, Reinhold Pub. Corp. [c.1961] 158p. illus. (part col.) 27cm. 61-5990 12.50
1. Water-color painting—Technique. 2. Architectural drawing. I. Title.

CHOMICKY, Yar G 751.4'22
Watercolor painting; media, methods, and materials [by]Yar G. Chomicky. Englewood Cliffs, N.J., Prentice-Hall [1967, c1968] xii, 196 p. illus. (part col.) 25 cm. [ND2133.C45] 68-12553
1. Water-color painting—Technique. I. Title.

CHOMICKY, Yar G. 751.4'22
Watercolor painting; media, methods, and materials [by] Yar G. Chomicky. Englewood Cliffs, N.J., Prentice-Hall [1967, c1968] xii, 196 p. illus. (part col.) 25 cm. [ND2133.C45] 68-12553
1. Water-color painting—Technique. I. Title.

COOPER, Mario. 751.4'22
Painting with watercolor. New York, Van Nostrand Reinhold [1971] 143 p. illus. (part col.) 29 cm. (Art-in-practice series) [ND2420.C64] 72-149253
1. Water-color painting—Technique. I. Title.

COOPER, Mario. 751.4'22
Painting with watercolor / Mario Cooper. New York : Galahad Books, [1975?] c1971. 143 p. : ill. (some col.) ; 29 cm. (Art-in-practice series) Includes index. [ND2420.C64 1975] 75-329623 ISBN 0-88365-328-1 : 15.00
1. Water-color painting—Technique. I. Title.

CRONEY, Claude. 751.4'22
My way with watercolor ... a three-value approach. Westport, Conn., North Light Publishers; distributed by Watson-Guptill Publications, New York [1973] 112 p. illus. (part col.) 31 cm. [ND2420.C76] 73-76261 ISBN 0-8230-3151-9 12.95
1. Water-color painting—Technique. I. Title. BIP

DE REYNA, Rudy, 1914- 751.4'22
Magic realist watercolor painting / by Rudy de Reyna. New York : Watson-Guptill, 1978. 159 p. cm. Includes index. Bibliography: p. [ND2422.D46] 78-8194 ISBN 0-8230-2957-3 : 18.50
1. Water-color painting—Technique. 2. Magic realism (Art) I. Title. BIP

DE REYNA, Rudy, 1914- 751.4'22
Painting in opaque watercolor. New York, Watson-Guptill Publications [1969] 160 p. illus. (part col.) 27 cm. [ND2133.D45] 69-12492 12.50
1. Water-color painting—Technique. I. Title. BIP

DIBBLE, George 751.422
Watercolor materials and techniques. New York, Holt [1966] xi. 148p. illus. (pt. col.) 19x25cm. [ND2135.D5] 66-15484 5.95
1. Water-color painting—Technique. 2. Artists materials. I. Title.

DOUST, Len A. 751.422
Watercolour drawing. New York, Warne [1960] viii, 48p. illus. (part col.) 22cm. (Doust colour sketch book) 60-2216 2.00 bds.,
1. Water-color painting— technique. I. Title.

FABRY, Alois. 751.422
Water-color painting is fun. New York, Viking Press [1960] 94 p. illus. 21 cm. (A Studio book) [ND2135.F3] 60-6790
1. Water-color painting—Technique. I. Title.

FLINT, Francis M. Russell. 751.42
Water-colour for beginners. London, New York, Studio Publications [1951] 71 p. mounted illus. (part col.) 26 cm. (The How to do it series, no. 40) [ND2135.F6] 51-5631
1. Water-color painting—Technique. I. Title. II. Series: How to do it series (London, The Studio) no. 40

GRUSKIN, Alan D 1904- 759.13
The water colors of Dong Kingman, and how the artist works. Introd. by William Saroyan, text by Alan D. Gruskin. New York, Studio Publications [1958] 136p. illus. (part col.) ports. 26cm. Artist's name in characters on t. p. [ND1839.D6G7] 751.42 58-6611
1. Dong, Kingman, 1911- 2. Water-color painting—Technique. I. Title.
Contents omitted.

GUPTILL, Arthur Leighton, 1891-1956. 751.42
Watercolor painting step-by-step. [1st ed.] New York, Watson-Guptill Publications [1957] 128 p. illus. 24 cm. [ND2133.G8] 56-13161
1. Water-Color painting—Technique. I. Title. BIP

GUPTILL, Arthur Leighton, 1891-1956. 751.4'22
Watercolor painting, step-by-step. Edited by Susan E. Meyer. [2d ed.] New York, Watson-Guptill Publications [1967] 271 p. illus. (part col.) 27 cm. [ND2133.G8 1967] 66-19738
1. Water-color painting—Technique. I. Meyer, Susan E. II. Title.

HAYES, Colin. 751.4'22
The technique of water-colour painting. London, Batsford; New York, Reinhold, 1967. 3-96p. col. front., illus., 2 col. plates, tables. 26cm. [ND2135.H33] 68-11988 10.95
1. Water-color painting—Technique. I. Title.

HILDER, Rowland. 751.422
Starting with watercolour. London, Studio Vista; New York, Watson-Guptill Publications [1966] 104 p. illus. (part col.) 19 cm. Bibliography: p. 103. [ND2133.H5] 67-10435
1. Water-color painting — Technique. I. Title. BIP

HILL, Adrian Keith Graham, 1895- 751.422
The beginner's book of watercolour painting, written and illustrated by Adrian Hill. New York, Emerson Books [1959] 77 p. illus. 23 cm. [ND2135.H6] 59-13625
1. Water-color painting—Technique. I. Title.

HILL, Tom, 1922- 751.4'22
Color for the watercolor painter / by Tom Hill. New York : Watson-Guptill Publications, 1975. 159 p. : ill. (some col.) ; 29 cm. Includes index. Bibliography: p. 157. [ND2420.H54 1975] 74-30127 ISBN 0-8230-0733-2 : 16.95
1. Water-color painting—Technique. 2. Color in art. 3. Artists' materials. I. Title. BIP

JOHNSTON, F. C. 751.422
To start you painting; an introduction to landscape London, Macmillan [dist. New York, St. Martins, 1964, c.1963] vii, 71p. illus. (pt. col.) 26cm. 64-289 ainting in water colours. 5.95 bds.,
1. Water-color painting—Technique. 2. Landscape painting—Technique. I. Title.

JONES, Barbara Mildred, 1912- 751.422
Water-color painting. Princeton, N. J., Van Nostrand [1960] 109p. illus. 26cm. [ND2135.J6 1960] 60-51711
1. Water-color painting—Technique. I. Title.

JONES, Barbara Mildred, 1912- 751.422
Water-color painting. Princeton, N. J., Van

Nostrand [1960] 109p. illus., (part col.) 26cm. 60-51711 5.75
1. Water-color painting—Technique. I. Title.

KAUTZKY, Theodore, 1896-1953. 751.42
Painting trees & landscapes in watercolor. New York, Reinhold [1952] 111 p. illus. 26 cm. [ND2240.K38] 52-10618
1. Water-color painting—Technique. 2. Trees in art. 3. Landscape painting—Technique. I. Title.

KAUTZKY, Theodore, 1896-1953. 751.422
Ways with watercolor. 2d ed., enl. New York, Reinhold [1963] 136 p. illus. (part col.) 32 cm. [ND2133.K3 1963] 63-19220
1. Water-color painting—Technique. I. Title. BIP

KENT, Norman, 1903- ed. 759.13
Watercolor methods. [By] Ralph Avery [and others] New York, Watson-Guptill Publications, 1955. 126p. illus. (part col.) ports. 27cm. [ND2133.K4] 751.42 55-13607
1. Water-color painting—Technique. I. Avery, Ralph, 1906- II. Title.

LEECH, Hilton, 1906-1969. 751.4'22
The joys of watercolor [by] Hilton Leech, with Emily Holmes. New York, Van Nostrand Reinhold Co. [1973] 111 p. illus. (part col.) 29 cm. [ND2420.L43 1973] 72-2663 ISBN 0-442-23473-2 12.50
1. Water-color painting—Technique. I. Holmes, Emily. II. Title.

MEYER, Susan E. 751.4'22
Watercolorists at work, by Susan E. Meyer and Norman Kent. New York, Watson-Guptill Publications [1972] 159 p. col. illus. 29 cm. [ND2420.M49 1972] 72-5315 ISBN 0-8230-5690-2 15.00
1. Water-color painting—Technique. I. Kent, Norman, 1903-1972, joint author. II. Title. BIP

MONTGOMERY, Paul, 1892- 751.42
Adventures in watercolor painting. New York, McGraw-Hill [1954] 88 p. illus. 21 x 25 cm. [ND2133.M65] 54-8101
1. Water-color painting—Technique. I. Title.

MUSACCHIA, John B., 1916- 751.42
Course in beginning watercolor, by John B. Musacchia, Henri A. Fluchere [and] Melvin J. Grainger. New York, Reinhold Pub. Corp. [1956] 75 p. illus. 27 cm. [ND2135.M8] 56-10984
1. Water-color painting—Technique. I. Title.

NICKEL, Carl. 751.4'22
Creating and painting in watercolor. [1st ed.] Garden City, N.Y., Doubleday, 1972. 130 p. illus. 22 x 28 cm. [ND2420.N5] 79-150909 7.95
1. Water-color painting—Technique. I. Title.

NOBLE, R P 751.42
Water colour painting. New York, Pitman Pub. Corp. [1954] 63p. illus. 19cm. (The Artist's handbooks, no. 1) Adapted from the author's A guide to water colour painting. [ND2135.N6 1954] 55-12604
1. Water-color painting—Technique. I. Title. II. Series.

O'HARA, Eliot, 1890- 751.422
Watercolor with O'Hara. New York, Putnam [1966] 163 p. illus., col. plates, port. 27 cm. [ND2135.O54] 65-20684
1. Water-color painting—Technique. I. Title.

OLSEN, Herbert Vincent, 1905- 751.422
Guide to watercolor landscape, by Herb Olsen. NewYork, Reinhold [c.1965] 128p. illus. (pt. col.) 32cm. [ND2240.O4] 65-19677 15.00
1. Water-color painting—Technique. 2. Landscape painting—Technique. I. Title.

OLSON, Herbert Vincent, 1905- 751.4'22
Herb Olsen's guide to watercolor landscape / by Herb Olsen. New York : Galahad Books, [1974?] c1965. 128 p. : ill. (some col.) ; 32 cm. First published by Reinhold Pub. Corp., New York. [ND2240.O4 1974] 73-90504 ISBN 0-88365-122-X : 17.50
1. Water-color painting—Technique. 2. Landscape painting—Technique. I. Title. II. Title: Guide to watercolor landscape.

OLSON, Herbert Vincent, 1905- 751.422
Painting children in watercolor [by] Herb Olsen [pseud.] New York, Reinhold Pub. Corp. [1960] 124 p. illus. 27 cm. [ND2190.O44] 60-15925
1. Water-color painting—Technique. 2. Figure Painting. 3. Children in Art. I. Title.

OLSON, Herbert Vincent, 1905- 751.42
Watercolor made easy [by] Herb Olsen [pseud.] New York, Reinhold [1955] 109 p. illus. 27 cm. [ND2135.O6] 55-6279
1. Water-color painting—Technique. I. Title. BIP

PEIRCE, Gerry. 751.422
Painting the Southwest landscape in watercolor. New York, Reinhold Pub. Corp. [1961] 160 p. illus. 27 cm. [ND2140.P4] 61-15355
1. Water-color painting—Technique. 2. Landscape painting—Technique. 3. Water-color painting—Southwest, New. I. Title.

PELLEW, John C., 1903- 751.4'22
Painting in watercolor, by John C. Pellew. New York, Watson-Guptill Publications [1969 or 70] 160 p. illus. (part col.) 29 cm. Bibliography: p. 158. [ND2133.P28] 76-87322 12.50
1. Water-color painting—Technique. I. Title.

PIKE, John, 1911- 751.4'22
John Pike paints watercolors / by John Pike. New York : Watson-Guptill, 1978. p. cm. Includes index. [ND2430.P54 1978] 78-17139 ISBN 0-8230-2577-2 : 22.50
1. Water-color painting—Technique. I. Title.

PIKE, John, 1911- 751.422
Watercolor. New York, Watson-Guptill Publications [1966] 175 p. illus. (part col.) 29 cm. [ND2133.P5] 66-18665
1. Water-color painting—Technique. I. Title.

PIKE, John, 1911- 751.4'22
Watercolor. New, enl. ed. New York, Watson-Guptill Publications [1973] 223 p. illus. (part col.) 29 cm. [ND2420.P54 1973] 73-5552 ISBN 0-8230-5651-1 15.00
1. Water-color painting—Technique. I. Title.

RICHMOND, Leonard. 751.42
From the sketch to the finished picture; water-colour painting. New York, Pitman Pub. Corp. [1954] 80 p. illus. 26 cm. [ND2133.R45] 54-11655
1. Water-color painting—Technique. I. Title.

RICHMOND, Leonard. 751.4'22
Fundamentals of watercolor painting, by Leonard Richmond and J. Littlejohns. New York, Watson-Guptill Publications [1970] 143 p. illus. (part col.) 29 cm. 1925 and 1936 editions published under title: The technique of water-colour painting. Bibliography: p. 140. [ND2133.R5 1970] 78-98153 15.00
1. Water-color painting—Technique. I. Littlejohns, John, 1874- joint author. II. Title. BIP

ROGERS, John, 1906- 751.422
Watercolor simplified. New York, Reinhold Pub. Corp. [1962] 111 p. illus. 27 cm. [ND2133.R6] 62-19490
1. Water-color painting—Technique. I. Title.

SCHIMMEL, William B 751.42
Water color, the happy medium. New York, Macmillan, 1958. 100p. illus. 26cm. [ND2135.S35] 58-5080
1. Water-color painting—Technique. I. Title.

SCHLEMM, Betty L., 1934- 751.4'22
Painting with light / by Betty L. Schlemm ; edited by Charles Movalli. New York : Watson-Guptill, 1978. 143 p. : ill. (some col.) ; 32 cm. Includes index. Bibliography: p. 142. [ND2420.S34 1978] 77-26082 ISBN 0-8230-3881-5 : 18.50
1. Water-color painting—Technique. 2. Painting—Technique. 3. Light in art. I. Movalli, Charles. II. Title. BIP

SCHMALZ, Carl. 751.4'22
Watercolor lessons from Eliot O'Hara, by Carl Schmalz. Paintings by Eliot O'Hara. Text by Carl Schmalz. New York, Watson-Guptill [1974] 176 p. illus. (part col.) 29 cm. Bibliography: p. 173. [ND2420.S35 1974] 73-21666 ISBN 0-8230-5666-X 15.95
1. Water color painting—Technique. I. O'Hara, Eliot, 1890-1969. II. Title. BIP

SCHMALZ, Carl. 751.4'22
Watercolor your way / by Carl Schmalz. New York : Watson-Guptill Publications, 1978. 152 p. : ill. (some col.) ; 29 cm. Includes index. Bibliography: p. 150. [ND2420.S36 1978] 78-644 ISBN 0-8230-5685-6 : 16.95
1. Water-color painting—Technique. I. Title. BIP

SIMON, Howard, 1902-1961 751.42
Watercolor. New York, Pitman [c.1963] unpaged. illus. (pt. col.) port. 20x26cm. (Pitman 42) 63-15305 1.00 pap.,
1. Water-color painting—Technique. I. Title.

SMITH, Jacob Getlar, 1898- 751.42
Watercolor painting for the beginner. Rev. ed. [New York, Watson-Guptill Publications [1957] 127 p. illus. 26 cm. [ND2133.S6 1957] 57-7807
1. Water-color painting — Technique. I. Title.

SMITH, Jacob Getlar, 1898-1958. 751.4'22
Watercolor painting for the beginner. [Rev. ed.] New York, Sterling Pub. Co. [1967] 96 p. illus. (part col.) 29 cm. [ND2133.S6 1967] 67-4156
1. Water-color painting—Technique. I. Title.

SMITH, Jacob Getlar, 1898-1958. 751.42
Watercolor painting for the beginner. [1st ed.] New York, Watson-Guptill Publications [1951] 127 p. illus. (part col.) 27 cm. [ND2133.S6] 51-3519
1. Water-color painting—Technique.

SWENEY, Fredric 751.422
Painting the American scene in watercolor. New York, Reinhold [1964] 160p. illus. (pt. col.) 32cm. Bibl. 64-22427 12.50
1. Water-color painting—Technique. 2. Landscape painting—Technique. 3. U.S.—Descr. & trav.—Views. I. Title.

SZABO, Zoltan, 1928- 751.4'22
Creative watercolor techniques. New York, Watson-Guptill Publications [1974] 174 p. illus. (part col.) 29 cm. Bibliography: p. 171. [ND2420.S92 1974] 73-22234 ISBN 0-8230-1119-4 15.95
1. Water-color painting—Technique. I. Title. BIP

SZABO, Zoltan, 1928- 751.4'22
Zoltan Szabo paints landscapes : advanced techniques in watercolor. New York : Watson-Guptill Publications, 1977. 175 p. : ill. (some col.) 32 cm. Includes index. Bibliography: p. 171. [ND2240.S95 1977] 77-622 ISBN 0-8230-5980-4 : 18.50
1. Water-color painting—Technique. 2. Landscape painting—Technique. I. Title. BIP

WHITAKER, Frederic. 751.422
Whitaker on watercolor. New York, Reinhold Pub. Corp. [1963] 160 p. illus. 27 cm. [ND2133.W57] 62-19492
1. Water-color painting—Technique.

WHITNEY, Edgar A. 751.422
Complete guide to watercolor painting [by] Edgar A. Whitney. [Rev. ed.] New York, Watson-Guptill Publications [1965] 175 p. illus. (part col.) 27 cm. First ed. published in 1958 under title: Watercolor: the hows and whys. Bibliography: p. 171-172. [ND2133.W63 1965] 65-25310
1. Water-color painting—Technique. I. Title. BIP

WHITNEY, Edgar A. 751.4'22
Complete guide to watercolor painting, by Edgar A. Whitney. New, enl. ed. New York, Watson-Guptill Publications [1974] 175 p. illus. (part col.) 27 cm. First ed. published in 1958 under title: Watercolor: the hows and whys. Bibliography: p. 171-172. [ND2420.W45 1974] 74-4330 ISBN 0-8230-0851-7 15.95
1. Water color painting—Technique. I. Title.

WHITNEY, Edgar A. 751.42
Watercolor: the hows and whys. [New York] Watson-Guptill [1958] 142 p. illus. 27 cm. Includes bibliography. [ND2133.W63] 58-9992
1. Water-color painting—Technique. I. Title.

WONG, Frederick, 1929- 751.4'22
Oriental watercolor techniques / by Frederick Wong. New York : Watson-Guptill Publications, 1977. p. cm. Includes index. Bibliography: p. [ND2460.W66 1977] 77-24976 ISBN 0-8230-3390-2 : 16.95
1. Water-color painting—Technique. 2. Water-color painting, Chinese. 3. Water-color painting, Japanese. I. Title.

WOOD, Robert E., 1926- 751.4'22
Watercolor workshop, by Robert E. Wood and Mary Carroll Nelson. New York, Watson-Guptill [1974] 174 p. illus. (part col.) 29 cm. [ND2420.W66 1974] 74-10938 ISBN 0-8230-5682-1
1. Water-color painting—Technique. I. Nelson, Mary Carroll, joint author. II. Title. BIP

WYETH, Paul. 751.4'22
How to paint in water-colours. Foreword by Frederick Beddington. London, Elek [1967,c.1958] 95p. illus. (pt. col.) 26cm. [ND2133.W9] 68-1955 6.25 bds.,
1. Water-color painting—Technique. I. Title.
American distributor: Intl. Pubns. Serv., New York. BIP

Water-color Painting—Technique—Juvenile Literature.

HAWKINSON, John, 1912- 751
More to collect and paint from nature. Chicago, A. Whitman, 1964. 40 p. illus. (part col.) 24 cm. [ND2137.H32] 64-7715
1. Water-color painting—Technique—Juvenile literature. 2. Zoology—Juvenile literature. I. Title.

HAWKINSON, John, 1912- 751.4'22
Pat, swish, twist and the story of Patty Swish / John Hawkinson ; photos., Sue Long. Chicago : A. Whitman, c1978. 48 p. : ill. (some col.) ; 24 cm. (Albert Whitman how-to series) The first part of the book presents watercolor illustrations of the adventures of a little deer; the second part gives instructions for painting watercolor pictures using the three basic strokes—pat, swish, and twist. [ND2440.H38] 78-1339 ISBN 0-8075-6372-2 lib.bdg. : 4.75
1. Water-color painting—Technique—Juvenile literature. I. Long, Sue. II. Title.

ROMBERG, Jenean. 751.4'22
Let's discover watercolor. New York, Center for Applied Research in Ecucation [1973, c1974] 64 p. illus. 28 cm. (Her Arts and crafts discovery units) A step-by-step introduction to the materials and techniques of watercolor painting. [ND2440.R65] 73-16362 ISBN 0-87628-531-0 3.95
1. Water-color painting—Technique—Juvenile literature. I. Title. BIP

ZAIDENBERG, Arthur, 1903- 751.4'22
How to paint with water colors; a book for beginners. New York, Vanguard Press [1968] 60 p. illus. 28 cm. [ND2137.Z3 1968] 66-28885 3.95
1. Water-color painting—Technique—Juvenile literature. I. Title.

Water-color painting, American—Catalogs.

PRIZE-WINNING water color; bk. 2 [Comp. by Margaret Harold. Fort Lauderdale, Fla., Allied Pubns., c.1964] 40p. illus. (pt. col.) ports. 34cm. 63-14994 1.95 pap., 751.42
1. Water color paintings, American—Catalogs. I. Harold, Margaret, comp.

PRIZE-WINNING water   751.42
colors, comp. by Margaret Harold. Fort
Lauderdale, Fla., Allied Pubns., c.1963.
40p. illus. (pt. col.) ports. 34cm. 63-14994
1.00 pap.,
1. Water color paintings, American—
Catalogs. I. Harold, Margaret, comp.

Water-colorists—Australia.

BERNALDO, Allan T.,   759.994 B
1900-
A lifetime with water colours :
recollections / by Allan T. Bernaldo.
Frankston, Australia : Heritage Book
Publications, 1976. 59 p. : ill. (chiefly col.)
; 27 cm. Includes index.
[ND2091.B47A25] 77-368972
1. Bernaldo, Allan T., 1900- 2. Water-
colorists—Australia—Biography. I. Title.

Water-colorists—Great Britain—
Biography.

MALLALIEU, Huon.   759.941 B
The dictionary of British water-colour
artists up to 1920 / H. L. Mallalieu.
Woodbridge [Eng.] : Antique Collectors'
Club, c1976. 298 p. ; 29 cm.
[ND1928.M27] 77-353075 ISBN 0-
902028-48-0 : £15.00
1. Water-colorists—Great Britain—
Biography. I. Antique Collector's Club. II.
Title. III. Title: British watercolour artists.

Water-colors.

MASTER watercolors of the   759.06
twentieth century. [Introd. by Werner
Haftmann; picture analyses by Gunter
Aust, others. Tr. by Maria Pelikan] New
York, Abrams [1965] 63p. illus., 12 col.
plates, ports. 32cm. [ND1798.M313] 65-
21829 17.50
1. Water-colors. 2. Art, Modern—20th
cent.

Water-colors, American.

CHACE, Robert.   759.13
Coastal reflections; 28 watercolors. Introd.
by Edward Weeks. Barre, Mass., Barre
Publishers, 1971. [63] p. col. illus. 23 x 29
cm. [ND1839.C5A43] 75-163876 ISBN 0-
8271-7116-1 12.50
I. Title.

GRUSKIN, Alan D 1904-   759.13
The water colors of Dong Kingman, and
how the artist works. Introd. by William
Saroyan, text by Alan D. Gruskin. New
York, Studio Publications [1958] 136p.
illus. (part col.) ports. 26cm. Artist's name
in characters on t. p. [ND1839.D6G7]
751.42 58-6611
1. Dong, Kingman, 1911- 2. Water-color
painting—Technique. I. Title.
Contents omitted.

PRIZE-WINNING water   751.73
colors; bk. 7. 1967. Ft. Lauderdale, Fla.,
Allied Pubns., 1967. v. col. illus., ports.
25cm. annual. Title varies Comp.: 1963-
M. Harold [ND-1808.P7] 63-14994 1.95
pap.,
1. Water-colors, American. I. Harold,
Margaret, comp.

PRIZE-WINNING water   751.73
colors; bk. 4 [Comp. by Margaret Harold
[Fort Lauderdale, Fla., Allied Pubns.,
c.1966] 1v. (unpaged) col. illus., ports.
35cm. Cover title [ND1808.P7] 63-14994
1.95 pap.,
1. Water-colors, American. I. Harold,
Margaret, comp.

Water-colors, American—Exhibitions.

ANDREW Crispo Gallery.   759.13
Ten Americans: Avery, Burchfield,
Demuth, Dove, Homer, Hopper, Marin,
Prendergast, Sargent, Wyeth. May 16-June
30. New York [1974] [128] p. illus. (part
col.) 27 cm. On spine: Masters of
watercolor. Includes bibliographical
references. [ND1808.A6 1974] 74-81596
10.80 (pbk.)
1. Water-colors, American—Exhibitions. I.
Title. II. Title: Masters of watercolor.

CALIFORNIA Watercolor   751.42
Society.
National exhibition of watercolor painting
[catalog] [n.p.] v. illus. annual.
[ND1808.C3] 57-33626
1. Water-colors, American—Exhibitions. I.
Title.

CONTEMPORARY   759.13'074'017
images in watercolor : [exhibition, Akron
Art Institute, March 14-April 25, 1976,
Indianapolis Museum of Art, June 29-
August 8, 1976, Memorial Art Gallery of
the University of Rochester, October 1-
November 14, 1976] / by Robert Doty.
Akron, Ohio : Akron Art Institute, c1976.
[48] p. : chiefly ill. (some col.) ; 21 cm.
Catalog. [ND1808.A1C65] 76-3204
1. Water-colors, American—Exhibitions. I.
Doty, Robert M. II. Akron, Ohio. Art
Institute. III. Indianapolis Museum of Art.
IV. Rochester, N.Y. University. Memorial
Art Gallery.

EIGHT American masters of   759.13
watercolor: Winslow Homer, John Singer
Sargent, Maurice B. Prendergast, John
Marin, Arthur G. Dove, Charles Demuth.
Charles E. Burchfield, Andrew Wyeth.
[Catalog prepd. by] Larry Curry.
[Exhibition] Los Angeles County Mus. of
Art. April 23-June 16, 1968, M. H. de
Young 28-Aug. 18, 1968 & Seattle Art
Mus., Sept. 5-Oct. 13, 1968. [Los Angeles?
1968] 1 v. Bibl. [ND1807.E5] 68-26993
3.50
1. Water-colors, American—Exhibitions. I.
Curry, Larry. II. Los Angeles Co., Calif.
Museum of Art, Los Angeles. III. De
Young Memorial Museum, San Francisco.
IV. Seattle. Art Museum.
Order from the M. H. deYoung Memorial
Museum, San Francisco, Calif.

EIGHT American masters of   759.13
watercolor: Winslow Homer, John Singer
Sargent, Maurice B. Prendergast, John
Marin, Arthur G. Dove, Charles Demuth,
Charles E. Burchfield, Andrew Wyeth [by]
Larry Curry. [Los Angeles] Los Angeles
County Museum of Art [1968] [90] p.
(chiefly illus. part col.) 21 x 24 cm. Based
on an exhibition at the Los Angeles
County Museum of Art. Bibliography: p.
[89] [ND1807.E5 1968b] 68-29482 5.95
1. Water-colors, American—Exhibitions. I.
Curry, Larry. II. Los Angeles Co., Calif.
Museum of Art, Los Angeles.

ELLIS, Ray G.   759.13
The watercolors of Ray G. Ellis. Foreword
by Norman Kent. From an exhibition at
Macculloch Hall Museum, Morristown,
N.J., 1971. [North Plainfield, N.J., Twin
City Press Corp., 1971] [63] p. (chiefly
illus. (part col.)) 23 x 29 cm.
[ND1839.E43A58 1971] 72-158983
I. Macculloch Hall Museum. II. Title.

JAMISON, Philip, 1925-   759.13
Watercolors - oils - drawings. [Exhibition]
March 2-22, 1969, main gallery, Duke
University Art Museum. [Durham, N.C.,
1969] [28] p. illus. (part col.), port. 27 cm.
[ND1839.J3A57] 76-244727
I. Duke University, Durham, N.C. Art
Museum.

NEW York.   759.1307401471
Metropolitan Museum of Art.
200 years of watercolor painting in
America, an exhibition commemorating the
centennial of the American Watercolor
Society, the Metropolitan Museum of Art,
December 8, 1966 to January 29, 1967.
[New York 1967] 64p. illus. 28cm.
Includes catalogue of the retrospective
exhibition organized by the Metropolitan
Mus. of Art, &catalogue of an exihibition
organized by the Amer. Watercolor Soc.
&held in the Metropolitan Mus. of Art.
Foreword signed by Stuart P. Feld.
Introduction to the AWS water colors
signed by Mario Cooper. [ND1805.N4]
67-636 2.00 pap.,
1. Water-colors, American—Exhibitions. I.
Feld, Stuart P. II. Cooper, Mario. III.
American Watercolor Society, New York.
IV. Title.

SAVAGE, Gail.   759.14'074'017311
Three New England watercolor painters :
[exhibition] / catalogue by Gail and
Norbert H. Savage and Esther Sparks.
[Chicago] : Art Institute of Chicago, 1974.
72 p. : ill. (some col.) ; 25 cm. Includes

paintings by J. Evans, J. H. Davis, and J.
A. Davis. [ND1810.S28] 74-21601
1. Evans, J. 2. Davis, Joseph H. 3. Davis,
J. A. 4. Water-colors, American—
Exhibitions. 5. Primitivism in art—New
England—Exhibitions. I. Savage, Norbert
H., joint author. II. Sparks, Esther, joint
author. III. Evans, J. IV. Davis, Joseph H.
V. Davis, J. A. VI. Chicago. Art Institute.
VII. Title.

TRANSPARENT watercolor   759.194
paintings by members of the West Coast
Watercolor Society.[Exhibition at the] Otis
Art Institute of Los Angeles County,
November 13 through December 23, 1966.
[Alhambra, Calif., Printed at the
Cunningham Press, 1966] 1 v. (unpaged)
illus. 23 cm. [ND1808.T7] 67-68060
1. Water-colors, American—Exhibitions. I.
West Coast Watercolor Society. II. Los
Angeles Co., Calif. Otis Art Institute, Los
Angeles.

Water-colors, American—Exhibitions—
Indexes.

MOURE, Nancy Dustin Wall.   759.13
The California Water Color Society: prize
winners 1931-1954, index to exhibitions
1921-1954. Los Angeles, 1973. [78] p. 28
cm. (Publications in Southern California
art, no. 1) Includes bibliographies.
[ND1808.M68] 73-174909
1. California Watercolor Society. 2. Watercolors, American—Exhibitions—Indexes. 3.
Painters, American—Directories. I. Title.
II. Series.

Water-colors, British—Exhibitions.

INTERNATIONAL Exhibitions   759.2
Foundation.
British watercolors, 1750-1850; a loan
exhibition from the Victoria and Albert
Museum circulated by the International
Exhibitions Foundation, 1966-1967.
[Washington? 1966] 24, [60] p. 100 illus.
27 cm. Introd. signed: Jonathan Mayne.
Circulated throughout the United States to
include the Museum of Fine Arts,
Houston, Texas, and seven other
participating museums. Bibliography: p. 24
(1st group) [ND1928.I5] 67-665
1. Water-colors, British — Exhibitions. I.
Mayne, Jonathan. II. Victoria and Albert
Museum, South Kensington. III. Houston,
Tex. Museum of Fine Arts. IV. Title.

RHODE Island School   758'.1'0942
of Design, Providence. Museum of Art.
Selection II: British watercolors and
drawings from the museum's collection.
[Providence, 1972] 1 v. (unpaged) illus. 27
cm. Catalog of the exhibition held Apr. 13-
May 14, 1972. [ND1928.R45 1972] 72-
78344
1. Water-colors, British—Exhibitions. 2.
Drawings, British—Exhibitions.

Water-colors. Chinese.

STAEHELIN, Walter   738.20951
August
The book of porcelain; the manufacture,
transport, and sale of export porcelain in
China during the eighteenth century [by]
Walter A. Staehelin, Illus. by a
contemporary ser. of Chinese watercolors.
Tr. from German by Michael Bullock.
New York, Macmillan [1966] 87p. 34
mounted col. illus. 33cm. Bibl.
[ND2068.S713 1966] 66-23194 25.00
1. Water-colors, Chinese. 2. Porcelain-
China—Hist. I. Title. II. Title: Procelain.

Water-colors, English.

CLIFFORD, Derek Plint.   759.2
Collecting English watercolours / Derek
Clifford. 2d ed. New York : St. Martin's
Press, 1976. ix, 142 p., [81] leaves of plates
: ill. (some col.) ; 29 cm. Bibliography: p.
[129]-142. [ND1928.C55 1976b] 75-34749
40.00
1. Water-colors, English. 2. Water-colors—
Collectors and collecting. I. Title.   BIP

CLIFFORD, Derek Plint.   759.2
Collecting English watercolours / Derek
Clifford. 2nd ed. London : J. Baker, 1976.
x, 142 p., [2] leaves, [161] p. of plates : ill.
(some col.), ports. ; 29 cm. Bibliography: p.

131-142. [ND1928.C55 1976] 76-365860
ISBN 0-212-97013-5 : £12.50
1. Water-colors, English. 2. Water-colors—
Collectors and collecting. I. Title.

Water-colors, English—Catalogs.

THOMAS, Denis.   759.2
The price guide to English water-colours,
1750-1900; edited by Denis Thomas, with
Ian Bennett. Woodridge, Antique
Collectors' Club, 1971. [6], x, 339 p.
chiefly illus. 21 x 27 cm. (Price guide
series) Bibliography: p. iv. [ND1928.T45]
72-193300 ISBN 0-902028-05-7 £4.25
1. Water-colors, English—Catalogs. I.
Bennett, Ian. II. Antique Collector's Club.
III. Title.

Water-colors, English—Exhibitions.

WILLIAM Hayes   759.2'074'0156565
Ackland Memorial Art Center.
English watercolors and drawings, 1700-
1900 : [exhibition] the William Hayes
Ackland Memorial Art Center, September
21-October 26, 1975. [Chapel Hill] : The
Center, [1975] [39] p. : ill. ; 23 cm.
[ND1928.W535 1975] 76-620841
1. Water-colors, English—Exhibitions. 2.
Drawings, English—Exhibitions. I. Title.

Water-colors—Exhibitions.

HALLMARK CARDS, inc.   751.42
An exhibition of 100 prizewinning
watercolors of the second international
Hallmark art award sponsored by the
Hallmark Greeting Card Company New
York? 1952] [68] p. (chiefly illus. (part col.
)) 26 cm. [ND1730.H33] 53-20209
1. Water-colors—Exhibitions. 2. Art—
Exhibitions, Traveling. 3. Jesus Christ—
Art. I. Title.

Water-colors, French.

DAULTE, Francois.   760'.0944
French watercolors of the 20th century.
Foreword by Andre Duneyer de Segonzac.
Translated from the French by Diana
Imber. New York, Viking Press [1968] 141
p. illus. (part col.) 30 cm. (A Studio book)
Translation of L'aquarelle francaise au 20e
siecle. Includes bibliographical references.
[ND1947.D313] 68-18114
1. Water-colors, French. 2. Painting,
Modern—20th century—France. I. Title.

Water-colors, French—Exhibitions.

MICHIGAN. University.   759.4
Museum of Art.
French watercolors, 1760-1860.
[exhibition] September 29-October 24, 196
Ann Arbor [1965] 1 v. (unpaged) illus. 26
cm. [ND1947.M5] 66-64350
1. Water-colors, French — Exhibitions. 2.
Painters, French. I. Title.

RHODE Island   741.9'44'07401452
School of Design, Providence. Museum
of Art.
Selection V : French watercolors and
drawings from the museum's collection, ca.
1800-1910 Providence : Museum of Art,
Rhode Island School of Design, [1975] 176
p. : ill. ; 26 cm. Includes bibliographical
references. [ND1947.R48 1975] 75-898
1. Water-colors, French—Exhibitions. 2.
Drawings, French—Exhibitions. I. Title:
French watercolors and drawings from the
museum's collection, ca. 1800-1910.

Water-colors, German—Catalogs.

COLOGNE. Wallraf-Richartz-   759.3
Museum.
German expressionist watercolors, from the
collections of the Wallraf-Richartz-
Museum, Cologne. Introd. by Horst Keller.
Washington, International Exhibitions
Foundation [1969] 21 p. (incl. 5 col. illus.),
[66] p. of illus. 22 cm. To be circulated at
the National Gallery of Art, Washington,
D.C. and other participating American
museums. [ND1951.C64] 76-97063
1. Water-colors, German—Catalogs. 2.
Expressionism (Art)—Germany. I. Keller,
Horst. II. U.S. National Gallery of Art.

SUBJECT INDEX

WATTEAU, JEAN ANTOINE

Water-colors, Japanese—Exhibitions.

BOWIE, Theodore Robert. 759.952'074'0172255
Japanese drawing / Theodore Bowie. Bloomington : Indiana University Art Museum, 1975. 165 p. : ill. (some col.) ; 26 cm. (Indiana University Art Museum publication ; no. 1975/1) "Additions and corrections" slip inserted. Includes catalogue of the exhibition held Feb. 9-Mar. 9, 1975. Bibliography: p. 53. [ND2071.B68] 75-622254
1. Water-colors, Japanese—Exhibitions. 2. Brush drawing. 3. Sumie. I. Indiana. University. Museum of Art. II. Title. III. Series: Indiana. University. Museum of Art. Publication ; no. 1975/1.

JAPANESE ink 759.952'074'014967
paintings from American collections : the Muromachi period : an exhibition in honor of Shujiro Shimada / edited by Yoshiaki Shimizu and Carolyn Wheelwright. Princeton, N.J. : Art Museum, Princeton University : distributed by Princeton University Press, c1976. 300 p. : ill. ; 29 cm. Exhibition held Apr. 25-June 13, 1976. Includes index. Bibliography: p. 280-291. [ND2071.J36] 75-33450 ISBN 0-691-03913-5 : 40.00 ISBN 0-691-03918-6 pbk. : 18.00
1. Shimada, Shujiro, 1907- 2. Water-colors, Japanese—Exhibitions. 3. Sumie—Exhibitions. 4. Painting, Japanese—Kamakura-Momoyama periods, 1185-1600. I. Shimizu, Yoshiaki, fl. 1967- II. Wheelwright, Carolyn. III. Princeton University. Art Museum.

Water gardens.

BEEDELL, Suzanne Mollie. 714
Water in the garden [by] Suzanne Beedell. Newton Abbot, David and Charles, 1973, [i.e.1974] 176 p. illus. 23 cm. Includes index. Bibliography: p. 173. [SB423.B43] 73-178494 ISBN 0-7153-5897-9
1. Water gardens. 2. Swimming pools. I. Title.
Distributed by David and Charles, Vermont, 7.95.

Water in landscape architecture.

CAMPBELL, Craig S., 1938- 714
Water in landscape architecture / Craig S. Campbell. New York : Van Nostrand Reinhold, 1978. 128 p. : ill. ; 29 cm. Includes index. Bibliography: p. 126. [SB475.8.C35] 77-24952 ISBN 0-442-21459-6 : 15.95
1. Water in landscape architecture. I. Title. BIP

JELLICOE, Susan. 714
Water; the use of water in landscape architecture [by] Susan and Geoffrey Jellicoe. New York, St. Martin's Press [1971] 137 p. illus. 26 cm. [SB472.J46 1971b] 75-154678 12.50
1. Water in landscape architecture. 2. Fountains. I. Jellicoe, Geoffrey Alan, 1900- joint author. II. Title.

WATER and landscape : 333.9'102
an aesthetic overview of the role of water in the landscape / R. Burton Litton, Jr., Robert J. Tetlow, principal investigators ... [et al.]. Port Washington, N.Y. : Water Information Center, 1974. xviii, 314 p. : ill. ; 24 cm. Originally prepared for the National Water Commission and submitted in 1971 as a report entitled An aesthetic overview of the role of water in the landscape. Bibliography: p. 299-314. [SB475.8.W37 1974] 74-79147 ISBN 0-912394-10-2 : 11.50
1. Water in landscape architecture. 2. Landscape. 3. Nature (Aesthetics) I. Litton, R. Burton. II. Tetlow, Robert J. III. Water Information Center, inc. IV. United States. National Water Commission. BIP

WATER and the landscape : 714
a Landscape architecture book / edited by Grady Clay. New York : McGraw-Hill, [1978] c1979. p. cm. Includes index. [SB475.8.W38] 78-19206 ISBN 0-07-036190-8 : 19.50
1. Water in landscape architecture. I. Clay, Grady.

Water-marks.

BRIQUET, Charles Moise, 1839-1918 676.2802703
Les filigranes. Dictionnaire historique des marques du papier des leur apparition vers 1282 jusqu'en 1600. Avec 39 figures dans le texte et 16.112 fac-similes de filigranes. ed. New York Hacker Art Bks., 1966. 4v. (xxiv, 836p.) illus., facsims., plates. 32cm. Bibl. [Z237.B845 1966] 66-8252 120.00 set,
1. Water-marks. I. Title. BIP

CHURCHILL, William Algernon, 1865- 676
Watermarks in paper in Holland, England, France, etc., in the XVII, and XVIII centuries and their interconnection, by W. A. Churchill. Amsterdam, M. Hertzberger 1967. 94, cdxxxii p. incl. front., illus. (pt. mounted) facsims. 31cm. Bibl. [Z237.C56] 35-16165 25.00
1. Water-marks. 2. Paper making and trade—Hist. I. Title.
Distributed by Abner Schram, 1860 Broadway, New York, N.Y. 10023.

FELIX, Ervin J., 1918- 769.56
The stamp collector's guidebook of worldwide watermarks and perforations, by Ervin J. Felix. Racine, Wis., Whitman Pub. Co. [1966] 256 p. (p. 247-256 blank for "Notes") col. illus. 20 cm. Cover title: Worldwide watermarks and perforations from 1840 to date. On spine: Watermarks and perforations. [HE6183.F4] 66-28511
1. Water-marks. 2. Perforations (Philately) I. Title. II. Title: Worldwide watermarks and perforations from 1840 to date. III. Title: Watermarks and perforations.

Water-marks—Bibliography.

HUNTER, Dard, 1883-1966. 016.676'27'0275
Hand made paper and its water marks: a bibliography. New York, B. Franklin [1968] 22 p. 23 cm. (Burt Franklin: bibliography & reference series #218) "Originally published ... 1916." [Z7914.P2H9 1967] 68-56722
1. Water-marks—Bibliography. 2. Paper making and trade—Bibliography. I. Title. BIP

WEINER, Jack, 1910- 016.676'28'027
Watermarking [by] Jack Weiner and Kathleen Mirkes. Introd. by William C. Krueger. Appleton, Wis., Institute of Paper Chemistry, 1972. iv, 102 p. 28 cm. (The Institute of Paper Chemistry. Bibliographic series no. 257) [Z7914.P2W3525] 72-89525
1. Water-marks—Bibliography. I. Mirkes, Kathleen, joint author. II. Title. III. Series: Appleton, Wis. Institute of Paper Chemistry. Bibliographic series no. 257.

Water resources development—Illinois.

SHEAFFER, John Richard 711.8
The water resource in northeastern Illinois: planning its use. Pred. by John R. Sheaffer, Arthur J. Zeizel, with Isabel Giachetti [others] Chicago, Northwestern Illinois Planning Commn., 1966. xiii, 182p. illus. (pt. col.) col. maps. 28cm. (Northeastern Illinois Metropolitae Area) Planning. Comm. Technical report no. 4 Bibl. [NA9000.N67 no.4] 66-65587 7.5o pap.,
1. Water resources development—Illinois. 2. Water supply—illinois. I. Zeizel, Arthur John, joint author. II. Title. III. Series.
400 W. Madison, Chicago, Ill., 60606.

Water skiing.

SPINNER, Stephanie. 767.1'7
Water skiing and surfboarding. Illus. by Irwin Greenberg. New York, Golden Pr. [1968] 32p. col. illus. 18cm. (Golden pocket guide) [GV840.S5S65] 68-15710 1.00
1. Water skiing. 2. Surf riding. I. Title.

Water-supply—New Mexico.

NEW Mexico. State Planning Office. 711'.8
Water and sewer area plans, Guadalupe County, New Mexico [and other counties] Santa Fe, 1967- v. illus., maps (part col.) 28 cm. Cover title: FHA water & sewer area plans, Guadalupe County, New Mexico [and other counties] Includes bibliographies. [HD1694.N6A5] 75-627154
1. Water-supply—New Mexico. 2. Sewerage—New Mexico. I. Title. II. Title: FHA water & sewer area plans, Guadalupe, New Mexico [and other counties]

Watercolor painting—Technique.

ZAIDENBERG, Arthur, 1903- 751.4
How to paint with water colors; a book for beginners. New York, Vanguard Press [1968] 60 p. illus. 28 cm. Introduction to painting with water colors, including a description of basic techniques and materials needed. [ND2137.Z3 1968] AC 68
1. Watercolor painting—Technique. I. Title. BIP

Watergate Affair, 1972- —Caricatures and cartoons—Exhibitions.

WATERGATE, the 760'.074'016947 s
unmaking of a President : Lexington, January 12-February 9, 1975 / organized and edited for the University of Kentucky Art Gallery by Richard B. Freeman. [Lexington : University of Kentucky Art Gallery, 1975] 96 p. : chiefly ill. ; 28 cm. (Graphics ; 17, 1975) Catalog of the exhibition held at the University of Kentucky Art Gallery. [NE45.K4K45 no. 17, 1975] [E860] 364.1'32 75-312669
1. Nixon, Richard Milhous, 1913- —Cartoons, satire, etc.—Exhibitions. 2. Watergate Affair, 1972- —Caricatures and cartoons—Exhibitions. 3. American wit and humor, Pictorial—Exhibitions. I. Freeman, Richard B., 1908- II. Series: Kentucky. University. Art Gallery. Graphics ; 17, 1975.

Watergate Affair, 1972- —Portraits.

WARSHAW, Howard. 741.9'73
Drawings of the Watergate hearings. Pref. by George Dangerfield. [Limited ed. Santa Barbara, Esther Bear Gallery, 1973] [95] p. illus. 22 cm. Cover title. [E859.W35] 74-153429
1. Watergate Affair, 1972- —Portraits. I. Title.

Waterman, George—Art collections.

RHODE Island School of Design, Providence. Museum of Art. 709'.73
The George Waterman Collection. [Exhibition] October 22-November 23, 1969. [Providence, 1969] [55] p. illus. (part col.) 22 cm. Includes bibliographies. [N6512.R45] 78-105670
1. Waterman, George—Art collections. 2. Art, American—Exhibitions. 3. Art, Modern—20th century—U.S.

Watford, Eng.—Description—Views.

ILLUSTRATED 942.5'892'00222
companion to the 'History of Watford' (and district) / edited by Peter Taylor. Watford : Lesley Enstone, 1976. 68 p. : of ill. (some col.), facsims., ports. ; 24 cm. Bibliography: p. 68. [DA690.W34144] 77-372678 ISBN 0-9505675-0-7 : £4.20
1. Watford, Eng.—Description—Views. 2. Watford, Eng.—Social life and customs—Pictorial works. I. Taylor, Peter, 1943- II. Title: History of Watford.

Watkins, Franklin Chenault, 1894-

NEW York. Museum of Modern Art. 759.13
Franklin C. Watkins, by Andrew Carnduff Ritchie. New York [1950] 48 p. illus. (part col.) ports. 26 cm. "Catalog of the exhibition, March 21 to June 11, 1950": p. 45-46. Bibliography, by Anne Bollmann: p. 47-48. [ND237.W354N4] 50-4888
1. Watkins, Franklin Chenault, 1894- 2. Paintings, American — Exhibitions. I. Ritchie, Andrew Carnduff. II. Title.

WOLF, Ben. 759.13
Franklin C. Watkins; portrait of a painter. Philadelphia, University of Pennsylvania Press [1966] 103 p. illus. (part col.) ports. (part col.) 29 cm. Bibliography: p. 103. [ND237.W354W6] 66-21766
1. Watkins, Franklin Chenault, 1894-

Watkins, Frederick Mundell, 1910-

HARVARD University. William Hayes Fogg Art Museum. 730
The Frederick M. Watkins Collection. [Cambridge, 1973] 180 p. illus. 25 cm. Catalogue of an exhibition held at the Fogg Art Museum, Jan. 31-March 14, 1973. Includes bibliographies. [NK613.C35H384] 72-97716
1. Watkins, Frederick Mundell, 1910- Art collections. 2. Art objects, Ancient—Exhibitions. I. Title.

Watkins, Frederick Mundell, 1910- —Art collections.

†HARVARD University. William Hayes Fogg Art Museum. 730
The Frederick M. Watkins Collection, Fogg Art Museum. [New York] : Garland Pub., [1977] c1973. 180 p. : ill. ; 25 cm. "The catalogue was published on the occasion of the exhibition, The Frederick M. Watkins Collection, January 31-March 14, 1973." Reprint of the ed. published by the Fogg Art Museum, Cambridge, Mass. Includes bibliographical references. [NK613.C35H384 1977] 77-9991 ISBN 0-8240-1959-8 : 35.00
1. Watkins, Frederick Mundell, 1910- —Art collections. 2. Art objects, Ancient—Exhibitions. I. Title.

Watson, Earnest Charles, 1892- —Art collections.

ELVEHJEM Art Center. 751.7'7'0954
Indian miniature painting; the Collection of Earnest C. and Jane Werner Watson. Madison, Elvehjem Art Center, University of Wisconsin; distributed by the University of Wisconsin Press [1971] xxviii, 153 p. illus. (part col.) 18 x 23 cm. Catalog prepared by Pramod Chandra. [ND1337.I5E4] 70-157396 ISBN 0-299-97005-1
1. Watson, Earnest Charles, 1892- —Art collections. 2. Watson, Jane (Werner) 1915- —Art collections. 3. Miniature painting, Indic—Catalogs. 4. Illumination of books and manuscripts, Indic—Catalogs. I. Chandra, Pramod. II. Title.

Watson, William R., 1887-1973.

WATSON, William R., 1887-1973. 706'.5 B
Retrospective : recollections of a Montreal art dealer / William R. Watson. Toronto ; Buffalo : University of Toronto Press, [1974] 77 p., [8] leaves of plates : ill. ; 23 cm. Includes index. [N8660.W37A37] 74-75586 ISBN 0-8020-2148-4 : 8.50
1. Watson, William R., 1887-1973. 2. Art dealers—Montreal—Correspondence, reminiscences, etc. I. Title. BIP

Watteau, Jean Antoine, 1684-1721.

BANKS, Oliver T. 759.4
Watteau and the north : studies in the Dutch and Flemish baroque influences on French rococo painting / Oliver T. Banks. New York : Garland Pub., 1977, i.e.1978 xiv, 302 p., [105] leaves of plates : ill. ; 21 cm. (Outstanding dissertations in the fine arts) Originally presented as the author's thesis, Princeton, 1975. Bibliography: p. 296-302. [ND546.B34 1977] 76-23602 ISBN 0-8240-2676-4 lib.bdg. : 45.00
1. Watteau, Jean Antoine, 1684-1721. 2. Painting, French—Dutch influences. 3. Painting, French—Flemish influences. 4. Painting, Baroque—Influence. 5. Painting, Rococo—France. I. Title. II. Series.

EIDELBERG, Martin P. 760'.092'4
Watteau's drawings : their use and significance / Martin P. Eidelberg. New York : Garland Pub., 1977. vi, xiv, 277 p., [52] leaves of plates : ill. ; 21 cm. (Outstanding dissertations in the fine arts) Thesis—Princeton. Bibliography : p. [271]-277. [NC248.W3E36] 76-23616 ISBN 0-8240-2687-X lib.bdg. : 40.00
1. Watteau, Jean Antoine, 1684-1721. 2.

Artists' preparatory studies—France. I. Title. II. Series. BIP

HUYGHE, Rene. 741.9'44
Watteau. [Translated by Barbara Bray] New York, G. Braziller [1970, c1968] 121 p. 58 illus. (part col.) 25 cm. (The Great draughtsmen) Translation of L'Univers de Watteau. [NC248.W3H813 1970] 75-97899 7.95
1. Watteau, Jean Antoine, 1684-1721. I. Title. BIP

POSNER, Donald. 759.4
Watteau: A lady at her toilet. New York, Viking Press [1973] 112 p. illus. (part col.) 23 cm. (Art in context) Includes bibliographical references. [ND553.W3P67 1973b] 72-84124 ISBN 0-670-75173-1 7.95
1. Watteau, Jean-Antoine, 1684-1721. Lady at her toilet. I. Watteau, Jean-Antoine, 1684-1721. II. Title.

SCHNEIDER, Pierre. 760'.0924
The world of Watteau, 1684-1721, by Pierre Schneider and the editors of Time-Life Books New York, Time, inc. [1967] 191 p. illus. (part col.) 31 cm. (Time-Life library of art) Bibliography: p. 185. [ND553.W3S35] 67-20332
1. Watteau, Jean Antoine, 1684-1721. 2. France—Social life and customs.—Pictorial works. I. Time-Life Books. II. Title. BIP

WATTEAU, Jean Antoine, 759.4
1684-1721.
The complete paintings of Watteau. Introd. by John Sunderland. Notes and catalogue by Ettore Camesasca. New York, H. N. Abrams [1971, c1968] 132 p. illus., facsims., 64 col. plates, ports. 32 cm. (Classics of the world's great art) Translation of L'opera completa di Watteau. Bibliography: p. 82. [ND553.W3A28] 77-92260 ISBN 0-8109-5525-3
I. Camesasca, Ettore, 1922- II. Title.

WATTEAU, Jean Antoine, 741.9'44
1684-1721.
The drawings of Antoine Watteau, by K. T. Parker. New York, Hacker Art Books, 1970. 49 p. 117 plates. 30 cm. Reprint of the 1931 ed. [NC248.W3P3 1970] 77-116365 25.00
I. Parker, Karl Theodore, 1895- BIP

WATTEAU, Jean Antoine, 741.9'44
1684-1721.
The drawings of Watteau [by] Malcolm Cormack. London, New York, Hamlyn, 1970. 44 p., 132 plates. illus. 32 cm. Bibliography: p. 44. [NC248.W3C67] 74-587081 ISBN 0-600-02557-8 £2.50
I. Cormack, Malcolm. II. Title.

WATTEAU, Jean Antoine, 741.9'0924
1684-1721.
The drawings of Watteau. Introd. by Stephen Longstreet. [1st ed.] Alhambra, Calif., Borden Pub. Co. [1966] 1 v. (chiefly illus.) 31 cm. (Master draughtsman series) [NC1055.W3L6] 67-2679
I. Longstreet, Stephen, 1907- II. Title.

Watts, George Frederick, 1817-1904.

CHESTERTON, Gilbert Keith, 759.2
1874-1936.
G. F. Watts. Freeport, N.Y., Books for Libraries Press [1973] p. Reprint of the 1904 ed. published by Duckworth, London, in series: The Popular library of art. [ND497.W3C5 1973] 73-4422 ISBN 0-518-19025-0
1. Watts, George Frederick, 1817-1904. I. Series: The Popular library of art. BIP

EWING, Lucy Elizabeth Lee. 759.2
George Frederick Watts, Sandro Botticelli, Matthew Arnold, by Lucie Lee Ewing. [Folcroft, Pa.] Folcroft Library Editions, 1973 [c1904] 64 p. illus. 22 cm. Reprint of the ed. published by Grafton Press, New York. [ND497.W3E9 1973] 73-8983 ISBN 0-8414-1910-8 (lib. bdg.)
1. Watts, George Frederick, 1817-1904. 2. Botticelli, Sandro, 1447?-1510. 3. Arnold, Matthew, 1822-1888. BIP

EWING, Lucy Elizabeth Lee. 759.2
George Frederick Watts, Sandro Botticelli, Matthew Arnold / by Lucie Lee Ewing. Norwood, Pa. : Norwood Editions, 1976 [c1904] 64 p., [8] leaves of plates : ill. ; 21 cm. Reprint of the ed. published by Grafton Press, New York. [ND497.W3E9 1976] 76-3712 ISBN 0-88305-548-1 : 10.00
1. Watts, George Frederick, 1817-1904. 2. Botticelli, Sandro, 1447?-1510. 3. Arnold, Matthew, 1822-1888.

Waud, Alfred Rudolph, 1828-1891.

RAY, Frederic. 741.9'73
Alfred R. Waud, Civil War artist / Frederic E. Ray. New York : Viking Press, 1974. 192 p. : ill. ; 28 cm. (A Studio book) Includes (p. [73]-[183]) a selection of Waud's sketches, chiefly from the collection in the Library of Congress, together with a smaller sampling of those of his brother, William Waud. Includes index. Bibliography: p. 188-189. [NC139.W38R39 1974] 73-20667 ISBN 0-670-11260-7 : 16.95
1. Waud, Alfred Rudolph, 1828-1891. 2. United States—History—Civil War, 1861-1865—Pictorial works.

Waugh, Frederick Judd, 1861-1940.

HAVENS, George 759.13 B
Remington, 1890-
Frederick J. Waugh, American marine painter, by George R. Havens. Orono, University of Maine Press, 1969. xii, 361 p. illus. (part col.), ports. 24 cm. (University of Maine studies, no. 89) Includes bibliographical references. [ND237.W36H3] 70-7555 7.00
1. Waugh, Frederick Judd, 1861-1940. I. Series: Maine. University. University of Maine studies, no. 89

NEW Jersey. State Museum, 759.13
Trenton.
Paintings by Frederick J. Waugh (1861-1940) from the Edwin A. Ulrich Collection. [Catalog. Trenton, 1968] [16] p. illus. 22 cm. Exhibition held Dec. 7, 1968-Feb. 9, 1969. [ND237.W36A52] 71-625613
1. Waugh, Frederick Judd, 1861-1940. 2. Ulrich, Edwin A.—Art collections. I. Title.

Wax-modeling.

BOLTON, Ethel Stanwood, 736'.93
1873-
Wax portraits and silhouettes. With an introd. by Charles Henry Hart. Boston, Massachusetts Society of the Colonial Dames of America, 1914. Detroit, Gale Research, 1974. 88 p. illus. 22 cm. [NK9580.B6 1974] 71-164115 ISBN 0-8103-3168-3
1. Wax-modeling. 2. Silhouettes. I. National Society of the Colonial Dames of America. Massachusetts. II. Title. BIP

ELISCU, Frank. 736'.93
Direct wax sculpture. Photos. by David Rosenfeld. [1st ed.] Philadelphia, Chilton Book Co. [1969] viii, 180 p. illus. (part col.) 27 cm. [NK9580.E4 1969] 71-102050
1. Wax-modeling. I. Title. BIP

MARKS, Mickey Klar. 736.93
Wax sculpturing. Sculptures by Frank Eliscu. Photos. by David Rosenfeld. New York, Dial Press [1963] 61 p. illus. 21 cm. [NK9580.M34] 63-20265
1. Wax-modeling. I. Title.

NEWMAN, Thelma R. 702.8
Wax as art form, by Thelma R. Newman. South Brunswick [N.J.] T. Yoseloff [1966] 318 p. illus. (part col.) 29 cm. Bibliography: p. 308-311. [NK9580.N4] 66-21605
1. Wax-modeling. 2. Encaustic painting. I. Title.

Wax-modeling—Juvenile literature.

DIVALENTIN, Maria 731.4'2
(Messuri) 1911-
Sculpturing with wax, by Maria and Louis DiValentin. New York, Sterling Pub. Co. [1973] 48 p. illus. 20 cm. (Little craft book series) Discusses the tools and techniques for sculpturing a variety of objects in wax. [NK9580.D58] 72-95214 ISBN 0-8069-5246-6 2.95
1. Wax-modeling—Juvenile literature. I. DiValentin, Louis, joint author. II. Title.
Library binding 2.69; ISBN 0-8069-5247-4.

Wax-modeling—United States.

SELLERS, Charles 736'.93'0924 B
Coleman, 1903-
Patience Wright, American artist and spy in George III's London / by Charles Coleman Sellers. 1st ed. Middletown, Conn. : Wesleyan University Press, c1976. x, 281 p., [12] leaves of plates : ill. ; 24 cm. Includes bibliographical references and index. [NK9582.W74S44] 76-7193 ISBN 0-8195-5001-9 : 14.95
1. Wright, Patience. 2. Wax-modeling—United States. I. Title.

Wax modellers—Biography—Dictionaries.

PYKE, E. J. 736'.93'0922
A biographical dictionary of wax modellers [by] E. J. Pyke. Oxford, Clarendon Press, 1973. lxvi, 216, [79] p. illus. 24 cm. Includes index. Bibliography: p. 164-186. [NK9580.P94] 73-174552 ISBN 0-19-817194-3
1. Wax modellers—Biography—Dictionaries. I. Title.
Distributed by Oxford University Press, N.Y., 64.00; Library binding 50.56.

Waxes—Bibl.

ROTH, Lillian 016.676
Waxes, waxing, and wax modifiers [by] Lillian Roth, Jack Weiner. Appleton, Wis., Inst. of Paper Chem., 1967. 307p. 28cm. (Appleton, Wis. Inst. of Paper Chem. Bibl. ser. no. 198) Suppl. 1 [Z7914.O3R6] 62-781 price unreported pap.,
1. Waxes—Bibl. I. Weiner, Jack, 1910- joint author. II. Title. III. Series. BIP

Waxworks.

GURNEY, Gene. 973'.074
America in wax : an armchair tour visiting the famous people and fascinating events, from the earliest explorers to the present, as captured in wax museums throughout the United States, Canada, and abroad / by Gene Gurney. New York : Crown Publishers, c1977. 140 p. : ill. ; 28 cm. Includes index. [GV1836.G87 1977] 76-43972 ISBN 0-517-52524-0 : 10.00
1. Waxworks. 2. United States—History—Miscellanea. I. Title.

Wayne, June, 1918—

BASKETT, Mary W. 709'.24
The art of June Wayne, by Mary W. Baskett. New York, H. N. Abrams [1969?] 99 p. illus. (part col.), ports. 22 x 23 cm. Bibliography: p. 98-99. [N6537.W33B3] 69-18329
1. Wayne, June, 1918- I. Title.

Weather in art.

WEATHER / 769'.4'3
under the general editorship of Harold H. Hart ; compiled by Pam Pollack. New York : Hart Pub. Co., c1977. 95 p. : all ill. ; 33 cm. (Hart picture archives) Bibliography: p. 95. [N8261.W42W4] 77-151876 ISBN 0-8055-1213-6 : 10.95 ISBN 0-8055-0306-4 pbk. : 4.95
1. Weather in art. 2. Pictures. I. Pollack, Pam. BIP

Weavers—United States.

HEISEY, John W. 746.9'7
A checklist of American coverlet weavers / compiled for the Abby Aldrich Rockefeller Folk Art Center by John W. Heisey ; edited and expanded by Gail C. Andrews and Donald R. Walters. Williamsburg, Va. : Colonial Williamsburg Foundation ; Charottesville : distributed by the University Press of Virginia, 1978. 149 p., [3] leaves of plates : ill. ; 26 cm. Includes index. Bibliography: p. 139-142. [TT848.H4] 77-15968 ISBN 0-87935-048-2 : 10.00
1. Weavers—United States. 2. Coverlets—United States. I. Andrews, Gail C. II. Walters, Donald R. III. Abby Aldrich Rockefeller Folk Art Collection, Williamsburg, Va. IV. Title. BIP

Weaving.

ALEXANDER, Marthann. 745.5202824
Weaving handcraft; 15 simple ways to weave. Bloomington, Ill., McKnight Pub. Co. [1954] 91 p. illus. 23 cm. [TT848.A66] 54-4170
1. Weaving. I. Title.

ATWATER, Mary (Meigs) 1878- 745.52
Recipe book, patterns for handweavers. Salt Lake City, Published by the M. M. Atwater Weavers' Guild; distributed by Wheelwright Lithographing Co. [1957] unpaged. illus. 28cm. [TT848.A82] 57-41435
1. Weaving. I. Title.

ATWATER, Mary Meigs, 1878- 745.52
The shuttle-craft book of American hand-weaving; being an account of the rise, development, eclipse, and modern revival of a national popular art, together with information of interest and value to collectors, technical notes for the use of weavers, & a large collection of historic patterns. Rev. ed. New York, Macmillan, 1951. xv, 341 p. illus. 23 cm. [TS1490.A8 1951] 51-10000
1. Weaving. 2. Textile industry and fabrics—U.S. 3. Textile design. I. Title. BIP

BLACK, Mary E 745.52
New key to weaving; a textbook of hand weaving for the beginning weave. Milwaukee, Bruce Pub. Co. [c1957] 571p. illus. 25cm. [TT848.B5 1957] 57-12564
1. Weaving. I. Title. BIP

BLUMENAU, Lili. 745.52
The art and craft of hand weaving, including fabric design. Drawings by Martin Norman. New York, Crown Publishers [1955] 136 p. illus. 24 cm. [TT848.B53] 55-7241
1. Weaving. I. Title.

BROWN, Hariette J. 745.52
Hand weaving for pleasure and profit. Illus. by Craig Kavafes, photos. by Robert J. Lecomte. New York, Harper [1952] 273 p. illus. 24 cm. [TT848.B74] 51-11889
1. Weaving. I. Title.

BROWN, Harriette J. 745.52
Hand weaving for pleasure and profit. Illus. by Craig Kavafes, photos. by Robert J. Lecomte. New York, Harper [1952] 273 p. illus. 24 cm. [TT848.B74] 51-11889
1. Weaving. I. Title.

CROWELL, Ivan Herrett, 745.52
1904-
Popular weaving crafts. Peoria, Ill., C. A. Bennett Co., [1949, '1950] 166 p. illus. 20 cm. [TT848.C7] 50-8054
1. Weaving. I. Title.

CYRUS, Ulla. 745.52
Manual of Swedish hand weaving. Translation by Viola Anderson. Boston, C. T. Branford Co. [1956] 271 p. illus. 24 cm. Translation of Handbok i vavning. [TS1490.C913] 56-14249
1. Weaving. I. Title: Swedish hand weaving. BIP

DAVISON, Marguerite 745.52
Porter.
A handweaver's pattern book. Layouts designed and line illus. drawn by Charles C. Denzler; photos, by E. Fletcher Brown. Rev. ed. Swarthmore, Pa. [1951] 217 p. illus. 28 cm. [TT848.D3 1951] 51-5695
1. Weaving. 2. Textile design. I. Title. BIP

DAVISON, Marguerite 745.52
Porter.
A handweaver's pattern book. Rev. ed. Layout and line illus. drawn by Charles C. Denzler; photographs by E. Fletcher Brown. Swarthmore, Pa. [1950] xvi, 215 p. illus. 28 cm. Bibliography: p. 203-209. [TT848.D3 1950] 50-7736
1. Weaving. 2. Textile design. I. Title.

FREY, Berta. 745.52
Designing and drafting for handweavers; basic principles of cloth construction. New York, Macmillan, 1958. 225 p. illus. 22 cm. [TT848.F7] 57-12522
1. Weaving. I. Title. BIP

GALLINGER, Osma Palmer Couch, 1895- 745.52
The joy of hand weaving; the complete step-by-step book of weaving. Scranton, International Textbook Co. [1950] xxi, 306 p. illus. 27 cm. Bibliography: p. 293-295. "Periodicals and bulletins on weaving": p. 301. [TS1490.G34] 50-6739
1. Weaving. I. Title.

GREER, Gertrude G. 745.52
Adventures in weaving. Peoria, Ill., C. A. Bennett Co. [1951] 425 p. illus. (part col.) diagrs. 26 cm. Bibliography: p. 406-412. [TT848.G7] 51-4961
1. Weaving. I. Title.

JUBILEE Guilds of Newfoundland. 746.1
Twenty-one years of weaving patterns [1936-1957. 1st ed. St. Johns 1958?] 186l. illus. 28cm. [TT848.J8] 61-38109
1. Weaving. I. Title. II. Title: Weaving patterns.

KIRBY, Mary, 1908- 745.52
Designing on the loom. London, New York, Studio Publications [1955] 86 p. illus. 26 cm. (The How to do it series, no. 57) [TS1629.K57] 55-14777
1. Weaving. 2. Looms. I. Title. **BIP**

OELSNER, Gustaf Hermann, 1845- 746.1'4
A handbook of weaves, translated and rev. by Samuel S. Dale, including a supplement on the analysis of weaves and fabrics and 1875 illustrations. N.Y., Dover Publications [1951] vii, 402. illus. 25 cm. [TS1490.O] A52
1. Weaving. 2. Textile industry and fabrics—Germany. I. Title. **BIP**

REGENSTEINER, Else, 1906- 746.1'4
Weaver's study course, ideas and techniques / Else Regensteiner. New York : Van Nostrand Reinhold Co., [1975] 144 p. : ill. ; 29 cm. Includes index. Bibliography: p. [141] [TT848.R44] 74-19755 ISBN 0-442-26871-8 : 16.95
1. Weaving. I. Title.

TIDBALL, Harriet. 746.1
Summer and winter, and other two-tie unit weaves. Lansing, Mich., Shuttle Craft Guild; distributed by Craft and Hobby Book Service, Big Sur, Calif., 1966. 58 p. illus. 27 cm. (Shuttle craft monograph 19) Includes bibliographical references. 68-21832
1. Weaving. I. Title. **BIP**

WHITE, Alice Violet 746.1
Weaving is fun. [Dist. New York, Taplinger, 1962, c.1959] 94p. illus. 62-1231 3.95 bds.,
1. Weaving. I. Title. **BIP**

WILLCOX, Donald J., 1933- 746.1'4
New design in weaving [by] Donald J. Willcox. New York, Van Nostrand Reinhold [1970] 128 p. illus. (part col.) 21 cm. [NK8904.W54 1970] 70-126868
1. Weaving. 2. Design, Decorative. I. Title.

Weaving—Patterns.

ANGSTADT, Jacob. 746.1'4
Jacob Angstadt, his weavers patron book. [Pittsford? N.Y.] : R. N. Holroyd, c1976. 96 p., [1] leaf of plates : ill. ; 29 cm. "Replica of an 18th century manuscript book owned and reproduced by Ruth N. Holroyd." [TS1490.A54] 76-9401
1. Weaving—Patterns. I. Title.

HOLROYD, Ruth N. 746.1'4
Jacob Angstadt designs, drawn from his weavers patron book / Ruth N. Holroyd, with Ulrike L. Beck. [Pittsford, N.Y.] : Holroyd, c1976. 28, [256] p. [2] leaves of plates : chiefly ill. ; 30 cm. [TS1490.H57] 76-9402
1. Angstadt, Jacob, 1809- 2. Weaving—Patterns. I. Beck, Ulrike L., joint author. II. Title.

Webb, Prescott, 1888-

SMITH, Cecil Bernard. 709.24
A salute to Walter Prescott Webb and "The search for William E. Hinds." Austin, Tex., 1961. xxiv,178 l. illus. 29 cm. [E175.5.W4S5] 62-3978
1. Webb, Prescott, 1888- I. Title.

Webb, William Snyder, 1882-1964.

SCHWARTZ, Douglas Wright, 1929- 917.69'03'1
Conceptions of Kentucky prehistory; a case study in the history of archeology [by] Douglas W. Schwartz [Lexington] Univ. of Ky. Pr. [1968,c.1967] viii, 133p. illus., maps, ports. 23cm. (Studies in anthropol., no. 6) Bibl. [E78.K3S26] 67-17848 6.00
1. Webb, William Snyder, 1882-1964. 2. Kentucky—Antiq. 3. Indians of North America—Kentucky—Antiq. I. Title. II. Series: Studies in anthropology (Lexington, Ky.) no. 6

Weber, Kem, 1889-1963.

GEBHARD, David. 720'.924
Kem Weber: the moderne in southern California 1920 through 1941. [Exhibition at] the Art Galleries, University of California, Santa Barbara, February 11 to March 23, 1969. Organized by David Gebhard and Harriette Von Breton. [Santa Barbara, Printed by Standard Print., 1969] 106 p. illus. 21 cm. Catalog. On spine: Kem Weber and the moderne. Includes bibliographical references. [NK1535.W4G4] 74-625366 4.75 (pbk)
1. Weber, Kem, 1889-1963. I. Von Breton, Harriette. II. California. University, Santa Barbara. Art Gallery. III. Title: Kem Weber and the moderne.

Weber, Max, 1881-1961.

THREE American modernist painters: 759.13'074'01471 Max Weber, with an introd. by Alfred H. Barr, Jr.; Maurice Sterne, by H. M. Kallen, with a note by the artist; Stuart Davis, by James Johnson Sweeney. Reprint ed. New York, Published for the Museum of Modern Art by Arno Press, 1969. 1 v. (various pagings) illus., ports. 29 cm. Reprint of 3 catalogs of exhibitions at the Museum of Modern Art, originally issued separately, 1930-1945. Includes bibliographies. [ND236.T44] 70-86440
1. Weber, Max, 1881-1961. 2. Sterne, Maurice, 1878-1957. 3. Davis, Stuart, 1894-1964. I. New York (City). Museum of Modern Art. Max Weber, retrospective exhibition, 1907-1930. 1969. II. New York (City). Museum of Modern Art. Maurice Sterne retrospective exhibition, 1902-1932. 1969. III. Sweeney, James Johnson, 1900- Stuart Davis. 1969. **BIP**

WEBER, Max, 1881-1961 709'.73
First comprehensive retrospective exhibition in the West of oils, gouaches, pastels, drawings, and graphic works by Max Weber (1881-1961); The Art Galleries, Univ. of Calif. at Santa Barbara, Feb 6 through March 3, 1968. Selected, coordinated by Ala Story. [Santa Barbara, The Art Galleries, Univ. of Calif. at Santa Barbara, 1968] 86p. illus. 27cm. The exhibition will be toured under the auspices of the Art Affiliates, UCSB, & presented at Calif. Palace of the Legion of Honor, Phoenix Mus. of Art [and] the Fine Arts Gallery of San Diego. Bibl. [ND237.W37S7] 68-63035 3.75 pap.,
I. Story, Ala. II. California. University, Santa Barbara. Art Gallery. III. California Palace of the Legion of Honor, San Francisco, IV. Phoenix, Ariz. Art Museum. V. San Diego, Calif. Fine Arts Gallery. VI. Title.

WEBER, Max, 1881-1961. 759.13
Max Weber. Text by Alfred Werner. New York, Abrams [1975] 200 p. illus. (part col.) 28 cm. Bibliography: p. [198] [ND237.W37W47] 74-9808 ISBN 0-8109-0540-X 37.50
1. Weber, Max, 1881-1961. I. Werner, Alfred, 1911- **BIP**

WEBER, Max, 1881-1961. 759.13
Max Weber, the years 1906-1916. [Exhibition] May 12-30, 1970. New York, Bernard Danenberg Galleries [1970?] 48 p. (chiefly illus., part. col.) 28 cm. [ND237.W37A52] 73-286240
I. Bernard Danenberg Galleries.

WEBER, Max, 1881-1961. 759.13
Max Weber, the years 1906-1916. [Exhibition] May 12-30, 1970. New York, Bernard Danenberg Galleries [1970?] 48 p. (chiefly illus., part. col.) 28 cm. [ND237.W37A52] 73-286240
I. Bernard Danenberg Galleries.

WEBER, Max, 1881-1961. 759.13
Max Weber: the years 1906-1916. [Exhibition] Nov. 8-29, 1970, Long Beach Museum of Art. [New York, 1970] 16 p. illus. (part col.) 28 cm. Exhibition organized by Bernard Danenberg Galleries, New York. [ND237.W37A53] 71-27601
I. Long Beach, Calif. Museum of Art. II. Bernard Danenberg Galleries.

WEBER, Max, 1881-1961. 759.13
Max Weber: the years 1906-1916. [Exhibition] Nov. 8-29, 1970, Long Beach Museum of Art. [New York, 1970] 16 p. illus. (part col.) 28 cm. Exhibition organized by Bernard Danenberg Galleries, New York. [ND237.W37A53] 71-27601
I. Long Beach, Calif. Museum of Art. II. Bernard Danenberg Galleries.

Wedding costume—Catalogs.

ODENRIDER, Ada Bridgman. 745.59'22
Wedding belles of dolls and costumes. [1st ed.] Seattle, 1969. 104 p. illus. (part col.), port. 22 cm. Cover title: Wedding belles, 1800-1969. [GT595.O4] 70-91824
1. Wedding costume—Catalogs. 2. Doll clothes—Catalogs. I. Title. II. Title: Wedding belles, 1800-1969.

Wedding photography.

ARIN, Michael Kenneth. 778.9'9'3925
Successful wedding photography, by Michael Arin. Philadelphia, Chilton Books [1967] 156 p. illus. (part. col.) 24 cm. [TR575.A7] 67-17796
1. Wedding photography. I. Title. **BIP**

FELTNER, Don, 1939- 658'.91'778993925
$54,000 a year in spare-time wedding photography / by Don Feltner, with Paul Castle Philadelphia : Studio Press, c1977. 191 p. : ill. ; 24 cm. [TR819.F44] 76-55673 ISBN 0-918368-03-0 : 15.00
1. Wedding photography. I. Castle, Paul, joint author. II. Title.

GUNN, Rocky. 778.9'9'3925
Wedding photography / Rocky Gunn. Los Angeles : Petersen Pub. Co., c1977. 80 p. : ill. ; 28 cm. (Petersen's how-to-photographic library) [TR819.G86] 77-74102 ISBN 0-8227-4019-2 pbk. : 3.95
1. Wedding photography. I. Title. **BIP**

STEIN, Barney. 778.9'9'3925
Wedding and party photography, by Barney Stein and Les Kaplan. 3d ed. Philadelphia, Chilton Book Co. [1968] 128 p. illus. 21 cm. [TR575.S76 1968] 67-21696
1. Wedding photography. I. Kaplan, Les, joint author. II. Title.

STEIN, Barney. 778.99392
Wedding and party photography, by Barney Stein and Les Kaplan. New Yori, Universal Photo Books [1961] 128 p. illus. 21 cm. (Universal photo books, U236) [TR575.S76] 61-8119
1. Wedding photography. I. Kaplan, Les, joint author. II. Title.

STOCKWELL, Bill H 778.92
Casuals; Bill Stockwell's many styles of wedding artistry. [Oklahoma City? 1965] vi, 165 p. illus. 29 cm. [TR575.S8] 65-15950
1. Wedding photography. I. Title.

SZASZ, Suzanne. 778'.9'3925
Modern wedding photography / Suzanne Szasz. Garden City, N.Y. : Amphoto, c1977. 160 p., [4] leaves of plates : ill. (some col.) ; 26 cm. [TR819.S96] 76-16680 ISBN 0-8174-2411-3 : 7.95
1. Wedding photography. I. Title. **BIP**

TYDINGS, Kenneth S 778.993925
Candid wedding photography guide. Philadelphia, Chilton Co., c1959. 103 p. 20 cm. (Modern camera guide series, 418) [TR575.T9] 59-10376
1. Wedding photography. I. Title. **BIP**

Wedgwood, Josiah, 1730-1795.

BROOKLYN Institute of Arts and Sciences. Museum. 738.37
The Emily Winthrop Miles collection: the work of Wedgwood and Tassie, by Jean Gorely and Marvin D. Schwartz. [Brooklyn] Brooklyn Museum, 1965. 63 p. illus. 23 cm. (Its Guides to the Museum's collections, 3) Bibliography: p. 62. [NK4335.B65] 65-19658
1. Wedgwood, Josiah, 1730-1795. 2. Wedgwood ware. 3. Tassie, James, 1735-1799. 4. Art objects — Catalogs. I. Miles, Emily (Winthrop) II. Gorely, Jean. III. Schwartz, Marvin D. IV. Title. V. Series.

BURTON, Anthony. 738.3'7 B
Josiah Wedgwood / Anthony Burton. New York : Stein and Day, [1976] p. cm. Includes index. Bibliography: p. [NK4210.W4B87] 76-6989 ISBN 0-8128-1907-1
1. Wedgwood, Josiah, 1730-1795. **BIP**

GRAHAM, John Meredith, 1905- 738.3'7
Wedgwood, by John Meredith Graham II and Hensleigh Cecil Wedgwood. New York, Arno Press, 1974 [c1948] 118 p. illus. 27 cm. Handbook and catalogue for the Brooklyn Museum exhibition: Wedgwood, a living tradition. Reprint of the ed. published by the Brooklyn Museum, Brooklyn Institute of Arts and Sciences, Brooklyn. [NK4335.G7 1974] 71-128384 ISBN 0-405-00878-3 12.50
1. Wedgwood, Josiah, 1730-1795. 2. Wedgwood ware—Exhibitions. I. Wedgwood, Hensleigh Cecil, 1908- joint author. II. Brooklyn Institute of Arts and Sciences. Museum. III. Title.

METEYARD, Eliza, 1816-1879. 738.3'7 B
The life of Josiah Wedgwood. New York, A. M. Kelley, 1971. 2 v. illus. 24 cm. (Reprints of economic classics) Reprint of the 1865-1866 ed. Includes bibliographical references. [NK4210.W4M6 1971] 78-183175 ISBN 0-678-00890-6
1. Wedgwood, Josiah, 1730-1795. 2. Wedgwood ware. 3. Pottery—England. I. Title.

SMILES, Samuel, 1812-1904. 738.3'7 B
Josiah Wedgwood, F.R.S., his personal history. Ann Arbor, Mich., Plutarch Press, 1971. xi, 304 p. 22 cm. Reprint of the 1894 ed. [NK4210.W4S7 1971] 71-141603
1. Wedgwood, Josiah, 1730-1795. 2. Wedgwood ware.

Wedgwood (Josiah) and Sons, ltd.

KELLY, Alison. 738.37
The story of Wedgwood. Compiled by Alison Kelly, in association with Josiah Wedgwood & Sons, ltd. New York, Viking Press [1963, c1962] 80 p. illus. (part col.) ports. (part col.) 22 cm. (A Studio book) Bibliography: p. 76-77. [NK4335.K4] 63-16712
1. Wedgwood (Josiah) and Sons, ltd. 2. Wedgwood ware. I. Title.

KELLY, Alison. 338.7'61'7380942464
The story of Wedgwood / compiled by Alison Kelly in association with Josiah Wedgwood & Sons, ltd. New York : Viking Press, 1975. 91 p., [27] leaves of plates : ill. (some col.) ; 26 cm. (A Studio book) Bibliography: [85]-86. [NK4335.K4 1975] 74-32530 ISBN 0-670-67594-6 : 12.95
1. Wedgwood (Josiah) and Sons, ltd. 2. Wedgwood ware. I. Wedgwood (Josiah) and Sons, ltd. II. Title.

Wedgwood, Thomas, 1771-1805.

LITCHFIELD, Richard Buckley, 1903- 770'.92'4 B
Tom Wedgwood; the first photographer. New York, Arno Press, 1973. xvi, 271 p. illus. 23 cm. (The Literature of Photography) Reprint of the 1903 ed. Includes bibliographical references. [TR140.W4L5 1973] 72-9217 ISBN 0-405-04924-2 17.00.
1. Wedgwood, Thomas, 1771-1805. 2. Coleridge, Samuel Taylor, 1772-1834. I. Title. II. Series.

Wedgwood ware.

BARNARD, Harry. 738.3'7
Chats on Wedgwood ware, by Harry Barnard. [1st ed. reprinted]; with a new introduction by Peter Walton. Wakefield, E. P. Publishing, 1973. [1], 260, [64] p., 2 leaves. illus., facsims., ports. 21 cm. Reprint of 1st ed., London Unwin, 1924. Includes index. [NK4335.B3 1973] 74-155163 ISBN 0-85409-799-6 £3.50
1. Wedgwood ware. I. Title. BIP

BEDFORD, John, 1907- 738.37
Wedgewood jasper ware. New York, Walker [1965, c1964] 64 p. illus., col. plates. 19 cm. (His Collectors' pieces, 1) [NK4335.B4 1965] 65-22130
1. Wedgwood ware. 2. Pottery—Collectors and collecting. I. Title.

BUTEN, Harry M 738.37
Wedgood and artists. Merion, Pa., Buten Museum of Wedgwood [1960] [14], 72p. illus. 28cm. Bibliography: 9th-12th prelim, pages. [NK4335.B73] 60-4348
1. Wedgwood ware. 2. Artists—Dictionaries. I. Buten Museum of Wedgwood, Merion, Pa. II. Title.

BUTEN, Harry M. 738.37
Wedgwood ABC but not middle E, by Harry M. Buten. [Deluxe ed.] Merton, Pa., Buten Museum of Wedgwood [1964] xv, 112 p. illus. 27 cm. Wedgwood jasperware medallion inset on cover. [NK4335.B72 1964] 65-1646
1. Wedgwood ware. I. Title.

BUTEN, Harry M 738.37
Wedgwood counterpoint. Merion, Pa., Buten Museum of Wedgwood [1962] 256p. illus. 28cm. [NK4335.B74] 62-4506
1. Wedgwood ware. I. Buten Museum of Wedgwood, Merion, Pa. II. Title.

GORELY, Jean. 738.37
Wedgwood. New York, Barrows [1950] 190 p. 97 illus. 15 cm. (Collectors' little-book library) [NK4335.G6] 50-8719
1. Wedgwood ware.

KELLY, Alison. 338.7'61'7380942464
The story of Wedgwood / compiled by Alison Kelly in association with Josiah Wedgwood & Sons, ltd. New York : Viking Press, 1975. 91 p., [27] leaves of plates : ill. (some col.) ; 26 cm. (A Studio book) Bibliography: [85]-86. [NK4335.K4 1975] 74-32530 ISBN 0-670-67594-6 : 12.95
1. Wedgwood (Josiah) and Sons, ltd. 2. Wedgwood ware. I. Wedgwood (Josiah) and Sons, ltd. II. Title.

KLAMKIN, Marian. 738.3'7
The collector's book of Wedgwood. Illustrated with photos. by Charles Klamkin. New York, Dodd, Mead [1971] 120 p. illus. (part col.) 25 cm. Bibliography: p. 114-117. [NK4335.K55 1971] 70-154063 ISBN 0-396-06368-3
1. Wedgwood ware. 2. Pottery—Collectors and collecting. I. Title.

MACHT, Carol. 738.37
Classical Wedgwood designs; the sources and their use and the relationship of Wedgwood jasper ware to the classical revival of the eighteenth century. New York, M. Barrows, 1957. xvi, 144 p. illus. 25 cm. Bibliography: p. 132-138. [NK4335.M3] 57-12188
1. Wedgwood ware. 2. Art, Ancient. I. Title.

MANKOWITZ, Wolf. 738.3'7
Wedgwood. New York, Dutton [1953] 283p. illus. (part col.) 31cm. Bibliography (p.[273]-[275]) [NK4335.M] A54
1. Wedgwood ware. I. Title.
Contents omitted.

METEYARD, Eliza, 1816-1879. 738.3'7
Wedgwood trio. Edited by Harry M. Buten. [Merion, Pa.] 1967. 280 p. illus. 31 cm. "Three books by ... the author] reprinted in their entirety in one volume by the Buten Museum of Wedgwood, Merion, Pennsylvania." Each book has also special t.p. Contents.Wedgwood and his works, 1873.--Memorials of Wedgwood, 1874.--Choice examples of Wedgwood art, 1879. Bibliographical footnotes. [Stet] 68-3960
1. Wedgwood ware. I. Title. II. Title: Wedgwood and his works. III. Title: Memorials of Wedgwood. IV. Title: Choice examples of Wedgwood art. BIP

METEYARD, Eliza, 1816-1879. 738.3'7 B
The life of Josiah Wedgwood. New York, A. M. Kelley, 1971. 2 v. illus. 24 cm. (Reprints of economic classics) Reprint of the 1865-1866 ed. Includes bibliographical references. [NK4210.W4M6 1971] 78-183175 ISBN 0-678-00890-6
1. Wedgwood, Josiah, 1730-1795. 2. Wedgwood ware. 3. Pottery—England. I. Title.

METEYARD, Eliza, 1816-1879. 738.2'7
The Wedgwood handbook; a manual for collectors. Treating of the marks, monograms, and other tests of the old period of manufacture. Also including the catalogues with prices obtained at various sales, together with a glossary of terms. Ann Arbor, Mich., Gryphon Books, 1971. xi, 427 p. illus. 22 cm. "Facsimile reprint of the 1875 edition." [NK4335.M6 1875a] 70-140320
1. Wedgwood ware. 2. Pottery—Marks. I. Title. BIP

REILLY, Robin. 738.3'7
Wedgwood jasper. [1st American ed.] New York, World Pub. Co. [1972] 80 p. illus. 22 cm. Bibliography: p. 80. [NK4335.R4 1972] 75-170320 5.95
1. Wedgwood ware. I. Title.

SMILES, Samuel, 1812-1904. 738.3'7 B
Josiah Wedgwood, F.R.S., his personal history. Ann Arbor, Mich., Plutarch Press, 1971. xi, 304 p. 22 cm. Reprint of the 1894 ed. [NK4210.W4S7 1971] 71-141603
1. Wedgwood, Josiah, 1730-1795. 2. Wedgwood ware.

Wedgwood ware—Exhibitions.

GRAHAM, John Meredith, 1905- 738.3'7
Wedgwood, by John Meredith Graham II and Hensleigh Cecil Wedgwood. New York, Arno Press, 1974 [c1948] 118 p. illus. 27 cm. Handbook and catalogue for the Brooklyn Museum exhibition: Wedgwood, a living tradition. Reprint of the ed. published by the Brooklyn Museum, Brooklyn Institute of Arts and Sciences, Brooklyn. [NK4335.G7 1974] 71-128384 ISBN 0-405-00878-3 12.50
1. Wedgwood, Josiah, 1730-1795. 2. Wedgwood ware—Exhibitions. I. Wedgwood, Hensleigh Cecil, 1908- joint author. II. Brooklyn Institute of Arts and Sciences. Museum. III. Title.

WEDGWOOD (Josiah) and Sons, ltd. 738.3'7
Early Wedgwood pottery, exhibited at 34 Wigmore Street, London, W. 1, 1951. [1st ed.] Barlaston, Eng., New York [1951] xii, 110 p. illus. (part col.) 21 cm. Bibliography: p. ix. [NK4335.W42 1951] 75-303992
1. Wedgwood ware—Exhibitions. I. Wedgwood, Josiah, 1730-1795. II. Title.

Weeds—Pictorial works.

HUNTER, Peter James Pierrepont, 1943- 633'.2
Hunter's guide to grasses, clovers and weeds: a useful and informative guide, by Peter J. P. Hunter. Chester, James Hunter Ltd. [1970] [4], 80 p. (chiefly illus., some col.). 21 cm. [QK98.H88 1970] 79-545409 ISBN 0-9501421-0-7 12/6
1. Weeds—Pictorial works. 2. Grasses—Pictorial works. 3. Clover—Pictorial works. 4. Seeds—Pictorial works. I. Title. II. Title: Guide to grasses, clovers and weeds.

Weeks and Gilson.

FIELD, Anne E. 748.2'9142'9
On the trail of Stoddard glass / by Anne E. Field. Dublin, N.H. : W. L. Bauhan, [1975] 110 p. : ill. ; 22 cm. Includes index. Bibliography: p. 101-102. [NK4027.S86F54] 73-153379 ISBN 0-87233-021-4 : 4.95
1. Weeks and Gilson. 2. Pottery—Stoddard, N.H. I. Title. BIP

Weights and measures, Arabic.

†BALOG, Paul. 681'.2
Umayyad, 'Abbasid, and Tulunid glass weights and vessel stamps / by Paul Balog. New York : American Numismatic Society, 1976. 322, lv p., : ill. ; 29 cm. (Numismatic studies ; no. 13) Includes indexes. Bibliography: p. 39-42. [CJ3413.B34] 77-359885 45.00
1. Weights and measures, Arabic. 2. Glass weights. I. Title. II. Series.
Publisher's address: Broadway at 156th St. NY NY 10032 BIP

Weil, Adolph—Art collections—Exhibitions.

GINGOLD, Diane J. 769'.94
Master prints from the fifteenth through eighteenth centuries : from the collection of Mr. and Mrs. Adolph Weil, Jr. : [exhibition] September 11 through November 6, 1977, Montgomery Museum of Fine Arts, Montgomery, Alabama, July 2 through August 14, 1978, Museum of Fine Arts, St. Petersburg, Florida. Montgomery, Ala. : Montgomery Museum of Fine Arts, 1977. 120 p. : ill. ; 28 cm. Catalog by D. J. Gingold. Includes index. [NE57.W44G56] 77-84545 ISBN 0-89280-007-0 pbk. : 9.00
1. Weil, Adolph—Art collections—Exhibitions. 2. Prints—15th century—Exhibitions. 3. Prints—16th century—Exhibitions. 4. Prints—17th century—Exhibitions. 5. Prints—18th century—Exhibitions. I. Montgomery Museum of Fine Arts. II. St. Petersburg, Fla. Museum of Fine Arts. III. Title. BIP

Weiner, Dan, 1919-1959.

WEINER, Dan, 1919-1959. 770'.92'4
Dan Weiner, 1919-1959 / [editors, Cornell Capa, Sandra Weiner]. New York : Grossman Publishers, 1974. 96 p. : chiefly ill. ; 23 cm. (ICP library of photographers ; v. 5) Bibliography: p. 96. [TR140.W42A33 1974] 72-11008 ISBN 0-670-25645-5 : 10.00. ISBN 0-670-25646-3 pbk : 5.95
1. Weiner, Dan, 1919-1959. 2. Photography, Artistic. I. Series: International Fund for Concerned Photography. ICP library of photographers ; v. 5.

Weiner, Lawrence.

WEINER, Lawrence. 818'.5'407
Lawrence Weiner / Westfal. Kunstverein Munster ; [Red., Klaus Honnef]. Munster : Westfal. Kunstverein, 1973. 117 p. ; 23 cm. (Jahresgabe-Westfalischer Kunstverein Munster ; 1972) English and German. [N6537.W35H66] 76-460664 DM25.00
1. Weiner, Lawrence. I. Honnef, Klaus. II. Westfalischer Kunstverein. III. Series: Westfalischer Kunstverein. Jahresgabe — Westfalischer Kunstverein Munster ; 1972.

Weiner, Ted—Art collections.

TEXAS. University. Art Museum. 709.04
An exhibition of sculpture and painting from the Collection of Mr. & Mrs. Ted Weiner at the Art Museum of the University of Texas, Austin, Texas, October 23 to November 27, 1966. [Austin, 1966] 54 p. illus. 22 cm. On cover: The collection of Mr. & Mrs. Ted Weiner. "A bibliography of modern sculpture": p. 53. [N6487.A87T49 1966] 74-187587
1. Weiner, Ted—Art collections. 2. Art, Modern—20th century—Exhibitions. I. Title. II. Title: The Collection of Mr. & Mrs. Ted Weiner.

Weir, Julian Alden, 1852-1919.

NEBRASKA. University. Sheldon Memorial Art Gallery. 769'.924
The etchings of J. Alden Weir. [Lincoln, 1967] [56] p. illus. 22 cm. (Monographs on American art, no. 1) Catalog of an exhibition held at the University of Nebraska Art Galleries Nov. 7-Dec. 3, 1967. "500 copies." Bibliography: p. [16] [NE2210.W37N4] 70-1488
1. Weir, Julian Alden, 1852-1919. I. Title. II. Series.

WEIR, Julian Alden, 1852-1919. 759.13
Paintings by Julian Alden Weir. [Washington, Phillips Collection] 1972. 30 p. illus. 26 cm. Catalog of a 1972 exhibition held at the Phillips Collection, Washington, D.C., May 6-June 8; the Columbus Gallery of Fine Arts, Columbus, Ohio, June 20-July 9; and the Brigham Young University Art Gallery, Provo, Utah, Sept. 1-Oct. 5. [ND237.W4P53] 72-82721
I. Phillips Collection, Washington, D.C. II. Columbus Gallery of Fine Arts, Columbus, Ohio. III. Brigham Young University, Provo, Utah. Art Gallery.

YOUNG, Dorothy (Weir) 927.5
The life & letters of J. Alden Weir. Edited with an introd.by Lawrence W. Chisholm. New Haven, Yale University Press, 1960. xxxii, 277 p. col. front., plates, ports. 26 cm. [ND237.W4Y6] 60-13128
1. Weir, Julian Alden, 1852-1919. I. Title.

YOUNG, Dorothy (Weir) 769'.924 B
The life and letters of J. Alden Weir. Edited with an introd. by Lawrence W. Chisolm. New York, Kennedy Graphics, 1971 [c1960] xxxii, 277 p. illus., ports. 24 cm. (Library of American art) Includes bibliographical references. [ND237.W4Y6 1971] 76-146157 ISBN 0-306-70097-2
1. Weir, Julian Alden, 1852-1919.

Weir, Robert Walter, 1803-1889.

CADET Fine Arts Forum of the United States Corps of Cadets. 759.13
Robert Weir, artist and teacher of West Point : [exhibition]. West Point, N.Y. : Cadet Fine Arts Forum of the United States Corps of Cadets, 1976. 95 p. : ill. (some col.) ; 21 x 28 cm. Bibliography: p. 92-95. [ND237.W413C3 1976] 76-23723
1. Weir, Robert Walter, 1803-1889. I. Weir, Robert Walter, 1803-1889. II. Title.

Weisgall, Nathalie—Art collections.

CROCKER Art Gallery, Sacramento, Calif. 707'.4'019454
The collecting muse : a selection from the Nathalie and Hugo Weisgall Collection. Sacramento, Calif. : E. B. Crocker Art Gallery, 1975. 68 p. : ill. ; 23 cm. Catalog of an exhibition held at the E. B. Crocker Art Gallery. [N5220.W58C76 1975] 75-25215
1. Weisgall, Nathalie—Art collections. 2. Weisgall, Hugo—Art collections. 3. Art—Exhibitions. I. Title.

Weiss, Harvey.

ROSENBERG (Paul) and Company, New York. 730'.924
Exhibition of recent sculpture by Harvey Weiss, February 2 to March 7, 1970. New York [1970] [8] p. (incl. cover) 5 illus. 26 cm. (Its Catalogue no. 165) [NB237.W416R6] 70-21140
1. Weiss, Harvey. I. Title. II. Series.

Welded sculpture.

BENTON, Suzanne. 731.4
The art of welded sculpture / Suzanne Benton ; with sculptural pieces, drawings, and photos. by the author. New York : Van Nostrand Reinhold, [1975] 148 p. : ill. (some col.) ; 25 cm. Includes index. Bibliography: p. 145-146. [NB1220.B46] 74-22513 ISBN 0-442-20692-5 : 12.95
1. Benton, Suzanne. 2. Welded sculpture. I. Title. BIP

Welding.

ALTHOUSE, Andrew Daniel. 671.52
Modern welding complete coverage of the welding field in one easy-to-use volume by Andrew D. Althouse, and Carl H. Turnquist and William A. Bowditch. Homewood, Ill., Goodheart-Willcox Co. [1965] 1 v. (various pagings) illus. (part col.) 27 cm. [TT211.A38] 65-20244
1. Welding. 2. Metals. I. Turnquist, Carl

FLEXNER, James Thomas, 1908- 759.13
America's old masters. Rev. [i.e. 2d] ed. New York, Dover [1967] 365p. illus., ports. 22cm. [ND207.F55 1967] 67-16702 2.75 pap.,
1. West, Benjamin, 1738-1820. 2. Copley, John Singleton, 1737-1815. 3. Peale, Charles Willson, 1741-1827. 4. Stuart, Gilbert, 1755-1828. 5. Painters, American. I. Title.
Contents Omitted.

GALT. JOHN, 1779-1839. 759.2
The life of Benjamin West (1816-1820) a facsimile reproduction with an introd. by Nathalia Wright. Gainesville, Fla., Scholars' Facsimiles & Reprints, 1960. ix p., facsim.: iv, 160, 251p. plates, ports. 23cm. (Scholars' facsimilies & reprints) Reproduction of copies in Ohio State University and Yale University Library, with title pages reading: [pt.] 1, The life, studies, and works of Benjamin West, Esq., composed from materials furnished by Himself. London, Printed for T. Cadell and W. Davies, 1820; pt. 2, The life and works of Benjamin West, Esq., subsequent to his arrival in this country. London, Printed for T. Cadell and W. Davies, 1820. 60-5041 8.50
1. West, Benjamin, 1738-1820. I. Title. BIP

PENNSYLVANIA Academy of the Fine Arts, Philadelphia. 759.13
Symbols of peace : William Penn's treaty with the Indians : an exhibition sponsored by the Pennsylvania Academy of the Fine Arts and Dickinson College : the Pennsylvania Academy of the Fine Arts, Philadelphia, Pennsylvania, May 12-September 26. Philadelphia : The Academy, 1976. [52] p. : ill. (some col.) ; 24 cm. Bibliography: p. [52] [ND237.W45P38 1976] 76-369124
1. West, Benjamin, 1738-1820. William Penn's treaty with the Indians. 2. West, Benjamin, 1738-1820—Adaptations—Exhibitions. I. Dickinson College, Carlisle, Pa. II. Title.

SNOW, Dorothea J., 1909- 92
Benjamin West, gifted young painter, by Dorothea J. Snow. Illustrated by George Buctel. Indianapolis, Bobbs-Merrill [1967] 200 p. col. illus. 20 cm. (Childhood of famous Americans) Biography of the "Father of American painting" who, as a Quaker, had to secure special permission from his townsmen to engage in his chosen profession of "making images." [ND237.W45S6] AC 67
1. West, Benjamin, 1738-1820. I. Buctel, George, illus. II. Title.

West, Benjamin, 1738-1820—Juvenile literature.

SNOW, Dorothea J., 1909- 92
Benjamin West, gifted young painter, by Dorothea J. Snow. Illus. by George Buctel. Indianapolis, Bobbs [1967] 200p. col. illus. 20cm. (Childhood of famous Americans) [ND237.W45S6] 67-17738 2.50
1. West, Benjamin, 1738-1820—Juvenile literature. I. Title. BIP

West, Benjamin, 1738-1820.

ALBERTS, Robert C. 759.13 B
Benjamin West : a biography / Robert C. Alberts. Boston : Houghton Mifflin, 1978. xvi, 525 p., [24] leaves of plates : ill. ; 24 cm. Includes index. Bibliography: p. [477]-507. [ND237.W45A86] 78-17241 ISBN 0-395-26289-5 : 20.00
1. West, Benjamin, 1738-1830. 2. Painters—United States—Biography. BIP

The West—Descr. & trav.—Views.

ATKESON, Ray. 779'.9'9179
Western impressions / photographed by Ray Atkeson. Portland, Or. : Beautiful West Pub. Co., 1977 printing. 144 p. : col. ill. ; 35 cm. [F595.2.A87] 78-102327 ISBN 0-915796-11-2 : 25.00
1. The West—Description and travel—1951- —Views. 2. Hawaii—Description and travel—1951- —Views. I. Title. BIP

BOREIN, Edward, 1873-1945. 767.2
Etchings of the West; edited by Edward S. Spaulding. [Santa Barbara memorial ed. Santa Barbara? Calif., 1950] 1 v. (unpaged) illus., plates (part col.) ports. 32 cm. [NE2210.B6S7] 51-1589
1. The West—Descr. & trav.—Views. I. Spaulding, Edward S. ed. II. Title.

MCCRACKEN, Harold, 1894- 759.13
Portrait of the Old West; with a biographical check list of western artists. Foreword by R. W. G. Vail. [1st ed.] New York, McGraw-Hill [1952] 232 p. illus., plates (part col.) 29 cm. Bibliographical footnotes. [ND225.M18] 52-9455
1. The West—Descr. & trav.—Views. 2. The West—Soc. life & cust. 3. Painters, American. I. Title.

MILLER, Alfred Jacob, 1810-1874 759.13
The West of Alfred Jacob Miller (1837), from the notes and water colors in the Walters Art Gallery. With an account of the artist by Marvin C. Ross. Rev. enl. ed. Norman, Univ. of Okla. Pr [1967, c1968] 208 (i.e.416), 1xxxiiip. illus. (pt. col.) 27cm. Bibl. [ND1839M54R6 1968] 67-15578 15.00
1. The West—Descr. & trav.—Views. I. Ross, Marvin Chauncey, 1904-. II. Waiters Art Gallery, Baltimore. III. Title. BIP

MUENCH, David. 779'.9'91780420922
Lewis and Clark : voyages of discovery / photography by David Muench ; text by Dan Murphy ; edited by Gweneth DenDooven. Las Vegas, Nev. : KC Publications, c1977. [64] p. : col. ill. ; 31 cm. Includes reproductions of photo-murals which are on permanent display at the Museum of Westward Expansion in St. Louis. [F592.7.M8] 76-57451 7.95 ISBN 0-916122-50-6 pbk. : 3.95
1. Lewis and Clark Expedition. 2. Lewis, Meriwether, 1774-1809. 3. Clark, William, 1770-1838. 4. The West—Description and travel—1951-—Views. I. Murphy, Dan. II. Museum of Westward Expansion. III. Title.

The West—Description and travel—Views.

HASSRICK, Peter H. 769'.92'4
Frederic Remington: paintings, drawings, and sculpture in the Amon Carter Museum and the Sid W. Richardson Foundation Collection, by Peter h. Hassrick. Foreword by Ruth Carter Johnson. [New York] Abrams [1973] 218 p. illus. (part col.) 32x35 cm. Bibliography: p. 215-218. [N6537.R4H38] 72-8852 ISBN 0-8109-0444-6 35.00
1. The West—Description and travel views. I. Remington, Frederic, 1861-1909. II. Amon Carter Museum of western art, Fort Worth, Tex. III. Sid W. Richardson Foundation.

MCINTYRE, Peter. 760'.0924
Peter McIntyre's West. Menlo Park, Calif., Lane Magazine & Book Co. [1970] 24 p. illus., 56 col. plates. 36 cm. [ND1108.M25A49] 79-115162 19.50
1. The West—Description and travel—Views. I. Title.

The West — Hist. — Pictorial works.

TILDEN, Freeman, 1883- 778.949978
Following the Frontier with F. Jay Haynes, pioneer photographer of the old West. [1st ed.] New York, Knopf, 1964. xi, 406, vii p. illus., map, ports. 26 cm. [TR140H39T5] 64-12327
1. The West — Hist. — Pictorial works. I. Haynes, Frank Jay. II. Title.

The West—History—Pictorial works.

REMINGTON, Frederic, 1861-1909. 741.9'73
101 Frederic Remington drawings of the Old West. Text by Irvin W. Hansom. Willmar, Minn., Printed by Color Press [1968] 203 p. illus. 29 cm. [NC1075.R4H3] 73-867 12.50
1. The West—History—Pictorial works. I. Hanson, Irvin W. II. Title. III. Title: Remington drawings.

The West in art.

AMON Carter Museum of Western Art, Fort Worth, Tex. 708'.1764'5315
Catalogue of the collection, 1972. Fort Worth [Tex., c1973] v, 602 p. illus. 23 cm. [N8214.5.U6A48 1973] 73-84472 ISBN 0-88360-000-5
1. Amon Carter Museum of Western Art, Fort Worth, Tex. 2. The West in art. 3. Art—Forth Worth, Tex.—Catalogs. I. Title.

AMON Carter Museum of Western Art, Fort Worth, Tex. 709'.2'4
Charles M. Russell; paintings, drawings, and sculpture in the Amon Carter Museum [by] Frederic G. Renner. [Rev. ed.] New York, H. N. Abrams [1974] 296 p. illus. (part col.) 31 x 35 cm. Bibliography: p. 291-292. [ND237.R75A72 1974] 74-5114 ISBN 0-8109-0466-7
1. Russell, Charles Marion, 1864-1926. 2. The West in art. I. Renner, Frederic Gordon, 1897-

AMON Carter Museum of Western Art, Fort Worth, Tex. 709.73
Charles M. Russell; paintings, drawings and sculpture in the Amon G. Carter collection: a descriptive catalogue, by Frederic G. Renner. Foreword by Ruth Carter Johnson. Austin, University of Texas Press [1966] xvi, 148 p. illus. (part col.) map., port. 30 cm. Bibliography: p. 143-144. [ND237.R75A72] 65-11152
1. Russell, Charles Marion, 1864-1926. 2. The West in art. I. Renner, Frederic Gordon, 1897-

AMON Carter Museum of Western Art, Fort Worth, Tex. 709'.2'4
Charles M. Russell: paintings, drawings, and sculpture in the Amon G. Carter Collection; a descriptive catalogue, by Frederic G. Renner. Foreword by Ruth Carter Johnson. Austin, University of Texas Press [1972, c1966] xvi, 148 p. illus. 30 cm. Bibliography: p. 143-144. [ND237.R75A72 1972] 72-192460 ISBN 0-292-73622-3 20.00
1. Russell, Charles Marion, 1864-1926. 2. The West in art. I. Renner, Frederic Gordon, 1897-

†AMON Carter Museum of Western Art, Forth Worth, Tex. 709'.2'4
Charles M. Russell : paintings, drawings, and sculpture in the Amon Carter Museum / by Frederic G. Renner ; foreword by Ruth Carter Johnson. New concise ed. New York : H. N. Abrams, 1976. 160 p. : ill. (some col.) ; 24 x 28 cm. Includes index. [ND237.R75A72 1976] 76-22656 ISBN 0-8109-2057-3 : 40.00
1. Russell, Charles Marion, 1864-1926. 2. Amon Carter Museum of Western Art, Fort Worth, Tex. 3. The West in art. I. Russell, Charles Marion, 1864-1926. II. Renner, Frederic Gordon, 1897-

BAIGELL, Matthew. 709.2'4
The western art of Frederic Remington / by Matthew Baigell. 1st ed. New York : Ballantine Books, 1976. p. cm. [N6537.R4B24] 76-9744 ISBN 0-345-25128-8 pbk. : 5.95
1. Remington, Frederic, 1861-1909. 2. The West in art. I. Title. BIP

BAIRD, Joseph Armstrong. 704.94'9'978
The West remembered : artists and images, 1837-1973 : selections from the Collection of Earl C. Adams, exhibited at the Old Mint, San Francisco, June 16, 1973, through September 15, 1973, and the Santa Barbara Museum of Art, November 10 to January 6 / compiled by Joseph A. Baird, Jr. ; photos. by Armando Solis. San Francisco : California Historical Society, 1973. 88 p. : ill. (some col.) ; 27 cm. Includes index. Bibliography: p. 85-87. [N8214.5.U6B34] 75-318276
1. Adams, Earl C.—Art collections. 2. The West in art. 3. Art, Modern—19th century—Exhibitions. 4. Art, Modern—20th century—Exhibitions. I. Santa Barbara, Calif. Museum of Art. II. California Historical Society. III. Title.

BAMA, James. 759.13
Western paintings : [exhibitions] / James Bama. New York : Coe Kerr Gallery, c1977. [44] p. : ill. (some col.) ; 28 cm. Held at the Coe Kerr Gallery, New York, March 15-April 16, 1977 and at the Buffalo Bill Historical Center, Cody, Wyoming, May 1-July 18, 1977. [ND237.B235C63] 77-151080
1. Bama, James. 2. The West in art. I. Coe Kerr Gallery. II. Buffalo Bill Historical Center. III. Title.

*BAMBA, James 759.13
The western art of James Bamba introduction by Ian Ballantine New York, Charles Scribner's Sons [1975] [6] p. [45] leaves of plates 45 col. ill. 29 cm. [ND1839] 10.00.
1. Bama, James. 2. The west in art. I. Title.
L.C. card no. for original edition: 75-7782.

BEELER, Joe. 709'.73
Cowboys and Indians; characters in oil and bronze. [1st ed.] Norman, Univ. of Okla. Pr. [1967] 80 1., xvii p. illus. (pt. col.) 26 cm. [ND237.B42A45] 67-24616 7.95
I. Title. BIP

BEELER, Joe. 759.13
Joe Beeler; shows at the C. M. Russell Gallery, July 14 through August 30, 1970, Great Falls, Montana. Introd. by Terry Melton. Comments by Joe Beeler. [Flagstaff, Ariz., Printed by Northland Press, 1970] 1 v. (unpaged) illus. 27 cm. [N6537.B44R8] 74-132848
1. The West in art. I. Russell (C. M.) Gallery.

BEELER, Joe. 741.9'73
The Joe Beeler sketch book / by Joe Beeler ; with a foreword by Frederic G. Renner. 1st ed. [Flagstaff, Ariz.] : Northland Press, [1974] x, 141 p. : ill. ; 28 cm. [NC139.B42A48] 72-79075 ISBN 0-87358-099-0 : 12.50
1. Beeler, Joe. 2. The West in art. I. Title. BIP

BOREIN, Edward, 1872-1945. 741.9'73
Drawings & paintings of the Old West [by] Edward Borein. Compiled with an introd. by Nicholas Woloshuk, Jr. Foreword by Harold McCracken. [1st ed.] Flagstaff, Ariz., Northland Press, 1968- v. chiefly illus. 31 cm. Contents.Contents.—v. 1. The Indians. [NC139.B64W64] 68-22584
1. Borein, Edward, 1872-1945. 2. The West in art. I. Woloshuk, Nicholas, 1924- II. Title.

BOREIN, Edward, 1872-1945. 769'.92'4
The etchings of Edward Borein. A catalogue of his work by John Galvin. Complied with the assistance of Warren R. Howell, in collaboration with Harold G. Davidson. San Francisco, J. Howell—Books, 1971. 1 v. (unpaged) illus. 32 cm. [NE2012.B6G3] 76-174984
1. Borein, Edward, 1872-1945. 2. The West in art. I. Galvin, John, ed.

BURNSIDE, Wesley M. 759.13
Maynard Dixon, artist of the West [by] Wesley M. Burnside. Provo, Utah, Brigham Young University Press [1973] xvi, 237 p. illus. (part col.) 28 x 34 cm. Developed from the author's thesis, Ohio State University, 1970. "250 limited special edition." Bibliography: p. 225-227. [ND237.D5B87] 73-18262 ISBN 0-8425-0912-7 28.95
1. Dixon, Maynard, 1875-1946. 2. The West in art. I. Dixon, Maynard, 1875-1946. II. Title.

CARTER, Denny T., 1940- 759.13 B
Henry Farny / by Denny T. Carter. New York : Watson-Guptil Publications, 1978. p. cm. Includes index. Bibliography: p. [ND237.F25C33 1978] 78-17999 ISBN 0-8230-2239-0 : 35.00
1. Farny, Henry Francois, 1847-1916. 2. The West in art. 3. Indians of North America—Pictorial works. I. Farny, Henry Francois, 1847-1916. BIP

DAVIDSON, Harold G., 1912- 769'.92'4 B
Edward Borein, cowboy artist; the life and works of John Edward Borein, 1872 [sic]-1945 [by] Harold G. Davidson. [1st ed.] Garden City, N.Y., Doubleday, 1974. 189 p. illus. (part col.) 32 cm. Includes bibliographical references. [N6537.B63D38 1974] 74-2063 ISBN 0-385-09607-0 25.00
1. Borein, Edward, 1873-1945. 2. The West in art. I. Borein, Edward, 1873-1945. II. Title.

SUBJECT INDEX THE WEST IN

EGGENHOFER, Nicholas, 1897- 741'.092'4
Eggenhofer : the pulp years / John M. Carroll ; introd. by Jeff Dykes. 1st ed. Fort Collins, Colo : Old Army Press, c1975. 145 p. : ill. (some col.) ; 29 cm. [NC975.5.E33C37] 75-333132 15.00
1. Eggenhofer, Nicholas, 1897- 2. The West in art. I. Carroll, John M.

EWERS, John Canfield. 759.13
Artists of the Old West [by] John C. Ewers. [Enl. ed.] Garden City, N.Y., Doubleday [1973] 240 p. illus. (part col.) 32 cm. "A Chanticleer Press edition." Bibliography: p. 238-240. [N6525.E9 1973] 73-79662 ISBN 0-385-04474-7 22.50
1. The West in art. 2. Artists, American—The West. 3. Indians of North America—The West—Pictorial works. I. Title.

FRONTIER 709'.78'074014461
America : the Far West / Department of American Decorative Arts and Sculpture, Museum of Fine Arts, Boston ; contributors, Jonathan L. Fairbanks ... [et al.]. Boston : Museum of Fine Arts, [1975?] 233 p. : ill. (some col.) ; 22 x 27 cm. Exhibition held Museum of Fine Arts, Boston, Jan. 23-Mar. 16, 1975; Denver Art Museum, April 19-June 1, 1975; The Fine Arts Gallery of San Diego, July 2-Aug. 17, 1975; William Rockhill Nelson Gallery of Art, Kansas City, Sept. 17-Nov. 2, 1975; Milwaukee Art Center, Dec. 5-Jan. 18, 1975. Bibliography: p. 229-233. [N8214.5.U6F76] 74-21765 ISBN 0-87846-086-1 : 29.50
1. The West in art. 2. Art, American—Exhibitions. I. Fairbanks, Jonathan L. II. Boston. Museum of Fine Arts. Dept. of American Decorative Arts and Sculpture.

GRANDEE, Joe Ruiz, 1929- 709'.24
The Old West; pictorialized by Joe Ruiz Grandee. [Exhibition] R. W. Norton Art Gallery, July 11-August 15, 1971. [1st ed. Shreveport, La.] R. W. Norton Art Gallery [1971] 14 p. illus. (part col.) 29 cm. Cover title. [N6537.G68A56] 79-171014 ISBN 0-9600182-5-5
1. The West in art. I. Norton (R. W.) Art Gallery. II. Title.

THE Great American West. 758
Fort Atkinson, Wils. : Home Library Pub. Co., c1976. 96 p. : chiefly ill. (some col.) ; 32 cm. Includes index. [ND1451.5.G7] 76-370803 4.98
1. The West in art. 2. Paintings, American. 3. Paintings, Modern—19th century—United States. I. Title.

HARMAN, Fred. 759.13
The great West in paintings. Introd. by Dean Krakel. [1st ed.] Chicago, Sage Books [1969] xiv, 185 p. (chiefly illus. (part col.)) 22 x 31 cm. [ND237.H313A46] 73-81966 30.00
1. The West in art. I. Title.

HARMSEN, Dorothy. 758
Harmsen's Western Americana; a collection of one hundred Western paintings with biographical profiles of the artists. Foreword by Robert Rockwell. Flagstaff, Ariz., Northland Press [1971] ix, 213 p. col. illus. 31 cm. Bibliography: p. 211-213. [ND210.H36] 79-134925 ISBN 0-87358-061-3 35.00
1. The West in art. 2. Paintings, American. 3. Paintings—Private collections—U.S. I. Title. BIP

HARRIS, Fred Red, 1910- 759.13
The Western paintings of Fred Red Harris. Foreword by Ben Barnes. Introd. by Ron Calhoun. Dallas, Tex., Taylor Pub. Co. [1971] 96 p. (chiefly illus. (part col.), port.) 16 x 24 cm. [ND237.H325A57] 72-155819
1. The West in art. I. Title.

HASSRICK, Peter H. 759.13
Frederic Remington; an essay and catalogue to accompany a retrospective exhibition of the work of Frederic Remington, by Peter H. Hassrick. Fort Worth [Tex.] Amon Carter Museum [1973] 48 p. illus. 22 cm. Includes bibliographical references. [N6537.R4H37] 72-96833 3.00
1. Remington, Frederic, 1861-1909. 2. The West in art. I. Amon Carter Museum of Western Art, Fort Worth, Tex. BIP

HASSRICK, Peter H. 709'.2'4
Frederic Remington : paintings, drawings, and sculpture in the Amon Carter Museum and the Sid W. Richardson Foundation collections / by Peter H. Hassrick ; foreword by Ruth Carter Johnson. New York : Abrams, [1975] p. cm. Bibliography: p. [N6537.R4H38 1975] 74-31085 ISBN 0-8109-2054-9
1. Remington, Frederic, 1861-1909. 2. The West in art. I. Remington, Frederic, 1861-1909. II. Amon Carter Museum of Western Art, Fort Worth, Tex. III. Sid W. Richardson Foundation.

HASSRICK, Peter H. 704.94'9'978
The way West / Peter Hassrick. New York : Abrams, [1977] p. cm. Includes index. Bibliography: p. [N8214.5.U6H3] 77-5625 ISBN 0-8109-1750-5
1. The West in art. 2. Art, American. 3. Art, Modern—19th century—United States. 4. Art, Modern—20th century—United States. I. Title. BIP

HILLS, Patricia. 759.13
The American frontier: images and myths. [Exhibition at] Whitney Museum of American Art, June 26 to September 16, 1973. [New York, Whitney Museum of American Art, 1973] 63 p. illus. 25 cm. Includes bibliographical references. [ND210.H46] 73-82576 3.00 (pbk.)
1. The West in art. 2. Paintings, American—Exhibitions. 3. Painting, Modern—19th century—United States. I. Whitney Museum of American Art, New York. II. Title.

HOUSTON, Tex. Museum of Fine Arts. 709'.78
Days on the range; artists in the American West. [Exhibition] Museum of Fine Arts, Houston, Feb. 5-Mar. 5, 1972. Foreword by Philippe de Montebello. Chronology and catalogue by Dennis Harrington. [Houston, c1972] 70 p. illus. 18 x 26 cm. [N8214.5.U6H6] 78-189136
1. The West in art. 2. Art—Exhibitions. I. Harrington, Dennis. II. Title.

HOWARD, James K. 709'.2'2 B
Ten years with the Cowboy Artists of America : a complete history and exhibition record / by James K. Howard ; foreword by Frederic G. Renner. 1st ed. Flagstaff [Ariz.] : Northland Press, c1976. x, 213 p. : ill. (some col.) ; 29 cm. Bibliography: p. 211-212. [N8214.5.U6H64] 75-43345 ISBN 0-87358-150-4 : 40.00
1. The West in art. 2. Cowboy Artists of America. 3. Artists—United States—Biography. I. Title. BIP

JACOB, Ned. 759.13
Ned Jacob. [Exhibition held at] the National Cowboy Hall of Fame & Western Heritage Center, March 4-May 14, 1972. [Boulder, Colo., Printed by Pruett Press, 1972] 107 p. (chiefly illus. (part col.)) 22 x 23 cm. [ND237.J18N37] 72-75508
1. Jacob, Ned. 2. The West in art. I. National Cowboy Hall of Fame and Western Heritage Center.

JOHNSON, Frank Tenney, 1874-1939. 759.13
Frank Tenney Johnson Western paintings. Text by Harold McCracken. Collection of the Exchange Bank & Trust Company, Dallas. [Dallas?] c1971. [24 p.] illus. 21 x 26 cm. [ND237.J72M3] 76-186380
1. Exchange Bank & Trust Company—Art collections. 2. The West in art. I. McCracken, Harold, 1894-

KENNEDY Galleries, inc., New York. 704.94'9'9178
An artists' gazetteer: beyond the Mississippi; the American West in nineteenth and twentieth century art. New York [1971] 64 p. illus. (part col.) 23 cm. (The Kennedy quarterly, v. 11, no. 1) [N8640.K4 vol. 11, no. 1] [N8214.5.W4] 70-29646 2.00
1. The West in art. 2. Art, Modern—19th century—Catalogs. 3. Art, Modern—20th century—Catalogs. I. Title. II. Title: Beyond the Mississippi. III. Series.

KENNEDY Galleries, inc., New York. 709'.73
Tradition and change; a memorial of the old West and a record of the new in paintings and bronzes. New York, 1963. 68-112 p. illus. 23 cm. (The Kennedy quarterly, v. 4, no. 2) [N8640.K4 vol. 4, no. 2] 73-11538
1. The West in art. 2. Art, American—Catalogs. I. Title. II. Series.

KENNEDY Galleries, inc., New York. 708'.147'1 s
Walking westward: an American journey; 19th and 20th century paintings, drawings and sculpture of the Western scene. [New York, 1972] 196-256 p. illus. (part col.) 24 cm. (The Kennedy quarterly, v. 11, no. 4) [N8640.K4 vol. 11, no. 4] [N8214.5] 760'.0973 72-192059 2.00
1. The West in art. 2. Art, Modern—19th century. 3. Art, Modern—20th century. I. Title. II. Series.

KENNEDY Galleries, inc., New York. 731.8'9'9178
The West in bronze; [catalogue] New York [1968] 28 p. illus. 21 cm. [NK7912.K45] 76-253531
1. The West in art. 2. Bronzes—United States—Catalogs. I. Title.

KUHN, Walt, 1877-1949. 759.13
An imaginary history of the West. Foreword by Fred S. Bartlett. [Fort Worth, Tex.,] Amon Carter Museum of Western Art [1964] i v. (unpaged) illus. (part col.) port. 22 x 26 cm. All pictures are from the collection of the Colorado Springs. Fine Arts Center. [ND237.K8A47] 64-20211
I. Title.

MCCARTHY, Frank C., 1924- 759.13
The western paintings of Frank C. McCarthy. Edited by Frank Storz. New York, Ballantine Books [1974] 1 v. (chiefly 45 col. plates) 24 x 29 cm. [ND237.M16A57] 74-164377 ISBN 0-345-23844-3 4.95 (pbk.)
1. McCarthy, Frank C., 1924- 2. The West in art. I. Title.

MCCRACKEN, Harold, 1894- 927.5
The Charles M. Russell book; the life and work of the cowboy artist. Garden City, N.Y., Doubleday, [1957] 236 p. illus., col. plates, ports. 35 cm. Bibliographical references included in "Notes" (p. 232-233) [ND237.R75M3] 759.13 57-11431
1. Russell, Charles Marion, 1864-1826. 2. The West in art. BIP

PALADIN, Vivian A. 704.94'9'9178
Second annual Rendezvous of Western Art, September-October, 1973. Compiled and edited by Vivian A. Paladin. Helena, Montana Historical Society [1973] 38 p. illus. 29 cm. Held at the Poindexter Gallery of Contemporary Art. [N6512.P28] 74-160956
1. The West in art. 2. Art, American—Exhibitions. 3. Art, Modern—20th century—United States. I. Montana Historical Society. II. Poindexter Gallery of Contemporary Art. III. Title. IV. Title: Rendezvous of Western Art.

POLLAND, Don, 1932- 730'.92'4
The Old West in miniature : sculpture / by Don Polland. Shreveport, La. : R. W. Norton Art Gallery, [1974] 23 p. : ill. (some col.) ; 28 cm. Cover title. Catalog of an exhibition held at the R. W. Norton Art Gallery, Shreveport, La., Oct. 13-Nov. 24, 1974. [NB237.P65N67] 74-24491
1. Polland, Don, 1932- 2. The West in art. I. Norton (R. W.) Art Gallery. II. Title. BIP

REED, Walt. 741'.092'4
Harold von Schmidt draws and paints the Old West. Foreword by Dean Krakel. Introd. by Harold McCracken. [1st ed.] Flagstaff [Ariz.] Northland Press [1972] xvii, 230 p. illus. (part col.) 32 cm. Bibliography: p. 225-230. [ND237.V66R44] 72-76376 ISBN 0-87358-095-8 40.00
1. Von Schmidt, Harold, 1893- 2. The West in art. I. Von Schmidt, Harold, 1893- Harold von Schmidt draws and paints the Old West. 1972. II. Title. BIP

REED, Walt. 759.13
John Clymer : an artist's rendezvous with the frontier West / by Walt Reed ; foreword by Harold McCracken. 1st ed. Flagstaff : Northland Press, c1976. xvii, 141 p. : ill. (some col.) ; 26 x 30 cm. [ND237.C576R43] 75-11164 ISBN 0-87358-151-2 : 40.00
1. Clymer, John, 1907- 2. The West in art. I. Clymer, John, 1907-

REMINGTON, Frederic, 1861-1909. 741.9'73
Drawings by Frederic Remington. New York, B. Franklin [1971] [65] p. (chiefly illus.) 27 x 36 cm. (Burt Franklin research & source works series 763. Art history and art reference series 31) Reprint of the 1897 ed. [NC139.R4A43 1971] 77-101991 ISBN 0-8337-2935-7
1. The West in art. I. Title.

REMINGTON, Frederic, 1861-1909. 759.13
Frederic Remington; selections from the Hogg Brothers collection, the Museum of Fine Arts, Houston. Text by Marjorie S. Thompson. [Houston, Museum of Fine Arts, 1973] [7] p., 14 plates (part col.) 22 x 26 cm. [ND237.R36T48] 73-81195
1. Remington, Frederic, 1861-1909. 2. Hogg family—Art collections. 3. Houston, Tex. Museum of Fine Arts. 4. West in art. I. Thompson, Marjorie S. II. Houston, Tex. Museum of Fine Arts. BIP

REMINGTON, Frederic, 1861-1909. 917.8'0022'2
The illustrations of Frederic Remington, with a commentary by Owen Wister. Edited with a concise biography and an account of Remington's work and career, by Marta Jackson. New York, Bounty Books [1970] 192 p. illus. 23 x 29 cm. [NC139.R4J3 1970] 70-75095
1. The West in art. I. Wister, Owen, 1860-1938. II. Jackson, Marta, ed. III. Title. BIP

REMINGTON, Frederic, 1861-1909. 741.9'73
173 drawings and illustrations. Selected and with an introd. by Henry C. Pitz. New York, Dover Publications [1972] xiii p., 140 p. of illus. 31 cm. [NC139.R4P57] 78-158963 ISBN 0-486-20714-5 3.95
1. Remington, Frederic, 1861-1909. 2. The West in art. I. Pitz, Henry Clarence, 1895- II. Title.

ROSSI, Paul A., 1929- 917.3'03
The art of the Old West, from the collection of the Gilcrease Institute. Selections and text by Paul A. Rossi and David C. Hunt. [1st ed.] New York, Knopf, 1971. 335 p. illus. (part col.) 32 cm. Bibliography: p. 332-335. [N8214.5.W4R6] 73-154901 ISBN 0-394-46669-1 30.00
1. The West in art. I. Hunt, David C., 1935- joint author. II. Thomas Gilcrease Institute of American History and Art, Tulsa, Okla. III. Title. BIP

RUSSELL, Charles Marion, 1864-1926. 741.9'73
C. M. Russell: boyhood sketchbook, by R. D. Warden. Introd. by Frederic G. Renner. [1st ed.] Bozeman, Mont., Treasure Products [1972] iv, 29 p. illus. 30 cm. Errata slip inserted. [NC139.R87W37] 72-88933
1. Russell, Charles Marion, 1864-1926. 2. The West in art. I. Warden, Robert D. II. Title. III. Title: Boyhood sketchbook.

RUSSELL, Charles Marion, 1864-1926. 709'.2'4
Charles M. Russell : centennial exhibition : [summer 1964 at Hammer Galleries]. New York : Hammer Galleries, [1964] 48 p. : ill. ; 27 cm. Cover title. [N6537.R88H35] 75-318274
1. Russell, Charles Marion, 1864-1926. 2. The West in art. I. Hammer Galleries, New York.

RUSSELL, Charles Marion, 1864-1926. 759.13
The CMR book. Text by John Willard. With foreword by Mike Mansfield. Seattle, Salisbury Press [1970] 64 p. illus. (part col.) 36 cm. Includes bibliographical references. [ND237.R75W54] 78-125897
1. Russell, Charles Marion, 1864-1926. 2. The West in art. I. Willard, John, 1915- II. Title.

RUSSELL, Charles Marion, 1864-1926. 759.13
The western art of Charles M. Russell / edited by Lanning Aldrich. New York : Ballantine Books, 1975. [95] p. : chiefly col. ill. ; 24 x 29 cm. [ND237.R75A57] 76-359873 ISBN 0-345-24734-5 pbk. : 5.95
1. Russell, Charles Marion, 1864-1926. 2. The West in art. I. Title.

SAMUELS, Peggy. 709'.2'2 B
The illustrated biographical encyclopedia of artists of the American West / Peggy and Harold Samuels. 1st ed. Garden City, N.Y. : Doubleday, 1976. p. cm. Includes index. Bibliography: p. [N8214.5.U6S25] 76-2816 ISBN 0-385-01730-8 : 25.00
1. The West in art. 2. Indians of North America—Pictorial works. 3. Artists—Biography. 4. Artists—United States—Biography. I. Samuels, Harold, joint author. II. Title. BIP

SANDS, John 759.13'074'019173
Porter, Mrs.
Today's artist and the West by members of the National Academy of Design. [Phoenix, Ariz., 1972] 25 p. 26 cm. Catalogue of an exhibition held March-May, 1972 at the Phoenix Art Museum and sponsored by the Western Art Associates. [N6512.S256] 72-186124
1. The West in art. 2. Art, American—Exhibitions. 3. Art, Modern—20th century—United States. I. New York (City). National Academy of Design. II. Phoenix, Ariz. Art Museum. III. Western Art Associates. IV. Title.

SCHRIEVER, George. 758
American masters in the West : selections from the Anschutz Collection : the Boise Gallery of Art, Boise, Idaho, April 26 to June 16, 1974, Utah Museum of Fine Arts, University of Utah, Salt Lake City, Utah, June 30 to September 1, 1974 / catalog text by George Schriever ; with an introd. by E. F. Sanguinetti. Boise, Idaho : Boise Gallery of Art, c1974. 48 p. : ill. (some col.) ; 22 x 28 cm. Includes index. [ND1441.5.S37] 76-359327
1. Anschutz, Philip—Art collections. 2. The West in art. 3. Paintings, American—Exhibitions. 4. Paintings, Modern—19th century—United States—Exhibitions. 5. Paintings, Modern—20th century—United States—Exhibitions. I. Boise Gallery of Art. II. Utah Museum of Fine Arts. III. Title.

SHAFER, L. E., 1907- 709'.2'4
Gus Shafer's West, by L. E. "Gus" Shafer, with the editorial assistance of Donald V. Bates. Foreword by John M. Christlieb. [1st ed.] Kansas City, Mo., Trail West [1973] x, 150 p. illus. (part col.) 29 cm. [N6537.S48A46] 73-85933 ISBN 0-914160-00-1 20.00
1. Shafer, L. E., 1907- 2. The West in art. I. Title.

SNIDOW, Gordon, 1936- 709'.73
Gordon Snidow, chronicler of the contemporary West. Foreword by Sam Gilluly. Introd. by Don Hedgpeth. [1st ed. Flagstaff, Ariz.] Northland Press [1973] x, 68 p. illus. (part col.) 21 x 25 cm. Catalog of an exhibition held at the Montana Historical Society, 6 Apr. thru 22 May, 1973. [N6537.S62M66] 73-78005 ISBN 0-87358-117-2 6.50 (pbk.)
1. Snidow, Gordon, 1936- 2. The West in art. I. Montana Historical Society. II. Title.

SOUTHERN Arizona 704.94'9'9178
Bank and Trust Co.
A collection of Western art. [Tucson, c1973] 53 p. illus. (part col.) 31 cm. [N8214.5.W4S68 1973] 74-157773
1. The West in art. 2. Art, American. I. Title.

STENZEL, Franz. 759.13
E. S. Paxson—Montana artist / by Franz R. Stenzel. Helena : Montana Historical Society, [1975?] 32 p. : ill. ; 27 cm. (Montana heritage series ; no. 14) Cover title. [ND237.P257S84] 75-328261 1.00
1. Paxson, E. S., 1852-1919. 2. The West in art. I. Title. II. Series.

TEXAS. University at 759.13
Austin. Art Museum.
Paintings from the C. R. Smith Collection. [Austin, 1970] xii, 40 p. illus. (part col.) 21 x 22 cm. Catalog of an exhibition presented jointly by the University Art Museum and the Humanities Research Center of the University of Texas, Dec. 4, 1969-Jan. 15, 1970. [ND210.T48] 73-171236
1. Smith, Cyrus Rowlett, 1899- —Art collections. 2. The West in art. 3. Paintings, American—Exhibitions. 4. Painting, Modern—19th century—United States. I. Texas. University at Austin. Humanities Research Center. II. Title. BIP

VON SCHMIDT, Harold, 1893 759.13
The Western art of Harold Von Schmidt / edited and with an introd. by Walt Reed. 1st U.S. ed. New York : Peacock Press/Bantam Book, 1976. [8] p., 44 leaves of plates : col. ill. ; 23 x 28 cm. [ND237.V66R45] 75-38078 6.95
1. Von Schmidt, Harold, 1893- 2. The West in art. I. Reed, Walt. II. Title.

WAKEFIELD, Robert. 759.13 B
Schwiering and the West. [1st ed. Aberdeen, S.D., North Plains Press, 1973] xvii, 207 p. illus. (part col.) 32 cm. [ND237.S4363W34] 73-77752 ISBN 0-87970-128-5 25.00
1. Schwiering, Conrad, 1916- 2. The West in art. I. Title. BIP

WEST, Hal, 1902-1968. 759.13
Hal West: Western gallery. With a biography of the artist and a special tribute by Jack Schaefer. [Santa Fe, N.M., Museum Press, 1971] 1 v. (unpaged) illus. 28 cm. Catalog of the exhibition held in the Museum of New Mexico. [ND237.W46S2] 73-198444
I. Santa Fe, N.M. Museum of New Mexico. II. Title. III. Title: Western gallery.

WESTERN Art 731.8'9'9178074019173
Associates.
The West in bronze; selected bronze sculpture from Arizona collections. [Phoenix? Ariz., 1971] [40] p. illus. 26 cm. Catalog of an exhibition held at the Phoenix Art Museum, May-July, 1971. [NK7912.W4] 71-28057
1. The West in art. 2. Bronzes, American—Exhibitions. I. Phoenix, Ariz. Art Museum. II. Title.

WESTERN art 759.13'074'019173
from the Eugene B. Adkins Collection; [exhibition] Phoenix Art Musuem, Western Art Associates, November 1971-January 1972. [Phoenix, Ariz., 1971] [40] p. illus. (part col.) 26 cm. [N8214.5.U6W4] 72-175442
1. Adkins, Eugene B.—Art collections. 2. The West in art. 3. Art—Exhibitions. I. Western Art Associates.

ZAIDENBERG, Arthur, 1903- 741.2
How to draw the Wild West. New York, Abelard-Schuman [1972] 64 p. illus. 27 cm. Step-by-step instructions for the beginning artists in drawing cowboys, Indians, stage coaches, covered wagons, and other Western scenes. [NC655.Z32] 71-156848 ISBN 0-200-71846-0
1. The West in art. 2. Drawing—Instruction—Juvenile literature. I. Title. BIP

The West in art—Bibliography.

DYKES, Jefferson 016.741'092'2
Chenowth, 1900-
Fifty great Western illustrators : a bibliographic checklist / by Jeff Dykes. [Flagstaff, Ariz.] : Northland Press, [1975] xiv, 457 p. : ill. (some col.) ; 30 cm. [Z5956.W45D94] [N8214.5.U6] 73-79780 ISBN 0-87358-114-8 : 35.00
1. The West in art—Bibliography. 2. Illustrators—United States—Bibliography. I. Title. BIP

The West in art—Catalogs.

HARMSEN, Dorothy. 704.94'9'978
American Western art : a collection of one hundred twenty-five Western paintings and sculpture with biographies of the artists / by Dorothy Harmsen ; foreword by Bill Harmsen. [Denver] : Harmsen Pub. Co., c1977. xiii, 256 p. : col. ill. ; 31 cm. On spine: Harmsen Collection, v. 2. Bibliography: p. 254-256. [N8214.5.U6H28] 77-80017 ISBN 0-9601322-1-X : 40.00
1. Harmsen, William—Art collections—Catalogs. 2. Harmsen, Dorothy—Art collections—Catalogs. 3. The West in art—Catalogs. 4. Art, Modern—19th century—Catalogs. 5. Art, Modern—20th century—Catalogs. 6. Artists—Biography. I. Title.
Available from Two Continents BIP

The West in art—Exhibitions.

AMON Carter Museum 704.94'9'978
of Western Art, Fort Worth, Tex.
Amon Carter Museum, 1961-1977 Forth Worth, Tex. : The Museum, c1977. 47 p. : chiefly ill. ; 23 cm. Catalogue of an exhibition on the occasion of the opening of the west wing of the museum. [N8214.5.U6A48 1977] 77-81806 ISBN 0-88360-028-5
1. The West in art—Exhibitions. 2. Art, American—United States—Exhibitions. BIP

TOLEDO. Museum of 704.94'9'978
Art.
Art of the American West : from the Collection of John and Margaret Hill, the Toledo Museum of Art, July 6-August 10, 1975 : [exhibition]. Toledo : The Museum, [1975] 16 p. : ill. ; 18 cm. Catalog. [N8214.5.U6T64 1975] 75-16064
1. Hill, John A., 1970- —Art collections. 2. Hill, Margaret M.—Art collections. 3. The West in art—Exhibitions. 4. Art, American—Exhibitions. I. Title.

WIEGHORST, Olaf, 1899- 759.13
A retrospective exhibition of Olaf Wieghorst : November 15, 1974-January 19, 1975 / presented by the National Cowboy Hall of Fame and Western Heritage Center, Oklahoma City, Oklahoma. Kansas City, Mo. : Lowell Press, c1974. 74 p. : ill. (some col.) ; 23 x 26 cm. [ND237.W64N37] 74-25549 ISBN 0-913504-21-1
1. Wieghorst, Olaf, 1899- 2. The West in art—Exhibitions. I. National Cowboy Hall of Fame and Western Heritage Center. II. Title.

The West in art—Juvenile literature.

GLUBOK, Shirley. 709'.73
The art of the old West. Designed by Gerard Nook. New York, Macmillan [1971] 48 p. illus. 26 cm. A survey of the Old West as it was captured in the paintings, sculpture, and photographs of such artists as Charles Nahl, Frederic Remington, Edward Curtis, Thomas Eakins, and William Henry Jackson. [N8214.5.U6G55] 79-123138
1. The West in art—Juvenile literature. I. Title. BIP

PETER, Adeline. 759.13
Frederic Remington, by Adeline Peter and Ernest Raboff. Garden City, N.Y., Doubleday [1973] [31] p. illus. (part col.) 29 cm. (Art for children) (A Gemini-Smith book) Introduces a selection of Frederic Remington's paintings and sculptures emphasizing social context and technical approach. Includes a brief biography of the artist. [ND237.R36P47] 73-75361 ISBN 0-385-05033-X 4.95
1. Remington, Frederic, 1861-1909—Juvenile literature. 2. The West in art—Juvenile literature. I. Raboff, Ernest Lloyd, joint author. II. Title.

West, Levon, 1900-1968.

MACNEIL, Neil, 1891- 769'.924
1969.
Levon West. Southampton, N.Y., Parrish Art Museum, 1968. [16] p. illus., port. 28 cm. [NE2012.W4M3] 73-286338
1. West, Levon, 1900-1968. I. Parrish Art Museum.

West Virginia—Antiquities.

MCMICHAEL, Edward V. 917.8963044
Introduction to West Virginia archaeology by Edward V. McMichael. Illustrations by Bettye J. Broyles and Paul W. Queen. 2d ed. rev. Morgantown, West Virginia Geological and Economic Survey, 1968. 68 p. illus., maps. 23 cm. (West Virginia. Geological Survey. Educational series) Cover title. Bibliography: p. 68. [E78.W6M3 1968] 71-650479
1. West Virginia—Antiquities. 2. Indians of North America—West Virginia—Antiquities. I. Title. II. Series.

West Virginia Arts and Humanities Council.

WEST Virginia 338.4'7'7009754
Arts and Humanities Council.
West Virginia Arts and Humanities Council : [pictorial report] / [text, Ewel Cornett, Mary Alice Stevens, Jim Andrews, photography, Betty Benjamin ... et al.]. [Charleston] : The Council, [1972?] [42] p., [1] fold. leaf of plates : ill. ; 23 cm. [NX24.W4W48 1972] 74-622980
1. West Virginia Arts and Humanities Council. I. Cornett, Ewel. II. Stevens, Mary Alice. III. Andrews, Jim. IV. Benjamin, Betty.

West Virginia. University. Library. West Virginia Collection.

WEST Virginia. 016.091
University. Library. West Virginia Collection.
Guide to manuscripts and archives in the West Virginia Collection [by] James W. Hess. Morgantown, West Virginia University Library, 1974. viii, 317 p. 23 cm. "Describes collections listed in the first two guides [i.e. 1959-65 ed.] and materials added through June 1972." [Z6621.W42W48 1974] 73-78072 ISBN 0-87012-144-8
1. West Virginia. University. Library. West Virginia Collection. 2. Manuscripts—West Virginia. I. Hess, James W. II. Title.

West, Walter Richard, 1912—

WAUGAMAN, Charles A. 759.11 B
Cheyenne artist: the story of Richard West, by Charles A. Waugaman. New York, Friendship Press [1970] 95 p. 18 cm. (Bold believers series) [E99.C53W3] 70-130779 ISBN 0-377-84211-7 1.50
1. West, Walter Richard, 1912- I. Title. BIP

Western Australia—Historic houses, etc.

WRIGHT, Ronald P. 728.8
Western landmarks; historic buildings of Western Australia. Drawings by H. Smeed. Perth, Paterson Brokensha [New Rochelle. N.Y., SportShelf, 1966] 67p. illus. 14x22cm. [DU377.W7] 61-48915 2.25 pap.,
1. Western Australia—Historic houses, etc. I. Smeed, Hubert, illus. II. Title.

Western comic books, strips, etc.—History and criticism.

HORN, Maurice. 741.5'973
Comics of the American West / Maurice Horn. New York : Winchester Press, c1977. p. cm. Includes index. Bibliography: p. Traces the history of Western comics and discusses the contributions made by comic strips and comic books to the mythology of the West. [PN6714.H67] 77-782 ISBN 0-87691-190-4 : 15.00
1. Western comic books, strips, etc.—History and criticism. I. Title. BIP

HORN, Maurice. 741.5'973
Comics of the American West / Maurice Horn. [South Hackensack, N.J.] : Stoeger Pub. Co., [1978], c1977. p. cm. (Stoeger sportsman's library) Reprint of the ed. published by Winchester Press, New York. Includes index. Bibliography: p. [PN6714.H67 1978] 77-90767 ISBN 0-88317-048-5 pbk. : 7.95
1. Western comic books, strips, etc.—History and criticism. I. Title.
Distributed by Follett

Westman, Barbara.

WESTMAN, Barbara. 759.13
A Beacon Hill Christmas / by Barbara Westman. Boston : Houghton Mifflin, 1976. 41 p. : col. ill. ; 27 cm. [ND237.W54A42] 76-18147 ISBN 0-395-24726-8 : 8.95
1. Westman, Barbara. 2. Christmas in art. 3. Beacon Hill, Boston—Pictorial works. 4. Boston in art. I. Title. BIP

Westminister, Eng. St. Stephen's Chapel.

HASTINGS, Maurice, 1896- 726.595
St. Stephen's Chapel and its place in the development of perpendicular style in England. Cambridge [Eng.] University Press, 1955. 256p. illus. 22cm. [NA5470.S6H3] 55-14058
1. Westminister, Eng. St. Stephen's Chapel. I. Title.

Westminster Abbey.

CARPENTER, Edward Frederick, 1910- ed. 942.13
A house of kings; the official history of Westminster Abbey. New York, John Day [c.1966] xix,491p. illus. (part. col.) facsims., ports. 26cm. Bibl. [DA687.W5C3] 66-19626 16.00
1. Westminster Abbey. I. Title.

LETHABY, William Richard, 1857-1931. 726'.77'1
Westminster Abbey & the kings' craftsmen; a study of mediaeval building, by W. R. Lethaby. New York, B. Blom, 1971. xvi, 382 p. illus., plans, port. 22 cm. Reprint of the 1906 ed. [NA5470.W5L6 1971] 69-13243
1. Westminster Abbey. I. Title. BIP

LETHABY, William Richard, 1857-1931. 726.5'09421'32
Westminster Abbey re-examined. New York, B. Blom, 1972. viii, 298 p. illus. 21 cm. Reprint of the 1925 ed. "Recent works on the Abbey": p. v-vi. [DA687.W5L4 1972] 69-13244
1. Westminster Abbey. BIP

TANNER, Lawrence Edward, 1890- 914.213
The story of Westminster Abbey. With a foreword by the Dean of Westminster. London, Chicago, R. Tuck [1953] 84p. illus. 19cm. [DA687.W5T3 1953] 54-44800
1. Westminster Abbey. I. Title.

WESTMINSTER 914.21'3'0485
Abbey. Norwich, Jarrold, [1967] [24] p. col. front., illus. (some col.). 14 cm. (A Jarrold Wensum series colour book) English text, introductions in English, French and German. [DA687.W5W43] 67-95167
1. Westminster Abbey. BIP

Westminster, Eng.—Descr.

NORRIE, Ian, 1927- ed. 914.213
The book of Westminster. Photos. by Edwin Smith. Drawings by Ronald Saxby. [London] High Hill Bks. [Chester Springs, Pa., Dufour, 1965, c.1964] xiii, 208p. illus., maps (on lining papers) 26cm. Bibl. [DA685.W5N65] 65-4357 6.95
1. Westminster, Eng.—Descr. I. Title.

Westminster, Eng. St. Margaret's Parish—Historic houses, etc.

FORREST, George Topham, 1872-1945. 914.21'32
The Parish of St. Margaret, Westminster. [Drawings, illustrations, and architectural descriptions by G. Topham Forrest] London, Published for the London County Council by B. T. Batsford, 1926- [New York, AMS Press, 1971- v. illus. 29 cm. (The Survey of London, v. 10,) [DA685.W57F672] 70-138272 ISBN 0-404-51660-2 (v. 10)
1. Westminster, Eng. St. Margaret's Parish—Historic houses, etc. 2. Architecture—Westminster, Eng. St. Margaret's Parish. I. Title. II. Series: Joint Publishing Committee Representing the London County Council and the London Survey Committee. Survey of London, v. 10, etc. BIP

Weston, Brett.

WESTON, Brett. 779'.092'4
Voyage of the eye / Brett Weston ; afterword by Beaumont Newhall. Millerton, N.Y. : Aperture, inc., c1975. 100, [3] p. : chiefly ill. ; 30 cm. Bibliography: p. [101] [TR654.W443 1975] 75-13610 ISBN 0-912334-83-5 : 17.50 pbk.: 9.50
1. Weston, Brett. 2. Photography, Artistic. I. Title.

Weston, Edward, 1886-1958.

WESTON, Edward, 1886-1958. 779'.092'4
Edward Weston: fifty years; the definitive volume of his photographic work. Illustrated biography by Ben Maddow. [1st ed. Millerton, N.Y., Aperture, Inc., 1973] 285 p. illus. 32 x 35 cm. Bibliography: p. 282-285. [TR653.W457 1973] 73-85262 ISBN 0-912334-38-X 40.00
1. Weston, Edward, 1886-1958. 2. Photography, Artistic. I. Maddow, Ben, 1909- II. Title.

Weston, Harold, 1894-1972.

MOUNT Holyoke Friends of Art. 759.13
The Mount Holyoke Friends of Art presents a retrospective exhibition of paintings by Harold Weston (1894-1972) September 8-October 8, 1975 [at the] John and Norah Warbeke Gallery, Art Building, Mount Holyoke College, South Hadley. [South Hadley, Mass.] : Mount Holyoke Friends of Art, c1975. 30 p. : ill. ; 23 cm. Bibliography: p. 11. [ND237.W55M68 1975] 75-330442
1. Weston, Harold, 1894-1972. I. Weston, Harold, 1894-1972. II. John and Norah Warbeke Gallery. III. Title.

Weston, Mass.—History.

RIPLEY, Emma F. 974.4'4
Weston, a Puritan town, by Emma F. Ripley. Illus. by Margaret F. Kronenberg. Weston, Mass., Benevolent-Alliance of the First Parish, 1961. 270, [1] p. illus. 25 cm. Bibliography: p. [271] [F74.W74R5] 974.4'82 74-289718
1. Weston, Mass.—History. 2. Weston, Mass.—Historic houses, etc. I. Title.

Weyden, Roger van der, 1400 (ca.) 1464.

DAVIES, Martin, 1908- 759.9493
Rogier van der Weyden; an essay, with a critical catalogue of paintings assigned to him and to Robert Campin. London, Phaidon, 1972. [5], 272, [11] p. illus. (some col.). 31 cm. Distributed in the U.S. by Praeger Publishers, Inc., New York. Bibliography: p. 186. [ND673.W4D3 1972b] 73-156118 ISBN 0-7148-1516-0 38.50
1. Weyden, Roger van der, 1400 (ca.) 1464. 2. Campin, Robert, d. 1444. I. Title. BIP

Whaling.

FORBES, Allan, 1874-1955. 759.13
Whale ships and whaling scenes as portrayed by Benjamin Russell. Presenting reproductions in color of the paintings of the foremost artist in that field. Edited byRalph M. Eastman, assisted by K. G. Rogers. Boston, Printed for the Second Bank-State Street Trust Co., 1955. 79p. illus. (part col.) group port. 23cm. [ND1839.R8F6] A55
1. Whaling. 2. Whalers. I. Russell, Benjamin, 1804-1885. II. Title.

Whaling—History.

MEYER, Charles Robert, 1926- 736'.6
Whaling and the art of scrimshaw / Charles R. Meyer. New York : H. Z. Walck, c1976. p. cm. Includes index. [SH383.M48] 74-25977 ISBN 0-8098-3924-5 : 9.95
1. Whaling—History. 2. Scrimshaws. I. Title. BIP

Whaling in art.

GRANT, Gordon, 1875- 741.9'73
Greasy luck; a whaling sketch book. New York, W. F. Payson [c1932] Jamaica, N.Y., Caravan Maritime Books, 1970. xiv, 126 p. col. illus. 27 cm. Companion volume to the author's Sail ho! [NC139.G68A45 1970] 76-21234
1. Whaling in art. I. Title. BIP

KENDALL, Whaling Museum, Sharon, Mass. 769.9
Kendall Whaling Museum prints, by M. V. & Dorothy Brewington. Sharon, Mass., 1969. vii, 209 p. illus., 6 col. plates. 30 cm. [NE957.K4] 70-107611
1. Whaling in art. 2. Prints—Sharon, Mass.—Catalogs. I. Brewington, Marion Vernon, 1902- II. Brewington, Dorothy.

Whips.

MORGAN, David W., 1925- 745.59'3
Whips and whipmaking, with a practical introduction to braiding, by David W. Morgan. Cambridge, Md., Cornell Maritime Press, 1972. xii, 132 p. illus. 24 cm. [TS1040.M59] 72-78240 ISBN 0-87033-170-1 6.00
1. Whips. 2. Braid. I. Title. BIP

Whistler, Anna Mathilda (McNeill) 1804-1881.

MUMFORD, Elizabeth, pseud. 759.13
Whistler's mother; the life of Anna McNeill Whistler. Ann Arbor, Mich., Plutarch Press, 1971. 256 p. 22 cm. Reprint of the 1940 ed. [ND237.W612M8 1971] 75-141655
1. Whistler, Anna Mathilda (McNeill) 1804-1881. I. Title.

Whistler, James Abbott McNeil, 1834-1903.

MACDONALD, Margaret F. 760'.092'4
Whistler : the graphic work : Amsterdam, Liverpool, London, Venice : an exhibition organised by Thos. Agnew & Sons, London, the Walker Art Gallery, Liverpool, and the Hunterian Art Gallery, University of Glasgow, in association with the Arts Council of Great Britain, 1976 / [selection and catalogue by Margaret MacDonald]. [Liverpool] : [Walker Art Gallery], [1976] 52 p., 8 p. of plates : ill., port. ; 25 cm. Bibliography: p. 11. [NE642.W47M3] 77-361141 ISBN 0-901534-42-0 : £0.75
1. Whistler, James Abbott McNeil, 1834-1903. I. Whistler, James Abbott McNeil, 1834-1903. II. Agnew (Thos.) & Sons, ltd., London. III. Liverpool. Public Libraries, Museums, and Art Gallery. Walker Art Gallery. IV. Glasgow. University. Hunterian Museum. V. Arts Council of Great Britain.

WHISTLER, James Abbott McNeill, 1834-1903. 759.13
The gentle art of making enemies. With an introd. by Alfred Werner. New York, Dover Publications [1967] xxii, 340 p. illus. 19 cm. "Unabridged and unaltered republication [with new introd.] of the second, enlarged edition published ... in 1892." [ND237.W6A3 1967] 67-24225
I. Title. BIP

WHISTLER, James Abbott McNeill, 1834-1903. 927.5
The gentle art of making enemies, as pleasingly exemplified in many instances, wherein the serious ones of this earth, carefully exasperated, have been prettily spurred on to unseemliness and indiscretion, while overcome by an undue sense of right. New York, Putnam, 1953. 340p. 21cm. [ND237.W6A3 1953] 54-558
I. Title.

Whistler, James Abbott McNeill, 1834-1903.

ART Reference Gallery. Art Appraisal Information Division. 760'.092'4
Price profile on lithographs by James Abbott McNeill Whistler. Montclair, N.J. [1973] vi, 45 p. 22 cm. Includes bibliographical references. [NE2312.W45A89] 73-159630 20.00
1. Whistler, James Abbott McNeill, 1834-1903. 2. Lithographs—Prices. I. Title.

ART Reference Gallery. Art Appraisal Information Division. 760'.092'4
Price profile on oils, drawings, watercolors, and pastels by James Abbott McNeill Whistler. Montclair, N.J. [1973] v, 13 p. 22 cm. [NE6537.W4A89] 73-163959 8.00
1. Whistler, James Abbott McNeill, 1834-1903. 2. Art—Prices. I. Title.

CARY, Elisabeth Luther, 1867-1936. 760'.092'4
The works of James McNeill Whistler / by Elisabeth Luther Cary. Boston : Longwood Press, 1977. p. cm. Reprint of the 1913 ed. [ND237.W6C3 1977] 77-6969 ISBN 0-89341-217-1 lib.bdg. : 35.00
1. Whistler, James Abbott McNeill, 1834-1903. I. Title. BIP

CARY, Elisabeth Luther, 1867-1936. 760'.092'4
The works of James McNeill Whistler; a study. With a tentative list of the artist's works. Boston, Milford House [1972] 301 p. illus. 22 cm. Reprint of the 1913 ed. [ND237.W6C3 1972] 72-77236 ISBN 0-87821-102-0 30.00
1. Whistler, James Abbott McNeill, 1834-1903. I. Title.

CARY, Elisabeth Luther, 1867-1936. 760'.0924 B
The works of James McNeill Whistler, a study. With a tentative list of the artist's works. Freeport, N.Y., Books for Libraries Press [1971] 302 p. illus., ports. 23 cm. Reprint of the 1907 ed. [ND237.W6C3 1971] 77-157328 ISBN 0-8369-5788-1
1. Whistler, James Abbott McNeill, 1834-1903. I. Title.

CINCINNATI. Art Museum. 769'.924
The Whistlers; a family reunion. [Cincinnati, 1965?] [19] p. illus. 26 cm. Catalog of an exhibition held January 9-31, 1965. [NE539.W5C5] 68-7039
I. Whistler, James Abbott McNeill, 1834-1903. II. Title.

EDDY, Arthur Jerome, 1859-1920. 759.13
Recollections and impressions of James A. McNeill Whistler. [2d ed.] New York, B. Blom, 1972. 296 p. illus. 21 cm. Reprint of the 1904 ed. Includes bibliographical references. [ND237.W6E3 1972] 71-173163
1. Whistler, James Abbott McNeill, 1834-1903. I. Title. BIP

FLEMING, Gordon H., 1920- 760'.092'4 B
The young Whistler, 1834-66 / by Gordon Fleming. London ; Boston : Allen & Unwin, 1978. 264 p., [8] leaves of plates : ill. ; 24 cm. Includes index. Bibliography: p. [247]-255. [ND237.W6F56] 77-30588 ISBN 0-04-927009-5 : 30.95
1. Whistler, James Abbott McNeill, 1834-1903. 2. Painters—United States—Biography. I. Title. BIP

FREER Gallery of Art, Washington, D. C. 709'.04'0740153
The Whistler Peacock room. Washington, 1962. vii, 22 p. illus. 24 cm. (Smithsonian Institution. Publication 4024 (rev.)) Includes an account of a portrait by Whistler, in the Peacock room, known as Rose and silver: the princess from the land of porcelain. Includes bibliographies. [N857.5A64] 63-60653
1. Whistler, James Abbott McNeill, 1834-1903. I. Title. BIP

GREGORY, Horace, 1898- 759.13
The world of James McNeill Whistler. New York, Nelson [1959] 255p. :illus. 22cm. [ND237.W6G7] 59-15544
1. Whistler, James Abbott McNeill, 1834-1903. I. Title. BIP

GREGORY, Horace, 1898- 759.13 B
The world of James McNeill Whistler. Freeport, N.Y., Books for Libraries Press [1969, c1959] 255 p. illus., ports. 23 cm. (Select bibliographies reprint series) [ND237.W6G7 1969] 70-80621
1. Whistler, James Abbott McNeill, 1834-1903. I. Title.

HOLDEN, Donald. 759.13
Whistler landscapes and seascapes. New York, Watson-Guptill Publications [1969] 87 p. 32 col. plates. 29 cm. "Bibliographical note": p. 10. [ND237.W6H6] 70-76573 17.50
1. Whistler, James Abbott McNeill, 1834-1903. I. Title. BIP

KENNEDY, Edward Guthrie, 1849-1932. 769'.92'4
The etched work of Whistler, illustrated by reproductions of the different states of the plates. Compiled, arr., and described by Edward G. Kennedy with an introd. by Royal Cortissoz. New York, Da Capo Press, 1974 [c1910] 3 v. illus. 39 cm. (v. 1: 29 cm.) (Library of American art) Corrected reprint of the ed. published by the Grolier Club, New York. Contents.Contents.—v. 1. Catalog/index.—v. 2. Numbers 1-190 [plates].—v. 3. Numbers 191-433 [plates]. [NE2012.W45K46 1974] 72-1778 ISBN 0-306-70503-6
1. Whistler, James Abbott McNeill, 1834-1903. I. Title. BIP

MCMULLEN, Roy. 759.13 B
Victorian outsider; a biography of J. A. M. Whistler. [1st ed.] New York, E. P. Dutton, 1973. 307 p. illus. 25 cm. Bibliography: p. 283-288. [ND237.W6M33] 72-94702 ISBN 0-525-22853-5 10.00
1. Whistler, James Abbott McNeill, 1834-1903. I. Title.

PEARSON, Hesketh, 1887- 927.5
The man Whistler. [1st American ed.] New York, Harper [1953, c1952] 276p. illus. 22cm. [ND237.W6P25 1953] 52-11694
1. Whistler, James Abbott McNeill, 1834-1903. I. Title. BIP

PEARSON, Hesketh, 1887-1964. 760'.092'4 B
The man Whistler / Hesketh Pearson ; introd. by Benny Green. New York : Taplinger Pub. Co., 1978. xviii, 198 p., [4] leaves of plates : ill. ; 23 cm. Includes index. Bibliography: p. 191-193. [ND237.W6P25 1978] 78-52949 ISBN 0-8008-5097-1 : 9.95
1. Whistler, James Abbott McNeill, 1834-1903. 2. Painters—United States—Biography. I. Title.

PENNELL, Elizabeth (Robins) 1855-1936. 759.13
The life of James McNeill Whistler, by E. R. and J. Pennell. Philadelphia, Lippincott, 1908. [New York, AMS Press, 1973] 2 v. illus. 24 cm. [ND237.W6P4 1973] 70-148285 ISBN 0-404-04988-5 47.50 per vol.
1. Whistler, James Abbott McNeill, 1834-1903. I. Pennell, Joseph, 1857-1926, joint author.
Set 95.00 BIP

PRIDEAUX, Tom. 759.13
The world of Whistler, 1834-1903, by Tom Prideaux and the editors of Time-Life Books New York, Time-Life Books [1970] 191 p. illus., col. plates, ports. 32 cm. (Time-Life library of art) Issued in a case. Bibliography: p. 187. [ND237.W6P7] 70-116437 7.95
1. Whistler, James Abbott McNeill, 1834-1903. I. Time-Life Books. II. Title. BIP

SUTTON, Denys 759.13
James McNeill Whistler; paintings, etchings, pastels & watercolours. [London] Phaidon Pr. [1966] 197p. illus. (pt. col.) 32cm. [ND237.W6S83] 66-8772 14.50
1. Whistler, James Abbott McNeill, 1834-1903. I. Title.
Available from N.Y. Graphic.

SUTTON, Denys 759.13
Nocturne: the art of James McNeill Whistler. Philadelphia, Lippincott, 1964 [c.1963] 153p. illus. (pt. col.) ports. (pt. col.) 26cm. Bibl. 64-22181 7.95
1. Whistler, James Abbott McNeill, 1834-1903. I. Title.

SWEET, Frederick Arnold, 1903- 759.13
James McNeill Whistler: paintings, pastels, watercolors, etching, lithographs; catalogue, by Frederick A. Sweet. [Chicago, Printed by H. L. Ruggles, 1968] 131 p. illus. (part col.), ports. 26 cm. Catalog of an exhibition held Jan. 13 to Feb. 25, 1968, at the Art Institute of Chicago and March 17 to April 28, 1968, at the Munson-Williams-Proctor Institute. Includes bibliographies. [ND237.W6S9] 68-15571
1. Whistler, James Abbott McNeill, 1834-1903. I. Chicago. Art Institute. II. Munson-Williams-Proctor Institute, Utica, N.Y. Museum of Art.

TAYLOR, Hilary. 760'.092'4 B
James McNeill Whistler / Hilary Taylor. New York : Putnam, c1978. 192 p. : ill. (some col.) ; 29 cm. Includes index. Bibliography: p. 186-187. [ND237.W6T35 1978] 78-50983 ISBN 0-399-12238-9 : 22.50
1. Whistler, James Abbott McNeill, 1834-1903. 2. Painters—United States—Biography.

WEINTRAUB, Stanley, 1929- 759.13 B
Whistler; a biography. New York, Weybright and Talley [1974] x, 498 p. illus. 25 cm. Bibliography: p. 469-481. [ND237.W6W44] 73-76570 ISBN 0-679-40099-0 12.50
1. Whistler, James Abbott McNeill, 1834-1903. BIP

WHISTLER, James Abbott McNeill, 1834-1903. 769'.92'4
Etchings and lithographs; exhibition [catalogue] New York, M. Knoedler & Co., 1973. 28 p. illus. 23 cm. [NE2012.W45K56] 74-173094
1. Whistler, James Abbott McNeill, 1834-1903. I. Knoedler (M.) and Company, inc. II. Title.

WHISTLER, James Abbott McNeill, 1834-1903. 769'.92'4
Etchings and lithographs by James A. McNeill Whistler : from the collection of the Herbert F. Johnson Museum of Arts, Cornell University : an exhibition circulated by the Gallery Association of New York State : [catalogue]. Ithaca, N.Y. : Herbert F. Johnson Museum of Arts, Cornell University, c1975. [16] p. : ill. ; 21 cm. Bibliography: p. [16] [NE2012.W45H47] 75-27820
1. Whistler, James Abbott McNeill, 1834-1903. I. Herbert F. Johnson Museum of Arts. II. Gallery Association of New York State. III. Title: Etchings and lithographs by James A. McNeill Whistler...

WHISTLER, James Abbott McNeill, 1834-1903. 769'.92'4
An exhibition of lithographs: December 2nd-January 12, 1974. Cold Spring Harbor, N.Y., Harbor Gallery [1973] [40] p. illus. 22 cm. Catalog. [NE2312.W45H37] 73-90046
1. Whistler, James Abbott McNeill, 1834-1903. I. Harbor Gallery. II. Title.

WHISTLER, James Abbott McNeill, 1834-1903. 769'.92'4
Selected etchings of James A. McN. Whistler / selected and introduced by Maria Naylor. New York : Dover Publications, c1975. xxxv p., [70] leaves of plates : ill. ; 31 cm. (Dover art collections) [NE2012.W45N39 1975] 73-86438 ISBN 0-486-23194-1 : 5.00
1. Whistler, James Abbott McNeill, 1834-1903. I. Naylor, Maria. II. Title. BIP

Whistler, Laurence, 1912—

WHISTLER, Laurence, 1912- 748.6
Pictures on glass; engraved by Laurence Whistler. Ipswich, Cupid Press, 1972. 32, 80 p., leaf (chiefly illus.) 28 cm. [NK5198.W4A53] 73-159846 ISBN 0-903575-00-0 £7.50
1. Whistler, Laurence, 1912- 2. Engraved glass—Great Britain. I. Title. BIP

Whitaker, Frederic.

LOVOOS, Janice. 759.13
Frederic Whitaker. Flagstaff, Ariz., Northland Press [1972] viii, 115 p. illus. (part col.) 30 cm. Bibliography: p. 114. [ND1839.W48L6] 77-188290 ISBN 0-87358-094-X 17.50
1. Whitaker, Frederic. BIP

White, Charles, 1918—

WHITE, Charles 1918- 741.9'0924
Images of dignity: the drawings of Charles White. Foreword by Harry Belafonte. Introd. by James Porter. Commentary by Benjamin Horowitz. [Los Angeles, Calif.] Ritchie [1967] vi, 121p. illus., port 29cm. [NC1075.W55H6] 67-15079 10.00
I. Horowitz, Benjamin. II. Title.
Distributed by Lane in Menlo Park, Calif.

WHITE, Charles, 1918- 760'.092'4
The work of Charles White : an American experience : an exhibition / organized by the High Museum of Art, Atlanta, Georgia, 1976. Atlanta : The Museum, 1976. 23 p. : ill. ; 21 cm. Catalogue of an exhibition held at the High Museum of Art, Atlanta, Sept. 4-Oct. 3, 1976, and at other museums, Oct. 23, 1976-Aug. 14, 1977. [N6537.W44H53] 76-26396
1. White, Charles, 1918- 2. Afro-Americans in art. I. High Museum of Art.

White, Jack, 1931—

WHITE, Jack, 1931- 759.13
Jack White. [Edited by Peg Weiss] Syracuse, N.Y., Everson Museum of Art [1974] [7] p. illus. (part col.) 23 cm. Cover title. Catalog of an exhibition, Dec. 15, 1973-Jan. 14, 1974. [ND237.W617W44] 74-77745
1. White, Jack, 1931- I. Weiss, Peg, ed. II. Everson Museum of Art of Syracuse and Onondaga County.

White, John, fl 1585-1503.

HULTON, Paul Hope. 741.973
The American drawings of John White, 1577-1590, with drawings of European and oriental subjects. By Paul Hulton & David Beers Quinn, with contributions by W. C. Sturtevant and others Pref by Edward Croft-murray London, Trustees of the British Museum; Chapel Hill, University of North Carolina Press, 1964. 2 v. illus. (part col.) facsims., maps (part col.) 40 cm. "Planned and produced by the John White Committee." Issued in a case. Contents.Contents.--v. 1. A catalogue raisonne and a study of the artist--v. 2. Reproductions of the originals in colour facsimile and of derivatives in monochrome. Bibliography: v. 1, p. 156-162. [NC242.W53H8] 64-4527
1. White, John, fl 1585-1503. I. Quinn, David Beers, joint author. II. Title.

*WHITE, John 759.2
The Americn drawings of John White, 1577-1590; with drawings of European and oriental subjects; 2v. By Paul Hulton, David Beers Quinn, Contribs. W. C. Sturtevant others Pref. by Edward Croft Murray. London, The Trustees of the Brit. Mus. [dist.] Chapel Hill, Univ. of N.C. Pr. [[1964] 2v. 454p. illus., col. plates. 29cm. Contents.v.1. A catalogue raisonne and a study of the artist.--v.2. Plates in colour facsimile and monochrome. 225.00 li0 colour facsimile and monochrome. 225.00 set, lim. ed.
I. Hulton, Paul. II. Quinn, David Beers. III. Title.

White, Katherine Coryton—Art collections.

THOMPSON, Robert Farris. 709'.67
African art in motion; icon and act in the Collection of Katherine Coryton White. [Catalog of an exhibition] National Gallery of Art, Washington, D.C.; Frederick S. Wight Art Gallery, University of California, Los Angeles. Los Angeles, University of California Press [1974] xv, 275 p. illus. (part col.) 28 cm. Bibliography: p. 243-249. [NX588.75.T47] 73-91679 ISBN 0-520-02685-3 20.00
1. White, Katherine Coryton—Art collections. 2. Arts, African—Exhibitions. 3. Arts—Africa, Sub-Saharan. I. United States. National Gallery of Art. II. Frederick S. Wight Art Gallery. III. Title.
Pbk. 9.95

White, Stanford, 1853-1906.

BALDWIN, Charles Crittenton, 1888- 720'.924 B
Stanford White, by Charles C. Baldwin. New York, Da Capo Press, 1971 [c1931] xii, 399 p. illus., ports. 24 cm. (Da Capo Press series in architecture and decorative art, v. 39) [NA737.W5B3 1971] 78-150512 ISBN 0-306-70138-3
1. White, Stanford, 1853-1906.

BALDWIN, Charles Crittenton, 1888- 720'.92'4 B
Stanford White / by Charles C. Baldwin ; with an introd. by Paul Goldberger. New York : Da Capo Press, 1976, c1931. p. cm. (A Da Capo paperback) Reprint, with new introd., of the ed. published by Dodd, Mead, New York. [NA737.W5B3 1976] 75-31800 ISBN 0-306-80031-4 : 20.00 pbk. : 4.95
1. White, Stanford, 1853-1906. BIP

White, Stephen.

WHITE, Stephen. 769'.92'4
Amish. [Chapel Hill? N.C., 1968-69] 3 v. illus. 30 cm. Issued in a case. Artist's proof ed. of 25: no. 1. [NE1112.W46A57] 74-176355 180.00
1. White, Stephen. 2. Amish in art. I. Title.

Whitefield, Edwin, b. 1816.

NORTON, Bettina A. 760'.092'4
Edwin Whitefield—North American scenery, faithfully delineated / Bettina A. Norton. Barre, Mass. : Barre Publishers, 1974, c1975. p. cm. Bibliography: p. [NC242.W54N67] 72-95109 ISBN 0-517-51731-0
1. Whitefield, Edwin, b. 1816. 2. United States in art. 3. Canada in art. I. Title.

Whitehall Palace.

CHARLTON, John, 1909- 724.1
The Banqueting House, Whitehall. London, H. M. S. O. [New York, Brit. Info., 1965] 66p. illus. (pt. col.) 27cm. At head of title: Ministry of Public Building and Works [NA7746.W4C5] 65-5352 1.70 pap.,
1. Whitehall Palace. I. Gt. Brit. Ministry of Public Building and Works. II. Title.

Whitlock, Brand, 1869-1934.

CRUNDEN, Robert Morse. 973.91 B
A hero in spite of himself: Brand Whitlock; in art, politics & war [by] Robert M. Crunden. [1st ed.] New York, Knopf, 1969. 479, xi p. port. 22 cm. Bibliographical references included in "Notes" (p. [437]-479) [CT275.W5518C7 1969] 73-79316 10.00
1. Whitlock, Brand, 1869-1934. I. Title.

Whitney, Gertrude Vanderbilt, 1877-1942.

FRIEDMAN, Bernard Harper, 1926- 704'.7 B
Gertrude Vanderbilt Whitney : a biography / by B. H. Friedman, with the research collaboration of Flora Miller Irving. 1st ed. Garden City, N.Y. : Doubleday, 1978. xi, 684 p., [32] leaves of plates : ill. ; 24 cm. Includes index. [N5220.W65F74] 77-26524 ISBN 0-385-12994-7 : 14.95
1. Whitney, Gertrude Vanderbilt, 1877-1942. 2. Art patrons—United States—Biography. I. Title. BIP

Whitney Museum of American Art, New York.

GINGOLD, Diane J. 759.13'074'016147
American painting, 1900-1939 : selections from the Whitney Museum of American Art: exhibition June 29 through August 8, 1976, Montgomery Museum of Fine Arts, Montgomery Alabama [Montgomery] : Montgomery Museum of Fine Arts, 1976. 110 p. : ill. ; 25 cm. Catalog prepared by D. J. Gingold. Includes index. Bibliography: p. 105-107. [ND212.G5] 76-21911 ISBN 0-89280-003-8
1. Whitney Museum of American Art, New York. 2. Paintings, American—Exhibitions. 3. Paintings, Modern—20th century—United States—Exhibitions. I. Montgomery Museum of Fine Arts. II. Title.

WHITNEY Museum of American Art, New York. 709'.73'07401471
Catalogue of the collection / [catalogue of paintings, watercolors, drawings and sculpture by Margaret McKellar, catalogue of prints by Elke Morger Solomon and Mariann Nowack]. New York : Whitney Museum of American Art, 1975. 237 p. : ill. (some col.) ; 28 cm. Includes indexes. [N6512W532 1975a] 74-79170
1. Whitney Museum of American Art,

New York. 2. Art, American—Catalogs. 3. Art, Modern—20th century—United States—Catalogs. 4. Art, Modern—20th century—Catalogs. 5. Art—New York (City)—Catalogs. I. McKellar, Margaret. II. Solomon, Elke Morger. III. Nowack, Mariann.

WHITNEY Museum 709'.73'07401471
of American Art, New York.
Selections from the permanent collection / Whitney Museum of American Art. Chicago : University of Chicago Press, 1977 p. cm. [N6512.W532 1977] 76-19074 ISBN 0-226-69818-1 12.50
1. Whitney Museum of American Art, New York. 2. Art, American—Catalogs. 3. Art, Modern—20th century—United States—Catalogs. 4. Art—New York (City)—Catalogs. I. Title. BIP

Whitney Studio Club.

WHITNEY Museum 759.13'074'01471
of American Art, New York.
The Whitney Studio Club and American art, 1900-1932 : [exhibition, Whitney Museum of American Art, New York, May 23-September 3, 1975]. New York : The Museum, [1975] 23 p. : ill. ; 26 cm. Cover title. "Catalogue of the exhibition:" p. 22-23. [N6512.W532 1975b] 75-325749
1. Whitney Studio Club. 2. Art, American—Exhibitions. 3. Art, Modern—20th century—United States—Exhibitions. I. Title.

Wichita Art Museum—Catalogue.

**CATALOGUE of the Roland* 708.1563
P. Murdock Collection [Witchita, Ks.,] Wichita Art Museum [1972] 237 p., illus., 24 cm. Includes Bibliographical reference [N529] 72-82939 pap. 4.00
1. Wichita Art Museum—Catalogue. I. Witchita Art Museum

Wicker furniture.

BAUSERT, John. 684.1'06
The complete book of wicker & cane furniture making / by John Bausert. New York : Drake Publishers, 1976. 123 p. : ill. ; 28 cm. [TT197.7.B38] 75-36148 ISBN 0-8473-1182-1 pbk. : 6.95
1. Wicker furniture. I. Title. II. Title: Cane furniture. BIP

CORBIN, Patricia. 749.2
All about wicker / Patricia Corbin. 1st ed. New York : Dutton, c1978. 121 p., [12] leaves of plates : ill. ; 21 cm. Includes index. [NK2712.7.C67 1978] 78-53095 8.95 ($11.25 Canada)
1. Wicker furniture. I. Title. BIP

SAUNDERS, Richard, 1947- 749.2'13
Collecting & restoring wicker furniture / by Richard Saunders. New York : Crown, c1976. p. cm. Includes bibliographical references and index. [TT197.7.S38] 76-14995 ISBN 0-517-52622-0 : 6.95
1. Wicker furniture. 2. Furniture—Repairing. I. Title. BIP

Wicker furniture—History.

THOMPSON, Frances, 1920- 749.2
The complete wicker book : the history of wicker furniture and accessories from antique to modern / Frances Thompson. Des Moines : WH Books, c1978. 98 p. : ill. ; 25 cm. [NK2712.7.T47] 76-58067 ISBN 0-87069-211-9 pbk. : 7.95
1. Wicker furniture—History. I. Title. BIP

Wickes, Forsyth, 1876-1964—Art collections.

BOSTON. Museum of Fine 708.144'61
Arts.
The Forsyth Wickes Collection, by Perry T. Rathbone. Boston, Museum of Fine Arts; distributed by New York Graphic Society, Greenwich, Conn. [1968] 111 p. illus. (part col.), port. 23 cm. [N5220.W68] 68-27635 8.50
1. Wickes, Forsyth, 1876-1964—Art collections. I. Rathbone, Perry Townsend, 1911- II. Title. BIP

Wide-angle photography.

LAHUE, Kalton C. 778.3'2
Wide-angle photography / by Kalton C. Lahue. Los Angeles : Petersen Pub. Co., c1977. 80 p. : ill. ; 28 cm. (Petersen's how-to photographic library) [TR687.L33] 77-74100 ISBN 0-8227-4014-1 pbk. : 3.95
1. Wide-angle photography. 2. Lenses, Photographic. I. Title. BIP

Widforss, Gunnar.

BELKNAP, Bill, 1920- 759.13
Gunnar Widforss: painter of the Grand Canyon [by] Bill Belknap and Frances Spencer Belknap. Flagstaff, Published for the Museum of Northern Arizona by the Northland Press, 1969. xx, 86 p. col. plates, port. 28 cm. [ND1998.W5B4] 79-94654 14.50
1. Widforss, Gunnar. I. Belknap, Frances Spencer, 1913- joint author. II. Flagstaff, Ariz. Museum of Northern Arizona.

Wiebach, Carl M. Heinz.

WIEBACH, Carl M. 728'.092'4 B
Heinz.
Escape from rat-race / by Carl M. Heinz Wiebach ; collaborator, Barbara Hopfinger ; ill. Hein Wiebach. Los Angeles : Cultural Exchange Center, c1975. 140 p. : ill. ; 23 cm. [NA781.W53] 75-16889
1. Wiebach, Carl M. Heinz. 2. Architects—Honduras—Roatan Island. 3. Bay Islands—Description and travel. I. Title.

Wieghorst, Olaf, 1899—

REED, William, 1929- 759.13 B
Olaf Wieghorst. With a foreword by Barry Goldwater. Flagstaff, Northland Press, 1969. xiv, 194 p. illus., plates (part col.), ports. (part col.) 29 cm. [ND237.W64R4] 72-94655 25.00
1. Wieghorst, Olaf, 1899-

WIEGHORST, Olaf, 1899- 759.13
A retrospective exhibition of Olaf Wieghorst : November 15, 1974-January 19, 1975 / presented by the National Cowboy Hall of Fame and Western Heritage Center, Oklahoma City, Oklahoma. Kansas City, Mo. : Lowell Press, c1974. 74 p. : ill. (some col.) ; 23 x 26 cm. [ND237.W64N37] 74-25549 ISBN 0-913504-21-1
1. Wieghorst, Olaf, 1899- 2. The West in art—Exhibitions. I. National Cowboy Hall of Fame and Western Heritage Center. II. Title.

Wiener, Grand Pa, 1886-1970.

BOCK, Joanne. 759.13
Pop Wiener, naive painter. [Amherst] University of Massachusetts Press, 1974. 157 p. illus. (part col.) 27 cm. Based on the author's thesis (M.A.) State University of New York, Cooperstown Museum Training Program, 1970. Bibliography: p. 149-152. [ND237.W644B62] 72-90499 20.00
1. Wiener, Grand Pa, 1886-1970. I. Wiener, Grand Pa, 1886-1970. II. Title.

Wigs.

WOODFORDE, John. 391'.5
The strange story of false hair. New York, Drake Publishers [1972] xv, 126 p. illus. 23 cm. Includes bibliographical references. [GT2310.W66 1972] 72-1240 ISBN 0-87749-249-2 5.95
1. Wigs. I. Title.

Wilborough, Eng.

BAKER, John, 1901- 630.1
Cottage by the springs. Frontispiece by H. B. Brabazon and illus. by Kenneth Lindley. New York, Roy Publishers [1961] 109 p. illus. 20 cm. [DA690.W605B3] 61-3905
1. Wilborough, Eng. I. Title.

Wild flowers.

WALCOTT, Mary Morris 581.97
(Vaux) 1860-1940.
Wild flowers of America. 400 flowers in full color based on paintings by Mary Vaux Walcott, with additional paintings by Dorothy Falcon Platt; edited with an introd. and detailed descriptions by H. w. Rickett. New York, Crown Publishers [1953] 71p., 400 col. plates. 31cm. 'The Mary Vaux Walcott color plates ... are reproduced ... from the ... portfolio set North American wild flowers. by Mary Vaux Walcott, as published by the Smithsonian Institution.' [QK112.W35] 53-9972
1. Wild flowers. 2. Botany—North America. 3. Wild flowers—Pictorial works. I. Platt, Dorothy Falcon. II. Rickett, Harold William, 1896- ed. III. Title. BIP

ZIM, Herbert Spencer, 582.13
1909-
Flowers; a guide to familiar American wildflowers, by Herbert S. Zim and Alexander C. Martin. Illustrated by Rudolf Freund. Sponsored by the Wildlife Management Institute. 134 paintings in full color. New York, Golden Press [1961? c1950] 157 p. illus. 20 cm. (A Golden nature guide) A guide to approximately 200 of the most commonly viewed American wildflowers, with 134 color paintings. Flowers are grouped by color. [QK112.Z5 1961] AC 68
1. Wild flowers. 2. Botany—Pictures and illustrations. I. Martin, Alexander Campbell, 1897- joint author. II. Freund, Rudolf, 1915- illus. III. Title.

Wild flowers—North America.

HYLANDER, Clarence John, 581.973
1897-
The Macmillan wild flower book. Descriptive text by Clarence J. Hylander; illus. by Edith Farrington Johnston. New York, Macmillan [1954] xv, 480 p. illus. (part col.) 28 cm. [QK112.H9] 54-7383
1. Wild flowers—North America. 2. Wild flowers—Pictorial works. I. Johnston, Edith Farrington, illus. II. Title. BIP

Wild flowers—North America—Pictorial works.

PRENTICE, Thurlow 582'.13'0974
Merrill, 1898-
Weeds & wildflowers of Eastern North America. From watercolors by T. Merrill Prentice, and text by Elizabeth O. Sargent. [Salem?] Peabody Museum of Salem [1973] [251] p. 114 col. plates. 30 cm. Errata slip inserted. [QK112.P7] 73-81957 ISBN 0-8271-7307-5 45.00
1. Wild flowers—North America—Pictorial works. 2. Weeds—North America—Pictorial works. I. Sargent, Elizabeth O. II. Peabody Museum of Salem, Salem, Mass. III. Title. BIP

Wild flowers.—Palestine.

VESTER, Bertha Hedges 759.95694
(Spafford) 1878-
Flowers of the Holy Land. 17 color reproductions of orig. watercolors. Biographical sketch by Lowell Thomas; note by Norman Vincent Peale. Kansas City, Mo., Hallmark Cards [dist. Garden City, N. Y., Doubleday, c.]1962. 64p. col. illus. 20cm. 62-14859 2.00 bds.,
1. Wild flowers.—Palestine. I. Title.

Wild flowers—Pictorial works.

BRUNSKILL, R. W. 728'.09427'8
Vernacular architecture of the Lake counties : a field handbook / by R. W. Brunskill. London ; Boston : Faber and Faber, 1978. 164 p. : ill. ; 21 cm. (Faber paperbacks) Includes index. Bibliography: p. 154-159. [NA995.L34B78 1978] 78-324736 ISBN 0-571-09460 : 14.95 ISBN 0-571-09459-7 pbk. : 7.95
1. Vernacular architecture—England—Lake District. I. Title.

EVERARD, Barbara. 582'.13
Wild flowers of the world. Paintings by Barbara Everard. Text by Brian D. Morley. Consultant editors: W. T. Stearn [and] Peter S. Green. [1st American ed.] New York, Putnam [1970] 432 p. col. illus., maps. 32 cm. Bibliography: p. 28-29. [QK98.E93 1970b] 79-116143 15.00
1. Wild flowers—Pictorial works. I. Morley, Brian Derek. II. Title.

FELSKO, Elsa. 582.13
A book of wild flowers, 160 watercolors. Pref. by C. D. Darlington, notes by Sheila Littleboy. [1st American ed.] New York, T. Yoseloff, [1956] xi, 231 p. col. plates. 25 cm. [QK98.F4] 56-3664
1. Wild flowers—Pictorial works. I. Title.

LINE, Les. 582.13
The Audubon Society book of wildflowers / by Les Line and Walter Henricks Hodge. New York : H. N. Abrams, 1978. 259 p. : ill. ; 32 cm. "A Chanticleer Press edition." Includes index. [QK98.L75] 78-6204 ISBN 0-8109-0671-6 : 37.50
1. Wild flowers—Pictorial works. 2. Botany—Ecology. I. Hodge, Walter H., 1912- joint author. II. National Audubon Society. III. Title. BIP

THOMPSON, Eloise 582.130973
(Reid)
Wildflower portraits. With botanical descriptions by Edna Wolf Miner. [1st ed.] Norman, University of Oklahoma Press [1964] xix p., 100 col. plates. 29 cm. [QK98.T47] 64-14622
1. Wild flowers — Pictorial works. 2. Wild flowers — U.S. I. Miner, Edna Wolf. II. Title.

Wild flowers—United States.—Identification.

HERSEY, Jean, 1902- 582'.13'0973
The Woman's day book of wildflowers / by Jean Hersey ; illustrated by Fritz Kredel. New York : Simon and Schuster, c1976. 160 p. : col. ill. ; 24 cm. Includes index. [QK115.H44 1976] 76-57 ISBN 0-671-22251-1 : 6.95
1. Wild flowers—United States—Identification. 2. Wild flowers—Canada—Identification. 3. Wild flower gardening. I. Title. BIP

LINN, Louis C. 582'.13'0973
Eastern North America's wildflowers / Louis C. Linn. 1st ed. New York : Dutton, c1977. p. cm. "A Sunrise book." Includes index. [QK115.L56] 77-4314 7.95
1. Wild flowers—United States—Identification. I. Title. BIP

ZIM, Herbert Spencer, 582.130973
1909-
Flowers; a guide to familiar American wildflowers, by Herbert S. Zim and Alexander C. Martin. Illustrated by Rudolf Freund. Sponsored by the Wildlife Management Institute. 134 paintings in full color. New York, Golden Press [1961? c1950] 157 p. illus. 20 cm. (A Golden nature guide) [QK112.Z5 1961] 61-8319
1. Wild flowers—United States.—Identification. 2. Botany—United States—Pictorial works. I. Martin, Alexander Campbell, 1897- joint author.

Wild flowers—United States—Pictorial works.

BISHOP, Bette. 582.13'022'2
Beautiful wildflowers; a garland of American wildflowers. With 20 watercolors by Nanae Ito. [Kansas City, Mo.] Hallmark Editions [1968] 61 p. illus. (part col.) facsims. 20 cm. "Lilies of the field, by Richard Rhodes": p. 49-61. [QK112.B5] 68-16435
1. Wild flowers—United States—Pictorial works. I. Ito, Nanae, illus. II. Title.

EVANS, Henry Herman, 582.13'0973
1918-
State flowers. Text and illustrations by Henry Evans. San Francisco [Printed at the Peregrine Press] 1968- v. col. illus. 51 cm. (His The Botanical prints series, v. 22, 26, 28) Printed for subscribers in an ed. of 40 copies, each print signed by the artist. Contents.Contents.—pt. 1. Alaska. Arizona. California. Hawaii. Idaho. Montana. Nevada. Oregon. Utah. Washington.—pt. 2. Alabama. Colorado. Kansas. Louisiana. Maryland. Minnesota. New Mexico. Ohio. Pennsylvania. Tennessee.—pt. 3. Delaware.

Massachusetts. Michigan. Missouri. New Hampshire. New Jersey. Rhode Island. Texas. Vermont. Virginia.—pt. 4. Arkansas. Maine. Mississippi. New York. North Carolina. West Virginia. Wisconsin. Wyoming. [QK98.E9] 70-222751
1. Wild flowers—United States—Pictorial works. I. Title.

FERGUSON, Mary. 582'.13'097
Wildflowers / Mary Ferguson, Richard M. Saunders. Toronto ; New York : Van Nostrand Reinhold, c1976. 192 p. : col. ill. ; 25 cm. Includes indexes. [QK112.F47] 76-23671 ISBN 0-442-29850-1 : 19.95
1. Wild flowers—United States—Pictorial works. 2. Wild flowers—Canada—Pictorial works. 3. Wild flowers—Pictorial works. I. Saunders, Richard Merrill, 1904- joint author. II. Title. BIP

RICKETT, Harold William, 1896- 582.130973
Wild flowers of the United States. General editor, William C. Steere. Collaborators: Rogers McVaugh [and others. 1st ed.] New York, McGraw-Hill [1966-73] 6 v. in 14 pts. illus., col. map (on lining papers) col. plates. 33 cm. "Publication of the New York Botanical Garden." Contents.Contents.—v. 1. The Northeastern States. 2 v.—v. 2. The Southeastern States. 2 v.—v. 3. Texas. 2 v.—v. 4. The Southwestern States. 3 v.—v. 5. The Northwestern States. 2 v.—v. 6. The central mountains and plains. 3 v. [QK115.R5] 66-17920
1. Wild flowers—United States—Pictorial works. I. Steere, William Campbell, 1907- ed. II. McVaugh, Rogers, 1909- III. New York (City). Botanical Garden. IV. Title. BIP

Wildenhain, Marguerite.

WILDENHAIN, Marguerite. 738'.092'4 B
The invisible core; a potter's life and thoughts. Photos. by Fran Ortiz. Palo Alto, Calif., Pacific Books [1973] 207 p. illus. 29 cm. [NK4210.W47A25] 72-80746 ISBN 0-87015-201-7 12.50
1. Wildenhain, Marguerite. 2. Potters—United States. I. Title. BIP

Wilder, Billy, 1906- —Art collections.

CALIFORNIA. University, Santa Barbara. Art Galleries. 707.4
A selection of paintings, drawings, collages and sculpture from the Collection of Mr. and Mrs. Billy Wilder. [Santa Barbara? 1966] 38 p. illus. (part col.) 22 x 25 cm. Exhibition held at the Art Gallery, University of California, Santa Barbara, Oct. 11-Nov. 13, 1966, and sponsored by the Committee on Arts and Lectures. Introduction by H. J. Seldis. [N5220.W738C3] 67-65132
1. Wilder, Billy, 1906- —Art collections. 2. Wilder, Billy, Mrs.—Art collections. 3. Art—Exhibitions. I. California. University, Santa Barbara. Committee on Arts and Lectures. II. Title.

Wiley, William T., 1937—

WILEY, William T., 1937- 709'.2'4
William T. Wiley. University Art Museum, Berkeley. Exhibition organized and catalogue compiled by Brenda Richardson. [Berkeley, Calif., University Art Museum, 1971] 73 p. illus. (part col.) 26 cm. On cover: Wizdumb. Bibliography: p. 52. [N6537.W47P52] 73-171042
1. Wiley, William T., 1937- I. Richardson, Brenda. II. California. University. Art Museum.

Wilke, Ulfert, 1907- —Art collections.

IOWA. University. Museum of Art. 707'.4'0177655
An artist collects : selections from five continents : [exhibition] the University of Iowa Museum of Art, Iowa City, Iowa, March 23, 1975, through May 3, 1975 / [selected by] Ulfert Wilke. [Iowa City] : The Museum, [1975] 147 p. : ill. (some col.) ; 29 cm. Errata sheet inserted. [N5220.W739I58 1975] 75-3924
1. Wilke, Ulfert, 1907- —Art collections. 2. Art—Exhibitions. I. Title.

IOWA. University. Museum of Art. 738.3'7
Calligraphic ceramics from eastern Iran : early Islamic pottery from the Collection of Ulfert Wilke : [exhibition] the University of Iowa Museum of Art, Iowa City, November 7 through December 15, 1974 / [Wendy Waldron]. [Iowa City] : The Museum, [1974?] 32 p. : ill. ; 28 cm. [NK4147.I58 1974] 75-624382
1. Wilke, Ulfert, 1907- —Art collections. 2. Pottery, Iranian—Exhibitions. 3. Pottery, Islamic—Iran—Exhibitions. 4. Paleography, Arabic (Cufic) in art. I. Wilke, Ulfert, 1907- II. Waldron, Wendy. III. Title.

William A. Farnsworth Library and Art Museum, Rockland, Me.

WILLIAM A. Farnsworth Library and Art Museum, Rockland, Me. 759.13'074'014153
American paintings and drawings in the William A. Farnsworth Library and Art Museum, Rockland, Maine. Rockland : The Library and Art Museum, c1975. 169 p. : ill. (some col.) ; 28 cm. [ND205.W515 1975] 75-324272
1. William A. Farnsworth Library and Art Museum, Rockland, Me. 2. Paintings, American—Catalogs. 3. Paintings—Rockland, Me.—Catalogs. 4. Drawings, American—Catalogs. 5. Drawings—Rockland, Me.—Catalogs. I. Title: American paintings and drawings ...

William and Mary College, Williamsburg, Va. — Portraits.

WILLIAM and Mary College, Williamsburg, Va. Earl Gregg Swem Library. 757.0838
Catalog of portraits in the library and in other buildings of William and Mary college, by E. G. Swem, Librarian. Williamsburg, Va., 1936. 62 p. illus. 23 cm. (Bulletin of the College of William and Mary, v. 30, no. 6) Cover title. [N7621.W55] 36-28139
1. William and Mary College, Williamsburg, Va. — Portraits. I. Swem, Earl Gregg, 1870-1965. II. Title.

William Rockhill Nelson Gallery of Art and Mary Atkins Museum of Fine Arts, Kansas City, Mo.

WILLIAM Rockhill Nelson Gallery of Art and Mary Atkins Museum of Fine Arts, Kansas City, Mo. 709'.51
The dragon's gate : exploring oriental art / William Rockhill Nelson Gallery of Art and Mary Atkins Museum of Fine Arts, Kansas City, Missouri, edited by Victoria R. Melcher and Dianne T. Deckert. 1st ed. Kansas City, Mo. : The Museum, 1976. 52 p. : ill. ; 22 x 28 cm. Includes index. Explores facets of Oriental art including sculpture, painting, and furniture. Includes suggestions for related activities. [N7340.W48 1976] 77-359560
1. William Rockhill Nelson Gallery of Art and Mary Atkins Museum of Fine Arts, Kansas City, Mo. 2. Art, Chinese. 3. Art appreciation. I. Melcher, Victoria R. II. Deckert, Dianne Turner. III. Title.

WILLIAM Rockhill Nelson Gallery of Art and Mary Atkins Museum of Fine Arts, Kansas City, Mo. 708'.178'411
Handbook of the collections in the William Rockhill Nelson Gallery of Art and Mary Atkins Museum of Fine Arts, Kansas City, Missouri. 5th ed. Kansas City, Mo., 1973. 2 v. illus. (part col.) 28 cm. Published in 1933 under title: Handbook of the William Rockhill Nelson Gallery of Art; in 1940 and 1949: The William Rockhill Nelson collection. Contents.Contents.—v. 1. Art of the Occident, edited by R. E. Taggart and G. L. McKenna.—v. 2. Art of the Orient, edited by R. E. Taggart, G. L. McKenna, and M. F. Wilson. [N582.K3A57 1973] 74-176114
1. William Rockhill Nelson Gallery of Art and Mary Atkins Museum of Fine Arts, Kansas City, Mo. 2. Art—Kansas, Mo.—Catalogs. I. Taggart, Ross E., ed. II. McKenna, George L., ed. III. Wilson, Marc F., ed. IV. Title.

Williams, G. Mennen, 1911- —Art collections.

AGA-OGLU, Kamer, 1903- 738'.095'074017435
The Williams collection of Far Eastern ceramics. Chinese, Siamese, and Annamese ceramic wares selected from the collection of Justice and Mrs. G. Mennen Williams in the University of Michigan Museum of Anthropology. Catalogue of an exhibition held in the West Gallery of the Horace H. Rackham School of Graduate Studies, Mar. 1-30, 1972. Ann Arbor, University of Michigan, Museum of Anthropology [1972] v, 73 p. illus. 27 cm. Bibliography: p. 73. [NK4163.A34] 72-197785
1. Williams, G. Mennen, 1911- —Art collections. 2. Pottery, Far Eastern—Exhibitions. 3. Porcelain, Far Eastern—Exhibitions. I. Michigan. University. Museum of Anthropology. II. Title. BIP

Williams, Guy, 1932—

WILLIAMS, Guy, 1932- 760'.092'4
The paper works: paintings, photographs, texts : University Art Galleries, University of California, Santa Barbara, January 5-February 6, 1977 / Guy Williams ; sponsored by the Art Affiliates, UCSB. Santa Barbara, Calif. : The Galleries, c1977. [44] p. : col. ill. ; 22 cm. Bibliography: p. [35] [N6537.W53C34] 76-620097
1. Williams, Guy, 1932- I. California. University, Santa Barbara. Art Galleries. II. Title.

Williams, Hiram.

STEPHENS, William B. 759.13
Hiram Williams, exploring the sources of his expression / William B. Stephens. [Memphis] : Memphis State University Press, c1978. viii, 132 p. : ill. (some col.) ; 24 cm. [ND237.W712S73] 79-101201 ISBN 0-87870-045-5 : 18.50
1. Williams, Hiram. 2. Painters—United States—Interviews. I. Title.

Williams, Thomas E., 1894—

CURTISS, Richard D. 686.2'092'4 B
Thomas E. Williams & the Fine Arts Press, by Richard D. Curtiss. Los Angeles, Dawson's Book Shop, 1973. xv, 119 p. ports., facsims. 25 cm. [Z232.W69C87] 73-85053 ISBN 0-87093-091-5
1. Williams, Thomas E., 1894- 2. Fine Arts Press. I. Title. BIP

Williams, William, 1727-1791.

DICKASON, David Howard. 759.13
William Williams: novelist and painter of colonial America, 1727-1791. Bloomington, Indiana University Press [1970] xii, 269 p. illus., ports. 23 cm. (Indiana University humanities series, no. 67) Includes bibliographical references. [PS875.W3Z65] 76-628292 ISBN 0-253-38667-5 6.75
1. Williams, William, 1727-1791. I. Series: Indiana. University. Indiana University humanities series, no. 67

WILLIAMS, John Francis, 1894- 759.13
The ancestor; the world of William Williams. Philadelphia, Dorrance [1971] xv, 184 p. illus., geneal. table, ports. 22 cm. Bibliography: p. 180-184. [ND237.W717W5] 79-137848 ISBN 0-8059-1517-6 5.00
1. Williams, William, 1727-1791. I. Title.

Williams, William, 1787-1850.

WILLIAMS, John Camp, 1859?-1929. 686.2'092'4
An Oneida County printer, William Williams, printer, publisher, editor, with a bibliography of the press at Utica, Oneida County, New York, from 1803-1838. New York, Scribner, 1906. Harrison, N.Y., Harbor Hill Books, 1974. xxvi, 211 p. illus. 22 cm. Bibliography: p. 18. [Z232.W7W7 1974] 74-14766 12.50
1. Williams, William, 1787-1850. 2. Printing—History—Utica, N.Y. 3. Utica, N.Y.—Imprints. I. Title.

Williamsburg, Va., in art.

DAVIS, Burke. 738.6
The Saint-Galy tiles of Williamsburg : a narrative history of early Virginia and the restoration of Colonial Williamsburg / text by Burke Davis. Milwaukee : W. H. Brady Co., c1974. 63 p. : ill. (some col.) ; 28 cm. Bibliography: p. 55-56. [NK4670.7.U53S243] 74-17781
1. Saint-Galy, Geza, 1908- 2. Colonial Williamsburg, inc. 3. Williamsburg, Va., in art. 4. Williamsburg, Va.—History—Pictorial works. 5. Williamsburg, Va.—Antiquities. 6. Tiles, American. I. Title.

Williamsburg, Va. — Public buildings.

WHIFFEN, Marcus. 724.173
The public buildings of Williamsburg, colonial capital of Virginia; an architectural history. Williamsburg, Va., Colonial Williamsburg [1958] xv, 269 p. illus., ports., map, plans. 26 cm. (Williamsburg architectural studies, v. 1) Bibliography: p. 235-240. [NA735.W5W47 vol. 1] 57-13499
1. Williamsburg, Va. — Public buildings. 2. Architecture, Colonial. I. Colonial Williamsburg, inc. II. Title. III. Series.

Williamsburg, Va.—Social life and customs.

JEFFREY, Tina C. 745.59'41
Williamsburg Christmas decorations, by Tina C. Jeffrey. Claude Jones Jr., consultant. Photos. by Del Wenzel, and the Colonial Williamsburg Foundations. [Williamsburg, Va., Jeffrey Pub. Co., 1972] 28 p. illus. (part col.) 23 cm. [F234.W7J4 1972] 73-153051
1. Williamsburg, Va.—Social life and customs. 2. Christmas decorations—Virginia—Williamsburg. I. Title.

Williamson, Clara Irene (McDonald) 1875—

VOGEL, Donald. 759.13
Aunt Clara; the paintings of Clara McDonald Williamson, by Donald and Margaret Vogel. Austin, Published for the Amon Carter Museum of Western Art by the University of Texas Press [1966] v, 119 p. illus. (part col.) 25 cm. "On the occasion of a retrospective exhibition of the artist's work at the Amon Carter Museum of Western Art, Fort Worth; the Oklahoma Art Center, Oklahoma City; the Marion Koogler McNay Art Institute, San Antonio; and the Dallas Museum of Fine Arts, Dallas." [ND237.W72V6] 66-28698
1. Williamson, Clara Irene (McDonald) 1875- I. Vogel, Margaret, joint author. II. Amon Carter Museum of Western Art, Fort Worth, Tex. III. Title. BIP

Willis, Robert, 1800-1875.

PEVSNER, Nikolaus, Sir, 1902- 720'.924
Robert Willis. North Hampton, Mass., Smith College, 1970. 27 p. illus. 22 cm. (Smith College studies in history, 46) "Remarks ... delivered at Smith College on 13 April 1968, as part of a celebration in honor of the sixty-fifth anniversary of Henry-Russell Hitchcock." [N7483.W47P4] 73-21611
1. Willis, Robert, 1800-1875. I. Hitchcock, Henry Russell, 1903- II. Series: Smith College studies in history, v. 46 BIP

Wilmette, Ill. Bahal Temple.

MCDANIEL, Allen Boyer, 1879- 726.2
The spell of the temple. New York, Vantage Press [1953] 96p. illus. 23cm. [NA4710.M2] 54-814
1. Wilmette, Ill. Bahal Temple. I. Title.

Wilmington, Del. Old Town Hall.

NELSON, Lee H v. 12
An architectural study of Old Town Hall built 1798-1800, Wilmington, Delaware. Prepared for the Historical Society of Delaware [by] Lee H. Nelson and Henry A. Judd. [Wilmington 1965. 1 v. 57 illus.,

plans. 28 cm. "Copy no 7 of twelve copies." [NA4433.W5N4] 66-45925
1. Wilmington, Del. Old Town Hall. I. Judd, Henry A., joint author. II. Delaware Historical Society. III. Title.

Wilson, Donald Roller, 1938—

WILSON, Donald Roller, 1938- 759.13
Donald Roller Wilson. An exhibition organized by the La Jolla Museum of Contemporary Art, July 13-Sept. 8, 1974. [La Jolla, Calif., La Jolla Museum of Contemporary Art, 1974] [28] p. illus. (part col.) 23 cm. Bibliography: p. [24] [ND237.W733L34] 74-83460
1. Wilson, Donald Roller, 1938- I. La Jolla Museum of Contemporary Art.

WILSON, Donald Roller, 1938- 759.13
Donald Roller Wilson; a mid-America invitational exhibition, fall, 1970-summer, 1971. [Kansas City, Mo., 1970] [24] p. illus., port. 22 cm. Text by Ralph T. Coe. "Sponsored by the Nelson Gallery-Atkins Museum, Kansas City, Missouri, and the City Art Museum of Saint Louis (organized by the Nelson Gallery of Art)." [ND237.W733C6] 77-23554
I. Coe, Ralph T. II. William Rockhill Nelson Gallery of Art and Mary Atkins Museum of Fine Arts, Kansas City, Mo. III. St. Louis. City Art Museum.

Wilson, Howard Stebbins, 1894-1958—Art collections.

NEBRASKA. University. Sheldon Memorial Art Gallery. 708'.178'411
The Howard S. Wilson memorial collection. [Catalogue of exhibition held Oct. 11 through Nov. 13, 1966. Lincoln, Printed by the F. Arnold Print. Co., 1966?] [48] p. illus. (1 col.), ports. 20 x 24 cm. Cover title. "First review in one place of all the paintings, drawings, and sculpture acquired [from 1959] to date." [N582.L5A57] 68-1052
1. Wilson, Howard Stebbins, 1894-1958—Art collections. 2. Art—Exhibitions. I. Wilson, Howard Stebbins, 1894-1958.

Wilson, Jack Turner—Art collections.

CATALOG of an exhibition of sculpture of India and Thailand. 730'.954
Lawrence University, Appleton, Wisconsin, Sept. 18-Oct. 27, 1968. [Appleton, Wis., Lawrence University, 1968] 51 p. illus. (part col.) 23 cm. Cover title. Pages 50-51, blank. Contents.Contents.—Part 1: Sculpture of India from the collection of Jack Turner Wilson.—Part 2: Sculpture of Thailand from the collection of John Adams Thierry. Includes bibliographies. [NB1000.C3] 73-729
1. Wilson, Jack Turner—Art collections. 2. Thierry, John Adams, 1913—Art collections. 3. Sculpture, Indic—Exhibitions. 4. Sculpture, Thai—Exhibitions. I. Lawrence University.

Winchester Cathedral.

CARBONELL, Dorothy. 746.4'4'09422735
Winchester Cathedral embroideries / written and compiled by Dorothy Carbonell. Winchester : Friends of Winchester Cathedral, 1975. 32 p. : ill., facsims. ; 22 cm. Bibliography: p. 32. [NK9244.W55C37] 75-326840 ISBN 0-903346-06-0 : £0.30
1. Winchester Cathedral. 2. Embroidery—England—Winchester. I. Title.

JERVIS, Simon. 914.22'735'04857
Woodwork of Winchester Cathedral / [by] Simon Jervis ; photographs by Murray Davison. Winchester : Friends of Winchester Cathedral, 1976. 39 p. : ill., plan ; 22 cm. Bibliography: p. 38-39. [NK9744.W56J47] 77-364704 ISBN 0-903346-10-9 : £0.50
1. Winchester Cathedral. 2. Wood-carving, Medieval—England—Winchester. 3. Wood-carving, English—England—Winchester. I. Title.

Winchester firearms.

†MADIS, George. 683'.42
The Winchester book / by George Madis. 1st ed. Brownsboro, Tex. : Art and Reference House, c1977. 638 p. : ill. ; 29 cm. [TS533.2.M3 1977] 77-155147 ISBN 0-910156-03-4 : 35.00
1. Winchester firearms. I. Title. BIP

WATROUS, George R. 683.4
The history of Winchester firearms, 1866-1975 / by George R. Watrous. 4th ed. - edited and rev. by Thomas E. Hall and James C. Rikhoff/history of winchester firearms eighteen sixty six nineteen seventy five New York : Winchester Press, [1975] p. cm. First-2d editions published under title: Winchester rifles and shotguns; 3d ed. published in 1966 under title: The history of Winchester firearms, 1866-1966. Includes index. [TS533.2.W37 1975] 75-9269 ISBN 0-87691-208-0 : 12.50
1. Winchester firearms. I. Title. BIP

WILSON, Robert Lawrence, 1939- 739.7'4'425
The book of Winchester engraving / by R. L. Wilson. 1st ed. Los Angeles : Beinfeld Pub., c1975. viii, 402 p. : ill. (some col., 5 fold.) ; 32 cm. Includes indexes. Bibliography: p. 394-397. [TS534.5.W54] 74-28671
1. Winchester firearms. 2. Engraving (Metal-work) I. Title.

Winchester rifle.

BUTLER, David F. 683'.42
Winchester '73 & '76; the first repeating centerfire rifles [by David F. Butler [New York] Winchester Press [1970] 95 p. illus. (part col.) 24 cm. Bibliography: p. 95. [TS536.B87] 71-99754 7.95
1. Winchester rifle. I. Title.

PARSONS, John E. 623.4423
The first Winchester; the story of the 1866 repeating rifle. New York, Morrow, 1955. 207 p. illus. 24 cm. [TS536.P3] 55-7621
1. Winchester rifle. I. Title.

PARSONS, John E 623.442
The first Winchester; the story of the 1866 repeating rifle. New York, Morrow, 1955 [i. e. 1960] 207p. illus. 25cm. [TS536.P3 1960] 60-12290
1. Winchester rifle. I. Title. BIP

STONE, George W. 683'.42
The Winchester 1873 handbook, by George W. Stone Arvada, Colo., Frontier Press [1973] 134 p. illus. 29 cm. [TS536.S76] 73-169365
1. Winchester rifle. I. Title.

WEST, Bill. 683.4
Winchester for over a century; the Winchesters I have owned or have come to my attention. Complete reference 1848-1965, all models. [1st ed. Whittier? Calif.] 1964- v. illus. 24 cm. Contents.Contents.—v. 1. Know your Winchesters. [TS536.W46] 64-66442
1. Winchester rifle. I. Title.

WEST, Bill 683.4
Winchester for over a century: the Winchesters I have known or have come to my attention; v.3. Complete reference 1885-1920 [Azusa, Calif., 91702, Author, 324 E. 13 St., c.1965] 1v. (various p.) illus. 24cm. Contents.v.3. The model 1885 Winchester single shot [TS536.W46] 64-66442 7.00
1. Winchester rifle. I. Title.

Winckelmann, Johann Joachim, 1717-1768.

LEPPMANN, Wolfgang. 913.03'1'0924 B
Winckelmann. [1st ed.] New York, Knopf, 1970. xx, 312, xii p. illus., ports. 22 cm. Bibliography: p. [309]-312. [N7483.W5L4] 70-118711 10.00
1. Winckelmann, Johann Joachim, 1717-1768.

Wind instruments.

BAINES, Anthony. 788.5
Woodwind instruments and their history. With a foreword by Adrian Boult. [1st ed.] New York, W. W. Norton [1957] 382 p. illus., music. 22 cm. Bibliography: p. 357-366. [ML930.B3] 57-8338
1. Wind instruments. I. Title. BIP

DAUBENY, Ulric. 788'.009
Orchestral wind instruments, ancient and modern; being an account of the origin and evolution of wind instruments from the earliest to the most recent times. Freeport, N.Y., Books for Libraries Press [1970] vi, 147 p. illus., 10 plates. 24 cm. Reprint of the 1920 ed. Bibliography: p. [vii] [ML930.D18 1970] 76-140354 ISBN 0-8369-5597-8
1. Wind instruments. I. Title. BIP

Wind instruments — Bibl.

U.S. Library of Congress. Music Division. 025.2
The Dayton C. Miller flute collection: a checklist of the instruments. Compiled by Laura E. Gilliam & William Lichtenwanger. Washington, 1961. vi. 115 p. illus., port. 23 cm. [ML128.W5U5] [Z663.37.D3] 016.784'0973 61-60077
1. Wind instruments — Bibl. I. Gilliam, Laura E., comp. II. Lichtenwanger, William, 1915- III. Title.

Wind instruments—Construction.

ROBINSON, Trevor. 788
The amateur wind instrument maker. [Amherst] University of Massachusetts Press, 1973. 115 p. illus. 27 cm. Bibliography: p. [113]-115. [ML930.R62] 72-90492 8.95
1. Wind instruments—Construction. I. Title. BIP

Windows.

BECKETT, Harold Edward. 721'.8
Windows : performance, design, and installation / by H. E. Beckett and J. A. Godfrey. New York : Van Nostrand Reinhold Co., [1974] x, 370 p. : ill. ; 31 cm. Includes index. Bibliography: p. [355]-364. [NA3020.B42 1974b] 73-221381 ISBN 0-442-20634-8 : 32.95
1. Windows. I. Godfrey, James Arthur, joint author.

COOK, Frank Palmer. 721'.8
Talk to me of windows; an entertaining story about windows, by F. Palmer Cook. [1st American ed.] South Brunswick, A. S. Barnes [1971, c1970] 128 p. illus., plans. 22 cm. [NA3020.C55 1971] 73-141570 ISBN 0-498-07857-4 6.95
1. Windows. I. Title.

WINDOWS and window walls, 721'.8
featuring timber construction; associate eds. H. M. Meier-Menzel, F. Hierl, K. Halmburger, tr. [from German] by P. B. A. Browning. London, Illiffe [1966] 120p. illus., plans. diagrs. 27cm. (Architect's detail lib., v.3) [NA3020.W513] 67-80293 11.50 bds.,
1. Windows. 2. Curtain walls. I. Series.
American distributor: Transatlantic, Levittown, N.Y.

Windows—Handbooks, manuals, etc.

WINDOW glass design guide 721'.8
/ edited by Denis Philip Turner. London : Architectural Press ; New York : Nichols Pub. Co., 1977. viii, 110 p. : ill. ; 31 cm. Includes index. Bibliography: p. 109-110. [TH2275.W56] 77-6739 ISBN 0-89397-028-X : 8.00
1. Windows—Handbooks, manuals, etc. 2. Glass—Handbooks, manuals, etc. I. Turner, Denis Philip. BIP

Windsor Castle. St. George's Chapel.

BLACKBURNE, Harry William, 1878- 726.6
The romance of St. George s Chapel, Windsor Castle, by Harry W. Blackburne and Maurice F. Bond. Foreword by E. K. C. Hamilton. [4th ed., rev. Windsor, Oxley, 1956] 90p. illus. 19cm. [NA5471.W73B6 1956] 57-41952
1. Windsor Castle. St. George's Chapel. I. Bond, Maurice Francis. II. Title.

BOND, Shelagh M ed. 726.8
The monuments of St. George's Chapel, Windsor Castle. [Windsor, Published for the Dean and canons of St. George's Chapel in Windsor Castle by Oxley, 1958] ix, 260p. 21 plates. 22cm. d(Historical monographs relating to St. George's Chapel, Windsor Castle) Bibliography: p. ivi-ix. [NA5471.W73B63] 59-41999
1. Windsor Castle. St. George's Chapel. I. Title. II. Series.

Windsor Great Park.

ROPER, Lanning. 712.5094212
The gardens in the Royal Park at Windsor. With a foreword by David Bowes Lyon. Garden City, N. Y., Doubleday, 1959. 127p. plates (part col.) ports., map. 29cm. [SB484.G7R6] 59-2156
1. Windsor Great Park. I. Title.

Windsor, House of—Art collections.

LONDON. Queen's Gallery, Buckingham Palace. 759.9492'074'021
Dutch pictures from the royal collection. [1st ed.] University Park, Pennsylvania State University Press [1971] 96 p. plates (part col.) 23 cm. Catalog of an exhibition held at the Queen's Gallery at Buckingham Palace in 1971. Introd. (p. 7-36) by O. Millar. Includes bibliographical references. [ND646.L64 1971b] 79-172996 ISBN 0-271-01109-2 6.50
1. Windsor, House of—Art collections. 2. Paintings, Dutch—Exhibitions. 3. Painting, Modern—17th-18th centuries—Netherlands. I. Millar, Oliver, 1923- II. Title. BIP

MILLAR, Oliver, 1923- 750'.74'02
The Queen's pictures / Oliver Millar. 1st American ed. New York : Macmillan, 1977. 240 p., [24] leaves of plates : ill. (some col.) ; 30 cm. Includes bibliographical references and index. [N5247.W56M54 1977] 76-30894 ISBN 0-02-584690-6 : 35.00
1. Windsor, House of—Art collections. 2. Paintings—England—Catalogs. I. Elizabeth II, Queen of Great Britain, 1926- II. Title. BIP

SCHILLING, Edmund, 1888- 741.9'4'0740229
The German drawings in the collection of Her Majesty the Queen at Windsor Castle, by Edmund Schilling; and, Supplements to the catalogues of Italian and French drawings, with a history of the Royal Collection of Drawings, by Anthony Blunt. London, New York, Phaidon [1971] viii, 239 p. illus., facsims. 31 cm. (The Drawings at Windsor Castle) "Distributors in the United States: Praeger Publishers Inc." Includes bibliographical references. [NC249.S3] 73-111053 ISBN 0-7148-1446-6 £8.50
1. Windsor, House of—Art collections. 2. Drawings, German—Catalogs. 3. Windsor Castle. I. Blunt, Anthony, Sir, 1907- II. Title.

Wine in art.

DALI, Salvador, 1904- 760'.092'4
Dali : the wines of gala / by Salvador Dali. New York : Abrams, [1977] p. cm. [N7113.D3A44] 77-8625 ISBN 0-8109-0802-6 : 50.00
1. Dali, Salvador, 1904- 2. Wine in art.

Winn, Robert K.—Art collections.

WINN, Robert K. 745'.0972
V. J. M. y J. : Viva Jesus, Maria y Jose : a celebration of the birth of Jesus : Mexican folk art and toys from the Collection of Robert K. Winn / foreword by Everett H. Jones ; photos. by Michael J. Smith. San Antonio : Trinity University Press, c1977. vii, 103 p. : col. ill. ; 23 cm. Bibliography: p. 101. [NK844.W5] 77-89457 ISBN 0-911536-68-X : 10.00
1. Winn, Robert K.—Art collections. 2. Folk art—Mexico. 3. Toys—Mexico. 4. Christian art and symbolism—Mexico. 5. Crib in Christian art and tradition. 6. Christmas—Mexico. I. Smith, Michael Jay, 1946- II. Title. III. Title: Viva Jesus, Maria y Jose. BIP

Winslow family—Portraits, etc.—Exhibitions.

BOWDOIN College. Museum of Art. 757'.9'074014461
The Winslows : pilgrims, patrons, and portraits : a joint exhibition at Bowdoin College Museum of Art and the Museum of Fine Arts, Boston / organized by Bowdoin College Museum of Art. [Brunswick, Me. : Bowdoin College, 1974] 40 p. : 20 ports. ; 23 cm. Includes bibliographical references. [ND1311.1.B68 1974] 75-327367
1. Winslow family—Portraits, etc.—Exhibitions. 2. Portraits, American—Exhibitions. I. Boston. Museum of Fine Arts. II. Title.

Winstanley, Henry, d. 1703.

WAYLAND, Virginia. 795.4'09
The Winstanley geographical cards. Pasadena, Calif., V. & H. Wayland [1967] 75 p. facsims. 25 cm. (The Wayland playing card monographs, no. 1) Bibliography: p. 75. [GV1235.W3] 68-2737
1. Winstanley, Henry, d. 1703. 2. Cards. 3. Geography—Early works. I. Title.

Winston, Lydia, 1897- —Art collections.

KRANNERT Art Museum. 769
Extensions of the artist; prints from the Collection of Lydia and Harry Lewis Winston (Mrs. Barnett Malbin) Champaign [1969] 52 p. illus., port. 28 cm. Exhibition held Oct. 12-Nov. 16, 1969. Contents.Contents.—Introduction, by M. B. Christison.—Reflections on art collecting as a creative process, by L. K. Winston.—Catalogue of the exhibition. [NE42.C45K72 1969] 72-629118
1. Winston, Lydia, 1897- —Art collections. 2. Winston, Harry Lewis—Art collections. 3. Prints—Exhibitions. I. Title.

SOLOMON R. Guggenheim Museum, New York. 709'.04
Futurism: a modern focus; the Lydia and Harry Lewis Winston Collection, Dr. and Mrs. Barnett Malbin. New York [Solomon R. Guggenheim Foundation, 1973] 251 p. illus. (part col.) 27 cm. Catalog of the exhibition held in the fall of 1973 at the Solomon R. Guggenheim Museum, New York. Bibliography: p. 232. [N6494.F8S64 1973] 73-86860 13.75
1. Winston, Lydia, 1897- —Art collections. 2. Winston, Harry Lewis—Art collections. 3. Futurism (Art)—Exhibitions. I. Title.

Winston, Lydia, 1897- —Art collections—Bibliography—Exhibitions.

DETROIT. Institute of Arts. 016.709'04
Documenting a collection ; About the designer/"illem Sandberg ; Twentieth-century graphics : chekc lists for three exhibitions selected from the Winston-Malbin Collection shown in conjunction with Cobra and Contrasts at the Detroit Institute of ARts, September 25-November 17, 1974. Detroit : Founders Society, Detroit Institute of Arts, 1974. 40 p. ; 26 cm. Includes bibliographies. [Z5935.5.D44 1974] [N6487] 75-317139
1. Winston, Lydia, 1897- —Art collections—Bibliography—Exhibitions. 2. Winston, Harry Lewis—Art collections—Bibliography—Exhibitions. 3. Sandberg, Willem Jacob Henri Berend, 1897- 4. Prints—Exhibitions. I. Title.

Winterthur Conference, 20th, 1974.

WINTERTHUR Conference, 20th, 1974. 745'.0974
Arts of the Anglo-American community in the seventeenth century : [twentieth annual Winterthur Conference, 1974] / edited by Ian M. G. Quimby. Charlottesville : Published for the Henry Francis du Pont Winterthur Museum [by] the University Press of Virginia, 1975. x, 299 p. : ill. ; 23 cm. (Winterthur Conference report ; 1974) Includes bibliographical references. [NK805.W53 1974] 74-22098 ISBN 0-8139-0612-1 pbk. : 4.50
1. Winterthur Conference, 20th, 1974. 2. Art industries and trade, Early American—Congresses. I. Quimby, Ian M. G., ed. II. Henry Francis du Pont Winterthur Museum. III. Title. IV. Series: Winterthur Conference. Report ; 1974. BIP

Winthrop, Grenville Lindall, 1864-1943—Art collections.

HARVARD University. William Hayes Fogg Art Museum. 708.144'4
Genville L. Winthrop; retrospective for a collector, Fogg Museum of Art, Cambridge, Massachusetts, January 23-March 31, 1969. Cambridge [1969] xix, 261 p. illus., port. 22 cm. "This catalogue has been prepared as a Museum course project by Dorothy W. Gillerman, Gridley McKim, and Joan R. Mertens." "Grenville L. Winthrop and his bequest: a brief bibliography of publications": p. xviii-xix. [N5220.W782H3] 77-76429
1. Winthrop, Grenville Lindall, 1864-1943—Art collections. 2. Art—Exhibitions. I. Gillerman, Dorothy W. II. McKim, Gridley. III. Mertens, Joan R. IV. Title.

Wire craft.

ABISCH, Roz. 745.56
The wire coat hanger book, over 150 intriguing uses, by Roz Abisch & Boche Kaplan New York, Drake Publishers [1974] p. cm. [TT214.3.A24] 74-6129 ISBN 0-87749-670-6 9.95
1. Wire craft. I. Kaplan, Boche, joint author. II. Title.

NEWMAN, Jay Hartley. 745.56
Wire art : metals, techniques, sculpture, collage, jewelry, mixed media / Jay Hartley Newman, Lee Scott Newman. New York : Crown Publishers, [1975] 248 p. : ill. ; 27 cm. Includes index. Bibliography: p. 239. [TT214.3.N48 1975] 74-32448 ISBN 0-517-51622-5 : 8.95
1. Wire craft. I. Newman, Lee Scott, joint author. II. Title.

Wire craft—Juvenile literature.

LIDSTONE, John. 745.56
Building with wire. Photos. by Roger Kerkham. New York, Van Nostrand [1972] 95 p. illus. 23 x 27 cm. Demonstrates various techniques and lists the necessary tools for creating wire sculpture. [TT214.3.L52] 70-149258
1. Wire craft—Juvenile literature. I. Kerkham, Roger, illus. II. Title. BIP

Wirecraft.

KRAMER, Jack, 1927- 745.56
Wirecraft : two dozen useful decorative projects for the house / John Highstone [i.e. J. Kramer] ; drawings by Michael Valdez, photos. by Matthew Barr and Clark Photo Graphics Studio, San Francisco. Boston : Houghton Mifflin, 1978. p. cm. [TT214.3.K7] 78-15538 ISBN 0-395-26297-6 : 10.95. ISBN 0-395-27396-X pbk. : 5.95
1. Wirecraft. I. Title.

Wisconsin in art.

WISCONSIN sketches. 741.9'73
Drawings by Aaron Bohrod. Words by Robert E. Gard. Edited by Mark E. Lefebvre. [1st ed. Madison, Wisconsin House, 1973] 1 v. (unpaged) illus. 23 x 27 cm. [NC139.B63W57] 73-89027 ISBN 0-88361-026-4 12.95
1. Bohrod, Aaron. 2. Wisconsin in art. 3. Wisconsin—Poetry. I. Bohrod, Aaron. II. Gard, Robert Edward. III. Lefebvre, Mark E., ed. BIP

Wise, Henry, 1653-1738.

GREEN, David. 927.12
Gardener to Queen Anne; Henry Wise (1653-1738) and the formal garden. London, New York, Oxford University Press, 1956. xx, 232p. illus., ports., facsims., plans, 28cm. Bibliography: p. [222]-225. [SB470.W5G7] 56-4101
1. Wise, Henry, 1653-1738. 2. Landscape gardening—Gt. Brit. I. Title.

Wit and humor, Pictorial.

ARNO, Peter 817'.5'4
Lady in the shower. New York, S.&S. [1967] 140p. (illus.) 29cm. All but one of the cartoons were first pub. in the New Yorker from 1956 to 1967. [NC1429.A64A49] 67-28037 4.95 bds.,
I. Title.

BAILEY, John Swartout, 1907- comp. 741.59
Great cartoonists of the world's foremost cartoonists. Edited by John Bailey. Sixth series. New York, Crown [1972] [136 p.] (chiefly illus.) 31 cm. [NC1355.B28] 72-84295 ISBN 0-517-500949 5.95
1. Wit and humor, Pictorial. I. Title.

BAILEY, John Swartwout, 1907- comp. 741.59
Great cartoons of the world, by the world's foremost cartoonists. Edited by John Bailey. New York, Crown Publishers [1967] 136 p. (chiefly illus.) 31 cm. [NC1355.B28] 67-27025
1. Wit and humor, Pictorial. I. Title. BIP

COPI. 741.5944
Chickens don't have chairs. Translated by Richard Seaver. New York, Grove Press [1969] 1 v. (unpaged) illus. 18 cm. Cartoons. Translation of Les poulets n'ont pas de chaises. [NC1499.C63A443] 78-81848 1.50
I. Title.

HANS, Marcie 741.59
The executive coloring book, by Marcie Hans, Dennis Altman, Martin A. Cohen, Funny Products [dist. New York, Pocket Bks., 1962, c.1961] unpaged. illus. 32cm. 2.98 pap.,
I. Title.

KHOSLA, Gopal Das, 1901- 757'.5
Grim fairy tales and other facts and fancies [by] G. D. Khosla. Bombay, New York, Asia Pub. House [c1966] viii, 176 p. 22 cm. Rs 12. "Originally published in The Times of India. The Tribune. The Indian express. The Illustrated weekly of India and Thought." [PR6061.H6G7] S A
I. Title. BIP

KURTZMAN. HARVEY. 741.5973
Jungle book; or, Up from the apes and right back down ... New York, Ballantine Books [1959] unpaged. illus. 18cm. (Ballantine books, 338K) [NC1429.K8A45] 59-11152
I. Title.

SCARFE, Gerald 741.5942
Gerald Scarfe's people; including Parliament and politicians, international affairs, Berlin, rest in peace, people, Egypt, miscellany, phantasmagoria, Paris collections, the Presidential election 1964, New York, the American way of life. New York, D. White [1966] [128] p. of illus. 31cm. [NC1479.S33A44 1966a] 66-17671 15.00
I. Title.

STEIG, William, 1907- 741.5973
The lonely ones. Introd. by William Saroyan. Foreword by Wolcott Gibbs. New York, Windmill Books [1970] 88 p. (chiefly illus.) 18 cm. [NC1429.S579 1970] 71-130218 2.95
I. Title.

Wit and humor, Pictorial—Renaissance, 1450-1600—Italy.

BAROLSKY, Paul, 1941- 709'.45
Infinite jest : wit and humor in Italian Renaissance art / Paul Barolsky. Columbia : University of Missouri Press, 1978. 224 p. : ill. ; 27 cm. Includes index. Bibliography: p. 217-222. [NC1523.B37] 77-15843 ISBN 0-8262-0241-1 : 34.00
1. Wit and humor, Pictorial—Renaissance, 1450-1600—Italy. 2. Italian wit and humor, Pictorial. I. Title. BIP

Wittamer-De Camps, L.—Art collections.

OOSTENS-WITTAMER, Yolande. 760'.09493
La Belle Epoque; Belgian posters, watercolors and drawings from the collection of L. Wittamer-De Camps. Introd. and catalogue by Yolande Oostens-Wittamer. Pref. by Emile Langui. Circulated by International Exhibitions Foundation, 1970-1971. [New York] Grossman [1970] 93 p. illus. (part col.) 23 x 28 cm. "Participating institutions: Library of Congress [and others]" [NC1807.B4O55] 71-134209
1. Wittamer-De Camps, L.—Art collections. 2. Posters, Belgian—Exhibitions. 3. Decoration and ornament—Art nouveau. I. International Exhibitions Foundation. II. Title.

Witte Memorial Museum, San Antonio.

WOOLFORD, Bess Carroll. 069.09764351
The story of the Witte Memorial Museum, 1922-1960, by Bess Carroll Woolford & Ellen Schulz Quillin. [San Antonio 1966] xiv, 374 p. illus., ports. 24 cm. [AM101.W546W6] 66-29912
1. Witte Memorial Museum, San Antonio. I. Quillin, Ellen (Schulz) 1892- II. Title.

WOOLFORD, Bess Carroll. 069.09764351
The story of the Witte Memorial Museum, 1922-1960, by Bess Carroll Woolford & Ellen Schulz Quillin. [San Antonio? 1966] xiv, 374 p. illus., ports. 24 cm. [AM101.W546W6] 66-29912
1. Witte Memorial Museum, San Antonio. I. Quillin, Ellen (Schulz) 1892- II. Title.

Wittgenstein, Ludwig, 1889-1951.

LEITNER, Bernhard, 1938- 720'.92'4
The architecture of Ludwig Wittgenstein: a documentation, with excerpts from the family recollections by Hermine Wittgenstein [English text edited by Dennis Young] Halifax, Press of the Nova Scotia College of Art and Design [1973] 127 p. illus. 28 cm. Distributed in the U.S.A. by Jaap Rietman, New York. Added t.p.: Die Architektur von Ludwig Wittgenstein. English and German. [NA1011.5.W5L45] 72-97706 ISBN 0-919616-00-3 9.95
1. Wittgenstein, Ludwig, 1889-1951. I. Title. II. Title: Die Architektur von Ludwig Wittgenstein. BIP

†LEITNER, Bernhard, 1938- 728.3'7'0924
The architecture of Ludwig Wittgenstein : a documentation = Die Architektur von Ludwig Wittgenstein : eine Dokumentation / Bernhard Leitner ; with excerpts from the Family recollections by Hermine Wittgenstein ; [English text edited by Dennis Young ; translation of excerpts from chapters V and VI of the Family recollections by Richard Ilgner]. New York : New York University Press, 1976. 127 p. : ill. ; 29 cm. Bibliography: p. 126. [NA1011.5.W5L45 1976] 76-150739 ISBN 0-8147-4968-2 : 22.50 ISBN 0-8147-4969-0 pbk. : 12.00
1. Wittgenstein, Ludwig, 1889-1951. 2. Vienna. Palais Stonborough. I. Wittgenstein, Hermine. Familienerinnerungen. English & German. Selections. 1976. II. Title. III. Title: Die Architektur von Ludwig Wittgenstein.

Wolf, Melvyn D., 1932- —Art collections.

FLINT Institute of Arts. 739'.533'0973
American pewter (c. 1730 - c.1870) in the Collection of Dr. and Mrs. Melvyn D. Wolf. [Loan exhibition Dec. 14, 1973-Jan. 13, 1974 [Flint, Mich., 1973] 40 p. illus. 26 cm. Includes bibliographical references. [NK8412.F55 1973] 73-92367
1. Wolf, Melvyn D., 1932- —Art collections. 2. Pewter, American—Exhibitions. I. Title.

Wolff, Bernard Pierre, 1930—

WOLFF, Bernard Pierre, 1930- 779'.2'0924
Friends and friends of friends / Bernard Pierre Wolff ; with an introd. by John Leonard. 1st ed. New York : E. P. Dutton, c1978. xviii, 121 p. : chiefy ill. ; 23 x 26

cm. [TR680.W64 1978] 78-55050 ISBN 0-525-47519-2 : 8.95
1. Wolff, Bernard Pierre, 1930- 2. Photography—Portraits. 3. Friendship—Pictorial works. I. Title. BIP

Wolves in art.

BEYER, Richard S., 1925- 761'.2
George Washington and the wolves / woodblock prints by Richard S. Beyer ; text by Jerome Hellmuth. Seattle : Madrona Publishers, [1977] p. cm. [NE1112.B49H44] 77-20798 ISBN 0-914842-23-4 pbk. : 3.95
1. Beyer, Richard S., 1925- 2. Wolves in art. 3. Wolves—United States. 4. United States—Social life and customs—Colonial period, ca. 1600-1775. I. Hellmuth, Jerome. II. Title.

Women architects—Juvenile literature.

GOLDREICH, Gloria. 720'.23
What can she be? An architect [by] Gloria and Esther Goldreich. Photos. by Robert Ipcar. New York, Lothrop, Lee & Shepard [1974] 48 p. illus. 24 cm. (Lothrop what can she be series) Introduces the various aspects of a career in architecture through a description of a woman architect's projects and daily work. [NA1997.G64 1974] 73-17710 ISBN 0-688-41579-2 3.95
1. Women architects—Juvenile literature. 2. Architecture as a profession—Juvenile literature. I. Goldreich, Esther, joint author. II. Ipcar, Robert, illus. III. Title.
Library binding; 3.78, ISBN 0-688-51579-7. BIP

Women architects—United States.

COLE, Doris. 720'.973
From tipi to skyscraper; a history of women in architecture. [Boston, i press; distributed by G. Braziller, New York, 1973] xi, 136 p. illus. 22 cm. (i press series on the human environment) Bibliography: p. 132-136. [NA1997.C57 1973] 73-80932 ISBN 0-913222-01-1 8.95
1. Women architects—United States. I. Title.

Women architects—United States—Addresses, essays, lectures.

WOMEN in American 720'.973
architecture : a historic and contemporary perspective : a publication and exhibition organized by the Architectural League of New York through its Archive of Women in Architecture / edited by Susana Torre. New York : Whitney Library of Design, 1977. 224 p. : ill. ; 29 cm. Includes index. Bibliography: p. 216-218. [NA1997.W65] 76-54960 ISBN 0-8230-7485-4 : 22.50
1. Women architects—United States—Addresses, essays, lectures. I. Torre, Susana, 1944- II. Architectural League of New York. BIP

Women architects—United States—Congresses.

WEST Coast Women's Design 720
Conference, University of Oregon, 1974.
Proceedings of the West Coast Women's Design Conference, April 18-20, 1974, University of Oregon. [Eugene? : s.n.], c1975. 120 p. : ill. ; 28 cm. Cover title. "Organized by the women students and faculty in environmental design at the School of Architecture and Allied Arts at the University of Oregon." Bibliography: p. 66. [NA1997.W47 1974] 76-620869
1. Women architects—United States—Congresses. I. Oregon. University. School of Architecture and Allied Arts.

Women architects—United States—Juvenile literature.

†FENTEN, D. X. 720'.23
Ms.—architect / by D. X. Fenten. 1st ed. Philadelphia : Westminster Press, c1977. 128 p. : ill. ; 21 cm. Includes index. Examines the traditionally subordinate place of women in architecture and discusses career opportunities for women as architects and in related jobs. [NA1997.F4] 77-7498 ISBN 0-664-32615-3 : 7.95
1. Women architects—United States—Juvenile literature. 2. Architecture—Vocational guidance—Juvenile literature. I. Title. BIP

Women architects—Washington, D.C.

WASHINGTON 720'.9753'0740153
women architects : an exhibition organized by Washington Women in Architecture and sponsored by the Interamerican Development Bank Gallery, August 2-13, 1976 : catalogue / designed and edited by Eileen Ross ... [et al.]. [Washington] : Washington Women in Architecture, c1976. [30] p. ; 22 cm. [NA735.W3W27] 76-379521
1. Women architects—Washington, D.C. 2. Architecture—United States—Exhibitions. 3. Architecture, Modern—20th century—United States—Exhibitions. I. Ross, Eileen. II. Washington Women in Architecture. III. Inter-American Development Bank. Gallery.

Women artists.

CALLEN, Anthea. 745
Women artists of the arts and crafts movement, 1870-1914 / Anthea Callen. New York : Pantheon Books, [1979] p. cm. Reprint of the ed. published by the Architectural Press, London, under the title: Angel in the studio. Includes index. Bibliography: p. [NK1149.5.C34 1979] 78-73646 ISBN 0-394-50667-7 : 20.00
1. Women artists. 2. Arts and crafts movement. I. Title. BIP

GOLDBERG, Dorothy (Kurgans) 704
The creative woman. Washington, R. B. Luce [dist. New York, McKay, c.1963] 204p. 21cm. 63-16690 3.95
I. Title.

NORTH Carolina. Museum 709'.2'2
of Art, Raleigh.
Women; a historical survey of works by women artists presented by the North Carolina Museum of Art and the Salem Fine Arts Center as part of the 200th anniversary celebration of Salem College and Academy, Winston Salem, North Carolina. [Raleigh, N.C., 1972] 58 p. illus. 26 cm. Catalog of an exhibition held at the Salem Fine Arts Center, Winston-Salem, N.C., Feb. 27-Mar. 19, 1972, and at the North Carolina Museum of Art, Raleigh, Mar. 25-Apr. 20, 1972. [N8354.N67] 72-611871
1. Women artists. 2. Art, Modern—Exhibitions. I. Salem Fine Arts Center. II. Title.

SYNDER-OTT, Joelynn, 1940- 700
Women and creativity / Joelynn Snyder-Ott. Millbrae, Calif. : Les Femmes Pub., c1978. xi, 144 p. : ill. ; 22 cm. Contents.—The female experience and artistic creativity.—Female iconography at Stonehenge.—A view form England.—Women in art.—A woman's place.—Art as vin in a yang society.—Angelica Kauffman: rival to Gainsborough.—500 years of birth in art forms, no one gives a damn!—Dialogue with a craftswoman.—Greativity/procreativity.—An art school for women.—Feminist art programs. Bibliography: p. 143-144. [N8354.S64] 77-77954 ISBN 0-89087-989-3 : 9.95
1. Women artists. 2. Women in art. I. Title.
Contents omitted BIP

WATERS, Clara Erskine 709'.2'2 B
Clement, 1834-1916.
Women in the fine arts, from the seventh century B.C. to the twentieth century A.D. / by Clara Erskine Clement Waters. Boston : Longwood Press, 1977 [c1904] p. cm. Reprint of the ed. published by Houghton, Mifflin, Boston. [N43.W3 1977] 77-9091 ISBN 0-89341-214-7 : 50.00
1. Women artists. I. Title.

WATERS, Clara Erskine 709'.2'2 B
Clement, 1834-1916.
Women in the fine arts, from the seventh century B.C. to the twentieth century A.D. / Clara Erskine Clement. New York : Hacker Art Books, 1974. li, 395 p., [31] leaves of plates : ill. ; 21 cm. Reprint of the 1904 ed., published by Houghton Mifflin, Boston. [N43.W3 1974] 73-92107 ISBN 0-87817-150-9 lib.bdg. : 17.50
1. Women artists. I. Title.

Women artists—Australia—South Australia—Biography.

BIVEN, Rachel. 709'.2'2 B
Some forgotten, some remembered : women artists of South Australia / written and compiled by Rachel Biven. Norwood, S.A. : Sydenham Gallery, 1976. [76] p. : ill. (part col.) ; 28 cm. [N7402.S6B58] 77-355746 ISBN 0-9597105-0-7
1. Women artists—Australia—South Australia—Biography. I. Title.

Women artists—Bibliography.

BACHMANN, Donna G., 016.709'2'2
1948-
Women artists : an historical, contemporary, and feminist bibliography / by Donna G. Bachmann and Sherry Piland. Metuchen, N.J. : Scarecrow Press, 1978. p. cm. [Z7963.A75B32] [N8354] 78-19182 ISBN 0-8108-1149-9 : 14.00
1. Women artists—Bibliography. I. Piland, Sherry, joint author. II. Title. BIP

Women artists—Biography.

PETERSEN, Karen, 1943- 709'.2'2 B
Women artists : recognition and reappraisal from the early Middle Ages to the twentieth century / Karen Petersen & J. J. Wilson. 1st ed. New York : Harper & Row, 1976. 212 p. : ill. ; 24 cm. (Harper colophon books ; CN 387) Includes index. Bibliography: p. 179-189. [N40.P45 1976] 75-39543 ISBN 0-06-090387-2 : 5.95
1. Women artists—Biography. I. Wilson, J. J., 1936- joint author. II. Title.

TUFTS, Eleanor. 709'.2'2 B
Our hidden heritage: five centuries of women artists. [New York] Paddington Press [1974] 256 p. illus. 29 cm. Bibliography: p. 247-251. [N43.T83] 73-20955 ISBN 0-8467-0026-3 12.95
1. Women artists—Biography. I. Title.

Women artists—Directories.

GUIDE to women's art 700'.25'73
organizations : groups, activities, networks, publications : painting, sculpture, drawing, photography, architecture, design, film and video, dance, music, theatre, writing, with a bibliography and resource list / Cynthia Navaretta, editor. New York : Midmarch Associates, 1979. 84 p. : ill. ; 22 cm. Bibliography: p. 65-76. [NX504.G84] 79-83876 ISBN 0-9602476-0-2 : 4.00
1. Arts, American—Directories. 2. Arts, Modern—20th century—United States—Directories. 3. Women artists—United States—Societies, etc.—Directories. I. Navaretta, Cynthia.

WOMEN'S History Research 709'.2'2
Center.
Female artists, past and present. Berkeley, Calif., c1972. 42 p. 28 cm. [N43.W65 1972] 74-184169 4.00
1. Women artists—Directories. 2. Women artists—Bibliography. I. Title. BIP

WOMEN'S History Research 709'.2'2
Center.
Female artists, past and present. [2d ed.]. [Berkeley, Calif. : Women's History Research Center, 1974] 158 p. ; 28 cm. Cover title. Includes bibliographies. [N43.W65 1974] 76-358991
1. Women artists—Directories. 2. Women artists—Bibliography. I. Title.

Women artists—History.

MUNSTERBERG, Hugo, 1916- 709'.2'2
A history of women artists / by Hugo Munsterberg. 1st ed. New York : C. N. Potter : distributed by Crown Publishers, [1975] ix, 150 p., [4] leaves of plates : ill. (some col.) ; 29 cm. Includes bibliographical references and index. [N8354.M86 1975] 75-19043 ISBN 0-517-52380-9 : 12.95
1. Women artists—History. I. Title.

Women artists—Interviews.

NEMSER, Cindy. 709'.2'2 B
Art Talk: conversations with 12 women artists New York, Scribner [1975] xiv, 367 p. illus. 24 cm. Bibliograpgy: p. 359-367. [N8354.N45] 74-11302 ISBN 0-684-13984-7 8.95
1. Women artists—Interviews. I. Title.

Women artists—United States.

COLLINS, Jimmie Lee, 709'.2'2 B
1934-
Women artists in America II / by J.L. Collins [Chattanooga, Tenn. : Collins], c1975. ca. 300 p. : ill. ; 24 cm. [N6536.C52] 75-327704 15.00
1. Women artists—United States. I. Title. BIP

WOMEN in the Arts 709'.73
(Organization)
Women choose women, January 12-February 18, 1973. An exhibition organized by Women in the Arts. New York, New York Cultural Center [1973] 127 p. illus. 23 cm. Exhibition held at the New York Cultural Center. [N6512.W59 1973] 72-97639
1. Women artists—United States. 2. Art, American—Exhibitions. 3. Art, Modern—20th century—United States. I. New York Cultural Center. II. Title.

Women artists—United States—Biography—Juvenile literature.

DAVIS, Mary Lee, 700'.92'2 B
1935-
Women in entertainment and the arts / by Mary L. Davis. Minneapolis : T. S. Denison, c1976. 12 p. ; 22 cm. (Her Women in American life series ; book 3) Brief sketches of the careers of women who have made significant contributions to the arts and the field of entertainment. [NX504.D38] 920 76-150795 ISBN 0-513-01499-3
1. Women artists—United States—Biography—Juvenile literature. 2. Arts, Modern—20th century—United States—Juvenile literature. I. Title. II. Series.

FOWLER, Carol. 709'.2'2 B
Art / by Carol Fowler. Minneapolis : Dillon Press, c1976. p. cm. (Contributions of women) Bibliography: p. Brief biographies of six prominent American women artists: Mary Cassatt, Grandma Moses, Georgia O'Keefe, Louise Nevelson, Helen Frankenthaler, and Suzanne Jackson. [N6536.F64] 920 76-3479 ISBN 0-87518-115-5
1. Women artists—United States—Biography—Juvenile literature. I. Title.

Women artists—United States—Juvenile literature.

BOWMAN, Kathleen. 700'.92'2 B
New women in art & dance / by Kathleen Bowman ; designed by Larry Soule. Mankato, Minn. : Creative Education, [1976] p. cm. Brief biographies of a sculptor, weaver. photographer, artist, and dancers, including Louise Nevelson, Charlene Burningham, Cynthia Gregory, Barbara Morgan, Martha Graham, Judith Jamison, and Marie Burton. [NX504.B6] 920 76-5457 ISBN 0-87191-510-3
1. Women artists—United States—Juvenile literature. 2. Arts, Modern—20th century—United States—Juvenile literature. I. Title. BIP

Women as artists—United States.

COLLINS, Jimmie Lee, 709'.2'2 B
1934-
Women artists in America; eighteenth century to the present, by J. L. Collins. [Chattanooga? Tenn., 1973] 1 v. (unpaged) illus. 24 cm. [N43.C64] 73-163882 15.00
1. Women as artists—United States. I. Title. BIP

Women as printers.

CLUB of Printing Women 396.5655
of New York.
Antique, modern & swash; a brief history

of women in printing. [New York, 1955] 60p. illus., ports. 23cm. [Z244.5.C55] 56-20184
1. Women as rpinters. I. Title.

Women—Caricatures and cartoons.

COLE, William, 1919- ed. 741.5
Women are wonderful! A history in cartoons of a hundred years with America's most controversial figure. Edited by William Cole and Florett Robinson. Boston, Houghton Mifflin, 1956. 196 p. illus. 29 cm. [NC1427.C58] 56-11806
1. Women—Caricatures and cartoons. I. Robinson, Florett, joint ed. II. Title.

Women in art.

CASSOU, Jean, 1897- 757.4
The female form in painting [by] Jean Cassou [and] Geoffrey Grigson. New York, Harcourt, Brace [1953] 64p. plates (part col.) 25cm. [ND1290.C38] 53-11218
1. Women in art. 2. Nude in art. 3. Painting. I. Grigson, Geoffrey, 1905- joint author. II. Title.

DORFMAN, Bruce, 1936- 741.9'73
Women. New York, Kennedy Galleries [1972] [8] p. col. illus. 28 cm. Catalog of the exhibition held Jan. 26-Feb. 12, 1972 at the Kennedy Galleries, New York. [N6537.D6K4] 72-176955
1. Women in art. I. Kennedy Galleries, Inc., New York.

FINCH College, New York. Museum of Art. Contemporary Study Wing. 704.94'24
The dominant woman. [Exhibition] December 13 through January 26, 1969. Foreword by Elayne H. Varian. Text by Walter Gutman. New York [1968] [24] p. illus. 28 cm. [N7632.F5] 68-59489
1. Women in art. 2. Art, Modern—20th century—Exhibitions. I. Gutman, Walter. II. Title.

GARLAND, Madge. 704.9424
The changing face of beauty; four thousand years of beautiful women. New York, M. Barrows, 1957. 223 p. illus. 29 cm. [N7630.G3] 57-4938
1. Women in art. 2. Beauty, Personal. 3. Costume—History. I. Title.

MATHEY, Jacques. [396.7] 743.44
Women; five centuries of master drawings. [Translated by Eveline Winkworth] New York, Harper [1951] 90 p. illus. 25 cm. (Master drawings) Harper's art library. [N7630.M34] 51-11215
1. Women in art. I. Title.

MODE, Heinz Adolph, 1913- 704.94'24'0954
The woman in Indian art [by] Heinz Mode. [Translated from the German by Marianne Herzfeld, rev. by D. Talbot Rice] New York, McGraw-Hill [1970] 51 p., 118 plates (part col.) illus., map. 28 cm. (The Image of woman) Translation of Die Frau in der indischen Kunst. [N7638.I5M613] 76-87838
1. Women in art. 2. Art, Indic. I. Title.

MOEN, Arve 704.9424
Edvard Munch: woman and Eros; graphic art and paintings. [Tr. by Christopher Norman] Oslo, Forlaget Norsk Kunstreproduksion [dist. Chester Springs, Pa., Dufour. 1963] 109, [3]p. illus. (pt. mounted col.) 33cm. Bibl. 15.00, bxd.
1. Munch, Edvard, 1863-1944. 2. Women in art. I. Title.

SCHNESSEL, S. Michael. 769'.92'4
A collector's guide to Louis Icart, by S. Michael Schnessel. [Princeton, N.J., distributed by The Exhumation, 1973] 48 p. (chiefly illus.) 28 cm. [NE2049.5.I25S36] 74-161988 5.95
1. Icart, Louis. 2. Women in art. I. Icart, Louis. II. Title.

WOMAN as sex object; 705 s studies in erotic art, 1730-1970. Edited by Thomas B. Hess and Linda Nochlin. [New York, Newsweek, 1972] 257 p. illus. (part. col.) 26 cm. (Art news annual, 38) Includes bibliographical references. [N1.A613 vol 38] [N7630] 760 72-197178 7.95
1. Women in art. 2. Sex in art. I. Hess, Thomas B., ed. II. Nochlin, Linda, ed. III. Title. IV. Series.

WORCESTER, Mass. Art Museum. 757'.4'0945
Woman as heroine. [Exhibition] September 15 through October 22, 1972. [Worcester, 1972] 63 p. illus. 23 cm. [N6916.W67] 73-172106
1. Women in art. 2. Art, Italian—Exhibitions. 3. Art, Baroque—Italy. I. Title.

Women painters.

NEILSON, Winthrop. 759
Seven women: great painters [by] Winthrop & Frances Neilson. [1st ed.] Philadelphia, Chilton Book Co. [1968, c1969] viii, 178 p. illus. (part col.), ports. 26 cm. Bibliography: p. 171-172. [ND38.N4] 68-57513 8.50
1. Women painters. 2. Painters—Biography. I. Neilson, Frances Fullerton, joint author. II. Title.

Women painters—Biography.

SPARROW, Walter Shaw, 1862- ed. 759
Women painters of the world : from the time of Caterina Vigri, 1413-1463, to Rosa Bonheur and the present day / edited by Walter Shaw Sparrow. New York : Hacker Art Books, 1976. 332 p. : ill. ; 29 cm. Reprint of the 1905 ed. published by F. A. Stokes, New York, which was issued as v. 3 of the Art and life library. Includes index. [ND38.S7 1976] 75-10526 lib.bdg. : 30.00
1. Women painters—Biography. 2. Painting—History. I. Title. II. Series: The Art and life library ; v. 3. BIP

Women painters—United States—Biography.

HENKES, Robert. 759.13 B
Eight American women painters / by Robert Henkes. New York : Gordon Press, 1976. p. cm. Includes index. Bibliography: p. [ND236.H46] 76-16131 ISBN 0-87968-457-7 lib.bdg. : 42.95
1. Women painters—United States—Biography. I. Title. BIP

Women—Pictorial works.

OLIVIER, Sigurd. 779'.24'0924
Gentlewoman : photographs / by Sigurd Olivier ; verse by Mark Swift. New York : Grosset & Dunlap, 1978 [112] p. : chiefly ill. ; 30 cm. [HQ1219.O37] 77-87807 ISBN 0-448-14577-4 : 14.95 ISBN 0-448-14578-2 pbk . : 5.95
1. Women—Pictorial works. I. Swift, Mark, 1946- II. Title.

Women—Portraits.

BEZ, Frank. 779'.24
ABC. Photos. [by] Frank Bez. Concept [by] Stephanie LeVanda. [Los Angeles?, 1967] [4] l., [26] plates in box. 29 cm. [TR680.B49] 67-8674
1. Women—Portraits. 2. Photography of women. I. LeVanda, Stephanie. II. Title.

GREEN, John D. 779'.24
Birds of Britain. Photography: John d Green. Art direction: David Tree. [Introduction and captions by Anthony Haden-Guest] New York, Macmillan, 1967. 1 v. (chiefly ports.) 36 cm. [TR680.G695] 67-22397
1. Women—Portraits. 2. Photography of women. 3. Women—Great Britain. I. Haden-Guest, Anthony. II. Title.

GRUBER, L. Fritz, ed. 779.25
Beauty; variations on the theme woman, by masters of the camera, past and present. Edited by L. Fritz Gruber. [Commentaries translated by Trevor Boon] London, New York, Focal Press [1965] 146 p. illus. 31 cm. [TR680.G72] 65-9071
1. Women — Portraits. 2. Photography of women. I. Title.

LANGE, Dorothea. 779'.24
Dorothea Lange looks at the American country woman; a photographic essay by Dorothea Lange with a commentary by Beaumont Newhall. Fort Worth [Tex.] Amon Carter Museum [1967] 72 p. illus. 27 cm. [TR680.L32] 67-18363
1. Women—Portraits. 2. Country life—United States—Pictorial works. I. Title: The American country woman. BIP

MACADAMS, Cynthia, 1939- 779'.24'0924
Emergence / photography by Cynthia MacAdams ; with an introd. by Kate Millett. New York : Chelsea House Publishers, 1977. p. cm. [TR681.W6M3] 77-24911 ISBN 0-87754-057-8 : 15.00
1. Women—Portraits. I. Title. BIP

RODELL, Fred, 1907- 779.0924
Her infinite variety, captured in color. [1st ed.] Garden City, N.Y., Doubleday [1966] 1 v. (chiefly col. illus.) 27 cm. [TR680.R67] 66-11399
1. Women—Portraits. I. Title.

Women—Psychology.

GINANDES, Carol, 1947- 779'.24'0924
Of women born : photographs / by Carol Ginandes. Carlisle, Mass. : Pentacle Press, [1976] p. cm. [HQ1206.G63] 76-4505 ISBN 0-916736-01-6 : 5.95
1. Women—Psychology. 2. Women—United States—Pictorial works. I. Title.

Women—Social conditions—Pictorial works.

WOMEN see woman 778.9'9'301412 / Cheryl Wiesenfeld ... [et al.], eds. ; art direction by Geri Davis ; introd. and text by Natalie Canavor. New York : Crowell, [1975] p. cm. [HQ1154.W885] 75-16410 ISBN 0-690-00965-8 : 12.50. ISBN 0-690-00972-0 pbk. : 5.95
1. Women—Social conditions—Pictorial works. I. Wiesenfeld, Cheryl. II. Canavor, Natalie.

Wonders.

STAGG, James. 720.222
Wonders of the world. London, Odhams [1966] 2-127 p. illus. 10 x 13 cm. (Hippo books, no. 23) 3/6 (B 66-5707) [G140.S75] 67-72752
1. Wonders. 2. Historic houses, etc. I. Title.

Wood.

OLSON, Delmar Walter, 1909- 684
Woods and woodworking for industrial arts. Englewood Cliffs, N. J., Prentice-Hall [1958] 235p. illus. 25cm. Includes bibliography. [TT180.O4] 58-9191
1. Wood. 2. Woodworking industries. I. Title.

Wood-carvers—United States—Biography.

BERKEY, Barry R. 745.59'3 B
Pioneer decoy carvers : a biography of Lemuel and Stephen Ward / Barry Robert Berkey, Velma Berkey, Richard Eric Berkey. Cambridge, Md. : Tidewater Publishers, 1977. p. cm. Includes index. Bibliography: p. [NK9797.B47] 77-13075 ISBN 0-87033-243-0 : 17.50
1. Ward, Lemuel T. 2. Ward, Stephen Wesley, 1895-1976. 3. Wood-carvers—United States—Biography. 4. Decoys (Hunting) I. Berkey, Velma A., joint author. II. Berkey, Richard, 1964- joint author. III. Title. BIP

Wood-carving.

ALLER, Doris, 1909- 736.4
Sunset wood carving book. [1st ed.] Menlo Park, Calif., Lane Pub. Co. [1951] 95 p. illus. 28 cm. [NK9704.A43] 51-13032
1. Wood-carving. I. Title.

BALL, Al 736.4
Wood carving for fun and profit; a handbook for woodworkers. Illustrated by the author. New York, Exposition Press [c.1959] 56p. 21cm. 2.50
I. Title. BIP

BENTHAM, Graeme. 731.4'62
Creative wood sculpture from natural form / [by] Graeme Bentham. Poole : Blandford Press, 1978. viii, 112 p., [4] p. of plates : ill. (some col.), port. ; 23 cm. Includes index. Bibliography: p. 110. [TT199.7.B46] 79-304206 ISBN 0-7137-0874-3 : 8.95
1. Wood-carving. I. Title.
Distributed by Sterling Pub., Co., 2 Park Ave., New York N NY 10016 BIP

BYERS, Ralph Eugene, 1910- 736.4
Wood carving with power tools. [1st ed.] Philadelphia, Chilton Co. [1959] 180 p. illus. 27 cm. (Arts and crafts series) [NK9704.B9] 59-9016
1. Wood-carving. 2. Power tools. I. Title.

COLLETTI, Jack J., 1907- 736'.4
The art of woodcarving / Jack J. Colletti. Englewood Cliffs, N.J. : Prentice-Hall, c1977. xvi, 138 p. ; 24 cm. (A Spectrum book ; S-CR-14) (The Creative handcrafts series) Includes index. Bibliography: p. 130-131. [TT199.7.C64] 76-56442 ISBN 0-13-049247-7 : 10.95. ISBN 0-13-049239-6 pbk. : 4.95
1. Wood-carving. I. Title.

GREEN, H. D. 736'.4
Carving realistic birds : a step-by-step manual with full-size patterns / by H. D. Green. New York : Dover Publicatons, 1977. 75 p. : ill. ; 28 cm. [TT199.7.G72] 76-55216 ISBN 0-486-23484-3 pbk. : 3.00
1. Wood-carving. 2. Birds—Models. I. Title. BIP

HANNA, Jay S. 736'.4
Marine carving handbook : the design and making of billetheads, trailboards, and other marine carvings / by Jay S. Hanna. Camden, Me. : International Marine Pub. Co., c1975. 92 p. : ill. ; 24 cm. [TT199.7.H36] 74-33147 ISBN 0-87742-052-1 : 6.95
1. Wood-carving. 2. Ships—Decoration. I. Title. BIP

HAYES, M. Vincent. 731.4'62
Artistry in wood; ideas, history, tools, techniques: carving, sculpture, assemblage, woodcuts, etc., by M. Vincent Hayes. Designed by Pat E. Hayes. New York, Drake Publishers [1972] 128 p. illus. 23 cm. Bibliography: p. 128. [NK9704.H34] 72-173734 ISBN 0-87749-130-5 8.95
1. Wood-carving. I. Title.

HOSLEY, David. 731.4'62
Simple wood sculptures / by David Hosley. New York : Drake Publishers, [1977] p. cm. [TT199.7.H67] 77-6928 ISBN 0-8473-1581-9 : 4.95
1. Wood-carving. I. Title.

HUNT, Walter Bernard, 1888- 736.4
Whittling with Ben Hunt. Milwaukee, Bruce Pub. Co. [1959] 160p. illus. 27cm. [NK9704.H84] 59-7568
1. Wood-carving. I. Title.

*KLAMKIN, Marian. 736.4
Wood carvings; North American folk sculptures [by] Marian Klamkin and Charles Klamkin. New York, Hawthorn Books, [1974]. 213 p. illus. 29 cm. [NK9920] 73-21309 ISBN 0-8015-8816-2. 14.95.
1. Wood-carving. I. Klamkin, Charles, joint author. II. Title.

LACEY, John L. 736.4
The Audubon book of bird carving, by John L. Lacey, as told to Tom Moore McBride. New York, McGraw-Hill [1951] vii, 124 p. illus., ports. 26 cm. Bibliography: p. 119-120. [NK9704.L25] 51-10468
1. Wood-carving. I. McBride, Tom Moore. II. Title. III. Title: Bird carving.

LACEY, John L 731
Book of woodcarving. New York, Prentice-Hall [1953] 108p. illus. 26cm. [NK9704.L26] 736.4 53-7957
1. Wood-carving. I. Title.

*LACEY, John L. 736.4
How to do wood carving. By John L. Lacey. New York, Arco Pub., [1975 c1954] 144 p. ill. 24 cm. [NK9704.L27] 74-33212 ISBN 0-668-03642-7 2.00 (pbk.)
1. Wood-carving. 2. Carving (Art industries.) I. Title.

LACEY, John L   731
How to do wood carving. New York, Arco Pub. Co. [c1954] 144p. illus. 26cm. (Arco handy books for better living) A Fawcett book, no. 248. [NK9704.L27] 736.4 54-12976
1. *Wood-carving.* 2. *Carving (Art industries)* I. *Title.*   **BIP**

LE MASTER, Richard,   745.59'3
1928-
Wildlife in wood / by Richard Le Master. Chillicothe, Ill. : Model Technology, c1978. 244 p. : ill. ; 25 x 32 cm. Includes index. [TT199.7.L45] 77-71565 ISBN 0-915498-49-9 : 19.95
1. *Wood-carving.* 2. *Decoys (Hunting)* 3. *Ducks.* 4. *Zoological models.* I. *Title.* **BIP**

LUBKEMANN, Chris.   736'.4
Branch craft : creative fun with twigs and branches / by Chris Lubkemann. New York : Drake Publishers, [1977] p. cm. [TT199.7.L8] 76-26195 ISBN 0-8473-1350-6 : 9.95. ISBN 0-8473-1401-4 pbk. : 5.95
1. *Wood-carving.* I. *Title.*

MCKELLIPS, Art.   736'.4
Woodcarving for beginners / Art McKellips. Forest Grove, Or. : Timber Press, 1977. ix, 69 p., [1] leaf of plates : ill. ; 28 cm. Stamped on t.p.: Exclusive distributor, ISBS, Forest Grove. Bibliography: p. 59. Introduces the tools and techniques of wood carving. Includes 10 patterns. [TT199.7.M33] 77-99159 ISBN 0-917304-11-X pbk. : 7.50
1. *Wood-carving.* I. *Title.*   **BIP**

MATTHEWS, John, 1933-   736'.4
Creative log sculpture. New York, Drake Publishers [1972] 91 p. illus. 20 x 26 cm. [TT199.7.M37 1972] 72-1257 ISBN 0-87749-250-6 5.95
1. *Wood-carving.* I. *Title.*

PARDEE, Caroline Julia,   927.364
1911-
The little boy who found a knife; the story of Ernest Warther, master carver. With a foreword by Henry C. Hagloch. Modern photography by Paul S. Somogy. [1st ed.] Dover, Ohio, Printed by Dover Daily Reporter, 1951. 65 p. illus. 23 cm. [TT188.P3] 51-7872
1. *Wood-carving.* 2. *Models and model making.* I. *Warther, Ernest, 1885-* II. *Title.*

SACK, Walter.   731.4'62
Woodcarving: designs, materials, techniques. [Translated from the German by Frank Bradley] New York, Van Nostrand Reinhold [1973] 96 p. illus. 21 cm. (A Reinhold craft paperback) Translation of *Holzschnitzen.* [TT199.7.S213] 73-162764 ISBN 0-442-29984-2 2.95
1. *Wood-carving.* I. *Title.*
ISBN 0-442-29984-2; 5.95 (cloth)

TANGERMAN, Elmer John,   731.4'62
1907-
The modern book of whittling and woodcarving [by] E. J. Tangerman. New York, McGraw-Hill [1973] 188 p. illus. 31 cm. [TT199.7.T36] 73-9994 ISBN 0-07-062670-7 10.00 7.95 (spiral bound)
1. *Wood-carving.* I. *Title.*
Spiral Bound ISBN 0-07-062676-9.   **BIP**

TANGERMAN, Elmer John,   736'.4
1907-
1001 designs for whittling and woodcarving / by E.J. Tangerman New York : McGraw-Hill, c1976. p. cm. Includes index. [TT199.7.T37] 76-7950 ISBN 0-07-062648-0 : 14.95
1. *Wood-carving.* 2. *Design, Decorative.* I. *Title.*

TANGERMAN, Elmer John,   736.4
1907-
Whittling and woodcarving. New York, Dover [1962, c.1936] 293p. illus. (T965) 1.75 pap.,
1. *Wood-carving.* I. *Title.*   **BIP**

UPTON, John, 1897-   •731 736.4
The art of wood carving. Princeton, N.J., Van Nostrand [1958] 130 p. illus. 27 cm. [NK9704.U65] 58-14222
1. *Wood-carving.* I. *Title.*

UPTON, John, 1897-   736'.4
A woodcarver's primer. New York, Drake Publishers [1973] 164 p. illus. 27 cm.

[TT199.7.U67] 73-4345 ISBN 0-87749-494-0
1. *Wood-carving.* I. *Title.*   **BIP**

WHEELER, William, 1895-   736'.4
Wood carving, by William Wheeler and Charles H. Hayward. New York, Drake Publishers [1974] p. cm. [TT199.7.W49 1974] 74-6469 ISBN 0-87749-709-5 3.95 (pbk.)
1. *Wood-carving.* I. *Hayward, Charles Harold, 1898- joint author.* II. *Title.* **BIP**

WHEELER, William, 1895-   736'.4
Woodcarving, by William Wheeler and Charles H. Hayward. New York, Drake Publishers [1972] 127 p. illus. 22 cm. Discusses the tools, equipment, and techniques used in carving wood, with sections on lettering, gilding, and selecting timber. [TT199.7.M49] 73-164542 ISBN 0-87749-270-0 5.95
1. *Wood-carving.* I. *Hayward, Charles Harold, 1898- joint author.* II. *Title.*

Wood-carving—Africa, West—Catalogs.

FAGG, William Buller.   732'.2
Miniature wood carvings of Africa [by] William Fagg. With a foreword by Josef Herman. [Greenwich, Conn.] New York Graphic Society [1971, c1970] 103, [1] p. 102 illus., map (on lining papers), 8 col. plates. 26 cm. A selection of sculptures from the Collection of Josef Herman. Bibliography: p. [104] [NK9789.F3 1971] 70-126289 ISBN 0-8212-0225-1 12.50
1. *Herman, Josef, 1911- —Art collections.* 2. *Wood-carving—Africa, West—Catalogs.* 3. *Miniature objects—Africa, West.* I. *Title.*

Wood-carving, African—Catalogs.

MERTON D. Simpson Gallery,   v. 12
New York.
African excellence. [New York, 1966] [16] p. (chiefly illus.) 23 cm. [NK9787.M4] 68-649
1. *Wood-carving, African—Catalogs.* 2. *Head in art.* I. *Title.*

Wood-carving, American.

BREWINGTON, Marion Vernon,   736.4
1902-
Shipcarvers of North America. Barre, Mass., Barre Pub. Co., 1962. xiv, 173 p. illus. 28 cm. Bibliography: p. 147-153. [NK9712.B7] 62-16848
1. *Wood-carving, American.* 2. *Wood-carving, Canadian.* 3. *Figureheads of ships.* 4. *Ships, Wooden.* I. *Title.* **BIP**

CHRISTENSEN, Erwin Ottomar,   736.4
1890-
Early American wood carving. [1st ed.] Cleveland, World Pub. Co. [1952] 149 p. illus. (part col.) 24 cm. Bibliography: p. 139-143. [NK9712.C47] 52-8444
1. *Wood-carving, American.* 2. *Folk art—U.S.* I. *Title.*   **BIP**

CHRISTENSEN, Erwin   736'.4'0973
Ottomar, 1890-
Early American wood carving, by Erwin O. Christensen. New York, Dover Publications [1972, c1952] 149 p. illus. 24 cm. Bibliography: p. 139-143. [NK9712.C47 1972] 77-189350 ISBN 0-486-21840-6 2.50
1. *Wood-carving, American.* 2. *Folk art—United States.* I. *Title.*

FRIED, Frederick.   736'.4'0973
Artists in wood; American carvers of cigar-store Indians, show figures, and circus wagons. [1st ed.] New York, C. N. Potter [1970] xiv, 297 p. illus. (part col.), facsims., ports. 31 cm. Bibliography: p. 279-287. [NK9712.F73 1970] 72-118295 15.00
1. *Wood-carving, American.* 2. *Folk art—U.S.* I. *Title.*

LALIBERTE, Norman.   745.510973
Wooden images [by] Norman Laliberte and Maureen Jones. New York, Reinhold Pub. Corp. [1966] 136 p. illus. (part col.) 27 cm. [NK9712.L3] 66-14435
1. *Wood-carving, American.* 2. *Folk art—United States.* I. *Jones, Maureen, joint author.* II. *Title.*

SEAL, Thomas C.   736'.4
The life and works of Emil Janel; an illustrated essay, by Thomas C. Seal. [San Francisco? 1973] viii, 81 p. illus. 32 cm. Bibliography: p. 81. [NK9798.J36S42] 73-166410
1. *Janel, Emil, 1896-* 2. *Wood-carving, American.*

Wood-carving, Asmat.

GERBRANDS, Adrianus   736'.4
Alexander, 1917-
Wow-Ipits. Eight Asmat woodcarvers of New Guinea. [by] Adrian A. Gerbrands. Tr. from Dutch by Inez Wolf Seeger. The Hague, Paris, Mouton, 1957. 192p. with illus. 26cm. (Art in its context; studies in ethno-aesthetics. Field reports, v. 3) Bibl. [NK9796.N4G43] 66-17949 13.00
1. *Wood-carving, Asmat.* I. *Title.* II. *Series.* Available from Humanities, New York. **BIP**

Wood-carving—England.

SMITH, John Colin   736'.4'0942
Dinsdale.
Church woodcarvings: a West Country study [by] J. C. D. Smith. New York, A. M. Kelley [1969] 112 p. illus. 26 cm. Bibliography: p. 101. [NK9743.S6] 79-77874
1. *Wood-carving—England.* 2. *Wood-carving, Medieval—England.* I. *Title.*

Wood-carving, English.

SMITH, John Colin   726'.593
Dinsdale.
A guide to church woodcarvings; misericords and bench-ends [by] J. C. D. Smith. Newton Abbot [Eng.] North Pomfret, Vt., David & Charles [1974] 112 p. illus. 25 cm. Bibliography: p. 107-108. [NK9743.S62] 74-185701 ISBN 0-7153-6562-2 11.50
1. *Wood-carving, English.* 2. *Wood-carving, Medieval—England.* 3. *Choir-stalls—England.* I. *Title.*   **BIP**

Wood-carving—Juvenile literature.

TORRE, Frank D.   736
It's easy to carve / by Frank D. Torre ; illustrations by Carol Inouye. 1st ed. Garden City, N.Y. : Doubleday, c1977. 156 p. : ill. ; 22 cm. Includes index. An introduction to the techniques and tools used in carving including complete directions for many different projects using wood, stone, and plastics. [TT199.7.T67] 76-2828 ISBN 0-385-11089-8 : 5.95. ISBN 0-385-11090-1 lib. bdg.
1. *Wood-carving—Juvenile literature.* 2. *Carving (Art industries)—Juvenile literature.* I. *Inouye, Carol.* II. *Title.* **BIP**

WEISS, Harvey.   731.4'6
Carving : how to carve wood and stone / by Harvey Weiss. Reading, Mass. : Addison-Wesley, c1976. 72 p. : ill. ; 28 cm. (The Beginning artist's library) "A Young Scott book." Introduces the tools and techniques for carving wood and stone. [TT199.7.W43] 75-2337 lib.bdg. : 6.50
1. *Wood-carving—Juvenile literature.* 2. *Stone-cutting—Juvenile literature.* 3. *Sculpture—Juvenile literature.* I. *Title.* **BIP**

Wood-carving—Karawari region.

THE Caves of   736'.4'0955
Karawari. [New York, D'Arcy Galleries, 1968] xix, 105 p. illus., map. 34 x 14 cm. Cover title. German, French, and English. [NK9791.K3C3] 68-25860
1. *Wood-carving—Karawari region.* 2. *Caves—New Guinea—Karawari region.* I. *D'Arcy Galleries, New York.*

Wood-carving, Maori.

BARROW, Tui Terence,   736'.4'09931
1923-
Maori wood sculpture of New Zealand [by] T. Barrow. Rutland [Vt.], C.E. Tuttle [1970, c1969] 162 p. 234 illus. (39 col.), ports. 30 cm. Bibliography: p. 161-162. [NK9793.B32 1970] 79-109412 15.00
1. *Wood-carving, Maori.* I. *Title.*

Wood-carving, Medieval—England—Winchester.

JERVIS, Simon.   914.22'735'04857
Woodwork of Winchester Cathedral / [by] Simon Jervis ; photographs by Murray Davison. Winchester : Friends of Winchester Cathedral, 1976. 39 p. : ill., plan ; 22 cm. Bibliography: p. 38-39. [NK9744.W56J47] 77-364704 ISBN 0-903346-10-9 : £0.50
1. *Winchester Cathedral.* 2. *Wood-carving, Medieval—England—Winchester.* 3. *Wood-carving, English—England—Winchester.* I. *Title.*

Wood-carving, Primitive—History—Juvenile literature.

PRICE, Christine, 1928-   736'.4
Arts of wood / by Christine Price. New York : Scribner, [1976] p. cm. An illustrated survey of everyday wooden artwork made by various primitive cultures. [NK9706.P74] 76-13886 ISBN lib.bdg. : 6.95
1. *Wood-carving, Primitive—History—Juvenile literature.* 2. *Wood-carving—History—Juvenile literature.* I. *Title.* **BIP**

Wood-carving, Romanesque—Auvergne.

CAHN, Walter.   726'.591
The Romanesque wooden doors of Auvergne / Walter Cahn. New York : Published by New York University Press for the College Art Association of America, 1974. xv, 168 p., [17] leaves of plates : ill. ; 29 cm. (Monographs on archaeology and fine arts ; 30) Includes bibliographical references and index. [NK9749.A3A953] 74-15291 ISBN 0-8147-1357-2
1. *Wood-carving, Romanesque—Auvergne.* 2. *Wood-carving—Auvergne.* 3. *Church doors—Auvergne.* I. *Title.* II. *Series.* **BIP**

Wood-carving—Technique.

BURK, Bruce.   731.4'62
Game bird carving. [New York] Winchester Press [1972] xi, 242 p. illus. 29 cm. Bibliography: p. 235-236. [NK9704.B86] 72-79365 ISBN 0-87691-080-0 12.50
1. *Wood-carving—Technique.* 2. *Decoys (Hunting)* I. *Title.*   **BIP**

CARTMELL, Ronald.   731.4'62
Wood sculpture. With diagrs. by the author. New York, Taplinger Pub. Co. [1970] 126 p. illus., map. 22 cm. Bibliography: p. 125. [NK9704.C3 1970] 79-109010 6.50
1. *Wood-carving—Technique.* I. *Title.* **BIP**

CROWELL, Ivan Herrett,   736'.4
1904-
Chip carving patterns and designs / Ivan H. Crowell. New York : Dover Publications, 1977. viii, 55 p. : chiefly ill. ; 28 cm. Published in 1945 under title: The brown book of traditional European and Polynesian chip carving designs. [TT199.7.C76 1977] 77-78511 ISBN 0-486-23532-7 pbk. : 1.75
1. *Wood-carving—Technique.* I. *Title.* **BIP**

DURST, Alan Lydiate, 1883-   736.4
Wood carving [by] Alan Durst. New York, Viking Press [1968] 80 p. illus. 26 cm. (A Studio book) [NK9704.D8 1968] 69-10593 5.95
1. *Wood-carving—Technique.* I. *Title.*

ENLOW, Harold L.   736'.4
Carving figure caricatures in the Ozark style / Harold L. Enlow ; with 22 drawings and 47 photos. by Wade Radford and the author. New York : Dover Publications, 1975. vii, 39 p. : ill. ; 28 cm. [NK9704.E54 1975] 74-17879 ISBN 0-486-23151-8 pbk. : 2.00
1. *Wood-carving—Technique.* 2. *Figurines—Ozark Mountain region.* I. *Title.*   **BIP**

GILLEY, Wendell.   736'.4
The art of bird carving; a guide to a fascinating hobby. Photos. by W. H. Ballard. Drawings by the author. [New ed. Heber City, Utah] Hillcrest Publications, 1972. 150 p. illus. 26 cm. First ed.

published in 1961 under title: Bird carving. [NK9704.G5 1972] 72-191159
1. Wood-carving—Technique. 2. Decoys (Hunting) I. Title.

GILLEY, Wendell. 736.4
Bird carving; a guide to a fascinating hobby. Photos. by W. H. Ballard. Drawings by the author. [1st ed.] Princeton [N. J.] Van Nostrand [1961] 115 p. illus. 24 cm. [NK9704.G5 1961] 61-65107
1. Wood-carving—Technique. I. Title.

GOTTSHALL, Franklin H. 736'.4
Wood carving and whittling for everyone / Franklin H. Gottshall. New York : Scribner, c1977. xiii, 145 p. : ill. ; 29 cm. Includes index. [TT199.7.G66] 77-23224 ISBN 0-684-14886-2 : 12.95
1. Wood-carving—Technique. I. Title.

GOTTSHALL, Franklin H. 736.4
Wood carving and whittling made easy. All drawings by the author. Photos. by the author and by his son, Bruce H. Gottshall. Milwaukee, Bruce Pub. Co. [1963] 128 p. illus. 26 cm. [NK9704.G6] 63-10891
1. Wood-carving—Technique. I. Title. BIP

GRAVENEY, Charles. 736'.4
Woodcarving for beginners. London, Studio Vista; New York, Watson-Guptill [1967] 104 p. front., illus, (some col.), table, diagrs, 19 cm. 10/6 (B 67-6428) Bibliography: p. 103. [NK9704.G7] 67-13740
1. Wood-carving—Technique. I. Title.

HANAUER, Elsie V. 736'.4
Handbook of woodcarving and whittling, by Elsie Hanauer. South Brunswick [N.J.] A. S. Barnes [1967] 80 p. illus. 22 cm. [NK9704.H25 1967] 67-16459
1. Wood-carving—Technique. I. Title.

HASLUCK, Paul Nooneree, 1854-1931. 736'.4
Manual of traditional wood carving / edited by Paul N. Hasluck. New York : Dover Publications, 1977. viii, 568 p. : ill. ; 24 cm. Reprint of the 1911 ed. published by Cassell, London under title: Wood carving. Includes index. [NK9704.H3 1977] 76-58574 ISBN 0-486-23489-4 : 7.95
1. Wood-carving—Technique. 2. Design, Decorative. I. Title. BIP

HOPPE, Heinrich. 731.4'62
Whittling & wood carving [by] H. Hoppe. [Translated by Eric Greweldinger] New York, Sterling Pub. Co. [1969] 48 p. illus. 20 x 20 cm. (Little craft book series) Translation of Schnitzen in Holz. [NK9704.H7313 1969] 69-19488
1. Wood-carving—Technique. I. Title. BIP

HUNT, Walter Bernard, 1888- 736'.4
Contemporary carving and whittling [by] W. Ben Hunt. Milwaukee, Bruce Pub. Co. [1967] 110 p. illus. 26 cm. [NK9704.H815] 67-19441
1. Wood-carving—Technique. I. Title.

HUNT, Walter Bernard, 1888-1970. 736.4
Let's whittle. Milwaukee, Bruce Pub. Co. [1962] 96 p. illus. 26 cm. [NK9704.H82] 61-17979
1. Wood-carving—Technique. I. Title.

MANNING, Frank, 1918- 736'.4
Creative chip carving. New York, Carlton [1967] 80p. illus. 24cm. [NK9704.M27] 66-28780 3.50
1. Wood-carving—Technique. I. Title.

MATTHEWS, John, 1933- 736'.4
Creative light wood carving [by] J. Matthews. New York, St. Martin's Press [1969, c1968] 96 p. illus. 19 x 25 cm. [NK9704.M43 1969] 70-9316
1. Wood-carving—Technique. I. Title.

MATTHEWS, John, 1933- 736'.4
Further creative light wood carving [by] J. Matthews. New York, St. Martin's Press [1970] 96 p. illus. 19 x 26 cm. First published in 1968 under title: Creative light wood carving. [NK9704.M43 1970] 73-145691
1. Wood-carving—Technique. I. Title.

MEILACH, Dona Z. 731.4'62
Contemporary art with wood; creative techniques and appreciation, by Dona Z. Meilach. New York, Crown [1968] 214 p. illus. (part. col.) 27 cm. [NK9710.M4] 68-9063 6.95
1. Wood-carving—Technique. 2. Art, Modern—20th century. I. Title. BIP

MOORE, Harris W. 736'.4
Chip carving : 25 projects with instructions and full-size patterns / by Harris W. Moore. [Rev. ed.]. New York : Dover Publications, 1976. 31 p. : chiefly ill. ; 28 cm. [TT199.7.M66 1976] 75-19755 ISBN 0-486-23256-5 : 1.50
1. Wood-carving—Technique. I. Title. BIP

RICH, Jack C. 731
Sculpture in wood [by] Jack C. Rich. New York, Oxford University Press, 1970. 155 p. illus. (part col.), map (on lining paper) 24 cm. Bibliography: p. 141-142. [NK9704.R35] 70-111647 9.95
1. Wood-carving—Technique. I. Title. BIP

†RICH, Jack C., 1914- 731.4'62
Sculpture in wood / Jack C. Rich. New York : Da Capo Press, [1977] c1970. 155 p. : ill. ; 24 cm. (A Da Capo paperback) Includes index. Bibliography: p. 141-142. [NK9704.R35 1977] 76-30520 ISBN 0-306-80052-7 pbk. : 4.95
1. Wood-carving—Technique. I. Title.

ROTTGER, Ernst. 736.4
Creative wood design. New York, Reinhold Pub. Corp. [1961, c1960] 94 p. (chiefly illus.) 22 cm. (His Creative play series, 2) [NK9704.R43 1961] 61-10979
1. Wood-carving—Technique. 2. Woodwork. I. Title.

SAYERS, Charles Marshall, 1892- 736'.4
The book of wood carving : technique, designs, and projects / by Charles Marshall Sayers. New York : Dover Publications, 1978, c1942. 118 p. : ill. ; 27 cm. Reprint, with new pref., of the ed. published by Caxton Printers, Caldwell, Idaho. [NK9704.S3 1978] 78-52156 ISBN 0-486-23654-4 pbk. : 3.00
1. Wood-carving—Technique. I. Title. BIP

SKINNER, Freda 736.4
Wood carving. Illus. by Constance Morton. New York, Sterling [1963, c.1961] 164p. illus. 19cm. 62-18635 3.95
1. Wood-carving—Technique. 2. Wood-carving—Hist. I. Title.

TANGERMAN, Elmer John, 1907- 736.4
Design and figure carving. New York, Dover publications [1964, c.1940] x, 288p. illus. 22cm. Bibl. [NK9704.T26] 64-18869 1.85 pap.,
1. Wood-carving—Technique. I. Title. BIP

TAWES, William I. 736'.4
Creative bird carving, by William I. Tawes. Cambridge, Md., Tidewater Publishers, 1969. xvi, 207 p. illus. (part col.) 26 cm. Bibliography: p. 203-204. [NK9704.T36] 79-107781 ISBN 0-87033-141-8 7.50
1. Wood-carving—Technique. I. Title. II. Title: Bird carving. BIP

WILLCOX, Donald, 1933- 731.4'62
Wood design. New York, Watson-Guptill Publications [1968] 143 p. illus. 25 cm. Bibliography: p. 137. [NK9704.W55] 68-12400
1. Wood-carving—Technique. I. Title. BIP

Wood-carving—Texas—Exhibitions.

MANSBENDEL, Peter, 1883-1940. 730'.92'4
Peter Mansbendel : a Swiss woodcarver in Texas : an exhibit / prepared by the University of Texas at San Antonio, Institute of Texan Cultures, 1977-1978. 1st ed. San Antonio : The Institute, c1977. [47] p. : ill. ; 25 cm. [NK9798.M35A4 1977] 77-154122
1. Mansbendel, Peter, 1883-1940—Exhibitions. 2. Wood-carving—Texas—Exhibitions. I. Institute of Texan Cultures.

Wood-carving—United States.

LAFFAL, Ken. 736'.4'0924 B
Vivolo and his wooden children / text and photography, Ken Laffal. Essex ; Conn. : Gallery Press, c1976. 144 p. : ill. (some col.) ; 24 cm. [NK9798.V58L33] 76-11492 ISBN 0-913622-04-4 : 11.95
1. Vivolo, John, 1886- 2. Wood-carving—United States. 3. Primitivism in art—United States. I. Vivolo, John, 1886- II. Title. BIP

Wood-carving—Zambia.

KELLER, Bonnie B. 736'.4
Wood carvers of Zambia, by Bonnie B. Keller. Livingstone, National Museums of Zambia, 1967. 57 p. illus. 19 cm. (National Museums of Zambia, special paper) Bibliography: p. 55-56. [NK9789.8.Z3K44] 78-981399
1. Wood-carving—Zambia. 2. Wood-carvers—Zambia. I. Title. II. Series: National Museums of Zambia. Special paper.

Wood-carvings, American.

EARNEST, Adele 736.4
The art of the decoy: American bird carvings. Drawings: Lou Schifferl. New York, Potter [dist. Crown, c.1965] 208p. illus. (pt. col.) maps, ports. 29cm. Bibl. [NK9712.E2] 65-24835 10.00
1. Wood-carvings, American. 2. Birds. I. Title.

ERNEST, Adele. 736.4
The art of the decoy: american bird carvings. Drawings: Lou Schifferl. New York, C.N. Potter [1965] 208 p. illus. (part col.) maps, ports. 29 cm. Bibliography: p. [199] [NK9712.E2] 65-24835
1. Wood-carvings, American. 2. Birds. I. Title.

Wood-engravers, English.

DOBSON, Austin, 1840-1921. 769'.924 B
Thomas Bewick and his pupils. London, Chatto and Windus, 1884; Detroit, Singing Tree Press, 1968. xviii, 232 p. illus., ports. 20 cm. [NE1212.B5D64 1968] 69-17340
1. Bewick, Thomas, 1753-1828. 2. Wood-engravers, English. I. Title. BIP

Wood-engravers—Great Britain—Correspondence, reminiscences, etc.

RAVERAT, Gwendolen Mary Darwin, 1885-1957. 769'.92'4 B
Period piece / Gwen Raverat. New York : Norton, 1976, c1952. p. cm. (The Norton library) [NE1147.6.R28A2 1976] 76-18933 ISBN 0-393-00822-3 pbk. : 3.95
1. Raverat, Gwendolen Mary Darwin, 1885-1957. 2. Wood-engravers—Great Britain—Correspondence, reminiscences, etc. 3. Cambridge, Eng.—Social life and customs. I. Title. BIP

Wood-engraving.

RUMPEL, Heinrich, 1912- 761'.2
Wood engraving. [English version by Frank Jellinek] New York, Van Nostrand Reinhold Co. [1974, c1972] 127 p. illus. 18 x 21 cm. (Craft and art) Bibliography: p. 123-124. [NE1225.R8513 1974] 73-8468 ISBN 0-442-29995-8 7.95
1. Wood-engraving.

Wood-engraving—17th century—History.

LEHMANN-HAUPT, Hellmut, 1903- 769'.94
An introduction to the woodcut of the seventeenth century / by Hellmut Lehmann-Haupt ; with a discussion of the German woodcut broadsides of the seventeenth century by Ingeborg Lehmann-Haupt. New York : Abaris Books, 1978 282 p. : ill. ; 29 cm. Includes index. Bibliography: p. 267-268. [NE1050.L43] 77-86220 ISBN 0-913870-49-8 : 48.50
1. Wood-engraving—17th century—History. I. Title. BIP

Wood-engraving, American.

WARD, Lynd Kendall, 1905- 769.924
God's man; a novel in woodcuts, by Lynd Ward. Cleveland, World Pub. Co. [1966, c1929] [3] l., 144 plates. 22 cm. [NE1215.W3A43 1966] 66-3415
1. Wood-engraving, American. I. Title. II. Title: A novel in woodcuts.

Wood-engraving, Australian—Catalogs.

DRAFFIN, Nicholas. 769'.994'0740994
Australian woodcuts and linocuts of the 1920s and 1930s / Nicholas Draffin. South Melbourne, Vic. : Sun Books, 1976. 80 p. : chiefly ill. (some col.) ; 29 cm. (Sun-academy series) [NE1190.3.D7] 77-365329 ISBN 0-7251-0224-1
1. Wood-engraving, Australian—Catalogs. 2. Linoleum block-printing, Australian—Catalogs. 3. Printmakers—Australia—Biography. I. Title.

Wood-engraving, British.

GARRETT, Albert. 769'.941
A history of British wood engraving / by Albert Garrett. Atlantic Highlands, N.J. : Humanities Press, c1978. 407 p. : ill. ; 28 cm. Includes bibliographical references and index. [NE1143.G37 1978] 77-19325 ISBN 0-391-00574-X : 120.00
1. Wood-engraving, British. I. Title. BIP

Wood-engraving, German—Catalogs.

THE German single-leaf woodcut, 1600-1700 : a pictorial catalogue / Dorothy Alexander, in collaboration with Walter L. Strauss. New York : Abaris Books, 1978. 2 v. (827 p.) : chiefly ill. ; 32 cm. (Aga Abaris graphics archive ; 2) Includes indexes. Bibliography: p. [807]-811. [NE1150.2.G47] 76-22305 195.00 769'.943'074
1. Wood-engraving, German—Catalogs. 2. Wood-engraving—17th century—Germany—Catalogs. I. Alexander, Dorothy. II. Strauss, Walter L. III. Title. IV. Series.

Wood-engraving—History.

CHATTO, William Andrew, 1799-1864. 761'.2'09
A treatise on wood engraving, historical and practical; with upwards of three hundred illustrations engraved on wood by John Jackson. The historical portion by W. A. Chatto. 2d ed., with a new chapter on the artists of the present day by Henry G. Bohn, and 145 additional wood engravings. London, H. G. Bohn, 1861. Detroit, Gale Research Co., 1969. xvi, 560, 561*-600*, 561-664 p. illus. 23 cm. Bibliographical footnotes. [NE1030.C5 1969] 69-16477
1. Wood-engraving—History. I. Jackson, John, 1801-1848. II. Bohn, Henry George, 1796-1884. III. Title. BIP

HIND, Arthur Mayger, 1880-1957 761.209
An introduction to a history of woodcut, with a detailed survey of work done in the fifteenth century; 2v. [Gloucester, Mass., P. Smith, 1963] 2v. (x1,838p.) illus., facsims. 21cm. (Dover bks. T952, 953 rebound) Bibl. 4.50 ea.,
1. Wood-engraving—Hist. 2. Illustrated books—15th and 16th cent. 3. Illustrated books—15th and 16th cent.—Bibl. I. Title.

HIND, Arthur Mayger, 1880-1957. 761.209
An introduction to a history of woodcut, with a detailed survey of work done in the fifteenth century. New York, Dover Publications [1963] 2 v, (xl, 838 p.) illus., facsims. 21 cm. "'t952-953." "An unabridged and unaltered republication of the work first published ... in 1935." Includes bibliographies. Bibliographical footnotes. [NE1030.H55 1963] 63-5621
1. Wood-engraving — Hist. 2. Illustrated books — 15th and 16th cent. 3. Illustrated books — 15th and 16th cent. — Bibl. I. Title. BIP

LALIBERTE, Norman. 761'.2'09
Twentieth century woodcuts; history and modern techniques [by] Norman Laliberte

SUBJECT INDEX WOOD-ENGRAVINGS, AMERICAN.

[and] Alex Mogelon. New York, Van Nostrand Reinhold [1971] 111 p. illus. (part col.) 22 cm. (An Art horizons book) [NE490.L3] 79-150507
1. Wood-engraving—History. 2. Wood-engraving—Technique. I. Mogelon, Alex, joint author. II. Title.

LINDLEY, Kenneth Arthur, 1928- 769'.942
The woodblock engravers [by] Kenneth Lindley. New York, Drake Publishers [1970] 128 p. illus. 22 cm. Bibliography: p. [125] [NE1080.L55 1970] 72-24026 ISBN 0-87749-057-0 5.95
1. Wood-engraving—History. I. Title.

WOODBERRY, George Edward, 1855-1930. 761.2'09
A history of wood-engraving. New York, Harper & Bros., 1883. Detroit, Gale Research Co., 1969. 221 p. illus., ports. 23 cm. Bibliography: p. [211]-215. [NE1030.W8 1969] 69-17490
1. Wood-engraving—History. 2. Wood-engraving—Bibliography. I. Title. BIP

Wood-engraving, Italian.

POLLARD, Alfred William, 1859-1944. 741.64
Italian book illustrations, chiefly of the fifteenth century. [Folcroft, Pa.] Folcroft Library Editions, 1973. 80 p. illus. 34 cm. Reprint of the 1894 ed. published by Seeley, London and Macmillan, New York, which was issued as no. 12 of The Portfolio; artistic monographs. [NE1152.P64 1973b] 73-11341 13.00
1. Wood-engraving, Italian. 2. Illustrated books—15th and 16th centuries. I. Title. II. Series: The Portfolio; monographs on artistic subjects, no. 12.

POLLARD, Alfred William, 1859-1944. 769'.945
Italian book illustrations, chiefly of the fifteenth century / by Alfred W. Pollard. Norwood, Pa. : Norwood Editions, 1976. 80 p., [9] leaves of plates : ill. ; 33 cm. Reprint of the 1894 ed. published by Seeley, London, and Macmillan, New York, which was issued as no. 12 of the Portfolio; artistic monographs. [NE1152.P64 1976] 76-10775 ISBN 0-8482-2076-5 lib. bdg : 12.50
1. Wood-engraving, Italian. 2. Illustrated books—15 and 16th centuries. I. Title. II. Series: The Portfolio, monographs on artistic subjects ; no. 12.

POLLARD, Alfred William, 1859-1944. 741.64
Italian book illustrations, chiefly of the fifteenth century. New York, B. Franklin [1973] 80 p. illus. 26 cm. (Burt Franklin bibliography & reference series, 486. Art history & reference series, 46) Reprint of the 1905 ed. published by Selley & Co., London, which was issued as no. 12 of The Portfolio; artistic monographs. [NE1152.P64 1973] 73-6633 ISBN 0-8337-4328-7 13.50
1. Wood-engraving, Italian. 2. Illustrated books—15th-16th centuries. I. Title. II. Series: The Portfolio; monographs on artistic subjects, no. 12.

Wood-engraving, Japanese.

MOORE, Keiko Hiratsuka. 761'.2
Moku-hanga; how to make Japanese woodblock prints. Washington, Acropolis Books [1973] 144 p. illus. 23 cm. Bibliography: p. 139-140. [NE1310.M567] 73-16597 ISBN 0-87491-358-6 5.95
1. Wood-engraving, Japanese. 2. Wood-engraving—Technique. I. Title.

Wood-engraving—Technique.

BANISTER, Manly Miles, 1914- 761'.2
Wood block cutting & printing / by Manly Banister ; photos, drawings, and prints by the author. New York : Sterling Pub. Co., c1976. 72 p. : ill. (some col.) ; 22 cm. Includes index. [NE1227.B27] 76-19813 ISBN 0-8069-5374-8 : 6.95 ISBN 0-8069-5375-6 lib.bdg. :
1. Wood-engraving—Technique. I. Title. BIP

BIGGS, John R. 736.4
The craft of woodcuts. New York, Sterling Pub. Co. [1963] 63 p. illus. 23 cm. [NE1225.B48 1963a] 63-2808
1. Wood-engraving—Technique. 2. Linoleum block-printing. I. Title.

BRABY, Dorothea. 761.2
The way of wood engraving. London, New York, Studio Publications [1953] 95 p. illus. 26 cm. (The How to do it series, no. 46) [NE1227.B69] 53-11497
1. Wood-engraving—Technique.

CHAMBERLAIN, Walter. 761'.2
Manual of woodcut printmaking and related techniques / Walter Chamberlain. New York ; Scribner, c1978. 184 p. : ill. (some col.); 25 cm. Includes index. Bibliography: p. 171-173. [NE1220.C48] 77-79902 ISBN 0-684-15355-6 : 13.95
1. Wood-engraving—Technique. I. Title.

CHAMBERLAIN, Walter. 761'.2
The Thames and Hudson manual of woodcut printmaking and related techniques / Walter Chamberlain. London : Thames & Hudson, 1978. 184 p. : ill. (some col.) ; 25 cm. (The Thames and Hudson manuals) Includes index. Bibliography: p. 171-173. [NE1225.C47] 78-309451 ISBN 0-500-67013-7 : 14.95
1. Wood-engraving—Technique. I. Title. II. Title: Woodcut printmaking.
Available from W. W. Norton, New York, NY Available from W. W. Norton, New York, NY

HAMMOND, Dorothy M. 745.1'075
Pictorial price guide to American antiques and objects made for the American market : almost 6000 objects in 300 categories illustrated and priced / by Dorothy Hammond. 2d ed. New York : Dutton, c1979. 224 p. : ill. ; 28 cm. Includes index. [NK805.H328 1979] 78-74223 ISBN 0-525-47517-6 : 8.95
1. Antiques—United States—Catalogs. 2. Americana—Catalogs. I. Title.

ROTHENSTEIN, Michael, 1908- 761.2
Linocuts and woodcuts; a complete block printing handbook. New York, Watson-Guptill Publications [1964, c1962] 104 p. illus. (part col.) 26 cm. Bibliography: p. ix. [NE1225.R6 1964] 64-14769
1. Wood-engraving—Technique. 2. Linoleum block-printing. I. Title.

ROTHENSTEIN, Michael, 1908- 761'.2
Linocuts and woodcuts, and related ways of print-making. [New York] Studio Books [c1962] x, 11-104 p. 26 cm. (A Studio handbook) Bibliography: p. ix. [NE1225.R6] 68-7413
1. Wood-engraving—Technique. 2. Linoleum block-printing. I. Title.

SANDER, David M. 761'.2
Wood engraving : an adventure in printmaking / by David M. Sander. New York : Viking Press, [1978] p. cm. (A Studio book) Bibliography: p. [NE1227.S27] 78-8097 ISBN 0-670-78083-9 : 12.50
1. Wood-engraving—Technique. I. Title. BIP

STERNBERG, Harry, 1904- 761'.2
Woodcut. Photography by Ted Davies. [New York?] Pitman Pub. Corp., c1962. unpaged. illus. 20 x 26 cm. (Pitman art books, 40) [NE1225.S8] 62-17739
1. Wood-engraving- Technique. I. Title.

YOSHIDA, Toshi, 1911- 761.2
Japanese print-making; a handbook of traditional & modern techniques [by] Toshi Yoshida, Rei Yuki. Pref. by Oliver Statler. Rutland, Vt., Tuttle [1966] 176p. illus. (pt. col.) 21cm. Bibl. [NE1310.Y63] 66-20674 10.00; bxd.
1. Wood-engraving—Technique. 2. Wood-engravings—Printing 3. Color prints. Japanese. I. Yuki, Rei, joint author. II. Title.

Wood-engraving, Venetian—Exhibitions.

ROSAND, David. 769'.945'31
Titian and the Venetian woodcut : a loan exhibition / introduction and catalogue by David Rosand, Michelangelo Muraro ; organized and circulated by International Exhibitions Foundation, 1976-1977. Washington : The Foundation, c1976. 315 p. : ill. ; 22 x 26 cm. Held at the National Gallery of Art, the Dallas Museum of Fine Arts, and the Detroit Institute of Arts. Bibliography: p. 28-31. [NE1152.4.V46R67] 77-351487
1. Tiziano Vecelli, 1477-1576. 2. Wood-engraving, Venetian—Exhibitions. I. Muraro, Michelangelo, joint author. II. International Exhibitions Foundation. III. United States. National Gallery of Art. IV. Dallas. Museum of Fine Arts. V. Detroit. Institute of Arts. VI. Title. BIP

Wood-engravings.

BEWICK, Thomas, 1753-1828 769.942
1800 woodcuts / by Thomas Bewick and his school; introd. by Robert Hutchinson New York, Dover [1962] xiv, 247p. illus. 31cm. (Pictorial archives) Bibl. 62-51830 10.00
I. Title.

FRASCONI, Antonio. 759.13
Woodcuts 1957. With comments by Antonio Frasconi, Joseph Blumenthal and Paul Bennett. Printed from the original wood blocks at the Spiral Press. New York, The Typophiles, 1957. 1 v. (unpaged, chiefly illus.) 19 cm. (Chap book in the Typophile series, 34) [[NE1215.F7A]] 60-1047
I. Title. II. Series. III. Series: The Typophiles, New York. Typophile chap books, no. 34

GIBBINGS, Robert [John] 769.942
Wood engravings, with some recollections by the artist. Edited by Patience Empson. Introd. by Thomas Balston. Chicago [1], Quadrangle Books [119 W. Lake St.] [1959] xliv, 355p. illus., col. plate, ports. 29cm. 60-91 20.00
I. Title.

GRIESHABER, Helmut A. P., 1909- 769.92
H. A. P. Grieshaber; woodcuts. [New York] Arts Inc., 667 Madison Ave. [1965, c.1964] 76, [28] p. of illus. (pt. fold., pt. col.) 38cm. HAP Grieshaber; woodcuts. Introd. by Margot Fuerst. [Tr. from German: Fritz Eichenberg, William Hubben [20] p. in pocket Bibl. [NE1217.G69F83] 65-16858 25.00 bds.,
I. Fuerst, Margot. II. Title.

HASSALL, Joan 769.942
The wood engravings of Joan Hassall. With an introd. by Ruari McLean. New York, Oxford University Press, 1960 [ ] 38p., 188 illus. 19cm. 60-4309 5.00
I. Title.

HOMER, Winslow, 1836-1910. 769'.924
The wood engravings of Winslow Homer. Edited with an introd. by Barbara Gelman. New York, Bounty Books [1969] xii, 204 p. (chiefly illus.) 23 x 29 cm. Bibliography: p. 198-204. [NE1215.H58G4 1969] 73-75096
I. Gelman, Barbara, ed. II. Title.

HYDE, Laurence. 761.2084
Southern cross; a novel of the South Seas told in wood engravings by Laurence Hyde, with a review of stories in pictures from earliest times. Introd. by Rockwell Kent. [1st ed.] Los Angeles, Ward Ritchie Press [1951] 255 p. (chiefly illus.) 19 cm. [NE1215.H9K4] 52-256
I. Title.

KAPLAN, Edith, 1919- 759.13
Voices of the revolution; fifteen color woodcuts. An anthology of poems with historical notes, edited by Helen Haynes. Pref. by Bayard Rustin. [Philadelphia, E. and J. Kaplan, 1967] 1 portfolio ([19] l., 15 col. plates) 39 x 48 cm. "350 copies ... No. 101." [NE1215.K3H3] 68-7290
I. Haynes, Helen, ed. II. Title.

LE Peintre graveur illustre: illustrations to Adam Bartsch's Le peintre graveur, volumes XII-XXI. [General editors: A. Hyatt Mayor and Anthony Blunt. Associate editor: Ann Percy] University Park, Pennsylvania State University Press, 1971- v. illus. 31 cm. [NE1055.P43] 77-29436 761'.2
1. Wood-engravings. I. Bartsch, Adam von, 1757-1821. Le peintre graveur. II. Mayor, Alpheus Hyatt, 1901- ed. III. Blunt, Anthony, Sir, 1907- ed.

STEINHARDT, Jacob, 1887- 769.943
The woodcuts of Jakob Steinhardt, chronologically arranged and fully reproduced. Ed. by Leon Kolb. Philadelphia, Jewish Pubn. [1962, c. 1959] x, 26p. [123]p. of illus. 32cm. 62-12950 10.00
I. Kolb, Leon, 1890- ed. II. Title.

STEINHARDT, Jacob, 1887- 769.943
The woodcuts of Jakob Steinhardt chronologically arranged and fully reproduced. Edited by Leon Kolb. [1st ed.] San Francisco, Genuart Co. [1959] x 26 p. [123] p. of illus. 32 cm. [NE1217.S75K6] 59-24455
I. Kolb, Leon, 1890- ed. II. Title.

STERNBERG, Harry 761.2
Woodcut. Photography by Ted Davies. New York, Pitman, c.1962. unpaged. illus. (pt. col.) 20x26cm. (40) 1.00 pap.,
I. Title. BIP

TUER, Andrew White, 1838-1900. 761'.2
1,000 quaint cuts; from books of other days, including amusing illustrations from children's story books, fables, chap-books, &c., &c.,; a selection of pictorial initial letters & curious designs & ornaments from original wooden blocks belonging to the Leadenhall Press. Edited by Andrew W. Tuer. London, Field & Tuer; New York, Scribner & Welford [1886] Detroit, Singing Tree Press, 1968. 170 p. illus. 29 cm. [NE1265.T8 1968] 68-31097
1. Wood-engravings. I. Leadenhall Press Limited, London. II. Title.

TUER, Andrew White, 1838-1900. 769
1,000 quaint cuts; from books of other days, including amusing illustrations from children's story books, fables, chap-books, &c., &c., a selection of pictorial initial letters & curious designs & ornaments from original wooden blocks belonging to the Leadenhall Press. [Reprinted.] London, Field & Tuer: New York, Scribnen & Welford. [New York, Art Direction Book Company, 1974, c1973]. 170 p. (chiefly illus.) 25 cm. Label mounted on half-title page: Hastings House, New York. [NE1080.T83 1973] 73-89743 ISBN 0-910158-15-0 13.50
1. Wood-engravings. I. Leadenhall Press Limited, London. II. Title.

Wood-engravings, American.

FERRO, Walter. 769'.924
Sunflower. Woodcuts by Walter Ferro. [Pound Ridge, N.Y., 1971] [10] l. (chiefly illus. (part col.)) 24 cm. "Twenty copies ... No. 2." Signed. [NE1112.F4A57] 70-25766
I. Title.

SMITH College. Museum of Art. 761.2
Winslow Homer: illustrator. Catalogue of the exhibition, with a checklist of wood engravings and a list of illustrated books, prepared by Mary Bartlett Cowdrey. Smith College, February 1951: Williams College, March 1951. Northampton, Mass., 1951. 66 p. plates. 23 cm. [NE1215.H58S5] 51-3173
1. Homer, Winslow, 1830-1910. 2. Wood-engravings, American. 3. Art, American — Exhibitions. I. Cowdrey, Mary Bartlett, 1910- II. Williams College. Lawrence Art Museum. III. Title.

WARD, Lynd Kendall, 1905- 769'.92'4
Storyteller without words; the wood engravings of Lynd Ward. With text by the artist. New York, Abrams [1974] 310, [73] p. (chiefly illus.) 28 cm. Bibliography: p. [383] [NE1112.W37A57] 70-163308 ISBN 0-8109-0541-8 25.00
1. Ward, Lynd Kendall, 1905- 2. Wood-engravings, American. I. Title.

[WARD, Lynd Kendall] 1905- 761
Wild pilgrimage. Cleveland, World [1967, c.1960] 5p. l., 95 pl. 22cm. A novel in woodcuts by Lynd Ward. [NE1215.W3A48] 6.50
1. Wood-engravings, American. I. Title.
Originally published in New York in 1932.

YANKEE Doodle, 784.7
by Richard Schackburg. Woodcuts by Ed Emberley. Notes by Barbara Emberley. Englewood Cliffs, N.J., Prentice [c.1965] [33]p. col. illus. 21x27cm. Orig. words sung by the English are generally attributed to Dr. Richard Schackburg. Arrangement by Charity Bailey for voice and piano, with chord symbols [NE1215.E4Y3] 65-15000 3.75
1. Schackburg, Richard, supposed author. II. Emberley, Ed, illus. BIP

Wood-engravings, American—Exhibitions.

BROOKLYN Institute of Arts and Sciences. Museum. 761.20838
American woodcuts, 1670-1950. A survey of woodcuts and wood-engravings in the United States. [By] Una E. Johnson. [Brooklyn, '1950] 55 p. illus. 22 cm. Catalog of an exhibition held in the Brooklyn Museum: p. 25-55. Bibliography: p. 24. [NE1010.B75] 51-3520
1. Wood-engravings, American—Exhibitions. I. Johnson, Una E. II. Title.

Wood-engravings—Catalogs.

HUGO, Thomas, 1820-1876. 016.769'922
The Bewick collector; a descriptive catalogue of the works of Thomas and John Bewick. New York, B. Franklin [1970] xxiii, 562 p. illus. 23 cm. (Burt Franklin bibliography & reference series, 314) (Art history & art reference, 33.) Reprint of the 1866 ed. [NE1112.B48H8 1970] 70-128113
1. Bewick, Thomas, 1753-1828. 2. Bewick, John, 1760-1795. 3. Wood-engravings—Catalogs. 4. Engravings—Private collections. I. Title. BIP

Wood-engravings, Chinese.

LOEHR, Max. 761'.2'0951
Chinese landscape woodcuts; from an imperial commentary to the tenth-century printed edition of the Buddhist canon. Cambridge, Mass., Belknap Press, 1968. xiv, 114, 40 p. illus. 28 cm. The four woodblock prints described are owned by the Fogg Art Museum, Harvard University. Includes bibliographical references. [NE1183.L6] 67-22868
1. Wood-engravings, Chinese. 2. Landscape painting, Chinese. I. Harvard University. William Hayes Fogg Art Museum. II. Title.

SPIEGELBERG, Frederic, 1897- 769.952
Zen, rocks, and waters. Introd. by Herbert Read. [New York] Pantheon Books [1961] 63 p. illus. 26 cm. Bibliography: p. 63 [NE1183.P64] 61-14771
1. Wood-engravings. Chinese 2. Wood-engravings, Japanese 3. Zen (Sect) I. Title.

Wood-engravings, Dutch.

SCHRETLEN, Martinus Joseph Antonius Maria, 1890- 769'.9492
Dutch and Flemish woodcuts of the fifteenth century, by M. J. Schretlen. With a foreword by M. J. Friedlander. New York, Hacker Art Books, 1969. viii, 71, 80 p. illus. 32 cm. Reprint of the 1925 ed. Bibliographical footnotes. [NE1153.A1S3 1969] 68-9013
1. Wood-engravings, Dutch. 2. Wood-engravings, Flemish. 3. Wood-engraving, Renaissance—Netherlands. I. Title. BIP

Wood-engravings—Exhibitions.

DOMJAN, Joseph. 1907- 769.973
Peacock festival; selected color woodcuts. Introd. by John F. Mills. [River Edge, N.J.] Art Edge [c1964] 80 p. illus. (2 col.) facsim., port. 31 cm. Catalog of the international exhibitions held 1962-1965 at Oahkosh Public Museum, and others. [NE1215.D6A53] 64-8130
I. Title. BIP

KANSAS. University. Museum of Art. 761'.2
1450-1550 the golden age of woodcut The woodcut revival:1800-1925. [Lawrence] 1968. 68 p. illus. 23 cm. (Miscellaneous publications of the Museum of Art, no. 70) Authors of parts one and two of this exhibition catalogue are respectively: J. L. Schrader, and Diane Johnson. Includes bibliographical references. [NE1010.K3] 68-65453
1. Wood-engravings—Exhibitions. I. Schrader, J. L. II. Johnson, Diane, 1943- III. Title. IV. Title: The woodcut revival: 1800-1925. V. Series: Kansas. University. Museum of Art. Miscellaneous publications, no. 70

Wood-engravings, German.

GEISBERG, Max, 1875-1943. 769'.943
The German single-leaf woodcut, 1500-1550 / Max Geisberg; rev. and edited by Walter L. Strauss. New York : Hacker Art Books, 1974. 4 v. (xvii, 1578 p.) : chiefly ill. ; 35 cm. Original ed. published under title: Der deutsche Einblatt Holzschnitt. Includes index. Bibliography: p. ix-xiii (vol. I) [NE1150.A1G413] 72-95115 295.00
1. Wood-engravings, German. 2. Wood-engraving, Renaissance—Germany. I. Strauss, Walter L., ed. II. Title. BIP

MASEREEL, Frans, 1889- 769'.924
Passionate journey (Mein Stundenbuch); 167 woodcuts. New York, Dover Publications [1971] 171 p. (chiefly illus.) 22 cm. Reprint of the 1920 ed. [NE1155.5.M3A513 1971] 75-182102 ISBN 0-486-22447-3 2.00
I. Title.

UPTON, Richard. 741.9
Eros—thanatos; German poems with woodcuts by Richard Upton. [Saratoga Springs, N.Y.] Erebus Press, 1968. 1 portfolio. 8 plates. 36 cm. Consists of 6 unsewn quires; each of 4 of the quires contains a poem in German with a translation into English by H. D., accompanied by 2 woodcuts. "One hundred copies are on Rising Line Marque paper ... number 95/100." [NE1217.U67A44] 70-1260 44.00
I. Title.

Wood-engravings, German—Catalogs.

THE German single-leaf woodcut, 1550-1600 : 769'.92'2 B
a pictorial catalogue / by Walter L. Strauss New York : Abaris Books, 1975. 3 v. (xv, 1429 p.) : chiefly ill. ; 32 cm. Addenda and errata slip inserted. Includes indexes. Contents.Contents.—v. 1. A-J.—v. 2. K-R.—v. 3. S-Z. Bibliography: p. 1409-1414. [NE1150.G47] 74-1620 195.00
1. Wood-engravings, German—Catalogs. 2. Wood-engravings, Renaissance—Germany—Catalogs. I. Strauss, Walter L. BIP

Wood-engravings, German—Exhibitions.

CASE Western Reserve University. 769'.943
German woodcuts of the early sixteenth century; an exhibition prepared by the students of Art History 515, Case Western Reserve University, Jane Glaubinger [and others] [Cleveland, 1972] [44] p. 28 cm. Catalog of an exhibition held at the Cleveland Museum of Art, May-July, 1972. Bibliography: p. [21] [NE651.C37 1972] 73-170307
1. Wood-engravings, German—Exhibitions. 2. Wood-engraving, Renaissance—Germany. I. Glaubinger, Jane. II. Cleveland Museum of Art. III. Title.

Wood-engravings, Japanese.

ISHIDA, Mosaku, 1894- 769.952
Japanese Buddhist prints. With the collaboration of Un'ichi Hiratsuka [and others] English adaptation by Charles S. Terry. New York, H. N. Abrams [1964] 195 p. illus., col. plates. 35 cm. [NE1184.I813] 64-20004
1. Wood-engravings, Japanese. 2. Color prints, Japanese. 3. Art, Buddhist. I. Terry, Charles S., ed. and tr. II. Title. BIP

MEISSNER, Kurt, 1885- 761'.2'0952
Japanese woodblock prints in miniature; the genre of surimono. Rutland, Vt., C. E. Tuttle Co. [1970] 143 p. 33 col. plates. 22 x 24 cm. Bibliography: p. 135-139. [NE1310.M35] 78-94024 12.50
1. Wood-engravings, Japanese. I. Title.

SHARAKU, fl.1794 761
Sharaku, a complete collection, v. 2. Reproduction by the Adachi institute of woodcut prints [Text by Teruji Yoshida. English translation by Jiro Harada. Edited by Toyohisa Adachi] Tokyo, Meijishobo [dist. Los Angeles, Perkins Oriental Books] 1960[ ] 2v. 1 col. plates in mats (issued in portfolio) 48cm. and 1 pam. 52p. 31cm. Each volume of plates accompanied by pamphlet of explanatory text. illus. (part col.) 100.00. bxd.
I. Title.

Wood-engravings, Renaissance.

AMMAN, Jost, 1539-1591. 761'.2'09031
293 Renaissance woodcuts for artists and illustrators. With a new introd.by Alfred Werner. New York, Dover Publications [1968] xviii, [6] p., 293 p. of illus. 21 cm. "Unabridged and unaltered republication of Jost Amman's Kunstbuchl[e]in, as published ... in 1599. The introduction ... includes new translations of all the original German text." [NE1245.A413 1968] 68-14561 3.00
1. Wood-engravings, Renaissance. I. Title.

CURIOUS woodcuts of fanciful and real beasts; 769*.9031
a selection of 190 sixteenth-century woodcuts from Gesner's and Topsell's natural histories [by] Konrad Gesner. New York, Dover Publications [1971] 111 p. illus. 31 cm. (Dover pictorial archives series) [NE962.A5C8 1971] 70-127357 ISBN 0-486-22701-4 3.00
1. Wood-engravings, Renaissance. 2. Animals in art. 3. Animals, Mythical, in art. I. Gesner, Konrad, 1516-1565. II. Topsell, Edward, 1572-1625? BIP

Wood-engravings, Renaissance—Exhibitions.

NEW Jersey. State Museum, Trenton. 769'.94'074014966
A selection of fifteenth and sixteenth century book prints from the National Gallery of Art; Rosenwald collection: [exhibition], April 30-July 5, 1971, New Jersey State Museum, Trenton. [Trenton : New Jersey State Museum, Dept. of Education, 1971] [24] p. : ill. ; 22 cm. Bibliography: p. [8] [NE1052.N5 1971] 75-313579
1. Rosenwald, Lessing Julius, 1891-—Art collections. 2. Wood-engravings, Renaissance—Exhibitions. I. United States. National Gallery of Art. II. Title.

Wood-engravings—Tibet.

WEINER, Douglas. 769'.9515
Tibetan and Himalayan woodblock prints. Introd. and captions by Douglas Weiner. New York, Dover Publications [1974] vii, [66] p. of illus. 41 cm. [NE1183.W37 1974] 73-89752 ISBN 0-486-22988-2 3.50 (pbk.)
1. Wood-engravings—Tibet. I. Title. BIP

Wood-engravings—U. S.—Catalogs.

PRINCETON University. Library. 761.2084
Early American book illustrators and wood engravers, 1670-1870;a catalogue of a collection of American books, illustrated for the most part with woodcuts and wood engravings in the Princeton University Library. With an introductory sketch of the development of early American book illustration,by Sinclair Hamilton. With a foreword by Frank Weitenkampf. Princeton, N. J., 1958. xlvii, 265p. illus., facsims. (1 fold. mounted) 29cm. [Z1023.P9 1958] 58-9784
1. Wood-engravings—U. S.—Catalogs. 2. Illustrated books—Bibl.—Catalogs. 3. Illustration of books—U. S.—Hist. I. Hamilton, Sinclair. II. Title.

Wood family.

FALKNER, Frank. 738.3'7
The Wood family of Burslem. [1st ed. reprinted] with a note on the author by Michael Robert Parkinson. Wakefield, E. P. Publishing, 1972. vi, v-xx, 118 p. 59 leaves (1 fold.) illus., coats of arms, geneal. table, map, ports. 29 cm. Reprint of 1st ed., published in 1912 by Chapman and Hall, London. Includes index. [NK4210.W6F3 1972] 74-162337 ISBN 0-85409-911-5 £4.00
1. Wood family. 2. Pottery, English. 3. Staffordshire pottery. I. Title.

Wood finishing.

COLLIER, John William, 1906- 684.1'0443
Wood finishing [by] John W. Collier. [1st ed.] Oxford, New York, Pergamon Press [1967] xxiii, 306 p. illus. 21 cm. (Pergamon series of monographs on furniture and timber, v. 6) Bibliography: p. 299. [TT325.C6 1967] 65-16852
1. Wood finishing. BIP

THE French polisher's manual; 684'.084
a description of French polishing methods and technique. 2d ed., rev. and enl. London, E. & F. N. Spon, 1946. [Kentfield, Calif., N. K. Gregg, 1971] 64 p. illus. 19 cm. (Gregg series of reprints on crafts and hobbies) [TT325.F72 1971] 76-163749 ISBN 0-912318-14-7
1. Wood finishing. BIP

GIBBIA, S. W. 698.3
Wood finishing and refinishing. New York, Van Nostrand [1954] 255 p. illus. 24 cm. [TT325.G5] 54-11405
1. Wood finishing. BIP

GIBBIA, S. W. 684.08'4
Wood finishing and refinishing [by] S. W. Gibbia. Rev. ed. New York, Van Nostrand Reinhold [1971] 271 p. illus. 24 cm. [TT325.G5 1971] 70-149255
1. Wood finishing. I. Title.

GROTZ, George 684.10443
Instant furniture refinishing and other crafty practices. Garden City, N.Y., Doubleday [c.]1966. 95p. illus. 21cm. [TT325.G86] 66-12826 1.95 pap.,
1. Wood finishing. 2. Furniture—Repairing. I. Title.

GROTZ, George. 684.10443
Instant furniture refinishing and other crafty practices. [1st ed.] Garden City, N. Y., Doubleday, 1966. 95 p. illus. 21 cm. [TT325.G86] 66-12826
1. Wood finishing. 2. Furniture—Repairing. I. Title. BIP

HAND, Jackson. 684.1'043
How to do your own wood finishing. New York, Popular Science Pub. Co. [1967] 170 p. illus. (part col.) 24 cm. (Popular science skill book) [TT325.H32] 67-10842
1. Wood finishing. I. Title. BIP

HAND, Jackson. 684.1'043
How to do your own wood finishing. New York, Barnes & Noble [1974, c1967] vii, 162 p. illus. 21 cm. (A Popular Science Skill book) [TT325.H32] ISBN 0-06-463353-5 2.50 (pbk.)
1. Wood finishing. I. Title.
L.C. card number for original edition: 67-10842.

HAYWARD, Charles Harold, 1898- 684.08'4
Staining and polishing: how to finish woodwork; staining; French, wax, and oil polishing; the cellulose finish; varnishing; lacquering. Edited by Charles H. Hayward. New York, Drake Publishers [1969, c1959] viii, 213 p. illus. 23 cm. [TT325.H39 1969] 71-24677
1. Wood finishing. 2. Stains and staining. I. Title.

HAYWARD, Charles Harold, 1898- ed. 698.3
Staining and polishing: how to finish woodwork; staining; French, wax, and oil polishing; the cellulose finish; varnishing; lacquering. Philadelphia, Lippincott [1959] 213p. illus: 23cm. *Woodworker handbooks) 'New and enlarged edition'--Dust jacket. [TT325] 59-65261

[TT174.5.W6M34 1973] 78-39354 ISBN 0-498-01179-8 8.95
1. Wooden toy making. I. Title. BIP

MATHIAS, Bob. 745.59'2
Simple wooden toymaking / Bob Mathias. London ; New York : Hamlyn, 1974. 80 p. : ill. (some col.) ; 26 cm. Includes index. [TT174.5.W6M37] 74-196362 ISBN 0-600-34446-0 : £1.50
1. Wooden toy making. I. Title. BIP

PARKER, Xenia Ley. 745.59'2
Wooden toys / Xenia Ley Parker. New York : Hawthorn Books, c1978. 193 p. : ill. ; 29 cm. Includes index. [TT174.5.W6P37 1978] 77-92312 ISBN 0-8015-4809-8 : 12.95
1. Wooden toy making. I. Title. BIP

PETERSEN, Grete. 745.59'2
Making toys with plywood. New York, Reinhold [1967] 88 p. illus. 23 cm. ([Reinhold Scandinavian craft series]) [TT185.P38] 66-24543
1. Wooden toy making. 2. Plywood craft. I. Title.

RYAN, Hugh M. 745.59'2
101 quality wooden toys you can make / Hugh M. & Judith Ryan. Blue Ridge Summit, Pa. : Tab Books, [1979] p. cm. Includes index. [TT174.5.W6R92] 78-26446 ISBN 0-8306-9830-2 : 9.95. ISBN 0-8306-1046-4 pbk. : 4.95
1. Wooden toy making. I. Ryan, Judith, joint author. II. Title.

SCHUTZ, Walter E. 745.59'2
How to make wooden toys and games / Walter E. Schutz. New York : Macmillan, 1975. 119 p. : ill. ; 26 cm. First published in 1966 under title: Toys for fun and how to make them. [TT174.5.W6S38 1975] 75-1331 ISBN 0-02-607530-X : 8.95 ISBN 0-02-081950-1 pbk. : 4.95
1. Wooden toy making. I. Title.

SCHUTZE, Rolf. 745.59'2
Making wooden toys. New York, Reinhold [1967] 88 p. illus. 23 cm. ([Reinhold Scandinavian craft series]) [TT185.S27] 66-24547
1. Wooden toy making. I. Title.

STEVENSON, Peter, 1941- 745.59'2
The art of making wooden toys. [1st ed.] Philadelphia, Chilton Book Co. [1971] 247 p. illus. (part col.) 27 cm. [TT185.S73 1971] 77-153136 ISBN 0-8019-5604-8 9.95
1. Wooden toy making. I. Title.

TOYS from wood : 745.59'2
original designs / by Brian Brooks, Albert Lain, and John Money ; edited by Peter Scaife. London : Evans, 1976. 104 p. : ill. ; 26 cm. [TT174.5.W6T68] 77-350815 ISBN 0-237-44806-8 : £4.95
1. Wooden toy making. I. Brooks, Brian. II. Lain, Albert. III. Money, John.

WOLVERTON, Ruth. 745.59'2
How to make wood learning toys / by Ruth Wolverton. Blue Ridge Summit, Pa. : G/L Tab Books, [1977] p. cm. Includes index. Bibliography: p. [TT174.5.W6W64] 77-24124 ISBN 0-8306-7915-4 : 9.95. ISBN 0-8306-6915-9 pbk. : 6.95
1. Wooden toy making. I. Title. BIP

Woodroffe, Patrick, 1940—

WOODROFFE, Patrick, 1940- 760'.092'44
"Mythopoeikon" : fantasies, monsters, nightmares, daydreams : the paintings, book-jacket illustrations, and record-sleeve designs of Patrick Woodroffe / with a commentary by the artist. [Limpsfield, Eng. : Dragon's World, c1976] 155 p. : chiefly col. ill. ; 30 cm. [NC1883.3.W66A55] 77-363167 ISBN 0-905071-09-3. ISBN 0-905071-08-5 pbk. : £3.95
1. Woodroffe, Patrick, 1940- 2. Grotesque in art. I. Title.

Woodwork.

ADAMS, Jeannette T. 684'.08
Arco's new complete woodworking handbook / by Jeannette T. Adams. Rev. ed. New York : Arco Pub. Co., 1975. ix, 739 p. : ill. ; 21 cm. Published in 1960 under title: Complete woodworking handbook. [TT180.A17 1975] 74-25024 ISBN 0-668-03822-5 : 8.95
1. Woodwork. I. Title. II. Title: New complete woodworking handbook.

ADAMS, Jeannette T 684.8
Complete woodworking handbook, by Jeannette T. Adams and Emanuele Stieri. Drawings by John G. Marinac. New York, Arco Pub. Co. [1960] 568p. illus. 23cm. [TT130.A17] 60-8584
1. Woodwork. I. Stieri, Emanuele, 1891- joint author. II. Title.

ADKINS, Jan. 684'.082
Toolchest. Written, designed, and illustrated by Jan Adkins. Carpenter in residence, Joseph Karson. New York, Walker [1973] 48 p. illus. 23 x 29 cm. [TT185.A34 1973] 72-81374 ISBN 0-8027-6153-4 4.95
1. Woodwork. 2. Tools. I. Title. BIP

BASSETT, Kendall T. 684
How to make objects of wood, by Kendall T. Bassett and Arthur B. Thurman in collaboration with Victor D'Amico. New York, Museum of Modern Art; distributed by Simon and Schuster [1952, c1951] 95 p. illus. 26 cm. (Art for beginners series, 3) [TT180.B25] 52-306
1. Woodwork. I. New York (City) Museum of Modern Art. II. Title.

BASSETT, Kendall T. 684
The pleasures of woodworking; a complete and authoritative guide for the home carpenter. With illus. by Alexander Williams. New York, Simon and Schuster [1954] 190 p. illus. 24 cm. [TT180.B253] 54-6667
1. Woodwork. I. Title.

BLANDFORD, Percy W. 684'.08
The woodworker's bible / by Percy W. Blandford. 1st ed. Blue Ridge Summit, Pa. : G/L Tab Books, 1976. 416 p. : ill. ; 22 cm. Includes index. [TT185.B62] 76-8647 ISBN 0-8306-6860-8 : 10.95. ISBN 0-8306-5860-2 pbk. :
1. Woodwork. I. Title. BIP

BOSTON. Museum of Fine Arts. 708.144
Illustrated handbook. Boston, 1964. xvi, 389 p. illus. (part col.) 23 cm. [N520.A56] 65-3479
I. Title.

BRIDGE, Paul. 684.08
Designs in wood [by] Paul Bridge and Austin Crossland. New York, Praeger [1969] 88 p. illus. 21 cm. [TT180.B74 1969] 77-95270 4.95
1. Woodwork. 2. Design. I. Crossland, Austin, joint author. II. Title.

CAPOTOSTO, Rosario. 684'.08
Complete book of woodworking / by Rosario Capotosto. New York : Outdoor Life; [distributed by] Harper & Row, [1975] vi, 441 p. : ill. ; 24 cm. "A Popular Science book." [TT180.C36] 74-27319 ISBN 0-06-010613-1 (Harper & Row) : 13.95
1. Woodwork. I. Title. BIP

DE CRISTOFORO, R. J. 684.08'3
Modern power tool woodworking [by] R. J. de Cristoforo. Raymond, Miss., Magna Publications [1967] 352 p. illus. 26 cm. 1953 ed. published under title: Power tool woodworking for everyone. [TT180.D33 1967] 66-30741
1. Woodwork. 2. Power tools. I. Title.

DE CRISTOFORO, R J 684
Power tool woodworking for everyone. New York, McGraw-Hill [1953] 283p. illus. 26cm. [TT180.D33] 53-5183
1. Woodwork. 2. Power tools. I. Title.

DURBAHN, Walter Edward, 1894- 684
Walt's workshop. [Chicago] General Pub. Co., Hobby Books Division, '1951. 144 p. illus. 22 cm. [TT180.D8] 52-273
1. Woodwork. I. Walt's workshop (Television program) II. Title.

EYERS, A. S. 684.08'2
Practical woodwork for laboratory technicians, by A. S. Eyers. [1st ed.] Oxford, New York, Pergamon Press [1970] vi, 168 p. illus. 20 cm. (Pergamon series of monographs in laboratory techniques, v. 4) [TT180.E9 1970] 79-117463
1. Woodwork. I. Title. BIP

FEIRER, John Louis. 684'.08
Wood : materials and processes / John L. Feirer. Peoria, Ill. : C. A. Bennett Co., c1975. 592 p. : ill. ; 24 cm. Includes index. [TT180.F43] 74-19847 ISBN 0-87002-126-5
1. Woodwork. I. Title. BIP

FINE woodworking 684'.08
techniques / selected by the editors of Fine woodworking magazine. Newton, Conn. : Taunton Press, c1978. 189 p. : ill. ; 31 cm. Includes index. [TT180.F56] 78-58221 ISBN 0-918804-02-7 : 13.95
1. Woodwork. I. Fine woodworking.
Distributed by Scribner, NYC BIP

GLENISTER, S H 745.51
Contemporary design in woodwork. New York, Studio-Crowell [1956] 96p. illus. 26cm. [NK9604.G5 1956] 57-2734
1. Woodwork. 2. Furniture. I. Title.

GRIMWOOD, Herbert H 731
An introduction to decorative woodwork for the use of schools, by Herbert H. Grimwood and Frederick Goodyear. With a foreword by Ernest Healey. [3d ed.] Peoria, Ill., C. A. Bennett Co. [1952] 239p. illus. 26cm. [NK9604.G7 1952] 736.4 52-14131
1. Woodwork. 2. Wood-carving. I. Goodyear, Frederick, joint author. II. Title. III. Title: Decorative woodwork.

GRONEMAN, Chris Harold, 1906- 684
General woodworking. New York, McGraw-Hill [1952] 220 p. illus. 25 cm. (McGraw-Hill publications in industrial arts) [TT197.G7] 51-12614
1. Woodwork. 2. Cabinet-work. I. Title.

GRONEMAN, Chris Harold, 1906- 684.8
General woodworking. 2d ed. New York, McGraw-Hill [1959] 248 p. illus. 25 cm. (McGraw-Hill publications in industrial arts) [TT197.G7 1959] 58-14350
1. Woodwork. 2. Cabinet-work. I. Title.

GRONEMAN, Chris Harold, 1906- 684
General woodworking. New York, McGraw-Hill [1955] 220p. illus. 24cm. (McGraw-Hill publications in industrial arts) Includes bibliography. [TT197.G7 1955] 55-7913
1. Woodwork. 2. Cabinet-work. I. Title. BIP

HAINES, Ray Edward. 684
Portable woodworking power tools [by] Ray E. Haines [and others] New York, Van Nostrand [1954] 148p. illus. 27cm. (The Home workshop series) [TT180.H33] 54-10379
1. Woodwork. 2. Power tools. I. Title.

HAND, Jackson. 684'.08
Modern woodworking / Jackson Hand. Reston, Va. : Reston Pub. Co., [1975] xii, 337 p. : ill. ; 25 cm. Includes index. [TT180.H34] 75-14468 ISBN 0-87909-492-3 : 12.95
1. Woodwork. I. Title. BIP

*HARWOOD, Mark. 745.51
Fun with wood, illustrated by Ron Brown. New York, Grosset and Dunlap [1975] 64 p. ill. 32 cm. [TT185] 74-3870 ISBN 0-448-11880-7 3.95.
1. Woodwork. I. Title.

HAYWARD, Charles Harold, 1898- 684
The complete book of woodwork. Philadelphia, Lippincott [1955] 344 p. illus. 22 cm. (Woodworker handbooks) [TT180.H386] 55-1411
1. Woodwork. I. Title. BIP

HAYWARD, Charles Harold, 1898- 684.08
Practical woodwork [by] Charles H. Hayward. New York, Emerson Books [1967, c1965] 192 p. illus. 22 cm. [TT180.H3884] 67-12954
1. Woodwork. I. Title. BIP

HAYWARD, Charles Harold, 1898- 684.08'2
Woodwork joints; kinds of joints, how they are cut and where used [by] Charles H. Hayward. New York, Drake Publishers [1970] vi, 176 p. illus. 23 cm. [TT180.H4 1970] 78-164540 ISBN 0-87749-042-2 5.50
1. Woodwork. I. Title. BIP

HERISKO, Clarence C 694.024
The Collier quick and easy guide to carpentry. [1st ed.] New York, Collier Books [1963] 126 p. illus., port. 28 cm. (A Collier Books original) "BL 29." [TT185.H398] 63-7965
1. Woodwork. 2. Carpentry. I. Title. II. Title: Quick and easy guide to carpentry.

HJORTH, Herman, 1883-1951. 684
Operation of modern woodworking machines [by] Herman Hjorth [and] William F. Holtrop. Milwaukee, Bruce Pub. Co. [1958] 176p. illus. 28cm. [TT180.H58] 58-12229
1. Woodwork. 2. Woodworking machinery. I. Holtrop, William F., joint author. II. Title.

HJORTH, Herman, 1883-1951. 684.083
Operation of modern woodworking machines [by] Herman Hjorth [and] William F. Holtrop. Milwaukee, Bruce Pub. Co. [1966] viii, 176 p. illus. 28 cm. [TT180.H58 1966] 66-26620
1. Woodwork. 2. Woodworking machinery. I. Holtrop, William F., joint author. II. Title. BIP

HOBBS, Harry J. 745.51
Veneer craft for everyone / Harry J. Hobbs; pattern drawings by Bill Mitchell. New York : Schribner, c1976. 154 p. : ill. ; 28 cm. Includes index. [TT200.H57] 75-45326 ISBN 0-684-14614-2 : 9.95
1. Woodwork. 2. Marquetry. 3. Veneers and veneering. I. Title. BIP

HOME craftsman. 684
Book of home woodwork projects everyone can make; simplified, fully illustrated instruction for beautiful pieces of furniture, ornamental shelves, racks, brackets, plaques, and novelties, window valances, toys, and scenic lamps, lawn and garden furnishings. Edited by Arthur Wakeling. New York, Home Craftsman Pub. Corp. [1953] 96p. illus. 29cm. (The Home craftsman series of woodworking manuals) [TT180.H63] 53-3922
1. Woodwork. I. Wakeling, Arthur, ed. II. Title. III. Title: Home wood-work projects.

HOME craftsman. 674.43
Book of selected wood turning projects; step-by-step illustrated instructions on how to make trays, woodenware, servers, shakers, bowls, and boxes, stands, tables, and other furniture... Edited by Milton Gunerman. New York, Home Craftsman Pub. Corp. [1952] 95p. illus. 29cm. (The Home craftsman series of woodworking manuals) [TT201.H65] 53-75
1. Woodwork. 2. Handicraft. I. Gunerman, Milton John, 1906- ed. II. Title.

THE Home mechanic's 680
handbook; an encyclopedia of tools, materials, methods, and directions. [Reprint ed.] Garden City, N. Y., Garden City Books [1954] 804p. illus. 22cm. [TT155.H68 1954] 54-946
1. Woodwork. 2. Metal-work. 3. Building—Repair and reconstruction.

HUNT, De Witt. 371.42684
Machine woodworking. Rev. by John L. Cermak. Oklahoma City, Harlow Pub. Corp., 1956. 280p. illus. 24cm. A revision of the author's A manual for machine woodworking. [TT185.H87 1956] 56-4642
1. Woodwork. I. Title.

HUNT, De Witt 684.8
Machine woodworking, by DeWitt Hunt and John L. Cermak. 3d ed. Oklahoma City, Harlow Pub. Corp. [1961] 289p. illus. 24cm. Revision of A manual for machine woodworking, published in 1925 as book 3 of A manual for hand woodworking. [TT185.H85 1961] 61-66556
1. Woodwork. I. Cermak, John L., joint author. II. Title.

KEABLE, J. E. 684.08
Woodworking [by] J. E. Keable [and] B. R. Leadbeatter. Sydney, New York, McGraw-Hill [1970] 475 p. illus., diagrs. 25 cm. Metric ed. published in 1974 under title: Australian woodworking, by B. R. Leadbeatter and J. E. Keable. [TT185.K36] 77-522985 5.95
1. Woodwork. I. Leadbeatter, B. R., joint author. II. Title.

LANGSNER, Drew. 684'.082
Country woodcraft / Drew Langsner. Emmaus, Pa. : Rodale Press, 1978. xv, 304 p. : ill. ; 19 x 23 cm. Includes index. Bibliography: p. 297-299. [TT200.L34] 78-780 ISBN 0-87857-200-7 : 12.95. ISBN 0-87857-201-5 pbk. : 9.95
1. Woodwork. 2. Agricultural implements. 3. Implements, utensils, etc. I. Title. **BIP**

LAURY, Jean Ray. 745.51
Wood applique. New York, Van Nostrand Reinhold Co. [1973] 96 p. illus. 21 cm. Lists the tools and gives instructions for creating decorative wood applique from scrap lumber, found objects, paint, and glue. [TT200.L37] 72-9707 ISBN 0-442-24695-1 8.95
1. Woodwork. 2. Applique. I. Title.

MAKE it from wood. 684.8
Greenwich, Conn., Fawcett Publications, c1962. 144p. illus. 24cm. (Fawcett book, no. 524) [TT185.M27] 62-52488
1. Woodwork. I. Fawcett Publications, inc.

MEILACH, Dona Z. 745.51
Creating small wood objects as functional sculpture / by Dona Z. Meilach ; consultant, Lawrence B. Hunter. New York : Crown Publishers, c1976. vii, 248 p., [4] leaves of plates : ill. ; 27 cm. Includes index. Bibliography: p. 238-241. [TT180.M38 1976] 75-37531 ISBN 0-517-51866-X : 10.95 ISBN 0-517-51867-8 pbk. :
1. Woodwork. 2. Treenware. I. Hunter, Lawrence B. II. Title.

MURPHEY, Wayne K. 674'.13
Wood as an industrial arts material [by] Wayne K. Murphey and Richard N. Jorgensen. New York, Pergamon Press [1974] viii, 164 p. illus. 24 cm. Includes bibliographies. [TS820.M8 1974] 73-16250 ISBN 0-08-017906-1 13.00
1. Woodwork. 2. Wood. I. Jorgensen, Richard N., joint author. II. Title. **BIP**

OAKLEY, W 680
The boy's workship companion; with illus. by the author. New York, Greenberg [1952] 218 p. illus. 21 cm. [TT160.O2] 52-5622
1. Woodwork. 2. Metal-work. I. Title.

PLATT, John, 1935- 684'.08
Step-by-step woodcraft : a complete introduction to the craft of woodworking / by John Platt ; conceived and edited by William and Shirley Sayles. New York : Golden Press, c1978. 64 p. : ill. ; 28 cm. (The Golden Press step-by-step craft series) Includes bibliographical references. [TT194.P55] 77-90814 2.95
1. Woodwork. I. Sayles, William. II. Sayles, Shirley. III. Title. IV. Title: Woodcraft.

POPULAR mechanics magazine. 684
How to use hand tools. [Chicago] Popular Mechanics Press [1955] 160p. illus. 24cm. [TT155.P825] 53-11872
1. Woodwork. 2. Carpentry—Tools. I. Title.

POPULAR mechanics magazine. 684
100 best woodworking projects Chicago, Popular Mechanics Press [1951] 144 p. illus. 24 cm. (Popular mechanics craftsman's library) [TT180.P58] 52-267
1. Woodwork. I. Title.

POPULAR science monthly. 680
Mammoth home workshop manual. New York, Popular Science Pub. Co. [1950] 512 p. illus. (part col.) 25 cm. [TT153.P6] 50-12285
1. Woodwork. 2. Metal-work. 3. Handicraft. I. Title.

PRACTICAL woodworking : 684'.08
a comprehensive guide to tools and materials, woodworking methods and things to make. [Revised ed.]. London ; New York : Hamlyn, 1973. 160 p. : ill. ; 29 cm. Includes index. [TT180.P72 1973] 75-324605 ISBN 0-600-37029-1 : £1.75
1. Woodwork.

SCHARFF, Robert. 684
Easy ways to expert woodworking. New York, McGraw-Hill [1956] 185p. illus. 26cm. [TT180.S37] 56-11726
1. Woodwork. 2. Woodworking machinery. I. Title.

SCIENCE and mechanics. 684.8
Woodworker's encyclopedia. v. 1- Chicago, Science and Mechanics Pub. Co., 1960- v. illus. 24 cm. (Science and mechanics handbook annual) Most articles reprinted from Science and Mechanics magazine. [TT180.W63] 61-2533
1. Woodwork. I. Title.

SHEA, John Gerald. 684
Woodworking for everybody, by John Gerald Shea and Paul Nolt Wenger. 2d ed. Scranton, Laurel Publishers: distributed by Grosset & Dunlap, New York [1953] 207p. illus. 29cm. [TT180.S47 1953] 52-6661
1. Woodwork. I. Wenger, Paul Nolt, joint author. II. Title.

SMITH, Robert Ernest, 1879- 684
Machine woodworking. [3d ed.] Bloomington, Ill., McKnight & McKnight Pub. Co. [1958] 203 p. illus. 27 cm. First ed. published in 1938 under title: Information and operation units in machine woodworking. [TT180.S5 1958] 58-2447
1. Woodwork. 2. Woodworking machinery. I. Title. **BIP**

SPIELMAN, Patrick E. 745.5
Modern projects in wood, metal, & plastics. Milwaukee, Bruce Pub. Co. [1964] 160 p. illus., diagrs. 25 cm. [TT155.S68] 63-16323
1. Woodwork. 2. Metal-work. 3. Plastics. I. Title.

STIERI, Emanuele, 1891- 684
Woodworking for the home craftsman. Drawings by John C. Marinac. New York, Barnes & Noble [1953, c1950] 376p. illus. 21cm. (Everyday handbook series, 246) [TT180] 53-12398
1. Woodwork. I. Title.

VERNON, Ralph J 684.8
Basic woodwork; a text for the first year of woodwork. Text ed. Austin, Tex., Steck Co. [1963] 144 p. illus. 29 cm. (The Steck industrial arts series) [TT185.V4] 63-4160
1. Woodwork. I. Title.

WAGNER, Willis H. 684'.08
Woodworking / by Willis H. Wagner ; Walter C. Brown, consulting editor. South Holland, Ill. : Goodheart-Willcox Co., [1975] 120 p. : ill. ; 27 cm. (Goodheart-Willcox's build-a-course series) Includes bibliographies and index. An introductory text for a basic course in woodworking, stressing hand tool operations, the importance of planning and design, and safe work habits. [TT180.W28] 74-22473 ISBN 0-87006-184-4 : 4.48
1. Woodwork. I. Title.

WAY, Robert Barnard, 1890- 684
Woodworking in home and garden, by R. Barnard Way and Noel D. Green. Illustrated by R. B. Way. Redhill, Surrey, Wells Gardner, Darton [1952] 134p. illus. 19cm. [TT185.W38] 53-23374
1. Woodwork. I. Green, Noel Dutton, 1890- joint author. II. Title.

WILLCOX, Donald J., 1933- 745.51
New design in wood [by] Donald J. Willcox. New York, Van Nostrand Reinhold Co. [1970] 119 p. illus. (part col.) 22 cm. Bibliography: p. 119. [NK9604.W54 1970] 73-126866
1. Woodwork. I. Title.

WOMAN'S day. 643
Workshop ideas. Greenwich, Conn., Fawcett Publications, c1961. 144 p. illus. 24 cm. (A Fawcett book, 499) [TT185.W65] 62-1919
1. Woodwork. I. Title.

WOOD, metal, and plastic 684'.08
/ edited by Saul Lapidus. New York : D. McKay Co., c1978. 247 p. : ill. ; 26 cm. "A Courier book." Includes index. [TT194.W66] 77-20262 ISBN 0-679-50757-4 : 12.50 ISBN 0-679-50808-2 pbk. : 6.95
1. Woodwork. 2. Metal-work. 3. Plastics craft. I. Lapidus, Saul. **BIP**

WOODWORKING / 684'.08
Wilbur R. Miller ... [et al.]. 1st ed. Bloomington, Ill. : McKnight Pub. Co., c1978. v, 122 p., [1] leaf of plates : ill. (some col.) ; 24 cm. (Basic industrial arts) Includes index. [TT180.W65] 78-533386 ISBN 0-87345-791-9 : 3.96
1. Woodwork. I. Miller, Wilbur R. II. Title. III. Series.

ZANCO, Manley Lawrence. 371.426
General shop projects. Bloomington, Ill., McKnight & McKnight Pub. Co., c1960. 111 p. illus. 23 cm. [[TT168]] A62
1. Woodwork. 2. Metal-work. I. Title.

Woodwork—Amateurs' manuals.

ADAMS, Florence. 643'.7
The woman's build-it & fix-it handbook / by Florence Adams. Chatsworth, Calif. : Major Books, c1973. 317 p. : ill. ; 18 cm. Abridged reprint of the 1973 ed. published under title: I took a hammer in my hand. Includes index. [TT185.A28] 75-20817 ISBN 0-89041-021-6 : 1.50
1. Woodwork—Amateurs' manuals. 2. Dwellings—Maintenance and repair—Amateurs' manuals. 3. Repairing—Amateurs' manuals. I. Title. **BIP**

ADDING storage space. 684.1'6
Los Angeles : Petersen Pub. Co., c1978. 95 p. : ill. ; 28 cm. (Petersen's fixit yourself books ; PN 8010) (Petersen home repair and maintenance guides) Includes index. [TT185.A33] 78-50828 ISBN 0-8227-8010-0 pbk. : 3.95
1. Woodwork—Amateurs' manuals. 2. Storage in the home. I. Petersen Publishing Company.

ALTON WALTER GEORGE. 684.08'8
Woodwork projects [by] W. G. Alton. New York, Taplinger [1967, i., 1968] 84p. illus. 19x25cm. [TT185] 67-24406 3.98
1. Woodwork—Amateur's manuals. I. Title.

BEALER, Alex W. 684'.082
Old ways of working wood, by Alex W. Bealer. Barre, Mass., Barre Publishers, 1972. 231 p. illus. 24 cm. Bibliography: p. 225-226. [TT185.B38] 72-80855 ISBN 0-8271-7221-4 12.50
1. Woodwork—Amateurs' manuals. I. Title. **BIP**

BETTER homes and gardens 684.1'6
family room projects you can build. Des Moines, Iowa : Meredith Corp., c1977. 96 p. : ill. ; 27 cm. (Better homes and gardens books) [TT195.B475] 77-74595 ISBN 0-696-00235-3 : 3.95
1. Woodwork—Amateurs' manuals. 2. Storage in the home. 3. Shelving (for books) I. Title: Family room projects you can build. **BIP**

BETTER homes and gardens 684.1'6
kitchen projects you can build. 1st ed. Des Moines, Iowa : Meredith Corp., c1977. 96 p. : ill. ; 27 cm. (Better homes and gardens books) [TT195.B477] 77-74598 ISBN 0-696-00250-7 : 3.95
1. Woodwork—Amateurs' manuals. 2. Storage in the home. 3. Shelving (for books) I. Title: Kitchen projects you can build. **BIP**

BOHR, Charles W. 684'.08
A variety of woodworking projects, by Charles W. Bohr. Cincinnati, Ohio, McCormick-Mathers Pub. Co. [1969] v, 113 p. illus. 27 cm. [TT185.B65] 73-153563
1. Woodwork—Amateurs' manuals. I. Title.

BRANN, Donald R. 684'.083
Scroll saw projects / by Donald R. Brann. Briarcliff Manor, N.Y. : Directions Simplified, 1975. 130 p. : ill. ; 23 cm. (Easi-bild home improvement library ; 756) (Easi-bild simplified directions) [TT185.B7] 75-3911 pbk. : 2.50
1. Woodwork—Amateurs' manuals. 2. Jig saws. I. Title. **BIP**

BURKE, Charles C. 684'.08
Woodworking for cave dwellers / Charles C. Burke. Blue Ridge Summit, Pa. : Tab Books, [1978] p. cm. Includes index. [TT185.B79] 78-12493 ISBN 0-8306-9877-9 : 10.95. ISBN 0-8306-1022-7 pbk. : 6.95
1. Woodwork—Amateurs' manuals. I. Title. **BIP**

ENDACOTT, G. W. 684'.08
Woodworking and furniture making for the home [by] G. W. Endacott. Illus. by the author. New York, Drake Publishers [1972] 220 p. illus. 23 cm. Bibliography: p. [214] [TT185.E48 1972] 73-175967 ISBN 0-87749-157-7 6.95
1. Woodwork—Amateurs' manuals. 2. Furniture making—Amateurs' manuals. I. Title.

ENDACOTT, G. W. 684'.08
Woodworking and furniture making for the home, [by] G. W. Endacott; illustrations by the author. Newton Abbot, David and Charles, 1971. 221, [4] p. illus., map. 23 cm. Bibliography: p. [216] [TT185.E48 1971] 72-183591 ISBN 0-7153-5387-X
1. Woodwork—Amateurs' manuals. 2. Furniture making—Amateurs' manuals. I. Title.
Available from Drake Pubs., 6.95, 0-87749-157-7.

ERDMANN, La Dora. 745.51
Driftwood: techniques and projects. New York, Drake Publishers [1974] 89 p. illus. 29 cm. [TT185.E7] 74-10177 ISBN 0-87749-717-6 12.95
1. Woodwork—Amateurs' manuals. I. Title.

HAYWARD, Charles Harold, 1898- 684.08
Carpentry for beginners; how to use tools, basic joints, workshop practice, designs for things to make, edited by Charles H. Hayward. New York, Emerson Books [1969, c1960] vi, 199 p. illus. 23 cm. [TT185.H39 1969] 73-77188 4.95
1. Woodwork—Amateurs' manuals. I. Title. **BIP**

HAYWARD, Charles Harold, 1898- 684'.08
Carpentry for beginners : how to use tools, basic joints, workshop practice, designs for things to make / edited by Charles Hayward. New York : Drake Publishers, 1978, c1960. vi, 201 p. : ill. ; 22 cm. (A Drake home craftsman's book.) First published in 1949. Includes index. [TT185.H39 1978] 77-18406 ISBN 0-8473-1684-X : 4.95
1. Woodwork—Amateurs' manuals. I. Title.

HAYWARD, Charles Harold, 1898- 684'.08
The complete book of woodwork [by] Charles H. Hayward. New York, Drake Publishers [1972, c1959] 344 p. illus. 23 cm. [TT185.H3915 1972] 70-178085 ISBN 0-87749-162-3 8.95
1. Woodwork—Amateurs' manuals. I. Title.

LEAVY, Herbert T. 684.08
Carpentry & storage projects; complete plans for storage walls and dividers, built-ins, dozens of money-saving projects for every room in the house; refresher course in the use of power tools, by Herbert T. Leavy. [Greenwich, Conn., Fawcett Publications, 1971] 112 p. illus. 24 cm. Cover title. [TT185.L43] 70-24071 1.25
1. Woodwork—Amateurs' manuals. 2. Storage in the home. I. Title.

MARTENSSON, Alf. 684'.08
Woodwork in easy steps / Alf Martensson. London : Studio Vista, 1976. 64 p. : ill. ; 28 cm. Bibliography: p. 64. [TT185.M298] 77-368563 ISBN 0-289-70740-4 : £1.95
1. Woodwork—Amateurs' manuals. I. Title.

MASON, Bernard Sterling, 1896-1953. 796.54 s
Woodcraft. Illus. by Frederic H. Kock. South Brunswick, A. S. Barnes [1973] 189 p. illus. 22 cm. (His Woodcrafts library, pt. 2) First published in 1939 as pt. 2 (p. 189-368) of the author's Woodcraft. [TT7.M37 pt. 2] [TT185] 796.54 72-6367 ISBN 0-498-01296-4 5.95
1. Woodwork—Amateurs' manuals. I. Title. II. Series.

NEWMAN, Thelma R. 684'.08
Woodcraft : basic concepts and skills / Thelma R. Newman. 1st ed. Radnor, Pa. : Chilton Book Co., c1976. xvii, 229 p., [4] leaves of plates : ill. ; 27 cm. (Chilton's creative crafts series) Includes index. Bibliography: p. 225. [TT185.N43 1976] 75-44325 ISBN 0-8019-6126-2 : 13.95 ISBN 0-8019-6127-0 pbk. : 7.95
1. Woodwork—Amateurs' manuals. I. Title. II. Series.

NICOL, William Dalziel. 372.5'5
Wood. [By] W. D. Nicol. Line drawings by Jennifer Nicol. Melbourne, New York, [etc.] Oxford University Press, 1966. xv, 100 p. illus., diagrs. 22 cm. (Experience with materials, book 3) (Aus 66-225) [TT185.N445] 68-79924

FEIRER, John Louis. 371.426884
Industrial arts woodworking. Peoria, Ill., C. A. Bennett [1950] 295 p. illus. 24 cm. [TT180.F42] 50-5694
1. Woodwork (Manual training) I. Title. BIP

FEIRER, John Louis. 684.8
Industrial arts woodworking [by] John L. Feirer. 2d ed. Peoria, Ill., C. A. Bennett Co. [1965] 432 p. illus. (part col.) maps. 25 cm. [TT180.F42 1965] 65-7002
1. Woodwork (Manual training) I. Title.

FEIRER, John Louis. 684'.08
Industrial arts woodworking [by] John L. Feirer. 2d ed. Peoria, Ill., C. A. Bennett Co. [1972] 432 p. illus. (part col.) 25 cm. [TT180.F42 1972] 72-175886 ISBN 0-87002-111-7
1. Woodwork (Manual training) I. Title.

FEIRER, John Louis. 684'.08
Industrial arts woodworking / John L. Feirer. 2d ed., rev. Peoria, Ill. : C. A. Bennett Co., c1977. 439 p. : ill. ; 25 cm. Includes index. [TT180.F42 1977] 77-373223 ISBN 0-87002-195-8 : 10.72
1. Woodwork (Manual training) I. Title.

FEIRER, John Louis. 684.8
Woodworking for industry: technology and practice. Peoria, Ill., C.A. Bennett [1963] 640 p. illus. 25 cm. [TT185.F4] 63-14887
1. Woodwork (Manual training) I. Title. BIP

FEIRER, John Louis. 684.08
Woodworking for industry: technology and practice [by] John L. Feirer. Rev. Peoria, Ill., C. A. Bennett Co. [1971] 672 p. illus. (part col.), plans (part col.) 24 cm. [TT185.F4 1971] 76-21896 ISBN 0-87002-053-6
1. Woodwork (Manual training) I. Title. BIP

FRYKLUND, Verne Charles, 1896- 371.426884
General shop bench woodworking [by] Verne C. Fryklund [and] Armand J. La Berge. [4th ed.] Bloomington, Ill., McKnight & McKnight [c1955] 152p. illus. 27cm. Previous editions published under title: General shop woodworking. [TT185.F75 1955] 55-14127
1. Woodwork (Manual training) I. La Berge, Armand John, 1891- joint author. II. Title. BIP

FRYKLUND, Verne Charles, 1896- 684.08
General shop woodworking [by] Verne C. Fryklund, Armand J. La Berge. [6th ed.] McKnight [dist. New York, Taplinger, 1965] 239p. illus. (pt. col.) 27cm. Bibl. [TT185.F75] 65-6480 4.80
1. Woodwork (Manual training) I. La Berge, Armand John, 1891- joint author. II. Title.

FRYKLUND, Verne Charles, 1896- 684'.08
General shop woodworking [by] Verne C. Fryklund [and] Armand J. La Berge. [7th ed.] Bloomington, Ill., McKnight & McKnight [1972] 240 p. illus. 27 cm. [TT185.F75 1972] 70-183260 ISBN 0-87345-031-0
1. Woodwork (Manual training) I. La Berge, Armand John, 1891- joint author. II. Title.

FRYKLUND, Verne Charles, 1896- 684.8
General shop woodworking [by] Verne C. Fryklund [and] Armand J. La Berge, [5th ed.] Bloomington, Ill., McKnight & McKnight Pub. Co. [1963] 238 p. illus. (part col.) 27 cm. Bibliography: p. 231-232. [TT185.F75] 64-1632
1. Woodwork (Manual training) I. La Berge, Armand John, 1891- joint author. II. Title.

GOTTSHALL, Franklin H. 371.426884
Making useful things of wood. Milwaukee, Bruce [1950] xii, 192 p. illus. 28 cm. [TT180.G63] 51-739
1. Woodwork (Manual training) I. Title.

GOTTSHALL, Franklin H. 371.426884
Woodwork for the beginner. Milwaukee, Bruce Pub. Co. [1952] 139 p. illus. 29 cm. [TT185.G76] 52-3582
1. Woodwork (Manual training) I. Title.

GREEN, John Nigel 684.088
Modern woodwork for pleasure. New York, Taplinger [1966,c.1965] 80p. illus. 20x26cm. [TT185.G768] 66-16976 3.95 bds.,
1. Woodwork (Manual training) I. Title.

GRONEMAN, Chris Harold, 1906- 684.08
General woodworking [by] Chris H. Groneman. 4th ed. New York, McGraw-Hill [1971] xiv, 434 p. illus. (part col.) 25 cm. (McGraw-Hill publications in industrial education) [TT180.G73 1971] 77-22380 ISBN 0-07-024952-0
1. Woodwork (Manual training) I. Title.

GRONEMAN, Chris Harold, 1906- 684'.08
General woodworking / Chris H. Groneman. 5th ed. New York : McGraw-Hill, [1976] xii, 404 p., [4] leaves of plates : ill. ; 25 cm. (McGraw-Hill publications in industrial education) Includes index. [TT180.G73 1976] 75-9819 ISBN 0-07-024985-7 : 9.76
1. Woodwork (Manual training) I. Title.

GRONEMAN, Chris Harold, 1906- 684.08
Technical woodworking [by] Chris H. Groneman [and] Everett R. Glazener. St. Louis, Webster Division, McGraw-Hill [1966] 474 p. illus. (part col.) map, plans. 25 cm. (McGraw Hill publications in industrial education) [TT180.G75] 66-5323
1. Woodwork (Manual training) I. Glazener, Everett Ruthven, 1921- joint author. II. Title. BIP

GRONEMAN, Chris Harold, 1906- 684'.08
Technical woodworking / Chris H. Groneman, Everett R. Glazener. 2d ed. New York : McGraw-Hill, [1976] xiii, 434 p. : ill. ; 25 cm. (McGraw-Hill publications in industrial education) Includes index. [TT180.G75 1976] 75-1071 ISBN 0-07-024964-4 : 12.94
1. Woodwork (Manual training) I. Glazener, Everett Ruthven, 1921- joint author. II. Title.

HACKETT, Donald F. 684.08
Modern wood technology [by] Donald F. Hackett [and] Patrick E. Spielman. Milwaukee, Bruce Pub. Co. [1968] x, 757 p. illus. 25 cm. [TT130.H28] 67-19792
1. Woodwork (Manual training) 2. Wood-using industries. I. Spielman, Patrick E., joint author. II. Title.

HAMMOND, James J. 684.08
Woodworking technology [by] James J. Hammond [and others. 2d ed.] Bloomington, Ill., McKnight & McKnight Pub. Co. [1966] xi, 427 p. illus. (part col.) 27 cm. Includes bibliographies. [TT185.H32 1966] 66-22783
1. Woodwork (Manual training) I. Title. BIP

HAMMOND, James J. 684'.08
Woodworking technology [by] James J. Hammond [and others. 3d ed.] Bloomington, Ill., McKnight & McKnight Pub. Co. [1972] xii, 457 p. illus. 27 cm. Bibliography: p. 439-442. [TT185.H32 1972] 70-163293 ISBN 0-87345-017-5
1. Woodwork (Manual training) I. Title. BIP

HAYNES, Frank A 684.0807
Learning woodwork; a scheme of work, by Frank A. Haynes, [1st ed.] Oxford, New York, Pergamon Press [1966] 89 p. illus. 27 cm. (The Commonwealth and international library. Applied arts and crafts division) [TT185.H38] 66-18392
1. Woodwork (Manual training) I. Title.

HJORTH, Herman, 1883-1951. 684.8
Basic woodworking processes. Rev. by Ewell W. Fowler. Milwaukee, Bruce Pub. Co. [1961] 224 p. illus. 23 cm. [TT185.H64 1961] 60-15479
1. Woodwork (Manual training) 2. Woodworking tools. I. Title. II. Title: Woodworking processes.

HOLTROP, William F 684.8
Principles of woodworking [by] William F. Holtrop and Herman Hjorth. [Rev. ed.] Milwaukee, Bruce Pub. Co. [1961] 600p. illus. 24cm. Earlier editions by Herman Hjorth. Includes bibliography. [TT185.H66 1961] 61-11832
1. Woodwork (Manual training) 2. Cabinet-work. I. Hjorth, Herman, 1883-1951, joint author. II. Title.

HUNT, De Witt. 371.426884
Hand woodworking, by De Witt Hunt and John Bruce Tate. 4th ed. Oklahoma City, Harlow Pub. Corp., 1956. 418p. illus. 24cm. Previous editions published under title: A manual for hand woodworking. [TT180.H8 1956] 57-18518
1. Woodwork (Manual training) I. Tate, John Bruce, joint author. II. Title.

HUNT, DeWitt. 684.8
Hard woodworking, by DeWitt Hunt and John Bruce Tate. 5th ed. Oklahoma City, Harlow Pub. Corp. [1962] 424 p. illus. 24 cm. Previous editions published under title: A manual for hand woodworking. Full name: DeWitt Talmadge Hunt. [TT180.H8] 62-46358
1. Woodwork (Manual training) I. Tate, John Bruce, joint author. II. Title.

KETTLESS, Alonzo William Percy. 684'.08
Modern woodwork [by] A. W. P. Kettless. London, Melbourne [etc.] Macmillan; New York, St. Martin's P., 1967- . v. illus., tables, diagrs. 25 cm. Contents.CONTENTS. -- v. 1. Design, techniques and construction. 12/6 (B 67-7531) [TT185.K4] 67-100244
1. Woodwork (Manual training) I. Title.

LA BERGE, Armand John, 1891- joint author. 684.8
General shop woodworking [by] Verne C. Fryklund [and] Armand J. La Berge, [5th ed.] Bloomington, Ill., McKnight & McKnight Pub. Co. [1963] 238 p. illus. (part col.) 27 cm. Bibliography: p. 231-232. [TT185.F75] 64-1632
1. Woodwork (Manual training) I. Title. BIP

MCGHEE, C. Douglas. 684.08
Woodwork notes, by C. Douglas McGhee. [1st ed.] Oxford, New York, Pergamon Press [1967] vii, 73 p. illus. 20 cm. (The Commonwealth and international library. Applied arts and crafts division) [TT185.M22 1967] 67-18956
1. Woodwork (Manual training) I. Title.

MADDEN, Ira C. 684.8
Woodworking for industrial arts, teaches students to think and to plan. Chicago, Goodheart-Willcox Co. [1962] 224 p. illus. 29 cm. [TT185.M24 1962] 62-10396
1. Woodwork (Manual training) I. Title.

MISSOURI. Division of Public Schools. 371.426884
Industrial arts, general woodwork. [Jefferson City] 1951. 82p. 28cm. (Missouri at work on the public school curriculum. Industrial education series) [Missouri. Dept. of Education] Publication no. 65. [TT185.M5 1951] 51-62506
1. Woodwork (Manual training) I. Title.

MORRIS, Floyd. 684.08'8
198 easy wood projects. South Holland, Ill., Goodheart-Willcox Co. [1970] 96 p. illus. 28 cm. [TT185.M66] 78-111282 ISBN 8-7006-1119-
1. Woodwork (Manual training) I. Title.

OLSON, Delmar Walter, 1909- 684
Woods and woodworking for industrial arts [by] Delmar W. Olson. 2d ed. Englewood Cliffs, N. J., Prentice-Hall [1965] 260 p. illus. 25 cm. (Prentice-Hall industrial arts series) Bibliography: p. 252-253. [TT180.O4 1965] 65-10093
1. Woodwork (Manual training) 2. Woodworking industries. I. Title.

PIEPENBURG, Robert E. 684.08
Designs in wood [by] Robert E. Piepenburg. New York, Bruce Pub. Co. [1969] 144 p. illus. 26 cm. Includes bibliographies. [TT185.P586] 77-78971
1. Woodwork (Manual training) I. Title. BIP

PROSSER, R. D. 684.08
Design development - wood; a complete course in woodwork. Class book; creative design, projects, timber, tools by R. D. Prosser. [Melbourne, Hall's Book Store, 1968] 2 v. (chiefly diagrs.) 39 cm. Each vol. accompanied by a Project guide, and two sets of Woodwork theory drawings. [TT180.P78] 74-427901 unpriced
1. Woodwork (Manual training) I. Title.

ROMERO, A. C. 684.088
Contemporary designs for wood [by] A. C. Romero. Milwaukee, Bruce Pub. Co. [1966] 79 p. illus. 24 cm. [TT180.R647] 66-10832
1. Woodwork (Manual training) I. Title.

THOMAS, Geoffrey William. 371.426884
Textbook of woodwork. Leeds, E. J. Arnold [1951] 160 p. illus. 24 cm. [TT180.T5] 51-38753
1. Woodwork (Manual training) I. Title.

TURNBULL, J. S. 371.426884
Modern woodworking projects. Illus. by Myron W. Graybill. New York, Macmillan [1953] 122 p. illus. 28 cm. [TT185.T8] 53-3563
1. Woodwork (Manual training) I. Title.

TUSTISON, Francis Elwood, 1886- 371.426884
Instructional units in hand woodwork [by] F. E. Tustion, Arthur G. Brown, and Louis Barocci. Rev. ed. Milwaukee, Bruce Pub. Co. [1954] 185p. illus. 27cm. [TT180.T8 1954] 54-14509
1. Woodwork (Manual training) I. Title. II. Title: Hand woodwork.

VAN TASSEL, Raymond, 1906- 684.8
Woodworking crafts. 2d ed. Princeton, N. J., Van Nostrand [1960] 196 p. illus. 22 cm. [TT185.V33 1960] 60-50781
1. Woodwork (Manual training) I. Title.

WAGNER, Willis H. 684.08
Modern woodworking; tools, materials, and procedures, by Willis H. Wagner. Homewood, Ill., Goodheart-Willcox Co. [1967] 1 v. (various pagings) illus. (part col.) plans. 29 cm. Includes bibliography. [TT185.W32] 67-13293
1. Woodwork (Manual training). I. Title. BIP

WAGNER, Willis H. 674'.8
Modern woodworking; tools, materials, and procedures, by Willis H. Wagner. South Holland, Ill., Goodheart-Willcox Co. [1970] 1 v. (various pagings) illus. (part col.), plans. 29 cm. Includes bibliography. [TT185.W32 1970] 71-14534
1. Woodwork (Manual training) I. Title.

WAGNER, Willis H. 684'.08
Modern woodworking : tools, materials, and processes / by Willis H. Wagner. South Holland, Ill. : Goodheart-Willcox Co., c1978. 432 p., [6] leaves of plates : ill. ; 29 cm. Includes index.. [TT185.W32 1978] 77-17976 ISBN 0-87006-246-8 : 10.20
1. Woodwork (Manual training) I. Title.

WAGNER, Willis H. 684'.08
Modern woodworking; tools, materials, and procedures, by Willis H. Wagner. South Holland, Ill., Goodheart-Willcox Co. [1974] p. Bibliography: p. [TT185.W32 1974] 74-8878 ISBN 0-87006-180-1 8.95
1. Woodwork (Manual training) I. Title.

WILLE, Milton W. 684.088
Art in wood [by] Milton W. Wille. Milwaukee, Bruce Pub. Co. [1966] 76 p. illus. 24 cm. [TT180.W527] 66-20486
1. Woodwork (Manual training) I. Title.

ZIMMERMAN, Fred W. 684'.08
Exploring woodworking : basic fundamentals / by Fred W. Zimmerman. South Holland, Ill. : Goodheart-Willcox Co., c1976. 208 p. : ill. ; 29 cm. Includes index. [TT180.Z54 1976] 75-31809 ISBN 0-87006-200-X : 6.64
1. Woodwork (Manual training) I. Title.

ZIMMERMAN, Fred W. 684'.08
Exploring woodworking; basic fundamentals, by Fred W. Zimmerman. South Holland, Ill., Goodheart-Willcox Co. [1972] 208 p. illus. 29 cm. [TT180.Z54] 75-187334
1. Woodwork (Manual training) I. Title.

Woodwork (Manual training)—Juvenile literature.

GRONEMAN, Chris Harold, 1906- 684'.08
Getting started in woodworking / Chris H. Groneman, John L. Feirer. New York : McGraw-Hill, c1979. iv, 108 p. : ill. ; 24 cm. Includes index. A beginning woodworking textbook for junior high school students including basic techniques using metric measurements, a glossary of

terms, and a variety of practice projects. [TT180.G74] 78-18271 ISBN 0-07-024997-0 pbk. : 4.40
1. Woodwork (Manual training)—Juvenile literature. I. Feirer, John Louis, joint author. II. Title. BIP

Woodwork (Manual training)—Pictorial works.

CRAMLET, Ross C. 684.08'07
Woodwork visualized, by Ross C. Cramlet. Rev. ed. Milwaukee, Bruce Pub. Co. [1967] 158 p. illus. 28 cm. [TT185.C82 1967] 67-19440
1. Woodwork (Manual training)—Pictorial works. I. Title.

MATTHEWS, John, 1933- 684.08'8
Pictorial woodwork [by] J. Matthews. Illustrated by J. D. Kerr. New York, St. Martin's Press [1969, c1963-67] 3 v. illus. 19 x 25 cm. Contents.Contents.—Background to wood, construction, finishes.—Tools and their correct use.—A guide to practical work. [TT185.M35 1969] 78-9212
1. Woodwork (Manual training)—Pictorial works. I. Title.

Woodwork Manual traning)

WAGNER, Willis H 684.8
Woodworking. Chicago, Goodheart-Wilcox Co. [1961] 112 p. illus. 27 cm. (Goodheart-Willcox's build-a-course series) [TT185.W33] 61-5340
1. Woodwork Manual traning) I. Title. BIP

Woodwork—New England.

MERAS, Phyllis. 680
A Yankee way with wood / by Phyllis Meras. Boston : Houghton Mifflin, 1975. 255 p. : ill. ; 29 cm. [TT180.M44] 75-14221 ISBN 0-395-20423-2 : 12.95
1. Woodwork—New England. 2. Wood-carving—New England. 3. Artisans—New England. I. Title. BIP

Woodwork—Study and teaching.

JARMAN, Christopher. 745.51
Teach your children woodwork / Christopher Jarman ; photos. by George Rousell. New York : Drake Publishers, 1974. 96 p. : ill. ; 21 cm. Bibliography: p. 95. [TT185.J37] 74-11762 ISBN 0-87749-722-2 : 6.95
1. Woodwork—Study and teaching. I. Rousell, George. II. Title. BIP

Woodworking tools.

ALBERS, Vernon Martin, 1902- 684'.08
How to use woodworking tools effectively and safely / by Vernon M. Albers. South Brunswick : A. S. Barnes, [1975] 190 p. : ill. ; 22 cm. Includes index. [TT186.A42] 74-9277 ISBN 0-498-01551-3 : 6.95
1. Woodworking tools. I. Title. BIP

DE CRISTOFORO, R. J. 684'.082
Handtool handbook for woodworking / by R. J. DeCristoforo. Tucson, AZ : H.P. Books, c1977. 184 p. : ill. ; 28 cm. Includes index. [TT186.D4] 77-89289 ISBN 0-912656-53-0 pbk. : 4.95
1. Woodworking tools. 2. Woodwork. I. Title. BIP

HAYWARD, Charles Harold, 1898- 684'.08
Tools for woodwork / Charles H. Hayward. New York : Drake Publishers, 1976, c1973. 127 p. : ill. ; 21 cm. (Drake home craftsman's book) Includes index. [TT186.H39 1976] 76-49681 ISBN 0-8473-1338-7 pbk. : 4.95
1. Woodworking tools. I. Title. BIP

JONES, David Thomas. 684'.08
Woodworking tools / by David T. Jones. Ed. 1. Scranton : International Correspondence Schools, c1976. 72, 3 p. : ill. ; 27 cm. "2180." [TT186.J66] 77-357158
1. Woodworking tools. 2. Woodworking machinery. I. Title.

KEBABIAN, Paul B. 621.9'08
American woodworking tools / text by Paul B. Kebabian ; photos. by Dudley Witney. 1st ed. Boston : New York Graphic Society, c1978. p. cm. Includes index. Bibliography: p. [TT186.K4] 78-7066 ISBN 0-8212-0731-8 : 24.95
1. Woodworking tools. I. Witney, Dudley. II. Title. BIP

SCHARFF, Robert. 684'.08
The complete book of home workshop tools / by Robert Scharff. New York : McGraw-Hill, c1979. ix, 438 p. : ill. ; 24 cm. (A Norback book) Includes index. [TT186.S3] 78-14822 ISBN 0-07-055042-5 : 16.95
1. Woodworking tools. 2. Power tools. I. Title. BIP

Woodworking tools—Catalogs.

†BUCK Brothers. 684'.082
Price list of chisels, plane irons, gouges, carving tools, nail sets, screw drivers, handles, &c. manufactured by Buck Brothers, Riverlin Works, Millbury, Mass. .... [Fitzwilliam, N.H. : K. Roberts Pub. Co., 1976] 128 p. : ill. ; 22 cm. Reprint of the 1890 ed. printed by C. Hamilton, Worcester, Mass.; with new commentary and bibliography. [TT186.B8 1976] 76-380151 ISBN 0-913602-19-1 : 8.75 pbk. : 6.00
1. Woodworking tools—Catalogs. 2. Chisels—Catalogs. I. Title: Price list of chisels, plane irons, gouges ...

Woodworking tools—Dictionaries.

BLACKBURN, Graham, 1940- 684'.082'028
The illustrated encyclopedia of woodworking handtools, instruments, & devices : containing a full description of the tools used by carpenters, joiners, and cabinet makers, with many examples of tools used by other woodworkers such as, woodsmen, sawyers, coach makers, wheelwrights, shipwrights, wainwrights, coopers, turners, pattern makers, and whittlers / written and illustrated by Graham Blackburn. New York : Simon and Schuster, [1974] 238 p. : ill. ; 29 cm. Bibliography: p. 237. [TT186.B52] 74-6541 ISBN 0-671-21874-3 : 8.95 ISBN 0-671-22152-3 pbk. : 3.95
1. Woodworking tools—Dictionaries. 2. Woodworking tools—History. I. Title. BIP

SALAMAN, R. A. 684'.082'03
Dictionary of tools used in the woodworking and allied trades, c. 1700-1970 / R. A. Salaman ; foreword by Joseph Needham. New York : Scribner, [19776]c1975. 545 p. : ill. ; 26 cm. Bibliography: p. 537-545. [TT186.S24 1975] 75-35059 ISBN 0-684-14535-9 : 47.50
1. Woodworking tools—Dictionaries. 2. Tools—Dictionaries. I. Title: Dictionary of tools used in the woodworking and allied trades ... BIP

Woodworking tools—History.

DUNBAR, Michael. 684'.082
Antique woodworking tools : a guuide to the purchase, restoration and use of old tools for today's shop / by Michael Dunbar. New York : Hastings House, [1977] p. cm. Includes index. [TT186.D86] 77-23350 ISBN 0-8038-5821-3 : 12.50
1. Woodworking tools—History. I. Title.

Woody plants—pictorial works.

SCHWARZENBACH, Hans, 1911- 715.084
Decorative trees and shrubs. Text by Hans Zaugg and Hans Coaz. Translated and adapted by Herbert L, Edlin. New York, Viking Press [1960] 1 v, (unpaged) 60 plates. 32 cm. (A Studio book) Translation of Unsere Gartenpflanzen. [SB435.S423] 60-2519
1. Woody plants—pictorial works. 2. Plants, Ornamental—Pictorial works. I. Zaugg, Hans. II. Coaz, Hans.

Wootton, Frank A. A.

WOOTTON, Frank A. A. 759.2
The aviation art of Frank Wootton / edited by David Larkin ; introd. by John Blake. 1st U.S. ed. Bearsville, N.Y. : Peacock Press, 1976. [16] p., [40] leaves of plates : ill. (some col.) ; 23 x 28 cm. [ND497.W77A43 1976] 76-15475 6.95
1. Wootton, Frank A. A. 2. Great Britain. Royal Air Force—Pictorial works. 3. Airplanes in art. I. Title. BIP

Worcester Cathedral.

NOAKE, Valentine. 942.47
The cathedral church of Worcester. With a foreword by W. E. Beck. Worcester [Eng.] Littlebury [1951] 96p. illus. 23cm. [DA690.W9N75] 53-21564
1. Worcester Cathedral. I. Title.

Worcester, Mass. Art Museum.

WORCESTER, Mass. Art Museum. 759.94'074'01443
European paintings in the collection of the Worcester Art Museum. Worcester, Mass. : The Museum, 1974. 2 v. (vii, 666 p.) : ill. ; 25 cm. Includes index. Contents.Contents.—[1] Text.—[2] Plates. [ND450.W67 1974] 73-90538
1. Worcester, Mass. Art Museum. 2. Paintings, European—Catalogs. 3. Paintings—Worcester, Mass.—Catalogs. I. Title.

WORCESTER, Mass. Art Museum. 708'.144'3
A handbook to the Worcester Art Museum. Worcester, Mass. : The Museum, [1973] 222 p. : ill. ; 21 cm. [N870.A76] 75-320885
1. Worcester, Mass. Art Museum. 2. Art—Worcester, Mass.—Catalogs. I. Title.

Worcester porcelain.

BEDFORD, John, 1907- 738.2'7
Old Worcester China. New York, Walker [1967, c1966] 63 p. illus., facsims., col. plate. 19 cm. (Collectors' pieces, 9) [NK4395.B4 1967] 67-11601
1. Worcester porcelain. I. Title.

SANDON, Henry. 738.27
The illustrated guide to Worcester porcelain, 1751-1793. New York, Praeger [1970, c1969] xvii, 96 p. illus. (part col.), plans, port. 26 cm. (The Illustrated guides to pottery and porcelain) Bibliography: p. 91-92. [NK4395.S18] 70-100037 15.00
1. Worcester porcelain. I. Title. II. Title: Worcester porcelain, 1751-1793.

SANDON, Henry. 738.2'7
Royal Worcester porcelain, from 1862 to the present day / Henry Sandon ; photos. by John and Joan Beckerley. 1st American ed. New York : C. N. Potter : distributed by Crown Publishers, 1975, c1973. xxix, 265 p., [64] leaves of plates : ill. (some col.) ; 26 cm. Includes index. Bibliography: p. 255-256. [NK4395.S19 1975] 74-25155 17.50
1. Worcester Royal Porcelain Company Ltd. 2. Worcester porcelain. I. Title. BIP

Worcester porcelain—Catalogs.

MANCHESTER, Eng. Art Gallery. 738.2'7
Transfer-printed Worcester porcelain at Manchester City Art Gallery : a catalogue / by Emmeline Leary and Peter Walton. [Manchester] : City of Manchester Cultural Services, [1976] 52 p. : ill., port. ; 20 x 21 cm. Includes index. Bibliography: p. 50-51. [NK4395.M33 1976] 77-361624 ISBN 0-901673-08-0 : £1.50
1. Manchester, Eng. Art Gallery. 2. Worcester porcelain—Catalogs. 3. Blue and white transfer ware—Catalogs. I. Leary, Emmeline. II. Walton, Peter, 1944- III. Title.

Worcester Royal Porcelain Company Ltd.

SANDON, Henry. 738.2'7
Royal Worcester porcelain, from 1862 to the present day / Henry Sandon ; photos. by John and Joan Beckerley. 1st American ed. New York : C. N. Potter : distributed by Crown Publishers, 1975, c1973. xxix, 265 p., [64] leaves of plates : ill. (some col.) ; 26 cm. Includes index. Bibliography: p. 255-256. [NK4395.S19 1975] 74-25155 17.50
1. Worcester Royal Porcelain Company Ltd. 2. Worcester porcelain. I. Title. BIP

Worde, Wynkyn de, d. 1534?

MORAN, James. 686.2'092'4 B
Wynkyn de Worde, father of Fleet Street / James Moran. 2d ed. London : Wynkyn de Worde Society, 1976. 52, [8] p., [1] fold. leaf of plates : ill. ; 20 cm. Originally published in 1960. Includes index. Bibliography: p. [53] [Z232.W87M6 1976] 77-357537 ISBN 0-85331-388-1 : £2.95
1. Worde, Wynkyn de, d. 1534? 2. Printing—England—London—History. I. Wynkyn de Worde Society. II. Title.

Words in art.

BING, Ilse. 741.9'43
Words as visions; logograms. Worte als Visionen. Mots comme visions. [1st ed.] New York, Drigh-Graph, inc. [1974] 1 v. (chiefly illus.) 22 x 28 cm. [NC251.B53A57] 73-90744 8.95
1. Bing, Ilse. 2. Words in art. I. Title.
Publisher's address: 75 E., 55 St., N.Y. 10019. BIP

Wordsworth, William, 1770-1850—Criticism and interpretation.

KROEBER, Karl, 1926- 759'.2
Romantic landscape vision: Constable and Wordsworth. [Madison] University of Wisconsin Press [1975] xi, 142 p. illus. 23 cm. Includes bibliographical references. [PR5892.N2K7] 74-5905 ISBN 0-299-06710-6 10.00
1. Wordsworth, William, 1770-1850—Criticism and interpretation. 2. Constable, John, 1776-1837. 3. Nature in literature. 4. Romanticism, English. 5. Landscape painting, English. 6. Romanticism in art—England. I. Title.

Wores, Theodore, 1858-1939.

WORES, Theodore, 1858-1939. 759.13
Theodore Wores, 1858-1939; a retrospective exhibition at Kennedy Galleries, inc., May 4 through June 1, 1973. [New York, Kennedy Galleries, 1973] 36 p. illus. 21 x 28 cm. [ND237.W86K46] 74-160782
1. Wores, Theodore, 1858-1939. I. Kennedy Galleries, inc., New York.

Workbenches.

BRANN, Donald R. 684'.08'028
How to build workbenches, by Donald R. Brann. Rev. ed. Briarcliff Manor, N.Y., Directions Simplified, 1972. 98 p. illus. 23 cm. (Easi-bild simplified directions, 672) First published in 1967 under title: How to build three workbenches. [TT197.5.W6B72 1972] 73-153310 1.50
1. Workbenches. 2. Furniture making—Amateurs' manuals. I. Title. BIP

Workshop receipts.

ABLER, Bill. 684'.08
The sensuous gadgeteer : bringing tools and materials to life / by Bill Abler. Philadelphia : Running Press, 1973. 113 p. : ill. ; 28 cm. Includes index. Bibliography: p. 111-113. [TT153.A24] 73-89457 ISBN 0-914294-04-0 : 3.95
1. Workshop receipts. 2. Woodworking tools. I. Title.

ABLER, Bill. 684'.08
Shop tactics : the common-sense way of using tools and working with woods, metals, plastic, and glass / by William Abler. Philadelphia : Running Press, c1976. p. cm. A revision of The sensuous gadgeteer, published in 1973. Includes index. Bibliography: p. [TT153.A24 1976] 76-28967 ISBN 0-914294-64-4 pbk. : 3.95. ISBN 0-914294-63-6 lib. bdg. : 9.80

TOY, Raymond S 769'.55
All known issues of World War II and post war (U.S. & allies) military currency... [by] Raymond S. Toy. Tucson, Ariz., Monitor Print Co. [1964] 51 p. illus. 22 cm. Cover title: World War II military currency. [HG353.5.T6] 65-9267
1. World War, 1939-1945 — Military currency. 2. Paper money — Catalogs. I. Title. II. Title: World War II military currency.

TOY, Raymond S 769.550216
All known issues of World War II and post war (U.S. & allies) military currency... [by] Raymond S. Toy. 2d illustrated ed. Tucson, Ariz., Monitor Offset Print. Co., 1965. 79 p. illus. 22 cm. Cover title: World War II allied military currency. [HG353.5.T6] 65-9715
1. World War, 1939-1945 — Military currency. 2. Paper money — Catalogs. I. Title. II. Title: World War II allied military currency.

TOY, Raymond S. 769'.55
All known issues of World War II and post war (U.S. & allies) military currency ... [by] Raymond S. Toy. 3d illustrated ed. San Diego, Malter-Westerfield Pub. Co., 1969. 86 p. illus. 22 cm. Cover title: World War II allied military currency. Fourth ed. (1974) published under title: World War II Allied military currency. [HG353.5.T6 1969] 72-169132 2.00
1. World War, 1939-1945—Military currency. 2. Paper money—Catalogs. I. Title. II. Title: World War II allied military currency.

TOY, Raymond S. 769.55
Axis military currency; all known issues of World War II are listed [by Raymond S. Toy and Bob Meyer] 1st ed. Tucson, Ariz., Monitor Offset Print. Co., 1967. 98 p. illus. 22 cm. Cover title: World War II Axis military currency. [HG353.5.T58] 67-5897
1. World War, 1939-1945—Military currency. 2. Paper money—Catalogs. I. Meyer, Bob, joint author. II. Title.

TOY, Raymond S. 769'.55
World War II allied military currency; a comprehensive, illustrated catalog of all military currencies used during or as a result of World War II, with valuations, background, and other numismatic information [by] Raymond S. Toy [and] Carlton F. Schwan. 4th ed. Portage, Ohio, C. F. Schwan [1974] xii, 110 p. illus. 21 cm. First-3d ed. published under title: All known issues of World War II and postwar (U.S. & Allies) military currency. [HG353.5.T6 1974] 74-79385
1. World War, 1939-1945—Military currency. 2. Paper money—Catalogs. I. Schwan, Carlton F., joint author. II. Title.

World War, 1939-1945—Pictorial works.

BRODIE, Howard 743.973
War drawings: World War II, Korea. Palo Alto, Calif., National Pr. [1963c.1962] 1.v. (unpaged) illus., plates. 39cm. 63-4241 15.00; 10.00pap.,
1. World War, 1939-1945—Pictorial works. 2. Korean War, 1950-1953—Pictorial works. I. Title.

CHRYSLER Corporation. 756
Significant war scenes by battlefront artists, 1941-1945; a collection of reflective paintings in which sixteen artists interpret war as they saw it around the world. [Detroit?] [1951] 32 p. col. illus. 34 x 45 cm. [ND1240.C52] 51-8137
1. World War, 1939-1945—Pictorial works. I. Title.

SABER, Clifford. 759.13
Desert rat sketch book, written and illustrated, on-the-spot, in full color by Clifford Saber. Forewords by Tom Lea and Stephen Galatti. [1st ed.] New York, Sketchbook Press, 1959. 187p. illus. 27x37cm. [ND1839.S3A45] 59-13535
1. World War, 1939-1945— Pictorial works. 2. World War, 1930-1945—Campaigns—Africa, North. 3. World War, 1939-1945—Personal narratives, American. 4. Gt. Brit. Army. 8th Army. I. Title.

World War, 1939-1945—Posters.

JUDD, Denis, 1938- 769'.4'994053
Posters of World War Two. New York, St. Martin's Press [1973] 160 p. illus. 29 cm. [D743.25.J82 1973] 73-80788 11.95
1. World War, 1939-1945—Posters. I. Title.

Worth, Charles Frederick, 1825-1895.

SAUNDERS, Edith. 926.46
The age of Worth, couturier to the Empress Eugenie. London, New York, Longmans, Green [1954] 218p. illus. 23cm. [TT505.W58S3] 55-1216
1. Worth, Charles Frederick, 1825-1895. 2. France—Court and courtiers. I. Title.

SAUNDERS, Edith. 926.46
The age of Worth, couturier to the Empress Eugenie. Bloomington, Indiana University Press, 1955. 218p. illus. 23cm. [TT505] 55-8084
1. Worth, Charles Frederick, 1825-1895. 2. France—Court and courtiers. I. Title.

Worth. Paris.

BROOKLYN Institute of Arts and Sciences. Museum. 687.12065
The House of Worth; [en exhibition held at the Brooklyn Museum from May 8 through June 24, 1962. Brooklyn, 1962] 56p. illus. 23cm. Includes bibliography. [TT505.W6B7] 62-40963
1. Worth. Paris. I. Title.

Wreaths.

ALDRICH, Dot. 745.92
Decorative wreaths & plaques Original drawings by Gen. Young. Approved by Great Outdoors Association. St. Petersburg, Fla., Great Outdoors Pub. Co. [1963] 80 p. illus. 28 cm. [SB449.3.D7A4] 63-3759
1. Wreaths. 2. Plaques, plaquettes. 3. Handicraft. I. Title.

Wren, Christopher, Sir, 1632-1723.

BOOTH, Arthur Harold. 720'.924
Sir Christopher Wren [by] Arthur H. Booth; drawings by Charles King. London, Muller, 1967. 125p. illus., plan, facsim., diagrs. 21 cm. (True bks.) Bibl. [NA997.W8B65] (B) 67-96582 3.75 bds.,
1. Wren, Christopher, Sir 1632-1723. II. Title.

DUTTON, Ralph, 1898- 720.942
The age of Wren. London, New York, Batsford [1951] 136 p. illus., ports. (1 col.) 25 cm. [NA997.W8D8] 720.81 A52
1. Wren, Sir Christopher, 1632-1723. 2. Architecture—England—Hist. I. Title.

HUTCHINSON, Harold Frederick. 720'.92'4 B
Sir Christopher Wren : a biography / by Harold F. Hutchinson. New York : Stein and Day, [1976] c1975. p. cm. Includes index. Bibliography: p. [NA997.W8H87 1976] 75-34324 10.00
1. Wren, Christopher, Sir, 1632-1723. BIP

HUTCHISON, Harold Frederick. 720'.92'4 B
Sir Christopher Wren : a biography / by Harold F. Hutchison. London : Gollancz, 1976. 191 p., leaf of plate, [16] p. of plates : ill., plan, ports. ; 23 cm. Includes index. Bibliography: p. [177]-181. [NA997.W8H87 1976b] 76-367374 ISBN 0-575-01876-3 : £5.00
1. Wren, Christopher, Sir, 1632-1723.

LANG, Jane. 726.6
Rebuilding St. Paul's after the great fire of London. London, New York, Oxford University Press, 1956. xi, 269p. illus., ports. 26cm. Bibliography: p. [257]- 261. [NA5470.S5L3] 56-14474
1. Wren, Christopher, Sir 1632-1723. 2. London. St. Paul's Cathedral. I. Title.

MURIEL, John St. Clair, 1909- 927.2
Wren: his work and times, by John Lindsey [pseud.] London, New York, Rich & Cowan [1951] 256 p. illus. ports. 22 cm. [NA997.W8M8] 52-9206
1. Wren, Sir Christopher, 1632-1723. I. Title.

SEKLER, Eduard Franz. 927.2
Wren and his place in European architecture. New York, Macmillan, 1956. 217 p. illus., 80 plates. 26 cm. Translated by Mr. and Mrs. Peter Murray. "Sir Christopher Wren: a selected bibliography": p. 195-202. Bibliographical footnotes. [NA997.W8S4 1956a] 56-4231
1. Wren, Christopher, Sir, 1632-1723.

SUMMERSON, John Newenham, 1904- 927.2
Sir Christopher Wren. New York, Macmillan [1953] 159p. illus. 19cm. (Brieg lives, no. 9) [NA997.W8S8] 53-12511
1. Wren, Christopher, Sir 1632-1723. I. Title.

SUMMERSON, John Newenham, Sir 1904- 927.2
Sir Christopher Wren. Hamden, Conn., Archon [dist. Shoe String] 1965[c.1953, 1965] 159p. illus., plans. port. 21cm. (Makers of hist.) [NA997.W8S8] 65-4284 4.00
1. Wren, Sir Christopher, 1632-1723. I. Title.

WEIR, Rosemary. 720.924 B
The man who built a city; a life of Sir Christopher Wren. [1st ed.] New York, Farrar, Straus & Giroux [1971] viii, 208 p. illus. 21 cm. (An Ariel book) Bibliography: p. 201. A biography of the seventeenth-century inventor, astronomer, and mathematician principally known for his architectural achievements such as the rebuilding of London's St. Paul's Cathedral. [NA997.W8W44] 92 74-161371 ISBN 0-374-35008-6 4.95
1. Wren, Christopher, Sir, 1632-1723. I. Title. BIP

WHINNEY, Margaret Dickens. 720.924 B
Christopher Wren [by] Margaret Whinney. New York, Praeger [1971] 216 p. illus., plans, ports. 22 cm. Bibliography: p. 206-208. [NA997.W8W48 1971b] 78-155448 8.95
1. Wren, Christopher, Sir, 1632-1723. I. Title.

WREN, Christopher, Sir 1632-1723. 720.942
Christopher Wren, 1632-1723 [by] Nikolaus Pevsner. New York, Universe Books [1960] [51]p. illus. (1 fold), port., plans, 17cm. (Universe architecture series) 60-12418 1.50 pap.,
I. Title.

Wren, Christopher, Sir, 1632-1723—Juvenile literature.

GOULD, Heywood. 720'.92'4
Sir Christopher Wren: Renaissance architect, philosopher and scientist. London, New York, Franklin Watts Ltd, 1970, [i.e. 1972] x, 3-216 p. illus., plans, ports. 23 cm. Bibliography: p. [208] [NA997.W8G6 1972] 73-154615 ISBN 0-85166-316-8 £1.25
1. Wren, Christopher, Sir, 1632-1723—Juvenile literature.

GOULD, Heywood. 720'.924 B
Sir Christopher Wren; Renaissance architect, philosopher, and scientist. New York, Watts [1970] x, 216 p. illus., ports. 22 cm. (Immortals of history) Bibliography: p. [208] A biography of the architect who helped rebuild London after the fire of 1666 and who redesigned St. Paul's Cathedral. [NA997.W8G6] 92 75-101752
1. Wren, Christopher, Sir, 1632-1723—Juvenile literature. I. Title.

Wright, Frank Lloyd, 1867-1959.

BROOKS, Harold Allen, 1925- 720'.977
The prairie school : Frank Lloyd Wright and his midwest contemporaries / H. Allen Brooks. New York : Norton, [1976], c1972. p. cm. (The Norton library) Includes index. Bibliography: p. [NA722.B7 1976] 76-16576 ISBN 0-393-00811-8 pbk. : 7.95
1. Wright, Frank Lloyd, 1867-1959. 2. Prairie School (Architecture) 3. Architecture, Modern—20th century—Middle West. I. Title. BIP

BROOKS, Harold Allen, 1925- 724.9
The prairie school; Frank Lloyd Wright and his midwest contemporaries [by] H. Allen Brooks. [Toronto, University of Toronto Press, 1972] xxiii, 373 p. illus. 23 cm. Bibliography: p. [349]-352. [NA722.B7 1972] 72-151363 ISBN 0-8020-5251-7 25.00
1. Wright, Frank Lloyd, 1867-1959. 2. Prairie School (Architecture) 3. Architecture—Middle West. 4. Architecture, Modern—20th century—Middle West. I. Title.

COWLES, Linn Ann. 720'.92'4 B
An index and guide to An autobiography, the 1943 edition, by Frank Lloyd Wright / prepared by Linn Ann Cowles. [Hopkins, Minn.] : Greenwich Design, c1976. 113 leaves ; 22 x 23 cm. [NA737.W7A323] 77-150602
1. Wright, Frank Lloyd, 1867-1959. An autobiography—Indexes. I. Title.

DEZZI Bardeschi, Marco. 720'.92'4
Frank Lloyd Wright; [translated from the Italian]. London, New York, Hamlyn, 1972. 94 p. illus. (some col.), ports. 32 cm. (Twentieth-century masters) Bibliography: p. 94. [NA737.W7D413 1972] 73-168581 ISBN 0-600-39205-8 £2.25
1. Wright, Frank Lloyd, 1867-1957.

EATON, Leonard K. 720'.922
Two Chicago architects and their clients: Frank Lloyd Wright and Howard Van Doren Shaw [by] Leonard K. Eaton, with an appendix by Elizabeth M. Douvan. Cambridge, Mass., MIT Press [1969] ix, 259 p. illus., plans, ports. 27 cm. Bibliography: p. 239-242. [NA736.E15] 69-12752 ISBN 0-262-05007-2 10.00
1. Wright, Frank Lloyd, 1867-1959. 2. Shaw, Howard Van Doren, 1869-1926. I. Title.

FORSEE, Aylesa. 720.973
Frank Lloyd Wright, rebel in concrete. Philadelphia, Macrae Smith [1959] 181 p. illus. 24 cm. [NA737.W7F6] 59-13256
1. Wright, Frank Lloyd, 1867-1959.

FRANK Lloyd Wright Home and Studio Foundation. Restoration Committee. 728.3'7'0924
The plan for restoration and adaptive use of the Frank Lloyd Wright home and studio / The Restoration Committee of the Frank Lloyd Wright Home and Studio Foundation. Chicago : University of Chicago Press, 1978. ix, 82 p. : ill. ; 28 x 39 cm. [NA7238.O28F7 1978] 78-67224 ISBN 0-226-90832-1 : 25.00
1. Wright, Frank Lloyd, 1867-1959—Homes and haunts. 2. Oak Park, Ill. Frank Lloyd Wright House. 3. Oak Park, Ill. Frank Lloyd Wright Studio. 4. Architecture—Illinois—Oak Park—Conservation and restoration. I. Title.

GUGGENHEIM, Solomon R., Foundation 708.1471
The Solomon R. Guggenheim Museum. Architect: Frank Lloyd Wright. New York [dist. Horizon Press] [c.1960] 72p. (chiefly illus., ports., one foldout) 26cm. 60-13748 3.95
1. Wright. Frank Lloyd, 2. Solomon R. Guggenheim Museum, New York. I. Title.

HANKS, David A. 745.4'49'24
The decorative designs of Frank Lloyd Wright / David A. Hanks. 1st ed. New York : Dutton, c1979. xx, [1], 232 p., [8] leaves of plates : ill. ; 24 cm. "Published in association with an exhibition originated by Renwick Gallery of the National Collection of Fine Arts, Smithsonian Institution, Washington, D.C." Includes index. Bibliography: 21st prelim. page. [NK1535.W74H36 1979] 78-55777 ISBN 0-525-08958-6 : 16.95. ISBN 0-525-47477-3 pbk. : 9.95
1. Wright, Frank Lloyd, 1867-1959. 2. Design, Decorative—United States. BIP

HITCHCOCK, Henry Russell, 1903- 720'.92'4
In the nature of materials, 1887-1941; the buildings of Frank Lloyd Wright. New foreword and bibliography by the author. New York, Da Capo Press, 1973 [c1942] xlix, 143 p. illus. 22 cm. (Da Capo Press series in architecture and decorative art, v.

28) Bibliography: p. xxxix-xlv. [NA737.W7H5 1973] 72-75322 ISBN 0-306-71283-0 18.50
1. Wright, Frank Lloyd, 1867-1959. I. Title.

HITCHCOCK, Henry Russell, 1903- 720'.92'4
In the nature of materials, 1887-1941 : the buildings of Frank Lloyd Wright / Henry-Russell Hitchcock new foreword and bibliography by the author New York : Da Capo Press, [1975] c1942. p. cm. (A Da Capo paperback) Reprint of the ed. published by Hawthorn Books, New York. Includes index. [NA737.W7H5 1975] 75-14322 ISBN 0-306-80019-5 pbk. : 5.95
1. Wright, Frank Lloyd, 1867-1959. I. Title. BIP

HOFFMANN, Donald. 728.3'7'0924
Frank Lloyd Wright's Fallingwater : the house and its history / by Donald Hoffmann ; with an introd. by Edgar Kaufmann, Jr. New York : Dover Publications, 1978. 98 p. : ill. ; 28 cm. Includes bibliographical references and index. [NA737.W7H6] 77-81471 ISBN 0-486-23671-4 pbk. 5.00
1. Wright, Frank Lloyd, 1867-1959. 2. Edgar J. Kaufmann House (Bear Run, Pa.) I. Title. BIP

JACOBS, Herbert Austin. 724.90924 B
Frank Lloyd Wright; America's greatest architect [by] Herbert Jacobs. [1st ed.] New York, Harcourt, Brace & World [1965] 223 p. illus., ports. 22 cm. Bibliographical references included in "Notes" (p. [214]-217) [NA737.W7J3] 65-25306
1. Wright, Frank Lloyd, 1867-1959.

JACOBS. HERBERT AUSTIN 724.90924
Frank Lloyd Wright: America's greatest architect. New York, Harcourt [c.1965] 223p. illus., ports. 22cm. Bibl. [NA737.W7J3] 65-25306 3.95
1. Wright. Frank Lloyd, 1869-1959. I. Title.

JAMES, Cary, 1935- 728.5'0924
The Imperial Hotel; Frank Lloyd Wright and the architecture of unity. Rutland, Vt., C. E. Tuttle Co. [1968] 46, [79] p. illus., 6 fold. plans. 27 cm. "Quotations from Frank Lloyd Wright": p. 23-46. Bibliography: p. [125] [NA737.W7J33] 68-25888 7.50
1. Wright, Frank Lloyd, 1867-1959. 2. Teikoku Hoteru. I. Title.

NADEN, Corinne J. 730'.924 B
Frank Lloyd Wright, the rebel architect, by Corinne J. Naden. Illustrated with photos. New York, F. Watts [1968] 147 p. illus., ports. 22 cm. (Immortals of engineering) Bibliography: p. 143-144. [NA737.W7N3] 68-10349
1. Wright, Frank Lloyd, 1867-1959.

NADEN, Corinne J. 720'.924 B
Frank Lloyd Wright, the rebel architect, by Corrine J. Naden. Illustrated with photos. New York, F. Watts [1968] 147 p. illus., ports. 22 cm. (Immortals of engineering) Bibliography: p. 143-144. During a professional career of sixty-six years Wright designed 600 buildings. His designs were uncluttered, his life chaotic. This is the story of the conflict. [NZ737.W7N3] 92 AC 68
1. Wright, Frank Lloyd, 1869-1959. I. Title.

RICHARDS, Kenneth G., 1926- 720'.924 B
Frank Lloyd Wright [by] Kenneth G. Richards. Chicago, Childrens Press [1968] 95 p. illus., ports. 29 cm. (People of destiny: a humanities series) Bibliography: p. 92. A biography of the man whose new concept of design revolutionized the development of American architecture in the twentieth century. [NA737.W7R5] 92 AC 68
I. Title.

SCULLY, Vincent Joseph, 1920- 720.973
Frank Lloyd Wright. New York, G. Braziller, 1960. 125 p. plates, port., plans. 26 cm. (The Masters of world architecture series) "Bibliographical note": p. 117-118. [NA737.W7S3] 60-6075
1. Wright, Frank Lloyd, 1867-1959. I. Title. II. Series.

SERGEANT, John, 1939- 728.6'4
Frank Lloyd Wright's Usonian houses : the case for organic architecture / by John Sergeant. New York : Whitney Library of Design, 1976. 207 p. : ill. ; 26 cm. Includes index. Bibliography: p. 203. [NA737.W7S4] 76-7281 ISBN 0-8230-7177-4 : 24.50
*1. Wright, Frank Lloyd, 1867-1959. 2. Usonian houses—United States. I. Title.*BIP

SMITH, Norris Kelly. 720.924 B
Frank Lloyd Wright; a study in architectural content. Englewood Cliffs, N.J., Prentice-Hall [1966] 178 p. illus. 21 cm. (A Spectrum book) Bibliographical footnotes. [NA737.W7S44] 66-23438
1. Wright, Frank Lloyd, 1867-1959. I. Title.

SPRAGUE, Paul E. 917.73'1
Frank Lloyd Wright and Prairie School architecture in Oak Park / Paul E. Sprague. 2d ed. Oak Park, Ill. : Oak Park Bicentennial Commission of the American Revolution ; Chicago : distributed by Follett Pub. Co., 1978. 96 p. : ill. ; 23 cm. On cover: Guide to Frank Lloyd Wright and Prairie School architecture in Oak Park. Includes index. [NA735.O24S67 1978] 78-54948 ISBN 0-695-81213-0 : 3.50
1. Wright, Frank Lloyd, 1867-1959. 2. Architecture—Illinois—Oak Park—Guide-books. 3. Prairie School (Architecture) I. Title.

STORRER, William Allin. 720'.92'4
The architecture of Frank Lloyd Wright, a complete catalog. Cambridge, Mass., MIT Press [1974] 1 v. (unpaged) illus. 21 cm. [NA737.W7S83 1974] 73-11300 ISBN 0-262-19097-4 15.00
1. Wright, Frank Lloyd, 1869-1959. I. Wright, Frank Lloyd, 1869-1959. II. Title.

TAFEL, Edgar. 720'.92'4 B
Apprentice to genius : years with Frank Lloyd Wright / Edgar Tafel. New York : McGraw-Hill, c1979. 228 p. : ill. (some col.) ; 29 cm. Includes index. [NA737.W7T33] 78-18504 ISBN 0-07-062815-7 : 19.50
1. Wright, Frank Lloyd, 1867-1959. 2. Tafel, Edgar. 3. Architects—United States—Biography. I. Title.

TAFEL, Edgar. 720'.92'4 B
Apprentice to genius : years with Frank Lloyd Wright / Edgar Tafel. New York : McGraw-Hill, c1979. 228 p. : ill. (some col.) ; 29 cm. Includes index. [NA737.W7T33] 78-18504 ISBN 0-07-062815-7 : 19.50
1. Wright, Frank Lloyd, 1867-1959. 2. Tafel, Edgar. 3. Architects—United States—Biography. I. Title. BIP

TWOMBLY, Robert C. 720'.92'4 B
Frank Lloyd Wright; an interpretive biography, by Robert C. Twombly. [1st ed.] New York, Harper & Row [1973] x, 373 p. illus. 22 cm. Bibliography: p. 343-362. [NA737.W7T94 1973] 72-9248 ISBN 0-06-014467-X 10.00
1. Wright, Frank Lloyd, 1867-1959.

TWOMBLY, Robert C. 720'.92'4
Frank Lloyd Wright; an interpretive biography by Robert C. Twombly. New York, Harper & Row [1974, c1973] x, 373 p. illus. 20 cm. (A Harper colophon book) Bibliography: p. 343-362. [NA737.W7T94 1974] ISBN 0-06-090359-7 3.95 (pbk.)
1. Wright, Frank Lloyd, 1867-1959. I. Title.
L.C. card number for hardbound ed.: 72-9248

TWOMBLY, Robert C. 720'.92'4 B
Frank Lloyd Wright, his life and his architecture / Robert C. Twombly. New York : Wiley, c1979. x, 444 p. : ill. ; 24 cm. "A Wiley-Interscience publication." Includes index. Bibliography: p. 423-434. [NA737.W7T95] 78-9466 ISBN 0-470-03400-2 : 19.95
1. Wright, Frank Lloyd, 1867-1959. 2. Wright, Frank Lloyd, 1867-1959—Influence. 3. Architects—United States—Biography. I. Title.

WILSON, Richard Guy, 1940- 720'.9777
The Prairie School in Iowa / Richard Guy Wilson, Sidney K. Robinson. 1st ed. Ames : Iowa State University Press, 1977. p. cm. Includes bibliographical references. [NA730.I8W54] 77-2788 ISBN 0-8138-0915-0 pbk. : 6.50
1. Wright, Frank Lloyd, 1867-1959. 2. Sullivan, Louis Henri, 1856-1924. 3. Prairie School (Architecture) 4. Architecture—Iowa. 5. Architecture, Modern—20th century—Iowa. I. Robinson, Sidney K., 1943- joint author. II. Title. BIP

WRIGHT, Frank Lloyd, 1867-1959. 720'.92'4 B
An autobiography / Frank Lloyd Wright. New York : Horizon Press, c1977. 620 p., [20] leaves of plates : ill. ; 24 cm. Includes index. [NA737.W7A3 1977] 72-86739 ISBN 0-8180-0222-0 : 17.50
1. Wright, Frank Lloyd, 1867-1959. 2. Architects—United States—Biography.

WRIGHT, Frank Lloyd, 1867-1959. 720.973
Drawings for a living architecture. [Introductory essays by Giuseppe Samona and A. Hyatt Mayor] New York, Published for the Bear Run Foundation and the Edgar J. Kaufman Charitable Foundation by Horizon Press, 1959. 255 p. illus. (part col.) group port. 30 x 35 cm. [NA737.W7A443] 59-10989
I. Title.

WRIGHT, Frank Lloyd, 1867-1959. 720.973
The drawings of Frank Lloyd Wright [by] Arthur Drexler. New York, Published for the Museum of Modern Art by Horizon Press [1962] 320 p. plates, plans. 30 cm. [NA737.W7D7] 62-11236
I. Drexler, Arthur. II. New York. Museum of Modern Art.

WRIGHT, Frank Lloyd, 1867-1959. 720'.22'2
Frank Lloyd Wright : fifty-nine drawings / compiled by the Frank Lloyd Wright Memorial Foundation. [Phoenix? Ariz.] : The Foundation, c1976. 2 p., 59 leaves : ill. ; 22 x 29 cm. [NA737.W7A453] 77-354138
1. Wright, Frank Lloyd, 1867-1959. I. Frank Lloyd Wright Foundation.

WRIGHT, Frank Lloyd, 1867-1959. 720'.924
Frank Lloyd Wright. Introd. and notes by Martin Pawley. With 68 photos. by Yukio Futagawa. New York, Simon and Schuster [1970- v. illus. (part col.), plans. 27 cm. (Library of contemporary architects) Volume 1 "first published in Japan in 1967 ... New texts have been provided for this English language edition." Contents.Contents.—1. Public buildings. Bibliography: v. 1, p. 127. [NA737.W7A448] 78-118015 ISBN 0-671-20689-3 (v. 1) 7.50 (v. 1)
I. Pawley, Martin. II. Futagawa, Yukio, 1932- illus.

WRIGHT, Frank Lloyd, 1867-1959. 730'.92'4
Nakoma-Nakomis : Winnebago Indian memorials : two sculptures by Frank Lloyd Wright, 1924, bronze edition, 1974. [Scottsdale, Ariz.] : Frank Lloyd Wright Foundation, [1974] [12] p. : ill. ; 23 cm. Cover title: Indian memorials. [NB237.W74F72] 75-304574
1. Wright, Frank Lloyd, 1867-1959. Nakoma. 2. Wright, Frank Lloyd, 1867-1959. Nakomis. I. Frank Lloyd Wright Foundation. II. Title. III. Title: Indian memorials.

WRIGHT, Frank Lloyd, 1867-1959. 726'.3'0924
Pfeiffer Chapel, Florida Southern College, Lakeland, Florida, 1938 : Beth Sholom Synagogue, Elkins Park, Pennsylvania, 1954 / Frank Lloyd Wright ; edited and photographed by Yukio Futagawa ; text by Bruce Brooks Pfeiffer. Tokyo : A.D.A. Edita, [1976] 39 p. : chiefly ill. ; 37 cm. (Global architecture ; 40) Text in English and Japanese. [NA737.W7F8735] 77-354934
1. Wright, Frank Lloyd, 1867-1959. 2. Ann Pfeiffer Chapel, Lakeland, Fla. 3. Beth Sholom Synagogue, Elkins Park, Pa. I. Futagawa, Yukio, 1932- II. Pfeiffer, Bruce Brooks. III. Title.

WRIGHT, Frank Lloyd, 1867-1959. 720'.22'2
Studies and executed buildings = Ausgefuhrte Bauten und Entwurfe / by Frank Lloyd Wright. Palos Park, Ill. : Prairie School Press, 1975. ca. 250 p. : chiefly ill. ; 24 x 38 cm. [NA737.W7A47] 75-27623 ISBN 0-87370-001-5 : 40.00
1. Wright, Frank Lloyd, 1867-1959. I. Title. II. Title: Ausgefuhrte Bauten und Entwurfe. BIP

WRIGHT, Frank Lloyd, 1869-1959. 720'.924
Frank Lloyd Wright: the early work. New York, Horizon Press, 1968. xvi, 140 p. illus. 34 cm. Translation of Ausgefuhrte Bauten, originally published 1911. [NA737.W7A4613] 68-54184 15.00

WRIGHT, Frank Lloyd, 1869-1959. 927.2
A testament. New York, Horizon Press [1957] 256 p. illus., plans. 31 cm. [NA737.W7A33] 57-14545 201 A0036399WRIGHT, Olgivanna

WRIGHT, Olgivanna Lloyd. 720.924 B
Frank Lloyd Wright: his life, his work, his words. New York, Horizon Press [1966] 224 p. illus., ports. 26 cm. Bibliography: p. 223-224. [NA737.W7W725] 66-26703
1. Wright, Frank Lloyd, 1867-1959.

WRIGHT, Olgivanna Lloyd. 927.2
Our house. New York, Horizon Press, 1959. 308 p. illus. 23 cm. Autobiographical. [NA737.W7W73] 59-9252
1. Wright, Frank Lloyd, 1867-1959. I. Title.

WRIGHT, Olgivanna Lloyd. 927.2
The roots of life. New York, Horizon Press, 1963. 256 p. 23 cm. [NA737.W7W736] 63-21570
1. Wright, Frank Lloyd, 1869-1959. I. Title. BIP

WRIGHT, Olgivanna Lloyd. 720.973
The shining brow; Frank Lloyd Wright. New York, Horizon Press, 1960. 300 p. illus., ports. 23 cm. [NA737.W7W74] 60-1926
1. Wright, Frank Lloyd, 1869-1959. I. Title. BIP

Wright, Frank Lloyd, 1867-1959—Catalogs.

STORRER, William Allin. 720'.92'4
The architecture of Frank Lloyd Wright : a complete catalog / William Allin Storrer. 2d ed. Cambridge, Mass. : MIT Press, c1978. p. cm. Includes indexes. [NA737.W7A4 1978] 78-1306 ISBN 0-262-19171-7 : 15.00
1. Wright, Frank Lloyd, 1867-1959—Catalogs. I. Wright, Frank Lloyd, 1867-1959. II. Title. BIP

Wright, Frank Lloyd, 1867-1959—Juvenile literature.

RANSOHOFF, Doris. 92
Frank Lloyd Wright; living architecture. Chicago, Britannica Books [1962] 190p. illus. 22cm. (Britannica bookshelf: Great lives for young Americans) [NA737.W7R3] 62-19372
1. Wright, Frank Lloyd, 1869-1959—Juvenile literature. I. Title.

RICHARDS, Kenneth G., 1926- 92 (j)
Frank Lloyd Wright [by] Kenneth G. Richards. Chicago, Childrens Press [1968] 95 p. illus., ports. 29 cm. (People of destiny: a humanities series) Bibliography: p. 92. [NA737.W7R5] 68-31305
1. Wright, Frank Lloyd, 1867-1959—Juvenile literature.

WILLARD, Charlotte. 720'.9'24 B
Frank Lloyd Wright, American architect. New York, Macmillan [1972] xiv, 183 p. illus. 21 cm. A biography of the man whose new concept of design revolutionized the development of American architecture in the twentieth century. [NA737.W7W54] 92 71-188775 5.95
1. Wright, Frank Lloyd, 1867-1959—Juvenile literature. I. Title.

RANSOHOFF, Doris. j 92
Living architecture: Frank Lloyd Wright. Chicago, Britannica Books [1962] 190 p. illus. 22 cm. (Britannica bookshelf: Great lives for young Americans) [NA737.W7R3] 62-19372
1. Wright, Frank Lloyd, 1869-1959 — Juvenile literature. I. Title.

SALSINI, Paul. 720'.92'4 B
Frank Lloyd Wright, the architectural genius of the twentieth century. Charlotteville, N.Y., SamHar Press, 1971. 32 p. 22 cm. (Outstanding personalities, no. 2) Bibliography: p. 31-32. A brief biography of the architect responsible for some of the most innovative structures of the twentieth century. [NA737.W7S27] 92 77-185658
1. Wright, Frank Lloyd, 1869-1959— Juvenile literature. I. Title.

Wright, Lloyd, 1890—

CALIFORNIA. University, Santa Barbara. Art Galleries. 720'.92'4
Lloyd Wright, architect; 20th century architecture in an organic exhibition. An exhibition organized by David Gebhard and Harriette Von Breton for the Art Galleries, University of California, Santa Barbara, Nov. 23 to Dec. 22, 1971. [Santa Barbara, 1971] 101 p. illus. 29 cm. Bibliography: p. 81. [NA737.W72C3] 73-634352
1. Wright, Lloyd, 1890- I. Gebhard, David. II. Von Breton, Harriette.

Wright, Patience.

SELLERS, Charles Coleman, 1903- 736'.93'0924 B
Patience Wright, American artist and spy in George III's London / by Charles Coleman Sellers. 1st ed. Middletown, Conn. : Wesleyan University Press, c1976. x, 281 p., [12] leaves of plates : ill. ; 24 cm. Includes bibliographical references and index. [NK9582.W74S44] 76-7193 ISBN 0-8195-5001-9 : 14.95
1. Wright, Patience. 2. Wax-modeling— United States. I. Title.

Wright, Virginia—Art collections.

CHAMBERS, Marlene. 759.13'074'018883
American art since 1960 : the Virginia and Bagley Wright Collection : Denver Art Museum, February 1-March 16, 1975 / [text by Marlene Chambers Denver : Denver Art Museum, 1975. [23] p. : ill. (some col.) ; 23 x 28 cm. Bibliography: p. [23] [N6512.C45] 74-33089 ISBN 0-914738-08-9
1. Wright, Virginia—Art collections. 2. Wright, Bagley—Art collections. 3. Art, American—Exhibitions. 4. Art, Modern— 20th century—United States. I. Denver. Art Museum. II. Title. III. Title: The Virginia and Bagley Wright collection.

Wrightsman, Charles B.—Art collections.

NEW York (City). Metropolitan Museum of Art. 739.2'274'07401471
Gold boxes : the Wrightsman collection / text by Clare Le Corbeiller ; photos. by Malcolm Varon. New York : Metropolitan Museum of Art, c1977. p. cm. Catalog of a permanent exhibit at the Metropolitan Museum of Art, New York. [NK7102.N4N476 1977] 77-23592 ISBN 0-87099-166-3 pbk. : 4.95
1. Wrightsman, Charles B.—Art collections. 2. New York (City). Metropolitan Museum of Art. 3. Gold boxes—New York (City)—Catalogs. 4. Goldwork, Rococo—New York (City)— Catalogs. I. Le Corbeiller, Clare. II. Varon, Malcolm. III. Title.

Writing.

FAIRBANK, Alfred J. 652
A book of scripts, by Alfred Fairbank. Rev. enl. ed. Baltimore, Md., Penguin Books [1968] 44 p. facsims., 80 plates. 20 cm. (Pelican books) Bibliography: p. 39-[42] [Z40.F3 1968b] 72-4662 1.95
1. Writing. I. Title.

FAIRBANK, Alfred J. 745.6'1
A book of scripts, by Alfred Fairbank. Revised and enlarged ed. Harmondsworth, Penguin, 1968. 47 p. 80 plates, illus., facsims. 20 cm. (Pelican books, A973) Bibliography: p. 39-[42] [Z40.F3 1968] 70-399628 10/-
1. Writing. I. Title. BIP

FAIRBANK, Alfred J. 745.6'197
A book of scripts / by Alfred Fairbank. [New ed.]. London : Faber, 1977. 47 p., 80 p. of plates : ill., facsims. ; 21 cm. Includes bibliographical references. [Z40.F3 1977] 77-378016 ISBN 0-571-10876-8 : 7.95 ISBN 0-571-11080-0 pbk. : 7.95
1. Writing. I. Title.

LINDEGREN, Erik, 1919- 745.6'1
An ABC-book / Erik Lindegren. Askim : E. Lindegren grafisk studio, [1976?] 199 p. : ill. ; 18 x 26 cm. "Supposed to be a compilation of the three parts of ABC of lettering and printing types ... but also a substitute for them." [Z40.L57] 77-556283
1. Writing. 2. Lettering. 3. Type and type-founding. I. Title.

Writing—History.

ETIEMBLE, Rene, 1909- 411.09
The Orion book of the written word. [Translated from the French, L'Ecriture, by Rebecca Abramson] New York, Orion Press [1961] 114 p. illus. (part col.) 20 x 22 cm. [Z40.E813] 61-14187
1. Writing—History. I. Title.

FAIRBANK, Alfred J. 745.6'1
The story of handwriting; origins and development [by] Alfred Fairbank. New York, Watson-Guptill [1970] 108 p. illus. (part col.) 22 cm. Bibliography: p. 102-103. [Z40.F33] 77-84820 7.95
1. Writing—History. 2. Penmanship. I. Title.

FRAENKEL, Gerd. 411.09
Writing systems. Boston, Ginn [1965] iii, 134 p. illus., maps. 21 cm. (New aspects of language, 2) A Ginn English monograph. [Z40.F7] 65-28532
1. Writing — Hist. I. Title. II. Series.

GOAMAN, Muriel. 411
How writing began; illus. by Neil Hyslop. London, Faber, 1966. Label mounted on t. p.: Sole dist. for the U. S. A. Transatlantic, New York. 46p. illus., table. 21cm. [Z40.G6] 68-87272 250
1. Writing—Hist.—Juvenile literature. I. Title.
Available from the publisher's Levittown, N. Y. office.

MORISON, Stanley, 1889-1967. 745.6'197
Politics and script: aspects of authority and freedom in the development of Graeco-Latin script from the sixth century B.C. to the twentieth century A.D.; edited and completed by Nicolas Barker. Oxford, Clarendon Press, 1972. [5], 361 p. illus., facsims. 28 cm. (The Lyell lectures, 1957) Lectures delivered in 1957, reworked and elaborated for publication. Bibliography: p. 341-345. [Z40.M67 1972] 72-194122 ISBN 0-19-818146-9 £6.00
1. Writing—History. 2. Paleography. 3. Lettering. I. Barker, Nicolas, ed. II. Title. III. Series. BIP

Writing—History—Juvenile literature.

ROBINSON, J. A. 001.54'3
Looking at language [by] J. A. Robinson. Line drawings by Constance and Brian Dear. London, Routledge & K. Paul [1974] x, 70 p. illus. 24 cm. (The Local search series) [Z40.R62] 74-185886 ISBN 0-7100-7589-8 5.75
1. Writing—History—Juvenile literature. I. Title.
Distributed by Routledge & Kegan Paul, Boston. BIP

TAYLOR, Margaret C. 411
Wht's yr nm? Written and illustrated by Margaret C. Taylor. [1st. ed.] New York, Harcourt, Brace & World [1970] 61 p. illus. 22 cm. Explains how written language began with the concept of symbols that evolved into the alphabet we know today. [Z40.T3] 70-94334 3.50
1. Writing—History—Juvenile literature. I. Title.

Writing in art.

NEW York. Museum of Modern Art 745.6
Lettering by modern artists. Dist., Garden City, N.Y., Doubleday [1964] 1v. (unpaged) illus. (pt. col.) facsims. 21x25cm. [N8265.N48] 64-18332 2.50 pap.,
1. Writing in art. 2. Art—Exhibitions. I. Title.

Writing, Italic.

AARON, William Metcalf. 745.6'197
Italic writing; a concise guide [by] W. M. Aaron. [1st American ed.] New York, Transatlantic Arts, 1971 [c1969] 110 p. illus. 22 cm. [Z43.A42 1971b] 77-151718 6.25
1. Writing, Italic. BIP

BOARDWELL, Robert. 745.6'197
Beginning calligraphy; a guide to italic writing. Introd. by Lloyd Reynolds. Beaverton, Or., Touchstone Press [1974] 115 p. illus. 28 cm. Bibliography: p. 115. [Z43.B69] 74-76842 ISBN 0-911518-24-X 4.95
1. Writing, Italic. I. Title.

EAGER, Fred. 652'.1
The italic way to beautiful handwriting, cursive & calligraphic. New York, Macmillan [1974] 113 p. illus. 29 cm. [Z43.E118 1974b] 74-10506 ISBN 0-02-534580-X
1. Writing, Italic. I. Title.

EAGER, Fred. 652'.1
The italic way to beautiful handwriting, cursive and calligraphic. New York, Collier Books [1974] p. cm. [Z43.E118 1974] 74-10505 ISBN 0-02-079990-X 2.95 (pbk.)
1. Writing, Italic. I. Title.

FAIRBANK, Alfred J. 745.6'197
A handwriting manual [by] Alfred Fairbank. [9th ed.] New York, Watson-Guptill Publications [1975] 144 p. illus. 23 cm. Bibliography: p. 92-94. [Z43.F16 1975] 74-14984 ISBN 0-8230-2185-8 8.50
1. Writing, Italic. I. Title. BIP

GOURDIE, Tom. 652.1
Italic handwriting. London, New York, Studio Publications [1955] 96 p. illus. 19 cm. [Z43.G68] 55-3419
1. Writing, Italic. BIP

GOURDIE, Tom. 652.1
Italic handwriting. [Rev. ed.] New York, Viking Press [1964] 96 p. illus. 19 cm. (A Studio book) [Z115.I 8G6 1964] 64-2567
1. Writing, Italic. I. Title.

RUDLAND, Peter. 652.1
From scribble to script. New York, J. De Graff [1956] 123p. illus. 23cm. [Z43] 57-2244
1. Writing, Italic. I. Title.

WARDROP, James, d.1957. 417
The script of humanism; some aspects of humanistic script, 1460-1560. Oxford, Clarendon Press, 1963. xiv, 57 p. 58 facsims. 28 cm. A series of lectures delivered in March 1952 at King's College, University of London, under the title: Some aspects of humanistic script, 1460-1560. Bibliographical footnotes. [Z115.I8W3] 63-5964
1. Writing, Italic. I. Title.

Writing, Italic—Juvenile literature.

EAGER, Fred. 745.6'197
Italic handwriting for young people / Fred Eager. New York : Macmillan, c1978. p. cm. Introduces basic techniques of italic handwriting. [Z43.E117 1978] 78-1944 ISBN 0-02-534570-2 : 7.95
1. Writing, Italic—Juvenile literature. I. Title. BIP

EAGER, Fred. 745.6'197
Italic handwriting for young people / by Fred Eager. New York : Collier Books, 1978. 116 p. : ill. ; 28 cm. Introduces basic techniques of italic handwriting. [Z43.E117 1978b] 78-1945 ISBN 0-02-079960-8 pbk. : 4.95
1. Writing, Italic—Juvenile literature. I. Title.

Wunder, Richard P.—Art collections.

WUNDER, Richard P. 720'.28
Architectural, ornament, landscape, and figure drawings / collected by Richard Wunder. Middlebury, Vt. : Middlebury College, 1975. 200 p. : ill. ; 28 cm. Catalogue of an exhibition. Includes bibliographical references and index. [NC15.M5M528] 74-28546 7.50
1. Wunder, Richard P.—Art collections. 2. Drawings—Exhibitions. 3. Artists' preparatory studies—Exhibitions. I. Middlebury College, Middlebury, Vt. II. Title.

Wunderman, Lester—Art collections.

LAUDE, Jean. 732'.2'096623
African art of the Dogon; the myths of the cliff dwellers. [Translation by Joachim Neugroschel] Foreword by Lester Wunderman. New York, Brooklyn Museum in association with the Viking Press [1973] 60, [71] p. illus. (part col.) 25 cm. (A Studio book) Issued in connection with an exhibition of L. Wunderman's private collection of Dogon art, organized by the Brooklyn Museum in 1973. "The catalogue": p. [65]-[129] Bibliography: p. [130]-[131] [N7399.M3L3 1973] 72-12060 ISBN 0-670-10928-2 10.00
1. Wunderman, Lester—Art collections. 2. Art, Dogon. I. Brooklyn Institute of Arts and Sciences. Museum. II. Title.

Wyatville, Jeffry, Sir, 1776-1840.

LINSTRUM, Derek. 720'.92'4
Sir Jeffry Wyatville: architect to the king. Oxford, Clarendon Press, [1973, c1972] xvi, 279 p., [3] fold. leaves. illus., geneal. table, plans, ports. 30 cm. (Oxford studies in the history of art and architecture) Bibliography: p. [270]-271. [NA997.W95L56] 73-154086 ISBN 0-19-817190-0
1. Wyatville, Jeffry, Sir, 1776-1840. I. Title. II. Series.
Distributed by Oxford University Press N.Y; 32.00.

Wyeth, Andrew, 1917-

ARIZONA. University. Art Gallery. 709.73
Andrew Wyeth; an exhibition of watercolors, temperas, and drawings, March 16 through April 14. Tucson [1963] 94 p. illus. (port col.) ports. 26 cm. Includes "Andrew Wyeth: Impressions for a portrait, text by Paul Horgan." [ND1839.W9A7] 63-63092
1. Wyeth, Andrew, 1917- I. Horgan, Paul, 1903- II. Title.

BUFFALO Fine Arts Academy. 759.13
Andrew Wyeth: temperas, water colors, and drawings. November 2-December 9, 1962. Buffalo, Buffalo Fine Arts Academy, Albright-Knox Art Gallery [c1962] 75 p. (chiefly illus. (part col.) ports.) 31 cm. [ND237.W93B8] 63-2363
1. Wyeth, Andrew, 1917- I. Title.

CORN, Wanda M., comp. 759.13
The art of Andrew Wyeth [by] Wanda M. Corn. Greenwich, Conn., New York Graphic Society [1975 c1973] 176 p. ill. 23 cm. by 30 cm. Includes index. Bibliography: p. 166-171. [ND237.W93C67] ISBN 0-8212-0685-0 9.95 (pbk.)
I. Title.
L.C. card no. for original edition: 72-93900.

CORN, Wanda M. 759.13
The art of Andrew Wyeth [by] Wanda M. Corn. With contributions by Brian O'Doherty, Richard Meryman [and] E. P. Richardson. Greenwich, Conn., Published for the Fine Arts Museums of San Francisco by the New York Graphic Society [1973] 176 p. illus. (part col.) 24 x

31 cm. Issued in connection with the exhibition held at the M. H. de Young Memorial Museum of the Fine Arts Museums of San Francisco, June 16-Sept. 3, 1973. Bibliography: p. 166-171. [ND237.W93C67 1973] 72-93900 ISBN 0-8212-0516-1 19.95
1. Wyeth, Andrew, 1917- I. De Young Memorial Museum, San Francisco. II. Title.

HARVARD University. 741.9'73
William Hayes Fogg Art Museum.
Andrew Wyeth: dry brush and pencil drawings; a loan exhibition organized by the Fogg Art Museum 1963. [Cambridge, 1963] [72] p. illus. 22 x 28 cm. Exhibition to be held at the Fogg Art Museum and other places. [NC139.W9H3] 63-1605
1. Wyeth, Andrew, 1917-

LOGSDON, Gene. 759.13 B
Wyeth people; a portrait of Andrew Wyeth as he is seen by his friends and neighbors. Illustrated with photos. by the author. Garden City, N.Y., Doubleday, 1971. 159 p. illus., ports. 22 cm. [ND237.W93L6] 75-147360 5.95
1. Wyeth, Andrew, 1917- I. Title.

PENNSYLVANIA Academy of 759.13
the Fine Arts, Philadelphia
Andrew Wyeth: temperas, watercolors, dry brush, drawings, 1938 into 1966; [exhibition] Pennsylvania Acad. of the Fine Arts, Philadelphia, Oct. 5-Nov. 27, 1966: Baltimore Mus. of Art, Dec. 11, 1966-January 27, 1967; Whitney Mus. of Amer. Art. New York, Feb. 6-April 12, 1967; the Art Inst. of Chicago, April 21-June 4, 1967. [New York, Abercrombie & Fitch, 1966] 111p. illus. (pt. col.) ports. (pt. col.) 26cm. Text by Edgar P. Richardson [ND237.W93P4] 66-27597 4.00 pap.,
1. Wyeth, Andrew, 1917- I. Richardson, Edgar Preston, 1902- II. Title.

WYETH, Andrew, 1917- 760'.0924
Andrew Wyeth [by] Richard Meryman. Boston, Houghton Mifflin, 1968. 174 p. illus. (part col.) 34 x 44 cm. [ND237.W93M4] 67-18254 75.00
I. Meryman, Richard, 1926-

WYETH, Andrew, 1917- 759.13
Andrew Wyeth. Introd. by David McCord. Selection by Frederick A. Sweet. Boston, Museum of Fine Arts [1970] 224 p. illus. (part col.) 22 x 28 cm. Centennial exhibition of the Museum of Fine Arts. [ND237.W93S95] 76-127419
I. Sweet, Frederick Arnold, 1903- ed. II. Boston. Museum of Fine Arts.

WYETH, Andrew, 1917- 759.13
Wyeth at Kuerners. Boston : Houghton Mifflin, 1976. viii, 324 p. : ill. (some col.) ; 26 x 34 cm. Includes index. [ND237.W93W93 (fol.)] 76-6171 ISBN 0-395-21990-6 : 75.00
1. Wyeth, Andrew, 1917- 2. Kuerner, Karl, 1898- —Portraits, etc. 3. Kuerner, Anna—Portraits, etc. 4. Farm life in art. I. Title.

Wyeth, Andrew, 1917- —Catalogs.

MORTENSON, C. Walter. 741.9'73
The illustrations of Andrew Wyeth : a check list / by C. Walter Mortenson. West Chester, Penn. : Aralia Press, 1977. 12 p., [1] leaf of plates : ill. (some col.) ; 22 cm. [NC975.5.M67A4 1977] 77-155056
1. Wyeth, Andrew, 1917- —Catalogs. I. Title.

Wyeth, Andrew, 1917- —Exhibitions.

WYETH, Andrew, 1917- 759.13
Two worlds of Andrew Wyeth : a conversation with Andrew Wyeth / by Thomas Hoving. Boston : Houghton Mifflin, 1978, c1976. p. cm. Originally published as the catalog of an exhibition held at the Metropolitan Museum of Art, New York. [ND237.W93A4 1978] 78-16545 ISBN 0-395-27089-8 : 25.00. ISBN 0-395-27080-4 pbk. : 10.00
1. Wyeth, Andrew, 1917- —Exhibitions. I. Hoving, Thomas Pearsall Field, 1931- II. New York (City). Metropolitan Museum of Art. III. Title. BIP

Wyeth, Andrew, 1917- —Juvenile literature.

BAKER, Donna. 759.13 B
Andrew Wyeth / by Donna and Eugene Baker. Chicago : Childrens Press, [1976] p. cm. (Artists in America) Includes bibliographical references. Biography of painter Andrew Wyeth, who maintains his family's artistic tradition yet has developed his own unique style. [ND237.W93B34] 92 76-8440 ISBN 0-516-03681-5
1. Wyeth, Andrew, 1917- —Juvenile literature. I. Baker., Eugene H., joint author. II. Title.

Wyeth, Carolyn.

WYETH, Carolyn. 759.13
Carolyn Wyeth : a retrospective exhibition, February 1-March 14, 1976, the R. W. Norton Art Gallery. Shreveport, La. : The Gallery, c1976. 23 p. : ill. (some col.) ; 28 cm. Cover title. [N6537.W88N67] 75-43579 ISBN 0-913060-08-9 pbk. : 2.00
1. Wyeth, Carolyn. I. Norton (R. W.) Art Gallery. BIP

Wyeth family.

WYETH, Newell Convers, 759.13
1882-1945.
The Wyeths; the letters of N. C. Wyeth, 1901-1945. Edited by Betsy James Wyeth. Boston, Gambit, 1971. xii, 858 p. illus. 25 cm. [ND237.W94A3] 73-137021 ISBN 0-87645-046-X 22.50
1. Wyeth family. I. Wyeth, Betsy James, 1921- ed. II. Title.

Wyeth, James, 1946—

WYETH, James, 1946- 759.13
James Wyeth, recent paintings : [exhibition at] Coe Kerr Gallery, Inc. ... New York, November 7-November 25, 1974 [and] Brandywine River Museum ... Chadd's Ford, Pennsylvania, November 29-January 5, 1975. [s.l. : s.n., 1974] [22] p. : chiefly ill. ; 21 cm. [ND237.W935C63] 74-196047
1. Wyeth, James, 1946- I. Coe Kerr Gallery. II. Brandywine River Museum.

Wyeth, James, 1946- —Exhibitions.

WYETH, James, 1946- 759.13
Jamie Wyeth : recent paintings : [exhibition] November 10th-December 3rd, 1977, Coe Kerr Gallery ... New York. New York : The Gallery, c1977. [23] p. : chiefly ill. ; 26 cm. Exhibition also held at Columbus Gallery of Fine Arts, Columbus, Ohio, Jan. 1978. [ND237.W935A4 1977] 77-155990
1. Wyeth, James, 1946- —Exhibitions. I. Coe Kerr Gallery. II. Columbus Gallery of Fine Arts, Columbus, Ohio.

WYETH, James, 1946- 759.13
Oils, watercolors, drawings. [Rockland, Me., Printed by Courier-Gazette, inc., 1969] [35] p. illus. 20 x 29 cm. "[Catalog of a loan] exhibition presented by the William A. Farnsworth Library and Art Museum, Rockland, Maine, July 11-September 8, 1969." [N6537.W9A53] 74-20842
I. William A. Farnsworth Library and Art Museum, Rockland, Me. II. Title.

Wyeth, Newell Convers, 1882-1945.

WYETH, Newell Convers, 741'.092'4
1882-1945.
N. C. Wyeth: the collected paintings, illustrations, and murals. By Douglas Allen and Douglas Allen, Jr. With a foreword by Paul Horgan and an introd. by Richard Layton. New York, Crown Publishers [1972] 335 p. illus. (part col.) 32 cm. "A bibliography of the published works of N. C. Wyeth": [193]-317. [ND237.W94A79 1972] 71-168323 ISBN 0-517-50054-X 29.95
1. Wyeth, Newell Convers, 1882-1945. 2. Wyeth, Newell Convers, 1882-1945—Bibliography. I. Allen, Douglas. II. Allen, Douglas, 1935- BIP

WYETH, Newell Convers, 759.13
1882-1945.
1966 summer exhibition : William H. Farnsworth Library and Art Museum, Rockland, Maine, July 20 - September 4. [Rockland, Me., William A. Farnsworth Library and Art Museum, c1966] [34] p. illus., port. 23 cm. Cover title: An exhibition of paintings from the world of N. C. Wyeth. [ND237.W94W48] 73-682
I. William A. Farnsworth Library and Art Museum, Rockland, Me. II. Title.

Wynter, Bryan, 1915-1975.

WYNTER, Bryan, 1915-1975. 759.2
Bryan Wynter, 1915-1975 : paintings, kinetics and works on paper : [catalogue of an exhibition held at the] Hayward Gallery, London, 5 to 30 August 1976. [London] : Arts Council of Great Britain, 1976. [28] p. : chiefly ill. (some col.), port. ; 30 cm. Bibliography: p. [21]. [N6797.W95H39] 77-361639 ISBN 0-7287-0100-6 : £1.50
1. Wynter, Bryan, 1915-1975. I. Hayward Gallery.

Wyoming—Description and travel—1951- —Views.

LAMB, Russell. 779'.9'91787043
Wyoming / [photos.] by Russell Lamb ; text by Archie Satterfield. Portland, Or. : Graphic Arts Center Pub. Co., c1978. 128 p. (p. 128 blank) : chiefly col. ill. ; 36 cm. [F762.L35] 78-51215 ISBN 0-912856-41-6 : 22.00
1. Wyoming—Description and travel—1951- —Views. I. Satterfield, Archie. II. Title.
Publisher's address : 2000 N.W. Wilson, Portland, OR 97209 BIP

X-ray photogrammetry.

HALLERT, Bertil. 621.36
X-ray photogrammetry. Basic geometry and quality. Amsterdam, New York, Elsevier Pub. Co., 1970. ix, 154 p. 23 cm. Bibliography: p. [149]-150. [TR750.H32] 74-88079 46.80
1. X-ray photogrammetry. I. Title. BIP

Xceron, Jean, 1890-

SOLOMON R. Guggenheim 759.9495
Museum, New York.
Jean Xceron. [Catalogue of exhibition 65/5, September-October, 1965] New York [1965] 59 p. illus. (part col.) ports. 26 cm. Bibliography: p. [52]-53. [ND237.X3S6] 65-26312
1. Xceron, Jean, 1890- I. Title.

Xerography.

COOK, W. A. 686'.44
Electrostatics in reprography, by W. A. Cook. London, New York, Focal P., 1970. 162 p. illus. 23 cm. (The reprographic library) [TR1045.C64] 76-551319 ISBN 0-240-50699-5 35/-
1. Xerography. I. Title. BIP

DESSAUER, John H., ed. 655.328
Xerography and related processes. Ed. by John H. Dessauer, Harold E. Clark. Chapters contrib. by members of the staffs of Res. and Engin. Div. Xerox Corp., and Applied Res. Div., Battelle Memorial Inst. New York, Focal [c.1965] 520p. illus. 25cm. (Focal lib.) Bibl. [TR1045.D4] 65-18645 38.00
1. Xerography. I. Clark, Harold Ernst, joint ed. II. Title. BIP

Xerox Corporation.

DESSAUER, John H. 658'.9'8644
My days with Xerox; the billions nobody wanted [New York Manor Bks. 1973? c.1971] 239 p. 18 cm. [TR1045.D39] pap., 1.50
1. Xerox Corporation. I. Title.

Yale-New Haven Hospital.

THOMPSON, John D. 725'51'09
The hospital : a social and architectural history / John D. Thompson and Grace Goldin. New Haven : Yale University Press, 1975. xxvii, 349 p. : ill. ; 29 cm. Includes index. Bibliography: p. 339-342. [RA967.T5] 74-19574 ISBN 0-300-01829-0 : 25.00
1. Yale-New Haven Hospital. 2. Hospitals—Design and construction—History. 3. Hospital wards. 4. Hospitals—Sociological aspects. 5. Hospital care. I. Goldin, Grace, joint author. II. Title. BIP

Yale University. Mabel Brady Garvan Collection.

YALE University. 681'.113'0973
Art Gallery.
The American clock, 1725-1865; the Mabel Brady Garvan and other collections at Yale University. Essay and technical notes by Edwin A. Battison. Commentary by Patricia E. Kane. Foreword by Charles F. Montgomery. Introd. by Derek de Solla Price. Greenwich, Conn., New York Graphic Society [1973] 207 p. illus. 27 cm. Bibliography: p. 204-205. [NK7492.Y34 1973] 72-93856 ISBN 0-8212-0493-9 16.95
1. Yale University. Mabel Brady Garvan Collection. 2. Clocks and watches, American. I. Battison, Edwin A. II. Kane, Patricia E. III. Title. BIP

Yale University. Mathematics Building.

MOORE, Charles 727'.4'51097468
Willard, 1925- comp.
The Yale Mathematics Building competition : architecture for a time of questioning / Charles W. Moore and Nicholas Pyle, editors. New Haven : Yale University Press, 1974. viii, 117 p. : ill. ; 23 x 29 cm. Includes index. [LD6342.M37M66] 73-77162 ISBN 0-300-01621-2 : 15.00
1. Yale University. Mathematics Building. 2. Architecture—Competitions. 3. Architecture—Designs and plans. I. Pyle, Nicholas, joint comp. II. Title. BIP

Yale University — Portraits.

YALE University. 704.942
Yale University portrait index 1701-1951 New Haven, Yale University Press, 1951. vii, 185 p. illus. 29 cm. [N590.A62] 51-11550
1. Yale University — Portraits. 2. Portraits — Catalogs. I. Title. BIP

Yang, Hanford—Art collections.

ALDRICH Museum of 709'.04
Contemporary Art.
Art of the 60's : selections from the collection of Hanford Yang. [exhibition: September 29 through December 22, 1968.] Ridgefield, Conn., 1968] [39] p. illus. 20 cm. [N6487.R5A43 1968] 74-156512
1. Yang, Hanford—Art collections. 2. Art, Modern—20th century—Exhibitions. I. Title.

Yaqui Indians—Rites and ceremonies.

DEGRAZIA, Ted Ettore, 759.13
1909-
De Grazia paints the Yaqui Easter; forty days of Lent in forty paintings, with a personal commentary. [Tucson] University of Arizona Press [1968] 92 p. col. illus., port. 24 x 32 cm. [ND237.D3337A44] 68-22334
1. Yaqui Indians—Rites and ceremonies. 2. Easter—Art. I. Title. II. Title: The Yaqui Easter. BIP

Yashica camera.

AHLERS, Arvel W., 1915- 770.282
The Yashica guide to picture taking fun for all, by Arvel W. Ahlers. New York, Popular Library [1966] 208 p. illus. (part col.) 18 cm. [TR263.Y3A35] 66-8899
1. Yashica camera. 2. Photography—Handbooks, manuals, etc. I. Title.

EMANUEL, Walter Daniel, 771.3'1
1908-
Yashica 35mm guide. how to use the Yashica 35J, Yashica Minister, Yashica Lynx, Lynx E and Yashica Electro models, by W. D. Emanuel. 2d ed. London, New York, Focal Press; distributed by

Amphoto, New York [1969] 72, [22] p. illus. 17 cm. (Focal camera guides) "The Yashica 35 mm. models" (22 p.) inserted between p. 16-17. [TR263.Y3E44 1969] 72-104669
1. Yashica camera. 2. Photography—Handbooks, manuals, etc. I. Title.

EMANUEL, Walter Daniel, 1908- 771.31
Yashica twin lens reflex guide, by W. D. Emanuel. London, New York, Focal Press [1964] 72 p. illus. 17 cm. (The Camera guide) [TR263.Y3E45] 65-29599
1. Yashica camera. 2. Twin-lens cameras. 3. Photography — Handbooks, manuals, etc. I. Title. II. Series. BIP

EMANUEL, Walter Daniel, 1908- 771.3'1
Yashica twin lens reflex guide: how to use the Yashica A, Yashica B, Yashica C, Yashica D, Yashica E Flash, Yashica 635, Yashica 44A, Yashica-MAT, Yashica 44LM, Yashica MAT LM, Yashica MAT EM and Yashica 24 and MAT 124 cameras, by W. D. Emanuel. 5th ed. London, New York, Focal, 1970. 72 p. illus. 17 cm. (The Camera guide) Distributed in U.S.A. by Amphoto, New York. [TR263.Y3E45 1970] 78-114434 ISBN 0-240-38817-8 13/-
1. Yashica camera. 2. Twin-lens cameras. 3. Photography—Handbooks, manuals, etc. I. Title.

JONAS, Paul. 771.31
Yashica Pentamatic guide. New York, Universal Photo Books [c1961] 128p. illus. 21cm. [TR263.Y3J6] 61-14257
1. Yashica camera. 2. Photography—Handbooks, manuals, etc. I. Title.

LOWELL, Richard 770.28
Yashica guide, 2d ed., rev New York, Amphoto-Universal [1963,c. 1959] 136p. illus. 20cm. 63-71 1.95pap.,
1. Yashica camera. I. Title. BIP

LOWELL, Richard. 770.28
Yashica guide. New York, American Photographic Book Pub. Co. [1958] 128p. illus. 20cm. (An Amphoto book) [TR263.Y3L6] 57-14987
1. Yashica camera. I. Title.

TYDINGS, Kenneth S. 771.31
Advanced Yashica guide. Rev. Philadelphia, Chilton Co., Book Division, c. 1958, 1959 95p. illus. 20cm. (Modern camera guide series, 424) 59-15196 1.95 pap.,
1. Yashica camera. 2. Photography—Handbooks, manuals, etc. I. Title.

TYDINGS, Kenneth S 771.31
Advanced Yashica guide. Rev. Philadelphia, Chilton Co., Book Division, c1959. 95 p. illus. 20 cm. (Modern camera guide series, 424) [TR263.Y3T9] 59-15196
1. Yashica camera. 2. Photography — Handbooks, manuals, etc. I. Title.

TYDINGS, Kenneth S. 771.3'1
The photo-visual guide to Yashica twin-lens reflex cameras [by] Kenneth S. Tydings and Shirley C. Tydings. New York, Amphoto [1971] 128 p. illus. 20 cm. (An Amphoto camera guide, 175) On spine: Yashica twin-lens reflex cameras. [TR263.Y3T92] 74-160804 ISBN 0-8174-0175-X 2.50
1. Yashica camera. 2. Photography—Handbooks, manuals, etc. I. Tydings, Shirley C., joint author. II. Title. III. Title: Yashica twin-lens reflex cameras. BIP

Yates, Norman, 1923—

YATES, Norman, 1923- 759.11
Norman Yates : drawings and paintings / [introd., Raymond Ouellet ; critique, George Melnyk ; photos., Doug Clark]. [Edmonton : Edmonton Art Gallery, 1976?] [20] p. : ill. ; 21 x 25 cm. [ND249.Y37A5] 77-366115
1. Yates, Norman, 1923-

Yearbury, Pauline Kahurangi.

YEARBURY, Pauline Kahurangi. 759.9931
The children of Rangi and Papa : the Maori story of creation / Pauline Kahurangi Yearbury. Christchurch : Whitcoulls, 1976. 36 p. : col. ill. ; 36 cm. [ND1108.Y4A43] 77-363030 ISBN 0-7233-0449-1 : 25.00
1. Yearbury, Pauline Kahurangi. 2. Creation in art. 3. Mythology, Maori—Poetry. I. Title. BIP

Yeats, Jack Butler, 1871-1957.

JACK B. Yeats; 759.9415
a centenary gathering, by Samuel Beckett/[and others] Edited with an introd. by Roger McHugh. [Dublin] Dolmen Press; [distributed by Humanities Press, New York, 1971] 114 p. illus. 21 cm. (Tower series of Anglo-Irish studies, 3) Contents.Contents.—The personality of Jack B. Yeats, by T. de V. White.—An interview with Jack Butler Yeats, by S. Oshima.—Six drawings by Jack B. Yeats for 'A lament for Art O'Leary.'—The paintings of Jack B. Yeats, by E. O'Malley.—MacGreevy on Yeats, by S. Beckett.—Hommage a Jack B. Yeats, by S. Beckett with a translation by R. Cohn.—Jack B. Yeats: promise and regret, by B. O'Doherty.—Mixed metaphors: Jack B. Yeats's writings, by M. G. Rose.—A chronology of major personal events, publications, and exhibitions, by M. Caldwell.—A bibliography of the published writings of Jack B. Yeats, by M. Caldwell (p. 110-114) [NX93.Y4J3] 72-188396 ISBN 0-85105-205-3 4.50 (pbk)
1. Yeats, Jack Butler, 1871-1957. I. Yeats, Jack Butler, 1871-1957. II. Beckett, Samuel, 1906-

Yeats, John Butler, 1839-1922.

GORDON, Robert, 1946- 759.9415 B
John Butler Yeats and John Sloan : the records of a friendship / [by] Robert Gordon ; with illustrations from the Corcoran Gallery of Art, the Delaware Art Museum and the collection of Michael B. Yeats. Dublin : Dolmen Press, 1978. 32 p., 8 p. of plates : ill., ports. ; 25 cm. (New Yeats papers ; 14) Distributed in the U.S. by Humanities Press, Atlantic Highlands, N.J. Includes bibliographical references. [ND497.Y43G67] 79-304358 ISBN 0-85105-322-X pbk. : 7.00
1. Yeats, John Butler, 1839-1922—Friends and associates. 2. Sloan, John, 1871-1951—Friends and associates. I. Yeats, John Butler, 1839-1922. II. Sloan, John, 1871-1951. III. Title. IV. Series. BIP

MURPHY, William Michael, 1916- 759.9415 B
Prodigal father : the life of John Butler Yeats, 1839-122 / William M. Murphy. Ithaca : Cornell University Press, 1978. 680 p. : ill. ; 25 cm. Includes index. Bibliography: p. [543]-547. [ND1329.Y43M86] 77-3122 ISBN 0-8014-1047-9 : 27.50
1. Yeats, John Butler, 1839-1922. 2. Portrait painters—Ireland—Biography. I. Title. BIP

Yelf Brothers.

DAISH, Alfred Newman. 665.4'422'8
Printers' pride, the House of Yelf at Newport, Isle of Wight, 1816-1966, by A. N. Daish. Newport (I. o. W), Yelf Bros., 1967. [12] 92 p. front., illus., 2 maps, facsims. 25 cm. 21/- (B67-20775) Bibliography: p. 85. [Z232.Y44D3] 68-78647
1. Yelf Brothers. I. Title.

Yellow.

WOLFF, Robert Jay, 1905- JUV
Hello, yellow! New York, Scribner [1968] [30] p. col. illus. 21 cm. Yellow is always happy and cheerful and it has many names. While not as bold as red, it stands out in any group of colors. [PZ7.W82127He] 701.8 AC 68
1. Yellow. 2. Color. I. Title.

Yirawala.

HOLMES, Sandra Le Brun. 759.994
Yirawala, artist and man. [Milton, Queensland] Jacaranda Press [1972] [xii], 92 p. illus. (part col.) 30 cm. [ND1105.Y57H64 1972] 73-331093 ISBN 0-7016-0582-0
1. Yirawala. I. Title.

Yokoyama, Talkan, 1868-

YOKOYAMA Taikan 759.952
(1868-) Text by Seiroku Noma English adaptation by Meredith Weatherby. [1st English ed.] Tokyo, Rutland, Vt., C. E. Tuttle Co. [1956] 1v. (unpaged) illus. (part col.) port. 18cm. (Kodansha library of Japanese art, no. 4) Title also in Japanese on t. p. Bibliography: [1] p. at end. [ND1059.Y6N6] 927.5 56-8489
1. Yokoyama, Talkan, 1868- I. Noma, Seiroku. II. Weatherby, Meredith, ed. and tr. III. Series.

York, Edward Palmer, 1865-1928.

SAWYER, Philip, 1868-1950. 927.2
Edward Palmer York; personal reminiscences by his friend and partner, Philip Sawyer, and a biographical sketch by Royal Cortissoz. Stonington [Conn.] Priv. print., 1951. 68 p. port. 25 cm. "One hundred copies printed." [NA737.Y6S3] 51-27372
1. York, Edward Palmer, 1865-1928. I. Title.

York, Pa.—Soc. life & cust.—Illustrations.

MILLER, Lewis, 1796-1882. 741.9'73
Lewis Miller, sketches and chronicles; the reflections of a nineteenth century Pennsylvania German folk artist. Introd. by Donald A. Shelley. [1st ed.] York, Pa., Historical Society of York County [c1966] xxii, 185 p. (chiefly col. illus., facsims., port.) 29 cm. Selected chiefly from the collections of the Historical Society of York County. Bibliography: p. 185. [NC1075.M5H5] 66-20888
1. York, Pa.—Soc. life & cust.—Illustrations. I. Historical Society of York County (Pennsylvania) II. Title.

Yorkshire, Eng. West Riding—Antiquities, Celtic.

JACKSON, Sidney. 732'.6
Celtic and other stone heads; foreword by Anne Ross. Bradford, S. Jackson c/o Percy Lund, Humphries and Co. Ltd. The County Press, Drummond Rd., 1973. 40 p. illus. 21 cm. [DA670.Y6J3] 75-331331 ISBN 0-9502906-0-2 £0.98
1. Yorkshire, Eng. West Riding—Antiquities, Celtic. 2. Celts—England—Yorkshire. West Riding. 3. Sculpture, Primitive. 4. Head (in religion, folk-lore, etc.) I. Title. II. Title: Stone heads.

Yorktown, Va. Thomas Pate House.

HATCH, Charles E. 917.55
The Thomas Pate House and Lot 42 in Yorktown, Colonial National Historical Park, Yorktown, Virginia, by Charles E. Hatch, Jr. [Washington] Division of History, Office of Archeology and Historic Preservation, 1969. iii, 44 p. illus. 26 cm. Includes bibliographical references. [NA7238.Z9Y65] 423 70-608518
1. Yorktown, Va. Thomas Pate House. I. Title.

Young, Arthur Henry, 1866-1943.

YOUNG, Arthur Henry, 1866-1943. 741.5'973 B
Art Young : his life and times / by Art Young ; edited by John Nicholas Beffel. Westport, Conn. : Hyperion Press, 1975, c1939. p. cm. Reprint of the ed. published by Sheridan House, New York. Includes index. [NC1429.Y57B43 1975] 75-352 ISBN 0-88355-255-8 : 28.50
1. Young, Arthur Henry, 1866-1943. BIP

Young, Owen D., 1874—

SZLADITS, Lola L. 016.09
Owen D. Young, book collector / by Lola L. Szladits ; with an introd. by Josephine Young Case. [New York] : New York Public Library : distributed by Readex Books, 1974. 47 p. : ill. ; 23 cm. Five hundred copies printed. [Z121.S93] 74-83044 ISBN 0-87104-253-3 pbk. : 5.00
1. Young, Owen D., 1874- 2. Bibliographic exhibitions. 3. Manuscripts—Exhibitions. BIP

Youngerman, Jack, 1926-

WORCESTER, Mass. Art Museum. 759.13
Paintings and drawings by Jack Youngerman. [Worcester, Mass., 196-. 16 p. illus. 28 cm. Exhibition held at the Worcester Art Museum No. 4, 1965 -- Jan. 2, 1966. [ND237.Y66W6] 67-68284
1. Youngerman, Jack, 1926- I. Title.

YOUNGERMAN, Jack, 1926- 759.13
Youngerman: recent paintings and sculptures, February 13, to March 10, 1971. [Exhibition at] the Pace Gallery. [New York, Pace Editions, 1971] [28] p. (chiefly illus.) 23 cm. Bibliography: p. [26] [N6537.Y68A58] 77-153475
I. Pace Gallery. II. Title.

Youth as artists.

THOMPSON, Beatrice Terzian. 741.973
Drawings by high school students [by] Beatrice Thompson. New York, Reinhold Pub. Corp. [1966] 110 p. (chiefly illus.) 27 cm. (An Art horizons book) [N352.T54] 66-11937
1. Youth as artists. 2. Drawings. I. Title.

Youth — Portraits.

HODGES, Charles Du Bois. 779.25
In search of young beauty. New York, A. S. Barnes [1964] 220 p. illus. 26 cm. [TR680.H63] 64-21361
1. Youth — Portraits. 2. Photography of youth. 3. Children — Portraits. 4. Photography of children. Title. I. Title.

Yoxall, Harold Waldo.

YOXALL, Harold Waldo. 659.1'9'39100924
A fashion of life [by] H. W. Yoxall. [1st American ed.] New York, Taplinger Pub. Co. [1967] viii, 269 p. illus., ports. 23 cm. Autobiographical. [TT505.Y6A3 1967] 67-12613
1. Yoxall, Harold Waldo. 2. Vogue. I. Title.

Yunkers, Adja, 1900—

UTAH Museum of Fine Arts. 759.13
Adja Yunkers. [Salt Lake City, 1969] [26] p. illus., port. 29 cm. Catalog of an exhibition held at the Utah Museum of Fine Arts, 9 Feb.-9 Mar., 1969. "Catalog printed in a quantity of 500." Contents.Contents.—Adja Yunkers, by E. B. Henning.—Adja Yunkers: the eye's edge, by S. Burton.—Catalog of the exhibition.—Selected chronology.—Partial bibliography (p. [24]-[25]) [N6537.Y8U8] 74-625776
1. Yunkers, Adja, 1900-

YUNKERS, Adja, 1900- 769'.924
Adja Yunkers; prints 1927-1967. [Text by Una E. Johnson. Catalogue by Jo Miller. Brooklyn, N.Y., Brooklyn Museum, 1969] 78 p. illus. (part col.), port. 24 cm. (American graphic artists of the twentieth century. Monograph no. 7) Bibliography: p. 76-78. [NE539.Y8J6] 74-82879
I. Johnson, Una E. II. Miller, Jo. III. Brooklyn Institute of Arts and Sciences. Museum. IV. Title. V. Series.

Zacualpa, Guatemala.

WAUCHOPE, Robert, 1909- 738.3
Zacualpa, El Quiche, Guatemala, an ancient provincial center of the Highland Maya / Robert Wauchope. New Orleans : Middle American Research Institute, Tulane University, 1975. xix, 303 p. : ill. ; 28 cm. (Publication - Middle American Research Institute, Tulane University ; 39) Bibliography: p. 301-303. [F1465.1.Z3W38] 76-357671

1. Zacualpa, Guatemala. 2. Indians of Central America—Guatemala—Pottery. I. Title: Zacualpa, El Quiche, Guatemala, an ancient provincial center ... II. Series: Tulane University of Louisiana. Middle American Research Institute. Publication ; 39.

Zadkine, Ossip.

JIANU, Ionel 730.944
Zadkine. Paris. Arted. Editions d'Art [dist. Greenwich, Conn., N.Y. Graphic. 1965, c.1964] 109p. 97 plates, port. 29cm. Bibl. [NB553.Z3J5] 65-673 12.50
1. Zadkine, Ossip. I. Title.

Zagat, Samuel, 1890-1962.

ZAGAT, Samuel, 1890-1962. 917.47'1'06924
Jewish life on New York's Lower East Side, 1912-1962. Ida R. Zagat, editor. New York, Rogers Book Service [1972] 107 p. illus. (part col.) 32 cm. Cover title: Zagat: drawings and paintings. [F128.9.J5Z33] 74-173433 15.00
1. Zagat, Samuel, 1890-1962. 2. Jews in New York (City)—Caricatures and cartoons. 3. World politics—20th century—Caricatures and cartoons. I. Zagat, Ida R. II. Title. III. Title: Zagat: drawings and paintings. BIP

Zagorsk, Russia. Gosudarstvennyi istoriko-khudozhestvennyi muzei.

ZAGORSK, Russia. Gosudarstvennyi istoriko-khudozhestvennyi muzei. 755'.2'09496
Zagorsk : ancient Russian painting in the collection of the Zagorsk Historical and Art Museum / [compiled by Tatiana Nikolajevna Manushina]. Moscow : Pub. House "Soviet Russia", 1976. 64 p. : col. ill. ; 20 cm. [N8189.R92Z349 1976] 77-474499 0.93rub
1. Zagorsk, Russia. Gosudarstvennyi istoriko-khudozhestvennyi muzei. 2. Icons, Russian—Catalogs. 3. Icons—Russian Republic—Zagorsk—Catalogs. I. Manushina, Tat'iana Nikolaevna. II. Title.

Zahn, Helga.

ZAHN, Helga. 739.27'092'4
Helga Zahn : a retrospective assessment, 1960-1976 : jewellery, prints, and drawings, 14 April-12 June 1976 / photography Ray Carpenter ... [et al.]. London : Crafts Advisory Committee, 1976. [25] p. : chiefly ill., port. ; 26 cm. [NK7398.Z33C37] 76-378314 £1.00
1. Zahn, Helga. 2. Jewelry—History—20th century—Exhibitions. I. Carpenter, Ray. II. Crafts Advisory Committee.

Zakharov, Feodor, 1882-

NORTH Carolina. Museum of Art, Raleigh. 741.9'73
Feodor Zakharov; a retrospective exhibition, May 2-30, 1965, North Carolina Museum of Art, Raleigh. [Raleigh, 1965] 58 p. illus. 26 cm. Bibliography: p. 56. [N6537.Z3N6] 66-64857
1. Zakharov, Feodor, 1882- I. Title.

Zale Corporation—Art collections.

FRIED, Henry B., 1907- 739.3
Cavalcade of time; a visual history of watches [by] Henry B. Fried. [1st ed. Dallas 1968] 126 p. col. illus. 23 cm. "From the private collection of the Zale Corporation." [NK7483.F7] 68-23804
1. Zale Corporation—Art collections. 2. Clocks and watches—Catalogs. I. Title. II. Title: A visual history of watches.

Zavaro, Albert, 1925—

ZAVARO, Albert, 1925- 759.9561
Zavaro: recent works. Chicago, R. S. Johnson-International Gallery, 1973. 20 p. (chiefly illus., part col.) 25 cm. Catalog of the exhibition held in the winter of 1973 at the R. S. Johnson-International Gallery, Chicago. [ND873.Z3J64] 72-97225
1. Zavaro, Albert, 1925- I. Johnson (R. S.)-International Gallery. II. Title.

Zeiss cameras.

TYDINGS, Kenneth S. 770.2
The Ziess Ikon 35 mm. guide. New York, Greenberg, 1955, c1953. 127p. illus. 20cm. (The Modern camera guide series) [TR263.Z4T9] 54-8492
1. Zeise cameras. I. Title.

Zemach, Margot—Juvenile literature.

ZEMACH, Margot. 741'.092'4 B
Self protrait : Margot Zemach. Reading, Mass. : Addison-Wesley, c1978. p. cm. A well-known illustrator of children's books talks about herself, her life, and her work. [NC975.5.Z45A4 1978] 92 78-17140 ISBN 0-201-09096-1 : 7.95
1. Zemach, Margot—Juvenile literature. 2. Illustrators—United States—Biography—Juvenile literature. I. Title.

Zen Buddhism.

FRANCK, Frederick, 1909- 741'.092'4
The Zen of seeing; seeing/drawing as meditation, drawn and handwritten by Frederick Franck. New York, Vintage Books [1973] xxi, 130 p. illus. 27 cm. [NC139.F72A58] 73-174195 3.45 (pbk.)
1. Franck, Frederick, 1909- 2. Zen Buddhism. I. Title. BIP

FRANCK, Frederick, 1909- 741'.092'4
The Zen of seeing : seeing, drawing as meditation / drawn and handwritten by Frederick Franck. 1st ed. New York : Knopf : distributed by Random House, 1973. xxi, 130 p. : ill. ; 28 cm. [NC139.F72A58 1973b] 74-184817 ISBN 0-394-48804-0 : 7.95
1. Franck, Frederick, 1909- 2. Zen Buddhism. I. Title.

Zerbe, Jerome, 1904—

GILL, Brendan, 1914- 779'.2'0924
Happy times. Text by Brendan Gill. Photos. by Jerome Zerbe. [1st ed.] New York, Harcourt Brace Jovanovich [1973] 288 p. illus. 32 cm. [TR140.Z47G54] 74-157920 ISBN 0-15-138480-0 25.00
1. Zerbe, Jerome, 1904- 2. United States—Biography—Portraits. I. Zerbe, Jerome, 1904- illus. II. Title.

Zerbe, Karl, 1903-

AMERICAN Federation of Arts. 707.4
Karl Zerbe, by H. W. Janson. New York [1961] 51 p. illus. (part col.) ports. 19 cm. "Retrospective exhibition circulated by the American Federation of Arts, opening April 7 [1961] Art Gallery, Boston University." Bibliography: p. 21-24. [ND588.Z4A7] 63-25206
1. Zerbe, Karl, 1903- I. Janson, Horst Woldemar, 1913- II. Title.

Zigrosser, Carl, 1891—

ZIGROSSER, Carl, 1891- 708'.0092'4 [B]
A world of art and museums / Carl Zigrosser. Philadelphia : Art Alliance Press, [1975] 309 p. ; 24 cm. Continuation and companion volume to My own shall come to me. Includes index. [N685.Z53] 74-75989 ISBN 0-87982-014-4 : 12.00
1. Zigrosser, Carl, 1891- 2. Philadelphia Museum of Art. I. Title. BIP

Zillis, Switzerland. St. Martinskirche.

MURBACH, Ernst. 759.9'494
The painted Romanesque ceiling of St. Martin in Zillis. Text by Ernst Murbach. Ed. and with photos. by Peter Heman. New York, Praeger [1967, i.e. 1968] 48p. illus., map, plans, 80col. plates. 26cm. Tr. of Zillis. Bibl. [ND2793.Z5M83 1967b] 67-29703 20.00
1. Zillis, Switzerland. St. Martinskirche. 2. Mural painting and decoration—Zillis, Switzerland. I. Heman, Peter. illus. II. Title.

Zimmerman, John, 1927—

CALLAHAN, Sean. 770'.92'2
Photographing sports, John Zimmerman, Mark Kauffman and Neil Leifer / text by Sean Callahan and Gerald Astor, with the editors of Alskog, inc. Los Angeles : Alskog, inc., c1975. 96 p. : ill. (some col.) ; 29 cm. (Masters of contemporary photography) Title on spine: Zimmerman & Kauffman: photographing sports. [TR821.C34] 75-12965 ISBN 0-690-00785-X : 8.95.
1. Zimmerman, John, 1927- 2. Kauffman, Mark. 3. Leifer, Neil. 4. Photography of sports. I. Astor, Gerald, 1926- joint author. II. Alskog, inc. III. Title. IV. Title: Zimmerman & Kauffman : photographing sports.

Zincography.

POE, Edgar Allan, 1809-1849. 686.2'314
Anastatic printing / as described by Edgar Allan Poe in 1845. Norwood, Pa. : Norwood Editions, 1976. p. cm. Reprint of the 1946 ed. published by Silver Quoin Press, Chicago. [NE2550.P63 1976] 76-10666 ISBN 0-8482-2073-0 : 6.50
1. Zincography. I. Title. BIP

Zogbaum, Wilfrid, 1915-1965.

ZOGBAUM, Wilfrid, 1915-1965. 730'.92'4
Wilfrid Zogbaum: sculpture, 1955-1964. [Exhibition] organized by the San Francisco Museum of Art, Apr. 28-July 1, 1973 [San Francisco, 1973] [20] p. illus. (part col.) 26 cm. [NB237.Z56S36] 73-164606
1. Zogbaum, Wilfrid, 1915-1965. I. San Francisco. Museum of Art. II. Title.

Zone system (Photography)

SALTZER, Joseph. 770'.28
A zone system for all formats / Joseph Saltzer. Garden City, N.Y. : Amphoto, [1978] p. cm. Includes index. [TR147.S24] 78-12888 ISBN 0-8174-2419-9 : 25.00
1. Zone system (Photography) I. Title. BIP

Zone system (Photography)—Handbooks, manuals, etc.

SALTZER, Joseph. 770'.28
Zone system calibration manual / Joseph Saltzer. Garden City, N.Y. : Amphoto, [1978] p. cm. Includes index. [TR150.S24] 78-13170 ISBN 0-8174-2421-0 : 9.95
1. Zone system (Photography)—Handbooks, manuals, etc. I. Title. BIP

Zoo animals—Pictorial works.

WINOGRAND, Garry, 1928- 779'.32
The animals. With an afterword by John Szarkowski. New York, Museum of Modern Art; distributed by New York Graphic Society, Greenwich, Conn. [1969] 43 p. (chiefly illus.) 20 x 22 cm. [QL77.5.W5] 68-54918
1. Zoo animals—Pictorial works. I. New York (City). Museum of Modern Art. II. Title. BIP

Zoological gardens—Design and construction—Bibliography.

LUPTON, David Walker. 016.3092'08 s
Zoo and aquarium design / David Walker Lupton. Monticello, Ill. : Council of Planning Librarians, 1978. 51 p. ; 29 cm. (Exchange bibliography - Council of Planning Librarians ; 1484) Cover title. [Z5942.C68 no. 1484] [Z7994.Z66] [QL76] 016.7275'59 78-105206 5.00
1. Zoological gardens—Design and construction—Bibliography. 2. Aquariums, Public—Design and construction—Bibliography. I. Title. II. Series: Council of Planning Librarians. Exchange bibliography; 1484.

Zoological illustration—History.

DANCE, S. Peter. 591'.022'2
The art of natural history : animal illustrators and their work / S. Peter Dance. Woodstock, N.Y. : Overlook Press, 1978. p. cm. Includes index. Bibliography: p. [QL46.5.D36 1978] 78-56076 ISBN 0-87951-077-3 : 49.50
1. Zoological illustration—History. I. Title. BIP

KNIGHT, David M. 743'.6'09
Zoological illustration : an essay towards a history of printed zoological pictures / David Knight. Folkstone, Eng. : Dawson ; Hamden, Conn. : Archon Books, 1977. xii, 204 p. : ill. ; 23 cm. Includes index. Bibliography: p. 189-201. [QL46.5.K54] 77-30385 ISBN 0-208-01720-8 (Archon Books) : 17.50
1. Zoological illustration—History. I. Title. BIP

Zoological speciments—Collection and preservation.

CLARK, James Lippitt, 1883- 069'.0924 B
In the steps of the great American museum collector Carl Ethan Akeley by James L. Clark. Illus. by Matthew Kalmenoff. New York, M. Evans; distributed in association with Lippincott, Philadelphia [1968] 127 p. illus. 21 cm. Bibliography: p. 127. A biography of the museum specialist who invented an inexpensive method of stuffing and displaying animals to make them look natural in a natural setting. [QL31.A5C6] 92 AC 68
1. Akeley, Carl Ethan, 1864-1926. 2. Zoological speciments—Collection and preservation. I. Kalmenoff, Matthew, illus. II. Title.

Zoology—Africa—Pictorial works.

HARM, Ray. 741.9'73
Ray Harm's African sketchbook. Edited by Robert Emmett McDowell. Louisville, Ky., Frame House Gallery [1973] xxix p., 80 plates (part col.) 29 x 40 cm. [QL336.H33 1973] 74-154467
1. Zoology—Africa—Pictorial works. 2. Botany—Africa—Pictorial works. I. Title. II. Title: African sketchbook.

Zoology—Pictorial works.

THE Animal kingdom / 591'.022'2
under the general editorship of Harold H. Hart ; compiled by Pam Pollack. New York : Hart Pub. Co., c1977. 399 p. : all ill. ; 32 cm. (Hart picture archives) Includes index. Bibliography: p. 391. [QL46.A46] 76-20916 ISBN 0-8055-1161-X : 29.95 ISBN 0-8055-1190-3 loose-leaf : 45.00 ISBN 0-8055-0300-5 pbk. : 14.95
1. Zoology—Pictorial works. 2. Zoological illustration—Pictorial works. I. Pollack, Pam.

AUSTERMAN, Miriam, 1923- 599'.05
Animals : unique moments / captured by Miriam Austerman. La Jolla, Calif. : Theorex, c1977. p. cm. Includes index. [QL46.A89] 77-11699 ISBN 0-916004-06-6 lib. bdg. : 9.00. ISBN 0-916004-05-8 pbk. : 4.95
1. Zoology—Pictorial works. I. Title. BIP

ENCYCLOPAEDIA Britannica 590.84
picture stories: We learn about animals. Prepared under the direction of the staff of Britannica junior. Chicago, Encyclopaedia Britannica, inc. [1954] 316p. illus. 20x28cm. A new ed. of Encyclopaedia Britannica picture stories: True nature series. [QL46.E55 1954] 54-3994
1. Zoology—Pictorial works. I. Britannica junior. II. Title: We learn about.

GRASSE, Pierre Paul, 1895- 596'.0022'2
Larousse animal portraits / [by] P. P. Grasse ; consultant editor, Maurice Burton ; [translated from the French by John Bailie]. London ; New York : Hamlyn, 1977. 174 p. : col. ill. ; 29 cm. Translation of Le plus beau bestiaire du monde. [QL46.G6613] 76-52344 ISBN 0-88332-076-2 (U.S.A.) : 19.95
1. Zoology—Pictorial works. 2. Birds—Pictorial works. I. Title.

Available from Larousse & Co., 572 Fifth Ave., New York, NY 10036 **BIP**

KUHN, Bob. 758'.3
The animal art of Bob Kuhn ... a lifetime of drawing and painting. [Westport, Conn., North Light Publishers; distributed by Watson-Guptill Publications, New York, 1973] 128 p. illus. (part col.) 27 x 34 cm. [QL46.5.K83] 73-82102 16.00
1. Zoology—Pictorial works. 2. Animal painting and illustration. I. Title. **BIP**

RUSSELL, Franklin, 1922- 591
Wild creatures : a pageant of the untamed / text by Franklin Russell ; photos. by Anthony Bannister ... [et al.] ; photos. assembled and edited by Milton Rugoff and Ann Guilfoyle. New York : Simon and Schuster, [1975] 178 p. : ill. (some col.) ; 31 cm. "A Chanticleer Press edition." [QL46.R87] 75-4417 ISBN 0-671-22098-5 : 35.00
1. Zoology—Pictorial works. I. Bannister, Anthony. II. Rugoff, Milton Allan, 1913- III. Guilfoyle, Ann. IV. Title. **BIP**

SCHUHMACHER, Eugen. 591
The last paradises; on the track of rare animals. Zoological appendix by Gerd Diesselhorst [and others] Translated by Gwynne Vevers and Winwood Reade. Garden City, N.Y., Doubleday, 1967. 315 p. col. illus., map (on lining papers) 28 cm. Translation of Die letzten Paradiese. [QL46.S3913] 67-17545
1. Zoology—Pictorial works. 2. Rare animals. I. Title.

TIME-LIFE Films. 596
Elephants & other land giants : based on the television series Wild, wild world of animals. [New York] : Time-Life Films, c1976. 128 p. : ill. ; 28 cm. (Wild, wild world of animals) Includes index. Bibliography: p. 126. [QL46.T57 1976] 76-1868 ISBN 0-913948-05-5 : 7.95
1. Zoology—Pictorial works. I. Title. II. Series.

Zoom lenses.

CLARK, Alan Dennis. 535'.08 s
Zoom lenses [by] A. D. Clark. With a pref. by W. D. Wright. New York, American Elsevier Pub. Co. [1973] ix, 89 p: illus. 26 cm. (Monographs on applied optics, no. 7) Includes bibliographical references. [TR270.C55 1973a] [TR270] 771.3'52 73-9905 ISBN 0-444-19555-6 17.00
1. Zoom lenses. I. Title. II. Series.

Zoppo, Marco, 1433-1478.

ARMSTRONG, Lilian. 759.5
The paintings and drawings of Marco Zoppo / Lilian Armstrong. New York : Garland, 1976. ix, 589 p., [25] leaves of plates : ill. ; 21 cm. (Outstanding dissertations in the fine arts) Originally presented as the author's thesis, Columbia. Bibliography: p. 431-449. [ND623.Z53A74 1976] 75-23779 ISBN 0-8240-1976-8 lib.bdg. : 40.00
1. Zoppo, Marco, 1433-1478. I. Title. II. Series. **BIP**

Zorach, William, 1887-

BAUR, John Ireland Howe, 730.973
1909-
William Zorach. New York, Published for the Whitney Museum of American Art by Praeger, 1959. 116p. illus., plates (part col.) 30cm. (Books that matter) Bbibliography: p. 112-114. [NB237.Z6B3] 59-10500
1. Zorach, William, 1887- I. Whitney Museum of American Art, New York. II. Title.

WHITNEY Museum of 730.973
American Art, New York.
William Zorach; exhibition and catalogue. Whitney Museum of American Art. Oct. 14-Nov. 29, 1959. The Joe and Emily Lowe Art Gallery, Miami, Jan. 1-31, 1960. The Columbus Gallery of Fine Arts, Mar. 3-31, 1960. The Contemporary Arts Center, Cincinnati, Apr. 20-May 30, 1960. [New York, 1959] [51] p. plates (part col.) 28 cm. "The text is a shorter version of that which appears in the book, William Zorach, by John I. H. Baur." Bibliography: p. [21]-[23] [NB237.Z6W48] 59-16946
1. Zorach, William, 1887- I. Title.

ZORACH, William, 1887- 760'.0924
1966.
Paintings, watercolors, and drawings, 1911-1922 [compiled by] Donelson F. Hoopes. [Brooklyn, Brooklyn Museum, 1968] vi, 71 p. illus. (part col.) 23 cm. "A special exhibition November 26, 1968-January 19, 1969 [at] the Brooklyn Museum." Bibliographical footnotes. [ND237.Z6H6] 68-59107
I. Hoopes, Donelson F. II. Brooklyn Institute of Arts and Sciences. Museum.

ZORACH, William, 1887- 730.924

1966.
William Zorach: memorial exhibition; sculpture, drawings and watercolors, February 28, 1969-March 30, 1969. New York, American Academy of Arts and Letters [1969] [18] p. illus. 26 cm. ([American Academy of Arts and Letters] Publication no. 253) Catalog of an exhibition held in the Museum of the American Academy of Arts and Letters. [AS36.A473 no. 253] 73-274067
I. American Academy of Arts and Letters. Museum. II. Title. III. Series.

Zorn, Anders Leonard, 1860-1920.

BOETHIUS, Gerda Axelina 759.85
Johnanna, 1890-
Zorn, Swedish painter and world traveller. With 84 reproductions of paintings, etchings, and drawings. [Tr. from Swedish by Albert Read] [dist. New York, Taplinger, 1961, c.1959] 155p. illus. (part col.) 27cm. 61-19871 12.50
1. Zorn, Anders Leonard, 1860-1920. I. Title.

Zox, Larry, 1936—

ZOX, Larry, 1936- 759.13
Larry Zox, by James Monte. [Catalog of the exhibition at the] Whitney Museum of American Art. New York [1973] 40 p. illus. 20 x 23 cm. Bibliography: p. 38-40. [ND237.Z65M66] 73-89035
1. Zox, Larry, 1936- I. Monte, James K. II. Whitney Museum of American Art, New York.

ZOX, Larry, 1936- 759.13
Zox 70. [Akron, Ohio, Akron Art Institute, 1971] [18] p. illus. (part col.) 18 x 23 cm. Exhibition held Feb. 7-March 21, 1971 at Akron Art Institute. Bibliography: p. [17] [ND237.Z65A75] 77-198437
I. Akron, Ohio. Art Institute. II. Title.

Zuccari, Taddeo, 1529-1566.

GERE, John A. 741.9'45
Taddeo Zuccaro, his development studied in his drawings [by] J. A. Gere. [Chicago] University of Chicago Press [1969] 239 p. 176 plates. 29 cm. [NC257.Z8G4 1969b] 77-79471 ISBN 0-226-28821-8
1. Zuccari, Taddeo, 1529-1566. I. Title.

Zuni Indians—Pictorial works.

WHITESIDE, Frank Reed, 759.13
1866-1929.
Frank Reed Whiteside, 1866-1929; the Zuni and the Indian country (The Zuni Indians—their life and tradition) [Phoenix, Ariz., 1971] [32] p. illus. 25 cm. Catalogue of an exhibition held at the Phoenix Art Museum, in cooperation with Western Art Associates, Jan.-Mar., 1971. [ND237.W623A45] 70-23555
1. Zuni Indians—Pictorial works. I. Phoenix, Ariz. Art Museum. II. Western Art Associates. III. Title: The Zuni and the Indian country.

Zurbaran, Francisco, 1598-1664.

BROWN, Jonathan. 759.6
Francisco de Zurbaran. New York, H. N. Abrams [1974] 158 p. illus. (part col.) 33 cm. (The Library of great painters) Bibliography: p. 157-158. [ND813.Z85B76] 73-10481 ISBN 0-8109-0549-3
1. Zurbaran, Francisco, 1598-1664.

PAINTINGS. 759.6
Complete ed. by Marin S. Soria. [New York] Phaidon Publishers; distributed by Garden City Books [1953] x, 199p. (p. [35]-[130] plates) illus. 9 mounted col. plates. 31cm. Bibliography: p. 190-192. [ND813.Z85S6] 927.5 54-10136
I. Zurbaran, Francisco, b. 1598. II. Soria, Marin Sebastian, ed.

ZURBARAN, Francisco, 927.5
b.1598.
Paintings. Complete ed. by Marin S. Soria. [New York] Phaidon Publishers; distributed by Garden City Books [1953] x, 199 p. (p.[35]-[130] plates) illus., 9 mounted col. plates. 31 cm. Bibliography: p. 190-192. [ND813.Z85S6] 759.6 54-10136
I. Soria, Martin Sebastian, ed.

ZURBARAN, Francisco, 1598- 759.6
1664.
Zurbaran, 1598-1664 / biography and critical analysis by Julian Gallego ; catalogue of the works by Jose Gudiol. New York : Rizzoli, 1977. 415 p. : ill. (some col.) ; 30 cm. Includes indexes. Bibliography: p. 411-415. [ND813.Z85A4 1977] 77-77657 ISBN 0-8478-0118-7 : 60.00
1. Zurbaran, Francisco, 1598-1664. 2. Painters—Spain—Biography. I. Gallego, Julian. II. Gudiol i Ricart, Josep. **BIP**

AUTHOR INDEX

G

Henry Francis du Pont Winterthur
  Museum. 478
Henry, Francoise. 151
Henry, Marguerite. 1009
Henry Morrison Flagler Museum, Palm
  Beach, Fla. 551
Henry, Stella (Vitty) 342
Hensel, John. 671
Henze, Anton. 320
Henzel, S. Sylvia. 363
Henzke, Lucile. 912
Hepler, Donald E. 30
Hepper, Alfred H B. 368
Hepworth, Barbara. 551
Hepworth, Thomas Cradock. 644
Herberholz, Barbara J. 202
Herberholz, Donald W. 200
Herbert, Alan. 335, 706
Herbert, Eugenia W. 108
Herbert F. Johnson Museum of Art. 149,
  551, 736, 849
Herbert, Gilbert. 602, 683
Herbert, John Alexander. 569
Herbert, Kevin. 106
Herbert, Lynden. 29
Herbert, Robert L. 235, 702, 803, 1003
Herbert, Sharon. 919
Herberts, Kurt. 633, 787
Herda, D. J. 865
Herdeg, Walter. 830, 1008
Herdeg, Walter. 1008
Herisko, Clarence C. 1122
Heritage Foundation. 1013
Herlihy, David. 886
Hermann, Bernard. 740
Hermann, Fritz. 798
Hermeren, Goran. 593
Hernandez, Anthony. 849
Herndon, Booton. 244
Herndon, William Henry. 658
Herr, Dan. 843
Herrad von Landsberg, d. 1195. 551
Herrick, Francis Hobart. 230
Herrigel, Gustie Luise. 460
Herriman, George. 351
Herring, Jan. 787
Herrington, Arthur William Sidney. 187,
  188
Herrmann, Frank. 121
Herrmann, Luke. 642, 1070
Herron, Gaylord Oscar. 551, 843
Hersey, George L. 515, 728, 810
Hersey, Jean. 1111
Hersey, John Brackett. 877
Hershfield, Harry. 353
Hershoff, Evelyn Glantz. 534
Hersk, Bernadette. 238
Herskovits, Melville Jean. 94
Herst, Herman. 901, 903
Herter, Christine. 406
Hertsch, Max. 899
Hertz, Louis Heilbroner. 175, 1066
Hertzberg, Robert E. 875
Hertzberg, Robert Edward. 534, 858, 875,
  889
Herz, Nat. 629
Hess, Albert Gunter. 725
Hess, Hans. 452, 523, 789, 890
Hess, John L. 564
Hess, Thomas B. 380, 657, 745, 768
Hesse, Eva. 551
Hesselgren, Sven. 75
Hessen, Beatrice. 906
Hessler, Gene. 814, 815
Hester, George M. 870
Hetherington, John Aikman. 660
Hetrich, George. 1061
Hetrick, Calvin. 525
Hetzer, Linda. 237, 360, 531, 614, 648,
  686, 699, 967
Hewison, Robert. 972
Hewitt Brothers. 338
Hewitt, Linda. 316, 481
Hewlett, Crockette W. 105
Hewlett, Maurice Raymond. 909
Hewlett-Woodmere Public Library. 884
Heyden, Doris. 581
Heydenreich, Ludwig Heinrich. 65, 651,
  723
Heydenryk, Henry. 883
Heyer, Paul. 28, 71
Heyerdahl, Thor. 127
Heyert, Elizabeth M. 856
Heyl, Bernard Chapman. 122
Heyman, Ken. 868
Heyman, Therese Thau. 273, 376, 712,
  849
Heyn, K. D. 900
Heyne, Carl J. 156
Heysen, Hans. 111
Hiatt, June. 1068
Hiatt, Noble W. 1013
Hibbard, Howard. 76, 214, 245, 282, 672
Hibben, Frank Cummings. 920
Hibbert, Christopher. 667
Hibbert, L J. 858

Hibbs, Ruth. 1033
Hibler, Harold E. 353
Hickey, Helen. 566
Hicklin, Frances. 297
Hickman, Peggy. 1010
Hicks, Clifford B. 279
Hicks, David. 597, 1048
Hicks, David. 463, 552
Hicks, Edward. 552
Hicks, G. A. 692
Hicks, Harmon T. 1044
Hicks, John. 852
Hicks, Wilson. 617
Hickson, Howard. 706
Hiett, Steve. 846
Higginbottom, Nick. 75, 292
Higgins, Alfred. 482
Higgins, Chester. 737
Higgins, Ian. 218
Higgins Ink Company, inc., Brooklyn. 692
Higgins, Reynold Alleyne. 122, 1046
Higgins, Richard Carter. 212, 224, 358
Higgins, Victor. 552
High Museum of Art. 87, 195, 641
Highland, Harold Joseph. 779, 858
Highwater, Jamake. 779
Hilberseimer, Ludwig. 69, 700
Hildebrand, Grant. 617
Hilder, Rowland. 1098
Hiler, Hilaire. 89, 787
Hiler, Hilaire. 5, 215, 363, 787
Hiley, Michael. 843, 1038
*Hill, Adrian. 406
Hill, Adrian Keith Graham. 19, 406, 407,
  409, 768, 785, 787, 1098
Hill, Amelia Leavitt. 460, 638
Hill, Anthony. 471
Hill, Arthur M. 534
Hill, Bessie May. 200
Hill, Beth. 589
Hill, Brian. 289
Hill, Cuthbert William. 904
Hill, David Octavius. 552, 843
Hill, Derek. 65
Hill, Draper. 499
Hill, Edward. 405
Hill, George Francis. 339, 749, 751, 752
Hill, George Henry. 832
Hill, Henry D. 1019
Hill, Jackson. 707
Hill, Levi L. 375, 552
Hill, Ralph Nading. 1087
Hill, Richard. 4
Hill, Robert. 504
Hill-Stead Museum, Farmington, Conn.
  134
Hill, Tom. 1097, 1098
Hillcourt, William. 269, 959
Hiller, Carl E. 81, 323
Hilles, Frederick Whiley. 955
Hillhouse, Marion Strong. 362
Hillier, Bevis. 873, 908, 919
Hillier, Florence Bell. 463
Hillier, Jack Ronald. 154, 349, 416, 546,
  547, 619, 623, 1087
Hillier, Mary. 401, 1066
Hilling, John B. 83
Hills, Pat. 647
Hills, Patricia. 495, 616, 793, 1107
Hillsmith, Fannie. 293
Hillson, Peter J. 836
Hillyer, Virgil Mores. 66, 143, 156, 994
Hils, Karl. 534
Hilton, Suzanne. 708
Hilton, Timothy. 373, 880, 924
Hilts, Leonard Finley. 486
Himel, Susan. 544
Himmelfarb, John. 553
Hinchcliffe, John. 968
Hinckley, F Lewis. 476, 480, 483
Hind, Arthur Mayger. 439
Hind, Arthur Mayger. 439
Hind, Arthur Mayger. 437, 438, 439, 558,
  666, 885, 951, 962, 1118
Hind, Charles Lewis. 308, 899
Hindman, Sandra. 249, 343, 678
Hindman, W C. 934
Hinds, James R. 1094
Hinds, Will. 1022
Hindson, Alice. 529
Hine, Lewis Wickes. 553, 843, 854, 1079
Hine, Robert V. 236, 1022
Hines, Millie. 293, 397
Hines, Thomas S. 283
Hingorani, Ratan Pribhdas. 785
Hinks, Roger Packman. 116, 296
Hinman, Bob. 1008
Hino, Arthur Mayger. 951
Hinson, Dolores A. 366, 944, 945
Hinwood, Tony. 354
Hiort, Esbjorn. 480, 916, 1012
Hipp, Hermann. 51
Hipple, Walter John. 9
Hiraga, Hoei. 465
Hirai, Kiyoshi. 302
Hirn, Yrjo. 5, 317
Hirota, Jozan. 260

Hirsch, Joseph. 553
Hirsch, Richard Teller. 1031
Hirsch, S. Carl. 662
Hirsch, Sylvia. 466
Hirschfeld, Albert. 298, 1051
Hirschl & Adler Galleries. 793, 794, 926
Hirsh, Diana. 1070
Hirsh, John C. 678
Hirshhorn Museum and Sculpture Garden.
  426
Hirst, Irene. 448
Hirst-Smith, Ann. 291
Hispanic Society of America. 743, 971
Historic American Buildings Survey. 67,
  72, 77, 80, 81, 83, 313, 553, 554, 1049,
  1076
Historic Towns and Cities Conference,
  York, Eng., 1968. 555
Historical Survey Associates. 745
Hitchcock, Anthony. 24
Hitchcock, Henry Russell. 33, 39, 61, 63,
  66, 68, 76, 78, 296, 488, 956, 1128, 1129
Hitomi, Junco. 272
Hitt, Henry C. 1019
Hix, Charles. 697
Hix, John. 502
Hixon, Orval. 440
Hixson, Richard F. 343
Hiyama, Yoshio. 458
Hjersman, Peter. 401
Hjorth, Herman. 1122, 1125
Hlasta, Stanley C. 1071
Ho, Wing Meng. 1015
Hoag, Edwin. 55
Hoag, John D. 65
Hoagland, Clayton. 407
Hoar, Frank. 824
Hoard, F E. 285
Hoban, Tana. 730, 831, 868
Hobbs, Eric. 354
Hobbs, Harry J. 1122
Hobbs, Jack A. 1089
Hobbs, Robert. 376
Hobbs, Robert Carleton. 2
Hobby Industry Association of America.
  534
Hobhouse, Hermione. 373, 665
Hobhouse, Penelope. 638
Hoblitzelle, Karl. 1012
Hobson, Burton. 332, 335, 337, 340, 341,
  354, 513, 750, 751, 901
Hobson, Robert Lockhart. 914
Hobson, Sarah. 243
Hochberg, Bette. 528
Hochman, Louis. 486, 490
Hochman, Shirley. 156
Hock, Fred William. 932
Hockney, David. 214, 556
Hoddinott, Ralph F. 321
Hodge, A. Trevor. 963
Hodgell, Murlin Ray. 448
Hodgell, Robert O. 21
Hodges, Charles Du Bois. 1132
Hodges, Lewis H. 397, 485
Hodgetts, Craig. 1031
Hodgkin, Howard. 556
Hodgkin, John Eliot. 918
Hodgson, Mary Anne. 294, 761
Hodgson, Pat. 854, 1093
Hodgson, Thomas Sherlock. 556
Hodin, Josef Paul. 91, 164, 628, 675, 720
Hodnett, Edward. 235
Hodson, Peter. 272
Hoeber, Arthur. 235
Hoefler, Richard Carl. 323
Hoegler, Rudolf G. 122
Hoelscher, Randolph Philip. 692
Hofer, Philip. 244, 574, 646
Hoff, August. 649
Hoff, Sydney. 297, 427
Hoff, Ursula. 159, 358, 806, 1087
Hofbauer, Charles. 556
Hofberg, Judith A. 157
Hoffman, John Jacob. 631
Hoffman, Walter James. 442
Hoffmann, Donald. 963, 1129
Hoffmann, Herbert. 85, 138, 139
Hoffmann, Hubert. 47
Hoffmann, Kurt. 50, 279, 447
Hoffmann, Marta. 667
Hoffsommer, Alan. 399
Hoffstot, Barbara D. 74
Hofmann, Armin. 519
Hofmann, Hans. 567
Hofmann, Hans. 91, 556, 557
Hofmann, Ruth B. 315
Hofmann, Werner. 68, 297, 445, 625, 801
Hofsinde, Robert. 240, 586, 587
Hofstadter, Albert. 5, 8
Hofstatter, Hans Hellmut. 60, 158
Hofsted, Jolyon. 911
Hofstede de Groot, Cornelis, 1863-1930.
  781
Hogarth, Burne. 19, 352, 353, 407, 453,
  528
Hogarth, Paul. 30, 566, 573, 575, 665,
  824

Hogarth, William. 8, 494, 557, 696, 822
Hogeboom, Amy. 230, 259
Hogg, Garry. 301, 553
Hogg, Ian V. 886, 887
Hogg, James. 189
Hoggett, Chris. 1027
Hohaus, Hermann. 995
Hohauser, Sanford. 708
Hohl, Reinhold. 498, 754, 1084
Hohlwein, Ludwig. 557
Hoke, John L. 865
Hoke, John L. 865
Hokinson, Helen Elna. 17
Holbein, Hans. 247, 557
Holborn, Mark. 491
Holbourne, David. 627
Holbrook, Stewart Hall. 95
Holbrook, Wallace W. 429
Holcomb, Grant. 95
Holden, Donald. 110, 1109
Holden, Geoffrey. 1014
Holden, Stan. 851
Holder, Fred W. 243
Holderbaum, James. 260, 985
Holderness, Esther R. 330
Holdgate, Charles. 739
Holiday, Ensor. 390
Holladay, Harriett MacDonald. 467
Holland, John. 834
Holland, Margaret. 1013
Holland, Nina. 529, 944
Holland, Ralph. 416
Holland, Viki. 865
Holland, Vyvyan Beresford. 517
Hollander, Anne. 363
Hollander, Annette. 534, 816
Hollander, Hans. 158
Hollander, Harry. 613
Hollen, Norma R. 419
Hollingsworth, Alvin C. 1021
Hollis, Daniel Walker. 322
Hollis, Harold Francis. 827
Hollis, Jay S. 461
Hollis, Nesta. 396, 627, 1003
Hollister, Paul M. 818, 1105
Hollmann, Clide Anne. 761
Hollmann, Eckhard. 643
Holloway, John Gifford Everett. 563
Holloway, Owen E. 574
Holloway, R. Ross. 139
Holloway, R. Ross. 139
Hollyhock, W. S. 693
Holm, Bill. 588
Holm, Bill. 588
Holm, Oscar William. 584
Holman, William R. 552
Holme, Bryan. 109, 304, 409, 521, 560,
  790
Holme, Charles. 843
Holme, Geoffrey. 298
Holme, Rathbone. 654
Holmes, Anita. 398
Holmes, Burton. 558, 1067
Holmes, Charles John. 88
Holmes, David. 238, 1036
Holmes, Edwin F. 1056
Holmes, John Guyscliffe. 658
Holmes, John M. 381, 827
Holmes, Kenneth. 313
Holmes, Sandra Le Brun. 1132
Holmes, Stewart Walker. 1036
Holmes, Wendy. 843
Holmstrom, John Gustaf. 253
Holroyd, Michael. 615
Holroyd, Ruth N. 20, 1103
Holst, Niels von. 121
Holstein, Jonathan. 366
Holt, Claire. 145
Holt, Don. 266, 564
Holt, Elizabeth Basye (Gilmore) 143, 144,
  162
Holt, Florrie Bell. 399
Holt, Verna W. 434
Holtje, Adrienne. 522
Holtrop, William F. 1125
Holtzapffel, John Jacob. 1070
Holub, Rand. 654
Holy, Ladislav. 686
Holyfield, Frank. 234, 558
Holz, Loretta. 158, 433, 707
Holzer, Hans W. 750
Hom, Jesper. 843
Homann-Wedeking, Ernst. 138
Home Builders Plan Service, Atlanta. 47
Home Building Plan Service, Portland, Or.
  47
Home craftsman. 477, 534, 1121, 1122,
  1127
Home Packaging Company, Los Angeles.
  498
Home Planners Clinic, Portland, Or. 47
Home Planners, inc., Detroit. 47, 48, 50
Homemaker's Encyclopedia, inc., New
  York. 597
Homer, William Innes. 96, 108, 550,
  1003, 1030
Homer, Winslow. 297, 1119

TITLE INDEX

J

O

ART BOOKS IN PRINT INDEX

The Art Books In Print Index lists entries for books on the visual arts currently available providing complete acquisitions information. Titles were selected from the BOOKS IN PRINT 1979-1980 database.

A

A. C. Goodwin. pap. 2.00. Mus Fine Arts Boston.

A. L. A. Portrait Index. 73.00 (ISBN 0-8337-2002-3). B Franklin.

Abbeys, Priories & Cathedrals. 5.95 (ISBN 0-85944-004-4). Transatlantic.

Abbott H. Thayer, Painter & Naturalist. 30.00 (ISBN 0-87233-015-X). Bauhan.

ABC of Flower Arranging. 6.95 (ISBN 0-8129-0635-7). Times Bks.

ABC of Lettering. 5th, rev., enl. ed. pap. text ed. 17.50 (ISBN 0-06-010329-9). Har-Row.

ABC's of Batik. 12.50 (ISBN 0-8019-6134-3); pap. 6.95 (ISBN 0-8019-6135-1). Chilton.

ABC's of Needlepoint. pap. 2.95 (ISBN 0-684-13513-2, SL 468). Scribner.

ABC's of Origami. bds. 4.50 (ISBN 0-8048-0000-6). C E Tuttle.

Abe Lincoln Grows Up. 6.95 (ISBN 0-15-201037-8). HarBraceJ.

Abe Lincoln Grows up. pap. 1.95 (ISBN 0-15-602615-5, AVB92). HarBraceJ.

Abe Lincoln: Log Cabin to White House. PLB 4.69 (ISBN 0-394-90361-7). Random.

Abie the Agent: An Original Compilation, First Collection of the Complete First Year of the Daily Strip, 1914-15. 14.50 (ISBN 0-88355-645-6); pap. 5.95 (ISBN 0-88355-644-8). Hyperion Conn.

About Alphabets. pap. 3.95 (ISBN 0-262-74003-6, 146). MIT Pr.

About Antiques. 12.50 (ISBN 0-8103-3921-8). Gale.

About Photography & Photographers. 14.00 (ISBN 0-405-04931-5). Arno.

About Prints. 41.75x (ISBN 0-19-211421-2). Oxford U Pr.

Abraham Rattner. 55.00 (ISBN 0-8109-0429-2). Abrams.

Abstract and Surrealist Art in America. 15.00 (ISBN 0-405-00729-9). Arno.

Abstract Painting & Sculpture in America. 14.00 (ISBN 0-405-01544-5). Arno.

Abstract Painting in the 70's: A Selection. pap. 3.50. Mus Fine Arts Boston.

Abstraction & Artifice in Twentieth Century Art. 18.50x (ISBN 0-19-817359-8). Oxford U Pr.

Abstraction & Empathy. text ed. 11.00 (ISBN 0-8236-0020-3). Intl Univs Pr.

Academies of Art, Past & Present. lib. bdg. 22.50 (ISBN 0-306-71603-8). Da Capo.

Academy: The Academic Tradition in American Art. 25.00 (ISBN 0-226-69412-7); 2 color fiches incl. U of Chicago Pr.

Accurate Perspective Simplified. text ed. 16.00 (ISBN 0-914214-01-2). Abak Pr.

Accurate Rifle. pap. 5.95 (ISBN 0-695-80564-9). Follett.

Accurate Rifle. 8.95 (ISBN 0-87691-102-5). Winchester Pr.

Acoustical Designing in Architecture. 21.95 (ISBN 0-471-49632-4). Wiley.

Acoustics, Noise & Buildings. 4th ed. 19.95 (ISBN 0-571-04952-4); pap. 12.95 (ISBN 0-571-04953-2). Merrimack Bk Serv.

Acropolis. 10.00 (ISBN 0-02-553980-9). Macmillan.

Acropolis. pap. 4.95 (ISBN 0-87011-085-3). Kodansha.

Acrylic Landscape Painting. pap. 9.95 (ISBN 0-8230-0051-6). Watson-Guptill.

Acrylic Painting Book. 22.50 (ISBN 0-8230-0067-2). Watson-Guptill.

Acrylic Painting for the Beginner. 13.95 (ISBN 0-8230-0060-5). Watson-Guptill.

Acrylic Portrait Painting. pap. 9.95 (ISBN 0-8230-0076-1). Watson-Guptill.

Acrylic Watercolor Painting. 18.50 (ISBN 0-8230-0100-8). Watson-Guptill.

Act of Creation. 9.95 (ISBN 0-02-565700-3); Danube ed. 7.95 (ISBN 0-02-565710-0, 56571). Macmillan.

Act of Drawing. 12.50 (ISBN 0-07-036349-8). McGraw.

Activities & Projects: India in Color. 7.95 (ISBN 0-8069-4550-8); PLB 7.49 (ISBN 0-8069-4551-6). Sterling.

Activities in Ceramics. pap. 3.96 (ISBN 0-87345-161-9). McKnight.

Actor & Architect. 7.50x (ISBN 0-8020-1309-0); pap. 2.50 (ISBN 0-8020-6103-6). U of Toronto Pr.

Adam Silver 1765-1795. 31.95 (ISBN 0-571-06466-3). Merrimack Bk Serv.

Adams' Revolvers. 29.95 (ISBN 0-214-20089-2, 8011). Barrie & Jenkins.

Adaptable Stage Costume for Women. pap. 13.85 (ISBN 0-87830-567-X). Theatre Arts.

Adapting American Antiques. 8.95 (80740). Glencoe.

Adena People. 12.50x (ISBN 0-87049-159-8). U of Tenn Pr.

Adobe Architecture. pap. 4.25 (ISBN 0-913270-12-1). Sunstone Pr.

Adolf Dehn Drawings. 22.00x (ISBN 0-8262-0100-8). U of Mo Pr.

Adolph Lewisohn Collection of Modern French Paintings & Sculptures. 25.00 (ISBN 0-405-00723-X). Arno.

Adriaen Coorte: A Unique Late Seventeenth Century Dutch Still-Life Painter. text ed. 24.75x (ISBN 90-232-1516-8). Humanities.

Advanced Furniture Construction. 7.95 (ISBN 0-498-01110-0). A S Barnes.

Advanced Photography. 29.95 (ISBN 0-8038-0450-4); pap. 18.95 (ISBN 0-8038-0396-6). Focal Pr.

Advanced Photography. rev., 4th ed. 29.95 (ISBN 0-8038-0483-0); pap. text ed. 19.95x (ISBN 0-8038-0484-9). Focal Pr.

Advances in the Psychophysical & Visual Aspects of Image Evaluation: Program Summary, Proceedings. pap. 15.00 (ISBN 0-89208-092-2). Soc Photo Sci & Eng.

Adventure in Architecture. text ed. 12.50 (ISBN 0-930558-01-4). Virgo Pr.

Adventure of Art. 25.00 (ISBN 0-517-50630-0). Potter.

Adventures in Color - Slide Photography. 10.95 (ISBN 0-87985-162-7, AE-8). Eastman Kodak.

Adventures in Crocheting. 9.95 (ISBN 0-385-08492-7). Doubleday.

Adventures in Making: Romance of Crafts Around the World. 5.95 (ISBN 0-8149-0361-4). Vanguard.

Adventures in Patchwork. 5.50 (ISBN 0-263-05591-4). Transatlantic.

Adventures in Retrieval: Han Murals & Shang Bronze Molds. pap. 8.50x (ISBN 0-674-00575-9). Harvard U Pr.

Adventures in Stitches. pap. 5.95 (ISBN 0-308-10177-4, F-118). T Y Crowell.

Adventures in the Arts: Informal Chapters on Painters, Vaudeville & Poets. 15.00 (ISBN 0-87817-071-5). Hacker.

Adventures in Toy-Making. 9.95 (ISBN 0-8008-0102-4); pap. 5.95 (ISBN 0-8008-0103-2). Taplinger.

Adventures in Western Art. 11.95 (ISBN 0-913504-35-1). Lowell Pr.

Adventures with Collage. 5.95 (ISBN 0-7232-6033-8). Warne.

Adventurous Crocheter. pap. 3.95 (ISBN 0-671-21755-0). S&S.

Adventurous Decade: Comic Strips in the Thirties. 8.95 (ISBN 0-87000-252-X). Arlington Hse.

Advertising Art in the Art Deco Style. 8.50 (ISBN 0-8446-5222-9). Peter Smith.

Advertising Art in the Art Deco Style. pap. 5.00 (ISBN 0-486-23164-X). Dover.

Advertising Directions. 8.50 (ISBN 0-910158-12-6); 8.50 (ISBN 0-910158-13-4); 8.50 (ISBN 0-910158-14-2). Art Dir.

Aegean Metalwork in the Early & Middle Bronze Age. 54.00x (ISBN 0-19-813213-1). Oxford U Pr.

Aeolic Style in Architecture: A Survey of Its Development in Palestine, the Halikarnassos Peninsula, & Greece, 1000-500 B.C. text ed. 27.50 (ISBN 0-691-03922-4). Princeton U Pr.

Aerial Discovery Manual. pap. 23.50 (ISBN 0-471-83170-0). Wiley.

Aerial Photography: The Story of Aerial Mapping & Reconnaissance. 5.95 (ISBN 0-02-550770-2). Macmillan.

Aesthetic Approach to Byzantine Art. 13.95. Dufour.

Aesthetic Attitude. 9.50 (ISBN 0-8046-0260-3). Kennikat.

Aesthetic Concepts & Education. 15.00 (ISBN 0-252-00082-X). U of Ill Pr.

Aesthetic Experience & Its Presuppositions. 15.00 (ISBN 0-8462-1093-2). Russell.

Aesthetic Motive. lib. bdg. 12.00 (ISBN 0-374-97127-7). Octagon.

Aesthetic Movement in England. 6.50 (ISBN 0-404-03091-2). AMS Pr.

Aesthetic Movement in England. lib. bdg. 6.45 (ISBN 0-8414-2068-8). Folcroft.

Aesthetic Quality: A Contextualistic Theory of Beauty. lib. bdg. 12.25x (ISBN 0-8371-4437-X, PEAQ). Greenwood.

Aesthetic Studies: Architecture & Poetry. 9.00 (ISBN 0-404-02765-2). AMS Pr.

Aesthetic Theories of French Artists: From Realism to Surrealism. pap. 2.45x (ISBN 0-8018-0216-4). Johns Hopkins.

Aesthetic Theories of Kant, Hegel & Schopenhauer. text ed. 10.00x (ISBN 0-391-00929-X). Humanities.

Aesthetic Thought of the French Enlightenment. 10.95x (ISBN 0-8229-3221-0). U of Pittsburgh Pr.

Aesthetics & Art Theory. pap. 4.95 (ISBN 0-525-47258-4). Dutton.

Aesthetics & Criticism. lib. bdg. 18.50x (ISBN 0-8371-6847-3, OSAC). Greenwood.

Aesthetics & History. 30.00 (ISBN 0-403-03882-0). Somerset Pub.

Aesthetics & Psychology. 6.00 (ISBN 0-8046-0736-2). Kennikat.

Aesthetics & Technology in Building. 11.00x (ISBN 0-674-00701-8). Harvard U Pr.

Aesthetics & the Arts. pap. text ed. 9.95 (ISBN 0-07-032215-5). McGraw.

Aesthetics & the Theory of Criticism. text ed. 14.50x (ISBN 0-226-38511-6). U of Chicago Pr.

Aesthetics & Theory of Art. text ed. 14.95x (ISBN 0-8143-1383-3). Wayne St U Pr.

Aesthetics for Dancers. 5.00x (243-25828). AAHPER.

Aesthetics from Classical Greece to the Present: A Short History. pap. 7.50 (ISBN 0-8173-6623-7). U of Ala Pr.

Aesthetics in Twentieth-Century Poland: Selected Essays. 15.00 (ISBN 0-8387-1100-6). Bucknell U Pr.

Aesthetics of Gyorgy Lukacs. 11.50x (ISBN 0-691-07205-1). Princeton U Pr.

Aesthetics: Problems in the Philosophy of Criticism. text ed. 15.50 (ISBN 0-15-501976-7). HarBraceJ.

Aesthetics Today: Selected Readings. 8.75 (ISBN 0-8446-2741-0). Peter Smith.

Affecting Presence: An Essay in Humanistic Anthropology. 8.95 (ISBN 0-252-00104-4). U of Ill Pr.

Affordable Houses Designed by Architects. 18.95 (ISBN 0-07-002341-7). McGraw.

Afghans: Traditional & Modern. 9.95 (ISBN 0-517-53104-6); pap. 4.95 (ISBN 0-517-53105-4). Crown.

Afo-A-Kom. 12.95 (ISBN 0-89388-134-1). Okpaku Communications.

African & Ancient Mexican Art: The Loran Collection. pap. 4.95 (ISBN 0-8048-1237-3). C E Tuttle.

African Art. pap. 7.95 (ISBN 0-19-519948-0). Oxford U Pr.

African Art in Cultural Perspective: An Introduction. new ed. 7.95x (ISBN 0-393-04368-1); pap. 3.45x (ISBN 0-393-09375-1). Norton.

African Crafts for You to Make. PLB 7.79 (ISBN 0-671-32130-7). Messner.

African Designs from Traditional Sources. pap. 3.50 (ISBN 0-486-22752-9). Dover.

African Designs from Traditional Sources. 7.50 (ISBN 0-8446-0295-7). Peter Smith.

African Fabric Crafts: Sources of African Design & Technique. 10.95 (ISBN 0-8008-0150-4). Taplinger.

African Images: Essays in African Iconology. text ed. 40.00x (ISBN 0-8419-0147-3). Holmes & Meier.

African Needlepoint Designs. pap. 2.00 (ISBN 0-486-23244-1). Dover.

African Negro Art. 15.00 (ISBN 0-405-01517-8). Arno.

African Primitives: Function & Form in African Masks & Figures. text ed. 17.50 (ISBN 0-8419-0048-5). Holmes & Meier.

African Sculpture. pap. 3.50 (ISBN 0-486-20396-4). Dover.

African Sculpture. 7.50 (ISBN 0-8446-0905-6). Peter Smith.

African Sculpture. pap. 5.95 (ISBN 0-691-01763-8, 201). Princeton U Pr.

African Sculpture Speaks. 4th rev. ed. pap. 8.95 (ISBN 0-306-80018-7). Da Capo.

African Textiles & Decorative Arts. 17.50 (ISBN 0-87070-228-9); pap. 7.95 (ISBN 0-87070-227-0). NYGS.

African Traditional Architecture. text ed. 12.50x (ISBN 0-8419-0287-9); pap. text ed. 9.75x (ISBN 0-8419-0336-0). Holmes & Meier.

Afro-American Artists: A Bio-Bibliographical Directory. 10.00 (ISBN 0-89073-007-5). Boston Public Lib.

After All: From Colonial Times to the 20th Century. 19.00x (ISBN 0-405-06085-8). Arno.

After Ninety. 17.50 (ISBN 0-295-95559-7); pap. 9.95 (ISBN 0-295-95333-0). U of Wash Pr.

After the Hunt. 38.50 (ISBN 0-520-02936-4). U of Cal Pr.

Aftermath. 10.25x (ISBN 0-19-211195-7). Oxford U Pr.

Agam. 55.00 (ISBN 0-8109-0294-X). Abrams.

Age of Barns. 16.95 (ISBN 0-308-70052-X). T Y Crowell.

Age of Dolls. pap. 7.50 (ISBN 0-910396-02-7). D S Coleman.

Age of Patronage: The Arts in England, 1660-1750. 16.50x (ISBN 0-8014-0684-6). Cornell U Pr.

Age of Rembrandt & Vermeer. pap. 17.50 (ISBN 0-7148-1973-5). Dutton.

Age of Surrealism. 6.00 (ISBN 0-8446-2078-5). Peter Smith.

Age of the Avant-Garde: An Art Chronicle of 1956-1972. 15.00 (ISBN 0-374-10238-4). FS&G.

Age of the Masters: A Personal View of Modern Architecture. 17.50 (ISBN 0-06-430369-1); pap. 6.95 (ISBN 0-06-430064-1, IN-64). Har-Row.

Ageless Borobudur. 15.00 (ISBN 90-6077-553-8). Hunter Hse.

Ageless Story of Jesus: Paintings & Engravings from the National Gallery of Art. 7.95 (ISBN 0-87491-008-0). Acropolis.

Agnolo Gaddi. 27.50x (ISBN 0-19-817339-3). Oxford U Pr.

Agony & Epitaph: Man, His Art & His Poetry. 7.50 (ISBN 0-8076-0544-1). Braziller.

Agora of Athens. 28.00x (ISBN 0-87661-214-1). Am Sch Athens.

Agrinion Hoard. pap. 5.50 (ISBN 0-89722-057-9). Am Numismatic.

AIA Guide to New York City. 6.95. Macmillan.

Aim for a Job in Cartooning. PLB 4.98 (ISBN 0-8239-0355-9). Rosen Pr.

Aim for a Job in Drafting. PLB 4.98 (ISBN 0-8239-0093-2). Rosen Pr.

Aim for a Job in Graphic Design & Art. PLB 4.98 (ISBN 0-8239-0480-6). Rosen Pr.

Air Guns & Air Pistols. new & enl. ed. 9.95 (ISBN 0-498-02042-8). A S Barnes.

Airborne Camera: The World from the Air & Outer Space. 12.50 (ISBN 0-8038-0335-4). Hastings.

Aircraft Photo Album. pap. 3.50 (ISBN 0-911852-50-6). Aviation.

Aisthetikos: Essays in Art, Architecture & Aesthetics. 18.95x (ISBN 0-8143-1560-7). Wayne St U Pr.

Al Nestler's Southwest. 12.50 (ISBN 0-87358-052-4). Northland.

Alaskan Paintings of Fred Machetanz. pap. 6.95 (ISBN 0-553-01061-1, M1060). Bantam.

Albers. pap. 3.95 (ISBN 0-452-00353-9, FM353). NAL.

Albert Pilavin Collection of Twentieth Century American Art. 6.00. Mus of Art RI.

Album of American Battle Art. lib. bdg. 29.50 (ISBN 0-306-70523-0). Da Capo.

Aldo's Dog House: Drawing in Perspective. 5.95 (ISBN 0-698-20458-1). Coward.

Alexander Phimister Proctor, Sculptor in Buckskin: An Autobiography. 17.50 (ISBN 0-8061-0912-2). U of Okla Pr.

Alexandre-Gabriel Decamps (1803-1860) lib. bdg. 105.00 (ISBN 0-8240-2714-0). Garland Pub.

Alexandria: A History & a Guide. 7.50 (ISBN 0-8446-0625-1). Peter Smith.

Alexandria: A History & a Guide. new ed. 10.00 (ISBN 0-87951-023-4). Overlook Pr.

Alfonso Ossorio. 55.00 (ISBN 0-8109-0352-0). Abrams.

Alfred Stieglitz: An American Seer. 35.00 (ISBN 0-89381-035-5); pap. 17.50 (ISBN 0-89381-036-3). Aperture.

Alhambra. 15.00 (ISBN 0-674-01556-8). Harvard U Pr.

Alice's World: The Life & Photography of an American Original: Alice Austen, 1866-1952. 22.50 (ISBN 0-85699-128-7). Chatham Pr.

Alkema's Complete Guide to Creative Art for Young People. 14.95 (ISBN 0-8069-5188-5); PLB 13.29 (ISBN 0-8069-5189-3). Sterling.

Alkema's Scrap Magic. 12.95 (ISBN 0-8069-5352-7); PLB 11.69 (ISBN 0-8069-5353-5). Sterling.

All About Upholstering. pap. 4.95 (ISBN 0-8015-0169-5). Hawthorn.

All About Wicker. pap. 8.95 (ISBN 0-525-47495-1). Dutton.

All Around Our Town. 12.00 (ISBN 0-930000-03-X); lib. bdg. 8.95 (ISBN 0-930000-04-8); pap. 6.95 (ISBN 0-930000-05-6). Mathom.

All-Around-the-House Art & Craft Book. pap. 3.95 (ISBN 0-395-19974-3). HM.

All Around the Town: A Walking Guide to Outdoor Sculpture of New York City. 6.95 (ISBN 0-684-15721-7). Scribner.

All-Bisque & Half-Bisque Dolls. 20.00 (ISBN 0-8407-4300-9). Nelson.

All Dolls Are Collectible. 12.95. Wallace-Homestead.

All Dolls Are Collectible. 12.95 (ISBN 0-517-53182-8). Crown.

All in Color for a Dime. pap. 1.50 (ISBN 0-441-01625-1). Ace Bks.

All-in-One Camera Book. 77th ed. pap. 6.95 (ISBN 0-8038-0451-2). Focal Pr.

All-in-One Camera Book. rev., 3rd ed. pap. 6.95 (ISBN 0-8038-0472-5). Focal Pr.

All the Best Rubbish. 10.00 (ISBN 0-06-011997-7). Har-Row.

Allart van Everdingen. lib. bdg. 58.00 (ISBN 0-8240-3223-3). Garland Pub.

Allegoriae Poeticae. Incl. Theologia Mythologica; Apotheoseos Tam Exterarum Gentium Quam Romanorum Deorum. lib. bdg. 66.00 (ISBN 0-8240-2053-7). Garland Pub.

Allover Patterns for Designers & Craftsmen. pap. 5.00 (ISBN 0-486-23179-8). Dover.

Allover Patterns for Designers & Craftsmen. 7.50 (ISBN 0-8446-5493-0). Peter Smith.

Alma-Tadema. encore ed. 5.95 (ISBN 0-684-16366-7). Scribner.

Almost Grown. 12.95 (ISBN 0-517-53327-8); pap. 5.95 (ISBN 0-517-53328-6). Harmony.

Along the Riverrun. 12.00 (ISBN 0-912020-09-1); pap. 7.75 (ISBN 0-912020-07-5). Scrimshaw Calif.

Along the Tokaido: Twelve Views by Utagawa Kunigoshi. pap. 4.95 (ISBN 0-87273-060-3). Bklyn Mus.

Alphabet & Elements of Lettering. rev. ed. 7.50 (ISBN 0-8446-2145-5). Peter Smith.

Alphabet & Elements of Lettering. pap. 3.50 (ISBN 0-486-20792-7). Dover.

Alphabet Art: Thirteen ABC's from Around the World. 8.95g (ISBN 0-590-07520-9). Schol Bk Serv.

Alphabets & Ornaments. pap. 5.00 (ISBN 0-486-21905-4). Dover.

Alphabets & Ornaments. 9.00 (ISBN 0-8446-2447-0). Peter Smith.

Alphabets Old & New for the Use of Craftsmen. 3rd ed. 9.50 (ISBN 0-8103-3301-5). Gale.

Alpine Country of the West. 25.00 (ISBN 0-912856-31-9). Graphic Arts Ctr.

Altair Design. pap. 2.95 (ISBN 0-394-82548-9). Pantheon.

Altair Design 3. pap. 2.95 (ISBN 0-394-83329-5). Pantheon.

Altair Design 4. pap. 2.95 (ISBN 0-394-83794-0). Pantheon.

Altar De Sacrificios Excavations: General Summary & Conclusions. pap. text ed. 5.00 (ISBN 0-87365-185-5). Peabody Harvard.

Alternative Natural Energy Sources in Building Design. pap. 7.95 (ISBN 0-442-22008-1). Van Nos Reinhold.

Alternative Photographic Processes. pap. 11.95 (ISBN 0-87100-136-5). Morgan.

Alvar Aalto: A Bibliography. 5.00. Coun Plan Lib.

Alvar Aalto & the International Style. cancelled. Watson-Guptill.

Alvin Langdon Coburn, Photographer: An Autobiography. pap. 6.00 (ISBN 0-486-23685-4). Dover.

Amateur Cabinetmaking. 7.95 (ISBN 0-498-01012-0); large type 6.95 (ISBN 0-498-01855-5). A S Barnes.

Amateur Furniture Construction. large type 7.95 (ISBN 0-498-01599-8). A S Barnes.

Amateur Photographer's Handbook. 8th ed. 12.95 (ISBN 0-690-05782-2). T Y Crowell.

Amateur Photomicrography. 15.95 (ISBN 0-8038-0455-5). Focal Pr.

Amateur Wind Instrument Maker. 10.00 (ISBN 0-87023-118-9). U of Mass Pr.

Amazon Indian Designs from Brazilian & Guianan Wood Carvings. 2.50 (ISBN 0-486-23040-6). Dover.

Amazon Indian Designs from Brazilian & Guianan Wood Carvings. 5.50 (ISBN 0-8446-5085-4). Peter Smith.

America & Alfred Stieglitz. lib. bdg. 17.00 (ISBN 0-374-96117-4). Octagon.

America & Lewis Hine. 25.00 (ISBN 0-89381-008-8). Aperture.

America As Art. 27.50 (ISBN 0-87474-900-X). Smithsonian.

America As Art. pap. 9.95 (ISBN 0-06-430090-0, IN-90). Har-Row.

America in Cross-Stitch. 12.95 (ISBN 0-13-024125-3). P-H.

America in Miniatures: How to Make Models of Early American Houses & Furniture. 10.00 (ISBN 0-15-105587-4). HarBraceJ.

America on Stone: The Other Printmakers to the American People. 150.00x (ISBN 0-405-07703-3). Arno.

American Academy in Rome, 1894-1969. 10.00x (ISBN 0-8139-0444-7). U Pr of Va.

American Advertising Posters of the Nineteenth Century. pap. 7.50 (ISBN 0-486-23356-1). Dover.

American & British Pewter: An Historical Survey. 11.95x (ISBN 0-87663-241-X); pap. 7.95 (ISBN 0-87663-949-X). Universe.

American Antique Furniture. pap. 8.95 ea.; pap. (ISBN 0-486-21599-7); pap. (ISBN 0-486-21600-4). Dover.

American Antique Glass. pap. 1.95 (ISBN 0-307-24363-X). Western Pub.

American Architects from the Civil War to the First World War: A Guide to Information Sources. 22.00 (ISBN 0-8103-1269-7). Gale.

American Architects from the First World War to the Present: A Guide to Information Sources. 22.00 (ISBN 0-8103-1270-0). Gale.

American Architectural Books: A List of Books, Portfolios, and Pamphlets on Architecture and Related Subjects Published in America Before 1895. lib. bdg. 12.50 (ISBN 0-306-70742-X). Da Capo.

American Architecture. 20.00 (ISBN 0-8180-0006-6). Horizon.

American Architecture: Westchester County, New York: Colonial to Contemporary. 30.00 (ISBN 0-88427-026-2). North River.

American Architecture & Art: A Guide to Information Sources. 22.00 (ISBN 0-8103-1255-7). Gale.

American Architecture & Other Writings. 20.00x (ISBN 0-674-01900-8). Harvard U Pr.

American Architecture for the Arts. 22.95x. Intl Schol Bk Serv.

American Architecture for the Arts. 22.95 (ISBN 0-917080-06-8). Handel & Sons.

American Architecture Since 1780: A Guide to the Styles. 15.00 (ISBN 0-262-23034-8). MIT Pr.

American Art & American Art Collections. lib. bdg. 135.00 (ISBN 0-8240-2241-6). Garland Pub.

American Art Directory, 1978. 47th ed. 42.50 (ISBN 0-8352-1037-5). Bowker.

American Art in the Barbizon Mood. 19.50 (ISBN 0-226-69413-5); 2 color fiches incl. U of Chicago Pr.

American Art in Upstate New York. pap. 3.00x (ISBN 0-914782-00-2). Buffalo Acad.

American Art Museums: An Introduction to Looking. 3rd, expanded ed. 15.00 (ISBN 0-06-013978-1). Har-Row.

American Art Nouveau Glass. 27.50 (ISBN 0-8407-4302-5). Nelson.

American Art Pottery. 20.00 (ISBN 0-8407-4301-7). Nelson.

American Artists. 9.50 (ISBN 0-404-01736-3). AMS Pr.

American Artists. facs. ed. 14.50 (ISBN 0-8369-1825-8). Arno.

American Artists. facs. ed. 13.50 (ISBN 0-8369-1311-6). Arno.

American Basketry & Woodenware: A Collector's Guide. 6.95 (ISBN 0-02-562970-0). Macmillan.

American Book Design & William Morris. 29.95 (ISBN 0-8352-0984-9). Bowker.

American Book-Plates. 20.00 (ISBN 0-405-08203-7). Arno.

American Bottles & Flasks & Their Ancestry. 29.95 (ISBN 0-517-53147-X). Crown.

American Brilliant Cut Glass. 14.95 (ISBN 0-517-52525-9). Crown.

American, British & Continental Pepperbox Firearms. 17.95 (ISBN 0-87015-158-4). Pacific Bks.

American Builder's Companion. 6th ed. 11.50 (ISBN 0-8446-1626-5). Peter Smith.

American Builder's Companion: Or, a System of Architecture Particularly Adapted to the Present Style of Building. 25.00 (ISBN 0-403-06628-X). Scholarly.

American Builder's Companion: Or, a System of Architecture, Particularly Adapted to the Present Style of Building. pap. 5.00 (ISBN 0-486-22236-5). Dover.

American Building: The Environmental Forces That Shape It. 2nd ed. pap. 7.50 (ISBN 0-8052-0503-9). Schocken.

American Building: The Historical Forces That Shaped It. 15.00 (ISBN 0-395-07680-3). HM.

American Building: The Historical Forces That Shaped It. 2nd. ed. pap. 5.95 (ISBN 0-8052-0392-3). Schocken.

American Buildings & Their Architects. Incl. The Colonial & Neo-Classical Styles. pap. (ISBN 0-385-01623-9); Progressive & Academic Ideals at the Turn of the Century. pap. (ISBN 0-385-05702-4); The Impact of European Modernism in the Mid-Twentieth Century. pap. (ISBN 0-385-05704-0). pap. 6.95 ea. Doubleday.

American Buildings & Their Architects. 12.95 (ISBN 0-385-12073-7). Doubleday.

American Circus Posters in Full Color. pap. 6.95 (ISBN 0-486-23693-5). Dover.

American Clock, 1725-1865: From the Mabel Brady Garvan & Other Collections at Yale University. 19.95 (ISBN 0-8212-0493-9). NYGS.

American Clocks & Clockmakers. 9.95 (ISBN 0-8231-3001-0). Branford.

American Colonial History Illustrated by Contemporary Medals (1894) 15.00x (ISBN 0-88000-004-X). Quarterman.

American Colonial Painting: Materials for a History. boxed 15.00x (ISBN 0-674-02250-5). Harvard U Pr.

American Colonial Paper House: To Cut Out & Color. spiral bdg. 7.95 (ISBN 0-684-14461-1). Scribner.

American Country Furniture: 1780-1875. 10.00 (ISBN 0-517-09737-0). Crown.

American Crewel Work. 9.95 (ISBN 0-02-567870-1). Macmillan.

American Crewel Work. pap. 5.95 (ISBN 0-02-011730-2). Macmillan.

American Cross-Stitch. 9.95t (ISBN 0-442-28514-0). Van Nos Reinhold.

American Cut Glass. 5.95. Warman.

American Cut Glass for the Discriminating Collector. 3rd ed. 20.00 (ISBN 0-916528-00-6). J M Pearson.

American Decorative Wall Painting: 1700-1850. pap. 7.50 (ISBN 0-525-47335-1). Dutton.

American Dictionary of Printing & Bookmaking. 19.00 (ISBN 0-8103-3345-7). Gale.

American Doll Artist. 15.95 (ISBN 0-89161-006-5). Athena Pub.

American Doll Artist. 6.95 (ISBN 0-87069-278-X). Wallace-Homestead.

American Eagle. 29.50 (ISBN 0-8212-0612-5). NYGS.

American Eagle in Art & Design. pap. 5.00 (ISBN 0-486-23604-8). Dover.

American Eagle in Art & Design: Three Hundred Twenty-One Examples. 12.50 (ISBN 0-8446-5671-2). Peter Smith.

American Engraved Powder Horns. 22.50. Ray Riling.

American Engravers Upon Copper & Steel. 47.50 (ISBN 0-8337-3378-8). B Franklin.

American Film Institute Guide to College Courses in Film & Television. pap. 9.75 (ISBN 0-87866-085-2). Petersons Guides.

American Firearms & the Changing Frontier. pap. 3.00 (ISBN 0-910524-01-7). Eastern Wash.

American Fireplace. 20.00 (ISBN 0-8407-4320-3). Nelson.

American Folk Decoration. pap. 5.00 (ISBN 0-486-22217-9). Dover.

American Folk Toys: How to Make Them. pap. 4.95 (ISBN 0-14-046209-0). Penguin.

American Furniture & Its Makers. 20.00 (ISBN 0-226-92139-5). U of Chicago Pr.

American Furniture Classics. 9.95 (ISBN 0-87069-133-3). Wallace-Homestead.

American Furniture of the Colonial Period. 6.95 (ISBN 0-87099-149-3). Metro Mus Art.

American Georgian Architecture. 29.50 (ISBN 0-306-70796-9). Da Capo.

American Glass Paperweights & Their Makers. rev. & enl. ed. 17.50 (ISBN 0-8407-4305-X). Nelson.

American Graphic Art. 15.00 (ISBN 0-8103-4020-8). Gale.

American Graphic Art. new & enl. ed. 18.50 (ISBN 0-384-66645-0). Johnson Repr.

American Guide to U.S. Coins. 5.95 (ISBN 0-671-27080-X). Trident.

American Guide to U.S. Coins: 1979 Edition. rev. ed. pap. 2.95 (ISBN 0-346-12362-3). Cornerstone.

American Guide to U.S. Coins: 1980 Edition. pap. 2.95 (ISBN 0-346-12402-6). Cornerstone.

American Hand Book of the Daguerreotype. 5th ed. 16.00 (ISBN 0-405-04919-6). Arno.

Ansel Adams: Images Nineteen Twenty-Three to Nineteen Seventy-Four. slipcased 100.00 (ISBN 0-8212-0600-1). NYGS.
Antelope Rises: Elimo Njau. pap. text ed. 1.95 (ISBN 0-89253-103-7). InterCulture.
Anthrophysical Form: Two Families & Their Neighborhood Environments. 9.75x (ISBN 0-8139-0393-9). U Pr of Va.
Anthropology & Art: Readings in Cross-Cultural Aesthetics. pap. 6.95x (ISBN 0-292-70313-9). U of Tex Pr.
Anthropology in Historic Preservation: Caring for Culture's Clutter. 17.50 (ISBN 0-12-408250-5). Acad Pr.
Anti-Rationalists. 20.00x (ISBN 0-8020-1955-2). U of Toronto Pr.
Anticlassicism in Greek Sculpture of the Fourth Century B.C. 18.50x (ISBN 0-8147-0971-0). NYU Pr.
Antietam: The Photographic Legacy of America's Bloodiest Day. 15.95 (ISBN 0-684-15659-8). Scribner.
Antipodean Manifesto: Essays in Art & History. 23.25x (ISBN 0-19-550477-1). Oxford U Pr.
Antique Alphabets. 7.00 (ISBN 0-911380-01-9). Signs of Times.
Antique American Country Furniture: A Field Guide. 9.95 (ISBN 0-397-01219-5); pap. 6.95 (ISBN 0-397-01267-5). Lippincott.
Antique & Unusual Thimbles. 15.00 (ISBN 0-498-02065-7). A S Barnes.
Antique Bottle Collector. pap. 2.95 (9271). HarBraceJ.
Antique Cameras. 12.95 (ISBN 0-7153-6840-0). David & Charles.
Antique Chinese Rugs. 7.50 (ISBN 0-8048-0025-1). C E Tuttle.
Antique Collector's Dictionary. pap. 1.95 (ISBN 0-668-01868-2). Arc Bks.
Antique Collector's Dolls. 17.95 (ISBN 0-89145-049-1). Collector Bks.
Antique Collector's Dolls: Second Series. 17.95 (ISBN 0-89145-021-1). Collector Bks.
Antique Collector's Handbook. rev ed. 10.25 (ISBN 0-600-00054-0). Intl Pubns Serv.
Antique Country Furniture of North America. 16.95 (ISBN 0-442-27544-7). Van Nos Reinhold.
Antique Dealers Pocketbook. 4.95 (ISBN 0-684-13828-X). Scribner.
Antique Fakes & Reproductions. rev. ed. 15.00 (ISBN 0-910872-07-4). Lee Pubns.
Antique Finishing for Beginners. 13.95 (ISBN 0-8230-0230-6). Watson-Guptill.
Antique Firearms. 14.95 (ISBN 0-89141-050-3). Presidio Pr.
Antique Furniture. lib. bdg. 8.95 (ISBN 0-668-04471-3); pap. 5.95 (ISBN 0-668-04482-9). Arco.
Antique Furniture for the Smaller Home. 4.50 (ISBN 0-668-01026-6). Arco.
Antique Furniture for the Smaller Home. pap. 0.95 (ISBN 0-668-01025-8). Arc Bks.
Antique Furniture Guide. 5.00. Warman.
Antique Furniture Repairs. 7.95 (ISBN 0-684-14720-3). Scribner.
Antique Guns from the Stagecoach Collection. lib. bdg. 3.50 (ISBN 0-668-01917-4). Arco.
Antique Guns in Color: Twelve Fifty to Eighteen Sixty-Five. 8.95 (ISBN 0-668-04467-5); pap. 6.95 (ISBN 0-668-04478-0). Arco.
Antique-Hunter's Handbook. 6.95 (ISBN 0-7153-7578-4). David & Charles.
Antique Jewelry Identification with Price Guide. plastic bdg. 6.95 (ISBN 0-87069-004-3). Wallace-Homestead.
Antique Jewelry Identification with Price Guide. plastic bdg. 6.95 (ISBN 0-87069-098-1). Wallace-Homestead.
Antique Paper Dolls: Nineteen Fifteen to Nineteen Twenty. pap. 2.00 (ISBN 0-486-23176-3). Dover.
Antique Pewter of the British Isles. 6.50 (ISBN 0-8446-0207-8). Peter Smith.
Antique Pewter of the British Isles. pap. 2.50 (ISBN 0-486-22706-5). Dover.
Antique Picture Frame Guide. 12.50. Wallace-Homestead.
Antique Restorer's Handbook: A Dictionary of the Crafts & Materials Used in Restoring Antiques & Works of Art. 8.95 (ISBN 0-385-05302-9). Doubleday.
Antique Shaving Mugs of the United States. softcover 17.95. Wallace-Homestead.
Antique Shaving Mugs of the United States. 17.95 (ISBN 0-9600680-1-5). R B Powell.
Antique Tin & Tole Ware: Its History & Romance. 27.50 (ISBN 0-8048-0026-X). C E Tuttle.
Antique Toys & Their Background. lib. bdg. 12.50 (ISBN 0-668-02484-4). Arco.
Antique Woodworking Tools: A Guide to the Purchase, Restoration & Use of Old Tools for Today's Shop. 12.50 (ISBN 0-8038-5821-3). Hastings.
Antique Works of Art from Benin. 10.00 (ISBN 0-8446-5654-2). Peter Smith.
Antique Works of Art from Benin. 20.00 (ISBN 0-87817-017-0). Hacker.
Antique Works of Art from Benin. pap. 5.00 (ISBN 0-486-23323-5). Dover.
Antique Works of Art from Benin, West Africa. facs. ed. 17.50 (ISBN 0-8369-8736-5). Arno.
Antiquers' of Glass Candy Containers. spiral bd. 12.75 (ISBN 0-9601150-0-5). R T Matthews.
Antiques: A Browser's Handbook. 10.95 (ISBN 0-06-013104-7). Har-Row.
Antiques & Collectibles: A Bibliography of Works in English, 16th Century to 1976. 37.50 (ISBN 0-8108-1092-1). Scarecrow.
Antiques for Amateurs on a Shoestring Budget. pap. 3.95 (ISBN 0-89104-063-3). A & W Pubs.
Antiques Guide to Decorative Arts in America 1600-1875. pap. 6.95 (ISBN 0-525-47334-3). Dutton.
Antiques Illustrated & Priced. 25.00 (ISBN 0-498-02109-2). A S Barnes.
Antiquing from A to Z. 8.95 (ISBN 0-671-22075-6). S&S.
Antiquing in New Jersey & Bucks County, Pennsylvania. 15.00 (ISBN 0-8135-0853-3); pap. 8.25 (ISBN 0-8135-0863-0). Rutgers U Pr.
Antiquities from the City of Benin & from Other Parts of West Africa in the British Museum. 75.00 (ISBN 0-87817-079-0). Hacker.
Antiquity Depicted: Aspects of Archaeological Illustration. 9.95 (ISBN 0-500-55010-7). Thames Hudson.
Antiquity Explained & Represented in Sculptures. lib. bdg. 132.00 (ISBN 0-8240-2085-5); lib. bdg. 60.00 ea. Garland Pub.
Antiquity of the Art of Painting. 32.50x (ISBN 0-300-00641-1). Yale U Pr.
Antoine Le Pautre: A French Architect of the Era of Louis XIV. 18.50x (ISBN 0-8147-0039-X). NYU Pr.
Antonin Raymond: An Autobiography. 27.50 (ISBN 0-8048-1044-3). C E Tuttle.
Antonio & Francesco Guardi: Their Life & Milieu: With a Catalogue of Their Figure Drawings. lib. bdg. 40.00 (ISBN 0-8240-1979-2). Garland Pub.
Antonio & Piero Pollaiuolo. 75.00 (ISBN 0-7148-1768-6). Dutton.
Antonio Gaudi. 7.95 (ISBN 0-8076-0107-1). Braziller.
Anuszkiewicz. 55.00 (ISBN 0-8109-0363-6). Abrams.
Anyone Can Make Big Money Buying Art. 7.95 (ISBN 0-02-610560-8, 61056). Macmillan.
Anyone Can Quilt. pap. 2.95 (ISBN 0-87502-039-9). Benjamin Co.
Anyone Can Sculpt. rev. ed. 14.95 (ISBN 0-06-014800-4). Har-Row.
Apartments for the Affluent: A Historical Survey of Buildings in New York. 34.50 (ISBN 0-07-001372-1). McGraw.
Apex Treasury of Underground Comics. pap. 5.95 (ISBN 0-8256-3042-8). Music Sales.
Aphrodisiac. pap. 4.95 (ISBN 0-517-52679-4). Crown.
Apocalyptic Vision: The Art of Franz Marc As German Expressionism. 17.50 (ISBN 0-06-435275-7). Har-Row.
Apollonio Di Giovanni. 38.50x (ISBN 0-19-817196-X). Oxford U Pr.
Apostle Bas-Relief at Saint-Denis. 21.00x (ISBN 0-300-01504-6). Yale U Pr.
Apotheoseos Tam Exterarum Gentium Quam Romanorum Deorum see Allegoriae Poeticae.
Application of Ornament. lib. bdg. 35.00x (ISBN 0-8240-2471-0). Garland Pub.
Application of Science in the Examination of Works of Art. 25.00 (ISBN 0-87846-071-3). NYGS.
Applications Manual for Paint & Protective Coatings: A Guide to Types of Coatings, Methods of Surface Preparation & Hand Application Techniques. 32.50 (ISBN 0-07-024970-9). McGraw.
Applications of Holography. 39.50 (ISBN 0-306-30526-7). Plenum Pub.
Applications of Holography. 16.50 (ISBN 0-471-14080-5). Krieger.
Applied & Decorative Arts: A Bibliographic Guide to Basic Reference Works, Histories, & Handbooks. lib. bdg. 15.00 (ISBN 0-87287-136-3). Libs Unl.
Applied Imagination. 3rd ed. pap. text ed. 6.95 (ISBN 0-684-16256-3). Scribner.
Applied Imagination. 3rd ed. pap. text ed. 6.95x (ISBN 0-684-41393-0). Scribner.
Applied Infrared Photography. pap. 4.50 (ISBN 0-87985-009-4, M-28). Eastman Kodak.
Applied Penmanship. 2nd ed. pap. text ed. 2.32 (ISBN 0-538-05780-7). SW Pub.
Applied Photographic Theory. 51.95 (ISBN 0-471-50600-1). Wiley.
Applied Photography. 46.95 (ISBN 0-8038-0457-1). Focal Pr.
Applied Police & Fire Photography. 21.50 (ISBN 0-398-03566-0). C C Thomas.
Applied Surveillance Photography. 12.25 (ISBN 0-398-03376-5). C C Thomas.
Applique & Reverse Applique. 3.95 (ISBN 0-8069-5274-1); PLB 4.59 (ISBN 0-8069-5277-6). Sterling.
Applique Old & New, Including Patchwork & Embroidery. pap. 2.50 (ISBN 0-486-23246-8). Dover.
Applique Old & New, Including Patchwork & Embroidery. 5.00 (ISBN 0-8446-5490-6). Peter Smith.
Appreciation of Byzantine Art. pap. 10.50x (ISBN 0-19-211923-0). Oxford U Pr.
Appreciation of Painting. facsimile ed. 15.50 (ISBN 0-8369-6671-6). Arno.
Appreciation of Stained Glass. 12.25x (ISBN 0-19-211913-3). Oxford U Pr.
Apprentice-Mechanical Trades. 6th ed. pap. 6.00 (ISBN 0-668-00571-8). Arco.
Apprentice to Genius: Architect. 19.95 (ISBN 0-07-062815-7). McGraw.
Approach to Architectural Design. 15.00x (ISBN 0-8020-1801-7). U of Toronto Pr.
Approach to Urban Planning. lib. bdg. 9.00x (ISBN 0-8371-2284-8, BRUP). Greenwood.
Approaches to Art in Education. text ed. 14.95. HarBraceJ.
Approaches to Collage. 9.95 (ISBN 0-8008-0280-2). Taplinger.
Approaching Design Through Nature: The Quiet Joy. 12.50 (ISBN 0-670-12980-1). Viking Pr.
Approved Practices in Beautifying the Home Grounds. 5th ed. 11.35 (ISBN 0-8134-2042-3, 2042); text ed. 8.50x. Interstate.
Arab Painting. 25.00 (ISBN 0-8478-0095-4); pap. 14.95 (ISBN 0-8478-0081-4). Rizzoli Intl.
Arab Painting. text ed. 22.50x (ISBN 0-8426-1097-9). Verry.
Arabesque: Decorative Needlework from the Holy Land. 12.95 (ISBN 0-442-20290-3). Van Nos Reinhold.
Arabic Geometrical Pattern & Design. pap. 4.50 (ISBN 0-486-22924-6). Dover.
Arabic Geometrical Pattern & Design. 6.50 (ISBN 0-8446-5104-4). Peter Smith.
Arabic Manuscripts in the Yale University Library. pap. 15.00 (ISBN 0-208-01103-X). Shoe String.
Archaeological Photography. 7.95x, UK (ISBN 0-8147-0388-7). NYU Pr.
Archaeological Studies Among the Ancient Cities of Mexico. pap. 28.00 (ISBN 0-527-01861-9). Kraus Repr.
Archaeologische Hermeneutik: Anleitung Zur Deutung Klassischer Bildwerke. facsimile ed. 24.00x (ISBN 0-405-07276-7). Arno.
Archaeology & Ceramics at the Marksville Site. pap. 4.00x (ISBN 0-932206-54-9). U Mich Mus Anthro.
Archaeology & the Colonial Gardener. pap. 1.95 (ISBN 0-87935-012-1). Williamsburg.
Archaeology of Amapa, Nayarit. 35.00 (ISBN 0-917956-01-X). UCLA Arch.
Archaeology of London. 9.95 (ISBN 0-8155-5033-2). Noyes.
Archaic & Archaistic Sculpture. 20.00x (ISBN 0-87661-211-7). Am Sch Athens.
Archaic & Classical Greek Coins. 65.00x (ISBN 0-520-03254-3). U of Cal Pr.
Archaic Corinthian Pottery & the Anaploga Well. 35.00x (ISBN 0-87661-072-6). Am Sch Athens.
Archaic Greek Gems: Schools & Artists in the Sixth & Early Fifth Centuries. 9.60x (ISBN 0-8101-0029-0). Northwestern U Pr.
Archaic Style in Greek Sculpture. text ed. 40.00x (ISBN 0-691-03920-8); pap. 13.50x (ISBN 0-691-10052-7). Princeton U Pr.
Archeology of the Death Valley Salt Pan. 25.50. Johnson Repr.
Archetypal World of Henry Moore. 12.50x (ISBN 0-691-09702-X). Princeton U Pr.
Archipenko: A Study of the Early Works, 1908-1920. lib. bdg. 49.00 (ISBN 0-8240-2712-4). Garland Pub.
Archipenko: International Visionary. 15.00 (ISBN 0-87474-080-0). Smithsonian.
Archipenko: The Sculpture & Graphic Art. 35.00x (ISBN 0-89158-500-1). Westview.
Architect & Community: Environmental Design in an Urban Society. text ed. 12.00x (ISBN 0-7206-0290-4). Humanities.
Architect & Sculptor in Classical Greece. 20.00 (ISBN 0-8147-0553-7). NYU Pr.
Architect & the Shelter Industry. pap. text ed. 3.00 (ISBN 0-913962-10-4). Am Inst Arch.
Architect As Developer. 27.50 (ISBN 0-07-050536-5). McGraw.
Architect: Chapters in the History of the Profession. 21.00 (ISBN 0-19-502067-7). Oxford U Pr.
Architect: Creating Man's Environment. 4.95 (ISBN 0-02-583530-0). Macmillan.
Architect in History. lib. bdg. 19.50 (ISBN 0-306-70584-2). Da Capo.
Architects. PLB 4.90 (ISBN 0-531-01041-4). Watts.
Architects & Man's Skyline. 5.95 (ISBN 0-396-06435-3). Dodd.
Architects' Data. text ed. 34.95x. Beekman Pubs.
Architects on Architecture. rev. ed. pap. 10.95. Walker & Co.
Architects on Architecture: New Directions in America. 19.95 (ISBN 0-8027-0019-5); pap. 12.95. Walker & Co.
Architectural Acoustics. 36.00 (ISBN 0-12-787145-4). Acad Pr.
Architectural & Building Trades Dictionary. 3rd ed. 15.10 (ISBN 0-8269-0402-5). Am Technical.
Architectural & Engineering Salesmanship. 14.95 (ISBN 0-471-03642-0). Wiley.
Architectural & Ornament Drawings: Juvarra, Vanvitelli, the Bibiena Family, & Other Italian Draughtsmen. pap. 8.95 (ISBN 0-87099-126-4). Metro Mus Art.
Architectural & Perspective Designs. pap. 5.00 (ISBN 0-486-21263-7). Dover.
Architectural & Perspective Designs. 7.00 (ISBN 0-8446-1676-1). Peter Smith.
Architectural Delineation: A Photographic Approach to Presentation. 29.95 (ISBN 0-07-008924-8). McGraw.
Architectural Development of the Greek Stoa. 39.00x (ISBN 0-19-813215-8). Oxford U Pr.
Architectural Drafting. 2nd ed. 11.65 (ISBN 0-07-004418-X). McGraw.
Architectural Drafting. 5th ed. text ed. 18.60 (ISBN 0-13-044123-6). P-H.
Architectural Drafting & Construction. text ed. 17.95x (ISBN 0-205-04221-X); instr's hndbk avail. (ISBN 0-205-04222-8). Allyn.
Architectural Drafting & Design. 3rd ed. text ed. 18.50x (ISBN 0-205-05624-5); tchr's manual avail. (ISBN 0-205-05625-3). Allyn.
Architectural Drafting: Functional Planning & Creative Design. 2nd ed. 18.25 (ISBN 0-8269-1042-4). Am Technical.
Architectural Drawing. 3rd ed. pap. text ed. 8.95 (ISBN 0-8403-1809-X). Kendall-Hunt.
Architectural Drawing. rev. ed. 9.00 (ISBN 0-02-829660-5). Glencoe.
Architectural Drawing & Light Construction. 2nd ed. 17.95 (ISBN 0-13-044578-9). P-H.
Architectural Drawing & Planning. 2nd ed. text ed. 15.95 (ISBN 0-07-023751-4). McGraw.
Architectural Drawing & Planning. 3rd ed. pap. text ed. 13.95 (ISBN 0-07-023771-9). McGraw.
Architectural Drawing Problems. 3rd ed. wkbk. 9.95 (ISBN 0-8403-1756-5). Kendall-Hunt.
Architectural Environment & Our Mental Health. 5.95 (ISBN 0-8180-0010-4). Horizon.
Architectural Graphic Standards. 6th ed. 55.00 (ISBN 0-471-70780-5). Wiley.
Architectural Graphics. 9.95x (ISBN 0-442-21530-4); pap. 5.50 (ISBN 0-442-21531-2). Van Nos Reinhold.
Architectural Graphics. 2nd ed. text ed. 16.50. Macmillan.
Architectural Heritage of Newport, Rhode Island: 1640-1915. 2nd ed. 25.00 (ISBN 0-517-09719-2). Potter.
Architectural Heritage of the Merrimack. 18.95 (ISBN 0-917890-13-2). Heritage Bk.
Architectural Illustration. 27.50 (ISBN 0-13-044610-6). P-H.
Architectural Illustration. text ed. 34.50 (ISBN 0-442-26274-4). Van Nos Reinhold.
Architectural Interior Systems: Lighting, Air Conditioning, Acoustics. 17.50x (ISBN 0-442-15664-2). Van Nos Reinhold.
Architectural Interpretation of History. 18.95 (ISBN 0-312-04812-2). St Martin.
Architectural Journey Through Long Island. 9.95 (ISBN 0-8046-9109-6). Kennikat.
Architectural Models. 25.00 (ISBN 0-8038-0012-6). Architectural.
Architectural Photography. 27.50 (ISBN 0-471-61312-6). Wiley.
Architectural Photography. 19.95 (ISBN 0-8174-0556-9). Amphoto.
Architectural Polychromy of the 1830's. lib. bdg. 52.00 (ISBN 0-8240-2733-7). Garland Pub.
Architectural Precast Concrete Drafting Handbook. ref. ed. 17.95 (ISBN 0-13-044602-5). P-H.
Architectural Presentation Techniques. 16.95 (ISBN 0-442-20361-6). Van Nos Reinhold.
Architectural Preservation in the United States, 1941-1975: A Bibliography of Federal, State, & Local Government Publications. lib. bdg. 42.00 (ISBN 0-8240-9937-0). Garland Pub.
Architectural Principles in the Age of Humanism. pap. 3.95 (ISBN 0-393-00599-2). Norton.
Architectural Rendering: The Technique of Contemporary Presentation. 2nd ed. 36.00 (ISBN 0-07-025628-4). McGraw.
Architectural Scale. 5.00 (ISBN 0-8076-0351-1). Braziller.
Architectural Sculpture in New York City. pap. 4.00 (ISBN 0-486-23120-8). Dover.
Architectural Sculpture in New York City. 7.50 (ISBN 0-8446-5203-2). Peter Smith.
Architectural Signing & Graphics. 32.50 (ISBN 0-8230-7051-4). Watson-Guptill.
Architectural Sketches & Flower Drawings by Charles Rennie Mackintosh. 13.95 (ISBN 0-8478-0074-1); pap. 7.95 (ISBN 0-8478-0084-9). Rizzoli Intl.
Architectural Space in Ancient Greece. pap. 5.95 (ISBN 0-262-54030-4). MIT Pr.

Art & Human Values. 13.95 (ISBN 0-13-046821-5). P-H.
Art & Ideas for Young People. 10.95x (ISBN 0-442-11361-7). Van Nos Reinhold.
Art & Illusion: A Study in the Psychology of Pictorial Presentation. 2nd ed. 22.00x (ISBN 0-691-09785-2); pap. 9.95 (ISBN 0-691-01750-6, 156). Princeton U Pr.
Art & Illustration Techniques. 18.95 (ISBN 0-8230-0272-1). Watson-Guptill.
Art & Indian Individualists. 35.00 (ISBN 0-87358-137-7). Northland.
Art & Industry. pap. 2.75x (ISBN 0-253-20032-6). Ind U Pr.
Art & Industry: The Principles of Industrial Design. 6.50 (ISBN 0-8446-2786-0). Peter Smith.
Art & Inquiry. text ed. 13.95x (ISBN 0-8143-1531-3). Wayne St U Pr.
Art & Instinct. lib. bdg. 5.00 (ISBN 0-8414-2929-4). Folcroft.
Art & Ireland. 13.50 (ISBN 0-8046-0776-1). Kennikat.
Art & Knowledge. 11.00 (ISBN 0-87752-208-1). Gordian.
Art & Life in New Guinea. 24.50 (ISBN 0-404-14119-6). AMS Pr.
Art & Literature in Fourth Century Athens. lib. bdg. 15.00x (ISBN 0-8371-0743-1, WEAL). Greenwood.
Art & Man. facsimile ed. 19.50 (ISBN 0-8369-1270-5). Arno.
Art & Morality. 9.00x (ISBN 0-8248-0256-X). U Pr of Hawaii.
Art & Music: An Introduction. pap. text ed. 11.95 (ISBN 0-15-503437-5); 4.95. HarBraceJ.
Art & Nonart. pap. text ed. 9.00 (ISBN 0-8191-0404-3). U Pr of Amer.
Art & Peoples of Black Africa. pap. 7.95 (ISBN 0-525-47364-5). Dutton.
Art & Philosophy. rev. ed. text ed. write for info. (ISBN 0-391-00645-2). Humanities.
Art & Politics: Cartoonists of the "Masses" & "Liberator". lib. bdg. 15.95x (ISBN 0-8371-6006-5, FRI). Greenwood.
Art & Politics of Thomas Nast. pap. 8.95 (ISBN 0-19-501929-6, GB437). Oxford U Pr.
Art & Practice of Silver Printing. 10.00 (ISBN 0-405-04933-1). Arno.
Art & Reproduction: Graphic Reproduction Techniques. 13.95 (ISBN 0-442-20550-3); pap. 8.95 (ISBN 0-442-20551-1). Van Nos Reinhold.
Art & Scholasticism & the Frontiers of Poetry. text ed. 9.95x (ISBN 0-268-00556-7); pap. 3.25x (ISBN 0-268-00557-5). U of Notre Dame Pr.
Art & Scholasticism: With Other Essays. facsimile ed. 10.50 (ISBN 0-8369-2241-7). Arno.
Art & Science of Medical Radiography. 5th ed. pap. text ed. 7.50 (ISBN 0-87125-034-9). Cath Health.
Art & Scientific Thought. 10.50 (ISBN 0-404-00593-4). AMS Pr.
Art & Society. rev. ed. pap. 3.95 (ISBN 0-8052-0132-7). Schocken.
Art & Society: Essays in Marxist Aesthetics. 13.50 (ISBN 0-85345-269-5, CL2695). Monthly Rev.
Art & Society: Essays in Marxist Aesthetics. pap. 5.95 (ISBN 0-85345-327-6, PB3276). Monthly Rev.
Art & Stained Glass. Softbound 3.95 (ISBN 0-385-08286-X). Doubleday.
Art & Technics. 11.00x (ISBN 0-231-01903-3); pap. 2.45 (ISBN 0-231-08509-5, 9). Columbia U Pr.
Art & Technique of Sumi-E. 19.50 (ISBN 0-8048-0031-6). C E Tuttle.
Art & the Aesthetic: An Institutional Analysis. 14.50x (ISBN 0-8014-0887-3). Cornell U Pr.
Art & the Camera. 13.00 (ISBN 0-405-04912-9). Arno.
Art & the Creative Consciousness. pap. text ed. 6.95 (ISBN 0-13-046706-5). P-H.
Art & the Creative Unconscious. 13.00 (ISBN 0-691-09706-2); pap. 3.95 (ISBN 0-691-01773-5, 240). Princeton U Pr.
Art & the Formation of Taste. lib. bdg. 35.00x (ISBN 0-8240-2458-3). Garland Pub.
Art & the Human Enterprise. 17.50 (ISBN 0-208-00753-9). Shoe String.
Art & the Industrial Revolution. 22.50x (ISBN 0-678-07510-7). Kelley.
Art & the Occult. 17.50 (ISBN 0-8076-0784-3); pap. 7.95 (ISBN 0-8076-0785-1). Braziller.
Art & the Reformation. 22.50 (ISBN 0-208-00738-5). Shoe String.
Art & the Romans. 10.00x (ISBN 0-87291-070-9). Coronado Pr.
Art & Theological Imagination. 12.95 (ISBN 0-8164-0397-X). Seabury.
Art & Visual Perception: A Psychology of the Creative Eye... the New Version. 15.00 (ISBN 0-520-02327-7); pap. 7.95 (ISBN 0-520-02613-6). U of Cal Pr.
Art, Another Language for Learning. pap. 7.95 (ISBN 0-590-09405-X). Schol Bk Serv.
Art Appreciation Made Simple. 2.95 (ISBN 0-385-01222-5). Doubleday.
Art, Artists & Art Education. perfect bdg. 11.95 (ISBN 0-8403-1427-2). Kendall Hunt.
Art As Art: The Writings of Ad Reinhardt. 14.95 (ISBN 0-670-13451-1). Viking Pr.
Art As Experience. pap. 3.95 (ISBN 0-399-50025-1). Paragon.
Art at Educational Institutions in the United States: A Handbook of Permanent, Semi-Permanent & Temporary Works of Art at Elementary & Secondary Schools, Colleges & Universities. 40.00 (ISBN 0-8108-0715-7). Scarecrow.
Art au Point de Vue Sociologique: Art from the Sociological Point of View. 11th ed. 24.00x (ISBN 0-405-06510-8). Arno.
Art Before Columbus. pap. 4.95 (ISBN 0-671-20506-4). S&S.
Art Career Guide. rev. & enl. ed. 9.95 (ISBN 0-8230-0251-9). Watson-Guptill.
Art Censorship: A Chronology of Proscribed & Prescribed Art. 20.00 (ISBN 0-8108-0455-7). Scarecrow.
Art Chronicles: 1954-1966. 15.00 (ISBN 0-8076-0755-X). Braziller.
Art, Crafts, & Architecture in Early Illinois. 19.50 (ISBN 0-252-00391-8). U of Ill Pr.
Art, Crafts, & Architecture in Early Illinois. pap. 10.00 (ISBN 0-252-00675-5). U of Ill Pr.
Art Criticism from a Laboratory. lib. bdg. 16.75x (ISBN 0-8371-4493-0, BUAC). Greenwood.
Art Criticism in the Sixties. pap. 2.95 (ISBN 0-8079-0008-7). October.
Art Crowd. 9.95 (ISBN 0-679-50332-3). McKay.
Art, Culture & Environment. 14.95 (ISBN 0-534-00472-5). Wadsworth Pub.
Art De France. pap. 25.00x. Wittenborn.
Art Deco: A Guide for Collectors. 14.95 (ISBN 0-517-50076-0). Potter.
Art Deco Architecture in New York, 1920-1940. 17.50x (ISBN 0-06-438850-6). Har-Row.
Art Deco Designs & Motifs. pap. 3.00 (ISBN 0-486-22826-6). Dover.
Art Deco Designs & Motifs. 6.75 (ISBN 0-8446-4575-3). Peter Smith.
Art Deco Interiors in Color. pap. 4.00 (ISBN 0-486-23527-0). Dover.
Art Deco Internationale. pap. 7.95 (ISBN 0-8256-3070-3, 030070). Music Sales.
Art Directors' Book of Type Faces. 3rd ed. flexible bdg. 9.95 (ISBN 0-668-04041-6). Arco.
Art Embroidery. lib. bdg. 35.00x (ISBN 0-8240-2462-1). Garland Pub.
Art Epochs & Their Leaders: A Survey of the Genesis of Modern Art. facsimile ed. 27.25 (ISBN 0-8369-5946-9). Arno.
Art Experience. 17.50 (ISBN 0-912158-60-3); pap. 4.95 (ISBN 0-912158-61-1). Hennessey.
Art Expression & Beauty. 12.50 (ISBN 0-88275-217-0). Krieger.
Art for Teachers of Children. 2nd ed. text ed. 15.95x (ISBN 0-675-08962-X). Merrill.
Art for the Millions: Essays from the 1930's by Artists & Administrators of the WPA Federal Art Project. pap. 9.95 (ISBN 0-8212-0659-1). NYGS.
Art for Today's Schools. 14.50 (ISBN 0-87192-001-8). Davis Mass.
Art for Young America. text ed. 15.96 (ISBN 0-87002-294-6). Bennett Co.
Art Forms & Civic Life in the Late Roman Empire. 11.00x (ISBN 0-691-03802-3); pap. 4.95 (ISBN 0-691-00305-X, 269). Princeton U Pr.
Art Forms from Photomicrography. pap. 4.50 (ISBN 0-486-20298-4). Dover.
Art from Clutter. PLB 9.66 (ISBN 0-8239-0341-9). Rosen Pr.
Art from Found Objects. 6.25 (ISBN 0-688-41646-2); PLB 6.00 (ISBN 0-688-51646-7). Lothrop.
Art from Recycled Materials. 9.95 (ISBN 0-87192-059-X). Davis Mass.
Art from Scrap. rev. ed. 5.95 (ISBN 0-87192-055-7). Davis Mass.
Art from Shells. pap. 5.95 (ISBN 0-517-50025-6). Crown.
Art from the Mayans to Disney. facsimile ed. 18.25 (ISBN 0-8369-1399-X). Arno.
Art Fundamentals. 12.95 (ISBN 0-87396-082-3). Stravon.
Art Fundamentals: Theory & Practice. 3rd ed. pap. text ed. 10.95x (ISBN 0-697-03231-0). Wm C Brown.
Art Galleries of Britain & Ireland: A Guide to Their Collections. 12.00 (ISBN 0-8386-1850-2). Fairleigh Dickinson.
Art Glass Nouveau. 42.50 (ISBN 0-8048-0032-4). C E Tuttle.
Art Glass Sampler. softbound 12.95 (ISBN 0-87069-171-6). Wallace-Homestead.
Art Glass Shades. 4.95; price guide 1.50. Wallace-Homestead.
Art Has Many Faces. 10.95 (ISBN 0-06-003180-8). Har-Row.
Art History: An Anthology of Modern Criticism. 7.50 (ISBN 0-8446-3044-6). Peter Smith.
Art History of Photography. 15.95 (ISBN 0-670-13437-6). Viking Pr.
Art-Idea. 15.00x (ISBN 0-674-04700-1). Harvard U Pr.
Art in America: A Brief History. pap. text ed. 6.50 (ISBN 0-15-503466-9). HarBraceJ.
Art in Architecture. 34.50 (ISBN 0-07-051365-1). McGraw.
Art in Business: The Philip Morris Story. 40.00 (ISBN 0-8109-0713-5). Abrams.
Art in Cartooning. pap. 9.95 (ISBN 0-684-16398-5). Scribner.
Art in Context. pap. text ed. 9.95 (ISBN 0-15-503469-3). HarBraceJ.
Art in East Africa: A Contemporary Guide to East African Art. text ed. 17.50x (ISBN 0-8419-0269-0). Holmes & Meier.
Art in East & West. pap. 2.95 (ISBN 0-8070-6685-0, BP188). Beacon Pr.
Art in England: Eighteen Hundred to Eighteen Thirty-Seven. lib. bdg. 50.00 (ISBN 0-87817-109-6). Hacker.
Art in Everyday Life. 4th ed. text ed. 13.95x (ISBN 0-02-344480-0, 34448). Macmillan.
Art in Flanders. 20.00 (ISBN 0-404-05397-1). AMS Pr.
Art in Indonesia: Continuities & Change. 38.50x (ISBN 0-8014-0188-7). Cornell U Pr.
Art in Israel. 10.00 (ISBN 0-8052-3605-8). Schocken.
Art in Its Fourth Dimension. 7.95 (ISBN 0-8022-2182-3). Philos Lib.
Art in Japanese Esoteric Buddhism. 17.50 (ISBN 0-8348-1001-8). Weatherhill.
Art in Needlework. lib. bdg. 35.00x (ISBN 0-8240-2473-7). Garland Pub.
Art in Needlework: A Book About Embroidery. 13.50 (ISBN 0-8103-3062-8). Gale.
Art in Our Time: 10th Anniversary Exhibition. 33.00 (ISBN 0-405-01554-2). Arno.
Art in Paper. 12.00 (ISBN 0-498-01489-4). A S Barnes.
Art in Primitive Societies. pap. 8.95 ref. ed. (ISBN 0-13-048108-4). P-H.
Art in Revolution. pap. 2.95 (ISBN 0-394-41562-0). Pantheon.
Art in Teaching Art. 25.00x (ISBN 0-8032-0948-7). U of Nebr Pr.
Art in the Armed Forces. lib. bdg. 33.00x (ISBN 0-8240-0438-8). Garland Pub.
Art in the Early Church. pap. 5.95 (ISBN 0-393-00493-7). Norton.
Art in the Early Church. rev. ed. 8.50 (ISBN 0-8446-2492-6). Peter Smith.
Art in the Elementary School: Drawing, Painting & Creating for the Classroom. pap. text ed. 6.95x (ISBN 0-697-03294-9). Wm C Brown.
Art in the Environment in the United States. 12.00 (ISBN 0-910642-02-8). Fundaburk.
Art in the Humanities. 2nd ed. pap. text ed. 7.50 (ISBN 0-13-046979-3). P-H.
Art in the Primary School. text ed. 7.25x (ISBN 0-631-11880-2). Humanities.
Art Institute of Chicago: 100 Masterpieces. 35.00 (ISBN 0-528-81033-2). Rand.
Art into Life. 7.50 (ISBN 0-8283-1125-0). Branden.
Art Is Action. 9.25 (ISBN 0-8046-1690-6). Kennikat.
Art Is Action. facsimile ed. 14.50 (ISBN 0-8369-1250-0). Arno.
Art Is Elementary: Teaching Visual Thinking Through Art Concepts. pap. text ed. 19.95x (ISBN 0-8425-1517-8). Brigham.
Art Lessons on a Shoestring: New Ideas for Practical Art Lessons in the Elementary School. 10.95 (ISBN 0-13-047407-X). P-H.
Art Lessons That Mirror the Child's World. text ed. 13.95 (ISBN 0-13-047423-1). P-H.
Art Library Manual. 24.50 (ISBN 0-85935-054-1). Bowker.
Art, Life & Nature in Japan. lib. bdg. 13.25x (ISBN 0-8371-4196-6, ANNJ). Greenwood.
Art-Life of William Morris Hunt. 15.00 (ISBN 0-405-08714-4). Arno.
Art Market in the Nineteen Sixties see Economics of Taste.
Art Materials, Techniques, Ideas: A Resource Book for Teachers. 11.95 (ISBN 0-87192-057-3). Davis Mass.
Art Metal & Enameling. text ed. 11.60 (ISBN 0-87002-157-5). Bennett Co.
Art Monograms & Lettering. 20th ed. 17.95 (ISBN 0-910222-02-9). Gem City Coll.
Art Monograms & Lettering. 18th ed. pap. 6.50 (ISBN 0-910222-03-7). Gem City Coll.
Art Museum As Educator. 35.00x (ISBN 0-520-03248-9); pap. 14.95 (ISBN 0-520-03249-7). U of Cal Pr.
Art Museum: Power, Money & Ethics. a Twentieth Century Fund Essay. 15.00 (ISBN 0-688-03390-3). Morrow.
Art Needs No Justification. pap. 1.95 (ISBN 0-87784-323-6). Inter-Varsity.
Art Nouveau & Art Deco Lighting. 25.00 (ISBN 0-671-24307-1). S&S.
Art Nouveau Belgium-France. 20.00 (ISBN 0-914412-11-6). Inst for the Arts.
Art Nouveau Designs in Color. 9.00 (ISBN 0-8446-5070-6). Peter Smith.
Art Nouveau Display Alphabets: One Hundred Complete Fonts. pap. 3.00 (ISBN 0-486-23386-3). Dover.
Art Nouveau Display Alphabets: 100 Complete Fonts from the Solotype Typographers Catalog. 6.50 (ISBN 0-8446-5521-X). Peter Smith.
Art Nouveau Jewellery & Fans. 8.00 (ISBN 0-8446-5067-6). Peter Smith.
Art Nouveau Postcards: The Posterist's Postcards. 11.95 (ISBN 0-89545-014-3); pap. 5.95 (ISBN 0-89545-015-1). Images Graphiques.
Art Nouveau Stained Glass Pattern Book. pap. 2.25 (ISBN 0-486-23577-7). Dover.
Art Nouveau Style in Jewelry, Metalwork, Glass, Ceramics, Textiles, Architecture & Furniture. 12.50 (ISBN 0-8446-5660-7). Peter Smith.
Art Now. 29.95 (ISBN 0-688-03201-X). Morrow.
Art Objects, Their Care & Preservation: A Handbook for Museums & Collectors. lib. bdg. 17.50 (ISBN 0-910938-56-3). McGilvery.
Art of a Vanished Race: The Mimbres Classic Black-on-White. pap. 5.95 (ISBN 0-916280-00-4). Dillon-Tyler Pubs.
Art of Africa. 6.95 (ISBN 0-06-022035-X); PLB 7.89 (ISBN 0-06-022036-8). Har-Row.
Art of America from Jackson to Lincoln. 6.95g (ISBN 0-02-736250-7). Macmillan.
Art of America in the Early Twentieth Century. 6.95g (ISBN 0-02-736180-2). Macmillan.
Art of America in the Gilded Age. 6.95g (ISBN 0-02-736100-4). Macmillan.
Art of America Since World War II. 7.95 (ISBN 0-02-736310-4, 73631). Macmillan.
Art of Ancient America. 6.95 (ISBN 0-517-50827-3). Crown.
Art of Ancient Cyprus. pap. 2.50. Mus Fine Arts Boston.
Art of Ancient Mexico. PLB 7.89 (ISBN 0-06-022034-1). Har-Row.
Art of Andrew Wyeth. pap. 11.95 (ISBN 0-8212-0685-0). NYGS.
Art of Andrew Wyeth. 27.50 (ISBN 0-8212-0516-1). NYGS.
Art of Architecture. 3rd ed. lib. bdg. 40.50x (ISBN 0-8371-5861-3, RIAA). Greenwood.
Art of Art for Children's Books. 6.95 (ISBN 0-517-02438-1). Potter.
Art of Attack. 24.00x (ISBN 0-7158-1212-2). Charles River Bks.
Art of Attack. text ed. 23.00x (ISBN 0-8277-5517-1). British Bk Ctr.
Art of Attack: Being a Study in the Development of Weapons & Appliances of Offence, from the Earliest Times to the Age of Gunpowder. 16.00x (ISBN 0-8476-6061-3). Rowman.
Art of Balcomb Greene. 27.50 (ISBN 0-8180-0125-9). Horizon.
Art of Beatrix Potter. 6th rev. ed. 25.00 (ISBN 0-7232-1457-3). Warne.
Art of Bernard Leach. 32.50 (ISBN 0-8230-0263-2). Watson-Guptill.
Art of Black Africa. 32.50 (ISBN 0-289-70289-5). Hacker.
Art of Black Africa. pap. 14.95 (ISBN 0-8478-0221-3). Rizzoli Intl.
Art of Blacksmithing. 11.95 (ISBN 0-308-10254-1). T Y Crowell.
Art of Blackwork Embroidery. 12.95 (ISBN 0-684-14330-5). Scribner.
Art of Bolivian Highland Weaving. 22.50 (ISBN 0-8230-0264-0). Watson-Guptill.
Art of Building Cities: City Building According to Its Artistic Fudamentals. 21.50 (ISBN 0-88355-817-3). Hyperion Conn.
Art of Byzantium & the Medieval West: Selected Studies. 22.50x (ISBN 0-253-31055-5). Ind U Pr.
Art of Calligraphy: A Practical Guide. pap. 6.95 (ISBN 0-684-15518-4). Scribner.
Art of Cartooning. 9.75 (ISBN 0-87396-072-6). Stravon.
Art of Chabana: Flowers for the Tea Ceremony. 12.00 (ISBN 0-8048-1111-3). C E Tuttle.
Art of Charles Prendergast. pap. 3.00 (ISBN 0-87846-141-8). Mus Fine Arts Boston.
Art of Charles Prendergast. pap. 3.00 (ISBN 0-8048-1269-1). C E Tuttle.
Art of China. 6.95 (ISBN 0-517-50833-8). Crown.
Art of Colonial America. 5.95g (ISBN 0-02-736070-9). Macmillan.
Art of Color. 48.00x (ISBN 0-442-24037-6). Van Nos Reinhold.
Art of Color & Design. 2nd ed. text ed. 22.50 (ISBN 0-07-024119-8). McGraw.
Art of Color Photography. 29.95 (ISBN 0-671-24274-1). S&S.
Art of Craftsmanship. pap. 3.50 (ISBN 0-87491-043-9). Acropolis.
Art of Crewel Embroidery. 13.95 (ISBN 0-87245-074-0). Textile Bk.
Art of Crewel Embroidery. pap. 4.95 (ISBN 0-517-50077-9). Crown.
Art of Cutwork & Applique. 19.50 (ISBN 0-8231-4256-6). Branford.
Art of Cyprus. 29.95 (ISBN 0-688-61003-X). Reynal.
Art of Decoration. lib. bdg. 35.00x (ISBN 0-8240-2466-4). Garland Pub.

Artists in Revolution: Portraits of the Russian Avant-Garde, 1905-1925. 15.00x (ISBN 0-253-31077-6). Ind U Pr.

Artists in String: String Figures, Their Regional Distribution & Social Significance. 18.50 (ISBN 0-404-14127-7). AMS Pr.

Artists in the Making. 19.75 (ISBN 0-12-785042-2). Acad Pr.

Artist's Notebook: Techniques & Materials. pap. text ed. 13.95 (ISBN 0-03-040726-5). HR&W.

Artists of America: S. T.,A Series of Biographical Sketches of American Artists. lib. bdg. 22.50 (ISBN 0-306-71169-9). Da Capo.

Artists of Early Michigan: A Biographical Dictionary of Artists Native to or Active in Michigan 1701-1900. text ed. 9.95x (ISBN 0-8143-1528-3). Wayne St U Pr.

Artists of Hawaii. 25.00 (ISBN 0-8248-0467-8). U Pr of Hawaii.

Artists of Hawaii: Nineteen Painters & Sculptors. 25.00 (ISBN 0-8248-0338-8). U Pr of Hawaii.

Artists of Terezin. pap. 7.95 (ISBN 0-8052-0609-4). Schocken.

Artists of the American West: A Biographical Dictionary. 15.00x (ISBN 0-8040-0607-5). Swallow.

Artists of the Old West. 14.95 (ISBN 0-385-04474-7). Doubleday.

Artist's Reminiscences. 14.50 (ISBN 0-8103-3522-0). Gale.

Artist's Silk Screen Manual. pap. 4.95 (ISBN 0-448-11593-X). G&D.

Artist's Voice. 10.95 (ISBN 0-06-012465-2). Har-Row.

Arts. 9.95 (ISBN 0-87140-579-2). Liveright.

Arts & Cognition. 16.50x (ISBN 0-8018-1843-5). Johns Hopkins.

Arts & Crafts at Home. pap. 1.95 (ISBN 0-87637-148-9). Hse of Collectibles.

Arts & Crafts Essays. lib. bdg. 35.00x (ISBN 0-8240-2483-4). Garland Pub.

Arts & Crafts for All Seasons. pap. 3.95 (ISBN 0-8224-0490-7). Fearon-Pitman.

Arts & Crafts for Children: Fifty-Two Projects for Children to Create on Their Own. pap. 5.95 (ISBN 0-8091-2114-X). Paulist Pr.

Arts & Crafts for Home, School & Community. pap. 8.95 (ISBN 0-8016-0615-2). Mosby.

Arts & Crafts for Physically & Mentally Disabled: The How, What & Why of It. 34.50 (ISBN 0-398-03783-3). C C Thomas.

Arts & Crafts in Britain & America. 25.00 (ISBN 0-8478-0184-5). Rizzoli Intl.

Arts & Crafts in New York, Eighteen Hundred to Eighteen Four: Advertisements & News Items from New York City Newspapers. 11.25x. U Pr of Va.

Arts & Crafts in Philadelphia, Maryland, & South Carolina, 1721-1785. lib. bdg. 35.00 (ISBN 0-306-71320-9). Da Capo.

Arts & Crafts Media Ideas for the Elementary Teacher. 12.95 (ISBN 0-13-047050-3). P-H.

Arts & Crafts Movement in America. 32.50x (ISBN 0-691-03883-X); pap. 9.95 (ISBN 0-691-03884-8). Princeton U Pr.

Arts & Crafts Objects Children Can Make for the Home. 13.95 (ISBN 0-13-047068-6). P-H.

Arts & Crafts of Ancient Egypt. pap. 8.00 (ISBN 0-915018-05-5). Attic Bks.

Arts & Crafts of India & Ceylon. 7.95 (ISBN 0-374-10616-9). FS&G.

Arts & Crafts of India & Ceylon. pap. 2.95 (ISBN 0-374-50340-0, N256). FS&G.

Arts & Crafts of the Austral Islands: A Special Exhibition, 17 December 1968 to 30 April 1969. pap. 2.00 (ISBN 0-87577-018-5). Peabody Mus Salem.

Arts & Crafts the Year Round. 29.00x (ISBN 0-8381-0213-1). United Syn Bk.

Arts & Crafts You Can Eat. 7.95 (ISBN 0-397-31491-4); pap. 2.75 (ISBN 0-397-31492-2). Lippincott.

Arts & Human Development: A Psychological Study of the Artistic Process. 20.50 (ISBN 0-471-29145-5). Wiley.

Arts & Ideas: New Brief Edition. pap. text ed. 14.95 (ISBN 0-03-089434-4). HR&W.

Arts & Religion: The Ayer Lectures of the Colgate-Rochester Divinity School, 1943. 20.75 (ISBN 0-8369-2889-X). Arno.

Arts & Signs. pap. text ed. 8.25x (ISBN 0-87750-188-2). Humanities.

Arts & the Art of Criticism. 22.50x (ISBN 0-87752-162-X). Gordian.

Arts & the People. pap. 5.00 perfect bound (ISBN 0-89062-000-8). Pub Ctr Cult Res.

Arts & the World of Business: A Selected Bibliography (Supplement I) pap. 5.00x (ISBN 0-911798-09-9). UCLA Mgmt.

Arts & the World of Business: A Selected Bibliography (Supplement 2) pap. 5.00x (ISBN 0-911798-16-1). UCLA Mgmt.

Arts Betrayed. 13.50x (ISBN 0-87663-322-X). Universe.

Arts Catalogue of New Jersey. 12.95 (ISBN 0-89529-064-2); pap. 9.95. Avery Pub.

Arts, Human Development, & Education. text ed. 12.60x (ISBN 0-8211-0414-4); ten or more copies 11.35x. McCutchan.

Arts in Boston. 7.50x (ISBN 0-674-04825-3); pap. 2.95 (ISBN 0-674-04832-6). Harvard U Pr.

Arts in Early American History. 9.50x (ISBN 0-8078-0940-3). U of NC Pr.

Arts in Greece. 6.00 (ISBN 0-8046-0719-2). Kennikat.

Arts in Higher Education. 8.95x (ISBN 0-87589-023-7). Jossey-Bass.

Arts in Montana. 10.00 (ISBN 0-87842-068-1). Mountain Pr.

Arts in Prehistoric Greece. pap. 12.95 (ISBN 0-14-056142-0). Penguin.

Arts in Society. lib. bdg. 25.00x (ISBN 0-405-12129-6). Arno.

Arts of a Vanished Era. pap. 5.00 (ISBN 0-295-95576-7). U of Wash Pr.

Arts of Black Africa. pap. 3.45 (ISBN 0-520-02358-7, CAL256). U of Cal Pr.

Arts of China. 17.50 (ISBN 0-8048-0039-1). C E Tuttle.

Arts of China. rev. ed. 20.00 (ISBN 0-520-03366-3); pap. 7.95 (ISBN 0-520-03367-1). U of Cal Pr.

Arts of China: Neolithic Cultures to the T'ang Dynasty. 75.00 (ISBN 0-87011-064-0). Kodansha.

Arts of Clay. reinforced bdg. 6.95 (ISBN 0-684-15120-0). Scribner.

Arts of David Levine. 25.00 (ISBN 0-394-50265-5). Knopf.

Arts of Japan. 18.95 (ISBN 0-07-044053-0); cassette 3.95 (ISBN 0-07-044054-9); recorder 19.95; 22.90 (ISBN 0-07-079265-8). McGraw.

Arts of Japan. 19.50 ea. (ISBN 0-87011-335-6) (ISBN 0-87011-336-4). Kodansha.

Arts of Japan: An Illustrated History. pap. 10.00 (ISBN 0-8048-0042-1). C E Tuttle.

Arts of Shinto. 12.50 (ISBN 0-8348-2706-9). Weatherhill.

Arts of Thailand: A Handbook of the Architecture, Sculpture, & Painting of Thailand. lib. bdg. 22.75x (IUAT). Greenwood.

Arts of the Ancient Greeks. text ed. 35.00 (ISBN 0-07-007850-5). McGraw.

Arts of the Anglo-American Community in the Seventeenth Century. pap. 4.50x (ISBN 0-8139-0612-1). U Pr of Va.

Arts of the Beautiful. lib. bdg. 14.50x (ISBN 0-8371-9294-3, GIAB). Greenwood.

Arts of the Environment. 12.50 (ISBN 0-8076-0620-0). Braziller.

Arts of the Hausa. 25.00 (ISBN 0-226-68899-2); 2 color fiches incl. U of Chicago Pr.

Arts of the Japanese Sword. 25.00 (ISBN 0-571-04723-8). Merrimack Bk Serv.

Arts of the South Pacific. 30.00 (ISBN 0-8076-0500-X). Braziller.

Arts of the South Seas. 24.00 (ISBN 0-405-01567-4). Arno.

Arts of West Africa (Excluding Music) facsimile ed. 18.25 (ISBN 0-8369-8908-2). Arno.

Arts of Wood. reinforced bdg. 6.95 (ISBN 0-684-14665-7). Scribner.

As Bees in Honey Drown: Elbert Hubbard & the Roycrofters. 10.00 (ISBN 0-498-01052-X). A S Barnes.

As I Remember. lib. bdg. 28.00x (ISBN 0-405-09660-7). Arno.

Asahi Pentax Guide. pap. 3.95 (ISBN 0-8038-0463-6). Focal Pr.

Asahi Pentax Way. 11th ed. 24.95 (ISBN 0-8038-0476-8). Focal Pr.

Asahi Pentax Way. rev., new, 11th ed. 24.95 (ISBN 0-8038-0466-0). Focal Pr.

Asian Art. pap. text ed. 4.95x (ISBN 0-697-03206-X). Wm C Brown.

Asian Art: Selections from the Collection of Mr. and Mrs. John D. Rockefeller, 3rd. pap. text ed. 30.00. Interbk Inc.

Asian Crafts. PLB 5.98 (ISBN 0-87460-148-7). Lion.

Ask Any Vegetable. 7.95 (ISBN 0-13-049759-2). P-H.

Ask Erica. 6.95 (ISBN 0-684-15296-7); pap. 2.50 (ISBN 0-684-15295-9). Scribner.

Aspects of Boston. 19.95 (ISBN 0-395-19418-0). HM.

Aspects of Boston. pap. 9.95 (ISBN 0-395-20549-2). HM.

Aspects of Classic Maya Rulership on Two Inscribed Vessels. pap. 3.00 (ISBN 0-88402-070-3). Dumbarton Oaks.

Aspects of "Official" Painting & Philosophic Art, 1789-1799. lib. bdg. 31.00 (ISBN 0-8240-1992-X). Garland Pub.

Aspen Art in the New Mexico Highlands. 5.95 (ISBN 0-89013-041-8). Museum NM Pr.

Assignments. 12.50 (ISBN 0-688-00027-4). Morrow.

Assisi Problem & the Art of Giotto: A Study of the Legend of St. Francis in the Upper Church of San Francesco, Assisi. 32.00x (ISBN 0-19-817166-8). Oxford U Pr.

At Home. pap. 10.95 (ISBN 0-87100-137-3). Morgan.

Athenian Black Figure Vases. pap. 7.95 (ISBN 0-19-519760-7). Oxford U Pr.

Athenian White Lekythoi: Patterns & Painters. 89.00x (ISBN 0-19-813214-X). Oxford U Pr.

Athens: Its History & Coinage Before the Persian Invasion. 25.00 (ISBN 0-89005-002-3). Ares.

Atlantic Brief Lives: A Biographical Companion to the Arts. 15.00 (ISBN 0-316-50451-3); pap. 4.95 (ISBN 0-316-50457-2). Little.

Atlas of Anatomy for Artists. 3rd ed. 6.95 (ISBN 0-486-20241-0). Dover.

Atlas of Animal Anatomy for Artists. rev. ed. pap. 5.00 (ISBN 0-486-20082-5). Dover.

Atlas of Animal Anatomy for Artists. 2nd rev. & enl. ed. 10.00 (ISBN 0-8446-2029-7). Peter Smith.

Atlas of Human Anatomy for the Artist. 14.95 (ISBN 0-19-500052-8); pap. text ed. 10.95x (ISBN 0-19-501020-5). Oxford U Pr.

Atlas of Photogrammetric Instruments. 85.50 (ISBN 0-444-40700-6). Elsevier.

Atomic Age: Decorative Designs of the Fifties. pap. 2.95 (ISBN 0-912300-64-7, 64-7). Troubador Pr.

Attainment of Delacroix. 37.50x (ISBN 0-8018-1048-5). Johns Hopkins.

Attention Getting Old Engravings. 19.50 (ISBN 0-910158-22-3). Art Dir.

Attic Bilingual Vases & Their Painters. lib. bdg. 72.00 (ISBN 0-8240-3220-9). Garland Pub.

Attic Black Figure Vase-Painters. lib. bdg. 40.00 (ISBN 0-87817-191-6). Hacker.

Attic Black-figured Neck-amphorae. 30.00 (ISBN 0-87099-134-5). Metro Mus Art.

Attic Black-Figured Pottery. 9.95 (ISBN 0-8155-5035-9). Noyes.

Attic Red-Figure Vase-Painters. 2nd ed. 125.00x (ISBN 0-19-813146-1). Oxford U Pr.

Attic Red-Figured Pottery. 9.95 (ISBN 0-8155-5049-9). Noyes.

Attic White-Ground: Its Development on Shapes Other Than Lekythoi. lib. bdg. 40.00x (ISBN 0-8240-2711-6). Garland Pub.

Auditorium Acoustics. 32.50 (ISBN 0-470-56284-6). Halsted Pr.

Audubon. 17.95 (ISBN 0-670-14053-8). Viking Pr.

Audubon Society Book of Wild Birds. 40.00 (ISBN 0-8109-0661-9). Abrams.

Audubon Society Book of Wildflowers. 40.00 (ISBN 0-8109-0671-6). Abrams.

Audubon: The Kentucky Years. 4.95 (ISBN 0-8131-0215-4). U Pr of Ky.

Audubon the Naturalist. 16.00 (ISBN 0-8446-2245-1). Peter Smith.

Audubon's Birds in Color for Decoupage. pap. 2.50 (ISBN 0-486-23492-4). Dover.

August Benziger Portrait Painter. 16.00. Benziger Sis.

August Sander. bds. 7.95 (ISBN 0-89381-007-X). Aperture.

Auguste Edouart's Silhouettes of Eminent Americans, 1839-1844. 22.50x (ISBN 0-8139-0632-6). U Pr of Va.

Augustus John. 17.95 (ISBN 0-03-013821-3). HR&W.

Augustus John. 34.50 (ISBN 0-404-14560-4). AMS Pr.

Aunt Clara: The Paintings of Clara McDonald Williamson. 14.00 (ISBN 0-88360-025-0). Amon Carter.

Australian Primitive Painters. 24.25x (ISBN 0-7022-1039-0). U of Queensland Pr.

Australian Traditional Bush Crafts. 10.95x (ISBN 0-8052-3654-6); pap. 6.95 (ISBN 0-8052-0560-8). Schocken.

Authentic American Johnboat: How to Build It, How to Use It. 7.95 (ISBN 0-679-50861-9). McKay.

Authentic Indian Designs. pap. 6.00 (ISBN 0-486-23170-4). Dover.

Authentic Indian Designs: 2500 Ils. from Reports of the Bureau of American Ethnology. 8.50 (ISBN 0-8446-5228-8). Peter Smith.

Authenticity in Art: The Scientific Detection of Forgery. 16.50x (ISBN 0-8448-0752-4). Crane-Russak Co.

Autobiographical Sketches. 14.95 (ISBN 0-236-40010-X). Merrimack Bk Serv.

Autobiography of an Idea. 7.50 (ISBN 0-8446-3032-2). Peter Smith.

Autobiography of an Idea. pap. 4.00 (ISBN 0-486-20281-X). Dover.

Autobiography of Colonel John Trumbull. lib. bdg. 32.50 (ISBN 0-306-71242-3). Da Capo.

Autobiography of James Gallier, Architect. lib. bdg. 20.00 (ISBN 0-306-71247-4). Da Capo.

Autobiography of Surrealism. 30.00 (ISBN 0-670-14235-2). Viking Pr.

Autobiography of Worthington Whittredge. 10.00 (ISBN 0-405-00874-0). Arno.

Available Light. pap. 3.95 (ISBN 0-8227-4003-6). Petersen Pub.

Avedon Photographs: 1947-1977. 50.00 (ISBN 0-374-23200-8). FS&G.

Avery Obituary Index of Architects & Artists. lib. bdg. 48.00 (ISBN 0-8161-0667-3). G K Hall.

Aviation Art of Frank Wootton. large format ed. pap. 6.95 (ISBN 0-553-01049-2). Bantam.

Aviation Art of Keith Ferris. pap. 8.95 (ISBN 0-553-01063-8, 01196-0). Bantam.

Avons Bottles: Research & History. 4th rev. ed. pap. 2.95 (ISBN 0-913772-01-1). Avons Res.

Awdrey-Gore Legacy. 4.95 (ISBN 0-396-06598-8). Dodd.

Awkward Embrace: The Creative Artist & the Institution in America. 15.00 (ISBN 0-394-49563-2). Knopf.

Aztec & Maya Papermakers. 25.00 (ISBN 0-87817-206-8). Hacker.

B

Baby Animals & Their Mothers. 5.95 (ISBN 0-8090-2010-6). Hill & Wang.

Babylonian Art. 20.00 (ISBN 0-404-15360-7). AMS Pr.

Background Patterns, Textures & Tints: Ninety-Five Plates for Artists & Designers. 6.00 (ISBN 0-8446-5492-2). Peter Smith.

Background Patterns, Textures & Tints. pap. 3.50 (ISBN 0-486-23260-3). Dover.

Background to Chinese Painting. pap. 3.95 (ISBN 0-8052-0117-3). Schocken.

Backstage at the Strips. pap. 6.95 (ISBN 0-89104-057-9). A & W Pubs.

Backstrap Weaving. 13.95 (ISBN 0-8230-0422-8). Watson-Guptill.

Bag Book. 10.95 (ISBN 0-442-22326-9); pap. 6.95 (ISBN 0-442-22327-7). Van Nos Reinhold.

Bag of Tricks: Fun Things to Make & Do with the Groceries. 5.95 (ISBN 0-8193-0449-2); PLB 5.41 (ISBN 0-8193-0450-6). Parents.

Baker's Clay. pap. 6.95 (ISBN 0-442-29486-7). Van Nos Reinhold.

Bakst. pap. 6.95 (ISBN 0-8478-0072-5). Rizzoli Intl.

Balinese Painting. pap. 1.50. Taylor Museum.

Ball of Clay. 6.25g (ISBN 0-8075-0557-9). A Whitman.

Ballet Art. 14.95 (ISBN 0-517-53454-1); pap. 6.95 (ISBN 0-517-53455-X). Potter.

Balsa Wood Craft. pap. 2.50 (ISBN 0-688-45526-3). Lothrop.

Baltimore Painted Furniture: 1800-1840. pap. text ed. 8.50 (ISBN 0-912298-32-4). Baltimore Mus.

Bamboo. 25.00 (ISBN 0-8348-0048-9). Weatherhill.

Band Weaving. 11.95 (ISBN 0-442-28404-7). Van Nos Reinhold.

Banners & Flags: How to Sew a Celebration. 16.95 (ISBN 0-15-110560-X); pap. 7.95 (ISBN 0-15-610678-7). HarBraceJ.

Bannerstone House: A Frank Lloyd Wright House, Springfield, Illinois. pap. 3.50 (ISBN 0-398-00299-1). C C Thomas.

Baptistery of Pisa. lib. bdg. 40.00 (ISBN 0-8240-3249-7). Garland Pub.

Barbara Morgan. new ed. 14.00 (ISBN 0-87100-034-2). Morgan.

Barbara Walker's Learn to Knit Afghan Book. pap. 4.95 (ISBN 0-684-14714-9, SL666). Scribner.

Barbizon Days. facs. ed. 18.25 (ISBN 0-8369-1194-6). Arno.

Barbizon Painters. facs. ed. 18.25 (ISBN 0-8369-1084-2). Arno.

Barefoot Abe. pap. 0.95 (ISBN 0-440-40639-0). Dell.

Barefoot in the Grass: The Story of Grandma Moses. 4.95 (ISBN 0-385-06032-7); PLB (ISBN 0-385-00454-0). Doubleday.

Bargello. 8.95 (ISBN 0-442-11248-3). Van Nos Reinhold.

Bargello Antics. 14.95 (ISBN 0-684-15995-3); pap. 8.95 (ISBN 0-684-15996-1). Scribner.

Bargello: Florentine Canvas Work. pap. 4.95 (ISBN 0-442-29481-6). Van Nos Reinhold.

Bargello Plus. 5.95 (ISBN 0-684-15715-2). Scribner.

Barkal Temples. 40.00. Mus Fine Arts Boston.

Barn: A Vanishing Landmark in North America. 27.50 (ISBN 0-8212-0488-2). NYGS.

Barn: A Vanishing Landmark in North America. pap. 10.95 (ISBN 0-89104-004-8). A & W Pubs.

Barnett Newman. 55.00 (ISBN 0-8109-1360-7). Abrams.

Barney Google: An Original Compilation. First Collection of the Complete First Year of the Daily Strip, 1919-1920. 15.95 (ISBN 0-88355-631-6); pap. 6.95 (ISBN 0-88355-630-8). Hyperion Conn.

Barns of California. 7.00 (ISBN 0-910312-02-8). Calif Hist.

Barns, Sheds & Outbuildings. 6.95 (ISBN 0-8289-0293-3). Greene.

Baron Bean: An Original Compilation, First Collection of the Complete First Year of the Daily Strip, 1916-1917. 14.50 (ISBN 0-88355-641-3); pap. 5.95 (ISBN 0-88355-640-5). Hyperion Conn.

Baron Dominique Vivant Denon, 1747-1825: Hedonist & Scholar in a Period of Transition. 12.00 (ISBN 0-8386-7470-4). Fairleigh Dickinson.

Baroness Pontalba's Buildings. pap. 3.25 (ISBN 0-911116-40-0). Pelican.

Better Homes & Gardens Needlepoint. 4.95 (ISBN 0-696-00475-5). Meredith Corp.
Better Photography. 2nd ed. 7.50x (ISBN 0-7182-0489-1). Intl Pubns Serv.
Better Photography for Amateurs. 10.95 (ISBN 0-13-075929-5). P-H.
Better Photography for Amateurs. pap. 4.95 (ISBN 0-8174-0183-0). Amphoto.
Between Silence & Light: Spirit in the Architecture of Louis I. Kahn. 15.00 (ISBN 0-394-50625-1); pap. 7.95 (ISBN 0-394-73687-7). Shambhala Pubns.
Bewick Collector. 28.50 (ISBN 0-8103-3491-7). Gale.
Bewick Collector. lib. bdg. 33.50 (ISBN 0-8337-1764-2). B Franklin.
Beyond Aesthetics: Investigations into the Nature of Visual Art. 25.00 (ISBN 0-500-01147-8). Transatlantic.
Beyond Basic Photography: A Technical Manual. pap. 7.95 (ISBN 0-316-37312-5). Little.
Beyond East & West. 15.95 (ISBN 0-8230-0485-6). Watson-Guptill.
Beyond Habitat. pap. 4.95 (ISBN 0-262-69036-5, MIT217). MIT Pr.
Beyond Metabolism: The New Japanese Architecture. 19.95 (ISBN 0-07-053893-X). Arch Rec Bks.
Beyond Modern Art. pap. 8.95 (ISBN 0-525-47370-X). Dutton.
Beyond Modern Sculpture: Effects of Science & Technology on Sculpture of This Century. 20.00 (ISBN 0-8076-0450-X); pap. 8.95 (ISBN 0-8076-0715-0). Braziller.
Beyond Stonehenge. 15.95 (ISBN 0-06-011786-9). Har-Row.
Beyond Tic Tac Toe: Seven Exciting & Challenging New Games to Play with Colored Pen or Pencil. pap. 2.95 (ISBN 0-394-83136-5). Pantheon.
Beyond Time & Place: Non-Realist Painting in the Nineteenth Century. 60.00 (ISBN 0-19-211446-8). Oxford U Pr.
Beyond Weaving. 16.95 (ISBN 0-8230-0486-4). Watson-Guptill.
Bible Through Stamps. 7.50 (ISBN 0-87068-397-7). Ktav.
Bibliographical Essays. 22.50 (ISBN 0-8337-2865-2). B Franklin.
Bibliography of American Numismatic Auction Catalogues, 1828-1875. 25.00x (ISBN 0-88000-072-4). Quarterman.
Bibliography of Bookplate Literature. 13.00 (ISBN 0-8103-3190-X). Gale.
Bibliography of Cartography. lib. bdg. 535.00 (ISBN 0-8161-1008-5). G K Hall.
Bibliography of Early American Architecture: Writings on Architecture Constructed Before 1860 in Eastern & Central U.S. 15.00 (ISBN 0-252-72680-4). U of Ill Pr.
Bibliography of Energy Conservation in Architecture: Keyword Searched. 50.00 (ISBN 0-915250-19-5). Environ Design.
Bibliography of the Arts of Africa. pap. 10.00 (ISBN 0-918456-05-3). African Studies Assn.
Bibliography of the Strawberry Hill Press. 2nd ed. 16.50 (ISBN 0-7129-0571-5). Dawson Pub.
Bibliography of Water Colour Painting & Painters. 20.00x (ISBN 0-8476-1313-5). Rowman.
Bibliotheca Americana Nova: A Catalogue of Books in Various Languages Relating to America, Printed Since 1700. 55.50 (ISBN 0-8337-2985-3). B Franklin.
Big Art: Megamurals & Supergraphics. lib. bdg. 15.90 (ISBN 0-89471-007-9); pap. 6.95 (ISBN 0-89471-006-0). Running Pr.
Big Bag Book: How to Make All Kinds of Carry-Alls. 14.95 (ISBN 0-684-15180-4); pap. 6.95 (ISBN 0-684-15179-0). Scribner.
Big Book of Applique: For Quilts & Banners, Clothes, Hangings, Gifts, & More. 17.50 (ISBN 0-684-15623-7). Scribner.
Big Book of Cats. 1.50 (ISBN 0-448-00339-2). G&D.
Big Book of Dolls. 12.95 (ISBN 0-8037-0580-8). Dial.
Big Book of Fabulous, Fun'filled Celebrations & Holiday Crafts. 14.95 (ISBN 0-03-040446-0). HR&W.
Big Felt Burger. 5.95 (ISBN 0-385-09899-5). Doubleday.
Big-Knot Macrame. 3.95 (ISBN 0-8069-5184-2); PLB 4.59 (ISBN 0-8069-5185-0). Sterling.
Big Name Hunting: A Beginner's Guide to Autograph Collecting. 4.95g (ISBN 0-671-65206-0). S&S.
Bigallo: The Oratory & Residence of the Compagnia Del Bigallo Della Misericordia in Florence. 15.00x (ISBN 0-8147-0370-4). NYU Pr.
Bigger & Better Enlarging. 10.95 (ISBN 0-8174-0579-8). Amphoto.
Bild und Lied: Archaologische Beitrage Zur Geschichte der Griechischen Heldensage. facsimile ed. 15.00x (ISBN 0-405-07277-5). Arno.
Bill Dean's Book of Balsa Models. rev. ed. pap. 3.95 (ISBN 0-668-02210-8). Arco.
Billy Bartram & His Green World. 6.50g (ISBN 0-374-30707-5). FS&G.
Biographical Index of American Artists. 11.00x (ISBN 0-8103-4251-0). Gale.
Biographical Index of American Artists. 35.00 (ISBN 0-87968-751-7). Gordon Pr.
Biographical Memoirs of Extraordinary Painters (1780) pap. 9.50 (ISBN 0-900891-13-0). Oleander Pr.
Biographical Memoirs of Extraordinary Painters. 8.00 (ISBN 0-8386-7367-8). Fairleigh Dickinson.
Bird Decoy: An American Art Form. A Catalog of Carvings Exhibited at the Sheldon Memorial Art Gallery, Lincoln Nebraska. 17.95 (ISBN 0-8032-0887-1). U of Nebr Pr.
Bird in Art. PLB 4.95 (ISBN 0-8225-0158-9). Lerner Pubns.
Bird, the Banner, & Uncle Sam: Images of America in Folk & Popular Art. 8.95 (ISBN 0-397-31690-9); pap. 5.95 (ISBN 0-397-31691-7). Lippincott.
Birdhouse Book: Building Houses, Feeders & Baths. pap. 8.95 (ISBN 0-914718-36-3). Pacific Search.
Birds. lib. bdg. 6.99. Silver.
Birds, Beasts, Blossoms & Bugs. 28.50 (ISBN 0-8109-0708-9); pap. 12.50 (ISBN 0-8109-9022-9). Abrams.
Birds, Beasts, Blossoms, & Bugs: The Nature of Japan. pap. 12.50. Freer.
Birds of America. 52.50 (ISBN 0-8446-1567-6); 7.50 ea. Peter Smith.
Birds of Field & Forest. new ed. 7.95 (ISBN 0-913948-13-6). Time-Life.
Birds of Field & Forest. PLB 8.97. Silver.
Birds of the Northern Forest. 35.00 (ISBN 0-395-07887-3). HM.
Birth & Development of Ornament. 17.50 (ISBN 0-8103-4026-7). Gale.
Birth of Greek Art. 30.00 (ISBN 0-8076-0502-6). Braziller.
Bischoff Kord & Kamotsuru Bottles. pap. 4.75. Borden.
Bison in Art: A Graphic Chronicle of the American Bison. pap. 14.50 (ISBN 0-87358-158-X). Amon Carter.
Bitters Bottles. 10.00 (ISBN 0-8407-4309-2); supplement 6.50 (ISBN 0-8407-4310-6). Nelson.
Bizarreries & Fantasies of Grandville. pap. 4.00 (ISBN 0-486-22991-2). Dover.
Black Aesthetic. 3.50 (ISBN 0-385-06951-0). Doubleday.
Black & Plain Pottery of the 6th, 5th & 4th Centuries B.C. 40.00x (ISBN 0-87661-212-5). Am Sch Athens.
Black & White. pap. 5.95 (ISBN 0-917960-01-7). Padma.
Black & White Photography: A Basic Manual. 7.95 (ISBN 0-316-37310-9); pap. 4.95 (ISBN 0-316-37311-7). Little.
Black Art in Houston: The Texas Southern University Experience. 20.00 (ISBN 0-89096-046-1). Tex A&M Univ Pr.
Black Artists of the New Generation. 9.95 (ISBN 0-396-07434-0). Dodd.
Black Dimensions in Contemporary American Art. 3.95 (ISBN 0-452-25041-2, Z5041). NAL.
Black Gods & Kings: Yoruba Art at Ucla. 18.50x (ISBN 0-253-31204-3). Ind U Pr.
Black Images: The Art of West Africa. PLB 6.95 (ISBN 0-385-07462-X). Doubleday.
Black Man in Art. PLB 4.95 (ISBN 0-8225-0163-5). Lerner Pubns.
Black Pilgrimage. PLB 6.96 (ISBN 0-688-51630-0). Lothrop.
Black Powder Gunsmithing. pap. 6.95 (ISBN 0-695-80659-9). Follett.
Black Woman. pap. 10.95 (ISBN 0-918696-05-4). Camera Graphic.
Blacksmiths. PLB 4.90 (ISBN 0-531-02901-8). Watts.
Blackwork Embroidery. pap. 3.00 (ISBN 0-486-23245-X). Dover.
Blackwork: The Art of Black-on-White Embroidery. 13.95 (ISBN 0-442-22792-2). Van Nos Reinhold.
Blain Village & the Fort Ancient Tradition in Ohio. 12.00x (ISBN 0-87338-090-8). Kent St U Pr.
Blake. lib. bdg. 10.75. Folcroft.
Blake. lib. bdg. 15.95 (ISBN 0-8383-1055-9). Haskell.
Blake: A Psychological Study. 35.00 (ISBN 0-87968-753-3). Gordon Pr.
Blake: A Psychological Study. lib. bdg. 20.00 (ISBN 0-8414-9574-2). Folcroft.
Blake & Antiquity. pap. 5.95 (ISBN 0-691-01802-2, 330). Princeton U Pr.
Blake & England. lib. bdg. 7.50 (ISBN 0-8414-7285-8). Folcroft.
Blake & Rossetti. 18.50. Porter.
Blake & Rossetti. lib. bdg. 23.95 (ISBN 0-8383-1054-0). Haskell.
Blake & Rossetti. lib. bdg. 17.50 (ISBN 0-8414-6782-X). Folcroft.
Blake As an Artist. 27.95 (ISBN 0-7148-1637-X). Dutton.
Blake Books: Annotated Catalogues of His Writings in Illuminated Printing, in Conventional Typography & in Manuscript & Reprints Thereof; Reproductions of His Designs: Books with His Engravings: Catalogues: Books He Owned; & Scholarly & Critical Works About Him. 95.00x (ISBN 0-19-818151-5). Oxford U Pr.
Blake Collection of Mrs. Landon K. Thorne. pap. 10.00. Pierpont Morgan.
Blake Dictionary: The Ideas & Symbols of William Blake. 25.00 (ISBN 0-87057-088-9). Brown U Pr.
Blake Dictionary: The Ideas & Symbols of William Blake, with a New Index by Morris Eaves. pap. 9.50 (ISBN 0-394-73688-5). Shambhala Pubns.
Blake Records. 53.00x (ISBN 0-19-811639-X). Oxford U Pr.
Blake Studies. lib. bdg. 24.95 (ISBN 0-8383-1050-8). Haskell.
Blake Studies: Essays on His Life & Work. 2nd ed. 31.50x (ISBN 0-19-812003-6). Oxford U Pr.
Blake's Composite Art: A Study of the Illuminated Poetry. text ed. 16.50 (ISBN 0-691-06348-6). Princeton U Pr.
Blake's Four Zoas: The Design of a Dream. 15.00x (ISBN 0-674-07645-1). Harvard U Pr.
Blake's Human Form Divine. 26.50x (ISBN 0-520-02065-0). U of Cal Pr.
Blake's Illustrations to the Divine Comedy. lib. bdg. 38.00x (ISBN 0-8371-9595-0, ROBIL). Greenwood.
Blake's Illustrations to the Poems of Gray. 33.00x (ISBN 0-691-06182-3). Princeton U Pr.
Blake's Innocence & Experience. lib. bdg. 45.00 (ISBN 0-8414-9350-2). Folcroft.
Blake's Innocence & Experience: A Study of the Songs & Manuscripts. 39.00 (ISBN 0-403-01275-9). Scholarly.
Blake's Job: William Blake's Illustrations of the Book of Job. 10.00 (ISBN 0-87057-096-X). Brown U Pr.
Blaue Reiter Almanac. 15.00 (ISBN 0-670-17355-X). Viking Pr.
Blaue Reiter Almanac. pap. 6.95 (ISBN 0-670-01931-3, D6). Penguin.
Block Printing on Textiles. pap. 12.95 (ISBN 0-8230-0502-X). Watson-Guptill.
Block Printing on Textiles. 12.95 (ISBN 0-8230-0501-1); sheet stock avail. Watson-Guptill.
Bloomingdale's Book of Home Decorating. 15.95 (ISBN 0-06-010948-3). Har-Row.
Blue & White Stoneware, Pottery, Crockery. pap. 7.95 (ISBN 0-89145-050-5). Collector Bks.
Blue & White: The Cotton Embroideries of Rural China. encore ed 5.95 (ISBN 0-684-16344-6). Scribner.
Blue & White Transfer Ware 1780-1840. 12.50 (ISBN 0-8048-0975-5). C E Tuttle.
Blue-China Book: Early American Scenes & History Pictured in the Pottery of the Time. 9.50 (ISBN 0-8446-0049-0). Peter Smith.
Blue-China Book: Early American Scenes & History Pictured in the Pottery of the Time. pap. 5.00 (ISBN 0-486-22749-9). Dover.
Blue Jeans. 6.64 (ISBN 0-671-32798-4). Messner.
Blue Mystery: The Story of the Hope Diamond. 7.95 (ISBN 0-87474-740-6); pap. 4.50 (ISBN 0-87474-165-3). Smithsonian.
Blueprint Reading & Sketching. pap. 3.96 (ISBN 0-87345-053-1). McKnight.
Blueprint Reading for the Construction Trades. text ed. 9.75 (ISBN 0-07-004405-8). McGraw.
Blueprint Reading for the Construction Trades. 2nd ed. pap. text ed. 10.75 (ISBN 0-07-004410-4); ans. key 1.50 (ISBN 0-07-004411-2). McGraw.
Blueprint Reading: Interpretation of Architectural Working Drawings. ref. ed. 14.95 (ISBN 0-13-079673-5). P-H.
Boat, a Bat & a Beanie: Things to Make from Newspaper. 6.75 (ISBN 0-688-41789-2); PLB 6.48 (ISBN 0-688-51789-7). Lothrop.
Boat Buff's Book of Embroidery: Needlepoint, Crewel, Applique. 12.95 (ISBN 0-684-16051-X). Scribner.
Boats & How to Draw Them. 3.95 (ISBN 0-8149-0319-3). Vanguard.
Bobbin Lace. 14.95 (ISBN 0-8230-0520-8). Watson-Guptill.
Bobbin Lace. pap. 9.95 (ISBN 0-8230-0521-6). Watson-Guptill.
Bobbin Lace, First Series: Les Dentelles Aux Fuseaux. rev. ed. 15.00 (ISBN 0-8103-3955-2); 25 corner patterns incl. Gale.
Bobbin Lace Making. 9.75 (ISBN 0-8231-5033-X). Branford.
Bobbin Lacemaking. 14.95 (ISBN 0-684-15032-8). Scribner.
Bobbin Lacemaking for Beginners. 3.95 (ISBN 0-7137-0817-4). Sterling.
Boden's Beasts. 3.95 (ISBN 0-8392-3045-1). Astor-Honor.
Body, Memory & Architecture. 15.00x (ISBN 0-300-02139-9); pap. 6.95 (ISBN 0-300-02142-9). Yale U Pr.
Bonanza Victorian: Architecture & Society in Colorado Mining Towns. 13.95 (ISBN 0-8263-0390-0). U of NM Pr.
Bonkei: Tray Landscapes. 14.95 (ISBN 0-87011-124-8). Kodansha.
Bonnard. 5.95 (ISBN 0-517-09889-X). Crown.
Bonnin & Morris of Philadelphia: The First American Porcelain Factory, 1770-1772. 8.00 (ISBN 0-8078-1200-5). U of NC Pr.
Book About Fans: The History of Fans & Fan-Painting. 11.00 (ISBN 0-8103-4049-6). Gale.
Book About Fans: The History of Fans & Fan-Painting. lib. bdg. 25.00 (ISBN 0-89341-204-X). Longwood Pr.
Book Design: Systematic Aspects. 17.50 (ISBN 0-8352-1044-8). Bowker.
Book Design: Text Format Models. 17.50 (ISBN 0-8352-1045-6). Bowker.
Book Illustrators in Eighteenth-Century England. 29.00x (ISBN 0-300-01895-9). Yale U Pr.
Book of American Clocks. 14.95 (ISBN 0-02-594590-4). Macmillan.
Book of American Figure Painters. lib. bdg. 55.00 (ISBN 0-8240-2235-1). Garland Pub.
Book of Architecture. 55.00 (ISBN 0-405-08951-1). Arno.
Book of Art. write for info (ISBN 0-7172-1301-3). Grolier Ed Corp.
Book of Art Nouveau Alphabets & Ornamental Designs. pap. 4.50 (ISBN 0-87663-958-9). Universe.
Book of Arts & Crafts. pap. 2.50 (ISBN 0-486-21472-9). Dover.
Book of Authentic Indian Life Crafts. rev. ed. 9.95 (ISBN 0-87874-012-0). Galloway.
Book of Autographs. 10.00 (ISBN 0-671-24258-X). S&S.
Book of Batik. rev. ed. 4.95 (ISBN 0-8008-0876-2). Taplinger.
Book of Buffalo Pottery. 10.00 (ISBN 0-517-53045-7). Crown.
Book of Color Photography. 17.95 (ISBN 0-394-41607-4). Knopf.
Book of Country Crafts. 3.98 (ISBN 0-498-06127-2). A S Barnes.
Book of Country Crafts: Large Type Editions Ser. 9.95 (ISBN 0-498-01601-3). A S Barnes.
Book of Craftsmen: The Story of Man's Handiwork Through the Ages. 14.00 (ISBN 0-8103-3960-9). Gale.
Book of Fairies. 15.00; pap. 8.95 (ISBN 0-345-28092-X). Ballantine.
Book of Hebrew Letters. 12.50 (ISBN 0-8276-0117-4, 436); pap. 5.95 (ISBN 0-8276-0118-2, 435). Jewish Pubn.
Book of Hours. 29.95 (ISBN 0-690-01654-9). T Y Crowell.
Book of Hours of Catherine of Cleves. pap. 2.75 (ISBN 0-87598-011-2). Pierpont Morgan.
Book of Hours of Emperor Maximilian the First. 49.50 (ISBN 0-913870-01-3). Abaris Bks.
Book of Kells. 65.00 (ISBN 0-394-49475-X). Knopf.
Book of Knitting & Crochet. 11.25 (ISBN 0-8231-5031-3). Branford.
Book of Landscape Design. pap. 3.25. Morrow.
Book of Miniatures: Furniture & Accessories. 13.95 (ISBN 0-8019-6366-4); pap. 7.95 (ISBN 0-8019-6366-4). Chilton.
Book of Ornamental Knots. 12.50 (ISBN 0-684-13409-8). Scribner.
Book of Ornamental Knots. pap. 6.95 (ISBN 0-684-15566-4); 12.50 (ISBN 0-684-13409-8). Scribner.
Book of Photography. 19.95 (ISBN 0-394-49818-6). Knopf.
Book of Posters. pap. text ed. 7.50 (ISBN 0-912242-07-8). Art Educ.
Book of Rookwood Pottery. 10.00 (ISBN 0-517-53046-5). Crown.
Book of Scripts. 2nd ed. 9.95 (ISBN 0-571-10876-8); pap. 5.95 (ISBN 0-571-11080-0). Merrimack Bk Serv.
Book of Signs. pap. 2.00 (ISBN 0-486-20162-7). Dover.
Book of Signs. 7.50 (ISBN 0-8446-0744-4). Peter Smith.
Book of Signs. lib. bdg. 9.50x (ISBN 0-88307-171-1). Gannon.
Book of Successful Home Plans. 12.00 (ISBN 0-912336-34-X); pap. 5.95 (ISBN 0-912336-35-8). Structures Pub.
Book of Successful Painting. pap. 4.95 (ISBN 0-912336-12-9). Structures Pub.
Book of Tapestry: History & Technique. 40.00 (ISBN 0-670-18015-7). Viking Pr.
Book of the Lantern. lib. bdg. 25.00x (ISBN 0-405-11132-0). Arno.
Book of Thel: A Facsimile & a Critical Text. 15.00 (ISBN 0-87057-127-3). Brown U Pr.
Book of Thel: A Facsimile & a Critical Text. 15.00 (ISBN 0-87104-236-3). NY Pub Lib.
Book of Trades in the Iconography of Social Typology. 3.00 (ISBN 0-89073-010-5). Boston Public Lib.
Book of Wood Carving: Technique, Designs & Projects. pap. 3.00 (ISBN 0-486-23654-4). Dover.
Book-Plates. 2nd ed. 17.25 (ISBN 0-8369-6914-6). Arno.

C

Crucifixion in American Painting. lib. bdg. 49.95 (ISBN 0-8490-1370-4). Gordon Pr.

Crusader Figural Sculpture in the Holy Land: Twelfth Century Examples from Acra, Nazareth & Belvoir Castle. 19.50 (ISBN 0-8135-0680-8). Rutgers U Pr.

Crusader Manuscript Illumination at Saint-Jean D'acre, 1275-1291. 38.50x (ISBN 0-691-03907-0). Princeton U Pr.

Cubism & Abstract Art. 20.00 (ISBN 0-405-01509-7). Arno.

Cubism & Abstract Art. pap. 6.95 (ISBN 0-87070-274-2). NYGS.

Cubism & Twentieth Century Art. pap. 11.95 (ISBN 0-13-195065-7). P-H.

Cubism & Twentieth Century Art. rev. ed. 18.50 (ISBN 0-8109-0767-4). Abrams.

Cubism-Futurism. pap. 4.95 (ISBN 0-06-430059-5, IN-59). Har-Row.

Cubist Cinema. 20.00x (ISBN 0-8147-4956-9); pap. 11.75 (ISBN 0-8147-4957-7). NYU Pr.

Cubist Painters. pap. 7.50 (ISBN 0-8150-0029-4). Wittenborn.

Cuddly Dolls & How to Dress Them. 8.50 (ISBN 0-8008-2090-8). Taplinger.

Cult of Elizabeth: Elizabethan Portraiture & Pageantry. 24.95 (ISBN 0-500-23263-6). Thames Hudson.

Cultural History of the American Revolution. 17.50 (ISBN 0-690-01079-6). T Y Crowell.

Cultural Policy & Arts Administration. pap. 5.95x (ISBN 0-674-17980-3). Harvard U Pr.

Cultural Policy in Costa Rica. pap. 3.25 (ISBN 92-3-101400-5, U773). Unipub.

Cultural Policy in Guyana. pap. 4.75 (ISBN 92-3-101511-7, U792). Unipub.

Cultural Policy in Indonesia. pap. 2.00 (ISBN 92-3-101128-6). Unipub.

Cultural Policy in Iran. pap. 2.65 (ISBN 9-231-01002-6). Unipub.

Cultural Policy in Jamaica. pap. 3.25 (ISBN 92-3-101521-4, U806). Unipub.

Cultural Policy in Kenya. pap. 3.30 (ISBN 92-3-101202-9). Unipub.

Cultural Policy in Liberia. pap. 2.65 (ISBN 92-3-101160-X). Unipub.

Cultural Policy in Nigeria. pap. 2.65 (ISBN 92-3-101029-8). Unipub.

Cultural Policy in Peru. pap. 4.75 (ISBN 92-3-101470-6, U787). Unipub.

Cultural Policy in Romania. pap. 3.30 (ISBN 92-3-101188-X). Unipub.

Cultural Policy in Senegal. pap. 2.00 (ISBN 92-3-101118-9). Unipub.

Cultural Policy in Sri Lanka. pap. 2.65 (ISBN 9-231-01004-2). Unipub.

Cultural Policy in the German Democratic Republic. pap. 3.30 (ISBN 92-3-101291-6). Unipub.

Cultural Policy in the Republic of Korea. pap. 2.65 (ISBN 92-3-101384-X). Unipub.

Cultural Policy in the Republic of Zaire. pap. 4.65 (ISBN 92-3-101317-3). Unipub.

Cultural Policy in Yugoslavia. pap. 2.75 (ISBN 92-3-100920-6). Unipub.

Cultural Policy of the United Republic of Tanzania. pap. 3.30 (ISBN 92-3-101179-0). Unipub.

Cultural Resource Development: A Planning Survey & Analysis. 19.95 (ISBN 0-275-55640-9). Praeger.

Cultural Resource Development: Planning Survey & Analysis. pap. 5.00x. Pub Ctr Cult Res.

Culture & the City: Cultural Philanthropy in Chicago from the 1880's to 1917. 16.00 (ISBN 0-8131-1344-X). U Pr of Ky.

Culture Consumers. 10.00 (ISBN 0-394-48261-1). Random.

Culture Gulch: Notes on Art & Its Public in the 1960's. 5.95 (ISBN 0-374-13332-8). FS&G.

Cup of Cold Water. 15.00, signed ltd ed; pap. 3.00. SBD.

Curious Woodcuts of Fanciful & Real Beasts: A Selection of 190 Sixteenth-Century Woodcuts from Gesner's & Topsell's Natural Histories. 6.50 (ISBN 0-8446-0109-8). Peter Smith.

Current Antique Furniture Style & Price Guide. 9.95 (ISBN 0-385-13165-8). Doubleday.

Current Coins of the World. 5.50. Wehman.

Current Techniques in Architectural Practice. 25.00 (ISBN 0-07-002324-7). Arch Rec Bks.

Current Values of Antique Glass. rev. ed. 8.95 (ISBN 0-910872-08-2). Lee Pubns.

Currier & Ives Prints: An Illustrated Check List. 12.50 (ISBN 0-517-02446-2). Crown.

Curtain Wall Construction. 38.50x (ISBN 0-89197-718-X). Irvington.

Curves of Life. 2nd ed. text ed. price not set (ISBN 0-8284-0290-6). Chelsea Pub.

Curves of Life. pap. 5.95 (ISBN 0-486-23701-X). Dover.

Custom Made. 14.95 (ISBN 0-06-012633-7). Har-Row.

Custom Make Your Own Shoes & Handbags. 10.00 (ISBN 0-517-53138-0); pap. 4.95 (ISBN 0-517-53139-9). Crown.

Cut & Engraved Glass. rev. ed. 13.95 (ISBN 0-688-01402-X). Morrow.

Cut & Engraved Glass of Corning, 1868-1940. pap. 5.00 (ISBN 0-87290-064-9). Corning.

Cut Glass Handbook & Price Guide. pap. 4.95. Wallace-Homestead.

Cut Glass Handbook & Price Guide. pap. 4.75 (ISBN 0-8015-1878-4). Hawthorn.

Cut Glass Handbook & Price Guide. 2nd ed. pap. 4.95 (ISBN 0-912220-04-X). Hotchkiss House.

Cut of Women's Clothes: 1600-1930. 32.45 (ISBN 0-87830-026-0). Theatre Arts.

Cutting up with Paper: A Craft Book. 6.75 (ISBN 0-688-40064-7); PLB 6.48 (ISBN 0-688-50064-1). Lothrop.

Cycles of Taste. 7.50 (ISBN 0-8462-0917-9). Russell.

Cyclopedia of Painters & Paintings. 350.00 (ISBN 0-8490-1697-5). Gordon Pr.

Cyclopedia of United States Postmarks & Postal History. 30.00x (ISBN 0-88000-063-5). Quarterman.

Cyclopedic Treasury of Arts & Crafts Activities Using Scrap Materials. 14.95 (ISBN 0-13-196600-6). P-H.

D

D. C. Super Heroes Poster Book. pap. 5.95 (ISBN 0-517-53329-4). Crown.

Dacia: An Outline of the Early Civilizations of the Carpatho-Danubian Countries. lib. bdg. 22.00x (ISBN 0-313-20798-4, PADA). Greenwood.

Dada Almanach. 7.50 (ISBN 0-89366-060-4). Ultramarine Pub.

Dada: Art & Anti-Art. pap. 7.95 (ISBN 0-19-520071-3). Oxford U Pr.

Dada, Surrealism & Their Heritage. pap. 8.95 (ISBN 0-87070-284-X). NYGS.

Daguerreotype in America. pap. 6.00 (ISBN 0-486-23322-7). Dover.

Daguerreotype in America. 3rd.rev. ed. 11.50 (ISBN 0-8446-5461-2). Peter Smith.

Daguerreotype in Germany: Original Anthology. lib. bdg. 30.00x (ISBN 0-405-09598-8). Arno.

Daisy Hooee Nampeyo. PLB 5.95 (ISBN 0-87518-141-4). Dillon.

Dal Pozzo-Albani Drawings of Classical Antiquities in the Royal Library at Windsor Castle. pap. 2.50 (ISBN 0-87169-562-6). Am Philos.

Dale Eldred: Sculpture into Environment. 35.00 (ISBN 0-7006-0159-7). Regents Pr KS.

Dali. 50.00 (ISBN 0-8109-0063-7). Abrams.

Dali. 12.95 (ISBN 0-517-53675-7). Crown.

Dali: The Wines of Gala. 50.00 (ISBN 0-8109-0802-6). Abrams.

Dancing Masks of Africa. reinforced bdg. 6.95 (ISBN 0-684-14332-1). Scribner.

Danse. 24.95 (ISBN 0-688-00248-X). Morrow.

Dante Gabriel Rossetti. lib. bdg. 12.50. Folcroft.

Dante Gabriel Rossetti As Designer & Writer. 12.50 (ISBN 0-404-05429-3). AMS Pr.

Dante Gabriel Rossetti: Painter & Man of Letters. 9.50 (ISBN 0-404-05468-4). AMS Pr.

Dante Gabriel Rossetti, Painter Poet of Heaven in Earth. 19.00 (ISBN 0-403-01101-9). Scholarly.

Daring Young Men: The Story of the American Pre-Raphaelites. 15.00 (ISBN 0-405-08444-7). Arno.

Darker Brother. 18.95 (ISBN 0-525-49502-9). Dutton.

Darkroom Dynamics: An Introduction to Creative Photographic Techniques. 17.95 (ISBN 0-930764-07-2). Curtin & London.

Darkroom Graphics. 14.95 (ISBN 0-8174-0573-9). Amphoto.

Darkroom Handbook: A Complete Guide to the Best Design, Construction & Equipment. 16.95 (ISBN 0-930764-08-0); pap. 10.95 (ISBN 0-930764-06-4). Curtin & London.

Darkroom Magic. 2nd ed. 11.95 (ISBN 0-8174-0509-7). Amphoto.

Darkroom Techniques. 8.95 (ISBN 0-13-197533-1). P-H.

Darkroom Techniques: The Darkroom Film Development, Basic Photo Chemistry. 8.95 (ISBN 0-13-197517-X). P-H.

Dartington Hall. 22.00x (ISBN 0-19-920030-0). Oxford U Pr.

Daumier & His World. 7.65x (ISBN 0-8101-0019-3). Northwestern U Pr.

Daumier on War. pap. 6.95 (ISBN 0-306-80079-9). Da Capo.

Daumier: One Hundred & Twenty Great Lithographies. 12.50 (ISBN 0-8446-5675-5). Peter Smith.

Davenport Pottery & Porcelain: 1794-1887. 10.00 (ISBN 0-8048-1079-6). C E Tuttle.

David Adler: The Architect & His Work. 20.00 (ISBN 0-87131-026-0). M Evans.

David Claypool Johnston, American Graphic Humorist, 1798-1865. 4.00 (ISBN 0-89073-028-8); pap. 2.00. Boston Public Lib.

David Hicks on Living with Taste. 12.95 (ISBN 0-02-551370-2). Macmillan.

David Hockney. 30.00 (ISBN 0-8109-1058-6). Abrams.

David to Delacroix. pap. 3.95 (ISBN 0-674-19401-2). Harvard U Pr.

Dawn of Bohemianism: The Barbu Rebellion & Primitivism in Neoclassical France. 18.50x (ISBN 0-271-00527-0). Pa St U Pr.

Dawn of Italian Painting, 1250-1400. 29.50x (ISBN 0-8014-1124-6); pap. 14.95x (ISBN 0-8014-9172-X). Cornell U Pr.

Dawns & Dusks: Taped Conversations with Diana MacKown. 12.95 (ISBN 0-684-14781-5); pap. 7.95 (ISBN 0-684-15895-7, SL 810). Scribner.

Day off. pap. 7.95 (ISBN 0-8212-0708-3). NYGS.

Daybooks of Edward Weston. 35.00 set (ISBN 0-912334-43-6); pap. 20.00x set (ISBN 0-912334-46-0). Aperture.

De Architectura: The Como 1521 Edition in Exact Photographic Reproduction. 75.00 (ISBN 0-405-09047-1). Arno.

De-Definition of Art. pap. 3.95 (ISBN 0-02-074680-6). Macmillan.

De Grazia Paints Cabeza de Vaca: The First Non-Indian in Texas, New Mexico, & Arizona, 1527-1536. 13.50 (ISBN 0-8165-0469-5). U of Ariz Pr.

De Grazia Paints the Yaqui Easter. 18.00 (ISBN 0-8165-0023-1). U of Ariz Pr.

De Kooning. 60.00 (ISBN 0-8109-0123-4). Abrams.

De Meyer. 25.00 (ISBN 0-394-49744-9). Knopf.

Dean Cornwell: Dean of Illustrators. 35.00 (ISBN 0-8230-1269-7). Watson-Guptill.

Death of Naturalistic Photography see **Naturalistic Photography for Students of the Art.**

Decade of Sculpture. 25.00 (ISBN 0-87982-007-1). Art Alliance.

Decade of Still Life. 35.00 (ISBN 0-299-04121-2). U of Wis Pr.

Decatur House. pap. 1.50 (ISBN 0-89133-001-1). Preservation Pr.

December Decorations. 6.95 (ISBN 0-02-769920-X, 76992). Macmillan.

Decent Exposures. pap. 6.00 (ISBN 0-914728-01-6). Wingbow Pr.

Deciphering the Maya Script. 34.50x (ISBN 0-292-71504-8). U of Tex Pr.

Decorated Chapels of the Meroitic Pyramids at Meroe & Barkal see **Royal Cemeteries of Kush.**

Decorated Firearms, 1540-1870, from the Collection of Clay P. Bedford. 25.00 (ISBN 0-87935-041-5). U Pr of Va.

Decorated Letter. 22.95 (ISBN 0-8076-0894-7); pap. 10.95 (ISBN 0-8076-0895-5). Braziller.

Decorated Stoneware Pottery of North America. 19.50 (ISBN 0-8048-0007-3). C E Tuttle.

Decorating. 7.95 (ISBN 0-7207-1036-7). Transatlantic.

Decorating: A Realistic Guide. 25.00 (ISBN 0-394-40700-8). Pantheon.

Decorating American Style. 19.95 (ISBN 0-8212-0603-6). NYGS.

Decorating Defined. 9.95 (ISBN 0-671-20525-0). S&S.

Decorating Made Simple. 2.50 (ISBN 0-385-01695-6). Doubleday.

Decorating with Confidence. 9.95 (ISBN 0-671-21518-3). S&S.

Decorating with Crochet. 14.95 (ISBN 0-395-20992-7). HM.

Decorating with Fabric. 9.95 (ISBN 0-88421-037-5). Butterick Pub.

Decorating with Fabric: An Idea Book. rev. ed. pap. 4.00. Lindahl.

Decorating with Flowers. 35.00 (ISBN 0-8109-0808-5). Abrams.

Decorating with Plants. 8.95 (ISBN 0-8094-2579-3). Time-Life.

Decorating with Plants. 12.95 (ISBN 0-394-42680-0). Pantheon.

Decorating with Plants: A House & Garden Book. pap. 6.95 (ISBN 0-394-73465-3). Pantheon.

Decorating with Stitches. 13.95 (ISBN 0-8231-5047-X). Branford.

Decorating with Wild Flowers. 12.95 (ISBN 0-87857-126-4). Rodale Pr Inc.

Decoration & Furniture of Town Houses. 20.00x (ISBN 0-8277-1319-3). British Bk Ctr.

Decoration of Houses. 14.95 (ISBN 0-393-04468-8); pap. 3.95 (ISBN 0-393-00840-1). Norton.

Decoration of Houses. facsimile ed. 21.00x (ISBN 0-405-06938-3). Arno.

Decorations for Holidays & Celebrations. 15.95 (ISBN 0-517-51593-8); pap. 8.95 (ISBN 0-517-51594-6). Crown.

Decorative Alphabets & Initials. 9.50 (ISBN 0-8446-0820-3). Peter Smith.

Decorative & Sculptural Ironwork. 14.95 (ISBN 0-517-52319-1); pap. 7.95 (ISBN 0-517-52731-6). Crown.

Decorative Antique Ironwork: A Pictorial Treasury. pap. 8.95 (ISBN 0-486-22082-6). Dover.

Decorative Antique Ironwork: A Pictorial Treasury. 12.50 (ISBN 0-8446-1939-6). Peter Smith.

Decorative Art & Modern Interiors: Themes in Nature. 29.95 (ISBN 0-688-03480-2). Morrow.

Decorative Art & Modern Interiors 1977. 24.95 (ISBN 0-442-27423-8). Van Nos Reinhold.

Decorative Art & Modern Interiors 1978. 29.95 (ISBN 0-442-27421-1). Van Nos Reinhold.

Decorative Art of British New Guinea: A Study in Papuan Ethnography. 39.50 (ISBN 0-404-14124-2). AMS Pr.

Decorative Art of Dried Flower Arrangement. 9.95 (ISBN 0-385-06665-1). Doubleday.

Decorative Art of Leon Bakst. 30.00 (ISBN 0-405-08234-7). Arno.

Decorative Art of the Amur Tribes. 42.50 (ISBN 0-404-58104-8). AMS Pr.

Decorative Art of the Indians of the North Pacific Coast. 7.00 (ISBN 0-404-11823-2). AMS Pr.

Decorative Arts of Sweden. pap. 5.00 (ISBN 0-486-21478-8). Dover.

Decorative Arts of Sweden. 10.00 (ISBN 0-8446-2745-3). Peter Smith.

Decorative Braiding & Weaving. 9.25 (ISBN 0-8231-7031-4). Branford.

Decorative Crafts. PLB 8.49 (ISBN 0-8172-1178-0). Raintree Pubs Ltd.

Decorative Design in Mexican Homes. 16.50 (ISBN 0-8038-0058-4). Architectural.

Decorative Designs of Frank Lloyd Wright. 16.95 (ISBN 0-525-08958-6); pap. 9.95 (ISBN 0-525-47477-3). Dutton.

Decorative Machine Stitchery: Designs. 9.95. Wehman.

Decorative Machine Stitchery: Designs, Techniques & Projects for Every Sewing Machine. pap. 5.95 (ISBN 0-88421-051-0). Butterick Pub.

Decorative Motives of Oriental Art. 50.00 (ISBN 0-87817-002-2). Hacker.

Decorative Music Title Pages: 201 Examples from 1500 to 1800. 8.00 (ISBN 0-8446-2079-3). Peter Smith.

Decorative Music Title Pages: 201 Examples from 1500-1800. pap. 5.00 (ISBN 0-486-21915-1). Dover.

Decorative Painting Using Patterns from Nature. 7.95 (ISBN 0-517-53395-2); pap. 4.95 (ISBN 0-517-53396-0). Crown.

Decorative Patterns of the Ancient World for Craftsmen. 3.00 (ISBN 0-486-22986-6). Dover.

Decorative Patterns of the Ancient World for Craftsmen. 6.00 (ISBN 0-8446-5074-9). Peter Smith.

Decorative Silhouettes of the Twenties for Designers & Craftsmen. pap. 3.50 (ISBN 0-486-23152-6). Dover.

Decorative Silhouettes of the Twenties for Designers & Craftsmen. 6.75 (ISBN 0-8446-5178-8). Peter Smith.

Decorative Techniques. PLB 11.49 (ISBN 0-8094-1763-4). Silver.

Decorative Thirties. 20.00 (ISBN 0-8027-0353-4). Walker & Co.

Decorative Thirties. pap. 7.95 (ISBN 0-02-000210-6). Macmillan.

Decorative Tole Painting: A Basic Course in Folk Art for Beginners & Craftsmen. 5.95 (ISBN 0-517-50130-9); pap. 3.95 (ISBN 0-517-50373-5). Crown.

Decorative Treasures from Papier-Mache. 6.95 (ISBN 0-8208-0334-0). Hearthside.

Decorative Twenties. 20.00 (ISBN 0-8027-0078-0, 11045); drawings 5.00. Walker & Co.

Decorative Twenties. pap. 7.95 (ISBN 0-02-000200-9). Macmillan.

Decorative Work of John la Farge. lib. bdg. 69.00 (ISBN 0-8240-2736-1). Garland Pub.

Decorative Work of Robert Adam. 11.50 (ISBN 0-85458-160-X). Transatlantic.

Decoupage Crafts. PLB 5.95 (ISBN 0-385-07791-2). Doubleday.

Decoupage for Young Crafters. 7.95 (ISBN 0-525-28614-4). Dutton.

Decoupage Workshop. 12.95 (ISBN 0-385-07702-5). Doubleday.

Decouverte de la Photographie en 1839. lib. bdg. 15.00x (ISBN 0-405-09600-3). Arno.

Decoys of the Atlantic Flyway. 17.95 (ISBN 0-87691-141-6). Winchester Pr.

Deep-Sea Photography. 25.00x (ISBN 0-8018-0270-9). Johns Hopkins.

Deerfield Embroidery: Traditional Patterns from Colonial Massachusetts. 7.95 (ISBN 0-684-15949-X). Scribner.

Degas. 5.95 (ISBN 0-517-00502-6). Crown.

Degas' Drawings. 9.00 (ISBN 0-8446-5022-6). Peter Smith.

Degas Pastels. pap. 8.95 (ISBN 0-8230-1276-X). Watson-Guptill.

Delacroix. 7.95 (ISBN 0-8076-0586-7). Braziller.

Delicate Wear. lib. bdg. 11.49 (ISBN 0-8094-1739-1). Silver.

Delirious New York: A Retroactive Manifesto for Manhattan. 35.00 (ISBN 0-19-520035-7). Oxford U Pr.

Dell Encyclopedia of Birds. 8.95 (ISBN 0-440-01785-8). Delacorte.

Demands of Art. 25.00 (ISBN 0-691-09722-4). Princeton U Pr.

Demons & Beasts in Art. PLB 4.95 (ISBN 0-8225-0165-1). Lerner Pubns.

Dictionary of Subjects & Symbols in Art. 2nd, rev. ed. 15.95 (ISBN 0-06-433316-7); pap. 6.95 (ISBN 0-06-430100-1, IN-100). Har-Row.
Dictionary of Terms in Art. 35.00 (ISBN 0-8490-0047-5). Gordon Pr.
Dictionary of Terms in Art. 12.50 (ISBN 0-8103-3071-7). Gale.
Dictionary of the Art of Printing. lib. bdg. 20.00 (ISBN 0-576-52390-9). Intl Pubns Serv.
Dictionary of the Art of Printing. 32.00 (ISBN 0-8337-3128-9). B Franklin.
Dictionary of Tools Used in the Woodworking & Allied Trades c. 1700-1970. 47.50 (ISBN 0-684-14535-9). Scribner.
Dictionary of World Pottery & Porcelain. 9.95 (ISBN 0-684-14962-1). Scribner.
Diderot's Thoughts on Art & Style. lib. bdg. 17.00 (ISBN 0-8337-4077-6). B Franklin.
Dimensions. 2nd ed. 14.95 (ISBN 0-07-002336-0). Arch Rec Bks.
Diners. pap. 7.95 (ISBN 0-8109-2078-6). Abrams.
Ding: The Life of Jay Norwood Darling. 10.95 (ISBN 0-8138-0010-2). Iowa St U Pr.
Dining & Drinking: Picture Archives Ser. 14.95 (ISBN 0-8055-1211-X); pap. 4.95 (ISBN 0-8055-0304-8). Hart.
Dinner Party. 24.95 (ISBN 0-385-14566-7); pap. 12.95 (ISBN 0-385-14567-5). Doubleday.
Direct Metal Sculpture: Creative Techniques & Appreciation. 9.95 (ISBN 0-517-02448-9). Crown.
Direct Wax Sculpture. 12.50 (ISBN 0-8019-5463-0). Chilton.
Directory for the Arts. 10.00 (ISBN 0-89062-061-X); pap. 6.00. Ctr for Arts Info.
Directory of American Silver, Pewter & Silver Plate. 9.95 (ISBN 0-517-50636-X). Crown.
Directory of Antique Furniture: The Authentic Classification of European & American Designs. 12.95 (ISBN 0-517-01170-0). Crown.
Directory of Architects for Health Facilities: 1979 Edition. pap. 12.00 (ISBN 0-87258-271-X, 1328). Am Hospital.
Directory of Art Libraries & Visual Resource Collections in North America. text ed. 39.95 (ISBN 0-918212-05-7). Neal-Schuman.
Directory of British Photographic Collections. 32.00 (ISBN 0-918696-00-3). Camera Graphic.
Disasters of War. 8.00 (ISBN 0-8446-2148-X). Peter Smith.
Disasters of War. pap. 3.50 (ISBN 0-486-21872-4). Dover.
Discover Acrylics with Frank Covino: An Academic Approach. 16.95 (ISBN 0-8230-1340-5). North Light Pub.
Discover Your Self Through Photography. pap. 9.95 (ISBN 0-87100-099-7, 259). Morgan.
Discovering Antiques. 7.95 (ISBN 0-498-01844-X). A S Barnes.
Discovering Embroidery. 4.95 (ISBN 0-263-69981-1). Transatlantic.
Discovering Oil Painting. 15.95 (ISBN 0-8230-1345-6). Watson-Guptill.
Discovering the Fun in First Day Covers. 2nd ed. pap. 2.95 (ISBN 0-89794-005-9). FDC Pub.
Discovering the Present. pap. 3.95 (ISBN 0-226-72681-9, P671). U of Chicago Pr.
Discovering the Present: Three Decades in Art, Culture, & Politics. 10.95x (ISBN 0-226-72680-0). U of Chicago Pr.
Discovery of the Lost Art Treasures of California's First Mission. 20.00 (ISBN 0-913938-20-3). Copley Bks.
Discovery of Tutankhamun's Tomb. 6.95 (ISBN 0-448-14546-4). G&D.
Disfarmer: The Heber Springs Portraits, 1939-46. 22.50 (ISBN 0-89169-003-4). Addison Hse.
Disguises You Can Make. PLB 6.96 (ISBN 0-688-51810-9). Lothrop.
Disintegration of Form in the Arts. 6.95 (ISBN 0-8076-0441-0); pap. 3.95 (ISBN 0-8076-0442-9). Braziller.
Disney Poster Book. pap. 6.95 (ISBN 0-517-52936-X). Harmony.
Disparates: Or, the Proverbs. 7.00 (ISBN 0-8446-0655-3). Peter Smith.
Distortions. 22.50 (ISBN 0-394-40890-X). Knopf.
Divine Comedy of Pavel Tchelitchew. 17.50 (ISBN 0-8303-0020-1). Fleet.
Divine Presence: Asian Sculptures from the Collection of Mr. & Mrs. Harry Lenart. pap. 4.50 (ISBN 0-87587-086-4). LA Co Art Mus.
Divine Vision. lib. bdg. 20.95 (ISBN 0-8383-0790-6). Haskell.
Divine Vision. 6.50 (ISBN 0-8274-2193-1). R West.
Dixon's Book of Photography. 12.50 (ISBN 0-241-02276-2). Transatlantic.
Do-It-Yourself Dinosaurs: Imaginative Toycraft for Beginners. 6.95 (ISBN 0-8008-2263-3). Taplinger.
Do-It-Yourself Gunsmithing. 14.95 (ISBN 0-06-010638-7). Har-Row.
Do-It-Yourselfer's Guide to Furniture Repair & Refinishing. 9.95 (ISBN 0-8306-7894-8); pap. 5.95 (ISBN 0-8306-6894-2). Tab Bks.
Do Your Own Thing with Macrame. 13.95 (ISBN 0-8230-1354-5). Watson-Guptill.
Dr. Church's "Hoax". 12.00. Graphic Crafts.
Documentary Photography. 9.95 (ISBN 0-8094-1046-X). Time-Life.
Documents, Famous & Infamous: Selected from the Berg Collection of English & American Literature. pap. 3.00 (ISBN 0-87104-240-1). NY Pub Lib.
Documents of the Spanish Vanguard. pap. 16.95x (ISBN 0-8078-9078-2). U of NC Pr.
Documents on Art & Taste in Australia: The Colonial Period, 1770-1914. 17.75x (ISBN 0-19-550473-9). Oxford U Pr.
Dog. pap. 2.95 (ISBN 0-671-24002-1). S&S.
Dogs Bodies. pap. 1.25 (ISBN 0-448-22975-7). Paddington.
Dogs Bodies. pap. 1.95 (ISBN 0-200-71727-8). Transatlantic.
Dog's Book of Birds. reinforced bdg. 5.95 (ISBN 0-684-15181-2). Scribner.
Doll Book. pap. 7.95 (ISBN 0-442-29555-3). Van Nos Reinhold.
Doll Collectors' Manual, 1973. 8.50. Doll Collect Am.
Doll House Book. 9.95 (ISBN 0-442-09550-3). Van Nos Reinhold.
Doll Houses. PLB 3.95 (ISBN 0-8225-0854-0). Lerner Pubns.
Doll Making. 10.95 (ISBN 0-442-24693-5). Van Nos Reinhold.
Doll Making: A Creative Approach. pap. 7.95 (ISBN 0-442-24702-8). Van Nos Reinhold.
Doll Repair. 11.95 (ISBN 0-87588-121-1); pap. 7.95 (ISBN 0-87588-122-X). Hobby Hse.
Dollhouse Book. pap. 6.95 (ISBN 0-442-29558-8). Van Nos Reinhold.
Dollhouse Construction & Restoration. 10.95 (ISBN 0-8019-6462-8, 6462); pap. 5.95 (ISBN 0-8019-6463-6, 6463). Chilton.
Dollhouse Furniture You Can Make. 12.00 (ISBN 0-498-01994-2). A S Barnes.
Dollhouse Idea Book. pap. 3.50 (ISBN 0-8015-2152-1). Hawthorn.
Dollhouse Magic: How to Make & Find Simple Dollhouse Furniture. 7.95 (ISBN 0-8037-2122-6); lib. bdg. 7.45 (ISBN 0-8037-2123-4). Dial.
Dollmaking for Everyone. 9.95 (ISBN 0-498-01867-9). A S Barnes.
Dolls & Puppets. 4.95 (ISBN 0-7153-6311-5). David & Charles.
Dolls & Toys at the Essex Institute. 4.95 (ISBN 0-88389-066-6). Essex Inst.
Dolls, Dolls, Dolls. 5.95 (ISBN 0-695-80483-9); lib. ed. 5.97 (ISBN 0-695-40483-0). Follett.
Dolls' Houses in America: Historic Preservation in Miniature. pap. 16.95 (ISBN 0-684-15627-X). Scribner.
Dolls in Color. plastic bdg. 6.95 (ISBN 0-87069-025-6). Wallace-Homestead.
Dolls in Miniature. 10.95 (ISBN 0-8019-6412-1); pap. 6.95 (ISBN 0-8019-6413-X). Chilton.
Dolls in National & Folk Costume. 10.95 (ISBN 0-8231-3033-9). Branford.
Dolls in National Costume. 5.95 (ISBN 0-8231-3023-1). Branford.
Dolls, Makers & Marks. 2nd ed. pap. 7.00 (ISBN 0-910396-01-9). D S Coleman.
Dolls, Puppedolls & Teddy Bears. 11.95 (ISBN 0-442-29541-3). Van Nos Reinhold.
Dolls the Wide World Over. 19.95 (ISBN 0-517-50307-7, 503077). Crown.
Dolls to Make for Fun & Profit. rev. & new ed. 9.95 (ISBN 0-397-00027-8). Lippincott.
Dome Notes. pap. 7.50 (ISBN 0-916342-01-8). Bookpeople.
Dome People. 5.25 (ISBN 0-689-30139-1). Atheneum.
Domestic & Artistic Life of John Singleton Copley, R.A. facs. ed. 20.50 (ISBN 0-8369-5368-1). Arno.
Domestic Architecture of the American Colonies & of the Early Republic. 11.00 (ISBN 0-8446-2374-1). Peter Smith.
Domestic Architecture of the American Colonies & of the Early Republic. pap. 6.00 (ISBN 0-486-21743-4). Dover.
Domestic Colonial Architecture of Tidewater Virginia. lib. bdg. 29.50 (ISBN 0-306-71190-7). Da Capo.
Dominican Architecture in Sixteenth Century Oaxaca. new ed. 12.95x (ISBN 0-87918-016-1). ASU Lat Am St.
Don Judd. 7.95 (ISBN 0-912158-72-7). Hennessey.
Don Martin Drops 13 Stories. pap. 1.50 (ISBN 0-446-88858-3). Warner Bks.
Don Quixote. lib. bdg. 5.00 (ISBN 0-8414-4430-7). Folcroft.
Donald Rogers Illustrated Handbook of Arts & Crafts Lesson Plans for the Elementary Teacher: An Innovative Classroom-Tested Approach. 12.95 (ISBN 0-13-218396-X). P-H.
Donatello. facsimile ed. 29.75 (ISBN 0-8369-6681-3). Arno.
Donkeys. 5.95 (ISBN 0-8090-2048-3). Hill & Wang.
Donkeys: Their Care & Management. text ed. 4.95x (ISBN 0-8277-2120-X). British Bk Ctr.
Don't Move--Improve! Hundreds of Ways to Make a Good House Better. 14.95 (ISBN 0-308-10314-9). T Y Crowell.
Doodle Book. pap. 1.25 (ISBN 0-02-078120-2). Macmillan.
Doonesbury Chronicles. 12.95 (ISBN 0-03-014906-1); pap. 6.95 (ISBN 0-03-015256-9). HR&W.
Doors. pap. 9.95 (ISBN 0-14-005105-8). Penguin.
Dore Bible Illustrations. pap. 5.00 (ISBN 0-486-23004-X). Dover.
Dore Bible Illustrations. 10.00 (ISBN 0-8446-5023-4). Peter Smith.
Dore Gallery. 15.00 (ISBN 0-668-03444-0). Arco.
Dore's Illustrations for Rabelais: A Selection of 252 Illustrations. pap. 5.00 (ISBN 0-486-23656-0). Dover.
Dorothea Lange Looks at the American Country Woman. 12.95 (ISBN 0-88360-027-7); pap. 9.95 (ISBN 0-88360-026-9). Amon Carter.
Dosso & Battista Dossi: Court Painters at Ferrara. 41.50 (ISBN 0-691-03850-3). Princeton U Pr.
Double Elephant Folio. 45.00 (ISBN 0-8389-0103-4). ALA.
Double Market: Art Theft & Thieves. 15.95 (ISBN 0-347-00042-8). Saxon.
Double Weave. 12.95 (ISBN 0-8230-1355-3). Watson-Guptill.
Doubleday Book of Interior Decorating & Encyclopedia of Styles. 16.95 (ISBN 0-385-03711-2). Doubleday.
Down the Emperor's Road with Hiroshige. 9.50 (ISBN 0-8048-0143-6). C E Tuttle.
Doyle Diary: The Last Great Conan Doyle Mystery. 12.95 (ISBN 0-448-22068-7). Paddington.
Drafting Made Simple. 2.50 (ISBN 0-385-01348-5). Doubleday.
Drafting Technology. pap. 9.20 (ISBN 0-8273-0063-8); instructor's guide 1.75 (ISBN 0-8273-0064-6). Delmar.
Draping for Fashion Design. 13.50 (ISBN 0-87909-210-6). Reston.
Drawing All Animals. pap. 5.95 (ISBN 0-308-10108-1, F99). T Y Crowell.
Drawing & Designing Children's & Teenage Fashions. 12.95x (ISBN 0-470-26592-2). Halsted Pr.
Drawing & Designing Menswear. 8.95 (ISBN 0-470-98897-5). Halsted Pr.
Drawing & Painting the Natural Environment. 12.95 (ISBN 0-87192-060-3). Davis Mass.
Drawing & Painting the World of Animals. 25.00 (ISBN 0-672-21458-X). Sams.
Drawing & Painting the World of Animals. 25.00 (ISBN 0-672-21457-1). Sams.
Drawing & Planning for the Industrial Arts. new ed. text ed. 11.56 (ISBN 0-87002-159-1); tchr's guide & charts, worksheets 5.60 (ISBN 0-87002-162-1). Bennett Co.
Drawing & Selling Cartoons. 2nd ed. pap. 1.95 (ISBN 0-448-11959-5). G&D.
Drawing Animals. pap. 1.95 (ISBN 0-448-00514-X). G&D.
Drawing Animals & Birds. pap. 4.95 (ISBN 0-8008-2268-4). Taplinger.
Drawing As a Means to Architecture. rev. ed. 15.00 (ISBN 0-914468-03-0); pap. 12.50x (ISBN 0-914468-04-9). Pepper Pub.
Drawing Birds. 2nd ed. pap. 1.95 (ISBN 0-448-00515-8). G&D.
Drawing Cats. pap. 1.95 (ISBN 0-448-00517-4). G&D.
Drawing Children. pap. 1.95 (ISBN 0-448-00518-2). G&D.
Drawing Dogs. pap. 1.95 (ISBN 0-448-00519-0). G&D.
Drawing Dogs & Puppies. PLB 5.90 s&l (ISBN 0-531-01452-5). Watts.
Drawing Dynamic Hands. 12.95 (ISBN 0-8230-1367-7). Watson-Guptill.
Drawing Faces & Expressions. pap. 1.95 (ISBN 0-448-00520-4). G&D.
Drawing File for Architects, Illustrators, & Designers. pap. 13.95 (ISBN 0-442-27878-0). Van Nos Reinhold.
Drawing Flowers. pap. 1.95 (ISBN 0-448-00521-2). G&D.
Drawing for Boys. pap. 1.95 (ISBN 0-448-00522-0). G&D.
Drawing for Girls. pap. 1.95 (ISBN 0-448-00539-5). G&D.
Drawing for Product Planning. text ed. 6.60 (ISBN 0-87002-037-4); student guide 1.08 (ISBN 0-87002-087-0); transparency masters 6.80 (ISBN 0-87002-077-3). Bennett Co.
Drawing for Young Artists. pap. 1.95 (ISBN 0-448-00523-9). G&D.
Drawing Funny Pictures. pap. 1.95 (ISBN 0-448-00574-3). G&D.
Drawing Hands. pap. 1.95 (ISBN 0-448-00524-7). G&D.
Drawing Horses. pap. 1.95 (ISBN 0-448-00525-5). G&D.
Drawing Horses & Foals. PLB 5.90 (ISBN 0-531-00379-5). Watts.
Drawing in Ink. 14.95 (ISBN 0-8230-1385-5). Watson-Guptill.
Drawing Lessons from the Great Masters. 17.95 (ISBN 0-8230-1400-2). Watson-Guptill.
Drawing of the Hand & Its Anatomy. 7.50. Borden.
Drawing Outdoors. pap. 7.95 (ISBN 0-8230-1417-7). Watson-Guptill.
Drawing Portraits. 14.50 (ISBN 0-8230-1430-4). Watson-Guptill.
Drawing Sea & Sky. pap. 1.50 (ISBN 0-448-00526-3). G&D.
Drawing the Female Figure. 13.95 (ISBN 0-8230-1370-7). Watson-Guptill.
Drawing the Figure from Top to Toe. pap. 5.95 (ISBN 0-308-10107-3, F98). T Y Crowell.
Drawing the Head & Hands. 12.95 (ISBN 0-670-28385-1). Viking Pr.
Drawing the Human Form. 16.95 (ISBN 0-442-20718-2); pap. 10.95 (ISBN 0-442-20717-4). Van Nos Reinhold.
Drawing the Human Head. 11.95 (ISBN 0-8230-1375-8). Watson-Guptill.
Drawing the Male Figure. 14.95 (ISBN 0-8230-1405-3). Watson-Guptill.
Drawing with Markers. 14.95 (ISBN 0-8230-1462-2). Watson-Guptill.
Drawings. 17.50 (ISBN 0-912158-62-X). Hennessey.
Drawings by American Architects. 44.95 (ISBN 0-471-46845-2). Wiley.
Drawings by Canaletto. pap. 3.00 (ISBN 0-486-21990-9). Dover.
Drawings by Canaletto. 5.00 (ISBN 0-8446-1807-1). Peter Smith.
Drawings by John Flaxman in the Huntington Collection. pap. 5.00 (ISBN 0-87328-047-4). Huntington Lib.
Drawings by Old Masters at Christ Church, Oxford. 125.00x (ISBN 0-19-817323-7). Oxford U Pr.
Drawings by Thomas Rowlandson in the Huntington Collection. 20.00 (ISBN 0-87328-065-2). Huntington Lib.
Drawings by Tintoretto. 4.50 (ISBN 0-8446-3077-2). Peter Smith.
Drawings by Wharton Esherick. 14.95 (ISBN 0-442-26967-6). Van Nos Reinhold.
Drawings for the Theatre. 13.50 (ISBN 0-87830-036-8). Theatre Arts.
Drawings from Stockholm. 9.00 (ISBN 0-87598-001-5); pap. 5.00 (ISBN 0-87598-013-9). Pierpont Morgan.
Drawings from the Collection of Lore & Rudolf Heinemann. pap. 7.50 (ISBN 0-87598-040-6). Pierpont Morgan.
Drawings from the Turner Shakespeare. 5.00 (ISBN 0-87328-059-8). Huntington Lib.
Drawings of Albrecht Durer: Selected. 6.75 (ISBN 0-8446-0593-X). Peter Smith.
Drawings of Antoine Watteau. buckram 30.00 (ISBN 0-87817-050-2). Hacker.
Drawings of Architectural Interiors. pap. 9.95 (ISBN 0-8230-7158-8). Watson-Guptill.
Drawings of Augustus John. treasure trove bdg. 6.47x; pap. 2.95. Borden.
Drawings of Degas. treasure trove bdg. 6.47x; pap. 2.95. Borden.
Drawings of Edouard Manet. 42.50x (ISBN 0-520-01547-9). U of Cal Pr.
Drawings of Florence. pap. 3.50 (ISBN 0-911070-02-8). Olivet.
Drawings of Frank Lloyd Wright. 20.00 (ISBN 0-8180-0019-8). Horizon.
Drawings of G. B. Tiepolo. 60.00 (ISBN 0-87817-030-8). Hacker.
Drawings of Gauguin. treasure trove bdg. 6.47x; pap. 2.95. Borden.
Drawings of George Bellows. treasure trove bdg. 6.47x; pap. 2.95. Borden.
Drawings of Georges Seurat. 10.00 (ISBN 0-8446-0254-X). Peter Smith.
Drawings of Hokusai. lib. bdg. 28.00x (ISBN 0-313-21074-8, BODH). Greenwood.
Drawings of Hokusai. treasure trove bdg. 6.47x; pap. 2.95. Borden.
Drawings of Ignacio Tirsch: A Jesuit Missionary in Baja California. 15.00 (ISBN 0-87093-227-6). Dawsons.
Drawings of Ingres. treasure trove bdg. 6.47x; pap. 2.95. Borden.
Drawings of James Cockburn. 25.00. Vanguard.
Drawings of John Ruskin. 32.50x (ISBN 0-19-817305-9). Oxford U Pr.
Drawings of John Singer Sargent in the Corcoran Gallery of Art. treasure trove bdg. 6.47x; pap. 2.95. Borden.
Drawings of Jossi Stern. treasure trove bdg. 6.47; pap. 2.95. Borden.
Drawings of La Lyre. treasure trove bdg. 6.47x; pap. 2.95. Borden.
Drawings of Lorrain. treasure trove bdg. 6.47x; pap. 2.95. Borden.
Drawings of Matisse. treasure trove bdg. 6.47x; pap. 2.95. Borden.
Drawings of Michelangelo. treasure trove bdg. 6.47x; pap. 2.95. Borden.
Drawings of Modigliani. treasure trove bdg. 6.47x; pap. 2.95. Borden.
Drawings of Morris Graves. 22.50 (ISBN 0-8212-0592-7). NYGS.
Drawings of Mucha: Seventy Works. pap. 4.00 (ISBN 0-486-23672-2). Dover.
Drawings of Paul Cezanne: A Catalogue Raisonne. 140.00 (ISBN 0-8212-0427-0). NYGS.

E

Easy Quillery: Projects with Paper Coils & Scrolls. 6.25 (ISBN 0-688-22130-0); PLB 6.00 (ISBN 0-688-32130-5). Morrow.
Easy Speaker Projects. pap. 3.95 (ISBN 0-672-21104-1). Sams.
Easy-to-Do Leathercraft Projects with Full Size Templates. pap. 2.25 (ISBN 0-486-23319-7). Dover.
Easy to Make Costumes for Stage & School. 8.95 (ISBN 0-8238-0205-1). Plays.
Easy-to-Make Dolls with Nineteenth-Century Costumes. pap. 2.75 (ISBN 0-486-23426-6). Dover.
Easy to Make Holiday Fun Things. pap. 1.25 (ISBN 0-448-14449-2). G&D.
Easy to Make Puppets. PLB 5.09 (ISBN 0-8178-5432-0). Harvey.
Easy to Make Puppets. pap. 6.95 (ISBN 0-8238-0178-0). Plays.
Easy Weaving. 6.75 (ISBN 0-688-40057-4); PLB 6.48 (ISBN 0-688-50057-9). Lothrop.
Eccentric Spaces. 8.95 (ISBN 0-394-40719-9). Knopf.
Eccentrics & Other American Visionary Painters. pap. 9.95 (ISBN 0-525-47500-1). Dutton.
Ecclesiastical Art in Germany During the Middle Ages. lib. bdg. 35.00 (ISBN 0-89341-359-3). Longwood Pr.
Ecclesiastical Crafts. 16.95 (ISBN 0-442-22966-6). Van Nos Reinhold.
Echoes of Silence. 14.95 (ISBN 0-87992-006-8). Light Impressions.
Eclipse of Symbolism. 14.95x (ISBN 0-87249-172-2). U of SC Pr.
Ecology & the Arts in Ancient Panama: On the Development of Social Rank & Symbolism in the Central Provinces. pap. 6.00 (ISBN 0-88402-069-X). Dumbarton Oaks.
Economic Benefits of Preserving Old Buildings. 9.00; pap. 6.00 (ISBN 0-89133-037-2). Preservation Pr.
Economics of Taste. Incl. Rise & Fall of Objets d'Art Prices Since 1750. text ed. o.p.; Art Market in the Nineteen Sixties. text ed. 26.50x (ISBN 0-214-65131-2). Humanities.
Economics of the Arts. 22.00x (ISBN 0-89158-613-X). Westview.
Ed Emberley's Drawing Book of Faces. 4.95g (ISBN 0-316-23609-8). Little.
Ed Emberley's Great Thumbprint Drawing Book. 4.95g (ISBN 0-316-23613-6). Little.
Edge of the Anvil. 9.95 (ISBN 0-87857-186-8); pap. 6.95 (ISBN 0-87857-195-7). Rodale Pr Inc.
Editing by Design: Word-&-Picture Communication for Editors & Designers. 18.50 (ISBN 0-8352-0692-0). Bowker.
Editorial & Political Cartooning. 12.95 (ISBN 0-87396-078-5). Stravon.
Edmund Dulac. 10.95 (ISBN 0-684-15470-6). Scribner.
Edo Painting - Sotatsu & Korin. 17.50 (ISBN 0-8348-1011-5). Weatherhill.
Educating Artistic Vision. text ed. 14.95x (ISBN 0-02-332120-2). Macmillan.
Education & Art: A Symposium. 49.00 (ISBN 0-518-10072-3). Arno.
Education in the Graphic Arts. 3.00 (ISBN 0-89073-025-3). Boston Public Lib.
Education of le Corbusier. lib. bdg. 40.00 (ISBN 0-8240-2732-9). Garland Pub.
Educational Change & Architectural Consequences. pap. 2.00 (ISBN 0-89192-050-1). Interbk Inc.
Educational Philosophy & Practice of Art Museums in the United States. 17.50 (ISBN 0-404-55942-5). AMS Pr.
Educreation. 16.50 (ISBN 0-08-011656-6); pap. 9.50 (ISBN 0-08-011655-8). Pergamon.
Educreation: Education for Creation, Growth & Change. new ed. text ed. 34.00 (ISBN 0-08-021475-4); pap. text ed. 19.00 (ISBN 0-08-021476-2). Pergamon.
Edvard Munch. pap. text ed. 7.95 (ISBN 0-19-519936-7). Oxford U Pr.
Edward Gordon Craig. 7.75 (ISBN 0-87830-042-2). Theatre Arts.
Edward Gordon Craig, Artist of the Theatre, 1872-1966. 10.00 (ISBN 0-87104-502-8). NY Pub Lib.
Edward Gordon Craig, Artist of the Theatre, 1872-1966: A Memorial Exhibition in the Amsterdam Gallery. 9.00 (ISBN 0-405-01749-9). Arno.
Edward Hicks, Painter of the Peaceable Kingdom. 39.00 (ISBN 0-527-30400-X). Kraus Repr.
Edward Hopper. concise ed. 17.50 (ISBN 0-8109-1061-6). Abrams.
Edward Johnston. pap. 6.95 (ISBN 0-8008-2367-2). Taplinger.
Edward Lear & His World. 9.95 (ISBN 0-684-15173-1). Scribner.
Edward Lear As a Landscape Draughtsman. 10.00x (ISBN 0-674-23950-4). Harvard U Pr.
Edward Sheriff Curtis: Visions of a Vanishing Race. 35.00 (ISBN 0-690-01162-8). T Y Crowell.
Edward Steichen. 7.95 (ISBN 0-89381-006-1). Aperture.
Edward Weston: The Flame of Recognition. new ed. 15.00 (ISBN 0-912334-02-9); pap. 9.50 (ISBN 0-912334-03-7). Aperture.
Edwardian Observer: Photographs of Leslie Hamilton Wilson. 22.50 (ISBN 0-517-53376-6). Crown.
Eero Saarinen. 6.95 (ISBN 0-8076-0199-3); pap. 3.95 (ISBN 0-8076-0391-0). Braziller.
Effanbee, the Dolls with the Golden Hearts. new ed. 14.95 (ISBN 0-913914-10-X). Trojan Pr.
Effective Architect. 22.95 (ISBN 0-13-240754-X). P-H.
Effects & Experiments in Photography. 17.95 (ISBN 0-8038-1938-2). Focal Pr.
Egg Art. 3.95 (ISBN 0-87749-476-2). Sterling.
Egg Craft. pap. 2.95 (ISBN 0-688-45512-3). Lothrop.
Egon Schiele's Portraits. 65.00 (ISBN 0-520-01726-9). U of Cal Pr.
Egon Schiele's Portraits. pap. 19.95 (ISBN 0-8076-0841-6). Braziller.
Egypt Before the Pharaohs. 15.95 (ISBN 0-394-41049-1). Knopf.
Egyptian Decorative Art. 13.00 (ISBN 0-405-08849-3). Arno.
Egyptian Designs in Modern Stitchery. 14.95 (ISBN 0-87690-316-2). Dutton.
Egyptian Objects in the Victoria & Albert Museum. pap. 19.50 (ISBN 0-85668-103-2). Intl Schol Bk Serv.
Egyptian Revival: Its Sources, Monuments, & Meaning, 1808-1858. 20.00 (ISBN 0-520-03324-8). U of Cal Pr.
Egyptian Sculpture. lib. bdg. 13.50x (ISBN 0-8371-4293-8, MUEG). Greenwood.
Egyptian Temples. 27.50 (ISBN 0-404-14719-4). AMS Pr.
Eight American Women Painters. lib. bdg. 42.95 (ISBN 0-87968-457-7). Gordon Pr.
Eighteenth & Nineteenth Century Maryland Silver in the Collection of the Baltimore Museum of Art. text ed. 25.00 (ISBN 0-912298-44-8); pap. text ed. 12.50 (ISBN 0-912298-37-5). Baltimore Mus.
Eisenstaedt's Album: Fifty Years of Friends & Acquaintances. 16.95 (ISBN 0-670-29078-5). Viking Pr.
Eisenstaedt's Guide to Photography. 17.95 (ISBN 0-670-29081-5). Viking Pr.
El Kurru see Royal Cemeteries of Kush.
Elaine Slater's Book of Needlepoint Projects. 14.95 (ISBN 0-03-017516-X). HR&W.
Elder Pliny's Chapters on the History of Art. 16.00 (ISBN 0-403-01152-3). Scholarly.
Electric Kiln Ceramics. 14.95 (ISBN 0-442-26961-7); pap. 8.95 (ISBN 0-442-26958-7). Van Nos Reinhold.
Electric Kiln Construction for Potters. 11.95 (ISBN 0-442-30134-0). Van Nos Reinhold.
Electrical Soldering. 2nd ed. 4.95 (ISBN 0-672-21411-3, 21411). Sams.
Electronic Flash. 2nd. ed. 4.95 (ISBN 0-8174-0447-3). Amphoto.
Electronic Flash Guide. 2nd ed. pap. 3.95 (ISBN 0-8038-1939-0). Focal Pr.
Electronic Flash Simplified. pap. 4.95 (ISBN 0-8174-0185-7). Amphoto.
Electronic Flash-Strobe. pap. 9.95 (ISBN 0-262-55008-3). MIT Pr.
Electrophotography. rev, 2nd ed. 77.95 (ISBN 0-470-75696-9). Halsted Pr.
Electrostatics in Reprography. 7.95 (ISBN 0-8038-1899-8). Focal Pr.
Elegant Decorating on a Limited Budget. 3.95 (ISBN 0-02-602180-3). Macmillan.
Elegant Doll House Book. pap. 4.50 (ISBN 0-914728-18-0). Wingbow Pr.
Elegant Japanese House. 80.00 (ISBN 0-8348-1500-1). Weatherhill.
Elementary Developing & Printing. 8.95 (ISBN 0-8174-0558-5). Amphoto.
Elementary Fashion Design & Trade Sketching. 10.00 (ISBN 0-87005-103-2). Fairchild.
Elementary Teacher's Art Ideas Desk Book. 12.95 (ISBN 0-13-260679-8). P-H.
Elements of a Pictorial Photograph. 16.00 (ISBN 0-405-04934-X). Arno.
Elements of Architecture. 16.00 (ISBN 90-221-0272-6). Walter J Johnson.
Elements of Color. 11.95 (ISBN 0-442-24038-4). Van Nos Reinhold.
Elements of Color: Study Material. 6.95 (ISBN 0-442-24036-8). Van Nos Reinhold.
Elements of Drawing. pap. 2.75 (ISBN 0-486-22730-8). Dover.
Elements of Drawing. 24.00 (ISBN 0-403-00307-5). Scholarly.
Elements of Dynamic Symmetry. pap. 3.00 (ISBN 0-486-21776-0). Dover.
Elements of Dynamic Symmetry. 7.50 (ISBN 0-8446-2193-5). Peter Smith.
Elements of Lettering. 2nd ed. text ed. 9.95 (ISBN 0-07-004775-8). McGraw.
Elements of Park & Recreation Administration. 4th ed. text ed. write for info. (ISBN 0-8087-0468-0). Burgess.
Elements of Stagecraft. pap. text ed. 10.95x (ISBN 0-88284-053-3). Alfred Pub.
Elements of the Art of Architecture. 6.50 (ISBN 0-670-29132-3). Viking Pr.
Elements of Weaving. 10.95 (ISBN 0-385-03473-3). Doubleday.
Elements of Weaving. pap. 5.95 (ISBN 0-385-12540-2). Doubleday.
Elie Nadelman. 65.00x (ISBN 0-87130-034-6). Eakins.
Elie Nadelman Drawings. buckram 15.00 (ISBN 0-87817-045-6). Hacker.
Ellsworth Kelly. 55.00 (ISBN 0-8109-0217-6). Abrams.
Elsa's Housebook: A Woman's Photojournal. pap. 5.95 (ISBN 0-87923-099-1). Godine.
Emaki: Picture Scrolls. pap. 3.95. Japan Pubns.
Emancipation & the Freed in American Sculpture. facsimile ed. 25.00 (ISBN 0-8369-8983-X). Arno.
Embattled Critic: Views on Modern Art. 19.50 (ISBN 0-8369-7309-7). Arno.
Emblem & Expression: Meaning in English Art of the Eighteenth Century. text ed. 25.00 (ISBN 0-674-24778-7). Harvard U Pr.
Embroidering with the Loom: Creative Combinations of Weaving & Stitchery. 14.95 (ISBN 0-442-22175-4). Van Nos Reinhold.
Embroidery. 12.95 (ISBN 0-442-23070-2); pap. 8.95 (ISBN 0-442-23071-0). Van Nos Reinhold.
Embroidery & Design on Patterned Fabric. 9.95 (ISBN 0-498-01679-X). A S Barnes.
Embroidery Design for Students of All Ages. 5.00 (ISBN 0-87245-207-7). Textile Bk.
Embroidery Designs from the Sea. 8.95 (ISBN 0-8008-2403-2). Taplinger.
Embroidery for the Church. 15.50 (ISBN 0-8231-4034-2). Branford.
Embroidery Magic on Patterned Fabrics. 5.95 (ISBN 0-684-15704-7). Scribner.
Embroidery of All Russia. 9.95 (ISBN 0-684-15184-7). Scribner.
Embroidery of Mexico & Guatemala. 6.95 (ISBN 0-684-15946-5). Scribner.
Emergence. 15.00 (ISBN 0-87754-057-8). Chelsea Hse.
Emergence & Growth of an Urban Region: The Developing Urban Detroit Area. 20.00x (ISBN 0-8143-1505-4). Wayne St U Pr.
Emergence & Growth of an Urban Region: The Developing Urban Detroit Area Vol. 3-A Concept for Future Development. 20.00x (ISBN 0-8143-1506-2). Wayne St U Pr.
Emotion in Art. facs. ed. 15.00 (ISBN 0-8369-0788-4). Arno.
Emphasis Art: A Qualitative Art Program for the Elementary School. 3rd ed. text ed. 15.95x (ISBN 0-690-00868-6). Har-Row.
Empire Furniture 1800 to 1825. 26.00 (ISBN 0-571-06666-6). Merrimack Bk Serv.
Empire State Building. 12.95 (ISBN 0-06-012172-6). Har-Row.
Empire Style Designs & Ornaments. pap. 4.00 (ISBN 0-486-22984-X). Dover.
Empire Style Designs & Ornaments. 7.50 (ISBN 0-8446-5004-8). Peter Smith.
Enameling on Metal. 11.95 (ISBN 0-8019-0166-9); pap. 6.95 (ISBN 0-8019-5702-8). Chilton.
Enamelist. pap. 3.50 (ISBN 0-308-10196-0, F-127). T Y Crowell.
Enamels of China & Japan. 10.00 (ISBN 0-396-06733-6). Dodd.
Enchanted World: The Magic of Pictures. 9.95 (ISBN 0-19-520130-2). Oxford U Pr.
Enclosing Behavior. 25.00 (ISBN 0-87933-069-4). DH&R.
Encyclopedia of American Cut & Engraved Glass: Geometric Conceptions. 25.00 (ISBN 0-916528-01-4). J M Pearson.
Encyclopedia of American Cut & Engraved Glass: Geometric Motifs. 30.00 (ISBN 0-916528-05-7). J M Pearson.
Encyclopedia of American Silver Manufacturers. 7.95. Wallace-Homestead.
Encyclopedia of American Silver Manufacturers: Their Marks, Trademarks, & History. new, rev. ed. 7.95 (ISBN 0-517-52145-8). Crown.
Encyclopedia of Australian Art. 39.95 (ISBN 0-09-081420-7). Merrimack Bk Serv.
Encyclopedia of Canvas Embroidery Stitch Patterns. rev. ed. 10.95 (ISBN 0-690-01665-4); pap. 6.95 (ISBN 0-690-01666-2). T Y Crowell.
Encyclopedia of Chinese Coins. 15.50 (ISBN 0-912706-04-X). Coole.
Encyclopedia of Comic Book Heroes: Batman. pap. 8.95 (ISBN 0-02-080090-8). Macmillan.
Encyclopedia of Comparative Letterforms for Artists & Designers. 21.50 (ISBN 0-910158-01-0). Art Dir.
Encyclopedia of Decorative Arts, 1890-1940. 35.00 (ISBN 0-442-22577-6). Van Nos Reinhold.
Encyclopedia of Duncan Glass. 17.50 (ISBN 0-682-48527-6). Exposition.
Encyclopedia of Embroidery Stitches, Including Crewel. pap. 4.95 (ISBN 0-486-22929-7). Dover.
Encyclopedia of Embroidery Stitches, Including Crewel. 9.00 (ISBN 0-8446-5232-6). Peter Smith.
Encyclopedia of Energy-Efficient Building Design: 391 Practical Case Studies. 150.00 (ISBN 0-915250-18-7). Environ Design.
Encyclopedia of Furniture. rev. ed. 12.95 (ISBN 0-517-03735-1). Crown.
Encyclopedia of Furniture Making. 14.95 (ISBN 0-8069-8302-7). Sterling.
Encyclopedia of Handweaving. pap. 4.95 (ISBN 0-308-10072-7). T Y Crowell.
Encyclopedia of Knitting & Crochet Stitch Patterns. 14.95 (ISBN 0-442-25117-3). Van Nos Reinhold.
Encyclopedia of Knots & Fancy Rope Work. 4th ed. 17.50 (ISBN 0-87033-021-7). Cornell Maritime.
Encyclopedia of Modern Architecture. 17.50 (ISBN 0-8109-0308-3). Abrams.
Encyclopedia of Ornament. 12.50 (ISBN 0-312-24920-9); pap. 5.50 (ISBN 0-312-24955-1). St Martin.
Encyclopedia of Photography. new ed. 139.50 set (ISBN 0-911744-55-X). Career Inst.
Encyclopedia of Practical Photography. 11.95 (ISBN 0-8174-3053-9); lib. bdg. 15.95 (ISBN 0-8174-3203-5). Amphoto.
Encyclopedia of Practical Photography. 11.95; lib. bdg. 15.95 (ISBN 0-8174-3206-X). Amphoto.
Encyclopedia of Practical Photography. 11.95 ea.; lib. bdg. 15.95 ea.; lib. bdg. (ISBN 0-8174-3200-0). Amphoto.
Encyclopedia of Practical Photography. 11.95 (ISBN 0-8174-3055-5); lib. bdg. 15.95 (ISBN 0-8174-3205-1). Amphoto.
Encyclopedia of Practical Photography. 11.95 (ISBN 0-8174-3052-0); lib. bdg. 15.95 (ISBN 0-8174-3202-7). Amphoto.
Encyclopedia of Practical Photography. 11.95 (ISBN 0-8174-3054-7); lib. bdg. 15.95 (ISBN 0-8174-3204-3). Amphoto.
Encyclopedia of Practical Photography. 11.95 (ISBN 0-8174-3051-2); lib. bdg. 15.95 (ISBN 0-8174-3201-9). Amphoto.
Encyclopedia of Practical Photography. 11.95 ea.; lib. bdg. 15.95 ea. (ISBN 0-8174-3061-X). lib. bdg. (ISBN 0-8174-3211-6) (ISBN 0-8174-3062-8). lib. bdg. (ISBN 0-8174-3212-4). Amphoto.
Encyclopedia of Practical Photography. 11.95 ea.; lib. bdg. 15.95 ea. (ISBN 0-8174-3057-1). lib. bdg. (ISBN 0-8174-3207-8) (ISBN 0-8174-3058-X). lib. bdg. (ISBN 0-8174-3208-6). Amphoto.
Encyclopedia of Practical Photography. 11.95 ea.; lib. bdg. 15.95 ea. (ISBN 0-8174-3063-6). lib. bdg. (ISBN 0-8174-3213-2) (ISBN 0-8174-3064-4). lib. bdg. (ISBN 0-8174-3214-0). Amphoto.
Encyclopedia of Practical Photography. 11.95 ea.; lib. bdg. 15.95 ea. (ISBN 0-8174-3059-8). lib. bdg. (ISBN 0-8174-3209-4) (ISBN 0-8174-3060-1). lib. bdg. (ISBN 0-8174-3210-8). Amphoto.
Encyclopedia of Rawhide & Leather Braiding. 12.00 (ISBN 0-87033-161-2). Cornell Maritime.
Encyclopedia of Small Antiques. 22.50 (ISBN 0-06-012795-3). Har-Row.
Encyclopedia of Small Spot Engravings. 24.95 (ISBN 0-911842-00-4). Valley Sun.
Encyclopedia of the Comic Book Heroes: Wonder Woman. 14.95 (ISBN 0-02-538710-3). Macmillan.
Encyclopedia of the Comic Book Heroes: Wonder Woman. pap. 7.95 (ISBN 0-02-080080-0). Macmillan.
Encyclopedia of Toys. 15.95 (ISBN 0-517-53027-9). Crown.
Encyclopedia of Victorian Needlework. pap. 6.00 ea. (ISBN 0-486-22800-2) (ISBN 0-486-22801-0). Dover.
Encyclopedia of Working with Glass. 17.50 (ISBN 0-379-00274-4). Oceana.
Encyclopedia of Working with Glass. 9.95 (ISBN 0-89345-003-0). Freedeeds Assocs.
Encyclopedia of World Art. 750.00 (ISBN 0-07-079788-9); guide 1.00. McGraw.
Encyclopedia of World Stamps, 1945-1975. 24.95 (ISBN 0-07-044595-8). McGraw.
Encyclopedia or Decorative Arts 1890-1940. 35.00 (ISBN 0-442-22577-6). Litton Educ Pub.
Enduring Art of Japan. pap. 4.95 (ISBN 0-394-17392-9, E579). Grove.
Enduring Image: American Painting from 1665. 15.00 (ISBN 0-690-26619-7). T Y Crowell.
Energies of Consciousness: Exploration in Acupuncture, Auras & Kirlian Photography. new ed. 22.50x (ISBN 0-677-05190-5). Gordon.
Energy & Form: An Ecological Approach to Urban Growth. pap. 8.95x (ISBN 0-262-61025-6). MIT Pr.
Energy & the Imagination: A Study of the Development of Blake's Thought. 18.50x (ISBN 0-19-811682-9). Oxford U Pr.
Energy Conservation Through Building Design. 19.50 (ISBN 0-07-068460-X). McGraw.

Frederic Remington: 173 Drawings & Illustrations. 10.00 (ISBN 0-8446-4601-6). Peter Smith.
Frederic Whitaker. 17.50 (ISBN 0-87358-094-X). Northland.
Frederick Law Olmsted & the American Environmental Tradition. 10.00 (ISBN 0-8076-0650-2); pap. 4.95 (ISBN 0-8076-0649-9). Braziller.
Frederick Law Olmsted, Landscape Architect: 1822-1903. 35.00 (ISBN 0-405-08829-9). Arno.
Frederick Law Olmsted: Partner with Nature. 4.95 (ISBN 0-396-07079-5). Dodd.
Free-Form Bargello. 14.95 (ISBN 0-684-15024-7); pap. 7.95 (ISBN 0-684-15055-7, SL719). Scribner.
Free Weaving. 6.95 (ISBN 0-684-15945-7). Scribner.
Freelance Photography. pap. 3.95 (ISBN 0-8227-0090-5). Petersen Pub.
Freer Chinese Bronzes. 30.00. Freer.
Freer Chinese Bronzes. 40.00. Freer.
Freer Chinese Bronzes: Cataloque. 40.00 (ISBN 0-87474-764-3). Smithsonian.
Freer Chinese Bronzes: Technical Studies. 30.00 (ISBN 0-87474-470-9). Smithsonian.
Freer Indian Sculptures. 12.00. Freer.
Freer Indian Sculptures. 15.00 (ISBN 0-87474-612-4). Smithsonian.
Frei Otto: Form & Structure. 32.75 (ISBN 0-89158-535-4). Westview.
French Cameo Glass. 25.00 (ISBN 0-87069-030-2). Wallace-Homestead.
French Decorative Art in the Huntington Collection. 7.50 (ISBN 0-87328-031-8). Huntington Lib.
French Drawings & Sketchbooks of the Eighteenth Century. 45.00 (ISBN 0-226-68795-3); 4 color fiches incl. U of Chicago Pr.
French Drawings & Sketchbooks of the Nineteenth Century. 150.00; 5 color fiches 70.00 (ISBN 0-226-68796-1); 7 color fiches 80.00 (ISBN 0-226-68798-8). U of Chicago Pr.
French Drawings of the Sixteenth & Seventeenth Centuries. 19.50 (ISBN 0-226-68794-5); 1 color fiche incl. U of Chicago Pr.
French Faience. 2nd ed. 19.95 (ISBN 0-571-04638-X). Merrimack Bk Serv.
French Furniture in Hungary. 3.75 (ISBN 0-8002-1433-1). Intl Pubns Serv.
French Opera Posters, 1868 - 1930. pap. 5.00 (ISBN 0-486-23306-5). Dover.
French Opera Posters, 1868-1930: Theatre National De L'opera Comique. 8.75 (ISBN 0-8446-5519-8). Peter Smith.
French Painters & Paintings from the Fourteenth Century to Post-Impressionism. 30.00 (ISBN 0-8044-3210-4); pap. 8.95 (ISBN 0-8044-6521-5). Ungar.
French Painting. rev. ed. pap. 5.00 (ISBN 0-486-22931-9). Dover.
French Painting. 3rd rev. ed. 8.50 (ISBN 0-8446-4839-6). Peter Smith.
French Painting. 12.50 (ISBN 0-8317-3566-X); pap. 6.95 (ISBN 0-8317-3567-8). Mayflower Bks.
French Painting Between the Past & the Present: Artists, Critics, & Traditions from 1848 to 1870. 22.50x (ISBN 0-691-03817-1); pap. 5.95 (ISBN 0-691-00306-8, 293). Princeton U Pr.
French Painting in the Sixteenth Century. 16.00 (ISBN 0-405-02226-3). Arno.
French Painting in the Time of Jean De Berry: The Limbourgs & Their Contemporaries. 70.00. Pierpont Morgan.
French Painting in the Time of Jean De Berry: The Limbourgs & Their Contemporaries. 70.00 (ISBN 0-8076-0734-7). Braziller.
French Paintings from the Collection of Mr. & Mrs. Paul Mellon & Mrs. Mellon Bruce. pap. 4.50. Natl Gallery Art.
French Pistols & Sporting Guns. 2.95 (ISBN 0-600-43594-6). Transatlantic.
French Polisher's Manual. pap. 4.00 (ISBN 0-918036-05-4, 20D11-D). Woodcraft Supply.
French Primitive Photography. 15.00 (ISBN 0-89381-044-4); pap. 10.00 (ISBN 0-89381-046-0). Aperture.
French Renaissance Fountains. lib. bdg. 52.00 (ISBN 0-8240-2713-2). Garland Pub.
French Rococo Book Illustration. 15.00 (ISBN 0-85458-140-5). Transatlantic.
French Satirical Drawings from "L'Assiette au Beurre". pap. 6.50 (ISBN 0-486-23583-1). Dover.
French Sculpture at the Beginning of the Gothic Period, 1140-1225. 40.00 (ISBN 0-87817-057-X). Hacker.
French Tapestry. 15.00 (ISBN 0-8231-3006-1). Branford.
French Undressing. pap. 4.95 (ISBN 0-515-04198-X). HarBraceJ.
Frick Collection: An Illustrated Catalogue. Incl. Paintings: American, British, Dutch, Flemish & German (ISBN 0-691-03859-7); Paintings: French, Italian & Spanish. 50.00x (ISBN 0-691-03859-7); Sculpture: Italian (ISBN 0-691-03866-X); Sculpture: Netherlandish, German, French & British. 50.00x (ISBN 0-691-03866-X); Furniture. price not set (ISBN 0-691-03867-8); Porcelains, Oriental & French. 35.00x (ISBN 0-691-03811-2); llimoges Painted Enamels, Oriental Rugs & English Silver. 40.00 (ISBN 0-691-03832-5); Prints, Drawings & Recent Acquisitions. write for info. (ISBN 0-691-03832-5). Princeton U Pr.
Friedel Dzubas. pap. 2.00. Mus Fine Arts Boston.
Friends & Friends of Friends. pap. 8.95 (ISBN 0-525-47519-2). Dutton.
Frog He Would A-Wooing Go. 3.50 (ISBN 0-8027-6026-0). Walker & Co.
From Abacus to Zeus: A Handbook of Art History. pap. text ed. 7.50 (ISBN 0-13-331686-6). P-H.
From Chalk to Bronze: A Biography of Waldine Tauch. 15.00 (ISBN 0-88319-037-0). Shoal Creek Pub.
From Croesus to Constantine: The Cities of Western Asia Minor & Their Arts in Greek & Roman Times. text ed. 15.00x (ISBN 0-472-08420-8). U of Mich Pr.
From Crossbow to H-Bomb. rev. enl. ed. pap. 2.95x (ISBN 0-253-20161-6). Ind U Pr.
From Cubism to Surrealism in French Literature. lib. bdg. 19.50x (ISBN 0-313-20112-9, LEFC). Greenwood.
From Early American Paint Brushes: Colony to New Nation. 5.95 (ISBN 0-8193-0477-8); PLB 5.41 (ISBN 0-8193-0478-6). Parents.
From El Greco to Pollock: Early & Late Works by European & American Artists. text ed. 12.00 (ISBN 0-912298-05-7). Baltimore Mus.
From Gunk to Glow. pap. 1.25. Random.
From Idea into House. 7.95 (ISBN 0-689-30144-8). Atheneum.
From Nudity to Raiment: An Introduction to the Study of Costume. 59.95 (ISBN 0-87968-156-X). Gordon Pr.
From Petals to Pinecones: A Nature Art & Craft Book. PLB 6.96 (ISBN 0-688-51594-0); pap. 2.95 (ISBN 0-688-45003-2). Lothrop.
From Realism to Reality in Recent American Painting. facs. ed. 11.00 (ISBN 0-8369-0173-8). Arno.
From Schinkel to the Bauhaus. pap. 12.50x (ISBN 0-8150-0012-X). Wittenborn.
From Sophocles to Picasso. lib. bdg. 14.75x (ISBN 0-8371-6469-9, OASP). Greenwood.
From Tepees to Towers: A Photographic History of American Architecture. 6.95 (ISBN 0-316-36396-0). Little.
From the Bosporus to Samarkand: Flat-Woven Rugs. pap. 7.95. Textile Mus.
From the Center: Feminist Essays on Women's Art. pap. 6.95 (ISBN 0-525-47427-7). Dutton.
From the Classicists to the Impressionists: A Documentary History of Art & Architecture in the 19th Century. 3.95 (ISBN 0-385-06683-X, A114C). Doubleday.
From the Ground Up: Observations on Contemporary Architecture, Housing, Highway Building, & Civic Design. pap. 1.65 (ISBN 0-15-634019-4, HB13). HarBraceJ.
From the Lands of the Scythians: Ancient Treasures from the Museums of the U.S.S.R. 3000 BC-100 BC. 17.50 (ISBN 0-87099-143-4). NYGS.
From the Picture Press. pap. 3.95 (ISBN 0-87070-334-X). Museum Mod Art.
From the Renaissance to Romanticism: Trends in Style in Art, Literature, & Music 1300-1830. 10.00x (ISBN 0-226-02837-2). U of Chicago Pr.
From the Renaissance to Romanticism: Trends in Style, in Art, Literature & Music, 1300-1830. pap. 3.95 (ISBN 0-226-02838-0, P186). U of Chicago Pr.
From Toulouse-Lautrec to Rodin: With Some Personal Impressions. facs. ed. 14.25 (ISBN 0-8369-0919-4). Arno.
Frontiers of Photography. 9.95 (ISBN 0-8094-1064-8). Time-Life.
Frostbite. pap. 10.95 (ISBN 0-87100-143-8, 2143). Morgan.
Frueh on the Theater: Theatrical Caricatures, 1906-1962. pap. 9.00 (ISBN 0-87104-235-5). NY Pub Lib.
Fruit & Vegetable Arrangements. rev. ed. 4.50 (ISBN 0-8208-0014-7). Hearthside.
Fruit Jars: A Collector's Manual with Prices. 8.95 (ISBN 0-8407-5615-1). Nelson.
Full-Color Floral Needlepoint Designs. pap. 2.00 (ISBN 0-486-23387-1). Dover.
Full-Color Russian Folk Needlepoint Designs Charted for Easy Use. pap. 2.25 (ISBN 0-486-23451-7). Dover.
Fun & Profit in Stamp Collecting. pap. 3.95 (ISBN 0-8015-2851-8, 7308). Hawthorn.
Fun Crafts. 5.50x (ISBN 0-85467-005-X). Intl Pubns Serv.
Fun in Photography. 9.95 (ISBN 0-8174-0564-X). Amphoto.
Fun Jewelry. lib. bdg. 2.45 incl. catalog cards (ISBN 0-87157-910-3); pap. 1.25 vinyl laminated covers (ISBN 0-87157-410-1). SamHar Pr.
Fun Projects for Dad & the Kids. pap. 3.95 (ISBN 0-668-01104-1). Arco.
Fun with Crewel Embroidery. 5.95 (ISBN 0-684-12894-2). Scribner.
Fun with Fabric Printing. 8.00 (ISBN 0-87245-231-X). Textile Bk.
Fun with Fabric Printing. 8.50 (ISBN 0-8008-3100-4). Taplinger.
Fun with Handcraft. pap. 1.00 (ISBN 0-8341-0250-1). Nazarene.
Fun with Handcraft: Forty-Four Projects for Group or Personal Enjoyment. pap. 1.25 (ISBN 0-8010-0628-7). Baker Bk.
Fun with Historical Costume. new ed. 11.50x (ISBN 0-7182-0092-6). Soccer.
Fun with Lines & Curves. PLB 6.48 (ISBN 0-688-51527-4); pap. 2.95 (ISBN 0-688-45527-1). Lothrop.
Fun with Next to Nothing: Handicraft Projects for Boys & Girls. PLB 7.89 (ISBN 0-06-020146-0). Har-Row.
Fun with Photography. pap. 1.95 (ISBN 0-531-02711-2). Watts.
Fun with Puppets. pap. 1.95 (ISBN 0-531-02802-X). Watts.
Fun with Shells. 4.82 (ISBN 0-397-31384-5). Lippincott.
Fun with String. pap. 1.75 (ISBN 0-486-23063-5). Dover.
Fun with String. 6.00 (ISBN 0-8446-5058-7). Peter Smith.
Fun with String Figures. pap. 1.50 (ISBN 0-486-22809-6). Dover.
Fun with String Figures. lib. bdg. 9.50x (ISBN 0-88307-550-4). Gannon.
Fun with Weaving. 5.75 (ISBN 0-688-22063-0); PLB 5.52 (ISBN 0-688-32063-5). Morrow.
Fun with Your Camera. PLB 3.99 (ISBN 0-394-90283-1). Random.
Functions of Painting. 10.00 (ISBN 0-670-33221-6). Viking Pr.
Functions of Painting. pap. 4.50 (ISBN 0-670-01945-3, D9). Penguin.
Fundamental Structure: Nature's Architecture. pap. 14.00x (ISBN 0-8122-1082-4). U of Pa Pr.
Fundamentals of Oil Painting. pap. 9.95 (ISBN 0-8230-2026-6). Watson-Guptill.
Fundamentals of Pastel Painting. pap. 9.95 (ISBN 0-8230-2051-7). Watson-Guptill.
Fundamentals of Watercolor Painting. pap. 9.95 (ISBN 0-8230-2076-2). Watson-Guptill.
Funk & Wagnall's Guide to the World of Stamp Collecting: The Joys of Stamp Collecting for the Beginning & Advanced Philatelist. 13.95 (ISBN 0-308-10330-0). T Y Crowell.
Funny Bags. 8.95 (ISBN 0-397-31549-X). Lippincott.
Funny Drawing Book. 5.50g (ISBN 0-8075-2681-9). A Whitman.
Furnishing Dolls' Houses. 22.50 (ISBN 0-8231-3029-0). Branford.
Furnishing the City. 27.50 (ISBN 0-07-039845-3). McGraw.
Furniture see Frick Collection: An Illustrated Catalogue.
Furniture & Accessories. new ed. lib. bdg. 2.45 incl. catalog cards; pap. 1.25 vinyl laminated covers (ISBN 0-87157-403-9). SamHar Pr.
Furniture & It's Makers of Chester County Pennsylvania. 35.00 (ISBN 0-916838-05-6). Schiffer.
Furniture Collector's Glossary. lib. bdg. 10.00 (ISBN 0-306-70968-6). Da Capo.
Furniture Finishing. 15.00 (ISBN 0-672-52349-3). Bobbs.
Furniture Masterpieces of Duncan Phyfe. 12.50 (ISBN 0-8446-0556-5). Peter Smith.
Furniture of Gerrit Thomas Rietveld. 16.95 (ISBN 0-8120-5201-3). Barron.
Furniture of Our Forefathers. 35.00 (ISBN 0-405-08975-9). Arno.
Furniture of Spanish New Mexico. 14.95 (ISBN 0-913270-67-9). Sunstone Pr.
Furniture of the Pilgrim Century. 20.00 (ISBN 0-8446-2672-4). Peter Smith.
Furniture of the Pilgrim Century. pap. 5.00 ea.; pap. (ISBN 0-486-21470-2); pap. (ISBN 0-486-21471-0). Dover.
Furniture of Williamsburg & Eastern Virginia, 1710-1790. 24.00 (ISBN 0-917046-05-6). VA Mus Fine Arts.
Furniture Past & Present: --A Complete Illustrated Guide. 14.95 (ISBN 0-385-07067-5). Doubleday.
Furniture Refinishing at Home. rev. ed. 11.95 (ISBN 0-8019-6144-0); pap. 6.95 (ISBN 0-8019-6145-9). Chilton.
Furniture Repair & Refinishing. text ed. 12.95 (ISBN 0-87909-273-4); pap. 6.95 (ISBN 0-87909-290-4). Reston.
Furniture Repair & Refinishing. pap. 1.95 (ISBN 0-8487-0378-2). Oxmoor Hse.
Furniture Treasury. 25.00 (ISBN 0-02-590980-0); 19.95 (ISBN 0-02-591040-X). Macmillan.
Furs. 9.95 (ISBN 0-8015-4310-X). Hawthorn.
Further Exploration of the Rowe Chavin Seriation & its Implications for North Central Coast Chronology. pap. 3.50 (ISBN 0-88402-056-8). Dumbarton Oaks.
Further Exploration of the Rowe Chavin Seriation & Its Implications for North Central Coast Chronology see Thread of Life: Symbolism of Miniature Art from Ecuador.
Further Steps in Drawing & Sketching. 3.95 (ISBN 0-7137-0560-4). Transatlantic.
Future of Architecture. 15.00 (ISBN 0-8180-0003-1). Horizon.
Future of Architecture. 3.95 (ISBN 0-452-00446-2, F446). NAL.
Futurism. 6.50 (ISBN 0-87070-326-9). NYGS.
Futurism & the Arts: A Bibliography, 1959-1973. 20.00x (ISBN 0-8020-2120-4). U of Toronto Pr.
Futurist Art & Theory. lib. bdg. 40.00 (ISBN 0-87817-192-4). Hacker.
Futurist Manifestos. 12.50 (ISBN 0-670-33338-7). Viking Pr.

G

G. F. Watts. lib. bdg. 25.00 (ISBN 0-8492-4019-0). R West.
Gallery Management. 8.95x (ISBN 0-8156-0127-1). Syracuse U Pr.
Gallery of American Samplers: The Theodore Kapnek Collection. 19.95 (ISBN 0-525-11130-1); pap. 10.95 (ISBN 0-525-47515-X). Dutton.
Gallery of Nazis. 12.00 (ISBN 0-8184-0256-3). Lyle Stuart.
Gallery of Presidents. pap. 4.95 (ISBN 0-87474-743-0). Smithsonian.
Gallery of Waterfowl & Upland Birds. text ed. 39.95 (ISBN 0-8227-8019-4). Petersen Pub.
Game Bird Carving. 15.00 (ISBN 0-87691-080-0). Winchester Pr.
Games You Can Build Yourself. 6.95 (ISBN 0-8069-5308-X); PLB 6.69 (ISBN 0-8069-5309-8). Sterling.
Garden: An Illustrated History. 22.50 (ISBN 0-670-33433-2). Viking Pr.
Garden & Patio Building Book. pap. 2.95 (ISBN 0-376-01212-9). Lane.
Garden Art of Japan. 17.50 (ISBN 0-8348-1014-X). Weatherhill.
Garden Design. 10.95 (ISBN 0-7207-0982-2). Merrimack Bk Serv.
Garden Design Illustrated. pap. 9.95 (ISBN 0-295-95608-9). U of Wash Pr.
Gardener--Assistant Gardener. 2nd ed. pap. 8.00 (ISBN 0-668-01340-0, 1341). Arco.
Gardener's Book of Needlepoint. 10.95 (ISBN 0-671-23015-8). S&S.
Gardening & Home Landscaping Guide. lib. bdg. 4.95 (ISBN 0-668-02021-0). Arco.
Gardens of Williamsburg. pap. 1.95 (ISBN 0-910412-89-8). Williamsburg.
Gardens That Care for Themselves: How to Grow Neater, Healthier Plants, Cut Your Outdoor Chores in Half. 10.95 (ISBN 0-385-11171-1). Doubleday.
Gardens Through the Ages. 17.50x (ISBN 0-333-90137-1). South Asia Bks.
Gargoyles & Grotesques: Paganism in the Medieval Church. 14.95 (ISBN 0-8212-0644-3). NYGS.
Gargoyles, Chimeres, & the Grotesque in French Gothic Sculpture. enl. & 2nd ed. lib. bdg. 39.50 (ISBN 0-306-71152-4). Da Capo.
Garland of Weights: Some Notes on Collecting Antique French Glass Paperweights for Those Who Don't. 15.00 (ISBN 0-374-16048-1). FS&G.
Gasoline Alley. pap. 3.95 (ISBN 0-380-00761-4, 30486). Avon.
Gatherings in Honor of Dorothy E. Miner. bds. 37.50. Walters Art.
Gaudier-Brzeska: A Memoir. pap. 3.95 (ISBN 0-8112-0527-4, NDP372). New Directions.
Gaudy Welsh China. softbound 12.95 (ISBN 0-87069-167-8). Wallace-Homestead.
Gauguin. 5.95 (ISBN 0-517-00499-2). Crown.
Gauguin. pap. 4.95 (ISBN 0-8109-2153-7). Abrams.
Geisha Story: With Doll & Flower Arrangements. brocade 5.50 (ISBN 0-8048-0205-X). C E Tuttle.
Gem Cutting Is Easy. 4.95 (ISBN 0-517-50020-5); pap. 3.95 (ISBN 0-517-50021-3). Crown.
Gem Identification. 12.95 (ISBN 0-8069-3078-0); PLB 11.69 (ISBN 0-8069-3079-9). Sterling.
Gem Testing. 10.95. Wallace-Homestead.
Gem Testing. 8th ed. text ed. 29.95x (ISBN 0-408-70127-7). Butterworths.
Gem Testing. 10.95 (ISBN 0-87523-082-2). Emerson.
Gems & Jewelry in Color. 7.95 (ISBN 0-02-533500-6, 53350). Macmillan.
Gemstone & Mineral Data Book. 8.95 (ISBN 0-87691-067-3). Winchester Pr.
Gemstone Carving. 12.50 (ISBN 0-8019-6192-0); pap. 6.95 (ISBN 0-8019-6193-9). Chilton.

Gothic Revival: An Essay in the History of Taste. pap. 5.95x (ISBN 0-06-430048-X, IN-48). Har-Row.
Gothic Revival & American Church Architecture: An Episode in Taste, 1840-1856. 20.00x (ISBN 0-8018-0612-7). Johns Hopkins.
Gothic Revival in Europe & Britain: Sources, Influences & Ideas. pap. 12.95 (ISBN 0-262-57050-5). MIT Pr.
Gothic Visionary Perspective. 18.00 (ISBN 0-691-06337-0). Princeton U Pr.
Gothic Vs. Classic: Architectural Projects in Seventeenth-Century Italy. 12.50 (ISBN 0-8076-0704-5); pap. 4.95 (ISBN 0-8076-0705-3). Braziller.
Gothick Taste. 30.00 (ISBN 0-8386-1746-8). Fairleigh Dickinson.
Gottingen Model Book. text ed. 35.00x (ISBN 0-8262-0261-6). U of Mo Pr.
Gould's Gold & Silver Guide to Coins. 8.95 (ISBN 0-8303-0077-5). Fleet.
Gould's Gold & Silver Guide to Coins. pap. 2.00 (ISBN 0-87980-037-2). Wilshire.
Gourd Craft. 12.95 (ISBN 0-517-52830-4); pap. 6.95 (ISBN 0-517-52831-2). Crown.
Gourmet Bouquet. pap. 5.95 (ISBN 0-88421-091-X). Butterick Pub.
Government Patronage of the Arts in Great Britain. 13.50x (ISBN 0-226-31743-9). U of Chicago Pr.
Gowland's Guide to Glamour Photography. 6.95 (ISBN 0-517-50189-9). Crown.
Goya & His Critics. 35.00x (ISBN 0-300-02011-2). Yale U Pr.
Goya & His Sitters. 10.00 (ISBN 0-87535-101-8). Hispanic Soc.
Goya & the Impossible Revolution. 15.00 (ISBN 0-394-49304-4). Pantheon.
Goya's Caprichos: Beauty, Reason & Caricature. lib. bdg. 34.50x (ISBN 0-8371-4465-5, LOGO). Greenwood.
Graded Lessons in Macrame, Knotting & Netting. pap. 2.75 (ISBN 0-486-22754-5). Dover.
Graded Lessons in Macrame, Knotting, & Netting. 5.00 (ISBN 0-8446-0285-X). Peter Smith.
Grading Coins: A Collection of Readings. pap. text ed. 9.95 (ISBN 0-930332-01-6). Essex Pubns.
Grading Techniques for Modern Design. new ed. 12.50 (ISBN 0-87005-102-4). Fairchild.
Graffiti & Dipinti. 35.00x (ISBN 0-87661-221-4). Am Sch Athens.
Grammar of the Arts. 17.50 (ISBN 0-404-03314-8). AMS Pr.
Grand Central...the World's Greatest Railway Terminal. 19.95 (ISBN 0-87095-071-1). Golden West.
Grand Old American Bottles. 25.00 (ISBN 0-87282-045-9). Century Hse.
Grandes Heures of Jean, Duke of Berry. 55.00 (ISBN 0-8076-0613-8). Braziller.
Grant Wood & Marvin Cone: Artists of an Era. 6.95 (ISBN 0-8138-1775-7). Iowa St U Pr.
Grants in Photography: How to Get Them. 12.50 (ISBN 0-8174-2445-8). Amphoto.
Graphic Art of Edvard Munch. 17.50 (ISBN 0-8212-0333-9). NYGS.
Graphic Art of Rolf Nesch. pap. 5.00 (ISBN 0-8143-1446-5). Wayne St U Pr.
Graphic Art of the Eskimos. 20.00 (ISBN 0-8466-9008-X, SJ172). Shorey.
Graphic Art of the Eskimos. 35.00 (ISBN 0-404-11651-5). AMS Pr.
Graphic Arts. new ed. text ed. 8.48 (ISBN 0-87002-177-X); tchr's guide avail. Bennett Co.
Graphic Arts. text ed. 4.40 (ISBN 0-87006-252-2). Goodheart.
Graphic Arts Encyclopedia. 21.95 (ISBN 0-07-061287-0). McGraw.
Graphic Arts Encyclopedia. 2nd ed. 19.50 (ISBN 0-07-061288-9). McGraw.
Graphic Communication. 17.95 (ISBN 0-471-09290-8). Wiley.
Graphic Communications. text ed. 12.64 (ISBN 0-87345-246-1); study guide 3.32; ans. key free (ISBN 0-687-01262-7). McKnight.
Graphic Design & Reproduction Techniques. rev ed. 15.95 (ISBN 0-8038-2654-0). Focal Pr.
Graphic Design Manual: Principles & Practice. pap. 6.95 (ISBN 0-442-23469-4). Van Nos Reinhold.
Graphic Effects by Photography. 14.95 (ISBN 0-8038-2661-3). Focal Pr.
Graphic Guide to Interior Design. pap. 5.95 (ISBN 0-442-29552-9). Van Nos Reinhold.
Graphic Photo Design. 14.95 (ISBN 0-8174-2434-2). Amphoto.
Graphic Problem Solving for Architects & Builders. 15.95 (ISBN 0-8436-0154-X); student ed. 12.00. CBI Pub.
Graphic Reproduction Photography. 19.50 (ISBN 0-8038-2651-6). Focal Pr.
Graphic Work of Kandinsky. 8.95 (ISBN 0-88397-051-1). Intl Exhibit Foun.
Graphic Work of M. C. Escher. rev. ed. 13.95 (ISBN 0-8015-3102-0). Hawthorn.
Graphic Works of Max Klinger. pap. 5.00 (ISBN 0-486-23437-1). Dover.
Graphic Works of Max Klinger. 12.50 (ISBN 0-8446-5592-9). Peter Smith.
Graphic Works of Odilon Redon. pap. 6.00 (ISBN 0-486-21996-8). Dover.
Graphic Worlds of Peter Bruegel the Elder: Reproducing Sixty-Four Engravings & a Woodcut After Designs by Peter Bruegel the Elder. pap. 6.00 (ISBN 0-486-21132-0). Dover.
Graphics, Analysis & Conceptual Design. 2nd ed. text ed. 22.95x (ISBN 0-471-53085-9). Wiley.
Graphics for Designers. pap. 7.95x (ISBN 0-8138-0760-3). Iowa St U Pr.
Graphics Master. 39.50 (ISBN 0-914218-02-6). D Lem Assocs.
Graphics of Communication: Typography-Layout-Design. 3rd ed. text ed. 13.95 (ISBN 0-03-089580-4). HR&W.
Graphicstudio U. S. F. An Experiment in Art & Education. pap. 8.95 (ISBN 0-87273-068-9). Bklyn Mus.
Graven Images: New England Stonecarving & Its Symbols, 1650-1815. pap. 12.50 (ISBN 0-8195-6040-5). Wesleyan U Pr.
Greasy Luck. 17.50 (ISBN 0-917368-02-9). Caravan-Maritime.
Great American Mansions & Their Stories. pap. 7.95 (ISBN 0-8038-2681-8). Hastings.
Great American Sculptures. lib. bdg. 33.00 (ISBN 0-8240-2229-7). Garland Pub.
Great Architecture of the World. 29.95 (ISBN 0-394-49887-9). Random.
Great Artists & Great Anatomists: A Biographical & Philosophical Study. 18.00 (ISBN 0-404-13291-X). AMS Pr.
Great Artists of China Decoration. lib. bdg. 29.95 (ISBN 0-911298-01-0). Salyer.
Great Ball Court of Chichen Itza, Yucatan, Mexico. lib. bdg. 44.00 (ISBN 0-8240-3221-7). Garland Pub.
Great Books in Great Editions. pap. cancelled. Huntington Lib.
Great British Gunmakers 1740-1790: The History of John Twigg & the Packington Guns. 70.00x (ISBN 0-85667-015-4). Biblio Dist.
Great Cartoons of the World: Fifth Series. 5.95 (ISBN 0-517-50719-6). Crown.
Great Cartoons of the World: Ninth Series. 6.95 (ISBN 0-517-52351-5). Crown.
Great Days in the Rockies: The Photographs of Byron Harmon 1906-1934. 15.95 (ISBN 0-19-540288-X). Oxford U Pr.
Great Draughtsmen from Pisanello to Picasso. 15.00x (ISBN 0-674-36200-4). Harvard U Pr.
Great Draughtsmen from Pisanello to Picasso. rev. ed. pap. 7.95x (ISBN 0-06-430029-3, IN-29). Har-Row.
Great Drawings of All Time. 375.00 (ISBN 0-87011-263-5). Kodansha.
Great Flower Painters: Four Centuries of Floral Art. 35.00 (ISBN 0-87951-008-0). Overlook Pr.
Great Gardens of Britain. 15.95 (ISBN 0-688-03246-X). Morrow.
Great Georgian Houses of America. pap. 7.50 ea. (ISBN 0-486-22491-0) (ISBN 0-486-22492-9). Dover.
Great Houses of New Orleans. 15.00 (ISBN 0-394-40716-4). Knopf.
Great Houses of San Francisco. 13.95 (ISBN 0-394-48380-4). Knopf.
Great Masters. facsimile ed. 24.00 (ISBN 0-8369-0604-7). Arno.
Great Masters in Art. facs. ed. 17.50 (ISBN 0-8369-0508-3). Arno.
Great Masters of Dutch & Flemish Painting. 17.50 (ISBN 0-8369-0222-X). Arno.
Great Masters of French Impressionism. 17.95 (ISBN 0-517-53447-9). Crown.
Great Masters of French Impressionism. 17.95 (ISBN 0-89660-030-0, ND547). Artabras.
Great Moments in Architecture. 11.95 (ISBN 0-395-25500-7); pap. 5.95 (ISBN 0-395-26711-0); prepack 71.40. HM.
Great News Photos & the Stories Behind Them. pap. 5.00 (ISBN 0-486-23667-6). Dover.
Great Paintings from the Metropolitan Museum of Art. 35.00 (ISBN 0-8109-0296-6). Abrams.
Great Paintings of All Time: 100 Masterpieces. 12.95 (ISBN 0-671-28996-9). S&S.
Great Photographers. 9.95 (ISBN 0-8094-1043-5). Time-Life.
Great Poster Trip: Art Eureka. 5.00; pap. 3.00. Am Fed Arts.
Great Prints & Printmakers. 35.00 (ISBN 0-8148-0682-1). L Amiel Pub.
Great Pyramid: A Miracle in Stone. pap. 2.50 (ISBN 0-8334-1735-5). Multimedia.
Great Railroad Paintings. large format ed. pap. 6.95 (ISBN 0-553-01048-4). Bantam.
Great Sporting Posters of the Golden Age. pap. 8.95 (ISBN 0-8117-2115-9). Stackpole.
Great Statuary of China. 20.00 (ISBN 0-226-74448-5). U of Chicago Pr.
Great Western Salt Works: Essays on the Meaning of Post-Formalist Art. 15.00 (ISBN 0-8076-0740-1); pap. 5.95 (ISBN 0-8076-0741-X). Braziller.
Greek & Roman Architecture. 2nd ed. 33.95 (ISBN 0-521-06104-0); pap. 10.95 (ISBN 0-521-09452-6). Cambridge U Pr.
Greek & Roman Art in the British Museum. pap. 6.95 (ISBN 0-8120-0903-7). Barron.
Greek & Roman Art: 3000 B.C. to A.D. 550. swedish ed. pap. 4.95 (ISBN 0-8152-0263-6, A263). T Y Crowell.
Greek & Roman Coins & the Study of History. lib. bdg. 10.75x (ISBN 0-8371-4283-0, MIGR). Greenwood.
Greek & Roman Coins in the Athenian Agora. pap. 1.50x (ISBN 0-87661-615-5). Am Sch Athens.
Greek & Roman Sculpture. lib. bdg. 35.00 (ISBN 0-89341-205-8). Longwood Pr.
Greek & Roman Sculpture in Gold & Silver. pap. 2.95. Mus Fine Arts Boston.
Greek Architecture. 7.95 (ISBN 0-8076-0175-6); pap. 5.95 (ISBN 0-8076-0337-6). Braziller.
Greek Art. 8.95 (ISBN 0-87663-169-3). Universe.
Greek Coins & Cities. 20.00 (ISBN 0-295-95534-1). U of Wash Pr.
Greek, Etruscan & Roman Art: The Classical Collection of the Museum of Fine Arts, Boston. 10.00; pap. 3.75. Mus Fine Arts Boston.
Greek Geometric Art. 25.00 (ISBN 0-7148-1411-3). Dutton.
Greek House: Its History & Development from the Neolithic Period to the Hellenistic Age. lib. bdg. 30.00 (ISBN 0-89341-248-1). Longwood Pr.
Greek Lamps & Their Survivals. 17.50x (ISBN 0-87661-204-4). Am Sch Athens.
Greek Myths: A Vase Painter's Notebook. 12.50x (ISBN 0-253-32635-4); pap. 3.50x (ISBN 0-253-32636-2). Ind U Pr.
Greek Painted Pottery. 2nd ed. 52.95x (ISBN 0-416-76170-4). Methuen Inc.
Greek Revival Architecture in America. pap. 5.00 (ISBN 0-486-21148-7). Dover.
Greek Revival Architecture in America. 8.75 (ISBN 0-8446-2196-X). Peter Smith.
Greek Sanctuaries. 19.95x (ISBN 0-312-34930-0). St Martin.
Greek Sculpture. pap. 6.95 (ISBN 0-226-09475-8, P436). U of Chicago Pr.
Greek Sculpture: A Critical Review. 15.00x (ISBN 0-226-09473-1). U of Chicago Pr.
Greek Sculpture & Roman Taste. text ed. 18.50x (ISBN 0-472-08940-4). U of Mich Pr.
Greek Temples. 23.00 (ISBN 0-405-02258-1). Arno.
Green Says Go. 5.95 (ISBN 0-316-23599-7). Little.
Green Wood House: How to Build & Own a Beautiful,Inexpensive House. rev. ed. 9.75; pap. 4.95. U Pr of Va.
Greene & Greene: Architects in the Residential Style. pap. 10.95 (ISBN 0-87100-134-9). Morgan.
Greene & Greene: Architects in the Residential Style. 15.00 (ISBN 0-88360-005-6). Amon Carter.
Greene & Greene: Architecture As a Fine Art. 24.95 (ISBN 0-87905-023-3). Peregrine Smith.
Greene & Greene: Furniture & Related Designs. 27.95 (ISBN 0-87905-060-8). Peregrine Smith.
Greene & Greene Guide. 8.00 (ISBN 0-9600780-1-0). J Strand.
Greenwich Village: A Photographic Guide. pap. 3.00 (ISBN 0-486-23114-3). Dover.
Grim Fairy Tales & Other Facts & Fancies. 4.50x (ISBN 0-210-26885-9). Asia.
Grotesque in Art & Literature. pap. 2.95 (ISBN 0-07-033407-2). McGraw.
Grotesque in Art & Literature. 7.50 (ISBN 0-8446-0731-2). Peter Smith.
Grotesque in Church Art. 9.50 (ISBN 0-8103-3077-6). Gale.
Grotesque in Photography. 20.00 (ISBN 0-671-40014-2); pap. 10.00 (ISBN 0-671-40016-9). Summit Bks.
Grounds Maintenance Handbook. 3rd ed. 29.50 (ISBN 0-07-012412-4). McGraw.
Group Zero: An American Exhibition. 4.00 (ISBN 0-405-00389-7). Arno.
Gruppe on Color. 19.50 (ISBN 0-8230-2155-6). Watson-Guptill.
Gruppe on Painting: Direct Techniques in Oil. 16.95 (ISBN 0-8230-2157-2). Watson-Guptill.
Guarding the Treasured Lands: The Story of the National Park Service. 4.95 (ISBN 0-397-30805-1). Lippincott.
Guatemalan Textiles Today. 24.50 (ISBN 0-8230-2158-0). Watson-Guptill.
Guennol Collection. 18.50 (ISBN 0-87099-144-2). Metro Mus Art.
Guide Book of Modern United States Currency. 3.00 (ISBN 0-307-09373-5). Western Pub.
Guide Book of United States Coins. 3.95 (ISBN 0-307-09051-5). Western Pub.
Guide to Aesthetics. pap. 3.45 (ISBN 0-89526-901-5). Regnery-Gateway.
Guide to Ancient Maya Ruins. 13.95 (ISBN 0-8061-1214-X); pap. 5.95 (ISBN 0-8061-1215-8). U of Okla Pr.
Guide to Ancient Mexican Ruins. 10.95 (ISBN 0-8061-1399-5); pap. 5.95 (ISBN 0-8061-1407-X). U of Okla Pr.
Guide to Antiques. pap. 1.95 (ISBN 0-346-12228-7). Cornerstone.
Guide to Architecture in Los Angeles & Southern California. pap. 11.95 (ISBN 0-87905-049-7). Peregrine Smith.
Guide to Architecture in San Francisco & Northern California. pap. 8.95 (ISBN 0-87905-010-1). Peregrine Smith.
Guide to Artifacts of Colonial America. 12.95 (ISBN 0-394-42754-8). Knopf.
Guide to Basic Information Sources in the Visual Arts. 14.95x (ISBN 0-87436-278-4). J Norton Pubs.
Guide to Business Principles & Practices for Interior Designers. 16.50 (ISBN 0-8230-7251-7). Watson-Guptill.
Guide to Cambridge Architecture: Ten Walking Tours. pap. 2.95 (ISBN 0-262-68017-3). MIT Pr.
Guide to Church Woodcarvings. 11.50 (ISBN 0-7153-6562-2). David & Charles.
Guide to Collecting & Selling Comic Books. pap. 2.00 (ISBN 0-87576-056-2). Pilot Bks.
Guide to Collecting & Selling Netsuke. 2.50 (ISBN 0-87576-061-9). Pilot Bks.
Guide to Collecting Currier & Ives. pap. 4.95. HarBraceJ.
Guide to Decoration in the Early American Manner. 6.75 (ISBN 0-8048-0224-6). C E Tuttle.
Guide to Drawing. 2nd ed. pap. text ed. 13.95 (ISBN 0-03-086565-4). HR&W.
Guide to English Country Houses. 6.95 (ISBN 0-668-02080-6). Arco.
Guide to Fashion Merchandise Knowledge. text ed. 17.00 (ISBN 0-87350-250-7). Milady.
Guide to Fashion Merchandise Knowledge. softcover 10.25 (ISBN 0-87350-253-1). Milady.
Guide to Federal Programs for Historic Preservation: 1976 Supplement. pap. 3.00 (ISBN 0-89133-039-9). Preservation Pr.
Guide to Flower Arranging. 4.00 (ISBN 0-8231-6017-3). Branford.
Guide to Handmade Knives & the Official Directory of the Knifemaker's Guild. pap. 9.50 (ISBN 0-916172-03-1). Janus Pr.
Guide to Handmade Knives & the Official Directory of the Knifemakers Guild. limited ed. 19.50 (ISBN 0-916172-06-6). Janus Pr.
Guide to Japanese Flower Arrangement. 8.75. Japan Pubns.
Guide to Japanese Flower Arrangement. 8.95 (ISBN 0-8048-1327-2). C E Tuttle.
Guide to Landscaping. pap. 1.95 (ISBN 0-8200-0403-0). Great Outdoors.
Guide to Marine Photography. 12.50 (ISBN 0-393-03182-9). Norton.
Guide to Mexican Art: From Its Beginnings to the Present. 13.50x (ISBN 0-226-24420-2); pap. 5.45 (ISBN 0-226-24421-0). U of Chicago Pr.
Guide to Museum Villages. pap. 5.95 (ISBN 0-8473-1656-4, 025995). Sterling.
Guide to Retouching Negatives & Prints. pap. 2.95 (ISBN 0-8174-0271-3). Amphoto.
Guide to Site & Environmental Planning. 22.95 (ISBN 0-471-74440-9). Wiley.
Guide to Site & Environmental Planning. 2nd ed. 20.00 (ISBN 0-471-04729-5). Wiley.
Guide to the Architecture of Washington, D. C. 2nd ed. 7.95 (ISBN 0-07-013286-0); pap. 6.95 (ISBN 0-07-013285-2). McGraw.
Guide to the Archives & Manuscript Collections of the American Philosophical Society. 4.50 (ISBN 0-87169-066-7). Am Philos.
Guide to the Art of Latin America. 15.00 (ISBN 0-405-03421-0). Arno.
Guide to the British Cathedrals. pap. 4.95 (ISBN 0-212-97007-0). Transatlantic.
Guide to the Care & Administration of Manuscripts. 2nd ed. pap. 3.00 (ISBN 0-910050-02-3). AASLH.
Guide to the Collecting & Care of Original Prints. 4.95 (ISBN 0-517-03805-6). Crown.
Guide to the Collection: Isabella Stewart Gardner Museum. 2nd ed. pap. 2.00 (ISBN 0-914660-02-0). I S Gardner Mus.
Guide to United States Beer Cans. pap. 9.95 (ISBN 0-915498-26-X). Greatlakes Liv.
Gum Bichromate Book: Contemporary Methods for Photographic Printmaking. pap. 7.95 (ISBN 0-87992-010-6). Light Impressions.
Gun Care & Repair. 10.95 (ISBN 0-87691-256-0). Winchester Pr.
Gun Collector's Digest. 2nd ed. pap. 7.95 (ISBN 0-695-80684-X). Follett.
Gun Collector's Fact Book. pap. 5.95 (ISBN 0-668-03782-2). Arco.
Gun Collector's Handbook of Values: 1977-78. rev. ed. 17.95 (ISBN 0-698-10825-6). Coward.
Gun Collector's Handbook of Values: 1980-81 Values. 13th rev. ed. pap. 9.95 (ISBN 0-698-11010-2). Coward.
Gun Digest Book of Exploded Firearms Drawings. 2nd ed. pap. 7.95 (ISBN 0-695-80842-7). Follett.

Hints on Household Taste in Furniture, Upholstery & Other Details. 7.50 (ISBN 0-8446-0610-3). Peter Smith.

Hiram Powers & His Ideal Sculpture. lib. bdg. 52.00 (ISBN 0-8240-2720-5). Garland Pub.

Hispanic Society of America: Catalogue of the Library. 675.00 (ISBN 0-87535-115-8); first supplement, 1970. 4 vols 360.00. Hispanic Soc.

Hispanic Society of America: Handbook of Museum & Library Collections. 5.00 (ISBN 0-87535-043-7). Hispanic Soc.

Historia Numorum. 37.50. S J Durst.

Historic American Buildings Survey: Catalog of the Measured Drawings & Photographs of the Survey in the Library of Congress, March 1, 1941. lib. bdg. 32.00 (ISBN 0-8337-1711-1). B Franklin.

Historic American Buildings Survey, District of Columbia Catalog, 9.75x (ISBN 0-8139-0618-0); pap. 3.50x (ISBN 0-8139-0665-2). U Pr of Va.

Historic American Buildings Survey, Virginia Catalog: A List of Measured Drawings, Photographs, & Written Documentation in the Survey. 20.00x (ISBN 0-8139-0518-4); pap. 6.95x (ISBN 0-8139-0708-X). U Pr of Va.

Historic Annals of the National Academy of Design. 32.50 (ISBN 0-306-71411-6). Da Capo.

Historic Architecture of Wales: An Introduction. text ed. 18.50x (ISBN 0-7083-0626-8). Verry.

Historic Architecture Sourcebook. new ed. 24.95 (ISBN 0-07-026755-3). McGraw.

Historic Buildings of Massachusetts. 14.95 (ISBN 0-684-14567-7). Scribner.

Historic Floral & Animal Designs for Embroiderers & Craftsmen. pap. 3.00 (ISBN 0-486-23526-2). Dover.

Historic Floral & Animal Designs for Embroiderers & Craftsmen. 6.50 (ISBN 0-8446-5564-3). Peter Smith.

Historic House Museums. 15.00 (ISBN 0-8103-3118-7). Gale.

Historic Houses Restored & Preserved. 25.00 (ISBN 0-8230-7275-4). Watson-Guptill.

Historic Houses Restored & Preserved. pap. 9.95 (ISBN 0-8230-7270-3). Watson-Guptill.

Historic Monuments of England & Wales. 14.50x (ISBN 0-460-04158-4). Biblio Dist.

Historic Ornament: A Pictorial Archive. pap. 6.00 (ISBN 0-486-23215-8). Dover.

Historic Ornament: A Pictorial Archive; 900 Fine Examples from Ancient Egypt to 1800 Suitable for Reproduction. 11.50 (ISBN 0-8446-5195-8). Peter Smith.

Historic Ornament: Treatise on Decorative Art & Architectural Ornament. lib. bdg. 60.00 (ISBN 0-89341-107-8). Longwood Pr.

Historic Pottery of the Pueblo Indians, 1660-1880. 27.50 (ISBN 0-8212-0586-2). NYGS.

Historic Property Owner's Handbook. 7.50 (ISBN 0-89133-059-3). Preservation Pr.

Historic Pueblo Indian Pottery. pap. 2.45 (ISBN 0-89013-029-9). Museum NM Pr.

Historic Virginia Gardens: Preservations by the Garden Club of Virginia. 20.00x (ISBN 0-8139-0604-0). U Pr of Va.

Historical Greek Coins. 10.00 (ISBN 0-89005-064-3). Ares.

Historical Needlework of Pennsylvania. 10.00. Schiffer.

Historical Nuggets: Bibliotheca Americana or a Descriptive Account of My Collection of Rare Books Relating to America. lib. bdg. 44.00 (ISBN 0-8337-3407-5). B Franklin.

Historical Outline of Architectural Science. 2nd, enl. ed. 17.00 (ISBN 0-444-00250-2). Elsevier.

Historical Roman Coins. 10.00 (ISBN 0-89005-065-1). Ares.

Historical Staffordshire: Illustrated Checklist. 15.00x (ISBN 0-915438-00-3). Arman Ent.

Historical Studies of Church-Building in the Middle Ages. 24.50 (ISBN 0-8369-5072-0). Arno.

Historical Studies of Church Building in the Middle Ages: Venice, Sienna, Florence. lib. bdg. 39.95 (ISBN 0-8490-1962-1). Gordon Pr.

Historical Studies of Church-Building in the Middle Ages: Venice, Siena, Florence. lib. bdg. 35.00 (ISBN 0-89341-361-5). Longwood Pr.

History & Antiquities of the Most Ancient Town & Borough of Colchester. text ed. 30.00x (ISBN 0-8277-1641-9). British Bk Ctr.

History & Decoration of the Ponte S. Angelo. 22.50x (ISBN 0-271-01101-7). Pa St U Pr.

History & Description of English Porcelain. 15.00x (ISBN 0-8277-1318-5). British Bk Ctr.

History & Description of English Porcelain. 17.50x (ISBN 0-85409-902-6). Charles River Bks.

History & Handbook of Photography. 2nd ed. 26.00 (ISBN 0-405-04943-9). Arno.

History & Practice of Daguerreotyping. 15.00 (ISBN 0-405-04894-7). Arno.

History & Practice of the Art of Photography. 6.95 (ISBN 0-87100-014-8). Morgan.

History & Technique of Lettering. pap. 4.50 (ISBN 0-486-20427-8). Dover.

History & Technique of Lettering. 8.50 (ISBN 0-8446-0821-1). Peter Smith.

History & Technique of Old Master Drawings: A Handbook. 50.00 (ISBN 0-87817-107-X). Hacker.

History of American Art. 2nd ed. pap. text ed. 16.95 (ISBN 0-03-089475-1). HR&W.

History of American Ceramics: The Studio Potter. 15.95 (ISBN 0-8403-1864-2). Kendall-Hunt.

History of American Graphic Humor: Vol. 1, 1747-1865. 36.00 (ISBN 0-8154-0161-2). Cooper Sq.

History of American Marine Painting. 25.00 (ISBN 0-316-94123-9). Little.

History of American Marine Painting. 25.00 (ISBN 0-87577-001-0). Peabody Mus Salem.

History of American Pewter. pap. 12.50 (ISBN 0-525-47467-6). Dutton.

History of Art. 2nd ed. pap. 3.25 (ISBN 0-06-460095-5, 95). B&N.

History of Art & Music. pap. text ed. 9.95 (ISBN 0-13-389312-X). P-H.

History of Art & Music. pap. 12.50 (ISBN 0-8109-9012-1). Abrams.

History of Art Criticism. pap. 4.25 (ISBN 0-525-47123-5). Dutton.

History of Art in Phrygia, Lydia, Caria, & Lycia. lib. bdg. 65.00 (ISBN 0-89341-213-9). Longwood Pr.

History of British Wood Engraving. text ed. 120.00x (ISBN 0-391-00574-X). Humanities.

History of Building. 8.95x. Beekman Pubs.

History of Building Types. 42.50 (ISBN 0-691-09904-9); pap. 17.50 (ISBN 0-691-01829-4). Princeton U Pr.

History of Caricature. 10.00 (ISBN 0-8103-4044-5). Gale.

History of Caricature & Grotesque in Literature & Art. 15.00 (ISBN 0-8044-2987-1). Ungar.

History of Caricature & Grotesque in Literature & Art. lib. bdg. 40.00 (ISBN 0-89341-353-4). Longwood Pr.

History of Collage. 16.95 (ISBN 0-02-630870-3). Macmillan.

History of Color Photography. 46.95 (ISBN 0-8038-8955-0). Focal Pr.

History of Composing Machines: A Complete Record of the Art of Composing Type by Machinery. 13.00 (ISBN 0-405-04726-6). Arno.

History of Decorative Art in Mughal Architecture. 12.00x (ISBN 0-8364-0413-0). South Asia Bks.

History of Doll Houses. 15.00 (ISBN 0-684-14538-3, SL630). Scribner.

History of Early Chinese Art. 150.00 (ISBN 0-87817-036-7). Hacker.

History of English Art in the Middle Ages. facsimile ed. 25.00 (ISBN 0-8369-5158-1). Arno.

History of Esthetics. rev. ed. lib. bdg. 29.25x (ISBN 0-8371-6207-6, GIHE). Greenwood.

History of Far Eastern Art. rev. ed. 35.00 (ISBN 0-8109-0113-7). Abrams.

History of Far Eastern Art. rev. ed. text ed. 19.95 (ISBN 0-13-390088-6). P-H.

History of Garden Art. lib. bdg. 120.00 (ISBN 0-87817-008-1). Hacker.

History of Glass in Japan. 75.00. Kodansha.

History of Glass in Japan. 60.00 (ISBN 0-87011-196-5). Corning.

History of Glass in Japan. 60.00x (ISBN 0-87011-196-5). U Pr of Va.

History of Gothic Art in England. 21.00x. Beekman Pubs.

History of Gothic Art in England. 25.00x (ISBN 0-7158-1022-7). Charles River Bks.

History of Gothic Art in England. text ed. 35.00x (ISBN 0-8277-3249-X). British Bk Ctr.

History of Graphic Art. 32.00x (ISBN 0-7158-1209-2). Charles River Bks.

History of Graphic Art. text ed. 20.00x (ISBN 0-8277-5507-4). British Bk Ctr.

History of Graphic Art. lib. bdg. 20.75x (ISBN 0-8371-2522-7, CLGA). Greenwood.

History of Greek Art. 85.00 set (ISBN 0-521-20277-9). Cambridge U Pr.

History of Greek Art. lib. bdg. 19.50x (ISBN 0-8371-4351-9, TAGA). Greenwood.

History of Hand Made Lace: Dealing with the Origin of Lace, the Growth of the Great Lace Centres, Etc. 17.50 (ISBN 0-8103-3935-8). Gale.

History of Impressionism. 32.50 (ISBN 0-87070-360-9). NYGS.

History of Indian & Indonesian Art. 25.00x (ISBN 0-8426-0393-X). Verry.

History of Indian & Indonesian Art. 10.00 (ISBN 0-8446-1895-0). Peter Smith.

History of Indian & Indonesian Art. pap. 6.00 (ISBN 0-486-21436-2). Dover.

History of Indian & Indonesian Art. 15.00x (ISBN 0-8002-1502-8). Intl Pubns Serv.

History of Indian Painting: Manuscript, Monghul & Deccani Traditions. 42.50x (ISBN 0-8364-0357-6). South Asia Bks.

History of Indian Painting: The Mural Tradition. 28.50x (ISBN 0-88386-786-9). South Asia Bks.

History of Italian Painting. rev. ed. lib. bdg. 38.25x (ISBN 0-8371-2534-0, MAIP). Greenwood.

History of Italian Painting, 1250-1800. 8.95 (ISBN 0-8008-3875-0). Taplinger.

History of Italian Renaissance Art. text ed. 19.95 (ISBN 0-13-392035-6). P-H.

History of Japanese Lacquerwork. 40.00 (ISBN 0-8020-2135-2). U of Toronto Pr.

History of Japanese Printing & Book Illustration. 50.00 (ISBN 0-87011-288-0). Kodansha.

History of Modern Art. 2nd ed. 19.95 (ISBN 0-13-390351-6). P-H.

History of Modern Art: Painting, Sculpture, & Architecture. rev. ed. 37.50 (ISBN 0-8109-0181-1). Abrams.

History of Mosaics. 30.00 (ISBN 0-87817-001-4). Hacker.

History of Ornament. lib. bdg. 47.50 (ISBN 0-8154-0450-6). Cooper Sq.

History of Painting in Italy, Umbria, Florence, & Siena from the Second to the Sixteenth Century. Incl. Early Christian Art; Giotto & the Giottesques; The Sienese, Umbrian & North Italian Schools; Florentine Masters of the Fifteenth Century; Umbrian & Sienese Masters of the Fifteenth Century; Sienese & Florentine Masters of the Sixteenth Century. 39.00 ea. (ISBN 0-403-03603-8); 195.00 (ISBN 0-403-00431-4). Scholarly.

History of Painting in North Italy. 125.00 set (ISBN 0-404-09290-X). AMS Pr.

History of Photography. 15.00 (ISBN 0-8446-5687-9). Peter Smith.

History of Photography. lib. bdg. 18.00x (ISBN 0-405-09611-9). Arno.

History of Photography. 24.95 (ISBN 0-385-12664-6). Doubleday.

History of Photography Written As a Practical Guide & an Introduction to Its Latest Developments. 11.00 (ISBN 0-405-04913-7). Arno.

History of Printed Textiles. 15.00 (ISBN 0-262-18043-X). MIT Pr.

History of Sculpture. lib. bdg. 23.25x (ISBN 0-8371-5681-5, CHHS). Greenwood.

History of Taste: An Account of the Revolutions of Art Criticism & Theory in Europe. lib. bdg. 27.25x (ISBN 0-8371-5207-0, CHHT). Greenwood.

History of the Art of Orissa. 17.50 (ISBN 0-88386-575-0). South Asia Bks.

History of the Christmas Card. 14.00 (ISBN 0-8103-3931-5). Gale.

History of the Comic Strip. 6.95 (ISBN 0-517-50303-4). Crown.

History of the Discovery of Photography. 18.00 (ISBN 0-405-04929-3). Arno.

History of the Gothic Revival. pap. text ed. 10.00 (ISBN 0-89257-035-0). Am Life Foun.

History of the Gothic Revival. 2nd ed. text ed. 39.25x (ISBN 0-7185-5033-1). Humanities.

History of the Handkerchief. 33.50 (ISBN 0-87245-499-1). Textile Bk.

History of the Metropolitan Museum of Art: With a Chapter on the Early Institutions of Art in New York. 27.00 (ISBN 0-405-02260-3). Arno.

History of the Monies Medals & Tokens of Monaco. write for info.; lib. bdg. 80.00x. S J Durst.

History of the Rise & Progress of the Arts of Design in the United States. rev. ed. 75.00 (ISBN 0-405-08470-6). Arno.

History of the Rise & Progress of the Arts of Design in the United States. Incl (ISBN 0-486-21695-0) (ISBN 0-486-21696-9) (ISBN 0-486-21697-7). pap. 7.50 ea. Dover.

History of the Royal Academy 1768-1968. 12.95 (ISBN 0-8008-3900-5). Taplinger.

History of the Skyscraper. lib. bdg. 75.00 (ISBN 0-306-70862-0). Da Capo.

History of the Staffordshire Potteries. 7.50 (ISBN 0-9600568-1-5). Weinstock.

History of the Torksey & Mansfield China Factories. 8.50. ARS Ceramica.

History of the Umbrella. 9.50 (ISBN 0-8008-3911-0). Taplinger.

History of the United States Capitol. lib. bdg. 65.00 (ISBN 0-306-71372-1). Da Capo.

History of Three Color Photography. 46.95 (ISBN 0-8038-8954-2). Focal Pr.

History of Valentines. 15.00 (ISBN 0-910872-10-4). Lee Pubns.

History of Winchester Firearms, 1866-1975. 15.00 (ISBN 0-87691-208-0). Winchester Pr.

History of Women Artists. 12.95 (ISBN 0-517-52380-9). Potter.

History of Wood-Engraving. 10.00 (ISBN 0-8103-3890-4). Gale.

History on Art's Side: Social Dynamics in Artistic Efflorescences. 15.00x (ISBN 0-8014-0715-X). Cornell U Pr.

History Preserved: A Guide to New York City Landmarks & Historic Districts. pap. 8.95 (ISBN 0-8052-0544-6). Schocken.

History, Principles & Practice of Symbolism in Christian Art. 35.00 (ISBN 0-8490-0364-4). Gordon Pr.

History, Principles, & Practice of Symbolism in Christian Art. 10.00 (ISBN 0-8103-3214-0). Gale.

Hobbit's Travels: Being the Hitherto Unpublished Travel Sketches of Sam Gamgee with Space for Notes. lib. bdg. 9.80 (ISBN 0-89471-041-9); pap. 3.95 (ISBN 0-89471-040-0). Running Pr.

Hobby Crafts. PLB 8.49 (ISBN 0-8172-1180-2). Raintree Pubs Ltd.

Hobby Gunsmithing. pap. 6.95 (ISBN 0-695-80361-1). Follett.

Hobbycraft Around the World. 6.70 (ISBN 0-8313-0097-3). Lantern.

Hobbycraft for Juniors. 6.70 (ISBN 0-8313-0096-5). Lantern.

Hobbycraft Toys & Games. 6.70 (ISBN 0-8313-0094-9). Lantern.

Hocus Focus: The World's Weirdest Cameras. PLB 5.90 (ISBN 0-531-00350-7). Watts.

Hogarth: His Art & His World. 14.95 (ISBN 0-8008-3916-1). Taplinger.

Hogarth, His Life, Art, & Times. abr ed. 30.00x (ISBN 0-300-01766-9). Yale U Pr.

Hogarth on High Life: The "Marriage a la Mode" Series from Georg Christoph Lichtenberg's Commentaries. 40.00 (ISBN 0-8195-4009-9). Wesleyan U Pr.

Hogarth's Literary Relationships. lib. bdg. 12.50 (ISBN 0-374-95852-1). Octagon.

Hohlwein Posters in Full Color. 10.00 (ISBN 0-8446-5527-9). Peter Smith.

Hokusai Sketchbooks: Selections from the Manga. 32.50 (ISBN 0-8048-0252-1). C E Tuttle.

Hokusai, the Old Man Mad with Painting. lib. bdg. 10.00 (ISBN 0-8414-7753-1). Folcroft.

Hokusai's Views of Mt. Fuji. 7.25 (ISBN 0-8048-0253-X). C E Tuttle.

Hole Thing: A Manual of Pinhole Fotography. new ed. pap. 2.95 (ISBN 0-87100-047-4). Morgan.

Holiday Cards for You to Make. 8.95 (ISBN 0-397-31574-0). Lippincott.

Holiday Craft & Fun. 7.50 (ISBN 0-397-30169-3). Lippincott.

Holiday Gifts, Favors, & Decorations That You Can Make. PLB 6.67 (ISBN 0-688-51616-5). Lothrop.

Holiday Hobbycraft. 6.70 (ISBN 0-8313-0093-0). Lantern.

Holiday Painter. 7.95 (ISBN 0-87523-128-4). Emerson.

Hollow Line in Dating Chinese Porcelains. l.t.d. ed. 20.00 (ISBN 0-930940-03-2); pap. 12.00 (ISBN 0-930940-00-8). Chinese Art App.

Holloware Techniques. 15.00 (ISBN 0-8230-2322-2). Watson-Guptill.

Hollywood Costume Design. 15.00 (ISBN 0-517-52637-9). Harmony.

Hollywood Glamor Portraits: One Hundred & Fifty Photos of Stars, 1926-1949. pap. 5.00 (ISBN 0-486-23352-9). Dover.

Holographic Interferometry. 27.50 (ISBN 0-471-90683-2). Wiley.

Holy Land. pap. 4.95 (ISBN 0-8010-0010-6). Baker Bk.

Home - It Takes More Than Money. pap. 6.95 (ISBN 0-8129-6269-9). Times Bks.

Home Darkroom. 2nd ed. pap. 4.95 (ISBN 0-8174-0555-0). Amphoto.

Home Dyeing with Natural Dyes. pap. 1.50 (ISBN 0-913664-00-6). Thresh Pubns.

Home Furnishing Self Help. 7.00 (ISBN 0-8108-0180-9). Scarecrow.

Home Guide to Lawns & Landscaping. 6.95 (ISBN 0-06-010689-1). Har-Row.

Home Guide to Lawns & Landscaping. pap. 3.95 (ISBN 0-06-010697-2, TD-275). Har-Row.

Home Gun Care & Repair. pap. 4.95. Stackpole.

Home Gunsmithing Digest. 2nd ed. pap. 7.95 (ISBN 0-695-81212-2). Follett.

Home Landscape: The Art of Home Landscaping. rev. & enl. ed. 13.95 (ISBN 0-07-018879-3). McGraw.

Home-Made Baby Toys. 8.95 (ISBN 0-395-25101-X); pap. 4.95 (ISBN 0-395-25410-8). HM.

Home Paint Book. pap. 1.95 (ISBN 0-8487-0403-7). Oxmoor Hse.

Home Planning & Architectural Drawing. text ed. 8.50 (ISBN 0-88275-400-9). Krieger.

Home Storage. pap. 1.95 (ISBN 0-8487-0386-3). Oxmoor Hse.

Home Workshop & Tool Handy Book. 2nd ed. 6.50 (ISBN 0-672-23208-1). Audel.

Homegrown Holography. 13.95 (ISBN 0-8174-2113-0); pap. 8.95 (ISBN 0-8174-2406-7). Amphoto.

Homemakers. PLB 4.90 (ISBN 0-531-01047-3). Watts.

Homeowner's Complete Outdoor Building Book. 12.50 (ISBN 0-06-010473-2). Har-Row.

Homeowners' Guide to Landscape Design. 9.95 (ISBN 0-914378-32-5); pap. 7.95 (ISBN 0-914378-27-9). Countryman.

Homeowner's Guide to Landscaping That Saves Energy Dollars. 10.95 (ISBN 0-679-50863-5); pap. 5.95 (ISBN 0-679-50866-X). McKay.

I

Inquiries into the Fundamentals of Aesthetics. pap. text ed. 7.95 (ISBN 0-262-63066-4). MIT Pr.
Inro & Other Miniature Forms of Japanese Lacquer Art. 30.25 (ISBN 0-8048-0263-7). C E Tuttle.
Inscriptional Work of Eric Gill. 13.95 (ISBN 0-304-92196-3). Dufour.
Inscriptions of Kourion. 25.00 (ISBN 0-87169-083-7). Am Philos.
Inscriptions: The Funerary Monuments. 25.00x (ISBN 0-87661-217-6). Am Sch Athens.
Inside Design: Creating Your Environment. text ed. 14.95x (ISBN 0-06-453508-8). Har-Row.
Inside Fashion Design. text ed. 14.95x (ISBN 0-06-453504-5); instructor's manual free (ISBN 0-06-453507-X). Har-Row.
Inside the World of Miniatures & Dollhouses: A Comprehensive Guide to Collecting & Creating. 17.95 (ISBN 0-679-50617-9); pap. 8.95 (ISBN 0-679-50620-9). McKay.
Inside Today's Home. 4th ed. text ed. 16.95 (ISBN 0-03-089480-8). HR&W.
Insider's Guide to Antiques, Art & Collectibles. pap. 3.95 (ISBN 0-346-12277-5). Cornerstone.
Insider's Guide to Antiques, Art & Collectibles. 9.95 (ISBN 0-385-06747-X). Doubleday.
Insiders: Rejection & Rediscovery of Man in the Arts of Our Time. d/1960 ed. 6.95x (ISBN 0-8071-0720-4). La State U Pr.
Insights in Art & Education. lib. bdg. 44.95 (ISBN 0-8490-1371-2). Gordon Pr.
Inspiration for Embroidery. 15.00 (ISBN 0-8231-4017-2). Branford.
Instances of Accessory Art. lib. bdg. 40.00 (ISBN 0-8240-2467-2). Garland Pub.
Instant Decorator. 27.50. Potter.
Instant Furniture. 12.95 (ISBN 0-442-27935-3); pap. 7.95 (ISBN 0-442-27934-5). Van Nos Reinhold.
Instant Furniture Refinishing & Other Crafty Practices. 2.50 (ISBN 0-385-03628-0). Doubleday.
Instant It Happened. 22.50 (ISBN 0-8109-0376-8). Abrams.
Instant Photo - Instant Art. pap. 5.95 (ISBN 0-8431-0423-6). Price Stern.
Instant Photography. 6.25 (ISBN 0-688-41741-8); PLB 6.00 (ISBN 0-688-51741-2). Lothrop.
Institute of American Indian Arts, Alumni Exhibition. pap. 3.25 (ISBN 0-88360-003-X). Amon Carter.
Intaglio Printmaking Techniques. 22.50 (ISBN 0-8230-2554-3). Watson-Guptill.
Intaglio Prints of Albrecht Durer: Engravings, Etchings, & Drypoints. lib. bdg. 45.00 (ISBN 0-87920-001-4). Kennedy Gall.
Intentions in Architecture. pap. 6.95 (ISBN 0-262-64002-3). MIT Pr.
Interaction of Color. rev ed. 13.00x (ISBN 0-300-01845-2); pap. 4.95 (ISBN 0-300-01846-0). Yale U Pr.
Interactive Computer Graphics in Architecture. 30.00 (ISBN 0-915250-21-7). Environ Design.
Interchangeable Lenses. pap. 3.95 (ISBN 0-8227-0107-3). Petersen Pub.
Interesting People: Eighty Years with the Great & Near-Great. 17.50 (ISBN 0-8061-0525-9). U of Okla Pr.
Interior Decorating with Plants. 14.95 (ISBN 0-02-623140-9). Macmillan.
Interior Decorating with Plants. pap. 8.95 (ISBN 0-02-012000-1). Macmillan.
Interior Design. spiral bdg. 5.95 (ISBN 0-8087-2305-7). Burgess.
Interior Design Careers. 5.96 (ISBN 0-13-392795-4); pap. text ed. 4.40 (ISBN 0-13-392787-3). P-H.
Interior Designer's Bedspread & Canopy Sketchfile. 13.50 (ISBN 0-8230-7290-8). Watson-Guptill.
Interior Designer's Drapery Sketchfile. 13.50 (ISBN 0-8230-7289-4). Watson-Guptill.
Interior Lighting for Environmental Designers. 26.95 (ISBN 0-471-65163-X). Wiley.
Interior Plantscaping. 24.95 (ISBN 0-07-022678-4). McGraw.
Interior Plantscaping. 22.95 (ISBN 0-07-022678-4). Arch Rec Bks.
Interiors & Interior Details. lib. bdg. 27.50 (ISBN 0-306-70747-0). Da Capo.
Intermediate Perspective. text ed. 6.00 (ISBN 0-682-40056-4). Exposition.
International Antiques Market. 30.00 (ISBN 0-498-01989-6). A S Barnes.
International Modern Glass. 30.00 (ISBN 0-684-15934-1). Scribner.
International Needlework Designs. 22.50 (ISBN 0-684-15169-3). Scribner.
International Sourcebook of Paper History. 17.50 (ISBN 0-208-01691-0). Shoe String.
International Style, Arts of Europe Around 1400: An Exhibition Catalogue. pap. 12.50. Walters Art.
International Who's Who in Art & Antiques. 2nd ed. 37.50x (ISBN 0-900332-37-9). Biblio Dist.
Interpretation of Aerial Photographs. 3rd ed. text ed. 16.95 (ISBN 0-8087-0130-4). Burgess.
Interrelated Arts in Leisure: Perceiving & Creating. 10.50 (ISBN 0-8016-0328-5). Mosby.
Interviews with Master Photographers. 10.00 (ISBN 0-448-22183-7). Paddington.
Intimate Journals. new ed. pap. 3.95 (ISBN 0-87140-016-2, L-016). Liveright.
Intrinsic Values of Gold Coins. pap. 14.99x ea. (ISBN 0-9601392-0-6) (ISBN 0-9601392-1-4). D Mason.
Introducing Candlemaking. 6.95 (ISBN 0-8008-4199-9). Taplinger.
Introducing Drawing Techniques. 7.50 (ISBN 0-8008-4174-3). Taplinger.
Introducing Needlepoint. 6.75 (ISBN 0-688-41550-4); PLB 6.48 (ISBN 0-688-51550-9). Lothrop.
Introducing Rushcraft. 6.25 (ISBN 0-8231-7009-8). Branford.
Introducing Soft Toy Making. 5.50 (ISBN 0-8231-5005-4). Branford.
Introduction to a History of Woodcut. 10.00 ea. Peter Smith.
Introduction to American Indian Art. lib. bdg. 15.00 (ISBN 0-87380-047-8). Rio Grande.
Introduction to Applied Drawing. rev. ed. pap. 3.72 (ISBN 0-87345-051-5). McKnight.
Introduction to Architecture. text ed. 23.50 (ISBN 0-07-059547-X). McGraw.
Introduction to Armenian Manuscript Illumination: A Picture Book. pap. 4.00. Walters Art.
Introduction to Art Activities. lib. bdg. 23.00x (ISBN 0-8371-2567-7, WIAA). Greenwood.
Introduction to Beauty. facs. ed. 14.25 (ISBN 0-8369-0152-5). Arno.
Introduction to Benin Art & Technology. 28.50x (ISBN 0-19-817191-9). Oxford U Pr.
Introduction to Breadcraft. 11.95 (ISBN 0-395-25770-0); pap. 5.95 (ISBN 0-395-25951-7). HM.
Introduction to Chinese Art & History. rev. & enl. ed. lib. bdg. 25.00x (ISBN 0-8371-6254-8, SICA). Greenwood.
Introduction to English Mediaeval Architecture. 2nd ed. 14.95 (ISBN 0-571-08331-5). Merrimack Bk Serv.
Introduction to European Painting. 10.00x (ISBN 0-210-34068-1). Asia.
Introduction to Furniture Making. pap. 4.95 (ISBN 0-8473-1339-5). Sterling.
Introduction to Home Furnishings. 3rd ed. text ed. 16.95 (ISBN 0-02-417090-9). Macmillan.
Introduction to Jewelry Casting. pap. 7.95 (ISBN 0-8096-1885-0). Assn Pr.
Introduction to Lace. pap. 1.50 (ISBN 0-8283-1042-4). Branden.
Introduction to Lalique Glass. 14.95 (ISBN 0-87069-238-0). Wallace-Homestead.
Introduction to Landscape Architecture. 27.00 (ISBN 0-444-00146-8); pap. text ed. 13.95 (ISBN 0-444-00171-9). Elsevier.
Introduction to Lettering. pap. 3.50 (ISBN 0-14-046329-1). Penguin.
Introduction to Literature & the Fine Arts. text ed. 6.00x (ISBN 0-87013-037-4). Mich St U Pr.
Introduction to Mechanical Drawing. new ed. pap. text ed. 5.20 (ISBN 0-205-06580-5, 3265803). Allyn.
Introduction to Modern Gunsmithing. pap. 2.95 (ISBN 0-06-463426-4). B&N.
Introduction to Music & Art in the Western World. 5th ed. pap. text ed. 10.95x (ISBN 0-697-03113-6); study guide 4.95x (ISBN 0-697-03114-4). Wm C Brown.
Introduction to Natural Dyeing. pap. 1.95 (ISBN 0-9600572-2-6). Thresh Pubns.
Introduction to Netsuke. 5.00 (ISBN 0-8048-0905-4). C E Tuttle.
Introduction to Paper Sculpture. 3.95 (ISBN 0-7137-0388-1). Sterling.
Introduction to Persian Art Since the Seventh Century A. D. lib. bdg. 22.50x (ISBN 0-8371-4315-2, POIP). Greenwood.
Introduction to Photographic Principles. pap. 3.00 (ISBN 0-486-21385-4). Dover.
Introduction to Photographic Principles. 2nd ed. 7.00 (ISBN 0-8446-2433-0). Peter Smith.
Introduction to Photography. 8.95 (ISBN 0-85242-050-1). Fountain Brit.
Introduction to Rembrandt. 12.95 (ISBN 0-06-430860-X). Har-Row.
Introduction to Textile Printing. 4th ed. text ed. 14.95 (ISBN 0-87245-575-0). Textile Bk.
Introduction to the Elements of Calligraphy. rev. 3rd ed. pap. 7.50 (ISBN 0-913718-08-4). St Heironymous.
Introduction to the Humanities: Painting, Sculpture, Architecture, Music & Literature. 10.00x (ISBN 0-06-480910-2). B&N.
Introduction to the Humanities: Painting, Sculpture, Architecture, Music & Literature. pap. 3.95 (ISBN 0-06-463277-6, 277). B&N.
Introduction to the Study of Chinese Painting. 42.50 (ISBN 0-404-56967-6). AMS Pr.
Introduction to the Study of Maya Hieroglyphs. 27.00 (ISBN 0-403-03615-1). Scholarly.
Introduction to the Study of the Maya Hieroglyphs. pap. 4.00 (ISBN 0-486-23108-9). Dover.
Introduction to the Study of the Maya Hieroglyphs. 9.00 (ISBN 0-8446-5226-1). Peter Smith.
Introduction to the Woodcut of the Seventeenth Century. 48.50 (ISBN 0-913870-49-8). Abaris Bks.
Introduction to Tudor Architecture. 21.00 (ISBN 0-403-07232-8). Somerset Pub.
Introductions to Modern Design: What Is Modern Design & What Is Modern Interior Design. 10.00 (ISBN 0-405-01537-2). Arno.
Introductions to the Collected Works of William Morris. 35.00 (ISBN 0-88211-046-2). Oriole Edns.
Introductory & Publications Photography. 3rd ed. 5.50x. Kenilworth.
Introductory Guide to Midwest Antiques. pap. 5.95. Greatlakes Liv.
Introductory Readings in Aesthetics. pap. text ed. 5.95 (ISBN 0-02-915260-7). Free Pr.
Invention of Printing: A Bibliography. lib. bdg. 32.00 (ISBN 0-8337-2342-1). B Franklin.
Inventive Fiber Crafts. 14.95 (ISBN 0-13-502468-4); pap. 6.95 (ISBN 0-13-502450-1). P-H.
Inventive Jewelry-Making. 10.95 (ISBN 0-442-27875-6). Van Nos Reinhold.
Inventive Paris Clothes 1909-1939: A Photographic Essay. 18.95 (ISBN 0-670-40067-X). Viking Pr.
Inverse Illusionism. pap. 1.50. Am Fed Arts.
Investigating Art. 14.95 (ISBN 0-236-31143-3). Merrimack Bk Serv.
Invisible Core: A Potter's Life & Thoughts. 12.95 (ISBN 0-87015-201-7). Pacific Bks.
Invisible Present: African Art & Literature. 10.00x (ISBN 0-06-432000-6). Har-Row.
Invitation to See: One Hundred Twenty-Five Paintings from the Museum of Modern Art. 12.50 (ISBN 0-87070-231-9). NYGS.
Iowa Catalog: Historic American Buildings Survey. 12.50 (ISBN 0-87745-091-9, 8288); pap. 8.95 (ISBN 0-87745-092-7, 8289). U of Iowa Pr.
Iridescent Glass. 6.50 (ISBN 0-87282-058-0). Century Hse.
Iridescent Stretch Glass. pap. 5.95. Borden.
Irish Art in the Romanesque Period 1020-1170 A.D. 28.50x (ISBN 0-8014-0526-2). Cornell U Pr.
Irish Blessing. pap. 5.95 (ISBN 0-03-021271-5). Winston Pr.
Irish Medieval Figure Sculpture 1200-1600: A Study of Irish Tombs with Notes on Costume & Armour. 85.00x (ISBN 0-85667-012-X). Biblio Dist.
Iron & Brass Implements of the English & American House. rev. & enl. ed. 27.50 (ISBN 0-85458-999-6). Herman Pub.
Is Your Contemporary Painting More Temporary Than You Think? 2nd ed. pap. 2.50 (ISBN 0-910790-00-0). Intl Bk Co IL.
Isabella Stewart Gardner & Fenway Court. 24.25 (ISBN 0-8369-6901-4). Arno.
Isabella Stewart Gardner & Fenway Court. 3rd ed. 6.00 (ISBN 0-914660-07-1). I S Gardner Mus.
Isamu Noguchi. 65.00 (ISBN 0-89659-003-8). Abbeville Pr.
Isamu Noguchi: The Life of a Sculptor. 6.89 (ISBN 0-690-45014-1). T Y Crowell.
Islam. 25.00 (ISBN 0-448-02027-0). G&D.
Islam & Tribal Art in West Africa. 18.95 (ISBN 0-521-20192-6). Cambridge U Pr.
Islamic Architecture. 42.50 (ISBN 0-8109-1010-1). Abrams.
Islamic Architecture in North Africa: A Photographic Survey. 60.00 (ISBN 0-208-01599-X). Shoe String.
Islamic Art. pap. 7.95 (ISBN 0-19-519926-X). Oxford U Pr.
Islamic Patterns. 24.75x (ISBN 0-8052-3627-9); pap. 9.95 (ISBN 0-8052-0537-3). Schocken.
Island Garden. 15.00 (ISBN 0-917890-06-X). Heritage Bk.
Island of the Pelicans. 5.00 (ISBN 0-916480-01-1). Creative Eye.
Israel's Money & Medals. 2nd ed. with supplement 25.00. Am Israel Numismatic.
Italian Baroque Stage: Documents by Giulio Troili, Andrea Pozzo, Ferdinando Galli-Bibiena, & Baldassare Orsini. 20.00x (ISBN 0-520-03006-0). U of Cal Pr.
Italian Chiaroscuro Woodcuts: Illustrations to the Italian Volumes of Bartsch's Le Peintre-Graveur. 29.50x (ISBN 0-271-00129-1). Pa St U Pr.
Italian Crafts: Inspirations from Folk Art. 7.95 (ISBN 0-87131-227-1). M Evans.
Italian Drawings in Oxford. 60.00 (ISBN 0-7148-1764-3). Dutton.
Italian Drawings in the Art Museum, Princeton University. 12.50 (ISBN 0-8079-0069-9). October.
Italian Followers of Caravaggio. 30.00x (ISBN 0-674-46900-3). Harvard U Pr.
Italian Landscape in Eighteenth Century England. 10.00 (ISBN 0-8462-0705-2). Russell.
Italian Landscape in Eighteenth Century England. 21.00x (ISBN 0-7146-2069-6). Biblio Dist.
Italian Maiolica. 2.95 (ISBN 0-600-43184-3). Transatlantic.
Italian Master Drawings, 1350-1800, from the Janos Scholz Collection. pap. 6.00 (ISBN 0-486-23257-3). Dover.
Italian Painters of the Renaissance. Incl. Venetian & North Italian Schools (ISBN 0-7148-1335-4); Florentine & Central Italian Schools (ISBN 0-7148-1336-2). pap. 4.95 ea. Dutton.
Italian Painters of the Renaissance. pap. 5.95 (ISBN 0-452-00455-1, F455). NAL.
Italian Paintings in the Walters Art Gallery. 75.00. Walters Art.
Italian Pictures of the Renaissance: Central Italian & North Italian Schools. 85.00 (ISBN 0-7148-1324-9). Dutton.
Italian Renaissance. pap. 1.95 (ISBN 0-448-00562-X). G&D.
Italian Renaissance Illuminations. 19.95 (ISBN 0-8076-0863-7); pap. 9.95 (ISBN 0-8076-0864-5). Braziller.
Italian Renaissance Painting. 7.95 (ISBN 0-7148-1745-7). Dutton.
Italian Romanesque Panel Painting. lib. bdg. 50.00 (ISBN 0-87817-180-0). Hacker.
Italian Sculpture of the Renaissance: The Charles Eliot Norton Lectures for the Years 1927-1928. lib. bdg. 24.00x (ISBN 0-8371-4498-1, MAIS). Greenwood.
Italian Sculpture: 1250-1700. 8.50 (ISBN 0-8008-4275-8). Taplinger.
Italian Villas & Palaces. pap. 6.95 (ISBN 0-500-20045-9). Transatlantic.
Italian Villas & Their Gardens. lib. bdg. 35.00 (ISBN 0-306-70817-5); pap. 8.95 (ISBN 0-306-80048-9). Da Capo.
Italian Villas Today. 18.50. Transatlantic.
Italic Handwriting. pap. 3.00 (ISBN 0-8008-4288-X). Taplinger.
Italic Handwriting for Young People. pap. 4.95 (ISBN 0-02-079960-8). Macmillan.
Italic Handwriting for Young People. cancelled (ISBN 0-02-534570-2). Macmillan.
Italic Writing. pap. 6.95 (ISBN 0-85458-311-4). Transatlantic.
Italy & Spain: 1600-1750. pap. 8.95 ref. ed. (ISBN 0-13-508101-7). P-H.
It's a Model World. 5.95 (ISBN 0-664-32515-7). Westminster.
It's Art Time: A Handbook of Art Awareness Activities for Teachers. text ed. 8.95 (ISBN 0-675-08702-3). Merrill.
It's Easy to Carve. pap. 1.95 (ISBN 0-89516-023-4). Condor Pub Co.
It's Easy to Carve. 5.95 (ISBN 0-385-11089-8); PLB (ISBN 0-385-11090-1). Doubleday.
It's Fun Making Things. 8.00 (ISBN 0-8002-1601-6). Intl Pubns Serv.
It's Fun to Make Things from Scrap Materials. pap. 3.50 (ISBN 0-486-21251-3). Dover.
It's Me, O Lord: The Autobiography of Rockwell Kent. lib. bdg. 39.50 (ISBN 0-306-77412-7). Da Capo.
It's Smart to Use a Dummy. 5.50 (ISBN 0-664-32500-9). Westminster.
Ivan Albright. 65.00 (ISBN 0-89659-002-X); limited ed. 1500.00 (ISBN 0-89659-015-1). Abbeville Pr.
I've Decided I Want My Seat Back. 10.00 (ISBN 0-06-012845-3). Har-Row.
Ivory Workers of the Middle Ages. 10.00 (ISBN 0-404-56537-9). AMS Pr.
Izapan-Style Art: A Study of its Form & Meaning see **Possible Focus of Andean Artistic Influence in Mesoamerica.**

J

J. B. Fischer von Erlach. 15.95x (ISBN 0-674-46988-7). Harvard U Pr.
J. M. Hanson. 9.75x (ISBN 0-8014-0469-X). Cornell U Pr.
Jack Levine. 55.00 (ISBN 0-8109-0245-1). Abrams.
Jacopo della Quercia, Sculptor. 31.50x (ISBN 0-300-01529-1). Yale U Pr.
Jacopo Della Quercia's Fonte Gaia. 20.50x (ISBN 0-19-817148-X). Oxford U Pr.
Jacopo Sansovino: Architecture & Patronage in Renaissance Venice. 22.50x (ISBN 0-300-01891-6). Yale U Pr.
Jacques Callot: Artist of the Theatre. 15.00x (ISBN 0-8203-0345-3). U of Ga Pr.
Jade Lore. 2nd ed. 25.00 (ISBN 0-89344-009-4). Ars Ceramica.
Jade of the East. 35.00 (ISBN 0-8348-1854-X). Weatherhill.
Jaina Iconography. 2nd ed. text ed. 21.00x. Verry.

Kinsey, Photographer. pap. 24.95 (ISBN 0-87701-107-9). Chronicle Bks.
Kinsey, Photographer: A Half Century of Negatives by Darius & Tabitha May Kinsey. boxed set 150.00; (ISBN 0-912020-35-0); (ISBN 0-912020-36-9). Scrimshaw Calif.
Kitchen. 25.00 (ISBN 0-8230-7320-3). Watson-Guptill.
Kitchen Book. 30.00 (ISBN 0-517-53131-3). Crown.
Kitchen Carton Crafts. PLB 6.00 (ISBN 0-688-51133-3); pap. 2.95 (ISBN 0-688-45005-9). Lothrop.
Kitchen Craft Workshop. 9.95. Wehman.
Kitchen Crafts. pap. 3.95 (ISBN 0-02-009430-2). Macmillan.
Kite Craft. pap. 4.95 (ISBN 0-517-51471-0). Crown.
Kiyonaga. pap. 12.95 (ISBN 0-87011-099-3). Kodansha.
Klamath Basin Petroglyphs. pap. 5.95 (ISBN 0-87919-078-7). Ballena Pr.
Knights in Armor. PLB 7.89 (ISBN 0-06-022038-4). Har-Row.
Knit Art. 10.50 (ISBN 0-442-21655-6); pap. 6.95 (ISBN 0-442-21656-4). Van Nos Reinhold.
Knit Your Own Norwegian Sweaters. pap. 2.50 (ISBN 0-486-23031-7). Dover.
Knit Your Own Norwegian Sweaters: Complete Instructions for 50 Authentic Sweaters, Hats, Mittens, Gloves, Caps, Etc. 5.00 (ISBN 0-8446-5175-3). Peter Smith.
Knitted Outfits for Teenage Dolls. 9.50 (ISBN 0-571-10453-3). Transatlantic.
Knitting. 8.95x (ISBN 0-8277-0264-7). British Bk Ctr.
Knitting & Crocheting Pattern Index. 7.50 (ISBN 0-8108-0998-2). Scarecrow.
Knitting & Crocheting Your Own Fashions of the Forties. 5.50 (ISBN 0-8446-5013-7). Peter Smith.
Knitting for Beginners. 7.95 (ISBN 0-397-31473-6); pap. 2.95 (ISBN 0-397-31474-4). Lippincott.
Knitting Made Easy. 4.95 (ISBN 0-385-09355-1). Doubleday.
Knock Vigorously to Be Heard. 4.00 (ISBN 0-8022-0211-X). Philos Lib.
Knots & Netting. 8.95 (ISBN 0-8008-4484-X). Taplinger.
Knots & Splices. pap. 1.25 (ISBN 0-668-01331-1). Arc Bks.
Knots & Splices. lib. bdg. 4.50 (ISBN 0-668-01330-3). Arco.
Knotting Crafts. 5.50x (ISBN 0-85467-020-3). Intl Pubns Serv.
Know How Book of Action Toys: Lots of Toys & Machines to Make & Work. 4.95 (ISBN 0-8069-8056-7); PLB 4.99 (ISBN 0-8069-8057-5). Sterling.
Know How Book of Paper Fun. 4.95 (ISBN 0-8069-8036-2); PLB 4.99 (ISBN 0-8069-8037-0). Sterling.
Know How Book of Print & Paint. 4.95 (ISBN 0-8069-8046-X); PLB 4.99 (ISBN 0-8069-8047-8). Sterling.
Know How Book of Puppets. 4.95 (ISBN 0-8069-8038-9); PLB 4.99 (ISBN 0-8069-8039-7). Sterling.
Know Your Antiques. 7.95 (ISBN 0-517-51321-8). Crown.
Knoxville: A Pictorial History. pap. 12.95 (ISBN 0-915442-46-9). Donning Co.
Knutty Knitting for Kids. 6.95 (ISBN 0-695-80739-0); lib. bdg. 6.99 (ISBN 0-695-40739-2). Follett.
Kodak Pocket Instamatic Camera Guide. pap. 2.95 (ISBN 0-87100-076-8). Morgan.
Konica Autoreflex Manual. 11.95 (ISBN 0-8174-0551-8). Amphoto.
Konica Guide. 10.95 (ISBN 0-8174-2501-2); pap. 6.95 (ISBN 0-8174-2121-1). Amphoto.
Korean Pottery & Porcelain of the Yi Period. 33.00 (ISBN 0-571-08404-4). Merrimack Bk Serv.
Kovel's Collector's Guide to American Art Pottery. 12.95 (ISBN 0-517-51676-4). Crown.
Kovels' Official Bottle Price List. 4th ed. pap. 8.95 (ISBN 0-517-53013-9). Crown.
Kovels' Official Bottle Price List: Third Edition. pap. 6.95 (ISBN 0-517-52189-X). Crown.
Kremlin of Moscow. 25.00 (ISBN 0-312-46095-3). St Martin.
Kubin's Dance of Death & Other Drawings. pap. 3.00 (ISBN 0-486-22884-3). Dover.
Kyoto Ceramics. 12.50 (ISBN 0-8348-2701-8). Weatherhill.

L

L. J. M. Daguerre: The History of the Diorama & the Daugerreotype. pap. 4.50 (ISBN 0-486-22290-X). Dover.
L. J. M. Daguerre: The History of the Diorama & the Daguerreotype. 2nd rev. ed. 7.50 (ISBN 0-8446-2120-X). Peter Smith.
Lace & Embroidery Collector. 12.00 (ISBN 0-8103-3663-4). Gale.
Lacquer & Crackle. 3.95 (ISBN 0-8069-5200-8); PLB 4.59 (ISBN 0-8069-5201-6). Sterling.
Lacquer of the West: The History of a Craft & an Industry, 1600-1950. 25.00 (ISBN 0-226-36315-5). U of Chicago Pr.
Lady Ottoline's Album. 12.50 (ISBN 0-394-48758-3). Knopf.
Lalique for Collectors. 7.95 (ISBN 0-684-15863-9). Scribner.
L'Amour Bleu. 65.00 (ISBN 0-8478-0129-2). Rizzoli Intl.
Lampmaking. 7.95 (ISBN 0-8473-1040-X). Sterling.
Lamps of the Roman Period, First to Seventh Century After Christ. 17.50x (ISBN 0-87661-207-9). Am Sch Athens.
Land of Israel. 40.00 (ISBN 0-500-24101-5). Thames Hudson.
Land, Sea & Sky: A Photographic Album for Artists & Designers. pap. 4.50 (ISBN 0-486-23249-2). Dover.
Land, Sea & Sky: A Photographic Album for Artists & Designers. 7.50 (ISBN 0-8446-5453-1). Peter Smith.
Land: Twentieth Century Landscape Photographs. 15.00 (ISBN 0-306-70753-5); pap. 7.95 (ISBN 0-306-80026-8). Da Capo.
Landmark History of New York. lib. bdg. 34.95 (ISBN 0-8490-2128-6). Gordon Pr.
Landmark History of New York. 7.00 (ISBN 0-87198-070-3). Friedman.
Landmarks in Nineteenth Century Painting. facs. ed. 13.50 (ISBN 0-8369-0186-X). Arno.
Landmarks of Liberty. 4.50 (ISBN 0-8437-3078-1). Hammond Inc.
Landmarks of Rochester & Monroe County: A Guide to Neighborhoods & Villages. 10.00 (ISBN 0-8156-0103-4); pap. 6.00 (ISBN 0-8156-0104-2). Syracuse U Pr.
Landscape. pap. 8.95 (ISBN 0-07-009780-1). McGraw.
Landscape & Figure Composition. 16.00 (ISBN 0-405-04915-3). Arno.
Landscape Architectural Site Construction Details. pap. 20.00 (ISBN 0-918436-01-X). Environ Des VA.
Landscape Architecture. 26.50 (ISBN 0-07-057391-3). McGraw.
Landscape Artist in America: The Life & Work of Jens Jensen. 15.00x (ISBN 0-226-18053-0). U of Chicago Pr.
Landscape Drawing & Painting. 9.95 (ISBN 0-670-41772-6). Viking Pr.
Landscape Gardening. lib. bdg. 9.99 (ISBN 0-8094-1090-7). Silver.
Landscape Gardening. 8.95 (ISBN 0-8094-1089-3); lib. bdg. avail. Time-Life.
Landscape into Art. rev. & enl. ed. 17.50 (ISBN 0-06-010781-2). Har-Row.
Landscape into Art. rev. & enl. ed. pap. 8.95 (ISBN 0-06-430088-9, IN-88). Har-Row.
Landscape into Cityscape: Frederick Law Olmsted's Plans for a Greater New York City. 22.50x (ISBN 0-8014-0125-9). Cornell U Pr.
Landscape It Yourself. pap. 8.95. HarBraceJ.
Landscape It Yourself: A Handbook for Home Gardeners. pap. 8.95 (ISBN 0-15-147689-6). HarBraceJ.
Landscape of Industry. 45.50 (ISBN 0-470-84440-X). Halsted Pr.
Landscape Painting for Beginners. pap. 3.95 (ISBN 0-8008-4543-9). Taplinger.
Landscape Painting in Oil. 16.95 (ISBN 0-8230-2609-4). Watson-Guptill.
Landscape Painting in Oils. pap. 1.95 (ISBN 0-448-00546-8). G&D.
Landscape Painting in Watercolor. 16.95 (ISBN 0-8230-2620-5). Watson-Guptill.
Landscape Painting Step-by-Step. pap. 9.95 (ISBN 0-8230-2616-7). Watson-Guptill.
Landscape Painting with a Knife. 18.95 (ISBN 0-8230-2632-9). Watson-Guptill.
Landscape Painting with a Knife. pap. 9.95 (ISBN 0-8230-2633-7). Watson-Guptill.
Landscape Painting with Markers. pap. text ed. 9.95 (ISBN 0-8230-2636-1). Watson-Guptill.
Landscape Sumi-E in Three Weeks. pap. 3.25 (ISBN 0-87040-075-4). Japan Pubns.
Landscape We See. 28.50 (ISBN 0-07-018882-3). McGraw.
Landscape Your Florida Home: With a Special Chapter on Landscaping Mobile Homes. 12.95 (ISBN 0-912458-08-9). E A Seemann.
Landscapes & Seasons of the Medieval World. 27.50 (ISBN 0-8020-2110-7). U of Toronto Pr.
Landscapes in the Hungarian National Gallery. 9.00x. Intl Pubns Serv.
Landscaping Principles & Practices. 12.95 (ISBN 0-442-23634-4). Van Nos Reinhold.
Landscaping: Principles & Practices. pap. text ed. 10.00 (ISBN 0-8273-1634-8); instructor's guide 1.35 (ISBN 0-8273-1635-6). Delmar.
Landscaping the Saudi Arabian Desert. 22.50 (ISBN 0-9601128-1-2). Delancey Pr.
Landscaping Your Home. pap. 1.95 (ISBN 0-8487-0285-9). Oxmoor Hse.
Landseer: The Victorian Paragon. 19.95 (ISBN 0-241-89432-8). David & Charles.
Language & Aesthetics: Contributions to the Philosophy of Art. 8.00x (ISBN 0-7006-0104-X). Regents Pr KS.
Language & Visual Form: The Personal Record of a Dual Creative Process. 10.00x (ISBN 0-292-78353-1). U of Tex Pr.
Language of Drawing. pap. 2.95 (ISBN 0-13-522748-8, S146). P-H.
Language of Drawing & Painting. 17.50 (ISBN 0-8462-1057-6). Russell.
Language of Painting. lib. bdg. 19.50x (ISBN 0-8371-2525-1, JOLP). Greenwood.
Language of Pattern: An Enquiry Inspired by Islamic Decoration. pap. 5.95x (ISBN 0-06-430050-1, IN-50). Har-Row.
Language of Post-Modern Architecture. rev. ed. pap. 13.50 (ISBN 0-8478-0167-5). Rizzoli Intl.
Laocoon. lib. bdg. 40.00 (ISBN 0-89341-475-1). Longwood Pr.
Lapidary for Pleasure & Profit. 7.95 (ISBN 0-668-04533-7, 4533). Arco.
Larousse Animal Portraits. 19.95 (ISBN 0-88332-076-2, 8090). Larousse.
Larry Bell. 4.95 (ISBN 0-912158-75-1). Hennessey.
Larry Rivers. 55.00 (ISBN 0-8109-0451-9). Abrams.
Larry Rivers: Drawings & Digressions. 30.00 (ISBN 0-517-53430-4). Potter.
Last Empire: Photography in British India 1855-1911. 25.00 (ISBN 0-912334-86-X); pap. 15.00 (ISBN 0-89381-018-5). Aperture.
Last Flower. pap. 3.50 (ISBN 0-06-090232-9, CN232). Har-Row.
Last Flower. lib. bdg. 5.95 (ISBN 0-89244-057-0). Queens Hse.
Last Flowering of the Middle Ages. 17.50 (ISBN 0-8046-0470-3). Kennikat.
Last Letters of Aubrey Beardsley. lib. bdg. 20.00 (ISBN 0-8414-4426-9). Folcroft.
Last of the Arctic. 19.95 (ISBN 0-88932-031-4). Pagurian.
Last Words on the History of the Title-Page. lib. bdg. 24.50 (ISBN 0-8337-2796-6). B Franklin.
Last Years of Rodin. lib. bdg. 19.95 (ISBN 0-8383-1945-9). Haskell.
Late Baroque & Rococo Architecture. 42.50 (ISBN 0-8109-1012-8). Abrams.
Late Georgian & Regency Furniture. 2.95 (ISBN 0-600-43575-X). Transatlantic.
Late Georgian & Regency Silver. 2.95 (ISBN 0-600-43203-3). Transatlantic.
Late Gothic Engravings of Germany & the Netherlands: 682 Copperplates from the Kritischer Katalog. 11.00 (ISBN 0-8446-4774-8). Peter Smith.
Late Nubian Settlement at Arminna West. 16.00. Univ Mus of U PA.
Late Nubian Settlement at Arminna West. 20.00. Penn-Yale Expedit.
Late Roman & Byzantine Solidi Found in Sweden & Denmark. pap. 6.00 (ISBN 0-89722-056-0). Am Numismatic.
Later Court Hands in England from the Fifteenth to the Seventeenth Century. 75.00 (ISBN 0-8044-5523-6). Ungar.
Later Work of Aubrey Beardsley. 17.50 (ISBN 0-306-70954-6). Da Capo.
Later Work of Aubrey Beardsley. 8.00 (ISBN 0-8446-1617-6). Peter Smith.
Later Work of Aubrey Beardsley. rev. ed. pap. 4.50 (ISBN 0-486-21817-1). Dover.
Latin American Architecture Since 1945. 23.00 (ISBN 0-405-01563-1). Arno.
Latin American Paintings & Drawings from the Collection of John & Barbara Duncan. pap. 2.00 (ISBN 0-913456-10-1). Interbk Inc.
Latin American Prints from the Museum of Modern Art. pap. 3.00 (ISBN 0-913456-24-1). Interbk Inc.
Latrobe, Jefferson, & the National Capitol. lib. bdg. 46.00x (ISBN 0-8240-2716-7). Garland Pub.
Laughing Camera. 5.95 (ISBN 0-8090-2120-X). Hill & Wang.
Laughing Camera. 5.95 (ISBN 0-8090-2121-8). Hill & Wang.
Laughing Camera for Children. 5.95 (ISBN 0-8090-2122-6). Hill & Wang.
Lautrec-Redon. 12.00 (ISBN 0-405-01527-5). Arno.
Lawrence. 18.50 (ISBN 0-404-00385-0). AMS Pr.
Layman's Handbook of Interior Design. 5.00 (ISBN 0-682-47363-4). Exposition.
Layout. 17.95 (ISBN 0-8230-2655-8). Watson-Guptill.
Le Corbusier. 10.00 (ISBN 0-88208-002-4). Lawrence Hill.
Le Corbusier & the Tragic View of Architecture. 13.95x (ISBN 0-674-51860-8). Harvard U Pr.
Le Corbusier & the Tragic View of Architecture. pap. 4.95 (ISBN 0-674-51861-6). Harvard U Pr.
Le Corbusier in Perspective. 8.95 (ISBN 0-13-527291-2); pap. 3.95 (ISBN 0-13-527283-1). P-H.
Leaded Glass: A Handbook of Techniques. 18.50 (ISBN 0-8230-2660-4). Watson-Guptill.
Learning About Nature Through Crafts. 4.95 (ISBN 0-8117-0938-8). Stackpole.
Learning Calligraphy: A Book of Lettering, Design & History. pap. 7.95 (ISBN 0-02-015550-6). Macmillan.
Learning from Las Vegas. rev. ed. 17.50x (ISBN 0-262-22020-2); pap. 9.95 (ISBN 0-262-72006-X). MIT Pr.
Learning from the Old Masters. 19.50 (ISBN 0-8230-2672-8). Watson-Guptill.
Learning How to Paint in Oils: Illustrated Step by Step on TV Storyboard. Softbound 3.95 (ISBN 0-385-05945-0). Doubleday.
Learning to Draw. 11.95 (ISBN 0-8230-2675-2). Watson-Guptill.
Learning to Look: A Handbook for the Visual Arts. 8.50x (ISBN 0-226-79148-3). U of Chicago Pr.
Learning to Look: A Handbook for the Visual Arts. pap. 3.95 (ISBN 0-226-79149-1, P78). U of Chicago Pr.
Learning to Paint. pap. 9.95 (ISBN 0-8230-2701-5). Watson-Guptill.
Leather As Art & Craft. 9.95 (ISBN 0-517-50574-6); pap. 6.95 (ISBN 0-517-50575-4). Crown.
Leather Braiding. 5.00 (ISBN 0-87033-039-X). Cornell Maritime.
Leather Tooling & Carving. pap. 2.50 (ISBN 0-486-23061-9). Dover.
Leather Tooling & Carving. 7.50 (ISBN 0-8446-5042-0). Peter Smith.
Leathercraft. text ed. 4.40 (ISBN 0-87006-234-4). Goodheart.
Leathercraft by Hand. pap. 2.50 (ISBN 0-06-463403-5). B&N.
Leathercraft Handbook. 6.95 (ISBN 0-912092-43-2). Educator Bks.
Leatherwork. 7.95 (ISBN 0-397-31692-5); pap. 3.95 (ISBN 0-397-31693-3). Lippincott.
Leatherwork: A Basic Manual. pap. 3.95 (ISBN 0-316-54450-7). Little.
Lectures on Art. 21.00 (ISBN 0-403-01233-3). Scholarly.
Lectures on Art. 25.00 set (ISBN 0-8274-2813-8). R West.
Lectures on Art. 22.50 (ISBN 0-404-06333-0) (ISBN 0-404-06334-9) (ISBN 0-404-06335-7). AMS Pr.
Lectures on Art - Poems. lib. bdg. 29.50 (ISBN 0-306-70414-5). Da Capo.
Leeds Old & New. pap. text ed. 9.00x (ISBN 0-8277-5117-6). British Bk Ctr.
Left-Handed Book. pap. 1.95 (ISBN 0-87131-156-9). M Evans.
Left-Handed Crochet. pap. 5.95 (ISBN 0-442-23590-9). Van Nos Reinhold.
Left-Handed Knitting. pap. 5.95 (ISBN 0-442-23585-2). Van Nos Reinhold.
Left-Handed Needlepoint. pap. 4.95 (ISBN 0-442-23597-6). Van Nos Reinhold.
Legacy of Beauty. 6.50 (ISBN 0-911432-15-9). State Ptg.
Legacy of Mark Rothko. 14.95 (ISBN 0-03-014751-4). HR&W.
Legacy of Mark Rothko. pap. 4.95 (ISBN 0-14-005205-4). Penguin.
Legends of the Madonna, As Represented in the Fine Arts. lib. bdg. 25.00. Folcroft.
Legends of the Madonna, As Represented in the Fine Arts. 15.00 (ISBN 0-8103-3114-4). Gale.
Legends of the Monastic Orders As Represented in the Fine Arts. 26.00 (ISBN 0-404-14767-4). AMS Pr.
Leger & the Avant-Garde. 36.50x (ISBN 0-300-01800-2). Yale U Pr.
Legibility of Print. facsimile ed. pap. 7.45 (ISBN 0-8138-2450-8). Iowa St U Pr.
Leica & Leicaflex Way. 27.95 (ISBN 0-8038-4303-8, 659). Focal Pr.
Leica Guide. 3.95 (ISBN 0-8038-4304-6). Focal Pr.
Leicaflex & Leicaflex SL Guide. pap. 2.95 (ISBN 0-8174-0172-5). Amphoto.
Leicaflex System of Photography. 10.95 (ISBN 0-8174-0539-9). Amphoto.
Lens & Shutter. PLB 7.95 (ISBN 0-201-09240-9). A-W.
Lens Guide. rev. ed. pap. 3.95 (ISBN 0-8038-4306-2). Focal Pr.
Lens in Action. pap. 8.95 (ISBN 0-8038-4296-1). Focal Pr.
Lens Mechanism Technology. 72.50x (ISBN 0-8448-0770-2). Crane-Russak Co.
Leonardo Da Vinci. 15.00x (ISBN 0-674-52450-0). Harvard U Pr.
Leonardo da Vinci on Painting: A Lost Book (Libro A) 25.00x (ISBN 0-520-00993-2). U of Cal Pr.
Leonardo da Vinci's Advice to Artists. 7.50 (ISBN 0-8407-6377-8). Elsevier-Nelson.
Leonardo-Studien. 71.00 (ISBN 3-11-005727-1). De Gruyter.
Leonardo's Legacy: An International Symposium. 30.00x (ISBN 0-520-00956-8). U of Cal Pr.
Less Than Sharp Show. pap. 3.95 (ISBN 0-932026-01-X). Chicago Contemp Photo.
Let Them Make Me a Sanctuary. text ed. 29.95x (ISBN 0-87441-316-8). Behrman.

Loggia del Capitaniato. 25.00x (ISBN 0-271-00089-9). Pa St U Pr.

Lombard Architecture. 150.00 (ISBN 0-87817-018-9). Hacker.

London Furniture Makers from the Restoration to the Victorian Era: 1660-1840. 11.00 (ISBN 0-8446-4752-7). Peter Smith.

London Goldsmiths, 1697-1837. 98.00 (ISBN 0-571-10550-5). Merrimack Bk Serv.

London Perceived. pap. 2.25 (ISBN 0-15-652970-X, HB103). HarBraceJ.

London Signs & Inscriptions. 9.50 (ISBN 0-8103-3496-8). Gale.

London's Historic Railway Stations. pap. 7.50 (ISBN 0-7195-3426-7). Transatlantic.

Long Ago in Florence: The Story of Della Robbia Sculpture. 5.50 (ISBN 0-688-41205-X); PLB 5.28 (ISBN 0-688-51205-4). Lothrop.

Longcase Clock. 29.95x. Beekman Pubs.

Longcase Clock. 2nd ed. 22.95 (ISBN 0-684-16247-4). Scribner.

Look Again. 6.95 (ISBN 0-02-744050-8). Macmillan.

Look Again. pap. 1.95 (ISBN 0-525-62331-0). Dutton.

Look at This. 6.95 (ISBN 0-02-777590-9, 77759). Macmillan.

Looking at Architecture. PLB 6.96 (ISBN 0-688-51553-3). Lothrop.

Looking at Architecture with Ruskin. 15.00 (ISBN 0-8020-2284-7). U of Toronto Pr.

Looking at Beasties. PLB 9.00 (ISBN 0-516-08823-8). Childrens.

Looking at Children. PLB 9.00 (ISBN 0-516-08825-4). Childrens.

Looking at Churches. 5.95 (ISBN 0-7153-7011-1). David & Charles.

Looking at Horses. PLB 9.00 (ISBN 0-516-08814-9). Childrens.

Looking at Language. 5.95 (ISBN 0-7100-7589-8). Routledge & Kegan.

Looking at Modern Painting. pap. 8.50x (ISBN 0-393-09534-7). Norton.

Looking at Photographs: One Hundred Pictures from the Collection of the Museum of Modern Art. 17.50 (ISBN 0-87070-514-8); pap. 9.95 (ISBN 0-87070-515-6). NYGS.

Looking at Pisa. 7.50x (ISBN 0-8002-1683-0). Intl Pubns Serv.

Looking into Houses. pap. 9.95. Watson-Guptill.

Looking into Houses. 22.50 (ISBN 0-8230-7358-0). Watson-Guptill.

Looney Tunes Poster Book. pap. 7.95 (ISBN 0-517-53680-3). Harmony.

Lootens on Photographic Enlarging & Print Quality. 8th ed. 13.95 (ISBN 0-8174-0467-8). Amphoto.

Lord Leighton. 50.00x (ISBN 0-300-01896-7). Yale U Pr.

Lords of the Underworld: Masterpieces of Classical Maya Ceramics. 45.00x (ISBN 0-691-03917-8). Princeton U Pr.

Lore & Lure of Hooked Rugs. 10.00 (ISBN 0-910940-04-5). Lincoln Hse.

Lorenzo Ghiberti. 55.00x (ISBN 0-691-03820-1). Princeton U Pr.

Los Angeles Barrio Calligraphy. 15.00 (ISBN 0-87093-170-9). Dawsons.

Lost Chicago. 20.00 (ISBN 0-395-20726-6). HM.

Lost Chicago. pap. 8.95 (ISBN 0-395-26468-5). HM.

Lost New York. pap. 7.95 (ISBN 0-8052-0328-1). Schocken.

Lost Pharaohs: The Romance of Egyptian Archaeology. lib. bdg. 16.00x (ISBN 0-8371-2260-0, COLP). Greenwood.

Lost Wax Bronze Casting: A Photographic Essay on This Antique & Venerable Art. 16.95 (ISBN 0-442-26099-7). Van Nos Reinhold.

Lost World of the Impressionists. 32.50 (ISBN 0-8212-0687-7). NYGS.

Lost Years: Mural Painting in New York City Under the Works Progress Administration's Federal Art Project 1935-1943. lib. bdg. 41.00 (ISBN 0-8240-3216-0). Garland Pub.

Lot's Wife & the Venus of Milo. 16.95 (ISBN 0-521-21677-X). Cambridge U Pr.

Louis Agassiz Fuertes & the Singular Beauty of Birds. 40.00 (ISBN 0-06-012775-9). Har-Row.

Louis C. Tiffany's Art Glass. 12.95 (ISBN 0-517-53068-6). Crown.

Louis C. Tiffany's Glass, Bronzes & Lamps: A Complete Collector's Guide. 11.95 (ISBN 0-517-50556-8). Crown.

Louis I. Kahn. 4.95 (ISBN 0-8076-0198-5); pap. 3.95 (ISBN 0-8076-0390-2). Braziller.

Louis I. Kahn: Romaldo Giurgola & Jaimini Mehta. 39.50 (ISBN 0-89158-502-8). Westview.

Louis Sullivan. 7.95 (ISBN 0-8076-0129-2); pap. 3.95 (ISBN 0-8076-0227-2). Braziller.

Louise Nevelson. cancelled (ISBN 0-8109-0339-3). Abrams.

Louise Nevelson. pap. 13.95 (ISBN 0-525-47439-0). Dutton.

Louisiana Cajuns. 14.95 (ISBN 0-8071-0363-2). La State U Pr.

Louisiana Capitol: Its Art & Architecture. 19.95 (ISBN 0-88289-082-4). Pelican.

Louisiana Duck Decoys. 24.95 (ISBN 0-88289-191-X). Pelican.

Louisiana Images, 1880-1920: A Photographic History. pap. 6.95 (ISBN 0-8071-0151-6). La State U Pr.

Louisiana's Art Nouveau: Pottery & Crafts of the Newcomb Style. 25.00 (ISBN 0-88289-112-X). Pelican.

Louvre Dialogues. 10.00 (ISBN 0-689-10386-7). Atheneum.

Love Above All & Other Drawings. pap. 3.00 (ISBN 0-486-22675-1). Dover.

Love Above All & Other Drawings. 5.50 (ISBN 0-8446-0122-5). Peter Smith.

Love, Sunrise & Elevated Apes. 5.95 (ISBN 0-393-08694-1, 8694); pap. 2.50 (ISBN 0-393-08699-2, 8699). Norton.

Lovely Hull Pottery. softbound 6.95 (ISBN 0-87069-084-1). Wallace-Homestead.

Lovely Hull Pottery: With Price Guide. softbound 6.95 (ISBN 0-87069-204-6); price guide 1.50 (ISBN 0-87069-209-7). Wallace-Homestead.

Lovers. 5.95 (ISBN 0-8090-2130-7). Hill & Wang.

Luca Signorelli. 19.00 (ISBN 0-403-00912-X). Scholarly.

Lucy's Bag Book. 12.95 (ISBN 0-395-26302-6); pap. 6.95 (ISBN 0-395-26473-1). HM.

Ludwig Mies Van Der Rohe. 7.95 (ISBN 0-8076-0108-X); pap. 3.95 (ISBN 0-8076-0222-1). Braziller.

Ludwig Mies van der Rohe. lib. bdg. 16.00 (ISBN 0-8240-9830-7). Garland Pub.

Luger Pistol. rev. ed. 9.50. Borden.

Lure of Antique Arms. 9.95 (ISBN 0-679-20299-4). Arma Pr.

Lure of Antique Arms. pap. 5.95 (ISBN 0-695-80928-8). Follett.

Lure of Antiques. pap. 2.45 (ISBN 0-7195-0516-X). Transatlantic.

Luxardo Bottles. pap. 4.75. Borden.

Luxor: A Guide to Ancient Thebes. 2nd ed. pap. text ed. 4.50x (ISBN 0-582-78065-9). Longman.

Lydian Houses & Architectural Terracottas. 14.00x (ISBN 0-674-53959-1). Harvard U Pr.

Lyonel Feininger: Caricature & Fantasy. 17.50x (ISBN 0-8143-1202-0). Wayne St U Pr.

Lysippos. lib. bdg. 27.75x (ISBN 0-8371-0119-0, JOLY). Greenwood.

M

M. H. Baillie Scott & the Arts & Crafts Movement: Pioneers of Modern Design. 35.00x (ISBN 0-8018-1112-0). Johns Hopkins.

McCall's Do It Yourself Traditional Decorating. 7.95 (ISBN 0-394-49065-7). Random.

Machine Stitchery. 10.50 (ISBN 0-8231-5046-1). Branford.

Machine Woodworking. rev. ed. text ed. 10.64 (ISBN 0-87345-010-8). McKnight.

McKim, Mead & White. 14.00 (ISBN 0-405-08877-9). Arno.

Mackintosh Watercolours. 20.00 (ISBN 0-8008-5044-0). Taplinger.

Mackintosh Watercolours. pap. cancelled (ISBN 0-8008-5043-2). Taplinger.

Macmillan Wild Flower Book. 19.95 (ISBN 0-02-557990-8). Macmillan.

Macrame. 7.95 (ISBN 0-671-27108-3). Trident.

Macrame Book. 14.95 (ISBN 0-684-12756-3). Scribner.

Macrame Made Easy. pap. 3.95 (ISBN 0-02-011170-3). Macmillan.

Madame Alexander Collector's Dolls. 19.95 (ISBN 0-89145-054-8). Collector Bks.

Madame Alexander Collector's Dolls. 19.95 (ISBN 0-517-25835-8). Crown.

Made in America. lib. bdg. 15.00 (ISBN 0-374-94626-4). Octagon.

Made in America. 7.00 (ISBN 0-8103-3396-1). Gale.

Made in Occupied Japan: A Collector's Guide. pap. 6.95 (ISBN 0-517-52661-1). Crown.

Made in the Renaissance. 6.95 (ISBN 0-525-34396-2). Dutton.

Made in West Africa. 9.95 (ISBN 0-525-34400-4). Dutton.

Made with Oak. pap. 5.95 (ISBN 0-8256-3052-5). Music Sales.

Maggie Lane's Needlepoint Pillows. encore ed. 4.95 (ISBN 0-684-16199-0); pap. 6.95 (ISBN 0-684-14724-6, SL672). Scribner.

Maggie Lane's Oriental Patchwork: Elegant Designs for Easy Living. 16.95 (ISBN 0-684-15621-0). Scribner.

Magic Crayon. 4.95 (ISBN 0-87460-003-0); PLB 4.59 (ISBN 0-87460-089-8). Lion.

Magic Doors. 10.95 (ISBN 0-201-05668-2); pap. 6.95 (ISBN 0-201-05669-0). A-W.

Magic Image: The Genius of Photography from 1839 to the Present Day. 19.95 (ISBN 0-316-08597-9). Little.

Magic Mirror of M. C. Escher. 15.00 (ISBN 0-394-49217-X). Random.

Magic Mirror of M. C. Escher. pap. 6.95 (ISBN 0-345-24243-2). Ballantine.

Magic of Light. 15.00. Theatre Arts.

Magic of Light: The Craft & Career of Jean Rosenthal, Pioneer in Lighting for the Modern Stage. 15.00 (ISBN 0-316-93120-9). Little.

Magic Pear. new ed. 2.95 (ISBN 0-8055-0352-8). Hart.

Magic Pen of Joseph Clement Coll. pap. 8.95 (ISBN 0-89134-009-2). North Light Pub.

Magic Realist Landscape Painting: Techniques in Oil, Watercolor, Egg Tempera, & Acrylic. 16.95 (ISBN 0-8230-2955-7). Watson-Guptill.

Magic Realist Painting Techniques. 17.95 (ISBN 0-8230-2956-5). Watson-Guptill.

Magic Realist Watercolor Painting. 18.50 (ISBN 0-8230-2957-3). Watson-Guptill.

Magic Worlds of Fantasy. 14.95 (ISBN 0-15-155102-2). HarBraceJ.

Magnificent Dreams: Burne-Jones & the Late Victorians. 12.95 (ISBN 0-7148-1827-5); pap. 6.95 (ISBN 0-7148-1909-3). Dutton.

Magnum in Parvo. 12.50 (ISBN 0-405-08589-3). Arno.

Magritte. 17.50 (ISBN 0-8212-0387-8); pap. 8.95 (ISBN 0-8212-0520-X). NYGS.

Magritte. 5.95 (ISBN 0-517-53009-0). Crown.

Magubane's South Africa. 12.95 (ISBN 0-394-50016-4); pap. 7.95 (ISBN 0-394-73565-X). Knopf.

Mahayana Buddhist Sculpture of Ceylon. lib. bdg. 40.00 (ISBN 0-8240-2685-3). Garland Pub.

Mail-Order Crafts Catalogue: Supplies, Kits, Finished Items, Publications, Home Study Courses, Organizations, Services. pap. 7.95 (ISBN 0-8019-5882-2). Chilton.

Maillol. 5.95 (ISBN 0-517-02688-0). Crown.

Maine & Its Role in American Art: 1740-1963. 8.00 (ISBN 0-910394-09-1). Colby.

Maine Made Guns & Their Makers. 22.00 (ISBN 0-913764-04-3). Maine St Mus.

Mainstreams of Modern Art. text ed. 18.95 (ISBN 0-03-005030-8). HR&W.

Mainstreams of Modern Art: David to Picasso. 29.95 (ISBN 0-671-44020-9). S&S.

Major European Art Movements 1900-1945: A Critical Anthology. pap. 9.95 (ISBN 0-525-47462-5). Dutton.

Major Themes in Japanese Art. 17.50 (ISBN 0-8348-1003-4). Weatherhill.

Make a Mobile. 7.95 (ISBN 0-87599-206-4). S G Phillips.

Make a Witch, Make a Goblin: A Book of Halloween Crafts. 6.95g (ISBN 0-590-07450-4). Schol Bk Serv.

Make & Furnish Your Own Miniature Rooms. 16.95 (ISBN 0-8015-4808-X). Hawthorn.

Make & Furnish Your Own Miniature Rooms. pap. 9.95 (ISBN 0-8015-4811-X). Hawthorn.

Make It with Burlap. PLB 6.00 (ISBN 0-688-50037-4). Lothrop.

Make It with Felt: An Art & Craft Book. PLB 6.00 (ISBN 0-688-50984-3). Lothrop.

Make It with Paper. 6.95 (ISBN 0-679-50263-7). McKay.

Make-It-Yourself Shoe Book. 10.00 (ISBN 0-394-41057-2); pap. 4.95 (ISBN 0-394-73303-7). Knopf.

Make Things Grandma Made. 6.95 (ISBN 0-8008-5052-1). Taplinger.

Make Things Sailors Made. 6.95 (ISBN 0-8008-5053-X). Taplinger.

Make Use of Your Garden Plants. 8.95 (ISBN 0-517-53198-4). Barre.

Make Your Choice: 80 Things to Make for Yourself & the Home. 7.50 (ISBN 0-263-05515-9). Transatlantic.

Make Your Garden New Again. 9.95 (ISBN 0-671-21949-9). S&S.

Make Your Own Antiques. pap. 5.95 (ISBN 0-316-33783-8). Little.

Make Your Own Chess Set. 8.95 (ISBN 0-13-547802-2); pap. 2.95 (ISBN 0-13-547786-7). P-H.

Make Your Own Dollhouses & Dollhouse Miniatures. pap. 8.95 (ISBN 0-8015-4799-7). Hawthorn.

Make Your Own Dollhouses & Dollhouse Miniatures. 16.95 (ISBN 0-8015-4801-2); pap. 8.95 (ISBN 0-8015-4799-7). Hawthorn.

Make Your Own Dolls. PLB 6.00 (ISBN 0-688-51570-3). Lothrop.

Make Your Own Doll's House. 8.95 (ISBN 0-442-21618-1). Van Nos Reinhold.

Make Your Own Miniature Rooms. pap. 8.95 (ISBN 0-87588-139-4). Hobby Hse.

Make Your Own Silk Flowers. 7.95 (ISBN 0-8069-5318-7); PLB 7.49 (ISBN 0-8069-5319-5). Sterling.

Make Your Own Thing: Games, Puzzles, Gimmicks & Gifts. PLB 7.29 (ISBN 0-671-32906-5). Messner.

Make Your Pet a Present. 6.75 (ISBN 0-688-41788-4); PLB 6.48 (ISBN 0-688-51788-9). Lothrop.

Makers of America: Stamps That Honor Them. PLB 7.29 (ISBN 0-671-32869-7). Messner.

Making a Dress. 3.95 (ISBN 0-8208-0314-6). Hearthside.

Making a Miniature House. 8.25x (ISBN 0-19-273090-8). Oxford U Pr.

Making American Folk Art Dolls. pap. 6.95 (ISBN 0-8019-6123-8). Chilton.

Making & Improving Plastic Models. 4.95 (ISBN 0-7153-6698-X). David & Charles.

Making Artist's Tools. 15.95 (ISBN 0-442-27903-5). Van Nos Reinhold.

Making Children's Furniture & Play Structures. 8.95 (ISBN 0-911104-24-0); pap. 3.95 (ISBN 0-911104-25-9). Workman Pub.

Making Clothes in Leather. 10.95 (ISBN 0-8008-5063-7). Taplinger.

Making Costumes for Parties, Plays & Holidays. PLB 6.00 (ISBN 0-688-30103-7). Morrow.

Making Designs by Chance. 5.75 (ISBN 0-688-20107-5); PLB 5.52 (ISBN 0-688-30107-X). Morrow.

Making Dollhouse Accessories: Patterns & Directions for Rooms, Furniture, Animal Companions, Utensils, & Vehicles for Full-Size Dolls. 8.95 (ISBN 0-517-52878-9); pap. 4.95 (ISBN 0-517-52879-7). Crown.

Making Dolls for Pleasure & Profit. 7.95 (ISBN 0-668-04534-5, 4534). Arco.

Making Furry Toys. 4.95 (ISBN 0-236-15424-9). Merrimack Bk Serv.

Making Gifts. PLB 3.95 (ISBN 0-8225-0867-2). Lerner Pubns.

Making Gifts from Oddments & Outdoor Materials. 8.95 (ISBN 0-8208-0069-4). Hearthside.

Making Glove Puppets. 12.95 (ISBN 0-8238-0144-6). Plays.

Making Historical Costume Dolls. 9.25 (ISBN 0-8231-3031-2). Branford.

Making It Legal: A Law Primer for the Craftmaker, Visual Artist, & Writer. pap. 6.95 (ISBN 0-07-015431-7). McGraw.

Making Jewelry. PLB 7.98 (ISBN 0-8393-0116-2). Raintree Child.

Making Jewelry. PLB 3.95 (ISBN 0-8225-0862-1). Lerner Pubns.

Making Jewelry & Sculpture Through Unit Construction. pap. 2.75 (ISBN 0-486-23678-1). Dover.

Making Lampshades. pap. 4.95 (ISBN 0-8473-1560-6). Sterling.

Making Leaf Rubbings. pap. 3.95 (ISBN 0-8289-0334-4). Greene.

Making Masks for School Plays. 7.95 (ISBN 0-8238-0131-4). Plays.

Making Mediterranean Furniture. pap. 3.95 (ISBN 0-668-04432-2). Arco.

Making Miniature Toys & Dolls. 9.95 (ISBN 0-442-22837-6); pap. 5.95 (ISBN 0-442-22838-4). Van Nos Reinhold.

Making Mobiles. 7.95 (ISBN 0-87523-167-5). Emerson.

Making Model Soldiers of the World. pap. 5.95 (ISBN 0-8120-0822-7). Barron.

Making Money in Autographs. 8.95 (ISBN 0-698-10747-0). Coward.

Making New Testament Toys. 7.95 (ISBN 0-8008-5078-5). Taplinger.

Making New Testament Toys. pap. 3.95 (ISBN 0-8015-4802-0). Hawthorn.

Making Nice Things Out of Straw. 7.95 (ISBN 0-679-20452-0). McKay.

Making Nonprojected Visuals & Displays. new ed. pap. 2.50 (ISBN 0-8054-3419-4). Broadman.

Making of Books. 5th ed. 24.00 (ISBN 0-571-04786-6). Merrimack Bk Serv.

Making Old Testament Toys. 7.95 (ISBN 0-8008-5079-3). Taplinger.

Making Old Testament Toys. pap. 3.95 (ISBN 0-8015-4804-7). Hawthorn.

Making Paper & Fabric Flowers. 4.95 (ISBN 0-8208-0317-0). Hearthside.

Making Paper Costumes. 8.95 (ISBN 0-8238-0147-0). Plays.

Making Paper Flowers. 3.95 (ISBN 0-8069-5130-3); PLB 4.59 (ISBN 0-8069-5131-1). Sterling.

Making Paper Flowers & Decorations. 7.95 (ISBN 0-8008-5057-2). Taplinger.

Making Photograms: The Creative Process of Painting with Light. 12.50 (ISBN 0-8038-4650-9). Focal Pr.

Making Photographs: A Workbook of Materials. 16.95 (ISBN 0-442-23156-3). Van Nos Reinhold.

Making Pictures Without Paint. 5.75 (ISBN 0-688-20068-0); PLB 5.52 (ISBN 0-688-30068-5). Morrow.

Making Pottery Figures. 6.75 (ISBN 0-85458-080-8); pap. 4.50 (ISBN 0-85458-081-6). Transatlantic.

Making Pottery Without a Wheel. 16.95 (ISBN 0-442-11024-3). Van Nos Reinhold.

Making Pottery Without a Wheel. pap. 5.95 (ISBN 0-442-20541-4). Van Nos Reinhold.

Making Puppets & Puppet Theatres. 7.95 (ISBN 0-8119-0242-0). Fell.

Making Puppets Come Alive: Method of Learning & Teaching Hand Puppetry. 9.95 (ISBN 0-8008-5074-2). Taplinger.

Mazeppa Legend in European Romanticism. 15.00x (ISBN 0-231-03825-9). Columbia U Pr.
Mazes & Labyrinths: Their History & Development. pap. 3.50 (ISBN 0-486-22614-X). Dover.
Mazes & Labyrinths: Their History & Development. 7.50 (ISBN 0-8446-0790-8). Peter Smith.
M.C. Escher Kaleidocycles. pap. 8.95 (ISBN 0-345-25686-7). Ballantine.
Meaning & Truth in the Arts. pap. 4.50x (ISBN 0-8078-4008-4). U of NC Pr.
Meaning in the Visual Arts. 3.50 (ISBN 0-385-09248-2, A59). Doubleday.
Meaning in the Visual Arts. new ed. 15.00 (ISBN 0-87951-024-2). Overlook Pr.
Meaning of Art. lib. bdg. 15.00 (ISBN 0-8495-4506-4). Arden Lib.
Meaning of Mannerism. text ed. 7.50x (ISBN 0-87451-068-6). U Pr of New England.
Meaning of Modern Art: A Philosophical Interpretation. 6.50x (ISBN 0-8101-0113-0). Northwestern U Pr.
Meaning of Modern Sculpture. 17.50 (ISBN 0-404-14757-7). AMS Pr.
Meaning of Unintelligibility in Modern Art. 8.00 (ISBN 0-88211-041-1). Oriole Edns.
Measure & Design in American Painting, 1760-1860. lib. bdg. 46.00 (ISBN 0-8240-2675-6). Garland Pub.
Measured Drawings of Early American Furniture. pap. 3.00 (ISBN 0-486-23057-0). Dover.
Measured Drawings of Early American Furniture. 9.00 (ISBN 0-8446-5233-4). Peter Smith.
Mechanical Composition. Incl. Line Composition (ISBN 0-08-013964-7); The Monotype Keyboard (ISBN 0-08-013965-5); Caster Metallurgy (ISBN 0-08-013966-3). pap. 2.00 ea. Pergamon.
Mechanical Drafting Essentials. 4th ed. text ed. 13.60 (ISBN 0-13-568931-7). P-H.
Mechanick Exercises on the Whole Art of Printing. pap. 7.95 (ISBN 0-486-23617-X). Dover.
Medallas De Proclamaciones y Juras De los Reyes De Espana En America. 30.00x (ISBN 0-88000-017-1). Quarterman.
Medallic Art of the United States, 1800-1972. pap. 3.00x (ISBN 0-9600182-9-8). Norton Art.
Medallic Portraits of Washington. lib. bdg. 29.50 (ISBN 0-915262-24-X). S J Durst.
Medals & Plaquettes from the Molinari Collection at Bowdoin College. 40.00x (ISBN 0-916606-00-7); pap. 17.50x (ISBN 0-8195-8039-2). Wesleyan U Pr.
Medardo Rosso. 13.00 (ISBN 0-405-01558-5). Arno.
Mediaeval Arabic Bookmaking & Its Relation to Early Chemistry & Pharmacology. pap. 1.00 (ISBN 0-87169-524-3). Am Philos.
Mediaeval Church Architecture of England. facsimile ed. 22.00 (ISBN 0-8369-6738-0). Arno.
Mediaeval Church Vaulting. 14.50 (ISBN 0-404-06836-7). AMS Pr.
Mediaeval Floor Tiles. 21.50 (ISBN 0-312-52570-2). St Martin.
Mediaeval Musical Relics of Denmark. 24.50 (ISBN 0-404-12952-8). AMS Pr.
Medical Photography; Clinical-Ultraviolet-Infrared. new ed. 14.95 (ISBN 0-87985-076-0, N-18). Eastman Kodak.
Medici Emerald. 8.95 (ISBN 0-525-15458-2). Dutton.
Medicine & the Artist. pap. 5.50 (ISBN 0-486-22133-4). Dover.
Medieval & Renaissance Miniatures from the National Gallery of Art. pap. 8.95. Natl Gallery Art.
Medieval Architecture. lib. bdg. 45.00 (ISBN 0-8240-2414-1). Garland Pub.
Medieval Architecture. 7.95 (ISBN 0-8076-0174-8); pap. 5.95 (ISBN 0-8076-0336-8). Braziller.
Medieval Art. lib. bdg. 45.00 (ISBN 0-8240-2415-X). Garland Pub.
Medieval Art from Private Collections: A Special Exhibition at the Cloisters. pap. 4.95 (ISBN 0-87099-161-2). Metro Mus Art.
Medieval Art from the Peace of the Church to the Eve of the Renaissance, 312-1350. lib. bdg. 19.50x (ISBN 0-8371-2554-5). Greenwood.
Medieval Cities. pap. 5.95 (ISBN 0-8076-0471-2). Braziller.
Medieval Latin Scientific Writings in the Barberini Collection: A Provisional Catalogue. 8.50x (ISBN 0-226-75766-8). U of Chicago Pr.
Medieval Pottery from Excavations. 18.95 (ISBN 0-312-52745-4). St Martin.
Medieval Structure: The Gothic Vault. 30.00x (ISBN 0-8020-1886-6). U of Toronto Pr.
Medieval Studies in Memory of A. Kingsley Porter. facs. ed. 70.00 (ISBN 0-8369-1044-3). Arno.
Medieval Theatre Costume. 7.45 (ISBN 0-87830-081-3). Theatre Arts.
Medinet Habu: The Eastern High Gate with Translations of the Texts Epigraphic Survey. lib. bdg. 72.00x (ISBN 0-226-62197-9, OIP94). U of Chicago Pr.
Meditations on a Hobby Horse: And Other Essays on the Theory of Art. pap. 5.95 (ISBN 0-7148-1830-5). Dutton.
Meet Miss Liberty. 4.50g (ISBN 0-02-770570-6). Macmillan.
Meeting of Eastern & Western Art from the Sixteenth Century to the Present Day. 17.50 (ISBN 0-8212-0543-9). NYGS.
Megalithic Architecture in Southern India. pap. 2.50x (ISBN 0-913134-97-X). Mus Anthro Mo.
Megaliths, Myths, & Men. pap. 4.95 (ISBN 0-06-090578-6, CN578). Har-Row.
Megaliths, Myths & Men: An Introduction to Astro-Archaeology. 13.95 (ISBN 0-8008-5187-0). Taplinger.
Meiji Western Painting. 12.50 (ISBN 0-8348-2708-5). Weatherhill.
Meissen China: An Illustrated History. pap. 7.50 (ISBN 0-486-21958-5). Dover.
Meissen Porcelain. 3.95 (ISBN 0-88254-337-7). Hippocrene Bks.
Melanesian Design: A Study of Style in Wood & Tortoiseshell Carving. 50.00 (ISBN 0-87817-021-9). Hacker.
Melanesian Design: A Study of Style in Wood & Tortoiseshell Carving. 95.00 (ISBN 0-404-50568-6). AMS Pr.
Melanesian Shell Money in Field Museum Collections. pap. 6.00 (ISBN 0-527-01879-1). Kraus Repr.
Melbourne Churches, 1836-1851. 32.50x (ISBN 0-522-83602-X). Intl Schol Bk Serv.
Melnikov: Solo Architect in a Mass Society. text ed. 25.00 (ISBN 0-691-03931-3). Princeton U Pr.
Memoir of an Art Gallery. 8.95 (ISBN 0-399-11847-0). Putnam.
Memoir of David Scott, R. S. A. 24.50 (ISBN 0-404-05646-6). AMS Pr.
Memoir of George Edmund Street, R. A. 1824-1881. 20.00 (ISBN 0-405-09007-2). Arno.
Memoir of Thomas Bewick: Written by Himself. 19.95x (ISBN 0-19-255413-1). Oxford U Pr.
Memoirs of a Dada Drummer. 16.50 (ISBN 0-670-46791-X). Viking Pr.
Memoirs of Giorgio De Chirico. 13.95x (ISBN 0-87024-125-7). U of Miami Pr.
Memorial of Horatio Greenough. 15.00 (ISBN 0-405-09033-1). Arno.
Memorials for Children of Change: The Art of Early New England Stonecarving. 22.50x (ISBN 0-8195-4061-7). Wesleyan U Pr.
Memorials of Edward Burne-Jones. 35.00 (ISBN 0-405-08334-3). Arno.
Memphite Tomb-Chapel of Mose. 36.00 (ISBN 0-85668-088-5). Intl Schol Bk Serv.
Men & Memories. 40.00 set (ISBN 0-8274-2723-9). R West.
Men & Monuments. facs. ed. 17.50 (ISBN 0-8369-1876-2). Arno.
Men at Work. pap. 3.00 (ISBN 0-486-23475-4). Dover.
Men at Work: Photographic Modern Men & Machines. 6.50 (ISBN 0-8446-5585-6). Peter Smith.
Men in Stitches. 13.95 (ISBN 0-442-23630-1). Van Nos Reinhold.
Men, Women, and Dogs. 8.95 (ISBN 0-396-07206-2). Dodd.
Mending & Restoring Upholstery & Soft Furnishings. 7.95 (ISBN 0-498-01742-7). A S Barnes.
Meroitic Funerary Inscriptions from Arminna West. 20.00. Penn-Yale Expedit.
Mervyn Peake. 10.95 (ISBN 0-312-53025-0). St Martin.
Mesopotamia. 29.50x (ISBN 0-88254-248-6). Hippocrene Bks.
Messiah: A Photographic Meditation on Handel's Messiah. pap. 5.95 (ISBN 0-03-045721-1). Winston Pr.
Metabolism in Architecture. 25.00 (ISBN 0-89158-734-9). Westview.
Metal & Wire Sculpture. 3.95 (ISBN 0-8069-5128-1); PLB 4.59 (ISBN 0-8069-5129-X). Sterling.
Metal Craft. pap. 2.95 (ISBN 0-915462-04-4). Paragraph Pr.
Metal-Crafting Encyclopedia. 14.95 (ISBN 0-8069-5336-5); lib. bdg. 13.29 (ISBN 0-8069-5337-3). Sterling.
Metal: Design & Technique. 35.00 (ISBN 0-442-21039-6). Van Nos Reinhold.
Metal Enameling. 8.95 (ISBN 0-517-02560-4). Crown.
Metal Jewelry Techniques. 18.95 (ISBN 0-8230-3036-9). Watson-Guptill.
Metal Projects. pap. 4.00 (ISBN 0-87006-238-7). Goodheart.
Metal Projects. pap. 4.00 (ISBN 0-87006-153-4). Goodheart.
Metal Techniques for Craftsmen. 19.95 (ISBN 0-385-03027-4). Doubleday.
Metal Thread Embroidery. 12.95 (ISBN 0-8008-5200-1). Taplinger.
Metal Thread Embroidery. rev. ed. 17.50 (ISBN 0-8230-3044-X). Watson-Guptill.
Metal Working. text ed. 4.40 (ISBN 0-87006-258-1). Goodheart.
Metallic Ornaments of the New York Indians. 12.00 (ISBN 0-404-11814-3). AMS Pr.
Metalsmithing for the Artist-Craftsman. 11.25 (ISBN 0-8019-0465-X). Chilton.
Metalsmiths. PLB 9.63 (ISBN 0-8094-1309-4). Silver.
Metalsmiths. 7.95 (ISBN 0-8094-1312-4); lib. bdg. avail. Time-Life.
Metalwork. rev. ed. ans. sheet avail 7.96; 10.60 (ISBN 0-87002-048-X). Bennett Co.
Metalwork & Enamelling. 4th ed. pap. 4.00 (ISBN 0-486-22702-2). Dover.
Metalwork & Enamelling: A Practical Treatise on Gold & Silversmiths' Work & Their Allied Crafts. lib. bdg. 11.50x (ISBN 0-88307-195-9). Gannon.
Metalwork & Enamelling: A Practical Treatise on Gold & Silversmiths' Work & Their Allied Crafts. 5th & rev. ed. 7.00 (ISBN 0-8446-0198-5). Peter Smith.
Metalwork Essentials. rev. ed. 6.00 (ISBN 0-02-829540-4). Glencoe.
Metalwork for Craftsmen: A Step by Step Guide with 55 Projects. pap. 3.00 (ISBN 0-486-22789-8). Dover.
Metalwork for Craftsmen: A Step-by-Step Guide with 55 Projects. 7.50 (ISBN 0-8446-0171-3). Peter Smith.
Metalworking. 3.96 (ISBN 0-87345-792-7); softbound 2.64 (ISBN 0-87345-784-6). McKnight.
Metalworking for Jewelry: Tools, Materials, Techniques. 15.95 (ISBN 0-442-26143-8). Van Nos Reinhold.
Metalworking for the Designer & Technician. pap. text ed. 13.95x (ISBN 0-910482-86-1). Drama Bk.
Metalworking Handbook: Principles & Procedures. lib. bdg. 12.50 (ISBN 0-668-03857-8). Arco.
Metamorphoseon...Ovidianarum. lib. bdg. 66.00 (ISBN 0-8240-2067-7). Garland Pub.
Metamorphosis of a Death Symbol: The Changing Meaning of the Transi Tomb in the Late Middle Ages & the Renaissance. 37.50x (ISBN 0-520-01844-3). U of Cal Pr.
Metamorphosis of the Gods. 15.00 (ISBN 0-385-00955-0). Doubleday.
Metaphorical Eye: Special Effects in Photography. 15.95 (ISBN 0-8174-0599-2). Amphoto.
Metaphysical Art. text ed. 7.95 (ISBN 0-19-520008-X). Oxford U Pr.
Method & Theory in Historical Archeology. 19.75 (ISBN 0-12-655750-0). Acad Pr.
Method of Lighting the Stage. 6.95 (ISBN 0-87830-082-1). Theatre Arts.
Methodenlehre der Kunstgeschichte: Ein Handbuch Fur Studierende. 20.50 (ISBN 0-8337-1639-5). B Franklin.
Methods & Materials of Painting of the Great Schools & Masters. pap. 6.00 ea.; pap. (ISBN 0-486-20718-8); pap. (ISBN 0-486-20719-6). Dover.
Methods of Architectural Programming. 20.00 (ISBN 0-87933-253-0). DH&R.
Methods of Construction of Celtic Art. 8.50 (ISBN 0-8446-4706-3). Peter Smith.
Methods of Teaching Shop & Technical Subjects. pap. text ed. 5.60 (ISBN 0-8273-0360-2). Delmar.
Metodologia para la Ensenanza De las Artes Industriales y la Educacion Vocacional Industrial. pap. text ed. 6.25 (ISBN 0-8477-2722-X). U of PR Pr.
Metric Pattern Cutting. 11.95 (ISBN 0-263-06119-1). Transatlantic.
Metropolitan Museum of Art, New York. 14.95 (ISBN 0-88225-241-0). Newsweek.
Metropolitan Museum of Art: Notable Acquisitions, 1965-1975. pap. 12.50 (ISBN 0-87099-141-8). Metro Mus Art.
Mexican American Artists. 15.00 (ISBN 0-292-75006-4); pap. 9.95 (ISBN 0-292-75048-X). U of Tex Pr.
Mexican Archaeology. 24.00 (ISBN 0-527-46850-9). Kraus Repr.
Mexican Archaeology. 20.00 (ISBN 0-87817-031-6). Hacker.
Mexican Architecture of the Sixteenth Century. lib. bdg. 60.00x (ISBN 0-8371-6256-4, KUMA). Greenwood.
Mexican Architecture of the Vice-Regal Period. lib. bdg. 34.95 (ISBN 0-8490-2233-9). Gordon Pr.
Mexican Architecture of the Vice-Regal Period. 19.75 (ISBN 0-404-03675-9). AMS Pr.
Mexican Art & the Academy of San Carlos, 1785-1915. 8.50x (ISBN 0-292-73303-8). U of Tex Pr.
Mexican Folk Retablos: Masterpieces on Tin. 28.50 (ISBN 0-8165-0322-2). U of Ariz Pr.
Mexican Homes of Today. 16.50 (ISBN 0-8038-0157-2). Architectural.
Mexican Interiors. 16.50 (ISBN 0-8038-0159-9). Architectural.
Mexican Jewelry. 9.95 (ISBN 0-292-73305-4). U of Tex Pr.
Mexican Landscape Architecture-from the Street & From Within. 27.50 (ISBN 0-8165-0327-3). U of Ariz Pr.
Mexican Masks. pap. 2.00 (ISBN 0-88360-004-8). Amon Carter.
Mexican Popular Arts: A Fond Glance at the Craftsmen & Their Handiwork in Ceramics, Textiles, Metals, Glass, Paint, Fibres, & Other Materials. 12.00x (ISBN 0-87917-034-4). Blaine Ethridge.
Mexican Popular Arts: Mexico Ser. lib. bdg. 34.95 (ISBN 0-8490-2239-8). Gordon Pr.
Mexican Tapestry Weaving. wrap-around spiral bdg., leatherette 9.95 (ISBN 0-9602098-0-8). J Arvidson.
Mexico Before Cortez: Art, History, & Legend. 6.00 (ISBN 0-8446-1669-9). Peter Smith.
Mexico Before Cortez: Art, History & Legend. rev. ed. 2.50 (ISBN 0-385-01068-0, 936). Doubleday.
Mi Fu & the Classical Tradition of Chinese Calligraphy. text ed. 30.00 (ISBN 0-691-03937-2). Princeton U Pr.
Michael Cardew. 25.00 (ISBN 0-87011-277-5). Kodansha.
Michael Naranjo. PLB 5.95 (ISBN 0-87518-111-2). Dillon.
Michelangelo: Six Lectures by Johannes Wilde. 23.50x (ISBN 0-19-817316-4); pap. 11.95x (ISBN 0-19-817346-6). Oxford U Pr.
Michelangelo's David: A Search for Identity. pap. 3.95 (ISBN 0-393-00735-9). Norton.
Michelangelo's Theory of Art. 17.50x (ISBN 0-8147-0084-5). NYU Pr.
Michelangelo's Three Pietas. 35.00 (ISBN 0-8109-0340-7). Abrams.
Michele Felice Corne: 1752-1845. pap. 3.00 (ISBN 0-87577-042-8). Peabody Mus Salem.
Michelozzo. lib. bdg. 95.00 (ISBN 0-8240-2678-0). Garland Pub.
Mickey Mouse: Fifty Happy Years. 12.95 (ISBN 0-517-52962-9). Harmony.
Mickey Mouse Make-It Book. 3.50 (ISBN 0-394-82555-1); PLB 4.39 (ISBN 0-394-92555-6). Random.
Micrographics 1900-1977: A Bibliography. PLB 19.00 (ISBN 0-933474-01-6). Minn Scholarly.
Microorganism Control. pap. 23.00 (ISBN 0-87010-051-3). Inst Paper Chem.
Mid-Georgian Silver. 2.95 (ISBN 0-600-43129-0). Transatlantic.
Middle-Earth Album. 14.95 (ISBN 0-671-24954-1); pap. 7.95 (ISBN 0-671-24928-2). S&S.
Middle Earth: The World of Tolkien Illustrated. pap. 6.95 (ISBN 0-87818-014-1). Centaur.
Middle Eastern Cities: A Symposium on Ancient, Islamic, & Contemporary Middle Eastern Urbanism. 14.50x (ISBN 0-520-03850-9). U of Cal Pr.
Mightier Than the Sword: Cartoon, Caricature, Social Comment. 7.50 (ISBN 0-15-253860-7). HarBraceJ.
Migration of Symbols. 21.00 (ISBN 0-8337-0762-0). B Franklin.
Military Buttons of the Gulf Coast 1711-1830. pap. write for info. Museum Mobile.
Military Miniatures: The Art of Making Model Soldiers. 15.00 (ISBN 0-8019-6721-X); pap. 8.50 (ISBN 0-8019-6722-8). Chilton.
Milkbottle Manual: A Collector's Pictorial Primer & Pricing Guide. pap. 4.95 (ISBN 0-911068-07-4). Old Time.
Mill & Mansion: A Study of Architecture & Society in Lowell, Massachusetts, 1820-1865. 19.00 (ISBN 0-8462-0866-0). Russell.
Milton & English Art. 15.00x (ISBN 0-8020-1708-8). U of Toronto Pr.
Mind & Art of Giovanni Battista Piranesi. 39.95 (ISBN 0-500-09122-6). Thames Hudson.
Mind & Art of Victorian England. 15.00x (ISBN 0-8166-0772-9). U of Minn Pr.
Mind & Image: An Essay on Art & Architecture. 22.50 (ISBN 0-8131-1323-7). U Pr of Ky.
Miniature Antique Furniture. 20.00 (ISBN 0-87098-049-1). Livingston.
Miniature Arms. 7.95 (ISBN 0-87691-011-8). Arma Pr.
Miniature Lamps. 18.95 (ISBN 0-8407-4315-7). Nelson.
Miniature Needlepoint & Sewing Projects for Dollhouses. 13.95 (ISBN 0-8015-5072-6). Hawthorn.
Miniature Needlepoint & Sewing Projects for Dollhouses. pap. 7.95 (ISBN 0-8015-5073-4). Hawthorn.
Miniature Painting in the Latin Kingdom of Jerusalem. 87.50 (ISBN 0-404-16249-5). AMS Pr.
Miniature Room Settings. 12.50 (ISBN 0-8019-6678-7); pap. 6.95 (ISBN 0-8019-6679-5). Chilton.
Miniature Shops: How to Design & Make Them. 12.00 (ISBN 0-498-01783-4). A S Barnes.
Miniature Vignettes: A How-to Book of Three-Dimensional Scenes. 6.95 (ISBN 0-684-15237-1). Scribner.

Mornings in Florence: Being Simple Studies of Christian Art for English Travellers. 27.50 (ISBN 0-403-00306-7). Scholarly.

Mosaic Knitting. 7.95 (ISBN 0-684-15961-9). Scribner.

Mosaic Making Techniques. encore ed. 3.95 (ISBN 0-684-16197-4); pap. 6.95 (ISBN 0-684-15356-4). Scribner.

Mosaic Techniques: New Aspects of Fragmented Design. 7.95 (025620). Crown.

Mosaics in Needlepoint. encore ed. 5.95 (ISBN 0-684-16201-6); pap. 7.95 (ISBN 0-684-15036-0, SL713). Scribner.

Mosaics in Roman Britain. 9.00x (ISBN 0-87471-158-4). Rowman.

Mosaics of Roman North Africa: Studies in Iconography & Patronage. 69.00 (ISBN 0-19-813217-4). Oxford U Pr.

Moscow: An Architectual History. 16.95 (ISBN 0-312-54888-5). St Martin.

Moscow Kremlin: Its History, Architecture, & Art Treasures. lib. bdg. 36.25x (ISBN 0-8371-5708-0, VOMK). Greenwood.

Mosque in Early Ottoman Architecture. 25.00x (ISBN 0-226-46293-5). U of Chicago Pr.

Most Beautiful Jewish Woman in the History of Mankind. deluxe ed. 42.50 (ISBN 0-930582-17-9). Gloucester Art.

Most Noble Art of Them All. 13.50x (ISBN 0-7022-1370-5). U of Queensland Pr.

Most Wonderful Dollhouse Book. 12.95 (ISBN 0-88421-076-6). Butterick Pub.

Mother & Child. new & rev. ed. 8.95 (ISBN 0-912020-23-7). Scrimshaw Calif.

Mother Goose in Stitches. 9.95 (ISBN 0-03-015201-1). HR&W.

Motion Picture Camera Techniques. pap. 8.95 (ISBN 0-8038-4700-9). Focal Pr.

Mount Rushmore. pap. 4.95 (ISBN 0-8061-0959-9). U of Okla Pr.

Mountain Artisans Quilting Book. 15.00 (ISBN 0-02-571260-8). Macmillan.

Mountain People, Mountain Crafts. 8.95 (ISBN 0-397-31498-1); pap. 3.95 (ISBN 0-397-31499-X). Lippincott.

Movements in Modern Art. 6.95 (ISBN 0-8180-0122-4). Horizon.

Movie-Star Portraits of the Forties: 163 Glamor Photos. pap. 6.00 (ISBN 0-486-23546-7). Dover.

Movie-Star Portraits of the Forties: 163 Glamour Photos. 10.00 (ISBN 0-8446-5594-5). Peter Smith.

Movietone Presents the 20th Century. 17.95 (ISBN 0-312-55055-3). St Martin.

Ms-Architect. 7.95 (ISBN 0-664-32615-3). Westminster.

Ms. Pinchpenny's Book of Interior Design. 12.95 (ISBN 0-442-26558-1). Van Nos Reinhold.

Much Loved Books. 7.95 (ISBN 0-87140-979-8). Liveright.

Much Loved Books: Best Sellers of the Ages. lib. bdg. 34.95 (ISBN 0-8490-2305-X). Gordon Pr.

Much of Jackson Pollock Is Vivid Wallpaper: An Essay in the Epistomology of Aesthetic Judgements. pap. text ed. 9.00x (ISBN 0-8191-0380-2). U Pr of Amer.

Mud Pie Dilemma: A Master Potter's Struggle to Make Art & Ends Meet. 14.95 (ISBN 0-917304-18-7). Intl Schol Bk Serv.

Mud, Space and Spirit: Handmade Adobes. pap. 7.95 (ISBN 0-88496-059-5). Capra Pr.

Mudra: A Study of Symbolic Gestures in Japanese Buddhist Sculpture. 20.00x (ISBN 0-691-09796-8). Princeton U Pr.

Muhammadan Architecture in Egypt & Palestine. lib. bdg. 17.50 (ISBN 0-306-70590-7). Da Capo.

Multiple Stage in Spain During the Fifteenth & Sixteenth Centuries. lib. bdg. 10.50x (ISBN 0-8371-5539-8, SHMS). Greenwood.

Multum in Parvo: An Essay in Poetic Imagination. 5.00 (ISBN 0-8076-0309-0). Braziller.

Mummies of Guanajuato. pap. 8.95 (ISBN 0-8109-2150-2). Abrams.

Munch. 7.95 (ISBN 0-7148-1799-6). Dutton.

Murals of Eugene Delacroix at Saint-Sulpice. 17.50x (ISBN 0-8147-0396-8). NYU Pr.

Murals Without Walls: Arshile Gorky's Aviation Murals Rediscovered. soft cover 7.95 (ISBN 0-932828-01-9). Newark Mus.

Muray's Celebrity Portraits of the Twenties & Thirties. pap. 5.00 (ISBN 0-486-23578-5). Dover.

Muses' Concord: Literature, Music & the Visual Arts in the Baroque Age. 12.95x (ISBN 0-253-33945-6). Ind U Pr.

Museum Cataloging in the Computer Age. 17.50 (ISBN 0-910050-12-0). AASLH.

Museum Collections of the Essex Institute. pap. 2.50 (ISBN 0-88389-070-4). Essex Inst.

Museum of Fine Arts, Boston: A Centennial History. 25.00 (ISBN 0-674-58875-4). Harvard U Pr.

Museum People. 8.95 (ISBN 0-13-606889-8). P-H.

Museums & Adult Education. lib. bdg. 8.50x (ISBN 0-678-07753-3). Kelley.

Museums in New York. pap. 5.95 (ISBN 0-8256-3112-2). Music Sales.

Museums of Yugoslavia. 14.95 (ISBN 0-88225-240-2). Newsweek.

Music, Acoustics & Architecture. lib. bdg. 33.00 (ISBN 0-88275-851-9). Krieger.

Music & Painting: A Study in Comparative Ideas from Turner to Schoenberg. pap. 4.95x (ISBN 0-06-430040-4, IN-40). Har-Row.

Music Engraving & Printing: Historical & Technical Treatise. lib. bdg. 17.50 (ISBN 0-306-70168-5). Da Capo.

Music Engraving & Printing: Historical & Technical Treatise. 18.00 (ISBN 0-405-08549-4). Arno.

Music in Prints: Fifty Two Prints Illustrating Musical Instruments from the 15th Century to the Present. 12.00 (ISBN 0-87104-124-3). NY Pub Lib.

Music Publishing in the Middle Western States Before the Civil War. pap. 4.00 (ISBN 0-911772-47-2). Info Coord.

Music 1900-1930 see New Arts.

Musical Comedy: A Story in Pictures. 12.00 (ISBN 0-8008-5460-8). Taplinger.

Musical Comedy in America: From the Black Crook Through Annie. write for info. (ISBN 0-87830-086-4); pap. write for info. (ISBN 0-87830-564-5). Theatre Arts.

Musical Instruments & Their Symbolism in Western Art. 24.95x (ISBN 0-300-02324-3); pap. 8.95 (ISBN 0-300-02376-6). Yale U Pr.

Musical Instruments in Art. PLB 4.95 (ISBN 0-8225-0160-0). Lerner Pubns.

Muslim Architecture of Egypt. lib. bdg. 250.00 (ISBN 0-87817-175-4). Hacker.

Mustard Seed Garden Manual of Painting: A Facsimile of the 1887-1888 Shanghai Edition. 20.00 (ISBN 0-691-09940-5); pap. 8.95 (ISBN 0-691-01819-7). Princeton U Pr.

Muybridge: Man in Motion. 18.50 (ISBN 0-520-02464-8). U of Cal Pr.

My Favorite Things. pap. 8.95 (ISBN 0-689-70548-4). Atheneum.

My Ivory Cellar. 6.50 (ISBN 0-8159-6217-7). Devin.

My Life in Sculpture. 10.00 (ISBN 0-670-50000-3). Viking Pr.

My Life with Sydney Laurence. 30.00 (ISBN 0-87564-010-9). Superior Pub.

My Threescore Years & Ten. 2nd ed. lib. bdg. 28.00 (ISBN 0-8240-2242-4). Garland Pub.

My Village, Sturbridge. 6.95 (ISBN 0-374-35110-4). FS&G.

My Way with a Camera. 15.95 (ISBN 0-8038-4701-7). Focal Pr.

My Way with Watercolor. 12.95. North Light Pub.

Mysteries of Chartres Cathedral. pap. 1.75 (ISBN 0-380-00386-4, 24596). Avon.

Mysteries of the Great Pyramids. pap. 2.25 (ISBN 0-380-00881-5, 31492). Avon.

Mysteries of the Mexican Pyramids. 22.50 (ISBN 0-06-014324-X). Har-Row.

Mystery of Masks. reinforced bdg. 7.95 (ISBN 0-684-15653-9). Scribner.

N

N. C. Wyeth. 29.95 (ISBN 0-517-50054-X). Crown.

Nagasaki Prints & Early Copperplates. 14.95 (ISBN 0-87011-311-9). Kodansha.

Nailsea Glass. 5.95 (ISBN 0-7153-6807-9). David & Charles.

Naked City. lib. bdg. 12.95 (ISBN 0-306-70724-1). Da Capo.

Namban Art. softbound 7.50 (ISBN 0-913304-01-8). Intl Exhibit Foun.

Namban Art of Japan. 17.50 (ISBN 0-8348-1008-5). Weatherhill.

Names on Trees: Ariosto into Art. 16.00 (ISBN 0-691-03914-3); pap. 5.95 (ISBN 0-691-00311-4). Princeton U Pr.

Nantucket Lightship Baskets. 2nd ed. 10.00 (ISBN 0-9600596-2-8); 5 or more 6.00. Deermouse.

Nara Picture Books. pap. 4.75 (ISBN 0-87093-045-1). Dawsons.

Narrative of Some of the Things of New Spain & of the Great City Temestitan Mexico. lib. bdg. 12.50 (ISBN 0-89341-276-7). Longwood Pr.

Narrative of Some Things of New Spain & of the Great City of Temestitan, Mexico. 10.00 (ISBN 0-527-19721-1). Kraus Repr.

Narrative Picture Scrolls. 12.50 (ISBN 0-8348-2710-7). Weatherhill.

Narrative Pictures: A Survey of English Genre & Its Painters. 22.00 (ISBN 0-405-08978-3). Arno.

National Exhibition Centre: Shop Window for the World. pap. 7.95x. Beekman Pubs.

National Gallery London. pap. 7.95 (ISBN 0-500-20161-7). Thames Hudson.

National Gallery of Art. 20.00 (ISBN 0-8109-1364-X); pap. 9.95 (ISBN 0-8109-2185-5). Abrams.

National Gallery of Art: Washington, D.C. 45.00 (ISBN 0-8109-0336-9). Abrams.

National Guide to Craft Supplies. 14.95 (ISBN 0-442-22704-3); pap. 7.95 (ISBN 0-442-22702-7). Van Nos Reinhold.

National Trust Book of British Castles. 20.00 (ISBN 0-399-12091-2). Putnam.

National Trust Guide to England, Wales, & Northern Ireland. rev. ed. 19.95 (ISBN 0-393-08813-8). Norton.

Native American Art in the Denver Art Museum. 40.00 (ISBN 0-295-95637-2); pap. 19.95 (ISBN 0-295-95638-0). Denver Art Mus.

Natural Collage: The Making of Pictures with Seeds, Leaves & Grasses. 3.95 (ISBN 0-684-15425-0). Scribner.

Natural Disasters & Educational Building Design. pap. 5.30. Unipub.

Natural History Drawings in the India Office Library. 17.00x. Biblio Dist.

Natural History Photography. 26.75 (ISBN 0-12-703950-3). Acad Pr.

Natural House. 9.95 (ISBN 0-8180-0007-4). Horizon.

Natural Man Observed: A Study of Catlin's Indian Gallery. 40.00 (ISBN 0-87474-918-2). Smithsonian.

Natural Paradise: Painting in America 1800-1950. 19.95 (ISBN 0-87070-505-9). NYGS.

Natural Solar Architecture: A Passive Approach. 14.95 (ISBN 0-442-29585-5); pap. 7.95 (ISBN 0-442-29586-3). Van Nos Reinhold.

Natural Way to Draw: A Working Plan for Art Study. 10.00 (ISBN 0-395-08048-7). HM.

Natural Way to Draw: A Working Plan for Art Study. pap. 5.95 (ISBN 0-395-20548-4). HM.

Naturalistic Photography for Students of the Art. 17.00 (ISBN 0-405-04905-6). Arno.

Naturalistic Photography for Students of the Art. 3rd ed. Incl. Death of Naturalistic Photography. 16.00 (ISBN 0-405-04906-4); pap. 4.95. Arno.

Naturally Powered Old Time Toys: How to Make Sun Yachts, Sail Cars, a Monkey on a String, & Other Moving Toys. 12.95 (ISBN 0-397-01308-6); pap. 6.95 (ISBN 0-397-01316-7). Lippincott.

Nature & Aesthetics of Design. 12.95 (ISBN 0-442-26651-0). Van Nos Reinhold.

Nature & Art of Motion. 12.50 (ISBN 0-8076-0289-2). Braziller.

Nature & Art of Workmanship. 17.95 (ISBN 0-521-06016-8); pap. 7.50 (ISBN 0-521-29356-1). Cambridge U Pr.

Nature & Function of Art, More Especially of Architecture. lib. bdg. 32.50 (ISBN 0-306-70898-1). Da Capo.

Nature & Imagination: The Work of Odilon Redon. 12.95 (ISBN 0-7148-1849-6); pap. 6.95 (ISBN 0-7148-1905-0). Dutton.

Nature & Ornament: Nature the Raw Material of Design. 12.50 (ISBN 0-8103-3328-7). Gale.

Nature & the Victorian Imagination. 25.00 (ISBN 0-520-03229-2). U of Cal Pr.

Nature Crafts. 4.50 (ISBN 0-02-558770-6). Macmillan.

Nature in Needlepoint. 9.95 (ISBN 0-671-22081-0). S&S.

Nature in Ornament. 12.50 (ISBN 0-8103-3207-8). Gale.

Nature in Ornament. lib. bdg. 35.00 (ISBN 0-8240-2472-9). Garland Pub.

Nature of Gothic: A Chapter from the Stones of Venice. lib. bdg. 35.00 (ISBN 0-8240-2450-8). Garland Pub.

Nature Photography Simplified. pap. 4.95 (ISBN 0-8174-0184-9). Amphoto.

Nature to Advantage Dress'd. spiral bdg. 3.75 (ISBN 0-87018-043-6). Ross.

Naturecraft. PLB 5.95 (ISBN 0-385-01190-3). Doubleday.

Nature's Candles. 9.95 (ISBN 0-498-01669-2). A S Barnes.

Nature's Harmonic Unity: A Treatise on Its Relation to Proportional Form. 25.00 (ISBN 0-405-08374-2). Arno.

Nature's Toyshop. 9.75 (ISBN 0-263-05595-7). Transatlantic.

Navaho Sandpainting: The Huckel Collection. 2nd ed. pap. 2.25. Taylor Museum.

Navaho Weaving, Its Technic & History. 12.00. Southwest Mus.

Navaho Weaving, Its Technic & History. 15.00 (ISBN 0-87380-017-6). Rio Grande.

Navajo & Hopi Weaving Techniques. 10.95 (ISBN 0-02-595500-4). Macmillan.

Navajo & Hopi Weaving Techniques. pap. 5.95 (ISBN 0-02-011850-3). Macmillan.

Navajo Pictorial Weaving. pap. 2.00 (ISBN 0-89013-103-1, CA1). Museum NM Pr.

Navajo Sandpainting Art. pap. 4.95 (ISBN 0-918080-20-7). Treasure Chest.

Navajo Shepherd & Weaver. 2nd ed. lib. bdg. 10.00 (ISBN 0-87380-032-X). Rio Grande.

Navajo Sketch Book. 2nd ed. 14.50 (ISBN 0-87358-036-2). Northland.

Navajo Techniques for Today's Weaver. 14.95 (ISBN 0-8230-3153-5). Watson-Guptill.

Navajo Textile Arts. 9.95 (ISBN 0-87905-040-3). Peregrine Smith.

Nazi Drawings. new ed. 14.95 (ISBN 0-87745-065-X). U of Iowa Pr.

Neapolitan Painting of the Seicento. lib. bdg. 40.00 (ISBN 0-87817-177-0). Hacker.

Neblette's Handbook of Photography & Reprography. 7th ed. 49.50x (ISBN 0-442-25948-4). Van Nos Reinhold.

Nebraska Photographic Documentary Project, 1975-1977. pap. 12.95 (ISBN 0-8032-5864-X). U of Nebr Pr.

Necessity of Art. 13.00 (ISBN 0-8369-1364-7). Arno.

Necessity of Art. pap. 2.95 (ISBN 0-14-055151-4). Penguin.

Necessity of Art: A Marxist Approach. pap. 2.95 (ISBN 0-14-055151-4). Penguin.

Needle Lace & Needleweaving: A New Look at Traditional Stitches. pap. 6.95 (ISBN 0-442-26057-1). Van Nos Reinhold.

Needlecraft Designs from Our Best Quilts. pap. 4.95 (ISBN 0-8487-0483-5). Oxmoor Hse.

Needlecraft Kingdom. pap. 4.95 (ISBN 0-8487-0413-4). Oxmoor Hse.

Needlecraft Manual. pap. 7.95 (ISBN 0-8473-1573-8). Sterling.

Needlepainting: A Garden of Stitches. 14.95 (ISBN 0-87140-593-8). Liveright.

Needleplay. 14.95 (ISBN 0-684-14362-3). Scribner.

Needlepoint. rev. ed. 14.95 (ISBN 0-684-14036-5). Scribner.

Needlepoint. PLB 4.90 (ISBN 0-531-02779-1). Watts.

Needlepoint Alphabet Book. 15.95 (ISBN 0-688-00197-1). Morrow.

Needlepoint Alphabet Sampler Book. pap. 2.75 (ISBN 0-486-23472-X). Dover.

Needlepoint Bargello. 12.95 (ISBN 0-684-13991-X). Scribner.

Needlepoint Book: 303 Stitches with Patterns & Projects. 18.95 (ISBN 0-13-610980-2); pap. 9.95 (ISBN 0-13-610972-1). P-H.

Needlepoint Designs After Illustrations by Beatrix Potter. pap. 1.50 (ISBN 0-486-20218-6). Dover.

Needlepoint Designs for Chair Covers. 15.95 (ISBN 0-442-22882-1). Van Nos Reinhold.

Needlepoint for Everyone. 13.95 (ISBN 0-06-005761-0). Har-Row.

Needlepoint from America's Great Quilt Designs. 10.95 (ISBN 0-911104-42-9); pap. 5.95 (ISBN 0-911104-41-0). Workman Pub.

Needlepoint Letters & Numbers. 10.00 (ISBN 0-385-09980-0). Doubleday.

Needlepoint Made Easy. pap. 1.95 (ISBN 0-06-463398-5). B&N.

Needlepoint on Plastic Canvas. 12.95 (ISBN 0-684-15534-6); pap. 6.95 (ISBN 0-684-15577-X, SL779). Scribner.

Needlepoint Pattern Book. 12.95 (ISBN 0-688-00241-2). Morrow.

Needlepoint Patterns for Signs & Sayings. pap. 4.95 (ISBN 0-517-52859-2). Crown.

Needlepoint Plaids. 7.95 (ISBN 0-517-52041-9); pap. 5.95 (ISBN 0-517-52042-7). Crown.

Needlepoint Primer. 12.95 (ISBN 0-8019-5830-X); pap. 7.95 (ISBN 0-8019-5836-9). Chilton.

Needlepoint Simplified. 3.95 (ISBN 0-8069-5178-8); PLB 4.59 (ISBN 0-8069-5179-6). Sterling.

Needlepoints to Go: Small Projects for Spare Moments. 10.95 (ISBN 0-395-20422-4). HM.

Needlery. 12.95 (ISBN 0-88421-045-6). Butterick Pub.

Needleweaving-Easy As Embroidery. Softbound 4.95 (ISBN 0-385-12543-7). Doubleday.

Needlework As Art. 25.95x. Beekman Pubs.

Needlework Book. 14.95 (ISBN 0-671-20842-X). S&S.

Needlework Book of Bible Stories. 6.95 (ISBN 0-15-256793-3). HarBraceJ.

Needlework Boutique. new ed. 12.95 (ISBN 0-87469-012-9). Rutledge Bks.

Needlework Classics: Nostalgic Designs from Butterick. 13.95. Wehman.

Needlework in Miniature. 10.95 (ISBN 0-517-52824-X); pap. 6.95 (ISBN 0-517-52825-8). Crown.

Needlework Nostalgia. 12.95. Wehman.

Needlework Patterns from the Metropolitan Museum of Art. 17.50 (ISBN 0-8212-0639-7). NYGS.

Needlework Patterns from the Metropolitan Museum of Art. pap. 9.95 (ISBN 0-8212-0736-9). NYGS.

Needlework Puppets. rev. ed. 6.95 (ISBN 0-8238-0179-9). Plays.

Needlework Stitches. 3.50 (ISBN 0-517-02516-7); pap. 1.95 (ISBN 0-517-50079-5). Crown.

Needleworker's Botany. 12.50 (ISBN 0-912274-81-6); pap. 5.95 (ISBN 0-912274-99-9). NH Pub Co.

Nefertiti Graffiti: Comments on an Exhibition. pap. 3.95 (ISBN 0-913696-29-3). Bklyn Mus.

Negro Artists. facsimile ed. 16.00 (ISBN 0-8369-8821-3). Arno.

Negro in American Culture. 2nd ed. 8.95 (ISBN 0-394-47943-2). Knopf.

Negro in Art: A Pictorial Record of the Negro Artist & of the Negro Theme in Art. lib. bdg. 15.00 buckram (ISBN 0-87817-013-8). Hacker.

Norman Rockwell's World of Scouting. 17.50 (ISBN 0-8109-1582-0). Abrams.

Norman's Natchez: An Early Photographer & His Town. 25.00 (ISBN 0-87805-078-7). U Pr of Miss.

Norris Embry. pap. text ed. 3.00 (ISBN 0-912298-49-9). Baltimore Mus.

North Carolina Collects: A Loan Exhibition of North Carolina Owned Art Objects. pap. 4.00x (ISBN 0-88259-034-0). NCMA.

North Italian Drawings. 15.00 (ISBN 0-8079-0102-4). October.

North Italian Painting of the Cinquecento: Piedmont, Liguria, Lombardy, Emilia. lib. bdg. 40.00 (ISBN 0-87817-171-1). Hacker.

Northwood, King of Carnival Glass. pap. 8.95 (ISBN 0-89145-070-X). Collector Bks.

Norwegian Romanesque Decorative Sculpture, 1090-1210. 11.50 (ISBN 0-85458-170-7). Transatlantic.

Nostalgic Treasures from America's Past. 9.95 (ISBN 0-87294-098-5). Country Beautiful.

Notations in Passing. 16.00x (ISBN 0-262-12067-4); pap. 4.95 (ISBN 0-262-62028-6). MIT Pr.

Notebook of John Smibert. 10.00. Mass Hist Soc.

Notebooks of Edgar Degas: A Catalogue of the Thirty-Eight Notebooks in the Bibliotheque Nationale & Other Collections. 125.00x (ISBN 0-19-817333-4). Oxford U Pr.

Notebooks of Leonardo Da Vinci. pap. 7.95 ea.; pap. (ISBN 0-486-22572-0); pap. (ISBN 0-486-22573-9). Dover.

Notes in Hand: Miniatures of My Notebook Pages. pap. 2.95 (ISBN 0-525-47325-4). Dutton.

Notes on a Century of Typography at the University Press Oxford, 1693-1794. 32.00x (ISBN 0-19-818138-8). Oxford U Pr.

Notes on American Artists 1754-1820. 20.50 (ISBN 0-8337-1906-8). B Franklin.

Notes on Prints. pap. 4.95 (ISBN 0-262-59003-4). MIT Pr.

Notes on Prints. lib. bdg. 19.50 (ISBN 0-306-70957-0). Da Capo.

Notes on the Merrymount Press & Its Work. lib. bdg. 25.00 (ISBN 0-87821-066-0). Milford Hse.

Notes on the Royal Academy Exhibition, 1868. 6.50 (ISBN 0-404-05418-8). AMS Pr.

Notes on the Synthesis of Form. 9.00x (ISBN 0-674-62750-4); pap. 3.50 (ISBN 0-674-62751-2). Harvard U Pr.

Notes on the Technique of Painting. 10.00. Exposition.

Notre-Dame of Noyon in the Twelfth Century: A Study in the Early Development of Gothic Architecture. pap. 3.95 (ISBN 0-393-00464-3). Norton.

Now You Need a Tool Box. PLB 4.58 (ISBN 0-8037-6740-4); pap. 1.50 (ISBN 0-8037-6751-X). Dial.

Nuclear Research Emulsions. Incl. Techniques & Theory. o.s.i (ISBN 0-12-078301-0); Particle Behavior & Emulsion Applications. 52.00 (ISBN 0-12-078302-9). Acad Pr.

Nude. 24.50 (ISBN 0-470-26426-8). Halsted Pr.

Nude & the Portrait: How to Pose & Paint Them. 7.95 (ISBN 0-87523-147-0). Emerson.

Nude in Western Art. pap. 9.95 (ISBN 0-7148-1668-X). Dutton.

Nude Landscapes. 10.00 (ISBN 0-8216-0129-6). Univ Bks.

Nude Male: A New Perspective. 12.95 (ISBN 0-448-23168-9). Paddington.

Nude Male: A New Perspective. pap. 8.95 (ISBN 0-14-005188-0). Penguin.

Nudes, My Camera & I. 21.95 (ISBN 0-8038-5057-3). Focal Pr.

Nudes of the 20's & 30's. pap. 3.95 (ISBN 0-312-57977-2). St Martin.

Numbers in Images: Illuminations of Numerical Meanings. 9.95 (ISBN 0-916832-00-7). Ilkon Pr.

Numismatic Art in America: Aesthetics & the United States Coinage. 20.00x (ISBN 0-674-62840-3). Harvard U Pr.

Numismatics. 11.95 (ISBN 0-19-885098-0). Oxford U Pr.

Numismatics. pap. 4.95 (ISBN 0-19-888098-7, GB440). Oxford U Pr.

Nuri see Royal Cemeteries of Kush.

Nymphets & Fairies: Three Victorian Children's Illustrators. pap. 3.95 (ISBN 0-312-58047-9). St Martin.

O

Obelisks of Egypt: The Skyscrapers of the Past. 12.95 (ISBN 0-684-14805-6). Scribner.

Object & Image: An Introduction to Photography. ref. ed. 15.95 (ISBN 0-13-628925-8). P-H.

Observation & Reflection: Claude Monet. 39.95 (ISBN 0-7148-1781-3). Dutton.

Observations. 18.75 (ISBN 0-8274-1722-5). R West.

Observer's Book of Flags. 3.95 (ISBN 0-684-14941-9). Scribner.

Observer's Book of Furniture. 3.95 (ISBN 0-684-15217-7). Scribner.

Observer's Book of Glass. 3.95 (ISBN 0-684-14940-0). Scribner.

Observer's Book of Old English Churches. 3.95 (ISBN 0-684-16031-5). Scribner.

Observer's Book of Postage Stamps. 3.95 (ISBN 0-684-15205-3). Scribner.

Observer's Book of Pottery & Porcelain. 3.95 (ISBN 0-684-15215-0). Scribner.

Observer's Book of Sewing. 3.95 (ISBN 0-684-14939-7). Scribner.

Obsolete Bank Notes of New England, 1922. 20.00x (ISBN 0-88000-006-6). Quarterman.

Occult Symbolism in France: Josephin Peladan & the Salons De la Rose-Croix. lib. bdg. 34.00 (ISBN 0-8240-2003-0). Garland Pub.

Occupational & Fraternal Shaving Mugs of the United States. pap. 17.50 (ISBN 0-9600680-3-1). R B Powell.

Ocean in the Sand: Japan-from Landscape to Garden. 15.00 (ISBN 0-394-50298-1); pap. 6.95 (ISBN 0-394-73628-1). Shambhala Pubns.

Oceanic Images. 15.00 (ISBN 0-8109-1466-2). Abrams.

Octagon House: A Home for All. pap. 4.00 (ISBN 0-486-22887-8). Dover.

Octave of Prayer. 12.50 (ISBN 0-912334-36-3); pap. 8.50 (ISBN 0-912334-37-1). Aperture.

Of All Things Most Yielding. pap. 6.95 (ISBN 0-345-24245-9). Ballantine.

Of Divers Arts. 17.50x (ISBN 0-691-09793-3, 224). Princeton U Pr.

Of Earth & Timbers Made: New Mexico Architecture. pap. 6.95 (ISBN 0-8263-0318-8). U of NM Pr.

Of Night & Day. 10.00 (ISBN 0-912020-31-8). Scrimshaw Calif.

Of the Decorative Illustration of Books Old & New. 16.50 (ISBN 0-8103-3299-X). Gale.

Of the Just Shaping of Letters. 6.50 (ISBN 0-8446-2016-5). Peter Smith.

Of the Just Shaping of Letters: From the Applied Geometry of Albrecht Durer, Book 3. pap. 2.50 (ISBN 0-486-21306-4). Dover.

Of Wind, Fog & Sail. 12.95 (ISBN 0-87701-018-8). Chronicle Bks.

Off-Loom Weaving: A Basic Manual. 7.95 (ISBN 0-316-76295-4); pap. 3.95 (ISBN 0-316-76296-2). Little.

Off Loom Weaving Book. 4.95 (ISBN 0-684-15950-3). Scribner.

Off the Board - into the Ground. plastic comb bdg. 14.95 (ISBN 0-8403-0136-7). Kendall-Hunt.

Off the Loom: Creating with Fibre. 8.95 (ISBN 0-670-52053-5). Viking Pr.

Off-Wheel Pottery Book. 3.95 (ISBN 0-684-14980-X). Scribner.

Off Your Rocker: A Complete Guide to Refinishing Furniture. softbound 3.95 (ISBN 0-87069-126-0). Wallace-Homestead.

Offguard: A Paparazzi Look at the Beautiful People. 12.95 (ISBN 0-07-022729-2); pap. 6.95 (ISBN 0-07-022733-0). McGraw.

Office of the Supervising Architect of Treasury: Its History, Activities & Organization. 14.00 (ISBN 0-404-57123-9). AMS Pr.

Official Guide to Bottles, Old & New. 4th rev. ed. pap. 8.95 (ISBN 0-87637-106-3). Hse of Collectibles.

Official Guide to Bottles, Old & New. pap. 6.95 (ISBN 0-87637-330-9). Hse of Collectibles.

Official Guide to Coin Collecting. pap. text ed. write for info. (ISBN 0-87637-238-8). Hse of Collectibles.

Official Guide to Collector Prints. pap. 5.95. Wallace-Homestead.

Official Guide to Popular Antiques & Curios. rev 5th ed. pap. 8.95. Wallace-Homestead.

Official Guide to Popular Antiques & Curios. 5th ed. pap. 5.00 (ISBN 0-87637-326-0). Hse of Collectibles.

Official Integral Precancel Type List & Handbook. 1.50. G W Noble.

Official Nikon Nikkormat Manual. 8th ed. 9.95 (ISBN 0-8174-2464-4). Amphoto.

Official Nikon Nikkormat Manual. 7th ed. 8.95 (ISBN 0-8174-0582-8). Amphoto.

Official Precancel Town & Type List. 2nd ed. 2.00. G W Noble.

Official Printed Dated Control Precancel Catalog. 4th ed. 3.00. G W Noble.

Official Washington D.C. Directory. 10.00 (ISBN 0-517-53029-5). Crown.

Ohio Art & Artists. 24.00 (ISBN 0-8103-4058-5). Gale.

Oil Lamps: The Kerosene Era in America. 28.50 (ISBN 0-87069-121-X). Wallace-Homestead.

Oil Painting. pap. 1.95 (ISBN 0-448-00542-5). G&D.

Oil Painting for the Beginner. rev. & enl. ed. 14.50 (ISBN 0-8230-3275-2). Watson-Guptill.

Oil Painting Outdoors. pap. 9.95 (ISBN 0-8230-3283-3). Watson-Guptill.

Oil Painting Step-By-Step. rev. & enl. ed. 18.95 (ISBN 0-8230-3290-6). Watson-Guptill.

Oil Sketches of Peter Paul Rubens: A Critical Catalogue. 75.00x (ISBN 0-691-03929-1). Princeton U Pr.

Okanagan. 11.95 (ISBN 0-19-540286-3). Oxford U Pr.

Olaf Wieghorst. 30.00 (ISBN 0-87358-045-1). Northland.

Old Age Among the Ancient Greeks. 19.50 (ISBN 0-404-05289-4). AMS Pr.

Old Age Among the Ancient Greeks: The Greek Portrayal of Old Age in Literature, Art & Inscriptions. lib. bdg. 23.50x (ISBN 0-8371-0637-0, RIOA). Greenwood.

Old America Comes Alive: Our Restored Villages from Colonial Williamsburg to Dodge City. PLB 7.95 (ISBN 0-381-99904-1, A57400). John Day.

Old American Glass: The Mills Collection at TCU. 3.00 (ISBN 0-912646-02-0). Tex Christian.

Old American Kitchenware: Seventeen Twenty-Five to Nineteen Twenty-Five. 15.00. Wallace-Homestead.

Old American Kitchenware 1725-1925. 15.00 (ISBN 0-8407-4317-3). Nelson.

Old Brooklyn Heights. pap. price not set (ISBN 0-486-23872-5). Dover.

Old Buildings, Gardens & Furniture in Tidewater, Maryland. 12.50 (ISBN 0-87033-075-6). Cornell Maritime.

Old China Book: Including Staffordshire, Wedgwood, Lustre, & Other English Pottery & Porcelain. pap. 3.95 (ISBN 0-8048-1126-1). C E Tuttle.

Old Chinese Snuff Bottles: Notes with a Catalogue of a Modest Collection. 10.00 (ISBN 0-8048-1220-9). C E Tuttle.

Old Derby China Factory. 17.50x (ISBN 0-85409-904-2). Charles River Bks.

Old English Furniture. rev. 7th ed. text ed. 15.00x (ISBN 0-8277-5083-8). British Bk Ctr.

Old English Porcelain: A Handbook for Collectors. rev. 3rd ed. 35.00 (ISBN 0-571-04902-8). Merrimack Bk Serv.

Old Furniture: Understanding the Craftsman's Art. 12.95 (ISBN 0-672-51894-5). Bobbs.

Old Furniture: Understanding the Craftsman's Art. pap. 5.95 (ISBN 0-316-79932-7). Little.

Old House Plans: Two Centuries of Domestic Architecture. pap. 4.95 (ISBN 0-87663-981-3). Universe.

Old Houses on Nantucket. 15.00 (ISBN 0-8038-0193-9). Architectural.

Old Lamps & New: Restoring & Decorating. 12.50. R Little.

Old Landmarks & Historic Personages of Boston. 15.00 (ISBN 0-8103-3582-4). Gale.

Old Landmarks & Historic Personages of Boston. pap. 3.95 (ISBN 0-8048-0993-3). C E Tuttle.

Old Master Drawings from Christ Church, Oxford. pap. 5.95 (ISBN 0-88397-061-9). Intl Exhibit Foun.

Old Master Paintings in Britain: An Index of Continental Old Master Paintings Executed Before C. 1800 in Public Collections in the United Kingdom. 42.50x (ISBN 0-85667-024-3). Biblio Dist.

Old Masters & New. facsimile ed. 18.25 (ISBN 0-8369-1403-1). Arno.

Old Masters in America. write for info. (ISBN 0-89659-050-X). Abbeville Pr.

Old New York in Early Photographs: Eighteen Fifty-Three to Nineteen Hundred & One. pap. 6.95 (ISBN 0-486-22907-6). Dover.

Old New York in Early Photographs, 1853-1901. 10.00 (ISBN 0-8446-5005-6). Peter Smith.

Old Philadelphia Houses on Society Hill, 1750-1840. 15.00 (ISBN 0-8038-0194-7). Architectural.

Old Printer & the Modern Press. 14.50 (ISBN 0-404-08838-4). AMS Pr.

Old Ranches of the Texas Plains. 27.50 (ISBN 0-89096-019-4). Tex A&M Univ Pr.

Old Rooms for New Living. 9.95 (ISBN 0-8038-5346-7). Hastings.

Old Sheffield Town. text ed. 17.50x (ISBN 0-8277-1518-8). British Bk Ctr.

Old Sleepy Eye. pap. 4.95; price guide 1.25. Wallace-Homestead.

Old Sturbridge Village in Color. 5.95 (ISBN 0-8038-5389-0). Hastings.

Old Table Silver. 17.50 (ISBN 0-8008-5725-9). Taplinger.

Old Testament in Art. PLB 4.95 (ISBN 0-8225-0168-6). Lerner Pubns.

Old Testament Miniatures. 60.00 (ISBN 0-8076-0513-1). Braziller.

Old Time Bottles Found in the Ghost Towns. rev. ed. pap. 2.95 (ISBN 0-911068-01-5, A666974). Old Time.

Old-Time Tools & Toys of Needlework. pap. 5.00 (ISBN 0-486-22517-8). Dover.

Old-Time Tools & Toys of Needlework. 8.00 (ISBN 0-8446-0292-2). Peter Smith.

Old Ways of Working Wood. 12.50 (ISBN 0-517-51742-6). Barre.

Old West in Miniature: Sculptures by Don Polland. pap. 2.00x (ISBN 0-913060-06-2). Norton Art.

Old Wooden Buildings. pap. 4.95 (ISBN 0-919654-90-8). Hancock Hse.

Oliver Madox Brown. 10.00 (ISBN 0-404-03503-5). AMS Pr.

Olmec Figure at Dumbarton Oaks. pap. 2.00 (ISBN 0-88402-035-5). Dumbarton Oaks.

Olmec Figure at Dumbarton Oaks see Olmec Paintings of Oxtotitlan Cave, Guerrero, Mexico.

Olmec Paintings of Oxtotitlan Cave, Guerrero, Mexico. pap. 2.50 (ISBN 0-88402-032-0). Dumbarton Oaks.

Olmec Paintings of Oxtotitlan Cave, Guerrero, Mexico. Bd. with Study of Olmec Iconography; Olmec Figure at Dumbarton Oaks. 8.00 (ISBN 0-88402-036-3). Dumbarton Oaks.

Olympus Guide. 10.95 (ISBN 0-8174-2449-0); pap. 6.95 (ISBN 0-8174-2104-1). Amphoto.

Olympus OM Camera Manual. 11.95 (ISBN 0-8174-2412-1). Amphoto.

Omani Silver. pap. text ed. 6.50x (ISBN 0-582-78070-5). Longman.

On Art & Architecture in the Modern World. text ed. 9.00 (ISBN 0-89257-027-X). Am Life Foun.

On Art & Artists. 13.00 (ISBN 0-527-43800-6). Kraus Repr.

On Art & the Mind. text ed. 15.00 (ISBN 0-674-63405-5). Harvard U Pr.

On Designing. pap. 5.95 (ISBN 0-8195-6019-7). Wesleyan U Pr.

On Drawing & Painting. 14.50 (ISBN 0-404-05406-4). AMS Pr.

On Mobile Streets: A Rumor of the City. pap. 5.95 (ISBN 0-930642-04-X). Easter Pub.

On Not Being Able to Paint. 2nd rev. ed. text ed. 12.50; pap. 4.95 (ISBN 0-8236-8202-1, 023820). Intl Univs Pr.

On Permanent View. pap. 2.95 (ISBN 0-87314-092-3). Peter Glenn.

On, Romanticism. 12.50x (ISBN 0-8147-7753-8). NYU Pr.

On the Aesthetic Education of Man, in a Series of Letters. 32.50x (ISBN 0-19-815359-7). Oxford U Pr.

On the Laws of Japanese Painting. pap. 4.50 (ISBN 0-486-20030-2). Dover.

On the Laws of Japanese Painting. 8.50 (ISBN 0-8446-0504-2). Peter Smith.

On the Loose. pap. 6.95 (ISBN 0-87156-264-2). Sierra.

On the Loose. pap. 4.95 (ISBN 0-345-24307-2). Ballantine.

On the Rationalization of Sight: De Artificiali Perspectiva. 2nd ed. lib. bdg. 19.50 (ISBN 0-306-71189-3). Da Capo.

On the Rationalization of Sight: With an Examination of Three Renaissance Texts on Perspective to Which Is Appended "De Artificiali Perspectiva" by Viator (Pelerin) pap. 2.95 (ISBN 0-306-80011-X). Da Capo.

On-The-Spot-Drawing. pap. 7.95 (ISBN 0-8230-3351-1). Watson-Guptill.

On the Trail of Stoddard Glass. pap. 4.95 (ISBN 0-87233-021-4). Bauhan.

On the Transmission of Photography. pap. 5.95 (ISBN 0-9600374-2-X). Images Pr.

On the True Precepts of the Art of Painting. 25.00 (ISBN 0-89102-054-3); pap. 9.95 (ISBN 0-89102-100-0). B Franklin.

Once Upon a Quilt: Patchwork Design & Technique. 10.95 (ISBN 0-442-24967-5); pap. 6.95 (ISBN 0-442-24966-7). Van Nos Reinhold.

Onderdonks: A Family of Texas Painters. 25.00 (ISBN 0-911536-57-4). Trinity U Pr.

One Hundred & One Patchwork Patterns. 8.50 (ISBN 0-8446-1711-3). Peter Smith.

One Hundred & One Patchwork Patterns. rev. ed. pap. 2.75 (ISBN 0-486-20773-0). Dover.

One Hundred Books About Bookmaking. lib. bdg. 9.00x (ISBN 0-8371-8546-7, LEOB). Greenwood.

One Hundred Drawings. pap. 3.50 (ISBN 0-486-22446-5). Dover.

One Hundred Master Drawings. lib. bdg. 23.25x (ISBN 0-8371-3989-9, MOMD). Greenwood.

One Hundred Title Pages: 1500-1800. lib. bdg. 35.00 (ISBN 0-89341-228-7). Longwood Pr.

One Hundred Years of Photographic History: Essays in Honor of Beaumont Newhall. 17.50 (ISBN 0-8263-0344-7). U of NM Pr.

One Hundred Years of Science Fiction Illustration. pap. 4.95 (ISBN 0-515-03863-6). HarBraceJ.

One Mind's Eye. pap. 12.95 (ISBN 0-8212-0732-6). NYGS.

One Mind's Eye: The Portraits and Other Photographs of Arnold Newman. 30.00 (ISBN 0-87923-094-0). Godine.

One-Piece Knits That Fit: How to Knit & Crochet One-Piece Garments. 15.95 (ISBN 0-442-23567-4). Van Nos Reinhold.

One Piece of Paper. 7.50 (ISBN 0-8008-5825-5). Taplinger.

One-Stitch Stitchery. 3.95 (ISBN 0-8069-5384-5); lib. bdg. 4.59 (ISBN 0-8069-5385-3). Sterling.

PAINTING TECHNIQUES OF THE

ART BOOKS 1950 - 1979

Painting Techniques of the Masters. rev. & enl. ed. 21.50 (ISBN 0-8230-3863-7). Watson-Guptill.
Painting the Head in Oil. 17.95 (ISBN 0-8230-3640-5). Watson-Guptill.
Painting the Nude. pap. text ed. 9.95 (ISBN 0-8230-3726-6). Watson-Guptill.
Painting the Seasons in Watercolor. 15.95 (ISBN 0-8230-3858-0). Watson-Guptill.
Painting with a Palette Knife. pap. 1.95 (ISBN 0-448-00592-1). G&D.
Painting with Cold Enamel. 2.95 (ISBN 0-87749-466-5). Sterling.
Painting with Light. 18.50 (ISBN 0-8230-3881-5). Watson-Guptill.
Painting with Oils. 12.95 (ISBN 0-87192-093-X). Davis Mass.
Painting with Stitches: A Guide to Embroidery, Needlepoint, Crochet & Macrame. 10.95 (ISBN 0-87192-080-8). Davis Mass.
Painting Without a Brush. 9.50 (ISBN 0-7134-0189-3). Hippocrene Bks.
Painting Women's Portraits. 16.95 (ISBN 0-8230-3882-3). Watson-Guptill.
Paintings & Drawings at the Shelburne Museum. pap. 12.50. Shelburne.
Paintings & Drawings of Dante Gabriel Rossetti (1828-1882) A Catalogue Raisonne. 78.00x (ISBN 0-19-817174-9). Oxford U Pr.
Paintings & Drawings of Marco Zoppo. lib. bdg. 50.00 (ISBN 0-8240-1976-8). Garland Pub.
Paintings & Drawings of the Gypsies of Granada. 12.50 (ISBN 0-8103-5003-3). Gale.
Paintings & Miniatures at the Historical Society of Pennsylvania. 20.00 (ISBN 0-910732-08-6). Pa Hist Soc.
Paintings & the Journal of Joseph Whiting Stock. 30.00 (ISBN 0-8195-4098-6). Wesleyan U Pr.
Paintings from Islamic Lands. 19.50x (ISBN 0-87249-138-2). U of SC Pr.
Paintings from the C. R. Smith Collection. pap. 6.00 (ISBN 0-87959-030-0). U of Tex Hum Res.
Paintings in the "Studiolo" of Isabella d'Este at Mantua. 17.50x (ISBN 0-8147-8751-7). NYU Pr.
Paintings of Cornelis Engebrechtsz. lib. bdg. 46.00 (ISBN 0-8240-2691-8). Garland Pub.
Paintings of Correggio. 85.00x (ISBN 0-8014-0973-X). Cornell U Pr.
Paintings of Girolamo Mazzola Bedoli. lib. bdg. 52.00 (ISBN 0-8240-3242-X). Garland Pub.
Paintings of Lucas Cranach. 85.00x (ISBN 0-8014-1061-4). Cornell U Pr.
Paints, Inks, & Dyes: The Story of Colors at Work. 6.50 (ISBN 0-8234-0240-1). Holiday.
Pairpoint Glass. 29.95 (ISBN 0-87069-218-6). Wallace-Homestead.
Palaces of Crete. 22.000 (ISBN 0-691-03524-5); pap. 6.95 (ISBN 0-691-00206-1, 154). Princeton U Pr.
Palaces of Kyoto. pap. 4.95 (ISBN 0-87011-059-4). Kodansha.
Palaces of Venice. 35.00 (ISBN 0-670-53724-1). Viking Pr.
Palazzo del Te in Mantua: Images of Love & Politics. text ed. 22.50x (ISBN 0-8018-1809-5). Johns Hopkins.
Palestinian Costume & Jewelry. pap. 14.95 (ISBN 0-8263-0490-7). U of NM Pr.
Palladio. rev. ed. pap. 4.95 (ISBN 0-14-020845-3). Penguin.
Palladio & Palladianism. 22.50 (ISBN 0-8076-0735-5). Braziller.
Palladio in America. pap. 7.95 (ISBN 0-8478-0169-1). Rizzoli Intl.
Palliser's Model Homes. pap. text ed. 4.00 (ISBN 0-89257-026-1). Am Life Foun.
Palliser's New Cottage Homes & Details. lib. bdg. 39.50 (ISBN 0-306-70744-6). Da Capo.
Palm Leaf Patterns: A New Approach to Clothing Design. pap. 4.95 (ISBN 0-915572-20-6). Panjandrum.
Pamper Your Possessions. 10.95 (ISBN 0-517-53617-X); pap. 4.95 (ISBN 0-517-53524-6). Barre.
Pandora's Box: The Changing Aspects of a Mythical Symbol. 2nd ed. 16.50 (ISBN 0-691-09809-3); pap. 6.95 (ISBN 0-691-01824-3). Princeton U Pr.
Pantheon: Design, Meaning & Progeny. 12.50x (ISBN 0-674-65345-9). Harvard U Pr.
Pantyhose Craft Book: Making Things from Run Pantyhose & Nylons. 10.95 (ISBN 0-8008-6235-X); pap. 5.95 (ISBN 0-8008-6234-1). Taplinger.
Paolozzi. 12.50 (ISBN 0-8109-4414-6). Abrams.
Paper Airplane Book. pap. 1.95 (ISBN 0-14-030925-X). Penguin.
Paper Airplane Book. PLB 6.50 (ISBN 0-670-53797-7). Viking Pr.
Paper Airplanes You Can Build & Fly. pap. 4.50 (ISBN 0-87749-689-7). Sterling.
Paper As Art & Craft. 9.95 (ISBN 0-517-50370-0); pap. 5.95 (ISBN 0-517-50378-6). Crown.
Paper-Bag Puppets. pap. 3.50 (ISBN 0-8224-5275-8). Fearon-Pitman.
Paper Bead Book. 9.95 (ISBN 0-679-20319-2); pap. 4.95 (ISBN 0-679-20378-8). McKay.
Paper Book. pap. 0.95 (ISBN 0-684-15770-5, SL380). Scribner.
Paper Collage. 10.50 (ISBN 0-8231-7035-7). Branford.
Paper Craft. pap. 2.95 (ISBN 0-915462-05-2). Paragraph Pr.
Paper Crafts. PLB 8.49 (ISBN 0-8172-1186-1). Raintree Pubs Ltd.
Paper Cut-Out Design Book. 15.95 (ISBN 0-916144-03-8); pap. 7.95 (ISBN 0-916144-04-6). Stemmer Hse.
Paper Cutting. 7.95 (ISBN 0-87599-224-2). S G Phillips.
Paper Dreams. 11.95x (ISBN 0-87663-287-8); pap. 6.95 (ISBN 0-87663-964-3). Universe.
Paper Faces. 8.95 (ISBN 0-8008-6250-3). Taplinger.
Paper Flowers. 11.95 (ISBN 0-8019-6414-8); pap. 6.95 (ISBN 0-8019-6415-6). Chilton.
Paper Folding & Paper Sculpture. 8.95 (ISBN 0-87523-155-1). Emerson.
Paper, Ink & Roller. PLB 7.95 (ISBN 0-201-09305-7). A-W.
Paper Money. 6.95 (ISBN 0-312-59570-0). St Martin.
Paper Money of Brasil. 2nd ed. pap. 5.00 (ISBN 0-916710-21-1). Obol Intl.
Paper Money of the United States. 9th ed. 17.50 (ISBN 0-87184-509-1). Coin & Curr.
Paper People. 9.95 (ISBN 0-8008-6255-4). Taplinger.
Paper Sculpture Step by Step. 9.50 (ISBN 0-7135-1718-2). Transatlantic.
Paper Straw Craft. 6.95 (ISBN 0-8069-5312-8); PLB 6.69 (ISBN 0-8069-5313-6). Sterling.
Paper Toy Making. pap. 1.75 (ISBN 0-486-21662-4). Dover.
Papercutting. 6.50 (ISBN 0-8008-6247-3). Taplinger.
Papercutting. PLB 4.95 (ISBN 0-385-09444-2). Doubleday.
Paperweights: Flowers Which Clothe the Meadows. pap. 20.00 (ISBN 0-87290-065-7). Corning.
Paperweights for Collectors. 27.50. Wallace-Homestead.
Paperweights for Collectors. 2nd ed. 27.50. Paperweight Pr.
Papier-Mache. 6.95 (ISBN 0-679-50069-3). McKay.
Papier Mache. 7.95 (ISBN 0-88332-068-1, 8033); pap. 4.95 (ISBN 0-88332-069-X, 8032). Larousse.
Papier Mache Crafts. 8.95 (ISBN 0-8069-5338-1); lib. bdg. 8.39 (ISBN 0-8069-5339-X). Sterling.
Paraguayan Paper Money. 10.00 (ISBN 0-916710-12-2); pap. 5.00. Obol Intl.
Pardon Me, Mr. President: The Cartoon Almanac for 1975. pap. 4.95 (ISBN 0-8129-0503-2). Times Bks.
Paris & the Arts, 1851-1896: From the Goncourt Journal. 17.50x (ISBN 0-8014-0655-2). Cornell U Pr.
Paris Through the Ages. 12.50 (ISBN 0-8076-0556-5). Braziller.
Parish Churches of England in Colour. 9.50 (ISBN 0-7137-0630-9). Transatlantic.
Parish of Chelsea. 57.50 (ISBN 0-404-51652-1). AMS Pr.
Parish of St. Margaret, Westminster. 57.50 (ISBN 0-404-51660-2). AMS Pr.
Parish of St. Pancras. 57.50 (ISBN 0-404-51669-6). AMS Pr.
Parish of St. Pancras. 57.50 (ISBN 0-404-51667-X). AMS Pr.
Park. 3.95 (ISBN 0-671-65028-9). S&S.
Park-Maker: A Life of Frederick Law Olmsted. 17.95 (ISBN 0-02-614440-9, 61444). Macmillan.
Park Planning Handbook: Fundamentals of Physical Planning for Parks & Recreation Areas. text ed. 20.50 (ISBN 0-471-15619-1). Wiley.
Parmigianino: His Works in Painting. lib. bdg. 29.95x (ISBN 0-8371-3717-9, FRPA). Greenwood.
Parnasse Francois: Titon Du Tillet & the Origins of the Monument to Genius. text ed. 25.00 (ISBN 0-300-02270-0). Yale U Pr.
Part 1: New Coptic Texts from the Monastery of Saint Macarius see Monasteries of the Wadi 'n Natrun: Metropolitan Museum of Art Egyptian Expedition Publications.
Part 2: the History of the Monasteries of Nitria & of Scetis see Monasteries of the Wadi 'n Natrun: Metropolitan Museum of Art Egyptian Expedition Publications.
Part 3: the Architecture & Archaeology see Monasteries of the Wadi 'n Natrun: Metropolitan Museum of Art Egyptian Expedition Publications.
Parthenon. 12.50 (ISBN 0-393-04373-8); pap. 4.95x (ISBN 0-393-09354-9). Norton.
Parthenon. 12.95 (ISBN 0-88225-026-4). Newsweek.
Parthian Art. 27.50x (ISBN 0-8014-1111-4). Cornell U Pr.
Participating in Architectural Competitions. 12.75 (ISBN 0-85139-514-7). Nichols Pub.
Parting at the Shore: Chinese Painting of the Early & Middle Ming Dynasty, 1368-1580. 32.50 (ISBN 0-8348-0128-0). Weatherhill.
Pascin: One Hundred Ten Drawings. 7.50 (ISBN 0-8446-4594-X). Peter Smith.
Passages in Modern Sculpture. 18.95 (ISBN 0-670-54133-8). Viking Pr.
Passenger Terminals & Trains. 10.00 (ISBN 0-89024-015-9). Kalmbach.
Passion of Christ see Iconography of Christian Art.
Passport. 17.95 (ISBN 0-394-50528-X). Random.
Passport. pap. 9.95 (ISBN 0-394-72861-0). Random.
Past Joys. ltd. signed ed. 45.00 (ISBN 0-87701-116-8); pap. 12.95 (ISBN 0-87701-115-X). Chronicle Bks.
Paste-up: Art Production for the New Art World. 12.95 (ISBN 0-442-29022-5); pap. 7.95 (ISBN 0-442-29021-7). Van Nos Reinhold.
Pastel: A Comprehensive Guide to Pastel Painting. 17.50 (ISBN 0-8230-3899-8). Watson-Guptill.
Pastels Are Great. 6.25g (ISBN 0-8075-6362-5). A Whitman.
Pastimes with String & Paper. pap. 3.95 (ISBN 0-8158-0169-6). Chris Mass.
Patchwork. 6.95 (ISBN 0-385-09681-X). Doubleday.
Patchwork & Applique. 14.95 (ISBN 0-8037-6854-0); pap. 7.95. Dial.
Patchwork, Applique, & Quilting Primer. PLB 6.00 (ISBN 0-688-51693-9). Lothrop.
Patchwork for Beginners. 9.95 (ISBN 0-8230-3925-0). Watson-Guptill.
Patchwork Patterns. 24.95 (ISBN 0-914440-26-8); pap. 15.95 (ISBN 0-914440-27-6). EPM Pubns.
Patchwork Plain & Fancy. pap. 2.95 (ISBN 0-425-03194-2). Berkley Pub.
Patchwork Point of View. 8.95 (ISBN 0-671-21957-X). S&S.
Patchwork Quilt Design & Coloring Book. pap. 8.95 (ISBN 0-88421-028-6). Butterick Pub.
Patchwork Quilt Designs for Needlepoint. pap. 1.50 (ISBN 0-486-23300-6). Dover.
Patchwork Quilts. 4.95 (ISBN 0-684-15240-1). Scribner.
Patchwork Simplified. 5.95 (ISBN 0-668-03321-5). Arco.
Patchwork Today. 5.75 (ISBN 0-8231-5010-0). Branford.
Patents for Inventions. lib. bdg. 90.00x (ISBN 0-405-09626-7). Arno.
Patrons & Artists in the Italian Renaissance. 7.95x (ISBN 0-87249-220-6); pap. 3.95x (ISBN 0-87249-221-4). U of SC Pr.
Patrons & Patriotism: The Encouragement of the Fine Arts in the United States, 1790-1860. 14.00x (ISBN 0-226-52772-7). U of Chicago Pr.
Patrons & Patriotism: The Encouragement of the Fine Arts in the United States, 1790-1860. pap. 5.75 (ISBN 0-226-52773-5, P611). U of Chicago Pr.
Pattern. pap. 9.95 (ISBN 0-306-80040-3); pap. 9.95 (ISBN 0-306-80041-1). Da Capo.
Pattern: A Historical Panorama. 15.00 (ISBN 0-8212-0665-6). NYGS.
Pattern: A Study of Ornament in Western Europe from 1180 to 1900. lib. bdg. 75.00 (ISBN 0-87817-151-7). Hacker.
Pattern & Design with Dynamic Symmetry. 7.50 (ISBN 0-8446-2021-1). Peter Smith.
Pattern & Design with Dynamic Symmetry. pap. 3.00 (ISBN 0-486-21756-6). Dover.
Pattern Design: An Introduction to the Study of Formal Ornament. 7.00 (ISBN 0-8446-0545-X). Peter Smith.
Pattern Drafting & Dressmaking. PLB 15.30 (ISBN 0-307-03309-0). Western Pub.
Pattern in Islamic Art. 20.00 (ISBN 0-87951-042-0). Overlook Pr.
Pattern Making by the Flat Pattern Method. 4th ed. spiral bdg. 8.95 (ISBN 0-8087-0856-2). Burgess.
Pattern Making Design: Skirts & Pants. pap. text ed. 4.40 (ISBN 0-8273-0583-4). Delmar.
Pattern Making Design: Sleeved & Tailored Garments. pap. text ed. 4.40 (ISBN 0-8273-0585-0). Delmar.
Pattern Making Design: Sleeveless Dresses. pap. text ed. 4.40 (ISBN 0-8273-0584-2). Delmar.
Patterned Backgrounds for Needlepoint. pap. 7.95 (ISBN 0-442-27480-7). Van Nos Reinhold.
Patterns for Guernseys, Jerseys & Arans: Fishermans' Sweaters from the British Isles. pap. 3.50 (ISBN 0-486-22703-0). Dover.
Patterns for Guernseys, Jerseys & Arans: Fisherman's Sweaters from the British Isles. 2nd & rev. ed. 7.00 (ISBN 0-8446-0273-6). Peter Smith.
Patterns for Patchwork Quilts & Cushions. pap. 5.95 (ISBN 0-8231-5050-X). Branford.
Patterns of Fashion: 1660-1860. 3rd rev. ed. text ed. 10.00x (ISBN 0-89676-026-X). Drama Bk.
Patterns of Fashion: 1860-1940. 3rd rev. ed. text ed. 10.00x (ISBN 0-89676-027-8). Drama Bk.
Patterns of Symmetry. 12.00x (ISBN 0-87023-232-0). U of Mass Pr.
Paul Delaroche: A Study in 19th Century French History Painting. lib. bdg. 46.00 (ISBN 0-8240-2741-8). Garland Pub.
Paul Gauguin. 12.95 (ISBN 0-07-069441-9). McGraw.
Paul Harris. 9.95 (ISBN 0-8109-0359-8). Abrams.
Paul Jenkins. 55.00 (ISBN 0-8109-0215-X). Abrams.
Paul Kane, the Columbia Wanderer: Sketches, Paintings & Comment, 1846-1847. pap. 3.95 (ISBN 0-87595-029-9). Oreg Hist Soc.
Paul Klee. 28.50 (ISBN 0-8109-0228-1). Abrams.
Paul Klee & Primitive Art. lib. bdg. 25.00 (ISBN 0-8240-2001-4). Garland Pub.
Paul Martin: Victorian Photographer. 24.95 (ISBN 0-292-76436-7). U of Tex Pr.
Paul Revere's Boston 1735-1818. 29.50 (ISBN 0-87846-088-8). NYGS.
Peacock Festival: Selected Color Woodcuts. pap. 8.00 (ISBN 0-933652-00-3). J Domjan.
Peanut Craft. 6.75 (ISBN 0-688-41567-9); PLB 6.48 (ISBN 0-688-51567-3). Lothrop.
Peanut Parade. PLB 7.29 (ISBN 0-671-32944-8). Messner.
Peasant Chic. pap. 7.95. Hawthorn.
Peasant Designs for Artists & Craftsmen. 6.75 (ISBN 0-8446-5610-0). Peter Smith.
Peasant Designs for Artists and Craftsmen. pap. 3.00 (ISBN 0-486-23478-9). Dover.
Pebble People Pets & Things. pap. 5.95 (ISBN 0-88421-038-3). Butterick Pub.
Pedagogical Sketchbook. 3.95 (ISBN 0-571-08618-7). Merrimack Bk Serv.
Pelican Guide to Gardens of Louisiana. pap. 2.95 (ISBN 0-88289-003-4). Pelican.
Pelican Guide to Historic Homes & Sights of Revolutionary America. Incl. New England. 3.25 (ISBN 0-88289-090-5). Pelican.
Pen & Ink Drawing. pap. 1.95 (ISBN 0-448-00550-6). G&D.
Pen & Ink Techniques. 11.95 (ISBN 0-8092-7439-6); pap. 5.95 (ISBN 0-8092-7438-8). Contemp Bks.
Pen Drawing & Pen-Draughtsmen. pap. 8.95 (ISBN 0-306-80064-0). Da Capo.
Pencil of Nature. lib. bdg. 40.00 (ISBN 0-306-71135-4). Da Capo.
Pencil, Pen & Brush. PLB 7.95 (ISBN 0-201-09311-1). A-W.
Pencil, Pen, & Brush. pap. 0.95 (ISBN 0-590-02229-6). Schol Bk Serv.
Pencil Sketching. pap. 5.95 (ISBN 0-442-29177-9). Van Nos Reinhold.
Pencil to Press: How This Book Came to Be. 6.00 (ISBN 0-688-51713-7). Lothrop.
Penguin Dictionary of Architecture. rev. ed. pap. 3.95 (ISBN 0-14-051013-3). Penguin.
Penland School of Crafts Book of Jewelry Making. 12.95 (ISBN 0-672-51967-4). Bobbs.
Penland School of Crafts Book of Pottery. 12.95 (ISBN 0-672-51968-2). Bobbs.
Penn's Countrie: Antique Collector's Guide to Pennsylvania & Surrounding Areas. pap. 1.95 (ISBN 0-87133-051-2). Franklin Pub Locust.
Pennsylvania. 27.50 (ISBN 0-912856-40-8). Graphic Arts Ctr.
Pennsylvania Dutch American Folk Art. rev. & enl. ed. pap. 4.00 (ISBN 0-486-21205-X). Dover.
Pennsylvania Dutch American Folk Art. rev. & enl. ed. 7.50 (ISBN 0-8446-2354-7). Peter Smith.
Pennsylvania Dutch Needlepoint Designs. pap. 1.50 (ISBN 0-486-23299-9). Dover.
Pennsylvania-German Decorated Chest. 25.00 (ISBN 0-87663-310-6). Universe.
Pennsylvania German Fraktur of the Free Library of Philadelphia: An Illustrated Catalogue. 60.00x (ISBN 0-911122-32-X). Phila Free Lib.
Pennsylvania German Illuminated Manuscripts: A Classification of Fraktur-Schriften & an Inquiry into Their History & Art. 8.50. Peter Smith.
Penny Whimsy. 35.00x (ISBN 0-88000-087-2). Quarterman.
Pennybanks. pap. 8.95 (ISBN 0-525-47468-4). Dutton.
Pens and Needles: Literary Caricatures Introduced & Selected by John Updike. 8.95 (ISBN 0-87645-006-0). Gambit.
People. pap. 9.95 (ISBN 0-14-005073-6). Penguin.
People & Buildings. text ed. 12.50x (ISBN 0-465-05456-0). Basic.
People & Spaces: A View of History Through Architecture. 14.95 (ISBN 0-670-54705-0). Viking Pr.
People in Focus. 14.95 (ISBN 0-8174-2429-6); pap. 8.95 (ISBN 0-8174-2107-6). Amphoto.
People of the Saints. 3.75. Taylor Museum.
People of the Willow: The Padlimiut Tribe of the Caribou Eskimo. 11.95 (ISBN 0-19-540271-5). Oxford U Pr.
People Who Make Things: How American Craftsmen Live & Work. 6.50 (ISBN 0-689-50012-2). Atheneum.
People's Architects. 8.95x (ISBN 0-226-70483-1). U of Chicago Pr.

Picasso's Private Drawings. 8.50 (ISBN 0-671-20383-5). S&S.
Picasso's Vollard Suite. pap. 6.95 (ISBN 0-8109-2076-X). Abrams.
Picasso's World of Children. 9.95 (ISBN 0-385-12627-1). Doubleday.
Pick-up Book of Cartoon-Style Illustrations. lib. bdg. 12.95 (ISBN 0-668-04665-1); pap. 9.95 (ISBN 0-668-04505-1). Arco.
Pickering Manuscript. pap. 3.00 (ISBN 0-87598-036-8). Pierpont Morgan.
Pictor Succensor: A Study of Salvator Rosa As Satirist, Cynic, & Painter. lib. bdg. 42.00 (ISBN 0-8240-3248-9). Garland Pub.
Pictorial Autobiography. rev. ed. text ed. 10.00x (ISBN 0-239-00179-6). Humanities.
Pictorial Calligraphy & Ornamentation. pap. 3.00 (ISBN 0-486-22788-X). Dover.
Pictorial Calligraphy & Ornamentation: 86 Plates Selected from the Work of Pedro Diaz Morante, Giuliano Sellari, & Leopardo Antonozzi. 7.00 (ISBN 0-8446-4548-6). Peter Smith.
Pictorial Cyclopedia of Photography. 29.95 (ISBN 0-8038-5874-4). Focal Pr.
Pictorial Cyclopedia of Photography. 25.95 (ISBN 0-8038-5855-8). Focal Pr.
Pictorial Encyclopedia of Birds. 10.00 (ISBN 0-517-00549-2). Crown.
Pictorial Encyclopedia of Plants & Flowers. 10.00 (ISBN 0-517-09540-8). Crown.
Pictorial History of English Architecture. 12.95 (ISBN 0-02-510500-0). Macmillan.
Pictorial History of Music. 18.95 (ISBN 0-393-02107-6). Norton.
Pictorial Journalism. 24.00 (ISBN 0-405-04945-5). Arno.
Pictorial Quilting. 17.50 (ISBN 0-498-01944-6). A S Barnes.
Pictorial Souvenirs of Britain. 15.00x (ISBN 0-7153-6660-2). State Mutual Bk.
Pictorial Souvenirs of Britain. 14.95 (ISBN 0-7153-6660-2). David & Charles.
Picture Book of Montana. rev. ed. 4.75g (ISBN 0-8075-9529-2). A Whitman.
Picture Framer's Handbook. 7.95 (ISBN 0-517-50058-2). Potter.
Picture Framing. pap. 1.95 (ISBN 0-448-00552-2). G&D.
Picture Framing Handbook. 6.95 (ISBN 0-912092-42-4). Educator Bks.
Picture Gallery. 50.00 (ISBN 0-316-51802-6). Little.
Picture History of Photography. concise ed. pap. 8.95 (ISBN 0-8109-2056-5). Abrams.
Picture History of Photography. rev. ed. 35.00 (ISBN 0-8109-0404-7); concise 17.50 (ISBN 0-8109-1462-X). Abrams.
Picture or Two: The Story of Ray Eyerly. pap. 6.25 (ISBN 0-915418-00-2). Oakwood Pr.
Picture Panorama of World Building. 15.00 (ISBN 0-263-06307-0). Transatlantic.
Picture Postcards. 15.00 (ISBN 0-396-06889-8). Dodd.
Picture Postcards in the United States. 15.95 (ISBN 0-517-52400-7). Potter.
Picture Postcards in the United States: 1893-1918. 15.95 (ISBN 0-517-52400-7). Crown.
Picture Researchers' Handbook. 15.00 (ISBN 0-684-14133-7). Scribner.
Picture Signs & Symbols. PLB 5.41 (ISBN 0-8193-0577-4). Parents.
Picture Sourcebook for Collage & Decoupage. pap. 4.00 (ISBN 0-486-23095-3). Dover.
Picture the Songs: Lithographs from the Sheet Music of 19th Century America. 25.00 (ISBN 0-8018-1814-1). Johns Hopkins.
Picture-Writing of the American Indians. 39.95 (ISBN 0-8490-0836-0). Gordon Pr.
Picture-Writing of the American Indians. 20.00 (ISBN 0-8446-4582-6). Peter Smith.
Picture-Writing of the American Indians. pap. 6.00 ea.; pap. (ISBN 0-486-22842-8); pap. (ISBN 0-486-22843-6). Dover.
Picturemaking: Easy-to-Make Pictures with Paint, Fabric, Paper, Yarn & Lots More. 9.95 (ISBN 0-88421-057-X). Butterick Pub.
Pictures & Patterns. PLB 7.98 (ISBN 0-8393-0117-0). Raintree Child.
Pictures by Maurice Sendak. boxed 25.00 (ISBN 0-06-025538-2); boxed & limited ed. 100.00 (ISBN 0-06-025539-0). Har-Row.
Pictures from the Douglas M. Duncan Collection. 15.00 (ISBN 0-8020-3322-9). U of Toronto Pr.
Pictures in Patchwork. 12.95 (ISBN 0-8069-5380-2); lib. bdg. 11.69 (ISBN 0-8069-5381-0). Sterling.
Pictures on Glass. limited ed. 30.00x (ISBN 0-8277-1222-7). British Bk Ctr.
Pictures with Pins. 9.95 (ISBN 0-668-04567-1). Arco.
Picturesque California Homes. pap. 14.95 (ISBN 0-912158-82-4). Hennessey.
Picturesque Garden in France. text ed. 30.00 (ISBN 0-691-03930-5). Princeton U Pr.
Picturesque Ideas on the Flight into Egypt. 5.00 (ISBN 0-87099-121-3). Metro Mus Art.
Picturesque Images from Taos & Santa Fe. pap. 12.95. Denver Art Mus.
Picturesque: Studies in a Point of View. 27.50x (ISBN 0-7146-1144-1). Biblio Dist.
Picturesque Views of Rural Occupations in Early Nineteenth-Century England. pap. 4.50 (ISBN 0-486-23547-5). Dover.
Picturing People. 12.95 (ISBN 0-8174-0576-3). Amphoto.
Picced Quilt: An American Design Tradition. pap. 9.95 (ISBN 0-8212-0686-9). NYGS.
Pieced Work & Applique Quilts at Shelburne Museum. pap. 7.50. Shelburne.
Pier Luigi Nervi. 7.95 (ISBN 0-8076-0106-3); pap. 3.95 (ISBN 0-8076-0223-X). Braziller.
Piet Mondrian's Early Career: The Naturalistic Periods. lib. bdg. 46.00x (ISBN 0-8240-2738-8). Garland Pub.
Pieter Aertsen, Joachim Beuckelaer & the Rise of Secular Painting in the Context of the Reformation. lib. bdg. 40.00 (ISBN 0-8240-2715-9). Garland Pub.
Pieter Brueghel's The Fair. 7.95 (ISBN 0-397-31698-4). Lippincott.
Pietro Da Cortona at the Pitti Palace: A Study of the Planetary Rooms & Related Projects. text ed. 50.00 (ISBN 0-691-03891-0). Princeton U Pr.
Pigozzi's Journal of the Seventies. 8.95 (ISBN 0-385-15104-7). Doubleday.
Pile Weaves: Twenty Six Techniques & How to Do Them. rev. ed. pap. 9.95 (ISBN 0-684-16085-4, SL843). Scribner.
Pilgrimage of Life. 18.50 (ISBN 0-8046-1692-2). Kennikat.
Pillow Making As Art & Craft. 12.95 (ISBN 0-517-52968-8); pap. 7.95 (ISBN 0-517-52969-6). Crown.
Pin & Thread Art. 8.95 (ISBN 0-8008-6452-2). Taplinger.
Pin It, Tack It, Hang It. 9.95 (ISBN 0-911104-61-5); pap. 4.95 (ISBN 0-911104-63-1). Workman Pub.
Pin Pictures with Wire & Thread. 3.95 (ISBN 0-8069-5340-3); PLB 4.59 (ISBN 0-8069-5341-1). Sterling.
Pin-up: A Modest History. pap. 6.95 (ISBN 0-87663-910-4). Universe.
Pinatas. 6.50 (ISBN 0-687-31436-4). Abingdon.
Pine Furniture of Early New England. 12.95 (ISBN 0-486-20145-7). Dover.
Pins, Picks, & Popsicle Sticks. PLB 7.95 (ISBN 0-03-017786-3). HR&W.
Pioneer Decoy Carvers: A Biography of Lemuel & Stephen Ward. 17.50 (ISBN 0-87033-243-0). Cornell Maritime.
Pioneer Pottery. pap. 6.95 (ISBN 0-312-61320-2). St Martin.
Pioneer Pottery. 15.00 (ISBN 0-312-61285-0, P24300). St Martin.
Pioneer Texas Buildings: A Geometry Lesson. 15.00 (ISBN 0-292-73699-1). U of Tex Pr.
Pioneers of Photography. 20.00 (ISBN 0-8109-0408-X). Abrams.
Pioneers: The Frontier Image. pap. 9.95 (ISBN 0-7148-1775-9). Dutton.
Piranesi: Etchings & Drawings. 19.95 (ISBN 0-8212-0577-3). NYGS.
Pissarro in Venezuela. pap. 2.00 (ISBN 0-913456-05-5). Interbk Inc.
Pistolsmithing. 14.95 (ISBN 0-8117-1265-6). Stackpole.
Pittsburgh Glass, 1797-1891: A History & Guide for Collectors. 30.00 (ISBN 0-395-20733-9). HM.
Place of Book Illumination in Byzantine Art. 28.50x (ISBN 0-691-03910-0). Princeton U Pr.
Place of Houses. pap. 7.95. HR&W.
Place of Houses. 17.95 (ISBN 0-03-007726-5). HR&W.
Place of the Arts in New Towns. pap. 3.00 (ISBN 0-89192-044-7). Interbk Inc.
Places of Musical Fame. PLB 3.95 (ISBN 0-8225-0055-8). Lerner Pubns.
Plain & Fancy: American Women & Their Needlework, 1700-1850. 14.95 (ISBN 0-03-015121-X). HR&W.
Plain Man's Guide to Second-Hand Furniture. 6.95 (ISBN 0-7181-0936-8). Transatlantic.
Plains Indian Art from Fort Marion. 18.50 (ISBN 0-8061-0888-6). U of Okla Pr.
Plains Indian Painting: A Description of Aboriginal American Art. 24.50 (ISBN 0-404-15533-2). AMS Pr.
Plains Rifle. 11.95 (ISBN 0-88227-015-X). Gun Room.
Plaiting Step-by-Step. 14.95 (ISBN 0-8230-4020-8). Watson-Guptill.
Plaiting Step-by-Step. pap. 9.95 (ISBN 0-8230-4021-6). Watson-Guptill.
Plan & Section Drawing. 13.95 (ISBN 0-442-26127-6); pap. 6.95 (ISBN 0-442-29178-7). Van Nos Reinhold.
Plan for Restoration & Adaptive Use of the Frank Lloyd Wright Home & Studio. 25.00 (ISBN 0-226-90832-1). U of Chicago Pr.
Plan Graphics. 2nd ed. text ed. 18.00 (ISBN 0-914886-07-X). PDA Pubs.
Plan Your Own Landscape. 12.95 (ISBN 0-448-14382-8); pap. 6.95 (ISBN 0-448-14383-6). G&D.
Planar Dimension: Europe, Nineteen Twelve to Nineteen Thirty-Two. new ed. pap. 12.95 (ISBN 0-89207-017-X). S R Guggenheim.
Planning Academic & Research Library Buildings. text ed. 27.50 (ISBN 0-07-041657-5). McGraw.
Planning & Design of Library Buildings. 2nd ed. 27.50 (ISBN 0-89397-019-0). Nichols Pub.
Planning & Planting the Small Garden Plot: A Practical Guide. 7.95 (ISBN 0-8037-7044-8). Dial.
Planning & Producing Slide Programs. 3rd ed. pap. 4.00 (S-30). Eastman Kodak.
Planning for Play. pap. 6.95 (ISBN 0-262-51013-8). MIT Pr.
Planning Manual for Academic Library Buildings. 9.00 (ISBN 0-8108-0680-0). Scarecrow.
Planning of Ornament. lib. bdg. 35.00x (ISBN 0-8240-2470-2). Garland Pub.
Planning the Community Hospital. lib. bdg. 18.50 (ISBN 0-88275-511-0). Krieger.
Planning the Special Library. pap. 9.75 (ISBN 0-87111-205-1). SLA.
Planning Your Bathroom. pap. 4.95 (ISBN 0-85072-026-5, 030078). Music Sales.
Planning Your Garden. 14.50x (ISBN 0-392-04148-0). Soccer.
Plant & Floral Woodcuts for Designers & Craftsmen. pap. 4.50 (ISBN 0-486-20722-6). Dover.
Plant & Floral Woodcuts for Designers & Craftsmen: 419 Illustrations from the Renaissance Herbal of Clusius. 7.50 (ISBN 0-8446-5170-2). Peter Smith.
Plant Sculptures: Making Miniature Indoor Topiaries. 5.95 (ISBN 0-688-22144-0); PLB 5.71 (ISBN 0-688-32144-5). Morrow.
Planters: Make Your Own Containers for Indoor & Outdoor Plants. pap. 3.95 (ISBN 0-345-25534-8). Ballantine.
Planting Design. 16.95 (ISBN 0-07-025402-8). McGraw.
Plants & Flowers to Decorate Your Home. 12.95 (ISBN 0-307-49335-0); pap. 5.95 (ISBN 0-307-49254-0). Western Pub.
Plants in the Landscape. text ed. 21.50x (ISBN 0-7167-0778-0). W H Freeman.
Plants of the World. o.p.; 19.95 (ISBN 0-525-18040-0); o.p. Dutton.
Plaster Mold & Model Making. pap. 6.95 (ISBN 0-442-21515-0). Van Nos Reinhold.
Plastic Furniture for the Home Craftsman. pap. 5.95 (ISBN 0-8473-1664-5, 028100). Sterling.
Plastic Modelling. 5.65 (ISBN 0-85059-153-8). Aztex.
Plasticrafts. 6.95 (ISBN 0-671-21496-9). S&S.
Plastics. text ed. 4.40 (ISBN 0-87006-239-5). Goodheart.
Plastics - Projects & Techniques. text ed. 11.96 (ISBN 0-87345-159-7). McKnight.
Plastics As an Art Form. rev. ed. pap. 8.95 (ISBN 0-8019-6563-2). Chilton.
Plastics As Sculpture. 11.95 (ISBN 0-8019-5767-2). Chilton.
Plastics for Jewelry. 19.50 (ISBN 0-8230-4027-5). Watson Guptill.
Plastics for Kinetic Art. 17.95 (ISBN 0-8230-4029-1). Watson-Guptill.
Plastics for the Craftsman: Basic Techniques for Working with Plastics. pap. 4.95 (ISBN 0-517-50100-7). Crown.
Plate Collecting: A Guide to a Fascinating Hobby. 17.95 (ISBN 0-8065-0478-1). Citadel Pr.
Play with Paper. 4.95g (ISBN 0-02-708240-7). Macmillan.
Playtime Crafts. PLB 8.49 (ISBN 0-8172-1182-9). Raintree Pubs Ltd.
Playtime Dishes. softbound 9.95 (ISBN 0-87069-212-7). Wallace-Homestead.
Pleasure Places. pap. 4.95 (ISBN 0-8256-3904-2). Music Sales.
Pleasures of Sketching Outdoors. rev. ed. pap. 4.00 (ISBN 0-486-22229-2). Dover.
Pleated Paper Folding. 6.95 (ISBN 0-571-10625-0); pap. 2.95 (ISBN 0-571-10882-2). Merrimack Bk Serv.
Plenty of Patches: An Introduction to Patchwork, Quilting & Applique. 7.95 (ISBN 0-690-01329-9); PLB 7.49 (ISBN 0-690-03836-4). T Y Crowell.
Plundered Past. pap. 5.95 (ISBN 0-689-70551-4, 234). Atheneum.
Pocket Book of American Pewter: The Makers & the Marks, a Handbook for Collectors. 2nd ed. pap. 4.50 (ISBN 0-89046-001-9). Herman Pub.
Pocket Dictionary of Art Terms. pap. 1.95 (ISBN 0-8212-1115-3). NYGS.
Poetry of Architecture. 15.00 (ISBN 0-404-05463-3). AMS Pr.
Poetry of Architecture. 29.00 (ISBN 0-403-00305-9). Scholarly.
Poetry of Architecture: Or, the Architecture of the Nations of Europe. 35.00 (ISBN 0-8490-0859-X). Gordon Pr.
Point & Pillow Lace: A Short Account of Various Kinds, Ancient & Modern, & How to Recognize Them. 15.00 (ISBN 0-8103-3912-9). Gale.
Point of View. 19.95 (ISBN 0-8195-5019-1); limited ed. 150.00 (ISBN 0-8195-8037-6). Wesleyan U Pr.
Pointed Spade Coins of the Chou Dynasty. 30.00x (ISBN 0-88000-012-0). Quarterman.
Police Photography. 21.00x (ISBN 0-85334-621-6). Intl Ideas.
Political Career of Peter Paul Rubens. 9.25 (ISBN 0-500-55007-7). Transatlantic.
Political Cartoonists. PLB 3.95 (ISBN 0-8225-0463-4). Lerner Pubns.
Politics & Script: Aspects of Athority & Freedom in the Development of Graeco-Latin Script from the Sixth Century B.C. to the Twentieth Century A.D. 21.00x (ISBN 0-19-818146-9). Oxford U Pr.
Politics in Art. PLB 4.95 (ISBN 0-8225-0170-8); pap. 3.95 (ISBN 0-8225-9950-3). Lerner Pubns.
Politics of Architecture: A History of Modern Architecture in Britain. 8.50x (ISBN 0-8020-1663-4). U of Toronto Pr.
Pollock. pap. 2.95 (ISBN 0-448-00473-9). G&D.
Polymetis. lib. bdg. 66.00 (ISBN 0-8240-2090-1). Garland Pub.
Pomerance Collection of Ancient Art. pap. 4.50 (ISBN 0-913696-03-X). Bklyn Mus.
Pompeii & Herculaneum: The Living Cities of the Dead. 45.00 (ISBN 0-8109-0418-7). Abrams.
Pompeo Leoni: Work in Marble & Alabaster in Relation to Spanish Sculpture. 1.50 (ISBN 0-87535-088-7). Hispanic Soc.
Pooh Craft Book. 6.95 (ISBN 0-525-37410-8). Dutton.
Pooh: His Art Gallery: Prints from the World of Pooh & the World of Christopher Robin. boxed 8.95 (ISBN 0-525-37433-7). Dutton.
Pop-Topping. 12.50 (ISBN 0-8019-6226-9); pap. 6.95 (ISBN 0-8019-6227-7). Chilton.
Popmooi: European Dolls to Make Yourself. lib. bdg. 8.95 (ISBN 0-87701-132-X); pap. 5.95 (ISBN 0-87701-131-1). Chronicle Bks.
Popular Art: The Example of Jean Charlot. pap. 4.95 (ISBN 0-88496-078-1). Capra Pr.
Popular Arts in America: A Reader. pap. text ed. 7.50 (ISBN 0-15-570743-4). HarBraceJ.
Popular Arts in America: A Reader. 2nd ed. pap. text ed. 7.50 (ISBN 0-15-570742-6). HarBraceJ.
Popular Arts of Colonial New Mexico. pap. 2.45 (ISBN 0-89013-086-8). Museum NM Pr.
Popular Arts of Spanish New Mexico. 34.95 (ISBN 0-89013-064-7). U of NM Pr.
Popular Mechanics Complete Book of Furniture. new ed. 8.95 (ISBN 0-910990-62-X). Hearst Bks.
Popular Mechanics Do It Yourself Encyclopedia. 89.25 (ISBN 0-910990-52-2). Hearst Bks.
Popular Prints of the Americas. write for info. Hispanic Soc.
Porcelain Marks of the World. 6.95 (ISBN 0-668-03403-3). Arco.
Porcelain of Paris, 1770-1850. 35.00 (ISBN 0-8027-0395-X). Walker & Co.
Porfirio Salinas. 25.00 (ISBN 0-914872-04-4). Austin Pr.
Porno-Graphics: The Shame of Our Art Museums. 2.95 (ISBN 0-394-42483-2). Random.
Portable Needlepoint Boutique. 10.95 (ISBN 0-8008-6416-6). Taplinger.
Portfolio of Architecture for Health. 22.00 (ISBN 0-87258-219-1, 2300). Am Hospital.
Portfolio of Low Expense Art Lessons: Featuring 43 Novel Display Techniques. 12.95 (ISBN 0-13-686469-4). P-H.
Portfolio Papers. facsimile ed. 17.75 (ISBN 0-8369-2504-1). Arno.
Portfolios of Ansel Adams. 19.50 (ISBN 0-8212-0723-7). NYGS.
Portrait in the Renaissance. 30.00 (ISBN 0-691-09795-X); pap. 9.95 (ISBN 0-691-01825-1). Princeton U Pr.
Portrait Life of Lincoln. facsimile ed. 18.25 (ISBN 0-8369-5560-9). Arno.
Portrait' Miniatures in Early American History: 1750-1840. pap. 3.00x (ISBN 0-913060-09-7). Norton Art.
Portrait of a Decade: Roy Stryker & the Development of Documentary Photography in the Thirties. 12.95 (ISBN 0-8071-0235-0). La State U Pr.
Portrait of a Decade: Roy Stryker & the Development of Documentary Photography in the Thirties. pap. 6.95 (ISBN 0-306-80058-6). Da Capo.
Portrait of a Shelter. 9.95 (ISBN 0-87784-866-1). Inter-Varsity.
Portrait of an Age. pap. 7.95 (ISBN 0-02-000820-1). Macmillan.
Portrait of Bristol. 10.50 (ISBN 0-7091-5435-6). Intl Pubns Serv.
Portrait of Iowa. 14.95 (ISBN 0-914828-01-0). Adams Minn.
Portrait of Liverpool. 10.50 (ISBN 0-7091-5575-1). Intl Pubns Serv.

Printing & Promotion Handbook: How to Plan, Produce, & Use Printing, Advertising & Direct Mail. 3rd ed. 24.95 (ISBN 0-07-041451-3). McGraw.

Printing As a Hobby. 10.95 (ISBN 0-918142-08-3); pap. 6.95 (ISBN 0-918142-07-5). Myriade.

Printing for Pleasure. 2nd rev. ed. 5.95 (ISBN 0-8092-7810-3). Contemp Bks.

Printing It! pap. 3.50 (ISBN 0-914728-03-2). Wingbow Pr.

Printing Layout & Design. pap. text ed. 6.20 (ISBN 0-8273-0374-2). Delmar.

Printing of Books. 18.25 (ISBN 0-8369-1931-9). Arno.

Printing Plant. PLB 4.90 s&l (ISBN 0-531-02207-2). Watts.

Printing Types: An Introduction. pap. 4.95x (ISBN 0-8070-6659-1, BP474). Beacon Pr.

Printing Unwins. 16.50 (ISBN 0-04-655013-5). Allen Unwin.

Printing with the Handpress. 11.50 (ISBN 0-88275-379-7). Krieger.

Printing Works Like This. 4.95x (ISBN 0-460-06414-2). Biblio Dist.

Printmaking. pap. 1.95 (ISBN 0-448-00563-8). G&D.

Printmaking in Britain: A General History from Its Beginnings to the Present Day. 24.50x, USA (ISBN 0-8147-2973-8). NYU Pr.

Printmaking Today: A Studio Handbook. 2nd ed. 15.00 (ISBN 0-03-073585-8). HR&W.

Prints & Books. 22.50 (ISBN 0-306-71288-1). Da Capo.

Prints & Drawings: A Pictorial History. 16.95 (ISBN 0-7148-1760-0). Dutton.

Prints & People. 20.00 (ISBN 0-87099-108-6). Hispanic Soc.

Prints & People: A Social History of Printed Pictures. 20.00 (ISBN 0-87099-108-6). NYGS.

Prints & Visual Communication. 17.50 (ISBN 0-306-71159-1). Da Capo.

Prints & Visual Communication. pap. 5.95 (ISBN 0-262-59002-6). MIT Pr.

Prints in & of America to 1850. pap. 4.50 (ISBN 0-8139-0323-8). U Pr of Va.

Prints, Maps & Drawings,1677-1822. 3rd ed. 2.00. Mass Hist Soc.

Prints of James Ensor. lib. bdg. 17.50 (ISBN 0-306-70439-0). Da Capo.

Prints of Reginald Marsh. 15.00 (ISBN 0-517-52493-7). Potter.

Prints of Rockwell Kent: A Catalogue Raisonne. 32.50 (ISBN 0-226-40623-7). U of Chicago Pr.

Prints of the Twentieth Century: A History. 13.95 (ISBN 0-19-519887-5); pap. 7.95 (ISBN 0-19-519888-3). Oxford U Pr.

Priscilla Hauser Book of Tole & Decorative Painting. 13.95 (ISBN 0-442-23236-5). Van Nos Reinhold.

Prison Architecture. 75.00x (ISBN 0-85139-547-3). Nichols Pub.

Prisoner of War Ship Models 1775-1825. 22.50 (ISBN 0-87021-858-1). Naval Inst Pr.

Prisons (Le Carceri) The Complete First & Second States. pap. 4.00 (ISBN 0-486-21540-7). Dover.

Private Houses - Graves in the Diyala Region. 40.00x (ISBN 0-226-62190-1, OIP88). U of Chicago Pr.

Private Presswork: A Bibliographic Approach to Printing As an Avocation. 12.50 (ISBN 0-498-01876-8). A S Barnes.

Prize Country Quilts. 14.95 (ISBN 0-8487-0444-4). Oxmoor Hse.

Problem Seeking: An Architectural Programming Primer. 15.95 (ISBN 0-8436-2172-9); text ed. 12.95. CBI Pub.

Problems in Aesthetics: An Introductory Book of Readings. 2nd ed. text ed. 16.95x (ISBN 0-02-425290-5). Macmillan.

Problems in Artistic Woodturning. pap. 7.50 (ISBN 0-918036-07-0, 20J61-D). Woodcraft Supply.

Problems in Mechanical Drawing. 4th ed. 8.70 (ISBN 0-07-037349-3); answer key 1.20 (ISBN 0-07-037355-8). McGraw.

Problems in Titian, Mostly Iconographic. 17.50 (ISBN 0-8147-0334-8). NYU Pr.

Problems of Art. pap. text ed. 3.95x (ISBN 0-684-15346-7). Scribner.

Problems of Design. 8.95 (ISBN 0-8230-7440-4). Watson-Guptill.

Problems of Design. pap. 9.95 (ISBN 0-8230-7439-0). Watson-Guptill.

Prodigal Father: The Life of John Butler Yeats, 1839-1922. 27.50x (ISBN 0-8014-1047-9). Cornell U Pr.

Prodigious Builders. pap. 7.95 (ISBN 0-15-674625-5). HarBraceJ.

Production for the Graphic Designer. 19.95 (ISBN 0-8230-4415-7). Watson-Guptill.

Production of Culture. pap. 4.50x (ISBN 0-8039-0734-6). Sage.

Production of Micro-Forms. lib. bdg. 13.00x (ISBN 0-8371-8235-2, HAPM). Greenwood.

Professional Cartooning: A Complete Course in Graphic Humor. cloth 12.50 (ISBN 0-88275-064-X). Krieger.

Professional Flower Arranging for Beginners. 6.95 (ISBN 0-668-03392-4). Arco.

Professional Furniture Refinishing for the Amateur. 8.95 (ISBN 0-06-013774-6). Har-Row.

Professional Handweaving on the Fly-Shuttle Loom. 16.50 (ISBN 0-442-20948-7). Van Nos Reinhold.

Professional Hungarian Artists Outside of Hungary. english ed. pap. 7.50. Hungarian Rev.

Professional Pattern Making for Designers of Women's Wear. 15.95 (ISBN 0-87245-545-9). Textile Bk.

Professional Patternmaking for Designer's of Women's Wear. spiral bdg. 12.95x (ISBN 0-916434-21-4). Plycon Pr.

Professional Perspective Drawing for Architects & Engineers. text ed. 27.50 (ISBN 0-07-009776-3). McGraw.

Professional Photographic Illustration Techniques. pap. 7.50 (ISBN 0-87985-190-2, 0-16). Eastman Kodak.

Professional Photography. 21.95 (ISBN 0-8038-5862-0). Focal Pr.

Professional Picture Framing for the Amateur. 6.95 (ISBN 0-8306-3674-9); pap. 3.95 (ISBN 0-8306-2674-3). TAB Bks.

Professional Practice of Architectural Detailing. 20.95 (ISBN 0-471-91715-X); tchrs'. manual avail. (ISBN 0-471-04173-4). Wiley.

Professional Skin Care Manual. 13.95 (ISBN 0-13-725358-3). P-H.

Profiles. deluxe ed. 15.00 signed, ltd., numbered (ISBN 0-916290-02-6); pap. 4.95 (ISBN 0-916290-01-8). Squarebooks.

Programmed Blueprint Reading. 3rd ed. text ed. 9.80 (ISBN 0-07-013063-9); tests 11.32 (ISBN 0-07-013064-7). McGraw.

Programs & Manifestoes on 20th-Century Architecture. 12.50x (ISBN 0-262-03039-X); pap. 4.95 (ISBN 0-262-53030-9). MIT Pr.

Programs of Promise: Art in the Schools. pap. text ed. 6.95 (ISBN 0-15-572150-X). HarBraceJ.

Progress in Art. pap. 9.95 (ISBN 0-8478-0168-3). Rizzoli Intl.

Projected Scenery: A Technical Manual. spiral bdg. 4.95x (ISBN 0-910482-08-X). Drama Bk.

Projects in General Metalwork. text ed. 11.96 (ISBN 0-87345-135-X). McKnight.

Projects in Wood Furniture. rev. ed. text ed. 12.96 (ISBN 0-87345-027-2). McKnight.

Prolegomena to the Study of Roman Art. text ed. 16.00 (ISBN 0-300-02268-9); pap. 4.95x (ISBN 0-300-02372-3). Yale U Pr.

Promenades of an Impressionist. 18.25 (ISBN 0-8369-1959-9). Arno.

Promoting & Selling Your Art. 10.95 (ISBN 0-8230-4422-X). Watson-Guptill.

Prophesying Peace: A Sequel to "Ancestral Voices". 10.95 (ISBN 0-684-15646-6). Scribner.

Providing for Future Change: Adaptability & Flexibility in School Building. 7.00 (ISBN 92-64-11487-4). OECD.

Provincial Token-Coinage of the 18th Century. 50.00x (ISBN 0-88000-107-0). Quarterman.

Prytaneion: Its Function & Architectural Form. 15.75x (ISBN 0-520-03316-7). U of Cal Pr.

Psychiatry & Psychology in the Visual Arts & Aesthetics: A Bibliography. 17.50x (ISBN 0-299-03500-X). U of Wis Pr.

Psycho-Birds. pap. 3.95 (ISBN 0-914378-41-4). Countryman.

Psycho-Cosmic Symbolism of the Buddhist Stupa. pap. 4.95 (ISBN 0-913546-36-4). Dharma Pub.

Psychoanalysis of Artistic Vision & Hearing. 3rd ed. lib. bdg. 22.50x (ISBN 0-8277-4846-9). British Bk Ctr.

Psychoanalytic Avenues to Art. text ed. 10.00x (ISBN 0-8236-4420-0). Intl Univs Pr.

Psychoanalytic Explorations in Art. text ed. 20.00x (ISBN 0-8236-4440-5). Intl Univs Pr.

Psychology & the Built Environment. 24.95 (ISBN 0-470-52149-X). Halsted Pr.

Psychology & Visual Aesthetics. 19.50x (ISBN 0-8448-0014-7). Crane-Russak Co.

Psychology for Architects. 17.95 (ISBN 0-470-13460-7). Halsted Pr.

Psychology of the Arts. 18.75 (ISBN 0-8223-0269-1); pap. 9.75. Duke.

Ptolemaic Oinochoai & Portraits in Faience: Aspects of the Ruler-Cult. 49.50x (ISBN 0-19-813211-5). Oxford U Pr.

Public Assembly Facilities: Planning & Management. 15.95 (ISBN 0-471-02437-6). Wiley.

Public Entrance Doors. pap. 6.00 (ISBN 0-309-00948-0). Natl Acad Sci.

Publication Design. 2nd ed. text ed. 12.95x (ISBN 0-697-04324-X). Wm C. Brown.

Pueblo Crafts. 8.00; pap. 6.00 (ISBN 0-910584-51-6). Filter.

Pueblo Crafts. 32.50 (ISBN 0-404-15737-8). AMS Pr.

Pueblo Designs: 176 Illustrations of the "Rain Bird". pap. 3.50 (ISBN 0-486-22073-7). Dover.

Pueblo Designs: 176 Illustrations of the Rain Bird. 5.50 (ISBN 0-8446-0206-X). Peter Smith.

Pueblo Indian Embroidery. 19.50 (ISBN 0-88307-512-1); pap. 8.95 (ISBN 0-88307-513-X). Gannon.

Pueblo Potter: A Study of Creative Imagination in Primitive Art. 55.00 (ISBN 0-404-50558-9). AMS Pr.

Pueblo Potter: A Study of Creative Imagination in Primitive Art. pap. 3.50 (ISBN 0-486-22875-4). Dover.

Pueblo Potter: A Study of Creative Imagination in Primitive Art. 6.50 (ISBN 0-8446-4622-9). Peter Smith.

Puffin Book of Lettering. pap. 1.95 (ISBN 0-14-049117-1). Penguin.

Pull Up a Chair. PLB 3.95 (ISBN 0-8225-0265-8). Lerner Pubns.

Pull up an Easel: How to Paint for Enjoyment. rev. ed. 8.95 (ISBN 0-498-01777-X). A S Barnes.

Pull up an Easel: How to Paint for Enjoyment. rev. large type ed. 9.95 (ISBN 0-498-01854-7). A S Barnes.

Pulled Thread Embroidery. 9.95 (ISBN 0-8008-6562-6); pap. 4.50 (ISBN 0-8008-6563-4). Taplinger.

Pulled Work on Canvas & Linen. 14.95 (ISBN 0-684-15786-1). Scribner.

Puppet Circus. 7.95 (ISBN 0-8238-0119-5). Plays.

Puppet-Making. 3.95 (ISBN 0-8069-5174-5); PLB 4.59 (ISBN 0-8069-5175-3). Sterling.

Puppets. 5.95 (ISBN 0-8231-3027-4). Branford.

Pure Land Buddhist Painting. 14.95 (ISBN 0-87011-287-2). Kodansha.

Put Your Best Foot Forward. 4.95 (ISBN 0-8054-5585-X). Broadman.

Puzzle of Architecture. 16.00x (ISBN 0-522-83539-2). Intl Schol Bk Serv.

Pyramid. 9.95 (ISBN 0-395-21407-6). HM.

Pyramid Odyssey. 10.00 (ISBN 0-8317-7160-7). Mayflower Bks.

Pyramids. 2nd ed. 12.00x (ISBN 0-226-23471-1). U of Chicago Pr.

Pyramids. 2.95 (ISBN 0-521-07240-9). Cambridge U Pr.

Pyramids. PLB 4.95 (ISBN 0-8225-1209-2). Lerner Pubns.

Pyramids of Egypt. pap. 3.95 (ISBN 0-14-020168-8). Penguin.

Pyramids of the New World. PLB 5.49 (ISBN 0-399-60526-6). Putnam.

Pyrography: The Art of Woodburning. 9.95 (ISBN 0-442-23241-1). Van Nos Reinhold.

Pythagorean Palaces: Magic & Architecture in the Italian Renaissance. 28.50x (ISBN 0-8014-0998-5). Cornell U Pr.

Q

Quaint Cuts in the Chap Book Style. 4.00 (ISBN 0-486-23020-1). Dover.

Quaint Cuts in the Chap Book Style. 6.00 (ISBN 0-8446-5020-X). Peter Smith.

Quebec & Related Silver at the Detroit Institute of Arts. 12.00 (ISBN 0-8143-1575-5). Wayne St U Pr.

Queen's Pictures. 17.98 (ISBN 0-02-584690-6, 58469). Macmillan.

Queer Thing, Painting: Forty Years in the World of Art. facsimile ed. 20.00 (ISBN 0-8369-2328-6). Arno.

Quest at Glastonbury: A Biographical Study of Frederick Bligh Bond. 8.50 (ISBN 0-912326-14-X). Garrett-Helix.

Quest for Ulysses. 19.95 (ISBN 0-7148-1616-7). Dutton.

Quest of the Colonial. 15.00 (ISBN 0-8103-3574-3). Gale.

Quick & Easy Holiday Costumes. 8.25 (ISBN 0-688-41809-0); PLB 7.92 (ISBN 0-688-51809-5). Lothrop.

Quick & Easy Quilting. lib. bdg. 7.95 (ISBN 0-8208-0343-X). Hearthside.

Quick Quilting. pap. 6.95 (ISBN 0-8473-1181-3). Sterling.

Quick Sketching. pap. 1.95 (ISBN 0-448-00543-3). G&D.

Quickest Way to Draw Well. pap. 3.95 (ISBN 0-14-046275-9). Penguin.

Quickpoint Book. 10.95; pap. 5.95 (ISBN 0-03-016896-1). HR&W.

Quiet Rebellion: The Making & Meaning of the Arts. 7.95 (ISBN 0-8180-1314-1). Horizon.

Quilt Design Workbook. 12.95 (ISBN 0-89256-004-5); pap. 6.95 (ISBN 0-89256-037-1). Rawson Wade.

Quilter's Companion. pap. 7.95 (ISBN 0-668-04605-8, 4605). Arco.

Quilter's Companion. lib. bdg. 12.95 (ISBN 0-668-02666-9). Arco.

Quilters: Women & Domestic Art. pap. 6.95 (ISBN 0-385-12039-7). Doubleday.

Quilting. pap. 8.95 (ISBN 0-684-16058-7, SL839). Scribner.

Quilting for Today. 4.95 (ISBN 0-263-05601-5). Transatlantic.

Quilting in Squares. 12.95 (ISBN 0-684-15501-X). Scribner.

Quilting Manual. 6.95 (ISBN 0-8208-0322-7). Hearthside.

Quilting Primer. 12.50 (ISBN 0-8019-5859-8); pap. 5.95 (ISBN 0-8019-5860-1). Chilton.

Quilting Primer. 2nd ed. 14.95 (ISBN 0-8019-6826-7); pap. 8.95 (ISBN 0-8019-6827-5, 6827). Chilton.

Quiltmaker's Handbook. 12.95 (ISBN 0-13-749416-5); pap. 6.95 (ISBN 0-13-749408-4). P-H.

Quiltmaking & Quiltmakers. pap. 4.50 (ISBN 0-308-10089-1). T Y Crowell.

Quilts & Coverlets. 10.95 (ISBN 0-442-24694-3); pap. 5.95 (ISBN 0-442-24703-6). Van Nos Reinhold.

Quilts in America. 24.95 (ISBN 0-07-047725-6). McGraw.

R

R. Brownell McGrew. 25.00 (ISBN 0-913504-43-2). Lowell Pr.

R. C. Gorman: The Lithographs. 35.00 (ISBN 0-87358-179-2). Northland.

Radical Perspectives in the Arts. pap. 2.45 (ISBN 0-14-021423-2). Penguin.

Radiographic Photography. 3rd ed. 27.00 (ISBN 0-397-60119-0). Lippincott.

Rags, Rugs & Wool Pictures. reinforced bdg. 5.95 (ISBN 0-684-13490-X). Scribner.

Railroad Station: An Architectural History. 30.00 (ISBN 0-300-00764-7). Yale U Pr.

Railroad Station: An Architectural History. 25.00x (ISBN 0-300-00764-7). Yale U Pr.

Railroad Station Planbook. pap. 4.00 (ISBN 0-89024-531-2). Kalmbach.

Rainbows of Life. pap. 6.95 (ISBN 0-06-090624-3, CN 624). Har-Row.

Rainy Day Magic: The Art of Making Sunshine on a Rainy Day. 5.95 (ISBN 0-87131-087-2). M Evans.

Raku Art & Technique. pap. 7.95 (ISBN 0-442-26949-8). Van Nos Reinhold.

Raku Handbook: A Practical Approach to Ceramic Art. 10.95 (ISBN 0-442-22092-8). Van Nos Reinhold.

Raku Pottery. pap. 6.95 (ISBN 0-02-011860-0). Macmillan.

Raku: Techniques for Contemporary Potters. 17.95 (ISBN 0-8230-4503-X). Watson-Guptill.

Ralph Adams Cram, American Medievalist. 8.00 (ISBN 0-89073-038-5). Boston Public Lib.

Ralph Earl: Recorder for an Era. 8.50 (ISBN 0-87395-020-8); microfiche 8.50 (ISBN 0-87395-120-4). State U NY Pr.

Ralph Eugene Meatyard: An Aperture Monograph. 15.00 (ISBN 0-912334-61-4); pap. 9.50 (ISBN 0-912334-62-2). Aperture.

Ramon Kelley Paints Portraits & Figures. 17.50 (ISBN 0-8230-4505-6). Watson-Guptill.

Ranch & Modern Homes. 3.00 (ISBN 0-911008-13-6). H Estes.

Randolph Caldecott Treasury. 30.00 (ISBN 0-7232-6139-3). Warne.

Raphael. 5.95 (ISBN 0-393-04244-8). Norton.

Raphael, His Life & Works. 42.50 (ISBN 0-8369-6852-2). Arno.

Rapid Perspective. 5.95 (ISBN 0-85458-050-6); pap. 3.75 (ISBN 0-85458-051-4). Transatlantic.

Rare & Expensive Postcards. 6.95 (ISBN 0-87069-087-6). Wallace-Homestead.

Rarities in Carnival Glass. pap. 8.95 (ISBN 0-89145-075-0). Collector Bks.

Rarities of the Musee Guimet. 19.50 (ISBN 0-87848-043-9). Weatherhill.

Rathbone Years: Masterpieces Acquired for the Museum of Fine Arts, Boston, 1955-1972 & for the St. Louis Art Museum, 1940-1955. pap. 6.50. Mus Fine Arts Boston.

Rauschenberg. pap. 3.95 (ISBN 0-452-00356-3, FM356). NAL.

Raven: A Collection of Woodcuts. slip-cased 100.00 (ISBN 0-88240-040-1). Alaska Northwest.

Ravenna Mosaics. 55.00 (ISBN 0-7148-1896-8). Dutton.

Raymond Duchamp-Villon. 7.50 (ISBN 0-8027-0241-4); pap. 3.50 (ISBN 0-8027-7073-8). Walker & Co.

Re-used Blocks from the Pyramid of Amenemhet I at Lisht. 20.00 (ISBN 0-87099-107-8). Metro Mus Art.

Reaching for Art. facs. ed. 12.25 (ISBN 0-8369-0408-7). Arno.

Readability of Certain Type Sizes & Forms in Sight-Saving Classes. 17.50 (ISBN 0-404-55883-6). AMS Pr.

Reader on the Library Building. 19.00 (ISBN 0-910972-11-7). IHS-PDS.

Reading & Detailing Assembly Drawings: Dies. 6.00 (ISBN 0-911168-10-9). Prakken.

Robert Henri & Five of His Pupils: Loan Exhibition of Paintings, April 5, to June 1, 1946. 14.00 (ISBN 0-8369-8081-6). Arno.

Robert Henri & His Circle. 32.50x (ISBN 0-8014-0498-3). Cornell U Pr.

Robert Hudson Tannahill Bequest to the Detroit Institute of Arts: A Catalogue Issued on the Occasion of the Exhibition. 14.95 (ISBN 0-8143-1445-7). Wayne St U Pr.

Robert Lehman Collection. pap. 7.50 (ISBN 0-87099-127-2). Metro Mus Art.

Robert Motherwell. 55.00 (ISBN 0-8109-0289-3). Abrams.

Robert Rohm, Christopher Sproat. pap. 1.50. Mus Fine Arts Boston.

Robert Salmon, Painter of Ship & Shore. 20.00 (ISBN 0-87577-040-1). Peabody Mus Salem.

Robert Vickrey: Artist at Work. 19.50 (ISBN 0-8230-4580-3). Watson-Guptill.

Robert Willis. pap. 3.00 (ISBN 0-87391-007-9). Smith Coll.

Robes of White Shell & Sunrise. pap. 7.50 (ISBN 0-914738-04-6). Denver Art Mus.

Rock & Stone Craft. 4.95 (ISBN 0-517-50353-0); pap. 3.95 (ISBN 0-517-50380-8). Crown.

Rock Art in New Mexico. pap. 8.50 (ISBN 0-8263-0372-2). U of NM Pr.

Rock Art of Africa. 25.00 (ISBN 0-498-01753-2). A S Barnes.

Rock Art of Africa. 25.00 (ISBN 0-87982-024-1). Art Alliance.

Rock Art of the Cobar Pediplain in Central Western New South Wales. text ed. 14.00x (ISBN 0-85575-049-9). Humanities.

Rock Art of Utah. pap. 10.00 (ISBN 0-87365-186-3). Peabody Harvard.

Rockefeller Center. 17.50 (ISBN 0-19-502317-X). Oxford U Pr.

Rockefeller Center. pap. 9.95 (ISBN 0-19-502404-4, GB544). Oxford U Pr.

Rockefeller Center: Architecture As Theatre. 19.95 (ISBN 0-07-003480-X). McGraw.

Rockingham Pottery. 8.50 (ISBN 0-8048-1121-0). C E Tuttle.

Rocks Begin to Speak. 10.95 (ISBN 0-916122-30-1). K C Pubns.

Rockwell Portrait. pap. 2.95 (ISBN 0-553-13206-7). Bantam.

Rockwell Portrait: An Intimate Biography. 12.95 (ISBN 0-8362-6602-1). Andrews & McMeel.

Rocky Mountains. 30.00 (ISBN 0-912856-16-5). Graphic Arts Ctr.

Rococo to Revolution: Major Trends in Eighteenth-Century Painting. pap. 7.95 (ISBN 0-19-519960-X). Oxford U Pr.

Rodin. 5.95 (ISBN 0-517-08266-7). Crown.

Rodin on Art. pap. 4.95 (ISBN 0-8180-0114-3). Horizon.

Rodin's Sculpture: A Critical Study of the Spreckles Collection. pap. 13.95 (ISBN 0-8048-1236-5). C E Tuttle.

Rodin's Sculpture: A Critical Study of the Spreckels Collection. new ed. 20.00 (ISBN 0-88401-023-6); pap. 13.95 (ISBN 0-88401-022-8). Fine Arts Mus.

Roentgen Furniture: Abraham & David Roentgen, European Cabinet Makers. 80.00x (ISBN 0-85667-003-0). Biblio Dist.

Roger Fry: A Biography. pap. 4.50 (ISBN 0-15-678520-X, HB338). HarBraceJ.

Rogier Van der Weyden. 50.00 (ISBN 0-7148-1516-0). Dutton.

Role of Culture in Leisure-Time in New Zealand. pap. 2.65 (ISBN 92-3-101041-7). Unipub.

Role of Vincent Van Gogh's Copies in the Development of His Art. lib. bdg. 34.00 (ISBN 0-8240-1984-9). Garland Pub.

Roll Call of the Iroquois Chiefs: A Study of a Mnemonic Cane from the Six Nations Reserve. 12.00 (ISBN 0-404-15536-7). AMS Pr.

Rollei Way. 9th ed. 21.95 (ISBN 0-8038-6354-3). Focal Pr.

Rolleiflex Guide. pap. 3.95 (ISBN 0-8038-6352-7). Focal Pr.

Roman Anniversary Issues: An Exploratory Study of the Numismatic & Medallic Commenmoration of Anniversary Years 49 B.C.-A.D.375. 10.00 (ISBN 0-915018-18-7). Attic Bks.

Roman Architecture. pap. 5.95 (ISBN 0-8076-0331-7). Braziller.

Roman Art. 40.00 (ISBN 0-670-60342-2). Viking Pr.

Roman Art & Architecture. pap. 7.95 (ISBN 0-19-519921-9). Oxford U Pr.

Roman Baroque Art. 60.00 (ISBN 0-87817-065-0). Hacker.

Roman Coins. 60.00 (ISBN 0-8109-1584-7). Abrams.

Roman Construction in Italy from Nerva Through the Antonines. 20.00 (ISBN 0-87169-096-9). Am Philos.

Roman Construction in Italy from Tiberius Through Flavians. 23.00 (ISBN 0-527-08870-6). Kraus Repr.

Roman Granaries & Store Buildings. 45.00 (ISBN 0-521-07724-9). Cambridge U Pr.

Roman Group Portraiture: The Funerary Reliefs of the Late Republic & Early Empire. lib. bdg. 52.00 (ISBN 0-8240-2703-5). Garland Pub.

Roman Historical Portraits. 35.00x (ISBN 0-8014-1011-8). Cornell U Pr.

Roman History from Coins. pap. 3.95 (ISBN 0-521-09549-2, 549). Cambridge U Pr.

Roman Imperial Art in Greece & Asia Minor. 25.00x (ISBN 0-674-77775-1). Harvard U Pr.

Roman Imperial Coins in the Hunter Coin Cabinet, University of Glasgow: Pertinax to Aemilian. 72.50x (ISBN 0-19-713306-1). Oxford U Pr.

Roman Imperial Sculpture: Up to the Death of Constantine. 12.00 (ISBN 0-85458-869-8). Transatlantic.

Roman Republican Coinage. 132.00 (ISBN 0-521-07492-4). Cambridge U Pr.

Roman Rococo Architecture from Clement XI to Benedict XIV (1700-1758) lib. bdg. 37.00x (ISBN 0-8240-2710-8). Garland Pub.

Roman Sculpture from Augustus to Constantine. 25.00 (ISBN 0-405-02230-1). Arno.

Roman Sources of Christian Art. lib. bdg. 22.00x (ISBN 0-8371-3430-7, SWCA). Greenwood.

Roman Stonecutter: An Introduction to Latin Epigraphy. 12.50x (ISBN 0-87471-196-7). Rowman.

Roman Temples of Lebanon: A Pictorial Guide. 2nd ed. 27.50x (ISBN 0-8002-1932-5). Intl Pubns Serv.

Roman Theater-Temples. lib. bdg. 21.00x (ISBN 0-313-20477-2, HATT). Greenwood.

Romance of Greeting Cards: An Historical Account of the Origin, Evolution, & Development. 15.00 (ISBN 0-8103-3903-X). Gale.

Romance of Symbolism & It's Relation to Church Ornament & Architecture. 14.00 (ISBN 0-8103-4302-9). Gale.

Romanesque Architecture. 42.50 (ISBN 0-8109-1024-1). Abrams.

Romanesque Architecture of the Order of Cluny. 42.00 (ISBN 0-404-02358-4). AMS Pr.

Romanesque Art in Europe. pap. 4.95 (ISBN 0-393-00687-5). Norton.

Romanesque Frescoes. lib. bdg. 26.25x (ISBN 0-8371-4707-7, ANRF). Greenwood.

Romanesque Goldsmith's Art in Hungary. 5.00x. Intl Pubns Serv.

Romanesque Sculpture from the Cathedral of Saint-Etienne, Toulouse. lib. bdg. 43.00 (ISBN 0-8240-2729-9). Garland Pub.

Romanesque Sculpture of the Pilgrimage Roads. 150.00 (ISBN 0-87817-020-0). Hacker.

Romanesque Wooden Doors of Auvergne. 18.50x (ISBN 0-8147-1357-2). NYU Pr.

Romanian Icons Painted on Glass. 25.00x (ISBN 0-393-04309-6). Norton.

Romantic England. 11.95 (ISBN 0-02-600100-4). Macmillan.

Romanticism & Realism. 13.95 (ISBN 0-07-055318-1). McGraw.

Romanticism & the Gothic Revival. 8.50 (ISBN 0-87752-000-3). Gordian.

Romanticism: The Culture of the Nineteenth Century. 6.95 (ISBN 0-8076-0314-7). Braziller.

Romischen Grabaltare der Kaiserzeit. facsimile ed. 19.00x (ISBN 0-405-07002-0). Arno.

Room Acoustics. 33.95 (ISBN 0-470-51105-2). Halsted Pr.

Room Acoustics. 2nd ed. 40.00x. Intl Ideas.

Room for Wonder: Indian Painting During the British Period, 1760-1880. 18.50 (ISBN 0-8478-0176-4). Rizzoli Intl.

Room for Wonder: Indian Painting During the British Period, 1760-1880. soft cover 8.00 (ISBN 0-917418-60-3). Am Fed Arts.

Room Outside: A New Approach to Garden Design. pap. 6.95 (ISBN 0-14-005077-9). Penguin.

Rooms for Living. pap. 4.95 (ISBN 0-8256-3077-0, 030077). Music Sales.

Roots & Routes of Art in the 20th Century. 17.50 (ISBN 0-8180-0123-2). Horizon.

Roots of Contemporary American Architecture: A Series of 37 Essays from Mid-19th Century to the Present. 7.50 (ISBN 0-8446-0215-9). Peter Smith.

Roots of Contemporary American Architecture. pap. 6.00 (ISBN 0-486-22072-9). Dover.

Roots of Life. 5.50 (ISBN 0-8180-0013-9). Horizon.

Rope Dolls. pap. 4.95 (ISBN 0-8473-1550-9). Sterling.

Rose Painting in Norway. 2 nd, rev ed. pap. 12.00x (N390). Vanous.

Rose Windows. 22.50 (ISBN 0-87701-121-4). Chronicle Bks.

Rosegarden & Labyrinth: A Study in Art Education. 16.75 (ISBN 0-7100-2046-5). Routledge & Kegan.

Rossetti: A Critical Essay on His Art. lib. bdg. 20.00 (ISBN 0-8414-4939-2). Folcroft.

Rossetti, Dante & Ourselves. lib. bdg. 17.95 (ISBN 0-8383-1917-3). Haskell.

Rossetti, Dante & Ourselves. lib. bdg. 10.75 (ISBN 0-8414-4531-1). Folcroft.

Rossetti Family, 1824-1854. 18.00 (ISBN 0-403-01261-9). Scholarly.

Rossetti-Leyland Letters: The Correspondence of an Artist & His Patron. 12.00 (ISBN 0-8214-0207-2). Ohio U Pr.

Rossetti Papers, 1862-1870. 17.50 (ISBN 0-404-05438-2). AMS Pr.

Rossettis. lib. bdg. 27.95 (ISBN 0-8383-1943-2). Haskell.

Royal Academy Exhibitors 1905-1970: A Dictionary of Artists & Their Work in the Summer Exhibitions of the Royal Academy of Arts. text ed. 45.00x (ISBN 0-8277-2683-X). British Bk Ctr.

Royal Academy Exhibitors 1905-1970: A Dictionary of Artists & Their Work in the Summer Exhibitions of the Royal Academy of Arts. text ed. 45.00x ea.; text ed. 350.00x (ISBN 0-8277-2675-9); (ISBN 0-8277-2684-8); (ISBN 0-8277-2677-5); (ISBN 0-8277-2678-3); (ISBN 0-8277-2680-5); (ISBN 0-8277-2681-3); (ISBN 0-8277-2682-1). British Bk Ctr.

Royal Academy of Arts: A Complete Dictionary of Contributors & Their Work from 1769-1904. 120.00x. Beekman Pubs.

Royal Academy of Arts: A Complete Dictionary of Contributors & Their Work from Its Foundation in 1769-1904. text ed. 300.00x (ISBN 0-8277-1411-4). British Bk Ctr.

Royal Cemeteries of Kush. Incl. El Kurru. 25.00; Nuri. 35.00; Decorated Chapels of the Meroitic Pyramids at Meroe & Barkal. 30.00; Royal Tombs at Meroe & Barkal. 35.00; West & South Cemeteries of Meroe. 35.00. Mus Fine Arts Boston.

Royal Crown Derby. 15.00 (ISBN 0-517-52814-2). Potter.

Royal Head from Ancient Egypt. pap. 0.50. Freer.

Royal Heritage: The Treasures of the Kings & Queens of England. 25.00 (ISBN 0-15-179011-6). HarBraceJ.

Royal Parks for the People. 9.95 (ISBN 0-7153-6454-5). David & Charles.

Royal Tombs at Meroe & Barkal see **Royal Cemeteries of Kush.**

Royal Worcester Porcelain from 1862 to the Present Day. 29.95 (ISBN 0-214-20106-6, 8070). Barrie & Jenkins.

RSVP Cycles. 15.00 (ISBN 0-8076-0557-3); pap. 6.95 (ISBN 0-8076-0628-6). Braziller.

Rub Book. 3.50g (ISBN 0-02-781590-0). Macmillan.

Rubbing Craft. pap. 4.95 (ISBN 0-8256-3062-2). Music Sales.

Rubens & Italy. 55.00 (ISBN 0-8014-1064-9). Cornell U Pr.

Rubens & the Counter Reformation: Studies in His Religious Paintings Between 1609 & 1620. lib. bdg. 37.00x. Garland Pub.

Rubies & Roses: Gems Portrayed in Flowers. 13.75 (ISBN 0-8048-0507-5). C E Tuttle.

Rufino Tamayo. 55.00 (ISBN 0-8109-0500-0). Abrams.

Rug Hooking & Braiding for Pleasure & Profit. pap. 4.95 (ISBN 0-308-10234-7). T Y Crowell.

Rug Making. 6.50 (ISBN 0-8231-5026-7). Branford.

Rug Weaving for Beginners. 9.95 (ISBN 0-8230-4616-8). Watson-Guptill.

Rugs & Wall Hangings. 14.95 (ISBN 0-684-14670-3). Scribner.

Rugs of Spain & Morocco. 19.00 (ISBN 0-226-69109-8); one color fiche incl. U of Chicago Pr.

Ruins of Altar De Sacrificios, Department of Peten, Guatemala: An Introduction. pap. text ed. 3.00 (ISBN 0-87365-177-4). Peabody Harvard.

Run for the Money. 4.95 (ISBN 0-316-15707-4). Little.

Run for the Money. pap. 1.25 (ISBN 0-671-29751-1). Archway.

Rural Architecture in the Chinese Taste. 12.50 (ISBN 0-405-08591-5). Arno.

Rural Crafts in Scotland. 8.75 (ISBN 0-7091-5460-7). Transatlantic.

Rural Pennsylvania Clothing: Being a Study of the Wearing Apparel of the German & Inhabitants in the Late 18th & Early 19th Century. 29.50 (ISBN 0-87387-064-6). Shumway.

Ruskin. lib. bdg. 12.50 (ISBN 0-8414-3530-8). Folcroft.

Ruskin & Brantwood. lib. bdg. 10.00. Folcroft.

Ruskin & His Circle. 15.00 (ISBN 0-404-02232-4). AMS Pr.

Ruskin & His Circle. 15.00 (ISBN 0-8274-1690-3). R West.

Ruskin and His Circle. lib. bdg. 17.50 (ISBN 0-8495-1308-1). Arden Lib.

Ruskin & His Circle. lib. bdg. 25.00 (ISBN 0-8482-0734-3). Norwood Edns.

Ruskin & Turner. 17.95 (ISBN 0-571-08497-4). Merrimack Bk Serv.

Ruskin, the Great Victorian. 19.50 (ISBN 0-208-00815-2). Shoe String.

Ruskin the Prophet & Other Centenary Studies. lib. bdg. 25.00 (ISBN 0-8414-9368-5). Folcroft.

Ruskin's Scottish Heritage. 11.00 (ISBN 0-252-72634-0). U of Ill Pr.

Ruskin's Venice. 12.95 (ISBN 0-8230-7445-5). Watson-Guptill.

Russia in Original Photographs: 1860-1920. 20.00 (ISBN 0-684-15274-6). Scribner.

Russian Art of the Avant Garde. 20.00 (ISBN 0-670-61257-X). Viking Pr.

Russian Artist. 5.95 (ISBN 0-02-540650-7). Macmillan.

Russian Icons: A Color Plate Book. 7.95 (ISBN 0-7148-1792-9). Dutton.

Russian Impact on Art. lib. bdg. 21.00x (ISBN 0-8371-2160-4, ALRA). Greenwood.

Russian Orders, Decorations & Medals. 2nd ed. 35.00. Quaker.

Russian Peasant Design Motifs for Needleworkers & Craftsmen. pap. 1.50 (ISBN 0-486-23235-2). Dover.

Russian Self-Portraits. pap. 6.95 (ISBN 0-06-010171-7, TD-293). Har-Row.

Rustic Furniture. 15.95 (ISBN 0-442-27974-4). Van Nos Reinhold.

S

S. Andrea in Mantua: The Building. 30.00x (ISBN 0-271-01186-6). Pa St U Pr.

Sacred & Legendary Art. 18.50 (ISBN 0-404-03551-5). AMS Pr.

Sacred Art of Tibet. 2nd ed. pap. 5.95 (ISBN 0-913546-01-1). Dharma Pub.

Sacred Circles: Two Thousand Years of North American Indian Art. pap. 12.95 (ISBN 0-295-95584-8). U of Wash Pr.

Sacred Fortress: Byzanine Art & Statecraft in Ravenna. 18.50x (ISBN 0-226-75977-6). U of Chicago Pr.

Safeguarding the School Board's Purchase of Architects' Working Drawings. 17.50 (ISBN 0-404-55474-1). AMS Pr.

Safeguarding Your Collection in Travel. pap. 3.25 (ISBN 0-910050-05-8). AASLH.

Sailing to Byzantium: An Architectural Companion. 11.95 (ISBN 0-87645-007-9). Gambit.

St. Martin Embroideries. 2.95 (ISBN 0-87099-071-3). Metro Mus Art.

Saints & Their Emblems. 22.00 (ISBN 0-403-04249-6). Somerset Pub.

Saints & Their Emblems. lib. bdg. 24.50 (ISBN 0-8337-0902-X). B Franklin.

Saints & Their Emblems. 14.00 (ISBN 0-8103-3032-6). Gale.

Sakkara: A Guide to the Necropolis of Sakkara & the Site of Memphis. pap. text ed. 5.95x (ISBN 0-582-78069-1). Longman.

Salem Interiors. 10.00 (ISBN 0-8038-6642-9). Hastings.

Salinas De los Nueve Cerros Guatemala: Preliminary Archaeological Investigations. pap. 5.95 (ISBN 0-87919-070-1). Ballena Pr.

Salomon de Brosse & the Development of the Classical Style in French Architecture from 1565 to 1630. 32.50x (ISBN 0-271-00140-2). Pa St U Pr.

Salons. 2nd ed. 3.95. French & Eur.

Salt-Glazed Ceramics. 17.95 (ISBN 0-8230-4630-3). Watson-Guptill.

Saltwater Flats: A Silent Film. 9.95 (ISBN 0-915090-00-7). Calif Street.

Salvador Dali. 16.00 (ISBN 0-405-01522-4). Arno.

Salvage Archaeology in Painted Rocks Reservoir, Western Arizona. pap. 4.95x (ISBN 0-8165-0273-0). U of Ariz Pr.

Sam Francis. 55.00 (ISBN 0-8109-0265-6). Abrams.

Sampler Book. spiral bdg. 9.95 (ISBN 0-517-53461-4). Crown.

Samplers & Stitches. 6.95 (ISBN 0-8208-0339-1). Hearthside.

Samplers & Tapestry Embroideries. pap. 4.00 (ISBN 0-486-22070-2). Dover.

Samplers & Tapestry Embroideries. 2nd ed. 6.50 (ISBN 0-8446-0149-7). Peter Smith.

Samuel Richardson: Master Printer. lib. bdg. 21.75x (ISBN 0-8371-9732-5, SASR). Greenwood.

San Francisco's Heritage in Art Glass. 27.95 (ISBN 0-87564-013-3). Superior Pub.

San Xavier Altarpiece. pap. 4.95x (ISBN 0-8165-0323-0). U of Ariz Pr.

Sand Art. 6.95 (ISBN 0-517-52475-9); pap. 4.95 (ISBN 0-517-52476-7). Crown.

Sand Creatures & Castles: How to Build Them. reinforced bdg. 5.95 (ISBN 0-03-014366-7). HR&W.

Sandcasting. text ed. 3.95 (ISBN 0-8225-0860-5). Lerner Pubns.

Sandpaintings of the Navajo Shooting Chant. pap. 6.00 (ISBN 0-486-23141-0). Dover.

Sandpaintings of the Navajo Shooting Chant. 11.50 (ISBN 0-8446-5231-8). Peter Smith.

Sandro Botticelli. Incl. Life & Work (ISBN 0-520-03372-8); Complete Catalogue (ISBN 0-520-03574-7). boxed set 120.00x. U of Cal Pr.

Sanford Robinson Gifford (1823-1880) lib. bdg. 66.00 (ISBN 0-8240-2737-X). Garland Pub.
Sanity of William Blake. pap. 7.95 (ISBN 0-8383-0097-9). Haskell.
Sanity of William Blake. lib. bdg. 5.50 (ISBN 0-8414-6156-2). Folcroft.
Santa Casa di Loreto: Problems in Cinquecento Sculpture. lib. bdg. 110.00x (ISBN 0-8240-2735-3). Garland Pub.
Santa Clara Pottery Today. pap. 5.95 (ISBN 0-8263-0322-6). U of NM Pr.
Santayana's Aesthetics: A Critical Introduction. lib. bdg. 13.00x (ISBN 0-8371-6696-9, SISB). Greenwood.
Santos: The Religious Folk Art of New Mexico. lib. bdg. 30.00 (ISBN 0-87817-169-X). Hacker.
Sargent Watercolors. pap. 8.95 (ISBN 0-8230-4641-9). Watson-Guptill.
Sasanian Remains from Qasr-i Abu Nasr: Seals, Sealings, & Coins. 12.50x (ISBN 0-674-78960-1). Harvard U Pr.
Satirical Etchings of James Gillray. pap. 5.00 (ISBN 0-486-23340-5). Dover.
Satirical Etchings of James Gillray. 10.00 (ISBN 0-8446-5579-1). Peter Smith.
Satsuma: An Illustrated Guide. softbound 7.95 (ISBN 0-87069-227-5). Wallace-Homestead.
Saul Steinberg. 25.00 (ISBN 0-394-50136-5); pap. 12.95 (ISBN 0-394-73591-9). Knopf.
Savage Hits Back. 10.00 (ISBN 0-8216-0147-4). Univ Bks.
Savage Messiah. pap. 2.95 (ISBN 0-380-01394-0, 12831). Avon.
Saw, Hammer & Paint: Woodworking & Finishing for Beginners. 6.75 (ISBN 0-688-20069-9); PLB 6.48 (ISBN 0-688-30069-3). Morrow.
Say It with Pictures: Graphic Communication with Illustration. 12.95 (ISBN 0-442-28642-2); pap. 7.95 (ISBN 0-442-28644-9). Van Nos Reinhold.
Scale Models in Balsa. pap. 2.95 (ISBN 0-8008-7000-X). Taplinger.
Scandinavian Art. 35.00 (ISBN 0-405-08735-7). Arno.
Scandinavian Design. 4.00 (ISBN 0-8184-0071-4). Lyle Stuart.
Scandinavian Knitting Designs. 17.95 (ISBN 0-684-14817-X). Scribner.
Scaylea on Photography. 19.95 (ISBN 0-87564-014-1). Superior Pub.
Scene. 18.00 (ISBN 0-405-08381-5). Arno.
Scene Design: A Guide to the Stage. pap. 3.00 (ISBN 0-486-23153-4). Dover.
Scene Design: A Guide to the Stage. 7.50 (ISBN 0-8446-5507-4). Peter Smith.
Scene Design & Stage Lighting. 4th ed. text ed. 14.95 (ISBN 0-03-020761-4). HR&W.
Scene Design for Stage & Screen. lib. bdg. 21.50x (ISBN 0-8371-8320-0, LASS). Greenwood.
Scenery for the Theatre. 2nd, rev. ed. 32.00 (ISBN 0-316-11754-4). Little.
Scenes from Childhood. 7.95 (ISBN 0-525-38820-6). Dutton.
Scepter of Egypt: A Background for the Study of Egyptian Antiquities in the Metropolitan Museum of Art, Part II: the Hyksos Period & the New Kingdom (1675-1080 B.C.) 16.95 (ISBN 0-87099-074-8); pap. write for info. (ISBN 0-87099-074-8). Metro Mus Art.
Scepter of Egypt: A Background for the Study of Egyptian Antiquities in the Metropolitan Museum of Art. Incl. From the Earliest Times to the End of the Middle Kingdom. o.p. (ISBN 0-87099-072-1); The Hyksos Period & the New Kingdom. 16.95 (ISBN 0-87099-074-8). NYGS.
Schiele in Prison. pap. 7.95 (ISBN 0-8212-0554-4). NYGS.
Schinkel's Berlin: A Study in Environmental Planning. 12.50x (ISBN 0-674-79095-2). Harvard U Pr.
Schiwetz Legacy: An Artist's Tribute to Texas, 1910-1971. 24.50 (ISBN 0-292-77502-4). U of Tex Pr.
Schoenhut Dolls & Toys: A Loving Legacy. pap. 8.95 (ISBN 0-89145-012-2). Collector Bks.
Scholar Painters of Japan: The Nanga School. lib. bdg. 30.00x (ISBN 0-405-06562-0). Arno.
Scholder - Indians. pap. 12.50 (ISBN 0-87358-092-3). Northland.
School Architecture. text ed. 15.00x (ISBN 0-391-00251-1). Humanities.
School Days: An Original Compilation. 14.95 (ISBN 0-88355-633-2); pap. 6.95 (ISBN 0-88355-632-4). Hyperion Conn.
Schwiering & the West. new ed. 25.00 (ISBN 0-87970-128-5). North Plains.
Science & Building: Structural & Environmental Design in the Nineteenth & Twentieth Centuries. 24.95 (ISBN 0-471-02738-3). Wiley.
Science & the Arts: A Study in Relationships from 1600-1900. 10.50 (ISBN 0-8386-1054-4). Fairleigh Dickinson.
Science from Wood. pap. text ed. 5.95 (ISBN 0-356-05073-4). Raintree Child.
Science Lecture Room. 25.00 (ISBN 0-521-06612-3). Cambridge U Pr.
Science of Photography. 3rd ed. 11.95 (ISBN 0-471-03440-0). Halsted Pr.
Scissor Cutting for Beginners. 6.50 (ISBN 0-03-039941-6). HR&W.
Scooters Are Groovy & You Can Build Your Own. PLB 4.58 (ISBN 0-8037-8168-7); pap. 1.95 (ISBN 0-8037-8135-0). Dial.
Scope of Total Architecture. pap. 1.25 (ISBN 0-02-000500-8). Macmillan.
Scottish Painting: 1837-1939. 29.95 (ISBN 0-02-548110-X). Macmillan.
Scrap Craft for Youth Groups. 9.95x (ISBN 0-381-97015-9, A68200). T Y Crowell.
Scrap Craft: One Hundred & Five Projects. pap. 3.00 (ISBN 0-486-21999-2). Dover.
Scrap Craft: 105 Projects. 5.50 (ISBN 0-8446-0572-7). Peter Smith.
Scrap Puppets: How to Make & Move Them. 7.95 (ISBN 0-03-018511-4). HR&W.
Scrap Wood Craft. 6.25 (ISBN 0-688-41791-4); PLB 6.00 (ISBN 0-688-51791-9). Lothrop.
Screen Printing Photographic Techniques. 8.50 (ISBN 0-911380-30-2). Signs of Times.
Screen Printing Techniques. 12.50 (ISBN 0-8008-7005-0). Taplinger.
Screen Printing Techniques. pap. 5.95 (ISBN 0-8008-7008-5). Taplinger.
Screenprinting: History & Process. pap. text ed. 9.95 (ISBN 0-03-045491-3). HR&W.
Scribes & Scholars: A Guide to the Transmission of Greek & Latin Literature. 2nd ed. pap. text ed. 8.95x (ISBN 0-19-814372-9). Oxford U Pr.
Scrimshander. rev ed. pap. 8.95 (ISBN 0-912300-92-2). Troubador Pr.
Scrimshaw & Scrimshanders: Whales & Whalemen. 39.95 (ISBN 0-910598-09-6). Flayderman.
Script Letter: Its Form, Construction & Application. 7.50 (ISBN 0-8446-3068-3). Peter Smith.
Scroll Saw Projects. lib. bdg. 5.95 (ISBN 0-87733-056-5); pap. 3.50 (ISBN 0-87733-756-X). Directions.
Sculpting in Steel & Other Metals. 12.50 (ISBN 0-8019-5829-6); pap. 6.95 (ISBN 0-8019-5835-0). Chilton.
Sculptor Giovanni Bologna. lib. bdg. 46.00x (ISBN 0-8240-2696-9). Garland Pub.
Sculptor Jules Dalou: Studies in His Style & Imagery. lib. bdg. 49.00 (ISBN 0-8240-2699-3). Garland Pub.
Sculptural Idea. 3rd ed. pap. text ed. price not set (ISBN 0-8087-1142-3). Burgess.
Sculptural Programs of Chartres Cathedral. pap. 3.95 (ISBN 0-393-00233-0). Norton.
Sculpture & Modeling for the Elementary School. 12.95 (ISBN 0-13-796755-1). P-H.
Sculpture & Sculptors of the Greeks. 4th ed. rev. & enl. ed. 42.50x (ISBN 0-300-01281-0). Yale U Pr.
Sculpture Casting. 9.95 (ISBN 0-517-50059-0). Crown.
Sculpture from Found Objects. 9.95 (ISBN 0-87192-056-5). Davis Mass.
Sculpture from Sardis: The Finds Through 1975. 30.00x (ISBN 0-674-79588-1). Harvard U Pr.
Sculpture in Britain: The Middle Age. rev. ed. 35.00 (ISBN 0-670-62432-2). Viking Pr.
Sculpture in Britain: 1530-1830. 42.00 (ISBN 0-670-62436-5). Viking Pr.
Sculpture in Fiberglass. 10.95 (ISBN 0-8230-4672-9). Watson-Guptill.
Sculpture in Modern America. lib. bdg. 22.75x (ISBN 0-8371-6213-0, SCSC). Greenwood.
Sculpture in Paper. rev. ed. pap. 6.95 (ISBN 0-8230-4699-0). Watson-Guptill.
Sculpture in Plastics. 22.50 (ISBN 0-8230-4701-6). Watson-Guptill.
Sculpture in Plastics. 12.50 (ISBN 0-8230-4700-8). Watson-Guptill.
Sculpture in Siam. 35.00 (ISBN 0-87817-081-2). Hacker.
Sculpture in the Huntington Collection. 5.00 (ISBN 0-87328-012-1). Huntington Lib.
Sculpture in the Netherlands, Germany, France, & Spain: 1400-1500. 50.00 (ISBN 0-670-62440-3). Viking Pr.
Sculpture in the Sun: Hawaii's Art for Open Spaces. pap. 7.95 (ISBN 0-8248-0526-7). U Pr of Hawaii.
Sculpture in Wood. pap. 4.95 (ISBN 0-306-80052-7). Da Capo.
Sculpture in Wood. 15.95 (ISBN 0-19-500081-1). Oxford U Pr.
Sculpture in Wood. 10.00 (ISBN 0-8166-0062-7); pap. 5.95 (ISBN 0-8166-0466-5, MP13). U of Minn Pr.
Sculpture Index: Sculpture of Europe & the Contemporary Middle East. 35.00 (ISBN 0-8108-0249-X). Scarecrow.
Sculpture Index: Sculpture of the Americas, the Orient, Africa, the Pacific Area & the Classical World. 40.00 (ISBN 0-8108-0311-9). Scarecrow.
Sculpture of a City: Philadelphia's Treasures in Bronze & Stone. 25.00 (ISBN 0-8027-0459-X). Walker & Co.
Sculpture of Africa. lib. bdg. 35.00 (ISBN 0-87817-210-6). Hacker.
Sculpture of David Smith: A Catalogue Raisonne. lib. bdg. 60.00 (ISBN 0-8240-9924-9). Garland Pub.
Sculpture of Edgar Degas. 27.50x (ISBN 0-691-03898-8); pap. 8.50 (ISBN 0-691-00318-1). Princeton U Pr.
Sculpture of Gaston Lachaise. 12.00x (ISBN 0-87130-016-8); pap. 6.00x (ISBN 0-87130-017-6). Eakins.
Sculpture of Isidore Konti, 1862-1938. pap. 8.00 (ISBN 0-89062-016-4). Pub Ctr Cult Res.
Sculpture of Jose De Creeft. signed & slipcased 250.00 (ISBN 0-306-70562-1); lib. bdg. 30.00 (ISBN 0-306-70294-0). Da Capo.
Sculpture of Matisse. pap. 3.50 (ISBN 0-87070-448-6). Museum Mod Art.
Sculpture of Taras. 18.00 (ISBN 0-87169-657-6). Am Philos.
Sculpture of Thailand. 30.00x (ISBN 0-405-06559-0). Arno.
Sculpture of the Orient. pap. 3.50 (ISBN 0-486-20018-3). Dover.
Sculpture of the Orient. 6.50 (ISBN 0-8446-4591-5). Peter Smith.
Sculpture of the Twentieth Century. 30.00 (ISBN 0-405-01570-4). Arno.
Sculpture of the World: A History. 15.00 (ISBN 0-670-62543-4). Viking Pr.
Sculpture of Tullio Lombardo: Studies in Sources & Meaning. lib. bdg. 41.00x (ISBN 0-8240-3256-X). Garland Pub.
Sculpture of Vincenzo Danti. lib. bdg. 55.00 (ISBN 0-8240-3252-7). Garland Pub.
Sculpture, Principles & Practice. 9.00 (ISBN 0-8446-4818-3). Peter Smith.
Sculpture: Processes & Principles. 16.50 (ISBN 0-06-438930-8); pap. 8.95 (ISBN 0-06-430091-9, IN-91). Har-Row.
Sculpture West & East: Two Traditions. 12.50 (ISBN 0-396-06703-4). Dodd.
Sculpture with a Torch. 10.00 (ISBN 0-8166-0294-8); pap. 4.95 (ISBN 0-8166-0491-6, MP17). U of Minn Pr.
Sculptured Hyacinths. 20.00 (ISBN 0-915736-02-0). C N Aronson.
Sculptured Needlepoint Stitchery. 14.95 (ISBN 0-684-15371-8). Scribner.
Sculptured Sandcast Candles. 11.25 (ISBN 0-8019-5748-6); pap. 6.95 (ISBN 0-8019-5749-4). Chilton.
Sculptures D'Afrique, D'Amerique, D'Oceanie see **Sculptures Negres.**
Sculptures Negres. Bd. with Sculptures D'Afrique, D'Amerique, D'Oceanie. 40.00 (ISBN 0-87817-056-1). Hacker.
Sculptures of el Tajin, Vera Cruz, Mexico. new ed. 12.50 (ISBN 0-8130-0306-7). U Presses Fla.
Sea-Stories see **Stones of Venice.**
Seaport: Architecture & Townscape of Liverpool. 9.50. Transatlantic.
Seaport City: New York in 1775. pap. 1.95. South St Sea Mus.
Seaport City: New York 1775. pap. 1.95 (ISBN 0-913344-20-6). Interbk Inc.
Search for the Gold of Tutankhamen. 8.95 (ISBN 0-442-80364-8). Van Nos Reinhold.
Search for the Gold of Tutankhamen. pap. 1.95 (ISBN 0-671-81072-3). PB.
Search for the Gold of Tutankhamen. pap. 2.50 (ISBN 0-671-83027-9). PB.
Seascape Painter's Problem Book. 16.95 (ISBN 0-8230-4737-7). Watson-Guptill.
Seascape Painting Step-By-Step. 15.00 (ISBN 0-8230-4740-7). Watson-Guptill.
Seascape Painting Step-by-Step. pap. 9.95 (ISBN 0-8230-4741-5). Watson-Guptill.
Season Sarcophagus in Dumbarton Oaks. 35.00 (ISBN 0-88402-001-0). Dumbarton Oaks.
Season Sarcophagus in Dumbarton Oaks. 49.00 (ISBN 0-384-21290-5); 25.00 ea. Johnson Repr.
Sebastiano Ricci. 80.00x. Westview.
Second Book of Modern Lace Knitting. 5.50 (ISBN 0-8446-4763-2). Peter Smith.
Second Book of Modern Lace Knitting. rev. ed. pap. 3.50 (ISBN 0-486-22905-X). Dover.
Second Norman Rockwell Poster Book. pap. 7.95 (ISBN 0-8230-4589-7). Watson-Guptill.
Second Painter's Problem Book: 20 More Problem Subjects & How to Paint Them. 18.50 (ISBN 0-8230-4749-0). Watson-Guptill.
Second Whole Kids Catalog. pap. 7.50 (ISBN 0-553-01084-0). Bantam.
Secret Affinities: Words & Images by Rene Magritte. 2.00 (ISBN 0-914412-12-4). Inst for the Arts.
Secret of the Good Samaritan Shilling: Supplemented with Notes on Other Genuine & Counterfeit Massachusetts Silver Coins. pap. 3.50 (ISBN 0-89192-291-1). Am Numismatic.
Secret Sculptures of Komo: Art & Power in Bamana (Bambara) Initiation Associations. pap. text ed. 3.95x (ISBN 0-89727-004-5). Inst Study Human.
Secrets of Eskimo Skin Sewing. pap. 4.95 (ISBN 0-88240-026-6). Alaska Northwest.
Secrets of the Stones: The Story of Astro-Archaeology. pap. 2.95 (ISBN 0-14-004491-4). Penguin.
See Inside a Roman Town. PLB 5.90 s&l (ISBN 0-531-09063-9). Watts.
Seeing Red. reinforced bdg. 5.95 (ISBN 0-684-12826-8). Scribner.
Seeing Through Clothes. 25.00 (ISBN 0-670-63174-4). Viking Pr.
Seguy's Decorative Butterflies & Insects in Full Color. pap. 5.00 (ISBN 0-486-23552-1). Dover.
Selected American Game Birds. 30.00 (ISBN 0-87004-213-0). Caxton.
Selected Drawings of Gian Lorenzo Bernini. pap. 5.00 (ISBN 0-486-23525-4). Dover.
Selected Etchings of James A. McN. Whistler. pap. 5.00 (ISBN 0-486-23194-1). Dover.
Selected Far Eastern Art in the Yale University Art Gallery: A Catalogue. 22.50x (ISBN 0-300-01297-7). Yale U Pr.
Selection of Etchings by John Sloan. pap. 10.00x (ISBN 0-8262-0059-1). U of Mo Pr.
Selection of Paintings, Drawings & Watercolors. 19.50 (ISBN 0-226-69181-0); 2 color fiches incl. U of Chicago Pr.
Selections from the Collection of Mr. & Mrs. Harry L. Dalton. pap. 1.50x (ISBN 0-88259-022-7). NCMA.
Selections from the Notebooks of Leonardo Da Vinci. pap. 3.95 (ISBN 0-19-281214-9, GB504). Oxford U Pr.
Selections from the Permanent Collection. 19.50 (ISBN 0-226-69818-1); 2 color fiches incl. U of Chicago Pr.
Self Portrait. pap. 5.95 (ISBN 0-07-051248-5). McGraw.
Self-Portrait in Art. PLB 4.95 (ISBN 0-8225-0154-6). Lerner Pubns.
Self-Portrait with Donors: Confessions of an Art Collector. 12.95 (ISBN 0-316-91803-2). Little.
Self Portraits of Great Artists. treasure trove bdg. 6.47; pap. 2.95. Borden.
Selling Antiques & Collectibles at Your Own Flea Market. 15.95 (ISBN 0-87294-058-6). Country Beautiful.
Selling Your Art Work: A Marketing Guide for Fine & Commercial Artists. 9.95 (ISBN 0-498-01105-4). A S Barnes.
Semaine De Bonte: A Surrealistic Novel in Collage. 2nd ed. pap. 5.00 (ISBN 0-486-23252-2). Dover.
Seneca Ray Stoddard, Versatile Camera Artist. 10.50 (ISBN 0-9601158-1-1). Adirondack Yes.
Sengai, the Zen Master. 15.00 (ISBN 0-8212-0319-3). NYGS.
Sense of Form in Art. pap. 3.95x (ISBN 0-8284-0153-5). Chelsea Pub.
Sense of Order: A Study in the Psychology of Decorative Art. 38.50 (ISBN 0-8014-1143-2). Cornell U Pr.
Sensitive Chaos: The Creation of Flowing Forms in Water & Air. 14.95x (ISBN 0-8052-3636-8); pap. 9.95 (ISBN 0-8052-0589-6). Schocken.
Sensitometric Testing Methods. 55.00 (ISBN 0-8038-8959-3). Focal Pr.
Sensuous Immortals. 40.00 (ISBN 0-262-16068-4). MIT Pr.
Seth Eastman's Mississippi: A Lost Portfolio Recovered. 10.00 (ISBN 0-252-00192-3). U of Ill Pr.
Setting in Clear Plastic. 4.95 (ISBN 0-8008-7070-0). Taplinger.
Seurat. pap. 7.95 (ISBN 0-19-519954-5). Oxford U Pr.
Seurat & the Evolution of the La Grande Jatte. lib. bdg. 18.25x (ISBN 0-8371-2361-5, RISE). Greenwood.
Seurat & the Science of Painting. pap. 8.95 (ISBN 0-262-58036-5). MIT Pr.
Seven Families in Pueblo Pottery. pap. 4.95 (ISBN 0-8263-0388-9). U of NM Pr.
Seven Lamps of Architecture. pap. 3.95 (ISBN 0-374-50188-2, N215). FS&G.
Seven Little Known Birds of the Inner Eye. 17.50 (ISBN 0-8048-0936-4). C E Tuttle.
Seven Matched Hollow Gold Jaguars from Peru's Early Horizon. pap. 3.00 (ISBN 0-88402-060-6). Dumbarton Oaks.
Seven Rock Art Sites in Baja California. pap. 8.95 (ISBN 0-87919-081-7). Ballena Pr.
Seven Soviet Arts. lib. bdg. 18.25x (ISBN 0-8371-4263-6, LOSA). Greenwood.
Seven Victorian Architects. 14.50 (ISBN 0-271-00500-9). Pa St U Pr.
Seven Wonders of the Ancient World. 5.95g (ISBN 0-02-782650-3). Macmillan.
Seventeen Black Artists. 7.95 (ISBN 0-396-06391-8). Dodd.
Seventeenth Century Art in Flanders & Holland. lib. bdg. 45.00 (ISBN 0-8240-2419-2). Garland Pub.
Seventeenth Century Art in Italy, France, & Spain. lib. bdg. 45.00 (ISBN 0-8240-2418-4). Garland Pub.
Seventeenth Century Dutch Drawings from American Collections. pap. 11.50 (ISBN 0-88397-064-3). Intl Exhibit Foun.
Sew-Fit Manual. 26.00 (ISBN 0-933956-03-7); tchrs. ed 21.50. Sew-Fit.

Sew-up Art: How to Do It, 26 Applique Projects. pap. 4.95 (ISBN 0-8256-3065-7). Music Sales.

Sewing Dictionary. 12.00 (ISBN 0-498-02147-5); pap. 5.95. A S Barnes.

Sewing for Fashion Design. ref. 12.95 (ISBN 0-87909-755-8). Reston.

Sewing for Twentieth Century Dolls. 17.50 (ISBN 0-89161-007-3). Athena Pub.

Sewing for Twentieth Century Dolls. 19.95 (ISBN 0-87069-276-3). Wallace-Homestead.

Sewing Machine As a Creative Tool. 10.95 (ISBN 0-13-807255-8); pap. 4.95 (ISBN 0-13-807248-5). P-H.

Sewing Sculpture. 12.50 (ISBN 0-87131-215-8); pap. 6.95 (ISBN 0-87131-236-0). M Evans.

Sewing the Easy Way. pap. 2.50 (ISBN 0-06-463420-5). B&N.

Sewing to Decorate Your Home. 6.95 (ISBN 0-385-12560-7). Doubleday.

Shadow Book. 5.95 (ISBN 0-15-272991-7). HarBraceJ.

Shadow of Light. lib. bdg. 29.50 (ISBN 0-306-70858-2); pap. 14.50 (ISBN 0-306-80066-7). Da Capo.

Shah Abbas & the Arts of Isfahan. 19.95 (ISBN 0-87848-041-2). Weatherhill.

Shake Hands with the Dragon. 12.50 (ISBN 0-8103-3765-7). Gale.

Shaker Furniture: The Craftmanship of an American Communal Sect. 8.00 (ISBN 0-8446-1537-4). Peter Smith.

Shaker Furniture: The Craftsmanship of an American Communal Sect. pap. 4.00 (ISBN 0-486-20679-3). Dover.

Shaker Miniature Furniture. pap. 7.95 (ISBN 0-442-27150-6). Van Nos Reinhold.

Shaker Reader. 12.95x (ISBN 0-87663-297-5); pap. 7.95 (ISBN 0-87663-969-4). Universe.

Shakespeare's Globe Playhouse: A Modern Reconstruction. pap. 8.95 (ISBN 0-684-15972-4). Scribner.

Shape & Form: Design Elements. 8.50 (ISBN 0-87192-064-6). Davis Mass.

Shape of Content. 4.50x (ISBN 0-674-80565-8); pap. 2.50 (ISBN 0-674-80570-4). Harvard U Pr.

Shape of Time: Remarks on the History of Things. 10.50x (ISBN 0-300-00643-8); pap. 2.95 (ISBN 0-300-00144-4, Y140). Yale U Pr.

Shaped Canvas: Constructing, Stretching, Painting. 6.95 (ISBN 0-8069-5360-8); PLB 6.69 (ISBN 0-8069-5361-6). Sterling.

Shapes & People. 7.95 (ISBN 0-8149-0662-1). Vanguard.

Shapes & Stories: A Book About Pictures. 7.95 (ISBN 0-8149-0311-8). Vanguard.

Shapes & Things. 6.95 (ISBN 0-02-744060-5). Macmillan.

Shapes of Structure. 8.75x (ISBN 0-19-217646-3); pap. 5.95x (ISBN 0-19-289075-1). Oxford U Pr.

Shaping of Art & Architecture in Nineteenth Century America. pap. 12.50 (ISBN 0-87099-024-1). Metro Mus Art.

Sharaku. pap. 12.95 (ISBN 0-87011-056-X). Kodansha.

Sharps Firearms. 34.95 (ISBN 0-695-80912-1). Follett.

Shearer Furniture Designs. 6.95. Transatlantic.

Sheet Magic: Games, Toys & Gifts from Old Sheets. 4.95g (ISBN 0-02-769870-X). Macmillan.

Shelf Book: Complete Do-It-Yourself Systems for Building Shelves in Living Rooms, Kitchens, Closets, Basements, Garages, Etc. lib. bdg. 9.80 (ISBN 0-89471-001-X); pap. 4.95 (ISBN 0-89471-000-1). Running Pr.

Shell Art: A Handbook for Making Flowers, Mosaics, Jewelry & Other Ornaments. 5.00 (ISBN 0-8446-5473-6). Peter Smith.

Shell Art: A Handbook for Making Shell Flowers, Mosaics, Jewelry. rev. ed. pap. 2.50 (ISBN 0-486-23255-7). Dover.

Shell Book of Country Crafts. 14.95 (ISBN 0-8038-6683-6). Hastings.

Shell-Heaps of the Lower Fraser River, British Columbia. 17.50 (ISBN 0-404-58120-X). AMS Pr.

Shellcraft. 5.00 (ISBN 0-8231-7016-0). Branford.

Shellcraft. 11.25 (ISBN 0-8019-5886-5); pap. 6.95 (ISBN 0-8019-5885-7). Chilton.

Shellcraft Animals. pap. 1.00 (ISBN 0-8200-0507-X). Great Outdoors.

Shellcraft Earrings. pap. 1.00 (ISBN 0-8200-0508-8). Great Outdoors.

Shelter. 20.00 (ISBN 0-394-48829-6); pap. 6.00 (ISBN 0-394-70991-8). Random.

Shelter. 20.00 (ISBN 0-394-48829-6); pap. 9.00 (ISBN 0-394-70991-8). Random.

Shepherd's Glossary of Graphic Signs & Symbols. 15.00 (ISBN 0-486-20700-5). Dover.

Shepherd's London. 23.00 (ISBN 0-8277-4807-8). British Bk Ctr.

Shining Brow: Frank Lloyd Wright. 5.95 (ISBN 0-8180-0014-7). Horizon.

Shino & Oribe Ceramics. 14.95 (ISBN 0-87011-284-8). Kodansha.

Ship & Sea in Art. PLB 4.95 (ISBN 0-8225-0153-8). Lerner Pubns.

Ship Models & How to Build Them. 8.95 (ISBN 0-690-73270-8). T Y Crowell.

Shipcarvers of North America. pap. 4.00 (ISBN 0-486-22168-7). Dover.

Shipcarvers of North America. 7.50 (ISBN 0-8446-4518-4). Peter Smith.

Ships & How to Draw Them. pap. 1.95 (ISBN 0-448-00533-6). G&D.

Ships in Art. 20.00x (ISBN 0-8002-1975-9). Intl Pubns Serv.

Shirley Temple Dolls & Collectibles. 17.95 (ISBN -089145-053-X). Collector Bks.

Shisha Mirror Embroidery: A Contemporary Approach. 13.95 (ISBN 0-442-27641-9). Van Nos Reinhold.

Shoes for Free People. pap. 4.95 (ISBN 0-913300-44-6). Unity Pr.

Shoots: A Guide to Your Family's Photographic Heritage. 7.95 (ISBN 0-89169-033-6). Addison Hse.

Shoots: A Guide to Your Family's Photographic Heritage. pap. 4.95 (ISBN 0-89169-012-3). Addison Hse.

Shop Drawings of Shaker Furniture & Woodenware. pap. 3.95 (ISBN 0-912944-29-3). Berkshire Traveller.

Shop Drawings of Shaker Furniture & Woodenware. pap. 3.95 (ISBN 0-912944-09-9). Berkshire Traveller.

Shop Drawings of Shaker Furniture & Woodenware. pap. 3.95 (ISBN 0-912944-45-5). Berkshire Traveller.

Shop on High Street: Toys & Games of Early America. 7.95 (ISBN 0-689-30622-9). Atheneum.

Shop Tactics: The Common-Sense Way of Using Tools & Working with Woods, Metals, Plastics & Glass. lib. bdg. 9.80 (ISBN 0-914294-63-6); pap. 3.95 (ISBN 0-914294-64-4). Running Pr.

Shopping Cart Art. 4.95g (ISBN 0-02-767230-1). Macmillan.

Shopping Cart Art. abr. ed. pap. 0.95 (ISBN 0-02-045100-8). Macmillan.

Shopping Towns USA. 18.95x (ISBN 0-442-12008-7). Van Nos Reinhold.

Short Course in Canon Photography. 14.95 (ISBN 0-930764-11-0); pap. 8.95 (ISBN 0-930764-01-3). Curtin & London.

Short Course in Minolta Photography. 14.95 (ISBN 0-930764-12-9); pap. 8.95 (ISBN 0-930764-02-1). Curtin & London.

Short Course in Nikon Photography. 14.95 (ISBN 0-930764-10-2); pap. 8.95 (ISBN 0-930764-03-X). Curtin & London.

Short Course in Photography. 14.95 (ISBN 0-930764-09-9); pap. 8.95 (ISBN 0-930764-00-5). Curtin & London.

Short Dictionary of Furniture. pap. 14.95 (ISBN 0-04-749009-8). Allen Unwin.

Short History of Painting in America. pap. 7.95x (ISBN 0-690-73376-3); pap. text ed. 6.50 (ISBN 0-690-73377-1). Har-Row.

Short History of Scene Design in Great Britain. 13.50x (ISBN 0-87471-178-9). Rowman.

Short Season: A Boston Celtics Diary, 1977-1978. 8.95 (ISBN 0-06-013451-8). Har-Row.

Shorthand Fashion Sketching. 15.95 (ISBN 0-87245-286-7). Textile Bk.

Shorthand Fashion Sketching. 4th ed. 12.50 (ISBN 0-87005-068-0). Fairchild.

Shoto Clay. pap. 2.00 (ISBN 0-8323-0133-7). Binford.

Should We Stop Teaching Art? lib. bdg. 35.00x (ISBN 0-8240-2478-8). Garland Pub.

Shrine of St. Peter & the Vatican Excavations. 32.00 (ISBN 0-404-16548-6). AMS Pr.

Shrines of Power: The Grand Tour. 15.95. HarBraceJ.

Shunga: The Art of Love in Japan. 30.00 (ISBN 0-448-23330-4). Paddington.

Shuttle-Craft Book of American Hand Weaving. 12.95 (ISBN 0-87245-026-0). Textile Bk.

Shuttle-Craft Book of American Hand-Weaving. rev. ed. 14.95 (ISBN 0-02-504380-3). Macmillan.

Sicily: A Sketch Book. 10.00 (ISBN 0-914016-52-0). Phoenix Pub.

Sidewalk Fossils. 5.95 (ISBN 0-8027-6228-X); PLB 5.83 (ISBN 0-8027-6233-6). Walker & Co.

Sidney's Appearance: A Study in Elizabethan Portraiture. 16.75 (ISBN 0-8369-8098-0). Arno.

Siena & Her Artists. lib. bdg. 25.00 (ISBN 0-89341-201-5). Longwood Pr.

Sienese Painter Paolo Di Giovanni Fei (c.1345-1411) lib. bdg. 34.00 (ISBN 0-8240-1997-0). Garland Pub.

Sienese Painting of the Trecento. 40.00 (ISBN 0-87817-087-1). Hacker.

Sight & Insight. 8.00 (ISBN 0-8046-0186-0). Kennikat.

Signature Book of Netsuke, Inro & Ojime Artists in Photographs. 85.00 (ISBN 0-917064-01-1). Reed Pubs.

Significant American Artists & Architects. PLB 9.25 (ISBN 0-516-05303-5). Childrens.

Signs & Graphics for Health Care Facilities. pap. 25.00 (ISBN 0-87258-179-9, 1262). Am Hospital.

Signs & Symbols Around the World. PLB 6.67 (ISBN 0-688-51249-6). Lothrop.

Signs & Symbols in Christian Art. 14.95 (ISBN 0-19-501168-6). Oxford U Pr.

Signs & Symbols in Christian Art. pap. 3.95 (ISBN 0-19-501432-4). Oxford U Pr.

Signs of Celebration. 2.50 (ISBN 0-570-03770-0, 12-2706). Concordia.

Signs, Symbols, & Ornaments. 11.95 (ISBN 0-442-27849-7). Van Nos Reinhold.

Silent Studio. 12.50 (ISBN 0-393-04442-4). Norton.

Silent Traveller in Boston. 7.50 (ISBN 0-393-08474-4). Norton.

Silhouettes: A Living Art. 8.95 (ISBN 0-312-72485-3). St Martin.

Silhouettes: How to Make & Use Them. 7.95 (ISBN 0-395-25060-9). HM.

Silk Pictures of Thomas Stevens. 50.00x (ISBN 0-682-40006-8). Exposition.

Silk Road & the Shoso-in. 17.50 (ISBN 0-8348-1022-0). Weatherhill.

Silk Screen. pap. 1.95 (ISBN 0-448-00556-5). G&D.

Silk-Screen As a Fine Art: A Handbook of Contemporary Silk-Screen Printing. pap. 8.95 (ISBN 0-442-21561-4). Van Nos Reinhold.

Silk Screen Printing. rev. ed. pap. 3.96 (ISBN 0-87345-205-4). McKnight.

Silk Screen Techniques. pap. 2.75 (ISBN 0-486-20433-2). Dover.

Silk Screen Techniques. 7.00 (ISBN 0-8446-0491-7). Peter Smith.

Silkscreening. 14.95 (ISBN 0-13-809996-0); pap. 6.95 (ISBN 0-13-809988-X). P-H.

Silver Coinage of Crete: A Metrological Note. pap. 5.00 (ISBN 0-916710-13-0). Obol Intl.

Silver Coinage of Massachusetts. 30.00x (ISBN 0-88000-005-8). Quarterman.

Silver Collecting for Amateurs. 14.50x (ISBN 0-392-04599-0). Soccer.

Silver Collector's Glossary & a List of Early American Silversmiths & Their Marks. 15.00 (ISBN 0-306-70969-4). Da Capo.

Silver Meditations. pap. 10.95 (ISBN 0-87100-101-2). Morgan.

Silver Spectrum: 20 Beautiful Hand-Wrought Jewelry Projects with Step-by-Step Instructions. pap. 3.95 (ISBN 0-8256-3809-7). Music Sales.

Silver Sunbeam. 13.50 (ISBN 0-87100-005-9). Morgan.

Silversmithing. pap. 5.95x (ISBN 0-19-289915-5). Oxford U Pr.

Silversmithing: A Basic Manual. pap. 6.95 (ISBN 0-316-38151-9). Little.

Silversmithing & Art Metal for Schools, Tradesmen, Craftsmen. 12.50 (ISBN 0-910280-04-5); pap. 8.95 (ISBN 0-910280-03-7). Bovin.

Silversmiths. PLB 4.90 (ISBN 0-531-01036-8). Watts.

Silversmiths of Lancaster, Pennsylvania 1730-1850. 9.50 (ISBN 0-915010-17-8). Sutter House.

Simple Decoupage: Having Fun with Cutouts. 5.50 (ISBN 0-688-22134-3); pap. 5.28 (ISBN 0-688-32134-8). Morrow.

Simple Furniture Making & Refinishing. 15.95 (ISBN 0-87909-765-5). Reston.

Simple Photogrammetry. 14.50 (ISBN 0-12-754650-2). Acad Pr.

Simple Printing Methods. 8.95 (ISBN 0-87599-192-0). S G Phillips.

Simple Printmaking. PLB 5.52 (ISBN 0-688-51735-8). Lothrop.

Simple Weaving. 6.95 (ISBN 0-8008-7200-2). Taplinger.

Simplified Design of Structural Steel. 4th ed. 17.50 (ISBN 0-471-66432-4). Wiley.

Simplified Furniture Design & Construction. 6.95 (ISBN 0-498-07345-9). A S Barnes.

Since Cezanne. facs. ed. 13.50 (ISBN 0-8369-0034-0). Arno.

Singer Magic Fusibles in Fashion Sewing. pap. 4.95 (ISBN 0-307-09876-1). Western Pub.

Singular Images. pap. 7.95 (ISBN 0-8212-0728-8). NYGS.

Sino-Iranica see Beginnings of Porcelain in China.

Sir Charles Eastlake & the Victorian Art World. text ed. 50.00 (ISBN 0-691-03902-X). Princeton U Pr.

Sir Christopher Wren. 10.95 (ISBN 0-8128-1893-8). Stein & Day.

Sir Ebenezer Howard & the Town Planning Movement. 14.00x (ISBN 0-262-13066-1). MIT Pr.

Sir Edward Burne-Jones: A Record & Review. 10.00 (ISBN 0-404-00733-3). AMS Pr.

Sir John Vanbrugh, Architect & Dramatist, 1664-1726. 19.00 (ISBN 0-527-95850-6). Kraus Repr.

Sir Joshua Reynolds. lib. bdg. 12.50 (ISBN 0-8414-7867-8). Folcroft.

Sirague City. 25.00 (ISBN 0-915756-00-5); pap. 10.00 (ISBN 0-915756-01-3). D McPhail.

Sisley: Q.L.P. 5.95 (ISBN 0-517-53321-9). Crown.

Sisters. 24.95; pap. 8.95 (ISBN 0-688-05166-9). Morrow.

Site Planning. 2nd rev. ed. 13.95x (ISBN 0-262-12050-X). MIT Pr.

Site Planning Standards. 27.50 (ISBN 0-07-016216-6). McGraw.

Site Selection & Development: Camps, Conferences, Retreats. spiral bdg. 12.50 (ISBN 0-8298-0126-X). Pilgrim NY.

Six Architects. facs. ed. 14.00 (ISBN 0-8369-1340-X). Arno.

Six Black Masters of American Art. 4.95 (ISBN 0-385-01211-X). Doubleday.

Six Essays. 23.00 (ISBN 0-384-14335-0). Johnson Repr.

Six Greek Sculptors. facs. ed. 17.50 (ISBN 0-8369-0468-0). Arno.

Six Greek Sculptors. lib. bdg. 40.00 (ISBN 0-89341-215-5). Longwood Pr.

Six Lectures on Architecture. facs. ed. 13.75 (ISBN 0-8369-0348-X). Arno.

Sixteenth Century Art & Architecture. lib. bdg. 45.00 (ISBN 0-8240-2417-6). Garland Pub.

Sixteenth Century Italian Drawings from the Collection of Janos Scholz. 15.00. Pierpont Morgan.

Sixty Photographs. 10.00 (ISBN 0-394-49892-5); pap. 5.95 (ISBN 0-394-73097-6). Knopf.

Sixty Years' Memories of Art & Artists. lib. bdg. 28.00 (ISBN 0-8240-2244-0). Garland Pub.

Sketch of Chester A. Harding, Artist. lib. bdg. 17.50 (ISBN 0-306-71711-5). Da Capo.

Sketchbook of Villard De Honnecourt. pap. 2.75x (ISBN 0-253-20117-9). Ind U Pr.

Sketches of Great Painters. facs. ed. 15.00 (ISBN 0-8369-0304-8). Arno.

Sketching & Painting: A Step by Step Introduction. pap. 8.95 (ISBN 0-312-72765-8). St Martin.

Sketching Landscape. pap. 1.95 (ISBN 0-448-00534-4). G&D.

Sketching Out of Doors. pap. 1.95 (ISBN 0-448-00535-2). G&D.

Skirts: Sew Your Own. pap. 7.95 (ISBN 0-07-027940-3). McGraw.

Skopas in Samothrace. pap. 5.00 (ISBN 0-87391-009-5). Smith Coll.

Skopas of Paros. 32.00 (ISBN 0-8155-5051-0). Noyes.

Skrebneski Portraits: A Matter of Record. 27.50 (ISBN 0-385-14623-X). Doubleday.

Sky Gods: The Sun & Moon in Art & Myth. 10.00x (ISBN 0-87663-187-1); pap. 6.95 (ISBN 0-87663-952-X). Universe.

Sky Hooks: The Autobiography of John Kane see John Kane, Painter.

Skyscraper Goes up. 4.95 (ISBN 0-394-82147-5); PLB 5.99 (ISBN 0-394-92147-X). Random.

Skyscraper Primitives: Dada & the American Avant-Garde, 1910-1925. 20.00x (ISBN 0-8195-4081-1). Wesleyan U Pr.

Skyscraper Style: Art Deco New York. 25.00 (ISBN 0-19-501873-7). Oxford U Pr.

Skyscraper Style: Art Deco New York Photographs by Cervin Robinson. pap. 10.95 (ISBN 0-19-502112-6, 478). Oxford U Pr.

Skystone & Silver: The Collector's Book of Southwest Indian Jewelry. 39.95 (ISBN 0-13-812834-0). P-H.

Slab, Coil, & Pinch: A Beginners Pottery Book. 5.75 (ISBN 0-688-22105-X); PLB 5.52 (ISBN 0-688-32105-4). Morrow.

Slapdash Decorating. pap. 3.95 (ISBN 0-671-33027-6). Wanderer Bks.

Slapdash Decorating. 6.25 (ISBN 0-688-41813-9); PLB 6.00 (ISBN 0-688-51813-3). Lothrop.

Sleeve Puppets. 8.50 (ISBN 0-8008-7237-1). Taplinger.

Slotted Sculpture from Cardboard. 6.25 (ISBN 0-688-41793-0); PLB 6.00 (ISBN 0-688-51793-5). Lothrop.

SLR Photographer's Handbook. pap. 7.95 (ISBN 0-912656-59-X). H P Bks.

Small Antique Furniture. 7th ed. text ed. 14.50x (ISBN 0-8277-5085-4). British Bk Ctr.

Small Camera Portraiture. pap. 3.95 (ISBN 0-8227-4018-4). Petersen Pub.

Small Dolls & Other Collectibles. pap. 6.95 (ISBN 0-8473-1665-3, 037900). Sterling.

Small Garden. 10.98 (ISBN 0-02-516700-6). Macmillan.

Small Garden in the City. 12.50 (ISBN 0-8076-0752-5). Braziller.

Small Gardens Are More Fun. 8.95 (ISBN 0-671-21142-0). S&S.

Small Gardens for City & Country: A Guide to Designing & Planting Your Own Property. 14.95 (ISBN 0-13-813063-9); pap. 8.95 (ISBN 0-13-813055-8). P-H.

Small House in the Sun. 12.50 (ISBN 0-8038-6704-2). Hastings.

Small Needlepoint Treasures: A Complete How-to Workbook for Making Quick Needlepoint Gifts. 15.95 (ISBN 0-688-03388-1); pap. 6.95 (ISBN 0-688-08388-9). Morrow.

Small-Space Gardens. pap. 3.95 (ISBN 0-376-03702-4). Lane.

Standard Modern Doll Identification & Value Guide. pap. 7.95 (ISBN 0-89145-013-0). Collector Bks.
Standard Textbook of Cosmetology. rev. ed. 10.60 (ISBN 0-87350-000-8). Milady.
Standards Relating to Architecture of Facilities. soft cover 7.59 (ISBN 0-88410-778-7); casebound 12.50 (ISBN 0-88410-249-1). Ballinger Pub.
Stanford White. pap. 4.95 (ISBN 0-306-80031-4). Da Capo.
Stanford White. lib. bdg. 29.50 (ISBN 0-306-70138-3). Da Capo.
Stanley Morison. 22.50x (ISBN 0-674-83425-9). Harvard U Pr.
Stanley Spencer at War. 25.00 (ISBN 0-571-11028-2). Merrimack Bk Serv.
Star-Spangled Fun! Things to Make, Do & See from American History. 5.95 (ISBN 0-8193-0817-X); PLB 5.41 (ISBN 0-8193-0818-8). Parents.
Star-Spangled Kitsch. pap. 4.95 (ISBN 0-87663-948-1). Universe.
Stars of the Twenties: 125 Photographs. 10.00 (ISBN 0-670-66836-2). Viking Pr.
Start to Draw. PLB 4.90 (ISBN 0-531-01799-0). Watts.
Starting Photography. 8.95 (ISBN 0-8038-6736-0); pap. 6.95 (ISBN 0-8038-6757-3). Hastings.
Starting to Paint Portraits. pap. 3.95 (ISBN 0-8008-7382-3). Taplinger.
Starting with Ceramics. 6.95 (ISBN 0-8069-5324-1); PLB 6.69 (ISBN 0-8069-5325-X). Sterling.
Starting with Papier Mache. 3.95 (ISBN 0-8069-5298-9); PLB 4.59 (ISBN 0-8069-5299-7). Sterling.
Starting with Stained Glass. 3.95 (ISBN 0-8069-5244-X); PLB 4.59 (ISBN 0-8069-5245-8). Sterling.
Starting with Watercolour. pap. 3.95 (ISBN 0-8008-7384-X). Taplinger.
State Arts Agencies in Transition. 7.95 (ISBN 0-89062-007-5). Pub Ctr Cult Res.
State Capitals Quilt Blocks: Fifty Patchwork Patterns from "Hearth & Home Magazine". pap. 2.25 (ISBN 0-486-23557-2). Dover.
State of the Art of Computer Aided Environmental Design. 50.00 (ISBN 0-915250-14-4). Environ Design.
Statue of Liberty. 8.95 (ISBN 0-399-20670-1). Putnam.
Statue of Liberty. 14.95 (ISBN 0-670-66854-0). Viking Pr.
Statue of Liberty. pap. 5.95 (ISBN 0-14-004513-9). Penguin.
Statue of Liberty Comes to America. PLB 4.48 (ISBN 0-8116-6505-4). Garrard.
Steichen: The Master Prints 1895-1914: the Symbolist Period. 35.00 (ISBN 0-87070-581-4). NYGS.
Stencil Craft. pap. 2.95 (ISBN 0-915462-02-8). Paragraph Pr.
Stenciling. 12.95 (ISBN 0-442-21055-8). Van Nos Reinhold.
Step-by-Step Guide to Landscaping & Gardening. text ed. 10.00 (ISBN 0-682-48084-3). Exposition.
Step-by-Step Guide to Photography. 15.95 (ISBN 0-394-41604-X). Knopf.
Step-by-Step Knifemaking. 10.95 (ISBN 0-87857-180-9); pap. 7.95 (ISBN 0-87857-181-7). Rodale Pr Inc.
Step-by-Step Sugar Artistry. 6.00 (ISBN 0-682-47741-9). Exposition.
Step Towards an Integrated Computer Aided Design System for the Architect-Planner. 25.00 (ISBN 0-915250-07-1). Environ Design.
Steps in Clothing Skills. text ed. 13.28 (ISBN 0-87002-265-2). Bennett Co.
Steranko History of the Comics. pap. 4.00 (ISBN 0-517-50758-7); pap. 6.00 (ISBN 0-517-50188-0). Crown.
Stereo-Realist Manual. 6.95 (ISBN 0-87100-054-7). Morgan.
Stereoscope, Its History, Theory & Construction. 9.95 (ISBN 0-87100-017-2). Morgan.
Steuben Glass. 3rd rev. ed. 8.50 (ISBN 0-8446-4634-2). Peter Smith.
Steuben Glass: A Monograph. 3rd rev. ed. pap. 4.00 (ISBN 0-486-22892-4). Dover.
Steven Caney's Playbook. 9.95 (ISBN 0-911104-37-2); pap. 4.95 (ISBN 0-911104-38-0). Workman Pub.
Stevengraphs & Other Victorian Silk Pictures. 40.00 (ISBN 0-8386-7880-7). Fairleigh Dickinson.
Sticks & Stones. rev. ed. pap. 2.50 (ISBN 0-486-20202-X). Dover.
Sticks & Stones: A Study of American Architecture & Civilization. 5.25 (ISBN 0-8446-0813-0). Peter Smith.
Sticks & Stones & Ice Cream Cones. 9.95 (ISBN 0-911104-29-1); pap. 4.95 (ISBN 0-911104-30-5). Workman Pub.
Sticks, Spools & Feathers. PLB 7.95. A-W.
Stiegel Glass. pap. 5.00 (ISBN 0-486-20128-7). Dover.
Stiegel Glass. 11.00 (ISBN 0-8446-2286-9). Peter Smith.
Still Life Drawing & Painting. pap. 4.95 (ISBN 0-448-11526-3). G&D.
Still-Life Painting in America. 25.00 (ISBN 0-87817-092-8). Hacker.
Still Life Painting Techniques. 12.50 (ISBN 0-7134-0635-6). Hippocrene Bks.
Stinson Beach Salt Marsh: The Form of Its Growth. pap. 12.00 (ISBN 0-918540-01-1). Stinson Beach.
Stitch by Stitch: Needlework for Beginners. 5.50 (ISBN 0-15-280350-5). HarBraceJ.
Stitch in Time: Victorian & Edwardian Needlecraft. 9.95 (ISBN 0-8008-7435-8). Taplinger.
Stitch with Style. pap. 7.50 (ISBN 0-914842-39-0). Madrona Pubs.
Stitchery Book. PLB 4.95 (ISBN 0-385-05550-1). Doubleday.
Stitchery for Children: A Manual for Teachers, Parents, & Children. pap. 7.95 (ISBN 0-442-22325-0). Van Nos Reinhold.
Stitchery, Needlepoint, Applique & Patchwork: A Complete Guide. pap. 5.95 (ISBN 0-14-046249-X). Penguin.
Stitches of Creative Embroidery. 9.95 (ISBN 0-442-11087-1). Van Nos Reinhold.
Stitches of Creative Embroidery. pap. 7.95 (ISBN 0-442-22318-8). Van Nos Reinhold.
Stock Photo & Assignment Source Book: Where to Find Photographs Instantly. pap. 19.95 (ISBN 0-8352-0879-6). Bowker.
Stone Age Painting in India. 17.50x (ISBN 0-300-01937-8). Yale U Pr.
Stone Mad: A Sculptor's Life & Craft. pap. 5.75 (ISBN 0-7100-8542-7). Routledge & Kegan.
Stone Shelters. pap. 7.95 (ISBN 0-262-51010-3). MIT Pr.
Stone Tools As Cultural Markers: Change, Evolution & Complexity. text ed. 30.00 (ISBN 0-391-00835-8); pap. text ed. 21.25x (ISBN 0-391-00836-6). Humanities.
Stonehenge. pap. 4.95 (ISBN 0-8467-0323-8). Two Continents.
Stones of Florence. 25.00 (ISBN 0-15-185079-8). HarBraceJ.
Stones of Florence. pap. 3.25 (ISBN 0-15-685080-X, HB60). HarBraceJ.
Stones of Venice. Incl. Foundation; Sea-Stories; Fall. lib. bdg. 104.00 (ISBN 0-8240-3278-0). Garland Pub.
Stoneware. pap. 3.95 (ISBN 0-307-43177-0). Western Pub.
Stoneware & Porcelain: The Art of High-Fired Pottery. 12.50 (ISBN 0-8019-0098-0); pap. 7.95 (ISBN 0-8019-5856-3). Chilton.
Stonework of the Maya. pap. 9.95 (ISBN 0-8263-0277-7). U of NM Pr.
Stopping the World. 5.95 (ISBN 0-385-11584-9). Doubleday.
Story-Lives of Master Artists. rev. ed. 5.50 (ISBN 0-397-30254-1). Lippincott.
Story of American Painting. 15.95 (ISBN 0-8109-0498-5); pap. 6.95 (ISBN 0-8109-2069-7). Abrams.
Story of American Painting: The Evolution of Painting in America from Colonial Times to the Present. 27.00 (ISBN 0-384-06955-X). Johnson Repr.
Story of American Photography: An Illustrated History for Young People. 16.95 (ISBN 0-316-77021-3). Little.
Story of Art. 13th ed. 19.95 (ISBN 0-7148-1841-0); pap. 10.95 (ISBN 0-7148-1820-8). Dutton.
Story of Bing & Grondahl Christmas Plates. loose leaf 12.00 (ISBN 0-911576-02-9). Viking Import.
Story of Coins. pap. 5.39 (ISBN 0-8178-3922-4). Harvey.
Story of Israel in Coins. pap. 2.00 (ISBN 0-87980-150-6). Wilshire.
Story of Jewelry. 29.95 (ISBN 0-688-00308-7). Morrow.
Story of Modern Art. rev. ed. 15.00 (ISBN 0-670-67492-3). Viking Pr.
Story of Our Gardens. 3.50 (ISBN 0-900406-04-6). Dufour.
Story of Painting for Young People. text ed. 7.95 (ISBN 0-8109-0491-8). Abrams.
Story of Photography. 11.95 (ISBN 0-87992-003-3); pap. 6.75 (ISBN 0-87992-002-5). Light Impressions.
Story of Photography. lib. bdg. 25.00 (ISBN 0-8495-4947-7). Arden Lib.
Story of Royal Copenhagen Christmas Plates. loose leaf 12.00 (ISBN 0-911576-01-0). Viking Import.
Story of Sculpture. 2nd ed. 6.95 (ISBN 0-571-04601-0). Merrimack Bk Serv.
Story of Spanish Painting. 17.50 (ISBN 0-404-01361-9). AMS Pr.
Story of the Armory Show. 10.00 (ISBN 0-8212-0104-2). NYGS.
Story of the Capitol. PLB 7.35 (ISBN 0-516-04604-7). Childrens.
Story of the Lincoln Memorial. PLB 7.35 (ISBN 0-516-04623-3). Childrens.
Story of the Statue of Liberty. PLB 7.35 (ISBN 0-516-04637-3). Childrens.
Story of the Totem Pole. 5.95 (ISBN 0-8149-0277-4). Vanguard.
Stove Book. pap. 5.95 (ISBN 0-312-76376-X). St Martin.
Stow Wengenroth, Artist-Lithographer: A Retrospective Exhibition. pap. 2.50x (ISBN 0-913060-10-0). Norton Art.
Stranger Stop & Cast an Eye. pap. 5.95 (ISBN 0-8289-0344-1). Greene.
Strasburg Manuscript: A Medieval Painters Handbook. 6.75. Transatlantic.
Straw Work & Corn Dollies. 8.95 (ISBN 0-670-67813-9). Viking Pr.
Strawcraft. 8.75 (ISBN 0-212-97010-0). Transatlantic.
Streamline: Decorative Designs of the Forties. pap. 2.95 (ISBN 0-912300-63-9, 63-9). Troubador Pr.
Streamlined Curtains & Covers. 2.95 (ISBN 0-312-76510-X, S65380). St Martin.
Streamlined Decade: Design in the Nineteen Thirties. pap. 7.95 (ISBN 0-8076-0793-2). Braziller.
Street Art. pap. 7.95 (ISBN 0-8256-3044-4). Music Sales.
Street Name Lettering in the British Isles. pap. 8.95 (ISBN 0-8230-4930-2). Watson-Guptill.
Streets for People. 14.95 (ISBN 0-385-04231-0). Doubleday.
String Art Encyclopedia. 12.95 (ISBN 0-8069-5362-4); PLB 11.69 (ISBN 0-8069-5363-2). Sterling.
String Art: Step-by-Step. 12.50 (ISBN 0-8019-6131-9); pap. 6.95 (ISBN 0-8019-6132-7). Chilton.
String Designs. 3.95 (ISBN 0-8069-5320-9); PLB 4.59 (ISBN 0-8069-5321-7). Sterling.
String Projects. PLB 4.95 (ISBN 0-385-02366-9). Doubleday.
String, Raffia & Material. 6.95 (ISBN 0-531-02004-5). Watts.
String Things You Can Create. 3.95 (ISBN 0-8069-5262-8); PLB 4.59 (ISBN 0-8069-5263-6). Sterling.
Stringcraft. 3.95 (ISBN 0-8069-5364-0); PLB 4.59 (ISBN 0-8069-5365-9). Sterling.
Strings on Your Fingers: How to Make String Figures. PLB 5.52 (ISBN 0-688-31582-8). Morrow.
Stroll Through Historic Salem. 7.95 (ISBN 0-8038-6689-5). Hastings.
Structural Design in Architecture. 21.95 (ISBN 0-13-853465-9). P-H.
Structure & Form in Japan. 22.50 (ISBN 0-8150-0019-7). Wittenborn.
Structure & Form in Modern Architecture. 22.50 (ISBN 0-88275-192-1). Krieger.
Structure in Nature Is a Strategy for Design. 45.00x (ISBN 0-262-16064-1). MIT Pr.
Structure of Aesthetics. 12.50x (ISBN 0-8020-5124-3). U of Toronto Pr.
Structure of Art. rev. ed. 12.50 (ISBN 0-8076-0596-4); pap. 5.95 (ISBN 0-8076-0595-6). Braziller.
Structure, Sign & Function: Selected Essays. 16.50x (ISBN 0-300-02108-9). Yale U Pr.
Stubbs. 7.95 (ISBN 0-7148-1808-9). Dutton.
Stucco from Chal Tarkhan-Eshqabad Near Rayy: Including Illustrations of the Excavated Ostraca from the Same Site. 45.00 (ISBN 0-85668-062-1). Intl Schol Bk Serv.
Student Journalist & Creative Photography. PLB 9.66 (ISBN 0-8239-0335-4). Rosen Pr.
Student Journalist & Photojournalism. PLB 4.98 (ISBN 0-8239-0125-4). Rosen Pr.
Studies & Executed Buildings. 40.00 (ISBN 0-87370-001-5). Prairie Sch.
Studies in Art, Architecture, & Design. 15.00 ea (ISBN 0-8027-0276-7) (ISBN 0-8027-0277-5). Walker & Co.
Studies in Classic Maya Iconography. 25.00 (ISBN 0-208-00833-0). Shoe String.
Studies in Classical & Byzantine Manuscript Illumination. 25.00x (ISBN 0-226-89246-8). U of Chicago Pr.
Studies in Early Impressionism. 35.00x (ISBN 0-300-01285-3). Yale U Pr.
Studies in Early Indian Painting. 35.00 (ISBN 0-210-22310-3). Asia.
Studies in East Christian & Roman Art. 31.00 (ISBN 0-384-38812-4). Johnson Repr.
Studies in Honor of Gertrude Rosenthal: Annual III. pap. text ed. 4.00 (ISBN 0-912298-27-8). Baltimore Mus.
Studies in Iconology: Humanistic Themes in the Art of the Renaissance. 9.50 (ISBN 0-8446-2696-1). Peter Smith.
Studies in Iconology: Humanistic Themes in the Art of the Renaissance. pap. 5.95 (ISBN 0-06-430025-0, IN-25). Har-Row.
Studies in Italian Renaissance Architecture. 17.50x (ISBN 0-262-12073-9). MIT Pr.
Studies in Late Medieval & Renaissance Painting in Honor of Millard Meiss. 75.00x set; Vol. I (ISBN 0-8147-4963-1); Vol. II (ISBN 0-8147-4978-X). NYU Pr.
Studies in Medieval Painting. pap. 3.95 (ISBN 0-306-80010-1). Da Capo.
Studies in Medieval Painting. lib. bdg. 29.50 (ISBN 0-306-70292-4). Da Capo.
Studies in Pre-Vesalian Anatomy: Biography, Translations, Documents. 18.00 (ISBN 0-87169-104-3). Am Philos.
Studies in Seicento Art & Theory. lib. bdg. 22.50x (ISBN 0-8371-4743-3, MAST). Greenwood.
Studies in the Arts & Architecture. 5.50 (ISBN 0-8046-0355-3). Kennikat.
Studies in the Psychology of Art. 10.00 (ISBN 0-405-05149-2). Arno.
Studies of Ancient Tollan: A Report of the University of Missouri Tula Archaeological Project. 10.00x (ISBN 0-913134-99-6). Mus Anthro Mo.
Studies on Modern Painters. facs. ed. 12.75 (ISBN 0-8369-0920-8). Arno.
Studies on Money in Early America. 27.50 (ISBN 0-89722-065-X). Am Numismatic.
Studio Art: A Resource for Artist-Teachers. 9.95 (ISBN 0-442-27433-5); pap. 4.95 (ISBN 0-442-27430-0). Van Nos Reinhold.
Studio Tips for Artists & Graphic Designers. pap. 4.95 (ISBN 0-442-22819-8). Van Nos Reinhold.
Studios & Styles of the Italian Renaissance. 30.00 (ISBN 0-8076-0504-2). Braziller.
Study in Aesthetics. lib. bdg. 18.75x (ISBN 0-8371-4794-8, RESA). Greenwood.
Study in Conservation. 11.95 (ISBN 0-85362-168-3); pap. 8.25 (ISBN 0-85362-172-1). Routledge & Kegan.
Study of Chiriquian Antiquities. 37.00 (ISBN 0-527-59220-X). Kraus Repr.
Study of Classic Maya Sculpture. 30.50 (ISBN 0-404-16275-4). AMS Pr.
Study of Education & Art. 12.95 (ISBN 0-7100-7648-7); pap. 5.00 (ISBN 0-7100-7775-0). Routledge & Kegan.
Study of Incunabula. 30.00 (ISBN 0-527-37100-9). Kraus Repr.
Study of Olmec Iconography see Olmec Paintings of Oxtotitlan Cave, Guerrero, Mexico.
Study of the Non-Profit Arts & Cultural Industry in New York State. pap. 4.00x spiral bound (ISBN 0-89062-013-X). Pub Ctr Cult Res.
Stumpwork: The Art of Raised Embroidery. 14.95 (ISBN 0-684-15360-2). Scribner.
Style for Living: How to Make Where You Live You. 12.50 (ISBN 0-385-08252-5). Doubleday.
Style in the Arts of China. pap. 4.25 (ISBN 0-14-021863-7). Penguin.
Styles in Painting: A Comparative Study. pap. 4.00 (ISBN 0-486-20760-9). Dover.
Styles in Painting: A Comparative Study. 5.50 (ISBN 0-8446-3230-9). Peter Smith.
Styles of Ornament. pap. 6.00 (ISBN 0-486-20557-6). Dover.
Styles of Ornament. 10.00 (ISBN 0-8446-2982-0). Peter Smith.
Stylistic Analysis of Arshile Gorky's Art from 1943-1948. lib. bdg. 43.00 (ISBN 0-8240-2719-1). Garland Pub.
Subsidized Muse. 14.95 (ISBN 0-521-21966-3). Cambridge U Pr.
Suburban Portraits. pap. 3.95 (ISBN 0-915864-07-X). Academy Chi Ltd.
Successful Coin Hunting. rev. ed. pap. 5.95 (ISBN 0-915920-30-1). Ram Pub.
Successful Landscaping. 12.00 (ISBN 0-912336-55-2); pap. 4.95 (ISBN 0-912336-56-0). Structures Pub.
Successful Photography. rev. ed. 11.95 (ISBN 0-13-864603-1). P-H.
Successful Shelves & Built-Ins. 12.00 (ISBN 0-912336-77-3); pap. 5.95 (ISBN 0-912336-78-1). Structures Pub.
Successful Studios & Work Centers. 12.00x (ISBN 0-912336-36-6); pap. 4.95x (ISBN 0-912336-37-4). Structures Pub.
Successful Wedding Photography. 10.95 (ISBN 0-8174-0461-9). Amphoto.
Successful Wood Book: Selection & Use, Fastening & Finishing. 12.00 (ISBN 0-912336-73-0); pap. 5.95 (ISBN 0-912336-74-9). Structures Pub.
Suggested Nicaraguan Pottery Sequence Based on the Museum Collection. pap. 2.50 (ISBN 0-934490-35-X). Mus Am Ind.
Suggestions in Design: Three Thousand Years of Ornaments, Styles Motifs. pap. 4.95 (ISBN 0-448-22615-4). Paddington.
Sumi-E: A Meditation in Ink. pap. 6.95 (ISBN 0-8473-1659-9, 043000). Sterling.
Sumi-E in Three Weeks. pap. 3.25 (ISBN 0-87040-121-1). Japan Pubns.
Summer & Winter. pap. 7.00 (ISBN 0-916658-19-8). HTH Pubs.
Summer Morn... Winter Weather. pap. 4.00 (ISBN 0-913994-23-5). Hippocrene Bks.
Sun-Warmed Nudes. 10.00. Elysium.
Sunrise Island: A Story of Japan & Its Arts. 5.95 (ISBN 0-8193-0523-5); PLB 5.41 (ISBN 0-8193-0486-7). Parents.
Sun's Birthday. Softbound 5.95 (ISBN 0-385-07412-3). Doubleday.
Sunshine & Shadow: The Amish & Their Quilts. 5.95 (ISBN 0-87663-236-3). Universe.
Sunshine at Midnight. 6.95 (ISBN 0-02-568300-4). Macmillan.

That Wilder Image: The Paintings of America's Native School from Thomas Cole to Winslow Homer. 8.00 (ISBN 0-8446-0093-8). Peter Smith.

Theater Design. 100.00 (ISBN 0-07-032086-1). McGraw.

Theater of the Bauhaus. pap. 7.95 (ISBN 0-8195-6020-0). Wesleyan U Pr.

Theater of the Mind. pap. 7.95 (ISBN 0-87100-106-3, 301). Morgan.

Theatre Art. 9.50 (ISBN 0-8154-0289-9). Cooper Sq.

Theatre Check List: A Guide to the Planning & Construction of Proscenium & Open Stage Theatres. pap. 5.95 (ISBN 0-8195-6005-7). Wesleyan U Pr.

Theatre in Action. 29.00 (ISBN 0-405-09074-9). Arno.

Theatre Lighting. 5.95x (ISBN 0-910482-18-7). Drama Bk.

Theatre Lighting Before Electricity. 16.00 (ISBN 0-8195-5021-3). Wesleyan U Pr.

Theatre Props. 10.95x (ISBN 0-910482-66-7). Drama Bk.

Theatres & Auditoriums. 38.50 (ISBN 0-88275-170-0). Krieger.

Theatres, Spaces, Environments: 18 Projects. 15.00 (ISBN 0-910482-63-2). Drama Bk.

Theatrical Photographs of Napoleon Sarony. pap. 8.50 (ISBN 0-87338-213-7). Kent St U Pr.

Theatrical Set Design: The Basic Techniques. 2nd ed. text ed. 18.95. Allyn.

Theatrical Set Design: The Basic Techniques. text ed. 13.95x (ISBN 0-205-02222-7, 4822226). Allyn.

Theatrical Style: A Visual Approach to the Theatre. 15.95 (ISBN 0-87484-227-1); pap. 9.95 (ISBN 0-87484-226-3). Mayfield Pub.

Theodore Robinson: 1852-1896. pap. text ed. 6.25 (ISBN 0-912298-33-2). Baltimore Mus.

Theologia Mythologica see Allegoriae Poeticae.

Theora Hamblett Paintings. 15.00 (ISBN 0-87805-069-8). U Pr of Miss.

Theories of Modern Art: A Source Book by Artists & Critics. pap. 6.95 (ISBN 0-520-01450-2, CAL168). U of Cal Pr.

Theory & Practice of Perspective. 16.00 (ISBN 0-405-09004-8). Arno.

Theory & Practice of the Photographic Art. 13.00 (ISBN 0-405-04942-0). Arno.

Theory of Beauty. lib. bdg. 30.00 (ISBN 0-8414-1805-5). Folcroft.

Theory of Fashion Design. 14.95 (ISBN 0-87245-041-4). Textile Bk.

Theory of Fashion Design. 16.95 (ISBN 0-471-10586-4). Wiley.

Theory of the Avant-Garde. 9.50x (ISBN 0-674-88215-6). Harvard U Pr.

There's a Sound in the Sea: A Child's-Eye View of the Whale. 10.95 (ISBN 0-912020-47-4); pap. 5.95 (ISBN 0-912020-46-6). Scrimshaw Calif.

They Built for Eternity. facsimile ed. 30.00 (ISBN 0-8369-2451-7). Arno.

Things I Remember. 13.50 (ISBN 0-8129-0575-X). Times Bks.

Things to Do. PLB 3.50 (ISBN 0-385-03683-3). Doubleday.

Things to Do in a Day. pap. 5.95 (ISBN 0-02-011870-8, 01187). Macmillan.

Things to Do in a Day. 8.95 (ISBN 0-02-578240-1, 57824). Macmillan.

Things to Make & Do for Columbus Day. PLB 6.90 s&l (ISBN 0-531-01274-3). Watts.

Things to Make & Do for Easter. PLB 6.90 (ISBN 0-531-01463-0). Watts.

Things to Make & Do for George Washington's Birthday. PLB 6.90 s&l (ISBN 0-531-02294-3). Watts.

Things to Make & Do for Halloween. PLB 4.90 (ISBN 0-531-01103-8). Watts.

Things to Make & Do for Valentine's Day. PLB 4.90 (ISBN 0-531-01187-9). Watts.

Things to Make & Do for Your Birthday. 3.95 (ISBN 0-531-02380-X); PLB 6.90 s&l (ISBN 0-531-01462-2). Watts.

Thinking with a Pencil. pap. 3.95 (ISBN 0-06-463206-7, 206). B&N.

Third Book of Virgil Finlay. 15.50. De La Ree.

Third Display of Old Maps & Plans. 5.00 (ISBN 0-911462-10-4). Sumac.

Third Harvest of Souvenir Spoons. 2nd ed. 13.50 (ISBN 0-911708-03-0). Greenwich Pr.

Thirteen Masterpieces of Mexican Archaeology. lib. bdg. 44.95 (ISBN 0-8490-1194-9). Gordon Pr.

Thirty-Two Adobe Houses of Old California. write for info. Southwest Mus.

This Book Is a Movie. pap. 3.25 (ISBN 0-440-50738-3). Dell.

This Business of Art. 12.50 (ISBN 0-8230-5360-1). Watson-Guptill.

This I Saw: The Life & Times of Goya. lib. bdg. 17.75x (ISBN 0-8371-6047-2, VATI). Greenwood.

This Is Baker's Clay. pap. 6.95 (ISBN 0-8473-1176-7). Sterling.

This Is Charleston. rev. ed. pap. 4.75 (ISBN 0-910326-04-5). Carolina Art.

This Is Edinburgh. 5.95g (ISBN 0-02-778180-1). Macmillan.

This Is Ephemera: Collecting Printed Throwaways. 7.00 (ISBN 0-8289-0322-0); pap. 3.95 (ISBN 0-8289-0323-9). Greene.

This Is Greece. 3.95 (ISBN 0-02-778260-3). Macmillan.

This Is Hong Kong. 5.95g (ISBN 0-02-778190-9). Macmillan.

This Is Ireland. 4.95g (ISBN 0-02-778350-2). Macmillan.

This Is Israel. 4.95g (ISBN 0-02-778340-5). Macmillan.

This Is Munich. 3.95g (ISBN 0-02-779410-5). Macmillan.

This Is New York. abr. ed. pap. 0.95 (ISBN 0-02-045160-1). Macmillan.

This Is New York. 5.95g (ISBN 0-02-779530-6). Macmillan.

This Is Paris. 3.95 (ISBN 0-02-779960-3). Macmillan.

This Is Rome. 5.95g (ISBN 0-02-780390-2). Macmillan.

This Is San Francisco. abr. ed. pap. 0.95 (ISBN 0-02-045170-9). Macmillan.

This Is San Francisco. 5.95g (ISBN 0-02-780830-0). Macmillan.

This Is Washington, D. C. 4.95 (ISBN 0-02-778240-9). Macmillan.

This Is Washington, D.C. abr. ed. pap. 2.25 (ISBN 0-02-045180-6). Macmillan.

Thomas Bewick & His Pupils. 7.80 (ISBN 0-8103-3523-9). Gale.

Thomas Bewick: Vignettes. 14.95 (ISBN 0-85967-410-X). Biblio Dist.

Thomas E. Williams & the Fine Arts Press. 12.50 (ISBN 0-87093-091-5). Dawsons.

Thomas Eakins Collection of the Hirshhorn Museum & Sculpture Garden. 25.00 (ISBN 0-87474-812-7). Smithsonian.

Thomas Eakins Collection of the Hirshhorn Museum & Sculpture Garden. 32.50 (ISBN 0-226-69102-0). U of Chicago Pr.

Thomas Eakins, His Life & Work. 15.00 (ISBN 0-404-02863-2). AMS Pr.

Thomas Gainsborough. 16.00 (ISBN 0-900963-69-7). State Mutual Bk.

Thomas Hart Benton. 60.00 (ISBN 0-8109-0132-3). Abrams.

Thomas Jefferson, Architect: Original Designs. 22.00 (ISBN 0-403-01047-0). Scholarly.

Thomas Jefferson Landscape Architect. 9.75x (ISBN 0-8139-0603-2). U Pr of Va.

Thomas Nast's Christmas Drawings. pap. 3.50 (ISBN 0-486-23660-9). Dover.

Thomas Nast's Christmas Drawings. 7.50 (ISBN 0-8446-5688-7). Peter Smith.

Thomas Woolner, R. A., Sculptor & Poet: His Life & Letters. 17.50 (ISBN 0-404-07030-2). AMS Pr.

Thomason Sketchbook: Drawings by John W. Thomason, Jr. 14.50 (ISBN 0-292-78414-7). U of Tex Pr.

Thoreau Country. 32.50 (ISBN 0-87156-140-9); pap. 9.95 (ISBN 0-87156-144-1). Sierra.

Thoreau MacDonald: A Catalogue of Design & Illustration. 20.00 (ISBN 0-8020-1959-5). U of Toronto Pr.

Thoughts on the American Flintlock Pistol. pap. 6.50 (ISBN 0-87387-070-0). Shumway.

Thoughts on the Kentucky Rifle in Its Golden Age. casebound 49.50 (ISBN 0-87387-048-4). Shumway.

Thoughts on the Meaning & Use of Pre-Hispanic Mexican Sellos. pap. 2.00 (ISBN 0-88402-017-7). Dumbarton Oaks.

Thread of Life: Symbolism of Miniature Art from Ecuador. Bd. with Further Exploration of the Rowe Chavin Seriation & Its Implications for North Central Coast Chronology; Man & a Feline in Mochica Art. 11.00 (ISBN 0-88402-061-4). Dumbarton Oaks.

Three Alexander Calders: A Family Memoir. 15.00 (ISBN 0-8397-8017-6). Eriksson.

Three American Modernist Painters. Incl. Max Weber; Maurice Stern; Stuart Davis. 13.00. Arno.

Three American Romantic Painters. Incl. Charles Burchfield, Early Watercolor; Florine Stettheimer; Franklin Watkins. 13.00. Arno.

Three Centuries of American Painting. 12.95 (ISBN 0-88401-011-2); pap. 2.95 (ISBN 0-88401-010-4). Fine Arts Mus.

Three Centuries of American Painting: From the Collection of the M. H. de Young Memorial Museum & the California Palace of the Legion of Honor. 12.45 (ISBN 0-8048-1242-X); pap. 2.95 (ISBN 0-8048-1244-6). C E Tuttle.

Three Classics of Italian Calligraphy: The Writing Books of Arrighi, Tagliente, Palatino. 7.50 (ISBN 0-8446-0829-7). Peter Smith.

Three Classics of Italian Calligraphy. pap. 4.00 (ISBN 0-486-20212-7). Dover.

Three Contemporary Chinese Painters: Chang Da-chien, Ting Yin-yung, Ch'eng Shih-fa. 10.00 (ISBN 0-295-95463-9). U of Wash Pr.

Three Decades of British Art, 1740-1770. 3.00 (ISBN 0-87169-063-2). Am Philos.

Three-Dimensional Decoupage. 9.95 (ISBN 0-8069-5322-5); PLB 9.29 (ISBN 0-8069-5323-3). Sterling.

Three-Dimensional Embroidery. 10.95 (ISBN 0-442-30075-1); pap. 5.95 (ISBN 0-442-30085-9). Van Nos Reinhold.

Three Generations of Twentieth-Century Art: The Sidney & Harriet Janis Collection of the Museum of Modern Art. 22.50 (ISBN 0-87070-400-1). Museum Mod Art.

Three Hundred Years of French Architecture, 1494-1794. facs. ed. 13.50 (ISBN 0-8369-5414-9). Arno.

Three Lectures on Aesthetic. pap. 1.70 (ISBN 0-672-60376-4, LLA154). Bobbs.

Three Maya Relief Panels at Dumbarton Oaks. pap. 2.00 (ISBN 0-88402-014-2). Dumbarton Oaks.

Three Places in New Inkland. pap. 5.95. Zartscorp.

Three Worlds of Leonid: Memoirs & Confessions. 13.95 (ISBN 0-465-08618-7). Basic.

Throne of the Third Heaven of the Nations Millenium General Assembly. pap. 1.50 (ISBN 0-89280-005-4). Montgomery Mus.

Through Camera Eyes. 10.95 (ISBN 0-8425-0435-4). Brigham.

Through England on My Knees. 12.00 (ISBN 0-498-01864-4). A S Barnes.

Through One's Eyes. 4.00 (ISBN 0-88445-002-3). Haddad's Fine Arts.

Through the Flower: My Struggle As a Woman Artist. pap. 4.50 (ISBN 0-385-12696-4). Doubleday.

Through the Flower: My Struggle As a Woman Artist. 8.95 (ISBN 0-385-09782-4); pap. 4.50 (ISBN 0-385-12696-4). Doubleday.

Through the Vanishing Point: Space in Poetry & Painting. 10.00 (ISBN 0-06-012914-X). Har-Row.

Throwing on the Potter's Wheel. 4.00. Prof Pubns Ohio.

Thurber & Company. 10.95 (ISBN 0-06-014305-3). Har-Row.

Tibetan & Himalayan Woodblock Prints. pap. 4.00 (ISBN 0-486-22988-2). Dover.

Tibetan & Himalayan Woodblock Prints. 7.50 (ISBN 0-8446-5089-7). Peter Smith.

Tides in English Taste, 1619-1800. 17.50x (ISBN 0-87471-005-7). Rowman.

Tie-Dyed Paper: An Easy New Craft. 12.95 (ISBN 0-8008-7702-0). Taplinger.

Tie Dyeing & Batik. 6.95 (ISBN 0-385-03626-4). Doubleday.

Tiffany Silver. 25.00 (ISBN 0-396-07547-9). Dodd.

Tiffany Touch. 10.95 (ISBN 0-394-46159-2). Random.

Tiffen Practical Filter Manual. pap. 5.95 (ISBN 0-8174-0180-6). Amphoto.

Tile Decorating with Gemma. 12.95 (ISBN 0-517-52950-5); pap. 6.95 (ISBN 0-517-52951-3). Crown.

Tile Panels of Spain, 1500-1650. 30.00 (ISBN 0-87535-110-7). Hispanic Soc.

Tilt: An Anthology of New England Women's Writing & Art. pap. 5.00 (ISBN 0-934678-02-2). New Victoria Pubs.

Time in a Frame: Photography & the Nineteenth-Century Mind. 17.95 (ISBN 0-8052-3674-0). Schocken.

Time in Eden. 15.00. Rho-Delta Pr.

Time-Saver Standards for Building Types. 45.00 (ISBN 0-07-016218-2). McGraw.

Timeless Theme: A Critical Theory Formulated & Applied. lib. bdg. 20.00 (ISBN 0-8414-2615-5). Folcroft.

Timeless Way of Building. 19.50 (ISBN 0-19-502402-8). Oxford U Pr.

Tin Can Book. pap. 6.95 (ISBN 0-451-79965-8, G9965). NAL.

Tina Modotti: A Fragile Life. 14.95 (ISBN 0-8467-0027-1). Brown Bk.

Tintoretto. lib. bdg. 23.50x (ISBN 0-8371-4501-5, NETI). Greenwood.

Tissue Paper Activities. pap. 1.95 (ISBN 0-87192-037-9). Davis Mass.

Tissue Paper Creations. 3.95 (ISBN 0-8069-5288-1); PLB 4.59 (ISBN 0-8069-5289-X). Sterling.

Titian & the Venetian Woodcut. soft bdg. 12.00 (ISBN 0-88397-067-8). Intl Exhibit Foun.

Titian's Assistants During the Later Years. lib. bdg. 46.00x (ISBN 0-8240-2689-6). Garland Pub.

Titian's Rape of Europa. 1.95 (ISBN 0-914660-08-X); pap. 0.95. I S Gardner Mus.

Tlingit Designs & Carving Manual. 9.95 (ISBN 0-87564-862-2); pap. 6.95 (ISBN 0-87564-861-4). Superior Pub.

To a Young Bird Artist: Selected Letters from Louis Agassiz Fuertes to George Miksch Sutton. 9.95 (ISBN 0-8061-1589-0). U of Okla Pr.

To Be a Woman in America, 1850-1930. 14.95 (ISBN 0-8129-0764-7); pap. 7.95 (ISBN 0-8129-6306-7). Times Bks.

To Grandfather's House We Go: A Roadside Tour of American Homes. 5.95 (ISBN 0-8193-0193-0); PLB 5.41 (ISBN 0-8193-0194-9). Parents.

To Keep Art Alive: The Effort of Kenneth Hayes Miller, American Painter (1876-1952) 15.00 (ISBN 0-87982-012-8). Art Alliance.

To See Is to Think: Looking at American Art. pap. 5.50 (ISBN 0-87474-177-7). Smithsonian.

Tobey. pap. 3.95 (ISBN 0-452-00352-0, FM352). NAL.

Today in Old Boston. PLB 6.60 (ISBN 0-516-03803-6). Childrens.

Tokens of the Eighteenth Century, Connected with Booksellers & Bookmakers (Authors, Printers, Publishers, Engravers, & Paper Makers) 7.50 (ISBN 0-8103-3368-6). Gale.

Tolstoi's Theory of Art. lib. bdg. 5.50 (ISBN 0-8414-4539-7). Folcroft.

Tolstoy on Art. lib. bdg. 33.95 (ISBN 0-8383-1459-7). Haskell.

Tomb of Nefer-Hotep at Thebes: Metropolitan Museum of Art Egyptian Expedition Publications. 39.00 (ISBN 0-405-02236-0). Arno.

Tomb of Nyhetep-Ptah at Giza & the Tomb of 'Ankhm' Ahor at Saqqara. pap. 15.00x (ISBN 0-520-09575-8). U of Cal Pr.

Tomb of Rekh-Mi-Re at Thebes: Metropolitan Museum of Art Egyptian Expedition Publications. 43.00 (ISBN 0-405-02267-0). Arno.

Tomb of Senebtisi at Lisht: Metropolitan Museum of Art Egyptian Expedition Publications. 29.00 (ISBN 0-405-02241-7). Arno.

Tombs of Iteti, Sekhem'ankh-Ptah, & Kaemnofert at Giza. pap. 11.00x (ISBN 0-520-09544-8). U of Cal Pr.

Tombstone Lettering in the British Isles. pap. 8.95 (ISBN 0-8230-5380-6). Watson-Guptill.

Tomorrow & Beyond. 19.95 (ISBN 0-89480-062-0, 1996); pap. 9.95 (ISBN 0-89480-055-8, 1988). Workman Pub.

Too Good to Eat! The Art of Dough Sculpture. pap. 4.95. Folk Art.

Toolchest: A Primer of Woodcraft. 6.95 (ISBN 0-8027-6153-4); lib. bdg. 6.85 (ISBN 0-8027-6154-2). Walker & Co.

Tools for Woodwork. pap. 4.95 (ISBN 0-8473-1338-7). Sterling.

Toothpick Sculpture & Ice-Cream Stick Art. 6.95 (ISBN 0-8069-5372-1); PLB 6.69 (ISBN 0-8069-5373-X). Sterling.

Top Outfits for Teenage Dolls. 9.95 (ISBN 0-8008-7768-3). Taplinger.

Topical Stamp Collecting. lib. bdg. 8.95 (ISBN 0-668-03754-7); pap. 5.95 (ISBN 0-668-03662-1). Arco.

Topics in American Art Since 1945. text ed. 12.95 (ISBN 0-393-04401-7); pap. text ed. 4.95x (ISBN 0-393-09237-2). Norton.

Tormented Genius: The Struggles of Vincent Van Gogh. 6.75 (ISBN 0-688-21605-6). Morrow.

Torres Straits Sculpture: A Study in Oceanic Primitive Art. lib. bdg. 44.00 (ISBN 0-8240-3228-4). Garland Pub.

Total Tote Bag Book: Designer Totes to Craft & Carry. 12.50 (ISBN 0-8008-7793-4); pap. 5.95 (ISBN 0-8008-7794-2). Taplinger.

Totems, Decoys, & Covered Wagons: Cardboard Constructions from Early American Life. PLB 6.00 (ISBN 0-688-51739-0). Lothrop.

Touchstone: Historical Essays on the Reigning Diversions of the Town. lib. bdg. 38.00 (ISBN 0-8240-0630-5). Garland Pub.

Tour of Old Sturbridge Village. rev. ed. pap. 1.50 (ISBN 0-8038-7128-7). Hastings.

Toward a National Taste: America's Quest for Aesthetic Independence. 12.00x (ISBN 0-8248-0340-X). U Pr of Hawaii.

Toward a People's Art. 12.95 (ISBN 0-525-22165-4); pap. 7.95 (ISBN 0-525-47426-9). Dutton.

Toward a Psychology of Art. 15.00x (ISBN 0-520-00038-2); pap. 4.95 (ISBN 0-520-02161-4, CAL242). U of Cal Pr.

Toward a Scientific Architecture. 12.50x (ISBN 0-262-06058-2). MIT Pr.

Toward the Transformation of Art. 6.50 (ISBN 0-8386-1382-9). Fairleigh Dickinson.

Towards a Cultural Policy for Honduras. pap. 4.75 (ISBN 92-3-101520-6, U875). Unipub.

Towards a Humane Architecture. 7.50 (ISBN 0-584-10301-8). Transatlantic.

Towards a Non-Oppressive Environment. 8.95x (ISBN 0-262-20038-4); pap. 4.95x (ISBN 0-262-70018-2). MIT Pr.

Town & Revolution: Soviet Architecture & City Planning 1917-1935. 15.00 (ISBN 0-8076-0554-9). Braziller.

Toymaker. 8.95 (ISBN 0-07-009604-X). McGraw.

Toymaking & Children's Furniture Simplified. pap. 3.50 (ISBN 0-87733-771-3). Directions.

Toys & Dolls. 24.50 (ISBN 0-8231-3032-0). Branford.

Toys & Gifts for You to Make. 8.25 (ISBN 0-8231-5022-4). Branford.

Toys for Your Delight. 9.95 (ISBN 0-263-70035-6). Transatlantic.

Toys from the Tales of Beatrix Potter. 17.95 (ISBN 0-7232-6098-2). Warne.

Toys from the Tales of Beatrix Potter. pap. 7.95 (ISBN 0-8015-7857-4). Hawthorn.

U

William Blake - Poet & Painter: An Introduction to the Illuminated Verse. pap. 6.95 (ISBN 0-226-31297-6, P795). U of Chicago Pr.
William Blake, Engraver. pap. 3.00 (ISBN 0-87811-014-3). Princeton Lib.
William Blake in This World. lib. bdg. 25.00. Folcroft.
William Blake in This World. lib. bdg. 24.95 (ISBN 0-8383-1732-4). Haskell.
William Blake in This World. lib. bdg. 30.00 (ISBN 0-8495-0440-6). Arden Lib.
William Blake: the Seer & His Visions. 12.95 (ISBN 0-517-52939-4); pap. 7.95 (ISBN 0-517-52940-8). Harmony.
William Blake's Circle of Destiny. lib. bdg. 15.00 (ISBN 0-374-96384-3). Octagon.
William C. A. Frerichs 1829-1905: A Retrospective Exhibition. pap. 3.00x (ISBN 0-88259-075-8). NCMA.
William Caxton. 13.45 (ISBN 0-8274-0486-7). R West.
William Caxton. 19.50 (ISBN 0-8337-2788-5). B Franklin.
William H. Jackson. 14.00 (ISBN 0-87100-045-8). Morgan.
William Hamilton's Anti-Social Register. pap. 3.95 (ISBN 0-14-004384-5). Penguin.
William Henry Bartlett 1809-1854: Artist, Author, & Traveller. 17.50 (ISBN 0-8020-1986-2). U of Toronto Pr.
William Henry Fox Talbot: Pioneer of Photography & Man of Science. 31.95 (ISBN 0-09-129600-5). Merrimack Bk Serv.
William Henry Jackson's Colorado. 27.95 (ISBN 0-87108-092-3); deluxe limited ed. 76.00 (ISBN 0-87108-093-1). Pruett.
William Hogarth: Paintings from the Collection of Mr. & Mrs. Paul Mellon. pap. 2.50. Natl Gallery Art.
William Morris. lib. bdg. 12.50. Folcroft.
William Morris. 12.75 (ISBN 0-405-08822-1). Arno.
William Morris. lib. bdg. 12.50 (ISBN 0-8414-2800-X). Folcroft.
William Morris & His Circle. lib. bdg. 6.75. Folcroft.
William Morris & His Circle. lib. bdg. 10.95 (ISBN 0-8383-1018-4). Haskell.
William Morris & His Work. lib. bdg. 6.50 (ISBN 0-8414-3544-8). Folcroft.
William Morris & the Art of the Book: A Pierpont Morgan Library Volume. 55.00 (ISBN 0-19-519910-3). Oxford U Pr.
William Morris & the Art of the Book. 55.00; pap. 27.50 (ISBN 0-87598-059-7). Pierpont Morgan.
William Morris & the Arts & Crafts. 35.00 (ISBN 0-8490-1306-2). Gordon Pr.
William Morris, Poet, Craftsman, Socialist. 29.00 (ISBN 0-403-07268-9). Scholarly.
William Morris to Whistler. lib. bdg. 25.00 (ISBN 0-8414-3534-0). Folcroft.
William Morris to Whistler. lib. bdg. 25.00 (ISBN 0-8495-0836-3). Arden Lib.
William Nicholson. 15.00 (ISBN 0-246-63804-4). Dufour.
William Sidney Mount. 40.00 (ISBN 0-8109-0315-6). Abrams.
William Strickland-Architect & Engineer 1788-1854. enl. ed. lib. bdg. 25.00 (ISBN 0-306-71235-0). Da Capo.
William Wetmore Story & His Friends. lib. bdg. 39.50 (ISBN 0-306-71249-0). Da Capo.
Williams Collection of Far Eastern Ceramics: Tonnancour Section. pap. 8.00x (ISBN 0-932206-75-1). U Mich Mus Anthro.
Williamsburg Collection of Antique Furnishings. pap. 3.95 (ISBN 0-87935-017-2). Williamsburg.
Willow Spokes & Wickerwork. 9.95 (ISBN 0-8117-1900-6). Stackpole.
Wilson's Photographics. 19.00 (ISBN 0-405-04951-X). Arno.
Winchester Book. 3rd ed. 35.00 (ISBN 0-910156-03-4). Art & Ref.
Wind on Your Cheek. 17.50 (ISBN 0-88395-015-4); partial lea. bdg. boxed 75.00. Freshet Pr.
Window Glass Design Guide. 12.00x (ISBN 0-89397-028-X). Nichols Pub.
Windows. 19.95 (ISBN 0-8092-7819-7). Contemp Bks.
Windows. pap. cancelled (ISBN 0-8092-7818-9). Contemp Bks.
Windsor Chairmaking. 9.95 (ISBN 0-8038-8077-4). Hastings.
Windsor Handbook. pap. 3.75 (ISBN 0-8048-1105-9). C E Tuttle.
Wings for Words: The Story of Johann Gutenberg & His Invention of Printing. 11.00 (ISBN 0-8103-3936-6). Gale.
Winnington Letters: John Ruskin's Correspondence with Margaret Alexis Bell & the Children at Winnington Hall. 25.00x (ISBN 0-674-95365-7). Harvard U Pr.
Winterthur Guide to American Needlework. 6.95 (ISBN 0-517-52785-5). Crown.
Winterthur Guide to Chinese Export Porcelain. 6.95 (ISBN 0-517-52784-7). Crown.
Wire Sculpture & Other Three Dimensional Construction. 8.95 (ISBN 0-87192-025-5). Davis Mass.
Wire, Wood & Cork. 6.95 (ISBN 0-531-02556-X). Watts.
Wisconsin Sketches. 12.95 (ISBN 0-88361-024-8). Stanton & Lee.
With Benefit of Architect. 7.95 (ISBN 0-02-620750-8). Macmillan.
With Camera in the Ghetto. 12.95 (ISBN 0-8052-3645-7). Schocken.
Without Our Past: A Handbook for the Preservation of Canada's Architectural Heritage. 17.50 (ISBN 0-8020-2239-1); pap. 5.50 (ISBN 0-8020-6298-9). U of Toronto Pr.
Without Rhetoric: An Architectural Aesthetic 1955-1972. 7.95x (ISBN 0-262-19119-9). MIT Pr.
Wolf & the Raven: Totem Poles of Southeastern Alaska. 2nd ed. pap. 5.95 (ISBN 0-295-73998-3). U of Wash Pr.
Wolf Huber Studies: Aspects of Renaissance Thought & Practice in Danube School Painting. lib. bdg. 52.00 (ISBN 0-8240-2725-6). Garland Pub.
Woman. 15.00 (ISBN 0-8076-0664-2). Braziller.
Woman to Woman. 14.95 (ISBN 0-385-13645-5). Doubleday.
Woman's Build-It & Fix-It Handbook. pap. 1.50 (ISBN 0-89041-021-6, 3021). Major Bks.
Woman's Day Book of Granny Squares & Other Carry-Along Crochet. pap. 4.95 (ISBN 0-671-22946-X). S&S.
Woman's Day Book of Soft Toys & Dolls. 12.50 (ISBN 0-671-22085-3). S&S.
Woman's Day Book of Weekend Crafts: More Than 100 Quick-to-Finish Projects. 11.95 (ISBN 0-395-26284-4). HM.
Woman's Day Book of Wildflowers. 6.95 (ISBN 0-671-22251-1). S&S.
Woman's Eye. 15.00 (ISBN 0-394-48678-1); pap. 7.95 (ISBN 0-394-70626-9). Knopf.
Women & Creativity. 9.95 (ISBN 0-89087-989-3); pap. 4.95 (ISBN 0-89087-926-5). Les Femmes Pub.
Women & Other Visions. pap. 9.95 (ISBN 0-87100-102-0, 399). Morgan.
Women Artists: An Historical, Contemporary & Feminist Bibliography. 14.00 (ISBN 0-8108-1149-9). Scarecrow.
Women Artists in America II. 15.00x (ISBN 0-8150-0899-6). Wittenborn.
Women Artists in America: 18th Century to the Present. 15.00x. Wittenborn.
Women Artists of the Arts & Crafts Movement, 1870-1914. 20.00 (ISBN 0-394-50667-7); pap. 10.95 (ISBN 0-394-73780-6). Pantheon.
Women Artists: Recognition & Reappraisal From the Early Middle Ages to the Twentieth Century. 12.50x (ISBN 0-8147-6567-X). NYU Pr.
Women Artists: Recognition & Reappraisal from the Early Middle Ages to the Twentieth Century. pap. 5.95 (ISBN 0-06-090387-2, CN387). Har-Row.
Women Artists, 1550-1950. 17.50 (ISBN 0-394-41169-2); pap. 11.95 (ISBN 0-394-73326-6). Knopf.
Women, Heroes, & a Frog. pap. 3.95 (ISBN 0-393-08624-0). Norton.
Women in American Architecture: A Historic & Contemporary Perspective. 25.00 (ISBN 0-8230-7485-4). Watson-Guptill.
Women in the Comics. 15.00 (ISBN 0-87754-056-X). Chelsea Hse.
Women Painters of Mithila. pap. 8.95 (ISBN 0-500-27093-7). Thames Hudson.
Women Painters of the World: From the Time of Caterina Vigri 1413-1463 to Rosa Bonheur & the Present Day. lib. bdg. 30.00 (ISBN 0-87817-184-3). Hacker.
Women Photograph Men. 15.95 (ISBN 0-688-03214-1); pap. 7.95 (ISBN 0-688-08214-9). Morrow.
Women We Wanted to Look Like. 14.95 (ISBN 0-312-88783-3). St Martin.
Wonder of Hands. 5.95 (ISBN 0-8193-0420-4); PLB 5.41 (ISBN 0-8193-0421-2). Parents.
Wonderful Webbers. 12.95. Elysium.
Wonderings. pap. 2.50 (ISBN 0-88489-041-4). St Marys.
Wonders of Gems. PLB 4.50 (ISBN 0-396-06403-5). Dodd.
Wonders of Light & Shadow. 9.00 (ISBN 0-405-04941-2). Arno.
Wonders of the Stereoscope. 25.00 (ISBN 0-394-40882-9). Knopf.
Wood & the Graver. 22.50. Potter.
Wood & the Graver. limited ed. 45.00; 22.50 (ISBN 0-517-52910-6). Potter.
Wood & Wood Grains: A Photographic Album for Artists and Designers. 3.50 (ISBN 0-486-22424-4). Dover.
Wood & Wood Grains: A Photographic Album for Artists & Designers. 6.75 (ISBN 0-8446-0040-7). Peter Smith.
Wood As an Industrial Arts Material. text ed. 16.50 (ISBN 0-08-017906-1); pap. text ed. 9.50 (ISBN 0-08-017907-X). Pergamon.
Wood Carver of Salem: Samuel McIntire, His Life & Work. 20.00 (ISBN 0-404-01786-X). AMS Pr.
Wood Carving. rev. ed. pap. 4.95 (ISBN 0-8069-8790-1). Sterling.
Wood Carving & Whittling for Everyone. 12.95 (ISBN 0-684-14886-2). Scribner.
Wood Carving & Whittling Made Easy. 6.95 (ISBN 0-02-544860-9). Macmillan.
Wood Design. 11.95 (ISBN 0-8230-5850-6). Watson-Guptill.
Wood Engraving: An Adventure in Printmaking. 14.95 (ISBN 0-670-78083-9). Viking Pr.
Wood Finishing. 9.00 (ISBN 0-08-011242-0). Pergamon.
Wood Finishing. pap. text ed. 5.60 (ISBN 0-87002-012-9). Bennett Co.
Wood Finishing & Refinishing. rev. ed. pap. 6.95 (ISBN 0-442-22668-3). Van Nos Reinhold.
Wood Finishing & Refinishing. 2nd ed. 11.95 (ISBN 0-442-22667-5). Van Nos Reinhold.
Wood Finishing-Plain & Decorative. 9.95 (ISBN 0-87749-024-4); pap. 4.95 (ISBN 0-87749-811-3). Sterling.
Wood Laminating. rev. ed. 11.96 (ISBN 0-87345-046-9). McKnight.
Wood: Materials & Processes. rev. ed. text ed. 15.96 (ISBN 0-87002-307-1). Bennett Co.
Wood, Metal & Plastic: A Creative Introduction to Methods & Materials. 12.50; pap. 6.95 (ISBN 0-679-50757-4). McKay.
Wood Sculpture. 6.50 (ISBN 0-8008-8470-1). Taplinger.
Wood Type Alphabets. pap. 3.50 (ISBN 0-486-23533-5). Dover.
Wood Type Alphabets: 100 Fonts. 7.50 (ISBN 0-8446-5590-2). Peter Smith.
Woodblock Cutting & Printing. 7.95 (ISBN 0-8069-5374-8); PLB 7.49 (ISBN 0-8069-5375-6). Sterling.
Woodcarver's Primer. 8.95 (ISBN 0-8069-8786-3); pap. 5.95 (ISBN 0-8069-8788-X). Sterling.
Woodcarving. 7.95 (ISBN 0-87749-270-0); pap. 4.95 (ISBN 0-8069-8790-1). Sterling.
Woodcarving for Beginners. pap. 7.95 (ISBN 0-917304-11-X). Intl Schol Bk Serv.
Woodcut. pap. 1.95 (ISBN 0-448-00549-2). G&D.
Woodcuts. new ed. 14.95 (ISBN 0-918266-09-2); pap. 3.95 (ISBN 0-918266-03-3). Smyrna.
Wooden Spoon Puppets. 10.95 (ISBN 0-8238-0204-3). Plays.
Wooden Toys. 12.95 (ISBN 0-8015-4809-8). Hawthorn.
Woodstock Craftsman's Manual. pap. 8.95 (ISBN 0-14-046340-2). Penguin.
Woodstock Handmade Houses. pap. 6.95 (ISBN 0-345-25592-5). Ballantine.
Woodturning. pap. 2.00 (ISBN 0-668-00983-7). Arc Bks.
Woodturning. text ed. 11.96. McKnight.
Woodturning Visualized. rev ed. pap. 7.20 (ISBN 0-02-813770-1). Glencoe.
Woodward's National Architect. text ed. 25.00 (ISBN 0-89257-017-2). Am Life Foun.
Woodwind Instruments & Their History. rev. ed. 11.95x (ISBN 0-393-09723-4). Norton.
Woodwork: A Basic Manual. 7.95 (ISBN 0-316-83655-9); pap. 3.95 (ISBN 0-316-83656-7). Little.
Woodwork Joints. rev. ed. pap. 4.95 (ISBN 0-8069-8806-1). Sterling.
Woodwork Joints: Kinds of Joints., How They Are Cut, & Where Used. pap. 4.95 (ISBN 0-8069-8806-1). Sterling.
Woodwork of Greek Roofs. 13.50 (ISBN 0-521-05280-7). Cambridge U Pr.
Woodwork Visualized. rev. ed. pap. text ed. 6.00 (ISBN 0-02-813790-6). Glencoe.
Woodworker's Bible. pap. 5.95 (ISBN 0-8306-5860-2). TAB Bks.
Woodworking. text ed. 4.40 (ISBN 0-87006-184-4). Goodheart.
Woodworking Factbook: Basic Information on Wood for Wood Carvers, Home Woodshop Craftsmen, Tradesmen & Instructors. 15.00 (ISBN 0-8315-0024-7). Speller.
Woodworking for Cave Dwellers. 10.95 (ISBN 0-8306-9877-9); pap. 6.95 (ISBN 0-8306-1022-7, 1022). Tab Bks.
Woodworking for Industry. text ed. 18.20 (ISBN 0-87002-242-3). Bennett Co.
Woodworking for Industry. rev. ed. cancelled (ISBN 0-87002-053-6). Bennett Co.
Woodworking for Industry: Technology & Practice. 29.95 (ISBN 0-684-16385-3). Scribner.
Woodworking for Kids. 6.95 (ISBN 0-385-11430-3); PLB (ISBN 0-385-11431-1). Doubleday.
Woodworking Technology. 4th, rev. ed. 14.64x (ISBN 0-87345-235-6, B83327). McKnight.
Woodworking Technology. rev. ed. text ed. 12.64 (ISBN 0-87345-017-5); study guide 3.32 (ISBN 0-87345-018-3); ans. key avail. McKnight.
Wool Toys. PLB 3.95 (ISBN 0-7232-1998-2). Warne.
Word in Stone: The Role of Architecture in the Nationalist Socialist Ideology. 19.50x (ISBN 0-520-02193-2). U of Cal Pr.
Word Shadows of the Great: The Lure of Autograph Collecting. 15.00 (ISBN 0-8103-3378-3). Gale.
Wordless Workshop. pap. 0.95 (ISBN 0-8008-8500-7). Taplinger.
Words & Pictures: An Introduction to Photojournalism. 18.00 (ISBN 0-405-04917-X); pap. 4.95. Arno.
Words & Pictures: On the Literal & the Symbolic in the Illustrations of a Text. pap. text ed. 15.00x. Mouton.
Words As Visions: Logograms. pap. 6.95. Ilkon Pr.
Words of the Earth. 15.00 (ISBN 0-87156-002-X). Sierra.
Work of Frei Otto. pap. 6.95 (ISBN 0-87070-333-1). Museum Mod Art.
Work of Our Hands: Jewish Needlecraft for Today. 10.00 (ISBN 0-8052-3502-7); pap. 5.95 (ISBN 0-8052-0489-X). Schocken.
Work of Robert Adam. 16.95 (ISBN 0-668-04535-3, 4535). Arco.
Work of Thomas W. Nason, N. A. 65.00 (ISBN 0-89073-012-1). Boston Public Lib.
Workbook of an Unsuccessful Architect. 8.95 (ISBN 0-85345-294-6, CL-2946). Monthly Rev.
Workbook of an Unsuccessful Architect. pap. 3.45 (ISBN 0-85345-332-2, PB3322). Monthly Rev.
Worker in Art. PLB 4.95 (ISBN 0-8225-0167-8). Lerner Pubns.
Working Big. pap. 6.95 (ISBN 0-442-24795-8). Van Nos Reinhold.
Working Drawing Handbook. 13.95 (ISBN 0-442-25283-8); pap. 6.95 (ISBN 0-442-25284-6). Van Nos Reinhold.
Working Plans for Working Decoys. 12.50 (ISBN 0-87691-286-2). Winchester Pr.
Working with Cardboard & Paper. PLB 7.95 (ISBN 0-201-09342-1). A-W.
Working with Copper. 7.95 (ISBN 0-8473-1078-7). Sterling.
Working with Gemstones. 8.95 (ISBN 0-668-03430-0). Arco.
Working with Leather. 7.95 (ISBN 0-87523-161-6). Emerson.
Working with Nature: A Practical Guide. 19.95 (ISBN 0-19-501667-X). Oxford U Pr.
Working with Odds & Ends. PLB 6.95 (ISBN 0-531-02678-7). Watts.
Working with Stained Glass: Fundamental Techniques & Applications. 10.95 (ISBN 0-690-89706-5). T Y Crowell.
Working with Stained Glass: Fundamental Techniques & Applications. pap. 3.95 (ISBN 0-308-10153-7, F112). T Y Crowell.
Working with the Wool: How to Weave a Navajo Rug. pap. 4.95 (ISBN 0-87358-084-2). Northland.
Works in Architecture of Robert & James Adam. 135.00. AMS Pr.
Works in Architecture of Robert & James Adam. 135.00 (ISBN 0-404-17233-4). AMS Pr.
Works in Architecture of Robert & James Adam. pap. price not set (ISBN 0-486-23810-5). Dover.
Works of Colonel John Trumbull. rev. ed. 25.00x (ISBN 0-300-00957-7). Yale U Pr.
Works of James Gillray. 40.00 (ISBN 0-405-08562-1). Arno.
Works of James McNeill Whistler. facsimile ed. 18.50 (ISBN 0-8369-5788-1). Arno.
Works of James McNeill Whistler. lib. bdg. 35.00 (ISBN 0-89341-217-1). Longwood Pr.
Works of William Blake, Poetic, Symbolic, & Critical. 100.00 (ISBN 0-404-08960-7); 35.00 ea. (ISBN 0-404-08961-5) (ISBN 0-404-08962-3) (ISBN 0-404-08963-1). AMS Pr.
Workshop Book of Knitting. 9.95 (ISBN 0-689-20696-8); pap. 4.95 (ISBN 0-689-70564-6). Atheneum.
Workshop Crafts. PLB 8.49 (ISBN 0-8172-1184-5). Raintree Pubs Ltd.
World As Non-Objectivity: Unpublished Writings 1922-25. pap. 42.50x (ISBN 0-8150-0894-5). Wittenborn.
World Between the Ox & the Swine: Dada Drawings by Hans Richter. 2.00. Mus of Art RI.
World Collectors Annuary. write for info., vol. 1-28, 1943-76 avail. (ISBN 9-0701-3904-9); 1977 100.00. Heinman.
World Encyclopedia of Comics. 42.50 set. Bowker.
World Encyclopedia of Comics. pap. 10.00 (ISBN 0-380-01735-0, 34249). Avon.
World History of Art. rev. ed. 35.00 (ISBN 0-671-22013-6). S&S.
World History of Art. 2nd rev. ed. lib. bdg. 18.50 (ISBN 0-531-05402-0). Watts.
World History of Art. 2nd rev ed. 35.00 (ISBN 0-88225-258-5). Newsweek.
World I Love to See. pap. 6.95 (ISBN 0-395-25400-0). HM.
World in My Camera. 15.00 (ISBN 0-8037-9732-X). Dial.
World of Abstract Art. 22.50 (ISBN 0-8150-0003-0). Wittenborn.

GEOGRAPHIC GUIDE TO MUSEUMS

This guide is arranged by institution name within country. Cross-references provide access from variant forms of the institution name, when applicable. Descriptive annotations of permanent collections were provided by the institution.

AFGHANISTAN

National Museum of Afghanistan.
Darul Aman, Kabul

ALBANIA

Museum of Archaeology & Ethnography.
Institute of Scientific Research in History & Linguistics of the State University of Tirana, Tirana

ALGERIA

Musee Archeologique.
Timgad

Musee d'Archeologie de Djemila.
Djemila Par Elalma Wilayatte (Setif)

Musee de Cherchell.
Place de la Mairie, Cherchell

Musee de Constantine.
Blvd. de la Republique, Constantine

Musee de Philippeville.
Phillippeville

Musee de Prehistoire et d'Ethnographie du Bardo.
3 Rue Franklin D. Roosevelt, Algiers
Permanent Collections:
Prehistory and ethnography.

Musee de Skikda.
Skikda

Musee de Tlemcen.
Mosquee de Sidi Bel-Hacene, Place d'Alger, Tlemcen

Musee des Antiquites de Tipasa.
Rue des Thermes, Tipasa

Musee du Temple de Minerva.
Rte. de Constantine, Place de Minerve, Tebessa

Musee du Theatre Antique de Guelma.
Theate Antique, Guelma

Musee Municipal.
19 Blvd. Zabana, Oran

Musee National des Antiquities.
Parc de la Liberte, Algiers, 60 56 37

Musee National des Beaux-Arts d'Alger.
Pl. Dares-Salaam, Algiers, 66 93 05

AMERICAN SAMOA

Haydon, Jean P. , Museum.
P.O. Box 1540, Pago Pago, 96799

ANGOLA

Museu de Angola.
Rua de Nossa Senhora da Muxima, CP 1267, Luanda, 3 40 54

Museu do Dundo.
Companhia de Diamantes de Angola, Dundo, Lunda

Museu Municipal de Nova Lisboa.
Av. Paiva Couceiro, Nova Lisboa

ARGENTINA

Brizuela, Laurearo, Museum. *See* Museo Provincial de Bellas Artes "Laureano Brizuela"

Caraffa, Emilio A., Museum. *See* Museo Provincial de Bellas Artes "Emilio A. Caraffa"

Centro de Arte y Communicacion.
Elpidio Gonzalez 4070, 1407 Buenos Aires

Centro de Artesanias Americanas.
Santa Clara del Mar

Cornet, Ramon, Museum. *See* Museo Provincial de Bellas Artes "Ramon Gomez Cornet"

Escuela Superior De Bellas Artes Ernesto De La Carcova.
Tristan Achaval Rodriguez 1701, 1107 Buenos Aires

Estudio Museo "Ramoneda".
Salta 214, Humahuaca

Guinazu, Emiliano, Museo. *See* Museo Provincial de Bellas Artes "Emiliaro Guinazu"

Instituto Interdisciplinario "Tilcara".
Belgrado 445, Tilcara 4624
Permanent Collections:
Archaeology, ethnography and folklore.

Martinez, Dr. E. Pedro, Museum of Fine Art. *See* Museo Provincial de Bellas Artes "Dr. Pedro E. Martinez"

Museo Arquitectonico de la Ciudad de Buenos Aires.
Sarmiento 1551, Buenos Aires

Museo Colonial e Historico "Enrique Uduando.
Lezica 917, Apdo. 96, Lujan

Museo Colonial, Historica y de Bellas Artes.
Calle 9 de Julio 1044, Corrientes Juana S.C. de Castillo Odena

Museo Colonial, Historico y de Bellas Artes.
Caseros 575, Salta

Museo de Arqueologi Calchaqui.
Colon 191, Cafayate

Museo de Arte Marino.
Callao 966, Buenos Aires

Museo de Arte Moderno de la Ciudad de Buenos Aires.
Av. Corrientes 1530, Piso 7, Buenos Aires

Museo de Arte Religioso "Juan de Tejeda".
Independencia 122, Cordoba

Museo de Arte Religioso "San Francisco Solano".
Av. Roca 716, Santiago del Estero

Museo de Artes Plasticas "Edoardo Sivori".
Av. Corrientes 1530, Piso 5, Buenos Aires, 46-9664
Permanent Collections:
Argentine painting and sculpture from the 19th and 20th centuries.

Museo de Artes Plasticas "Mercedes Tomasa de San Martin de Balcarce".
Pueyrredon 502, San Martin

Museo de Bellas Artes.
Av. Moreno 232, Tres Arroyos

Museo de Bellas Artes "Ceferino Carnacini".
America 151, Villa Ballester

Museo de Bellas Artes de Coronel Pringles.
San Martin 857, Coronel Pringles

Museo de Bellas Artes de la Boca.
Pedro de Mendoza 1835, Buenos Aires

Museo de Bellas Artes de la Escuela del Distrito Escolar XII "General Urquiza".
Yerbal 2370, Buenos Aires

Museo de Bellas Artes de Lincoln.
Alem 1950, Lincoln

Museo de Bellas Artes de Lujan.
San Martin y Lavalle Lujan

Museo de Bellas Artes "Octavio de la Colina".
Copiapo 245, la Rioja

Museo de Calcos.
Ave. Tristan Achaval
Rodriguez 1701, Buenos Aires

**Museo de la Basilica del Rosario
de la Reconquista y Defensa de
Buenos Aires.**
Defensa 422, Buenos Aires

**Museo de Motivos Populares
Argentinos "Jose Hernandez".**
Av. del Libertador General San
Martin 2373

Museo de Nueva Pompeya.
Av. Saenz 1260, Buenos Aires

**Museo del Convento de San
Francisco.**
Amenabar 2567, Santa Fe

Museo del Grabado.
Florida 588, Buenos Aires

**Museo del Instituto Nacional
Sanmartiniaro.**
Sanchez de Bustamente y Av.
A. M. de Aguado, Buenos
Aires

**Museo "Dorotea Caleano de
Sugo".**
Dr. Aberastain 872, Sur, San
Juan

**Museo Escolar de Artes
"Fernando Fader".**
Cuenca 5040, Buenos Aires

Museo Folklorico Regional.
Ave. San Martin 55, Humahaca
Permanent Collections:
Silversmith art, fabrics, tobacco
pouches, stirrups, religious
statues, colonial painting,
ceremonial objects, costumes,
carnival masks, witchcraft
amulets and talismans,
ironwork, precious stones and
pottery.

**Museo "Fray Jose de la
Quintana".**
Fray Jose de la Quintana y San
Juan, Corrientes

**Museo Historico de la Ciudad de
Buenos Aires, "Brigadier
General Cornelio de Saavedra".**
Avda. Gral. Paz y
Republiquetas 6309, Buenos
Aires

**Museo Historico del Convento de
San Carlos.**
Belgrano 430, San Lorenzo

Museo Historico Eclesiastico.
Jose Cubas 3543, Buenos Aires

Museo Historico Provincial.
3 de Febrere y San Martin,
Santa Fe

**Museo Historico Provincial de
Rosario "Dr. Julio Mare".**
Parque Independencia, Rosario

**Museo Historico Regional de
Colon.**
Calle 12 de Abril No. 120,
Colon

**Museo Historico y de Arte
Sagrado.**
General Lopez y San
Geronimo, Santa Fe

**Museo Internacional de la
Caricatura y Humorismo
"Severo Vaccaro".**
Estadosunidos 2162, Buenos
Aires

Museo "Iramain".
Entre Rios 27, San Miguel de
Tucuman

Museo Jesuitico.
Ruinas Jesuiticas de San
Ignacio, San Ignacio

Museo Jesuitico.
Convento e Iglesia de San
Isidro, Jesus Maria

**Museo Jesuitico Numismatico
"Domingo F. Sarmiento".**
Av. Sarmiento s/no, San
Ignacio

Museo "Juan B. Ambrosetti".
Rioja 3383, Mar del Plata

Museo Judio.
Liberated 773, Buenos Aires

**Museo Municipal de Arte
Decorativo, "Firma y Odilo
Estevez".**
Sante Fe 748, Rosario

**Museo Municipal de Arte Espanol
"Enrique Larreta".**
Juramento 2291, Buenos Aires

**Museo Municipal de Arte
Hispano-Americano "Isaac
Fernandez Blanco".**
Suipacha 1422, Buenos Aires

**Museo Municipal de Arte
Morderno.**
San Martin 1143, Mendoza

**Museo Municipal de Artes
Plasticas.**
San Martin 799, Avellaneda

**Museo Municipal de Artes
Plasticas de Chivilcoy.**
Bolivar 319, Chivilcoy, 3813
Permanent Collections:
Historic Museum Francisco
Castagnino; Plastic Arts
Museum "Pompeo Poggio;"
Municipal Historical File,
Library and Place Room;
Archaeological Museum "Dr.
Osvaldo Menaghin."

**Museo Municipal de Artes
Visuales.**
Rivadavia 498, Esq. Pringles,
Quilmes

Museo Municipal de Bellas Artes.
Colon 149, Rio Cuarto

Museo Municipal de Bellas Artes.
Alsina 65, Bahia Blanca

Museo Municipal de Bellas Artes.
San Martin 555, Rafaela

Museo Municipal de Bellas Artes.
Calle 53 No. 840, la Plata

Museo Municipal de Bellas Artes.
An. Luro 2440 piso 7, la Plata

**Museo Municipal de Bellas Artes
de Tandil.**
Chacabuco 357, Tandil

**Museo Municipal de Bellas Artes
"Dr. Genero Perez.**
Av. General Paz 33, Cordoba

**Museo Municipal de Bellas Artes
Juan B. Castagnino.**
Avda Pellegrini, 2202, Parque
Independencia, Rosario

**Museo Municipal de Bellas Artes
y Arte Nacional.**
Av. Alvear 3273, Buenos Aires

Museo Nacional de Arte Oriental.
Av. del Libertador Gral. San
Martin 1902, Piso 1, Buenos
Aires

Museo Particular "Sormani".
Av. 9 de Julio 695, Este, San
Juan

**Museo Pedagogico de Artes
Visuales.**
San Martin 468, Galvez

Museo Provincial.
Hipolito Yrigoyen 160, Santa
Rosa

Museo Provincial de Bellas Artes.
Congreso 56, San Miguel de
Tucuman

Museo Provincial de Bellas Artes.
Congresso 56, San Miguel de
Tucuman

**Museo Provincial de Bellas Artes
"Dr. Pedro E. Martinez".**
Laprida y Buenos Aires, Parana

**Museo Provincial de Bellas Artes
"Emiliaro Guinazu".**
Mayor Drumond, Lujan de
Cuyo

**Museo Provincial de Bellas Artes
"Emilio A. Caraffa".**
Pl. Espana, Cordoba

**Museo Provincial de Bellas Artes
"Franklin Rawson".**
Av. Libertador Gral. San
Martin 315, Oeste, San Juan

**Museo Provincial de Bellas Artes
"Laureano Brizuela".**
Republica 318, Catamarca

**Museo Provincial de Bellas Artes
"Ramon Gomez Cornet".**
Independencia 222, Santiago
del Estero

**Museo Provincial de Bellas Artes
"Rosa Galisteo de Rodriguez".**
4 de Enero 1510, Santa Fe

**Museo Regional de Pintura "Jose
A. Terry".**
Rivadavia 451, Tilcara

Museo "San Roque".
Alsina 340, Buenos Aires

**Museo y Archivo Historico de
Neuquen.**
Brown 162, Neuquen

Museo y Salon Municipal.
Av. 9 de Julio Esq. Avellaneda,
San Francisco

**National Museum of Decorative
Art.**
Ave. del Libertador 1902,
Buenos Aires

Palacio del Mate.
Rivadavia 324, Posadas

Rawson, Franklin, Museum. *See*
**Museo Provincial de Bellas
Artes "Franklin Rawson"**

**Rodriguez, Rosa Galisteo de,
Museum.** *See* **Museo Provincial
de Bellas Artes "Rosa Galisteo
de Rodriguez"**

Sivori Museum. *See* **Museo de
Artes Plasticas "Edoardo Sivori"**

Terry, Jose A., Museum. *See*
**Museo Regional de Pintura
"Jose A. Terry"**

AUSTRALIA

Art Gallery of New South Wales.
Art Gallery Rd., 2000 Sydney

Art Gallery of South Australia.
North Terrace, Adelaide 5000,
08 2238911

Bendigo Art Gallery.
42 View St., Bendigo, Vic., 43
4991
Permanent Collections:
The Collection includes
paintings, sculptures, prints and
decorative arts, an outstanding
collection of 19th century
European narrative paintings,
the Dr. J. A. S. N. Scott
Collection of European and
Australian paintings, English
furniture, fine silver and
European porcelain as well as a
representative collection of
Australian mainstream art from
c. 1840 to the present.

**Castlemaine Art Gallery &
Historical Museum.**
Lyttleton St., Castlemaine, Vic.
3450

Geelong Art Gallery.
Litttle Malop St., Geelong, Vic.
3220

Leighton Gallery of Art.
Leighton House, 346-348 Little
Collins St., Melbourne, Vic.

**Museum of Applied Arts &
Science.**
659-795 Harris St., Broadway,
2007 Sydney

**Museum of Modern Art & Design
of Australia.**
180 Flinders St., Melbourne,
Vic. 3000

National Gallery of Victoria.
180 St. Kilda Rd., Melbourne
3004, 62 7411 NATGALVIC
Permanent Collections:
Departments of Australian art,
Asian art, prints and drawings,
photography, decorative arts,
European painting and
sculpture before 1800,
European and American art
after 1800.

Nicholson Museum of Antiquities.
University of Sydney, Sydney,
NSW 2006, 692-2812
Permanent Collections:
Near Eastern, Egyptian,
Cypriot, Greek and Roman,
European art

**Power Gallery of Comtemporary
Art.**
Power Institute of Fine Arts,
University of Sydney, Nsw
2006

Queen Victoria Museum.
Wellington St., 7250
Launceston

Queensland Art Gallery.
M.I.M. Bldg., 160 Ann St.,
Brisbane, Qld. 4000

**State Library of Tasmania
Museum of Fine Arts.**
91 Murray St., Hobart, Tas.
7000

**Tasmanian Museum & Art
Gallery.**
GPO Box 1164M, 7001 Hobart

War Memorial Gallery of Fine Arts.
University of Sydney, Parrametta Rd., Sydney NSW 2006

Western Australian Art Gallery.
Beaufort St., 6000 Perth

AUSTRIA

Abteilung Fur Kunstgewerbe Am Landesmuseum Joanneum.
Neutorgasse 45, A-8010 Graz

Abteilung Schloss Eggenberg am Landesmuseum Joanneum.
Eggenberger Allee 90, A-8020 Graz

Alte Backstube (Josefstadter Heimatmuseum)
Langegasse 34, A-1010 Wien

Alte Galerie am Landesmusem Joanneum.
Neutorgasse 45, A-8010 Graz

Anton-Museum.
Landst. 65, A-3910 Zwetti

Augustiner-Chorherrenstift und Stifts-Sammlungen.
Haus 1, A-8250 Vorau

Austrian Gallery.
Prinz Eugen-Str. 27, Postfach 12, A-1037 Vienna

Barockmuseum.
Schloss Heiligenkreuz, A-3665 Gutenbrunn

Beethoven-Wohnung (Eroicahaus)
Doblinger Hauptstrasse 92, Wien 19

Beethoven-Wohnung (Heiligenstadter Testament)
Probusgasse 6, Wien 19

Beethoven-Wohnung (Pasqualatihaus)
Molkerbastei 8, Wien 1

Benediktinerabtei und Abteimuseum.
A-8732 Seckau

Benediktinerinnenstift am Nonnberg und Stiftssammlungen.
Nonnberggasse 2, A-5020 Salzburg

Benediktinerstift Melk.
A-3390 Melk, 02752/2312

Benediktinerstift mit Stiftssamlungen.
A-4650 Lambach

Benediktinerstift und Kunstsammlungen.
A-5152 Michaelbeuren

Benediktinerstift und Stiftssammlungen.
A-3591 Altenburg

Bezirksheimatmuseum.
Schloss Porcia, Edlingstr. 13 A-9800 Spittal/Drau, 33 123
Permanent Collections:
Ethnology and handicrafts.

Bezirksmuseum.
Johann-Fischer-Gasse 18 und 20, A-5280 Braunau

Bild-und Tonarchiv am Landesmuseum Joanneum.
Sackstr. 17, A-8010 Graz

Bischofliches Diozesanmuseum.
Herrenstr. 36, A-4000 Linz

Bischofliches Diozesanmuseum.
Haus am Dom, Lidmanskygasse 10, A-9020 Klagenfurt

Bundessammlungen Alter Stimobel (Bundesmobilienverwaltung)
Mariahilfer Str. 88, A-1070 Wien

Burg Bernstein.
Schloss, A-7434 Berstein

Burg Kreuzenstein mit Burgsammlungen.
Leobendorf, A-2100 Korneuburg

Burg Schlaining.
Rochusplatz 1, A-7461 Stadtschlaining

Burg und Burgsammlungen.
Burg Riegersburg, A-8333 Riegersburg (Steiermark)

Burgenkundliches Museum.
A-8011 Graz, Burgergasse 2

Burgenkundliches Museum.
Schloss Alt-Kainach, A-8573 Barnbach

Burgenlandisches Landesmuseum.
Museumsgasse 1-5, A-7000 Eisenstadt

Burgmuseum.
Burg, A-4600 Wels

Burgmuseum.
Burg Seebenstein, A-2824 Seebenstein

Burgmuseum Klam.
A-4352 Klam, Dipl. -Ing.

Burgmuseum und Heimatmuseum Wartburg.
Ruine Lichtenegg, A-8661 Wartburg im Murztal

Chorherrenstift St. Florian.
A-4490 St. Florian

Dekanatsmuseum.
A-8967 Haus Im Ennstal

Diozesan-Museum.
Domplatz 1, A-3100 St. Polten

Diozesan-und Heimatmuseum.
Schloss Strassburg, A-9341 Strassburg

Diozesanmuseum.
Hoforatorium der Domkirche, A-8010 Graz

Donaumuseum.
Schloss, A-2404 Petronell

Dorfmuseum.
St. Peter, A-9863 Rennweg

Eroicahaus. *See Beethoven-Wohnung (Eroicahaus)*

Erzbischofliches Dom-und Diozesanmuseum.
Stephansplatz 6, A-1010 Wien

Erzherzog Johann Museum.
Jagdschloss, A-8635 Brandhof

Festenburg mit Kernstock-Museum.
Schloss Festenburg, A-8251 Bruck A.D. Lafnitz

Figarohaus. *See Mozart-Wohnung (Figarohaus*

Freilichtmuseum Teurnia.
Bendesstrasse, St. Peter im Holz

Galeria im Gerichtsgebaude-Heimatmuseum.
Bezirksgericht, A-3040 Neulengbach

Galerie Graf Czernin.
Friedrich-Schmidt-Platz 4, A-1080 Vienna

Gauermann-Gedenkstatte.
Scheuchenstein, A-2761 Miesenbach

Gebertshaus. *See Schubert-Museum (Geburtshaus*

Gemaldegalerie der Akademie der Bildender Kunst in Wien.
Schillerplatz 3, A-1010 Wien, 57 95 16
Permanent Collections:
European painting from 15th to 18th century, main works by Bouts, Bosch, Botticelli, Titian, Rubens, van Dyck, Guardi, Baroque Netherlandish landscape painters like Ruisdaal, van Goyen and Asselijn.

Gemeindemuseum.
Kleberhaus, A-6867 Schwarzenberg

Geymuller-Schlossel Sammlung Sobek.
Khevenhullerstr. 2, A-1180 Vienna

Glasmuseum Gmund.
Stadtplatz 34, Rathaus, A-3950 Gmund

Graf Harrach'sche Familiensammlung.
Schloss Rohrau, A-2471-Rohrau, 02164/253

Graphische Sammlung Albertina.
Augustinerstrasse 1, 1010 Vienna

Graphisches Kabinett des Stiftes Gottweig.
Stift Gottweig, A-3511 Furth bei Gottweig

Gurlitt, Wolfgang, Museum. *See Neue Galerie der Stadt Linz-Wolfgang-Gurlitt Museum*

Haenel-Pancera Familien-Museum.
Ischl-Kaltenbach, Ville Haenel, Concordiastr.

Haydn-Wohnhaus.
Haydngasse 19, Wien 6

Heiligenstadter Testament. *See Beethoven-Wohnung (Heiligenstadter Testament)*

Heimat-und Goldbergbaumuseum.
Schloss Grosskircheim, A9843 Dollach

Heimat-und Schlossmuseum.
Burg Gussing, A-7540 Gussing

Heimatmuseum.
A-8330 Feldbach

Heimatmuseum.
A-5642 Bad Gastein

Heimatmuseum.
Schloss, A-2304 Orth

Heimatmuseum.
Ellenbogen 181, A-6870 Bezau

Heimatmuseum.
Rathausplatz, A-3264 Gresten

Heimatmuseum.
Eibiswald 36, A-8552 Eibiswald

Heimatmuseum.
Im Pfarrhof, A-2253 Weikendorf

Heimatmuseum.
Gemeindehaus, A-5731 Hollersbach

Heimatmuseum.
Untere Marktstr. 8, A-6410 Telfs

Heimatmuseum.
Schloss Freundsberg, Burggasse 24

Heimatmuseum.
Franz-Lehar-Kai 8, A-4820 Bad Ischl

Heimatmuseum.
Hauptplatz 1, Gemeindeamt, A-2130 Langenzersdorf

Heimatmuseum der Stadt.
Kirchgasse 6, A-8707 Leoben

Heimatmuseum Friesach.
Furstenhofgasse 115, A-9360 Friesach

Heimatmuseum in der Schattenberg.
Burg, A-6800 Feldkirch

Heimatmuseum Kitzbuhel.
Hinterstadt 32, A-6370 Kitzbuhel

Heimatmuseum Mittelweiherburg.
Wasserschloss, A-6971

Heimatmuseum Pochlarn.
Regensburger St., A-3380 Pochlarn

Heimatmuseum und Folterkammer.
Hauptstr. 1, A-3650 Poggstall

Historisches Museum der Stadt Wien.
Karlsplatz, Vienna 4

Hofburg und Silberne Kapelle.
Rennweg 1, A-6020 Innsbruck

Husslik-Museum.
Enzersdorf 1, A-8761 Pols

Innviertler Volkskundehaus und Galerie der Stadt Ried.
Kirchenplatz 13, A-4910 Ried

Josefstadter Heimatmuseum. *See Alte Backstube (Josefstadter Heimatmuseum)*

Kaiser-Franz-Josef-Museum fur Handwerk und Volkskunst.
Hochstr. 51, A-2500 Baden bei Wien, 0 22 52/41 00

Kaiser-Villa.
Jainzen 38, A-4820 Bad Ischl

Karntner Landesgalerie.
Burggasse 8, A-9020 Klagenfurt

Kartner Freilichtmuseum.
A-9063 Maria Saal, (04223)
352

**Kollegiatstift und
Stiftssammlungen.**
A-5163

**Konventsmuseum der
Barmherzigen Bruder.**
Taborstr. 16, A-1020 Wien

**Kostumsammlung der Akademie
der Bildenden Kunste.**
Schillerplatz 3, A-1010 Vienna

Krahutetz-Museum.
Krahuletzplatz 1, A-3730
Eggenburg

**Kunst-und Schatzkammer des
Stiftes Zwettl.**
A-3534 Stift Zwettl

**Kunstausstellung Stift
Herzogenburg.**
Stiftsgasse 3, A-3103
Herzogenburg

Kunstgewerbemuseum.
Schloss, A-2404 Petronell
Permanent Collections:
Furniture, porcelain, glass,
textiles, metalwork, ivory,
history of the castle and its
proprietor.

Kunsthistorische Sammlungen.
Scholoss Ambras, A-6020
Innsbruck

Kunsthistorisches Museum.
1 Burgring 5, A-1010 Vienna

**Kunsthistorisches Museum der
Abtei Admont.**
Benediktinerabtei, A-8911
Admont

**Kunsthistorisches Museum
(Sammlungen des Stifts St.
Lambrecht)**
Hauptstr, 1, A-8813 St.
Lambrecht

**Kunstkammer des
Serritenklosters.**
Theresienstr. A-6020 Innsbruck

**Kunstsammlungen des
Benediktinerstiftes w
Seitenstetten.**
Am Klosterberg 1, A-3353
Seitenstetten, 07477/2300
Permanent Collections:
Collection of paintings,
sculpture and prehistoric,
Greek and Roman relics.

**Kunstsammlungen des
Benediktinerstifts.**
A-9470 St. Paul

**Kunstsammlungen Palais
Schwarzenberg.**
Rennweg 2, A-1030 Vienna

**Kupferstichkabinett der Akademie
der Bildenden Kunste.**
Schillerplatz 3, A-1010 Vienna

Kusthistorisches Museum.
Burgring 5, A-1010 Vienna

Landesgalerie.
Schloss, A-7000 Eisenstadt

Landesmuseum fur Karrten.
Museumgasse 2, A-9010
Klagenfurt

Lehar-Museum.
Franz-Lehar-Kai 8, A-4820 Bad
Ischl

Lungauer Heimatmuseum.
Tamsweg 133, A-5580
Tamsweg Dipl. -Ing

**Middleheim-Openluchtmuseum
voor Beeldhouwkundt.**
Middelheimlaan 61, B-2000
Antwerp

Mozart-Wohnung (Figarohaus)
Domgasse 5, Wien 1

**Musee Communal de la
Ceramique.**
Rue Charles Lapierre 29, B-
5220 Andenne

Museen der Stadt Wien.
Magistratsabteilung 10, A-1040
Wien, 42 804
Permanent Collections:
History Museum of the City of
Vienna, Clock Museum, Roman
Ruins under the Hohen
Market, Beethoven Residence
(Pasqualatihaus), Beethoven
Residence (Heiligenstadter
Testament), Beethoven
Residence (Eroicahaus), Johann
Strauss Residence, Schubert
Residence, Haydn Residence,
Virgil Chapel and the Historic
Ceramic Collection from
Vienna, and Mozart Residence
(Figarohaus).

Museum Carnuntinum.
Badgasse 42, A-2405 Bad
Deutsch Altenburg

Museum der Stadt Ennst.
Hauptplatz 19, A-4470 Enns

Museum der Stadt Gmunden.
Kammerhofgasse, A-4810
Gmunden

Museum der Stadt Hall.
Oberer Stadtplatz, Rathaus, A-
6060 Solbad Hall

Museum der Stadt Krems.
A-3500 Krems

Museum der Stadt Modling.
Josef Deutsch-Platz 2, A-2340
Modling, 02236/4153
Permanent Collections:
History of Modling and its
district; prehistory, Roman
times, time of the migrations; 2
graves from early 5th century
AD; Langobard cemetary,
largest cemetary of Avars in
Austria (497); Middle Ages,
Modern Times; Folklore of
Modling and its district; natural
history of Modling.

Museum der Stadt Poysdorf.
Brunnerstr. 3, A-2170
Poysdorf, 02552
Permanent Collections:
Geology and paleontology,
early history, city history,
viniculture.

Museum der Stadt Villach.
Widmanngasse 38, A-9500
Villach

**Museum der Stiftspfarrkirche
Maria Saal.**
A-9063 Maria Saal

**Museum des Chorherrenstiftes
Klosterneuburg.**
Stiftplatz 1, A-3400
Klosterneuburg

**Museum des Zwanzigst
Jahrhunderts.**
Schweizergarten, 1010 Vienna

Museum Hallstatt.
Markt, A-4830 Hallstatt

**Museum Mayer van den Bergh
(Kunsthistorische Musea)**
Lange Gasthuisstraat 19, B-
2000 Antwerpen

**Museum Mittelalterlicher
Osterreischer Kunst
(Osterreichischer Galerie)**
Orangerie des Belvedere,
Rennweg 6A, A-1030 Vienna

**Neue Galerie am Landesmuseum
Joanneum.**
Sackstrasse 16 8010 Graz

**Neue Galerie der Stadt Linz-
Wolfgang-Gurlitt Museum.**
Hauptplatz 8, A-4000 Linz,
0732/70104

**Neue Galerie (Kunsthistorisches
Museum)**
Reitschulgasse 2 (Stallburg), A-
1010 Vienna

Neues Museum.
Alte Hofmuhle, Muhlenring 2

**Niederosterreichisches
Landesmuseum.**
Herrengasse 9, A-1010 Vienna

**Oberosterreichischer
Landesmuseum.**
Schloss Bruck, A-9900 Lienz

**Oberosterreichisches Jagdmuseum
Schloss Hohenbrunn.**
Hohenbrunn 1, A-4490 St.
Florian, 07224/533

Ost Tiroler Heimatmuseum.
Scholss Bruck, A-9900 Lienz

Osterreichische Galerie:
Oberes Belvedere, Prinz-Eugen-
Str. 27, Postfach 12, A-1030
Wien

**Osterreichisches Barockmuseum
(Osterreichische Galerie)**
Unteres Belvedere, Rennweg
6a, A-1030 Vienna

**Osterreichisches Museum fur
Angewandte Kunst.**
Stubenring 5, A-1010 Vienna

**Osterreichisches Museum Fur
Volkskunde.**
Laudongasse 19, A-1010 Wien
Permanent Collections:
Traditional folk culture.

**Paramentenkammer der
Wallfahrtskirche.**
Sonntagsberg, A-3332 Rosenau,
Sonntagsberg

Pasqualatihaus. *See* **Beethoven-
Wohnung (Pasqualatihaus)**

**Photogeschichtliche Sammlung
Frank.**
Arenbergstr. 10, A-5020
Salzburg

Pielachtaler Heimatmuseum.
Markt 6, A-3203

**Praemonstratenser Chorherrenstift
Wilten.**
Klostergasse 7, A-6020
Innsbruck

Reichersburg.
Stift Reichersburg, A-4981
Reichersburg

**Romische Ruinen Unter dem
Hohen Market.**
Hoher Markt 3, Wien 1

**Saltzburger Museum Carolina
Augusteum.**
Museumsplatz 6, Postfach 525,
A-5010 Salzburg

**Salzburger Dommuseum
(Salzburger Museum Carolino
Augusteum)**
Domplatz, Postfach 525, A-
5010 Salzburg

Salzburger Residenzgalerie.
Residenzplatz 1, A-5010
Salzburg Postfach 527
Permanent Collections:
European painting from the
16th-19th centuries.

**Sammlung Altosterreichischer
Volksmajolika Schloss
Gobelsburg (Osterreichisches
Museum fur Volkskunde Wien)**
A-3551 Gobelsburg

**Sammlung Religiose Volkskunst
(Osterreichisches Museum fur
Volkskunde)**
Johannegasse 8, A-1010 Vienna

Sammlungen der Burg.
Burg Hochosterwotz, A-9314
Launsdorf

Sammlungen der Schottenabtei.
Freyung 6, A-1010 Vienna

Sammlungen des Stiftes Schlagl.
Schlagl Nr. 1, A-4160 Aigen

**Sammlungen des Stifts
Heiligenkreuz.**
Stift Heiligekreuz, A-3453
Reidling

Sammlungen Schloss Tratzberg.
Schloss Tratzberg, A-6200
Jenbach

**Schatzkammer der
Gnadenbasilika.**
Kardinal Eugene Tisserant-
Planz, A-8630 Mariazell

**Schatzkammer der
Wallfahrtskirche Maria
Langegg.**
Maria Langegg, A-3642
Aggsbach Dorf

**Schatzkammer der
Wallfahrtskirche Maria Taferl.**
A-3672 Maria Taferl

**Schatzkammer des Deutschen
Ordens.**
Singenstr. 7, A-1010 Vienna

**Schausammlung der Ehemaligen
Hoftafel-und Silberkammer
(Bundesmobilienverwaltung)**
Hofburg, A-1010 Vienna

Schloss Hellbrunn.
Hellbrunn, A-5020 Salzburg

Schloss Hohenbrunn. *See*
**Oberosterreichisches
Jagdmuseum Schloss
Hohenbrunn**

Schloss Hohenems.
Schloss, A-6845 Hohenems

Schloss Rohrau. *See* **Graf Harrach'sche Familiensammlung**

Schloss-Sammlung.
Schloss Hollenegg- A-8530 Deutschlandsberg

Schloss Schonbrunn.
A-1130 Vienna

Schloss und Schloss-Sammlungen.
Unternberg, Moosham, A-6670 Mauterndorf

Schlossammlungen.
Schloss Loosdorf, A-2133 Loosdorf

Schlossammlungen Forchtenstein.
Schloss Forchtenstein, A-7210 Mattersburg

Schlossbergmuseum.
Glockenturm, Schlossberg, A-8010 Graz

Schlossmuseum.
A-2115 Ernstbrunn

Schlossmuseum.
Schloss, A-2116 Niederlies

Schlossmuseum.
A-2092 Riegersburg (Niederosterreich)

Schlossmuseum Burg Rosenburg.
A-3573 Rosenburg

Schlossmuseum Greillenstein.
Schloss Greillenstein, A-3592 Rohrenbach

Schlossmuseum im Rittersal.
Burg Maria Stein, A-6322 Kirchbichl

Schubert-Museum (Geburtshaus)
Nussdorfer Strasse 54, Wien 9

Schuberts Sterbezimmer.
Kettenbruckengasse 6, Wien 4

Rollett Museum der Stadtgemeinde Baden.
Weikersdorfer Platz 1, A-2500 Baden bei Wien, 0 22 52/35 1 23

Stadtisches Museum.
Schlossgasse, A-4780 Scharding

Stadtmuseum, Furstlich Starhembergisches Familienmuseum und Heimatmuseum.
Schloss Starhemberg, Kirchplatz 1 A-4070 Eferding

Stadtmuseum Gmund.
Hauptplatz (Altes Rathaus), A-3950 Gmund

Stadtmuseum Graz (Palais Khuenburg)
Sackstr. 18, A-8010 Graz

Stadtmuseum Linz.
Bethlehemstr. 7, A-4020 Linz, 0732/70272
Permanent Collections:
Archaeology, history and cultural history of Linz.

Steirischer Burgenverein. *See* **Burgenkundliches Museum**

Steirisches Volkskundemuseum am Landesmuseum Joanneum.
Paulustorgasse 13, A-8010 Graz

Stiftssammlung.
Zisterzienserstift, A-4073 Wilhering

Stiftssammlungen.
Benediktinerstift, A-4550 Kremsmunster

Stiftssammlungen der Benediktinererzabtei St. Peter.
A-5020 Salzburg

Strauss, Johann, Wohung:
Praterstrasse 54, Wien 2

Tiroler Landesmuseum Fredinandeum.
Museumstr. 15, A-6020 Innsbruck

Tiroler Volkskunstmuseum.
Universitatsstr. 2, A-6020 Innsbruck

Uhrenmuseum.
Schulhof 2, Wien 1

Ungarisches Museum.
Schloss Hart, A-8650 Kindberg

Virgilkapelle und Sammlung Historischer Keramik aus Wien.
Stephansplatz, U-Bahn-Station, Wien 1

Vorarlberger Landesmuseum.
Kornmarkt 1, A-6900 Bregenz

Votivsammlungen der Wallfahrtskirche St. Martin.
A-5092 St. Martin

Votivschatz der Wallfahrtskirche St. Erhard.
A-2624 Breitenau

Wachaumuseum.
Teisenhoferhof, A-3610 Weissenkirchen

Webereimuseum.
A-4170 Haslach

Werner-Berg-Galarie.
Stadtplatz, A-9150 Bleiburg

Wolfgany-Gurlitt-Museum, Neue Galerie der Stadt Linz.
Hauptplatz 8, A-4020 Linz

Zisterzienserstift Neukloster und Stiftsmuseum.
Stift, A-2700 Wiener Neustad

Zisterzienserstift und Stiftssammlungen.
A-6422 Stams

Zisterzienserstift und Stiftssammlungen.
A-3180 Lilienfeld

BANGLA DESH

Balda Museum of Art & Archaeology.
Dacca

Dacca Museum.
Ramna Rd., Dacca

BELGIUM

Arentshvis. *See* **Brangwyn Museum**

Baretta-Museum.
Grote Markt 1, B-8480 Veurne

Beginhuisjemuseum.
Monasterium de Wijngaard, Oud-Begijnhof 30, B-8000 Bruges

Bequinage d'Anderleeht.
Rue du Chapelain 4, B-1070 Brussels

Bibliotheque Royale Albert I, Cabinet des Estampes, Calchographie.
Blvd. De l'Empereur 4, B-1000 Brussels

Braecke, Pieter, Museum.
Hoogstraat, B-8450, Nievwpoort

Brangwyn Museum.
Dyver 16, B-8000 Bruges

Cabinet des Estampes et Dessins.
Parc de la Boverie 3, B-4000 Liege

Chateau De Jehay. *See* **Musee Historique et Prehistorique de Jehay**

Chateau de Lexhy.
Lexhy, B-4230 Horizon-Hozemont

Da Vinci-Museum.
Norbertijnenabdij, Tongerlo, B-3180 Westerlo

Diocesaan Museum.
Schoutestraat, B-2800 Mechelen

Etnografisch Museum.
Kloosterstraat 11, B-2000 Antwerp

Faikin-Museum.
Stadhuis, B-2410 Herentals

Gemeentemuseum.
Gemeenteplein, B-3620 Rekem

Groeningmuseum.
Dyver 12, B-8000 Bruges

Gruuthusemuseum.
Dyver 17, B-8000 Bruges

Hotel-Museum Merghelynck.
Merghelynckstraat 2, B-8900 Ieper

Institut Archeologique du Luxembourg.
Rue des Martyrs 13, B-6700 Arlon, 063-21 52 36

Internationaal Cultureel Centtrum.
Meir 50, 2000 Antwerp

Kerkschatmuseum.
Hoofdkerk, B-2700 Sint-Niklaas

Koninklijk Museum voor Schone Kunsten.
Plaatsnijderstraat 2, 2000 Antwerp, (031) 38-78-01
Permanent Collections:
Old Masters paintings, sculpture and graphic arts; Modern paintings, sculpture and graphic arts.

Lectere Museum. *See* **Musee Leon Lectere**

Lode Craeybeck Documentation Center.
Middelheimlaan 61, 020 Antwerp

Maagdenhuismuseum. *See* **Openbaar Centrum voor Maatschappelijk Welzijn van Antwerpen**

Maison de Gretry et Son Musee.
Rue des Recollets 34, B-4000 Liege

Maison d'Erasme.
Rue Du Chapitre 31, B-1070 Bruxelles

Memling Museum.
St. Janshospitaal Mariastraat 38 B-8000 Brugge

Meunier, Constantin, Museum.
See **Musee Constantin Meunier**

Musee Archeologique de la Province de Namur.
Rue du Port, B-5000 Namur

Musee Athois.
Rue de Pintamont 45, B-7800 Ath

Musee Communal.
Rue Van Keerbergen, B-5200 Huy

Musee Communal Alexandre-Louis Martin.
Place Communale 52, B-6508 Carnieres

Musee Communal "Chateau Gilson".
Rue De Bouvy 13, B-7100 La Louviere

Musee Communal des Beaux Arts.
Hotel de Ville, Place Charles II, B-6000 Charleroi

Musee Constantin Meunier.
Rue de l'Abbaye 59, B-1000 Brussels

Musee Curtius.
Quai de Maestricht 13, B-4000 Liege, 041-23 20 68
Permanent Collections:
Archaeology and decoraive arts.

Musee d'Ansembourg.
Feronstree 114, B-4000 Liege
Permanent Collections:
Decorative arts of Liege from the 18th century.

Musee d'Archeologie.
Rue de Bruxelles 27, B-1400 Nivelles

Musee d'Art Ancien.
Rue de la Regence 3, B-1000 Brussels

Musee d'Art Moderne.
Place Royal 1, B-1000 Brussels

Musee d'Art Religieux & d'Art Mosan.
6, Rue Bonne Fortune, B-4000 Liege, 041-237980 EXT. 348
Permanent Collections:
Sculptures, paintings, textiles, manuscripts, glass from the 18th-19th centuries.

Musee de la Commission d'Assistance Publique.
Rue Haute 298 A, B-1000 Brussels

Musee de la Poterie.
Kasteel, B-4730 Raeren

Musee de la Ville d'Eau.
Villa de la Reine, Ave. Reine Astrid, B-4880 Spa

Musee de l'Ancienne Abbaye.
B-4970 Stavelot

Musee de l'Art Wallon.
Parc de la Boverie 3, B-4000 Liege

Musee des Beaux-Arts de la Ceramique.
Rue Renier 17-19, B-4800 Verviers

Musee des Beaux-Arts de la Ville de Liege.
Rue de l'Acadamie 34, B-4000 Liege

Musee d'Histoire et d'Archeologie et des Arts Decoratifs.
Rue des Carmes 8, B-7500 Tournai

Musee Diocesain et Tresor de la Cathedrale Saint-Aubain.
Place du Chapitre, B-5000 Namur

Musee d'Ixelles.
Rue Jean Van Volsem 71, B-1050 Brussels

Musee du Chanonie Puissant "Vieux Logis" - "Attacat".
Rue de Notre-Dame Debonnaire, Rue des Sars, B-7000 Mons

Musee du Cinema - Filmmuseum.
Rue Baron Horta 9, Bruxelles, 02/513 41 55 23022 CINETK B
Permanent Collections:
Chinese shadows, panoramas, polyoramas, magic lanterns, zoogroscope, alethoscope, kaleidoscope, thaumatrope, anorthoscope, phenakisticopes, zootropes, praxinoscope, choreutoscopes, zoopraxiscope, fusil de marey, tachyscope, electrotachyscope, kinora, feuilleteurs, phonoscope, mutoscope, kinetoscope, and other inventions from the 18th and 19th centuries.

Musee du Verre.
Quai de Maestricht 13, B-4000 Liege

Musee du Vieux-Cimitiere.
Rue Henry Leroy 17, B-7400 Soignies

Musee Ducal.
Rue du Petit 1, B-6830 Bouillon

Musee Felicien Rops.
Hotel Gaiffier D'Hestroy B-5000 Namur

Musee Gaumais.
Rue d'Arlon 38-40, B-6760 Virton

Musee Historique et Prehistorique de Jehay.
Kasteel van Jehay, B-5262 Jehay-Bodegnee

Permanent Collections:
Historical collection, archaeological collections, contemporary sculptures of Count Guy Von Den Steen.

Musee Horta.
25, Rue Americaine, B-1060 Brussels, 02-537.16.92
Permanent Collections:
Museum of Architecture and Decorative Arts.

Musee Leon Lectere.
Ave. Franklin Roosevelt 50, B-1000 Brussels

Musee National du Cinema.
Rue Baron Horta 9, B-1000 Brussels

Musee Regional d'Art et d'Histoire.
Fue I. Saintrant 3, B-5000 Namur

Musee Royal de Mariemont.
Chaussee de Mariemont, B-6510 Morlanwelz-Mariemont, 064 22 12 43
Permanent Collections:
Art from Italy, Greece, Egypt, Middle East and Far East; regional archaeology; porcelain from Tournai; rare books.

Musee Schott.
Rue du Chene 27, B-1000 Brussels

Musee Wiertz.
Rue Vautier 62, B-1040 Brussels

Musees Communaux des Beaux-Arts et d'Archeologie.
Beaux Arts-Rue Renier, 17 Verviers

Musees d'Archeologie et d'Arts Decoratifs.
13, Quai de Maastricht, 4000 Liege
Permanent Collections:
The collections of the Musee Curtius, Musee d'Ansembourg and Musee du Verre.

Musees Royaux d'Art et d'Histoire.
10 Parc du Cinquantenaire, 1040 Brussels

Musees Royaux des Beaux-Arts de Belgique.
Rue du Musee 9, Brussels

Musem Jules Dhondt-Dhaenens.
Museumlaan 12, B-1200 Deurle

Museum der Oude Mechelsekunstambachten "De Zalm".
Zoutwerf 5, B-2800 Mechelen

Museum Felix de Boeck.
Gemeentehuis, B-1620 Drogenbos

Museum Mayer van den Bergh.
Lange Gasthuisstraat 19, B-2000 Antwerp, 013-32 42 37
Permanent Collections:
Paintings, drawings, sculpture, manuscripts, European decorative arts, Chinese and Japanese porcelain, textiles, prints, plaquettes, etc.

Museum Modest Huys.
Modest Huyslaan 44, B-9780 Zulte

Museum O. L. Vrouw Ter Potterie.
Potterierei 79, B-8000 Bruges

Museum of Applied Arts & Crafts.
Pl. N. Vlaskovski, Trojan

Museum Plantin-Moretus.
Vrijdagmarkt 22, Antwerp

Museum Smidt van Gelder.
Belgielei 91, 2000 Antwerp

Museum van de St. Salvators-Kathedraal.
Steen-En-Zuidzanstraat, B-8000 Bruges

Museum van de Sint-Sebastiaans-Gilde.
Carmersstraat 176, B-8000 Bruges

Museum van het Heilig Bloed.
Basiliek van het Heilig Bloed, Burg 13, B-8000 Bruges

Museum Vleeshuis.
Vleeshouwersstraat 38-40, B-2000 Antwerp

Museum voor Religieuze Kunst.
Begijnhof 39, B-3800 Sint-Truiden, 011/67 65 79
Permanent Collections:
Religious art; mural paintings.

Museum voor Schone Kunsten.
Citadelpark, B-9000 Gent

Museum voor Schone Kunsten.
Vlanderenstraat 66, B-8400 Oostende

Museum voor Schone Kunsten.
Kasteel van Egmont, Heldenlaan, B-9620 Zottegem

Museum voor Schone Kunsten van Latem en Leistreek.
E. Clausplein 2, B-9800 Deinze

Museum voor Sierkunst.
Jan Breydelstraat 7, B-9000 Gent

Museum Wuyts-Van Campen en Baron Caroly.
Fl. van Cauwenberghstraat 14, B-2500 Lier

Mussee Communal des Beaux Arts.
Rue Neuve 9, B-7000 Mons

Nationaal Vlasmuseum.
Stijn Streuevelslaan, B-8500 Kortrijk

Openbaar Centrum voor Maatschappelijk.
Rijselstraat 38, B-8900 Ieper

Openbaar Centrum voor Maatschappelijk Welzijn van Antwerpen.
Lange Gasthuisstraat 33, B-2000 Antwerp, 32 98 35-31 09 70

Openluchtmuseum voor Beeelhouwkurst, Middleheim.
Middlehemlaan 61, 2020 Antwerp

Ostmuseum.
Begijihnof, B-2320 Hoogstraten

Oudheidkunde Museum van de Bijloke.
Godshuizenlaan 2, B-90000 Gent

Oudheidkundige Museum van het Sint-Jans-Hospital.
Kerkstraat 39, B-8351 Damme

Pavillon Chinois.
Ave. Praet 44, B-1000 Brussels

Pieter Braecke Museum. *See* Braecke, Pieter, Museum

Provinciaal Gallo-Romeins Museum.
Kielenstraat 15 B-3700 Tongeren

Provinciaal Museum Sterckshof.
Hooftvunderlei 160, B-2100 Deurne, 031-240207 OR 031-247176
Permanent Collections:
Arts and crafts, photography, silver collection, legacy of Pierre Lunden.

Provincial Gallo-Romeins Museum.
Kielenstraat 15, B-3700 Tongeren

Rijksdomein van Gaasbeek.
B-1682 Gaasbeek

Rops, Felicien, Museum. *See* Musee Felicien Rops

Rubenianium (Kunsthistorische Musea)
Belgielai 91, B-2000 Antwerp

Rubenianum.
Belgielei 91, B 2000 Antwerp

Rubenshuis (Kuntshistorische Musea)
Rubenstraat 9/11, B-2000 Antwerp

St. Baafskathedral.
St. Baffsplein, B-9000 Gent

Salle Wittert.
Bibliothek van de Rijksuniversiteit, Place Cockerill 1, B-4000 Liege

Schatkamer van O.L. Vrouwbasilick.
Markt, O. L. Vrouwstraat, B-3700 Tongern

Schoeiselmuseum.
Wijngaardstraat, 9, B-8700 Izegem

Sint Baafsabij.
Gandestraat, B-9000 Gent

Sint Franciscusmuseum.
Minderbroederstraat 5, B-3800 Sint-Truiden

Slot van Laarne.
Slot, B-9270 Laarne

Stadsbestur.
Kasteelstraat 16-18, B-9700 Oudenaarde

Stadsmusuem Hof van Busleyden.
Fr. de Merodestraat 67, B-2800 Mechelen

Stedelijk Museum.
Savoyestraat 6, B-3000 Leuven

Stedelijk Museum.
Stadthuisplein 9, B-3700 Tongeren

Stedelijk Museum.
Stadhuis, Grote Markt, B-3290 Diest

Stedelijk Museum Sint-Niklaas.
Zamanstraat 49, B-2700 Sint-
Niklaas, 031-760753
Permanent Collections:
Art collection Mathys-Vanneste
donation, Mercator Collection,
archaeological collection.

**Stedelijk Museum voor Schone
Kunsten.**
Broelkaai 6, B-8500 Kortrijk

**Stedelijk Museum voor
Volkskunde, Oude Ambachten
en Regionale Geschiendenis.**
Zamanstraat 49, B-2700 Sint-
Niklaas

Stedelijke Musea.
Dyver, 12, 8000 Bruges, 050-
3399 11

**Tresor de la Cathedrale Notre-
Dame.**
Place de l'Eveche, B-7500
Tournai

Tresor de la Cathedrale St. Paul.
Rue Bonne Fortune 6, B-4000
Liege, 041-320426 OR 041-
323759

**Tresor de la Collegiale Notre-
Dame.**
Quai de Namur, B-5200 Huy

**Tresor de la Collegiale Sainte-
Waudrau.**
Place du Chapitre, B-7000
Mons

**Tresor de l'Eglise Primaire de
Saint-Sebastian.**
Rue de l'Eglise, B-4970
Stavelot

Tresor du Frere Hugo d'Oiginies.
Convent des Soeurs de N.D.,
Rue 1 Belliart 17, B-5000
Namur

BOLIVIA

Museo "Casa de Murillo".
Calle Jaen 790, La Paz

Museo de Colonial "Charchs".
Bolivar 401, Sucre

Museo del Ateneo de Bellas Artes.
Sucre

Museo Nacional de Arqueologia.
Calle Tihaunacu 93, Casilla
Official 64, la Paz

Museo Nacional de Arte.
Socabaya 485, la Paz

BOTSWANA

Musee d'Art Negre.
Centre Catholique Universitaire
de Yaounde, BP 876 Yaounde

National Museum & Art Gallery.
Independence Ave., P.O. Box
114, Gaborone

Petit Musee d'Art Camerounais.
Monastere Benedictin de Mont
Febe BP 1178, Yaounde

BRAZIL

Casa de Rui Barbosa.
Rua Sac Clemente, 134,
Botafogo, Rio De Janeiro

**"Imperial Imandade de Nossal
Senhora da Gloria do Outerio"
Museum.**
Praca Nossa Senhora da Gloria,
135, Rio de Janeiro

**Musee de Arte Moderna do Rio
de Janeiro.**
Av. Infante Don Henrique, 85,
C.P. 44, Rio de Janeiro

Museu Antonio Parreiras.
Rua Tiradentes, 47, Niteroi

Museu Arquidocesano de Mariana.
Frei Durao, Mariana

Museu da Curia Metropolitana.
Arcebispado, Porto Alegre

Museu da Curia Metropolitana.
Praca Clovis Bevilacqua, 37,
Sao Paulo

**Museu da Orden Terceira da Sao
Francisco da Penitencia.**
Largo Da Carioca, 5, Rio
Pardo

Museu da Republica.
Rua do Catete, Rio de Janeiro

Museu de Arte Antiga.
Instituto Feminino da Bahia,
Rua Monsenhor Flaviano, 2,
Salvador

Museu de Arte Contemporanea.
Fundacao Armando Ivares
Penteado, Rua Alagos, 903, Sao
Paulo

**Museu de Arte Contemporanea da
Universidade de Sao Paulo.**
Ibirapuera Parc, C.Pp. 22031,
Sao Paulo

Museu de Arte da Bahia.
Rua Joana Angelica, 198,
Salvador

Museu de Arte de Sao Paulo.
Ave. Paulista 1578, Sao Paulo

**Museu de Arte de Universidade do
Ceara.**
Av. Visconde de Cauipe, 2854,
Fortaleza

Museu de Arte e Historia.
Casa de Gonzaga, Rua do
Ouvidor 9, Ouro Preto

Museu de Arte Moderna.
Rua Sete de Abril, 230, Sao
Paulo

Museu de Arte Moderna.
Beira-Mar Ave., Box 44, Rio
de Janeiro

**Museu de Arte Moderna da Bahia
e Museu de Arte Popular.**
Rua Desembargardor Castelo
Branco, 1, Salvador

**Museu de Arte Moderna de Sao
Paulo.**
Parque Ibirapuera, Sao Paulo

Museu de Arte Sacra.
Ladeira de Santa Teresa, C.P.
12, Salvador

**Museu de Arte Sacra de Sao
Paulo.**
Av. Tiradentes, 676, Sao Paulo

Museu Diocesano Dom Inocencio.
Rua Joao Luiz Alves, 76,
Campanha

Museu do Cenvento de S. Antonio.
Largo de Carioca, Rio de
Janeiro

Museu do Estado.
Av. Rui Barbosa, 960, Recife

Museu Dom Vital.
Convento da Penha, Praca
Dom Vital, Recife

**Museu Historico da Cidade Do
Rio de Janeiro.**
Estrada Santa Marinha, s-n,
Rio de Janeiro

Museu Nacional de Belas Artes.
Ave. Rio Branco 199, Rio de
Janeiro

**Piratini Museu Historico
Farroupilha.**
Coronel Manoel Pedroso, 77,
Piranitni

Popular Arts Museum.
Av. Rui Barbosa S/N
Flamengo, Rio de Janeiro

Religious Art Museum.
Rua Santa Luzia, 206, Rio de
Janeiro

**"Veneravel e Arquiepiscopal
Ordem Terceira de Nossa
Senhora do Monte do Carmo"
Museum.**
Rua do Carmo, 46, Rio de
Janeiro

BULGARIA

Galeria.
Vidin

Galeria.
Bul. Lenin 7, Sliven

Galeria.
Ul. Bayer, Stara Zagora

Galeria.
Ul. Georgi Dimitrov, Vraca

Galeria.
Bul. 9 Septemvri, Paradzik

Galeria.
Ul. Dr. Samenhoff 13, Plovdiv

Galeria.
Ul. Car Osvoboditel 1,
Haskovo

Galeria.
Ul. Ljuben Karavelov 3,
Kjustendil

Galeria (Okrasen Naraden Musei)
Ul. Sredec 6, Ruse

Gradska Huodosestvena Galeria.
Ul. Serdika 1, Sofija

Hudosestvena Galeria.
Ul. Vassil-Kolarov, Plovdiv

Musei "Bojanna Carkva".
Ul. Bratja Buxton 53, Bojana,
Sofija

**Museum of Wood Carving &
Mural Paintings.**
Ul. Petko Slavejkov 27a,
Trjavna

**Nationalen Arheologiceski
Museum.**
Str. Saedinenie 1, Plovdir 4001,
2-43-39
Permanent Collections:
Permanent collections include
exhibits entitled "Thracian Art
in the Bulgarian Lands" and
"One Thousand Years of
Bulgarian Irons."

**Nationalen Musei Rilski
Manastir.**
Rila

Nationalna Hudosestvena Galeria.
Moskovska 6, Sofija

**Vazrozdenski Musei "Ilarion
Makariopolski" (Ilarion-
Makariopolski-Museum of
Renaissance)**
Ul. Karsovska, Elena, Tarnovo

**Zentralen Cerkovnoistouceski-
Arheologiceski Musei.**
Pl. Lenin 19, Sofija

BURMA

Mon Museum.
Moulmein

Museum in the Peace Pagoda.
Institute of Advanced Buddistic
Studies, Kaba-Aye Pagoda
Compound, Rangoon

**National Museum of Art &
Archaeology.**
Jubilee Hall, Pagoda Rd.,
Rangoon

State Gallery.
Mandalay

State Library & Museum.
West Moat, Mandalay

CAMBODIA

Musee Poveal.
Battambang

**Museum National de Phnom
Penh.**
Phnom Penh

CAMEROON

Foyer Culturel de Dschang.
Centre de Jeunesse, BP 10,
Dschang

Musee de Diamare.
Maroua

**Musee des Arts et des Traditions
Bamoun.**
BP 71 Foumban (Bamoun)

CANADA

Acadia University Art Gallery:
P.O. Box 28, Wolfville, N.S.

Alberta Art Foundation.
Eleventh Floor, 10004 104th
Ave., Edmonton, AB

Alberta College of Art Gallery.
1301 16th Ave. N.W., Calgary
AB T2M OL4

Allied Arts Council.
8, 503A Third Ave., S.E.,
Medicine Hat, AB T1A 2M2

Allied Arts Council of Lethbridge.
The Bowman Arts Centre, 811
Fifth Ave. S., Lethbridge, AB
T1J OV2

Architects Association of New Brunswick.
C/O Freda M. Large, Exec.
Secy., P.O. Box 910, Rothesay,
Saint John, NB E0G 2W0

Archives of the Canadian Rockies.
111 Bear St., Banff, Alberta

Art Gallery of Brant.
20 Ava Rd., Brantford, Ont.

Art Gallery of Brant, Inc.
76 Dalhousie St., P.O. Box
1747, Brantford, ON N3T5V7

Art Gallery of Greater Victoria.
1040 Moss St., Victoria, BC
V8V 4P1, Tel 604-384-4101
Permanent Collections:
Canadian art, European
decorative arts, Asian art,
prints and drawings,
contemporary art of British
Columbia.

Art Gallery of Hamilton.
Main St. West at Forsyth,
Hamilton ON L8P4S8

Art Gallery of Nova Scotia.
6152 Coburg Rd. (P.O. Box
2262), Halifax, NS B3J 3C8

Art Gallery of Ontario.
Grange Park, Toronto, ON
M5T 1G4

Art Gallery of Windsor.
445 Riverside Dr., Windsor,
ON N9A 6T8

Art Gallery of Windsor.
Williestead Park, Windsor, Ont.
N8Y 2K7

Art Metropole.
241 Yonge St., Toronto, ON,
M5B 1N8

Arts & Letters Club of Toronto.
14 Elm St., Toronto, 0N M5G
1G7

Association des Graveurs du Quebec:
5131 Ave. Durocher, Montreal,
PQ H2V 3X7

Association des Musees Canadiens:
331 Copper St., Suite 400,
Ottawa, ON, 52P OG5

Association of Canadian Industrial Designers:
55 University, Toronto, 0N
M5J 2H7

Banff Centre, Walter Phillips Gallery.
P. O. Box 1020, Banff, AB,
TOL OCO

Basilian Fathers.
Box 379, Mundare, AB T0B
3H0

Beaverbrook Art Gallery.
703 Queen St., (Box 605),
Fredericton, NB E3B 5A6

Bibliotheque Centrale de l'Outaouias.
Chemin Freeman, P.O. Box
938, Hull, P.Q.

Black Creek Pioneer Village.
The Metropolitan & Region
Conservation Authority, 1000
Murray Ross Pkwy., Toronto,
Ont.

Boucher, Pierre, Museum.
Seminaire Saint-Joseph, Trois-
Rivieres,P.Q.

Brandon Allied Arts Council.
1036 Louise Ave., Brandon,
MB R7A 0Y1

Brant County Museum.
57 Charlotte St., Brantford, 0N
N3T 2W6

Burnaby Art Gallery.
6344 Gilpin St., Burnaby, BC
V5G 2J3

Calgary Artists Society.
C/o Zaidee Finch, Secy, 3728
35th Ave. S.W., Calgary , AB
T3E 1A5

Campbell, Grace, Gallery. *See*
John M. Cuelenaere Library;
Grace Campbell Gallery

Canadian Artists' Representation.
C/O Giuseppe Albi, Exec.
Secy., 309-12708 90th St.,
Edmonton, AB T5E 3L5

Canadian Conference of the Arts.
3 Church St., Suite 47,
Toronto, ON M5E 1M2

Canadian Crafts Council.
16-46 Elgin St., Ottawa, 0N
K1P 5K6

Canadian Crafts Council.
46 Elgin St., Suite 16, Ottawa,
ON K1P 5K6, 613-235-8200

Canadian Guild of Potters.
C/O Gordon Barnes, Pres., 11
Catherine Ave., Aurora, ON
L4G 1K4

Canadian Museums Assn.
331 Cooper St., Suite 400,
Ottawa, ON K2P 0G5

Canadian Society for Education Through Art.
University of Regina, Regina
SK S4S O42

Canadian Society for Education Through Art.
Faculty of Education, Univ. of
Regina, SK S4S OA2

Canadian Society of Painters in Watercolour.
C/O Julius Griffith, Secy.,
Hillsdale Ave. W., Toronto,
ON M5P 1G3

Canadian Society of Painters in Watercolour.
C/o Julius Griffith, Secy., 102
Hillside Ave. W., Toronto 0N
M5P 2G3

Canadiana Gallery.
14 Queen's Park Crescent,
Toronto, Ont.

Centennial Art Gallery of Nova Scotia.
Halifax Citadel, P.O. Box 2262,
Halifax, N.S.

Center for Experimental Art & Communication.
15 Duncan St., Toronto, 0N
M5H 3H1

Centre Culturel Confederatif.
219 Blvd. Panoramique,
Mistassini, P.Q.

Centre Culturel de Trois Rivieres.
1425 Place de l'Hotel de Ville,
Trois Rivieres PQ

Chateau de Ramezay Antiquarian & Numismatic Society.
290 Notre Dame St. E.,
Montreal, PQ H2V 1C5

Chauvin House.
Tadoussac, P.Q.

Colborne Lodge.
High Park, Toronto, Ont.

Community Arts Council of Chilliwack.
Box 53, Chillwack, BC V2P
6H7

Community Arts Council of Vancouver.
315 W. Cordova St.,
Vancouver, BC V6B 1E5

Compton County Historical Museum & Society.
Eaton, P.Q.

Concordia University, Sir George Williams Art Galleries:
1455 De Maisonneuve Blvd.,
Montreal, PQ H3G 1M8

Confederation Centre Art Gallery & Museum.
P.O. Box 848, Charlottetown,
PE C1A 7L9

Cowansville Art Center.
225 Main St., Cowansville,
P.Q.

Craftsmen's Assn. of British Columbia:
801 - 207 W. Hastings St.,
Vancouver, BC V6B 1H7

Dalhousie University Art Gallery:
University Ave., Halifax, NS
B34 3J5

Dartmouth Heritage Museum.
Wyse Rd., Dartmouth, NS

Dauphin Allied Arts Centre.
104 First Ave. N. W., Dauphin,
MB

Department of Culture, Government of Province of Alberta.
CN Tower, 10004 104th Ave.,
Edmonton, AB T5J CK5

Donly, Eva Brook, Museum.
109 Norfolk St. S., Simcoe,
Ont.

Dorval Cultural Centre.
1401 Lakeshore Dr., Dorval,
PQ H9S 2E5

Dundurn Castle.
Dundurn Park, York Blvd.,
Hamilton, 0N L8R 3H1

Dunlop Art Gallery. *See* Regina
Public Library; Dunlop Art
Gallery

Edmonton Art Gallery.
2 Sir Winston Churchill Square,
Edmonton, AB T5J 2C1, 403-
429-6781

Edmonton Weavers' Guild.
13816 110th A Ave.,
Edmonton, AB T5M 2M9

Edward P. Taylor Reference Library. *See* Taylor, Edward P.,
Reference Library

Etherington, Agnes, Art Center.
See Queen's University, Agnes
Etherington Art Center

Eva Brook Donly Museum. *See*
Donly, Eva Brook, Museum

Eye Level Gallery.
Marble Bldg., 1672 Barrington
St., Halifax, NS

Federation des Centres Culturels de la Province de Quebec.
1415 Jarry E., Montreal, PQ
H2E 2Z7

Fort George National Historic Park.
P.O. Box 787, Niagara-on-the-
Lake, Ont

Fortress of Louisbourg National Historic Park.
P.O. Box 160, Louisbourg, N.S.

Stratford.
54 Romeo St. N., Stratford ON
N5A 4S9

Gananoque Museum.
10 King St. E., Ganoque, Ont.

Glenbow Museum.
Ninth Ave. & First St., S.E.,
Calgary AB T2G OP3, 264-
8300

Greater Vancouver Artists Gallery.
555 Hamilton St., Vancouver,
BC V6B 2R1, 604-687-1345

Guilde Canadienne des Metiers d'Art Quebec.
2025 Peel St., Montreal, PQ
H3A 1T6

Halifax Citadel National Historic Park.
C/o Royal Bank Bldg., 5161
George St., Halifax, N.S.

Hastings County Historical Society Museum.
257 Bridge St. E., Belleville,
Ont.

International Pavilion of Humor.
Man & His World, Montreal
PQ H3C 1AO
Permanent Collections:
Strip, editorial and gag cartoons
from Canada, Europe and
America; humorous sculptures
from many countries and films.

John M. Cuelenaere Library; Grace Campbell Gallery.
125 125th St. E., Prince Albert,
SK S6V 1B7

Jordan Historical Museum of the Twenty.
Vintage House, Main St.,
Jordan, 0N L0R 1S0

Keillor House Museum.
1813 Middleton Rd.,
Dorchester, N.B.

Kelowna Centennial Museum & National Exhibit Centre.
470 Queensway Ave., Kelowna,
BC V1Y 6S7

Killarney Museum.
414 Williams Ave., Killarney,
Man.

Kings County Museum.
Hampton, Kings County, N.B.

Kinnoull Historial Museum.
Colinton, Alberta

Kitchener-Waterloo Art Gallery.
43 Benton St., Kitchener, ON
N2G 3H1

Kootenay School of Art Gallery.
2001 Silver King Rd., Nelson,
B.C. V1L 1C8

La Maison des Arts, La Sauvegarde.
160 Est, Rue Notre Dame,
Montreal, P.Q.

Societe des Arts de Chicoutimi.
534 Jaques-Cartier Rue,
Chicoutimi, PQ G7H 1Z5

Societe des Decorateurs Ensembliers du Quebec.
Studio G, 451 St. Sulpice St.,
Montreal, PQ

LaCalvet House.
Angle des Rues Bonsecours et
Saint Paul, Montreal, P.Q.

Lachine Cultural Center.
100 laSalle Rd., Lachine, P. O.

Lakehead Visual Arts.
C/o Robert Boorman, Pres.,
301 S. Vickers St., Thunder
Bay, 0N P7E 1J6

Langley Centennial Museum.
9135 King St., Fort Langley,
B.C.

Laurentine University Museum & Arts Centre:
John St. at Nelson, Sudbury,
ON P3E 2C6

Laurier House.
335 Laurier Ave. E., K1N 6R4
Ottawa
Permanent Collections:
Furnishings and memorabilia
belonging to three Canadian
prime ministers: Sir Wilfred
Laurier, William Lyon
Mackenzie and Lester Bowles
Pearson.

Le Centre d'Art de Perce.
Perce PQ GOC 2 LO

Le Comite des Arts d'Arvida.
CP 53, Arvida, PQ G7S 4K6

Le Front des Artistes Canadiens.
44-221 McDermott Ave.,
Winnipeg, MB R3B 0S2

Le Musee Regional de Rimouski.
35 W. St. Germain Rimouski
PQ G5L 4B4

Leon-Owens, Anne, Gallery. *See*
Nova Scotia College of Art & Design, Anne Leon-Owen Gallery

Lloydminster Barr Colony Museum Committee.
C/O City Hall, 5011 49 Ave.,
Lloydminster SK S9V 0T8

London Public Library & Art Museum.
305 Queens Ave., London ON,
N6B 1X2

London Regional Art Gallery.
355 Ridout St. N., London
N6A 2N8

L'Universite Laval, Ecole des Arts Visuels, Cite Universitaire.
Quebec PQ 61K 7P4

Luxton Museum.
Banff, Alberta

Lyceum Club & Women's Assn. of Canada.
23 Prince Arthur Ave. 5,
Toronto, 0N

McCord Museum.
690 Sherbrooke St. W.,
Montreal, P.Q.

Mackenzie House.
82 Bond St., Toronto, Ont.

McLaughlin, Robert, Gallery.
Civic Centre, Oshawa 0N L1J
3Z3, 416-576-3000

McMichael Canadian Collection.
Kleinburg, ON LOJ 1CO

Maillou House.
17, Rue Saint-Louis, Quebec,
P.Q.

Manisphere Group of Artists.
C/o Ellen B. Cringan, 82
Cordova St., Winnipeg, MB
R3N 0Z8

Manitoba Association of Architects:
10-177 Lombard Ave.,
Winnipeg, MB R3B 0W9

Marie de l'Incarnation Center & Museum.
12 Rue Donnaconna, CP 760,
Quebec H3C 2V2

Maritime Art Assn.
C/O Frank Gillard, Treas., 40
West Lane, Moncton, NB E1C
6T7

Medicine Hat Public Library.
414 First St. S.E., Medicine
Hat AB T1A 0A8

Memorial University of Newfoundland, Arts & Culture Center:
Saint John's, NF

Monastere des Augustines de l'Hotel-Dieu de Quebec.
32 Rue Charlevoix, Quebec,
P.Q.

Montreal Military & Maritime Museum. *See* **Society of the Montreal Military & Maritime Museum**

Montreal Museum of Fine Arts.
3400 Ave. Du Musee,
Montreal PQ H3G 1K3, 514-
285-1600 MONTMUSE
MONTMUSE

Moose Jaw Art Museum.
Crescent Park, Moose Jaw SK
S64 4N6

Mount Allison Univ., Owens Art Gallery.
Owens Art Gallery, York St.,
Sackville, NB E0A 3C0

Mount Saint Vincent Univ. Art Gallery.
Bedford Hwy.-Seton Acad.
Ctr., Halifax, NS B3M 2J6

Musee d'Art Contemporain.
Cite du Havre, H3C 3R4,
Montreal

Musee d'Art de Joliette.
145 Wilfrid Corbeil, Joliette,
PQ J6E 4T4

Musee d'Art de Saint-Laurent.
615, Blvd. Sainte-Croix, Ville
Saint-Laurent, P.Q. H4L 3X7

Musee de l'Eglise Notre-Dame.
43 St. Sulpice St., H2Y 2V5
Montreal

Musee des Augustins.
21 Rue de Metz, 31000
Toulouse

Musee du College Bourget.
65 Rue St. Pierre, P.O. Box
1000, Rigaud, P.Q.

Musee du Quebec.
Parc des Champs de Bataille,
Quebec PQ G1S 1C8

Musee du Seminaire de Quebec.
6, Rue de l'Universite, CP 460,
Quebec

Musee Historique de Vaudreuil.
431 Blvd. Roche, CP 121,
Darion, Vaudreuil PQ J7V 2N3

Musee Kateri Tekakwitha.
Mission Saint Francois Xavier,
CP 70, Caughnawaga, PQ J0L
1B0

Museum of African & Oceanian Arts RGD.
1180 Bleury, Montreal 111,
P.Q.

Museum of Northern British Columbia, Prince Rupert Museum of Art.
McBride St. & First Ave., P.O.
Box 669, Prince Rupert, BC
V8J 3S1

Museum of Prehistoric Archaeology.
1260 Rue Royale, P.O. Box
500, Trois-Rivieres, P.Q.

Museum of Ukrainian Culture.
202 Ave. M.S. Saskatoon, Sask.

National Film Board of Canada.
Tunney's Pasture, 150 Kent St.,
Ottawa ON K1A & ON1

National Gallery of Canada.
Lorne Bldg., Elgin & Slater Sts.,
Ottawa, ON K1A OM8
Permanent Collections:
European painting, sculpture
and decorative arts; Traditional
American art; contemporary
art; early Canadian painting,
sculpture and decorative arts;
Contemporary Canadian art;
drawings (non-Canadian); prints
(non-Canadian); Canadian
prints and drawings;
photographs.

National Museum of Man.
Metcalfe & McLeod Sts.,
Ottawa, 0N K1A 0M8

National Museums of Canada.

New Brunswick Craft School.
Woodstock Rd., E3B 5H1 New
Brunswick

Niagara Falls Art Gallery & Museum.
Queen Elizabeth Way, Niagara
Falls, Ont.

Nicolet Seminary Museum.
Seminaire de Nicolet, Nicolet,
P. Q.

Nightingale Arts Association:
A Space, 85 St. Nicholas St.,
Toronto, 0N M4Y 1W8

Notre Dame Church Museum.
430, Rue Saint-Sulpice,
Montreal, P.Q.

Nova Scotia Association of Architects:
Suite 630, 5991 Spring Garden
Rd., Halifax, NS B3H 1Y6

Nova Scotia College of Art & Design, Anne Leon-Owen Gallery.
Anne Leonowens Gallery, 153
Granville St., Halifax, NS B3J
3J6

Nutana Collegiate Institute Memorial Library & Art Gallery.
411 11th St. E., Saskatoon SK
S7N 0E9

Oak Hall.
Portage Rd., C/O The Niagara
Parks Commission, Box 150,
Niagara Falls, ON, L2E 6T2

Oakville Public Library & Centennial Gallery.
120 Navy St., Oakville, ON,
16J 2Z4

Odanak Museum.
Odanak, P.Q.

Ontario Association of Architects:
50 Park Rd., Toronto, 0N
M4M 2N5

Ontario Association of Art Galleries:
38 Charles St. E., Toronto, 0N
M4Y 1T3

Ontario College of Art.
Gallery Seventy Six, 100
McCaul St., Toronto, 0N M5T
1W1

Ontario Crafts Council.
346 Dundas St. W., Toronto ,
0N M5T 1G5

Ontario Society of Artists.
8 York St., Toronto, 0N M5J
1R2

Open Space Gallery Secession Gallery of Photography.
510 Fort St., (P.O. Box 5207,
Sta. B) Victoria, BC V8R 6N4

Order of Architects of Quebec.
1825 Dorchester Blvd., W.,
Montreal PQ 43H 1R4

Ottawa Public Library.
120 Metcalfe St., Ottawa, 0N
K1P 5M2

Parry Sound Public Library.
29 Mary St., Parry Sound, ON
P2A 1E3

Peace Region Arts Society.
P.O. Box 297, Spirit River, AB
T0H 3G0

Peel Museum & Art Gallery.
7 Wellington St. E., Brampton,
ON L6W 1Y1

**Peninsula & St. Edmunds
Township Museum.**
Tobermory, Ont.

**Peres Redemptoristes Basilique
Sainte Anne.**
Basilique Sainte Anne, PQ
GQA 1CO

Peter Whyte Gallery.
Box 160 Banff, Alberta T0L
0C0

Phillips, Walter, Gallery. *See*
Banff Centre, Walter Phillips
Gallery

Pierre Boucher Museum. *See*
Boucher, Pierre, Museum

Place des Arts.
166 King Edward St.,
Coquitlam, BC V3K 4T2

Prince George Art Gallery.
2820 15th Ave., Prince George,
BC V2L 3P1

**Prince of Wales Northern
Heritage Center.**
Yellowknife, N.W.T. X1A 2L9,
Tel 403-873-7551
Permanent Collections:
Winnifred Marsh Collection of
Watercolors; Don Cardinal
Collection of Oils; Inuit
sculpture; Bishop Fleming
Collection of miniature ivories;
historical memorabilia; N.W.T.
natural history and ethnology
collections.

Prince Rupert Art Club.
C/o Ms. Johnan C. Woodland,
Secy., 658 Seventh Ave. E.,
Prince Rupert, BC V8J 2J6

Prince Rupert Museum of Art.
See Museum of Northern
British Columbia, Prince Rupert
Museum of Art

**Printing & Drawing Council of
Canada.**
C/O Univ. of Calgary Art
Dept., 2920 24th Ave. N.W.,
Calgary, AB T2N 1N4

**Professional Art Dealers Assn. of
Canada Inc.**
65 Queen St. W., Suite 1800,
Toronto, ON M5H 2M5

Provincial Archives of Alberta.
Historical Resources Division,
12845 - 102 Ave., Edmonton,
AB T5N 0M6

**Provincial Archives of British
Columbia.**
655 Belleville St., Victoria, BC
V8V 1X4

Provincial Archives of Manitoba.
200 Vaughan St., Winnipeg,
MB R3C 1T5

Public Archives of Canada.
395 Wellington St., Ottawa, 0N
K1A 0N3

Public Archives of Nova Scotia.
Cobury Rd., Halifax, NS B3K
5K5

**Queen's University, Agnes
Etherington Art Center:**
Queen's Univ., Agnes
Etherington Center, 613-547-
6551

**R. Tait McKenzie Memorial
Museum.**
Mill of Kintail, R.R. 1, K0A
1A0 Almonte, Ontario

**Regina Public Library; Dunlop
Art Gallery.**
2311 Twelfth Ave., Regina SK
S4P 0N3

Richmond Arts Centre.
767 Minoru Gate, Richmond,
BC V6Y 1R8

Robert McLaughlin Gallery. *See*
McLaughlin, Robert, Gallery

Rodman Hall Arts Centre.
109 St. Paul Crescent, Saint
Catharines, 0N L2S 1M7

**Rothmans Art Gallery of
Stratford.**
54 Romeo St., Stratford, Ont

**Royal Architectural Institute of
Canada.**
151 Slater St., Suite 1104,
Ottawa, ON K1P 5H3

Royal Canadian Academy of Arts.
601-11 Yorkville Ave.,
Toronto, ON, M4W 1L3

Royal Ontario Museum.
100 Queen's Park, Toronto, 0N
M5S 2C6, 416-978-3641
Permanent Collections:
Collections in Greek and
Roman, Near and Far Eastern
and European (decorative arts,
textiles and costumes) and
Canadiana departments;
Chinese Collection (with
extensive research library)
covering the entire range of art
and archaeology; Ethnology
collection with an emphasis on
the American Indian; North
American archaeology
collection; collections in
entomology, invertebrate
zoology, geology, ichtyology
and herpetology, invertebrate
paleontology, mammology,
minerology, ornithology,
vertebrate paleontology;
collections relating specifically
to music, philately, Canadian
textiles and costumes.

**Saidye Bronfman Centre of the
YM-YWHA.**
5170 Cottage St., Catherine
Rd., Montreal, P.Q.

Saint Joseph's Oratory.
3800 Queen Mary Ch,
Montreal PQ H3V 1H6

St. Mary's District Museum.
177 Church St. S., St. Mary's,
Ont

**Sarnia Public Library & Art
Gallery.**
124 Christina St. S., Sarnia,
ON, N7T 2M6

Saskatchewan Arts Board.
200 Lakeshore Dr., Regina SK
S4S 0A4

Permanent Collections:
Collection of paintings,
drawings, prints, sculpture,
ceramics and crafts.

Saskatchewan Assn. of Architects.
226 20th St., E., Saskatoon SK
S7K 0A6

**Saskatoon Gallery & Conservatory
Corporation.**
950 Spadina Cfescent E., P.O.
Box 569, Saskatoon SK S7K
3L6

Sculptor's Society of Canada.
21 Dunblaine Ave., Toronto
ON M5M 2R6

**Shevchenko, Taras H., Museum &
Memorial Park Foundation
(Oakville)**
1363 Dundas St. W., Oakville,
0N 16J4Z2

**Shevchenko, Taras H., Museum &
Memorial Park Foundation
(Toronto)**
42 Roncesvalles Ave., Toronto.
Ont.

Sibbald Point Provincial Park.
Eildon Hall, R.R. 2, Stuton
West, 0N L0E 1R0

Simcoe County Museum.
R.R. 2, Minesing, Ont.

**Simon Fraser University, Simon
Fraser Gallery:**
Simon Fraser Gallery, Centre
for the Arts, Academic
Quadrangle 3004, Burnaby, BC
V5A 1S6

**Societe des Artistes Professionels
du Quebec.**
4545 St. Denis, Montreal PQ

Society of Canadian Artists.
45 Brixham Terrace,
Downsview, Ont M3M 2R9

**Society of the Montreal Military
& Maritime Museum.**
431 Blvd. Roche, Vaudreuil,
PQ J7V 2N3

South Peace Art Society.
10100 13th St., Dawson Creek,
BC V1G 3W7

South Rawdon Museum.
R.R. 1, Mount Uniacke, N.S.

**Sunbury Shores Arts & Nature
Centre, Inc.**
139 Water St., (P.O. Box 100),
Saint Andrews, NB E0G 2X0

Surrey-Centennial Museum.
17679 60th Ave., P.O. Box
1006, Sta. A, Cloverdale, Ont.

**Taras H. Shevchenko Museum &
Memorial Park Foundation
(Oakville).** *See* Shevchenko,
Taras H., Museum & Memorial
Park Foundation (Oakville)

**Taras H. Shevchenko Museum &
Memorial Park Foundation
(Toronto).** *See* Shevchenko,
Taras H., Museum & Memorial
Park Foundation (Toronto)

**Taylor, Edward P., Reference
Library.**
317 Dundas St. W., M5T 1G4
Toronto

Thames Arts Centre.
75 William St. N., Chatham,
0N N7M 4L4

**Thomson, Tom, Memorial Gallery
& Museum of Fine Art.**
840 First Ave. W., P. O. Box
312, Owen Sound, Ont., 519-
376-1932
Permanent Collections:
Collections are mostly
Canadian, except prints; also
Native Canadian, Indian and
Innuit; emphasis on Tom
Thomson, Canada's most
famous landscape artist, who
grew up near Owen Sound; 3rd
largest collection of his works
on permanent display.

Todmorden Mills.
67 Pottery Rd., Toronto, Ont.

Ukrainian Arts & Crafts Museum.
10611 110 Ave., Edmonton,
AB T5H 1H7

Ukrainian Arts & Crafts Museum.
620 Spadina Ave., Toronto 12,
Ont. M5S 2H4

**Ukrainian Arts & Crafts Museum
of the Ukrainian Women's Assn.
of Canada, Manitoba Branch.**
1175 Main St., Winnipeg, Man.

Ukrainian Folk Art Museum.
154 E. 10th Ave., Vancouver,
B.C.

**University of Alberta, University
Art Gallery & Museum:**
Ring House One, Edmonton,
AB T6G 2E2

**University of British Columbia,
Museum of Anthropology:**
Main Library Bldg., Fine Arts,
Vancouver, BC V6T 1W5

**University of Calgary, Art
Gallery:**
2920 24th Ave. N.W., Calgary
AB T2N 1N4

University of Guelph:
Guelph, Ontario N1G 2W1,
Tel 519-824-4120
Permanent Collections:
Historical and contemporary
collection.

**University of Lethbridge Art
Gallery:**
4401 University Dr.,
Lethbridge, AB T1K 3M4

University of Manitoba Gallery:
111 School of Art, Winnipeg,
MB R3T 2N2

**University of Regina, Norman
Mackenzie Art Gallery:**
College & Scarth Sts., Regina,
SK S4S 0A2

**University of Saskatchewan,
Saskatchewan Art Dept.
Gallery:**
Saskatoon SK S7N 0W0

**University of Sherbrooke Cultural
Center, Art Gallery:**
Sherbrooke PQ J1K 2R1

**University of Toronto, Hart
House:**
7 Hart House Circle, Toronto,
ON M5S 1A1, 416-978-2453
Permanent Collections:
Historic and contemporary
Canadian art

University of Victoria, Maltwood Art Museum & Gallery:
Finnerty Rd., P.O. Box 1700, Victoria BC V8W 2Y2
Permanent Collections:
University of Victoria collection of Modern Canadian artists; Maltwood Memorial Collection of Decorative Arts including collections of Katherine Maltwood sculpture.

University of Waterloo, Arts Center Gallery:
Waterloo ON N2L 3G1

University of Western Ontario, McIntosh Art Gallery:
1151 Richmond St., London, 0N N6A 3K7

Upper Canada Village.
P. O. Box 740, Morrisburg, Ont.

Vancouver Art Gallery.
1145 W. Georgia St., Vancouver, BC V6E 3H2, Tel 604-682-5621

Vancouver City Archives.
1150 Chestnut St., Vancouver, BC V6J 3J9

Vernon Museum, Art Gallery & Archives.
3009 32nd Ave., Vernon, B.C.

Village of St. Maurice Ironworks.
Rue des Forges, Trois-Rivieres, P. Q.

Visual Arts Ontario.
8 York St., Toronto, ON M5 1R2

West Vancouver Visual Arts Society.
C/o Norma Sorensen, Pres., 993 Sinclair, West Vancouver, BC V7V 3W1

Western Canada Art Assn., Inc.
C/O Center for the Arts, Simon Fraser University, Burnaby, BC V5A 1S6

White Rock Painting & Sketch Club.
Art Centre, Marine Dr., P.O. Box 85, White Rock, BC

Winnipeg Art Gallery.
300 Memorial Blvd., Winnipeg, MB R3C 1V1

Winnipeg Sketch Club.
434 Assiniboine Ave., Winnipeg, MB R3C 0Y1

Wolfville Historical Museum.
175 Main St., Wolfville, N.S.

Woodstock Public Library & Art Gallery.
445 Hunter St., Woodstock, 0N N4S 4G7

York University Art Gallery:
Ross Bldg. N 145, 4700 Keele St., Downsview ON M3J 1P3

CAPE VERDE

Museo de Arte Popular.
Plaza de la Catedral, Havanna

Museo Historico de las Ciencias "Carlos J. Finlay".
Cuba 460, Apdo. 70, Havana 1

Museo Nacional.
Palacio de Bellas Artes, Animas entre Zuluta y Monserrate, Havana

Museo Napoleonico.
San Miguel y Ronda, Havana

Museos des Artes Decorativos.
Calle 17 No. 502, Vedado, Havana

CHAD

Musee National Tchadien.
1, Place de l'Independence, BP 503, Ndjamena

CHILE

Museo de Arte Popular Americano.
University of Chile, Cerrosanta Lucia, Santiago

Museo Nacional de Bellas Artes.
Parque Forestal S/N, Casilla 3209, Santiago

CHINA, MAINLAND

Fouliang Ceramics Museum.
Fouliang

Nanking Museum.
Nanking

Shanghai Museum.
Shanghai

CHINA, REPUBLIC OF

National Art Gallery of Taiwan.
Nan Hai Rd., Taipei

National Museum of History.
49 Nan Hai Rd., Taipei

National Palace Museum.
Wai-Shuang-Hsi, Shih-Lin, 111 Taipei, 88 20 21-4
Permanent Collections:
Calligraphy and paintings numbering 14,987, some dating from the Chin Dynasty (265-419 A.D.) onwards; bronzes numbering 4,402, items dating from the Shang Dynasty (960-1279 A.D.) onwards; jade, 3,894 items; sculpture, 105 items; enamel ware, 1,927 items; lacquer ware, 421 items; rare books, 149,544 volumes; official documents of the Ch'ing Dynasty, 350,000 leaflets.

COLOMBIA

Colombian Institute of Culture; Museum of Colonial Art.
Carrera 6, No, 9-77 Bogota

Museo Arquidiocesano de Arte Religioso.
Calle 4, No. 4-56, Popayan

Museo de Arte Colonial.
Calle 4a No. 9-13, Popayan

Museo de Arte Colonial.
Alcaldia Municipal, Villa de Leiva

Museo de Arte Colonial.
Carrera 6a., No. 9-77, Bogota, 2-41-60-17
Permanent Collections:
Paintings, drawings, sculpture, decorative wood carving, furniture, silverwork from the Spanish period in "Nueva Granada" (today Columbia and Ecuador) from the 16th, 17th, 18th and 19th centuries.

Museo de Arte "La Tertulia".
Ave. Colombia No. 5-105 Oeste, Cali

Museo de Arte Moderno.
Extension Cultural del Tolima, Ibague

Museo de Arte Moderno.
Palacio de la Inquisicion, Plaza de Bolivar, Cartagena

Museo de Arte Moderno.
Planetario Distrital, Parque de la Independencia, Carrera 6a, No. 24-55, Bogota

Museo de Arte Religioso de la Catedral de San Nicolas.
Catedral de San Nicolas, Rio Negro

Museo de Arte Religioso del Desierto de la Candelaria.
Rapuira

Museo de Arte Religioso "Tiberio de J. Salazar y Herrara".
Catedral de Sonson, Sonson

Museo de Artes Graficas.
Carrera 15 No. 56 sur, Bogota

Museo de Cucuta.
Calle 13 No. 3-67, Cucuta

Museo de Museos Colsubsidio.
Carrera 3 No. 17-23, Bogota

Museo de Santa Clara.
Calle 9 No. 8-31, Bogota

Museo de Zea.
Carrera 53 No. 51-74, Medellin

Museo Del Oro.
Banco De la Republica, Calle 16, No. 5-41, Bogota

Museo Eclesiastico Colonial.
Iglesia Parroquial, Carrera 11 No. 16-82, Tunja

Museo Efrain Martinez.
Carrera 3, Via Sur, el Refugio, Popayan

Museo Franciscano.
Carrera 6 No. 9-03, Cali

Museo Nacional.
Carrera 7 No. 28-66, Bogota

Museo San Francisco.
Calle 4a, Carrera 9a, Popayan

Museo San Pedro Claver.
Carrera 4 No. 30-01, Cartagena

Museu del Carmen.
Plazuela del Carmen, Villa de Leiva

Museum of Colonial Art. *See* **Colombian Institute of Culture; Museum of Colonial Art**

Sala Romulo Carvajal.
Casa de la Cultura, Sonson

COSTA RICA

Galeria de la Facultad de Bellas Artes.
Universidad de Costa Rica, San Jose

Galeria la Casa del Arista.
San Jose

Galeria Teatro Nacional.
San Jose

Museo Nacional de Costa Rica.
Avenidas 0 y 2, Calles 15-17, Apdo. 749 San Jose

CYPRUS

"Argo" Gallery.
Princess Zena De Tyras Palace, Nicosia

Cyprus Museum.
Museum St., Nicosia

Famagusta Munincipal Art Gallery.
16th June St., P.O. Box 41, Famagusta

Folk Art Museum.
P.O. Box 1436, Nicosia

Museum of Byzantine Icons.
Nicosia

CZECHOSLOVAKIA

Alsova Jihoceska Galerie.
CS-373 41 Hluboka Nad Vltavcu

Alsova Jihoceska Gallerie.
Nam. Rude Armady, Bechyme

Bohuns, Peter M., Galeria.
Tranovskeho 3, CS-031 01 Liptovsky Mikulas, 227 58
Permanent Collections:
Ancient Slovak art, art in the Lipton Region from the 19th and 20th century.

Cerveny Klastor (Vychodo-Slovenske Muzeum, Kosice)
Pieniny, CS-059 06 Cerveny Klastor-Kupele

Cyprian Majernik Galeria.
Hurbanovo Nam. 5 CS-800 00 Bratislava

Expozice Historickeho Nabytku (Umeleckoprumislove Muzeum, Praha)
Zamek Hruby Rohozec U Turnevo, CS-511 01 Turnov

Expozice Soudobe Tapiserie (Umeleckoprumyslove Muzeum, Praha)
Statni Zamek, CS-37701 Jindrichuv Hradec

Galeria Hlavneho Mesta SSR Bratislavy.
Dibrovovo Nam. 11, 894 16 Bratislava
Permanent Collections:
Exposition of Gothic art, Klarisky Church; exposition of central European art from the 17th to 19th centuries, Mirbach's Palace; exposition of English tapestries and old European painting, Primatial Palace.

Galeria Vytvarneho Umenia Presov.
Slovenskej Repuliky Rad 137, CS-080 02 Presov

Galerie.
Dum Umeni CS 695 00 Hodonin

Galerie Benedikta Rejta.
Pivovarska Ul. CS-44001 Louny

Galerie M. Ladych.
Gottwaldovo Nabr., CS-110 00 Prague 1

Galerie U Recickych.
Vodickova 10, CS-110 00 Prague

Galerie Umeni.
Puskinova Stezka 6, CS-360 00 Karlovy Vary

Galerie Vytvarneho Umeni.
Michalska 7, CS-412 01 Litomerice

Galerie Vytvarneho Umeni v Chebu.
Spalicek Nam., CS-350 01 Cheb

Galerie Vytvarneho Umeni.
Ockova 5, CS-413 01 Roudnice Nad Labem

Jeneweinova Galerie (Oblastni Muzeum)
Vlassky Dvur, CS-284 00 Kutna Hora

Krajska Galerie.
Dum Umeni, CS-700 00 Ostrava

Krajska Galerie.
Ziskova Nam. 35, CS-500 00 Hradec Kralove

Ladych Gallery. See Galerie M. Ladych

Lesnicke Drevarske A Pol'Ovnicke Muzem.
Hrad, CS-969 72

Liptovske Muzeum.
Park Obracov Mieru 8, CS-034 00 Ruzomberok

Metska Galeria v Bratislave.
Primacialny Palac, Radnica Ul. 1 CS-800 00 Bratislava

Moravska Galeria v Brne.
Husova Ulice 14, 662 26 Brno
Permanent Collections:
Applied arts from the Middle Ages until the present.

Muzeum.
CS-059 55 Zdiar

Muzeum a Hrad.
Hrad, CS-911 00 Trencin

Muzeum Na Zamke Telc (Muzeum Vysoginy Jihlava)
Zamek CS-588 56 Telc

Muzeum Nabytkv (Umeleckoprumyslove Muzeum, Praha)
U Jablonneho, Zamek Lemberk, CS-110-00 Prague

Muzeum Porcelanu.
Statni Zamek, CS-431 51 Klasterec Nad Ohri

Muzeum Skla.
CS-468 22 Zelezny Brod

Muzeum Skla.
CS-512 46 Harrachov v Krkoncsida

Muzeum Skla a Bizuterie.
CS-46600 Jablonec Nad Nisou, Jiraskova Ul. 4
Permanent Collections:
Historical and contemporary glass, costume jewelry and jewels.

Muzeum Vsociny v Jihlave.
Nam. Mirv 98, CS-586 00 Jihlava

Nabytkove Muzeum.
CS-053 21 Markusovce

Naprstkovo Muzeum Asijskych, Afrikych a Amerikych Kultur.
Bettemske Nam. 1, CS-110 00 Prague 1

Narodni Galerie v Praze.
Hradcanske Namesti, 15, 1 Hradcany, Prague

Oblastna Galerie v Banskej Bystrici.
Nam. Ca 25, CS 97400 Banska Bystrica

Oblastni Galerie.
U Tiskarny 1, CS-460 00 Liberec

Oblastni Galerie.
Hyniasova Ul. 13, S-770 00 Olomouc

Oblastni Galerie Vytvarneho Umeni.
Dum Umeni, CS-760 00 Gottwaldov

Oblastni Muzeum. See Jeneweinova Galerie (Oblastni Muzeum

Oblastni Muzeum.
Palackeho Tr/III, CS-290 01 Podebrady

Obuvnicke Muzeum N.P. Svit.
CS 760 00 Gottwaldov

Okresni Muzeum v Kromerizi.
Snemovni Nam. 1, CS-767 00 Kromeriz

Oravske Muzeum.
CS-027 41 Oravsky Podzamok

Peter M. Bohuns Gallery. See Bohuns, Peter M., Galeria

Povazske Muzeum a Galeria.
Budatinsky Hrad CS-010 00 Zilina

Sarisske Muzeum.
Radnica, C-S-085 01 Bardejov

Sbrika Ceskeho Socharstvi (Narodni Galerie v Praze)
CS-225 01 Zbraslav Nad Vltavou

Severoceska Galerie Vytvarnelho Umeni.
Michalska 7, 412 47 Litomerice
Permanent Collections:
Roman and Gothic art of the North-Bohemian County from the 12th-15th century; Renaissance and Baroque art; paintings and sculptures; 19th and 20th century modern

Czechoslovakian sculptures in the garden.

Severoceske Muzeum.
Leninova Ul. 11, CS-460 00 Liberec

Slezske Muzeum.
Tyrsova 1, CS-746 46 Opava, 3464 MUSEUM OPAVA

Slovenska Narodne Muzeum.
Vajanskeho Nabr 2, CS-800 00 Bratislava, 300-94
Permanent Collections:
Prehistory and evolution; archaeology of Slovakia; History and building of the castle in Bratislava; coins and medal of Slovakia; Ethnography collection.

Solvenska Narodna Galeria.
Razusovo Nabrezie 2, 89013 Bratislava

Statni Zidovske Muzeum.
Jachymova 3, 110 01 Prague

Statny Hrad.
Hrad CS-01856 Cerveny Kamen

Statny Kastiel.
CS-049 21 Betliar

Stedoslovenske Muzeum.
CS-974 00 Banska Bystrica, Thurzov Dom, Nam, Narodneho Povstania

Stredoceska Galerie v Praze.
Husova 229, CS-150 00 Prague

Umeleckoprumyslove Muzeum.
Prague 1, Ul.17, Listopadu 2
Permanent Collections:
Museum of decorative arts: glass, majolica, china, pottery and ceramics.

Vychodoceska Galerie.
Zamek 3, CS-530 00 Pardubice

Vychodoslovenska Galeria v Kosiciach.
Leninova Ul. 78 CS-040 00 Kosice

Zapadoslovenske Muzeum.
Klastorik, Saldovnicka 1, CS-91700 Trnava

Zapodoceska Galerie v Plzni.
Kopeckeho Sady 2, CS-300 00 Plzen

Zemplinske Muzeum.
Sztaray Hrad, CS-071 01 Michalovce

DENMARK

Aarhus Kuntsmuseum.
Vennelystparken, 8000 Aarhus

Arhus Permanente Udstilling.
J.M. Morsgade 13, DK-8000 Arhus

Bakkehusmuseet.
Rahbeks Alle 23, DK-1801-Kobenhaven-V

David Collection.
Kronprinsessegade 30, DK-1306 Copenhagen
Permanent Collections:
Islamic art and European 18th century decorative art.

Den Hirschprungske Samling.
Stockholmsgade 20, DK-2100 Kobenhavn-C

Det Danske Kunstindustrimuseum.
Bredgade 68, 1260 Copenhagen

Esbjerg Kunstforenings Samling.
Kunstpavillionen, Haunegarde, DK-6700 Ebsjerg

Faaborg Museum.
Gronnegade, DK-5600 Faborg
Permanent Collections:
Paintings by Danish painters in the period 1875-1925; mostly painters from the isle of Funen.

Fyns Stifts Kunstmuseum.
Jemebanegade 13, DK-5000 Odense

Horsens Kunst Museum.
Sundvej 1a, DK-8700 Horsens

Internationalt Kunstnerhjem.
DK-8500 Grena

J.F. Willumsens Museum. See Willumsens, J.F., Museum

Kobenhaven Museum for Moderne Kunst.
Nikolajgade 22, DK-1067 Kobenhavn-V

Kobenhavns Bymuseum.
Vesterbrogade 59, 1620 Copenhagen

Kunstmuseet.
Storgade 9, DK-4180 Soro

Louisiana Museum of Modern Art.
Gammel Strandvel 13, 8050 Humlebaek

Malerismalingen Pa Nivagaard.
Niva

Museet Pa Koldinghus Slot.
Koldinghus Slot, DK-6000 Kolding

Museet Pa Sonderborg Slot.
DK-6400 Sonderborg

Nationalhistoriski Museum Pa Frederiksborg.
Frederiksborg Slot, DK-3400 Hillerod

Nationalmuseet.
Prinsens Palace, Frederiksholms Kanal 12, Copenhagen

Nodiyllands Kunstmuseum.
Kong Christians Alle 50, 9000 Aalborg

NY Carlsberg Glypothek.
Dantes Plads, 1556 Copenhagen

Ordrupgaard Collection.
Vilvorcevej 110, 2920 Charlottenund

Oregaard-Museum.
Orehoj Alle 2, DK-2900 Hellerup

Reventlow-Museet.
Pederstrup Pr. Torrig L. 4943

Ribe Kunstmuseum.
St. Nicoljgade 10, DK-6760 Ribe

Rosenborg Slot (De Danske Kongers Kronologiske Samling Pa Rosenborg)
Oster Voldgade 4A, DK-1350 Copenhagen, 01 15 32 86
Permanent Collections:
A summer palace for King Christin IV, the castle is in Renaissance style. Collections contain the Crown Jewels, royal costumes and ancient arms, family portraits and various other art objects. An ivory coronation chair and life size silver lions are on view in Banquet Hall, internationally renowned collection of Venetian glass; one of the largest collections of silver furniture in Europe; fine collections of ivory and porcelain (Royal Copenhagen, Sevres and Meissen). Oldest and most celebrated treasure is the Oldenburg Horn, made in Germany circa 1470. It is a Gothic drinking horn mounted in silver gilt and ornately encrusted with reliefs of battlements, shield bearers and other figures.

Rudolph Tegners Museum. *See* **Tegners, Rudolph, Museum**

Silkeborg Kunstmuseum.
Hostrupsgade 41, DK-8600 Silkeborg

Skagens Museum.
Brondumsvej DK-9900 Skagen

Statens Museum for Kunst.
Solvgade, 1307 Copenhagen

Tegners, Rudolph, Museum.
Museumsvej 19, DK-3120 Dronningnmolle

Thingbaek Kalkminer.
Thingbaek DK-9520 Skorping
Permanent Collections:
Museum is a permanent exhibition of two Danish sculptors, A.J. Bundgaard and C.J. Bonnesen. Cement sculptures by the priest Anton Laier.

Thorvaldsen Museum.
Porthuscade 2, 1213 Copenhagen, (01) 121532
Permanent Collections:
Works by the Danish sculptor Bertel Thorvaldsen, paintings from the 19th century and antiquities (Greek, Etruscan and Roman).

Thorvaldsen-Samlingen Pa Nyso.
Nyso pr. Praesto, DK-4720 Praesto

Tonder Museum.
Kongevej 55, DK-6720 Tonder

Vejen Museum.
DK-6600 Vejen

Vejle Kunstmuseum.
DK-7100 Vejle

Willumsens, J.F., Museum.
DK-3600 Frederikssund, (O3) 31 07 73
Permanent Collections:
Works of J.F Willumsens and his collection of old foreign art.

DOMINICAN REPUBLIC

Galeria Nacional de Bellas Artes.
Santo Domingo

Museo Arqueologico y Galerias de Arte del Banco Central del Ecuador.
Plaza Bolivar, Av. 10 de Agosto y Briseno, Quito

Museo Nacional.
Paul P. Harris, Santo Domingo

EAST GERMANY

Agyptisches Museum.
D-1000 Berlin 19, Schlosstr. 70

Agyptisches Museum Des Agyptologischen Instituts der Karl-Marx-Universitat Leipzig.
DDR-701 Leipzig, Schillerstr. 6

Albrechtsburg.
DDR-825 Meissen, Domplatz 1

Altmarkisches Museum-Ausstellung Am Dom.
DDR-35 Stendal, Strasse der Freundschaft 48

Altmarkisches Museum-Ausstellung Monchskirchhof.
DDR-35, Monchskirchhof 1

Angermuseum-Bereich Kunst.
DDR-5 Erfurt, Anger 18

Antiken-Sammlung (Staatliche Museen Zu Berlin)
DDR-102 Berlin, Bodestr. 1-3

Archaologisches Museum des Archaologischen Instituts der Karl-Marx-Univ. Leipzig.
DDR-701 Leipzig, Universitatsstr. 3-5

Barlach, Ernst, Gedenkstatte.
DDR-26 Gustrow, Getrudenkapelle

Barockmuseum Schloss Moritzburg.
DDR-8105 Moritzburg

Bildergalerie.
DDR-15 Potsdam, Park Sanssouci

Buchdruckermiuseum.
DDR-4407 Oraniebaum

Burgruine und Heimat Museum.
DDR-9202 Frauenstein, Schloss

Chinesisches Teehaus.
DDR-15 Potsdam, Park Sanssovci

Domschatz.
DDR-36 Halberstadt, Dom

Dornburger Schlosser.
DR-6904 Dornburg

Ernst Barlach Gedenkstatte. *See* **Barlach, Ernst, Gedenkstatte**

Feudalmuseum.
DDR-37 Werigerode, Schloss

Fritz-Rentsch-Gedenkstatte.
DDR-48 Naumburg, Neidschuzerstr. 19

Frohnauer-Hammer.
DDR-9301 Frohnau, Technisches Museum

Fruhchristlich-Byzantinische Sammlung, Bode-Museum (Staaliche Museen Zu Berlin)
DDR-102 Berlin, Bodestr. 1-3, Museumsinsel

Galerie Junge Kunst.
DDR-12 Frankfurt (Oder), am Rathaus

Gemaldegalerie Alte Meister (Staatliche Kunstsammlungen Dresden)
DDR-801 Dresden

Gemaldegalerie Neue Meister (Staatliche Kunstsammlungen Dresden)
DDR-801 Dresden, Albertinium, Georg-Treu-Platz 3

Goschenhaus.
DDR-724 Grimma 3, Schillerstr. 25

Grunes Gewolbe (Staatliche Kunstsammlungen Dresden)
DDR-801 Dresden, Albertinum

Heimat Museum.
DDR-6222 Geisa, Schloss

Heimat-und Schlossmuseum.
DDR-54 Sondershausen, Schloss

Heimatmuseum.
DDR-437 Kothen, Museumsstr. 4-5

Heimatmuseum.
DDR-925 Mittweida, Kirchberg 3 - 5

Heimatmuseum.
DDR-372 Blankenburg, Schnappelberg 6

Heimatmuseum.
DDR-521 Arnstadt, Schlossplatz 1, Schloss

Heimatmuseum.
DD8r-5812 Waltershausen, Schloss Tenenberg

Heimatmuseum im Hasenhaus.
DDR-9382 Augustburg, Schloss Augustburg

Heimatmuseum und Naturalien-Kabinett.
DDR-9613 Waldenburg, Geschwister-Scholl-Pl. 1

Heimatstube.
DDR-9933 Bad Elster, Kurhaus-Sudflugel

Islamisches Museum (Staatliche Museen zu Berlin)
DDR-102 Berlin, Bodestr. 1-3

Kaisertrutz (Staatliche Kunstsammlungen)
DDR-89 Gorlitz, Demianiplatz 1

Keramisches Museum.
DDR-6522 Burgel, Altes Badertor

Kloster Unser Lieben Frauen.
DDR-301 Magdeburg

Kreis-Heimatmuseum.
DDR-784 Senftenberg, Schloss

Kreis-Heimatmuseum.
DDR-203 Demmin, Ernst-Thalmann-Str. 23

Kreismuseum Burg Kriebstein.
DDR-9251 Kriebethal

Kreismuseum Burg Mildenstein.
DDR-732 Leisnig, Burglein 6

Kulturhistorisches Museum.
DR-25 Rostock, Im Steintor

Kulturhistorisches Museum.
DDR-23 Stralsund, Monchstr. 25-27

Kulturhistorisches Museum.
DDR-20 Neubrandenburg, Treptower St. 38

Kulturhistorisches Museum.
DDR-301 Magdeburg, Otto-Von-Guericke-St. 68/73

Kulturzentrum Knochenstampfe.
DDR-9151 Dorfchemnitz, am Anger 1

Kunstgalerie, Orangerie (Stadtische Museen Gera)
DDR-65 Gera, Dimitroffallee 4

Kunsthalle.
DDR-25 Rostock, Am Schwanenteich

Kupferstich-Kabinett (Staatliche Kunstammlungen Dresden)
DDR-801 Dresden, Guntzstr. 34a, Albertinium

Landschaftsmuseum der Duber Heide.
DDR-7282 Bad Duben, Burg Duben

Markisches Museum.
DDR-102 Berlin, Bodestr. 1-3

Meininger Museum, Schloss Elisabethenburg.
DDR-601 Meiningen

Meyenburg-Museum.
DDR-20 Nordhausen, Alexander-Puschikin-St. 31

Museum der Bildenden Kunst.
DDR-701 Leipzig, Georgi-Dimitroff-Platz 1

Museum des Kunsthandwerks, Grassi-Museum.
DDR-701 Leipzig, Johannis Platz 1 - 11

Museum fur Bergmannische Volkskunst.
DDR-9412 Schneeberg, Rosa-Luxemburg-Platz 1

Museum fur Deutsche Geschicte.
DDR-108 Berlinem unter den Linden 2

Museum fur Glaskunst.
DDR-6426 Lauscha, Oberlandstr. 10

Museum fur Kulturgeschichte (Stadtische Museen Gera)
DDR-65 Gera, Strasse der Republik 2

Museum fur Kunst-und Kultur Geschicte (Stadtmuseum)
DDR-86 Bautzen, Platz der Roten

ECUADOR

Museum fur Kunsthandwerk
(Staatliche Kunstsamlungen
Dresden)
DDR-8057 Dresden, Schloss
Pillnitz, Wasserpalais

Museum fur Naturkunde und
Vorgeschicte.
DDR-45 Dessau, August-Bebel-
Str. 32

Museum fur Volkskunst
(Staatliche Kunstsammlungen
Dresden)
DDR-806 Dresden, Kockestr. 1

Museum im Schloss Bernburg.
DDR-435 Bernburg, Schlosstr.
24

Nagel, Otto, House. See Otto-
Nagel-Haus.

Neue Kammern.
DDR-15 Potsdam, Park
Sansoucci

Neues Palais.
DDR-15 Potsdam, Park
Sanssouci

Oberjausitzer-Heimat-und
Damastmuseum.
DDR-8802 Grosschonau,
Schenaustri-Kupterhaus

Orangerie.
DDR-15 Potsdam, Park
Sanssouci

Ostasiatische Sammlung
(Staatliche Museen zu Berlin)
DDR-101 Berlin, Markisches
Ufer

Otto-Nagel-Haus.
Ddr-101 Berlin,Markisches U
Fer

Parkanlagen Sanssouci.
DDR-15 Potsdam

Porzellansammlung (Staatliche
Kunstsammlungen Dresden)
DDR-801 Dresden, Zwinger

Romische Bader.
DDR-15 Potsdam, Park
Sanssouci

Rote Spitzen (Schlossmuseum und
Spiekartenmuseum)
DDR-74 Altenburg, Ernst-
Thalmann-Platz 5

Schloss Belvedere.
DDR-53 Weimar

Schloss Charlottenhof.
DDR-15 Potsdam, Park
Sanssouci

Schloss Luisium.
DDR-4508 Dessau-Waldersee

Schloss Sanssouci.
DDR-15 Potsdam Park
Sanssouci

Schloss Tiefurt.
DDR-53 Weimar, Haupstr. 14

Schloss-und Heimatmuseum.
DDR-8246 Lauenstein, Schloss

Schlossberg Museum, Stadt-und
Kulturgeschichtliche Sammlung.
DDR-90 Karl-Marx-Stadt,
Schlossberg 12

Schlossmuseum.
DDR-9291 Rochsburg

Schlossmuseum.
DDR-9316 Schlettau, Schloss

Schlossmuseum.
DDR-43 Quedlinburg,
Schlossberg 1

Schlossmuseum.
DDR-8301 Weesenstein, Burg
Wessenstein

Schlossmuseum - Staatliche
Kunstsammulungen Weimar.
DDR-53 Weimar, Burgplatz 4

Schlossmuseum Heidecksburg.
DDR-682 Rudolstadt,
Schlossbezirk 1-3

Schlossmuseum-Kunstsammlungen.
DDR-58 Gotha, Schloss
Friedenstein

Schlossmuseum (Museum der
Stadt Arnstadt)
DDR-521 Arnstadt,
Schlossplatz 1

Skulpturensammlung (Staatliche
Kunstammlungen Dresden)
DDR-801 Dresden, Georg-
Treu-Platz

Skulpturensammlung (Staatliche
Museen zu Berlin)
DDR-102 Berlin, Bodestr. 1-3

Spreewaldmuseum Lubbenau mit
Volkspark.
DDR-7543 Lubbenau

Staaliche Schlosser und Garten
Worlitz.
DDR-4414 Worlitz

Staatliche Bucher-und
Kupferstichsammlung.
DDR-66 Greiz, Sommerpalais,
Leninpark

Staatliche Galerie Moritzburg.
DDR-402 Halle, Friedemann-
Bach-Platz 5

Staatliche Galerie-Schloss
Georgium (Staatliche
Kunstsammlung der Stadt
Dessau)
DDR-45 Dessau Puschinallee
100

Staatliche Kunstsammlungen
Dresden.
DDR-801 Dresden,
Albertinum, Georg-Treu-Platz

Staatliche Porzellan-Manufaktur
Meissen, Schauhalle.
DDDR-825 Meissen, Leninstr.

Staatliches Lindenau-Museum.
DDR-74 Altenburg, Ernst-
Thalmann-Str. 5

Staatliches Museum Schloss
Magiskau (Staatliche
Kunstsammlung der Stadt
Dessau)
DDR-4506 Dessau

Staatliches Museum Schwerin.
DDR-27 Schwerin, am Alter
Graben

Stadt-und Berbaumuseum.
DDR-92 Freiberg, am Dom 1-3

Stadt-und Kreismuseum.
DDR-825 Meissen,
Rathenauplatz 3

Stadtische Kunstsammlungen.
DDR-90 Karl-Marx-Stadt,
Theaterplatz 1

Stadtische Kunstsammlungen
Augsburg.
D-8900 Augsburg, Maxilianstr.
46

Stadtisches Heimat-und
Kermikmuseum.
DDR-142 Velten, Karl-Marx-
St. 79

Stadtisches Kunstgewerbe-und
Heimatmuseum.
DDR-657 Zeulenfoda,
Aumaische St. 30

Stadtisches Museum.
DDR-95 Zwickau, Lessingstr.

Stadtisches Museum.
DDR-49 Zeitz, Schloss
Moritzburg

Stadtisches Museum und
Kunstsammlung.
DDR-961 Glauchau, Schloss
Hinterglauchau

Stadtmuseum.
DDR-88 Zittzu, Klosterstr. 3

Topfermuseum.
DDR-723 Kohren-Sahlis,
Ernst-Thalmann-Str. 14

Voderasiatisches Museum
(Staatliche Museen zu Berlin)
DDR-102 Berlin, Bodestr. 1-3

Vogtlandisches Bauernmuseum.
DDR-9931 Landwust 48

Volskundemuseum.
DDR-209 Templin, Prenzlauer
Tor

Wartburg-Stifttung.
DDR-59 Eisenach

Weissgerbermuseum.
DDR-797 Doberlung-
Kirchhain, Potsdamer Str. 18

Werkmuseum fur Keramik.
DDR-8252 Coswig, Rosa-
Luxemburg-Platz 13

Wittumspalais.
DDR-53 Weimar, am Palais 3

Zinnsammlung (Staatliche
Kunstsammlungen Dresden)
DDR-801 Dresden, Zwinger

ECUADOR

Caamano, Alberto Mena, Museum
of Art. See Museo de Arte
"Alberto Mena Caamano"

Museo de Arte "Alberto Mena
Caamano".
Palacio del Antiquo Cuartel de
la Real Audiencia de Quito,
Apdo. 399, Quito

Museo de Arte Colonial, Casa de
la Cultura Ecuatoriana.
Calles Cuenca y Mejia 915
2550 Quito, 219-297

Museo de Arte e Historia de la
Ciudad.
Espejo 1147, Apdo. 399, Quito
Hugo Moncayo

EGYPT

Al-Gawhara Palace Museum.
The Citadel, Cairo

Coptic Museum.
St. George St., Cairo, 841766
Permanent Collections:
Stones section, textiles, icons,
metals, ivory and bones,
manuscripts, woods, fresco and
Ethiopian section.

Egyptian Museum.
Sh Selim Hassan, Cairo

Greco-Roman Museum.
Museum St., Alexandria

Mouktar Museum.
Shari Kasr El-Nil 4, Cairo

Musee Du Caire. See Egyptian
Museum

Museum of Fine Arts & Cultural
Center.
Menascha St., Alexandria

Museum of Islamic Art.
Ahmed Maher Sq., Cairo

University of Alexandria, Museum
of the Faculty of Arts:
Alexandria

ETHIOPIA

Addis Ababa University, Museum
of the Institute of Ethiopian
Studies:
P.O. Box 1176, Addis Ababa

Museum of the Holy Trinity
Church of Ethiopia.
Like Sultanate Hapte Mariam,
P.O. Box 3137, Addis Ababa

National Museum.
King George VI St., P.O. Box
76, Addis Ababa

FINLAND

Anderson, Amos, Taidemuseo.
Yrjonkatu 27, SF-00100
Helsinki 10

Anjala Kart Anomuseo.
SF-46910 Anjala

Arabian Museo.
Hameentie 135, SF-00560
Helsinki 56

Ateneumin Taidemuseo.
Kaivokatu 2-4, SF-00100
Helsinki 10

Cedercreutzin, Emil, Museo.
SF-29210 Merstola, Harjavalta
Permanent Collections:
Artists' home, studio and
sculpture room, 2 exhibition
halls of Finnish art (paintings
and sculptures of early 20th
century), the Temple to the
Spirit of the Earth
(ethnographic collections).

Cygnaeuksen Galleria.
Kalliolinnantie 8, 00140
Helsinki, 656 928

Permanent Collections:
Art collection of Frederick
Cygnaeus.

Cygnaeus Gallery. *See*
Cygnaeuksen Galleria

Didrichsenin Taidemuseo.
Kuusilahdenkuja 3, SF-00340
Helsinki
Permanent Collections:
Collection of modern gold and
silversmithing.

Emil Cedercreutzin Museo. *See*
Cedercreutzin, Emil, Museo

Emil Wilkstromin Museo. *See*
Wilkstromin, Emil, Museo

Etela-Karjalan Museo.
Linnoitus, F-53900
Lappeenranta

Gallen-Kallelan Museo.
Tarvaspaa SF-02600
Leppavaara, Espoo

**Gosta Serlachius Fine Arts
Foundation.**
SF-35800 Mantta, 934-477490,
477489 22122 SERLA SF
Permanent Collections:
Finnish and Scandinavian art
from the 19th and 20th
centuries. Works of the Italian
and Spanish Renaissance and
Baroque masters; Dutch art
from the 17th century.

Hameenlnnan Taidemuseo.
Viipurintie 2, SF-13200
Hemeenlinna

Hiekan Taidemuseo.
Pirkankatu 6, SF-33210
Tampere 21

Iittalan Lasitehtaan Museo.
SF-14500 Iittala

Imatran Taidemuseo.
SF-55100 Imatra

Joensuun Taidemuseo.
Rantakatu 8, F-80100 Joensuu
10
Permanent Collections:
Turtiainien Art Collection, the
Okkonen Art Collection and
the Cederberg Art Collection.

Johnnes Haapasalon Museo.
Risimaenkatu 5, SF-550100
Mikkeli 10

Karhulan Tehtaan Museo.
William Ruthinkatu SF-48600
Karhula

Kuntsin Taidekoelma.
Ravikatu, SF-65140 Vaasa 14

Lahti Art Museum.
Vesijavenkatu 11, SF-15111
Lahti 11, 918-182233
Permanent Collections:
Old and modern Finnish art; a
collection of posters.

Lahti Historical Museum.
Lahdenkatu 4, P.B. 115, SF-
15110 Lahti 11, 918/1811
Permanent Collections:
A special collection of French
and Italian art as well as arts
and crafts from the Middle
Ages to about 1800; local
ethnographical collections;
Finnish arts and crafts and
Finnish medals.

Luostarinmaen Kasityolaismuseo.
Luostarinmaki, SF-20700 Turku
70

Museet "Ett Hem".
Biskopgaten 14, SF-20500
Turku 50
Permanent Collections:
A total number of 1,522 objects
in the residence of Consul
Alfred Jacobson, (1841-1931).
Art collection of approximately
120 pieces.

Nelimarkka-Museo.
Pekkola, SF-62900 Alajarvi

Ortodoksinen Kirkkomuseo.
Karjalankatu 1, SF-70300
Kuopio 30

Oulon Taidemuseo.
Asemakstu 18, SF-90100 Oulu
10

Pampereen Kaupunginmuseo.
Hatanpaan Kartano SF-33100
Tampere

Pohjanman Museo.
Museokatu 3, SF-65100 Vaasa
10

Porvoon Museo.
Valikatu 11, SF-06100 Porvoo
10, 915-140589
Permanent Collections:
Paintings, sculpture and
graphics.

Rauman Taidemuseo.
Kuninkaankatu 37, SF-26100
Rauma 10

Sinbebyrchoff in Taidekokoelmat.
Bulevardi, 40 SF-00120
Helsinki

Suomen Kansallismuseo.
Mannerheiminte P.O. Box 913,
10 Helsinki

Suomen Lasimuseo.
Koulukatu 14, SF-11100
Riihimaki 10

Suomen Rakennustaiteen Museo.
Puistokatu 4, SF-00140,
Helsinki 14
Permanent Collections:
Museum of Finnish
Architecture originates from
the photographic archives
founded in 1949 by the
Association of Finnish
Architects. At present the
museum has four departments:
Archives, Library, Exhibition
and Research. The
photographic archives
collection consists of about
60,000 black and white
photographs and drawing
copies of Finnish architecture.
The slide collection consists of
some 10,000 slides, both black
and white and color, on
Finnish architecture; also
original drawings and
competition projects.

Tampereen Nykytaiteen Museo.
Palomaentie 23, SF-33230
Tampere 23

Tampereen Taidemuseo.
Puutarhakatu 34, SF-33210
Tampere 23

Turun Taidemuseo.
Puolalanpuisto, 10 Turku

Varkauden Kaupungin Museot.
Vesitorni, F-78200 Varkaus

Waino Aaltosen Museo.
Itainen Rantakatu 38, SF-20810
Turku 8

**Walter Runebergin
Veistoskokelma.**
Aleksanterinkatu 5, SF-06100
Porvoo

Wilkstromin, Emil, Museo.
Visavuori SF-37700 Tarttila,
Saaksmaki

FRANCE

Abbaye.
F-86250 Charroux

Abbaye de Conques.
F-12320 St-Cyprien-Sur-
Dourdou

Abbaye de Jumieges.
C/O Caisse Nationale des
Monuments Historiques et des
Sites, Paris 75004, 274-22-22

Abbaye de la Sauve-Majeure.
C/O Caisse National des
Monuments Historiques et des
Sites, Paris 75004, 274-22-22

Abbaye de Montmajour.
C/O Caisse Nationale des
Monuments Historiques et des
Sites, Paris 75004, 274-22-22

Abbaye de Noirlac.
C/O Caisse Nationale des
Monuments Historiques et des
Sites, Paris 75004, 274-22-22

Abbaye de Silvacane.
C/O Caisse Nationale des
Monuments Historiques et des
Sites, Paris 75004, 274-22-22

Abbaye du Bec-Hellouin.
C/O Caisse Nationale des
Monuments Historiques et des
Sites, Paris 75004, 274-22-22

Abbaye du Thoronet.
C/O Caisse Nationale des
Monuments Historiques et des
Sites, Paris 75004, 274-22-22

Aicard, Jean, Museum (La Garde).
See **Musee Jean Aicard**

**Aicard, Jean, Museum (Sollies-
Pont).** *See* **Musee Jean Aicard**

**Ancienne Abbaye de Saint-
Germain.**
F-89000 Auxerre

Annexe du Musee Fabre.
Hotel du Cabrieres-Sabatier
d'Espeyran, F-34000
Montpellier

Arbaud, Paul, Museum. *See*
Musee Paul Arbaud

Barthe, Edoard, Museum. *See*
Musee Edouard-Barthe

Bibliotheque Nationale.
Cabinet des Medailles, 58 Rue
de Richelieu, F-75084 Paris
Cedex 02, 266-62-62

Bois Preau. *See* **Musee du
Chateau de Bois Preau**

Boudin, Eugene, Museum. *See*
Musee Eugene Boudin

Bron.
C/O Caisse Nationale des
Monuments Historiques et des
Sites, Paris 75004, 274-22-22

**Cabinet Des Estampes et
Bibliotheque Des Musees.**
2 Place Du Rohan, F-67000
Strasbourg

**Caisse Nationale des Monuments
Historiques et des Sites.**
Hotel de Sully, 62 Rue Saint-
Antoine, Paris 75004, 277-59-
20
Permanent Collections:
Art collections belonging to a
number of French historic
monuments.

Cathedrale.
F-11000 Carcassonne

Cathedrale de Reims.
C/O Caisse Nationale Des
Monuments Historiques et Des
Sites, Paris 75004, 274-22-22

Cathedrale de Tours.
C/O Caisse Nationale des
Monuments Historiques et des
Sites, Paris 75004, 274-22-22

Cathedrale Notre-Dame.
F-05200 Embrum

Cazin, Charles, Museum. *See*
Musee Charles Cazin

Centre Georges Pompidou. *See*
**Musee d'Art Moderne
(Beaubourg), Centre National
d'Art et de Culture George
Pompidou**

Chambord.
C/O Caisse Nationale des
Monuments Historiques et des
Sites, 274-22-22

Chapelle.
F-91490 Milly-la-Foret

Chapelle des Moines.
Berze-la-Ville, F-71112 Sologny

Chapelle du Rosaire.
Ave. Henri-Matisse, F-06140
Vence

Charreton, Victor, Museum. *See*
Musee Victor Charreton

**Chartreuse de Champmol Musee
des Beaux-Arts.**
Hopital Psychiatrique, Ave.
Albert 1e, F-21000 Dijon

Chateau.
F-71530 Cormatin

Chateau.
Ciron, F-79100 Thouars

Chateau d'Ancy-le-Franc.
F-89160 Ancy-le-Franc

Chateau d'Azay-le-Ferron.
Mezieres-En-Brenne

**Chateau de Beaumont sur
Vingeanne.**
Beaumont-Sur-Vingeanne, F-
21310 Mirabeau-Sur-Beze

Chateau de Bussy-Rabutin.
Bussy-le-Grand, F-21150 Les
Laumes

Chateau de Champs-Sur-Marne.
F-94 Champs-Sur-Marne, Seine
et Marne

Chateau de Chateaudun.
F-28200 Chateaudun

Chateau de Clermont-En-Genevois.
F-74150 Rumilly

Chateau De Gien. *See* Musee
Internationale de la Chasse

Chateau de Langeais.
F-37130 Langeais

Chateau de Montrottier.
F-74000 Annecy

Chateau De Saumur. *See* Musee
d'Arts Decoratifs, Chateau de
Saumur

Chateau De Sceaux. *See* Musee de
l'Ile de France

Chateau de St-Aubin-Sur-Loire.
St-Aubin-Sur-Loire

Chateau de Talcy.
C/O Caisse Nationale des
Monuments Historiques et des
Sites, Paris 75004, 274-22-22

Chateau de Thoisy-la-Berchere.
Thoisy-la-Berchere

Chateau de Tourlaville.
F-50100 Cherbourg

Chateau de Vincennes.
C/O Caisse Nationale des
Monuments Historiques et des
Sites, Paris 75004, 274-22-22

Chateau du Haut-Koenigsbourg.
C/O Caisse Nationale des
Monuments Historiques et des
Sites, Paris 75004, 274-22-22

Chateau-Musee de Blois.
Chateau, F-41000 Blois

Cocteau, Jean, Museum.
Quai Napoleon III, F-06500
Menton

Collection Charles de l'Escalopier.
Bibliotheque Municipale, 50
Rue de la Republique, F-8000
Amiens

Collection Mainssieux.
Hotel de Ville, F-38500 Vorin

Collegiale Notre-Dame.
Place Maufoux, F-21200
Beaune

Compiegne. *See* Musee National
du Chateau de Compiegne

Conciergerie.
C/O Caisse Nationale des
Monuments Historiques et des
Sites, Paris 75004, 274-22-22

Conde Museum. *See* Institut de
France, Musee Conde, Chantilly

Coucy.
C/O Caisse Nationale des
Monuments Historiques et des
Sites, Paris 75004, 274-22-22

Courbet, Gustave, Museum. *See*
Musee d'Ornans

D'Aboville, Jeanne, Museum. *See*
Musee Jeanne d'Aboville

Davoine, Rene, Museum. *See*
Musee Rene Davoine

Dechelette, Joseph, Museum. *See*
Musee Joseph Dechelette

Delacroix, Eugene, Museum. *See*
Musee Eugene Delacroix

Depot Lapidaire.
Chateau Comtal, F-11000
Carcassonne

**Dubouche, Adrien, Musee
National.** *See* Musee National
Adrien-Dubouche

Dupuy, Paul, Museum. *See* Musee
Paul Dupuy

Eglise Collegiale Notre-Dame.
F-30400 Villeneuve-les-
Avignon

Eglise des Cordeliers.
Grand-Rue, F-54000 Nancy

Enserune.
C/O Caisse Nationale des
Monuments Historiques et des
Sites, Paris 75004, 274-22-22

Fondation Ephrussi de Rothschild.
DDR-101 Berlin, Markisches U
Fer

Fondation Maeght.
F-O6570 St-Paul

Fondation Theodore Reinach.
F-06310 Beaulieu-Sur-Mer

Fontainebleau. *See* Musee
National du Chateau de
Fontainebleau

Fragonard Museum. *See* Musee
Fragonard

Francisque Mandet Museum. *See*
Mandet, Francisque, Museum

Galerie des Arts.
9 Ave. Marcelin-Maurel, F-
06140 Vence

Girodet Museum. *See* Musee
Girodet

Glanum.
Caisse Nationale des
Monuments Historiques et des
Sites, Paris 75004, 274-22-22

Goya Museum. *See* Musee Goya

Grand Trianon.
Versailles

Granet Museum. *See* Musee
Granet

Greuze Museum. *See* Musee
Greuze

Grimaldi Museum. *See* Musee
Grimaldi

Henner, J. J., Museum. *See*
Musee J.-J.Henner

Henry, Thomas, Museum. *See*
Musee Thomas Henry

Hopital.
F-25290 Ornans

Hopital.
Quai de l'Hopital, F-71100
Chalon-Sur-Saone

Hotel de Sully.
C/O Caisse Nationale des
Monuments Historiques et des
Sites, Paris 75004, 274-22-22

Hotel Gouin.
25 Rue de Commerce, F-37000
Tours

Hotel Jacques Coeur.
Place Jacques-Coeur, F-18000
Bourges

Hotel Lallemant.
Rue Bourbonnoux, F-18000
Bourges

Hotel St-Vic.
F-18200 St-Amand-Montrond

Ingres Museum. *See* Musee Ingres

**Institut de France, Musee Conde,
Chantilly.**
60500 Paris

**Jacquemart, Andre, Museum
(Paris).** *See* Musee Jacquemart-
Andre

**Jacquemart, Andre, Museum
(Senlis).** *See* Musee Jaquemart-
Andre

Jouglet, Theophile, Museum. *See*
Musee Theophile Jouglet

Labit, George, Museum. *See*
Musee George Labit

Landowsky, Paul, Museum. *See*
Musee Paul Landowsky

Laronze, Jean, Museum. *See*
Musee Jean Laronze

Leger, Fernand, Museum. *See*
Musee Fernand Leger

L'Escalopier Collection. *See*
Collection Charles de
l'Escalopier

Maison de Renoir.
Collettes, F-06800 Cagnes-Sur-
Mer

Malmaison. *See* Musee National
de Vallauris, Musee National
Picasso

Mandet, Francisque, Museum.
Rue de l'Hotel-De-Ville, F-
63200 Riom
Permanent Collections:
Museum situated in a beautiful
"hotel" of the 18th century.
Collection includes paintings
and art objects. Represented
are Flemish and Dutch schools
from the 17th and 18th
century; Spanish, German and
Italian works; French painting
of the 17th, 18th and 19th
century. There are also rooms
containing contemporary
sculpture and painting.

Matisse, Henri, Museum. *See*
Musee Henri Matisse

Matisse Museum. *See* Musee
Matisse

Mont-Saint-Michel.
C/O Caisse Nationale des
Monuments Historiques et des
Sites, Paris 75004, 274-22-22

Moreau, Gustave, Museum. *See*
Musee Gustave Moreau

Musee.
F-86310 St-Savin

Musee.
F-65000 Luz-Saint-Sauveur

Musee.
Rue Sallier, F-21210 Saulieu

Musee.
Hotel de Ville, F-55200
Commercy

Musee.
Mairie, F-42260 St.-Germain-
Laval

Musee.
Rue du Musee, F-71140
Bourbon-Lancy

Musee.
4 Place des Ormeaux, F-26000
Valence

Musee.
Place des Freres-Mounet, F-
84100 Orange

Musee Africain.
Ile d'Aix

Musee Africain.
150 Cours Gambetta, F-69361
Lyon, 16(78) 58-45-70

Musee Alsacien.
25 Quai Saint-Nicolas, F-67000
Strasbourg

Musee Antoine Lecuyer.
28, Rue Antoine-Lecuyer. F-
02100 St-Quentin, (23) 62 39
71
Permanent Collections:
Pastels of Maurice Quentin de
la Tour; Faiences from the 18th
century; ivories; tapestries;
paintings from the 17th through
20th centuries.

Musee Archeologioue.
Cathedale, F-83600 Frejus

Musee Archeologique.
Mairie, F-32800 Eauze

Musee Archeologique.
Hotel Babou de la Bourdaisiere
Place Foire-Lerci, F-37000
Tours

Musee Archeologique.
Batiment des Benedictins, Place
de la Cathedrale St. Benigne,
F-21000 Dijon

**Musee Archeologique du
Nivernais.**
Porte du Croux, F-58000
Neverrs

Musee Archeologique Municipal.
32, Rue Georges Ermant, F-
02000 Laon, 23 22 05
Permanent Collections:
Very important Antiquities
collection (Egypt, Greece,
Anatolia). Regional
archaeology; prehistory; Gallo-
Roman, Merovingian and
Medieval collections of jewels,
armes, ceramics, glass, bronzes
and tools. Painting from the
15th to the 20th century.
Diptych of the Master of the
Hours of Rohan; copies of lost
works by the brothers Le Nain
(born in Laon) and works by J-
S. Berthelemy (born in Laon).

Musee Archeologique Regional.
St-Pere, F-89450 Vezelay

Musee Armenien en France.
59 Ave. Foch, F-75016 Paris

Musee Atger.
2 Rue Cardinal de l'Ecole-De-Medecine

Musee Bargoin.
45, Rue Ballainvilliers, F-63000 Clermont-Ferrand, (73)-91-37-31

Musee Baron-Martin.
Chateau, F-70100 Gray

Musee Benoit-De-Puydt.
Rue du Musee, F-59270 Bailleul

Musee Bertrand.
Rue Descente-Des Cordeliers, F-36000 Chateauroux

Musee-Bibliotheque Municipal.
Villa Garnier, F-77160 Provins

Musee Bonnat.
5 Rue Jacques-Laffitte, F-641001 Bayonne

Musee Borely.
Chateau Borely, Ave. Clot-Bey, F-13008 Marseille

Musee Bossuet.
5 Pl Charles de Gaulle, F-7100 Meaux, 434-84-45
Permanent Collections:
Archaeology, art and history.

Musee Boucher de Perthes.
Rue du Beffroi, F-80100 Abbeville, (22) 24 08 49
Permanent Collections:
Prehistory and archaeology of the valley of the Somme; sculpture of northern France from the 15th-18th centuries; painting of the French school and of the Low Countries from the 16th-18th centuries; ceramics and objects of art from the 12th-18th centuries.

Musee Bourdelle.
16 Rue Antoine-Bourdelle, F-75015 Paris

Musee Calvet.
65 Rue Joseph-Vernet, F-84000 Avignon

Musee Cantini.
19 Rue Grignan, F-13006 Marseille

Musee Carnavalet.
23 Rue De Sevigne, F-75003 Paris, 272-21-13/278.03.59
Permanent Collections:
History of Paris; French furniture of the 17th and 18th centuries and French paintings from the 16th to 20th centuries.

Musee Carnavelet.
23 Rue de Sevigne, F-75003 Paris

Musee Central.
2 Rue du Haut-Poirier, F-57000 Metz

Musee Cernuschi.
7 Ave. Valasquez, F-75008 Paris

Musee Chabrand.
Blvd. de la Liberation, F04400 Barcelonnette

Musee Chapu.
334 Rue Chapu, F-77350 le-Mee-Sur-Seine

Musee Charles Cazin.
Hotel de Ville, F-83230 F83230 Bormes-les-Mimosas

Musee Cheret.
33 Ave. des Beaumettes, F-06000 Nice

Musee Claustral.
Cloitre, F-82200 Moissac

Musee Cognacq-Jay.
25 Blvd. Des Capucines, F-75002 Paris

Musee Conde.
Chateau, F-60500 Chantilly

Musee Crozatier.
Jardin Henri-Vaenay, 43012 le Puy

Musee d'Ales.
F-30100 Ales

Musee d'Annecy.
F-74000 Annecy

Musee d'Antiquite.
Rue Antoine-Lecuyer, F-02100 St-Quentin

Musee d'Antiquites Gallo-Romaines.
Aoste, F-38810

Musee d'Aquitaine.
Cours D'Albert, F-33000 Bordeaux

Musee d'Archeologie.
Ave. des Arenes, No. 164, F-06000 Nice

Musee d'Arras.
Ancienne Abbaye de Saint-Vaast, 22 Rue Paul Doumer, F-84000

Musee d'Art Chretien.
Saint-Andre-le-Bas, F-38200 Vienne

Musee d'Art d'Industrie.
Place Louis Comte, F-42000 St-Etienne

Musee d'Art et d'Archeologie.
F-32000 Auch

Musee d'Art et d'Archeologie.
Place de l'Hotel-De-Ville, F-47000 Agen

Musee d'Art et d'Archeologie.
20 Blvd. du Marechal-Leclerc, F-83100 Toulon

Musee d'Art et d'Histoire.
3 Rue Verrier, F-03200 Vichy

Musee d'Art et d'Histoire.
Palais des Archeveques, F-11100 Narbonne, (68) 32 31 60
Permanent Collections:
Painting, sculpture and ceramics.

Musee d'Art et d'Industrie.
Saint-Etienne, 32-64-41

Musee d'Art Juif.
2 Rue des Saules, F-75018 Paris, 257 84 15
Permanent Collections:
Cultural and popular art objects, including a collection of objects from North Africa; a unique collection of synagogue

models from various countries dating from the 12th to the 19th century, notably Eastern and Central Europe; sculpture comprising a very rare series of castings and reproductions of stone tombs from Jewish cemetaries in Prague and Czernovitz; synagogical paintings and mosaics; contemporary art paintings, drawings, lithographs, engravings and sculpture from Jewish artists (Chagall, Mane-Katz, Benn and Lipschitz).

Musee d'Art Moderne.
F-06800 Cagnes-Sur-Mer

Musee d'Art Moderne.
Rue Joseph-Parayre, F-66400 Ceret

Musee d'Art Moderne (Beaubourg), Centre National d'Art et de Culture George Pompidou.
75191 Rue Des Archives, Paris 277 1233, CNAC GP 212 726 PARIS

Musee d'Art Provencal.
5 Place des Heros, Chateau-Gomber

Musee d'Art Regional.
F-89119 Viller-St.-Benoit

Musee d'Art Sacre.
Catherdale Saint-Siffrein, F-84200 Carpentras

Musee d'Arts Decoratifs, Chateau de Saumur.
Chateau, F-49400 Saumur, (41) 51 30 46

Musee Dauphinois.
30 Rue Gignoux, F-38000 Grenoble

Musee de Bagnols-Sur-Ceze.
Mairie, F-30200 Bagnols-Sur-Ceze, (66) 89 60 02

Musee de Bretagne.
20 Quai Emile-Zola, F-350000 Rennes

Musee de Chaumont.
Place du Palais, F-52200 Chaumont

Musee de Comminges.
Place de la Cathedrale, F-31510 St-Bertrand-De-Comminges

Musee de Dieppe.
Chateau, F-76200 Dieppe

Musee de Folklore et des Moulins.
6 Place de l'Ancien-Palais, F-0300 Moulins

Musee de la Benedictine.
110 Rue Theagene-Boufart, F-76400 Fecamp

Musee de la Castree.
Le Suquet, F-06400 Cannes

Musee de la Chapelle Saint-Jean.
Grand-Rue, F-68100 Mulhouse

Musee de la Dentelle a la Main.
F-63220 Arlanc-En-Livradois

Musee de la Faience.
Mairie, F-04360 Moustiers-Saint-Marie

Musee de la Fondation Smith-Lesouef.
14 Bis Rue Charles VII, F-94130 Nogent-Sur-Marne

Musee de la Grange aux Dimes.
F-77160 Provins

Musee de la Maison d'Oze.
Place de la Magdeleine

Musee de la Mode et du Costume.
Palais Galliera, 10, Ave. Pierre 1er de Serbie, 75116 Paris, 720-85-46
Permanent Collections:
Collections comprise close to 4,000 complete costumes and more than 25,000 pieces, illustrating men's and children's fashions from 1735 to the present day.

Musee de la Peinture et Musee la Place.
F-14950 Beaumont-En-Auge

Musee de la Princerie.
16 Rue de Belle-Vierge, F-55107 Verdun

Musee de la Renaissance.
Chateau, F-37190 Azay-le-Rideau

Musee de la Societe Archeologique et Historique de la Charente.
44 Rue de Montmoreau, F-16000 Angouleme

Musee de la Societe d'Archeologie.
F-59440 Avesnes-Sur-Helpe

Musee de la Societe des Amis de Thann.
Halle Auble, F-68800 Thann

Musee de la Tapisserie de la Reine Mathilde.
Rue Lambert-Leforesier, F-14400 Bayeux

Musee de la Tour du Moulin.
Rue de la Tour, F-71110 Marcigny

Musee de l'Abbaye de Graville.
Rue de l'Abbaye, F-76600 le Havre

Musee de l'Abbaye de Sept-Fontaines.
Sept-Fontaines

Musee de l'Ain.
63, Boulevard de Brou, F-01000 Bourg-En-Bresse, (74) 22 22 31
Permanent Collections:
Fine arts, history of the city with two rooms dedicated to celebrated men born in the city. Also "La Volaille dans l'Art," sculpture, decorative arts, prehistory, popular traditions.

Musee de l'Ancien Hopital Saint-Roch.
F-36100 Issoudun

Musee de l'Ancienne Douane.
Pont du Corbeau, F-67000 Strasbourg

Musee de l'Annonciade.
Place Georges Grammont, F-83990 St-Tropez, 97 04 01

Musee de l'Avallonais.
7 Rue de Odebert, F-89200
Avallon

**Musee de l'Ecole Superieure des
Beaux-Arts.**
14 Rue Bonaparte, F-75006
Paris

Musee de l'Emperi.
Chateau, F-13300 Salon-De-
France
Permanent Collections:
Military arts and history
housed in the oldest fortress in
Provence built along the 10th,
13th and 16th centuries.
National collection covers
history of French armies.
Among 10,000 authentic pieces
of the collection are flags,
decorations, swords, fire arms,
guns, uniforms and their
equipment harnesses, drawings
and paintings.

**Musee de l'Histoire de France,
Archives Nationales.**
Rue des Francs-Bourgeois, F-
75003 Paris
Permanent Collections:
Permanent collection of 71
major documents from the
history of France from the
Merovingians until the Second
World War and a permanent
collection of documents from
the French Revolution.

Musee de l'Hopital.
Place de l'Hopital, F-69000
Lyon

Musee de l'Hopital.
Rue Irma-Masson, F-52300
Joinville

Musee de l'Hospice.
F-30400 Villeneuve-les-
Avignon

Musee De L'Hospice Comtesse.
32 Rue De La Monnaie, F-
59000 Lille

Musee de l'Hotel de Ville.
F-62140 Hesdin

Musee de l'Hotel de Ville.
F-04400 Barcelonnette

Musee de l'Hotel de Ville.
F-50120 Equeurdreville-
Heinneville

Musee de l'Hotel-Dieu.
Rue De l'Hotel Dieu, F-21200
Beaune

Musee de l'Ile de France.
Chateau de l'Ile de France, F-
92330 Sceaux

Musee de l'Impression sur Etoffes.
3 Rue des Bonnes-Gens, F-
68100 Mulhouse
Permanent Collections:
Textile collection.

Musee de Limur.
31 Rue Thiers, F-56000 Vannes

Musee de l'Oeuvre Notre-Dame.
Place du Chateau, F-67000
Strasbourg

Musee de Melun.
5 Rue du Franc-Murier, F-
77000 Melun

Musee de Meudon.
11 Rue de Pierres, F-92190
Meudon

Musee de Peinture.
Hotel de Ville, F-61000
Alencon

Musee de Peinture.
Ancien Eveche, Court des
Tribunaux, F-14400 Bayeux

**Musee de Peinture et de
Sculpture.**
Place de Verdun, F-38000
Grenoble

Musee de Picardie.
48 Rue de la Republique, F-
80000 Amiens
Permanent Collections:
Archaeology, art and natural
history.

Musee de Pontoise. *See* **Musee
Tavet-Delacour**

Musee de St-Lo.
Place de l'Hotel de Ville, F-
5000 St-Lo

Musee de Tesse.
2 Rue de Tesse, F-72000 le
Mans

Musee del'Opera.
Place Charles-Garnier, F-75009
Paris

Musee d'Ennery.
59 Ave. Foch, F-75016 Paris

Musee Denon.
Place de l'Hotel-De-Ville, Rue
Boichot, F-71100 Chalon-Sur-
Saone

**Musee Departemental et
Municipal.**
Place du Colonel-Laussedat, F-
03000 Moulins

**Musee Departmental de l'Oise-
Beauvais.**
1 Rue de Musee, F-60000
Beauvais, 445-13-60
Permanent Collections:
Regional ceramics, sculptures,
Italian and French paintings,
engravings, archaeology,
paleontology and minerology.

**Musee Departmental des
Antiquites de la Seine-Maritime.**
198 Rue Beauvoisine, F-76000
Rouen

Musee Departmental des Vosges.
Place Lagarde, F-88000 Epinal

**Musee des Amis du Vieux St-
Etienne.**
13 Bis, Rue Bambetta, F-42100
St-Etienne

Musee des Antiques.
Blvd. Admiral Courbet, F-
30033 Nimes

Musee des Antiquites Nationales.
Chateau, F-78100 St-Germain-
En-Laye

**Musee des Arts Africains et
Oceaniens.**
293 Ave. Daumesnil, F-75012
Paris
Permanent Collections:
Arts of Black Africa, Mahgreb
and Oceania.

**Musee des Arts & Traditions
Populaires du Terroir
Marseillais.**
5 Place des Heros, Chateau-
Gombert, 13013 Marseille, (91)
68 14 38

Permanent Collections:
Costume collection, archives,
photographs, paintings,
iconography, reconstructed
rooms, religious art,
mannequins, library and work
instruments.

Musee des Arts Decoratifs.
39 Rue Bouffard, F-33000
Bordeaux

Musee des Arts Decoratifs.
2 Place du Chateau, F-67000
Strasbourg

**Musee des Arts Decoratifs ou
Musee de l'Ecole Nancy.**
38 Rue Sergent-Blandan, F-
54000 Nancy

Musee des Arts Decoratifs, Paris.
See **Union Central des Arts
Decoratifs- Musee des Arts
Decoratifs**

Musee Des Augustins.
21 Rue De Metz, 31000
Toulouse

Musee des Beaux-Arts.
F-12000 Rodez

Musee des Beaux-Arts.
F-38200 Vienne

Musee des Beaux-Arts.
F-51200 Epernay

Musee des Beaux-Arts.
Cours Bosquet, F-6400 Pau

Musee des Beaux-Arts.
Place du Palais de Justice

Musee des Beaux-Arts.
3 Rue du Musee, F-79000
Niort

Musee des Beaux-Arts.
Hotel de Ville, F21200 Beaune

Musee des Beaux-Arts.
Place de Herce, F-53000 Laval

Musee des Beaux-Arts.
3 Place Stanislas, F-54000
Nancy

Musee des Beaux-Arts.
Rue Victor-Hugo, F-17100
Saintes

Musee des Beaux-Arts.
Blvd. Watteau, F-59300
Valenciennes

Musee des Beaux-Arts.
Place du Chateau, F-67000
Strasbourg

Musee des Beaux-Arts.
Palais de Longchamp, F-13004
Marseille

Musee des Beaux-Arts.
63 Rue de l'Arsenal, F-17300
Rochefort

Musee des Beaux-Arts.
Blvd. Alsace-Lorraine, F-32300
Mirande

Musee des Beaux-Arts.
1 Place de la Republique,
45000 Orleans

Musee des Beaux-Arts.
10 Rue Georges Clemenceau,
F-44000 Nantes

Musee des Beaux-Arts.
1 Place de la Republique, F-
45000 Orleans

Musee des Beaux-Arts.
Hotel de Ville, Place Saint-
Corentin, F-29000 Quimper

Musee des Beaux-Arts.
Hotel Fabregat, Place de la
Revolution, F-34500 Beziers

Musee des Beaux-Arts.
Hotel Fabregat, Place de la
Revolution, F-25000 Besancon

Musee des Beaux-Arts.
Hotel de Ville, Place du
Marechal-Leclerc, F-86000
Poitiers

Musee des Beaux-Arts.
Rue Gargolleau, Hotel De
Crussol d'Uzes, F-17000 la
Rochelle

Musee des Beaux-Arts.
1 Rue de Verdun, F-11000
Carcassonne
Permanent Collections:
Paintings.

Musee des Beaux-Arts.
10 Rue du Musee, 49000
Angers
Permanent Collections:
Sculpture, paintings, drawings
and engravings.

Musee des Beaux-Arts.
Chateau de Caen, F-14000
Caen, (31) 81 78 63
Permanent Collections:
Painting, engraving, art objects,
ceramics, furniture and
tapestries.

Musee des Beaux-Arts.
18 Place Francois Sicard,
37000 Tours, 47 05 68 73
Permanent Collections:
Greek ceramics; Italian and
Flemish paintings from the
15th and 16th century;
paintings from 17th, 18th, 19th
and 20th century; sculpture
from 17th, 18th and 19th
century; 20th century drawings;
stamps and ceramics; furniture
from the 17th and 18th
century.

**Musee des Beaux-Arts, Chateau
des Rohan.**
2 Place du Chateau, 67000
Strasbourg

**Musee des Beaux-Arts de
Bordeaux.**
20 Cours d'Albert, F-33000
Bordeaux

Musee des Beaux-Arts de Dijon.
Place de la Sainte-Chapelle,
21000 Dijon

**Musee des Beaux-Arts de
Dunkerque.**
Place du General de Gaulle, F-
59140 Dunkerque
Permanent Collections:
French, Dutch, Flemish and
Italian paintings of the 16th-
20th centuries; local history
collection; boat models; natural
history gallery.

**Musee des Beaux-Arts de la
Ceramique.**
Square Verdrel, F-76000 Rouen

Musee des Beaux-Arts et d'Archeologie.
21 Rue Chretien-De-Troyes, F-10000 Troyes

Musee des Beaux-Arts et d'Archeologie.
34 bis Grand-Rue, F-62200 Boulogne-Sur-Mer

Musee des Beaux-Arts et d'Archeologie.
20 Quai Emile Zola, F-35100, (99) 30 59 66
Permanent Collections:
French and foreign paintings from the 15th century to the present; French and foreign drawings from the 15th century to the present; Egyptian, Greek and Roman archaeology; primitive arts and art from the Far East.

Musee des Beaux-Arts et de la Dentelle.
25 Rue Richelieu, F-62000 Calais

Musee des Beaux-Arts et Musee d'Archeologie.
Chateau, F-21500 Montbard

Musee des Beaux-Arts Lille.
Place de la Republique 59000 Lille, (20)-57 01 84-57 17 64

Musee des Beaux-Arts, Palais St. Pierre.
20 Place des Terreaux, 69001 Lyon

Musee des Moulages D'Art Antique.
15 Quai Claude-Bernard, F-69000 Lyon

Musee Des Moulages D'Art Medieval et Moderne.
Faculte Des Lettres, 72 Rue Pasteur, F-69000 Lyon

Musee des Moulages du Moyen-Age.
14 Rue Cardinal de Cabrieres, F-34000 Montpellier

Musee des Ponchettes.
77 Quai des Etats-Uais, F-06300 Nice

Musee des Tapisseries.
Chateau d'Angers, F-49000 Angers

Musee des Tapisseries et Pavillon de Vendome.
13 Rue de la Molle, F-13100 Aix-En-Provence
Permanent Collections:
The museum installed in 1910 in the Palace des Archeveques d'Aix, presents the rich collection of tapestries of the 17th and 18th century used by the Archeveques to decorate the palace. This collection has become the property of the State and permits one to follow the evolution of the art of tapestry for more than 2 centuries. It is divided into 4 groups: 1)Les Grotesques, 2)L'Histoire de Don Quichotte, 3)Les Jeux Russiens, 4)Les Verdures des Flandres.

Musee des Thermes et De L'hotel Cluny. *See Musee des Thermes et de l'Hotel Cluny*

Musee des Thermes et de l'Hotel Cluny.
6 Place Paul-Painleve, F-75005 Paris

Musee des Vins de Touraine.
16 Rue Nationale, 37000 Tours, 47 61 81 24
Permanent Collections:
Social, cultural and economic aspects of viniculture. Art related items include signs, plaques and coat of arms from the Poussin school (17th century).

Musee D'Espelosin.
Rochecorbon, F-37210 Vouray

Musee Despiau-Wlerick.
Donjon la Cataye, F-40000 Mont-De-Marsan

Musee d'Histoire de la France Comte.
Palais Granvelle, 96 Grand Rue, F-25000 Besancon

Musee Diocesain d'Art Religieux.
68 Rue Royale, F-59000 Lille

Musee Dobree.
Place Jean-V., F-44000 Nantes

Musee d'Ornans.
Rue de la Froidiere, F-25290 Ornans

Musee du Berry.
Hotel Cujas, Rue des Avenes, F-18000 Bourges

Musee du Cellier.
Ecole Nationale des Arts et Metiers, F-71250 Cluny

Musee du Chateau.
Chateau, F-35500 Vitre

Musee du Chateau de Bois Preau.
Rueil-Malmaison

Musee du Compagnonnage.
8 Rue Nationale, F-37000 Tours, (47) 61 81 94
Permanent Collections:
Handicrafts.

Musee du Conservatoire National des Arts et Metiers.
292 Rue Saint-Martin, F-75008 Paris

Musee du Docteur Faure.
Blvd. des Cotes, F-73100 Aix-les-Bains

Musee du Farinier.
Ecole Nationale des Arts et Metiers, F-71250 Cluny

Musee du Haubergier.
Rue de Haubergier, F-60300 Senlis

Musee du Hieron.
Route de Charolles, F-71600 Paray-le-Monial

Musee du Jeu de Paume.
Place de la Concorde, 75001 Paris, 260 12 07
Permanent Collections:
Impressionist collections.

Musee du Louvre.
Palais du Louvre, Place du Carrousel, 75041 Paris

Musee du Pays Brignolais.
Palais des Comtes de Provence, F-83170 Brignoles

Musee du Perigord.
Cours Tourny, F-24000 Perigueux, 53-53-16-42
Permanent Collections:
Prehistoric and Gallo-Roman archaeology; ethnogaphy; natural history; popular arts; Middle Ages; fine arts.

Musee du Petit Palais.
Place du Palais des Papes, 4000 Avignon, 86 44 58
Permanent Collections:
Italian painting from the end of 13th century to the beginning of the 16th century; Provencal painting, 14th-15th century; Provencal sculpture, 12th-15th century.

Musee du Petit Palais (Municipal Museum)
Ave. W Churchill, Paris

Musee du Prieure du Vieux-Logis.
59 Ave. Saint-Barthelemy, F-0600 Nice

Musee du Tissu d'Art et du Costume Ancien.
F-59200 Tourcoing

Musee du Vieux Chateau.
Rue Gautier-Ier, F-77140 Nemours

Musee du Vieux-Chateau, Laval.
Place de la Tremoille, Laval, (43) 53 39 89

Musee du Vieux-Chinon.
8 Rue Voltaire, F-37500 Chinon

Musee du Vieux Marseille.
Maison Diamentee, F-13000 Marseille

Musee du Vieux Queyras.
Place de la Mairie, F-05470 Aiguilles

Musee du Vieux Toulon.
69 Cours Lafayette, F-83100 Toulon

Musee du Vieux Toulouse.
7 Rue Dumay, F-31500 Toulouse

Musee du Vin Bourgogne.
Rue D'Enfer, 21200 Beaune
Permanent Collections:
History of wine and of wine production from antiquity through the 19th century. Art related items include bottles, glasses, tapestries by Jean Lurcat and Michel Tourliere.

Musee Dunois.
F-45190 Beaugency

Musee d'Unterlinden.
1 Place d'Unterlinden, F-68000 Colmar

Musee Duplessis.
234 Bd. Albin-Durand, F-84200 Carpentras

Musee Edouard-Barthe.
Hotel de Ville, Montblanc, F-34290 Servian

Musee Ernest Rupin.
15 Rue du Docteur-Massenat, F-19100 Brive-la-Gaillarde

Musee et Bibliotheque.
Rue de l'Ancienne-Comedic, F-21140 Semur-En-Auxois

Musee Eugene Boudin.
Place Erik Satie, F-14600 Honfleur

Musee Eugene Delacroix.
6 Place Furstenberg, F-75006 Paris

Musee Fabre.
13 Rue Montpellierat, F-34000 Montpellier

Musee Fernand Leger.
F-06410 Biot

Musee Fesch.
F-20000 Ajaccio

Musee Fontenille Mondiere.
10 Rue Barante, F-63300 Thiers

Musee Fragonard.
2 Rue Mirabeau, F-06130 Grasse

Musee Francais de la Photographie.
Mairie, F-91570 Bievres, 941 10 60
Permanent Collections:
History of Photography, techniques, artistry, illustrations, cinema.

Musee Garret.
F-70000 Vesoul

Musee Gaston-Coute.
Mairie, F-45130 Meung-Sur-Loire

Musee George Labit.
43 Rue des Martyrs de la Liberation, F-31500 Toulouse

Musee Girodet.
Hotel de Ville, F-45200 Montargis

Musee Goya.
Hotel de Ville, F-81100 Castres

Musee Granet.
Place Saint-Jean-De-Malte, F-13100 Aix-En-Provence

Musee Greuze.
Rue du College, F-71700 Tournus

Musee Grimaldi.
Chateau, F-06600

Musee Grobet-Labadie.
140 Blvd. Longchamp, F-13000 Marseille

Musee Guimet.
Place D'Iena, F-75016 Paris

Musee Guimet.
Blvd. des Belges, F-69000 Lyon

Musee Gustave Moreau.
Rue la Rochefoucault, F-75009 Paris

Musee Henri Matisse.
Hotel de Ville, F-59360 le Cateau

Musee Henri Rousseau.
F-53000 Laval

Musee Hippolyte de Parieu.
8 Place de la Paix, F-15000 Aurillac

Musee Historique.
F-50116 Le Mont-Saint-Michel

Musee Historique.
Place de la Reunion, F-68100
Mulhouse

Musee Historique.
Halle aux Bles, Place du
Marche, F-67210 Obernai, (88)
95 61 31

**Musee Historique de Troyes et de
la Champagne.**
Hotel de Vauluisant, F-10000
Troyes

Musee Historique des Tissus.
34 Rue de la Charite, F-69002
Lyon, (78) 37 15 05
Permanent Collections:
Collections among the richest
in the world recount 2,000
years of the history of the
fabric, especially silk fabric.
Main features of this unique set
are, first and foremost, Lyon
silk fabrics from the 17th to
20th century. Also, the bequest
of Copt fabrics and tapestries;
fabrics dating back before 1,000
A.D. and coming from the
Byzantine and Islamic
civilizations of the
Mediterranean basin; Italian
and Spanish silk fabrics from
the 14th-18th century. Persia
and Turkey, of the "Classical"
period (16th-18th century),
hold a privileged position with
an internationally famous
collection of carpets. Far
Eastern charm and delicacy
appear in several rooms as well
as dress (vestments and
costumes).

**Musee Historique et
Archeologique De l'Orleanais.**
Square Abbe-Desnoyers, Rue
Sainte-Catherine, F-45000
Orleans

Musee Historique Lorrain.
64 Grand-Rue, F-44000 Nancy

Musee Hotel Sandelin.
14 Rue Carnot, F-62500 St-
Omer

Musee Hyacinthe Rigaud.
Rue du Musee, F-66000
Perpignan

**Musee Industriel et Commercial,
Art et Metiers, Bibliotheque
Technique.**
2 Rue du Lombard, F-59000
Lille

Musee Ingres.
19 Rue de la Mairie, F-82000
Montauban

**Musee International de l'Image
Vie.**
Place Legarde, F-88000 Epinal

**Musee Internationale de la
Chasse.**
Chateau de Gien, F-45500
Gien, (38)67 24 11
Permanent Collections:
Paintings, tapestries, engravings
and arms presenting the
evolution of the hunt and and
the arts which it has inspired
from prehistory to the present.

Musee J.-J.Henner.
43 Ave. de Villiers, F-75017
Paris

Musee Jacquemart-Andre.
158 Blvd. Haussman, F-75008
Paris

Musee Jaquemart-Andre.
Abbaye De Chaalis, Ontaine
Chaalis, F-60305 Senlis

Musee Jean Aicard.
F-83210 Sollies-Pont

Musee Jean Aicard.
Les Lauriers Roses, F-83130 La
Garde

Musee Jean Laronze.
Rue du Chateau, F-71120
Charolles

Musee Jeanne d'Aboville.
Place de l'Esplanade F-02800
la Fere

Musee Jeanne d'Art.
C/O Hotel de Ville de Riom,
63200 Riom
Permanent Collections:
Collections include arms,
prehistoric documents, money,
faiences, "la charte
d'Alphonisme"; also a letter
signed by jean   d'Arc
addressed to her dear friends of
the city of Riom in 1492.

Musee Joseph Dechelette.
F-42300 Roanne

Musee Jourdain.
Palace Jean-Jaures, F-39400
Morez

Musee "La Folie Marco".
30 Rue Dr. Sultzer, F-67140
Barr

Musee Lamartine.
Hotel Senece, Rue Sigorgne, F-
71000 Macon

Musee Lambinet.
54 Blvd. de la Reine, F-78000
Versailles, 950-30-32
Permanent Collections:
Liturgical objects from the
Middle Ages; Works from the
18th century including
sculptures of Houdon; Armes
of N. N. Boutet; history of the
city of Versailles; documents on
the Revolution; drawings and
engravings.

Musee Lannelongue.
F-32410 Castera-Verduzan

Musee Lansyer.
Rue Lansyer, F-37600 Loches

Musee Lapidaire.
Ruines de l'Abbaye, F-76118
Jumieges

Musee Lapidaire d'Art Chretien.
Rue Blaze, F-13200 Arles

Musee Lapidaire d'Art Paien.
Place de la Republique, F-
13200 Arles

Musee Lapidaire Romain.
Saint-Pierre, F-38200 Vienne

Musee leBlanc-Duvernoy.
Rue d'Egleny, F-89000 Auxerre
Permanent Collections:
Fayences, tableaux, Greek
pottery and Merovingian
objects, member of the
Museums of Auxerre

Musee Ligier Richier.
Bibliotheque Municipale, F-
55300 St-Mihiel

Musee Lombart.
Rue du Musee, F-80600
Doullens

**Musee Lyonnais des Arts
Decoratifs.**
30-32 Rue de la Charite, F-
69000 Lyon, 37 15 05
Permanent Collections:
Recreation of French 18th
century salons with first-rate
furniture, objets d'art and
decorative pieces. There is
furniture made by the best 18th
century Parisian cabinet-makers
and a remarkable collection of
clocks, carpets and tapestries;
16th and 17th century Lyon
earthware, china and
silverware. Thus, the ambience
of an 18th century home is
established. The collection of
15th and 16th century Italian
majolicas, one of the most
important in France, is present
at the museum. The Middle
Ages and Renaissance are
represented by the Limoges
enamels, liturgical pieces,
ivories and some internationally
known tapestries ("Titus and
Vespasian," "Petrarchs
Triumphs" and "Presenting
Jesus with Fruit"). There is an
important collection of French,
Italian, German, Flemish and
Dutch drawings from the 16th-
19th centuries also located in
the museum.

Musee Magnin.
5 Rue Bons-Enfants, F-21000
Dijon

Musee Maraichin.
F-85800 St-Gilles Croix-De-Vie

Musee Marly.
"Le Chenil". F-78160 Marly-le-
Roi

Musee Marmottan.
2 Rue Louis-Boilly, F-75016
Paris

Musee Massey.
Jardin Massey, F-65000 Tarbes

Musee Matisse.
Ave. des Arenes, No. 164, F-
06000 Nice, 53 17 70
Permanent Collections:
Works of Henri Matisse
including paintings, sculpture,
drawings, engravings, maquettes
for the Chapelle de Vence,
gouaches decoupees, stained
glass, illustrated books and
personal objects belonging to
the artist.

Musee Millet.
F-77630 Barbizon

Musee Minal.
Place de l'Eglise, F-70400
Hericourt

Musee Municipal.
F-58210 Varzy

Musee Municipal.
F-59500 Douai

Musee Municipal.
F-77 Coulommiers

Musee Municipal.
F-52100 St-Dizier

Musee Municipal.
B.P. 102, 06503 Menton

Musee Municipal.
Mairie, F-37400 Amboise

Musee Municipal.
45 Rue Rigault, F-89100 Sens

Musee Municipal.
Place Carnot, F-27300 Bernay

Musee Municipal.
Rue du College, F-39100 Dole

Musee Municipal.
Blvd. Gassendi, F-04000 Digne

Musee Municipal.
Rue des Vignes, F-29210
Morlaix

Musee Municipal.
Mairie, F-77400 Lagny-Sur-
Marne

Musee Municipal.
Hotel de Ville, F-40500 St-
Sever

Musee Municipal.
54 Rue Emile-Zola, F-46000
Cahors

Musee Municipal.
15 Rue de l'Epee, F-59400
Cambrai

Musee Municipal.
Rue de Friedland, F-16000
Angouleme

Musee Municipal.
Abbaye de la Trinite, F-41100
Vendome

Musee Municipal.
11 Rue Camille-Buffardel, F-
26150 Die

Musee Municipal.
6 Rue Charles-Corbeau, F-
27000 Evreux

Musee Municipal.
Rue du Mont-De-Piete, F-
59380 Bergues

Musee Municipal.
Ave. de la Senatorerie, F-23000
Gueret

Musee Municipal.
Place Perraud, F-39000 Lons-
le-Saunier

Musee Municipal.
Hotel de la Bellegarde, F-58500
Clamecy

Musee Municipal.
Place Godart, F-51000
Chalons-Sur-Marne

Musee Municipal.
Hotel de Ville, F-71600 Paray-
le-Monial

Musee Municipal.
21 Rue Alexandre-Legros, F-
76400 Fecamp

Musee Municipal.
29 Cloitre Notre-Dame, F-
28000 Chartres

Musee Municipal.
Rue de la Poste, F-53200
Chateau-Gontier

Musee Municipal.
2 Rue de la Congregation, F-
02200 Soissons

Musee Municipal.
9 Rue de la Republique, F-83000 Draguignan

Musee Municipal.
15 Rue Victor-Hugo, F-38300 Bourgoin-Jaillieu

Musee Municipal.
Pl. Maurice Berteaux, F-78100 St-Germain en Laye

Musee Municipal.
Chateau, Place Verte, F-59163 Conde-Sur-l'Escault

Musee Municipal.
Chateau, Place General de Gaulle, F-67700 Saverne

Musee Municipal Antoine Vivenel.
2 Rue d'Austerlitz, F-60200 Compiegne

Musee Municipal Charbonneau-Lassay.
Rue De Martrey, F-86200 Loudon

Musee Municipal d'Art et d'Histoire.
Place du Musee, F-28100 Dreux

Musee Municipal d'Art et d'Histoire.
4 Place de la Legion d'Honneur, F-93200 St-Denis, 820 63 83

Musee Municipal de Cognac.
40 Blvd. Denfert-Rochereau, F-16100 Cognac, (45) 82 01 23
Permanent Collections:
Regional archaeology, history and ethnography along with painting, sculpture and decorative arts of Europe, 16th-20th century.

Musee Municipal de Limoges.
Place de la Cathedrale, F-87000 Limoges

Musee Municipal de Vierzon.
24 Rue des Changes, 24 Vierzon, (36) 75.29.93
Permanent Collections:
Archaeology from the Gallo-Roman period through the Middle Ages; porcelain; ceramics; local history.

Musee Municipal des Beaux-Arts.
2 Rue Paul-Doumer, Square Winston-Churchill, F-59200 Tourcoing

Musee Municipal des Ursulines.
5 Rue des Ursulines, F-71000 Macon

Musee Municipal Paul Valery.
F-34200 Sete

Musee Municipale.
2 Rue Quesnel-Moriniere, F-50200 Coutances

Musee Napoleonien.
Ile d'Aix

Musee National Adrien-Dubouche.
Place Winston-Churchill, F-87000 Limoges

Musee National de Ceramique de Sevres.
Place De la Manufacture, F-92310 Sevres

Musee National de la Maison Bonaparte.
Ajaccio
Permanent Collections:
Art and history collections relating to Napoleon as well as the furnishings of the chateau itself.

Musee National de la Renaissance.
Ecouen

Musee National de Prehistoire.
Chateau, F-24620 les Eyzies-De-Tayac

Musee National De Vallauris, Musee National Picasso.
Place De la Liberation; F-06220 Vallauris

Musee National des Arts et Traditions Populaires.
6 Route Du Mahatma Gandhi, F-75116 Paris

Musee National des Granges De Port-Royal.
Magny-les-Homeaux, F-78470 St.-Remy-les-Chevreuse

Musee National des Monuments Francais.
Palais de Chaillot, Place du Trocadero, F-75116 Paris

Musee National du Chateau de Compiegne.
F-60200 Compiegne

Musee National du Chateau de Fontainebleau.
F-77300 Fontainebleau

Musee National du Chateau de Pau.
2 Rue du Chateau, F-6400 Pau

Musee National du Chateau de Versailles.
F-78000 Versailles

Musee National du Message Biblique Marc Chagall.
Ave. du Docteur Menard, F-06000 Nice

Musee National Picasso. *See* Musee National De Vallauris, Musee National Picasso.

Musee Nationale.
Chateau, F-78600 Maisons-Laffitte

Musee Nissim de Camondo.
Rue de Monceau, F-75008 Paris

Musee Paul Arbaud.
2A Rue 4-Septembre, F-13100 Aix-En-Provence

Musee Paul Dubois-Alfred Boucher.
Rue Alfred Boucher, F-10400 Nogent-Sur-Seine

Musee Paul Dupuy.
13 Rue de la Pleau, F-31500 Toulouse

Musee Paul Landowsky.
14 Rue Max-Blondat, F-92100 Boulogne Billancourt

Musee Picasso
F-06600 Antibes

Musee Pierre Tauziac.
Montcaret, F-24230 Velines

Musee Pince.
32 bis rue Lenepveu, 49000 Angers
Permanent Collections:
Greek, Roman and Egyptian antiquities; Japanese art; Chinese art.

Musee Prehistorique.
Miln-le-Rouzic, F-11000 Carnac-Ville

Musee Reattu.
10, Rue du Grand-Prieure, F-13200 Arles

Musee Regional.
Place Richepanse, F-57400 Sarrebourg

Musee Regional Auvergne.
10 Bis Rue Delille, 63200 Riom
Permanent Collections:
A museum dedicated to the ancestors of Auvergne. Collections present the history of Auvergne and include regional and popular arts.

Musee Rene Davoine.
32 Rue Rene Davoine, F-71120 Charolles

Musee Rene Princeteau.
Mairie de Libourne, F-33500 Libourne

Musee Rodin.
77 Rue de Varenne, F-75007 Paris, 705.01.34-555.17.61

Musee Rodin.
Villa des Brillants, Ave. Auguste-Rodin, F-92190 Meudon

Musee Rolin.
3, Rue des Bancs, F-71400 Autun, 85-52-09-76

Musee Roybet-Foud.
Blvd. Saint-Denis, F-92400 Courbevoie

Musee Saint-Denis.
8, Chanzy, 51100 Reims

Musee Saint-Jean.
4 Boulevard Arago, 49000 Angers
Permanent Collections:
Edifice from the 12th century with tapestries "Le Chant du Monde" of Jean Lussat.

Musee Sarret-De-Grozon.
F-39600 Arbois

Musee Savoisien.
Square de Lannoy-De-Bissy, Chambery 73000
Permanent Collections:
Fine arts, ethnology and archeology.

Musee Sobirats.
112 Rue du College, F-84200 Carpentras

Musee St-Raymond.
Place St-Sernin, F-31500 Toulouse

Musee Tavet-Delacour.
Rue Lemercier, F-95300 Pontoise, 031 93 00

Permanent Collections:
Freundlich Donation, Charles Oulmont Library.

Musee Theodore Rousseau.
F-77630 Barbizon

Musee Theophile Jouglet.
Ave. Anatole-France, F-59410 Anzin

Musee Thomas Henry.
Hotel de Ville, F-50100 Cherbourg

Musee Toulouse-Lautrec.
Palaise de la Berberie, Albi

Musee Vasarely.
BP 4, F-84220 Gordes

Musee Victor Charreton.
15 Rue Victor-Hugo, F-38300 Bourgoin-Jaillieau

Musee Vivenel.
Rue du Grand-Ferre, F-60200 Compiegne

Musee Vulliod Saint-Germain.
3 Rue A.P.-Allies, F-34120 Pezenas

Musee Westercamp.
3 Rue du Musee, F-67160 Wissembourg

Musees d'Angers.
10 Rue du Musee, 49000 Angers, (41) 886465

Musees d'Auxerre.
Auxerre, (86) 52-69-45 OR 52-43-59
Permanent Collections:
Includes Musee d'Art, Musee d'Histoire Naturelle, Musee Leblanc-Duvernoy and Ancienne Abbaye Saint-Germain.

Musees de la Ville de Troyes.
Troyes
Permanent Collections:
Includes Musee de la Bonneterie, Musee Historiques de Troyes et de la Champagne, Musee d'Histoire Naturelle, Musee des Beaux-Arts et d'Archeologie

Musees Departmentaux de Loire-Atlantique.
Place Jean V, F-44000 Nantes

Musse Ochier.
Rue de l'Abbatiale, F-71250 Cluny

Nohan.
C/O Caisse Nationale des Monuments et des Sites, Paris 75004, 274-22-22

Nouveau Musee des Beaux-Arts.
Blvd. J.F. Kennedy, F-6600 Le Havre

Orangerie des Tuileries.
Place de la Concorde, Pavillon de l'Orangerie F-75001 Paris

Palais des Papes d'Avignon.
C/O Caisse Nationale des Monuments Historiques et des Sites, Paris 75004, 274-22-22

Palais Synodal ou Officialite.
F-89100 Sens

Pantheon.
C/O Caisse Nationale des
Monuments Historiques et des
Sites, Paris 75004, 274-22-22

Picasso Museum. *See* **Musee
Picasso**

Pierrefonds.
C/O Caisse Nationale des
Monuments Historiques et des
Sites, Paris 75004, 274-22-22

Princeteau, Rene, Museum. *See*
Musee Rene Princeteau

Reinach, Theodore, Foundation.
See **Fondation Theodore
Reinach**

Rigaud, Hyacinthe, Museum. *See*
Musee Hyacinthe Rigaud

Rodin Museum. *See* **Musee Rodin**

**Rothschild, Ephrussi De,
Foundation.** *See* **Fondation
Ephrussi de Rothschild**

Rousseau, Henri, Museum. *See*
Musee Henri Rousseau

Rousseau, Theodore, Museum. *See*
Musee Theodore Rousseau

Rupin, Ernest, Museum. *See*
Musee Ernest Rupin

Sainte-Chapelle.
Caisse Nationale des
Monuments Historiques et des
Sites, Paris 75004, 274-22-22

Salle des Mariages.
Mairie, F-06500 Menton

**Societe Archeologique de
Montpelier.**
5 Rue des Tresoriers-De-
France, Hotel de Lunaret, F-
34000 Montpellier
Permanent Collections:
Regional prehistory, regional
antiquity, Greek antiquities,
Middle Ages, 16th, 17th and
18th centuries.

Synagogue.
Rue Hebraique, F-84300
Cavaillon

Tauziac, Peirre, Museum. *See*
Musee Pierre Tauziac

Toulouse-Lautrec Museum. *See*
Musee Toulouse-Lautrec

Tresor de la Cathedrale.
F-10000 Troyes

**Tresor de la Cathedrale Saint-
Andre.**
Place de la Cathedrale, F-
33000 Bordeaux

**Tresor de la Cathedrale St.-
Etienne.**
Place de la Republique, F-
89100 Sens

Tresor de l'Eglise.
F-34440 Nissan-les-Enserume

**Union Central des Arts
Decoratifs- Musee des Arts
Decoratifs.**
107 Rue De Rivoli, 75001
Paris, 260-32-14

**Union Central des Arts
Decoratifs-Bibliotheque des Arts
Decoratifs.**
107rue de Rivoli, 75001 Paris

Valery, Paul, Municipal Museum.
See **Musee Municipal Paul
Valery**

Versailles. *See* **Musee National du
Chateau de Versailles**

**Vivenel, Antoine, Municipal
Museum.** *See* **Musee Municipal
Antoine Vivenel**

GHANA

Ghana National Museum.
P.O. Box 3343 Accra

GREECE

A. Goulandris Private Collection.
See **Goulandris, A., Private
Collection**

A. Iolas Private Collection. *See*
Iolas, A., Private Collection

A. Kounopis Private Collection.
See **Kounopis, A., Private
Collection**

A. Melas Private Collection. *See*
Melas, A., Private Collection

A. Sohos Museum. *See* **Sohos, A.,
Museum**

Acropolis Museum.
Acropolis, Athens

Agora Museum.
Stoa of Attalos II, Athens

**Amphiareion-Archaeological
Museum.**
Amphiaraos Ruins, Kalamos

**Antonopouleion Archaeological
Museum.**
Pylos, Messinia

Archaelogical Museum.
38 Filellinon St., Piraeus

**Archaeological & Folklore
Collection.**
Village Hall Aiani Kozani

Archaeological Collection.
Symi

Archaeological Collection.
Astros

Archaeological Collection.
Tanagra

Archaeological Collection.
Nea Anchialos

Archaeological Collection.
Bezesteni, Serrai

Archaeological Collection.
Library Dimitsana

Archaeological Collection.
Gymnasium, Megara

Archaeological Collection.
Mosque, Monemvassia

Archaeological Collection.
Village Hall, Tilos

Archaeological Collection.
Town Hall, Istriaia

Archaeological Collection.
Traianoupolis (Loutros)

Archaeological Collection.
Primary School, Katerini

Archaeological Collection.
Primary School, Katapola

Archaeological Collection.
Municipal Library, Lefkas

Archaeological Collection.
Elis Site, Kalyvia Ilidos

Archaeological Collection.
Girls' Orphanage, Kastoria

Archaeological Collection.
Main Square, Kastelli Kisamou

Archaeological Collection.
Trapeza Tis Parigoritissas Arta

Archaeological Collection.
Kosti Adosidi Pasha St.,
Neapolis

Archaeological Collection.
Mourdzinos Tower
Kardamly/Messina

Archaeological Collection.
Main Square, Public Library,
Kozani

Archaeological Collection.
Mayor's Residence, Molyvos
(Lesvos)

Archaeological Collection.
Primary School, Neos Skopos,
Serrai

Archaeological Collection.
Town Hall, Loutra Aidipsou
(Euboea)

Archaeological Collection.
Church of St. Antony at
Kastro, Sifnos

Archaeological Collection.
Papakonstandinou Mansion,
Lindos (Rodos)

Archaeological Collection.
Archaeological Site,
Mavromation, Messinia

Archaeological Collection.
Municipal Library, Prefecture
Offices, Lamia

Archaeological Collection.
Town Hall & Primary School,
Mandraki (Nissyros)

Archaeological Collection.
Iakovateios Public Library,
Lixouri (Kefallinia)

**Archaeological Collection of
Edessa.**
Yeni Cami, Mosque, Edessa

Archaeological Museum.
Tinos

Archaeological Museum.
Delos

Archaeological Museum.
Thira

Archaeological Museum.
Samos

Archaeological Museum.
Tegea

Archaeological Museum.
Kampos

Archaeological Museum.
Sikyon

Archaeological Museum.
Kavala

Archaeological Museum.
Skyros

Archaeological Museum.
Eressos

Archaeological Museum.
Mykonos

Archaeological Museum.
Thassos

Archaeological Museum.
Thermon

Archaeological Museum.
Salamis

Archaeological Museum.
Agrinion

Archaeological Museum.
Thyrreion

Archaeological Museum.
Chaironela

Archaeological Museum.
Plaka, Milos

Archaeological Museum.
Mosque, Chios

Archaeological Museum.
Vathy (Ithaki)

Archaeological Museum.
Garitsa, Corfu

Archaeological Museum.
Myrina (Limnos)

Archaeological Museum.
Myrina (Limnos)

Archaeological Museum.
Chora Trifylias

Archaeological Museum.
Eretria, Euboea

Archaeological Museum.
Palaia Korinthos

Archaeological Museum.
Gymnasium, Naxos

Archaeological Museum.
Gymnasium, Paros

Archaeological Museum.
Stavros (Ithaki)

Archaeological Museum.
Eynardeion Aigina

Archaeological Museum.
Mosque Kastellorizon

Archaeological Museum.
Sparti (Peleponnesus)

Archaeological Museum.
Argostolion, Kefallinia

Archaeological Museum.
1 Threpsiafi St., Thivai

Archaeological Museum.
Demeter Sanctuary, Elefsis

Archaeological Museum.
Artemis Sanctuary, Vravron

Archaeological Museum.
Palio Tapitouryion, Kalymnos

Archaeological Museum.
Vassilissis Olgas St., Argos

Archaeological Museum.
Despoina Sanctuary, Lykosoura

Archaeological Museum.
St. Francis Monastery, Chania

Archaeological Museum.
Asclepios Sanctuary, Epidavros

Archaeological Museum.
Archaeological Site, Samothraki

Archaeological Museum.
Yiokaleion Foundation,
Karystos

Archaeological Museum.
Near Phaneromeni Church,
Trikala

Archaeological Museum.
Near Altis, Olympia
(Peleponnesus)

Archaeological Museum.
Municipal Library, Platanos
(Leros)

Archaeological Museum.
Benakis Mansion, Benaki St.
Kalamata

Archaeological Museum.
42 Mezonos St., Patrai
(Peleponnesus)

Archaeological Museum.
21 el. Venizelou Ave., Chalkis,
Euboea

Archaeological Museum.
Plateia Syntagmato, Nafplion,
Peleponnesus

Archaeological Museum.
Arkadiou & Konstantinou
Paleologou Sts., Rethymnon
(Crete)

**Archaeological Museum of
Heraclion.**
Heraclion

Archaeological Museum of Pella.
Archaeological Site, Pella
(Macedonia)

**Archaeological Museum of
Rhodos.**
Museum Sq., Old Town, Rodos

**Archaeological Museum of
Thessaloniki.**
Plateia X an Thessaloniki,
(031) 830538
Permanent Collections:
Prehistoric - Classical Greek
and Roman sculpture, pottery,
jewelry and metalwork
including Vergina finds (Tomb
of Philip II).

Archaeological Museum of Veroia.
47 Anixeos St., Veroia

Archaeology Museum.
Kos

Archaeoogical Museum of Delphi.
Delphi, 0265-82313
Permanent Collections:
Pottery from early Helladic to
Hellenistic periods; Bronzes
from Geometric to Roman
periods; Sculpture from Archaic
to Roman periods; Gold and

Ivory Exhibits, 7th-5th
centuries B.C.

**Art Gallery of the Municipality &
Town of Mesolongion.**
Town Hall, Mesolongion

**Athanassakeion Archaeological
Museum.**
1 Athanassaki St., Volos

**Bassias, E., Historical & Folklore
Museum.**
Koryaleneios Library,
Argostolion

Benaki Museum.
1, Odos Koumbari, Athinai -
138
Permanent Collections:
Ancient Greek Art, chiefly
jewelry; Byzantine and Post-
Byzantine art; Icons,
manuscripts and minor crafts,
Greek popular art, costumes
and embroideries; Greek
historical relics; collections of
Islamic art and Chinese
porcelain; textiles and
embroideries from Near East
and Far East. A collection of
watercolors, engravings and
sketches. Historic archives
department, photographic
archives department and
library.

Benakis, L., Private Collection.
4 Neofytou Vamba St., Athens

Binos, H., Private Collection.
2 Harilaou Trikoupi St.,
Mytilini (Lesvos)

Byzantine Collection.
Royal Palace, Corfu

Byzantine Collection.
Mosque Chalkis, Euboea

**Byzantine Collection of
Katapoliani.**
Paros

Byzantine Museum.
Solomou Sq., Zakynthos

Byzantine Museum.
22 Vassilissis Sofias Ave.,
Athens

Byzantine Museum.
Church of the Panagia
Evangelistria, Tinos

**Byzantine Museum of the
Metropolis of Samos & Ikaria.**
Biship's Palace, Samos

Chozoviotissa Monastery.
Katapola

City Gallery.
YMCA Bldg., Thessaloniki

Collection of Agion Panton.
Cloister Varlaam, Meteora

Collection of Agios Stephanos.
Meteora

Collection of Boy's Gymnasium.
Secondary School, Chios

**Collection of Ecclestical Paintings
& Relics of Orthodoxy.**
Municipal Library, Lefkas

**Collection of Metropolis of
Xanthi.**
Bishop's Palace, Xanthi

**Collection of the Agathonos
Monastery.**
Near Ypati

**Collection of the Agia Laora
Monastery.**
Near Kalvryta

**Collection of the Arkadi
Monastery.**
Rethymnon (Crete)

**Collection of the Church of Agia
Marina.**
Kissos/Pilion

**Collection of the Church of the
Evangelistra.**
Kastron Agiou Georgiou

**Collection of the Church of the
Holy Apostles.**
Parga

**Collection of the Church of the
Koimissi Tis Theotokou.**
Panagitsa Pellis

**Collection of the Church of the
Panagia.**
Agiassos

**Collection of the Church of the
Panagia.**
Samarina, Grevena

**Collection of the Kavala
Metropolis.**
Bishop's Palace, Kavala

**Collection of the Koroni
Monastery.**
Near Karditsa

**Collection of the Likion Ton
Ellinidon, Rethymnon Branch.**
Prokymea el. Venezelou,
Rethymnon (Crete)

**Collection of the Mega Spileon
Monastery.**
Near Kalavryta

**Collection of the Mega Spileon
Monastery of St. Ignatios.**
Limonos Near Kalloni

**Collection of the Metropolis of
Kefallinia.**
Bishop's Palace, Argostolion,
Kefallinia

**Collection of the Metropolis of
Monemvassia & Sparti.**
Bishop's Palace, Sparti,
Peleponnesus

Collection of the Monastery.
Nea Moni

**Collection of the Monastery of
Agii Saranda.**
Sparti, Peleponnesus

**Collection of the Monastery of
Agios Andreas.**
Peratata, Kefallinia

**Collection of the Monastery of
Agios Nikolaos.**
Near Apoikia

**Collection of the Monastery of
Ossios Loukas.**
Near Steiri (Boeotia)

**Collection of the Monastery of
Ossios Nikanov.**
Zavorda

**Collection of the Monastery of
Profitis Ilias.**
Near Pyrgos (Thira)

**Collection of the Monastery of St.
John the Divine, Ypsilou.**
Antrissa

**Collection of the Monastery of the
Evangelismos Tis Thetokou.**
Agallianos, Mt.
Karafildzanakas, Skiathos

**Collection of the Monastery of the
Evangelistria.**
Skopelos

**Collection of the Monastery of the
Koimissis Tis Theotokou.**
Zerbitsa

**Collection of the Monastery of the
Odigtria Gonia.**
Kolymvari, Crete

**Collection of the Monastery of the
Timios Stravros.**
Mavradzei, Samos

**Collection of the Olympiotissa
Monastery.**
Elasson

**Collection of the Panagia
Tourlian.**
Ano Mera, Mykonos

**Collection of the Proussou
Monastery.**
Near Karpenission

**Collection of the Rendina
Monastery.**
Near Karditas

**Collection of the Tatarna
Monastery.**
Near Karpenission

**Decorative Arts Collection of the
Museum of Rhodes.**
Argyrokastrou Sq., Old Town,
Rodos

**E. Bassias Historical & Folklore
Museum. See Bassias, E.,
Historical & Folklore Museum**

**E. Kandis Private Collection. See
Kandis, E., Private Collection**

**E. Kaskines Private Collection.
See Kaskines, E., Private
Collection**

**E. Kastrinoyannis Private
Collection. See Kastrinoyannis,
E., Private Collection**

**E. Koutlidis Private Collection.
See Koutlidis, E., Private
Collection**

Ecclesiastical Collection.
Church of St. Nicholas,
Naoussa

Ecclesiastical Museum.
Mitropolitou Anthinmou St.
Joakeimideion Boys'
Orphanage, Komotini

**Ecclesiastical Museum of the
Metropolis of Trikki & Stagoi.**
Bishop's Palace, Trikala

**Eleftheriadis, T., Private
Collection.**
Petra (Lesvos)

**Exhibition of Contemporary Greek
Painters.**
Town Hall, Amfissa

Musee National de Conakry.
BP 561, Conakry

HAITI

Centre d'Art.
Rue de la Revolution, Port-Au-Prince

HONDURAS

Museo Regional de Arqueologia y Colonial.
Comayagua, P.M. Osmin Rivera Ortega

HONG KONG

Fung Ping Shan Museum of Chinese Art & Archaeology.
Institue of Oriental Studies of the University of Hong Kong

Hong Kong Museum of Art.
City Hall, Edinburgh Place

HUNGARY

Andras, Joza, Muzeum.
Egyhaz u. 15, P.O. Box 57, H-4401 Nyiregyhaza

Budapesti Torteneti Muzeum. *See* Kiscelli Muzeum (Budapesti Torteneti Muzeum

Egry Jozsef Emlekmuzeum.
Egry Jozsef Setany 12, H-8261 Badacsony

Ferenczy Muzeum.
Marx Ter 6, P.O. Box 103, H-2001 Szentendre, 92-73
Permanent Collections:
Permanent Collection of the Ferenczy family; Margit Kovacs Ceramics Collection; permanent collection of Jeno Barcsay; Museum of Bela Czabel; Memorial Museum of Jeno Kerenyi.

Gorogkeleti Szerb Egyhazmuveszeti Gyujtemeny.
Engels u. 5, H-2000 Szentendre

Hansagi Muzeum.
Lenin u. 101, H-9200 Mosonmagyarovar

Herman Otto Muzeum. *See* Otto, Herman, Muzeum

Hopp Ferenc Keletazsiai Muveszeti Muzeum.
Nepkoztarsasag Utja 103, H-1062 Buda Pest

Iparmuveszeti Muzeum.
Ulloi u. 33-37, P.O. Box 4, H-1450 Budapest, 175-222
Permanent Collections:
Masterpieces of European applied art. The Museum of Applied Arts, 1872-1972.

Janus Pannonius Muzeum.
Szechenyi ter 12, P.O. Box 158, H-7601 Pecs, 72/15222
Permanent Collections:
Modern Magyar Keptar (Gallery of Modern Hungarian Art), Csontvary Muzeum (works of Csontvary Kosztka Tivadar), Vasarely Muzeum

(Works of Victor Vasarely), Zsolnay Muzeum (Zsolnay Ceramics), Vitz Muzeum (Works of Bela Vitz), Gador Muzeum (Ceramics of Istvan Gador).

Joza Andras Muzeum. *See* Andras, Joza, Muzeum

Jozef, Katona, Muzeum.
Bethlen ter 75, P.O. Box 6, H-6001 Kecskemet

Katona Jozef Muzeum. *See* Jozef, Katona, Muzeum

Kereszteny Muzeum.
Berenyi Zsigmond u. 2, H-2500 Esztergom, ESZTERGOM 764
Permanent Collections:
Hungarian Gothic and Renaissance panel paintings, paintings by Italian masters, 13th-18th century paintings by foreign and Hungarian masters, 13th-19th century works of applied art, tapestries, Oriental rugs, Hungarian embroideries, ceramics, goldsmiths' work, numismatic collection and engravings.

Kina Muzeum (Iparmuvszeti Muzeum)
Gorkij Fasor 12, H-1068 Budapest

Kiscelli Muzeum (Budapesti Torteneti Muzeum)
Kiscelli u. 108, H-1037 Budapest

Koszta Jozaf Muzeum.
Szechenyi Liget 187, H-6600 Szentes

Liszr Ferenc Museum.
Majus 1. ter 1, P.O. Box 68, H-9401 Sopron

Magyar Nemzeti Galeria.
Dizsa Gyorgy Ut 41, 1062 Budapest

Magyar Nemzeti Galeria.
Budavari Palota, 1250 Budapest, P.O. Box 31 Budapest

Mora Ferenc Muzeum.
Roosevelt ter 1-3, P.O. Box 474, H-6701 Szeged

Mucsarnok.
Doza Gyorgy Ut 36, H-1134 Budapest

Munkacsy Mihaly Muzeum.
Szechenyi U. 9, H-5601 Bekescsaba

Nepmuveszeti Muzeum.
H-8710 Balatonszentgyorgy

Orszagos Zsido Vallasi Es Torteneti Gyujtemeny.
Dohany u. 2, H-1077 Budapest

Otto, Herman, Muzeum.
Szabadsag ter 3, P.O. Box 4, H-3501 Miskolc

Pannanhalmi Foapatsag Gyujtemenye.
Var 1, H-9090 Pannonhalma

Reformatus Kollegiumi Es Egyhazmuveszeti Muzeum.
Kalvin Ter 16, H-4001 Debrecen

Rippl-Ronai Muzeum.
Rippl-Ronai ter 1, P.O. Box 70, H-7401 Kaposvar

Szepmuvezeti Muzeum.
1146 Budapest, XIV Dozsa Gyorgy Ut 41

Tornyaijanos Muzeum.
Szanto Kovacs Janos u. 16, P.O. Box 2, H-6801 Hodmezovasarhely

Visky Karoly Muzeum.
Hunyadi u. 23, H-6300 Kalocsa

ICELAND

Listafn Einars Jonssonar.
Eiriksgata, P.O. Box 1051, Reyjavik, 13797
Permanent Collections:
Sculptures and painting, Einar Jonsson (1874-1954).

Thjodminjasafn.
Sudurgata, P.O. Box 1439, Reykjavik

INDIA

Amreli Archaeological & Art Museum.
Amreli, Gujarat

Andhra Kesari Yuvajana Samiti Museum.
Rajahmundry-2, Dist. East Godavari Andhra Pradesh

Archaeologial Museum & Picture Gallery.
Trichur Kerala

Archaeological Museum.
Hampi, Mysore

Archaeological Museum.
Biljapur, Mysore

Archaeological Museum.
Jhalawar, Rajasthan

Archaeological Museum.
Dampier Park, Mathura, Uttar Pradesh

Archaeological Museum for Chalcolithic Antiquities.
Ahar Near Udaipur, Rajasthan

Arts & Crafts Museum.
M.S. University of Baroda, Lokmanya Tilak Rd., Baroda,, Gujarat

Assam State Museum.
Gauhati-1 Assam

Asutosh Museum of Indian Art.
Univ. of Calcutta, Centenary Bldg., Calcutta-7000 12, West Bengal

Bangiya Sahitya Parisad Chitrasala.
243/1 Acharya Prafulla Chandra Rd., Calcutta-16 West Bengal

Bharat Kala Bhavan.
Banaras Hindu Univ., Varanasi-221005 Uttar Pradesh

Bharata Itihasa Samshodhaka Mandala Museum.
1321 Sadashiva, Poona-2 Maharashtra

Bhuri Singh Museum of Archaeology & Art.
Chamba, Himachal Pradesh

Birla Academy of Art & Culture Museum.
108-109 Southern Ave., Calcutta-700029 West Bengal

Central Archaeologial Museum.
Gujari Mahal, Fort Gwalior, Madhya Pradesh

Central Museum.
Museum Rd., Nagpur, Maharashtra

Crafts Museum.
Thapar House, 124 Janparth, New Delhi-1

Damerla Rama Rao Memorial Art Gallery.
Parade Grounds E, Rajahnmurdry Andra Pradesh

Dhar Museum of Arts & Crafts.
Dhar, Madhya Pradesh

Dogra Art Gallery.
Jammu, Jammu & Kashmir

Fort St. George Museum.
Fort St. George, Madras

Ganga Golden Jubilee Museum.
Bikaner, Rajasthan

Gaya Museum.
Riverside Rd., Gaya, Bihar

Government Museum & Art Gallery.
Sector 10-C, Chandigarh 160011

Government Museum of Art.
Srimanthi Bhavan, Mangalone, Mysore

Governmental Archaeological & Art Museum.
Alwar, Rajasthan

Haraprasad Sastri Museum.
Sanskrit College, Calcutta, West Bengal

Haryana Prantiya Puratatva Sangrahalaya.
Gurukul Jhajjar, Dist. Rohtak, Haryana

Heras Institute of Indian History & Culture.
Mahapalika Marg, Bombay 400 001, 266661
Permanent Collections:
Indian stone sculptures, metal images, woodwork, paintings, Mesopotamian seals, old and rare books and maps.

History Museum.
Ahmednagar College, Ahmednagar Maharashtra

Indian Institute of Art in Industry, Crafts Museum.
17 Park St., Calcutta-16, West Bengal

Indian Museum.
27 Jawaharlal Nehru Rd., Calcutta 700013

Indore Archaeological Museum.
Bombay Agra Rd., Indore-1, Madhya Pradesh

Junagadh Museum.
Sakker Baug, Junagadh-362001, Guarat, 745

INDONESIA

Permanent Collections:
Miniature paintings, old manuscripts, archaeological finds, old coins, bronzes, inscriptions, sculptures; stone memorial plates, silver utensils, carpets, glassware, stuffed animals, wooden objects, folk art, textiles, marble replicas and historical reference library.

Kannada Research Institute: Museum of Art & Archaeology.
Karnatak University Chotamahabalesh War Dharwar-580003, Mysore

Madras Government Museum.
Pantheon Rd., Egmore, Madras-8, 86274
Permanent Collections:
Archaeology, art, anthropology, ethnology, numismatics, zoology, botany and geology.

Maharaja Banaras Museum.
Fort Ram Nagar, Varanasi, Uttar Pradesh

Maharaja Sawaii Man Singh II Museum.
City Palace Jaipur 302002 Rajasthan, 74146
Permanent Collections:
Paintings, manuscripts, early printed books, arms and weapons, textiles and costumes, royal paraphernalia, transport, etc.

Mandan-Kala Bhavana.
Visva Bharati Univ., Kala-Bhavana Santinikenta-731235, West Bengal

Municipal Museum.
Allahabad, Uttar Pradesh

Musee d'Art et d'Archeologie.
18 Rue Docteur Villett, Tanarive

Museum & Art Gallery.
Univ. of Burdwan, Burdwan, West Bengal

Museum & Picture Gallery.
Sayaji Park, 5, Baroda, 390005

Museum of Art & Archaeology.
Vallabh Vidya Nagar Gujarat

Museum of Fine Arts.
Punjab University Chandigarh Punjab

Museum of the Central Glass & Ceramic Research Institute.
Calcutta, West Bengal

Nagarjunakonda Archaeological Museum.
Nagarjunakonda, Dist. Guntur, Andrha Pradesh

National Academy of Art.
Rabindra Bhavan, Ferozeshan Rd., 110001 New Delhi

National Gallery of Modern Art.
Dr. Zkir Husain Rd., New Delhi 110003

National Museum of India.
Janpath 11, New Delhi

Patel, Sardar V., Museum.
Sonifalia, Surat-395001, Gujarat

Prince of Wales Museum of Western India.
M. G. Rd., Fort, 400 023, Bombay, Maharashtra, 244484/244519
Permanent Collections:
Art, archaeology, painting and natural history.

Rajputana Museum of Archaeology.
Ajmer, Rajasthan

Rana Pratap Museum.
City Palace, Udaipur, Rajasthan

Salar Jung Museum.
Pathergatti Rd., Hyderbad-2 Andhra Pradesh

Sardar V. Patel Museum. *See* **Patel, Sardar V., Museum**

Shri Bhavani Museum & Library.
Aundh Dist. Satara, Maharashtra

Sibsagar College Museum.
Sibsagar College, P.O. Box Joysagar, Dist. Sibsagar, Assam

Sri Chitra Art Gallery- Gallery of Asian Paintings.
Trivandrum, Kerala

Sri Neenakshi Sudereswara Temple Museum.
Madurai Madras

State Archaeological Gallery.
33 Chittaranjan Ave., Calcutta-13 West Bengal

State Archeological Museum.
Public Gardens, Hyderabad, Andhra Pradesh 500004

State Chandradhari Museum.
Station Rd., Mansarobar Dighi House, Darbhanga Bihar

State Museum.
Benarasibagh, Lucknow, Uttar Pradesh

Taj Mahal & Fort of Akbar.
Agra, Uttar Pradesh

Tanjore Art Gallery.
Palace Bldg., Tanjore, Madras

University of Baroda, Museum of the Department of Archaeology & Ancient History:
Lokmanya Tilak Rd., Baroda, Gujrat

Venkata Vidya Sadan Museum of Art & Archaeology.
Rewa Vindhya Pradesh

Victoria Memorial Hall.
1 Queens Way, Calcutta-16 West Bengal

Watson Museum.
Jubilee Garden, Rajkot, Gujarat

INDONESIA

Museum Puri Lukisan Ratnawartha.
Ubud, Bali

Museum Radya Pustaka.
Sols, Surakarta Java

Nawab Salarjung Museum of Art.
Nawab Salarjung Andhra Pradesh

Patna Museum.
Patna-Gaya-Rd., Buddha Marg, Patna-1, Bihar

Sanur Museum.
Sanur, Bali

IRAN

All Saviour's Cathedral Museum.
Diocese of the Armenians in Iran & India, P.O. Box 4, New Julfa-Isfahan
Permanent Collections:
The museum houses and displays more than 700 ancient Armenian manuscripts, 450 paintings, miniatures and antique tombs. Portraits made by Armenian artists.

Astaneh QODS Museum.
Mashhad

Javaherat Saltanati Museum.
(Crown Jewels of Iran), Bank Markazi Iran, Ferdowis Ave., P.O. Box 632, Teheran, THN 21-2359 MARZABANK

Mohitshenasi Museum.
Bandar Abbas

Museum of the Mausoleum of Iman Raza.
Meched

Muze-Ye Honarhaye Melli.
Kamal-Ol-Mulk St., Teheran

Muze-Ye Honarhaye Tazini.
Amir Kabir St., Teheran

Myandoab Museum.
Myandoab

Napier Museum.
Dept. of Museums & Zoos, Trivandrum, Kerala

State Museum.
Chembukavu, Trichur, Kerala

IRAQ

Babylon Museum.
Babylon

Iraq Museum.
Museum Square, Baghdad, 36121-5 ANTIQUITY

Mosul Museum.
Dawassa, Mosul

National Museum of Modern Art.
Kifah St., Baghdad

IRELAND

Bunratty Castle & Museum.
Bunratty, Co. Clare

Charlemont House. *See* **Lane, Hugh, Municipal Gallery of Art; Charlemont House**

Lane, Hugh, Municipal Gallery of Art; Charlemont House.
Parnell Square 1, Dublin

Limerick Municipal Art Gallery & Museum.
Pery Sq., Limerick

National Gallery of Ireland.
Merrion Square W, 2 Dublin

National Museum of Ireland.
Kildare St., 2, Dublin

Westport House.
Westport, Co. Mayo

ISRAEL

Beit Immanuel.
18 Hibbat-Zion St., Ramat-Gan

Beit Shean Museum.
1 D St., Beit Shean

Beit Uri Verami Nechushtan.
Ashdot Yaakov Kibbutz

Bezalel National Art Museum.
(Israel Museum) Jerusalem

Ceramics Museum.
(Museum Haaretz) Ramat-Aviv, Tel-Aviv

Chagall House.
Painters & Sculptors Assn. of Israel, 24 Uno Ave., Haifa

Clark, Herbert E., Collection of Near Eastern Antiquities.
David Hamelech St., yMCA Bldg., Jerusalem

Crusader Church.
Lazarite Monastery, Resurrection Church Abu-Gosh

Ethnologial Museum & Folklore Archives.
Shabtay Levy Str. 26, Haifa 5333, 523-255
Permanent Collections:
Jewish ethnology: costumes, jewels, etc. Jewish ceremonial art, Black African sculptures and masks, Ecuadorian Indian costumes, Portuguese folk art and Yugoslavian folk costumes.

Greek Orthodox Patriarchiate.
St. Dimitri St., Jerusalem

Haaretz Museum.
P.O. Box 17068, Tel-Aviv 61170

Haaretz Museum (Glass Museum)
Ramat-Amiv, Tel-Aviv

Herbert E. Clark Collection of Near Eastern Antiquities. *See* **Clark, Herbert E., Collection of Near Eastern Antiquities**

Herzliya Museum.
Bar Ilan St., Herzliya, 03-981011
Permanent Collections:
Paintings, graphics and sculpture, especially of Israeli artists. Some European artists.

Israel, Wilfrid, House for Art & Oriental Studies.
Hazorea Kibbutz, Post Hazorea 30060

Israel Museum.
P.O. Box 1299 Hakirya, 91000 Jeruselum

Israel Museum, Billy Rose Art Garden.
Jerusalem

Jerusalem Artists House.
Beit Ha' Omanim, 12 Shmuel Managid St., Jerusalem

L.A. Mayer Memorial Institute for Islamic Art. *See* **Mayer, L.A., Institute for Islamic Art**

Mayer, L.A., Institute for Islamic Art.
2 Palmach St., Jerusalem

Mishkan Le' Omanut Museum of Art.
Ein Harod 18965

Modern Art Gallery.
Eilat

Municipal Museum Glicenstein.
P.O. Box 1006, Safes

Museum Dor Vador.
58 King George St., Hechal Shifomo Jerusalem

Museum Hanita.
Byzantine Church, Hanita

Museum of Ancient Art.
26 Shabetai Levi St., Haifa, 254604
Permanent Collections:
Sculpture, Egyptian collection, pottery, coins, jewelry, seals, plaster copies of Greek sculptures and Islamic collection.

Museum of Ethnography and Folklore.
(Museum Haaretz) Ramat-Aviv, Tel-Aviv

Museum of Modern Art.
26 Shabtai Levi St., Haifa

Muze-Ye Iran Bastan.
Ghawan Saltaneh, Teheran

Negev Museum.
Atzma'uth St., Municipality Beersheba

Polombo Museum.
Mt. Zion, P.O. Box 8110, Jerusalem

Rose, Billy, Art Garden. *See* **Israel Museum, Billy Rose Art Garden**

Rybak Museum.
Ramat Joseph, Hadaci St., Bat-Yam

Tel-Aviv Museum.
Helena Rubinstein Pavilion, 6 Tarsat St., Tel-Aviv

Tiberias Museum of Antiquities.
On the Sea Front, P.O. Box 283, Tiberias

Titotkin Museum of Japanese Art.
89 Hanassi Ave., Haifa 34 642

Wilfrid Israel House for Art & Oriental Studies. *See* **Israel, Wilfrid, House for Art & Oriental Studies**

Yad-Lebanim Memorial Center.
Habanim St., Rehovot

Youth Wing of the Israel Museum.
Jerusalem

ITALY

Albertina Collection. *See* **Galleria dell'Accademia Albertina**

Antiquarium.
I-66040 Altino

Antiquarium.
Nei Locali dell'Edificio Romano, I-06031 Bevagna

Antiquarium.
Via Marco Mario 22, I-800053 Castelammare di Stabia

Antiquarium degli Scavi.
Megara Hyblaea, I-96011 Augusta

Antiquarium della Cattedrale.
Annesso Alla Cattedrale, I-800053 Castellamara Di Stabia

Antiquarium di Villa Aurea.
Villa Aurea, I-92100 Agrigento

Appartamenti Monumentali.
Palazzo Pitti, Piazza Pitti, 1, 50125 Florence

Archivo di Stato di Siena.
Via Bachi di Sotto 52, I-53100 Siena

Bailo, Luigi, Civic Museum. *See* **Museo Civico Luigi Bailo**

Basilica San Apollinare in Classe.
I-48100 Ravenna

Basilica San Vitale.
Via San Vitale, I-48100 Ravenna

Biblioteca della Sopritendenza.
Piazza S. Agostino, Modena

Biblioteca-Pinacoteca Comunale, Museo della Fauna e della Flora dell'Appennino.
I-62028 Sarnano (Macerata), Piazza Perfetti

Cabinetto dei Disegni Stampe.
Nel Palazzo degli Uffizi, I-501000 Florence

Camera di S. Paolo.
Via Melloni, I-43100 Parma

Camposanto.
Piazza Duomo, I-56100 Pisa

Cappelle Medicee.
S. Lorenzo, I-50123 Florence

Casa Buonarroti.
Via Ghibellina 70, I-50122 Florence

Casa Romei.
Via Savonarola 30, I-44100 Ferrara

Casa Vasari.
Via XX Settembre 59, I-52100 Arezzo

Casina Cinese.
Parco della Favorita, I-90146 Palermo

Castromediano, Sigismundo, Museum. *See* **Museo Provinciale "Sigismundo Castromediano"**

Cavoti, Pietro, Museum. *See* **Museo d'Arte "Pietro Cavoti"**

Cenacolo della Grazie.
Piazza Santa Maria della Grazie, I-20123 Milano

Cenacolo di Foligno e Galleria "Feroni".
Via Faenza 42, I-50123 Firenze

Cenacolo di Ognissanti.
Piazza Ognissanti 42, I-50123 Florence

Cenacolo di San Salivi.
Via Andrea del Sarto 16, I-50135 Florence

Cenacolo di Sant'Apollonia.
Via XXVII Aprile 1, I-50100 Florence

Cenacolo di Santo Spiritto e Fondazion "Salvore Romano".
Piazza Santo Spiritto, I-50125 Florence

Chiostri Monumentali di Santa Maria Novella e Cappella degli Spagnoli.
Piazza Santa Maria Novella, I-50123 Firenze

Chiostro della Scalzo.
Via Camillo Cavour 69, I-50129 Florence

Civiche Raccolte Archeologiche e Numismatiche di Milano.
Castello Sforzesco, I-20121 Milan, (02) 620 83119

Civiche Raccolte de Arte Applicata.
Piazza Castello, 20122 Milan

Civico Museo di Storia de Arte.
Via della Cattedrale 15, I-34121 Trieste

Civico Museo Ingauno.
Piazza San Michele, I-17031 Albenga

Civico Museo "Morpurgo".
Via Imbriani 5, I-34122 Trieste

Civico Museo Revoltella - Galleria d'Arte Moderna.
Via Armando Diaz 27, Trieste

Civico Museo Sartorio.
Largo Papa Giovanni XXIII 1, I-34123 Trieste

Collezioni Comunali d'Arte.
Palazza del Comune, I-40126 Bologna

Cordici, Antonio, Museum. *See* **Museo "Antonio Cordici"**

Eusebio Museum. *See* **Museo Archaeologico "Federico Eusebio"**

Fattori, Giovanni, Civic Museum. *See* **Museo Civico "Giovanni Fattori"**

Ferrari, Giulio, Civic Museum. *See* **Museo Civico "Giulio Ferrari"**

Fondazione "Horne". *See* **Horne, Herbert Percy, Fondazione**

Gabinetto Nazionale delle Stampe.
Via della Lungara 230, I-00165 Rome

Galeria d'Arte.
Palazzo Casali, I-52044 Cortona

Galeria Nazionale d'Arte Moderna.
Viale della Belle Arti, 131, I-00197 Rome

Galleria "Anna e Luigi Parmeggiani".
Corso Cairoli 2, I-42100 Reggio Emilia

Galleria Borghese.
Piazzale Scipione, Borghese 00197 Rome

Galleria Civica di Arte Moderna.
Via Aldo Casotti, Villa Serra, I-16167 Genova-Nervi

Galleria Colonna.
Palazzo Colonna, Via della Pilotta 17, I-00187 Rome

Galleria Comunale.
Palazzo Pretorio, I-50047 Prato

Galleria Comunale d'Arte.
Viale Regina Elena, Giardini Pubblici, I-09100 Cagliari

Galleria Comunale d'Arte Moderna.
Palazzo Collicola, I-06049 Spoleto

Galleria Comunale d'Arte Moderna.
Palazzo di San Pantaleo 10, I-00186 Rome

Galleria Comunale d'Arte Moderna.
Piazz della Constituzione 6, I-40100 Bologna

Galleria Corsini.
Via di Parione 10, I-50123 Florence

Galleria d'Arte.
Palazzo della Provincia, I-66100 Chieti

Galleria d'Arte.
Piazza Edmondo de Amicis 2, I-34170 Gorizia

Galleria d'Arte Antica.
Piazza Liberta 7, I-34132 Trieste

Galleria d'Arte del Colegio Alberoni.
Via Emilia Parmense 77, I-29100 Piacenza

Galleria d'Arte Moderna.
Villa Reale, I-20100 Milano

Galleria d'Arte Moderna.
Via dei Musei 81, I-25100 Brescia

Galleria D'arte Moderna.
Via Rigaste Redentore, I-37100 Verona

Galleria d'Arte Moderna.
Palazzo Pitti, Piazza Pitti, 1, 50125 Florence

Galleria d'Arte Moderna Carlo Rizzada.
Via del Paradiso, I-32032 Feltre

Galleria d'Arte Moderna di Palazzo PiHi.
Piazza PiHi 1, I-50125 Florence

Galleria d'Arte Moderna "Ricci Oddi".
Via S. Siro 13 I-29100 Piacenza

Galleria d'Arte Sacra Contemporanea.
Cittadella Christana, I-06081 Assisi

Galleria d'Arte Sacra dei Contemporanei.
Via Giovanni Terruggia 14, I-20162 Milan

Galleria Degli Uffizi.
Piazzale Degli Uffizi, 50125 Florence

Galleria del Palazzo Reale.
Via Balbi 10, I-16126 Genoa

Galleria della Accademia.
Via della Accademia, I-50122 Florence

Galleria della Antiche Ceramiche Abruzzesi.
Palazzo del Barone Giacomo Acerbo, I-65014 Lereto Aprutino

Galleria della Collegiata.
Collegiatta di Sant'Andrea, I-50053 Empoli

Galleria dell'Acamedia Carrara.
Piazza Giacomo Carrara 82, I-24100

Galleria dell'Accademia.
Campo della Carita, I-30121 Venice

Galleria dell'Accademia Albertina.
Via Accademia della Science 6, I-10123 Turin

Galleria dell'Accademia di Belle Arti.
Via Bellini 37, I-80135 Naples

Galleria dell'Accademia di San Luca.
Piazza dell'Accademia di S. Luca 77, I-00187 Rome

Galleria dell'Accademia "Tadini".
Piazza Garibaldi 1, I-24065 Lovere

Galleria di Palazzo Bianco.
Via Garibaldi 11, 16100 Genda

Galleria di Palazzo Rosso.
Via Garibaldi 18, I-16124 Genoa

Galleria Doria Pamphilj.
Piazza de Collegio Romano 1a, I-00186 Rome

Galleria e Museo del Palazzo Ducale.
Piazza Sordello, 46100 Mantua

Galleria e Museu Mediovale e Moderno.
Palazza di Guilio III, Via San Lorentino 8, I-52100 Arezzo

Galleria "Giannoni".
Palazzo del Broletto, I-28100 Norvara

Galleria Giorgio Franchetti alla Ca'd'Oro.
I-30100 Venice

Galleria Nazionale.
Palazzo Pilotta, Via della Pilotta 4, I-43100 Parma

Galleria Nazionale d'Arte Antica.
Palazzo Corsini, Via della Lungara 10, I-00165 Rome

Galleria Nazionale d'Arte Antica.
Palazzo Barberini, Via Quattre Fontane 13, I-00184 Rome

Galleria Nazionale della Sicilia.
Via Allora 6, I-90133 Palermo

Galleria Nazionale delle Marche.
Palazzo Ducale, Piazza Duca Federico 1, I-61029 Urbino

Galleria Nazionale dell'Umbria.
Palazzo del Priori, Corso Vannuci, 06100 Perugia

Galleria Nazionale di Palazzo Spinola.
Piazza di Pellicceria 1, I-16123 Genoa, 206.870-205.590

Galleria Ospedale degli Innocenti.
Piazzo della SS. Annunziata 12, I-50100 Florence

Galleria Palatina di Palazzo Pitti.
Piazza Pitti 1, I-50125 Florence, 214579

Galleria Pallavicini.
Palazzo Pallavicini, Via XIIV Maggio 45, I-00100 Rome

Galleria Querini Stampalia.
San Zaccaria 4778, I-30122 Venice

Galleria Sabauda.
Via Accademia delle Science 6, I-10123 Turin

Galleria Spada.
Piazza Capodiferro 3, I-00186 Rome

Gallerina e Museo Estense.
Piazza S Agostino, Milan

Gipsoteca.
Castello, I-70122 Bari

Horne, Herbert Percy, Fondazione.
Via Del Benci 6, I-50122 Firenze, 283348

Lalit Kala Akademi.
Rabindra Bhavan, Ferozeshan Rd., 110001 New Delhi

Mattese, Giovanni, Civic Museum.
See Museo Civico "Giovanni Mattese"

Mausoleo di Galla Placidia.
I-48100 Ravenna

Monumenti Musei E Gallerie Pontifice.
Vatican City

Mostra Permanente dei Cimeli della Biblioteca Marciana.
Piazzetta S. Marco 7, Libreria Vecchia, I-30124 Venezia

Musei Capitolini.
Piazza del Campidoglio 1471, 00100 Rome

Musei Civici.
Piazza Mosca 8, I-61100 Pesaro

Musei Civici.
Piazza della Motta 4, I-21100 Varese

Musei Civici.
Piazza Medaglie d'Oro 1, I-22100 Como

Museo "Ala Ponzone".
Via Uglino Dati 2, I-26100 Cremona

Museo "Alessi".
Piazza Duomo, I-94100 Enna

Museo Annesso alla Basilica di San Domenico.
Piazza San Domenico 13, I-40124 Bologna

Museo Annesso alla Chiesa dei SS Pietro e Paolo.
I-53022 Buonconvento

Museo Annesso Alla Societa di Esecutori di Pie Disposizioni.
Via Roma 71, I-53100 Siena

Museo Annesso all'Opificio di Pietre Dure.
Via degli Alfani 78, I-50121 Florence

Museo Antoniano.
Annesso alla Basilica, I-35100 Padova

Museo "Antonio Cordici".
Piazza Umberto I, I-91016 Erice

Museo Archaeologico "Federico Eusebio".
Presso il Liceo Govone, I-12051 Alba

Museo Archelogico Nazionale.
Piazza Cavour, I-80135 Naples

Museo Archeologico.
Via Roma 1, I-33100 Aquileia

Museo Archeologico.
Via della Sapienza, I-53100 Siena

Museo Archeologico.
Palazza dell'Ateneo, I-70122 Bari

Museo Archeologico.
Piazza Cittadella, I-24100 Bergamo

Museo Archeologico.
Casa del Popolo, I-58040 Vetulonia

Museo Archeologico.
Piazzetta S. Marco 17, I-30124 Venice

Museo Archeologico.
Palazzo di Bellino, Corso Alfieri, I-14100 Asti

Museo Archeologico al Teatro Romano.
Via Rigaste Redentore, I-37100 Verona

Museo Archeologico Mecenate.
Via Margaritone, Convento di San Bernardo, I-52100 Arezzo

Museo Archeologico Nazionale.
Piazza Olivella, I-90133 Palerma

Museo Archeologico Nazionale.
Via XX Settembre 124, I-44100 Ferrara

Museo Archeologico Nazionale.
Piazza Indipendenza 7, I-09001 Cagliari

Museo Archeologico "Oliveri".
Palazzo Almerici, Via Mazza 97, I-61100 Pesaro

Museo Archeologico Provinciale.
Via San Benedetto, I-84100 Salerno

Museo Arcivescovile.
Plaza dell'Arcivescovado 1, I-48100 Ravenna

Museo "Aurelio Castelli".
Via dell'Osservanza 7, I-53100 Siena

Museo Bandini.
Via Givannidupre, I-50014 Fiesole

Museo Bardini.
Piazza De'Mozzi 1, I-50125 Florence

Museo Barracco.
Corso Vittorio Emanuele 168, I-00186 Rome

Museo "Borgona".
Via Antonio Borgogna 1, I-3100 Vercelli

Museo Camuno.
Via Garibaldi 6, I-25043 Breno

Museo Capitolare.
Piazza San Rufino, I-06081 Assisi

Museo Capitolare.
Via Fabio Filzi 4, I-00049 Velletri

Museo Capitolare.
Ammesso al Duomo, I-06012 Citta di Castello

Museo Capitolare.
Annesso alla Cattedrale, Via Roma, I-64032 Atri, 085-87241
Permanent Collections:
Paintings from the 16th century to 18th century, pottery (17th and 18th century), silvers (17th and 18th centuries), wood carvings (15th-20th century), codices (11th-15th century) and incunabula.

Museo Capitolare della Cattedrale.
Piazza del Duomo, I-51100 Pistoia

Museo Civico.
I-92027 Licata

Museo Civico.
I-07017 Ploaghe

Museo Civico.
Via Garibaldi 74, Monselice

Museo Civico.
Via Portica 2, I-06081 Assisi

Museo Civico.
Via Provesi 41, I-43011 Busseto

Museo Civico.
Corso Umberto I 63, I-20075 Lodi

Museo Civico.
Corso Cavour 8, I-70051 Barletta

Museo Civico.
Corso Garibaldi, I-20051 Legnano

Museo Civico.
Via Lorenzo Luzzo, I-32032 Feltre

Museo Civico.
Palazzo Comunale, I-51100
Pistoia

Museo Civico.
Palazzo Comunale, I-00049
Velletri

Museo Civico.
Palazzo del Popolo, I-63100
Ascoli

Museo Civico.
Via del Duomo 20, I-06049
Spoletto

Museo Civico.
Loggia del Capitano, I-31011
Asolo

Museo Civico.
Via S. Maria 11, I-86042
Baranello

Museo Civico.
Palazzo Gottifredo, I-03011
Alatri

Museo Civico.
Nella Rocca, I-38066 Riva del
Garda

Museo Civico.
Via Pietro Micca 38, I-13051
Biella

Museo Civico.
Via Cacciatori Alpi 9, I-12100
Cuneo

Museo Civico.
Piazza del Duomo 16, I-32100
Belluno

Museo Civico.
Palazzo Comunale, I-52046
Lucaignano

Museo Civico.
Via Archiginnasio 2, I-40124
Bologna

Museo Civico.
Piazza Santo Stefano, I-51017
Pescia

Museo Civico.
Via Ludovico Grossi 28, I-
46019 Viadana

Museo Civico.
Via Museo 4, I-36061 Bassano
del Grappa

Museo Civico.
Via Contessa Matilde 1, I-
67010 Bazzano

Museo Civico.
Piazza dell'Annunziata, I-67039
Sulmona

Museo Civico.
Piazza Matteotti, I-58024
Massa Marittima

Museo Civico.
Via Cassa di Risparmio 14, I-
39100 Bolzano

Museo Civico.
Torrione del Castello, I-26026
Pizzighettone

Museo Civico.
Via del Museo Civico, I-90018
Termini Imerese

Museo Civico.
Chiesa di Santa Maria della
Verita I-0110 Viterbo

Museo Civico.
Chiesa Di Santa Marie Della
Verita I-0110 Viterbo

Museo Civico.
Piazza Martiri 23, Maggio, I-
10053 Canosa di Puglia

Museo Civico.
Palazza dell Scuole, Via Roma,
I-12041 Bene Vagienna

Museo Civico.
Palazzo Chiericati, Piazza
Matteotti, I-36100 Vicenza

Museo Civico.
Palazzo Communale, Via Ricci
15, I-53045 Montepulciano

Museo Civico Archeologico.
Piazza del Municipio 383, I-
92100 Agrigento

**Museo Civico dei Monumenti
Genovesi.**
Piazza R. Negri, Nell'ex Chiesa
di S. Agostino, I-16123 Genoa

**Museo Civico di Archeologia
Ligure.**
Villa Durazzo Pallavicini, I-
16155 Genova-Pegli

Museo Civico di Arte Antica.
Palazzo Madam, I-10125 Turin

**Museo Civico di Etnografia e
Folklore Calabrese "R. Corso".**
Palazzo Municipale, I-89015
Palmi

Museo Civico di Padua.
Piazza del Santo, 10 Padua

**Museo Civico di Storia e Arte
Mediovale e Moderna.**
Palazzo dei Musei, Piazza S.
Agostino 337, I-41100 Modena

Museo Civico di Torino.
Via Magenta, 31 10128 Torino,
541-822

**Museo Civico e Galleria d'Arte
Antica e Moderna.**
Castello, I-33100 Udine

Museo Civico "Giovanni Fattori".
Piazza Belle Arti 1, I-57100
Livorno

Museo Civico "Giovanni Mattese".
I-80075 Forio d'Ischia

Museo Civico "Giulio Ferrari".
Nel Castello dei Pio, Piazza dei
Martiri, I-41012 Carpi

Museo Civico Luigi Bailo.
Borgo Cavour, I-31100 Treviso

Museo Comunale.
I-00019 Tivoli

Museo Comunale.
Palazzo Ducale, I-61049
Urbania

Museo Correale di Terranova.
Via Correale 50, I-80067
Sorrento

Museo d'Arte Antica.
Castello Sforzesco, Milan

**Museo d'Arte d'Ammobiglia-
Mento.**
Nella Villa Ex Reale, I-10040
Stupinigi

**Museo d'Arte Industriale e
Galleria Davia Bargellini.**
Via Maggiore 44, I-40125
Bologna

Museo d'Arte Moderna.
Palazzo Pesaro a San Stae, I-
30100 Venice

**Museo d'Arte Orientale "Eduardo
Chiossone".**
I-16100 Genoa

Museo d'Arte "Pietro Cavoti".
Via Umberto I 30, I-73013
Galatina

Museo d'Arte Sacra.
I-53042 Chianciano

Museo d'Arte Sacra.
Via Collegiata 1, I-53041
Asciano

Museo d'Arte Sacra.
Via IV Novembre, I-55041
Camaiore

**Museo de Arte Estremo Orientale
e di Etnografia.**
Via Mose Bianchi 94, I-20149
Milano

Museo de Capodimonte.
Reggia di Capodimonte, Naples

Museo degli Argenti.
Palazzo Pitti, I-50125 Florence

Museo degli Argenti.
C/O Palazzo PiHi, 50125
Florence

Museo degli Arredi Sacri.
Via de Santuario, I-01030
Castel Sant'Elia

Museo del Castello.
I-00062 Bracciano

Museo del Castello.
Castello Visconteo, I-27100
Pavia

Museo del Cenedese.
Piazza Marcantonio Flaminio,
I-31029 Vittorio Veneto

Museo del Corallo.
Piazza L. Palomba 6, I-80059
Torre del Greco

Museo del Duomo.
Piazza del Duomo, I-04024
Gaeta

Museo del Duomo.
Piazza del Duomo 12, I-20122
Milan

Museo del Duomo.
Via Nicola Monterisi 2, I-
84100 Salerno

Museo del Marmo.
Presso l'Accademia di Belle
Arti, I-54033 Carrara

Museo del Palazzo Comunale.
I-60047 Sassoferrato

Museo del Sannio.
Piazza Matteotti, I-82100
Benevento

**Museo del Santurio di Nostra
Signora Misericordia.**
Piazza Santuario 6, I-17100
Savona

**Museo del Seminario
Arcivescovile.**
Piazza S. Francesco, I-53100
Siena

**Museo del Tesoro della
Cattedrale.**
Piazza S. Eusebio, I-13100
Vercelli

Museo del Tesoro di San Lorenze.
Annesso alla Cattedrale, I-
16123 Genoa

Museo dell Abbazia.
I-03020 Casamari

Museo dell Badia Greca.
Croso del Popolo 128, I-00046
Grotta-Ferrata

Museo dell Istituto Statale d'Arte.
Piazzetta Salazar 6, I-80132
Napoli

Museo della Badia.
I-84013 Cava dei Tirreni

**Museo della Basilica di Santa
Maria degli Angeli.**
Annesso alla Basilica, I-06081
Assisi

**Museo della Basilica di Santa
Maria della Grazie.**
Piazza Masaccio 9, I-52027 San
Giovanni Valdarno

**Museo della Capella di Santa
Maria della Pieta dei Sangro.**
Via dei Sanctis 19, I-80100
Naples

**Museo della Casa Fiorentina
Antica.**
Via Portarossa 13, I-50123
Florence

Museo della Cattedrale.
Annesso alla Cattedrale, I-
67039 Sulmona

Museo della Cattedrale.
Nel Palazzetto a Fianco della
Chiesa, I-24024 Gandino

Museo della Ceramica.
Via Roma 10, I-95041
Caltagirone

Museo della Cetosa.
Palazzo Ducale, I-27100 Pavia

**Museo della Chiesa di Santa
Maria Maggiore.**
I-06038 Spello

Museo della Collegiata.
I-29014 Castell'Arquato

**Museo della Congregazione dei
Pardi Armeni.**
Mechitarisi di Venezia, Isola

**Museo della Fauna e della Flora
dell'Appennino.** *See* Biblioteca-
Pinacoteca Comunale, Museo
della Fauna e della Flora
dell'Appennino

Museo della Prepositura.
I-51010 Montecatini
Valdinievole

Museo della Rocca dei Sanvitale.
I-43012 Fontanellato

Permanent Collections:
Frescoes, arms, pictures and
furniture.

Museo della Sibaritide.
Via Taranto, I-87070 Sibari
Stazione

Museo della Villa Bettoni.
I-25080 Bogliaco

**Museo dell'Abbazia di San
Colombano.**
Piazza Santa Fara, I-29022
Bobbio

Museo dell'Accademia Etrusca.
Palazzao Casali, I-52044
Cortona

**Museo dell'Accademia Ligustica di
Belle Arti.**
Piazza de Ferrari 5, I-16128

Museo dell'Arte Serica.
Scuolo di Setifico, I-22100
Como

Museo delle Terme. *See* **Museo
Nazionale Romano**

Museo dell'Eta Cristiani.
Via Piamarta 4, I-25100 Brescia

Museo dell'Opera del Duomo.
I-44100 Ferrara

Museo dell'Opera del Duomo.
Piazza del Duomo, I-53100
Siena

Museo dell'Opera del Duomo.
Piazza del Duomo 49, I-50047
Praro

Museo dell'Opera del Duomo.
Piazza del Duomo 9, I-50122
Florence

Museo dell'Opera del Duomo.
Palazzo dei Canonici, I-06100
Perugia

Museo dell'Opera del Duomo.
Palazzo dei Papi, Piazza del
Duomo, I-05018 Orvieto

Museo dell'Opera di Santa Croce.
Piazza Santa Croce 6, I-50122
Florence

Museo Demidof.
San Martino, I-57037
Portoferraio

Museo di Antichita.
Via Accademia della Science 6,
I-10123 Turin

Museo di Arte Cinese.
Via San Martino 8, I-43100
Parma

**Museo di Arte Estremo Orientale
e di Etnografia.**
Via Mose Bianchi 94, I-20149
Milano

Museo di Arte Sacra.
Via Matteo Bonello 2, I-90134
Palermo

Museo di Arte Sacra.
Annesso alla Basilica, I-53037
San Gimignano

Museo di Castello Ursino.
Piazza Federico di Svezia, I-
95121 Catania

Museo di Castelvecchio.
Corso Cavour, I-37100 Verona

Museo di Convento Dominicano.
Piazza XVI Maggio, I-96017
Noto

Museo di Diefenbach.
Convento Certosa, I-41012
Capri

Museo di Milano.
Via Sant'Andrea 6, Milan

Museo di Palazzo Venezia.
Piazza Venezia 3, I-00187
Rome

Museo di Roma.
Palazzo Braschi, Piazza di S.
Pantaleo 10, I-00186 Rome

Museo di S. Pancrazio.
Annesso alla Basilica di San
Pancrazio I-00100 Rome

Museo di San Marco.
Piazza San Marco, I-50121
Florence

Museo di San Petronio.
Piazza Galvani 5, I-40124
Bologna

Museo di Sant Antonio.
Annesso alla Basilica, I-29100
Piacenzo

Museo di Santo Stefan.
Via Santo Stefan 24, I-40125
Bologna

Museo di Schifanoia.
Via Scandiana 23, I-44100
Ferrara, 0532/32303

Museo Diocesano.
I-87067 Rome

Museo Diocesano.
Via del Duomo, I-60100
Ancona

Museo Diocesano.
Via Alboino 2, I-39042
Bressanone

Museo Diocesano.
Annesso al Duomo, I-92100
Agrigento

Museo Diocesano.
Piazza S. Giuseppe, I-67100
l'Aquila

Museo Diocesano.
Piazza del Duomo, Chiesa del
Geso, I-52044 Cortona

Museo Diocesano d'Arte Sacra.
Annesso alla Cattedrale, I-
53026 Pienza

Museo Diocesano di Arte Sacra.
Annesso al Seminario, I-53024
Montalcino

Museo Diocesano di Arte Sacre.
Via Roma, I-56048 Volterra

Museo Diocesano Teatino.
Corso Marrucino, I-66100
Chieti

Museo Diocesano Tridentino.
Palazzo Pretorio Piazza del
Duomo, I-38100 Trento

**Museo Duca di Martina alla
Floridiana.**
Via Cimarosa 77, I-80127
Naples

Museo e Pinacoteca Civica.
Piazza Carrara, I-05100 Terni

Museo e Pinacoteca Civica.
Palazzo del Popolo, I-06059
Todi

Museo e Pinacoteca Civici.
Via Tripoli 8, I-15100
Alessandria

**Museo e Pinacoteca Civici "Luigi
Sturzo".**
Via Roma 10, Caltagirone

Museo e Pinacoteca Comunali.
Viale Bovio 1-64100 Teramo

Museo e Pinacoteca Comunali.
Palazzo della Signoria, I-60035
Jesi

Museo e Pinacoteca Comunali.
Piazza della Signoia, I-06024
Gubbio

Museo Etnografico.
Via San Martino 8, I-43100
Parma

Museo Etnologico Missionario.
Via S. Francesco, Convento
Francescano, I-50014 Fiesole

Museo Fantoni.
Via Andrea Fantoni 1, I-24020
Rovetta

Museo "Gianettino Luxoro".
Via Campolungo, Villa Luxoro,
I-16167 Genova-Nervi

**Museo Internazionale della
Caricatura.**
Palazzo Parisani-Bezzi, Via
della Pace 20, I-62029
Tolentino

**Museo Internazionale delle
Ceramiche.**
V. Campidori N. 2, I-48018
Faenza, 0546/21240

Museo Irpino.
Corso Europa, I-83100
Avellino

Museo Lapidario Marscano.
Palazza Municipale, I-67051
Avezzano

Museo Malatestino.
Piazza XX Settembre, I-610322
Fano

Museo Marciano.
Piazza S. Marco, I-30124
Venice

Museo Marino Marini.
Villa Reale, I-20100 Milan

Museo "Miniscalchi Erizzo".
Via S. Mammaso 2, I-37100
Verona

Museo Missionario Francesano.
Presso la Basilica di San
Nicola, I-62029 Tolentino

**Museo "Mons. Domenico
Mambrini".**
Via Ferdinando Zannetti 14, I-
47010 Galatea

Museo Multscher.
Piazza Mitra 112, I-39049
Vipiteno

Museo Napoleonico.
Piazza di Ponte Umberto, I-
00186 Rome

Museo Nazionale.
Via S. Vitale 11, I-48100
Ravenna

Museo Nazionale.
Corso Umberto 41, I-74100
Taranto

Museo Nazionale.
Viale della Liberta 461, I-98100
Messina

Museo Nazionale.
Palazzo del Bergello, Via del
Proncosolo, I-50122 Florence

Museo Nazionale 'Arte Orientale.
Via Merulana 248, I-00185
Roma

Museo Nazionale Atestino.
Castello di Umbertino da
Carrara, I-35042 Este

Museo Nazionale dell Marche.
Piazza del Senato 2, I-70100
Ancona

Museo Nazionale dell'Artiganato.
Piazza della Liberia 1, I-50129
Florence

Museo Nazionale di Adria.
Piazzale degli Etruschi 2, I-
45011 Adria, 21612
Permanent Collections:
Fragments of Attic vases with
black and red figures; tombs
from pre-Roman times and
from the Roman Necropolis of
Adria. Collection of glass, guns,
coins.

Museo Nazionale di Antichita.
Villa Comunale, I-66100 Chieti

**Museo Nazionale di Palazzo
Bellomo.**
Via Giuseppe Capodieci 14, I-
96100 Siracusa

**Museo Nazionale di Reggio
Calabria.**
Piazza de Nava 26, I-89100
Reggio Calabria

Museo Nazionale di San Martino.
Piazzele San Martino, 80100
Naples

Museo Nazionale di San Mateo.
Convento di San Mateo,
Lungarno Mediceo, 56100 Pisa

Museo Nazionale di Villa Guinigi.
Via della Quarqonia, 55100
Lucca

**Museo Nazionale Etrusco di Villa
Giulia.**
Piazzale di Villa Giulia 9, I-
00196 Rome

Museo Nazionale G A Sanna.
Viale delle Terme di
Diocleziano, 00185 Rome

Museo Nazionale Romano.
Viala delle Terme di
Diocleziano, 00185 Rome

Museo Nazionale Tarquiniese.
I-01016 Tarquinia

Museo Orientale a Ca'pesaro.
I-30100 Venice

Museo Ostiense.
I-00050 Ostia Antica

Museo Paleocristiano.
Piazza Monsatero, I-33100
Aquileia

Museo "Piersanti".
Via Umberto I 11, I-62024
Matelica

Museo Pinacoteca Civico.
Via L. Sparapani 10, I-62032
Camerino

Museo Pogliaghi.
I-21100 Varese

Museo Poldi Pezzoli.
Via Manzoni 12, 20121 Milan

Museo Pomarici.
I-70024 Gravina di Puglia

**Museo Principe Deigo Aragonia
Pignatelli Cortes.**
Riveria di Chiaia 200, I-80121
Naples

Museo Provinciale Campano.
Via Museo Campano, I-81043
Capua

**Museo Provinciale "Francesco
Ribezzo".**
Piazza del Duomo, I-72100
Brindisi

**Museo Provinciale "Sigismundo
Castromediano".**
Palazzo, Del Governo, I-13100
Lecce

Museo Romano.
Via dei Musei 57, Brescia

Museo Sacro di Sant'Ambrogio.
Piazza Sant'Ambrogio 15, I-
20123 Milan

Museo Scipione Gentili.
Via Matteotti 5, I-62026
Sanginesio

Museo Silva.
Palazzo Silva, Via del Museo,
I-28037 Dormodossola

Museo Storico Provinciale.
Borgo Castello 15, I-34170
Gorizia

Museo Tuscolano.
Palazzo Vescovile, I-00044
Frascati

Museo Vetrario.
A San Donato, I-30121
Murano

Museum of Modern Art.
Via Ercole d'Este, I-44100
Ferrara

Nobile Collegio del Cambio.
Corso Vannucci, I-06100
Perugia

Oratorio dell'Annunziata.
Via Borga die Sotto, I-44100
Ferrara

Palazzina di Marfisa d'Este.
Corso Giovecca 170, I-44100
Ferrara

**Palazzo Apostolico e Archivio
Storico.**
I-60025 Loreto

Palazzo Borromeo.
Isola Bella, I-28049 Stresa

Palazzo Chigi-Saracini.
Via di Citta 89, I-53100 Siena

Palazzo Davanzati. *See* **Museo
della Casa Fiorentina Antica**

Palazzo dei Normanni.
Corso Vittorio Emanule, I-
90133 Palermo

Palazzo del Te.
I-46100 Mantova

Palazzo della Ragione.
Tra Piazza delle Erbe e Piazza
della Frutta, I-35100 Padova

Palazzo Ducale.
Piazza S. Marco, I-30124
Venice

Palazzo Ex Reale.
Castello Moncalieri, I-10100
Torino

Palazzo Farnese.
Piazza Cattadella, I-29100
Piacenza

Palazzo Publico.
Piazza del Campo, I-53100
Siena

Palazzo Reale.
I-81100 Caserta

Palazzo Reale.
Piazza Plebiscito 1, I-80132
Naples

Palazzo Strozzi.
Piazza Davanzati, I-50123
Florence

Palazzo Vecchio.
Piazza dell Signoria, I-50122
Florence

Pinacoteca.
Coros Alfieri 117, I-14100 Asti

Pinacoteca.
Via Sacro Monte, I-13019
Varallo

Pinacoteca.
Palazzo Comunale, I-33170
Pordenone

Pinacoteca.
Palazzo del Popolo, I-53037
San Gimignano

Pinacoteca.
Annessa alla Chiesa di S.
Verdiana, I-50051
Castelfiorentino

Pinacoteca Ambrosiana.
Piazza Pio XI, 2, 20123 Milan

Pinacoteca "Bindi".
Via Garibaldi, I-64021
Giulianova

Pinacoteca Civica.
Villa Reale, I-20052 Monza

Pinacoteca Civica.
Via Matteotti, I-44042 Cent

Pinacoteca Civica.
Via Mentana 9, I-40054 Budrio

Pinacoteca Civica.
Via Quarda Superiore 7, I-
17100 Savona

Pinacoteca Civica.
Palazio del Municipio, I-62019
Recanati

Pinacoteca Civica.
Palzza Communale, I-63100
Ascoli Piceno

**Pinacoteca Civica e Museo degli
Arazzi.**
Piazza Umberto di Savoia 3, I-
60044 Fabriano

**Pinacoteca Civica "Francesco
Podesti" Galeria Comunale
d'Arte Moderna.**
Palazzo Bosdari, Via Pizzecolli
17, I-60100 Ancona, 071-23632
Permanent Collections:
Paintings and sculptures from
the 12th century to the 19th
century. In the modern and
contemporary section there are
works, photos, video tapes and
projects of this century from
Italian and foreign artists.

Pinacoteca Comunale.
Via Roma, I-63047
Montifortino

Pinacoteca Comunale.
Palazzo Comunale, I-06039
Trevi

Pinacoteca Comunale.
Palazzo Trinci, I-06034 Foligno

Pinacoteca Comunale.
Piazza dei Priori, I-05035
Narni

Pinacoteca Comunale.
Via Porta Guelfa, I-06031
Bevagna

Pinacoteca Comunale.
Palazzo del Comune, I-63023
Fermo

Pinacoteca Comunale.
Via Gambalunga 27, I-47037
Rimini

Pinacoteca Comunale.
Palazza del Comune, I-06081
Assisi

Pinacoteca Comunale.
Piazza dei Consoli, I-06053
Deruta

Pinacoteca Comunale.
Via Calai 39, I-06023 Gualdo
Tadino

Pinacoteca Comunale.
Palazzo Communale, I-52037
Sansepolcro

Pinacoteca Comunale.
Corso della Republica 72, I-
47100 Forli

Pinacoteca Comunale.
Palazzo Communale, I-62027
San Severino Marche

Pinacoteca Comunale.
Via della Cannoniera 22, I-
06012 Citta di Castello

Pinacoteca Comunale.
Piazza del Municipo 1, I-52043
Castiglion Fiorentino

Pinacoteca Comunale.
Palazzo del Commune, Piazza
dei Priori, I-56048 Volterra

Pinacoteca Comunale.
Piazza Caprera 3, Chiesa di
San Francesco, I-06025 Nocera
Umbra

Pinacoteca Comunale "Foresiana".
I-57037 Portoferraio

Pinacoteca "De Napoli".
Corso Garibaldi 9, I-70038
Terlizzi

**Pinacoteca dell'Accademia dei
Concordi.**
Piazza Vittorio Emanuele 14, I-
45100 Rovigo

**Pinacoteca dell'Accademia di
Belle Arti.**
Via Baccarini 3, I-48100
Ravenna

**Pinacoteca dell'Accademia
Zelantea.**
Via Marche di San Guiliano 15,
I-95024 Acireale

Pinacoteca di Brera.
Via Brera 28, 20121 Milan

Pinacoteca e Museo Civico.
Piazza Cavour, I-06084 Bettona

Pinacoteca e Museo Civico.
Via S. Maria dell'Angelo 2, I-
48018 Faenza

Pinacoteca e Museo Civico.
Piazza Vittorio Veneto 6, I-
62100 Macerata

Pinacoteca "Malaspina".
Piazza Petrarca 2, I-27100
Pavia

**Pinacoteca Manfrediana e
Raccolte del Seminario
Patriarcale.**
Via Campo della Salute 100, I-
30123 Venice

Pinacoteca Municipale.
Via S. Agata 19, I-66100 Chieti

Pinacoteca Nazionale.
Via Belle Arti 56, I-40126
Bologna

Pinacoteca Nazionale.
Palazzo del Governo, Piazza
Napoleone, 55100 Lucca

Pinacoteca Nazionale.
Palazzo dei Diamanti, Via
Ercola d'Este, I-44100 Ferrara

Pinacoteca Nazionale Siena.
Via del Capitano, 1 Siena, 41
246
Permanent Collections:
Painting from the 13th-18th
centuries.

Pinacoteca Provinciale.
Palazza della Provincia, I-
70122 Bari

Pinacoteca "Rambaldi".
Piazza San Sebastiano, I-18010
Col di Rodi

Pinacoteca "Repossi".
Via Bernarino Varisco 9, I-
25032 Chiari

Pinacoteca "Rizzi".
Via dei Cappuccini 4, I-16039
Sestri Levante

Pinacoteca "Stuard".
Via G. Cavestro 14, I-43100
Parma

Pinacoteca Tosio e Martinengo.
Palazzo Martinengo da Barco,
Via Martinengo da Barco 1, I-
25100 Bresci

Pitti Palace. *See* **Galleria Palatina
di Palazzo Pitti**

**Qaudreria dei Virtuosi al
Pantheon.**
Nell'Attico del Pantheon, I-
00100 Rome

**Quadreria della Casse Depositi e
Prestiti.**
I-00100 Rome

Quadreria di Villa d'Este.
I-00019 Tivoli

Raccolta Archaeologica.
Palazzo Comunale, I-05022
Amelia

Raccolta Comunale.
Palazzo Comunale, I-06046
Norcia

Raccolta d'Arte Comunale.
Via Emilia 80, I-40026 Imola

**Raccolta d'Arte Contemporanea
Alberto della Regione.**
Piazza della Signoria 5, I-50122
Florence

Raccolta d'Arte dei Domenicani.
I-18018 Taggia

Raccolta d'Arte Pagliara.
Corso Vittorio Emanuele
Cariati, I-80132 Naples

**Raccolta delle Stampe Achille
Bertarelli.**
Castello Sforzesco, Milan

**Raccolte Archaeologiche e
Numismatiche.**
Castello Sforzesco & Corse,
Magenta 15, Milan

**Raccolte D'Arte dell'Ospedale
Maggiore.**
Via Francesco Sforza 32, Milan

**Raccolte del Settecento
Veneziano.**
A Ca'Rezzonico, I-30123
Venice

Raccolte di Palazzo Tursi.
Via Garibaldi 9, I-16124 Genoa

Ribezzo, Francesco, Museum. *See*
**Museo Provinciale "Francesco
Ribezzo"**

Sala del Collegio della Mercanzia.
Corso Vannucci 15, I-06100
Perugia

Sale d'Arte Antica.
Via Solferino 38, I-53042
Chianciano Terme

Scuola del Santo.
Piazza del Santo, Santo, I-
35100 Padova

Scuola di San Rocco.
Via S. Lucia, I-35100 Padova

**Scuola Grande Arciconfra Ternita
di S. Maria del Carmelo.**
Campos Margherita, I-30123
Venice

**Scuola Grande di S. Giovanni
Evangelista.**
Campo della Salute, I-30123
Venice

Scuola Grande di San Rocco.
Campo San Rocco, I-30125
Venice

**Suola Dalmata dei SS. Giorgio e
Trifone.**
Calle dei Furlani, Sant'Antonin,
I-30122 Venice

Tesero dell Duomo.
Piazza Duca Federico, I-61029
Urbino

Tesoro del Duomo.
I-34073 Grado

Tesoro del Duomo.
I-03012 Anagni

Tesoro del Duomo.
I-27029 Vigevano

Tesoro del Duomo.
Via Lepanto, I-98100 Messina

**Tesoro del Sacro Convento di S.
Francesco.**
Annesso alla Basilica, I-06081
Assisi

**Tesoro della Basilica di San
Giovanni.**
Via Duomo, I-20052 Monza

Tesoro della Cattedrale.
I-11100 Aosta

Tesoro della Cattedrale.
I-90100 Palermo

**Tesoro della Collegiata di
Sant'Oro.**
I-11100 Aosta

**Tesoro dell'Abbazia di San
Silvestro.**
I-41015 Nonantola

Tesoro di San Marco.
Presso la Basilica di San
Marco, I-30125 Venice

Villa Carlotta.
Via Regina, Tremezzo

Villa della Farnesina.
Via della Lungara, I-00165
Rome

Villa Medica.
I-57030 Poggio a Caiano

Villa Pasani.
I-30039 Stra

IVORY COAST

**Musee de la Cote d'Ivoire et
Centre des Sciences Humaines.**
P.O. Box 1600 Abidjan

New Stanley Art Gallery.
New Stanley Hotel, Kimathi St.
P.O. Box 75, Nairobi

Paa Ya Paa Art Gallery.
Sadler House, Koinange St.,
P.O. Box 49646 Nairobi

JAPAN

Aichi Art Gallery.
8-8 Hisayacho, Higashi-ku,
Nagoya, Aichi Pref.

**Aizu Memorial Exhibition Room
of Oriental Arts.**
Waseda University, Totsuka-
cho, Shinjuku-ku, Tokyo

Akita City Art Museum.
6, Uena Ka-Jo, Senshu Park,
Akita City

Akita Prefectural Art Museum.
3-7 Chiaki-Meitoku-Cho, Akita
City

Arita Ceramic Museum.
3-Ku Arita, Matsuura-Gun,
Saga Pref.

**Art Gallery of the Tokiwayama
Foundation.**
1993 Fueta, Kamakura,
Kanagawa Pref.

**Association of the Tomei Art
Preservation.** *See* **Kyusei Atami
Art Museum**

**Association of the Tomei Art
Preservation.** *See* **Kyusei
Hakone Art Museum**

Atami Art Museum.
26-1 Momoyama-Cho, Atami,
Shizuoka Pref.

Beppu Municipal Museum of Art.
Uedanoyu, Beppu, Oita Pref.

**Beppu University Ancient Culture
Museum:**
Kamegawa, Rikushoen, Beppu
Oita Pref.

Bridgestone Bijutsukan.
1-1 Kybashi, Chuo-ku, Tokyo

Chorakuji Collection.
Shi-Chiken-Cho, Shimoda-
Machi, Kamo-Gun, Shizuoka
Pref.

Crafts Gallery.
Kitanomaru Koen, Tokyo

Daigo-Ji Treasure Hall.
Daigo-ji , Daigo-Higashioji-
machi, Fushima-"Ku, Kyoto

Domoto Art Museum.
Kamiyagi-cho, Hirano, Kita-ku,
Kyoto

Ehime Cultural Hall.
Fukiage Park, Yamazato-Dori,
Imabari, Ehime Pref.

**Ehime Prefectural Local Art
Museum.**
19 Ichiban-cho, Matsuyama,
Ehime Pref.

Fujii Yurin-Kan Museum.
44 Ensyojimachi, Okazaki,
Sakyo-ku, Kyoto

Fujita Art Museum.
10-32 Amijimacho,
Miyakojima-Ku, Osaka Pref.
534, 6-351-0582
Permanent Collections:
Scroll-painting "Murasaki
Shikibu Nikki E-kotoba," Fan
paper album of Hoke-kyo
Sutra, Scroll-painting "Hsuan-
chang Sanstsang," Portrait of
Yakamochi, Tea-bowl, Yohen
Temmoku, Kochi Ogame Kogo
(incense container), Kokushi
Nasu Chai-ire (tea caddy),
Yuteki Temmoku Chawan (tea
bowl), Goshomaru kurohake
chaan, Title Sekiyo (tea bowl).

**Fukui Prefectural Okajima Art
Memorial Hall.**
1 Hoei Nakamachi, Fukui City

Fukuoka Art Museum.
Fuku-oka-ken Bunka Kaikan, 1-
Go 2, 5-Chome, Tenjin,
Fukuoka City

Fukuzawa Memorial Hall.
Nakatsu-shi, Oita Pref.

**Gallery of Horyu-Ji Treasures,
Tokyo National Museum.**
Ueno-Park, Taito-ku, Tokyo

**General Nogi Memorial
Collection.**
Momoyama, Fushima-ku,
Kyoto

Ginkakuji (Jishoji) Silver Temple.
Ginkakuji-cho, Sakyo-ku,
Kyoto

Goryu Buddhistic Museum.
Hayashi, Gonai-mura, Koto-
gun, Okayama Pref.

**Goryu Shrine Historical
Collection, Goryu-Jinja
Kokokan.**
Kamiotsu-Machi, Fukae-Shi,
Nagasaki Pref.

Gotoh Art Museum.
3-9-25 Kami-Noge, Setagaya-
Ku, Tokyo

Gyokudo Art Museum.
75 Mitake, Ome-shi, Tokyo

Gyokusenji Collection.
Kakizaki, Shimoda-machi,
Kamo-gun, Shizuoka Pref.

Hakone Open-Air Museum.
Ninotaira, Hakone-machi,
Kanagawa Pref.

Hakone Shrine Treasure House.
86 Oshiba, Motohakone,
Hakone-Machi, Kanagawa Pref.

Hakutsuru Fine Art Museum.
1-1-6 Sumiyoshi-Yamate,
Higashinada-Ku, Kobe, Hyogo
Pref. 658

Hara Castle Memorial Hall.
Minamitakaki-Gun, Oe,
Minamianima-Machi, Nagasaki
Pref.

Hatakeyama Museum.
67 Saru-machi, Shiba
Shirogane, Minatoku, Tokyo

Heijo Shrine Museum.
Saki-machi, Nara City

Hikone Castle Collection.
Kinkame-cho, Hikone, Shiga
Pref.

Hirado Kanko Historical Hall.
Okubo-Cho, Hirado, Nagasaki
Pref.

Hokkaido Museum of Art.
North 1, West 5, Sapporo,
Hokkaido, 060

**Hokkaido University, Ainu
Museum in Memory of Dr. John
Batchelor:**
Botanical Garden, Nishi 8-
Chrome, Kita Sanjo, Sapparo,
Hokkaido

Homma Art Museum.
12, Hamabata-machi, Sakata,
Yamagata Pref.

Hommyo-Ji Treasure House.
Hommyo-ji, Hanazono-cho,
Kumamoto City

**Hyogo Prefectural Museum of
Modern Art.**
3-8-30 Harada-dori, Nada-ku,
Kobe, Hyogo Pref., 078-801-
1591
Permanent Collections:
Sculptures and prints of
Western Modern Art.

Ibaraki Prefectural Art Museum.
Bunka Senta, Semba-Machi,
Saeki-Gun, Hiroshima

Idemitsu Art Gallery.
3-1-1, Marunouchi, Chiyodo-
Ku, Tokyo 100, (03) 213-3111
Permanent Collections:
Oriental art; ceramics
(Japanese, Chinese, Korean,
Thai, Siamese, Iranian, Turkish,
etc.), Chinese Bronzes and
Jade, Japanese paintings,
Calligraphic works (Chinese
and Japanese, mainly of Zen
monks), Lacquer wares
(Chinese and Japanese) and
Utensils for Tea Ceremony.

**Iga Art & Industry Institute
Musem.**
6, 1-Marunouchi, Ueno-shi,
Mie Pref.

Ii Art Museum.
Hikone-jo, Konki-machi,
Hikone, Shiga Pref.

Ikeno Taiga Art Museum.
57 Matsuobankoku-cho, Ukyo-
ku, T. Kyoto

Ishibashi Art Museum.
Ishibashi Bunka Senta, Nonaka-
Cho, Kurume, Fukuoka Pref.

Ishikawa Prefectural Art Museum.
1-1 Kenroku-cho, Kanazawa,
Ishikawa Pref.

Itsuo Art Museum.
1965 Tateishi-cho, Ikeda-shi,
Osaka Pref.

**Japan-China Peace Negotaitions
Memorial Hall.**
Amidaji-machi, Shimoneseki,
Yama-guchi Pref.

Japan Handicraft Museum.
3-169 Shinkawa, Naniwa-ku,
Osaka City

Japanese Craft Museum.
4-3-33 Komaba-cho, Meguro-
ku, Tokyo

Japanese Sword Museum.
4-25-10- Yoyogi, Shibuya-ku,
Tokyo

Jingu Museum of Antiquties.
Kuratayama, Ise, Mie Pref.

Jirocho Memorial Collection.
872 Shimoshimizu, Shimizu-shi,
Shizuoka Pref.

**Joyo Memorial Museum of Meiji
the Great.**
Tokodai, Oari-marchi,
Higashi'ibaraki-gun, Ibaraki
Pref.

**Kagoshima Municipal Art
Museum.**
134 Yamashita-machi,
Kagashima City

Kaisendo Museum.
277 Tanaka, Toka-machi,
Kaminiyama, Yamagata Pref.

Kakurin-Ji Treasure House.
Kakurin-ji, Kakogawa, Hyogo
Pref.

**Kanagawa Prefectural Museum of
Modern Art.**
1051 Yukinoshita, Kamakura,
Kanagawa Pref.

**Kanshin-Ji Treasur House
(Kanshin-Ji Reihokan)**
Kanshin-Ji, Teramoto, Kawachi
Nagaro, Osaka City

**Kasama Municipal Museum of
Art.**
Sahaku-Park, Kasama-Shi,
Ibaraki Pref.

Kasuga Shrine Treasure House.
Kasuga Shrine, Kasugano-
machi, Nara City

**Katei-Gakko-Museum of Local
History.**
Engaru-machi, Monbetsu-gun,
Hokkaido, Pref.

Kibi Archaeological Collection.
183 Jitokatayama, Yamate-
mura, Tsukubo-gun, Okayama
Pref.

Kikusi Handicraft Museum.
2911 Komatsu, Kawanishi-
machi, Yamagata Pref.

Kinsuien Art Museum.
1006-1 Matogahama Kaigan,
Beppu, Oita Pref.

**Kitano Temman-Gu Treasure
House.**
Kitano, Temman-Gu, Kitano
Bakuro-Cho, Kamikyo-Ku,
Kyoto

Kobe City Museum.
1-35 Kumachi-machi, Fukiai-
ku, Kobe, Hyogo Pref.

Kofuku-Ji Treasure Hall.
Kofuku-ji, 59 Noborioji-cho,
Nara City

Kokuritsu Seiyo Bijutsukann.
Ueno Park, Taito-ku, 110
Tokyo

Koryu-Ji Treasure Hall.
Koryu-jim Futohata
Hachigaoka-machi, Ukyo-ku,
Kyoto

Kotohira Shrine Museum.
Kotohira-gu, Kotohira-machi,
Nakatada-gun, Kagawa Pref.

Koyasan Reihokan.
Koyasan, Koyacho, Ito-gun,
Tokyo

Koyasan Treasure House.
Koyasan, Koya-machi, Ito-gun,
Wakayama Pref.

Kozo-Ji Museum.
Kozo-ji, 553-2 Setoda-cho,
Setoda-machi, Hiroshima Pref.

**Kumano Hayatama Shrine
Treasure House.**
Kumano Hayatama Shrine,
Shingu-machi, Shingu,
Wakayama Pref.

**Kunozan Tosho-Gu Treasure
House.**
Kunozan, 390 Nekoya,
Shizuoka City

Kuon-Ji Treasure House.
Kuon-ji, Minobu-machi,
Yamanashi Pref.

Kurashiki Folk Art Museum.
Maegami-cho, Kurashiki,
Okayama Pref.

Kyoto City Art Museum.
Okazaki Park, Sakyo-ku, Kyoto

**Kyoto Kokuritsu Kindai
Bijutsukan.**
Enshoji-cho, Okazaki, Sakyo-
ku, Kyoto

Kyoto National Museum.
527 Chaya-Machi,
Higashiyama-Ku, Kyoto

**Kyoto Prefectural Exhibition
Hall.**
Hangi-cho, Shimogamo, Kyoto

Kyusei Atami Art Museum.
26-1 Momoyama-Cho, Atami-
Shi, Shizvoka-Ken
Permanent Collections:
National treasures, cultural
properties and important art
objects. Approximately 2,000 in
total.

Kyusei Hakone Art Museum.
1300 Gora, Hakone, Kanagawa-
Ken, 0460-2-2623
Permanent Collections:
Oriental ceramic art objects.

Masaoka Memorial Collection.
Higashikyuban-cho, Sendai,
Miyagi Pref.

Matsumoto Folk Art Museum.
Shimoganai, 4-1 Marunouchi,
Marsumoto, Nagano Pref.

Matsunaga Memorial Hall.
943 Itabashi, Odawara,
Kanagawa Pref.

**Meiji Shrine, Memorial Picture
Gallery.**
9 Kasumigaoka, Shinjuku-ku,
Tokyo

**Meiji the Great Memorial Hall of
Tama.**
Renko-ji, Tama-mura,
Minamitamagun, Tokyo

**Memorial Hall of the Emperor
Meiji's Temporary Headquarters
at Akashi.**
Precincts of Komyoji Temple
Kajiyamachi Akashi-Shi, Hyogo
Pref.

**Metropolitan Komaba High
School Art Museum.**
660-8, Kamineguro, Meguro-ku,
Tokyo

Misawa Collection.
Osawa, Tajiri-machi, Onda-gun,
Miyagi Pref.

**Mitsukini & Nariaka Tokugawa
Memorial Collection.**
Tokiwa Park, Mito, Ibaraki
Pref.

**Musee National d'Art Occidental.
See National Museum of
Western Art**

Museum of Calligraphy.
125 Negishi-cho, Ueno,
Taitoku, Tokyo

**Nagaoka Museum of
Contemporary Art.**
2-1 Sakanoue-machi, Nagaoka,
Niigata Pref.

**Nagasaki Prefectural Museum of
Art.**
2 Tateyama-cho, Nagasaki City

Nagoya Castle Treasure House.
1-1 Hon-maru, Naka-ku,
Nagoya, Aichi Pref.

Nakoso Art Museum.
Irritabane, Sekiden-cho,
Nakoso-shi, Fukushima Pref.

Nara Art Museum.
Isuien Park, 74 Suimon-cho,
Nara City

Nara Kokuritsu Hakubutsukan.
50 Noboriojicho, Nara Park,
Nara

Nata-Dera Treasure House.
Nata-Dera, Nata-Machi,
Komatsu, Ishikawa Pref.

National Film Center.
7-6, 3-Chrome Kyobashi,
Chuo-Ku, 1104 Tokyo

National Museum of Modern Art.
Enshoji-cho, Sakyoku, Okazaki

National Museum of Western Art.
Veno-Koen Taito-Ku Tokyo
Permanent Collections:
European art

Neesima Memorabilia Room.
Gembu-cho, Kamikyo-ku,
Kyoto

Neiraku Museum.
50 Suimon-cho, Nara City

Nezu Museum of Art.
6-5-36 Minami-aoyama,
Minato-ku, Tokyo

Niigata B.S.N. Art Museum.
2 Igaku-cho, Niigata City

Nikko Tosho-Gu Treasure House.
Nikkosan, Nikko, Tochigi Pref.

Ninna-Ji Treasure House.
Ninna-ji, Omuro Ouchi, Ukyo-
ku, Kyoto

Nippon Mingei-Kan.
861 Komabamachi, Meguro-ku,
Tokyo

Nishimura Art Museum.
297 Yokoyama, Kikko Park,
Iwakuini-shi, Yamaguchi Pref.

Nogi Memorial Collection. *See*
**General Nogi Memorial
Collection**

Nyorin-Ji Treasure House.
Nyoirin-ji, Tono-o,
Yoshinoyama, Yoshina, Nara
Pref.

Ogasawara Memorial Hall.
Nishidera-machi, Karatsu-shi,
Saga Pref.

Ohara Bijitsukan.
1-1-15 Chuo, Kurashiki

Ohara Pottery Hall.
312-, 1-chome Shinkawa-cho,
Kurashiki, Okayama Pref.

Okayama Art Museum.
78 Uchisange, Okayama City

Okura Shukokan Museum.
3 Akasaka-Aoi-cho, Minato-ku,
Tokyo

Old Ceramics Hall.
Korakuen, Furukyo-machi,
Okayama City

Osaka Municipal Museum of Fine Arts.
Tennoji-ku, Osaka City

Rikuzentakada Municipal Museum.
Kesen'numa-machi, Rikuzentakada-shi, Iwate Pref.

Rinno-Ji Jokodo Treasure House.
Nikkosan, Nikko, Tochigi Pref.

Rokuzan Art Gallery.
5095- 1 Hodaka, Hodaka-machi, Minami-Azumi-gun, Nagano Pref.

Ryoanji Temple.
Ryoanjigoryo-machi, Ukyo-ku, Kyoto

Ryokan Memorial Gallery.
Kami 12-1, 12sha, Komeda, Izumozaki-Machi, Santo-Gun, Niigate Pref.

Saga Prefectural Museum.
1-15 Jonai, Saga City

Saitama Prefectural Museum of Art.
Bessho Park, 1005 Bessho, Urawa-shi, Saitama Pref.

Sano Art Museum.
1-43 Nakada-Cho, Mishima, Shizuoka Pref.

Sanuki Folk Art Museum.
Ritsurin Park, Ritsurin-cho, Takamatsu, Kagawa Pref.

Seicho-Ji Tomioka Tessai Gallery.
Seicho-ji Yoneya Kiyoshi, Takarazuka, Hyogo Pref.

Seisonkaku.
37, 1-chrome, Dewa-machi, Kenroku Park, Kanazawa, Ishikawa Pref.

Seto Ceramics Exhibition Hall.
Kurasho-cho, Seto, Aichi Pref.

Shoko Shuseikan Memorial Collection.
Iso, Yoshino-cho, Kagoshima City

Shoshoin Treasure House.
Zoshi-cho, Nara City

Sumitomo Collection.
25 Shimo Miyanomae-cho, Shikagatani, Sakyo-ku, Kyoto, 075-771-7227
Permanent Collections:
Bronzes of Ancient China.

Suntory Museum of Art.
1-10 Marunouchi, Chiyodo-ku, Tokyo

Suwa Municipal Art Museum.
Nakahama-machi, Suwa-shi, Nagano Pref.

Tajimi Municipal Old Ceramics Exhibition Hall.
Chamber of Commerce, Shin-machi, Tajimi, Gifu Pref.

Takaoka City Art Museum.
Kojo Park, Sadazuka-Cho, Takaoka, Toyama Pref.

Tamazawa Treasure House.
Myohogeji Tamazawa, Mishima, Shizuoka Pref.

Tekisui Art Museum.
60 Yama-Ashiya-Cho, Ashiya, Hyogo Pref.

Tenri Gallery.
Tokyo Tenrikyokan, 19, 1-chome, Nishiki-cho. Kanda, Chivoda-ku, Tokyo

Tibetan Collection at the Kotoku-Ji.
Kotoku-ji, Tabo-cho, Hanamaki, Iwate Pref.

To-Ji Treasure House.
To-ji, Kujo-dori, Nishi Kujo-machi, Minami-ku, Sendai, Miyaji Pref.

Tokiwayama Foundation. *See* **Art Gallery of the Tokiwayama Foundation**

Tokoname Ceramic Research Center.
7-22 Okujou, Tokoname-Shi Aichi Pref. 479, 05693-5-3970
Permanent Collections:
Jar with scratched pattern, natural ash glaze (Heian period); vase for sutra case, wood ash glaze (Heian period); long necked vase with wide mouth, natural ash glaze (late Heian period); partially fired vase with three carved horizontal lines (late Heian period); jar, wood ash glaze (Komokura period); large jar with double-fold lip, wood ash glaze (Kamakura period); water jar with engraved ornament "Fushiki" type (Muromachi period); small jar, natural ash (Momogama period); lipped bowl (Ido period); teapots imitating the Chinese-I-hsing red stone ware (Edo period); about 100 Old Tokonome wares and about 10,000 valuable objects for archaeologists of Old Tokonome ware.

Tokugawa Art Museum, the Tokugawa Reimeikai Foundation.
27, Tokugawa-Cho 2-Chome Higashi-Ku, Nagoya, Aichi Pref., 052-935-6262
Permanent Collections:
Entire collection of the Tokugawa family, "The Tokugawa Collection." About 12,000 treasures such as various swords, No costumes, picture scrolls, hanging scrolls, calligraphies, potteries and lacquer-wares, etc. One of the most famous national treasures which the museum owns is the Picture Scrolls of Tales of Genji.

Tokyo Kokuritsu Hakubutsukan.
13-9 Ueno Park, Daito-ku, Tokyo

Tokyo Kokuritsu Kindai Bijutsukan.
3 Kitanomaru Koen, Chiyoda-ku, 102 Tokyo

Tokyo Metropolitan Museum of Art.
Ueno-Park, Taito-ku, Tokyo

Tokyo-To Bijutsukan.
Ueno-Park, Daito-ku, 110 Tokyo

Tokyo University of Arts Museum:
Ueno-Park, Taito-Ku, Tokyo

Tottori Folk Art Museum.
124 Kawara-cho, Tottori City

Treasure Hall of the Chishakuin Temple.
Higashi-Kawaramachi, Higashiyama-ku, Kyoto

Treasure Hall of the Kamakuragu (Kamakuragu Homotsu Chinretsujo)
Precincts of Kamakiragu Shrine, Nikaido, Kamakura, Kanagawa Pref.

Treasure Hall of the Kashima Shrine.
Precincts of Kashima Shrine, Kashima-machi, Ibaraki Pref.

Treasure Hall of the Kasugataisha Shrine.
Kasugataisha-gu, Kasugano-cho, Nara City

Treasure Hall of the Rakuhoji Temple.
Motoki, Yamato-mura Makabe-gun, Ibaraki Pref.

Treasure Hall of the Todaiji Temple.
406 Zoshi-cho, Nara City

Treasure Hall of the Yogen-in Temple.
Sanjusangendo-Mae, Yamato-Oji, Shichijo Higashiyama-Ku, Kyoto

Treasure House of the Chimanji Temple.
Chiba, Shimada-shi, Shizuoka Pref.

Treasure House of the Chusonji Temple.
Hirizumi-machi, Iwate Pref.

Treasure House of the Chuzenji Temple.
Lake-Side of Chuzenjiko, Nakaguji, Nikko, Tochigi Pref.

Treasure House of the Daitonomiya-Kamakuragau-Shrine.
318 Kamakura Nikaido, Kamakura Pref.

Treasure House of the Dazaifu-Tenmangu Shrine.
Precincts of Dazaifu-Tenmangu Shrine, Dazaifu-Machi, Tsukushi-Gun, Fukuoka Pref.

Treasure House of the Dewasanzan Shrine.
Haguro-Machi, Higashi-Agawa-Gun, Yamagata Pref.

Treasure House of the Eiheiji Temple.
Precincts of Eiheiji Temple, Eiheiji-Cho

Treasure House of the Hakozaki Shrine.
Nakozaki-machi, Fukuoka City

Treasure House of the Horyuji Temple.
Aza Horyuji, Ikaruga-machi, Ikoma-gun Nara Pref.

Treasure House of the Hotoku Ninomiya Shrine.
Precincts of Hotoku Ninomiya Shrine, 1-chome, Saiwai, Odawara, Kanagawa Pref.

Treasure House of the Hyohogeji Temple.
Tamasawa, Mishima, Shizuoka Pref.

Treasure House of the Itsukushima Shinto Shrine.
Miyajima-machi, Saeki-gun, Hiroshima Pref.

Treasure House of the Izumo O'oyashiro.
195 Kiuzuki, O'oyasiro-machi, Hikawa-gun, Shimane Pref.

Treasure House of the Kanrantei.
Matsushima, Miyagi Pref.

Treasure House of the Kanshinji Temple.
Precincts of Kanshinji Temple, Teramoto Kochi-nagano-shi, Osaka Pref.

Treasure House of the Kikuchi Shrine.
Precincts of Kikuchi Shrine, Waifu, Kikuchi-shi, Kumamoto Pref.

Treasure House of the Kodaiji Temple.
Shimokawara-machi, Higashiyama-ku, Kyoto

Treasure House of the Miho Shrine.
Precincts of Miho Shrine, Miho, Shimizushi Pref.

Treasure House of the Myohoin Temple.
Daibutsu Myohoinmae-machi, Higashiyama-ku, Kyoto

Treasure House of the Nayaji-Temple.
Precincts of the Nayaji Temple, Navamachi, Komatsu, Ishikawa Pref.

Treasure House of the O'oyashiro.
195 Kiuzuki, O'oyashiro-machi, Hakawa-gun, Shimane Pref.

Treasure House of the Rengeoin Temple.
Diabutsu Myohoinmae-machi, Higashiyama-ku, Kyoto

Treasure House of the Shido Temple.
Precincts of Shido Temple, Shido-machi, Okawa-gun, Kagawa Pref.

Treasure House of the Shoren-in Temple.
Sanjobo-Machi, Awadaguchi, Higashiyama-Ku, Kyoto

Treasure House of the Toyokuni Shrine.
Precincts of Toyokuni Shrine, Shomenchaya-machi, Yamato-oji, Higashiyama-ku, Kyoto

Treasure House of the Tsukubasan Shrine.
On Mt. Tsukubasan, Tsukuba-machi, Ibaraki Pref.

Treasure House of the Wanibuchiji Temple.
Precincts of Wanibuchiji Temple, Bessho-machi, Hirata-shi, Shimane Pref.

Treasure House of the Yahiko Shrine.
Precincts of Yahiko Shrine, Yahiko, Yahiko-mura, Nishikambara-gun, Niigata Pref.

Treasure House on Chikufujima
Islands.
(Chikufujima Homotsukan)
Chikujima Higashi-Asai-Gun,
Shiga Pref.

Treasure of the Choshoji Temple.
Shioki-Machi, Ikukata-Gunn,
Ibaraki Pref.

Treasures of the Rokuonji Temple.
Kinkakuji-cho, Kitaku, Kyoto

Tsurugaoka Hachiman-Gu
Treasure House.
Tsurugaoka Hachiman-gu,
Yukinoshita, Kamakura,
Kanagawa Pref.

Uesugi Shrine Treasure House.
Uesugi-jinja, Minami Horibata-
machi, Yonezawa,
Yamagatapref.

Wakayama Prefectural Art
Museum.
Wakayama-jo, Ichiban-cho,
Wakayama City

Waseda University, Gallery of
Asian Art:
1-647 Tozuka-Machi, Shijuku-
Ku, Tokyo

Yahata Municipal Art Museum.
4-Chrome, Hon-Machi, Yahata,
Kukuoka Pref.

Yakushiji Temple.
Nishi-no-Kyo-machi, Nara City

Yamagata Art Museum.
1-63 Ote-machi, Yamagata City

Yamatane Museum of Art.
2-30 Kabuto-cho, Nihonbashi,
Chuo-ku, Tokyo

Yamato Bunkakan Museum.
1-11-6, Gakuen-Minami, Nara
City

Yashima-Dera Treasure House.
Yashima Yamaue, Takamatsu,
Kagawa Pref.

Yoshimizu-Jinja Collection.
Yoshimizu-jinja, Yoshinoyama,
Yoshino, Nara Pref.

Yurinkan Collection.
44, Okazaki, Enshojimachi,
Sakyo-Ku, Kyoto

Zenko-Ji Jodo Section Treasure
House.
Zenko-ji, Motoyoshi-cho,
Nagano City

Zenko-Ji Tendai Section Treasure
House.
Zenko-ji, Motoyoshi-cho,
Nagano City

Zentsu-Ji Treasure House.
Zentsu-ji, Zentsuji, Kagawa
Pref.

Zuigan-Ji Museum.
Zuigan-ji, Matsushima-machi,
Matsushima, Mivagi Pref.

JORDAN

Islamic Museum.
Amman

KENYA

Fort Jesus Museum.
Nkrumah Rd., P.O. Box 82412
Mombasa

National Museum of Lamu.
P.O. Box 48 Lamu

KOREA, NORTH

State Central Fine Arts Museum.
Pyongyang

KOREA, SOUTH

Ewha Women's Univ.
Seoul

Gyunbok Art Gallery.
Gyungbok Palace, Seoul

National Museum of Korea.
Kyong Bok Palace, 1 Sejongro,
Chongro-Ku Seoul

LEBANON

American University of Beirut,
Archeological Museum
Beirut

Musee des Beaux-Arts.
BP 3939, Beirut

National Museum of Lebanon.
Rue de Dumas, Beirut

LIBERIA

Tubman Centre of African Culture.
Robertsport, Cape Mount

LIBYA

Archaeological Museum.
Es Saray El-Hamara, Tripoli

Department of Antiquities for the
Eastern Region:
Beida

Leptis Magna Museum of
Antiquities.
Homs

Museum of Antiquities.
(Dept. of Antiquities for the
Eastern Region, Beida) Cyrene

Museum of Apollonia (Dept. of
Antiquitites for the Eastern
Region Beida)
Apollonia

Museum of Tocra (Department of
Antiquities for the Eastern
Region, Beida)
Tocra

Sabratha Museum of Antiquities
(Directorate General of
Antiquities, Tripoli)
Sabratha

LIECHTENSTEIN

Gemaldeaustellung aus den
Bestanden der Furstl.
Liechtensteinischen Gemalde-
Galerie.
Haupstr., FL-9490 Vaduz

Liechtensteinische Staatliche
Kunstsammlung.
Kunstsammlung Englander Bau,
Fl-9490 Vaduz

Sammlungen des Regierden
Fursten von Liechtenstein.
Schloss Fl-940 Vaduz

Vereinigung der Mund-und
Fussmalen den Kunstler E.V.
Kasperigasse 112, Fl-9490
Vaduz

LUXEMBOURG

Galerie Municipale de Peinture de
la Ville de Luxembourg.
18 Ave. de l'Arsenal,
Luxembourg

MALAGASY REPUBLIC

Musee Folklorique, Archeologique,
Paleontologique et Fauntistique
(Institut de Recherches
Scientifiques a Madagascar)
Parc de Tsimbazaza, Tanarive

Museum D'Art et D'Archeologie.
18 Rue Docteur Villett,
Tanarive

Salle des Beaux Ats.
Palais de la Reine, Tananarive

MALAYSIA

Museum of Asian Art.
Univ. of Malaya, Kuala
Lumpur 22-11

National Museum of Malaysia.
Damansara Rd., Kuala Lumpur

MALTA

Inquisitor's Palace.
Vittoriosa

National Museum.
Auberge De Provence,
Kingsway, Valletta

MEXICO

Galerias del Palacio de Bellas
Artes.
Angela Peralta y Av. Juarez,
Mexico

Museo Arqueologico de
Teotihuacan.
Piramides, Teotihuacan

Museo Arqueologico de Yucatan.
Calle 60 y 65, Merida

Museo Colonial.
Converto de Agustinos, Yuriria

Museo Colonial e Santa Monica.
Av. Poniente 103, Puebla

Museo de Antropologia de la
Universidad Veracurzana.
Av. Jalapa, Apdo. 191, Jalapa

Museo de Arte "Jose Luis Bello y
Gonzalez".
Ave 3 Poniente 302, Puebla

Museo de Arte Moderno.
Bosque de Chapultec, 5 Mexico
City

Museo de Arte Popular.
Prolongation de Hidalgo s-n,
Toluca

Museo de Arte Popular Poblano.
Calle 3 Norte 1203, Puebla

Museo de Artes Populares.
Ensenanza y Alcantarillas s/n,
Patzcuaro

Museo de las Bellas Artes.
Santos Degollado 102, Toluca

Museo de las Culturas.
Moneda 13, Mexico

Museo de San Carlos.
Puente de Alvarado; 50, 1
Mexico City

Museo del Estado.
Guadalajara

Museo del Instituto Mexicano-
Norteamericano de Relaciones
Culturales.
Hamburgo 115, Mexico

Museo Etnografico de Esculturas
de Cera.
Seminario No. 4 Esquina Con
Guatemala, Mexico

Museo Etnografico y
Arqueologico.
Tzintzuntzan

Museo "Frida Kahlo".
Londres 127-Coyoacan, Mexico

Museo "Jose Clemente Orozco".
Aurelio Aceves 27, Guadalajara
Berta Valdivia

Museo Nacional de Antropologia.
Ave. Paseo de la Reforma y
Gandhi S/N, 10 Mexico City

Museo Nacional de Artes y
Industriales Populares.
Ave. Juarez 44, 1 Mexico City

Museo Nacional de Historia.
Castillo de Chapultepec,
Mexico City

Museo Regional de Antropologia e
Historia de Tepic.
Mexico-91. Norte, Tepic

Museo Regional de Arqueologico y
Colonial.
Palacio del Obispado, Apdo
Postal 566 Monterrey

Museo Regional de Oaxaca.
Independencia 33, Oaxaca

National Viceroyalty Museum.
Tepotzotlan

Orozco Museum. See Museo "Jose
Clemente Orozco"

Pinacoteca Virreinal de San
Diego.
Dr. Mora 7, Mexico

Salon de la Plastica Mexicana.
Harve 7, Mexico

Universidad de las Americas.
P.O. Box 100, Santa Catarina
Martir, Cholula

MONACO

Musee National des Beaux-Arts.
Rue des Genetes, Monte-Carlo

MONGOLIA

Fines Arts Museum.
Ulan Bator

Museum of Religion.
Ulan Bator

MOROCCO

**Galerie d'Exposition de la
Direction des Musees.**
Bab-el-Rouah, Rabat

Musee de Dar Jamai.
Sebbaghine 1, Meknes

Musee de Dar Si Said.
Rue de la Bahia, Riad Ziotun
Kdim BP 475, Marrakech

Musee des Oudaia.
Kasbah des Oudaia, Rabat

MOZAMBIQUE

Museu Historico Militar.
Praca 7 de Marco, CP 2033,
Lourenco Marques

NAMIBIA

Art Gallery Windhoek.
John Meinert/Leutwein St.,
P.O. Box 994 Windhoek

NEPAL

Museum - Picture Gallery.
Lal Baithak (Bhaktapur Darbar)

National Museum of Nepal.
Museum Rd., Chhauni
Katmandu

Woodwork Museum.
Palace of Fifty-Five Windows,
Bhaktapur Bhadgaon

NETHERLANDS

Aartsbisschoppelijk Museum.
Agnietenstraat 1, Utrecht

Beiaad-En Klokken Museum.
Raadhus, Berdijk 20, Asten

Bisschoppelijk Museum.
Grote Martk 19, Breda

**Bisschoppelijk Museum voor
Religieuze Kunst.**
Jansstraat 79, Haarlem

Bolten Collection. *See* **Collectie
D.H.G. Bolten**

Bonger Collection. *See* **Collectie
A. Bonger**

Bonnefantenmuseum.
Bonnefantenstraat 4, Maastricht

Botke Collection. *See* **Collectie
T.J. Botke**

Centraal Museum.
Maliebaan 42, Utrecht

Centraal Museum.
Agnietenstraat 1, Utrecht

Chabot Museum.
Oude Raaduhuislaan 4,
Hillegersberg Rotterdam

Citroen Collection. *See* **Collectie
Citroen**

Collectie A. Bonger.
Grott Have, Almen

Collectie A. Schwarz.
Westelijk Halfrond 441,
Amstelveen

Collectie A. Veltman.
Koningslaan 37, Bussum

**Collectie C. E. A. A. en E. M. C.
Gravin van Rechteren Limpurg.**
Kasteel Rechteren, Dalfsen (O.)

Collectie Citroen.
Kalverstraat 1, Amsterdam

Collectie D.H.G. Bolten.
Statenlaan 4, The Hague

Collectie Dr. B. Slingenberg.
Keizersgracht 414, Amsterdam

Collectie Douairiere.
Mr. G. C. D. Baron van
Hardenbroek,
Kasteelhardenbroek, Cothen
(O.)

**Collectie E. Baron van Zuylen van
Nijevelt van de Haar.**
Kasteel de Haar, Post Vleuten,
Haarzuilens (U.)

Collectie E. Proehl.
Koningslaan 17, Amsterdam

Collectie Erven.
G. J. G. C. Graaf van
Albenburg Bentinck

Collectie Erven Jhr.
Berlicum (N.B.)

**Collectie F. Baron van Heeckern
van Walien.**
Prinses Margrietstraat 24,
Amsterdam

Collectie H.H.F. Salomon.
Noordeinde 80, The Hague

Collectie Ir. C. Th. F. Thurkow.
Plain 1813, The Hague

Collectie J.G. Wurfbain.
De Geldersche Toren
Spankeren (G.)

**Collectie Jhr. Mr. W.E. van
Weede.**
Kasteel Bingerden, Angerlo
(G.)

**Collectie Mr. H.K. de Raaf Brand
van Straaten.**
De Sphinx, Bronsteeweg 1,
Vijfhuizen (N.H.)

**Collectie Mr. H.N.C. Baron van
Tuyll van Serookerken van
Heeze en Leende.**
Kasteel Heeze, Heeze (N.B.)

Collectie Six.
Amstel 218, Amsterdam

Collectie T.J. Botke.
Bredestraat 5, Maastricht

Collectie Victor De Stuers.
De Wiersse, Vorden (G.)

Collection H. Jungeling.
Vlaarding Sekade 57,
Schipluiden (Z.H.)

De "Goudse Glazen".
St. Janskerk Gouda

"De Hallen" (Vishal en Vleeshal)
Grote Markt, Haarlem

De Schotse Huizen.
Kade 25-27, Veere

de Stuers Collection. *See* **Collectie
Victor De Stuers**

De Waag.
Middendam 7, Monnikendam
(N.H.)

Dordrechts Museum.
Museumstraat 40, Dordrecht
3311 XP, 078-171121
Permanent Collections:
Mainly Dutch paintings from
17th century to present day
together with prints and
drawings and a small number of
sculptures.

Frans Halsmuseum.
Groot Heiligland 62, Haarlem,
023-319180
Permanent Collections:
Frans Hals' group portraits of
the militia and governors,
survey of the Haarlem school
of painting from the 16th
century until 1850. Period
rooms, old pharmacy, doll
house, Haarlem silver and
manuscript with watercolors of
tulips by Judith Leyster, Dept.
of Modern Art.

Fries Museum.
Turfmarkt 24, Leeuwarden

**Gemeentelijke Van Reekum
Galerij.**
Churchillplein 2, 7314 bz
Apeldorn, 055-219155

Gemeentemuseum.
Kerkplein 6, Woerden (Z.H.)

Gemeentemuseum Arnhem.
Utrechtseweg 87, 6812 AA
Arnhem

**Gemeentemuseum het
Markiezenhof.**
Steenbergsestraat 6, Bergen Op
Zoom

Gmeentemuseum Maassluis.
Zuiddijk 16 Maassluis (Z.H.)

**Goltziusmuseum, Museum van
Gesichiedenis en Kunst.**
Goltziusstraat 21, Venlo (L.)

Groninger Museum.
Praediniussingel 59, Groningen
9711 AG, 050-172929

Haags Gemeentemuseum.
Stadhouderslaan 41, P.O. Box
72, 2076 The Hague

Hannema-de Stuers Fundatie.
Kasteel het Nyenhuis, Heind
(O.)

Het Klooster Ter Apel.
Boslaan 3 Ter Apel

Het Waaierkabinet.
Prinsengracht 1083,
Amsterdam, 234416
Permanent Collections:
Collection of approximately
400 fans of 3 centuries,
specifically European (French).

Het Zakkendragershuisje.
Voorstraat 13-15 Delfshaven
Rotterdam

Historisch Museum.
Korte Hoogstraat 31,
Rotterdam

Huis Bergh.
Hof Van Berg 12, 's-
Heerenberg (G)

Iconografisch Bureau.
Sophialaan 9,'s-Gravenhage

Joods Historisch Museum.
Waaggebouw, Nieumarkt 4,
Amsterdam 1012 CR, 020-
242209

Jungeling Collection. *See*
Collection H. Jungeling

Kardinal van Rossum-Museum.
Wittem (L.)

Kasteel Middachten.
Rentambt Middachten, De
Steeg

Kasteel-Museum Sypesteyn.
Nieuw-Loosdrechtsedijk 150,
Loosdrecht 1231 LC, 02158-
3208
Permanent Collections:
Paintings (portraits of members
of the Family Van Sypesteyn u.
w., the great Dutch statesman
Johan de Witt), early Dutch
furniture, glass, silver,
sculpture, clocks, watches,
China porcelain, European
porcelain, Dutch 18th century
porcelain, special Loosdrecht
porcelain, Dutch and German
earthenware (including Delft
Blue), ironwork from the 16th
century onwards, all kinds of
arms (swords, crossbows,
fireguns), etc.

Kasteel Ophemert.
Dreef 2, Ophemert (G)

Kasteel Soelen.
Zoelen

Kerkmuseum.
Janum

Klokken Museum.
St. Odradastraat, Alem, (Maas)

**Koninklijk Kabinet van
Schilderijen.** *See* **Mauritshaus
Royal Picture Gallery,
Koninklijk Kabinet van
Schilderijen**

Koornmarktspoort.
Ijsselkade 1, Kampen (O.)

Kristiansands Billedgalleri.
Radhusgatan 7-9, Postboks 164,
N-4601 Kirstiansand S.

Lips' Brandkasten-En Slotenmuseum.
Merwedestraat 48, Dordrecht

Martin Van Rossum Museum. *See* Van Rossum, Martin, Museum

Mauritshaus Royal Picture Gallery, Koninklijk Kabinet van Schilderijen.
Korte Vijverberg 8, The Hague

Museum Boymans-Van Beuningen.
P.O. Box 2277, 3015 Rotterdam

Museum Bredius.
Prinsegracht 6, P.O. Box 72, 2076 The Hague

Museum de Ghulden Roos.
Molnestraat 2, Roosendaal

Museum Dinghuis Deurne.
Haageind 39, Deurne (N.B.)

Museum Fodor.
Keizersgacht 609, Amsterdam

Museum Herengracht.
Amsterdam; Fundatie van den Santheuvel, Sobbe

Museum "Het Rembrandthuis".
Jodenbreestraat 4-6, 1001 Amsterdam, 020-249486
Permanent Collections:
Rembrandt's graphic work, etchings and drawings.

Museum in de Stifkerk.
Gemeentehuis, Thorn (L.)

Museum Nieuwenkamp.
Voorhaven 137, Edam (N.H)

Museum Paul Tetar Van Elven.
Koornmarkt 67, Delft; Ihr

Museum van Baaren.
Oude Gracht 317, Utrecht

Museum voor Nieuwe Religeuze Kunst.
Lange Nieuwstraat 38, Utrecht

National Glasmuseum Leerdam.
Lingedijki 28, Leerdam (Z.H.)

Nederlands, Goud-, Zilveren Klokkenmuseum.
Achter de Dom 12, Utrecht

Nederlands Museum van Knipkunst.
Westeind 6, Westerbork (D.)

Nijmeegs Museum "Commanderie van St. Jan".
Franse Plaats 3, 6511 VS Nijmegen, 080-22.91.93

Noordbrabants Museum.
Bethaniestaat 4, 5211 LJs'-Hertogenbosch, 073-138712
Permanent Collections:
Art and history from the Province of Noord-Brabant, from antiquity to the present day: archaeology, painting, sculpture, religious art, folklore.

Occo Hofje.
Nieuwe Keizersgracht 94, Amsterdam

Oud-Katholiek Museum.
Mariahoek 9, Utrecht

Oudheidkundige Verzameling van de Gemeente.
Gemeentehuis Grote Markt 1 Sluis

Panorama Mesdag.
Zeestrat 65B, The Hague, 070-642563

Prentenkabinet der Rijksuniversiteit.
Rapenburg 65, Leiden

Pier Pander Museum.
Prinsentuin, P.O. Box 805 Leeuwarden

Princessehof Museum. *See* **Vereniging van Vrienden van het Princesshof**

Proehl Collection. *See* Collectie E. Proehl

Rembrandthuis. *See* Museum "Het Rembrandthuis"

Rijksmuseum.
Stadhouderskada 42, 1071 ZD, Amsterdam, 020-73 21 21
Permanent Collections:
Dutch paintings, 16th-19th century, sculpture and decorative arts, Dutch history, print room, Asiatic art.

Rijksmuseum, Afd. Aziatische Kunst.
Hobbemastraat 19, Amsterdam

Rijksmuseum, Afd. Beeldhouwkunst en Kunstrijverheid.
Stadhouderskade 42, Amsterdam

Rijksmuseum Hendrik Willem Mesdag.
Laan van Meerdervoort 7F, The Hague

Rijksmuseum Het Catharijneconvent.
Nieuwe Gracht 63, 3512 LG Utrecht, 030-313835

Rijksmuseum Kroller-Muller.
P. O. Box 1, 6730 AA Otterlo
Permanent Collections:
Paintings from 19th and early 20th century (particularly a collection of Vincent Van Gogh), drawings (17th-20th century), sculpture (19th and 20th century).

Rijksmuseum Twente.
Lasondersingel 129, Enschede

Rijksmuseum van Bilderbeek-Lamaison.
Dordrecht

Rijksmuseum Vincent Van Gogh.
Paulus Potterstraat 7, 1071 CX Amsterdam

Rijksmusuem van Oudheden.
Rapenburg 28, Leiden

Rijksprentenkabinet, Rijksmuseum.
Jan Luykenstraat 1 A, Amsterdam

Salomon Collection. *See* Collectie H.H.F. Salomon

Schatkamer van de O.L. Vrouwebasiliek.
O.L. Vrouweplein 8, Maastricht

Schatkamer van de St. Servaaskerk.
Keizer Karelplein 6, Maastricht

Schultehuis.
Brink 6, Diever (D.)

Schwarz, A., Collection. *See* Collectie A. Schwarz

Singer Museum.
(Stichting Singer Memorial Foundation), Oude Drift 1, Laren (N.H.)

Singraven.
Denekamp (O.)

Slingenberg Collection. *See* Collectie Dr. B. Slingenberg

Sonja Henies Og Niels Onstadts Stiftelser.
Kunstsentret N-1311 Hovikodden

Stedelijk Museum.
Hoogstraat 12, Schiedam (Z.H.)

Stedelijk Museum Alkmaar.
Doelenstraat 3, Alkmaar

Stedelijk Museum-Amsterdam.
Paulus Potterstraat 12, 1071 CX Amsterdam, 73 21 66 STEMUSEA
Permanent Collections:
Modern art.

Stedelijk Museum de Lakenhal.
Oude Singel 28-32, 2312 RA Leiden

Stedelijk Museum "Het Catharina-Gasthuis".
Oosthaven 10, Gouda

Stedelijk Museum het Prinsenhof.
St. Agathaplein 1, Delft

Stedelijk van Abbemuseum.
Bilderdijklaan 10, P.O. Box 235, 5600 AE Eindhoven
Permanent Collections:
20th century Avant-garde art

Stedelijk van Rekum Galerij.
Churchillplein 2, Apeldoorn

Stichting Nijmeegs Museum.
Grote Markt, Waaggebouw P.O. Box 578 Nijmegen

Stichting Stedelijk Museum van Vainen.
Museumzal in Het Stadhuis Voorstraat 30, Vianan (Z.H.)

Stichting Tegelmuseum "It Noflik Ste".
6731 BH Otterlo Eikenzoom 10, 08382-519

Stichting Willem van der Vorm.
Westersingel 66, Rotterdam

Teylers Museum.
Spaarne 16, Damstraat 21, 2011 HA Haarlem
Permanent Collections:
Dutch paintings, 19th and early 20th century drawings; Dutch, Italian and French school (16th-19th century); historical physical instruments (18th and

19th century); fossils and minerals.

Thurkow Collection. *See* Collectie Ir. C. Th. F. Thurkow

Van Abbe Museum. *See* Stedelijk van Abbemuseum

Van Elven, Paul, Museum. *See* Museum Paul Tetar Van Elven

Van Gogh Museum. *See* Rijksmuseum Vincent Van Gogh

Van Harinxma Thoe Slooten Stichting.
Harinxma-State, Beetsterzwaag, Gem.

Van Heeckern Van Walien Collection. *See* Collectie F. Baron van Heeckern van Walien

Van Nijevelt Van de Haar Collection. *See* Collectie E. Baron van Zuylen van Nijevelt van de Haar

Van Rechteren Collection. *See* Collectie C. E. A. A. en E. M. C. Gravin van Rechteren Limpurg

Van Rossum, Martin, Museum.
Nonnenstraat 7, Zaltbommel (G.)

Van Straaten Collection. *See* Collectie Mr. H.K. de Raaf Brand van Straaten

Van Tuyll Van Serooskerhen Van Heeze en Leende Collection. *See* Collectie Mr. H.N.C. Baron van Tuyll van Serookerken van Heeze en Leende

Van Weede Collection. *See* Collectie Jhr. Mr. W.E. van Weede

Veltman, A., Collection. *See* Collectie A. Veltman

Vereniging van Vrienden van het Princesshof.
Grote Kerkstraat 9-15, Leeuwarden
Permanent Collections:
Primarily ceramics; specialized in Oriental ceramics, tiles and modern ceramics. The approach is to exhibit and study flow of techniques, ideas and trends between East and West; and to identify common trade ceramics, ceramic industrial design, etc.

Westfries Museum.
Rode Steen 1, Kerkstraat 10, 1900 Hoorn

Westlands Streekmuseum.
Heilige Geest Hofje 7, Naaldwijk (Z.H.)

Wurfbain Collection. *See* Collectie J.G. Wurfbain

NEW ZEALAND

Aigantighe Art Gallery.
49 Wai-iti Rd., Timaru, Canterbury

Anderson Park Art Gallery.
P.O. Box 755, Invercangill

Art Gallery & Museum.
18 Stout St., Gisborne, Auckland

Auckland City Art Gallery.
Kitchener St., 1 Auckland

Bishop Suter Art Gallery. *See*
Suter, Bishop, Art Gallery

Dunedin Public Art Gallery.
P.O. Box 566 Dunedin

Govett-Brewster Art Gallery.
Queen St., P.O. Box 647, New Plymouth

Hawkes Bay Art Gallery & Museum.
Post Box 429 Napier

Manawatu Art Gallery.
Corner Grey & Carroll Sts., P.O. Box 565, Palmerston N., Wellington

National Art Gallery of New Zealand.
Buckle St., Wellington, 859-703 NATART
Permanent Collections:
Beauchamp Bequest, Monrad, Ilott, Rex Nan Kivell, Harold Wright, Smyth, Rita Angus Estate, National Art Gallery Collection, New Zealand painting.

Sarjeant Gallery.
P.O. Box 637, Wanganui

Suter, Bishop, Art Gallery.
Queen's Gardens, Bridge St., Nelson

Theomin Gallery (Olveston)
42 Royal Terrace, Dunedin, Otago

Waihi Arts Centre & Museum.
Kenny St., Waihi, Auckland

Waikato Art Museum.
150 London St., P.O. Box 937, Hamilton

Wairarapa Arts Center.
Bruce St., P.O. Box 633, Masterton

NIGERIA

Jos Museum.
Jos (Plateau Province, Northern Region)

Museum of Ife Antiquities.
Enuwa Square, Ife, Oyo, Western Region

Museum of the Institute of African Studies.
University of Ife, Jos (Plateau Province, Northern Region)

NORWAY

Bergen Billedgallerie "Permanenten".
Permanenten N-5000 Bergen

City of Oslo Art Collection, Munch Museum.
P.O. Box 2812 Kampen, 5, Oslo, 67-37-74

De Sandvigske Samlinger.
Maihaugen, N-2600, Lillehammer, 062 50 135

Permanent Collections:
Open-air museum and permanent indoor section for old crafts.

Det Faste Galleri. *See*
Trondhjems Kunstforening-Trondelag Kunstgalleri

Domkirkens Skulptursamling.
Bispegatan 3-5, N-7000 Trondheim

Drammens Museum, Fylkesmuseum for Buskerud.
Konnerudgaten 7, N-3000 Drammen

Historisk Museum.
Universitetet i Bergen, Frieles gate 3, Postboks 2632, N-5000 Bergen

Ingebbright Vik's Museum.
Oystese

Kunstindustrimuseet i Oslo.
St. Olvas Gate 1, Oslo

Kunstnerns Hus.
Vengelandsveien 17, Oslo

Lillehammer Bys Malerisamling.
Kirkegaten 69, 2600 Lillehammer

Munch Museum. *See* **City of Oslo Art Collection, Munch Museum**

Nasjonalgalleriet.
Universitetsgaten 13, 1 Oslo, 20 04 04
Permanent Collections:
Painting, sculpture, prints and drawings.

Njorsk Sjofartmuseum.
Bygodoynes, 2 Oslo

Nordenfjeldske Kunstindustrimusem.
Munkegata 5, N-7000 Trondheim

Norsk Folkemuseum.
Bygdoy, 2 Oslo

Norsk Folkmuseums Bibliotek.
Museumsveien 10, Oslo

Norwegian National Gallery. *See*
Nasjonalgalleriet

Rasmus Meyers Samlinger.
Lars Hilles Gate 8, N-5000 Bergen

Riksgalleriet.
Fornebu Hovegard, Lysaker, Postboks 8147 Oslo 1

Rolf E. Stenerson's Donation. *See*
Stenersons, Rolf E., Donation

Stavanger Art Gallery.
Stavanger Art Association, Madlaveien 33, N-4000 Stavanger

Stenersons, Rolf E., Donation.
Toyengata 53, Oslo 5

Sunnhordland Folkemuseum Og Sogelag.
N-5400 Stord

Trondhjems Kunstforening-Trondelag Kunstgalleri.
N-7000 Trondheim, 26671
Permanent Collections:
About 1500 pieces of art.

Universitetets Samling Av Nordiskek Oldsaker.
Frederiksgate 2, 1 Oslo

Vestlandske Kunstinustrimuseum.
Nordal Brunasgate 9, 5000 Bergen

Vigeland-Museet (Oslo Kommuneskuntsamlinger)
Nobelsgate 32, Oslo, 02 442306
Permanent Collections:
Gustav Vigeland's sculptures, drawings and woodcuts.

Vigeland-Parken (Oslo Kommuneskuntsamlinger)
Sogn, Oslo 8, 02 442306

PAKISTAN

Aiwen E-Rifaf Museum & Art Gallery.
Karachi

Art Gallery Society of Contemporary Art.
Rawalpindi Gallery of Modern Art, 25 Civil Lines, Taxila District

Industrial & Commercial Museum.
Dept. of Industries, Bank Sq., Lahore

Lahore Museum.
Shahrah-E-Quaid-E-Azam Lahore

National Museum of Pakistan.
Burns Garden, Karachi

Peshawar Museum.
Grand Trunk Rd., Peshawar, 72252 72252
Permanent Collections:
Gandhara Art, Terracotta, stucco, seals, coins belonging to Indo-Greek, Scythian, Parthian, Kushan and Sassanians manuscripts, paintings, arms, weapons, jewelry, dresses and wooden effigies, etc.

PANAMA

Museo Nacional de Panama.
Esquina Ave. Cuba y Calle 30, Panama City

PARAGUAY

Museo Botanico y Zoologico.
Presidente Franco Esq. A Juan e O'Leary, Asuscion

Museo de Arte Moderno.
Ministerio de Educacion, Chile 415, Asuncion

Museo de Ceramica y Bellas Artes "Julian de la Herreria".
Estados Unidos 1120, Asuncion

PERU

Centro de Arte.
Ricardo Palma 246, Miraflores, Lima

Merino, Ignacio, Gallery. *See*
Pinacoteca Municipal "Ignacio Merino"

Museo Amano.
Retiro 131, Mirafloes, Lima

Museo Arqueologico Bruning.
8 de Octubre 469, Lambayeque

Museo Arqueologico "Frederico Galvez Durard" de la Gran Unidad Escolar "Santa Isabel".
Huancas 251, Apdo. 189, Huancayo

Museo Arqueologico "Rafael Larco Herrera".
Ave. Bolivar 1515, Pueblo Libre, Lima

Museo de Arte.
Paseo Colon 125, Lima

Museo de Arte Italiano.
Paseo Colon 125, Lima

Museo Historico Regional de Ayacucho.
Jiron 28 de Julio No. 106, Ayacucho

Museo Historico Regional de Cuzco.
Dalle Heladeros, Cuzco

Museo Nacional de Historia.
Plaza Bolivar, Pueblo Libre, Lima

Museo Nacional de la Cultura Peruana.
Avenida Alfonso Ugarte 650, Apdo 3048 Lima

Museo "Oro del Peru" y "Armas Antiguas".
Belen 1058, Huerta de San Antonio, Apdo 988, Lima

Pinacoteca Municipal "Ignacio Merino".
Paseo Colon 125, Lima

PHILIPPINES

Ateneo Art Gallery.
Ateneo de Manila University, Manila

Cultural Center of the Philippines Art Gallery.
Roxas Blvd., Manila

Lopez Memorial Museum & Library.
10 Lancaster Ave., Pasay City D-720

National Museum of the Philippines, Gallery of Arts.
Manila

Rizal Shrine at Fort Santiago.
Port Santiago, Manila

Rizal Shrine in Dapitan.
Dapitan, Zamboanga

University of Santo Thomas Museum of Art & Sciences:
Calle Espana, Manila
Permanent Collections:
Natural history mostly of the Philippines; ethnology of the Philippine cultures as well as Chinese, Japanese, Vietnamese, Thai and European related cultures; painting; sculpture; applied art mainly of the Philippines; numismatics; philately; portraits; relics; archaeology.

POLAND

Biblioteka Jagiellonska.
Ul. Mickiewicza 22, Krakow

Biblioteka Kornicka Polskiej Akademii Nauk-Dzial Muzealny.
Kornik, Woj. Poznan

Centrale Muzeum Morskie w Gdansku.
Ul.Szeroka 67/68, 80-835 Gdansk, 31 69 38
Permanent Collections:
History of Shipbuilding, History of Maritime shipping and Trade, History of Inland Shipping, History of Fishing, History of Marine Arts.

Czartoryski Library & Archives.
Ul Sw Marka 17, Cracow

Dom Jana Matejki.
Ul Florianska 41, Cracow

Gabinet Grafiki Biblioteki Zakladu Norodowego im Ossolinskich Pan.
Ul. Szewska 37, Wroclaw

Gabinet Rycin Biblioteki Uniwersyteckiej w Warsawie.
Ul. Krakowskie Przedmiescie 32, Warszawa
Permanent Collections:
Prints and drawings 15th through the 20th century.

Galeria Malarstawa Polskiego w XIX.
Rynek Glowny, Sukiennice, Cracow

Galeria Polskiego Malarstwa Rzezby.
Pl. Szczepanski 9, Kamienica Szolayskich, Cracow

Galeria Sztuki Polskiej w XX.
Al Trzeciego Maja 1, Cracow

Kamienca Szolayskich.
Pl. Szczepanski Krakow

Kamienica Pod Gwiazda.
Rynek Staromiejski 35, Torun, Woj. Bydgoszcz

Kuznia Wodna (Muzeum Techniki w Warszawie)
Stara Kuznica, Woj. Kielce

Muzeum.
Oporow woj. Lodz

Muzeum.
Zamek, Leczyca, woj. Lodz

Muzeum.
Zamek, Ul. Zamkowa 9, Lublin

Muzeum.
Lidzbark Warminski, woj Olsztyn

Muzeum.
Zamek, Ul. Katedralna 1, Kwidzyn

Muzeum.
Ul. Nowotki 12, Radom, woj Kielce

Muzeum.
Ul. Lubelska 55, Chelm, woj. Lublin

Muzeum.
Ul. Chopina 12, Raciborz, woj. Opole

Muzeum.
Ul. Dominikanska 2, Sieradz, woj. Lodz

Muzeum.
Ul. Marcinkowskiego 1, Nysa, woj Opole

Muzeum.
Ul. Wodna 3/5, Grudziadz, wol Bydgoszcz

Muzeum.
Ul. Wigilijna 11/12, Elblag, woj. Gdansk

Muzeum.
Zamek, Ul. Zamkowa 2, Lancut, woj. Rzeszow

Muzeum.
Ul. Dolnych Walow 8a, Gliwice, woj. Katowice

Muzeum.
Ul. Wzgorze 16a, Bielsko-Biala, woj. Katowice

Muzeum.
Zamek Ksiazat Pomorskiech Ul. Zamkowa 4, Darlowo, Woj. Koszalin

Muzeum.
Ratusz, Budynek B. Pl. Im. Dra W. Bieganskiego, Czestochowa, woj. Katowice

Muzeum Archeologiczne.
Ul. Mariacka 25/26, Gdansk

Muzeum Archeologiczne.
Palac Gorkow, Ul. Wodna 27, Poznant, 582-51

Muzeum Archeologiczne i Etnograficzne w Lodzi.
Pl. Wolnosci 14, Lodz 91-415, 339-13
Permanent Collections:
Archaeological objects from the Paleolithic to 16th century A.D., mainly from central Poland; ethnographical folk culture of Poland, mid-19th century to present day exhibits from South America, East Asia, subtropical Africa; numismatics (Ancient, Medieval and Modern coins from various countries) and Medieval and Modern coins from Poland; coin hoards, medals, decorations and paper money.

Muzeum Archidiecezjalne.
Ul. Lubranskiego 1, Poznan

Muzeum Archidiecezjalne we Wroclawiu.
Ul. Kanonia 12, 50-238 Wroclaw

Muzeum Baroku Polskiego.
Lowicz, woj. Lodz

Muzeum Budowlane.
Ul. Gornoslaska 31, Warsaw

Muzeum Budownictwa Ludowego.
Ul. Traugutta 3, Sanok' woj. Rzeszow, 2493

Muzeum Diecezjalne.
Pelplin, woj. Gdansk

Muzeum Diecezjalne.
Pl. Katedralny 5, Tarnow, woj. Krakow

Muzeum Diecezjalne.
Ul. Dlugosza 9, Sandomierz, woj. Kielce

Muzeum Diecezjalne.
Plac T. Czackiego 2, 37-700 Przemysl, 27-92

Muzeum Diecjalne.
Ul. Tumska 3a, Plock, woj. Warsaw

Muzeum Etnograficzne.
Pl. Wolnica 1, Krakow

Muzeum Etnograficzne (Muzeum Narodowe)
Ul. Kazimierza Wielkiego 33, Wroclaw

Muzeum Gornoslaskie.
Pl. E. Thalmanna 2, Bytom

Muzeum Historycznoartystyczne.
Ul. Zamkowa 2, Sanok, woj.

Muzeum Im. Leona Wyczolkowskiego.
Al. 1 Maja 4, Bydgoszcz

Muzeum Kaszubskie.
Ul. Koscierska 1, Kartuzy, woj. Gdansk

Muzeum Kujawskie.
Ul. Stowackiego 1a, Wloclawek

Muzeum Kultry i Sztuki Lodowej (Muzeum Narodowe)
Ul. Grobla 25, Poznan

Muzeum Manieryzmu.
Zorawina, woj. Wroclaw

Muzeum Mazowieckie w Plocku.
Ul. Tumska 2, Plock, woj. Warsaw, 28-31
Permanent Collections:
Art nouveau and the history of the Masovian region.

Muzeum Mazurskie.
Ul. Zamkowa 2, Olsztyn

Muzeum Miejskie.
Ul. Kniewskiego 24, Tarnow

Muzeum (Muzeum Diecjlnego w Tarnowie)
Szczyrzyc, woj. Krakow

Muzeum (Muzeum Narodowego w Pozananiu)
Rogalin, woj. Poznan

Muzeum (Muzeum Narodowego w Warszawie)
Rynek Kosciuszki 4, Lowicz

Muzeum Narodowe Oddzial w Lowiczu.
Rynek Kosciuszki 4, 928
Permanent Collections:
Polish Baroque art, painting of Josef Chelmonski and Stanislaw Noakowski, regional history and ethnography, rural architecture of Lowicz country.

Muzeum Narodowe w Gdansku.
Ul. Torunska 1, 80-822 Gdansk, 31-40-31, 31-11-25

Muzeum Narodowe w Kielcach.
Pl. Partyzantow 3-5, 25-303 Kielce, 482-61, 467-64
Permanent Collections:
Polish painting and graphic art of the 17th-20th century, especially an old Polish "Sarmatian" portrait from 17th-18th century; landscape painting from the 19th and 20th century; painting of the Polish Modernism period; so called Young Poland - Art Nouveau; Goldsmithery, antique furniture from the 17th to 19th century, glass from the 18th and 19th century; "Cmielow" porcelain from the 19th to 20th century: arms and armor from the 16th-20th century; decorated stone tiles from Bodzentyn Castle in Kielce province from the 15th-16th century; folk arts and handicrafts from the region, especially sculpture from the 19th and 20th century.

Muzeum Narodowe w Krakowie.
Ul. Manifestu Lipcowego 12, Krakow, 254-34
Permanent Collections:
Gallery of Polish painting and sculpture (14th-18th century), Gallery of Polish painting and sculpture (19th-20th century), the Czartoryski's Collection, the Matejkos House.

Muzeum Narodowe w Poznaniu.
Al. Marcinkowskiego 9, Poznan 61-745, 580-11, 559, 69
Permanent Collections:
Medieval art, Polish and European painting from the 14th-20th centuries, decorative art, musical instruments, popular art, numismatics, printing, sculpture from the 14th-20th centuries and historical documents library.

Muzeum Narodowe w Szczecinie.
Ul. Staromlynska 27, Szczecin

Muzeum Narodowe w Warsawie.
Al Jerozolimskie 3, Warsaw 00-495, 21-10-31

Muzeum Narodowe we Wroclawiu.
Plac Powstancow Warszawy 5, Wroclaw 50-153

Muzeum Okregowe.
Ul. 3 Maja 19, Rzeszow

Muzeum Okregowe.
Rynek Kosciuszki, Bialystok

Muzeum Okregowe.
Rynek Staromiejski 1, Torun, woj. Bydgoszcz

Muzeum Parafialne.
Dobra, woj. Krakow

Muzeum Piastow Slaskich.
Pl Zamkowy 1, Brzeg woj. Opole

Muzeum Plakatu w Wilanowie.
02-958 Warsaw, Wilanow-Palac, 42-26-06

Muzeum Pomorskie.
Ul. Rzenznicka 25, Gdansk

Muzeum Pomorza Srodkowego.
Slupsk, woj. Koszalin

Muzeum Regionalne.
Ul. Kromera 2, Biecz, woj Rzeszow

Muzeum Rzemiose Artystycznych.
Gora Przemyslawa 1, Poznan

Muzeum Rzemiosla.
Ul. Pocwale 11, Warsaw

Muzeum Slaska Opolskiego.
Maly Rynek 7, Copole

Muzeum Slezy.
Ul. Armii Czerwonej 9,
Sobotka, woj. Wroclaw

Muzeum Sztuki Sakralnej.
Istebna na Kubalonce woj.
Katowice

Muzeum Tkactwa.
Andrychow, woj. Krakow

**Muzeum Uniwersytetu
Jagiellonskiego.**
Ul. Sw. Anny 8, Krakow

**Muzeum w Wilanowie (Muzeum
Narodowego w Warszawic)**
Warsaw

Muzeum Wnetrz Zabytkowych.
Pszcyna, woj. Katowice, 30-37
Permanent Collections:
Historic interiors, 16th-19th
century, with fine paintings,
furniture, sculpture, porcelain,
silver, carpets, etc. Department
of Armor and Hunting
Trophies from 16th to 20th
century. Also 300 miniatures
from the 17th-20th century.

Muzeum Zamkowe.
(Panstwowych Zbiorow Sztuki
Na Wawelu, Krakow)

Muzeum Ziemi Klodzkiej.
Pl. Boleslawa Chrobrego 22,
Klodzko, woj. Wroclaw

Muzeum Ziemi Przemyskiej.
Pl. Czackiego, Przemysl, woj.
Rzeszow

National Museum of Ethnography.
See **Panstwowe Muzeum
Etnograficzine**

Nieborow.
Nieborow I Arkadia, woj. Lodz

**Nowy Gmach (Muzeum Narodowe
w Krakowie)**
A1. Trzeciego Maja 1, Krakow

**Oddzial im Emeryka
Huttenczapskiego (Muzeum
Narodowe w Krakowie)**
Ul. Manifestu Lipcowego 10,
Krakow

**Oddzial Muzeum Budownictwa w
Sanoku.**
Ulucz, woj. Rzeszow

**Panstwowe Muzeum
Etnograficzine.**
Kredytowa 1, Warsaw, 26-81-
78, 27-66-69
Permanent Collections:
Non-European culture: Africa,
Australia, Oceania, Indonesia,
Latin America, South America;
Polish Folk Culture: crafts,
weaving and regional costumes,
art and folklore.

**Panstwowe Zbiory Sztuki Na
Wawelu.**
Wawel 5, Cracow

Punkt Muzealny.
Dorbra Szlachecka, woj.
Rzeszow

Punkt Muzealny.
(Muzeum Bodownictwa
Ludowego Wsanoku) Haczow

Skarbiec Na Jasnel Orze.
Klasztor Panlinow, Ul.
Kordeckiego Czestochowa, woj.
Katowice

**Sukiennice (Muzeum Narodowe w
Krakowie)**
Ryenk Glowny, Krakow

**Wawelu Castle State Art
Collections.** *See* **Panstwowe
Zbiory Sztuki Na Wawelu**

Zbiory Czartoryskich.
Ul Pijarska 15, Cracow

**Zbiory Graficzine Biblioteki
Narodowej.**
Pl. Kranskich 5, Warsaw

**Zbiory Graficzne Biblioteki
Polskiej Akademij Nauk.**
Ul. Slawkowska 17, Krakow

**Zbiory Panstwowej Wyzszej
Szkoly Sztok Plastycznych.**
Ul. Traugutta 19/20, Wroclaw

PORTUGAL

**Biblioteca-Museu Municipal de
Albano Sandoeira.**
Convento Goncalo, Amarante
(Duoro Litoral)

Calouste Gulbenkian Museum.
Ave. de Berna, Lisbon, 735131
Permanent Collections:
Calouste Gulbenkian art
collection covering the period
2800 B.C. to the 20th century,
antique classical and Oriental
art, Egyptian, Assyrian, Greek,
Roman, Islamic, and Far
Eastern art; European painting,
sculpture, illuminated
manuscripts, tapestries and
fabrics, furniture, gold and
silver, jewelry, glass, medals.

Casa Museu dos Patudos. *See*
**Instituicao Jose Relvas, Casa
Museu dos Patudos**

Gomes, Cesar, Museu. *See* **Museu
Cesar Gomes**

**Instituicao Jose Relvas, Casa
Museu dos Patudos.**
Casa de Patudos, Alpiaca, 5 42
06
Permanent Collections:
Collections of painting,
sculpture, tapestry and
ceramics.

Museo de Escultura Camparada.
Convento, Mafra

Museo de Escultura Comparado.
Rua do Bispo 21, Madeira

Museu.
Azambuja

Museu.
Casa do Barbosa Macieis, Rua
Manuel Espregueira, Viana do
Castelo (Minho)

Museu Almeida Moreira.
Largo Do Soar De Cima, Viseu
Permanent Collections:
Furniture of the following
styles: Dutch, Empire,
Renaissance, D. Joao V, Louis
XV, D. Jose and Baroque; tin
from the 18th and 19th
century, Portuguese silver from
the 18th and 19th century,
English earthenware,
Portuguese ceramics; fayences
and porcelain (Portuguese,
Chinese, Dutch, Delft, Italian

and Spanish), contemporary
Portuguese painting, art and
history library.

Museu Arqueologico.
Sao Joao d'Alporao, Santarem

Museu Arqueologico do Carmo.
Largo do Carmo, 1200 Lisbon

**Museu Arqueologico Infante D.
Henrique.**
Praca Afonso III, Faro

**Museu Biblioteca "Conde de
Castro Guimaraes".**
Cascais

Museu Cesar Gomes.
Maderia

Museu de Alberto Sampaio.
Rua Alfredo Guimaraes,
Guimaraes

**Museu de Arte Sacra da
Misericordia.**
Rua de Misericordia, Lisbon

Museu de Evora.
Lango Conde Vila Flor, Evora
7000

Museu de "Grao Vasco".
Paco dos Tres Escaloes, Viseu
Permanent Collections:
The Museum occupies 3 floors
with the following collections:
Portuguese furniture from the
17th-18th century; Portuguese
sculpture from the 13th-18th
century (stone, wood, ivory and
terra-cotta). Portuguese
engraving from the Baroque
period through the 18th
century; Portuguese ceramics
from the 16th-17th century and
the 19th century. There are
examples from the factories of
Lisbon, Porto, Viara do Castelo
Massarelos, Vale do Pudade,
Carninha, Coimbra and
Estremoz. China Porcelain
from 17th to 18th century;
Portuguese silverware from the
17th, 18th and 19th century,
French and English silver,
Portuguese tapestries from the
17th and 18th century, French,
Italian, English and Japanese
liturgical vestments designed in
velvet, brocaded and bordered
with silk and gold from the
16th, 17th and 18th century;
Numismatics; Paintings
including the 16th century
School of Vasco Fernandes, of
Grao Vasco da Tradicao and
his collaborators; 14 panels
representing the life of Christ;
foreign painting includes
French, German, Spanish,
Italian and Flemish schools;
contemporary Portuguese
painting.

Museu de Jose Malhoa.
Caldas de Rainha
(Estremadura)

Museu de Lamego.
5100 Lamego

Museu de Sao Rogue.
Largo Trindade Coelho, Lisbon

Museu do Abade de Bacal.
Rua Serpa, Braganca

**Museu-Escola de Artes
Decorativas.**
Largo das Portas do Sol 2,
Lisbon

Museu Etnologico.
Dormitorio, Jeronimus-Cloister,
Belem, Lisbon

Museu Nacional de Arte Antiga.
Rua das Janelas Verdes, Lisbon
1293, 664151, 672725
Permanent Collections:
Painting (Portuguese and
foreign), sculpture, ornamental
art (goldsmith's art, ceramics,
furniture and textiles--
Portuguese, European and
Oriental).

**Museu Nacional de Arte
Contemporanea.**
Rua Serpia Pinto 6, Lisbon

**Museu Nacional de "Machado de
Castro".**
Largo da Feira, Coimbra

**Museu Nacional de Soares dos
Reis.**
Rua D. Manuel II, Porto

Museu Rafael Bordalo Pinheiro.
Campo Grande, 382, Lisbon

Museu Regional.
Converto Nossa Senhora da
Conceiacao Largo do Porvir,
Beja

Museu Regional de Aveiro.
Aveiro

**Museu Regional "Francisco
Tavares Proenca Junior".**
Castelo Branco

Museu Santo Antonio.
Ermida de Santo Antonio
Doalto, Faro

Muzeul Manastirii Agapia.
Agapia

**Pinheiro, Rafael Bordalo,
Museum.** *See* **Museu Rafael
Bordalo Pinheiro**

Sampaio, Alberto, Museum. *See*
Museu de Alberto Sampaio

PUERTO RICO

Ateneo Puertorriqueno.
Ponce de Leon Stop 1, San
Juan

House of Books.
Calle del Cristo 255, San Juan,
00901

Institute of Puerto Rico Culture.
Apartado 4184, San Juan,
00905

Museo de Arquitectura Colonial.
Fortaleza 319, San Juan

Museo de Arte.
Luis A. Ferre Foundation,
Apdo. 1492, Ponce

Museo de Arte Popular.
Calle Cristo San Juan

Museo de Arte Religioso.
Hermita Porta Coeli, San
German

Museo de Bellas Artes.
Calle del Santo Cristo de la
Salud 253 San Juan

Ponce Art Museum.
P. O. Box 1492, Ponce, 00731

University of Puerto Rico Museum of Archaeology, History & Art:
Rio Piedras

REUNION

Musee des Beaux-Arts Leon Dierx.
Rue Sainte Marie et Rue de Paris, BP 395, Saint-Denis

RHODESIA

Bulawayo Art Gallery.
Grey St., P.O. Box 1993, Bulawayo

National Gallery of Rhodesia.
Post Box 8155, Salisbury

RUMANIA

Cabinet de Stampe al Bibliotechii Academiei R. C. Romania.
Calea Victoriei 125, Bucuresti

Cas "Hagi Prodan".
Str. Democratie 2, Ploiesti

Colectia de Arta Comparata Slatineanu.
(Muzeul de Istorrie a Municipiului Bucuresti)

Colectia "Ion Minulescu".
Bd. Gh. Marinescu 19, Bucuresti

Colectia Memoriala "I. Iser".
Bd. N. Balcescu 9, Bucuresti

Colectia "Moise M. Weinberg".
Str. Alex. Sahia 36 Bucuresti

Grigorescu, Nicolae, Memorial Museum. *See* **Muzeul Memorial "Nicolae Grigorescu"**

Iser, I., Memorial Collection. *See* **Colectia Memoriala "I. Iser"**

Muzeul Banatului.
Plata Huniade 1, Timisoara

Muzeul Brukenthal.
Piata Republicii 4-6, Sibiu

Muzeul "Cecilia Si Frederic Stock" (Muzeul de Arta al Municipiului Bucuresti "Anastasie Simu")
Berevoiesti

Muzeul "Cornel Medrea" (Muzeul de Arta al Munici Piului Bucuresti "Anastasie Simu")
Str. Gen. Budisteanv 16, Bucuresti

Muzeul de Archeologie Tecuci.
Str. 23 August 36, Tecuci

Muzeul de Arta al Academei R. S. Romania - Colectia George Oprescu.
Str. Dr. Clunet 16, Bucuresti

Muzeul de Arta al Municipiului Bucuresti "Anastasie Simu".
Str. Biserica Amzei 9, Bucuresti

Muzeul de Arta al R. S. Romania.
Str. Stirbei Voda 1, Bucuresti

Muzeul de Arta Babadag.
Babadag

Muzeul de Arta Braila.
Str. Galati, Braila

Muzeul de Arta Brincoveneasca-Mogos Aia.
Mogosoaia/Bucuresti

Muzeul de Arta Cluj-Napuca.
Piata Libertatii 30, Cluj-Napoca

Muzeul de Arta Crajova.
Calea Unirii 15, Crajova

Muzeul de Arta Din Iasi.
Str. Palatului 1, Iasi

Muzeul de Arta Din Ploiesti.
Bd. Gheorgghiu-Dej 1, Ploiesti

Muzeul de Arta Feudala "Ing. D. Minovici al Academiei R.S.R.
Str. Dr. Minovici 3, Bucuresti 18

Muzeul de Arta Limanu.
Limanu

Muzeul de Arta Medgidia.
Medgidia

Muzeul de Arta Populara al R.S. Romania.
Calea Victoriei 107, Bucuresti

Muzeul de Arta Populara "Dr. N. Minovici" (Muzeul de Istorie al Municipiului Bucuresti)
Str. Dr. N. Minovici 1, Bucuresti 18

Muzeul de Arta Romaneasca Moderna Si Contemporana.
Str. Republicii 141, Galati

Muzeul de Arta Tirgu Mures.
Piata Eroilor Sovietici 1, Tirgu Mures

Muzeul de Arta Topalu.
Topalu

Muzeul de Istorie al R. S. Romania.
Calea Victoriei 12, Bucuresti

Muzeul de Istorie Nationala si Arheologie.
Piata Ovidiu, 12, 8700 Constanta, 139 25; 145 62; 145 83
Permanent Collections:
Archaeology; numismatics; glass vessels; Janagra statuettes; pottery; ancient art; edifice with mosaics; collection of curiosities; Mercurius; Medieval, modern and contemporary history.

Muzeul de Istorie Satu Mare.
Piata Libertatii 21, Satu Mare

Muzeul de Istorie Si Arheologie Alba Iulia.
Str. Mihai Viteazul 12-14, Alba Iulia, Jud. Hunedoara

Muzeul de Istorie Si Arta.
Str. Manasesti 42, Bacau

Muzeul de Istorie Suceava.
Str. Stefan del Mare 33, Suceava

Muzeul Din Caracal.
Str. Negru Voda 1, Caracal, jud. Olt

Muzeul Din Sebes.
Parcul 8 Mai 4, Sebes

Muzeul Din SF. Gheorghe.
Str. 16 Februarie 10, Sf. Gheorghe

Muzeul "Dr. Dona" (Muzeul de Arta Municipiuli Bucuresti "Anastasie Simu")
Str. Eneral Dona 12-14, Bucuresti 7

Muzeul Etnografic Din Radauti.
Str. Bogdan Voda 2, Radauit

Muzeul Ion Jalea.
Constanta

Muzeul Judetean Arad.
Piata Enescu 1, Anad

Muzeul Judetean Botosani.
Calea Nationala 251, Botosani

Muzeul Judetean Maramures.
Str. 1 Mai 8, Baia Mare

Muzeul Judetean Tirgu Mures.
Str. Horia 24, Piata Tnandafirilor 11, Tingu Mures

Muzeul Manastirii Cozia.
Cozia

Muzeul Manastirii Horezu.
Horez

Muzeul Memorial "Nicolae Grigorescu".
Str. 23 August 170, Cimpina, jud. Prahova

Muzeul Memorial "Theodor Aman" (Muzeul de Arta al Municipiuliu Bucuresti "Anastasie Simu")
Str. C.A. Rosetti 8, Bucuresti

Muzeul Minastirii Dealu.
Tirgoviste

Muzeul Mixt Orasenesc Cimpulung.
Str. Republicii 5, Cimpulung Muscel, Jud. Arges

Muzeul Peles.
Str. Peles 2, Sinaia

Muzeul Pictor Gheorghe Tattarascu (Muzeul de Arta al Municipiului Bucuresti "Anastasie Simu")
Str. Domnita Anastasia 7, Bucuresti

Muzeul Toma Stelian.
Sos. Kisseleff 8, Bucuresti

Muzeul Zambaccian (Muzeul de Arta al Municipiului Bucuresti "Anastesi Simu")
Str. Muzeal Zambaccian 21, Bucuresti

Muzeuul Pinacoteca si Gliptoteca Alex. Aman.
Str. Kogalniceanu 9, Craiova, jud. Dolj

Muzuel "Cecilia Si Frederic Storck" (Muzeul De Arta Al Municipiului Bucuresti "Anastasie Simu")
Str. Vasile Alecsandri 16, Bucuresti 1

Oprescu, George, Collection. *See* **Muzeul de Arta al Academei R. S. Romania - Colectia George Oprescu**

Weinberg, Moise M., Collection. *See* **Colectia "Moise M. Weinberg"**

RWANDA

Ecole d'Art de Nyundo.
BP 177, Nyundo/Gisenyi

SAN MARINO

Museo Civico.
Via Carduccil-47031 San Marino

SENEGAL

Musee d'Art Africain de Dakar.
Institut Fondamental d'Afrique Noire, Place Tacher BP 206, Dakar

SINGAPORE

National Museum of Singapore.
Stamford Rd., Singapore 6

University of Singapore Art Museum:
Bukit Timah Rd., Singapore

SOUTH AFRICA

Bryant, Ann, Art Gallery.
12 St. Lukas Rd., East London

Durban Art Gallery.
P.O. Box 4085, Durban 4000
Permanent Collections:
Oil paintings, watercolors and drawings of the following: South African school, English 19th and 20th century, French 19th and 20th century, Dutch and Flemish 17th century, South African, French and English sculpture.

Engelenburg House Art Collection.
Hamilton & Ziervogel Sts. P.O. Box 538, Pretoria

Fehr, William, Collection.
Castle of Good Hope, P. O. Box 1, Cape Town, 458711
Permanent Collections:
Oil paintings, seascapes and early views of the Cape; Cape furniture, silver, glass, brass and copper; Chinese and Japanese porcelain. Another section of the museum is housed at Rust en Vreugd, built in 1777, and contains watercolors, drawings and prints of South African interest.

Gordon, Julius, Africana Centre.
Verveld House, Long St., Riversdale

Groot Constantia Manor House.
P.O. Box 645, Cape Town, 74 1067
Permanent Collections:
17th, 18th and 19th century South African and European furniture, paintings, ceramics, glassware, maps and graphics. Also Chinese and Japanese ceramics. Wine Museum housed in 18th century wine cellar containing drinking vessels from antiquity to present.

Hester Rupert Art Museum. *See* Rupert, Hester, Art Museum

Humphreys, William, Art Gallery.
Post Box 455, Kimberley

Jewish Museum of the South African Jewish Board of Deputees.
4th Floor, Sheffield House, Main & Kruis St, P.O. Box 1180, Johannesburg

Johannesburg Art Gallery.
Joubert Park Johannesburg, 725-3130
Permanent Collections:
Dutch, French and English art from the 17th-19th century; South African Collection; International Modern Collection, print cabinet with works ranging from Durer and Rembrandt to the present day; Decorative arts (small collections of furniture, ceramics and textiles).

Julius Gordon Africana Centre. *See* Gordon, Julius, Africana Centre

King George VI Art Gallery.
One Park Dr 6001, Port Elizabeth

Koopmans de Wet House.
35 Strand St., Cape Town, 412068
Permanent Collections:
Furnished as a late 18th century house.

Michaelis Collection, Old Town House.
Greenmarket Square, Cape Town

Oude Pastorie Museum.
Main St., Paarl

Pretoria Art Museum.
Aredia Park, Schoeman St. 0089 Pretoria

Rupert, Hester, Art Museum.
Church St., Graaff-Reinet

South African Cultural History Museum.
Old Supreme Court, 49 Adderley St., P.O. Box 61, Cape Town

South African National Gallery.
Government Ave., P.O. Box 2420, 8000 Cape Town, 451628 SANGAL
Permanent Collections:
South African paintings, sculpture, prints and drawings, European paintings (mainly Dutch, French, Flemish and English), European sculpture (mainly English), foreign prints and drawings.

Tatham Art Gallery.
Post Box 321 3200 Pietermartzburg
Permanent Collections:
Paintings, graphics, objets d'art, sculpture, Oriental carpets, glass and porcelain.

William Fehr Collection. *See* Fehr, William, Collection

William Humphreys Art Gallery. *See* Humphreys, William, Art Gallery

SPAIN

Biblioteca-Mueso Soler y Palet.
Fuente Vieja, 28, Tarrasa, Prov. Barcelona

Casa y Museo del Greco.
Calle de Samuel Levi, Toledo

Coleccion Arqueologica Municipal.
Jerez de la Frontera, Prov. Cadiz

Colleciones del Real Monasterio.
El Escorial, Prov. Madrid

Frederico Mares Museo. *See* Mares, Frederico, Museum

Instituto de Valencia de Don Juan.
Calle de Fortuny, 43, Madrid

Mares, Frederico, Museum.
Condes de Barcelona, 10, Barcelona
Permanent Collections:
Sculpture and "artes suntuarias."

Museo Archaeologicum Diocesanum.
Solsona, Lerida

Museo Arquelogico Provincial.
Oviedo

Museo Arqueologico.
Plaza de la Catedral, Ibizia, Baleares

Museo Arqueologico.
Plazuelo de Santa Clara 5, Merida, Prov. Badajoz

Museo Arqueologico Artistico Episcopal.
Vich, Prov. Barcelona

Museo Arqueologico de Barcelona.
Parque de Montjuich, Barcelona

Museo Arqueologico de la Alhambra.
Granada

Museo Arqueologico de Toledo.
Toledo

Museo Arqueologico del Monasterio.
Monasterio de Santo Domingo de Silos, Prov. Burgos

Museo Arqueologico Municipal "Camilio Visedo Molto".
Plazuelo del Carbo, Alcoy

Museo Arqueologico Nacional.
Calle de San Marcos, Lugo

Museo Arqueologico Provincial.
Palencia

Museo Arqueologico Provincial.
Alcazaba, Malaga

Museo Arqueologico Provincial.
La Galera, Badajoz

Museo Arqueologico Provincial.
Plaza de Mina, Cadiz

Museo Arqueologico Provincial.
Palacio Episcopal, Orense

Museo Arqueologico Provincial.
Calle de la Calera, Burgos

Museo Arqueologico Provincial.
Carrera del Darro, Granada

Museo Arqueologico Provincial.
Convento de San Marco, Leon

Museo Arqueologico Provincial.
Plaza de la Cattedral, Huesca

Museo Arqueologico Provincial.
Plaza de Santo Cruz, Valladolid

Museo Arqueologico Provincial.
Iglesia del Monasterio de San Pedro de Galligans

Museo Arqueologico Provincial de Cordoba.
Plaza de Jeronimo Paez, 7, Cordoba

Museo Arqueologico y de Bellas Artes.
Murcia

Museo Balaguer.
Villanueva y Geltru, Prov. Barcelona

Museo Catedralicio.
Leon

Museo Catedralicio.
Zamora

Museo Catedralicio.
Huesca

Museo Catedralicio.
Burgos

Museo Catedralicio.
Badajoz

Museo Catedralicio.
Segovia

Museo Catedralicio.
Granada

Museo Cerralbo.
Ventura Rodriguez 17, Madrid

Museo Comarcal.
Cervera, Prov.

Museo Comarcal y de Vino.
Palacio de los Reyes de la Corona de Aragon, Villafranca del Panaces, Prov. Barcelona

Museo de America.
Ave. Reyes Catolicos, Cuidad Universitaria, Madrid 3

Museo de Arte Moderno.
Olot, Prov. Gerona

Museo de Arte Moderno.
Palacio de la Ciudadela, Barcelona

Museo de Arte Popular.
Avila

Museo de Artes Contemporaneo de Toledo.
Toledo

Museo de Artes Decorativas.
Rambla, Palacio de la Virreina, Barcelona

Museo de Bellas Artes.
Plaza de Mina, Cadiz

Museo de Bellas Artes.
San Agustin, Segovia

Museo de Bellas Artes.
Tres Cruces, 85, Sabadell, Prov. Barcelona

Museo de Bellas Artes de Cataluna.
Palacio Nacional, Parque de Montjuich, Barcelona

Museo de Belles Artes.
Plaza de las Naciones, Bilbao

Museo de Gomellano.
Gumiel de Izan, Prov. Burgos

Museo de Historia de la Ciudad.
Plaza del Ray, Barcelona

Museo de la Camara Santa.
Oviedo

Museo de la Capilla Real.
Granada

Museo de la Casa de Cultura.
Enrique Granados, 17, Mataro, Prov. Barcelona

Museo de la Casa de los Tiros.
Calle de Pavaneras, Granada

Museo de la Catedral.
Plaza de la Catedral, Avila

Museo de la Catedral.
Roda de Isabena, Prov. Huesca

Museo de la Colegiata.
Manresa, Prov. Barcelona

Museo de la Encarnacion.
Plaza de la Encarnacion, Madrid

Museo de la Fundacion Duque de Lerma.
Toledo

Museo de la Mezquita.
Calle de Velazquez Bosco 15, Cordoba

Museo de la Real Academia de Bellas Artes de San Fernando.
Acala 13, Madrid

Museo de las Descalzes Reales.
Madrid

Museo de Mallorca, Seccion Bellas Artes.
Lonja, Palma de Mallorca

Museo de Pintura y Sales de Escultura.
Akala, 13, Madrid

Museo de Pontevedra.
Calle Pasanteria, Apdo 104, Pontevedra

Museo de Reproducciones Artisticas.
Ciudad Universitaria, Madrid

Museo de Reproducciones Artisticas de Bilbao.
Bilbao

Museo de Santa Cruz.
Sevilla

Museo de Santa Cruz.
Hospital de Santa Cruz, Cervantes, 3, Toledo

Museo del Cabildo Insular.
Las Palmas de Gran Canarias

Museo del Cau Ferrat.
Sitges, Prov. Barcelona

Museo del Colegio del Patriarca.
Calle de la Nave, Valencia

Museo del Duque de Alba.
Martires de Alcale, Madrid

Museo del Instituto de Estudios Iberdenses.
Lerida

Museo del Prado.
Calle de Felipe IV, Madrid

Museo del Santisimo Sacramento.
Daroca, Zaragoza

Museo del Seminario.
Lerida

Museo del Seminario Diocesano.
Logrono

Museo Diocesano.
Astorga

Museo Diocesano.
Zaragoza

Museo Diocesano.
Salamanca

Museo Diocesano.
Tarragona

Museo Diocesano.
Santiago de Compostela

Museo Diocesano.
Plaza de Espana 2, Gerona

Museo Diocesano.
Palacio Arzobispal, Valencia

Museo Diocesano.
C. Jaime Conquistador, 67, Lerida

Museo Diocesano.
Palacio Episcopal, Palma de Mallorca

Museo Diocesano.
Seminario Conciliar, Calle de la Disputacion, Barcelona

Museo Diocesano de Arte Sacra.
Oriheula, Prov. Alicante

Museo Espanol de Arte Contemporaneo.
Calvo Sotelo, 20. Madrid

Museo Etnologico.
Alfonos XII, 68, Madrid

Museo Historico de Vizcayo.
Calle de la Cruz, Bilbao

Museo Lazaro Galdiano.
Serrano, Madrid

Museo Martimo.
Palma de Mallorca

Museo Monasterio de las Huelgas.
Burgos

Museo Municipal.
Fuencarral, Madrid

Museo Municipal.
Figueras, Prov. Gerona

Museo Municipal.
Villadoris, 1, Manresa, Prov. Barcelona

Museo Municipal.
Calle de Jose Carchano, 8, Jativa, Prov.

Museo Municipal Cau de la Costabrava.
Plaza del Horno, 4, Palamos, Prov. Gerona

Museo Municipal de Arte y Museo Gotico.
Calle de Santo Domingo, Pollensa, Baleares

Museo Municipal de Castrelos.
Pazo de Castrelos, Vigo, Prov. Pontevedra

Museo Municipal de Mallorca.
Mallorca

Museo Municipal de Pinturas.
Calle de Rubio, Santander

Museo Municipal de San Telmo.
San Sebastian

Museo Municipal Prim-Rull.
San Juan, 27, Reus, Prov. Tarragona

Museo Nacional de Artes Decorativas.
Montalban, 12, Madrid

Museo Nacional de Ceramica.
Palacio del Marque de Aquas, Valencia

Museo Nacional de Escultura.
Cadenas de San Gregorio, 1, Valladolid

Museo Nonasterio de Tordesillas.
Valladolid

Museo Parroquial.
Santa Gadea del Cid, Prov. Burgos

Museo Parroquial de San Pueblo.
Zaragoza

Museo Picasso.
Montcada, 15-17, Barcelona 3

Museo Provincial.
Ansoleaga, Pamplona

Museo Provincial.
Calle de San Marcos, Lugo

Museo Provincial.
Paseo de Fray Francisco Vitorio, Vitorio

Museo Provincial Arqueologico y Etnologico de Bellas Artes.
Plaza de las Veletas, Caceres

Museo Provincial de Albacete.
Ave. de Jose Antonia 3, Albacete

Museo Provincial de Bellas Artes.
Logrono

Museo Provincial de Bellas Artes.
Badajoz

Museo Provincial de Bellas Artes.
Granada

Museo Provincial de Bellas Artes.
Puerta Del Sol, Jaen

Museo Provincial de Bellas Artes.
San Agustin 6, Malaga

Museo Provincial de Bellas Artes.
Santa Clara 17, Zamora

Museo Provincial de Bellas Artes.
Plaza del Museo, Seville

Museo Provincial de Bellas Artes.
Plaza del Potro, Cordoba

Museo Provincial de Bellas Artes.
Calle de Panaderas, la Coruna

Museo Provincial de Bellas Artes.
Plaza de Jose Antonio, 6, Zaragoza

Museo Provincial de Bellas Artes.
Disputacion Provincial, Castellon de la Plana

Museo Provincial Textil.
Parque de Vallparadis, Tarrasa

Museo Romanico de las Benedictinas.
Jaca, Prov. Huesca

Museo Romantico y Hogar Ochocentista.
San Gaudencio, Sitges

Museo Tesoro del Monasterio.
Lluch, Mallorca

Museo y Tesoro Catedralicio.
Toledo

Museu de Bellas Artes de Valencia.
Calle de San Pio V, 9 Valencia

Museum of the Romantic Epoch.
San Mateo 13, 4 Madrid

Museuo de Bellas Artes.
Patio de Escuelas, 2, Salamanca

Palacio del Marques de San Feliz.
Oviedo

Palacio Real de Aranjuez.
Aranjuez

Prado. *See* **Museo del Prado**

SRI LANKA

Art Gallery.
Green Path, Colombo

Colombo National Museum.
P.O. Box 854, 7 Colombo, 94768

Museum of Archaeology.
Anuradhapura
Permanent Collections:
Stone sculptures from the 3rd century A.D., original mural paintings, frescoes dating from the 8th century to the 11th century A.D., coins from the 3rd century B.C., bronzes from the 2nd century A.D., pottery from pre-Christian times and inscriptions from the 2nd century B.C.

SWEDEN

Arkiv for Dekorattiv Konst.
Finngt. 2, S-223 62 Lund

Boras Konstmuseum.
S-500 00 Boras

Carl Larsson Garden. *See* **Larsson, Carl, Garden**

Dalarnas Museum Med Konsthallen.
Stigaregt. 2-4, S-791 01 Falun

Drottningholms Slott.
S-170 11 Drottningholm

Eldhs Studio Museum.
Logebodavagen 10, S-113 47 Stockholm

Eskilstuna Konstmuseum.
Kirkogt., S-632 20 Eskilstuna

Goteborgs Konstmuseum.
Gotaplatsen 412-56, Gothenburg, 031-18 95 37
Permanent Collections:
Old Master paintings, especially Dutch and Flemish; Swedish 17th century painting and sculpture; Scandinavian art (19th-20th century); French art (19th-20th century); contemporary international art.

Gotlands Fornsal.
Strandgt. 12-14, Office: Mellangt. 19, Box 83, S-621 01 Visby, 0498/173 60

Gustav III Antiksamling.
Kungl. slottet, S-111 30 Stockholm

Hallwylska Museet.
Hamngt. 4, S-111 47 Stockholm

Halsinglands Museum.
Storgt. 31, S-824 00 Hudiksvall

Helsingborgs Museum, Vikingberg Art Museum.
S. Storgt. 31, S-252 23 Helsingborg, 042-11 15 50
Permanent Collections:
Swedish 19th and 20th century art, a few foreign artists from the 17th and 18th century and Provincial art from the 20th century.

Jamtlands Lans Museum.
Museiplan, S-831 00 Ostersund

Jonkopings Lans Museum.
Box 2133, S-550 02 Jonkoping

Kalmar Konstmuseum.
Slottsvagen 1, S-381 00 Kalmar

Kalmar Lans Museum.
Kalmar Slott, S-381 00 Kalmar

Konsthallen.
Ostra Agatan 19, S-753 22 Uppsala

Kristianstads Museum.
Nya Boulevarden 9, S-0291 00 Kristianstad

Kulturhistoriska Museet.
Adelgt. 1A, Box 1095, S-223 50 Lund

Kulturhistoriska Museet Murberget.
S-871 00 Harnosand

Kungl. Akademiem for de Fria Konsterna, Konstsamling.
Fredsgt. 12, Box 16317, S-103 26 Stockholm

Kungl Myntkabinettet Statens Museum for Mynt.
P.O. Box 5405 Stockholm, S-114-84
Permanent Collections:
Swedish coin history; coins from the Swedish possessions; history of Swedish medal art; history of medal art.

Kungliga Slottet.
S-111 30 Stockholm

Landskrona Kulturnamd.
Slottsgatan, S-261 31
Landskrona, 0418-79000
Permanent Collections:
Sturm-Art, modern Swiss art,
paintings by Nell Walden,
sculptures by Anders Jonsson,
Ethnological collection from
Nell Walden and Swedish
paintings from the beginning of
the 20th century.

Lansmuseet Linkoping.
Box 232, S-581 02 Linkoping,
073/115 7 70
Permanent Collections:
Art, specifically 17th to 18th
century Dutch, Flemish and
Swedish; Swedish archaeology;
Egyptian Collection; furniture,
clothes and a set of
embroidered tapestries; cultural
history.

Larsson, Carl, Garden.
S-790 15 Sundborn

Liljevalchs Konsthall.
Djurgardsvagen 60, S-11521
Stockholm

**Lunds Universitets Historisk A
Museum.**
Kraftstorg 1. Box 1135, S-223
50 Lund

Lunds Universitets Konstmuseum.
Universitetshuset, Box 1135, S-
221 04 Lund

Malmo Museum.
Malmohus, S-211 20 Malmo

Millesgarden.
Carl Millesvag 2, S-181 34
Lidingo 1

**Museum for Klassika
Fornsakerantik-Samlingen
(Universitets Samlingar i
Gustavianum)**
Institut for Antikens Kultur
Och Samhallsliv, S-752 20
Uppsala

Nationalmuseum.
Box 16 176, Stockholm, S-103-
24, 08/24 42 00

Nordiska Museet.
Djurgarden, S-115 21
Stockholm

Norrkopings Museum.
Kristianaplatsen, S-602 34
Norrkoping

Oppenheimers Konsthall.
Tonnersjo, S-310 31 Eldsberga

Orebro Lans Museum.
Slottparken, S-705 90 Orebro

**Ostasiatiska Museet, Museum of
Far Eastern Antiquities.**
Box 16381, S-103 27
Stockholm, 08/24 42 00
Permanent Collections:
Chinese Stone Age, Chinese
Ceramics T'ang-Ming, Chinese
Applied Arts, Korean Art,
Japanese Art, Chinese Bronze
Age, Chinese Ceramics Ch'ing,
Chinese Sculpture, Indian
Sculpture, Chinese Paintings.

Prins Eugens Waldemarsudde.
Djurgarden, S-115 21
Stockholm

Rohsska Konstslojdmuseet.
37-39 Vasagatan, Gothenburg

Rottneros Park.
Rottneros Park, S-680 12
Rottneros, 0565/60035
Permanent Collections:
Park open to the public
containing about 100
sculptures.

Skoklosters Slott.
S-190 60 Balsta

Sodermanlands Lansmuseum.
Nykopinghus, S-611 01
Nykoping

Statens Historiska Museum.
P.O. Box 5405, Stockholm
S114-84

Surahammars Bruksmuseum.
S-735 00 Surahammar

Sveriges Arkitekturmuseum.
Skeppsholmen, S-111 49
Stockholm

Swedish State Portrait Gallery.
Gripsolm Castle, Mariefred, S-
150-30

Thieska Galleriet.
Djurgarden, S-115 25
Stockholm

**Trelleborgs Museum Och Axel
Ebbes Konsthall.**
Ostergt. 52, S-231 00
Trelleborg

**Uppsala Universitets
Konstsamling.**
Domkyrkoplan 7, S-752 20
Uppsala

Varmlands Museum.
Box 335, S-651 05 Karlstad

Vasteras Konstmuseum.
S-271 87 Vasteras

**Vikingsberg Art Museum. *See*
Helsingborgs Museum,
Vikingberg Art Museum**

Ystads Konstmuseum.
St. Knuts torg, S-271 00 Ystad

Zornmuseet.
S-792 00 Mora

SWITZERLAND

Aargauer Kunsthaus.
Rathausplatz, CH-5000 Aarau

Abegg-Stiftung Bern.
CH-3132 Riggisberg
Permanent Collections:
Exquisite works of applied art
from antiquity of the Near
East, European Middle Ages
and the Renaissance. Choice
examples of artifacts in gold,
silver, bronze, crystal, enamel,
ivory, ceramics, textiles,
sculpture and painting.

**Altertumssammlung der
Beneditinerabtei.**
CH-6390 Engelberg

Antikenmuseum.
St. Albangraben 5, CH-4051
Basel, 061/22 22 02

**Archaologische Sammlung der
Universitat Zurich.**
Ramistr. 73, CH-8006 Zurich,
01/229 2275 UNIZ 54864
Permanent Collections:
Egyptian, Syrian, Greek and

Roman art. Collection of
plaster casts of original
antiquities.

**Barfusserkirche (Historisches
Museum Basel)**
Barfusserplatz, CH-4000 Basel

**Baur Collection. *See* Collections
Baur**

Bundner Kunstmuseum.
Postplatz, 7000 Chur, 081/22
17 63
Permanent Collections:
Bundner Art Collection

**Burnand, Eugene, Museum. *See*
Musee Eugene Burnand**

Cabinet des Estampes.
2 Place du Rohan, F-67000
Strasbourg

Centre de Corbusier.
Hoschgasse 8, CH-8000 Zurich

Chateau.
CH-1663 Gruyeres

**Chateau de Coppet et Musee des
Suisses au Service Etranger.**
Chateau, CH-1296 Coppet

Chateau d'Oron.
CH-1699 Oron-le-Chatel

Collections Baur.
Rue Munier-Romilly 8, CH-
1206 Geneva, 022 46 17 29
Permanent Collections:
Chinese art, ceramics, jades,
tobacco flagons, Japanese art,
ceramics, netsuke, laquers and
sword guards.

Diozesanmuseum.
CH-6430 Schwyz

Domschatz.
St-Ursen-Kathedrale, CH-4500
Solothurn

**Forel, Alexis, Museum. *See* Musee
Alexis Forel**

Fricktaler Museum.
Marktgasse 12, CH-4310
Rheinfelden

**Furstenzimmer Kloster St.
Johann.**
Frauenkloster St. Johan, CH-
7531 Mustair

Gewerbemuseum.
Spalenvorstadt 2, CH-4000
Basel

Gewerbemuseum.
Kirchplatz 14, CH-8400
Winterthur

Gewerbemuseum im Kornhaus.
Zeughausgasse 2, CH-3011
Bern

**Graphische Sammlung der
Eidgenossische Technischen
Hochschule.**
Ramistr. 101, CH-8092 Zurich,
01/32-62-11
Permanent Collections:
Graphics from the 15th
through the 20th centuries.

Haller, Hermann, Studio.
Hoeschgasse, Ecke Bellerivestr.
CH-8008 Zurich

Heimatmuseum.
Am Herrenberg, Breynhaus,
CH-8640 Rapperswil

Heimatmuseum.
Haupstr. 16, CH-4153 Reinach
Permanent Collections:
Folklore collection.

Heimatmuseum Appenzell.
Hauptgasse, Rathaus, CH-9050
Appenzell

**Hermann Haller Studio. *See*
Haller, Hermann, Studio**

Historisches Museum.
Blumensteinwig 12, CH-4500
Solothurn

**Historisches Museum im
Landvogteischloss.**
Landvogteischloss, CH-5400
Baden

Ikonenmuseum.
Haus Klostermatt, CH-5742
Kolliken

Industrie-und Gewerbemuseum.
Vadianstr. 2, CH-9000 St.
Gallen
Permanent Collections:
A collection of laces and a
collection of embroideries.

Kantonale Historische Sammlung.
Schloss Lenzburg, CH-5600
Lenzburg, 064/51 43 92
Permanent Collections:
Historical interiors, arms, tin,
glass and ceramics.

Keramische Sammlung.
Zunfhaus Zur Meisen, CH-8000
Zurich

**Kunstgewerbemuseum der Stadt
Zurich.**
Ausstelungsstr. 60, CH-8000
Zurich, 01 42 67 00

Kunsthalle Basel.
Klostergasse 5/Steinenberg 7,
CH-4051 Basel

Kunsthaus.
Museumsstr., CH-8750 Glarus

Kunsthaus Zurich.
Box 8024 Zurich 8001

Kunstmuseum.
Kirchgasse 8, CH-4600 Olten

Kunstmuseum Bern.
Hodlerstrasse 12, CH-3011
Berne

Kunstmuseum Luzern.
Robertt Zund-Str. 1, CH-6000
Luzern, 041 23 92 42
Permanent Collections:
Swiss art from 16th-20th
centuries., Lucerne masters,
European Expressionist art
from the 20th century.

Kunstmuseum St. Gallen.
Museumstrasse 50, CH-9000
Saint Gallen, 071 23 56 23
Permanent Collections:
Fine arts from the 19th and
20th centuries.; graphic arts.

Kunstmuseum Winterthur.
Museumstrasse 52, CH-8400
Winterthur

Kunstsammlung der Stadt Thun.
Sstaatsstr., Thunerhof, CH-
3600 Thun

Kuntsmuseum Solothurn.
Werkhofstrasse 30, Solothurn

Muraltengut.
Seetr. 203, Ch-8000 Zurich

Musee Alexis Forel.
Grand-Rue 54, CH-1110
Morges

Musee Ariana.
Ave. de la Paix 10, CH-1202
Geneva

Musee Cantonal des Beaux-Arts.
Place de la Majorie, CH-1950
Sion

Musee Cantonal des Beaux-Arts.
Palais de Rumine, Place de la
Riponne, CH-1000 Lausanne,
012-22 83 22-33
Permanent Collections:
Paintings, drawings, stamps and
sculptures from Vaudois artists
from 15th century to present
day. Principal artists are the
brothers Sablet, Ducros,
Gleyre; Auberjonois, Bieler,
Bocion, Bosshard, Borgeaud,
Chavannes, David, Steinlen,
Hermanjat, Soutter, Vallotton
and Buchet. Also a small
collection of Swiss painting,
Genevoise school: Anker,
Hodler, G. Giacometti; Foreign
art from the Dutch school,
17th-18th century, and French
school, 17th century: Gericault,
Courbet, Cezanne, Degas,
Marouet, Matisse, Bonnard,
Renoir and Utrillo.
Contemporary paintings and
sculpture along with a small
group of Gothic sculptures,
Egyptian sculptures and art of
the Far East are also present.

Musee d'Art et d'Histoire.
Rue Pierre-Aeby 227, CH-1700
Fribourg

Musee d'Art et d'Histoire.
Quai Leopold Robert, CH-2000
Neuchatel

Musee d'Art et d'Histoire.
Cabinet des Estampes, 5
Promenade du Pin, 1204
Geneva

Musee d'Art Moderne.
Petit Palais, 2 Terrasse Saint-
Victor, CH-1206 Geneva

Musee de la Cathedrale.
Cathedrale, CH-1000 Lausanne

Musee de l'Athenee.
Rue de l'Athenee, CH-1200
Geneva

Musee de Mon Repos.
Parc Mon Repos, CH-1000
Lausanne

**Musee des Arts Decoratifs de la
Ville de Lausanne.**
Ave. Villamont 4, CH-1000
Lausanne

Musee des Beaux-Arts.
Rue Marie Anne Calame 6,,
CH-1400 Le Loche

**Musee des Beaux-Arts et Societe
des Amis des Arts.**
33 Rue Des Musees, 2300 La
Chaux de Fonds

Musee Eugene Burnand.
"Le Grand-Air" Le Bourg, CH-
1510 Moudon

**Musee Historique de l'Ancien
Eveche.**
Place de la Cathedrale 2, CH-
1000 Lausanne

**Musee Historique et des
Porcelaines.**
Chateau, B.P. 91, CH-1260
Nyon

Musee Jean-Jacques-Rousseau.
Bibliotheque Publique et
Universitaire de Geneve,
Promenade des Bastions, CH-
1211 Geneva

Musee Jenisch.
Ave. de la Gare 2, CH-1800
Vevey

Musee Jurassien Delemont.
Grand-Rue, CH-2800
Delemont

Musee Jurassien des Beaux Arts.
Rue de l'Hotel-De-Ville 9, CH-
2740 Moutier

Musee Vela.
Ugo Cleis, CH-6853 Lig

Museo d'Arte Contemporanea.
Castello, CH-6600 Locarno

Museo di Bella Arti.
Villa Ciani, CH-6900 Lugano

Museo Vela.
CH-6853 Ligornetto TI
Permanent Collections:
The museum constructed
between 1863-1865 by architect
Isidoro Spinelli of Sagno, was a
residential mansion with studio
and show-room of the sculptor
Vincenzo Vela. After the
necessary alterations to the
building to serve its new
purpose, the following rooms
have been retained with their
original fittings: the library (II
and III), the reception room
(XVIII and XIX) on the upper
story. The art collections
include: by Vincenzo Vela,
drawings and terracotta models
("Bozzetti"); a large number of
original plaster casts. By
Lorenzo Vela, sculptures in
marble, terracotta and plaster;
some paintings. By Spartaco
Vela, paintings, drawings, some
ceramics and graphic art. In the
upper story and in the former
living quarters, paintings, water
colours and drawings are on
show, mainly by
contemporaries and friends of
the Velas of Lombard and
Piedmont origin.

**Museum der Kathedrale Chur-
Domsplatz.**
Hof 18, CH-7000 Chur

Museum des Kantons Thurgau.
Haus Sonnenberg, CH-8500
Frauenfeld

**Museum fur Volkekunde und
Schweizerisches Museum fur
Volkskunde Basel.**
P.O. Box 1048, 4001 Basel

Museum Rietberg Zurich.
Gablerstrasse 15, CH-8002
Zurich

Museum zu Allerheiligen.
Klosterplatz, CH-8200
Schaffhausen

Museum zur Hohen Eich.
Schonenbergstr. 22, CH-8820
Wadenswil

Napoleon-Museum.
Schloss, CH-8268 Arenenberg
Permanent Collections:
A museum of living styles,
where the monumental style of
Napoleon I, the delicate taste
of the Romantic, the world of
the rich bourgeoisie at the
advent of the Second Empire
and the neo-Baroque splendor
at its end unite to form a vivid
picture of the whole 19th
century.

Offentliche Kunstsammlung.
Bernerhaus, CH-Frauenfeld

**Offentliche Kunstsammlung-
Kunstmuseum.**
St. Albangraben 16, CH-4010
Basel

**Oskar Reinhart Foundation. See
Reinhart, Oskar, Stiftung**

Panorama der Stadt Thun.
Schadaupark, CH-3600 Thun

Pinacoteca Cantonale Giovanni.
CH-6862 Rancate

Pinakothek Thyssen-Bornemisza.
Villa Favorita, CH-6976
Castagnola di Lugano

Prieure de Romainmotier.
CH-1349 Romainmotier

Ratisches Museum.
Hofstr. 1, CH-7000 Chur

Reinhart, Oskar, Stiftung.
Stadthasstr. 6, CH-8400
Winterthur, 052 84 51 72
Permanent Collections:
About 600 works by German,
Swiss and Austrian artists of
the 18th, 19th and 20th
centuries. Centers of interest:
Romanticism (Friedrick, Runge,
Schwind, Spitzweg, Blechen,
Calame); Realism and Idealism
(Anker, Lund, Menn, Thoma,
Leibl, Feuerbach, Bocklin,
Marees); modern Swiss art
(Hodler, Segantini, Amiet, G.
Giacometti, Auberjonois, M.
Gubler).

Rousseau, Jean Jacques, Museum.
See Musee Jean-Jacques-
Rousseau

**Sammlung Oskar Reinart "Am
Romerholz".**
Halcenstr. 95, CH-8400
Winterthur, 052-23 41 21
Permanent Collections:
Former residence of Oskar
Reinhart, built by Genevan
architect Maurice Turrettini. A
choice selection of pictures and
drawings of Old Masters
(Cranach, Holbein, Bruegel,
Rembrandt, Rubens, Poussin,
Chardin, El Greco, Goya) and
a considerable number of works
from great French painters and
sculpters of the 19th century,
including Ingres, Delacroix,
Daumier, Corot, Courbet,
Manet, Renoir, Cezanne, Van
Gogh and Maillol.

Sammlung der Benediktinerabtei.
CH-8840 Einsiedeln

**Sammlung Jakob Bryner und
Konrad Kellenberger.**
Rathaus, CH-8400 Winterthur

**Sammlungen im Kloster
Wettingen.**
CH-5430 Wettingen

**Schloss Lenzburg. See Kantonale
Historische Sammlung**

Schlossmuseum.
Schloss, CH-3653 Oberhofen
am Thunersee

**Schweizerisches
Kleinmeistermuseum.**
Schadaupark, Kunstsammlung,
CH-3600 Thun

Schweizerisches Landesmuseum.
P.O. Box 2760, Zurich CH-
8023

**Schweizerisches Museum fur
Volkskunde im Museum fur
Volkerkunde.**
Augustinergasse, CH-4000
Basel

Segantini-Museum.
Suvrettastr., CH-7500 St.
Moritz, 082-34454 OR 082-
33147
Permanent Collections:
Paintings of Giovanni
Segantini.

Skulpturhalle.
Mittlere Str. 17, CH-4056
Basel

Stablistubli.
Zeughaus, CH-5200 Brugg

Stadtmuseum.
Hofplatz, CH-9500 Wil

Stiftsschatz.
CH-6215 Beromunster

Stiftsschatz.
Hofkirche, CH-6000 Lucerne

Stiftung Sammlung E.G. Buhrle.
Zollikerstr. 172, CH-8000
Zurich

Tresor de l'Abbaye.
Abbaye, CH-1890 St-Maurice

**Zentralbibliothek Zurich,
Graphische Sammlung.**
Zahringerplatz 6, CH-8000
Zurich

SYRIA

Bosra Museum.
Bosra

National Museum of Aleppo.
Aleppo

National Museum of Damascus.
Reda Saeed St., Damascus

TANZANIA

Kibo Art Gallery.
Kilimanjaro, Marangu, P.O.
Box 98, Moshi

THAILAND

Cloister of Bodhi-Baum Museum.
Bangkok

Cloister of the Fifth King Museum.
Bangkok

Lopburi National Museum.
Phra Narai Rajanives Palace

Monastery of Phra Boromadhat.
Chainat

National Museum.
Lampun

National Museum.
Nagara Pathama

National Museum.
6 Na Phra-drhart Rd., Bandkok 2

Suan Pakkad Palace.
Bangkok

TRINIDAD & TOBAGO

National Museum & Art Gallery.
117 Frederick St., Port-of-Spain

TUNISIA

Musee Archeologique de Sousse.
Kasbah de Sousse, Sousse

Musee d'Art et Tradition Populaire.
Mahdia

Musee d'Art et Tradition Populaire.
5 Rue Sisiali Ennouri, Sfax

Musee d'Art Islamique.
Kairouan

Musee d'Art Islamique du Ribat.
Sousse

Musee d'Art Islamique du Ribat.
Monastir

Musee National du Bardo.
Le Bardo

TURKEY

Aya Sofya Musei.
Sultanahmet, Istanbul

Ethnographical Museum.
Ankara

Istanbul Arkeoloji Muzelrei.
Sultanahmet, Istanbul

Kariye Cami.
Istanbul

Museum of Fine Arts.
Istanbul

Museum of Mosaics.
Misis

Museum of Turkish & Islamic Art.
Sifahane Cad. 6, Istanbul-Suleymaniy, 22 18 88
Permanent Collections:
Islamic calligraphy 7th-9th centuries, Anatolian, Persian and Caucasian carpets, Islamic metalwork, Islamic pottery and Islamic woodcarving.

Topkapi Palace Museum.
Sultanahmed, Istanbul

Turk Ve Islam Eserleri Muzesi.
Sulymaniye 6, Sifahane St.

Turkish Ceramics Museum.
Konya

U S S R

Andrei Rublov Museum of Ancient Russian Art. *See* Rublov, Andrei, Museum of Ancient Russian Art

Armenian State Picture Gallery.
Ul. Spandaryana 2, Erevan, Armenian SSR

A.V. Shchusev Architectural Museum of the State Committee of Building & Architecture.
Kalininsky Prosp. 5, Moskva V.I. Baldin

Azerbaijan R. Mustafaev State Art Museum. *See* Mustafaev, Azerbaijan R., State Art Museum

Belorussian State Art Museum.
Ul. Lenina 40, Minsk, Byelorussian SSR

Cathedral of St. Basil.
Moskva

Dnepropetrovsk State Art Museum.
Ul. Shevchenko 21, Dneppropetrovsk, Ukrainian SSR

Folk Art Museum.
Ul. Stanislavskogo 7, Moskav

Georgian State Art Museum.
Ul. Ketskhoveli 1, Tbilisi, Georgian SSR

Georgian State Picture Gallery.
Pr. Rustaveli 3, Tbilisi, Georgian SSR

Gorky State Art Museum.
Nab. im Zhdanova 3, Gorky

Great Kremlin Palace.
Kremlin, Moscow

History & Art Museum at Zagorsk.
Zagorsk, Moskovskaya Obl.

Karelian Museum of Fine Arts.
Pr. K. Marxa 8, Petrozavodsk

Kaunas M.K. Chiurleins State Art Museum.
Ul. S. Neres 45, Kaunas, Lithuanian SSR

Kazakh T.G. Shevchenko State Art Gallery.
Ul. Sovietskaya 22, Alma-Ata, Kazakh SSR

Kharkov State Art Museum.
Sovnarkomovskaya Ul. 11, Kharkov Ukrainian SSR

Kiev State Museum of Russian Art.
Ul. Repina 9, Kiev, Ukrainian SSR

Kiev State Museum of Ukrainian Art.
Ul. Kirova 6, Kiev, Ukrainian SSR

Kiev State Museum of Western & Oriental Art.
Ul. Repina 15, Kiev Ukrainian SSR

Kirghiz State Musem of Fine Art.
Ul. Pervomaiskaya 90, Frunze, Kirghiz SSR

Kolomya State Museum of Folk Art.
Teatralnaya Ul. 25, Kolomya, Ivanov-Frankivska

Komi Art Museum.
Ul. Kommunisticheskaya 6, Siktivkar

Kostroma Museum of Fine Arts.
Pr. Mira 1, Kostroma

Krasnoy-Arsk Picture Gallery.
Ul. Krasnoyarskogo 68, Krasnoyarsk

Kremlin Armoury.
Kremlin, Moscow

Kremlin Cathedrals.
Sorbonya Pl., Moscow

Kremlin Museums.
Kremlin, Moscow

Kuibyshev Art Museum.
Palace of Culture, Pl Kuibysheva, Kuibyshev

Kursk Art Gallery.
Ul. Sovietskaya 3, Kursk

Latvian State Museum of Fine Arts.
Pl.Pionerov 3, Riga, Latvian Ssr

Lithuanian State Art Museum.
Ul. Gorkogo 55, Vilnius, Lithuanian SSR

Lvov State Museum of Ukrainian Art.
Ul. Dragomanova 42, Lvov, Ukrainian SSR

Lvov State Picture Gallery.
Ul. Stefanika 3, Lvov, Ukrainian SSR

Minsk State Museum.
Ul. Lenina 20, Minsk

Moldavian State Art Museum.
Ul. Lenina 115, Kischev, Moldavian SSR

Morvian Art Gallery.
Ul. Sovietskaya 29, Saransk

Museum of Classical Archaeology of the Tartu State Univ.
Ulikooli 18, Tartu, Estonian SSR

Museum of Sculpture.
Pl. A. Nevskogo 1, Leningrad

Museum of Soviet Fine Arts.
Pr. Truda 50, Komsomolsk-On-Amur

Museum Palaces & Parks in Pavlovsk.
Ul. Revolutsoi 20, Pavlovsk, Leningrad-Skaya Obl

Museum Palaces & Parks in Pushkin.
Komsomolskaya 7, Pushkin, Leningradskaya Obl

Mustafaev, Azerbaijan R., State Art Museum.
Ul. Chkalova 9, Baku, Azerbaija SSR

Novodevichy Monastery Museum.
Smolensky Cathedral, Moscow

Odessa State Museum of Western & Eastern Art.
Ul. Pushkinskaya 9, Odessa, Ukrainian SSR

Odessa State Picture Gallery.
Ul. Korolenko 5, Odessa, Ukrainian SSR

Omsk Fine Art Museum.
Ul. Lenina 23, Omsk

Orenburg Fine Art Museum.
Ul. Pravdy 6, Orenburg

Orloskaya Art Gallery.
Ul. Saltikava-Sedrina, Orel

Perm State Art Museum.
Komsomolsky Prosp. 2, Perm

Poltava Art Museum.
Ul. Dzerdzhiskogo 11, Poltava

Riga Art Museum.
U. Gorkogo 10a, Riga

Rublov, Andrei, Museum of Ancient Russian Art.
Ul. Pryamikova 10, Moskva

Ryazan Regional Art Museum.
Kremlin 11, Ryazan

Saint Issac's Cathedral (State Museum of the History of Leningrad)
Leningrad

Sarayov A.N. Radishchev State Art Museum.
Pl. Radishcheva 39, Saratov

State Hermitage Museum.
M. Dvortsovaya Nab. 34, Leningrad B.B. Piotrovsky

State Museum of Ceramics.
St. Kuskovo, Moscow

State Museum of Latvian & Russian Art.
Ul. Gorkogo 10, Riga, Latvian SSR

State Museum of Oriental Art.
16 Obukha St., Moscow

State Museum of Palekh Art.
Ul. Bakanova 50, Palekh, Ivanovskaya Obl

State Pushkin Museum of Fine Arts.
Volkhonka 12, Moscow

State Russian Museum.
Inzhernernaya 4, Leningrad V.A. Pushkarev

State Tretyakov Gallery.
Lavrushensky per. 10, Moskva P.I. Lebedev

Stavropol Museum of Fine Art.
Ul. Dzerzhinskogo 115, Stavropol

Summer Garden & Museum Palace of Peter the Great.
Leningrad

Sumy State Art Museum.
Ul. Lenina 67, Sumy, Ukrainian SSR

Sverdlovsk Regional Picture Gallery.
Ul. Vasneia 11, Sverdlovsk

Tallinn State Art Museum.
Kadriorg Palace, Weizenbergi 37, Tallinn, Estonian SSR

Tambov Picture Gallery.
Ul. Sovietskaya 59, Tambov

Tartu Art Museum.
Vallikraavi 14, Tartu, Estonian SSR

Tatar State Museum of Fine Arts.
Ul. K. Marka 64, Kazan

Tobolsk Picture Gallery.
Pl. Knasnaya 2, Tobolsk

Tula Art Museum.
Ul. Englelsa 144, Tula

Turkmen State Museum of Fine Art.
Pr. Svobody 84, Ashkhabad, Turkmenian Ssr

Tyumen Picture Gallery.
Ul. Repbulic 29, Tyumen

Ukrainian Museum of Folk & Decorative Art.
Ul. Yanvarskogo Vosstaniya 21, Kiev

Uzbek State Museum of Art.
Ul. Proletarskaya 16, Tashkent, Uzbek SSR

Vologda Picture Gallery.
Pl. Kremlina 3, Vologda

Vologodsky Historical Museum.
Pl. Kremlin 1, Vologda

Vorenezh Art Museum.
Ul. Plekhanovskaya 29, Voronez

Yakutsk Museum of Fine Arts.
Ul. Maxima Ammosova 14, Yakutsk

UGANDA

Markerere Art Gallery.
Markerere School of Fine Art, P.O. Box 7062 Kampala

Nommo Gallery.
52 Kampala Rd., P.O. Box 16132, Kampala

UNITED KINGDOM

Abbey Art Center & Museum.
89 Park Rd., New Barnet, Herts.

Abbot Hall Gallery & Museum of Lakeland Life & Industry.
Kendal, Cumbria LA9 5AL, KENDAL 22464
Permanent Collections:
Abbot Hall was built in 1759 reputedly to the design of John Carr of York. The ground floor rooms now contain collections of 18th century English pictures, furniture and objets d'art. The upper floor has been converted into galleries for the display of temporary

exhibitions and the permanent collection of 20th century British painting and sculpture.

Aberdeen Art Gallery.
Schoolhill, Aberdeen AB9 1FQ, 53517
Permanent Collections:
Works of art from the 17th century onwards. Most representative in the fields of Scottish artists, British painting in the 19th and 20th centuries and modern painting and sculpture. Small collection of 19th century French works. Extensive collection of etchings by James McBey. Also drawing and watercolor collection and modern print collection.

Air Gallery.
125-129 Shaftesbury Ave., WC2H 8AD London

Alfred East Art Gallery.
Sheep St., Kettering, Northants

Alnwick Castle.
Estates Office, Alnwick Castle, Northumberland

Altrincham Museum & Art Gallery.
George St., Altrincham, Cheshire

American Museum in Britain.
Claverton Manor, BA2 7BD Bath, BATH (0225) 60503
Permanent Collections:
Eighteen completely furnished rooms showing domestic life in America from the 17th to 19th century. Galleries of silver, glass, pewter, quilts: sections devoted to the American Indian and the opening of the West. Folk Art Gallery, American Gardens, Conestoga Wagon and Indian tepee.

Ancient House Museum.
White Hart St., Thetford, THETFORD 2599
Permanent Collections:
A museum of Thetford and Breckland life, natural history and antiquities. It is housed in a fine 15th century timber framed building which was probably the home of a wealthy merchant. There is a richly carved ceiling in the principal room.

Apsley House. *See* Wellington Museum, Apsley House

Arbroath Art Gallery.
Hill Terrace, Arbroath, Angus

Arbuthnot Museum & Art Gallery.
St. Peter St., Peterhead AB4 6QD, Aberdeenshire

Arlington Mill.
Bibury, Cirencester, Glos.

Armagh County Museum.
The Mall East, Armagh, N. Ireland BT61 9BE

Art Gallery.
Princess Alexandra Walk, Huddersfie HD1 2SU, Yorks.

Art Gallery & Museum.
Moss St., Bury, Lancs.

Art Gallery & Museum.
Union St. Oldham, Lancs.

Art Gallery & Museum.
George St. Perth, Scotland

Art Gallery & Museum.
Bird St., Lichfield WS13 6PA

Art Gallery & Museum.
Spring Gardens Lane, Keighly BD20 6LH

Art Gallery & Museum.
Central Library, Oriel Rd., Bootle L20 6AG

Arthur Segal Collection. *See* Segal, Arthur, Collection

Ascott (National Trust Property)
Leighton Buzzard, Bucks.

Ashmolean Museum of Art & Archaeology. *See* Oxford University Ashomolean Museum of Art & Archeology

Astley Cheetham Public Library & Art Gallery.
Trinity St. Stalybridge SK15 2BN Cheshire

Astley Hall Museum & Art Gallery.
Astley Park, Chorley, Lancs.

Athenaeum (City of Manchester Art Gallery)
Princess St., Manchester M1 4HR

Atkinson Art Gallery.
Lord St.,Southport, Merseyside PR8 1DH
Permanent Collections:
Over 1500 works of art (oils, watercolors, prints, drawings, English glass and Chinese ceramics). Primarily British art from the 18th-20th centuries.

Bagshaw Art Gallery.
Market Place, Batley, Yorks.

Balston, Thomas, Collection of Staffordshire Portrait Figures.
Stapleford Park Nr. Melton Mowbray LE14 2SF Leicester

Bangor Art Gallery.
Old Canonry, Bangor, Wales

Bantock House.
Bantock Park, Merridale Rd., Wolverton, Staffs.

Barber Institute of Fine Arts.
Univ. of Birmingham-Edgbaston Park Rd., Birmingham B15 2TS

Bargate Guildhall Museum.
High St., Southampton

Barnard Castles. *See* Bowes Museum

Beecroft Art Gallery.
Station Rd., Southend-on-Sea SSO 7RA

Berwick-Upon-Tweed Museum & Art Gallery.
Marygate, Berwick-Upon-Tweed, Northumberland TD 15 1BT, BERWICK 7320
Permanent Collections:
Burrell Collections (Art Gallery). Miscellaneous ceramics, brass, bronze and local history.

Bethnal Green Museum.
Cambridge Heath Rd., London E2 9PA

Birmingham Museums & Art Gallery.
Chamberlain Square, Birmingham B3 3DH, 021-235 4051
Permanent Collections:
Paintings, sculpture, drawings, watercolors, archaeology and natural history.

Blackburn Museum & Art Gallery.
Library St., Blackburn, Lancs., BLACKBURN 667130
Permanent Collections:
Hart Collection of Medieval manuscripts, early printed books and ancient coins; Lewis Collection of Japanese Prints; Municipal Collection of Fine and Decorative Arts; East Lancashire Regiment Collection of Militaria.

Blickling Hall.
Aylsham, Norfolk

Bolling Hall Museum.
Bolling Hall Rd. Bradford BD4

Bourough Museum, Art Gallery & Archives.
Oaklands, Stade St., Hythe, Kent

Bowes Museum.
Barnard Castle, County Durham, TEESDALE (0833) 37139
Permanent Collections:
Paintings of most Continental schools and the English school including works by El Greco, Goya, Sassetta, Tiepolo, Boucher and Gainsborough; porcelain (Sevres, Meissen) and Italian, French and Dutch glazed earthenware; tapestries, costumes, embroidery, sculpture, carvings, illuminated manuscripts, book bindings, an important series of French and English period rooms, toys, dolls, models, musical instruments, archaeology and local history.

Breamore House.
Breamore, Hants.

Bridewell Museum.
Bridewell Alley, Norwich, NORWICH 22233 EXT. 639
Permanent Collections:
Housed in medieval merchants house, art related items include examples of Norwich-made textiles and decorative ironwork.

Bridlington Art Gallery & Museum.
Sewerby Hall, Bridington, Yorks.

Brierley Hill Glass Museum.
Moor St. Brierley Hill, Staffs.

British Library.
Great Russell St., WC1B 3DG London

British Museum.
6 Bedford Square, London, WC1B 3RA, 01-323-1234

Brodick Castle & Gardens (National Trust for Scotland)
Bute, Nr. Brodick Pier, Isle of Arran, Scotland

Broomsfield Museum.
Broomfield Park, Palmers Green, London N13

Buckland Abbey.
Nr. Yelverton, Plymouth, Devon

Burrows Toy Museum.
York St., Bath, BATH (0225) 4019 OR 61819
Permanent Collections:
Museum is devoted to a collection of children's playthings. The collection records the pastimes of children over the past century and a half. Books, games, mechanical and constructional toys, dolls, doll houses, carriages and accessories - the prosperity and poverty, the charm and inventiveness of this age is reflected in the toys on display.

Burton Agnes Hall.
Driffield, Yorks.

Burton Art Gallery.
Kingsley Rd., Bideford, Devon

Buscot House (National Trust)
Buscot, Berks.

Camphill Museum.
Queen's Park, Glasgow, S.1

Cannon Hall Museum & Art Gallery Yorks.
Cannon Hall, Cawthorne, Barnsley, Yorks.

Castle Museum & Art Gallery.
Nottingham NG1 6EL

Cecil Higgins Art Gallery. *See* **Higgins, Cecil, Art Gallery**

Central Museum & Art Gallery.
Guildhall Rd., Northampton

Chambers Institution Museum & Art Gallery.
High St., Peebles, Scotland

Cheltenham Art Gallery & Museum Service.
Clarence St., Cheltenham GL50 3JT

Chiddingstone Castle.
Chiddingstone Near Edenbridge, Kent

Christ Church Picture Gallery.
Canterbury Quadrangle, Oxford OX1 1DP, (0865) 42102
Permanent Collections:
Old Master paintings and drawings.

Christchruch Mansion (Ipswich Museums & Art Galleries)
Ipswich IP1 3QH, Suffolk

Christchurch Mansion. *See* **Ipswich Museums & Art Galleries**

Churchill Gardens Museum.
3 Venn's Lane, Hereford HR4 9AU

City Art Gallery.
Municipal Buildings, Leeds LS1 3AA

City Art Gallery & Museum.
Peel Park, Salford, M54WU

City Art Gallery & Museum.
Cartwright Hall, Lister Park, Bradford BD9 4DZ

City Museum & Art Gallery.
Brunswick Rd., Gloucester

City Museum & Art Gallery.
Museum Rd., Old Portsmouth PO1 2LJ, Hants.

City Museum & Art Gallery.
Broad St., Hanely Stoke-on-Trent ST1 4HS, Staffs.

City Museum & Art Gallery.
Priestgate, Peterborough, PE1 1LF, 0733-43329
Permanent Collections:
Geology, natural history, local history, archaeology, social history and paintings and drawings.

City Museums & Art Galleries.
Kingston-Upon-Hull HU1 3RA

City of Bristol Museum & Art Gallery.
Queens's Road, 8S8 1RL Bristol, 0272 299771
Permanent Collections:
Fine and applied and Oriental Art; Archaeological and Ethnological Collection; Social History; History of Science and Technology.

Colchester & Essex Museum.
The Castle, Colchester C01 1TJ, Essex

Coleridge Museum.
St. Augustine's College, Canterbury, Kent

Commonwealth Institute.
Kensington High St., London W8 6NQ

Cooper Art Gallery.
Church St., Barnsley, Yorks.

Courtauld Institute Galleries.
Woburn Square, London WC1E 7HU

Craigievar Castle (National Trust for Scotland)
Craigievar Castle, Aberdeenshire, Scotland

Crathes Castle.
Crathes Castle, Kincardineshire, Scotland

Curtis Museum (Hampshire County Museum Service)
High St., Alton, Hants.

Cyfarthfa Castle Art Gallery &Museum.
Cyfartha Park Merthyr Tydfil Glam

David, Percival, Foundation of Chinese Art.
53 Gordon Square London WC1H OPD
Permanent Collections:
Chinese ceramics.

Deal Town Hall.
High St., Deal, DEAL 4963
Permanent Collections:
Local Belgic and Roman pottery; Cinque Ports Baron's robes.

Dean & Chapter Library.
Durham DH1 3EH, 0385-62489
Permanent Collections:
Treasures from Durham Cathedral.

Delgatie Castle.
Turriff AB5 7TD, Co. of Aberdeen, Scotland

Derby Museums & Art Gallery.
The Strand, Derby DE1 1BS, DERBY 31111 EXT 782
Permanent Collections:
Paintings and drawings by Joseph Wright of Derby, 1734-1797.

Dick Institute. *See* **Museum & Art Gallery**

Dickens House Museum.
Victoria Parade, Broadstairs, THANET 62853
Permanent Collections:
Dickens relics, furniture and Victoriana.

Dover Museum.
Ladywell, Dover CT16 1DQ, DOVER 201066
Permanent Collections:
Large collection includes items of local and national interest.

Dulwich College Picture Gallery.
College Rd., London SE 21 7LD
Permanent Collections:
Alleyn Collection, Cartwright Collection, Desenfans-Boureois Collection, Linley Gift and Fairfax-Murray Gift.

Dundee Museum & Art Gallery.
Albert Square, DD1 1DA Dundee, 25492

Dunimarle Castle.
Culross, Fife

Durham Cathedral.
The Treasury, the College, Durham DH1 3EH
Permanent Collections:
Durham Cathedral treasury.

Durham Light Infantry Museum & Arts Centre.
Aykley Heads, Durham DH1 5TU

Dyson Perrins Museum. *See* **Perrins, Dyson, Museum**

Ealing College Gallery.
83 The Ave., London W1S

Eastnor Castle.
Ledbury, Herefordshire
Permanent Collections:
Tapestries, arms and armour, antique furniture, pictures

Edward Pease Public Library & Art Gallery. *See* **Pease, Edward, Public Library & Art Gallery**

Elizabeth Castle.
Jersey, C.I.

Elizabethan House.
32 New St., Plymouth, Devon

Elizabethan House Museum.
4 South Quay, Great Yarmouth, Norfolk, GREAT YARMOUTH 55746
Permanent Collections:
A wealthy merchant built this house in 1596. Although it has a late Georgian front, it contains 16th century panellrooms, one with a magnificent plaster ceiling. Other rooms have features from later periods, some containing furniture and exhibits illustrating domestic life in the 19th century. There are displays of Victorian children's toys, Lowestoft porcelain and a collection of

18th and 19th century drinking glasses.

Fenton House (National Trust)
Hampstead Grove, London NW3

Firle Place.
Lewes, Sussex

Fitz Park & Art Gallery.
Fitz Park, Keswick CA12 4NF Cumbria

Forty Hall Museum.
Forty Hall, Enfield EN2 9HA, Middx., 01-363 8196
Permanent Collections:
Paintings, drawings, prints, ceramics, glass, woodwork, metalwork, needlework, material illustrating local history.

Foundling Hospital Art Treasures.
Thomas Coram Foundation, 40 Brunswick Square, London WC1

Gainsborough's House.
Gainsborough St., Sudbury, Suffolk

Gallery of the Royal Scottish Academy.
The Mound & Princess St., Edinburgh EH2 2EL

Gefrye Museum.
Kingsland Rd., London E2 8EA

Glasgow Museums & Art Galleries.
Kelvingrove, G3 8AG Glasgow

Glynde Place.
Glynde, Nr. Lewes, Sussex

Goodwood House.
Goodwood Near Chichester, Sussex

Grange Art Gallery & Museums.
The Green, Rottingdean BN2 7HA Brighton

Graves Art Gallery.
Surrey St., Sheffield S1 1XZ
Permanent Collections:
For information see Sheffield City Art Galleries.

Gray Art Gallery & Museum.
Clarence Rd., Hartlepool TS24 8BT, Cleveland

Great Hall Gallery.
University College of Wales-Penglais, Aberystwyth, Cardiganshire

Greenock Art Gallery. *See* **McLean Museum & Greenock Art Gallery**

Greenwich Theatre Art Gallery.
Kings St., London EC2

Grundy Art Gallery.
Queen St., Blackpool FY1 2PX

Guildhall.
Guildhall Lane, Leicester

Guildhall Art Gallery.
King St., London EC2
Permanent Collections:
Guildhall permanent collection of paintings and sculpture and Guildhall Library collection of prints and drawings.

Gulbenkian Museum of Oriental Art & Archaeology.
School of Oriental Studies, the University, Elvert Hill, Durham DH1, 3TH

Hampton Court Palace.
Hampton Court, Middx

Harewood House.
Harewood, Leeds LS17 9LQ

Harris Museum & Art Gallery.
Market Square Preston PR1 2PP, Lancs.

Harrogate Art Gallery.
Public Library, Victoria Ave., Harrogate, Yorks.

Harvington Hall.
Nr. Kidderminister, Words.

Hatton Gallery.
The University Newcastle-Upon-Tyne NE1 7RU

Hauteville House.
Maison de Victor Hugo, 38 Hauteville, Saint Peter, Port Guernsey

Haworth Art Gallery.
Haworth Park, Manchester Rd., Accrington, Lancs.

Heaton Hall.
Heaton Park, Prestwich, Manchester M25 55W

Henry Reitlinger Bequest. *See* **Reitlinger, Henry, Bequest**

Herbert Art Gallery & Museum.
Jordan Well, Coventry CV1 5RG, (0203) 25555, 2662
Permanent Collections:
Visual arts, social history, natural history, industry and transport.

Heveningham Hall.
Halesworth, Suffolk

Higgins, Cecil, Art Gallery.
Castle Close, Bedford MK40 3NY

Higham Place Gallery. *See* **Lain Art Gallery & Museum & Higham Place Gallery**

Hill of Tarvit (National Trust for Scotland)
Hill of Tarvit, Fife, Scotland

Hirsch Collection (Branch of Brtish Museum)
Great Russell St., London WC1

Hitchin Museum & Art Gallery.
Paynes Park, Hitchin SG 5 1EQ Herts.

Hogarth's House.
Hogarth Lane, Great West Ed., Chiswick, London W4

Holburne of Menstrie Museum (University of Bath)
Great Pulteney St., Bath BA2 4DB, (0225) 66669
Permanent Collections:
Housed in the Sydney Hotel built in 1796-7, the museum contains a fine collection, mainly assembled by Sir Thomas Holburne, as well as possessing one of the choicest collections of silver in the country. The arts of the 18th century are well represented by porcelain, paintings, miniatures,

glass, silhouettes and furniture. The Crafts Study Centre opened at the Holburne in June 1977. The collection covers a wide range of 20th century craftwork, including printed and woven textiles, pottery, furniture and calligraphy.

Hopetoun House.
South Queensferry, West Lothian, EH30 9SL, Scotland

Hove Museum of Art.
19 New Church Rd., Hove BN3 4AB, Sussex

Hunterian Museum and University Art Collections.
Univ. of Glasgow, Glasgow G12 8 Q Q, 041-339 8855 EXT. 5XX 7430
Permanent Collections:
Particular strengths: James McNeill Whistler oils, pastels, watercolors, drawings; and prints; Charles Rennie Mackintosh furniture, watercolors and drawings; Scottish late 19th and early 20th century paintings, watercolors and drawings; Old Master 19th and 20th century prints; Dutch and Flemish 17th century paintings; 18th century portraits.

Huntly House Museum.
142 Canongate, Edinburgh EH 8DD

Ickworth House (National Trust)
Bury St. Edmunds, Suffolk

Instituto Nazionale per la Grafica Calcografia.
Via della Stamperia 6, I-00187 Rome, 6798958-6794916

Inverness Museum & Art Gallery.
Castle Wynd, Inverness, IV2 3ED, Scotland, 0463-37114
Permanent Collections:
Archeology, social history, decorative arts, fine art, geology, minerology, natural history.

Ipswich Museums & Art Galleries.
Main Museum, High St., Ipswich IP1 3QH, Suffolk, IPSWICH 213761
Permanent Collections:
The Museum includes geology, prehistory, archaeology of Suffolk from earlier times to the Medieval period, Natural History, Ethnography. The Christchurch Mansion includes a country house collection of furniture, pictures, bygones, ceramics, paintings by Gainsborough, Constable and other Suffolk artists; 20th century works (paintings, drawings, sculptures and prints).

Iveagh Bequest. *See* **Kenwood, The Iveagh Bequest**

James Guthrie Orchard Art Gallery.
31 Beach Crescent, Broughty Ferry, Dundee

Jersey Museums at Pier Road & Lahougue Bie & Barreau Art Gallery.
La Societe Jersiaise, 9 Pier Rd., St. Helier, Jersey, C.I.

Kellie Castle & Gardens (National Trust for Scotland)
Kellie Castle, Nr. Pittenweem, Fife, Scotland

Kenwood, The Iveagh Bequest.
Hampstead Lane, London NW3 7JR, 01-348 1286
Permanent Collections:
Old Master paintings and British 18th century paintings; Georgian shoebuckles; jewelry.

Kidderminster Art Gallery & Museum.
Market St., Kidderminster DY10 1AB, Worcs.

Knole House.
Sevenoaks, Kent

La Hougue Bie & Barreau Art Gallery. *See* **Jersey Museums at Pier Road & Lahougue Bie & Barreau Art Gallery**

Lady Lever Art Gallery.
Port Sunlight L62 5EQ Wirral, Merseyside

Lain Art Gallery & Museum & Higham Place Gallery.
Higham Place Newcastle-Upon-Tyne NE1 8AG

Lancaster Museum & Art Gallery.
Old Town Hall, Market Square, Lancaster

Lauriston Castle.
2A Cramond Rd. South, Edinburgh EH4 5QD

Leamington Spa Art Gallery.
Avenue Rd., Leamington Spa, Warwickshire

Leicester Museum & Art Gallery.
New Walk, Leicester LE1 6TD, (0533) 539111
Permanent Collections:
Important collection of 18th, 19th and 20th century British paintings, watercolors, drawings, prints and sculpture; collection of works by the German Expressionists; 19th and 20th century French art; large collection of French, Italian, German and Flemish fine prints.

Leighton Hall.
Carnforth, Lancs.

Leighton House Art Gallery & Museum.
12 Holland Park Rd., London W14
Permanent Collections:
Nineteenth century British painting and prints; drawings by Lord Leighton; pottery by William de Morgan.

Lewis Textile Museum.
Exchange St., Blackburn, Lancs.

Lillie Art Gallery.
Staton Rd., Milngavie, Dunbartonshire

Lincoln Cathedral Treasury of Diocesan Plate.
The Cathedral, Lincoln

Lincolnshire Museums, Usher Gallery.
Lincoln Rd., LN2 1NN Lincoln, LINCOLN 27980
Permanent Collections:
Watercolors by Peter De Wint;

paintings of local interest; watches, ceramics, glass, enamels, miniatures, silver and costumes.

Little Moreton Hall (National Trust Property)
Congleton, Cheshire

London Museum.
Kensington Palace, London W8 4PX

Longford Hall Art Gallery.
Longford Park, Edge Lane, Stretford, Lancs.

Longleat House.
Longleat BA12 7NN, Nr. Warminster Wilts.

Losely House.
Guildford, Surrey

Lotherton Hall.
Aberford, Nr. Leeds, Yorks.

Luton Museum & Art Gallery.
Wardown Park, Luton, Beds.

Lyme Hall.
Lyme Park, Disley Nr. Stockport, Cheshire

McLean Museum & Greenock Art Gallery.
9 Union St., Greenock, Renfrewshire, (0475) 50 23741
Permanent Collections:
Mixed collections including the following subjects: Fine art, (painting, prints, sculpture), including the Caird Collection of works of art; Decorative art, (glassware, porcelain, needlework, etc.); natural history, geology, archaeology, Egyptology, local history, science and technology, medals, coins and tokens, posters, model shops, ethnography, photography.

Maidstone Museum & Art Gallery.
Saint Faith's St., Maidstone, Kent ME14 1LH
Permanent Collections:
Foreign oil paintings; British oil paintings and watercolors; sculpture; English, Continental and Oriental ceramics and jewelry, 17th-20th century.

Manchester City Art Galleries.
Mosley St., Manchester

Manor House Museum & Art Gallery.
Castle Yard, Yorks.

Manx Museum, Library & Art Gallery.
Douglas, Isle of Man

Mappin Art Gallery.
Weston Park, S10 2TP Sheffield, 0742-26281
Permanent Collections:
For information see Sheffield Art Galleries.

Martin Ware Pottery Collection.
District Library, Osterley Park Rd., Ealing, London

Melrose Abbey Museum.
Melrose, Roxburghshire

Mercer Museum & Art Gallery.
Mercer Park, Clayton-le-Moors, Lancs.

Michelham Priory.
Upper Dicker, Nr. Hailsham,
Sussex

Middlesbrough Art Gallery.
Linthorpe Rd., Middlesbrough,
Cleveland

Minories Gallery (Victor Batte-Lay Trust)
74 High St., Colchester C01
1UE

Morris, William, Gallery.
Lloyd Park, Forest Rd.,
Walthamstow, London F17
4PP, 01-527-5544 EXT. 390
Permanent Collections:
All aspects of the work of
William Morris, the pre-
Raphaelites and the arts and
crafts movement. Sculpture by
Rodin and other late 19th
century artists. Books from the
Private Presses, 19th century
prints and drawings as well as
all aspects of the work of Frank
Brangwyn (etchings,
lithographs, oil paintings, etc.).

Moss, Fletcher, Museum.
Old Parsonage Wilmslow Rd.,
Didsbury, Manchester M2O
8AU

Muncaster Castle & Bird Gardens.
Ravenglass CA18 1RQ
Cumbria

Museum & Art Galleries.
High St. Paisley PA1 2BA,
Renfrewshire

Museum & Art Gallery.
Wardown Park, Luton LU2
7HA

Museum & Art Gallery.
Broadway, Letchworth, Herts.

Museum & Art Gallery.
Leeming St. Mansfield, Notts.

Museum & Art Gallery.
St.Jame's Rd., Dudley, Worcs.

Museum & Art Gallery.
Checure Rd., Doncaster, Yorks.

Museum & Art Gallery.
Rivesley Park Nuneator CV11
5TU

Museum & Art Gallery.
St. Matthew's., Rugby,
Warwickshire

Museum & Art Gallery.
Boulevard Weston-Super-Mare
Somerset

Museum & Art Gallery.
Guild St., Burton-Upon-Trent,
Staffs.

Museum & Art Gallery.
Tullie House, Castle St.,
Carlisle CA3 8TR

Museum & Art Gallery.
Fairfield Rd., Kingston-Upon-
Thames, Surrey

Museum & Art Gallery.
The Mansion, Crow Nest Park,
Dewsbury, Yorks.

Museum & Art Gallery.
Dick Institute, Elmbank Ave.,
Kilmarnock, Ayrshire

Museum & Art Gallery.
Castle Hill House, Priory Ave.,
High Wycombe, Bucks.

Museum & Art Gallery.
John's Place, Cambridge Rd.,
Hastings TN34 1FT, Sussex

Museum of Antiquities of the University & The Society of Antiquaries of Newscastle-Upon-Tyne.
Dept. of Archaeology of the
University of Newcastle-Upon-
Tyne NE1 7RU

Museum of Costume.
Assembly Rooms, Alfred St.,
Bath, Somerset, BATH(0225)
61111
Permanent Collections:
One of the largest displays of
costume in the world, founded
on the famous collection of
Mrs. Langley Moore, and now
greatly enlarged and enriched
by donations from many
sources. In the Panorama
Room, fashionable Victorians
appear in Bath settings; there is
an Underwear Room; one for
every kind of headgear, and
another for dolls and children's
toys as well as a superb
collection of jewelry covering
200 years. The Modern Room
brings haute couture of the
20th century up to date with
models of the present year.

Museum of Modern Art.
30 Pembroke St. Oxford OX1
1BP

Museum of the Society of Friends of Dunblane Cathedral.
The Cross, Dunblane,
Perthshire

Museum of Welsh Antiquities.
Ffordd Gwynedd, Bangor,
Wales

Museums & Art Gallery.
Civic Center, Bolton, Lancs.

Museums & Art Gallery.
War Memorial Grounds,
Kirkcaldy, Fife, KY1 1YG,
0592 60732
Permanent Collections:
Scottish painting, 1750-1940,
with collections of William
McTaggart and S. J. Peploe.
Some modern art.

National Gallery.
Trafalgar Square, WC2N 5DN
London

National Gallery of Scotland.
The Mound EH2 2EL
Edinburgh, (031) 556 8921
Permanent Collections:
Paintings (some sculpture) and
graphic art of the 14th through
19th centuries.

National Museum of Wales.
Cardiff

National Portrait Gallery.
2 St. Martin's Place, London
WC2H OHE, 01-930-1552
Permanent Collections:
Records (portraits) of famous
British men and women.

National Toy Museum. *See*
**Rottingdean Grange Art Gallery
& Museum & National Toy
Museum**

Newark Museum & Art Gallery.
Appleton Gate, Newark, Notts.
NG24 1JY

Nicholson Institute Art Gallery.
Stockwell St., Leek ST13 6
DW Staffs.

Norfolk Museums Service.
C/0 Norfolk County Council,
Castle Museum, Norwich NR1
3JU, NORWICH 22233 EXT.
639
Permanent Collections:
Provides information on the
collections of the museums of
Norfolk County.

Normanby Hall.
Normanby, Nr. Sounthorpe,
Linds.

Norwich Castle Museum.
Norwich, NORWICH 22233
EXT, 639
Permanent Collections:
The Castle Keep is the oldest
part of the building and
contains displays of medieval
objects, armour, guns, coins,
two of the Norwich
Snapdragons and Egyptian
mummies. Museum galleries
contain displays of natural
history, art, social history and
archaeology. A new gallery of
ceramics and glass has recently
been completed.

Nostell Priory.
Nostell, Nr. Wakefield WF4
1QD, Yorks.

Number One Royal Crescent:
Bath, BATH (0225) 28126
Permanent Collections:
A Georgian House as it was.
The house was bought and
handed over to Bath
Preservation Trust in 1968 for
the fulfilment of a long-
cherished idea, the creation of
an authentic Georgian interior.

Old Glasgow Museum (Glasgow Museum & Art Galleriers)
People's Palace, Glasgow
Green, Glasgow S.E.

Osterley Park House, (Victoria & Albert Museum, London)
Isleworth, Middx.

Oxford University Ashomolean Museum of Art & Archeology:
Beaumont St., OX1 2DH
Oxford

Packwood House (National Trust Property)
Hockley Heath Near Solihull,
Warwickshire

Parc Howard Museum & Art Gallery.
Llanelly, Carms.

Passmore Edwards Art Gallery.
Smain Rd. Newlyn, Cornwall

Pease, Edward, Public Library & Art Gallery.
Crown St., Darlington, Co.
Durham

Penwith Society of Arts.
Back Rd. West, Saint Ives.,
Cornwall

Percival David Foundation of Chinese Art. *See* **David,
Percival, Foundation of Chinese
Art**

Perrins, Dyson, Museum.
Royal Worcester Co. Ltd.,
Severn St., Worcester 20272,
WORCESTER 20272
Permanent Collections:
Porcelains made at Worcester,
covering the whole history of
production from 1751 to the
present day. Comprises the
finest collection of Worcester
porcelain in the world.

Petworth House.
Petworth, Sussex

Piccots End Medieval Wall Paintings.
Piccot's End, Hemel
Hempstead, Herts.

Plymouth City Museum & Gallery.
Drake Circus, PL4 8AJ
Plymouth

Polesdan Lacey (National Trust Property)
Dorking, Surrey

Pollok House, (Glasgow Museums & Art Galleries)
2060 Pollokshaws Rd., Glasgow
G43 1AT
Permanent Collections:
Stirling Maxwell Collection of
Paintings and Sculpture,
Furniture, Silver, Glass,
Ceramics, mostly 18th century.

Powis Castle.
Welshpool, Montgomeryshire

Preston Manor.
Preston Park, BN1 6SD
Brighton

Public Library, Art Gallery & Museum.
Champney Rd., Beverley,
Yorks.

Public Library, Museum & Art Gallery.
Grace Hill, Folkestone, Kent

Puttenden Manor.
Lingfield, Surrey

Queens Gallery.
Buckingham Palace, Lord
Chamberlain's Office, St. James
Palace, SW1 London

Queen's Park Art Gallery.
Queen's Park, Harpuhey,
Manchester M9 ISH

Raby Castle.
Staindrop, Darlington, Co.,
Durham

Rapallo House Museum & Art Gallery.
Ferm Bach Rd., Llandudno,
Wales

Reading Museum & Art Gallery.
P.O. Box 17, Town Hall,
Reading RG1 1QN

Red House Museum, Art Gallery & Gardens.
Quay Rd., Christchurch, Dorset
BH23 1BU

Reitlinger, Henry, Bequest.
Oldfield, Riverside,
Maidenhead SL6 8DN

Richborough Castle.
Richborough, Kent

Rochdale Museum & Art Gallery.
Esplanade, Rochdale, Lancs.

Roman Baths and Museum.
Pump Room, Bath, BATH
(O225) 61111
Permanent Collections:
The finest Roman remains in
Britain. The treasures include
mosaics, sculptured stones and
the famous gilt-bronze head of
the goddess Minerva.

Rossendale Museum.
Whitaker Park, Rawtenstall,
Rossendale BB4 6RE, 07062
7777
Permanent Collections:
Rossendale Collection, British
birds, fine arts, furniture and
ceramics.

**Rotherham Municipal Museum &
Art Gallery.**
Clifton Park, Rotherham,
Yorks.

Rothesay Museum.
8 Bath Rd., Bournemouth,
Hants.

**Rottingdean Grange Art Gallery &
Museum & National Toy
Museum.**
The Grange, Rottingdean BN2
7HA, Sussex

Royal Academy of Arts.
Burlington House, Picadilly,
London W1V ODS

Royal Albert Memorial Museum.
Queen St., Exeter EX4 3RX,
0392 56724
Permanent Collections:
British oil paintings, watercolors, prints, drawings and
sculpture.

**Royal Art Collection, Windsor
Castle.**
Windsor, Berks.

Royal Cambrian Academy of Art.
"Plas Mawr", High St.,
Conway, Wales

Royal College of Art.
Kensington Gore, SW7 2EU
London

Royal Crown Derby Museum.
Osmaston Rd., Derby DE3
1HS

**Royal Holloway College Picture
Gallery.**
Royal Holloway College (Univ.
of London) Egham Hill, Egham
TW20 0EX, Surrey

**Royal Institute of British
Architects Drawings Collection.**
66 Portland Place London W1

Royal Museum and Art Gallery.
High St., Canterbury,
CANTERBURY 52747
Permanent Collections:
Local history, archaeology and
natural history; fine and
decorative art; Buffs
Regimental Museum

**Royal Pavillion Art Gallery and
Museums.**
Church St. BN1 1UE Brighton,
603005 BRIGHTON

Royal Scottish Museum.
Chambers St., EH1 1JF
Edinburgh, 031-225-7534
SCOTMUS

Permanent Collections:
Decorative arts and sculpture
(pre-1900) of Europe and the
Orient, archaeology,
ethnography, geology, zoology,
science and technology.

**Royal Shakespeare Theatre
Picture Gallery & Museum.**
Waterside, Stratford-Upon-
Avon, Warwickshire

**Royal Society of Painters in
Water Colours.**
26 Conduit St., London W1R
9TA

Ruskin Gallery.
Bembridge School, Bembridge,
Isle of Wight

**Russel-Cotes Art Gallery &
Museum.**
East Cliff, Bournemouth,
Hants.

Rutland County Museum.
Catmos St., Oakham, Rutland
LE15 6HW, OAKHAM (0572)
3654
Permanent Collections:
Archaeology, social history,
folk life, trade tools, local crafts
relating to former county of
Rutland.

**Saint Andrews Cathedral
Museum:**
St. Andrews, Fife, Scotland

St. Anne's Chapel Museum.
Parish Churchyard, High St.,
Barnstaple, Devon

**Saint Helen's Museum & Art
Gallery:**
St. Helen's, Merseyside WA10
1DY
Permanent Collections:
Geology, Palaentology,
Archaeology, Egyptology, Fine
and Decorative arts, militaria,
clocks and watches, cameras
and exhibits illustrative of local
mining, glass, clay pipe, pill
earthenware and mineral water
manufactures.

**St. Mary's Tower (Corporation of
the City of Dundee Art Galleries
& Museums Dept.)**
Kirk Stile, Nethergait, Dundee
DD1 4DG

St. Peter Hungate.
Princes St., Norwich,
NORWICH 22233 EXT. 639
Permanent Collections:
This handsome 15th century
church is noted for its fine
hammer bean roof and the
Norwich painted glass in the
east and west windows. The
displays illustrate the theme of
art and craftsmanship in the
service of Christianity. The
exhibits, which range in date
from the 9th to 20th century,
include medieval illuminated
religious books, vestments,
monumental brasses,
communion plate, more stands
and types of musical
instruments played in churches.
Many of the objects shown are
from Norfolk, but there are
also items from overseas.

**Salisbury & South Wiltshire
Museum.**
42 St. Ann St., Salisbury,
Wilts., SALISBURY 4465
Permanent Collections:
Architecture, local history,
ceramics, costume, prints and
drawings.

Samlesbury Hall.
Preston New Rd., Samlesbury,
Prestonn PR5 OUP

Samlesbury Old Hall.
Samlesbury, Nr. Blackburn,
Lancs.

Scarborough Art Gallery.
The Crescent, Scarborough,
Yorks.

Scottish Arts Council Gallery.
19 Charlotte Square, Edinburgh
EH2 4DF, 031-226 6051

**Scottish National Gallery of
Modern Art.**
Royal Botanic Garden, EH3
5LR Edinburgh, (031) 332
3754
Permanent Collections:
Twentieth century painting,
sculpture and graphic art.

**Scottish National Portrait
Gallery.**
1 Queen St., EH2 1JD
Edinburgh, (031) 556 8921
Permanent Collections:
Portraits of eminent Scots
(16th century to present day);
photographs; paintings;
sculpture; prints; drawings;
medals etc.; paintings of
Scottish topography.

**Scunthorpe Museum & Art
Gallery.**
Oswald Rd., Scunthorpe, Lincs.

Segal, Arthur, Collection.
1 England Lane, London NW3

Sheffield City Art Galleries.
Surrey St., S1 1XZ Sheffield
Permanent Collections:
European Old Masters; English
painting from the 17th century;
19th century French painting;
English, European and
American painting; sculpture
and prints of the 20th century.

Shell Museum.
Glandford, Norfolk

Shipley Art Gallery.
Prince Consort Rd. South,
Gateshead NE8 4JB

Shrewsbury Borough Art Gallery.
Castle Gates, Shrewsbury, SY1
2AS

Sir John Soane's Museum. *See*
Soane, Sir John, Museum

Smith Art Gallery & Museum.
Albert Place, Stirling FK8
2RQ, Scotland

Soane, Sir John, Museum.
13 Lincoln's Inn Fields,
London WC2

South London Art Gallery.
Peekham Rd., SE5 8UH
London

Southampton Art Gallery.
Civic Centre, Commercial Rd.,
Southampton

Spencer, Stanley, Gallery.
King's Hall, High St.,
Cookham-on-Thames, Berks.

Spode Museum.
Spode Limited, Spode Works,
Stoke-on-Trent, Staffs.

Stanley Spencer Gallery. *See*
Spencer, Stanley, Gallery

Stockport Art Gallery.
Wellington Rd. S., Stockport,
Cheshire

Stourhead House.
Stourton, Nr, Warminster,
Wilts.

Strangers Hall Museum.
St. Benedicts St., Norwich,
NORWICH 22233 EXT. 639
Permanent Collections:
The museum is in a house
which has been the home of
prosperous citizens of Norwich
from the Middle Ages to within
living memory. The undercroft
was built about 1320 and the
oldest parts of the great hall
date from the 15th century.
Alterations have been made to
the house since Tudor times
and the rooms are furnished in
the styles of various periods
from the 16th century onwards.
Art related items include 15th
century tapestries, a chandelier
of 18th century Irish glass,
Norwich shop signs and
displays of toys and costumes.

Sudley Art Gallery & Museum.
Mossley Hill Rd., Liverpool
L18 8BX

**Sunderland Museum & Art
Gallery.**
Borough Rd., Sunderland SR2
1PP

Swindon Museum & Art Gallery.
Bath Rd., Swindon, Wilts.

Tate Gallery.
Millbank, SW1P 4RG London

Temple Newsam House.
Leeds LS1S OAE, LEEDS
647321/641358
Permanent Collections:
Paintings, watercolors, prints,
sculpture, furniture, English
ceramics, Oriental ceramics,
silver and costume.

The Greek Museum.
University, Newcastle-Upon-
Tyne NE1 7RU, 0632 28511
EXT. 3966
Permanent Collections:
Greek and Etruscan antiquities.

The Vyne.
Sherborne St., Basingstoke,
Hants.

The Wernher Collection.
Luton Hoo, Luton Beds.
Permanent Collections:
Old Master paintings, English
and French furniture, English
and French Porcelain, Flemish
and French Tapestries, English
Silver Gilt, German
Renaissance Silver Gilt,
Medieval Ivories, Limoges
Enamels, Renaissance Bronzes,
Renaissance Jewelry, Italian
Maiolica, Isnik Pottery (small
collection), late Medieval wood
carvings (small collection),
Faberge jewelry, clocks,

portraits and mementoes of the
Russian Imperial Family.

Thetford Art Gallery.
Guildhall, Market Place,
Thetford

**Thomas Balston Collection of
Staffordshire Portrait Figures.
See Balston, Thomas, Collection
of Staffordshire Portrait Figures**

**Torre Abbey Art Allery &
Conference.**
Kings Dr., Torquay, Devon

Totems Museum.
High St., Arundel, Sussex

Towneley Hall Art Gallery.
Burnley, Lancs.
Permanent Collections:
Oil paintings, watercolors,
ceramics, glass, furniture,
natural history, militaria, local
crafts, bygones and industries.

Towner Art Gallery.
Borough Lane, Eastbourne,
Sussex

Traquair House.
Traquair, Innerleithen,
Peebleshire

Treasure's House.
Minster Yard, York

**Tudor Barn Art Gallery. See Well
Hall, Tudor Barn Art Gallery**

Tudor House Museum.
Bugle St., Southampton

**Tunbridge Wells Municipal
Museum & Art Gallery.**
Civic Centre, Mount Pleasant,
Tunbridge Wells , Kent,
TUNBRIDGE WELLS 26121
EXT. 171
Permanent Collections:
Local history and natural
history; toys and dolls;
domestic bygones; Tunbridge
ware; the Ashton Bequest and
the Pamela McDowall
Collection.

Turner House.
Plymouth Rd. Penarth, Glam.,
South Wales

Ulster Museum.
National Museum of Northern
Ireland Botanic Gardens,
Belfast BT9 5AB

University Art Gallery.
Dept. of Fine Art, Portland
Bldg. University Park
Nottingham NG7 2RD

**University of Aberdeen, Marischal
College, Anthropological
Museum:**
Aberdeen AB9 1AS

**University of Cambridge;
Fitzwilliam Museum:**
Trumpington St., CB2 1RB
Cambridge, (0223)69789

**University of Manchester
Whitworth Art Gallery:**
Whitworth Park, M15 6ER
Manchester

**Upton House (National Trust
Property)**
Edgehill, Warwickshire

**Usher Gallery. See Lincolnshire
Museums, Usher Gallery**

Victoria & Albert Museum.
Cromwell Rd., SW7 2RL
London
Permanent Collections:
Collections include Medieval
art, Gothic art, Gothic
Tapestry court, Italian
Renaissance art, Continental
High Renaissance art;
Continental art 1600-1800,
British art 1500-1700, British
art 1750-1900, Far Eastern art,
Islamic art, Indian art, Costume
court, musical instruments
gallery, Tapestry cartoons of
Raphael, collection of
Constable, British oil paintings,
Ionides Collection, water
colors, architecture, sculpture,
embroideries, miniatures,
jewelry, furniture, clocks,
cutlery, enamels, woodwork,
lace, ivories, engravings,
posters, carpets, stained glass,
vestments, lithographs,
manuscripts, watches, ironwork,
arms and armor, metalwork,
ceramics, Indian section, prints
and drawings, textiles and the
National Art Library.

Victoria Art Gallery.
Bridge St., Bath BA2 4AT,
0225-61111
Permanent Collections:
17th-19th century paintings;
British 20th century paintings,
drawings and prints; Kimball
Collection of late 19th century
and contemporary prints,
English pottery and porcelain;
collection of antique English
drinking glasses; antique
watches, coins, tokens and
British Delft.

Victoria Street Art Gallery.
14 Victoria St., Nottingham
NG1 2EX

Waddesdon Manor.
National Trust, Waddesdon
Manor, Aylesbury, Bucks.
HPI8 OJH, (029 665) 211 &
282
Permanent Collections:
The James D. Rothschild
Bequest to the National Trust;
French 17th and 18th century
decorative art, English 18th
century portraits, Dutch and
Flemish 17th century pictures,
medieval manuscripts,
European arms and armor of
the 16th and 17th century,
Majolica, glass and French 18th
century books.

Wakefield Art Gallery.
Wentworth Terrace, Wakefield,
WF1 3QW, WAKEFIELD
70211 EXT. 8031

**Walker Art Gallery, Merseyside
County Council.**
William Brown St., L3 8EL
Liverpool, 051-227-5234

Wallace Collection.
Manchester Square WIM 6BN,
935-0687
Permanent Collections:
Old Master paintings,
sculpture, French furniture,
European arms and armor,
Oriental arms and armor,
Italian Majolica, Sevres
porcelain, goldsmith's work,
English and French 19th
century paintings and
watercolors.

Wallington Hall (National Trust)
Cambo, Morpeth
Northumberland

Walsall Museum & Art Gallery.
Lichfield St., Walsall WS1
1TR, WALSALL 21244
Permanent Collections:
The Garman-Ryan Collection
of Fine Art.

**Warrington Museum & Art
Gallery.**
Bold St., Warrington WA1
1JG, Cheshire

Watts Gallery.
Compton, Nr. Guildford;
Surrey

Wedgwood Museum.
Barlaston, Staffs.

Wedgwood Museum.
Stoke-on-Trent, Staffs.

Wednesbury Art Gallery.
Holyhead Rd., Wednesbury
WS10 7DF, West Midlands
Permanent Collections:
Edwin Richards Collection of
Oils and Watercolors.

**Well Hall, Tudor Barn Art
Gallery.**
Eltham London SE9

**Wellington Museum, Apsley
House.**
149 Piccadilly, W1V 9FA
London

Welsh Folk Museum.
Near Cardiff, Saint Fagans

Wesley House & Museum.
47 City Rd. London C1Y 1AU

**West Park Museum & Art
Gallery.**
Presbury Rd. Macclesfield,
Cheshire

Weston Park.
Weston Park, Shifnal,
Shropshire

Whitby Museum & Art Gallery.
Plannett Park, Whitby, Yorks.

Whitechapel Art Gallery.
Whitechapel High St., London
E1 7QX

Wigan Museum & Art Gallery.
Station Rd., Wigan, Lancs.

Wightwick Manor.
Compton, Wolverhampton,
Staffs.

**Williamson Art Gallery &
Museum.**
Slatey Rd., Claughton,
Birkenhead, L43 4UE

**Willis Museum & Art Gallery
(Hampshire County Museum
Service)**
New St., Basingstoke, Hants.

Wilton House Art Collection.
Wilton House, Wilton SP2 0BJ,
Nr. Salisbury, Wilts.

**Windsor Castle. See Royal Art
Collection, Windsor Castle**

Woburn Abbey Art Gallery.
Woburn, Beds.

Wolverhampton Art Gallery.
Lichfield St., WV1 1DU
Wolverhampton, (0902) 24549
Permanent Collections:
18th, 19th and 20th century oil
paintings and watercolors,
English enamels, Oriental
ivory, metalwork, weapons,
English Jappaned ware, 18th
and 19th century ceramics,
English and foreign dolls, cut
steel jewelry, 19th century
locks and keys, 19th century
steel animal traps and other
industrial items.

Wool House Museum.
The Wool House, Bugle St.,
Southampton

**Worcestershire Regimental
Museum.**
Foregate St., Worcester WR1
1DT

**Worshipful Company of
Goldsmiths Goldsmith's Hall.**
Foster Lane, EC2 London

Worthing Museum & Art Gallery.
Chapel Rd., Worthing BN11
1HD, Sussex, WORTHING
204226
Permanent Collections:
Regional archaeology, toys,
dolls and juvenilia. English
paintings, ceramics and glass;
English costume (1750-1950);
domestic equipment.

York City Art Gallery.
Exhibition Square, YO1 2EW
York

Yorkshire Museum.
Museum Gardens, York YO1
2DR

UNITED STATES

**Abby Aldrich Rockefeller Folk
Art Center. See Rockefeller,
Abby Aldrich, Folk Art Center**

Abilene Fine Arts Museum.
Box 1858, Abilene, TX 79604

Academy of Professional Artists.
Four Daniel Rd., Saint Louis,
MO 63124

Academy of the Arts.
P.O. Box 605, Easton, MD
21601

**Academy of the Museum of
Conceptual Art.**
75 Third St., San Francisco,
CA 94103

**Ackerman, Louise Sloss, Fine Arts
Library.**
Van Ness at McAllister, San
Francisco, CA 94102

Adams State College Museum.
ES Bldg., Alamosa, CO 81101

**Addison Gallery of American Art.
See Phillips Academy, Addison
Gallery of American Art**

**Adelphi University Fine Arts
Library:**
Garden City, NY 11530

**Adirondack Lakes Center for the
Arts.**
Blue Mountain Lake, NY
12812

Adirondack Museum of the Adirondack Historical Assn.
Blue Mountain Lake, NY 12812

Advocates for the Arts.
405 N. Hilgard Ave., Los Angeles, CA 90024

Agecroft Association, Agecroft Hall:
4305 Sulgrave Rd., Richmond, VA 23221

Ages of Man Foundation.
Sheffield Rd., Amenia, NY 12501

Agnes Scott College, Dalton Gallery.
College Ave. & Chandler St., Decatur, GA 30030

Akron Art Institute.
69 E. Market St., Akron, OH 44308 Tel 216-376-9185
Permanent Collections:
Post 1850 art work; the Edwin C. Shaw Collection of Paintings.

Alabama Museum of Photography.
4322 Glenwood Ave., Birmingham, AL 35222

Alabama State Dept. of Archives & History.
624 Washington Ave., Montgomery, AL 36130

Alaska Artist Guild.
P.O. Box 1888, Anchorage, AK 99501

Alaska Association for Fine Arts:
P.O. Box 2786, Fairbanks

Alaska State Museum.
Pouch FM, Juneau, AK 99811

Albany County Historical Assn.
9 Ten Broeck Pl., Albany, NY 12210

Albany Institute of History & Art.
125 Washington Ave., Albany, NY 12203 Tel 518-463-4478
Permanent Collections:
Fine and decorative arts relating to New York State.

Albert K. Mitchell Collection of Western Art, Lovelace Foundation for Medical Education & Research.
5200 Gibson Blvd. S.E., Albuquerque, NM 87108

Albion College, Bobbitt Visual Arts Center.
Albion, MI 49224

Albrecht Art Museum.
2818 Frederick Blvd., St. Joseph, MO 64506

Albright-Knox Art Gallery.
1285 Elmwood Ave., Buffalo, NY 14222 Tel 716-882-8700

Albuqerque Public Library Fine Arts Dept.
423 Central, N.E., Albuquerque, NM

Albuquerque Art Council.
5900 Domingo Rd., N.E., Albuquerque, NM 87108

Albuquerque Museum of Art & History & Science.
P.O. Box 1293, Albuquerque, NM 87101

Aldrich Museum of Contemporary Art.
258 Main St., Ridgefield, CT 06877

Alford House. *See* **Anderson Fine Arts Center, Alford House**

Alice T. Miner Colonial Collection. *See* **Miner, Alice T., Colonial Collection**

Alle-Kiski Museum.
224 E. Seventh Ave. & Lock St., Tarentum, PA 15084

Allegheny College, Bowman, Megahan & Penelec Galleries.
Meadville, PA 16335

Allen Knight Maritime Museum. *See* **Knight, Allen, Maritime Museum**

Allen Memorial Art Museum. *See* **Oberlin College , Allen Memorial Art Museum**

Allen Shivers Museum & Library. *See* **Shivers, Allen, Museum & Library**

Allentown Artmuseum.
P.O. Box 117, Allentown, PA 18105

Allied Artists of America, Inc.
1083 Fifth Ave., New York, NY 10028

Allied Arts Council of the Yakima Valley.
5000 W. Lincoln Ave., Yakima, WV 98908

Allied Arts of Seattle.
107 S. Main St., Seattle, WA 98104

Allis, Charles, Art Library.
1630 E. Royall Place, Milwaukee, WI 53202

Allyn, Lyman, Museum.
100 Mohegan Ave., New London, CT 06320

Alverno College Gallery.
3401 S. 39th St, Milwaukee, WI 53215

Alverthorpe Gallery.
511 Meetinghouse, Jenkintown, PA 19046

Amarillo Art Center.
2200 S. Van Buren, P.O. Box 447, Amarillo, TX 79178

American Abstract Artists.
218 W. 20th St., New York, NY 10011

American Academy & Institute of Arts & Letters.
633 E. 155th St., New York, NY 10032

American Academy in Rome.
633 E. 65th St., New York, NY 10021

American Art Society.
810 S. Lucerne Blvd., Los Angeles, CA 90005

American Artists Professional League, Inc.
215 Park Ave. S., New York, NY 10003

American Association of Museums.
1055 Thomas Jefferson St., N.W., Washington, DC 20007

American Association of University Press:
2401 Virginia Ave., N.W., Washington, DC 20037

American Baptist Historical Society.
1106 S. Goodman St., Rochester, NY 14620

American Ceramic Society.
65 Ceramic Dr., Columbus, OH 43214

American Color Print Society.
C/o Philadelphia College of Art, Broad & Pine Sts., Philadelphia, PA 19102

American Council for Arts in Education.
41 E. 65th St., New York

American Council for the Arts.
570 Seventh Ave., New York, NY 10018

American Craft Museum.
44 W. 53rd St., New York, NY 10019

American Federation of Arts.
41 E. 65th St., New York, NY 10021

American Fine Arts Society.
215 W. 57th St., New York, NY 10019

American Heritage Wax Museum.
98 W. Stetson Dr., Scottsdale, AZ 85251

American Institute of Architects.
1735 New York Ave., N.W., Washington, DC 20006

American Institute of Architects Foundation; The Octagon.
179 New York Av. N.W., Washington, DC 20006 Tel 202-638-3105
Permanent Collections:
The Octagon, a historic house museum, was built by Colonel John Taylor III in 1797-1800. Used as a temporary White House during the War of 1812, the house today has been restored to its original condition and contains American and English furnishings from the period 1785-1828. It contains a small number of the original family pieces.

American Institute of Graphic Arts.
1059 Third Ave, New York, NY 10021 Tel 212-752-0813

American International Sculptors Symposium.
799 Greenwich St., New York, NY 10014

American Jewish Historical Society.
2 Thornton Rd., Waltham, MA 02154 Tel 617-891-8110

Permanent Collections:
Collection of paintings, daguerrotypes and artifacts.

American Museum of Natural History.
Central Park W. at 79th, New York, NY 10024

American Numismatic Assn.
N. Cascade Ave., P.O. 2366, Colorado Springs, CA 80903
Permanent Collections:
U.S. and foreign coins and paper money, medals and tokens; numismatically related items.

American Numismatic Society.
Broadway at 155th St., New York, NY 10032 Tel 212-234-3130 "*NUMISMA" NEW YORK

American Red Cross.
17th & D Sts., N.W., Washington, DC 20006

American Society for Asthetics.
Storrs, CT 06268

American Society of Bookplate Collectors & Designers.
1206 N. Stoneman Ave., 15, Alhambra, CA 91801

American Society of Contemporary Artists.
C/O Rose Betensky, 66 Hayloft Place, Roslyn Heights, NY 11577

American Society of Interior Designers.
730 Fifth Ave., New York, NY 10019

American Swedish Institute.
2600 Park Ave., Minneapolis, MN 55411

American Swedish Historical Foundation Museum.
1900 Pattison Ave., Philadelphia, PA 19145

American University, Watkins Art Gallery, Dept. of Art:
Massachusettts & Nebraska Aves., N.W., Washington, DC 20016

American Watercolor Society.
1083 Fifth Ave., New York, NY 10028

Amerind Foundation, Inc.
P.O. Box 248, Dragoon, AZ 85609
Permanent Collections:
Fulton-Hayden Memorial Art Gallery and Museum of the Amerind Foundation.

Amerind Research Library.
P.O. Box 248, Dragoon, AZ 85609

Amherst College, Mead Art Museum.
Mead Art Bldg., Amherst, MA 01002 Tel 413-542-2142

Amherst Historical Society.
Amity St., Amherst, MA 01002

Amon Carter Museum of Western Art. *See* **Carter, Amon, Museum of Western Art**

Anacostia Neighborhood Museum.
2405 Martin Luther King Jr.
Ave., S.E., Washington, DC
20008

**Anchorage Historical & Fine Arts
Museum.**
121 W. Seventh Ave.,
Anchorage, AK 99501

**Ancient & Horonable Artillery
Co. of Massachusetts.**
Faneuil Hall, Boston, MA
02109

Ancient Buried City.
P.O. Box 155, Wickliffe, KY
42087

**Or, Resources in Contemporary
Arts.**
1525 10th Ave., Seattle, WA
98122

Anderson Center for the Arts. See
Hartwick College Fine Arts
Museum, Anderson Center for
the Arts

**Anderson Fine Arts Center, Alford
House.**
226 W. Historical Eighth St.,
Anderson, IN 46016
Permanent Collections:
Primarily American art
(extensively Indiana and
regional artists).

Anderson Gallery. See Virginia
Commonwealth Univ., Anderson
Gallery

**Anderson House Museum; Society
of the Cincinnati.**
2118 Massachusetts Ave.,
N.W., Washington, DC 20008

Andover Historical Society.
97 Main St., Andover, MA
01810

Andover Historical Society.
Fifth & Mulberry, Andover, IL
61233

**Andrew Johnson Memorial
Commission.** See Johnson,
Andrew, Memorial Commission

Andrew-Safford House.
13 Washington Square, Salem,
MA 01970

Andrews County Musem.
211 N. W. Second St., P. O.
Box 2139, Andrews, TX 79714

**Angelo State University Houston,
Harte University Center:**
Box 11027, San Angelo, TX
76901

Anglo-American Art Museum. See
Louisiana State Univ., Anglo-
American Art Museum

**Anna Marie College, St. Luke's
Gallery.**
Moll Art Center Sunset Lane,
Paxton, MA 01612

Annie S. Kemerer Museum. See
Kemerer, Annie S., Museum

Anoka County Historical Society.
Anoka, MN 55303

**Anson County Historical Society,
Inc.**
210 E. Wade St., Wadesboro,
NC 28170
Permanent Collections:
The Society owns and operates

two historical houses: the
Boggan-Hammond House (18th
century) and the Alexander
Little Wing (19th century).
These are museums and have
collections of 18th and 19th
century period furnishings and
artifacts. Listed on the National
Register of Historical Places.

**Antioch College, Noyes, Read &
Gray Galleries.**
Yellow Springs, OH 45387

**Antiquarian & Landmarks Society,
Inc. of Connecticut.**
394 Main St., Hartford, CT
06103 Tel 203-247-8996
Permanent Collections:
The Society owns seven
historic house museums which
are furnished with antique
furniture, paintings, silver, toys,
ceramics, porcelains,
woodenware, wrought iron,
clocks, samplers, embroideries,
old fabrics, pewter, lighting
fixtures, musical instruments,
carpeting, etc. All houses open
to the public.

Arabian Horse Museum.
P.O. Box 307, Barnesville, MD
20703

Archie Bray Foundation. See
Bray, Archie, Foundation

**Architectural League of New
York.**
41 E. 65th St., New York, NY
10021

Archives of American Art.
Eighth & G Sts., N.W., New
York, NY 10021

Arco Center for Visual Art.
505 S. Flower St., Los Angeles,
CA 90071

Arizona Arts Guild.
8912 N. Fourth St., Phoenix,
AZ 85020

Arizona Historical Society.
949 E. Second St., Tucson, AZ
85719

Arizona Museum, Inc.
1001 W. Van Buren, Phoenix,
AZ 85007

**Arizona State University;
University Art Collections,
Mathews Center:**
Tempe, AZ 85281

Arizona Watercolor Assn.
8122 N. Eighth Ave., Phoenix,
AZ 85021

Arkansas Arts Center.
P.O. Box 2137, Little Rock,
AK 72203 Tel 501-372-4000

**Arkansas History Commission,
Old State House (West Wing)**
300w. Markham St., Little
Rock, AK 72201

**Arkansas State Univ. Art Gallery,
Jonesboro.**
Box 846, State University, AK
72467

**Arkansas Territorial Capitol
Restoration.**
214 E. Third St., Little Rock,
AR 72201

Arkansas Territorial Restoration.
Territorial Square, Little Rock,
AK 72201

**Arlington House, The Robert E.
Lee Memorial.**
Arlington National Cemetery,
Arlington, VA 22101

Arms Museum.
648 Wick Ave., Youngstown,
OH 44502

**Armstrong Museum of Art &
Archaeology.** See Olivet College,
Armstrong Museum of Art &
Archaeology

Arnot Art Museum.
235 Lake St., Elmira, NY
14901

**Aroostook Historical & Art
Museum of Houlton.**
109 Main St., Houlton, ME
04730

**Art & Education Council of
Greater St. Louis.**
607 N. Grand, Saint Louis,
MO 63103

**Art Association of Jacksonville;
David Strawn Art Gallery:**
331 W. College, Jacksonville,
IL 62650

Art Association of Newport:
76 Bellevue Ave., Newport, RI
02840

**Art Association of Richmond,
McGuire Memorial Hall:**
Whitewater Blvd., IN 47374
Permanent Collections:
American art; Indian art; art of
Richmond, Indiana; European
and Oriental art.

Art Barn.
143 Lower Cross Rd.,
Greenwich, CT 06830

Art Center.
Box 5396, Waco, TX 76708

Art Center.
125 Macomb St., Mount
Clemens, MI 48043

Art Center Inc.
120 S. Saint Joseph St., South
Bend, IN 46601

Art Center of New Jersey.
16 Washington St., East
Orange, NJ 07017

**Art Commission-City and County
of San Francisco.**
165 Grove St., San Francisco,
CA 94102

**Art Commission of the City of
New York.**
City Hall, New York, NY
10007

Art Complex Inc. at Duxbury.
189 Alden St., Box 1411,
Duxbury, MA 02332

**Art Dealers Association of
America.**
575 Madison Ave., New York,
NY 10022

Art Directors Club Inc.
488 Madison Ave., New York,
NY 10022

**Art Gallery of California State
College, Dominguez Hills.**
1000 E. Victoria, Dominguez
Hills, CA 90747

Art Information Center Inc.
189 Lexington Ave., New
York, NY 10016

**Art Institute of Boston, MacIvor
Reddie Gallery.**
700 Beacon St., Boston, MA
02215

Art Institute of Chicago.
Michigan Ave. at Adams St.,
Chicago, IL 60603 Tel 312-
443-3533

**Art Institute of Pittsburgh
Gallery.**
536 Penn Ave., Pittsburgh, PA
15222

Art League of Houston.
1953 Montrose Blvd., Houston,
TX 77006

**Art League of Manatee County
Art Center.**
209 Ninth St., W., Bradenton,
FL 33505

Art Museum of South Texas.
1902 N. Shoreline, Corpus
Christi, TX 78402

Art Patrons League of Mobile.
Box 8055, Mobile, AL 36608

Art Research Center.
922 E. 48th St., Kansas City,
MO 64110 Tel 816-531-2067
Permanent Collections:
Art multiples presented by
group members or exhibiting
artists. Primarily an
experimental artists group,
creating and exhibiting serial,
systematic and programmatic
art forms. Exhibitors are local,
national and foreign artists.

Art Research Service.
P.O. Box 95, Chappaqua, NY
10514

Art Students League of New York.
215 W. 57th St., New York,
NY 10019

Artemisia Fund & Gallery.
9 W. Hubbard St., Chicago, IL
60610

Artist-Craftsmen of New York.
130 E. 28th St, New York, NY
10016

**Artists Association of Nantucket;
Kenneth Taylor Gallery:**
Nantucket, MA 02554

Artists Equity Assn., Inc.
3726 Albemarle St., N.W.,
Washington, DC 20016

**Artists Equity Association of New
York.**
1780 Broadway, New York,
NY 10019

Artists Guild Inc. of New York.
25 W. 36th St., New York,
10018

Artists Space.
105 Hudson St., New York,
NY 10013

Artists Technical Research Institute, Inc.
207 W. 106th St., New York, NY 10025

Arts & Crafts Assn. of Meriden.
P.O. Box 348, Meriden, CT 06450

Arts & Crafts Center.
Mellon Park, 5th & Shady Aves., Pittsburgh, PA 15232

Arts & Humanities Council of Tuscaloosa County.
Box 1117, Tuscaloosa, AL 35401

Arts & Science Center.
14 Court St., Nashua, NH 03060

Arts Club of Chicago.
109 E. Ontario St., Chicago, IL 60611

Arts Club of Washington; James Monroe House.
2017 Eve St., N.W., Washington, DC 20006

Arts Council Inc.
610 Coliseum Dr., 27106

Arts Council of Spartansburg County.
385 S. Spring St., Spartansburg, SC 29301

Arts Council of the Midcolumbia Region.
P..Box 735, Richland, WA 99352

Arts Council of Topeka.
215 E. Seventh St., Topeka, KS 66603

Arts for Living Center.
Seventh & Washington Sts., P.O. Box 5, Burlington, IA 52601

Arts Museum of South Texas.
P.O. Box 1010, Corpus Christi, TX 78403

Ashburnham Historical Society, Inc.
77 Main St., Ashburnham, MA 01430

Ashbury College Student Center Gallery.
Lexington Ave., Wilmore, KY 40390

Asheville Art Museum, Civic Center Complex.
Haywood St., Asheville, NC 28801

Ashland College Art & Humanities, Gallery.
College Ave., Ashland, OH 44805

Ashland Museum.
500 W. Second St., Ashland, WI 54806

Asia Foundation Gallery.
550 Kearny St., San Francisco, CA 94108

Asia Society Inc., Asia House Gallery.
112 E. 64th St, New York, NY 10021

Asian Art Museum of San Francisco.
Golden Gate Park, San Francisco, CA 94118 Tel 415-558-2993 SANCENOR
Permanent Collections:
The Avery Brundage Collection with over 10,000 objects spanning an area from Iran to Japan to Mongolia to Indonesia.

Associated Artists of New Jersey.
Pittstown, NJ 08867

Associated Artists of Pittsburgh Arts & Crafts Center.
Fifth & Shady Aves., Pittsburgh, PA 15232

Associated Artists of Winston-Salem.
601 Coliseum Dr., Winston-Salem, NC 27106

Association for Preservation of Virginia Antiquities:
2705 Park Ave., Richmond, VA 23220

Association for the Preservation of Tennessee Antiquities.
680-690-Adams Ave., Memphis, TN 38105

Association of American Editorial Cartoonists:
475 School St., S.W., Washington, DC 20024

Association of Art Museum Directors.
P.O. Box 620 Lenox Hill Station, New York, NY 10021

Association of Collegiate Schools of Architecture.
1735 New York Ave., N.W., Washington, DC 20006

Association of Honolulu Artists:
P.O. Box 10202, Honolulu, HI 96816

Association of Junior Leagues Inc.:
825 Third Ave., New York, NY 10022

Association of Medical Illustrators:
6650 N.W. Hwy., Suite 112, Chicago, IL 60631

Athenaeum of Philadelphia.
219 S. 6th St., Philadelphia, PA 19106

Athens Art Association, Unitarian Universalist Fellowship Church:
834 Prince Ave., Athens, GA 30601

Atkins Museum of Fine Arts. *See Nelson, William Rockhill, Gallery of Art; Atkins Museum of Fine Arts*

Atkyns, Lee, Studio Gallery.
Box 120 Rte. 2, Duncanville, PA 16635

Atlanta Art Workers Coalition.
1280 Peachtree St., N. E., Atlanta, GA 30309

Atlanta College of Art Library.
1280 Peachtree St. N.E., Atlanta, GA 30309

Atlanta Museum.
537039 Peachtree St., N. E., Atlanta, GA 30308

Atlanta Public Library, Fine Arts Dept.
10 Pryor St., S. W., Atlanta, GA 30303

Atlantic Christian College, Case Art Gallery.
Wilson, NC 28401

Attleboro Museum Inc.
199 County St., Attleboro, MA 02703

Aubbell Trading Post National Historic Site.
P.O. Box 298, Ganado, AZ 86505

Audubon Artists Inc.
1083 Fifth Ave., New York, NY 10028

Audubon Memorial State Park.
Louisiana State Hwy. 965, St. Francisville, LA 70775

Audubon Wildlife Sanctuary.
Mill Grove, Box 25, Audubon, PA 19407

Augusta Richmond County Museum.
540 Telfair St., Augusta, GA 30901

Austin Arts Center. *See Trinity College, Austin Arts Center*

Austin College; Ida Green Gallery.
Sherman, TX 75090

Austin Peay State Univ. Art Department, Margaret Fort Trahern Gallery.
Clarksville, TN 37040

Automation House. *See Once Gallery Inc., Automation House*

Avery Brundage Collection. *See Asian Art Museum of San Francisco*

Avila College Art Gallery, Whitfield Continuing Education.
Kansas City, MO 11901

Babson Library Art Gallery. *See Springfield College, Babson Library Art Gallery*

Bacone College Museum.
Atalea Lodge, Muskogee, OK 74401

Baker Furniture Museum.
E. Sixth St., Holland, MI 49423

Baldwin-Wallace College, Art Gallery.
95 E. Bagley Rd., Berea, OH 44017

Ball State University Art Gallery:
Muncie, IN 47306

Baltimore Maritime Museum.
Pier 4, Pratt St., Baltimore, MD 21202

Baltimore Museum of Art.
Art Museum Dr., Baltimore, MD 21218 Tel 310-396-7101
Permanent Collections:
The major collections of the Baltimore Museum of Art span primarily the 17th century to the present time, although there are excellent examples from the earlier periods, such as an outstanding group of mosaics from Antioch, offering the

opportunity to compare and better understand the various modes of creative expression throughout history. Collections include: Jacob Epstein Collection; American Wing; T. Harrison Garrett Collection of Graphic Art; Blanche Adler Collection of Graphic Art; Collection of Oriental Art; Collection of Maryland Silver; Mary Frick Jacobs Collection; Antioch Mosaics; Elise Agnus Daingerfield Collection; Cone Collection; Saidie A. May Collection; The Abram Eisenberg Collection; Edward Joseph Gallagher III Memorial Collection; Wurtzburger Collection of Primitive Art; The Thomas E. Benesch Memorial Collection; The Nelson and Juanita Grief Gutman Memorial Collection; The William Woodward Collection; The George A. Lucas Collection.

Balzekas Museum of Lithuanain Culture.
4012 S. Archer Ave., Chicago, IL 60032

Bard College, W. C. Proctor Art Center.
Annandale-on-Hudson, NY 12504

Barn Gallery Associates, Inc.
Shore Rd. & Bourne's Lane, Ogunquit, ME 03907

Barnes County Historical Museum.
County Courthouse, Valley City, ND 58072

Barnum Museum.
820 Main St., Bridgeport, CT 06604

Barre Historical Society, Inc.
Common St., Barre, MA 01005

Bartlett Memorial Historical Museum.
2149 St. Lawrence Ave., WI 53511

Bartow-Pell Mansion Museum & Garden.
Pelham Bay Park, New York, NY 10464

Basin, Judith, Museum.
Stanford, MT 59479

Bass Museum of Art.
2100 Collins Ave., Miami Beach, FL 33139
Permanent Collections:
John and Johanna Bass Collection.

Bassist Institute.
923 S.W. Taylor St., Portland, OR 97205

Bastrop County Museum.
704 Main St., Bastrop, TX 78602

Bates College, Treat Gallery.
Lewiston, ME 04240

Bates, Richard, House. *See Oswego County Historical Society*

Bath Maine Museum.
963 Washington St., Bath, ME 04530

Battle Creek Civic Art Center.
265 E. Emmett St., Battle
Creek, MI 49017

**Baylor University, Armstrong
Browning Library:**
P.O. Box 6336, Waco, TX
76706

**Baylor University, Dept. of Fine
Arts:**
Waco, TX 76703

Beal-Maltbie Shell Museum.
Rollins College, P.O. Box 31,
Winter Park, FL 32789

Beaumont Art Museum.
1111 Ninth St., Beaumont, TX
77702

Beaumont Arts Council.
3360 Beard St., Beaumont, TX
77703

**Beaver College, Fuller Gallery of
Art.**
Church & Limcklin Pike,
Glenside, PA 19038

Bedford Gallery. *See* **Longwood
College, Bedford Gallery**

Belchertown Historical Assn.
Maple St., Belchertown, MA
01007

Belcourt Castle.
Bellevue Ave., Newport, RI
02840

Bellegrove.
P.O. Box 137, Middletown, VA
22645

Bellingrath Gardens & Home.
Box 60, Theodore, AL 36582

**Beloit College, Theodore Lyman
Wright Art Center.**
Beloit, WI 53511

Benedicta Arts Center.
College of St. Benedict, St.
Joseph, MN 56374

Bennington Museum.
W. Main St., Bennington, VT
05201

**Benton County Historical
Museum.**
P.O. Box 591, Prosser, WA
99350

**Berea College Art Department
Gallery.**
Berea, KY 40404

Bergen Community Museum.
E. Ridgewood & Fairview
Aves., Paramus, NJ 07652

Bergen Museum of Local History.
7547 Lake Rd., Bergen, NY
14416

Bergstrom Art Center & Museum.
165 N. Park Ave, Neenah, WI
54956

Berkeley Art Center.
1275 Walnut St., Berkeley, CA
94709

**Berkeley Public Library, Art &
Music Section.**
2090 Kitredge St., Berkeley,
CA 94704

**Berks Art Alliance, Wyomissing
Institute of Art Building.**
Trent & Belmont St., Reading,
PA 19610

**Berkshire Athenaeum Music &
Arts Dept.**
One Wendell Ave., Pittsfield,
MA 01201

**Berlin Art and Historical
Collection.**
Berlin, MA 01503

Besser, Jesse, Museum.
491 Johnson St., Alpena, MI
49707

**Bethany College, B. Sandzen
Memorial Gallery.**
401 N. First St., Lindsborg, KS
67456

**Beverly Hills Public Library, Fine
Arts Library.**
444 N. Fexfod Dr., Beverly
Hills, CA 90210

Beverly Historical Society.
117 Cabot St., Beverly, MA
01915

Bigelow House.
918 Glass, Olympia, WA
98506

Bingham, George Caleb, House.
State Historic Site, Arrow
Rock, MO 65320

Birmingham-Bloomfield Art Assn.
1516 S. Cranbrook Rd.,
Birmingham, MI 48009

Birmingham Gallery.
1025 Haynes St., Birmingham,
MI 48011

Birmingham Museum of Art.
2000 Eighth Ave., N.,
Birmingham, AL 35203 Tel
205-254-2565
Permanent Collections:
Samuel H. Kress collections of
European Old Masters;
European and British Master
Paintings; sculpture and
decorative arts from the 16th-
19th centuries and 19th-20th
century American art. Also the
greatest collection of
Wedgwood in the country
which includes 1400 pieces
mostly from the 18th century.
There is a sizable Oriental and
Asiatic art collection along with
art of the West featuring twelve
bronzes by Remington; Pre-
Columbian and American
Indian art collection; Ancient
Near Eastern archaeology and
artifacts, particularly the Rives
Collection of Ancient
Palestinian Artifacts; the
Francis Oliver Collection of
European and English
Ceramics; European and
American silver; the Tribal Arts
Collection; prints; graphics;
photographs; textiles; costumes;
lace; large 19th century
German cast-iron decorative art
objects.

Birmingham Public Library.
2020 Seventh Ave.,
Birmingham, AL 35203

Bishop Hill Historic Site.
P.O. Box 0, Bishop Hill, IL
61419

Bishop's Palace.
1402 Broadway, Galveston, TX
77550

Bixby Memorial Library.
Vergennes, VT 05491

Black, Colonel, Mansion. *See*
Colonel Black Mansion

Black Hawk State Park.
1500 47th Ave., Rock Island,
IL 61201

**Black Hills Art Center, Little
Gallery.**
Spearfish, SD 57783

Black Kettle Museum.
Cheyenne, OK 73628

**Blackhawk Mountain School of
Art, the Gallery.**
251 Main St., Black Hawk, CO
80422

Blacksburg Regional Art Assn.
2501 Capistrano St.,
Blacksburg, VA 24060

**Blair Museum of Lithophanes &
Carved Waxes.**
2243 Ashland Ave., Toledo,
OH 43620

Blanden Art Gallery.
920 Third Ave., S., Ft. Dodge,
IA 50501

Bleak House. *See* **Confederate
Memorial Hall "Bleak House"**

Bloom House.
P.O. Box 472, Trinidad, CO
81082

Bloomington-Normal Art Assn.
202 E. Washington, Withers
Public Library, Bloomington, IL
61761

**Bloomsburg State College, Haas
Gallery of Art.**
Bakeless Center for the Arts,
Bloomsburg, PA 17815 Tel
717-389-2607

B'nai B'rith Exhibit Hall.
1640 Rhode Island Ave., N.W.,
Washington, DC 20036

**Bob Jones University, Museum &
Art Gallery.**
Wade Hampton Blvd.,
Greenville, SC 29614 Tel 803-
242-5100, 275

Bobbitt Visual Arts Center. *See*
**Albion College, Bobbitt Visual
Arts Center**

Bock Sculpture Collection. *See*
**Greenville College; Richard W.
Bock Sculpture Collection**

Boehm Gallery. *See* **Palomar
Community College, Boehm
Gallery**

Boise Gallery of Art.
C/O Julia Davis Park, Box
1505, Boise, ID 83701

Bolduc House.
Main St., Ste. Genevieve, MO
63670

**Boone Oriental Library Fine Arts
Collection.** *See* **Monmouth
College; Boone Oriental Library
Fine Arts Collection**

Boothbay Region Art Gallery.
Brick House, Oak St.,
Boothbay Harbor, ME 04538

Boscobel Restoration, Inc.
Rte. 9-D, Garrison-on-Hudson,
NY 10524

**Boston Architectural Center
Library.**
320 Newbury St., Boston, MA
02115

**Boston Art Committee of the City
of Boston.**
334 Boylston St., Boston, MA
02116

Boston Athenaeum.
10 1/2 Beacon St., Boston, MA
02108 Tel 617-227-0270
Permanent Collections:
Books, manuscripts, maps,
prints, photographs, paintings,
sculpture and decorative arts.

Boston Printmakers.
299 High Rock St., Needham,
MA 02192

Boston Public Library.
Copley Square, Boston, MA
02117

Boston Watercolor Society.
748 First Parish Rd., Scituate,
MA 02066

Bostonian Society. *See* **Old State
House, Bostonian Society**

**Bowan, Megahan & Penelec
Galleries.** *See* **Allegheny
College, Bowman, Megahan &
Penelec Galleries**

**Bowdoin College Museum of Art
& Peary-MacMillan Arctic
Museum.**
Brunswick, ME 04011

Bowen Bible Lands Museum. *See*
**Bob Jones University, Museum
& Art Gallery**

Bower's Museum.
2002 N. Main St., Santa Ana,
CA 92706 Tel 714-836-6550

**Bowling Green State Univ., Fine
Arts Gallery, School of Art.**
Bowling Green, OH 43403

Bowne House Historical Society.
37-01 Bowne St., Flushing, NY
11354

**Bradford Brinton Memorial
Ranch Museum.** *See* **Brinton,
Bradford, Memorial Ranch
Museum**

Bradley University Gallery:
Division of Art, Peoria, IL
61625

**Braintree Historical Society, Inc.
General Sylanus Thayer
Birthpace.**
786 Washington St., Braintree,
MA 02185

Braithwaite Fine Arts Gallery.
See **Southern Utah State
College, Braithwaite Fine Arts
Gallery**

Brand Library & Art Center.
1601 W. Mountain St.,
Glendale, CA 91201

Brandeis University, Rose Art Museum:
415 South St., Waltham, MA 02154

Brandywine River Museum.
P.O. Box 141, Chadds Ford, PA 19317

Brattleboro Museum & Art Center.
P.O.Box 800, Brattleboro, VT 05301

Braun Research Library.
P.O. Box 42128, Highland Park Station, Los Angeles, CA 90042

Bray, Archie, Foundation.
2915 Country Club, Helena, MT 59601

Breezewood Foundation Museum & Garden.
3722 Hess Rd., Monkton, MD 21111

Brick Store Museum.
P.O. Box 177, Kennebunk, ME 04043

Bridgeport Art League.
528 Clinton Ave., Bridgeport, CT 06605

Brigham City Museum Gallery.
P.O. Box 583, Brigham City, UT 84302

Brigham Young University; B.R. Larsen Gallery:
Harris Fine Arts Center, Provo, UT 84602

Brinton, Bradford, Memorial Ranch Museum.
P.O. Box 23, Big Horn, WY 82833

Bristol Art Museum.
Wardwell St., Bristol, RI 02809

Brockton Art Center, Fuller Memorial.
Oak St., Brockton, MA 02401

Brockton Public Library System, Municipal Gallery.
304 Main St., Brockton, MA 02401

Bronson, Silas, Library.
267 Grand St., Waterbury, CT 06702

Bronx Museum of the Arts.
851 Grand Concourse, Bronx, NY 10451

Brookgreen Gardens.
Murrells Inlet, SC 29576 Tel 803-237-4218
Permanent Collections:
Mid 19th and 20th century sculpture by American sculptors, either native born or naturalized citizens. At present the collection includes 408 sculptures by 184 sculptors.

Brooklyn Institute of Arts & Science.
200 Eastern Pkwy., Brooklyn, NY 11238

Brooklyn Museum.
188 Eastern Parkway, Brooklyn, NY 11238 Tel 212-638-5000

Brooklyn Public Library.
Grand Army Plaza, Brooklyn, NY 11238

Brooks Memorial Art Gallery.
Overton Park, Memphis, TN 38112 Tel 901-726-5266

Broussard, J. R., Memorial Gallery.
Old State Capital, P.O. Box 44247, Baton Rouge, LA 70804

Brown, John, Cabin.
Tenth & Main Sts., Osawatomie, KS 66064

Brown, Orlando, House.
202 Wilkinson St., Frankfort, KY 40601

Brown County Art Gallery.
Artist Dr., P.O. Box 443, Nashville, IN 47448

Brown, Jean, Archives. See Tyringham Institute, Jean Brown Archives

Brown University, Bell Gallery:
64 College St., Providence, RI 02912

Browning, Armstrong, Library. See Baylor University, Armstrong Browning Library

Brownson Art Gallery. See Manhattanville College, Brownson Art Gallery

Brownville Fine Arts Assn.,Carraige House Art Gallery.
Main St., Brownville, NE 68321

Brownville Historical Society, Inc.
Third & Main, P.O. Box 186, Brownville, NE 68321

Bruce Museum, Bruce Park.
Steamboat Rd., Greenwich, CT 06830

Brueckner Museum of Starr Commonwealth for Boys.
26 Mile Rd., Albion, MI 49224

Brush & Platte Club.
P.O. Box 466, Cooperstown, NY 13326

Bryn Mawr College, Art & Archaeology Library.
Thomas Library, Bryn Mawr, PA 19010

Buck Hill Art Assn.
Buck Hill Falls, PA 18323

Bucknell University; Ellen Clark Bertrand Library:
Lewisburg, PA 17837

Bucks County Community College Hicks Art Center.
Fine Arts Dept. Swamp Rd., Newtown, PA 18940

Bucks County Historical Society; Mercer Museum.
Pine & Ashland Sts., Doylestown, PA 18901

Buena Park Historical Society.
Manchester at Whitaker, Buena Park, CA 90620

Buffalo Bill Memorial Assn.
P.O. Box 1020, Cody, WY 82414

Buie, Mary, Museum.
510 University Ave., Oxford, MS 38555

Bundy Art Gallery.
P.O. Box 19, Waitsfield, VT 05673

Burchfield Center.
1300 Elmwood Ave., Buffalo, NY 14222

Burleson, General Edward, Museum.
Aquarene Springs, P.O. Box 2330, San Marcos, TX 78666

Burlington County Historical Society.
457 High St., Burlington, NJ 08016

Burpee Art Museum. See Rockford Art Assn., Burpee Art Museum

Bush House. See Salem Art Association, Bush House, Bush Barn Art Center

Buten Museum of Wedgwood.
246 N. Bowman Ave., Merion, PA 19066 Tel 215-664-9069
Permanent Collections:
Includes examples of these ten basic varieties of Wedgwood: Queen's Ware, Majolica, Variegated Ware, Pearl Ware, Bone China, Jasper, Black Basalt, Cane Ware, Rosso Antico and Parian.

Butterfield Trail Historical Museum.
Russell Springs, KS 67755

C. Cowles Memorial Museum. See Eastern Washington State Historical Society; C. Cowles Memorial Museum

C. H. Macnider Museum. See Macnide, C. H., Museum

C. M. Russel Museum. See Russel, C. M., Museum

C. W. Post Center, Long Island Univ. Art Gallery.
Greenvale, NY 11548

Caldwell College Art Gallery.
Caldwell, NJ 07006

Calhoun County Museum.
P.O. Box 435, St. Matthews, SC 29135

California College of Arts & Crafts, Meyer Library.
Broadway & College Aves., Oakland, CA 94618

California Fair & Expo Art Show.
1600 Exposition Bldg., Sacramento, CA 95815

California Historical Society.
2090 Jackson St., San Francisco, CA 94109

California Museum of Science & Industry.
700 State Dr., Expo. Park, Los Angeles, CA 90037

California National Water Color Society.
1323 Columbia Dr., Glendale, CA 91205

California Palace of the Legion of Honor.
Lincoln Park, San Francisco, CA 94121

California Polytechnic State University, Shakespeare Press Museum:
Califorina Polytechnic State University, San Luis Obispo, CA 93407

California State College San Bernadino.
5500 State College Pkwy., San Bernadino, CA 92407

California State College, Stanislaus.
800 Monte Vista, Turlock, CA 95380

California State Univ., Fullerton, Art Gallery.
Normal & Salem Sts., Chico, CA 95929

California State Univ., Los Angeles Fine Arts Gallery.
5151 State University Dr., Los Angeles, CA 90032

California State Univ., Northridge, Gallery.
18111 Nordhoff St., Northridge, CA 91330

California State University, Fullerton; Art Gallery.
800 N. State College Blvd., Fullerton, CA 92634

California State University, Long Beach.
1250 Bellflower Blvd., Long Beach, CA 90840

Calvin College Center Gallery.
Grand Rapids, MI 49506

Cambridge Art Assn.
23 Garden St., Cambridge, MA 02138

Camden College of Arts and Sciences. See Rutgers, The State Univ. of New Jersey, Camden College of Arts and Sciences

Camden County Historical Society.
Park Blvd. & Euclid Ave., Camden, NJ 08103

Campbell House Museum.
1508 Locust St., St. Louis, MO 63103

Campbell Museum.
Campbell Pl., Camden, NJ 08101 Tel 609-964-4000
Permanent Collections:
Soup tureens of the 18th century.

Campus Martius Museum & Ohio River Museum.
601 Second St., Marietta, OH 45750

Canajoharie Library & Art Gallery.
Erie Blvd., Canajoharie, NY 13317

Cantigny War Memorial Museum of the First Division.
Rte. 4, P.O. Box 195, Wheaton, IL 60187

Canton Art Institute.
1001 Market Ave., N., Canton, OH 44702

Cape Ann Historical Assn.
27 Pleasant St., Gloucester, MA 01930

Capital University, Schumacher Gallery:
2199 E. Main St., Columbus, 43209

Caravan of East & West Inc., Caravan House Galleries.
132 E. 65th St., New York, NY 10021

Cardinal Stritch College; Studio San Lamino.
6801 N. Yates Rd., Milwaukee, WI 53217

Carlyle House.
121 N. Fairfax St., Alexandria, VA 22314

Carmel Mission Basilica.
3080 Rio Rd., Carmel, CA 93921

Carnegie Center of the Arts Elliott Square.
109 S. Palouse, Walla Walla, WA 99362

Carnegie Institute Museum of Art.
4400 Forbes Ave., Pittsburgh, PA 15213 Tel 412-622-3200
Permanent Collections:
American and European painting and sculpture, antiquities, Oriental and decorative arts, prints, drawings, photographs and film. Also Italian, Flemish, Dutch and other old masters, 19th and 20th century art and an important collection of Impressionist and Post-Impressionist paintings and American art.

Carnegie Library of Pittsburgh, Art Room Music & Art Department.
4400 Forbes Ave., Pittsburgh, PA 15213

Carnegie Mellon Univ., Forbes St. Gallery.
5200 Forbes Ave., Pittsburgh, PA 15213

Carolina Art Assn., Gibbes Art Gallery.
135 Meeting St., Charleston, SC 29401
Permanent Collections:
Collections owned by the Association since founding in 1857. Collection reflects taste in Charleston and in South Carolina and consists of portraits of famous individuals, both in oil and in miniature (on ivory) and a few sculptures. Supplementing this is a collection of Japanese wood block prints of the Ukiyo-e school, a collection of Oriental objects, and a contemporary collection of paintings, prints, sculptures and photographs.

Carpenter Center Visual Arts.
19 Prescott St., Cambridge, MA 02138

Carriage House Art Gallery. *See* Brownville Fine Arts Assn.,Carraige House Art Gallery

Carriage House Gallery. *See* Utah State Division of Fine Art, Carriage House Gallery

Carroll Mansion.
800 E. Lombard St., Baltimore, MD 21202 Tel 301-396-4980
Permanent Collections:
The mansion is an early 19th century Baltimore townhouse museum furnished in the Empire style, attempting to relay information on Charles Carroll of Carrollton, the Caton family and Baltimore and Maryland history. The furnishings belong to the Peale Museum Collection and include items from the Hambelton Collection, donations from the Jacob and Annita France Foundations, G. Leiper Carey III and other prominent Baltimoreans.

Carson, Kit, Memorial Foundation, Inc.
P.O. Box B, Taos, NM 87571

Carter, Amon, Museum of Western Art.
P.O. Box 2365, Fort Worth, TX 76101 Tel 817-738-1933
Permanent Collections:
American paintings, sculpture, prints and photos.

Carter's Grove Plantation.
Goodwin Bldg., Williamsburg, VA 23185

Cartwright Foundation for Religious Art. *See* Cathedral Museum; Cartwright Foundation for Religious Art; Cathedral Church of St. John

Carver, George Washington, Museum. *See* Tuskegee Institute, National Historic Site, George Washington Carver Museum

Casa Amesti.
516 Polk St., Monterey, CA 93940

Casa Hove.
723 Toulouse St., New Orleans, LA 70130

Case Art Gallery. *See* Atlantic Christian College, Case Art Gallery

Castelton Historical Society.
Main St., Castleton, VT 05735

Catharine Lorillard Wolfe Art Club, Inc.. *See* Wolfe, Catharine Lorillard, Art Club, Inc

Cathedral Museum; Cartwright Foundation for Religious Art; Cathedral Church of St. John.
Amsterdam Ave. at 112 St., New York, NY 10025

Catholic University of America; Humanities Division; Mullen Library:
Michigan Ave., Washington, DC 20064

Catkins-Slater Metropolitan Museum of Art.
866 Third Ave., Seattle, WA 98105

Cavalry Museum.
12901 Gateway W., El Paso, TX 79935

Cayuga Museum of History & Art.
203 Genesee St., Auburn, NY 13021

Cazenovia College, Chapman Art Center Gallery.
Cazenovia, NY 13055

Cedar Rapids Art Center.
324 Third St. S.E., Cedar Rapids, IA 52401

Center Art Assn., Inc.
Fisher Community Center, Marshalltown, IA 50158

Center for Creative Photography, Univ. of Arizona Library.
843 E. University, Tucson, AZ 85710 Tel 602-626-4636
Permanent Collections:
Numerous photographic archives including those of Ansel Adams, Wynn Bullock, Harry Callahan, Aaron Siskind, W. Eugene Smith and Frederick Sommer. Significant major holdings in 20th century photography, primarily American.

Center for Inter-American Relations Art Gallery.
680 Park Ave., New York, NY 10021

Central Connecticut State College Museum.
1615 Stanley St., New Britian, CT 06050

Central Florida Community College Art Collection.
P.O. Box 1388, 3001 College Rd., Ocala, FL 32670

Central Missouri State Univ.; Grinstead Gallery.
Warrensburg, MO 64093

Central Texas Area Museum, Inc.
Main & Front Sts., Salado, TX 76571

Central Washington Univ., Sara Spungeon Gallery.
Ellensburg, WA 98926

Central Wyoming Museum of Art.
104 Rancho Rd., Casper, WY 82601

Chadron State College Arts Gallery.
Tenth & Main Sts., Chadron, NE 69337

Chaffee Art Gallery. *See* Rutland Area Art Assn. Inc., Chaffee Art Gallery

Chalet of the Golden Fleece.
618 Second St., New Glarus, WI 53574

Chapman Art Center Gallery. *See* Cazenovia College, Chapman Art Center Gallery

Chapter House, Wiltwyck Chapter.
Crown & Green Sts., Kingston, NY 12401

Chariton County Historical Society Museum.
S. Weber St., Salisbury, MO 65281

Charles A. Wustum Museum of Fine Arts. *See* Wustum, Charles A., Museum of Fine Arts

Charles Allis Art Library. *See* Allis, Charles, Art Library

Charles & Emma Frye Art Museum. *See* Frye, Charles & Emma, Art Museum

Charles B. Goddard Center for the Visual & Performing Arts. *See* Goddard, Charles B., Center for the Visual & Performing Arts

Charleston Art Gallery of Sunrise.
755 Myrtle Rd., Charleston, WV 25314

Charleston Museum.
121 Rutledge Ave., Charleston, SC 29401 Tel 803-722-2996
Permanent Collections:
Natural history, anthropology, silver, decorative arts, porcelain, clothing, weaponry, prints, maps, manuscripts, rare books and some paintings.

Charlotte Nature Museum.
1658 Sterling Rd., Charlotte, NC 28209

Chatham College Art Gallery.
Woodland Rd., Pittsburgh, PA 15232

Chemung County Historical Society, Inc.
Historical Center, 304 William St., Elmira, NY 14901

Cherokee National Historical Society.
P.O. Box 515, Tahlequah, OK 74464

Cherokee Strip Historical Society & Henry S. Johnston Library.
W. Ditch Witch Rd., Perry, OK 73077

Cherokee Strip Museum.
1201 Maple, 508 Seventh St., Alva City Library Bldg., Alva, OK 73717

Cherry County Historical Society.
Eleanor Dr., Valentine, NE 69201

Chesapeake Bay Maritime Museum.
P.O. Box 636, St. Michaels, MD 21663

Chester County Historical Society.
225 N. High St., West Chester, PA 19380

Chesterwood.
Box 248, Stockbridge, MA 01262

Chicago Architecture Foundation, Glessner House.
1800 S. Prairie Ave., Chicago, IL 60616

Chicago Art Dealers Assn.
646 N. Michigan Ave., Chicago, IL 60611

Chicago Historical Society.
Clark St. at North Ave., Chicago, IL 60614 Tel 312-642-4600

Chicago Public Library, Cultural Center, Special Collections Division.
78 E. Washington St., Chicago, IL 60602 Tel 312-269-2926
Permanent Collections:
Grand Army of the Republic

Memorial Collection: Civil War manuscripts, photographs, graphics, scrapbooks, sheet music, weapons, military uniforms, accessories and flags; World's Columbian Exposition Collection: books, photographs, ephemera, manuscripts; Chicago Theatre Arts Collection: scrapbooks, programs, ephemera; World War I and World War II posters; Chicago Public Library Permanent Art Collection; Plitt Theatre Sheet Music Collection; Chicagoana; Chicago authors and imprints; Archives of Chicago Public Library and Gordman Theatre.

Chief Plenty Coups State Monument.
Box 35, Pryor, MT 59066

Children's Museum.
67 E. Kirby, Detroit, MI 48202

Children's Museum.
The Jamaica Way, Boston, MA 02130

Children's Museum of Indianapolis.
3010 N. Meridian St., Indianapolis, IN 46208

Chillicothe Restoration Foundation.
P.O. Box 921, Chillicothe, OH 45601

China House Gallery. *See* China Institute in America; China House Gallery

China Institute in America; China House Gallery.
125 E. 65th St., New York, NY 10021 Tel 212-744-8181

Chinqua-Penn Plantation House.
Rte 3, P.O. Box 437, Reidsville, NC 27320

Christ Church Windsor Mills.
Wiswell at Maryfield Rd., Windsor, OH 44099

Chrysler Art Museum.
Corner Commercial & Center Sts., Provincetown, MA 02657

Chrysler Museum at Norfolk.
Olney Rd. & Mowbray Arch, Norfolk, VA 23510 Tel 804-622-1211

Chung-Cheng Cultural Center. *See* Saint John's University Art Gallery; Chung-Cheng Cultural Ctr

Church of Jesus Christ of Latter Day Saints Arts & Sites Division.
Salt Lake City, UT 84150
Permanent Collections:
Art and artifacts relating to Mormon history and culture; some ethnographic objects; American Indian and South Pacific archaeological items; Pre-Columbian, Mezo-American and South American items also.

Churchill County Museum.
S. Maine St., Fallon, NV 89406

Cincinnati Art Club.
1021 Parkside Place, Cincinnati, OH 45202

Cincinnati Art Museum.
Eden Park, Cincinnati, OH 45202 Tel 513-721-5204
Permanent Collections:
Visitors are offered some 118 galleries which review the visual arts of almost every major civilization of the world over the past 5,000 years through paintings, sculpture, prints, drawings, playing cards, costumes, decorative arts, photographs and musical instruments.

Cincinnati Institute of Fine Arts.
2649 Erie Ave., Cincinnati, OH 45208

City College of City New York; Eisner Hall Art Gallery.
133 St & Convert Ave, New York, NY 10031

City County Pioneer Museum.
304 Locust St. P.O. Box 92, Sweetwater, TX 79556

City of Holyoke Museum; Wistariahurst.
238 Cabot St., Holyoke, MA 01040

City of Los Angeles, Municipal Arts Dept.
Rm. 1500, City Hall, Los Angeles, CA 90012

City of Rockville Municipal Art Gallery.
603 Edmonston Dr., Rockville, MD 20851

Civic Fine Arts Assn.
235 W. 10th St., Sioux Falls, SD 57102

Clallam County Historical Society.
2800 Hurricane Ridge Rd., Port Angeles, WA 98362

Claremont Colleges. *See* Galleries of the Claremont Colleges

Clark, Kate Freeman, Art Gallery.
College, Holly Springs, MS 38635

Clark County Historical Society Memorial Hall.
Springfield, OH 45504

Clark University Gallery in the Little Center for Visual & Performing Arts.
950 Main St., Worcester, MA 01610

Clarke Memorial Museum, Inc.
240 E. St., Eureka, CA 95501

Classical School Gallery.
607 McKnight St., Albuquerque, NM 87102 Tel 505-843-7749
Permanent Collections:
New Mexico items, Flegellanti Santos, Art of the Southwest and E. W. Deming.

Claypool-Young Art Gallery. *See* Morehead State Univ., Claypool-Young Art Gallery

Clearwater Art Assn.
P.O. Box 1482, Orofino, ID 83544

Clemson University, Rudolf E. Lee Gallery:
College of Architecture, Clemson, SC 29631

Clermont.
R. R. 1, County Rd. 6, Germantown, NY 12526

Cleveland Institute of Art.
11141 E. Blvd., University Circle, Cleveland, OH 44106

Cleveland Museum of Art.
11150 E. Blvd, Cleveland, OH 44106 Tel 216-421-7340
MUSART CLEVELAND

Cleveland Museum of Natural History.
Wade Oval, University Circle, Cleveland, OH 44106 Tel 216-231-4600
Permanent Collections:
Mammals, birds, reptiles, minerals, rocks, gems, fishes, fossils, Hamann-Todd Osteological Collection, live animals, plant and ethnographic materials, etc.

Clinton Art Assn. Gallery.
708 25th Ave., N., P.O. Box 132, Clinton, IA 52732

Clinton Historical Museum Village.
P.O. Box 5005, Clinton, NJ 08809

Cliveden.
Germantown Ave., Philadelphia, PA 19144

Cloisters.
Fort Tyron Park, New York, NY 10040

Cloisters. *See* International Center of Medieval Art; The Cloisters

Clover Lawn, the David Davis Mansion.
Davis Ave., Bloomington, IL 61701

Cody Country Art League.
836 Sheridan Ave., Cody, WY 82414

Coe College Art Galleries.
1221 First Ave. N.E., Cedar Rapids, IA 52402

Cohasset Historic House.
Elm St., Cohasset, MA 02025

Cohen, Morris Raphael, Library, Art Division.
135th St. & Convent, New York, NY 10031

Cohen Memorial Museum of Art. *See* G. Peabody College for Teachers, Cohen Memorial Museum of Art

Colby Community College; Northwest Kansas Cultural & Art Center.
1255 S. Range, Colby, KS

Colby Museum of Art.
Waterville, ME 04901

Cole County Historical Museum.
109 Madison St., Jefferson, MO 65101

Colgate Univ., Picker Art Gallery; Charles A. Dana Arts Center:
Hamilton, NY 13346

College Art Association of America:
16 E. 52nd St., New York, NY 10027

College of Idaho, Jewett Exhibition Center.
Caldwell, ID 83605

College of Marin Art Gallery.
Kentfield, CA 94904

College of Saint Elizabeth; Mahoney Library.
Convent Station, NJ 07961

College of Saint Rose Art Gallery.
432 Western Ave., Albany, NY 12203

College of Southern Idaho Art Gallery.
Box 1238, Twin Falls, ID 83301

College of the Americas; Museum of the Americas.
Rt.14, Brookfield, VT 05036

College of the Ozarks Art Dept. Library.
610 Johnson St., Clarksville, AK 72830

College of William & Mary, Dept. of Fine Arts.
Williamsburg, VA 23185

College of Wooster Art Center Museum.
University St., Wooster, OH 44691

Colonel Black Mansion.
Ellsworth, ME 04605

Colonial Burlington Foundation, Inc.
Wood St., Burlington, NJ 08016

Colonial Dames of America Chapter II.
Lemon Hill Mansion, East River & Sedgely Drives, Philadelphia, PA 19130

Colonial National Historical Park.
P.O. Box 210, Yorktown, VA 23490

Colonial Williamsburg Foundation.
P.O. Box Drawer C, Williamsburg, VA 23185 Tel 804-229-1000
Permanent Collections:
Important collection of objects relating to life in an 18th century English colony in America. Includes furniture, household accessories, ceramics, silver, pewter, brass, textiles, paintings, prints, tools and other miscellaneous objects. Collections extend to 17th and 19th century for study purposes. Many of the decorative arts groupings are highly important museum-quality collections, especially textiles, ceramics and Virginia furniture. Also the Abby Aldrich Rockefeller Folk Art Collection which contains 1800 objects dating from late 18th century to about 1900.

Colorado Historical Society.
1300 Broadway, Denver, CO 80203

Colorado Women's College; Lyle True Gallery.
Montview at Quebec, Denver, CA 80204

Columbia County Courthouse Museum.
45 S. 21st, St. Helena, OR 97051

Columbia Historical Society.
1307 New Hampshire Ave., N. W., Washington, DC 20036

Columbia Museum of Art & Science.
1112 Bull St., Columbia, SC 29201 Tel 803-799-2810
Permanent Collections: Classical art including Greek artifacts; Samuel H. Kress Collection of Renaissance Paintings; Barringer Collection of Decorative Arts; Scotese Collection of Contemporary Graphics; Hammond Collection of English Paintings; Spanish Colonial Collection; Newhoff Collection of English Furniture; European and American paintings and decorative arts and a very famous collection of South Carolina dispensary bottles.

Columbia River Maritime Museum.
1618 Exchange St., Astoria, OR 97103

Columbus Chapel, Boal Mansion & Museum.
Rte. 322, Boalsburg, PA 16827

Columbus Museum of Art.
480 E. Broad St., Columbus, OH 43215

Columbus Museum of Arts & Crafts, Inc.
1251 Wynnton Rd., Columbus, GA 31906

Commission of Fine Arts.
708 Jackson Place, N.W., Washington, DC 20006

Community College of Baltimore Art Dept.
2901 Liberty Heights Ave., Baltimore, MD 21215

Community Gallery of Lancaster County.
13 W. Grant St., Lancaster, PA 17603

Community Museum. *See* New Museum Community Museum of Brooklyn Inc.

Concord Antiquarian Society Museum.
200 Lexington Rd., Box 146, Concord, MA 01742

Concord Art Association:
15 Lexington Rd., Concord, MA 01742

Concord College Alexander Arts Center.
Athens, WV 24712

Concordia Historical Institute.
801 Lemur Ave., St Louis, MO 63105

Condordia College; Koenig Art Gallery.
800 N. Columbia Ave., Seward, NE 68434

Confederate Memorial Hall "Bleak House".
3148 Kingston Pike, Knoxville, PA 37919

Connecticut Historical Society Library.
1 Elizabeth St., Hartford, CT 06115

Connecticut Valley History Museum.
194 State St., Springfield, MA 01103

Conner Prairie Pioneer Settlement & Museum.
30 Conner Lane, Noblesville, IN 46060

Constitution Island Assn.
P.O. Box 41, West Point, NY 10996

Contemporary Art Center of Hawaii.
605 Kapiolani Blvd., Honolulu, HI 96813 Tel 808-525-8047

Contemporary Art Workshop.
542 W. Grant Place, Chicago, IL 60614

Contemporary Arts Center.
115. E. Fifth St., Cincinnati, OH 45202 Tel 513-721-0390

Contemporary Arts Foundation.
609 Robert S. Kerr Ave., Oklahoma City, OK 73102

Contemporary Arts Museum.
5216 Montrose, Houston, TX 77006

Contemporary Crafts Assn. & Gallery.
3934 S.W. Corbett, Portland, OR 97201

Cookeville Art Center. *See* Cumberland Art Society, Cookeville Art Center

Cooper, Lewis Jr., Memorial Library & Art Center.
200 S. Sixth St., Opelika, AL 36801

Cooper Gallery. *See* Cooper School of Art, Cooper Gallery

Cooper-Hewitt Museum Smithsonian Institution; National Museum of Design.
New York, NY 10028

Cooper School of Art, Cooper Gallery.
2341 Carnegie Ave. S.E., Cleveland, OH 44115

Cooperstown Art Assn.
22 Main St., Cooperstown, NY 13326

Coos Art Museum.
515 Market Ave., Coos Bay, OR 97420

Copper King Mansion.
219 W. Granite, Butte, MT 59701

Copper Village Museum & Arts Center.
P.O. Box 29, Anaconda, MT 59711

Coppini Academy of Fine Arts.
115 Melrose Pl., San Antonio, TX 78212

Coquille Valley Art Assn.
Fairview Rte., Box 625, Coquille, OR 97423

Corbit-Sharp House.
Main St., Odessa, DE 19730

Corcoran Gallery of Art.
17th St. & New York Ave., N.W., Washington, DC 20006 Tel 202-638-3211
Permanent Collections: Collection of American Art, the William A. Clark Collection and the Walker Collection.

Corinth, Lovis, Memorial Foundation.
120 Broadway, New York, NY 10005 Tel 212-964-4424

Cornell, George D. & Harriet W., Fine Arts Center. *See* Rollins College; George D. & Harriet W. Cornell Fine Arts Center

Cornell College Armstrong Gallery.
Mt. Vernon, IA 52314

Cornell University, Herbert F. Johnson Museum of Art:
Ithaca, NY 14853

Corning Museum of Glass.
Corning Glass Center, Corning, NY 14830 Tel 607-937-5371
Permanent Collections: Glass, ancient and contemporary.

Johnson, Herbert F., Museum of Art. *See* Cornell University, Herbert F. Johnson Museum of Art

Cornish Institute of Allied Arts; Cornish Gallery.
710 Eroy, Seattle, WA 98102

Corporate Council for the Arts.
421 Skinner Bldg., Seattle, WA 98101

Corry Area Historical Society.
Mead Ave. P.O. Box 107, Corry, PA 16407

Cortland County Historical Society Inc.
25 Homer Ave., Cortland, NY 13045

Cortland Free Library Art Gallery.
32 Church St., Cortland, NY 13045

Cosanti Foundation.
6433 Doubletree Rd., Scottsdale, AZ 85253

Costume & Textile Study Center.
School of Home Economics DL-10, University of Washington, Seattle, WA 98195

Cottonwood County Historical Society.
812 Fourth Ave., Windom, MN 56101 Tel 507-831-1134
Permanent Collections: Medical, telephone, clothing, mounted African specimens of big game, 1800 furniture, Depression collection, spinning wheels, looms and a research library.

Council of American Artist Societies.
215 Park Ave. S., New York, NY 10003

Council of Delaware Artists.
803 W. Du Pont Rd., Westover Hills, Wilmington, DE 19807

Council of Ozark Artists & Craftsmen, Inc.
Arts Center of the Ozarks, P.O. Box 725, Springdale, AK 72764

Courtney Art Gallery. *See* Jersey City State College; Courtney Art Gallery, Dept. of Art.

Couturier Galerie.
1814 Newfield Ave., Stamford, CT 06903

Cowley County Historical Society.
1011 Mansfield St., Winfield, KS 67156

Craft & Folk Art Museum.
5814 Wilshire Blvd., Los Angeles, CA 90036
Permanent Collections: Small collection of traditional Japanese toys.

Craft Center Gallery.
25 Sagamore Rd., Worcester, MA 01605

Craft Center Museum.
80 Danbury Rd., Wilton, CT 06897

Craftsmen's Guild of Mississippi.
Mississippi Crafts Center, P.O. Box 22886, Jackson, MS 39205

Cragfont Project Summer County Assn. for Preservation of Tennessee Antiquities.
Hwy. 25, Gallatin, TN 37066

Cranbrook Academy of Art Museum.
500 Lone Pine Rd., Bloomfield Hills, MI 48103 Tel 313-645-3312
Permanent Collections: Paintings and ceramics; contemporary art from all media.

Crapo, William W., Gallery. *See* Swain School of Design; William W. Crapo Gallery

Creative Arts Guild.
Old Firehouse on Pentz St., Dalton, GA 30720

Creighton University Fine Arts Gallery:
2500 California St., Omaha, NE 68178

Cripple Creek District Museum, Inc.
E. Bennet Ave., Cripple Creek, CO 80813

Crocker, E. B. , Art Gallery.
216 O St., Sacramento, CA 95814

Crosby County Pioneer Memorial Museum.
010 Main (U.S. 82) on Plains Trail, P. O. Box 386, Crosbyton, TX 79322

Crossett Art League.
125 Main, Crossett, AK 71635

Cuban Museum. *See* Museum of Arts & Sciences, Cuban Museum, Planetarium

Cumberland Art Society, Cookeville Art Center.
186 S. Walnut, Cookeville, TN 38501

Cummer Gallery of Art; DeEtte Holder Cummer Museum Foundation.
829 Riverside Ave., Jacksonville, FL 32204

Cunningham Memorial Art Gallery.
1930 R St., Bakersfield, CA 93301

Currier Gallery of Art.
192 Orange St., Manchester, NH 03104

Cypress College of Fine Arts Gallery.
9200 Valley View St., Cypress, CA 90630

Czech American Historical Society. *See* **Herman, Augustine, Czech American Historical Society**

Dacotah Prairie Museum.
P.O. Box 395, Aberdeen, SD 57401

Dade County Art Museum, Vizcaya Museum & Gardens.
3251 S. Miami Ave., Miami, FL 33129
Permanent Collections:
American realization of an Italian Renaissance villa and gardens. Fine period furniture, textiles, sculpture and decorative appointments shown in architectural settings.

Daemen College Dun Scotus Gallery.
4380 Main St., Amherst, NY 14226

Dakota Art Gallery, Dakota Artists Guild.
Dahl Fine Arts Ctr., Rapid City, SD 47701

Dali, Salvador, Museum.
24050 Commerce Park Rd., Beachwood, OH 44122
Permanent Collections:
Dali paintings, watercolor and graphics from 1917 to the present (93 oils).

Dallas Historical Society, Hall of State.
P.O.Box 26038, Dallas, TX 75226

Dallas Museum of Fashion.
2300 Stemmons Freeway, Dallas, TX 75207

Dallas Museum of Fine Arts.
P.O. Box 26250, Dallas, TX 75226

Dallas Public Library Fine Arts Division.
1954 Commerce St., Dallas, TX 75201

Dalles Art Assn., Dalles Art Center.
Fourth & Washington, The Dalles, OR 97058

Dalton Gallery. *See* **Agnes Scott College, Dalton Gallery**

Damon Memorial Historical Museum.
P.O. Box 66, Soldotna, AK 99669

Dana House. *See* **Woodstock Historical Society, the Dana House**

Danbury Scott-Fanton Museum & Historical Society, Inc.
43 Main St., Danbury, CT 06810

Danforth Museum.
123 Union Ave., Framingham, MA 01701

Daniel Boone Home, Daniel Boone Shrine Assn., Inc.
Hwy. F, Defiance, MO 63341

Daniel Boone Regional Library.
P.O. Box 1267, Columbia, MO 65205

Dartmouth College Museum & Galleries.
Hopkins Center, Hanover, NH 03755

Daughters of the American Revolution Museum.
Memorial Continental Hall, 1776 D. St., N.W., Washington, DC 20006

Daughters of Utah Pioneers.
300 N. Main St., Salt Lake City, UT 84103

Davenport Municipal Art Gallery.
1737 W. 12th. St., Davenport, IA 52804

Davidson College Art Gallery.
P.O. Box 2495, Davidson, NC 28036

Davis, J. M., Gun Museum.
P.O. Box 966, Claremore, OK 74017

Day County Museum.
Day County Court House, Webster, SD 57274

Dayton Art Institute.
P.O. Box 941, Dayton, OH 45401

De Young Museum Library.
Golden Gate Park, San Francisco, CA 94118

Deadwood Gulch Art Gallery.
665 Historic Main St., Deadwood, SD 57732

Dearborn Historical Museum.
915 Brady St., Dearborn, MI 48124

Decatur House.
748 Jackson Pl., N.W., Washington, DC 20006

Decker Gallery. *See* **Maryland Institute College of Art, Decker Gallery**

Decordova & Dana Museum & Park.
Sandy Pond Rd., Lincoln, MA 01773

Dedham Historical Society.
612 Higg St., Dedham, MA 02026

Deer Isle-Stonington Historical Society.
Deer Isle, ME 04627

Deerfield Academy, Hilson Gallery, Dept. of Fine Arts.
Deerfield, MA 01342 Tel 413-722-0241
Permanent Collections:
The Charles P. Russell Collection.

Deland Museum.
449 E. New York Ave., P.O. Box 941, De Land, FL 32720

Delaware Art Museum.
2301 Kentmere Pkwy., Wilmington, DE 19806 Tel 302-571-9590
Permanent Collections:
American painting and sculpture; Samuel and Mary R. Bancroft Jr. Pre-Raphaelite Collection; Howard Pyle and American Illustration; John Sloan.

Delaware County Historical Society.
P.O. Box 1036, Widner College, PA 19013

Delta State University; F.L. Wright Art Center:
Box D-2, Cleveland, MS 38733

Deluce Gallery. *See* **Northwest Missouri State Univ., Deluce Gallery**

Denison University Art Gallery:
Granville, OH 43023

Denver Art Museum.
100 W. 14th Ave. Parkway, Denver, CO 80204 Tel 303-575-5582
Permanent Collections:
Native Arts (American Indian, African, Oceanic); New World Art (Pre-Columbian and Spanish Colonial); American Art (up to 1945); European Art (Ancient Mediterranean and European up to 1945); Asian Art; Contemporary Art (post-1945); costumes and textiles.

Denver Artists Guild.
355 Ingalls St., Lakewood, Denver, CA 80226

Department of Library & Archives.
Third Floor, State Capitol, Phoenix, AZ 85007

Department of State Diplomatic Reception Room.
2201 C. St., N.W., Washington, DC 20520

Des Moines Art Center.
Greenwood Park, Des Moines, IA 50312

Desert Caballeros Western Museum.
Box 1446, Wickenburg, AZ 85358

Detroit Artists Market.
1452 Randolf St., Detroit, MI 48226

Detroit Historical Museum.
5401 Woodward, Detroit, MI 48202

Detroit Institute of Arts.
5200 Woodward Ave., Detroit, MI 48202 Tel 313-833-7900
DETINARTS

Detroit Public Library Fine Arts Dept.
5201 Woodward Ave., Detroit, MI 48202

DeYoung Memorial Museum. *See* **Fine Art Museums of San Francisco, M.H. de Young Memorial Museum**

Dezign House III.
1701 E. 12th St., Cleveland, OH 44114

Diablo Valley College Museum.
321 Golf Club Rd., Pleasant Hill, CA 94523

Diamond M Foundation Museum.
P.O. Box 1149, Snyder, TX 79549

Dickinson State College, Mind's Eye Gallery.
Dept. of Art, Dickinson, ND 58601

Dimock Gallery. *See* **George Washington Univ., the Dimock Gallery**

Divison of Archives, History & Records Management.
401 E. Gaines St., Tallahassee, FL 32304

Dixie College, Southwest Utah Art Gallery.
St. George, UT 84770

Dixon County Historical Society.
Allen, NE 68710

Dixon Gallery & Gardens.
4339 Park Ave., Memphis, TN 38117 Tel 901-761-5250
Permanent Collections:
Collection composed of French and American Impressionists and related schools and 18th and 19th century British portraits and landscapes.

Dr. Matthew Hall House.
State Historic Site, Arrow Rock, MO 65320

Dodge County Old Settlers & Historical Society.
Dodge Center, MN 55927

Dossin Great Lakes Museum.
Belle Isle, Detroit, MI 48202

Douglas Art Assn.. *See* **Douglas Art Association**

Douglas Art Association.
P.O. Box 256, Douglas, AZ 85607

Douglas County Historical Museum.
906 E. Second St., Superior, WI 54880

Downey Museum of Art.
10419 S. Rives Ave., Downey, CA 90241

Drew Univ. College Art Gallery. *See* **Drew University College Art Gallery**

Drew University College Art Gallery.
Madison, NJ 07940

Drexel University Art Gallery & Museum Collection:
Chestnut & 32nd Sts., Philadelphia, PA 19104

Drummer Boy Museum.
Rte. 6A, Brewster, MA 02631

Du Sable Museum of African American History.
740 E. 56th Place, Chicago, IL 60637

Dubuque Art Assn., Flora Park Barn Gallery.
Dubuque, IA 52001

Duke University Art Museum.
College Station, P.O. Box 6877, Durham, NC 27708

Dulin Gallery of Art.
3100 Kingston Pike, Knoxville, TN 37919

Dumbarton House.
2715 Que St., N.W., Washington, DC 20007

Durand Art Collection. See Yankton College, Durand Art Collection

Dwight D. Eisenhower Presidential Library. See Eisenhower, Dwight D., Presidential Library

Dyckman House & Museum.
204th & Broadway, New York, NY 10053

E. B. Crocker Art Gallery. See Crocker, E. B. , Art Gallery

E. M. Parker Indian Museum. See Parker, E. M., Indian Museum

Eagle Americana Shop & Gun Museum.
R.D. 1, Stratford, PA 17579

Eagle, Clara M., Gallery. See Murray State Univ., Clara M. Eagle Gallery, Price Doyle Fine Arts Center

Earlham College, Leeds Gallery.
National Rd., W., Richmond, IN 47374

Early American Museum.
E. Silver Springs Blvd., P.O. Box 188, Silver Springs, FL 32688

East Carolina University, Wellington B. Gray Gallery, School of Art:
Greenville, NC 27834

East Lyme Historical Society, Inc.
Romagna Court, Niantic, CT 06357

East Tennessee Univ., Carroll Reede Museum.
Johnson City, TN 37601

East Texas State Univ., Little Gallery Art Dept.
Commerce, TX 75428

Eastern Illinois Univ., Paul Turner Sargent Gallery.
Lincoln & Seventh Sts., Charleston, IL 61920

Eastern Michigan Univ., Still Gallery.
Ypsilanti, MI 48197

Eastern New Mexico Univ. Art Gallery.
Liberal Arts Bldg. 101, Portales, NM 88130

Eastern Washington State Historical Society; C. Cowles Memorial Museum.
2316 W. 1st.Ave., Spokane, WA 99204

Eastman, George, House. See International Museum of Photography, George Eastman House

Eccles Community Art Center.
2580 Jefferson Ave., Ogden, UT 84401

Edgecliff College, Emery Gallery.
2220 Victory Pkwy., Cincinnati, OH 45206

Edwin A. Ulrich Museum; Wave Crest on the Hudson. See Ulrich, Edwin A., Museum; Wave Crest on the Hudson

Edwin Smith Historical Museum. See Smith, Edwin, Historical Museum

Edwin Wolters Memorial Museum & Library. See Wolters, Edwin, Memorial Museum & Library

Egner Fine Arts Center. See Findlay College; Egner Fine Arts Center

Eisenberg Museum. See Southern Baptist Seminary, Eisenberg Museum

Eisenhower, Dwight D., Presidential Library.
Abilene, KS 67410

Eissner Hall Art Gallery. See City College of City New York; Eisner Hall Art Gallery

El Camino College Art Gallery.
16007 Crenshaw Blvd., Torrance, CA 90506

El Monte Historical Museum.
3100 N. Tyler Ave., El Monte, CA 91731

El Museo del Barrio.
1230 Fifth Ave., Suite F, New York, NY 10029

El Paso Museum of Art.
1211 Montana, Elpaso, TX 79902

Elbert Hubbard Library Museum. See Hubbard, Elbert, Library Museum

Elder Gallery. See Nebraska Wesleyan Univ., Elder Gallery

Electronic Arts Intermix, Inc.
84 Fifth Ave. Room 403, New York, NY 10011

Elgin Academy; Laura Davidson Sears Fine Arts Gallery.
350 Park T., Elgin, IL 60120

Elisabet Ney Museum. See Ney, Elisabet, Museum

Elizabeth Prewitt Taylor Memorial Library. See Taylor, Elizabeth Prewitt, Memorial Library

Elizabeth Slocum Gallery. See Slocum, Elizabeth, Gallery

Ella Sharp Museum. See Sharp, Ella, Museum

Elliot Museum.
Rte. 5, Hutchinson Island, Stuart, FL 33494

Ellison, John, House. See Knox Headquarters-The John Ellison House

Ellsworth Memorial Assn.
778 Palisado Ave., Windsor, CT 06095

Elmer Belt Library of Valencia.
405 Hilgard Ave., Los Angeles, CA 90024

Elmira College Hamilton Art Gallery.
Park Pl., Elmira, NY 14901

Elwood, Walter, Museum & Art Gallery.
300 Guy Park Ave., Amsterdam, NY 12010

Emerald Empire Arts Assn.
421 N. A, Springfield, OR 97477

Emery Gallery. See Edgecliff College, Emery Gallery

Endless Caverns Museum of Art.
Endless Caverns, New Market, VA 22844

Ephrata Cloister.
632 W. Main St., Ephrata, PA 17522

Erie Art Center.
338 W. 6th St., Erie, PA 16507

Erie District Library Center.
3 S. Perry Square, P.O. Box 1631, Erie, PA 16507

Erie Public Museum and Planetarium.
356 W. Sixth St., Erie, PA 16507

Erlander Home Museum.
404 S. Third St., Rockford, IL 61108

Ernest Thompson Seton Memorial Library & Museum. See Seton, Ernest Thompson, Memorial Library & Museum

Essex Art Association, Inc.
P.O. Box 193, Essex, CT 06426

Essex Institute.
132 Essex St., Salem, MA 01970

Essex Institute.
132-4 Essex St., Salem, MA 01970
Permanent Collections:
First floor: Auditorium and John A. McCarthy Gallery devoted to changing displays of objects from the Institute's diverse collections and loan exhibitions. Second floor: more permanent installations including portrait gallery and main gallery containing 3 early period rooms set up in 1907 and believed to be the first in the U.S. Special collections of clocks, ceramics, military uniforms and weapons, dolls, toys, glassware, buttons, silver pewter, early lighting devices, architectural fragments, sculpture, tools, wearing apparel and China trade objects, furniture and paintings.

Eugene Field Museum. See Field, Eugene, Museum

Eureka Springs Guild of Artists & Crafts People.
P.O. Box 182, Eureka Springs, AK 72632

Evanston Art Center.
2603 Sheridan Rd., Evanston, IL 60201

Evansville Museum Art & Science.
411 S.E. Riverside Dr., Evansville, IN 47713

Everhart Museum.
Nay Aug Park, Scranton, PA 18510

Everson Museum of Art.
401 Harrison St., Syracuse, NY 13202 Tel 315-474-6064
Permanent Collections:
American painting, sculpture, ceramics, video and Oriental art.

Exhibitionists, Inc.
92-20 Union Hall St., Jamaica, NY 11432

Exploratorium.
3601 Lyon St., San Francisco, CA 94123

Fairbanks House.
511 East St., Dedham, MA 02026

Fairbanks Museum & Planetarium.
Main & Prospect Sts., St. Johnsbury, VT 05819

Fairfield Historical Society.
636 Old Post Rd., Fairfield, CT 06430

Fairfield Public Library Museum, Fairfield Art Assn.
Court & Washington, Fairfield, IA 52556

Fairmount Park Art Assn.
Box 7646, Philadelphia, PA 19101

Fairview Museum of History & Art.
Fairview, UT 84629

Faison, Nathaniel W., Home & Museum.
822 S. Jefferson, La Grange, TX 78945

Fall River Historical Society.
451 Rock St., Fall River, MA 02720

Farmington Museum; Starley-Whitman House.
37 High St., Farmington, CT 06032

Farnsworth, W. A., Library & Art Museum.
19 Elm St. Box 466, Rockland, ME 04841

Farrar-Mansur House.
On the Common, Weston, VT 05161

Fashion Institute of Technology Galleries.
277 W. 27th St., New York, NY 10001

Faulkner Memorial Art Wing. See Santa Barbara Public Library, Faulkner Memorial Art Wing

Favell Museum of Western Art & Indian Artifacts.
P.O. Box 165, Klamath Falls, OR 97601

Federal Art Association of New Jersey Inc.:
31 Pershing Blvd., Lavalette, NJ 08735

Federal Arts Council of Richmond, Inc.
5 N. Sixth St., Richmond, VA 23219

Federal Design Council.
P.O. Box 7537, Washington, DC 20044

Federation of Modern Painters & Sculptors.
340 W. 72nd St., New York, NY 10023

Fenimore House.
Lake Rd., Cooperstown, NY 13326

Fenimore House. See New York State Historical Assn., Fenimore House

Fenimore House. See Historical Society of Early American Decoration Inc., Fenimore House

Fenster, Rebecca & Gershon, Gallery of Jewish Art.
1719 S. Owasso Ave., Tulsa, OK 74120

Ferguson Library.
96 Brand St., Stamford, CT 06901

Field, Eugene, Museum.
634 S. Broadway, St. Louis, MO 63102

Field Museum of National History.
Roosevelt Rd. at Lake Shore Dr., Chicago, IL 60605 Tel 312-238-8867
Permanent Collections:
Anthropology, Botany, Geology, Paleontology and Zoology.

Filson Club.
118 W. Breckinridge St., Louisville, KY 40203

Finch College Museum of Art.
New York, NY 10021

Findlay College; Egner Fine Arts Center.
1000 N. Main St., Findlay, OH 45840

Fine Art Museums of San Francisco, M.H. de Young Memorial Museum.
Golden Gate Park, San Francisco, CA 94118 Tel 415-558-2887
Permanent Collections:
European painting, sculpture and decorative arts; American painting, sculpture and decorative arts; European and American graphic arts; art of Africa, Oceania and the Americas.

Fine Arts Association; AKA School of Fine Arts:
38660 Mentor Ave., Willoughby, OH 44094

Fine Arts Center of Clinton.
119 W. Macon St., Clinton, IL 61727

Fine Arts Club, Valley City State College.
P.O. Box 1319, Valley City, ND 58072

Fine Arts Federation of New York.
44 W. Ninth St., Room 20, New York, NY 10011

Fine Arts Gallery of San Diego.
P.O. Box 2107, San Diego, CA 92112

Fine Arts Museum of the South.
P.O. Box 8404, Mobile, AL 36608 Tel 205-342-4642
Permanent Collections:
Main collection is of 19th century American art including Chase, Robinson, Bierstadt, Moran, American Primitive painters and others. Also 19th century American prints. The museum has a Southern Heritage gallery containing Southern furniture, Southern paintings and folk art. European paintings include Tissot, Renoir and Picasso. Also a very good African collection.

Fisher, Jonathan, Memorial, Inc.. See Parson Fisher House; Jonathan Fisher Memorial Inc

Fisk University Museum:
18th & Jackson Sts., Nashville, TN 37203

Fiske Kimball Fine Arts Library.
Bayly Dr., Charlottesville, VA 22903

Fitchburg Art Museum.
Merriam Pkwy., Fitchburg, MA 01420

Five Civilized Tribes Museum.
Agency Hill, Honor Heights Dr., Muskogee, OK 74401

Flagler, Henry Morrison, Museum.
Whitehall Way, Palm Beach, FL 33480 Tel 305-655-2833

Flagler, Henry Morrison, Museum. See Palm Beach County Historical Society, Henry Morrison Flagler Museum

Flint Institute of Arts.
1120 E. Kearley St., Flint, MI 48503

Flint Public Library.
1026 E. Kearley St., Flint, MI 48502

Flora Park Barn Gallery. See Dubuque Art Assn., Flora Park Barn Gallery

Florence Griswold House. See Lyme Historical Society Inc., Florence Griswold House

Florence Museum.
600 Spruce St., Florence, SC 29501

Florida Arts Group Inc.
6 South St., Saint Augustine, FL 32084

Florida Atlantic Univ. Art Gallery.
Boca Raton, FL 33431

Florida Gulf Coast Art Center, Inc.
Ponce de Leon Blvd., Clearwater, FL 33516

Florida Southern College; Melvil Art Gallery.
Spivey Fine Arts & Humanities Bldg., Lakeland, FL 33801

Florida State Univ. Art Gallery, Fine Arts Bldg.
Tallahassee, FL 32306

Flynt, Helen Geier, Fabrik Hall.
The Street, Deerfield, MA 01342

Folger Coffee Company Museum.
330 W. Eighth St., Kansas City, MO 64105

Folger Shakespeare Library.
201 E. Capitol St., S.E., Washington, DC 20003

Foothills Art Center Inc.
809 15th St., Golden, CO 80401

Forbes Street Gallery. See Carnegie Mellon Univ., Forbes St. Gallery

Forest Lawn Museum.
1712 Glendale Ave., Glendale, CA 91209

Fort Belknap Museum & Archives.
P.O. Box 68, New Castle, TX 76372

Fort Bridger State Museum.
State Office Bldg., Cheyenne, WY 82001

Fort Concho Restoration Museum.
716 Burges St., San Angelo, TX 76901

Fort Fisher & Homer Garrison Memorial Museum.
Interstate 35 W., Box 1370, Waco, TX 76703

Fort Hays State Univ. Visual Arts Center.
Hays, KS 67601

Fort Kearney Museum.
311 S. Central Ave., Kearney, NE 68847

Fort Lauderdale Museum of Art.
426 E. Las Olas Blvd., Ft. Lauderdale, FL 33301 Tel 305-463-5184

Fort LeBoeuf Memorial.
P.O. Box 16, Waterford, PA 16441

Fort Loudoun Assn.
Rte. 1, Vonore, TN 37885

Fort McHenry National Monument & Historic Shrine.
Baltimore, MD 21230

Fort Meade Museum.
Griffin Ave., Bldg. 4674, Fort George Meade, MD 20755

Fort Monroe Casemate Museum.
P.O. Box 341, Fort Monroe, VA 23351

Fort Mount Hope.
Burgoyne Rd., Ticonderoga, NY 12883

Fort Okanogan Historical Museum.
Brewster, WA 98812

Fort Ontario.
P. O. Box 102, Oswego, NY 13126

Fort Peck Fine Arts Council.
Glasgrow, MT 59230

Fort Smith Art Center.
423 N. Sixth St., Fort Smith, AK 72901

Fort Ticonderoga.
P.O. Box 390, Ticonderoga, NY 12883

Fort Ticonderoga Museum.
Ticonderoga, NY 12883

Fort Vancouver National Historic Site.
Vancouver, WA 98661

Fort Walla Walla Museum Complex.
P.O. Box 1616, Walla Walla, WA 99362

Fort Wayne Fine Arts Foundation.
324 Penn Ave., Ft. Wayne, IN 46805

Fort Wayne Museum of Art.
1202 W. Wayne St., Ft. Wayne, IN 46804

Fort Western Museum.
Bowman St., Augusta, ME 04330

Fort Worth Art Museum.
1309 Montgomery, Fort Worth, TX 76107 Tel 817-738-9215
Permanent Collections:
Paintings, sculpture, drawings, prints, objects and photographs.

Fort Worth Public Library Arts Department.
300 Taylor St., Fort Worth, TX 76102

Fort Wright College Art Gallery.
W. 4000 Randolph Rd., Spokane, WA 99204

Foster, Ralph, Museum. See School of the Ozarks, Ralph Foster Museum

Foundation for Historic Restoration in Pendleton Area.
P.O. Box 444, Pendleton, SC 29670

Foundry.
899 Waimanu St., Honolulu, HI 96813

Fowler Museum.
9215 Wilshire Blvd., Beverly Hills, CA 90210

Franciscan Monastery.
12th & Jefferson Dr., Washington, DC 20560

Franklin D. Roosevelt Library & Museum. See Roosevelt, Franklin D., Library & Museum

Franklin Furnace Archives.
122 Franklin St., New York, NY 10013 Tel 212-925-4671

Permanent Collections:
Franklin Furnace Artist's Book
Archive

**Franklin Mint Corporation
Museum.**
Franklin Center, PA 19091

Frederick S. Wight Art Galleries.
See Wight, Frederick S., Art
Galleries

Frederick Thompson Foundation.
See Thompson, Frederick,
Foundation

**Free Library of Philadelphia Print
& Picture Department.**
Logan Square, Philadelphia, PA
19103   Tel 215-686-5403
Permanent Collections:
Pictures in all media, original
works of art as well as
reproductions. Universal subject
coverage, current events as
well as history, geography,
science, biography and fine
arts. 1,123,498 items in total of
which approximately 800,000
are for loan to registered
borrowers. Specialties:
Philadelphia history, portrait
prints, costume pictures and
Napoleonica.

Free Public Library.
11 S. Broad St., Elizabeth, NJ
07202

**Free Public Library Art & Music
Dept.**
P.O. Box 2448, Trenton, NJ
08608

Freeport Art Museum. *See*
Highland Area Arts Council,
Freeport Art Museum

Freer Gallery of Art.
C/O Smithsonian Institution,
12th St. at Jefferson Dr., S.W.,
Washington, DC 20560 Tel
202-381-5344

**French Institute, Alliance
Francaise Library.**
22 E. 60th St., New York, NY
10022

French Legation.
802 San Marcos St., Austin,
TX 78702

Fresno Arts Center.
3033 E. Yale, Fresno, CA
93703

Frick Art Museum.
7227 Reynolds St., Pittsburgh,
PA 15208 Tel 412-371-7766
Permanent Collections:
Italian Renaissance, French
18th century paintings;
Decorative Arts, 18th century;
16th century Italian small
bronzes; Chinese 18th century
porcelains; Russian 17th and
18th century Parcel-gilt silver;
15th and 16th century French
and Flemish tapestries; 18th
century French period room
and 18th century sculpture.

Frick Art Reference Library.
10 E. 71st St., New York, NY
10021

Frick Collection.
One E. 70th St., New York,
NY 10021 Tel 212-288-0700
Permanent Collections:
Paintings (14th to 19th
century); Renaissance bronzes;

18th century French sculpture;
French, Italian and English
furniture; Oriental porcelain;
French porcelains; Limoges
enamels; English silver;
Oriental rugs; prints and
drawings.

Friends Historical Library. *See*
Swarthmore College, Friends
Historical Library

Friends of Arrow Rock, Inc.
Main St., Arrow Rock, MO
65320

Friends of Contemporary Art.
1336 Stout St., Second Floor,
Denver, CO 80202

Friends of Photography.
P.O. Box 239, Carmel, CA
93921

**Friends of the Caleb Pusey House,
Inc.**
15 Race St., Upland, PA 19015

Frontier Museum. *See* Williams
County Historical Society,
Frontier Museum

Frontier Times Museum.
P.O. Box 313, Bandera, TX
78003

**Frostburg State College, Fine Arts
Gallery I.**
Frostburg, MD 21532

Fruitlands Museums.
Prospect Hill, Harvard, MA
01451

**Frye, Charles & Emma, Art
Museum.**
P.O.Box 3005, Seattle, WA
98114

Fuller Gallery of Art. *See* Beaver
College, Fuller Gallery of Art

**G. Peabody College for Teachers,
Cohen Memorial Museum of
Art.**
Box 513, Nashville, TN 37203

Gale Private Museum.
300 Viking Dr., Valley City,
ND 58072

Galeria de la Faza.
2851 24th St., San Francisco,
CA 94110

Galesburg Civic Art Center.
114 E. Main St., Galesburg, IL
61401

**Galleries of Ivy School of
Professional Art.**
University Ave., Pittsburgh, PA
15214

**Galleries of the Claremont
Colleges.**
C/O Montgomery Art Gallery,
Pomona College, Claremont,
CA 91711 Tel 714-621-8000
Permanent Collections:
Scripps College: The Phil Dike
Watercolor Collection (20th
century U.S.); The General and
Mrs. Edward Clinton Young
Collection of American
Paintings (19th-20th century);
The Fred and Mary Marer
Collection of Ceramics
(contemporary ceramics--one of
the foremost collections of its
kind in the U.S.); The Dorothy
Adler Routh Cloisonne
Collection (Chinese and

Japanese enamels); The Edward
Nagel Collection (misc.
ancient, medieval and
renaissance art; non-Western
art); The Mrs. Frederick S.
Bailey and Mrs. James W.
Johnson Collections of
Japanese Prints; The Dr.
William B. Pettus Collection of
Chinese Painting. Other
collections: oriental and Near
Eastern costumes and textiles;
American prints and drawings;
ancient ceramics. Pomona
College: the Norton Simon
Collection (graphic art of
Goya); the June Wayne
Collection (contemporary U.S.
graphic art); the Culley
Collection (U.S. graphic art of
the 1920's-1940's); the C. E.
Merrill Trust (contemporary
U.S. graphics); the Kress
Collection (early Renaissance
painting); other collections:
European and American prints;
U.S. and European painting.
Claremont University Center:
Native American ceramics
(historic and pre-Columbian),
beadwork, basketry.

Gallery of African Art.
1621 21st St., N.W.,
Washington, DC 20009

Gallery of Contemporary Art.
500 S. Main St., Winston-
Salem, NC 27101

Gallery of Prehistoric Art.
20 E. 12th St., New York, NY
10003 Tel 212-674-5389
Permanent Collections:
Over 60 serigraphs (or
silkscreens) representing the
earliest known paintings of
man. These renderings in size,
color and quality accurately
represent the work of artists
20,000-40,000 years ago.

Gallery of Stell & Shevis.
82 Elm St., Camden, ME
04843

Gallier House.
1118-32 Royal St., New
Orleans, LA 70116

Galloway House & Museum.
336 E. Pioneer Rd., Fond Du
Lac, WI 54935

**Gallup Museum of Indian Arts &
Crafts.**
103 W. 66th, P.O. Box 1395,
Gallup, NM 87301

Gardiner Art Gallery. *See*
Oklahoma State University,
Gardiner Art Gallery

**Gardner, Isabella Stewart,
Museum.**
280 The Fenway, 2 Palace Rd.,
Boston, MA 02115 Tel 617-
566-1401
Permanent Collections:
Collections of Mrs. Isabella
Stewart Gardner. Strengths are
in Italian Renaissance painting
and 17th century Dutch
painting and also include
everything from Classical and
Medieval sculpture to tapestries
and 19th and 20th century
prints and drawings. The
museum itself is built in the
style of a Venetian palazzo
with central courtyard and its
interior windows, columns,
fireplaces and doorways are all

from various European
churches and buildings of many
different periods and styles.

**Garrison, Homer, Memorial
Museum.** *See* Fort Fisher &
Homer Garrison Memorial
Museum

**Gaston County Art & Historical
Museum.**
P.O. Box 429, Dallas, NC
28304

Gautier's Plantation Home.
Highway 90, Gautier, MS
39553

Gavilan College Art Gallery.
5055 Santa Therese Blvd.,
Gilroy, CA 95020

Gay Nineties Museum.
532 N. Chestnut St., Barnsville,
OH 43713

**General Adam Stephen Memorial
Assn., Inc..** *See* Stephen,
General Adam, Memorial Assn.,
Inc

**General Bissell Home, Jefferson
Barracks Historical Park.**
7900 Forsythe, Clayton, MO
63105

**General Edward Burleson
Museum.** *See* Burleson, General
Edward, Museum

**General Federation Women's
Clubs.**
1734 N. St., N.W.,
Washington, DC 20036

**General Services Administration,
Public Building Service Fine
Arts Program.**
18th & F. St., N.W.,
Washington, DC 20405

**Geneva Historical Society &
Museum.**
543 S. Main St., Geneva, NY
14456

George Caleb Bingham House.
See Bingham, George Caleb,
House

George F. Harding Museum. *See*
Harding, George F. Museum

**George Walter Vincent Smith Art
Museum.** *See* Smith, George
Walter Vincent, Art Museum

**George Washington Birthplace
National Monument.** *See*
Washington, George, Birthplace
National Monument

George Washington Museum. *See*
Washington, George, Museum

**George Washington Univ., the
Dimock Gallery.**
730 21st St., N.W.,
Washington, DC 20037

**Georgetown University Art &
History Museum:**
P.O. Box 1595, Hova Station,
Washington, DC 20007

Georgia Historical Society.
501 Whitaker St., Savannah,
GA 31401

**Georgia Institute of Technology,
College of Architecture Library.**
225 N. Ave. N.W., Atlanta,
GA 30332

Georgian Court College Gallery.
Lakewood Ave., NJ 08701

Germantown Historical Society Museums.
5214 Germantown Ave., Philadelphia, PA 19144

Geronimo Springs Museum.
325 Main St., P.O. Box 1029, Truth or Consequences, NM 87901

Gertrude Herbert Institute of Art. *See* **Herbert, Gertrude, Institute of Art**

Getty, J. Paul, Museum.
17985 Pacific Coast Hwy., Malibu, CA 90265 Tel 213-459-2306
Permanent Collections:
Greek and Roman art; French 18th century Decorative arts; Renaissance through early 20th century Western painting.

Ghost Ranch.
Carson National Forest, General Delivery, Abiquiu, NM 87510

Gibson Society Inc.
137 Beacon St., Boston, MA 02116

Gilbert Stuart Birthplace. *See* **Stuart, Gilbert, Birthplace**

Gilcrease, Thomas, Institute of American History & Art.
1400 N. 25th West Ave., Tulsa, OK 74127

Gilmore, Genevieve & Donald, Art Center. *See* **Kalamazoo Institute of Arts; Genevieve & Donald Gilmore Art Center**

Gilpin County Arts Assn.
Eureka St., Central City, CA 80427

Girard, Stephen, Collection.
Corinthian & Girard Aves., Philadelphia, PA 19121

Glebe House.
Hollow Rd., Woodbury, CT 06798

Glessner House. *See* **Chicago Architecture Foundation, Glessner House**

Gloucester County Historical Society.
58 N. Broad St., Woodbury, NJ 08096

Goddard, Charles B., Center for the Visual & Performing Arts.
First & D Sts., S. W., Ardmore, OK 73401

Goodhue County Historical Society.
1166 Oak St., Red Wing, MN 55066

Gore Place Society.
52 Gore St., Waltham, MA 02154

Goschenhoppen Folklife Library & Museum.
Rte. 63, Vernfield, PA 18973

Goucher College, Kraushaar Audit Lobby Gallery.
Dulaney Valley Rd., Towson, MD 21204

Governor Bent Museum.
Bent St., Taos, NM 87571

Governor Hogg Shrine State Park.
518 S. Main St., P.O. Box 137, Quitman, TX 75783

Governor Stephen Hopkins House. *See* **Hopkins, Governor Stephen, House**

Grand Central Art Gallery, Biltmore Hotel.
43rd St. & Madison Ave., New York, NY 10017 Tel 212-867-3344
Permanent Collections:
Wide offering of representational art by more than 100 of the gallery's contemporary artists in all mediums. There is also a large offering of fine late 19th-early 20th century art by American masters who worked in the Impressionist and Realist traditions.

Grand Prairie Art Council, Inc.
P.O. Box 65, Stuttgart, AK 72160

Grand Rapids Art Museum.
230 E. Fulton, Grand Rapids, MI 49503

Grand Rapids Public Library Music & Art Dept.
Library Plaza N.E., Grand Rapids, MI 49503

Grands Rapids Public Museum.
54 Jefferson Ave., Grand Rapids, MI 49502

Grant County Historical Society.
742 Basin St., N.W., P.O. Box 1141, Ephrata, WA 98823

Granville Historical Museum.
420 E. Broadway, Granville, OH 43023

Great Lakes Historical Society.
480 Main St., Vermillion, OH 44089

Greater Fall River Art Assn.
80 Belmont St., Fall River, MA 02720

Greater Gary Arts Council.
504 Bradway Suite 1037, Gary, IN 46402

Greek Council House & Museum.
Council Square, Okmulgee, OK 74442

Green Country Art Center.
1825 E. 15th St., Tulsa, OK 74104

Green Hill Art Gallery.
712 Summit Ave., Greensboro, NC 27405

Greene County Historical Society.
R.D. 2, Waynesburg, PA 15370

Greenfield Village & Henry Ford Museum.
Dearborn, MI 48121

Greensboro Historical Museum, Inc.
130 Summit Ave., Greensboro, NC 27401

Greenville Art Center.
802 Evans St. S., Greenville, NC 27834

Greenville College; Richard W. Bock Sculpture Collection.
Greenville, IL 62246

Greenville County Museum of Art.
420 College St., Greenville, SC 29601

Greenwich Art Society & Art Center.
449 Pemberwick Rd, Greenwich, CT 06830

Griffin. *See* **Magdalene Charlton Memorial Museum & Griffin Memorial House**

Griffiths Art Gallery. *See* **Saint Lawrence University, Griffiths Art Gallery**

Grigon Home.
Augustine St., Kaukauna, WI 54130

Grinstead Gallery. *See* **Central Missouri State Univ.; Grinstead Gallery**

Grolier Club.
47 E. 60th St., New York, NY 10022

Grossmont College Gallery.
8800 Grossmont College Dr., El Cajon, CA 92020 Tel 714-465-1700, 450
Permanent Collections:
Art Department collection: primarily prints, photographs and ceramics. One Tom Holland painting, one Jim Wayne glass sculpture, one Anton Mauve drawing, two medieval illuminated manuscript pages. Prints include etchings, silkscreen prints and lithographs.

Guggenheim, John Simon, Memorial Foundation.
90 Park Ave., New York, NY 10013

Guggenheim, Solomon, Museum.
1071 Fifth Ave., New York, NY 10028 Tel 212-860-1300
Permanent Collections:
Solomon R. Guggenheim Collection, The Peggy Guggenheim Collection and the Justin K. Thannhauser Collection.

Guild Hall of East Hampton Museum Section.
158 Main St., East Hampton, NY 11937

Guild of Book Workers.
1059 Third Ave., New York, NY 10021

Guild of Boston Artists.
162 Newbury St., Boston, MA 02116

Guild of South Carolina Artists.
1112 Bull St., Columbia, SC 29201

Gunston Hall Planation.
Gunston Rd., Lorton, VA 22079

Guy Park House.
366 W. Main St., Amsterdam, NY 12010

Haas Gallery of Art. *See* **Bloomsburg State College, Haas Gallery of Art**

Hackaday Center for the Arts.
Flathead Valley Art Assn., Box 83, Kalispell, MT

Hackley Art Museum.
296 W. Webster, Muskegon, MI 49440

Haggin Gallery. *See* **Pioneer Museum & Haggin Gallery**

Hagley Museum.
P.O. Box 3630, Wilmington, DE 19807

Hall of Fame of the Trotter.
240 Main St., Goshen, NY 10924

Hall of Presidents.
1050 S. 21st St., Colorado Springs, CO 80904

Hallmark Cards Inc. Creative Library.
25th & McGee, Kansas City, MO 64141

Hallmark Gallery.
720 Fifth Ave. at 56th St., New York, NY 10019

Hamilton College.
Edward W. Root Center, Clinton, NY 13323

Hamline University Galleries.
Dept. of Art, Saint Paul, MN 55104

Hammond-Harwood House.
19 Maryland Ave., Annapolis, MD 21401

Hammond Museum Inc., Hammond Castle.
80 Hesperus Ave., Glouchester, MA 01930

Hammond Museum; Museum of Humanities.
Deveau Rd., North Salem, NY 10560

Hampson Museum State Park.
Dept. of Parks & Tourism, P.O. Box 32, Wilson, AR 72395 Tel 501-655-4741
Permanent Collections:
Archaeological collection from the late Mississippian period.

Hampton Center for Arts & Humanities.
22 Wine St, Hampton, VA 23669
Permanent Collections:
Archaeology collection from the city of Hampton.

Hampton Institute, College Museum.
Hampton, VA 23668

Hampton National Historic Site.
535 Hampton Lane, Towson, MD 21204

Hand Work Shop Inc.
7 N. Sixth St., Richmond, VA 23223

Handforth Gallery. *See* **Tacoma Public Library, Handforth Gallery**

Hanson, John, Memorial Museum.
6701 Oxon Hill Rd., Oxon Hill, MD 20021

Harbor College Art Gallery.
1111 Figueroa Pl., Los Angeles, CA 90036

Harding, George F. Museum.
86. E. Randolp St., Chicago, IL 60601

Hardy, Marcellite, Memorial Museum.
Old Southern Bank of Kentucky Bldg., 296 S. Main St., Russellville, KY 42276

Hargate Art Center. *See* St. Paul's School, The Art Center in Hargate

Harlow Gallery. *See* Kennebec Valley Art Assn., Harlow Gallery

Harmonie Associates, Inc.
Old Economy, 14th & Church Sts., Ambridge, PA 15003

Harper Art Association, Inc.:
E. 12th St., Harper, KS 67058

Harris County Heritage Society.
110 Bagby, Houston, TX 77002

Harris Swift Museum of Religious & Ceremonial Arts & Library of Rare Books.
526 Vine St., Chattanooga, TN 37403

Harrison County Historical Museum.
P.O. Box 23, Marshall, TX 75670

Harry S. Truman Library & Museum. *See* Truman, Harry S., Library & Museum

Hart, William S., Museum.
241551 N. Newhall Ave., Newhall, CA 91321

Harte University Center. *See* Angelo State University Houston, Harte University Center

Hartford Art School.
200 Bloomfield Ave., West Hartford, CT 06117

Hartland Art Council.
P.O. Box 127, Hartland, MI 48029

Hartnell College Gallery.
156 Homestead Ave., Salinas, CA 93901

Hartwick College Fine Arts Museum, Anderson Center for the Arts.
Oneonta, NY 13820

Harvard Semitic Museum.
6 Divinity Ave., Cambridge, MA 02138

Harvard University Busch-Reisinger Museum:
29 Kirkland St., Cambridge, MA 02138

Harvard University, Dumbarton Oaks Research Library & Collections:
1703 32nd St., N.W., Washington, DC 20560

Harvard University, Fogg Art Museum:
Cambridge, MA 20138

Hastings Museum.
1330 N. Burlington Ave., Hastings, NE 68901

Haverhill Public Library.
99 Main St., Haverhill, MA 01830

Hawaii State Library Fine Arts-Audiovisual Section.
478 S. King St., Honolulu, HI 96813

Hayden Gallery. *See* Massachusetts Institute of Technology; Hayden Gallery

Haystack Mountian School of Crafts Gallery.
Deer Isle, ME 04627

Heard Museum.
22 E. Monte Vista, Phoenix, AZ 85004 Tel 602-252-8848
Permanent Collections:
Southwest Indian paintings; primitive art (African, Oceanian, Pre-Columbian); Mexican folk art.

Hebrew Union College Museum.
3101 Clifton Ave., Cincinnati, OH 45220
Permanent Collections:
Archaeology and Judaica. Within Judaica Collection there are 1500 textiles, 4000 prints and drawings , a large collection of Jewish ceremonial objects and a collection of archaeology. Four major collections include the Joseph Hamburger collection of coins and medals, the predominantly Anglo-Jewish collections of Israel Solomons and Dr. Louis Grossman etchings, engravings, medals and seals, and the Kirschstein Collection of ceremonial art.

Hebrew Union College, Skirball Museum.
3077 University Ave., Los Angeles, CA 90007 Tel 213-749-3424

Heckscher Museum.
Prime Ave., Huntington, NY 11743 Tel 516-271-4440
Permanent Collections:
American and European paintings, sculpture, drawings and prints from the 16th through 20th centuries. Included are works by Blakelock, Durand, Dore, Eakins, Inness, T. Moran, Cranach, Courbet, G. Grosz and T. Rosenthal among others.

Helen Geier Flynt Fabrik Hall. *See* Flynt, Helen Geier, Fabrik Hall

Hendrik Kip House. *See* Kip, Hendrik, House

Henren, Harry D., Gallery. *See* Lindenwood Colleges; Harry D. Henren Gallery Dept. of Art

Henry, O., Museum.
409 E. Fifth St., Austin, TX 78701

Henry B. Plant Museum. *See* Plant, Henry B., Museum

Henry Morrison Flagler Museum. *See* Flagler, Henry Morrison, Museum

Henry S. Lane Home. *See* Lane, Henry S., Home

Herbert, Gertrude, Institute of Art.
506 Telfair St., Augusta, GA 30901

Heritage Foundation Museum.
7637 N. Shore Rd., Norfolk, VA 23505

Heritage Garden Village.
Hwy. 190, P.O. Box 666, Woodville, TX 75979

Heritage Plantation of Sandwich.
Grove & Pine Sts., Sandwich, MA 02563

Herman, Augustine, Czech American Historical Society.
700 N. Collington Ave., Baltimore, MD 21205

Hermann, Grover M., Fine Arts Center. *See* Marietta College, Grover M. Hermann Fine Arts Center

Herrett Arts & Science Center Inc.
1220 Kimberley Rd. E., Five Points, Twin Falls, ID 83301

Heward-Washington House.
87 Church St., Charleston, SC 29401

Heye Foundation; Museum of the American Indian.
Broadway at 155th St., New York, NY 10032

Hickory Museum of Art Inc.
P.O. Box 2572, Hickory, NC 28601 Tel 704-327-8576
Permanent Collections:
American art, chiefly from 1850 to 1950, mainly Hudson River, American, Impressionist, Regionalist and American Scene schools. Smaller groups of European works including Turner, J. Rousseau, Tintoretto. Pre-Columbian items, of which most are Peruvian pottery, are also present.

Higgins, John Woodman, Armory Museum.
100 Barber Ave., Worcester, MA 01601 Tel 617-853-6015
Permanent Collections:
Over 100 suits of armor and related artifacts including paintings, stained glass, statues, tapestries, wood carvings, etc.

High Museum of Art.
1280 Peachtree St., N.E., Atlanta, GA 30309
Permanent Collections:
Ralph K. Uhry Collection of Prints, Francis and Emory Cocke Collection of English Ceramics, Fred and Rita Richman Collection of African Art, J. J. Haverty Collection of American Paintings, Samuel H. Kress Collection, High Museum Collection of Photographs, High Museum Collection of Paintings, High Museum Decorative Arts Collection.

High Plains Museum.
423 Norris Ave., McCook, NE 69001

Highland Area Arts Council, Freeport Art Museum.
511 S. Liberty, Freeport, IL 61302

Hill Country Arts Foundation.
P.O. Box 176, Ingram, TX 78025

Hill-Stead Museum.
671 Farmington Ave., Farmington, CT 06032 Tel 203-677-9064
Permanent Collections:
French Impressionist paintings, silver, rugs, porcelains, etc.

Hillendale Museum.
Hillendale & Hickory Hill Rds., P.O. Box 129, Mendenhall, PA 19357

Hillforest Historical Foundation, Inc.
213 Fifth St., P.O. Box 276, Aurora, IN 47001

Hillsbourough County Museum.
1101 E. River Core, P.O. Box 8311, Tampa, FL 33674

Hilson Gallery. *See* Deerfield Academy, Hilson Gallery, Dept. of Fine Arts

Hinds Junior College; Marie Hull Gallery.
Raymond, MS 39154

Hirshhorn Museum & Sculpture Garden.
Eighth & Independence Aves., S.W., Washington, DC 20560

Hispanic Society of America.
613 W. 155th, New York, NY 10032 Tel 212-926-2234
Permanent Collections:
Collection includes paintings, sculpture and examples of the decorative arts.

Historic Alexandria Foundation, Inc.
1007 Kings St., P.O. Box 524, Alexandria, VA 22314

Historic Annapolis Inc.
18 Pinkney St., Annapolis, MD 21401

Historic Cherry Hill.
S. Pearl St., Albany, NY 12202

Historic Deerfield.
The Street, Deerfield, MA 01346

Historic Hope Foundation.
Windsor, NC 27983

Historic Landmarks Foundation.
3402 Blvd. Place, Indianapolis, IN 46208

Historic New Orleans Collection, Kemper & Leila Williams Foundation.
533 Royal St., New Orleans, LA 70130 Tel 504-523-7146

Historic Pensacola Preservation Board; West Florida Museum of History.
205 E. Zaragoza St., Pensacola, FL 32501

Historic Schaefferstown Museum.
N. Market St., Schaefferstown, PA 17088

Historic Towne of Smithville.
New York Rd., U.S. Rte. 9, Smithville, NJ 08201

Historical Burlington County Prison Museum.
128 High St., Mt. Holly, NJ 08060

Historical Museum of the Gunn Memorial Library.
Wykeham Rd., Washington, CT 06793

Historical Museum of the Wabash Valley.
1411 S. Sixth St., Terre Haute, IN 47802

Historical Society of Delaware Museum; Old Hall Town.
Sixth & Market Sts., Wilmington, DE 19801

Historical Society of Early American Decoration, Inc.
C/o NYSHA, Cooperstown, NY 13326

Historical Society of Early American Decoration Inc., Fenimore House.
Cooperstown, NY 13326

Historical Society of Haddonfield.
343 King's Hwy. E., Haddonfield, NJ 08033

Historical Society of Kent County.
P.O. Box 665, Chestertown, ND 21620

Historical Society of Michigan.
2117 Washtenaw Ave., Ann Arbor, MI 48104

Historical Society of New Mexico.
Palace of the Governors, P.O. Box 2087, Santa Fe, NM 87501

Historical Society of Old Newbury.
98 High St., Newburyport, MA 01950

Historical Society of Olde Northfield.
P.O. Box 99, Northfied, OH 44067

Historical Society of Pennsylvania.
1300 Locust St., Philadelphia, PA 19107 Tel 215-732-6200

Historical Society of Princeton.
158 Nassau St., Princeton, NJ 08540

Historical Society of Quincy & Adams County.
425 S. 12th St., Quincy, IL 62301

Historical Society of Rockland County.
Kings Hwy., Orangeburg, NY 10962

Historical Society of Saratoga Springs Museum & Walworth Memorial Museum.
Canfield Casino, Congress Park, P.O. Box 216, Saratoga Springs, NY 12866

Historical Society of the Tarrytowns, Inc.
1 Grove St., Tarrytown, NY 10591

Historical Society of the Townawandas, Inc.
113 Main St., Tonawanda, NY 14150

Historical Society of Western Pennsylvania.
4338 Bigelow Blvd., Pittsburgh, PA 15213

Historical Society of York County.
250 E. Market St., York, PA 17403

History Center & Museum.
Main & Portage Sts., Center of Village Park, Westfield, NY 14787

Hoffman Gallery. *See* School of Arts & Crafts Society of Portland, Hoffman Gallery

Hofstra University, Emily Lowe Gallery:
Hempstead Turnpike, Hempstead, NY 11550

Home of Franklin D. Roosevelt National Historic Site.
Hyde Park, NY 12538

Homer Museum.
Bartlett St., P.O. Box 682, Homer, AK 99603

Honolulu Academy of Arts.
900 S. Beretania St., Honolulu, HI 96814 Tel 808-538-3693
Permanent Collections:
Ancient to Contemporary art; extensive Asian art collect1on and James A. Michener Collection of Japanese Prints.

Honolulu House Museum.
P. O. Box 15, Marshall, MI 49068

Hood River County Museum.
Court House, State St., Hood River, OR 97031

Hoosier Salon Patrons Assn., Hoosier Salon Art Gallery.
951 N. Delware, Indianapolis, IN 46202

Hope Historical Society Museum.
High St., Hope, NJ 07844

Hope Lodge.
Old Bethlehem Pike, Fort Washington, PA 19034

Hopewell Museum.
28 E. Broad St., Hopewell, NJ 08525

Hopewell Museum.
28 E. Broad St., Hopewell, NJ 08525

Hopkins, Governor Stephen, House.
Corner Hopkins & Benefit Sts., Providence, RI 02903

Housatonic Museum of Art.
510 Barnum Ave., Bridgeport, CT 06608 Tel 203-579-6440
Permanent Collections:
Extensive holdings in ethnographic art. Contemporary art includes works by Rodin, Renoir, Matisse, Chagall, Miro, DeChirico, Cassat, Avery, Shinn, Lindner, Rivers, Shahn, Vaserly, Warhol, Derain, Marisol, Rauschenberg, Baskin, Lichtenstein, Katz, Wesselman, Jenkins, Nagouchi, Ossorio, Dine, John Singer Sargent, Christo, Dubuffet, Klimt, Giacometti, Dohanos and others.

House in the Horseshoe State Historic Site.
P.O. Box 503, Sanford, NC 27330

House of the Seven Gables Settlement Assn.
54 Turner St., Salem, MA 01970

Houston Antique Museum.
201 High St., Chattanooga, TN 37403

Houston Public Library; Fine Arts & Record Department.
500 McKinney, Houston, TX 77002

Howard University Gallery of Art:
Sixth & Fairmont Sts., N.W., Washington, DC 20001

Howe, Oscar, Cultural Center.
119 W. Third St., Mitchell, SD 57301

Howe Architecture Library.
College of Architecture, Planning & Design Sciences, Tempe, AZ 85281

Hoyt Institute of Fine Arts.
124 E. Leasure Ave, New Castle, PA 16105

Hubbard, Elbert, Library Museum.
571 Main St., Village Hall, East Aurora, NY 14052

Hudson County Court House, Board of Chosen Freeholder.
595 Newark Ave., Jersey City, NJ 07302

Hudson River Museum.
511 Warburton Ave., Trevor Park on Hudson, Yonkers, NY 10701 Tel 914-963-4550

Hudson Valley Art Assn.
C/O Rayma Spaulding, 15 Minivale Rd., Stamford, CT 06907

Hulihee Palace.
P.O. Box 949, Kailua-Kona, HI 96740

Hull, Marie, Gallery. *See* Hinds Junior College; Marie Hull Gallery

Humboldt Arts Council.
P.O. Box 221, Eureka, CA 95501

Humley Museum.
50 Broad St., Charleston, SC 29401

Hunter Museum of Art.
10 Bluff View, Chattanooga, TN 37403
Permanent Collections:
Approximately 1,000 pieces including paintings, sculpture, prints, ceramics, fabrics, etc.

Hunterdon Art Center.
7 Center St., Clinton, NJ 08826

Huntington Free Library. *See* Museum of the American Indian, Huntington Free Library

Huntington Galleries.
Park Hills, Huntington, WV 25701 Tel 304-529-2701
Permanent Collections:
Gifts of Herbert L. Fitzpatrick,

Mrs. Henry Norwels, George L. Bagby, Alex E. Booth Jr., Major and Mrs. Henry Dourif, William C. Estler and Mrs. R. K. Van Zandt; the Herman P. Dean Collection of Antique Firearms; the Daywood Collection; pure nickel coins of the World.

Huntington Library, Art Gallery & Botanical Gardens.
1151 Oxford Rd., San Marino, CA 91108

Huntsville Museum of Art.
700 Monroe St., S.W., Huntsville, AL 35801

Hutchinson Art Assn.
C/O Mrs. Laura Barr, 321 E. First St., Hutchinson, KS 67501

Hyde Collection.
161 Warren St., Glens Falls, NY 12801

Idaho State University, John B. Davis Gallery of Fine Arts:
Pocatello, ID 83209

Illinois Pioneer Heritage Center.
315 W. Main, Monticello, IL 61856

Illinois State Museum of Natural History & Art.
Spring & Edwards Sts., Springfield, IL 62706
Permanent Collections:
Natural history and science. Art sub-division includes a focus on the art of Illinois. Collection includes paintings, sculpture, prints and watercolors of Illinois artists from 1820 to the present. Decorative arts from America, Europe and the Orient. Highlights include a clock collection dating from 1600-1930; French paperweights mostly from mid-19th century; American and European glassware, ancient through 20th century; Dolls; Oriental items; Inro Netske; porcelain; ceramics; American textiles, 1800 to present; American woven coverlets; Depression era glassware; Illinois costumes; quilts and gun collection.

Illinois State University, University Museum:
Normal, IL 61761

Illinois Valley Museum.
R.R. No. 1, Morris, IL 60450

Illinois Wesleyan Univ., Merwin Gallery.
Bloomington, IL 61701

Imperial Calcasieu Museum.
204 W. Sallier St., Lake Charles, LA 70601

Independence Museum. *See* Ladies Library & Art Assn., Independence Museum

Independence National Historical Park.
313 Walnut St., Philadelphia, PA 19106

Indian Arts & Crafts Board.
U.S. Dept. of Interior, Room 4004, Washington, DC 20240

Indian House Memorial, Inc.
Main St., Deerfield, MA 01342

Indiana Central Univ., L. Ransburg Art Gallery.
1400 E. Hana Ave., Indianapolis, IN 46227

Indiana State Museum.
202 N. Alabama St., Indianapolis, IN 46204

Indiana State Univ., Truman Gallery.
Terre Haute, IN 47809

Indiana University Art Museum:
Fine Arts 007, Bloomington, IN 47401 Tel 812-337-0607
Permanent Collections:
Collections from the West: Ancient Art (Egypt, Greece, Italy, Hellenistic and Roman), Early Christian, Medieval, Renaissance, 17th-20th century; the East: Ancient Near East, Islamic, Southeast Asia, India, China, Japan; Primitive World: Africa, Oceania; the New World: Pre-Columbian, American Indian; Media: paintings, drawings, prints, sculpture, photographs, minor arts and textiles.

Indiana University of Pennsylvania, Kipp Gallery:
Indiana, PA 15701

Indianapolis Marion Co. Public Library.
40 E. St. Clair St., Indianapolis, IN 46204

Indianapolis Museum of Art.
1200 W. 38th St., Indianapolis, IN 46208

Industrial Designers Society of America.
1750 Old Meadow Rd., McLean, VA 22101

Institute for Advanced Studies in Comtemporary Art.
6361 Elmhurst Dr., San Diego, CA 92120

Institute for Art & Urban Resources.
108 Leonard, New York, NY 10013

Institute for the Arts.
Stockton St. & University Blvd., Houston, TX 77001

Institute of American Indian Arts Museum.
Cerillos Rd., Santa Fe, NM 87501 Tel 505-988-6281
Permanent Collections:
Collections of contemporary Indian arts and crafts; paintings, sculpture, beadwork, ceramics, printed textiles, woven textiles, jewelry, drawings, prints and ethnographical materials. Approximately 8,000 items from Indian tribes throughout the U.S., Alaska and Canada.

Institute of Contemporary Art.
955 Boylston St., Boston, MA 02115

Institute of the Great Plains, Museum of the Great Plains.
P.O. Box 68, Lawton, OK 73501

Intermuseum Conservation Assn.
Allen Bldg., Oberlin, OH 44074

International Center of Medieval Art; The Cloisters.
Fort Tryon Park, New York, NY 10040

International Center of Photography.
1130 Fifth Ave., New York, NY 10028

International Council of Museum Committee of the American Assn. of Museums.
1055 Thomas Jefferson St., Washington, DC 20007

International Foundation for Art Research.
24 E. 81st St., New York, NY 10028

International Museum of Photography, George Eastman House.
900 East Ave., Rochester, NY 14607

Irene Leache Museum. *See* Leach, Irene Museum

Iron Work Farm in Action, Inc.
P.O. Box 11, Acton, MA 01720

Iroquois County Historical Society Museum.
Old Courthouse , Second & Cherry Sts., Watseka, IL 60970

Isabella Stewart Gardner Mansion. *See* Gardner, Isabella Stewart, Museum

Islesford Museum.
Acadia National Park, P.O. Box 1, Bar Harbor, ME 04609

J. K. Ralston Museum & Art Center. *See* Ralston, J. K., Museum & Art Center

J. M. Davis Gun Museum. *See* Davis, J. M., Gun Museum

J. Paul Getty Museum. *See* Getty, J. Paul, Museum

J. R. Broussard Memorial Gallery. *See* Broussard, J. R., Memorial Gallery

Jack London State Historical Park.
P.O. Box 358, Glen Ellen, CA 95441

Jackson, Sheldon, Museum.
P.O. Box 479, Sitka, AK 99835
Permanent Collections:
Ethnographic collections from Alaskan native groups: Tlingit, Haida, Aleut, Athabascan and Eskimo.

Jackson County Historical Society.
201 N. Main St., Independence, MO 64050

Jackson Homestead.
527 Washington St., Newton, MA 02158

Jackson's Mill Museum.
Weston, WV 26452

Jacksonville Art Museum.
4160 Blvd. Center Dr., Jacksonville, FL 32201

Permanent Collections:
Contemporary art, Oriental porcelains.

Jacksonville Museum Arts & Sciences.
1025 Gulf Dr., Jacksonville, FL 32207

Jacksonville Public Library Art & Music Dept.
122 N. Ocean St., Jacksonville, FL 32201

Jacques Marchais Center of Tibetan Arts. *See* Marchais, Jacques, Center of Tibetan Arts, Inc

James Madison Univ., Sawhill Duke Fine Arts Ctr.
Duke Fine Arts Ctr., Harrisburg, VA 22801

James Monroe Law Office Museum & Memorial Library.
908 Charles St., Frederickburg, VA 23669

Japan House Gallery. *See* Japan Society Inc., Japan House Gallery

Japan Society Inc., Japan House Gallery.
333 E. 47th St., New York, NY 10017

Jasper Rd. Art Museum. *See* Westfield Athenaem, Jasper Rd. Art Museum

Jay, John, Homestead.
P.O. Box AH, Katonah, NY 10536

J.B. Speed Art Museum. *See* Speed, J.B., Art Museum

Jekyll Island State Park Authority.
201 Old Plantation Rd., Jekyll Island, GA 31520

Jelet Museum of History & Arts.
5439 Library St., Brewerton, NY 13029

Jersey City Museum.
427 Jersey Ave., Jersey City, NJ 07302
Permanent Collections:
19th century furniture, four centuries of household objects, 19th and 20th century paintings and drawings (American), archaeological artifacts and the August Will Collection of paintings, drawings and sculpture.

Jersey City Public Library Fine Arts Dept.
678 Newark Ave., Jersey City, NJ 07306

Jersey City State College; Courtney Art Gallery, Dept. of Art.
2039 Kennedy Blvd., Jersey City, NJ 07307

Jesse Besser Museum. *See* Besser, Jesse, Museum

Jewish Museum.
1109 Fifth Ave., New York, NY 10028

John & Mabel Ringling Museum of Art. *See* Ringling, John and Mable, Museum of Art

John Brown Cabin. *See* Brown, John, Cabin

John F. Kennedy Center for the Performing Arts. *See* Kennedy, John F., Center for the Performing Arts

John F. Kennedy Memorial Center. *See* Kennedy, John F., Memorial Center

John Hanson Memorial Museum. *See* Hanson, John, Memorial Museum

John Hopkins Univ. Archaeological Collection.
Charles & 34th St., Baltimore, MD 21218

John Jay Homestead. *See* Jay, John, Homestead

John Michael Kohler Arts Center. *See* Kohler, John Michael, Arts Center

John Paul Jones House. *See* Jones, John Paul, House

John Simon Guggenheim Memorial Foundation. *See* Guggenheim, John Simon, Memorial Foundation

John Strong Mansion. *See* Strong, John, Mansion

John Wesley Powell Memorial Museum. *See* Powell, John Wesley Memorial Museum

John Woodman Higgins Armory Museum. *See* Higgins, John Woodman, Armory Museum

John Wornall House. *See* Wornall, John, House

Johnester Art Gallery.
Abbot Academy, Andover, MA 01810

Johnson, Andrew, Memorial Commission.
P.O. Box 1881, Raleigh, NC 27602

Johnson, Martin & Osa Memorial Safari Museum.
16 S. Grant, Chanute,, KS 66720
Permanent Collections:
Photographs and movies of the South Seas (New Hebrides and Solomon Islands), Africa and Borneo by Martin and Osa Johnson; artifacts from these areas which were brought back by them; West African Art Collection.

Johnson County Historical Society, Inc.
Third & Lincoln Sts., Tecumseh, NE 68450

Johnson Gallery. *See* Middlebury College; Johnson Gallery

Johnson, Grace Phillips, Art Gallery. *See* Phillips University, Grace Phillips Johnson Art Gallery

Johnson-Humrickhouse Memorial Museum.
Sycamore & 3rd Sts., Coshocton, OH 43812

Johnston, Henry S., Library. *See* **Cherokee Strip Historical Society & Henry S. Johnston Library**

Johnston National Scouting Museum.
Rtes. 1 & 130, North Brunswick, NJ 08902

Jones, John Paul, House.
54 Court St., Portsmouth, NH 03801

Jones Library Inc.
43 Amity St., Amherst, MA 01002

Jonson Gallery-Univ. of New Mexico.
1909 Las Lomas Rd., N.E., Albuquerque, NM 87106

Josephine D. Randall Jr. Museum. *See* **Randall, Josephine D. Jr., Museum**

Joslyn Art Museum.
2200 Dodge St., Omaha, NE 68102

Judah L. Magnas Memorial Museum. *See* **Magnas, Judah L., Memorial Museum**

Judith Basin Museum. *See* **Basin, Judith, Museum**

Junior Art Gallery.
301 York St., Louisville, KY 40203

Junior Arts Center.
4814 Hollywood Blvd., Los Angeles, CA 90027

Junior Center of Arts & Science.
3612 Webster St., Oakland, CA 94609

Justin Smith Morill Homestead. *See* **Morill, Justin Smith, Homestead**

Kalamazoo Institute of Arts; Genevieve & Donald Gilmore Art Center.
314 S. Park St., Kalamazoo, MI 49006

Kalamazoo Public Museum.
315 S. Rose St., Kalamazoo, MI

Kamuela Museum.
Kawaihae-Kohala Junction, Rte. 25-26, P.O. Box 507, Kamuela, HI 96743

Kansas City Art Institute; Kemper Gallery.
4415 Warwick, Kansas City, MO 64111

Kansas City Public Library Art & Music Dept.
311 E. 12th St., Kansas City, MO 64106

Kansas State Historical Society Museum.
120 W. Tenth St., Topeka, KS 66612

Kansas State Univ., Paul Weigel Library, College of Architecture & Design.
Manhattan, KS 66506

Kansas Watercolor.
1545 Willow Rd., Wichita, KS 67208

Kappa Pi International Art Fraternity.
P.O. Box 7843, Midfield, Birmingham, AL 35228

Kate Freeman Clark Art Gallery. *See* **Clark, Kate Freeman, Art Gallery**

Katonah Gallery.
28 Bedford Rd., Katonah, NY 10536

Kauai Museum.
P.O. Box 248, Lihue, HI 96766

Kaysville Community Art League, LeConte Stewart Art Gallery.
611 Crestwood Rd., Kaysville, UT 84037

Kean College of New Jersey; College Gallery.
Morris Ave., Union, NJ 08063

Kearny Cottage Historical Society.
39 Catalpa Ave., Perth Amboy, NJ 08861

Keene State College; Thorn-Sagendorph Art Gallery.
Appian Way, Keene, NH 03431

Kelly-Griggs House Museum.
1248 Jefferson St., Red Bluff, CA 96080

Kelsey Museum Ancient & Mediaeval Archaeology.
434 S. State St., Ann Arbor, MI 48109

Kemerer, Annie S., Museum.
427 N. New St., Bethlehem, PA 18018

Kemper & Leila Williams Foundation. *See* **Historic New Orleans Collection, Kemper & Leila Williams Foundation**

Kemper Gallery. *See* **Kansas City Art Institute; Kemper Gallery**

Kendall Art Gallery. *See* **San Angelo Art Club, Kendall Art Gallery**

Kendall Whaling Museum.
27 Everett St. Box297, Sharon, MA 02066

Kenmore.
1201 Washington Ave., Fredericksburg, VA 22401

Kennebec Valley Art Assn., Harlow Gallery.
P.O. Box 213, Hallowell, ME 04347

Kennedy, John F., Center for the Performing Arts.
Washington, DC 20566

Kennedy, John F., Memorial Center.
1308 16th Ave. S., Nashville, TN 37212

Kenosha Public Museum.
5608 10th Ave., Kenosha, WI 53140

Kent Art Association Inc., Gallery:
P.O. Box 385, Kent, CT 06759

Kent State University School of Art Gallery:
Kent, OH 44242

Kentucky Guild of Artists & Craftsmen Inc.
P.O. Box 291, Berea, KY 40403

Kentucky Historical Society Museum.
P.O. Box H, Frankfort, KY 40602

Kentucky Museum. *See* **Western Kentucky Univ., Kentucky Museum**

Keokuk Art Center.
Box 871, Keokuk, IA 52632

Kern County Museum.
3801 Chester Ave., Bakersfield, CA 93301

Kerr Museum.
P.O. Box 588, Poteau, OK 74953

Ketterer Art Center.
35 N. Grand, Bozeman, MT 59715

Key West Art & Historical Society.
S. Roosevelt Blvd., Key West, FL 33040

Kiah Museum.
505 W. 36th St., Savannah, GA 31401

Kimbell Art Museum.
P.O. Box 9440, Fort Worth, TX 76107 Tel 817-332-8451 KIMBART
Permanent Collections:
Arts of Asia, Africa, Pre-Columbian America and Europe through the early 20th century (painting, sculpture, graphics and ceramics).

King, Emma B., Library. *See* **Shaker Museum & Emma B. King Library**

King County Arts Commission.
King County Administration Bldg., Seattle, WA 98102

King, Martin Luther, Memorial Library. *See* **Public Library of the District of Columbia, Martin Luther King Memorial Library**

Kingsport Fine Arts Center.
Church Circle, Kingsport, TN 37660

Kip, Hendrik, House.
Kip House (Duchess County), Fishskill, NY 12524

Kirk, Samuel, Museum, Inc.
225 Holiday St., Baltimore, MD 21218

Kirkland Art Center.
Clinton, NY 13323

Kirkpatrick Center. *See* **Omniplex, Kirkpatrick Center**

Kit Carson Memorial Foundation Inc.. *See* **Carson, Kit, Memorial Foundation, Inc**

Kitsap County Historical Museum.
837 Fourth St., Bremerton, WA 98310

Klamath Art Assn.
P.O. Box 955, Klamath Falls, OR 97601

Klamath County Museum.
1451 Main St., Klamath, OR 97601

Klapper, Paul, Library. *See* **Queen's College Art Collection, Paul Klapper Library**

Klickitat County Historical Society.
127 W. Broadway, Goldendale, WA 98620

Knickerbocker Historical Society, Inc.
Schaghticoke, NY 12154

Knight, Allen, Maritime Museum.
P.O. Box 805, Monterey, CA 93940 Tel 403-375-2553
Permanent Collections:
Large private collection of maritime artifacts and relics. Collection includes many sailing ship models, steering wheels, bells, blocks, compasses, lanterns, scrimshaw, navigation instruments, ship nameboards and and other parts of old ships. There are prints and paintings of ships; literally thousands of ship pictures. Comprehensive maritime library.

Knox Headquarters-The John Ellison House.
Rte. 94, at Forge Hill Rd. P.O. Box 207, Vails Gate, NY 12584

Koenig Art Gallery. *See* **Condordia College; Koenig Art Gallery**

Kohler, John Michael, Arts Center.
608 New York Ave., Sheboygan, WI Tel 414-458-6144

Kohler Art Library.
800 University Ave., Madison, WI 53706

Koshare Indian Museum, Inc.
18th & Santa Fe, La Junta, CO 81050

Kraushaar Audit Lobby Gallery. *See* **Goucher College, Kraushaar Audit Lobby Gallery**

Kutztown State College, Sharadin Art Gallery.
Kutztown, PA 19530

L & N Railroad Depot Gallery. *See* **Singing River Art Assn. Inc**

La Crosse Historical Society.
123 S. 22nd St., La Crosse, WI 54601

La Jolla Museum of Contemporary Art.
700 Prospect St., La Jolla, CA 92037

La Mamelle Inc.
Box 3123 Rinson, San Francisco, CA 94119

La Salle College Art Gallery.
20th & Olney Ave., Philadelphia, PA 19141

Lac Qui Parle Historical Society.
City Hall, 404 Sixth Ave., Madison, MN 56256

Ladies Library & Art Assn., Independence Museum.
123 N. Eighth, Independence, KS 67301

Lafayette Art Center.
101 S. Ninth St., Lafayette, IN 47901

Laguna Beach Museum of Art.
Pacific Coast Hwy. at Cliff Dr., Laguna Beach, CA 92651

Laguna Gloria Art Museum.
P.O. Box 5568, Austin, TX 78763

Lahaina Arts Society.
649 Wharf St., Lahaina, HI 96761

Lake County Historical Society.
8095 Mentor Ave., Mentor, OH 44060

Lake County Historical Society & Railroad Museum.
415 Eighth Ave., Two Harbors, MN 55616

Lake George Institute of History, Art & Science.
Canada St., Lake George, NY 12845

Lake Placid School Art Gallery.
Saranac Ave., Lake Placid, NY 12946

Lake Region Art Assn.
P.O. Box 11, Devils Lake, NC 58601

Lakeview Center for Arts & Sciences.
1125 W. Lake Ave., Peoria, IL 61614

Lambert Castle. *See* Passaic Community Historical Society; Lambert Castle

Lamont Gallery. *See* Phillips Exeter Academy, Lamont Gallery

Lampe Gallery of Fine Art, Lampe School of Art.
3920 Old Gentilly Rd., New Orleans, LA 70130

Lampham-Patterson House.
626 N. Dawson St., Thomasville, GA 31792

Lamson, Herbert H., Library. *See* Plymouth State College, Herbert H. Lamson Library

Lancaster County Art Assn., Art Center.
22 Vine St., Lancaster, PA 17602

Landmark Conservators.
67-616 E. Desert View Ave., Desert Hot Springs, CA 92240

Landmark Inn.
Florence & Florella St., Castroville, TX 78009

Landmark Society of Western New York.
130 Spring St., Rochester, NY 14608

Lane, Henry S., Home.
212 S. Water St., Crawfordsville, IN 47922

Langston University Art Gallery:
Langston, OK 73050

Las Vegas Art League; Las Vegas Art Museum.
3333 W. Washington, Las Vegas, NV 89107

LaSalle County Historical Museum.
P.O. Box 577, Utica, IL 61373

Latin Quarter Art Gallery; Ybor City Chamber of Commerce.
1509 Eight Ave., Tampa, FL 33605

Laura Musser Art Gallery & Museum. *See* Musser, Laura, Art Gallery & Museum

Lauren Rogers Library & Museum of Art. *See* Rogers, Lauren, Library & Museum of Art

Lavis Art Gallery. *See* Stephens College, Lewis James & Nellie Stratton Lavis Art Gallery

Le Sueur County Historical Society Museum.
306 W. Lake St., Waterville, MN 56096

Leach, Irene Museum.
C/o Mrs. Charles Dalton Jr., 556 Mowbray Arch, Norfolk, VA 23507

League of New Hampshire Craftsmen.
205 N. Main St., Concord, NH 03301

LeConte Stewart Art Gallery. *See* Kaysville Community Art League, LeConte Stewart Art Gallery

Lee Atkyns Studio Gallery. *See* Atkyns, Lee, Studio Gallery

Lee County Library.
219 Madison St., Tupelo, MS 38801

Lee Hall Gallery. *See* Northern Michigan Univ., Lee Hall Gallery

Lee, Robert E., Memorial. *See* Arlington House, The Robert E. Lee Memorial

Leeds Gallery. *See* Earlham College, Leeds Gallery

Leffert's Homestead.
Prospect Park, Flatbush Ave., Near Willinck Gate, Brooklyn, NY 11215

Leffingwell Inn.
348 Washington St., Norwich, CT 06360

Lehigh Univ. Galleries, Fine Arts Bldg.. *See* Lehigh University Galleries, Fine Arts Bldg

Lehigh University Galleries, Fine Arts Bldg.
Chandler-Ullman Hall, Rm. 17, Bethlehem, PA 18015

Lemhi County Historical Museum.
Salmon, ID 83467

Lemoyne Art Foundation.
125 N. Gadsden St., Tallahassee, FL 32301

Lenawee County Historical Society, Inc.
4380 Evergreen Dr., P.O. Box 511, Adrian, MI 49221

Lenox China Museum.
Prince & Meade Sts., Trenton, NJ 08605

Leroy House.
23 E. Main St., LeRoy, NY 14482

Levere Memorial Foundation.
1856 Sheridan Rd., Evanston, IL 60204

Lewis Cooper Jr. Memorial Library & Art Center. *See* Cooper, Lewis Jr., Memorial Library & Art Center

Liberty Hall Museum.
218 Wilkinson St., Frankfort, KY 40601

Library of Congress.
First St. Between E. Capitol St. & Independence, Washington, DC 20540

Licking County Historical Society.
P. O. Box 535, Newark, OH 43055

Lighthouse Gallery Inc.
100 Waterway Rd., Tequesta, FL 33458

Lighthouse Museum.
South End of Water St., Stonington, CT 06378

Lightner Museum of Hobbies.
King St., St. Augustine, FL 32084

Lincoln Center for the Performing Arts; Amsterdam, Plaza & Main Galleries.
1865 Broadway, New York, NY 10023

Lincoln Community Arts Council.
Rm. 508 Lincoln Center Bldg., Lincoln, NE 68508

Lincoln County Cultural & Historical Assn.
Wiscasset, ME 04578

Lincoln Memorial Shrine.
P.O. Box 751, Redlands, CA 92373 Tel 714-793-6622

Lindenwood Colleges; Harry D. Henren Gallery Dept. of Art.
St. Charles, MO 63301

Litchfield Historical Society.
Litchfield, CT 06759 Tel 203-567-5862
Permanent Collections:
American art, furniture, costumes, pottery.

Little Art Gallery. *See* North Canton Public Library, Little Art Gallery

Little Gallery. *See* Siena Heights College, Little Gallery

Little Gallery. *See* Black Hills Art Center, Little Gallery

Little Gallery Art Dept.. *See* East Texas State Univ., Little Gallery Art Dept

Little Gallery of Arts.
155 E. Main St., Vernal, UT 84078

Little Salmon River Canyon Museum.
Pollock, ID 83547

Living Arts & Science Center, Inc.
362 Walnut St., Lexington, KY 40508

Lizzadro Museum of Lipidary Art.
220 Cottage Hill Ave., Elmhurst, IL 60126

Loch Haven Art Center.
2416 N. Hills Ave., Orlando, FL 32803 Tel 305-896-4231
Permanent Collections:
101 20th century American graphics, pre-Columbian collection, small African collection, various American paintings (O'Keefe and Sheeler).

Lockerbie Street Home of James Whitcomb Riley.
528 Lockerbie St., Indianapolis, IN 46202

Lockwood-Mathews Mansion Museum.
295 West Ave., Norwalk, CT 06360

Lone Mountian College Art Department Gallery.
2800 Turk Blvd., San Francisco, CA 94118

Long Beach Art Assn.
111 W. Park Ave., Long Beach, NY 11561

Long Beach Museum of Art.
2300 E. Ocean Blvd., Long Beach, CA 90803

Long Beach Public Library.
101 Pacific Ave., Long Beach, CA 90802

Long Branch Historical Museum.
1260 Ocean Ave., Long Beach, NJ 07740

Long Island Historical Society.
128 Pierrepont St., Brooklyn, NY 11201

Long Island Univ. Art Gallery. *See* C. W. Post Center, Long Island Univ. Art Gallery

Longfellow's Wayside Inn.
Wayside Inn Rd. off Rte. 20, South Sudbury, MA 01776

Longmeadow Historical Society.
697 Longmeadow St., Longmeadow, MA 01106

Longview Museum & Arts Center.
Box 562, Longview, TX 75601 Tel 214-753-8103
Permanent Collections:
Collection of contemporary regional artists, consisting of oils, acrylics, prints, sculpture, drawings and watercolors.

Longwood College, Bedford Gallery.
Pine St., Farmville, VA 23901

Lorado Taft Museum Studios. *See* Taft, Lorado, Museum Studios

Lord House.
Main St., Conway, NH 03818

Lorenzo.
Ledyard Ave., R.D. 2, Cazenovia, NY 13055

Loretto-Hilton Center Gallery. *See* Webster College, Loretto-Hilton Center Gallery

Los Almos Art Council.
223 El Viento, Los Alamos,
NM 87544

Los Angeles Art Assn. & Galleries.
825 N. La Cienega Blvd., Los
Angeles, CA 90069

Los Angeles County Museum of Art.
5905 Wilshire Blvd., Los
Angeles, CA 90036
Permanent Collections:
Egyptian, Oriental, Indian and
Classical antiquities including
glass and textiles; Medieval and
Renaissance paintings,
sculpture, decorative arts,
stained glass and tapestries;
European paintings and
sculpture; Contemporary,
Modern American and
European art, costumes and
textiles; Decorative Arts;
American Art; prints, drawings
and photographs.

Los Angeles Institute of Contemporary Art.
20220 S. Robertson Blvd., Los
Angeles, CA 90034

Los Angeles Trade-Technical College Library.
400 W. Washington Blvd., Los
Angeles, CA 90015

Los Nogales Museum.
Corner of S. River & Live Oak
Sts., Seguin, TX 78155

Lotos Club.
5 E. 66th St., New York, NY
10021

Louis Comfort Tiffany Foundation.
See Tiffany, Louis Comfort,
Foundation

Louise Sloss Ackerman Fine Arts Library. *See* Ackerman, Louise
Sloss, Fine Arts Library

Louisiana Art Commission.
100 N. Blvd., Old State
Capitol, Baton Rouge, LA
70801

Louisiana Arts & Science Center.
100 S. River Rd., P.O. Box
3373, Baton Rouge, LA 70821
Tel 504-344-9463
Permanent Collections:
Eskimo Soapstone carvings and
graphics; North American
Indian crafts; Francois Brochet
sculpture and lithographs; Ivan
Mestrovic sculpture; Black and
White photography; Egyptian
tapestries. Free brochures
available on all permanent
collections.

Louisiana State Exhibit Museum.
3015 Greenwood Rd.,
Shreveport, LA 71109

Louisiana State Museum.
751 Chartres St., New Orleans,
LA 70118

Louisiana State Univ., Anglo-American Art Museum.
114 Memorial Tower, Baton
Rouge, LA 70803 Tel 504-
388-4003
Permanent Collections:
British and American paintings,
prints, drawings, decorative arts
and period panelings.

Louisville School of Art.
100 Park Rd., Anchorage, KY
40223 Tel 502-245-8836

Loveland Museums.
503 Lincoln, Loveland, CO
80537

Lovely Lane Museum. *See* United
Methodist Historical Society,
Lovely Lane Museum

Lovis Corinth Memorial Foundation. *See* Corinth, Lovis,
Memorial Foundation

Lowell Art Association; Whistler House & Parker Gallery:
243 Worthen St., Lowell, MA
01852

Lower Cape Fear Historical Society, Inc.
118 S. Fourth St., Wilmington,
NC 28401

Lowie, R. H., Museum of Anthropology.
103 Kroeber Hall, Univ. of
California, Berkeley, Berkeley,
CA 94720

Loyola Marymount Univ., Malone Art Gallery.
Loyola Blvd. at W. 80th, Los
Angeles, CA 90045

Loyola University of Chicago; Martin D'Arcy Gallery of Art:
6525 N. Sheridan Rd., Chicago,
IL 60626 Tel 312-274-3000
Permanent Collections:
Medieval, Renaissance and
Baroque art, especially
sculpture and objects in gold,
silver, bronze, enamel, ivory,
textiles, etc.

Luna-Mimibres Museum.
301 S. Silver Rd., P.O. Box
1617, Deming, NM 88030

Lundhurst.
635 S. Broadway, Tarrytown,
NY 10591

Lutz Junior Museum.
126 Cedar St., Manchester, CT
06040

Lycoming College, Art Center Gallery.
Williamsport, PA 17701

Lycoming County Historical Society & Museum.
858 W. Fourth St.,
Williamsport, VA 17701

Lyle True Gallery. *See* Colorado
Women's College; Lyle True
Gallery

Lyman Allyn Museum. *See* Allyn,
Lyman, Museum

Lyme Art Association, Inc.
P.O. Box 222, Old Lyme, CT
06371

Lyme Historical Society Inc., Florence Griswold House.
96 Lyme St, Old Lyme, CT
06371 Tel 203-434-5542
Permanent Collections:
Old Lyme Art Colony
Collection, McCurdy Salisbury
China Collection and the Clara
Champlain Griswold Toy
Collection.

Lynchburg Fine Arts Center.
1815 Thomson Dr., Lynchburg,
VA 24501

Lyons, Harrye, Design Library.
See North Carolina State Univ.,
Harrye Lyons Design Library

Mabee-Gerner Museum. *See* St.
Gregory's Abbey & College, The
Mabee-Gerner Museum

Macalester College Galleries.
1600 Grand St., Saint Paul,
MN 55101

McAllen International Museum.
P.O. Box 2495, McAllen, TX
78501

MacArthur Memorial.
One MacArthur Sq., Norfolk,
VA 23510

McCallum Museum.
City Park, Sibley, IA 51249

McCormick, R.R., Museum.
Rte. 4, P.O. Box 195, Wheaton,
IL 60187

McCully House Doll Museum.
240 California St., Jacksonville,
OR 97530

McGuire Memorial Hall. *See* Art
Association of Richmond,
McGuire Memorial Hall

McHenry County Historical Society, Inc.
Old Union School, 205 E.
Main St., Woodstock, IL 60098

McIntire Garrison.
York, ME 03909

Mackay House.
1822 Broad St., Augusta, GA
30904

McLean County Art Assn.
210 W. Washington St.,
Bloomington, IL 61701

McMurray College, Amy Graves Ryan Fine Arts Center.
Box 8, Abilene, TX 79605
Permanent Collections:
Collection includes a Picasso
lithograph, a Jack Levine
lithograph, an Adolph Dehn
watercolor, a Peter Hurd
watercolor, a David Brownlow
oil, a Frielander lithograph, a
Jack Garver watercolor, a
Woody Big Bow tempera and a
Carolyn Walker oil, etc.

McNamara-O'connor Historical and Fine Arts Museum.
502 N. Liberty St., Victoria,
TX 77901

McNay, Marion Koogler, Art Institute.
6000 N. New Braunfels St.,
San Antonio, TX 78209

Macnide, C. H., Museum.
225 Second St., S.E., Mason
City, IA 50401

McPherson Museum.
1130 E. Euclid, McPherson,
KS 67460

Madison Art Center Inc.
720 E. Gorham St., Madison,
WI 53703 Tel 608-257-0158

Madison County Historical Society.
435 Main & Grove, Oneida,
NY 13421

Magdalene Charlton Memorial Museum & Griffin Memorial House.
N. Pine St., Tomball, TX
77375

Magee Museum.
698 W. Main St., Bloomsburg,
PA 17815

Magnas, Judah L., Memorial Museum.
2911 Russel St., Berkeley, CA
94705

Mahoney Library. *See* College of
Saint Elizabeth; Mahoney
Library

Main Line Center of the Arts.
Old Buck Rd. & Lancaster,
Haverford, PA 11041

Maine Coast Artists.
Russell Ave., Box 147,
Rockport, ME 04856

Maine Historical Society.
485 Congress St., Portland, ME
04111

Maitland Art Center Research Studio.
231 W. Packwood Ave.,
Maitland, FL 32751

Malden Public Library.
36 Salem St., Malden, MA
02148 Tel 617-324-0218
Permanent Collections:
110 oil paintings, 150 etchings,
1000 prints.

Malki Museum.
Morongo Indian Reservation,
11-795 Fields Rd., Banning,
CA 92220

Malone Art Gallery. *See* Loyola
Marymount Univ., Malone Art
Gallery

"Man Full of Trouble" Tavern.
127-129 Spruce St.,
Philadelphia, PA 19106

Manchester Historical Society.
Union St., Manchester, MA
01944

Manchester Institute of Arts & Sciences.
148 Concord St., Manchester,
NH 03104

Manhattanville College, Brownson Art Gallery.
Purchase, NY 10577

Mankato State University; Nichols Gallery:
Manato, MI 56001

Mansfield Art Center, Mansfield Fine Arts Guild.
700 Marion Ave., Mansfield,
OH 44903

Mansfield Historical Society Museum.
Rte. 32 & S. Eagleville Rd.,
Storrs, CT 06268

Marathon County Historical Society.
403 McIndoe St., Wausau, WI
54401

Marble Exhibit.
Main St., Proctor, VT 05765

Marblehead Arts Assn., Inc.
Eight Hooper St., Marblehead,
MA 01945

**Marcellite Hardy Memorial
Museum.** *See* Hardy, Marcellite,
Memorial Museum

**Marchais, Jacques, Center of
Tibetan Arts, Inc.**
338 Lighthouse Ave., Staten
Island, NY 10306

Marias Museum of History & Art.
229 Maple Ave., Shelby, MT
59474

**Marietta College, Grover M.
Hermann Fine Arts Center.**
Marietta, OH 45750

Marin Art & Garden Society.
P.O. Box 203, Ross, CA 94957

Mariners Museum.
1 Museum Dr., Newport News,
VA 23606
Permanent Collections:
Collections of carvings,
paintings, prints, ceramics and
scrimshaw; international in
scope.

Marion Art Center.
Main St., Marion, MA 02739

**Marion College Art Dept., Alison
Mansion.**
3200 Cold Spring Rd.,
Indianapolis, IN 46222

**Marion Koogler McNay Art
Institute.** *See* McNay, Marion
Koogler, Art Institute

**Maritime Museum Assn. of San
Diego.**
1306 N. Harbor Dr., San
Diego, CA 92101

Mark Twain Memorial. *See*
Twain, Mark, Memorial

Marlpit Hall.
137 Kings Hwy., Middletown,
NJ 07748

**Marquette University; Marquette
Art Gallery:**
134 Coughlin Hall, Milwaukee,
WI 53217

**Marshall County Historical
Museum Inc.**
317 W. Monroe, Plymouth, IN
46563

Martello Gallery & Museum.
S. Roosevelt Blvd., Key West,
FL 33040

**Martin & Osa Johnson Memorial
Safari Museum.** *See* Johnson,
Martin & Osa Memorial Safari
Museum

Martin Memorial Library.
159 E. Market St., York, PA
17401

Mary Buie Museum. *See* Buie,
Mary, Museum

Mary S. Robinson Art Library.
See Robinson, Mary S., Art
Library

Maryhill Museum of Art.
Star Route 677, Box 23,
Goldendale, WA 98620

Maryhill Museum of Fine Arts.
Star Rte. 677, P.O. Box 23,
Maryhill, WA 98620

**Maryland Historical Society
Museum.**
201 W. Monument St.,
Baltimore, MD 21201

**Maryland Institute College of Art,
Decker Gallery.**
1300 Mt. Royal Ave.,
Baltimore, MD 21239

**Maryville College Fine Arts
Center Gallery.**
Maryville, TN 37801

Massachusetts Historical Society.
1154 Boylston St., Boston, MA
02115

**Massachusetts Institute of
Technology; Hayden Gallery.**
Rm. 14W-111, Cambridge, MA
02139

Massillon Museum.
212 Lincoln Way E., Massillon,
OH 44646

Masur Museum of Art. *See* Twin
City Art Foundation, Masur
Museum of Art

Mattatuck Historical Society.
119 W. Main St., Waterbury,
CT 06702

**Maude L. Kerns Art Center,
Henry Korn Gallery.**
1910 E. 15th Ave., Eugene,
OR 97403

Maui Historical Society.
P.O. Box 1018, Wailuku, HI
96793

**Maurice Spertus Museum of
Judaica.** *See* Spertus, Maurice,
Museum of Judaica

**Maxwell Museum of
Anthropology, Univ. of New
Mexico.**
Corner of University & Roma,
N.E., Albuquerque, NM 87131
Tel 505-277-4404
Permanent Collections:
Collections from all over the
world but with chief emphasis
on the Southwest. Major
collections of Navajo weaving,
Mimbres pottery, historic and
prehistoric Pueblo pottery,
Hopi Rachinas, North
American Indian basketry as
well as Arctic and Southwest
Indian prehistoric materials.

Mayflower Society House.
4 Winslow St., Plymouth, MA
02360

Mead Art Museum. *See* Amherst
College, Mead Art Museum

Meadow Brook Art Gallery. *See*
Oakland University, Meadow
Brook Art Gallery

Meadows Museum. *See* Southern
Methodist Univ., Meadows
Museum

Mellette Memorial Assn.
421 Fifth Ave., N.W.,
602watertown, N.W.
Watertown, SD 57201

Melvil Art Gallery. *See* Florida
Southern College; Melvil Art
Gallery

**Memphis Academy of Arts, Frank
T. Tobey Gallery.**
Overton Park, Memphis, TN
38112

**Memphis State University
Campus, E. H. Little Gallery:**
Memphis, TN 38111

Mendocino Art Center Gallery.
45200 Little Lake St., P.O. Box
36, Mendocino, CA 95460

Mendocino County Museum.
400 E. Commercial St., Willits,
CA 95490

Mercer Museum. *See* Bucks
County Historical Society;
Mercer Museum

Meridian Museum of Art.
Box 5773, 25th Ave. at
Seventh St., Meridian, MS
39301

Merrick Art Gallery.
5th Ave. & 11th St., P.O. Box
312, New Brighton, PA 15066

**Merrimack Valley Textile
Museum.**
800 Massachusetts Ave., North
Andover, MA 01845 Tel 617-
686-0191
Permanent Collections:
Machines, tools, documents,
pictures, books and textiles
which tell the story of
America's textile industry from
1750 to 1950.

Merwin Gallery. *See* Illinois
Wesleyan Univ., Merwin
Gallery

Metropolitan Arts Commission.
430 S.W. Morrison, Portland,
OR 97204

**Metropolitan Cultural Arts
Center.**
1530 Russell Ave., N.,
Minneapolis, MN 55411

Metropolitan Museum of Art.
Main Bldg., Fifth Ave. at 82nd
St., New York, NY 10028

**Metropolitian Museum & Art
Center.**
1212 Anastasia Ave., Coral
Gables, FL 33134

Meyer Library. *See* California
College of Arts & Crafts, Meyer
Library

Miami Art Center, Inc.
7867 N. Kendall Dr., Miami,
FL 33156

**Miami-Dade Community College;
South Campus Art Gallery.**
11011 S.W. 104th St., Miami,
FL 33176

Miami Museum of Modern Art.
381 N.E. 20th St., Miami, FL
33137

Miami Purchase Assn.
812 Dayton St., Cincinnati, OH
45214

Miami University Art Center:
Rowan Hall, Oxford, OH
45056

**Michigan Historical Commission
Museum.**
505 N. Washington Ave.,
Lansing, MI 48933

**Michigan State Univ., Kresge Art
Center Gallery.**
Kresge Art Center, East
Lansing, MI 48824

**Mid Fairfield County Youth
Museum.**
10 Woodside Lane, P. O. Box
165, Westport, CT 06880

Mid-Southern Watercolorists.
6632 Waverly Pl., Little Rock,
AK 72207

**Middle East Exhibits & Training,
Inc.**
1761 N. St., N.W.,
Washington, DC 20036

**Middle Tennessee State Univ.,
Photographic Gallery.**
Murfreesboro, TN 37132 Tel
615-898-2491
Permanent Collections:
300 uncatalogued photographs.

**Middleborough Historical Assn.,
Inc.**
Jackson St., Middleborough,
MA 02346

**Middlebury College; Johnson
Gallery.**
Middlebury, VT 05753

**Middlebury Historical Society
Museum.**
22 S. Academy St., Wyoming,
NY 14591

**Middlesex County Historical
Society.**
151 Main St., Middletown, CT
06457

Middletown Fine Arts Center.
116 S. Main St., Middletown,
OH 45042

**Midland Art Coucil of the
Midland Center for Arts.**
1801 W. St. Andrews, Midland,
MI 48640

**Midlands Exposition Center South
Carolina State Historical
Museum.**
1615 Blanding St., Columbia,
SC 29202

Midwest Art History Society.
C/O Northwestern University,
Evanston, IL 60201

Mifflin County Historical Society.
53 N. Pine St., Lewistown, PA
17044

**Millikin University, Kirkland
Gallery; Kirkland Fine Arts
Center:**
Decatur, IL 62522

Mills College.
Seminary & Macarthur Blvd.,
P.O. Box 9973, Oakland, CA
94607

Mills College Art Gallery.
Seminary & MacArthur Blvd.,
Oakland, CA 94613

Mills House Art Gallery.
12732 Main St., Garden Grove,
CA 92640

**Mills Museum (Ogden L. Mills
Estate)**
Rte. 9, Staatsburg, NY 12580

Milwaukee Area Technical College; Kronquist Craft Gallery.
1015 N.6th St., Milwaukee, WI 53203

Milwaukee Art Center.
750 N. Lincoln Memorial Dr., Milwaukee, WI 53202 Tel 414-271-9508
Permanent Collections:
Ancient art to the present with emphasis on 19th and 20th century art and American art.

Milwaukee Public Library; Art & Music Dept.
814 W. Wisconsin Ave., Milwaukee, WI 53233

Milwaukee Public Museum.
800 Wells St., Milwaukee, WI 83233 Tel 414-278-2700
Permanent Collections:
Pre-Columbian Art and Archaeology.

Mind's Eye Gallery. *See Dickinson State College, Mind's Eye Gallery*

Miner, Alice T., Colonial Collection.
P. O. Box 334, Chazy, NY 12921

Minerva Area Historical Society.
City Hall, Minerva, OH 44657

Miniature Arts Society of New Jersey.
200 Chestnut St., Nutley, NJ 07110

Miniature Painters Sculptors & Gravers Society of Washington, D.C.
1711 Mass. Ave. N.W., Washington, DC 20036

Minneapolis College Art & Design Library & Media Center.
200 E. 25th St., Minneapolis, MN 55404

Minneapolis Institute of Arts.
2400 Third Ave S., Minneapolis, MN 55404 Tel 612-870-3176 MINNART
Permanent Collections:
Paintings, decorative arts, pre-Columbian arts, Oriental arts, prints, drawings, books on the history of books and printing, Gale Collection of Japanese prints, Pillsbury Collection of bronzes.

Minneapolis Public Library & Information Center; Art, Music & Film Dept.
300 Nicollett Hall, Minneapolis, MN 55401

Minnesota Historical Society.
690 Cedar St., Saint Paul, MN 55101

Minnesota Museum of Art, Permanent Collection Gallery.
305 St. Peter St., St. Paul, MN 55102 Tel 612-224-7431
Permanent Collections:
Chinese, Japanese and Korean art; African Art; Contemporary drawings and prints,; Contemporary Crafts; Contemporary Japanese prints and sculpture.

Minot Art Gallery, Minot Art Assn.
P.O. Box 325, Minot, ND 58701

Mint Museum of Art.
501 Hemstead Pl., P. O. Box 6011, Charlotte, NC 28207

Miramar Museum.
2217 Cedar Springs Rd., Dallas, TX 75201

Mission San Luis Rey.
4050 Mission Ave., San Luis Rey, CA 92068

Mississippi Art Colony.
C/O Alex M. Loeck; 2741 38th St., Meridian, MS 39301

Mississippi Dept. of Archives & History.
P.O. Box 571, Jackson, MS 39205

Mississippi Museum of Art.
P.O. Box 1330, Jackson, MS 39205 Tel 601-354-3538
Permanent Collections:
19th and 20th century American art. Regional Mississippi artists as well as those of national and international acclaim, mostly early 20th century to the present.

Mississippi University for Women; Art Gallery & Museum.
Fine Arts Bldg., Cleveland, MS 38733

Missouri State Museum.
State Capitol, Jefferson City, MO 65101

Mitchell County Historical Museum.
N. Seventh, Osage, IA 50461

Mitchell Museum.
P.O. Box 923, Mt. Vernon, IL 62864

Mobile Art Assn., Inc.. *See Mobile Art Association, Inc*

Mobile Art Association, Inc.
39 Alverson Rd., Mobile, AL 36608

Moffatt-Ladd House.
154 Market St., Portsmouth, NH 03801

Mohawk-Caughnawaga Museum.
R.D. 1, P.O. Box 6, Fonda, NY 12068

Mohawk Valley Museum.
620 Memorial Pkwy., Utica, NY 13501

Monastery Cloister of Saint Bernard.
16711 W. Dixie Hwy., N. Miami Beach, FL 33160

Monmouth College; Boone Oriental Library Fine Arts Collection.
Monmouth, IL 61462

Monmouth County Historial Assn.
70 Court St., Freehold, NJ 07728

Monmouth Museum & Cultural Center; Brookdale Community College.
Newman Springs Rd., Lincroft, NJ 07738

Monroe City-County Fine Arts Council.
1555 S. Raisinville Rd., Monroe, MI 48161

Monroe County Historical Society.
Ninth & Main St., Stroudsburg, PA 18360

Monroe, James House. *See Arts Club of Washington; James Monroe House*

Montalvo Center for the Arts.
P.O. Box 158, Saratoga, CA 95070

Montana Historical Society.
225 N. Roberts, Helena, MT 59601

Montana State Univ., Museum of the Rockies.
Bozeman, MT 59717

Montclair Art Museum.
P.O. Box X, Montclair, NJ 07042 Tel 201-746-5555
Permanent Collections:
American paintings; the Rand Collection of American Indian Art; American and European prints, drawings, sculptures, tapestries and needlepoint; Whitney Silver Collection; Chinese snuff bottles, costumes and accessories.

Monterey Historical & Art Assn.
P.O. Box 805, Monterey, CA 93940

Monterey Peninsula Museum of Art.
559 Pacific St., Monterey, CA 93940

Montgomery Museum of Fine Arts.
440 S. McDonough St., Montgomery, AL 36104 Tel 205-834-3490
Permanent Collections:
19th and 20th century American paintings; American and European drawings and prints.

Monticello.
Thomas Jefferson Memorial Foundation, VA 22902

Montville Historical Museum.
Taylortown Rd., Montville, NJ 07045

Monument House.
Park Ave., Groton, CT 06340

Moore College of Art Gallery.
20th & Race Sts., Philadelphia, PA 19104

Moravian Historical Society, Whitefield House Museum.
210 E. Center St., Nazareth, PA 18064

Moravian Museum of Bethlehem.
66 W. Church St., Bethlehem, PA 18018

Mordecai Square Historical Society, Inc.
1 Mimosa St., Raleigh, NC 27604

Moreau Gallery. *See Saint Mary's College, Moreau Gallery Art Dept*

Morehead State Univ., Claypool-Young Art Gallery.
Morehead, KY 40351

Morgan, Pierpont, Library.
29 E. 36th St., New York, NY 10016

Morgan State Univ. Gallery of Art.
Cold Spring Lane & Hillen, Baltimore, MD 21212

Morill, Justin Smith, Homestead.
Stafford, VT 05072

Morris-Butler Museum of High Victorian Decorative Arts.
Indianapolis, IN 46202

Morris-Jumel Mansion.
160th St. & Edgecombe Ave., New York, NY 10032

Morris Library.
South College Ave., Newark, DE 19711

Morris Museum of Arts & Science.
P.O. Box 125, Morristown, NJ 07961

Morris Museum of Arts & Sciences.
P.O. Box 125, Convent, NJ 07960

Morris Raphael Library Art Division. *See Cohen, Morris Raphael, Library, Art Division*

Morton Homestead.
Pennsyvania Rte. 420, Prospect Park, PA 19076

Mount Clare Mansion.
Carroll Park, Baltimore, MD 21230

Mount Holyoke College Art Museum.
South Hadley, MA 01075 Tel 413-538-2245

Mount Mary College; Tower Gallery.
2900 Menomonee River Pkwy., Milwaukee, WI 53222

Mount St. Mary's College Art Gallery.
12001 Chalon Rd., Los Angeles, CA 90049

Mount San Antonio College Art Gallery.
1100 N. Grand Ave., Walnut, CA 91789

Mount Vernon.
Mount Vernon, VA 22121

Mount Vernon Ladies Assn. of the Union.
Mount Vernon, VA 22121 Tel 703-780-2000
Permanent Collections:
Furniture, china, silver, paintings, prints, books and other memorabilia belonging to George and Martha Washington at Mount Vernon.

Mount Vernon Public Library.
28 S. First Ave., Mt. Vernon, NY 10550

Mount Wachusett Community College Art Galleries.
Green St., Gardner, MA 01440

Moxlan Gallery. *See* Transylvaina College, Moxlan Gallery

Muckenthaler Cultural Center.
1201 W. Malvern, Fullerton, CA 92633

Muhlenberg College Center for the Arts.
24th & Chew Sts., Allentown, PA 18104

Muir House.
Corner Second & Atlanta Sts., Brownville, NE 68321

Multnomah County Library, Henry Failing Art & Music.
Dept. 801 S.W. 10th Ave., Portland, OR 97205

Municipal Art Commission.
City Hall, 415 E. 11th St., Kansas City, MO 64106

Municipal Art Society of Baltimore City.
135 E. Baltimore St., Baltimore, MD 21202

Municipal Art Society of New York.
30 Rockefeller Plaza, New York, NY 10020

Munson Gallery.
33 Whitney Ave., New Haven, CT 06511

Munson-Williams-Proctor Institute, Museum of Art.
318 Genesee St., Utica, NY 13502
Permanent Collections:
Proctor collection of paintings, furniture and decorative arts; Root collection of American 20th century paintings, furniture and decorative arts; collection of American paintings, sculpture, furniture and decorative arts; ancient and archaic art; prints, drawings and watercolors.

Murray State Univ., Clara M. Eagle Gallery, Price Doyle Fine Arts Center.
Murray, KY 42071

Museo de San Elizario.
San Elizario, TX 78949

Museum.
P.O. Box 3131, Greenwood, SC 29646

Museum of African Art.
316-332 A St., N.E., Washington, DC 20002 Tel 202-547-7424

Museum of American Architecture & Decorative Arts.
7502 Fondren Rd., Houston Baptist College, Houston, TX 77036

Museum of American Comedy.
6 Hazelton Circle, Briarcliff, NY 10510

Museum of American Folk Art.
49 W. 53rd St., New York, NY 10019

Museum of American Treasures.
1315 E. Fourth St., National City, CA 92050

Museum of Anthropology.
Department of Anthropology, Washington State University, Pullman, WA 99163

Museum of Antiquities & Art, Hotel Arner.
Glenn Grove & Plumley Pl., Cathedral City, CA 92234

Museum of Art of Ogunquit.
Shore Rd., Ogunquit, ME 03907

Museum of Art, Science & Industry.
4450 Park Ave., Bridgeport, CT 06604

Museum of Arts & History.
1115 Sixth St., Port Huron, MI 48060

Museum of Arts & Sciences, Cuban Museum, Planetarium.
1040 Museum Blvd., Daytona Beach, FL 32014

Museum of Arts & Sciences Inc.
4182 Forsyth Rd., Macon, GA 31204 Tel 912-477-3232
Permanent Collections:
A collection of approximately 100 pieces of artwork, both two and three dimensional. Most mediums of painting and printing are present in the collection. Some of the more renowned artists whose works are in the collection are Salvador Dali, Alexander Calder and James Whistler.

Museum of Bronx History. *See* Valentine-Varian House, Museum of Bronx History

Museum of Cartoon Art.
384 Field Point Rd., Greenwich, CT 06830

Museum of City of New York.
1220 Fifth Ave., New York, NY 10029

Museum of Contemporary Art.
237 E. Ontairo St., Chicago, IL 60611

Museum of Early Southern Decorative Arts.
Drawer F, Salem Station, Winston-Salem, NC 27108 Tel 919-722-6148
Permanent Collections:
Ceramics, furniture, paintings, metals and textiles in period settings prior to 1820 which were made south of Maryland.

Museum of Fine Arts.
P.O. Box 2826, Houston, TX 77005

Museum of Fine Arts.
49 Chestnut St., Springfield, MA 01103

Museum of Fine Arts.
465 Huntington Ave., Boston, MA 02115 Tel 617-267-9300

Museum of Fine Arts.
255 Beach Dr. N., St. Petersburg, FL 33701 Tel 813-896-2667

Museum of History & Industry.
2161 E. Hamlin St., Seattle, WA 98112

Museum of International Folk Art. *See* Museum of New Mexico, Museum of International Folk Art

Museum of Local History.
Town Hall, Main Canada Dr., Chestertown, NY 12817

Museum of Modern Art.
11 W. 53rd St., New York, NY 10019 Tel 212-956-6100
MODERNART
Permanent Collections:
Paintings, sculpture, drawings, prints and illustrated books, architecture and design, film and photography.

Museum of Modern Art of Latin America.
17th & Constitution N.W., Washington, DC 20006

Museum of National Center of Afro-American Artists.
122 Elm Hill Ave., Dorchester, MA 02121

Museum of New Mexico, Museum of Fine Arts.
Santa Fe, NM 87501

Museum of New Mexico, Museum of International Folk Art.
P.O. Box 2087, Santa Fe, NM 87503 Tel 505-827-2544

Museum of Northern Arizona.
Rte. 4, Box 720, Flagstaff, AZ 86001
Permanent Collections:
Anthropology, geology, biology of Colorado Plateau, 4,000 piece Pueblo pottery collection.

Museum of Old Dolls & Toys.
1530 Sixth St., N.W., U.S. 17 North, Winterhaven, FL 33880

Museum of Philadelphia Civic Center.
Civic Center Blvd. at 34th, Philadelphia, PA 19104

Museum of Texas Technical Univ.
P.O. Box 4499, Lubbock, TX 79409

Museum of the American Indian. *See* Heye Foundation; Museum of the American Indian

Museum of the American Indian, Huntington Free Library.
9 Westchester Square, Bronx, NY 10461
Permanent Collections:
40,000 volumes on the archaeology and ethnology of the Indians of the entire Western Hemisphere.

Museum of the Americas. *See* College of the Americas; Museum of the Americas

Museum of the Great Plains.
P. O. Box 68, Lawton, OK 73502 Tel 405-353-5676

Museum of the Great Plains. *See* Institute of the Great Plains, Museum of the Great Plains

Museum of the Hudson Highlands.
The Blvd., Cornwall on Hudson, NY 12520

Museum of the National Center of Afro-American Artists.
122 Elm Hill Ave., Dorchester, MA 02121

"Museum of the North & the South".
Rte. 1, P.O. Box 361, Kingsley Lake, Starke, FL 32091

Museum of the Plains Indians.
P.O. Box 400, Browning, MT 59417

Museum of the Southwest.
1705 W. Missouri, Midland, TX 79701

Museum of the Tamworth Historical Society, Inc.
Center of the Village, Tamworth, NH 03886

Museum of the United States Department of the Interior.
C St.- 18th & 19th Sts. N.W., Washington, DC 20240

Museum of York County.
Rte. 4, Box 211, Mt. Gallant Rd., Rock Hill, SC 29730

Museum Society of Petersburg.
Front St., Petersburg, AK 99833

Museum Without Walls, RCEDA.
P.O. Box 45 Morris Ave., Friendsville, MD 21531

Museums at Stony Brook.
Rte. 25A, Stony Brook, NY 11790

Music & Art Foundation.
710 E. Roy St., Seattle, WA 98102

Musser, Laura, Art Gallery & Museum.
1314 Mulberry Ave, Muscatine, IA 52761

Mystic Art Association, Inc.
P.O. Box 259, Mystic, CT 06355

Mystic Seaport Museum, Inc.
Greemanville Ave., Mystic, CT 06355

Nasson College, Anderson Learning Center.
Braden St., Springvale, ME 04083

Natchez Trace Parkway.
R.R. 5, N.T. 143, Tupelo, MS 38801

Nathaniel W. Faisson Home & Museum. *See* Faison, Nathaniel W., Home & Museum

National Academy of Design.
1083 Fifth Ave., New York, NY 10028
Permanent Collections:
American art since 1825; paintings, sculptures, graphic arts, architectural drawings and photographs.

National Air & Space Museum.
Seventh St. & Independence Ave. S.W., Washington, DC 20560

National Architectural Accrediting Board Inc.
1735 New York Ave. N.W., Washington, DC 20006

National Art Education Assn.
1916 Association Dr., Reston,
VA 22091

National Art League.
44-21 Douglaston Pkwy.,
Douglaston, NY 11360

National Art Museum of Sports.
4 Penn Plaza, New York, NY
10001

**National Association of Women
Artists Inc.:**
41 Union Square, New York,
NY 10003

National Cartoonists Society.
9 Ebony Court, Brooklyn, NY
11229

National Collection Fine Arts.
Eighth & G Sts., N.W.,
Washington, DC 20560

**National Council for Arts &
Education.**
743 Fifth Ave., New York, NY
10022

**National Council of Architectural
Registration Boards.**
1735 New York Ave., N.W.,
Suite 700, Washington, DC
20006

**National Cowboy Hall of Fame &
Western Heritage Center.**
1700 N.E. 63rd St., Oklahoma
City, OK 73111

National Endowment for the Arts.
2401 E St. N.W., Washington,
DC 20560

National Gallery of Art.
Constitution Ave. & Sixth St.,
N.W., Washington, DC 20565
Tel 202-737-4215

**National Geographic Society-
Explorers Hall.**
17th & M Sts., N.W.,
Washington, DC 20036

**National Hall of Fame for Famous
American Indians.**
Hwy. 62, Box 808, Anadarko,
OK 73005

**National History Museum of Los
Angeles County.**
900 Exposition Blvd., Los
Angeles, CA 90007

National Infantry Museum.
Bldg. 396, Baltzell Ave., Ft.
Benning, GA 31905

**National Institute of Arts &
Letters.**
633 E. 155th St., New York,
NY 10032

National Museum of Design. *See*
**Cooper-Hewitt Museum
Smithsonian Institution;
National Museum of Design**

**National Museum of History &
Technology, Smithsonian
Institution.**
Constitution Ave., 12th & 14th
Sts., N.W., Washington, DC
20560

National Museum of Racing, Inc.
Union Ave, Saratoga Springs,
NY

**National Park Service; Federal
Hall National Memorial.**
26 Wall St., New York, NY
10017

National Portrait Gallery.
F St. at Eighth, N.W.,
Washington, DC 20560 Tel
202-381-6428
Permanent Collections:
Portraits in a vast range of
media, of men and women who
have made significant
contributions to the history,
development and culture of the
United States.

National Sculpture Society.
777 Third Ave., New York,
NY 10017 Tel 212-838-5218

**National Socety of the Colonial
Dames of America in the State
of North Carolina.**
224 Market St., Wilmington,
NC 28401

**National Society Daughters of the
American Revolution Museum.**
1776 D St., N.W., Washington,
DC 20006

**National Society of Children of
American Revolution Museum.**
1776 D St., N.W., Washington,
DC 20006

**National Society of Colonial
Dames of America in the State
of Maryland.**
Mt. Clare Mansion, Carroll
Park, Baltimore, MD 21230

**National Society of Mural
Painters.**
1083 Fifth Ave., New York,
NY 10021

**National Society of Painters in
Casein & Acrylic Inc.**
1083 Fifth Ave., New York,
NY 10028

**National Trust for Historic
Preservation.**
740-748 Jackson Place, N.W.,
Washington, DC 20006

National Watercolor Society.
401 Cascada Way, Los
Angeles, CA 90049

**Nationial Trust for Historic
Preservation.**
740-748 Jackson Place, N.W.,
Washington, DC 20006

**Native American Painting
Reference Library.**
Box 32504, Oklahoma City,
OK 73132 Tel 405-721-5743
Permanent Collections:
Lithographs, photo-offset
lithographs, silkscreens and
pochoirs of Native American
paintings organized into
travelling educational exhibits
for schools and libraries.

Navajo National Monument.
Tonalea, AZ 86044

Navajo Tribal Museum.
Box 308, Window Rock, AZ
85615 Tel 602-871-6457

Naval Amphibious Museum.
Naval Amphibious Base, Little
Creek, Norfolk, VA 23521

Nebraska State Capitol.
1449 K St., Lincoln, NE 68509

**Nebraska Wesleyan Univ., Elder
Gallery.**
50th & Huntington, Lincoln,
NE 68504

Nelson, Richard L., Gallery.
Dept. of Art, Univ. of
California, Davis, Davis, CA
95616

**Nelson, William Rockhill, Gallery
of Art; Atkins Museum of Fine
Arts.**
4525 Oak St., Kansas City,
MO 64111 Tel 816-561-4000
NELTRUST

**Nelson Pioneer Farm & Crafts
Museum.**
R.R. 1, P.O. Box 578,
Oskaloosa, IA 52577

Nelville Public Museum.
129 S. Jefferson, Green Bay,
WI 54301

Neville Public Museum.
129 S. Jefferson St., Green
Bay, WI 54301

New Bedford Whaling Museum.
18 Johnny Cake Hill, New
Bedford, MA 02740
Permanent Collections:
Implements, gear and
decorative arts of the American
whaling industry; paintings and
prints of New Bedford artists;
furniture and decorative arts of
the New Bedford area.

**New Britian Museum of American
Art.**
56 Lexington St, New Britian,
CT 06050

New Castle Historical Society.
2 E. Fourth St., New Castle,
DE 19720

**New Glarus Historical Society,
Inc.**
Sixth Ave. & Seventh St., New
Glarus, WI 53574

New Hampshire Art Assn., Inc.
24 W. Bridge St., Manchester,
NH 03105

**New Hampshire Historical
Society.**
30 Park St., Concord, NH
03301 Tel 603-225-3381
Permanent Collections:
New Hampshire decorative arts
and historical artifacts.

New Haven Paint & Clay Club.
51 Trumbull St., New Haven,
CT 06510

**New Jersey Historical Society
Museum.**
230 Broadway, Newark, NJ
07104
Permanent Collections:
New Jersey fine and decorative
arts, costumes and textiles,
prints, photographs, furniture,
coins, currency, housewares,
patent models, Yarnell
Maritime Collection, Alofsen

and Stoudinger Collections of
technical drawings by Fulton,
Latrode, etc.

New Jersey State Museum.
205 W. State St., Trenton, NJ
08625

New Jersey Watercolor Society.
554 Bloomfield Ave.,
Bloomfield, NJ 07003

**New London County Historical
Society.**
11 Blinman St., New London,
CT 06320

**New Mexico Art League; Ken
Roberts Gallery.**
3401 Juan Tabo N.E.,
Albuquerque, NM 87111

**New Mexico Highlands University
Art Gallery.**
National Ave., Las Vegas, NM

New Mexico State Univ. Museum.
P.O. Box 3564, Las Cruces,
NM 88001

New Milford Historical Society.
6 Aspetuck Ave., New Milford,
CT 06776

New Museum.
65 Fifth Ave., New York, NY
10003 Tel 212-741-8962

**New Museum Community
Museum of Brooklyn Inc.**
1530 Bedford Ave., Brooklyn,
NY 11216 Tel 212-774-2968

New Orleans Museum of Art.
P.O. Box 19123, New Orleans,
LA 70179 Tel 504-488-2631
Permanent Collections:
Old master paintings of various
schools; Kress Collection of
Italian Renaissance and
Baroque painting; Chapman H.
Hyams Collection of Barbizon
and Salon paintings; Pre-
Columbian masterworks from
Mexico, Central and South
America; Latin Colonial
painting and sculpture; works
of Edgar Degas; 20th century
European art, featuring
Surrealism and the school of
Paris; Chinese and Japanese
art; African art; photography
and graphics; Melvin P. Billups
Glass Collection; 19th and 20th
century United States and
Louisiana painting and
sculpture; Latter-Schlesinger
Collection of European portrait
miniatures.

New Orleans Public Library.
219 Loyola Ave., New Orleans,
LA 70140

**New School for Social Research
Art Center.**
65 Fifth Ave., New York, NY
10003

**New York Chamber of Commerce
and Industry.**
65 Liberty St., New York, NY
10005

New York Historical Society.
170 Central Park West, New
York, NY 10024 Tel 212-873-
3400
Permanent Collections:
American portraits, American
Silver, American landscapes
and genre, original watercolors
by John James Audobon for

Birds of America, paperweights, period furniture, John Roger's sculpture, American toys, American folk art.

New York Institute of Technology.
Wheatley Rd., Old Westbury, NY 11568

New York Public Library.
Fifth Ave. & 42nd St., New York, NY 10018

New York Society of Architects.
101 Park Ave., New York, NY 10017

New York State College of Ceramics at Alfred Univ.
State St., Alfred, NY 14802 Tel 607-871-2411
Permanent Collections:
Silverman Collection of modern glass

New York State Historic Trust.
Parks & Recreation Executive Dept., Albany, NY 12266

New York State Historical Assn., Fenimore House.
P.O. Box 391, Cooperstown, NY 13326 Tel 607-547-2533
Permanent Collections:
American folk art; American academic art - 19th century (Fenimore House), Agricultural tools and implements (The Farmer's Museum).

New York State Library.
State Education Bldg., Albany, NY 12234

New York University Art Collection:
100 Washington Square East, New York, NY 10003

Newark Museum.
49 Washington St., P.O. Box 540, Newark, NJ 07101 Tel 201-733-6600
Permanent Collections:
American painting and sculpture, American decorative arts, Oriental Collections, Classical (Greek, Roman, Egyptian) Collection, Ethnology Collection (African, American Indian).

Newport Clock Museum.
43 Park St., Newport, NH 03801

Newport Harbor Art Museum.
850 San Clemente Dr., Newport Beach, CA 92660

Newport Historical Society.
82 Touro St., Newport, RI 02840

Newtown Historic Assn., Inc.
Court St. & Centre Ave., Newtown, PA 18940

Ney, Elisabet, Museum.
304 E. 44th St., Austin, TX 78751 Tel 512-458-2255
Permanent Collections:
Nineteenth century sculptures in plaster, marble and bronze by German-American sculptress Elisabet Ney. Also furnishings, tools, letters and memorabilia related to her.

Niagara County Community College Art Gallery.
3111 Saunders Settlement Rd., Sanborn, NY 14132

Nicholas Roerich Museum. *See* **Roerich, Nicholas, Museum**

Ninety-Second Street Ymha-Ywha, Weill Art Gallery:
1395 Lexington Ave., New York, NY 10028

No Man's Island Historical Society.
Sewell St., Goodwell, OK 73939

Nobles County Art Center Gallery.
416 12th St., P.O. Box 281, Worthington, MN 56187

Nodena Site.
Nodena Plantation, Wilson, AR 72395

Nome Arts Council.
Box 233, Nome, AK 99762

Nome Museum.
Front St., Nome, AZ 99762

Norstrand Visual Arts Gallery & Fine Arts Center. *See* **Wayne State College, Norstrand Visual Arts Gallery & Fine Arts Center**

North Andover Historical Society.
153 Academy Rd. P.O. Box 266, North Andover, MA 08145

North Canton Public Library, Little Art Gallery.
185 N.Main St., North Canton, OH 44720

North Carolina Art Society.
107 E. Morgan St., Raleigh, NC 27601

North Carolina Central Univ., Museum of Arts.
Fayetteville St., Durham, NC 27707

North Carolina Council.
Drawer F, Salem Station, Winston-Salem, NC 27108

North Carolina Museum of Art.
Raleigh, NC 27611 Tel 919-733-7568
Permanent Collections:
European and American painting and scultpure; ancient art; African, Pre-Columbian, Oceanic art; Samuel H. Kress Collection.

North Carolina Office of Archives & History.
109 E. Jones St., Raleigh, NC 27602

North Carolina State Univ., Harrye Lyons Design Library.
Brooks Hall, Raleigh, NC 27650

North River Community Gallery. *See* **Northeastern Illinois Univ., North River Community Gallery**

North Shore Art League.
Winnetka Community House 620 Lincoln, Winnetka, IL 60093

North Shore Arts Assn., Inc.
Rear 197 E. Main St., Gloucester, MA 01930

North Texas State Univ. Art Gallery.
N. Texas Box 5098, Denton, TX 76203

Northampton Historical Society.
58 Bridge St., Northampton, MA 01060

Northborough Historical Society, Inc.
Main St., Northborough, MA 01532

Northeastern Illinois Univ., North River Community Gallery.
3307 W. Bryn Mawr, Chicago, IL 60659

Northeastern Nevada Museum.
1515 Idaho St., P.O. Box 503, Elko, NV 89801

Northern Arizona Univ. Art Gallery.
Box 6021, Flagstaff, AZ 86331

Northern Arizona Univ. Art Gallery.
Kip House (Dutchess County), Flagstaff, AZ 86001

Northern Bible Society.
715 W. Superior St., Duluth, MI 55802

Northern Illinois Univ., Swen Parson Gallery.
Dekalb, IL 60115 Tel 815-753-0292, 38-*C
Permanent Collections:
Pfaelger Collection, NIU Foundation Collection, Student Association Collection and Art Department Collection.

Northern Indiana Historical Society.
112 S. Lafayette Blvd., South Bend, IN 46601

Northern Michigan Univ., Lee Hall Gallery.
Marquette, MI 49855

Northern Oklahoma College.
1220 E. Grand, Tonkawa, OK 74653

Northern Virginia Fine Arts Assn.
201 Prince St., Alexandria, VA 22314

Northwest Missouri State Univ., Deluce Gallery.
Maryville, MO 64468

Northwestern College, Ramaker Library Art Gallery.
101 Seventh St. S.W., Orange City, IA 51041

Northwestern University Library Art Collection:
Evanston, IL 60201

Norton, R.W., Art Gallery.
4700 Block of Creswell Ave., Shreveport, LA 71106 Tel 318-865-4201
Permanent Collections:
American and European paintings, drawings, sculpture and decorative arts; Frederic Remington and Charles M. Russell Collections; Numismatics; antique firearms.

Norton Gallery & School of Art.
1451 S. Olive Ave., West Palm Beach, FL 33401

Norton Simon Inc. Museum of Art. *See* **Simon, Norton, Inc. Museum of Art**

Norwich Free Academy.
108 Crescent St., Norwich, CT 06360

Norwood Historical Society, Inc.
93 Day St., Norwood, MA 02062

Noyes, Read & Gray Galleries. *See* **Antioch College, Noyes, Read & Gray Galleries**

Nutley Historical Society Museum.
65 Church St., Nutley, NJ 07110

O. Henry Museum. *See* **Henry, O., Museum**

Oak Ridge Community Art Center.
P.O. Box 105, Oak Ridge, TN 37830

Oakland University, Meadow Brook Art Gallery:
Rochester, MI

Oakley, Violet, Memorial Foundation.
627 St. George's Rd., Philadelphia, PA 19119

Oatlands.
P. O. Box 352, Leesburg, VA 22075

Oberlin College , Allen Memorial Art Museum.
Main & Lorain Sts., Oberlin, OH 44074

Occidental College, Thorne Hall.
1600 Campus Rd., Los Angeles, CA 00041

Ocean City Historical Museum.
409 Wesley Ave., Ocean City, NJ 08226

Oceanport Historical Society.
Oceanport Municipal Bldg., Oceanport, NJ 07757

Octagon. *See* **American Institute of Architects Foundation; The Octagon**

Octagone Center for Arts.
232 1/2 Main, Ames, IA 50010

Odel Mar College, Dept. of Art Gallery.
Baldwin at Avers, Corpus Christi, TX 78404

Oglebay Institute Mansion Museum.
Oglebay Park, Wheeling, WV 26003

Ohio Historical Society.
1982 Velma Ave., Columbus, OH 43211

Ohio State Univ., Gallery of Fine Art.
128 N. Oval Mall, Columbus, OH 43210 Tel 614-422-2395
Permanent Collections:
Contemporary collections.

Ohio University, A. G. Trisolini Memorial Gallery.
48 E. Union St., Athens, OH 45701

Ohio Wesleyan University, Department of Fine Arts.
Humphreys Art Hall, Delaware, OH 43015

Ojai Valley Art Center.
113 S. Montgomey, Ojai, CA 93023

Okanogan County Historical Society.
County Court House, Okanogan, WA 98840

Oklahoma Art Center.
Plaza Circle Fair Park, 3113 Pershing Blvd., Oklahoma City, OK 73107 Tel 405-946-4477
Permanent Collections:
Primarily 20th century American art; some Indian art.

Oklahoma Historical Society, Division of Museums.
Historical Bldg., Oklahoma City, OK 73105

Oklahoma Museum of Art.
7316 Nichols Rd., Oklahoma, OK 73120 Tel 405-840-2759

Oklahoma State University, Gardiner Art Gallery.
Morrill & Knoblock Sts., Stillwater, OK 74074

Olana State Historic Site.
P. O. Box 199, Hudson, NY 12534
Permanent Collections:
Nineteenth century American art collection of F.E. Church, 19th century decorative arts collection, archival collection, 19th century mansion and landscaped estate.

Old Agency House.
P. O. Box 84, Portage, WI 53901

Old Barracks.
S. Willow St., Trenton, NJ 08608

Old Blandford Church & Interpretation Center.
319 S. Crater Rd., Petersburg, VA 23803

Old Bohemia Historical Society, Inc.
P.O. Box 61, Warwick, MD 21912

Old Castle Museum.
Fifth St., Baldwin City, KS 66006

Old Constitution House.
N. Main St., Windsor, VT 05089

Old Court House.
State Historic Site, Arrow Rock, MO 65320

Old Dominion University Gallery:
Hampton Blvd., Norfolk, VA 23508

Old Dutch Parsonage.
38 Washington Pl., Somerville, NJ 08876

Old Economy Village.
14th & Church Sts., Ambrige, PA 15003

Old Fort Harrod Mansion Museum.
Old Fort Harrod State Park, Harrodsburg, KY 40330

Old Frontier Museum.
Oskaloosa, KS 66066

Old Gaol Museum.
York St. & Lindsay Rd., York, ME 03909

Old House.
Main Rd., Cutchogue, NY 11935

Old Jail Museum and Felker House.
Vienna, MO 65582

Old Parsonage.
Newington, NH 03801

Old Place Plantation.
Highway 90, Gautier, MO 39553

Old Slave Mart Museum.
6 Chalmers St., Charleston, SC 29401

Old Spanish Fort & Museum.
4602 Fort St., Pascagoula, MS 39567

Old State House, Bostonian Society.
206 Washington St., Boston, MA 02109

Old State House in Newport, Rhode Island, Inc.
Washington Square, Newport, RI 02840

Old Stone Church.
194 14th St., Osawatomie, KS 66064

Old Sturbridge Village.
Sturbridge, MA 01566

Olde Princess Anne Days, Inc.
Mansion St., Princess Anne, MD 21853

Olivet College, Armstrong Museum of Art & Archaeology.
Olivet, MI 49076

Omniplex, Kirkpatrick Center.
2100 N.E. 52nd, Oklahoma City, OK 73111

Once Gallery Inc., Automation House.
49 E. 68th St., New York, NY 10021

Ononadaga Historical Assn.
311 Montgomery St., Syracuse, NY 13202

Ontario City Library.
215 East C St., Ontario, CA 91764 Tel 714-984-2758
Permanent Collections:
Special collection of 16,000 pictures and photographs on almost every conceivable subject including copies of the world's most famous art.

Orange County Community of Museums & Galleries.
101 Main St., P.O. Box 527, Goshen, NY 10924

Orange County Public Library.
11200 Stanford Ave., Garden Grove, CA 92640

Orange Johnson House.
956 High St., P.O. Box 355, Worthington, OH 43085

Orchard Lake Schools Galeria.
Orchard Lake, MI 48033

Orchard Park Historical Society.
5800 Armor Rd., Orchard Park, NY 14127

Oregon College of Education.
Gallery 107, Monmouth, OR 97361

Oregon Historical Society.
1230 S.W. Park Ave., Portland, OR 97205

Oregon State Univ. Horner Museum, Gill Coliseum.
26th near Western, Corvallis, OR 97331

Oregon Trail Museum.
P.O. Box 427, Gering, NE 69341

Organization of American States, General Secretariat.
17th & Constitution, N.W., Washington, DC 20006

Orlando Brown House. See Brown, Orlando, House

Osborn Foundation. See World Museum Art Center, Osborn Foundation

Oscar Howe Cultural Center. See Howe, Oscar, Cultural Center

Oshkosh Public Museum.
1331 Algoma Blvd, Oshkosh, WI 54901

Ossining Historical Society Museum.
196 Croton Ave., Ossining, NY 10562

Oswego County Historical Society.
Richardson-Bates House, 135 E. Third St., P.O. Box 1072, Oswego, NY 13126

Otis Art Institute Gallery.
2410 Wilshire Blvd., Los Angeles, CA 90057

Otis House. See Society for Preservation of New England Antiquities, Otis House

Our House Memorial.
434 First Ave., Gallipolis, OH 45631

Overland Trail Museum.
1320 S. Fourth Ave., Sterling, CO 80751

Owatonna Arts Center.
P.O. Box 134, Owatonna, MN 55060 Tel 507-451-4540
Permanent Collections:
Local artists and the Marianne Young World Costume Collection

Oysterponds Historical Society.
Village Lane, Orient, NY 11957

Pace University; Art Gallery.
Bedford Rd., Pleasantville, NY 10510

Pacific Center for Western Historical Studies. See University of the Pacific, Pacific Center for Western Historical Studies

Pacific Grove Art Center.
568 Lighthouse Ave., Drawer 700, Pacific Grove, CA 93950

Pacific Northwest Arts & Crafts Assn.
10310 N.E. Fourth St., Bellevue, WA 98004

Pacific University Museum:
Forest Grove, OR 97116

Pacificulture-Asia Museum.
46 N. Los Robles Ave., Pasadena, CA 91101

Pack Memorial Public Library.
Haywood St., NC 28801

Paducah Art Guild.
P.O. Box 634, Paducah, KY 42001

Paine Art Center & Arboretius.
1410algona St., P.O. Box 1097, Oshkosh, WI 54901

Paint 'n' Pallette Club.
204 N. Huber St., Anamosa, IA 52202

Painters & Sculptors Society.
340 W. 28th St., New York, NY 10001

Palestine Institute Museum, Pacific School of Religion.
1798 Scenic Av., Berkley, CA 94709

Palette & Chisel Academy of Fine Arts.
1012 N. Dearborn St., Chicago, IL 60610

Palisades Interstate Park Commission; Senate House State Historic Site.
296 Fair St., Kingston, NY 12401

Palm Beach County Historical Society, Henry Morrison Flagler Museum.
Whitehall Way, Palm Beach, FL 33480

Palm Springs Desert Museum.
P.O. Box 2288, Palm Springs, CA 92262

Palo Alto Cultural Center.
1313 Newell Rd., Palo Alto, CA 94303

Palo Alto Jr. Museum & Zoo.
1451 Middlefield Rd., Palo Alto, CA 94301

Palomar Community College, Boehm Gallery.
1140 W. Mission Rd., San Marcos, CA 92069

Palos Verdes Art Center.
5504 W. Crestridge Rd., Rancho Palos Verdes, CA 90274

Panhandle-Plains Historical Society Museum.
2401 4th Ave., Canyon, TX 79015

Paper Mill Playhouse.
Brookside Dr., Millburn, NJ 07041

Parker, E. M., Indian Museum.
247 E. Main St., Brookville, PA 15825

Parker & Russell Silver Shop.
The Street, Deerfield, MA 01342

Parker Historical Society of Clay County.
300 E. Third St., Spencer, IA 51301

Parkersburg Art Center.
P. O. Box 131, Parkersburg, WV 26101

Parrish Art Museum.
25 Jobs Lane, Southampton, NY 11968

Parson Fisher House; Jonathan Fisher Memorial Inc.
Blue Hill, ME 04614

Parsons Museum.
1808 Washington Ave., Parsons, KS 67357

Parsons School of Design.
66 Fifth Ave., New York, NY 10011

Pasadena City College Art Gallery.
1570 E. Colorado Blvd., Pasadena, CA 91106

Pasadena Historical Society Museum.
470 W. Walnut St., Pasadena, CA 91103

Passaic Community Historical Society; Lambert Castle.
P.O. Box 1729, Paterson, NJ 07509

Passaic County Historical Society.
P.O. Box 1729, Paterson, NJ 07509

Paterson Memorial Museum.
210 N. Bridge St., Smithville, MO 64089

Patterson Library.
40 S. Portage St., Westfield, NY 10996

Paul Sargent Gallery. *See* Sargent, Paul, Gallery

Payson Gallery. *See* Westbrook College, Joan Whitney Payson Gallery

Peabody, Robert S., Foundation for Archaeology.
Corner of Phillips & Main St., Andover, MA 01810

Peabody Museum of Archaeology & Ethnology.
Harvard Univ., 11 Divinity Ave., Cambridge, MA 02138

Peabody Museum of Salem.
East India Square, Salem, MA 01970

Peale Museum, Municipal Museum of the City of Baltimore.
225 Holliday St., Baltimore, MD 21202 Tel 301-396-3523
Permanent Collections:
Hambleton Collection of Historic Prints of Baltimore; John Dubas Photographic Collection, Baltimore 1910-1965; A. Aubrey Bodine Photographic Collection, 1920-

1965; Photo-Baltimore '77, by six photographers; Robert Harris Photographic Collection, 1900-1925; Peale Museum Collection of paintings, prints, photographs and maps.

Peary-MacMillan Arctic Museum. *See* Bowdoin College Museum of Art & Peary-MacMillan Arctic Museum

Pejepscot Historical Society.
12 School St., Brunswick, ME 04011

Pemaquid Group of Artists.
Lighthouse Park, Bristol, ME 04539

Pen & Brush Inc.
16 E. Tenth St., New York, NY 10003

Penebscot Maine Museum.
Church St., Searsport, ME 04974

Peninsula Arts Assn.
Box 6438, Newport News, VA 23606

Penn, William, Memorial Museum. *See* Pennsylvania Historical & Museum Commission, William Penn Memorial Museum

Pennsbury Manor.
R. D. 9, Morrisville, PA 19067

Pennsylvania Academy of Fine Arts.
Broad & Cherry Sts., Philadelphia, PA 19102

Pennsylvania Department of Education, Division of General Education, Arts in Education Program.
Box 911, Harrisburg, PA 17126

Pennsylvania Farm Museum of Landis Valley.
2451 Kissel Hill Rd., Lancaster, PA 17601

Pennsylvania Historical & Museum Commission, William Penn Memorial Museum.
Box 1026, Harrisburg, PA 17120

Pennsylvania State Univ. Museum of Art.
University Park, PA 16802

Pensacola Art Center.
407 S. Jefferson St., Pensacola, FL 32501

Pensacola Historical Museum.
405 Adams St., Pensacola, FL 32501

Pensacola Museum of Art.
407 S. Jefferson St., Pensacola, FL 32501

Peoria Art Guild.
1831 N. Knoxville, Peoria, IL 61603

Percy H. Whiting Art Center. *See* Whiting, Percy H., Art Center

Permanent Collection Gallery. *See* Minnesota Museum of Art, Permanent Collection Gallery

Perry County History Museum.
S. Columbus St., Somerset, OH 43783

Pete Kitchen Museum.
Pete Kitchen Ranch, Nogales, AZ 85621

Peterborough Historical Society.
Grove St., P. O. Box 58, Peterborough, NH 03458

Petersham Historical Society, Inc.
N. Main St., Petersham, MA 01366

Pettigrew Museum.
131 N. Duluth Ave., Sioux Falls, SD 57104

Pettis County Museum.
502 E. Fourth St., Sedalia, MO 65301

Phelps County Historical Society.
1020 Sherman St., Holdrege, NE 68949

Phetteplace Museum.
115 Inlay Ave., Wauzeka, WI 53826

Philadelphia Art Alliance.
251 S. 18th St., Philadelphia, PA 19103

Philadelphia Art Commission.
1329 City Hall Annex, Philadelphia, PA 19107

Philadelphia College of Art.
Broad & Spruce Sts., Philadelphia, PA 19102 Tel 215-893-3100

Philadelphia Maritime Museum.
321 Chestnut St., Philadelphia, PA 19106 Tel 215-925-5439

Philadelphia Museum of Art.
26th & Pkwy., Box 7646, Philadelphia, PA 19101

Philadelphia Sketch Club.
235 S. Camac St., Philadelphia, PA 19107

Philbrook Art Center.
2727 S. Rockford Rd., Tulsa, OK 74114
Permanent Collections:
Kress Collection of Italian Renaissance Art; Laura Clubb Collection of 19th century paintings (American and European); Clark Field Collection of Southwestern Indian Baskets and Pottery; Gussman Collection of African Art; Gillert Collection of Southeast Asian Ceramics; Tabor Collection of Chinese Art; also collections of contemporary American Indian paintings, Indian cultural material, some decorative arts.

Philip H. & A.S.W. Rosenbach Foundation Museum. *See* Rosenbach, Philip H. & A.S.W., Foundation Museum

Philipse Manor Hall, State Historic Site.
P.O. Box 496, Warburton Ave. & Dock St., Yonkers, NY 10702
Permanent Collections:
American portraits and furniture from the 18th and 19th centuries.

Phillips Academy, Addison Gallery of American Art.
P.O. Box 48, Andover, MA 01810

Phillips Collection.
1600-1612 21st St., N.W., Washington, DC 20009 Tel 202-387-2151
Permanent Collections:
19th and 20th century European and American painting, with special emphasis on Impressionism and modern European painting, notable "units" of Bonnard, Daumier, Klee, Braque, Dove, Maria, O'Keeffe, Knaths, many others.

Phillips County Museum.
623 Pecan St., Helena, AK 72342

Phillips Exeter Academy, Lamont Gallery.
Exeter, NH 03833

Phillips Historical Society.
Pleasant St., P. O. Box 55, Phillips, ME 04966

Phillips University, Grace Phillips Johnson Art Gallery:
University Station, Enid, OK 73701

Phoenix Art Museum.
1625 N. Central Ave., Phoenix, AZ 85004

Piatt Castles.
Rural Rte. 2, West Liberty, OH 43357

Pierpont Morgan Library. *See* Morgan, Pierpont, Library

Pilgrim Society.
75 Court St., Plymouth, MA 02360

Pilgrim Society, Pilgrim Hall.
75 Court St., Plymouth, MA 02360 Tel 615-746-1620
Permanent Collections:
Pilgrim artifacts

Pimeria Alta Historical Society.
Grand Ave. P. O. Box 2281, Nogales, AZ 85621

Pioneer Museum.
Hwy. A, Wild Rose, WI 54984

Pioneer Museum & Haggin Gallery.
1201 N. Pershing Ave., Stockton, CA 95203

Pioneer Town.
7A Ranch Resort, Box 259, Rte. 1, Wimberly, TX 78676

Pioneer Village.
Minden, NE 58959

Pioneer Washington Restoration Foundation.
Washington, AR 71862

Pioneer Woman Statue, Museum & State Park.
701 Monument Rd., Ponca City, OK 74601

Pittsburg Historical Society.
Civic Ave., Pittsburg, CA 94565

Pittsburgh Plan for Art, Gallery.
407 S. Craig St., Pittsburgh, PA 15213

Plains Art Museum.
521 Main Ave., Moorehead, MN 56560
Permanent Collections:
Works by Rosenquist, Scholder,

Jimenez, Warhol, Lichtenstein, Dali, etc.

Plains Indians & Pioneer Historical Foundation.
Box 1167, 73801

Plant, Henry B., Museum.
401 W. Kennedy Blvd., Tampa, FL 33606

Plantation Museum, Inc.
P.O. Box 38, Scott, AR 72142

Plastic Club, Art Club for Women.
247 S. Comac St., Woodward, OK 19107

Plymouth Antiquarian Society.
27 N. St., Plymouth, MA 02360

Plymouth Plantation, Inc.
Warren Ave., Plymouth, MA 02360

Plymouth State College, Herbert H. Lamson Library.
Plymouth, NH 03264

Polish Museum of America.
Chicago, IL 60622

Polk Public Museum.
800 E. Palmetto, Lakeland, FL 33801

Polynesian Cultural Center.
Laie, HI 96762

Pomona College Art Gallery.
College & Bonita St., CA 91711

Ponca City Art Assn.
Box 1394, 819 E. Central, Ponca City, OK 74601

Ponca City Cultural Center & Museum.
1000 E. Grand Ave., Ponca City, OK 74601

Poncho Villa Museum. See Villa, Poncho, Museum

Pontiac Creative Arts Center.
47 Williams St., Pontiac, MI 48053

Pope Country Historical Society Museum.
S. Hwy. 104, Glenwood, MN 56334

Pope-Leighey House.
Mount Vernon, VA 22121

Port Chester Public Library.
1 Haselo Av., Port Chester, NY 10573

Portage County Historical Society.
6459 N. Chestnut, Ravenna, OH 44266

Portland Art Assn., Portland Art Museum, Museum Art School.
1219 S.W. Park Ave., Portland, OR 97225

Portland Center for Visual Arts.
117 N. W. Fifth Ave., Portland, OR 97209

Portland Children's Museum.
3037 S.W. Second Ave., Portland, OR 97201

Portland Society of Art, Museum of Art.
111 High St., Portland, ME 04101

Portland State Univ. White Gallery.
P.O. Box 751, Portland, OR 97207

Portsmouth Athenaeum.
9 Market Square, Portsmouth, NH 03801

Portsmouth Naval Shipyard Museum, Inc.
2 High St., P.O. Box 248, Portsmouth, VA 23705

Potsdam Public Museum.
Civic Center, Potsdam, NY 13676 Tel 315-265-6910
Permanent Collections:
Burnap collection of English pottery.

Pottsgrove Mansion.
W. King St., Pottstown, PA 19464

Pottstown Area Artists Guild.
P.O. Box 512, Pottstown, PA 19464

Poultney Historical Society Museum.
The Green, East Poultney, VT 05741

Powell, John Wesley Memorial Museum.
6 N. Seventh Ave., Page, AZ 86040

Powell, Ray E., Museum.
313 Division, Grandview, WA 98930

Powhatan House & Museum.
5427 Ave. O, P.O. Box 3271, Galveston, TX 77550

Pratt Institute Library.
Brooklyn, NY 11205

Presbyterian Historical Society.
425 Lombard St., Philadelphia, PA 19147

Preservation Society of Newport County.
Washington Square, Newport, RI 02840

Presidental Museum.
622 N. Lee, Odessa, TX 79761

Priestley House.
Priestly Ave., Northumberland, PA 17857

Princeton Antiques Bookservice; Art Marketing Reference Library.
2915-17 Atlantic Ave., Atlantic City, NJ 08401
Permanent Collections:
Post card photo collection (1/2 million index filed).

Princeton University Art Museum:
Princeton, NJ 08544 Tel 609-452-3787
Permanent Collections:
Collections run the gamut from ancient to contemporary art and, geographically, concentrate on the Mediterranean regions, Western Europe, China, and the United States.

Principia College, School of Nations Museum.
Elsah, IL 62028

Print Club.
1614 Latimer St., Philadelphia, PA 19103

Print Council of America, National Gallery of Art.
Constitution Ave. at Sixth St., N.W., Washington, DC 20565

Printed Matter Inc.
7 Lispenard St., NY 10013

Printmaking Workshop.
114 W. 17th St., New York, NY 10011

Proctor, W. C., Art Center. See Bard College, W. C. Proctor Art Center

Professional Artists Guild.
P.O. 11, Roslyn Heights, NY 11577

Providence Art Club.
11 Thomas St., Providence, RI 02903

Providence Athenaeum.
251 Benefit St., Providence, RI 02903

Providence Public Library, Art & Music Department.
150 Empire St., Providence, RI 02906

Providence Water Color Club.
6 Thomas St., Providence, RI 02903

Provincetown Art Assn. & Museum.
460 Commercial St., Provincetown, MA 02657

Public Library of Charlotte & Mecklenburg County.
310 N. Tryon St., Charlotte, NC 28202

Public Library of the District of Columbia, Martin Luther King Memorial Library.
901 G St. N.W., Washington, DC 20001

Pueblo Metropolitan Museum.
419 W. 14th St., Pueblo, CO 81003

Pullen Alaska Museum.
Seattle Ctr. Food Circus, Seattle, WA 98109

Purdue University Galleries:
Creative Bldg. 1, W. Lafayette, IN 47907

Purdy, Jacob, House. See Washington's Headquarters in White Plains Known As Jacob Purcy House

Putnam Cottage.
243 E. Putnam Ave., Greenwich, CT 06830

Putnam Museum.
1717 W. 12th St., Davenport, IA 52804

Quakertown Historical Society.
44 S. Main St., Quakertown, PA 18951

Queen Anne's County Historical Society.
S. Commerce St., P. O. Box 296, Centreville, MD 21617

Queen Emma Summer Palace.
2913 Pali Hwy., Honolulu, HI 96817

Queen's College Art Collection, Paul Klapper Library.
Kissena Blvd. & L. I. Expwy., Flushing, NY 11367 Tel 212-520-7243
Permanent Collections:
Study collection touching on a wide range of European art history and some Oriental and primitive pieces. Large collection of ancient and antique glass; WPA prints.

Queens Museum.
New York City Bldg., Flushing Meadow Park, Flushing, NY 11368 Tel 212-592-2405

Queensboro Society of Art & Allied Crafts, Inc.
90-22 155th St., Queens, NY 11421

Quigley Hall Art Gallery. See Western State College, Quigley Hall Art Gallery

Quincy Art Center.
1515 Jersey St., Quincy, IL 62301

Quincy College Gallery.
1831 College Ave., Quincy, IL 62301

Quincy Society of Fine Arts.
1624 Main St., Quincy, IL 62301

R. H. Lowrie Museum of Anthropology. See Lowie, R. H., Museum of Anthropology

R. W. Norton Art Gallery. See Norton, R.W., Art Gallery

Racine Art Assn.
2519 Northwestern Ave., Racine, WI 53404

Rahr Civic Center & Public Museum.
610 N. 80th St., Manitowac, MI 54220

Rahr-West Museum & Civic Center.
Park St. at N. 8th, Manitowoc, WI 54220

Ralston, J. K., Museum & Art Center.
P.O. Box 50, Sidney, MT 59270

Ramaker Library Art Gallery. See Northwestern College, Ramaker Library Art Gallery

Randall, Josephine D. Jr., Museum.
199 Museum Way, San Francisco, CA 94114

Randolph County Indiana Historical Museum.
416 S. Meridian St., Winchester, IN 47394

Randolph-Macon Women's College Collection of American Art.
2500 Rivermont Ave., Lynchburg, VA 24503 Tel 804-846-7392
Permanent Collections:
Paintings, drawings, prints and sculpture by American artists of the 19th and 20th centuries.

Ransburg, L., Art Gallery. See Indiana Central Univ., L. Ransburg Art Gallery

Rappahannock County Historical Society.
Avon Hall, Washington, VA 22747

Rawleigh Museum.
223 E. Main St., Freeport, IL 61032

Rawls, Walter C., Museum.
Courtland, VA 23837

Ray E. Powell Museum. See Powell, Ray E., Museum

Reading Historical Society.
Reading, VT 05062

Reading Public Museum & Art Gallery.
500 Museum Rd., Reading, PA 19611

Rebecca & Gershon Fenster Gallery of Jewish Art. See Fenster, Rebecca & Gershon, Gallery of Jewish Art

Reddie, MacIvor, Gallery. See Art Institute of Boston, MacIvor Reddie Gallery

Redding Museum & Art Center.
P.O. Box 427, Redding, CA 96001

Redington Museum, Waterville Historical Society.
64 Silver St., Waterville, ME 04901

Redlands Art Assn.
12 E. Vine St., Redlands, CA 92373

Redwood Library & Athenaeum.
50 Bellevue Ave., Newport, RI 02840

Reed College Art Gallery.
3202 S.W. Woodstock Blvd., Portland, OR 97202

Reede, Carroll, Museum. See East Tennessee Univ., Carroll Reede Museum

Regis College, L.J. Walters Jr. Gallery.
235 Wellesley St., Weston, MA 02193

Rehoboth Art League.
P.O. Box 84, Rehoboth, DE 19971

Religious America Museum.
Van Lieu's Rd., Ringoes, NJ 08551

Remington Art Museum.
303 Washington St., Ogdensburg, NY 13669 Tel 315-393-2425
Permanent Collections:
Largest single collection of Remington's works on exhibit. Other permanent exhibits are

Parish Collection of Better furniture, the Sharp Collection of period glass, china, silver and cameos, collection of 19th century American and European paintings; exhibit of paintings by Frank Rosseel, a collection of first studies in plaster by Edwin Deming and several pieces of sculpture by Sally James Farnham.

Rensselaer County Historical Society.
59 Second St., Troy, NY 12180

Rensselaer Newman Foundation, Chapel & Cultural Center.
2125 Burdett Ave, Troy, NY 12180

Reynolda House Inc.
P.O. Box 11765, Winston-Salem, NC 27106

Rhode Island College Art Center Gallery.
600 Mount Pleasant Ave., Providence, RI 02908

Rhode Island College Art Department Gallery.
Knight Campus, 400 E. Ave., Warwick, RI 02886

Rhode Island Historical Society.
52 Power St., Providence, RI 02906

Rhode Island School of Design, Museum of Art.
224 Benefit St., Providence, RI 02903 Tel 401-331-3511
Permanent Collections:
American drawings and watercolors, British watercolors and drawings, contemporary graphics, glass, American paintings, classical bronze, classical jewelry, classical sculpture, classical vases, Nancy Sayles Day Collection of Latin American Art, Albert Pilavin Collection of 20th century art.

Rice University Institute for the Arts:
1892 Box 1892, Houston, TX 77001

Richard Gallery & Almond Tea Gallery.
2250 Front St., Cuyahoga Falls, OH 44221

Richard L. Nelson Gallery. See Nelson, Richard L., Gallery

Richard Sparrow House Assn., Inc.
42 Summer St., Plymouth, MA 02360

Richland County Museum.
51 Church St., Lexington, OH 44904

Richmond Art Center.
Civic Center, 25th & Barrett Ave., Richmond, CA 49804

Ricketts Memorial Museum.
Hamilton, MT 59840

Rifle Creek Museum.
R.R. 1, Rifle, CO 81650

Ringling, John and Mable, Museum of Art.
Box 1838, Sarasota, FL 33578 Tel 813-355-5101

Ringwood Manor House Museum.
P.O. Box 1304, Ringwood, NJ 07456

Rio Hondo College Art Gallery.
3600 Workmen Mill Rd., Whitter, CA 90608

Ripon College Art Gallery.
Harwood Union Bldg., Ripon, WI 54971

Riverside Art Center & Museum.
3425 Seventh, Riverside, CA 92501

Riverside County Art & Cultural Center.
9401 Oak Glen Rd., Cherry Valley, CA 92223

Riverside Municipal Museum.
3720 Orange St., Riverside, CA 92501

Riverside Museum.
310 Riverside Dr., New York, NY 10025

Roanoke Fine Arts Center.
302 23rd St., S.W., Roanoke, VA 24014

Roanoke Historical Society.
P.O. Box 1904, Roanoke, VA 24008

Roberson Center.
30 Front St., Binghamton, NY 13905

Robert Louis Stevenson House.
530 Houston St., Monterey, CA 93940

Robert Mills Historic Columbia Foundation.
1616 Blanding St., Columbia, SC 29201

Robert P. Strathearn Historical Park. See Strathearn, Robert P., Historical Park

Robert S. Peabody Foundation for Archaeology. See Peabody, Robert S., Foundation for Archaeology

Roberts Art Gallery. See Santa Monica High School, Roberts Art Gallery

Roberts Room, Towson State Univ.
Fine Arts Bldg., Towson, MD 21204

Robinson, Mary S., Art Library.
809 15th St., Golden, CO 80401

Rochester Art Center.
320 E. Center St., Rochester, MN 55901

Rochester Historical Society.
485 East Ave., Rochester, NY 14607

Rochester Public Library, Rundell Gallery.
115 South Ave., Rochester, NY 14604

Rock County Historical Society.
440 N. Jackson St., P.O. Box 890, Janesville, WI 53545

Rockbridge County Historical Society.
7 Randolph St., Lexington, VA 24450

Rockefeller, Abby Aldrich, Folk Art Center.
P.O. Drawer C, Williamsburg, VA 23185
Permanent Collections:
For information see Colonial Williamsburg Foundation.

Rockford Art Assn., Burpee Art Museum.
737 N. Main St., Rockford, IL 61103

Rockport Art Assn., Old Tavern.
12 Main St., Rockport, MA 01966

Rockville Municipal Art Gallery. See City of Rockville Municipal Art Gallery

Rockwell-Corning Museum.
Baron Steuben Pl., Corning, NY 14830 Tel 607-937-5386
Permanent Collections:
Western American art and artifacts; Indian, cowboy and landscape paintings by famous American artists including Remington, Russell, Bierstadt, Leigh, Sharp, Rungius and Catlin; Pueblo pottery, Navajo rugs, bronzes, firearms, Plains Indians beadwork. Collection also includes the largest collection of Frederick Carder Steuben glass and Victorian toys.

Rocky Mount Arts & Crafts Center.
Old Nashville Rd., P.O. Box 4031, Rocky Mount, NC 27801

Rocky Mountain School of Art.
1441 Ogden St., Denver, CO 80218

Roerich, Nicholas, Museum.
319 W. 107th St., New York, NY 10025 Tel 212-864-7752
Permanent Collections:
Nicholas Roerich paintings

Roger Williams Park Museum. See Williams, Roger, Park Museum

Rogers, Lauren, Library & Museum of Art.
P.O. Box 1180, Laurel, MS 39440
Permanent Collections:
American paintings and sculpture; Georgian silver; ethnic baskets.

Rogers, Will, Memorial & Museum:
P.O. Box 157, Claremore, OK 74017

Rogers House Museum Gallery.
Snake Row, Ellsworth, KS 67439

Rolfe-Warren House.
Surry, VA 23883

Rollins College; George D. & Harriet W. Cornell Fine Arts Center.
Holt Ave., Winter Park, FL 32789
Permanent Collections:
19th century American portraits and landscapes; European Old Master paintings, (Italian, French, Dutch, English); Bronzes, including 19th century French bronzes, 1200 watch keys; collection of late 19th century and early

20th century Hungarian and East European paintings.

Roosevelt, Franklin D., Library & Museum.
Albany Post Rd., Hyde Park, NY 12538

Roosevelt County Museum.
Portales, NM 88130

Roosevelt, Franklin, Home. *See* **Home of Franklin D. Roosevelt National Historic Site**

Ropes Mansion.
318 Essex St., Salem, MA 01970

Rosenbach, Philip H. & A.S.W., Foundation Museum.
2010 DeLancy Pl., Philadelphia, PA 19103 Tel 215-732-1600
Permanent Collections:
British and American Literature, Americana, Marianne Moore Collection, Maurice Sendak Collection.

Rosenberg Library.
2301 Sealy, Galveston, TX 77550

Rosicrucian Egyptian Museum & Art Museum.
Park & Naglee, San Jose, CA 95191
Permanent Collections:
Egyptian, Babylonian and Assyrian artifacts

Roswell Museum & Art Center.
11th & Main Sts., Roswell, NM 88201

Rotch Library of Architecture & Planning.
77 Massachusetts Ave., Cambridge, MA 02138

Rothschild Interpretive Center.
C/O Washington State Parks & Recreation Commission, P.O. Box 1128, Olympia, WA 98504

Rouge Valley Art Assn.
P.O. Box 763, 40 S. Bartlett, Medford, OR 97501

Rouke Art Gallery.
523 S. Fourth St., Moorehead, MN 56560

Rowayton Arts Center.
145 Rowayton Ave., CT 06853

R.R. McCormick Museum. *See* **McCormick, R.R., Museum**

Ruggles House Society.
Bar Harbor, ME 04609

Rundell Gallery. *See* **Rochester Public Library, Rundell Gallery**

Rusk County Heritage Assn.
313 E. Main St., P. O. Box 510, Henderson, TX 75662

Ruskin Art Club.
800 S. Plymouth Blvd., Los Angeles, CA 90005

Russel, C. M., Museum.
1201 4th Ave., Great Falls, MT 59401

Russell Sage College, New Gallery, Schacht Fine Arts Center.
Troy, NY 12180

Rutgers, The State Univ. of New Jersey, Camden College of Arts and Sciences.
Camden, NJ 08102

Rutgers, the State University of New Jersey, Fine Arts Collection.
Voorhees Hall, Hamilton St., New Brunswick, NJ 08903 Tel 201-932-7237
Permanent Collections:
Collection of close to 6,000 paintings, prints and sculptures. A general survey of the history of art of the western world with its strongest areas, those of 19th and early 20th century English, French and American paintings and graphics.

Rutland Area Art Assn. Inc., Chaffee Art Gallery.
16 S. Main St., Rutland, VT 05701

Rutler Institute of American Art.
524 Wick Ave., Youngstown, OH 44502

Ryan Fine Arts Center. *See* **McMurray College, Amy Graves Ryan Fine Arts Center**

Saginaw Art Museum.
1126 N. Michgian Ave., Saginaw, MI 48602

Saguache County Museum.
Highway 285, Saguache, CO 81149

Saint Anselm's College Chapel Arts Center.
Manchester, NH 03102

Saint Augustine Art Assn. Gallery.
22 Maine St., St. Augustine, FL 32084

Saint Augustine Historical Society, Oldest House & Museum.
14 St. Frances St., St. Augustine, FL 32084

Saint Bernard Foundation & Monastery:
16711 W. Dixie Hwy., Miami Beach, FL 33160

Saint Bonaventure Univ. Art Collection.
Friedsam Memorial Library, Saint Bonaventure, NY 14778 Tel 716-375-2323
Permanent Collections:
200 works of art and approximately 100 Chinese porcelains and American Indian pottery and rugs.

Saint Cloud State University; Atwood Center Gallery.
Atwood Center, Saint Cloud, MN 56301

St. Edward's University. Fine Arts Exhibit Program.
Austin, 78704

Saint Francis Home. *See* **Wilkin County Historical Society-Saint Francis Home**

Saint-Gaudens National Historic Site.
Saint Gaudens Rd., Windsor, VT 05089

Saint Gertrude's Museum.
College of Saint Gertrude, Cottonwood, ID 83522

St. Gregory's Abbey & College, The Mabee-Gerner Museum.
1900 W. MacArthur Dr., Shawnee, OK 74801
Permanent Collections:
Paintings, prints, artifacts, (Egyptian, Babylonian, Grecian, Roman, African, North and South American Indian, Polynesian, Japanese and Chinese).

Saint John's Art Gallery.
114 Orange St., Wilmington, DE 28401

Saint John's University Art Gallery; Chung-Cheng Cultural Ctr.
Grand Central & Utopia, Jamaica, NY 11439

Saint Johnsbury Athenaeum:
30 Main St., St. Johnsbury, VT 05819

Saint Joseph Museum.
11th & Charles, Saint Joseph, MO 65401

Saint Lawrence University, Griffiths Art Gallery.
Romoda Dr., Canton, NY 13617

Saint Louis Art Museum:
Forest Park, St. Louis, MO 63110 Tel 314-721-0067

Saint Louis Artists Guild.
227 E. Lockwood, Saint Louis, MO 63319

Saint Louis Public Library Art Dept.
1301 Olive St., Saint Louis, MO 63105

St. Luke's Gallery. *See* **Anna Marie College, St. Luke's Gallery**

Saint Mary's College, Moreau Gallery Art Dept.
Notre Dame, IN 46556

Saint Paul Council of Arts & Sciences.
30 E. Tenth St., Saint Paul, MN 55101

St. Paul's School Art Center in Hargate.
Concord, NH 03301

St. Paul's School, The Art Center in Hargate.
Concord, NH 03301

St. Peter's College Art Gallery.
Kennedy Blvd., Jersey City, NJ 07306

Salem Art Association, Bush House, Bush Barn Art Center.
600 Mission St. S.E., Salem, OR 97301

Salem County Historical Society.
79-83 Market St., Salem, NJ 08079

Salida Museum.
Swimming Pool Bldg., 410 W. Rainbow Blvd., Salida, CO 81201

Salinas Valley Museum.
1150 N. Main St., Salinas, CA 93901

Salisbury Historical Society.
Salisbury, NH 03268

Salisbury House.
4025 Tonawanda Dr., Des Moines, IA 50312

Salmagundi Club.
47 Fifth Ave., New York, NY 10003

Salt Lake City Public Library.
Fine Art Dept., 209 E. 51st., Salt Lake City, UT 84111

Salvador Dali Museum. *See* **Dali, Salvador, Museum**

Sampson Art Gallery. *See* **Theil College, Sampson Art Gallery**

Samuel Kirk Museum, Inc.. *See* **Kirk, Samuel, Museum, Inc**

San Angelo Art Club, Kendall Art Gallery.
Box 3362, San Angelo, TX 76901

San Antonio Art League.
310 W. Ashby, San Antoino, TX 78209

San Antonio Museum Assn., Whitte Memorial Museum.
3801 Broadway, San Antonio, TX 78029
Permanent Collections:
Early Texas Furniture and Decorative Arts.

San Antonio Public Library, Art, Music & Films Department.
203 S. St.& Marys St., San Antonio, TX 78202

San Bernardino Art Assn.
P.O. Box 2272, San Bernardino, CA 92406

San Buena Ventura Mission Museum.
225 E. Main St., Ventura, CA 93001

San Carlos Cathedral.
550 Church St., Monterey, CA 93940

San Diego State Univ. Art Gallery.
5402 College Ave., San Diego, CA 92182

San Fernando Valley Historical Society.
10940 Sepulveda Blvd., Mission Hills, CA 91340

San Francisco Art Institute.
800 Chestnut St., San Francisco, CA 94133

San Francisco Maritime Museum, Photogaph Dept.
At the Foot of Polk St., San Francisco, CA 94109
Permanent Collections:
Approximately 150,000 photographic items including glass negatives, nitrate negatives, original safety film negatives, copy negatives, albumen prints, gelatin chloride prints, collodion prints, cyanotypes, modern black and white prints; West Coast and Maritime history.

San Francisco Museum of Modern Art.
Van Ness at McAllister, San Francisco, CA 94102 Tel 415-863-2890
Permanent Collections:
Painting and sculpture.

San Francisco Plantation House.
Hwy. 44, River Rd., Reserve, LA 70084

San Joaquin County Historical Museum.
11793 N. Micke Grove Rd., P.O. Box 21, Lodi, CA 95240

San Jose Mission.
6539 San Jose Dr., San Antonio, TX 78214

San Jose Museum of Art.
110 S. Market St., San Jose, CA 95113

San Jose State Univ. Art Gallery.
San Jose, CA 95192

San Juan County Historical Society Museum.
P.O. Box 154, Silverton, CO 81433

San Luis Obispo Historical Museum.
696 Monterey St., San Luis Obispo, CA 93401

San Mateo County Historical Assn.
1700 W. Hillsdale Blvd., San Mateo, CA 94402

San Miguel Historical Society.
Telluride, CO 81435

San Miguel Mission.
Mission St., San Miguel, CA 93451

Sanchez Adobe.
Linda Mar Blvd., Pacifica, CA 94044

Sandersen, B. Memorial, Gallery. *See* **Bethany College, B. Sandzen Memorial Gallery**

Sandhill Woman's Exchange.
Pinehurst, NC 28374

Sandwich Glass Museum.
Rte. 130, 129 Main St., P.O. Box 103, Sandwich, MA 02563

Sandwich Historical Society.
704 N. Main St., Sandwich, IL 60548

Sandwich Historical Society.
Maple St., Center Sandwich, NH 03227

Sandy Bay Historical Society & Museum, Inc.
40 King St., Rockport, MA 09166

Sanford Museum & Planetarium.
117 E. Willow St., Cherokee, IA 51012

Sangre de Cristo Arts & Conference Ctr.
210 N. Santa Fe, Pueblo, CO 81003

Santa Barbara Museum of Art.
1130 State St., Santa Barbara, CA 93101 Tel 805-963-4364
Permanent Collections:
American and European paintings, sculpture, drawings,

prints; Oriental sculpture, paintings and ceramics; Greek and Roman art; Henry Eichheim Collection of Oriental Musical Instruments; Alice F. Schott Doll Collection.

Santa Barbara Public Library, Faulkner Memorial Art Wing.
Box 1019, Santa Barbara, CA 93102

Santa Cruz Art League.
526 Broadway, Santa Cruz, CA 95060

Santa Cruz Public Library; Art, Music & Film Dept.
Church St., Santa Cruz, CA 90405

Santa Cruz Valley Art Assn. *See* **Tubac Center for the Arts, Santa Cruz Valley Art Assn**

Santa Monica College Art Gallery.
1900 Pico Blvd., Santa Monica, CA 90405

Santa Monica High School, Roberts Art Gallery.
601 Pico Blvd, Santa Monica, CA 90405

Santa Rosa Junior College Art Gallery.
1501 Mendocino Ave., Santa Rosa, CA 95401

Sarasota Art Assn. Civic Center.
707 N. Tamiami Trail, Sarasota, FL 33577

Sargent, Paul, Gallery.
Lincoln at Seventh, Charleston, IL 61920

Sargent, Paul Turner, Gallery. *See* **Eastern Illinois Univ., Paul Turner Sargent Gallery**

Savery Art Gallery. *See* **Talladega College, Savery Art Gallery**

Sawhill Duke Fine Arts Center. *See* **James Madison Univ., Sawhill Duke Fine Arts Ctr**

Sayville Historical Society.
Sayville, NY 11782

Scalamandre Museum of Textiles.
950 Third Ave., New York, NY 10022

Scantic Academy Museum, East Windsor Historical Society, Inc.
Scantic Rd., Rte. 191, Warehouse Point, CT 06088

Scarborough Historical Museum.
U.S. Rte. 1, Scarborough, ME 04074

Schacht Fine Arts Center. *See* **Russell Sage College, New Gallery, Schacht Fine Arts Center**

Schenectady County Historical Society.
32 Washington Ave., Schenectady, NY 12305

Schenectady Museum.
Nott Terrace Heights, Schenectady, NY 12308

Schminck Memorial Museum.
128 South E. St., Lakeview, OR 97630

Schofield Barracks Tropic Lighting History Center.
25th Infantry Division Hdqs, Honolulu, HI 69857

School Art League of New York.
131 Livington St., Brooklyn, NY 11201

School of American Research.
P.O. Box 2188, Santa Fe, NM 87501

School of Arts & Crafts Society of Portland, Hoffman Gallery.
616 N.W. 18th Ave., Portland, OR 97209

School of Associated Arts.
344 Summit Ave., Saint Paul, MN 55102

School of the Ozarks, Ralph Foster Museum.
Ralph Foster Museum, Point Lookout, MO 65726

School of Visual Arts Library.
209 E. 23rd St., New York, NY 10010

Schuyler County Historical Society, Inc.
R.D. 1, Watkins Glen, NY 14891

Schuyler Mansion.
27 Clinton St., Albany, NY 12202

Scituate Historical Society.
121 Maple St., Scituate, MA 02066

Scottish Rite Temple.
1733 16th St., N.W., Washington, DC 20009

Scotts Bluff National Monument.
National Park Service, P.O. Box 427, Gering, NE 69341

Scottsdale Arists League.
P.O. Box 1071, Scottsdale, AZ 85252

Sculptors Guild Inc.
10 E. 53rd St., New York, NY 10022

Sculpture Center.
167 E. 69th St., New York, NY 10028

Sears, Laura Davidson, Fine Arts Gallery. *See* **Elgin Academy; Laura Davidson Sears Fine Arts Gallery**

Seattle Art Museum.
Volunteer Park, Seattle, WA 98112
Permanent Collections:
Chinese, Japanese, Indian, Modern, European, and Ethnic art; photography, prints and drawings of the Pacific Northwest.

Seattle Public Library Art & Music Dept.
1000 Fourth Ave., Seattle, WA 98104

O Museum of History & Industry.
2161 E. Hamlin St., Seattle, WA 98112

Sellor's Memorial Museum.
312 N. Elm, Ainsworth, NE 69210

Seneca County Museum.
28 Clay St., Tiffin, OH 44883

Seneca Falls Historical Society Museum.
55 Cayuga St., Seneca Falls, NY 13148

Sequoia & Kings Canyon National Parks.
Three Rivers, CA 93271

Seton, Ernest Thompson, Memorial Library & Museum.
Philmont Scout Ranch and Explorer Base, Cimarron, NM 87114

Seton Hall Univ., Art Center Building.
S. Orange Ave., South Orange, NJ 07079

Shadows-on-the-Teche.
117 E. Main St., P.O. Box 254, New Iberia, LA 70560

Shaftsbury Historical Society, Inc.
P.O. Box 101, R.R. 1, Shaftsbury, VT 05262

Shaker Community, Inc.
Rte. 20, Pittsfield, Hancock, MA 01201

Shaker Historical Society.
3486 Lee Rd., Shaker Heights, OH 44120

Shaker Museum.
Sabbathday Lake, Poland Spring, ME 04274

Shaker Museum & Emma B. King Library.
Shaker Museum Rd., Old Chatham, NY 12136 Tel 518-794-9100
Permanent Collections:
Shaker furniture, tools, machines, textiles, crafts and other artifacts representing the complete range of the Shaker's communal life, work and worship. Library collections: imprints, approximately 500 manuscripts pertaining to accounts, biography, business correspondance, covenants, deeds and real estate, diaries and travels, visions, etc., maps, photographs, music.

Shakertown at Pleasant Hill Kentucky.
Rte. 4, Harrodsburg, KY 40330

Shakespeare Press Museum. *See* **California Polytechnic State University, Shakespeare Press Museum**

Shanker Community Inc.
P.O. Box 898, Pittsfield, MA 01201

Sharadin Art Gallery. *See* **Kutztown State College, Sharadin Art Gallery**

Sharon Arts Center Inc.
R.F.D. 2 Box 361, Peterborough, NH 03458

Sharp, Ella, Museum.
3225 Fourth St., Jackson, MI 49203

Shasta State Historical Monument.
P.O. Box 507, Shasta, CA 98607

Shawano County Historical Society, Inc.
524 N. Franklin St., Shawano, WI 54166

Shelburne Museum.
Shelburne, VT 05482 Tel 802-985-3344

Sheldon Art Museum.
1 Park St., Middlebury, VT 05753 Tel 802-388-6956
Permanent Collections:
Nineteenth century paintings, prints, furniture and furnishings, pewter, china, glassware, canes, tools, kitchen equipment, needlework, clothing, quilts and coverlets, dolls, clocks, hair wreaths and jewelry, sewing machines, locks and keys, pianos, maps, letters, diaries, account books, newspapers, old and regional books.

Sheldon Jackson Museum. *See* **Jackson, Sheldon, Museum**

Sheldon Museum & Cultural Center.
Box 236, Haines, AK 99827

Sheldon Swope Art Gallery. *See* **Swope, Sheldon, Art Gallery**

Sheldon's Museum.
P.O. Box 236, Haines, AK 99827

Sheyenne Valley Arts & Crafts Assn.
P.O. Box 52, Fort Ransom, ND 58202

Shiloh Museum.
118 W. Johnson Ave., Springdale, AR 72764

Shippensburg Historical Society Museum.
W. King St., Library Bldg., Shippensburg, PA 17257

Ships of the Sea Museum.
503 E. River St., Savannah, GA 31401

Shirley Plantation.
Rte. 2, P.O. Box 57, Charles City, VA 23030

Shivers, Allen, Museum & Library.
302 N. Charlton, Woodville, TX 75979

Shrewsbury House Museum.
301 W. First St., Madison, IN 47250

Sidney Historical Assn.
P.O. Box 173, Sidney, NY 13838

Siena Heights College, Little Gallery.
Studio Angelico, 1257 Siena Heights Dr., Adrian, MI 49221

Sierra Arts Foundation.
P.O. Box 2814, Reno, NV 89505

Sierra Nevada Museum of Art.
549 Court St., Reno, NV 89501

Silas Bronson Library. *See* **Bronson, Silas, Library**

Silver City Museum.
312 W. Broadway, Silver City, NM 88061

Silverado Museum.
P.O. Box 409, Saint Helena, CA 94574

Silvermine Guild School of the Arts.
1037 Silvermine Rd., New Canaan, CT 06840

Simi Valley Historical Society.
1938 Third St., Simi, CA 93065

Simon, Norton, Inc. Museum of Art.
3440 Wilshire Blvd., Los Angeles, CA 90005

Simon's Rock Early College, Fine Arts Division, Studio Arts Dept, 30
Alford Rd., Great Barrington, MA 01230

Simpson College Gallery.
Indianola, IA 50125

Singing River Art Assn. Inc.
L & N Railroad Depot Gallery, P.O. Box 262, Pascaugoula, MS 39567

Sioux City Art Center.
513 Nebraska St., Sioux City, IA 51104

Sioux City Public Museum.
2901 Jackson St., Sioux City, IA 51104

Sioux Indian Museum.
P.O. Box 1504, Rapid City, SD 57709

Sioux Lookout D.A.R. Log Cabin Museum.
Memorial Park, North Platte, NE 69101

Siskiyou County Museum.
910 S. Main St., Yreka, CA 96097

Skidmore College Art Gallery.
N. Broadway, Saratoga Springs, NY 12866

Skinner Museum.
35 Woodbridge St., South Hadley, MA 01075

Skirball Museum. *See* **Hebrew Union College, Skirball Museum**

Skirball Museum of Hebrew Union College.
Jewish Institute of Religion, 3077 University Ave., Los Angeles, CA 90007

Slabsides.
West Park, NY 12493

Sleepy Hollow Restorations.
P.O. Box 245, Tarrytown, NY 10591

Slocum, Elizabeth, Gallery.
Art Dept., Johnson City, TN 37601

Smith, Edwin, Historical Museum.
Six Elm St., Westfield, MA 01085

Smith, George Walter Vincent, Art Museum.
222 State St., Springfield, MA 01103

Smith College Museum of Art.
Fine Arts Center, Northhampton, MA 01060 Tel 413-584-2700, 2236; 740
Permanent Collections:
Total collection: 15,000 objects.

Smith-Mason Gallery & Museum.
1207 Rhode Island Ave., N.W., Washington, DC 20005

Smithsonian Institution.
1000 Jefferson Dr., S.W., Washington, DC 20560

Society for Preservation of Historic Landmarks.
York, ME 03909

Society for Preservation of New England Antiquities.
141 Cambridge St., Boston, MA 02114

Society for Preservation of New England Antiquities, Otis House.
141 Cambridge St., Brewster, MA 02114

Society for the Preservation of Long Island Antiquities.
N. Country Rd., P.O. Box 206, Setauket, NY 11733

Society of American Graphic Artists, Inc.
Rm. 1214, 32 Union Square, New York, NY 10003 Tel 212-260-5706

Society of Animal Artists Inc.
151 Carroll St., City Island, Bronx, NY 10464

Society of Illustrators.
128 E. 63rd St., New York, NY 10021

Society of Medalists.
Danbury, CT 06810

Society of North American Artists.
P.O. Box 37072, Millard Sta., Omaha, NE 68137

Society of the Four Arts.
Four Arts Plaza, Palm Beach, FL 33480

Socorro Art League.
1212 North Dr., N.W., Socorro, NM 87801

Soho Center for Visual Artists.
110-114 Prince St., New York, NY 10012

Solomon R. Guggenheim Museum. *See* **Guggenheim, Solomon, Museum**

Somers Historical Society.
Elephant Hotel, Somers, NY 10589

Somerset Historical Center.
R.D. 2, Somerset, PA 15501

Sonoma State College Art Gallery.
1801 E. Cotati Ave., Rohnert Park, CA 94928

Sordoni Art Gallery. *See* **Wilkes College, Sordoni Art Gallery**

South Arkansas Art Center.
110 E. Fifth St., El Dorado, AK 71730

South Carolina Arts Commission.
829 Richland St., Columbia, SC 29201

South Carolina Department of Parks, Recreation and Tourism.
P.O. Box 1358, Columbia, SC 29202

South County Art Assn.
Helme House, 1319 Kingstown Rd., Kingston, RI 02852

South Dakota Univ., South Dakota Memorial Art Center.
Medary Ave. at Harvey Dunn, Brookings, SD 57006

South Street Seaport.
203 Front St., New York, NY 10038

South Texas Art Mobile.
P.O. Box 8183, Corpus Christi, TX 78412

Southeast Alaskan Regional Arts Council.
P.O. Box 678, Sitka, AK 99835

Southeast Arkansas Arts & Science Center.
Civic Center, Pine Bluff, AK 71601

Southeast Missouri State Univ. Art Collections.
Kent Library, Cape Girardeau, MO 63701 Tel 314-651-2000

Southeastern Center for Contemporary Art.
750 Marguerite Dr., Winston-Salem, NC 27106

Southeastern College Art Conference.
P.O. Box 1022, Chapel Hill, NC 27514

Southern Alleghenies Museum of Art.
P.O. Box 8, Loretto, PA 15940 Tel 814-472-6400

Southern Artists Assn., Fine Arts Center.
815 Whitington Ave., Hot Springs, AK 71901

Southern Baptist Seminary, Eisenberg Museum.
2825 Lexington Rd., Louisville, KY 40206

Southern Highland Handicraft Guild.
P.O. Box 9545, Asheville, NC 28805

Southern Illinois Univ. Museum & Art Galleries.
Faner Hall Rm. 2469, Carbondale, IL 62901

Southern Methodist Univ., Meadows Museum.
Dallas, TX 75275 Tel 214-692-2516
Permanent Collections:
Spanish paintings from late Gothic to 20th century masters.

Southern Oregon College, Stevenson Union Art Gallery.
Ashland, OR 97520

Southern Oregon Historical Society.
P.O. Box 480, Jacksonville, OR 97530

Southern Plains Indian Museum.
P.O. Box 749, Anadarko, OK
73005

**Southern Utah State College,
Braithwaite Fine Arts Gallery.**
Cedar City, UT 84720

Southern Vermont Art Center.
Manchester, VT 05254

**Southold Historical Society &
Museum.**
Main Rd. & Maple Lane,
Southold, NY 11971

**Southwest Commercial College
Art Gallery.**
900 Otay Lakes Rd., Chula
Vista, CA 92010

Southwest Craft Center.
300 Augusta St., San Antonio,
TX 78205

**Southwest Missouri Museum
Assn.**
1111 Broodside Dr, Springfield,
MO 65807

Southwest Museum.
P.O. Box 42128, Highland Park
Station, Los Angeles, CA
90042

Southwest Utah Art Gallery. *See*
**Dixie College, Southwest Utah
Art Gallery**

Spanish Governor's Palace.
105 Military Plaza, San
Antonio, TX 78205

**Spartanburg County Art Assn.,
The Gallery.**
385 S. Spring St., Spartanburg,
SC 29301

**Spartanburg County Regional
Museum.**
501 Otis Blvd., Spartanburg,
SC 29302

**Spectrum Friends of Fine Art,
Inc.**
5304 Elmer Dr., Toledo, OH
43615

Speed, J.B., Art Museum.
P.O. Box 8345, Louisville, KY
40208

**Spertus, Maurice, Museum of
Judaica.**
618 S. Michigan Ave., Chicago,
IL 60605 Tel 312-922-9012
Permanent Collections:
Jewish ceremonial art, Bernard
and Rochelle Zell Holocaust
Memorial, Room of the
Generations.

Spiva Art Center Inc.
Newman & Duquesne Rds.
Missori Southern Fine Arts
Bldg., Joplin, MO 64801

Spotsylania Historical Assn., Inc.
P.O. Box 64, Spotslyvania
County, VA 22533

**Springfield Art & Historical
Society.**
9 Elm St., Springfield, VT
05156

**Springfield Art Assn. of Edwards
Place.**
700 N. Fourth St., Springfield,
IL 62702

Springfield Art Center.
107 Cliff Park Rd., Springfield,
OH 45501
Permanent Collections:
Predominantly 19th and 20th
century American art.

Springfield Art League.
220 State St., Springfield, MA
01103

Springfield Art Museum.
1111 Brookside Dr.,
Springfield, MO 65807

**Springfield College, Babson
Library Art Gallery.**
263 Alden St., Springfield, MA
01109

Springfield Historical Society.
126 Morris Ave., Springfield,
NJ 07081

Springs Historical Society.
Springs, PA 15562

Springvale Museum of Art.
126 E. 400 South, Springvale,
UT 84663

Stamford Historical Society, Inc.
713 Bedford St., Stamford, CT
06901

**Stamford Museum & Nature
Center.**
High Ridge & Scofield Rds.,
Stamford, CT 06903

Stan Hywet Hall Foundation, Inc.
714 N. Portage Path, Akron,
OH 44303

**Stanford University, Museum of
Art, T.W. Stanford Art Gallery:**
Museum Way & Lomita,
Stanford, CA

Stanley Hall Gallery.
University of Missouri Dept. of
Housing & Interior, Columbia,
MO 65211

**Stanley House & Stevenson
House.** *See* **Tyron Palace
Restoration, Stanley House &
Stevenson House**

**Star-Spangled Banner Flag House
Assn., Inc.**
844 E. Pratt St., Baltimore,
MD 21202

Stark Museum of Art.
P.O. Box 1897, Orange, TX
77630 Tel 713-883-6661
Permanent Collections:
Western Collection, American
Indian Collection, European
paintings, porcelains by
Dorothy Doughty and Edward
Marshall Boehm, Steuben glass,
Egyptian and Roman
antiquities.

Starley-Whitman House. *See*
**Farmington Museum; Starley-
Whitman House**

State Capitol Museum.
211 W. 21st Ave., Olympia,
WA 98501

**State Education Department,
State University of New York,
State Education Bldg.**
Albany, NY 12234

**State Historical Society of
Missouri.**
Hitt & Lowry Sts., Columbia,
MO 65201

**State Historical Society of
Wiconisn.**
816 State St., Madison, WI
53706

**State University of New York at
Albany, Art Gallery:**
1400 Washington Ave., Albany,
NY 12222

**State University of New York at
Binghampton, Art Gallery:**
Binghamton, NY 13901

**State University of New York at
Buffalo Gallery:**
Room 106 Talbert Hall,
Amherst, NY 14260

**State University of New York at
Cortland, Art Slide Library:**
Cortland, NY 13045

**State University of New York at
Fredonia, M.C. Rockefeller Arts
Center Gallery:**
Fredonia, NY 14063

**State University of New York at
Geneseo, Fine Arts Gallery:**
Geneseo, NY 14454

**State University of New York at
New Paltz, Art Gallery:**
Smiley Art Bldg., New Paltz,
NY 12561

**State University of New York at
Oneonta, Fine Arts Center:**
Oneonta, NY 13820

**State University of New York at
Oswego, Tyler Art Gallery:**
Oswego, NY 13126

**State University of New York at
Potsdam, Art Gallery:**
Potsdam, NY 13676

**State University of New York at
Purchase, Neuberger Museum:**
Purchase, NY 10577

**State University of New York at
Stony Brook, Art Gallery:**
Stony Brook, NY 11794

**Staten Island Ferry, Maritime
Museum.**
St. George Ferry Term Bldg.,
Staten Island, NY 10301

Staten Island Historical Museum.
302 Center St., Staten Island,
NY 10306

**Staten Island Institute of Arts &
Sciences.**
75 Stuyvesant Pl., St. George,
Staten Island, NY 10301

**Stearns County Historical
Museum.**
Box 702, St.Cloud, MN 56301
Tel 612-253-8424

**Stephen, General Adam, Memorial
Assn., Inc.**
P. O. Box 862, Martinsburg,
WV 25401

Stephen Foster Center.
P.O. Box 265, White Springs,
FL 32096

Stephen Girard Collection. *See*
Girard, Stephen, Collection

**Stephens College, Lewis James &
Nellie Stratton Lavis Art
Gallery.**
Columbia, MO 65201

**Sterling, Francine & Sterling, Art
Museum.**
P.O. Box 8, Williamstown, MA
01267 Tel 413-458-8109

**Sterling & Francine Clark Art
Institute.** *See* **Sterling, Francine
& Sterling, Art Museum**

Stetson University Art Gallery:
Deland, FL 32720

Stevenson, Robert Louis, House.
See **Robert Louis Stevenson
House**

Stevenson Union Art Gallery. *See*
**Southern Oregon College,
Stevenson Union Art Gallery**

Still Gallery. *See* **Eastern
Michigan Univ., Still Gallery**

**Stockbridge Historical Society
Inc.**
Main St., Stockbridge, MA
01262

Stockbridge Mission House Assn.
Box 422, Stockbridge, MA
01262

Stonington Historical Society.
P.O. Box 103, Stonington, CT
06378

Store Front Museum.
162-02 Liberty Ave., Jamaica,
NY 11433

Storm King Art Center.
Mountainville, NY 10953

Stoughton Historical Society.
112 S. Page St., Stoughton, WI
53589

Stowe-Day Foundation.
77 Forest St., Hartford, CT
06105 Tel 203-522-9258

Stowe-Day Library.
77 Forest St., Hartford, CT
06105

Stradling Museum of the Horse.
Box 413, Patagonia, AZ 85624

**Stratford Hall Plantation, Robert
Lee Memorial Assn., Inc.**
Stratford, VA 22558

Stratford Historical Society.
967 Academy Hill, Straford,
CT 06497

**Strathearn, Robert P., Historical
Park.**
137 Strathearn Pl., P.O. Box
351, Simi Valley, CA 93065

Strausburg Museum.
E. King St., Strausburg, VA
22657

Strawberry Banke.
Hancock & Washington St.,
Portsmouth, NH 03801

Strong, John, Mansion.
R.F.D. 3, Vergennes, VT 05491

Strong Museum.
7000 Allen Creek Rd.,
Rochester, NY 14618

Stuart, Gilbert, Birthplace.
Gilbert Stuart Rd.,
Saunderstown, RI 02874

Studio Museum in Harlem.
2033 Fifth Ave., New York,
NY 10035

Sturdivant Hall.
713 Mabry St., P.O. Box 1205, Selma, AL 36701

Suffolk Museum & Carriage House.
Stony Brook, NY 11790

Summit Art Center Inc.
68 Elm St., Summit, NJ 07901

Summit County Historical Society.
550 Copley Rd., Akron, OH 44320

Sumter Gallery of Art.
421 N. Main St., P.O. Box 1316, Sumter, SC 29150

Sun Museum.
Alcova, WY 82620

Sunset Trading Post Old West Museum.
Rte. 1, Sunset, TX 76270

Supplementary Educational Center Art Gallery.
314 N. Ellis St., Salisbury, NC 28144

Swain School of Design; William W. Crapo Gallery.
19 Hawthorn St., New Bedford, MA 02740

Swansboro Historical Assn. Inc.
P.O. Box 21, Swansboro, NC 28584

Swarthmore College, Friends Historical Library.
Swarthmore, PA 18031

Sweet Briar College; Babcock Art League.
Sweet Briar, VA 24595 Tel 804-381-5451
Permanent Collections:
Teaching collection with a selection of paintings, prints, drawings and sculpture from the Middle Ages to the present. The major holdings are 20th century works from all of the above media.

Sweetwater Community Fine Arts Center.
400 C St., Rock Springs, WY 82901

Swen Parson Gallery. *See* **Northern Illinois Univ., Swen Parson Gallery**

Swope, Sheldon, Art Gallery.
25 S. Seventh St., Terre Haute, IN 47807

Synagogue Architecture Library. *See* **Union of American Hebrew Congregations; Synagogue Architecture Library**

Syracuse University, Joe & Emily Lowe Art Gallery:
College Place, Syracuse, NY 13210

Table Rock Historical Society & Museum.
Table Rock, NE 68447

Tacoma Art Museum.
12th & Pacific Aves., Tacoma, WA 98402

Tacoma Public Library, Handforth Gallery.
1102 Tacoma Ave. S., Tacoma, WA 98402

Taft, Lorado, Museum Studios.
6016 Ingleside Ave., Chicago, IL 60637

Taft Museum.
316 Pike St., Cincinnati, OH 45202

Talisman Gallery.
307 Delaware, Bartlesville, OK 74003

Talladega College, Savery Art Gallery.
627 W. Battle St., Talladega, AL 35160

Tallahassee Junior Museum.
3945 Museum Dr., Tallahassee, FL 32304

Tampa Bay Art Center.
320 North Blvd., Tampa, FL 33606

Tantaquidgeon Indian Museum.
1819 Norwich-New London Turnpike, Uncasville, CT 06382

Taos Art Association, Inc., Stables Gallery:
P.O. Box 198, Taos, NM 87571

Tappantown Society.
P.O. Box 71, Tappan, NY 10983

Taylor, Elizabeth Prewitt, Memorial Library.
P.O. Box 2137, Little Rock, AK 72203

Taylor University Chronicle, Tribune Art Gallery:
Upland, IN 46989

Telfair Academy Arts & Sciences.
121 Barnard St. P.O. Box 10081, Savannah, GA 31401

Temple B'rith Kodesh Museum.
131 Elmwood Ave., Rochester, NY 14618

Temple Museum of Jewish Religious Art & Music.
University Circle & Silver Park, Cleveland, OH 44106

Temple University, Tyler School of Art Library.
Beech & Penrose Ave., Philadelphia, PA 19126

Tennent Art Foundation Gallery.
203 Prospect St., Honolulu, HI 96813

Tennessee Botanical Gardens & Fine Arts Center.
Cheekwood, Nashville, TN 37205

Tennessee Fine Arts Center. *See* **Tennessee Botanical Gardens & Fine Arts Center**

Tennessee Historical Society.
403 7th Ave., N., Nashville, TN 37219

Tennessee State Museum.
War Memorial Bldg., Nashville, TN 37219

Tennessee Valley Art Center.
P.O. Box 474, Tuscumbia, AL 35674

Territorial Statehouse.
50 W. Capital Ave., Fillmore, UT 84631

Texas A & I University Art Gallery:
Art Dept., Santa Gertrudis, Kingsville, TX 78363

Texas Christian Univ. Student Center Gallery.
P.O. Box 292-80A, Fort Worth, TX 76129

Texas Ranger Museum.
124 N. St. Marys, Falfurrias, TX 78355

Texas Women's University Art Galleries:
TWU Sta. Box 22995, Denton, TX 72011

Textile Museum.
2320 "S" St., N.W., Washington, DC 20008 Tel 202-667-0441
Permanent Collections:
The museum possesses approximately 9,000 textiles and 700 rugs. Textiles and rugs from countries influenced by Islamic culture are especially well represented; (Spain, Egypt, Turkey, Iran and India). In addition there are rugs from the Caucasus and China, and textiles from Indonesia, East Asia, North and West Africa; also Greek island embroideries. The Greco-Roman and Coptic textiles are also of the first rank.

Thayer, General Sylanus, Birthplace. *See* **Braintree Historical Society, Inc. General Sylanus Thayer Birthpace**

Theil College, Sampson Art Gallery.
College Ave., Greenville, PA 16125

Thomas College.
W. River Rd., Waterville, ME 04961

Thomas Gilcrease Institute of American History & Art. *See* **Gilcrease, Thomas, Institute of American History & Art**

Thomas Waterman Wood Art Gallery. *See* **Wood, Thomas Waterman, Art Gallery**

Thompson, Frederick, Foundation.
441 E. 20th St., New York, NY 10010

Thorn-Sagendorph Art Gallery. *See* **Keene State College; Thorn-Sagendorph Art Gallery**

Tiffany, Louis Comfort, Foundation.
1083 Fifth Ave., New York, NY 10028

Timken Art Gallery.
Balboa Park, San Diego, CA 92101

Tioga County Historical Society Museum.
110-112 Front St., Oswego, NY 13827

Tioga Point Museum.
724 S. Main St., P.O. Box 143, Athens, PA 18810

Tippecanoe Co. Historical Museum.
909 S. St., Lafayette, IN 47901

Tiverton Historical Society.
3908 Main Rd., Tiverton, RI 02878

Toledo Artists Club.
1456 Sylvania Ave., Toledo, OH 43612

Toledo Federation of Art Societies.
P.O. Box 5588, Toledo, OH 43613

Toledo Museum of Art.
Box 1013, Toledo, OH 43697 Tel 419-255-8000
Permanent Collections:
Art from Ancient Egypt to the 20th century. Over 700 American and European paintings and an extensive collection of glass. Also sculpture, prints, photographs, decorative arts and tapestries.

Tombstone Courthouse, State Historic Park.
219 Toughnut St. P.O. Box 216, Tombstone, AZ 85638

Tome Parish Museum.
P.O. Box 397, Tome, NM 87060

Tomoka State Park Museum.
N. Beach St., Ormand Beach, FL 32074 Tel 904-677-9463
Permanent Collections:
Paintings and sculpture by Fred Dana Marsh.

Topeka Public Library Gallery of Fine Arts.
1515 W. Tenth St., Topeka, KS 66604
Permanent Collections:
Collections in the areas of glass, pottery, Kansas artists and miscellaneous prints, drawings, paintings, mostly American. Also a collection of 190 Ashanti bronze gold weights and West African wood masks.

Topsfield Historical Society.
27 Prospect St., Topsfield, MA 01983

Torrington Historical Society, Inc.
P.O. Box 353, Torrington, CT 06790

Tougaloo College Art Collections.
Tougaloo, MS 39174

Tower Gallery. *See* **Mount Mary College; Tower Gallery**

Town of Bethlehem Historical Assn.
Clapper Rd. & Rte. 144, Selkirk, NY 12158

Town of Ontario Historical Society.
115 Ridge Rd., Ontario, NY 14519

Town of Yorktown Museum.
1886 Hanover Rd., Yorktown Heights, NY 10598

Towson State Univ. Art Gallery.
York Rd., Towson, MD 21204

Trahern, Margaret Fort, Gallery. *See* **Austin Peay State Univ. Art Department, Margaret Fort Trahern Gallery**

Trail End Museum.
400 Clarendon St., P.O. Box 186, Sheridan, WY 82801

Traill County, North Dakota Historical Society.
Hillsboro, ND 58045

Trails Museum.
Rte. 2, P.O. Box 37, Ogallala, NE 69153

Transylvaina College, Moxlan Gallery.
Mitchell Fine Arts Center, Lexington, KY 40508

Traphagen School of Fashion Museum Collection.
257 Park Ave. S., New York, NY 10010
Permanent Collections:
Small, private collection of approximately 1,000 costumes plus textiles and fashion accessories of many cultures; buttons, dolls, jewelry, brass houshold objects and handmade chests from many lands.

Treasure Island Museum.
587 N. State St., St. Ignace, MI 49781

Treat Gallery. *See* **Bates College, Treat Gallery**

Trent, William, House.
539 S. Warren St., Trenton, NJ 08611

Trenton Historical Museum.
306 St. Joseph St., Trenton, MI 48183

Tribal House of the Bear.
Wrangell, AL 99929

Trinidad State Junior College Museum.
600 Prospect St., Trinidad, CO 81082

Trinity College, Austin Arts Center.
Summit St., Hartford, CT 06106

Trisolini, A.G., Memorial Gallery. *See* **Ohio University, A. G. Trisolini Memorial Gallery**

Triton Museum of Art.
1505 Warburton Ave., Santa Clara, CA 95050 Tel 408-248-4585
Permanent Collections:
Paintings by Theodore Wores and the Vivian Elmer Collection.

Trube House.
1627 Sealy Ave., Galveston, TX 77550

Truman, Harry S., Library & Museum.
Independence, MO 64050

Truman Gallery. *See* **Indiana State Univ., Truman Gallery**

Truxtun-Decatur Naval Museum.
1610 H St., N.W., Washington, DC 20006

Tryon Palace Restoration Complex.
613 Pollock St., New Bern, NC 28560

T.T. Wentworth Junior Museum. *See* **Wentworth, T.T., Junior Museum**

Tubac Center for the Arts, Santa Cruz Valley Art Assn.
Box 1314, Tubac, AZ 84540

Tubac Presidio State Historic Park.
P.O. Box 1296, Tubac, AZ 85640

Tucson Art Center, Inc.
325 W. Franklin, Tucson, AZ 85705

Tucson Museum of Art.
235 W. Alameda, Tucson, AZ 85701 Tel 602-624-2333
Permanent Collections:
Fine arts, crafts, textiles, furnishings and artifacts representing Tucson's Latin American heritage, including a large collection of Pre-Columbian objects. Also works reflecting trends in American art and contemporary Southwestern crafts; 19th and 20th century American and European paintings, sculpture and graphics; Spanish colonial art and artifacts.

Tucumcari Historical Research Institute.
416 S. Adams, Tucumcari, NM 88401

Tufts University, Gallery Eleven, Cohen Fine Arts Center:
Talbot Ave., Medford, MA 02155

Tulane University, Newcomb Art Dept., Exhibit Gallery:
60 Newcomb Pl., New Orleans, LA 70118

Tullahoma Fine Arts Center.
410 S. Jackson, Tullahoma, TN 37388

Turner Museum.
Torrington Library, 12 Dycoeton Pl., Torrington, CT 06790

Tuskegee Institute, National Historic Site, George Washington Carver Museum.
Tuskegee, AL 36088 Tel 205-727-6391
Permanent Collections:
Included are paintings, sketches, handcrafted pottery and various types of needlework, macrame and weaving all by George Washington Carver. Natural history collections of scientific interest are also present. The collection is currently expanding to include furnishings and artifacts relating to the history of Tuskegee Institute and the Booker T. Washington family.

Twain, Mark, Memorial.
351 Farmington Ave., Hartford, CT 06105

Twin City Art Foundation, Masur Museum of Art.
1400 S. Grand St., Monroe, LA 71201

Tyler Museum of Art.
1300 S. Mahon Ave., Tyler, TX 75701

Tyringham Art Galleries.
Tyringham Rd., Tyringham, MA 01264

Tyringham Institute, Jean Brown Archives.
Shaker Seed House, Tyringham, MA 01264

Tyron Palace Restoration, Stanley House & Stevenson House.
611 Pollock St., New Bern, NC 28560

Ulrich, Edwin A. , Museum of Art. *See* **Wichita State Univ., Edwin A. Ulrich Museum of Art**

Ulrich, Edwin A., Museum; Wave Crest on the Hudson.
Albany Post Rd., Hyde Park, NY 12538 Tel 914-229-7107
Permanent Collections:
Exhibits of three generations of the Waugh family.

Ulster County Community College, Visual Arts Gallery.
Stone Ridge, NY 12484

Union Mills Homestead.
Westminster R.D. 2, Union Mills, MD 21157

Union of American Hebrew Congregations; Synagogue Architecture Library.
838 Fifth Ave., New York, NY 10021

Union University Art Guild:
Hwy. 45 Bypass, Jackson, TN 38301

United Methodist Church Commission on Archives & History.
P.O. Box 488, Lake Junaluska, NC 28745

United Methodist Historical Society, Lovely Lane Museum.
2200 St. Paul St., Baltimore, MD 21218
Permanent Collections:
Baltimore Conference archives, United Methodist and Predecessor General Conferences, Washington Conference archives, Letters of John Wesley, Journals of Early Methodist Preachers, Artifacts Memorabilia of American Methodists.

United States Memorial Museum Navy Combat Art Gallery, Washington Naval Yard.
Ninth St. & M St. S.E., Washington, DC 20390

U. S. Military Academy, West Point Museum.
West Point, NY 10996

U. S. Naval Academy Museum.
Annapolis, MD 21402

United States Senate Commission on Art & Antiquities.
Rm. S-411, U.S. Capitol Bldg., Washington, DC 20510

University Gallery, University of Tennessee at Chattanooga.
Baldwin St., Chattanooga, TN 37401

University Museum, Univ. of South Carolina.
Sumter & Pendleton Sts., Columbia, SC 29208

University of Akron University Galleries.
Akron, OH 44325

University of Alabama Art Museum.
Box F, University, AL 35486

University of Alabama, University Art Gallery.
Tuscaloosa, AL 35486

University of Alaska Museum:
Fairbanks, AK 99701

University of Arizona Museum of Art.
Olive & Speedway Sts., Tucson, AZ 85721 Tel 602-626-2173
Permanent Collections:
Samuel H. Kress Collection, C. Leonard Pfeiffer Collection, Gallagher Memorial Collection and miscellaneous collections

University of Arkansas, Fine Arts Center Gallery.
Garland St., Fayetteville, AK 72701

University of California at Los Angeles, Museum of Cultural History.
405 Hilgard Ave., Los Angeles, CA 90024 Tel 213-825-4361 ; 00
Permanent Collections:
Objects representing contemporary, historic and prehistoric cultures of Africa, Oceania, the Americas, Asia, the Near East and Europe.

University of California, Berkeley, Univ. Art Museum.
2626 Bancroft Way, Berkeley, CA 94720

University of California, Davis, The Gallery.
Fourth Floor, Memorial Union, Davis, CA 95616

University of California, Irvine Art Gallery.
Irvine, CA 92717

University of California, Los Angeles, Grunwald Center for the Graphic Arts.
405 Hilgard Ave., Los Angeles, CA 90024

University of California, Riverside, University Art Galleries & California Museum of Photography.
3401 Watkins Dr., Riverside, CA 92521

University of California, San Diego, Mandeville Art Gallery:
B-027, La Jolla, CA 92093

University of California-Santa Barbara, Art Museum.
Santa Barbara, CA 93106 Tel 805-961-2951
Permanent Collections:
Sedgwick collection of Italian, Flemish, Dutch and German paintings; Morgenroth Collection of Renaissance medal and plaquettes; Dreyfus Collection of Luristan bronzes, Near Eastern ceramics and Pre-Columbian art; American paintings, sculptures, graphics, architecture and archaeology; archives of architecture in California.

University of Chicago, Bergman Gallery.
5811 S. Ellis, Chicago, IL 60637

University of Cincinnati, Tangeman University Center Art Gallery.
403 Tangeman Center, Cincinnati, OH 45221

University of Colorado, Henderson Building Fine Arts Gallery.
Boulder, CO 80309

University of Colorado Museum.
University of Colorado Mailroom, Boulder, CO 80302

University of Colorado, Permanent Collection of the Dept. of Fine Arts.
Boulder, CO 80309

University of Connecticut, Jorgensen Gallery.
Wilmington, CT 06268

University of Connecticut, William Benton Museum of Art.
Storrs, CT 06268

University of Delware, Student Center Art Gallery.
Newark, CT 19711

University of Evansville, Krannert Gallery.
Box 329, Evansville, IN 47702

University of Florida, University Gallery.
Gainesville, FL 32611 Tel 904-392-0201
Permanent Collections:
Folk art of the Andes; art of India; Pre-Columbian ceramics; miniatures and small sculptures from India; African sculptures; Archives of Florida; Photography.

University of Georgia; Georgia Museum of Art.
Jackson St., Athens, GA 30602
Tel 404-542-3254
Permanent Collections:
Eva Underhill Holbrook Collection of American Art; graphics, paintings and sculpture; Kress Study Collection.

University of Hawaii at Manoa Art Gallery.
2535 the Mall, Honolulu, HI 96822

University of Houston, Sarah Campbell Blaffer Gallery.
4800 Calhoun, Houston, TX 77004 Tel 713-749-1329

University of Idaho Museum.
Moscow, ID 83843

University of Illinois at Urbana-Champaign World Heritage Museum.
484 Lincoln Hall, Urbana, IL 61801

University of Illinois, Krannert Art Museum.
500 Peabody Dr., Champaign, IL 61820

University of Iowa Museum of Art.
Riverside Dr., Iowa City, IA 52242 Tel 319-353-3266

University of Kansas, H. Foresman Spencer Museum of Art.
1301 Mississippi, Lawrence, KS 66045 Tel 913-864-4710

University of Kentucky Art Museum.
213 Kinkead Hall, Lexington, KY 40506
Permanent Collections:
Ancient Greek, Roman, Medieval, Renaissance and 17th-20th century collections.

University of Louisville, A. R. Hite Art Institute.
Belknap Campus, Louisville, KY 40208

University of Maine at Orono Art Collection.
Carnegie Hall, Orono, ME 04473

University of Maine at Portland-Gorham, Art Gallery.
Gorham Campus, Gorham, ME 04038

University of Maine, Augusta, Gallery.
University Heights, Augusta, ME 04330

University of Maine, Mashias Art Gallery.
Machias, ME 04654 Tel 207-255-3313
Permanent Collections:
The Marin Collection

University of Maryland, College Park, Art Gallery.
College Park, MD 20742

University of Massachusetts, Amherst, University Gallery.
Fine Arts Center, Amherst, MA 01003 Tel 413-545-3670
Permanent Collections:
Primarily 20th century American drawings, prints and photographs.

University of Miami, Love Art Museum.
1301 Miller Dr., Coral Gables, FL 33146

University of Michigan Museum of Art, Alumni Memorial Hall.
525 S. State St., Ann Arbor, MI 48109
Permanent Collections:
Far Eastern art including Indian, Near Eastern and Western art from the 6th century A.D.

University of Minnesota, Coffman Union Gallery.
Minneapolis, MN 55455

University of Minnesota, Duluth, Tweed Museum of Art.
Duluth, MI 55812

University of Minnesota, Student Center Galleries.
2017 Burford, Saint Paul, MN 55108

University of Minnesota, University Gallery.
Northrop Memorial Auditorium, Minneapolis, MN 55455 Tel 612-373-3424

University of Mississippi, University Gallery.
Fine Arts Center, University, MS 38677

University of Mississippi, University Museum.
University Ave. & Fifth St., Oxford, MS 38677

University of Missouri, Columbia Museum of Art & Archaeology.
1 Pickard Hall, Columbia, MO 65201 Tel 314-882-3591
Permanent Collections:
Paintings, sculpture, graphics, archaeology of tne Near East, Egypt and the Mediterranean; Ethnology of Middle and South America, Africa and Oceania; South and Southeast Asian, Chinese and Japanese art.

University of Montana Gallery of Visual Arts.
Turner Hall & University Center Art Gallery, Missoula, MT 59801

University of Montevallo Art Gallery.
Montevallo, AL 35115
Permanent Collections:
19th and 20th century prints; paintings.

University of Nebraska, Lincoln; Sheldon Memorial Art Gallery.
Lincoln, NE 68588

University of Nebraska, Omaha, Art Galleries.
133 S. Elmwood Rd., Omaha, NE 68101

University of Nevada, Las Vegas, Art Gallery.
4505 Maryland Pkwy., Las Vegas, NV 89109

University of New Hampshire Art Galleries, Paul Creative Arts Center.
Durham, NH 03824

University of New Mexico, Harwood Foundation.
Box 766, Taos, NM 87571

University of New Mexico, University Art Museum, Fine Arts Center.
Albuquerque, NM 87131

University of North Carolina at Chapel Hill, William Hayes Ackland Memorial Art Center.
Columbia & Franklin Sts., Chapel Hill, NC 27514

University of North Carolina at Greensboro, Weatherspoon Art Gallery.
Greensboro, NC 27412

University of North Dakota.
Box 8136 University Station, Grand Forks, ND 58202

University of Northern Colorodo, John Mariani Art Gallery, Dept. of Fine Arts.
Greeley, CO 80639

University of Northern Iowa, Gallery of Art.
27th St. at Hudson Rd., Cedar Falls, IA 50613 Tel 319-273-6114

University of Notre Dame Art Gallery.
Notre Dame, IN 46556 Tel 219-283-4266

University of Oklahoma Museum of Art.
410 Boyd St., Norman, OK 73019

University of Oregon, Museum of Art.
Eugene, OR 97403

University of Pennsylvania, University Museum.
33rd & Spruce Sts., Philadelphia, PA 19104

University of Pittsburgh, University Art Gallery.
Pittsburgh, PA 15260

University of Redlands, Peppers Art Center.
1200 W. Colton Ave., Redlands, CA 92373

University of Rhode Island Gallery.
Kingston, RI 02881

University of Rochester Memorial Art Gallery.
490 University Ave., Rochester, NY 14607

University of San Diego, Founders Gallery.
Alcala Park, San Diego, CA 92110

University of Santa Clara, De Saisset Art Gallery & Museum.
Santa Clara, CA 95053
Permanent Collections:
D'Berger Collection of 18th century French Boulle furniture and ivories; 17th century tapestries; Sevre, Meissen, Royal Vienna Beehive, Royal Crown Austria, Capodimonte porcelains; Mountfort Collection of 19th century oil porcelains; Kalb Collection of 17th and 18th century graphics including Hogarth, Huret, Engelbrecht and Durer; Robinson Collection of African Artifacts; Oriental Collection, T'ang dynasty through 19th century; California Mission and Indian Collection; 20th century artists: Wynn Bullock, David Bottini, Fletcher Benton, Robert Fried and Harold Paris; collection of videotapes including Douglas Davis, Lynda Benglis, Terry Fox, Joel Glassman and the California New Deal Art Repository.

University of South Alabama, Ethnic American Slide Library.
University Blvd., Mobile, AL 36688

University of South Carolina, McKissick Museums.
Columbia, SC 29208

University of South Dakota, W. H. Over Museum.
W.H. Over Museum, Vermillion, SD Tel 605-677-5228
Permanent Collections:
Natural history, ethnology and history of South Dakota. Special collections include the David and Elizabeth Clarke Memorial Collection of Dakota (Sioux) Artifacts and the Stanley J. Morrow Collection of Photographs (1868-1883).

University of South Florida, College of Fine Arts Galleries.
4204 E. Fowler Ave., Tampa, FL 33620

University of Southern California-University Galleries.
823 Exposition Blvd., Los Angeles, CA 90007

University of Southern Colorado, Belmont Campus, Creative & Performing Arts Center.
2200 Bonfort Ave., Pueblo, CT 81001

University of Southwestern Louisiana Art Center.
P. O. Drawer 4-4290, University of Southwestern Louisiana Station, Lafayette, LA 70504

University of Tennessee at Chattanooga Art Gallery.
Baldwin St., Chattanooga, TN 37401

University of Texas at Arlington, University Art Gallery.
Fine Arts Bldg., Arlington, TX 76019

University of Texas at Austin, University Art Museum.
23rd at San Jacinto, Austin, TX 78712 Tel 512-471-7324
Permanent Collections:
James A. Michener Collection of 20th century art, 20th century Latin American art, C. R. Smith Collection of Western art and a print collection.

University of Texas at El Paso, Dept. of Art Galleries.
El Paso, TX 79968

University of the Pacific, Pacific Center for Western Historical Studies.
Stockton, CA 95204

University of the Pacific, University Center Gallery
3601 Pacific Ave., Stockton, CA 95211

University of the South Gallery of Fine Arts.
Guerry Hall, Sewanee, TN 37375

University of Utah; Utah Museum of Fine Arts.
101 Art & Architectural Center, Salt Lake City, UT 84112

University of Vermont, Robert Hull Fleming Museum.
Burlington, VT 05401
Permanent Collections:
Paintings, prints and drawings; sculpture, decorative arts; ethnographic art including African, American Indian, Pre-Columbian and Oceanic items.

University of Virginia Art Museum, T. H. Bayly Memorial Bldg..
Rugby Rd., Charlottesville, VA 22903

University of Washington, Henry Art Gallery.
Seattle, WA 98195

University of West Florida Art Gallery.
Pensacola, FL 32504

University of Wisconsin-Eau Claire, Foster Art Gallery Fine Arts Center.
100 Water St., Eau Claire, WI 54301 Tel 715-836-3277

University of Wisconsin-Madison, Memorial Union.
800 Langdon St., Madison, WI 53706

University of Wisconsin-Milwaukee, Fine Arts Gallery.
School of Fine Arts, 3200 Downer Ave., Milwaukee, WI 53201

University of Wisconsin-Oshkosh, Allen Priebe Gallery.
Oshkosh, WI 54901

University of Wisconsin-River Falls, Gallery.
Cascade St., River Falls, WI 54022

University of Wisconsin-Stout; Gallery Two Hundred Nine.
Art Dept., Menomonie, WI 54751

University of Wyoming Art Museum.
Box 3138, University Station, Laramie, WY 82071 Tel 307-766-2374
Permanent Collections:
European and American paintings, sculpture and graphics primarily from the 19th and 20th centuries.

Upper Room Devotional Library & Museum.
1908 Grand Ave., Nashville, TN 37203

Utah Division of State History.
Suite 1000, Crane Bldg., 307 W. 200 S., Salt Lake City, UT 84101

Utah State Division of Fine Art, Carriage House Gallery.
609 E. South Temple St., Salt Lake City, UT 84114

Vachel Lindsay Assn.
502 S. State St., Springfield, IL 62704

Valdosta State College Art Gallery.
N. Patterson St., Valdosta, GA 31601

Valentine Museum.
1015 E. Clay St., Richmond, VA 23219

Valentine-Varian House, Museum of Bronx History.
3266 Bainbridge Ave., Bronx, NY 10467

Valley Art Center Inc.
842 6th St., P.O. Box 65, Clarkston, WA 99403

Valparaiso University, Sloan Galleries of American Paintings & Henry F. Mollering Memorial Library:
Valparaiso, IN 46383

Van Cortland Museum, Van Cortland Park.
W. 246th St. & Broadway, Bronx, NY 10471

Van Riper-Hopper House-Wayne Museum.
533 Berdan Ave., Wayne, NJ 07470

Vandalla Statehouse Memorial.
315 W. Gallatin St., Vandalia, IL 62471
Permanent Collections:
The building is a former statehouse used by Illinois and the permanent collections are period (1830's) pieces displayed as functioning state offices.

Vanderbilt Mansion National Historic Site.
Hyde Park, NY 12538

Vanderbilt University Art Gallery:
Box 1801-B, Nashville, TN 37235

Vann House.
U.S. Hwy. 76, Spring Place, GA 30705

Varner-Hogg State Park.
1702 N. 17th St., West Columbia, TX 77486

Vassar College Art Gallery.
Raymond Ave., Poughkeepsie, NY 12601 Tel 914-452-7000, 2645

Ventura County Pioneer Museum.
77 N. California St., Ventura, CA 93001

Verde Valley Art Assn., Inc.
P.O. Box 985, Jerome, AZ 86331

Vermilion County Museum Society.
116 N. Gilbert St., Danville, IL 61832

Vermont State Craft Center at Frog Hollow.
Frog Hollow Rd., Middlebury, VT 05753

Vernon Historians, Inc.
Maple Glen Farm, Vernon, VT 05354

Vesterheim Norwegian-American Museum.
5002 W. Water St., Decorah, IA 52101

Veteran Car Museum.
2030 S. Cherokee, Denver, CO 80223

Victoria Society of Maine Women.
Victoria Mansion, 109 Danforth St., Portland, ME 04101

Vilas County Museum & Historical Society, Inc.
Sayner, WI 54560

Villa, Poncho, Museum.
Lima St., Columbus, NM 88029

Village Art Center Gallery, Inc.
39 Grove St., New York, NY 10014

Violet Oakley Memorial Foundation. *See* Oakley, Violet, Memorial Foundation

Virginia Beach Arts Center.
P.O. Box 884, Virginia Beach, VA 23452

Virginia Commonwealth Univ., Anderson Gallery.
907 1/2 W. Franklin St., Richmond, VA 23284

Virginia Historical Society.
428 N. Blvd., P.O. Box 7311, Richmond, VA 23221

Virginia Museum of Fine Arts.
Blvd. & Grove, Richmond, VA 23221 Tel 804-257-0818
Permanent Collections:
Paintings, sculptures, prints, drawings, decorative arts, objects from Ancient Egypt, Classical Greece and Rome, Medieval Byzantium, the Orient, India, Pre-Columbian South America, Medieval Europe, Renaissance and Baroque Italy, France and Germany, Impressionist France, the contemporary world as well as 18th century America.

Virginia Polytech Institute & State University Art Gallery.
20 Owens Hall, Blacksburg, VA 24061

Visual Artists & Galleries Assn., Inc.
1 World Trade Center Suite 1535, New York, NY 10048

Viterbo College Museum.
815 S. Ninth St., La Crosse, WI 54601

Vizcaya Museum & Gardens. *See* Dade County Art Museum, Vizcaya Museum & Gardens

W. A. Farnsworth Library & Art Museum. *See* Farnsworth, W. A., Library & Art Museum

Wadsworth Atheneum.
600 Main St., Hartford, CT 06103

Walker Art Center.
Vineland Place, Minneapolis, MN 55403

Walker Museum.
Route 5, Fairlee, VT 05045

Walker Museums.
Minnesota Ave., Walker, MN 56484

Wallace House.
38 Washington Pl., Somerville, NJ 08876

Wallingford Art League.
P.O. Box 163, Wallingford, CT 06492

Walnut Creek Civic Arts Gallery.
1445 Civic Dr., Walnut, CA 94596

Walter C. Rawls Museum. *See* Rawls, Walter C., Museum

Walter Elwood Museum & Art Gallery. *See* Elwood, Walter, Museum & Art Gallery

Walters Art Gallery.
600 N. Charles St., Baltimore, MD 21201 Tel 301-547-9000
Permanent Collections:
Egyptian art; Ancient East, Minoan and Mycenaean art; Greek, Etruscan and Roman art; Near-Eastern art; Coptic art; Byzantine art; pre-Romanesque and Romanesque; early Gothic art; later Gothic

art; Renaissance sculpture and decorative arts; manuscript illumination; incunabula; Italian painting; Renaissance and Northern Renaissance art; 17th, 18th and 19th century art; Far-Eastern art; Ancient American art; 19th century American art.

Walters, L.J. Jr., Gallery. *See* **Regis College, L.J. Walters Jr. Gallery**

Walworth Memorial Museum. *See* **Historical Society of Saratoga Springs Museum & Walworth Memorial Museum**

Wapello County Historical Museum.
402 Chester Ave., Ottumwa, IA 52501

Warner House.
150 Daniel St., Portsmouth, NH 03801

Warren County Historical Society.
P.O. Box 427, 210 Fourth Ave., Warren, PA 16365

Warren County Historical Society Museum.
Harmon Hall, S. Broadway, P.O. Box 233, Lebanon, OH 45036

Warsaw Historical Museum.
15 Perry Ave., Warsaw, NY 14569

Warwick Arts Foundation, Buttonwoods School.
W. Shore Rd., Warwick, RI 02886

Warwick Historical Society.
Main St., Warwick, NY 10990

Waseca County Historical Society.
Corner Fourth St.& Second Ave., N.E., Waseca, MN 56093

Washburn University, Mulvane Art Center:
17th & Jewell, KS 66621

Washington, George, Birthplace National Monument.
Washington's Birthplace, VA 22575

Washington, George, Museum.
King St. at Callahan Dr., Alexandria, VA 22301

Washington & Jefferson College Commons Gallery.
Lincoln St., Washington, PA 15301

Washington & Lee University, Dupont Gallery:
Lexington, VA 24450

Washington Art Association.
Washington Depot, CT 06793

Washington County Historical Society, Inc.
307 E. Market St., Salem, IN 47167

Washington County Museum of Fine Arts.
P.O. Box 423, Hagerstown, MD 21740

Washington State Historical Society.
315 N. Stadium Way, Tacoma, WA 98403

Washington State Univ., Museum of Art.
Pullman, WA 99164 Tel 509-335-1910

Washington University Gallery of Art:
P. O. Box 1189, Saint Louis, MO 63130 Tel 314-889-5490
Permanent Collections:
19th and 20th century European and American painting and sculpture, modern American painting, ancient coins and Greek vases, Old Master prints and drawings.

Washington's Headquarters in White Plains Known As Jacob Purcy House.
60 Park Ave., P.O. Box 1776, White Plains, NY 10601

Waterloo Art Assn.
420 W. 11th St., Waterloo, IA 56702

Waterloo Library & Historical Society.
85 Queen St., Waterloo, NY 13165

Waterloo Municipal Gallery.
225 Cedar St., Waterloo, IA 50704

Watertown Historical Society.
22 DeForest St., Watertown, CT 06795

Watertown Historical Society.
919 Charles St., Watertown, WI 53094

Watkins Gallery.
Massachusetts & Nebraska Aves., N.W. Washington, DC 20014

Watkins Institute.
Sixth Ave. at Church St., Nashville, TN 37219

Watson Gallery. *See* **Wheaton College, Watson Gallery**

Waukesha County Historical Society Museum.
101 W. Main St., Waukesha, WI 53186

Wayne Art Center.
413 Maplewood Ave., Wayne, PA 19087

Wayne County Historical Museum.
1150 N. "A" St., Richmond, IN 47374

Wayne County Historical Society.
810 Main P.O. Box 446, Honesdale, PA 18431

Wayne County Historical Society Museum.
546 E. Bowman St., Wooster, OH 44691

Wayne Museum. *See* **Van Riper-Hopper House-Wayne Museum**

Wayne State College, Norstrand Visual Arts Gallery & Fine Arts Center.
Wayne, NE 68787

Wayne State University, McGregor Memorial Community Arts Gallery:
450 W. Kirby at Cass, Detroit, MI 48824

Webster College, Loretto-Hilton Center Gallery.
130 Edgar Rd., Saint Louis, MO 63119

Weidler Art Gallery. *See* **Westmar College, Weidler Art Gallery**

Weigel, Paul, Library. *See* **Kansas State Univ., Paul Weigel Library, College of Architecture & Design**

Weill Art Gallery. *See* **Ninety-Second Street Ymha-Ywha, Weill Art Gallery**

Wellesley College Museum.
Wellesley, MA 02181 Tel 617-235-0320
Permanent Collections:
European and American paintings, drawings, sculpture (Greek through 20th century), African sculpture and Chinese ceramics.

Wellesley Historical Society, Inc.
210 Washington St., Wellesley Hills, MA 02181

Wenham Historical Assn. & Museum.
132 Main St., Wenham, MA 01984

Wentworth, T.T., Junior Museum.
8382 Palafax Hwy., P.O. Box 806, FL 32594

West Baton Rouge Museum.
845 N. Jefferson Ave., Port Allen, LA 70767

West Bend Gallery of Fine Arts.
300 S. Sixth Ave., P. O. Box 426, West Bend, WY 53095

West Hills Unitarian Fellowship.
8470 S.W. Oleson Rd., Portland, OR 97223

West Point Museum. *See* **U. S. Military Academy, West Point Museum**

West Virginia University Galleries; A & B Evandale Campus.
Morgantown, WV

Westbrook College, Joan Whitney Payson Gallery.
716 Stevens Ave., Portland, ME 04103 Tel 207-797-9546
Permanent Collections:
28 works by Chagall, Courbet, Daumier, Degas, Gaugin, Glackens, Homer, Ingres, Marquet, Monet, Picasso, Prendergast, Renoir, Reynolds, Rousseau, Sargent, Sisley, Soutine, Van Gogh, Whistler and Wyeth.

Western Association of Art Museums.
P.O. Box 9989, Oakland, CA 94613

Western Camera Museum, Inc.
3636 Main St., Riverside, CA 92501

Western Colorado Center for the Arts, Inc.
1803 N. Seventh, Grand Junction, CO 81501

Western Illinois Univ. Art Gallery.
Garwood Hall, Macomb, IL 61455

Western Kentucky Univ., Kentucky Museum.
Bowling Green, KY 42101
Permanent Collections:
American, Colonial and Federal furniture, Kentucky, American and European art, historical tools, implements, furnishings, textiles, Native American artifacts.

Western Maryland College, Gallery One.
Dept. of Art, Westminster, MD 21157

Western Montana College Art Gallery.
Billon, MT 59725

Western Reserve Historical Society.
10825 E. Blvd., Cleveland, OH 44106 Tel 216-721-5722
Permanent Collections:
Wallace Cathcart Shaker Collection, Gries Chinese Export Porcelain Collection, William Palmer Civil War Collection, Charles Hubbell aviation paintings, Nord Fan Collection, Phyllis Peckham Costume Collection.

Western Rhode Island Civic Historical Society.
365 Plainfield St., Providence, RI 02909

Western State College, Quigley Hall Art Gallery.
Gunnison, CO 81230

Western States Art Foundation.
428 E. Eleventh Ave., Denver, CO 80203

Western Woodcarvings.
Hwy. 16 Box 747, Custer, SD 57730

Westfield Athenaem, Jasper Rd. Art Museum.
6 Elm St., Westfield, MA 01085

Westmar College, Weidler Art Gallery.
Lemars, IA 51031

Westminster College Art Gallery.
New Wilmington, PA 16142

Westmoreland County Museum of Art.
221 N. Main St., Greenburg, PA 15601

Westover.
Charles City Country, Charles City, VA 23030

Wethersfield Properties of the National Society of the Colonial Dames of America.
211 Main St., Wethersfield, CT 06109

Whatcom Museum of History & Art.
121 Prospect St., Bellevue, WA 98225

Wheaton College, Watson Gallery.
E. Main St., Norton, MA 02766

Wheaton Museum of Glass.
Wheaton Village, Millville, NJ 08332

Wheelwright Museum of the American Indian.
P.O. Box 5153, Santa Fe, NM 87502
Permanent Collections:
Articles from Native American culture. Artifacts are divided into following categories: pottery; stone; jewelry; horn and bone; basketry; textiles and articles of clothing, wood, reed, bark, feather and quill; musical instruments and recordings; ceremonial foot, arm and headgear; casts; molds; vegetal products; special inventions; implements of war; articles of transportation; games, toys, dolls and novelties; drug artifacts and pipes; artwork and maps.

White Gallery. *See* Portland State Univ. White Gallery

White House.
1600 Pennsylania Ave. N.W., Washington, DC 20500 Tel 202-456-1414
Permanent Collections:
American period furniture from the late 18th and 19th century; American, European and Chinese decorative arts; collections of Presidential porcelain and glassware; portraits of Presidents and First Ladies and other national notables; late 18th, 19th and early 20th century American paintings and prints; presidential and White House memorabilia.

Whitefield House Museum. *See* Moravian Historical Society, Whitefield House Museum

Whitely, William, State Park & Shrine.
Stanford, KY 40484

Whiting, Percy H., Art Center.
401 Oak St., Fairhope, AL 36532

Whitney Museum of American Art.
945 Madison Ave., New York, NY 10021 Tel 202-794-0600
Permanent Collections:
19th and 20th century American art: paintings, watercolors, drawings, sculptures and prints.

Whitte Memorial Museum. *See* San Antonio Museum Assn., Whitte Memorial Museum

Wichita Art Assn., Inc.
9112 E. Central, Wichita, KS 67206

Wichita Art Museum.
619 Stackman Dr., Wichita, KS 67203 Tel 316-268-4621
Permanent Collections:
Roland P. Murdock Collection of American Art; M. C. Naftzger Collection of Charles M. Russell paintings, drawings and sculpture; L. S. and Ida L. Naftzger Collection of Prints; Gwendolyn Houston Naftzger Collection of Edward Boehm and Dorothy Doughty Porcelain Birds; Kurdian Collection of Pre-Columbian artifacts; Ed L. and Faye Davison Collection of Paintings (primarily Southwestern artists); Robert B. Frizzell Collection

(Blake's "Book of Job" and Goya's "Los Caprichos"); Powell Collection of Oriental Ivories; Mrs. Cyrus M. Beachy Doll Collection; Clare Hannum Collection (Indian baskets and weaving); Paul Edwards Collection (contemporary ceramics); Florence Naftzger Evans Collection (porcelains and faience).

Wichita Falls Museum & Art Center.
Two Eureka Circle, Wichita Falls, TX 76308

Wichita Historical Museum Assn.
3751 E. Douglas Ave., Wichita, KS 67218

Wichita Public Library.
223 S. Main, Wichita, KS 67202

Wichita State Univ., Edwin A. Ulrich Museum of Art.
McKnight Art Center, Wichita, KS 67208
Permanent Collections:
Edwin A. Ulrich Collection of American Art; the Wichita State University Sculpture Collection; the University Collection Of European Art; the University Collection of Contemporary American Art; the University Collection of Ancient Art of the Americas; the University Collection of Southwestern Art; the University Print Collection; the University Study Collection; the Joan Miro mural, "Personnages Oiseaux."

Wickland.
U.S. Hwy. 62, Bloomfield Rd., Bardstown, KY 40004

Wicomico Historical Society.
309 Gay St., Salisbury, MD 21801

Wight, Frederick S., Art Galleries.
405 Hilgard Ave., Los Angeles, CA 90024

Wilber Czech Museum.
P.O. Box 217, Wilber, NE 68465

Wilkes College, Sordoni Art Gallery.
150 S. River St., Wilkes-Barre, PA 18703
Permanent Collections:
Nineteenth century European paintings and sculpture.

Wilkin County Historical Society-Saint Francis Home.
Breckenrige, MN 56520

Willamette University, Putnam University Center.
900 State St., Salem, OR 97301

Willet Stained Glass Studio.
10 E. Moreland Ave., Philadelphia, PA 19118

William S. Hart Museum. *See* Hart, William S., Museum

William Trent House. *See* Trent, William, House

William Whitely State Park & Shrine. *See* Whitely, William, State Park & Shrine

Williams, Roger, Park Museum.
Roger Williams Park, Providence, RI 02905

Williams College, Museum of Art.
Main St., Willamstown, MA 01267
Permanent Collections:
Representative works from nearly every period of art history, including Assyrian bas-reliefs; the Bolles-Rogers collection of ancient gold; medieval sculpture and stained glass; Renaissance paintings from the Kress collection; Spanish and Italian Baroque paintings; the Lehman collection of French 19th century paintings; a collection of watercolors by Homer, Hopper, Prendergast, Marin, Demuth and others; the Lawrence H. Bloedel Collection of Modern American Art; African sculpture; Asian painting and Sculpture.

Williams County Historical Society, Frontier Museum.
Williston, ND 58801

Williamsburg. *See* Colonial Williamsburg Foundation

Wilmar Lapidary Museum.
232 & Pineville Rd., Bucks County, Pineville, PA 18946

Wilmette Historical Museum.
825 Green Bay Rd., Wilmette, IL 60091

Wilmington-New Hanover Museum.
814 Market St., Wilmington, NC 28401

Wilson, Woodrow, Birthplace Foundation.
20 N. Coalter St., Box 24, Stauton, VA 24401

Wilson, Woodrow, Boyhood Home.
1750 Hampton St., Columbia, SC 29201

Wilson Printing House.
The Street, Deerfield, MA 01342

Wilson-Warner House.
Main St., Odessa, DE 19730

Wilton.
S. Wilton Rd., Richmond, VA 23226

Wilton Historical Society.
150 Danbury Rd., Wilton, CT 06897

Winchendon Historical Society, Inc.
50 Pleasant St., Winchedon, MA 01475

Winchester Frederick County Historical Society.
610 Tennyson Ave., Winchester, VA 22601

Wind River Valley Artists Guild.
Box 26, Lubois, WY 82513

Windward Artists Guild.
P.O. Box 851, Kailua, HI 96734

Wine Museum of San Francisco.
633 Beach St., San Francisco, CA 94109 Tel 415-673-6990

Permanent Collections:
The Christian Brothers collection of graphic and decorative arts.

Winterthur Museum & Gardens.
Rte. 52, Winterthur, DE 19735
Permanent Collections:
The museum contains more than 100 domestic interiors displaying what has been called the largest and richest assemblage of American arts ever brought together. Furniture, textiles, silver, pewter, porcelain, earthenware, paintings and prints are arranged in an attempt to relate features of design, period and place of manufacture. Furnishings range in date from 1650 to 1850, but the collection is especially rich in American furniture of the Queen Anne, Chippendale and Federal periods.

Winthrop College of Art.
Rock Hill, SC 29733

Wistariahurst. *See* City of Holyoke Museum; Wistariahurst

Witte Memorial Museum.
3801 Broadway, San Antonio, TX 78209

Wolfe, Catharine Lorillard, Art Club, Inc.
802 Broadway, New York, NY 10003

Wolfeboro Historical Society.
S. Main St., Wolfeboro, NH 03894

Wolters, Edwin, Memorial Museum & Library.
609 E. Ave. 1, Shiner, TX 77984

Women in Arts Foundation, Inc.
435 Broome St., New York, NY 10013

Women's Art Registry of Minnesota.
414 First Ave N., Minneapolis, MN 55401

Women's City Club of Boston.
40 Beacon St., Boston, MA 02108

Women's City Club of Cleveland.
320 Superior Ave. N.E., Cleveland, OH 44114

Women's Slide Registry.
105 Hudson, New York, NY 10013

Wood, Naomi, Collection at Woodford Mansion.
Fairmount Park, 33rd & Dauphin Sts., Philadelphia, PA 19132 Tel 215-229-6115

Wood, Thomas Waterman, Art Gallery.
Main St., Montpelier, VT 05602

Wood Art Gallery.
135 Main St., Montpelier, VT 05602
Permanent Collections:
Oils and watercolors by Thomas Waterman Wood (1823-1903).

Woodlawn.
Mount Vernon, VA 22121

Woodlawn Plantation.
9000 Richmond Hwy., Rte. 1,
Fairfax County, VA 22309

Woodmere Art Gallery.
9201 Germantown Ave.,
Philadelphia, PA 19118

**Woodrow Wilson Birthplace
Foundation.** *See* Wilson,
Woodrow, Birthplace
Foundation

Woodrow Wilson Boyhood Home.
See Wilson, Woodrow, Boyhood
Home

Woodrow Wilson House.
2340 S St. N.W., DC 20008

**Woodstock Historical Society, the
Dana House.**
26 Elm St., Woodstock, VT
05091 Tel 802-457-1822
Permanent Collections:
Dana House with furnished
period rooms, costumes, library,
manuscript and photograph
archives, dolls and toys, tools
and farm implements in the
attached barn. Also a special
collection of etchings of John
Taylor Arms.

Woolaroc Museum.
Rte. 3, Bartlesville, OK 74003

Wooster Community Art Center.
Ridgebury Rd., Danbury, CT
06810

Worcester Art Museum.
55 Salisbury St., Worcester,
MA 01608 Tel 617-799-4406

Art Center, Osborn Foundation.
Box 7572, Tulsa, OK 74105

Wornall, John, House.
61th Terr. & Wornall Rd.,
Kansas City, MO 64113

**Wright State University, Fine
Arts Gallery:**
Dayton, OH 45435

**Wright, Theodore Lyman Art
Center.** *See* Beloit College,
Theodore Lyman Wright Art
Center

**Wustum, Charles A., Museum of
Fine Arts.**
2519 N. Western Ave., Racine,
WI 53404

**Wyandot County Historical
Society.**
130 S. Seventh St., Upper
Sandusky, OH 43351

Wyoming Council on the Arts.
200 W. 25th St., State of
Wyoming Offices, Cheyenne,
WY 82002

**Wyoming Historical & Geological
Society.**
69 S. Franklin St., Wilkes-
Barre, PA 18701

Wyoming State Art Gallery.
Barrett Bldg., Cheyenne, WY
82002

**Yakima Valley Museum &
Historical Assn.**
2105 Tieton Dr., Yakima, WA
98902

Yale University Art Gallery:
1111 Chapel St., P.O. Box
2006, Yale Station, New
Haven, CT 06520 Tel 203-
436-0574
Permanent Collections:
Oriental collections of Near
and Far Eastern art;
Department of prints, drawings,
watercolors, paintings and
sculpture (European and
American); Italian paintings;
Trumball Collection of
Revolutionary pictures and
miniatures; Mabel Brady
Garvar Collection of American
painting and decorative arts;
European paintings; Edwin
Austin Abbey Collection.

**Yankton College, Durand Art
Collection.**
James Lloyd Library, Yankton,
SD 57078

Yellowstone Art Center.
401 N. 27th St., Billings, MT
59101

Yellowstone County Museum.
Logan Field, P.O. Box 959,
Billings, MT 59103

Yellowstone National Park.
Yellowstone Park, WY 82190

Yesteryears Museum.
Main & River Sts., Sandwich,
MA 02563

**Yonkers Public Library, Fine Arts
Dept.**
1500 Central Park, Yonkers,
NY 10710

York Academy of Arts.
625 E. Philadelphia St., York,
PA 17403

York Institute Museum.
375 Main St., Saco, ME 04072

Yorker Yankee Village.
R.D.1, P.O. Box 349, Watkins
Glen, NY 14891

Yosemite Museum Collections.
National Park Service, P.O.
Box 577, Yosemite National
Park, CA 95389

**Youngstown State University,
Kilcawley Center Art Gallery:**
410 Wick Ave., Youngstown,
OH 44555

Youth Cultural Center.
815 Columbus Ave., Waco, TX
76702

Yuma Art Center.
P.O. Box 1471, Yuma, AZ
85364

Zanesville Art Center.
620 Military Rd., Zanesville,
OH 43701

Zigler Museum.
411 Clara St., Jennings, LA
70546

URUGUAY

Museo de Arte Industrial.
San Salvador 1674, Montevideo

Museo del Indio.
Calle 25 de Mayo 315,
Tacuarembo

**Museo del Instituto Geologico del
Uruguay.**
Montevideo

Museo Departmental de San Jose.
San Jose de Mayo

Museo Municipal de Bellas Artes.
Ave. Millan 4015, Montevideo

**Museo Nacional de Artes
Plasticas.**
Tomas Giribaldi 2283, Parque
Rodo, Apdo 271, Montevideo

**Museo Nacional de Artes
Plasticas.**
Tomas Giribaldi 2283 Esq Julio
Herrera y Reissig, Parque
Rodo, Montevideo

**Museo y Archivo Historico
Municipal.**
Juan Carlos Gomez 1362,
Montevideo

VATICAN CITY

**Cappele, Sale e Gallerie
Affrescate.**
C/O Musei Vaticani, Vatican

**Collezione d'Arte Religiosa
Moderna.**
C/O Musei Vaticani, Vatican

Musei Vaticani.
Vatican City
Permanent Collections:
Classsical Antiquities, Oriental
Antiquities, Etruscan/Italic
Antiquities, Early Christian
Art, Byzantine, Medieval and
Modern Art, Missionary,
Ethnological, Modern Religious
Art.

**Museo Chiaramonti e Braccio
Nuovo.**
C/O Musei Vaticani, Vatican

Museo Gregoriano Egizio.
C/O Musei Vaticani, Vatican

Museo Gregoriano Etrusco.
C/O Musei Vaticani, Vatican

Museo Gregoriano Profano.
C/O Musei Vaticani, Vatican

Museo Missionario-Etnologico.
Musei Vaticani, Vatican

Museo Pio Clementino.
C/O Musei Vaticani, Vatican

Museo Pio Cristiano Lateranense.
C/O Musei Vaticani, Vatican

Museo Profano.
C/O Musei Vaticani, Vatican

Museo Sacro.
C/O Musei Vaticani, Vatican

Pinacoteca Vaticana.
C/O Musei Vaticani, Vatican

Vatican Museums. *See* Musei
Vaticani

VENEZUELA

Michelena, Arturo, Museum. *See*
Museo Arturo Michelena

Museo Arturo Michelena.
Esquina de Urapal 82, la
Pastoria, Caracas 101

Museo de Arte Colonial.
Ave. Quinta Anauco, Panteon
y Calle Gamboa, San
Bernardino, Caracas, 101

**Museo de Arte Moderno "Jesus
Soto".**
Ave. Germania y Mario
Briceno Iragorry, Ciudad
Bolivar

Museo de Bellas Artes.
Parque Sucre, Los Caobos, 105,
Caracas

**Museo de Bellas Artes de
Caracas.**
Los Caobos, Caracas 105

Museo de la Tradicion.
Juncal 3-45, Barcelona

Museo "Emilio Boggio".
Esquina de las Monjas, Caracas
101

Museo Fundacion "John Boulton".
Bolivar 180, la Guaira, Caracas

**Museo Pedagogico de Historia del
Arte.**
Instituto de Arte, Faculdad de
Humanidades y Educacion,
Ciudad Universitaria, Caracas

Museo "Talavera".
Calle Bolivar 103, Ciudad
Bolivar

VIETNAM

Fine Arts Museum.
Hanoi

**National Museum of Cham
Sculpture.**
Da-Nang

National Museum of Viet-Nam.
Botanical Garden, Saigon

Royal Museum.
Hue

WEST GERMANY

A. Paul Weber Haus. *See* Weber,
A. Paul, Haus

Ahrgau-Museum.
D-5483 Bad Nevenahr-
Ahrweiler, Altenbaustr. 5

**Akademisches Kunstmuseum der
Universitat Bonn.**
D-5300 Bonn, am Hofgarten
21, 02221/737282 OR 737738
Permanent Collections:
Original antique works of the
Mediterranean; plaster casts of
classical sculpture.

Allgauer Heimatmuseum.
D-8960 Kempten, Grosser
Kornhausplatz 1

Alte Pinakothek.
Barerstr 27, Munich

**"Altes Haus" des Saarland-
Museums.**
D-6600 Saarbrucken, Altes
Haus, St. Johanner Markt 24

**Altes Schloss Meersburg mit
Schlossmuseum, Kunst und
Kulturgeschichtliche
Sammlungen.**
D-7758 Meersburg

Altonaer Museum im Hamburg.
D-20000 Hamburg 52, Baron-
Voght-Str. 50, Jenisch-Park

**Antiken und Abgussammlung der
Philipps-Universitat.**
D-3550 Marburg, Beigenstr. 11

Antikenmuseum.
D-1000 Berlin 19, Schlossstr. 1

**Archaeologisches Institut der
Universitat Heidelberg.**
D-6100 Heidelberg, Marstallhof
4

Archaologische Sammlung.
D-2300 Kiel, Dusternbroaker
Weg 1-7, Kunsthalle

**Archaologische Sammlung der
Universitat Erlangen-Nurnberg.**
D-8250 Erlangen, Kochstr. 4

**Archaologisches Museum der
Universitat Munster.**
D-4400 Munster, Domplatz
20/22
Permanent Collections:
Classical Antiquity Collection.

Asein-Museum.
D-3590 Bad Wildungen, Laustr.
26

**Athiopien-Haus Schloss
Bauschlott.**
D-7531 Neulingen-Bauschlott,
Haupstr. 70

Augustinermuseum.
D-7800 Freiburg I. Br.,
Augustinerplatz

Badisches Landesmuseum.
D-7500 Karlsruhe, Schloss,
0721/26921
Permanent Collections:
Egyptian, Greek, Etruscan and
Roman artwork. Archaeology,
sculptures and handicrafts from
the Middle Ages to the present
day. Turkish trophy collection,
coin collection, folklore and
"Jugenstil" collection.

Barlach, Ernst, Gedenkstatte.
D-2418 Ratzeburg, Barlachplatz
3

Barlach, Ernst, Haus.
D-2000 Hamburg 52, Klein-
Flottbek, Baron-Voght-Str. 50a,
Jenisch-Park
Permanent Collections:
Paintings, sculptures and prints
by Ernst Barlach

**Bartholomaus-Schmucker-
Heimatmuseum.**
D-8222 Ruhpolding,
Jagdschhloss, Schlosstr.

**Bayerischen
Staatsgemaldessammlungen.**
2 Meiserstr. 10, 8000 Munich
2, 5591/291

**Bayerischer Verwaltung der
Staatlichen Schlosser, Garten
und Seen.**
Postfach 38 0120, 8000
Munchen 38, 089 1208 227
Permanent Collections:
Collections of Bavarian palaces
and castles including
Nymphemburg,
Neuschwanstein, Linderhof,
Herrenchiemsee, Castle at
Nuremburg, Castle at
Aschaffensburg, Residenz
Munich, Residenz Wurzburg,
Plassenburg ob Kulmbach, and

Ehrenburg at Coburg and
others.

Bayerisches Nationalmuseum.
Prinzregentenstrasse 3, 22
Munich

Behnhaus-Museum.
D-2400 Lubeck, Konigstr. 11

Bergisches Museum.
D-5652 Burg/Wupper, Schloss,
Schlossplatz 1

Berlin-Museum.
D-1000 Berlin 61, Lindenstr.
14

Besteckmuseum.
D-5000 Cologne 1, Burgmauer
68

Bildergalerie.
D-8859 Bertoldsheim, Schloss

Bischofliches Diozesan-Museum.
D-4400 Munster, Domplatz 20-
22

Bischofliches Diozesanmuseum.
D-4500 Osnabruk,
Domportikus

**Bischofliches Dom-und Diozesan-
Museum.**
D-6500 Mainz Domstr. 3

**Bischofliches Dom-und Diozesan-
Museum.**
D-5500 Trier, Banthusstr. 6

Bleikeller im St. Petri-Dom.
D-2800 Bremen, Am Markte

**Bonner Bildungsmuseum-Kasimer
Hagen Sammlung.**
D-5300 Bonn, Wilelmstr. 34

Braith-Mali-Museum.
D-7950 Biberach, Museumstr. 2

Brucke-Museum.
D-1000 Berlin 33, Bussardsteig
9

Brunsbutteler Heimatmuseum.
D-2212 Brunsbuttel, Am Markt
12

**Buchbindermuseum, Abteilung des
Gutenbergs Museum.**
D-6500 Mainz, Leibfrauenplatz
5

Bundespostmuseum.
D-6000 Frankfurt 70,
Schaumainkai 53, (0611) 61 02
31

Burghof-Museum.
D-4770 Soest, Burghofstr. 22

Busch, Wilhelm, Museum. *See*
Wilhelm-Busch-Museum

City Art Gallery.
Grabbeplatz 4, (Postfach 1120),
Dusseldorf

Clemens-Sels-Museum.
D-4040 Neuss. im Obertor

Couven-Museum.
D-5100 Aachen, Huhnermarkt
17

**Design Center Stuttgart des
Landesgewbeamtes Baden-
Wurttemberg.**
Kanzleistr. 19, 7000 Stuttgart

Deutsche Barockgalerie.
D-8900 Augsburg,
Maxmilianstr. 45, Schaezler-
Palais

Deutsches Brotmuseum.
D-7900 Ulm, Furstenkerstr.
17

Deutsches Elfenbeinmuseum.
D-6122 Erbach, Otto-Glenz-
Str. 1

Deutsches Goldschmiedehaus.
D-6450 Hanau 1, Altstatter
Markt 6
Permanent Collections:
Collection of modern gold and
silversmithing.

Deutsches Jagdmuseum.
D-8000 Munich 2,
Neuhauserstr. 53

Deutsches Klingenmuseum.
D-5650 Solingen 1,
Wuppertaler Str. 160

**Deutsches Korb-und
Flechtmuseum.**
D-8626 Michelau, Bismarckstr.
4, Stolzel-Haus

Deutsches Ledermuseum.
D-6050 Offenbach Am Main,
Frankfurter Str. 86, (06 11) 81
30 21
Permanent Collections:
European arts and crafts, shoe
collection from Europe and all
over the world, shadow
puppets, arts and crafts of
African nomads, arts and crafts
of North American Indians.

**Deutsches Schloss-und
Beschlagemuseum.**
D-5620 Velbert, Rathaus,
Thomasstr. 1

Deutsches Tapeten-Museum.
D-3500 Kassel, Schloss
Wilhelmshohe

Deutsschordenmuseum.
D-6900 Bad Mergentheim,
Schloss

**Neue Sammlung-Staatliches
Museum fur Angewandte Kunst.**
D-8000 Munich 22, Prinz-
Regenstr. 3

Diozesan-Museum.
D-7407 Rottenburg am Neckar

Diozesanmuseum.
D-8050 Freising, Domberg 21

Diozesanmuseum.
D-8833 Eichstatt, Leonrodpl. 3

Diozesanmuseum Freising.
D-8400 Regensburg 1,
Frustliches Schloss
Emmeransplatz, Postfach 142,
08161/2432
Permanent Collections:
Sculpture, paintings (12th
through 20th century), religious
art, folk art.

Dithmarscher Landesmuseum.
D-2223 Meldorf, Butjestr. 4

**Dr. Otto Bloss-Gedenkstatte-und
Werkstattsammlung.**
D-8630 Coburg, Callenberger
Str. 70

Dom-Museum.
D-6400 Fulda, Domplatz 1

Dom-Museum.
D-4232 Xanten 1, Kapitel 8

**Dom-Museum und Dom-
Schatzkammer.**
D-4400 Munster, Domplatz 32

Dom-und Diozesan-Museum.
D-6720 Speyer, Domplatz

Domschatz.
D-8050 Freising, Dom

Domschatz.
D-8833 Eichstatt,
Kapitelsaristei

**Domschatz und Museum des St.-
Petri-Domes.**
D-3580 Frirzlar, Dr. Jestadt-
Platz 11

Domschatzkammer.
D-5500 Trier, Dom

Domschatzkammer.
D-4300 Essen, Burgplatz 2

Domschatzkammer.
D-5000 Cologne, Roncalliplatz
2

**Domschatzkammer des Aachener
Domes.**
D-5100 Aachen, Domhof 4a

**Domschatzkammer und
Dombaumuseum.**
D-4950 Minden, Grosser
Domhof 10

Droste-Hulshoff-Museum.
D-4410 Roxel, Burg Hulshoff
Frtr. V. Droste-Hulshoff

Elfenbein-Museum.
D-6968 Walldurn, Burgst.

Ernst, Karl, Osthaus Museum.
D-5800 Hagen, Hochstr. 73
Permanent Collections:
Twentieth century art.

Ernst Barlach Gedenkstatte. *See*
Barlach, Ernst, Gedenkstatte

**Erzbischofliches Diozesan-
Museum.**
D-5000 Koln 1, Roncalliplatz
2, (0221) 24 45 46

Erzbischofliches Diozesanmuseum.
D-4790 Paderborn, Im Dom

Erzbischofliches Diozesanmuseum.
D-8390 Passau, Schloss
Oberhaus

Erzbischofliches Diozesanmuseum.
479 Paderborn, Postfach 1480
Permanent Collections:
Christian art of all centuries.

**Escuela Superior de Bellas Artes
"Ernesto de la Carcova".**
D-8600 Bamberg, Domplatz 5

Falkenhof-Museum.
D-4440 Rheine, Teife Str.

**Fertung Marienberg mit
Rundkirche, Furstgarten.**
D-8700 Wurzburg, Festung
Marienberg

Fichtelgebirgs-Museum Wunsiedel.
D-8592 Wunsiedel, Spitalhof 1-
2

Filialmuseum Lustheim. *See*
**Meissener Porzellan-Sammlung
Stiftung Ernst Scheider**

Formsammlung in der Werkkunsteschule.
D-3330 Braunschweig, Boitzemer Str. 230

Forschungesstelle fur Papier-Geschicte.
D-8000 Munchen 26, Postfach

Frankenwald-Heimat-Museum.
D-8640 Kronach, Veste Rosenberg 1

Frankfurter Goethe-Museum.
D-6000 Frankfurt, Freises Deutsches Hoch-Stift, Grosser Hirschagraben 23, 0611/28 28 24

Frankisch-Homenlohesches Heimatemuseum.
D-7180 Crailsheim, Lange Str.

Fugger-Museum.
D-8943 Babenhausen, Schloss

Furst Thurn und Taxis Schlossmuseum.
D-8400 Regensburg 1, Furstliches Schloss, Emmeransplatz, P.O. Box 211, 0941 51041

Furstlich Furstenbergische Sammlungen und Schlossmuseum.
D-7710 Donaveschingen, Karlplatz 7

Furstlich Furstenbergisches Schlossmuseum.
D-7710 Donaueschingen, Schloss

Furstlich Hohenzollernsches Museum.
D-7480 Sigmaringen, Schloss

Furstlich Oettingen-Wallerstein's'sche Bibliothek und Kunstsammlung, Schloss Harburg.
D-8856 Harburg
Permanent Collections:
Illuminated manuscripts from the 8th-16th century; goldsmith's work; enamel and ivory work; carpets and wood sculpture from the 15th and 16th century.

Furstlich Ysenburg-und Budingenesches Schlossmuseum.
D-6470 Budingen, Schloss

Furstluch-Lippisches Residenzschloss.
D-4930 Detmold, Schloss, 05231-22507
Permanent Collections:
Historic settings; Gobelin tapestries, porcelain, glass, weapons and arms, furniture and portraits.

Gablonzer Galerie.
D-8950 Kaufbeuren-Neugablonz, Marktgasse

Galeria des Zwanzigst Jahrhunderts.
D-8400 Regensburg

Galerie der Stadt Stuttgart.
D-7000 Stuttgart, Schlossplatz 2

Galerie Kunstlerglide Buslat.
D-7531 Bauscholott Schloss

Gaubodenmuseum.
D-8440 Straubing, Fraunhoferstr. 9

Gemaldeausstellung Frauenchiemsee.
D-8211 Frauenchiemsee

Gemaldegalerie.
D-4967 Buckebung, Schloss

Gemaldegalerie.
D-1000 Berlin 33, Arnimallee 23/27

Gemaldegalerie Alte Meister und Antikenabteilung.
D-3500 Kassel, Schloss Wilhelmshohe

Gemaldegalerie-Stiftung Pommern.
D-2300 Kiel, Schloss, Rantzaubau, Danische Str. 44

Gemaldegalerie und Graphische Sammlung Kunsthalle zu Kiel.
D-2300 Kiel, Dusternbrooker Weg 1-7

Gemaldesammlung im Paula-Becker-Modersohn-Haus.
D-2800 Bremen, Bottcherstr. 8-10

Gemaldessammlung der Universitat Erlangen-Nurnberg.
D-8520 Erlangen, Schlossgarten 1

Georg-Kolbe-Museum.
D-1000 Berlin 19, Sensburger Allee 25

Gerhard Marcks Stiftung. *See* **Marcks, Gerhard, Stiftung**

Germanische Nationalmuseum.
Postfach 95 80, 8500 Nurnberg 11

Gewerbemuseum.
D-8500 Nurnberg, Gewerbemuseumplatz 2

Gipsformerei.
D-1000 Berlin 19, Sophie-Charlotte-Str. 17/18

Glasmuseum.
D-5308 Rheinbach, Vor dem Voigtstor 23

Glyptothek.
D-8000 Munich 2, Konigsplatz 3

Goethehaus. *See* **Frankfurter Goethe-Museum**

Gottfried-Neukam-Kunst-Sammlungen.
D-8640 Kronach, Veste Rosenberg 1

Graf-Luxburg-Museum.
Schloss Aschach, D-8731 Aschach

Graphische Sammlung.
D-8900 Augsbuurg, Maximlianstr. 46, Schaezler-Palais

Graphische Sammlung der Universitats Erlangen-Nurnberg.
Universitatsbibliothek, D-8520 Erlangen, Universitatsstr. 4

Graphische Sammlung Joseph Heller in der Staadtsbibliothek Bamberg.
D-8600 Bamberg, Domplatz 8

Gronegau-Museum.
D-4520 Melle, Wallgarten 2

Grossherzogliche Porzellansammlung Im Prinz Georgs-Palais.
D-6100 Darmstadt, im Schlossgarten

Hamburger Kunsthalle.
Glockengiesserwal, 2 Hamburg, 24 82 51
Permanent Collections:
Paintings (all schools from the 14th to the 20th century), sculpture (primarily 19th and 20th century), prints and drawings (all schools from 14th to 20th century), ancient coins, medals (all schools from 15th to 20th century).

Hansjakobmuseum.
D-7612 Haslach, Hansjakobstr. 13

Heimat-und Spessartmuseum.
D-8770 Lohr am Main, Schlossplatz 1

Heimat-und Wallfahrtsmuseum.
D-6968 Walldurn, Haus "Zum Guldenen Engel"

Heimathaus.
D-8340 Pfarrkirchen, Stadtplatz 1, Postfach 69

Heimathaus Munsterland.
D-8180 Telgte

Heimatkindliche Sammlungen.
D-4630 Bochum, an der Kemnade 10

Heimatkundliche Sammlungen.
D-8952 Marktoberdorf, Eberle-Kobl-Str. 20, Rathaus

Heimatmuseum.
D-8872 Burgau, Schloss

Heimatmuseum.
D-5485 Sinzig, Schloss

Heimatmuseum.
D-7850 Lorrach, Burghof 5

Heimatmuseum.
D-7890 Waldshut, Kaiserstr.

Heimatmuseum.
D-5138 Heinsberg, Hochst. 21

Heimatmuseum.
D-8980 Oberstdorf, Oststr. 13

Heimatmuseum.
D-7930 Ehingen, Kasemengasse 2

Heimatmuseum.
D-8399 Rotthalmunster, Rathaus

Heimatmuseum.
D-8870 Gunzburg, Rathaugasse

Heimatmuseum.
D-2370 Rendsburg, Altes Rathaus

Heimatmuseum.
D-8170 Bad Tolz, Schlossplatz 2

Heimatmuseum.
8970 Immenstadt, Klosterplatz 3

Heimatmuseum.
D-8931 Obernzell, Schlossplatz 2

Heimatmuseum.
D-8474 Oberviechtach, Marktplatz

Heimatmuseum.
D-2150 Buxtehude, St.-Petri-Platz

Heimatmuseum.
D-8930 Schwabmunchen, Museumstr. 18

Heimatmuseum.
D-8908 Krumbach, Heinrich-Sinzstr. 5

Heimatmuseum.
D-7700 Uberlingen, Krummebergstr. 30

Heimatmuseum.
E-8953 Obergunzburg, Altes Pfarrhaus

Heimatmuseum.
D-8080 Furstenfeldbruck, Altes Rathaus

Heimatmuseum.
D-8950 Kaufbeuren, Kaisergaschen 12-14

Heimatmuseum.
D-8090 Wasserburg, Herrengasse 15 U. 17

Heimatmuseum.
D-8052 Moosburg, Stadtplatz 13, Rathaus

Heimatmuseum.
D-8068 Pfaffenhofen, Haptplatz, Rathaus

Heimatmuseum.
D-80258 Erding, Rathaus, Landshuter Str. 1

Heimatmuseum.
D-6320 Alsfeld, Hochzeitshaus am Marktplatz

Heimatmuseum.
D-3428 Duderstadt, Oberkirche 3 H. Blaschke

Heimatmuseum.
D-8162 Schiliersee, Schradlhaus, Rathausstr. 1

Heimatmuseum.
D-8850 Donauworth, im Ried 103, Hintermeierhaus

Heimatmuseum.
D-8898 Schrobenhausen 1, Lenbachstr. 22, Postfach 1380

Heimatmuseum.
Berchtesgaden, Schloss Adelsheim, Schroffenbergallee 6

Heimatmuseum der Stadt.
D-8948 Mindelhelm, Haubestr. 2

Heimatmuseum der Stadt Calw und Herman-Hesse Gedenkstatle.
D-7260 Calw, Bischofstr. 48

Heimatmuseum Friedburg Schloss.
D-8904 Friedburg, Bierweg 15

Heimatmuseum im Schloss Ratibor.
D-8542 Roth

Heimatmuseum "Steinernes Haus".
D-6967 Buchen, Kellereistr. 29

Heimatmuseum und Kustgewerbe-Sammlung.
Burg Franenberg, D-5100 Aachen, Bismarckstr. 68

Heimatschau der Stadt.
D-5202 Hennef 1, Katharineenturm

Herrenhaus Altenhof.
D-2330 Altenhof, Post Eckernforde

Herzog Anton Ulrich Museum.
Museumstrasse 1, D-33 Braunschweig, Brunswick, (05 31) 4 93 78/4 95 89

Herzog Anton Ulrich Museum Burg Dank Warderode.
D-3300 Braunschweig, Burgplatz 4

Hessisches Landesmuseum.
D-6100 Darnstadt, Freidensplatz 1

Hetjens Museum.
C-4000 Dusseldorf, Palais Nesselrode, Schulstr. 4

Hildesheimer Domschatz.
D-3200 Hildesheim, Domhof 16

Historische Fraunhofer Glashutte.
D-8714 Benediktebeuern., Fraunhofer Str. 126

Historisches Museum der Stadt Koln Abteilung Kolnisches Stadtmuseum.
Zeughaustrasse 1-3, Cologne, 66 23 88
Permanent Collections:
Graphics; coin collection.

Historisches Museum in der Stadt Bamberg.
D-8600 Bamberg, Domplatz 7

Historisches Stadtmuseum.
D-8263 Burghausen, Burg

Hochster Museum Heimatmuseum.
D-6230 Frankfurt 80, Schlossplatz

Hoesch, Leopold, Museum.
D-5160 Duren

Hoffmann Von Fallersleben-Museum.
D-3183 Fallersleben, Schlosspl. 5

Hohenlohe-Museum Schloss Neuenstein.
D-7113 Neuenstein, Schlosstr. 49
Permanent Collections:
Weapons, furniture (15th-20th century), porcelain, oil paintings, engravings, Gobelin tapestries. Original kitchen from the 15th century (1485).

Huldigungssaal.
D-3380 Goslar, im Rathaus

Ikonenmuseum.
D-88771 Autenried, Schloss

Ikonenmuseum.
D-4350 Recklinghausen, Kirchplatz 2a

Jagdschloss Schachen.
D-8100 Garmisch-Partenkirchen

Jenish-Haus. *See Altonaer Museum im Hamburg*

Jerusalemhaus.
D-6330 Wetzlar

Justinus-Kerner-Haus.
D-7102 Weinsberg, Ohringer Str. 3

Kaiser Wilhelm Museum.
D-4150 Krefeld, Karlsplatz 35

Kaiserburg Nurnberg.
D-8500 Nurnberg, auf der Burg 13

Karl-Ernst-Osthaus Museum. *See Ernst, Karl, Osthaus Museum*

Katharinenkirche.
D-2400 Lubeck, Konigstr.

Kaulbachmuseum der Stadt Arolsen.
D-3548 Arolsen, Kaulbachstr. 3

Keramiksammlung.
D-7081 Baldern, Schloss

Kestner-Museum.
Trammplatz 3, 3000 Hannover

Kirchenmuseum.
D-7614 Gegenbach, Pfarrei

Kirchenschatz.
D-77880 Sackingen, St. Fridolinsmunster

Kirchenschatz St. Johann.
D-4500 Osahbruck, Johannisstr.

Kleine Galerie.
C-7967 Bad Waldsee, im Elisabethenbad

Kloster-Kunstsammlung.
D-2308 Preetz

Kloster Wienhausen
D-7962 Wienhause, am der Kirche 1

Klosterkirche.
D-7902 Blaubeuren, Klosterhof 2

Klostermuseum.
D-8942 Ohobeuren, Postfach 45

Kolbe, George, Museum. *See Georg-Kolbe-Museum*

Konigspesel.
D-2251 Hallig Hooge, Hanswarft

Kreis-Heimatmuseum.
D-5130 Geilenkirchen, Vogteistr. 2

Kreis und Heimatmuseum auf dem Bogenberg.
D-8443 Bogenberg, Post Bogen

Kreis-und Stadtmuseum.
D-8800 Ansbach, Schaitbergerstr. 10

Kreisheimatmuseum.
D-4791 Wewelsburg, Burg

Kreisheimatmuseum.
D-3330 Helmstedt, Botticherstr. 2

Kreismuseum.
D-2418 Ratzeburg Domhof 13

Kreismuseum.
D-4558 Bersenbruck, Stifthof 4

Kreismuseum.
D-5450 Neuweid 1, Raiffeisenplatz 1a

Kubin-Archiv.
D-2000 Hamburg 11, Alter Fischmarkt 3

Kulturhistorisches Museum.
D-4800 Bielefeld, Welle 61

Kunstausstellungen im Spendhaus.
D-7410 Reutling En Spendhausstr. 8

Kunstbibliothek.
Jobens-Strasse 2, Berlin

Kunstgewerbemuseum.
D-1000 Berlin 19, Schloss Charlottenburg

Kunstgewerbemuseum der Stadt Koln.
Eigelsteintorburg, 5000 Cologne, 2 21 38 60
Permanent Collections:
Handicrafts from the Middle Ages to the present.

Kunstgussmuseum.
D-3270 Rendsburg, Ahlmann Gmbh, Gluck-Auf-Allee

Kunsthalle Bielefeld.
D-4800 Bielefeld, Artur-Ladebeck-Str. 5, 05 21/51 24 79
Permanent Collections:
Art museum of the 20th century.

Kunsthalle Bremen.
Am Wall 207, D-28 Bremen, (0421) 32 4785
Permanent Collections:
Paintings from the 15th to 20th centuries; sculpture from the 19th and 20th centuries; drawings and prints from the 15th to the 20th centuries; illustrated books.

Kunsthalle Koln.
Josef-Haubrich-Hof 1, Cologne

Kunsthalle Nurnberg.
D-8500 Nurnberg, Lorenzer Str. 32

Kunsthaus Heylshof.
D-6520 Worms, Stephansgasse 9

Kunstmuseum.
D-4000 Dusseldorf, Ehrenhof 5

Kunstsammlung der Nicolaikirche.
D-4192 Kalkar

Kunstsammlung der Universitat Gottingen.
D-3400 Gottingen, Hospitalstr. 10

Kunstsammlung Nordrhein-Westfalen.
Jacobostr 2, Schloss Jagerhof, 4 Dusseldorf

Kunstsammlungen.
D-7133 Maulbronn, im Kloster

Kunstsammlungen der Veste Coburg.
D-8630 Coburg, Veste Coburg, 95055/56
Permanent Collections:
Glass, ceramics, arms collections, coins, medallions, autographs, handicrafts, paintings, plastics, carriages, sleighs and historic rooms.

Kunstsammlungen im Kloster Lune.
Lune, D-3140 Luenburg

Kunstsammlungen im Schloss Rheinstein.
D-6531 Trechtlinghausen

Kunstsammlung Lorenzkapelle Rottweil.
D-7210 Rottweil, Postfach 108

Kunstverein Braunschweig, Haus Salve Hospes.
D-3300 Braunschweig, Lessingplatz 12, (0531) 495 56

Kunstverein Konstanz.
D-7750 Konstanz, Wessenbergstr. 41

Kupferstickabinett.
DDR-1000 Berlin 33, Schloss Charlottenburg

Kurfurstliches Haus mit Lapidarium.
D-6143 Lorsch, Kloster

Kurpfalzisches Museum.
D-6900 Heidelberg, Hauptstr. 97

Landesmuseum fur Kunst und Kulturgeschichte.
D-2900 Oldenburg, Schloss

Landschaftsmuseum.
D-8650 Kulmbach, Bauergasse 2, Postfach 1969

Landwirtschaftliche Gertesammlung.
D-8580 Bayreuth 8

Lehmbruck, Wilhelm, Museum. *See* **Wilhelm-Lehmbruck-Museum**

Lehrgalerie der Volkshochschule Erlangen.
D-8520 Erlangen, Friedrischstr. 17

Lenbachmuseum.
D-8898 Schrobenhausen 1, Ulrich-Peisser-Gasse 1, Postfach

Leopold-Hoesch-Museum. *See* **Hoesch, Leopold, Museum**

Liebieghaus, Museum Alter Plastik.
Schamainkai 71, Frankfurt 6000, 638907
Permanent Collections:
Egyptian, Greek, Roman, Medieval, Baroque, Rococco, Classic and East Asian sculpture.

Limburg Domschatz.
D-6250 Limburg, Rossmarkt

Limburger Diozesan-Museum.
D-6250 Limburg, Schloss

Lippisches Landesmuseum.
D-4930 Detmold, Ameide 4

Lobdengau-Museum im Bischofshof.
D-6802 Ladenburg

Lokalmuseum.
D-8852 Ain, Kirchplatz 143

Ludwig-Roselius-Museum. *See* **Roselius-Haus**

Mainfrankisches Museum.
D-8700 Wurzburg, Festung
Marienberg, 0931/43016
Permanent Collections:
Medieval and Baroque painting;
sculpture from the Middle Ages
and the Baroque period;
prehistory; city history; arts
and crafts and folk art.

Marcks, Gerhard, Stiftung.
D-2800 Bremen, am Wall 208,
0421 32 72 00
Permanent Collections:
Sculpture, prints and graphics.

Markisches Museum.
D-5810 Witten, Husemannstr.
12
Permanent Collections:
German paintings, drawings
and graphics since 1900.

Marstallmuseum.
C/O Schloss Nymphenburg,
Munich, 089 1208 227.

**Martin von Wagner Museum der
Universitat Wurzburg.**
D-8700 Wurzburg,
Residenz/Sudflugel, 0931 31
866
Permanent Collections:
Antiquities collection and
painting gallery.

Maximillan-Museum.
D-8900 Augsburg, Philippine-
Welser Str. 24

**Meissener Porzellan-Sammlung
Stiftung Ernst Scheider.**
D-8042 Oberschleissheim,
Schloss Park, Lustheim, 22 25
91, 22 25 92
Permanent Collections:
2,000 pieces of 18th century
Meissen porcelain.

Mittelmosel-Museum.
D-5580 Traben-Trarbach,
Moselstr.

Mittelrhein Museum.
D-5400 Koblenz, Florinsmarkt
15

Mittelrheinisches Landesmuseum.
D-6500 Mainz, Grosse Bleiche
49/51

Mobelsammlung.
D-7912 Weissenborn,
Kirchplatz, Post-Fach 3,

**"Moderne Galerie" des Saarland-
Museums.**
D-6600 Saarbrucken,
Bismarckstr. 13-15

Morgner, Wilhelm, Haus. *See*
Wilhelm-Morgner-Haus

Muiska-Museum.
Metzstrasse 31, 80 D-8000
Munich, 4484145
Permanent Collections:
Collection Frankenberg;
Kolawole's Motion-Art.

Munchner Stadtmuseum.
D-8000 Munich 2, St.-Jakobs-
Platz 1

**Museen fur Kunst und Kultur-
Geschichte der Hansestadt
Lubeck.**
D-2400 Lubeck, Duvekenstr.
21

Museum.
D-8450 Amberg,
Eichenforstgasse 2

Museum Abtei Liesborn.
D-7723 Liesborn, Abteiring 8,
P.O. Box 87

Museum Altes Rathaus.
D-7730 Villengen,
Rathausgasse 1

Museum auf der Willibaldsburg.
D-8833 Eichstatt

Museum Bochum.
D-4630 Bochum, Kortumstr.
147

Museum Bottinger Haus.
8600 Bamberg

Museum der Grafschaft Mark.
Burg Altena, D-5990 Altena

Museum der Stadt Koln.
An der Rechtschule, Cologne

Museum der Stadt Regensburg.
D-8400 Regensburg,
Dachauplatz 2-4

Museum des Kreises Plon.
D-2320 Plon, Schlossberg 3

Museum des Siegerlandes.
D-5900 Siegen, Oberes Schloss

Museum Folkwang.
D-4300 Essen 1, Bismarckstr.
64/66

**Museum fur Abgusse Klassischer
Bildwerke.**
D-8000 Munich 2, Meiserstr.
10

**Museum fur Bauerliche und
Sakrale Kunst.**
D-8222 Ruhpolding, Pfarrgasse
2

Museum fur Deutsche Volkskunde.
D-1000 Berlin 33, im Winkel
6-8

Museum fur Indische Kunst.
0-1000 Berlin 33, Takustr 40

Museum fur Islamische Kunst.
D-1000 Berlin 33, Takustr, 40

**Museum fur Kunst und Gewerbe
Hamburg.**
D-2000 Hamburg 1,
Steintorplatz, 24 825 26 30
Permanent Collections:
Sculpture and applied art of
Europe from the Midddle Ages
to present; antique art, art of
the distant north, graphics
collection, folk art collection,
collection of photographic
history.

**Museum fur Kunst und
Kulturgeschicte der Stadt
Dortmundt.**
D-4628 Cappenberg, Schloss

Museum fur Kunsthandwerk.
Schaumankai 15,6 Frankfurt

Museum fur Moderne Keramik.
D-6705 Deidesheim
Permanent Collections:
Modern ceramics from nearly
80 German potters and a few
examples from potters from
abroad.

Museum fur Ostasiatische Kunst.
D-1000 Berlin 33, Takustr. 40

Museum fur Ostasiatische Kunst.
Universitatstrasse 100, 5000
Cologne, 40 50 38

Permanent Collections:
Art from China, Japan and
Korea.

Museum fur Volkerkunde.
D-1000 Berlin 33, Arnimallee
23-27

**Museum fur Vor-und
Fruhgeschichte.**
D-1000 Berlin 19, Schloss
Charlottenburg

**Museum fur Vor-und
Fruhgeschicte.**
D-6000 Frankurt, Justinianstr.
5

Museum im Stadt Turm.
D-8492 Furth I. Wald,
Schlossplatz

**Museum Katharinehof und
Muhlentrum.**
D-4193 Kranenburg,
Muhlenstr. 7, Postfach 106

Museum Ludwig. *See* **Wallraf-
Richartz-Museum, Museum
Ludwig**

**Museum Rade im Naturpark
Oberalster.**
D-2111 Rade, im Naturpark
Oberalster

Museum Schloss Lembeck.
D-4274 Lembeck

Museum Villeroy & Boch.
D-66442 Mettlach, Saaruferstr.

Museum Wasserburg.
D-4294 Anholt

Nationalgalerie.
D-1000 Berlin 30, Potsdamer
Str. 50

Nationalgalerie.
C/O Staatliche Museen
Preussicher Kulturbesitz, Berlin

Neue Galerie.
D-3500 Kassel, Schone
Aussicht 2

Neue Galerie-Sammlung Ludwig.
D-5100 Aachen,
Komphausbadstrasse 19, RUF
47 25 61

**Neue Pinakothek und
Staatsgalerie Moderne-Kunst.**
Prinzergentenstr 1, Munich

Neue Residenz Bamberg.
D-8600bamberg Domplatz 8

**Neue Sammlung im Oberhaus-
Museum.**
D-8390 Passau, Schloss
Oberhaus

Neuenstein. *See* **Hohenlohe-
Museum Schloss Neuenstein**

Neues Schloss Bayreuth.
D-8580 Bayreuth, Ludwigstr.
21

**Neues Schloss und Ludwig II-
Museum.**
D-8210 Herrenchiemsee

**Neuses Schloss Schleissheim und
Staatsgalerie.**
D-8042 Oberschleissheim,
Max-Emanuel-Platz 1

**Niedersachsishes Landesgalerie
und Stadtische Galerie.**
Hannover, am Maschpark 5

Nolde, Emil und Ada, Museum.
See **Stiftung Seebull Ada und
Emil Nolde**

Oberhausmuseum.
D-8390 Passau, Schloss
Oberhaus

**Oldenburger Stadtmuseum-
Stadtische Kunstsammlungen.**
D-2900 Oldenberg,
Raiffeisenstr. 32/33, Postfach
1187, (0441) 1 45 38
Permanent Collections:
Theodor-Francksen Collection,
which includes two villas
decorated in 19th century style,
The Bernhard Winter
Collection (an Oldenburgian
painter of the 19th century),
Elise Bamberger Collection of
European and Asian Art,
Gallery of Modern Times
(paintings and sculptures made
by Oldenburgian artists in the
20th century).

**Oskar Schlemmer-Archiv,
Staatsgalerie Stuttgart.**
D-7000 Stuttgart, Konrad-
Adenauer-Str. 32

Ostdeutsche Galerie.
D-8400 Regensburg, Dr.
Johann-Maier-Str. 5

**Palais Papius, Sammlung
Europaischer Wohnkultur.**
D-6330 Wetzlar,
Kornblumengasse 1

**Paramenten-und Schatzkammer
der Benedictinerabtei.**
D-8351 Niederaltaich

Paula-Becker-Modersohn-Haus.
Bottcherstrasse D-2800 Bremen
Permanent Collections:
Thirty paintings of Paula
Becker-Modersohn.

Pfalzgalerie.
D-6750 Kaiserslautern,
Museumsplatz 1, Postfach 2860

Pfalzmuseum.
D-8550 Forchheim,
Kapellenstr. 16, Pfalz

**Porzellansammlung der Stadt
Frankenthal.**
D-6710 Frankenthal, Rathaus

Prinz-Johann-Georg-Sammlung.
D-6500 Mainz, Binger Str. 26

Rat fur Formgebrung.
D-6100 Darmstadt, Eugen-
Bracht-Weg 6

**Rautenstrauch-Joest Museum fur
Volkekunde der Stadt Koln.**
Ubierring 45, Cologne, 31 10
65/66
Permanent Collections:
European folk culture and art.

**Regionales Heimatmuseum fur das
Renchtal.**
7603 Oppenau, Rathaus

Regionalmusem.
D-4420 Alsfeld, Rittergasse 3
bis 5

Reisengebirgssammlung.
D-8952 Marktoberdof, Eberle-
Kogl-Str. 11, Martinsheim

Rekenbert-Museum.
D-6710 Frankenthal, Stadt,
Verwaltungs-Gebade III

Residenz Ansbach mit Keramiksammlung und Gemaldegalerie.
D-8800 Ansbach, Residenz

Residenz Ellingen.
D-8836 Ellingen

Residenz Wurzburg.
D-8700 Wurzburg, Residenzplatz 2

Residenzmuseum Munchen.
D-8000 Munich 22, Max-Joseph-Platz 3

Rheinisches Landesmuseum Bonn.
Colmanstrasse 14-16, D-5300 Bonn

Rhonmuseum.
D-8741 Fladungen, Rathau, Postfach 13

Romerhaus Schwarzenacker.
D-6650 Homburg

Romisch-Frankisches Museum.
D-5480 Remagen

Romisch-Germanisches Museum.
D-5170 Julich, Markt 1, P.O. Box 209

Romisch-Germanisches Museum.
Roncalliplatz 4, Cologne, 2 21 44 38/45 90
Permanent Collections:
European prehistory, mosaics, Roman glass collection, gold collection, coin collection.

Roselius-Haus.
D-2800 Bremen, Bottcherstr. 4, Postfach 697

Ruhr-Universitat Bochum, Instit fur Archaologie.
D-4630 Bochum-Querenburg, Universitats-Str., 0234-7004738

St. Annen-Museum.
D-2400 Lubeck St. Annen-Str. 15

St. Nikolaus Hospital.
D-5550 Bernkastel-Kues, Cusanusstr.

Sammlung des Archaologischen Instituts der Eberhard-Karls-Universitat Tubingen.
D-7400 Tubingen, Nauklerstr. 2, 07071/29 60 94
Permanent Collections:
Greek and Roman Antiquities, Numismatics.

Sammlung des Archaologischen Instituts der Universitat Gottingen.
D-3400 Gottingen, Nikolausbergerweg 15

Sammlung Deutsches Plakat-Museum.
D-4300 Essen, Bismarckstr. 64/66, Steeler Str. 29

Sammlung Ruhr-Universitat Bochum, Institut Fur Archaologie.
D-4630 Bochum-Querenburg, Universitats-Str.
Permanent Collections:
Museum of Classical Antiquity, Museum of Contemporary Art, Museum of Greek, Roman and Medieval Coins.

Sammlungen, Domvorhalle.
D-3380 Goslar, Kaiserbleck 10

Sammlungen Jagdschloss Grunewald.
D-1000 Berlin 33, Jagdschloss Grundwald

Sammlungen Schloss Bellevue.
D-1000 Berlin, Tiergarten

Sauerland-Museum.
D-5770 Arnsberg

Schackgalerie.
Prinzregenterstr. 9 Munich

Schatzkammer.
D-8262 Altotting, Kapellplatz 4

Schatzkammer der Residenz Munchen.
D-8000 Munich 22, Residenzstr. 1

Schatzkammer und Religienkappelle.
Kloster Andechs, D-8131 Erling-Andechs

Schaumburgisches Heimatmuseum.
D-3260 Rinteln, Eulenburg

Schelfenhaus.
D-8712 Volkach, Schelfengasse 1

Schleswig-Holsteinisches Landesmuseum.
Schleswig, Schloss Gottorf

Schloss Ahrensburg.
D-2070 Ahrensburg, Lubecker Str. 1

Schloss Augustusburg.
D-5040 Bruhl, Schlosstr. 6

Schloss Benrath.
D-4000 Dusseldorf, Benrather Scholballee

Schloss Charlottenburg.
D-1000 Berlin 19, Luisenplatz

Schloss der Grafen von Schonborn.
D-8602 Pommersfelden, Post Steppach

Schloss Ehrenburg.
D-8630 Coburg

Schloss Eremitage zu Bayreuth.
Bayreuth

Schloss Eutin.
D-2420 Eutin

Schloss Falkenlust.
D-5040 Bruhl, Schlobstr. 6

Schloss Glienicke.
D-1000 Wannsee, Koniginstr.

Schloss Harburg. *See* **Furstlich Oettingen-Wallerstein'sche Bibliothek und Kunstsammlung, Schloss Harburg**

Schloss Hohenschwangau.
D-8959 Hohenschwangau

Schloss Linderhof.
D-8103 Linderhof

Schloss mit Kunstausstellung.
D-6830 Schwetzingen

Schloss Neuschwanstein.
D-8959 Neuschwanstein

Schloss Nymphenburg.
D-8000 Munchen 19, Schloss Nymphenburg

Schloss Pruun.
D-8421 Pruun

Schloss Rastatt mit Schlosskirche.
D-7750 Rastatt 22-Forch

Schloss Tegle.
D-1000 Berlin 27, Adelheidallee 19/21

Schloss Wolfegg.
D-7962 Wolfegg

Schloss, Zweigmuseum des Badischen Landesmuseums.
D-7520 Bruchsal

Schlossmuseum.
D-8471 Winklarn

Schlossmuseum.
D-7090 Ellwagen

Schlossmuseum.
D-8751 Mespelbrunn

Schlossmuseum.
D-2392 Glucksburg, Schloss

Schlossmuseum.
D-7140 Ludwigsburg, Schloss

Schlossmuseum.
Burg Lichetenstein, D-7411 Honau

Schlossmuseum.
D-8240 Berchtesgaden. Schlossplatz 2

Schlossmuseum.
D-8481 Thumsenreuth, Post Reuth B. Erbendorf

Schlossmuseum der Stadt Aschaffenberg.
D-8750 Aschaffenberg, Schlossplatz

Schlossmuseum (Wurttembergisches Landesmuseum, Stuttgart)
D-6992 Weikersheim

Schmuckmuseum.
D-7530 Pforzheim, Reuchlinhaus, Jahn-Str. 42

Schnutgen Museum.
Cacilienstr. 29, Cologne, 2 21 23 10
Permanent Collections:
Art of the Middle Ages through the Baroque period.

Schwarzwaldmuseum.
D-7291 Lossburg

Schwarzwaldsammlung-Magdalenenbergmuseum.
D-7730 Villingen-Schwenningen

Skulpturengalerie.
D-1000 Berlin 33, Arnimallee 23-27

Sommerschloss mit Rokoko-Hofgarten.
D-8702 Veitshochheim

Staatgalerie Fussen.
D-8958 Fussen, Magnusplatz 10, Hohes Schloss

Staatliche Antikensammlungen und Glyptothek.
D-8000 Munich 2, Konigsplatz 1, 28 30 46 & 28 30 47

Staatliche Graphische Sammlung.
Meiserstr. 10, D-8000 2 Munich

Staatliche Kunsthalle.
Hans Thoma Str. 2-4, D-7800 Karlsruhe, 0721/135 3355
Permanent Collections:
Ancient German painting; Dutch painting, 16th-18th century; French painting, 17th-20th century; German painting from Baroque period to the present. Sculpture from the 15th and 16th centuries. Graphics from the 19th and 20th century through the present

Staatliche Munzsammlung.
D-5000 Munich 2, Residenzstr. 1, (089) 22 72 21/22
Permanent Collections:
Coins and medals, gems (Intaglios, cameos), paper money and primitive money.

Staatliche Museen Preussicher Kulturbesitz Berlin.
Stauffenbergstrasse 41, 30 Berlin
Permanent Collections:
Includes collections of the State Museums Foundation for Cultural Treasures: Kunstgewerbemuseum, Antikenmuseum, Gemaldegalerie, Kunstbibliothek, Kupferstichkabinett, Nationalgalerie, Gipsformerei, Museum fur Deutsch Volkskunde, Agyptisches Museum, Museum fur Islamische Kunst, Skulpturengalerie, Museum fur Indische Kunst, Museum fur Ostasiatische Kunst, Museum fur Volkerkunde, Museum fur Vor und Fruhgeschichte.

Staatliche Sammlung Agyptischer Kunst.
Meiserstr 10, D-8000 2 Munich, (089) 5591-350
Permanent Collections:
Egyptian, Coptic and Meroitic art.

Staatliches Klosterschloss.
D-7401 Bebenhausen, Kloster

Staatliches Museum fur Volkerkunde.
D-8000 Munich 22, Maxmilienstr. 42

Staatlichliche Graphische Sammlung.
Schlosstr. Johannisburg, D-8750 Aschaffenburg

Staatsgalerie.
D-8300 Landshut, Staatsresidenz

Staatsgalerie.
D-8900 Augsburg, Maxilianstr. 46

Staatsgalerie.
D-8400 Regensburg, Dachauplatz 2-4

Staatsgalerie.
D-7000 Stuttgart, Konrad-Adenauer-Str. 32

Staatsgalerie.
Schloss St. Johannisburg. D-8750 Aschaffenburg

Staatsgalerie Bayreuth im Neuen Schloss Bayreuth.
D-8580 Bayreuth, Ludwigstr. 21

Staatsgalerie Burghausen.
D-8263 Burghausen, Burg

Staatsgalerie im Oberhaus Museum.
D-8390 Passau, Schloss Oberhaus

Staatsgalerie in der Neuen Residenz.
D-8600 Bamberg, Domplatz 8

Staatsgalerie in der Residenz, Europaische Barockgalerie.
D-8800 Ansbach

Staatsgalerie Ingolstadt.
D-8070 Ingolstadt, Paradeplatz

Staatsgalerie Moderner Kunst.
D-8000 Munchen 22, Haus der Kunst, Westflugel, Prinzregentenstr. 1

Staatsgalerie Plassenburg.
D-8650 Kulmbach

Stadelisches Kunstinstitut und Stadtische Galerie.
Durerstrasse 2, D-6000 Frankfurt

Stadische Kunstsammlungen.
D-8990 Lindau, Markplatz 6

Stadt-Und Kreis-Heimatmuseum.
D-3340 Wolfenbuttel, Schlossplatz

Stadt-und Kreismuseum.
D-8300 Landshut, Stadtresidenz, Altstadt 79

Stadtarchiv und Stadtische Sammlungen.
D-8360 Lauf, Rudolfshofer Str. 13

Stadtgeschichtliches Museum.
D-4030 Ratingen, Speestr. 21

Stadtgeschichtliches Museum Dusseldorf.
D-4000 Dusseldorf, Backerstr. 7/9

Stadtische Galerie.
D-8700 Wurzburg, Hofstr.3

Stadtische Galerie "Die Fahre".
D-7968 Saulgau, Schulstr. 6

Stadtische Galerie im Lenbachhaus.
Luisenstrasse 33, 2 Munich

Stadtische Galerie Roesenheim.
D-8200 Rosenheim, Max-Bram-Platz 2

Stadtische Galerie Schloss Oberhausen.
D-4200 Oberhausen, Sterkrader Str. 48

Stadtische Graphische Sammlung.
D-8500 Nurnberg, Burg 2 (Kaiserstallung)

Stadtische Kunsthalle Dusseldorf.
Grabbeplatz 4, Dusseldorf 1

Stadtische Kunsthalle Mannheim.
D-6800 Mannheim 1, Moltkestr. 9

Stadtische Kunsthalle Recklinghausen.
D-4350 Recklinghausen, Franz-Grosse-Perdekamp-Str., 58 73 95
Permanent Collections:
International art since 1945.

Stadtische Kunstsammlungen.
D-8520 Erlangen, Marktplatz 1

Stadtische Kunstsammlungen.
D-7500 Karlsruhe 1, Zahringerstr. 96-98, P.O. Box 6260

Stadtische Sammlung.
D-8480 Weiden, Unterer Markt 23

Stadtische Sammlungen.
D-4140 Rheinhausen, Handelstr. 8 Ebbers

Stadtisches Bodensee-Museum.
D-7990 Friedrichshafen 1, Kirchplatz 2, P.O. Box 129

Stadtisches Gustav-Lubcke-Museum.
D-4700 Hamm, Museumsstr. 2

Stadtisches Heimatmuseum.
D-7620 Wolfach

Stadtisches Heimatmuseum.
D-5830 Schwelm, Schloss Martfeld

Stadtisches Heimatmuseum.
D-2067 Reinfeld, Neuer Garten 9

Stadtisches Heimatmuseum, Wurmgau-Museum.
D-8130 Starnberg, Possenhofenerstr. 9

Stadtisches Kramer-Museum.
D-4152 Kempen 1, Burgstr. 19, 02152/5 25 26

Stadtisches Krugemuseum.
D-8581 Creussen, am Rennsteig 8

Stadtisches Kunsthaus.
D-4290 Bocholt, Salierstr. 6

Stadtisches Kunstmuseum Bonn.
Rathausgasse 7, D-5300 Bonn

Stadtisches Museum.
D-8670 Hof, Hallplatz 3

Stadtisches Museum.
D-5500 Trier, Simeonstift

Stadtisches Museum.
D-8120 Weilheim, Marienplatz 1

Stadtisches Museum.
D-4330 Mulheim, Leineweberstr. 1

Stadtisches Museum.
D-4500 Osanbruck, Heger-Tor-Wall 27

Stadtisches Museum.
D-5090 Leverkusen, Schloss Morsbroich

Stadtisches Museum.
D-2380 Schleswig, Frierichstr. 7 bis 11

Stadtisches Museum.
D-4550 Monghengladbach, Bismarckstr. 97

Stadtisches Museum.
D-8720 Schweinfurt, Martin-Luther-Platz 12

Stadtisches Museum.
D-3400 Gottingen, Ritterplan 7/8, Postfach 31

Stadtisches Museum.
D-8940 Memmingen, Zangmeisterstr. 8, Postfach 2240

Stadtisches Museum.
D-7070 Schwabisch Gmund, Johannisplatz 3, im Prediger

Stadtisches Museum Flensburg.
D-2390 Flensburg, Lutherplatz 1

Stadtisches Museum Haus Koekkoek.
D-4190 Kleve, Kavarinerstr. 33
Permanent Collections:
Painting and sculpture of the Lower Rhine (12th-20th centuries).

Stadtisches Museum "Haus Kupferhammer".
D-4788 Warstein, Belecker Landstr.

Stadtisches Museum im Vogthaus.
D-7980 Ravensburg, Charlottenstr., Postfach 2180

Stadtisches Museum, Schloss Rheydt.
4050 Munchengladbach 2, Schloss Rheydt
Permanent Collections:
Renaissance and Baroque museum and city history collection.

Stadtisches Reiss-Museum.
D-6800 Mannheim, C 5. (Zeughaus), P.O. Box 2203

Stadtmuseum.
D-8920 Schongau, Blumenstr. 2

Stadtmuseum.
D-8540 Schwabach, Pfarrgasse 8

Stadtmuseum.
D-8150 Furth. Schloss Burgfarnbach

Stadtmuseum.
D-8860 Nordlingen, Vordere Gerbergasse 1

Stadtmuseum.
D-8580 Bayreuth, Ludwigstr., Neues Schloss

Stadtmuseum Rottweil.
D-7210 Rottweil, Haupstr. 21

Stadtresidenz Landshut.
D-8300 Landshut

State Museums, Foundation for Prussian Cultural Treasures. *See* **Staatliche Museen Preussicher Kulturbesitz Berlin**

Steintormuseum.
D-4180 Goch, am Steintor

Stiftsmuseum.
D-8750 Aschaffenburg, Stiftsplatz

Stiftung Ernst Scheider.
D-4000 Dusseldorf, Schloss Jagerhof, Jacobistr. 2

Stiftung Heimathaus Traustein.
D-8220 Traunstein, Stadtplatz 2-3, Post-Fach 1829

Stiftung Seebull Ada und Emil Nolde.
D-2261 Neukirchen uber Niebull, Seebull, (Schlesw.), 04664/3 64

Stuck-Jugendstil-Museum.
D-8000 Munich 80, Stuck-Villa, Prinzregentenstr. 60

Stukk-Museum.
D-1000 Berlin 44, Karl-Marx-Str. 17

Suermondt-Ludwig-Museum der Stadt Aachen.
Wilhemstrassee 18, 51000 Aachen

Sylter Heimatmuseum.
D-2286 Keitum

Textilmuseum.
Frankenring 20, D-4150 Krefeld, 770357
Permanent Collections:
Textiles.

Topferei-Museum.
D-51631 Angerweje, Pastoratsweg 1

Topferstube mit Keramikmuseum.
D-8182 Bad Wiessee, Anton-Von-Rieppel-Str. 21

Ubersee-Museum.
D-2800 Bremen, Bahnhofsplatz 13, 0421/397 8357

Ulmer Museum.
D-7900 Ulm, Neue Str. 92 bis 96

Vestisches Museum.
D-4350 Recklinghausen, Franz-Grosse-Perdekamp-Str.
Permanent Collections:
Early and primitive history; city history; Ecclesiastical art; furniture; handicrafts; coin collection; weapons; folklore; geology collection.

Von der Heydt-Museum.
D-5600 Wuppertal 1, Turmhof

Von Wagner, Martin, Museum der Universitat Wurzburg. *See* **Martin von Wagner Museum der Universitat Wurzburg**

Vonderau-Museum.
D-6400 Fulda, Stadtschloss und Universitatsplatz

Waffensammlung der Bottcherstrasse GMBH.
D-2800 Bremen, Bottcherstr. 4

Wallraf-Richartz-Museum, Museum Ludwig.
An der Rechtschule, Cologne, 2 21 23 70
Permanent Collections:
Ancient and modern art; graphics collection; art and museum library.

Weber, A. Paul, Haus.
D-2418 Ratzeburg, am Domhof

Werdenfelser Museum.
D-8100 Garmisch-Partenkirchen, Ludwig-Str. 47

Westallgauer Heimatmuseum.
D-8999 Weiler, Haus Nr.11

Westfalisches Freilichtmuseum Bauerliche Kulturdenkmale.
D-4930 Detmold, Krummes Haus

Westfalisches Landesmuseum fur Kunst und Kulturgeschichte.
D-4400 Munster, Domplatz 10

Wilhelm-Busch-Museum.
D-8000 Hannover,
Georgengarten

Wilhelm-Hack-Museum.
D-6700 Ludwigshafen, Berliner
Strasse 23, 0621-5043044
Permanent Collections:
Arts and crafts from the Celtics
to the Frankonians; Medieval
art; painting, sculpture and
graphic arts of the 20th
century.

Wilhelm-Lehmbruck-Museum.
D-4000 Duisburg, Dusseldorfer
Str. 51

Wilhelm-Morgner-Haus.
D-4770 Soest, Thomastr.

Wuppertaler Uhrenmuseum.
D-5600 Wuppertal 1,
Poststr.11, 0202/45 60 47
Permanent Collections:
Collection of clocks, watches,
insignia and antique rugs.

**Wurttembergisches
Landesmuseum.**
D-7000 Stuttgart 1, Altes
Schloss, Schiller-Platz 5

Zahringer Museum.
D-7570 Baden-Baden, Neues
Schloss

YUGOSLAVIA

Arkade-Rastavni Salon.
Trg Revolucije 18, YU-61000
Ljubijana

**Crkva-Muzej Na Oplencu-
Zadusbina Tetra I.
Karadordevica.**
YU-34360 Oplenac Kod Topole

Dijecezanski Muzej.
Rtg Strosmajerov 6, YU-54400
Djakovo

**Dijecezanski Muzej Zagrebacke
Nadbiskupije.**
Kaptol 28, YU-41000 Zagreb

Dolenjski Muzej.
Ul. Muzejska 7, YU-68000
Novo Mesto

Franjevacki Samostan Sv. Franje.
Trg Vranjanina 1, YU-57000
Zadar

Galerija.
Ul. Lvretska 11, YU-58000
Split

**Galerija Akad, Kipara Rista
Stijevica.**
YU-81000 Titograd

Galerija Benko Horvat.
Rokov Perijov 4, YU-41000
Zagreb

Galerija "Branislav Deskovic".
YU-58420 Bol, Otok Brac

**Galerija Decjeg Likovnog
Stvaralastva.**
Ul. Admirala Gepota 12, YU-
11000 Belgrade

Galerija Fresaka.
Ul. Cara Urosa 20, YU-11000
Belgrade

Galerija Idrija.
Trg. Svobode, YU-65280 Idrija
Milan Bozic

Galerija Jaki.
YU-63331 Nazarje

Galerija Likovnih Umjetnosti.
Bul. Jna 9, YU-54000 Osijek,
054-27 534
Permanent Collections:
Painting in Slawonia from the
18th through the 20th century.

Galerija "Loza".
Trg. Titov 1, YU-66000 Koper

Galerija Maksimilijana Vanke.
YU-50260 Korcula

Galerija Matice Srpske.
Trg Prolterskih Brigada 8, YU-
21000, Novi Sad

Galerija Meblo.
Ul. Leninova 4, YU-65000
Nova Gorica

Galerija Mestrovic.
Setaliste Mose Pijade 46, YU-
58000 Split

Galerija "Milan Konlovic".
Trg. Bratsava I Jedinstva 2,
YU-25000

Galerija "Milene Pavlovic-Barili".
Ul. Voja Dulica 8, YU-12000
Pozarevac Smiljana Stojanovic-
Guleski

Galerija Naivih Umjetnika.
YU-43323 Hlebina

Galerija Primitivne Umjetnosti.
Cirilomentodska 3, Katarin Trg
2, 41000 Zagreb

Galerija Save Sumanovica.
Ul. Lenjinova 7, YU-22240 Sid

**Galerija Savremene Likovne
Umetnosti.**
Ul. Ina 45/1, YU-21000 Novi
Sad

Galerija Silka.
YU-52273 Motovun

Galerija Slika "Vjekoslav Karas".
YU-47000 Karlovac

**Galerija Srpske Akademije Nauka
i Umetnosti.**
Knez Mihalova 35, YU-11000
Belgrade

Galerija Suvremene Umjetnosti.
Katarinin Trg 2, P.O. Box 233,
41000 Zagreb

Galerija Umetnosti Vinkovci.
Ul. JNA 3, YU-5600 Vinkovic

Galerija v Mestni Hisi.
Trq. Titov 44, YU-64001 Kranj

Galerija v Presernovi Hisi.
Ul. Presernova 7, YU-64001
Kranj

Galerije Grada Zagreba.
Rokov Perivoj 4, YU-41000
Zagreb

Gliptoteka "Jazu".
Ul. Medvedgradska 2, YU-
41000 Zagreb

Gorenjski Muzej.
Trg. Titov 4, YU-64001 Kranj

**Graficka Zbirka Nacionalne
Sveucilisne Biblioteke.**
Trg. Marulicev 21, YU-41000
Zagreb

Ivan Mestrovic Studio. *See*
Mestrovic, Ivan, Studio

**Jugoslavenska Galerija
Reprodukcha i Umetnickih
Dela.**
Ul. Dositejeva 1, YU-11000
Belgrade

Kabinet Grafike "Jazu".
Ul. Brace Kavurica 1, YU-
41000 Zareb

Katedralina Zbirka.
Biskupi Dvor. YU-58450 Hvart

Malagalerija.
Trg Solobode 7, YU-23000
Zrenjanin

Manastirska Riznica.
YU-38322 Decane

Manastirska Riznica.
YU-38205 Gracanica

Manastirski Muzej.
Marastir Cetinijski, YU-81250
Cetinja

**Memorijalna Galerija Akad.
Slikare Velisa Lekovic.**
YU-81350 Bar

**Memorijalna Zbirka Antuna
Masle.**
Ul. N. Bozidarevia 11, YU-
50000 Dubrovnik

**Memoryalna Galerija Djure
Tiljka.**
YU-58485 Komiza otok Vis

Mestni Muzej.
Ul. Gosposka 15, YU-61000
Ljubljana

Mestrovic, Ivan, Studio.
Mletacka 8, 41000 Zagreb

Moderna Galerija.
Ul. Dolac 1, YU-51000 Rijeka

Moderna Galerija.
Ul. Miljana Vukovar 27, YU-
81000 Titograd

Moderna Galerija.
Tomisceva 14, YU-6100
Ljubljana, 21-709
Permanent Collections:
Paintings, sculptures, prints and
drawings.

Moderna Galerija "Jazu".
Ul. Brace Kavurica, YU-41000
Zagreb

**Musej Na Sovrementa Umetnost
Skopje.**
Samoilova bb YU-91001 Skopje,
235 244

Museum of Modern Art.
USCE SAVE BB, 11071
Belgrade

Muzei Primenjene Umetnosti.
Ul. Vuka Karadzica 18, YU-
11000 Belgrade

Muzej Evolucije u Krapini.
YU-41230 Krapina

Muzej Grada Zagreba.
Ul. Opaticka 20, YU-41000
Zagreb

**Muzej Naivne Umetnoste
"Ilijanum".**
Ul. Leninova 5, YU-2240 Sid

**Muzej-Riznica Stare Srpske
Parvoslavne Crkve.**
Ul. Marsala Tita 87, YU-71000
Sarajevo

Muzej Za. Umjetnost i Obrt.
Trg Marsala Tita 10, YU-41000
Zagreb

**Muzejiska Zbirka Pri Katolickoi
Parohiji.**
YU-24410 Horgos

**Muzejska Zbirka "Anka
Gvozdanovic".**
Zgb. Visoka 8, YU-41000
Zagreb

**Muzejska Zbirka
Dominkanskogsamostana.**
Izmedu Vrata Od Ploca 5, YU-
50000 Dubrovnik

**Muzejska Zbirka i Stara Apoteka
Male Brace.**
Placa 2, YU-50000 Dubrovnik

**Muzejska Zbirka Kapucinskog
Samostana.**
YU-51288 Karlobag

Muzejska Zibirka.
YU-52210 Rovinj

**Muzejske Zbirka Franjevackog
Samostana.**
YU-58260 Imotski

Muzje Branka Sotre.
YU-79430 Stolac

**Muzje Franjevackog Samostana
Fojnica.**
YU-71270 Fojnica

Muzje Srpske Pravoslavne Crkve.
Ul. 73 Juli 55, YU-11000
Belgrade

Napotnikova Galerija.
Osnova Sola Biba Rock, YU-
663325 Sostanj

Narodna Galerija.
Prezihova Vlica 1-Pp 432, YU-
61001 Ljublana

Narodni Muzej.
Ul. Poljana V. Gortana B.B.,
Zadar

Narodni Muzej.
Trg. Rebublike 1, YU-11000
Belgrade

Narodni Muzej Kragujevac.
Ul. Vuka Karadzica 1, YU-
3400 Kragujevec

Opatska Riznica Sv. Marka.
YU-50260 Korcula

**Privatna Galerija Umjetnickih
Silka Mirka Komosare.**
YU-71000 Sarajevo

Rastavni Salon Rotov.
Trg. Rotovski 1, YU-62000
Maribor

**Razstavni Paviljon Dusana
Kvedra.**
YU-62250 Ptuj

Riznica Katedrale Split.
Ul. Kraj Sv. Duje 5, YU-58000
Split

Riznica Katedrale Sv. Vlaha.
Bikupija, YU-5000 Dubrovnik

Riznica Katedrale u Sakristiji Katedrale.
YU-58220 Trogir

Riznica Manastira Studenica.
YU-36350 Raska

Riznica Pecke Patrijarsije.
YU-38300 Pec

Riznica Zagrebacke Katedrale.
Kaptol 31, YU-4100 Zagreb

Savremena Galerija Umetnick Kolonije Ecka.
YU-23203 Ecka lkod Zrenjanina

Slikarski Kolonija.
V. Nemanjina 16, YU-24400 Senta

Spomen-Zbirka Palvla Beljanskog.
Ul. Bukoveva, yU-50210 Cavtat

Spomen-Zbirka Vlaha Bukovca.
Ul. Bukoveva, YU-50210 Cavtat

Stalna Izlozba Crkvene Umejetonoste.
Ul. Stomorica B.B. YU-57000 Zadar

Stalna Izlozba Stilskog Naejestaja.
18. i 19. St. Dvorac u Celarevu, YU-21413 Celarevo

Strossmayerova Galerija Starik Majstora.
Zrinjski Trg 11, 41000 Zagreb

Umejetnicka Galerija.
Dom Kulture-Rondo, YU-79000 Mostar

Umetnicka Galerija Nadezde Petrovic.
Ul. Cara Cusana 4, YU-32000 Cacak

Umetnicka Zbirka Flogel.
Ul. Marsala Tita 21, YU-11000 Belgrade

Umetnostna Galerija.
Ul. Strossmayerva 6, YU-62000 Maribor

Umetnostni Paviljon.
YU-62380 Slovenj Gradec

Umjetnicka Galerija.
YU-75000 Tuzia

Umjetnicka Galerija.
YU-78000 Banja Luka

Umjetnicka Galerija.
Put. F. Supilia 45, YU-50000 Dubrovnik

Umjetnicka Galerija.
Ul. M. Vojnovica 11, YU-81340 Hercegnovi

Umjetnicka Galerija.
Daw-Pasin Aman. P.P. 278, P.O. Box 278, YU-91000 Skopje

Umjetnicka Galerija Bosne i Hercegovine.
Ul. Ina 38, YU-771000 Sarajevo

Umjetnicka Galerija Crne Gore.
Trg Revolucije 14, YU-81250 Centinja

Umjetnicki Paviljon.
Tomislavob Trg 22, YU-41000 Zagreb

Zavicajna Galerija.
Petrovaradin-Tvrdjava, YU-21000 Novi-Sad

Zbirka Bauer i Galerija Umjetnina.
Marsala Tita 19, YU-56230 Vukovar

Zbirka Bratovstine Gospe Od Utjehe.
YU-50260 Korcula

Zbirka Bratovstine Sv. Roka.
YU-50260 Korcula

Zbirka Crkve Gospe Od Skrpjela.
YU-81336 Perast

Zbirka Crkve Sv. Nikole.
YU-81336 Perast

Zbirka Crkvene Umjetnosti.
Pri Biskupskom Orginarijatu, YU-59000 Sibenik

Zbirka Dr. Grigijevic Emilana i Jelisaveta.
Radomira Putnika Venac 36, YU-25000 Sombor

Zbirka Eparhije Banatski.
Eparhija Banatska, YU-26300 Vrsac

Zbirka Ikona.
Pravoslavne Parohije u Crkvi Uznesanja, YU-59000 Sibenik

Zbirka Ikona Bratovstine Svih Svetih.
YU-50260 Korkula

Zbirka Ikona i Portreta.
Srpskwe Pravoslavne Drkve, Ul. Od Puca 2, YU-5000 Dubrovnik

Zbirka Katedrale sv. Trifuna.
Katedrale sv. Trifuna, YU-81330 Kotor

Zbirka Keramike.
Keramnica Industija Liboje

Zbirka Pri Samostanu sv. Frane.
YU-59000 Sibenik

Zbirka Pri Samostanu Sv. Lovre.
YU-59000 Sibenik

Zbirka Strane Umetnosti.
Ul. Dunavska 29, YU-21000 Novi Sad

Zbirka Umetnina u Opatiji sv. Ivana Krstitelja.
YU-58220 Trogir

Zbirka Umjetnina Franjevackog Samostana.
YU-58450 Hvar

Zbirka Zupne Crkve.
YU-81335 Prcanj

ZAIRE

Academie des Beaux-Arts.
Ave. des Victimes de la Rebellion, BP 8249, Kinshasa

ZAMBIA

Art Centre Foundation Ltd.
P.O. Box 198, Lusakat

PERMANENT COLLECTION CATALOG INDEX

This index is arranged alphabetically by title, with headings for institution name. These headings also provide the location of the institutions. Cross-references are included for variant forms of institution names, when applicable.

Thirty (30)-Luvulta Meidan Paiviimme. 1977. write for info. Amos Anderson.
Thirty (30)-Luvulta Meidan Paiviimme. 1969. write for info. Amos Anderson.
Thirty (30) Vuotta Suomalaista Taidetta. 1976. write for info. Amos Anderson.
Ulkomaista Nykygrafiikkaa Amos Andersonin Taidemuseon Kokoelmista. write for info. Amos Anderson.
Ung Finsk Konst. 1970. write for info. Amos Anderson.

ANGLO-AMERICAN ART MUSEUM
see Louisiana State Univ., Anglo-American Art Museum

ANTIKENMUSEUM
Berlin, Germany, West.
Romisches Im Antikenmuseum. (Ger.). DM.35.00. Blaschker Verlag.

ANTIQUARIAN AND LANDMARKS SOCIETY INC. OF CONNECTICUT
Hartford, Connecticut.
Images of Connecticut Life. Ronna L. Reynolds. (Illus., 120 photos, 9 maps, 15 line drawings). 1978. $6.50. Antiq Land Soc.

ARCHAEOLOGICAL MUSEUM OF CORFU
Corfu, Greece.
Guide to the Museum of Joanni. G. Dontas. (Gr., Eng. & Fr.). write for info. Genl Dir Antiq.

ARCHAEOLOGICAL MUSEUM OF DELPHI
Delphi, Greece.
Delphi. Basil Petrakos. Ed. by Clio Editions Athens. Tr. by Giuliano Vacalopoulou. (Clio Editions). (Illus., color, b&w, Gr., Eng., Fr., Ger. & It.). 1975. pap. Dr.130.00. Delphi.
Delphi, the Museum. Petros Themelis. Ed. by Ekdotike Athenon AE. (Ekdotike Athenon AE). (Illus., color, Eng., Fr & Ger.). 1979. pap. Dr.150.00. Delphi.

ARCHAEOLOGICAL MUSEUM OF HERACLION
Heraclion, Greece.
Guide to the Archaeological Museum of Heraclion. N. St. Alexiou & N. Platon. (Gr., Eng., Fr & Ger.). write for info. Genl Dir Antiq.

ARCHAEOLOGICAL MUSEUM OF THESSALONIKI
Thessaloniki, Greece.
Treasures of Ancient Macedonia. Ed. by Greek Archaeological Service. Tr. by K. T. Sigada. (Illus., Gr. & Eng.). 1979. pap. $10.00. Greek Arch Serv.

ARCHAOLOGISCHE SAMMLUNG DER UNIVERSITAT ZURICH
Zurich, Switzerland.
Arbeiter Des Jenseits: Aegyptishe Totenfiguren. H. Schlogl & M. Sguaitamatti. Ed. by Archaologische Sammlung der Universitat. (Zurcher Archaologische Hefte Ser., 2). (Illus., 13, Ger.). 1977. 9.00 F. Arch Zurich.
Fruhgeschichtlicher Furst Aus Dem Iraq. M. Muller. Ed. by Archaologische Sammlung der Univeritat Zurich. (Zurcher Archaologische Hefte Ser., 1). (Illus., 9, Ger.). 1976. 9.00 F. Arch Zurich.
Geschenk Des Nils. Hermann Schlogl. (Ausstellunskataloge Ser). (Illus., 114, Ger. & Fr.). 1978. 48.00 F. Arch Zurich.
Lieblinge der Meermadchen. C. Isler-Kerenyi. Ed. by Archaologische Sammlung der Universitat. (Zurcher Archaologische Hefte Ser., 3). (Illus., 39, Ger.). 1978. 9.00 F. Arch Zurich.
Stamnoi. C. Isler-Kerenyi. (Illus., 86). 1977. 50.00 F. Arch Zurich.

ARCHAOLOGISCHES MUSEUM DER UNIVERSITAT MUNSTER
Munster, Germany, West.
Boreas. Ed. & intro. by Werner Fuchs. (Illus., 37 plates, Ger.). 1978. DM.48.00. Arch Munster.
Grieschische Vasen Des Archaologischen Museums der Universitat Munster. Klaus Stahler. Ed. by Werner Fuchs. (Illus., 13 plates, Ger.). 1978. DM.5.00. Arch Munster.
Klaus Stahler: Grab und Psyche Des Patroklos. Klaus Stahler. (Illus., 13, 4 plates, Ger.). 1967. DM.10.00. Arch Munster.
Klaus Stahler: Eine Unbelcannte Pelike Des Eucharides. Klaus Stahler. Ed. by Jost Trier & Heine Gallwitzer. (Ger.). 1967. DM.32.00. Bohnlau Verlag.
Zwei Klassiche Met Openkopfe. Klaus Stahler. Ed. by Werner Fuchs. (Boreas Ser., No. 2). (Illus., 1 plate, Ger.). DM.1.00. Arch Munster.

ARCHIVO DI STATO DI SIENA
Siena, Italy.
Tavolette Della Biccherna E Della Gabella E D'Altre Magistrature Dell'Antico Stato Senese Conservate Presso L'Archivo Di Stato Di Siena. Ubaldo Morandi. Ed. by Monte Dei Paschi Di Siena. (Illus., 103 color photos, It.). 1964. write for info. Archi Siena.

ARENTSHUIS
see Brangwynmuseum

ART ASSN. OF RICHMOND, MCGUIRE MEMORIAL FOUNDATION
Richmond, Indiana.
Art in Richmond, 1898-1978. Sara Gaar Laughlin. Ed. by Marcia Lemon. (Illus., 80). 1978. pap. $5.00. Art Richmond.

ART GALLERY OF GREATER VICTORIA
Victoria, Canada.
Art of Lithography. Robert Amos & Louis Goldich. (Collections of the Art Gallery of Greater Victoria Ser., No. 11). (Illus., 21 b&w). 1978. pap. Can.$0.50 (ISBN 0-88885-026-3). Art Gal Vict.
Arts of Tibet: Painting. Douglas Henderson. Ed. by Chris Bitten. (Collections of the Art Gallery of Greater Victoria Ser., No. 6). (Illus., 12 b&w). 1977. pap. Can.$0.50. Art Gal Vict.
British & European Decorative Arts. Colin Graham. (Collections of the Art Gallery of Greater Victoria Ser., No. 7). (Illus., 20 b&w). 1977. pap. Can.$0.50. Art Gal Vict.
Canadian Block Print: Woodcuts, Linocuts, Stonecuts, Wood Engravings. Robert Amos. (Collections of the Art Gallery of Greater Victoria Ser., No. 9). (Illus., 18 b&w). 1977. pap. Can.$0.50 (ISBN 0-88885-002-6). Art Gal Vict.
Chinese Ceramics Handbook. Mary Tregear. (Collections of the Art Gallery of Greater Victoria Ser). (Illus., 48 b&w). 1978. pap. Can.$2.00 (ISBN 0-88885-032-8). Art Gal Vict.
Etching Revival, 1852-1936. Robert Amos. (Collections of the Art Gallery of Greater Victoria Ser., No. 8). (Illus., 16 b&w). 1977. pap. Can.$0.50. Art Gal Vict.
German Expressionism. Robert Amos. (Collections of the Art Gallery of Greater Victoria Ser., No. 13). (Illus., 28 b&w). 1978. pap. Can.$0.50 (ISBN 0-88885-036-0). Art Gal Vict.
H. Mortimer-Lamb: Paintings. Colin Graham. (Collections of the Art Gallery of Greater Victoria Ser., No. 10). (Illus., 9 b&w). 1978. pap. Can.$0.50 (ISBN 0-88885-016-6). Art Gal Vict.
Mark Tobey in Victoria. Colin Graham. (Collections of the Art Gallery of Greater Victoria Ser., NO. 2). (Illus., 10 b&w). 1975. pap. Can.$0.50. Art Gal Vict.
Nineteenth Century English Watercolours & Drawings. Robert Amos. (Collections of the Art Gallery of Greater Victoria Ser., No. 3). (Illus., 12 b&w). 1976. pap. Can.$0.50. Art Gal Vict.
Pehr. Colin Graham. (Collections of the Art Gallery of Greater Victoria Ser., No. 4). (Illus., 8 b&w). 1977. pap. Can.$0.50. Art Gal Vict.
Ukiyoe: Glimpses into the Floating World; Japanese Woodblock Prints. Patricia Wright. Ed. by Robert Amos. (Collections of the Art Gallery of Greater Victoria Ser., No. 5). (Illus., 19 b&w). 1977. pap. Can.$0.50. Art Gal Vict.

ART GALLERY OF ONTARIO
Toronto, Canada.
Art Gallery of Ontario: The Canadian Collection. Compiled by Helen Bradfield. (Illus., 64 color plates, 436 b&w). 1970. Can.$3.99. McGraw-Hill Canada.
Drawings in the Collection of the Art Gallery of Ontario. Notes by Walter Vitzthum & Mario Amaya. (Illus., 19 b&w). 1970. pap. Can.$1.50. Art Gal Ontario.
Handbook: Catalogue Illustre. Intro. by Richard Wattenmaker & William Withrow. (Illus., 25 color plates, 240 b&w, Eng. & Fr.). 1974. Can.$10.00; pap. Can.$5.00. Art Gal Ontario.

ART GALLERY OF SOUTH AUSTRALIA
Adelaide, Australia.
Bulletin of the Art Gallery of South Australia. (Illus., 5 color, 39 b&w). 1977. pap. Aus.$4.00. Gal S Austral.
Bulletin of the Art Gallery of South Australia. (Illus., 3 color, 50 b&w). 1978. pap. Aus.$4.00. Gal S Austral.
Master Prints & Drawings from the Collection. Alison Carroll. (Illus., 44 b&w). 1978. pap. Aus.$3.00. Gal S Austral.
Picture Book: Selected Works from the Collection. Intro. by John Bailey. (Illus., 48 color, 87 b&w). 1972. pap. Aus.$9.50. Gal S Austral.

ART INSTITUTE OF CHICAGO
Chicago, Illinois.
American Rooms in Miniature. Mrs. James W. Thorne. (Illus., b&w). 1974. pap. $2.50. Chicago Inst.
Art Institute of Chicago. John Maxon. (Illus., 33 color, 265 b&w). 1977. pap. $6.95. Chicago Inst.
Art Institute of Chicago: One Hundred Masterpieces. (Illus., 100 color, 26 b&w). 1978. $35.00. Chicago Inst.
Art Institute of Chicago: The Stock Exchange Trading Room. John Vinci. (Illus., 8 color, 37 b&w). 1977. pap. $4.95. Chicago Inst.
Classical Presence in American Art. Milo Naeve. (Illus., 24 color, 23 b&w). 1978. pap. $2.50. Chicago Inst.
Department of Textiles at the Art Institute of Chicago. Christa C. Mayer. (Illus., 30 b&w). 1978. pap. $2.50. Chicago Inst.
European Portraits 1600-1900 in the Art Institute of Chicago. (Illus., 8 color, 54 b&w). 1978. pap. $10.00. Chicago Inst.
European Rooms in Miniature. Mrs. James W. Thorne. (Illus., b&w). 1976. pap. $2.50. Chicago Inst.
First One Hundred Years. (Illus., 11 color, 327 b&w). 1977. pap. $15.00. Chicago Inst.
Museum Studies, No. 9. Ed. by John Maxon & Anselmo Carini. (Illus., 30 b&w). 1978. pap. $5.00. Chicago Inst.
Photographs from the Julian Levy Collection: Starting with Atget. David Travis. (Illus., 55 b&w). 1976. pap. $6.95. Chicago Inst.

ART RESEARCH CENTER
Kansas City, Missouri.
Art Research Center Tenth Anniversary Catalog. Ed. by Art Research Center. (Illus., 15 b&w photos & line reprods.). 1977. pap. $10.00. New Circle.
Matrix: International Exhibition, 1973, Prints and Drawings Parameters: Continuous Field - 2 vs. 3-D Ambiguity. Ed. by Art Research Center. (Illus., 49 b&w reprods. of prints & drawings, Eng. & Fr.). 1973. pap. $5.00. New Circle.
TELIC: International Exhibition. 1979. pap. $10.00. New Circle.

ASIAN ART MUSEUM OF SAN FRANCISCO
San Francisco, California.
Bronze Vessels of Ancient China in the Avery Brundage Collection. Rene-Yvon D'Argence. (Handbook Ser). (Illus., 61 plates, 63 figs.). 1977. pap. $10.00. Mus Society.
Chinese Jades in the Avery Brundage Collection. Rene-Yvon D'Argence. (Handbook Ser). (Illus., 81 color plates). pap. $10.00. Mus Society.
Chinese, Korean & Japanese Sculpture in the Avery Brundage Collection. Ed. by Rene-Yvon D'Argence & Diana Turner. (Illus., 228 plates). 1974. $65.00. Kodansha.
Decade of Collecting. Intro. by Rene-Yvon D'Argence. (Illus., 8 color plates, color frontis). $14.00; pap. $9.00. Mus Society.

ASSOCIATION OF TOMEI ART FOUNDATION
see Kyusei Atami Art Museum

ATKINS MUSEUM OF FINE ARTS
see William Rockhill Nelson Gallery of Art

ATKINSON ART GALLERY
Southport, United Kingdom.
Literal Landscape: A Selection of Victorian Oils from the Permanent Collections of the Atkinson Art Gallery, Southport. Andrew W. Moore. (Illus., 4 b&w). 1979. pap. 0.50 d. Atkinson Gal.
Selection of Victorian Paintings from the Permanent Collections of the Atkinson Art Gallery, Southport, 1878-1978. Andrew W. Moore. (Illus., 15 b&w). 1978. pap. 0.50 d. Atkinson Gal.

BADISCHES LANDESMUSEUM KARLSRUHE
Karlsruhe, Germany, West.
Alte Textilien. Eva Zimmermann. (Illus., Ger.). 1957. DM.3.00. Karlsruhe Bad.
Barocke Bildwerke. Eva Zimmermann. (Illus., Ger.). 1964. DM.3.00. Karlsruhe Bad.
Bildkatalog. (Illus., 24 color, 364 b&w, Ger.). 1975. DM.25.00. Karlsruhe Bad.
Glasgemalde Des Badischen Landesmuseums. Arthur Von Schneider. (Ger.). 1950. DM.25.00. Karlsruhe Bad.
Griechische Vasen. Jurgen Thimme. (Illus., Ger.). 1975. DM.5.00. Karlsruhe Bad.
Jugendstil. Irmela Franzke. (Illus., 24 color, 155 b&w, Ger.). 1978. DM.18.00. Karlsruhe Bad.
Medaillen der Renaissance & Des Barock. Freidrich Wielandt. (Illus., Ger.). 1969. DM.3.00. Karlsruhe Bad.
Phonizische Elfenbeine. Jurgen Thimme. (Illus., Ger.). 1973. DM.3.00. Karlsruhe Bad.
Porzellanfiguren. Walther Franzius. (Illus., Ger.). 1977. DM.6.00. Karlsruhe Bad.
Rundgang Durch das Badische Landesmuseum. (Illus., Ger.). 1976. DM.6.00. Karlsruhe Bad.
Turkenbeute. Ernst Petrasch. (Illus., Ger.). 1977. DM.5.00. Karlsruhe Bad.

BALTIMORE MUSEUM OF ART
Baltimore, Maryland.
And Eagles Swept Across the Sky: Indian Textiles of the North American West. Dena Katzenberg. (Illus., 124, 9 color). 1977. pap. $12.00. Baltimore Mus.
Edward Joseph Gallagher III Memorial Collection. Pref. by Israel Rosen. (Illus., 36). 1964. pap. $1.00. Baltimore Mus.
Eighteenth & Nineteenth Century Maryland Silver in the Collection of the Baltimore Museum of Art. Jennifer Goldsborough. Ed. by Ann Harper. (Illus., 220). 1975. $25.00; pap. $12.50. Baltimore Mus.
Oval Room from Willow Brook. William Elder, 3rd. (Illus., 19). 1966. pap. $1.00. Baltimore Mus.
Picasso Drawings & Watercolors, 1899-1907, in the Collection of the Baltimore Museum of Art. Victor Carlson. (Illus., 51, 5 color). 1977. $25.00; pap. $15.00. Baltimore Mus.
Robert Mills' Waterloo Row: Baltimore, 1816. William Elder, 3rd. (Illus., 16). 1971. pap. $1.70. Baltimore Mus.
Saidie A. May Collection. Intro. by Jane Cone. (Illus., 128, 5 color). 1972. pap. $3.50. Baltimore Mus.
The George A. Lucas Collection. Gertrude Rosenthal & Victor Carlson. (Illus., 26). 1965. pap. $2.00. Baltimore Mus.
Thomas Edward Bensch Memorial Collection. Intro. by Charles Parkhurst. (Illus., 43). 1970. pap. $1.70. Baltimore Mus.
Two Hundred Objects in the Baltimore Museum of Art. Gertrude Rosenthal. (Illus., 200). 1955. pap. $2.00. Baltimore Mus.
Wurtzburger Collection of African Sculpture. Paul Wingert. (Illus., 34, map). 1954. pap. $1.50. Baltimore Mus.
Wurtzburger Collection of Oceanic Art. Paul Wingert & Douglas Fraser. (Illus., 48, 1 color, map). 1956. pap. $1.50. Baltimore Mus.
Wurtzburger Collection of Pre-Columbian Art. Notes by George Kubler et al. (Illus., 57, 1 color, map). 1958. pap. $1.50. Baltimore Mus.

BARLACH, ERNST, HAUS
Hamburg, Germany, West.
Ernst Barlach Haus, Stiftung Hermann F. Reemtsma Plastiken, Handzeichnungen und Autographen. Isa Lohmann-Siems. Ed. by Ernst Barlach Haus. (Ger.). 1977. pap. DM.18.00. Ernst Barlach.

BASS MUSEUM OF ART
Miami Beach, Florida.
Bass Museum of Art. (Illus.). pap. write for info. Bass Mus.

BAUR COLLECTION
Geneva, Switzerland.
Chinese Jades, Vol. 5. Pierre-Francis Schneeberger. Ed. by Collections Baur, Geneve. Tr. by Katherine Watson. (Illus., 23 color, 106 b&w, 23 line drawings, Eng. & Fr.). 1976. 200.00 F. Baur Collect.
Netsuke (Selected Pieces, Vol. 6. Marie-Therese Coullery & Martin Newstead. Ed. by Baur Collections, Geneve. Tr. by Katherine Watson. (Illus., 8 color plates, 1200 pieces, 897 signatures, Eng. & Fr.). 200.00 F. Baur Collect.

BAYERISCHE STAATSGEMALDESAMMLUNGEN
Munich, Germany, West.
Bayerische Staatsgemaldesammlungen: Jahresbericht. (Illus., Ger.). 1978. pap. write for info. Bayer Staats.

BAYERISCHER VERWALTUNG DER STAATLICHEN SCHLOSSER, GARTEN UND SEEN
Munich, Germany, West.
Altes Residenztheater Munchen. Herbert Brunner. (Ger.). 1969. DM.2.00. Bayer Verwal.
Aschaffenburg Castle. Erich Bachmann. 1976. DM.2.00. Bayer Verwal.
Ausstellungskatalog. Markgrafin W. Von Bayreuth. (Ger.). 1959. DM.1.00. Bayer Verwal.
Befreiungshalle Kelheim. Manfred F. Fischer. (Ger.). 1978. DM.2.00. Bayer Verwal.
Burg Lauenstein. Elmar D. Schmid & Horst H. Stierhof. (Ger.). 1976. DM.2.00. Bayer Verwal.
Burg Trausnitz-Landshut. Herbert Brunner & Elmar D. Schmid. (Ger.). 1975. DM.2.50. Bayer Verwal.
Burg Zu Burghausen. Elmar D. Schmis & Von Hohenzollern. (Ger.). 1978. DM.2.50. Bayer Verwal.
Burg Zwernitz und Sanspareil Bei Bayreuth. Erich Bachmann. (Ger.). 1970. DM.1.50. Bayer Verwal.
Castles in Bavaria. 1977. DM.1.00. Bayer Verwal.
Chateaux En Baviere. (Fr.). 1977. DM.1.00. Bayer Verwal.
Festschrift Zur Wiedereroffnung Des Alten Residenzmuseums. (Ger.). DM.2.50. Bayer Verwal.
Festschrift Zur Wiedereroffnung Des Alten Residenztheaters. (Ger.). DM.2.50. Bayer Verwal.
Konig Ludwig II: Sein Leben in Bildern. Hans Rall & Michael Petzet. (Illus., 6 color, 70 b&w, Ger.). DM.6.30. Schnell & Steiner.
Kroninsignien Des Konigreiches Bayern. Hans Ottomeyer. (Illus., 4 color, 34 b&w, Ger.). DM.9.80 (ISBN 3-7954-0707-9). Schnell & Steiner.
Kurfurst Max Emanuel der "Blaue Konig". Hans Rall & Hojer. (Illus., 40 b&w, Ger.). DM.12.80 (ISBN 3-7954-0706-0). Schnell & Steiner.
Margravial Opera House Bayreuth. Luisa Hager & Albrecht Miller. 1973. DM.1.50. Bayer Verwal.
Markgrafliches Opernhaus in Bayreuth. Luisa Hager & Albrecht Miller. (Ger.). 1978. DM.1.50. Bayer Verwal.
Old Residence-Theatre (Cuvillies-Theatre) Munich. Herbert Brunner. 1978. DM.3.00. Bayer Verwal.
Prospekt Schlosser und Burgen in Bayern. (Ger., Eng. & Fr.). 1977. DM.1.00. Bayer Verwal.

Coins of the Macedonians. Martin Price. (Illus., 16 plates, map). 1974. pap. E1.50. British Mus.
Coins of the Roman Republic in the British Museum, 3 vols. H. A. Grueber. (Illus., 123 plates). 1970. E45.00. British Mus.
Collectors & Collections: The British Museum Yearbook 2: 1976. Ed. by British Museum. (Illus., 4 color plates, 219 b&w). 1977. E10.00, cased. British Mus.
Corpus Vasorum Antiquorum: Fascicules. R. M. Cook. (Illus., 38 plates). 1954. E10.00, folders of texts & reproductions. British Mus.
Cuneiform Texts from Babylonian Tablets at the British Museum, Pt. 7. (Illus., 50 plates). 1961. E4.00. British Mus.
Cuneiform Texts from Babylonian Tablets in the British Museum, Pt. 3. (Illus., 50 plates). 1961. E4.00. British Mus.
Cuneiform Texts from Babylonian Tablets in the British Museum, Pt. 5. (Illus., 50 plates). 1959. E4.00. British Mus.
Cuneiform Texts from Babylonian Tablets in the British Museum, Pt. 8. 1961. E4.00. British Mus.
Cuneiform Texts from Babylonian Tablets in the British Museum, Pt. 9. (Illus., 50 plates). 1962. E4.00. British Mus.
Cuneiform Texts from Babylonian Tablets in the British Museum, Pt. 10. (Illus., 50 plates). 1962. E4.00. British Mus.
Cuneiform Texts from Babylonian Tablets in the British Museum, Pt. 11. (Illus., 50 plates). 1962. E4.00. British Mus.
Cuneiform Texts from Babylonian Tablets in the British Museum, Pt. 12. (Illus., 50 plates). 1962. E4.00. British Mus.
Cuneiform Texts from Babylonian Tablets in the British Museum, Pt. 13. (Illus., 50 plates). 1963. E4.00. British Mus.
Cuneiform Texts from Babylonian Tablets in the British Museum, Pt. 14. (Illus., 50 plates). 1964. E4.00. British Mus.
Cuneiform Texts from Babylonian Tablets in the British Museum, Pt. 18. (Illus., 50 plates). 1964. E4.00. British Mus.
Cuneiform Texts from Babylonian Tablets in the British Museum, Pt. 19. 1965. E4.00. British Mus.
Cuneiform Texts from Babylonian Tablets in the British Museum, Pt.20. (Illus., 50 plates). 1966. E4.00. British Mus.
Cuneiform Texts from Babylonian Tablets in the British Museum, Pt. 21. (Illus., 50 plates). 1966. E4.00. British Mus.
Cuneiform Texts from Babylonian Tablets in the British Museum, Pt. 22. (Illus., 50 plates). 1966. E4.00. British Mus.
Cuneiform Texts from Babylonian Tablets in the British Museum, Pt. 23. (Illus., 50 plates). 1967. E4.00. British Mus.
Cuneiform Texts from Babylonian Tablets in the British Museum, Pt. 24. (Illus., 50 plates). 1967. E4.00. British Mus.
Cuneiform Texts from Babylonian Tablets in the British Museum, Pt. 25. (Illus., 50 plates). 1967. E4.00. British Mus.
Cuneiform Texts from Babylonian Tablets in the British Museum, Pt. 26. (Illus., 50 plates). 1968. E4.00. British Mus.
Cuneiform Texts from Babylonian Tablets in the British Museum, Pt. 27. (Illus., 50 plates). 1968. E4.00. British Mus.
Cuneiform Texts from Babylonian Tablets in the British Museum, Pt. 28. (Illus., 50 plates). 1969. E4.00. British Mus.
Cuneiform Texts from Babylonian Tablets in the British Museum, Pt. 29. (Illus., 50 plates). 1971. E4.00. British Mus.
Cuneiform Texts from Babylonian Tablets in the British Museum, Pt. 30. (Illus., 50 plates). 1971. E4.00. British Mus.
Cuneiform Texts from Babylonian Tablets in the British Museum, Pt. 31. (Illus., 50 plates). 1972. E4.00. British Mus.
Cuneiform Texts from Babylonian Tablets in the British Museum, Pt. 32. (Illus., 50 plates). 1973. E5.00. British Mus.
Cuneiform Texts from Babylonian Tablets in the British Museum, Pt. 33. (Illus., 50 plates). 1973. E5.00. British Mus.
Cuneiform Texts from Babylonian Tablets in the British Museum, Pts. 34-37. (Illus., 200 plates). 1977. E16.00. British Mus.
Cuneiform Texts from Babylonian Tablets in the British Museum, Pts. 38-41. (Illus., 200 plates). 1977. E16.00. British Mus.
Cuneiform Texts from Babylonian Tablets in the British Museum, Pt. 50. (Illus., 50 plates). 1972. E4.00. British Mus.
Cuneiform Texts from Babylonian Tablets in the British Museum, Pt. 51. (Illus., 73 plates). 1972. E7.00. British Mus.
Cuneiform Texts from Babylonian Tablets in the British Museum, Pt. 52. (Illus., 61 plates). 1976. E7.00. British Mus.
Cuneiform Texts from Babylonian Tablets in the British Museum, Pt. 53. (Illus., 219 plates). 1979. write for info. British Mus.
Cuneiform Texts from Babylonian Tablets in the British Museum, Pt. 54. (Illus., 139 plates). 1979. write for info. British Mus.
Cuneiform Texts from Babylonian Tablets in the British Museum: Index to Parts 1-50. C. B. Walker. 1975. E7.50, cased. British Mus.
Cuneiform Texts from Cappadocian Tablets in the British Museum, Pt. 6. P. Garelli. (Illus., 58 plates). 1975. E8.00, cased. British Mus.
Cuneiform Texts from Cappadocian Tablets in the British Museum, Pt. 5. Sidney Smith & D. J. Wiseman. (Illus., 50 plates). 1959. E6.00, cased. British Mus.
Dance of Death: German Medals of the First World War. Mark Jones. (Illus., monochrome). 1978. pap. E1.25. British Mus.
Descriptive Catalogue of Playing & Other Cards in the British Museum. W. H. Willshire. (Illus., 23 plates). 1975. E35.00, cased. British Mus.
Divine Kingship in Africa. William Fagg. (Illus., 36). 1978. pap. E2.25. British Mus.
Drawings by Michelangelo. J. A. Gere. (Illus., 144). 1975. E5.00, cased; pap. E2.50. British Mus.
Early Celtic Masterpieces from Britain in the British Museum. John Brailsford. (Illus., 10 color plates, 137 b&w). 1975. E5.50, cased; pap. E3.25. British Mus.
Early Islamic Stamped Glass Objects. A. H. Morton. 1979. write for info. British Mus.
Early Medieval Art in the British Museum. Ernst Kitzinger. (Illus., 48 b&w). 1969. pap. E1.00. British Mus.
English Copper, Tin & Bronze Coins in the British Museum, 1558-1958. C. Wilson Peck. (Illus., 50 plates). 1970. E20.00. British Mus.
Etruscan Bronze Utensils. Sybille Haynes. (Illus., 16 plates, 4 color). 1974. E2.25, cased; pap. E1.50. British Mus.
Etruscan Sculpture. Sybille Haynes. (Illus., 16 plates, 5 color). 1971. pap. E1.50. British Mus.
Excavations at Sutton Hoo: Prehistoric to Anglo-Saxon. I. H. Longworth & I. A. Kinnes. 1979. write for info. British Mus.
Excavations in Cyprus. A. S. Murray et al. (Illus., 14 plates). 1970. E15.00. British Mus.
Facsimile of the Ku K'ai-Chih Scroll Painting "Admonitions of the Instructresses of the Ladies in the Palace". (Illus.). 1966. E30.00, contained in a wooden box. British Mus.
Fifty Masterpieces of Ancient Near Eastern Art. R. D. Barnett & D. J. Wiseman. (Illus., 57, 5 color plates). 1969. pap. E1.75. British Mus.
Fifty Masterpieces of Classical Art in the British Museum. Photos by John Webb. (Illus., 50 color plates). 1970. E10.00, cased. British Mus.
Flint Implements. Ed. by British Museum. 1975. E2.75, cased; pap. E1.75. British Mus.
Flowers in Art from East & West. Paul Hulton & Lawrence Smith. (Illus., 32 color, 150 b&w). 1979. E7.95; pap. E4.95. British Mus.
French Landscape Drawings & Sketches of the Eighteenth Century. Roseline Bacou et al. (Illus., 8 color plates, 60 b&w). 1977. E6.95, cased; pap. E4.50. British Mus.
From Manet to Toulouse-Lautrec: French Lithographs, 1860-1900. Frances Carey & Antony Griffiths. (Illus., 11 color, 60 b&w). 1978. E7.50, cased; pap. E3.95. British Mus.
Frozen Tombs: The Culture & Art of the Ancient Tribes of Siberia. (Illus., 13 color plates, 22 b&w, 3 maps). 1978. E7.50, cased; pap. E4.95. British Mus.
Gainsborough & Reynolds in the British Museum. Compiled by Timothy Clifford et al. (Illus., 48 b&w). 1979. E7.95, cased; pap. E4.95. British Mus.
Gold & Silver in the Late Roman World. Kenneth Painter. (Illus., monochrome). 1977. pap. 0.50p. British Mus.
Gonds of Central India. Ed. by Shelagh Weir. (Illus., b&w). 1973. pap. E1.50. British Mus.
Greek & Roman Art in the British Museum. B. F. Cook. (Illus., 150 b&w, color frontis). 1976. E5.50; pap. E2.75. British Mus.
Greek & Roman Portrait Sculpture. R. P. Hinks. (Illus., 74 b&w). 1976. E4.95, cased; pap. E3.25. British Mus.
Greek & Roman Pottery Lamps. D. M. Bailey. (Illus., 4 color plates, 16 b&w). 1972. pap. E1.50. British Mus.
Greek Bronze Age. R. A. Higgins. (Illus., 4 color plates, 16 b&w). 1977. E2.25, cased; pap. E1.50. British Mus.
Greek Gods & Heroes. Ann Birchall & P. E. Corbett. (Illus., 73). 1978. E5.50, cased; pap. E2.95. British Mus.
Greek Terracotta Figures. R. A. Higgins. (Illus., 4 color plates, 16 b&w). 1969. E1.50. British Mus.
Greek Theatre. Judith Swadding. (Illus., 16 b&w). 1977. pap. 0.60p. British Mus.
Hawaii. Dorota Starzecka. (Illus., 5 color plates, 15 b&w). 1975. pap. E2.25. British Mus.
Heralds & Ancestors. Anthony Wagner. (Illus., 16 color plates, 31 b&w). 1978. E6.95, cased; pap. E3.95. British Mus.
Hieratic Papyri in the British Museum: Abu Sir Papyri. P. Posener-Krieger & J. L. De Cenival. (Fifth Ser). (Illus., 225 b&w). 1968. E20.00, cased. British Mus.
Hieratic Papyri in the British Museum: Oracular Amuletic Decrees of the Late New Kingdom, 2 vols. I. E. S. Edwards. (Fourth Ser). (Illus., 92 b&w). 1960. E20.00, cased. British Mus.
Hieroglyphic Texts from Egyptian Stelae Etc. in the British Museum, Pt. 1. T. G. James. (Illus., 42 b&w). 1961. E10.00, cased. British Mus.
Hieroglyphic Texts from Egyptian Stelae Etc. in the British Museum, Pt. 9. T. G. James. (Illus., 51 b&w). 1970. E12.00, cased. British Mus.
Historical Guide to the Sculptures of the Parthenon. Ed. by British Museum. (Illus., frontis). 1975. E2.50, cased; pap. E1.50. British Mus.
Hod Hill: Antiquities from Hod Hill in the Durden Collection, Vol. 1. J. W. Brailsford. (Illus., 14 b&w, 15 line drawings). 1962. E4.00. British Mus.
Hod Hill: Excavations Carried Out Between 1951 & 1958 for the Trustees of the British Museum, Vol. 2. Ian Richmond. (Illus., 48 b&w, 71 line drawings). 1968. E12.00. British Mus.
Hunters & Gatherers. James Woodburn. (Illus., color, b&w). 1970. pap. E1.50. British Mus.
Illustrations of Old Testament History. R. D. Barnett. (Illus., 76). 1977. E4.50, cased; pap. E2.25. British Mus.
Introduction to Ancient Egypt. Ed. by T. G. H. James. 1980. E8.50, cased; pap. E4.95. British Mus.
Inventaria Archaeologica: Early & Middle Bronze Age Grave-Groups & Hoards from Scotland, 5th Set. Ed. by Stuart Piggott & Margaret Stewart. 1958. pap. E1.00 ten cards. British Mus.
Inventaria Archaeologica: Late Bronze Age Finds in the Heathery Burn Cave, Co. Durham, 9th Set. Ed. by D. Britton & I. H. Longworth. 1968. pap. E1.00 ten cards. British Mus.
Inventaria Archaeologica: Middle Bronze Age Hoards from Southern England, 7th Set. Ed. by M. A. Smith. 1959. pap. E1.00 ten cards. British Mus.
Japanese Birds & Flowers. Ed. by British Museum. (Illus., 12 color plates). 1978. pap. E1.95. British Mus.
Jeweller's Art: An Introduction to the Hall Grundy Gift to the British Museum. Hugh Tait & Charlotte Gere. (Illus., 24 color plates, 96 b&w). 1978. pap. E3.95. British Mus.
Jewellery Through 7000 Years. Ed. by British Museum. (Illus., 27 color plates, 470 b&w). 1976. E7.50, cased; pap. E3.50. British Mus.
Jewellry from the Classical Lands. Reynold Higgins. (Illus., 16 plates, 4 color). 1976. E2.25, cased; pap. E1.50. British Mus.
Lewis Chessman. Michael Taylor. (Illus., b&w). 1978. pap. 0.60p. British Mus.
List of Fragments Rejoined in the Kuyunjik Collection of the British Museum. Ed. by British Museum. 1960. E5.00, cased. British Mus.
Lubaantun, 1926-70. Norman Hammond. (Illus., b&w, line drawings). 1972. pap. E1.50. British Mus.
Malay Shadow Puppets: The Wayang Siam of Kelantan. Amin Sweeney. (Illus., b&w). 1979. pap. E1.50. British Mus.
Man Before Metals. Ed. by British Museum. (Illus., 25 b&w). 1979. pap. E1.25. British Mus.
Maya Hieroglyphs Without Tears. Eric Thompson. (Illus., b&w). 1979. E2.50, cased; pap. E1.50. British Mus.
Maya Jades. Adrian Digby. (Illus., 16 b&w, color frontis). 1972. E2.25, cased; pap. E1.50. British Mus.
Medals of the French Revolution. Mark Jones. (Illus., 20 b&w). 1977. pap. 0.60p. British Mus.
Medals of the Sun King. Mark Jones. (Illus., monochrome). 1978. pap. E1.25. British Mus.
Medieval Tiles: A Handbook. Elizabeth Eames. (Illus., 4 color plates, 16 b&w). 1976. E2.50, cased; pap. E1.50. British Mus.
Mildenhall Treasure. K. S. Painter. (Illus., 37 b&w, 14 line drawings). 1977. pap. E1.75. British Mus.
Moore: Poems Lithographs. John Russell. (Illus., 26). 1974. pap. E1.00. British Mus.
Mystery of the Aegina Treasure. Reynold Higgins. 1979. write for info. British Mus.
Netsuke: The Miniature Sculpture of Japan. Richard Barker & Lawrence Smith. (Illus., 7 color plates, 650 b&w). 1979. E9.95. British Mus.
Nomads of Eastern Siberia. Tom Blagg. (Illus., 20 b&w). 1978. 0.60p. British Mus.
Parthenon Frieze. Martin Frobertson & Alison Frantz. (Illus., monochrome, line drawings). 1975. pap. E1.95. British Mus.
Pisanello's Medallion of the Emperor John VIII Palaeologus. Roberto Weiss. (Illus., 16 plates). 1966. pap. E1.50. British Mus.
Portland Vase. D. E. Haynes. (Illus., 16 plates, color frontis). 1975. E2.50, cased; pap. E1.50. British Mus.
Portrait Painting from Roman Egypt. A. F. Shore. (Illus., 16 plates, 4 color plates). 1972. pap. E1.50. British Mus.
Potter's Art in Africa. William Fagg & John Picton. (Illus., 32). 1978. pap. E2.25. British Mus.
Prehistoric & Roman Studies. Ed. by G. De Sieveking. (Illus., 91 b&w, color frontis). 1971. pap. E5.00. British Mus.
Principal Coins of the Romans: The Principate, 31 BC-AD 296, Vol. 2. R. A. Carson. (Illus., 1658). 1979. write for info. British Mus.
Principal Coins of the Romans: The Republic, C. 290-31 BC, Vol. 1. R. A. Carson. (Illus., 638). 1978. E15.00. British Mus.
Raffles Gamelan. William Fagg. (Illus., color, b&w). 1970. pap. E1.50. British Mus.
Roman Sculpture from Cyrenaica: Corpus Signorum Imperii Romani II, 1. Janet Huskinson. (Illus., 56 b&w, 2 maps). E20.00, cased. British Mus.
Rosetta Stone. E. A. Wallis Budge. (Illus., frontis). 1976. pap. 0.35p. British Mus.
Rubens: Drawings & Sketches. John Rowlands. (Illus., color, b&w). 1977. E6.95, cased; pap. E4.95. British Mus.
Sculptures from Amaravati in the British Museum. Douglas Barrett. (Illus., 48 b&w). 1954. E6.00, cased. British Mus.
Sculptures of Ashburnipal. R. D. Barnett. (Illus., 78 plates, 14 figs.). 1976. write for info. British Mus.
Sculptures of Tiglath-Pileser III (745-727 BC) R. D. Barnett & M. Falkner. (Illus., 1 color plate, 129 plates). 1962. E15.00, cased. British Mus.
Sir Hans Sloane & Ethnography. Ed. by William Fagg. (Illus., color, b&w). 1970. pap. E1.50. British Mus.
Sketches of Amerindian Tribes, 1841-1843. Edward Goodall. (Illus., 63 color plates, 6 monochrome plates, 1 map). 1977. E4.95. British Mus.
Smoking Pipes of the North American Indian. J. C. King. (Illus., 44 b&w, maps). 1977. pap. E1.75. British Mus.
South Italian Vase Painting. A. D. Trendall. (Illus., 4 color plates, 16 b&w). 1976. E2.50, cased; pap. E1.50. British Mus.
Stein Von Rosette. E. A. Wallis Budge. (Illus., 4). 1978. pap. 0.95p. British Mus.
Sutton Hoo Ship Burial: A Handbook. Rupert Bruce-Mitford. (Illus., 8 color plates, 91 b&w). 1979. E7.50, cased; pap. E4.50. British Mus.
Sutton Hoo Ship Burial: Arms, Armor & Regalia, Vol. 2. Rupert Bruce-Mitford. (Illus., 27 color plates, 550 half-tone & line drawings). 1978. E50.00, cased. British Mus.
Sutton Hoo Ship Burial: Excavations, Background, the Ship, Dating & Inventory, Vol. 1. Rupert Bruce-Mitford. (Illus., 13 color plates, 424 half-tones & line drawings, 16 foldouts, 84 halftone coin illus., 37 tables). 1975. E45.00, cased. British Mus.
Sylloge of Coins of the British Isles: The Hiberno-Norse Coins in the British Museum. R. H. M. Dolley. (Illus., 14 plates). 1966. E15.00. British Mus.
Textiles of Baluchistan. M. G. Konieczny. (Illus., 48 plates including 10 color, 12 line drawings, 1 map). 1979. write for info. British Mus.
The Free-Standing Sculptures of the Mausoleum at Halicarna Ssus in the British Museum. G. B. Waywell. (Illus., 194 b&w, 62 line drawings). 1978. E45.00. British Mus.
Thracian Treasures from Bulgaria. Ed. by British Museum. (Illus., 8 color plates, 120 b&w, map). 1976. E5.50, cased; pap. E2.50. British Mus.
Travels in Asia Minor. Richard Chandler. Ed. by Edith Clay. (Illus., 16 plates, color frontis). 1971. E5.00. British Mus.
Tribal Image: Wooden Figure Sculpture of the World. William Fagg. (Illus., 80). 1978. pap. E2.25. British Mus.
Turner in the British Museum: Drawings & Watercolors. Andrew Wilton. (Illus., 35 color plates, 220 monochrome). 1975. E6.25, cased; pap. E3.75. British Mus.
Turquoise Mosaics from Mexico. Elizabeth Carmichael. (Illus., color, b&w). 1970. pap. E1.50. British Mus.
Twelve British Landscapes. Ed. by British Museum. (Illus., 12 color plates). 1979. write for info. British Mus.
Two Thousand Years of British Coins & Medals. John Kent. (Illus., 382). 1978. E3.50, cased; pap. E2.50. British Mus.
Ur Excavations: Middle-Babylonian Legal Documents & Other Texts, Vol. 7. O. R. Gurney. (Texts Ser). (Illus., 79 plates). 1974. E9.00, cased. British Mus.
Ur Excavations: The Old Babylonian Period, Vol. 7. Leonard Woolley & Max Mallowan. (Archaeological Ser). (Illus., 129 plates, 44 figs.). 1976. E45.00, cased. British Mus.

PERMANENT COLLECTION CATALOG INDEX CHRISTCHURCH MANSION

Water Newton Early Christian Silver. K. S. Painter. (Illus., 35 b&w, 11 line drawings). 1977. pap. E1.75. British Mus.
Wealth of the Roman World A. D. 300-700. J. P. C. Kent & K. S. Painter. (Illus., 12 color plates, 269 b&w, 5 maps). 1977. E5.00; pap. E1.95. British Mus.
Works of Jacques le Moyne De Morgues: A/Huguenot Artist in France, Florida & England, 2 vols. Paul Hulton. (Illus., 144 plates, 16 color facsims.). 1977. E75.00 set, slipcased. British Mus.

BRON
Paris, France.
Bron. Francois Marhey. Ed. by Caisse Nationale. (Cathedrales-Eglises Ser). (Illus., 47 b&w, Fr.). 1978. 15.00 F. (ISBN 2-85822-005-0). Caisse Nation.

BROOKGREEN GARDENS
Murrells Inlet, South Carolina.
Brookgreen Gardens Sculpture. Beatrice Proske. (Illus., 169 b&w). 1968. $6.95. Brookgreen.

BROOKLYN MUSEUM
Brooklyn, New York.
Along the Tokaido: Twelve Views by Utagawa Kuniyoshi. Amy Poster. (Illus., 22 color). pap. $4.95 (ISBN 0-87273-060-3). Brooklyn Mus.
American Interiors 1675-1885. Marvin D. Schwartz. (Illus., 97; 20 color). pap. $4.95 (ISBN 0-87273-016-6). Brooklyn Mus.
American Painting in the Brooklyn Museum Collection. (Illus., 74). pap. $2.00 (ISBN 0-87273-023-9). Brooklyn Mus.
Ancient Egyptian Glass & Glazes in the Brooklyn Museum. Elizabeth Riefstahl. (Wilbour Monographs, Vol. 1). (Illus., 126; 26 color). $9.00 (ISBN 0-913696-04-8). Brooklyn Mus.
Brief Guide to the Department of Egyptian & Classical Art. Intro. by Bernard V. Bothmer. (Illus., 57; 4 color, 3 maps). pap. $4.00 (ISBN 0-913696-24-2). Brooklyn Mus.
Brooklyn Museum American Paintings: A Complete Illustrated Listing of Works in the Museum's Collection. (Illus., 1000; 4 color). pap. $9.95 (ISBN 0-87273-074-3). Brooklyn Mus.
Brooklyn Museum Aramaic Papyri: New Documents of the Fifth Century B.C. from the Jewish Community at Elephantine. Ed. & intro. by Emil G. Kraeling. (Illus., 50). 1969. $18.00 (ISBN 0-405-00873-2). Brooklyn Mus.
Brooklyn Museum Handbook. Thomas S. Buechner. Ed. by Axel Von Saldern. (Illus., 267; 26 color). pap. $5.95 (ISBN 0-87273-007-7). Brooklyn Mus.
Brooklyn Museum Japanese Ceramics. Robert Moes. (Illus., 78). pap. $5.00 (ISBN 0-87273-073-5). Brooklyn Mus.
Changing Fashions 1800-1970. Elizabeth A. Coleman. (Illus., 56; 8 color). pap. $4.50 (ISBN 0-87273-012-3). Brooklyn Mus.
Coptic Textiles in the Brooklyn Museum. Deborah Thompson. (Wilbour Monographs, Vol. 2). (Illus., 52; 16 color, 1 map). $11.00 (ISBN 0-913696-11-0). Brooklyn Mus.
Corpus of Hieroglyphic Inscriptions in the Brooklyn Museum: From Dynasty I to the End of Dynasty XVIII, Pt. 1. T. G. H. James. (Wilbour Monographs, Vol. 6). (Illus., 117; 1 color). $10.00 (ISBN 0-913696-16-1). Brooklyn Mus.
Curator's Choice: Durer to Dubuffet. Jo Miller. (Illus., 9). pap. $0.75 (ISBN 0-87273-052-2). Brooklyn Mus.
Five Years of Collecting Egyptian Art, 1951-1956. Pref. by Edgar C. Schenck & John D. Cooney. (Illus., 171). 1969. $15.00. Brooklyn Mus.
Frieda Schiff Warburg Memorial Sculpture Garden. Frederick Fried. (Illus., 13). pap. $0.75 (ISBN 0-87273-031-X). Brooklyn Mus.
Greek & Latin Inscriptions in the Brooklyn Museum. Ed. by Kevin Herbert. (Wilbour Monographs, Vol. 4). (Illus., 72; 2 color). $8.00 (ISBN 0-913696-13-7). Brooklyn Mus.
House of Worth. Robert Riley. (Illus., 24). pap. $2.50 (ISBN 0-87273-013-1). Brooklyn Mus.
Indonesian Art. Rochelle Estrin & Arline Meyer. (Illus., 16). pap. $0.75 (ISBN 0-87273-019-0). Brooklyn Mus.
Jan Martense Schenk House. Marvin D. Schwartz. (Illus., 26). pap. $2.00 (ISBN 0-87273-018-2). Brooklyn Mus.
King of the World: Ashur-nasir-pal II of Assyria. Samuel M. Paley. (Illus., 64, 1 color). $20.00 (ISBN 0-87273-003-4). Brooklyn Mus.
Lace with the Delicate Air. Dassah Saulpaugh. (Illus., 22). pap. $0.75 (ISBN 0-87273-014-X). Brooklyn Mus.
Late Egyptian & Coptic Art: An Introduction to the Collections in the Brooklyn Museum. John D. Cooney. (Illus., 79). 1974. $9.00 (ISBN 0-913696-23-4). Brooklyn Mus.
Masterpieces of American Painting from the Brooklyn Museum. (Illus., 47). pap. $6.00 (ISBN 0-87273-059-X). Brooklyn Mus.
Papyrus of the Late Middle Kingdom in the Brooklyn Museum. Ed. by William C. Hayes. (Wilbour Monographs, Vol. 5). (Illus., 28). 1972. $8.00 (ISBN 0-913696-15-3). Brooklyn Mus.
Primitive Art of the Pacific Islands. Jane P. Powell & Martin L. Friedman. (Illus., 13). pap. $0.50. Brooklyn Mus.
Wilbour Library Acquisitions Lists. pap. $1.00 ea. Brooklyn Mus.

BROOKS MEMORIAL ART GALLERY
Memphis, Tennessee.
Art Today Collection. Intro. by Mildred Hudson & John Whitlock. (Illus., color, b&w). 1977. pap. $5.00. Murdock Print.
Samuel H. Kress Collection. Frwd. by Robert McKnight. (Illus., 2 color, 27 b&w). 1958. pap. $1.00. Murdock Print.
Selections from the American Collection. Compiled by Joseph Czestochowski. (Illus., 1 color,133 b&w). 1975. pap. $2.00. Brooks Memorial Art Gal.
Sixty Paintings. Intro. by Robert McKnight. (Illus., 60). 1966. pap. $1.00. Brooks Memorial Art Gal.

BUNDESPOSTMUSEUM
Frankfurt, Germany, West.
Bundespostmuseum. (Illus.). pap. write for info. Bundespostmus.

BUNDNER KUNSTMUSEUM CHUR
Chur, Switzerland.
Bundner Kunstsammlung Chur: Neueingange 70-71. Hans Hartmann. Ed. by Kunsthaus Chur. (Illus., 1, Ger.). 1971. write for info. Kunstmus Chur.
Bundner Kunstsammlung: Die Ausgestellten Werke. Emil Hungerbuhler & Hans Christoph Von Tavel. Ed. by Kunsthaus Chur. (Illus., 188, 16 color, Ger.). 8.00 F. Kunstmus Chur.

BURGENKUNDLICHES MUSEUM
Graz, Austria.
Burgenkundliches Museum Alt-Kainach. Pfeifer Egon. Ed. by Steirischer Burgenverein. (Ger.). 1977. write for info. Burgenkun Mus.

BUSCH REISENGER MUSEUM
see Harvard Univ., Busch Reisenger Museum

CAIRO MUSEUM
see Egyptian Museum

CAISSE NATIONAL DES MONUMENTS HISTORIQUES ET DES SITES
Paris, France.
Chartreuse De Villenueve les Avignon. H. Cingria et al. Ed. by Caisse Nationale. (Abbayes En France Ser: Provence). (Illus., 52 b&w, Fr.). 1977. 18.00 F. (ISBN 2-85822-003-4). Caisse Nation.
Citi De Carcassonne. Francois Grimal. Ed. by Caisse Nationale. (Chateaux, Forteresses, Villes Fortifiees Ser: Languenoc). (Illus., 11 color, 59 b&w, Fr.). 1966. 30.00 F. Caisse Nation.
Tapisseries D'Angers. Rene Planchenault. Ed. by Caisse Nationale. (France, Objets D Art Ser). (Illus., 26 b&w, Fr.). 1978. 15.00 F. Caisse Nation.

CALOUSTE GULBENKIAN MUSEUM
Lisbon, Portugal.
Arte Do Livro Frances Dos Seculos XIX E XX. Maria A. Chico & Maria F. Leite. Ed. by Calouste Gulbenkian Foundation. (Illus., 8 color, 45 b&w, Port.). 1976. pap. Esc.75.00. Gulbenkian Mus.
Arte Francesa Do Seclo XVIII Da Coleccao Calouste Gulbenkian - Objets D'Art Francais De la Collection Calouste Gulbenkian. Pierre Verlet. Ed. by Calouste Gulbenkian Foundation. Tr. by Dagoberto L. Markl. (Illus., 23 color, 32 b&w, Fr.). 1969. Esc.350.00. Gulbenkian Mus.
Arte Francesa Do Seclo XVIII Da Coleccao Calouste Gulbenkian - Objets D'Art Francais De la Collection Calouste Gulbenkian. Pierre Verlet. Ed. by Calouste Gulbenkian Foundation. Tr. by Dagoberto L. Markl. (Illus., 23 color, 32 b&w, Port.). 1971. Esc.250.00. Gulbenkian Mus.
Artes Plasticas Francesas De Watteau a Renoir. Ed. by Calouste Gulbenkian Foundation. (Illus., 4 color, 103 b&w, Eng.). 1964. pap. Esc.40.00. Gulbenkian Mus.
Artes Plasticas Francesas De Watteau a Renoir. Ed. by Calouste Gulbenkian Foundation. (Illus., 4 color, 103 b&w, Port.). 1964. pap. Esc.30.00. Gulbenkian Mus.
Catalogue of the Calouste Gulbenkian Collection of Greek Coins, 2 vols. E. S. Robinson & M. Castro Hipolito. Ed. by Calouste Gulbenkian Foundation. (Illus., 42 b&w). 1971. Esc.1200.00. Gulbenkian Mus.
Francesco Guardi. Rudolfo Pallucchini. Ed. by Calouste Gulbenkian Foundation. (Illus., 20 color, Fr.). 1977. pap. Esc.250.00. Gulbenkian Mus.
Francesco Guardi. Rudolfo Pallucchini. Ed. by Calouste Gulbenkian Foundation. (Illus., 20 color, Eng.). 1977. pap. Esc.250.00. Gulbenkian Mus.
Francesco Guardi. Rudolfo Pallucchini. Ed. by Calouste Gulbenkian Foundation. (Illus., 20 color, Port.). 1977. pap. Esc.150.00. Gulbenkian Mus.
Moedas Gregas: Coleccao Calouste Gulbenkian. Mario Hipolito. Ed. by Calouste Gulbenkian Foundation. (Illus., 20 b&w, Port.). 1976. pap. Esc.20.00. Gulbenkian Mus.
Museu Calouste Gulbenkian. Ed. by Calouste Gulbenkian Foundation. (Port.). 1975. pap. Esc.30.00. Gulbenkian Mus.
Persian Art. Richard Ettinghausen. Ed. by Calouste Gulbenkian Foundation. Tr. by Fernando Moser. (Illus., 32 color, 14 b&w, Eng.). 1972. Esc.450.00. Gulbenkian Mus.
Persian Art. Richard Ettinghausen. Ed. by Calouste Gulbenkian Foundation. Tr. by Fernando Moser. (Illus., 32 color, 14 b&w, Port.). 1972. Esc.450.00. Gulbenkian Mus.
Rendas Da Coleccao Calouste Gulbenkian. Ed. by Calouste Gulbenkian Foundation. (Illus., 9 b&w, Port., Fr. & Eng.). 1978. pap. write for info. Gulbenkian Mus.
Tecidos Da Coleccao Calouste Gulbenkian. Ed. by Calouste Gulbenkian Foundation. (Illus., 8 color, 66 b&w, Port., Fr. & Eng.). 1978. pap. write for info. Gulbenkian Mus.

CAMPBELL MUSEUM
Camden, New Jersey.
Campbell Museum Collection. (Illus., color, b&w). 1972. $4.00. Campbell Mus.

CARNEGIE INSTITUTE, MUSEUM OF ART
Pittsburgh, Pennsylvania.
Catalogue of Painting Collection Museum of Art, Carnegie Institute. Ed. by Herdis Teilman. (Illus., 98 color plates). 1973. $12.00; pap. $9.00. Carnegie.
Introduction to the Collections of the Museum of Art, Carnegie Institute. David T. Owsley et al. (Illus., 89 b&w). 1977. $1.25.,pamphlet. Carnegie.

CAROLINA ART ASSN., GIBBES ART GALLERY
Charleston, South Carolina.
Selections from the Collection of the Carolina Art Association. Martha Severns. (Illus., 136 b&w). 1977. pap. $4.50 (ISBN 0-910326-09-6). Carolina Art.

CARTER, AMON, MUSEUM OF ART
Fort Worth, Texas.
Alfred Jacob Miller. Ron Tyler. (Amon Carter Museum Collection Ser). (Illus., 10 b&w). 1972. pap. $0.25. Amon Carter.
Amon Carter Museum of Western Art: Catalogue of the Collection, 1972. Ed. by Peter H. Hassrick. (Illus., 600 b&w). 1973. pap. $12.50 (ISBN 0-88360-000-5). Amon Carter.
Amon Carter Museum, 1961-1977. Amon Carter Museum. (Illus., 41 b&w). 1977. pap. $3.50 (ISBN 0-88360-028-5). Amon Carter.
Anton Schonborn: Western Forts. Franz Stenzel. (Amon Carter Museum Collection Ser). (Illus., 11 b&w). 1972. pap. $0.25. Amon Carter.
Armor Exhibition. J. R. Philpott, Jr. (Illus., 16 color, 22 b&w). 1978. pap. write for info. Asheville Mus.
Bonaparte Audubon Prints. Amon Carter Museum. (Amon Carter Museum Collection Ser). (Illus., 14 b&w). 1972. pap. $0.25. Amon Carter.
Buffalo & the Artists. Larry Barsness. (Amon Carter Museum Collection Ser). (Illus., 18 b&w). 1977. pap. $0.25. Amon Carter.
Charles M. Russell. John A. Diffily. (Amon Carter Museum Collection Ser). (Illus., 15 b&w). 1972. pap. $0.25. Amon Carter.
Charles M. Russell: Paintings, Drawings & Sculpture in the Amon Carter Museum Collection. Frederic C. Renner. (Illus., 80 color, 240 b&w). 1974. $40.00. Amon Carter.
Charles M. Russell: Paintings, Drawings & Sculptures in the Amon G. Carter Collection. Frederic G. Renner. (Illus., 36 color, 259 b&w). 1966. $20.00. Amon Carter.
Contemporary Eskimo Prints. Helga Goetz. (Amon Carter Museum Collection Ser). (Illus., 13 b&w). 1977. pap. $0.25. Amon Carter.
Currier & Ives. Ron Tyler. (Amon Carter Museum Collection Ser). (Illus., 15 b&w). 1972. pap. $0.25. Amon Carter.
Frederic Remington. Peter H. Hassrick. (Amon Carter Museum Collection Ser). (Illus., 13 b&w). 1972. pap. $0.25. Amon Carter.
Frederic Remington: Paintings, Drawings & Sculpture in the Amon Carter Museum & the Sid W. Richardson Foundation Collections. Peter H. Hassrick. (Illus., 60 color, 94 b&w). 1973. $35.00. Amon Carter.
Illusions of Reality. Alfred Frankenstein. (Amon Carter Museum Collection Ser). (Illus., 7 b&w). 1977. pap. $0.25. Amon Carter.
Leonard Baskin Indian Drawings. Leonard Baskin & Peter H. Hassrick. (Amon Carter Museum Collection Ser). (Illus., 10 b&w). 1972. pap. $0.25. Amon Carter.
Western City Views. John W. Reps. (Amon Carter Museum Collection Ser). (Illus., 27 b&w). 1972. pap. $0.25. Amon Carter.
William H. Holmes: Panoramic Art. William H. Goetzmann. (Amon Carter Museum Collection Ser). (Illus., 20 b&w). 1977. pap. $0.25. Amon Carter.

CASA MUSEU DOS PATUDOS
see Instituicao Jose Relvas, Casa Museu Dos Patudos

CATHEDRALE DE REIMS
Paris, France.
Cathedrale De Reims. M. Eschapasse. Ed. by Caisse Nationale. (Cathedrales-Eglises Ser: Champagne). (Illus., 2 color, 50 b&w, Fr.). 1977. 18.00 F. Caisse Nation.

CATHEDRALE DE TOURS
Paris, France.
Cathedrale De Tours. Dominique Hervier. Ed. by Caisse Nationale. (Cathedrales-Eglises Ser). (Fr.). write for info. Caisse Nation.

CEDERCREUTZIN, EMIL, MUSEUM
Harjavalta, Finland.
Temple to the Spirit of the Earth. Ritva Kava & Henry Nordberg. Tr. by Maritta Jarvinen & Liisa Rasanen. (Illus., Finnish, Eng., Swed., Ger., Fr. & Rus.). 1976. Fmk.10.00. Emil Ceder Mus.

CENTER FOR CREATIVE PHOTOGRAPHY, UNIV. OF ARIZONA LIBRARY
Tucson, Arizona.
Center: Photographs from the Collection of the Center for Creative Photography. Peter MacGill. 1977. pap. $1.00. Ctr Creative Photo.
Contemporary Photography in New Mexico: Nine Photographers. Terence Pitts & Rene Verdugo. (Illus., 10 photos). 1978. pap. $2.00. Ctr Creative Photo.
Guides to the Collections of the Center for Creative Photography. Ed. by Terence Pitts. (Guide Ser). 1979. pap. $2.00. Ctr Creative Photo.

CENTRALE MUZEUM MORSKIE
Gdansk, Poland.
Polska Grafika Marynistyczna. Boleslaw Roginski. 1965. write for info. Muz Morskie.

CENTRE GEORGES POMPIDOU
see Musee D'Art Moderne (Beaubourg), Centre National D'Art et De Culture Georges Pompidou

CHAMBORD
Paris, France.
Chambord. T. Imbert. Ed. by Caisse Nationale. (Chateaux, Demeures, Hotels Ser). (Illus., 42 b&w, Fr.). 1978. 15.00 F. Caisse Nation.

CHATEAU DE SAUMUR
see Musee D'Arts Decoratifs, Chateau De Saumur

CHATEAU DE SCEAUX
see Musee De L'Isle De France

CHATEAU DE TALCY
Paris, France.
Chateau De Talcy. Jacques Houlet. Ed. by Caisse Nationale. (Chateaux, Demeures, Hotels Ser: Loire). (Illus., 31 b&w, Fr.). 1967. write for info. Caisse Nation.

CHATEAU DE VINCENNES
Paris, France.
Chateau De Vincennes. Francois Enaud. Ed. by Caisse Nationale. (Chateaux, Forteresses, Villes Fortifiees: Paris). (Illus., 40 b&w, Fr.). 1965. 18.00 F. Caisse Nation.

CHATEAU DU HAUT-KOENIGSBOURG
Paris, France.
Chateau Du Haut Koenigsbourg. Hans Haug. Ed. by Caisse Nationale. (Chateaux, Forteresses, Villes Fortifiees Ser: Alsace). (Illus., 1 color, 25 b&w, Fr.). 1964. 16.00 F. Caisse Nation.

CHICAGO PUBLIC LIBRARY, CULTURAL CENTER, SPECIAL COLLECTIONS DIVISION
Chicago, Illinois.
One Hundred Important Additions to the Civil War & American History Research Collection: An Exhibition of Acquisitions, 1974-1978. Thomas Orlando. (Illus., 22). 1978. pap. $2.50. Chi Pub Lib.
Take up the Sword of Justice: An Exhibition of British World War I Posters from the Special Collections of the Chicago Public Library. Marie Gecik & Thomas Orlando. (Illus., 6 b&w). 1976. pap. write for info. Chi Pub Lib.
Treasures of the Chicago Public Library: A Contribution Toward a Descriptive Catalog. Compiled by Thomas Orlando & Marie Gecik. (Illus., 37 b&w). 1977. $12.50. Chi Pub Lib.

CHORHERRENSTIFT ST. FLORIAN
St. Florian, Austria.
Stift St. Florian. Karl Rehberger. (Illus., 6 color, 8 b&w). pap. write for info. St. Florian.

CHRIST CHURCH PICTURE GALLERY
Oxford, United Kingdom.
Drawings by Old Masters at Christ Church, Oxford. James B. Shaw. Ed. by Henry Chadwick. (Illus., 890 halftone plates). 1976. E60.00 (ISBN 0-19-817323-7). Oxford U Pr.
Paintings by Old Masters at Christ Church, Oxford. James B. Shaw. (Illus., 6 color, 178 b&w). 1967. E10.00. Phaidon Pr.

CHRISTCHURCH MANSION
see Ipswich Museums and Art Galleries

CHRYSLER MUSEUM AT NORFOLK
Norfolk, Virginia.
American Native Painting of the 18th & 19th Centuries: One Hundred Eleven Masterpieces from the Collection of Edgar William & Bernice Chrysler Garbisch. Frwd. by John Walker. (Illus., 111). 1968. $3.50. Chrysler Mus.
American Native Paintings of the 18th & 19th Centuries: Twenty Two Masterpieces from the Collection of Edgar William & Bernice Chrysler Garbrisch. Pref. by Lloyd Goodrich. (Illus., 22). $3.00. Chrysler Mus.
Chinese Art in the Chrysler Museum. Shirley Ganse. (Illus., 18). 1976. $1.00. Chrysler Mus.
Chrysler Art Museum of Provincetown, Inaugural Exhibition. Bertina Manning. (Illus., 75). 1958. $7.50. Chrysler Mus.
Gift of American Native Paintings from the Collection of Edgar William & Bernice Chrysler Garbisch: Forty Eight Masterpieces. (Illus., 48). 1975. $3.50. Chrysler Mus.
Hawthorne Retrospective. Frwd. by Joseph Hawthorne. (Illus., 89). 1961. $7.50. Chrysler Mus.
Italian Renaissance & Baroque Paintings from the Collection of Walter P. Chrysler, Jr. Frwd. by Henry Caldwell. (Illus., 58, 10 color plates). 1968. $8.50. Chrysler Mus.
Three Hundred Years of American Art in the Chrysler Museum. Dennis Anderson. (Illus., 307, 10 color plates). 1976. $10.00. Chrysler Mus.
Tiffany Collection from the Chrysler Museum at Norfolk. Paul Doros. (Illus., 150, 60 color). 1977. $10.00. Chrysler Mus.

CINCINNATI ART MUSEUM
Cincinnati, Ohio.
Art Conservation: The Race Against Destruction. E. Batchelor et al. (Illus., 4 color plates, 33 b&w photos & diags.). 1978. pap. $5.00. Cincinnati Mus.
Art of the First Americans. C. R. Shine et al. (Illus., 6 color plates, 150 b&w). 1976. pap. $10.00. Cincinnati Mus.
Cincinnati Art Museum Handbook. Ed. by B. L. Zimmerman & C. R. Shine. (Illus., 404 b&w photos, floor plans). 1975. $10.00; pap. $5.00. Cincinnati Mus.
French Drawings, Watercolors & Pastels: 1800-1950. Kristin L. Spangenberg. (Illus., 12 color plates, 88 b&w photos). 1978. pap. $17.50. Cincinnati Mus.
Ladies, God Bless 'Em. Carol Macht et al. (Illus., 52 b&w). 1976. pap. $3.00. Cincinnati Mus.
Sculpture Collection of the Cincinnati Art Museum. Ed. & intro. by P. R. Adams. (Illus., 163 b&w). 1970. $7.50. Cincinnati Mus.
Spanish Paintings in the Cincinnati Art Museum. M. F. Rogers, Jr. (Illus., 4 color plates, 37 b&w photos). 1978. pap. $7.50. Cincinnati Mus.

CITY MUSEUM AND ART GALLERY
Peterborough, United Kingdom.
Descriptive Catalogue of the John Clare Collection. Margaret Granger. (Illus., 11 photos). 1973. pap. E1.75. Peterborough.
Guide Catalogue to Archaeological Collections in the Peterborough Museum. Miranda J. Green. (Illus., 32 drawings). 1977. pap. E1.00. Peterborough.

CITY OF BRISTOL MUSEUM AND ART GALLERY
Bristol, United Kingdom.
Catalogue of Paintings. (Illus., 10 color, 40 b&w). 1970. pap. E1.25. Bristol Art Gal.
Delftware. Cleo Witt. (Illus., 20 halftones). pap. 0.40p. Bristol Art Gal.

CIVICHE RACCOLTE ARCHEOLOGICHE E NUMIMATICHE DI MILANO
Milan, Italy.
Cinquecentine Della Biblioteca. R. La Guardia. (Cataloghi Della Biblioteca). (It.). 1978. $6.60. Arch Num Milan.
Civica Raccolta Egizia. G. Lise. (Guide Della Raccolte). (It.). 1976. $1.60. Arch Num Milan.
I Longobardi E la Lombardia. (Cataloghi Di Mostre Organizzate). (It.). 1978. $1.60. Arch Num Milan.
I Longobardi E la Lombardia, Saggi. (Cataloghi Di Mostre Organizzate). (Illus., It.). 1978. $10.00. Arch Num Milan.
Medaglia Polacca Contemporanea. (Cataloghi Di Mostre Organizzate). (It.). 1974. $0.85. Arch Num Milan.
Moneta Della Sicilia Antica. E. A. Arslan. (Cataloghi Del Gabinetto Numismatico). (Illus., It.). 1976. $6.60. Arch Num Milan.
Monetazione Punica. E. Acquaro. (Cataloghi Del Gabinetto Numismatico). (It.). 1979. $7.50. Arch Num Milan.
Monete Dell'Impero Romano, Vol. 1, Da Augusto A Traiano. (Cataloghi Del Gabinetto Numismatico). (Illus., It.). 1938. $25.00. Arch Num Milan.
Monete Dell'Impero Romano, Vol. 2, Da Adriano Ad Elio Cesare. (Cataloghi Del Gabinetto Numismatico). (Illus., It.). 1940. $20.85. Arch Num Milan.
Monete Di Ostrogoti, Longobardi E Vandali. E. A. Arslan. (Cataloghi Del Gabinetto Numismatico). (Illus., It.). 1978. $7.50. Arch Num Milan.
Monete Di Traiano. G. G. Belloni. (Cataloghi Del Gabinetto Numismatico). (Illus., It.). 1973. $12.50. Arch Num Milan.
Monete Greche del 6 al 2 sec. aC, per la 14 Settimana Dei Musei. (Cataloghi Di Mostre Organizzate Dalla Direzione Raccolta Archeologiche E Numismatiche). (Illus., It.). 1971. $1.25. Arch Num Milan.
Monete Romane Dell'Eta Repubblicana. G. G. Belloni. (Cataloghi Del Gabinetto Numismatico). (Illus., It.). 1960. $20.85. Arch Num Milan.
Tesoretto Di Vigevano. E. A. Arslan. (Cataloghi Di Mostre Organizzate). (Illus., It.). 1976. $0.85. Arch Num Milan.

CLARK, STERLING AND FRANCINE, ART INSTITUTE
Williamstown, Massachusetts.
Drawings from the Clark Art Institute. Egbert Haverkamp-Begemann. (Illus.). 1964. $20.00. Clark Art Inst.
Illustrated List of Paintings. (Illus.). 1973. $5.00. Clark Art Inst.

CLASSICAL SCHOOL GALLERY
Albuquerque, New Mexico.
New Mexico Santos. (Illus., 37 color, b&w). 1978. $10.00. Am Classical C.

CLEVELAND MUSEUM OF ART
Cleveland, Ohio.
European Paintings Before 1500. Wolfgang Stechow et al. (Catalogue of Paintings Ser). (Illus., 29 color plates, 179 b&w). 1974. $30.00 (ISBN 0-910386-19-6). Ind U Pr.
Handbook of the Cleveland Museum of Art. Cleveland Museum of Art. (Illus., 1624 b&w). 1978. $20.00 (ISBN 0-910386-31-5). Ind U Pr.
Selected Works: The Cleveland Art Museum. Cleveland Art Museum. (Illus., 32 color plates, 126 b&w). 1966. $12.50, slipcased (ISBN 0-910386-12-9). Ind U Pr.

CLOISTERS
New York, New York.
Cloisters: The Building & the Collection of Medieval Art in Fort Tryon Park. James J. Rorimer. (Illus., 112). 1969. pap. $3.95 (ISBN 0-87099-050-0). Metro Mus Art.

COLLECTIONS BAUR
see Baur Collection

COLLEZIONE D'ARTE RELIGIOSA MODERNA
Vatican, Vatican City.
Musei Vaticani, Collezione Vaticana D'arte Religiosa Moderna. V. Mariani et al. (Illus., 780 b&w, It., Eng., Fr., Ger. & Span.). 1974. L.25.00. Silvana Edit.

COLOMBO NATIONAL MUSEUM
Colombo, Sri Lanka.
Guide to the Ratnapura National Museum. (Illus., 15 b&w). 1968. pap. Rs.2.25. Colombo Mus.
Illustrated Guide to the Colombo Museum: Ground Floor Galleries, Pt. 1. De Silva. (Illus., 163, 41 color). 1976. pap. Rs.20.00. Colombo Mus.

COLONIAL WILLIAMSBURG FOUNDATION
Williamsburg, Virginia.
Asahel Powers: Painter of Vermont Faces. Nina Little. (Illus., 2 color, 54 b&w). 1973. pap. $4.00 (ISBN 0-87935-015-6). Williamsburg.
Beardsley Limner & Some Contemporaries: Post Revolutionary Portraiture in New England, 1785-1805. Christine Schloss. (Illus., 4 color, 30 b&w halftones). 1972. pap. $3.50 (ISBN 0-87935-005-9). Williamsburg.
Charles Bridges & William Dering: Two Virginia Painters, 1735-1750. Graham Hood. (Illus., 9 color plates, 76 b&w). 1978. $15.00 (ISBN 0-87935-047-4). U Pr of Va.
Checklist of American Coverlet Weavers. John Heisey. Ed. by Gail Andrews & Donald Walters. (Illus., 10 color, 118 b&w, 2 drawings, 1 map). 1978. $10.00 (ISBN 0-87935-048-2). U Pr of Va.
Chelsea Porcelain at Williamsburg. John Austin. Ed. & intro. by Graham Hood. (Williamsburg Decorative Arts Ser). (Illus., 78 color plates, 73 b&w). 1977. $30.00 (ISBN 0-87935-023-7). U Pr of Va.
Copperplate Textiles in the Williamsburg Collection. Ruth Cox. (Illus., 10 plates). 1965. pap. $0.95 (ISBN 0-910412-36-7). U Pr of Va.
Eighteenth Century Prints in Colonial America: To Educate & to Decorate. Joan Dolmetch. (Illus., 108 b&w). 1979. $10.95 (ISBN 0-87935-049-0). U Pr of Va.
English & Oriental Carpets at Williamsburg. Mildred Lanier. Ed. & intro. by Graham Hood. (Williamsburg Decorative Arts Ser). (Illus., 57 color photos, 6 b&w). 1975. $17.50 (ISBN 0-87935-021-0). U Pr of Va.
English Silver at Williamsburg. John Davis. Ed. & intro. by Graham Hood. (Williamsburg Decorative Arts Ser). (Illus., 1050 b&w). 1976. $15.00 (ISBN 0-87935-027-X); pap. $11.00 (ISBN 0-87935-028-8). U Pr of Va.
Gallery Guide: The Abbey Aldrich Rockefeller Folk Art Collection. Beatrix Rumford. (Illus., 29 color, 2 b&w halftones). 1976. pap. $3.00 (ISBN 0-87935-033-4). Williamsburg.
New England Furniture at Williamsburg. Barry Greenlaw. Ed. by Graham Hood. (Williamsburg Decorative Arts Ser). (Illus., 8 color photos, 183 b&w). 1974. $10.00 (ISBN 0-87935-020-2); pap. $5.95 (ISBN 0-87935-019-9). U Pr of Va.
Paintings of James Sanford Ellsworth: Itinerant Folk Artist, 1802-1873. Lucy Mitchell. (Illus., 2 color, 268 b&w, 1 map). 1974. pap. $7.00 (ISBN 0-87935-025-3). Williamsburg.
Rebellion & Reconciliation: Satirical Prints on the Revolution at Williamsburg. Joan Dolmetsch. Ed. & frwd. by Graham Hood. (Williamsburg Decorative Arts Ser). (Illus., 101 b&w). 1976. $12.95 (ISBN 0-87935-032-6). U Pr of Va.
Williamsburg Collection of Antique Furnishings. Intro. by Carlisle Humelsine. (Williamsburg Decorative Arts Ser). (Illus., 216 color photos). 1973. $6.95 (ISBN 0-87935-018-0); pap. $3.95 (ISBN 0-87935-017-2). HR&W.

COLUMBUS MUSEUM OF ART
Columbus, Ohio.
American Paintings in the Ferdinand Howald Collection. Marcia Tucker. (Illus., 4 color, 112 b&w). 1969. $7.50; pap. $3.50. Columbus Mus.
Catalog of the Collection. (Illus., 300 b&w). 1979. $7.50. Columbus Mus.
Frederick W. Schumacher Collection. Maurice Cope & John D. Farmer. (Illus., 12 color, 131 b&w). 1976. $25.00; pap. $15.00. Columbus Mus.
Two Hundred Selections from the Permanent Collection. (Illus.). 1979. pap. $2.50. Columbus Mus.

COMPIEGNE
see Musee National Du Chateau De Compiegne

CONCIERGERIE
Paris, France.
Concielgerie. Roger Weigert. Ed. by Caisse Nationale. Tr. by Anne Dorny. (Chateaux, Demeures, Hotels Ser). (Illus., 32 b&w, Fr.). 1977. $18.00. Caisse Nation.

COPTIC MUSEUM
Cairo, Egypt.
Cairo's Ancient Coptic Churches. Raouf Habib. Ed. by Dept. of Antiquities, Coptic Mus. (Illus., 55 b&w, Arabic & Eng.). 1967. P.T.125.00, Arabic ed.; P.T. 144.00. Eng. ed. Coptic Mus.
Coptic Museum & the Fortress of Babylon. Victor Girgis & Pahor Labib. Ed. by General Organization for Government Printing Offices, Cairo. (Illus., 28 b&w). 1975. P.T.50.00. Coptic Mus.
Coptic Museum: General Guide. Raouf Habib. Ed. by Dept. of Antiquities, Coptic Mus. (Illus., 83 b&w, Arabic.). 1966. P.T.175.00. Coptic Mus.
Illustrated Paintings: Icons. Victor Girgis & Pahor Labib. Ed. by Coptic Museum. (Illus., 61 b&w, Arabic.). 1965. P.T.144.00. Coptic Mus.
Textiles of the Coptic Museum. Soaad Maher & Heshmat Mesieha. Ed. by Dept. of Antiquities, Coptic Mus. (Illus., 77 b&w, 1 map, Arabic.). 1957. write for info. Coptic Mus.

CORCORAN GALLERY OF ART
Washington, D.C.
Catalogue of the Collection of American Paintings in the Corcoran Gallery of Art: Painters Born from 1850 to 1910, Vol. 2. Dorothy W. Phillips. (Illus., 9 color, 116 b&w). 1973. $14.50; pap. $10.00. Corcoran.
Catalogue of the Collection of American Paintings in the Corcoran Gallery of Art: Painters Born Before 1850, Vol. 1. Hermann W. Williams, Jr. (Illus., 42 b&w). 1966. $10.00; pap. $7.50. Corcoran.
William A. Clark Collection. Ed. by Edward J. Nygren. (Illus., 5 color, 105 b&w). 1978. pap. $9.00. Corcoran.

CORINTH, LOVIS, MEMORIAL FOUNDATION
New York, New York.
Lovis Corinth: Eine Dokumentation. Thomas Corinth. (Illus., 187 photos, Ger.). 1979. $185.00 (ISBN 3-8030-3025-0). Ernst Wasmuth.

CORNING MUSEUM OF GLASS
Corning, New York.
Corning Flood: Museum Under Water. John Martin. (Illus., 120 b&w). 1977. pap. $6.00 (ISBN 0-87290-063-0). Corning.
Cut & Engraved Glass of Corning,1868-1940. Jane Spillman & Estelle Farrar. (Illus., 112 b&w). 1977. pap. $5.00 (ISBN 0-87290-064-9). Corning.
English Nineteenth Century Cameo Glass. (Illus., 27 b&w). 1963. pap. $1.50 (ISBN 0-87290-056-8). Corning.
German Enameled Glass. Axel Von Saldern. (Illus., 167, 37 color). 1965. pap. $25.00 (ISBN 0-87290-057-6). Corning.
Glass from the Corning Museum of Glass: A Guide to the Collections. (Illus., 129, 20 color). 1974. pap. $3.50 (ISBN 0-87290-050-9). Corning.
Glassmaking: America's First Industry. Jane Spillman. (Illus., 34, 6 color). 1976. pap. $1.40 (ISBN 0-87290-062-2). Corning.
History of Glass in Japan. 1973. $60.00 (ISBN 0-87290-059-2). Corning.
Index: Journal of Glass Studies, 1959-1973, Vols. 1-15. Ed. by Marie-Anne Honeywell. 1976. pap. write for info. (ISBN 0-87290-061-4). Corning.
Journal of Glass Studies, 1972-1978, Vols. 14-20. Ed. by John Martin. (Illus.). 1972-1978. pap. $15.00 ea. Corning.
New Glass: A Worldwide Survey. (Illus., 196 color, 67 b&w). 1979. pap. $20.00 (ISBN 0-87290-069-X). Corning.
Paperweights: Flowers Which Clothe the Meadows. Paul Hollister & Dwight Lanimon. (Illus., 306 color, b&w). 1978. pap. $20.00 (ISBN 0-87290-065-7). Corning.
Survey of Glassmaking from Ancient Egypt to the Present. Compiled by Charleen Edwards. (Illus., 2 microfiche of 168 transparencies). 1977. pap. $26.00 (ISBN 0-226-68902-6). Corning.
Tales from a King's Book of Kings. (Illus., 52). 1973. pap. $1.00. Corning.
Victorian Glass: British Glass of the Victorian Period from the Victoria & Albert Museum, London. 1973. pap. write for info. Corning.

COTTONWOOD COUNTY HISTORICAL SOCIETY
Windom, Minnesota.
Cottonwood County History, 1870-1970. Cottonwood County Historical Society. (Illus., photo). 1970. $5.00. Cottonwood.

COUCY
Paris, France.
Coucy. Francois Enand. Ed. by Caisse Nationale. (Illus., 56 b&w, Fr.). 1978. 18.00 F. (ISBN 2-85822-008-5). Caisse Nation.

COURBET, GUSTAVE, MUSEUM
see Musee D'Ornans

CRANBROOK ACADEMY OF ART MUSEUM
Bloomfield Hills, Michigan.
Creative Spirit of Cranbrook: The Early Years. Ed. by Elizabeth Gaidos. (Illus., 18 b&w photos). 1972. pap. $3.50. Cranbrook.
Historic Fiberworks: Cranbrook. Ed. by Rosalyn Chat. (Illus., 44 b&w photos). 1974. pap. $3.50. Cranbrook.

CYGNAEUKSEN GALLERIA
Helsinki, Finland.
Cygnaeuksen Galleria: Cygnaei Galleri. Ed. by Seppo Niinivaara. (Illus., Swed. & Finnish.). 1975. Fmk.1.00. Cygnaeus.

CYGNAEUS GALLERY
see Cygnaeuksen Galleria

DA VINCI-MUSEUM
Westerlo, Belgium.
Cene. pap. write for info. Da Vinci Mus.

DALI, SALVADOR, MUSEUM
Cleveland, Ohio.
Dali--Picasso...Picasso--Dali. A. Reynolds Morse. (Illus., 97 b&w). 1973. pap. $9.95. Reyn Morse Foun.
Dali: A Panorama of His Art. A. Reynolds Morse. (Illus., 58 color plates, 476 b&w). 1974. $35.00. Reyn Morse Foun.
Guide to Works by Salvador Dali in Public Museum Collections, 1974. A. Reynolds Morse. (Illus., 154 b&w). 1974. deluxe ed. $7.95; pap. $6.95. Reyn Morse Foun.

DANA HOUSE
see Woodstock Historical Society, the Dana House

D'ARCY, MARTIN, GALLERY OF ART
see Loyola Univ., Martin D'Arcy Gallery of Art

DAVID, PERCIVAL, FOUNDATION OF CHINESE ART
London, United Kingdom.
Illustrated Catalogue of Celadon Wares. Margaret Medley. (Illus., 12 plates, halftone). 1977. pap. E2.00. Sch Ori Afr St.
Illustrated Catalogue of Ch'ing Enamelled Ware in the Percival David Foundation. Lady David. (Illus., 12 plates, halftone). 1973. pap. E2.00. Sch Ori Afr St.
Illustrated Catalogue of Ming & Ch'ing Monochrome in the Percival David Foundation of Chinese Art. Margaret Medley. (Illus., 14 plates, halftone). 1973. pap. E2.00. Sch Ori Afr St.
Illustrated Catalogue of Ming Polychrome Wares. Margaret Medley. (Illus., 16 plates, halftone). 1978. E2.50. Sch Ori Afr St.
Illustrated Catalogue of Underglaze Blue & Copper Red Decorated Porcelains in the Percival David Foundation of Chinese Art. Margaret Medley. (Illus., 16 plates, halftone). 1976. pap. E2.00. Sch Ori Afr St.

Dolls & Toys at the Essex Institute. Madeline Merrill & Richard Merrill. Ed. by Bryant Tolles, Jr. & Anne Farnam. (Essex Institute Museum Booklet Ser). (Illus., 59 sepia tone). 1976. pap. $4.95. Essex Inst.
Gardner-Pingree House. Gerald Ward. Ed. by Anne Farnam & Bryant Tolles, Jr. (Essex Institute Historic House Booklet Ser). (Illus., 10 halftone). 1976. pap. $2.00 ea. (ISBN 0-88389-063-1). Essex Inst.
John Tucker Daland House. Bryant Tolles, Jr. Ed. & frwd. by Anne Farnam. (Essex Instittute Historic House Booklet Ser). (Illus., 10 halftone). 1978. pap. $2.00 ea. (ISBN 0-88389-065-8). Essex Inst.
John Ward House. Barbara Ward & Gerald Ward. Ed. by Anne Farnam & Bryant Tolles, Jr. (Essex Institute Historic House Booklet Ser). (Illus., 11 halftone). 1976. pap. $2.00 ea. (ISBN 0-88389-059-3). Essex Inst.
Museum Collections of the Essex Institute. Huldah Payson. Ed. by Anne Farnam & Bryant Tolles, Jr. (Essex Institute Museum Booklet Ser). (Illus., 55 b&w). 1978. pap. $2.50 (ISBN 0-88389-070-4). Essex Inst.
Peirce-Nichols House. Gerald Ward. Ed. by Anne Farnam & Bryant Tolles, Jr. (Essex Institute Historic House Booklet Ser). (Illus., 11 halftone). 1976. pap. $2.00 ea. (ISBN 0-88389-062-3). Essex Inst.
Prints at the Essex Institute. Bettina Norton. Ed. by Anne Farnam & Bryant Tolles, Jr. (Essex Institute Museum Booklet Ser). (Illus., 51 b&w). 1978. pap. $4.95 (ISBN 0-88389-069-0). Essex Inst.

EVERSON MUSEUM OF ART
Syracuse, New York.
Century of Ceramics in the United States, 1878-1978. Garth Clark & Margie Hughto. 1979. $20.00; pap. $12.95. Everson Mus.
Chinese Art from the Cloud Wampler & Other Collections. Celia Carrington Riely. (Illus., 79 photos). 1968. pap. $5.50. Everson Mus.
Everson Museum of Art Introduction to the Collections. Peg Weiss. (Illus., 95 photos). 1978. pap. $5.00. Everson Mus.

FAABORG MUSEUM
Faaborg, Denmark.
Illustreret Katalog for Faaborg Museum. Leo Swane & Kirsten Rasmussen. Ed. by Faaborg Museum. (Illus., 76 b&w photos, 1 drawing, Danish.). 1950. pap. Kr.15.00. Faaborg Mus.

FEHR, WILLIAM, COLLECTION
Cape Town, South Africa.
Treasures at the Castle of Good Hope: Skatte Indie Kasteel De Goede Hoop. William Fehr & Elizabeth Paap. (Illus., 25 color, 204 b&w, Eng. & Afrik.). 1978. R.9.50 (ISBN 0-620-03011-9). Fehr Coll.

FERENCZY MUSEUM
Szentendre, Hungary.
Barcsay Collection at Szentendre. Katalin Petenyi. (Illus., 14 color, 77 b&w, Hung., Eng., Ger., Fr. & Rus.). 1978. pap. 85.00 Ft. Pest Count Mus.
Collection Catalog of the Ferenczy Family. Vanda M. Varhelyi. (Illus., 3 color, 59 b&w, Hung.). 1978. pap. 40.00 Ft. Pest Count Mus.
Czobel Museum. Ed. by Julia Gergelyne. (Illus., 1 color, 23 b&w, Hung., Eng., Ger., Fr. & Rus.). 1979. pap. 30.00 Ft. Pest Count Mus.
Jeno Kerenyi. Ed. by Ferenc Hann. (Illus., 22 b&w, Hung.). 1978. pap. 18.00 Ft. Pest Count Mus.
Margit Kovacs Collection. Katalin Petenyl. (Illus., 3 color, 200 b&w, Hung., Eng., Ger., Fr. & Rus.). 1977. pap. 35.00 Ft.; pap. 2.00 Ft., suppl. Pest Count Mus.

FIGAROHAUS
see Mozart-Wohnung (Figarohaus)

FILIALMUSEUM LUSTHEIM
see Meissner Porzellan-Sammlung Stiftung Ernst Schneider

FINE ARTS MUSEUMS OF SAN FRANCISCO, M. H. DE YOUNG MEMORIAL MUSEUM
San Francisco, California.
European Works of Art in the M. H. De Young Memorial Museum. Fine Arts Museum of San Francisco. (Illus., 16 color, 98 b&w). 1966. $2.95 (ISBN 0-88401-005-8). Fine Arts Mus San Fran.
Five Centuries of Tapestry. Anna G. Bennet. (Illus., 19 color, 154 b&w). 1976. $9.95 (ISBN 0-88401-019-8). Fine Arts Mus San Fran.
Four Centuries of French Drawings in the Fine Arts Museums of San Francisco. Phyllis Hattis. (Illus., 8 color, 500 b&w). 1977. $20.00; pap. $13.95 (ISBN 0-88401-026-0). Fine Arts Mus San Fran.
Rodin's Sculpture: A Critical Study of the Spreckles Collection. Jacques De Caso & Patricia B. Sanders. (Illus., 168 b&w). 1977. $20.00 (ISBN 0-88401-023-6); pap. $13.95 (ISBN 0-88401-022-8). Fine Arts Mus San Fran.
Three Centuries of American Painting. F. Lanier Graham. (Illus., 7 color, 58 b&w). 1971. $12.95 (ISBN 0-88401-011-2). Fine Arts Mus San Fran.
Traditional Art of Africa, Oceania & the Americas. Jane Dwyer & Edward Dwyer. 1973. $3.95 (ISBN 0-88401-014-7); pap. $9.95 (ISBN 0-88401-013-9). Fine Arts Mus San Fran.

FITZWILLIAM MUSEUM
see Univ. of Cambridge, Fitzwilliam Museum

FLAGLER, HENRY MORRISON, MUSEUM
Palm Beach, Florida.
Henry Morrison Flagler Museum. Jean Flagler Matthews. (Illus.). 1975. pap. $1.00. Flagler Mus.

FOGG ART MUSEUM
see Harvard Univ., Fogg Art Museum

FONDAZIONE HORNE
see Horne, Herbert Ray, Fondazione

FONTAINEBLEAU
see Musee National Du Chateau De Fontainebleau

FORT WORTH ART MUSEUM
Fort Worth, Texas.
Drawings: An Exhibition of the Collection of the Fort Worth Art Museum. Fort Worth Art Mus. (Illus., 19 b&w photos). 1974. pap. $3.00. Fort Worth Mus.
Paintings & Sculpture: Selections from the Collection of the Fort Worth Art Museum. Fort Worth Art Mus. (Illus., 53 color, b&w photos). 1974. pap. $5.00. Fort Worth Mus.
Prints: Catalog of the Collection of the Fort Worth Art Museum. Fort Worth Art Mus. (Illus., 92 b&w photos). 1974. pap. $3.00. Fort Worth Mus.

FRANKFURTER GOETHE-MUSEUM
Frankfurt, Germany, West.
Dichter der Deutschen Romantik. (Illus., 16, Ger.). 1976. DM.15.00. Frank Goethe.
Frankfurter Goethe Museum. Ernst Beutler & Helga Haberland. Ed. by Freies Deutsches Hochstift. (Fuhrer Ser). (Illus., 8, Ger.). 1961. DM.2.00. Frank Goethe.
Goethe Museum in Rom. Detley Luders. Ed. by Freies Deutsches Hochstift. (Fuhrer Ser). (Illus., 16, 1 plan, 1 color, Ger., Eng. & It.). 1973. DM.2.00. Frank Goethe.
Goethehaus in Frankfurt Am Main. Ernst Beutler. Ed. by Freies Deutsches Hochstift. (Fuhrer Ser). (Illus., 2, 4 plates, 1 color, Ger., Eng., Fr. & Jap.). 1978. DM.2.00. Frank Goethe.
Im September 1978 Erscheint: Katalog der Ausstellung Zu Clemens Brentanos 200. Geburtstag. (Illus., 30, Ger.). 1978. DM.20.00. Frank Goethe.
Junge Goethe. (Illus., 23, Ger.). 1974. DM.5.00. Frank Goethe.
Katalog Samlichter Gemalde Des Freien Deutschen Hochstifts. write for info. Frank Goethe.
Katalog Samlichter Handschriften Des Freien Deutschen Hochstifts. write for info. Frank Goethe.
Rudolf Borchardt. (Ger.). 1967. DM.1.00. Frank Goethe.

FRANKLIN FURNACE ARCHIVE, INC.
New York, New York.
Franklin Furnace Artists' Book Bibliography. Ed. by Franklin Furnace Archive. (Vol. 2). 1978. $5.00. Printed Matter.
Franklin Furnace Artists' Book Bibliography. Ed. by Franklin Furnace Archive. (Vol. 1). 1977. $5.00. Printed Matter.

FRANS HALSMUSEUM
Haarlem, Netherlands.
Frans Halsmuseum Haarlem. H. P. Baard. (Dutch, Eng., Fr. & Ger.). 1969. pap. fl.7.50. Frans Halsmuseum.

FREER GALLERY OF ART
Washington, D.C.
Ancient Glass in the Freer Gallery of Art. Richard Ettinghausen. (Illus., 2 color, 97 b&w). 1962. pap. $1.50. Freer.
Arts of Asia at the Time of American Independence. (Illus., 44). 1976. pap. $3.00. Freer.
Eugene & Agnes E. Meyer Memorial Exhibition. (Illus., 32). 1971. pap. $3.00. Freer.
Freer Chinese Bronzes. Rutherford J. Gettens. (Vol. 2). (Illus., 13 color). 1969. $20.00. Freer.
Freer Chinese Bronzes. John A. Pope et al. (Vol. 1). (Illus., 8 color, 108 b&w). 1967. $40.00. Freer.
Freer Gallery of Art. (Illus., 9). 1978. pap. $0.50. Freer.
Freer Gallery of Art, 1 China 1971. (Illus., 131). 1971. $15.00. Freer.
Freer Gallery of Art, 2 Japan 1971. (Illus., 128). 1971. $15.00. Freer.
Freer Indian Sculptures. Aschwin Lippe. (Illus.). 1970. $12.00. Freer.
James McNeill Whistler, a Biographical Outline Illustrated from the Collection of the Freer Gallery of Art. Burns A. Stubbs. (Illus., 28). 1965. pap. $1.50. Freer.
Japanese Lacquer. Ann Yonemura. (Illus., 80). 1979. pap. $9.00. Freer.
Lohans & a Bridge to Heaven. Wen Fong. (Illus.). 1958. pap. $2.00. Freer.
Masterpieces of Chinese & Japanese Art: Freer Gallery of Art Handbook. (Illus., 36 color, 232 b&w). 1976. pap. $5.00. Freer.
Paintings, Pastels, Drawings, Prints & Copper Plates by & Attributed to American & European Artists, Together with a List of Original Whistleriana in the Freer Gallery of Art. Burns A. Stubbs. (Illus., 30). 1967. pap. $2.00. Freer.
Two Early Chinese Bronze Weapons with Meteoritic Iron Blades. Rutherford J. Gettens & Roy S. Clarke, Jr. (Illus., 29). 1971. pap. $5.00. Freer.
Whistler Peacock Room. (Illus.). 1972. pap. $0.50. Freer.

FRICK ART MUSEUM
Pittsburgh, Pennsylvania.
Treasures of the Frick Art Museum. Walter Read Hovey. 1975. $17.50. Frick Art Mus.

FRICK COLLECTION
New York, New York.
Frick Collection: An Illustrated Catalogue, Enamels, Rugs & Silver, Vol. 8. Philippe Verdier et al. Ed. by Joseph Focarino. (Illus., 10 color, 100 b&w). 1977. $40.00. Frick.
Frick Collection: An Illustrated Catalogue, Paintings, 2 vols. Ed. by Joseph Focarino & Bernice Davidson. (Illus., 18 color, 200 b&w). 1968. $50.00 set. Frick.
Frick Collection: An Illustrated Catalogue, Porcelains, Vol. 7. John A. Pope & Marcelle Brunet. Ed. & tr. by Joseph Focarino. (Illus., 15 color, 100 b&w). 1974. $35.00. Frick.
Frick Collection: An Illustrated Catalogue, Sculpture, 2 vols. John Pope-Hennesey & Terence Hodgkinson. Ed. by Joseph Focarino. (Illus., 15 color, 150 b&w). 1970. $50.00 set. Frick.
Guide to the Galleries. Edgar Munhall. Ed. by Joseph Focarino. (Illus., 8 color, 97 b&w). 1979. $4.00 (ISBN 0-912114-10-X). Frick.
Handbook of Paintings. Frick Collection. Ed. by Joseph Focarino. (Illus., 8 color, 169 b&w). 1979. $5.00 (ISBN 0-912114-09-6). Frick.

FUJITA ART MUSEUM
Osaka, Japan.
Illustrated Catalogue, Masterpieces in the Fujita Museum of Art: Arts & Crafts, Vol. 1. Ed. by Sueji Umehara & Cultural Properties Protection Commission. (Illus., 88 color, monochrome, Jap. & Eng.). 1954. 6000.00 Yen. Fujita.
Illustrated Catalogue, Masterpieces in the Fujita Museum of Art: Tea Ceremony Implements, Vol. 2. Ed. by Sueji Umehara & Cultural Properties Protection Commission. (Illus.) 66 color, monochrome, Jap. & Eng.). 1954. 5000.00 Yen. Fujita.

FURST THURN UND TAXIS SCHLOSSMUSEUM
Regensburg, Germany, West.
Beitrage Zur Geschichte, Kunst und Kulturpflege Im Hause Thurn und Taxis. (Illus., 104). 1978. DM.98.00 (ISBN 3-7847-1512-5). Furstlic Haus.
Beitrage Zur Kunst und Kulturpflege Des Hauses Thurn und Taxis. (Illus., 119). 1963. DM.48.00 (ISBN 3-7847-1501-X). Furstlic Haus.
Furstliche Marstall in Regensburg. (Illus., 117). 1966. DM.32.00 (ISBN 3-7847-1504-4). Furstlic Haus.
Max Piendl: Die Furstl. Wirkteppiche und Ihre Geschichte. (Illus., 51). 1978. DM.8.00. Furstlic Haus.
Max Piendl: Ein Jahrhundert Schlossbaugeschichte Regensburg, 1812-1912. (Illus., 51). write for info. (ISBN 3-7847-1513-3). Furstlic Haus.
Schloss Thurn und Taxis Regensburg. DM.3.00. Furstlic Haus.

FURSTLICH-LIPPISCHES RESIDENZSCHLOSS
Detmold, Germany, West.
Furstliche Residenzschloss Detmold. Gerhard Peters. Ed. by Armin Prinz Zur Lippe. (Illus., 17 color, 34 b&w, Ger.). 1979. DM.8.00. Furstlich Ver.
Furstliche Residenzschloss Detmold: Ein Kleiner Fuhrer. Ed. by Furstliche Verwaltung Detmold, Schloss. (Illus., 21 b&w, Ger.). DM.2.00. Furstlich Ver.

GABINET RYCIN BIBLIOTEKI UNIWERSYTECKIEJ W WARSAWIE
Warsaw, Poland.
Catalogue Des Dessins De Cabinet Des Estampes De la Bibliotheque De L'Universite De Varsovie: Dessins D'Architecture, Decoratifs, et Divers Des XVIII et XIXs, Vol. 1, Varsaviana. Teresa Sulerzyska & Stanislawa Sawicka. Ed. by University Library, Warsaw. (Illus., 111, Pol.). 1967. write for info. Panst Wyd Nauk.
Catalogue Des Dessins Du Cabinet Des Estampes De la Bibliotheque De L'Universite De Varsovie: Dessins D'Architecture, Decoratifs, et Divers Des XVIII et XIXs, Vol. 2, Localites Diverses. Teresa Sulerzyska & Stanislawa Sawicka. Ed. by University Library, Warsaw. (Illus., 103, Pol.). 1969. write for info. Panst Wyd Nauk.
Catalogue Des Dessins Du Cabinet Des Estampes De la Bibliotheque De L'Universite De Varsovie: Dessins D'architecture, Decoratifs, et Divers Des XVIII et XIXs, Vol. 3, Varia. Teresa Sulerzyska & Stanislawa Sawicka. Ed. by University Library, Warsaw. (Illus., 232, Pol.). 1972. write for info. Panst Wyd Nauk.
Dessins Des Costumes Turc De la Collection Du Roi Stanislas Auguste Du Cabinet Des Estampes De la Bibliotheque De L'Universite De Varsovie. Alina Mrozowska & Tadeusz Majda. Ed. by University Library. (Acta Bibliothecae Universitatis Varsoviensis Ser). (Illus., 62 b&w, Pol.). 1973. write for info. Wyd Uni Warsz.
Dessins Des Costumes Turc De la Collection Du Roi Stanislas Auguste Du Cabinet Des Estampes De la Bibliotheque De L'Universite De Varsovie. Alina Mrozowska & Tadeusz Majda. Ed. by University Library. (Acta Bibliothecae Universitatis Varsoviensis Ser). (Illus., 51 b&w, Pol.). 1978. pap. write for info. Wyd Uni Warsz.
Gravure Dans L'ecole De Rubens Au Cabinet Des Estampes, Vol. 10. Elzbieta Budzinska. Ed. by University Library, Warsaw. (Acta Bibliothecae Universitatis Varsoviensis). (Illus., 24, Pol.). 1975. pap. write for info. Wyd Uni Warsz.

GALERIA HLAVNEHO MESTA SSR BRATISLAVY
Bratislava, Czechoslovakia.
Exposition of Central-European Art from the 17th Century to the 19th Century. Zelmira Grajciarova & Andrej Lohnert. Ed. by Galeria Hl. Mesta SSR Bratislavy. Tr. by Bratislava Information And Publicity Servis. (Mala Galeria Ser). (Illus., 12 color, Slovak, Rus., Eng., Ger., Fr., Hung. & Bulgarian.). 1979. write for info. Gal Bratislav.
Exposition of English Tapestries and Old-European Painting. Andrej Lohnert. Ed. by Galeria Hl. Mesta SSR Bratislavy. Tr. by Bratislava Information And Publicity Servis. (Mala Galeria Ser). (Illus., 12 color, Slovak, Rus., Eng., Ger., Fr., Hung. & Bulgarian.). 1980. write for info. Gal Bratislav.
Exposition of Gothic Art. Zelmira Grajciarova. Ed. by Galeria Hl. Mesta SSR Bratislavy. Tr. by Bratislava Information And Publicity Servis. (Mala Galeria Ser). (Illus., 12 color, Slovak, Rus., Eng., Ger., Fr., Hung. & Bulgarian.). 1979. write for info. Gal Bratislav.

GALERIJA LIKOVNIH UMJETNOSTI
Osijek, Yugoslavia.
Eighteenth Century in Slawonia. Ivy Lentic et al. Ed. by Galerija Likovnih Umjetnosti, Osijek. Tr. by Marija Malbasa. (Illus., 40 b&w photos, Croate & Ger.). 1971. 100.00 din. Gal Liko Umje.
Guide to the Permanent Collection. Oto Svajcer et al. Ed. by Galerija Likovnih Umjetnosti, Osijek. (Illus., 80 b&w photos, Croate, Fr. & Ger.). 1979. 100.00 din. Gal Liko Umje.

GALLERIA BORGHESE
Rome, Italy.
Galleria Borghese. Paola Della Pergola. (It.). L.1200.00. Ediz Arnaud.
Galleria Borghese. Luciana Ferrara. L.6000.00. Inst Geo Agos.
Galleria Borghese. Luciana Ferrara. (It.). L.3500.00. Inst Geo Agos.
Galleria Borghese-I Dipinti: Cataloghi Dei Musei E Gallerie D'Italia, Vol. 1. Paola Della Pergola. (It.). L.8000.00. Lib Del Stato.
Galleria Borghese-I Dipinti: Cataloghi Dei Musei E Gallerie D'Italia, Vol. 2. Paola Della Pergola. (It.). L.16000.00. Lib Del Stato.
Galleria Borghese in Roma: Itinerari Dei Musei, Gallerie E Monumenti D'Italia. Paola Della Pergola. L.2000.00. Lib Del Stato.
Galleria Borghese in Roma: Itinerari Dei Musei, Gallerie E Monumenti D'Italia. Paola Della Pergola. (It.). L.2000.00. Lib Del Stato.
Galleria Borghese in Roma: Itinerari Dei Musei, Gallerie E Monumenti D'Italia. Paola Della Pergola. (Fr.). L.2000.00. Lib Del Stato.
Galleria Borghese in Roma: Itinerari Dei Musei, Gallerie E Monumenti D'Italia. Paola Della Pergola. (Ger.). L.2000.00. Lib Del Stato.
Galleria Borghese in Roma: Itinerari Dei Musei, Gallerie E Monumenti D'Italia. Paola Della Pergola. (Span.). L.2000.00. Lib Del Stato.
Tesori Della Galleria Borghese. Luciana Ferrara. (It., Fr., Eng. & Ger.). L.1200.00. Martello Edit.
Villa Borghese. Paola Della Pergola. (It.). L.26000.00. Lib Del Stato.

GALLERIA DORIA PAMPHILJ
Rome, Italy.
Catalogo Sommario Della Galleria Doria Pamphilj in Roma. (It.). 1979. write for info. Doria Pamphilj.

GALLERIA NAZIONALE DI PALAZZO SPINOLA
Genoa, Italy.
Galleria Nazionale Di Palazzo Spinola a Genova. Pasquale Rotondi. (Illus., 24 color, 108 b&w, It.). 1967. write for info. Gal Spinola.

Ingres' Sculptural Style: A Group of Unknown Drawings. Phyllis Hattis. (Illus., 72 b&w). 1973. $5.25. Fogg Art Mus.
Memorial Exhibition: Works of Art from the Collection of Paul J. Sachs. Agnes Mongan. (Illus., 106 b&w). 1965. $4.00. Fogg Art Mus.
Salmantine Lanterns: Their Origin & Development. Carl K. Hersey. (Illus., 86 b&w). 1937. $7.00. Fogg Art Mus.
Selections from the Collection of Freddy & Regina Homburger. Agnes Mongan. (Illus., 81 b&w). 1971. $4.00. Fogg Art Mus.
Theatrical Drawings & Watercolors by George Grosz. Ed. by Hedy B. Landman. (Illus., 60 b&w). 1973. $2.00. Fogg Art Mus.
Three American Painters: Kenneth Noland, Jules Olitski, Frank Stella. Michael Fried. (Illus., 21 b&w). 1965. $4.00. Fogg Art Mus.
Traditions of Japanese Art: Selections from the Kimiko & John Powers Collection. John M. Rosenfield & Shujiro Shimada. (Illus., 16 color, 184 b&w). 1970. $25.00. Fogg Art Mus.
Wash & Gouache: A Study of the Development of the Materials of Watercolor. Marjorie B. Cohn. (Illus., 6 color, 19 b&w). 1977. $7.50. Fogg Art Mus.

HAYDN-WOHNHAUS
Vienna, Austria.
Haydn-Museum: Haydn Wohn & Sterbehaus. Eigenverlag der Museen der Stadt Wien. Tr. by John Whitten. (Illus., 4 b&w, Ger. & Eng.). 1978. pap. S.30.00. Museen Wien.

HEARD MUSEUM
Phoenix, Arizona.
Dancing Kachinas: Original Paintings by Cliff Bahnimptewa. $2.00. Heard Mus.
Fred Harvey Fine Arts Collection. Harvey et al. $7.50. Heard Mus.
Kachinas, a Hopi Artist's Documentary: Original Paintings by Cliff Bahnimptewa. Barton Wright. $125.00, deluxe limited edition; Heard Mus.
Kachinas: An Evolving Hopi Art Form? Jon T. Erickson. $8.95. Heard Mus.
Kachinas, the Coldwater Collection at the Heard Museum. Barton Wright. (Illus.). $9.95; pap. $5.95. Heard Mus.
Navajo Textiles from the Read Mullan Collection. $10.00. Heard Mus.
Pima Indian Basketry. H. Thomas Cain. $1.50. Heard Mus.
Pueblo Shields. Barton Wright. $9.50. Heard Mus.
Story of Navajo Weaving. Kate Peck Kent. $3.00. Heard Mus.

HEBREW UNION COLLEGE, SKIRBALL MUSEUM
Los Angeles, California.
Centennial Sampler. Intro. by Nancy Berman. (Illus., 15 b&w photos). 1976. pap. $2.50. Hebrew Un Col.
Peter Krasnow: A Retrospective Exhibition of Paintings, Sculpture & Graphics. Joseph Hoffman. (Illus., 16b&w). 1977. $3.00. Hebrew Un Col.
Walk Through the Past. Nancy Berman & Joe Seger. (Illus., 60 b&w photos). 1974. pap. $6.95. Hebrew Un Col.

HECKSCHER MUSEUM
Huntington, New York.
Catalogue of the Collection. Raymond Pisano & Carol Tabler. Ed. & intro. by Katherine Lochridge. (Illus., 8 color, 88 b&w). 1979. $18.00; pap. $14.00. Heckscher Mus.

HEIMATMUSEUM
Reinach, Switzerland.
Heimat-Museum Reinach. E. Feigenwinter. Ed. by Heimat-Museum Reinach. (Illus., 16, Ger.). write for info. Mus Reinach.

HENRY MORRISON FLAGLER MUSEUM
see Flagler, Henry Morrison, Museum

HERAS INSTITUTE OF INDIAN HISTORY AND CULTURE
Bombay, India.
Treasures of the Heras Institute. Kalpana Desai. (Illus., 122, monochrome). 1976. $20.00. Abhinav Pubns.

HERBERT ART GALLERY AND MUSEUM
Coventry, United Kingdom.
City of Coventry Archaeology & Development. Margaret Rylatt et al. (Illus., 15 maps & diag.). 1977. pap. 0.80p. Herbert Gal.
Collection of Motor Vehicles. Peter Mitchell. (Illus., 50 color photos). 1977. E5.80. Herbert Gal.
Visual Arts, Catalogue of the Permanent Collection. P. Day & R. A. Clarke. 1977. pap. 0.85p. Herbert Gal.

HERZLIYA MUSEUM
Herzliya, Israel.
Herzliya Museum in Its New Home. Pref. by Eugen Davilla. (Illus., 33 b&w, 7 photos, Heb. & Eng.). 1975. free. Herzliya Mus.

HERZOG ANTON ULRICH-MUSEUM
Braunschweig, Germany, West.
Franzosische Kunst Des Barock. Sabine Jacob & Rudiger Klessmann. (Illus., Ger.). 1975. DM.6.00. Anton Ulrich.
Furstenberger Porzellan. Bodo Hedergott. (Illus., Ger.). 1972. DM.6.00. Anton Ulrich.
Geschichte Des Herzog Anton Ulrich Museums in Braunschweig. August Fink. (Illus., Ger.). 1967. DM.8.00. Anton Ulrich.
Herzog Anton Ulrich Museum Braunschweig. Rudiger Klessmann. (Illus., Ger.). 1978. DM.162.00. Anton Ulrich.
Italienische Bronzen. Sabine Jacob. (Illus., Ger.). 1972. DM.6.00. Anton Ulrich.
Italienische Majolika: Katalog der Sammlung, Herzog Anton Ulrich Museums Braunschweig 1979. Johanna Lessmann. (Illus., Ger.). 1979. DM.180.00. Anton Ulrich.
Kunst Des Mittelalters. Bodo Hedergott. (Illus., Ger.). 1971. DM.6.00. Anton Ulrich.
Kunsthefte Des Herzog Anton Ulrich Museums. August Fink. (Illus., Ger.). 1951. DM.1.00. Anton Ulrich.
Meisterwerke Im Herzog Anton Ulrich Museum. (Illus., Ger.). 1973. DM.3.50. Anton Ulrich.
Rembrandt und Sein Kreis. Rudiger Klessmann. (Illus., Ger.). 1973. DM.6.00. Anton Ulrich.
Verzeichnis der Gemalde Vor 1800-1976. (Illus., 6 color, 104 b&w, Ger.). 1976. DM.14.50. Anton Ulrich.

HICKORY MUSEUM OF ART
Hickory, North Carolina.
Permanent Collection: The Hickory Museum of Art. Pamela Whitener. (Illus., 47 b&w photos). 1978. pap. $5.00. Hickory Mus.

HIGGINS, JOHN WOODMAN, ARMORY MUSEUM
Worcester, Massachusetts.
Catalogue on the Permanent Collection: The John Woodman Higgins Armory Catalogue of Armor. Stephen V. Granscay. (Illus.). 1961. $7.50. Higgins Mus.
John Woodman Higgins Memorial Library Catalogue of Books. Ed. by Erveen C. Lundberg. Higgins, Mrs. John. (Illus., photos). 1968. pap. $1.50. Higgins Mus.

HIGH MUSEUM OF ART
Atlanta, Georgia.
American Paintings in the High Museum of Art. Bruce W. Chambers. (Illus., 17 color, 28 b&w). 1975. pap. $10.00. High Mus Art.
Italian Paintings & Northern Sculpture from the Samuel H. Kress Collection. Reginald Poland. (Illus., 28 b&w, 4 color). 1958. pap. $3.00. High Mus Art.
Prints of the High Museum: Image & Process. Irving L. Finkelstein. Ed. by Kelly Morris & Paula Hancock. (Illus., 8 color, 20 b&w). 1978. pap. $4.00. High Mus Art.

HILL-STEAD MUSEUM
Farmington, Connecticut.
Hill-Stead Museum. Jean Harris. (Illus., 1 color, 18 b&w). 1966. pap. $1.25. Hill Stead Mus.

HILSON GALLERY
see Deerfield Academy, Hilson Gallery

HISPANIC SOCIETY OF AMERICA
New York, New York.
Anna Hyatt Huntington, 1876-1973, Small Bronzes & Sketches. Beatrice Proske. (Illus., 8 b&w). 1974. pap. $0.75. Hispanic Soc.
Catalogue of Laces & Embroideries in the Collection. Florence May. (Illus., 120 b&w). 1936. $5.00 (ISBN 0-87535-038-0). Hispanic Soc.
Catalogue of Paintings, 14th & 15th Centuries, in the Collection. Elizabeth Du Gue Trapier. (Illus., 95 b&w). 1930. $5.00 (ISBN 0-87535-028-3). Hispanic Soc.
Catalogue of Sculpture, 13th to 15th Centuries, in the Collection. Beatrice Proske. (Illus., 328 b&w). 1932. $5.00 (ISBN 0-87535-030-5). Hispanic Soc.
Catalogue of Sculpture, 16th to 18th Centuries, in the Collection. Beatrice Proske. (Illus., 168 b&w). 1930. $6.00 (ISBN 0-87535-027-5). Hispanic Soc.
Catalogue Of Paintings, 19th & 20th Centuries, in the Collection. Elizabeth De Gue Trapier. (Illus., 342 b&w). 1932. $12.00 (ISBN 0-87535-031-3). Hispanic Soc.
Hispanic Society of America: Museum & Library Collections. The Hispanic Society of America. (Illus., 597 b&w ports., maps & facsims). 1938. $5.00 (ISBN 0-87535-043-7). Hispanic Soc.
History of the Hispanic Society of America, Museum & Library, 1905-1954, with a Survey of the Collection. The Hispanic Society of America. (Illus., 432 b&w). 1954. $10.00 (ISBN 0-87535-080-1). Hispanic Soc.
Martin Rico y Ortega in the Collection. Elizabeth De Gue Trapier. (Illus., 958 b&w). 1937. $5.00 (ISBN 0-87535-042-9). Hispanic Soc.
Sculpture by Anna Hyatt Huntington. Beatrice Proske. (Illus., 15 b&w). 1957. pap. $0.50. Hispanic Soc.
Sigillate Pottery of the Roman Empire. Alice Frothingham. (Illus., 124). 1937. $3.00 (ISBN 0-87535-041-0). Hispanic Soc.

HISTORICAL SOCIETY OF PENNSYLVANIA
Philadelphia, Pennsylvania.
One Hundred & Fifty Years of Collecting by the Historical Society of Pennsylvania. Nicholas B. Wainwright. (Illus.). 1974. $10.00 (ISBN 0-910732-09-4). Winchell Co.
Paintings & Miniatures at the Historical Society of Pennsylvania. Nicholas B. Wainwright. (Illus., 3 color plates, 200 b&w photos). 1974. $20.00 (ISBN 0-910732-08-6). Winchell Co.

HOESCH, LEOPOLD, MUSEUM
Duren, Germany, West.
Moderne Kunst. Heinrich Appel. Ed. by Leopold-Hoesch Museum. (Ger.). write for info. Leopold Hoesch.
Moderne Kunst. Heinrich Appel. Ed. by Leopold-Hoesch Museum. (Ger.). write for info. Leopold Hoesch.
Moderne Kunst: Leopold-Hoesch Museum, Duren,1955. Frwd. by Heinrich Appel. (Illus., Ger.). 1955. pap. write for info. Leopold Hoesch.
Moderne Kunst: Leopold-Hoesch Museum, Duren, 1965. Intro. by Hubert Lentz. (Illus., color, b&w, Ger.). 1965. pap. write for info. Leopold Hoesch.

HOHENLOHE-MUSEUM, SCHLOSS NEUENSTEIN
Neuenstein, Germany, West.
Schloss Neuenstein. Prince Constantine Zu Hohenlche-Langenburg. Ed. by Deutscher Kunstverlag, Munchen. (Ger. & Eng.). DM.1.50. Neuenstein.

HONOLULU ACADEMY OF THE ARTS
Honolulu, Hawaii.
Academy Album: A Pictorial Selection of Works of Art in the Collection. Honolulu Academy. (Illus., 140 b&w). 1968. pap. $2.50. Honolulu Aca.
Ancient Chinese Bronzes, Ceramics & Jade in the Collection. Robert J. Poor. (Illus., 53 b&w). 1979. pap. $6.00. Honolulu Aca.
Honolulu Academy of Arts Journal: A Selection of American Paintings in the Collection, Vol. 1. Charles Sellers et al. Ed. by Gertrude Rosenthal & Mary C. Dickerman. (Illus., 9 color, 20 b&w). 1974. pap. $3.50. Honolulu Aca.
Honolulu Academy of Arts Journal: American & European Masterworks of the Nineteenth & Twentieth Centuries from the Collection, Vol. 3. Lincoln F. Johnson & Victor I. Carlson. Ed. by Gertrude Rosenthal & Mary Dickerman. (Illus., 8 color, 33 b&w). 1978. pap. $3.50. Honolulu Aca.
Honolulu Academy of Arts Journal: Selection of Chinese Art in the Collection, Vol. 2. Robert D. Jacobson & Marylin Rhie. Ed. by Robert J. Poor & Howard A. Link. (Illus., 37 b&w). 1977. pap. $3.50. Honolulu Aca.

HOPETOUN HOUSE
South Queensferry, United Kingdom.
Hopetoun House Guide Book. (Illus., 24 color, 8 b&w, Eng., Ger., Fr. & It.). 1979. write for info. Hopetoun Hse.

HORNE, HERBERT RAY, FONDAZIONE
Florence, Italy.
Catalogo Illustrato Delle Foudeziou Horne Fireure, 1921. Carlo Gamba. Ed. by Giannini Borgo & S. Jecopo. (Illus., 23 b&w, It.). 1921. write for info. Fond Horne.
Illustrated Catalogue of the Horne Museum. Carlo Gamba. Ed. by Castrucci & Son. (Illus., 21 b&w). 1926. write for info. Fond Horne.
Museo Horne a Firenze. Filippo Rossi. (Illus., 166 b&w, 1 color, It.). 1966. write for info. Fond Horne.
Museo Horne a Tirenze. Carlo Gamba. Ed. by Acura Della Soprintendenza Alle Gallerie Di Firenze. (Illus., 40 b&w, It., Eng. & Fr.). 1961. L.500.00. Fond Horne.

HOTEL DE SULLY
Paris, France.
L'Hotel De Sully. J. Houlet. Ed. by Caisse Nationale Des Monuments Historiques. (Chateaux, Demeures, Hotels Ser). (Illus., 24 b&w, Fr.). 1974. 12.00 F. Caisse Nation.

HUNTERIAN MUSEUM AND UNIVERSITY ART COLLECTIONS
Glasgow, United Kingdom.
Glasgow University's Pictures. Andrew M. Young. (Illus., 4 color, 103 b&w). 1973. pap. E2.00. Colnaghi Co.
Muirhead Bone in Glasgow: Etchings & Drypoints from the Leonard Gow Collection on the Glasgow University Print Room. Andrew M. Young. 1973. pap. 0.20p. U Glasgow Pr.
The Smillie Collection: University of Glasgow. Hamish Miles. (Illus., 29 b&w). 1963. 0.60p. U Glasgow Pr.

HUNTINGTON FREE LIBRARY
see Museum of the American Indian, Huntington Free Library

HUNTINGTON GALLERIES
Huntington, West Virginia.
New American Glass: Focus West Virginia 1978. Roberta Emerson & G. Eason Eige. Ed. by Janet Dooley. (Illus., 4 color). 1978. pap. $2.50. Huntington.
New American Glass: Focus West Virginia 1976. Roberta Emerson & Joel Meyers. Ed. by Barbara Koenig. (Illus., 59 color & b&w photos). 1976. pap. $5.00. Huntington.
Twenty-Five at the Huntington Galleries. G. Eason Eige & Roberta Emerson. Ed. by Barbara Koenig. (Illus., 27 color & b&w photos). 1977. pap. $5.00. Huntington.

HUNTLY HOUSE MUSEUM
Edinburgh, United Kingdom.
Huntly House Guide. 0.85p. Huntly House.

IDEMITSU ART GALLERY
Tokyo, Japan.
Ancient Chinese Art & Craft. Idemitsu Art Gallery. (Illus., 4 color plates, 196 monochrome plates, Jap.). 1978. pap. 1000.00 Yen. Idemitsu Gal.
Catalogue of the Special Exhibition Commemorating the 10th Anniversary of the Idemitsu Collection. Idemitsu Art Gallery. (Illus., 23 color plates, 218 monochrome plates, Jap. & Eng.). 1976. pap. 2000.00 Yen. Idemitsu Gal.
Ceramics of the Yuan & Ming Dynasties. Idemitsu Art Gallery. (Illus., 6 color plates, 172 monochrome plates, Jap. & Eng.). 1977. pap. 1500.00 Yen. Idemitsu Gal.
Chinese Bronzes. Yuzo Sugimura. Ed. by Idemitsu Art Gallery. (Idemitsu Art Gallery Ser., 3). (Illus., 10 color plates, 21 monochrome plates, Jap.). 1966. 4000.00 Yen. Idemitsu Gal.
Chinese Ceramics, Vol. 1. Fujio Koyama. Ed. by Idemitsu Art Gallery. (Idemitsu Art Gallery Ser., 2). (Illus., 19 color plates, 38 monochrome plates, Jap.). 1971. 6500.00 Yen. Idemitsu Gal.
George Rouault. Idemitsu Art Gallery. (Illus., 8 color plates, 115 monochrome plates, Jap. & Fr.). 1973. pap. 1000.00 Yen. Idemitsu Gal.
Hand-Painted Ukiyo-e. Sadao Kikuchi. Ed. by Idemitsu Art Gallery. (Idemitsu Art Gallert Ser., 9). (Illus., 21 color plates, 41 monochrome plates, Jap & Eng.). 1976. 9500.00 Yen. Idemitsu Gal.
Itaya Hazan, a Japanese Modern Potter. Sensaku Nakagawa. Ed. by Idemitsu Art Gallery. (Idemitsu Art Gallery Ser., 5). (Illus., 20 color plates, 33 monochrome plates, Jap.). 1969. 4000.00 Yen. Idemitsu Gal.
Ko-Garatsu Ware, Vol. 1. Wasaburo Mizumachi. Ed. by Idemitsu Art Gallery. (Idemitsu Art Gallery Ser., 6). (Illus., 5 color plates, 172 monochrome plates, Jap.). 1973. 7500.00 Yen. Idemitsu Gal.
Ko-Garatsu Ware, Vol. 2. Wasaburo Mizumachi. Ed. by Idemitsu Art Gallery. (Idemitsu Art Gallery Ser., 7). (Illus., 33 color plates, 119 monochrome plates, Jap.). 1973. 7500.00 Yen. Idemitsu Gal.
Masterpieces of the Idemitsu Art Gallery: Ceramics & Other Crafts, Vol. 2. Idemitsu Art Gallery. (Illus., 8 color plates, 76 monochrome plates, Jap. & Eng.). 1969. pap. 1000.00 Yen. Idemitsu Gal.
Masterpieces of the Idemitsu Art Gallery: Paintings & Calligraphy, Vol. 1. Idemitsu Art Gallery. (Illus., 8 color plates, 49 monochrome plates, Jap. & Eng.). 1968. pap. 1000.00 Yen. Idemitsu Gal.
Minuyo-no-Tomo: Album of Exemplary Calligraphy Composed of Works by Celebrated Calligraphers. Kyozo Koresawa. Ed. by Idemitsu Art Gallery. (Idemitsu Art Gallery Ser., 8). (Illus., 12 color plates, 217 monochrome plates, Jap.). 1973. 7000.00 Yen. Idemitsu Gal.
Persian Pottery. Tsugio Mikami. Ed. by Idemitsu Art Gallery. (Idemitsu Art Gallery Ser., 4). (Illus., 10 color plates, 60 monochrome plates, Jap.). 1966. 4000.00 Yen. Idemitsu Gal.
Sam Francis. Idemitsu Art Gallery. (Illus., 10 color plates, 51 monochrome plates, Jap. & Eng.). 1974. pap. 1000.00 Yen. Idemitsu Gal.
Sengai, a Japanese Zen Monk. Shokin Furuta. Ed. by Idemitsu Art Gallery. (Idemitsu Art Gallery Ser., 1). (Illus., 6 collotype plates, 59 monochrome plates, Jap.). 1966. 4000.00 Yen. Idemitsu Gal.
Tanomura Chikuden, a Japanese Literrati Painter. Idemitsu Art Gallery. (Illus., 6 color plates, 38 monochrome plates, Jap.). 1978. pap. 1000.00 Yen. Idemitsu Gal.
Treasures of the Orient. Idemitsu Art Gallery. (Illus., 51 color plates, 379 monochrome plates, Jap. & Eng.). 1979. pap. 3000.00 Yen. Idemitsu Gal.

INDIANA UNIV. ART MUSEUM
Bloomington, Indiana.
Art of the Surimono. Theodore Bowie & James T. Kenney. Ed. by Pamela Buell. (Illus., 8 four-color seperation, & 111 b&w). 1979. pap. $15.00. In U Art Mus.
Indiana Art Museum Guide to the Collection. Ed. by Linda Baden. (Illus., 300 duotones & 24 four-color seperation). 1980. pap. $12.00. In U Art Mus.

INDUSTRIE UND GEWERBEMUSEUM
St. Gallen, Switzerland.
Eleganz in Schwarz: Spitzen Vom 1800 Bis Heute. Weber Marianne. Ed. by Industrie & Gewerbemuseum. (Illus., 43 photos., Ger.). 1979. 5.00 F. Indus St Gallen.

Spitzen, Laces & Dentelles. Stettbacher. Ed. by Industrie & Gewerbemuseum. (Illus., 75 drawings, Ger., Fr. & Eng.). 1962. 5.00 F. Indus St Gall.

INSTITUICAO JOSE RELVAS, CASA MUSEU DOS PATUDOS
Alpiarca, Portugal.
Roteiro Da Casa Museu Dos Patudos. (Illus., 18 b&w, Port.). 1960. Esc.40.00. Jose Relvas.

INSTITUT ARCHEOLOGIQUE DU LUXEMBOURG
Arlon, Belgium.
Arts et Metiers Gallo-Romains Au Musee D'Arlon. J. Moreau-Marechal. Ed. by Institut Archeologique Du Luxembourg. (Guide Nos. 2 Ser). (Illus., 27, Fr.). 1977. 100.00 F. Inst Arch Lux.
Het Luxemburgs Museum Van Aarlen. Louis Lefebvre. Ed. by Institut Archeologique Du Luxembourg. Tr. by Dirk Van De Meulebroecke. (Illus., 32, Dutch.). 1977. 80.00 F. Inst Arch Lux.
Sculptures Gallo-Romaines Du Musee D'Arlon. Louis Lefebvre. Ed. by Institut Archeologique Du Luxembourg - Arlon. (Guide No. 1 Ser). (Illus., 56, Fr.). 1975. 120.00 F. Inst Arch Lux.

INSTITUTE OF AMERICAN INDIAN ARTS MUSEUM
Santa Fe, New Mexico.
Institute of American Indian Arts Alumni Exhibition. Lloyd K. New & Peter Hassrock. (Illus., photos). 1964. free. IAIA Mus.
One with the Wind. Charles Dailey & Lloyd K. New. (Exhibition). (Illus., photos). 1976. pap. free. IAIA Mus.

INSTITUTO INTERDISCIPLINARIO TILCARA
Tilcara, Argentina.
Analisis Comparativo De un Mito Mashco. Mario Califano. Ed. by Norberto Pelissero. (Entregas Del "I. T." No. 3 Ser). (Span.). 1979. Arg.$4000.00. Inst Tilcara.
Aspectos De la Vegetacion De Altura y el Jardin Botanico De Tilcara. Horacio A. Difrieri. Ed. by Norberto Pelissero. (Entregas Del "I. T." No. 2 Ser). (Span.). 1978. Arg.$3000.00. Inst Tilcara.
Chuas y Mochilas, Prehistoricas En la Puna y Quebrada De Humahuaca. Norberto Pelissero. (Entregas Del "I. T." No. 4 Ser). (Span.). 1979. Arg.$1500.00. Inst Tilcara.
Geomorfologia De la Quebrada De Juella. Norberto Pelissero. (Entregas Del "I.T."No. 1 Ser). (Span.). 1977. Arg.$2000.00. Inst Tilcara.
Museo Arqueologico De Tilcara: Antecedentes, Funciones, Guia. Eduardo Casanova. (Number 2 Ser). (Span.). 1974. Arg.$5000.00. Inst Tilcara.
Pucara De Tilcara: Antecedentes, Reconstruccion, Guia. Eduardo Casanova. (Number One Ser). (Span.). 1978. Arg.$3000.00. Inst Tilcara.

INSTITUTO NAZIONALE PER LA GRAFICA CALCOGRAFIA
Rome, Italy.
Catalogo Dei Disegni Della Calcografia. Luigi Salerno. Ed. by De Luca. (It.). 1972. write for info. Calco Nazion.
Catalogo Generale Delle Stampe Della Calcografia. Carlo A. Alberto. Ed. by Instituto Nazionale per la Grafica Calcografia. (It.). 1972. write for info. Calco Nazion.

INTERNATIONAL PAVILION OF HUMOUR
Montreal, Canada.
Cartoonist of the Year. Ed. by International Pavilion of Humour. (Illus., 34 cartoons). pap. Can.$10.00. Int Pav Humor.
International Salon of Cartoons. Ed. by Intl. Pavilion of Humour. (Illus., 700 cartoons, Fr. & Eng.). 1979. pap. Can.$20.00. Int Pav Humor.

INVERNESS MUSEUM AND ART GALLERY
Inverness, Scotland.
Annual Report 1978. (Illus., 12 half-tones). 1979. 1.00 d. (ISBN 0-906575-01-X). Inverness Mus.
Inverness Silversmiths. Margaret O. MacDougall. 1977. 20.00 d. Inverness Mus.

IPARMUVESZETI MUZEUM
Budapest, Hungary.
Europai Butorok a 15th to 18th Szazadban. Ferenc Batari. Ed. by Nepmuvelesi Es Propaganda Iroda. (Illus., Hung. & Ger.). pap. 20.00 Ft. Iparmuveszeti.
Iparmuveszeti Muzeum Gyujtemenei. Ed. by Pal Miklos. (Illus., 162 color, 105 b&w, Eng., Ger., Fr. & Rus.). 1980. 280.00 Ft. Corvina.

IPSWICH MUSEUMS AND ART GALLERIES
Ipswich, United Kingdom.
Africa: A Guide to the Ipswich Collections. 0.35p. Ipswich Mus.
Gainsborough 250. 0.25p. Ipswich Mus.
Guide Sheets to the Archaeology, Natural History & Geological Departments of the Museum. 0.10p. Ipswich Mus.
Handlist of 19th Century Suffolk Artists on Display. 0.12p. Ipswich Mus.
John Constable Bicentenary: Drawings & Further Mezzotints from the Collections, Vol. 5. 0.30p. Ipswich Mus.

IRAQ MUSEUM
Baghdad, Iraq.
Treasures of the Iraq Museum. Faraj Basmachi. (Illus., 296 b&w, Arabic.). 1972. pap. ID.6000.00. Iraq Mus.
Treasures of the Iraq Museum. Faraj Basmachi. Tr. by Abd Noor. (Illus., 296 b&w). 1976. pap. ID.6000.00. Iraq Mus.

ISABELLA STEWART GARDNER MUSEUM
see Gardner, Isabella Stewart, Museum

IVEAGH BEQUEST
see Kenwood, the Iveagh Bequest

J. B. SPEED ART MUSEUM
see Speed, J. B., Art Museum

J. F. WILLUMSENS MUSEUM
see Willumsens, J.F., Museum

J. PAUL GETTY MUSEUM
see Getty, J. Paul, Museum

JACKSON, SHELDON, MUSEUM
Sitka, Alaska.
Catalogue of the Ethnological Collections in the Sheldon Jackson Museum. Erna Gunther. (Illus., 127 color, b&w photos). 1976. pap. $5.50. Shel Jack Col.
Sheldon Jackson Museum. Erna Gunther & Esther Billman. (Illus., 29 b&w photos). $1.00. Shel Jack Col.

JACKSONVILLE ART MUSEUM
Jacksonville, Florida.
Celebration of the Art of the Oriental Potter. Kamer Aga Oglu. 1973. pap. write for info. Jacks Art Mus.

JANUS PANNONIUS MUZEUM
Pecs, Hungary.
Csontvary Muzeum: Works of Csontvary Kosztka Tivadar. Ferenc Romvary & Eva Hars. (Illus., Hung., Eng. & Ger.). 1977. pap. $2.00. Pannonius Muz.
Gador Muzeum, Siklos-Var: Ceramics Works of Istvan Gador in Fort of Siklos. Ed. by Ferenc Romvary & Ilona Herceg. (Illus., 85 b&w photos, Hung., Serbian & Ger.). 1977. write for info. Pannonius Muz.
Modern Magyar Keptar. Ferenc Romvary. Tr. by Gyorgy Adorjan. (Illus., 149 photos., Hung., Eng. & Ger.). 1973. pap. $2.00. Pannonius Muz.
Uitz Muzeum, Pecs: Works of Bela Uitz. Bela Uitz et al. (Illus., 71 photos, Hung.). 1978. write for info. Pannonius Muz.
Vasarely Muzeum: Works of Victor Vasarely. Eva Hars. (Illus., 6 color, 84 b&w photos, Hung. & Fr.). 1976. pap. $2.00. Pannonius Muz.
Zsolnay Muzeum: Ceramics of Zsolnay Fabrik. Eva Hars. (Illus., 5 color, 53 b&w, Hung., Eng. & Ger.). 1977. write for info. Pannonius Muz.

JERSEY CITY MUSEUM
Jersey City, New Jersey.
August Will: Scenes of Old Jersey City. Cynthia Sanford & Eileen MacMahon. (Illus., 40 b&w). 1976. pap. $2.50. Jersey City Mus.

JEWISH MUSEUM
New York, New York.
Fabric of Jewish Life: Textiles from the Jewish Museum Collection. Barbara Kirshenblatt-Gimblett. (Vol. 1). (Illus., 22 color plates, b&w). 1977. pap. $7.50. Jewish Mus.

JOENSUUN TAIDEMUSEO
Joensuu, Finland.
Art Gallery of Joensuu. (Illus., 4 b&w, Finnish, Swed., Eng., Ger., Fr. & Rus.). pap. Fmk.2.00. Joensuun.

JOHANN STRAUSS-WOHNUNG
see Strauss, Johann, Wohnung

JOHANNESBURG ART GALLERY
Johannesburg, South Africa.
Catalogue List of Johannesburg Art Gallery Collections. P. M. Erasmus. (Eng. & Afrik.). 1968. pap. R.0.20. Johannesburg.

JOHN AND MABEL RINGLING MUSEUM OF ART
see Ringling, John and Mabel, Museum of Art

JOHN WOODMAN HIGGINS ARMORY MUSEUM
see Higgins, John Woodman, Armory Museum

JOHNSON, MARTIN AND OSA, SAFARI MUSEUM
Chanute, Kansas.
Cultural Heritage of Africa. Pascal J. Imperato. (Illus., 12 photos). 1974. pap. $2.00. Safari Mus Pr.

JOODS HISTORISCH MUSEUM
Amsterdam, Netherlands.
Jewish Historical Museum Handbook. Judith C. Belinfante. Ed. by Jewish Historical Museum. Tr. by Gary Schwartz. (Illus., 56 color, Dutch & Eng.). 1978. pap. 23.00 F. Joh Enschede.

KAISERBURG NURNBERG
Nurnberg, Germany, West.
Chateau Imperial De Nuremberg. Erich Bachmann. (Fr.). 1969. DM.2.00. Bayer Verwal.
Imperial Castle Nuremberg. Erich Bachmann. 1978. DM.2.50. Bayer Verwal.
Kaiserburg Nurnberg. Erich Bachmann. (Ger.). 1978. DM.2.00. Bayer Verwal.

KARL-ERNST-OSTHAUS MUSEUM
Hagen, Germany, West.
Aus Dem Kunsbesitz der Stadt Hagen. (Illus., 10 color). DM.20.00. Karl Ernst.
Malerei, Plastik, Objekte & Kunsthandwerk Eigenbesitzkatalog 2, 1961-1973. Karlerndt Osthaus Museum Hagen. (Illus., 18 color, 70 b&w, Ger.). 1974. pap. DM.10.00. Karl Ernst.
Silber Henry Van De Veldes Im Karl Ernst Osthaus Museum. Herta Hesse-Frielinghaus. Ed. by Karl Ernst Osthausmuseum Hagen. (Sonderveroffentlichungen Heft 1). (Illus., 15 b&w, Ger.). pap. DM.5.00. Karl Ernst.

KARNTNER FREILICHTMUSEUM
Karntner, Austria.
Karntner Freilichtmuseum in Maria Saal. Karl Eisner & Oskar Moser. (Illus., photos, drawings & 1 plan, Ger.). 1979. S.20.00. Karntner Frei.

KENWOOD, THE IVEAGH BEQUEST
London, United Kingdom.
Catalogue of Paintings. Intro. by Sir Anthony Blunt. (Illus., 16 b&w). 1972. pap. 0.50p. Kenwood.
Georgian Shoe Buckles. Bernard Hughes. (Illus., 81). 1972. pap. 0.30p. Kenwood.
Iveagh Bequest, Kenwood. Sir John Summerson. (Illus., 8 b&w). 1977. pap. 0.25p. Kenwood.
Jewellery from the Hull Grundy Collection. Lindsay Stainton. (Illus., 20 b&w). 1976. pap. 0.35p. Kenwood.
Suffolk Collection, Ranger's House, Blackheath, Catalogue of Paintings. John Jacob & Jacob Simon. (Illus., 54). 1974. pap. E1.00. Kenwood.

KERESZTENY MUZEUM
Esztergom, Hungary.
Esztergomi Kereszteny Muzeum. Andras Mucsi. (Illus., 65 b&w, Hung.). 1975. pap. 28.00 Ft. Kereszteny Muz.
Gothic and Renaissance Panel Paintings in the Esztergom Christian Museum. Andras Mucsi. Ed. by Kereszteny Muzeum. Tr. by Agnes Zador. (Illus., 48 b&w, Eng. & Fr.). 1974. 28.00 Ft. Kereszteny Muz.
Katalog der Alten Gemaldegalerie Des Christlichen Museums Zu Esztergom. Andras Mucsi. Tr. by Renate Messing. (Illus., 65 b&w, Ger.). 1975. 50.00 Ft. Kereszteny Muz.

KIMBELL ART MUSEUM
Fort Worth, Texas.
Kimbell Art Museum: Catalogue of the Collection. D. M. Robb, Jr. et al. Ed. by S. Spieckerman. (Kimbell Publication One). (Illus., 75 color, 137 b&w). 1972. $25.00. Kimbell Art.
Kimbell Art Museum: Handbook of the Collection. D. M. Robb, Jr. & N. Holland. Ed. by S. Spieckerman. (Kimbell Publications Four). (Illus., 250 b&w). 1979. pap. write for info. Kimbell Art.

KIRKCALDY MUSEUM AND ART GALLERY
Kirkcaldy, United Kingdom.
Kirkcaldy Art Gallery Catalogue. (Illus., 2 b&w). 1970. pap. 0.10p. Kirkcaldy.

KONINKLIJK MUSEUM VOOR SCHONEKUNSTEN
Antwerpen, Belgium.
Catalogue Descriptif: Maitres Anciens. Ed. by Koninklijk Museum. 1970. 50.00 F. Konin Mus Art.
Catalogus Schildeijen 19de En 20 Ste Eeuw. Ed. by Koninklijk Museum. 1977. 300.00 F. Konin Mus Art.

KOOPMANS DE WET HOUSE
Cape Town, South Africa.
Short Introduction to the Koopmans De Wet House. Intro. by E. A. Horner. (Illus., 2 plans (linedrawing), 6 sketches, Eng. & Afrik.). 1976. pap. R.0.30 (ISBN 0-620-02084-9). SA Cult Hist Mus.

KUNSTBIBLIOTHEK
Berlin, Germany, West.
Architektur in Darstellung und Theorie. (Ger.). DM.13.00. Blaschker Verlag.
Engel. (Ger.). DM.10.00. Blaschker Verl.
Fritz Hoger. (Ger.). DM.19.00. Blaschker Verlag.
Gerd Hartung. (Ger.). DM.1.00. Blaschker Verlag.
H. H. Palitzsch. (Ger.). DM.11.00. Blaschker Verl.
Hans Grisebach Kunstkatalog. (Ger.). DM.10.00. Blaschker Verl.
Katarina Wilczynski. (Ger.). DM.8.00. Blaschker Verlag.
Mittelalterl. Handschriften. (Ger.). DM.10.00. Blaschker Verlag.
R. J. Schmitt. (Ger.). DM.5.00. Blaschker Verlag.
Signale und Zeichen Von Stankowski. (Ger.). DM.7.00. Blaschker Verlag.
Suddeutsche Entwurfzeichnungen. (Ger.). DM.10.00. Blaschker Verlag.
Walter Tafelmaier. (Ger.). DM.10.00. Blaschker Verlag.
Werbung Fur Moderne Theater. (Ger.). DM.8.00. Blaschker Verl.

KUNSTGEWERBEMUSEUM
Berlin, Germany, West.
Ausgewahlte Werke, Vol. 1. (Ger.). DM.30.00. Blaschker Verlag.
Bronzer und Plaketten, Vol. 3. (Ger.). DM.52.00. Blaschker Verlag.
Europaisches Kunsthandwerk, Vol. 4. (Ger.). DM.30.00. Blaschker Verlag.
Fayancen. (Ger.). DM.16.00. Blaschker Verlag.
Goldschmiedewerke der Renaissance. (Ger.). DM.59.00. Blaschker Verlag.
Historismus. (Ger.). DM.46.00. Blaschker Verlag.
Kleinodien. (Ger.). DM.10.00. Blaschker Verlag.
Werke Um 1900. (Ger.). DM.70.00. Blaschker Verlag.
Zwanzig Jahre Neuerwerbung. (Ger.). DM.15.00. Blaschker Verlag.

KUNSTGEWERBEMUSEUM DER STADT KOLN
Cologne, Germany West.
Figurliches Porzellan. (Wissenschaftliche Katalog Ser., Vol. 5). (Ger.). DM.14.00. Mus Koln.
Glas. (Wissenschaftliche Kataloge Ser., Vol. 1). (Ger.). DM.15.00. Mus Koln.
Keramik. (Wissenschaftliche Katalog Ser., Vol. 7). (Ger.). DM.25.00. Mus Koln.
Kleinodien. (Ger.). 1976. DM.6.00. Mus Koln.
Kunstgewerbemuseum der Stadt Koln, Ausfuhrliche Illustrierte Geschicte Des Museums Mit Einer Auswahl Seiner Schonsten Sammlungsstucke. (Ger.). DM.16.00. Mus Koln.
Majolika. (Wissenschaftliche Kataloge Ser., Vol. 2). (Ger.). write for info. Mus Koln.
Sammlung Kasimir Hagen. (Ger.). 1963. DM.2.00. Mus Koln.
Seidengewebe Des 13.-18. Jh. (Wissenschaftliche Kataloge Ser., Vol. 8). (Ger.). DM.22.00. Mus Koln.
Steinzeug. (Wissenschaftliche Kataloge Ser., Vol. 4). (Ger.). DM.22.00. Mus Koln.
Verborgene Schatze Aus 7 Jahrhunderten. (Ger.). 1978. DM.40.00; pap. DM.33.00. Mus Koln.
Zinn. (Wissenschaftliche Kataloge Ser., Vol. 3). (Ger.). DM.10.00. Mus Koln.

KUNSTGEWERBEMUSEUM DER STADT ZURICH
Zurich, Switzerland.
Aussereuropaische Textilien. Erika Billeter & Renate Jacques. Ed. by Kunstgewerbemuseum Zurich. (Illus., 2 color, 324 b&w, Ger.). 1963. 10.00 F. Kunst Zurich.
Europaische Textilien. Erika Billeter. Ed. by Kunstgewerbemuseum Zurich. (Illus., 3 color, 272 b&w, Ger.). 10.00 F. Kunst Zurich.
Keramik. Erika Billeter & Rudolf Schnyder. Ed. by Kunstgewerbemuseum Zurich. (Illus., 6 color, 298 b&w, Ger.). 1965. 12.00 F. Kunst Zurich.

KUNSTGEWERBEMUSEUM SCHLOSS PETRONELL
Petronell, Austria.
Kunstgewerbemuseum Im Schloss Petronell: Katalog Mit Geschichte Des Schlosses. Werner Kitlitschka & Franz Windisch-Graetz. Ed. by Otto Abensperg-Traun. (Illus., 29 b&w, Ger.). 1965. write for info. Kunst Petron.

KUNSTHALLE BREMEN
Bremen, Germany, West.
Bild und Buch, das Illustrierte Buch Vom 15. Jahrhundert Bis Zur Gegenwart: Aus der Sammlung der Kunsthalle Bremen. Jurgen Schultze & Annemarie Winther. Ed. by Kunsthalle Bremen. (Kupferstichkabinett der Kunsthall Bremen Ser). (Illus., 172 b&w, Ger.). 1979. pap. DM.23.00. Kunst Bremen.
Katalog der Gemalde Des 19. und 20. Jahrhunderts in der Kunsthalle Bremen, 2 vols. Gerhard Gerkens & Ursula Heiderich. Ed. by Kunsthalle Bremen. (Illus., 679 b&w, Ger.). 1973. pap. DM.47.00. Kunst Bremen.
Katalog der Medaillen und Plaketten Des 19. und 20. Jahrhunderts in der Kunsthalle Bremen. Ulrike Kocke. Ed. by Kunsthalle Bremen. (Illus., 325 b&w, Ger.). 1975. pap. DM.24.00. Kunst Bremen.

KUNSTHALLE DER STADT BIELEFELD
Bielefeld, Federal Republic of Germany.
Abstakte Kunst Aus Paris. R. Von Gindertael. (Illus., 11, Ger. & Fr.). 1964. DM.1.00. Kunst Bielefe.
Alf Welski: Radierungen. Intro. by H. G. Gmelin. (Illus., 6, Ger.). 1972. DM.1.00. Kunst Bielefe.
Alfred Kubin, 1877-1959. Ch. Brockhaus. (Illus., 77, Ger.). 1977. DM.10.00. Kunst Bielefe.
Auf der Suche Nach Dem Schatten. H. Muck & B. Hatz. (Illus., 38, Ger.). 1978. DM.6.00. Kunst Bielefe.
Bielefelder Kunsthalle. Henry-Russel Hitchcock. (Illus., 41, 3 color, Ger.). 1974. DM.4.00. Kunst Bielefe.
Bruno Krenz: Feldbau. E. Franz. (Illus., 38, Ger.). 1978. DM.6.00. Kunst Bielefe.
Cecil M. Michaelis: Gemalde, Kinetische Objekte. William S. Hayter & A. Parinaud. (Illus., 6, Ger. & Fr.). 1973. DM.1.00. Kunst Bielefe.
Detlef Kappeler. H. G. Gmelin et al. (Illus., 39, 2 color, Ger.). 1973. DM.1.00. Kunst Bielefe.
Deutsche Kunst Des XVI. Jahrhunderts: Kleinplastik und Holzschnitte. P. Metz. (Illus., 12, Ger.). 1962. DM.1.00. Kunst Bielefe.
Dieter Krieg. (Illus., 31, Ger.). 1972. DM.2.00. Kunst Bielefe.
Erlauterungen Zu Gemalde und Plastiken: Kunsthalle Bielefeld. E. Franz et al. (Illus., 37, Ger.). 1978. DM.12.00. Kunst Bielefe.

Erlauterungen Zu Gemalde und Plastiken: Kunsthalle Bielefeld. Erich Franz et al. Ed. by Kunsthalle der Stadt Bielefeld. (Illus., 37 b&w, Ger.). DM.12.00. Kunst Bielefe.
Ermin Graumann: Malerei und Grafik. R. Von Gindertael. (Illus., 179, 5 color, Ger. & Fr.). 1966. DM.1.00. Kunst Bielefe.
Ernst Ludwig Kirchner Aus Privatbesitz. Ernst L. Kirchner. (Illus., 63, 23 color, Ger.). 1969. DM.3.00. Kunst Bielefe.
Felix H. Man: Sechzig Jahre Fotographie. Felix H. Man. (Illus., 97, Ger.). 1978. DM.16.00. Kunst Bielefe.
Frank Stella: Werke, 1958-1976. G. Boehm et al. (Illus., 86, 8 color, Ger.). 1977. DM.25.00. Kunst Bielefe.
Frank Stella: Werke, 1958-1976, Didaktische Texte. R. Jorn & M. Pauseback. (Illus., 21, Ger.). 1977. DM.3.00. Kunst Bielefe.
Friedel Dzubas: Gemalde. C. Greenberg et al. (Illus., 15, 3 color, Ger. & Eng.). 1977. DM.10.00. Kunst Bielefe.
Fuhrer Durch das Bauernhofmuseum Bielefeld. J. Schepers. (Illus., 17, Ger.). DM.2.00. Kunst Bielefe.
Fur Joachim Wolfgang Von Moltke. (Illus., 69, 1 color, Ger.). 1974. DM.4.00. Kunst Bielefe.
Georg A. Mathey: Buchkunst und Graphik. H. M. Elster. (Illus., 10, 6 color, Ger.). 1965. DM.1.00. Kunst Bielefe.
George Rickey: Kinetische Objekte, Material und Technik. George Rickey & U. Weisner. (Illus., 48, Ger.). 1976. DM.5.00. Kunst Bielefe.
Gerhard Knorre. W. Hadecke. (Illus., 10, 3 color, Ger.). 1962. DM.1.00. Kunst Bielefe.
Gerhard Marcks. Intro. by J. W. Von Moltke. (Illus., 6, Ger.). 1963. DM.1.00. Kunst Bielefe.
Gerri Benner: Amsterdam. P. Leo. (Illus., 28, 1 color, Ger.). 1961. DM.1.00. Kunst Bielefe.
Giuseppe Spagnulo: Skulpturen. E. Franz et al. (Illus., 52, Ger.). 1978. DM.12.00. Kunst Bielefe.
Gotische Kunst in Bielefeld, 1250-1500. U. Niemann & I. Eckert. (Illus., 55, Ger.). 1964. DM.1.00. Kunst Bielefe.
Grafik Design Bdg. (Illus., 95, Ger.). 1970. DM.1.00. Kunst Bielefe.
Graphik Des 20. Jahrhunderts Aus Eigenem Besitz. E. Franz. (Illus., 65, 5 color, Ger.). 1978. DM.16.00. Kunst Bielefe.
Gustav H. Wolff, 1886-1934. A. Holthusen et al. (Illus., 23, Ger.). 1971. DM.2.00. Kunst Bielefe.
Hannah Hoch: Fotomontagen und Gemalde. H. G. Gmelin. (Illus., 17, 1 color, Ger.). 1973. DM.4.50. Kunst Bielefe.
Hanno Edelmann. G. Guhr. (Illus., 15, 1 color, Ger.). 1961. DM.1.00. Kunst Bielefe.
Heinz Beier. Intro. by U. Weisner. (Illus., 63, 16 color, Ger.). 1974. DM.8.00. Kunst Bielefe.
Henri Gaudier-Brzeska, 1891-1915. Henri Gaudier-Brzeska. Ed. by H. S. Ede & U. Weisner. (Illus., 38, Ger.). 1969. DM.2.00. Kunst Bielefe.
Hermann Stenner, 1891-1914. G. Vriesen & H. Hildebrandt. (Illus., 28, 2 color, Ger.). 1956. DM.2.00. Kunst Bielefe.
Historisches Museum Welle 61. O. Corsdress. (Illus., 39, Ger.). 1966. DM.5.00. Kunst Bielefe.
Hubertus Von Pilgrim: Graphik und Plastik. W. Weber et al. (Illus., 52, Ger.). 1966. DM.1.00. Kunst Bielefe.
Jimmy Ernst: Gemalde und Gouachen. E. Pinder & E. Stunke. (Illus., 8, 1 color, Ger.). 1964. DM.1.00. Kunst Bielefe.
Kathe Kollwitz an Dr. Heinrich Becker: Briefe. (Illus., 8, Ger.). 1967. DM.2.50. Kunst Bielefe.
Kunst und Theater. H. Becker. (Illus., 20, Ger.). 1954. DM.1.00. Kunst Bielefe.
Kunsthalle der Stadt Bielefeld: Gemalde. H. Becker. (Illus., 121, 27 color, Ger.). 1968. DM.5.00. Kunst Bielefe.
Kunsthalle der Stadt Bielefeld: Gemalde. Heinrich Becker & Ulrich Weisner. Ed. by Kunsthalle der Stadt Bielefeld. (Illus., 121, 27 color, Ger.). 1968. DM.5.00. Kunst Bielefe.
Kunsthalle der Stadt Bielefeld: Plastik. (Illus., 131, Ger.). 1968. DM.5.00. Kunst Bielefe.
Kunsthalle der Stadt Bielefeld: Plastik. Ulrich Weisner. Ed. by Kunsthalle der Stadt Bielefeld. (Illus., 131 b&w, Ger.). 1968. DM.5.00. Kunst Bielefe.
Kunstler Aus Bielefeld und Ostwestfalen. (Illus., 7, Ger.). 1977. DM.4.00. Kunst Bielefe.
Lil Michaelis: Grafik, Collagen. William S. Hayter & A. Parinaud. (Illus., 12, Ger. & Fr.). 1973. DM.1.00. Kunst Bielefe.
Louis Cane: Werke, 1968-1978. Louis Cane et al. (Illus., 158, 12 color, Ger.). 1978. DM.25.00. Kunst Bielefe.
Lucien Clerque: Einhundert Fotos. Intro. by E. Billeter. (Illus., 28, Ger.). 1971. DM.1.00. Kunst Bielefe.
Lukas Cranach der Altere, 1472-1553: Grafik. H. G. Gmelin. (Illus., 28, Ger.). 1972. DM.5.50. Kunst Bielefe.
Macke,1887-1914: Aquarell-Ausstellung. G. Vriesen & E. Pinder. (Illus., 262, 6 in color, Ger.). 1957. DM.5.00. Kunst Bielefe.
Maler Hermann Stenner. Gustav Vriesen. (Illus., 19, 1 color, Ger.). 1957. DM.1.00. Kunst Bielefe.
Max Beckmann: Druckgraphik. E. Pinder. (Illus., 32, Ger.). 1963. DM.1.00. Kunst Bielefe.
Munzfunde. E. Pinder. (Illus., 10, 4 color, Ger.). 1959. DM.1.00. Kunst Bielefe.
Otto Kraft: Ein Weg. T. Ebeling & H. Grafenstein. (Illus., 22, 9 color, Ger.). 1977. DM.10.00. Kunst Bielefe.
Paul Klee: Spate Arbeiten, 1934-1940. E. Franz. (Illus., 36, 10 color, Ger.). 1978. DM.12.00. Kunst Bielefe.
Peter Gallaus: Gemalde, Aquarelle und Zeichnungen. R. Voss. (Illus., 11, 1 color, Ger.). 1972. DM.1.00. Kunst Bielefe.
Pranas Domsaitis, 1880-1965. E. Freitag. (Illus., 20, 2 color, Ger.). 1970. DM.1.00. Kunst Bielefe.
Reg Butler. Intro. by R. Melville. (Illus., 14, Ger.). 1958. DM.1.00. Kunst Bielefe.
Reinhold Voss: Gemalde, Grafik und Materialbilder. Intro. by P. Pieper. (Illus., 8, Ger.). 1978. DM.4.00. Kunst Bielefe.
Richard Hamilton: Studien, 1937-1977. Richard Hamilton et al. (Illus., 198, 11 color, Ger.). 1978. DM.25.00. Kunst Bielefe.
Rupert Shephard: Gemalde, Aquarelle, Zeichnungen und Grafik. A. Wilton. (Illus., 12, Ger. & Fr.). 1973. DM.1.00. Kunst Bielefe.
Schrecken Des Krieges. Intro. by H. G. Gmelin. (Illus., 40, Ger.). 1972. DM.3.00. Kunst Bielefe.
Sieben Aus Prag: Jiri Anderle, Jiri John, Alena Kucerova, Zdenek Sklenar, Pavel Sudolak, Karel Vysusil & Vladimir Preclik. E. Petrova. (Illus., 14, Ger.). 1971. DM.1.00. Kunst Bielefe.
Sonia Delaunay. Robert Delaunay & Sonia Delaunay. Ed. by G. Vriesen. (Illus., 29, 5 color, Ger.). 1958. DM.5.00. Kunst Bielefe.
Stanley William Hayter: Grafiken. J. W. Von Moltke & G. Syamken. (Illus., 6, 1 color, Ger.). 1968. DM.1.00. Kunst Bielefe.
Stiftungen Fur Kunsthaus und Museum, 1962-1965: Auswahl. (Illus., 9, 2 color, Ger.). 1965. DM.1.00. Kunst Bielefe.
Thyra Hamann-Hartmann: Textile Flachenkunst. Intro. by A. Meyer Zu Eissen. (Illus., 10, 2 color, Ger.). 1972. DM.1.00. Kunst Bielefe.
Werke der Griechischen Antike. K. Stahler. (Illus., 9, Ger.). 1977. DM.8.00. Kunst Bielefe.
Wessel: Helle Bilder. Intro. by O. Mauer. (Illus., 15, Ger.). 1970. DM.1.00. Kunst Bielefe.
Willi Pramann: Gegenstand und Abstraktion. Intro. by H. Wilmsmeyer. (Illus., 11, Ger.). 1972. DM.1.00. Kunst Bielefe.
Woldemar Winkler: Gemalde, Aquarelle und Zeichnungen. Intro. by H. G. Gmelin. (Illus., 9, Ger.). 1972. DM.1.00. Kunst Bielefe.
Wolfgang Tumpel. Intro. by H. G. Gmelin. (Illus., 24, Ger.). 1973. DM.2.50. Kunst Bielefe.
Zeichnungen Von Theo Ortmann: Bielefeld 1902, Amsterdam 1941. Intro. by U. Weisner. (Illus., 52, 1 color, Ger.). 1967. DM.1.00. Kunst Bielefe.
Zwanzig Lehrer der Hamburger Hochschule Fur Bildende Kunste. Immanuel Kant & James Ensor. Ed. by K. Gruber et al. (Illus., 128, Ger.). 1976. DM.8.00. Kunst Bielefe.
Zwischen Den Dingen. H. Muck. (Illus., 35, Ger.). 1974. DM.4.00. Kunst Bielefe.

KUNSTMUSEUM BERN
Bern, Switzerland.
Aus der Sammlung. (Ger.). 1960. 5.00 Fr. Kunst Bern.
Hermann & Margrit Rupf-Stiftung. (Ger.). 1969. 12.00 Fr. Kunst Bern.
Hugo Wagner: Gemalde Des 1500 & 1600. (Ger.). 1977. 25.00 Fr. Kunst Bern.
Kunstmuseum, I: Italienisch Malerei 1300-1600. (Ger.). 1974. 15.00 Fr. Kunst Bern.
Paul Klee: Handzeichnungen I, Kindheit Bis 1920. (Ger.). 1973. 95.00 Fr. Kunst Bern.
Paul Klee Im Kunstmuseum Bern. (Ger.). 1970. 6.00 Fr. Kunst Bern.
Schenkung Nell Walden. (Ger.). 1967. 3.00 Fr. Kunst Bern.
Schenkung Otto Nebel. (Ger.). 1971. 2.50 Fr. Kunst Bern.

KUNSTMUSEUM LUZERN
Lucerne, Switzerland.
Luzerner Kunstmuseum: Ein Fuhrer Durch Die Sammlung. Adolph Reinle. (Ger.). 5.00 F. Kunstmus Luz.

KUNSTMUSEUM ST. GALLEN
St. Gallen, Switzerland.
Katalog der Gemalde und Plastiken. Rudolf Hanhart. Ed. by Kunstverein St. Gallen. (Illus., Ger.). 1977. pap. 10.00 F. Kunst St Gallen.
Katalog der Zeichnungen und Aquarelle, 1979. Rudolf Hanhart. Ed. by Kunstverein St. Gallen. (Illus., 30). 1979. pap. 4.00 F. Kunst St Gallen.
Katalog der Zeichnungen und Aquarelle, 1978. Rudolf Hanhart. Ed. by Kunstverein St. Gallen. (Illus., 30, Ger.). 1978. pap. 4.00 F. Kunst St Gallen.

KUNSTSAMMLUNGEN DER VESTE COBURG
Coburg, Germany, West.
Ausgewahlte Werke, Kataloge der Kunstsammlungen der Veste Coburg I. H. Maedebach et al. (Uberarbeitete Auflage, 2). (Illus., 26 color, 128 b&w, Ger.). 1978. pap. DM.15.00. Kunst Coburg.
Creussener Steinzeug: Kataloge der Kunstsammlungen der Veste Coburg VI. E. Klinge. (Auflage 1977). (Illus., 141 b&w, Ger.). 1977. pap. DM.10.00. Kunst Coburg.
Lucas Cranach, 1472-1553: Kataloge der Kunstsammlungen der Veste Coburg IV. H. Maedebach & M. Maedebach-Gebhardt. (Auflage, 1). (Illus., 4 color, 34 b&w, Ger.). 1978. pap. DM.8.00. Kunst Coburg.
Meisterwerke Europaischer Graphik, Fifteenth to Eighteenth Century: Kataloge der Kunstsammlungen der Veste Coburg, V. H. Maedebach & M. Maedebach. (Auflage 1975). (Illus., 366 b&w, Ger.). 1975. pap. DM.23.00. Kunst Coburg.
Veste Coburg, Kleiner Kunstfuhrer, 871. H. Maedebach. (Auflage 6). (Illus., Ger.). 1978. pap. DM.2.00. Schnell Steiner.

KUPFERSTICHKABINETT
Berlin, Germany, West.
Bilder Einer Grossen Stadt. (Ger.). DM.32.00. Blaschker Verlag.
Durer Zeichnungen. (Ger.). DM.22.00. Blaschker Verl.
Holland, Landschaftszeichng. (Ger.). DM.26.00. Blaschker Verlag.
Rubens. (Ger.). DM.32.00. Blaschker Verlag.
Tizian und Sein Kreis. (Ger.). DM.22.00. Blaschker Verlag.
Vom Spaten Mittelalter Bis Zu David. (Ger.). DM.52.00. Blaschker Verlag.

KYUSEI ATAMI ART MUSEUM
Atami-shi, Japan.
Selected Catalogue, Vol. 1. Kyusei Hakone Art Museum & Kyusei Atami Art Museum. (Jap.). 1978. 3000.00 Yen. Messianica.
Selected Catalogue: Japanese & Chinese Ceramics, Vol. 2. Kyusei Hakone Art Museum & Kyusei Atami Art Museum. (Jap.). 1978. 3000.00 Yen. Messianica.
Selected Catalogue: Ukiyoe, Vol. 3. Kyusei Hakone Art Museum & Kyusei Atami Art Museum. (Jap.). 1978. 2700.00 Yen. Messianica.

KYUSEI HAKONE ART MUSEUM *Hakone, Japan.*
Selected Catalogue of the Hakone Art Museum, Vol. 2. (Illus., 43 color, 154 b&w, Jap. & Eng.). 1976. write for info. Hakone Mus.

LAHTI ART MUSEUM *Lahti, Finland.*
Ionowa-Kokoelma. Ed. by Ulla Korhonen. (Illus., 14 b&w, Finnish.). 1976. Fmk.8.00. Lahti Art Mus.
Lahden Taidemuseo Veistokset. Ed. by Ulla Korhonen. (Illus., b&w, Finnish.). 1975. Fmk.8.00. Lahti Art Mus.
Lahden Taidemuseon Kokoelmat. Ed. by Heikki Liimatta. (Illus., 8 b&w, Finnish.). 1952. write for info. Lahti Art Mus.

LAHTI HISTORICAL MUSEUM *Lahti, Finland.*
Medal Collection. Ed. by Historical Museum of Lahti. (Illus., b&w, Finnish.). pap. Fmk.8.00. Lahti Hist.

LANDSKRONA KULTURNAMND
Landskrona, Sweden.
Anders Jonsson. Vanna Beckman et al. (Illus., 5 b&w, Swed.). 1975. pap. Kr.5.00. Landskrona.
Bondemalning Pa Glas, Modernt Maleri. Sven B. Ek. (Illus., 5 b&w, Swed.). 1972. pap. Kr.2.00. Landskrona.
Etnografica. Sven B. Ek & Agneta Barle. (Illus., 8 b&w, Swed.). pap. Kr.3.00. Landskrona.
Nell Walden: Introduction till Nell Walden's Donation. Sven B. Ek & Margareta Alin. (Illus., 2 color, 3 b&w, Swed.). 1970. pap. Kr.2.00. Landskrona.
Sturmkonstnarer Och Schweizisk Nukonst. Margareta Alin & Sandor Kuthy. (Illus., 3 b&w, Swed. & Ger.). pap. Kr.2.00. Landskrona.

LANG ART GALLERY, SCRIPPS COLLEGE
see Galleries of the Claremont Colleges

LANSMUSEET LINKOPING
Linkoping, Sweden.
Yearbok: Ostergotland Meddelanden 1978. Lansmuseet. (Illus., 50 b&w, Swed.). 1978. Kr.40.00. Linkoping Lans.

LAUREN ROGERS LIBRARY AND MUSEUM OF ART
see Rogers, Lauren, Library and Museum of Art

LEICESTER MUSEUM AND ART GALLERY
Leicester, United Kingdom.
African Art Catalogue. 1978. 0.20p. Leicestershire.
Belgrave Hall Guide. 1978. 0.35p. Leicestershire.
Ben Marshall-John Leech Catalogue. 1978. 0.35p. Leicestershire.
Collection of Ceramics. 1978. 0.35p. Leicestershire.
Collection of Paintings. 1978. 0.40p. Leicestershire.
Daniel Lambert Booklet. 1978. 0.25p. Leicestershire.
Ellesmere Catalogue. 1978. 0.25p. Leicestershire.
Ernest Gimson & the Cotswold Group of Craftsmen. Annette Carruthers. (Illus., 7 color, 96 b&w). 1978. E2.50. Leicestershire.
Japanese Collection. 1978. 0.35p. Leicestershire.
John Flower. 1978. 0.15p. Leicestershire.
Leicestershire Hunting Pictures. 1978. 0.35p. Leicestershire.
Local Portraits. 1978. 0.35p. Leicestershire.
Lowesby Pottery Collection Catalogue. 1978. E1.00. Leicestershire.
Manor House, Donington-le-Heath Guide Book. 1978. 0.20p. Leicestershire.
Marinot Glass Collection Catalogue. 1978. E1.00. Leicestershire.
Mary Linwood Catalogue. 1978. 0.05p. Leicestershire.
Sir George Beaumont Catalogue. 1978. 0.60p. Leicestershire.
Watercolours & Drawings. 1978. 0.30p. Leicestershire.

LEIGHTON HOUSE ART GALLERY AND MUSEUM
London, United Kingdom.
Catalogue of Permanent Exhibition: High Victorian Art. Intro. by William Gaunt. (Illus., 16 b&w). 1979. pap. E1.00. Ken Chels Libs.

LEOPOLD-HOESCH-MUSEUM
see Hoesch, Leopold, Museum

LIBRARY OF CONGRESS
Washington, D.C.
American Prints in the Library of Congress: A Catalog of the Collection. LC 73-106134. 1970. $37.50. Johns Hopkins.
American Revolution in Drawings & Prints: A Checklist of 1765-1790 Graphics in the Library of Congress. Ed. by Donald H. Cresswell. LC 73-17405. 1975. $14.35. Su Docs.
Bronze Doors of the Library of Congress. 1962. free. LC.
Canterbury Pilgrims: Mural Paintings by Ezra Winter. LC 46-27985. 1975. free. LC.
Captain John Smith's Map of Virginia. LC 72-8536. (Illus., map facsim.). 1972. $1.75. LC.
Catalog of Broadsides in the Rare Book Division. LC 72-6563. 1972. $425.00. G K Hall.
Chevalier Delibere. Olivier De Lamarche. LC 47-32974. 1946. free. LC.
Civil War Maps. LC 61-60061. 1961. $16.75. Greenwood.
Civil War Maps. LC 61-60061. 1961. $7.95; $10.00, with Hotchkiss map collection; pap. $5.95. Sterling.
Civil War Photographs, 1861-1865. Ed. by Hirst D. Milhollen & Donald H. Mugridge. LC 61-60002. 1961. $3.00. LC Photo.
Collection of John Boyd Thacher in the Library of Congress: Autographs Relating to the French Revolution, Vol. 3. LC 31-26001. 1931. free. LC.
Collection of John Boyd Thacher in the Library of Congress: Catalogue of John Boyd Thacher Collection of Incunabula, Vol. 1. LC 31-26001. 1915. free. LC.
Costumes of France in the Library of Congress. LC 76-608412. 1977. $4.75. Su Docs.
Descriptive List of Treasure Maps & Charts. LC 73-15994. 1973. $1.50. Su Docs.
Gutenberg Bible. LC 72-7352. (Illus., facsim.). 1972. $1.75. LC Inf.
List of Maps of America in the Library of Congress: Preceded by a List of Works Relating to Cartography. P. Lee Phillips. LC 1-24175. 1901. $42.50. B Franklin.
Nineteenth Book: Tesoro De Poveri. Lessing J. Rosenwald. LC 62-60686. 1961. $1.50. LC Inf.
Rare Book Division: A Guide to Its Collections & Services. LC 64-60071. 1965. $1.15. Su Docs.
Some Guides to Special Collections in the Rare Book Division. LC 74-10534. 1974. free. LC.
Two Rebuses from the American Revolution, in Facsimile. LC 73-603400. (Illus., plates). 1973. $1.00. LC Inf.
Visit from St. Nicholas. Clement Clarke Moore. LC 77-350692. (Illus., facsim.). 1976. $1.50. LC Inf.

LIEBIGHAUS MUSEUM ALTER PLASTIK
Frankfurt, Germany, West.
Abenteuer Des Odysseus. W. Nold. (Ger.). 1977. pap. free. Liebieghaus.
Agypteraktion. W. Nold. (Ger.). 1976. pap. free. Liebieghaus.
Als Die Romer. W. Nold. (Ger.). 1978. pap. free. Liebieghaus.
Antike Kleinkunst. F. Eckstein & A. Legner. (Ger.). 1969. pap. DM.4.00. Liebieghaus.
Antike Plastik. F. Eckstein & A. Legner. (Ger.). 1973. pap. DM.5.00. Liebieghaus.
Bildwerke Aus Dem Liebieghaus. A. Legner. (Ger.). 1967. pap. DM.3.50. Liebieghaus.
Bildwerke der Barockzeit. A. Legner. (Illus., Ger.). 1963. pap. DM.3.50. Liebieghaus.
Faltblatter Zur Agyptischen Kunst. P. C. Bol. (Ger.). 1978. pap. DM.4.50. Liebieghaus.
Faltblatter Zur Agyptischen Kunst. A. Krug. (Ger.). 1976. pap. DM.4.50. Liebieghaus.
Faltblatter Zur Agyptischen und Griechischen Kunst. A. Krug. (Ger.). 1978. pap. DM.8.50. Liebieghaus.

MUNSON-WILLIAMS-PROCTOR INSTITUTE, MUSEUM OF ART
Utica, New York.
Edward Wales Root Bequest. (Illus., 21 b&w). 1961. pap. $0.50. Munson Williams.
European Prints: Thirteenth to Twentieth Century. (Illus., 9 b&w). 1953. pap. $0.25. Munson Williams.
Paintings, Drawings & Sculptures in the Munson-Williams-Proctor Institute. (Illus., 7 b&w). 1961. pap. $0.50. Munson-Williams.
MUSEE AFRICAIN
Ile d'Aix, France.
Musee Africain. (Petits Guides Des Grands Musees Ser). (Fr.). 3.50 F. Reunion.
MUSEE ANTOINE LECUYER
Saint-Quentin, France.
Collection Des Pastels De Maurice-Quentin Delatour a Saint-Quentin. Elie Fleury & Gaston Briers. (Illus., 16 b&w, Fr.). 1954. write for info. Mus Lecuyer.
Pastels De Maurice-Quintin De la Tour Musee De Saint-Quentin. Robert Haye. (Illus., 22 color, 7 b&w, Fr.). 1978. write for info. Mus Lecuyer.
MUSEE ARCHEOLOGIQUE MUNICIPAL
Laon, France.
Guide Catalogue Du Musee Archeologique De Laon. A. N. Rollas. Ed. by Musee Archeologique Municipal. (Illus., Fr.). 1975. 5.00 F. Mus De Laon.
MUSEE BARGOIN
Clermont-Ferrand, France.
Bronzes Figures Antiques. Stephanie Boucher. Ed. by Clermont-Ferrand. (Illus., 76 b&w, Fr.). 1978. 10.00 F. Mus Bargoin.
Carle Vanloo, 1705-1765. Marie-Catherine Sahut. Ed. by Clermont-Ferrand. (Illus., 631 b&w, Fr.). 1977. 50.00 F. Mus Bargoin.
Dix Annees De Recherches Archeologiques En Auvergne. Jean-Pierre Daugas. Ed. by Clermont-Ferrand. (Illus., 14 b&w, Fr.). 1976. 5.00 F. Mus Bargoin.
Fetes De la Revolution. J. P. Bouillon et al. Ed. by Clermont-Ferrand. (Illus., 61 b&w, Fr.). 1974. 8.00 F. Mus Bargoin.
Guide Du Musee Bargoin: Archeologie. Jean-Claude Ruiz. Ed. by Clermont-Ferrand. (Illus., 25 b&w, Fr.). 1976. 5.00 F. Mus Bargoin.
Guide Du Musee Bargoin: Beaux Arts. Marie Hallopeau. Ed. by Clermont-Ferrand. (Illus., 27 b&w, Fr.). 1976. 5.00 F. Mus Bargoin.
Habitat Rural En Basse Auvergne. Pierre Bonnaud & Jean-Paul Leclerque. Ed. by Clermont-Ferrand. (Illus., 36 b&w, Fr.). 1977. 8.00 F. Mus Bargoin.
Hommage a Louis Chauvignier. Marie Hallopeau. Ed. by Clermont-Ferrand. (Illus., 38 b&w, Fr.). 1977. 5.00 F. Mus Bargoin.
Jules Laurens on Auvergne. Marie Hallopeau. Ed. by Clermont-Ferrand. (Illus., 61 b&w, Fr.). 1975. 8.00 F. Mus Bargoin.
Lurcat. Christiane Maranden. Ed. by Clermont-Ferrand. (Illus., 1, Fr.). 1972. 2.00 F. Mus Bargoin.
Monnaies. M. Maimjones et al. Ed. by Clermont-Ferrand. (Illus., 3 b&w plates, Fr.). 1972. 5.00 F. Mus Bargoin.
Picasso. Marie Hallopeau. Ed. by Clermont-Ferrand. (Illus., 4 b&w, Fr.). 1974. 3.00 F. Mus Bargoin.
Prosper Marilhat. Marie Hallopeau. Ed. by Clermont-Ferrand. (Illus., 20 b&w, Fr.). 1973. 5.00 F. Mus Bargoin.
Ralph Stackpole, un Americain En Auvergne. Marie Hallopeau. Ed. by Clermont-Ferrand. (Illus., 24 b&w, Fr.). 1978. 10.00 F. Mus Bargoin.
Thomas Degeorge, 1786-1854: Fr. Michele Juillard. Ed. by Clermont-Ferrand. (Illus., 40 b&w). 1978. 10.00 F. Mus Bargoin.
MUSEE BONNAT
Bayonne, France.
Musee Bonnat. (Illus., Fr.). 9.00 F. Reunion.
MUSEE BOSSUET
Meaux, France.
Ancien Palais Episcopal et le Musee Bossuet. Jean-Claude Ruiz. Ed. by Musee Bossuet. (Illus., 1 color, 25 b&w photos, Fr.). 1978. 10.00 F. Bossuet.
MUSEE CANTONAL DES BEAUX-ARTS
Lausanne, Switzerland.
Promenade Au Musee Cantonal Des Beaux-Arts De Lausanne. Jacques-Edouard Berger & Renee Canova. Ed. by Musee Cantonal Des Beaux-Arts Lausanne. (Illus., 36 color, Fr.). 1971. pap. 14.00 F. Mus Cant Laus.
MUSEE CARNAVALET
Paris, France.
Bulletin Du Musee Carnavalet. Musee Carnavalet Conservatin. (Illus., b&w, Fr.). pap. write for info. Mus Carnavalet.
Collection Henriette Bouvier Leguee Au Musee Carnivalet. Musee Carnavalet Curator. (Illus., 96 b&w, Fr.). 1968. pap. 10 00.00 F. Mus Carnavalet.
MUSEE CURTIUS
Liege, Belgium.
Aspect De la Verrerie Contemporaine. (Illus., Fr.). 1958. 110.00 F. Mus Liegeois.
Catalogue Des Armes Du Musee Curtius. J. Gaier-Lhoest. (Ger.). 1963. 110.00 F. Mus Liegeois.
Musee Curtius a Liege. Joseph Philippe. (Illus., Fr.). 1976. 100.00 F. Mus Liegeois.
Prehistoire a Travers les Collections Du Musee Curtius De Liege. Marcel Otte. (Illus., Fr.). 1978. 450.00 F. Mus Liegeois.
Sculpteurs et Ornemanistes De L'Ancien Pays De Liege. (Illus., Fr.). 1958. 140.00 F. Mus Liegeois.
Verres Romains Tardifs et Merovingiens Du Musee Curtius. Michel Vanderhoeven. (Illus., Fr.). 1958. 110.00 F. Mus Liegeois.
MUSEE D'ANSEMBOURG
Liege, Belgium.
Musee D'Ansembourg. Joseph Philippe. (Illus., Fr.). 1976. 100.00 F. Mus Liegeois.
MUSEE D'ARLON
see Institut Archeologique Du Luxembourg
MUSEE D'ART
see Institut Archeologique Du Luxembourg
MUSEE D'ART ET D'HISTOIRE
Narbonne, France.
Catalogue De la Ceramique Au Musee De Narbonne. Paul Paloque. Ed. by Musee De Narbonne. (Fr.). 1951. 10.00 F. Mus Art Narbo.
Catalogue Descriptif et Annote Des Peintures et Sculptures Du Musee De Narbonne. Louis Berthomieu. Ed. by Edouard Privat. (Illus., 48 photos, Fr.). 1923. 20.00 F. Mus Art Narbo.
MUSEE D'ART JUIF
Paris, France.
Connaissez-Vous le Musee D'Art Juif? (Fr.). pap. write for info. Mus D'Art Juif.
MUSEE D'ART MODERNE (BEAUBOURG), CENTRE NATIONAL D'ART ET DE CULTURE GEORGES POMPIDOU
Paris, France.
Lipchitz. Nicole Barlier. (Illus., 96 b&w, Fr.). 1978. 48.00 F. (ISBN 2-85850-071-1). Pompidou.
Matisse. Isabelle Fontaine. (Illus., 30 color, 65 b&w, Fr.). 1979. 130.00 F. Pompidou.
MUSEE D'ART RELIGIEUX ET D'ART MOSAN
Liege, Belgium.
Art De L'Enluminure Au Musee Diocesain De Liege. F. Pirenne. Ed. by Vaillant-Carmanne. (Illus., Fr.). 1976. 30.00 F. Mus Mosan.
MUSEE D'ARTS DECORATIFS, CHATEAU DE SAUMUR
Saumur, France.
Chateau De Saumur: Musee D'Arts Decoratifs. Monique Jacob. Ed. by Ville De Saumur. (Illus., 777 photos, 8 color, Fr.). 1965. 15.00 F. Siraudeau.
MUSEE DE BAGNOLS-SUR-CEZE
Bagnols-sur-ceze, France.
Musee De Bagnols-Sur-Ceze: Catalogue-Guide. Jacqueline Bretegnier-Andre. (Illus., Fr.). pap. write for info. Mus Bagnols.
Musee De Bagnols-Sur-Ceze: Donation George et Adele Bagnols. (Illus., Fr.). pap. write for info. Mus Bagnols.
MUSEE DE CLUNY
Paris, France.
Musee Des Thermes et De l'Hotel De Cluny: Guide Du Musee. (Petits Guides Des Grands Musees Ser., No. 3). (Ger., Fr., Eng., Span. & It.). 3.50 F., ea. lang. Reunion.
Musee Des Thermes et De l'Hotel De Cluny. (Illus., Fr. & Eng.). 27.00 F., Fr. ed. .; 33.00 F., Eng. ed. Reunion.
MUSEE DE L'AIN
Bourg-en-Bresse, France.
Acquisitions De 1945 a 1975. Francoise Baudson. Ed. by Visages De l'Ain. (Tire a Part De Visages De l'Ain Ser). (Fr.). write for info. Mus De L'Ain.
MUSEE DE LA MODE ET DU COSTUME
Paris, France.
Elegance et Creation, Paris 1945-1975. Madeleine Delpierre. Ed. by Musee De la Mode et Du Costume. (Illus., 27 color, 260 b&w, Fr.). 25.00 F. Mus Mode Cost.
Modes Enfantines 1750-1950. Madeleine Delpierre. Ed. by Musee De la Mode et Du Costume. (Illus., 37 b&w, Fr.). 1979. 17.00 F. Mus Mode Cost.
Secrets d'elegance 1750-1950. Madeleine Delpierre. Ed. by Musee De la Mode et Du Costume. (Illus., 36 b&w, color cover, Fr.). 1978. 15.00 F. Mus Mode Cost.
Vingt Ans Apres, Principaux Enrichissements 1956-1976. Madeleine Delpierre. Ed. by Musee De la Mode et Du Costume. (Illus., 98 b&w, Fr.). 12.00 F. Mus Mode Cost.
MUSEE DE L'ANNONCIADE
Saint-Tropez, France.
Catalogue De la Collection Du Musee De L'Annonciade, Saint-Tropez. Alain Mousseigne. Ed. by Saint-Tropez Cogolin. (Illus., Fr.). 1977. 30.00 F. L'Annonciade.
Catalogue De L'Exposition Henri Manguin. Alain Mousseigne. (Illus., Fr.). 1975. 25.00 F. L'Annonciade.
Catalogue De L'Exposition le Drapeau, 1972-1977. Alain Mousseigne. (Illus., Fr.). 1977. 20.00 F. L'Annonciade.
MUSEE DE LA SOCIETE ARCHEOLOGIQUE DE MONTPELIER
Montpelier, France.
Ceramique Corinthienne et Etrusco-Corinthienne. Annie-Fe Laurens. Ed. by Societe Archeologique De Montpellier. (Illus., 150 photos., Fr.). 1974. write for info. Soc Arch Mont.
MUSEE DE L'HISTOIRE DE FRANCE, ARCHIVES NATIONALES
Paris, France.
Catalogues Des Musee: Batiments, Vol. 1. Jean-Pierre Babelon. Ed. by Imprimeris Nationale. (Fr.). 5.00 F. Mus Hist Franc.
Catalogues Des Musee: Sixteenth, Seventhteenth & Eighteenth Centuries, Vol. 3. Jean-Pierre Babelon. Ed. by Imprimeris Nationale. 4.00 F. Mus Hist France.
Catalogues Des Musees: Moyen Age, Vol. 2. Jean-Pierre Babelon. Ed. by Imprimeris Nationale. (Fr.). 4.00 F. Mus Hist France.
Catalogues Du Musee: Revolution Francais, Vol. 4. Jean-Pierre Babelon. Ed. by Imprimeris Nationale. 6.00 F. Mus Hist France.
MUSEE DE L'ISLE DE FRANCE
Chateau De Sceaux, France.
Affiches De L'ile De France Hier et Aujourd Hui. Corinne Henry. Ed. by Presses Artistiques. (Illus., 73 b&w, Fr.). 1975. 25.00 F. Sceaux.
Donation Millet: Two Hundred Pieces De Faience De Choisy. Maddy Aries. Ed. by Presses Artistiques. (Illus., 2 color, 27 b&w, Fr.). 1979. 25.00 F. Sceaux.
Musiciens De L'ile De France. Corinne Henry & Georges Poisson. Ed. by Presses Artistiques. (Fr.). 1973. 15.00 F. Sceaux.
Voltaire Voyageurs De L'Europe. Corinne Henry & Francoise Wasserman. Ed. by Presses Artistiques. (Illus., 40 b&w, Fr.). 1978. 25.00 F. Sceaux.
MUSEE DE L'IMPRESSION SUR ETOFFES
Mulhouse, France.
Musee De L'Impression Sur Etoffes De Mulhouse. Ed. by Souete Industrielle De Mulhause. (Illus., color, b&w, Fr.). 1975. 30.00 F. Mus Etoffes.
Toiles De Nantes Des 18th et 19th Siecles. Conservateurs Du Musee. (Fr.). 1977. 35.00 F. Mus Etoffes.
MUSEE DE PONTOISE
see Musee Tavet-Delacour
MUSEE DEPARTEMENTAL DE L'OISE-BEAUVAIS
Beauvais, France.
Arthur De Gobineau et le Departement De L'oise. Marie-Jose Salmon. Ed. by Musee Departemental De L'oise-Beauvais. (Illus., 49 b&w photos, F.). 1978. 20.00 Fr. Mus De L'oise.
Auguste Delaherche, 1857-1940: Musee Departemental De L'oise-Beauvais. Marie-Jose Salmon. Ed. by Musee Departemental De L'oise. (Illus., Fr.). 1973. 15.00 F. Mus De L'oise.
Beauvais Par Ceux Qui L'ont Vu: Musee Departemental De L'oise Beauvais. Marie-Jose Salmon. Ed. by Musee Departemental De L'oise-Beauvais. (Illus., photos, Fr.). 1977. 15.00 F. Mus De L'oise.
Musee Departemental De L'oise-Beauvais. Simon Cammas & Monique Quesnot. (Illus., 3 b&w, Fr.). 1967. write for info. Mus De L'oise.
Peintures Italiennes (1700-1800) Du Musee Departemental De L'oise. Marie-Jose Salmon. Ed. by Musee Departemental De L'oise. (Illus., 17 b&w photos, Fr.). 1971. 15.00 F. Mus De L'oise.
Pierres et Bois Sculptures XII Au XVI Siecle Du Musee Departemental De L'oise. Marie-Jose Salmon & Pierrette Bonnet-Laborderie. Ed. by Musee Departemental De L'oise. (Illus., 87 b&w photos, Fr.). 1975. write for info. Mus De L'oise.
Roger Vieillard - Anita De Caro. Marie-Jose Salmon. Ed. by Musee Departemental De L'oise. (Illus., 23 b&w, Fr.). 1978. 15.00 F. Mus De L'oise.
Sculpteur Max Blondat, (1872-1925), Du Modern Style L'art Deco Au Musee Departemental De L'oise. Marie-Jose Salmon. Ed. by Musee Departemental De L'oise-Beauvais. (Illus., 26 b&w photos, Fr.). 1979. 10.00 F. Mus De L'oise.
Thomas Couture, 1815-1879: Musee Departmental De l'Oise. Marie-Jose Salmon. Ed. by Musee Departemental De L'oise-Beauvais. Tr. by V. Bouton. (Illus., 20 photos, 2 b&w plates, Fr.). 1972. 15.00 F. Mus De L'oise.
MUSEE DES ANTIQUITES NATIONALES
Saint-Germain-en-Laye, France.
Age De Bronze Dans la Region De Paris. J. P. Mohen. (Illus., 713 drawings, 31 photos, Fr.). 250.00 F. Reunion.
Art Mobilier Prehistorique: Collection Piette. Marthe Chollot. (Illus., Fr.). 230.00 F. Reunion.
Musee Des Antiquites Nationales De Saint-Germain-en-Laye: Age Du Bronze et Du Fer. (Illus., Fr.). 6.00 F. Reunion.
Musee Des Antiquites Nationales De Saint-Germain-en-Laye: Antiquites Gallo-Romaines et Merovingiennes. (Illus., Fr.). 6.00 F. Reunion.
Musees Des Antiquites Nationales. (Petits Guides Des Grands Musees Ser., No. 10). (Fr.). 3.50 F. Reunion.
MUSEE DES ARTS AFRICAINS ET OCEANIENS
Paris, France.
Musee Des Arts Africains et Oceaniens: Art Africain. (Petits Guides Des Grands Musees Ser., No. 29). (Fr.). 3.50 F. Reunion.
Musee Des Arts Africains et Oceaniens: Art Islamique Au Maghreb. (Petits Guides Des Grands Musees Ser., No. 28). (Fr.). 3.50 F. Reunion.
Musee Des Arts Africains et Oceaniens: Arts Maghrebin, Africain et Oceanien. (Petits Guides Des Grands Musees Ser., No. 17). (Fr.). 3.50 F. Reunion.
Musee Des Arts Africains et Oceaniens: Aquarium. (Petits Guides Des Grands Musees Ser., No. 18). (Fr.). 3.50 F. Reunion.
MUSEE DES ARTS DECORATIFS
see Union Central Des Arts Decoratifs-Musee Des Arts Decoratifs
MUSEE DES BEAUX-ARTS
Angers, France.
Cent Dessins Des Musees D'Angers. Viviane Huchard & Alastair Laing. (Illus., 100 reprods., Fr. & Eng.). 1978. 30.00 F. Mus D'Angers.
MUSEE DES BEAUX ARTS
Caen, France.
Acquisitions Recentes: Musee Des Beaux Arts et Collection Mancel. (Illus., 8). 1969. 3.00 F. Mus Caen.
Autour De Rubens: Choix D'Estampes De la Collection Manuel. (Illus., 48). 1977. 20.00 F. Mus Caen.
Collection Mancel. (Illus., 8). 1964. 5.00 F. Mus Caen.
Gravures Italiennes Des XVe et XVIe Siecles. (Illus., 17). 1976. 8.00 F. Mus Caen.
Guide Du Musee Des Beaux Arts. F. Debaisieux. Ed. by Musee Des Beaux Arts. (Illus., 67, Fr.). 1971. 3.00 F. Mus Caen.
Hommage a Bernard Mancel. (Illus., 7). 1972. 12.00 F. Mus Caen.
Jacques Callot: Choix D'Estampes. F. Debaisieux. Ed. by Musee Des Beaux Arts. (Illus., Fr.). 1971. write for info. Mus Caen.
Portrait Peint Dans les Collections Du Musee. (Illus., 9). 1969. 3.00 F. Mus Caen.
Raimondi et Son Entourage. F. Debaisieux. Ed. by Musee Des Beaux Arts. (Illus., 17 b&w, Fr.). 1976. write for info. Mus Caen.
MUSEE DES BEAUX-ARTS DE DUNKERQUE
Dunkerque, France.
Catalogue Des Peintures Du Musee De Dunkerque. Guy Blazy. Ed. by Imprimerie Vanwormhoudt - Dunkerque. (Illus., 10, Fr.). 1976. 25.00 F. Mus Dunkerque.
Guide Des Collections Navales. Christian Pfister. Ed. by Imprimerie Vanwormhoudt - Dunkerque. (Fr.). 1973. 10.00 F. Mus Dunkerque.
MUSEE DES BEAUX-ARTS DE LILLE
Lille, France.
Collection D'Alexandre Leleux. H. Oursel. Ed. by Musee Des Beaux-Arts De Lille. (Grands Noms Grandes Figures Du Musee De Lille Ser.). (Illus., 90 b&w, Fr.). 1974. 20.00 F. Mus Art Lille.
Donation Masson a Lille: Oeuvres Impressionistes. H. Oursel. Ed. by Revue Du Louvre et Des Musees De France. (Illus., 28, Fr.). 1977. 10.00 F. Mus Art Lille.
MUSEE DES BEAUX ARTS DE TOURS
Tours, France.
Chateau Du Plessis les Tours. Sophie De Sudvirat. (Illus., 35 b&w, Fr.). 1977. 9.00 F. Mus Tours.
Inventaire Des Collections Publiques Francaises: Tours, Peintures Du XVIIIe Siecle. Boris Lossky. (Illus., 207 b&w, Fr.). 1962. 32.00 F. Mus Tours.
Musee Des Beaux Arts, Ancien Palais Des Archeveques, Guide Summaire. Marie De Villechenon & Sophie De Sudviraut. (Illus., 31 b&w photos, Fr.). 1975. 10.00 F. Mus Tours.
MUSEE DES BEAUX-ARTS ET D'ARCHEOLOGIE
Rennes, France.
Bulletin - Des Amis Du Musee De Rennes: Catalogue Des Peintures De L'Ecole Francaise Du XVIIeme Siecle, No. 3. Francois Bergot & Patrick Ramade. Ed. by Imprimerie Simon. (Illus., 53 b&w, Fr.). 1979. 50.00 F. Mus Rennes.
Dessins De la Collection Du President De Robien. Francois Bergot. (Illus., 52 b&w, Fr.). 25.00 F. Mus Rennes.

Collection Privees Audomaroises. (Fr.). 1971. 8.00 F. Mus Hot Sande.
Enrique Marin. (Fr.). 1977. 8.00 F. Mus Hot Sande.
Faience De Saint-Omer. (Fr.). 1976. 8.00 F. Mus Hot Sande.
Francois Chifflart. (Fr.). 1972. 8.00 F.,Mus Hot Sande.
Helmut Kolle. (Fr.). 1969. 8.00 F. Mus Hot Sande.
Henry Lhotellier. (Fr.). 1977. 8.00 F. Mus Hot Sande.
Leon Belly. (Fr.). 1977. 8.00 F. Mus Hot Sande.
Musee Hotel Sandelin De Saint-Omer. (Fr.). 1971. 8.00 F. Mus Hot Sande.
Orfevrerie De Saint-Omer. (Fr.). 1975. 8.00 F. Mus Hot Sande.
Pelayo. (Fr.). 1978. 8.00 F. Mus Hot Sande.
Saint-Omer et le 17e Siecle. (Fr.). 1977. 8.00 F. Mus Hot Sande.
Subira Puig. (Fr.). 1976. 8.00 F. Mus Hot Sande.
Yves De Coetlogon. (Fr.). 1974. 8.00 F. Mus Hot Sande.

MUSEE INTERNATIONAL DE LA CHASSE
Gien, France.
Musee International De la Chasse. Intro. by Bertrand Gretaire. (Illus., 6 color, 28 b&w). write for info. Mus Int Chasse.

MUSEE MAGNIN
Dijon, France.
Musee Magnin. (Petits Guides Des Grands Musees Ser., No. 37). (Fr.). 3.50 F. Reunion.

MUSEE MATISSE
Nice, France.
Henri Matisse, Sculpture. Colette Audibert. Ed. by Musee Matisse - Ville de Nice. (Illus., 60 b&w, Fr.). 1974. pap. 15.00 F. Mus Matisse.

MUSEE MUNICIPAL
Soissons, France.
Soissons: Ancienne Abbaye Saint-Leger Musee Municipal. (Illus., Fr.). pap. write for info. Mus Soissons.

MUSEE MUNICIPAL DE COGNAC
Cognac, France.
Catalogue Sommaire Des Peintures, Sculptures et Objets D'Art Exposes. Pauline Reverchon. Ed. by Musee Municipal De Cognac. (Illus., 4 b&w, Fr.). 1963. 2.00 F. Cognac.
Maurice Marinot, 1882-1960: Donation De Peintures, Dessins, Verreries Par Florence Marinot. Pauline Reverchon. Ed. by Musee Municipal De Cognac. 1979. write for info. Cognac.
Musee De Cognac Dans la Vie De la Cite. Pauline Reverchon. Ed. by Musee De Cognac. (Illus., 2 color, 16 b&w, Fr. & Eng.). 1965. 5.00 F. Cognac.

MUSEE NAPOLEONIEN
Ile d'Aix, France.
Musee Napoleonien: Fondation Gourgaud. (Petits Guides Des Grands Musees Ser., No. 21). (Fr.). 3.50 F. Reunion.

MUSEE NATIONAL ADRIEN DUBOUCHE
Limoges, France.
Musee Adrien Dubouche. (Illus., Fr.). 10.00 F. Reunion.

MUSEE NATIONAL D'ART OCCIDENTAL
see National Museum of Western Art

MUSEE NATIONAL DE LA MAISON BONAPARTE
Ajaccio, France.
Musee National De la Maison Bonaparte. Yvan David. (Illus., Fr.). 1968. 6.00 F. Reunion.
Musee National De la Maison Bonaparte. Yvan David. (Illus., Fr.). 1976. 4.00 F. (ISBN 2-7118-0328-7). Reunion.

MUSEE NATIONAL DE LA RENAISSANCE
Ecouen, France.
Musee National De la Renaissance. (Petit Guides Des Grands Musees Ser., No. 42). (Fr.). 3.50 F. Reunion.

MUSEE NATIONAL DES ARTS ET TRADITIONS POPULAIRES
Paris, France.
Arts et Traditions Populaires: Guide d'Orientation Documentaire. (Illus., Fr.). 5.50 F. Reunion.
Musee Des Arts et Traditions Populaires: Guide Du Musee. (Petits Guides Des Grands Musees Ser., No. 25). (Ger. & Fr.). $3.50, ea. lang. Reunion.
Systeme Descriptif Des Objets Domestiques. (Fr.). 100.00 F. Reunion.

MUSEE NATIONAL DES GRANGES DE PORT-ROYAL
Magny-les-Hameaux, France.
Musee Des Granges De Port-Royal. (Petits Guides Des Grands Musees Ser., No. 22). (Fr.). 3.50 F. Reunion.
Musee National Des Granges De Port-Royal Des Champs. (Illus., Fr.). 9.00 F. Reunion.

MUSEE NATIONAL DES MONUMENTS FRANCAIS
Paris, France.
Musee Des Monuments Francais. (Petits Guides Des Grands Musees Ser., No. 1). (Fr.). 3.50 F. Reunion.
Musee Des Monuments Francais: Renaissance. (Illus., Fr.). 2.50 F. Reunion.
Musee Des Monuments Francais: Temps Modernes XVIIe, XVIIIe et XIXe Siecles. (Fr.). 2.50 F. Reunion.

MUSEE NATIONAL DU CHATEAU DE COMPIEGNE
Compiegne, France.
Appartements Historiques Du Chateau De Compiegne. (Petits Guides Des Grands Musees Ser., No. 16). (Fr.). 3.50 F. Reunion.
Musee De la Voiture et Du Tourisme. (Petits Guides Des Grands Musees Ser., No. 2). (Fr.). 3.50 F. Reunion.

MUSEE NATIONAL DU CHATEAU DE FONTAINEBLEAU
Fontainebleau, France.
Musee Du Chateau De Fontainebleau. (Illus., Fr. & Eng.). 22.00 F., Fr. ed. ; 22.00 F., Eng. ed. Reunion.
Musee Du Chateau De Fontainebleau. (Petits Guides Des Grands Musees Ser., No. 7). (Ger., Fr., Eng., Span. & It.). 3.50 F., ea. lang. Reunion.

MUSEE NATIONAL DU CHATEAU DE MALMAISON
Rueil-Malmaison, France.
Inventaire Apres Deces De l'Imperatrice Josephine a Malmaison. Serge Grandjean. (Illus., 26 plates, Fr.). 32.00 F. Reunion.
Malmaison, le Chateau et Son Histoire, les Appartements et les Collections. Gerard Hubert. (Illus., Fr & Eng.). 1977. 12.00 F. Malmaison.
Musee De Bois-Preau. Gerard Hubert & Nicole Hubert. (Illus., 1, Fr.). 1971. 5.50 F. Malmaison.
Musee Du Chateau De Malmaison: Appartements De Josephine. (Fr.). 3.00 F. Reunion.
Musee National Du Chateau De Malmaison. Gerard Hubert. (Petits Guides Des Grands Musees Ser., No. 11). (Illus., Fr., Eng. & Ger.). 1973. 4.00 F. Malmaison.

MUSEE NATIONAL DU CHATEAU DE VERSAILLES
Versailles, France.
Grand Trianon: Meubles et Objets d'Art, Vol. 1. Denise Ledoux-Lebard. (Fr.). 135.00 F. Reunion.
Jardins De Versailles et De Trianon. (Petits Guides Des Grands Musees Ser., No. 38). (Fr.). 3.50 F. Reunion.
Musee Du Chateau De Versailles. (Petits Guides Des Grands Musees Ser., No. 23). (Fr., Ger., Span., Eng., It. & Jap.). 3.50 F., ea. lang. Reunion.
Musee Du Chateau De Versailles: Musee De l'Histoire De France: XIXe Siecle. (Illus., Fr.). 6.00 F. Reunion.
Musee Du Chateau De Versailles: Musee De l'Histoire De France: XVIIe et XVIIIe Siecles. (Illus., Fr.). 6.00 F. Reunion.
Salles De l'Empire. (Petits Guides Des Grands Musees Ser., No. 43). (Fr.). 3.50 F. Reunion.
Trianons. (Petits Guides Des Grands Musees Ser., No. 24). (Fr., Ger., Eng., Span., It & Jap.). 3.50 F., ea. lang. Fr. Reunion.

MUSEE NATIONAL DU MESSAGE BIBLIQUE MARC CHAGALL
Nice, France.
Maquettes et Esquisses Pour L'oeuvre Monumentale Marc Chagall. (Fr.). 22.00 F. Reunion.
Marc Chagall Peintures Bibliques Recentes 1966-1976. (Illus., Fr.). 20.00 F. Reunion.
Message Biblique Marc Chagall. Pref. by Jean Chatelain. (Illus., 1 original lithograph, Fr. & Eng.). 300.00 F., deluxe Fr. ed. ; 300.00 F., deluxe Eng. ed. . Reunion.
Musee Du Message Biblique Marc Chagall. (Petits Guides Des Grands Musees Ser., No. 5). (Fr., Ger & Eng.). 3.50 F., ea. lang. Reunion.
Musee National Du Message Biblique Marc Chagall. (Illus., Fr., Eng. & Ger.). 55.00 F.; pap. 35.00 F., ea. lang. Reunion.
Trente Peintres Du XVIIe Siecle Francais. (Illus., Fr.). 20.00 F. Reunion.

MUSEE PINCE
Angers, France.
Art Chinois-Art Japonais. H. De Morant. (Fr.). 1966. 20.00 F. Mus D'Angers.
Etains. (Illus., 111 b&w reprods., Fr.). 10.00 F. Mus D'Angers.
Route Du Tokaido, D'Hiroshioe. Madeline David. (Illus., 4 color reprods., 32 b&w reprods., Fr.). 1978. 30.00 F. Mus D'Angers.

MUSEE RODIN
Paris, France.
Albums "Danse". (Illus., 24). 39.00 F. Musee Rodin.
Albums 24 Dessins et Aquarelles. (Illus.). E68.00. Musee Rodin.
Guide Musee Rodin. E4.00. Musee Rodin.
Rodin: Jianou, Vol. 1. (Fr. & Eng.). 15.00 F. Musee Rodin.
Rodin: Jianou et C. Goldscheider, Vol. 1. (Fr. & Eng.). 150.00 F. Musee Rodin.
Rodin Museum of Paris. 130.00 F. Musee Rodin.
Rodin Par Descharnes. 188.00 F. Musee Rodin.
World of Rodin. 113.00 F. Musee Rodin.

MUSEE ROLIN
Autun, France.
Bronzes Figures Antiques. Lebel & Boucher. 70.00 F. Rolin Mus.
Figurines Gallo-Romaines. H. Vertet & G. Vuillemot. 15.00 F. Rolin Mus.
Guide Du Musee. G. Vuillemot. (Fr. & Ger.). 5.00 F. Rolin Mus.
Peintre Adrien Guignet. 20.00 F. Rolin Mus.
Renaissance a Autun. G. Vuillemot. 5.00 F. Rolin Mus.

MUSEE ROYAL DE MARIEMONT
Morlanwelz-Mariemont, Belgium.
Antiquites Egyptiennes, Grecques, Etrusques, Romaines et Gallo-Romaines du Musee de Mariemont. B. Van De Walle & P. Leveque. (Illus., 65, Fr.). 1952. 280.00 F. Mus Mariemont.
Collections d'Archeologie Regionale du Musee de Mariemont, 2 vols. G. Faider-Feytmans. (Illus., 151, Fr.). 1100.00 F. Mus Mariemont.
Porcelaines de Tournai du Musee de Mariemont. Christiane Deroubaix. (Illus., 68, Fr.). 1958. 675.00 F. Mus Mariemont.

MUSEE SAINT-JEAN
Angers, France.
Chant Du Monde. Jean Lursat. (Illus., 10 b&w, Fr., Eng. & Ger.). write for info. Mus D'Angers.
Hopital Saint Jean. Viviane Huchard. (Fr. & Eng.). 1975. 5.00 F. Mus D'Angers.

MUSEE SAVOISIEN
Chambery, France.
Archeologia-Prehist. Savoie. 15.00 F. Mus Savoisien.
Archeologie En Savoie. 6.00 F. Mus Savoisien.
Art Baroque En Savoie. 6.00 F. Mus Savoisien.
Art En Savoie. (Prehist. Ser. a). 20.00 F. Mus Savoisien.
Art En Savoie. (Antiquities Ser. B). 20.00 F. Mus Savoisien.
Art En Savoie. (Objets Du Musee Savoisien Ser. E). 20.00 F. Mus Savoisien.
Art et Liturgie Au Moyen Age. 15.00 F. Mus Savoisien.
Art Roman En Savoie. 6.00 F. Mus Savoisien.
Costumes De Savoie. 6.00 F. Mus Savoisien.
Nouvelle Peinture En France. 7.00 F. Mus Savoisien.
Realisme En Allemagne. 11.00 F. Mus Savoisien.

MUSEE TAVET-DELACOUR
Pontoise, France.
Aquarelles et Dessins Du Musee De Pontoise. Jacques Foucart. Ed. by Musee De Pontoise. (Fr.). 1971. pap. write for info. Mus Pontoise.
Bibliotheque, Musee Pontoise Donation Charles Oulmont. Ed. by Musee De Pontoise. (Illus., 9 b&w, Fr.). 1960. pap. 10.00 F. Mus Pontoise.
Donation Freundlich Au Musee De Pontoise. Otto Freundlich & Max Jacob. Ed. by Musee De Pontoise. (Illus., Fr.). 1974. pap. 20.00 F. Mus Pontoise.

MUSEEN DER STADT WIEN
Vienna, Austria.
Fuhrer Durch Die Schausammlung Des Historischen Museums der Stadt Wien. Historischen Museum. (Illus., 8 color, 32 b&w, Ger.). 1975. S.70.00. Museen Wien.

MUSEES D'ARCHEOLOGIE ET D'ARTS DECORATIFS
Liege, Belgium.
Antiquites Egyptiennes et Verres Du Proche-Orient Ancien Des Musees Curtius et Du Verre a Liege. M. Malaise. (Fr.). 1971. 275.00 F. Mus Liegeois.
Antiquites Egyptiennes et Verres Du Proche-Orient Ancien Des Musees Curtius et Du Verre a Liege. M. Malaise. (Illus., Fr.). 1971. 275.00 F. Mus Liegeois.
Musees Curtius et D'Ansembourg. Joseph Philippe. (Illus., Fr.). 1955. 85.00 F. Mus Liegeois.
Musees D'Archeologie et D'Arts Decoratifs De la Ville De Liege. Joseph Philippe. (Illus., Fr.). 1975. 20.00 F. Mus Liegeois.
Tresors Des Musees Liegeois. Joseph Philippe. (Illus., Fr.). 1976. 325.00 F. Mus Liegeois.
Verres Romains Des Musees Curtius et Du Verre. Michel Vanderhoeven. (Illus., Fr.). 1961. 110.00 F. Mus Liegeois.

MUSEES D'AUXERRE
Auxerre, France.
Cones. Pauy. (Fr.). 50.00 F. Mus D'Auxerre.
Faiences De L'Auxerrois. Sineau & Societe Des Amis Des Musees D'Auxerres. (Illus., Fr.). 1978. 60.00 F. Mus D'Auxerre.
Florilege. Societe Des Amis Des Musees D'Auxerre. (Illus., tableaux, Fr.). 10.00 F. Mus D'Auxerre.
Gaviel: Epuise. Ed. by Societe Des Amis Des Musees D'Auxerre. (Fr.). write for info. Mus D'Auxerre.
Monnaies De Bourgogne. George Lelong & Pierre Cuillier. (Fr.). 1970. 5.50 F. Mus D'Auxerre.
Rapaces. Pauy & Gravier. (Fr.). 1975. 6.00 F. Mus D'Auxerre.

MUSEES DE LA VILLE DE TROYES
Troyes, France.
Musee De la Bonneterie. M. Dubuisson. (Illus., 10 b&w plates, Fr.). 3.50 F. Mus Troyes.
Musee De la Bonneterie: Numero Special De la Vie En Champagne. (Illus., 15 b&w, Fr.). 6.00 F. Mus Troyes.
Musee Historique De Troyes et De la Champagne. M. Dubuisson. (Illus., 13 b&w plates, Fr.). 5.00 F. Mus Troyes.
Musees De Troyes. M. Dubuisson. (Illus., 2 color plates, 9 b&w plates, Fr.). 2.50 F. Mus Troyes.
Orry et Natoire: Orry & Natoire. (Illus., 10 b&w, Fr.). 10.00 F. Mus Troyes.
Pharmacie-Musee De L'Hotel-Dieu-le-Comte. (Illus., 9 color plates, 40 b&w, Fr.). write for info. Mus Troyes.
Sculptures Medievales. M. Dubuisson. (Illus., 13 b&w plates, Fr.). 4.00 F. Mus Troyes.

MUSEES ROYAUX DES BEAUX-ARTS DE BELGIQUE
Brussels, Belgium.
Permanent Collections: One Hundred Masterpieces of Ancient Art. (Fr., Dutch, Eng. & Ger.). 250.00 F. Mus Roy Belgique.

MUSEET ETT HEM
Turku, Finland.
Museet Ett Hem. Rolf Nummelin. Tr. by Margaret Jokinen. (Swed. & Finnish.). 1971. Kr.3.00. Ett Hem Mus.

MUSEI VATICANI
Vatican, Vatican City.
Papstlichen Sammlungen Im Vatikan und Lateran. Wolfgang Helbig. Ed. by Hermine Speier. (Fuhrer Durch Die Offentlichen Sammlungen Klassischer Altertumer in Rom Ser). (Ger.). 1963. write for info. Ernst Wasmuth.
Vasi Italioti Ed Etruschi a Figure Rossi E Di Eta Ellenistica. Aurthur D. Trendall. (Vasi Antichi Dipinti Del Vaticano, 3 Ser). (Illus., 20 b&w, It.). 1976. L.20000.00. Vatican.
Vasi Italioti Ed Etruschi a Figure Rosse, Vol. 1. Aurthur D. Trendall. (Illus., 38 b&w, It.). 1953. L.10000.00. Vatican.
Vasi Italioti Ed Etruschi a Figure Rossi, Vol. 2. Arthur D. Trendall. (Illus., 68 b&w, It.). 1955. L.25000.00. Vatican.

MUSEO ARCHEOLOGICO NAZIONALE DI NAPOLI
Naples, Italy.
Arti Decorative Del Museo Nazionale Di Napoli E a Pompei. V. Spinazzola. (It.). write for info. Mus Arc Napoli.
Catalogo Del Museo Nazionale Di Napoli, Colleziona Santangelo. G. Fiorelli. (It.). write for info. Mus Arc Napoli.
Catalogo Della Raccolta Epigrafica, I, Iscrizioni Greche Ed Italiche. G. Fiorelli. (It.). write for info. Mus Arc Napoli.
Catalogo Della Raccolta Epigrafica, II, Iscrizioni Latine. G. Fiorelli. (It.). write for info. Mus Arc Napoli.
Catalogo Della Raccolta Pornografica. G. Fiorelli. (It.). write for info. Mus Arc Napoli.
Catalogo Delle Armi. G. Fiorelli. (It.). write for info. Mus Arc Napoli.
Catalogo Delle Oreficerie Del Museo Nazionale Di Napoli. L. Breglia. (It.). write for info. Mus Arc Napoli.
Ceramiche Delle Fabbriche Tarde. A. Rocco. (It.). write for info. Mus Arc Napoli.
Creficeria, Toreutica, Glittica, Vitraria, Ceramica in Itinerari Dei Musei E Monumenti. G. Pesce. (It.). write for info. Mus Arc Napoli.
Gemme Medice Del Museo Nazionale Di Napoli, in Riv.1st Arch. E St. Dell 'arte. G. Pesce. (It.). write for info. Mus Arc Napoli.
Gli Ori E le Ambre Del Museo Nazionale Di Napoli. V. Siviero. (It.). write for info. Mus Arc Napoli.
Guida Del Museo Nazionale Di Napoli. A. De Franciscis. (It.). write for info. Mus Arc Napoli.
Guida Illustrata Del Museo Nazionale Di Napoli. A. Ruesch. (It.). write for info. Mus Arc Napoli.
Medagliere, Monete Romane. G. Fiorelli. (It.). write for info. Mus Arc Napoli.
Monete Del Medio Evo E Moderne. G. Fiorelli. (It.). write for info. Mus Arc Napoli.
Museo Nazionale Di Napoli. B. Maiuri. (It.). write for info. Mus Arc Napoli.
Pitture Murali E Mosaici Del Museo Nazionale Zu Neapel. C. Elia. (It.). write for info. Mus Arc Napoli.
Pompei. Gennaio-Marzo Parigi. (It.). write for info. Mus Arc Napoli.
Terrecotte Figurate Del Museo Nazionale Di Napoli. A. Levi. (It.). write for info. Mus Arc Napoli.
Vasi Di Stile Attico a Figure Nere. A. Adriani. (It.). write for info. Mus Arc Napoli.

MUSEO ARQUEOLOGICO DE TOLEDO
Toledo, Spain.
Museo Arqueologico De Toledo. Manuel Jorge Aragoneses. Ed. by Ministerio De Educacion y Ciencia. (Illus., 43 b&w, Span.). 1958. 50.00 ptas. Pat Nac Mus.

MUSEO CAPITOLARE
Atri, Italy.
Antiche Ceramiche D'Abruzzo Nel Museo Capitolare Di Atri. Franceschilli Vincenzo. Ed. by Bruno Trubiani. (Illus., 32 color, 92 b&w, It.). 1976. pap. $6.00. Capitolare Atri.

Westafrikanische Plastik 2. (Ger.). DM.22.00. Blaschker Verlag.
Westafrikanische Plastik 3. (Ger.). DM.30.00. Blaschker Verlag.
Westafrikansche Masken. (Ger.). DM.13.00. Blaschker Verlag.
Westmexikanische Keramik. (Ger.). DM.26.00. Blaschker Verlag.

MUSEUM FUR VOR UND FRUHGESCHICTE
Berlin, Germany, West.
Eisenverhuttung Vor 2000 Jahren. (Ger.). DM.14.00. Blaschker Verlag.
Fruhe Eauern und Schriftkulturen. (Ger.). DM.6.00. Blaschker Verl.
Steinzeit und Fruhe Stactkultur. (Ger.). DM.6.00. Blaschker Verlag.

MUSEUM HET REMBRANDT-HUIS
Amsterdam, The Netherlands.
Rembrandt Etchings & Drawings in the Rembrandt House. P. Filedkok. Ed. by P. W. Van Doorne & K. G. Boon. Tr. by Gary Schwartz. (Illus., 106 photos.). 1972. pap. fl.10.00. Rembrandt-Huis.

MUSEUM IN DER WILLIBALSDBURG
Eichstatt, Germany, West.
Willibaldsburg Eichstatt. Manfred S. Fischer. (Ger.). 1977. DM.1.50. Bayer Verwal.

MUSEUM LUDWIG
see Wallraf-Richartz-Museum

MUSEUM MAYEN VAN DEN BERGH
Antwerp, Belgium.
Beknopte Gids. H. Nieuwdorp. Ed. by Museum Mayer Van Den Bergh. (Dutch, Fr., Eng. & Ger.). 1979. pap. 50.00 F. Van Den Bergh.
Catalogus Museum Mayer Van Den Bergh, Vol. 1. J. De Coo. Ed. by Museum Mayer Van Den Bergh. (Illus., 29 color, 38 b&w, Dutch.). 1978. pap. 300.00 F. Van Den Bergh.
Catalogus Museum Mayer Van Den Bergh, Vol. 2. J. De Coo. Ed. by Museum Mayer Van Den Bergh. (Illus., 6 color, 471 b&w, Dutch.). 1969. pap. 300.00 F. Van Den Bergh.

MUSEUM OF AFRICAN ART
Washington, D.C.
African Art in Washington Collections. Intro. by Warren Robbins. (Illus., 114). 1973. $5.00. Mus Afr Art.
African Art: The Dehavenon Collection. (Illus., 6 color plates, 290 photos). 1971. $15.00. Mus Afr Art.
Language of African Art. (Illus., 57). 1976. $5.00. Mus Afr Art.
Sculptor's Eye: The African Art Collection of Chaim Gross. Intro. by Arnold Rubin. (Illus., 118). 1976. $8.00. Mus Afr Art.
Survey of Zairian Art: The Bronson Collection. Joseph Cornet. (Illus., 207). 1978. $78.60. Mus Afr Art.
Traditional Art of the Nigerian Peoples: The Ratner Collection. Intro. by Henry J. Drewal. (Illus., 57). 1977. $6.50. Mus Afr Art.

MUSEUM OF ARCHAEOLOGY
Anuradhapura, Sri Lanka.
Illustrated Guide to the Museum of Archaeology, Anuradhapura, Sri Lanka. Jayantha Uduwara. (Illus., 19 b&w). 1962. Rs.3.50. Mus Anuradhap.

MUSEUM OF EARLY SOUTHERN DECORATIVE ARTS
Winston-Salem, North Carolina.
Museum of Early Southern Decorative Arts. Jan Hind. (Illus., 25 color, 124 b&w). 1979. $10.00; pap. $7.50. Mus South Deco.

MUSEUM OF FINE ARTS
Boston, Massachusetts.
American Paintings in the Museum of Fine Arts, 2 vols. Intro. by Perry T. Rathbone. LC 68-27634. (Illus., 24 color plates, 607 b&w). 1968. $30.00, boxed. Mus Fine Arts.
American Pewter in the Museum of Fine Arts, Boston. Intro. by Jonathan Fairbanks. (Illus., 320 b&w). 1974. pap. $5.95 (ISBN 0-87846-080-2). Mus Fine Arts.
American Silver in the Museum of Fine Arts, Boston, 2 vols. Kathryn C. Buhler. (Illus., 650 b&w photos). 1972. $45.00, slipcase (ISBN 0-87846-064-0); pap. $20.00. Mus Fine Arts.
Ancient Egypt. William S. Smith. LC 60-13944. (Illus., 4 color plates, 130 b&w). 1960. pap. $4.50. Mus Fine Arts.
Ancient Glass in Museum of Fine Arts, Boston. Axel Von Saldern. LC 67-31751. (Illus., 7 color plates, 63 b&w). 1968. pap. $2.95. Mus Fine Arts.
Catalogue of Greek Coins. Frwd. by Agnes Brett & Mary Comstock. 1955. $35.00 (ISBN 0-915018-04-7). Mus Fine Arts.
Charles B. Hoyt Collection of Chinese Art, Vol. 1. Hsien-Ch'I Tseng & Robert P. Dart. (Illus., 40 color, 128 b&w). 1964. $22.00 (ISBN 0-87846-059-4). Mus Fine Arts.
Charles B. Hoyt Collection of Chinese Art, Vol. 2. Hsien-Ch'I Tseng & Robert P. Dart. LC 66-1343. (Illus., 44 color , 107 b&w). 1972. $38.00 (ISBN 0-87846-059-4). Mus Fine Arts.
Corot to Braque. Ann L. Poulet. LC 79-1719. (Illus., 69 color plates, 12 b&w). 1979. $19.50 (ISBN 0-87846-134-5); pap. $11.95. Mus Fine Arts.
Corpus Vasorum Antiquorum, No. 14. Herbert Hoffmann et al. (Illus., 17, 58 collotype plates, 51 profile drawings). 1973. $30.00, boxed (ISBN 0-87846-065-9). Mus Fine Arts.
Corpus Vasorum Antiquorum, No. 19. Marion True et al. (Illus., 50 collotype plates). 1978. $40.00, boxed (ISBN 0-87846-122-1). Mus Fine Arts.
Forsyth Wickes Collection. Perry T. Rathbone. (Illus., 17 color plates, 70 b&w). 1968. $9.50; pap. $3.00. Mus Fine Arts.
Greek, Etruscan & Roman Art. Mary Comstock & Cornelius Vermeule. (Illus., 4 color, 289 b&w). 1972. pap. $3.75. Mus Fine Arts.
Greek, Etruscan & Roman Bronzes in the Museum of Fine Arts, Boston. Mary B. Comstock & Cornelius Vermeule. (Illus., 800 b&w). 1971. $35.00 (ISBN 0-87846-060-8). Mus Fine Arts.
M & M Karolik Collection of American Watercolors & Drawings, 1800-1875, 2 vols. Henry P. Rossiter. LC 62-21319. (Illus., 35 color plates, 564 b&w). 1962. $30.00, boxed. Mus Fine Arts.
Monet in the Museum of Fine Arts, Boston. Intro. by John Walsh, Jr. & Jan Fontein. LC 77-90530. (Illus., 39 color plates). 1977. pap. $5.00 (ISBN 0-87846-121-3). Mus Fine Arts.
Museum of Fine Arts Handbook. Ed. by Museum of Fine Arts. LC 75-21769. (Illus., 12 color plates, 512 b&w). 1975. pap. $3.50. Mus Fine Arts.
Sculpture in Stone in the Museum of Fine Arts, Boston. Mary Comstock & Cornelius Vermeule. (Illus., 465 b&w). 1976. $35.00 (ISBN 0-87846-103-5); pap. $15.00. Mus Fine Arts.
Tapestries of Europe & of Colonial Peru in the Museum of Fine Arts, Boston. Adolph Cavallo. LC 67-17672. (Illus., 41 color plates, 127 b&w). 1968. $17.50, boxed. Mus Fine Arts.
Western Art in the Museum of Fine Arts. Adolph S. Cavallo et al. LC 74-10138. (Illus., 110 color plates, 44 b&w). 1971. $27.50 (ISBN 0-87846-054-3). Mus Fine Arts.

MUSEUM OF FINE ARTS
Istanbul, Turkey.
Istanbul Resim Heykel Muzesi. Devrim Erbil. (Illus., 50 b&w, Turk.). pap. P.T.12.50. Mus Fi Art Ist.
Istanbul Resim Ve Heykel Muzesi. Nurullah Berk. (Sanat Kitaplari Ser., 1). (Illus., 140 color, 6 b&w, Turk. & Eng.). 1972. $1.00. Mus Fi Art Ist.

MUSEUM OF INTERNATIONAL FOLK ART
Museum of New Mexico, Museum of International Folk Art.
Palestinian Costume & Jewelry. Yedida Stillman. 1979. $14.95. U of NM Pr.

MUSEUM OF IOANNINA
Ioannina, Greece.
Brief Guide to the Museum of Joannina. I. P. Vokotopoulou. (Gr.). write for info. Genl Dir Antiq.

MUSEUM OF MODERN ART
New York, New York.
Matisse in the Collection of the Museum of Modern Art. John Elderfield. (Illus., 34 color, 240 b&w). 1978. $25.00 (ISBN 0-87070-470-2); pap. $12.50 (ISBN 0-87070-471-0). Museum Mod Art.
Miro in the Collection of the Museum of Modern Art. William S. Rubin. (Illus., 22 color, 113 b&w). 1973. $17.50 (ISBN 0-87070-463-X); pap. $8.95 (ISBN 0-87070-462-1). Museum Mod Art.
Painting & Sculpture in the Museum of Modern Art: Catalog of the Collection 1977. Alicia Legg. 1977. pap. $6.95 (ISBN 0-87070-544-X). Museum Mod Art.
Painting & Sculpture in the Museum of Modern Art 1929-1967. Alfred H. Barr, Jr. (Illus., 1195 b&w). 1977. $40.00 (ISBN 0-87070-540-7). Museum Mod Art.
Picasso in the Collection of the Museum of Modern Art. William S. Rubin. (Illus., 49 color, 258 b&w). 1972. $15.00 (ISBN 0-87070-537-7). Museum Mod Art.

MUSEUM OF MODERN ART, HYOGO
Kobe, Japan.
Foriegn Prints in the Collection of Museum of Modern Art, Hyogo. (Illus., 488, Eng. & Jap.). 1977. $7.50. Hyogo Mod Mus.

MUSEUM OF NEW MEXICO, MUSEUM OF FINE ARTS
Santa Fe, New Mexico.
Museum of New Mexico, Museum of Fine Arts: Handbook of the Collection. (Illus.). 1974. free. Mus Nm Arts.

MUSEUM OF THE AMERICAN INDIAN, HUNTINGTON FREE LIBRARY
Bronx, New York.
Dictionary Catalog of the American Indian Collection. Ruth N. Wilcox. $350.00 (ISBN 0-8161-0065-9). G K Hall.

MUSEUM OF THE GREAT PLAINS
Lawton, Oklahoma.
Historical Guide to Wagon Hardware & Blacksmith Supplies. Ed. by Towana Spivey. (Illus.). 1979. write for info. Mus Great Plai.
Women's World: A Patchwork in Time & Space. Maryruth Prose & Barbara McQuitty. (Illus., 17 photos). 1978. pap. $1.50. Mus Great Plai.

MUSEUM RIETBERG ZURICH
Zurich, Switzerland.
Aegyptische Textilien. Peter. (Illus., 2 color, 149 b&w, Ger.). 1976. 20.00 F. Mus Rietberg.
Afrikanische Skulpturen. Leuzinger. (Illus., Ger.). 1978. 28.00 F. Mus Rietberg.
Chinesische Skulpturen. Siren. (Illus., Ger.). 1959. 20.00 F. Mus Rietberg.
Indische Skulpturen. Lohuizen. (Illus., 116 b&w, Ger.). 1961. 28.00 F. Mus Rietberg.
Japanische Holzschnitte. Brasch. (Illus., Ger.). 1965. 20.00 F. Mus Rietberg.
Kunst der Indianer Amerikas. Haberland. (Illus., Ger.). 1971. 28.00 F. Mus Rietberg.
Kunst der Sudsee. Buhler. (Illus., Ger.). 1969. 28.00 F. Mus Rietberg.
Wegleitung. Leuzinger. (Illus., 94 b&w, Ger.). 10.00 F. Mus Rietberg.

MUSEUM VOOR RELIGIEUZE KUNST
Sint-Truiden, Belgium.
Cologne Cathedral. Walter Schulten. (Illus.). pap. write for info. Greven Verlag.
Kostbarkeiten in Koln. Walter Schulten. (Illus., Ger.). 1978. pap. write for info. Greven Verlag.
Oude Kunst Uit De Verzameling Van De Vrienden Van Het Begijnhof Te Sint-Truiden. C. G. De Dijn. (Illus., Dutch.). 1974. pap. write for info. Documentatie.
Oude Muurschilderingen Van De Bigijnhofkerk Te Sint-Truiden. M. Buyle & C. G. De Dijn. (Kunst & Oudheden in Limburg). (Illus., 31 b&w, Dutch.). 1974. 100.00 F. Documentatie.
Treasury of Cologne Cathedral. (Illus.). pap. write for info. Greven Verlag.

MUZEJ NA SOVREMENATA UMETNOST SKOPJE
Skopje, Yugoslavia.
Izlozeni Grafiki Od Kolekcija Na Msu. Ljubica Damjanovska & Sonja Abadzieva Dimitrova. Ed. by Musej Na Sovremenata Umetnost Skopje. (Illus., 26 b&w, Macedonian & Fr.). 1970. pap. write for info. Muz Skopje.
Izlozeni Sliki I Skulpturi Od Kolekcijata Na Msu. Ljubica Damjanovska & Sonja Abadzieva Dimitrova. Ed. by Muzej Na Sovremenata Umetnost Skopje. (Illus., 74 b&w, Macedonian & Fr.). 1970. pap. 30.00 din. Muz Skopje.
Prilig Kon II Varijantata Na Postojanata Postavka Vo Muzejot Na Sovremenata Umetnost - Skopje. Ljubica Damjanovska. Ed. by Musej Na Sovremenata Umetnost Skopje. (Macedonian & Fr.). 1976. pap. write for info. Muz Skopje.

MUZEUL DE ISTORIE NATIONALA SI ARCHEOLOGIE CONSTANTA
Constanta, Romania.
Goutica. (Rumanian.). 40.00 lei. Muz Constanta.
Guide Book for the Museum. (Fr., Eng., Ger., Rus. & Rumanian.). 3.00 lei. Muz Constanta.

MUZEUM ARCHEOLOGICZNE I ETNOGRAFICZNE W LODZI
Lodz, Poland.
Japonski Strj Naodowy W Zbiorach Muzeum Archeologicznego I Etnograficznego W Lodz. Maria Halina Czurko. Ed. by I. Lechowa & T. Laszczemska. (Illus., 60 drawings & photos, 2 color plates, Pol.). 1980. pap. write for info. Muz Arch Lodz.
Katalog Garncarstwa Ludowego Woj. Rzeszowskiego. Ed. by Janina Krajewska. (Illus., 128 b&w photos, Pol., Rus., Fr. & Eng.). 1952. pap. 17.00 Zl. Muz Arch Lodz.

MUZEUM ARCHIDIECEZJALNE WE WROCLAWIU
Wroclaw, Poland.
Katalog Nabytkow Muzeum Archidiecezjalnego we Wroclawiu w Latach 1973-1977: Archiwa, Biblioteki i Muzea Koscielne. Jozef Pater. (Pol.). 1977. write for info. Muz Arch Wroc.
Medale Papiezy w Zbiorach Muzeum Archidiecezjalnego we Wroclawiu: Colloquium Salutis. Wincenty Urban. (Pol.). 1974. write for info. Muz Arch Wroc.
Muzeum Archidiecezjalne we Wroclawiuoraz Katalog Jego Zbiorow: Archiwa, Biblioteki i Muzea Koscielne. Wincenty Urban. (Pol.). write for info. Muz Arch Wroc.
Nabytki Muzeum Archidiecezjalnego we Wroclawiu w 1978 Roku: Wroclawskie Wiadomosci Koscielne. Jozef Pater. (Pol.). 1979. write for info. Muz Arch Wroc.
Zachowane Monety i Medale Biskupow Wroclawskich w Muzeum Archidiecezjalnym we Wroclawiu: Archiwa, Biblioteki i Muzea Koscielne. Wincenty Urban. (Pol.). 1977. write for info. Muz Arch Wroc.
Zbiory Medalierskie w Muzeum Archidiecezjalnym we Wroclawiu w 1978 Roku: Wroclawskie Wiadomosci Koscielne. Wincenty Urban. (Pol.). 1979. write for info. Muz Arch Wroc.

MUZEUM BUDOWNICTWA LUDOWEGO
Sanok, Poland.
Musee De L'Architecture Populaire De Sanok. (Illus., Fr. & Rus.). 1976. pap. write for info. Muz Bud Lud.
Museum of Folk Building at Sanok. (Illus., Eng. & Ger.). 1976. pap. write for info. Muz Bud Lud.
Muzeum Budownictwa Ludowego W Sanoku. (Illus., Pol.). 1978. pap. write for info. Muz Bud Lud.

MUZEUM MAZOWIECKIE W PLOCKU
Plock, Poland.
Moneta Sredniowieczna Na Ziemiach Polskicht. Elzbieta Jedrysek-Migdalska. Ed. by Masovian Museum. (Illus., 35 b&w, Pol.). 1979. write for info. Mazowieckie.
Szkto Katalog Zbiorow Secesyi Muzeum Mazowieckiego W Plocku. Krzysztof Kornacki. Ed. by Masovian Museum. (Illus., 20 color, 349 b&w, Pol.). 1978. write for info. Mazowieckie.

MUZEUM NARODOWE W KIELCACH
Kielce, Poland.
Muzeum Swietokryyskie w Kielcach, Zbiory Malarstwa Polskiego. Katalog. Barbara Modrzejewska & Alojzy Oborny. Ed. by Muzeum Swietokrzyskie. Tr. by Jan Prokop. (Illus., 8 color plates, 121 b&w photos, Pol.). 1971. 100.00 Zl. Muz Narod Kiel.
Portret Sarmacki, Ze Zbiorow Muzeum Narodowego w Kielcach: Katalog. Wieslawa Ozdoba-Kosierkiewicz. Ed. by National Museum in Kielce. (Illus., 10 b&w photos, Pol.). 1977. pap. 20.00 Zl. Muz Narod Kiel.
Wspolczesna Rzezba Ludowa Ze Zbioroow Muzeumm Narodowego w Kielcach. Barbara Katarzyna Erber. Ed. by National Museum in Kielce. (Illus., 42 b&w photos, Pol.). 1978. pap. 40.00 Zl. Muz Narod Kiel.

MUZEUM NARODOWE W KRAKOWIE
Krakow, Poland.
Amulety Egipskie. Joachim Sliwa. Ed. by National Museum in Cracow. (Male Katalogi Zabytkow Wybranych Ser., NR 6). (Illus., 73 b&w, Pol.). 1976. 40.00 Zl. Muz Narod Kra.
Bron Palna Europejska. Adam Labinowicz. Ed. by Muzeum Narodowe W Krakowie. (Male Katalogi Zabytkow Wybranych Ser., Nr 1). (Illus., 59 b&w, Pol.). 1966. 20.00 Zl. Muz Narod Kra.
Ikony. Janina Klosinska. Ed. by National Museum in Cracow. (Katalogi Zbiorow Tom Ser., I). (Illus., 6 color, 216 b&w, Pol. & Fr.). 1973. 220.00 Zl. Muz Narod Kra.
Katalog Dokumentow Pergaminowych Biblioteki Czartoryskich W Krakowie 1148-1506. Waclawa Szelinska & Janina Tomaszewicz. Ed. by National Museum in Cracow. (Pol.). 1975. 250.00 Zl. Muz Narod Kra.
Katalog Galerii Malarstwa I Rzezby Polskiej Wieku 20. Helena Blum et al. Ed. by National Museum in Cracow. (Illus., 64 b&w, Pol.). 1963. write for info. Muz Narod Kra.
Laka Japonska. Zofia Alberowa. Ed. by National Museum in Cracow. (Male Katalogi Zabytkow Wybrnych Ser., NR 3). (Illus., 60 b&w, Pol.). 1968. 25.00 Zl. Muz Narod Kra.
Stare Srebra. Jadwiga Bujanska. (Male Katalogi Zabytkow Wybranych Ser., NR 4). (Illus., 43 b&w, Pol.). 1972. 25.00 Zl. Muz Narod Kra.
Ubiory I Akcesoria Mody Wieku 19. Maria Rychlewska & Maria Taszycka. Ed. by National Museum Cracow. (Male Katalogi Zabytkow Wybranych Ser., NR 2). (Illus., 50 b&w, Pol.). 1967. 25.00 Zl. Muz Narod Kra.
Uzbrojenie Dawnej Japonii. Maria Dzieduszcka & Stanislaw Kobielski. (Male Katalogi Zabytkow Wybranych Ser., Nr 5). (Illus., 48 b&w, Pol.). 1974. 40.00 Zl. Muz Narod Kra.

MUZEUM NARODOWE W POZNANIU
Poznan, Poland.
Katalog Instrumentow Muzycznych. Zdzislaw Szulc. Ed. by Muzeum Wielkopolskie. (Illus., 20, Pol.). 1949. write for info. Muz Narod Poz.
Malarstwo Flamandzkie XVII-XVIII W. Katalog Zbiorow: Flemish Painting. Anna Dobrzycka. Ed. by Muzeum Narodowe. (Illus., 41, Pol.). 15.00 Zl. Muz Narod Poz.
Malarstwo Holenderskie XVII-XVIII W. Katalog Zbiorow: Dutch Painting. (Illus., 117, Pol.). 1958. 20.00 Zl. Muz Narod Poz.

MUZEUM NARODOWE W SZCZECINIE
Szczecin, Poland.
Andezej Zywicki, 1928-1970. (Illus., Pol.). 1977. pap. write for info. Muz Narod Szc.
Budownictwo Okretowe. (Illus., Pol.). pap. write for info. Muz Narod Szc.
Moderne Polsk Kunst Fra Ostersokysten. Jadwiga Najdowa. (Illus., color, b&w, Pol.). 1978. pap. write for info. Muz Narod Szc.
Plastyka Gotycka Na Pomorzu Zachodnim. (Pol.). 1962. pap. write for info. Muz Narod Szc.
Polish Maritime Graphic Art. Jadwiga Najdowa. 1974. pap. write for info. Muz Narod Szc.
Portret W Malarstwie, Pomorza Zachodniego. (Pol.). 1978. pap. write for info. Muz Narod Szc.
Przewodnik Po Wystawie. (Illus., Pol.). pap. write for info. Muz Narod Szc.

Masterpieces of Chinese Jade in the National Palace Museum: Supplement. (Illus., 50 color plates, Chin., Jap. & Eng.). $10.50. Nat Palace Mus.
Masterpieces of Chinese Miniature Crafts in the National Palace Museum. (Illus., 50 color plates, Chin., Jap. & Eng.). $10.50. Nat Palace Mus.
Masterpieces of Chinese Painting in the National Palace Museum. (Illus., 50 color plates, Chin., Jap. & Eng.). $10.50. Nat Palace Mus.
Masterpieces of Chinese Painting in the National Palace Museum: Supplement. (Illus., 50 color plates, Chin., Jap. & Eng.). $10.50. Nat Palace Mus.
Masterpieces of Chinese Porcelain in the National Palace Museum. (Illus., 50 color plates, Chin., Jap. & Eng.). $10.50. Nat Palace Mus.
Masterpieces of Chinese Porcelain in the National Palace Museum: Supplement. (Illus., 50 color plates, Chin., Jap. & Eng.). $10.50. Nat Palace Mus.
Masterpieces of Chinese Portrait Painting in the National Palace Museum. (Illus., 50 color plates, Chin., Jap. & Eng.). $10.50. Nat Palace Mus.
Masterpieces of Chinese Seal in the National Palace Museum. (Illus., 50 color plates, Chin., Jap. & Eng.). $10.50. Nat Palace Mus.
Masterpieces of Chinese Silk Tapestry & Embroidery in the National Palace Museum. (Illus., 50 color plates, Chin., Jap. & Eng.). $10.50. Nat Palace Mus.
Masterpieces of Chinese Tibetan Buddhist Altar Fittings in the National Palace Museum. (Illus., 50 color plates, Chin., Jap. & Eng.). $10.50. Nat Palace Mus.
Masterpieces of Chinese Writing Materials in the National Palace Museum. (Illus., 50 color plates, Chin., Jap. & Eng.). $10.50. Nat Palace Mus.
Masterpieces of Ju-I Scepter in the National Palace Museum. (Illus., 50 color plates, Chin., Jap. & Eng.). $10.50. Nat Palace Mus.
Masterpieces of Snuff Bottle in the National Palace Museum. (Illus., 50 color plates, Chin., Jap. & Eng.). $10.50. Nat Palace Mus.
Ming Dynasty. (Select Chinese Paintings in the National Palace Museum Collection Ser., Vols. 7 & 8). (Illus., 5 color plates, 46 b&w plates). $18.50 ea. Nat Palace Mus.
Select Chinese Rare Books & Historical Documents in the National Palace Museum. (Illus., 50 color plates, Chin., Jap. & Eng.). $10.50. Nat Palace Mus.
Selection of Masterworks in the National Palace Museum. (Illus., 150 color, b&w plates, Chin. & Eng.). $4.00. Nat Palace Mus.
Selection of Tapestry & Embroidery of the National Palace Museum, 2 vols. & 2 supplementary vols. (Chin., Jap. & Eng.). $316.00 set. Nat Palace Mus.
Series of Select Chinese Painting in the National Palace Museum, 10 vols. (Illus., 5 color, 45 b&w, Chin.). write for info. Nat Palace Mus.
Series of Select Chinese Painting in the National Palace Museum Collection, Vol. 1. (Illus., 5 color, 45 b&w, Chin.). $19.55. Nat Palace Mus.
Series of Select Chinese Painting in the National Palace Museum Collection, Vol. 2. (Illus., 5 color, 45 b&w, Chin.). $19.55. Nat Palace Mus.
Series of Select Chinese Painting in the National Palace Museum Collection, Vol. 3. (Illus., 5 color, 45 b&w, Chin.). $19.55. Nat Palace Mus.
Series of Select Chinese Painting in the National Palace Museum Collection, Vol. 4. (Illus., 5 color, 45 b&w, Chin.). $19.55. Nat Palace Mus.
Series of Select Chinese Painting in the National Palace Museum Collection, Vol. 5. (Illus., 5 color, 45 b&w, Chin.). $19.55. Nat Palace Mus.
Series of Select Chinese Painting in the National Palace Museum Collection, Vol. 6. (Illus., 5 color, 45 b&w, Chin.). $19.55. Nat Palace Mus.
Series of Select Chinese Painting in the National Palace Museum Collection, Vol. 7. (Illus., 5 color, 45 b&w, Chin.). $19.55. Nat Palace Mus.
Series of Select Chinese Painting in the National Palace Museum Collection, Vol. 8. (Illus., 5 color, 45 b&w, Chin.). $19.55. Nat Palace Mus.
Series of Select Chinese Painting in the National Palace Museum Collection, Vol. 9. (Illus., 5 color, 45 b&w, Chin.). $19.55. Nat Palace Mus.
Series of Select Chinese Painting in the National Palace Museum Collection, Vol. 10. (Illus., 5 color, 45 b&w, Chin.). $19.55. Nat Palace Mus.
Southern Sung Dynasty. (Select Chinese Paintings in the National Palace Museum Collection Ser., Vols. 3 & 4). (Illus., 5 color plates, 46 b&w plates). $18.50 ea. Nat Palace Mus.
T'ang, Five Dynasties & Northern Sung Dynasty. (Select Chinese Paintings in the National Palace Museum Collection Ser., Vols. 1 & 2). (Illus., 5 color plates, 46 b&w plates). $18.50 ea. Nat Palace Mus.
Three Hundred Masterpieces of Chinese Painting in the National Palace Museum, 6 vols. (Illus., 43 color chromolithographic plates & collotypeprinting, Chin. & Eng.). $211.00 set. Nat Palace Mus.
Yuan Dynasty. (Select Chinese Paintings in the National Palace Museum Collection Ser., Vols. 5 & 6). (Illus., 5 color plates, 46 b&w plates). $18.50 ea. Nat Palace Mus.

NATIONAL PORTRAIT GALLERY
London, United Kingdom.
Concise Illustrated Catalogue of National Portrait Gallery Portraits. K. K. Yung. (Illus., 5 color, 500 b&w). 1980. write for info. Nat Port Gal Lon.

NATIONAL PORTRAIT GALLERY, SMITHSONIAN INSTITUTION
Washington, D.C.
Permanent Collection Illustrated Checklist. Compiled by Linda T. Neumaier & Marvin Sadik. (Illus., 1267 b&w photos). 1978. $25.00; pap. $5.50. Smithsonian.

NATIONALGALERIE
Berlin, Germany, West.
Antoni Tapies. (Ger.). DM.26.00. Blaschker Verlag.
Beuys-Richtkrafte. (Ger.). DM.26.00. Blaschker Verlag.
Drei Berliner Kunstler: Fussmann, Hoffmann und Waldenburg. (Ger.). DM.8.00. Blaschker Verlag.
Drei Berliner Kunstler: Horst, Hirsig und Sax V. Dulmann. (Ger.). DM.12.00. Blaschker Verlag.
E. W. Nay. (Ger.). DM.13.00. Blaschker Verlag.
Freunde Danken Haftmann. (Ger.). DM.30.00. Blaschker Verlag.
Geschicte das Nationalgalerie. (Ger.). DM.8.00. Blaschker Verlag.
Jim Dine. (Ger.). DM.15.00. Blaschker Verlag.
Kleiner Fuhrer Durch Die Nationalgalerie. (Ger.). DM.8.00. Blaschker Verlag.
Nationalgalerie und Ihre Stifter. (Ger.). DM.8.00. Blaschker Verlag.
Willi Baumeister. (Ger.). DM.19.00. Blaschker Verlag.

NATIONALMUSEUM
Stockholm, Sweden.
Aldre Nordiska Malningar Och Skulturer. (Illus., 292). 1952. Kr.18.00; pap. Kr.5.00. Nationalmuseum.
Aldre Utlandska Malningar Och Skulturer. (Illus., 301). 1958. Kr.23.50; pap. Kr.18.00. Nationalmuseum.
Carl Larsson I Nationalmuseum. Gertrud Serner. 1947. Kr.3.50. Nationalmuseum.
Drawings of John Tobias Sergel. Per Bjurstrom & Ulf Cederlof. (Illus., 4 microfiches). 1979. pap. write for info. (ISBN 0-226-69420-8). Nationalmuseum.
Franska 1800-Talsmalare. Ragnar Hoppe. 1936. Kr.3.50. Nationalmuseum.
French Drawings: Sixteenth & Seventeenth Centuries. Per Bjurstrom. (Illus., 297). 1976. Kr.345.00 (ISBN 91-38-02345-8). Nationalmuseum.
German Drawings. Per Bjurstrom. (Illus., 232). 1972. Kr.295.00 (ISBN 91-38-01352-5). Nationalmuseum.
Graverade Glas I Nationalmusei Samlingar. Carl Hernmarck. 1946. Kr.3.50. Nationalmuseum.
Italian Drawings. Per Bjurstrom. (Illus., 210). 1979. Kr.355.00 (ISBN 91-38-03982-6). Nationalmuseum.
Malningar Pa Nationalmuseum. Britta Birnbaum. (Illus., 40 color, Eng. & Ger.). 1976. pap. Kr.28.00. Nationalmuseum.
Nationalmusei Guider. Kr.2.00. Nationalmuseum.
Nationalmusei Guider. (Swed.). Kr.2.00. Nationalmuseum.
Nationalmusei Guider. (Tyska.). Kr.2.00. Nationalmuseum.
Porslinsfabriken I Meissen Och Dess Produkter I Nationalmuseum. Carl Hernmarck. 1930. Kr.3.50. Nationalmuseum.
Svenskt Silver 1580-1800 I Nationalmusei Samlingar. Carl Hernmarck. 1951. Kr.8.00. Nationalmuseum.

NEUE GALERIE DER STADT LINZ WOLFGANG-GURLITT-MUSEUM
Linz, Austria.
Museum Permanent Collection. (Illus., 100 color, 250 b&w, Ger.). 1979. write for info. Neue Gal Linz.

NEUE RESIDENZ BAMBERG
Bamberg, Germany, West.
Neue Residenz Bamberg. Erich Bachmann & Albrecht Miller. (Ger.). 1974. DM.2.00. Bayer Verwal.

NEUES SCHLOSS BAYREUTH
Bayreuth, Germany, West.
Neues Schloss Bayreuth. Erich Bachmann. (Ger.). 1972. DM.2.00. Bayer Verwal.

NEUES SCHLOSS SCHLEISHEIM UND STAATSGALERIE
Oberschleissheim, Germany, West.
Neues Schloss Schleissheim. Gerhard Hojer. (Ger.). 1976. DM.2.00. Bayer Verwal.

NEUES SCHLOSS UND LUDWIG-II MUSEUM
Herrenchiemsee, Germany, West.
Chateau De Herrenchiemsee. Michael Petzet. (Fr.). 1976. DM.2.00. Bayer Verwal.
Herrenchiemsee Palace. Michael Petzet. 1975. DM.2.00. Bayer Verwal.
Neues Schloss Herrenchiemsee. Michael Petzet & Gerhard Hojer. (Ger.). 1976. DM.2.00. Bayer Verwal.

NEW JERSEY HISTORICAL SOCIETY
Newark, New Jersey.
Historic American Buildings Survey of New Jersey: Catalog of Measured Drawings, Photographs & Written Documents in the Survey. William B. Bassett. Ed. by John Poppeliers. (Illus.). 1977. $13.95; pap. $9.95. NJ Hist Soc.
New Jersey Medicine in the Revolutionary Era, 1763-1787. Ed. by Robert C. Morris. (Illus., 5 photos). 1976. pap. $2.00. NJ Hist Soc.
Wayne B. Yarnall Maritime Collection at the New Jersey Historical Society. Compiled by Alan D. Frazer. 1979. pap. $4.50. NJ Hist Soc.

NEW ORLEANS MUSEUM OF ART
New Orleans, Louisiana.
Art Collection of Mr. & Mrs. Chapman H. Hyams. Robert B. Mayfield. (Illus., 41, 3 color plates). 1964. pap. $1.00. New Orleans Mus.
Decade of Glass Collecting: Selections from the Melvin Billups Collection. Paul N. Perrot. LC 62-17708. (Illus., 100). 1962. pap. $1.50. New Orleans Mus.
Diverse Images: Photographs from the New Orleans Museum of Art. Intro. by Tina Freeman & E. John Bullard. (Illus., 96). 1979. $19.95 (ISBN 0-8174-2484-9); pap. $9.95 (ISBN 0-8174-2156-4). New Orleans Mus.
Early Views of the Vieux Carre, Guide to the French Quarter, New Orleans. Barbara Byrnes & James B. Byrnes. (Illus., 35, 28 color). 1965. pap. $2.50. New Orleans Mus.
English & Continental Portrait Miniatures, the Latter-Schlesinger Collection. Pamela P. Bardo. LC 78-59762. (Illus., 187, 2 color plates). 1978. pap. $7.95 (ISBN 0-89494-006-6). New Orleans Mus.
Guide to the Permanent Collection of the New Orleans Museum of Art. write for info. New Orleans Mus.
Peruvian Painting. Pal Kelemen. LC 78-172508. (Illus., 49). pap. $4.50. New Orleans Mus.
Richard Claque. Roulhac Toledano. LC 74-25157. (Illus., 98, 4 color plates). 1974. pap. $6.95. New Orleans Mus.
Samuel H. Kress Collection. William E. Suida & Paul Wescher. LC 66-25871. (Illus., 31). 1966. pap. $1.50. New Orleans Mus.
Thirty Years of J. L. Steg, 1948-1978. Alan Fern. LC 78-59762. (Illus., 23). 1978. pap. $7.95 (ISBN 0-89494-006-6). New Orleans Mus.

NEW YORK COLLEGE OF CERAMICS AT ALFRED UNIV.
Alfred, New York.
Modern Glass at Alfred: The Silverman Collection. Alexander Silverman. (Illus., 38 b&w photos). 1959. pap. $1.00. Ceramics Alfred.

NEW YORK HISTORICAL SOCIETY
New York, New York.
Catalogue of American Portraits in the New York Historical Society, 2 vols. New York Historical Society. Ed. by Wendy Shadwell. (Illus., 2 color plates, 930 b&w). 1974. $50.00 (ISBN 0-300-01477-5). Yale U Pr.

NEW YORK STATE HISTORICAL ASSN.
Cooperstown, New York.
Informal Guide to the Museums of the New York State Historical Association. Frederick L. Rath, Jr. & Minor Thomas, Jr. (Illus., 3 color, 175 b&w). 1975. $1.95. NY Hist Assn.

NEWARK MUSEUM
Newark, New Jersey.
Additions to the Museum's Collection of American Paintings & Sculpture, 1956-1960. Wm. H. Gerdts. (Newark Museum Quarterly Ser: Vol. 13, Nos. 1 & 2). (Illus.). 1961. pap. $0.25. Newark Mus.
Additions to the Museum's Collection of Painting & Sculpture: European, American, Since 1950. (Newark Museum Quarterly Ser: Vol. 8, Nos. 2 & 3). (Illus.). 1956. pap. $0.25. Newark Mus.
American Folk Art. Elinor Bradshaw. (Newark Museum Quarterly Ser: Vol. 19, Nos. 3 & 4). (Illus.). 1967. pap. $1.00. Newark Mus.
American Quilts in the Newark Museum Collection. Phillip H. Curtis. (Newark Museum Quarterly Ser: Vol. 25, Nos. 3 & 4). (Illus., 1 color, 29 b&w). pap. $3.00. Newark Mus.
Ancient Glass at the Newark Museum from the Eugene Schaefer Collection. Susan H. Auth. (Illus., 10 color, 552 b&w). 1977. $15.95; pap. $9.95. Newark Mus.
Art Nouveau Glass. Yolanda Digaetano. (Newark Museum Quarterly Ser: Vol. 23, Nos. 2 & 3). (Illus.). 1971. pap. $1.00. Newark Mus.
Art of Africa. Deborah Waite. (Newark Museum Quarterly Ser: Vol. 21, Nos. 1 & 2). (Illus.). 1969. pap. $1.00. Newark Mus.
As the Seasons Turn: Southwest Indian Easel Painting & Related Arts. Anne Spencer & Fearn Thurlow. (Newark Museum Quarterly Ser: Vol. 28, No. 2). (Illus., 1 color, 23 b&w). 1977. pap. $2.00. Newark Mus.
Coptic Art. Susan H. Auth. (Newark Museum Quarterly Ser: Vol. 29, No. 2). (Illus., 54 b&w, 5 drawings). 1978. pap. $2.00. Newark Mus.
Eighteenth to Twentieth Century Paintings & Sculpture Acquired Since 1944. (Newark Museum Quarterly Ser: Vol. 2, Nos. 3 & 4). (Illus.). 1950. pap. $0.25. Newark Mus.
Japanese Netsuke & Ojime from the Herman & Paul Jaehne Collection. Barbra Okada. (Newark Museum Quarterly Ser: Vol. 27, Nos. 1 & 2). (Illus., 100 netsuke, 50 ojime). 1976. $10.00; pap. $4.00. Newark Mus.
John H. Ballantine House. Phillip Curtis. (Newark Museum Quarterly Ser: Vol. 27, No. 4). (Illus., 5 color, 31 b&w). 1976. pap. $3.00. Newark Mus.
Tibet: A Lost World-The Newark Museum of Tibetan Art & Ethnography. Valrae Reynolds. LC 78-66376. (Illus., 11 color, 101 b&w). 1978. $17.50 (ISBN 0-253-13790-X); pap. $8.00. Newark Mus.
Two Thousand Years of Chinese Ceramics. Valrae Reynolds & Phillip Curtis. (Newark Museum Quarterly Ser: Vol. 28, Nos. 3 & 4). (Illus., 6 color, 63 b&w). 1977. pap. $4.00. Newark Mus.

NICHOLSON MUSEUM OF ANTIQUITIES
Sydney, Australia.
Handlist to the Classical Collection. (Illus., maps). 1979. Aus.$1.50. U of Sydney.
Handlist to the Egyptian Collection. (Illus., maps). 1974. Aus.$1.00. U of Sydney.
Handlist to the European Collection. (Illus., map). 1976. Aus.$1.00. U of Sydney.
Handlist to the Near Eastern Collection. (Illus., map). 1979. Aus.$1.00. U of Sydney.
Handlist to the New Gallery. 1978. Aus.$1.50. U of Sydney.

NIJMEEGS MUSEUM COMMANDERIE VAN ST. JAN
Nijmegen, Netherlands.
Stedelijke Munt Van Nijmegen. (Catalogi Van Het Kunstbezit Van De Gemeente Nijmegen Ser., No. 2). (Dutch.). 1979. pap. write for info. Nijmeegs Mus.
Vrede Van Nijmegen. Ed. by Nijmeegs Mus. (Catalogi Van Het Kunstbezit Van De Gemeente Nijmegen Ser., No. 1). (Illus., 259, Dutch.). pap. fl.12.50. Nijmeegs Mus.

NOHANT
Paris, France.
Nohant. Georges Lubin. Ed. by Caisse Nationale Des Monuments Historique. (Chateaux, Demeures, Hotels Ser). (Illus., 52 b&w, Fr.). 1976. 18.00 F. (ISBN 2-85822-000-X). Caisse Nation.

NOLDE, EMIL UND ADA, MUSEUM
see Stiftung Seebull Ada und Emil Nolde

NOORDBRABANTS MUSEUM
S'-Hertogenbosch, Netherlands.
Noordbrabants Museum. Margriet Van Boven & Jan Van Laarhoven. Tr. by Patricia Wardle. (Illus., 60 color, 10 b&w, Dan. & Eng.). 1979. pap. fl.16.00. Joh Enschede.

NORFOLK MUSEUMS SERVICE
Norwich, United Kingdom.
Lynn Silver. James Gilchrist & J. B. Inglis. 0.50p. Norfolk Mus.
Munnings: Pictures from the Sir Alfred Munnings Art Museum. Norma Watt. 0.50p. Norfolk Mus.
Norwich Society of Artists, 1805-1833. Miklos Rajnai. E7.00. Norfolk Mus.
Paintings and Drawings. 0.30p. Norfolk Mus.
Treasure of the Norwich Museums. 0.60p. Norfolk Mus.
Treasures of the Yarmouth Museums. Rachel M. Young. 0.60p. Norfolk Mus.

NORTH CAROLINA MUSEUM OF ART
Raleigh, North Carolina.
Acquisitions from North Carolina Annuals, 1946-1966. Ed. by North Carolina Museum of Art. (Illus., 42 b&w). 1967. pap. $1.50 (ISBN 0-88259-031-6). NCMA.
American Paintings Since 1900 from the Permanent Collection. Ed. by North Carolina Museum of Art. (Illus., 2 color, 74 b&w). 1967. pap. $1.50 (ISBN 0-88259-032-4). NCMA.
British Paintings to 1900, Vol. 2. North Carolina Museum of Art. (Catalogue of Paintings Ser). (Illus., 52). 1969. pap. $1.50 (ISBN 0-88259-042-1). NCMA.
Catalogue of Paintings: American Paintings to 1900, Vol. 1. North Carolina Museum of Art. (Catalogue of Paintings Ser). (Illus., 1 color, 63 b&w). 1969. $3.00 (ISBN 0-88259-052-9); pap. $1.50. NCMA.

Exhibition Number One from the Permanent Collection. Ed. by North Carolina Museum of Art. (Illus., 31 color, 39 b&w). 1970. pap. $5.00 (ISBN 0-88259-053-7). NCMA.

Masterpieces in the North Carolina Museum of Art. Ed. by North Carolina Museum of Art. (Illus., 16 color). 1972. pap. $1.75 (ISBN 0-88259-063-4). NCMA.

Robert F. Phifer Collection. Ed. by North Carolina Museum of Art. pap. $3.00 (ISBN 0-88259-069-3). NCMA.

Selections from British & American Painting & Sculpture. Ed. by North Carolina Museum of Art. (Illus., 15 color, 26 b&w). 1967. pap. $1.75 (ISBN 0-88259-036-7); plus slides 9.00, (ISBN 0-88259-069-3). NCMA.

NORTHERN ILLINOIS UNIV., SWEN PARSON GALLERY
Dekalb, Illinois.

Pfaelzer Collection Catalog. Jerry D. Meyer & Joshua Kind. (Illus., 1 color, 109 b&w). 1975. pap. free. N I U Art Dept.

NORTON, R.W. GALLERY
Shreveport, Louisiana.

American Sculpture: A Tenth Anniversary Exhibition. R. W. Norton Art Gallery. (Illus., 2 color, 86 b&w). 1976. pap. $3.00 (ISBN 0-913060-11-9). R W Nort Gal.

American Silver & Pressed Glass. R. W. Norton Art Gallery. (Illus., 77 b&w). 1967. pap. $2.50 (ISBN 0-9600182-0-4). R W Nort Gal.

Artistry in Arms: The Art of Gunsmithing & Gun Engraving. R. W. Norton Art Gallery. (Illus., 28 b&w). 1971. pap. $2.50 (ISBN 0-9600182-4-7). R W Nort Gal.

Charles M. Russell, 1864-1926: Paintings & Sculpture in the R. W. Norton Art Gallery Collection. R. W. Norton Art Gallery. (Illus., 25 color, 142 b&w). 1979. pap. $8.00 (ISBN 0-913060-15-1). R W Nort Gal.

Frederic Remington, 1861-1909: Paintings, Drawings & Sculpture in the R. W. Norton Art Gallery Collection. R. W. Norton Art Gallery. (Illus., 26 color, 56 b&w). 1979. pap. $7.00 (ISBN 0-913060-14-3). R W Nort Gal.

Medallic Art of the United States, 1800-1972. R. W. Norton Art Gallery. (Illus., 5 color, 118 b&w). 1972. pap. $3.00 (ISBN 0-9600182-9-8). R W Nort Gal.

Portrait Miniatures in Early American History, 1750-1840. R. W. Norton Art Gallery. (Illus., 12 color, 46 b&w). 1976. pap. $3.00 (ISBN 0-913060-09-7). R W Nort Gal.

NORWICH CASTLE MUSEUM
Norwich, United Kingdom.

Bronze Age Metalwork in Norwich Castle Museum. Archaeology Dept. 0.75p. Norfolk Mus.

Guide to the Castle Museum. 0.25p. Norfolk Mus.

J. S. Cotman Drawings of Normandy in Norwich Castle Museum. Miklos Rajnai & Marjorie Allthorpe-Guyton. E3.50. Norfolk Mus.

J. S. Cotman: Early Drawings in Norwich Castle Museum. E4.50. Norfolk Mus.

John Thirtle, 1777-1839: Drawings in Norwich Castle Museum. Marjorie Allthorpe-Guyton. E3.00. Norfolk Mus.

Lowestoft Porcelain in Norwich Castle Museum, Vol. 1. Sheenah Smith. E5.00. Norfolk Mus.

Norwich Castle: Fortress for Nine Centuries. Barbara Green. 0.40p. Norfolk Mus.

OBEROSTERREICHISCHES JAGDMUSEUM, SCHLOSS HOHENBRUNN
St. Florian, Austria.

OO. Jagdmuseum: Schloss Hohenbrunn. (Illus., Ger. & Eng.). pap. write for info. Schloss Hohen.

OCTAGON
see American Institute of Architects Foundation, the Octagon

OHIO STATE UNIV., GALLERY OF FINE ART
Columbus, Ohio.

Acquisitions, 1976-1978: Contemporary Collection Interim Catalogue. Ed. by Betty Collings. (Illus., 18 photos of art works). 1978. $4.00. Oh State Gal.

OLANA STATE HISTORIC SITE
Hudson, New York.

Olana Custom & Receipt. L. E. McLean. (Illus., line drawings). 1974. pap. $3.00. Olana.

OLDENBURGER STADTMUSEUM-STADTISCHE KUNSTSAMMLUNGEN
Oldenburg, Germany, West.

Alteren Bestande Privaten Charakters der Stadtischen Kunstsammlungen. Wilhelm Gilly. Ed. by Oldenburg Stadtmuseum. (Illus., 30 color, 48 b&w, Ger.). 1964. DM.24.50. Oldenburger.

Antike Vasen & Terrakotten, 7, Vorchristliches Bis 1, Nachchristliches Jahrhundert. Wilhelm Gilly. Ed. by Oldenburger Stadtmuseum. (Illus., 80 b&w, Ger.). 1978. pap. DM.10.00. Oldenburger.

Oldenburger Stadtmuseum Fuhrer Durch Die Stadtischen Kunstsammlungen. Wilhelm Gilly. Ed. by Oldenburger Stadtmuseum. (Illus., 5 color, 78 b&w, Ger.). 1977. pap. DM.10.00 (ISBN 3-920557-22-0). Oldenburger.

OPENBAAR CENTRUM VOOR MAATSCHAPPELIJK WELZIJN
Antwerp, Belgium.

Museum Maagdenhuis. (Illus., 6 b&w). write for info. Maagdenhuis.

OSTASIATISKA MUSEET, MUSEUM OF FAR EASTERN ANTIQUITIES
Stockholm, Sweden.

Arkeologiska Fynd Fran Folkrepubliken Kina. 1974. Kr.20.00. Ostasiatiska.

Bondemaleri Fran Huhsien. 1976. Kr.2.00. Ostasiatiska.

Celadon: Jade (National Museum) Kr.20.00. Ostasiatiska.

Chinese Art from the Collection of King Gustav VI Adolf. 1967. Kr.10.00. Ostasiatiska.

Famille Rose. Kr.3.00. Ostasiatiska.

Geishas & Samurais: Japanese Woodblock Prints. Kr.3.00. Ostasiatiska.

Gustaf VI Adolfs Gava. 1975. Kr.5.00. Ostasiatiska.

Kinasamlares Gava: Axel Och Nora Lundgrens Samling Av Kinesisk Keramik, Bronser Och Maleri. (Illus.). 1978. Kr.25.00. Ostasiatiska.

Kinesisk Kost Under 5,000 Ar. 1977. Kr.25.00. Ostasiatiska.

Konst Fran Thailand. 1975. Kr.10.00. Ostasiatiska.

Korean Ceramics. 1966. Kr.10.00. Ostasiatiska.

Kvinna I Kina. 1976. Kr.10.00. Ostasiatiska.

Lam Oi: Kinesiskt Maleri. 1969. Kr.5.00. Ostasiatiska.

Li Li-Ta: Kinesisk Kalligraf. 1972. Kr.2.00. Ostasiatiska.

Nya Arkeologiska Fynd Och Konstskatter Fran Korea. Kr.2.00. Ostasiatiska.

Sengai: Museum of Modern Art. (Fr.). Kr.20.00. Ostasiatiska.

Soo-Nam Song. 1975. Kr.10.00. Ostasiatiska.

Stengods Ur Flammor. 1974. Kr.10.00. Ostasiatiska.

Traditional Korean Room. Kr.5.00. Ostasiatiska.

Wajang: Skuggspel Fran Java. 1969. Kr.10.00. Ostasiatiska.

OTIS ART INSTITUTE GALLERY
Los Angeles, California.

American Indian Arts. (Illus., 12 color, 23 b&w, 2 sepia tone). 1973. $1.50. Otis Art Gal.

Ancient Art of China & the Modern Paintings of George Chann. Frwd. by Wen-Shan Huang. (Illus., 27 b&w). 1965. $1.00. Otis Art Gal.

Andean Arts. Jack L. Larson. (Illus., 19 b&w). 1967. $1.00. Otis Art Gal.

Antoine Bourdelle. Frwd. by F. M. Hinkhouse. (Illus., 12 b&w). 1964. $1.00. Otis Art Gal.

Artist Collects. Frwd. by Jarvis Barlow. (Illus., 7 sepia tone). 1960. $1.00. Otis Art Gal.

Containers: Baskets, Bottles, Boxes & Bowls. Frwd. by Wayne Long. (Illus., 23 b&w). 1965. $1.00. Otis Art Gal.

Contemporary African Art. Frwd. by Jean Wohlford. (Illus., 20 b&w). 1969. $1.50. Otis Art Gal.

Contemporary New Guinea Art. Frwd. by Ulli Beier. (Illus., 18 b&w). 1971. $1.50. Otis Art Gal.

Etruscan Art. Frwd. by Alfred E. Stendahl. (Illus., 56 b&w, map). 1963. $1.50. Otis Art Gal.

Indonesian Art. (Illus., 6 b&w). 1961. $1.00. Otis Art Gal.

Kachinas. (Illus., 36 b&w). 1967. $1.50. Otis Art Gal.

Southwest American Indian Art. (Illus., 6 b&w). 1959. $1.00. Otis Art Gal.

Vernon Mona Lisa. Wayne Long. (Illus., 1 color, 1 b&w, 13 sepia tone). 1964. $1.00. Otis Art Gal.

Wayne Long Ethnic Art Collection. Frwd. by Wayne Long. (Illus., 80 sepia tone). 1970. $2.25. Otis Art Gal.

OUDE PASTORIE-MUZEUM
Paarl, South Africa.

Oude Pastorie-Museum. (Illus., 1 color, 9 b&w, Ger. & Eng.). pap. write for info. Oude Pastorie.

PALAIS DES PAPES D'AVIGNON
Paris, France.

Palais Des Papes D'Avignon. S. Gagniere. Ed. by Caisse Nationale. (Chateaux, Demeures, Hotels Ser: Vallee Du Rhone). (Illus., 3 color, 66 b&w, Fr.). 1977. 22.00 F. Caisse Nation.

PALAZZO DAVANZATI
see Museo Della Casa Fiorentina Antica Di Palazzo Davanzati

PALAZZO PITTI
see Galleria Palatina Di Palazzo Pitti

PANORAMA MESDAG
The Hague, Netherlands.

Panorama Mesdag. (Illus., 13 b&w). 1977. pap. 2.00 F. Mesdag.

PANSTOWE MUZEUM ETNOGRAFICZNE
Warsaw, Poland.

Guide to the Exhibitions. (Illus., 48, Eng., Fr. & Rus.). 1976. 15.00 Zl. Panst Muz Etno.

National Museum of Ethnography in Warsaw: History, Collections & Expositions. (Illus., 48, Pol., Rus. & Eng.). 1973. 30.00 Zl. Panst Muz Etno.

PANTHEON
Paris, France.

Pantheon. Pierre Chevallier & Daniel Rabreau. Ed. by Caisse Nationale Des Monuments Historiques. Tr. by Kathleen Wilson. (Cathedrales-Eglises Ser). (Illus., Fr. & Eng.). 1977. 18.00 F. (ISBN 2-85822-001-8). Caisse Nation.

PASQUALATIHAUS
see Beethoven-Wohnung (Pasqualatihaus)

PAULA-BECKER-MODERSOHN-HAUS
Bremen, Germany, West.

Gemalde Im Paula Becker-Modersohn-Haus. (Ger.). DM.50.00. Paula Becker.

Paula Becker-Modersohn: Bilder Aus der Sammlung Roselius. (Illus., 8 color, Ger.). DM.11.00. Paula Becker.

Paula Becker-Modersohn Zum Hundersten Geburtstag. (Illus., 32 color, 79 b&w, Ger.). 1976. DM.35.00. Paula Becker.

PAYSON GALLERY OF ART
see Westbrook College, Joan Whitney Payson Gallery of Art

PEALE MUSEUM, MUNICIPAL MUSEUM OF THE CITY OF BALTIMORE
Baltimore, Maryland.

PictoCat: A Picture History of Baltimore from the Collections of the Peale Museum. Wilbur Hunter & Marion Sinwell. (Illus., 1512 frames of pictures). 1978. $45.00, 16mm. positive microfilm. Peale Mus.

PERCIVAL DAVID FOUNDATION OF CHINESE ART
see David, Percival, Foundation of Chinese Art

PERMANENT COLLECTION GALLERY
see Minnesota Museum of Art

PERRINS, DYSON, MUSEUM
Worcester, United Kingdom.

Flight & Barr Worcester Porcelain, 1783-1840. Henry Sandon. (Illus.). 1978. 11.50 d. Barrie and Jen.

Royal Worcester Porcelain from 1862. Henry Sandon. (Illus.). 1979. 16.00 d. Barrie and Jen.

Worcester Porcelain, 1751-1793. Henry Sandon. (Illus.). 1978. 10.00 d. Barrie and Jen.

PESHAWAR MUSEUM
Peshawar, Pakistan.

Buddha Story in Peshawar Museum. Fidaullah Sehrai. (Illus., 72 photos). 1978. pap. Rs.35.00. Peshawar Mus.

PETER M. BOHUNS GALERIA
Liptovsky Mikulas, Czechoslovakia.

Galeria Petra Michala Bohuna, Katalog Zbierok. Vojtech Mensatoris. (Illus., 64 color, 32 b&w, Slovak.). 1978. 20.00 Kcs. Peter M Bohuns.

PHILADELPHIA COLLEGE OF ART
Philadelphia, Pennsylvania.

Alice Aycock. Janet Kardon. (Illus., 8 b&w reprods.). 1978. pap. $5.00. Phila Col Art.

George Trakas. Janet Kardon. (Projects for PCA Ser., 2). (Illus., 6 b&w reprods.). 1977. pap. $5.00. Phila Col Art.

Point. Janet Kardon. (Illus., 13 b&w reprods.). 1978. pap. $5.00. Phila Col Art.

Seventies Painting. Janet Kardon. (Illus., 12 b&w reprods.). 1978. pap. $5.00. Phila Col Art.

Siah Armajani. Janet Kardon. (Projects for PCA Ser., 3). (Illus., 7 b&w reprods.). 1978. pap. $5.00. Phila Col Art.

Time. Janet Kardon. (Illus., 21 b&w reprods.). 1977. pap. $6.00. Phila Col Art.

PHILBROOK ART CENTER
Tulsa, Oklahoma.

African Sculpture: Collection of the Philbrook Art Center. Intro. by Donald Humphrey. (Museum of Art Ser.,Vol. 12, No. 2). (Illus., 6 b&w). 1969. pap. $1.00. U of Ok Mus Art.

American Art: The Philbrook Collection. Linda Pinkerton. (Illus., 10 b&w). 1976. pap. $3.00. U of Ok Mus Art.

American Indian Paintings: From the Collection of Philbrook Art Center. Jeanne Snodgrass. pap. $1.00. U of Ok Mus Art.

Indian Pottery of the Southwest, Post Spanish Period. Intro. by Donald Humphrey. (Illus., 23 b&w plates). 1970. pap. $1.50. U of Ok Mus Art.

Villa Philbrook. Raakel Vesanen. (Illus., 36 b&w, sepia tone). 1976. pap. $3.00. U of Ok Mus Art.

PHILLIPS COLLECTION
Washington, D.C.

Duncan Phillips & His Collection. Marjorie Phillips. (Illus., 25 color, 185 b&w). 1970. $15.00. Phillips Coll.

Phillips Collection. Duncan Phillips. (Illus., 10 color, 315 b&w). 1952. $5.00. Phillips Coll.

PIERREFONDS
Paris, France.

Pierrefonds. Louis Grodecki. Ed. by Caisse Nationale. (Chateaux Forteresses Ser). write for info. Caisse Nation.

PILGRIM SOCIETY, PILGRIM HALL
Plymouth, Massachusetts.

History As Art: Selections from the Pilgrim Hall Museum. L. D. Geller. (Pilgrim Society Booklet Ser). (Illus., 39 b&w photos). 1970. pap. $0.75. Pilg Soc.

PINACOTECA AMBROSIANA
Milano, Italy.

Pinoteca Ambrosiana: Catalogo a Cura Di Antonia Falchetti. (Illus., 244). 1969. L.6000.00. Ambrosiana.

PINACOTECA CIVICA FRANCESCO PODESTI E GALLERIA COMUNALE D'ARTE MODERNA
Ancona, Italy.

Pinoteca Civica Di Ancona. Giuseppe Marchini. Ed. by Pinoteca Civica Di Ancona. (Illus., 50 color, b&w, It.). 1979. L.5000.00. Fran Podesti.

PINACOTECA NAZIONALE SIENA
Siena, Italy.

Nostra Di Opere D'Arte Restaurate Delle Provincie Di Siena E Di Grosseto, Luglio-Ottobre 1979. Piero Torriti. (Catalogo Ser). (It.). 1979. write for info. Pina Naz Siena.

Pinoteca Nazionale Di Siena, I Dipinti Dal XIII Al XV Secolo. Piero Torriti. (Illus., 487, It.). 1977. L.40000.00. Pina Naz Siena.

Pinoteca Nazionale Di Siena, I Dipinti Dal XV Al XVIII Secolo. Piero Torriti. (Illus., 508, It.). 1978. L.40000.00. Pina Naz Siena.

PINACOTECA VATICANA
Vatican, Vatican City.

I Dipinti Dal X Secolo Fino a Giotto. Wolfgang F. Volbach. (Catalogo Della Pinacoteca Vaticana Ser). (Illus., 107 b&w, It.). 1979. write for info. Vatican.

I Fiorentini E I Senesi Del Trecento. Wolfgang F. Volbach. (Catalogo Della Pinacoteca Vaticana, II). (It.). write for info. Vatican.

PLAINS ART MUSEUM
Moorehead, Minnesota.

Kertesz & Harbutt: Sympathetic Explorations. Ed. by Magnum Photos. LC 78-59643. 1978. pap. $7.50. Plains Art Mus.

PODESTI, FRANCESCO, GALLERIA
see Pinacoteca Civica Francesco Podesti E Galleria Comunale D'Arte Moderna

POLLOK HOUSE (GLASGOW MUSEUMS AND ART GALLERIES)
Edinburgh, United Kingdom.

Pollok House Catalogue of Paintings & Sculpture. (Illus., 19 b&w). 1977. pap. 0.50 p. Glasgow Mus.

PORVOON MUSEO
Porvoon, Finland.

Porvoon Museon Taidekokoelmat. Ed. by Marja Supinen. (Illus., 30 color, b&w, Finnish & Swed.). 1980. write for info. Porvoon Mus.

POTSDAM PUBLIC MUSEUM
Potsdam, New York.

Burnap Collection on the Potsdam Public Museum. Adelle Little. (Illus., 169, photos). 1975. pap. $1.50. Potsdam Pub Mus.

PRADO
see Museo Del Prado

PRINCE OF WALES MUSEUM OF WESTERN INDIA
Bombay, India.

Animal in Indian Art. Sadashiv Gorakshkar. (Illus., 346 monochrome). 1979. Rs.15.00. Prin Wales Mus.

Dawn of Civilization in Maharashtra. M. Deshpanda et al. (Illus.). 1975. Rs.45.00. Prin Wales Mus.

Stone Sculpture in the Prince of Wales Museum. Moti Chandra. (Illus., 167 b&w). 1974. pap. Rs.20.00. Prin Wales Mus.

PRINCESSEHOF MUSEUM
see Vereniging Van Vrienden Van Het Princessehof

PRINCETON UNIV. ART MUSEUM
Princeton, New Jersey.

Art Museum. pap. write for info. Prince U Art Mus.

Contemporary Sculpture. pap. write for info. Princeton U.

PROVINCIAAL MUSEUM STERCKSHOF
Deurne, Belgium.

Lefaat Pierre Lunden: Catalogus. A. Claessens-Pere. (Illus., Dutch.). 1977. pap. 200.00 F. Mus Sterckshof.

QUEENS COLLEGE OF THE CITY UNIVERSITY OF NEW YORK ART COLLECTION
Flushing, New York.

Ancient & Antique Glass in the Queens College Art Collection. Manzari et al. Ed. & intro. by Irene Winter. (Illus., 62 color, b&w). 1976. pap. $3.50. Queens Coll Pr.

Queens College Art Collection & First Supplement. (Illus., 15 b&w). 1960. pap. $3.00. Queens Coll Pr.

QUEEN'S UNIV., AGNES ETHERINGTON ART CENTER
Kingston, Canada.

Catalogue of the Permanent Collection of Paintings, Drawings & Sculpture. Compiled by Frances Smith & Ralph Allen. (Illus., 275). $8.00. Etherington.

Supplement. 1976. $0.50. Etherington.

RANDOLPH-MACON WOMAN'S COLLEGE COLLECTION OF AMERICAN ART
Lynchburg, Virginia.
Catalogue of the Collection of American Art at Randolph-Macon Woman's College. Mary Frances Williams. (Illus., 11 color plates, 108 b&w). 1977. $15.00 (ISBN 0-8139-0591-5). U of Va Pr.
RAUTENSTRAUCH-JOEST MUSEUM FUR VOLKEKUNDE DER STADT KOLN
Cologne, Germany, West.
Ostafrika: Figur und Ornament. (Ger.). 1975. DM.4.00. Mus Koln.
San Blas Cuna: Ein Indianerstamm in Panama. (Ger.). 1977. DM.10.00. Mus Koln.
REINHART, OSKAR, FOUNDATION
see Stiftung Oskar Reinhart
REMINGTON ART MUSEUM
Ogdensburg, New York.
Frederic Remington Memorial Collection Catalog. write for info. Remington.
RESIDENZ ANSBACH
Ansbach, Germany, West.
Residenz Ansbach. Erich Bachmann. (Ger.). 1978. DM.2.00. Bayer Verwal.
RESIDENZ ELLINGEN
Ellingen, Germany, West.
Residenz Ellingen. Erich Bachmann. (Ger.). 1976. DM.2.50. Bayer Verwal.
RESIDENZ MUNCHEN
Munich, Germany, West.
Ancien Theatre De la Residence a Munich. Herbert Brunner. (Fr.). 1960. DM.1.50. Bayer Verwal.
Residence-Museum Munich. Hans Thoma & Herbert Brunner. (Ger.). 1975. DM.3.50. Bayer Verwal.
Residenz Munchen. Herbert Brunner & Gerhard Hojer. (Ger.). 1976. DM.3.00. Bayer Verwal.
RESIDENZ WURZBURG
Wurzburg, Germany, West.
Residenz Wurzburg. Erich Bachmann & Rolf Kultzen. (Ger.). 1978. DM.2.50. Bayer Verwal.
RHODE ISLAND SCHOOL OF DESIGN, MUSEUM OF ART
Providence, Rhode Island.
Albert Pilavin Collection of 20th Century American Art, Vol. 1. (Illus., 4 color plates, 15 b&w). 1969. $6.00. Mus of Art RI.
Albert Pilavin Collection of 20th Century American Art, Vol. 2. LC 70-19905. (Illus., 4 color plates, 16 b&w). 1973. $3.00. Mus of Art RI.
American Drawings & Watercolors from the Museum's Collection. (Selection Ser., 1). (Illus., 60). 1972. $1.50. Mus of Art RI.
American Paintings from the Museum's Collection, C, 1800-1930. Patricia Mandel. LC 77-70393. (Selection Ser., 7). (Illus., 105 b&w photos). 1977. $22.00; pap. $18.00. Mus of Art RI.
British Watercolors & Drawings from the Museum's Collection. LC 72-78344. (Selection Ser., 2). (Illus., 119). 1972. $6.50. Mus of Art RI.
Catalogue of the Classical Collection: Bronzes. David G. Mitten & James Loeb. LC 75-18670. (Illus., 290 b&w). 1975. $15.00. Mus of Art RI.
Catalogue of the Classical Collection: Jewelry. Tony Hackens. LC 76-16947. (Illus., 330). 1976. $10.00. Mus of Art RI.
Catalogue of the Classical Collection: Sculpture. Brunilde S. Ridgway. LC 72-79496. (Illus., 177 b&w). 1973. $10.00; pap. $8.00. Mus of Art RI.
Catalogue of the Classical Collection: Vases. LC 76-45537. 1976. $10.00. Mus of Art RI.
Contemporary Graphics from the Museum's Collection. LC 73-76521. (Selection Ser., 3). (Illus., 66 b&w). 1973. $5.00. Mus of Art RI.
Corpus Vasorum Antiquorum: USA Fascicule 2, Providence Fascicule 1. Stephen B. Luce. (Illus., 31 b&w). 1933. $4.00. Mus of Art RI.
Glass from the Museum's Collection. LC 73-94132. (Selection Ser., 4). (Illus., 73 b&w). 1974. $6.50. Mus of Art RI.
Nancy Sayles Day Supplementary Catalogue. Daniel Robbins. (Illus., 15). 1968. $1.00. Mus of Art RI.
RIJKSMUSEUM
Amsterdam, Netherlands.
All the Paintings of the Rijksmuseum in Amsterdam. Pieter Van Thiel et al. Ed. by Amsterdam Rijksmuseum & Gary Schwartz. Tr. by Marianne Buikstra-De Boer et al. (Illus., 5000 b&w, Eng. & Dutch.). 1976. fl.195.00. Gary Schwartz.
Beeldhouwkunst in Het Rijksmuseum. Jaap Leeuwenberg & Willy Halsema-Kubes. Tr. by A. Van Schendel. (Illus., 500 b&w, Dutch.). 1973. fl.75.00. Staatsuitgeverij.
Netherlandish Drawings of the Fifteenth & Sixteenth Centuries. K. G. Boon. Tr. by Margot Muntz. (Illus., 600 b&w). 1978. fl.150.00. Staatsuitgeverij.
RIJKSMUSEUM HET CATHARIJNECONVENT
Utrecht, Netherlands.
Tekst En Uitleg. H. L. Defoer et al. (Illus., 100, Dutch.). 1979. fl.15.00. Rijks Het Cat.
RIJKSMUSEUM KROLLER-MULLER
Otterlo, Netherlands.
Beeldhouwwerken Van Het Rijksmuseum Kroller-Muller. (Illus., 90). 1973. fl.10.00. Kroller-Muller.
Christo. E. Joosten. (Illus., 38, Dutch & Eng.). 1977. fl.7.50. Kroller-Muller.
Drawings, 19th & 20th Century, of the Rijksmuseum Kroller-Muller. (Illus., 400, Dutch.). 1968. fl.9.75. Kroller-Muller.
Dubuffet: Jardin d'Email. (Illus., 32, Dutch, Fr. & Eng.). 1974. fl.9.75. Kroller-Muller.
Kroller-Muller Museum. (Illus., 135, 120 color, Dutch, Eng. & Ger.). 1977. fl.24.50. Kroller-Muller.
Lipscitz in Otterlo. A. M. Hammacher. (Illus., 55, Dutch & Eng.). 1977. fl.7.50. Kroller-Muller.
Nieuwbouw-Extension, 1970-1977. (Illus., 70, Dutch & Eng.). 1977. fl.10.75. Kroller-Muller.
Paintings of the Rijksmuseum Kroller-Muller. (Illus., 117 b&w, Dutch & Eng.). 1969. fl.9.75. Kroller-Muller.
Schilderijen Van Het Rijksmuseum Kroller-Muller. (Illus., 117). 1970. fl.9.75. Kroller-Muller.
Sculptures of the Rijksmuseum Kroller-Muller. (Illus., 90 b&w, Dutch & Eng.). 1970. Fl. $10.00. Kroller-Muller.
Vincent Van Gogh, Catalogue of 276 Works in the Collection of the Rijksmuseum Kroller-Muller. (Dutch-Eng. Ed. & Fr. -Ger. Ed.). fl.4.50. Kroller-Muller.
RINGLING, JOHN AND MABEL, MUSEUM OF ART
Sarasota, Florida.
Italian Paintings Before 1800. Peter Tomory. (Illus., 18 color, 120 b&w). 1976. $28.50. Ringling Mus Art.
Masterworks on Paper: Prints & Drawings from the Ringling Museums, 1400-1900. $2.00. Ringling Mus Art.
ROBERT HULL FLEMING MUSEUM
see Univ. of Vermont, Robert Hull Fleming Museum
ROBERT MCLAUGHLIN GALLERY
see McLaughlin, Robert, Gallery
ROCKWELL-CORNING MUSEUM
Corning, New York.
The Painters' West. Paul E. Rivard. (Illus., 61 color, b&w). 1976. $10.50; pap. $4.50. Rockwell Corning Mus.
ROERICH, NICHOLAS, MUSEUM
New York, New York.
Guggenheim Museum: Justin K. Thannhauser Collection. Vivian Barnett. (Illus., 51 color plates, b&w). 1978. $24.50 (ISBN 0-89207-016-1). Allanheld & Schram.
Kandinsky at the Guggenheim Museum. Intro. by Thomas Messer. LC 72-77738. (Illus., 26 color, 121 b&w). 1972. $6.00. Allanheld & Schram.
Klee at the Guggenheim Museum. Louise A. Svendsen. (Illus., 21 color plates, 45 b&w). 1977. pap. $6.95 (ISBN 0-89207-006-4). Allanheld & Schram.
Nicholas Roerich, 1874-1974. Jawaharlal Nehru et al. (Illus., 10 color, 11 b&w). 1974. $5.00. Nicholas Roerich Mus.
Solomon R. Guggenheim Museum Collection: Paintings, 1800-1945, 2 vols. Angelica Rudenstine. (Illus., 32 color, 550 b&w). 1976. $85.00 (ISBN 0-89207-002-1). Allanheld & Schram.
ROGERS, LAUREN, LIBRARY AND MUSEUM OF ART
Laurel, Mississippi.
Gibbons Georgian Silver Collection. Ed. by Donald D. Crawford. pap. $2.50. Lauren Rogers.
ROMISCH GERMANISCHES MUSEUM
Julich, Germany, West.
Romisch Germanisches Museum, Julich. Frwd. by W. Scharenberg. (Illus.). 1967. pap. write for info. Rom Ger Julich.
ROMISCHE RUINEN UNTER DEM HOHEN MARKT
Vienna, Austria.
Romische Ruinen Unter Dem Hohen Markt, Wegweiser. Eigenverlag der Museen der Stadt Wien. (Illus., 3 b&w, Ger. & Eng.). 1974. pap. S.7.00. Museen Wien.
ROMISCH-GERMANISCHES MUSEUM
Cologne, Germany, West.
Funf Taschenbucher Im Schuber Zusammengefasst. (Ger.). DM.16.00. Mus Koln.
Glaser der Antike. (Ger.). DM.24.00. Mus Koln.
Poblicius-Grabmal. (Ger.). DM.4.00. Mus Koln.
Romer: Illustrierte, Vol. 1. (Ger.). DM.8.00. Mus Koln.
Romer: Illustrierte, Vol. 2. (Ger.). DM.8.00. Mus Koln.
Romer: Illustrierte, Vol. 3. (Ger.). write for info. Mus Koln.
Romer: Illustrierte I und II. (Illus., Ger.). DM.12.00. Mus Koln.
Romische Kleinkunst. (Ger.). DM.18.00. Mus Koln.
Romische Wandmalerei der Nordwestlichen Provinzen. (Ger.). DM.4.00. Mus Koln.
Romischer Alltag in Koln. (Ger.). DM.4.00. Mus Koln.
Steinzit in Koln. (Ger.). DM.4.00. Mus Koln.
Zur Religionsgeschicte Des Romischen Kolns. (Ger.). DM.4.00. Mus Koln.
ROSELIUS-HAUS
Bremen, Germany, West.
Roselius-Haus in der Bottcherstrasse, Bremen. Ernst Redaktion. (Illus., Ger.). 1975. DM.2.00. Roselius Haus.
ROSENBACH, PHILIP H. AND A.S.W., FOUNDATION
Philadelphia, Pennsylvania.
Early American Maps & Views. Clive E. Driver. (Illus., 51 b&w, map & view reprods.). 1972. pap. $3.50. Rosenbach Foun.
Peruvian & Other South American Manuscripts in the Rosenbach Foundation, 1536-1914. David M. Szewczyk. (Illus., 10 b&w manuscript facsims.). 1977. $10.00. Rosenbach Foun.
Selection from Our Shelves: Books, Manuscripts & Drawings from the Philip H. & A. S. W. Rosenbach Foundation Museum. Clive Driver. (Illus., 88 b&w). 1973. pap. $12.50. Rosenbach Foun.
ROSENBORG SLOT (DE DANSKE KONGERS KRONOLOGISKE SAMMLING PA ROSENBORG)
Copenhagen, Denmark.
Rosenborg: Official Guide. (Illus., 6 b&w). 1979. pap. Kr.10.00. Rosenborg.
Rosenborg: Vejledning. (Dan.). 1975. pap. Kr.6.00. Rosenborg.
Tresors Des Rois De Danemark. H. D. Schepelern et al. (Illus., 4 color plates, Fr.). 1978. Kr.15.00 (ISBN 87-87646-01-3). Rosenborg.
ROSSENDALE MUSEUM
Rossendale, United Kingdom.
Hollands En Duits Porcelain in Kasteel Sypesteyn Te Loosdrecht. M. A. Heukensfeldt Jansen & A. L. Den Blaauwen. Ed. by Vriends Van De Nederlandse Ceramiek. (Mededelingenblad Van De Vrienden Van De Nederlandse Ceramiek Ser., No. 42). (Illus., 166 color, b&w photos, Dutch.). 1966. pap. fl.10.00. Sypesteyn.
Inventaris Van Het Familiearchief Van Sypesteyn. S. M. Van Zanten Jut. (Dutch.). 1969. pap. fl.25.00. Sypesteyn.
Portretten Op Het Kasteel Sypesteyn Te Loosdrecht. F. G. Van Kretschmar. (Illus., 36 photos, Dutch.). 1969. pap. fl.5.00. Sypesteyn.
Rossendale Museum. Jon Elliott. (Illus., 4 photos). 1979. pap. 0.25 d. Rossendale.
ROTTNEROS PARK
Rottneros, Sweden.
Catalogue of Rottneros Park. Rottneros Park. (Swed., Eng. & Ger.). Kr.6.00. Rottneros.
ROYAL ALBERT MEMORIAL MUSEUM
Exeter, United Kingdom.
Catalogue of Oil Paintings, Watercolours, Prints, Drawings & Sculpture. C. J. Baker. (Illus., 17 half tone). 1979. pap. 2.75 d. Exeter Mus Serv.
ROYAL ONTARIO MUSEUM
Toronto, Canada.
Canadian Watercolours & Drawings in the Royal Ontario Museum, 2 vols. Mary Allodi. (Illus., 30 color, 400 b&w). 1974. $30.00, slipcased (ISBN 0-88854-159-7). Royal Ont Mus.
Chinese Art in the Royal Ontario Museum. Royal Ontario Mus., Far Eastern Dep't. (Illus., 12 color, 189 b&w). $10.95 (ISBN 0-88854-140-6). Royal Ont Mus.
Chinese Jades in the Royal Ontario Museum. Doris Dohrenwend. (Illus., 2 color, 240 b&w). 1971. $8.95 (ISBN 0-88854-075-2). Royal Ont Mus.
Etruscan & Italian Collections in the Royal Ontario Museum, Toronto: A Survey. John W. Hayes. (Illus., 61 b&w photos). 1975. pap. $3.00. Royal Ont Mus.
Far Eastern Collection. Henry Trubner. (Illus., 12 color, 130 b&w). 1968. $5.50 (ISBN 0-88854-076-0). Royal Ont Mus.
Images of Eighteenth Century Japan: Ukiyoe Prints from the Sir Edmund Walker Collection. David Waterhouse. (Illus., 8 color, 151 b&w). 1975. $14.95 (ISBN 0-88854-170-8); pap. $9.95 (ISBN 0-88854-170-8). Royal Ont Mus.
Loch Collection of Cypriote Antiquities. Neda Leipen. (Illus., 123 b&w photos). 1966. pap. $1.50 (ISBN 0-88854-049-3). Royal Ont Mus.
Menzies Collection of Shang Dynasty Oracle Bones: The Text, Vol. II. Hsu Chin-Hsiung. (Illus., 5 plates, Chin. Text & Eng. Pref.). 1977. $20.00 (ISBN 0-88854-023-X). Royal Ont Mus.
Menzies Collection of Shang Oracle Bones: A Catalogue, Vol. I. Hsu Chin-Hsiung. (Illus., 264 plates of rubbings). 1972. $15.00 (ISBN 0-88854-022-1). Royal Ont Mus.
Roman & Pre-Roman Glass in the Royal Ontario Museum: A Catalogue. John Hayes. (Illus., 43 plates, 21 b&w drawings recording 670 artifacts). 1975. $15.00 (ISBN 0-88854-027-2). Royal Ont Mus.
Roman Pottery in the Royal Ontario Museum. John Hayes. (Illus., 40 plates, 13 b&w drawings recording 369 artifacts). 1976. $13.50 (ISBN 0-88854-172-4). Royal Ont Mus.
ROYAL PAVILION ART GALLERY AND MUSEUM
Brighton, United Kingdom.
African Carvings with an Addendum on African Sculpture & the Modern Movement in Art. George Bankes. (Illus., 33 b&w photos). 1975. pap. E1.50. Royal Pavilion.
Eskimos & Indians, the North American Collections in Brighton Museum. George Bankes. (Information Sheet Ser., 2). (Illus., 11 photos). pap. 0.15p. Royal Pavilion.
Guide to the Booth & Related Bird Collections. (Information Sheet Ser., 1). (Illus., 12 line drawings). pap. 0.80p. Royal Pavilion.
Illustrated Guide & Introduction to the Collections in the Art Gallery & Museum Brighton. (Illus., 8 color, 35 b&w photos). 1975. pap. 0.50p. Royal Pavilion.
Man Who Invented the Seaside. Jean Garratt. (Information Sheet Ser., 1). (Illus., 5 photos, 1 line drawing). pap. 0.10p. Royal Pavilion.
Preston Manor, Brighton. pap. 0.15p. Royal Pavilion.
Royal Pavillion, Brighton Guide & Regency Exhibition Catalogue. John Dinkel & John Morley. (Illus., 80 photos). 1979. pap. 0.70p. Royal Pavilion.
ROYAL SCOTTISH MUSEUM
Edinburgh, United Kingdom.
Ancient American Art. Dale Idiens. (Illus., 28 b&w photos). 1971. 40.00 d. Royal Scot Mus.
Arms & Armour in the Royal Scottish Museum. A. V. Norman. (Illus., 29 b&w photos). 1972. 60.00 d. Royal Scot Mus.
Catalogue of Northern Athapaskan Indian Artifacts in the Collection of the Royal Scottish Museum, Edinburgh. Dale Idiens. 1979. write for info. Royal Scot Mus.
Catalogue of the Ancient Greek Coins in the Royal Scottish Museum. N. K. Rutter. write for info. Royal Scot Mus.
English Glass. Intro. by W. Cyril Wallis & Revel Oddy. (Illus., 26 b&w photos). 1964. pap. 0.20 d. Royal Scot Mus.
Playfair Collection & the Teaching of Chemistry at the University of Edinburgh, 1713-1858. R. G. Anderson. (Illus., 56 b&w photos). 1978. pap. 4.50 d. Royal Scot Mus.
Samplers. Naomi E. Tarrant. (Illus., 49 b&w photos). 1978. pap. 5.50 d. (ISBN 0-900733-17-9). Royal Scot Mus.
Traditional African Sculpture. Dale Idiens. (Illus., 31 b&w photos). 1969. 15.00 d. Royal Scot Mus.
RUHR-UNIVERSITAT BOCHUM, INSTITUT FUR ARCHAOLOGIE
Bochum-Querenburg, Germany, West.
Antiken der Sammlung Julius C. und Margot Funcke. Norbert Kunisch. (Illus., 160 b&w, Ger.). 1972. DM.14.00. Ruhr Uni Boch.
Plastik: Antike und Moderne Kunst der Sammlung Dierichs in der Ruhr-Universitat Bochum. Max Imdahl & Norbert Kunisch. (Illus., 90 color, b&w, Ger.). 1979. DM.25.00. Paul Dierichs.
RUTGERS, THE STATE UNIVERSITY OF NEW JERSEY, FINE ARTS COLLECTION
New Brunswick, New Jersey.
Fine Arts Collection of Rutgers, the State University: A Selection. (Illus., 55 b&w photos). 1966. pap. $2.00. Rutgers U Pr.
RUTLAND COUNTY MUSEUM
Rutland, United Kingdom.
Horseshoes of Oakham Castle. T. H. Clough. (Illus., 13 photos). 1978. pap. 0.40p. (ISBN 0-85022-041-6). Leicestershire.
R.W. NORTON GALLERY
see Norton, R.W. Gallery
ST. BAAFSKATHEDRAAL
Gent, Belgium.
De St. Baafskathedraal Gent. Roger Van De Wielle. Ed. by St. Baafskathedraal. (Illus., 5 color, 16 b&w photos, Netherlands, Fr., Ger. & Eng.). 100.00 Fr. St. Baafskathe.
Het Lam Gods. A. L. Dierick. (Illus., 24 color photos, Netherlands, Fr., Ger., Eng. & Span.). 200.00 Fr. St. Baafskathe.
SAINT GREGORY'S ABBEY AND COLLEGE, THE MABEE-GERRER MUSEUM
Shawnee, Oklahoma.
Catalogue of St. Gregory's Art Gallery & Museum. 1942. pap. write for info. Mabee Gerner.
ST. JOHNSBURY ATHENEUM
St. Johnsbury, Vermont.
Catalogue of the Collection: The St. Johnsbury Athenaeum & Art Gallery. St. Johnsbury Athenaeum. (Illus.). pap. $1.00. St Johns Ath.

STAATLICHE ANTIKENSAMMLUNGEN UND GLYPTOTHEK
Munich, Germany, West.
Antikensammlungen Am Konigsplatz in Munchen. D. Ohly. (Ger.). write for info. Staat Ant Gly.
Attische Vasenbilder der Antikensammlungen in Munchen Nach Zeichnungen Von Karl Reichhold: Bilder Auf Schalen, Vol. 2. F. W. Hamdorf. 1976. write for info. Staat Ant Gly.
Attische Vasenbilder der Antikensammlungen in Munchen Nach Zeichnungen Von Karl Reichhold: Bilder Auf Krugen, Vol. 1. M. Ohly-Dunn. 1975. write for info. Staat Ant Gly.
Glyptothek Munchen: Grieschische und Romische Skulpturen. D. Ohly. (Ger.). 1974. write for info. Staat Ant Gly.
Griechische und Romische Bronzewerke. M. Maass. 1979. write for info. Staat Ant Gly.
Guide to the Munich Antikensammlungen. D. Ohly. write for info. Staat Ant Gly.
Munich Glyptothek: Greek & Roman Sculpture. D. Ohly. 1974. write for info. Staat Ant Gly.
Tempel und Heiligtum der Aphaia Auf Aegina. D. Ohly. 1977. write for info. Staat Ant Gly.

STAATLICHE KUNSTHALLE KARLSRUHE
Karlsruhe, Germany, West.
Deutsche Zeichnungen Des 19 Jahrhundert. Rudolf Theilmann. Ed. by Staatliche Kunsthalle. (Illus., Ger.). 1978. DM.40.00. Kunst Karlsru.
Katalog Alte Meister. Jau Lauts. Ed. by Staatliche Kunsthalle. (Illus., Ger.). 1966. DM.27.00. Kunst Karlsru.
Katalog: Neue Meister, Text und Bildband. Jau Lauts & Werner Zimmermann. Ed. by Staatliche Kunsthalle Karlsruhe. (Illus., Ger.). 1977. DM.39.00. Kunst Karlsru.

STAATLICHE MUSEEN PREUSSISCHER KULTURBESITZ, BERLIN
Berlin, Germany, West.
Agyptisches Museum. (Ger.). DM.32.00. Blaschker Verlag.
Kleiner Fuhrer Durch das Museum. (Ger.). DM.2.00. Blaschker Verlag.
Papyri Aus Hermupolis. (Ger.). DM.130.00. Blaschker Verlag.

STAATLICHE MUNZSAMMLUNG
Munich, Germany, West.
Antike Gemmen in Deutschen Sammlungen. Brandt et al. Ed. by Staatliche Munzsammlung Munchen. (Illus., plates, Ger.). DM. 120.00, 1968 ed. DM. 190.00, 1970 ed. DM. 220.00. 1972 ed. Prestel Verlag.
Bauten Roms Auf Munzen und Medaillen. Kuthmann et al. Ed. by Staatliche Munzsammlung Munchen. (Illus., 409, Ger.). 1973. pap. DM.18.00. Prestel Verlag.
Sylloge Nummorum Graecorum. Franke et al. Ed. by Deutsches Archaologisches Institut, Berlin. (Illus., Ger.). 1968. write for info. Gebruder Mann.

STAATLICHE SAMMLUNG AGYPTISCHER KUNST
Munich, Germany, West.
Staatliche Sammlung Agyptischer Kunst. Dietrich Wildung. Ed. by Staatliche Sammlung Agyptischer Kunst. (Illus., color, b&w, Ger.). 1976. pap. DM.17.00. Staat Agyp Kun.

STAATSGALERIE PLASSENBURG
Kulmbach, Germany, West.
Plassenburg Ob Kulmbach. Erich Bachmann. (Ger.). 1978. DM.2.00. Bayer Verwal.

STADTISCHE KUNSTHALLE RECKLINGHAUSEN
Recklinghausen, Germany, West.
Kunstschatze in Recklinghausen. 1972. write for info. Aurel Bongers.

STADTISCHE SAMMLUNGEN, ARCHIVO-ROLLETT MUSEUM DER STADT BADEN
Baden bei Wien, Austria.
Baden Bei Wien, Stadtische Sammlungen. (Ger.). write for info. Rollet Mus.

STADTISCHES KRAMER-MUSEUM
Kempen, Germany, West.
Fuhrer Durch das Museum Fur Niederrheinische Sakralkunst in der Paterskirche Zu Kempen. Carsten Sternberg. Ed. by Kramer-Museum Kempen. (Illus., 12 color, 90 b&w, Ger.). 1979. DM.10.00. Kramer Mus.

STADTISCHES MUSEUM
Mulheim, Germany, West.
Stadtisches Museum, Mulheim an der Ruhr. (Illus., color, b&w, Ger.). 1974. pap. write for info. Mus Mulheim.
Stadtisches Museum, Mulheim an der Ruhr. (Illus., color, b&w, Ger.). 1970. pap. write for info. Mus Mulheim.

STADTISCHES MUSEUM HAUS KOEKKOEK
Kleve, Germany, West.
Catalogue of Painting, Sculpture & Drawings at the Stadt-Museum, Haus Koekkoek. Guido De Werd. (Illus., 140, Ger.). 1974. pap. DM10.00. Haus Koekkoek.
Klerisches Silber, 1400-1900. Guido De Werd & Ellen Ihne. (Illus., 120, Ger.). pap. DM10.00. Haus Koekkoek.

STADTISCHES MUSEUM, SCHLOSS RHEYDT
Rheydt, Germany, West.
Stadtisches Museum Schloss Rheydt Monchengladbach. Eva Brues. Ed. by Stadt Monchengladbach. (Illus., 9 color, 80 b&w, Ger.). 1979. pap. DM.6.00. Stad Mus Rheydt.

STADTMUSEUM LINZ
Linz, Austria.
Mittelalter - Renaissance - Barock. Renate Maier & Georg Wacha. (Stadtmuseum Linz - Katalog der Schausammlung 2 Ser). (Illus., 116 b&w, Ger.). 1974. pap. DM.100.00. Stadtmus Linz.
Urgeschichte - Romerzeit - Fruhgeschichte. Renate Kux-Julg & Max Kandelhart. Ed. by Georg Wacha. (Illus., 400 photos, Ger.). 1975. pap. DM.250.00. Stadtmus Linz.

STADTRESIDENZ LANDSHUT
Landshut, Germany, West.
Stadtresidenz Landshut. Hans Thoma & Herbert Brunner. (Ger.). 1969. DM.2.00. Bayer Verwal.

STALNA IZLOZBA CRKVENE UMJETNOSTI
Zadar, Yugoslavia.
Permanent Exhibition of Church Art, Zadar. 1978. pap. write for info. Stalna Izlozb.

STARK MUSEUM OF ART
Orange, Texas.
Stark Museum of Art: The American & British Birds of Dorothy Doughty. Henry Sandon. Ed. by Anne Hecht. LC 78-55438. (Illus., 4 color, 7 b&w). 1978. pap. $2.50. Stark Mus Art.
Stark Museum of Art: The Steuben Glass Collection. Isobel Beers. Ed. by Anne Hecht. LC 78-55439. (Illus., 4 color, 7 b&w). 1978. pap. $2.50. Stark Mus Art.
Stark Museum of Art: The Western Collection 1978. Julie Schimmel. Ed. by Anne Hecht. LC 78-55440. (Illus., 33 color, 74 b&w). 1978. pap. $10.00. Stark Mus Art.

STATE ARCHAEOLOGICAL MUSEUM
Hyderabad, India.
Bahmini Coins in the Andhra Pradesh Government Museum. Abdul Wali Khan. (Museum Ser). 1963. Rs.18.00. Mus Andhra Prad.
Catalogue of Arms & Armour. M. L. Gam. (Museum Ser). 1975. Rs.30.00. Mus Andhra Prad.
Catalogue of Ikshvaku Coins. R. Subrahmanyam. (Museum Ser). 1962. Rs.3.00. Mus Andhra Prad.
Catalogue of Roman Coins in the Andhra Pradesh Government Museum. Parameswarilal Gupta. (Museum Ser). 1966. Rs.14.00. Mus Andhra Prad.
Catalogue of Yadava Coins in the Andhra Pradesh Government Museum. R. Subrahmanyam. (Museum Ser). 1965. Rs.4.00. Mus Andhra Prad.
Copper Plate Inscriptions of Andhra Pradesh Government Museum, Vol. 1. N. Ramesan. (Archaeological Ser). 1962. Rs.15.00. Mus Andhra Prad.
Copper Plate Inscriptions of Andhra Pradesh State Museum, Vol. 2. N. Ramesan. (Archaeological Ser). 1970. Rs.15.00. Mus Andhra Prad.
Eastern Chalukyan Coins in Andhra Pradesh Government Museum. M. Rama Rao. (Archaeological Ser). 1963. Rs.3.50. Mus Andhra Prad.
Guide Book to the State Museum, Hyderabad. (Museum Ser). 1976. Rs.12.00. Mus Andhra Prad.
Punch-Marked Coins in Andhra Pradesh Government Museum. P. L. Gupta. (Museum Ser). 1960. Rs.5.00. Mus Andhra Prad.
Qutub Shahi Coins in Andhra Pradesh Government Museum. Abdul Wali Khan. (Museum Ser). 1961. Rs.5.00. Mus Andhra Prad.
Satavahana Coins in Andhra Pradesh Government Museum. M. Rama Rao. (Museum Ser). 1961. Rs.3.50. Mus Andhra Prad.
Select Gold & Silver Coins in Andhra Pradesh Government Museum. M. Rama Rao. (Archaeological Ser). 1963. Rs.2.50. Mus Andhra Prad.
Select Stone Inscriptions of Andhra Pradesh Government Museum. P. B. Desai. (Archaeological Ser). 1962. Rs.5.00. Mus Andhra Prad.
Vishnukundin Coins in Andhra Pradesh Government Museum. M. Rama Rao. (Archaeological Ser). 1963. Rs.5.00. Mus Andhra Prad.

STATENS MUSEUM FOR KUNST
Copenhagen, Denmark.
Abstrakte. (Illus., Danish.). 1961. write for info. Statens Mus.
Aeldre Dansk Skulptur. (Illus.). 1977. write for info. Statens Mus.
Albrecht Durer. Erik Fischer & Marianne Rorup. (Illus., Danish.). 1971. write for info. Statens Mus.
Asger Jorns Grafik. (Lommebog Ser., No. 2). (Illus., Danish.). 1976. write for info. Statens Mus.
Astrid Noack. Erik Thommesen. (Illus., Danish.). 1964. write for info. Statens Mus.
Billedudvalg, 2 vols. Ed. by Else Lofthus. (Danish.). 1970. write for info. Statens Mus.
Catalogue of Old Foreign Paintings. (Illus.). 1951. write for info. Statens Mus.
Dan Sterup-Hansen. Jan Garff. (Lommebog Ser., No. 5). (Illus., Danish.). 1977. write for info. Statens Mus.
Dansk Kunst I 1970'erne. (Danish.). 1976. write for info. Statens Mus.
Dansk Malere I Rom I Det 19. Arhundrede. Ed. by Harald Olsen. (Illus., Danish.). 1977. write for info. Statens Mus.
Dansk Malerkunst. Ed. by Marianne Brons et al. 1970. write for info. Statens Mus.
Fra Ole Kielberg's Verden. Erik Fischer. (Lommebog Ser., No. 4). (Illus., Danish.). 1977. write for info. Statens Mus.
G. B. Piranesi: Three Drawings. Erik Fischer. (Lommebog Ser., No. 6). (Illus.). 1978. write for info. Statens Mus.
Herbert Melbyes Samling. Erik Fischer. (Illus., Danish, Eng. Intro.). 1977. write for info. Statens Mus.
Hollandske Tegninger Og Tryk. Jan Garff. (Lommebog Ser., No. 1). (Illus., Danish, Eng. Intro.). 1976. write for info. Statens Mus.
Host, Rude, Scharff Og Nordiske Samtidige. (Danish.). 1971. write for info. Statens Mus.
Inge Schioler. Nils Ryndel. (Illus., Danish.). 1970. write for info. Statens Mus.
Italiensk Inspiration. Ed. by Inger Nielsen. (Illus., Danish.). 1967. write for info. Statens Mus.
Karl Isakson. Ed. by Jan Garff. (Illus., Danish.). 1974. write for info. Statens Mus.
Lorenz Frolich, 1820-1908. Ed. by Hanne Westergaard. (Illus., Danish.). 1971. write for info. Statens Mus.
Moderne Udenlansk Kunst. Compiled by Hanne Finsen. (Illus., Fr.). 1964. write for info. Statens Mus.
N. A. Abildgaard Tegninger. Ed. by Bente Skovgaard. (Illus.). 1978. write for info. Statens Mus.
Nyere Dansk Skulptur, 2 vols. Ed. by Marianne Brons et al. (Illus.). 1974. write for info. Statens Mus.
Omkring Orfeus. Palle Nielsen. (Lommebog Ser., No. 7). (Illus., Danish.). 1978. write for info. Statens Mus.
Tegninger of Jens Juel. Ed. by Ellen Poulsen. (Illus., Danish, Eng. Intro.). 1975. write for info. Statens Mus.

STEDELIJK MUSEUM-AMSTERDAM
Amsterdam, Netherlands.
Rietveld (Furniture) Harold Plantenga. Ed. by Stedelyk Mus. Tr. by Yvonne Paternotte-Limburg. (From the Collection of the Stedelyk Ser). (Illus., 5 color, 72 b&w, Dutch & Eng.). 1977. pap. write for info. Stedelyk Mus.
Stedelyk Museum, 1963-73. Ed. by Stedelyk Museum. Tr. by Ina Rike & Yvonne Paternotte-Limburg. (From the Collection of the Stedelyk Ser). (Illus., 48 color, 93 b&w, Dutch & Eng.). 1977. pap. fl.25.00. Stedelyk Mus.
Werkman, Druksel Prints & General Printed Matter. Jan Martinet. Tr. by James Brockway & Ina Rike. (From the Collection of the Stedelyk Ser). (Illus., 27 color, 350 b&w, Dutch & Eur.). 1977. pap. fl.25.00. Stedelyk Mus.

STEDELIJK MUSEUM SINT-NIKLAAS
Sint-Niklaas, Belgium.
Catalogus Mathys-Vanneste. Jules Mathys & Herman Nauts. (Illus., 1 color front, 214 b&w, Dutch.). 1974. 150.00 F. Stads Sint-Nik.

STEDELIJK MUSEUM VOOR SCHONE KUNSTEN
Kortrijk, Belgium.
Aanwinsten Vande Musea Kortrijk 1966-1976. P. Debrabandere. (Illus., 15, Dutch.). 1977. 120.00 Fr. Mus Kortrijk.
Kataloog Herdenking Roeland Savery. P. Debrabandere. (Illus., 32, Dutch.). 1976. 150.00 Fr. Mus Kortrijk.
Kortrijks Zilver. P. Debrabandere. (Illus., 5, Dutch.). 1979. 150.00 Fr. Mus Kortrijk.

STEDELIJK VAN ABBE MUSEUM
Eindhoven, Netherlands.
Painting in the Twentieth Century. W. Leering Van Moorsel. Tr. by I. Finley. (Illus., 36 color, Dutch, Eng., Ger. & Fr.). 1969. fl.10.00. Knorr Hirth.
Zonder Titel. R. H. Fuchs. (Illus., 24 b&w, Dutch.). 1976. fl.2.50. Van Abbe Mus.

STEDELIJKE MUSEA
Bruges, Belgium.
Catalogus Aanwinsten 1965. V. Vermeersch. (Illus., 15 plates, Dutch.). 1966. 50.00 F. Stedelijke Mus.
Catalogus Koetsen in Het Brugse Stadsbeeld, Tentoonstelling 1970. D. Devos & A. Janssens De Bisthoven. (Illus., 31 plates). 40.00 F. Stedelijke Mus.
Catalogus Schatten Voor Brugge, Aanwinsten 1966-1972. A. Janssens De Bisthoven et al. (Illus., 7 color, 129 b&w, Dutch & Fr.). 20.00 F. Stedelijke Mus.
Catalogus Schenking Herssens (Voorwerpen in Faience, Porselein En Tin, Meubels, Koperwerk En Oudvlaamse Huisraad) V. Vermeersch. (Dutch.). 1977. 200.00 F. Stedelijke Mus.

STEIRISCHER BURGENVEREIN
see Burgenkundliches Museum

STERLING AND FRANCINE CLARK ART INSTITUTE
see Clark, Sterling and Francine, Art Institute

STIFTUNG OSKAR REINHART
Winterthur, Switzerland.
German & Austrian Painters. Peter Vignau-Wilberg. Ed. by Swiss Institute for Art Research. (Catalogues of Swiss Museums & Collections Ser., 3-II). (Illus., 16 color, 138 b&w, Ger.). 1979. 35.00 F. Orell Fussli Verlag.
Stiftung Oskar Reinhart, Winterthur. Franz M. Zelger. Ed. by Scheizerische Gesellschaft Fur Kunstgeschichte. (Schweizerische Kunstfuhrer Ser). (Illus., 1 color, 49 b&w). 1974. 4.00 F. Oskar Reinhart.
Stiftung Oskar Reinhart, Winterthur: Katalog, Gemalde, Aquarelle & Zeichnungen, Skulpturen. Lisbeth Stahelin. Ed. by Stiftung Oskar Reinhart. (Illus., 8 color, 44 b&w, Ger.). 1971. pap. 10.00 F. Oskar Reinhart.
Swiss Painters After Ferdinand Hodler. Franz M. Zelger. Ed. by Swiss Institute for Art Research. (Catalogues of Swiss Museums & Collections Ser., 3-III). (Illus., 16 color, 126 b&w, Ger.). 35.00 F. Orell Fussli Verlag.
Swiss Painters of the Eighteenth & Nineteenth Centuries. Franz M. Zelger. Ed. by Swiss Institute for Art Research. (Catalogue of Swiss Museums & Collections Ser., 3-I). (Illus., 16 color, 174 b&w, Ger.). 1977. 35.00 F. (ISBN 3-280-00933-2). Orell Fussli Verlag.

STIFTUNG SEEBULL ADA UND EMIL NOLDE
Seebull, Germany, West.
Emil Nolde: Aquarelle. (Illus., Ger.). 1973. write for info. Nolde Mus.
Emil Nolde: Aquarelle & Handzeichnungen. (Illus., Ger.). 1975. DM.25.00. Nolde Mus.
Emil Nolde: Aquarelle & Handzeichnungen. (Illus., Ger. & Eng.). 1974. DM.32.00. Nolde Mus.
Emil Nolde: Aquarelle & Zeichnungen. (Illus., Ger.). 1972. DM.7.50. Nolde Mus.
Emil Nolde: Blumen & Tiere. (Illus., Ger. & Eng.). 1972. DM.86.00. Nolde Mus.
Emil Nolde: Das Abendmahl. (Illus., Ger.). 1964. DM.3.20. Nolde Mus.
Emil Nolde: Das Eigene Leben. (Illus., Ger.). 1974. DM.28.00. Nolde Mus.
Emil Nolde: Gemalde, Aquarelle, Graphik. (Illus., Ger.). 1978. DM.18.00. Nolde Mus.
Emil Nolde: Graphik. (Illus., Ger.). 1975. DM.23.00. Nolde Mus.
Emil Nolde: Das Graphische Werk, Vol. 1. (Illus., Ger.). 1971. write for info. Nolde Mus.
Emil Nolde: Das Graphische Werk, Vol. 2. (Illus.). 1971. write for info. Nolde Mus.
Emil Nolde: Holzschnitte. (Illus., Ger.). 1957. DM.8.80. Nolde Mus.
Emil Nolde: Jahre der Kampfe, 1902-1914. (Illus., Ger.). 1971. DM.28.00. Nolde Mus.
Emil Nolde: En Kunsterns Kampar, 1902-1914. (Illus., Ger.). 1967. DM.16.00. Nolde Mus.
Emil Nolde: Landschaften. (Illus., Ger. & Eng.). 1977. DM.68.00. Nolde Mus.
Emil Nolde: Malerier, Akvareller, Graphik. (Illus., Ger.). 1973. write for info. Nolde Mus.
Emil Nolde: Reisen-Achtung-Befreiung, 1919-1946. (Illus., Ger.). 1978. DM.28.00. Nolde Mus.
Emil Nolde: Ungemalte Bilder. (Illus., Ger. & Eng.). 1971. DM.86.00. Nolde Mus.
Emil Nolde: Ungemalte Bilder, 1938-1945. (Illus., Ger.). 1973. DM.32.00. Nolde Mus.
Emil Nolde Von Werner Haftmann. (Illus., Ger.). 1975. DM.74.00. Nolde Mus.
Emil Nolde: Welt & Heimat. (Illus., Ger.). 1971. DM.28.00. Nolde Mus.
Hundertjahrige. (Illus., Ger.). 1967. DM.5.50. Nolde Mus.

STOWE-DAY FOUNDATION
Hartford, Connecticut.
Illustrated Catalogue of Known Portraits by Jared B. Flagg, 1820-1899. Helen Perkins. (Illus., 91 b&w photos). 1972. pap. $4.00 (ISBN 0-917482-00-X). Stowe Day.

STRANGER'S HALL MUSEUM
Norwich, United Kingdom.
Guide to Strangers' Hall Museum. 0.15p. Norfolk Mus.

STRAUSS, JOHANN, WOHNUNG
Vienna, Austria.
Johann Strauss-Wohnung. Eigenverlag der Museen der Stadt Wien. Tr. by John Whitten. (Illus., 4 b&w, Ger. & Eng.). 1978. pap. S.30.00. Museen Wien.

SUMITOMO COLLECTION
Kyoto, Japan.
Sen-Oku Hakko-Kan: Sumitomo Collection. Takayasu Higuchi. (Jap.). 1976. 800.00 Yen. Sumitomo.
Shin-Shu Sen-Oku Sei-Sho: The Collection of Old Bronzes of Sumitomo. Sueji Umehara. (Jap.). 1971. write for info. Sumitomo.

SUOMEN KANSALLISMUSEO
Helsinki, Finland.
Armfelt-Museo Suomenlinna. Kr.2.00, Finnish ed. (ISBN 951-9074-09-0); Kr.2.00, Swed. ed. (ISBN 951-9074-13-9). Suomen Kans.
Finlands Kyrkor 7 Suomen Kirkot. Ed. by Natl. Mus. Finland. (Illus., 233 b&w). Kr.76.00 (ISBN 951-9074-03-1). Suomen Kans.
Finlands Kyrkor 8 Suomen Kirkot. Natl. Mus. Finland. (Illus., 211 b&w). Kr.114.00 (ISBN 951-9074-12-0). Suomen Kans.
Folk Costumes & Textiles. (Illus., 9 color, 6 b&w, 13 drawings, Finnish.). Kr.10.00 (ISBN 951-9074-35-X). Suomen Kans.
Kivikausi. (Illus., 12 b&w). Kr.1.00, Finnish ed. (ISBN 951-9074-00-7); Kr.1.00, Swed. ed. (ISBN 951-9074-01-5). Suomen Kans.
Kuvat Kuniaan. Ed. by Natl. Mus. Finland. (Illus., 128 b&w). Kr.7.00 (ISBN 951-9074-33-3). Suomen Kans.
Lasia Suomen Kansallismuseon Kokoelmista. Sirkka Kopisto. (Illus., 2 color, 247 b&w, Finnish & Eng.). Kr.20.00 (ISBN 951-9074-30-9). Suomen Kans.
Louhisaari Villnas. (Illus., 4 drawings). Finnish ed.; Kr.1.50, Swed. ed. Kr.1.50, Suomen Kans.
National Museum of Finland. (Illus., 11 b&w). 1974. Kr.3.00, Finnish ed. (ISBN 951-9074-05-8); Kr.3.00, Swed. ed. (ISBN 951-9074-07-4); Suomen Kans.
Pukkilan Kartano - Ja Ajokalumuseo. (Illus., 4 drawings). 1972. Kr.1.50, Finnish ed.; Kr.1.50, Swed. ed. Suomen Kans.
Seurasaaren Ulkomuseo. (Illus., 36 b&w, 12 plans & maps). Kr.3.00, Finnish ed. (ISBN 951-9074-32-5); Kr.3.00, Swed. ed. (ISBN 951-9074-40-6). Suomen Kans.
Tradition und Volkskunst in Finnland. Pirkko Sihvo. (Illus., 2 color, 57 b&w). Kr.20.00. Suomen Kans.

SWEET BRIAR COLLEGE
Sweet Briar, Virginia.
Prints from the Sweet Briar Collection. Barbara Behrens & Cannie Crysler. Ed. by Ruth Firm & Aileen Laing. (Illus., 36 b&w). 1978. pap. free. Sweet Briar.

SWEN PARSON GALLERY
see Northern Illinois Univ., Swen Parson Gallery

TATE GALLERY
London, United Kingdom.
Age of Charles I. (Illus., 258; 9 color). pap. $4.95. Barron.
Ben Nicholson. (Illus., 63; 13 color). $4.95. Barron.
Caspar David Friedrich, 1774-1840. William Vaughan & Helmut Borsch-Supan. (Illus., 128; 10 color). $11.95. Barron.
Child of Six Could Do It! George Melly & J. R. Glaves-Smith. (Illus., 114). pap. $3.95. Barron.
Constable: Landscape Watercolours & Drawings. Ian Fleming-Williams. (Illus., 198; 12 color). pap. $29.95. Barron.
Constable: Paintings, Watercolours & Drawings. Leslie Parris & Ian Fleming-Williams. (Illus., 350; 6 color). pap. $10.95. Barron.
Eduardo Paolozzi. Frank Whitford. (Illus., 239; 1 color). $3.95. Barron.
Elizabethan Image: Paintings in England, 1540-1620. Roy Strong. (Illus., 127; 12 color). $4.95. Barron.
Henry Fuseli, 1741-1825. (Illus., 304; 81 color). pap. $7.95. Barron.
Henry Moore Gift. (Illus., 83; 7 color). pap. $6.95. Barron.
Henry Moore: Graphics in the Making. Pat Gilmour. (Illus., 58; 12 color). pap. $7.95. Barron.
Illustrated Catalogue of Acquisitions: Illustrated Catalogue of Acquisitions. (Illus., 115). pap. $10.95. Barron.
John Constable. (Barron's-The Tate Gallery Little Art Book Ser). (Illus., 36; 9 color). pap. $1.95. Barron.
John Latham. Terry Measham. (Illus., 29). pap. $3.50. Barron.
Julio Gonzalez. (Illus., 42). pap. $2.95. Barron.
Kasimir Malevich. A. Nakov. (Illus., 20). pap. $4.95. Barron.
Landscape in Britain c. 1750-1850. Leslie Parris. (Illus., 280; 10 color). $9.95. Barron.
Late Richard Dadd, 1817-86. Patricia Allderidge. (Illus., 230; 16 color). pap. $6.95. Barron.
Leger & Purist Paris. (Illus., 127; 8 color). pap. $3.95. Barron.
Optical & Kinetic Art. (Barron's-The Tate Gallery Little Art Book Ser). (Illus., 36; 9 color). pap. $1.95. Barron.
Paul Nash, Paintings & Watercolors. (Illus., 99; 14 color). pap. $8.95. Barron.
Pre-Raphaelites. (Barron's-The Tate Gallery Little Art Book Ser). (Illus., 36; 9 color). pap. $1.95. Barron.
Richard Smith. (Illus., 111; 8 color). pap. $5.95. Barron.
Robert Morris. Michael Compton & David Sylvester. (Illus., 109). $3.95. Barron.
Surrealists. (Barron's-The Tate Gallery Little Art Book Ser). (Illus., 36; 9 color). pap. $1.95. Barron.
Tate Gallery. (Illus., 203; 83 color). pap. $6.95. Barron.
Turner: Early Works. (Barron's-The Tate Gallery Little Art Book Ser). (Illus., 36; 9 color). pap. $1.95. Barron.
Turner: Later Works. (Barron's-The Tate Gallery Little Art Book Ser). (Illus., 36; 9 color). pap. $1.95. Barron.
Warhol. (Illus., 87; 18 color). $5.95. Barron.
William Blake. Martin Butlin. (Illus., 380; 17 color). $18.95; pap. $11.95. Barron.
William Blake. (Barron's-The Tate Gallery Little Art Book Ser). (Illus., 36; 9 color). pap. $1.95. Barron.
William Turnbull. (Illus., 178; 18 color). pap. $5.95. Barron.

TEMPLE NEWSAM HOUSE
Leeds, United Kingdom.
Concise Catalogue of Paintings, Water Colours, Prints, Drawings & Sculpture in the Leeds Collection. Miranda Strickland-Constable & Alexander Robinson. 1976. pap. E1.00. P L Humphries.
Creamware & Other English Pottery at Temple Newsam House, Leeds. Peter Walton. (Illus., 16 color, 450 b&w). 1976. E42.00 (ISBN 0-905564-00-6). P L Humphries.
Furniture at Temple Newsam House & Lotherton Hall. Christopher Gilbert. (Illus., 14 color, 680 b&w). 1978. E60.00 (ISBN 0-9503334-1-7). P L Humphries.

TENNESSEE BOTANICAL GARDENS AND FINE ARTS CENTER
Nashville, Tennessee.
One Hundred Works from the Permanent Collection. Intro. by Walter Sharp. 1965. pap. write for info. Tenn Fine Ctr.

TENNESSEE FINE ARTS CENTER
see Tennessee Botanical Gardens and Fine Arts Center

TEXTILE MUSEUM
Washington, D.C.
Caucasian Rugs from Private Collections. Patricia L. Fiske. (Illus., 37 b&w). 1976. $2.50. Textile Mus.
Early Caucasian Rugs. Charles Ellis. (Illus., 16 color, 21 b&w). 1975. $12.50. Textile Mus.
From the Bosporus to Samarkand: Flat Woven Rugs. Anthony N. Landreau & W. R. Pickering. (Illus., 9 color, 104 b&w). 1969. $5.00. Textile Mus.
Masterpieces in the Textile Museum. Louise W. Mackie & Ann Pollard Rowe. (Illus., 35 b&w). 1976. $2.50. Textile Mus.
Oriental Rug Collection of Jerome & Mary Jane Straka. Jerome A. Straka & Louise W. Mackie. (Illus., 77 color, 52 b&w). 1978. $12.50. Textile Mus.
Prayer Rugs. Richard Ettinghausen et al. (Illus., 32 color, 28 b&w). 1974. $28.00; pap. $9.00. Textile Mus.
Prayer Rugs from Private Collections. Patricia L. Fiske. (Illus., 33 b&w). 1974. $2.50. Textile Mus.
Splendid Symbols: Textiles & Traditions in Indonesia. Mattiebelle Gittinger. (Illus., 7 color, 177 b&w). 1978. $15.00. Textile Mus.
Splendor of Turkish Weaving. Louise W. Mackie. (Illus., 4 color, 44 b&w). 1974. $5.00. Textile Mus.
Turkish Rugs. Ralph S. Yohe & H. McCoy Jones. (Illus., 5 color, 6 b&w). 1968. $3.95. Textile Mus.
Turkish Rugs: The Rachel B. Stevens Memorial Collection. Barbara C. Fertig. (Illus., 21 color, 15 b&w). 1972. $4.00. Textile Mus.
Warp-Patterned Weaves of the Andes. Ann Pollard-Rowe. (Illus., 7 color, 146 b&w). 1977. $9.95. Textile Mus.

TEXTILMUSEUM
Krefeld, Germany, West.
Gebilddamast. Renate Jaques. (Illus., Ger.). 1968. DM.12.00. Textil Krefeld.
Seimle, Velvets, Velours. Ruth Gusthaus & Carl Wolfgang-Schumann. Ed. by Textil Museum Krefeld. (Illus., 10 color, 90 b&w, Ger., Eng. & Fr.). 1979. DM.20.00. Textil Krefeld.
Stofle, 1900. Brijitte Monzel. Ed. by Textil Museum Krefeld. (Illus., 15 color, 85 b&w, Ger.). 1977. DM.15.00. Textil Krefeld.

TEYLERS MUSEUM
Haarlem, Netherlands.
Cent Dessins Du Musee Teyler. I. Q. Altena. (Illus., 100 b&w, Fr.). 1972. pap. fl.20.00. Teylers Mus.
Drawings from the Teylers Museum. I. Q. Altena & P. W. Jackson. (Illus., 118 b&w). 1970. pap. fl.20.00. Teylers Mus.
Two Hundred Jaar Verzamelen: Hoogtepunten der Tekenkunst. J. H. Van Borssum Buisman. (Illus., 40 b&w, Dutch.). 1978. pap. fl.7.00. Teylers Mus.

THORVALDSEN MUSEUM
Copenhagen, Denmark.
Thorvaldsens Museum. Sigurd Schultz & Dyveke Helsted. Ed. by Thorvaldsen Museum. (Illus., 49, Danish, Eng., Fr. & Ger.). 1959. pap. Kr.10.00. Thorvaldsen.
Thorvaldsens Museum Katalog. Dyveke Helsted et al. Ed. by Thorvaldsen Museum. (Illus., 88, Danish.). 1975. pap. Kr.15.00. Thorvaldsen.

TIROLER LANDESMUSEUM
Innsbruck, Austria.
Albin Egger-Lienz, 1868-1926: Malerei und Grafik. E. Egg. Ed. by G. Ammann. (Illus., 97 color, Ger.). 1976. S.70.00. Tirol Lan Mus.
Alfred Kubin - Wilde Tiere. Ed. by G. Ammann. (Illus., 31 pen & ink drawings, Ger.). 1977. S.5.00. Tirol Lan Mus.
Alte Kostume in Figurinen. Ed. by E. Egg. (Ger.). 1970. S.5.00. Tirol Lan Mus.
Barock in Kitzbuhel. Ed. by E. Egg & G. Ammann. (Illus., 67, Ger.). 1971. S.20.00. Tirol Lan Mus.
Christian, 1895-1944. Ed. by G. Ammann. (Illus., 9, Ger.). 1976. S.20.00. Tirol Lan Mus.
Einhundertfunfzig Jahre Bibliothek Des Ferdindeums: Handschriften, Drucke, Karten, Urkunder, Siegal, Heraldik und Genealogie. Ed. by O. Kostenzer & M. Pizzinini. (Illus., 12, Ger.). 1973. S.20.00. Tirol Lan Mus.
Einhundertfunfzig Jahre Tiroler Landesmuseum Ferdinandeum. E. Egg. (Illus., color, Ger., Fr. & Eng.). 1973. S.+15.00. Tirol Lan Mus.
Franz Lettner: Malerei und Grafik. Ed. by E. Egg. (Illus., Ger.). 1969. S.15.00. Tirol Lan Mus.
Friedrich Hell, 1869-1957: Malerei. Ed. by A. Weiler. (Illus., 6). 1970. S.10.00. Tirol Lan Mus.
Fuhrer Durch das Tiroler Landeskundliche Museum in Zeughaus. Ed. by E. Egg. (Illus., 24, Ger.). 1973. S.10.00. Tirol Lan Mus.
Hans Pontiller: Plastik. Ed. by E. Egg. (Illus., Ger.). 1964. S.15.00. Tirol Lan Mus.
Hilde Goldschmidt: Malerei und Grafik. Ed. by G. Ammann. (Illus., 9, Ger.). 1977. S.20.00. Tirol Lan Mus.
Jagd und Kunst, Zum 100: Jubilaum Des Tiroler Landesjagdschutzvereines. Ed. by E. Egg. (Illus., 64, Ger.). 1975. S.20.00. Tirol Lan Mus.
Johannes Itten, 1888-1967: Malerei. Frwd. by Kristian Sotriffer. (Illus., Ger.). 1967. S.15.00. Tirol Lan Mus.
Josef Anton Koch, 1768-1839: Grafik, Aus Den Sammlungen der Akademiebibliothek Wien. Ed. by H. Hutter. (Illus., 16, Ger.). 1968. S.15.00. Tirol Lan Mus.
Karl Plattner: Grafik. Ed. by E. Egg & G. Ammann. (Illus., 5, Ger.). 1976. S.10.00. Tirol Lan Mus.
Katalog der Gemaldesammlung. Ed. by J. Ringler. (Illus., Ger.). 1928. S.20.00. Tirol Lan Mus.
Mineralien Aus Aller Welt. Ed. by J. Ladurner. (Illus., 6, Ger.). 1978. S.15.00. Tirol Lan Mus.
Nach 1900: Zeichnungen, Pastelle, Aquarelle und Collagen Moderner Meister Aus Dem Besitz Des Museums Grenoble. Ed. by W. Kirschl. (Illus., 78, Ger.). 1972. S.30.00. Tirol Lan Mus.
Osterreichischen Ausgrabungen in Sayala, Agyptisch-Nubien, 1961-1966. Ed. by K. Kromer. (Illus., 34, Ger.). 1978. S.30.00. Tirol Lan Mus.
Paul Troger: Der Maler Des Osterreichischen Barock. Ed. by E. Egg & W. Aschebrenner. (Illus., 37, 5 color, Ger.). 1962. S.20.00. Tirol Lan Mus.
Plastik Des 20. Jahrhunderts in Tirol. Ed. by G. Ammann. (Illus., 78, Ger.). 1978. S.20.00. Tirol Lan Mus.
Portrat Nach 1945 in Tirol: Malerei und Grafik. Ed. by G. Ammann. (Illus., Ger.). 1977. S.30.00. Tirol Lan Mus.
Schutzen - Scheiben - Schatze: Geschichte Des Tiroler Schutzenwesens. Ed. by E. Egg. (Illus., 48, Ger.). 1975. S.35.00. Tirol Lan Mus.
Stiftung Emanuel und Sofie Fohn: Malerei und Grafik. Ed. by E. Egg. (Illus., 7, Ger.). 1970. S.10.00. Tirol Lan Mus.
Tiroler Freiheitskampf, 1809: Zeitgenossiche Bilder und Dokumente. Ed. by E. Egg. (Illus., 16, Ger.). 1959. S.5.00. Tirol Lan Mus.
Tiroler Maler Sehen Frankreich: Malerei und Grafik. Ed. by E. Egg. (Illus., Ger.). 1969. S.15.00. Tirol Lan Mus.
Tiroler Standschutzen: Vierhundert Jahre Landesverteidigung in Tirol. Ed. by E. Egg & O. Gschliesser. (Illus., 12, Ger.). 1965. S.20.00. Tirol Lan Mus.
Venezianische Kupferstecher Von Mantegna Bis Tiepolo: Aus Dem Museo Correr in Venedig. Ed. by T. Pignatti. (Illus., 8, Ger.). 1970. S.10.00. Tirol Lan Mus.
Werner Scholz: Malerei und Grafik. Ed. by G. Ammann. (Illus., 8, Ger.). 1973. S.10.00. Tirol Lan Mus.
Wilhelm Nikolaus Prachensky: Gemalde und Aquarelle. Ed. by E. Egg. (Illus., 8, Ger.). 1977. S.10.00. Tirol Lan Mus.
Zinnfiguren: Entwicklung der Zinnfiguren und Darstellung Historicher Ereignisse. Ed. by E. Kroner-Grimm. (Illus., 20, Ger.). 1978. S.10.00. Tirol Lan Mus.

TOKUGAWA ART MUSEUM, THE TOKUGAWA REIMEIKAI FOUNDATION
Tokyo, Japan.
Chaire: Tea Caddy, One of the Instruments of the Tea Ceremony. C. Okuda et al. Ed. by Tokugawa Reimeikai Foundation & Nezu Institute of Fine Arts. (Illus., 12 color plates, 247 b&w plates, Jap.). 1977. 2000.00 Yen. Tokugawa.
Fukko Yamato-E: Paintings by Tanaka Totsugen & Other Artists of the Fukko Yamato-E Group. M. Kinoshita. Ed. & intro. by Tokugawa Reimeikai Foundation. (Illus., 19 color plates, 114 b&w plates, Jap.). 1978. 1500.00 Yen. Tokugawa.
Genji Monogatari Emaki: Scenes from the Tale of Genji. Y. Tokugawa et al. Ed. by Tokugawa Reimeikai Foundation. (Illus., 27 color plates, 55 b&w plates, Jap.). 1975. 1300.00 Yen. Tokugawa.
Higashi-Yama Gomotsu: Masters of the Ashikagas in the Muromachi Period. C. Okuda et al. Ed. by Tokugawa Reimeikai Foundation & Nezu Institute of Fine Arts. (Illus., 18 color plates, 145 b&w plates, Jap.). 1976. 2000.00 Yen. Tokugawa.
Meihin Zuroku: Selected Art Objects of the Tokugawa Art Museum, Nagoya. Y. Tokugawa. Ed. by Tokugawa Reimeikai Foundation. (Illus., 23 color plates, 396 b&w plates, Jap. & Eng.). 1976. 1800.00 Yen. Tokugawa.
Mino Koto: Old Potteries of the Mino District. C. Okuda et al. Ed. by Tokugawa Reimeikai Foundation & Nezu Institute of Fine Arts. (Illus., 12 color plates, 114 b&w plates, Jap.). 1971. 2000.00 Yen. Tokugawa.
Ryukyu Shikki: Ryukyu Lacquer Arts. Y. Tokugawa & H. Arakawa. Ed. by Tokugawa Reimeikai Foundation & Nezu Institute of Fine Arts. (Illus., 27 color plates, 94 b&w plates, Jap. & Eng.). 1978. 2000.00 Yen. Tokugawa.
Sunpu-Owakemono Token & Sengoku-Busho Gazou: Swords Left by Tokugawa Iyeyasu & Warrior's Portraits & Letters. Y. Tokugawa et al. Ed. by Tokugawa Reimeikai Foundation. (Illus., 4 color plates, 166 b&w plates, Jap.). 1974. 1400.00 Yen. Tokugawa.
The Tokugawa Collection: No Robes & Masks. Y. Tokugawa & S. Okochi. Ed. by Japan Society. Tr. by Louise Cort & Monica Bethe. (Illus., 24 color plates, 145 b&w plates). 1977. 10000.00 Yen (ISBN 0-913304-08-5). Tokugawa.

TOLEDO MUSEUM OF ART
Toledo, Ohio.
American Painting. Susan Strickler. Ed. by William Hutton. 1979. write for info. Toledo Mus.
Art in Glass. Intro. by Otto Wittmann. (Illus., 9 color, 191 b&w). 1969. pap. $3.95. Toledo Mus.
European Paintings. Intro. by Otto Wittmann. (Illus., 12 color, 453 b&w). 1976. $22.50 (ISBN 0-271-01249-8); pap. $12.95 (ISBN 0-271-01248-X). Toledo Mus.
Guide to the Collections. Intro. by Otto Wittmann. (Illus., 38 color, 362 b&w). 1976. pap. $3.95. Toledo Mus.
Toledo Museum of Art. Cedric G. Boulter & Kurt T. Luckner. (Corpus Vasorum Antiquorum, U. S. A. Fasc. 17 Ser). (Illus., 60). 1976. $30.00. Toledo Mus.

TOM THOMSON MEMORIAL GALLERY AND MUSEUM OF FINE ART
Owen Sound, Canada.
Permanent Collection, 1978. Ed. by James Logan & Catherine Harrison. (Illus., 25 b&w). 1979. pap. Can.$2.50. Tom Thomson.

TOUGALOO COLLEGE ART COLLECTIONS
Tougaloo, Mississippi.
Tougaloo College Art Collection. Ed. by Ronald Schnell. (Illus., 4 color, 43 b&w). 1977. pap. $10.00. Tougaloo.

TOWNELEY HALL ART GALLERY AND MUSEUMS
Burneley, United Kingdom.
Catalogue of Oil Paintings & Watercolors in the Permanent Collection. Susan Bourne. 1978. 0.40p. Burnley Boro Coun.
Childrens Furniture, 1600-1900. Susan Bourne. (Illus., 8 b&w photos). 1977. pap. 0.30p. Burnley Boro Coun.
Introduction to the Architecture of Towneley Hall. Susan Bourne. (Illus., 14 b&w photos). 1979. pap. E1.50. Burnley Boro Coun.
Regiments of Lancashire. Susan Bourne. (Illus., 9 b&w photos). 1973. pap. 0.12p. Burnley Boro Coun.

Towneley Hall Art Gallery & Museums Official Guide & Handbook. 0.30p. Burnley Boro Coun.
Twentieth Century British Sculpture. Susan Bourne. 1975. pap. 0.10p. Burnley Boro Coun.

TRESOR DE LA CATHEDRALE ST. PAUL
Liege, Belgium.
Tresor De la Cathedrale St. Paul a Liege. Pierre Colman. (Illus., 24 photos, Fr.). 1968. pap. $105.00. Cath St Paul.

TRITON MUSEUM OF ART
Santa Clara, California.
Catalog of the Paintings by Theodore Wores in the Permanent Collection of the Triton Museum of Art. Donna Thomas & Andrea Glanz. (Illus., 3 b&w photos). 1976. pap. $0.50. Triton Mus Art.

TRONDHJEMS KUNSTFORENING, TRONDELAG KUNSTGALLERI
Trondheim, Norway.
Trondhjems Kunstforening, Det Faste Galleri. (Illus., 127 b&w photos, Norwegian.). 1954. write for info. Det Faste Galleri.

TUNBRIDGE WELLS MUNICIPAL MUSEUM AND ART GALLERY
Tunbridge Wells, United Kingdom.
Ashton Bequest. Rupert Qunnis. 1952. 0.06p. Tunbridge.
Pamela McDowall Collection of Cartoon Collages. 1978. 0.10p. Tunbridge.

UHRENMUSEUM
Vienna, Austria.
Uhrenmuseum. (Illus., 14 color, 47 b&w, Ger.). 1979. S.80.00. Museen Wien.

ULRICH, EDWIN A., MUSEUM, WAVE CREST ON-THE-HUDSON
Hyde Park, New York.
Complete Biography of Frederick J. Waugh. Havens. (Illus., 32). 1968. pap. $9.00. Ed Ulrich Mus.
Frederick Waugh's Paintings of the Sea, No. 153. (Illus., 60 color). 1974. $2.00. Ed Ulrich Mus.
Landscape Painting with a Knife. Coulton Waugh. (Illus., 150). 1974. $17.00. Ed Ulrich Mus.

UMELECKOPRUMYSLOVE MUZEUM
Prague, Czechoslovakia.
Arts & Crafts 1860-1900. Jarmila Brozova. (Museum Collections Ser). (Illus., 10 color, 310 b&w, Czech. & Ger.). 1975. pap. 60.00 Kcs. Umeleck Muz.
Bohemian Glass of the 17th & 18th Centuries. E. Poche & D. Hejdova. (Glass Collection Ser). (Illus., 47 b&w photos, Czech. & Eng.). 1970. pap. 50.00 Kcs. Umeleck Muz.
Bohemian Glass 1800-1860. Jarmila Brozova. (Glass Collection Ser). (Illus., 10 color, 184 b&w photos, Czech. & Ger.). pap. 60.00 Kcs. Umeleck Muz.
Clocks & Watches from the Museum of Decorative Arts in Prague. Libuse Uresova. (Museums Collections Ser). (Illus., 10 color, 214 b&w photos, Czech. & Eng.). 1977. pap. 45.00 Kcs. Umeleck Muz.
Czech Cubist Interior. Olga Herbenova & Milena Lamarova. (Museums Collection Ser). (Illus., 3 color photos, 143 b&w, Czech. & Eng.). 1973. pap. 35.00 Kcs. Umeleck Muz.
Delft Ceramics. Jana Kybalova. (Ceramics Collections Ser). (Illus., 9 color photos, 108 b&w, Czech. & Eng.). 1973. pap. 30.00 Kcs. Umeleck Muz.
Goldsmithwork of the Barocco Time. Libuse Uresova. (Museum Collections Ser). (Illus., 2 color, 188 b&w photos, Czech. & Ger.). 1974. pap. 40.00 Kcs. Umeleck Muz.
Italian Maiolica. Jirina Vydrova. (Great Era of the Italian Art of the Flame Ser). (Illus., 4 color, 182 b&w photos & 39 drawings, Czech. & Eng.). 1973. pap. 30.00 Kcs. Umeleck Muz.
Ninety & One Chair. Olga Herbenova. (Collection of Furniture Ser). (Illus., 89 b&w, Czech. & Eng.). 1972. pap. 30.00 Kcs. Umeleck Muz.
Tapestry of the 16th to the 18th Centuries. Jarmila Blazkova. (Museum Collections Ser). (Illus., 2 color, 151 b&w photos, Czech. & Eng.). 1977. pap. 35.00 Kcs. Umeleck Muz.
Textiles from the Barocco Time-Paramenta. Milena Zeminova. (Museums Collection of Textiles Ser). (Illus., 2 color, 104 b&w photos, Czech. & Ger.). 1974. pap. 40.00 Kcs. Umeleck Muz.
Venetian Glass. Karel Hettes. (Great Era of the Italian Art of the Flame Ser). (Illus., 4 color, 58 b&w photos, 19 drawings, Czech. & Eng.). 1973. pap. 30.00 Kcs. Umeleck Muz.

UNION CENTRAL DES ARTS DECORATIFS-MUSEE DES ARTS DECORATIFS
Paris, France.
Affiches De Cafe-Concert. Intro. by Genevieve Gaetan-Picon. (Illus., 5 color, 47 b&w, Fr.). 1977. 25.00 F. Arts Deco.
Annees 25. Intro. by Francoi Mathey. (Illus., 48 b&w, Fr.). 1966. 30.00 F. Arts Deco.
Antagonisme 2: L'Objet. (Illus., 157 b&w, Fr.). 1962. 35.00 F. Arts Deco.
Arman: Accumulations Renault. (Illus., 10 color, 34 b&w, Fr.). 1969. 25.00 F. Arts Deco.
Art Armenien De L'Ourartou a Nos Jours. Intro. by Martiros Sarian & Vadime Elisseeff. (Illus., 8 color, 120 b&w, Fr.). 1970. 25.00 F. Arts Deco.
Belle Epoque. Intro. by Andre Conquet. (Illus., 80, Fr.). 1964. 25.00 F. Arts Deco.
Broderie Au Passe et Au Present. Nadine Gasc. (Illus., 11 color, 27 b&w, Fr.). 1977. 30.00 F. Arts Deco.
Bronzes Du Monde Iranien. A. S. Melikian-Chirvani. (Illus., 4 color, 80 b&w, Fr.). 1973. 20.00 F. Arts Deco.
Cent Ans: Cent Chef D'oeuvres. (Illus., 99 b&w, Fr.). 1964. 20.00 F. Arts Deco.
Cesar-Daum. Ed. by Jacques Daum & Francois Mathey. (Illus., 2 color, 20 b&w, Fr.). 1969. 15.00 F. Arts Deco.
Charles Loupot, Affichiste, 1892-1962. Alain Weill. (Illus., Fr.). 1978. 30.00 F. Arts Deco.
Chasse a L'Anamorphose. Intro. by Jurgis Baltrusaitis. (Illus., 8 color, 62 b&w, Fr.). 1976. 35.00 F. Arts Deco.
Cinquartenaire De L'Exposition De 1925. Ed. by Yvonne Brunhammer. (Illus., 8 color, 12 b&w, Fr.). 1976. 20.00 F. Arts Deco.
Des Dorelotiers Aux Passementiers. (Illus., 23 color, 45 b&w, Fr.). 1973. 30.00 F. Arts Deco.
Des Tapisseries Nouvelles. (Illus., 73 b&w, Fr.). 1975. 15.00 F. Arts Deco.
Donation Jean Dubuffet. Intro. by Eugene Petit. (Illus., 138 b&w, Fr.). 1967. 15.00 F. Arts Deco.
Equivoques. Pref. by Francois Mathey. (Illus., 140 b&w, Fr.). 1973. 35.00 F. Arts Deco.
Ernest Chaplet, 1835-1909. (Illus., 8 color, 86 b&w, Fr.). 1976. 50.00 F. Arts Deco.
Fernand Leger. Intro. by Jacques Guerin. (Illus., 8 color, 200 b&w, Fr.). 1956. 40.00 F. Arts Deco.
Georges Melies. Intro. by Georges Melies & Madeleine Melies. (Illus., 8 color, 16 b&w, Fr.). 25.00 F. Arts Deco.
Jean Dubuffet: Parachiffres, Mondanites et Autres Peintures 1975. Pref. by Gaetan Picon. (Illus., 4 color,25 b&w, Fr.). 1976. 20.00 F. Arts Deco.
Jouets Americains. Robert Debre & Inez McClintock. (Illus., 13 color, 38 b&w, Fr.). 1977. 20.00 F. Arts Deco.
Machines Celibataires. (Illus., Fr. & Ger.). 1976. 50.00 F. Arts Deco.
Marc Chagall. Intro. by Jacques Guerin. (Illus., 13 color, 170 b&w, Fr.). 1959. 50.00 F. Arts Deco.
Matisse. Intro. by Jacques Lassaigne. (Illus., 13 color, 12 b&w, Fr.). 1961. 35.00 F. Arts Deco.
Niko Pirosmanachvili. (Illus., 4 color, 28 b&w, Fr.). 1969. 15.00 F. Arts Deco.
Picasso. Intro. by Maurice Jardot. (Illus., 130 b&w, Fr.). 1955. 35.00 F. Arts Deco.
Portraits D'Helena Rubinstein. (Illus., 6 color, 6 b&w, Fr.). 1977. 7.50 F. Arts Deco.
Retrospective Jean Dubuffet. Pref. by Gaetan Picon. (Illus., 11 color, 182 b&w, Fr.). 1960. 45.00 F. Arts Deco.
Retrospective Marc Tobey. Pref. by Francois Mathey. (Illus., 6 color, 85 b&w, Fr.). 1961. 45.00 F. Arts Deco.
Science Fiction. (Illus., 90 b&w, Fr.). 1968. 20.00 F. Arts Deco.
Siecle De Photographie De Niepoe a Man Ray. Andre Jammes & L. Roosens. (Illus., 32 b&w, Fr.). 1965. 30.00 F. Arts Deco.
Sucre D'Art. Jean-Marie Lhote & David Guy. (Illus., 18 color, 64 b&w, Fr.). 1978. 18.00 F. Arts Deco.
Tapisseries De le Corbusier. Charles Goerg & Francois Mathey. (Illus., 6 color, 49 b&w, Fr.). 1975. 30.00 F. Arts Deco.
Trois Sculpteurs: Cesar, Roel D'Haese & Tinguely. Francois Mathey et al. (Illus., 53 b&w, Fr.). 1965. 20.00 F. Arts Deco.
Trois Siecles D'Affiches Francaises. Pref. by Robert Bordaz & Jean Casanova. (Illus., 10 color, 144 b&w, Fr.). 1978. 25.00 F. Arts Deco.
Trois Siecles De Papiers Peints. Intro. by Eugene Petit. (Illus., 9 color, 61 b&w). 1967. 40.00 F. Arts Deco.
Victor Regnault. Pref. by Pierre Gassmann. (Illus., Fr.). 1978. 15.00 F. Arts Deco.
Yves Klein. Pierre Restany & Paul Wember. (Illus., 9 color, Fr.). 1969. 25.00 F. Arts Deco.

UNIV. OF ARIZONA, MUSEUM OF ART
Tucson, Arizona.
C. Leonard Pfeiffer Collection of American Paintings & Drawings. Intro. by Richard Harvill & William Steadman. (Illus., 4 color, 99 b&w). 1969. pap. $3.00. U of Ariz Mus.
Retablo of the Cathedral of Ciudad Rodrigo by Fernando Gallego from the Samuel H. Kress Collections at the University of Arizona. Robert M. Quinn. Tr. by Renato I. Rosaldo. (Illus., 1 color, 26 b&w, Eng. & Span.). 1960. pap. $1.00. U of Ariz Mus.
Samuel H. Kress Collection at the University of Arizona. Intro. by R. M. Quinn. (Illus., 1 color, 26 b&w). 1957. pap. $1.00. U of Ariz Mus.
Vault Show I: Selections from the Museum of Art at the University of Arizona. (Illus., 59 b&w). 1977. pap. $0.50. U of Ariz Mus.

UNIV. OF BRITISH COLUMBIA, MUSEUM OF ANTHROPOLOGY
Vancouver, Canada.
Indian Masterpieces from the Walter & Marianne Koerner Collection in the Museum of Anthropolgy, University of British Columbia. $4.95. U Brit Colum.
Northwest Coast Indian Artifacts from the H. R. Macmillan Collection in the Museum of Anthropology, University of British Columbia. $4.95. U Brit Colum.

UNIV. OF CALIFORNIA, LOS ANGELES, MUSEUM OF CULTURAL HISTORY
Los Angeles, California.
Art & Material Culture of the Zulu-Speaking Peoples. Carolee Kennedy. (UCLA Museum of Cultural History Pamphlet Ser., Vol. I, No. 3). (Illus., 27 b&w, 1 map). 1979. pap. $1.50. Mus Cult Hist.
Balega & Other Tribal Arts from the Congo. Ralph Altman. (Illus., 22 b&w). 1963. pap. $2.50. Mus Cult Hist.
Black Gods & Kings: Yoruba Art at UCLA. Robert Thompson. (Illus., 416 b&w, 2 maps). 1971. pap. write for info. Ind U Pr.
Decade in Retrospect: Works from Asia, Europe, the Near East, Africa, North & South America, Indonesia & Oceania, Drawn from Museum Collections. Charles E. Young. (Illus., 4 color, 54 b&w). 1974. pap. $6.00. Mus Cult Hist.
George G. Frelinghuysen Collection at UCLA: Objects from Africa, Indonesia, the South Seas & Asia. Frwd. by Franklin Murphy & Jay Frierman. (Illus., 35 b&w). 1968. pap. $4.00. Mus Cult Hist.
Lithuanian Folk Art. Victoria Feldon & Marija Gimbutas. (Illus., 32 b&w). 1966. pap. $4.00. Mus Cult Hist.
Loom, the Needle & the Dye Pot. Patricia Altman. (UCLA Museum of Cultural History Pamphlet Ser.,Vol. I, No. 1). (Illus., 14 b&w). 1977. pap. $1.50. Mus Cult Hist.
Masterpieces from the Sir Henry Wellcome Collection at UCLA. (Illus., 3 color plates, 129 b&w). 1965. pap. $6.00. Mus Cult Hist.
Natalie Wood Collection of Pre-Columbian Ceramics from Chupicuaro, Guanajuato, Mexico at UCLA. Muriel Weaver et al. (Occasional Papers of the Museum & Laboratories of Ethnic Arts & Technology Ser., No. 1). (Illus., 8 color plates, 404 b&w, 3 maps, 1 chart). 1969. pap. $22.50. Mus Cult Hist.
Near East: In UCLA Collections. Lois Brooks et al. (Illus., 20 b&w). 1969. pap. $4.00. Mus Cult Hist.
Warao Basketry: Form & Function. Johannes Wilbert. Ed. by Raul Lopez. (Occasional Papers of the Museum of Cultural History Ser., No. 3). (Illus., 1 color plate, 83 b&w, 1 map). 1975. pap. $11.50. Mus Cult Hist.

UNIV. OF CAMBRIDGE, FITZWILLIAM MUSEUM
Cambridge, United Kingdom.
Augustus Edwin John, OM 1878-1961. 1978. 0.60p. Fitzwilliam.
Catalogue of Paintings, Vol. 1. H. Gerson & J. W. Goodison. (Illus., 211, Dutch & Flemish.). 1960. E9.00; pap. E3.95 Fitzwilliam.
Catalogue of Paintings, Vol. 1. J. W. Goodison & Denys Sutton. (Illus., 211, Fr., Ger. & Span.). 1960. E9.00; pap. E3.95. Fitzwilliam.
Catalogue of Paintings: British School, Vol. 3. J. W. Goodison. (Illus., 64 plates). 1977. E18.00. Fitzwilliam.
Catalogue of Paintings: Italian Schools, Vol. 2. J. W. Goodison & G. H. Robertson. (Illus., 64 plates). 1967. E9.00. Fitzwilliam.
Catalogue of the Beddington Collection of Colour Prints. Frederick C. Daniels. 1959. 0.50p. Fitzwilliam.
Catalogue of the Greek & Roman Sculpture. L. Budde & R. V. Nicholls. (Illus., 62 plates). 1964. E7.50. Fitzwilliam.
Corpus Vasorum Antiquorum, Fitzwilliam Museum: Fascicules 1 & 2, 2 vols. Winifred Lamb. (Illus.). 1936. E8.00. Fitzwilliam.
Drawings by George Romney from the Fitzwilliam Museum. P. Jaffe. E2.95. Fitzwilliam.
European Drawings from the Fitzwilliam Museum. 1976. E8.00. Fitzwilliam.
Fourty Exhibits of Outstanding Interest: A Tour of the Fitzwilliam. (Illus., 6 color plates). 1979. 0.50p. Fitzwilliam.
Gainsborough, English Music & the Fitzwilliam. 1977. E1.00. Fitzwilliam.
Glass at the Fitzwilliam Museum. 1978. E12.95; pap. E3.95. Fitzwilliam.
Handbook to the Museum. (Illus., 16 plates). 1971. 0.50p. Fitzwilliam.
Handlist of Additional Manuscripts, 4 vols. F. Wormald & Phyllis M. Giles. 1966. 0.50p. Fitzwilliam.
Illuminated Manuscripts in the Fitzwilliam Museum. F. Wormald & Phyllis M. Giles. (Illus., 32). 1966. 0.95p. Fitzwilliam.
J. M. W. Turner: Exhibition of Drawings from the Collection of the Fitzwilliam Museum. Malcolm Cormack. (Illus., 4 color, 36 b&w). 1975. E2.00. Fitzwilliam.
John Constable: Exhibition of Drawings from the Collection of the Fitzwilliam Museum. Reg Gadney. (Illus., 8 color, 46 b&w). 1976. E2.25. Fitzwilliam.
Landscapes from the Fitzwilliam. Malcolm Cormack & Duncan Robinson. 1974. E2.00. Fitzwilliam.
William Blake: An Illustrated Catalogue of Works in the Fitzwilliam Museum. Ed. by David Bindman. (Illus., 75). 1971. 5.00p. Fitzwilliam.

UNIV. OF CONNECTICUT, WILLIAM BENTON MUSEUM OF ART
Storrs, Connecticut.
American Decorative Tiles, 1870-1930. (Illus., 51 b&w). 1979. $4.50 (ISBN 0-918386-23-3). William Benton.
Bulletin, Vol. 1, No.2. Richard P. Giarniero. (Illus., 6 b&w). 1973. pap. $0.75 (ISBN 0-918386-10-1). William Benton.
Bulletin, Vol. 1, No. 3. (Illus., 9 b&w). 1974. pap. $0.75 (ISBN 0-918386-14-4). William Benton.
Bulletin, Vol. 1, No. 4. (Illus., 7 b&w). 1976. pap. $0.75 (ISBN 0-918386-19-5). William Benton.
Bulletin, Vol. 1, No. 5. (Illus., 6 b&w, 5 diag.). 1977. pap. $0.75 (ISBN 0-918386-24-1). William Benton.
Bulletin, Vol. 1. No. 6. (Illus.). 1978. pap. $0.75 (ISBN 0-918386-25-X). William Benton.
Landauer Collection of Kathe Kollwitz Prints & Drawings. Intro. by Joseph Kuntz. (Illus., 30 b&w). 1968. $2.50 (ISBN 0-918386-04-7). William Benton.

UNIV. OF FLORIDA, UNIV. GALLERY
Gainesville, Florida.
Folk Arts & Crafts of the Andes. Intro. by Robert Ebersole & Roy Craven. (University Gallery Bulletin Ser., No. 2). (Illus., 29 b&w, 1 map). 1978. $3.00. U Gal U Fla.
Jamini Roy & Bengali Folk Art. Intro. by Thomas Needhams & Roy Craven. (Illus., 2 color, 34 b&w). 1971. $3.00. U Gal U Fla.
Pre-Columbian Pottery of Peru. Intro. by Elsbeth Gordon & Roy Craven. (University Gallery Bulletin Ser., No. 1). (Illus., 36 b&w, 1 map, 1 chart). 1975. $3.00. U Gal U Fla.

UNIV. OF GEORGIA, GEORGIA MUSEUM OF ART
Athens, Georgia.
Alice Neel: The Woman & Her Work. Cindy Nemser. (Illus., 92 b&w). 1975. pap. $7.50. U of Ga Pr.
Georgia Museum of Art Bulletin: Alfred H. Holbrook, T. Addison Richards & an Engraving by the Master i.e, Vol. 1, No. 1. Ethel Moore & Louis T. Griffith. (Fall 1974 Ser). (Illus., 22 b&w). 1974. pap. $1.50. U of Ga Pr.
Georgia Museum of Art Bulletin: Jean Charlot - Paintings, Drawings & Prints, Vol. 2, No. 2. Lester C. Walker, Jr. & John Charlot. Ed. by Ethel Moore. (Fall 1976 Ser). (Illus., 61 b&w). 1977. pap. $4.50. U of Ga Pr.
Georgia Museum of Art Bulletin: John Taylor Arms, Thirty-Nine Years of Etched Memories, Vol. 1, No. 2 & 3. S. William Pelletier. Ed. by Ethel Moore. (Winter-Spring 1975 Ser). (Illus., 21 b&w). 1975. pap. $3.00. U of Ga Pr.
Georgia Museum of Art Bulletin: Robert Henri & Sissy; Goya in the Fantastic Tradition; and Elihu Vedder: American Old Master, Vol. 2, No. 1. George Ehrlich & Irving L. Finkelstein. Ed. by Ethel Moore. (Spring 1976 Ser). (Illus., 18 b&w). 1976. pap. $1.50. U of Ga Pr.
Highlights from the Collections: Georgia Museum of Art. Ed. by William D. Paul, Jr. (Illus., 28 b&w). 1968. pap. $2.00. U of Ga Pr.
Philip Pearlstein. Linda Nochlin. (Illus., 82 b&w). 1970. pap. $7.50. U of Ga Pr.
University Collects: Georgia Museum of Art, the University of Georgia. Pref. by William D. Paul, Jr. & Stuart P. Feld. (Illus., 44 b&w). 1969. pap. $3.50. U of Ga Pr.

UNIV. OF GUELPH, ART MUSEUM
Guelph, Canada.
Permanent Collection Catalogue: University of Guelph. (Illus.). 1979. write for info. U of Guelph.

UNIV. OF IOWA, MUSEUM OF ART
Iowa City, Iowa.
Accessions 1970-1971. (Illus., 1 color, 54 b&w). 1971. $1.00. U IA Mus Art.
Accessions 1971-1972. (Illus., 8 color, 52 b&w). 1973. $1.00. U IA Mus Art.
Accessions 1973. (Illus., 6 color, 38 b&w). 1973. $1.00. U IA Mus Art.
African Sculpture: The Stanley Collection. Christopher D. Roy. (Illus., 4 color, 196 b&w). 1979. $14.00. U IA Mus Art.
Alcock Collection of Silver Plate. Harlan Sifford. (Illus.). 1978. $3.00. U IA Mus Art.
Face to Face: Self-Portraits in the Museum Collection. Joann Moser. (Illus.). 1979. $2.50. U IA Mus Art.

Kashmir Shawl. John Irwin. (Monograph Ser., No. 29). E2.30 (ISBN 0-11-290164-6). V & A.
Late Antique & Byzantine Art. (Illustrated Booklet Ser., No. 12). 0.30p. V & A.
Leighton's Frescoes in the Victoria & Albert Museum. R. Ormond. 0.70p. V & A.
Limoges Painted Enamels. R. Pinkham. (Small Colour Book Ser., No. 5). 0.40p. (ISBN 0-11-290186-7). V & A.
Listening Eye: Teaching in an Art Museum. 0.25p. V & A.
Looking at the Tudor Period. Madeleine Mainstone & Arete Swartz. 0.15p. V & A.
Masterpiece by Hubert Gerhard. Michael Baxandall. 0.13p. V & A.
Matisse Lithographs. Susan Lambert. 0.55p. V & A.
Mediaeval Near Eastern Pottery. (Small Picture Book No. 42). 0.15p. V & A.
Medici Casket. R. W. Lightbown. 0.08p. V & A.
Mid-Georgian Domestic Silver. (Small Picture Book No. 28). 0.65p. (ISBN 0-11-290254-5). V & A.
Ming Porcelains. John Ayers. (Small Colour Book Ser., No. 17). 0.40p. (ISBN 0-11-290260-X). V & A.
Monti's Allegory of the Risorgimento. Anthony Radcliffe. 0.13p. V & A.
Musical Instruments at the Victoria & Albert Museum. Carole Patey. 0.95p. (ISBN 0-11-290274-X). V & A.
Nineteenth Century Papier-Mache. (Small Colour Book Ser., No. 4). 0.40p. (ISBN 0-11-290185-9). V & A.
Nonsense Alphabet, by Edward Lear. (Small Picture Book Ser., No. 32). (Illus., facsim.). 0.40p. (ISBN 0-11-290156-5). V & A.
Norfolk House Music Room. Desmond Fitz-Gerald. 0.75p. V & A.
Notes on Carpet-Knotting & Weaving. 1969. 0.50p. (ISBN 0-11-290034-8). V & A.
Orange Wrappers. Frances Hicklin. (Illus., color wallchart). 0.50p. V & A.
Paintings at Apsley House. C. M. Kauffmann. (Large Picture Book Ser., No. 23). 0.53p. V & A.
Paintings of the Sikhs. W. G. Archer. (Monograph Ser., No. 31). E3.15. V & a.
Paintings, Water-colours & Miniatures. C. M. Kauffmann. E1.15 (ISBN 0-905209-10-9). V & A.
Persian Oil Paintings. B. W. Robinson. (Small Colour Book Ser., No. 20). 0.40p. (ISBN 0-11-290268-5). V & A.
Persian Paintings. B. W. Robinson. (Large Picture Book Ser., No. 6). 0.43p. V & A.
Photography & the South Kensington Museum. John Physick. 0.60p. V & A.
Playing Cards. Frances Hicklin. (Small Colour Book Ser., No. 12). 0.35p. (ISBN 0-11-290234-0). V & A.
Pop Art. Elizabeth Bailey. (Small Colour Book Ser., No. 13). 0.35p. (ISBN 0-11-290235-9). V & A.
Portrait Drawings. (Small Picture Book Ser., No. 12). 0.23p. (ISBN 0-11-290092-5). V & A.
Puppets. Caroline Goodfellow. (Small Colour Book Ser., No. 15). 0.40p. (ISBN 0-11-290256-1). V & A.
Queen Anne Domestic Silver. (Small Picture Book Ser., No. 25). 0.15p. (ISBN 0-11-290063-1). V & A.
Raphael Cartoons. John White. (Large Colour Book Ser., No. 1). 0.95p. (ISBN 0-11-290135-2). V & A.
Rediscovered English Reliquary Cross. John Beckwith. 0.08p. V & A.
Regency Domestic Silver. (Small Picture Book Ser., No. 33). 0.25p. (ISBN 0-11-290104-2). V & A.
Rodin Sculptures. Jennifer Hawkins. (Monograph Ser., No. 30). E2.25 (ISBN 0-11-290210-3). V & A.
Rood-Loft from Hertogenbosch. Charles Avery. 0.40p. V & A.
S. W. Hayter's Graphic Work. 0.03p. V & A.
Samplers. Donald King. (Large Picture Book Ser., No. 14). E3.00 (ISBN 0-11-290149-2). V & A.
Samuel Cooper's Pocket-Book. Graham Reynolds. 0.95p. V & A.
Sanchi Torso. John Irwin. E1.25. V & A.
Scandinavian Silver. (Small Picture Book No. 47). 0.13p. V & A.
Sculpture from Troyes in the Victoria & Albert Museum. Charles Avery. E1.20. V & A.
Shah Jahan Cup. Robert Skelton. 0.08p. V & A.
Sizergh Castle Room. (Monographs on Panelled Rooms in the Museum Ser., No. 4). 0.19p. V & A.
Sketches by Thornhill in the Victoria & Albert Museum. E. de N. Mayhew. (Monograph Ser., No. 19). 0.63p. V & A.
Sketching Society 1799-1851. Jean Hamilton. 0.50p. V & A.
Some Main Streams & Tributaries in European Ornament from 1500 to 1750. Peter Ward-Jackson. 0.20p. V & A.
South German Sculpture 1480-1530. Michael Baxandall. (Monograph Ser., No. 26). E1.25 (ISBN 0-11-290163-8). V & A.
Spitalfields Silks. Natalie Rothstein. (Small Color Book Ser., No. 6). 0.40p. (ISBN 0-11-290208-1). V & A.
State Bed from Erthig. John Hardy & Sheila Landi. 0.35p. V & A.
Summary Catalogue of British Paintings. 0.65p. V & A.
Swords & Daggers. John Hayward. (Illustrated Booklet Ser., No. 3). 0.35p. (ISBN 0-11-290077-1). V & A.
Synopsis of Nineteenth Century Women's Fashion. (Illus.). 0.03p. V & A.
Teapots in Pottery & Porcelain. (Small Picture Book Ser., No. 9). 0.65p. (ISBN 0-11-290242-1). V & A.
Textiles & Dress. E1.15 (ISBN 0-905209-09-5). V & A.
Thomas Gainsborough's Exhibition Box. Jonathan Mayne. 0.08p. V & A.
Three Presentation Swords. Claude Blair. 0.60p. V & A.
Tibetan Art. John Lowry. E2.00 (ISBN 0-11-290109-3). V & A.
Tibetan Tangkas. John Lowry. (Small Colour Book Ser., No. 18). 0.40p. (ISBN 0-11-290264-2). V & A.
Tortoiseshell Cabinet & Its Precursors. Simon Jervis. 0.10p. V & A.
Toys. Caroline Goodfellow. (Small Colour Book Ser., No. 8). 0.35p. (ISBN 0-11-290220-0). V & A.
Tudor & Jacobean Miniatures. Graham Reynolds. (Small Colour Book Ser., No. 2). 0.40p. (ISBN 0-11-290117-4). V & A.
Tudor Domestic Silver (1500-1800) (Illustrated Booklet Ser., No. 15). 0.40p. (ISBN 0-11-290042-9). V & A.
Turkish Pottery. (Small Picture Book No. 21). 0.25p. (ISBN 0-11-290103-4). V & A.
Twentieth Century British Water-Colours from the Tate Gallery & the Victoria & Albert Museum. (Illustrated Booklet Ser., No. 8). 0.23p. V & A.
Two Garden Sculptures by Antonio Corradini. Terence Hodgkinson. 0.10p. V & A.
Venetian Embroidered Altar Frontal. Donald King. 0.10p. V & A.
Victoria & Albert Museum Brief Guide. 0.45p. V & A.
Victoria & Albert Museum Bulletin. 0.38p. V & A.
Victoria & Albert Museum Guia Concisa. 0.35p. V & A.
Victoria & Albert Museum Guida Breve. 0.35p. V & A.
Victoria & Albert Museum Guide Sommaire. 0.35p. V & A.
Victoria & Albert Museum Kurzer Fuhrer. 0.35p. V & A.
Victorian Engravings. Hilary Beck. E1.30. V & A.
Victorian Glass. Betty O'Looney. 0.50p. (ISBN 0-11-290133-6). V & A.
Waltham Abbey Room. (Monographs on Panelled Rooms in the Museum No. 6). 0.19p. V & A.
Wedgwood. (Small Picture Book Ser., No. 45). 0.25p. (ISBN 0-11-290131-X). V & A.
Wellington Monument. John Physick. 0.75p. V & A.
Wellington Plate (Portuguese Service) Charles Oman. (Monograph Ser., No. 4). 0.18p. V & A.

VIGELAND MUSEET
Oslo, Norway.
Guide to the Vigeland Sculpture Park. T. Wikborg. Ed. by The Vigeland Museum. (Illus., 25 b&w, Eng. & Norwegian.). 1978. pap. $1.75. Vigeland Mus.
Vigeland Museum. Tone Wikborg. Ed. by The Vigeland Museum. Tr. by L. Coll. (Illus., 42 b&w, Eng. & Norwegian.). 1972. pap. $1.20. Vigeland Mus.

VIRGILKAPELLE UND SAMMLUNG HISTORISCHER KERAMIK AUS WIEN
Vienna, Austria.
Stephansplatz & Virgilkapellen. Eigenverlag der Museen der Stadt Wien. (Illus., 7 b&w, Ger.). 1979. pap. S.12.00. Museen Wien.

VIRGINIA MUSEUM OF FINE ARTS
Richmond, Virginia.
Ancient Art in the Virginia Museum of Fine Arts. Helen Reed. (Illus., 10 color, 150 b&w). 1973. $10.95. Va Mus Arts.
European Art in the Virginia Museum of Fine Arts. Paul L. Grigaut. (Illus., 12 color, 300 b&w). 1966. $4.00 (ISBN 0-8139-0426-9). Va Mus Arts.
Faberge: A Catalog of the Lillian Thomas Pratt Collection of Russian Imperial Jewels. Parker Lesley. (Illus., 250 color). 1976. $22.50 (ISBN 0-917046-00-5). Va Mus Arts.

WADDESDON MANOR
Aylesbury, United Kingdom.
Waddesdon Catalogue of Furniture, Clocks & Gilt-Bronzes, 2 vols. Geoffrey De Bellaigue. Ed. by Anthony Blunt. (James De Rothschild Collection at Waddesdon Manor Ser). (Illus., 48 color plates, 560 b&w plates, 135 illus. of marks & signatures). 1974. $140.00. National Trust.
Waddesdon Catalogue of Glass Enamels. R. J. Charleston et al. Ed. by Anthony Blunt. (James A. De Rothschild Collection at Waddesdon Manor Ser). (Illus., 24 color plates, 244 b&w plates, 9 line drawings). 1977. $104.00. National Trust.
Waddesdon Catalogue of Gold Boxes. Serge Grandjean et al. (James A. De Rothschild Collection at Waddesdon Manor Ser). (Illus., 32 color plates, 270 b&w plates, 230 illus. of marks & signatures). 1975. $104.00. National Trust.
Waddesdon Catalogue of Illuminated Manuscripts. L. M. J. Delaisse et al. (James A. De Rothschild Collection at Waddesdon Manor Ser). (Illus., 49 color plates, 449 b&w plates, 68 diags.). 1977. $104.00. National Trust.
Waddesdon Catalogue of Meissen & Oriental Porcelain. R. J. Charleston & John Ayers. Ed. by Anthony Blunt. (James A. De Rothschild Collection at Waddesdon Manor Ser). (Illus., 30 color plates, 122 b&w plates, 28 illus. of marks). 1971. $74.00. National Trust.
Waddesdon Catalogue of Sculpture. Terence Hodgkinson. Ed. by Anthony Blunt. (James A. De Rothschild Collection at Waddesdon Manor Ser). (Illus., 9 color plates, 182 b&w plates). 1970. $54.00. National Trust.
Waddesdon Catalogue of Arms, Armour & Base-Metalwork. Claude Blair. Ed. by Anthony Blunt. (James A. De Rothschild Collection at Waddesdon Manor Ser). (Illus., 2 color plates, 225 b&w plates, 120 illus. of marks). 1974. $57.00. National Trust.

WADSWORTH ATHENEUM
Hartford, Connecticut.
Catalogue of the Paintings from the Netherlands & the German-Speaking Countries, 15th-19th Centuries. Ed. by E. Haverkamp-Begemann. (Illus., 228 b&w). $18.00; pap. $12.00. Wadsworth Ath.
English Silver: The Elizabeth B. Miles Collection. Intro. by Elizabeth Miles. (Illus., 2 color, 175 b&w). 1976. $12.00. Wadsworth Ath.
Glass: American & European Glass in the Wadsworth Atheneum. Intro. by Dwight Lanmon. (Illus., 8 color, 150 b&w). 1976. $10.00. Wadsworth Ath.
Handbook of the Hudson River School: Nineteenth Century American Landscapes in the Wadsworth Atheneum. Compiled by & intro. by Theodore E. Stebbins, Jr. (Illus., 8 color, 73 b&w). 1976. $7.50. Wadsworth Ath.
John Trumbull: Five Paintings of the Revolution. Irma B. Jaffe. (Illus., 3 color, 22 b&w). 1975. $5.00. Wadsworth Ath.
Three Centuries of Costume in the Atheneum's Collections. Intro. by J. Herbert Callister. (Illus., 8 color, 64 b&w). 1977. $7.00. Wadsworth Ath.

WAKEFIELD ART GALLERY
Wakefield, United Kingdom.
Acquired for Wakefield 1974-1977. 1977. 0.15p. Wakefield.
Handlist of the Permanent Collection of Paintings, Watercolours, Drawings, Prints and Sculptures. 1975. 0.10p. Wakefield.
Paintings, Watercolours, Drawings, Prints and Sculptures Acquired with the Assistance of the Wakefield Permanent Art Fund 1924-1975. 1975. 0.10p. Wakefield.

WALKER ART GALLERY, MERSEYSIDE COUNTY COUNCIL
Liverpool, United Kingdom.
Early English Drawings & Watercolours. (Illus., 16 b&w plates). 1968. 0.35p. Walker Art Gal.
English Watercolours from the Collection of C. F. J. Beausire. (Illus., 24 b&w plates). 1970. 0.25. p. Walker Art Gal.
Foreign School Catalogue. (Illus.). 1977. E2.50; E5.00, plates. Walker Art Gal.
Lady Lever Collection Port Sunlight. (Illus., 30 b&w). 1978. 0.50p. Walker Art Gal.
Merseyside Painters, People & Places. Mary Bennett. (Illus.). 1978. E3.00; E4.00, plates. Walker Art Gal.
Old Master Drawings & Prints. (Illus., 16 b&w plates). 1967. 0.25p. Walker Art Gal.
Pictures in the Walker Art Gallery. (Illus., 34 color & b&w). 1974. 0.70p. Walker Art Gal.
Sudley. (Illus., 64 b&w). 1971. 0.50p. Walker Art Gal.

WALLACE COLLECTION
London, United Kingdom.
Catalogue of Ceramics I: Pottery, Maiolica, Faience & Stoneware. A. V. Norman. (Illus., 3 color, 271 b&w). 1976. pap. E4.00. Wallace Col.
European Arms & Armor, 2 vol. James Mann. (Illus.). 1962. pap. E2.50. Wallace Col.
Furniture. F. J. Watson. (Illus., 120 b&w). 1976. pap. E3.00. Wallace Col.
Oriental Arms & Armour. Guy F. Laking. 1978. pap. E1.00. Wallace Col.
Pictures & Drawings. F. J. Watson. (Illus., 450 b&w). 1968. pap. E2.00. Wallace Col.
Sculpture. J. G. Mann. (Illus., 99 b&w). 1931. E1.00. Wallace Col.
Summary Illustrated Catalogue of Pictures. John Ingamells. (Illus., 788 b&w). 1979. pap. E2.00. Wallace Col.

WALLRAF-RICHARTZ-MUSEUM
Cologne, Germany, West.
F. E. Walther: 2. Werksatz. (Ger.). 1977. DM.12.00. Mus Koln.
Fotographische Kunstlerbildnisse. (Ger.). 1977. DM.5.00. Mus Koln.
J. Cuevas. (Ger.). 1978. DM.3.00. Mus Koln.
Rodschenko: Fotografien. (Ger.). 1978. DM.20.00. Mus Koln.
Rom in Fruhen Photographien (1846-1878) (Ger.). 1978. DM.22.00. Mus Koln.
Unmittelbar und Unverfalscht: Fruhe Druckgraphik Des Expressionismus. (Ger.). 1976. DM.10.00. Mus Koln.
Wallraf-Richartz-Museum: Ausgewahlte Handzeichnungen und Aquarelle, Vol. 4. (Ger.). 1967. DM.10.00. Mus Koln.
Wallraf-Richartz-Museum: Band 1 Bis Band 10 Geschlossen. (Ger.). DM.60.00. Mus Koln.
Wallraf-Richartz-Museum: Bildwerke Seit Etwa 1800, Vol. 2. (Ger.). 1965. DM.8.00. Mus Koln.
Wallraf-Richartz-Museum: Bildwerke und Objekte, Neuzugange Seit 1965, Vol. 9. (Ger.). 1973. DM.10.00. Mus Koln.
Wallraf-Richartz-Museum: Deutsche Gemalde Von 1550-1800, Vol. 10. (Ger.). 1973. DM.10.00. Mus Koln.
Wallraf-Richartz-Museum: Deutsche und Niederlandische Gemalde Bis 1500, Vol. 5. (Ger.). 1969. DM.10.00. Mus Koln.
Wallraf-Richartz-Museum: Gemalde Des 19. Jh, Vol. 1. (Ger.). 1964. DM.10.00. Mus Koln.
Wallraf-Richartz-Museum: Gemalde Des 20. Jh. Bis 1912, Vol. 7. (Ger.). 1975. DM.18.00. Mus Koln.
Wallraf-Richartz-Museum: Italienische, Franzosische und Spanische Gemalde, Vol. 6. (Ger.). 1973. DM.10.00. Mus Koln.
Wallraf-Richartz-Museum: Malerei Des 20. Jh. Ab 1913, Vol. 8. (Ger.). 1977. DM.15.00. Mus Koln.
Wallraf-Richartz-Museum: Niederlandische Gemalde Von 1550-1880, Vol. 3. (Ger.). 1967. DM.10.00. Mus Koln.
Worte Werden Bilder: Bildertexte und Buchobjekte Von 1900 Bis Heute. (Ger.). 1972. DM.8.00. Mus Koln.

WALSALL MUSEUM AND ART GALLERY
Walsall, United Kingdom.
Garman-Ryan Collection. 1976. 1.00 d. Walsall Mus.

WALTERS ART GALLERY
Baltimore, Maryland.
Armenian Manuscripts in the Walters Art Gallery. Sirarpie Der Nersessian. Ed. by Ursula McCracken. (Illus., 8 color plates, 493 b&w). 1973. $60.00. Walters Art.
Catalogue of Japanese Lacquers in the Walters Art Gallery. Martha Boyer. Ed. by Dorothy Miner. (Illus., 1 color plate, 416 b&w). 1970. $30.00. Walters Art.
Catalogue of the American Works of Art, Including French Medals Made for America. Edward S. King & Marvin L. Ross. Ed. by Dorothy E. Miner. (Illus., 2 b&w plates). 1956. pap. $3.50. Walters Art.
Catalogue of the Italian Majolica in the Walters Art Gallery. Joan Von Erdberg & Marvin Ross. Ed. by Dorothy Miner. (Illus., 64 b&w plates). 1952. $10.00. Walters Art.
Catalogue of the Painted Enamels of the Renaissance in the Walters Art Gallery. Philippe Verdier. Ed. by Dorothy Miner. (Illus., 8 color plates, 312 b&w). 1967. $30.00. Walters Art.
Italian Paintings in the Walters Art Gallery, 2 vols. Federico Zeri. Ed. by Ursula McCracken. (Illus., 8 color plates, 503 b&w). 1976. $75.00 set. Walters Art.
West of Alfred Jacob Miller (1837), from the Notes & Watercolors in the Walters Art Gallery. Marvin Ross. (Illus., 8 color plates, 208 b&w plates). $35.00. Walters Art.

WASHINGTON STATE UNIV., MUSEUM OF ART
Pullman, Washington.
Works on Paper: American Art, 1945-1975. Rosalind Krauss. (Illus., 58 b&w). 1977. $5.00. Wash Art Cons.

WASHINGTON UNIV. GALLERY OF ART
St. Louis, Missouri.
Ancient Collections in Washington University. Sarantis Symenonoglou & Kevin Herbert. (Illus., 87 b&w). 1973. pap. $1.00. Wash U Gal.
Charles Parsons Collection of Paintings. Graham Beal. (Illus., 72 b&w). 1977. pap. $5.00. Wash U Gal.
Development of Modernist Painting: Jackson Pollock to the Present. Robert Buck, Jr. (Illus., 21 color plates). 1969. pap. $6.00. Wash U Gal.
Leonard Baskin: Images of Man. Arline Leven. (Illus., 16 b&w). 1978. pap. $2.50. Wash U Gal.

KEY TO PUBLISHERS' AND DISTRIBUTORS' DIRECTORY

A & W Pubs
A & W Pubs., Inc.
95 Madison Ave., New York, NY 10016
(0-89479)
A & W Visual Library
See A & W Pubs
A Harvey
Harvey, Arnold, Associates
P.O. Box 89, Commack, NY 11725
(0-913014)
A L Kerth
Kerth, A. L.
Jericho Run, Buckland Valley Farms,
Washington Crossing, PA 18977
(0-9601188)
A S Barnes
Barnes, A. S., & Co., Inc.
P.O. Box 421, Cranbury, NJ 08512
(0-498)
A-W
Addison-Wesley Publishing Co., Inc.
Jacob Way, Reading, MA 01867
(0-201)
A-W Childrens. A-W.
Addison-Wesley Children's Books. Imprint of
Addison-Wesley Publishing Co., Inc.
A Whitman
Whitman, Albert, & Co.
560 W. Lake St., Chicago, IL 60606
(0-8075)
A Wofsy Fine Arts
Wofsy, Alan, Fine Arts
150 Green St., San Francisco, CA 94111
(0-915346)
AA. U of Mich Pr.
Ann Arbor Books. Imprint of Univ. of
Michigan Press.
AAHPER
American Alliance for Health, Physical
Education & Recreation, Affiliate of National
Education Assn.
1201 16th St., N. W., Washington, DC
20036
(0-88314)
AASLH
American Assn. for State & Local History
1400 Eighth Ave., S., Nashville, TN 37203
(0-910050)
Abak Pr
Abak Press
500 Pepper Ridge Rd., Stamford, CT 06905
(0-914214)
Abaris Bks
Abaris Books, Inc.
24 W. 40th St., New York, NY 10018
(0-913870; 0-89835)
Abbeville Pr
Abbeville Press Inc.
505 Park Ave., New York, NY 10022
(0-89659)
Abbot Hall Gal
Abbot Hall Gallery & Museum of Lakeland
Life & Industry
Kendal, Cumbria LA9 5AL,
United Kingdom
Abegg-Stiftung
Abegg-Stiftung Bern
CH-3132 Riggisberg, Switzerland
Abelard
Abelard-Schuman Ltd.
(0-200)
c/o Harper & Row Pubs., Keystone
Industrial Park, Scranton, PA 18512
Aberdeen Gal
Aberdeen Art Gallery
Schoolhill, Aberdeen AB9 1FQ,
United Kingdom
Abhinav Pubns
Abhinav Publications
E-37 Hans Khas, New Delhi 110 016, India

Abingdon
Abingdon Press
Orders to:
Customer Service Dept., 201 Eighth Ave.
S., Nashville, TN 37202
(0-687)
Abrams
Abrams, Harry N., Inc, Subs. of Times Mirror
Co.
110 E. 59th St., New York, NY 10022
(0-8109)
Acad Pr
Academic Press, Inc.
111 Fifth Ave., New York, NY 10003
(0-12)
Academy Chi Ltd
Academy Chicago, Ltd.
360 N. Michigan Ave., Chicago, IL 60601
(0-915864)
Ace Bks
Ace Books, Div. of Charter Communications
Inc.
(0-441)
Grosset & Dunlap, 51 Madison Ave., New
York, NY 10010
ACEI
Assn. for Childhood Education International
3615 Wisconsin Ave., N.W., Washington,
DC 20016
(0-87173)
Acoma Bks
Acoma Books
P.O. Box 4, Ramona, CA 92065
(0-916552)
Acropolis
Acropolis Books
2400 17th St. N.W., Washington, DC
20009
(0-87491)
Adams Minn
Adams Press
Orders to:
Lerner Publications Co., 241 First Ave. N.,
Minneapolis, MN 55401
(0-914828)
Addison Hse
Addison House
Morgan's Run, Danbury, NH 03230
(0-89169)
Adirondack Yes
Adirondack Yesteryears, Inc.
Lake St. Extension-Drawer 209, Saranac
Lake, NY 12983
(0-9601158)
Adler
Adler's Foreign Books, Inc.
162 Fifth Ave., New York, NY 10010
(0-8417)
Aesthetic Realism
Aesthetic Realism Foundation & Terrain
Gallery
141 Greene St., New York, NY 10012
(0-911492)
African Studies Assn
African Studies Assn.
Epstein Bldg., Brandeis Univ., Waltham,
MA 02154
(0-918456)
Africana. Holmes & Meier.
Africana Pub. Imprint of Holmes & Meier
Pubs., Inc.
Agathon
Agathon Press Inc.
15 E. 26th St., New York, NY 10010
(0-87586)
AHM Pub
AHM Publishing Corp.
3110 N. Arlington Heights Rd., Arlington
Heights, IL 60004
(0-88295)

Aka U Bonn
Akademisches Kunstmuseum der Universitat
Bonn
D-5300 Bonn, am Hofgarten 21,
West Germany
Akron Art Ins
Akron Art Institute
69 E. Market St., Akron, OH 44308
United States
ALA
American Library Assn.
50 E. Huron St., Chicago, IL 60611
(0-8389)
Alaska Northwest
Alaska Northwest Publishing Co.
130 Second Ave. S., Edmonds, WA 98020
(0-88240)
Albany Hist & Art
Albany Institute of History & Art
125 Washington Ave., Albany, NY 12210
Aldine
See Beresford Bk Serv
Alfred Pub
Alfred Publishing Co., Inc.
15335 Morrison St., Sherman Oaks, CA
91403
(0-88284)
All Sav Cath
All Saviour's Cathedral Museum
Diocese of the Armenians in Iran & India,
P.O. Box 4, New Julfa-Isfahan, Iran
Allanheld & Schram
Allanheld & Schram
36 Park St., Montclair, NJ 07042
(0-8390)
Allen Unwin
Allen & Unwin, Inc.
Orders to:
P.O. Box 978, Edison, NJ 08817
(0-04; 0-86861)
Allyn
Allyn & Bacon, Inc.
Orders to:
College Division, Rockleigh, NJ 07647
(0-205)
Alpine Bk Co
Alpine Book Co., Inc.
527 Madison Ave., New York, NY 10022
(0-933516)
Am Antiquarian
American Antiquarian Society
(0-912296)
Univ. Press of Virginia, P.O. Box 3608,
University Sta., Charlottesville, VA 22903
Am Classical Coll Pr
American Classical College Press
P.O. Box 4526, Albuquerque, NM 87106
(0-913314; 0-89266)
Am Fed Arts
American Federation of Arts
41 E. 65th St., New York, NY 10021
(0-917418)
Am Hospital
American Hospital Assn.
Orders to:
P.O. Box 96003, Chicago, IL 60693
(0-87258)
Am Ind Mus
See Mus Am Ind
Am Indus Arts
American Industrial Arts Assn., Inc.
1201 Sixteenth St., N.W., Rm 230,
Washington, DC 20036
Am Inst Arch
American Institute of Architects
1735 New York Ave., N.W., Washington,
DC 20006
(0-913962)
Am Israel Numismatic
American Israel Numismatic Assn.
P.O. Box 370, Boca Raton, FL 33432
(0-9601658)

Am Jewish Hist Soc
American Jewish Historical Society
2 Thornton Rd., Waltham, MA 02154
(0-911934)
Am Lib Pub Co
American Library Publishing Co., Inc.
275 Central Park, W., New York, NY
10024
(0-87729)
Am Life Foun
American Life Foundation & Study Institute
P.O. Box 349, Watkins Glen, NY 14891
(0-89257)
Am Mus Natl Hist
American Museum of Natural History
Central Park W. at 79th St., New York,
NY 10024
(0-913424)
Am Numismatic
American Numismatic Society
Broadway at 155th St., New York, NY
10032
(0-89722)
Am Philos
American Philosophical Society
104 S. Fifth St., Philadelphia, PA 19106
(0-87169)
Am Sch Athens
American School of Classical Studies at
Athens
(0-87661)
c/o Institute for Advanced Study,
Princeton, NJ 08540
Am Technical
American Technical Society
5608 Stony Island Ave., Chicago, IL 60637
(0-8269)
Am Welding
American Welding Society
2501 N. W. Seventh St., Miami, FL 33125
(0-87171)
Ambrosiana
Pinacoteca Ambrosiana
Piazza Pio XI, 2, 20123 Milan, Italy
American Numismatic
American Numismatic Assn.
818 North Cascade, Colorado Springs, CO
80903
(0-89637)
Amon Carter
Amon Carter Musuem of Western Art
P.O. Box 2365, Fort Worth, TX 76113
Amos Anderson
Anderson, Amos, Taidemuseo
Yrjonkatu 27, SF-00100 Helsinki 10,
Finland
Amphoto
American Photographic Book Publishing Co.,
Inc.
750 Zeckendorf Blvd., Garden City, NY
11530
(0-8174)
AMS Pr
AMS Press, Inc.
56 E. 13th St., New York, NY 10003
(0-404)
Anch. Doubleday.
Anchor Books. Imprint of Doubleday & Co.,
Inc.
Anchor Pr. Doubleday.
Anchor Press. Imprint of Doubleday & Co.,
Inc.
Anchorage
Anchorage Press
P. O. Box 8067, New Orleans, LA 70182
(0-87602)
Andrews & McMeel
Andrews & McMeel, Inc.
6700 Squibb Rd., Mission, KS 66202
(0-8362)
Anglo Am Mus
Louisiana State Univ., Anglo-American Art
Museum
114 Memorial Tower, Baton Rouge, LA
70803
ANSI
American National Standards Institute
1430 Broadway, New York, NY 10018
Antelope Island
Antelope Island Press
P.O. Box 31508, San Francisco, CA 94131
(0-917946)
Antiq Land Soc
Antiquarian & Landmarks Society
394 Main St., Hartford, CT 06103

Anton Ulrich
Herzog Anton Ulrich Museum
Museumsstrasse 1, D-33 Braunschweig,
Brunswick, West Germany
Aperture
Aperture, Inc.
Elm St., Millerton, NY 12546
(0-89381; 0-912334)
Applied Arts
Applied Arts Pubs, Div. of Sowers Printing
Co.
Box 479, Lebanon, PA 17042
(0-911410)
Aqua Educ
Aquarian Educational Group
30188 Mulholland Hwy., Agoura, CA
91301
(0-911794)
Arc Bks
Arc Books
(0-668)
Arco Publishing Inc., 219 Park Ave., S.,
New York, NY 10003
Arch Munster
Archaologisches Museum der Universitat
Munster
D-4400 Munster, Domplatz 20/22,
West Germany
Arch Num Milan
Civiche Raccolte Archeologiche e
Numismatiche di Milano
Castello Sforzesco, I-20121 Milan, Italy
Arch Rec Bks
Architectural Record Books
1221 Ave. of Americas, 41st Floor, New
York, NY 10020
(0-915404)
Arch Zurich
Archaologische Sammlung der Universitat
Zurich
Ramistr. 73, CH-8006 Zurich, Switzerland
Archer Edns
Archer Editions Press
P.O. Box 562, Danbury, CT 06810
(0-89097)
Archi Siena
Archivo di Stato di Siena
Via Bachi di Sotto 52, I-53100 Siena, Italy
Architectural
Architectural Book Publishing Co.
Hastings House Pubs., Inc., 10 E. 40th St.,
New York, NY 10016
Archway
Archway Paperbacks
(0-671)
c/o Pocket Books, 1230 Avenue of the
Americas, New York, NY 10020
Arco
Arco Publishing, Inc.
219 Park Ave., S., New York, NY 10003
(0-668)
Arden Lib
Arden Library
Mill & Main Sts., Darby, PA 19023
(0-8495)
Ardis Pubs
Ardis Pubs.
2901 Heatherway, Ann Arbor, MI 48104
(0-88233)
Ares
Ares Pubs., Inc.
612 North Michigan Ave., Suite 216,
Chicago, IL 60611
(0-89005)
Argus Comm
Argus Communications
7440 Natchez Ave., Niles, IL 60648
(0-913592)
Ark Arch Surv
Arkansas Archaeological Survey
Fayetteville, AR 72701
Arlington Hse
Arlington House Pubs.
165 Huguenot St., New Rochelle, NY
10801
(0-87000)
Arma Pr
Arma Press
Rte. 139, North Branford, CT 06471
Arman Ent
Arman Enterprises, Inc.
P.O. Box 3331, Danville, VA 24541
(0-915438)
Arnall
Arnall, Franklin
P.O. Box 531, Mentone, CA 92359
(0-914638)

Arno
Arno Press
3 Park Ave., New York, NY 10016
(0-405)
Ars Ceramica
Ars Ceramica, Ltd.
(0-89344)
Dist. by:
Keramos, P.O. Box 7500, Ann Arbor, MI
48107
Art Alliance
Art Alliance Press
P.O. Box 421, Cranbury, NJ 08512
(0-87982)
Art & Image
Art et Image
28 Rue Gassendi, Paris, 75014, France
Art & Ref
Art & Reference House
Brownsboro, TX 75756
(0-910156)
Art Dir
Art Direction Book Co.
(0-910158)
Advertising Trade Pubns., Inc., 19 W. 44th
St., New York, NY 10036
Art Educ
Art Education, Inc.
28 E. Erie St., Blauvelt, NY 10913
(0-912242)
Art Gal Ontario
Art Gallery of Ontario
Grange Park, Toronto, ON M5T 1G4,
Canada
Art Gal Vict
Art Gallery of Greater Victoria
1040 Moss St., Victoria, BC V8V 4P1,
Canada
Art History
Art History Pubs.
Rte. 2, Red Wing, MN 55066
(0-9600002)
Art Richmond
Art Assn. of Richmond, McGuire Memorial
Hall
Whitewater Blvd., IN 47374
Artabras
Artabras, Inc.
505 Park Ave., New York, NY 10022
(0-89660)
Artisan Pr
Artisan Press
Bookpeople, 2940 Seventh St., Berkeley,
CA 94710
Arts Deco
Union Central des Arts Decoratifs- Musee des
Arts Decoratifs
107 Rue De Rivoli, 75001 Paris, France
Ash Lad Pr
Ash Lad Press
P.O. Box 396, Canton, NY 13617
(0-915492)
Asheville Mus
Asheville Art Museum
Civil Center, Asheville, NC 28801
Asia
Asia Publishing House
141 E. 44th St., New York, NY 10017
(0-210)
ASP
American Society of Photogrammetry
105 N. Virginia Ave., Falls Church, VA
22046
Assn Pr
Association Press
(0-8096)
c/o Follett Publishing Co., 1010 W.
Washington Blvd., Chicago, IL 60607
Assoc Bk
Associated Booksellers
P.O. Box 6361, Bridgeport, CT 06606
(0-87497)
Astor-Honor
Astor-Honor, Inc.
48 E. 43rd St., New York, NY 10017
(0-8392)
ASU Lat Am St
Arizona State Univ., Center for Latin
American Studies
Tempe, AZ 85281
(0-87918)
Atavistic Pr
Atavistic Press
4586 32nd St., San Diego, CA 92116
(0-915718)

Athena Pub
Athena Publishing Co.
2016 Clay, N. Kansas City, MO 64116
(0-89161)
Atheneum
Atheneum Pubs.
(0-689)
Dist. by:
Book Warehouse, Inc., Vreeland Ave., Boro of Totowa, Paterson, NJ 07512
Atkinson Gal
Atkinson Art Gallery
Lord St.,Southport, Merseyside PR8 1DH, United Kingdom
Atlantis
Atlantis Editions
11 East 73rd St., New York, NY 10021
Attic Bks
Attic Books Ltd.
P.O. Box 38, South Salem, NY 10590
(0-915018)
Audel
Audel, Theodore
(0-672)
Dist. by:
Bobbs-Merrill, 4300 W. 62nd St., Indianapolis, IN 46206
Augsburg
Augsburg Publishing House
426 S. Fifth St., Minneapolis, MN 55415
(0-8066)
Aurel Bongers
Verlag Aurel Bongers
Hubertusstr. 13, Postfach 220, D-4350 Recklinghausen, West Germany
(3-7647)
Aurora Pubs
Aurora Pubs.
1503 Laurel St., Nashville, TN 37203
(0-87695)
Austin Pr
Austin Press, Div. of Lone Star Pubs. Inc.
P.O. Box 9774, Austin, TX 78766
(0-914872)
Avant-Garde
Avant-Garde Media, Inc.
251 W. 57th St., New York, NY 10019
(0-913568)
Avery Pub
Avery Pub. Group, Inc.
89 Baldwin Terrace, Wayne, NJ 07470
(0-89529)
Aviation
Aviation Book Co.
P.O. Box 4187, Glendale, CA 91202
(0-911720; 0-911721)
Avon
Avon Books
959 Eighth Ave., New York, NY 10019
(0-380)
Avons Res
Avons Research Pubns.
P.O. Box 9321, Glendale, CA 91206
(0-913772)
Aztex
Aztex Corp.
(0-89404)
Dist. by:
E. P. Dutton, 2 Park Ave., New York, NY 10016
B Franklin
Franklin, Burt, Pub.
(0-89102)
Dist. by:
Lenox Hill Publishing & Distributing Corp., 235 E. 44th St., New York, NY 10017
B Jones U
Jones, Bob, University Press
Wade Hampton Blvd,, Greenville, SC 29614
B West
West, Bill
536 E. Ada Ave., Glendora, CA 91740
(0-911614)
Baker Bk
Baker Book House
P.O. Box 6287, Grand Rapids, MI 49506
(0-8010)
Baker Gallery
Baker Gallery Press
P.O. Box 1920, Lubbock, TX 79408
(0-912196)
Bale Bks
Bale Books
P.O. Box 2727, New Orleans, LA 70176
(0-912070)

Ballantine
Ballantine Books, Inc, Div. of Random House, Inc.
Orders to:
400 Hahn Rd., Westminster, MD 21157
(0-345)
Ballena Pr
Ballena Press
P.O. Box 1366, Socorro, NM 87801
(0-87919)
Ballinger Pub
Ballinger Publishing Co.
17 Dunster St., Harvard Square, Cambridge, MA 02138
(0-88410)
Baltimore Mus
Baltimore Museum of Art
Orders to:
The Museum Shop, Art Museum Dr., Baltimore, MD 21218
(0-912298)
B&N
Barnes & Noble Books, Div of Harper & Row Pubs., Inc.
Orders to:
Harper & Row Pubs., Inc., Keystone Industrial Park, Scranton, PA 18512
(0-389)
Banner. Exposition.
Banner. Imprint of Exposition Press, Inc.
Bantam
Bantam Books, Inc.
414 E. Golf Rd., Des Plaines, IL 60016
(0-553)
Banyan Bks
Banyan Books
7575 S.W. 62 Ave., Suite B, South Miami,, FL 33143
(0-916224)
Bard. Avon.
Avon Bard Books. Imprint of Avon Books.
Barre
Barre Publishing Co.
Valley Rd., Barre, MA 01005; 1 Park Ave., New York, NY 10016
Barrie and Jen
Barrie & Jenkins
24 Highbury Crescent, London N51 RP, United Kingdom
Barron
Barron's Educational Series, Inc.
113 Crossways Park Dr., Woodbury, NY 11797
(0-8120)
Basic
Basic Books, Inc.
10 E. 53rd St., New York, NY 10022
(0-465)
Basil Blackwell
See Biblio Dist
Bass Mus
Bass Museum of Art
2100 Collins Ave., Miami Beach, FL 33139
Bauhan
Bauhan, William L., Inc.
Old County Rd., Dublin, NH 03444
(0-87233)
Baur Collect
Collections Baur
Rue Munier-Romilly 8, CH-1206 Geneva, Switzerland
Bayer Nat Mus
Bayerisches Nationalmuseum
Prinzregentenstrasse 3, 22 Munich, West Germany
Bayer Staats
Bayerischen Staatsgemaldessammungen
2 Meiserstr. 10, 8000 Munich 2, West Germany
Bayer Verwal
Schloss Pruun
D-8421 Pruun, West Germany
BBM Assocs
See Calif Street
Beacon Pr
Beacon Press, Inc.
Harper & Row Pubs., Inc., Keystone Industrial Park, Scranton, PA 18512
(0-8070)
Beaufort
Beaufort Book Co., Inc.
808 Bay St., Box 1127, Beaufort, SC 29902
(0-910206)
Beautiful Am
Beautiful America Publishing Co.
P.O. Box 608, Beaverton, OR 97075
(0-89802; 0-915796)

Beaverbrook
Beaverbrook Art Gallery
703 Queen St., (Box 605), Fredericton, NB E3B 5A6, Canada
Beck'sche Ver
Beck'sche Verlagsbuchhandlung
Wilhelm Str. 9, D-8000 Munich 40, West Germany
(3-406)
Beekman Pubs
Beekman Pubs., Inc.
38 Hicks St., Brooklyn Heights, NY 11201
(0-8464)
Behrman
Behrman House, Inc.
1261 Broadway, New York, NY 10001
(0-87441)
Benaki Mus
Benaki Museum
1, Odos Koumbari, Athinai - 138, Greece
Bendigo
Bendigo Art Gallery
42 View St., Bendigo, Vic., Australia
Benjamin Co
Benjamin Co., Inc.
485 Madison Ave., New York, NY 10022
(0-87502)
Bennett Co
Bennett, Chas. A., Co., Inc.
809 W. Detweiler Dr., Peoria, IL 61615
(0-87002)
Benson
Benson, W. S., & Co.
P.O. Box 1866, Austin, TX 78767
(0-87443)
Benziger
See Glencoe
Benziger Sis
Benziger Sisters Publishers
466 E. Mariposa St., Altadena, CA 91001
Beresford Bk Serv
Beresford Book Service
1525 E. 53rd St., Suite 431, Chicago, IL 60615
(0-202)
Berg
See Larlin Corp
Bergling
See Gem City Coll
Berkshire Traveller
Berkshire Traveller Press
Pine St., Stockbridge, MA 01262
(0-912944)
Berwick Coun
Berwick Borough Council
Berwick-Upon-Tweed, United Kingdom
Beta Bk
Beta Book Co.
2801 Camino Del Rio S., San Diego, CA 92124
(0-89293)
Bezirksheimat
Bezirksheimatmuseum
Schloss Porcia, Edlingstr. 13 A-9800 Spittal/Drau, Austria
Biblio Dist
Biblio Distribution Centre
81 Adams Dr., P.O. Box 327, Totowa, NJ 07512
Biblo
Biblo & Tannen Booksellers & Pubs., Inc.
63 Fourth Ave., New York, NY 10003
(0-8196)
Binford
Binford & Mort Pubs.
2536 S.E. 11th Ave., Portland, OR 97202
(0-8323)
Biobooks
See Sullivan Bks Intl
Birds' Meadow Pub
Birds' Meadow Publishing Co., Inc.
17 Court St., Farmington, ME 04938
Birmingham Mus
Birmingham Museums & Art Gallery
Chamberlain Square, Birmingham B3 3DH, United Kingdom
Bishop Mus
Bishop Museum Press
P.O. Box 19000-A, Honolulu, HI 96818
(0-910240)
Bklyn Mus
Brooklyn Museum
Pubns. & Marketing Services, 188 Eastern Pkwy., Brooklyn, NY 11238
(0-87273; 0-913696)

Black Sparrow
Black Sparrow Press
P.O. Box 3993, Santa Barbara, CA 93105
(0-87685)
Blackburn Mus
Blackburn Museum & Art Gallery
Library St., Blackburn, Lancs.,
United Kingdom
Blackburn Rec
Borough of Blackburn Recreation Dept.
Library St., Blackburn BB1 7AJ,
United Kingdom
Blaine Ethridge
Blaine Ethridge Books
13977 Penrod St., Detroit, MI 48223
(0-87917)
Blair
Blair, John F., Pub.
1406 Plaza Dr., Winston-Salem, NC 27103
(0-910244; 0-89587)
Blaschker Ver
Blaschker Verlag GmbH
Lutzowstr. 105, 1000 Berlin 30,
West Germany
Bloch
Bloch Publishing Co.
915 Broadway, New York, NY 10010
(0-8197)
Bloomsburg
Bloomsburg State College, Dept. of Art
Bloomsburg, PA 17815
Bobbs
Bobbs-Merrill Co., Inc, A Thomas Audel Co.
4300 W. 62nd St., Indianapolis, IN 46206
(0-672)
Boise St Univ
Boise State Univ.
Dept. of English, Boise, ID 83725
(0-88430)
Bohnlau Verlag
Bohnlau Verlag
Koln, West Germany
Bookpeople
Bookpeople
2940 Seventh St., Berkeley, CA 94710
Books Marcus
Books Marcus
P.O. Box 188, Ojai, CA 93023
(0-916020)
Bookworks
Bookworks
Dist. by:
Random House, Inc., 400 Hahn Rd.,
Westminster, MD 21157
Borden
Borden Publishing Co.
1855 W. Main St., Alhambra, CA 91801
(0-87505)
Bossuet
Musee Bossuet
5 Pl Charles de Gaulle, F-7100 Meaux,
France
Boston Public Lib
Boston Public Library
P.O. Box 286, Boston, MA 02117
(0-89073)
Bovin
Bovin Publishing
68-36 108th St., Forest Hills, NY 11375
(0-910280)
Bowers Mus
Bowers Musuem
2002 N. Main St., Santa Ana, CA 92706
Bowes Mus
Bowes Museum
Barnard Castle, County Durham,
United Kingdom
Bowker
Bowker, R. R., Co, A Xerox Publishing Co.
P.O. Box 1807, Ann Arbor, MI 48106
(0-8352)
Bowmar
See Bowmar-Noble
Bowmar-Noble
Bowmar/Noble Publishers, Inc.
4563 Colorado Blvd., Los Angeles, CA
90039
(0-8372; 0-8107)
Branden
Branden Press, Inc.
P.O. Box 843-Brookline Village, 21 Station
St., Boston, MA 02147
(0-8283)
Branford
Branford, Charles T., Co.
19 Calvin Rd., P.O. Box 16, Watertown,
MA 02172
(0-8231)

Braziller
Braziller, George, Inc.
One Park Ave., New York, NY 10016
(0-8076)
Brigham
Brigham Young Univ. Press
206 University Press Bldg., Provo, UT
84602
(0-8425)
Bristol Art Gal
City of Bristol Museum & Art Gallery
Queens's Road, 8S8 1RL Bristol,
United Kingdom
British Bk Ctr
British Book Center
Fairview Park, Elmsford, NY 10523
(0-8277)
British Mus
British Museum
6 Bedford Square, London, WC1B 3RA,
United Kingdom
Broadman
Broadman Press
127 Ninth Ave., N., Nashville, TN 37234
(0-8054)
Brooke Hse
Brooke House Pubs., Inc.
9010 Reseda Blvd., Suite 226, Northridge,
CA 91324
(0-912588)
Brookgreen
Brookgreen Gardens
Rte. 1, Box 3, Murrels Inlet, SC 29576
Brooklyn Mus
Brooklyn Museum
188 Eastern Parkway, Brooklyn, NY 11238
United States
Brooks Memorial Art Gal
Brooks Memorial Art Gallery
Overton Park, Memphis, TN 38112
United States
Brown Bk
Brown Book Co.
120 Secatogue Ave., Farmingdale, NY
11735
(0-910294)
Brown U Pr
Brown Univ. Press
194 Meeting St., Box 1881, Providence, RI
02912
(0-87057)
Bruce Pub Co
See Glencoe
Bucknell U Pr
Bucknell Univ. Press
P.O. Box 421, Cranbury, NJ 08512
(0-8387)
Buffalo Acad
Buffalo Fine Arts Academy
Albright-Knox Art Gallery, 1285 Elmwood
Ave., Buffalo, NY 14222
(0-914782)
Bundespostmus
Bundespostmuseum
D-6000 Frankfurt 70, Schaumainkai 53,
West Germany
Bureau Issues
Bureau Issues Assn.
59 W. Germantown Pike, Norristown, PA
19401
(0-930412)
Burgenkun Mus
Burgenkundliches Museum
A-8011 Graz, Burgergasse 2, Austria
Burgess
Burgess Publishing Co.
7108 Ohms Lane, Minneapolis, MN 55435
(0-89469)
Burnley Boro Coun
Burnley Borough Council
Burnley, Lancs., United Kingdom
Busch Reisin
Busch-Reisinger Museum
C/O Harvard University, Cambridge, MA
02138
Busn. P-H.
Business & Professional Div. Imprint of
Prentice-Hall, Inc.
Buten Mus
Buten Museum of Wedgwood
246 N. Bowman Ave., Merion, PA 19066
(0-912014)
Butterick Pub
Butterick Publishing, Div. of American Can
Co.
P.O. Box 1914, Altoona, PA 16603
(0-88421)

Butterworths
Butterworths Pub., Inc.
10 Tower Office Park, Woburn, MA 01801
C B Pub & Dist
C. B. Publishing & Distributing, Inc.
(0-89241)
Independent Publishers Group, 14
Vanderventer Ave., Port Washington, NY
11050
C C Thomas
Thomas, Charles C., Pub.
301-327 E. Lawrence Ave., Springfield, IL
62717
(0-398)
C E Tuttle
Tuttle, Charles E., Co., Inc.
P.O. Drawer F, Rutland, VT 05701
(0-8048)
C N Aronson
Aronson, Charles N., Writer-Publisher
11520 Bixby Hill Road, Arcade, NY 14009
(0-915736)
Cahners
See CBI Pub
Caisse Nation
Service Commericial De La Caisse Nationale
Des Monuments Historiques et Des Sites
Grand Palais, Porte F, Cours-La-Reine,
75008 Paris, France
Calco Nazion
Instituto Nazionale per la Grafica Calcografia
Via della Stamperia 6, I-00187 Rome,
United Kingdom
Calif Hist
California Historical Society
2090 Jackson St., San Francisco, CA 94109
(0-910312)
Calif Street
California Street
723 Dwight Way, Berkeley, CA 94710
(0-915090)
Cambridge U Pr
Cambridge Univ. Press
510 North Ave., New Rochelle, NY 10801
(0-521)
Camera Graphic
Camera/Graphic Press Ltd.
P.O. Box 1702, F.D.R. Sta., New York, NY
10022
(0-918696)
Camerawork
See NFS Pr
Campana Art
Campana, D. M. , Art Co.
P.O. Box 355, Rte. 2, Box 30, Salem, WI
53168
Campbell Mus
Campbell Museum
Campbell Pl., Camden, NJ 08101
United States
Capitolare Atri
Museo Capitolare
Annesso alla Cattedrale, Via Roma, I-64032
Atri, Italy
Capra Pr
Capra Press
P.O. Box 2068, Santa Barbara, CA 93120
(0-912264; 0-88496)
Caratzas Bros
See C B Pub & Dist
Caravan Bks
Caravan Books
P.O. Box 344, Delmar, NY 12054
(0-88206)
Caravan-Maritime
Caravan-Maritime Books
87-06 168th Place, Jamaica, NY 11432
(0-917368)
Carcanet
See Dufour
Career Inst
Career Institute, Inc, Div. of Singer
Communications Corp.
1500 Cardinal Dr., Little Falls, NJ 07424
(0-911744)
Carnation
Carnation Press
P.O. Box 101, State College, PA 16801
(0-87601)
Carnegie
Carnegie Institute Museum of Art
4400 Forbes Ave., Pittsburgh, PA 15213
United States
Carnegie Inst
Carnegie Institution of Washington
1530 "P" St., N.W., Washington, DC 20005
(0-87279)

Carolina Art
Carolina Art Assn.
135 Meeting St., Charleston, SC 29401
(0-910326)

Carrier Pigeon
Carrier Pigeon
75 Kneeland St. Rm. 309, Boston, MA
02111
(0-932870)

Cassandra Pubns
Cassandra Pubns., Noe Valley Poets Workshop
143 Moffitt St., San Francisco, CA 94131

Cath Health
Catholic Health Assn.
1438 S. Grand Blvd., St. Louis, MO 63104
(0-87125)

Cath Hospital
See Cath Health

Cath St Paul
Tresor de la Cathedrale St. Paul
Rue Bonne Fortune 6, B-4000 Liege,
Belgium

Caxton
Caxton Printers, Ltd.
P.O. Box 700, Caldwell, ID 83605
(0-87004)

CBI Pub
CBI Publishing Co. Inc, Member of the
Wadsworth Publishing Group
51 Sleeper St., Boston, MA 02210
(0-8436)

CCPr. Macmillan.
Crowell-Collier Press. Imprint of Macmillan
Publishing Co., Inc.

Cellar
Cellar Book Shop
18090 Wyoming, Detroit, MI 48221

Centaur
Centaur Books, Inc.
799 Broadway, New York, NY 10003
(0-87818)

Centennial Photo Serv
Centennial Photo Services
P.O. Box 36, Grantsburg, WI 54840
(0-931838)

Century Hse
Century House, Inc.
Old Irelandville, Watkins Glen, NY 14891
(0-87282)

Ceramics Alfred
New York State College of Ceramics at Alfred
Univ
Alfred, NY 14802

Chain Store Pub
See Lebhar Friedman

Chandler & Sharp
Chandler & Sharp Pubs., Inc.
11A Commercial Blvd., Novato, CA 94947
(0-88316)

Charles Hardy
Charles E. Hardy
1 Cecil Rd., Barnard Castle DL12 8NP,
United Kingdom

Charles River Bks
Charles River Books
59 Commercial Wharf, Boston, MA 02110
(0-89182)

Chatham Pr
Chatham Press, Inc.
(0-85699)
Dist. by:
The Devin-Adair Co., Old Greenwich, CT
06870

Chatto-Bodley-Jonathan
See Merrimack Bk Serv

Chelsea Hse
Chelsea House Pubs.
70 W. 40th St., New York, NY 10018
(0-87754)

Chelsea Pub
Chelsea Publishing Co.
432 Park Avenue S., Rm. 503, New York,
NY 10016
(0-8284)

Chi Pub Lib
Chicago Public Library
78 E. Washington St., Chicago, IL 60602

Chicago Contemp Photo
Chicago Center for Contemporary
Photography
Columbia College, 600 S. Michigan Ave.,
Chicago, IL 60605
(0-932026)

Chicago Hist
Chicago Historical Society
Clark St. at North Ave., Chicago, IL 60614
(0-913820)

Chicago Inst
Art Institute of Chicago
Michigan Ave. at Adams St., Chicago, IL
60603

Chicago Review
Chicago Review Press, Inc.
215 W. Ohio St., Chicago, IL 60610
(0-914090)

Chicago Visual Lib. U of Chicago Pr.
Chicago Visual Library. Imprint of Univ. of
Chicago Press.

Chicorel Lib
See Am Lib Pub Co

Childrens
Childrens Press, Inc.
1224 W. Van Buren St., Chicago, IL 60607
(0-516)

Chilton
Chilton Book Co.
School, Library Services, 201 King of
Prussia Rd., Radnor, PA 19089
(0-8019)

Chinese Art App
Chinese Art Appraisers Assn.
Box 734, 625 Post St., San Francisco, CA
94109
(0-930940)

Chr Classics
Christian Classics, Inc.
205 Willis St., Westminister, MD 21157
(0-87061)

Chris Mass
Christopher Publishing House (Mass)
53 Billings Rd., North Quincy, MA 02171
(0-8158)

Christian Herald
Christian Herald Books
40 Overlook Dr., Chappaqua, NY 10514
(0-915684)

Chronicle Bks
Chronicle Books/Prism Editions, Div. of
Chronicle Publishing Co.
870 Market St., Suite 915, San Francisco,
CA 94102
(0-87701)

Chrysler Mus
Chrysler Museum at Norfolk
Olney Rd. & Mowbray Arch, Norfolk, VA
23510

Cincinnati Mus
Cincinnati Art Museum
Eden Park, Cincinnati, OH 45202
United States

Citadel Pr
Citadel Press, Subs. of Lyle Stuart, Inc.
120 Enterprise Ave., Secaucus, NJ 07094
(0-8065)

Claitors
Claitors Publishing Division
3165 S. Acadian at Interstate 10, Box 239,
Baton Rouge, LA 70821
(0-87511)

Clark Art Inst
Clark Art Institute
Wiliamstown, MA 01267

Cloudburst
See Madrona Pubs

Cognac
Musee Municipal de Cognac
40 Blvd. Denfert-Rochereau, F-16100
Cognac, France

Coin & Curr
Coin & Currency Institute, Inc.
116 W. 32nd St., New York, NY 10001
(0-87184)

Colby
Colby College Press
Library, Waterville, ME 04901
(0-910394)

Collector Bks
Collector Books
P.O. Box 3009, Paducah, KY 42001
(0-89145)

Collectors
Collectors Club, Inc.
22 E. 35th St., New York, NY 10016
(0-912574)

Collier. Macmillan.
Collier Books. Imprint of Macmillan Publishing
Co., Inc.

Collins Pubs
Collins, William, Pubs., Inc.
2080 W. 117th St., Cleveland, OH 44111;
200 Madison Ave., Suite 1405, New York,
NY 10016

Collins-World
See Collins Pubs

Colnaghi Co
Colnaghi & Co. Ltd.
Glasgow, United Kingdom

Colo Assoc
Colorado Associated Univ. Press, Univ. of
Colorado
1424 15th St. Univ. of Colorado, Boulder,
CO 80309
(0-87081)

Colombo Mus
Colombo National Museum
P.O. Box 854, 7 Colombo
Sri Lanka

Columbia U Pr
Columbia Univ. Press
Orders to:
136 S. Broadway, Irvington-on-Hudson, NY
10533
(0-231)

Columbus Mus
Columbus Museum of Art
480 E. Broad St., Columbus, OH 43215

Comm Whi Hse
Committee for the Preservation of the White
House
1100 Ohio Dr., S.W., Washington, DC
20242

Concordia
Concordia Publishing House
3558 S. Jefferson Ave., St. Louis, MO
63118
(0-570)

Condor Pub Co
Condor Pub. Co., Inc.
29 E. Main St., Westport, CT 06880
(0-89516)

Congreve Pub
Congreve Publishing Co., Inc.
375 Park Ave., New York, NY 10022
(0-930186)

Contemp Bks
Contemporary Books, Inc.
180 N. Michigan Ave., Chicago, IL 60601
(0-8092)

Coole
Coole, Arthur B.
219 S. Williams St., Denver, CO 80209
(0-912706)

Cooper Sq
Cooper Square Pubs., Inc.
59 Fourth Ave., New York, NY 10003
(0-8154)

Copley Bks
Copley Books
P.O. Box 957, 7776 Ivanhoe Ave., La Jolla,
CA 92038
(0-913938)

Coptic Mus
Coptic Museum
St. George St., Cairo, Egypt

Corcoran
Corcoran Gallery of Art
17th St. & New York Ave. N.W.,
Washington, DC 20006

Cornell Maritime
Cornell Maritime, Press, Inc.
P.O. Box 456, Centerville, MD 21617
(0-87033)

Cornell U Pr
Cornell Univ. Press
124 Robets Place, P.O. Box 250, Ithaca,
NY 14850
(0-8014)

Corner
Corner Book Shop
102 Fourth Ave., New York, NY 10003
(0-910442)

Cornerstone
Cornerstone Library, Inc, Div. of Simon &
Schuster, Inc.
Simon & Schuster, Inc., 1230 Avenue of the
Americas, New York, NY 10020
(0-346)

Corning
Corning Museum of Glass, Inc.
5 Denison Pkwy., E., Corning, NY 14830
(0-87290)

Coronado Pr
Coronado Press, Inc.
P.O. Box 3232, Lawrence, KS 66044
(0-87291)

Corvina
Corvina Publishing House
H-1364 Budapest 4, Box 108, Hungary

COS. B&N.
College Outline Series. Imprint of Barnes &
Noble Books.

Cottonwood
Cottonwood County Historical Society
812 Fourth Ave., Windom, MN 56101
United States

Coun Biology Eds
Council of Biology Editors
American Institute of Biological Sciences,
1401 Wilson Blvd., Arlington, VA 22209
(0-914340)

Coun Plan Lib
Council of Planning Librarians
P.O. Box 229, Monticello, IL 61856

Country Beautiful
Country Beautiful Corp.
24198 W. Bluemound Rd., Waukesha, WI
53186
(0-87294)

Countryman
Countryman Press, Inc.
Taftsville, VT 05073
(0-914378)

Coward
Coward, McCann & Geoghegan, Inc, A
Member of the Putnam Publishing Group
1050 W. Wall St., Lyndhurst, NJ 07071
(0-698)

Cranbrook
Cranbrook Academy of Art Museum
500 Lone Pine Rd., Bloomfield Hils, MI
48013

Crane-Russak Co
Crane, Russak & Co., Inc.
3 E. 44th St, New York, NY 10017
(0-8448)

Creative Bks
Creative Books
P.O. Box 5162, Carmel, CA 93921
(0-914606)

Creative Comp
Creative Computing
P.O. Box 789M, Morristown, NJ 07960
(0-916688)

Creative Ed
Creative Education, Inc.
123 S. Broad St., Mankato, MN 56001
(0-87191)

Creative Eye
Creative Eye Press
P.O. Box 620, Sonoma, CA 95476
(0-916480)

Crescendo
See Taplinger

Crown
Crown Pubs., Inc.
1 Park Ave., New York, NY 10016
(0-517)

Ctr Appl Res
Center for Applied Research in Education,
Inc., The, Subs. of Prentice-Hall
Orders to:
P.O. Box 130, W. Nyack, NY 10995
(0-87628)

Ctr Creative Photo
Center for Creative Photography
843 E. University, AZ 85719

Ctr for Arts Info
Center for Arts Information
152 W. 42nd St., New York, NY 10036

Curtin & London
Curtin & London, Inc.
6 Vernon St., Somerville, MA 02145
(0-930764)

Cygnaeus
Cygnaeuksen Galleria
Kalliolinnantie 8, 00140 Helsinki, Finland

D Lem Assocs
Lem, Dean, Associates, Inc.
P.O. Box 46086, Los Angeles, CA 90046
(0-914218)

D McPhail
McPhail, David
242 Trinity Ave., Berkeley, CA 94708

D Mason
Mason, D.
7546 Cowan Ave., Los Angeles, CA 90045
(0-9601392)

D S Coleman
Coleman, Dorothy S.
4315 Van Ness St., Washington, DC 20016
(0-910396)

Da Capo
Da Capo Press, Inc.
227 W. 17th St., New York, NY 10011
(0-306)

Da Vinci Mus
Da Vinci-Museum
Norbertijnenabdij, Tongerlo, B-3180
Westerlo, Belgium

David & Charles
David & Charles, Inc.
P.O. Box 57, North Pomfret, VT 05053
(0-7153)

David Collection
David Collection
Kronprinsessegade 30, DK-1306
Copenhagen, Denmark

Davis Mass
Davis Pubns., Inc.
50 Portland St., Worcester, MA 01608
(0-87192)

Dawson Pub
Dawson Publishing
(0-7129)
Shoe String Press, Inc., P.O. Box 4327, 995
Sherman Ave., Hamden, CT 06514

Dawsons
Dawson's Book Shop
535 N. Larchmont Blvd., Los Angeles, CA
90004
(0-87093)

De Gruyter
De Gruyter, Walter, Inc.
200 Saw Mill River Rd., Hawthorne, NY
10532
(3-11)

De La Ree
De La Ree, Gerry, Publisher
7 Cedarwood Lane, Saddle River, NJ
07458

Dean & Chapter
Durham Cathedral
The Treasury, the College, Durham DH1
3EH, United Kingdom

Deerfield
Deerfield Academy
Deerfield, MA 01342

Deermouse
Deermouse Press
4 Berkeley Place, Cambridge, MA 02138
(0-9600596)

Del Art Mus
Delaware Art Museum
2301 Kentmere Pkwy., Wilmington, DE
19806

Delacorte
Delacorte Press
c/o Dell Publishing Co., 1 Dag
Hammarskjold Plaza, 245 E. 47th St., New
York, NY 10017

Delancey Pr
Delancey Press
P.O. Box 754, Cooper Station, New York,
NY 10003
(0-9601128)

Dell
Dell Publishing Co., Inc.
1 Dag Hammarskjold Plaza, 245 E. 47th
St., New York, NY 10017
(0-440)

Delmar
Delmar Pubs, Div. of Litton Educ. Pub., Inc.
7625 Empire Dr., Florence, KY 41042
(0-8273)

Delphi
Archaeoogical Museum of Delphi
Delphi, Greece

Delta. Dell.
Delta Books. Imprint of Dell Publishing Co.,
Inc.

Demetrius-Victor
See C B Pub & Dist

Denison
Denison, T. S., & Co., Inc.
9601 Newton Ave. S., Minneapolis, MN
55431
(0-513)

Denver Art Mus
Denver Art Museum
100 W. 14th Ave. Pkwy., Denver, CO
80204
(0-914738)

Deseret Bk
Deseret Book Co.
40 E. South Temple, P.O. Box 30178, Salt
Lake City, UT 84125
(0-87747)

Det Faste Galleri
Trondhjems Kunstforening-Trondelag
Kunstgalleri
N-7000 Trondheim, Norway

Det Inst Arts
Detroit Institute of the Arts
5200 Woodward Ave., Detroit, MI 48202

Deut Ledermus
Deutsches Ledermuseum
D-6050 Offenbach Am Main, Frankfurter
Str. 86, West Germany

Devin
Devin-Adair Co., Inc.
143 Sound Beach Ave., Old Greenwich, CT
06870
(0-8159)

DH&R
Dowden, Hutchinson & Ross, Inc.
(0-87933)
Dist. by:
Academic Press, Inc., 111 Fifth Ave., New
York, NY 10003

Dharma Pub
Dharma Publishing
5856 Doyle St., Emeryville, CA 94608
(0-913546; 0-89800)

Dial
Dial Press
1 Dag Hammarskjold Plaza, 245 E. 47th
St., New York, NY 10017
(0-8037)

Didrichsen Mus
Didrichsenin Taidemuseo
Kuusilahdenkuja 3, SF-00340 Helsinki,
Finland

Dillon
Dillon Press, Inc.
500 S. Third St., Minneapolis, MN 55415
(0-87518)

Dillon-Tyler Pubs
Dillon-Tyler Pubs.
P.O. Box 971, Woodland, CA 95695
(0-916280)

Directions
Directions Simplified, Inc, Div. of Easi-Bild
Pattern Co., Inc
529 N. State Rd., P.O. Box 215, Briarcliff
Manor, NY 10510
(0-87733)

Dixon Gal
Dixon Gallery & Gardens
4339 Park Ave., Memphis,
TN 38117

Documentatie
Museum voor Religieuze Kunst
Begijnhof 39, B-3800 Sint-Truiden, Belgium

Dodd
Dodd, Mead & Co.
79 Madison Ave., New York, NY 10016
(0-396)

Doll Collect Am
Doll Collectors of America, Inc.
Dist. by:
Hazel Toon, 167 Round Cove Rd.,
Chatham, MA 02633

Dolmen Pr. Humanities.
Dolmen Press. Imprint of Humanities Press,
Inc.

Dolp. Doubleday.
Dolphin Books. Imprint of Doubleday & Co.,
Inc.

Donning Co
Donning Co. Pubs.
5041 Admiral Wright Rd., Virginia Beach,
VA 23462
(0-915442; 0-89865)

Dorchester Savings
Dorchester Savings Bank
572 Columbia Rd., Boston, MA 02125

Dordrechts Mus
Dordrechts Museum
Museumstraat 40, Dordrecht 3311 XP,
Netherlands

Doria Pamphilj
Galleria Doria Pamphilj
Piazza de Collegio Romano 1a, I-00186
Rome, Italy

Dorrance
Dorrance & Co.
35 Cricket Terrace, Ardmore, PA 19003
(0-8059)

Doubleday
Doubleday & Co., Inc.
501 Franklin Ave., Garden City, NY 11530
(0-385)

Douglas-West
Douglas-West Pubs., Inc.
7060 Hollywood Blvd., Los Angeles, CA
90028
(0-913264)

Dover
Dover Pubns., Inc.
180 Varick St., New York, NY 10014
(0-486)

Drama Bk
Drama Book Specialists (Pubs.)
150 W. 52nd St., New York, NY 10019
(0-910482; 0-89676)

Dream Place
Dream Place Pubns.
P.O. Box 9416, Stanford, CA 94305
(0-930486)

Dufour
Dufour Editions, Inc.
Chester Springs, PA 19425
(0-8023)

Duke
Duke Univ. Press
6697 College Sta., Durham, NC 27708
(0-8223)

Dunconor Bks
Dunconor Books
P. O. Box 2000, Crested Butte, CO 81224
(0-918820)

Dundee Mus
Dundee Museum & Art Gallery
Albert Square, DD1 1DA Dundee,
United Kingdom

Dunlap Soc
Dunlap Society
Lake Champlain Rd., Essex, NY 12936
(0-89481)

Durrell
Durrell Pubns., Inc.
P. O. Box 743, Mast Cove Lane,
Kennebunkport, ME 04046
(0-911764)

Dutton
Dutton, E. P.
2 Park Ave., New York, NY 10016
(0-525)

E A Seemann
Seemann, E. A., Publishing, Inc.
P.O. Box K, Miami, FL 33156
(0-912458; 0-89530)

Eakins
Eakins Press Foundation
155 E. 42nd St., New York, NY 10017
(0-87130)

Easter Pub
Easter Publishing Co.
P.O. Box 1244, Mobile, AL 36601
(0-930642)

Eastern Wash
Eastern Washington State Historical Society
W. 2316 First Ave., Spokane, WA 99204
(0-910524)

Eastman Kodak
Eastman Kodak Co.
Orders to:
343 State St., Dept. 454, Rochester, NY
14650
(0-87985)

Eastnor
Eastnor Castle
Ledbury, Herefordshire, United Kingdom

Ed Mus Nation
Editions Des Musees Nationaux
10, Rue De L'Abbaye, Paris 60, France

Ed Tecnicos
See French & Eur

Ed Ulrich Mus
Ulrich, Edwin A., Museum
Albany Post Rd., Hyde Park, NY 12538

Edinburgh Univ Pr.
See Biblio Dist

Ediz Arnaud
Edizioni Arnaud
Via XXVII Aprile 13, I-50129 Firenze,
Italy

Edmonton Gal
Edmonton Art Gallery
2 Sir Winston Churchill Square, Edmonton,
AB T5J 2C1, Canada

Eduardo Sivori
Museo de Artes Plasticas "Edoardo Sivori"
Av. Corrientes 1530, Piso 5, Buenos Aires,
Argentina

Educator Bks
Educator Books, Inc.
Drawer 32, 10 N. Main, San Angelo, TX
76901
(0-912092)

Eerdmans
Eerdmans, Wm. B., Publishing Co.
255 Jefferson Ave., S.E., Grand Rapids, MI
49503
(0-8028)

Egyptian Mus
Egyptian Myuseum
Sh Selim Hassan, Cairo, Egypt

EH. B&N.
Everyday Handbooks. Imprint of Barnes &
Noble Books.

Einars Jonsson
Listafn Einars Jonssonar
Eiriksgata, P.O. Box 1051, Reyjavik,
Iceland

Elliots Bks
Elliot's Books
P.O. Box 6, Northford, CT 06472
(0-911830)

Elsevier
Elsevier-North Holland Pub. Co.
52 Vanderbilt Ave., New York, NY 10017
(0-444; 0-7204)

Elsevier-Nelson
Elsevier/Nelson Books
2 Park Ave., New York, NY 10016
(0-525)

Elsevier Sci
See Elsevier

Elysium
Elysium Growth Press
5436 Fernwood Ave., Los Angeles, CA
90027
(0-910550)

Emerson
Emerson Books, Inc.
Reynolds Lane, Buchanan, NY 10511
(0-87523)

Emil Ceder Mus
Cedercreutzin, Emil, Museo
SF-29210 Merstola, Harjavalta, Finland

Encino Pr
Encino Press
510 Baylor St., Austin, TX 78703
(0-88426)

Ency Brit Ed
Encyclopaedia Britannica Educational Corp,
Affiliate of Encyclopaedia Britannica, Inc.
425 N. Michigan Ave., Chicago, IL 60611
(0-87827)

Eng Life Pubns
English Life Publications
The Strand, Derby DEI 1BS,
United Kingdom

Environ Des VA
Environmental Design Press, Div. of
Educational & Research Management, Inc.
P.O. Box 2187, Reston, VA 22090
(0-918436)

Environ Design
Environmental Design & Research Ctr.
142 Lowell Ave., Newtonville, MA 02160
(0-915250)

EPM Pubns
EPM Pubns.
P.O. Box 490, McLean, VA 22101
(0-914440)

Eriksson
Eriksson, Paul S., Pubs.
(0-8397)
Independent Publishers Group, 14
Vanderventer Ave., Port Washington, NY
11050

Ernst Barlach
Barlach, Ernst, Haus
D-2000 Hamburg 52, Klein-Flottbek,
Baron-Voght-Str. 50a, Jenisch-Park,
West Germany

Ernst Wasmuth
Verlag Ernst Wasmuth
Furst Str. 133, 7400 Tubingen,
West Germany

Erz Dioz Pade
Erzbischofliches Diozesanmuseum
479 Paderborn, Postfach 1480,
West Germany

Essex Inst
Essex Institute
132 Essex St., Salem, MA 01970
(0-88389)

Essex Pubns
Essex Pubns.
P.O. Box 2745, Boston, MA 02208
(0-930332)

Estate Bk
Estate Book Sales
2824 Pennsylvania Ave., N.W., Washington,
DC 20007

ETC Pubns
ETC Pubns.
Pubns. Dept., P.O. Drawer 1627-A, Palm
Springs, CA 92263
(0-88280)

Etherington
Queen's Univ.
Queen's Univ., Agnes Etherington Center,
Canada

Ett Hem Mus
Museet "Ett Hem"
Biskopgaten 14, SF-20500 Turku 50,
Finland

Everson Mus
Everson Museum of Art
401 Harrison St., Syracuse, NY 13202

Exeter Mus Serv
Exeter Museums Service
Queen St., Exeter EX4 3RX,
United Kingdom

Exposition
Exposition Press, Inc.
900 S., Oyster Bay Rd., Hicksville, NY
11801
(0-682)

F Cass Co
See Biblio Dist

F M Roberts
Roberts, F.M., Enterprises
P.O. Box 608, Dana Point, CA 92629
(0-912746)

Faaborg Mus
Faaborg Museum
Gronnegade, DK-5600 Faborg, Denmark

Faber & Faber
See Merrimack Bk Serv

Faenza
Museo Internazionale delle Ceramiche
V. Campidori N. 2, I-48018 Faenza, Italy

Fairchild
Fairchild Books & Visuals
7 E. 12th St., New York, NY 10003
(0-87005)

Fairleigh Dickinson
Fairleigh Dickinson Univ. Press
P.O. Box 421, Cranbury, NJ 08512
(0-8386)

Faxon
Faxon, F. W., Co., Inc.
15 Southwest Park, Westwood, MA 02090
(0-87305)

FDC Pub
F.D.C. Publising Co.
P.O. Box 206, Stewartsville, NJ 08886
(0-89794)

Fearon
See Fearon-Pitman

Fearon-Pitman
Fearon-Pitman Pubns., Inc.
6 Davis Dr., Belmont, CA 94002
(0-8224)

Fehr Coll
Fehr, William, Collection
Castle of Good Hope, P. O. Box 1, Cape
Town, South Africa

Fell
Fell, Frederick, Publishers, Inc.
386 Park Ave., S., New York, NY 10016
(0-8119)

Feminist Pr
Feminist Press
SUNY/College at Old Westbury, Box 334,
Old Westbury, NY 11568
(0-912670)

Fenimore Bk
Fenimore Book Store
Lake Rd., Cooperstown, NY 13326

Ferry Pr
See SBD

Fertig
Fertig, Howard, Inc.
80 E. 11th St., New York, NY 10003
(0-8335)

Field Mus
Field Museum of Natural History
Roosevelt Rd., at Lake Shore Dr., Chicago,
IL 60605
(0-914868)

Filsinger & Co
Filsinger & Co., Ltd.
150 Waverly Place, New York, NY 10014
(0-916754)

Filter
Filter Press
P.O. Box 5, Palmer Lake, CO 80133
(0-910584)

Fine Arts Mus
Fine Arts Museums of San Francisco
Golden Gate Park, San Francisco, CA
94118

Fireside. S&S.
Fireside Paperbacks. Imprint of Simon &
Schuster, Inc.

Fitzwilliam
Univ. of Cambridge, Fitzwilliam Museum
Trumpington St., CB2 1RB Cambridge,
United Kingdom
Flagler Mus
Flagler, Henry Morrison, Museum
Whitehall Way, Palm Beach,
FL 33480
Flash Bks. Music Sales.
Flash Books. Imprint of Music Sales Corp.
Flayderman
Flayderman, N., & Co., Inc.
Squash Hollow Rd., New Milford, CT
06776
(0-910598)
Fleet
Fleet Press Corp.
160 Fifth Ave., New York, NY 10010
(0-8303)
Focal Pr
Focal Press, Inc.
Hastings House Pubs., Inc., 10 E. 40th St.,
New York, NY 10016
Fogg Art Mus
Fogg Art Museum
Cambridge, MA 02138
Folcroft
Folcroft Library Editions
P.O. Box 182, Folcroft, PA 19032
(0-8414)
Folk Art
Folk Art Studios
P.O. Box 162, El Toro, CA 92630
(0-930310)
Follett
Follett Publishing Co, Div. of Follett Corp.
1010 W. Washington Blvd., Chicago, IL
60607
(0-695)
Fond Horne
Horne, Herbert Percy, Fondazione
Via Del Benci 6, I-50122 Firenze, Italy
Fordham
Fordham Univ. Press
University Box L, Bronx, NY 10458
(0-8232)
Fort Worth Mus
Fort Worth Art Museum
1309 Montgomery, Fort Worth,
TX 76107
Fortress
Fortress Press
2900 Queen Lane, Philadelphia, PA 19129
(0-8006)
Fountain Brit
Fountain Press
(0-85242)
Dist. by:
Hastings House Pubs., Inc., 10 E. 40th St.,
New York, NY 10016
Fountain Hse East
Fountain House East
Box 99298, Jeffersontown, KY 40299
(0-914736)
Fran Podesti
Pinacoteca Civica "Francesco Podesti" Galeria
Comunale d'Arte Moderna
Palazzo Bosdari, Via Pizzecolli 17, I-60100
Ancona, Italy
Franciscan Herald
Franciscan Herald Press
1434 W. 51st St., Chicago, IL 60609
(0-8199)
Frank Goethe
Frankfurter Goethe-Museum
D-6000 Frankfurt, Freises Deutsches
Hoch-Stift, Grosser Hirschagraben 23,
West Germany
Franklin Pub Locust
Franklin Publishing Co.
2047 Locust St., Philadelphia, PA 19103
(0-87133)
Frans Halsmuseum
Frans Halsmuseum
Groot Heiligland 62, Haarlem, Netherlands
Franz Steiner
Franz-Steiner Verlag GMBH
Friedrichstrasse 24, Postfach 5529, D-6200,
Wiesbaden, West Germany
(3-515)
Free Pr
Free Press, Div. of Macmillan Publishing Co.,
Inc.
(0-02)
Macmillan Co., Riverside, NJ 08370

Freedeeds Assocs
Freedeeds Associates
(0-89345)
Multimedia Publishing Co., 72 Fifth Ave.,
New York, NY 10011
Freer
Freer Gallery of Art, Smithsonian Institution
12th & Jefferson Dr., S.W., Washington,
DC 20560
French & Eur
French & European Pubns., Inc.
115 Fifth Ave., New York, NY 10003
(0-8288)
Freshet
Freshet Press, Inc.
90 Hamilton Rd., Rockville Centre, NY
11570
(0-88395)
Frick
Frick Collection
1 E. 70th St., New York, NY 10021
Frick Art Mus
Frick Art Museum
7227 Reynolds St., Pittsburgh, PA 15208
United States
Friedman
Friedman, Ira J., Inc, Div. of Kennikat Press,
Inc.
90 S. Bayles Ave., Port Washington, NY
11050
(0-87198)
Friend Pr
Friendship Press
P.O. Box 37844, Cincinnati, OH 45237
(0-377)
Friends Earth
Friends of the Earth, Inc.
124 Spear, San Francisco, CA 94105
(0-913890)
Frontier Pr Co
Frontier Press Co.
P.O. Box 1098, Columbus, OH 43216
(0-912168)
FS&G
Farrar, Straus & Giroux, Inc.
19 Union Square, W., New York, NY
10003
(0-374)
Fujita
Fujita Art Museum
10-32 Amijimacho, Miyakojima-Ku, Osaka
Pref. 534, Japan
Fundaburk
Fundaburk, Emma Lila, Pub.
Luverne, AL 36049
(0-910642)
Furstlic Haus
Furst Thurn und Taxis Schlossmuseum
D-8400 Regensburg 1, Furstliches Schloss,
Emmeransplatz, P.O. Box 211,
West Germany
Furstlich Ver
Furstluch-Lippisches Residenzschloss
D-4930 Detmold, Schloss, West Germany
G K Hall
Hall, G. K., & Co.
70 Lincoln St., Boston, MA 02111
(0-8161)
G W Noble
Noble, Gilbert W.
P.O. Box 931, Winter Park, FL 32789
(0-911036)
Gal Aca Venice
Galleria dell'Accademia
Campo della Carita, I-30121 Venice, Italy
Gal Bratislava
Galeria Hlavneho Mesta SSR Bratislavy
Dibrovovo Nam. 11, 894 16 Bratislava,
Czechoslovakia
Gal Claremont
Galleries of the Claremont Colleges
C/O Montgomery Art Gallery, Pomona
College, Claremont,
CA 91711
Gal Liko Umje
Galerija Likovnih Umjetnosti
Bul. Jna 9, YU-54000 Osijek, Yugoslavia
Gal Ljubljana
Moderna Galerija
Tomisceva 14, YU-6100 Ljubljana,
Yugoslavia
Gal S Austral
Art Gallery of South Australia
North Terrace, Adelaide 5000, Australia
Gal Spinola
Galleria Nazionale di Palazzo Spinola
Piazza di Pellicceria 1, I-16123 Genoa,
Italy

Gale
Gale Research Co.
Book Tower, Detroit, MI 48226
(0-8103)
Gallery Pr
Gallery Press
98 N. Main St., Essex, CT 06426
(0-913622)
Galloway
Galloway Pubns.
2940 N.W. Circle Blvd., Corvallis, OR
97330
(0-87874)
Gambit
Gambit
27 North Main St., Meeting House Green,
Ipswich, MA 01938
(0-87645)
G&D
Grosset & Dunlap, Inc.
51 Madison Ave., New York, NY 10010
(0-448)
Gannon
Gannon, William
P.O. Box 2610, Santa Fe, NM 87501
(0-88307)
Garden Way Pub
Garden Way Publishing Co.
Charlotte, VT 05445
(0-88266)
Gardner Mus
Gardner, Isabella Stewart, Museum
2 Palace Rd., MA 02115
Garland Pub
Garland Publishing, Inc.
136 Madison Ave., 2nd Floor, New York,
NY 10016
(0-8240)
Garlic Pr
Garlic Press
533 Rialto Ave., Venice, CA 90291
(0-932798)
Garrard
Garrard Publishing Co.
1607 N. Market St., Champaign, IL 61820
(0-8116)
Garrett-Helix
Garrett Pubns.-Helix Press
Taplinger Publishing Co., 200 Park Ave,
S., New York, NY 10003
(0-912326)
Gary Schwartz
Gary Schwartz
Herengrach 22, Postbos 162, Maarsen,
Netherlands
Gateway Ed Ltd
See Regnery-Gateway
Gaylord Prof Pubns
Gaylord Professional Pubns, Div. of Gaylord
Bros., Inc.
Orders to:
P.O. Box 4901, Syracuse, NY 13221
(0-915794)
GB. Oxford U Pr.
Galaxy Books. Imprint of Oxford Univ. Press,
Inc.
Gebruder Mann
Gebruder Mann Verlag
Lindenstr. 76, Postfach 110303, D-1000
Berlin 61, West Germany
Gem City Coll
Gem City College Press
700 State St., Quincy, IL 62301
(0-910222)
Gemalde Wien
Gemaldegalerie der Akademie der Bildender
Kunst in Wien
Schillerplatz 3, A-1010 Wien, Austria
Gembooks
Gembooks
P. O. Box 808, Mentone, CA 92359
(0-910652)
Gemological
Gemological Institute of America
1660 Stewart St., Santa Monica, CA 90404
(0-87311)
Genl Dir Antiq
Archaeological Museum
Garitsa, Corfu, Greece
Gerhard Marcks
Marcks, Gerhard, Stiftung
D-2800 Bremen, am Wall 208,
West Germany
German Natl
Germanische Nationalmuseum
Postfach 95 80, 8500 Nurnberg 11,
West Germany

Glasgow Mus
Pollok House, (Glasgow Museums & Art Galleries)
2060 Pollokshaws Rd., Glasgow G43 1AT, United Kingdom

Glenbow Mus
Glenbow Museum
Ninth Ave. & First St., S.E., Calgary AB T2G OP3, Canada

Glencoe
Glencoe Publishing Co., Inc.
(0-02)
Dist. by:
Macmillan Co., Riverside, NJ 08075

Glenn Vargas
Vargas, Glenn
85-159 Ave. 66, Thermal, CA 92274
(0-917646)

Glide
See New Glide

Globe Pequot
Globe Pequot Press
Old Chester Rd., Box Q, Chester, CT 06412
(0-87106)

Gloucester Art
Gloucester Art Press
P.O. Box 4526, Albuquerque, NM 87196
(0-930582)

Godine
Godine, David R., Pub., Inc.
306 Dartmouth St., Boston, MA 02116
(0-87923)

Golden Gate. Childrens.
Golden Gate. Imprint of Childrens Press, Inc.

Golden Pr. Western Pub.
Golden Press. Imprint of Western Publishing Co., Inc.

Golden West
Golden West Books
P. O. Box 8136, San Marino, CA 91108
(0-87095)

Goodheart
Goodheart-Willcox Co., Inc.
123 W. Taft Dr., South Holland, IL 60473
(0-87006)

Goodyear
Goodyear Publishing Co.
Orders to:
Salt Lake City, UT 84118
(0-87620)

Gordian
Gordian Press, Inc.
85 Tompkins St., Staten Island, NY 10304
(0-87752)

Gordon
Gordon & Breach Science Pubs., Inc.
1 Park Ave., New York, NY 10016
(0-677)

Gordon Pr
Gordon Press Pubs.
P.O. Box 459, Bowling Green Sta., New York, NY 10004
(0-87968)

Gosta Serlach
Gosta Serlachius Fine Arts Foundation
SF-35800 Mantta, Finland

Goteborgs Konst
Goteborgs Konstmuseum
Gotaplatsen 412-56, Gothenburg, Sweden

Gotham
Gotham Book Mart
41 W. 47th St., New York, NY 10036
(0-910664)

Grand Central
Grand Central Art Galleries, Inc.
43rd St. & Madison Ave., New York, NY 10017

Grant Dahlstrom
Dahlstrom, Grant, /Castle Press
516 N. Fair Oaks Ave., Pasadena, CA 91103

Graphic Arts Ctr
Graphic Arts Center Publishing Co.
2000 N.W. Wilson, Portland, OR 97209
(0-912856)

Graphic Crafts
Graphic Crafts, Inc.
P.O. Box 248, 300 Beaver Valley Pike, Willow Street, PA 17584

Great Outdoors
Great Outdoors Publishing Co.
4747 28th St., N., St. Petersburg, FL 33714
(0-8200)

Greatlakes Liv
Greatlakes Living Press
180 N. Michigan Ave., Chicago, IL 60601
(0-89635; 0-915498)

Greek Arch Serv
TAP-Greek Archaeological Service
Phillelinon 17 Str., Athens, Greece

Greek Mus
The Greek Museum
University, Newcastle-Upon-Tyne NE1 7RU, United Kingdom

Green Tiger
Green Tiger Press
7458 La Jolla Blvd., La Jolla, CA 92037
(0-914676)

Greene
Greene, Stephen, Press
Fressenden Rd. at Indian Flat, P.O. Box 1000, Brattleboro, VT 05301
(0-8289)

Greenwich Pr
Greenwich Press
335 Bleecker St., New York, NY 10014
(0-911708)

Greenwillow
Greenwillow Books, Div. of William Morrow & Co., Inc.
William Morrow & Co., Inc., Wilmor Warehouse, 6 Henderson Dr., West Caldwell, NJ 07006
(0-688)

Greenwood
Greenwood Press, Inc.
51 Riverside Ave., Westport, CT 06880
(0-8371; 0-313)

Greven Verlag
Greven Verlag
Neve Weyerstr. 1-3, Postfach 100947, D-5000, Koln, West Germany
(3-7743)

Grolier Ed Corp
Grolier Educational Corp, Subs. of Grolier, Inc.
Sherman Turnpike, Danbury, CT 06816
(0-7172)

Grolier Inc
See Grolier Ed Corp

Groninger Mus
Groninger Museum
Praediniussingel 59, Groningen 9711 AG, Netherlands

GS
Girl Scouts of the USA
National Equipment Service, 830 Third Ave., New York, NY 10022
(0-88441)

Guappones Pubs
Guappone's Pubs.
R.D. One, Box Ten, McClellandtown, PA 15458

Guildhall
Guildhall Art Gallery
King St., London EC2, United Kingdom

Gulbenkian Mus
Calouste Gulbenkian Museum
Ave. de Berna, Lisbon, Portugal

Gun Hill
Gun Hill Publishing Co.
P.O. Box 187B, Yazoo City, MS 39194
(0-9600228)

Gun Room
Gun Room Press
127 Raritan Ave., Highland Park, NJ 08904
(0-88227)

H Christian
Hans Christians Verlag
Kleine Theaterstr. 10, D-200 Hamburg 36, West Germany
(3-7672)

H Estes
Estes, Hiawatha, & Associates
P.O. Box 404-RR, Northridge, CA 91328
(0-911008)

H P Bks
H. P. Books
341 Ponce de Leon Ave., N.E., Rm. 416, Tucson, AZ 85703
(0-912656; 0-89586)

H Reichner
Reichner, Herbert
Main St., Stockbridge, MA 01262; Shaker Hill, Enfield, NH 03740
(0-9601520)

H S Dakin
Dakin, H. S., Co.
3101 Washington St., San Francisco, CA 94115
(0-930420)

Hacker
Hacker Art Books
54 W. 57th St., New York, NY 10019
(0-87817)

Haddad's Fine Arts
Haddad's Fine Arts, Inc.
P.O. Box 3016 C, Anaheim, CA 92803; 3855 E. Mira Loma Ave., Anaheim, CA 92803
(0-88445)

Hafner
Hafner Press, Div. of Macmillan Publishing Co., Inc.
(0-02)
Dist. by:
Collier-Macmillan Distribution Ctr., Riverside, NJ 08075

Hakone Mus
Kyusei Hakone Art Museum
1300 Gora, Hakone, Kanagawa-Ken, Japan

Halldin Pub
Halldin, A. G., Publishing Co.
Indiana, PA 15701

Halsted Pr
Halsted Press, Div. of John Wiley & Sons, Inc.
605 Third Ave., New York, NY 10016

Hamburg Kunst
Hamburger Kunsthalle
Glockengiesserwal, 2 Hamburg, West Germany

Hammond Inc
Hammond, Inc.
515 Valley St., Maplewood, NJ 07040
(0-8437)

Hancock Hse
Hancock House Pubs., Ltd.
12008 First Ave., S., Seattle, WA 98168
(0-919654; 0-88839)

Handel & Sons
Handel & Sons Publishing, Inc.
14001 Goldmark, Suite 242, Dallas, TX 75240
(0-917080)

Handelsdruk
Handelsdrukkerij
Leeuwarden, Netherlands

HarBraceJ
Harcourt Brace Jovanovich, Inc.
757 Third Ave., New York, NY 10017
(0-15)

Harmony
Harmony Book
Dist. by:
Crown Pubs., Inc., One Park Ave., New York, NY 10016

Hart
Hart Associates
12 E. 12th St., New York, NY 10003
(0-8055)

Harv. HarBraceJ.
Harvest Books. Imprint of Harcourt Brace Jovanovich, Inc.

Harvard U Pr
Harvard Univ. Press
Customer Service, Harvard Univ. Press, 79 Garden St., Cambridge, MA 02138
(0-674)

Harvey
Harvey House, Pubs, Div. of E. M. Hale & Co.
128 W. River St., Chippewa Falls, WI 54729
(0-8178)

Harvey Assoc
See A Harvey

Haskell
Haskell House Pubs., Inc.
P.O. Box FF, Blythebourne Sta., Brooklyn, NY 11219
(0-8383)

Hastings
Hastings House Pubs., Inc.
10 E. 40th St., New York, NY 10016
(0-8038)

Haus Koekkoek
Stadtisches Museum Haus Koekkoek
D-4190 Kleve, Kavarinerstr. 33, West Germany

Hawaiian Serv
Hawaiian Service, Inc.
P.O. Box 2835, Honolulu, HI 96803
(0-930492)

Hawthorn
Hawthorn Books, Inc.
E. P. Dutton, 2 Park Ave., New York, NY 10016
(0-8015)

HC. HarBraceJ.
Harcourt Brace Jovanovich, Inc., College Dept. Imprint of Harcourt Brace Jovanovich, Inc.

Heard Mus
Heard Museum
22 E. Monte Vista, Phoenix, AZ 85004
United States
Hearst Bks
Hearst Books, Div. of Hearst Magazines
P.O. Box 1406, Radio City Sta., New York,
NY 10019
(0-910992; 0-87851; 0-910990)
Hearthside
Hearthside Press, Inc.
Ingram Book Co., 347 Redwood Dr.,
Nashville, TN 37217
(0-8208)
Hebrew Pub
Hebrew Publishing Co.
80 Fifth Ave., New York, NY 10011
(0-88482)
Hebrew Un Coll
Hebrew Union College
3077 University Ave., Los Angeles, CA
90007
Heckscher Mus
Heckscher Museum
Prime Ave., Huntington, NY 11743
Heidelberg Pubs
Heidelberg Pubs., Inc.
1003 Brown Bldg., Austin, TX 78701
(0-913206)
Heineman
Heineman, James H., Inc., Pub.
475 Park Ave., New York, NY 10022
(0-87008)
Heinman
Heinman, William S.
1966 Broadway, New York, NY 10023
(0-88431)
Helios Vt
Helios
Pawlet, VT 05761
(0-87931)
Hennessey
Hennessey & Ingalls, Inc.
10814 W. Pico Blvd., Los Angeles, CA
90064
(0-912158)
Herbert Gal
Herbert Art Gallery & Museum
Jordan Well, Coventry CV1 5RG,
United Kingdom
Heritage Bk
Heritage Books, Inc.
3602 Maureen Lane, Bowie, MD 20715
(0-917890)
Herman Pub
Herman Publishing
45 Newbury St., Boston, MA 02116
(0-89046; 0-89047)
Hermon
Sepher-Hermon Press, Inc.
175 Fifth Ave., New York, NY 10010
(0-87203)
Herzliya Mus
Herzliya Museum
Bar Ilan St., Herzliya, Israel
Hickory Mus
Hickory Museum of Art
P.O. Box 2572 (Third St. & First Ave.,
N.W.), Hickory, NC 28601
Hidden Hse-Flash. Music Sales.
Hidden House/Flash. Imprint of Music Sales
Corp.
Higgins Mus
Higgins, John Woodman, Armory Museum
100 Barber Ave., Worcester, MA 01606
High Mus Art
High Museum of Art
1280 Peachtree St., N.E., Atlanta, GA
30309
Hill & Wang
Hill & Wang, Inc, Div. of Farrar, Straus &
Giroux, Inc.
19 Union Square, New York, NY 10003
(0-8090)
Hill Stead Mus
Hill-Stead Museum
671 Farmington Ave., Farmington, CT
06032
Himalaya Hse
Himalaya House
5190 Parfet, Wheat Ridge, CO 80033
(0-89654)
Hippocrene Bks
Hippocrene Books, Inc.
171 Madison Ave., New York, NY 10016
(0-88254)

Hispanic Soc
Hispanic Society of America
613 W. 155th St., New York, NY 10032
(0-87535)
HM
Houghton Mifflin Co.
Orders to:
Wayside Road, Burlington, MA 01803
(0-395)
Hobby Hse
Hobby House Press
4701 Queensbury Rd., Riverdale, MD
20840
(0-87588)
Hobby Pub Serv
Hobby Publishing Service
1318 Seventh St., N.W., Albuquerque, NM
87102
(0-917922)
Holiday
Holiday House, Inc.
18 E. 53rd St., New York, NY 10022
(0-8234)
Holmes & Meier
Holmes & Meier Pubs., Inc.
30 Irving Place, New York, NY 10003
(0-8419)
HoltC. HR&W.
Holt College Department. Imprint of Holt,
Rinehart & Winston, Inc.
Home Econ Educ
Home Economics Education Assn.
1201 Sixteenth St., N.W., Rm. 232,
Washington, DC 20036
Honolulu Aca
Honolulu Academy of the Arts
900 S. Beretania St., Honolulu, HI
Hopetoun Hse
Hopetoun House
South Queensferry, West Lothian, EH30
9SL, Scotland, United Kingdom
Horizon
Horizon Press Pubs.
156 Fifth Ave., New York, NY 10010
(0-8180)
Horn Bk
Horn Book, Inc.
Park Square Bldg., 31 St. James Ave.,
Boston, MA 02116
(0-87675)
Hotchkiss House
Hotchkiss House, Inc.
18 Hearthstone Rd., Pittsford, NY 14534
(0-912220)
Howard Doyle
Doyle, Howard A., Publishing Co.
P.O. Box 310, Cambridge, MA 02139
(0-87299)
Howell-North
Howell-North Books
1050 Parker St., Berkeley, CA 94710
(0-8310)
HR&W
Holt, Rinehart & Winston, Inc.
383 Madison Ave., New York, NY 10017
(0-03)
Hse of Collectibles
House of Collectibles, Inc.
Suite 120, 773 Kirkman Rd, Orlando, FL
32811
(0-87637)
HTH Pubs
HTH Pubs.
P.O. Box 468, Freeland, WA 98249
(0-916658)
Humanities
Humanities Press, Inc.
Atlantic Highlands, NJ 07716
(0-391)
Hungarian Rev
American Hungarian Review
5410 Kerth Rd., St. Louis, MO 63128
(0-911862)
Hunter Ariz
Hunter Publishing Co.
P.O. Box 9533, Phoenix, AZ 85068
(0-918126)
Hunter Hse
Hunter House Inc.
748 E. Bonita Ave., Suite 105, Pomona,
CA 91767
(0-89793)
Huntington
Huntington Galleries
Park Hills, Huntington, WV 25701

Huntington Lib
Huntington Library Pubns.
1151 Oxford Rd., San Marino, CA 91108
(0-87328)
Huntly House
Huntly House Museum
142 Canongate, Edinburgh EH 8DD,
United Kingdom
Hutchinson
See Merrimack Bk Serv
Hyogo Mod Mus
Hyogo Prefectural Museum of Modern Art
3-8-30 Harada-dori, Nada-ku, Kobe, Hyogo
Pref., Japan
Hyperion Conn
Hyperion Press, Inc.
45 Riverside Ave., Westport, CT 06880
(0-88355)
I S Gardner Mus
Isabella Stewart Gardner Museum
2 Palace Rd., Boston, MA 02115
(0-914660)
IAIA Mus
Institute of American Arts Museum
Cerrillos Rd., Santa Fe, NM 87501
Idemitsu Gal
Idemitsu Art Gallery
3-1-1, Marunouchi, Chiyoda-Ku, Tokyo
100, Japan
IHS-Library & Educ Div
See IHS-PDS
IHS-PDS
Information Handling Services/PDS Hard
Copy Publishing
15 Inverness Way E., P.O. Box 1154,
Englewood, CO 80150
(0-910972; 0-89847)
Ilkon Pr
Ilkon Press
210 Riverside Dr., Apt 6-G, New York,
NY 10025
(0-916832)
Ill St Hist Soc
Illinois State Historical Society
Old State Capitol, Springfield, IL 62706
(0-912226)
Images Graphiques
Images Graphiques, Inc.
37 Riverside Dr., New York, NY 10023
(0-89545)
Images Pr
Images Press
P.O. Box 9444, Berkeley, CA 94709
(0-9600374)
In U Art Mus
Indiana University Art Museum
Bloomington, IN 47401
Ind U Pr
Indiana Univ. Press
Tenth & Morton Sts., Bloomington, IN
47401
(0-253)
Indus St Gall
Industrie-und Gewerbemuseum
Vadianstr. 2, CH-9000 St. Gallen,
Switzerland
Info Coord
Information Coordinators, Inc.
1435-37 Randolph St., Detroit, MI 48226
(0-911772)
Inst Arch Lux
Institut Archeologique du Luxembourg
Rue des Martyrs 13, B-6700 Arlon,
Belgium
Inst for the Arts
Institute for the Arts, Rice Univ.
P.O. Box 1892, Houston, TX 77001
(0-914412)
Inst Geo Agos
Instituto Geografico De Agostini
Corso Delle Vittorie, 91 Novara, Italy
Inst Paper Chem
Institute of Paper Chemistry
P.O. Box 1039, Appleton, WI 54911
(0-87010)
Inst Study Human
Institute for the Study of Human Issues (ISHI)
3401 Market St., Suite 252, Philadelphia,
PA 19104
(0-89727; 0-915980)
Inst Tilcara
Instituto Interdisciplinario "Tilcara"
Belgrado 445, Tilcara 4624, Argentina
Int Pav Humor
International Pavilion of Humor
Man & His World, Montreal PQ H3C
1AO, Canada

Inter-Varsity
Inter-Varsity Press
P.O. Box F, Downers Grove, IL 60515
(0-87784; 0-8308)
Interbk Inc
Interbook, Inc.
13 E. 16th St., New York, NY 10003
(0-913456; 0-89192)
InterCulture
InterCulture Associates
Quaddick Rd., P.O. Box 277, Thompson,
CT 06277
(0-88253; 0-89253)
Interface Calif
Interface California Corp.
(0-915580)
Stein & Day Pubs., Scarborough House,
Briarcliff Manor, NY 10510
Interstate
Interstate
19-27 N. Jackson St., Danville, IL 61832
(0-8134)
Intl Bk Co IL
International Book Co.
332 S. Michigan Ave., Chicago, IL 60604
(0-910790)
Intl Ctr Environment
International Center for Environmental
Research
141 Emerald Bay, Laguna Beach, CA
92651
(0-914704)
Intl Exhibit Foun
International Exhibitions Foundation
1729 "H" St., N.W., Suite 310, Washington,
DC 20006
(0-88397)
Intl Ideas
International Ideas Inc.
1627 Spruce St., Philadelphia, PA 19103
(0-89563)
Intl Marine
International Marine Publishing Co.
21 Elm St., Camden, ME 04843
(0-87742)
Intl Pub Co
International Pubs. Co.
381 Park Ave., S., Suite 1301, New York,
NY 10016
(0-7178)
Intl Pubns Serv
International Pubns. Service
114 E. 32nd St., New York, NY 10016
(0-8002)
Intl Schol Bk Serv
International Scholarly Book Services, Inc.
(ISBS, Inc.)
P.O. Box 555, Forest Grove, OR 97116
Intl Univs Pr
International Universities Press, Inc.
315 Fifth Ave., New York, NY 10016
(0-8236)
Inverness Mus
Inverness Museum & Art Gallery
Castle Wynd, Inverness, IV2 3ED,
Scotland, United Kingdom
Iowa St U Pr
Iowa State Univ. Press
South State Ave., 112 C Press Office,
Ames, IA 50010
(0-8138)
Iparmuveszeti
Iparmuveszeti Muzeum
Ulloi u. 33-37, P.O. Box 4, H-1450
Budapest, Hungary
Ipswich Mus
Ipswich Museums & Art Galleries
Main Museum, High St., Ipswich IP1 3QH,
Suffolk, United Kingdom
Iraq Mus
Iraq Museum
Museum Square, Baghdad, Iraq
Irvington
Irvington Pubs.
551 Fifth Ave., New York, NY 10017
(0-89197)
Island Pub
Island Publishing House
P.O. Drawer 758, Manteo, NC 27954
(0-916424)
ITA
See Fearon-Pitman
Ivy Pr
Ivy Press Inc., The
7515 Greenville, Suite 800, Dallas, TX
75231
(0-933372)

J Arvidson
Arvidson, J., Press
P.O. Box 4022, Helena, MT 59601
(0-9602098)
J-B Pubs
J-B Publishing Co.
430 Ivy Ave., Crete, NE 68333
(0-916170)
J Domjan
Domjan, Joseph
West Lake Rd., Tuxedo Park, NY 10987
(0-933652)
J Halliburton
Halliburton, John
2217 Belmont Blvd., Apt B, Nashville, TN
37212
J J Augustin
Augustin, J. J., Inc., Pub.
Locust Valley, NY 11560
(0-87439)
J M Pearson
Pearson, J. Michael
P.O. Box 402844, Ocean View Sta., Miami
Beach, FL 33140
(0-916528)
J Norton Pubs
Norton, Jeffrey, Pubs., Inc.
145 E. 49th St., New York, NY 10017
(0-88432)
J Palmer
Palmer, J., Pub.
P.O. Box 498, 86 Friend St., Amesbury,
MA 01913
J Paul Getty
Getty, J Paul, Museum
17985 Pacific Coast Hwy., Malibu, CA
90265
J Strand
Strand, Janann
P.O. Box 2725D, Pasadena, CA 91105
(0-9600780)
Jaap Rietman
Rietman, Jaap
157 Spring St., New York, NY 10012
(0-930034)
Jacks Art Mus
Jacksonville Art Museum
4160 Blvd. Center Dr., Jacksonville, FL
32201
Janus Pr
Janus Press
P.O. Box 578, Rogue River, OR 97537
(0-916172)
Japan Pubns
Japan Pubns. Trading Center (U.S.A.), Inc.
(0-87040)
Dist. by:
Harper & Row Pubs., Inc., Keystone
Industrial Park, Scranton, PA 18512
Jefren Pub
Jefren Publishing Co.
7851 Mission Center Court, Suite 120, San
Diego, CA 92108
(0-917244)
Jehay
Musee Historique et Prehistorique de Jehay
Kasteel van Jehay, B-5262 Jehay-Bodegnee,
Belgium
Jenkins
Jenkins Publishing Co.
P.O. Box 2085, Austin, TX 78767
(0-8363)
Jersey City Mus
Jersey City Museum
472 Jersey Ave., Jersey City, NJ 07302
Jesuit Bks
Jesuit Books
Seattle University, Seattle, WA 98122
(0-913452)
Jeu De Paume
Musee du Jeu de Paume
Place de la Concorde, 75001 Paris, France
Jewelers Circular
Jewelers' Circular Keystone
Chilton Way, Radnor, PA 19089
(0-931744)
Jewish Mus
Jewish Museum
1109 Fifth Ave., New York, NY 10028
Jewish Pubn
Jewish Publication Society of America
117 S. 17th St., Philadelphia, PA 19103
(0-8276)
Joensuun
Joensuun Taidemuseo
Rantakatu 8, F-80100 Joensuu 10, Finland

Joh Enschede
Joh. Enschede & Zonen B. V.
P.O. Box 114, Haarlem 2000 AC,
Netherlands
Johannesburg
Johannesburg Art Gallery
Joubert Park Johannesburg, South Africa
Johns Hopkins
Johns Hopkins Univ. Press
Baltimore, MD 21218
(0-8018)
Johnson Repr
Johnson Reprint Corp, Subs. of Harcourt,
Brace & Jovanovich, Inc.
111 Fifth Ave., New York, NY 10003
(0-384)
Jonathan David
Jonathan David Pubs., Inc.
68-22 Eliot Ave., Middle Village, NY
11379
(0-8246)
Jose Relvas
Instituicao Jose Relvas, Casa Museu dos
Patudos
Casa de Patudos, Alpiaca, Portugal
Josef Preyer
HL Josef Preyer
Adolf Schwayer-Gasse 2, Poysdorf A-2170,
Austria
Jossey-Bass
Jossey-Bass Inc., Pubs.
433 California St., San Francisco, CA
94104
(0-87589)
Judaic Heritage
Judaic Heritage Society
866 United Nations Plaza, New York, NY
10017
Judd
Judd & Detweiler, Inc.
261 Madison Ave., New York, NY 10016
Just Above Midtown
Just Above Midtown, Inc.
50 W. 57th St., New York, NY 10019
Juveniles. S&S.
Juvenile Books. Imprint of Simon & Schuster,
Inc.
K C Pubns
K C Pubns.
P.O. Box 14883, Las Vegas, NV 89114
(0-916122)
Kalmbach
Kalmbach Publishing Co.
1027 N. Seventh St., Milwaukee, WI 53233
(0-89024)
Karl Ernst
Ernst, Karl, Osthaus Museum
D-5800 Hagen, Hochstr. 73,
West Germany
Karlsruhe Bad
Badisches Landesmuseum
D-7500 Karlsruhe, Schloss, West Germany
Karneke
Karneke Pubs
P.O. Box 3371, Santa Monica, CA 90404
Karntner Frei
Karntner Freilichtmuseum
A-9063 Maria Saal, Austria
Kelley
Kelley, Augustus M., Pubs.
300 Fairfield Rd., P.O. Box 1308, Fairfield,
NJ 07006
(0-678)
Ken Chels Libs
Kensington & Chelsea Public Libraries
London, W8, United Kingdom
Kendall-Hunt
Kendall/Hunt Publishing Co.
2460 Kerper Blvd., Dubuque, IA 52001
(0-8403)
Kendall Strachan
Kendall & Strachan
164 Pietermaritz St., Pietermaritzburg,
South Africa
Kenilworth
Kenilworth Press
421 W. Grant Ave., Eau Claire, WI 54701
Kennedy Gall
Kennedy Galleries
40 W. 57th St., New York, NY 10019
(0-87920)
Kennikat
Kennikat Press, Corp.
90 S. Bayles Ave., Port Washington, NY
11050
(0-8046)

Kent St U Pr
Kent State Univ. Press
Kent, OH 44242
(0-87338)
Kenwood
Kenwood, The Iveagh Bequest
Hampstead Lane, London NW3 7JR,
United Kingdom
Kereszteny Muz
Kereszteny Muzeum
Berenyi Zsigmond u. 2, H-2500 Esztergom,
Hungary
Kimbell Art
Kimbell Art Musuem
Will Rogers Rd., W., P.O. Box 9440, Fort
Worth, TX 76107
(0-912804)
King
King, Dale Stuart, Pub.
2002 N. Tucson Blvd., Tucson, AZ 85716
(0-912762)
Kirkcaldy
Museums & Art Gallery
War Memorial Grounds, Kirkcaldy, Fife,
KY1 1YG, United Kingdom
Kluwer Boston
Kluwer Boston, Inc.
160 Old Derby St., Hingham, MA 02043
Knopf
Knopf, Alfred A., Inc, Subs. of Random
House, Inc.
400 Hahn Rd., Westminster, MD 21157
(0-394)
Knorr Hirth
Knoor & Hirth Verlag
D-3167 Ahrbeck Vor Hanover,
West Germany
(3-7821)
Kodansha
Kodansha International
10 E. 53rd St., New York, NY 10022
Konin Mus Art
Koninklijk Museum voor Schone Kunsten
Plaatsnijderstraat 2, 2000 Antwerp, Belgium
Kramer Mus
Stadtisches Kramer-Museum
D-4152 Kempen 1, Burgstr. 19,
West Germany
Kraus Repr
Kraus Reprint Co, U.S. Div. of
Kraus-Thomson Organization, Ltd.
Rte. 100, Millwood, NY 10546
(0-527)
Krause Pubns
Krause Pubns., Inc.
700 E. State St., Iola, WI 54945
(0-87341)
Krieger
Krieger, Robert E., Pub. Co., Inc.
645 New York Ave., Huntington, NY
11743
(0-88275; 0-89874)
Kroller-Muller
Rijksmuseum Kroller-Muller
P. O. Box 1, 6730 AA Otterlo, Netherlands
Ktav
Ktav Publishing House, Inc.
75 Varick St., New York, NY 10013
(0-87068)
KTO Pr
K T O Press, Div. of Kraus-Thomson
Organization Ltd.
Rte. 100, Millwood, NY 10546
(0-527)
Kunst Bern
Kunstmuseum Bern
Hodlerstrasse 12, CH-3011 Berne,
Switzerland
Kunst Bielefe
Kunsthalle Bielefeld
D-4800 Bielefeld, Artur-Ladebeck-Str. 5,
West Germany
Kunst Bremen
Kunsthalle Bremen
Am Wall 207, D-28 Bremen,
West Germany
Kunst Coburg
Kunstsammlungen der Veste Coburg
D-8630 Coburg, Veste Coburg,
West Germany
Kunst Hamburg
Museum fur Kunst und Gewerbe Hamburg
D-2000 Hamburg 1, Steintorplatz,
West Germany
Kunst Karlsru
Staatliche Kunsthalle
Hans Thoma Str. 2-4, D-7800 Karlsruhe,
West Germany

Kunst Petron
Kunstgewerbemuseum
Schloss, A-2404 Petronell, Austria
Kunst St Gallen
Kunstmuseum St. Gallen
Museumstrasse 50, CH-9000 Saint Gallen,
Switzerland
Kunst Zurich
Kunstgewerbemuseum der Stadt Zurich
Ausstelungsstr. 60, CH-8000 Zurich,
Switzerland
Kunstmus Chur
Bundner Kunstmuseum
Postplatz, 7000 Chur, Switzerland
Kunstmus Luz
Kunstmuseum Luzern
Robertt Zund-Str. 1, CH-6000 Luzern,
Switzerland
L Amiel Pub
Amiel, Leon, Pub.
31 W. 46th St., New York, NY 10036
(0-8148)
L Sweetman
Sweetman, Leonard
1712 Fisherville Rd., Coatesville, PA 19320
(0-9600518)
LA Co Art Mus
Los Angeles County Museum of Art
5905 Wilshire Blvd., Los Angeles, CA
90036
(0-87587)
La State U Pr
Louisiana State Univ. Press
Baton Rouge, LA 70803
(0-8071)
Lahti Art Mus
Lahti Art Museum
Vesijavenkatu 11, SF-15111 Lahti 11,
Finland
Lahti Hist
Lahti Historical Museum
Lahdenkatu 4, P.B. 115, SF-15110 Lahti
11, Finland
Landesmus Muns
Westfalisches Landesmuseum fur Kunst und
Kulturgeschichte
D-4400 Munster, Domplatz 10,
West Germany
Landskrona
Landskrona Kulturnamd
Slottsgatan, S-261 31 Landskrona, Sweden
Lane
Lane Publishing Co.
Willow & Middlefield Rds., Menlo Park,
CA 94025
(0-376)
L'Annonciade
Musee de l'Annonciade
Place Georges Grammont, F-83990
St-Tropez, France
Lantern
Lantern Press, Inc. Pubs.
354 Hussey Rd., Mount Vernon, NY 10552
(0-8313)
Large Print Bks. G K Hall.
Large Print Books Series. Imprint of Hall, G.
K., & Co.
Larlin Corp
Larlin Corp.
P.O. Box 1523, Marietta, GA 30061
(0-910220; 0-89783)
Larousse
Larousse & Co., Inc.
572 Fifth Ave., New York, NY 10036
(0-88332)
Latin Am Ctr
See UCLA Lat Am Ctr
Lauren Rogers
Rogers, Lauren, Library & Museum of Art
P.O. Box 1108, Laurel, MS 39440
Lawrence Hill
Hill, Lawrence, & Co., Inc.
520 Riverside Ave., Westport, CT 06880
(0-88208)
LC
Library of Congress, Central Services Division
Washington, DC 20540
LC Inf
Library of Congress, Information Office
Washington, DC 20540
LC Photo
Library of Congress, Photoduplication Service
Washington, DC 20540
LE. Dell.
Laurel Editions. Imprint of Dell Publishing
Co., Inc.

Lebhar Friedman
Lebhar-Friedman Books, Subs. of
Lebhar-Friedman, Inc.
425 Park Ave, New York, NY 10022
(0-912016)
Lee Pubns
Lee Pubns.
105 Suffolk Rd., Wellesley Hills, MA
02181
(0-910872)
Leicester. Humanities.
Leicester Univ. Press. Imprint of Humanities
Press, Inc.
Leicestershire
Rutland County Museum
Catmos St., Oakham, Rutland LE15 6HW,
United Kingdom
Leopold Hoesch
Hoesch, Leopold, Museum
D-5160 Duren, West Germany
Lerner Bks
See Lerner Pubns
Lerner Pubns
Lerner Publications Co.
241 First Ave., N., Minneapolis, MN
55401
(0-8225)
Les Femmes Pub
Les Femmes Publishing
231 Adrian Rd., Millbrae, CA 94030
(0-89087)
LFL. Dell.
Laurel Leaf Library. Imprint of Dell Publishing
Co., Inc.
Lib Bost Athe
Library of the Boston Atheneum
10 1/2 Beacon St., Boston, MA 02108
Lib Del Stato
Libreria Dello Stato
Piazza Verdi, 10 Roma, Italy
Libs Unl
Libraries Unlimited, Inc.
P.O. Box 263, Littleton, CO 80160
(0-87287)
Liebieghaus
Liebieghaus, Museum Alter Plastik
Schamainkai 71, Frankfurt 6000,
West Germany
Light Impressions
Light Impressions Corp.
P.O. Box 3012, Rochester, NY 14614
(0-87992)
Lincoln Hse
Lincoln House
Old Sturbridge Village, Sturbridge, MA
01566
(0-910940)
Lindahl
Lindahl, Judy
3211 N.E. Siskiyou, Portland, OR 97212
Linkoping Lans
Lansmuseet Linkoping
Box 232, S-581 02 Linkoping, Sweden
Lion
Lion Press
(0-87460)
Dist. by:
Sayre Publishing, Inc., 111 E. 39th St.,
New York, NY 10016
Lippincott
Lippincott, J. B., Co.
521 Fifth Ave., New York, NY 10017
(0-397)
Litch Hist Soc
Litchfield Historical Society
P.O. Box 385, Litchfield, CT 06759
Little
Little, Brown & Co.
Orders to:
200 West St., Waltham, MA 02154
(0-316)
Little Glass
Little Glass Shack
3161 56th St., Sacramento, CA 95820
(0-911508)
Litton Educ Pub
Litton Educational Publishing, Inc.
135 W. 50th St., New York, NY 10020
(0-442)
Liveright
Liveright Publishing Corp, Subs. of W. W.
Norton Co., Inc.
500 Fifth Ave., New York, NY 10036
(0-87140)

Livingston
Livingston Publishing Co.
Orders to:
Harrowood Books, 3943 N. Providence
Rd., Newton Sq., PA 19073
(0-87098; 0-915180)
Livingston Pr
Livingston Press
Independent Pubs. Group, 14 Vanderventer
Ave., Port Washington, NY 11050
(0-915772)
Longman
Longman Inc.
19 W. 44th St., Suite 1012, New York, NY
10036
Longview Mus
Longview Museum & Arts Center
Box 562, Longview, TX 75601
Longwood Pr
Longwood Press, Ltd.
P.O. Box 101, Kennebunkport, ME 04046
(0-89341)
Lorenz Pr
Lorenz Press, Inc, Div. of Lorenz Industries,
Subs. of Internat'l Entertainment Corp.
(0-89328)
Independent Publishers Group, 14
Vanderventer Ave., Port Washington, NY
11050
Lothrop
Lothrop, Lee & Shepard Co, Div. of William
Morrow & Co., Inc.
William Morrow & Co., Inc., Wilmor
Warehouse, 6 Henderson Dr., West
Caldwell, NJ 07006
(0-688)
Louisville Sc
Louisville School of Art
100 Park Rd., Anchorage, KY 40223
Lowell Pr
Lowell Press
115 E. 31st St., Box 1877, Kansas City,
MO 64141
(0-913504)
Lyle Stuart
Stuart, Lyle, Inc.
120 Enterprise Ave., Secaucus, NJ 07094
(0-8184)
M Annenberg
Annenberg, Maurice
P.O. Box 190 South Rd., Pikesville, MD
21208
M Evans
Evans, M., & Co., Inc.
(0-87131)
E. P. Dutton, 2 Park Ave., New York, NY
10016
M Luff
Luff, Moe
12 Greene Rd., Spring Valley, NY 10977
(0-9600162)
M P Davison
Davison, Marguerite P.
P.O. Box 263, Swarthmore, PA 19081
(0-9603172)
M Robertson
See Biblio Dist
Maagdenhuis
Openbaar Centrum voor Maatschappelijk
Welzijn van Antwerpen
Lange Gasthuisstraat 33, B-2000 Antwerp,
Belgium
Mabee Gerner
St. Gregory's Abbey & College, The
Mabee-Gerner Museum
1900 W. MacArthur Dr., Shawnee, OK
74801 United States
McClain
McClain Printing Co.
212 Main St., Parsons, WV 26287
(0-87012)
McCutchan
McCutchan Publishing Corp.
P.O. Box 774A, 2526 Grove St., Berkeley,
CA 94701
(0-8211)
McElderry Bk. Atheneum.
McElderry Book. Imprint of Atheneum Pubs.
McGill-Queens U Pr
McGill-Queens Univ. Press
Orders to:
University of Toronto Press, 33 E. Tupper
St., Buffalo, NY 14203
(0-7735)
McGilvery
McGilvery, Laurence
P.O. Box 852, La Jolla, CA 92037
(0-910938)

McGraw
McGraw-Hill Book Co.
1221 Ave. of the Americas, New York, NY
10020
(0-07)
McGraw-Hill Canada
McGraw-Hill Company of Canada Ltd.
Grange Park, Toronto M5T 1G4, Canada
McKay
McKay, David, Co., Inc.
2 Park Ave., New York, NY 10016
(0-679)
McKnight
McKnight Publishing Co.
(0-8008)
Dist. by:
Taplinger Publishing Co., 200 Park Ave., S.,
New York, NY 10003
McKnight Ctr
McKnight Fine Arts Ctr.
Box 46, Wichita State University, Wichita,
KS 67208
Macmillan
Macmillan Publishing Co., Inc.
Orders to:
Riverside, NJ 08075
(0-02)
Made. Doubleday.
Made Simple Books. Imprint of Doubleday &
Co., Inc.
Madras Gov Mus
Madras Government Museum
Pantheon Rd., Egmore, Madras-8, India
Madrona Pr
Madrona Press, Inc.
P.O. Box 3750, Austin, TX 78764
(0-89052)
Madrona Pubs
Madrona Pubs., Inc.
2116 Western Ave., Seattle, WA 98121
(0-914842)
Magnet Bks. Fell.
Magnet Books, Inc. Imprint of Fell, Frederick,
Publishers, Inc.
Maharaja Sawai
Maharaja Sawaii Man Singh II Museum
City Palace Jaipur 302002 Rajasthan, India
Maidstone
Maidstone Museum & Art Gallery
Saint Faith's St., Maidstone, Kent ME14
1LH, United Kingdom
Maine Antique
Maine Antique Digest, Inc.
P.O. Box 358, Waldoboro, ME 04572
(0-9171312)
Maine St Mus
Maine State Museum Pubns.
State House, Augusta, ME 04333
(0-913764)
Major Bks
Major Books
Orders to:
Kable News, Inc., 777 Third Ave., New
York, NY 10017; Dist. by: Major Books,
18-39 128th St., College Point, NY
(0-89041)
Malden Lib
Malden Library
36 Salem St., Malden, MA 02148
Malmaison
Musee National de Vallauris, Musee National
Picasso
Place de la Liberation, F-06220 Vallauris,
France
Mara
Mara Books, Inc.
1318 Second Street, Santa Monica, CA
90401
(0-87787)
Mariners Mus
Mariners Museum
Museum Dr., Newport News, VA 23606
(0-917376)
Marquette
Marquette Univ. Press
1131 W. Wisconsin Ave., Rm. 006,
Milwaukee, WI 53233
(0-87462)
Marquis
Marquis Who's Who, Inc.
Orders to:
4300 W. 62nd St., Indianapolis, IN 46206
(0-8379)
Martello Edit
Martello Editore
Via Piave, 1-Milano, Italy
Mason Charter
See Van Nos Reinhold

Mass Hist Soc
Massachusetts Historical Society
1154 Boylston St., Boston, MA 02215
Master Pr
Master Press
P. O. Box 432, Dayton, OR 97114
(0-9600818)
Mathom
Mathom Pub. Co.
219 W. First St., Oswego, NY 13126
(0-930000)
Mattole Pr
Mattole Press
P.O. Box 22324, San Francisco, CA 94122
(0-916854)
Mayfield Pub
Mayfield Publishing Co.
285 Hamilton Ave., Palo Alto, CA 94301
(0-87484)
Mayflower Bks
Mayflower Books, Inc.
575 Lexington Ave., New York, NY 10022
Mazowieckie
Muzeum Mazowieckie w Plocku
Ul. Tumska 2, Plock, woj. Warsaw, Poland
Md Hist
Maryland Historical Society
201 W. Monument St., Baltimore, MD
21201
Mead Art Mus
Mead Art Museum
Amherst, MA 01002
Meadows Mus
Meadows Museum
Dallas, TX 75275
Meredith Corp
Meredith Corp.
Better Homes & Gardens Books, 1716
Locust, Des Moines, IA 50336
(0-696)
Merrill
Merrill, Charles E., Publishing Co, Div. of Bell
& Howell Co.
1300 Alum Creek Dr., Columbus, OH
43216
(0-675)
Merrimack Bk Serv
Merrimack Book Service, Inc.
99 Main St., Salem, NH 03079
Merrimack Mus
Merrimack Valley Textile Museum
800 Massachusetts Ave., North Andover,
MA 01845
Mesdag
Panorama Mesdag
Zeestrat 65B, The Hague, Netherlands
Messianica
Messianica General Co., Ltd.
27-1 Momoyama-Cho, Atami-Shi,
Shizuoka-Ken, Japan
Messner
Messner, Julian, A Simon & Schuster Div. of
Gulf & Western Corp.
1230 Ave. of the Americas, New York, NY
10020
(0-671)
Met Mus Art
See Metro Mus Art
Meth U Pr
See SMU Press
Methuen Inc
Methuen Inc.
(0-416)
Dist. by:
Transworld Distribution Services, Inc., 80
Northfield Ave., Raritan Center, Edison,
NJ 08817
Metro Bks
Metro Books, Inc.
3110 N. Arlington Heights Rd., Arlington
Heights, IL 60004
(0-8411)
Metro Mus Art
Metropolitan Museum of Art
5th Ave. and 82nd St., New York, NY
10028
(0-87099)
Mich St U Pr
Michigan State Univ. Press
1405 S. Harrison Rd., 25 Manly Miles
Bldg., East Lansing, MI 48824
(0-87013)
Michael Joseph
See Merrimack Bk Serv
Mid Tenn St U
Middle Tennessee State Univ. Photographic
Gallery
Box 305, Murfreesboro, TN 37132

Milady
Milady Publishing Corp.
3839 White Plains Rd., Bronx, NY 10467
(0-87350)

Milford Hse
Milford House
P.O. Box 101, Kennebunkport, ME 04046
(0-87821)

Milwauk Ctr
Miwaukee Art Center
750 N. Lincoln Memorial Dr., Milwaukee,
WI 53202

Milwaukee Pub Mus
Milwaukee Public Museum
800 Wells St., Milwaukee, WI 83233
United States

Minn Hist
Minnesota Historical Society
1500 Mississippi St., St. Paul, MN 55101
(0-87351)

Minn Scholarly
Minnesota Scholarly Press, Inc.
P.O. Box 224, Mankato, MN 56001

Minneapolis Inst Arts
Minneapolis Institute of Arts
2400 Third Ave., S., Minneapolis, MN
55404
(0-912236)

MIT Pr
MIT Press
28 Carleton St., Cambridge, MA 02142
(0-262)

Model Tech
Model Technology, Inc.
323 W. Cedar, Chillicothe, IL 61523
(0-9601840)

Modern Bks
Modern Books & Crafts, Inc.
(0-913274)
Dist. by:
Associated Booksellers, 147 McKinley
Ave., Bridgeport, CT 06606

Monad Pr
Monad Press
(0-913460)
Dist. by:
Pathfinder Press, 410 West St., New York,
NY 10014

Mont Hist Soc
Montana Historical Society
225 N. Roberts, Helena, MT 59601

Montclair Art
Montclair Art Museum
3 S. Mountain Ave., P.O. Box X,
Montclair, NJ 07042

Montgomery Mus
Montgomery Museum of Fine Arts
440 S. McDonough St., Montgomery, AL
36104
(0-89280)

Monthly Rev
Monthly Review Press
62 W. 14th St., New York, NY 10011
(0-85345)

Moore Pub Co
Moore Publishing Co.
P.O. Box 3036, W. Durham Sta., Durham,
NC 27705
(0-87716)

Mor-Mac
Mor-Mac Publishing Co., Inc.
P.O. Box 984, Fairborn, OH 45324
(0-912178)

Morav Gal Brne
Moravska Galeria v Brne
Husova Ulice 14, 662 26 Brno,
Czechoslovakia

Morehouse
Morehouse-Barlow Co.
78 Danbury Rd., Wilton, CT 06897
(0-8192)

Morgan
Morgan & Morgan, Inc.
145 Palisades St., Dobbs Ferry, NY 10522
(0-87100)

Morriss Prin
Morriss Printing Co. Ltd.
1745 Blanshard, Victoria, Canada

Morrow
Morrow, William, & Co., Inc.
Orders to:
Wilmor Warehouse, 6 Henderson Dr., West
Caldwell, NJ 07006
(0-688)

Mosby
Mosby, C. V., Co.
11830 Westline Industrial Dr., St. Louis,
MO 63141
(0-8016)

Mountain Pr
Mountain Press Publishing Co., Inc.
P.O. Box 2399, Missoula, MT 59806
(0-87842)

Mouse Pr
Mouse Press
(0-913968)
Dist. by:
Light Impressions Corp., P.O. Box 3012,
Rochester, NY 14614

Mouton
Mouton Pubs, Div. of Walter De Gruyter, Inc.
200 Saw Mill River Rd., Hawthorne, NY
10532

Mowbray Co
Mowbray Co. Pubs
222 W. Exchange St., Providence, RI
02903
(0-917218)

Mss Info
Mss Information Corp.
P.O. Box 985, Edison, NJ 08817
(0-8422)

Muiska Mus
Muiska-Museum
Metzstrasse 31, 80 D-8000 Munich,
West Germany

Multimedia
Multimedia Publishing Corp.
72 Fifth Ave., New York, NY 10011
(0-8334)

Munson Williams
Munson-Williams-Proctor Institute
310 Genesee St., Utica, NY 13502

Murdock Print
Murdock Printing Co
430 Monroe Ave., Memphis, TN 38103

Mus Afr Art
Museum of African Art
316-332 A St., N.E., Washington, DC
20002 United States

Mus African Art
Museum of African Art, Frederick Douglass
Institute
316-332 A St. N.E., Washington, DC
20002

Mus Am China Trade
Museum of the American China Trade
215 Adams St., Milton, MA 02186

Mus Am Ind
Museum of the American Indian
Broadway at 155th St., New York, NY
10032
(0-934490)

Mus Andhra Prad
State Archeological Museum
Public Gardens, Hyderabad, Andhra
Pradesh 500004, India

Mus Anthro MO
Univ. of Missouri, Museum of Anthropology
104 Swallow Hall, Columbia, MO 65211
(0-913134)

Mus Anuradhap
Museum of Archaeology
Anuradhapura, Sri Lanka

Mus Arc Napoli
Museo Archelogico Nazionale
Piazza Cavour, I-80135 Naples, Italy

Mus Art Antiga
Museu Nacional de Arte Antiga
Rua das Janelas Verdes, Lisbon 1293,
Portugal

Mus Art Lille
Musee des Beaux-Arts Lille
Place de la Republique 59000 Lille, France

Mus Art Narbo
Musee d'Art et d'Histoire
Palais des Archeveques, F-11100 Narbonne,
France

Mus Art Rioja
Museo de Bellas Artes "Octavio de la Colina"
Copiapo 245, la Rioja, Argentina

Mus Bagnols
Musee de Bagnols-Sur-Ceze
Mairie, F-30200 Bagnols-Sur-Ceze, France

Mus Bargoin
Musee Bargoin
45, Rue Ballainvilliers, F-63000
Clermont-Ferrand, France

Mus Bourgogne
Musee du Vin Bourgogne
Rue D'Enfer, 21200 Beaune, France

Mus Caen
Musee des Beaux-Arts
Chateau de Caen, F-14000 Caen, France

Mus Campagnon
Musee du Compagnonnage
8 Rue Nationale, F-37000 Tours, France

Mus Cant Laus
Musee Cantonal des Beaux-Arts
Palais de Rumine, Place de la Riponne,
CH-1000 Lausanne, Switzerland

Mus Carmo
Museu Arqueologico do Carmo
Largo do Carmo, 1200 Lisbon, Portugal

Mus Carnavalet
Musee Carnavalet
23 Rue De Sevigne, F-75003 Paris, France

Mus Chivilcoy
Museo Municipal de Artes Plasticas de
Chivilcoy
Bolivar 319, Chivilcoy, Argentina

Mus Civ Modena
Museo Civico di Storia e Arte Mediovale e
Moderna
Palazzo dei Musei, Piazza S. Agostino 337,
I-41100 Modena, Italy

Mus Civ Torin
Museo Civico di Torino
Via Magenta, 31 10128 Torino, Italy

Mus Col Bogota
Museo de Arte Colonial
Carrera 6a., No. 9-77, Bogota, Colombia

Mus Cult Hist
Museum of Cultural History
405 Hilgard Ave., Los Angeles, CA 90024

Mus D'Angers
Musees d'Angers
10 Rue du Musee, 49000 Angers, France

Mus D'Art Juif
Musee d'Art Juif
2 Rue des Saules, F-75018 Paris, France

Mus d'Auxerre
Musees d'Auxerre
Auxerre, France

Mus De l'Ain
Musee de l'Ain
63, Boulevard de Brou, F-01000
Bourg-En-Bresse, France

Mus De Laon
Musee Archeologique Municipal
32, Rue Georges Ermant, F-02000 Laon,
France

Mus De L'oise
Musee Departmental de l'Oise-Beauvais
1 Rue de Musee, F-60000 Beauvais, France

Mus Della Rocca
Museo della Rocca dei Sanvitale
I-43012 Fontanellato, Italy

Mus D'Ornans
Musee d'Ornans
Rue de la Froidiere, F-25290 Ornans,
France

Mus Dunkerque
Musee des Beaux-Arts de Dunkerque
Place du General de Gaulle, F-59140
Dunkerque, France

Mus Etoffes
Musee de l'Impression sur Etoffes
3 Rue des Bonnes-Gens, F-68100
Mulhouse, France

Mus Fi Art Ist
Museum of Fine Arts
Istanbul, Turkey

Mus Fine Arts Boston
Museum of Fine Arts, Boston
465 Huntington Ave., Boston, MA 02115
(0-87846)

Mus Fior Antica
Museo della Casa Fiorentina Antica
Via Portarossa 13, I-50123 Florence, Italy

Mus Folk Reg
Museo Folklorico Regional
Ave. San Martin 55, Humahaca, Argentina

Mus Fran Photo
Musee Francais de la Photographie
Mairie, F-91570 Bievres, France

Mus Great Plains
Museum of the Great Plains, Pubns. Dept.
601 Ferris, P.O. Box 68, Lawton, OK
73502
(0-911728)

Mus Hist France
Musee de l'Histoire de France, Archives
Nationales
Rue des Francs-Bourgeois, F-75003 Paris,
France

Mus Hot Sande
Musee Hotel Sandelin
14 Rue Carnot, F-62500 St-Omer, France

Mus Int Chasse
Musee Internationale de la Chasse
Chateau de Gien, F-45500 Gien, France
Mus Koln
Verwaltung der Museen der Stadt Koln
Kolumbasttr. 5, 5000 Cologne 1,
West Germany
Mus Kortrijk
Stedelijk Museum voor Schone Kunsten
Broelkaai 6, B-8500 Kortrijk, Belgium
Mus Lamego
Museu de Lamego
5100 Lamego, Portugal
Mus Laval
Musee du Vieux-Chateau, Laval
Place de la Tremoille, Laval, France
Mus Lecuyer
Musee Antoine Lecuyer
28, Rue Antoine-Lecuyer. F-02100
St-Quentin, France
Mus Liegeois
Musee du Verre
Quai de Maestricht 13, B-4000 Liege,
Belgium
Mus Mariemont
Musee Royal de Mariemont
Chaussee de Mariemont, B-6510
Morlanwelz-Mariemont, Belgium
Mus Matisse
Musee Matisse
Ave. des Arenes, No. 164, F-06000 Nice,
France
Mus Mode Cost
Musee de la Mode et du Costume
Palais Galliera, 10, Ave. Pierre 1er de
Serbie, 75116 Paris, France
Mus Mosan
Musee d'Art Religieux & d'Art Mosan
6, Rue Bonne Fortune, B-4000 Liege,
Belgium
Mus Mulheim
Stadtisches Museum
D-4330 Mulheim, Leineweberstr. 1,
West Germany
Mus NM Arts
Museum of New Mexico, Museum of Fine
Arts
P.O. Box 2087, Santa Fe, NM 87501
Mus Northern Ariz
Museum of Northern Arizona
Rte. 4, Box 720, Flagstaff, AZ 86001
(0-89734)
Mus of Art RI
Museum of Art Rhode Island School of Design
Milford House, Inc., 85 Newbury St.,
Boston, MA 02116
Mus Pontoise
Musee Tavet-Delacour
Rue Lemercier, F-95300 Pontoise, France
Mus Reinach
Heimatmuseum
Haupstr. 16, CH-4153 Reinach, Switzerland
Mus Rennes
Musee des Beaux-Arts et d'Archeologie
20 Quai Emile Zola, F-35100, France
Mus Rietberg
Museum Rietberg Zurich
Gablerstrasse 15, CH-8002 Zurich,
Switzerland
Mus Roy Belgique
Musees Royaux des Beaux-Arts de Belgique
Rue du Musee 9, Brussels, Belgium
Mus Savoisien
Musee Savoisien
Square de Lannoy-De-Bissy, Chambery
73000, France
Mus Schifanoia
Museo di Schifanoia
Via Scandiana 23, I-44100 Ferrara, Italy
Mus Society
Museum Society Bookshop
C/O de Young Museum, Golden Gate
Park, San Francisco, CA 94118
Mus Soissons
Musee Municipal
2 Rue de la Congregation, F-02200
Soissons, France
Mus South Deco
Museum of Early Southern Decorative Arts
Salem Station, Drawer F, Winston-Salem,
NC 27108
Mus Sterckshof
Provinciaal Museum Sterckshof
Hooftvunderlei 160, B-2100 Deurne,
Belgium

Mus Sys
Museum Systems
817 N. La Cienaga Blvd., Los Angeles, CA
90069
Mus Tiss Lyon
Musee Historique des Tissus
34, Rue de la Charite, F-69002 Lyon,
France
Mus Tours
Musee des Beaux-Arts
18 Place Francois Sicard, 37000 Tours,
France
Mus Troyes
Musees de la Ville de Troyes
Troyes, France
Mus Vins Tour
Musee des Vins de Touraine
16 Rue Nationale, 37000 Tours, France
Musee Rodin
Musee Rodin
77 Rue de Varenne, F-75007 Paris, France
Museen Wien
Historisches Museum der Stadt Wien
Karlsplatz, Vienna 4, Austria
Museo Vela
Museo Vela
CH-6853 Ligornetto TI, Switzerland
Museu Nac Bel
Museu Nacional de Belas Artes
Ave. Rio Branco 199, Rio de Janeiro, Brazil
Museum Mobile
Museum of the City of Mobile
355 Government St., Mobile, AL 36602
(0-914344)
Museum Mod Art
Museum of Modern Art
Customer Sales Service, 11 W. 53rd St.,
New York, NY 10019
(0-87070)
Museum NM Pr
Museum of New Mexico Press
P.O. Box 2087, Santa Fe, NM 87503
(0-89013)
Museum of NM Pr
See Museum NM Pr
Music Sales
Music Sales Corp.
(0-8256)
Quick Fox, Inc., 33 W. 60th St., New
York, NY 10023
Muz Arch Lodz
Muzeum Archeologiczne i Etnograficzne w
Lodzi
Pl. Wolnosci 14, Lodz 91-415, Poland
Muz Arch Wroc
Muzeum Archidiecezjalne we Wroclawiu
Ul. Kanonia 12, 50-238 Wroclaw, Poland
Muz Bud Lud
Muzeum Budownictwa Ludowego
Ul. Traugutta 3, Sanok' woj. Rzeszow,
Poland
Muz Constanta
Muzeul de Istorie Nationala si Arheologie
Piata Ovidiu, 12, 8700 Constanta, Rumania
Muz Lowiczu
Muzeum Narodowe Oddzial w Lowiczu
Rynek Kosciuszki 4, Poland
Muz Morskie
Centrale Muzeum Morskie w Gdansku
Ul.Szeroka 67/68, 80-835 Gdansk, Poland
Muz Narod Kielce
Muzeum Narodowe w Kielcach
Pl. Partyzantow 3-5, 25-303 Kielce, Poland
Muz Narod Kra
Muzeum Narodowe w Krakowie
Ul. Manifestu Lipcowego 12, Krakow,
Poland
Muz Narod Poz
Muzeum Narodowe w Poznaniu
Al. Marcinkowskiego 9, Poznan 61-745,
Poland
Muz Narod Szc
Muzeum Narodowe w Szczecinie
Ul. Staromlynska 27, Szczecin, Poland
Muz Naz Adria
Museo Nazionale di Adria
Piazzale degli Etruschi 2, I-45011 Adria,
Italy
Muz Skla Bizu
Muzeum Skla a Bizuterie
CS-46600 Jablonec Nad Nisou, Jiraskova
Ul. 4, Czechoslovakia
Muz Skopje
Musej Na Sovrementa Umetnost Skopje
Samoilova bb yU-91001 Skopje, Yugoslavia
Muz Wnetrz
Muzeum Wnetrz Zabytkowych
Pszczyna, woj. Katowice, Poland

Myriade
Myriade Press, Inc., The
Seven Stony Run, New Rochelle, NY
10804
(0-918142)
N Ill U Pr
Northern Illinois Univ. Press
515 Garden Rd., DeKalb, IL 60115
(0-87580)
Nasjonal Norway
Nasjonalgalleriet
Universitetsgaten 13, 1 Oslo, Norway
Nat Acad of Des
National Academy of Design
1083 Fifth Ave., New York, NY 10028
Nat Gal Art
National Gallery of Art
Constitution Ave. & Sixth St., N.W.,
Washington, DC 20565 United States
Nat Gal Art Nz
National Art Gallery of New Zealand
Buckle St., Wellington, New Zealand
Nat Gal Can
National Gallery of Canada
Lorne Bldg., Elgin & Slater Sts., Ottawa,
ON K1A OM8, Canada
Nat Gal Scot
National Gallery of Scotland
The Mound EH2 2EL Edinburgh,
United Kingdom
Nat Gal Vict
National Gallery of Victoria
180 St. Kilda Rd., Melbourne 3004,
Australia
Nat Mus Racing
National Museum of Racing
Union Ave., Saratoga Springs, NY 12866
Nat Mus West
Kokuritsu Seiyo Bijutsukann
Ueno Park, Taito-ku, 110 Tokyo, Japan
Nat Palace Mus
National Palace Museum
Wai-Shuang-Hsi, Shih-Lin, 111 Taipei,
China, Republic of
Nat Port Gal Lon
National Portrait Gallery
2 St. Martin's Place, London WC2H OHE,
United Kingdom
National Trust
Waddesdon Manor
National Trust, Waddesdon Manor,
Aylesbury, Bucks. HPI8 OJH,
United Kingdom
Nationalmuseum
Nationalmuseum
Box 16 176, Stockholm, S-103-24, Sweden
Natl Acad Sci
National Academy of Sciences
Printing & Publishing Office, 2101
Constitution Ave., Washington, DC 20418
(0-309)
Natl Art Ed
National Art Education Assn.
1916 Association Dr., Reston, VA 22091
Natl Fire Prot
National Fire Protection Assn.
470 Atlantic Ave., Boston, MA 02110
(0-87765)
Natl Gallery Art
National Gallery of Art
Sixth St. & Constitution Ave., N.W.,
Washington, DC 20565
(0-89468)
Natl Geog
National Geographic Society
17th & "M" Sts., N.W., Washington, DC
20036
(0-87044)
Natl Learning
National Learning Corp.
212 Michael Dr., Syosset, NY 11791
(0-8373)
Natl Textbk
National Textbook Co.
8259 Niles Center Rd., Skokie, IL 60076
(0-8442)
Natural Hist
Natural History Press
Doubleday & Co., Inc., 501 Franklin Ave.,
Garden City, NY 11530
Natural History Bks
Natural History Books
5239 Tendilla Ave., Woodland Hills, CA
91364
Naturegraph
Naturegraph Pubs., Inc.
P.O. Box 1075, Happy Camp, CA 96039
(0-911010; 0-87961)

Naval Inst Pr
Naval Institute Press
Annapolis, MD 21402
(0-87021)

Nazarene
Nazarene Publishing House
P.O. Box 527, Kansas City, MO 64141
(0-8341)

NC Archives
North Carolina Division of Archives & History
109 E. Jones St., Raleigh, NC 27611

NCMA
North Carolina Museum of Art
Raleigh, NC 27611
(0-88259)

Neal-Schuman
Neal-Schuman Pubs., Inc.
64 University Place, New York, NY 10003
(0-918212)

Nelson
Nelson, Thomas, Inc.
Orders to:
407 Seventh Ave., S., Nashville, TN 37203
(0-8407)

Nelson-Hall
Nelson-Hall Inc.
111 N. Canal, Chicago, IL 60606
(0-911012; 0-88229)

Neue Gal Linz
Neue Galerie der Stadt Linz-Wolfgang-Gurlitt
Museum
Hauptplatz 8, A-4000 Linz, Austria

Neuenstein
Hohenlohe-Museum Schloss Neuenstein
D-7113 Neuenstein, Schlosstr. 49,
West Germany

New Circle
New Circle Pubns., Art Research Ctr.
922 E. 48th St., Kansas City, MO 64110

New Directions
New Directions Publishing Corp.
(0-8112)
Dist. by:
W. W. Norton Co., 500 Fifth Ave., New
York, NY 10036

New Eng Pub
New England Pub. Co.
200 Glendale Rd., Stratford, CT 06497
(0-932268)

New English Art
New English Art Gallery
Charles & Liberty Sts., Rochester, NH
03867
(0-913064)

New Glide
New Glide Pubns.
330 Ellis St., Rm. 404, San Francisco, CA
94102
(0-912078)

New Orleans Mus
New Orleans Museum of Art
P.O. Box 19123, New Orleans, LA 70179
United States

New Republic
New Republic Books
(0-915220)
Dist. by:
Simon & Schuster, 1230 Ave. of the
Americas, New York, NY 10020

New Victoria Pubs
New Victoria Pubs. Inc.
7 Bank St., Lebanon, NH 03766

New Viewpoints. Watts.
New Viewpoints. Imprint of Watts, Franklin,
Inc.

Newark Mus
Newark Museum
P.O. Box 540, 43-49 Washington St.,
Newark, NJ 07101

Newbury Bks Inc
Newbury Books, Inc.
Box 29, Topsfield, MA 01983
(0-912728)

Newsweek
Newsweek
444 Madison Ave., New York, NY 10022
(0-88225)

NFS Pr
NFS Press
P.O. Box 31040, San Francisco, CA 94131
(0-917986)

NH Pub Co
New Hampshire Publishing Co.
P.O. Box 70, Somersworth, NH 03878
(0-912274; 0-89725)

Nicholas Roerich Mus
Roerich, Nicholas, Museum
319 W. 107th St., New York, NY 10025
United States

Nichols Pub
Nichols Publishing Co.
P.O. Box 96, New York, NY 10024
(0-89397)

Nijmeegs Mus
Nijmeegs Museum "Commanderie van St. Jan"
Franse Plaats 3, 6511 VS Nijmegen,
Netherlands

NIU Art Dept
Northern Illinois Univ. Art Dept.
Dekalb, IL 60115

NJ Hist Soc
New Jersey Historical Society
230 Broadway, Newark, NJ 07104

NM Philatelist
See Hobby Pub Serv

Noble
See Bowmar-Noble

Nolde Mus
Stiftung Seebull Ada und Emil Nolde
D-2261 Neukirchen uber Niebull, Seebull,
(Schlesw.), West Germany

Noonday. FS&G.
Noonday Press. Imprint of Farrar, Straus &
Giroux, Inc.

Norfolk Mus
Norfolk Museums Service
C/0 Norfolk County Council, Castle
Museum, Norwich NR1 3JU,
United Kingdom

Norm Mack Gal
Saskatchewan Arts Board
200 Lakeshore Dr., Regina SK S4S OA4,
Canada

North Am Pub Co
North American Publishing Co.
401 N. Broad St., Philadelphia, PA 19108
(0-912920)

North Central
North Central Publishing Co.
Riverview Industrial Park, 274 Fillmore
Ave., E., St. Paul, MN 55107

North Holland. Elsevier.
North-Holland. Imprint of Elsevier-North
Holland Pub. Co.

North Light Pub
North Light Pubs.
(0-89134)
Van Nostrand Reinhold, 450 W. 33rd St.,
New York, NY 10001

North Plains
North Plains Press
P.O. Box 1950, Aberdeen, SD 57401
(0-87970)

North River
North River Press, Inc.
P.O. Box 241, Croton-on-Hudson, NY
10520
(0-88427)

Northland
Northland Press
P.O. Box N, Flagstaff, AZ 86002
(0-87358)

Northwestern U Pr
Northwestern Univ. Press
1735 Benson Ave., Evanston, IL 60201
(0-8101)

Northwood Inst
Northwood Institute Press
3225 Cook St., Midland, MI 48640
(0-87359)

Norton
Norton, W. W., & Co., Inc.
500 Fifth Ave., New York, NY 10036
(0-393)

Norton Art
Norton, R. W., Art Gallery
4747 Creswell Ave., Shreveport, LA 71106
(0-913060; 0-9600182)

NortonC. Norton.
Norton College Division. Imprint of Norton,
W. W., & Co., Inc.

Norwood
See Norwood Edns

Norwood Edns
Norwood Editions
P.O. Box 38, Norwood, PA 19074
(0-88305; 0-8482)

Nostalgia Pr
Nostalgia Press, Inc.
P.O. Box 293, Franklin Square, NY 11010
(0-87897)

NY Hist Assn
New York State Historical Assn
Lake Rd., Cooperstown, NY 13326

NY Pub Lib
New York Public Library
Orders to:
Readex Books, 101 Fifth Ave., New York,
NY 10003
(0-87104)

NYGS
New York Graphic Society, Ltd.
(0-8212)
Dist. by:
Little, Brown & Co., 200 West St.,
Waltham, MA 02154

NYGS CT
New York Graphic Society in Greenwich
140 Greenwich Ave., Greenwich, CT 06830

NYU Pr
New York Univ. Press
113-15 University Place, New York, NY
10003
(0-8147)

Oakwood Pr
Oakwood Press, The
P.O. Box 541, McMinnville, OR 97128
(0-915418)

Obol Intl
Obol International
8 S. Michigan Ave., Chicago, IL 60603
(0-916710)

Oceana
Oceana Pubns.
75 Main St., Dobbs Ferry, NY 10522
(0-379)

Octagon
Octagon Books
19 Union Square W., New York, NY 10003
(0-374)

October
October House
P.O. Box 454, Stonington, CT 06378
(0-8079)

OECD
Organization for Economic Cooperation &
Development
1750 Pennsylvania Ave., Suite 1207BP,
N.W., Washington, DC 20006

Oh State Gal
Ohio State Univ Gallery of Fine Arts
128 N. Oval Mall, Columbus, OH 43210

Ohio St Pr
Ohio State Univ. Press
Hitchcock Hall, Rm. 316, 2070 Neil Ave.,
Columbus, OH 43210
(0-8142)

Ohio U Pr
Ohio Univ. Press
Scott Quadrangle, Athens, OH 45701
(0-8214)

Okpaku Communications
Okpaku Communications
444 Central Park, W., New York, NY
10025
(0-89388)

Olana
Olana State Historic Site
P. O. Box 199, Hudson, NY 12534

Old Time
Old Time Bottle Publishing Co.
611 Lancaster Dr., N.E., Salem, OR 97301
(0-911068)

Oldenburger
Oldenburger Stadtmuseum-Stadtische
Kunstsammlungen
D-2900 Oldenberg, Raiffeisenstr. 32/33,
Postfach 1187, West Germany

Oleander Pr
Oleander Press
210 Fifth Ave., New York, NY 10010
(0-902675; 0-900891)

Olivet
Olivet College Press
(0-911070)
Bill Whitney, P.O. Box 20, Mott Academic
Ctr., Olivet, MI 49076

One Hund One Prods
101 Productions
(0-912238; 0-89286)
Charles Scribner's Sons, Book Warehouse,
Vreeland Ave., Totowa, NJ 07512

Oreg Hist Soc
Oregon Historical Society
1230 S.W. Park Ave., Portland, OR 97205
(0-87595)

Oreg St U Pr
Oregon State Univ. Press
101 Waldo Hall, Oregon State University,
Corvallis, OR 97331
(0-87071)
Orell Fussli
Orell Fussli Verlag
Nuschelerstr. 22, CH-8022 Zurich,
Switzerland
Oriel. Routledge & Kegan.
Oriel Press. Imprint of Routledge & Kegan
Paul, Ltd.
Orient Bk Dist
Orient Book Distributors
P.O. Box 100, Livingston, NJ 07039
(0-89684)
Orient Longman. South Asia Bks.
Orient Longman. Imprint of South Asia Books.
Oriole Edns
Oriole Editions
19 W. 44th St., New York, NY 10036
(0-88211)
Oskar Reinhart
Reinhart, Oskar, Stiftung
Stadthasstr. 6, CH-8400 Winterthur,
Switzerland
Ostasiatiska
Ostasiatiska Museet, Museum of Far Eastern
Antiquities
Box 16381, S-103 27 Stockholm, Sweden
Otis Art Gal
Otis Art Institute Gallery
2401 Wilshire Blvd., Los Angeles, CA
90057
Otterden
Otterden Press
111 Plymouth Rd., Hillsdale, NJ 07642
(0-918868)
Oude Pastorie
Oude Pastorie Museum
Main St., Paarl, South Africa
Our Sunday Visitor
Our Sunday Visitor, Inc.
200 Noll Plaza, Huntington, IN 46750
(0-87973)
Outer Straubville
Outer Straubville Press
Book People, 2940 Seventh St., Berkeley,
CA 94710
Overlook Pr
Overlook Press
(0-87591)
c/o Viking Press, 625 Madison Ave, New
York, NY 10022
Owlswick Pr
Owlswick Press
P.O. Box 8243, Philadelphia, PA 19101
(0-913896)
Oxford U Pr
Oxford Univ. Press, Inc.
Orders to:
16-00 Pollitt Dr., Fair Lawn, NJ 07410
(0-19)
Oxmoor Hse
Oxmoor House, Inc.
Orders to:
P.O. Box C-59, Birmingham, AL 35283
(0-8487)
P Elek
See Merrimack Bk Serv
P Fanlac
Pierre Fanlac, Editeur
12 Rue du Professeur Peyrot, F-24000
Perigueux, France
P-H
Prentice-Hall, Inc.
Englewood Cliffs, NJ 07632
(0-13)
P L Humphries
Percy Lund Humphries
Drummond Rd., Bradford B D8 8DH,
United Kingdom
P Rosen
Rosen, Pauline
658 Main St., Placerville, CA 95667
(0-9600214)
Pa Hist Soc
Historical Society of Pennsylvania
1300 Locust St., Philadelphia, PA 19107
(0-910732)
Pa St U Pr
Pennsylvania State Univ. Press
215 Wagner Bldg., University Park, PA
16802
(0-271)

Pacific Bks
Pacific Books, Pubs.
P.O. Box 558, Palo Alto, CA 94302
(0-87015)
Pacific Coast
Pacific Coast Pubs.
4085 Campbell Ave., Menlo Park, CA
94025
(0-87465)
Pacific Search
Pacific Search Press
222 Dexter Ave. N., Seattle, WA 98109
(0-914718)
Paddington
Paddington Press, Ltd.
Grosset & Dunlap, 51 Madison Ave., New
York, NY 10010
(0-448)
Padma
Padma Press
P.O. Box 56, Oatman, AZ 86433
(0-917960)
Pagurian
Pagurian Press
(0-88932; 0-919364)
Baker & Taylor, 1515 Broadway, New
York, NY 10036
Palazzo Pitti
Galleria Palatina di Palazzo Pitti
Piazza Pitti 1, I-50125 Florence, Italy
Panjandrum
Panjandrum Books
(0-915572)
Dist. by:
Publisher's Group West, 5855 Beaudry,
Emeryville, CA 94608; Robert Rainer
Assocs, 318 Happ Rd., Northfield, IL
60093; Como Sales, Inc., 799 Broadway,
New York, NY 10013; Ralph Woodward,
New England Books & Arts, P.O. Drawer
1, Concord, MA 01742; Book People, 2940
Seventh St., Berkeley, CA 94710; Book
House Northwest, 2900 S.E. Stork St.,
Portland, OR 97214; Ingram Book Co., 347
Reedwood Dr., Nashville, TN 37217; WIP,
P.O. Box 66285, Houston, TX 77006
Panjandrum Pr
See Panjandrum
Pannonius Muz
Janus Pannonius Muzeum
Szechenyi ter 12, P.O. Box 158, H-7601
Pecs, Hungary
Panst Muz Etno
Panstwowe Muzeum Etnograficzine
Kredytowa 1, Warsaw, Poland
Panst Wyd Nauk
Panstwowe Wydawnictwo Naukowe
Ul. Miodowa 10, P-00-251 Warsaw, Poland
Pantheon
Pantheon Books, Div. of Random House, Inc.
Orders to:
Random House, Inc., 400 Hahn Rd.,
Westminster, MD 21157
Paperweight Pr
Paperweight Press
761 Chestnut St., Santa Cruz, CA 95060
(0-87833)
Paragon
Paragon Book Reprint Corp.
14 E. 38th St., New York, NY 10016
(0-8188)
Paragraph Pr
Paragraph Press
204 Circle Dr., P.O. Box 1107, Felton, CA
95018
(0-915462)
Parents
Parents Magazine Press
52 Vanderbilt Ave., New York, NY 10017
(0-8193)
Parker. P-H.
Parker Publishing Co. Imprint of Prentice-Hall,
Inc.
Parr AZ
Parr of Arizona
3903 N. 16th St., Phoenix, AZ 85016
Past in Glass
Past in Glass
515 Northridge Dr., Boulder City, NV
89005
(0-9600212)
Pat Nac Mus
Patronato Nacional De Museos
Generalisimo, No. 39, Madrid, Spain

Pathmark Bks
Pathmark Books, Inc.
P.O. Box 115, Newton Upper Falls, MA
02164
(0-913390)
Paul Dierichs
Paul Dierichs KG
Frankfurter Str. 168, Postfach 61-62,
D-3500 Kassel, West Germany
Paula Becker
Paula-Becker-Modersohn-Haus
Bottcherstrasse D-2800 Bremen,
West Germany
Paulist-Newman
See Paulist Pr
Paulist Pr
Paulist Press
1865 Broadway, New York, NY 10023
(0-8091)
Payson Gal
Payson Gallery of Art
C/O Westbrook College, Portland, ME
PB
Pocket Books, Inc, Div. of Simon & Schuster,
Inc.
1230 Ave. of the Americas, New York, NY
10020
(0-671)
PDA Pubs
PDA Publishers Corp.
P.O. Box 3075, 1200 S. Sharon Chapel Rd.,
W. Lafayette, IN 47906
(0-914886)
Peabody Harvard
Peabody Museum of Archaeology &
Ethnology, Harvard Univ.
11 Divinity Ave., Cambridge, MA 02138
(0-87365)
Peabody Mus Salem
Peabody Museum of Salem
East India Square, Salem, MA 01970
(0-87577)
Peace & Pieces
See SF Arts & Letters
Peacock. Bantam.
Peacock. Imprint of Bantam Books, Inc.
Peale Mus
Peale Museum
225 Holliday St., Baltimore, MD 21202
Peek Pubns
Peek Pubns.
Orders to:
P.O. Box 11065, Palo Alto, CA 94306
(0-917962)
Pelican
Pelican Publishing Co., Inc.
630 Burmaster St., Gretna, LA 70053
(0-911116; 0-88289)
Pelican. Penguin.
Pelican Books. Imprint of Penguin Books, Inc.
Pendel Hill
See Pendle Hill
Pendle Hill
Pendle Hill Pubns.
Pendle Hill, 338 Plush Mill Rd,
Wallingford, PA 19086
(0-87574)
Penguin
Penguin Books, Inc.
625 Madison Ave., New York, NY 10022
(0-14)
Penn-Yale Expedit
Pubns. of the Pennsylvania-Yale Expedition to
Egypt, Yale Univ.
c/o Peabody Museum of Natural History,
Pubns. Office, New Haven, CT 06520
Pentalic Corp
See Taplinger
Penumbra Projects
Penumbra Projects
(0-916416)
Dist. by:
Light Impressions Corp., P.O. Box 3012,
Rochester, NY 14614
Pepper Pub
Pepper Publishing
2901 E. Mabel, Tucson, AZ 85716
(0-914468)
Pequot
See Globe Pequot
Peregrine. Penguin.
Peregrine Books. Imprint of Penguin Books,
Inc.
Peregrine Smith
Peregrine Smith, Inc.
P.O. Box 667, 1877 E. Gentile St., Layton,
UT 84041
(0-87905)

Perfect Graphic
Perfect Graphic Arts
14 Dearborn Dr., Old Tappan, NJ 07675
(0-911126)

Pergamon
Pergamon Press, Inc.
Maxwell House, Fairview Park, Elmsford,
NY 10523
(0-08)

Persea Bks
Persea Books, Inc.
225 Lafayette St., New York, NY 10012
(0-89255)

Peshawar Mus
Peshawar Museum
Grand Trunk Rd., Peshawar, Pakistan

Pest Count Mus
Ferenczy Muzeum
Marx Ter 6, P.O. Box 103, H-2001
Szentendre, Hungary

Peter Glenn
Glenn, Peter, Pubns., Inc.
17 E. 48th St., New York, NY 10017
(0-87314)

Peter M Bohuns
Bohuns, Peter M., Galeria
Tranovskeho 3, CS-031 01 Liptovsky
Mikulas, Czechoslovakia

Peter Smith
Smith, Peter, Publisher Inc.
6 Lexington Ave., Magnolia, MA 01930
(0-8446)

Peterborough
City Museum & Art Gallery
Priestgate, Peterborough, PE1 1LF,
United Kingdom

Petersen Pub
Petersen Publishing Co.
6725 Sunset Blvd., Los Angeles, CA 90028
(0-8227)

Petersons Guides
Peterson's Guides Inc.
Orders to:
Peterson's Guides Order Dept., P.O. Box
978, Edison, NJ 08817
(0-87866)

Petit Palais
Musee du Petit Palais
Place du Palais des Papes, 4000 Avignon,
France

Petrocelli-Charter
See Van Nos Reinhold

Phaeton
Phaeton Press, Inc.
Gordian Press, 85 Tompkins St., Staten
Island, NY 10304
(0-87753)

Phaidon
See Dutton

Phaidon. Dutton.
Phaidon. Imprint of Dutton, E. P.

Phaidon Pr
Phaidon Press
Littlegate Ho, St. Ebbe's St, Oxford OXi
ISQ, London, United Kingdom
(0-7148)

Phi Delta Kappa
Phi Delta Kappa, Inc.
8th & Union, P.O. Box 789, Bloomington,
IN 47401
(0-87367)

Phila Col Art
Philadelphia College of Art
Broad & Spruce Sts., Philadelphia, PA
19102

Phila Free Lib
Free Library of Philadelphia
Rare Book Dept., Logan Square,
Philadelphia, PA 19103
(0-911132)

Philip Wilson
Philip Wilson & Co.
Russell Chambers, Covent Garden, London
WC2E 8AA, United Kingdom

Phillips Coll
Phillips Collection
1600-1612 21st St., N.W., Washington, DC
20009

Philos Lib
Philosophical Library, Inc.
15 E. 40th St., New York, NY 10016
(0-8022)

Phoenix Pub
Phoenix Publishing
Canaan, NH 03741
(0-914016)

Photo-Optical
Society of Photo-Optical Instrumentation
Engineers
P.O. Box 10, 405 Fieldston Rd.,
Bellingham, WA 98225
(0-89252)

Pierpont Morgan
Pierpont Morgan Library
29 E. 36th St., New York, NY 10016
(0-87598)

Pilg Soc
Pilgrim Society
75 Court St., Plymouth, MA 02360

Pilgrim NY
Pilgrim Press, The
Seabury Service Center, Somers, CT 06071
(0-8298)

Pilot Bks
Pilot Books
347 Fifth Ave., New York, NY 10016
(0-87576)

Pina Naz Siena
Pinacoteca Nazionale Siena
Via del Capitano, 1 Siena, Italy

Pioneer Pr
Pioneer Press, Inc.
P.O. Box 684, Union City, TN 38261
(0-913150)

Piper
Piper Publishing, Inc.
Blue Earth, MN 56013
(0-87832)

Pitkin Pics Ltd
Pitkin Pictorials Ltd,
11 Wyfold Rd., London SW6 6SG,
United Kingdom

Pitman
See Fearon-Pitman

Plains Art Mus
Plains Art Museum
521 Main Ave., Moorhead, MN 56560

Playboy
Playboy Press, Div. of P.E.I. Books, Inc.
(0-87223)
Harper & Row Pubs., Inc., Keystone
Industrial Park, Scranton, PA 18512

Playboy Pr Pbks
Playboy Press Paperbacks, Div. of P.E.I.
Books, Inc.
747 Third Ave., New York, NY 10017
(0-87216)

Plays
Plays, Inc.
8 Arlington St., Boston, MA 02116
(0-8238)

Plenum Pr. Plenum Pub.
Plenum Press. Imprint of Plenum Publishing
Corp.

Plenum Pub
Plenum Publishing Corp.
227 W. 17th St., New York, NY 10011
(0-306)

Plycon Pr
Plycon Press
P.O. Box 220, 340 The Village, No. 105,
Redondo Beach, CA 90277
(0-916434)

Pomerica Pr
Pomerica Press, Ltd.
(0-918732)
Caroline House Pubs., Box 161,
Thornwood, NY 10964

Pompidou
Musee d'Art Moderne (Beaubourg), Centre
National d'Art et de Culture George
Pompidou
75191 Paris Cedex 04, France

Popular Lib
Popular Library, Inc, Unit of CBS Pubns.
1515 Broadway, New York, NY 10036
(0-445)

Porter
Porter, Bern
22 Salmond Rd., Belfast, ME 04915
(0-911156)

Porvoon Mus
Porvoon Museo
Valikatu 11, SF-06100 Porvoo 10, Finland

Post-Era
Post-Era Books
Box 150, 119 S. First Ave., Arcadia, CA
91006
(0-911160)

Potsdam Pub Mus
Potsdam Public Museum
Civic Center, Potsdam, NY 13676

Potter
Potter, Clarkson N., Inc.
(0-8247)
Dist. by:
Crown Pubs., 419 Park Ave., S., New York,
NY 10016

Prado
Museo del Prado
Calle de Felipe IV, Madrid, Spain

Praeger
Praeger Pubs, Div. of Holt, Rinehart &
Winston/CBS
383 Madison Ave., New York, NY 10017
(0-275)

Prairie Sch
Prairie School Press
12509 S. 89th Ave., Palos Park, IL 60464
(0-87370)

Prakken
Prakken Pubns., Inc.
416 Longshore Dr., Ann Arbor, MI 48107
(0-911168)

Prehist Gal
Gallery of Prehistoric Art
20 E. 12th St., New York, NY 10003

Preservation Pr
Preservation Press, National Trust for Historic
Preservation
1785 Massachusetts Ave., N. W.,
Washington, DC 20036
(0-89133)

Presidio Pr
Presidio Press/Neff, McNally & Kane
Orders to:
Presidio Press Distribution Center, P.O.
Box 978, Edison, NJ 08817
(0-89141)

Prestel Verlag
Prestel Verlag
Mandlstr 26, D-8000 Munich 40,
West Germany
(3-7913)

Prestressed Concrete
Prestressed Concrete Institute
20 N. Wacker Dr., Chicago, IL 60606

Price Stern
Price, Stern, Sloan, Pubs., Inc.
410 N. La Cienega Blvd., Los Angeles, CA
90048
(0-8431)

Prin Wales Mus
Prince of Wales Museum of Western India
M. G. Rd., Fort, 400 023, Bombay,
Maharashtra, India

Prince U Art Mus
Princeton Univ. Art Museum
Princeton, NJ 08540

Princeton Lib
Princeton Univ. Library
Richard M. Ludwig, Princeton, NJ 08544
(0-87811)

Princeton U Pr
Princeton Univ. Press
41 William St., Princeton, NJ 08540
(0-691)

Printed Matter
Printed Matter, Inc.
7 Lispenard St., New York, NY 10013
(0-89439)

Prof Pubns Ohio
Professional Pubns., Inc.
1609 Northwest Blvd., Columbus, OH
43212

Prometheus Bks
Prometheus Books
1203 Kensington Ave., Buffalo, NY 14215
(0-87975)

Pruett
Pruett Publishing Co.
3235 Prairie Ave., Boulder, CO 80301
(0-87108)

Pub Ctr Cult Res
Publishing Center for Cultural Resources, Inc.
152 W. 42 St., New York, NY 10036

Puffin. Penguin.
Puffin Books. Imprint of Penguin Books, Inc.

Putnam
Putnam's, G. P., Sons
390 Murray Hill Pkwy., East Rutherford,
NJ 07073
(0-399)

Quadrangle
See Times Bks

Quaker
Quaker Press
P.O. Box 305, Rehoboth, DE 19971
(0-911200)

Quarterman
Quarterman Pubns., Inc.
5 S. Union St., Lawrence, MA 01843
(0-88000)

Queens Coll Pr
Queens College Press
Editorial Services, Flushing, NY 11367
(0-930146)

Queens Hse
Queens House
One Edgewood Ave., Larchmont, NY
10538
(0-89244)

Quick Fox. Music Sales.
Quick Fox. Imprint of Music Sales Corp.

R A Green
Green, Robert Alan, Publisher
214 Key Haven Rd., Key West, FL 33040
(0-9600266)

R B Powell
Powell, Robert Blake
P.O. Box 833, Hurst, TX 76053
(0-9600680)

R H Flem Mus
Fleming, Robert Hull, Museum
Burlington, VT 05401

R Little
Little, Ruth
3430 34th St., Lubbock, TX 79410
(0-9600062)

R McLaughlin
McLaughlin, Robert, Gallery
Civic Centre, Oshawa 0N L1J 3Z3, Canada

R Marek
Marek, Richard, Pubs., Inc, Subs. of G.P.
Putnam's Sons
200 Madison Ave., New York, NY 10016
(0-399)

R P Long
Long, Robert P.
634 Bellmore Ave., East Meadow, NY
11554
(0-9600064)

R T Matthews
Matthews, Robert T.
2400 Pfefferkorn Rd., West Friendship,
MD 21794
(0-9601150)

R W Grant
Grant, R.W.
P.O. Box 2060, Hanover, MA 02339
(0-9601218)

R W Nort Gal
Norton, R W , Gallery
4747 Creswell Ave., Shreveport, LA 71106

R West
West, Richard
Box 6404, Philadelphia, PA 19145

Radio City
Radio City Book Store
324 W. 47th St., New York, NY 10036
(0-911202)

Rainbow Bks
Rainbow Books, Inc.
675 Dell Rd., Carlstadt, NJ 07072
(0-89508)

Raintree Child
Raintree Childrens Books, Div. of
MacDonald-Raintree, Inc.
205 W. Highland Ave., Milwaukee, WI
53203
(0-8393)

Raintree Pubs Ltd
Raintree Pubs., Ltd.
205 W. Highland Ave., Milwaukee, WI
53203
(0-8172)

Ram Pub
Ram Publishing Co.
P.O. Box 38464, Dallas, TX 75238
(0-915920)

Rand
Rand McNally & Co.
P.O. Box 7600, Chicago, IL 60680
(0-528)

Random
Random House, Inc.
400 Hahn Rd., Westminster, MD 21157
(0-394)

Rather Pr
Rather Press
3200 Guido St., Oakland, CA 94602

Rawson Assocs
See Rawson Wade

Rawson Wade
Rawson, Wade Pubs., Inc.
(0-89256)
Atheneum Pubs., 122 E. 42nd St., New
York, NY 10017

Ray Riling
Riling, Ray, Arms Book Co.
P.O. Box 18925, 6844 Gorsten St.,
Philadelphia, PA 19119

Readers Digest Pr
Reader's Digest Press
(0-88349)
McGraw-Hill Book Co., 1221 Ave. of the
Americas, New York, NY 10020

Reed
Reed, A. H. & A. W., Books
(0-589)
Dist. by:
Charles E. Tuttle, Inc., 28 S. Main St.,
Rutland, VT 05701

Reed Pubs
Reed Pubs.
P. O. Box 10667, 4999 Kahala Ave.,
Honolulu, HI 96816
(0-917064)

Regents Pr KS
Regents Press of Kansas
366 Watson Library, Lawrence, KS 66045
(0-7006)

Regnery
See Contemp Bks

Regnery-Gateway
Regnery/Gateway, Inc.
Box 207, South Bend, IN 46624
(0-89526)

Reidel Pub
See Kluwer Boston

Reilly & Lee
See Contemp Bks

Reinhart Col
Sammlung Oskar Reinart "Am Romerholz"
Halcenstr. 95, CH-8400 Winterthur,
Switzerland

Rembrandt Huis
Museum "Het Rembrandthuis"
Jodenbreestraat 4-6, 1001 Amsterdam,
Netherlands

Remington
Remington Art Museum
303 Washington St., Ogdensburg, NY
13669

Reston
Reston Publishing Co., Inc.
(0-87909; 0-8359)
Prentice-Hall, Inc., Englewood Cliffs, NJ
07632

Reunion
Services Commerciaux de la Reunion des
Musees Nationaux
10 Rue De LAbbaye, F-75006 Paris, France

Review & Herald
Review & Herald Publishing Assn.
Takoma Park, Washington, DC 20012
(0-8280)

Reward. P-H.
Reward Books. Imprint of Prentice-Hall, Inc.

Reyn Morse Foun
Reynolds Morse Foundation
21709 Chagrin Blvd., Cleveland, OH 44122
(0-934236)

Reynal
Reynal & Co.
(0-688)
Dist. by:
William Morrow & Co., Order Dept., 6
Henderson Dr., West Caldwell, NJ 07006

Rho-Delta Pr
Rho-Delta Press
8831 Sunset Blvd., Suite 203, P.O. Box
69540, Los Angeles, CA 90069
(0-913770)

RI Hist Soc
Rhode Island Historical Society
52 Power St., Providence, RI 02906
(0-932840)

Rijks Het Cat
Rijksmuseum Het Catharijneconvent
Nieuwe Gracht 63, 3512 LG Utrecht,
Netherlands

Ringling Mus Art
Ringling, John & Mabel, Museum of Art
P.O. Box 1838, Sarasota, FL 33578

Rio Grande
Rio Grande Press, Inc.
P.O. Box 33, Glorieta, NM 87535
(0-87380)

Rizzoli Intl
Rizzoli International Pubns., Inc.
712 Fifth Ave., New York, NY 10019
(0-8478)

RK Edns
RK Editions
P.O. Box 73, Canal St., New York, NY
10013
(0-932360)

Robin & Russ
Robin & Russ Handweavers
533 N. Adams St., McMinnville, OR 97128

Rockhill Nelson
William Rockhill Nelson Trust
4525 Oak St., Kansas City, MO 64111

Rockwell Corning Mus
Rockwell-Corning Museum
Baron Steuben Place, Corning, NY 14830

Rocky Mtn Arms
Rocky Mountain Arms & Antiques
6288 S. Pontiac, Englewood, CO 80111
(0-914346)

Rodale Pr Inc
Rodale Press, Inc.
33 E. Minor St., Emmaus, PA 18049
(0-87857)

Rogers Bk
Rogers Book Service
217 W. 18th St, Box V, New York, NY
10011
(0-911268)

Rolin Mus
Musee Rolin
3, Rue des Bancs, F-71400 Autun, France

Rollet Mus
Stadtische Sammlungen, Archiv/Rollett
Museum der Stadtgemeinde Baden
Weikersdorfer Platz 1, A-2500 Baden bei
Wien, Austria

Rom Ger Julich
Romisch-Germanisches Museum
D-5170 Julich, Markt 1, P.O. Box 209,
West Germany

Roselius Haus
Roselius-Haus
D-2800 Bremen, Bottcherstr. 4, Postfach
697, West Germany

Rosen Pr
Rosen, Richards, Press, Inc.
29 E. 21st St., New York, NY 10010
(0-8239)

Rosenbach Found
Rosenbach, Philip H. & A.S.W., Foundation
2010 De Lancey Place, Philadelphia, PA
19103

Rosenborg
Rosenborg Slot (De Danske Kongers
Kronologiske Samling Pa Rosenborg)
Oster Voldgade 4A, DK-1350 Copenhagen,
Denmark

Ross
Ross & Haines, Inc.
639 E. Lake St., Wayzata, MN 55391
(0-87018)

Rossendale
Rossendale Museum
Whitaker Park, Rawtenstall, Rossendale
BB4 6RE, United Kingdom

Rottneros
Rottneros Park
Rottneros Park, S-680 12 Rottneros,
Sweden

Routledge & Kegan
Routledge & Kegan Paul, Ltd.
9 Park St., Boston, MA 02108
(0-7100)

Rowman
Rowman & Littlefield, Inc, Div. of Littlefield,
Adams, & Co.
81 Adams Dr., Box 327, Totowa, NJ 07512
(0-87471; 0-8476)

Royal Ont Mus
Royal Ontario Museum
100 Queen's Park, Toronto, 0N M5S 2C6,
Canada

Royal Pavilion
Royal Pavillion Art Gallery and Museums
Church St. BN1 1UE Brighton,
United Kingdom

Royal Scot Mus
Royal Scottish Museum
Chambers St., EH1 1JF Edinburgh,
United Kingdom

Ruhr Uni Boch
Ruhr-Universitat Bochum, Instit fur
Archaologie
D-4630 Bochum-Querenburg,
Universitats-Str., West Germany

Rumbleseat
Rumbleseat Press, Inc.
3835 Scott St., San Francisco, CA 94123
(0-913444)
Running Pr
Running Press
38 S. 19th St., Philadelphia, PA 19103
(0-89471)
Rushlight Club
Rushlight Club
Orders to:
21 Claire Rd, Vernon, CT 06066
(0-917422)
Russell
Russell & Russell, Pubs, Div. of Atheneum
Pubs.
122 E. 42nd St., New York, NY 10017
(0-8462)
Rutgers U Pr
Rutgers Univ. Press
30 College Ave., New Brunswick, NJ
08903
(0-8135)
Rutledge Bks
Rutledge Books, Inc.
(0-87469)
Dist. by:
Larousse & Co., Inc., 572 Fifth Ave., New
York, NY 10036; Charles Scribner's Sons,
597 Fifth Ave., New York, NY 10017
S Alleghenies
Southern Alleghenies Museum of Art
P.O. Box 8, Loretto, PA 15940
S G Phillips
Phillip's, S. G., Inc.
305 W. 86th St., New York, NY 10024
(0-87599)
S Ill U Pr
Southern Illinois Univ. Press
P.O. Box 3697, Carbondale, IL 62901
(0-8093)
S J Durst
Durst, Sanford J.
133 E. 58th St., New York, NY 10022
(0-915262)
S Meth U Pr
See SMU Press
S R Guggenheim
Guggenheim, Solomon R., Foundation
1071 Fifth Ave., New York, NY 10028
(0-89207)
SA Cult Hist Mus
Groot Constantia Manor House
P.O. Box 645, Cape Town, South Africa
SA Nat Gal
South African National Gallery
Government Ave., P.O. Box 2420, 8000
Cape Town, South Africa
Safari Mus Pr
Safari Museum Press
16 S. Grant, Chanute, KS 66720
Sage
Sage Pubns., Inc.
275 S. Beverly Dr., Beverly Hills, CA
90212
(0-8039)
Saifer
Saifer, Albert, Pub.
P.O. Box 239 W.O.B., West Orange, NJ
07052
(0-87556)
Sals Wilt Mus
Salisbury & South Wiltshire Museum
42 St. Ann St., Salisbury, Wilts.,
United Kingdom
Salyer
Salyer Publishing Co.
3111 19th St., N.W., Oklahoma City, OK
73107
(0-911298)
Salz Residenz
Salzburger Residenzgalerie
Residenzplatz 1, A-5010 Salzburg Postfach
527, Austria
SamHar Pr
SamHar Press, Div. of Story House Corp.
Charlotteville, NY 12036
Sams
Sams, Howard W., & Co, Inc, Subs. of ITT
4300 W. 62nd St., Indianapolis, IN 46206
(0-672)
San Ant Mus
San Antonio Museum Assn.
3801 Braodway, San Antonio, TX 78209

San Fran Mod
San Francisco Museum of Modern Art
Van Ness Ave. at McAllister St., San
Francisco, CA 94102
San Jacinto
San Jacinto Publishing Co.
P.O. Box 66254, Houston, TX 77006
(0-911982)
Sand Dollar
Sand Dollar Press
1222 Solano Ave., Albany, CA 94706
Sandlapper Pr
See Sandlapper Store
Sandlapper Store
Sandlapper Store, Inc.
Box 841, 101 W. Main, Lexington, SC
29072
(0-87844)
S&S
Simon & Schuster, Inc.
1230 Ave. of the Americas, New York, NY
10020
(0-671)
Santa Barbara Mus
Santa Barbara Museum of Art
1130 State St., Santa Barbara, CA 93101
Sat Rev Pr
See Dutton
Saxon
Saxon House
Atheneum Pubs., 122 E. 42nd St., New
York, NY 10017
SBD
SBD: Small Press Distribution
1636 Ocean View Ave., Kensington, CA
94707
(0-914068)
Scarecrow
Scarecrow Press, Inc, Subs. of Grolier
Educational Corp.
52 Liberty St., Box 656, Metuchen, NJ
08840
(0-8108)
Sceaux
Musee de l'Ile de France
Chateau de l'Ile de France, F-92330
Sceaux, France
Sch Ori Afr St
School of Oriental & African Studies, Univ. of
London
Malet St., London WC1E 7HP,
United Kingdom
Schiffer
Schiffer Publishing Ltd.
P.O. Box E, Exton, PA 19341
(0-916838)
Schleiger
Schleiger, Arlene
4416 Valli Vista Rd, Colorado Springs, CO
80915
(0-9600098)
Schloss Hohen
Oberosterreichisches Jagdmuseum Schloss
Hohenbrunn
Hohenbrunn 1, A-4490 St. Florian, Austria
Schloss Rohrau
Graf Harrach'sche Familiensammlung
Schloss Rohrau, A-2471-Rohrau, Austria
Schnell & Steiner
Schnell & Steiner
Von-der-Pfordten-Str. 15, Postfach 210260,
D-8000 Munich 21, West Germany
(3-7954)
Schocken
Schocken Books, Inc.
200 Madison Ave., New York, NY 10016
(0-8052)
Schol Facsimiles
Scholars' Facsimiles & Reprints
P.O. Box 344, Delmar, NY 12054
(0-8201)
Scholarly
Scholarly Press Inc.
19722 E. Nine Mile Rd., Saint Clair
Shores, MI 48080
(0-403)
Scot Art Coun
Scottish Arts Council Gallery
19 Charlotte Square, Edinburgh EH2 4DF,
United Kingdom
Scott F
Scott, Foresman & Co.
1900 E. Lake Ave., Glenview, IL 60025
(0-673)
ScribJ. Scribner.
Scrib-C. Imprint of Scribner's, Charles, Sons.

Scribner
Scribner's, Charles, Sons
Shipping & Service Ctr., Vreeland Ave.,
Totowa, NJ 07512
(0-684)
ScribT. Scribner.
Scrib-T. Imprint of Scribner's, Charles, Sons.
Scrimshaw Calif
Scrimshaw Press (California)
6040 Claremont Ave, Oakland, CA 94618
(0-912020)
Se Mo State U
Southeast Missouri State Univ.
Cape Girardeau, MO 63701
Segantini Mus
Segantini-Museum
Suvrettastr., CH-7500 St. Moritz,
Switzerland
Select Bks
Select Books
5969 Wilbur Ave., Tarzana, CA 91356
(0-910458)
Seton Art
Seton Hall University Art Center
Art Center Building, South Orange, NJ
07079
Sew-Fit
Sew/Fit Publishing Co.
905 Hillgrove, Suite 6, La Grange, IL
60525
SF Arts & Letters
San Francisco Arts & Letters Foundation
P.O. Box 99394, San Francisco, CA 94109
(0-914024)
SF Bk Co
San Francisco Book Co., Inc.
2311 Fillmore St., San Francisco, CA
94115
(0-913374)
SF Center Vis Stud
San Francisco Center for Visual Studies
900 Alabama St., San Francisco, CA 94110
(0-930976)
Shaker Mus
Shaker Museum
Shaker Museum Rd., Old Chatham, NY
12136
Shambala Pubns
See Shambhala Pubns
Shambhala Pubns
Shambhala Pubns., Inc.
(0-87773)
Random House, Inc., 400 Hahn Rd.,
Westminster, MD 21157
Shanghai People
Shanghai People's Art Publishing Co.
Shanghai, China, Mainland
Sharon Hill
Sharon Hill Books
P.O. Box 67, Sharon Hill, PA 19079
(0-932062)
Sheffield Gals
Sheffield City Art Galleries
Surrey St., S1 1XZ Sheffield,
United Kingdom
Shel Jack Col
Sheldon Jackson College
P.O. Box 479, Sitka, AK 99835
Shelburne
Shelburne Museum, Inc.
Shelburne, VT 05482
Shelter Pubns
See Random
Shengold
Shengold Pubs., Inc.
45 W. 45th St., New York, NY 10036
(0-88400)
Sheridan
Sheridan House, Inc.
175 Orawaupum St., White Plains, NY
10606
(0-911378)
Shirjieh Pubs
Shirjieh Pubs.
P.O. Box 259, Menlo Park, CA 94025
(0-912496)
Shoal Creek Pub
Shoal Creek Pubs.
P.O. Box 9737, Austin, TX 78766
(0-88319)
Shoe String
Shoe String Press, Inc.
P.O. Box 4327, 995 Sherman Ave.,
Hamden, CT 06514
(0-208)

Shorey
Shorey Pubns.
110 Union St., Seattle, WA 98111
(0-8466)

Shoshoin
Shoshoin Treasure House
Zoshi-cho, Nara City, Japan

Shumway
Shumway, George
R.D. 7, Box 388B, York, PA 17402
(0-87387)

Sierra
Sierra Club Books
(0-87156)
Charles Scribner's Sons, Book Warehouse,
Vreeland Ave., Totowa, NJ 07512

Sigga Pr
Sigga Press
P.O. Box 178, George's Mills, NH 03751
(0-916348)

Signs of Times
Signs of the Times Publishing Co.
407 Gilbert Ave., Cincinnati, OH 45202
(0-911380)

Silvana Edit
Silvana Editorials
Via Francesco Ferruccio 15, I-20145
Milano, Italy

Silver
Silver Burdett Co, Div. of General Learning
Co.
250 James St., Morristown, NJ 07960
(0-382)

Silvermine
Silvermine Pubs.
Comstock Hill, Silvermine, Norwalk, CT
06850
(0-87231)

Siraudeau
Siraudeau Cie
6 Pl. De La Visitation, F-49000, Angers,
France (2-85672)

SLA
Special Libraries Assn.
235 Park Ave., S., New York, NY 10003
(0-87111)

Sleepy Hollow
Sleepy Hollow Restorations, Inc.
(0-912882)
Independent Publishers Group, 14
Vanderventer Ave., Port Washington, NY
11050

Smith Col Art
Smith College Museum of Art
Northampton, MA 01063

Smith Coll
Smith College, Pubns.
(0-87391)
Neilson Library, Office of the Director of
Technical Services, Northampton, MA
01063

Smithsonian
Smithsonian Institution Press
P.O. Box 1579, Washington, DC 20013
(0-87474)

SMU Press
Southern Methodist Univ. Press
Dallas, TX 75275
(0-87074)

Smyrna
Smyrna Press
P.O. Box 1803, GPO, Brooklyn, NY 11202
(0-918266)

Soc Arch Mont
Societe Archeologique de Montpelier
5 Rue des Tresoriers-De-France, Hotel de
Lunaret, F-34000 Montpellier, France

Soc Photo Sci & Eng
Society of Photographic Scientists & Engineers
1411 "K" St., N.W., Suite 930, Washington,
DC 20005
(0-89208)

SOLARC
SOLARC - Solar Energy in Architecture
P.O. Box 18024, Irvine, CA 92713

Some Place
Some Place
2990 Adeline St., Berkeley, CA 94703
(0-916896)

Somerset Pub
Somerset Pubs, Div. of Scholarly Press, Inc.
19722 E. Nine Mile Rd, St. Clair Shores,
MI 48080

Sordoni Gal
Wilkes College Sordoni Art Gallery
150 S. River St., Wilkes-Barre, PA 18703

South Asia Bks
South Asia Books
P.O. Box 502, Columbia, MO 65201
(0-88386; 0-8364)

South St Sea Mus
South Street Seaport Museum
(0-913344)
Dist. by:
Interbook, Inc., 545 8th Ave., New York,
NY 10018

Southwest Mus
Southwest Museum
P.O. Box 128, Highland Park Sta., Los
Angeles, CA 90042

Spec. P-H.
Spectrum Books. Imprint of Prentice-Hall, Inc.

Speed Art Mus
Speed, J.B., Art Museum
P.O. Box 8345, Louisville, KY 40208
United States

Speller
Speller, Robert, & Sons, Pub., Inc.
Orders to:
P.O. Box 461, Times Square Sta., New
York, NY 10036
(0-8315)

Spertus Col Pr
Spertus College Press
618 S. Michigan Ave., Chicago, IL 60605

Spring Art Ctr
Springfield Art Center
107 Cliff Park Rd., Springfield, OH 45501

Springer Pub
Springer Publishing Co., Inc.
200 Park Ave., S., New York, NY 10003
(0-8261)

Springer-Verlag
Springer-Verlag New York, Inc.
175 Fifth Ave., New York, NY 10010
(0-387)

Squarebooks
Squarebooks
P.O. Box 144, Mill Valley, CA 94941
(0-916290)

St Baafskathe
St. Baafskathedral
St. Baffsplein, B-9000 Gent, Belgium

St. Florian
Chorherrenstift St. Florian
A-4490 St. Florian, Austria

St Heironymous
St. Heironymous Press, Inc.
P.O. Box 9431, Berkeley, CA 94709
(0-913718)

St Johns Ath
St. Johnsbury Atheneum
St. Johnsbury, VT 05819

St Louis Art Mus
St. Louis Art Museum
Forest Park, St. Louis, MO 63110
United States

St Louis Pub Lib
St. Louis Public Library, Pubns. Dept
1301 Olive St., St. Louis, MO 63103

St Martin
St. Martin's Press, Inc.
175 Fifth Ave., New York, NY 10010
(0-312)

St Mary's
St. Mary's College Press
Winona, MN 55987
(0-88489)

ST Pubns
See Signs of Times

Staat Agyp Kun
Staatliche Sammlung Agyptischer Kunst
Meiserstr 10, D-8000 2 Munich,
West Germany

Staat Ant Gly
Staatliche Antikensammlungen und Glyptothek
D-8000 Munich 2, Konigsplatz 1,
West Germany

Staatsuitgeverij
Staatsdrukkerij en Uitgeverijbedrijf
Chr. Plantijnstr. 1, The Hague, Netherlands

Stackpole
Stackpole Books
Cameron & Keller Sts., Harrisburg, PA
17105
(0-8117)

Stad Mus Rheydt
Stadtisches Museum, Schloss Rheydt
4050 Munchengladbach 2, Schloss Rheydt,
West Germany

Stads Sint-Nik
Stadsbestur Van Sint-Niklaas
Markt, Sint-Niklaas, 2700, Belgium

Stadtmus Linz
Stadtmuseum Linz
Bethlehemstr. 7, A-4020 Linz, Austria

Stalna Izlozb
Stalna Izlozba Crkvene Umejetonoste
Ul. Stomorica B.B. YU-57000 Zadar,
Yugoslavia

Stanford U Pr
Stanford Univ. Press
Stanford, CA 94305
(0-8047)

Stanton & Lee
Stanton & Lee Pubs., Inc.
Orders to:
Sauk City, WI 53583
(0-88361)

Stark Mus Art
Stark Museum of Art
712 Green Ave., P.O. Box 1897, Orange,
TX 77630

State Mutual Bk
State Mutual Book & Periodical Service, Ltd.
521 Fifth Ave., New York, NY 10017

State Ptg
State Printing Co.
1305 Sumter St., Columbia, SC 29201
(0-911432)

State U NY Pr
State Univ. of New York Press
P.O. Box 4830, Hampden Sta., Baltimore,
MD 21211
(0-87395)

Statens Mus
Statens Museum for Kunst
Solvgade, 1307 Copenhagen, Denmark

Stedelijke Mus
Stedelijke Musea
Dyver, 12, 8000 Bruges, Belgium

Stedelyk Mus
Stedelijk Museum-Amsterdam
Paulus Potterstraat 12, 1071 CX
Amsterdam, Netherlands

Stein & Day
Stein & Day
Scarborough House, Briarcliff Manor, NY
10510
(0-8128)

Steinerbooks. Multimedia.
Steiner. Imprint of Multimedia Publishing
Corp.

Stemmer Hse
Stemmer House Pubs., Inc.
2627 Caves Rd., Owings Mills, MD 21117
(0-916144)

Sterling
Sterling Publishing Co., Inc.
2 Park Ave., New York, NY 10016
(0-8069)

Stift Melk
Benediktinerstift Melk
A-3390 Melk, Austria

Stinson Beach
Stinson Beach Press
P.O. Box 475, Stinson Beach, CA 94970
(0-918540)

Stonehill Pub Co
Stonehill Publishing Co., Inc.
(0-88373)
Dist. by:
Farrar, Straus & Giroux, Inc., 19 Union
Square, New York, NY 10003

Stonehouse
Stonehouse Pubns.
Sweet, ID 83670
(0-9603236)

Stowe-Day
Stowe-Day Foundation
77 Forest St., Hartford, CT 06105
(0-917482)

Stravon
Stravon Educational Press
845 Third Ave., New York, NY 10022
(0-87396)

Street Fiction
Street Fiction Press
201 E. Liberty St., Ann Arbor, MI 48104
(0-914908)

Structures Pub
Structures Publishing Co.
P.O. Box 1002, Farmington, MI 48024
(0-912336)

Studio Three Thousand
Studio 3000
P.O. Box 122, Ansonia Sta., New York,
NY 10023
(0-915100)

Sturtz Verlag
Sturtz Verlag Wurzburg
Beethovenstr. 5, Wurzburg 8700,
West Germany
Su Docs
Superintendent of Documents, U.S.
Government Printing Office
Washington, DC 20402
Sullivan Bks Intl
Sullivan Books International
515 Weldon Ave., Oakland, CA 94610
(0-913620)
Sumac
Sumac Press
613 N. 22nd St., La Crosse, WI 54601
(0-911462)
Sumitomo
Sumitomo Collection
25 Shimo Miyanomae-cho, Shikagatani,
Sakyo-ku, Kyoto, Japan
Summit Bks
Summit Books, Div. of Simon & Schuster, Inc.
1230 Ave. of the Americas, New York, NY
10020
Sun Pub
Sun Publishing Co.
P.O. Box 4383, Albuquerque, NM 87106
(0-914172; 0-89540)
Sunstone Pr
Sunstone Press, The
P.O. Box 2321, Santa Fe, NM 87501
(0-913270)
Suomen Kans
Suomen Kansallismuseo
Mannerheiminte P.O. Box 913, 10 Helsinki,
Finland
Superior Pub
Superior Publishing Co.
708 Sixth Ave., N., Box 1710, Seattle, WA
98111
(0-87564)
Sutter
Sutter Publishing Co.
Orders to:
2303 S. Milton Ave., Overland, MO 63114
(0-9600120)
Sutter House
Sutter House
77 Main St., P.O. Box 212, Lititz, PA
17543
(0-915010)
SW Pks Mnmts
Southwest Parks & Monuments Assn.
P.O. Box 1562, Globe, AZ 85501
(0-911408)
SW Pub
South-Western Publishing Co.
5101 Madison Rd., Cincinnati, OH 45227
(0-538)
Swallow
Swallow Press
811 W. Junior Terrace, Chicago, IL 60613
(0-8040)
Sweet Briar
Sweet Briar College, Dept. of Art History
Sweet Briar, VA 24595
Sycamore Island
Sycamore Island Books
Caroline House, P.O. Box 161, Thornwood,
NY 10594
Sypesteyn
Kasteel-Museum Sypesteyn
Nieuw-Loosdrechtsedijk 150, Loosdrecht
1231 LC, Netherlands
Syracuse U Pr
Syracuse Univ. Press
1011 E. Water St., Syracuse, NY 13210
(0-8156)
TAB Bks
TAB Books
Blue Ridge Summit, PA 17214
(0-8306)
Taplinger
Taplinger Publishing Co., Inc.
200 Park Ave., S., New York, NY 10003
(0-8008)
Tats
Tat's, Inc.
230 Newport Ctr. Dr., Newport Beach, CA
92660
(0-911478)
Taylor Museum
Taylor Museum
Dist. by:
Colorado Springs Fine Arts Ctr., 30 W.
Dale St., Colorado Springs, CO 80903

Teach'em
Teach'em, Inc.
625 N. Michigan Ave., Chicago, IL 60611
(0-931028)
Telos Pr
Telos Press Ltd.
(0-914386)
c/o Washington Univ., Dept. of Sociology,
St. Louis, MO 63130
Temple U Pr
Temple Univ. Press
Philadelphia, PA 19122
(0-87722)
Tenn Fine Ctr
Tennessee Fine Arts Center
Cheekwood, Nashville, TN 37205
Terra Magica. Hill & Wang.
Terra Magica Books. Imprint of Hill & Wang,
Inc.
Tex A&M Univ Pr
Texas A & M Univ. Press
Drawer "C", College Sta., TX 77843
(0-89096)
Tex Christian
Texas Christian Univ. Press
Box 30783, Fort Worth, TX 76129
(0-912646)
Tex Tech Pr
Texas Tech Press
Room 118, Texas Tech University Library,
Texas Tech University, Lubbock, TX 79409
(0-89672)
Tex Western
Texas Western Press, Univ. of Texas at El
Paso
El Paso, TX 79968
(0-87404)
Textil Krefeld
Textilmuseum
Frankenring 20, D-4150 Krefeld,
West Germany
Textile Bk
Textile Book Service
1447 E. Second St., Box 907, Plainfield, NJ
07061
(0-87245)
Textile Mus
Textile Museum
2320 "S" St., N.W., Washington, DC 20008
(0-87405)
Teylers Mus
Teylers Museum
Spaarne 16, Damstraat 21, 2011 HA
Haarlem, Netherlands
Thames Hudson
Thames & Hudson
(0-500)
W.W. Norton, & Co., Inc., 500 Fifth Ave.,
New York, NY 10036
Theatre Arts
Theatre Arts Books
153 Waverly Place, New York, NY 10014
(0-87830)
Theobald
Theobald, Paul, & Co.
5 N. Wabash Ave., Chicago, IL 60602
(0-911498)
Theophrastus
Theophrastus
P.O. Box 458, Little Compton, RI 02837
(0-913728)
Theorex
Theorex
8327 La Jolla Scenic Dr., La Jolla, CA
92037
(0-916004)
Third Pr
See Okpaku Communications
Thomas Rae
Thomas Rae Ltd.
Greenock, Renfrewshire, United Kingdom
Thorvaldsen
Thorvaldsen Museum
Porthuscade 2, 1213 Copenhagen, Denmark
Thresh Pubns
Thresh Pubns.
3027 Gateway Rd, P.O. Box 580, Bethel
Island, CA 94511
(0-9600572; 0-913664)
Time Bks
See Times Bks

Time-Life
Time-Life Books, Div. of Time, Inc.
(0-8094)
Dist. by:
Little, Brown & Co., 34 Beacon St., Boston,
MA 02106; Morgan & Morgan Co., 400
Warburton Ave., Hastings on Hudson, NY
10706
Times Bks
Times Books, Div. of The New York Times
Co.
(0-8129)
Dist. by:
Harper & Row, Keystone Industrial Park,
Scranton, PA 18512
Tirol Lan Mus
Tiroler Landesmuseum Fredinandeum
Museumstr. 15, A-6020 Innsbruck, Austria
Tokugawa
Tokugawa Art Museum, the Tokugawa
Reimeikai Foundation
27, Tokugawa-Cho 2-Chome Higashi-Ku,
Nagoya, Aichi Pref., Japan
Toledo Mus
Toledo Museum of Art
Box 1013, Monroe St. at Scottwood,
Toledo, 43697
Tom Thomson
Thomson, Tom, Memorial Gallery & Museum
of Fine Art
840 First Ave. W., P. O. Box 312, Owen
Sound, Ont., Canada
Touchstone Bks. S&S.
Touchstone Bks. Imprint of Simon & Schuster,
Inc.
Tougaloo
Tougaloo College Museum
Tougaloo, MS 39174
Transatlantic
Transatlantic Arts, Inc.
N. Village Green, Levittown, NY 11756
(0-693)
Treasure Chest
Treasure Chest Pubns
Orders to:
P.O. Box 5250, Tucson, AZ 85903
(0-918080)
Trident
Trident Press, Div. of Simon & Schuster, Inc.
630 Fifth Ave., New York, NY 10020
(0-671)
Trinity U Pr
Trinity Univ. Press
715 Stadium Dr., San Antonio, TX 78284
(0-911536)
Triton Mus Art
Triton Museum of Art
1505 Warburton Ave., Santa Clara, CA
95050
Trojan Pr
Trojan Press, Inc.
310 E. 18th St., North Kansas City, MO
64116
(0-913914)
Troubador Pr
Troubador Press
385 Fremont St., San Francisco, CA 94105
(0-912300; 0-89844)
Tunbridge
Tunbridge Press
P.O. Box 345, New York, NY 10021
(0-911538)
Turquoise Bks
Turquoise Books
1202 Austin Bluffs Pkwy., Colorado
Springs, CO 80907
(0-917834)
Twayne
Twayne Pubs, Div. of G. K. Hall
(0-8057)
Dist. by:
G. K. Hall & Co., 70 Lincoln St., Boston,
MA 02111
Two Continents
Two Continents Publishing Group, Inc.
171 Madison Ave., New York, NY 10016
(0-8467)
Tyndale
Tyndale House Pubs.
336 Gundersen Dr., Wheaton, IL 60187
(0-8423)
U Brit Colum
Univ. of British Columbia, Museum of
Anthropology
Main Library Bldg., Fine Arts, Vancouver,
BC V6T 1W5, Canada
U Cal Grad Sch Mgmt
See UCLA Mgmt

U Delaware Pr
Univ. of Delaware Press
(0-87413)
c/o Associated Univ. Presses, Inc., P.O.
Box 421, Cranbury, NJ 08512

U Gal U Fla
University Gallery, Univ. of Florida
Gainesville, FL 32611

U Gal U Mass
University Gallery, Univ. of Massachusetts,
Amherst
Amherst, MA 01003

U Glasgow Pr
Univ. of Glasgow Press
Glasgow G12 8QG, United Kingdom
(0-85261)

U IA Mus Art
Univ. of Iowa Museum of Art
Riverside Dr., Iowa City, IA 52242

U Maine Orono
Univ. of Maine at Orono Press
PICS Building, Univ. of Marine at Orono,
Orono, ME 04469
(0-89101)

U Mich Mus Anthro
Univ. of Michigan, Museum of Anthropology,
Pubns. Dept.
4009 Museums Bldg., 1109 Geddes, Ann
Arbor, MI 48109
(0-932206)

U of Ala Pr
Univ. of Alabama Press
Box 2877, University, AL 35486
(0-8173)

U of Ariz Mus
Univ. of Arizona Museum of Art
Speedway & Olive, Tucson, AZ 85705

U of Ariz Pr
Univ. of Arizona Press
P.O. Box 3398, Tucson, AZ 85722
(0-8165)

U of Cal Pr
Univ. of California Press
2223 Fulton St., Berkeley, CA 94720
(0-520)

U of Chicago Pr
Univ. of Chicago Press
11030 S. Langley Ave., Chicago, IL 60628
(0-226)

U of Ga Pr
Univ. of Georgia Press
Terrell Hall, Athens, GA 30602
(0-8203)

U of Guelph
Univ. of Guelph
Guelph, Ontario N1G 2W1, Canada

U of Ill Pr
Univ. of Illinois Press
54 E. Gregory Dr., P.O. Box 5081, Sta. A,
Champaign, IL 61820
(0-252)

U of Iowa Pr
Univ. of Iowa Press
214 Graphic Services Bldg., Iowa City, IA
52242
(0-87745)

U of Kansas
Univ. of Kansas, Spencer Museum
Lawrence, KS 66045

U of Mass Pr
Univ. of Massachusetts Press
P.O. Box 429, Amherst, MA 01002
(0-87023)

U of Miami Pr
Univ. of Miami Press
(0-87024)
Dist. by:
Texas Press Services, P.O. Box 7877,
Austin, TX 78712

U of Mich Pr
Univ. of Michigan Press
P.O. Box 1104, Ann Arbor, MI 48106
(0-472)

U of Minn Pr
Univ. of Minnesota Press
2037 University Ave. S.E., Minneapolis,
MN 55455
(0-8166)

U of Mo Pr
Univ. of Missouri Press
107 Swallow Hall, Columbia, MO 65211
(0-8262)

U of NC Pr
Univ. of North Carolina Press
P.O Box 2288, Chapel Hill, NC 27514
(0-8078)

U of Nebr Pr
Univ. of Nebraska Press
901 N. 17th St., Lincoln, NE 68588
(0-8032)

U of NM Pr
Univ. of New Mexico Press
Albuquerque, NM 87131
(0-8263)

U of Notre Dame Pr
Univ. of Notre Dame Press
(0-268)
Harper & Row Pubs., Keystone Industrial
Park, Scranton, PA 18512

U of Ok Mus Art
Univ. of Oklahoma, Museum of Art
2727 S. Rockford Rd., Tulsa, OK 74152

U of Okla Pr
Univ. of Oklahoma Press
1005 Asp Ave., Norman, OK 73019
(0-8061)

U of Oreg Bks
Univ. of Oregon Books
(0-87114)
Dist. by:
University Business Office, 148 Oregon
Hall, VO, Eugene, OR 97403

U of Pa Contemp Art
Univ. of Pennsylvania, Institute of
Contemporary Art
34th & Walnut Sts., Philadelphia, PA 19104
(0-88454)

U of Pa Pr
Univ. of Pennsylvania Press
3933 Walnut St., Philadelphia, PA 19104
(0-8122)

U of Pittsburgh Pr
Univ. of Pittsburgh Press
127 N. Bellefield Ave., Pittsburgh, PA
15260
(0-8229)

U of PR Pr
Univ. of Puerto Rico Press
P.O. Box X, U.P.R. Sta., Rio Piedras, PR
00931
(0-8477)

U of Queensland Pr
Univ. of Queensland Press
Technical Impex Corp., 5 South Union St.,
Lawrence, MA 01843

U of RI Pr
See U Pr of New Eng

U of S Cal Pr
Univ. of Southern California Press
Student Union 400, Univ. of Southern
California, Los Angeles, CA 90007
(0-88474)

U of SC Pr
Univ. of South Carolina Press
Columbia, SC 29208
(0-87249)

U of Sydney
Nicholson Museum of Antiquites
University of Sydney, Sydney, NSW 2006,
Australia

U of Tenn Pr
Univ. of Tennessee Press
293 Communications Bldg., Knoxville, TN
37916
(0-87049)

U of Tex Hum Res
Univ. of Texas, Humanities Research Ctr.
P.O. Box 7219, Austin, TX 78712
(0-87959)

U of Tex Pr
Univ. of Texas Press
P.O. Box 7819, University Sta., Austin, TX
78712
(0-292)

U of Toronto Pr
Univ. of Toronto Press
Orders to:
33 E. Tupper St., Buffalo, NY 14203
(0-8020)

U of Utah Pr
Univ. of Utah Press
Salt Lake City, UT 84112
(0-87480)

U of Va Pr
Univ. of Virginia Press
Lynchburg, VA 24503

U of Wash Pr
Univ. of Washington Press
Seattle, WA 98105
(0-295)

U of Wis Pr
Univ. of Wisconsin Press
114 North Murray St., Madison, WI 53715
(0-299)

U of Wy Mus
Univ. of Wyoming Art Museum
Box 3138, University Sta., Laramie, WY
82071

U Pr of Amer
University Press of America
4710 Auth Place, S.E., Washington, DC
20023
(0-8191)

U Pr of Hawaii
Univ. Press of Hawaii
2840 Kolowalu St., Honolulu, HI 96822
(0-8248)

U Pr of Idaho
Univ. Press of Idaho, Div. of the Idaho
Research Foundation, Inc.
University Sta., Box 3368, Moscow, ID
83843
(0-89301)

U Pr of Ky
Univ. Press of Kentucky
Lexington, KY 40506
(0-8131)

U Pr of Miss
Univ. Press of Mississippi
3825 Ridgewood Rd., Jackson, MS 39211
(0-87805)

U Pr of New Eng
Univ. Press of New England
P.O. Box 979, Hanover, NH 03755
(0-87451)

U Pr of Va
Univ. Press of Virginia
P.O. Box 3608, University Sta.,
Charlottesville, VA 22903
(0-8139)

U Presses Fla
Univ. Presses of Fla.
15 N.W. 15th St., Gainesville, FL 32603
(0-8130)

U Santa Clara
Univ. of Santa Clara
Santa Clara, CA 95053

U Sherbrooke
Univ. of Sherbrooke Cultural Center, Art
Gallery
Sherbrooke PQ J1K 2R1, Canada

UAHC
Union of American Hebrew Congregations
838 Fifth Ave., New York, NY 10021
(0-8074)

UCLA Arch
Univ. of California, Los Angeles, Institute of
Archaeology
405 Hilgard Ave., Los Angeles, CA 90024
(0-917956)

UCLA Lat Am Ctr
Univ. of California, Latin American Center
405 Hilgard Ave., Los Angeles, CA 90024
(0-87903)

UCLA Mgmt
UCLA, Grad, School of Management, GSM
Pubns. Services
405 Hilgard Ave., Los Angeles, CA 90024
(0-911798)

Ultramarine Pub
Ultramarine Publishing Co., Inc.
P.O. Box 599, Midtown Sta., New York,
NY 10018
(0-89366)

Umeleck Muz
Umeleckoprumyslove Muzeum
Prague 1, Ul.17, Listopadu 2,
Czechoslovakia

Ungar
Ungar, Frederick, Publishing Co., Inc.
250 Park Ave. S., New York, NY 10003
(0-8044)

Unicorn Pr
Unicorn Press
P.O. Box 3307, Greensboro, NC 27402
(0-87775)

Union Coll
Union College Press
(0-912756)
c/o Syracuse Univ. Press, 1011 E. Water
St., Syracuse, NY 13210

United Church Pr
See Pilgrim NY

United Syn Bk
United Synagogue Book Service
155 Fifth Ave., New York, NY 10010
(0-8381)

Unity Pr
Unity Press
235 Hoover Road, Santa Cruz, CA 95065
(0-913300)

Univ Bks
University Books, Inc, Div. of Lyle Stuart, Inc.
120 Enterprise Ave., Secaucus, NJ 07094
(0-8216)

Univ Microfilms
University Microfilms International, A Xerox Publishing Co.
300 N. Zeeb Rd., Ann Arbor, MI 48106
(0-8357)

Univ Mus of U PA
University Museum, Univ. of Pennsylvania
33rd & Spruce Sts., Philadelphia, PA 19104

Univ Tubingen
Sammlung des Archaologischen Instituts der Eberhard-Karls-Universitat Tubingen
D-7400 Tubingen, Nauklerstr. 2,
West Germany

Universe
Universe Books, Inc.
381 Park Ave., S., New York, NY 10016
(0-87663)

Universitet
Universitetsforlaget
(82-00)
Columbia Univ. Press, 136 S. Broadway,
Irvington-on-Hudson, NY 10533

University. Exposition.
University. Imprint of Exposition Press, Inc.

Urban Land
Urban Land Institute
1200 18th St., N.W., Washington, DC 20036
(0-87420)

Urizen Bks
Urizen Books, Incorporated
(0-89396; 0-916354)
E. P. Dutton & Co. Inc., 201 Park Ave., S.,
New York, NY 10003

US Comm Unicef
U. S. Committee for UNICEF
331 E. 38th St., New York, NY 10016

Usher Gal
Lincolnshire Museums, Usher Gallery
Lincoln Rd., LN2 1NN Lincoln,
United Kingdom

Utah St Hist Soc
Utah State Historical Society
307 W. Second St., Salt Lake City, UT 84101
(0-913738)

Utah St U Pr
Utah State Univ. Press
UMC 05, Logan, UT 84322
(0-87421)

V & A
Victoria & Albert Museum
Cromwell Rd., SW7 2RL London,
United Kingdom

Va Mus Arts
Virginia Museum of Fine Arts
Blvd. & Grove, Richmond, VA 23221
United States

VA Mus Fine Arts
Virginia Museum of Fine Arts
Boulevard & Grove Ave., Richmond, VA 23221
(0-917046)

Vallentine Mitchell
See Biblio Dist

Valley Sun
Valley of the Sun Publishing Co.
Box 4276, Scottsdale, AZ 85258
(0-911842)

Van Abbe Mus
Stedelijk van Abbemuseum
Bilderdijklaan 10, P.O. Box 235, 5600 AE
Eindhoven, Netherlands

Van Den Bergh
Museum Mayer van den Bergh
Lange Gasthuisstraat 19, B-2000 Antwerp,
Belgium

Van Nos Reinhold
Van Nostrand Reinhold Co, Div. of Litton
Educational Publishing, Inc.
Lepi Order Processing, 7625 Empire Dr.,
Florence, KY 41042
(0-442)

Vance Biblios
Vance Bibliographies
P.O. Box 229, Monticello, IL 61856

Vanderbilt U Pr
Vanderbilt Univ. Press
2505(Rear) West End Ave., Nashville, TN 37203
(0-8265)

Vanguard
Vanguard Press, Inc.
424 Madison Ave., New York, NY 10017
(0-8149)

Vanous
Vanous, Arthur, Co.
P.O. Box A, River Edge, NJ 07661

Vassar Gal
Vassar College Art Gallery
Raymond Ave., Poughkepsie, NY 12601

Vatican
Museo Chiaramonti e Braccio Nuovo
C/O Musei Vaticani, Vatican, Vatican City

Ver Von Zabern
Verlag Philipp Von Zabern
P.O. Box 4065, Mainz D-6500,
West Germany

Verry
Verry, Lawrence, Inc.
Mystic, CT 06355
(0-8426)

Vestal
Vestal Press Ltd.
P.O. Box 97, 320 N. Jensen Rd., Vestal,
NY 13850
(0-911572)

Video-Info
Video-Info Pubns.
P.O. Box 1507, Santa Barbara, CA 93102
(0-931294)

Vigeland Mus
Vigeland-Parken (Oslo
Kommuneskuntsamlinger)
Sogn, Oslo 8, Norway

Viking Import
Viking Import House, Inc.
412 S.E. Sixth St., Ft. Lauderdale, FL 33301
(0-911576)

Viking Pr
Viking Press, Inc.
625 Madison Ave., New York, NY 10022
(0-670)

Vin. Random.
Vintage Trade Books. Imprint of Random
House, Inc.

Virgo Pr
Virgo Press
P.O. Box 402651, Miami Beach, FL 33140
(0-930558)

Von Wagner
Martin von Wagner Museum der Universitat
Wurzburg
D-8700 Wurzburg, Residenz/Sudflugel,
West Germany

VoyB. HarBraceJ.
Voyager Books. Imprint of Harcourt Brace
Jovanovich, Inc.

W C Darrah
Darrah, William Culp
R.D. 1, Gettysburg, PA 17325
(0-913116)

W D Farmer
Farmer, W. D., Residence Designer, Inc.
P.O. Box 49463, Atlanta, GA 30359
(0-931518)

W G Arader
Arader, W. Graham, III
1000 Boxwood Court, King of Prussia, PA 19406

W H Freeman
Freeman, W. H., & Co.
660 Market St., San Francisco, CA 94104
(0-7167)

W J Johnson
See Walter J Johnson

W Kaufmann
Kaufmann, William, Inc.
1 First St., Los Altos, CA 94022
(0-913232)

W S Sullwold
Sullwold, William S., Publishing, Inc.
18 Pearl St., Taunton, MA 02780
(0-88492)

Wadsworth
See Wadsworth Pub

Wadsworth Atheneum
Wadsworth Atheneum
25 Atheneum Square, N., Hartford, CT 06103

Wadsworth Pub
Wadsworth Publishing Co., Inc.
10 Davis Dr., Belmont, CA 94002
(0-534)

Wagoner
Wagoner, George
4318 Glenridge Dr., Carmichael, CA 95608
(0-9600178)

Wakefield
Wakefield Art Gallery
Wentworth Terrace, Wakefield, WF1 3QW,
United Kingdom

Walck
Walck, Henry Z., Inc, Div. of David McKay
Co. Inc.
Promotion Dept., 2 Park Ave., New York,
NY 10016
(0-8098)

Walker & Co
Walker & Co.
720 Fifth Ave., New York, NY 10019
(0-8027)

Walker Art Gal
Walker Art Gallery, Merseyside County
Council
William Brown St., L3 8EL Liverpool,
United Kingdom

Wallaby. PB.
Wallaby. Imprint of Pocket Books, Inc.

Wallace Col
Wallace Collection
Manchester Square WIM 6BN,
United Kingdom

Wallace-Homestead
Wallace-Homestead Book Co.
1912 Grand Ave., Des Moines, IA 50305
(0-87069)

Walsall Mus
Walsall Museum & Art Gallery
Lichfield St., Walsall WS1 1TR,
United Kingdom

Walter J Johnson
Johnson, Walter J., Inc.
355 Chestnut St., Norwood, NJ 07648
(0-8472)

Walters Art
Walters Art Gallery
600 N. Charles St., Baltimore, MD 21201
(0-911886)

Wanderer Bks
Wanderer Books, Div. of Simon & Schuster
1230 Ave. of the Americas, New York, NY 10020
(0-671)

Warman
Warman, E. G., Publishing,Inc.
540 Morgantown Rd., Uniontown, PA 15401
(0-911594)

Warne
Warne, Frederick, & Co., Inc.
101 Fifth Ave., New York, NY 10003
(0-7232)

Warner Bks
Warner Books, Inc.
Independent News Co., 75 Rockefeller
Plaza, New York, NY 10019
(0-446)

Warner Pr
Warner Press Pubs.
P.O. Box 2499, 1200 E. Fifth St.,
Anderson, IN 46011
(0-87162)

Wash & Lee. Norton Art.
Washington & Lee Univ. Imprint of Norton, R.
W., Art Gallery.

Wash Art Cons
Washington Art Consortium
C/O Museum of Art, Washington State
University, Pullman, WA 99164

Wash St Hist Soc
Washington State Historical Society
315 N. Stadium Way, Tacoma, WA 98403
(0-917048)

Wash U Gal
Washington Univ. Gallery of Art
Steinberg Hall, Box 1189, St. Louis,

Washingtonian
Washingtonian Books
1828 L St., N.W. Suite 200, Washington,
DC 20036
(0-915168)

Water Info
Water Information Center, Inc.
The North Shore Atrium, 6800 Jericho
Turnpike, Syosset, NY 11791
(0-912394)

Watson-Guptill
Watson-Guptill Pubns., Inc.
2160 Patterson St., Cincinnati, OH 45214
(0-8230)

Watts
Watts, Franklin, Inc, Subs. of Grolier Inc.
730 Fifth Ave., New York, NY 10019
(0-531)

Wayne St U Pr
Wayne State Univ. Press
The Leonard N. Simons Bldg., 5959
Woodward Ave., Detroit, MI 48202
(0-8143)
Wayne State U Pr
Wayne State Univ., McGregor Memorial
Community Arts Gallery
450 W. Kirby at Cass, Detroit, MI 48824

Weatherhill
Weatherhill, John, Inc.
(0-8348)
Dist. by:
Charles E. Tuttle, Co., Inc., 28 S. Main St.,
Rutland, VT 05701
Weatherman
Weatherman, Hazel Marie
(0-913074)
c/o Glassbooks, Inc., Rte. 1, Box 357A,
Ozark, MO 65721
Wednesbury
Wednesbury Art Gallery
Holyhead Rd., Wednesbury WS10 7DF,
West Midlands, United Kingdom
Wehman
Wehman Brothers, Inc.
Ridgedale Ave., Morris County Mall, Cedar
Knolls, NJ 07927
(0-911604)
Weinstock
Weinstock, Beatrice C.
14 Brook Bridge Rd., Great Neck, NY
11021
(0-9600568)
Wellesley Mus
Wellesley College Museum
Wellesley, MA 02181
Wen Wu Pub
Wen-Wu Publishing Company
Shanghai, China, Mainland
Wesleyan U Pr
Wesleyan Univ. Press
55 High St., Middletown, CT 06457
(0-8195)
Westermann
Westermann, Georg, Verlag
Georg-Westermann-Allee 66, Postfach
3320, D-3300 Braunschweig,
West Germany
Western Pub
Western Publishing Co., Inc.
Dept. M, 1220 Mound Ave., Racine, WI
53404
(0-307)
Western Res
Western Reserve Historical Society
10825 E. Blvd., Cleveland, OH 44106
United States
Westminster
Westminster Press
Orders to:
Order Dept., P.O. Box 718 Wm. Penn
Annex, Philadelphia, PA 19105
(0-644)
Westview
Westview Press
5500 Central Ave., Boulder, CO 80301
(0-89158)
Weybright
See McKay
Wheelwright
Wheelwright Museum of the American Indian
Box 5153, Santa Fe, NM 87502
White Hse Assn
White House Historical Assn.
New Executive Office Bldg., Washington,
DC 20506
Whitney
Whitney Museum of American Art
945 Madison Ave., New York, NY 10021
Whitney Lib. Watson-Guptill.
Whitney Library. Imprint of Watson-Guptill
Pubns., Inc.

Whitston Pub
Whitston Publishing Co., Inc.
P.O. Box 958, Troy, NY 12181
(0-87875)
Wichita Art Mus
Wichita Art Museum
619 Stackman Dr., Wichita, KS 67203
Wideview Bks
Wideview Books
Dist. by:
Harper & Row Pubs., Inc., Keystone
Industrial Park, Scranton, PA 18512
Wideview Pr
See Wideview Bks
Wiley
Wiley, John, & Sons, Inc.
605 Third Ave., New York, NY 10016
(0-471)
Wilhelm Hack
Wilhelm-Hack-Museum
D-6700 Ludwigshafen, Berliner Strasse 23,
West Germany
Will Morris Gal
Morris, William, Gallery
Lloyd Park, Forest Rd., Walthamstow,
London F17 4PP, United Kingdom
William Benton
William Benton Museum of Art
Storrs, CT
Williams Art
Williams College Museum of Art
Lawrence Hall, Williamstown, MA 01267
Williamsburg
Colonial Williamsburg Foundation
Orders to:
Merchandising Dept., Williamsburg, VA
23185
(0-910412; 0-87935)
Willumsens Mus
Willumsens, J.F., Museum
DK-3600 Frederikssund, Denmark
Wilshire
Wilshire Book Co.
12015 Sherman Rd., North Hollywood, CA
91605
(0-87980)
Wilson
Wilson, H. W.
950 University Ave., Bronx, NY 10452
(0-8242)
Winchell Co
Winchell Company
1315 Cherry St., Philadelphia, PA 19107
Winchester Pr
Winchester Press
205 E. 42nd St., New York, NY 10017
(0-87691)
Windmill. Dutton.
Windmill Books. Imprint of Dutton, E. P.
Wine Mus San Fran
Wine Museum of San Francisco
633 Beach St., San Francisco, CA 94109
Wingbow Pr
Wingbow Press
(0-914728)
Dist. by:
Bookpeople, 2940 Seventh St., Berkeley,
CA 94710
Winnipeg Art
Winnipeg Art Gallery
300 Memorial Blvd.,
Winnipeg, MB R3C 1V1
Canada
Winship Pr
Winship Press
P.O. Box 859, Mercer Univ., Sta., Macon,
GA 31207
(0-915430)
Winston Pr
Winston Press, Inc.
430 Oak Grove, Suite 203, Minneapolis,
MN 55403
(0-03)

Winterthur
Winterthur Museum
Winterthur, DE 19735
(0-912724)
Wittenborn
Wittenborn, George, Inc.
1018 Madison Ave., New York, NY 10021
(0-8150)
Wm C Brown
Brown, William C., Co., Pubs.
2460 Kerper Blvd., Dubuque, IA 52001
(0-697)
Woburn Pr
See Biblio Dist
Wolverhampton
Wolverhampton Art Gallery
Lichfield St., WV1 1DU Wolverhampton,
United Kingdom
Women's Hist
Women's History Research Center, Inc.
2325 Oak St., Berkeley, CA 94708
(0-912374)
Wood Art Gal
Wood Art Gallery
Montpelier, VT 05682
Woodcraft Supply
Woodcraft Supply Corp.
313 Montvale Ave., Woburn, MA 01801
(0-918036)
Workman Pub
Workman Publishing Co., Inc.
1 W. 39 St., New York, NY 10018
(0-911104; 0-89480)
Worthing Mus
Worthing Museum & Art Gallery
Chapel Rd., Worthing BN11 1HD, Sussex,
United Kingdom
Writers Digest
Writers Digest Books
9933 Alliance Rd., Cincinnati, OH 45242
(0-911654)
Wuppertaler
Wuppertaler Uhrenmuseum
D-5600 Wuppertal 1, Poststr.11,
West Germany
Wurtt Lan Mus
Wurttembergisches Landesmuseum
D-7000 Stuttgart 1, Altes Schloss,
Schiller-Platz 5, West Germany
Wyd Uni Warsz
Wydawnictwa Uniwersytetu Warszawskiego
Ul. Obonza 8, Warsaw, Poland
Wyden. McKay.
Wyden, Peter H., Inc. Imprint of McKay,
David, Co., Inc.
Yale U Anthro
Yale Univ. Pubns. in Anthropology
P.O. Box 2114, Yale Sta., New Haven, CT
06520
(0-913516)
Yale U Pr
Yale Univ. Press
Orders to:
92A Yale Sta., New Haven, CT 06520
(0-300)
Yankee Bks
Yankee Books
Dublin, NH 03444
(0-911658)
Yankee Bookmen
See Heritage Bk
Yankee Inc
See Yankee Bks
YB. Dell.
Yearling Books. Imprint of Dell Publishing
Co., Inc.
Zartscorp
Zartscorp, Inc. Books
267 W. 89th St., New York, NY 10024
Zondervan
Zondervan Publishing House
1415 Lake Dr., S.E., Grand Rapids, MI
49506
(0-310)